The Dictionary of Art · volume thirty-four

The Dictionary of Art

CONSULTING EDITOR Hugh Brigstocke

EDITOR Jane Turner

34

Index

GROVE

The Dictionary of Art

edited by JANE TURNER, in thirty-four volumes, 1996

This edition is distributed within the United Kingdom and Europe by Macmillan Publishers Limited, London, and within the United States and Canada by Grove's Dictionaries Inc., New York.

Text keyboarded by Wearset Limited, Sunderland, England
Database management by Pindar plc, York, England
Imagesetting by William Clowes Limited, Suffolk, England
Printed in the United States of America by RR Donnelley & Sons Company, Willard, Ohio

British Library Cataloguing in Publication Data

The dictionary of art
1. Art - Dictionaries 2. Art - History - Dictionaries
I. Turner, Jane
703

ISBN 1-884446-00-0

Library of Congress Cataloging in Publication Data

The dictionary of art / editor, Jane Turner.
p. cm.
Includes bibliographical references and index.
Contents: 1. A to Anckerman
ISBN 1-884446-00-0 (alk. paper)
1. Art—Encyclopedias.
I. Turner, Jane, 1956–
N31.D5 1996 96–13628
703—dc20 CIP

Contents

Introduction vii

The Dictionary, Volume Thirty Four:
Index 1

Appendix: Non-Western Dynasties and Peoples 1077

Introduction

This index comprises a selective listing of references in the *Dictionary of Art.* It has been compiled to be useful and accessible, enabling readers to locate both general and highly specific information quickly and easily. The following discussion outlines the logic behind the compilation of the index and explains what is indexed, how information has been alphabetized, the structure of subheadings and the function of cross-references within the index.

Numbers in **bold** refer to volume numbers, which are followed by specific page references. An asterisk (*) designates the main article (or sub-article) on that subject. Page numbers in *italics* refer to illustrations. A first-level illustration reference in a biographical entry (following the person's name rather than a subheading) indicates a portrait of the individual or a family tree. Colour plate references appear as large roman numerals after the appropriate volume number.

I. Coverage.

The range of entries cited in the index is as comprehensive as that covered by articles in the *Dictionary*, including, for example, artists, patrons, artistic groups, sites, cities, countries, cultures, peoples, periodicals, art forms, materials, techniques and technical terms, iconography, religions, art theories and abstract concepts such as authenticity. References to artists cite for the most part only substantial or significant discussions, not each passing mention. In the same way, specific references to a patron's activity as a collector or patron (e.g. when commissioning a building) have been indexed, but not a brief mention as the subject of a portrait or dedicatee of a book. Buildings are also indexed on the basis of substantial and meaningful discussions. Museums are extensively indexed, both for their architecture and their collections. References to collections under a museum entry indicate acquisitions of a significant nature (an important bequest, for instance); citations of the museum simply as the location of a work of art have not been indexed. All modern countries are included in the index, as are ancient cultures (e.g. Etruscan), regions (e.g. Bactria) and kingdoms (e.g. Gandhara). Art produced in a particular area before the existing country was established is indexed under the modern country name (e.g. Italy, Germany and Belgium (not Flanders)).

II. Headings.

1. PEOPLE. Most names of individuals are entered under the surname, with some exceptions. Some artists, for example, are so well known by their given names that they are always referred to as such and have been indexed under that name: e.g. **M**ichelangelo (Buonarroti), **R**aphael (Sanzio), **R**embrandt (van Rijn) and **T**itian (Vecellio). Medieval European names (to *c.* 1500) are indexed under the given name when it is followed by a name indicating a place of origin, domicile, patronym or profession (e.g. **G**iovanni da Pisa, **H**ans von Worms).

Compound Anglo-Saxon names are indexed under the first part of the name if hyphenated, under the last part if not (e.g. **C**aiger-Smith, Alan; **T**albot, William Henry Fox). Compound Danish names, which are not hyphenated, are entered under the first part of the surname (e.g.

Haugen Sørensen, Jørgen). Spanish and Portuguese individuals with double or triple surnames are also indexed under the first part of the surname (e.g. **A**lva de la Canal, Ramon; **S**andoval y Rojas, Bernardo de).

East Asian names are entered under the surname, which in Chinese and Korean names always comes before the given name and in Japanese names did until 1868, when the Western convention of placing surnames last was adopted. Post-1868 Japanese names are indicated with a comma after the surname (e.g. **T**ange, Kenzō). Islamic names are entered under the first given name (e.g. **M**uhammad ibn al-Zayn), with the exception of modern Turkish names, which follow the Western convention of surname last (e.g. **G**ezer, Hüseyin).

Names with prefixes are treated in various ways. Americanized and anglicized names are entered under the prefix (e.g. **D**e Kooning, Willem; **D**u Maurier, George). Belgian names (after 1830) are also indexed under the prefix (e.g. **D**e Ligne, Jean). Flemish names (before 1830), as well as Dutch and early Netherlandish ones, are indexed under the part of the name following the prefix (e.g. **G**ogh, Vincent van); exceptions to this are the prefixes Ver and Ter, which are usually elided with the rest of the name and thus form part of the surname (e.g. **V**erbrugghen, Henricus-Franciscus). French names are indexed under the prefix when this consists of an article or a contraction of a preposition and article (e.g. **D**u Cerceau, Baptiste Androuet; **L**e Nain, Louis; **L**a Chausse, Michel-Ange de). Names with the prefixes de and d' without articles are indexed under the last part of the name (e.g. **A**lembert, Jean Le Rond d'; **T**roy, François de); elided prefixes are entered under **D** (e.g. **D**elafosse, Jean-Charles).

German, Austrian and German-Swiss names are indexed under the prefix if this consists of an article or a contraction of a preposition and article (e.g. **V**om und Zum Stein, Karl; **Z**ur Mühlen, Rudolf Julius von); if the prefix is a preposition or a preposition followed by an article, it is entered under the part of the name following the prefix (e.g. **G**oethe, Johann Wolfgang von; **H**ildebrandt, Johann Lukas von). Scandinavian names with a prefix of Scandinavian or German origin are indexed under the word following the prefix (e.g. **B**reda, Carl Fredrik von); if the prefix is of French origin, the name is entered under the prefix (e.g. **D**e la Vallée, Simon).

Some early Italian names include a preposition that is not a prefix (de', d', degli', dei', de li); these are indexed under the name following the particle (e.g. **M**edici, Lorenzo de'). Early modern Italian names (*c.* 1500-*c.* 1800) are also entered under the name following the prefix (e.g. **S**arto, Andrea del). Modern Italian names (from *c.* 1800) are indexed under the prefix (e.g. **D**e Chirico, Giorgio; **D**ella Valle, Angel). When a Spanish or Portuguese individual has a given name immediately followed by a prefix and another name or names, he or she is indexed under the name following the prefix (e.g. **A**lmada e Melo, João de).

Islamic prefixes are not treated as part of the surname, and names are alphabetized under the word following the prefix, even though the entry starts with the prefix (e.g. al-**M**ansur).

A distinction is made in the index between rulers, who hold complete dominion over their lands, and nobles, who usually owe fealty to a ruler. Rulers and their consorts are indexed under the first name (which is usually anglicized in accordance with R. F. Tapsell's *Monarchs, Rulers, Dynasties and Kingdoms of the World*, London, 1983). Members of the nobility are usually entered under the title name, with the exception of British nobility, who are indexed under their family name (e.g. **B**oyle, Richard, 1st Earl of Cork). Extensive cross-references are provided between dynastic and aristocratic names and titles. Chinese, Japanese and Korean emperors are indexed under their first names or reign names (e.g. **M**eiji, Emperor). Nobles, such as shoguns, are entered under the family name (e.g. **T**okugawa, Ieyasu, Shogun); where a title exists but no family name, the noble is entered under his or her title (e.g. **Z**eng, Yi, Marquis of). Indian rulers (emperors, maharajas and rajas) are indexed under the given name (e.g. **A**kbar, Emperor (Mughal)), as are Islamic rulers (e.g. **M**urad I, Sultan).

Artists and patrons with identical or very similar names are differentiated by their dates of birth and death in brackets following the name, together with any common identifying epithets (e.g. the elder).

2. PLACES AND BUILDINGS. Modern country names follow United Nations conventions, with the exception of Myanmar, referred to herein as Burma. Sites and cities are indexed under the first word of their own names, not under the country or culture; where the place name begins with the prefix al-, el- or Tell, it is entered under the word following the prefix (e.g. **H**alaf, Tell; el-**K**ab).

Archaeological sites that are no longer inhabited are indexed under their ancient names (modern villages that have grown up around a site are not considered part of it). Sites of archaeological interest that have continued to be inhabited, often undergoing name changes, are indexed under their modern names, with a cross-reference from the ancient form (e.g. **P**ressburg *see* BRATISLAVA; **C**onstantinople *see under* ISTANBUL). When an ancient site is part of a major city, a second-level subheading (*see also* §III, 3 below) citing the ancient name is sometimes used for references to the ancient foundation, original layout and general construction, for example:

Istanbul
    Constantinople [for references to its founding].

All other references, including those to art production or buildings at the ancient site, are indexed under other second-level headings, for example:

Istanbul
    ecclesiastical buildings
        Hagia Sophia.

Villages and towns that were once separate entities but are now part of large cities have been indexed under their individual names, not the name of the modern city. **S**aint-Denis Abbey and **V**incennes, for instance, are indexed under those names, not under **P**aris. Exceptions are the metropolitan boroughs of London, which are indexed under **L**ondon. Cities and towns in the USA are followed by their state abbreviations, British places by their county abbreviations. When two or more places are known by the same name, the entry is followed by the name of the region or country in brackets, for example:

Philadelphia (Lydia)
Philadelphia (Palestine) *see* AMMAN
Philadelphia (PA; USA).

Buildings located in a town or city are indexed under the name of the town, for example:

Vicenza
    Villa Rotunda;

those that are not situated in a town or city are entered under their own names (e.g. **C**hatsworth House). Secular buildings are usually referred to in the vernacular when that language is considered to be widely known (English, French, German, Spanish and Italian). A building name in another language is usually translated into English unless its similarity to the name in one of these familiar languages makes its meaning obvious. Ecclesiastical buildings are excepted from this rule, and the type of building (e.g. church, abbey, convent, monastery) is almost always given in English. Dedications to saints in languages other than French, German, Spanish and Italian are translated into English.

3. GROUPS. Societies, partnerships, businesses and other groups are indexed under the main name in the title, excluding articles, first names and initials; for example, the firm of

Roger Smith & Gale is indexed as **S**mith, Roger, & Gale; The Five is indexed as **F**ive, The. Names of academies, art schools and institutes are entered under their location, for example:

Lisbon
    Academia de Belas-Artes.

4. WORKS OF ART. References to works of art are found under the name of the artist, though individual titles have not been indexed in most cases. Those works that have acquired a nickname (particularly from a previous owner or former location) are indexed, especially if the artist is unknown (e.g. **P**hoenix Jewel; **P**ortland Vase; **V**enus de Milo). A portrait of an individual is cited by means of a picture reference in *italics* following that person's main index entry. Tombs and monuments are indexed under their locations.

III. Structure.

Long index entries are divided into a number of subheadings, under which references to particular aspects of the subject are cited. In addition, information may appear under more than one index heading, enabling the reader to conduct a search with a particular emphasis. For example, information on albums produced in China can be found under the entry on **C**hina or under **A**lbums. The first will provide not only references to Chinese albums but also to other Chinese art forms; the last will refer to the same pages discussing Chinese albums and will also cite information on album production elsewhere, as well as having cross-references to associated art forms (e.g. butterfly books).

1. ARTISTS. An extensive entry for an artist includes subheadings that are intended to direct the reader to specific aspects of the artist's production or other activities; some examples are listed below:

Smith, John
    assistants
    attributions
    collaboration
    commentaries
    copies
    dealing
    exhibitions
    forgeries
    groups and movements
    house
    methods
    patrons and collectors
    personal collection
    productions
    pupils
    reproductive prints by others
    restorations by others
    sponsors
    studio
    teachers
    works
    workshop
    writings.

Attributions refers to current or former, correct or incorrect attributions. *Collaboration* includes instances in which the individual was commissioned by another artist or architect to execute a design, as well as citations of simple collaboration with another artist, jointly designing or executing a project. *Commentaries* refers to important writings about the artist. *Copies* indicates works specifically commissioned from other artists or those recording lost or destroyed originals. *Dealing* refers to the artist's activities as a dealer in works of art to other people. *Groups and movements* refers to collective groups or styles with which the artist has been associated, formally, informally or posthumously. *House* indicates the artist's own house; it may have been designed, decorated or commissioned by the artist. *Patrons and collectors* refers to people who commissioned, bought or collected the artist's work. *Personal collection* refers to works of art by others belonging to the artist; these works may have been used by the artist as aids to production, or they may have been bought for his or her own art collection. *Productions* cites the artist's involvement in the production of a theatrical performance (including opera and ballet). *Sponsors* indicates the financial support of an artist by a patron, without necessarily any reference to works commissioned. *Studio* refers to the artist's studio and its decoration, not to works produced there; *workshop* refers to the production of an artist's workshop. *Works* is replaced in some cases by individual terms refering to art form or medium. *Writings* refers to works written by the artist.

2. PATRONS AND COLLECTORS. Terms listed beneath the entry for a patron or collector refer to the art forms that were commissioned or acquired (e.g. paintings, prints, sculpture, furniture). General references to the individual's collection, across a variety of forms or media, are grouped under the term *collections*. *Sponsorship* refers to financial patronage (e.g. paying for an artist's travels or studies).

3. CITIES AND SITES. These entries include references to art production and activity as well as buildings (extant and destroyed) within a location (*see also* §II, 2 above). Large entries may be subdivided with the following examples:

Metropolis
- art forms and materials
- churches / other ecclesiastical buildings / Islamic religious buildings
- fountains
- government buildings
- monuments
- museums
- palaces
- temples
- tombs
- villas.

4. COUNTRIES AND CULTURES. Subheadings under these entries are self-explanatory and provide an outline of the *Dictionary*'s coverage of art production in a particular country, region or historical period or by a particular people. The nationality of art production is determined by the place in which the work was produced and originally located; for example, an artist of Estonian birth producing art in France for the French court is deemed to have produced French, not Estonian art.

5. ART FORMS, MATERIALS AND TECHNIQUES. Long entries in these categories are subdivided using examples listed below:

art forms: **P**orcelain
- conservation
- display
- historical and regional developments
- materials [includes any components of an art form]

technical examination
techniques
types

materials: **S**ilver
conservation
historical and regional traditions
patinas
technical examination
techniques
uses

techniques: **C**arving
historical and regional traditions
materials
types
uses.

IV. Cross-references.

The index contains numerous cross-references to direct the reader from variant spellings of a word or from similar terms. A term or name in LARGE AND SMALL CAPITAL LETTERS following *see*, *see also* or *see under* refers the reader to an index heading in the main alphabetical sequence. An arrow (→) indicates that the term is to be found under a subheading following the main entry; for example, for the cross-reference

Taj Mahal *see under* AGRA → tombs

the index entry is

Agra
tombs
Taj Mahal.

For the cross-reference

Florence
palazzi
Palazzo Bargello *see* museums → Museo Nazionale del Bargello

the index entry is

Florence
museums
Museo Nazionale del Bargello.

V. Appendices.

The index is followed by lists of non-Western dynasties and peoples; for further information on these, the reader should consult the main index entry for the dynastic or tribal name or the relevant culture, country or civilization entry.

Index

Numbers in **bold** refer to volume numbers, which are followed by specific page references. An asterisk (*) designates the main article (or sub-article) on that subject. Page numbers in *italics* refer to illustrations. A first-level illustration reference in a biographical entry (following the person's name rather than a subheading) indicates a portrait of the individual or a family tree. Colour plate references appear as large roman numerals after the appropriate volume number.

10+ group **31** 747
103 Grupo **21** 381
10th Street school **1** 78
12/15 **25** 434
1328, Master of **4** 274; **20** 695, 786–7*
 works **20** *696*
1346, Master of **20** 696
14, De **23** 226, 603
1402, Master of **20** 652
1419, Master of **16** 661; **20** 787–8*
 works **20** *787*
1446, Master of **10** 381
1456, Master of **20** 788*
1462, Master of *see* WEIBERMACHT, MASTER OF THE
1473, Master of **20** 788–9*
1482, Master of **3** 555; **19** 727
1499, Master of **3** 553; **10** 713; **20** 789*
14th Street school **21** 606
1500, Master of the Prayerbooks of *c. see* PRAYERBOOKS OF C. 1500, MASTER OF THE
1515, Master of (i) (Italian) **9** 308; **20** 789*
1515, Master of (ii) (Portuguese) **1** 213; **25** 295; **26** 252
1518, Master of *see* MERTENS, JAN (1470-1518)
1520s Hours Workshop **20** 789–90*
1527, Master of **1** 167
1540s, Master of the **20** 790*; **22** 924
1922 Group **12** 637
1930 Society *see* SENKYŪHYAKU SANJŪ KYŌKAI
2, Magister **28** 497
20 Artesanos Contemporáneos **6** 600
291 **8** 435; **24** 428, 432, 710; **29** 656; **31** 490
291 Gallery **29** 655, 656; **31** 490*
29 November, Cooperative of Handicraft Works **8** 862
2RC Editrice **20** 607
2 X 2 **17** 833
¡30-30! **1** 739; **21** 388; **26** 266
35mm *see under* CAMERAS → types; FILM → types
36 Artists **33** 487
391 **8** 435, 436; **18** 862; **24** 428, 710; **31** 490
3 Vergulden Astonnekens **22** 881
400-day clocks *see under* CLOCKS → types
41 **8** 437
43 Group **29** 461, 468; **33** 74
4D Company **11** 834
4F + R **19** 155
54 Group **1** 636
75 H.P. **26** 716
7 & 5 Society **10** 257; **14** 590; **23** 103; **28** 506*
 exhibitions **23** 103; **33** 744
 members **9** 9; **14** 401, 613; **17** 632; **22** 139; **23** 103; **24** 839; **33** 342
7 Arts **3** 399, 564, 587; **4** 577; **5** 44; **24** 439
8, De *see* ARCHITECTENGROEP DE 8
8 en Opbouw, de **2** 318; **14** 693; **21** 156; **24** 449
8 March Carpet Enterprise **1** 545
8th Street Club **17** 619
900 **16** 680

A

A, Painter **13** 511
Aa, Dirk van der **33** 262
Aa, Jan van der **2** 696
Aa, van der (family) **25** 810
A.A.A. *see* ALLIED ARTISTS' ASSOCIATION; AMERICAN ABSTRACT ARTISTS
A.A.A.-Anderson Galleries **24** 183
A.A.A. Gallery **24** 183
Aachen **1** 1–5*; **5** 792; **9** *507, 510*; **11** 653; **12** *361*, 379; **19** 709
 art forms and materials
  bronze **26** 685
  cupboards **12** 423
  enamel **13** 169
  furniture **12** 425
  gems **12** 255
  icons **19** 787
  ivory-carvings **5** 809
  manuscripts **1** 1*; **5** 800, 802; **11** 529; **30** 486
  metalwork **5** 805; **12** 452; **23** 656; **26** 683
  painting **12** 382
  pilgrim badges **12** 455; **24** 808, 809
  rock crystal **5** 811
  sculpture **12** 398
  silk **9** 664; **12** 464
 Cathedral *see* Palace → Palatine Chapel
 Couven-Museum **19** 779
 foundry **5** 806
 Gateway **5** 794
 Ludwig Forum für Internationale Kunst **17** 517
Aachen—cont.
 Ludwig-Stiftung für Kunst und Internationale Verständigung GmbH **19** 779
 Neue Galerie **1** 34
 Palace **1** 1–2*, *2*; **5** 794
  Palatine Chapel **1** 2–4*, *3*; **3** 541; **5** 794; **6** 459, 460; **7** 256, 382; **11** 507; **12** 363, 471; **26** 574
   ambo **25** 723
   capitals **1** 110
   chandeliers **6** 442; **26** 686
   dome **9** 84
   doors **4** 688; **9** 152; **23** 537, 658, 889
   gems **12** 255
   ivory-carvings **23** 660
   metalwork **5** 806; **8** 412; **13** 162
   mosaics **5** 799; **7** 275; **9** 569; **22** 165
   oliphants **16** 526
   orders (architecture) **23** 485
   pulpit **7** *825*, 826
   rock crystal **16** 541; **26** 485
   sceptres **26** 81
   sculpture **1** 4*; **5** 796; **13** 100, 214
   Shrine of Charlemagne **8** 261; **22** 44; **28** 630; **30** 467
   Shrine of the Virgin **22** 270; **28** 630, IV2
   situlae **28** 806
   throne **30** 779
Aachen
 Palace
  Palatine Chapel—cont.
   tomb of Charlemagne **7** 267; **22** 42, 43; **31** 121
   Treasury **1** 4–5*
   vaults **32** 88, 89
   wall paintings **5** 797; **23** 649
   westwork **5** 795; **33** 106–7
  Royal Hall **5** 794; **14** 73; **26** 575
   see also Rathaus
  Treasury *see under* PALATINE CHAPEL
  weathervane **33** 8
 Rathaus **12** 363, 394; **26** 255–6
 St Foillan **13** 117
 Suermondt-Ludwig-Museum **19** 779
Aachen, Hans von (1552-1615) **1** 5–7*; **8** 390; **22** 839; **25** 432
 groups and movements **26** 728
 patrons and collectors **5** 9; **12** 387; **13** 912, 914, 916; **29** 429; **32** 6
 pupils **16** 63
 reproductive prints by others **1** 663; **22** 272; **27** 502, 503
 works **1** *5, 6*; **12** 389, 494; **32** 730
Aachen, Johann von (*fl* 1540) **26** 407
Aachen Altar, Master of the **20** 611–12*, 802
 teachers **20** 692
 works **12** 384; **20** *611*, 692
Aachen Gospels *see under* GOSPEL BOOKS → individual manuscripts
Aachen Situla **28** 806
AACR *see* ANGLO-AMERICAN CATALOGING RULES
Aadnes, Peter **23** 225
Aagaard Andersen, Gunnar **1** 7*; **8** 736; **25** 26
Aaiuna
 Instituto de Enseñanza Media **33** 98
 Instituto de Villa Cosneros **33** 98
Aal **13** 143
Aalbers, A. F. **15** 770
à alentours tapestries *see under* TAPESTRIES → types
Aalesund **23** 221
Aalls, Niels **28** 348
Aalmis, J.
 works **30** *879*
Aalsmeer Church **22** 821
Aalto, (Hugo) Alvar (Henrik) **1** 7–11*; **11** 92, 104, 526; **31** 461
 architecture **4** 790; **11** 92, *93*; **14** 372
  civic centres **31** 243
  exhibition architecture **10** 684; **11** 88; **12** 380
  libraries **1** 125; **19** 320; **32** 746
  museums **22** 365
  pavilions (buildings) **1** *9*
  sanatoria **14** 783; **15** *886*
  sports centres **29** 427
  theatres **30** 684
  town halls **1** *10*
Aalto, (Hugo) Alvar (Henrik)
 architecture—cont.
  university buildings **4** 475; **31** 693; **33** 428
  villas **32** 556
 collaboration **19** 407; **23** 118
 furniture **6** 391; **8** 803, *803*; **11** 100, 104; **21** 363; **33** 331
 glass **11** 106
 groups and movements **11** 842; **15** 885, 886; **21** 783; **23** 498
 patrons and collectors **28** 548
 pupils **13** 842
 staff **10** 492; **14** 613; **18** 237; **26** 260; **31** 776
 teachers **19** 408
Aaltonen, Matti **31** 461
Aaltonen, Wäinö (Waldemar) **1** 11–12*
 pupils **31** 885
 teachers **33** 96
 works **11** 100, 106
Aaltonen, Wäinö, Museum *see under* TURKU
AAM **24** 439
Aanensen (family) **14** 483
A-ane-pada, King of Ur **31** 508
Aarau **30** *124*, 135, 143
Aarau Gradual *see under* GRADUALS → individual manuscripts
Aardenburg, St Bavo **22** 819
Aarlen **3** 566
Aarnio, Eero **6** 392; **11** 104
AARON **7** 680

Aaron, Michel **5** 878
Aarschot, Dukes of *see* CHIMAY, Princes of
Aarschot, Onze Lieve Vrouw **7** 703; **13** 100
Aarts, Johannes Josephus **1** 12*
Aarts, Joseph **22** 746
A(tomic) A(bsorption) S(pectrometry) *see under* TECHNICAL EXAMINATION → types
Aas, Nils (Sigurd) **1** 12–13*; **23** 231
Aasen, Knut **23** 602
Aasland, Sverre **18** 390; **23** 222
A(rt and) A(rchitecture) T(hesaurus) **1** 13*; **4** 25; **6** 78
Abacco, Antonio *see* LABACCO, ANTONIO
abaci (capitals) **1** 13*; **22** 213, *213*; **23** 482
  Corinthian **23** 478, 479, 482
  Doric **13** *378*; **23** 478
  Early Gothic **22** 218
  Ionic **13** *393*; **23** 478
  Late Gothic **22** 220, 222
  Romanesque **22** 216
abaci (counting frames) **17** 399
Abada, Tell
  houses **14** 128; **21** 270, *280*, 281
  iron **21** 270
Abadan Museum **12** 834
Abadel (family) **33** 358
Abadía **4** 566
Abadie, Paul, the elder (1783-1868) **1** 13
Abadie, Paul, the younger (1812-84) **1** 13–14*; **2** 727; **20** 523
  groups and movements **26** 704
  works **2** 89, 320, *321*; **7** 258
Abadiya **10** 59
Abahuda, Speos of Horemheb **9** 833; **23** 280
Abaj Takalik **1** 14–15*; **13** *758*; **20** *882*
  sculpture **16** 806; **20** 885; **23** 416
  Stele 3 **29** 620
  Stele 5 **29** 620
Abak **15** 61
Abakanowicz, Magdalena **1** 15*; **25** 116, 133
  works **10** 875; **11** 54; **30** 329, *330*
Abakelia, T. **12** 322
Abakuás **8** 231
Abakwariga **17** 680
abalone shells *see under* SHELLS → types
Abaneri **1** 15–16*; **15** *279*
  Harshatmata Temple **15** 270, 487, *487*
Abano, Pietro d' *see* PIETRO D'ABANO
Aba-Novák, Vilmos **1** 16*
  collaboration **2** 416
  groups and movements **14** 901; **30** 211
  pupils **3** 110
Abaqa, Khan (*reg* 1265-82) (Ilkhanid) **16** 193; **30** 262
Abaquesne, Masséot **9** 387; **11** 604; **22** 31; **24** 148; **30** 885
Abarca, Agustín **6** 597; **13** 9
Abarca de Bolea, Buenaventura de Urrea, 9th Conde de Aranda *see* ARANDA, BUENAVENTURA DE URREA ABARCA DE BOLEA, 9th Conde de
Abarca de Bolea, Pedro Pablo, 10th Conde de Aranda *see* ARANDA, 10th Conde de
Abargar *see* KALA-I MUG
Abarquh **1** 16*; **16** *105*
  Gunbad-i 'Ali **16** 160; **22** 321; **31** 112, *112*
  muqarnas (architecture) **16** 161
  portals **16** 194
Abarshahr *see* NISHAPUR
Abart, Franz **15** 144
Abárzuza **29** 335
Abas, Felipe **13** 245, 252
Abascal, Valentín **12** 53
Abashevo culture **28** 321
abata **13** 417
Abatan Odefunke Ayinke Ija **1** 329
Abate, Alberto **16** 683
Abate, Giovanni dell' **1** 17
Abate, Giulio Camillo dell' **1** 19; **20** 674
Abate, Nicolò dell' **1** 17–19*; **11** 260, 532, 656; **15** 137
  attributions **3** 487; **10** 525; **11** 265
  collaboration **11** 260, 572; **25** 580
  groups and movements **11** 262, 263, 266
  interior decoration **22** 413; **24** 133
  paintings
    frescoes **1** *17*; **4** 276; **6** 506; **10** 130
    genre **12** 288
    landscape **1** *18*; **16** 667; **18** 708
  patrons and collectors **24** 330; **31** 850
  reproductive prints by others **30** 787
  tapestries **11** 639
Abati, Pietro degli **19** 673
Abayi Philippe **3** 728
Abbadie, Antoine d' **9** 464
'Abbas I, Shah (*reg* 1588-1629) (Safavid) **1** *92*; **7** 155; **15** *586*; **16** 76; **27** 514*
  architecture **2** 377; **5** 722; **16** 78, 79, 230–31, *231*; **17** 830; **20** 105, 548; **25** 830
  carpets **2** 438; **16** 475, 479; **27** 513
  collections **28** 635
  furniture **30** 784
  gardens **12** 82
  jade **16** 528
  manuscripts **16** 338, 339, 545, 552, *552*; **22** 264; **26** 434; **27** 506
  paintings **28** 568
  porcelain **2** 377; **16** 424
  pottery **4** 172; **16** 424; **27** 513
  regalia **16** 538
  textiles **16** 449
  urban planning **16** 231, 265; **27** 512
  wall paintings **16** 253
'Abbas II, Shah (*reg* 1642-66)(Safavid) **16** 254
  architecture **16** 80, 231; **20** 548
  manuscripts **16** 339
  painters **2** 29
  paintings **16** 535; **28** 566
'Abbas I, Pasha (*reg* 1848-54) (Muhammad 'Ali's Line) **5** 399; **10** 90, 92; **23** 816
'Abbasi, Shaykh *see* SHAYKH 'ABBASI
Abbasid **1** 19–20*; **3** 51; **16** 111
  architecture **5** 722
  banners **11** 146
  palaces **23** 814, 815
  silk **28** 716
  thrones **30** 784
  see also:
    AL-AMIN, Caliph
    AL-MAHDI, Caliph
    AL-MA'MUN, Caliph
    AL-MANSUR, Caliph
    AL-MUNTASIR, Caliph
    AL-MUQTADIR, Caliph
    AL-MUSTANSIR, Caliph
    AL-MUSTA'SIM, Caliph
    AL-MU'TASIM, Caliph
    AL-MUTAWAKKIL, Caliph
    AL-MUTI, Caliph
    AL-NASIR, Caliph
    AL-WATHIQ, Caliph
    AL-ZAHIR, Caliph
    HARUN AL-RASHID, Caliph
    'ISA IBN MUSA
Abbasid scripts *see under* SCRIPTS → types
'Abbas II, Khedive (*reg* 1892-1914) (Muhammad 'Ali's Line) **16** 389
Abbasiyya **23** 815
'Abbas Mirza (Qajar) **22** 261
Abbati, Giuseppe **2** 106; **16** 678; **19** 870, 871; **20** 482; **28** 705
Abbatini, Guido Ubaldo **1** 20–21*; **3** 834
  works **3** 832; **16** *764*; **26** 810
Abbatt, Marjorie **31** 255
Abbatt, Paul **31** 255
Abbatt Toys **14** 571
Abbaye de Créteil **1** 21*, 650; **8** 243; **12** 805; **20** 385; **25** 747; **26** 558
Abbe, James (Edward) **1** 21–2*
Abbeloos, Daniel
  works **3** *608*
Abbeme, Louise **10** 782
Abbenante, Francesco **28** 388
Abbeville **11** 652
  Bagatelle **6** 508
  St Wulfram **11** 511
Abbeville, Bernard d', Bishop of Amiens *see* BERNARD D'ABBEVILLE, Bishop of Amiens
Abbeville Books **1** 71
Abbey, Edward Austin **1** 22–3*
  groups and movements **27** 557
  works **1** *22*; **4** 364, 477; **20** 18; **22** 335
Abbey, John Roland **1** 23*; **20** 631
Abbey, The **18** 64
Abbey Dore (Hereford & Worcs) **7** 353
  chapter house **6** 465
  Holy Trinity and St Mary **1** 768; **28** 294
Abbey Folk Park **29** 516
Abbey of Dilighem, Master of the **20** 612*
abbeys *see* MONASTERIES
Abbey St Bathans (Borders), Tomb of the Prioress **28** 241
Abbia Cinema **5** 523
Abbiati, Filippo **4** 427; **5** 290; **20** 95; **21** 527
Abbondi, Antonio *see* SCARPAGNINO, ANTONIO
Abbot, Ann **31** 266
Abbot, Jonathas **4** 725, 726
Abbot, R. Atkinson **2** 705
Abbotsford (Borders) **5** 169; **10** 298; **26** 85; **28** 248, *286*, 287, 288
  collections **9** 31
  furniture **4** 806
Abbott, Berenice **1** 23–4*; **2** 663; **12** 215; **24** 674
Abbott, George **8** 82
Abbott, Henry **10** 94
Abbott, John White **1** 24*; **31** 233
Abbott, Lemuel Francis **1** 24*; **13** 615; **20** 477
Abbottabad **15** 712
Abbot Walther Bible *see under* BIBLES → individual manuscripts
Abboud, Chafic **19** 8
ABC: Beiträge zum Bauen **7** 293; **27** 214; **28** 122; **29** 531; **30** 128
Abd, Tell al- *see* UBAID, TELL AL-
'Abd al-'Aziz, Khan (*reg* 1540-52) (Shaybanid) **5** 138; **6** 236; **15** 681; **16** 334, 342–3; **20** 109; **21** 722; **28** 566; **31** 702
'Abd al-'Aziz II, King (*reg* 1902-53) (Saudi) **27** 876
'Abd al-'Aziz, Sultan *see* ABDÜLAZIZ, Sultan
'Abd al-'Aziz al-Irbili **29** 553
'Abd al-'Aziz ibn Marwan **5** 395
'Abd al-'Aziz ibn Sharaf al-Din Tabrizi **6** 246
'Abd al-Halim, Halim **16** 243
  works **16** *242*
'Abd al-Hamid II, Sultan *see* ABDÜLHAMID II, Sultan
'Abd al-Hamid Lahauri **1** 461, 462
'Abd al-Haq Shirazi *see* AMANAT KHAN
'Abd al-Hayy **1** 24–5*; **15** 681; **16** 286, 318, 876
  attributions **16** 320; **17** 688
  works **16** 314
'Abd al-Hayy 'Ali
  works **16** *353*
'Abd al-Husayn **15** 899; **16** 534
'Abd al-Jabbar ibn 'Ali **16** 307
'Abd al-Jalil Čelebi *see* LEVNI
'Abd al-Karim (*fl* 1236) **2** 648
'Abd al-Karim (*fl* 1460s-90s) **16** 286
'Abd al-Karim Ma'mur Khan **15** 363, 365, 372
'Abdallah (*fl* 1412-31; calligrapher) **16** 864
'Abdallah (*fl* 1417-33; architect in Uzbekistan) **6** 203
Abdallah (*fl* 1479; architect in Spain) **18** 681
'Abd Allah, Amir (*reg* 888-912) (Umayyad) **7** 843
'Abdallah, Caliph (*reg* 1885-98) **23** 290; **29** 895
'Abdallah, Sultan (*reg* 1557-74)(Sa'di) **11** 49; **27** 506
'Abdallah, Sultan (*reg* 1729-57) ('Alawi) **16** 240
'Abdallah II, Khan (*reg* 1583-98) (Shaybanid) **6** 204; **16** 235, 236, *237*, 238
'Abdallah Ahmad **16** 497
'Abdallah al-Shirazi **16** 335
Abdallah Bayani **16** 285
Abdallah de Medina **7** 492
'Abdallah ibn al-Fadl **16** 309
'Abdallah ibn al-Rabi' **16** 523
'Abdallah ibn Mahmud al-Naqqash **16** 497
'Abdallah Jin **16** 238
'Abdallah Khan **1** 25*; **16** 343
  works **16** 535; **22** 260; **25** 770; **30** 415
'Abd Allah Muzahhib
  works **18** *70*
'Abdallah Sayrafi **1** 25*; **14** 260; **16** 284, 349
'Abdallah Shirazi **15** 578
'Abdallah Tabbakh **16** 285, 864
'Abdallah Zakhir **16** 360
Abdalla Nirqi, North Church **23** 287
'Abd al-Latif **15** 899; **16** 534
'Abd al-Latif, Sultan *see* 'ABD AL-'AZIZ, Khan
'Abd al-Latif 'Abbasi **15** 681
'Abd al-Latif Kanu **3** 69
'Abd al-Latif Mufiz **3** 69
'Abd al-Majid ibn Mas'ud **2** 892; **20** 401
'Abd al-Majid Taliqani **16** 287
'Abd-al-Malik, Caliph (*reg* 685-715) (Umayyad)
  coins **21** *505*
  dress **16** 455
  mosques **16** 146, 255; **17** 495, 496; **21** 505
  sculpture **16** 246; **23** 562
'Abd al-Malik al-Tha'alibi
  works **16** *361*
'Abd al-Mu'min, Khan (*reg* 1598) (Shaybanid) **16** 236, 237
'Abd al-Mu'min ibn Muhammad al-Khuvayyi **16** 329
'Abd al-Rahim **8** 542, *543*; **16** 286, 345
'Abd al-Rahim ibn 'Abdallah al-Rashidi **16** 374
'Abd al-Rahim Khan-i Khanan **15** 373, 593–5*; **16** 345; **20** 49
'Abd al-Rahman, King (*reg* 1880-1901) (Barakzay) **17** 717
'Abd al-Rahman I, Amir (*reg* 756-88) (Umayyad) **7** 843, 845; **20** 156; **22** 193; **29** 262; **31** 573
'Abd al-Rahman II, Amir (*reg* 822-52) (Umayyad) **7** 843, 844, 845; **16** 157, 158; **28** 510
'Abd al-Rahman III al-Nasir, Caliph (*reg* 912-61) (Umayyad) **31** 573*
  architecture **7** 843
    fortifications **28** 518
    minarets **21** 626
    mosques **7** 845; **16** 188
    palaces **16** 187; **20** 49; **29** 262
  interior decoration **29** 297
  sculpture **16** 246
  wall paintings **16** 253
'Abd al-Rahman al-Sufi *see* AL-SUFI
'Abd al-Rahman ibn Zayyan **16** 525
'Abd al-Rahman Katkhuda **5** 399
'Abd al-Rahman Khwarazmi **16** 286
'Abd al-Raji *see* JAVAD AL-IMAMI
'Abd al-Rashid, Sultan (1050-3) (Ghaznavid) **1** 208; **12** 513; **16** 292
'Abd al-Rashid Dailami **15** 681
'Abd al-Rasul, Aḥmad **10** 91
'Abd al-Rasul, Muhammad **10** 91
'Abd al-Razzaq Samarqandi **16** 196
'Abd al-Samad **1** 25–7*; **15** 579, 681; **16** 344; **22** 262
  patrons and collectors **16** 344
  pupils **8** 534
  works **1** *26*; **15** 578, *579*, 583; **21** 723
'Abd al-Vahid **16** 424
Abdar Rahman al-Zainal **31** 584
Abdel Moneim Abu Bakr **14** 462
Abdera **13** 420, 586, 587
Abderrahman **24** 280
'Abdin Bey **5** 398
Abdinghof Monastery **26** 683
Abdon and Sennon, Master of **5** 550
Abdülaziz, Sultan (*reg* 1861-76) (Ottoman) **16** 227, 586; **23** 638, 644*
Abdul Aziz bin Muhammad al-Khalifa **3** 69
Abdul Aziz Farman Farmaian and Associates **2** 378
Abdülcelil Çelebi *see* LEVNI
Abdul Elah al-Arab **3** 69
Abdul Fatah, Sultan of Banten (*reg* 1651-82) **15** 805
Abdul Ghani al-Ani **14** 217
Abdülhamid I, Sultan (*reg* 1774-89) (Ottoman) **32** 879
Abdülhamid II, Sultan (*reg* 1876-1909) (Ottoman) **8** 532; **16** 227; **22** 250
Abdul Hosein **15** 903
Abdul Karim (*fl c.* 1630-50) **15** 640
Abdulkarim (*fl* 1830-40) **23** 824
Abdulkarim, Salah **27** 876
Abdul Karim Orayid **3** 69
Abdulla **5** 320
Abdulla, Mohammed Ahmed **29** 897
'Abdullah (*fl* 1540s) **16** 343; **28** 568
Abdullah (*b* 1915) **15** 808
Abdullah, Basuki **15** 818
Abdullah, Fatima Shaaban **30** 301
Abdullah, Jalal ben **31** 426
Abdullah, Jamal **1** 317
Abdullah al-Jaber al-Sabah, Shaykh (*reg* 1815-36) (al-Sabah) **18** 541
Abdullah al-Muharraqi **3** 69
Abdullah Ariff **20** 172
Abdullah brothers **16** 591
'Abdullah Buhari **16** 350
Abdullahi Bayero, Emir **17** 778
'Abdullah ibn 'Ali al-Mail **25** 776
Abdullah of Amasya **16** 285

'Abdullah Qutb Shah, Ruler (*reg* 1626-72) (Qutb Shahi) **15** 48
Abdullah Zühdü **22** 385
Abdulla Nirqui Cathedral **7** 280
Abdul Latif Mohidin **20** 171, 172
Abdullayev, Abdulkhak **31** 783
Abdullayev, G. G. **2** 895
Abdullayev, Lutfulla **31** 783
Abdullayev, M. G. **2** 896, 897
Abdullayev, Sagdulla (Asadullayevich) **31** 783
Abdullayeva, G. A. **2** 898
Abdul Malik, Fu'ad **9** 766
Abdülmecid, Prince (1868-44) (Ottoman) **2** 634; **16** 537
Abdülmecid I, Sultan (*reg* 1839-61) (Ottoman)
  architecture **11** 329; **16** 227, 595, 611; **17** 491; **21** 33
  paintings **1** 750
Abdülmennan Ağa, Sinan *see* SINAN (ii)
Abdul Qadir al-Rayis **31** 584
Abdulrahim **2** 900
Abdurakhmanov, F. G. **2** 895; **12** 37
Abdurakhmanov, N. G. **2** 896
Abdurashidov, Shukhrat **31** 783
AB Durotapet **32** 817
Abdur Qadir Badaoni **15** 691
Abdur Rahim **31** 152
Abdusametov, Dot **30** 253
Abdus Ṣamad *see* 'ABD AL-SAMAD
Abe (Côte d'Ivoire) **8** 22
Abe (family) **14** 565
Abe, Eishirō **17** 359, 406; **21** 634, 635
Abe, Fusajirō **17** 429
Abe, Shuya **23** 777
Abebe, Bekele **10** 577
Abéché **1** *394*
  Museum **6** 382
à bec towers *see under* TOWERS → types
Abedin, Zainul **1** 27*
  patrons and collectors **3** 170
  works **3** 168, *168*; **23** 799
Abeele, Albijn Van den *see* VAN DEN ABEELE, ALBIJN
Abeele, Pieter van **1** 27*; **20** 923
Abegg **16** 753
Abegg Painter **17** 911
Abeille, Joseph **3** 822; **12** 276; **30** 127
Abei Rekidō **17** 413
Abe Kenshū **17** 413
Abel, Adolf **27** 315; **29** 874
Abel, Alexandre-Denis *see* ABEL DE PUJOL, ALEXANDRE (1785-1861)
Abel, Carl Friedrich **1** 125
Abel, David **17** 402
Abel, Florian **2** 800; **7** 554
  works **2** *800*
Abel, Josef **1** 27-8*; **8** 372
Abela, Eduardo **1** 28*; **8** 233
Abela, Giovanni Francesco **20** 219
Abelam **23** 713; **24** 66, 67, 68, 69, 70, 72
  sculpture **24** *71*
Abelardo **27** 750
Abel de Pujol, Alexandre (1785-1861) **1** 28*
  collaboration **8** 40; **21** 412
  pupils **6** 514; **8** 598; **13** 828; **19** 282; **27** 142
Abel de Pujol, Alexandre (1816-84) **1** 28
Abelen, Peter **14** 48; **25** 838; **29** 869
Abella, Francisco Alvarado *see* ALVARADO ABELLA, FRANCISCO
Abella, Josep Serra i *see* SERRA I ABELLA, JOSEP
Abels, Jacob **23** 590
Abemayor (family) **10** 91
Abemayor, Michel **10** 91
Aben, Ben **1** 636
Abengourou **1** *386*; **8** 23
Abe no Uchimaro **23** 596
Abeokuta **1** 251, 319, 349; **23** *129*; **33** 559
Aber, Ita **17** 580
Aberaeron (Dyfed) **32** 782
Aberconway, Henry Duncan McLaren, 2nd Baron *see* MCLAREN, HENRY DUNCAN, 2nd Baron Aberconway
Abercorn, James Hamilton, 1st Duke of *see* HAMILTON, JAMES, 1st Duke of Abercorn
Abercorn, James Hamilton, 8th Earl of *see* HAMILTON, JAMES, 8th Earl of Abercorn
Abercrombie, Lascelles **1** 29
Abercrombie, (Leslie) Patrick **1** 29*; **26** 460
  collaboration **1** 163; **14** 686
  works **12** 229; **19** 577; **31** 731, *732*
Aberdeen (Grampian) **1** 29-30*, *30*; **28** *222*, 273
  Art Gallery **1** 30; **28** 273
    James McBey Art Reference Library **28** 275
  Arts Centre **28** 229
  art schools **28** 274
  Assembly Rooms **2** 617; **28** 228
  Brig o' Balgownie **4** 801
  churches **9** 681
  craftsmen and artists **28** 250
  Gray's School of Art **28** 275
  King's College Chapel **28** 224, 250
  North Church *see* Arts Centre
  pottery **28** 258
  prints **28** 239
  Robert Gordon University **28** 232
  St Nicholas **28** 250
  Town Hall **28** 288
  Town House **28** 228, *229*
  Trinity Hall **28** 251
  University **7** 566
  urban planning **28** 229
Aberdeen, George Gordon, 4th Earl of *see* GORDON, GEORGE, 4th Earl of Aberdeen
Aberdeen, Ishbel Maria Gordon, Countess of *see* GORDON, ISHBEL MARIA, Countess of Aberdeen
Aberfeldy Bridge (Tayside) **4** 804
Åberg, Johan **11** 103
  works **11** *103*
Abergavenny (Gwent)
  St Mary's **32** 786
  town walls **31** 710
Abergen, Antonis van *see* OBBERGHEN, ANTONIS VAN
Aberlady Cross (Lothian) **2** 69
Aberlemno **24** 737
Aberlenc, René **27** 307
Aberli, Johann Ludwig **1** 31*; **3** 823; **30** 133
  assistants **13** 871
  collaboration **4** 84
  pupils **13** 663; **33** 13
  works **20** 914
Aberli style *see under* ENGRAVINGS → types; ETCHINGS → types
Abernethy (Tayside) **26** 591
Abe Ryōzan **17** 413
Aberystwyth (Dyfed) **32** *780*
  Castle **21** 564
  Castle House **32** 783
  National Library of Wales **32** 791
  University of Wales **32** 791
Abeysinghe, Stanley **29** 468
Abgar V, King of Edessa (*reg* 4 BC-AD 50) **20** 251
Abha **27** 875
Abhai Singh, Maharaja of Marwar (*reg* 1724-49) (Rajput) **15** 614
Abhānagari *see* ABANERI
Abhayakaragupta **15** 221, 224
Abhira *see* NIPA
'Abid **1** 31*; **2** 235; **15** 589
  works **15** 588, 589; **16** 345
Abidin, Zainal Mik **20** 172
  works **16** *288*
Abidjan **1** *386*, 427
  Institut National des Arts **8** 23
  Musée National **8** 23
Abildgaard, Nicolai Abraham **1** 31-4*; **7** 805; **8** 734, 760
  house **8** 728
  pupils **5** 885; **9** 700; **11** 779; **27** 338; **30** 763
  reproductive prints by others **7** 410
  works **1** *32*, *33*; **8** 745-6, *746*; **30** 763
Abingdon (Oxon)
  Abbey **2** 66, 75
  Town Hall **24** *804*; **31** 239
Abingdon, Alexander of *see* ALEXANDER OF ABINGDON
Abingdon Sword **33** 89
Abinger Castle (Surrey) **6** 53; **21** 562
Abiriba **15** 111, 114
Abiseo *see* GRAN PAJATÉN
Abkan culture **23** 277
Abkhazeti **12** 316
ablaq masonry *see under* MASONRY → types
Ableitner, Balthasar **22** 302; **25** 672; **33** 276, 296
Ablin, Yevgeny (Moiseyevich) **27** 425
Abnakee (rugs) **27** 317
Abnaki (people) **22** 552
Abney Hall (Ches) **10** 281
abnormal hieratic script *see under* SCRIPTS → types
Åbo *see* TURKU
Aboba *see* PLISKA
Aboleda, Carlos **23** 905
Abolikhin, Konstantin **27** 431
Āboliņš, Valdis **1** 34*
Ābols, Ojārs
Abomey *see* AGBOME
Abondance Abbey **7** 456
Abondio, Alessandro **1** 34, 36*
  patrons and collectors **13** 911
  teachers **1** 35
  works **25** 22
Abondio, Antonio **1** 34, 35*; **16** 749; **20** 920
  pupils **20** 190
  works **1** *35*; **12** 260; **13** *911*; **25** 22; **28** 666; **33** 3
Abonuteichos **27** 1
Aboriginal Arts Board **20** 419
Aboriginal Australia **1** 36-68*, *37*; **25** 481
  anthropology **2** 137
  architecture **1** 49-50*
  axes **1** 37
  bags **1** 52
  bark **1** 49, 50, 52
  baskets **1** 52; **3** 331, 332
  batik **1** 64
  body arts **1** 45-7*, *46*, 57, 59, *60*
  body ornaments **1** 52-3*
  bone **4** 314
  boomerangs **1** 54
  ceramics **1** 44
  cicatrices **1** 45
  cloaks **1** 56*
  clubs (weapons) **1** 55
  collections **1** 66*; **33** 534
  containers **1** 52
  craftsmen and artists **1** 38-9*
  dating methods **1** 40
  domes **1** 49-50
  erotic art **10** 474
  exhibitions **1** 67*
  feathers **1** 53
  headdresses **1** 53
  historiography **1** 67-8*
  linocuts **1** *65*
  logs **1** 48-9
  masks **1** 44, 61
  museums **1** 66-7*
Aboriginal Australia—cont.
  necklaces **1** 53
  painting **1** 60-61, 63-4*; **2** 752; **3** 331
    acrylic **1** *63*, 63-4, *64*
    bark **1** 50-51*, *51*, 58, *59*, 59-60, 61, 63; **10** 474
  pandanus **1** 52
  pendants (jewellery) **1** 52
  pigments **1** 39, 50
  pipes (musical) **1** 53*
  pipes (smoking) **1** 53
  posts **1** *47*, 47-8
  pottery **1** 64
  reeds **1** 53
  regions **1** 54-5*
    Cape York Peninsula **1** 61-2*, *62*
    Central Australia **1** 56-7*
    Eastern Arnhem Land **1** *60*, 60-61*
    Kimberleys **1** 57-8*
    South-east Australia **1** 55-6*
    Western Arnhem Land **1** 58-60*, *59*
  religion **1** 37-8*
  representation **1** 38*
  rock art **1** 40-42*; **10** 474; **25** 822
    Bradshaw figures **1** 57
    engraving **1** 40; **22** 229
    painting **1** 38, *41*, 41, *42*, *57*, 57-9, 61; **19** 368-9; **31** 133, 511, *511*; **32** 802, *803*
    stencilling **29** 627
  sand **1** 44-5*, *45*
  sand drawings **1** 56
  sculpture **1** 42-5*, *45*, *62*
  seeds **1** 53
  shells **1** 52
  shelters **1** 49, *49*
  shields **1** 54, *55*, 56
  skins **1** 56*
  spears **1** 53-4
  string **1** 52
  swords **1** 54
  textiles **1** 64; **2** 768
  tree-carvings **1** 56*
  weapons **1** 53-4*, *54*, 55-6*
  wood **1** *55*
  wood-carvings **1** 42-3*, *43*, *44*, 52, *53*, *55*, 56, *62*
  see also AUSTRALIA; TASMANIA
abosomfie *see* SHRINES (i) (CULT)
About, Edmond (François Valentin) **1** 69*
Abovyan, Khatchatur **2** 444
Abovyan, Ruben **2** 433
Abqayq **2** 267
Abraham, Jakob **12** 263
Abraham, Master **25** 110; **26** 684
Abraham, Philipp **12** 263
Abraham, Pol **1** 69-70*; **20** 584; **24** 826
Abraham, Robert **1** 733, 734
Abraham ben Judah ibn Hayyim **1** 70*; **17** 661; **20** 325
Abraham ben Yom Tov ha-Kohen **17** 564
Abraham Conat **17** 565
Abraham ibn Ezra **2** 650
Abraham of Kütahya **16** 420, 421
Abraham of Kütahya ware *see under* POTTERY → wares
Abrahams, Carl (*b* 1913) **1** 70*; **16** 884
Abrahams, Charles (1816-85) **2** 752
Abrahams, Ivor **23** 782
Abrahamstrup *see* JÆGERSPRIS
Abramo, Lívio **1** 70*; **24** 102
  pupils **4** 141; **17** 585
  works **24** 98
Abramov, Ayala Zacks *see* ZACKS ABRAMOV, AYALA
Abramović, Marina **24** 408; **28** 452
Abramovitz, Max **14** 199-200
Abrams, Harry N(athan) **1** 70-71*
Abra(ha)mson, Abraham **12** 263
Abramtsevo **1** 71-2*; **20** 232; **22** 178; **27** 408, 438
  architecture **32** 73
  members **6** 529; **18** 389; **20** 222; **25** 145, 146; **26** 218; **33** 487
  Museum-Estate **1** *71*, 72
  pottery **27** 410
  stage design **19** 276
  wood-carvings **27** 442
Abrantes, Marquês de Fontes e *see* FONTES E ABRANTES, Marquês de
Abraq, Tell **2** *246*
  jewellery **2** 264
  pottery **2** 266, *267*, 267
  seals **2** 271
  stone vessels **2** 271
abrasives
  materials
    agate **7** 11
    carborundum **7** 11; **29** 706
    diamonds **16** 859; **29** 706
    emery **12** 786; **16** 859; **21** 241; **29** 706
    flint **16** 859
    garnets **7** 11; **16** 859
    haematite **16** 859
    jadeite **21** 241
    loess **16** 859
    pumice **29** 706
    pyrite **16** 859
    quartz **7** 11; **16** 859
    quartz sand **21** 241
    sand **1** 761; **29** 706
    sandstone **1** 761; **16** 859
    slate **16** 859
    tungsten **29** 706
  uses
    amber **1** 761
    conservation **6** 334
    glass **12** 786
    hardstones **14** 168; **21** 241
    jade **7** 11; **16** 859
    stone **29** 706*
Abreha Atsbehj Church **1** 315
Abreu, José Francisco de **1** 72*; **32** 540
Abreu, Mario (*b* 1919) **1** 72*
Abreu, Mário de (*fl* 1939) **4** 658
Abreu do Ó, Manuel **1** 72*
Abreu do Ó, Sebastião **1** 72*
Abri Blanchard **25** 476, 485, 493
Abri Bourdois *see under* ANGLES-SUR-L'ANGLIN
Abricci, Gianni **1** 578
Abri Pataud **25** 485
Abritus *see* RAZGRAD
Abrosimov, P. V. **11** 244
ABS **25** 26
Absalon, Bishop **7** 802; **8** 723
absidiole *see under* CHAPELS → types
Absolon, John (1815-95) **1** 73
Absolon, John de Mansfield (*c.* 1843-79) **1** 73*
Absolon, Karel **9** 80; **25** 467
absolute schilderkunst **3** 704
Abstract American Artists (AAA) **20** 568
Abstract art **1** 73-81*; **2** 488; **7** 630, 698; **15** 829; **21** 341, 892; **28** 201; **30** 170
  art forms
    drawings **9** *758*
    painting **8** *635*; **26** 221, 224; **29** 670
      Australia **2** *751*; **17** 618; **20** 140; **32** 770
      Bolivia **4** 263
      Canada **19** 878
      Denmark **19** 799
      England **10** 258; **24** *229*
      Finland **11** *97*
      France **1** *74*; **8** *657*; **9** *334*; **12** *806*; **14** *206*; **20** *816*, *827*, *831*; **25** *148*; **29** 95; **30** 231; **32** *577*; **33** *305*

Abstract art
art forms
painting—cont.
Germany **10** 694; **14** 694; **17** *763*, *765*, *767*; **22** *379*, *701*
Japan **18** 55
Jordan **9** 452
Mexico **10** 866
Netherlands, the **21** 775; **22** *853*
New Zealand **23** 60
Paraguay **24** 99
Russia **12** 894, *895*
Switzerland **1** *77*; **12** 563; **18** *112*; **32** VIII2
United States of America **1** *549*; **2** *857*; **8** *871*; **9** 202; **17** *892*; **21** *856*; **25** 360; **26** *126*; **29** 670; **31** *605*
prints **27** 392
sculpture
Australia **2** *754*
Austria **2** 804
Belgium **3** *574*
Bolivia **4** *265*
England **5** *790*
Japan **17** 136–7
Norway **14** 229; **23** 231
Spain **23** *629*
Switzerland **30** 138–9
United States of America **1** *80*; **23** *29*
collections **26** 58
exhibitions **33** 744
regional traditions
Denmark **4** 62
Germany **10** 696; **33** 635
Iceland **1** 468
Russia **20** 192
Spain **21** 705
United States of America **31** 605
Uruguay **30** 275
Abstract Expressionism **1** 78, 83–8*, 131; **4** 75; **7** 636; **10** 258; **13** 616, 801; **18** 718; **21** 776; **25** 584; **31** 607
catalogues **6** 80
collections **16** 820; **21** 135; **23** 7; **28** 314; **31** 665, 667
dealers **16** 906
exhibitions **21** 606
historiography **31** 672
members
Baziotes, William **3** 436
De Kooning, Willem **8** 633
Frankenthaler, Helen **11** 729
Goodnough, Robert **13** 1
Gottlieb, Adolph **13** 214
Held, Al **14** 326
Hofmann, Hans (Georg Albert) (1880-1966) **14** 633
Kline, Franz (Rowe) **18** 132
Marca-Relli, Conrad **20** 384
Motherwell, Robert **22** 205
Newman, Barnett **23** 27
Pousette-Dart, Richard **25** 384
Rodríguez Larraín, Emilio **24** 510
Rothko, Mark **27** 219
Still, Clyfford **29** 663
Thieler, Fred **30** 731
Tomlin, Bradley Walker **31** 138
paintings **1** *86*, *87*; **8** *634*; **11** *730*; **13** *215*; **14** *633*; **18** *133*; **22** *206*; **23** *29*; **27** *220*, *221*; **29** *663*
see also PAINTING → types → colour field
Abstract Group **14** 902; **20** 518
abstraction **1** 88–9*; **2** 543; **10** 137
abstraction, geometric **1** 79; **14** 164
Brazil **4** 719
France **1** 89; **8** 246; **18** 526
Iceland **24** 572
Portugal **18** 746
Abstraction, Lyrical **1** 77; **2** 543, 544; **20** 815; **30** 231; **33** 620
Abstraction-Création **1** *89*, 89–90*; **2** 490; **7** 772; **8** 659, 697; **11** 550, 569; **20** 97; **21** *854*; **24** 144; **25** 447, *447*; **30** 135, 234
members **1** 76; **6** 342; **21** 855
Buchheister, Carl **5** 75
Calder, Alexander **5** 423
Doesburg, Theo van **9** 64
Erni, Hans **10** 465
Fernandez, Louis **10** 904
Foltýn, František **8** 393
Fontana, Lucio **11** 281
Freundlich, Otto **11** 768
Gabo, Naum **11** 877
Glarner, Fritz **12** 771
Gleizes, Albert **12** 807
Gorin, (Albert) Jean **13** 10
Hélion, Jean **14** 329
Hepworth, Barbara **14** 401
Herbin, Auguste **14** 437
Kobro, Katarzyna **18** 181
Kupka, František **18** 526
Licini, Osvaldo **19** 330
Martyn, Ferenc **20** 518
Nicholson, Ben **23** 103
Okamoto, Tarō **23** 385
Paalen, Wolfgang **23** 697
Pevsner, Antoine **24** 574
Reth, Alfred (1884-1966) **26** 255
Sartoris, Alberto **27** 853
Schwitters, Kurt (Herman Edward Karl Julius) **28** 198
Seligmann, Kurt **28** 385
Soldati, (Anton) Atanasio **29** 31
Stażewski, Henryk **29** 582
Täuber-Arp, Sophie **30** 234
Valmier, Georges **31** 832
Vantongerloo, Georges **31** 890
Veronesi, Luigi **32** 358
Vézelay, Paule **32** 395
Villon, Jacques **32** 577
Vordemberge-Gildewart, Friedrich **32** 696
Werner, Theodor **33** 83
Abstraction-Création: Art non-figuratif **21** 855; **24** 428, 442; **32** 754
abstract-reële schilderkunst see NEO-PLASTICISM
Abstrakten, Die **25** 447
Abstrakten Hannover, Die **5** 75; **32** 695
Abstrakter Tanz **30** 686
Absurd, Theatre of the **17** 449
Abt, Hendrik Willemsz. **14** 94
Abt, Otto **13** 726
Abtai Khan **5** 106
Abu (Egypt) *see* ELEPHANTINE
Abu (India) *see* MT ABU
Abu (*fl* 18th cent.) **15** 609
Abu ʿAbdallah Muhammad Pasha **20** 105
Abu al-Fazl *see* ABU'L-FAZL
Abu al-Hol *see under* MEMPHIS (EGYPT)
Abu ʿAli Muhammad ʿAli ibn Muqla *see* IBN MUQLA
Abu-al-Saheli **23** 824
Abu Bakr, Caliph (*reg* 632-4) (Orthodox Caliphs) **18** 239
Abu Bakr ibn Muhammad **16** 497; **29** 822
Abu Bakr ibn Yusuf **16** 496
Abu Bakr Muhammad ibn Rafiʿ **16** 292
Abu Bakr Sandal **16** 290
Abu Dhabi **2** *246*; **31** 584
al-Ain Museum **2** 275; **31** 585
al-Husn Palace **31** 584
reliefs **2** 253–4
Women's Craft Centre **31** 585
see also UNITED ARAB EMIRATES
Abu Dulaf **16** 152; **22** 194
Abu Dulaf, mosque of *see under* SAMARRA'
Abueva, Napoleon **24** 620
Abu Fadl Muhallabi **16** 491
Abu Fana **7** 820
Abū-Ghosh Church **17** 504
Abu Ghurab **1** 90–91*; **9** *774*
inscriptions **10** 82
obelisks **23** 329
sun temples **10** 80, 81
Temple of Neuserre **1** *91*, 97; **9** 828, 830, 831; **10** 93; **30** 433
altar **1** 691
wall paintings **9** 809
Temple of Userkaf **1** 96, 97; **9** 830
Abu Habba, Tell *see* SIPPAR
Abu Hafs ʿUmar al-Murtada, Ruler (*reg* 1248-66) (Almohad) **1** 682; **16** 357
Abu Harb Bakhtiyar ibn Muhammad **8** 482; **16** 160; **28** 748
Abu Hawam, Tell **1** 865
Abu Hoda **23** 287; **29** 386
Abu Hureyra **21** 269, 280; **30** 182
Abu Ibrahim **16** 372
Abu Ibrahim Ahmad, Governor (*reg* 856-63) (Aghlabid) **16** 488; **17** 731; **21** 629; **31** 423
Abu ʿInan Faris, Ruler (*reg* 1348-59)(Marinid) **16** 218, 291; **20** 57, 430
Abuja **23** *129*, 135
Pottery **5** 731
Abu Jaʿfar Ahmad ibn Sulayman al-Muqtadir bi-llah **16** 189
Abu Jaʿfar Muhmmad **16** 259
Abu Khanafis **18** 20
Abu'l-ʿAbbas Ahmad ibn Muhammad al-Sufyani **16** 356
Abu'l-ʿAbbas Valgin ibn Harun **16** 372
Abularach, Rodolfo **1** 91*
Abu'l-Asvar Shavur I, Ruler (*reg* 1049-67) (Shaddadid) **12** 37
Abu Layth al-Siqilli **28** 511
Abu'l-Fadl Bayhaqi **16** 398
Abu'l-Fath Muhammad ibn Sultan weapons **16** *506*
Abu'l-Fazl
writings **31** 793
on dress **15** 690
on enamel **15** 710
on jewellery **15** 701
on metalwork **15** 712
on painters **3** 319; **15** 207
on weapons **15** 678
Abu'l-Hasan **1** 31, 91–2*; **2** 235; **15** 208, 584, 586, 587, 589, 590
collaboration **20** 284
patrons and collectors **15** 745
works **1** *92*; **15** 587; **16** 345; **30** 785
Abu'l-Hasan ʿAli I, Ruler (*reg* 1331-48) (Marinid) **16** 218, 440; **20** 430; **25** 832; **28** 634, 635
Abu'l-Hasan ʿAli ibn Hilal al-Bawwab *see* IBN AL-BAWWAB
Abu'l-Hasan Ghaffari *see* GHAFFARI, ABU'L-HASAN
Abu'l-Hasan Mustawfi Ghaffari *see* GHAFFARI, ABU'L-HASAN MUSTAWFI
Abu'l-Hassan Khan **1** 637
Abul-Hassan Yussuf ibn Firuz **23** 893
Abu'l-Mutahhar al Adzi **16** 398
Abu'l-Qasim **1** 93*, 97; **16** 100, 295
Abu'l-Qasim al-Zayyani **16** 240
Abu'l-Qasim Babur, Sultan (*reg* 1449-57) (Timurid) **16** 286, 332
Abu'l-Qasim ibn Saʿd ibn Muhammad al-Isʿirdi **16** 379
Abu'l Qasim Jamal al-Din ʿAbdallah **1** 98*; **16** 133, 394, 409, 412
Abu'l-Qasim Kashani **4** 687
Abu'l-Qasim Mahmud ibn Sanjar Shah **16** 380
Abu'l Rayhan Muhammad al-Biruni *see* AL-BIRUNI
Abu'l-Wafa' al-Buzajani **16** 133
Abu Mansur Bakhtakin **16** 435
Abu Maʿshar **2** 650
Abu Mina **1** 93–4*, *94*; **7** *819*; **9** *507*
Baptistery **3** 191; **7** 302; **9** 533
capitals **7** 821
church **7** 820
pilgrim flasks **7** 826
St Menas **7** 820; **20** 520; **31** 280
Abu Muhammad Ism'il **16** 525
Abu Muslim **23** 815
Abu Nasr **16** 399
Abu Nasr al-Basri **16** 399
Abu Rawash **1** 94–5*; **9** *774*, 813
pyramid of Radjedef **1** 94–5; **9** 779
Aburto, Alvaro **21** 380
Abu Sahl **16** 545
Abu Saʿid, Sultan (*reg* 1317-35) (Ilkhanid) **14** 430; **15** 134; **16** 200, 443
Abu Saʿid ibn Kuchkunji **27** 677
Abu Saʿid Mirza, Sultan (*reg* 1459-69) (Timurid) **15** 698
Abu Saʿid ʿUthman, Ruler (*reg* 1310-31) (Marinid) **16** 387, 440
Abu Salabikh **1** 853
Abu Saybi **2** 249
Abu Sefa, Tell *see* SILE
Abu Shahrein, Tell *see* ERIDU
Abu Shujaʿ Inju Takin **16** 530
Abu Sifain Monastery, St Mercurius **7** 262
Abu Simbel **1** 95–6*; **9** *774*; **23** *276*
inscriptions **9** 784
limestone **9** 813
reliefs **9** 799
sculpture **22** 42
temples **2** 323; **9** 833; **10** 65, 81, 90; **23** 279, 280; **29** 386
Great Temple **1** *95*, 95–6; **22** 722; **23** 279; **25** 874
colossal statues **9** 862, 863; **24** *663*
reliefs **22** *512*
sculpture **10** 741
Small Temple **1** 96; **10** 83; **22** 722; **23** 279; **25** 874
statue of Nefertari **25** 875
Abusir **1** 96–7*; **9** *774*
gargoyles **12** 150
inscriptions **10** 82
necropolis **9** 779
pyramids **10** 80; **25** 763
Complex of Neferirkare **1** 96; **25** 763
Complex of Neuserre **1** 96; **25** *761*, 763
Complex of Raneferef **1** 96; **10** 47
Complex of Sahure **1** 96; **9** *814*, 871; **30** 433
quartzite **9** 813
sarcophagi **9** 821
sculpture **9** 863
tomb of Ptahshepses **1** 97
tomb of Shepseskare **1** 97
Abu Tahir (family) **1** 97*; **16** 412
Abu Tahir Husayn ibn Ghali ibn Ahmad **2** 380
Abu Tahir ibn Abi Husayn **1** 97
Abu Tahir ibn Muhammad Hamza ibn al-Hasan **1** 97
Abu Yaʿqub Yusuf, Ruler (*reg* 1286-1307) (Marinid) **16** 218
Abu Yaʿqub Yusuf, Ruler (*reg* 1163-84) (Almohad) **28** 511
Abu Yaʿqub Yusuf, Ruler (*reg* 1286-1307) (Marinid) **20** 430
Abu Yusuf Yaʿqub, Ruler (*reg* 1258-86) (Marinid) **20** 430
Abu Yusuf Yäqub al-Mansur, Ruler (*reg* 1184-99) (Almohad) **1** 682; **16** 191; **25** 832; **28** 511
Abu Zaidan **10** 60
Tomb 32 **9** *866*
Abu Zakariya, Ruler (*reg* 1228-49) (Hafsid) **14** 27; **16** 219
Abu Zayd **1** 98–9*
collaboration **1** 97
works **16** 409, 410, *410*; **21** 506
Abyana, Maydan Mosque **16** 492
Abydos **1** *99*, 99–101*; **9** 773, *774*, 778; **30** 699
art forms and materials
amulets **10** 38
coins **27** *98*
figurines **10** 47, *59*, 60
funerary equipment **10** 59
furniture **10** 50; **30** 775
glass **10** 56
ivory **10** 59
jewellery **10** 32
mummies **22** *285*, 286
palettes **23** 848
reliefs **9** *828*, 879, 881
sculpture **9** 856, 861, 866, 875, 879
shabti containers **10** 20
shabtis **10** 18
wall paintings **9** 810
cenotaphs **1** 100; **6** 170
excavations **10** 80; **24** 561
houses **9** 850, 851
necropoleis **9** 843; **22** 716
Osireion **1** 101; **9** 861
sacred lake **27** 496
reliefs of Ammenemes III **1** 793
Shunet el-Zebib **9** 825, 844
Middle Fort **9** 844
stelae **9** 877; **29** 614, 615, 616
stele of Ahmose **9** 882
stele of Iahnefer **9** 879
stele of Nakhte **9** 879
stele of Wadj **1** *99*; **9** 868
temples **10** 65
Temple of Kentimentiu **9** 828, 829
Temple of Ramesses II **1** 101; **9** 835, 903; **25** 874
Temple of Sethos I **1** 100–101; **9** 783, 835, 903; **10** 79, 83; **28** 494; **30** 433
paintings **9** 805
reliefs **1** *100*, 100–101; **9** 807, 864, 886
wall paintings **9** 903
tombs **1** 99–100; **9** 779, 838, 839, 840, 842; **10** 72; **22** 488
Djer **10** 29, 50
Khasekhemwy **10** 72
Peribsen **29** 614
Tomb B10 **22** 509
Wadj **9** 838
Abydos ware *see under* POTTERY → wares
AC, Monogrammist **7** 369
acacia
historical and regional traditions
Egypt, ancient **6** 559
Islamic **16** 500
Japan **17** 354
Netherlands, the **33** IV2
Yemen **16** 500
uses
cabinets (ii) (furniture) **33** IV2
chests **6** 559
doors **16** 500
dyes **17** 354
Acacus **1** *376*; **19** 323
Academia Theodoro Palatina *see under* MANNHEIM
Academician **23** 228, 600; **32** 515
works **23** *228*
Academicus, Icarus **29** 762
Académie Carmen **22** 252
Académie de France *see under* ROME → academies
Académie des Inscriptions **7** 545
Académie Matisse **4** 888; **21** 820; **25** 744; **27** 360; **29** 604
Académie Ranson *see under* PARIS → academies and art schools
academies **1** 101–8*; **2** 365, 369, 523; **6** 79; **7** 382, 562; **10** 675, 676; **21** 759; **29** 855
Belgium **19** 547

academies—cont.
China 7 148, 151
England 10 249; 19 620
France 8 788; 19 *34*; 20 135
Germany 3 400; 9 *459*; 28 343
Italy 16 *779*; 24 733
Mexico 21 404
Netherlands, the 22 907*
Norway 23 602
Romania 5 *73*
Russia 25 *791*; 27 442
Scotland 20 *22*; 28 235
United States of America 23 630
Yugoslavia 8 181
Academy Architecture and Annual Architectural Review 24 446
Academy Board *see under* BOARDS
academy exhibitions *see* EXHIBITIONS → types → fine arts
academy figures 1 101, 108–9*; 9 222; 21 759
see also DRAWINGS → forms → life-drawings
Academy Painter 13 521
Acaia, Ludovico, Duke of 17 444
Acámbaro 30 341
Açana *see* ATCHANA, TELL
Acanceh 29 828, 829
acanthus 1 109–12*, *109*, *110*, *111*; 13 415; 23 478, 534; 26 369
Acanthus Master *see* KLUKSTAD, JACOB BERSVEINSSON
acanthus style 23 229
Acar, Kuzgun 31 455
Acatzingo Monastery 21 374, *374*
Accademia Ambrosiana *see* MILAN → academies → Accademia del Disegno
Accademia di Bacchio Brandin *see under* ROME, VATICAN → Palace → Cortile del Belvedere (great)
Accademia di Belle Arti di Brera *see under* MILAN → academies
Accademia di Brera *see* MILAN → academies → Accademia di Belle Arti di Brera
Accademia Clementina *see under* BOLOGNA → academies
Accademia Columbaria *see under* FLORENCE → academies
Accademia *Crucifix* 8 211, *211*, 212
Accademia degli Desiderosi *see* BOLOGNA → academies → Accademia degli Incamminati
Accademia del Disegno
members
Florence
academies 31 54
Accademia Ercolanese di Archeologia *see under* ERCOLANO
Accademia Etrusca *see under* CORTONA
Accademia Fiorentina *see under* ROME → academies
Accademia degli Incamminati *see under* BOLOGNA → academies
Accademia Leonardi Vinci *see under* MILAN → academies
Accademia del Naturale *see* BOLOGNA → academies → Accademia degli Incamminati
Accademia dei Pensieri *see under* ROME → academies
Accademia della Virtù *see under* ROME → academies
Accaioli, Niccolo 5 894
Accame, Antonio 9 173
Accame, Pietro 9 173
Accardi, Carla 1 112*
groups and movements 7 782; 9 168; 11 314; 16 681; 26 777
Acceptus 1 112–13*; 26 626; 27 120
Acciaioli, Alessandro 5 360
Acciaiuoli, Margherita 4 404
acciajatura *see* ENGRAVINGS → types → steel
Acciauoli, Angelo, Cardinal 20 621
accident in art 2 488
Accino da Lecco 25 466
Accolti, Benedetto, Cardinal 11 193; 17 812
Accolti, Francesco 28 702
Accolti, Pietro 1 113*; 6 570
Acconci, Vito (Hannibal) 1 113*; 10 483; 24 408
accordion books *see under* BOOKS → forms
accords 10 91
accounts boxes *see under* BOXES → types
Accra 1 *386*
fort 21 597
Ghana National Museum 1 437; 12 510; 22 367
Loom Gallery 12 510
Accrocca, Elio Filippo 26 777
Accursio, Mariangelo 11 839
A. C. Documentos de actividad contemporánea 12 177; 24 452; 29 273, 321; 31 184
Aceh 15 *752*, 788, 794, 811
Acemhöyük 1 113–15*, *821*, 826, 894
architecture 1 830; 4 772
furniture 1 835
ivory-carvings 1 832, 869
Sarıkaya Palace 1 *114*, 114; 23 806
seals 1 856, 863
Aceramic Neolithic *see under* ANATOLIA, ANCIENT; CYPRUS, ANCIENT → periods
Acerbi, Francesco degli 20 323
Acerenza, Cathedral of the Assumption and S Canio 16 626; 26 580, 627
Acero, Vicente 5 368
works 5 *368*
acetate 7 432
acetic acid 24 649
Acevedo, Alonso de Fonseca y, Archbishop of Toledo *see* FONSECA Y ACEVEDO, ALONSO DE, Archbishop of Toledo
Acevedo, de 31 347
Acevedo, Manuel Hernández *see* HERNÁNDEZ ACEVEDO, MANUEL
Acevedo, Raúl Lerena *see* LERENA ACEVEDO, RAÚL
Acevedo y Zúñiga, Manuel de, 6th Conde de Monterrey *see* MONTERREY, MANUEL, 6th Conde de
Aceves Navarro, Gilberto 1 115*
Achadaeus Psalter *see under* PSALTERS → individual manuscripts
Achaea, William II of Villehardouin, Prince of *see* WILLIAM II OF VILLEHARDOUIN, Prince of Achaea
Achaean *see* MYCENAEAN
Achaemenid 1 115–18*, *852*; 10 133; 15 900, 907; 21 275*; 30 178
altars 1 690
apadanas 2 213; 15 912
architecture 1 116; 15 911–12
chariots 6 *479*
coins 1 116, 117, 203, 888*, *888*; 13 586
dress 1 *884*, 886–7*
friezes 2 213
glass 1 868
gold 1 118; 21 III1
harnesses 14 180
iconography 1 117
inscriptions 1 *116*
ivory-carvings 1 872
jewellery 1 118, 875
Achaemenid—cont.
metalwork 1 117, 118, *118*; 15 919
monuments 22 42
painting 1 118; 10 *151*, 151
palaces 1 116; 23 807
patronage 1 116–18
phialai 1 118, *118*
portraits 1 117
pottery 6 255
propaganda 1 115
religion 33 706
rock reliefs 1 *116*, 117; 6 *479*; 15 916; 24 *220*
sculpture 1 116; 15 *914*, 914–15; 21 302
seals 1 116, 117–18, 858, *863*, 864
silver 1 *118*, *888*
textiles 1 118
thrones 30 774
trade 1 118
trappings 14 180
see also IRAN, ANCIENT
Achaemenid, Cyrus I *see* CYRUS I
Achao 6 *590*, 592
Achard, Jean-Alexis 14 188
Achardus 7 371
Achchaveli 16 864
Aché 24 93
Achebe, Chinua 15 56; 23 139
Acheloos Painter 13 511; 32 27*
Achenbach, Andreas 1 119*; 9 460; 12 394; 18 800
frames 11 463, *463*
groups and movements 9 460
pupils 4 232; 13 776
teachers 28 104
Achenbach, Oswald 1 119*; 18 204; 22 316; 28 104
Achibal Gardens 12 74; 15 364
Achiki 17 214
Achilles Painter 13 511, 521, 524, 536; 32 28*, 48
pupils 13 521; 32 62
teachers 32 34
works 6 II1; 13 521, *522*, 550
Achkar, Yvette 19 8
Achmim *see* AKHMIM
Achomawi 22 549, 641, 659
Acho Yoshitori 33 318
Achremčyk, Ivan 3 529
Achtenhagen, Karl Ludwig 21 66
Achtermann, (Theodor) Wilhelm 1 119–20*
Achtschellinck(x), Lucas 2 875; 3 561; 21 427; 31 793
Achyutadeva Raya, Ruler (*reg* 1530-42) (Vijayanagara) 15 329
Aciaga, Martín de 10 499
acid-gold process 21 697
acid rain 29 708
acids 10 320, 548–9; 25 614
see also MORDANTS (i) (ACID)
Acier *see under* TYPE-FACES
Acier, Michel Victor 21 65
Acigné, Pierre d' *see* PIERRE D'ACIGNÉ
Aci i D'Allà, D' 3 219
Açık Saray 5 674, 675
Acioli, Luiz 5 912
Acireale, S Sebastiano 28 657
Acişi Abbey 14 883
Ačis Ilaek 18 495
Acke, Johan Axel Gustaf 30 81
Acke, Victor 3 579, 587
Acker, Ernest 10 658
Acker, Hans 1 120*; 13 188
Acker, Jakob 13 187
Acker, John 14 223
Acker, Peter 23 204
Ackerman, James 29 880
Ackerman, Phyllis 16 548; 25 234
Ackermann (*fl* early 19th cent.) 10 677; 25 627
Ackermann (*fl* 1860) 22 304
Ackermann, Arthur, & Son Ltd 1 121
Ackermann, Christian 10 539; 29 119; 30 276
Ackermann, Max 1 120*; 29 875
Ackermann, Rudolph, sr (1764-1834) 1 120–21*; 4 362; 19 699; 24 446; 25 623; 28 879
assistants 8 27
engravings 19 *593*
groups and movements 10 142
pattern books 25 712
printmakers 6 535; 8 21; 14 536; 25 710; 27 279, 601; 29 491; 30 39; 31 777; 32 419
Repository of Arts, The 4 806; 10 296; 13 206; 24 273; 25 759
staff 12 270
treatises 19 483
Ackermann, Rudolph, jr (*fl* 1822) 1 121
Ackermann & Co. 25 626
Ackersloot, Outgert (Arisz.) 1 121
Ackersloot, Willem (Outgertsz.) 1 121*; 32 140
works 27 508
ACME 19 591; 30 870
Acmeism 1 121*
Acolmán
Augustinian Monastery 21 375
Museo Colonial de Acolmán 21 396
Acolti, Stefano 1 457
ACOM *see* ASOCIACIÓN COLOMBIANA DE MUSEOS
Acoma (NM) 22 567, 568, 668, 676
blankets 22 *623*
pottery 22 607–8, *607*
S Estevan 31 *589*
acorns 7 45
Acort, Daviso de *see* DUCART, DAVIS
Acosta, Francisco de 32 176
Acosta, Jorge R. 30 452; 31 418
Acosta, Wladimiro 1 121–2*
Acosta León, Angel 8 234
Acosta Tupac Inca, Sebastián 4 264
acoustics 1 122–6*, *123*, *124*; 30 662, 667
ACP *see* ARCHITECTS' CO-PARTNERSHIP
Acqua, Cristoforo dall'
works 32 *410*
Acqua Fresca, Matteo 2 456
Acquarossa 1 126–7*; 10 *583*, 638, 640; 16 *620*
houses 10 *598*, 599
plaques 10 594
tiles 1 *126*
Acquasparta, Federico Cesi, Duca d' 6 360*
Acquasparta, Matteo d', Cardinal *see* MATTEO D'ACQUASPARTA, Cardinal
Acquaviva, Giovanni 20 428
Acquaviva, Michel Victor 4 395
Acquaviva d'Aragona, Andrea Matteo III, Duca d'Atri *see* ATRI, ANDREA MATTEO III ACQUAVIVA D'ARAGONA, Duca d'
Acquaviva d'Aragona, Giangirolamo II, Conte di Conversano *see* CONVERSANO, GIANGIROLAMO II ACQUAVIVA D'ARAGONA, Conte di
Acquaviva d'Aragona, Trojano, Cardinal 4 560; 11 815; 32 70
Acrae 6 70
Acre *see under* 'AKKO
Acrocorinth *see under* CORINTH
acro-elephantine sculpture *see under* SCULPTURE → types
acrography 25 611
acrolithic sculpture *see under* SCULPTURE → types
acroliths 27 29, 32
Acropolis *see under* ATHENS
Acropolis 606, Painter of 32 28–9*
works 13 508, *509*
acroteria 1 127–8*; 8 *689*; 10 *434*; 13 390, 391, 426, 432; 23 *429*
see also FINIALS (ARCHITECTURAL)
Acroyd, John 23 687
acrylic 5 34; 6 336; 25 23, 26, 27*
regional traditions
England 17 *529*
Guatemala 13 766
United States of America 22 336
uses
conservation 28 339
consolidants 7 747
frames 8 129
grounds 13 707*
jewellery 17 *529*, 530
lacquer 18 612
murals 22 336
paints 1 129, 130; 25 24–5
see also PAINTS → types → polymer colour
resins 28 339
secco paintings 28 339
acrylic paintings *see under* PAINTING → forms
Acryloid B72 *see* PARALOID B72
Acta historiae artium Academiae scientiarum Hungricae 24 424
Acte, Metilla
sarcophagus 22 *411*
actinolite 21 241
Action *see* AKUSHON
Action Art Society *see* KŌDŌ BIJUTSU KYŌKAI
action painting 1 78, 131*; 25 585, 645; 27 163; 31 607
Australia 31 412
United States of America 1 78, 83, 86
Action Surréaliste 24 428
Activists (Aktivizmus) 1 131–2*; 10 109; 13 840; 14 901; 20 103, 104
members 18 142; 20 849; 22 730; 31 541
Activities 17 806
Acton (Middx), All Saints
effigy of Robert de Bures 19 *580*
Acton Beauchamp (Hereford & Worcs), St Giles 2 70
Actopan
Augustinian Monastery 21 375
S Miguel 21 375
Actual 10 543
ACT-UP/New York 12 218
Acudoğu, Ratip Aşir 1 132*; 31 454
acuity perspective *see under* PERSPECTIVE → types
Acumincum *see* STARI SLANKAMEN
Acuña, Cosme de 20 57
Acuña, Cristobal de 29 193
Acuña, José María 29 295
Acuña, Julio 25 701
Acuña, Luis 5 203; 28 724
Acuña, Luis Alberto 7 609
Acuña, Miguel de 7 607
Acyutappa, Ruler (*reg* 1560-1600) (Nayaka) 22 702
Ada, Abbess 12 382
Ada, Princess 25 *576*
Adachi, Chōka 17 381, 382
Adachi Museum of Art 12 101
Adad-Nirari I (*reg* 1305-1274 BC) 2 637, 639
Adad-Nirari III (*reg* 810-783 BC) 2 640; 21 288, 298–9; 23 151, 153
Ada Eledisi 15 107
Ada Gospels *see under* GOSPEL OOKS → individual manuscripts
Ada group *see* COURT SCHOOL OF CHARLEMAGNE
Adalaj, Rudabai Vav 15 349; 29 635, 636
Adalbero, Bishop of Laon (977-1030) 18 757

Adalbero, Bishop of Metz (*d* 1005) 23 660
Adalbero, Saint 18 668
Adalbert I, Archbishop of Mainz 9 687; 20 128
Adalbertus *see* TYLKOWSKI, WOJCIECH
Adam (*fl* 12th cent.) 7 351
Adam (*fl* 1956) 18 118
Adam (i) (family) 28 246
collaboration 7 416
patrons and collectors 28 269
works 19 571; 28 227
Adam (iii), Albrecht 1 141*
pupils 14 768; 28 186
works 12 393
Adam (iii), Benno 1 141
Adam (iii), Eugen 1 141
Adam (i), François-Gaspard-Balthazar 1 132, 133*
Adam (iii), Franz 1 141; 4 671; 12 603
Adam (iii), Heinrich 1 141
Adam, Henri-Georges 1 142*; 11 569, 644; 30 329
pupils 31 159
works 3 461; 7 696, *697*; 19 92
Adam (i), Jacob-Sigisbert 1 132–3*
Adam (ii), James 1 134, 141*; 10 641, 642–3; 13 541
assistants 4 333; 8 267, 839; 26 337
collaboration 1 134, 136; 28 227
dealing 8 474
groups and movements 22 734
illustrated writings 32 652
teachers 7 415
works 1 *137*; 4 540; 6 60; 7 747; 8 576; 10 276, 342; 24 273; 25 192; 31 714
Adam (ii), John 1 134*
collaboration 28 227, 246
groups and movements 23 860
patrons and collectors 24 390
works 10 276; 28 227, 228
Adam (iii), Julius 1 141
Adam (i), Lambert 1 132
Adam (i), Lambert-Sigisbert 1 132–3*; 11 559
collaboration 1 133
competitions 7 672
patrons and collectors 23 517; 25 150
pupils 7 450; 12 636; 18 804
works 1 *133*; 11 560–61; 22 34; 32 372
Adam, Leonhard 1 67; 2 136
Adam (i), Nicolas-Sébastien 1 132, 133*
collaboration 1 132; 11 560
patrons and collectors 4 331
works 22 455; 32 372
Adam, Paul 1 21, 142*
Adam, Peter 1 896
Adam (iii), Richard Benno 1 141–2*
Adam (ii), Robert 1 134–40*; 7 384; 10 293, 351, 641; 13 301, 541; 19 426; 20 867; 28 *243*
aquatints 2 240
architecture 1 *139*; 10 233; 23 362; 28 288
architectural decorations 10 265; 30 502
bridges 3 371; 4 801
chimney-pieces 6 605; 27 469
country houses 8 48; 9 12; 27 656; 28 227
Gosford House (Lothian) 28 227; 33 565
Inveraray Castle (Strathclyde) 6 60
Kedleston Hall (Derbys) 1 *136*; 7 339
Kenwood House (London) 13 836
Luton Hoo (Beds) 29 796
Osterley Park House (Middx) 7 339
Adam (ii), Robert
architecture
country houses—cont.
Stowe (Bucks) 4 422; 13 637
Strawberry Hill (Middx) 32 825, *826*
gate lodges 12 176
houses 1 *137*; 8 62; 14 744; 33 55
mausolea 20 867, 868; 25 766
orders (architecture) 23 489
pavilions 24 290
porticos 25 266
prisons 25 636
public buildings 9 723; 12 773
sarcophagi 5 767
tombs 6 165
town halls 5 287
universities 9 723; 25 35
urban planning 9 723; 28 227; 31 714, 716
assistants 4 333; 5 907; 6 323; 8 839; 11 431; 16 24; 26 337; 33 442
bookbindings 4 353
candlesticks 5 612
carpets 5 839
collaboration 1 134; 28 227, 246; 29 835
drawings 9 30; 28 242; 29 417
fireplace furnishings 10 341; 11 119, *119*; 16 60; 28 263
fonts (baptismal) 11 255
frames 9 13; 11 429
furniture 7 172; 10 293, 295; 20 468
beds 10 353, *354*
cabinets 9 27, 29
chairs 6 390; 10 295, *295*, 296
commodes 7 659; 15 165
console tables 7 747
sideboards 28 665
sofas 10 295
groups and movements 2 163; 12 332; 13 199; 22 734, 736, 738, 740; 23 210, 859
interior decoration 1 111; 9 31; 10 276, 277, 637; 19 316; 23 544; 28 28, 245, *247*; 29 835
carpets 10 279, 358
festoons 11 34
glass 5 349; 10 277
mirrors 21 721
paintings 1 *138*; 5 687; 10 642–3, *643*; 13 702; 25 192
pedestals 24 317
stucco 9 16; 28 246–7
tapestries 9 30; 10 277
metalwork 10 342; 23 544
monuments 5 767; 27 469
patrons and collectors
Child, Robert 3 173
Clerk, John, 1st Baron Eldin (1757-1832) 7 419
Curzon, Nathaniel, 1st Baron Scarsdale 8 281
Dundas, Lawrence 9 392
Garrick, David 12 164
Kennedy, David, 10th Earl of Cassillis 28 269
Petty, William (Fitzmaurice), 2nd Earl of Shelburne and 1st Marquess of Lansdowne 24 570
Smithson (Percy), Hugh, 1st Duke and 2nd Earl of Northumberland 10 361; 24 390
Soane, John 28 908
Weddell, William 10 365; 33 20
Wernher, Julius 33 84
Williams-Wynn, Watkin, 4th Baronet, of Wynnstay (1749-89) 26 463; 32 790; 33 209
pattern books 24 273
silver 4 540; 10 333, *333*
sponsors 1 533
teachers 7 415; 18 661
Adam (ii), Robert—cont.
writings 2 358; 7 415; 10 276
illustrated 3 308; 32 652; 33 721
Adam, Shehata 33 481
Adam (i), Sigisbert 1 132
Adam (ii), William (1689-1748) 1 134*; 7 409; 28 274
collaboration 28 227, 269
groups and movements 23 860
patrons and collectors 7 418
pupils 1 134; 28 885
works 9 729; 28 227, 228, 246, 252, 269; 29 796; 31 239; 32 553
Adam (ii), William (1738-1822) 1 134
Adam (i), William (1751-1839) 1 134
Adamankottai, Chennaraya Perumal 15 646
Adamawa 22 286–7
body arts 1 *345*
Adamczewska, Hanna *see* WEJCHERT, HANNA
Adam d'Arogno 5 550
Adam de Sudbury 12 800
Adametz, Hans 3 393
Adami, Carlo 14 895
Adami, Valerio 1 143*; 16 682; 21 528
dealers 20 75
teachers 11 844
Adamino di San Giorgio 4 816; 32 344
Adamklissi, Tropaeum Trajani 26 906, *906*
Adamnan, Saint 13 808
Adam of Basing 13 195; 23 460
Adam of Corfe 4 692
Adam of Hartington 7 420
Adam of Meaux 7 351
Adam of St Victor 32 416
Adamos, Andy 8 364
Adamov, Arthur 32 423
Adamov Church 2 800
Adamovic (family) 11 33
Adamovich, Mikhail 27 413
works 27 *414*
Adamovich, Vladimir (Dmitriyevich) 27 378
Adams, Ansel (Easton) 1 143–4*; 24 656; 26 390
groups and movements 13 710
pupils 5 671; 7 917
works 1 *144*
Adams, Clinton 1 145*; 19 492; 20 606
Adams, Edward Dean 31 650
works 31 *650*
Adams, George
works 28 *211*
Adams, Henry 26 342
Adams, Herbert 7 875; 31 612
Adams, Holden & Pearson 14 674
Adams, John 29 116
Adams, John Quincey 23 *765*
Adams, Kim 5 572
Adams, Lewis B. 32 173
Adams, Luke 23 69
Adams, Mark 1 145–6*; 31 660
works 1 *146*; 31 661
Adams, Maurice B(ingham) 1 146*
collaboration 10 239
groups and movements 25 805
works 2 756; 12 144
Adams, Michael 31 528
Adams, Monni
works 1 *246*
Adams, Percy 14 673
works 14 *674*
Adams, Pieter 22 828
Adams, Richard (*fl* 1829-31) 2 395
Adams, Richard E. W. (*fl* 1962) 26 411
Adams, R. McC. 16 550
Adams, Robert (i) (1917-84) 1 146–7*
Adams, Robert (ii) (*b* 1937) 1 147*; 23 37
Adams, Tate 1 147*
Adams, Thomas 31 729
works 31 *729*
Adams, William (*fl* late 18th cent.) 10 307, 308
Adams, William (1806-85) 8 580
Adams, William, & Sons (Potters) Ltd 7 798
Adams, William Y. 10 81
Adam-Salomon, Antoine-Samuel 1 147–8*; 24 661
Adams & Co. 22 744
Adamski, Hans-Peter 9 72
Adamson, Amandus 1 148*; 3 197; 10 539; 30 202, 277
Adamson, E. 27 423
Adamson, Gordon Sinclair 1 148
Adamson, James 5 667
Adamson, John 1 148*; 14 539
Adamson, Joy 17 907, 908
Adamson, Robert 1 148; 2 119; 14 539–40*
works 14 *539*
Adamson Associates 1 148–9*
Adamstett, Andreas 33 274
Adams & Thompson 11 808
Adán, Juan 1 149*; 4 565; 29 293
Adán, Miguel 23 683
Adana 9 564; 16 473; 17 500
Adão, Manuel Carneiro *see* CARNEIRO ADÃO, MANUEL
Adaro Magro, Eduardo 1 149*
Adbadari 15 265
Adbülfettah 21 50
Adbülmecid 21 50
Adcote (Salop) 28 *562*
Adda, Crespi d' *see* CRESPI D'ADDA
Adda, Ferdinando d', Cardinal 32 402
Adda, Giacomo d' 1 608; 27 498; 31 897
Addahamiti-Inshushinak (*reg c.* 650 BC) 30 29
Addams, Charles 5 759
Addams, Clifford 33 142
Addams, Jane 2 572
Addaura 1 149–50*; 16 *621*; 23 840; 25 *470*; 28 653
rock art 1 *149*
Addis, John M(ansfield) 1 150*; 6 924
Addis Ababa 1 *379*
Africa Hall 10 567
architecture 10 567
Church of Elfren Gabre'el 10 567
Church of Entoto Ragriel 10 567
collections 10 578
Empress Menen Handicraft School 10 573, 578
Filwola thermal baths 10 567
Fine Arts School 10 573, 578
Guenet Leul palace *see* University
house of Ras Biru *see* Museum
Jubilee Palace *see* National Palace
Menelik Mausoleum 10 567
Municipality Building 10 567
Museum 10 567
National Bank 10 567
National Museum 10 578
National Palace 10 567
Organization of African Unity Hall 1 433
palace of Emperor Menelik 10 567
Parliament Building 10 567
St George 10 567
sculpture 10 577
Trinity Church 10 567
University 10 567
Museum of the Institute of Ethiopian Studies 10 578
Addison, Edward 30 278
Addison, G(eorge) H(enry) M(ale) 2 739; 23 327; 31 763
Addison, Joseph 1 150*; 12 128; 13 300
groups and movements 12 128; 24 741; 29 889
works 13 300
illustrated 30 759
translated 12 122
Addison Gallery of American Art *see under* ANDOVER (MA)
additive architecture *see under* ARCHITECTURE → types
Addy, S. O. 32 274
Adebayo and Adebayo 15 56
Adegbite 12 508
Adejimi, Muri 18 640
Adekhsan 21 585
Adelaide 1 *37*, 151–2*, *151*; 2 *736*
ANZ Bank 2 739
architecture 2 738
Art Gallery of South Australia 2 770; 14 508; 29 241
Carrick Hill 2 771
ceramics 2 760
Elder Park Bandstand 18 73
Flinders University of South Australia 2 772
Art Museum 1 152; 2 771
General Post Office 2 739
Government House 2 738
Jam Factory Craft Workshops 2 764
Magistrates' Court House 18 887
painting 2 745
parliament buildings 2 738
Royal South Australian Society of Arts 1 152
School of Arts 2 772
South Australian Museum 1 66, 151; 23 57
Town Hall 2 738
Adelaide, Duchess of Saxe-Meiningen (*fl* 1860s) 5 78
Adelaide, Queen of Great Britain (1792-1849) 8 886
Adelaide Henrietta of Savoy, Electress of Bavaria (1636-76) 3 229; 33 83, 276
Adelaide of Savoy, Duchesse de Bourgogne *see* BOURGOGNE, MARIE-ADELAÏDE OF SAVOY, Duchesse de
Adelaide of Savoy, Master of 20 612–13*, 735
works 20 *612*, 723
Adela Investment 24 515
Adelard of Bath 2 348
Adelbold, Bishop of Utrecht 2 349; 22 817
Adelborg, Louise 30 100, 884
Adelcrantz, C(arl) F(redrik) 1 152*; 11 91; 29 689; 30 88
collaboration 26 99
groups and movements 13 864
patrons and collectors 14 692; 29 691
works 11 91; 29 691; 30 72, *676*, 677
Adelcrantz, Göran Josuae 1 152; 14 177; 29 685; 30 71
Adèle de Champagne, Queen of France (*d* 1206) 25 220
Adeler, Max 11 804
Adelfia 27 827
Adelhausen Abbey 12 463, 465; 26 144
Adeline, Jules 10 209
Adelph Painter 32 37
Adelricus 30 486
works 30 *487*
Adelung, Friedrich von 27 440
Adem, Seyyid 2 883
Ademar of Chabanais 10 724, 725; 24 269
Ademollo, Carlo 1 152*; 28 318
Ademollo, Luigi 1 152
Ademuwagun Adesida II 1 *353*
Aden 6 *623*
architecture 33 519
collections 1 896

Aden—cont.
ivory-carvings **16** 523
National Archaeological Museum **33** 520
National Ethnographical Museum **33** 520
textiles **16** 438
Aden, Alonso **1** 443
Adena culture **1** 153; **22** 617; **31** 116
Adena Mound (OH) **1** 153*; **22** *544*, 571, 572
effigies **1** *153*
Adeodatus (*fl* 1166) **13** 713
Adeodatus I, Bishop of Torcello (*reg c.* 700) **31** 161
Adeodatus II, Bishop of Torcello (*reg* 864-67) **31** 161
Ader, Bas Jan **22** 853
Aders, Carl **1** 153*
Adharbayjan *see* AZERBAIJAN
Adharbod **16** 288
Adhémar, Jean **1** 154*; **28** 528
adhesives **1** 154–7*; **11** 141
historical and regional traditions
Greece, ancient **13** 483
Indian subcontinent **15** 551
Japan **17** 209
Vietnam **32** 488
uses
ceramics **6** 335–6
conservation **1** 157*; **6** 335–6; **7** 730, 737; **17** 209; **24** 7
frescoes **11** 764
glass **12** 797
gold leaf **1** 156
marquetry **20** 466
panel paintings **24** 4, 7
paper **1** 156; **24** 53
pigments **15** 551
plywood **1** 156
pottery **13** 483
wallpaper **32** 813
waxes **33** 6
wood **1** 156; **33** 338
see also CONSOLIDANTS; FIXATIVES; GLUES
Adhicchatrā *see* AHICHCHHATRA
adhiṣṭhāna **15** 242*
Adi **15** 733
Adichalanur **15** 677
Adichanallur **4** 853
Adickes, Franz **3** 769
ADI-FAD (Agrupació del Disseny Industrial -Sociedad de Foment de les Arts Decoratives) **29** 322
Adil, Ömer
works **31** *455*
'Adilabad *see under* DELHI
Adılcevaz *see* KEFKALESI
al-'Adil I, Sultan (*reg* Damascus 1196-1218; Egypt 1200-18) (Ayyubid) **2** 888; **5** 403
'Adil Shahi **1** 157*
see also:
'ALI 'ADIL SHAH I, Ruler
'ALI 'ADIL SHAH II, Ruler
IBRAHIM 'ADIL SHAH II, Ruler
ISMA'IL 'ADIL SHAH, Ruler
JAHAN BEGAM
MUHAMMAD 'ADIL SHAH, Ruler
SIKANDAR 'ADIL SHAH, Ruler
Adimari Cassone, Master of the **11** 388; **28** 70
Adimari Hours *see under* BOOKS OF HOURS → individual manuscripts
Adimari Wedding **29** 360
Adio Zande **33** 610
Adisham (Kent), Church of the Holy Innocents **11** 420
Adishi **12** 326
Adishi Gospels *see under* GOSPEL BOOKS → individual manuscripts
Aditya I, Ruler (*reg c.* 871-907) (Chola) **18** 514
Adityasena, Ruler (*reg c.* 650-75) (Later Gupta) **15** 281
ādivāsī see TRIBAL ART
Adivisomapalli **15** 534
Adıyaman **1** 823; **16** 411
Adjib **27** 810
Adjmi, Morris **27** 192, 193
works **27** *192*
Adjuma **11** 878
ADLAN *see* AMICS DEL ART NOU
Adlard, Henry
works **24** *275*
Adler, Dankmar **1** 157–9*
collaboration **5** 124; **6** 573; **10** 683; **14** 787; **19** 365; **28** 833; **29** 913; **31** 594
groups and movements **6** 577, 578
patrons and collectors **27** 565
works **1** *158*; **30** 678; **31** *594*
Adler, (Johann Heinrich) Friedrich (1827-1908) **1** 159–60*; **4** 505
pupils **12** 506; **19** 327
teachers **2** 478
Adler, Friedrich (1878-?1942) **22** 306
Adler, Iosef **26** 725
Adler, Jane Bodenheimer **26** 472
Adler, Jankel **1** 160*; **12** 777
Adler, Michael **30** 129
Adler, Rose **9** 196; **11** 673
Adler Petersen, Lene **8** 736
Adler & Sullivan **1** 158–9; **5** 274; **6** 573; **29** 913
restorations by others **33** 29
staff **12** 632; **25** 737; **33** 400
works **1** *158*; **23** 359; **29** *914*
Adlhart, Jakob **27** 665
Adlung, Jakob **22** 374
administrative buildings **14** 580
Admiraal, Siem **15** 818
Admiral, Joanne L' *see* L'ADMIRAL, JOANNE
Admiralty Islands **23** 728, 732; **24** *64*, 82
wood-carvings **24** *83*
Admont Abbey **1** 160–61*; **2** *776*, 781, 824
library **19** 316
manuscripts **2** 790, 791; **26** 675
sculpture **2** 801
Admont Bible *see under* BIBLES → individual manuscripts
Admont *Virgin and Child* **2** 798
Adnan, Etel **19** 8
Ådnes, Peder **23** 231
Adnet **11** 644
Adnet, Henry **11** 619; **21** 70
works **28** I2
Adnet, Jacques **11** 601
adobe **4** 767*
historical and regional traditions
Africa **1** 305
Algeria **1** 305
Australia **32** 308
Chimú **29** *168*
China **6** 691
Inca **29** 164
Mesoamerica, Pre-Columbian **4** 796
Moche (culture) **4** 796
Morocco **1** 305
Native North Americans **22** 567
New Zealand **32** 308
Nigeria **1** 305
Peru **29** *168*
South America, Pre-Columbian **4** 796; **29** 160, 162, *168*
United States of America **4** 786; **22** 567; **31** 588
materials
straw **4** 767
techniques
moulding **4** 767
uses
architecture **32** 308
houses **6** 691
pyramids **29** 160
relief sculpture **29** *168*
Adoian, Vosdanig Manoog *see* GORKY, ARSHILE
Adolf, Duke of Holstein-Gottorp (*reg* 1533-86) **13** 682
Adolf I, Count of Berg (*reg* 1101-52) **12** 471
Adolf Frederick, King of Sweden (*reg* 1751-71) **14** 17, 230, *648*, 692; **30** 94, 343
Adolfov Glassworks **8** 410
Adolfsson, Wilke **30** 103
Adolphe of Burgundy **5** 212; **13** 26
Adoni **15** 540
Ador, Jean-Pierre **27** 584
Adornes, Jan **4** 161
Adorni, Francesco **18** 733
Adorno (family) **4** 919
Adorno, Gretel **3** 731
Adorno, Theodor W. **3** 731; **8** 826; **20** 527; **28** 917
Adprint Ltd **23** 8
Adrada de Haza Church **26** 642
Adrar des Iforas **1** 370, *371*
Adreani, Aldo **16** 649
Adria **10** *583*, 592; **26** 869
Adriaensens, Jan **8** 463
Adriaenssen, Alex(ander) **1** 161*; **5** 352; **32** 713
Adriaenssen, Niclaes **1** 161
Adriaenssen, Vincent **1** 161
Adriaen van den Houte **20** 752
Adrian (1903-59) **9** 292
Adrian I, Pope (*reg* 772-95) **1** 652; **5** 801; **26** 754, 820, 824, 833
Adrian IV, Pope (*reg* 1154-59) **31** 121
Adrian VI, Pope (*reg* 1522) **10** 521; **23** 582; **28** 216
Adrian, Agustín de **2** 386
Adrian-Nilsson, Gösta **1** 161*
Adriano Fiorentino **1** 161–2*; **11** 217
patrons and collectors **33** 112
works **1** *162*; **3** *861*; **29** 568
Adrianople *see* EDIRNE
Adrianov, Alexander V. **4** 603
Adrichem, Aelbrecht Adriansz. van **22** 200
Adsett, Sandy **1** 162–3*; **20** 359
Adshead, S(tanley) D(avenport) **1** 29, 163*; **10** 239; **23** 248
Adsuara, Juan **29** 295
Aduard Church **4** 777
'Adud al-Dawla, Amir (*reg* 949-83) (Buyid) **16** 160, 272, 372, 373, 492; **19** 316
Adulis **1** 314, *379*; **10** 565
Aduma **11** 878; **18** 401
Ad Usus Publicus **8** 758
advanced works *see* OUTWORKS
advertisements **2** 372; **7** 650–56; **9** 494; **10** 419; **14** 690; **24** 650, 671, 678
England **10** *420*
India, Republic of **15** 177
United States of America **15** 824
Advisomanapalli **15** 301
Adygeya **27** 432, 433; **28** 323; **30** 770
Adygey region **27** 433
Adylov, Sabir (Rahimovich) **31** 782
Adynamische Groep **28** 103
adyta **1** 163*; **13** *376*, 377, 398
adzes
historical and regional development
Austral Islands **25** 896
Cook Islands **23** 735
Egypt, ancient **9** 821
Japan **17** *49*
Java **29** 227
Pacific Islands **23** 712, *712*
Prehistoric art **29** 227
Society Islands **23** *712*
South-east Asia **29** 227
materials
basalt **23** *712*
hardstones **29** 227
adzes
materials—cont.
sennit **23** *712*
wood **23** *712*
Adzhina Tepe **1** 163–4*, *164*; **6** *182*; **30** *252*, 440
Monastery **6** 200, 222, *232*
sculpture **6** 195, 221, *221*
wall paintings **6** 232
Aebi, Hans **2** 401, 546
Aech'un *see* SIN MYŎNG-YŎN
Aeclanum Macellum **19** 889
aediculae **1** 164*
aedicular frames *see under* FRAMES → types
Aedo Calderón, Ignacio de **6** 45
AEG (Allgemeine Elektrizitäts-Gesellschaft) **2** 566
advertisements **9** 86
architecture **8** 825; **28** 192
design **12** 472
designers **8** 802; **15** 823; **31** 497
factories **3** 511, *512*, 512–13, 795; **10** 697; **21** 780, *780*
kettles **15** *823*
logos **15** 824
Aegean **1** 165*; **8** 154
bronze **8** 262
carts **21** 691
cemeteries **2** 304–5
chariots **6** 479
chronologies **25** 472
limestone **8** 262
sculpture **8** 262
terracotta **8** 262
trade **21** 652–3
see also CYCLADIC; GREECE, ANCIENT; HELLADIC; MYCENAEAN; PHILISTINE
Aegeri, Carl *see* EGERI, CARL VON
Aegina *see* AIGINA
Aegina Marbles **12** 476
Aegistratus **21** 577
Aeglantyne table **20** 467
Aelewaeters (family) **3** 600
Aelfeah **33** 234
Aelfwine **2** 77; **33** 233
Aelia Capitolina **14** 22
Aelius Aristides **26** 925
Aelmis (family) **22** 881
Aelsinus **2** 77; **33** 233
Aelst, Evert van **1** 165; **33** 266
Aelst, Nicholas van **10** 389
Aelst, Pieter Coecke van *see* COECKE VAN AELST, PIETER
Aelst, Pieter van **1** 165*; **5** 49; **30** 317
patrons and collectors **16** 867
works **5** 47; **21** 16; **25** 902; **30** 315, II1
Aelst, Pieter van Edingen *see* EDINGEN AELST, PIETER VAN
Aelst, Willem van **1** 165–6*
patrons and collectors **28** 169
pupils **11** 228; **27** 454
teachers **28** 169
works **1** *165*; **11** 228; **22** 843; **29** 668
Aeltlin, Lienhard **31** 568
Aemilia Ars **16** 731
Aemilius Paulus **26** 764
Aenaria *see* PITHEKOUSSAI
Aeneas Tacitus **21** 577
Aengp'orŭmel *see* ART INFORMEL → Korea
Aeolis **13** 502
Aep, Jan **27** 256
Aeppli, Eva **30** 140
aeraria **26** 867
aerial perspective *see under* PERSPECTIVE → types
aerial photography *see* PHOTOGRAPHY → uses → surveys, photographic
Aernhofer, Hans (*fl* 1550-52) **22** 299
Aernhofer, Hans (*d* 1621) **22** 302; **33** 271
Aéro Club **24** 515
aerographs *see* AIRBRUSHES
aeronautical views *see* BIRD'S-EYE VIEWS
Aeropittura **1** 166*; **8** 771; **9** 191; **11** 80, 867; **16** 680; **20** 428
Aéroports de Paris **1** 495
Aerschot, Charles de Cröy, Duc de **26** 490
Aerssen van Sommelsdijk, Cornelis van **24** 103
Aert de Glaesmakere *see* ARNOULT DE NIMÈGUE
Aertgen van Leyden **1** 166–7*
attributions **1** *167*
patrons and collectors **23** 883
reproductive prints by others **9** 79
teachers **10** 216
works **19** 759
Aerts, Hendrick **19** 564
Aerts, Roch **12** 147
Aerts, Willem **3** 545
Aertsen, Niclaes **13** 234
Aertsen, Pieter **1** 168–9*, 799; **4** *895*
pupils **3** 887; **29** 740, 741
reproductive prints by others **20** 812
works **1** *169*, 658, 806; **3** 558; **8** 666; **12** 288; **22** 838, *838*; **29** 666
Aertsz., Hendrick **8** 663
Aertsz., Jan *see* AMSTEL, JAN VAN
Aertsz., Jan Terwen **22** 857
Aeschbacher, Hans **1** 170*; **30** 139
Aeschylus **1** 450; **13** 489, 550; **15** 149; **30** 650
Aesica brooch **6** 162
Aesop **1** 420; **4** 360; **10** 723
Aesslinger, Hans **1** 170*; **22** 302; **33** 271
Aesthetic Humanism **32** 483
Aesthetic Movement **1** 170–71*; **2** 475, 530, 569; **9** 19; **10** 254; **12** 216; **15** 895; **22** 51; **23** 504; **26** 743; **32** 415; **33** 137, 180
architecture **10** 238; **12** 840
etchings **33** *140*
exhibitions **19** 413
frames **11** *433*, 435–6, *436*
furniture **33** 155
interior decoration **1** *171*; **2** 755; **10** 282–3; **28** 249; **33** 139
ornament **23** 547
portraits **33** *139*, *141*
textiles **19** 311
writings **2** 530
see also ART FOR ART'S SAKE
aesthetics **1** 171–83*; **2** 835; **7** 563; **10** 207; **11** 310, 315; **14** 406–7; **22** 686; **29** 889
Africa **1** 230–34*, 235–40*
Akan **1** 238
Asante **1** 235, 238
Baule **1** 235, 238
Britain **10** 101; **24** 740
Byzantine **9** 622
China **6** 769, 771, 795–8
Chokwe **1** 236
Dan (Africa) **1** 236
Early Christian (*c.* AD 250-843) **9** 622
Edo (Africa) **1** 239
England **24** 257
18th cent. **7** 795; **25** 572–3
19th cent. **14** 263
20th cent. **19** 61
Epicureanism **1** 176
Fang **1** 237
France
16th cent. **31** 197
18th cent. **1** 898; **3** 386; **9** 327; **25** 799
19th cent. **4** 124; **8** 661; **10** 183–4; **14** 396
20th cent. **18** 587; **27** 853–4

aesthetics—cont.
Germany
18th cent. 3 411–12; 14 99, 446; 17 800–802; 21 121; 28 94, 109; 29 921–2
19th cent. 8 899; 14 298, 434; 28 56, 73, 160–61
20th cent. 19 457
Greece, ancient 1 175–6*; 13 375, 412, 413; 33 461–2
4th cent. BC 25 31–2
5th cent. BC 13 467
Guro 1 236
Ibibio 1 237
Idoma 1 236
Indian subcontinent 7 634; 15 206
Islamic 15 206
Italy
Mannerism 19 546–7
Renaissance 32 20
15th cent. 10 747; 11 56; 30 745
16th cent. 23 127
20th cent. 8 182–3
Japan 17 335
Kongo 1 236
Lega 1 236
Mende (Sierra Leone) 1 236
Native North Americans 22 561–2
Nicaragua 23 85
Nuba 1 237
Pacific Islands 23 713–14*, 714
Papua New Guinea 23 713, 714
Rome, ancient 1 176*; 26 924
Russia 25 38
Rwanda 1 237
Spain 21 128; 23 578–9, 628
Stoicism 1 176
Tibet 30 809
United States of America 8 839; 27 787
Yoruba 1 235, 239; 33 553–4
18th cent. 26 736–7
20th cent. 10 686; 14 304; 18 739; 31 97
see also ART CRITICISM; BEAUTY; MANUALS; TREATISES
Aethelbald, King of Mercia (reg 716-57) 25 743
Aethelbert, Archbishop of York 33 546
Aethelwald, Bishop of Lichfield 15 875
Aethelwold, Saint, Bishop of Winchester 1 183–4*; 33 234
architecture 2 66; 10 165; 24 544
manuscripts 2 74, 75, 75; 20 330; 28 487; 33 8
wall paintings 2 73
Aethiopia see NUBIA
Aetion 1 184*; 13 551
Aetius 23 375
Aetokremnos see AKROTIRI-AETOKEMNOS
Afāmiya see APAMEIA
Afanas'ev, Aleksey 30 361
Afanasev, Andrey 27 420
Afan de Ribera, Ferdinand 18 624
Afan de Rivera, Karlo 4 462
Afandou 26 289
Panagia Katholiki 26 295
Afar, Tell 21 280
Afars 1 343; 9 50
Afars and the Issas, French Territory of the see DJIBOUTI
al-Afdal 16 432; 31 21, 22
Afdal al-Husayni 15 681
Afer, Publius Terentius see TERENCE
Affandi 15 807, 808, 818; 33 538
Affecter 13 509; 32 29*
affiches lacérées 8 609
affichistes 8 609
Affleck, Desbarats, Dimakopoulos, Lebensold, Sise 1 184; 32 108
Affleck, Lewis G. 1 185
Affleck, Ray(mond Tait) 1 184*; 5 562; 22 36; 23 632
Affleck, Thomas 1 184–5*; 24 602; 31 626
Afflighem Abbey 3 542
Afflighem Abbey, Master of the see JOSEPH SEQUENCE, MASTER OF THE
Affonso, Sara 1 676
Affry, Adèle d', Duchessa di Castiglione Colonna see MARCELLO
Affry, Comte d' 18 628
Afganla, B. 2 897
Afghanistan 1 185–212*, 186; 6 181; 16 105
appliqué 10 872
arches 2 294; 16 167, 168, 168
architectural decorations 16 169
architecture 1 189–93*, 208*
brick 16 169
Buddhism 1 191–3*
Ghurid 16 169
Islamic 1 207–8*; 16 166–9*, 195–200*
Prehistoric 1 189–90*
Timurid 16 195–8
art history 1 210–11*
book covers 12 III1; 16 358
brass 16 378
brick 16 169
bronze 1 207; 16 366, 375
buckets 16 366
burnishing 1 207
calligraphy 16 276, 354
carpets 1 209*; 16 466
clay 1 193, 196, 197, 197, 198, 199, 202
coins 1 203–5*, 204; 15 687
collections 1 211–12*
columns 16 168
copper 16 366
crochet 30 549
dress 1 208
embroidery 1 209–10
epigraphy 16 166, 169
ewers 16 375, 378
felt 10 872, 874
gardens 16 197–8
garnets 1 206
gilding 12 III1; 29 825
glues 1 202
gold 1 204, 205, 206; 16 375
gypsum 1 202
historiography 1 210–11*
houses 1 208
iconography 1 188–9*, 198, 206
ikat 30 554
inlays 16 366, 375, 378
inscriptions 1 187; 16 166, 169
interior decoration 1 208, 209
ivory-carvings 1 195; 3 501
iwans 16 167
jewellery 1 205*, 210*
kaolin 1 202
Korans 16 290
lacquer 1 210
languages 1 187–8*; 15 198
lapis lazuli 1 185, 850; 14 168; 24 XII1
leather 12 III1; 16 358
limestone 1 193, 194
manuscript illumination 1 208*; 16 122, 290, 552
marble 1 198–9
mausolea 16 166
metalwork 1 205–7*
mihrabs 16 163
minarets 16 166, 167
miniatures (manuscript illumination) 16 324, 326; 20 VI
mosques 16 166
moulds 1 198; 29 825
mud-bricks 16 168
museums 1 211–12*
painting 1 208*
fresco 16 169
lorry 1 208
Afghanistan
painting—cont.
murals 1 209
wall 1 200–203*, 201, 202
palaces 1 189; 16 167
papercuts 16 354
plaster 29 824–5*
polychromy 1 198
pottery 1 207*, 210*; 16 407
religion 1 188–9*
reliquaries 1 206
schist 1 193, 195, 197
scripts 16 166, 169
sculpture 1 193*, 194–9*, 208*, 487; 29 824
bronze 1 207
Buddhism 1 197, 197–8*, 198, 199, 207
colossal statues 3 149
Hellenistic 1 197
Hinduism 1 199
Prehistoric 1 193–4*, 194
seals 1 850; 16 552
silver 1 204, 204, 210; 16 366, 375, 378
snuff-boxes 1 210
soldering 21 325
squinches 16 168–9
stucco 1 193, 196, 197–8; 16 163; 29 824–5*, 825
stupas 1 191–2, 192, 198; 3 113
synagogues 17 551
tempera 1 200, 202
tents 30 473
terracotta 16 166, 169
textiles 1 209–10*; 16 451
tiles 16 169
tin 1 850; 4 849
tombs 16 163
trade
coins 1 203
ivory 1 195
lapis lazuli 1 185; 9 814; 10 28; 12 246; 15 902; 21 272
pigments 15 551
ultramarine 24 790
wood-carvings 1 210
woodwork 1 210*
see also BACTRIA
Afikpo 1 386; 15 111
Afinger, Bernhard 1 212*; 26 23
Aflalo, Roberto 8 181*
Afokpella
costumes 1 270
Afong Lai see LAI, AFONG
Afonso, João 1 212*; 25 300
Afonso, Jorge 1 212–13*; 26 252
assistants 20 758
attributions 19 656; 25 295; 31 102
patrons and collectors 2 872
pupils 11 65; 19 655; 32 98
Afonso, Matondo 2 87
Afonso, Nadir 25 300
Åfors Group 30 103
Afrasiab see SAMARKAND
Africa 1 213–440*, 214, 255, 376, 379, 381, 386, 407
adobe 1 305
aesthetics 1 230–34*, 235–40*
altars 1 690
aluminium 1 411
amber 1 350
amulets 1 348
animal subjects 1 238
anklets 1 292, 351
anthropology 2 137
anvils 1 365
appliqué 1 299, 425
aprons 1 297, 418–19*, 419
archaeology 21 480–81
arches 1 315
architectural decorations 1 312–14, 313, 317–18, 318
architecture 1 304–21*, 306, 307, 377, 406, 410–11, 414*, 421–2*; 25 172
brick 1 377; 4 792–3*
Islamic 1 315–18*
Africa
architecture—cont.
megalithic 21 43*
military 21 596–7*
stone 1 377
trabeated construction 1 306
armlets 1 293
art criticism 2 519
art history 1 436*; 2 533
art legislation 1 251
art market 1 251, 252–3*
axes 1 361
bamboo 1 307, 310, 367
banknotes 3 181, 182
bark 1 293, 295, 306
basalt 1 292
baskets 1 310–11, 424; 3 331, 332
Angola 1 296
United States of America 1 426
Zaïre 1 296
basketwork 1 295–6*, 296; 3 332
beads 1 295, 296–8*, 347, 349, 350, 420; 12 440
Kenya 1 297, 350, 411
Kuba (iii) (Zaïre) 1 352, 353–4
Luba 1 325
Sudan 1 367
Yoruba 1 298
beadwork 1 349, 350, 410, 418–19*, 419; 4 I3
beds 1 366
bellows (furnaces) 1 287
blades 1 361
body arts 1 254–6*, 285, 288–9, 289, 297, 342–7*, 343, 344, 345, 409, 409
bone 1 296
bowls 1 356
boxes 1 366
tobacco-boxes 1 367*
bracelets 1 292, 296, 350, 351
brass 1 265, 287, 350, 351, 363; 4 854
brick 1 305, 377; 4 792–3*
Islamic 1 315, 317
bronze 1 287, 350; 4 854–5*
burial practices 1 257–9*
buttons 1 295
calabashes 1 302
cane 1 311; 3 331
canopies (ii) (textile coverings) 1 354
caricatures 5 761*
carnivals 1 423*
carving 1 303, 428
caves 1 304
cedar 1 307
cement 1 331–2*, 332
ceramics 1 285–6*, 328–30*, 378
Chad Republic 1 330
Mangbetu 1 329
Zaïre 1 329
chairs 1 366
chests 1 366; 33 III2
churches 1 314, 314–15
cicatrices 1 344–5, 346, 346
cladding 1 307
clay 1 285, 296, 367, 418; 29 827
laterite 1 305; 29 827
cloaks 1 424
coins 1 362
collections 1 438–9*
erotic art 10 487
sculpture 7 562; 13 826; 22 360
colour 7 635*
combs (hair) 1 423
compounds 1 311–12
copper 1 286, 287, 288, 296, 350, 411
coral 1 305, 350
cornelian 1 350
costumes 1 268, 270
cotton 1 218, 229, 251, 293, 424, 425; 9 III2; 30 VIII1
craftsmen and artists 1 242, 243–5*, 243, 244, 251, 286, 300, 303, 312, 338, 396
crowns 1 298, 353
crucifixes 1 228, 406
Africa—cont.
currency 1 362–3*; 12 440
cushion covers 1 218
cutlery 1 326
dealing 1 438–9*
divination instruments 1 355–8*, 356
dolls 1 419; 31 261
fertility 1 420
doors 1 314, 383, 427; 9 164–5*
drawings 1 431
dress 1 295, 347–9*, 348, 388
dung 29 827
dyeing 1 294, 303; 9 III2
dyes 1 294, 295, 299, 343
earplugs 1 351, 367
earrings 1 351
earth 1 284*; 9 164
education (art) 1 431
eggshells 1 350
embroidery 1 229, 295, 296, 299, 349
engraving 1 302–3, 302, 303
erotic art 10 473–4
etchings 1 429
ethnography 21 480
exhibitions 1 437–8*; 31 490
façades 1 317
fans 10 778–9*
feathers 1 296, 349, 405
fences 1 311
fibres 1 293*, 295–6*, 355, 405
figurines 1 271–3*, 330
Benin Republic 1 272
Cameroon 1 277
Congo, Republic of 1 275
Ghana 1 272
Nigeria 1 270
Senufo 1 281
Zaïre 1 269
finials (architectural) 1 328
footwear 1 349*
forgeries 1 434–6*
fortifications 1 311; 21 596–7*
forts 1 318
frames 1 306
fringes 1 300
funerary objects 1 257–8*, 339
funerary urns 18 218
fur 1 295, 296
furnaces 1 287, 287
furniture 1 365–6*
gesture 1 264–6*
glass 1 233, 296, 297, 297
gneiss 1 292
gold 1 286, 288, 296, 350
gourds 1 302–4*, 302, 303, 367, 382
granaries 1 310, 310–11
grasses 1 295, 306, 307, 308, 426; 3 331
guns 1 362
gypsum 1 305
hair 1 307, 404
hairstyles 1 342–3, 343
hangings 1 307
harnesses 14 183*
harps 1 359
hats 1 296, 349
headbands 1 351
headdresses 1 254, 349*, 351, 386, 391
headrests 1 366, 403, 411, 411, 416, 416–17*
hedges 21 597
henna 1 343
hides 1 295, 299, 307, 411
historiography 1 235, 436*
horns 1 326
houses 1 295, 305–7, 308, 311–14, 313, 318, 318, 319, 320, 421; 4 792
Basle Mission 1 319
bungalows 1 318
farmhouses 1 318
Islamic 1 308, 315–16
mbari 1 314, 331
Pètési 1 319
prefabricated 1 318

Africa—cont.
human figures **1** 321–2
huts **1** *306*, 307–8, *311*
iconoclasm **1** 228
iconography **1** 260–64*, 271–9*, 280–84*, 312, 334–6, 352
ikat **1** 294
impressing **1** 286
indigo **1** 294; **7** 635
iroko-wood **33** III2
iron **1** *233*, 286, 287, 288, 296, *297*, 350, 385
ivory **1** *219*, 292–3*, *293*, 325–8*, *326*, *327*, 350, 351, 352, *356*
ivory-carvers **1** 292
ivory-carvings **1** 292–3
Benin, Kingdom of **1** *293*, *327*
Sierra Leone **1** *326*
jars **1** 310–11
jewellery **1** 350–51*
kaolin **1** 343
kilns **1** 305
knitting **18** 158
knives **1** 361, *361*
kohl **1** 344
lead **1** 287
leather **1** *218*, 295, 299–300*, *300*, *322*, 349, *349*, *355*, *410*; **3** 331; **10** 778
leaves **1** *384*
libraries **1** 439*
limestone **1** 305
locust-beans **1** 305
looms **1** 250, 294, *294*
lost-wax casting **1** 288
malachite **1** 287
manuscript illumination **1** *380*
masks **1** 256*, *268*, *273*, 273–4, 278–9, *279*, 290, 296, 298, 301, 333–42*, *335*, *336*, *337*, *338*, *339*, *341*, 382, 384, 389–90, *390*, *399*, *405*, 405–6, 409–10, 423*
Bwa **1** *384*
Chamba (ii) (Africa) **6** *406*
Congo, Republic of **1** *399*
Islamic **1** 229
Kuba (iii) (Zaïre) **1** *301*
Mende (Sierra Leone) **1** *237*
Mossi **1** *384*
Nigeria **1** *239*, *241*
Sierra Leone **1** *237*
Western Equatoria **1** 398–9
Yoruba **1** *239*, *241*
Zaïre **1** *301*
masonry **1** 305
mats **1** 296, 306, 308, 366
mazes **21** 597
measures **1** 363–4
medical centres **1** *320*
meeting-houses **1** *309*, 310, *314*
metal **1** 286–8*, *322*
metalwork **1** 287–8, 400
metalworkers **1** 246, 286
mirrors **1** *219*
mixed-media **1** 300–302*, *301*
monasteries **1** 314–15
mosaics **1** 377–8
mosques **1** 229, *316*, 316–17
moulds **1** 285
mud **1** 284–5*, 295, 305, 307, 330–31*, 409; **9** 164
mud-bricks **4** 792, *792*
museums **1** 437*
musical instruments **1** 302, 358–60*, *359*; **22** 375
necklaces **1** 350, *350*
nuts **1** 296
oils **1** 305
open-mould casting **1** 288
painting **1** 303, 380, 399–400, 425*, 430–31
acrylic **1** *432*
genre **1** *432*
landscape **1** *430*
United States of America **1** *426*
wall **1** *246*, 289, *290*, 313, 411
20th cent. **7** I2
paints **1** 285, 288–90*

Africa—cont.
palaces **1** 242, 308–9, 314, 315; **23** 824–5*
palisades **21** 597
palm leaves **1** 295, *296*, 305–7; **3** 331
papyrus **1** 310
parapets **1** 308
patronage **1** 240–43*, 251*, 433–4
pendants (jewellery) **1** 367
periodicals **24** 429–30*
periods
Prehistoric **25** 468
photoarchives **1** 439*
photography **10** 580
pigments **7** 635
pipes (smoking) **1** 367–8*, *367*
plaster **1** 305; **29** 827–8*
plastic **1** 295
poles **1** 306, 307, 410
polychromy **25** 172
porches **1** 308
portraits **1** *226*, 267–71*, 354–5
posubans **1** 314
pots **1** 417–18*
cooking **1** 369
Mangbetu **1** *329*
water **1** 369, *369*
Zaïre **1** *329*
pottery **1** 246, 285–6, *286*, 406, 424*, 428; **31** 261
pyxides (boxes) **1** 326
quilts **1** 424, *425*
raffia **1** 293, 294, *294*, 295, 296, 336, *382*; **3** 331
reeds **1** 307, 311
regalia **1** 241–2, *242*, 351–5*, *352*, *353*, *355*
regions **1** 376*
Central **1** 400–406*, *401*
East **1** 406–11*, *407*
Guinea Coast **1** 386–93*
North-east **1** 378–80*
Northern **1** 376–8*
Southern **1** *413*, 413–19*
Western Equatoria **1** 393–400*, *394*
Western Sudan **1** 380–86*
religion **1** 226–30*, 421; **8** 229–31
rings **1** 351
ritual objects **1** 242–3, 257; **18** *220*
rituals **1** 257–9*, *260*, 338–9
robes **1** *353*
rock art **1** 370–75*, 378, 402, 408
painting **1** *220*, *374*, *375*, *376*
Prehistoric **1** *220*
San **27** 695–8
roofs **1** 305, *306*, 307, 308, 320
roots **1** 295
salts **1** 326, *326*, *327*
sand **29** 827
sandstone **1** 305
scarification **1** 344–6, *345*, 409; **10** 474
screens (i) (architectural) **1** 313
screens (ii) (furniture) **1** 291
sculpture **1** *219*, 257–8*, 278, 285, 300–301*, 321–32*, *332*, 378, 385–6, 418, 422–3*, 427–8
architectural **1** 314
display **22** 360
equestrian **1** 280–81*
figure **1** 230–34, 321–5*, 382, 396–8, *397*, *398*, 402–5, 410, 415–16
Bamana **1** *323*
Baule **1** *233*, *324*
Chokwe **1** *404*
Dogon **1** *322*
Fang **1** *232*
Kongo **1** *233*; **18** *217*, *219*, *220*
Luba **1** *325*
Mangbetu **1** *404*
Sapi culture **1** *388*
Tsonga **1** *415*
Kalabari Ijo **1** *247*
stone **18** *217*, *219*

Africa
sculpture—cont.
United States of America **1** *422*
wood **1** 321–5*, *322*
Bamana **1** *323*
Baule **1** *233*, *324*
Chokwe **1** *404*
Fang **1** *232*
Gabon **1** *397*, *398*
Kissi **1** *359*
Kongo **1** *233*; **18** *220*
Luba **1** *325*
Mangbetu **1** *404*
Tsonga **1** *415*
United States of America **1** *422*
Zande **1** *359*
20th cent. **1** 251
Yoruba **4** I3
seeds **1** 296
shells **1** 295, 296, 362; **28** 581
shelters **1** 306
shields **1** 299, 362*, 411, *412*; **3** 332
shirts **1** 348, *349*
shrines (i) (cult) **1** 289, 309–10, 313, 331, *332*
silk **1** 293
silver **1** 350, 351
sinew **1** 295
sisal **1** 296
skins **1** 295, 418
calfskin **1** 299
goatskin **1** 299, 307, *307*
sheepskin **1** 299
skirts **1** *410*
slaves **3** 60; **4** 707–8; **5** 753; **7** 603; **9** 115; **16** 880; **30** 13
sledges **1** 296
slit-drums **22** 375
slit-gongs **1** *359*, 360*
snuff-boxes **1** 351, 367*
soapstone **1** 292, *388*
sound and art **29** 96
spears **1** 362
spinning (textile) **1** 294
spoons **1** *291*, 326, *368*, 368–9*
staffs **1** *265*, *278*, *355*, *402*, 417, *417*
steel **1** *247*, 287
stone **1** 292*, 296, 305, 350, 377; **18** *217*, *219*
stone-carvings **1** 292, 429
stools **1** 353, 365–6, *366*
straw **1** 307
stucco **29** 827–8*
swords **1** 361
symbolism (critical term) **1** 260–64*
tables **1** 366
talc **1** 292
tattoos **1** 344–5, 346–7
teeth **1** 296
tembes **1** 311
temples **1** 309–10
tents **1** 307, *307*
terracotta **1** *221*, *222*, 285; **18** *218*; **30** *508*, 508–9*
textiles **1** 348–9, 378, 406, 423–4*, 428; **23** 131; **30** 562
thatch **1** 306, 307, 308
threads **1** 343
thrones **1** *352*, 353
timber structures **1** 306
tools **1** 291, *364*, 364–5*
tourist art **1** 239, 251, *252*, 252–3, *253*
trade **1** 248–51*
beads **1** 297
cornelian **1** 350
dress **1** 347
feathers **1** 250
ivory **1** 250
metal **1** 250
silk **1** 249
slaves **1** 249–50*
textiles **1** 250
trappings **14** 183*
trays **1** *356*

Africa—cont.
trousers **1** 348
trumpets **1** 292
tunics **1** *229*
umbrellas **1** 354
universities **1** 319
verandahs **1** 308
wall decorations **1** 312
walls **1** 305, 306, 307
waxes **33** 1
weapons **1** 361–2*
weaving **1** 246, 250, 293–5*, *294*
weights **1** 277–8, *363*, 363–4, 428
whisks **10** 779
women **1** 246–7*, 256, 340
women artists **1** *246*, 246–7*
wood **1** 251, 291–2*, 295, 305–7, 321–5*, 365, *402*, 402, *403*, *404*, *415*; **9** 164
Asante **1** *390*
Baga **1** *391*
Bamana **1** *323*
Baule **1** *233*, *324*
Cameroon **1** *277*
Congo, Republic of **1** *399*
Dan (Africa) **1** *368*
Dogon **1** *322*
Fang **1** *232*
Gabon **1** *399*
Ibibio **1** *273*
Kenya **1** *411*, *412*
Kissi **1** *359*
Kongo **1** *233*, *275*; **18** *220*
Kuba (iii) (Zaïre) **1** *269*
Lobi **1** *272*
Luba **1** *325*, *355*
Mbete **1** *398*
Mossi **1** *384*
Nigeria **1** *427*
Nupe **1** *383*
Senufo **1** *281*
Shona **1** *416*
Surinam **1** *423*
United States of America **1** *422*
Yoruba **1** *270*, *356*
Zande **1** *359*
wood-carvers **1** 246
wood-carvings **1** *252*, *253*, *291*, 291–2, *366*, 414*; **9** 66; **33** 325
wool **1** 293
wraps **1** 348
Africa, German East *see* RWANDA
Africa, South *see* SOUTH AFRICA
Africana *see under* COLLECTIONS → types
African American art **1** 440–46*; **31** 606
exhibitions **1** 446
houses **1** 440
marble **1** *441*
painting **1** *443*, *445*; **9** 199
portraits **1** 440
prizes (artists') **3** 185
screenprints **1** *444*
sculpture **1** 440, *441*; **19** 286
African-American Museum Association **32** 890
African Arts **1** 436; **24** 425, 430
African Commune of Bad Relevant Artists *see* AFRICOBRA
African Heritage **17** 908
africano *see* MARBLE → types → *Marmor luculleum*
African Union of Architects **23** 427
Africanus, Constantius *see* CONSTANTIUS AFRICANUS
Africa Proconsularis *see* TUNISIA
AfriCobra (African Commune of Bad Relevant Artists) **1** 445
Afrikaners *see* BOERS
Afro (Basaldella) **1** 446*; **21** 704; **26** 777
groups and movements **13** 727; **16** 681; **26** 777
works **19** 491
Afro-American art *see* AFRICAN AMERICAN ART

Afro-Caribbean culture
Bahamas, the **3** 59–60*, *60*
Caribbean Islands **5** 752–4*, *753*, *754*
Cuba (Caribbean) **5** 752
Dominican Republic **5** 752; **9** 115, *116*
Haiti **14** 55–6*, *56*
Jamaica **16** 880–82*, *881*
Puerto Rico **5** 752; **25** 699–700*
Trinidad and Tobago **31** 331–3*, *332*
Afrox Limited **29** 121
Afroz, Meher **23** 800
Afshar, Muhammad Hasan *see* MUHAMMAD HASAN AFSHAR
Afshar carpets *see under* CARPETS → types
Afsharid, Nadir Shah *see* NADIR SHAH, Ruler
Afshuta Mosque **16** 502
Afsin, Ribat-i Eshab-i Kehf **16** 185
AFT **24** 449
Afterimage **24** 434
Afula **17** 854
Afyon
Ak Mescid **16** 202
congregational mosque **16** 497; **22** 323
Great Mosque **16** 202
Kubbeli Mosque **16** 202
mosque of Gedik Ahmed Pasha **16** 206
Afzal **1** 446–7*
Ağa, Davud **16** 223, 595
Aga Alesker Safarogly **2** 901
Agababayeva, T. **2** 898
Agababov, T. **2** 898
Agabiti, Pietro Paolo **1** 447*
Agache, Donat-Alfred **1** 447*; **31** 729
collaboration **24** 128; **25** 658
staff **26** 109
teachers **18** 664
works **16** 587
Agache, Roger **32** 544
Agade **1** 508; **21** 268, 272
Agades **1** *381*
congregational mosque **1** 316
Agadez **31** 406, 407
Agadir
Groupe Scolaire **1** 319
Post Office **1** 319
Agaie **23** 303
Aga Khan, Sadruddin, Prince *see* SADRUDDIN AGA KHAN, Prince
agalma *see* SCULPTURE → types → cult statues
agalmatolite **27** *437*
Agam, Yaacov **1** 448*
dealers **26** 193, 194
groups and movements **23** 448, 449
methods **19** 395
works **3** 462; **29** 97
Agamedes **13** 389
Agamemnon *see* QUAY, PIERRE-MAURICE
Agano **1** 448*; **17** *11*
Agano ware *see under* POTTERY → wares
Aga-Oglu, Mehmet **16** 549
Agapiti, Pietro Paolo *see* AABITI, PIETRO PAOLO
Agar, Charles, Archbishop of Cashel and Dublin **22** 147
Agar, Charles d' **1** 449; **26** 473
Agar, Eileen **1** 448–9*; **10** 257, 268; **30** 22
Agar, Jacques d' **1** 449*; **8** 733; **19** 583
Agar, Madeline **7** 644
Agarabi **24** 75
agar-agar **11** 142
Agarak' **2** 435
Agard, Antoine **6** 76
Agard, Frank **2** 152
Agar Dinka
huts **1** *306*

Agar-Ellis, George James, 1st Baron Dover 10 146*; 14 270
Agar Ellis, Welbore see ELLIS, WELBORE AGAR
Agasias of Ephesos 4 407; 13 466
Agasse, Jacques-Laurent 1 449–50*; 12 276
  collaboration 20 592
  patrons and collectors 14 146; 21 91
  works 1 *449*; 2 105; 28 714; 30 133
Agassiz, Alexander 26 342
Agassiz, Louis 29 221
agate 14 167
  historical and regional traditions
    China 7 4, 90, 91, 109, 111, *111*
    England 10 347, *347*
    Etruscan 12 249
    France 11 *636*
    Germany 12 *459*; 14 167
    Greece, ancient 12 247, *247*
    Indian subcontinent 15 697–8*
    Iran, ancient 15 902
    Italy 14 I1
    Portugal 25 312
    Rome, ancient 12 250
    Russia 10 *721*
    South America, Pre-Columbian 29 155
    Tibet 30 839
  types
    Iceland agate see OBSIDIAN
    moss 14 II1; 17 525
    onyx see ONYX
    sardonyx see SARDONYX
  uses
    abrasives 7 11
    beads 30 839
    bowls 14 II1
    boxes 10 347
    burnishing 12 622
    crowns 7 111, *111*
    ewers 11 *636*
    jewellery 7 109, 111; 17 525, 529
    necklaces 7 4
    paternoster beads 17 520
    pietre dure 14 I1
    scarabs 12 *247*, 249
    seals 12 247
    snuff-boxes 10 *347*; 12 *459*
    watches 7 443
Agate, C. Gustave 28 281
Agatharchos 1 450*; 13 548, 551, 553; 15 135
  works 13 550
  writings 31 298
Agathyrsae 28 320
Agay Shipwreck 16 503
Agbarho 9 736
Agbome 1 284, *386*; 3 728; 11 246
  currency 1 363
  Musée Historique 3 728; 11 246
  royal palace 11 246
Agbon 9 736
A & G Development Consultants Inc 1 463
Agea, Juan 21 378, 403
Agea, Ramón 21 378, 403
Agedatami 11 826
Agedincum see SENS
Agee, James 10 656; 19 280
Ageladas 1 450*; 22 402; 25 177
Agelii, John Gustaf see AGUÉLI, IVAN (GUSTAVE)
Agellio, Giuseppe 33 587
Agen
  aqueduct 2 242
  Cathedral 26 584
  St Caprais 6 467
Age of Reason see ENLIGHTENMENT, THE
Ager Church 6 556
Ageyev, L. 18 84
Agg, James 5 418
Aggabodhi IV, King of Sri Lanka (*reg* 667-85) 25 169
Aggersborg 8 721; 32 532
Aggházy, Gyula 30 210
aggogoo see GONGS → types → double
Agha, Zubeida 1 450–51*; 23 799, 801
Aghadjanyan, Stephan 2 431, 432
Agha Muhammad, Shah (*reg* 1779-97) (Qajar) 12 82; 16 539; 21 589; 22 262
Aghapur 15 449
Aghdam 2 *890*
  congregational mosque 2 893
Aghjots' Monastery
  St Step'anos 2 435
Aghlabid 1 451*; 23 815
  see also:
    ABU IBRAHIM AHMAD, Governor
    IBRAHIM IBN AL-AGHLAB, Governor
    IBRAHIM II, Governor
    ZIYADAT ALLAH, Governor
Aght'amar 1 451–2*; 2 *423*, 426; 9 *512*
  Church of the Holy Cross 1 451–2; 2 444; 7 256
  reliefs 2 434, *434*, 435, 442
  sculpture 2 434
  wall paintings 2 429, *429*
  Sourb Khatch see Church of the Holy Cross
Aghts'
  hypogeum 2 433
  mausoleum 2 425, 434
Aghupuk 22 189
Aghurmi 28 810
  Oracle Temple 9 834
Agibiciu Church 25 341
AGIC see ARCHITECTURAL GROUP FOR INDUSTRY AND COMMERCE
Agighiol 25 *471*; 26 *705*; 30 771
  helmets 30 770, *770*, 772
  tomb 1 452*; 30 770
Agilqiyya 24 602
Agilulf 19 549
Agilulfing, Liutpirc, Duchess of Bavaria see LIUTPIRC, Duchess of Bavaria
Agilulfing, Otilo, Duke of Bavaria see OTILO, Duke of Bavaria
Agilulfing, Tassilo III, Duke of Bavaria see TASSILO III, Duke of Bavaria
Agin, Aleksandr (Alekseyevich) 18 138
Agincourt, Pierre d' see PIERRE D'AGINCOURT
Agion Oros see MT ATHOS
agitprop 1 452–3*; 6 529; 20 *887*; 22 178; 25 653; 27 284
Aglamova, L. 2 898
Aglaophon (grandfather) 25 176
Aglaophon (grandson) 25 176
Ağlasun see SAGALASSOS
Aglia, Antonio degli, Bishop of Florence 26 444
Agliate, SS Pietro e Paolo 23 649; 26 577
Agliè, Conte d' 31 449
Agliè, Filippo d' 28 10
Agliè Castello
  church 21 431
  Galleria di Ponente 16 720
Aglio see ALLIO
Aglio, Agostino 25 193
Aglionby, William 10 249; 24 741
Agneesens, Edouard (-Joseph-Alexandre) 1 453*; 5 44
Agnellus, Bishop of Ravenna 1 764; 29 816
Agnes, Duchess of Aquitaine see AGNES OF BURGUNDY, Countess of Anjou
Agnes, Queen of Hungary (1281-1364) 29 512
Agnesi, Giovanni Battista 20 371
Agnesini, Francesco 1 631
Agnes of Burgundy, Countess of Anjou (*fl* 11th cent.) 27 552
Agnes of Meissen (*d* 1203) 12 468
Agnetti, Vincenzo 6 21; 20 352
Agnew, Geoffrey 10 367
Agnew, Lockett 1 454
Agnew, Morland 1 454
Agnew, Thomas (1794-1871) 1 453–4*; 3 245; 10 679, 887; 18 906; 20 238; 29 634
Agnew, Thomas (1827-83) 1 453
Agnew, Tho(ma)s & Sons 10 366; 22 112
  catalogues 6 80
  exhibitions 10 679
  paintings 10 367; 13 836; 21 604; 22 351; 29 486
  photographs 10 887
  prints 21 604
Agnew, William 1 453, 454*; 7 548; 13 666; 19 427; 30 464; 32 795
Agniolo di Cosimo di Mariano Tori see BRONZINO, AGNOLO
Agnisy, Jean Grolier, Vicomte d' see GROLIER, JEAN, Vicomte d'Agnisy
Agnolo, Andrea d' see SARTO, ANDREA DEL
Agnolo, Baccio d' see BACCIO D'AGNOLO
Agnolo, Giuliano di Baccio d' see BAGLIONE, GIULIANO
Agnolo, Polo di see POLO DI AGNOLO
Agnolo del Moro, dell' see ANGOLO DEL MORO, DELL'
Agnolo di Domenico di Donnino 26 816
Agnolo di Lippo di Polo 1 454
Agnolo di Papi, Micele see MICELE AGNOLO DI PAPI
Agnolo di Polo 1 454*; 32 366
Agnolo di Tura 19 669, 670
Agnolo di Ventura 1 457; 2 389; 7 359
Agocchi, Giovanni Battista see AGUCCHI, GIOVANNI BATTISTA
Agocchiari, Barnaba see BARNABA DA MODENA
agorai 1 455*; 2 *684*; 8 154; 13 380, 381, *381*, 419
  see also FORA
Agorakritos 1 455*; 13 453, 455
  attributions 2 684
  works 2 685; 8 262; 13 454; 24 205; 26 287
Agost 15 59
Agostín, Antonio 15 83
Agostinho da Piedade 27 644
Agostinho de Jesus 4 715
Agostini, Alfredo 2 397
Agostini, Angelo 1 455*
Agostini, Ippolito 27 121
Agostini, Leonardo 2 162; 12 4; 21 27
Agostini, Niccolò degli 23 680
Agostino, Fra 3 307; 24 26
Agostino, Domenico d' see DOMENICO D'AGOSTINO
Agostino, Gaetano D' see D'AGOSTINO, GAETANO
Agostino, Giovanni d' see GIOVANNI D'AGOSTINO
Agostino (di Antonio) di Duccio 1 455–6*
  attributions 20 767
  collaboration 24 247; 30 497
  patrons and collectors 20 27, 160
  works 1 *456*; 10 743; 24 520; 26 399, 400
Agostino di Giovanni 1 457*; 2 389; 13 93; 24 854; 28 684
Agostino di Marsiglio 28 682
Agostino Veneziano see MUSI, AGOSTINO DEI
Agosto, Jacopo 25 443
Agouti 21 585
Agra 1 458–62*; 15 196, *261*, *360*; 16 *105*
  Agra Fort 1 460–62*, *461*; 15 196, 362–3, 365, *655*; 16 239; 21 591
    Akbari Mahal 1 461
    Anguri Bagh 12 74
    congregational mosque 1 462; 15 365, 366
    Divan-i 'Am 1 461–2
    gardens 12 74
    Jahangiri Mahal 1 461; 15 196, 362–3; 22 258; 23 818
    Khas Mahal 1 461
    Machchi Bhavan 1 461
    Moti Masjid see congregational mosque
    Muthamman Burj 1 461
    Nagina Masjid 1 461
    Shish Mahal 1 461
  art forms and materials
    architecture 8 674; 15 409
    brocades 15 662
    carpets 15 682; 16 485
    enamel 16 515
    manuscripts 15 595
    paintings 15 544, 596, 597
    tiles 15 686
    weapons 15 678
  gardens 12 73; 15 361, 364
    Ram Bagh 12 73; 15 364
  halls 14 77
  Kachpura Mosque 15 362
  tombs
    Chini ka Rauza 15 374, 686
    Taj Mahal 1 *459*, 459–60*; 15 196, 365–6; 16 141, 239; 18 71; 20 570; 22 258; 31 112, 114
      arches 2 294
      dome 9 83
      gardens 12 74; 16 129
      metalwork 16 389
    tomb of Arjumand Banu Begum see Taj Mahal
    tomb of I'timad al-Daula 1 460*; 15 364, *364*; 29 526
      gardens 12 74
    tomb of J. W. Hessing 31 115
    tomb of Mahmud of Ghazna 16 492
    tomb of Mulla Shukrulla Shirazi see Chini ka Rauza
    tomb of Shah Jahan see Taj Mahal
Agrab, Tell 1 *849*, 893; 9 46*; 21 *267*, 303, 552
  see also DIYALA REGION
Agrate, Gianfrancesco d' 1 462; 33 586
Agrate, Marco d' 1 462*; 21 533
Agreda, Esteban de 1 462*
Agrest, Diana 1 463*
Agresti da Forlì, Livio 26 818; 28 658
Agricola, Christoph Ludwig 1 463*
Agricola, Filippo 31 172
Agricola, Georgius 4 682; 8 416, 823; 15 827; 28 737
Agricola, Gioacchino 4 407
Agricola, Karl 11 789; 21 643
Agricola, Lorenz 12 495
Agricola, Luigi 5 367
Agricola, Rudolf 14 868
Agridia, Hagios Philon 8 358
Agrigento
  Akragas 1 511–12*; 13 *362*; 26 *886*
  architecture 28 654
  bouleuterion 4 530
  busts 13 583
  catacombs 6 70
  coins 28 654
  figurines 13 579, 580, 581
  fortifications 21 556
  Oratory of Phalaris 20 864
  sanctuary 13 *416*
  sculpture 22 402
Agrigento—cont.
  S Nicola 28 656
  temples 1 511; 13 374, 416
    Olympieion see Temple of Olympian Zeus
    Temple of Concord 28 655
    Temple of Herakles 1 511
    Temple of Hera Lakinia 10 414; 13 545; 33 639
    Temple of Olympian Zeus 1 511, *511*; 2 695; 7 502; 13 373, 374, 391, 415, 451
  Tomb of Theron 20 863
  town walls 21 556
Agrigento Painter 13 521
Agrinion Archaeological Museum 13 534
Agrippa(, Marcus Vipsanius) 1 463*
  architecture 2 668, 685; 5 375; 7 354; 23 619; 26 750, 751, 792, 890, 891; 32 632
  art policies 13 555
  hydraulic works 11 339
  paintings 9 13; 27 54
  sculpture 27 31
Agrippa, Lucius Julius 2 214
Agrippina the elder 14 II2
Agrippina the younger 14 II2; 26 891
Agripppa, Cornelio 11 270
Agris 25 542
  Grotte des Perrats 6 157
Agroha
  sculpture 15 *484*
A-group culture 23 277
  sculpture 23 *278*
Agrupació del Disseny Industrial-Societat de Foment de les Art Decoratives see ADI-FAD
Agrupación Courbet 2 542; 9 104; 21 705
Agrupación de Acuarelistas de Catalonia 32 903
Agrupación del Diseño Industrial (ADI) see ADI-FAD
Agrupación Espacio 19 387; 24 505
Agua Blanca 1 464*; 20 316; 29 *136*
Aguada culture 29 190
Água de Peixes 25 291
Aguado, Antonio López see LÓPEZ AGUADO, ANTONIO
Aguado, Martín López see LÓPEZ AGUADO, MARTÍN
Aguado Bejarano, Antonio Cabral y see CABRAL Y AGUADO BEJARANO, ANTONIO
Aguado de la Sierra, Miguel 1 464*
Aguado y Ramírez de Estemoz, Alejandro, Marqués de Las Marismas del Guadalquivir see LAS MARISMAS DEL GUADALQUIVIR, Marqués de
aguana 24 515
Aguas Buenas ware see under POTTERY → wares
Aguascalientes
  Cathedral 21 377
  Instituto Nacional de Estadistica, Geografía e Informática 21 381
  S Antonio 21 379
Aguayo, Pablo Burchard see BURCHARD AGUAYO, PABLO
Agucchi, Giovanni Battista 1 464–5*; 5 755; 9 88; 26 771
  pupils 3 673
  writings 9 7, 93
Agucchi, Girolamo, Cardinal 9 88
Agudo, Gil 29 342
Agudo, José de Madrazo y see MADRAZO Y AGUDO, JOSÉ DE
Aguéli, Ivan (Gustave) 1 465–6*; 30 81
Aguéli Museum see under SALA
Agüero, Benito Manuel de 20 900

Agüero, Juan Miguel de **2** 375; **21** 154, 375, 401
works **21** *376*
Agüero, Leopoldo Torres *see* TORRES AGÜERO, LEOPOLDO
Agueros, Jack **18** 833
Aguesca, Jerónimo **1** 466
Aguesca, Lorenzo **1** 466
Aguesca, Teresa **1** 466
Aguiar, Francisco Marcelino de Souza *see* MARCELINO DE SOUZA AGUIAR, FRANCISCO
Aguiar, João José de **1** 466*; **10** 728; **25** 301
Aguila, Diego del *see* DIEGO DEL AGUILA
Aguila, Pietro **11** 24
Aguilar **22** 607
Aguilar, Alonso de **24** 395; **29** 336
Aguilar, Carlos **13** 771
Aguilar, Fidel **23** 260
Aguilar, José de **21** 393
Aguilar, José Manuel de **9** 112
Aguilar, José María **1** 149
Aguilar, Juan de Herrera *see* HERRERA AGUILAR, JUAN DE
Aguilar, Mauricio **10** 154
Aguilar, Pablo *see* SERRANO, PABLO
Aguilar, Ricardo **14** 716
Aguilar, T. N. **16** 886
Aguilar, Tomás de **32** 135
Aguilar, Vincent D' *see* D'AGUILAR, VINCENT
Aguilar de Campóo **26** 609
S Miguel **26** 642
Aguilar de la Frontera **29** 337
Aguilar Ponce, Luis **1** 467*
Aguilar's Furnishing Warehouse **16** 886
Aguilera, Enrique de, Marqués de Cerralbo **29** 355
Aguilera, Marcos de **22** 507
Aguilera Cerni, Vicente **1** 620; **10** 443
Aguilera Silva, Gerardo **1** 467*
Aguilonius, Franciscus **1** 467*
assistants **15** 45
collaboration **3** 545
works **1** 113; **2** 192
Aguirre, Andrés Ginés de *see* GINÉS DE AGUIRRE, ANDRÉS
Aguirre, Francisco de **6** 591
Aguirre, Juan Antonio **29** 287
Aguirre, Juan de **13** 764
Aguirre Aristiguieta, Miguel **23** 629
Aguiton **31** 339
Agul **27** 432
Aguntum, Cathedral of Holy Andreas **2** 776
Agurcia, Ricardo **14** 716
Agurto Calvo, Santiago **24** 505
Agustín, Antonio, Archbishop of Tarragona **1** 467–8*; **29** 353
Ágústsson, Hörður **1** 468*; **15** 70
Aguyari, José **28** 810
Agvaan Balden **21** 873
Agvaandorz **21** 882
Agvanhaidub **21** 873
Agylla *see* CERVETERI
Aha **9** *776*, *828*; **10** 60; **27** 810
Ahab **27** 669, 670
el-Ahaiwah **10** 80
Ahalya Bai **2** 881
Ahalyabai Holkar **10** 148
Ahanakht **3** 848
Ahar **15** 598; **31** 518–19
Archaeological Museum **31** 519
cenotaphs **15** 389, 491
Jaina temple **15** 322
screens (i) (architectural) **15** 263
sculpture **15** 497
Aharoni, Y. **18** 596
Ahaw **20** 886
AHCI (*Arts and Humanities Citation Index*) **4** 26
Ahde-Kjäldman, Aili-Salli **19** 643
Ahed, M. A. **23** 801
Ahenny **1** 468*; **16** *5*
crosses **8** *196*, 196; **15** 876
Ahgupuk, George **22** 596
Ahhotpe (*d c.* 1550-30 BC) **1** 469*; **9** 879; **10** 31
axes **10** 41
coffin **9** 879; **10** 10
daggers **9** 818
exhibition **10** 94
jewellery **10** *31*
sarcophagus **10** 90
Ahichchhatra **1** 469*; **15** *261*
ivory **15** 695
plaques **30** 510
reliefs **15** 719
sculpture **15** 413, 441, 449
temple **15** 257
terracotta **15** 455
Ahinposh **1** 206; **15** 700
stupa **1** 211
Ahir **15** 176
Ahiram, King of Byblos (*reg c.* 1000 BC) **5** 332; **22** 511; **24** 642; **30** 187, 193
Ahlat **16** 411
fortifications **21** 586
tomb of Bayindir **16** 204; **31** 113
Ahlatlibel **1** 856
Ahlberg, Hakon **1** 470*; **3** 25; **30** 75, 92
Ählberg-Kriland, Gudrun **15** 142
Ahlers-Hestermann, Friedrich **1** 470*; **25** 744
Ahlgrén, Lauri **11** 97
Ahlmann, Lis **21** 791
Ahlschlager, Walter **7** 326
Ahlsén, Erik **1** 470–71
Ahlsén, Tore **1** 470–71
Åhlström, Betzy **30** 102
Ahmad (*fl* ?12th cent.) **5** 172; **6** 246
Ahmad (*fl* 1815-50) **1** 471*; **16** 534, 535
Ahmad (*fl* 1880) **16** 81
Ahmad, Sultan (*reg* 1382-1410) (Jalayrid) **1** 24; **6** 172; **16** 294, 318, 502
Ahmad I, Ruler (*reg* 1081-9) (Qarakhanid) **28** 636; **30** 489
Ahmad I Wali, Ruler (*reg* 1422-36) (Bahmani) **3** 66; **4** 35; **12** 82; **15** 356, 357, 572; **20** 105
Ahmad II al-Mansur, Sultan (*reg* 1578-1603) (Sa'di) **16** 240; **21** 585, 703; **23** 816
Ahmadabad **1** 471–3*; **15** *279*, *597*; **16** *105*
art forms and materials
architecture **7** 695; **15** 168, 195, 347, 349, 409; **19** 47
brocades **15** 662, 663
manuscripts **15** 566, 595
paintings **15** 674
textiles **15** 664, 669
Bhadra **15** 347
caravanserais **15** 372
Gandhi Institute of Labour Studies **15** *168*, 169
houses **32** *323*
Kasturbhai Lalbhai collection **15** 742
L. D. Institute of Indology **15** 184
mosques
Ahmad Shahi Mosque **15** 347, *348*
congregational mosque **1** *472*; **15** 348, 681; **16** 201
Haybat Khan Mosque **15** 347
Jami' Masjid *see* congregational mosque
Sayyid 'Alam Mosque **15** 347–8
Sidi Sayyid Mosque **15** 349
museums
Calico Museum of Textiles **1** 471; **15** 182
Gandhi Memorial Museum **7** 882, *882*; **15** 169
History Museum **1** 471
Ahmadabad
museums—cont.
Museum Gujarat Vidya Sabha **1** 471
Museum of Tribal Research and Training Institute **1** 471
Sanskar Kendra Museum and Cultural Centre **1** 471, 473; **22** 365
N. C. Mehta Collection **15** 182, 742
Shreyas Folk Art Museum **1** 471; **15** 182
National Institute of Design **15** 180
School of Architecture **15** 169, 180
Shah-i Bagh **15** 371
stepwells
Asapura Vav **29** 636
Dada Harir Vav **29** 636
Mata Bhavani Vav **29** 635, 636
Swaminarayana Temple **15** 541
Tin Darvaza **7** 361; **15** 347, 350
tomb of Ahmad Shah **15** 347
tomb of Rani Sipari **15** 349
tomb of Wajih al-Din **15** 371
Ahmad al-Khurasani **10** 832; **16** 525
Ahmad al-Suhrawardi **1** 473*; **16** 283; **33** 503
Ahmadi
works **16** *312*
Ahmad ibn 'Ali al-Maqrizi **16** 172
Ahmad ibn Ayub al-Hafiz al-Nakhchivani **2** 892; **3** 223
Ahmad ibn Basu **4** 784; **28** 511
Ahmad ibn Husayn ibn Basu **13** 285; **16** 386
Ahmad ibn Ibrahim **9** 41
Ahmad ibn Ibrahim al-Gazi, Imam of Harar **10** 565
Ahmad ibn 'Isa **16** 497
Ahmad ibn Khurasan **31** 423
Ahmad ibn Mas'ud *see* AL-RUMI
Ahmad ibn Muhammad-Mahdi **1** 638
Ahmad ibn Tulun, Governor (*reg* 868-84) (Tulunid) **5** 395; **16** 155; **21** 626; **31** 421
Ahmad Jalayir, Sultan (*reg* 1382-1410) (Jalayirid) **1** 24, 583; **16** 272, 319, 876–7*
Ahmad Karahisarı **1** 473*
patrons and collectors **23** 641
teachers **14** 103
works **16** 285, 604
Ahmad Khalid Yusuf **20** 172
Ahmad Khan Bangash, Nawab of Farrukhabad (*reg* ?1749-71) (Rohilla) **15** 592
Ahmad Khan Dunbuli **1** 638
Ahmad Moustafa **16** 288
Ahmad Musa **1** 474*; **16** 314, 318, 319
Ahmadnagar **15** *637*
calligraphy **15** 681
Farah Bakhsh **15** 381
Feria Bagh Palace **15** 373
fortifications **15** 380
Hasht Bihisht **15** 381, 382
painting **15** *637*, 637–8*
textiles **15** 664
Ahmad Qassim Sini **3** 68, 69
Ahmad Shah I, Sultan (*reg* 1411-42) (Sultans of Gujarat) **1** 471, 472; **15** 347, 409
Ahmad Shah ibn Sulayman Shah **9** 41
Ahmad Shah Mangujak **16** 183
Ahman ibn Muhammad al-Faraghani **2** 316
Ahmar, Tell *see* TIL BARSIP
Ahmed I, Sultan (*reg* 1603-17) (Ottoman) **16** 349, 350, 388, 499, 605, 610; **18** 509; **21** 50; **30** 784
Ahmed III, Sultan (*reg* 1703-30) (Ottoman) **12** 77; **14** 27; **16** 350; **23** 643*
architecture **12** 84; **16** 123, 226, *226*, 610; **23** 638
Ahmed, Anna Molka **23** 800
Ahmed, Bashir **23** 800
Ahmed, Iqbal **23** 800
Ahmed, Jalaluddin **23** 804
Ahmed, Tayyeba **23** 801
Ahmed, Zahin **23** 801
Ahmedabad *see* AHMADABAD
Ahmed Dalgıc **1** 474*; **16** 223, 595; **28** 768
Ahmed ibn Hasan Kalibî Fânî **16** 498
Ahmed Khan **23** 801
Ahmed Nakşi **1** 474–5*; **16** 350
Ahmed Pasha **18** 509
Ahmed Usta **1** 474
Ahmet, Ali **1** 475*; **16** 536, 591; **31** 453
works **16** 537
Ahmet Fethi Pasa **31** 456
Ahmet Gazi **16** 202
Ahmose (*reg c.* 1539-*c.* 1514 BC) **1** 469; **9** *777*, 880, 882; **10** 56, 61
Ahmose (son of Ebana) **17** 714
Ahmose, Prince **9** 879
Ahmose Nefertari **10** 10
Ahmose Pennekhbet **10** 31
Ahnas *see* HERAKLEOPOLIS MAGNA
Ahoada **15** 109
Ahobilam, Narashimha Temple **15** 331
Ahorn, Lucas **26** 742; **30** 765
Ahrbom, Nils **1** 475*
Ahrbom & Zimdahl **2** 603
Åhrén, Uno **1** 475*; **13** 31; **30** 75, 92
collaboration **20** 437
works **30** 91
Ahrend Group **18** 435
Ahrends, Bruno **3** 796
Ahrends, Burton & Koralek **1** 476*; **9** 323
Ahrends, Peter **1** 476*
Ahrens & Company **17** 378
Ahronson, Paula **16** 568
Ahsa' Oasis **27** 875
Ahtna **22** 546, 612
Ahualulco **21** 217; **31** 118
Åhus **30** 103
Ahwaz, Jondi Shapour University **15** 897
Ahyi, Paul **31** 74
works **31** *74*
Ai **1** 476*; **16** *565*; **30** *180*
cups **30** 184
fortifications **21** 553
temple **30** 188
AIA *see* ARTISTS INTERNATIONAL ASSOCIATION
A(merican) I(nstitute of) A(rchitects) *see under* NEW YORK → institutes
Aiala, Josefa de *see* AYALA (E CABRERA), JOSEFA DE
AIC *see* AMERICAN INSTITUTE FOR CONSERVATION
Aicard, Raymond **22** 505
Aichbauer, Johann Georg **25** 443
Aicher, Otl **4** 61; **12** 480; **15** 826
Aicher-Scholl, Inge **12** 480
Aichinger, Franz Xaver **13** 330
Aida, Takefumi **1** 477*; **2** 363; **17** 91, 92; **30** 260
Aigai (i) (Turkey) **1** 477*; **13** *363*, 405, 406
Aigai (ii) (Greece) *see* VERGINA
Aigai Takāku *see* TAKĀKU AIGAI
Aigen, Karl **4** 662
Aigina **1** 477–82*; **9** *511*; **13** *363*, 501; **14** *332*, 336; **23** 490
architecture **1** 478–9*
bronzes **13** 572
chamber **13** 383
Aigina—cont.
coins **13** 585
fibulae **10** 591
houses **14** 338, 339
National Archaeological Museum **13** 470, 542
Omorphi Ekklisia *see* St Theodore
pins **13** 600
pottery **13** 358, 485, 488; **14** 337, 342
St Theodore **1** 481–2; **9** 584
Sanctuary of Aphaia
jewellery **13** 600
propylon **25** 657
Temple of Aphaia **1** 478–9, *479*; **7** 502; **13** 378, *378*, 391, 397, *397*, 400, 414, 415, 432, *448*, 449
acroteria **1** 128
altar **27** 713
entasis **10** 415
pediment **13** 425; **24** 317, 318
proportions **2** 351
restoration **7** 739
sculpture **1** *480*, 480–81; **12** 474; **13** 451; **29** 396, *713*
trophy **31** 368
sculpture **1** 479–81*; **13** 468, 469, 470
stelae **1** 481
synagogue **17** 543, 559
Temple of Apollo **1** 478, 480; **13** 425
walls **14** 338
White House **14** 336
Aigina, Anaxagoras of *see* ANAXAGORAS OF AIGINA
Aigina, Glaukias of *see* GLAUKIAS OF AIGINA
Aigina Treasure **1** 478; **21** 687
Aigner, Chrystian Piotr **1** 482*; **25** 99, 141; **32** 871
patrons and collectors **8** 372; **25** 364
works **18** 693; **25** 99
Aigner, Josef Matthäus **1** 775
aigrettes **17** 523, 524, 527, 529
Aigueperse, Sainte-Chapelle **27** 551
Aigues-Mortes **1** *482*, 482–3*; **11** *505*, 511; **20** 572
Aiguier, Louis Auguste Laurent **33** 674
Aiguille Aimantée, L' **20** 414
Aiguillon, Marie-Madeleine de Vignerot, Duchesse d' **26** 348, 349; **27** 315; **32** 864
Aiha, Martti **11** 101
Aihole **1** 483–5*; **6** 404; **15** *294*
architecture **15** 325
craftsmen and artists **15** 324
Hallibasappa Gudi **15** 527
Huchchappayya Gudi **15** 526
Huchchappayya Math **15** 526, *527*
Huchchimalli Gudi **15** 298
Konti Gudi Shrine 1 **15** 526
Konti Gudi Shrine 2 **15** 527
Konti Gudi Shrine 3 **15** 527
reliefs **15** 227
rock reliefs **15** 477
sculpture **1** 485; **15** 526
temples **15** 293, 295, 298, 300, 302, 526
Durga Temple **15** 300, 526; **29** 526
Gaudar Gudi **15** 300, 526
Jaina cave temples **15** 293
Lad Khan Temple **14** 77; **15** 300, 526; **29** 526
Mallikarjuna Temple **15** 300
Meguti Temple **15** 295, 526
Ravana Phadi **15** 293, 295
shrine **1** *485*
south temple **1** *484*
Temple 10 **15** 300
Temple 52 **15** 527
Temple 53 **15** 527

Ai Hsüan *see* AI XUAN
Aija **29** *156*, 170
stone-carvings **29** *170*
Aikawa, Nichirō *see* AI MITSU
Aiken, John **16** 18
Ai Khanum **1** *186*, 211, 485–8*, *486*; **3** 32; **6** *182*, 197, 209; **11** 335; **15** 906, 912
architecture **1** 190; **6** 196; **28** 383
coins **1** 188; **6** 187
fortifications **21** 591
gymnasium **1** 487; **13** 406
inscriptions **1** 187
ivory-carvings **6** 270
metalwork **1** 206; **6** 237
mosaics **13** 565
sculpture **1** 193, 194–5, *487*, 488; **6** 212–13*; **28** 383
stucco **29** 824, 825
town walls **21** 558
wall paintings **1** 200
Aikman, William **1** 488*; **9** 724
patrons and collectors **4** 611; **7** 417; **28** 269
pupils **22** 190
reproductive prints by others **18** 570
teachers **21** 34
works **28** 235
Aila **22** 698
Ailesbury, Thomas Bruce, 2nd Earl of *see* BRUCE, THOMAS, 2nd Earl of Ailesbury
Aillaud, Emile **1** 489*
works **24** 131, *131*
Aillaud, Gilles **1** 489; **10** 443; **11** 552
Aimaq **1** 209
Aime, St Maurice **7** 253
Aimerich, Jaume **29** 333
works **29** *333*
Aimilianos of Cyzicus, Bishop of Constantinople **9** 638
Ai Mitsu **1** 489–90*
works **17** *206*, 207
Aimo, Domenico **1** 490*
collaboration **27** 747
works **4** 280; **16** 843; **30** 515
Aimone, Count of Savoy (*reg* 1329-43) **17** 457
Aimone Dux *see* DUX, AIMONE
Ain, Gregory **1** 490–91*; **2** 383; **19** 701
Ainai, Geoffroi d' *see* GEOFFROI D'AINAI
ā'inakārī see under ARCHITECTURE → techniques
Ain Dara **1** 491*; **30** *180*
sculpture **1** 833; **30** 187, 189
temple **1** 816
Ain el-Helweh **28** 667
Ain Gev **30** 191
Ain Ghazal **1** 491–2*; **30** *180*
figurines **30** 182
sculpture **1** *492*; **30** 181, 182, 188, 192
skulls **30** 181
statuettes **17** 655
Ain Karim, St John **9** 549
Ain Mallaha
beads **30** 181
shelters **30** 191
stone **23** 532; **30** 181
wall paintings **30** 198
Ainmuller, Max **29** 506
Aïn Qarwash **16** 218
Ain Sakhri **10** 472; **30** 181, 192
Ainslie, Bill **29** 109
Ainsworth, William **4** 885
Aintab *see* GAZIANTEP
Ain Tarakiwa **18** 20
Ainu **1** 493*; **17** 19, 317, 425, 433, 630
bark **1** 493
dress **1** 493, *493*; **17** *356*; **30** VII2
houses **1** 493
nettles **1** 493
tattoos **17** 414
Ainu—cont.
textiles **17** 356*
tourist art **1** 493
wands **1** 493
wood-carvings **1** 493
'Ain Zarba **16** 155
Aiolic capitals *see under* CAPITALS → types
Aiolic order *see under* ORDERS (ARCHITECTURAL) → types
Aiolis **13** 497
AIR **19** 591
Airard, Abbot of Reims **26** 122
airbrushes **1** 493–4*; **24** 656
air-conditioning **3** 537; **7** 734, 735, 736*; **28** 831
Aires de Sá e Meneses, Rodrigo, Marquês de Fontes *see* FONTES E ABRANTES, Marquês de
Aire-sur-la-Lys **13** 211
Airikiṇa *see* ERAN
Airoldi, Abbot of Monte Oliveto Maggiore **28** 702
airports **1** 494–6*, *495*; **11** *868*; **16** *11*; **27** *477*
air-pumps **28** *211*
Airpurah **15** 787
Aïrtam *see* AYRTAM
air-twists *see under* GLASS → techniques
Airvauld Abbey, Tomb of Petrus a Fonte Salubri **31** 121
Airvault **26** 600; **32** 90
Aischines Painter **13** 523
Aislabie, John **22** 138; **29** 861
Aislabie, William **11** 348; **29** 861, 862
aisles **1** 496*; **17** 65
Aisne, Abbaye de Prémontré **29** 524
Aisne Valley school **29** 17
Aison **13** 523; **32** 29–30*, 41, 56
Aispachaca **6** 380
Aistersheim Palace **2** 779
Aistulf, King of the Lombards (*reg* 749-56) **23** 193
Aitchison, Craigie **19** 246
Aitchison, George **10** 282; **19** 104; **22** 59; **23** 504; **30** 504
Aitiyev, Gapar **18** 568
Aitken, William Maxwell, 1st Baron Beaverbook **1** 496*; **5** 588
Aitsinger, M. **14** 644
'Aitun, Tell **24** 635
Aitutaki **7** 790; **23** 735
Aitzema, Lieuwe van **32** 232
Aiud, Bethlen Reformed College **26** 724
Aiun **1** *376*
Aivalli *see* AIHOLE
Aivazovsky, Ivan **18** 502; **31** 312
aiwan *see* IWAN
Aix, Lauthier d' **12** 266
Aix Annunciation, Master of the **6** 469; **7** 542; **10** 716; **11** 531; **20** 613–14*, 708
works **13** 675; **20** *613*, 708; **21** 338; **25** 795
Aix-en-Provence **1** 497–8*; **9** *510*; **11** *505*
Bibliothèque de l'Institut d'Art Moderne **11** 674
Cathedral of St Sauveur **1** 497; **11** 531
Baptistery **3** 192; **7** 256; **9** 533
paintings **11** *800*
sculpture **26** 603
Chambre des Comptes de Provence **8** 499
Cours à Carosses *see* Cours Mirabeau
Cours Mirabeau **1** *497*; **31** 718
Ecole Municipale de Dessin **1** 497; **11** 665
Fondation Vasarely **1** 498; **32** 10
Hôtel de Châteaurenard **8** 525
Hôtel de Maurel de Pontèves **11** *515*
Aix-en-Provence—cont.
Hôtel de Ville **8** 499
Musée des Beaux Arts *see* Musée Granet
Musée Granet **1** 497; **11** 665; **13** 309
Musée des Tapisseries **30** 332
Oratorian chapel **8** 525
painting **11** 531
Palais Comtal **24** 828
Palais de Justice **18** 887–8
sculpture **26** 603
silk **11** 644, 646
Aix-la-Chapelle *see* AACHEN
Aix-les-Bains, Musée Archéologique **19** 216
Aix Panels, Master of the **11** 398
Ai Xuan **6** 799
Aizanoi **1** 498*; **13** *362*; **26** *908*
bath-gymnasium **3** 375
stadium **29** 488
Temple of Zeus **1** 498; **23** 483
Aizelin, Eugène-Antoine **1** 498–9*
Aizenberg, Roberto **1** 499*; **2** 400
Aizpitarte, Martín **24** 501
Aizpurna, José María **12** 177
Aizpúrua, José Manuel de **15** 885; **29** 273
Aizu **17** 356, 357
Aizu-Hongō **17** 353
aizurie see under PRINTS → types → *ukiyoe*
Aizu Wakamatsu, Shōjōji **17** 100, 118
Ajaccio, Musée Fesch **11** 32
Ajalbert, Jean **3** 462
'Ajami **16** 417
'Ajami ibn Abu Bakr **2** 892; **22** 445–6
Ajanta **1** *499*, 499–501*; **5** 95; **15** 195, 257–9, *276*, *285*; **21** 847
caityas **1** 500–501*
Cave 1 **15** 207, 230, 258, 543, 555–6, *556*, *557*, *558*; **30** 784
Cave 2 **15** 543, *554*, 557
Cave 7 **15** 258
Cave 9 **1** 500; **15** 557
Cave 10 **1** 500; **15** 543, 553, 557
Cave 11 **15** 543
Cave 16 **15** 543, 555, 739; **31** 798
Cave 17 **15** 258, 543, 554, 555; **31** 798; **32** *322*
Cave 19 **1** *500*, 500–501; **15** *258*, 258, 464, *464*, 555
Cave 26 **1** 501; **15** 258, 464
Cave 244 **15** 258
Cave Lower 6 **15** 553
halls **14** 77
pilasters **15** 277
pillars **15** 277
sculpture **15** 416, 464–5, 548
temples **15** 275; **30** 437
vihāras **1** 501*
wall paintings **3** 378; **10** 484; **12** 72; **13** 3, 812; **15** 252, 548, 549, 553–7, 670, 671, 674, 677, 690, 701, 739; **22** 516; **23** 817; **24** 790; **26** 138
Ajatashatru, King (*reg c.* 491-59 BC) (Saisunaga) **24** 264; **25** 867
Ajaw **20** 886
Ajax Painter
works **13** 499, *499*
Ajayagarh **15** 497
Ajayameru *see* AJMER
Ajayapala, Ruler (*reg* mid-12th cent.) (Chahamana) **1** 502
Ajdabiya **19** 323
Ajit Singh, Maharaja of Marwar (*reg* 1707-24) (Rajput) **15** 390
Ajit Singh, Ruler of Ghanerao (*reg* 1800-56) (Rajput) **15** 615
Ajjul, Tell el- **1** 501–2*, 857; **16** *565*; **30** *180*
gold **1** 874
jewellery **1** 874
Ajlun, al-Rabad Castle **17** 655
'Ajman **31** 584
Museum **2** 275; **31** 585
'Ajman—cont.
see also UNITED ARAB EMIRATES
Ajmer **1** 502*; **15** *279*, *360*, 371; **16** *105*
Arha'i Din ka Jhompra Mosque **1** 502, *502*; **15** *241*, 338, 349, 680; **16** 168; **20** 226
congregational mosque **15** 207, 241, 371
fort **15** 371
Mayo College **15** 403, *404*
mosques **15** 339
painting **15** 609–10*
palace **15** 371, *371*
Rajputana Museum of Archaeology **1** 502; **15** 182
sculpture **15** 542
shrine of Mu'in al-Din Chisti **15** 371
tomb of 'Abd Allah Khan **15** 372
Ajuda **12** 125; **25** *288*
Akaana Shrine **17** 129
Akabori, Chausuyama Burial Mound **17** 56, 104
Akademiai értesítö **24** 440
Akaemachi **18** 538
Aka group **12** 509
Akaike
Kamanokuchi kiln **1** 448; **30** 258
Saruyama Hongama kiln **1** 448
Akajuk **10** 123
Akama **17** 388
Akamaru *see* GAMBIER ISLANDS
Akamatsu (family) **14** 551
akamatsu (red pine) *see under* PINE → types
Akamatsu, Rinsaku **17** 294; **27** 506
Akan **1** 392, 503*, 514–15; **2** 584, 585; **8** 21; **14** 55
aesthetics **1** 238
Akua'ba **1** 503
banners **1** 503
body arts **1** 288, 342
brass **2** 590
bronze **1** 288
ceramics **1** 392
chairs **1** 291
combs (hair) **2** 590*
forowa **2** 590
gold **1** 392; **8** 22
kuduo **2** 589
mythology **1** 281
pipes (smoking) **2** 590
portraits **1** 268
pots **1** 329
regalia **2** 588
sculpture **1** 257, 274, 278, 330, 392, 503; **2** 588
shirts **1** 348
terracotta **1** 257, 503; **2** 589; **30** 509
textiles **1** 295
weights **1** 274, 277–8, 363, 392; **2** 590
wood **1** 291; **2** 590
akane **9** 492
Akanji, Adebisi **1** 332
Akanthos **13** 586; **22** 225
Akanthou **8** 365
Akaroa **23** 51, *52*
Langlois-Eteveneaux House **23** 53
Akasegawa, Genpei **14** 568; **22** 742; **30** 256
Akashi **17** 21
Akasztott ember **24** 440
Akati Akpele Kendo **11** 246
works **11** *246*
Akator, Azii **12** 509
Akawaio **13** 874
basketwork **3** *331*
Akbar, Emperor (*reg* 1556-1605) (Mughal) **3** 904; **10** 827; **15** *546*, *582*, 587, 712; **16** 865; **22** 258; **30** 338
albums **1** 582
architecture **10** 826; **15** 372; **16** 239; **23** 804; **31** 793
Akbar, Emperor (*reg* 1556-1605) (Mughal)—cont.
art policies **15** 207, 722, 740; **17** 922
brocades **15** 662
calligraphy **15** 207
carpets **15** 682; **23** 802
cities **15** 196, 409, 410
coins **15** 689
collections **15** 740
dress **15** 690, 691
fortifications **18** 17
forts **1** 460, 502; **15** 371; **18** 646; **21** 591
jade **15** 699; **16** 860
jewellery **15** 701
manuscripts **8** 535; **10** 817; **15** 228, 546, 575, 577, 578, 579–84, 745; **16** 272, 344–5; **17** 512; **22** 517
'Abd al-Samad **1** 26
Basawan **3** 319
Bishan Das **4** 90
Daulat **8** 542
Farrukh Chela **10** 817
Mahesh **20** 106
Manohar (*fl c.* 1580-1620) **20** 284
Mir Sayyid 'Ali **21** 722
Miskin **21** 726, 727
Mukund **22** 269
Nanha **22** 457
Ramdas **25** 873
Ṭūṭīnāma **16** 345
palaces **10** 827; **23** 818
portraits **15** 231
shawls **15** 665
sponsorship **1** 26; **8** 534
tents **15** 716; **30** 471
tombs **1** 502; **8** 679; **15** 362–3; **28** 710, *710*, *711*
weapons **15** 678
Akbarabad *see* AGRA
Akbarnagar *see* RAJMAHAL
Akberg, Arnold **10** 539, 542
Ak-Beshim **1** 504*; **6** *182*; **18** *567*, 568
Akbulut, Ahmet Ziya **16** 537
Akcaalan **16** 418
Akçakale *see* KORDYLE
Ak-Chin (AZ), Eco Museum **22** 671
Akchunkur **6** 223
Akdik, Ahmed Kamil **2** 883; **23** 695; **27** 683
Aken, Alexander van **1** 505
Aken, Arnold van **1** 505
Aken, Jan van **27** 518
Aken, Jeroen van *see* BOSCH, HIERONYMUS
Aken, Joseph van **1** 504–5*; **9** 211–12; **25** 882
collaboration **14** 841, 842; **24** 735
works **9** 245; **14** 842
Ake-Ptolemais *see* 'AKKO
Åkerblom, Matti **11** 90
Akeredolu, Justus **23** 137
Åkermarck, Petter **30** 97
Akerö **30** 71
Akers, Benjamin Paul **29** 583
Akersloot, Willem *see* ACKERSLOOT, WILLEM (OUTGERTSZ.)
Akha **5** 262; **30** 623
appliqué **5** 248
basketwork **30** 630
dress **18** 774; **30** 626–7*
drums (musical instruments) **30** *637*
gates **30** 639
jewellery **5** 250; **30** 634
musical instruments **30** 637
wood-carvings **30** 639
Akhad Keble Kerbalai Huseinoghly **2** 899
Akhalgori Hoard **1** 505*; **12** *317*, 328, 330; **25** *471*

Akhali Shuamta 25 341
Church of the Birth of the Mother of God 25 344
Akhaltsikhe Museum 12 332
Ak Han 16 247
AKhChU see ASSOCIATION OF ARTISTS OF RED UKRAINE
Akhenaten (reg c. 1353–c. 1336 BC) 1 505*; 9 777, 782, 860, 861, 883, 884; 10 80
architecture 1 755; 9 833, 841, 851; 11 231; 23 279–80, 807; 30 433, 691
dress 10 44
ideology 9 798
jewellery 10 31
reliefs 9 884; 29 33
sculpture 3 523; 9 855, 883; 30 794
shabtis 10 18
stelae 2 656; 29 616
Akhetaten see AMARNA, (TELL) EL-
Akhhotpe 27 812; 31 107
tomb 27 811
Akhisar see THYATEIRA
Akhlamabad Dam 16 198
Akhlaq, Zahoor ul- 1 506*; 23 800, 801
Akhmadov, Shamsudin 27 433
Akhmarov, Chingiz 31 782
Akhmatova, Anna 1 121; 27 581
Akhmedbekov, A. 2 893; 3 88
Akhmedov, A. (fl 1925) 27 422
Akhmedov, Abdulla (Ramazanovich) (b 1929) 1 506*; 31 459
Akhmedov, Anvar (Kamilovich) 31 783
Akhmedov, G. 27 422
Akhmetzhanov, Kaliolla 17 867
Akhmim 1 506–7*; 7 819; 9 774; 26 921
coffins 10 12
dress 9 640
headrests 10 53
mummies 22 284
mummy cases 10 14
reliefs 9 874
silk 9 640, 663, 665, 665, 666; 16 431
speoi 9 833
tapestries 30 IV2
temples 29 386
textiles 7 826
Akhna 8 325, 342
Akhnur 1 199; 15 458, 483
sculpture 15 482
Akhodar, Surya Temple 15 267, 268
Akhor-i Rustam 15 916
Akhpet 27 812
AKhR see ASSOCIATION OF ARTISTS OF THE REVOLUTION
Akhrarov, I. 29 821
Akhratan 23 282
Akhriyev, Khadjibekir 27 433
AKhRR see ASSOCIATION OF ARTISTS OF REVOLUTIONARY RUSSIA
Akhsikath 10 896
Akhsu 2 890
congregational mosque 2 891
Akhsyket 6 245, 246
Akhtala Church 12 323
Akhtar, Saeed 23 799
Akhtopoli 25 338
Akhumukhamedov, Shamukkhamed 31 459
Akhundov, I. (fl c. 1935) 2 896
Akhundov, I. G. (fl 1960s) 2 897
Akhunov, Orif Abdur-raufovich 30 253
Akhverdiyev, G. 2 896
Akhvlediani, Yelena 1 507*; 12 326, 332
Akhy 9 856
Akiba Kōan 14 704
Akihide 17 402
Akihira, Fujiwara no see FUJIWARA NO AKIHIRA
Akihiro, Fujiwara no see FUJIWARA NO SHUNZEI
Akimov, Ivan (Akimovich) 27 579; 31 536
Akimov, Nikolay (Pavlovich) 1 507*; 27 396, 581
Akinari Ueda see UEDA AKINARI
Akinidad, Prince 21 160
Akinsemoyin, Kunle 32 86
Akio Suzuki see SUZUKI, AKIO
Akira Kanayama see KANAYAMA, AKIRA
Akira Kurosaki see KUROSAKI, AKIRA
Åkirkeby 26 639
sculpture 26 640
Akis, Timothy 23 736
Akishev, K. K. 16 577*
Akita 17 370
Akita school 14 565; 23 347
Akitek MAA Sdn Bhd 20 169
Akizato Ritō 17 417
Akjoujt 1 376
Akkad 1 508, 509; 3 11; 21 267, 268
Akkadian (language) 1 851, 853, 854
Akkadian (people) 1 507–10*; 21 267
bronze 4 850
busts 1 510
copper 1 510; 2 639
craftsmen and artists 1 508
limestone 1 509
metalwork 1 509–10
patronage 1 508
religion 21 277
scripts 1 508
sculpture 1 509; 2 639; 21 294*
seals 1 510, 860–61; 21 277
stelae 1 508–9, 509
writing 15 905; 20 361
Akkadian period see under MESOPOTAMIA → periods
Akkale Church 9 590
Akkatu see AKKAD
Akkerman, Ben 1 510*; 22 852
'Akko 16 104; 17 500, 505, 506; 28 383; 30 179
Acre 16 565
icons 9 627
Knights Hospitaller compound 18 151
manuscripts 8 219; 17 506
paintings 17 505, 506
portals 9 161; 16 209
refectory of the Order of St John 18 152
Akl, Said 19 8
Ak-mechet' see KYZL-ORDA
Akner Monastery 2 430
Ako, Jakupa 23 736, 737
Akok, Mahmut 1 520
Akola, Siddheshvara Temple 15 316
Akolo, Jimo 1 432
Ákos see ACIŞI
Akosombo, Volta Dam 1 320
Akota 15 487
Akotantos, Angelos 8 157; 24 263; 25 331, 332
works 25 332
Akoustolith 13 757
Akovitika 14 338
Akpakpa, Sacré-Coeur 3 728
Akpan, Sunday Jack 1 332
works 1 332
Akpan Chukwu 15 61
Ak-Peshin see AK-BESHIM
Akplodjegou, Kuevi Kangui 31 74
Akragas 16 621
Akragas see under AGRIGENTO
Akra Mound 15 446
Akropolites, Constantinos 15 77
Akropolitissa, Tornikia 15 77
Akrotiri (Cyprus) see AKROTIRI-AETOKREMNOS
Akrotiri (Greece) 8 304, 309, 310, 313, 323; 30 711–13
architecture 8 306, 309; 30 712
bronzes 8 323
Delta 2 8 318
ewers 8 314
gardens 12 67
House of the Ladies 8 319
pottery 30 712, 712
stone vessels 8 317; 21 689
urban planning 8 310–11
vase paintings 30 712, 712
wall paintings 8 307, 318, 319, 320; 21 654, 659; 30 712, 713
West House 8 309, 318, 319–20, 320
Xeste 3 8 309, 318, 319
Xeste 4 8 319
Akrotiri-Aetokremnos 8 328
Aksakov, Sergey 1 71
Aksamitov, D. V. 18 39
Aksaray
Archaeological Museum 1 114
carpets 15 682
manuscripts 16 329
palaces 16 204
Pertevniyal Mosque 16 227
wall paintings 5 676
Zincirli Madrasa 16 204
Akşehir 9 592
mosque of Ferruh Shah 16 183
tomb of Seyyid Mahmud Hayrani 16 204
Aksel, Malik 31 454
Aksha
church 23 287
Temple of Ramesses II 10 803; 23 280
Ak Sipil 6 296
Aksmanavati see LUCKNOW
Aksu 28 719
Aksum 1 379, 512–13*; 9 507
architecture 1 314, 378; 10 564–5
basilica 10 566
Cathedral of Maryam Syon 1 315; 10 565, 576
churches 10 565
Enda Mika'el 10 564
Enda Semon 10 564
mausoleum 10 565
sculpture 10 576
stelae 10 565
Ta'aka Maryam 10 564
Tomb of the False Door 10 565
Aktam 10 896
Akte see MT ATHOS
Ak Tepe II 6 244
Aktion, Die 10 869; 14 845; 23 456; 24 427, 445, 585; 26 266; 28 90, 169
Aktionen 24 403, 408
Aktionismus 1 513–14*; 2 798, 804, 837; 22 279; 28 344; 32 447
collections 29 16
members 5 30; 22 256; 23 163
Aktivizmus see Activists
Aktyubinsk 17 865
Akua'ba see under FIGURINES → types
Akuapem 1 503
Akumal 6 97
Akurgal, E. 28 893
Akuriyo 30 12
Akushon (Action) 17 206, 758; 18 191
Akwete 23 134
Akweya 15 102
Akyab see SITTWE
Akye 1 503, 514–15*; 8 21
gold 1 515
ivory-carvings 1 515
pots 1 328
pottery 8 22
regalia 1 514–15
sculpture 1 514, 515
staffs 1 514
wood-carvings 1 515
Akylbekov, Sabyrbek 18 568
AKZ 23 426
Ål 23 218
church 8 730; 23 223
Kulturhuset 22 808
wall paintings 23 223
Ala 13 120
'Ala' al-Dawla (1417-60) 16 528
'Ala al-Dawla Muhammad (fl 1037) 21 584
'Ala' al-Din Ahmad II, Ruler (reg 1436-58) (Bahmani) 15 713
'Ala' al-Din 'Ali ibn 'Abd al-Karim see ALI ACEMI
'Ala al-Din Kayqubadh I, Sultan (reg 1219-37) (Saljuq of Anatolia) 5 722; 16 186; 18 233
'Ala' al-Din Muhammad, Sultan (reg 1214-5) (Ghurid) 4 99
'Ala al-Din Muhammad Shah I, Sultan (reg 1296-1316) (Khalji) 8 672, 677, 678; 15 340; 18 16
Alabanda 5 742
bouleuterion 4 530; 13 407
alabaster (gypsum) 1 515–20*; 29 698
historical and regional traditions 1 517–20*
Arabia 2 248, 256, 272
Assyrian 2 641; 10 742; 21 297
Byzantine 9 657
Denmark 11 219
Egypt, ancient 10 54; 22 690; 25 762; 27 824
England 1 516, 517, 517, 519, 520, 707; 10 227, 260, 261; 13 84; 25 183
Etruscan 10 593
France 1 516; 17 459; 33 28
Germany 1 516; 21 72; 22 280
Gothic 1 517, 519; 3 456; 13 84; 17 459; 22 280; 33 28
Iran, ancient 15 913
Italy 1 516; 10 593
Mesopotamia 1 516; 9 45; 21 293, 297; 28 21, 22
Minoan 1 517
Netherlands, the 3 456; 21 858; 22 858; 29 571
Poland 25 114
Portugal 6 452
Prehistoric art 15 913
Punic 25 733
Romanesque 10 227
Rome, ancient 27 15
Spain 1 516; 29 841
Sumerian 9 45
Syria-Palestine 5 186
United States of America 1 516
uses
altarpieces 1 518–19, 519, 707; 6 452; 25 183
altars 21 858
busts 17 459
chests 10 54
effigies 1 518
façade decoration 10 742
figurines 5 186; 9 45; 28 22
Keenes cement 1 516
moulds 6 327
Parian cement 1 516
plaster 1 516
plates 9 657
portals 29 841
pyramids 25 762
reliefs 2 641; 21 297
relief sculpture 32 493
sarcophagi 27 824
sculpture
Arabia 2 256
Denmark 11 219
England 10 260
France 1 766
Germany 21 72
Iran, ancient 15 913
Netherlands, the 3 456; 22 858
Poland 25 114
Rome, ancient 27 15
statuettes 22 690; 29 571
tombs 1 517, 520; 10 261; 13 84
alabaster (gypsum)
uses—cont.
urns 10 593
vases 21 293
vessels 2 272
weepers 33 28
windows 2 248
alabaster (limestone)
historical and regional traditions 1 516
Egypt, ancient 1 516; 9 812–13*, 814; 21 109; 29 X1
uses
relief sculpture 22 280
sarcophagi 1 516, 516
sculpture 25 733; 29 X1
sphinxes 21 109
alabaster-carvings 1 517–18*; 23 258; 32 493
alabastra 1 520*
historical and regional traditions
Ancient Near East 1 867
Cyprus, ancient 1 868
Egypt, ancient 10 48
Greece, ancient 13 475, 477, 569, 569
Helladic 14 344
Mycenaean 14 344
materials
faience (i) (glass) 10 48
glass 12 VIII1
silver 13 569
Al 'Abeid, Tel
temple of Ninkhursag 22 159
Alabyan, Karo 22 174; 28 747; 32 695
Alacahisar Church 9 590
Alaca Höyük 1 520–22*, 821, 849; 14 591; 31 456
axes 1 834
bronzes 1 521, 521–2; 4 850
figurines 1 825
Gateway 1 831
gold 1 521, 874
inscriptions 24 690
ivory-carvings 1 869
jewellery 1 884
metalwork 1 824, 834, 835, 835
palace 1 826
pins 1 834
pottery 1 838
reliefs 1 522*, 829, 832
ritual objects 1 825
sculpture 1 827; 29 395
standards (flags) 1 521
swords 1 834
tombs 1 521, 521–2*, 824, 828, 834, 893
Alacalá de Henares, Convento de las Bernardes 22 507
Alacaluf 29 128
à la Capucine polishing see FRENCH POLISHING
Alaçatı see CAN HASAN
Alacuás 29 324
Aladrén y Mendívil, Luis 1 523*
alae 26 865
see also WINGS (THEATRE)
Alaeddin see ACEM ALI
à la façon de Venise glass see under GLASS → types
Alagar Koil, Kallalagar Temple 15 646
Alago 15 101
Alagona (family) 23 841
Alahan Monastery 1 523–4*; 3 191; 9 512
Basilica 1 523
East Church 9 537
sculpture 9 591
Alain 1 524*
Alain de Lille see ALANUS DE INSULIS
Alaja Hüyük see ALACA HÖYÜK
Alajo Pottery 5 731
Alakaroyil 15 227
Alakilise Church 9 590; 19 840
Alalakh see ATCHANA, TELL
Alaleona, Paolo 32 716

Alamán, Lucas 21 265
Alamandini, Ercole 1 628
Alamanni (family) 31 533
Alamanni, Luigi 29 742
Alamanno 3 808
Alamanno, Pietro see ALEMANNO, PIETRO
Alambra 8 330, 334
Alameda de Osuna 12 125; 13 242; 29 293
el-Alamein 9 848
Ala Miliara Church 8 222
Alamilla, Jesús 32 571
El Alamito 29 190
Alamito culture 29 190
  sculpture 29 190
Alamos, Tatiana 6 600
Alampur 1 525*; 15 294
  sculpture 15 534, 535, 537
  temples 6 404; 15 293, 299, 300, 534
    Garuda Brahma Temple 15 535
    Kumara Brahma Temple 15 534
    Padma Brahma Temple 15 535
    Sangameshvara Temple 15 299
    Svarga Brahma Temple 15 229, 534, 535
    Tarka Brahma Temple 15 298
    Vishva Brahma Temple 15 299, 535
  West Gate 15 535
Alamut 1 525*; 16 105
Alan 9 640, 668; 11 151; 27 368, 432; 28 324, 326
Alandia, Miguel 4 263
Åland Islands 11 87, 87, 88, 93
Alani see ALAN
Alano de Rupe 9 108
Alantansi, Eliezer 4 18; 17 565
à l'antique see under JEWELLERY → techniques
Alanus de Insulis 1 653
Alanya 27 632
  fortifications 16 186
  Karamanid Caravanserai 16 205
  palaces 16 204
  Sitti Zeynip cloister 16 204
  town walls 21 583
à la poupée see under PRINTING → processes
Alarco, Rosa 24 517
Alarcón, Eusebio 32 146
Alarcón, Pedro Antonio (1833-91) 31 827
Alarcón, Pedro de (fl 1619-26) 23 905
Alarcón, Rodrigo de Tapia y see TAPIA Y ALARCÓN, RODRIGO DE
Alarcón, Sérvulo Gutiérrez see GUTIÉRREZ ALARCÓN, SÉRVULO
Alari-Bonacolsi, Pier Jacopo di Antonio see ANTICO
Alarma, Salvador 29 308
alarm clocks see under CLOCKS → types
A La Ronde (Devon), Shell Gallery 28 581, 581
Alart du Hameel 1 525-6*; 28 595; 31 322
Ala-Safat 21 43
Alaşehir see PHILADELPHIA (LYDIA)
à la sévigné 17 526
Alaska
  amulets 1 816
  carving 22 573-4, 575-6
  combs (hair) 22 574
  dolls 31 259, 260
  ivory 16 796; 31 254, 259
  ivory-carvings 22 574
  leather 31 260
  masks 22 545, 573
  toys 31 254
  trade
    fur 22 546
  wood-carvings 22 573
Alaskan Movement 22 596
Alaškevič, Jozep 19 498
Alassa 8 354
Alaškevič, Jazep 3 528
Alatri
  macellum 19 888
  masonry 20 571
  temple 10 593; 23 480
Alaungpaya, King (reg 1752-60) (Konbaung) 5 238
Alaux, Jean 4 527; 11 261, 413; 12 830
Alaux, Jean-Paul 4 526
Alava, Juan de 1 526*; 12 619
  collaboration 7 679; 26 299; 27 603
  groups and movements 25 31
  patrons and collectors 9 112; 11 250
  works 13 70; 25 23; 27 603, 794; 28 518; 29 265
Alaverdi 25 341
  Cathedral 12 320
Alaverdi Gospels see under GOSPEL BOOKS → individual manuscripts
Alavoine, Jean-Antoine 1 527*
  pupils 13 231
  works 3 288; 6 139; 9 337; 11 523; 27 247, 251; 29 413
'Alawal Khan 27 858
'Alawi 1 527*; 16 119, 291; 25 833
  see also:
    AL-RASHID, Sultan
    'ABDALLAH, Sultan
    HASAN II, King
    ISMA'IL, Sultan
    MUHAMMAD III, Sultan
Alay Han 16 247
Alayla see THOMAS RESERVOIR
Alb, Mihu de la Crişul see MIHU DE LA CRIŞUL ALB
Alba, Duques de 1 528*
  architecture 29 299
  collections 4 566; 5 845
  metalwork 29 342
  paintings 11 872; 15 838; 22 21
Alba, 14th Duque de (1794-1835) 1 528-9*, 742; 29 20
Alba, 17th Duque de (1878-1953) 1 528, 529*
Alba, Catalina Méndez de Haro y Guzmán, Duquesa de 1 528; 5 845
Alba, Fernando Alvárez de Toledo, 3rd Duque de 2 411; 29 289
Alba, Fernando Alvárez de Toledo, 6th Duque de 1 528; 4 453; 5 182
Alba, Fernando Alvárez de Toledo, Gran-Duque de, Governor of the Netherlands 1 528; 18 5; 22 65; 30 518
Alba, Francisco Alvárez de Toledo, 10th Duque de 1 528
Alba, Joaquin de 5 751
Alba, José Alvárez de Toledo y Gonzaga, 17th Duque de (1756-96) 1 528; 2 173; 32 566
Alba, Macrino d' 1 529-30*
  works 1 530
Alba, Maria Teresa Cayetana Silva y Alvárez y Toledo, 13th Duquesa de 1 528, 528
Albacete, Museo de Albacete 23 837
Albacini, Carlo 4 181; 10 812; 20 517; 25 8; 30 268
Alba de Tormes
  Convento de Carmelitas Descalzas 14 8; 26 148
  Santiago Apóstol 26 642
Alba Fucens
  basilica 3 328
  macellum 19 888, 889
  S Pietro 7 921, 922; 9 152
  theatre 26 873
  urban planning 27 3
Alba Iulia 1 530-31*; 26 705, 906
  Bathyaneum Library 26 724
  Cathedral of St Michael 1 530; 14 883; 26 638, 706
    Lázói Chapel 14 885; 26 707, 712
    sculpture 26 710
    tympanum 14 891
  fortifications 26 708
  fortress 26 713
  Metropolitan church 26 722
  palace 14 885
  sculpture 14 894
  Triumphal Arch 14 894
Alba Madonna 1 528; 5 71; 12 839; 25 906
Albán, Antonio 9 712
Albán, Casimiro 9 712
Albán, Nicolás 9 712
Albanese, Francesco 1 531*
Albanese, Giovanni Battista 1 531*; 32 411
Albanese, Girolamo 1 531-2*
Albanese collection 3 321
Albani (family)
  collections 16 769
  paintings 20 394; 28 379
  sculpture 4 886; 16 771; 31 63
Albani, Alessandro, Cardinal 1 532-3*; 29 724; 33 241
  architecture 16 772, 772; 20 392; 22 361, 735; 26 780
  catalogues 32 237
  collections 10 93; 13 605; 25 411; 26 774, 840, 847
  dealing 2 829
  drawings 8 474; 14 144
  groups and movements 2 164
  interior decoration 10 643; 16 717
  medals 6 341; 15 862
  paintings 2 27; 16 677; 19 525; 21 132
  porcelain 8 202
  prints 25 631
  sculpture 2 169; 4 621; 6 97; 9 23; 13 303; 20 392; 27 46, 115
Albani, Annibale, Cardinal 20 392; 31 893
  drawings 12 536
  paintings 1 629; 3 920; 23 348; 29 888
  sculpture 19 459
Albani, Francesco 1 103, 533-6*; 4 277; 23 294; 26 773
  assistants 9 88; 12 23
  book illustrations 18 735
  collaboration 5 864, 865, 867; 20 586; 26 196; 32 593
  frames 11 386, 394, 396, 396
  interior decoration 5 870
  paintings 1 535, 536, 596; 15 137; 20 841; 21 26
  patrons and collectors
    Condé, Henry II de Bourbon, Prince de (1588-1646) 7 699
    Créquy, Charles de Blanchefort de 19 238
    Einden, van den (family) 10 115
    Ferdinando, 6th Duke of Mantua (reg 1612-26) 12 912, 913
    Filomarino, Ascanio, Cardinal 11 81
    Franzone, Agostino (i) (fl 1678) 11 739
    Giori, Angelo, Cardinal 12 680
    Giustiniani (i), Vincenzo, Marchese 12 764
    Lanier, Nicholas 18 747
    Louis XIV, King of France (reg 1643-1715) 4 552
    Peretti (-Montalto), Alessandro, Cardinal 24 399
    Pourtalès-Gorgier, James-Alexandre, Comte de 25 383
    Sampieri (family) 27 693
Albani, Francesco
  patrons and collectors—cont.
    Savoy, Maurice of, Cardinal 28 9
    Sebregondi, Nicolo 28 337
    Spencer, John, 1st Earl Spencer 29 381
    Tallard, Marie-Joseph d'Hostun, Duc de 30 274
    Temple-Nugent-Brydges-Chandos-Grenville, Richard, 1st Duke of Buckingham and Chandos 13 637
    Uffelen, Lucas van 31 526
  pupils 7 307; 21 806; 27 487; 29 32, 388; 30 349
  reproductions in porcelain 21 64
  reproductive prints by others 2 709; 18 812; 24 712
  teachers 5 851
Albani, Giovanni Francesco, Cardinal see CLEMENT XI, Pope
Albania 1 537, 537-47*
  architecture 1 538-9*, 539; 16 228; 32 290, 293
  carpets 1 544-5, 545
  ceramics 1 543*
  churches 1 538, 541-2
  collections 1 545-6*
  education (art) 1 546-7*
  exhibitions 1 546
  felt 1 544
  furniture 1 541-3*
  glass 1 543*
  guns 1 543-4; 8 862
  heritage 1 546
  houses 1 539; 16 228
  interior decoration 1 541-3*, 542
  külliye 1 538
  linocuts 21 78
  metalwork 1 543-4*
  miniatures (manuscript illumination) 1 539
  mosques 1 538, 542
  museums 1 545-6*
  painting 1 539-41*, 540, 542; 15 103
  sculpture 1 541*, 541
  silk 1 544
  silver 1 543
  textiles 1 544-5*
  women artists 1 540
Albani Hours see under BOOKS OF HOURS → individual manuscripts
Albano, Ray 24 623
Albano Laziale
  catacomb of St Senator 6 71
  nymphaeum 13 703
  S Maria della Rotunda 26 896
  Villa of Domitian 26 870, 896
Alba-Novák, Vilmos 14 159
Albany (NY)
  architecture 31 589
  court-house 18 887
  First Church 33 8
  Institute of History and Art 23 883
  New York State Capitol 10 104; 15 20; 26 340
Albany, Louisa Maria von Stolberg, Countess of see STUART, LOUISA MARIA VON STOLBERG, Countess of Albany
Albany, Robert Stewart, 1st Duke of see STEWART, ROBERT, 1st Duke of Albany
Albany Club 25 629
Albardi, Giuseppe 21 747
Alba Real, José Vega y Verdugo, Conde de 26 251
albarelli see under JARS → types
Albarelli, Giovanni 5 432
Albares, Cayetano 2 402
albarium see under ROME, ANCIENT → stucco
Albarracín 29 364, 365
Albarracín, Pedro de Lugo see LUGO ALBARRACÍN, PEDRO DE
Alba tapestry workshop 25 131
Albelda 29 275
Albemarle, George Monck, 1st Duke of see MONCK, GEORGE, 1st Duke of Albemarle
Alben 5 150
Albenga 1 547*; 9 510; 16 618
  Baptistery 1 547; 3 189; 7 256; 9 533
  Civico Museo Inguano 1 547
  Museo Navale Romano 1 547
Alberca Church 29 261
Alberdingk Thijm, Josephus Albertus 1 547*; 3 618; 22 828
Albergati, Niccolò, Cardinal 10 707
Alberghetti, Giovanni 5 537; 12 576; 26 478
Albergotti, Marchese 31 524
Alberi, Francesco 17 442
Alberic (fl 930) 26 754
Alberic of Montecassino (fl 1030) 8 800
Alberini, Giorgio 22 384
Albermann, Wilhelm 1 548*; 8 39
Alberola, Jean-Michel 11 553
Alberoni, Cardinal 8 12
Albers, Anni 1 548, 549-50*; 30 327; 31 660
  groups and movements 4 109; 12 470
  pupils 26 26
  works 11 54
Albers, Josef 1 548-9*; 7 637; 24 407; 30 201; 31 607
  collaboration 20 606, 607; 28 480
  dealers 26 193
  groups and movements 1 77, 90, 772; 3 403; 4 109; 12 396; 23 449
  methods 7 630; 28 202, 203
  patrons and collectors 9 189; 18 498; 28 167
  pupils
    Anuszkiewicz, Richard 2 208
    Bill, Max 4 60
    Chase-Riboud, Barbara 6 500
    Davidson, Bruce 8 568
    Feininger, T(heodore) Lux 10 863
    Henri, Florence 14 393
    Hesse, Eva 14 490
    Hicks, Sheila 14 512
    Johnson, Ray(mond Edward) 17 621
    Noland, Kenneth 23 183
    Rauschenberg, Robert 26 26
    Seidler, Harry 28 374
    Sharon, Arieh 28 556
    Snelson, Kenneth 28 899
  works 1 549; 7 638, VIII2(c); 10 178; 19 492; 28 300; 33 363
Albersdorf 11 253
Albert, Archduke of Austria, Regent of the Netherlands (reg 1599-1621) 13 900, 901, 915, 917*; 14 2
  architecture 11 501; 32 115
  fountains 6 95
  medals 17 643
  metalwork 5 52
  paintings 3 558, 613; 4 913; 7 413; 22 7; 25 382; 27 291
    allegorical 2 104; 4 915
    landscape 1 687
    religious 7 368; 19 650; 27 288
  sponsorship 9 409
  tapestries 1 686; 28 899
Albert, Duke of Saxony (reg 1464-1500) 2 480; 21 62; 33 110-12*, 110
Albert, Prince of Saxe-Coburg-Gotha (1819-61) 10 252, 362, 370; 11 238; 14 143, 148-9*; 15 821; 33 110
  architecture 2 541; 3 689; 4 170; 8 249; 11 360; 26 18; 27 656; 30 534
  cameos 27 878
  ceramics 12 487

Albert, Prince of Saxe-Coburg-Gotha (1819-61)—cont.
coats of arms 14 409
decorative works 33 449
drawings 9 229
etchings 25 630
exhibitions 10 678, 679
furniture 28 255
interior decoration 25 193; 28 248
paintings 5 78; 9 682; 14 147
genre 21 69
history 7 801; 27 173
landscape 13 891
murals 22 328
mythological 9 475; 10 252
religious 7 839
sculpture 9 25; 19 878; 30 703, 742; 33 449
silver 10 335
teachers 8 652
Albert I, Duke of Bavaria-Straubing (reg 1347-1404) 14 38; 22 835, 900–901
Albert II, Bishop of Meissen 21 62
Albert II, Duke of Austria (reg 1298-1358) 13 900; 32 440
Albert II, Duke of Bavaria (reg 1438-61) 20 746; 24 36
Albert II, Holy Roman Emperor (reg 1437-39) 17 828; 20 614
Albert III, Duke of Austria (reg 1358-95) 16 908; 21 424
Albert III, Duke of Bavaria (reg 1463-1508) 25 90
Albert IV, Duke of Bavaria (reg 1463-1508) 27 148
Albert V, Duke of Austria see ALBERT II, Holy Roman Emperor
Albert V, Duke of Bavaria (reg 1550-79) 2 199; 12 475, 577, 811; 14 618; 18 521; 21 484, 484; 28 189; 29 375; 33 271–4*, 272
architecture 8 432; 9 750; 22 299, 307
collections 2 161; 12 475, 476; 15 145; 29 738
enamel 10 194
gold 22 305
hardstones 27 814, 815
metalwork 12 446
miniatures (manuscript illumination) 19 706
models 2 336
paintings 12 387
plaques 11 279
rock crystal 21 529
sculpture 1 170; 9 22; 12 577
wall paintings 4 207, 208
Albert VI, Duke of Styria (1424-63) 17 827
Albert, Brother see CHMIELOWSKI, ADAM
Albert, Charles 21 86; 32 924
Albert, Gilbert 17 530
Albert, Josef 7 575; 25 618
Albert, Tótila 1 550*
Al'bert, Yury 27 398
Albert Achilles, Elector of Brandenburg (reg 1471-86) 14 648
Albertalli, Johann see ALBERTHAL, HANS
Albert d'Ailly, Joseph d', Duc de Chaulnes see CHAULNES, JOSEPH D'ALBERT D'AILLY, Duc de
Albert de Luynes, Jeanne-Baptiste d', Comtesse de Verrue see VERRUE, JEANNE-BAPTISTE, Comtesse de
Alberthal, Hans 1 550*; 18 533
collaboration 18 533; 22 919
works 8 874; 12 369, 370; 32 821; 33 592
Alberti (family) 29 405
Alberti, Alberto 1 550, 551
Alberti, Alessandro 1 551–2*
Alberti (da Ferrara), Antonio (di Guido) 1 553–4*
translated writings 20 488
works 1 554; 11 3
Alberti, Berto see ALBERTI, ALBERTO
Alberti, Cherubino 1 551–3*; 26 770
collaboration 4 813; 27 711
patrons and collectors 1 553, 595; 26 818
works 1 551, 552; 11 762
Alberti, Chiara 1 551
Alberti, Durante 1 551; 26 823
Alberti, Giovanni 1 551, 552–3*
collaboration 1 551; 2 493; 4 813
patrons and collectors 1 595; 26 818
works 1 552; 11 762; 20 840
Alberti, Giuseppe 5 180; 31 677
Alberti, Leandro 1 554–5*; 9 111; 13 808; 29 739
Alberti, Leon Battista 1 555–68*, 556; 2 313; 7 621; 9 103; 11 178; 12 111, 112; 14 868, 869; 20 623; 23 753; 24 278, 731; 26 399, 848; 31 740
architecture 7 254, 257, 527; 14 874; 16 628, 629, 630; 23 539; 24 804; 25 265; 27 733; 33 246
arches 11 2
chapels 1 563; 26 398, 399
churches 1 456, 564, 565, 566, 567; 10 784; 11 178, 209; 12 906; 23 492; 26 185, 398–9
orders (architecture) 23 486
palaces 20 318
palazzi 1 562; 10 784; 11 178; 23 836
piers (ii) (masonry) 24 752
attributions 27 182
collaboration 12 710; 20 917
drawings 2 328, 329
inscriptions 2 166
methods 5 519; 28 202; 29 437
patrons and collectors
Gonzaga (family) 20 318
Ludovico II, 2nd Marchese of Mantua (reg 1444-78) 11 204; 12 903, 906; 20 319
Malatesta, Sigismondo Pandolfo 20 160; 24 247; 31 351
Medici (family) 16 763
Nicholas V, Pope (reg 1447-55) 23 97; 26 804
Rucellai, Giovanni (di Paolo di Messer Paolo) 11 209; 27 306, 307
pupils 11 684
sculpture 5 826; 10 784
writings 12 905; 16 781; 22 378; 28 201
on architecture 11 840; 13 33; 16 629, 631; 20 567; 22 413; 24 746; 31 295; 32 638
bridges 4 804
churches 16 629
drawings 2 328
fortifications 21 578
gates 7 359
orders (architecture) 22 378; 23 486, 487
temples 2 356; 27 236
villas 12 110, 111; 32 550
on artists 29 853
on beauty 1 178; 23 292
on coffering 7 527
on contrapposto 7 783
on decorum 8 612, 613
on display of art 9 14
on gardens 12 110
on gesture 12 503, 695
on human proportions 14 871, 874
on interior design 16 711
on modelli 21 762
on models 2 336
Alberti, Leon Battista writings—cont.
on painting 1 840; 7 627; 10 130, 690; 11 184; 13 139; 15 86; 16 658; 18 704; 24 90; 31 299, 768; 32 805
chiaroscuro 6 569; 19 352
history 14 581–2
istorie 16 613–14; 25 71
light 19 354
perspective 16 658; 24 487, 487
squaring up 29 437
on proportion 2 345, 354–6*; 7 382; 21 758; 28 201
on sculpture 31 302
on stucco 29 812, 813
translated 3 293; 19 204
Alberti, Maria Ancilla 1 551
Alberti, Matteo 19 204
Alberti, Michele 8 504
Alberti, Pier Francesco 1 551
Alberti, Romano 1 551; 33 720
Alberti archive see under FLORENCE → museums → Uffizi
Albertinelli, Mariotto (di Biagio di Binolo) 1 569–72*; 3 306
collaboration 3 302, 304–5; 5 129; 24 27
pupils 11 703; 15 862; 25 222
teachers 24 771; 27 176
works 1 570, 571; 3 303; 12 556
Albertini, Francesco 1 572*
works 11 838; 13 808; 26 848
Albertis, Sebastiano De see DE ALBERTIS, SEBASTIANO
Alberto (fl 1169-70; Modena Cathedral) 21 774
Alberto (1190-1208; Modena Cathedral, Massaro) 5 549
Alberto (1895-1962) 1 573*; 5 613; 20 68; 29 295
Alberto, 11th Marchese of Ferrara (reg 1361-93) 3 298; 10 518
architecture 10 519; 11 2, 6
interior decoration 16 711
Alberto I, Captain General of Verona (reg 1277-1301) 28 28*
Alberto, Bernardo de 2 213
Alberto, Giovanni di see GIOVANNI DI ALBERTO
Alberto da Campione I (fl before 1244) 5 549
Alberto da Campione II (fl 1404) 5 551; 13 95; 21 533
Alberto da Egna 14 416
Alberto da Piacenza 2 593; 7 542
Alberto di Sozio 8 211
Albert of Brandenburg, Archbishop of Magdeburg see HOHENZOLLERN, ALBERT OF BRANDENBURG, Cardinal, Elector-Archbishop of Mainz
Albert of Hohenzollern-Ansbach, Duke of Prussia (reg 1525-68) 1 762; 17 740
Albertolli, Alberto 1 573
Albertolli, Fedele 1 573
Albertolli, Ferdinando 1 573, 575*
Albertolli, Francesco Saverio 1 573
Albertolli, Giacomo 1 573, 575*
Albertolli, (Giuseppe) Giocondo 1 573, 574–5*; 21 527
collaboration 24 25, 758
patrons and collectors 4 471
reproductive prints by others 1 575
works 1 574, 575; 16 719; 29 833
Albertolli, Grato 1 573, 574; 24 25
Albertolli, Michele 1 573
Albertolli, (Stefano) Raffaele 1 573, 575*
Albertoni, Angelo Paluzzi degli see ALTIERI, ANGELO
Albertoni, Baldassare Paluzzi, Marchese 21 805
Albertoni, Gasparo Paluzzo degli see ALTIERI, GASPARO
Albertoni, Paluzzo Paluzzi degli, Cardinal see ALTIERI, PADRONE, Cardinal
Alberto Scoto 24 695
Albertotype 7 575
Albertrandi, Antoni 25 105
Albert & Robert 32 816
Albertslund 8 729
Albert the Great 1 176; 30 744
Albert the painter 1 576*; 30 76, 115
works 30 76, 77
Albertus 7 595
Albertus Magnus 12 107, 109; 14 432
Albert von Passau, Bishop 20 695
Alberty, Roberto 25 702
Albertype Company 2 734
Albertype process see under PHOTOGRAPHY → processes
Albi 1 576–8*; 11 505
Cathedral of Ste Cécile 1 576–8*, 577; 4 780; 11 155, 511, 555; 13 43; 32 92
choir-stalls 7 192
rood screen 13 79; 28 292, 292
great tower 6 54
houses 4 780
La Berbie 4 780
Musée Toulouse-Lautrec 1 576; 20 351; 31 214
Palais de la Berbie see Musée Toulouse-Lautrec
sculpture 13 79
Albiker, Karl 1 578*; 12 407
Albingaunum see ALBENGA
Albini, Alfred 1 578*; 8 177
Albini, Franco 1 578*; 16 721; 21 363
collaboration 3 438; 8 600
pupils 13 213; 24 697
works 16 650, 775
Albini, Rudolf 3 428
works 3 429
Albini, William II of see WILLIAM II OF ALBINI
Albinus, Bernhard Siegfried 1 842; 21 6
works 1 843
Albio 24 199
Albion press see under PRESSES → types
Albisola 1 578–9*; 16 618, 735
albitic jadeite see under JADE → types
Albium Ingaunum see ALBENGA
Albizu, Olga 18 832; 25 701
Albizzi (family) 26 446
Albizzo di Piero 12 538
Albon, Jacques d', Maréchal de Saint-André see SAINT-ANDRÉ, JACQUES D'ALBON, Maréchal de
Ålborg 8 720
Carl Christiansen factory 16 828
Cathedral 4 781
Nordjyllands Kunstmuseum 1 10; 2 370; 8 759
Vor Frue Kirke 8 737, 737
Ålborg Room see under COPENHAGEN → museums → Nationalmuseet
Alborno, Pablo 24 98, 101
Albornoz, Carrillo de 8 253
Albornoz, Egidio, Cardinal 2 18, 620; 4 275; 23 584; 29 422
Albotto, Francesco 20 415
Alboy, Maurice 24 605
Albrecht, Adolph von 15 87
Albrecht, Augustin 1 579
Albrecht, Balthasar Augustin 1 579*; 22 302; 33 277
Albrecht, Benedikt 1 579
Albrecht, Conrad Adolph von 13 279
Albrecht, Gretchen 1 579*; 23 61
Albrecht, Herzog von Brunswick-Grubenhagen 26 563
Albrecht II, Archbishop of Magdeburg 20 87
Albrecht Altar, Master of the 2 792; 17 827; 20 614*; 32 441
albrechtd. 29 98
Albrechtsburg, Johann Konrad Albrecht von 11 134, 135
Albrecht von Nürnberg 30 136
Albret, Charlotte d', Duchesse de Valentinois see VALENTINOIS, CHARLOTTE D'ALBRET, Duchesse de
Albricus 15 83
Albright, Adam Amory 1 579
Albright, Harrison 33 408
Albright, Ivan (le Lorraine) 1 579–80*; 31 607
Albrizzi, Giambattista 13 741; 33 721
book illustrations 32 501
paintings 24 706
printmakers 6 91; 24 707, 708, 894; 32 501
Albrizzi, I.
works 26 232
albs 9 642; 32 387*
Albufereta, La see LA ALBUFERETA
Albukasem de Baldac see IBN BUTLAN
album amicorum 1 580, 584–5*
Albumasar see ABU MA'SHAR
Album Derand 8 775
albumen 1 155; 12 769*; 19 386; 23 783
etchings 10 560
gilding 1 156; 12 621
manuscript illumination 13 136; 20 347
mortars (building) 19 386
paints 23 783; 32 898
paper 24 55
pastiglia 24 248
photography 24 647, 648
tempera 30 425
varnishes 32 2, 3
albumen plates see under PHOTOGRAPHIC PLATES → types
albumen prints see under PHOTOGRAPHIC PRINTS → types
Album Ingaunum see ALBENGA
albums 1 580–84*
historical and regional traditions
Buddhism 1 581–2
China 1 580, 580–81; 6 762, 791; 22 234
Indian subcontinent 1 582–3*, 583; 15 547, 585–6, 586; 22 235–6
Iran 16 318–19
Iraq 16 318–19
Islamic 1 583–4*; 16 271, 272, 283, 318–19; 22 235–6
Japan 1 580, 581–2
Korea 1 580, 581
Nepal 22 786, 795
individual manuscripts
Amir Ghayb Beg Album (Istanbul, Topkapı Pal. Lib., H. 2161) 21 722; 22 390
Anwan Album (Senoku Hakkokan) 6 801, 802
Arenberg Album (Liège, Cab. Est. & Dessins) 2 382; 19 548
Berlin Album (Berlin, Staatsbib.) 16 286, 345; 17 923; 22 235
Churchill Album (London, BM, Or. MS. 4938) 2 235; 22 260
Davis Album (New York, Met., MS. 30. 95. 174) 1 643; 22 263
Diez Albums (Berlin, Staatsbib. Preuss. Kultbes., Orientabt., Diez A. fol. 70-72) 26 4
Fitzwilliam Album 3 319
Freshfield Album (Cambridge, Trinity College Library, O.17.2) 9 595

albums
individual manuscripts—cont.
Gerolamo di Giovanni Pennacchi *see* GIROLAMO DI GIOVANNI PENNACCHI 22 236
Gulshan Album (Tehran, Gulistan Pal. Lib.) 2 235; 16 345, 346; 17 923; 22 235
Hermitage Album 16 339, 340
Jahangir Album 9 461
Johnson Album 15 642
Kevorkian Album (New York, Met., MS. 55. 121. 10) 3 91–2; 8 543; 15 589; 16 286; 18 4
Minto Album (Dublin, Chester Beatty Lib., MS. 7; London, V&A, I.M. 8 to 28-1925) 1 582; 8 543; 13 235, 236; 15 589; 16 346; 22 236
Muraqqa'-i gulshan *see* GULSHAN ALBUM
St Bruno Album (Paris, Louvre) 19 247
St Petersburg Album (St Petersburg, Hermitage, E-14) 1 643; 22 263, 264
Shah Jahan Album, Late 15 589; 16 346
van Caloen album (Loppem, Sticht. van Caloen) 12 612
Wantage Album (London, V&A) 15 589; 22 236
Ya'qub Beg Albums (Istanbul, Topkapı Pal. Lib., H 2153 and H. 2160) 8 533; 28 811
types
accordion-folded *see* BOOKS → forms → accordion-books
butterfly books *see under* BOOKS → forms
stitched-bound books *see under* BOOKS → forms
uses
calligraphy 1 580–82
cartes-de-visite 24 649
drawings 9 11, 26
paintings 1 580–82
photographs 24 649
prints 1 582
sketches 1 582
see also BOOKS; MANUSCRIPTS; TABLETS
Albuquerque (NM), Indian Pueblo Community Center 22 671
Albuquerque, Duque de 29 303
Albuquerque, Afonso de (1453-1515) 7 493; 12 826; 15 401; 20 168
Albuquerque, Afonso de (1500-80) *see* ALBUQUERQUE, BRÁS DE
Albuquerque, Brás de 1 586*; 12 114
Albuquerque, Fernando Barbara de 22 534
Albuquerque, Marcelo 9 117
Albury Park (Surrey) 3 174; 12 128; 32 552
Albuzzi, Antonio Francesco 5 444
Alcahisar Church 19 840
Alcalá (family) 29 353
Alcalá, 1st Duque de (1509-71) 26 306*; 28 519
Alcalá, 3rd Duque de (1583-1637) 26 307*; 28 515
architecture 23 683; 28 519
paintings 4 210; 12 169; 21 35; 23 704; 26 310; 32 99
sponsorship 26 310
Alcalá Bibles *see under* BIBLES → types
Alcalá de Henares 1 586–7*, *587*; 29 *258*
Archbishop's Palace 2 529; 8 78
ceilings 2 *529*
Augustinian monastery 29 45
Colegio Málaga 29 269
colleges 7 566
Alcalá de Henares—cont.
Las Bernardas 22 67
magistral church 29 336, 337
Parainfo 2 529
pottery 16 411
silver 29 *334*
University 7 345; 29 267; 31 674
Chapel of S Ildefonso 2 529; 22 256
Paraninfo Hall 22 256
Alcalá-Zamora, María de la Salud Madrid *see* SALUD MADRID ALCALÁ-ZAMORA, MARÍA DE LA
Alcalde del Rio, Hermilio 6 46
Alcañices, Marqués de 19 657
Alcaniz, Miguel *see* ALCANYIS, MIGUEL
Alcántara, Antonio de 31 427
Alcántara, Diego de 10 499, 535; 29 267
Alcantara, Pedro d', 9th Conde de Aranda *see* ARANDA, PEDRO D'ALCANTARA, 9th Conde de
Alcántara Bridge 26 884, *908*; 27 7
Alcántara Téllez Girón, Pedro de, Duque de Osuna *see* OSUNA, PEDRO DE ALCÁNTARA TÉLLEZ GIRÓN, Duque de
Alcántara Téllez Girón y Pacheco, Pedro de *see* OSUNA, 9th Duque de
Alcanyis, Miguel 1 587–8*; 20 621, 622
Alcaraz 5 834; 29 347
Alcaraz, Francisco Salzillo y *see* SALZILLO Y ALCARAZ, FRANCISCO
Alcaraz, Hernando Toribio de *see* TORIBIO DE ALCARAZ, HERNANDO
Alcaudete 9 596
alcazaba *see* QAṢABA
Alcázar *see under* TOLEDO
Alcázar, Luis Paret y *see* PARET (Y ALCÁZAR), LUIS
Alce 6 97
Alcester 2 82
Alcherius, Johannes 1 588*; 7 525
Alchi 1 588–9*; 15 *264*; 30 *806*
architecture 15 311
Assembly Hall *see* Dukhang
Dukhang 15 311, 561, 562; 30 816, 832
sculpture 30 823
stupas 30 817
temples 30 816
Lhakhang Soma 15 561, 562; 30 832
Lotsawa Lhakhang 15 561, 562; 30 816
Manjushri Lhakhang 15 561; 30 816
New Temple *see* Lhakhang Soma
Sumtsek Lhakhang 15 311, 561–2; 30 832, *832*, 846
Temple of the Great Translator *see* Lotsawa Lhakhang
Three-tiered Temple *see* Sumtsek Lhakhang
wall paintings 15 561, *562*; 30 824, 831, 832
Alchiero, Johannes *see* ALCHERIUS, JOHANNES
Alchimavičius, Kazimieras 19 498
Alchymia 22 869, 877
Alciati, Andrea 1 589*, 656; 10 175
works 10 173, 174; 15 83, 149
illustrated 4 358; 10 *174*
Alciati, Enrique 1 589*
collaboration 26 425
works 21 379, 403
Alcíbar, José de 13 730; 21 384
Alcina, José 7 163; 15 832
Alciras, Master of 29 277
Alcoa Steam Ship Company 5 746
Alcobaça, Pedro of, Frei *see* PEDRO (OF ALCOBAÇA), Frei
Alcobaça Abbey 1 589–91*; 7 350; 9 104; 16 51; 20 326; 25 *288*, 289, 306, 317; 30 879
cloister 7 455
manuscripts 25 295
refectory 1 *590*
royal tombs 26 611
sculpture 25 301
silver 25 312
silver-gilt 13 166
tomb of Inês de Castro 1 590; 13 102; 25 300, *301*
tomb of Peter I 1 590; 13 *101*, 102; 25 300
Alcobendas, S Pedro Mártir 9 113
Alcock, Edward 18 906
Alcock, John, Bishop of Ely 10 168
Alcock, Rutherford 9 295; 17 440
alcohol 7 747; 10 560; 32 2, 898
see also BUTANOL; DIACETONE ALCOHOL; ETHANOL; ISOPROPANOL
Alcolea, Carlos 13 6
Alcora factory 2 284; 29 328, 329
works 29 *328*
Alcoverro y Amorós, José 1 591*
alcoves 17 *75*, 76; 19 262, 316
Alcubierre 21 37
Alcuéscar, Lucía del Trampal 29 261
Alcuin of York, Abbot of Tours 5 779, 800; 31 227; 32 636; 33 541, 546
Aldana, Juan de 2 386, 387; 24 503
Aldao, Luis 22 97
Aldborough (N. Yorks) 27 60
Aldegrever, Christoph 1 591
Aldegrever, Heinrich 1 591–4*; 2 455; 10 385; 22 315
groups and movements 19 501
reproductive prints by others 5 888; 14 682; 19 661
works 1 *592*, *593*; 12 386, 421; 25 604; 27 256; 30 87
Aldenberg, Stephan 12 209
Aldeneik Church 3 552
Aldenham, Henry Hucks Gibbs, 1st Baron *see* GIBBS, HENRY HUCKS, 1st Baron Aldenham
Alden & Harlow 5 781
alder 14 905; 24 248; 33 324
Aldermaston Pottery 5 389
Aldermaston Service Station 28 488
Aldernese IV, King (*reg* 881/8-923) 30 306
Aldersey, Laurence 10 78
Aldershot Clubhouse 26 18
Aldgate Pottery 10 303
Aldine Press 14 616, 867
Aldini, Antonio 12 584
Aldobrandini (family) 5 705, 708; 9 89; 14 426; 25 387; 26 748
Aldobrandini, Cinzio, Cardinal *see* PASSERI, CINZIO, Cardinal
Aldobrandini, Ippolito, Cardinal *see* CLEMENT VIII, Pope
Aldobrandini, Olimpia, Princess of Rossano 3 198; 25 563; 27 864
Aldobrandini, Pietro (i) (*d* 1587) 2 493
Aldobrandini, Pietro (ii), Cardinal (1571-1621) 1 594–6*
architecture 11 740; 18 669; 26 758; 32 547
art policies 16 768
decorative works 26 834
frescoes 26 197
gardens 12 115
paintings 1 534; 2 493; 3 353; 5 705; 10 522, 525; 11 4; 26 196
Aldobrandini Tazze 1 595; 29 415
Aldobrandini Wedding 1 594; 2 170; 13 629; 24 330; 31 50
Aldred 19 409; 20 329
Aldred, Obed 19 734
Aldrich, Abby *see* ROCKEFELLER, ABBY ALDRICH
Aldrich, Chester H. 8 652–3*
Aldrich, Henry 1 596–7*
groups and movements 23 857
works 23 687, 690; 31 234
Aldrich, Nelson, Associates 27 613
Aldrich, Nelson Wilmarth 26 488
Aldrophe, Alfred-Philibert 17 547
Aldrovandi, Carlo Filippo, Conte 1 597
Aldrovandi, Filippo 1 597
Aldrovandi, Giovanni Francesco 1 597; 4 276; 21 433
Aldrovandi, Pompeo 1 597; 12 30; 13 626
Aldrovandi, Ulisse 1 597*; 2 103; 4 276; 13 541
assistants 7 857; 11 803
personal collection 12 558; 16 770
works 2 105; 10 174; 12 21, 911; 19 374; 26 848
Aldrovandini, Tommaso 4 320; 5 281; 8 159; 29 32
Aldunate Avaria, Manuel 6 593
Alea, Tomás Gutiérrez 20 892
Aleandri, Ireneo 29 640
aleatoric art *see* CHANCE IN ART
Alebić, Josip 4 462
Alechinsky, Pierre 1 597–8*; 3 565
groups and movements 5 45; 7 489; 17 518
works 19 491
Alee, John *see* LEE, JOHN
Alegre, Manuel de Araújo Porto *see* PORTO ALEGRE, MANUEL DE ARAÚJO
Alegrete, Marquês d' 25 820
Alegría, Ricardo 25 703
Aleijadinho, O *see* LISBOA, ANTÔNIO FRANCISCO
Aleksandrov, G. I. 11 245
Aleksandrovich, Mikhail, Grand Duke 21 99
Aleksandrowicz, Jan 25 124
Aleksandrowicz, Konstanty 25 105
Aleksey, Metropolitan 8 *909*
Aleksey, Tsar of Moscow (*reg* 1645-76) 26 729
architecture 3 530; 18 207; 22 170; 29 778
glass 27 414
metalwork 11 714; 28 187
Alekseyev, Aleksandr (Alekseyvich) 32 164
Alekseyev, Fyodor (Yakovlevich) 1 598–9*; 18 38
works 1 *599*
Alekseyeva-Batanova, Yekaterina (Ivanovna) 27 417
Aleksey of Lys'k 31 557
Aleksić, Borivoje 4 461
Aleksić, Dragan 8 437
Aleksi-Meskhishvili, V. 12 320
Aleksiun, Jan 25 108
Alemagna, Giovanni d' *see* GIOVANNI D'ALEMAGNA
Alemagna, Rigo d' *see* RIGO D'ALEMAGNA
Alemán, Enrique 13 191; 28 518; 31 92
works 13 *191*
Alemán, Gaspar 29 340
Alemán, Juan (*c.* 1398-*c.* 1468) 1 599–600*; 29 289
works 9 748; 13 107; 31 90, 92
Alemán, Juan (*fl* 1506-13) 1 600
Aleman, Melchior *see* SITTOW, MICHEL
Alemán, Rodrigo 1 600*
patrons and collectors 21 125
works 3 847; 7 363; 13 123; 21 725; 25 23; 31 88, 92
Alemania, Giletto de *see* GILETTO DE ALEMANIA
Alemania, Teodorico de *see* TEODORICO DE ALEMANIA
Alemanno, Lodovico, Cardinal 13 96; 16 843
Alemanno, Pietro 1 600*; 2 594; 8 171
Alemans 14 182; 21 500; 23 537
fibulae 21 *502*
Alemany, C. B. 31 655
Alemany, J. 20 516
Alemany, Pere 14 858
Alemão, João 13 125
Alembert, Jean Le Rond d' 24 787
works 10 206, 401; 22 357
illustrated 24 268; 32 767
on architecture 4 163
on caricatures 5 760
on engraving 10 *392*
on furniture 11 595
on leather 19 *1*
on paper 24 38
on squaring up 29 437
on taste 22 21
Alen, William Van *see* VAN ALEN, WILLIAM
Alencastre, Juan Antonio 29 347
Alençon
lace 11 650; 18 589, *589*, 591
Musée des Beaux-Arts 14 577
Musée Municipal 6 545
Notre-Dame 13 60; 22 220
Alençon, François de Valois, Duc d' 2 160; 21 345
Alençon, Jean II, Duc d' 18 686
Alençon, Jeanne, Comtesse d' 5 895
Alençon, Marguerite de Valois, Duchesse d' 21 638
Alenza y Nieto, Leonardo 1 600*
patrons and collectors 18 899
works 29 284, *284*
Aleotti, Giovanni Battista 1 601*
attributions 3 744
collaboration 3 89; 11 3
patrons and collectors 3 743, 744; 10 524; 24 833
pupils 20 94
works 1 *601*; 11 3; 22 166; 30 666, 667
writings 11 343
Aleotti, Vincenzo 1 601
Aleppo 1 602–3*, *821*, *849*; 9 *513*; 16 *104*; 28 *719*, 721; 30 177, 178, *180*
art forms and materials
architecture 16 207, 208, 211, 228; 32 314
glass 12 IV1; 16 519, *521*
inscriptions 1 893
jewellery 27 103
manuscripts 16 308, 350
masonry 16 180
muqarnas (architecture) 22 323
printing 16 360
silk 16 445
textiles 16 441
baths 3 375
caravanserais 5 723; 16 228
Khan al-Gumruk 5 723
Khan al-Qadi 16 211
churches 9 539
craftsmen and artists 16 182
fortifications 21 582, 587; 33 614
Bab Antakiya 21 582
Bab Qinnasrin 21 587
Citadel 21 582, *583*, 587; 32 309
gardens 12 78
Maqam Ibrahim 16 490
revetments 16 381
houses 16 263, 270
Islamic religious buildings
'Adiliyya Mosque 16 221
portico 16 222
congregational mosque (16th/17th cent.) 16 222
Firdaws Madrasa 1 602; 16 180, *181*; 20 56
gardens 12 78
mihrab 1 *603*
muqarnas (architecture) 22 323

Aleppo
Islamic religious buildings—cont.
Great Mosque **16** 146, 179, 496; **21** 627
mosaics **16** 255
*khānaqāh*s **18** 17
Khusraw Pasha mosque complex **16** 228
madrasas **20** 56
musalla **22** 354
Shadbakhtiyya Madrasa **22** 323
al-Utrush Mosque **16** 211
Zahiriyya Madrasa **16** 180
Madina **16** 260
markets **16** 261, 262; **20** 438
Matbakh al-ʿAjami **16** 182
minbars **21** 629
National Museum **1** 603; **21** 310; **30** 178, 199
Palace of al-ʿAziz Muhammad **16** 182
synagogue **17** 550
trade **30** 179
urban planning **16** 241, 261, 262, 263
Alert Bay **22** *544*
cemetery **22** *579*
Aleš, Mikoláš **1** 604*; **25** 433
collaboration **29** 885; **33** 635
groups and movements **20** 254
works **8** 392, 400; **25** 433
Aleši, Andrija *see* ALESSI, ANDREA
Alesia **21** 559; **27** 85
Alesio, Mateo Pérez de *see* PÉREZ DE ALESIO, MATEO
Alessandri (family) **19** 443
Alessandria **21** 581
Dispensario Antitubercolare **4** 790; **15** 886; **16** 650
Palazzo Ghilini *see* Palazzo del Governo
Palazzo del Governo **1** 622
Alessandro (*fl* 1580) **14** 885
Alessandro, 3rd Duke of Parma (*reg* 1586-92) and Governor of the Netherlands **24** *696*
architecture **23** 745; **24** 193
paintings **7** 368; **32** 115; **33** 252
Alessandro, Duke of Florence (*reg* 1531-7) **14** *2*; **21** 7, *8*, 19*
dies (ii) (stamps) **6** 140
interior decoration **3** 15
medals **32** 393
military architecture **27** 744
sculpture **3** 158; **19** 551; **31** 320
Alessandro, Antonio d' **16** 736
Alessandro, Gennero **16** 736
Alessandro, Giuseppe **16** 736
Alessandro da Padova *see* PADOVANO, ALESSANDRO
Alessi **8** 805; **13** 326; **27** 192; **29** 547
Alessi, Andrea **1** 604*; **31** 359
collaboration **12** 667; **23** 92; **31** 359
works **8** 175, 178; **31** 359
Alessi, Galeazzo **1** 605–9*; **21** 517; **26** 769, 823; **27** 499
architecture **10** 499; **24** 520; **31** 897–8, 899
churches **1** *607*; **3** 354; **16** 634; **29** 372
grottoes **13** 703
palaces **1** *608*; **4** 748; **26** 819; **31** 878; **32** 767
villas **1** *606*; **12** 116, 281; **32** 547, *548*
assistants **19** 806; **25** 226
attributions **28** 460
patrons and collectors **3** 249; **5** 455; **27** 877
teachers **5** 672
Alesso di Andrea **11** 888
Aletić, Ivo **8** 180
aletoscopio *see under* PHOTOGRAPHY → instruments
Aletri *see* ABELIKOU-ALETRI
Aleut **22** 545, 638, 645, 655, 668
Aleu y Teixidor, Andrés **1** 610*; **10** 727
Alewijn, Cornelis **22** 828
Alewijn, Frederick **32** 589
Alexanco, José Luis **1** 610*; **29** 297
Alexander (*fl* 2nd cent.) **27** 1
Alexander (*fl* 1197) **18** 757
Alexander, Master (*fl c.* 1460s) **28** 854
Alexander, Mme **31** 261
Alexander, Bishop of Lincoln **7** 351; **19** 402, 404; **26** 614
Alexander, King of Poland (*reg* 1501-6) **25** 134
Alexander I, Emperor of Russia (*reg* 1801-25) **4** 302; **8** 580; **24** 388; **26** 733*; **27** 579; **30** 63
architecture **5** 521; **10** 219; **11** 92; **22** 25
collections **10** 819; **27** 439
interior decoration **29** 552
paintings **4** 304; **5** 68
Alexander I, King of Scotland (*reg* 1107-24) **29** 678
Alexander I, Voivode of Moldavia (*reg* 1400-32) **15** 55
Alexander II, Emperor of Russia (*reg* 1855-81) **4** 42; **15** 842; **19** 109; **26** 734*; **33** 581, 669
Alexander II, Pope (*reg* 1061-73) **19** 765
Alexander, Bishop of Aelia **17** 489
Alexander III, Emperor of Russia (*reg* 1881-94) **1** 148; **10** 722; **21** 98; **26** 734*
architecture **21** 177
paintings **28** 672
Alexander III, King of Macedon *see* ALEXANDER THE GREAT, King of Macedon
Alexander III, King of Serbia and Yugoslavia (*reg* 1929-34) **28** 439
Alexander IV, King of Macedon (*reg* 323-10 BC) **9** *778*; **27** 691
Alexander IV, Pope (*reg* 1254-61) **23** 460
Alexander VI, Pope (*reg* 1492-1503) **4** 409–10*; **26** *817*
altarpieces **23** 605
architecture **4** 409; **7** 366, 541; **24** 731, 732; **26** 756, 795, 800, 811, 831; **27** 739; **31** 815
frescoes **26** 817
gold **28** 260
interior decoration **31** 188
paintings **16** 660; **24** 829, 830; **31** 815
sculpture **2** 140; **4** 646, 737
swords **2** 453
Alexander VII, Pope (*reg* 1655-67) **6** 584–5*; **12** 648
architecture **3** 835; **7** 912; **13** 338; **16** 638, 639; **17** 510; **25** 862; **26** 759, 814; **29** 251
coats of arms **14** 417
collections **16** 763
frescoes **26** 818
metalwork **8** 202
paintings **12** 648; **13** 656; **20** 374, 375; **21** 54, 808
sculpture **3** 832, 833; **4** 433; **11** 739; **26** 810; **28** 677, 681
stucco **29** 830
teachers **12** 12
Alexander VIII, Pope (*reg* 1689-91) **11** 275; **13** 626; **27** 593; **32** 8
Alexander, Christopher **1** 610–11*; **6** 552; **30** 391; **31** 735
Alexander, Cicely **33** *139*
Alexander, Daniel Asher **25** 39
Alexander, David Asher **2** 324
Alexander, Esther Frances **1** 611
Alexander, Francesca *see* ALEXANDER, ESTHER FRANCES
Alexander, Francis **1** 611*
Alexander, James, 1st Earl of Caledon **15** 165
Alexander, John **28** 235
Alexander, John White **1** 611–12*; **9** 468; **11** 322; **25** 5
Alexander, P. **6** 363; **20** 89
Alexander, Robert **20** 487
Alexander, Robert E. **23** 10
Alexander, Samuel **10** 851
Alexander, W. C. **33** 139, 143
Alexander, William **1** 612*
Alexander Couza, Prince of Romania (*reg* 1859-66) **26** 718; **30** 202
Alexander & Cunliffe **32** 904
Alexander Master (*fl c.* 1420-50) **20** 615*
Alexander Mosaic **13** 551, 605; **22** 514; **25** 205, *206*
Alexander of Abingdon **1** 612*
works **8** 198; **13** 81; **31** 164
Alexander of Abonouteichos **4** 113
works **4** *113*
Alexander of Malonnes **25** 95
Alexander of Neckham *see* ALBRICUS
Alexander Papers **10** 356
Alexander Romance, Master of the *see* ALEXANDER MASTER
Alexander Sarcophagus **27** 825; **28** 668
Alexanderson, Gustav **10** 463
Alexandersson, Carl **10** 462
Alexander's Wall **24** 215
Alexander the Carpenter **7** 420
Alexander the Great, King of Macedon (*reg* 336-323 BC) **1** 612–14*; **3** 11; **9** *778*; **14** 429; **15** 908; **28** 668; **30** 178
architecture **1** 614; **3** 65; **9** 785, 852; **13** 391, 404; **23** 430; **25** 576; **28** 383; **30** 692; **31** 501
military **21** 591
coins **1** 204; **10** 608; **13** 588, *588*
gems **12** 248
paintings **2** 217; **13** 375, 551
sculpture **5** 604; **13** 439, 440; **19** 852, 853; **29** 567
siege engines **21** 557
urban planning **1** 614
Alexander von Buren *see* PASQUALINI, ALEXANDER (i)
Alexandr **3** 224
Alexandra, Queen of Great Britain (1844-1925) **8** 753; **14** 363, 523; **17** 527; **31** 307
Alexandra Fyodorovna, Empress of Russia (1798-1860) **14** 654; **28** 103
Alexandra Fyodorovna, Empress of Russia (1872-1918) **8** 531; **10** 722; **11** 894; **12** 606
Alexandre **10** 781
Alexandre, Arsène **1** 613–14*
Alexandre, José **28** 516
Alexandre, Maxime **30** 20
Alexandre, Paul **21** 786
Alexandre de Paris **26** 563
Alexandre II, King of Kakheti (*reg* 1574-1605) **12** 331
Alexandretta *see* ISKENDERUN
Alexandria (Egypt) **1** *376*, 612, 614–20*; **7** *819*; **9** *507*, *774*, 785, 852; **13** *362*, 368, 416; **16** *104*; **26** *921*
art forms and materials
architecture **1** 614–15*; **2** 428; **16** 208; **26** 920
bone-carvings **7** 825
books **23** 692
capitals **1** *615*; **7** 821; **13** 391
carpets **16** 470
coins **16** 510
faience (i) (glass) **10** 48
figurines **13** 581
furniture **13** 592
glass **10** 55, 58, 59; **13** 594; **16** 519; **26** 855; **27** 72; **28** 384
hardstones **14** 169
ivory **9** 647
jewellery **10** 33
Alexandria (Egypt)
art forms and materials—cont.
manuscripts **9** 619
marble **13** 434
metalwork **16** 369
mosaics **1** 616–17*, *617*; **13** 557, 558, 559, 560, 565–6, *566*; **22** 155
orders (architecture) **23** 484
painting **1** *618*, 618–19*; **12** 287; **27** 57
pigments **23** 785
pottery **1** 617–18*; **13** 539
sculpture **1** 616*; **13** 462, 463, 465; **26** 292
silk **9** 667
stucco **29** 814
tapestries **9** 767
textiles **1** 881; **16** 431, 432, 441; **31** 21
Caesareum **1** 615; **23** 330, 331
collections **13** 555
College of Fine Arts **9** 768
factories **16** 441
fortifications **20** 230; **21** 587
gardens **12** 68
gymnasium **13** 406
Hadra cemetery **13** 491
Library *see under* museums → Museum (Ptolemaic)
monopteros **21** 892
Mouseion *see* museums → Museum (Ptolemaic)
museums
Graeco-Roman Museum **1** 615, 620; **9** 768; **10** 92; **13** 470
Museum (Ptolemaic) **1** 615; **2** 364, 365; **13** 404; **22** 354–5
Library **19** 312; **26** 557
Museum of Fine Arts **1** 620; **9** 768
palace (Ptolemaic) **13** 407
Pharos lighthouse **1** 615; **19** 360
Ramleh-Casino **22** 270
Sanctuary of the Muses *see* museums → Museum (Ptolemaic)
Serapeion **19** 312
tombs **9** 842; **13** 404
Alabaster Tomb **13** 407
Karmouz catacomb **7** 822
Kom el-Shuqafa catacomb **6** 69, 70
reliefs **9** 897
urban planning **1** 613, 614–15
water-clock **13** 382
Alexandria (VA; USA) **31** 649
Assembly House **2** 618
Alexandria, Heron of *see* HERON OF ALEXANDRIA
Alexandria, Pappos of *see* PAPPOS OF ALEXANDRIA
Alexandria Eschate *see* KHODZHENT
Alexandrian, Sarane **30** 23
Alexandrian Library *see under* ALEXANDRIA (EGYPT) → museums → Museum (Ptolemaic)
Alexandrian World Chronicle *see under* CHRONICLES → individual manuscripts
Alexandria Oxiana *see* AI KHANUM
Alexandria Troas **31** 354
bath-gymnasium **3** 375
Alexandrino, Pedro *see* CARVALHO, PEDRO ALEXANDRINO
Alexandrium **17** 556
Alexandroni, A. **33** 507
Alexandros Athenaios **27** 52
Alexandros of Antioch on the Meander **13** 466; **32** 236
works **13** *466*
Alexandroupolis, Metropolis of St Nicholas **9** 627
Alex Gordon Partnership **32** 791
Alexii, Andreas *see* ALESSI, ANDREA
Alexios I, Emperor of Byzantium (*reg* 1081-1118) **7** 591; **9** 657; **16** 582; **18** 211; **28** 439
Alexios II, Grand Komnenos (*reg* 1297-1330) **31** 304
Alexios III, Grand Komnenos (*reg* 1349-90) **31** 304
Alexios the Grand Stratopedarch **9** 629
Alexis Gritchenko Foundation *see under* NEW YORK → foundations
Alexis Master (*fl* 1120-30) **10** 244; **20** 331; **26** 671, 672
works **26** *672*
Alexius (family) **7** 922
Alexius, Master (*fl* 1508) **28** 855
Alexy, Janko **28** 853
Alexy, Károly **14** 896
Alfani, Domenico (di Paride) **1** 620*; **25** 908; **31** 898, 899
Alfani, Orazio **1** 620
Alfanus, Archbishop of Salerno **22** 12; **26** 625
Alfanus of Termoli **3** 235
Alfarano, Tiberio **26** 800
alfardón mig tiles *see under* TILES → types
alfardón tiles *see under* TILES → types
Alfarería Artística Mexicana **7** 784
Alfaro, Anastasio **13** 771
Alfaro, Andreu **1** 620–21*; **29** 296; **31** 816
Alfaro, Brooke **1** 621*; **23** 905
Alfaro, Cristóbal de **29** 334
Alfaro, Matías de Arteaga y *see* ARTEAGA Y ALFARO, MATÍAS DE
Alfaro, Miguel Angel **24** 96
Alfaro Siqueiros, David *see* SIQUEIROS, DAVID ALFARO
Alfaro y Gómez, Juan de **1** 621*; **29** 358
Alfei, Francesco di Bartolomeo **1** 621–2*; **11** 688; **20** 740
Alfeld an der Leine, Fagus Factory **4** 788; **8** 247; **10** 749; **12** 792; **13** 687; **21** 780; **26** 15
Alfelt, Else **7** 488; **8** 736; **24** 315, 316
Alfieri, Count **20** 389
Alfieri, A. **30** 221
Alfieri, Benedetto Innocente **1** 622–4*; **31** 444
architecture **21** 519; **31** 898
cathedrals **12** 277
palazzi **1** *622*; **16** 716, 719; **17** 709, 710; **18** 729; **26** 500
reconstructions **21** 824
theatres **1** 125; **30** 667
collaboration **4** 423; **31** 446
interior decoration **28** 19
patrons and collectors **28** 18
Alfieri, Bernard **19** 424
Alfieri, Vittorio **10** 726; **23** 87
Alfonso (*fl c.* 1450) **14** 135
Alfonso (photographic firm) **1** 624*
Alfonso, Count of Barcelona *see* ALFONSO II, King of Aragon
Alfonso, King of Germany *see* ALFONSO X, King of Castile-León
Alfonso I, 3rd Duke of Ferrara, Modena and Reggio (*reg* 1505-34) **10** 517, *518*, 522–3*; **26** 459; **29** *408*
architecture **11** 3
drawings **12** 750
paintings **9** 183; **11** 4; **16** 667; **23** 96; **24** 342; **29** 860
mythological **3** 306, 660; **10** 130, 443; **14** 870; **16** 665; **21** 438, 443; **22** 413; **25** 71; **32** 192
religious **31** 34
productions **2** 412
rock crystal **16** 745

Alfonso I, 3rd Duke of Ferrara, Modena and Reggio (*reg* 1505-34)—cont.
  sculpture 3 496; 11 4; 16 693; 19 559; 29 25
  weapons 11 4
Alfonso I, King of Kongo *see* NZINGA MVEMBA ALFONSO I, King of Kongo
Alfonso I, King of Naples (*reg* 1435-58) 2 275, 276*; 10 747
  altarpieces 7 543; 21 13
  architecture 22 470, *486*; 24 782; 27 521
  manuscripts 4 764
  metalwork 29 332
  paintings 2 178; 7 543; 10 747; 16 658, 834
    frescoes 19 180
    religious 2 179; 10 713; 19 443, 444; 23 160; 33 118
  sculpture 16 67; 23 415; 24 28
  tiles 30 886
Alfonso I, King of Portugal (*reg* 1112-85) 1 589; 7 531
Alfonso II, 5th Duke of Ferrara, Modena and Reggio (*reg* 1559-97) 10 *518*, 524*
  architecture 1 601, 637; 3 89
  ceramics 24 252
  collections 19 373
  paintings 2 389; 9 187; 18 869
  porcelain 16 736
  tapestries 11 5
Alfonso II, King of Aragon (*reg* 1162-96) 26 676
Alfonso II, King of Asturias (*reg* 791-842) 2 653, 654*
  architecture 2 652–3; 23 681, 682; 31 19
  decorative works 23 682
  gold 2 654
Alfonso II, King of Naples (*reg* 1494-95) 2 275, 277*; 10 868; 20 112, 114; 30 496
  architecture 12 656; 22 470, 471
  sculpture 20 906
Alfonso III, 7th Duke of Modena and Reggio (*reg* 1628-9) 10 *518*, 525–6*
Alfonso III, King of Asturias (*reg* 866-910) 2 653, 654*
  architecture 2 653; 27 793
  decorative works 23 682
  manuscripts 20 330
  metalwork 5 808
Alfonso IV, 9th Duke of Modena and Reggio (*reg* 1658-62) 4 455; 10 *518*, 527*; 29 775
Alfonso IV, King of Aragon (*reg* 1327-36) 3 339
Alfonso IV, King of Portugal (*reg* 1325-57) 28 499
Alfonso V, King of Aragon and Sicily *see* ALFONSO I, King of Naples
Alfonso V, King of León (*reg* 999-1028) 19 171
Alfonso V, King of Portugal (*reg* 1438-61) 2 869, 871*; 25 304, 312
  architecture 11 210
  paintings 10 713; 12 890; 25 295
  sculpture 24 848
Alfonso VI, King of Castile-León (*reg* 1065-1109) 31 822
  architecture 7 473, 474; 14 508; 19 175; 27 793
  chairs 29 297
  interior decoration 29 297
  metalwork 23 683; 26 689
Alfonso VI, King of Portugal (*reg* 1656-83) 4 *631*, 632, 633–4*; 25 306
Alfonso VII, King of Castile (*reg* 1126-57) 7 350; 16 437
Alfonso VIII, King of Castile (*reg* 1158-1214) 5 201, 205, 664; 7 350; 8 252; 22 255; 25 22
Alfonso X, King of Castile-León (*reg* 1252-84), King of Germany (*reg* 1257-73) 1 624*
  architecture 5 202, 367; 7 843; 28 518; 31 86
  manuscripts 13 144; 16 455; 29 275, 298, *852*; 31 88
  stained glass 19 174
  writings 2 650
Alfonso XI, King of Castile-León (*reg* 1312-50) 7 177; 13 732; 22 255; 28 516, 518
Alfonso XII, King of Spain (*reg* 1874-85) 29 343
Alfonso XIII, King of Spain (*reg* 1886-1931) 30 784
Alfonso, Juan 13 732
Alfonso, Luís 1 625*
Alfonso, Rodrigo *see* RODRIGO ALFONSO
Alfonso of Castile 16 440
Alfonso the Chaste, King of Asturias *see* ALFONSO II, King of Asturias
Alfonso the Great, King of Asturias *see* ALFONSO III, King of Asturias
Alfonso the Magnanimous *see* ALFONSO I, King of Naples
Alfonso the Wise *see* ALFONSO X, King of Castile-León, King of Germany
Alfonzo, Carlos 18 835
Alford 10 316
Alford, A. & A., Co. 14 590
Alford, Arba 14 590
Alford, John Hume Egerton, Viscount *see* EGERTON, JOHN HUME, Viscount Alford
Alfraganus *see* AHMAN IBN MUHAMMAD AL-FARAGHANI
Alfred, Duke of Saxe-Coburg-Gotha (*reg* 1893-1900) 6 563
Alfred, King of Wessex *see* ALFRED THE GREAT, King of Wessex
Alfred Jewel 2 80; 10 194, 322, 346; 17 IV1; 33 89
Alfred the Great, King of Wessex (*reg* 871-99) 2 80, 82; 21 562; 23 684; 29 852; 33 89–90*
  architecture 2 64; 33 224
  coins 7 534
  writings 33 232
Alfterer Donnerstagsgesellschaft 10 825
Algardi, Alessandro 1 625–31*; 2 163; 4 277; 9 92; 16 699; 26 773, 842
  assistants 2 92; 11 17
  attributions 11 740; 20 214
  collaboration 3 835; 13 655, 814; 19 768; 26 823
  furniture 16 727; 26 780
  groups and movements 3 266
  medals 21 805
  patrons and collectors
    Aragón, Pascual de, Archbishop of Toledo 31 89
    Bird, Francis 4 79
    Coke, Thomas, 1st Earl of Leicester of the 1st creation (1697-1759) 7 540
    Francesco I, 8th Duke of Modena and Reggio (*reg* 1629-58) 10 526
    Franzone, Agostino (i) (*fl* 1678) 11 739
    Franzone, Agostino (ii) (*d* 1705) 11 739
    Franzone, Giacomo, Cardinal 11 739
    Innocent X, Pope (*reg* 1644-55) 23 898, 899
    Jesuit Order 17 509
    Ludovisi, Ludovico, Cardinal 19 779
    Pamphili (family) 23 898; 29 830
Algardi, Alessandro
  patrons and collectors—cont.
    Pamphili, Camillo, Prince 23 899
    Sacchetti (family) 27 486
  pupils 4 666; 13 814, 825; 16 855; 25 851
  reproductive prints by others 25 77
  sculpture 16 698
    altarpieces 1 712; 18 735; 29 251
    altars 3 198
    architectural 26 834
    busts 1 *630*; 21 804; 26 *773*
    relief 1 *629*, *711*
    religious 1 *626*; 2 92; 7 356; 23 472
    restorations 25 456
    statuettes 29 570
    tombs 1 *627*; 26 810; 27 831; 31 128
  teachers 5 851
Algarotti, Bonomo 1 633
Algarotti, Francesco 1 632–3*; 12 475; 32 196; 33 115
  collaboration 30 520
  dealing 14 314; 23 175; 24 706; 25 2; 30 857, 859; 33 714
  personal collection 18 626; 30 520; 32 615
  works 1 124; 19 354, 534; 31 296
    illustrated 24 705
Algaze, Mario 18 835
Algemisí, S Jaime Apostol 11 490; 26 300
Algeria 1 *214*, 376, 633–6*; 16 *103*
  adobe 1 305
  architectural decorations 1 317; 16 190
  architecture 1 305, 634
    Early Christian (*c.* AD 250-843) 30 727
    Fatimid 16 170
    Hammadid 16 170
    Islamic 16 170–71*, 187*, 190, 217–19*
    Marinid 16 217
    megalithic 21 43
    Ottoman 16 229
    vernacular 32 309–11*
    Wattasid 16 217
    Zayyanid 16 217
    Zirid 16 170
  calligraphy 1 *636*
  carpets 16 486
  collections 1 636; 16 448
  copper 16 394
  coral 7 834
  curtains 16 448
  domes 16 190
  dress 16 458
  earthenwares 16 427
  education (art) 1 635
  embroidery 16 448
  fortifications 1 311
  hats 16 459
  headdresses 16 448, 459
  headscarves 16 459
  houses 16 218–19
  jewellery 16 532
  kerchiefs 16 448
  mosaics 27 *63*
  mosques 16 190, 217–18
  muqarnas (architecture) 16 170, 190
  museums 1 636
  painting 1 634–6, *635*
  plaster 1 305
  pottery 16 404, 427
  prints 1 *636*
  purple 16 448
  red lead 16 393
  robes 16 459
  rock art 1 *220*, *372*, *373*, *376*, 634
  sculpture 1 634–6
  stone 1 305
  stucco 16 190
  synagogues 17 551
Algeria—cont.
  tents 30 473
  textiles 1 636; 16 448*
  theatres 14 564
  towns 28 757
  trade
    ribbons 16 448
  turbans 16 459
  woodwork 16 494
  see also NORTH AFRICA; NUMIDIA
Algeyer, Valentin 13 315
Alghisi, Galasso 1 636–7*; 10 524
  reproductive prints by others 30 803
  works 19 688
  writings 21 579
Algiardi collection 3 321
Algiers
  Bab ʿAzzun 16 262
  Bardo Museum of Ethnography and Prehistory 1 636
  Beylerbey Palace 16 229
  congregational mosque 16 190, 493
  embroidery 1 636
  Fort de l'Etoile 21 585
  Fort d'Eluj Ali 21 585
  fortifications 21 585
  Fort l'Empereur 21 585
  guns 16 509
  Jamiʿ al-Jadid *see* mosque of the Fishermen
  kasba 1 634
  Main Post Office 1 634
  markets 16 262
  medina 1 634
  minbars 21 629
  mosque of the Fishermen 16 229
  Musée National des Antiquités Algériennes et d'Art Musulman 1 636; 16 558
  Museum of Fine Arts 1 636
  Museum of Popular Arts and Traditions 1 636
  New Mosque *see* mosque of the Fishermen
  sculpture 27 31
  souk 1 634
  urban planning 16 260, 261, 262
Algon (Delaware) 22 552, 627
Algon (New England) 22 552
Algon (North Carolina) 22 552
Algon (Virginia) 22 552
Algonquin 22 627, 628, 650, 663, 670
Algonquin Legend Painters 22 597
Algrem, Bertil 32 534
Alguacil Blázquez, Casiano 1 637*
Alhadeff, Maurice 33 596
Alhambra *see under* GRANADA (SPAIN)
Alhazen *see* IBN AL-HAYTHAM
Alhilali, Neda 11 54
Alhuseyni, Shams Anwari 15 899
ʿAli (*fl* 1242-65) 1 97–8*
  works 1 *98*
ʿAli (*fl* 1435) 2 892
Ali (*fl* 17th cent.) 2 899
ʿAli (*fl* 1800-20) 1 637*; 16 515
  works 16 528
ʿAli (Bahrain) 2 249; 3 69
Ali, Pasha of Buda 15 16
ʿAli, Abbas 23 801
Ali, Ahmet *see* AHMED, ALI
ʿAli, Karima 9 767
  works 9 *767*
Alì, Luciano 30 176
al-ʿAli, Mahmoud (*b* 1942) 16 1
ʿAli, Maqsood 23 800
ʿAli, Mohammad (*b* 1951) 23 801
ʿAli, Naheed Raza 23 800
ʿAli, Shakir 1 637–8*; 23 800
  patrons and collectors 23 804
  pupils 1 506
  works 23 799
Ali, Wijdan 1 638*; 17 655
Ali Acemi 1 638*
ʿAli ʿAdil Shah I, Ruler (*reg* 1557-79) (ʿAdil Shahi)
  architecture 4 51; 15 381, 382; 25 211
  paintings 15 638
  walls 4 51
ʿAli ʿAdil Shah II, Ruler (*reg* 1656-72) (ʿAdil Shahi) 15 640
ʿAli Akbar (*fl* 1613/14) 27 859
ʿAli Akbar (*fl* 1846) 16 426
  works 16 *426*
Aliamet, François-Germain 24 820
Aliamet, Jacques 12 515; 14 85; 19 11, 641
ʿAli Asghar 16 337; 26 433
ʿAli Ashraf 1 638*
  pupils 16 81; 22 260, 262
  works 16 534
ʿAli Barid, Ruler (*reg* 1543-79) (Barid Shahi) 3 238
Alibek Guseynzade 2 896
Alibert, J. P. 16 860
ʿAli Bey 20 914
Alibrandi, Girolamo 28 656
alicatados 30 882
Alice, University of Fort Hare De Beer's Centenary Art Gallery 29 122
Alicea, José 25 702
Alice Springs 1 *37*, 66; 2 *736*
ʿAli Dada, Nayyar 18 647
ʿAli Dawlat, Ruler of Maraş (*reg* 1479-1515) 30 478
ʿAli de Gomara 4 784; 28 511
Alí de Lerma 7 492; 18 681
Alidosi, Cardinal 27 737
Alief, George 17 654
Alien Comic 24 409
Aliense *see* VASSILACCHI, ANTONIO
Alifanti, Mircea 26 710
Alif Khan Bhukai 8 848
Aligarh 1 639*; 15 *261*
Aligernus, Abbot of Montecassino 22 9
Alighieri, Dante 1 639–40*, 654; 9 *96*; 14 868; 16 780; 32 343
  commentaries 12 244
  works 2 518; 12 681; 15 82
    illustrated 1 *640*; 9 48; 10 819; 20 658; 23 743; 24 639
    on hell 15 82
    on manuscripts 13 137
    translated 2 514; 24 639; 27 185
Alighieri, Jacopo di Dante 1 654
Alighiero e Boetti *see* BOETTI, ALIGHIERO
alignments 25 505*
Aligny, Théodore Caruelle d' 1 641–2*
  patrons and collectors 23 522
  pupils 6 519; 26 38
  works 1 *641*
Ali Hakem, A. M. 21 160
Ali Hassan Algabir 25 777
Ali Haydar Bey 27 683
ʿAli ibn Abu Tahib, Caliph (*reg* 656-61) (Orthodox Caliphs) 16 278
ʿAli ibn Ahmad al-Maqrizi 16 143
ʿAli ibn Ahmad al-Warraq 16 281; 33 686
ʿAli ibn Ahmad ibn ʿAli al-Husayni 1 98
ʿAli ibn al-Dimishqi 10 430; 16 202
ʿAli ibn al-Hasan ibn Hibatallah 16 309
ʿAli ibn al-Nahi 16 491
ʿAli ibn Amir Beg Shirvani 16 347
ʿAli ibn Hasan al-Sultani 16 320
  works 16 *286*
ʿAli ibn Husayn ibn Muhammad 16 382
ʿAli ibn Ilyas al-Tabrizi al-Bavarji 16 876
Aʿli ibn Isa 16 398
ʿAli ibn Karmakh 12 512
ʿAli ibn Kasirat al-Mawsili 16 382

ʿAli ibn Makki **16** 496
ʿAli ibn Muhammad ʿAli Shahab al-Ghuri **16** 390
ʿAli ibn Muhammad al-Nisibini **16** 364
ʿAlī ibn Muḥammad ibn Abī Tāhir *see* ʿALI (*fl* 1242-65)
ʿAli ibn Salama **16** 491
ʿAli ibn Shadhan al-Razi **16** 290
ʿAli ibn Tashufin **31** 66
ʿAli ibn ʿUthman **16** 497
ʿAli ibn Yusuf, Ruler (*reg* 1106-43) (Almoravid) **1** 683; **16** 436
ʿAli Ibrahim **16** 553
Alikhanov, Racyl (Alixanovich) **27** 423
Alikianos, Hagios Ioannis Ermitis **8** 155
Aliki Sanctuary **30** 645
Ali Kosh **15** 903, 913, 918
ʿAli Mardan Khan **8** 675; **15** 366; **24** 541
Alimbekova, M.
works **18** *569*
Alimbrot, Louis *see* LODEWIJK VAN HALLYNCKBROOT
ʿAli Mirza, Sultan **16** 328
Alimov, Mirzorahmat **30** 253
Alimpy **1** 642*; **18** 37; **31** 554
ʿAli Muhammad Isfahani **1** 642–3*; **16** 394, 426
ʿAli Naqi **16** 232; **28** 566
Alinari (family) **16** 777
Alinari, Arturo Mélida y *see* MÉLIDA Y ALINARI, ARTURO
Alinari, Enrique Mélida y *see* MÉLIDA Y ALINARI, ENRIQUE
Alinari, Fratelli, Editori Fotografichi **1** 643*; **11** 190; **24** 667
Alinari, Giuseppe **1** 643*; **2** 365; **16** 678; **26** 232, 233
Alinari, José Ramón Mélida y *see* MÉLIDA Y ALINARI, JOSÉ RAMÓN
Alinari, Leopoldo **1** 643*; **2** 365; **16** 678; **26** 232, 233
Alinari, Romualdo **1** 643*; **2** 365; **16** 678; **26** 232, 233
Alinari, Vittorio **1** 643
Alinari photograph collection *see under* FLORENCE → museums → Museo della Fotografia Fratelli Alinari
Alinda **5** 742
stoa **2** 297; **13** 406
Alio (ii), Johann Paul *see* ALLIO (ii), PAOLO
Aliotto degli Embriachi, Baldassare di Simone d' *see* EMBRIACHI, BALDASSARE DI SIMONE D'ALIOTTO DEGLI
Ali Pasha Tepelenë **1** 545; **5** 313; **15** 890
Alipheira **21** 45
Alípio Barrio, Artur **4** 720
Aliprandi, Antonio **31** 816
Aliprandi, Gerolamo **6** 355
ʿAli Qapu Palace *see under* ISFAHAN
Ali Quli Aga **16** 265
ʿAliquli Jabbadar **1** 643*; **16** 339, 340, 533
ʿAliquli Khuvayyi **16** 342
Alirajpur Shiva Temple **15** 323
ʿAli Raza **15** 608
works **15** *608*
Alisal, José María Casado del *see* CASADO DEL ALISAL, JOSÉ MARÍA
Alişar Hüyük **1** 644*, *821*; **31** 456
architecture **1** 826
pins **1** 834
pottery **1** 824, 838
seals **1** 856
Alise-Sainte-Reine *see* ALESIA
ʿAlishah **16** 193; **30** 222
ʿAlishir Navaʾi **1** 644–5*; **30** 917
architecture **14** 430; **16** 196, 197, 198; **20** 548
calligraphy **29** 919
manuscripts **16** 286, 326
Alisjahbana, Takdir **15** 808
Alison, Archibald **1** 180; **2** 358; **24** 742; **31** 300
Alison, Richard **12** 598
Ali Usküdari **16** 350
ʿAlivardi Khan Mahabat Jang Ghazi, Nawab of Bengal (*reg* 1740-56) **15** 379, 592, 634, 711
Ali Vasfi **21** 50
Alix, Jean **6** 436
Alix, Pierre-Michel **1** 645*; **12** 153; **27** 484
Alix, Yves **1** 645–6*
Alixandre, Guillaume **16** 854
Alix de Vienne **4** 608
Aliyev, Fikrat Rza-ogly **31** 459
Aliyev, K. **2** 902
Aliyev, Nagi **2** 899
Aliyev, Sarkhan **2** 899
alizarin **9** 491
historical and regional traditions
China **7** 45
Indian subcontinent **15** 667–8
uses
dyes **7** 45; **9** 493; **15** 667–8; **30** 558, 559, 560
glazes **12** 623
pigments **18** 655, 656; **23** 786; **24** 796
Alkamenes **1** 646*; **13** 423, 450, 453, 596
attributions **23** 432; **25** 178
works **2** 682, 686; **13** 453–4
Alkborough (Humberside)
Julian's Bower **18** 585
St John the Baptist **18** 584
Alkema, Wobbe (Hendrik) **1** 646–7*; **22** 854
Alken (family) **2** 106
Alken, George **1** 647
Alken, Henry (Thomas) (1785-1851) **1** 647*
Alken, Henry, jr (1810-94) *see* ALKEN, SAMUEL HENRY (GORDON)
Alken, Samuel (1756-1815) **1** 647*; **18** 618
Alken, Samuel (1784-*c.* 1825) **1** 647
Alken, Samuel Henry (Gordon) (1810-94) **1** 647
Alken, Sefferien (1717-82) **1** 647; **11** 429, 431
Alken, Sefferien (1821-73) **1** 647
Alken, Sefferien John **1** 647
Alkibiades **1** 450; **13** 568
Alkım, Bahadır **1** 894
Alkmaar
Castle **22** 822
choir-stalls **22** 856
Raadhuis **10** 660
St Laurenskerk **17** 699; **22** 836, 837
tiles **22** 881
Alkmaar, Master of **20** 615*; **22** 836
works **11** 440; **31** 703, *703*
Alkmaionid (family) **13** 373
Alksnis, Ādams **12** 825; **18** 850
Alksnis, Jānis
alkyd paint *see under* PAINTS → types
alkyds **6** 336; **23** 793; **32** 2
All **26** 642
Allaberdy, Khaky **31** 459
Alladin, M. P. **31** 335
Alladio, Gian Giacomo de *see* ALBA, MACRINO D'
Allahabad **1** 647–8*; **15** *261*, *285*, *360*
architecture **15** 409
fort **15** 362; **17** 857
inscription **15** 475
Khusrau Bagh **15** 364
Allahabad—cont.
law courts **18** 890
Museum **1** 648; **15** 181
tomb of Shahi Begum **15** 364
Allah Quli Khan **16** 237, 238
Allahvardi Khan **12** 82; **16** 230; **20** 548; **27** 514
Allah Yar **16** 236
Allal, Muhammad ibn **22** 129
Allan, Bryce J. **19** 733
Allan, Charles **16** 889
Allan, Coline **28** 261
Allan, David **1** 648–9*; **28** 274
collaboration **28** 236
pupils **5** 884
teachers **11** 338; **14** 109; **28** 274
works **7** 785; **28** 235
Allan, George William **17** 771
Allan, Hugh **28** 258
Allan, Maxwell **28** 244
Allan, William **1** 649–50*; **9** 725; **28** 274
groups and movements **23** 504
patrons and collectors **27** 358
pupils **14** 208; **18** 856; **23** 106
teachers **22** 531
works **28** 238
Alland, Alexander **2** 138
Allander Pottery **28** 258
all'antica **1** 650*; **2** 165–6*
alla porcellana ware *see under* POTTERY → wares
alla prima painting *see under* PAINTING → techniques
Allar, André **28** 349
Allard (family) **2** 696
Allard, Jean **12** 135
Allard, Petrus **22** 895
Allard, Roger (-Charles-Félix) **1** 650*
groups and movements **1** 21; **25** 747
illustrated works **22** 92
Allardt, Hugo **25** 10
Allart du Hameel *see* ALART DU HAMEEL
Allauad (family) **19** 397
Allauad, François **19** 397
Allaume, Jacques **29** 917, 918
Allcard, John **24** 295
Alleaume **26** 598
Allebé, August **1** 650–51*; **22** 850, 908
pupils **19** 31
Arntzenius, Floris **2** 487
Derkinderen, Antoon (Johannes) **8** 778
Haverman, Hendrik Johannes **14** 245
Looy, Jacobus van **19** 654
Marius, G(erharda) H(ermina) **20** 437
Nibbrig, F(erdinand) Hart **23** 78
Tholen, Willem Bastiaan **30** 735
Verkade, Jan **32** 258
Veth, Jan Pieter **32** 392
Witsen, Willem (Arnold) **33** 266
works **1** *651*; **22** 848
allées **12** 61
allegorical drawings *see under* DRAWINGS → types
allegorical paintings *see under* PAINTINGS → types
allegorical sculpture *see under* SCULPTURE → types
allegories **1** 651–61*, *653*, *654*; **10** 174; **12** 287; **15** 89, 94–6; **22** 412, 414, 686; **23** 769
Belgium **30** *316*, II1
Byzantine **9** 519–20*
Christianity **1** 653; **25** 650
Early Christian (*c.* AD 250-843) **9** 519–20*
England **30** XII
France **30** II2
Greece, ancient **1** 651–2; **22** 411
Italy **1** 654–7*, 659; **30** *319*
Rome, ancient **1** 652, *652*
allegories—cont.
see also ICONOGRAPHY; ICONOLOGY; SYMBOLISM (CRITICAL TERM)
allegories of art **1** 662–4*, *663*; **21** *760*
Allegra **16** 780
Allegrain, Christophe-Gabriel **1** 664, 665*; **9** *400*; **11** 561
pupils **21** 544; **28** 568
Allegrain, Etienne **1** 664–5*
patrons and collectors **32** 372
works **8** 24; **12** *122*
Allegrain, Gabriel (1679-1748) **1** 664; **9** 153
Allegrain, Gabriel (1733-*d* after 1779) **1** 664
Allegrain, Jean-Baptiste **1** 664
Allegret, Jacques **2** 699
Allegri, Antonio *see* CORREGGIO
Allegri, Lorenzo **7** 885
Allegri, Mariotto **22** 800
Allegrini, Flaminio **1** 665
Allegrini, Francesco **1** 665–6*
Allélit *see* HÉBERT (i), HÉLÉNA
Allemagne, Henri d' **16** 555
Alleman *see* DEUTSCH
Allemand, Antoine d' **17** 545
Allemand, Siegmund l' **7** 368
Allen (family) **24** 599; **33** 91
Allen, Arthur **4** 786; **31** 589
Allen, Charles J. **19** 506
Allen, Edward John Milner **28** 273
Allen, Ellen Gordon **17** 382
Allen, Ethan **31** 632
Allen, James **33** 58
Allen, John **25** 317, 318
Allen, Louis **1** 66; **21** 733
Allen, Olive *see* BILLER, OLIVE ALLEN
Allen, Ralph **10** 233; **33** 340
Allen, Robert **19** 734
Allen, Thomas **33** 22
Allen, W. R. (Jim) **23** 63
Allende (family) **28** 884
Allen Jack and Cottier **2** 743; **30** 161
Allenstein *see* OLSZTYN
Allentown *Madonna* **5** 129
Allert, Henrik **11** 106
Allerton, Isaac **23** 25
Allerton Hall (Lancs) **12** 597
Alley, P. B. **32** 904
Allgemeine Bauzeitung mit Abbildungen **11** 319; **13** 204; **24** 438
Allgemeine deutsche Bibliothek **23** 108
Allgemeine Elektrizitäts-Gesellschaft *see* AEG
Allgemeines Künstler-Lexikon **20** 483
Allgemeines Lexikon der bildenden Künstler von der Antike bis zur Gegenwart *see* THIEME-BECKER
Allgemeines Magazin für die bürgliche Baukunst **24** 443
Alliance Photo **9** 71
Alliance Provinciale des Industries d'Art *see* ECOLE DE NANCY
Allianz **1** 666*; **30** 135, 139
members **4** 216; **12** 771; **13** 267
Allianz Vereinigung Moderner Schweizer Künstler **19** 541
Allied Architects **32** 892
Allied Architects Association **19** 700
Allied Artists' Association (A.A.A.) **1** 666*; **5** 516; **12** 652; **27** 359
members **2** 691; **12** 644; **13** 9; **27** 269
Alligator group pottery *see under* POTTERY → wares
All India Fine Arts and Crafts Society (AIFACS) **8** 677; **15** 657
All-India Handicrafts Board **15** 173
Allingham, Helen **1** 666–7*; **4** 87; **10** 254
Allingham, William **8** 828; **14** 849
Allington (Kent) **8** 138
Allio (ii) (family) **12** 404; **32** 435
Allio (iv) (family) **32** 435
Allio (i), Andrea (*fl* 1551-8) **1** 667
Allio (iv), Andrea, III (*fl* 1641) **1** 669; **25** 443
Allio (iv), Andrea, V (*fl* 1671-78) **1** 669
Allio (iv), Benedikt, II **1** 669
Allio (i), Domenico, I **1** 667*
works **2** 779, 780; **13** 329
Allio (ii), Donato-Felice **1** 667–8*
assistants **13** 661
pupils **12** 356; **13** 661
works **2** 783; **11** 134; **18** 140; **32** 458
Allio (iv), Francesco **1** 669
Allio (i), Gianmaria **1** 667
Allio (iv), Giovanni Battista, I, de Lowenthal (1644-1716) **1** 669
Allio (iv), Giovanni Battista, II (*fl* 1685-94) **1** 669
Allio (ii), Giovanni Battista, III (1690-1753) **1** 667, 668*
Allio (i), Martino (*fl* 1520) **1** 667
Allio (iv), Martino, II, de Lowenthal (1654-1701) **1** 669
Allio (iii), Matteo di Guaro Allio **1** 668, 669
Allio (ii), Paolo, I **1** 667–8*; **18** 447; **29** 838
collaboration **5** 773
pupils **1** 668
Allio (iv), Pietro **1** 669
Allio (ii), Sebastiano Domenico **1** 667, 668
Allio (iii), Tommaso **1** 668, 669
Alliprandi, Giovanni Battista **1** 669–70*; **6** 526
collaboration **17** 776
patrons and collectors **8** 378; **29** 422
works **8** 426; **18** 505, *505*; **25** 427
Alliprandi, Lorenzo **1** 669
Alliston, James **9** 296
Allita Amaya pottery *see under* POTTERY → wares
Allnet, Jean-Baptiste **11** 627
Alloa **28** 259
St John's Episcopal Church **28** 243
Allom, Thomas **2** 333; **4** 526; **19** 505; **25** 635; **33** 9
Allongé, Auguste **6** 471
Allonne Church
buttresses **5** *318*
Allori, Alessandro (di Cristofano di Lorenzo del Bronzino) **1** 670–71*; **16** 664
assistants **3** 101; **5** 317
collaboration **4** 859; **5** 317; **11** 194
drawings **25** 59, 558
cartoons **11** 194; **16** 757
paintings **1** *670*; **30** 358
altarpieces **8** 274; **11** 213
frescoes **11** 893; **27** 849
patrons and collectors **12** 897; **23** 87; **25** 77, 690; **27** 648
pupils **1** 671; **7** 311
tapestries **30** 319
teachers **4** 859
Allori, Cristofano **1** 670, 671–3*
patrons and collectors **21** 28
pupils **8** 497; **20** 908; **22** 190
teachers **7** 311
works **1** *672*, *673*; **11** 214; **16** 673; **23** 380
Allot, H. N.
works **25** *403*
allotment gardens *see under* GARDENS → types
Allotria **5** 290
Allouard, Henri-Emile **8** 41
all-over painting *see under* PAINTING → types

Alloway, Lawrence 15 166; 17 694; 25 231; 28 804, 839
alloys 4 849; 21 319*
historical and regional development
Buddhism 22 *787*
China 6 829–30*
Egypt, ancient 30 *396*
Indian subcontinent 15 706
Japan 17 318
Nepal 22 *787*
technical examination 30 *396*, 397, 408
types
baitong 5 612; 10 341; 11 *119*; 21 319
bell metal *see* speculum metal
bidri 4 687; 15 174; 21 330
brass *see* BRASS
Britannia metal 10 343; 24 578, 579; 31 652
bronze *see* BRONZE
Brunei brass 5 11
Corinthian bronze 21 329–30
Dutch metal 24 61
French pewter *see* hard metal
German silver 21 319
gilding metal 4 680
guanin 5 747
gunmetal 4 680, 681
hakudō 17 318
hard metal 24 578
hesmen kem 21 329
high-tin 16 363
irogane 21 330
latten plate 4 692
Monel metal 31 654
Muntz metal 4 680
paktong *see baitong*
pewter *see* PEWTER
pinchbeck *see* PINCHBECK
Princes metal 10 341
Rupert's metal 10 341
sahari see sawari
sawari 17 318
Schlagmetall 12 621, 627
shakudō 17 318; 21 330
shibuichi 17 318
speculum metal 21 319
Sterling silver 21 319
tumbaga 7 507; 13 291; 21 253, 332; 28 651; 29 211, *212*; 32 238
white metal *see* Britannia metal
yellow metal *see* Muntz metal
uses
gilding 12 621, 627
All-Russian Central Executive Committee 23 630
All Saints' Convent (Herts) 9 739
Allsopp, Disa 2 152
Allsteel Corporation 28 799
Allston, Washington 1 673–5*; 4 477
groups and movements 26 740
patrons and collectors 12 645
pupils 13 621; 22 149
teachers 18 66; 33 93
works 1 *674*; 31 601, *601*
Allston Club 15 20
All-Union Alliance of Association of Proletarian Architects *see* VOPRA
All-Union Committee for Artistic Affairs 27 581
All-Union Council for Craft Cooperatives *see* VESKOPROMSOVET
Allward, Walter 5 570
Allwood, Thomas 14 146
Alm, Johan 11 95
Alma, Petrus 1 675*; 21 775; 22 854
Alma Ata *see* ALMATY
Almada, Rodrigo Fernandes d' *see* FERNANDES D'ALMADA, RODRIGO
Almada e Melo, João de 1 675*; 25 293
Almada e Mendonça, Francisco de 1 675*
Almada Negreiros(, José Sobral de) 1 676*; 30 882
works 22 332; 25 299, *299*
Almadén de la Plata 27 13
Almagro, Corral de las Comedias 30 663
Almagro, Diego de 6 589; 9 708; 25 828
Almagro, Martin 19 704
Almain, Steven *see* HASCHENPERG, STEFAN VON
Almakerék *see* MĂLÎNCRAV
Al'manakh 24 428
Almanius 26 689
Almansa, Martin Enríquez de, Viceroy of Peru 3 470
Almaraz, Hugo 4 260; 18 778
Almășanu, Virgil 1 676*
Alma-Tadema, Anna 1 678
Alma-Tadema, Laura (Theresa) 1 677, 678*; 11 435
Alma-Tadema, Lawrence 1 676–8*; 14 588; 23 295
collaboration 30 680
dealers 12 30
groups and movements 17 440; 23 504
patrons and collectors 14 132; 25 639; 30 359
personal collection 22 373
pupils 1 678
reproductive prints by others 4 126; 12 30; 19 734
studio 29 856
teachers 32 853
works 1 *677*; 10 254, 480; 11 *433*, 435, 436; 18 100; 22 416, 848
Almaty 1 678*; 6 *182*; 17 *865*, 866
Archaeology Museum of the Kazakh Academy of Sciences 6 284
architecture 17 866
Central Museum of Kazakhstan 6 284
fort 17 866
Kasteyev Museum of the Art of Kazakhstan 1 678; 6 284
Kazakh Academy 17 867
Kazakh Theatre of Drama 17 867
Medeo sports centre 17 867
Palace of Pioneers 17 867
T. G. Shevchenko Art Gallery *see* Kasteyev Museum of the Art of Kazakhstan
Almeida, Belmiro (Barbosa) de 1 678–9*; 4 717
Almeida, Brás de 8 11
Almeida, Feliciano de 1 679*
Almeida, Francisco d' 19 468
Almeida, Isabella d' 3 280
Almeida, João 4 715
Almeida, João Anastacio Botelho de *see* BOTELHO DE ALMEIDA, JOÃO ANASTACIO
Almeida, Jorge de, Bishop of Coimbra 1 679*; 7 531; 23 414
Almeida, José Baptista de 1 680
Almeida, José de 1 679–80*
patrons and collectors 4 635
pupils 19 893
works 12 762; 18 578; 19 459
Almeida, José Simões de *see* SIMÕES DE ALMEIDA, JOSÉ
Almeida, Leopoldo de 25 302
Almeida, Luis José de 25 314
Almeida, Sebastião Inácio de 1 680*; 19 467; 25 310; 26 52; 30 881
Almeida, Tomás de, Patriarch of Lisbon 1 680*
Almeida, Valentim de 1 680–81*; 30 881
Almeida Crespo, Cirilo 19 659
Almeida e Mello e Castro, João de 32 425
Almeida e Silva, João Charters de *see* CHARTERS DE ALMEIDA E SILVA, JOÃO
Almeida Furtado, Tadeu d' 28 735
Almeida Júnior, José Ferraz de 1 681*; 4 717, 726
Almeida Saldanha, Eduardo de 22 245
Almeida Sobrinho, Simões 8 74
Almeloveen, Jan van 1 681*
Almenar, Maria de *see* MARIA DE ALMENAR
Almenas, Conde de las 29 308
Almeni (family) 11 180
Almeni, Sforza 8 511; 32 14
Almería
Alcazaba 16 189
Cathedral 13 211
citadel 16 215
embroidery 10 181
factories 16 436
metalwork 16 368
pottery 29 323
stelae 29 618
Sumadihiyya 12 79
textiles 29 349
Almerico, Paolo, Cardinal 32 411
Almerie 31 735
Almeyda, Giuseppe Damiani *see* DAMIANI ALMEYDA, GIUSEPPE
Almgren, Andreas 30 112
Almgren, K. A. 30 115
Almi, Bartolommeo di Francesco 22 805
Almloveen, Jan van 27 518
Almodóvar del Rio Castle 6 *58*
Almohad 1 681–2*; 16 114
architecture 20 470; 28 510, 511
see also:
ABU HAFS ʿUMAR AL-MURTADA, Ruler
ABU YAʿQUB YUSUF, Ruler
ABU YUSUF YAʿQUB AL-MANSUR, Ruler
Almonacid, Sebastián de *see* SEBASTIÁN DE ALMONACID
Almonte, Rosamund War Memorial 5 570
Almoravid 1 682–3*; 16 114
see also:
ʿALI IBN YUSUF, Ruler
YUSUF IBN TASHUFIN, Ruler
Almoster, S Maria 13 125
Almourol 18 153
Almqvist, Osvald 1 683–4*; 3 784; 29 686; 30 75
alms-dishes 24 580
Almshouse of the Seven Electors, Master of the *see* AMSTERDAM DEATH OF THE VIRGIN, MASTER OF THE
almshouses 10 230; 19 509
almuces 32 389*
Almy, Mary 20 282
Alne (N. Yorks), St Mary 26 614
Alnö 11 252; 30 83
Alnwick (Northumb.)
Castle 3 *209*, 209; 6 53, 55; 9 144; 21 549
carpets 11 575
furniture 12 *831*, 832
gems 12 266
paintings 10 367; 23 467; 24 390; 29 425
landscape 3 207; 7 394
portraits 3 208; 9 484; 24 390; 31 41; 32 575
religious 12 706; 25 899
vedute 5 598
St Michael 9 269
Alocco, Marcel 30 6
Alodia 23 287
aloe 12 623; 15 549
Alogism 18 22
Aloi, Master 5 911; 13 106
Aloi, Peter, II 3 599
Alois (-Joseph) I, Prince of Liechtenstein: (*reg* 1781-1805) 19 338*
Alois (-Joseph) II, Prince of Liechtenstein (*reg* 1836-58) 1 687; 2 814; 19 338–9*
Aloja, Vincenzo 14 17
Alomar, Cristian Cirici *see* CIRICI ALOMAR, CRISTIAN
Alono de Cartagena, Bishop of Burgos 13 107
Alons, Cor 22 868, 876
Alonso, Andrés 29 334
Alonso, Luis 25 702
Alonso, Raúl 1 684*; 2 400
Alonso de Burgos, Bishop of Palencia 7 614
Alonso de Cartagena, Archbishop of Burgos 1 684*; 5 201; 14 578
architecture 5 203; 7 614
Alonso de Sedano 1 684*
Alonso de Vozmediano 28 709
Alonso Pimental, María Josefa de la Soledad *see* OSUNA, 9th Duquesa de
Alonso Rochi, Alejandro 23 81
Alor 15 *751*, 789, 814, 816
Alós, Angelina 29 329
Alós, Juan Bautista 29 329
Alotia *see* ALWA
Aloul, Jean 5 666
Aloy, Master 29 289
alpaca hair *see under* HAIR → types
alpanasi 15 242*
alpanāsikā see NĀSIKĀ
Alpár, Ignác 14 61, 889; 25 829; 31 796
Alp Arslan, Sultan (*reg* 1063-72) (Saljuq) 16 546
Alpaslan, Ali 23 391; 31 454
Alpatov, Mikhail (Vladimirovich) 1 684–5*; 27 441, 444
Alpera 29 365
Alpers, Svetlana 2 538; 15 96; 31 673
Al'pert, Maks (Vladimirovich) 1 685*; 28 567; 33 631
Alpha 19 727
alphabetic script *see under* SCRIPTS → types
alphabets 28 303
Ancient Near East 1 850, 855*, 893
Arabic 16 273, *274*, 278
Armenia (Europe) 2 430
Canaanite 5 556
Coptic 10 1
Egypt, ancient 10 1, 4
Etruscan 10 591
Germany 10 592
Greece, ancient 10 1, 591; 13 490; 24 641
Iberia (peninsula) 12 889
Islamic 16 273, *274*, 278
Italy 10 591
Korea 18 247; 28 381
Phoenician 1 *854*, 855, *857*; 5 331; 24 641; 30 187
Scandinavia 10 592
Spain 12 889
Syria-Palestine 30 187
United States of America 7 292
see also SCRIPTS
Alphand, (Jean-Charles-) Adolphe 1 685–6*; 24 127, 174
assistants 8 572
collaboration 14 238; 24 126
works 11 523, *524*
Alphand, Jean-Claude 24 179
Alphen, Oscar 22 853
Alphen, Smeth van 14 146
Alphen aan de Rijn Church 22 821
Alphington (Devon), St Michael 11 252
Alphonse, Maître 19 *340*
Alphonso Psalter *see under* PSALTERS → individual manuscripts
Alpi, Judith 12 918
Alpini, Prospero 10 78
Alpirsbach, Abbey Church of St Benedict 1 724; 12 364, 419; 14 569, *569*; 26 574
Alpoim, José Fernandes Pinto 4 710, 711; 23 669; 26 412
Alpuente 29 323
Alpuy, Julio 30 275
Als, Peder 1 686*; 8 734
Alschuler, Alfred S. 17 547
Alsemberg 25 725
Alsen 12 255
Al Shabu, Omar 19 310
Alshekh, Eliezer 23 16
Als Ik Kan 21 167; 22 136; 31 875
Alsina, Ramón Martí *see* MARTÍ ALSINA, RAMÓN
Alsium 6 352; 10 601
Alskog 13 190
memorial stone 32 522, *522*
sculpture 26 647
Alsloot, Denijs van 1 686–7*
collaboration 4 916; 7 414
patrons and collectors 3 613; 13 917
works 5 43
Alsop & Lyall 5 732
Alsórákos *see* RACOS
Alspach 26 633
Alstad Memorial Stone 26 409; 32 522
Alston, Charles 1 442, 443; 22 335
Alston, Richard 30 688
Alt, Jakob 1 687; 4 39
works 4 *40*
Alt, Rudolf (von) 1 687–8*; 2 796
groups and movements 28 343
patrons and collectors 19 339
works 1 *688*; 32 444
Alta Emps *see* ALTEMPS
Alta Gracia 23 *79*
pottery 23 *83*
Altai Uriankhai 21 876, 877
Altamíra (Mexico) 5 411
Altamira (Spain) 1 688–9*, *689*; 6 469; 25 *470*, 474, 476, 477, 478, 479, 483, 484, 487; 29 *258*, 422
Altamira (family) 1 690; 29 353
Altamira, Joaquín Ventura Osorio Moscoso y Guzmán, 10th Conde de 1 689–90*
Altamira, María Ignacia Alvarez de Toledo, Condesa de 1 690
Altamira, Vicente Joaquín Osorio Moscoso y Guzmán, 11th Conde de 1 689–90*
Altamirano, Alba Arturo Pacheco *see* PACHECHO ALTAMIRANO, ALBA ARTURO
Altamouras, Ioannis 1 690*; 13 352
Altamura, Francesco Saverio 16 678; 22 480
Altamura, Saverio 19 870; 28 318
Altamura Painter 13 522; 32 59
altarcloths 1 697
altar crosses *see under* CROSSES → types
Altar de Sacrificios 1 700, 706*; 13 *758*; 20 *882*; 21 247
Altare 16 740
altar frontals *see* ANTEPENDIA
Altar of Domitius Ahenobarbus 16 684; 27 23, *23*, 29
Altar of Duke Ratchis 19 549–50, *550*
Altar of Encamp 11 *479*
altarpieces 1 697, 698, 707–12*; 7 562; 9 14; 23 381; 24 6; 25 462
conservation 24 7
historical and regional traditions
Argentina *see* RETABLES

altarpieces
historical and regional traditions—cont.
Austria **2** 799
Baroque **31** *678*
Gothic **11** *806*
15th cent. **23** *707, 708*
Beguines **3** *503*
Belgium
Baroque **3** *263*
Early Netherlandish style **3** *641*; **10** *704*; **17** *675*; **21** *104*; **30** *165*
Gothic **4** *416*; **13** 110
Renaissance **7** *424*; **8** *86*
15th cent. **25** 183
Benin, Kingdom of **3** *721*
Bolivia *see* RETABLES
Brazil *see* RETABLES
Byzantine **5** 300
Catalonia *see* RETABLES
Colombia *see* RETABLES
Cuba *see* RETABLES
Czech Republic **33** *212*
Denmark **8** 730–31, 732, 735, 738; **11** *467*
Dominican Order **25** 463
Ecuador *see* RETABLES
England **1** 707; **11** 420–21
France **1** 707
Gothic **13** *109*; **20** *742, 762*
15th cent. **20** *451*
Germany **1** 710; **12** 401; **18** 714
Baroque **8** *627*
Gothic **1** *709*; **11** 450–53; **12** 383; **13** 131; **23** *254*; **29** *730*
Gothic: Early Gothic **12** 400
Gothic: Late Gothic **26** *371, 372*
Renaissance **4** *759*; **13** *721, 722*
Rococo **1** *712*
14th cent. **3** *865, 866*
15th cent. **7** *722, 724*; **20** *192*; **22** *188*; **33** *301, 630*
16th cent. **19** *106*; **20** *611*; **31** *286*; **33** *31*
17th cent. **5** *607*; **27** *725*; **32** *772*
18th cent. **28** *145*
Gothic **12** 626; **13** 127, 130–31, 170; **24** 3
Austria **11** *806*
Belgium **4** *416*; **13** 110
Catalonia **14** *858*
England **11** 420–21
France **13** *109*; **20** *742, 762*
Germany **1** *709*; **11** 450–53; **12** 383; **13** 131; **23** *254*; **29** *730*
Germany: Early Gothic **12** 400
Germany: Late Gothic **26** *371, 372*
Holy Roman Empire (before 1648) **13** 116
Italy **7** *329, 334*; **9** *342, 347*; **13** 130, 146, *146*; **20** *728*; **32** *213*
Italy: Gothic (Late) **7** II1; **19** *680, 681*
Italy: International Gothic **12** *299, 300, 301*
Late Gothic **18** 827
Netherlands, the **13** 110–11, *114*
Norway **11** 465; **13** 143, *144*
Poland **29** *727*
Slovakia **19** 281; **28** *854*
Spain **11** *481*
Sweden **13** 120; **23** *255*; **30** 83
Switzerland **11** *452*
Guatemala *see* RETABLES
Holy Roman Empire (before 1648) **13** 116
Hungary **14** *894*; **30** *206*

altarpieces
historical and regional traditions—cont.
Italy **1** 707, 708–9, 710–12; **11** 379–81; **15** 85; **24** 4, 5; **27** 495–6; **32** 213
Baroque **1** *711*; **9** *90*; **11** *681*; **13** *815*; **20** *904*; **22** *478*
Gothic **7** *329, 334*; **9** *342, 347*; **13** 130, 146, *146*; **20** *728*; **32** *213*
Gothic: International Gothic **12** *299, 300, 301*
Gothic: Late Gothic **7** II1; **19** *680, 681*
Mannerism **1** *710*; **3** *486*; **12** *673*; **31** *38*
Order of Poor Clares **25** *229*
Renaissance **2** *32, 180*; **3** *663, 917*; **4** *284*; **7** *738*; **8** *4*; **9** *99*; **11** *28, 701*; **12** *162*; **19** *181, 441, 711, 713, 785*; **20** *312, 531, 787*; **21** *904, 905*; **22** *477, 798, 799, 800*; **24** *286, 526, 761*; **26** *445, 457*; **27** *495, 860, 861*; **31** *533*; **32** *104*; **33** *634*
Renaissance: High Renaissance **3** *304, 305*
13th cent. **25** *229*
14th cent. **1** *709*; **5** *164*; **7** *337*; **12** *689*; **28** *366*
15th cent. **4** *730*; **12** *714*; **20** *739*; **29** *550*
16th cent. **2** *128*; **31** *54, 55*
Mexico *see* RETABLES
Netherlands, the **1** 710; **3** *503*; **4** *149*; **13** 110–11, *114*
Norway **11** 465; **13** 143, *144*
Order of Poor Clares **25** *229*
Peru *see* RETABLES
Poland **25** 110; **29** *727*
Portugal *see* RETABLES
Romanesque **1** *708*
Slovakia **19** 281; **28** *854*
Spain *see* RETABLES
Sweden **13** 120; **23** *255*; **30** 77, 83
Switzerland **11** *452*
Yoruba **33** 557
materials
alabaster (gypsum) **1** 518–19, *519*, 707; **6** *452*; **25** 183
battens **24** 5
bone **10** *179*
brass **3** *721*
canvas **24** 3
enamel **13** 170; **32** *213*
frames **11** 374, 379–81, 420–21; **24** 4, 5
gems **32** *213*
gold **32** *213*
gold leaf **12** 623
ivory **1** 707; **13** *174, 177*; **16** 799
lime-wood **8** *627*; **12** *401*; **19** *106*; **26** *371*; **29** *727, 730*; **33** *31*
marble **1** *711, 712*; **7** *334*; **11** *28*; **13** *815*; **20** *728*; **24** *286*
oak **11** *467*
panel paintings **1** 708
sandstone **26** *372*
sculpture **1** 711
stone **1** 707, 709, *709*
stucco **1** 707
tempera **12** 383
terracotta **1** 707; **26** *445*
wood **1** 707, 709; **23** *255*
techniques
gilding **1** *708*; **12** 625, 626; **13** *109*
inlays **10** *179*
polychromy **13** *109*
tracery **28** 133

altarpieces—cont.
types
diptychs **9** 3–5*, 14
Belgium **12** *847*
Byzantine **9** 623
Carolingian **9** 3
Crusaders **9** 4
Early Christian (*c*. AD 250-843) **5** 809; **9** 3
England **9** 4, *4*
France **9** 3, 4
Germany **9** 4; **11** *451*; **13** *177*
Gothic **9** 3, *4*; **11** *451*; **13** *177*
Italy **9** 4
Netherlands, the **9** 4; **20** *636*
Rome, ancient **18** *826*; **26** 862
Spain **9** 4
14th cent. **9** *4*
Flügelaltar **1** 709; **11** 230*; **28** 133
Flügelretabel **28** 133
heptatychs **31** 534
Kanzelaltar **1** 711
pentaptychs **24** 370*
polyptychs **1** 709; **9** 14; **25** 183–4*
Austria **23** *709*
Belgium **20** *667*
Byzantine **9** 623
England **1** *519*
Germany **12** *383*; **20** *758*; **29** *772*
Gothic **13** 130
Gothic: England **1** *519*
Gothic: Germany **12** *383*
Gothic: Italy **4** *31*; **7** *333*; **9** *345*; **11** *380, 382*; **13** *129*, 139; **20** *675*
Gothic: Slovakia **19** *281*
Italy **13** 130; **24** 5; **25** 183–4, *184*; **27** *766*
Italy: Gothic **4** *31*; **7** *333*; **9** *345*; **11** *380, 382*; **13** *129*, 139; **20** *675*
Italy: Renaissance **8** *168, 170*; **9** *100, 102*; **21** *145*; **32** *654, 656*
Italy: 14th cent. **12** *702*; **20** *760*; **24** *32*
Italy: 15th cent. **3** *697*
Netherlands, the **31** 344
Slovakia **19** *281*
Spain **25** 184
Schnitzaltar **28** 133–4*
Austria **28** 133
Germany **1** 710; **28** *133*, 133
tetraptychs **25** 183
triptychs **9** 14; **31** 343–5*
Belgium: Baroque **27** *290*
Belgium: Early Netherlandish style **3** *739*; **4** *591*; **8** *551*; **12** *845*; **20** *668*; **21** *101, 103*; **31** *343, 344*; **33** *119, 122*
Belgium: Renaissance **5** *625*; **11** *441*; **21** *353*; **23** *525*
Byzantine **9** 623
England **25** 183
France **13** *174*; **20** *731*
Germany **25** 183; **31** 344
Germany: Renaissance **5** *200*; **8** *116*
Germany: 15th cent. **7** *723*; **19** *528*
Germany: 16th cent. **12** *401*; **18** *511*; **31** *287*
Gothic: France **13** *174*
Gothic: Italy **3** *696*; **4** *32*; **7** *335*; **10** *179*; **16** *825*; **32** *228*
Italy **31** 344
Italy: Gothic **3** *696*; **4** *32*; **7** *335*; **10** *179*; **16** *825*; **32** *228*
Italy: Renaissance **5** *307*; **9** *101*; **30** *232*
Italy: 14th cent. **8** *442*; **21** *112*; **23** *323*

altarpieces
types
triptychs—cont.
Italy: 15th cent. **1** *530*; **4** *620*; **18** *698*
Italy: 16th cent. **29** *28*
Netherlands, the **10** *217*; **31** 344
Netherlands, the: Early Netherlandish style **4** *446, 447, 448*; **20** *656*
Netherlands, the: Renaissance **19** *761*
Norway **23** 224
Wandelaltar **28** 133
see also PREDELLAS; RETABLES; SHRINES (ii) (ALTARPIECES)
altars **1** 690–707*; **7** 262–3, 281
historical and regional traditions
Achaemenid **1** 690
Africa **1** 690
Ancient Near East **1** 690*
Austria **1** 698; **27** *661*
Aztec **1** 701
Belgium **1** 698
Benin, Kingdom of **3** 721, *721*
Benin Republic **3** 728
Buddhism **1** 701
China **1** 703; **5** *112*
Japan **1** 703–4
Korea **1** 704
Lamaism **1** 704–5*
Mongolia **1** 705
Tibet **1** 704–5*
Vietnam **1** 706
Byzantine **1** 694*; **9** 656
Carolingian **5** 807, *807*, 808; **7** 263–4
Central Asia, Western **6** *243*
Chimú **1** 701
China **1** 701–3*, *702*; **6** *704*
Buddhism **1** 703; **5** *112*
Confucianism **1** 703
Daoism **1** 703; **6** 786
Christianity **1** 693, 698–9*, *699*, 700*
Confucianism **1** 703, 704
Coptic **1** 694
Cuba (Caribbean) **8** 230
Daoism **1** 703; **6** 786
Early Christian (*c*. AD 250-843) **1** 693–4*, *693*; **7** 278; **9** 656
Egypt, ancient **1** 691*
Ethiopia **1** 694
Etruscan **1** 692*
France **1** 693, *693*
Germany **1** 698, 699; **12** 461
Expressionism **9** *239*
Gothic **17** *741*
Mannerism **33** *738*
Rococo **19** *364*
Romanesque **10** *113*; **26** *535*
12th cent. **26** 534
17th cent. **17** *689, 690*
Gothic **2** *481*; **11** *479*; **13** 168; **17** *741*
Greece, ancient **1** 691–2*, *692*; **13** 376, 380, 393, 406, 417; **27** 712–13
Hellenistic **24** *412*
Hinduism **1** 701, 706
Inca **1** 701
Indian subcontinent **1** 705*; **4** 793; **15** 237*, 731
Indonesia **1** 706
Italy **1** 698, *695*
Baroque **1** *699*; **5** *533*; **19** *374*; **32** *195*
Carolingian **5** *807*
Gothic **2** *481*; **13** 168
Roman **26** *890*; **27** *23*
14th cent. **1** *696*
16th cent. **32** *649*
Japan **1** 703–4*, *704*
Java **1** 706
Khmer **1** 706
Korea **1** 704*, 705
Laos **18** 777
Maya **1** 700; **28** 640

altars
historical and regional traditions—cont.
Mesoamerica, Pre-Columbian **1** *700*, 700–701*; **25** 764; **31** 505
Mexico **1** *700*
Minoan **1** 691*
Moche (culture) **1** 701
Mongolia **1** 705*
Mycenaean **1** 691*
Native North Americans **1** 701*
Nazca **1** 701
Netherlands, the **1** 699; **21** *858*
Olmec **1** 700; **23** 417
Poland **25** 114
Portugal **30** 881
Romanesque **10** *113*; **26** *535*
Romania **26** 711, 718
Rome, ancient **1** 693*, 696; **26** *787*, 787–8, *890*; **27** *23*, 23–4, 712–13
Sardinia **27** 836
shamanism **1** 704, 705
Shinto **1** 703, *704*
South America, Pre-Columbian **1** 701*
South-east Asia **1** 705–6*
Spain **11** *479*
Tibet **1** 704–5*
Toltec **1** 701
Vietnam **1** 706
Yoruba **33** 556
materials
alabaster (gypsum) **21** *858*
amber **1** 762
brick **1** 698; **4** 793
bronze **5** *533*; **6** *243*; **26** *535*
enamel **10** *113*; **13** 168
gilding **26** *535*
hardstones **12** 461
iron **3** 728
ivory **29** IX1
marble **1** 698, *702*; **27** *23*; **32** *195*
porphyry **29** IX1
silver **9** 656
silver-gilt **5** *807*
stone **1** *692, 693*, 693, 694; **6** *704*
wood **1** 693, 694, 698; **17** *741*; **18** 777
reuse **1** 696
types
antimensia **1** 694
block **1** 694, 695, 696, 698
box **1** 694, 695, 698, 699
funerary **27** *34*
Gnadenaltar **12** 822*
organ **1** 700
portable **1** 697*, 699*; **28** 638; **29** IX1
pulpit **1** 700
sarcophagus **1** 695, 698
table **1** 693, 695, 698
altar sets **7** 86, *86*, 101
Alta Vista **1** 713*; **21** *193, 372*
mines **1** 713
skull racks **31** 505
Altay **27** 436
Altdeutsch style **1** 713*
Altdorf **30** *124*
fountains **30** 136
St Martin **30** 146
University **31** 674
Altdorf, Johan Coenraad **22** 896
Altdorfer, Albrecht **1** 713, 714–20*; **3** 387; **8** 595; **10** 385; **22** 302; **26** 87
assistants **1** 720
attributions **20** 690, 691
book illustrations **12** 385
collaboration **19** 131; **28** 58; **29** 433; **33** 353
drawings **8** *514*; **9** 221
groups and movements **2** 792; **8** 513, 514; **14** 835; **18** 705; **26** 189
methods **33** 353

Altdorfer, Albrecht—cont.
paintings **2** 340; **12** 387
battle **12** *388*
history **12** 387; **18** 705; **20** 278; **22** 302
religious **1** *717*, *718*
patrons and collectors **4** 243; **9** 185, 200; **13** 902, 903; **15** 145; **33** 84, 271, 275
pilgrim badges **24** 809
prints
etchings **1** *716*; **10** 549, 550; **25** 606
woodcuts **2** 792; **12** 387; **25** 598; **33** 353
pupils **21** 484; **23** 617
stained glass **27** 256
Altdorfer, Erhard **1** 713, 720–21*
attributions **12** 366
groups and movements **8** 514
works **1** *721*; **33** 365
Altdorfer, Ulrich **1** 713
Altemps (family) **32** 612
Altemps, Giovanni Angelo, Duca **1** 596, 721–2
Altemps, Marcus Sitticus, Cardinal **1** 721*; **11** 740; **19** 631, 632; **25** 7; **26** 834
Alten, Hans van **32** 709
Altena, J(ohan) Q(uirijn) van Regteren **1** 722*
Alten-Allen, Folbert van
works **32** *435*
Altenberg (Hesse), Premonstratensian Abbey **12** 462
Altenberg (Nordrhein-Westfalen) **14** 425
Cistercian monastery **12** 365, 471
frescoes **31** *357*
St Mariä Himmelfahrt **13** 49; **29** 503
stained glass **29** 502
Altenbourg, Gerhard **1** 722*
Altenburg (Germany)
collections **12** 481
Schloss **32** 92
Staatliches Lindenau-Museum **30** 731
stonewares **12** 428, 430
Altenburg Abbey (Austria) **2** 783; **15** 139; **22** 297
Altenloh, E. & R. **3** 602
Altenloh, Robert **3** 602
Altenmarkt, St Ämilian **2** 799
Altenmarkt im Pongau, Unsere Liebe Frau **13** 90
sculpture **13** *90*
Altenstadt, St Michael **26** 634
Altenstetter, David **2** 718; **12** 445, 456
works **12** *456*, III2
Alterberger, Thomas **28** 649
alternating systems **1** 722–4*, *723*; **26** 569, 571
Alteršperger, Petr **8** 395
Altet, Joan **29** 337
Altet, Ramón **29** 337
Altfried, Bishop of Hildesheim **10** 514; **14** 531
Althan, Conte d' (*fl* 1728) **29** *42*
Althann (family) **3** 488; **11** 130; **27** 233
Althann, Gundacker Louis Joseph, Graf von **1** 724*
architecture **1** 668; **11** 134, 135; **13** 921; **32** 460
Althans, Carl Ludwig **12** 374
Altherr, Heinrich **1** 724*
Altherr, Paul **1** 724
Altheus Reliquary **9** 660
Althorp House (Northants) **29** 381
books **29** 380
Brington Lodges **12** 176
collections **2** 722; **10** 364; **33** 375
dairy **8** 461
frames **11** 422, 423
furniture **23** 544; **29** 806
Althorp House (Northants)—cont.
paintings **2** 93
animal subjects **29** 381, 424
landscape **27** 150; **29** 380; **32** 700
portraits **8** 454; **19** 122; **20** 378; **25** 816, 843; **26** 394; **28** 50; **29** 380, 381; **31** 871
religious **29** 381
plate **26** 558
silver **14** 161
Althrey Hall (Flints) **32** 782, 784
Althusser, Louis **28** 927
Altichiero (di Domenico da Zevio) **1** 724–7*; **5** 871; **13** 149; **23** 753
collaboration **2** 849
patrons and collectors **16** 710; **32** 343
pupils **31** 104
works **1** *726*, *727*; **5** 871; **9** *260*, 261; **16** 657; **24** 559; **28** 29; **32** 341
Altieri (family)
architecture **26** 748; **27** 194
paintings **13** 650; **20** 375, 588
Altieri, Angelo **1** 727
Altieri, Emilio *see* CLEMENT X, Pope
Altieri, Gasparo **1** 727; **7** 399; **10** 753
Altieri, Padrone, Cardinal **1** 728
Altieri Claudes **1** 727
Altin 1 **1** *186*, 190
Altin 10 **1** 190
Altınbeser, Ismail Hakkı **23** 391
Altin Dilyar Tepe **1** *186*, 190; **6** 186
Alting, J. Carpentier **30** 15
Altini, Eustatie **1** 728*; **26** 713
Altintaş, Mar Azaziel **31** 435
Altıntepe (Turkey) **1** *728*, 728–30*, *821*, 894; **23** 807
figurines **1** *729*
halls **1** 730
ivory-carvings **1** 870, 872
sanctuary **31** 700
temple **1** 729*, 830, 831
tombs **1** 729–30*
wall paintings **1** 830, 839; **31** 700
Altinum **32** 182
Altissimo, Cristofano (di Papi) dell' **1** 730*; **7** 623; **16** 771
Altivole
Barco della Regina **7** 862; **32** 545
Villa Cornaro *see* Barco della Regina
Altlerchenfeld parish church *see under* VIENNA → ecclesiastical buildings
Altmäe, Riina **30** 276
Altman, Benjamin **1** 730–31*
collections **12** 474; **16** 554, 769; **28** 384
paintings **2** 180; **9** 467
Altman, Daniel **8** 384
Al'tman, Natan (Isayevich) **1** 731*; **9** 747; **17** 577; **27** 394
groups and movements **16** 818; **22** 508; **31** 583; **33** 380
works **27** 413, 578, 580, *581*
Altman, Sybrand **28** 77
Altman Carpet **15** 683
Altman *Madonna and Child* **20** 313
Altmann, Abbot of Niederalteich **18** 477
Altmann, Bishop of Passau **2** 777
Altmünden glass factory **12** 440, 897
Altmünster Church **2** 800
El Alto **18** 777
Alto, Monsù **19** 524
Alto Alentejo **27** 13
Altobello, Francesco Antonio **1** 731–2*; **27** 149
Alto de El Purutal **27** 700
Alto de Lavaderos **27** 700
Alto de Lavapatas **27** 700
Alto de los Idolos **27** 700
Altoluogo *see* SELÇUK
Altomonte, Andreas **1** 732; **6** 363; **32** 435
Altomonte, Bartolomeo **1** 732, 733*; **2** 795
paintings **1** 161, *659*, 660; **13** 279; **15** 139; **27** 553, 554
altarpieces **29** 75
Altomonte, Franz Lorenz **1** 732
Altomonte, Giacomo **1** 732
Altomonte, Martino **1** 732–3*; **32** 875
collaboration **1** 733; **19** 378
paintings **2** 794; **27** 665
altarpieces **13** 888; **14** 900
battle **25** 105
ceiling **27** 553
frescoes **32** 443, 458
religious **1** *732*
wall **19** 497
patrons and collectors **2** 828; **28** 15
pupils **1** 733
teachers **29** 789
works **14** 309
Altomünster Convent **11** 127; **12** 372
Alton, Eduard d' **20** 526
Altona
Jewish cemetery **17** 555
Villa Donner **25** 172
Alton Diptych **30** 267
Alton Towers (Staffs) **1** 733–4*; **10** *225*; **11** 243; **30** 267
frames **11** 432
Alton Towers Ltd. **1** 734
Alton Towers Triptych **31** 499
Altoon, John **19** 702
Altorf, Johan Coenraad **1** 734*
Altorfer, Erhard *see* ALTDORFER, ERHARD
Altos **24** 100
Altötting **12** 371
St Michael **32** 821
SS Philipp and Jakob **13** 158, 177
Wallfahrtskirche **12** 371
Altounian **10** 91
Altoviti, Bindo **1** 734–5*; **6** *144*
decorative works **27** 648
paintings **5** 789; **32** 11, 12
sculpture **21** 768
Altoviti, Guglielmo **20** 124
Altoviti, Jacopo **27** 486
Altson, Aby **14** 307
Altstetten **25** 542
Alttrier **19** 826
Altumvillare *see* HAUTVILLERS
Altuna Memorial Stone **32** 522
Altun Ha **1** 735*; **3** 622, *622*; **20** *882*
metalwork **21** 252
Structure A-5 **21** 214
Structure A-6 **21** 214
Structure B-4, 2nd **21** 214
Structure B-4, 2nd A **21** 215
tombs **20** 883
Alt-Wiener school **18** 419
Altwies **19** 826
Altxerri **25** 478
Altyn Tepe (Turkmenistan) **1** 735*; **6** *182*, 185, 209; **31** *458*
architecture **6** 195; **32** 320
metalwork **6** 272
pottery **6** 255
sculpture **6** 237
statuettes **6** 275
Altyre **28** 229
Aludenuya **29** 460
Aluku **11** 759, 760; **30** 13
alum **19** 6
historical and regional traditions
Byzantine **9** 665
China **7** 632
Early Christian (*c.* AD 250-843) **9** 665
Egypt **16** 431
Egypt, ancient **10** 61
alum
historical and regional traditions—cont.
Indian subcontinent **15** 667, 668
Islamic **16** 431
Mesoamerica, Pre-Columbian **21** 261
uses
consolidants **7** 748
dyeing **30** 557, 560, 561
glazes **12** 803
leather **10** 61; **19** 2
mordants (iii) (dyeing) **9** 665; **15** 667, 668; **21** 261; **30** 559
paper **24** 56
pigments **7** 632; **18** 655
plaster **29** 812
size **28** 813
stucco **29** 813
tanning **19** 1
alumina **6** 324, 329; **18** 655, 656
Aluminia Fajancefabrik **7** 807; **8** 748; **18** 462; **28** 847
aluminium **1** 735–9*; **21** 320
historical and regional traditions
Africa **1** *411*
China **7** 115
England **12** *610*, 613; **24** *34*
Hausa **1** 247
Japan **1** *737*, *738*; **17** 213
Kenya **1** *411*
Laos **18** 775
Netherlands, the **22** *896*
Russia **27** *397*
United States of America **31** 654
Venezuela **32** 171, *171*
uses
architecture **1** 736–7*, *737*; **32** 171, *171*
calligraphy **17** 213
coins **7** 539
conservation **24** 7
dyes **9** 490, 491
furniture **31** 654
gilding **12** 621, 623
headrests **1** *411*
jewellery **17** 530; **18** 775; **22** *896*
paint tubes **23** 787
panel paintings **24** 7
paper **7** 115
printing plates **10** 548
sculpture **1** 737–8*, *738*; **12** *610*, 613; **24** *34*; **27** *397*
spoons **1** 247
supports **31** 283
waxes **33** 2
Aluminium Français **24** 476
aluminium hydroxide **24** 789
aluminium oxides **1** 761; **6** 897
aluminium salts **7** 45; **24** 106
Alunda **25** 513
church **30** 865
Alunno, l' *see* NICCOLÒ DA FOLIGNO
Alunno di Domenico *see* BARTOLOMEO DI GIOVANNI
Aluthnuvara **29** 450
Aluvihara **5** 97; **29** 442
Alva de la Canal, Ramón **1** 739*; **21** 405
groups and movements **10** 543; **21** 387
pupils **23** 370
Alvani, St John the Baptist **25** 344
Alvarado, Antonio **1** 739*; **23** 905
Alvarado, Mario Urteaga *see* URTEAGA ALVARADO, MARIO
Alvarado, Pedro de **10** 153
Alvarado Abella, Francisco **8** 18
Alvarado Lang, Carlos **1** 739*; **21** 388
collaboration **5** 651
pupils **3** 688; **22** 104
Alvarado Stele **29** 619
Alvard, Julian **2** 545
Alvares, Afonso **1** 740*
attributions **25** 317
patrons and collectors **2** 873, 874, 875
Alvares, Afonso—cont.
pupils **1** 740
teachers **2** 501
works **1** 740; **2** 501; **10** 664; **25** 291
Alvares, Baltazar **1** 740–41*
works **1** *740*; **7** 531; **20** 462; **25** 291
Alvares, Manuel **30** 799
Alvares da Cunha, António **24** 321
Alváres de Toledo, Fernando, Gran-Duque de Alba *see* ALBA, FERNANDO, Gran-Duque de
Alvares Pereira de Melo, Nuno, Duque de Cadaval *see* CADAVAL, NUNO ALVARES PEREIRA DE MELO, Duque de
Alvárez **11** 662
Alvarez, Aníbal **1** 149; **24** 225
Alvarez, Antonio de **14** 714
Alvarez, Augusto H. **1** 743*; **21** 380, 381
groups and movements **15** 887
works **21** 381, 403
Alvarez, Domingo **1** 741
Alvarez, Francisco (*fl* 1552-68) **3** 7; **20** 69; **29** 334
Alvarez, Francisco (*fl* 1785-1813) **13** 767
Alvarez, José Antonio Caro *see* CARO ALVAREZ, JOSÉ ANTONIO
Alvarez, José Luis **12** 53
Alvarez, Manuel (16th cent.) **3** 847
Alvarez, Manuel (1727-97) **6** 68; **31** 89
Alvarez, Mariano **29** 343
Alvarez, Mario Roberto **1** 743*; **2** 397
Alvarez, Ricardo Borrero *see* BORRERO ALVAREZ, RICARDO
Alvarez Bouquel, Aníbal **1** 743*
Alvarez Bravo, Manuel **1** 743–4*; **21** 388; **24** 676
collaboration **4** 740
groups and movements **30** 21
pupils **19** 657
works **24** *676*
Alvarez Calderón, José **24** 505
Alvarez Capra, Lorenzo **1** 149, 798; **26** 521
Alvarez Carneiro, Fernando **32** 172
Alvarez Cubero, José **1** 741–3*
patrons and collectors **1** 529
works **1** *741*, *742*; **3** 199; **20** 67; **29** 21, 294, *294*
Alvarez de la Peña, Manuel Francisco **1** 744*
patrons and collectors **4** 562
teachers **5** 784
works **1** 742; **29** 293
Alvarez de Sotomayor, Fernando **1** 529; **4** 127; **6** 597; **13** 9; **18** 665
Alvárez de Toledo, Ferdinando, 3rd Duque de Alba *see* ALBA, FERDINANDO ALVÁREZ DE TOLEDO, 3rd Duque de
Alvárez de Toledo, Fernando, 6th Duque de Alba *see* ALBA, FERNANDO, 6th Duque de
Alvárez de Toledo, Francisco, 10th Duque de Alba *see* ALBA, FRANCISCO, 10th Duque de
Alvárez de Toledo, Juan **1** 526; **9** 112
Alvarez de Toledo, María Ignacia *see* ALTAMIRA, MARÍA IGNACIA ALVAREZ DE TOLEDO, Condesa de
Alvarez de Toledo, Pedro, Marqués de Villafranca *see* VILLAFRANCA, PEDRO ALVAREZ DE TOLEDO, Marqués de
Alvárez de Toledo y Gonzaga, José *see* ALBA, JOSÉ ALVÁREZ DE TOLEDO Y GONZAGA, 17th Duque de
Alvarez Ijjasz Murcia **1** 744–5*

Alvárez Ordóñez, Fernando 5 603; 7 696
works 7 *695*
Alvárez Ordóñez, Joaquin 5 603; 7 696
works 7 *695*
Alvarez Pereira, Cecilia 1 744
Alvarez Tabio 8 232
Alvarez Tabio, Emma 8 233
Alvarez y Priego, Jose 15 837
Alvaro, Bishop of Fez 24 848
Alvaro de Castro, Fernando *see* CASTRO, FERNANDO DE
Alvaro d'Évora *see* PIREZ, ALVARO
Alvaro di Pietro *see* PIREZ, ALVARO
Alvaro Portugallo 13 150
Alvastra 25 502
Monastery 13 50; 30 66, 117
Älvdalen 30 113
Alvelar, Francisco Gomes d' *see* GOMES D'ALVELAR FRANCISCO
Alvera, Alessandro 2 810
Alves Cargaleiro, Manuel 30 882
Alves de Souza, Wladimir 26 414
Alves Ferreira, José Mamede 26 65
Alves Macomboa, Manuel *see* MACOMBOA, MANUEL ALVES
Alves Martins, Manuel 24 395
Alves Narciso, Cicero 27 809
Alves Pereira de Lemos, António 10 729
Alviani, Getulio 1 745*; 10 416
Alviano, Bartolomeo d' 31 316
Alvim, Fernando 2 87
Alvinc 15 1
Alvino, Enrico 1 745–6*; 7 339; 8 483
Alvise, Alberto 10 725
Alvise, Bartolo d' 16 740
Alvise, Giovanni 10 725
Al Vista *see under* CAMERAS → types
Alwalton 19 403
Alwar 15 694, 713
City Palace 15 182
Alwa ware *see under* POTTERY → wares
Alxenor 13 440; 22 700
Alyoshin, Pavel F. 31 552
Alzano Maggiore, S Martino 29 831
Alzate, Antonio 33 472
Alzate, José Antonio 21 262
Alzibar, José de 32 173
AM, Master 10 383
Amada, Temple of Tuthmosis III and Amenophis II 23 279
Amadas, Robert 1 746*; 10 323; 33 306
Amadei, Giuliano 1 768*
Amadeo (de Souza-Cardoso) 1 746*; 2 62; 25 299
Amadeo, Giovanni Antonio 1 746–9*; 21 524
architecture 16 630; 26 502
cathedrals 4 645; 29 23
chapels 3 771, 772, *772*
churches 6 357; 19 185
hospitals 11 72
assistants 4 817; 26 289
attributions 26 289
collaboration 4 643, 645, 817; 9 75; 11 691; 20 302; 21 532; 26 289; 29 24, 25
patrons and collectors 3 249; 7 568; 28 532
pupils 11 856; 26 288
sculpture 21 533; 30 501
architectural 24 285
façade decoration 10 743; 20 302, 303; 24 286, 287
reliefs 1 *748*; 24 286; 25 19
tombs 1 *747*; 16 562; 27 830
Amadeo Fiorentino 11 217
Amadeus I, 1st Duke of Savoy *see* AMADEUS VIII, Count of Savoy
Amadeus VI, Count of Savoy (*reg* 1343-83) 3 362; 7 178; 28 1
Amadeus VII, Count of Savoy (*reg* 1383-91) 17 460
Amadeus VIII, Count of Savoy (*reg* 1391-1434) 17 444; 28 1, *2*, 3–4*
decorative works 3 188
manuscripts 3 188; 18 684; 28 1
paintings 33 287
sculpture 7 405
Amadeus of Savoy, King of Spain (*reg* 1870-73) 23 415
Amadi, Francesco 12 298
Amadio, Giuseppe 25 212
Amadio da Milano 10 519; 31 431
Amadlozi Press 18 514; 29 110
Amado, Maria Celia 26 60
Amado Blanco, Luis 24 334
Amador, Manuel E(ncarnación) 1 749*; 23 904
Amador de los Ríos, José 1 149, 749–50*
Amador Lira, Genaro 23 81, 85
Amager 8 755
Amaghu *see* NORAVANK'
Amagi 17 355
Amago 16 812
Amahata 17 388
Amak Tam 20 886
Amakusa Island 17 241
āmalaka 15 242*
āmalasāraka see ALPANĀSĪ
Amalekite Master 33 240
Amalfi
Cathedral of Monte Sant'Angelo 9 154; 26 619, 626
doors 9 581, 600
Cathedral of S Andrea 16 626
coral 16 750
ivory-carvings 16 526; 26 698
oliphants 23 401, *401*; 26 698
Amalfi, Maurus of *see* MAURUS OF AMALFI
Amalfi, Pantaleone of *see* PANTALEONE OF AMALFI
Amalia, Queen of Portugal (1863-1951) 4 629; 5 902
Amalia of Bavaria 30 459
Amalia von Solms, Princess of Orange (1602-75) 15 40; 22 902; 23 463, *463*, 465–6*
architecture 14 45; 22 825, 902; 25 324
collections 22 904
decorative works 13 337
drawings 29 799
interior decoration 15 40
paintings 7 832; 11 226; 14 584, 731; 17 649; 19 348, 349; 22 94; 25 370; 30 788
porcelain 9 28
Amalia Wilhelmina, Holy Roman Empress (1673-1742) 25 2
Amalienborg Palace *see under* COPENHAGEN → palaces
Amalienburg pavilion *see under* MUNICH → Schloss Nymphenburg
Amalric Frères 30 148
Amalric I, King of Jerusalem (1162-74) 3 882
Amalricus Augerius 13 627
Amalteo, Pomponio 1 750*; 13 658; 25 251
Amama, Franz von 8 762
Amami 27 469, 471
Aman, Johann 2 785; 5 82; 25 155; 32 460
Aman, Theodor 1 750–51*; 5 73; 14 588; 26 724, 725
pupils 2 21; 12 316; 26 714
works 26 714
Aman, Theodor, Museum *see under* BUCHAREST → museums
Amanaka Shinten'ō 17 199
Aman Allah, King (*reg* 1919-29) (Barakzay) 17 717
Amanat Khan 15 363, 365, 680
Amand, Saint 12 516, 520
Amandi, S Juan 3 443
Amandry, P. 2 406
Amangeldyyev, Aman 31 459
Amangeldyyev, Char 31 459
Amanikhabale 23 284
Amanishakheto, Queen (early 1st cent.) 10 93; 23 283, 285
Amanitore 23 283
Aman-Jean, Edmond (-François) 1 751*
assistants 31 145
collaboration 20 603
groups and movements 3 156
pupils 23 872
works 19 490
Amano, Yoshitaro 24 517
Amans, Jacques 23 32
Amapa 1 751–2*; 2 904; 21 *193*, *372*
metalwork 21 200
El-Amara 9 *774*; 23 *276*
temple 23 282
Amaral, Antonio Henrique 1 752*; 4 719
Amaral, Keil do 1 752*
Amaral, Olga de 7 610; 11 54; 30 329
Amaral, Tarsila do *see* TARSILA
Amarante, Carlos Luis Ferreira 1 752–3*
works 4 629, *629*; 23 453; 25 293
Amarante, S Gonçalo 17 596
amaranth 11 595
Amarapura 1 753*; 5 *221*; 29 *225*
architecture 5 237, 238
bells 5 253
Kyauk-taw-gyi 5 233, 244
Naga-yon 5 233
palace 5 235
Pato-daw-gyi 5 234; 23 556
Phaya-nga-zu 5 233
sculpture 5 241
temples 5 233
textiles 5 247, 248, 263
Tham-bude-hpaya 5 234, *234*
wood-carvings 5 261
Amarasekera, A. C. G. S. 29 467
Amarasinghe, Asoka 29 455
Amarasinghe, Nihal 29 456
Amarathian period *see* EGYPT, ANCIENT → periods → Naqada I
Amaravati 1 753–5*; 15 194, *294*
Archaeological Museum 1 753
Great Stupa 1 753–4, *754*; 15 249
ivory 15 695
reliefs 5 *88*, *95*; 15 248, 249, 250, 413, 438, 439, *454*
sculpture 5 94; 10 898; 15 220, 412, 416, 453, 476, 535, 744; 30 510
stucco 29 824
stupas 15 303; 19 717; 22 516
Amara West 9 848; 23 280
Amarbayasgalant Monastery 21 872, 875
Amar Chand 15 613
Amari
Hagia Anna 8 156
Hagia Paraskevi 25 334
Amari, Michele 16 547
Amari Valley 8 155
Amarkantak 15 291
Amarna, (Tell) el- 1 505, *755*, 755–6*; 9 *774*, 782, 844, *853*, 883
boxes 10 53
busts 10 93; 22 *723*; 29 814
chairs 10 53
craftsmen and artists 30 794
excavations 10 80, 81; 11 732; 33 373
frit 11 794
gardens 12 67
glass 10 55, 57
Great Temple 9 832, *833*
jewellery 10 31
letters *see* AMARNA LETTERS
masks 5 298; 10 68
Amarna, (Tell) el-—cont.
North Palace
Green Room 9 809, 902–3
paintings 24 798
palaces 23 807
pottery 8 330; 10 *24*
reliefs 1 505; 9 884, *884*; 22 722
sacred lake 27 496
sculpture 1 505; 3 523; 9 884
stelae 29 616
Temple of the Aten
altar 1 691
reliefs 9 884
temples 9 832–3; 30 433
textiles 9 823; 10 74, 75
tombs (private)
Meryre 9 *840*
Meryre I 9 805
Meryre II 9 826; 33 246
Tutu (el-Amarna) 9 840
tombs (royal)
Akhenaten (*reg c.* 1353-*c.* 1336 BC) 9 841
Ay (*reg c.* 1323-*c.* 1319 BC) 9 826, 840; 10 61
urban planning 1 755; 9 851–2
wall paintings 9 805, 808, 810, 898, *902*, 902–3
workshops 9 791
Amarna Letters 1 755, 853, 869, 893; 9 781, 782; 10 54; 17 836; 21 274, 730
Amarna period *see under* EGYPT, ANCIENT → periods
Amarna style 1 505, 755, 756*; 3 523; 9 782, 884
sculpture 9 853; 25 *880*
Amar Singh II, Rana of Mewar (*reg* 1698-1710) (Rajput) 15 599, 600, *600*
Amaseia 4 113
Amashukeli, E. 12 322
Amasis (*reg* 570-526 BC) 2 690; 8 458; 9 *777*; 21 121; 24 602; 27 593; 30 296
Amasis (*fl c.* 550 BC) 13 509; 32 30, 53
Amasis Painter 13 508; 32 30*
patrons and collectors 13 542
pupils 32 65
works 9 247; 13 509, *510*
Amastini (family) 12 264; 24 734
Amastini, Angelo Antonio 1 756; 12 262
Amastini, Carlo de Giovanni 1 756*
Amastini, Niccolò 1 756*; 12 264
Amastris 4 113
Amasya 1 756–7*; 16 *104*
architecture 16 183
bazaar 16 206
Burmalı Minare Mosque 16 183
Gök Madrasa 16 186
Gök Medrese Mosque 16 183
külliye 18 509
manuscripts 16 330
Mosque of Bayezid Pasha 1 756; 16 206
Mosque of Mehmet Pasha 1 756
Mosque of Yürgüç Pasha 1 756
silk 16 445
Amat, Hernan 6 523; 29 219
Amat (y Junyent), Manuel (de) 1 757*; 24 502, 503
Amateur Photographer, The 24 739
Amateur Photographic Exchange Club *see* EXCHANGE CLUB
Amateur Photographic Print, The 10 669
amateurs 6 771; 7 561
Amathus 1 757*; 8 *325*, 331; 13 *362*
basilica 8 357; 29 816
coins 8 349
pottery 8 348
Sanctuary of Aphrodite 8 342
sarcophagi 8 341
Temple of Aphrodite 8 337
wall paintings 8 356
Amati, Carlo 1 758*
patrons and collectors 16 647
works 4 248; 7 258; 21 532; 25 155
Amati, Nicolò 8 135
Amatitlán 21 259
Museo Municipal 13 769
Amato, Giacomo 1 758*; 28 477
Amato, Giovann' Angelo d' 15 147
Amato, Paolo 1 758–9*
works 23 841, *842*
Amatrice, Cola dell' *see* COLA DELL'AMATRICE
Amatuni (family) 25 686
Amatus of Montecassino 8 800
Amaury-Duval, Eugène-Emmanuel 1 759*; 11 671
collaboration 3 736
pupils 11 798
teachers 15 839
works 1 *759*
Amauta 24 435
Amaysa 16 303
Amazonas 29 171
amazonite 16 857; 21 241
Ambae 31 890
Ambala 8 673
Ambalavao 20 36
Ambalo 7 602
Ambar 31 434
'Ambar 'Ali Khan 15 380
Ambarnath 1 760*; 15 *276*, 316
Mahadeva Temple 15 493
Ambasz, Emilio 1 760*
Ambato 9 *709*
Ambatomainty 20 40
Ambedkar, Bhimrao 5 93; 15 406
Ambedkar Buddhism *see under* BUDDHISM → sects
Ambelakia, Georgios Schwartz Mansion 32 *294*
Ambelikou-Aletri 8 330, 353
amber 1 760–62*; 12 268; 26 244
historical and regional traditions
Africa 1 350
Anglo-Saxon 1 761; 3 442
Armenia (Europe) 1 762
Burma 1 761
Celtic 1 761
China 1 761; 7 89, 90, 91, 110, 111, *111*
Denmark 8 752, *753*; 31 *481*
Dominican Republic 1 761
England 1 761, 762
Etruscan 1 761; 10 635
France 1 761
Germany 1 *762*; 6 558; 28 168
Greece, ancient 1 761, *761*
Indian subcontinent 1 762
Insular art 15 *872*
Inuit 1 761
Ireland 15 *872*
Italy 10 635
Japan 17 398
Merovingian 1 761
Mesoamerica, Pre-Columbian 1 761
Mexico 1 761
Mongolia 3 441
Mycenaean 1 761
Native North Americans 1 761
Netherlands, the 1 761
Norway 1 761
Poland 1 762
Prehistoric art 16 615; 25 546
Romania 1 761; 7 90
Rome, ancient 1 761
Sicily 1 761
South America, Pre-Columbian 1 761
Spain 29 302
Teutonic Order 1 762
Thailand 3 441
Turkey 1 762
United States of America 1 761, 762
Viking 1 761

amber—cont.
  techniques
    abrasion 1 761
    polishing 1 761
    pressing 1 761, 762
  uses
    altars 1 762
    amphorae 1 761
    amulets 1 761
    beads 1 761, 762; 3 440, 441, 442; 7 110
    bowls 1 762
    brooches 1 761; 15 *872*
    cabinets (ii) (furniture) 1 762
    candlesticks 1 762
    caskets 1 762; 29 302
    chandeliers 31 *481*
    chess sets 6 555, 558
    crowns 7 110, 111, *111*
    cruets 1 762
    earrings 1 761
    figurines 1 761, *761*, *762*
    flasks 1 761
    game-boards 1 762
    game-pieces 1 761
    glazes 23 792
    goblets 1 762
    hairpins 1 761
    inlays 1 761
    interior decoration 1 762
    jewellery 1 350, 761, 762; 7 111
    knife-handles 8 285
    lamps 1 762
    mirror handles 1 761
    necklaces 1 761, 762; 8 *753*
    netsuke 17 398
    paternoster beads 1 761; 17 520
    plaques 1 761
    plates 1 762
    portraits *see under* PORTRAITS → media
    radios 1 762
    reliefs 1 762
    saddlery 1 762
    scarabs 1 761
    snuff bottles 1 761
    tankards 1 762
    thrones 1 762
    varnishes 32 1
    veneers 1 762
    vernis Martin 18 611
    watches 7 443
    writing sets 1 762
Amber (India) *see* AMER
Amberd Castle 2 436
Amberg, St Martin 12 365
Amberg, Adolf 1 762–3*; 12 436
Amberg, H. C. 26 305
Amberger, Christoph 1 763–4*; 2 716
  pupils 12 648
  works 1 *763*; 9 274; 12 387
Ambergris Caye 3 *622*
Ambert, Henry 2 112
Ambla 10 *536*
  church 10 536
Ambling, Carl Gustav (von) *see* AMLING, CARL GUSTAV (VON)
Ambohimanga 1 *413*; 20 40
Amboise
  Château 6 59, 504; 11 571; 23 809; 31 844, *844*
    gardens 12 110, 112
  Pagode de Chanteloup 7 168
Amboise, d' (family) 29 25
Amboise, Charles I d' (*d c.* 1503) 1 765
Amboise, Charles II d', Comte de Chaumont (1473-(1511) 1 765, 766–7*
  architecture 19 185; 21 517
  interior decoration 29 25
  sculpture 29 24
Amboise, Georges I d', Cardinal (1460-1510) 1 765–7*
  architecture 3 924; 8 684; 11 512, 556, 726, 904; 27 246
  fountains 11 341
  gardens 12 112
Amboise, Georges I d', Cardinal (1460-1510)—cont.
  interior decoration 29 25
  manuscripts 9 386; 20 744
  paintings 29 25
  sculpture 11 556, 660; 19 230; 23 709; 27 251
  stone-carvings 11 399
Amboise, Georges II d', Cardinal (1487-1550) 1 766*; 13 634
Amboise, Jacques d', Bishop of Clermont-Ferrand 1 765
Amboise, Louis I d', Bishop of Albi (*d* 1503) 1 577, 765
Amboise, Louis II d' (1477-1517), Cardinal 1 765
Amboise, Pierre d' (*d* 1505), Bishop of Poitiers 1 765
Amboise, Pierre II d' (*d* 1473) 1 765
Ambon 3 331; 15 810
  Fort Victoria 21 596
ambos 1 764–5*; 28 141
  Byzantine 1 764; 9 590
  Early Christian (*c.* AD 250-843) 7 278; 9 590
  Italy 7 *919*
  Mesopotamia 1 764
  Syria 1 764
Ambositra 20 36
amboyna
  historical and regional traditions
    Belgium 3 584
    England 10 279, 291, 297
    Indonesia 15 813
    Korea 33 IV1
  uses
    boxes 33 IV1
    furniture 3 584; 10 297; 15 813
    inlays 10 291
Ambra, Cavaliere 21 53
Ambrakia *see* ARTA (GREECE)
Ambras 2 793
Ambras, Schloss *see under* INNSBRUCK
Ambriz 1 *401*
Ambrogi, Domenico degli 11 839
Ambrogiana, Villa dell' *see* VILLA DELL' AMBROGIANA
Ambrogini, Angelo *see* POLIZIANO, ANGELO
Ambrogio 13 15
Ambrogio, Pietro di Giovanni d' *see* PIETRO DI GIOVANNI D'AMBROGIO
Ambrogio da Cermenate 20 675
Ambrogio da Marliano 25 465
Ambrogio da Milano *see* BAROCCI, AMBROGIO (D'ANTONIO)
Ambrogio da Predis 13 904; 31 847
Ambrogio da Urbino *see* BAROCCI, AMBROGIO (D'ANTONIO)
Ambrogio di Baldese 7 457; 23 95
Ambrogio Grifi 21 525
ambroid 1 762
Ambrose, Saint, Bishop of Milan 7 217; 9 642, 665; 11 174; 21 514, 534
Ambrosi, Gustinus 2 803
Ambrosi, Pietro di Giovanni *see* PIETRO DI GIOVANNI D'AMBROGIO
Ambrosini, Floriano 4 273; 9 111; 20 898
Ambrosio da Bindo 9 112
ambrotypes *see under* PHOTOGRAPHIC PLATES → types
Ambrym 31 890, 891
ambulatories 1 767–8*
  historical and regional traditions
    Britain 1 768
    France 1 767, *767*
    Germany 1 768
    Gothic 2 *864*
    Greece, ancient 13 379
    Romanesque 1 767, *767*; 8 223; 26 571
ambulatories
  historical and regional traditions—cont.
    Spain 2 *864*
  types
    double 1 768
ambulatory basilicas *see under* CHURCHES → types
AMC (Archives and Manuscript Control) 2 367
Amden 21 409
Amdo 30 808, 846
Amedeo (*fl* 1467) 22 801
Amedeo, Ser 22 801
Amedeo de Francesco *see* MEO DA CAPRINO
Ameishi 17 732
Amelia, Piermatteo (Lauro de' Manfredi) d' *see* PIERMATTEO (LAURO DE' MANFREDI) D'AMELIA
Amelia Elizabeth, Landgravine of Hesse-Kassel (*fl c.* 1626-39) 28 671
Amelias 24 57
Amelin, Albin 10 805; 30 81
Ameline, J.-F. 1 844
Amélineau, Emile 10 80
Amelot, Jean-Baptiste, Vicomte de Bisseuil *see* BISSEUIL, JEAN-BAPTISTE AMELOT, Vicomte de
Amelot de Gournay, Michel *see* GOURNAY, MICHEL AMELOT DE
Amelsfoort, Quirinus van 18 156
Amelung, John Frederick 1 769*; 10 852; 26 227; 31 642
Amelung, John Frederick Magnus 1 769
Amelung, Walter 6 77
Amenemhab 9 839, 840
Amenemhet 9 840
Amenemhet I *see* AMMENEMES I
Amenemhet II *see* AMMENEMES II
Amenemhet III *see* AMMENEMES III
Ameneminet 27 812
Amenemnisu (*reg c.* 1045-*c.* 1040 BC) 9 *777*
Amenemope (*reg c.* 998-*c.* 989 BC) 9 *777*; 10 74; 22 285
Amen glasses *see under* GLASSES → types
Amenhotpe, son of Hapu 1 769–70*; 9 826, 835, 858
  works 1 770
Amenirdis
  tomb 9 *839*
Amenmesse (*reg c.* 1203-*c.* 1200 BC) 9 *777*
Amenoff, Gregory 20 609
Amenophis I (*reg c.* 1514-*c.* 1493 BC) 9 *777*; 10 56
  faience (i) (glass) 10 48
  jewellery 10 31
  reliefs 9 882; 10 87
  sculpture 9 880, 885
Amenophis II (*reg c.* 1426-*c.* 1400 BC) 9 *777*, 860, 903, 904; 10 *58*, 80
  architecture 9 832; 23 279; 25 776
  glass 10 57
  sculpture 9 860
  textiles 1 880; 10 75, *75*
  wall paintings 10 7
Amenophis III (*reg c.* 1390-*c.* 1353 BC) 1 770*; 9 *777*, 861; 10 80; 30 689
  architecture 1 769; 2 657; 9 830, 831, 851; 14 462; 17 714; 20 231; 23 279, 807; 29 33; 30 692
  glass 10 57
  plaques 10 7
  reliefs 2 690; 9 881, 882
  scarabs 28 34, *34*
  sculpture 3 523; 9 853, 862, 863; 14 462; 23 *279*, 280; 25 874
  shrines (i) (cult) 12 227
Amenophis III (*reg*—cont.
  stelae 12 227
  wall paintings 9 898
Amenophis IV (*reg c.* 1353-*c* 1336 BC) *see* AKHENATEN
Amer (India) 1 770–71*; 15 *279*, *597*; 16 *105*
  Amber Fort 32 804
  enamel 15 711
  fortifications 21 590
  Ganesha Pol 15 372; 23 819, *819*
  gardens 12 75
  Jagat Shiromani Temple 15 371, 385
  Jai Mahal 15 372
  Man Singh Palace 1 770–71; 15 371, 386, 387, 389, 609
    carpets 15 683
  manuscript illumination 15 609
  Maunbari 12 75
  Shila Mata temple 15 372
  wall paintings 15 544, 609
Amer (Spain), S María 26 580
Amerbach (family) 3 336; 14 665; 25 21
Amerbach, Basilius 1 771*; 13 267; 30 131, 146, 152, 153, 154
Amerbach, Bonifacius 1 771*; 30 131, 154
Amerbach, Johannes 1 771*; 3 335; 30 131, 152, 153, 154, 487
America, United States of *see* UNITED STATES OF AMERICA
American Abstract Artists 1 771–2*; 9 503; 26 126; 31 607, 614
  collections 12 15
  members 1 84; 4 282; 6 111; 8 896; 12 771; 18 813; 22 749; 26 356
American Airlines 17 850; 32 501
American Amateur Photographer 24 432; 29 655
American Arabic typeface *see under* TYPEFACES
American Architect and Building News 2 333; 24 432
American Art 24 433
American Art Alliance 32 890
American Art Association *see* SOCIETY OF AMERICAN ARTISTS
American Art Association Gallery *see* A.A.A. GALLERY
American Artist Group 22 596
American Artists' Congress 1 772*; 23 48
American Art Journal 24 433
American Art Review 24 423, 431
American Art-Union 4 72; 25 629; 31 662, 664; 33 371
American Association of Museums 32 890
American Ballet company 19 844
American Bank Note Company 3 182; 17 597
American Builder and Journal of Art 24 432
American Ceramic Society 4 73; 31 638
American China Co. 18 169
American China Manufactory *see* TUCKER CHINA FACTORY
American Comic Almanach 5 758
American Encaustic Tiling Co. 26 287; 30 887
American Export lines 20 10
American Express 13 811
American Flint Glass Manufactory 29 654; 31 642
  works 31 *641*
American Historical Association 2 533
American Horologe Co. 15 822
American Impressionism *see under* IMPRESSIONISM → regional traditions
American Imprints on Art Through 1865 4 23
American Institute for Conservation (AIC) 7 744
American Institute of Architects (A.I.A.) *see under* NEW YORK → institutes
American Magazine of Art 24 433
American Philosophical Society 21 264
American Pottery Manufacturing Co. 1 772*; 31 636
American Print Alliance 25 629
American Renaissance 18 627
American Romanesque 2 756; 24 296
American Scene painting 1 772–3*; 20 476; 26 90; 31 606; 33 343
  works 1 *773*
American School of Architecture *see* ROME → academies → American Academy
American Society of Painters in Pastel 6 500
American Society of Watercolour Painters *see* AMERICAN WATERCOLOR SOCIETY
American Sociological Association 2 533
American System of Manufactures 15 821–3; 20 593
American Tapestry Alliance 31 661
American Terra Cotta Company 21 650
American Water Color Society (1850) *see* NEW YORK WATER COLOR SOCIETY
American Watercolor Society (1866) 32 903
American Wood Paper Co. 24 41
America's Cup 12 163
Américo de (Figueiredo e) Melo, Pedro 1 774*; 4 717, 726
Ameringius, Petrus *see* HEYDEN, PIETER VAN DER
Amerling, Friedrich von 1 774–5*; 2 796; 5 85; 32 444
  exhibitions 2 546
  patrons and collectors 19 339
  pupils 26 501
  works 1 *774*
Amero, Emilio 21 388
Ameron, H. J. van 24 892
Amerongen
  Castle 12 132; 22 826, 872
  tomb of Goert van Reede and Geertruyt van Nijenrode 22 857
Amerongen, Folpard van *see* FOLPARD VAN AMERONGEN
Amerongen, Jan van *see* JAN VAN AMERONGEN
Amersfoort 1 775*; 22 *813*
  glass 22 884
  houses 32 *284*
  Onze Lieve Vrouw 13 62
  pewter 22 893
  St Joriskerk 22 819, 820
Amersfoortse Tapijtfabriek 7 552; 22 900
Amersham (Bucks), High and Over 2 600; 10 241
Amery, Leopold 16 555
Ames (family) 23 422
Ames, Ezra 1 775–6*
Ames, Frederick Lothrop 25 806; 26 341, 343; 29 870
Ames, Kenneth 32 328
Amesbury House (Wilts) 8 45; 32 552
Ames Carpet 15 682
amethyst 12 I; 14 167
  historical and regional traditions
    China 7 91
    Egypt, ancient 10 29
    England 17 *528*
    France 26 *147*

amethyst
historical and regional traditions—cont.
Gothic **26** *147*
Islamic **16** *507*
Mesoamerica, Pre-Columbian **21** 241
Mixtec **21** 737
Ottoman **16** *507*
uses
bowls **14** *171*
helmets **16** *507*
jewellery **10** 29; **17** 524, *528*
reliquaries **26** *147*
Ametller Rotllan, Blas **1** 776*
Ametrano, Francesco Antonio **5** 693; **28** 389
Amfora Factory **8** 406
Amfreville **6** 157
Amhada
painting **8** *462*
Amhara **10** 564, 566
Amherst, Jeffrey, 1st Baron Amherst **15** 653
Amherst, William, Lord **10** 91
Amherst of Hackney, William Tyssen-Amherst, 1st Baron *see* TYSSEN-AMHERST, WILLIAM, Baron Amherst of Hackney
Amic des arts, L' **3** 219; **24** 452
amices **9** 642; **32** 387*
Amici, Giuliano di Scipione **16** 746
Amici, Luigi **10** 435
Amicis, Edmondo de **33** 469
Amico, Alicia d' **10** 747
Amico, G. B. **31** 296
Amico, Luis d' **10** 747
Amico di Sandro **19** 445
Amiconi, Jacopo *see* AMIGONI, JACOPO
Amics del Art Nou (ADLAN) **3** 219; **10** 909; **12** 889; **29** 286
Amida **9** 46, *512*, *513*
church (5th-6th cent.) **9** 539
fortifications **31** 434
St Thomas (7th-9th cent.) **9** 543
Amidaji (Shiga Prefecture) **17** 124
Amidaji (Yamaguchi Prefecture) **17** 131
Amidei, Fausto **24** 842
al-Amidi, Hamid *see* AYTAÇ, HAMID
Amiens **1** 777–82*; **11** *504*
architecture **26** 905
Cathedral of Notre-Dame **1** 777–9*, *778*; **7** 267–8; **11** 153, 510, *510*; **13** 39, 40; **14** 518, 519; **26** 44
altarpieces **11** 399
ambulatory **7** 267
arches **2** 292
buttresses **20** *581*, 581–3, *582*
chapels **11** 511
choir **1** *778*; **11** 510; **13** 42; **26** 45, 46
choir-stalls **7** 190, 192; **13** 126
façade **11** 555
Labyrinth **7** 275; **18** 584; **26** 453
La Grange chapels **13** 59; **32** 93
metalwork **11** 614
mouldings **22** 217, 218, 220, 222
nave **13** 41; **14** 518, 519; **20** 577, *582*; **26** 44
piers (ii) (masonry) **13** 40; **24** 751; **26** 44
pinnacles **24** *825*
reliefs **6** 389; **13** 42, 140
restoration **2** 320
roof **27** 130
sculpture **1** 779–81*, *781*; **13** 72, 74, 75, 77
shrine of St Firminus **28** 630
stained glass **1** 781*; **13** 141
tomb of Bishop Evrard de Fouilloi **31** 123
tomb of Evrard de Fouilloy **7** 267; **11** 623
tomb of Geoffroy d'Eu **7** 267
Amiens
Cathedral of Notre-Dame—cont.
tracery **7** 860; **13** 41; **31** 271, *272*, 273
Treasury **13** 158
vaults (ceiling) **14** 80; **20** 582
cotton **11** 649
manuscripts **1** 782*
museums **11** 668
Musée des Beaux-Arts **3** 277; **8** 123
Musée Napoléon *see* Musée de Picardie
Musée de Picardie **8** 879; **11** 667; **25** 749, 750
pilgrim badges **24** 808
St Germain **11** 154
tapestries **1** 782*; **11** 642
Amiens, Master of **2** 204; **3** 493; **11** 532; **20** 615*
Amiens, Colin d' *see* DIPRE, NICOLAS (*fl* 1465)
Amiens, John of *see* JOHN OF AMIENS
Amiens, Nicolas d' *see* DIPRE, NICOLAS (*fl* 1495)
Amiens 200, Master of **19** 340, 341
Amies, Hardy **9** 294
Amiet, Cuno **1** 782–3*; **3** 824; **30** 134
groups and movements **4** 891; **10** 694
works **22** 330
Amiet, Pierre **21** 276
Amighetti, Francisco **1** 783*; **8** 17
Amigo *see* KURAMA, FODE
Amigó, Eudaldo **29** 307
Amigo, Jaume **29** 268
Amigó, Ximo **31** 816
Amigoni, Jacopo **1** 784–5*; **15** 138; **16** 676; **22** 302
collaboration **11** 172
patrons and collectors **4** 561; **5** 792; **10** 806; **14** 143; **33** 277
pupils **29** 398; **32** 759; **33** 721
reproductive prints by others **3** 308; **6** 91; **32** 689
works **1** *785*; **7** 446; **10** 277; **18** 146; **24** 865; **28** 110
Amin (Indian subcontinent) **15** 427
al Amin (bookbinder) **16** 356
al-Amin, Caliph (*reg* 809-13) (Abbasid) **16** 432
Amin, Husayn Yusuf **9** 766; **12** 222
'Aminabad Carvanserai **5** 723
Amin al-Dawla **12** 82
Amindzhanov, Asror Tashpulatovich **30** 253
a-mi-ni-so *see* AMNISOS
Amino, Leo **4** 109
Amio, Domenico *see* AIMO, DOMENICO
Amiot, Jean-Nicolas **1** 785
Amiot, Laurent **1** 785–6*; **5** 585
Amiotte, Arthur **22** 655
Amiranashvili, Shalva **1** 786*
Amir Chupan **33** 482
Amir Dawlatyar **1** 474
Amir Ghayb Beg **22** 390
Amir Ghayb Beg Album *see under* ALBUMS → individual manuscripts
'Amir II, Ruler (*reg* 1488-1517) (Tahirid) **16** 214
Amir Khalil **30** 921
Amirkhanov, A. **2** 894
Amir Khusraw **15** 571
works **15** *571*
Amirola, Eugenio Llaguno y *see* LLAGUNO Y AMIROLA, EUGENIO
Amirov, Fikret **2** 897, *897*
Amir Ruhallah *see* MIRAK
Amis, Domenico de *see* AIMO, DOMENICO
Amis, Stanley Frederick **14** 812
Ami school **1** 776*
members **1** 776; **17** 173
patrons and collectors **17** 173
works **1** *776*
Amis de l'Art Japonais, Les **32** 394
Amis de l'URSS, Les **17** 669
Amisfield Tower **28** 224; **31** 230
Amish **31** 658
Amisus **4** 110
architecture **4** 113
coins **4** *686*
figurines **13** 581
sculpture **4** 113
terracottas **27** 111
Amiternum **27** 100
Amlapura **15** 776, 806
Amlash region **1** 786*; **15** *897*, *901*, 902, 921, 922
forgeries **1** 896
metalwork **1** 894
pottery **1** *786*
sculpture **1** 896
Amling, Carl Gustav (von) **1** 786–7*; **22** 302
Ammaedara, Arch of Septimius Severus **31** 350
Amman **1** 787*; **13** *362*; **16** *104*; **17** 655; **26** *915*; **30** *180*
architecture **17** 654
Basman Palace **17** 654
Department of Culture and Arts Institute of Fine Arts **17** 655
Haya Centre **17** 654
Housing Bank Complex **17** 654
al-Husayni Mosque **6** 171; **16** 241
Institute of Music and Painting **17** 654
Jordan Archaeological Museum **17** 656; **30** 199
King Abdullah Mosque **17** 654
Martyr's Memorial **17** 654
mosaics **16** 256
Municipality Building **17** 654
National Gallery of Fine Arts **1** 638; **17** 655
Parliament Building **17** 654
pottery **16** 396
Roman theatre **23** 349; **26** 916, 918
Royal Court **17** 654
Royal Cultural Centre **17** 654
sculpture **1** 794; **27** 16
Temple of Hercules **26** 918
theatre **30** 652
Turkish Embassy **17** 654
Amman, Jost **1** 787–9*; **11** 48; **12** 386; **23** 310; **30** 131
book illustrations **29** 628
collaboration **4** 207
drawings **1** *788*
engravings **24** *106*
glass **8** 407
manuscript illumination **29** 747
paintings **29** 665
pupils **17** 885
woodcuts **12** *621*; **24** 38; **25** 621; **33** 354, *355*
Amman, Josua **1** 788
Ammanati, Bartolomeo **1** 789–92*; **3** 700; **11** 187; **23** 293, 754; **24** 112; **26** 769, 779
architecture
bridges **4** 801; **11** 179
churches **11** 208
courtyards **11** 214
grottoes **13** 703
palazzi **11** 213; **19** 764; **23** 836
villas **32** *547*
assistants **9** 181; **30** 531
attributions **4** 286; **31** 820; **32** 692
collaboration **19** 560; **21** 452; **27** 204; **32** 13
competitions **7** 672
frames **11** 391
patrons and collectors
Camaldolese Order **5** 451
Cosimo I, Grand Duke of Tuscany (*reg* 1569- 74) **3** 160; **6** 146; **11** 213; **16** 633; **21** 21
Ammanati, Bartolomeo
patrons and collectors—cont.
Ferdinando I, Grand Duke of Tuscany (*reg* 1587-1609) **32** 546
Francesco I, Grand Duke of Tuscany (*reg* 1574-87) **21** 22; **29** 861
Julius III, Pope (*reg* 1550-55) **16** 634; **22** 6; **32** 504, 546
Pucci, Pandolfo di Roberto (1509-60; patron) **25** 690
Salviati (family) **27** 648
Salviati, Jacopo **27** 648
Vasari, Giorgio (1511-74) **32** 22
pupils **5** 735; **24** 112
sculpture **16** 695
architectural **9** 340; **32** 222, 223
fountains **11** 342; **16** 695, 696; **22** 44
monumental **1** *790*, *791*
statuettes **29** 569
teachers **29** 496
workshop **16** 696
Ammann, Gustav **23** 9
Ammann, Othmar Hermann **4** 803; **12** 615; **23** 43; **29** 250
Ammann and Whitney **30** 468
Ammannati, Bartolomeo *see* AMMANATI, BARTOLOMEO
Ammannati, Giovanni **16** 723
Ammannati, Jacopo **24** 732
Ammenemes (*c.* 1971-26 BC) **9** 823, 838, 900
Ammenemes I (*reg c.* 1938-1908 BC) **9** *776*, 780, 830, 874; **11** 231; **18** 238; **19** 470; **21** 554; **25** 763
architecture **19** 470
reliefs **9** 877
sculpture **9** 874
Ammenemes II (*reg c.* 1876-*c.* 1842 BC) **9** *776*, 875, 877
architecture **8** 456; **9** 831; **10** 80; **14** 462
Ammenemes III (*reg* 1844-1797 BC) **1** 793*, *793*; **9** 875–6
architecture **8** 456; **9** 830; **10** 80, 759; **14** 251; **23** 807; **25** 763
jewellery **10** 30
sculpture **9** 862, 879; **10** 35
Ammenemes IV (*reg c.* 1770-*c.* 1760 BC) **1** 793; **9** *776*, 830
Ammerdown (Somerset) **12** 141
Ammersoyen Castle **22** 822
Ammisaduqqa, King of Babylonia (*reg* 1646-26 BC) **1** 853
Ammochostos *see* FAMAGUSTA
Ammon **1** 794*; **30** *180*, 189
sculpture **30** 194
seals **1** 857
trade **30** 179
ammonia **4** 687; **9** 492; **12** 628
ammonites **15** 729
Amnisos **1** 794*; **8** 153; **13** *362*; **21** *651*
House of the Lilies **1** 794
jewellery **21** 686
wall paintings **21** 659, 674
Amoaku, Kwamina
works **1** *332*
Amo-'Astarte **28** 668
Amoda, Olu **23** 138
Amoedo, Rodolfo **4** 717; **32** 613
Amoghavajra (705-74) **5** 109
Amoghavarsha I, Ruler (*reg* 814-73) (Rashtrakuta) **26** 4
Amohini **15** 443
Amol ware *see under* POTTERY → wares
Amorbach
Abbey Church **13** 853
library **19** 316
Amorgos **1** 795*; **8** *304*, 324; **13** *363*
bronzes **8** 323
marble **29** 701
silver **8** 322, *322*
Amorini, Agostino degli **7** 927
Amorini, Antonio Bolognini *see* BOLOGNINI AMORINI, ANTONIO
Amorite **1** 795*; **3** 12; **21** 278; **30** 192
Amorós, Francesc **29** 306, 319
Amorós, José Alcoverro y *see* ALCOVERRO Y AMORÓS, JOSÉ
Amorós, Rosa **29** 330
Amorosi, Antonio (Mercurio) **1** 795–6*
collaboration **12** 533; **20** 394
teachers **12** 533
Amorosi, Pietro **19** 686
Amorsolo, Fernando C. **20** 274; **24** 622
Amory, John Heathcoate **5** 195; **10** 367
Ámos, Imre **1** 796*
groups and movements **10** 650; **14** 901; **30** 207
patrons and collectors **30** 212
works **30** 207
Amos, L. A. **7** 859
Amoura, Aziz **17** 655
Amour de l'art, L' *see* PROMÉTHÉE
Amoy *see* XIAMEN
Amozoc **21** 330
Ampach, Christian Leberecht, Baron von **26** 98
Ampang Tinggi **20** 167
Ampharete Stele **2** 687
Amphiaraos Painter **10** 614
amphiboles **21** 241
amphibolite **21** 241
Amphikrates **2** 681
Amphipolis **19** 880; **21** 556
churches **7** 255; **9** 590
coins **13** 587
Lion Tomb **31** 109
mosaics **9** 566
amphiprostyle temples *see under* TEMPLES → types
Amphissa, Hagios Sotirios **9** 547
amphitheatres **1** 796–8*
Rome, ancient **1** 796–7*; **21** 559; **26** 863, 864, 892, 904; **27** 712; **29** 521
Augustan **26** 873, 891
Flavian **26** 895
France **2** *418*; **23** 147; **26** 874
Greece **26** 910
Italy **1** *797*; **25** 198, 748; **26** 789–91*, 888, 889, *894*; **27** 781; **32** 340
Spain **30** *347*
see also STADIA
Amphitrite Painter **13** 538
Amphlett Island **24** 81
Amphora **22** 883
amphorae **1** 798*
historical and regional traditions
Byzantine **9** 632
Central Asia, Western **6** *256*
China **6** 827, 875, *876*, 888
Cyprus, ancient **8** 348
Early Christian (*c.* AD 250-843) **9** 632
Etruscan **10** *594*, 612
Greece, ancient **13** 474, 475, 478, 491, 504, *514*, 514, *591*
Attica **13** *517*, *519*, *522*
Euboia **13** 516
Orientalizing style **13** *501*, *503*
Proto-Attic **13** *501*
Prehistoric art **6** *876*
Rome, ancient **12** *787*; **26** 880, 903; **27** 106
Scythian **28** *324*
Sogdiana **6** *256*
Ukraine **28** *324*
materials
amber **1** 761
bronze **6** 827
glass **12** *787*

amphorae
materials—cont.
pottery **6** *256*; **9** 632; **10** *594*; **13** *492*, *494*, *495*, *501*, *503*, *507*, *510*, *514*, *517*, *519*, *522*, *591*; **27** 106
silver-gilt **28** *324*
types
belly **13** 475, *475*
belly-handled **13** 492, *494*
neck **13** 475, *475*, 491, *492*, *495*, 495, *507*, *510*, 518; **22** 716*
Nolan **13** 475, 536
one-piece **13** 475, *475*, 501
Panathenaic **13** 478, 479, 484, 485, 486, 491, 539
shoulder-handled **13** 491, *494*
transport **13** 474
Type A **32** 43, *44*
uses
domes **26** 903
vaults (ceiling) **26** 903
amphoriskoi **1** 798*; **13** *475*, 477, 536, *593*
Ampurias *see* EMPORIAE
Ampurias, Master of **20** 616*
Ampzing, Samuel **1** 121; **2** 342; **27** 508; **28** 309; **32** 140
ʿAmq *see* AMUK REGION
el-Amra **9** 849; **10** 59
models **9** *849*
Amratian *see* NAQADA
Amreli **15** 450
Amri **33** 538
ʿAmr ibn Layth, Amir (*reg* 879-901) (Saffarid) **23** 161; **28** 616
Amrit **24** 642; **30** *180*
shrine **24** 642
Amritananda **15** 224
Amrit Pal, Ruler (*reg* 1757-78) (Pahari) **15** 632
Amritsar **1** 798*; **15** *264*, *619*
caravanserai of Amanat Khan **15** 375
carpets **16** 485
garden **15** 375
Golden Temple *see* Haramandir
Harmandir **1** 798; **15** 375, *375*, 405; **28** 711
shawls **15** 666
textiles **15** 664
wool **15** 665
Amrit Stele **30** *189*, 194
Amrol **15** 287
Rameshvara Mahadeva **15** 287
Amrullah, Sultan **15** 818
Amsadong **18** 249, *250*, 297
amṣas **21** 545
Amsler, Arnold **33** 736
Amsler, Samuel **7** 870
Amsler en Ruthardt **14** 688
Amstel, Cornelis Ploos van *see* PLOOS VAN AMSTEL, CORNELIS
Amstel, Jan van **1** 799*; **4** *895*; **14** 381; **20** 792; **21** 167
Amsterdam **1** 799–814*, *800*; **22** *813*
academies and art schools
Gerrit Rietveld Academie **22** 908; **26** 379
Instituut voor Kunstnijverheidsonderwijs *see* Gerrit Rietveld Academie
Koninklijke Academie van Beeldende Kunsten **1** 808; **22** 907, 908
Quellinusschool **22** 829, 860
Rijksacademie van Beeldende Kunsten **22** 848, 850, 908
Rijkschool voor Kunstnijverheid **22** 908
Rijksmuseumsschool *see* Quellinusschool
Rijksnormaalschool **22** 908
Stadstekenacademie *see* Koninklijke Academie van Beeldende Kunsten
Amsterdam—cont.
Algemeene Maatschappij van Levensverzekering en Lijfrente **8** 778; **22** 829
American Hotel **22** 830
Amstel Hotel **14** 786; **22** 828; **23** 670, *671*; **26** 190
art forms and materials
architecture **22** 825, 826, 830, 832
books **17** 565; **21** 636
brass **22** 894, 895
bronze **22** 894
cartography **20** 364
ceramics **22** 878
diamonds **17** 522
engravings **10** 391
faience (ii) (ceramics) **25** 309
fans **10** 781
furniture **1** 811*
gables **11** 875
glass **22** 884
gold **22** 889, 897
guns **2** 463
Haggadot **17** 565
interior decoration **1** 802
ketubbot **18** 3
lacquer **18** 614
leather **19** 4
marks **1** 810
metalwork **1** 810–11*
mezzotints **21** 415
murals **22** 333
painting **22** 836, 841–3*
pattern books **24** 274
pewter **1** 810; **22** 893; **24** 579
pigments **24** 795
portraits **1** *807*
scrolls **21** 48
silk **22** 899
silver **22** 885, 887, 888, 891
silver-gilt **1** *811*
stained glass **27** 255
tapestries **22** 897; **30** 318
textiles **22** 899
tiles **22** 881; **30** 878
art market **2** 558
Begijnhof **8** 778
Betondorp *see* housing → Watergraafsmeer
Beursgebouw *see* Koopmansbeurs
botanic garden **4** 483
Burgerweeshuis **22** 832; **30** 391
collections **17** 582; **22** 904
Concertgebouw **7** 687
ecclesiastical buildings
Luthersekerk **23** 502
Maria Magdalenakerk **8** *299*
monastery of St Andries **22** 836
Mozes en Aaron Kerk **22** 828
Nieuwe Kerk **2** 732; **9** 179; **22** 820, 844
metalwork **22** 894
tomb of Commander Jan van Galen **22** 858
Nieuwezijdskapel **22** 821
Noorderkerk **22** 824
Onze Lieve Vrouwe Onbevlekt Ontvangen *see* Posthoorn Kerk
Oude Kerk **1** 811–12*, *812*; **13** 62; **22** 820, 821, 894
Posthoorn Kerk **13** 203
Ronde Kerk *see* Nieuwe Kerk
Westerkerk **4** 785; **18** 9; **22** 824
Zuiderkerk **18** 9; **22** 824
education (art) **3** 617
Exchange **10** 668; **22** 824
see also Koopmansbeurs
Felix Meritis Society building **22** 827
Gemeente Archief **2** 25; **19** 258
guilds **1** 806, 807
Haarlemmerpoort **22** 828
Henri Polaklaan Union Building **3** *787*
houses **1** 800–801; **4** 785
Daniel Soyhier House **32** *589*
Amsterdam
houses—cont.
Herengracht 130 **32** 708
Herengracht 168 *see* Nederlands Theater Instituut
Huis met de Hoofden **1** *802*; **22** 823
Huis Schuylenburch **22** 826
Huis Wassenaer-Obdam **22** 826
Keizersgracht 177 **5** 542
Keizersgracht 672-4 *see* museums → Museum van Loon
Rembrandthuis *see under* museums
housing
Burgesweeshuis **10** *715*
Dijkgraafplein housing complex **18** 138
Het Scheep housing complex **18** *126*
Landlust **21** 156
Muzenhof housing block **8** 669, *670*
P. L. Takstraat **1** *814*
Watergraafsmeer **13** 321, 632
see also tenements
Hubertushuis **22** 832
Kloveniersdoelen **22** 842
Koninklijk Paleis **1** 812–13*; **3** 267, 570; **4** 302; **13** 236; **22** 824–5, 842, 858–9, 866, 871; **25** 812; **31** 239, *239*
collections **1** 807
frescoes **11** 170
furniture **22** 873
interior decoration **10** 187; **25** 810
paintings **4** 250, 846; **18** 11; **19** 349; **23** 675; **26** 168; **33** 261
Raadzaal **4** 846
Koopmansbeurs **3** 787; **4** 788; **10** *668*, 669; **13** 204; **16** 55; **21** 779; **22** 828, 829, *830*, 861; **30** 506
murals **8** 778; **14** 691; **31** 148
see also Exchange
Maagdenhuis **22** 827
museums
Allard Pierson Museum **21** 692
Collectie Six **28** 810
Dutch Maritime Museum *see* Nederlands Historisch Scheepvaartsmuseum
Historisch Museum **11** 233; **17** 841; **19** 832; **22** 906
Joods Historisch Museum **17** 581, 582; **22** 906
Koninklijk Museum *see* Rijksmuseum
Museum Overholland **22** 906
Museum van Aziatische Kunst *see under* Rijksmuseum
Museum van Loon **1** 802; **9** 179
Nederlands Historisch Scheepvaartsmuseum **1** 802; **29** 530
Rembrandthuis **22** 906; **26** 177
drawings **26** 167, 168
paintings **26** 154
prints **26** 177
Rijksmuseum **1** 803, 808; **4** 305; **8** 299; **13** 203; **14** 202; **21** 39; **22** 357, 364, 829, *829*, 906; **30** 504
archives **2** 371
Chinese collection **7** 155
collections **22** 906
directors **2** 229; **24** 745
drawings **2** 25; **26** 177
etchings **26** 177
exhibitions **29** 516
Japanese collection **17** 434
library **22** 909
miniatures **29** 548
Museum van Aziatische Kunst **15** 744; **22** 795
paintings **8** 887; **32** 708
Amsterdam
museums
Rijksmuseum—cont.
photographs **33** 90
portraits **19** 749
prints **1** 12; **2** 136; **14** 563; **20** 693
Rijksprentenkabinet *see* Rijksprentenkabinet
Sri Lankan collection **29** 478
stained glass **29** 516
tapestries **30** 332
textiles **7** 53
Van Heteren collection **14** 42
wallpaper **2** 25
Rijksmuseum Vincent van Gogh **12** 861; **22** 906; **26** 379
Rijksprentenkabinet **22** 906
collections **1** 722; **2** 619; **14** 635; **15** 42, 741; **25** 649; **26** 527; **30** 412
directors **1** 722; **2** 229; **14** 635
drawings **32** 708
Stedelijk Museum **1** 803; **22** 852, 906; **27** 714; **33** 48
archives **2** 371
collections **20** 195; **32** 708
Groenendijk Collection **19** 768
library **22** 909
Tropenmuseum **1** 438; **29** 240
Van Gogh Museum *see* Rijksmuseum Vincent van Gogh
Zoölogisch Museum **14** 817
Nederlands Theater Instituut **22** 209; **33** 262
Olympic Stadium **29** 489
Oud Leyerhoven II **30** 504
Paleis voor Volksvlijt **22** 828; **23** 670
Rijksuniversiteit Library **10** 422; **22** 909
Royal Palace *see* Koninklijk Paleis
Scheepvaarthuis **1** *804*; **10** 698; **21** 58; **22** 861, 867
schools **14** 484
Openluchtschool voor het Gezonde Kind **11** *840*, 841; **22** 831; **28** 158
Stadhuis (1648-) *see* Koninklijk Paleis
stations
Amstelstation **25** 857
Centraal Station **22** 829; **30** 504
Metro stations **21** 350
studios **22** 908
synagogues **17** 544, 548
Jacob Obrechtplein synagogue **17** 548
Portuguese synagogue **1** 813*; **17** 545
ark **17** 570
Talmud Torah synagogue **17** 544
tenements **30** 458
see also housing
Tentoonstellingen van Levende Meesters **7** 677
theatres **30** 665
Leidseplein theatre *see* Schouwburg
Schouwburg **30** 665, 676, 677; **33** 268
Tuschinski Theatre **22** 867, 900; **30** 506
trade **24** 48
Tuschinski Cinema **7** 328
urban planning **7** 293; **9** 746; **31** 714–15
Vincent van Gogh Foundation **12** 861
warehouses **32** 860
Brouwersgracht 272-4 **32** 860
Prinsengracht 219-233 **32** 860
workshops **22** 860
Zeemagazijn *see* museums → Nederlands Historisch Scheepvaartsmuseum
Zoo **33** 698
Amsterdam, Jacob Cornelisz. von *see* CORNELISZ. VAN OOSTSANEN, JACOB
Amsterdam Cabinet, Master of the *see* HOUSEBOOK MASTER
Amsterdam Death of the Virgin, Master of the **20** 616*
Amsterdam Impressionists **14** 47; **22** 850, 851
works **22** *850*
Amsterdam Machzor *see under* MACHZORS → individual manuscripts
Amsterdamsche Joffers **1** 809
Amsterdam school (*fl* 1880s) **19** 654; **32** 392
Amsterdam school (*fl* 1915-30) **1** 814–15*; **4** 788, 789; **22** 875
brick **4** 790
furniture **22** 875
housing **1** *804*, *814*; **3** 788; **18** 126; **21** 58
interior decoration **22** 867–8
members **4** 106, 484; **10** 698; **18** 436, 618
urban planning **1** 804
villas **32** 696
Amsterodamus, Theodorus Bernardus *see* BARENDSZ, DIRCK
Amuda, Tell
sculpture **15** *33*
Amuk period *see under* SYRIA-PALESTINE → periods
Amuk region **1** 815–16*, *821*, 839; **30** *180*
bronze **30** 194
pottery **1** 816
sculpture **1** 815
seals **1** 856, 858, 862
Amul **16** 491; **31** 113
amulet boxes *see under* BOXES → types
Amulet of Charlemagne *see* TALISMAN OF CHARLEMAGNE
amulets **1** 816–19*; **8** 835; **17** 518
historical and regional traditions
Africa **1** 348
Alaska **1** 816
Ancient Near East **1** 817, 855, *856*, 859
Antilles, Lesser **5** 746, 747
Aztec **1** 818
Buddhism **1** 818; **30** 845
Carolingian **5** 807
China **1** 818; **7** 6, 107, 145
Christianity **1** 818
Coptic **1** 818
Egypt, ancient **1** 817, *817*; **3** 441; **10** 3, 20*, 38–9*, *39*, 47, 69–70; **22** 285
Early Dynastic (*c.* 2925-*c.* 2575 BC) **10** 47
Predynastic (*c.* 6000-*c.* 2925 BC) **9** 864; **10** 29, 60
England **17** 516
Gnosticism **1** 818; **12** 251–2*, *252*
Greece, ancient **1** 816, 817; **14** 360
Greenland **13** 620
Helladic **14** 360
Hinduism **1** 818
Indonesia **1** 817
Inuit **1** 816, 818
Islamic **1** 818; **17** 516
Italy **17** 574
Jewish art **1** 817; **17** 574
Mesoamerica, Pre-Columbian **21** 243, 248
Mesopotamia **1** *856*
Mixtec **21** 243, 248
Native North Americans **22** 573, 652
Phoenician **24** 645; **25** 734
Punic **25** 734, 735
Rome, ancient **1** 816, 817; **12** 251–2*, *252*; **26** 485
Scotland **17** 516

amulets
historical and regional traditions—cont.
Spain 17 514, 515, 515
Tibet 30 839, 840, 845
Tuareg 31 406
materials
amber 1 761
blackstone 1 856
bloodstone (chalcedony) 1 817
bone 10 60; 21 248
coral 1 817; 7 834, 835
cornelian 1 817; 10 38; 12 251
diamonds 1 818
faience (i) (glass) 10 3, 47; 25 734
feathers 22 652
feldspar 10 38
frit 10 47
glass 25 734
gold 3 441; 10 38, 39
haematite 12 251, 252, 252
hardstones 10 3
ivory 10 60
jade 1 818; 7 6, 107
jasper 1 817; 10 38; 12 251
jet 1 816; 17 514, 515, 515–16
lapis lazuli 10 38
onyx 12 251
rock crystal 26 485
rubies 1 817
sapphires 1 816, 818
turquoise 10 38
types
design amulets see SEALS → types → seal amulets
Amun, cult of 30 690, 696
Amund 1 819*; 30 76
Amuntefnakht 9 842
Amur cork oak see under OAK → types
Amuzgo 21 736
Aṁvaranātha see AMBARNATH
AMY Architects 15 56; 18 639
Amyklai 13 496; 29 367
Sanctuary of Apollo 29 367
Throne of Apollo 1 692
Amykos Painter 13 525
works 13 526
Amyot, Laurent see AMIOT, LAURENT
Amyrtaios 9 778
An (family) 33 439
'Ana 16 153
congregational mosque 16 152
Anacapri, S Michele Arcangelo 16 735
Anadarko (OK)
St Patrick's Mission School 22 594
Southern Plains Indian Museum and Crafts Center 14 801
Anadolou see ANATOLIA, ANCIENT; TURKEY
Anadolu Hisar 16 206; 21 585
Anadolu Kavak 21 586
anagama see KILNS → types → tunnel
Anaglypha Hadriani 27 38
Anaglypha Trajani see ANAGLYPHA HADRIANI
Anaglypta 32 813, 816
Anagni 1 819–20*; 16 620
Cathedral of S Maria 1 820; 7 921, 922
antependia 16 759
chasubles 16 759
crypt 15 85
frescoes 1 819
sculpture 26 624
textiles 12 462; 23 461
throne 2 348; 30 777
wall paintings 26 653
Anagni, First Master of 1 819
works 1 819
Anagni, Second Master of 1 819
works 1 819
Anagni, Third Master of 1 819
works 1 819
Anago 4 707; 16 880; 33 553
Anahilapataka see PATAN (i) (INDIA)
Anaikodai 29 474
Anaimali, Narasimha Cave 15 303
'Ana Island 14 21, 22
Anak
Tomb 2 18 353
Tomb 3 18 318–19, 328, 373
Tomb of Michon 18 353
Anaka see ARNORAJA
Anak Agung Gedé Meregeg 15 808
Anak Agung Gedé Soberat 15 808
Ana Kai Tangata 9 675
Anakles (fl 6th cent. BC) 23 145
Anakles (fl c. 480-70 BC) 12 247
Anakopia, St Simon Cananeus 12 319
Anakottei 16 864
Anakreon 13 489
Analatos Painter 13 500, 501; 32 30–33*
Anales del Instituto de Arte Americano e Investigaciones Estéticas 24 435
Anales del Instituto de Investigaciones Estéticas 24 435
Analipsis 13 534; 14 354
Analytical Art 24 429
Analytical Art, Masters of see MASTERS OF ANALYTICAL ART
Analytical Cubism see under CUBISM → types
Ana-Maria, Queen of Bulgaria (fl c. 1220-40) 32 149
Aname 31 891
An Amida Butsu see KAIKEI
anamorphosis 14 669; 24 491*; 25 479; 28 313; 29 437
Ananatuba 20 372
Anand, Mulk Raj 4 291
Ananda (fl c. 1st cent. BC) 15 431
Ananda (Burma) see under PAGAN
Anandadeva 3 905
Ananda Muni Shakya 22 785
Ānandapura see VADNAGAR
Anangapala, Ruler (reg c. 993) (Rajput) 8 671
Ananikyan, Hakob 2 433
Anan'in, Ya. A. 29 551
Anan'ino culture 27 367
Anant 1 820*
Anantasayanagudi 14 125
Anantavarman Codaganga, Ruler (reg 1077-1147) (Eastern Ganga) 25 738
Ananuri see under VARDZIA
Anap-chi 18 250
Anaplus, St Michael 9 537
anarchism 13 323; 30 170
Anasazi 1 820*; 21 174; 22 550, 554, 566; 28 898
architecture 5 658; 22 566–7
blankets 22 622
jewellery 22 642
pottery 22 600, 601, 602; 23 565
robes 22 622
textiles 22 623
Anastasi, Giovanni 10 90, 92, 93, 94
Anastasia, Duchess of Mazovia (fl mid-12th cent.) 26 687
Anastasia, Queen of Hungary (fl c. 1050) 9 653
Anastasios I, Emperor of Byzantium (reg 491-518) 9 540, 636, 654; 31 434
coins 9 636
Anastasius, Cardinal (d c. 1125) 26 826
Anastasius, Consul of Rome (c. 517) 18 824
Anastasius IV, Pope (reg 1153-54) 31 121
Anastasov, Rodoljub 1 820*; 19 884
anastylosis 2 323
anathyrosis 13 387
Anatolia see TURKEY
Anatolia, ancient 1 820–40*, 821; 9 512
animal subjects 1 834–5
architecture 1 823, 824, 826, 830–32*; 21 552–3*
basalt 1 829
beige stone 1 857
bit hilani 1 831
brass 1 836
bronze 1 521, 521–2, 825, 834, 835, 836
carpets 2 437
chariots 6 478
chronologies 1 852, 853
collections 1 839*
copper 1 822, 834
arsenical 1 834
electrum 1 834
exhibitions 1 839–40*
felt 10 873
figurines 1 823, 825, 825, 832, 834
forgeries 1 839
fortifications 1 831; 21 552–3*
glass 1 865–6*
gold 1 521, 834, 836, 874
hangings 9 490
human figures 2 504
iconography 1 828–30*, 834–5
inscriptions 1 827, 828, 830; 33 684
iron 1 834, 836
ivory-carvings 1 832
jewellery 1 834, 836, 876
kilims 9 490
languages 1 854
limestone 1 833
looms 30 546
masonry 1 826, 831
metal 21 302
metalwork 1 827, 834, 835–6*, 836
Bronze Age 1 826
Phrygian 1 836*
Prehistoric 1 824–5, 834–5*, 835
Urartian 1 836*
mud-bricks 1 823
museums 1 839*
orthostats 1 831; 33 685
painting 1 118, 838–9*; 2 504, 504; 6 74
palaces 1 824, 826; 23 806–7*
pebbles 22 159
periods 1 823*, 825*
Aceramic Neolithic (c. 8000-c. 6800 BC) 1 852
Assyrian Colony period 1 825
Assyrian Trading Colonies (c. 1920-c. 1740 BC) 1 852
Bronze Age 1 824–7*
Byzantine 1 852
Ceramic Neolithic (c. 6800-c. 5800 BC) 1 852
Chalcolithic 1 824*
Chalcolithic (c. 5800-c. 3400 BC) 1 852
Early Bronze Age (c. 3400-c. 2000 BC) 1 852
Graeco-Roman (332 BC-AD 395) 1 852
Iron Age 1 827–8*
Late Bronze Age (c. 1700-c. 1200 BC) 1 852
Mesolithic 1 823*
Mesolithic (before c. 8000 BC) 1 852
Middle Bronze Age (c. 2000-c. 1700 BC) 1 852
Neolithic 1 823–4*
Palaeolithic 1 823*
pots 18 513
pottery 1 644, 826, 837*; 5 615; 18 513
Black-and-red-on-buff ware 1 838
Brown-on-buff ware 1 837, 838
Cappadocian ware 1 823, 824, 838
Anatolia, ancient
pottery—cont.
Dark-on-light style 1 826
Fantastic style 1 823, 824, 837
Old Hittite ware 1 826, 838; 15 159–60
Prehistoric 1 823, 824, 837, 837–8*; 14 14
Red-on-buff ware 1 838
Toprakkale ware 1 838
religion 1 828–30*
rock art 1 823
rock reliefs 1 827, 828, 829, 832–3*
scripts
alphabetic 1 830
cuneiform 1 830
hieroglyphic 1 827, 855; 17 810
sculpture 1 827, 832*
animal subjects 1 835
architectural 1 832–3*; 17 810
cult statues 8 261
monumental 1 832–3*, 833
Prehistoric 1 823
reliefs 1 522; 5 729; 14 592; 17 810; 33 685
seals 1 826; 2 504
cylinder 1 828, 850, 859, 863; 2 504
stamp 1 827, 855, 856–7, 857
silver 1 824, 834, 835, 836
standards (flags) 1 521
stelae 29 614
stone 1 823
tablets 1 859
temples 1 826; 24 265; 30 432
textiles 1 881
tin 1 850
tombs 1 521–2
trade 1 822–3, 825; 2 639; 9 786; 21 273
flint 1 824
obsidian 1 824
pottery 8 345
weapons 1 834, 835
writing 1 828
see also ANCIENT NEAR EAST; CAPPADOCIA; TROAD
anatomical studies 1 840–45*, 841, 842, 843; 28 205, 206
see also MEDICAL BOOKS
anatomy 1 101; 26 401; 28 205*; 29 424; 32 381
Anatsui, El 12 509; 23 138
Anau 2 599; 6 209
complex of Shaykh Jamal al-Din 6 203
Anavarza Castle 2 427
Anavysos Kouros 13 447
Anawrahta, King of Burma (reg 1044-77) (Pagan) 5 223; 23 761
Anaxagoras of Aigina 1 481, 845*; 13 553
Anaxandra 13 552
Anaxilas 26 288
Anaya, Fernando López see LÓPEZ ANAYA, FERNANDO
Anaya, Franklin 21 3
Anazarba Castle see ANAVARZA CASTLE
Anba' 16 149
al-Anbar 3 51; 16 277
Ança 26 611
Ancaiani (family) 29 422
Ancaster 10 227
Anceau, Pierre 4 536
Ancelet 25 691
Ancelet, Gabriel Auguste 32 83
Anceschi, Giovanni 2 528; 13 728
Ancher, Cardinal 31 385
Ancher, Anna (Kirstine) 1 845, 846*
groups and movements 8 735; 18 470; 28 814
teachers 18 544
Ancher, Helga 1 845
Ancher, Michael (Peter) 1 845–6*
groups and movements 8 735; 18 470; 28 814
Ancher, Michael (Peter)—cont.
works 1 846
Ancher, Mortlock, Murray & Woolley 22 339; 33 373
Ancher, Mortlock & Woolley 33 373
Ancher, Sydney (Edward Cambrian) 1 846–7*; 2 742; 30 160, 161
Ancheta, Juan de 1 847*; 29 290; 32 98
Ancheval (family) 22 452
An Ch'i see An Qi
Anchialos see POMORIE
Anchieta, Juan de see ANCHETA, JUAN DE
Anchi Kaigetsudō see KAIGETSUDŌ ANCHI
Anchi Monastery 12 328
Anchin Abbey 3 641; 26 668
anchor beams see under BEAMS → types
Anchor Building Bricks 31 258
Anchorites 24 82
An Chung-sik 1 847–8*; 18 57, 59, 193
pupils 33 534
Anciau de Cens 25 694
Ancient Near East 1 848–96*, 849; 21 267
alabastra 1 867
alphabets 1 850, 855*, 893
altars 1 690*
amulets 1 817, 855, 856, 859
apadanas 24 483
archaeology 1 851–3*
architectural decorations 1 879*
architecture 1 851; 4 771; 21 287, 552–4*
armlets 1 876
armour 1 887
basketwork 1 879
beads 1 864, 883
beakers 1 866
beds 1 890
beige stone 1 857
bells 1 891
blackstone 1 856
body arts 1 855
bowls 1 867, 878
boxes 24 336, 336
bracelets 1 875
brass 4 681
brick 1 879; 4 769, 771
bronze 9 150; 21 711; 30 774; 31 530
casemates 21 552
ceramics 1 877
chairs 1 890; 30 774
chalcedony 1 858
chariots 6 479–80*
chronologies 1 851–3*, 852; 14 335
citadels 24 482
clay 4 771; 20 326
coins 1 888–9*, 888
collections 1 895–6*
containers 1 878
coral 1 876
cornelian 1 873, 873
cotton 1 880
craftsmen and artists 1 859
cream stone 1 856
damask 30 551
dating methods 1 851–3*
dealing 1 895–6*
doors 9 150*
dress 1 883–8*, 884
drums (musical instruments) 1 891
dyeing 1 880
earrings 1 874, 876
earthenwares 1 877
elephant tusks 1 868
faience (i) (glass) 1 877–9*, 878; 31 531
figurines 10 461; 31 530
flax 1 879
forgeries 1 875, 896*

Ancient Near East—cont.
fortifications 21 552–4*, 553
furniture 1 866, 867, 890*
gardens 12 66*
courtyard 12 66
garnets 1 876
glass 1 864–8*, 867, 877; 12 785; 28 384
gold-glass 1 867
mosaic 1 865, 866
glazes 1 877; 4 769; 6 333
goblets 1 878
gold 1 873–5, 873, 876; 21 III1; 31 531
gold leaf 1 867
greenstone 1 859
gypsum 29 814
harps 1 891
headdresses 1 873, 883, 884, 885
helmets 1 883
hippopotamus teeth 1 868
human figures 2 504
iconography 1 859
ideograms 1 853
inlays 1 865, 867, 869; 24 336, 336
inscriptions 1 854, 855, 859, 860, 891, 895; 2 299
interlace 15 881, 882
irrigation systems 12 66
ivory 1 868–9*; 14 353; 30 774
ivory-carvings 1 866–7, 869–72*, 869, 870, 871, 872, 890; 16 797; 24 336, 336; 29 395; 31 531
jasper 1 857
jewellery 1 872–6*, 873, 877, 879
jugs 1 867
lapis lazuli 1 873, 873
libraries 19 311*
limestone 22 511; 29 614
logograms 1 853
looms 1 880
lutes 1 891
lyres 1 890–91
marbling 1 865
mats 1 879
metalwork 1 853, 874
mirrors 21 711*
mosaics 1 889–90*; 27 64
moulds 1 865
mud-bricks 4 772; 23 806
musical instruments 1 890–91*
narratives 22 510–11*, 511
necklaces 1 873
ornament 23 532*
painting 2 504, 504; 12 511; 27 57; 30 197
palaces 23 806–7*
palettes 1 867
papyrus 1 854
pearls 1 876
pendants (jewellery) 1 855, 877
periods
Aceramic Neolithic 1 852
Akkadian (c. 2340-c. 2113 BC) 1 852
Assyrian Trading Colonies (c. 1920-c. 1740 BC) 1 852
Babylonian (c. 747-c. 539 BC) 1 852
Bronze Age 1 852
Ceramic Neolithic 1 852
Chalcolithic 1 852
Early Bronze Age 1 852
Early Dynastic (c. 2900-c. 2340 BC) 1 852
Elamite (c. 3500-c. 7th cent. BC) 1 852
Epipalaeolithic 1 852
Graeco-Roman (332 BC-AD 395) 1 852
Halaf (c. 5500-c. 4500 BC) 1 852
Hassuna (c. 6000-c. 5000 BC) 1 852
Late Bronze Age 1 852
Mesolithic 1 852
Middle Assyrian (c. 1363-c. 1157 BC) 1 852

Ancient Near East
periods—cont.
Middle Bronze Age 1 852
Neo-Assyrian (c. 883-c. 612 BC) 1 852
Neolithic 1 852
Old Babylonian (c. early 19th cent.-c. 1595 BC) 1 852
pre-Pottery Neolithic 1 852
proto-Hassuna (before c. 6000 BC) 1 852
Samarra (c. 5500-c. 5000 BC) 1 852
Ubaid (c. 5th millennium BC) 1 852
Ur III (c. 2112-c. 2004 BC) 1 852
Uruk (c. 4000-c. 2900 BC) 1 852
pictographs 1 853, 854
pigments 1 877, 878, 880
pins 1 884
pipes (musical) 1 891
plaques 1 865, 870, 879
plaster 29 814–16*
pottery 6 333; 22 341; 24 336
printing 1 855
propaganda 25 650
ramparts 4 772
rediscovery 1 891–5*
reeds 20 326
rings 1 857, 864, 874, 876
rock crystal 26 485
ruin mounds 1 851
sarcophagi 27 825*
scarabs 1 857*, 857
scripts 1 850, 854–5*
alphabetic 1 851, 893
cuneiform 1 850, 851, 853–4*, 854, 893, 895; 24 481
demotic 1 854
hieratic 1 854
hieroglyphic 1 855
Indus Valley 1 854
Pehlevi 1 858
Proto-Canaanite 1 855
Proto-Sinaitic 1 855
Ugarit 1 855
sculpture
cult statues 8 261
relief 4 769; 22 511; 25 880; 26 134; 31 530
seals 1 855*, 868, 877–8, 883, 886; 2 504
conoid 1 857
cylinder 1 853, 856, 858–60*, 859, 861, 862–3, 874; 2 504; 22 510
ring 1 857
seal amulets 1 856
stamp 1 855–8*, 856, 857, 858, 864
stamp-cylinder 1 863
Sumerian 10 802
votive 1 859
sewing 1 879
shells 1 869
signatures 1 859
silk 1 880, 882; 30 551, 552
silver 1 873, 888
soapstone 1 856, 857
sphinxes 29 394–5*, 395
spinning (textile) 1 880
stelae 24 335; 29 613–14*, 614
stone 9 150
stone-carvings 24 335
stools 30 774
straw 4 771
stucco 29 813, 814–16*
styluses 20 326
surveyors 30 25
syllabograms 1 853
tablets 1 859, 859
tapestries 1 880
tells 1 851*
temples 30 431–2*
terracotta 9 150
textiles 1 855, 856, 879–83*, 882; 30 774
thrones 1 890; 30 774*

Ancient Near East—cont.
tokens 1 855
trade 1 850–51, 869, 872, 876, 880–81, 882
turquoise 1 873
vases 1 867
villages 2 639
weaving 1 879, 880, 882; 30 552
wool 1 880
writing 1 851, 853–5*, 854, 893; 10 1; 20 326
writing-tablets 1 851, 865, 868, 895; 19 311; 20 326
see also ANATOLIA, ANCIENT; EGYPT, ANCIENT; IRAN, ANCIENT; MESOPOTAMIA; NABATAEA; SYRIA-PALESTINE
Ancients 1 897*; 5 444; 10 252; 23 884
members 4 121; 26 353
Ancients and Moderns, Quarrel of the 1 897–8*; 2 171; 7 840; 21 778; 24 170
Ancier, Fernand Gauthiot d' see GAUTHIOT D'ANCIER, FERNAND
Ancino, Pietro 2 456
Anckerman, Daniel 1 898–9*; 29 840; 30 85
El Ancón (Mexico) 21 260
Ancón (Panama) 23 902
Canal Administration building 23 904
Ancón (Peru) 13 229; 23 703
cemetery 28 651
Ancona 2 1–2*; 16 620; 26 886
Arch of Trajan 10 742; 26 868, 897; 31 349
Cathedral of S Ciriaco 16 625
coins 7 535
ketubbot 18 3
Lazaretto 31 894
Loggia dei Mercanti 2 2
Museo Archeologico Nazionale delle Marche 2 2
Palazzo Ferretti 30 801
Pinacoteca Comunale 2 2
synagogue 17 545
Ancona, Andrea d' see LILLI, (GIOVANNI) ANDREA
Ancona, Cyriac of see CYRIAC OF ANCONA
Ancona, Nicola d' see BERTUZZI, NICOLA
Ancona, Paolo D' see D'ANCONA, PAOLO
Anconitano, l' see BERTUZZI, NICOLA
Ancora, Pietro 22 714
Ancourt, Edward 19 489; 20 603
Ancram (NY) 31 652
Ancram, Robert Kerr, 1st Earl of see KERR, ROBERT, 1st Earl of Ancram
Ancus Marcius 23 619
Ancy-le-Franc Château 11 513, 572, 656; 25 790; 28 467, 468; 32 551
Chambre de Diane 13 700
gardens 12 113
Ancyra see ANKARA
aṇḍa 15 242*
Andachtsbilder 2 2–4*, 3; 8 595, 836; 27 499
Germany 2 3; 24 776
Gothic 13 115, 116, 129
Holy Roman Empire (before 1648) 13 115, 116
Andahuaylillas 24 498
aṇḍaka see ANDA
Andalusia (PA) 13 611
andalusī script see under SCRIPTS → types
Andamandans 29 445
Andaman Islands 10 580
Andarznāma 16 295
Andechs 24 36
Abbey 22 305

Andechs-Istrien, Berchtold V, Markgraf von 15 863
Andeli, Jean d' see JEAN D'ANDELI
Andenne 3 588, 590, 591
Anderberg, Axel 30 73
Andere, Das 19 651
Anderen, De 9 62; 29 397; 33 154
Anderle, Jiří 2 4*
Anderlini, Pietro 11 20
Andernach 25 490, 492
Liebfrauenkirche 26 633
Andernos-les-Bains 9 510, 530
Andersen, A. 17 479
Andersen, David 23 236
Andersen, Gunnar Aagaard see AAGAARD ANDERSEN, GUNNAR
Andersen, Hans see BRENDEKILDE, H(ANS) A(NDERSEN)
Andersen, Hans Christian 11 798
Andersen, Hendrick Christian 10 689; 33 150
Andersen, Just 8 751, 752
Andersen, Lorents 23 238
Andersen, Mogens 8 755
Andersen, Nils 9 427
Andersen, Robin Christian 2 876; 14 33; 23 2
Andersen, Troels 8 762
Andersen Nordmand, Peder 8 733
Andersen Riber, Lauritz 8 733
Anders målare see LARSSON, ANDERS
Anderson, A. Hamilton 5 696
Anderson, Alexander 2 4*
Anderson, Amos 11 112
Anderson, Amos, Museum of Art see under HELSINKI
Anderson, Beckwith and Haible 3 682
Anderson, Colin 22 751
Anderson, Domenico 2 5
Anderson, Elizabeth Garrett 5 66
Anderson, Enfred 19 501
Anderson, Forster and Wilcox 33 205
Anderson, George 3 61
Anderson, James 2 4–5*; 16 777
Anderson, James, photograph collection see under FLORENCE → museums → Museo della Fotografie Fratelli Alinari
Anderson, J. McVicar 29 768
Anderson, John (c. 1612-17) 16 897
Anderson, John, 1st Viscount Waverley (1882-1958) 2 560
Anderson, Lars 17 368
Anderson, Laurie 2 5*
groups and movements 10 882
works 24 403, 408, 409
Anderson, Margaret 8 435
Anderson, Millbank 14 813
Anderson, Paul 24 739
Anderson, (William) Peirce 5 274, 275; 13 271
Anderson, Robin 17 907
Anderson, (Robert) Rowand 2 5*
assistants 4 37, 884
groups and movements 28 289
pupils 19 689; 21 731; 28 173
staff 31 375
works 12 775; 28 230, 249, 250, 272; 29 797
Anderson, Rowand, Paul & Partners 29 379
Anderson, Sophie 6 451
Anderson, Stanley 10 397
Anderson and Anderson 33 602
Anderson & Hannaford 5 126
Anderson-Pelham, Charles, 1st Earl of Yarborough 12 598; 23 189
Andersson, Johann Gunnar
ceramics 6 925
collections 7 156
excavations 3 186; 7 159; 19 640, 894; 20 142; 25 782
Andersson, Petter 30 110

Andersson, Torsten 30 81
Andersson, Willy 30 103
Anderton, George 14 131
andesite (volcanic) see under LIMESTONE → types
Andhra see SATAVAHANA
Andino, Cristóbal de 29 290, 339
Andino, Dante Lazarroni see LAZARRONI ANDINO, DANTE
Andino, Silvestre 25 701
Andiparos see ANTIPAROS
andirons 11 118–19; 31 653
Andizhan 31 781, 782
Museum 6 283
textiles 16 451; 31 783
Andjar see 'ANJAR (LEBANON)
Andlau, Peter Hemmel von see HEMMEL VON ANDLAU, PETER
Andlau Abbey Church 2 6*; 11 504; 26 633
Andō, Hidetake 17 267
Ando, Tadao 2 6–7*; 17 53, 92; 23 595
works 2 7; 17 92
Andoche 5 364
Andō Denzen 17 165
Andō Hiroshige 2 7–9*; 9 738; 17 287–8
book illustrations 17 273, 290
collaboration 17 290; 31 53
groups and movements 31 764
paintings 17 177
patrons and collectors 10 487
prints 2 9; 15 129; 17 288; 31 53, 81
pupils 17 290
teachers 17 288; 31 766
Ando Kaigetsudō see KAIGETSUDŌ ANDO
Andokides 13 484; 32 31, 40, 54, 65
Andokides Painter 13 517; 32 31*
pupils 13 519; 23 145
works 13 517, 517–18; 32 54
Andong 18 248, 250
calligraphy 18 329
Iosan sŏwŏn 18 271
pagodas 4 795; 23 775
Pongjŏng Temple 18 254, 265, 268, 268
Yich'ŏn 18 293
Andoni-Ibeno 15 61
Andonov, Nikolay 27 397
Andonov Papradiški, Dimitrija 19 884
Andorra 2 9–10*; 29 258
Andorra la Vella
Casa de la Vall see Museo de Arte e Historia de Andorra
Museo de Arte e Historia de Andorra 2 10
Andover (MA), Addison Gallery of American Art 31 668
Andra 24 82
Andrada, Ramón 10 498
Andrade, Alfredo (Cesare Reis Freire) de 2 10*; 16 678
groups and movements 28 318
works 12 284
Andrade, Carlos Endara see ENDARA ANDRADE, CARLOS
Andrade, Domingo de 5 911; 12 56; 18 598; 29 270
Andrade, Jaime 2 10–11*; 9 713
patrons and collectors 9 714
works 2 387; 9 714
Andrade, José zan see ZAN
Andrade, Lázario di 10 569
Andrade, Manuel Costa see COSTA ANDRADE, MANUEL
Andrade, Manuel Gomes de see GOMES DE ANDRADE, MANUEL
Andrade, Mário de 4 725, 727, 729; 27 808; 30 348
Andrade, Oswald de 4 717; 28 394; 30 348; 33 317
Andrae, J. V. 31 720
Andrae, Walter 1 889, 892; 3 9, 10; 14 224; 18 797; 28 47

Andras, Catherine **2** 11*
Andrault, Michel **2** 11
Andrault and Parat **2** 11*; **6** 534
Andravida **2** 11*
André, Albert **2** 12*; **31** 853
André, Carl **2** 12–13*; **21** 124; **30** 201
 groups and movements **1** 80; **21** 645
 patrons and collectors **32** 623
 works **1** 738; **2** *12*; **15** 869; **21** *646*; **31** 615
André, Charles **2** 13
André, C. K. **8** 424
André, Edouard (*b* 1827) **1** 685; **24** 179
André, Edouard (-François) (1833-94) **16** 851*
André, Emile **2** 13*, 564; **22** 456
André, François **2** 13
André, Gaspar **19** 847
Andre, Hans **15** 866
André, Jean **2** 13–14*; **4** 391
André, Johann Anton **19** 481, 482; **28** 404
André, Jules **13** 732
André, Louis-Jules **2** 14*
 pupils **5** 875; **8** 626; **18** 664; **26** 338
André, Matyáš **6** 363
André, Peter Friedrich **19** 483
André, Philipp **6** 402; **19** 482
André, Piètre **2** 14*; **31** 842
André, Yves-Marie **2** 15*
Andrea, Benedetto di Domenico d' *see* BENEDETTO DI DOMENICO D'ANDREA
Andrea, Giuliano di ser *see* GIULIANO DI SER ANDREA
Andrea (di Giusto), Giusto d' *see* GIUSTO DI ANDREA (DI GIUSTO)
Andrea, John de **23** 297
Andrea, Paolo d' *see* PAOLO D'ANDREA
Andréa, Pat **14** 43
Andrea, Petrus *see* PETRUS ANDREA
Andrea, Ristoro di *see* RISTORO DI ANDREA
Andrea, Salvi d' *see* SALVI D'ANDREA
Andrea, Zohan **24** 271
Andrea Alovigi d'Assisi *see* INGEGNO, L'
Andrea da Bologna *see* ANDREA DEI BRUNI
Andrea (di Guido) da Fiesole **2** 15*; **13** 96
Andrea da Firenze (i) (*fl* 1343-77) **2** 15–16*; **24** 860
 works **1** 654; **2** *16*; **3** 249; **9** 108; **11** 196; **16** 655; **24** 855
Andrea da Firenze (ii) (1388-1455) **2** 17*; **24** 731
Andrea d'Agnolo *see* SARTO, ANDREA DEL
Andrea da Murano **2** 17–18*; **32** 225, 655
Andrea da Pontedera *see* PISANO (ii), ANDREA
Andrea da Trebisonda **26** 815
Andrea da Treviso **1** 531; **30** 914
Andrea de Fesulis *see* ANDREA (DI GUIDO) DA FIESOLE
Andrea de Giusto **9** 96
Andrea dei Bruni **2** 18*; **20** 695; **32** 626
Andrea del Castagno *see* CASTAGNO, ANDREA DEL
Andrea de Lodi **12** 906
Andrea del Sarto *see* SARTO, ANDREA DEL
Andrea del Verrocchio *see* VERROCCHIO, ANDREA DEL
Andrea di Andreas **7** 922
Andrea di Bartolo *see* CINI, ANDREA DI BARTOLO
Andrea di Bartolo di Simone di Bargiella *see* CASTAGNO, ANDREA DEL
Andrea di Bonaiuto *see* ANDREA DA FIRENZE (i)
Andrea di Cione *see* CIONE, ANDREA DI
Andrea di Cosimo *see* FELTRINI, ANDREA (DI GIOVANNI DI LORENZO)
Andrea di Giusto (Manzini) **2** 19*; **12** 765
 attributions **20** 532
 collaboration **13** 260; **20** 748
 teachers **20** 533
Andrea di Jacopo d'Ognabene **2** 19*; **24** 874
Andrea di Nerio **2** 19*, 389; **29** 403, 404
Andrea di Niccolò (di Giacomo) **2** 20*; **29** 362
Andrea di Niccolò da Durazzo *see* ALESSI, ANDREA
Andrea di Nino **24** 876
Andrea di Onofrio **2** 17
Andrea Doria see under SHIPS → named vessels
Andreae, August Heinrich **14** 212; **27** 334, 335
Andreae, Hieronymus **33** 353
Andrea Manfredi da Faenza **4** 279
Andreani, Aldo **20** 321; **23** 263
Andreani, Andrea **2** 20*; **32** 407; **33** 365, 367
Andreas **7** 922; **25** 865
Andreas, Andrea di *see* ANDREA DI ANDREAS
Andreas, Archbishop of Bari **3** 234
Andreasi, Ippolito **2** 20–21*; **20** 321
 collaboration **12** 558
 patrons and collectors **29** 738
 works **12** *754*, 909; **31** 35; **32** 404
Andreas Johannis **8** 731
Andreas Martini *see* ÖRJAN THE PAINTER
Andrea (di) Vanni (d'Andrea Salvani) **2** 21*; **28** 676
 patrons and collectors **27** 359
 pupils **24** 28
André d'Ypres **20** 703
Andree, Adolphus Wilhelmus (*b* 1799) **2** 21
Andree, Adolphus William (*fl* 1860-80) **2** 21
Andree, A(dolphus) W(illiam) (1869-1910) **2** 21*
Andrée, Johannes H. **22** 884
Andreescu, Ioan **2** 21–2*; **26** 714, 723
Andreev, Aleksandr **5** 156
Andreini, Pietro Andrea **2** 22*; **12** 661; **21** 27
Andreini, Roggio **19** 51
Andreino degli Impicchati *see* CASTAGNO, ANDREA DEL
Andreis, António Carlos **27** 800
Andreith, Anton **5** 667
Andrejević, Mileta **28** 451
Andrejević-Kun, Djordje **28** 451
Andreoli, Giorgio **2** 22–3*; **13** 773; **16** 734; **22** 111
Andreoli, Giovanni **2** 22
Andreoli, Salimbene **2** 22
Andreoli, Ubaldo **2** 23
Andreoli, Vincenzo **2** 23
Andreoni, Luis **22** 24; **31** 753
Andreozzi, Antonio Francesco **6** 86; **11** 23; **24** 696
Andres, Johan *see* ANHTONI, GIOVANNI
Andrés, Juan Francisco **1** 466
Andrés de Arriba, Manuel **29** 342
Andrés de Nájera **2** 23*; **14** 609; **32** 493
Andrés de San Juan *see* ANDRÉS DE NÁJERA
Andresen, Andreas **2** 23*
Andreu **13** 169
Andreu, Paul **24** 132
Andréu, Ramon **12** 739
Andreville *see* ANDRAVIDA
André Virgin, Master of the **20** 616*
Andrew (*fl* 1418) **19** 750; **31** 557
Andrew, Prince of Liechtenstein (*reg c.* 1694) **5** 295
Andrew I, King of Hungary (*reg* 1046-60) **14** 883
Andrew III, King of Hungary (*reg* 1290-1301) **16** 745
Andrew Lundy's Primer **28** 234
Andrews, Benny **1** 445
Andrews, Emily J. Harding **10** 878
 works **10** *877*
Andrews, Frances **11** *907*
Andrews, George T. **14** 863; **33** 545
Andrews, Gordon **2** 759
Andrews, John (*fl* 1577) **10** 273
Andrews, John (Hamilton) (*b* 1933) **2** 23*; **5** 602
 works **2** 743; **5** 562; **7** 896
Andrews, Michael **2** 23–4*; **19** 246; **23** 249
Andrews, Robert **11** *907*
Andrews, Roy Chapman **21** 885
Andrews, Thomas **17** 516
Andrews, William **18** 5; **19** 431
Andrews & Jacques **14** 517; **28** 193
Andrey **25** 343
Andreyev, Leonid **23** 391
Andreyev, Nikolay (Andreyevich) (i) (1873-1932) **2** 24*; **22** 173; **27** 392
Andreyev, Nikolay (Platonovich) (ii) (1882-1947) **2** 24*; **27** 394
Andreyev, Pyotr **27** 420
Andrey I Bogolyubsky, Prince of Suzdal'-Vladimir (*reg* 1157-75) **27** 369, 437; **31** 554
Andri, Ferdinand **2** 803; **28** 344
Andriake **9** 537; **19** 837
Andrianampoinimerina **20** 40
Andriantopoieion **11** 140
Andries (family) **2** 201
Andries, Frans **2** 25; **3** 588; **29** 326
Andries, Guido (*d* 1541) **2** 24–5*; **30** 878
 works **2** 201; **3** 575, 588
 workshop **10** 273
Andries, Guido (1535/41-*c.* 1587) **2** 25
Andries, J. **17** 471
Andries, Jaspar **2** 25; **10** 303; **30** 877
Andries, Jodocus **17** 471
Andries, Joris **2** 25; **30** 878
Andries, Lucas **2** 25
Andriessen, Anthonie **2** 25*
Andriessen, Christiaan **2** 25
Andriessen, Jurriaan **1** 807, 808; **2** 25*; **22** 847
 assistants **2** 25; **13** 295
 collaboration **23** 299
 patrons and collectors **12** 620
 pupils **31** 368; **32** 693
Andriessen, Mari **22** 861
Andrieu, Master *see* BEAUNEVEU, ANDRÉ
Andrieu, Bertrand **2** 25–6*; **8** 770; **12** 177; **20** 924
Andrieu, Pierre **8** 644, 645; **24** 838
Andrijić, Josip **9** 330
Andrijić, Nikola **9** 330
Andrijić, Petar **9** 331
Andriolis, Elviras **19** 498
Andriti, Andrea **13** 163
Andriyevsky, V. A. **27** 409
Androkydes of Kyzikos **13** 545, 548, 551, 554
Androna **9** 540
andrones **13** 383, 386, 556; **23** 434
Andronicos, Manolis **2** 26*
Andronikos I, Emperor of Byzantium (*reg* 1183-85) **9** 638
Andronikos II, Emperor of Byzantium (*reg* 1282-1328) **9** 629
Andronikos of Kyrrhos **2** 26*, 668
Andronov, Nikolay **28** 919
Andronovo culture **28** 321
Andropolis **7** 825
Andros **8** *304*; **13** *363*, 497
 Museum of Modern Art, B. & E. Goulandris Foundation **13** 359
Androuet Du Cerceau *see* DU CERCEAU
Andrup, Otto **8** 762
Andrzejewski, Marian **25** 409
Åndsindustri **24** 451
Andújar **27** 107
Anecameca **27** 499
Anedjib **9** *776*
Anegondi **14** 125
 Uchhayappa *maṭha* **15** 648
Aneho **1** *386*
 Museum **31** 74
Aneityum **31** 890, 891
Anemospilia Temple **1** 691; **2** 305
Anemurium **9** 564, 565
 church **9** 565
Anesi, Paolo **2** 26–7*
 assistants **21** 831
 patrons and collectors **3** 840
 pupils **33** 714
Anesi, Pietro **2** 26
Anet, Claude **16** 555
Anet Château **2** *27*, 27–8*; **4** 780; **6** 506; **11** *504*, 514, 572, 656; **19** *691*, 691–2; **24** 117
 Cabinet des Singes **28** 776
 Chapel **6** 506; **19** *691*
 frontispiece **9** *312*
 gardens **12** 120, 122
 interior decoration **8** 856
 locks **16** 59
 sculpture **6** 142; **11** 265
 tapestries **11** 639
Anfray, Francis **1** 512, 513
aṅga **15** 243*
Angami **15** 733
Angang-Eltz, Burgkapelle **7** 299
Angarano **16** 735
Angas, George French **1** 152; **2** 745; **23** 57
Angaur *see* NGEAUR
Angawi, Sami **27** 875
Ang Chan I, King of Cambodia (*reg c.* 1510-60) **2** 56
Ang Chan II, King of Cambodia (*reg* 1806-34) **5** 481
Ang Duong **5** 504
Angel, Abraham **21** 388
Ángel, Miguel **2** 397
Angel(o), Pedro **2** 28*
Angel, Philips (i) (1616-83) **2** 28–9*
Angel, Philips (ii) (1618-64) **2** 28, 29*; **14** 584
Angel Card, Abraham **2** 29*
Angel Cuadros, Miguel *see* CUADROS, MIGUEL ANGEL
Angelelli, Massimiliano Malvezzi, Marchese *see* MALVEZZI ANGELELLI, MASSIMILIANO, Marchese
Angeles Ortiz, Manuel **2** 29–30*; **29** 286
Angeletti, Pietro **4** 407
Angeli (family) **9** 638
Angeli, Filippo d' *see* NAPOLETANO, FILIPPO
Angeli, Franco **26** 778
Angeli, Giuseppe **24** 707, 894
Angeli, Heinrich von **2** 30*
 patrons and collectors **14** 148, 656
 pupils **13** 215; **18** 387
Angelico, Fra **2** 30–40*; **7** 905; **16** 661; **26** 765
 assistants **3** 99; **13** 259; **27** 729
 copies **18** 527
 frames **11** 381, 382, 384
 methods **11** 184; **24** 492
Angelico, Fra—cont.
 paintings **19** 442
  frescoes **16** 659; **26** 184
   Cappella di S Brizio (Cathedral of the Assumption, Orvieto) **23** 586; **24** 523; **28** 702
   Chapel of Nicholas V (Vatican Palace, Rome) **2** *38*; **26** 765, 817
   Monastery of S Marco (Florence) **2** *36*, *37*; **7** 218, 457; **9** 109; **21** 468; **27** 495; **32** *807*
  panel **2** *32*, *33*; **22** 521, *522*
   altarpieces **1** 711; **2** *32*; **6** 466; **9** 98, 109; **11** 185; **19** 681; **24** 520
 patrons and collectors
  Altman, Benjamin **1** 731
  Bardini, Stefano **3** 228
  Chalandon, Georges, the elder (*fl* 1890s) **6** 393
  Cosimo, Lord of Florence (*reg* 1434-64) **21** 10
  Dominican Order **9** 112
  Fesch, Joseph, Cardinal **11** 32
  Gondi, Bartolomeo **12** 897
  Henry, Bon-Thomas **14** 395
  His de La Salle, (Aimé-Charles-) Horace **14** 577
  Leopold I, King of Belgium (*reg* 1831-65) **7** 490
  Lerma, Francisco Gómez de Sandoval y Rojas, Duque de **27** 723
  Nicholas V, Pope (*reg* 1447-55) **23** 97
  Straus, Percy Selden **29** 763
  Strozzi, Palla (di Nofri) **29** 781
  Wicar, Jean-Baptiste (-Joseph) **33** 154
 pupils **9** 96; **12** 712; **13** 259; **29** 785
 reproductive prints by others **2** 576
 restorations by others **17** 644; **19** 677
Angelini, Costanzo **2** 40*
 collaboration **14** 114; **32** 689
 pupils **4** 333; **22** 78, 97
Angelini, Francesco Maria **1** 597
Angelini, Giandomenico **13** 275
Angelini, Giuseppe **4** 181; **24** 845, 846
Angelini, Luigi **3** 770
Angelini, Orazio **18** 778; **22** 481
Angelini, Tito **2** 40; **9** 177; **22** 480
Angelion **8** 458, 688; **17** 742
Angélique, Mère *see* ARNAULD, JACQUELINE MARIE ANGÉLIQUE
Angelis, Desiderio de **22** 481
Angelis, Domenico de **24** 734; **25** 8
Angelis, Giovanni de **24** 734
Angelis, Sabatino de **12** 612
Angelis, S. de & Son **29** 573
Angell, Samuel **13** 612; **28** 385
Angell, Truman O. **22** 126; **27** 642; **30** 450
Angellini, Giuseppe **1** 466
Angellis, Pieter **2** 40–41*; **3** 562
Ângelo, António **2** 41*; **25** 307, 814
Angelo, Filippo d' *see* NAPOLETANO, FILIPPO
Angelo, Francesco d' **28** 367
Angelo, Jacomo de Flandria de *see* JACOMO DE FLANDRIA DE ANGELO
Angelo, Lodovico di *see* LODOVICO DI ANGELO
Angelo, Nicolaus de *see* NICOLAUS DE ANGELO
Angelo da Lecco **9** 75
Angelo da Orvieto **2** 41–2*
 works **13** 772, *773*
Angelo da Tivoli **31** 57

Angelo (di Pietro) del Macagnino (da Siena) 2 42*; 10 519; 13 755; 31 429
Angelo de Lodensanis 25 249
Angelo de Paolo 23 109
Ângelo (César Cardoso) de Sousa 2 42*
Angelo di Lippo 31 513
Angelo di Marco 28 745
Angelo di Pietro d'Assisi 2 42*
Angeloni, Francesco 2 42–3*; 3 673; 5 866
Angeloni, Giovanni 7 412; 25 411; 31 679
Angeloni, Vincenzo 31 679
Angelos, Isaak II, Emperor of Byzantium *see* ISAAK II ANGELOS, Emperor of Byzantium
Angelot de la Presse 31 842
Angelrot, Balthasar 14 666
Angeluccio 2 43*; 6 347; 7 399; 21 483
Angelus de Trivio 9 304
Ang Eng, King of Cambodia (*reg* 1779-96) 5 481
Angennes, d' (family) 25 872
Angennes, Catherine de Vivonne d', Marquise de Rambouillet *see* RAMBOUILLET, Marquise de
Angennes, Charles d', Marquis de Rambouillet *see* RAMBOUILLET, CHARLES D'ANGENNES, Marquis de
Angennes, Julie Lucine d' 17 449
Anger, Kenneth 10 688
Anger, Roger 25 211
Angera, Master of 21 523
Angeren, Antoon Derkzen van *see* DERKZEN VAN ANGEREN, ANTOON
Angerer, Victor 18 127
Angermair, Christoph 2 43–5*; 12 460; 22 302
  patrons and collectors 33 274
  pupils 24 543
  teachers 8 626
  works 2 *44*, *45*; 12 460, *460*
Angermeyer, Johann Adalbert 5 338; 8 391
Angers 2 45–51*; 11 *504*
  Château et Galerie de l'Apocalypse 2 48–9*, *49*; 8 278; 21 565; 30 331; 31 478
    collections 30 332
    tapestries 11 155; 14 75
    see also APOCALYPSE TAPESTRIES
  ecclesiastical buildings
    Benedictine Abbey 26 670
    Cathedral of St Maurice 2 46*, *46*; 11 513; 13 37; 26 570; 32 94
      doors 11 624
      sculpture 2 47*, *47*; 13 73
      stained glass 13 180; 26 471, 702; 29 501
      tapestries 2 51; 11 639
      textiles 30 313
      tomb of Renné I and Isabella of Lorraine 13 79
      wall paintings 13 142
    Notre-Dame-de-Ronceray 26 599
    St Aubin 2 47–8*; 26 599
      capitals 26 599
      chapter house 6 467
      cloister 7 454
      wall paintings 26 657
    St Martin 26 599
    St Maurille 3 191
    St Serge 2 48*; 11 510; 13 37; 14 82; 22 218
    Toussaints church 32 92
  Hôpital St Jean *see* Musée Jean Lurçat
  Hôtel Pincé 11 512
  manuscripts 31 290
Angers—cont.
  Musée des Beaux-Arts 2 46; 11 665
    catalogues 17 667
    collections 6 535; 8 564; 17 667; 19 154, 510
    directors 19 153
  Musée Jean Lurçat 2 45; 30 907
  Musée Turpin de Crissé 2 46; 31 478
  painting 11 531
  sculpture 13 79
  silver 11 616
Angerstein, John Julius 2 51*
  collections 5 71; 10 369; 19 588, 624; 32 774
  paintings 2 559; 5 63; 10 365; 18 893
Angés, Juan de 17 693
Anghel, Gheorghe 2 51–2*; 26 716
Anghelache, Laurentiu 26 719
Anghelu Ruju 2 52*; 16 *620*; 25 *470*
  tombs 25 507; 27 834
Anghiari, Antonio da *see* ANTONIO DA ANGHIARI
Angicourt, Pierre d' *see* PIERRE D'ANGICOURT
Angilbert 5 794; 7 263, 302; 11 509; 27 588
Angilbert II, Archbishop of Milan (*reg* 824-59) 5 807; 21 522; 26 144
Angillis, Pieter *see* ANGELLIS, PIETER
Angiolini, Carolina 3 49
Angiolosa, Conte 14 367
Angiviller, Charles-Claude de Flahaut de la Billarderie, Comte d' 2 52–3*; 4 554; 7 496; 11 540, 658; 20 135; 23 778; 28 521
  cartoons 3 639
  drawings 8 814
  frames 11 411
  paintings 2 702; 8 561; 9 417; 18 642, 643; 19 217; 24 136, 583; 30 46
  sculpture 3 844; 4 798; 5 380; 7 450; 8 631; 11 561, 562; 12 862; 17 683; 22 45, 210; 23 795; 26 551; 29 733
Angkeiakmin 24 73, 74
Angkola 15 794
Angkor 2 *54*, 54–61*; 5 *458*, 460; 6 *418*, *623*; 15 79; 29 224, *225*; 30 446
  Ak Yom 5 466, 472
  Angkor Thom 2 55, 56, 60*; 5 479, 480, 494, 495, 496; 21 595
    Bayon 2 56, 60–61; 5 476, 479–80, *479*
      reliefs 5 495, 496, *496*, 508; 23 823
      sculpture 5 496, 497
    Elephant Terrace 5 496
    gateways 2 *60*
    Prasat Chrung 2 60
    Prasat Suor Prat 2 61
    reliefs 5 498
    Royal Palace 2 61; 5 496
    Royal Square 2 60, 61; 5 480
    Royal Terrace 2 61; 5 495
    Terrace of the Leper King 5 495
  Angkor Vat 2 55, 56, 57–9*, *58*; 5 460, 462, *473*, 473, 474, 475, 476, 481, 498; 29 237
    galleries (ii) (corridors) 5 *475*
    reliefs 5 490–92*, *492*, 493, 498, 499, 503, 508; 23 556
    sculpture 5 499
    stupas 5 481
  art forms and materials
    architecture 29 237
    reliefs 5 487, 504; 29 231
    sculpture 5 486–90, 508
    stucco 29 826
  Baksei Chamkrong 2 55; 5 468, 469
Angkor—cont.
  Banteay Kdei 2 55; 5 477, *477*, 489
  Banteay Samré 2 55; 5 473, 474, 493
  Banteay Srei 2 55, 57*; 5 *458*, 461, *470*, 470–71, 493
    sculpture 5 487–9, *488*
  Baphuon 2 55; 5 472, 490
  Chau Say Tevoda 2 55; 5 473, 474, 476, 493, 494
  East Baray 2 55; 5 467
  East Mebon 2 55; 5 469–70, 471, 486
  Jayatataka 2 55
  Jayendranagari 2 55
  Mangalartha 2 56; 5 480
  Nagarajayashri 2 55
  Neak Pean 2 56; 5 477, *478*, 495, 496
  North Khleang 2 55; 5 471, 489
  Phimeanakas 2 55; 5 471, 472, 474, 489
  Phnom Bakheng 2 54, *56*, 56–7*; 5 467–8, 486
  Prasat Ak Yom 5 464
  Prasat Bat Chum 5 470
  Prasat Kravan 2 55; 4 796; 5 468, 487, *487*
  Prasat Lak Nan 5 470
  Prasat Prei Prasat 5 486
  Prasat Sralau 5 471, 489
  Preah Khan 2 59–60*; 5 462, 477, 495, 497
  Preah Palilay 5 473, 474, 475, 496
  Preah Pean 5 498
  Preah Pithu 2 55; 5 473, 480, 498
  Pre Rup 2 55; 5 *469*, 469–70, 471
  shrines (i) (cult) 28 639
  South Khleang 2 55; 5 471, 489
  Ta Keo 2 55; 5 *458*, *471*, 471–2, 489
  Ta Prohm 2 55; 5 *458*, 462, 477, *478*, 481, 495, 496
  Temple 486 5 480, 498
  Temple 487 *see* Mangalartha
  Thommanon 2 55; 5 473, 474, 475, 476, 492, 493
  water supply 5 459, 472
  West Baray 5 464, 472
  West Mebon 2 55; 5 472, 490
  Yashodharagiri *see* Phnom Bakheng
  Yashodharapura 2 54, 60; 5 *458*, 467
  Yashodharatataka *see* East Baray
Angkor Borei 5 *458*, 461; 29 826
Anglada-Camarasa, Hermen(egild) 2 62*; 3 219; 29 285
  patrons and collectors 31 757
  pupils 8 267; 13 695, 836
Anglada Camarasa, Hermengildo 4 127
angle bastions *see under* BASTIONS → types
angle buttresses *see under* BUTTRESSES
angled perspective *see* SCENA PER ANGELO
angle-fillet mouldings *see under* MOULDINGS → types
Anglemont, Privat d' 31 373
Angler, Gabriel 20 747, 772
Angleria, Pedro Martir de 21 252
angle roll mouldings *see under* MOULDINGS → types
Anglés, Juan 31 674
Anglés, Juan Carlos 2 62*
Anglés, Miquel Joan 29 267
Anglesea, Charles Paget, 6th Marquess of *see* PAGET, CHARLES, 6th Marquess of Anglesea
Anglesey (Gwynedd)
  Britannia Bridge 4 802; 16 53
  Llanbano church 32 786
  Llaniestyn church 32 786
  Menai Straits Bridge 4 803; 7 693; 30 422
Anglesey Abbey (Cambs) 3 477; 7 399; 10 365; 21 541
Angles-sur-l'Anglin 2 63*; 11 *505*; 25 *470*, 477
  Abri Bourdois 2 63
  Cave Taillebourg 2 63
  rock art 10 472; 25 477, 487
Angleur 27 90
Anglicanism *see under* CHRISTIANITY → sects
Anglicus, Bartholomeus *see* BARTHOLOMEUS ANGLICUS
Anglo-American Cataloging Rules (AACR) 4 22
Anglo-American Corporation 29 121; 33 603
Anglois, Guillermo 4 564; 12 923
Anglo-Japanese style *see* JAPONISME
Anglona Church 3 443
Anglo-Saxon 2 63–84*
  acanthus 1 *111*
  amber 1 761; 3 442
  arches 2 *65*, 296
  architectural decorations 2 65, 71
  architecture 2 64–7*
  beadwork 3 442
  bookbindings 4 347, 348
  borders (manuscript) 20 338
  brass 4 688
  bronze 9 253
  brooches 2 79, 80, *80*; 9 253; 10 322
  buckles 2 79
  carpenters 2 64
  caskets 2 *81*
  cathedrals 33 *234*
  cemeteries 30 43
  churches 2 65–7, *65*, *66*, *67*; 10 227; 21 *887*
  clasps 10 322; 30 *44*
  coins 4 688; 7 533, 534
  copper 10 338, *338*
  crosses 2 68–9, *69*, 70, 71; 10 322; 27 *453*
  dress 9 253, *253*
  dyes 2 83
  embroidery 2 83, *84*
  enamel 2 79; 17 IV1; 30 44, *44*
  filigree 2 79; 10 322
  forts 21 560
  garnets 10 322; 30 *44*
  gilding 10 338
  glass 10 322
  gold 2 79, 83, *84*; 10 322; 17 IV1
  halls 10 226; 14 73–4
  harnesses 14 182
  helmets 10 *338*; 14 412
  herbals 14 432
  houses 2 64
  initials (manuscript) 5 *641*
  iron 10 *338*
  ivory 2 82, *82*
  ivory-carvings 2 80–82*, *81*, *82*
  jewellery 2 79*; 26 303
  knives 8 *283*
  manuscript illumination 2 72, 74–8*, *76*; 10 242–3*; 20 II; 25 676
  manuscripts 20 330
  masonry 2 64, 65; 20 571
  masons 2 64
  metalwork 2 79–80*; 30 44
  miniatures (manuscript illumination) 2 *75*, *77*; 3 *710*
  monasteries 2 66
  monuments 10 259
  mouldings 2 67
  niello 2 *80*; 10 322, 381
  ornament 23 537
  painting 2 72–4*, *73*
  pendants (jewellery) 10 322
  pins 2 79
  portraits 17 IV1
  Psalters 25 676; 32 517
  rings 2 79
  scripts 28 305
  sculpture 2 68–72*; 10 259
  silk 2 *84*
Anglo-Saxon—cont.
  silver 2 79, *80*; 10 322; 31 316–17
  spinning (textile) 2 83
  stained glass 2 83*
  stoles (ecclesiastical) 2 *84*
  stone-carvings 2 68–72*, *69*, *70*, *71*
  stripwork 29 775–6, *776*
  styles
    Style I 2 79
    Style II 2 79
    Trewhiddle 2 79
  swords 2 452
  textiles 2 83–4*
  timber structures 2 64, 66
  title-pages 31 48
  trappings 14 182
  urban planning 2 66
  weaving 2 83
  whetstones 30 *45*
  wood 2 64, 67
  wool 9 253
  workshops 29 851
  wrist-clasps 9 253
  see also ENGLAND
Ängman, Jacob 30 108
  works 30 *108*
Ango, Jean-Robert 2 84*
Angola 1 *214*; 2 85–7*; 11 880
  architecture 2 85–6*
  basketwork 1 296, *296*
  beads 7 *197*, *198*
  clubs (weapons) 7 *199*
  cotton 2 *87*
  fibres 7 *198*
  figurines 2 *86*
  hair 7 *197*
  hangings 2 *87*
  houses 1 320
  masks 1 296; 7 *198*
  painting 1 313; 2 86–7*
  palm leaves 1 *296*
  photography 10 580
  sculpture 1 359; 2 86*; 7 *197*, *198*
  weaving 2 87*
  wire 7 *197*
  wood 2 *86*; 7 *197*, *198*
Angolan Diamond Company (DIAMANG) 2 87
Angolo del Moro, Battista dell' 2 88*; 5 617; 31 161; 32 343
  collaboration 25 1
  patrons and collectors 10 805; 12 910; 32 348
  pupils 2 88
  works 5 31; 32 223
Angolo del Moro, Giulio dell' 2 88–9*
Angolo del Moro, Marco dell' 2 88*
Angoras 30 539
Angosciola *see* ANGUISSOLA
Angostura, Fort of S Francisco 32 169
Angot, Jean-Robert *see* ANGO, JEAN-ROBERT
Angoulême 2 89*; 11 *505*
  Cathedral of St Pierre 2 89*; 11 510; 26 570, 584, 600
    restoration 2 320, *321*
    sculpture 13 73; 26 599
Angoulême (family) 18 680; 30 529
Angoulême, Charles de Valois, Comte d' 4 569; 11 639; 14 422; 19 233; 30 529; 31 *833*
Angoulême, Diane d' 21 345
Angoulême, Jean de Valois, Comte d' 31 *833*
Angoulême, Louis (-Antoine) de Bourbon, Duc d' 12 153; 18 69
Angoulême, Louise of Savoy, Comtesse d' 8 115; 11 639; 12 837; 14 422; 30 529
Angoulême, Marguerite of Rohan, Comtesse d' 20 647
Angra, Monte Brasil 25 291

Angra do Heroísmo, Câmara Municipal **25** 293
Angran, Louis-Auguste, Vicomte de Fontpertuis **2** 90*
Angrand, Charles **2** 90*; **13** 323; **19** 10; **22** 745, 747
Angrand, Léonce (-Marie-François) **2** 90*; **24** 508
Angren Museum **6** 283
Angrer Portrait, Master of the **26** 105
Angry **26** 74
Angry Penguins **2** 749, 769; **24** 437
Angst, Caspar **33** 736
Angualasto culture **29** 191
Anguera, Josep Ribas i *see* RIBAS I ANGUERA, JOSEP
Anguiano, Raúl **2** 90*; **30** 275
Anguier, François **2** 91*; **11** 559; **26** 772
assistants **26** 91
patrons and collectors **4** 303
pupils **7** 422; **12** 725; **20** 480
teachers **13** 825
works **2** *91*; **11** 559
Anguier, Guillaume **2** 91; **12** 828, 832
Anguier, Honoré **2** 91
Anguier, Michel **2** 91, 92*; **11** 559; **26** 772
collaboration **2** 91; **11** 575
patrons and collectors **11** 356; **12** 727; **20** 895
pupils **7** 422; **12** 725
teachers **1** 629, 631; **13** 825
works **2** *91*; **11** 559; **13** 783; **24** 160; **26** 566; **29** 571, *572*, 833; **32** 97
Anguilla **2** 144
see also ANTILLES, LESSER; LEEWARD ISLANDS
Anguillara, Giovanni Andrea dell' **15** 82; **23** 680
Anguillara, Mura di S Stefano **26** 870, 878, 900
Anguissola, Anna-Maria **2** 92, 93
Anguissola, Elena **2** 92, 93
Anguissola, Europa **2** 92, 93
Anguissola, Leander **32** 436, 458
Anguissola, Lucia **2** 92, 94*
Anguissola, Minerva **2** 92
Anguissola, Sofonisba **2** 92, 93–4*, *93*; **8** 135; **16** 668, 780; **33** 308
attributions **2** 94
patrons and collectors **23** 577
pupils **2** 94
works **16** 668
Anguk Temple **18** 292
Angulo, Ludovico d' *see* LUDOVICO D'ANGULO
Angulo Iñiguez, Diego **12** 889
Angus, Craibe **12** 776; **28** 272
Angus, Peggy **33** 552
Angus, Rita (Catherine) **2** 94*; **7** 211; **23** 60; **33** 58
Angussola *see* ANGUISSOLA
Angyal, Béla **15** 12
Anhak Palace **18** 260
Anhalt, Amalia van **22** 872
Anhalt, Leopold III, Duke of *see* ANHALT-DESSAU, (LEOPOLD III FREDERICK) FRANCIS, Prince of
Anhalt-Dessau, Anna Wilhelmine of **8** 816
Anhalt-Dessau, (Leopold III Frederick) Francis, Prince of (*reg* 1756-1817) **2** 94–5*; **23** 410
architecture **12** 374; **33** 380
gardens **12** 134; **13** 199; **33** 380
paintings **23** 410
parks **12** 472
sculpture **6** 171
Anhalt-Dessau, Franz, Duke of **6** 98
Anhalt-Dessau, Henrietta Catharina, Princess of **8** 816; **23** 465
Anhalt-Dessau, Joachim Ernst, Prince of (*reg* 1918) **8** 816
Anhalt-Dessau, Leopold I, Prince of **8** 816
Anhalt-Zerbst, Sophie Friederike Auguste von *see* CATHERINE II, Empress of Russia
Anham **5** 114
Anhegger, Mualla Egüpoğlu **16** 611
Anhilvada *see* PATAN (i) (INDIA)
Anholt, Wasserschloss **23** 789
Anhtoni, Giovanni **2** 95*; **33** 622
Anhui **2** 95–6
Anhui school **2** 95–6*
members **8** 457; **14** 722, 820; **33** 467, 653
works **2** *96*
Anhui School of Seal Carvers **7** 130
An Hwi-Jun **18** 259
anhydrite **10** 66, 74; **29** 698*
Ani (scribe) **9** 905
Ani (Armenia) **2** 97–8*, *423*, 426; **9** *512*
Cathedral of the Mother of God **2** 97, *97*, 444
ceramics **2** 439
Church of the Holy Apostles **2** 427
Church of the Holy Saviour **2** 429
embroidery **2** 443
metalwork **2** 441
St Grigor **2** 426, 429
al-Ani, Abdul Ghani **16** 1
Ani, Book of the Dead for *see* BOOK OF THE DEAD FOR ANI
Aniambossou Armand **3** 728
Aniane Church **11** 653
Anianus II, Bishop of Bangor **25** 808
Aniba **10** 81; **23** *276*, 278
fortress **9** 845, 847
tomb of Pennut **23** 280
Anichini, Alvise **2** 98
Anichini, Andrea **2** 98
Anichini, Callisto **2** 98
Anichini, Francesco **2** 98*; **12** 257, 258
Anichini, Luigi **2** 98*; **10** 523
Anichini, Pietro **2** 98
works **25** *411*
Anicia Juliana **2** 98–9*
architecture **9** 513, 523, 537; **16** 580
manuscripts **8** 885; **9** 520, 617; **14** 432; **16** 307, 588; **21** 5
aniconism *see* ICONOCLASM
Anidi, Obiora **23** 138
works **23** *138*
Anige *see* ARNIKO
Anikiejčyk, Anatoly (Aleksandrovich) **21** 697
Anikin, Anatoly **27** 435
Anikov Dish **6** 206, 240
Anikushin, Mikhail (Konstantinovich) **2** 99*; **17** 753; **27** 397, 581; **29** 388
Anilco Temple **30** *450*
anilines **4** 724; **17** 277; **22** 661; **30** 562; **32** 816
animal black *see* BONE BLACK
animal carpets *see under* CARPETS → types
animal fibres *see under* FIBRES → types
Animal-Head Scroll, Master of the **2** 462
animalier sculpture *see under* SCULPTURE → types
animal necropoleis *see under* NECROPOLEIS → types
Animal style **2** 100–102*; **6** 242; **21** 882; **27** 367; **30** 769, 772
Central Asia, Eastern **6** 313
Central Asia, Western **6** 260, 261
Mongolia **21** 878, 883, 885
Russia **2** *101*
Scythian **2** *101*; **28** 319, 321
animal subjects **2** 99–100, 102–7*
Africa **1** *238*
Anatolia, ancient **1** 834–5, *835*
Arabia **2** *265*
Belgium **32** 252
Baroque **4** *916*
16th cent. **14** *619*
17th cent. **2** *104*; **4** *222*; **17** *918*
Britain **2** 105–6; **4** *363*
Canada **7** *644*
China **6** 799, *800*, *802*; **17** *587*; **19** *370*; **26** *211*
Egypt, ancient **7** XII; **9** 865, 867; **29** 34
England **29** 424–6
Gothic **3** *879*; **24** *270*
Romanesque **26** *617*
18th cent. **29** *425*, *810*
19th cent. **1** *449*; **18** *722*, *723*; **32** *326*
Etruscan **10** 593
France **2** 105; **29** 426
Rococo **8** *71*
Romanticism **2** *107*; **3** *313*, *315*
18th cent. **14** *846*; **23** *668*
19th cent. **2** *100*; **24** *141*
Germany **2** *103*; **4** *132*; **20** *381*
Gothic **3** *879*
Greece, ancient **13** 493, 501, 505, 506
Hurrian **15** *33*
Indian subcontinent **15** *585*; **20** *301*
Iran, ancient **15** 907–8
Islamic **16** *311*
Italy
Etruscan **10** 593
Mannerism **12** *572*
Renaissance **24** *861*
18th cent. **19** *634*
19th cent. **10** *835*
Japan **17** *185*
Korea **18** *377*; **33** *527*
16th cent. **18** 51; **33** *524*
19th cent. **14** *724*
Netherlands, the **10** *732*; **14** *707*; **26** *162*
Prehistoric art **1** *835*
Romanesque **26** *617*
Sudan **1** 237, *238*
Sweden **19** *379*
Syria **16** *311*
Syria-Palestine **15** *33*
Urartian **1** *836*
Yemen **2** *265*
animation **9** 10
animism **6** 625; **18** 252; **24** 609*
Animist style **5** 45
Aninas (family) **10** 620
Anis, Albert **21** 421
Anisfel'd, Boris (Izrailovich) **2** 108*
Anishinabe
works **22** *643*
Anisimov, Aleksandr **27** 381
Anisimov, Artemi **33** 600
Anita Grande **9** 679
Anitli
churches **9** 543; **31** 435
el-Hadra church **31** 435, *435*
manuscripts **31** 436
Mar Sovo **31** 434
Monastery of the Theotokos **31** 434, 435
SS Sergius and Bacchus **31** 435
Anitta, Prince of Kanesh **1** 825
Aniwa **25** 181
Anjaneri **15** 317
Temple 8 **15** 317
Anjar (India) **15** 671
'Anjar (Lebanon) **2** 108*; **16** *104*, 148; **19** 8
'Anjar (Syria) **16** 256
Anji Bridge **4** 800, *800*; **6** 644; **29** 905
Anjou (House of) **2** 108*
Anjou, Fulk III Nerra, Count of *see* FULK III NERRA, Count of Anjou
Anjou, Fulk IV Rechin, Count of *see* FULK IV RECHIN, Count of Anjou
Anjou, Geoffrey I, Count of *see* GEOFFREY I, Count of Anjou
Anjou, Geoffrey V Plantagenet, Count of *see* GEOFFREY V PLANTAGENET, Count of Anjou
Anjou, Henry de Valois, Duc d' *see* HENRY III, King of France
Anjou cross *see* CROSSES → types → Papal
Anjou I. (First House of) **2** 109*; **11** 655; **14** 410
coats of arms **14** 418
Anjou I., Charles, Comte d' *see* CHARLES I, King of Naples and Sicily
Anjou I., Charles I, King of Naples and Sicily *see* CHARLES I, King of Naples and Sicily
Anjou I., Charles II, King of Naples and Jerusalem *see* CHARLES II, King of Naples and Jerusalem
Anjou I., Charles III, King of Naples *see* CHARLES III, King of Naples
Anjou I., Charles Robert, King of Hungary *see* CHARLES ROBERT OF ANJOU, King of Hungary
Anjou I., Elizabeth, Queen of Hungary *see* ELIZABETH, Queen of Hungary
Anjou I., Joanna I, Queen of Naples *see* JOANNA I, Queen of Naples
Anjou I., Louis I, King of Hungary and Poland *see* LOUIS I, King of Hungary and Poland
Anjou I., Mary, Queen of Naples *see* MARY OF HUNGARY, Queen of Naples
Anjou I., Robert, King of Naples and Jerusalem *see* ROBERT, King of Naples and Jerusalem
Anjou II. (Second House of) **2** 111*
Anjou II., Charles, Comte de Maine *see* MAINE, CHARLES D'ANJOU, Comte de
Anjou II., Charles III, Comte d' *see* CHARLES III, Count of Anjou
Anjou II., Joanna II, Queen of Naples *see* JOANNA II, Queen of Naples
Anjou II., Louis I, Duke of Anjou *see* LOUIS I, Duke of Anjou, King of Naples, Sicily and Jerusalem
Anjou II., Louis II, Duke of Anjou *see* LOUIS II, Duke of Anjou, King of Naples, Sicily and Jerusalem
Anjou II., Louis III, Duke of Anjou *see* LOUIS III, Duke of Anjou
Anjou II., René I, Duke of Anjou *see* RENÉ I, Duke of Anjou & Lorraine, King of Naples, Sicily and Jerusalem
Anjou II., Yolande of Aragon, Duchess of *see* YOLANDE OF ARAGON, Duchess of Anjou
Anjuman Mimaran **18** 647
ANK '64 **18** 780; **32** 593
Ankara **2** 115–16*; **9** *507*, *512*; **16** *104*; **24** 689; **26** *908*
Ahi Elvan Mosque **16** 497
Alâeddin Mosque **16** 497
architecture **24** 690; **31** 452
Arslanhane Mosque **16** 202, 248, 497
minbar **16** 497, *498*
Atatürk Mausoleum **31** 452, *452*
bath-gymnasium **3** 375
baths **26** 913
bronze **1** 836
caravanserais **16** 266
Ankara—cont.
Cathedral **13** 355
Directorate of Turkish State Railways building **31** 452
Etimesgüt Armed Units Mosque **16** 242
exhibitions **31** 454
finials (scrolls) **17** 569
fortifications **9** 554, 555; **16** 186; **21** 562
Gazi Teachers' College **31** 455
Genabi Ahemd Pasha Mosque **16** 221
Hacettepe University **31** 456
Hacı Bayram Mosque **16** 498
Iş Bankası Tower **31** 453
Kurşunlu Caravanserai *see* Museum of Anatolian Civilizations
Middle East Technical University **31** 452
Ministry of Health building **31** 452
mohair **16** 445
Museum of Anatolian Civilizations **1** 114, 839; **14** 14; **31** 456
Museum of Ethnography **16** 557; **31** 456
rock reliefs **1** 833; **24** *691*
St Clement **7** 252; **9** 542
sculpture **24** 690
shops **16** 266
Temple of Rome and Augustus **26** 913
towers **9** 555
town walls **16** 266; **21** 583
tumuli **24** 691
Turkish Cultural Research Institute **31** 456
Turkish Historical Society building **5** 633; **31** 452, *453*
Turkish Language Society building **31** 453
Yörük Dede Tomb **16** 204
Anker, (Samuel) Albert **2** 116*; **3** 824; **17** 886; **30** 125
collaboration **8** 607; **22** 186
pupils **3** 20
teachers **12** 810
works **30** 134
Anker, Alfons **19** 773
Anker, Herman van den **25** 214
Anker, Peter **31** 279
Ankermann, Bernhard **10** 580
Ankeveen **13** 110
Ankh **9** 866
Ankh-haf **9** 870
Ankhmahor **9** 872
Ankhnesneferibre **10** 13
Ankhor **9** 843
Ankhorkawy **9** 840
Ankhpakhered **9** 860
Ankhtifi **9** 874, 899–900; **21** 744
wall paintings **21** *745*
Ankhwennefer (*reg* 199-186 BC) **9** *778*
Ankhyraous **9** 555
Ankiewicz, Julian **32** 872
anklets **1** 292, 351; **6** 312
Ankokuji **17** 132
Ankpa **15** 109
An Kyŏn **2** 117*; **18** 314, 329; **29** 18
patrons and collectors **33** 536
An Kyu-ŭng **18** 300
Anlamani **23** 282
Anmatyerre **1** 64
Anna, Duchess of Bavaria (1420-74) **20** 746
Anna, Queen of Poland (1523-96) **13** 774; **25** 132
Anna, Alessandro d' **30** 451
Anna, Baldassare d' **2** 117
Anna, Daniele d' **2** 117
Anna, Giovanni d' **2** 117; **31** 38
Anna, Margit **1** 796; **10** 650
Anna, Martin d' **2** 117
Anna, Vito d' **20** 283

Anna Amalia, Duchess of Saxe-Weimar (1739-1807) 33 110, 110, 116*
architecture 32 375
paintings 5 286
sculpture 18 107
el-'Annāba 1 634; 12 78; 23 299
Cathedral 9 569, 570
double basilica 9 535
Hippo Regius 9 510; 14 564*
House of Isguntus 27 63
marble 27 13
markets 19 888, 889; 26 871, 919
monopteros 21 893
Annaberg 2 117–18*; 12 361
Annenkirche 2 117–18, 118; 12 365, 366; 13 58; 14 81; 29 65
Beautiful Portal 20 798
Anna Ivanovna, Empress of Russia (reg 1730-40) 4 62; 27 575; 28 41, 464, 465
Annalen der bildenden Künste für die österreichischen Staaten 24 438
Annales 24 439
Annales archéologiques 8 868; 11 521; 13 204, 208; 24 422
Annales d'histoire de l'art et d'archéologie 24 439
Annali 24 447
Annals of the Fine Arts 10 151; 19 587; 24 422
Annals of the Four Masters 24 562
Annam see VIETNAM
Anna Maria Luisa de' Medici, Electress Palatine (1667-1743) 21 7, 9, 31*; 31 187; 33 272
architecture 25 322
cameos 12 547
collections 11 189; 16 772
gems 12 262
paintings 4 65; 11 874
sculpture 6 86; 11 322; 22 5; 24 697; 30 851
Anna Maria Sforza, Duchess of Ferrara, Modena and Reggio (fl 1520s) 16 751
Annan 2 767
Annan, James Craig 2 119–20*; 24 674
Annan, John 2 119
Annan, Richard 2 118
Annan, Thomas 2 118, 119*; 24 672
Annan, T. & R. 2 118, 119
Annan and Swann 18 127
Annandale, James Johnstone, 2nd Marquis see JOHNSTONE, JAMES, 2nd Marquis Annandale
Annandale Imitation Realists 2 120*, 751; 4 882; 18 689
Annang 15 61, 63, 64, 65
textiles 15 64
Annan & Sons 2 119
Anna of Hanover, Princess of Orange (1709-59) 14 42; 21 148; 22 905
Annapolis (MD) 2 120–21*, 121; 31 587, 721
Chase-Lloyd House 10 849; 29 842
Hammond-Harwood House 29 842
Post Office 7 619
theatre 30 677
urban planning 2 120–21
William Paca House 29 842
Ann Arbor (MI), University of Michigan
collections 17 435; 31 666
Museum of Art 6 826
Stearns Collection 22 377
annatto 4 724; 12 623
Anne, Archduchess of Austria and Duchess of Bavaria (1528-90) 12 455; 21 484
Anne, Duchess of Brittany (1476-1514) see ANNE OF BRITTANY, Queen of France
Anne, Holy Roman Empress (1585-1618) 13 847
Anne, Queen of England (reg 1702-14)
architecture 17 634
gardens 12 128; 33 257
gold 26 558
interior decoration 32 359
paintings 2 41; 7 286; 8 454; 18 145; 19 63; 31 786
stage design 17 637
throne 10 291
Anne, Queen of Serbia (c. 1196-1227) 28 454
Annear, Harold Desbrowe 2 122*, 740
Annear, James 23 65
Anne Catherine Constance, Electress Palatine (fl c. 1592) 32 6
Anne Catherine Gonzaga, Archduchess (1566-1621) 2 44; 29 387
Anne de Valois, Duchess of Bourbon (1460/61-1522) 4 542, 543, 545–7*; 31 833
architecture 4 545
books 4 545
manuscripts 7 597
paintings 20 731
sculpture 4 546
Anneessens, Frans 2 122
Anneessens, Jan Andries 2 122*; 3 546
Annenkov, Yury (Pavlovich) 2 122–3*; 4 156; 27 394
Anne of Austria, Queen of France (1601-66) 4 543; 6 434; 20 138
architecture 6 508; 12 747; 20 291; 24 118, 159
bronze 11 626
frescoes 21 498
furniture 11 587
interior decoration 2 92; 11 573, 574; 20 467; 25 70; 28 506
jewellery 17 523
manuscripts 17 449
opera 31 165
paintings 3 449; 6 434; 11 722; 13 701; 17 2; 18 580; 20 860; 21 803; 23 512; 25 70; 26 349, 566; 30 530; 31 908; 32 718
sculpture 2 92; 19 76; 27 821
silver 11 617, 618
stucco 20 480; 29 833
Anne of Austria, Queen of Spain (1549-80) 14 2; 29 334, 350
Anne of Beaujeu, Duchess of Bourbon (fl c. 1470) 20 732
Anne of Bohemia, Queen of England (1365-94) 8 412
Anne of Brittany, Master of see UNICORN HUNT, MASTER OF THE
Anne of Brittany, Queen of France (1477-1514) 4 571, 828; 9 94; 31 833, 845–6*
architecture 22 464
manuscripts 4 569, 570, 571; 20 778; 25 405; 31 834
metalwork 11 616
sculpture 7 595; 17 485
tapestries 20 776
Anne of Burgundy, Duchess of Bedford (d 1432) 18 685
Anne of Denmark, Queen of England and Scotland (1574-1619) 29 797, 798*
architecture 10 360; 13 623
gardens 12 126
miniatures 23 408
paintings 12 515
stage design 17 633, 637
Anne of France (fl c. 1460-1522) see ANNE, Duchess of Bourbon
Anne of Hungary, Holy Roman Empress (1503-47) 13 908
Anne of Lusignan, Duchess of Savoy (fl c. 1434) 18 684
Annes, Álvaro 5 421
Annes, Vicente 5 421
Annesley 7 233
Annesly, David 19 591
Annex Marchestens 21 533
Annfield Pottery 28 257
Annibaldi, Riccardo 2 483
Annibale, Marchese 4 560
Annichini see ANICHINI
Anniga, Ruler (reg 923-40) (Nolamba) 23 182
Annigeri, Amriteshvara Temple 15 325
Annigoni, Pietro 2 123*; 11 191; 24 278
Annink, Ed 22 877
Annio of Viterbo 10 636, 638
Annio of Viterbo see GIOVANNI NANNI
Anno 23 652, 653
Annobal Rufus 19 221
Annoni, Ambrogio 22 105
Annosuke Shikata see SHIKATA ANNOSUKE
Annuals of the Fine Arts or Repository of Painting, Sculpture, Architecture and Engraving 24 446
annular crypts see under CRYPTS → types
annular vaults see under VAULTS (CEILING) → types
annulet 2 123*
Annunciation of the Monte, Master of the 20 901
Annunciation to the Shepherds, Master of the 9 52; 16 673; 20 616–17*
works 20 617
Annuss, Augusts
Anonimo Gaddiano see MAGLIABECHIANO, ANONIMO
Anonimo Magliabechiano see MAGLIABECHIANO, ANONIMO
Anonimo Magliabechiano Codex see CODICES → individual manuscripts → Codex Magliabechiano
Anonymous Valesianus 9 557
anorthosite gneiss see under LIMESTONE → types
Anouilh, Jean 9 373
Anovelo da Imbonate 2 123*
Anoyira 8 329
Anozie, Isaiah 15 116
Anozie, Jonah 15 116
Anozie, Richard 15 116
Anpyŏng, Prince see YI YŎNG
An Pyŏng-ŭi 18 264
An Qi 2 124*; 7 153; 12 52; 19 298
Anquetin, Louis 2 124*; 3 812
dealers 19 10
groups and movements 7 451, 452
patrons and collectors 12 191
Anraadt, Pieter van 2 124–5*
Anreiter von Zirnfeld, Karl Wendelin 9 57; 16 737
works 16 737
Anreith, Anton 5 662; 29 111; 30 728
Anrep, Boris 1 121; 4 168
Anri, Master see EGAS CUEMAN
Anrion, Adrien-Joseph 2 125*; 8 699
Ansa, Queen (fl 753) 4 747
Ansães, S Salvador 26 611
Ansaldi, Innocenzio 2 125*
Ansaldo, (Giovanni) Andrea 2 125–7*
assistants 11 16
collaboration 11 14
patrons and collectors 4 811; 29 411
pupils 2 619; 3 34
restorations by others 11 9, 16
works 2 126
Ansano di Matteo see SANO DI MATTEO
Ansano di Pietro di Mencio see SANO DI PIETRO
al-Ansary, A. R. 2 275
Ansbach 2 127*; 12 361, 471
faience (ii) (ceramics) 12 430, 431
Orangery 12 373
porcelain 2 127; 12 433; 22 882
Residenz 5 348, 349; 12 373; 26 257; 30 885
tiles 30 885
Ansbach (House of) 3 20; 12 369
Ansbach, Georg Friedrich, Markgraf von 11 886; 31 311
Ansbach, Johann Friedrich, Markgraf von 4 203
Ansbach, Karl Alexander, Markgraf von 2 127
Anschütz, Hermann 6 532; 7 175, 181; 8 618; 14 768; 19 97; 20 809; 29 389
Anschütz, Ottomar 24 669
Ansdell, Richard 2 127–8*; 19 507; 27 460
Anse aux Meadows, L' 5 558
Ansedonia see COSA
Ansegis, Abbot of Fontanella 21 835
Anselevicius, Evelyn 30 329
Anselin, Jean-Louis 5 440
Anselm, Archbishop of Canterbury 5 642; 8 222, 224; 26 588, 589
Anselmi, Michelangelo 2 128*; 22 805
collaboration 24 200; 27 122
works 2 128; 3 487; 24 193, 196
Anselmo, Giovanni 2 129*, 527
Anselmo, Pompeo d' 1 620
Anselmo da Baggio see ALEXANDER II, Pope
Anselmo da Campione 2 129; 5 549*; 21 774; 26 621
works 21 774
Anselm of Laon 1 653; 29 500
Anselmus 2 129*; 5 549
Anseramo da Trani 2 129*; 3 235
Ansgar (fl 1940s) 14 234
Ansgar, Archbishop of Ribe (801-65) 14 100; 26 304
Anshan see under MALYAN, TALL'I
Anshelm, Thomas 2 130*
An Shigao 5 107
Anshutz, Thomas (Pollock) 2 130*; 24 600; 31 603
pupils 5 422; 8 577, 708; 12 769; 14 393; 20 421; 28 842
works 15 830
Ansiaux, Antoine 31 374
Ansidei *Madonna* 25 897, 899; 30 427
Ansim Temple 18 311
Ansingh, M. E. G. (Lizzy) 28 188
An-Ski, S. 17 581
Ansoald, Bishop of Poitiers 25 86
Anson, Thomas 29 806
Ansorena, Celestino 29 338
Anspach, Jules 5 41; 30 47
Anspert, Bishop of Milan 21 534
Anstett, François-Antoine 11 606; 23 113
Anstett, François-Michel 23 113
Anstice, Robert 7 480
Anstruther-Thomson, Clementine 19 61
Ansuino da Forlì 2 130–31*; 20 305; 25 9
Ansúrez, Pedro, Conde de 31 822
antae see under PILASTERS → types
Antaimoro 1 269; 20 36
Antaios (son of Aischrion) 8 691; 13 557, 558
Antakya 2 156–9*, 158; 26 902, 916; 28 721; 30 180
Antioch 1 816, 849; 2 155–6*; 9 512, 513; 13 362; 16 104, 263, 264; 26 914, 915; 28 719; 30 180
Antakya—cont.
architecture 14 465
banners 11 146
Cathedral of St Peter 9 539, 548
churches 9 539, 541
coins 17 502
Constantinian Villa 7 763; 9 567
fortifications 9 554; 21 562
glass 16 518
Golden Octagon 7 255
Hatay Museum 1 839
manuscripts 7 246; 9 620; 17 506
marks 9 654
mosaics 2 157, 157–8*; 9 563, 567
palace 9 557, 567
pottery 16 397
St Babylas 9 540, 541; 31 280
St Theodore 3 190
sculpture 2 156, 157*; 13 429
stamps 9 655
textiles 1 881; 16 441
Tyche see TYCHE OF ANTIOCH
Antal, Frederick 2 131*; 14 901; 28 917, 926
works 2 536; 20 528
Antaldi (family) 18 895
Antaldi, Antaldo, Marchese 33 345
Antalya 26 908
Arch of Hadrian 26 913
carpets 16 470
fortifications 9 555; 16 186
Hamidid Yivli Minare Mosque 16 202
town walls 21 583
Antandroy 20 35, 36, 37, 39
Antanosy 1 269; 20 35, 37
works 20 38
Antaradus 27 85
antarāla 15 243*
antarapaṭṭa 15 243*
Antas 25 733
Antay, Joaquín López see LÓPEZ ANTAY, JOAQUÍN
Ant chairs see under CHAIRS → types
antefixes 2 131*
Britain 26 878
Etruscan 10 603
Germany 26 878
Greece, ancient 2 131*, 131; 13 390
Rome, ancient 2 131; 26 878
Antegnati, Graziadio 12 911
Antelami, Benedetto 2 132–3*; 16 687; 24 195; 26 579, 619, 620, 621
assistants 19 518
attributions 2 132, 420
pupils 11 5; 23 101
reliefs 1 530; 24 193, 194–5, 194, 195, 196; 26 595
sculpture 3 192; 16 687
thrones 30 778
Antell, H. F. 11 111
Antella, Oratorio di S Caterina 29 405
Antella, Donato dell' 12 706
Antella, Francesco dell' 20 495
Antenor 2 133*
copies 2 685
works 8 696; 10 649; 13 439, 450; 18 460; 32 58
Antenor Kore 13 447
Anteo group 4 262, 263; 15 144; 22 335; 29 51, 894
antependia 1 696, 708; 2 133*
historical and regional traditions
Austria 2 823
Germany 12 462, 466, 469; 23 657
Gothic 11 466; 13 130, 135, 143, 144; 24 3
Italy 11 379
Norway 11 466; 13 135, 143, 144; 23 223–4
Ottonian 23 657, 657
Peru 24 511
Romanesque 29 275

antependia
historical and regional traditions—cont.
Spain 11 479; 29 275, *349*
materials
embroidery 29 *349*
gold 23 *657*
linen 2 *823*
silver 24 511
Antequera (i) (Spain) 2 133*; 25 *470*, 508; 29 *258*
fortifications 21 584, 585
Hospital de S Juan de Dios 14 782
marble 27 13
S María 29 267
Antequera (ii) (Mexico) *see* OAXACA
Antes, Horst 2 134*; 12 397; 17 818; 18 31
Antheaume (family) 11 628
Antheil, Georges 10 137, 687
Anthelme, Prior 5 894
anthemia 2 *134*, 134–5*
see also PALMETTES
Anthemios of Tralles 2 135*
works 16 592, *592*
Anthes, Rudolf 10 93
Anthoine, Jan-Baptiste 9 486; 32 706
Anthoni, Jakob 33 275
Anthoni, Johan *see* ANHTONI, GIOVANNI
Anthonissen, Arnoldus van 32 673
Anthonissen, Hendrick van 25 248; 32 673
Anthonissen, Reynier 31 881
Anthonisz., Adriaen 1 801
Anthonisz., Aert 32 734
Anthonisz., Cornelis 1 658; 2 135–6*
reproductive prints by others 19 343
works 1 658, 800, *800*, 806; 2 *136*; 20 424; 25 605, 621; 33 354
Anthony (Medieval painter) 31 557
Anthony, Duke of Lorraine (*reg* 1508-44) 19 696
Anthony, King of (Lower) Navarre (*reg* 1555-62) 4 *543*
Anthony, Master *see* TOTO DEL NUNZIATA, ANTONIO
Anthony, Mme 25 *670*
Anthony, Derick 14 546
Anthony, Earle C. 20 889
Anthony, E. & H. T., Co. 16 821
Anthony, Georges 8 *890*
Anthony, Henry T. 10 669
Anthony, J. B. 28 595
Anthony, Vincentius 19 58
Anthony à Wood 33 147
Anthony de Caraman 21 798
Anthony of Herakleia 28 458
Anthony of Novgorod 9 657
Anthoons, Willy 3 574; 17 518
Anthropological Associaton of Japan *see* NIHON JINRUIGAKKAI
anthropology 2 136–8*, 534; 10 578, 580; 19 275
Aboriginal Australia 2 137
Africa 2 137
Native North Americans 2 137; 22 673–4
Papua New Guinea 2 137
United States of America 22 673–4
anthropomorphism 30 171
Anthropos 24 430
Anthroposophical Society 29 607
anthroposophy 2 138*; 21 851; 30 168
antiaris 33 325
Anti-art Society *see* HANBIJUTSU
Antibes, Musée Antibes 24 724
Antić, Ivan 28 445
Antichak 2 138–9*; 15 *279*, 281
reliefs 15 719
Antichak—cont.
sculpture 15 499
Vikramashila Vihara 5 96; 15 281, *545*, 571
Antichi, Prospero 2 139*
works 9 340, 706; 27 486; 29 82
Antichità viva: Rassegna d'arte 24 449
Antico 2 139–41*; 20 322; 29 568
patrons and collectors 3 522; 10 521; 12 907–8; 13 920; 20 318; 29 763
works 2 *140*, *141*; 3 690; 5 300; 6 103; 20 918
Antidotos 10 649; 13 546, 551; 23 141
Antiek 24 450
Antifaschistische Gesellschaft 14 833
Antigna, (Jean-Pierre-) Alexandre 2 142*; 11 545
works 2 *142*; 11 545
Antigna, André-Marc 2 142
Antigna, Hélène-Marie *see* PETTIT, HÉLÈNE-MARIE
Antigó, Joan 2 142–3*
Antigó, Miguel 2 142
Antigó, Rafael 2 142
Antigonia *see* IZNIK
Antigonids 13 588
Antigonos 2 518; 13 554; 16 85*; 24 413; 25 45
Antigonos Gonatas, King of Macedon (*reg* 285-39 BC) 27 692
Antigonos Monophthalmos 16 809
Antigua (island) 2 144; 5 *745*
carnivals 5 788
ceramics 2 146, 152
libraries 2 153
metalwork 2 152
museums 2 153, 154
see also ANTILLES, LESSER; LEEWARD ISLANDS
Antigua (city) 2 143–4*; 13 *758*
architecture 13 760–61
Casa de Chamorro 13 761
Casa de los Leones 13 761
Centro de Investigaciones de Mesoamérica (CIRMA) Library 13 769
ecclesiastical buildings
Belén church 13 760
Cathedral 2 *143*; 13 760
Cathedral of S José 13 760
Colegio de Cristo Crucificado 13 761
convent 13 764
El Calvario 13 761
El Carmen 13 761
Hospital de S Pedro Apóstol 13 760
La Compañía 13 761
La Merced 13 761; 26 251
La Recolección *see* Colegio de Cristo Crucificado
S Ana 13 761
Santa Cruz 13 761
S Clara 13 761
S Francisco 13 760
S José 13 761
S Rosa de Lima 13 761
S Teresa 13 761
furniture 13 768
marks 13 768
metalwork 13 767
Museo Colonial 2 143; 13 769; 25 877
Museo del Libro Antiguo 2 143; 13 769
Museo de Santiago 2 143; 13 769
Palacio Real 13 761
pedestals 13 *767*
pottery 13 768
Real Cabildo 13 761
textiles 13 766
Universidad de S Carlos 13 761
Antikvariát 8 424
Antikythera 13 460, 594; 27 29
Antilias, Armenian Catholicate of Cilicia 2 444
Antilles, Greater 2 144–5*; 5 744, 746*
figurines 2 *145*
stone 2 *145*
Antilles, Lesser 2 144–54*; 5 746; 29 198–201*
amulets 5 746, 747
architecture 2 147–9*
barracks 2 148
batik 2 151
body ornaments 5 746, 747
carnivals 2 146–7, 153
cellarets 2 151, *151*
ceramics 2 144, 146, 152*
chairs 2 151
charcoal 5 746
churches 2 148
collections 2 144, 153–4*
costumes 2 *146*
cotton 2 144, 151; 5 747
couches 2 151
decorative arts 2 150–52*
dress 5 747
education (art) 2 154*
figurines 2 144
fortifications 2 148
furniture 2 150–51
galleries (iv) (art) 2 153
gold 2 152
hardstones 29 198–9
headdresses 2 147
houses 2 146, *147*, 147
interior decoration 2 150–51*
jewellery 2 152*
kaolin 5 746
libraries 2 153
masks 2 147
metalwork 2 152*
museums 2 153–4*
painting 2 146, 149*, *150*
paints 5 746
patronage 2 152–3*
pendants (jewellery) 5 747
pottery 2 145; 5 746, 747; 29 198, 200
rock art 2 145
sculpture 2 152
stone-carvings 29 200
textiles 2 151–2*
tourist art 2 153
trade 2 150; 5 747
wood-carvings 29 200
Antilles, Netherlands 2 144, 148; 5 *745*
see also ANTILLES, LESSER
Antímano, Nuestra Señora del Rosario 32 169
Antimenes Painter 32 31–2*, 65
works 12 286; 13 *510*, 510–11, *591*
antimensia see under ALTARS → types
antimony
alloys 21 319; 24 578
uses
glass 10 55; 13 594; 30 408
glazes 16 394
pigments 24 798
antimony oxides 10 192
antimony sulphides 12 782
Antin(, Duc) d' 2 154–5*; 4 550; 11 538; 19 141; 20 135; 23 515
architecture 18 815
competitions 7 570; 24 135
paintings 8 813; 14 584; 23 195
sculpture 8 72
Antin, Eleanor 2 155*; 10 879; 24 409
Antinis, Robertas 19 499
Antinoë *see* ANTINOÖPOLIS
Antinoöpolis 1 882; 2 155*; 7 *819*; 26 *921*
glass 16 519
ivory-carvings 7 826
sculpture 7 821
silk 9 663
stelae 7 821
Antinoöpolis—cont.
textiles 7 826; 27 114, *114*
Antinori, Giovanni 3 644; 25 8; 27 801
Antinous 27 37
Antioch (i) (Antakya) *see under* ANTAKYA
Antioch (ii) (Psidia) 2 159–60*; 9 *512*; 13 *362*; 26 *908*; 28 382, 383
agora 28 383
architecture 26 913; 28 384
collections 13 555
Epiphania 28 384
glass 28 384
mosaics 13 561; 27 64
sculpture 13 463; 28 383
Temple of Augustus and Mên 26 913
Temple of Zeus 28 383, 384
Antioch, Plain of *see* AMUK REGION
Antioch, Principality of 17 500
Antioch Cup 25 665
Antiochia Margiana *see* MERV (TURKMENISTAN) → Gyaur-Kala
Antioch-on-the-Chrysorrhoas *see under* JERASH
Antiochos I Soter (*reg* 281-261 BC) 15 912
Antiochos I Theos, King of Commagene (*reg c.* 69-*c.*36 BC) 13 466; 22 731, *731*, 732; 24 217
Antiochos III, King of Syria (*reg* 223-187 BC) 8 477; 28 382
Antiochos IV Epiphanes, King of Syria (*reg* 175-163 BC) 2 668, 688; 8 3; 13 405, 465; 17 493; 28 383, 384
Antiochos VI Epiphanes, King of Syria (*reg* 145-142 BC) 5 298
Antiochos Philopappos 2 668
Antiope Group 13 511
Antioquia 7 *601*, 603, 605
S Barbara 7 605
Antiparos 2 160*; 8 *304*, 324; 13 *363*; 32 294
Antiphanes 2 160*
Antiphellos *see* KAŞ
Antiphilos 2 160*; 13 552
works 1 619; 12 287; 13 547; 29 665
Antiphonals 7 188; 28 486, 487
individual manuscripts
Beaupré Antiphonal (Baltimore, MD, Walters A.G., MSS W. 759-62) 7 188, 189, *189*
Corvinian Antiphonal 14 904
see also CHOIR-BOOKS; GRADUALS
Antiphonaries 13 130
Antiphonitis Monastery 2 426
Antiphon Painter 13 521; 32 61
Antipodean group 2 161*, 750
antiquarian societies 2 161–5*
antiquaries 2 161–5*
Antique, the 2 165–71*
antique glass *see under* GLASS → types
antique lace *see under* LACE → types
Antique Master 7 383
antiques 10 284
antique scripts *see under* SCRIPTS → types
antiquities 15 183–4
Antiquity, Late *see* LATE ANTIQUITY
Antiquity and Art see SENATNE UN MĀKSLA
Antiquorum 30 153
anti-seismic construction *see under* ARCHITECTURE → techniques
Antissa 19 234, *234*
Antistius 27 111
Antivari *see* STARI BAR
antlers 14 763
historical and regional traditions
Japan 17 297, 401
Native North Americans 14 *746*
Prehistoric art 16 615; 25 472, 488, 491, 493
United States of America 14 *746*
techniques
engraving 25 491
uses
batons 25 493
figurines 25 488
glues 15 850
helmets 14 *746*
netsuke 17 401
spear-throwers 25 493
tools 16 615; 25 472, 493
Antoine, André 4 325; 30 682, 685
Antoine, Jacques-Denis 2 172–3*
works 2 *172*, 337; 3 823; 4 455; 22 454; 25 267
Antoine, Pierre-Joseph 8 889
Antoine de Chourses 11 726
Antoine de Compiègne 1 588
Antoine de Lonhy 20 775
Antoine of Burgundy 3 555; 5 206, 212*; 7 243; 20 617
Antoine of Burgundy, Master of 19 727; 20 617–18*; 24 606
attributions 14 389
patrons and collectors 3 555
Antoine Rolin, Master of 26 556
Antokol, SS Peter and Paul 29 839
Antokol'sky, Mark (Matveyevich) 2 173*; 17 576, 580; 27 390
groups and movements 20 232
pupils 12 653; 28 57
Antol
Château 28 850
Museum 28 857
Antolić, V. 19 883
Antolínez (y Sarabia), Francisco 2 173–4*
patrons and collectors 1 690; 5 792; 27 793
Antolínez, José 2 174*; 29 282
patrons and collectors 18 899; 27 792
teachers 26 438
Antolini, Giovanni Antonio 2 174–5*
illustrated writings 1 575
patrons and collectors 16 647
pupils 12 583; 23 259
works 5 622; 12 659; 21 520
Antologia 11 189
Antologia romana 24 447
Antomaria Parodi, Domenico di 24 203, 835; 28 79
Antona, Nicolás de *see* NICOLÁS DE ANTONA
Antonakakis, Dimitris 2 175*; 13 351
Antonakakis, Suzana (Maria) 2 175*; 13 351
Antonakos, Stephen 22 748
Antonelli, Alessandro 2 176–7*; 21 172
works 2 *177*; 16 648; 31 442
Antonelli, Bautista 2 176; 8 231; 23 903; 25 700; 26 501
works 25 *700*
Antonelli, Costanzo 2 177
Antonelli, Cristóbal Garavalli 2 176
Antonelli, Juan Bautista, the elder (1530-88) 2 143, 175; 13 760; 26 501; 30 518
Antonelli, Juan Bautista, the younger (1585-1649) 2 176; 5 886; 32 168
Antonelli, Juan Bautista (great nephew of Antonelli the younger) 2 176
Antonello, Jacopo di *see* JACOBELLO D'ANTONIO

Antonello da Messina (c. 1430-79) 2 178–82*; 5 127; 16 824; 25 138; 27 617, 658; 28 656; 32 190
attributions 7 543
collaboration 16 824
methods 12 501; 16 658; 23 376; 26 186
paintings
altarpieces 2 180; 27 495
genre 12 287
portraits 2 181
religious 2 179, 182; 5 443; 16 835; 29 859
patrons and collectors 3 239; 5 9, 845; 7 895; 15 158; 22 696; 25 383; 29 46
pupils 9 102; 21 904
restorations by others 24 343
teachers 7 543; 10 713
Antonello da Messina (1466-1535) see SALIBA, ANTONIO DE
Antonello di Giovanni degli Antonii see ANTONELLO DA MESSINA (c. 1430-79)
Antonescu, Petre 2 183*; 3 124; 5 74; 26 709
Anton-Florian, Prince of Liechtenstein (reg 1719-21) 23 606
An Tong-suk 18 60
Anton Günther, Count of Oldenburg (reg 1603-67) 12 494; 14 312; 22 317; 29 371
Antonia, Guido di Meo d' 10 652
Antoniani, Francesco 31 446
Antoniani, Silvio 24 399
Antonianos of Aphrodisias 27 37
works 27 38
Antoniazzo Romano 2 183–4*; 26 765, 766
attributions 3 876; 20 679
collaboration 21 97, 98
patrons and collectors 12 147; 21 125; 23 575; 26 766; 28 530
works 19 788
Antonibi, Bernardino 16 725
Antonibon, Giovanni Battista 23 262; 32 200
Antonibon, Pasquale 16 738; 23 262
Antonie, Lee 26 282
Antonii, Antonello di Giovanni degli see ANTONELLO DA MESSINA (c. 1430-79)
Antonin 25 99
Antonine Proserpina Sarcophagus 1 4; 22 42
Antonine Wall 14 23; 21 559; 26 906
Antonini, Antonio 2 397
Antoninus Pius, Emperor of Rome (reg 138-61) 2 184*; 9 896; 16 685; 23 619; 27 45
architecture 26 794, 795, 899–900*
sculpture 27 37, 39
Antonio (fl 14th cent.) 1 726
Antonio (fl 1463) 22 800
Antonio, Master (fl 1482-8) 21 125
Antonio, Angelito 24 623
Antonio, Battista d' see BATTISTA D'ANTONIO
Antonio (Tucci), Biagio d' see BIAGIO D'ANTONIO (TUCCI)
Antonio, Gasparino di see GASPARINO DI ANTONIO
Antonio, Jacobello d' see JACOBELLO D'ANTONIO
Antonio, Jacopo di see JACOPO DI ANTONIO
Antonio (di Ancona), Nicola di Maestro see NICOLA DI MAESTRO ANTONIO (DI ANCONA)
Antonio, Salvo d' see SALVO D'ANTONIO
Antonio da Anghiari 11 382; 24 759, 760
Antonio da Brescia 20 918
Antonio da Bufalo 1 531
Antonio (Leonelli) da Crevalcore 2 184–5*
Antonio da Fabriano 2 185*; 29 665
Antonio da Giovanni di Ser Francesco 33 350
Antonio dalla Casa 4 31
Antonio da Mercatello Bencivenni see BENCIVENNI, ANTONIO (DA MERCATELLO)
Antonio da Negroponte see FALIER, ANTONIO
Antonio da Pisa 11 198, 892
Antonio da Rimpacta 20 418
Antonio da Saluzzo, Archbishop 21 529
Antonio da Trento 2 185*; 10 799
works 24 200; 33 366, 366, 367
Antonio da Viterbo 11 683; 20 124; 26 817; 32 628
Antonio de Beatis 24 249
Antonio del Balzo 2 139
Antonio del Branca 19 442
Antonio del Massaro see PASTURA, IL
António de Santa Clara 30 799
Antonio di Agostino di ser Giovanni see ANTONIO DA FABRIANO
Antonio di Banco 22 461, 462
Antonio di Biagio 20 531
Antonio di Cristoforo da Firenze 3 260
Antonio di Domenico 20 413
Antonio di Duccio 1 455
Antonio di Francesco da Venezia see ANTONIO VENEZIANO
Antonio di Gregorio 13 293
Antonio di Lorenzo 4 32
Antonio di Maso 4 32
Antonio di Niccolò di Lorenzo (di Domenico) 2 186*
Antonio di Piergiovanni di Lorenzo da Settignano 31 190
Antonio di ser Cola 24 232
Antonio di Vincenzo 4 279, 280; 13 66, 96; 30 515
works 4 279
António Florentim 2 870
Antonio Juan, Lord of Tous see TOUS, ANTONIO JUAN, Lord of
Antonio Lombardi see LOMBARDI, ANTONIO
Antonio Maria da Milano 31 316
Antonio Maria da Villafora 2 186*; 4 397; 32 198
Antonios 21 345; 22 228; 25 335
Antonios I Kassimatas, Patriarch of Constantinople 9 638
Antonio Veneziano 2 187*
collaboration 2 16
patrons and collectors 28 656
pupils 29 549
works 2 187; 21 72; 24 855, 860
Antonis, Master see OBBERGHEN, ANTONIS VAN
Antonissen, Henri-Joseph 7 900; 23 438
Anton Maria da Carpi 7 323; 28 340
Antón Martínez de Bruselas 14 134
Anton of Worms see WOENSAM, ANTON
Antonov, I. P. 33 518
Antonov, Z. 1 507
Anton Ulrich, Duke of Brunswick-Wolfenbüttel (reg 1685-1714) 33 53–4*
architecture 18 242; 33 293
faience (ii) (ceramics) 5 30
paintings 19 707; 27 133
Antony House (Cornwall) 4 600; 10 785; 14 268; 15 44; 33 375
Antoshchenko-Olenev, Valentin 17 867
Antrakt 24 428
Antran 25 536
Antreasian, Garo 19 492; 20 606
Antri Mosque 15 372
Antropov, Aleksey (Petrovich) 2 188*; 27 388, 442, 578
collaboration 19 278
patrons and collectors 31 312
pupils 19 278
Anttila, Eva 11 110
Antubam, Kofi 12 508, 509
Antunes, Bartolomeu 2 188*; 30 881
Antunes, João 2 188–90*
patrons and collectors 4 634
works 2 189; 4 629; 20 411; 25 292, 292; 29 100; 31 1
Antunes Ribeiro, Paulo 2 190*; 7 884; 26 60
Antúnez, Nemesio 2 190–91*; 6 598; 9 204
Antunović, Ljupko 4 462
An Túr Gloine see TOWER OF GLASS
Antwerp 2 191–204*, 191; 3 539
Academie voor Schone Kunsten see Koninklijke Academie voor Schone Kunsten
Algemeen Ziekenhuis Stuivenberg 14 783
art forms and materials 2 201
alabaster (gypsum) 8 738
altarpieces 8 731
altars 25 111
armour 2 471
brass 3 603
brick 3 588
cabinets (ii) (furniture) 3 582, 610
cartography 20 364
ceramics 2 201*; 3 588
citadel 21 570
costumes 30 665
diamonds 2 201; 17 522
embroidery 3 609
engravings 2 196, 196; 3 558; 10 389
faience (ii) (ceramics) 2 201; 3 588
fortifications 21 570, 577
furniture 3 598
gables 11 875
glass 3 593
gold 2 201–2*
jewellery 2 201; 17 522
lace 3 610
lacquer 18 614
leather 19 4
maiolica 22 878
marks 2 198–9
metalwork 2 201; 3 601, 603
tapestries 2 198, 199
metalwork 3 596, 597–8, 602
monstrances 3 598
objects of vertu 2 201*
painting 2 195; 3 554, 556, 557, 558, 560, 562, 615; 18 705, 706–7
cabinet pictures 5 351, 352
murals 22 329
panel paintings 24 6, 6
still-lifes 29 668
pattern books 3 581
pewter 3 603; 24 578
pottery 3 589
printing 6 595
prints 25 625
sculpture 3 569, 570, 572; 13 112
shields 2 473
silver 2 201–2*; 3 597, 598, 599, 600
stage design 30 665
stained glass 27 255; 29 504
stoves 3 588
Antwerp
art forms and materials—cont.
tapestries 2 197–200*, 198, 200; 3 576, 606, 607; 25 137; 30 317, 320
tiles 30 877, 878, 880
title-pages 4 360
urban planning 31 714
art market 2 558; 3 615
auction houses 2 559
Beurs 2 194; 3 548; 10 668
Boerentoren 3 551
craftsmen and artists 2 194
Den Passer 3 579
ecclesiastical buildings
Jesuit church see St Carolus Borromeus
Onze Lieve Vrouwe Cathedral 2 191, 202–3*, 202, 231; 3 542, 567, 613; 7 192; 13 61, 62; 22 220
altarpieces 3 263, 263; 21 353–4; 27 290
engravings 2 196
sculpture 13 99, 99
spire 29 414
tomb of Isabel of Bourbon 13 160
St Andrieskerk 3 545; 25 728
St Augustinuskerk 1 699; 2 725; 3 545
St Carolus Borromeus 1 467; 2 192, 192; 3 263, 545, 613; 15 45
paintings 3 558
textiles 3 609
St Jacobskerk 7 192; 13 63; 33 197
St Joriskerk 3 548
St Just
Chapel of the Virgin 13 211
St Pauluskerk 3 545; 7 300, 703
St Vincentiusgesticht 4 788
education (art) 3 617
exchange see Beurs
Exposition Internationale, 1894 15 883
Exposition Universelle, 1885 15 883
festivals 23 769
galleries (iv) (art) 9 15
Grote Markt 3 572
guilds 2 194; 3 596; 25 625
Handschoenmarkt 13 160
houses
Jordaenshuis 3 546, 576; 17 649
Osterriethuis 3 577
Rockoxhuis see under museums
Rubenshuis see under museums
Vleeshuis see under museums
Koninklijke Academie voor Schone Kunsten 2 196; 3 617; 4 586
library 3 619
Koninklijke Nederlandsche Schouwburg 3 547
Koninklijk Paleis 3 546
Middelheim see museums → Openluchtmuseum voor Beeldhouwkunst Middelheim
museums
Etnografisch Museum 29 240
Koninklijk Museum voor Schone Kunsten 2 194, 196, 197; 3 616; 33 244
collections 2 516; 3 615; 10 491
library 3 618
paintings 8 632
Museum Mayer van den Bergh 2 196; 3 617
Nationaal Scheepvaartmuseum 2 192; 3 616
Openluchtmuseum voor Beeldhouwkunst Middelheim 2 197; 3 617
library 3 618
Antwerp
museums—cont.
Plantin-Moretus Museum 2 193, 196; 3 616; 25 17
catalogues 27 137
Provinciaal Museum voor Fotografie 3 616
Rockoxhuis 14 381; 26 490
Rubenianum 2 370; 3 619; 5 187
Rubenshuis 2 193, 193, 196, 549, 550; 3 546, 583, 617; 9 22; 31 856
collections 8 464
furniture 3 583
Vleeshuis 2 192; 3 544, 616
roof 30 910
Staats Bank 3 549, 549, 613
Stadhuis 2 192, 203, 203–4*; 3 545; 10 745; 11 875; 17 700; 18 886; 31 238
interior decoration 3 579
paintings 3 562; 17 3; 26 490; 27 290; 29 892
Stadsbibliotheek 3 618
theatres 30 665
trade
paintings 16 766
paper 24 48
water supply 31 711
Zoo 33 698
Antwerp, Albert Cahen, Count of 20 240
Antwerp Adoration, Master of the 2 204; 20 618*
Antwerp Bible see under BIBLES → individual manuscripts
Antwerp blue see under PIGMENTS → types
Antwerpen, Johannes van see HEEM, JAN DAVIDSZ. DE
Antwerp Mannerism 2 194, 204–6*, 205; 3 492; 10 326; 13 22, 23; 20 618, 750; 23 678
see also GOTHIC → styles → Late Gothic
Antwerp Sketchbook see under SKETCHBOOKS → individual manuscripts
ANUM see ASSOCIATION OF INDEPENDENT UKRANIAN ARTISTS
Ānumakoṇḍa see HANAMKONDA
Anunciação, Tomás José da 2 206–7*; 25 298
pupils 4 385; 19 879; 32 98
sponsors 4 638
works 28 781
Anup Singh, Maharaja of Bikaner (reg 1669-98) 15 608
Anuradhapura 2 207, 207–8*; 29 440
Abhayagiri Vihara 2 207–8; 29 442, 447, 474
sculpture 29 458
stupa 29 457, 457
architecture 29 446, 449
Dakkhina stupa 29 457, 475
exhibitions 29 478
Folk Museum 29 478
Isurumini 29 446
Jetavana Vihara 2 207–8; 29 442, 447, 476
stupa 29 446, 457, 472
Kuccaveli 29 457
Lankarama 29 447
Lohapasada 29 474
Maha Ilupallama 29 457
Mahavihara 2 207–8; 5 97; 29 447
metalwork 29 474
Mirisavati Vihara 2 207–8; 29 447
monasteries 29 448, 462
Ran-masu-uyana 29 448
Royal Palace 29 448
Ruvanveliseya 29 457, 459, 474, 475
sculpture 29 457, 459
Shiva Devale 1 29 448
shrines (i) (cult) 29 442, 448
stupas 5 98; 29 441, 447, 865

Anuradhapura—cont.
Thuparama **29** 447, *447*, 865
trade **20** 302
Vessagiriya **29** 446
anuratha *see* PRATIRATHA
Anuszkiewicz, Richard **2** 208*
collaboration **20** 607
groups and movements **1** 79; **23** 449
teachers **1** 549
works **7** 637, VII2(b)
Anuta **25** 181
anvils **1** 365
Anwa, Mahadeva Temple **15** 316
Anwan Album *see under* ALBUMS → individual manuscripts
Anwar, Ajaz **23** 800
Anwari Alhuseyni, Shams *see* ALHUSEYNI, SHAMS ANWARI
Anxi **28** *719*, 720
Anyang (China) **2** 208–9*; **6** *615*; **7** 150; **28** 603
altars **1** 702
architecture **6** 646, 685
bronze **4** 852; **6** *837*, 840; **7** 55, *55*
cemeteries **6** 694
chariots **6** 481
coins **7** 72, *72*
inscriptions **6** 737, *738*, 767
iron **7** 99
ivory-carvings **7** 102
jade **7** 3, 107
lacquer **7** 12
mirrors **21** 714
oracle bones **2** *208*; **6** 625, 836
pottery **6** 869
sculpture **6** 726, 733, 734
tomb of Zhang Sheng
furniture **7** 35
sculpture **29** 906
urban planning **6** 663
wall paintings **6** 773
see also XIAOTUN; XIBEIGANG
Anyang (Korea) **18** 343; **19** 804
Anyi (China) **6** 663
Anyi (people) **1** 392, 503, 514; **8** 21, 22
An Yŏng-bae **18** 264
Anyor **15** 441; **20** 819
Anyue **30** 443
Anýž, Franta **8** 414, 416
Anza **25** 499, 517
Anza, Antonio **23** 341
Anzan *see* MALYAN, TALL'I → Anshan
Anzeiger für schweizerische Geschichte und Altertumskunde/Indicateur d'histoire et d'antiquités suisses **24** 453
Anzi **13** 526
Anzinger, Siegfried **32** 447
Anzio **26** 292
Anzures, Pedro **29** 893
Anzy-le-Duc Priory **13** 73; **26** 584, 601, 602
Aohan **7** 23
Ao Ietsugu **17** 323
Aoki, Jitsusaburō **17** 421
Aoki, Shigeru **2** 211*; **17** 204
Aoki, Tomitarō *see* HARA, SANKEI
Aoki Mokubei **2** 210–11*; **17** 258, 399; **18** 60, 555; **23** 196, 594
works **2** *210*; **17** 191; **18** 538, 554–5
Aoki Renzan **18** 88
Ao Naga **15** 733
Aore **1** 317
Aorsi **28** 324
Aosta **2** 211–12*; **9** *510*; **16** *618*; **27** *4*
arch **31** 349
Augusta Praetoria **2** 212*; **26** *886*; **27** 3, 4, *4*
Cathedral **5** 427; **16** 722; **23** 650; **26** 702
gates **7** 358
orders (architecture) **23** 484
Aosta—cont.
Roman theatre **23** 349; **26** 891, 895
S Orso **2** 212*; **7** 455; **23** 649; **26** 620
theatre **26** 904
Aostalli (family) **25** 438
Aostalli, Andrea Maria **2** 212
Aostalli, Antonio **2** 212
Aostalli, Francesco **2** 212
Aostalli, Giovanni Battista **2** 212, 213; **19** 500; **24** 462
Aostalli, Giovanni Maria **2** 212; **4** 58
Aostalli, Pietro **2** 212
Aostalli, Stefano **2** 212
Aostalli, Ulrico **2** 212
castles **2** 212–13; **6** 59; **12** 149; **19** 500; **24** 108, 462; **25** 438
palaces **27** 285
Aouanrhet **1** *373*
aouchem *see* TATTOO GROUP
Aowin **1** 503
Apa **25** 526
Apache **22** 550, 554, 567, 629, 673
architecture **22** 567
basketwork **22** 661, *662*
dress **22** 634
leather **22** 655
pottery **22** 605
Apache (Chiricahua) **14** 801; **22** 665
Apache (Cibecue) **22** 661
Apache (Kiowa) **22** 551
Apache (Lipan) **22** 551
Apache (Mescalero) **22** 661
apadanas *see under* HALLS → types
Apameia **2** 213–14*; **9** *513*; **26** *915*, 916, 917; **30** 178
churches **9** 539
coins **4** *686*; **17** 533
mosaics **2** 214*; **9** 567; **17** 535; **27** 64, *65*
Roman theatre **2** 214
stucco **27** 72
synagogue **17** 543, 559
Triclinium Building **9** 567
Apano Symi, Hagios Georgios **8** 156; **25** 334
APAO (Associazione per l'Architettura Organica) **16** 650; **25** 792
Apap, Vincent **2** 215; **20** 214
Apap, Willie **2** 214–15*; **20** 213
aparajedor *see* WARDENS
Aparicio Inglada, José **2** 215*; **29** 283; **30** 417
collaboration **10** 134
pupils **10** 134; **20** 58; **21** 126
Aparicio Stele **21** 187
Aparici y Soriano, Federico **2** 215*; **26** 520; **29** 272
Apartis, Thanassis **2** 215*; **13** 354; **19** 727
apartments **2** 216*; **30** 457
Austria **30** *885*
Canada **5** *563*
Colombia **7** *606*
Denmark **8** *728*
Egypt, ancient **9** 852
England **6** *409*; **7** *483*; **11** *808*
France **11** *519*; **24** *128*, *129*; **27** *880*
Germany **21** *783*; **25** *839*
Hungary **14** 907
Islamic **16** 241
Japan **21** *317*
Mozambique **13** *781*
Netherlands, the **1** *814*; **19** 116; **22** *831*
Russia **27** *380*
United States of America **7** 436; **22** *53*; **31** *597*
see also INSULAE; TENEMENT BUILDINGS
Apartoglou, Thanassis *see* APARTIS, THANASSIS
Apasa **10** 423
Apa Tani **15** 733
Apátfalva **15** 2
apatite **14** 167
Apatourios of Alabanda **27** 50
Apáty, Sándor **15** 2
Apatzingán **21** 719
Ape *see* PELLEGRINI, CARLO
Apeiranthos **8** *304*
Ayia Kyriaki **9** 575; **22** 700
museum **8** 323
ape italiana delle belle arti, L' **24** 447
Apel, Otto **2** 216–17*; **30** 684
Apeldoorn **22** 884
Centraal Beheer **14** 484, *484*; **22** 832; **23** 360
Rijksmuseum Paleis Het Loo *see under* HET LOO
Apellániz, Juan Maria **25** 483
Apelles **1** 613; **2** 217–18*, 364; **13** 544, 551; **14** 868; **25** 44
attributions **13** 546
collaboration **21** 75
competitions **13** 546
methods **13** 551, 554; **21** 757
patrons and collectors **2** 726; **13** 375
teachers **13** 549; **23** 900
works **1** 651; **13** 549; **15** 84, 86; **16** 613; **18** 393; **25** 44
writings **13** 554
Apelli & Varesio **21** 824
Apengeter, Hans **13** 161
Apergis, Achilleas **2** 218*; **13** 355
Aperia **27** 812
Aperture **24** 434; **33** 147
Apéry **8** 480
Aphendrika
Asomatos Church **8** 358
Hagios Giorgios **8** 358
Panagia **8** 358
Aphrodisias **2** 218–21*, *219*; **5** 742; **9** *512*; **13** *362*; **26** *908*
architecture **2** 219*
bath-gymnasium **3** 375; **26** 912
capitals **19** 223
inscriptions **27** 29
marble **26** 911; **27** 13; **29** 702
mosaics **9** 564, 565
Museum **27** 115
odeion **23** 350
palace **9** 557
reliefs **2** *220*; **27** 31
sculptors **26** 855
Sculptors' Studio **29** 707
sculpture **2** 220–21*; **13** 467; **27** 28, 45
Sebasteion **27** 31
Aphrodisios Libyos **27** 28
Aphrodite Euploia **10** 675; **13** 434, 459; **18** 148; **23** 291; **25** 45
copies **13** 573; **18** *148*; **23** *291*; **31** 61
display **9** 20; **18** 147
Aphrodite Group **13** 578, 582
Aphrodite Kallypygos **27** 46
Aphrodite of Knidos *see* APHRODITE EUPLOIA
Aphrodite Painter **13** 532
Aphrodito **16** 146
Aphsad, Vishnu Temple **15** 281
Apian, Philipp **1** 788; **12** 811, 814; **33** 271
Apin, Mochtar **15** 808
Apindji **11** 878
Aplahanda, King of Carchemish (*reg* early 18th cent. BC) **1** 115
Aplomata **8** *304*
cemetery **22** 698
tombs **8** 311, 322, 323; **22** 698
Aply, Jeanine **10** 838
Apocalypse, Master of the (*fl* 1357) **17** 821
Apocalypse Master (*fl* 1408–20) *see* BERRY APOCALYPSE, MASTER OF THE
Apocalypses **2** 221–4*; **4** 3; **20** 341
historical and regional traditions
England **13** 136; **14** 423
Germany **2** *223*
Apocalypses
historical and regional traditions—cont.
Gothic **13** 130, 136
Netherlands, the **4** *144*
individual manuscripts
Bamberg Apocalypse (Bamberg, Staatsbib., MS. Bibl. 140) **12** 382; **23** 652, 654; **28** 25
Douce Apocalypse (Oxford, Bodleian Lib., MS. Douce 180) **10** 245; **13** 141, *141*; **20** 332, *348*; **21** 550; **25** 14
Gulbenkian Apocalypse (Lisbon, Mus. Gulbenkian, MS. LA 139) **13** 138
Lambeth Apocalypse (London, Lambeth Pal. Lib., MS. 209) **10** 245; **13** 121, 141; **14** *415*
Lorvão Apocalypse (Lisbon, Arquiv. N.) **25** 295
Trier Apocalypse (Trier, Stadtbib., MS. 23) **5** 801
Trinity College Apocalypse (Cambridge, Trinity Coll., MS. R. 16. 2) **25** 13
Valenciennes Apocalypse (Valenciennes, Bib. Mun., MS. 99) **5** 801; **15** 875
types
Beatus **2** 222
Apocalypse Tapestries **2** 49–51*, *50*, 112; **3** 362, 605; **11** 637; **13** 196, 197; **24** 133
Apocaucus, Alexis, Grand Duke **21** 5
Apocrypha Drawings, Master of the **30** 486; **33** 239
apodyteria **2** 224*; **10** 670
Apoil, Suzanne **28** 524
Apokaphos, Alexios **25** 331
Apokaukos, John **30** 718
Apol, Louis **2** 224*
Apolakkia **26** *289*, 294
Hagios Giorgios Varda **26** 293
Apolima **27** 683
Apollinaire, Guillaume **2** 224–6*; **8** 244, 602, *604*, 656; **13** 826; **18** 862; **23** 569–70, 694; **24** 427; **25** 6; **27** 307; **30** 25; **32** 327
groups and movements **8** 240, 245; **11** 865; **25** 747; **28** 347; **30** 18
personal collection **1** 438
works **2** *226*, 616; **7** 630, 698; **11** 865; **12** 497; **16** 818; **23** 333; **24** 405; **26** 51
illustrated **5** 669; **8** 606, 773, 775; **9** 372, 373; **17** 725; **20** 399; **24** 726; **25** 450
translated **6** 167
Apollini Sacrum Master *see* MARRADI, MASTER OF
Apollinopolis *see* EDFU
Apollo (*fl* 4th cent. AD) **3** 420
Apollo (Belgium) **3** 565
Apollo (England) **24** 423, 424, 446; **30** 42
Apollo, Benson **17** 908
Apollo 11 cave **27** 696
Apollo and Daphne Legend, Master of the **29** 361, 362
Apollo Association *see* AMERICAN ART-UNION
Apollo Belvedere **2** 226–7*; **7** 726; **13** 303, 468
casts **7** 562; **11** 661
censorship **26** 286
collectors **2** 559; **27** 46, 272
discovery **2** 168; **26** 767
display **2** 162; **9** 20; **13** 605; **16** 770; **26** 846; **27** 114, 273; **28** 755
original Greek model **13** 470
Apollodoros (*fl* 410 BC) **2** 227*; **13** 548, 553, 554
attributions **23** 900
works **13** 550, 553
Apollodoros (*c.* 61 BC) **15** 82
Apollodoros of Damascus (*fl* AD 103–25) **2** 227*, 312; **14** 22; **16** 623; **26** 866, 884, 885, 896, 925
architecture **26** 897
baths **3** 375; **26** 897
bridges **26** 885; **30** 900
columns **26** 791
fora **26** 785, 896
forts **2** 1
patrons and collectors **26** 856
writings **21** 577; **26** 924
Apollo Fountain **12** 401
Apollon **20** 152; **27** 439, 580; **32** 724; **33** 486
Apollona **22** 698, 699
Apollonia (Bulgaria) *see* SOZOPOL
Apollonia (Cirenaica) *see* MARSA SUSA
Apollonia (Crete) **8** 154
Apollonia (Illyria) **1** *537*, 538; **2** 227*
architecture **26** 907
pottery **13** 534
Apollonia (Libya) **27** 18
Apollonia Group **17** 911
Apollonio, Santo d' *see* SANTO D'APOLLONIO
Apollonio di Giovanni (di Tomaso) **2** 228–9*
attributions **6** 3
patrons and collectors **6** 503; **28** 270
works **2** *228*; **6** 2, 3, 4; **29** 360
workshop **6** *2*; **16** 660
Apollonios (*fl* ? 2nd cent. BC) **2** 229*; **25** 45
copies **10** 812
works **13** 470; **26** 292
Apollonios (*fl* 1st cent. BC) **3** 690
Apollonis **24** 412
Apollonius (*fl c.* 1300–20) **11** 199
Apollo of Piombino **13** 470
Apollo Sauroktonos **25** *456*
Aponte, Pedro de *see* PEDRO DE APONTE
Apophis **6** 170
apophyge **2** 229*
AP Originals **22** 876
Apostles, Master of the Miracle of the *see* MIRACLES OF THE APOSTLES, MASTER OF THE
Apostool, Cornelis **2** 229*
Apostu, Gheorghe **26** 716
Apotheosis Ivory **18** 826
APOYO (Assocation for the Conservation of Cultural Patrimony of the Americas) **7** 744
appareilleur *see* WARDENS
Appel, (Christiaan) Karel **2** 230–31*; **22** 851, 854, 861
dealers **16** 820
groups and movements **7** 489, 758; **9** 188; **17** 658; **22** 852; **27** 137
patrons and collectors **22** 332; **33** 254
works **2** *230*; **10** 483; **19** 491; **22** 852; **29** 97
Appel, Michael **11** 731
Appelby, Malcolm **28** 262
Appelman, Barend **3** 42
Appelmans, Jan **2** 202, 231
Appelmans, Peter **2** 202, 231–2*
Appelmaus, Jean **3** 542
Appenay, Logan **10** *578*
Appenzell **30** *124*, 141, 151
Appert, A. **4** 80
Appia, Adolphe **30** 682, 685
Appian **9** 618
Appian, Adolphe (-Jacques-Barthélemy) **2** 232*; **9** 309; **21** 896
Appian, Jean-Louis **2** 232
Appian, Louis **19** 847
Appiani (family) **12** 405; **21** 565

Appiani, Andrea 2 232–3*; 14 586; 21 527
collaboration 31 268
groups and movements 32 256
methods 10 199
patrons and collectors 3 452; 4 300, 471
pupils 5 783
reproductive prints by others 3 309
teachers 31 268
works 2 *233*; 16 677, 719, 728; 18 885; 20 90; 21 527, *528*
Appiani, Giuseppe 2 233–4*; 26 498; 32 467
Apple, Billy 2 234*
Apple, Jacki 24 409
Applebroog, Ida 2 234*
Apple Goblet 12 442
Appleton 29 98
Appleton, Thomas (Gooch) 2 234–5*
Appleton, Thomas Gold 21 612
Appleyard, Donald 31 735
application lace *see under* LACE → types
applied art 27 394; 30 382
applied art education *see under* EDUCATION (ART) → types
Applied Arts Quarterly 24 431
appliqué 2 235*; 30 562
historical and regional traditions
Afghanistan 10 872
Africa 1 299, *425*
Belgium 3 610
Bhutan 3 915
Buddhism 30 846
Burma 5 248*, *249*
Central Asia, Western 6 250, 251
China 7 14, 19, 144
England 10 *182*
Greece, ancient 13 540
India, Republic of 15 175, 176
Indonesia 15 792, 795
Islamic 16 466
Italy 16 759
Japan 17 *356*; 30 VII2
Java 15 792
Mongolia 21 878
Native North Americans 22 648, 654
Nigeria 1 299
Spain 29 349
Sumatra 15 795
Thailand 30 *626*
Tibet 30 846
United States of America 1 *425*; 30 VI3; 31 658
materials
felt 10 872
lacquer 7 14, 19
leather 1 299; 21 878
paints 29 349
quills 22 648
silk 10 *182*
wallpaper 32 817
uses
carpets 16 466
dress 6 251; 22 648
embroidery 3 610; 6 250; 10 *182*; 16 759
hangings 5 *249*
pottery 13 540
quilts 1 *425*; 30 VI3
robes 30 VII2
rugs 27 316
skirts 30 *626*
terracottas 29 475
tunics 30 *626*
turbans 30 *626*
see also PATCHWORK
Apponyi, Georg 11 33
Apport, L' 17 518
apprentices 2 523; 9 38; 20 561; 28 498
China 7 147
Egypt, ancient 9 790
England 19 532; 20 562
apprentices—cont.
France 11 585
Germany 19 532; 20 563
Italy 12 169; 16 777
Venezuela 32 172, 180
Appuna *Virgin* 26 647; 30 83
Apraiz, Julián de 32 630
Apraksin 27 439
Apraksin, Fyodor, Count 26 7
Apries (*reg* 589-570 BC) 9 *777*, 849, 852; 10 68; 23 807
Apriķi Church 18 848
Aprile (family) 31 89
Aprile, Antonio 12 114
Aprile, Carlo d' 28 476
aprons
historical and regional traditions
Africa 1 *297*, 418–19*, *419*
Byzantine 9 643
China 7 76, 145
Early Christian (*c.* AD 250-843) 9 643
Guyana 3 441; 13 875
Kenya 1 *297*
Mesoamerica, Pre-Columbian 21 249
Native North Americans 22 655
Ndebele 1 418
Tibet 3 442
Zulu 1 348; 3 442; 33 724
materials
beads 1 *297*; 3 442; 13 875
beadwork 3 441, 442
feathers 21 249
leather 22 655
techniques
beadwork 1 *419*
embroidery 7 145
Aprosio, Angelico 11 53
Apsadh 15 499; 29 824
Apsarades (family) 21 343
Apsarades, Nektarios 15 890; 21 344
Apsarades, Theophanis 15 890; 21 344
apses 2 235*; 22 161
France 5 371
Gothic 2 347
Romanesque 5 371
Rome, ancient 22 161; 26 923
Apsevdis, Theodoros 8 359
apsidal houses *see under* HOUSES → types
apsidiole *see* CHAPELS → types → absidiole
Apt 11 606
APT *see* ASSOCIATION FOR PRESERVATION TECHNOLOGY
Apt, Ulrich 2 715, 716; 4 758, 759; 12 387
Aptera 8 154
apteral 2 235*
Apukhtin, Viktor (Olegovich) 31 783
Apuleius 22 413; 25 46
Apulia, Nicolaus de *see* NICCOLÒ DELL'ARCA
Apulia, Robert Guiscard, Duke of *see* ROBERT GUISCARD, Duke of Apulia
Apulia, Roger Borsa, Duke of *see* ROGER BORSA, Duke of Apulia
Apulum 1 530
Apuna (family) 10 623
Apurle 30 447
APZ Painter 13 532
Aqa Abu al-Qasim Beg 15 373
Aqab, Tell 30 196
Aqaba 17 500
Aqa Baba 16 81
Aqa Buzurg 2 235*; 16 534
Aqa Mirak 2 235*
patrons and collectors 27 514
pupils 28 536
works 16 333, 334, 335
Aqa Riza (i) (*fl c.* 1580-1610) 1 31, 91; 2 235–6*
pupils 12 561
works 15 584
Aqa Riza (ii) (*c.* 1565-1635) *see* RIZA
Aqar Quf 2 236–7*; 17 837; 21 *267*
architecture 21 287
royal palace 1 865; 23 806
sculpture 17 *837*
wall paintings 21 308
ziggurat 2 *236*; 21 286; 33 675
al-Aqib 30 914
Aq Kupruk II 1 185, *186*, 193
Aqqoyunlu 2 237*; 16 117
see also:
KHALIL, Sultan
UZUN HASAN, Sultan
YA'QUB BEG, Sultan
ZAYNAL BEG
Aqua, Andrea dell' 25 63; 33 605
Aqua, Cristoforo dall' 32 501
Aquae Granni *see* AACHEN
Aquae Sulis *see under* BATH
Aquae Tarbellicae *see* DAX
aquamanilia *see under* EWERS → types
aquamarines 12 270, I
historical and regional traditions
Byzantine 9 *653*
Early Christian (*c.* AD 250-843) 9 *653*
Egypt 9 *653*
Russia 10 *721*
uses
fonts (baptismal) 11 *251*
jewellery 9 *653*; 10 *721*; 17 524
a quartieri ware *see under* POTTERY → wares
aquatints 2 238–41*; 10 548; 13 706; 25 597, 614, 619; 26 231, 742; 32 894
France 4 330
historical and regional traditions
Britain 2 240
England 2 *238*; 9 *287*; 10 252; 11 906
France 2 239; 24 *724*
Indian subcontinent 15 210
Ireland 6 *64*
Netherlands, the 25 *50*
South Africa 29 110
Spain 13 *243*; 20 *604*
Sweden 11 173
United States of America 31 599, 602
types
sugarbite *see* ETCHINGS → types → lift-ground
uses
book illustrations 2 241; 4 362
aqueducts 2 241–3*
historical and regional traditions
Britain 2 242
Byzantine 2 242; 9 560
Early Christian (*c.* AD 250-843) 9 560
France 2 242
Greece, ancient 13 381
Iran 16 231
Islamic 2 242; 16 224, 231
Italy 2 242
Mexico 2 242
Ottoman 16 224
Portugal 10 *165*
Rome, ancient 7 353; 11 339, 802–3; 26 864, 890; 27 6*, 7*
Greece 26 910
North Africa 26 919
Spain 2 *242*, 242; 28 *368*
Turkey 16 224
United States of America 2 242
materials
cast iron 2 242
wood 2 242
techniques
centering 6 178
Aquicum 5 86
Aquila, Andrea dell' 32 646, 648, 650
Aquila, L' *see* L'AQUILA
Aquila, Leonoro dell' 4 620; 28 461
Aquila, Pietro 10 140
Aquila, Silvestro dell' *see* SILVESTRO (DI GIACOMO DA SULMONA) DELL' AQUILA
Aquila de Rakerspurga, Johannes *see* JOHANNES AQUILA DE RAKERSPURGA
Aquilano *see* CESURA, POMPEO
Aquilar, Heather 2 151
Aquileia 2 243–4*; 9 *510*; 26 *886*
Baptistery 3 189; 9 533; 11 251
Cathedral of S Maria 2 243; 9 529, 680; 16 625; 26 578, 653
capitals 26 622
mosaics 2 *243*; 7 271; 9 563, 569; 27 60
throne 30 777
wall paintings 23 649
churches 3 329
coins 7 535
gems 12 250
glass 27 74
Mausoleum 13 407; 21 892
mosaics 9 563; 22 161
Aquileia, Patriarchs of *see* GRIMANI
Aquilés, Julio de 7 488; 29 299
Aquilio, Antonio di *see* ANTONIAZZO ROMANO
Aquinas, Thomas *see* THOMAS AQUINAS
Aquincum *see under* BUDAPEST
Aquino, Francisco Avalos de, Viceroy of Sicily *see* AVALOS DE AQUINO, FRANCISCO, Viceroy of Sicily
Aquino, Lucio 24 99
Aquino, S Maria della Libera 16 626
Aquirre, Julie 23 84
Aquisgranum *see* AACHEN
Aquitanian marble *see under* MARBLE → types
Ara, K. H. 4 290
Ara Basilica 2 425
Arabatchi 16 485
Arab Club 17 654
arabesques 2 244–5*, *245*; 13 700; 16 133; 23 557
Arabesque style 2 245*; 32 IV1
see also DIRECTOIRE STYLE; ETRUSCAN STYLE; POMPEIAN REVIVAL
Arabia 2 245–75*, *246*; 26 *852*
alabaster (gypsum) 2 248, *256*, 272
alabaster vessels 2 272
architectural decorations 2 255
architecture 2 247–50*
Islamic 16 229
military 21 588
trabeated construction 31 269
beach-rock 2 248
bronze 2 258–9
caravanserais 21 548
churches 2 252*
coins 2 260–63*, *262*
copper 2 264–5
doublures 16 356
dress 1 887
exhibitions 2 275*
fortifications 2 250–51*; 21 588
glass 2 263*
graves 2 248–50
guidebooks 13 811
houses 2 247–8; 16 270–71
iconography 2 254, 257
incense burners 2 269
iron 16 *506*
jewellery 2 263–4*
limestone 2 *257*
masonry 2 248
metalwork 2 264–6*, *265*
mosaics 16 256
mosques 16 229
museums 2 275*
painting 2 274–5*
Arabia—cont.
palaces 2 250*
palm leaves 2 247
pottery 2 266–9*, *267*
Barbar ware 2 267
BI-ware 2 268
Chain-ridged ware 2 267
Namord ware 2 267
Pseudo-Barbar ware 2 268
rock art 2 269–70*
sandstone 2 *254*
sculpture 2 253*, *257*
bronze 2 258–9*
figure 2 256–8, *257*
relief 2 253–6*, *254*, *256*
stone 2 253*, 256–8*
terracotta 2 260*
seals 2 270–71*
stelae 2 255
stone 2 253–8, 271–3
stone vessels 2 271–3*
stucco 2 273*
sword guards 16 *506*
temples 2 251–3*, *252*
tents 30 471
terracotta 2 260
trade 26 855
wood 2 248
windows 2 248
wine sets 2 265
wood 2 248
see also BAHRAIN; KUWAIT; NABATAEA; OMAN; QATAR; SAUDI ARABIA; UNITED ARAB EMIRATES; YEMEN
Arabia Porcelain Factory 11 105, 106; 30 884
production 11 *106*
Arabic 16 273, *274*, 277–8
see also under SCRIPTS → types
Arabissos Church 9 654
Arabs 1 229, 633; 6 188; 16 107; 19 323; 29 440; 30 470
Arabshahi, Mas'ud 15 898; 27 810
Arab Society of Fine Arts (Syria) 30 177
Arab-Swahili 20 35
Arab-type mosques *see under* MOSQUES → types
Arachosian 1 886
Aracoeli *Madonna* 20 774
Aracs 14 891
Arad (Israel) 30 179, *180*
architecture 30 191
fortifications 17 553
pottery 30 *197*
seals 1 862
temple 17 539; 30 184
textiles 1 881
Arad (Romania) 26 *705*
Arad Regional Museum 26 724
fortifications 26 708
Arad, Ron 10 300
Aradeon, David 18 640
Aradhe 9 736
Aradus 1 888
Aragats, Holy Trinity 2 426
Aragay, Josep 29 329
Aragel, Moses 17 536
Aragon (House of) 1 766; 2 275*; 12 115
Aragon, Alfonso I, King of Naples (*reg* 1435-58) *see* ALFONSO I, King of Naples
Aragon, Alfonso II, King of Naples *see* ALFONSO II, King of Naples
Aragon, Alfonso IV, King of *see* ALFONSO IV, King of Aragon
Aragon, Beatrice of, Queen of Hungary *see* BEATRICE OF ARAGON, Queen of Hungary
Aragon, Catherine of, Queen of England *see* CATHERINE OF ARAGON, Queen of England
Aragon, Charles of, Duke of Terranova *see* TERRANOVA, CHARLES OF ARAGON, Duke of

Aragon, Ferdinand I, King of Naples *see* FERDINAND I, King of Naples
Aragon, Ferdinand II, King of Aragon and Sicily *see* FERDINAND II, King of Aragon and Sicily
Aragon, Francisco Borja y *see* BORJA Y ARAGON, FRANCISCO
Aragon, Frederick IV, King of Naples *see* FREDERICK IV, King of Naples
Aragon, Isabella, Queen of Castile-León *see* ISABELLA, Queen of Castile-León
Aragon, Joanna, Queen of Castile *see* JOANNA, Queen of Castile
Aragon, John II, King of *see* JOHN II, King of Aragon
Aragon, John of **5** 697
Aragon, Louis **2** 279*; **9** 196; **11** 549; **16** 808
 collaboration **19** 83
 groups and movements **4** 753; **8** 438, 439, 605; **30** 17, 18, 19, 20, 21, 22; **31** 503, 852
 works **24** 405
Aragon, Maria of Navarre, Queen of *see* MARIA OF NAVARRE, Queen of Aragon
Aragón, Martín Gurrea y, Duque de Villahermosa *see* VILLAHERMOSA, MARTÍN GURREA Y ARAGÓN, Duque de
Aragón, Pascual de, Archbishop of Toledo **31** 89
Aragón, Pedro Antonio de, Duque de Segorbe y Cardona *see* SEGORBE Y CARDONA, Duque de
Aragon, Peter I, King of *see* PETER I, King of Aragon
Aragon, Sancho, King of *see* SANCHO, King of Aragon
Aragon, Yolande of, Duchess of Anjou *see* YOLANDE OF ARAGON, Duchess of Anjou
Aragona, Giovanni d', Cardinal *see* GIOVANNI D'ARAGONA, Cardinal
Aragon and Sicily, Alfonso V, King of *see* ALFONSO I, King of Naples
Aragona Pignatelli Cortes, Museu Diego d' *see under* NAPLES → museums
aragonite **21** 241, *243*
 see also MEXICAN ONYX
Aragón y Pino, Gasper Galcerán de Gurrea, Conde de Guimerá *see* GUIMERÁ, GASPER GALCERÁN DE GURREA ARAGÓN Y PINO, Conde de
Aragua **32** 178
Aragusuku **27** 470
Arai, Alberto T. **2** 280*; **21** 380; **33** 493
Arai Hakuseki **14** 428; **17** 364, 425
Āraišu **18** 846
Ara Juang **15** 733
Arak
 carpets **15** 899; **16** 482, 483
 pottery **16** 396, 412, *413*
Arakan **2** 280–82*, *282*; **5** *221*, 225
 architecture **5** 236, 237
 coins **5** 255
 sculpture **5** 238, 241
 shrines (i) (cult) **2** *281*
 textiles **5** 247
Arakawa, Shūsaku **2** 282–3*; **17** 207; **19** 493; **22** 742
Arakawa, Toyozō **17** 266
Arakcheyev, Aleksey, Baron **29** 554
Arak'elyan, Sedrak **2** 432
Araki (family) **17** 186
Araki, Nobuyoshi **2** 283*
Araki, Takako **17** 268
Araki Genkei **17** 186
Araki Genyū **17** 186, 187
Araki Jogen **17** 186–7*
 works **17** *187*
Aralaguppe **23** 182
 Kalleshvara Temple **15** 530
 stele **15** 530
Araldi, Alessandro **5** 913; **7** 887
Arali, Joaquín **1** 741
Aralica, Stojan **28** 451
Aramaean **1** 828, *852*; **2** 283*; **3** 12; **14** 592; **21** 274*; **30** 187, 189, 194
 iconography **1** 830
 reliefs **17** *810*
Aramaic **1** 855; **21** 274
Aramatelqo **23** 282
Arambasić, Dragomir **28** 453
Arambo
 drums (musical instruments) **22** *377*
Araña, La *see* LA ARAÑA
Arana Borica, Mañuel **24** 181
Aranchi, Carlos **2** 386; **24** 503
Aranda **1** 46, 56, 63, 64
Aranda, 10th Conde de **2** 283–4*; **29** 328
Aranda, Buenaventura de Urrea Abarca de Bolea, 9th Conde de **2** 283
Aranda, Ginés Martínez de *see* MARTÍNEZ DE ARANDA, GINÉS
Aranda, José Jiménez *see* JIMÉNEZ ARANDA, JOSÉ
Aranda, Juan de **16** 863
Aranda, Pedro d'Alcantara, 9th Conde de **29** 328
Aranda de Duero **29** 333
Aranda school **22** 449
Arandia, Juan de **31** 822
Arango, Débora **7** 609; **22** 727; **33** 316
Arangoiti, Ramón Rodríguez *see* RODRÍGUEZ ARANGOITI, RAMÓN
Aranha **17** 512
Aranha, Lázaro Leitão **20** 403
Arani **4** *255*, 264
 church **4** 258
Arani, Master of **4** 264
Aran islands **20** 571
Aranjuez **31** 719
 Palace **2** *284*, 284–5*; **14** 473; **29** *258*, 267, 271
  architecture **31** 93
  bedroom of Isabella II **29** 306, *307*, 319
  Capilla Real **13** 922; **29** 343
  Casa de Infantes **32** 564
  Casa del Labrador **9** 23; **29** 272, 305
   Gabinete de Platino **29** 305, *305*
   interior decoration **10** 187; **11** 494; **29** *316*
   sculpture **1** 742
  Fountain of Hercules and Antaeus **29** 293
  fountains **9** 22
  furniture **29** 315, 342
  Gabinete de la Porcelana **5** 348; **9** 29; **13** 646; **29** 304, 329
   collections **4** 564; **20** 69
  gardens **1** 462; **2** 284–5; **12** 124; **32** 564–5
   sculpture **4** 588
  interior decoration **11** 494; **29** 304
  metalwork **29** 342
  paintings **4** 564; **10** 730
  Sala de Conversación **12** 587
  sculpture **29** 291
  textiles **29** 348
  theatre **21** 133
 S Pascal **15** 139
Aranya Prathet **30** 599
Aranyosmedgyes *see* MEDIESU AURIT
Araos, Jerry **24** 620
Araoz, Andrés de **3** 452
Araoz, Juan de **3** 452
Ara Pacis *see under* ROME
Arapaho **22** 551, 616, 650, 669, 673
Arapaj **9** 566
Arapesh **24** 67, 68
Ara Pietatis *see under* ROME
Arapov, Anatoly **4** 178
'Araq el-Emir *see* 'IRAQ AL-AMIR
Araraquara University **4** 714
Ararat Trust **16** 576
Arata, Giulio Ulisse **16** 648; **24** 696; **27** 788
Arata Isozaki *see* ISOZAKI, ARATA
Arathoon, Hilary **12** 53
Arato, José **2** 399
Aratos of Sikyon (271-213 BC) **13** 546; **21** 75; **23** 900
Aratus of Soli (*fl* 315-240 BC) **2** 649; **5** 801; **22** 412
Araucano **2** 394; **29** 132
Araujo, Ceferino **2** 285*
Araujo, César de *see* POUSÃO, HENRIQUE
Araujo, Diego Fernández de *see* FERNÁNDEZ DE ARAUJO, DIEGO
Araújo, Emanoel **4** 709
Araújo, José Álvares de **2** 285–6*; **26** 254; **31** 813; **32** 535
Araújo, Manuel Francisco de **4** 710
Araújo, Marceliano de **2** 286*; **4** 629
Araújo Lemos, Carlos de **10** 729
Araújo Lima, João **10** 729
Araújo Porto Alegre, Manuel de *see* PORTO ALEGRE, MANUEL DE ARAÚJO
Arausio **11** *505*; **26** *904*
Arausio *see under* ORANGE
Arawak **2** 144–5; **13** 877; **31** 330
 architecture **2** 147; **14** 55; **30** 13
 carvings **8** 229
 dress **30** 13
 ethnic groups **7** 602; **9** 113; **11** 758; **13** 874; **14** 54; **29** 191; **30** 12; **31** 330, 331
 jewellery **1** 818
 pottery **11** 758
 vernacular art **32** 166
Arawak Taíno *see* TAÍNO
Araya **32** *165*, 168
Arazzeria Barberini (Rome) **3** 207; **16** 758; **26** 778; **30** 322
Arazzeria Medicea (Florence) **5** 317; **11** 193–4; **16** 757, 758; **21** 19; **30** 319, 322, 324
 designers
  Allori, Cristofano **1** 671
  Butteri, Giovanni Maria **5** 317
  Cigoli, Lodovico **7** 311
  Dandini, Vincenzo (1609-75) **8** 498
  Ferretti, Giovanni Domenico **11** 20
  Sagrestani, Giovanni Camillo **27** 522
  Salviati, Francesco (Cecchino) **27** 650
  Schut, Cornelis, I (1597-1655) **28** 179
  Stradanus, Joannes **29** 740
  Vignali, Jacopo **32** 500
 production **11** *193*; **16** 757; **21** 21
 weavers **5** 605; **11** 47
Arbaiza, Diego López de *see* LÓPEZ DE ARBAIZA, DIEGO
Arbaji **23** 290
Arbanassi **5** 147
 Church of the Nativity **5** 148
Arbasia, Cesare **29** 300; **32** 620
Arbaud, Paul **26** 240
Arbaut, P. d' **19** 847
ARBED steelworks **19** 825
Arbeiter-Fotograf **3** 121
Arbeitsgemeinschaft Schweizer Keramiker **30** 144
Arbeitsgruppe 4 **2** 287–8*
 members **14** 693
Arbeitsgruppe 4—cont.
 works **2** 789, *789*
Arbeitskreis für Hausforschung **32** 274
Arbeitsrat für Kunst **2** 288*; **3** 795, 801; **12** 378
 members **10** 697; **19** 773; **21** 781
  Bartning, Otto **3** 292
  Gropius, Walter (Adolf Georg) **13** 687
  Heckel, Erich **14** 285
  Hilberseimer, Ludwig (Karl) **14** 524
  Meidner, Ludwig (Baruch) **21** 55
  Meyer, Adolf (1881-1929) **21** 407
  Pechstein, (Hermann) Max **24** 312
  Schmidt-Rottluff, Karl **28** 125
  Schmitthenner, Paul **28** 126
  Taut, Bruno **30** 370
  Taut, Max **30** 371
Arbela **21** 277
Arbel Synagogue **17** 542
Arber, Thomas **5** 314
Arbër Glassworks **1** 543
Arbeteta **29** 331
Arbien, Hans **23** 225
ARBKD *see* ASSOZIATION REVOLUTIONÄRER BILDENDER KÜNSTLER DEUTSCHLANDS (ASSO)
Arboe **8** 196
Arboga **30** 77
Arbois, St Just **13** 100
Arbois, Jean d' *see* JEAN D'ARBOIS
Arboleda, Carlos **2** 288*
El Arbolillo **21** 254
Arbore, Luca **9** 210
Arborea **27** 836
Arbore Church **9** 210
Arboreus, Heinrich **12** 811
arbor vitae see under CROSSES → types
Arbós y Ayerbe, Manuel **2** 288
Arbós y Tremanti, Fernando **2** 288–9*
arbours **12** 61, 109, 126
Arbrissel, Robert d' *see* ROBERT D'ARBRISSEL
Arbroath (Tayside)
 Abbey **28** 241, 250, 267
 Abbots' House **28** 250
 Methodist Church **21** 347
 Patrick Allen Frazier School of Art **28** 275
 St Vigeans Museum **24** 738
Arbuda *see* MT ABU
Arbudagiri *see* MT ABU
Arburo (y) Morell, José **2** 289*
Arbury Hall (Warwicks) **19** 123; **23** 21; **29** 835, *836*
Arbus, Allan **2** 289
Arbus, André-Léon **11** 601
Arbus, Diane **2** 289*; **18** 476; **24** 679
Arbuthnot, Malcolm **24** 738, 739
Arbutus Berry **6** 164
Arc, St Martin **13** 113
Arca, Niccolò dell' *see* NICCOLÒ DELL' ARCA
arcades **2** 290*; **9** 21
 historical and regional traditions
  Austria **2** 778
  Byzantine **9** 524, 549
  Early Christian (*c.* AD 250-843) **9** 524
  Indian subcontinent **13** *882*
  Italy **26** 888, *888*, *894*
  Romanesque **26** 569
  Rome, ancient **2** 242, *242*; **26** 888, *888*, *894*
  Spain **1** 743; **2** *242*
 materials
  metal **1** 743
  mouldings **22** 215, 218
  tracery **31** 271
arcades—cont.
 types
  blind **4** 141*, *141*
  dwarf galleries *see* GALLERIES (ii) (CORRIDORS)
  triforia see TRIFORIA
 see also COLONNADES; GALLERIES (ii) (CORRIDORS)
Arcagnuolo *see* CIONE, ANDREA DI
Arcangelo, Allan D' *see* D'ARCANGELO, ALLAN
Arcangelo del Sellaio **16** 847
Arcangelo di Cola da Camerino **2** 290–91*
 collaboration **24** 539
 works **2** *290*
Arcangelo di Jacopo, Jacopo di *see* JACOPO DEL SELLAIO
Arcas **10** 136
Arcay, Wilfredo **28** 300
Arc de Triomphe de l'Etoile *see under* PARIS
Arce, Diego Martínez de *see* MARTÍNEZ DE ARCE, DIEGO
Arce, Gaspar Núñez de *see* NÚÑEZ DE ARCE, GASPAR
Arce, José de **2** 291*; **22** 4
Arce, Manuel Maples *see* MAPLES ARCE, MANUEL
Arce, Mario Pérez de *see* PÉREZ DE ARCE, MARIO
Arce, Pedro de **2** 291*; **29** 353; **32** 132
Arceo, Juan **20** 274; **24** 622
Arcés, José **8** 231
Arcetri, Villa la Gallina **13** 541; **32** 549
Arc-et-Senans **31** 713
 Saline de Chaux **19** *56*, 56–7; **23** 490
Arceuil, St Denis **13** 39
Arce y Ceballos, Gregorio Vázquez de *see* VÁZQUEZ DE ARCE Y CEBALLOS, GREGORIO
Archaeológiaia közlemények **24** 440
Archaeológiai értesítö **24** 440
archaeological collections *see under* COLLECTIONS → types
archaeological jewellery *see under* JEWELLERY → types
Archaeological Studies in Korea see CHOSŎN KOGO YŎNJU
Archaeological Survey of India (ASI) **15** 183, 184, 747; **24** 436; **30** 261; **31** 902
Archaeological Survey of India Reports **24** 437
archaeology **2** 298–304*, *303*, 534; **4** 75; **8** 369, 370, 793; **10** 208
 historical and regional traditions
  Africa **21** 480–81
  Ancient Near East **1** 851–3*
  Aztec **21** 211
  China **1** 150; **7** 157–60*
  Crete **4** 607; **14** 275
  Egypt, ancient **2** 299, 300; **8** 763; **10** 79*
  France **6** 95; **8** 868
  India, Republic of **15** 183
  Iraq **3** 629; **21** 310
  Ireland **16** 36
  Islamic **16** 550
  Italy **14** 867; **31** 61
  Japan **17** 425–7*; **22** 148; **23** 440
  Korea **18** 381–2*
  Mali **21** 480–81
  Maya **2** 300
  Mesoamerica, Pre-Columbian **21** 263
  Mesopotamia **2** 299, 300
  Middle Niger cultures **21** 480–81*
  Minoan **2** 300; **4** 607
  Mongolia **21** 885–6*
  Native North Americans **22** 671–3*, *672*
  Norway **23** 227

archaeology
historical and regional traditions—cont.
Pakistan **23** 804–5
Peru **2** 300; **23** 702
Rome, ancient **32** 544*
Tibet **30** 847*
Tunisia **31** 426–7*
United States of America **2** 299; **22** 671–3*
techniques
dating methods **2** 301–4*, *302*; **24** 561
photography **2** 300, *300*; **9** 341; **24** 662
surveys **2** 301; **22** 673
types
marine **7** 160
Archaeology see KOGOHAK
archaism **6** 865, 866; **27** 29, 31
Archambaud de Saint-Antonin **11** 655
Archambault, Louis **5** 571
Archambo, Peter **2** 304*; **10** 329; **19** 593
pupils **14** 382
works **10** 330
Archanes **2** 304–5*; **8** 153; **13** *362*; **21** *651*
cemetery **21** 664
ivory-carvings **21** 681, 682
palace **21** 658
rings **21** 691
sculpture **21** 679
seals **21** 682
wall paintings **21** 674
Archangel Michael Ivory **18** 825
Archangelos **26** *289*, 294
Archar **5** 145
Archatos
Panagia **22** 700
Panagia stis Giallous **22** 700
arch bridges *see under* BRIDGES → types
arch door tombs *see under* TOMBS → types
Arche, Anton Alois **2** 305*; **18** 467; **23** 424
Arche, Henri d' **14** 852
Arche, L' **3** 675; **11** 322; **14** 283
Archelaos of Macedon **13** 561
Archelaos of Priene **13** 465
Archer, Frederick Scott **24** 649
Archer, John Lee **2** 306*, 738
Archer, Mildred (Agnes) **2** 306*
Archer, Thomas **2** 306–7*; **8** 47; **28** 878
collaboration **4** 218
patrons and collectors **6** 115, 116, 117, 515; **30** 267
works **2** *307*; **4** 85; **10** 232, *232*; **13** 645
Archer, William George **2** 305–6*; **15** 212, 653, 742
Archerius, Johannes *see* ALCHERIUS, JOHANNES
Archermos of Chios **2** 308*; **5** 185; **7** 169; **8** 689
arches **2** 292–8*, *292*; **20** 567; **22** 211; **32** 86
historical and regional traditions
Afghanistan **16** 167, *168*
Africa **1** 315
Anglo-Saxon **2** *65*
Assyrian **2** 297*
Byzantine **4** 774
Central Asia, Western **16** 167
Christianity **2** 297*
Early Christian (*c.* AD 250-843) **2** 297
Egypt, ancient **2** 296*
England **2** *65*; **14** 198; **16** *54*
Etruscan **2** 297
France **7** *694*
Germany **3** *791*, 793, 795
Greece, ancient **2** 297*; **13** 403, 404; **26** 909
Hittite **2** 296*
arches
historical and regional traditions—cont.
Indian subcontinent **2** 297*; **8** 269; **15** 387; **16** 201
Islamic **1** 315; **2** 297–8*; **16** 142, 167, *168*, 190, 201
Italy **26** 887, *887*
Maya **21** 213
Mesoamerica, Pre-Columbian **21** *205*
Morocco **16** 190
Mycenaean **2** 296*
Rome, ancient **2** 297*; **26** 863, 877, 890, *892*, 922, 923, 924; **27** 41
Greece **26** 909
Italy **26** 887, *887*
Syria **2** 297
Syria **2** 297
Syria-Palestine **30** 190
Venezuela **32** 168
materials
brick **2** 296; **4** 767, 769, 774, 787; **26** 877
cast iron **3** 793
concrete **2** 297
limestone **26** *891*
marble **7** *920*
masonry **20** *574*, 574–5*, *583*
mouldings **22** 212, *212*, 213, *213*, 214, 215, 216, 217, 218, 219, 220, 222
mud-bricks **2** 296
plaster **31** 351
stone **2** 296, 297
wrought iron **16** *54*
techniques
centering **6** 178
types
basket **2** 292*, *293*
blind **2** 292*
bow-string **22** 532
catenary **2** 292*
ceremonial *see* PAILOU
commemorative **31** 349
containing **2** 292*, *293*
corbelled **2** 292–4*, *293*, 296; **21** *205*
see also false
curtain **2** 294*, 480
cusped **2** *293*, 294*
depressed *see* basket
diaphragm **2** *293*, 294*
drop *see* basket
equilateral **2** 294*
false **2** 294*
see also corbelled
flat **2** *293*, 294*; **20** 574, *574*
four-centred **2** *293*, 294*
funicular **20** 575
honorific *see* MONUMENTS → types → triumphal arches
horseshoe **2** *293*, 294*; **15** 317, *326*, 327; **16** 158, 168, 188, *188*; **21** 548
interlace **2** *293*, 294*
inverted **2** 294*
see also strainer
joggled **2** *293*, 294*
keel **2** 295*; **16** 176
keyhole *see* horseshoe
lancet **2** 295*
nodding **2** *293*, 295*
ogee **2** *293*, 295*; **13** 46, 54; **16** 239; **23** 368*; **32** 207
parabolic *see* catenary
plate-bande *see* flat
pointed **2** *293*, 295*, 298*; **13** 35, 51; **16** 150, 153; **20** *583*
polygonal **21** 376
proscenium **17** 330; **25** 658; **30** 650, 658, 666, 680
ramping **2** *293*, 295*
rear-arches **2** 295*
relieving **2** *293*, 295*
round **2** *293*, 295*, 297, 298*
segmental **2** *293*, 295*
arches
types—cont.
shouldered **2** *293*, 295*
skew **2** *293*, 295*
stilted **2** *293*, 295–6*
strainer **2** 296*
see also inverted
surbased **2** 296*
transverse **2** *293*, 296*
trefoil **2** *293*, 296*
triangular **2** *293*, 296*
triple **7** 917; **26** 868
triumphal *see* MONUMENTS → types
Tudor **2** *293*, 296*
two-centred **2** *293*, 296*
see also lancet; pointed
two-tiered **2** *293*, 296*
voussoir **2** 292; **20** 573, *574*, 574–5*
zakomary **27** 368, 369–70; **33** 600*
Archibald, George **4** 479
Archibald, J. F. **2** 769
Archibald, John S(mith) **1** 29; **2** 308*
Archibald & Schofield **6** 513
Archibras, L' **24** 428
archiepiscopal crosses *see under* CROSSES → types
Archigram **2** 308–9*; **7** 788; **19** 897; **31** 734
works **2** *309*
Archimedes **2** 349; **13** 561; **21** 558
Archinto (family) **20** 95
Archinto, Alberigo **2** 310
Archinto, Carlo (*d* 1665) **2** 310
Archinto, Carlo (1670-1732) **2** 310
Archinto, Filippo, Archbishop of Milan **2** 309
Archinto, Francesco **2** 309; **25** *466*
Archinto, Giovanni, Cardinal **2** 310
Archinto, Giuseppe (*d* 1476) **2** 309
Archinto, Giuseppe, Archbishop of Milan (1651-1712) **2** 310
Archinto, Giuseppe (1783-1861) **2** 310
Archinto, Orazio **2** 310
Archinto, Ottavio **2** 310
Archinto alle Forbici, Giuseppe, Conte **25** 74
Archipenko, Alexander **2** 310–11*
exhibitions **3** 801; **32** 774
groups and movements **8** 240, 243; **10** 696; **11** 568; **21** 775; **27** 307
patrons and collectors **16** 570, 571; **20** 97; **31** 565
pupils **5** 571; **7** 405; **10** 893; **23** 669; **28** 887
works **2** *311*; **12** 407; **19** 491; **23** 333; **29** 576
Archis: Tijdschrift voor architectur, stedebouw en beeldende kunst **24** 450
Architect *see* ZODCHIY
architect, De **24** 450
Architecta **2** 317–18*; **19** 643
Architectengroep de 8 **13** 679; **22** 868; **23** 663
391 **2** 318*
members **4** 216, 221; **9** 746; **10** 163; **21** 156; **23** 450; **29** 531
architects **2** 311–17*, 362; **20** 559, 560, 573; **28** 497
Australia **4** 167
China **2** 317*
Egypt, ancient **2** 312; **9** 790, 826*
England **2** 314–15
Finland **11** 90; **31** 461
France **2** 313–14, 315
Greece, ancient **2** 312; **13** 394–5*, 408
Inca **29** 135
architects—cont.
Indian subcontinent **2** 317*; **15** 207, 245
Mughal **15** 208
Iran **16** 232
Islamic **2** 316*; **16** 143*, 220–21, 232, 241
Italy **2** 313; **16** 637
Japan **2** 317*; **17** 51–3*, 65
Ottoman **2** 316; **16** 220–21
Rome, ancient **2** 312–13; **26** 864, 884–5*
Scandinavia **14** 151
South America, Pre-Columbian **29** 135
United States of America **2** 315–16; **10** 850
Architect's and Mechanic's Journal **24** 431
Architects Bureau **23** 799
Architects' Club (London) **27** 715
Architects' Club (Prague) **2** 314; **8** 251; **12** 834; **18** 434, 439, 569; **27** 283; **29** 553; **31** 491
Architects Collaborative, The *see* TAC
Architects' Co-Partnership **2** 318*; **23** 134
collaboration **2** 578
staff **23** 426; **32** 86
works **10** 242; **14** 863; **18** 639; **23** 135; **32** 783
architects' guilds *see under* GUILDS → types
Architects' Partnership (Zimbabawe) **33** 678
Architects' Partnership, The (Bahamas) **3** 61
Architects' Research Foundation *see* STICHTING ARCHITECTEN RESEARCH
Architects Yearbook **9** 297
Architectura **24** 449; **32** 779
Architectural Association of Kenya **22** 387
architectural blueprints *see* BLUEPRINTS (ARCHITECTURE)
architectural competitions *see under* COMPETITIONS → types
architectural decorations **14** 419–20
historical and regional traditions
Afghanistan **16** 169
Africa **1** 312–14, *313*, 317–18, *318*
Algeria **1** 317; **16** 190
Ancient Near East **1** 879*
Anglo-Saxon **2** 65, 71
Arabia **2** 255
Buddhism **18** 337, 766*; **30** 842
Byzantine **6** 564; **9** 527, 543, 547
Cambodia **5** 464, 475–6*
Central Asia, Eastern **6** 319
Central Asia, Western **6** 205–8*; **16** 169, 239, 245
Chimú **6** *441*
China **7** 143
Cistercian Order **4** 782
Egypt **1** 317; **16** *176*, 176–7, 244, *259*
England **6** 564; **10** 227, 228; **14** *420*; **30** *504*
Etruscan **1** 127; **10** 587; **32** *119*
Ghana **1** 312
Greece **4** 774; **9** 547
Greece, ancient **23** 533–4
Hausa **1** 317, *318*
Indian subcontinent **15** 262, 342, 354, 374–5, 680, 719
Iran **16** 165, 194–5, 233, *233*, *234*, *244*, *249*; **21** 718
Iraq **16** *247*
Islamic **16** 133, 142–3*, 146, 243–7*, 248–54*, 255*, 256*, 257–60*, 395; **22** 154
Afghanistan **16** 169
Africa **1** 317–18
Algeria **16** 190
architectural decorations
historical and regional traditions
Islamic—cont.
Central Asia, Western **16** 169, 239, 245
Egypt **16** *176*, 176–7, *259*
Ghaznavid **12** 513
Indian subcontinent **15** 342, 354, 680
Iran **16** 165, 194–5, 233, *233*, *234*, *244*, *249*; **21** 718
Iraq **16** *247*
Morocco **16** 190, 191, 250
Ottoman **16** 221
Spain **16** *189*
Syria **16** 146, 245, *255*
Turkey **16** 186, 221, 245
Umayyad (Syria) **16** 145
Italy **1** 127; **10** 587; **32** *119*
Jewish art **17** 542
Korea **18** 337
Laos **18** 766*
Mali **1** 317
Maori **20** *355*, *356*
Mesopotamia **4** 771, *771*
Mexico **25** II1
Morocco **16** 190, 191, 250
Nabataea **22** 419
Ndebele **1** 313, *313*
Nigeria **1** *318*
Nubia **1** 317
Ottoman **16** 221
Peru **6** *441*
Poland **4** 782
Romanesque **6** 564; **10** 228
Rome, ancient **23** 534–5; **26** 878, 916*; **27** 9
South Africa **1** 313, *313*
South America, Pre-Columbian **6** *441*
Spain **16** *189*; **32** *619*
Sri Lanka **29** 475, 477–8*
Swahili **1** 317
Syria **16** 146, 245, *255*
Tibet **30** 842, 846
Turkey **16** 186, 221, 245
United States of America **30** *507*
Visigothic **32** *619*
materials
brick **1** 317; **4** 769, 771, *771*, 774, 782; **15** 262; **16** 143, 165, 169, 195, 199, 239, 250
calligraphy **15** 338, 354
earthenwares **18** 337
faience (i) (glass) **1** 879*
glass **16** 221
glazes **16** 194
heraldry **16** 247
inscriptions **12** 513; **16** 147, 176, *176*, 243, 248, 257–60*, *259*
mirrors **16** 257
mosaics **16** 199, 248, 250, 255*, *255*; **22** 158
plaster **16** 142
sculpture **16** 239
shells **21** 259
stained glass **16** 256*
stone **16** 142
stucco **16** 165, *189*, 190, 215, *244*, 250
terracotta **10** 266; **15** 719; **16** 143, 166, 169, 245, *247*; **27** 9; **30** *504*, *507*; **32** *119*
tiles **15** 338, 342; **16** 143, 169, 206, 215, 221, *234*, 239, 248–50*, *249*; **25** 292, II1
wood **16** 142; **29** 477–8
techniques
painting **16** 221
see also FAÇADE DECORATION
Architectural Design **30** 392
architectural drawings *see under* DRAWINGS → types
architectural education *see under* EDUCATION (ART) → types

Architectural Forum **22** 728; **24** 433
architectural geometry *see* GEOMETRY (ARCHITECTURE)
Architectural Group for Industry and Commerce (AGIC) **23** 10
architectural history **11** 168; **24** 575; **28** 917
  Belgium **28** 61
  Denmark **8** 820
  England **2** 64; **10** 897; **23** 860; **33** 211
  France **9** 351, 420
  Romania **12** 547
  United States of America **22** 283
Architectural Institute of Japan **30** 364
Architectural Iron Works **3** 35; **12** 221; **16** 54
Architectural Library, The **30** 384
architectural manuals *see under* MANUALS → types
architectural models *see under* MODELS → types
architectural orders *see* ORDERS (ARCHITECTURE)
architectural paintings *see under* PAINTING → types
architectural periodicals *see under* PERIODICALS → types
architectural publications
  Britain **12** 333
  England **5** 538–9; **14** 66; **22** 211
  France **19** 144
  Italy **27** 762
  United States of America **14** 115–16
Architectural Record **24** 433
architectural refinements *see* REFINEMENTS (ARCHITECTURE)
Architectural Review **8** 256; **10** 377; **19** 872; **23** 22; **24** 446; **31** 735; **33** 219
architectural sculpture *see under* SCULPTURE → forms
Architectural Society **10** 374
architectural theories *see under* THEORIES
architecture **2** 361–3*; **20** 567; **28** 645
  conservation **2** 318–25*; **7** 729; **29** *713*
  criticism **13** 409; **15** 169; **32** 563
  dating methods **20** 881; **21** 40; **22** 212
  heritage *see* HERITAGE (ARCHITECTURE)
  historical and regional traditions
    Aboriginal Australia **1** 49–50*
    Achaemenid **15** 911–12
    Afghanistan **1** 189–93*, 207–8*; **16** 166–9*, 195–200*
    Africa **1** 304–21*, 377, 406, 410–11, 414*, 421–2*; **4** 792–3*; **25** 172
      Islamic **1** 315–18*
    Albania **1** 538–9*, *539*; **16** 228
    Algeria **1** 305, 634; **16** 170–71*, 187*, 190, 217–19*, 229; **30** 727
    Anasazi **5** 658
    Anatolia, ancient **1** 823, 824, 826, 830–32*
    Ancient Near East **1** 851; **4** 771; **21** 287
    Anglo-Saxon **2** 64–7*
    Angola **2** 85–6*
    Antilles, Lesser **2** 147–9*
    Arabia **2** 247–50*; **16** 229
    Argentina **1** 743; **2** 394–7*
    Armenia (Europe) **2** 425–8*
    Assyrian **18** 27; **21** 287–90
    Augustinian Canons **21** 375
    Australia **2** 736–43*; **4** 786, 788; **10** 852
    Austria **2** 776–89*; **4** 777
      Baroque **2** 780–83*
      Gothic **2** 777–8; **13** 56
      Jesuit Order **2** 781

architecture
  historical and regional traditions
    Austria—cont.
      Renaissance **2** 778–80*
      20th cent. **24** *327*
    Azerbaijan **2** 891–4*
    Aztec **2** 905*
    Bactria **6** 196, 197–8*
    Bahamas, the **3** 60–61*
    Bahmani **16** 201
    Bahrain **3** 68*
    Balearic Islands **3** *105*, 105–6
    Bali (Indonesia) **15** 772–3
    Bamana **3** 136*
    Bamum **3** 151–2*
    Bangladesh **3** 167–8*
    Barbados **2** 148
    Barnabites **27** 160
    Belarus' **3** 525–7*; **4** 783
    Belgium **2** 194; **3** 540–51*; **4** 790
      Gothic **3** 542–4; **13** 61–3*
      Jesuit Order **17** 511
      Romanesque **31** 220
    Belize **3** 622–3*
    Benin Republic **1** 261; **3** 728*
    Berber **1** 305, 377; **3** 754–5*; **20** 861
    Bhutan **3** 913*
    Bijogo **4** 55*
    Bolivia **4** 256–9*, 260–61*; **17** 513
    Bosnia **4** 459–60*; **16** 228
    Brazil **3** 66; **4** 709–10*, 711–15*
      Neo-classicism **4** 710–11*
      neo-colonial style **2** 903
      20th cent. **32** 855
    Britain **4** 770, 778–80*, 786–7, 788, 789; **7** 693; **12** 791
      Indian subcontinent **15** 401
      Sri Lanka **29** 453–4*
      United States of America **31** 589–90
    Brunei **5** 11*
    Buddhism
      Afghanistan **1** 191–3*
      Bactria **6** 198
      Burma **5** 233*
      Central Asia, Eastern **6** 297
      Central Asia, Western **6** 198
      Champa **6** 421–2*; **9** 133
      China **6** 666–71*
      Indian subcontinent **15** 311, 406
      Indonesia **15** 758
      Japan **14** 773; **17** 71–5*
      Korea **18** 261, 266–8*
      Malaysia **20** 165*
      Maldives, Republic of **20** 188
      Sarawak **20** 165
      Sri Lanka **29** 446–8*, 449
      Thailand **30** 576–7
      Tibet **30** 815–21
      Vietnam **6** 421–2*; **9** 133
    Bulgaria **5** 145*, 146–50*; **9** 551–2
    Burma **5** 224–32*, 233*, 234–8*
    Byzantine **4** 773–4*; **9** 523–8*, 542*, 543–7*, 549*, 550–53*, 556–9*, 560–61*; **18** 390
      Bulgaria **5** 147; **9** 551–2
      Cappadocia **5** 673*
      Crete **8** 155
      Georgia **9** 548–9
      Greece **7** 170; **9** 545–7*, 550–51*
      Macedonia (ii) (former Yugoslavia) **19** 882
      Mesopotamia **9** 538–41*, 542–3*
      Palestine **9** 538–41*, 542–3*, 547–9*
      Rhodes (island) **26** 293*
      Serbia **9** 552–3
      Syria **9** 538–41*, 542–3*, 547–9*
      Turkey **9** 536–7*, 542*, 543–5, 549–50*
      Ukraine **31** 546

architecture
  historical and regional traditions—cont.
    Cambodia **5** 463–72*, 473–80*, 481–3*
    Cameroon **1** 307, 312; **5** 523*
    Canaanite **5** 557*
    Canada **5** 558–63*, 572–4*
      Native North Americans **22** 563–5*
      20th cent. **22** *37*
    Cappadocia **5** 673*, 675*
    Caribbean Islands **5** 749–50*
    Carmelite Order **19** 566
    Carolingian **5** 793–6*; **6** 482
      France **11** 509*; **12** 485; **27** 539
      Germany **12** 362–3*; **26** 100
      Switzerland **27** 554
    Carthusian Order **5** 894–5*
    Catalonia **5** 734
    Central Asia, Eastern **6** 295–7*
    Central Asia, Western **6** 195–201*, 202–3*
      Bactria **6** 196, 197–8*
      Buddhism **6** 198
      Ghurid **16** 169
      Islamic **6** 201–2*, 204–5*; **16** 142, 153–4*, 158–61*, 166–9*, 195–200*, 235–9*, *236*, 264
      Khwarazm **6** 199*
      Khwarazmshah **16** 158
      Naqshbandiyya **16** 235
      Parthian **6** *198*, 198–9*
      Qarakhanid **16** 158, 258
      Samanid **16** 158
      Shaybanid **16** 220, 235
      Sogdiana **6** 200, 201
      Timurid **6** 202; **16** 195–8
    Champa **6** 420–21*, 422–5*; **9** 133
    Chassey culture **25** 502
    Chavín culture **6** 522*
    Chicano **18** 832
    Chile **6** 591–5*
    China **6** 631, 637–45*, *647*, 648, 662–6*, 679–92*, 693–6*; **12** 313; **19** 865; **25** 171
      Buddhism **6** 666–71*
      Christianity **6** 677–8*
      Confucianism **6** 674–6*
      Daoism **6** 671–4*
      Islamic **6** 676–7*
      Prehistoric **6** 684–5
      20th cent. **28** *551*
    Chokwe **1** 406
    Christianity **6** 677–8*; **26** 907, 923
      see also CHURCHES; MONASTERIES
    Cistercian Order **7** 350–51*; **26** 381
      Denmark **8** 722
      England **10** 227; **13** 43–4; **26** 590
      France **13** 37–8
      Germany **4** 776; **12** 471; **13** 47–8, 57
      Gothic **13** 35, 37–8, 50, 51, 57
      Ireland **16** 7; **21** 87
      Italy **13** 51; **16** 627
      Netherlands, the **4** 777
      Poland **25** 95
      Portugal **25** 289
      Romanesque **26** 590, 592
      Sardinia **27** 836
      Scandinavia **13** 50
      Spain **13** 50; **29** 263
    Colombia **7** 603–5*
    Confucianism **6** 674–6*; **18** 266, 269–71*
    Coptic **7** 819*
    Costa Rica **8** 16–17*
    Côte d'Ivoire **8** 22
    Creole **13** 878
    Crete **8** 154
      Byzantine **8** 155
      Hellenistic **8** 154

architecture
  historical and regional traditions
    Crete—cont.
      Minoan **8** 153; **18** *210*; **21** 658–9, 661–5*
      Roman **8** 154–5
      Venetian **8** 156
    Croatia **8** 175–7*; **26** 594
    Cuba (Caribbean) **8** 231–3*
    Cycladic **8** 309, 310–11*, *310*
    Cyprus **8** 357–8*, 361–3*, 364–5*
    Cyprus, ancient **8** 333–7*
    Czech Republic **4** 782, 783; **8** 375–81*; **24** *109*
      Gothic **8** 376–7; **13** 56, 57
      Romanesque **8** 376; **26** 594
      18th cent. **23** *425*
    Daoism **6** 671–4*, *672*
    Denmark **8** 721–9*
      Gothic **13** 50, 56; **26** 304
      Romanesque **26** 304, 592–3*
      Viking **32** *533*
    Dogon **1** 260, 312; **9** 68–9*
    Dominica **2** 148
    Dominican Order **4** 782; **19** 566
      Denmark **8** 723
      Germany **13** 57
      Gothic **13** 52, 57
      Ireland **16** 7
      Italy **13** 52
      Mexico **21** 375
      Poland **25** 95
    Dominican Republic **9** 116–17*
    Early Christian (*c.* AD 250–843) **9** 523–8*, 534, 538*, 542*, 553*, 556–8*, 561*, 731–2; **25** 171
      Algeria **30** 727
      Armenia (Europe) **2** 428
      Cappadocia **5** 673*
      Cyprus **8** 357–8*
      Greece **9** 538*
      Ireland **16** 6
      Italy **16** 623–5*
      Mesopotamia **9** 538–41*, 542–3*
      North Africa **9** 535
      Palestine **9** 538–41*, 542–3*
      Rhodes (island) **26** 293*
      Syria **9** 538–41*, 542–3*
      Turkey **9** 536–7*, 542*
    Easter Island **23** 715
    Ecuador **9** 710–11*
    Egypt **9** 764–5*
      Ayyubid **16** 172, 173, 175
      Coptic **7** 819*
      Fatimid **16** 172–5
      Islamic **16** 141, 155–6*, 172–7*, 207–13*, 229
      Mamluk **16** 207–13, 257
      Ottoman **16** 229
      Tulunid **16** 149
    Egypt, ancient **9** 773, 775, 824–6*, 827–35*, 836–8*, 842–3*, 849*, 850–53*, *852*, *853*; **10** 84; **13** 405; **25** 171, 761; **26** 920; **27** 811
      Early Dynastic (*c.* 2925–*c.* 2575 BC) **9** 850*
      Graeco-Roman (332 BC–AD 395) **9** 842*
      Late Period (664–332 BC) **9** 841–2*
      Middle Kingdom (*c.* 1966–*c.* 1630 BC) **9** 838*
      New Kingdom (*c.* 1539–*c.* 1075 BC) **9** 839–41*
      Old Kingdom (*c.* 2575–*c.* 2130 BC) **9** 850*
      Predynastic (*c.* 6000–*c.* 2925 BC) **9** 837*, 849–50*
    Elamite **15** 909–10
    El Salvador **10** 153

architecture
  historical and regional traditions—cont.
    England **4** 770–71; **10** 226–31*, 235–9*, 240, 242*; **23** *688*, 809; **30** 365–6, 501–4, 506–7; **33** 204
      Anglo-Saxon **2** 64–7*
      Cistercian Order **10** 227; **13** 43–4; **26** 590
      Gothic **10** 228; **13** 35, 43–7*, 53–6*, 136; **19** 402; **31** 284
      Gothic: Decorated style **13** 54
      Gothic: Early English style **9** 669–70
      Gothic: Early Gothic **13** 43
      Gothic: Perpendicular style **13** 55; **24** 465
      Gothic: Rayonnant style **13** 47
      Gothic Revival **6** *561*
      Modernism **19** *747*
      Norman *see* Romanesque
      Romanesque **2** 67; **19** 600; **23** 211; **26** 587–90*
      Transitional style **31** 284
      Viking **32** 533, 534
      19th cent. **16** 53–4
      20th cent. **2** *309*; **4** *158*
    Eritrea **10** 564–7*
    Estonia **10** 536–8*
    Ethiopia **10** 564–7*
    Etruscan **10** 596–602*; **16** 622; **26** 851
    Finland **11** 88*, 89*, 92–3*, *93*; **30** 284
    Fon **3** 728
    France **4** 780*, 790; **7** 531, 693; **9** 464; **11** 508–11*, 515*, 519–24*, 525–8*; **27** 879
      Carolingian **11** 509*; **12** 485; **27** 539
      Cistercian Order **13** 37–8
      Gothic **11** 510–11*; **13** 35, 36–43*, 50, 59–61*; **27** 539; **31** 284
      Gothic: Flamboyant style **9** 48; **13** 59
      Gothic: High Gothic **13** 39; **14** 518
      Gothic: Late Gothic **8** 789
      Gothic: *opus francigenum* **13** 42
      Gothic: Rayonnant style **13** 41–3*, 59
      Indian subcontinent **15** 401
      Iron Age **25** 538
      Jesuit Order **17** 511
      Mannerism **11** 514
      Merovingian **11** 509*; **25** 85, 88
      Neo-classicism **19** 725
      Prehistoric **25** 502–3*
      Renaissance **11** 511–14*
      Roman **11** 509*; **26** 904
      Romanesque **4** 780; **11** 509–10*; **23** 211; **26** 571, 582–6*; **27** 566; **31** 224
      United States of America **31** 589
      18th cent. **20** 416
      19th cent. **16** 53; **32** *595*
    Franciscan Order **11** 711–12; **19** 566
      Denmark **8** 723
      Gothic **13** 52
      Ireland **16** 7
      Italy **13** 52
      Mexico **21** 373, 375; **33** 571
      Sardinia **27** 836
      United States of America **22** 567; **31** 588
    French Guiana **11** 757–8*
    Gabon **11** 879*
    Gambia, The **12** 32*
    Georgia **9** 548–9; **12** 318–20*
    Germany **4** 776–7*; **12** 362–76*, 471, 472
      Baroque **12** 370, 389
      Cameroon **5** 523
      Carolingian **12** 362–3*; **26** 100

architecture
historical and regional traditions
Germany—cont.
Cistercian Order **4** 776; **12** 471; **13** 47–8, 57
Dominican Order **13** 57
Gothic **12** 362; **13** 35, 47–9, 56–8*; **20** 87; **31** 284
Gothic: Early Gothic **12** 364–5
Gothic: High Gothic **13** 49
Gothic: Late Gothic **12** 365–6*; **13** 58
Gothic: Rayonnant style **13** 56–7*
Jesuit Order **17** 511
Namibia **22** 450
Nazism **22** 711*
Neo-classicism **12** 374
Neue Sachlichkeit **21** 782
Ottonian **12** 363–4*
Premonstratensian Canons **12** 471
Renaissance **12** 366–8*
Renaissance Revival **12** 376
Romanesque **12** 363–4*; **17** 482; **26** 571–5*
Rundbogenstil **12** *167*
Transitional style **31** 284
20th cent. **12** 378–81*
Ghana **1** 312; **12** 508*
Gothic **12** 497; **13** 35–53*; **24** 347; **25** 172
Austria **2** 777–8; **13** 56
Belarus' **3** 526
Belgium **3** 542–4; **13** 61–3*
Cistercian Order **13** 35, 37–8, 43–4, 47–8, 50, 51, 57
Czech Republic **8** 376–7; **13** 56, 57
Denmark **13** 50, 56; **26** 304
Dominican Order **13** 52, 57
Early Gothic **31** 284
England **10** 228; **13** 35, 43–7*, 53–6*, 136; **19** 402; **31** 284
England: Decorated style **13** 54
England: Early English style **9** 669–70
England: Early Gothic **13** 43
England: Perpendicular style **13** 55
England: Rayonnant style **13** 47
France **11** 510–11*; **13** 35, 36–43*, 50, 59–61*; **27** 539; **31** 284
France: Flamboyant style **9** 48; **13** 59
France: High Gothic **13** 39; **14** 518
France: Late Gothic **8** 789
France: *opus francigenum* **13** 42
France: Rayonnant style **13** 41–3*, 59
Franciscan Order **13** 52
Germany **12** 362; **13** 35, 47–9, 56–8*; **20** 87; **31** 284
Germany: Early Gothic **12** 364–5
Germany: High Gothic **13** 49
Germany: Late Gothic **12** 365–6*; **13** 58
Germany: Rayonnant style **13** 56–7*
Holy Roman Empire (before 1648) **13** 47–9*
Hungary **13** 56
Ireland **9** 321; **13** 56; **16** 7
Italy **13** 35, 51–3*, 63–6*; **16** 627*
Italy: Rayonnant style **13** 65
Lithuania **13** 58; **19** 495
maniera tedesca **13** 35
Netherlands, the **13** 61–3*; **22** 819–21*
Norway **31** 363
opus francigenum **13** 35; **23** 462*

architecture
historical and regional traditions
Gothic—cont.
Poland **12** 823; **13** 56, 57; **31** 394
Poland: *Backsteingotik* **24** 347
Portugal **3** 362; **13** 70–71*; **25** 289–90
Portugal: Manueline style **13** 71
Sardinia **27** 836
Scandinavia **13** 50*, 56–8*
Scotland **13** 56
Slovakia **28** 849
Slovenia **28** 858–9
Spain **13** 35, 50–51*, 66–70*; **19** 171; **29** 263, 265
Spain: Flamboyant style **13** 68
Spain: Hispano-Flemish style **13** 69–70
Sweden **13** 50, 56
Switzerland **30** 125–6
Transitional style **31** 283–4
Greece **9** 538*, 542*, 545–7*, 550–51*; **13** 348–51*
Byzantine **7** 170
Greece, ancient **13** 368, 373–4*, 375*, 376–82*, 383–98*, 399, 400–404*, 405–7*, 408–17*, 418–21*; **25** 171; **29** 805
Archaic **13** *367*
Classical **2** 666; **13** *367*
Dark Age (*c.* 1050–*c.* 750 BC) **13** *367*
Hellenistic **13** *367*
Ionia **15** 893, 894
Italy **16** 622
Roman **13** *367*; **26** 908–11*
Greenland **32** 533
Grenada **2** 148
Guatemala **13** 760–63*; **24** *744*
Guyana **13** 875*, 877
Haiti **14** 56*
Halaf culture **30** 737
Hausa **1** 249; **4** 793; **14** 233*; **23** 127, 134
Helladic **14** 336, 338–41*
Herzegovina **4** 459*
Hinduism **15** 758; **20** 165*; **29** 448
Hittite **1** 826, 831*; **20** 540*
Holy Roman Empire (before 1648) **13** 47–9*; **26** 570, 571–5*
Honduras **14** 712–13*, 714*
Huari culture **14** 828*
Huastec **14** 829
Hungary **13** 56; **14** 883–91*; **26** 594
Iceland **15** 71–2*; **32** 533
Igbo **23** 134
Inca **15** 162–3*; **29** 166
India, Republic of **15** 167–9*, *168*
Indian subcontinent **3** 194; **4** 793–4*; **15** 209*, 212, 234–5*, 236–41*, 242*, 245*, 248–52*, 253*, 257–60*, 266–75*, 309*, 317–22*, 359*, 374*, 395–400*, 405–8*, 548, 721; **25** 292
Andhra Pradesh **15** 293*, 295, 324*, 328*
Avadh **15** 376–8*
Bengal **15** 351–3*, 378–80*; **16** 201
Buddhism **15** 311, 406
Chalukyas of Badami **15** 293–300
Chalukyas of Kalyana **15** 324
Chalukyas of Vengi **15** 301
Chandella **15** 290
Chola **15** 331–4*
Colonial period **15** 242*, 401–4*
Deccan **15** 355–8*, 380–85*

architecture
historical and regional traditions
Indian subcontinent—cont.
Gujarat **15** 311–15*, 347–9*, 393–5*; **16** 201
Gupta **15** 252–7*
Gurjara-Pratihara **15** 288, 738
Haihaya **15** 290–91
Himachal Pradesh **15** 309*, 310
Indus civilization **15** 246–7*
Islamic **4** *51*; **8** 670; **15** 207, 234, 241–2*, 260, 306–7*, 308–9*, 336–7*, 338–59*, 387; **16** 166, 192, 201*, 239*
Kachchhapaghata **15** 292–3
Karnataka **15** 293–302*, 324–8*
Kashmir **15** 264–6*
Kerala **15** 306*, 336*, 358*
Kosala **15** 283–4*
Ladakh **15** 311*
Madya Pradesh **15** 285–93*, 322–4*
Maharashtra **15** 275–9*, 315–17*
Malwa **15** 353–5; **16** 201
Maratha period **15** 393–5
Mughal **8** 679; **15** 207, 359–67*, 368–73*, 384, 388–9; **16** 220
Pallava period **15** 302–4
Paramara **15** 291–2
Prehistoric **15** 245–6*, 247*
Punjab **15** 374–5*
Rajasthan **15** 311–15*, 349–51*, 385–90; **16** 201
Rajput **15** 385–93*
Rashtrakuta **15** 300
Sikhism **15** 375
Sind **15** 338
Solanki **15** 311
Sultanate **15** 339–46*
Tamil Nadu **15** 302–5*, 331–4*, 358–9*
Uttar Pradesh **3** 908; **15** 260–64*
Vijayanagara period **15** 328–31*, 335–6*
Yadava **15** 315–17
20th cent. **15** 242
Indonesia **15** 758–68*, 769–70*, 771–5*, 806
Buddhism **15** 758
Hinduism **15** 758
Islamic **15** 768*
Indus civilization **4** 772; **15** 246–7*
Iran **4** 791; **15** 897–8*; **16** 142, 150, 153–4*, 158–65*, 166, 192–200*, 220, 229–35*, 248, 249, 264*
Iran, ancient **15** 909–13*, *911*
Iraq **16** 1, 149, 150–53*, *150*, 158, 182*, 192, 243
Ireland **16** 6–12*
Cistercian Order **16** 7; **21** 87
Dominican Order **16** 7
Early Christian (*c.* AD 250-843) **16** 6
Franciscan Order **16** 7
Gothic **9** 321; **13** 56; **16** 7
Romanesque **5** 915, 916; **7** 459; **12** 807–8; **16** 7; **26** 592*
18th cent. **12** *44*
Irian Jaya **23** 715
Islamic **4** 791–2; **16** 133, 134, 140–43*, 144–5*, 149–50*, 158*, 170*, 179, 182, 215*, 220*, 230, 241, 243–7*, 248–54*, 255*, 256*, 257–64*, 267–71*, 491–2; **25** 171
Abbasid **16** 149–50*
Afghanistan **1** 207–8*; **16** 166–9*, 195–200*
Africa **1** 315–18*

architecture
historical and regional traditions
Islamic—cont.
Albania **16** 228
Algeria **16** 170–71*, 187*, 190, 217–19*, 229
Arabia **16** 229
Azerbaijan **2** 891–2
Bosnia **16** 228
Central Asia, Western **6** 201–3*; **16** 142, 153–4*, 158–61*, 166–9*, 195–200*, 235–9*, *236*, 264
China **6** 676–7*
Egypt **16** 141, 155–6*, 172–7*, 207–13*, 229
Empire style **16** 227
Fatimid **16** 170*
Indian subcontinent **4** *51*; **8** 670; **15** 207, 234, 241–2*, 260, 306–7*, 308–9*, 336–59*, 387; **16** 166, 192, 201*, 239*
Indonesia **15** 768–9*
Iran **4** 791; **16** 142, 150, 153–4*, 158–65*, 166, 192–200*, 229–35*, 264*
Iraq **16** 149, *150*, 150–53*, 158, 182*
Java **15** 768–9*
Jordan **16** 155
Macedonia (ii) (former Yugoslavia) **16** 228
Malaysia **20** 165–6*
Morocco **16** 157–8*, 187*, 190–91*, 217–19*, 239–41*
North Africa **16** 190*
Orientalism **16** 227
Ottoman **16** 143, 199, 201, 205–7*, 220–29*, *228*, 265–7*
Pakistan **16** 166–9*
Philippines **24** 610–11*
Sicily **16** 171–2*
Spain **16** 157–8*, 187–91*, 215*; **29** 287–8
Syria **4** 791; **16** 145–9*, 155–6*, 178–82*, 207–13*, *228*, 228–9
Tajikistan **16** 166
Tunisia **16** 156–7*, 170–71*, 219–20*, 229
Turkey **16** 183*, 186*, 201–2*, 205–7*, 221*, 265–7*
Umayyad (Syria) **16** 145–9*
Uzbekistan **16** 166
Yemen **16** 177–8*, 207, 213–15*, 229
Israel **16** 564–7*; **30** 187
Italy **4** 774–6*, 790; **16** 622–7*, 636–43*; **30** 501
Baroque **16** 636–9*; **20** *541*; **32** 217
Cistercian Order **13** 51; **16** 627
Dominican Order **13** 52
Early Christian (*c.* AD 250-843) **16** 623–5*
Etruscan **10** 596–602*; **16** 622
Franciscan Order **13** 52
Futurism **16** 648*
Gothic **13** 35, 51–3*, 63–6*; **16** 627*
Greece, ancient **16** 622
Mannerism **16** 634–5*
Neo-classicism **16** 643–8*
Neo-Liberty **16** 650*
Post-modernism **16** 651*
Razionalismo **3** *438*; **16** 649–50*
Renaissance **4** 642, 652; **16** 628–35*
Rococo **16** 639
Roman **16** 623; **26** 886–9*
Romanesque **16** 625–7*; **26** 575–80*
stile liberty **16** 648*
13th cent. **23** 585

architecture
historical and regional traditions
Italy—cont.
20th cent. **16** 648–51*
Jamaica **16** 882–3*
Japan **17** 23, 45–7*, 50–53*, 57–9*, 60–64*, 65–70*, 71*, 75–83*, 86*; **31** *79*; **33** 539
Buddhism **14** 773; **17** 71–5*
Prehistoric **17** 53–6*
Shinto **17** 74
Java **15** 762, 768–70*, 772*
Jesuit Order
Argentina **2** 394
Austria **2** 781
Belgium **17** 511
Bolivia **17** 513
France **17** 511
Germany **17** 511
Paraguay **17** 513
Jewish art **17** 538–9*, 540–53*
Jordan **16** 155; **26** 918*
Jorwe culture **15** 247
Kassite **21** 286
Kazakhstan **17** 866–7*
Kenya **17** 906*
Khmer **30** 578–81*
Khwarazm **6** 199*
Kiribati **23** 717
Knights Hospitaller **14** 779; **17** 490; **18** 599; **28** 428
Rhodes (island) **26** 294, *294*
Knights Templar **18** 599; **28** 428
Kongo **1** 406
Korea **18** 260–61*, 262–8*, 269–81*
Kuba (iii) (Zaïre) **18** 489*
Kulli culture **15** 245–6
Kuwait **18** 540–41*
Kyrgyzstan **18** 568*
Laos **18** 764*, 766–7*
Lengyel culture **25** 498
Lesotho **19** 241
Levant **30** 184
Liberia **19** 310*
Linear Pottery culture **25** 498, 500
Lithuania **4** 782, 783; **13** 58; **19** 495–7; **25** 96
Lobi **19** 522*
Luba **1** 406
Luxembourg (country) **19** 826–7
Maasai **1** 306, 411
Macedonia (ii) (former Yugoslavia) **16** 228; **19** 882–3*
Malaysia **20** 165–6*, 167–9*
Maldives, Republic of **20** 188–9
Mali **1** 260, 312, 315; **20** 198*
Malta (Republic of) **20** 210–12*, *212*
Malwa culture **15** 247
Mande **1** 422
Mangbetu **1** 406; **20** 268
Maori **20** 355–6; **23** 53–4, 715, 717
Marinid **21** 73
Marquesas Islands **20** 462
Mauritania **20** 861–2
Maya **3** 623; **7** 484; **20** 883, 884; **21** 207, 700; **24** *744*; **31** *778*, 778
Merovingian **11** 509*; **21** 163*; **25** 85, 88
Mesoamerica, Pre-Columbian **7** 484; **21** 204–12*, *210*, 213, 216*, 700
Classic (*c.* AD 250–*c.* 900) **21** 216–17*
Guatemala **24** *744*
Huastec **14** 829
Maya **20** 881; **21** 212–16*
Mexico **30** *483*; **31** 98–9, *778*
Olmec **23** 416–18
Pre-Classic (*c.* 2000 BC–*c.* AD 250) **21** 216*
Toltec **31** 98–9

architecture
historical and regional traditions
Mesoamerica, Pre-Columbian—cont.
West Mexico **33** 102
Mesopotamia **12** 212; **21** 280–81*, 283–7*
Byzantine **9** 538–41*, 542–3*
Early Christian (*c.* AD 250-843) **9** 538–41*, 542–3*
Halaf culture **30** 737
Neo-Assyrian (*c.* 883-*c.* 612 BC) **21** 287–90*
Neo-Babylonian (*c.* 627-539 BC) **21** 291*
Parthian **21** 291–2*
Samarra (*c.* 5500-*c.* 5000 BC) **21** *280*
Ubaid (*c.* 5th millennium BC) **21** *280*
Uruk (*c.* 4000-*c.* 2900 BC) **21** 281–2*
Mexico **7** *695*; **18** 832; **21** 374*, 375, 378–82*; **30** *483*; **33** 571
Pre-Columbian **31** *778*
Minoan **8** 153; **18** *210*; **21** 658–9, 661–5*
Mitannian **21** 286
Moche (culture) **21** 749
Moldova **21** 810–11*
Mongolia **21** 873–5*
Montenegro **22** 16*
Morocco **16** 157–8*, 187*, 190–91*, 217–19*, 220, 239–41*, 250; **22** 128
Mozambique **22** 245*
Mycenaean **4** 772; **14** 338, 339–41*; **29** 367
Nabataea **22** 418*; **26** 917–18*
Namibia **22** 450
Native North Americans **22** 563–5*, 566–73*, 670–71*
Nazism **12** 379; **22** 711*; **29** 378
Ndebele **1** 414
Nepal **22** 758, 759–66*, 792–3
Netherlands, the **4** 777–8*, 785–6; **22** 815–27*, 828–31*, 832*
Cistercian Order **4** 777
Dutch Classicism **22** 824
Gothic **13** 61–3*; **22** 819–21*
Mannerism **22** 823–4
Neo-classicism **22** 827
Premonstratensian Canons **4** 777
Renaissance **4** 732; **22** 822–3*
Romanesque **22** 816–18*
South Africa **29** 102
Sri Lanka **29** 452–3*
United States of America **31** 589
New Caledonia **23** 17
New Guinea **23** 715
New Zealand **22** *468*; **23** 53–4*, 55–7*, 717
Nicaragua **23** 80–81*
Niger **23** 127
Nigeria **23** 134–5*
North Africa **9** 535; **16** 190*; **26** 920*
Northern Ireland **3** 536; **16** 39–40*
Norway **4** 781; **23** 218–19*, 220–22*
Gothic **31** 363
Romanesque **26** 593*
Viking **23** 219
Olmec **23** 416–18; **27** 756
Oman **23** 436*
Ostionoid culture **29** 200
Ottoman **8** 364; **16** 143, 199, 201, 205–7*, 220–29*, *228*, 265–7*, 604; **19** 882–3; **23** 638–9
Ottonian **12** 363–4*; **23** 645*; **26** 571
Pacific Islands **23** 715–18*
Pakistan **16** 166–9*; **23** 798–9*

architecture
historical and regional traditions—cont.
Palau **23** 715, 717
Palestine **9** 538–41*, 542–3*, 547–9*; **26** 917*
Panama **23** 903*, 904*
Papua New Guinea **23** 716–17; **24** 66–8*, 77
Paraguay **17** 513; **24** 93–7*
Parthian **6** 198–9*; **15** 912; **21** 291–2*; **24** 215–17*
Pende **1** 406
Peru **24** 500–506*
Philippines **20** *274*; **24** 610–15*
Philistine **24** 634*
Phoenician **24** 641–2*; **31** 426
Phrygian **1** 831
Poland **4** 783; **24** 347, 698; **25** 94–100*
Cistercian Order **25** 95
Dominican Order **25** 95
Gothic **12** 823; **13** 56, 57; **24** 347; **31** 394
Romanesque **25** 94; **26** 594
15th cent. **23** 399
Portugal **4** 784–5*, 790; **18** 390; **25** 171, 288–94*; **29** 452
Brazil **4** 709
China **19** 865
Cistercian Order **25** 289
Gothic **3** 362; **13** 70–71*; **25** 289–90
Indian subcontinent **15** 401; **25** 292
Manueline style **13** 71; **20** 325–6*; **25** 290–91*
Romanesque **25** 289
Sri Lanka **29** 452*
Uruguay **7** 614–15
Prehistoric art **25** 498
Afghanistan **1** 189–90*
Anatolia, ancient **1** 823, 824, 826
Balearic Islands **3** *105*, 105–6
Bronze Age **25** 519–24*
Chassey culture **25** 502
China **6** 684–5
Cyprus, ancient **8** 333–4*
France **25** 502–3*
Indian subcontinent **15** 245–6*, 247*
Iron Age **25** 535–9*
Korea **18** 260*, 271*
Linear Pottery culture **25** 500
Neolithic **25** 498–509*
Sardinia **25** 522
Starčevo-Körös-Criş culture **25** 499
Premonstratensian Canons **4** 777; **12** 471
Puerto Rico **25** 700–701*; **29** 200
Punic **25** 732–3*
Qatar **25** 776*
Rhodes (island) **26** 295*
Byzantine **26** 293*
Early Christian (*c.* AD 250-843) **26** 293*
Knights Hospitaller **26** 294, *294*
Romanesque **26** 568–71*, 587–90*, 593–4*
Belarus' **3** 526
Belgium **31** 220
Catalonia **5** 734
Cistercian Order **26** 590, 592
Croatia **8** 175; **26** 594
Czech Republic **8** 376; **26** 594
Denmark **26** 304, 592–3*
England **2** 67; **19** 600; **23** 211; **26** 587–90*
France **4** 780; **11** 509–10*; **23** 211; **26** 571, 582–6*; **27** 566; **31** 224
Germany **12** 363–4*; **17** 482; **26** 571–5*

architecture
historical and regional traditions
Romanesque—cont.
Holy Roman Empire (before 1648) **26** 570, 571–5*
Hungary **26** 594
Ireland **5** 915, 916; **7** 459; **12** 807–8; **16** 7; **26** 592*
Italy **16** 625–7*; **26** 575–80*
Netherlands, the **22** 816–18*
Norman *see* England; France; Sicily
Norway **26** 593
Ottonian **26** 571
Poland **25** 94; **26** 594
Portugal **25** 289
Russia **26** 594
Sardinia **27** 836
Scandinavia **26** 592–3*
Scotland **26** 591*
Sicily **16** 171, 626–7; **28** 655
Slovakia **28** 849
Slovenia **28** 857–8
Spain **26** 580–82*; **29** 262–3
Sweden **26** 592–3*
Transitional style **31** 283
Wales **26** 587–90*
Romania **26** 706–10*
Rome, ancient **4** *771*, 772; **7** 691–2; **12** 497; **13** 404, 412; **25** 171; **26** 854, 855–6, 863–4*, 865*, 867–84*, 886*, 889–91*, 893–908*, 911–18*, 922*, 924–5*; **27** 1–7*
Christianity **26** 907
Crete **8** 154–5
Cyprus **8** 337*
Egypt, ancient **26** 920
France **11** 509*; **26** 904
Greece **26** 908–11*
Ionia **15** 894
Italy **16** 623; **26** 886–9*
Jordan **26** 918*
Nabataea **26** 917–18*
North Africa **26** 920*
Palestine **26** 917*
Republican **26** 886–9*
Spain **26** 904
Syria **26** 916–17*, 918*
Turkey **26** *923*
Rössen culture **25** 498
Russia **4** 783; **18** 104; **27** 368–81*
Empire style **29** 554
Romanesque **26** 594
19th cent. **16** 53
20th cent. **27** *578*
Ryūkyū Islands **27** 470
St Kitts **2** 148
St Lucia **2** 148
Samoa **23** 715, 717, 718
Sarawak **20** 165
Sardinia **25** 522; **27** 836
Sasanian **15** 912–13; **21** 292–3*
Saudi Arabia **27** 875–6*
Scandinavia **4** 780–81*; **23** 222; **31** 363
Cistercian Order **13** 50
Gothic **13** 50*, 56–8*
Romanesque **26** 592–3*
Viking **32** 532–4*, *533*
Scotland **2** 5; **4** 788; **12** *773*; **27** 171; **28** 223–32*
Gothic **13** 56
Neo-classicism **25** *36*
Romanesque **26** 591*
19th cent. **28** 288–9*
Seleucid **13** 405
Senegal **28** 405*
Serbia **28** 439–42*, 444–5*
Byzantine **9** 552–3
19th cent. **3** *620*
Shakers **28** 539–40*
shamanism **18** 268
Shinto **17** 74
Shona **1** 414

architecture
historical and regional traditions—cont.
Sicán culture **28** 652
Sicily
Baroque **16** 640–41
Islamic **16** 171–2*
Norman *see* Romanesque
Romanesque **16** 171, 626–7; **28** 655
Sierra Leone **28** 691*
Sikhism **15** 375
Singapore **28** 771–4*
Slovakia **28** 849–50*
Slovenia **28** 857–60*
Society Islands **28** 922
Sogdiana **6** 197, 200, 201
Somalia **29** 56
South Africa **29** 102, 104–7*; **30** 728
South America, Pre-Columbian **29** 138–40*, 159–60, 161–7*, *163*, 192
Chavín culture **6** 522*
Puerto Rico **29** 200
Sicán culture **28** 652
Tairona **30** 240
Spain **4** 784–5*, 790; **25** 171; **29** 261–4*, 271–3*
Almohad **16** 187, 190–91*
Almoravid **16** 187, 190
Baroque **29** 268–71*
Cistercian Order **13** 50; **29** 263
Gothic **13** 35, 50–51*, 66–70*; **19** 171; **29** 263, 265
Gothic: Flamboyant style **13** 68
Gothic: Hispano-Flemish style **13** 69–70
Islamic **16** 157–8*, 187*, 189–91*, 215–17*; **29** 287–8
Mozarabic **22** *247*
Nasrid **16** 215
Philippines **24** 611–14
Renaissance **29** 264–8*
Roman **26** 904
Romanesque **26** 580–82*; **29** 262–3
Umayyad **16** 149, 157, 187–9*
20th cent. **20** *516*; **29** 273–4*
Sri Lanka **29** 441, 446–51*, 452–6*
Buddhism **29** 446–8*, 449
Hinduism **29** 448
Starčevo-Körös-Criş culture **25** 499
Sudan **29** 895–6*
Sumatra **15** 771–2*
Sumerian **29** 924*
Surinam **30** 14–15*
Swahili **1** 315, 410; **30** 56–7*
Sweden **30** 66–7*, 68–75*
Gothic **13** 50, 56
Romanesque **26** 592–3*
Switzerland **4** 777, 789; **30** 125–9*
Carolingian **27** 554
Gothic **30** 125–6
Modernism **29** *603*
Syria **13** 405
Byzantine **9** 538–41*, 542–3*, 547–9*
Early Christian (*c.* AD 250-843) **9** 538–41*, 542–3*
Egypt **16** 207*
Islamic **4** 791; **16** 145–9*, 155–6*, 182*, 207–13*
Mamluk **16** 207–13
Ottoman **16** *228*, 228–9
Roman **26** 916–17*, 918*
Umayyad **16** 145–9*, 243
Syria-Palestine **30** 184, 187, 190*, 191–2*
Tairona **30** 240
Tajikistan **16** 166; **30** 252*
Tarascan **30** 340*
Teutonic Order **26** 706

architecture
historical and regional traditions—cont.
Thailand **2** 884; **30** 574–5*, 576–81*, 582–4*, 585–8*, 589–92*
Tiahuanaco **30** 796
Tibet **30** 812, 814–21*
Toltec **31** 98–9
Tonga (Pacific Islands) **23** 715
Trinidad and Tobago **31** 333–5*
Tuareg **1** 305
Tunisia **16** 149, 156–7*, 170–71*, 219–20*, 229; **31** 424*, 426
Turkey **31** 452–3*
Aqqoyunlu **16** 201, 202
Beylik **16** 202*
Byzantine **9** 536–7*, 542*, 543–5*, 549–50*
Early Christian (*c.* AD 250-843) **9** 536–7*, 542*
Islamic **16** 183*, 186*, 201–2*, 205–7*, 221–7*, 265–7*
Ottoman **16** 205–7*, 221–7*, 265–7*, 604
Qaraqoyunlu **16** 201, 202
Roman **26** *923*
Saljuqs of Anatolia **16** 183
Turkmenistan **31** 458–9*
Uganda **31** 528
Ukraine **31** 546–9*, 550*, 551–3*
Byzantine **31** 546
United Arab Emirates **31** 584*
United States of America **4** 786, 788, 789; **12** 221; **30** 505, 507; **31** 588*, 589, 590–94*, 596–8*, 662
Colonial period **31** 588–90*
Franciscan Order **22** 567; **31** 588
Mexico **18** 832
Native North Americans **22** 563–5*, 566–70*
Philippines **24** 614–15
19th cent. **3** 35; **9** 205; **16** 54; **18** *844*; **27** *642*; **29** 651
Urartian **1** 831; **31** 699–700*
Uruguay **7** 614–15; **31** 752–4*
Uzbekistan **16** 166; **31** 782*
Vanuatu **31** 891–2*
Venda **1** 414; **32** 154*
Venetian Empire **8** 156; **32** 159
Venezuela **32** 166, 167–72*
Vietnam **6** 420–21*, 423–5*; **9** 133; **32** 471–8*
Viking **8** 721; **23** 219; **32** 532–4*, *533*
Wales **26** 587–90*; **32** 779–84*; **33** *208*
West Mexico **21** 216–17*; **33** 102*
Yemen **16** 177–8*, 207, 213–15*, 229; **33** 519–20
Yoruba **23** 134; **33** 554–5*
Zambia **33** 602*
Zimbabwe **13** *336*; **33** 678
Zulu **1** 414
historiography *see under* HISTORIOGRAPHY → types
lighting **19** 361–8*, *367*
materials
adobe **32** 308
aluminium **1** 736–7*, *737*; **32** 171, *171*
bamboo **1** 307; **3** 913; **7** 605; **29** 226
bark **1** 306
basalt **9** 538; **26** 880, 916
bitumen **16** 269
bone **25** 473
brick **2** 362; **4** 767*, *769*, 769–72*, *770*, *771*, 774*, 781–3*, 785–90*; **15** 168; **16** 154, 244; **26** 911
Afghanistan **16** 169

architecture
materials
brick—cont.
Africa **1** 377; **4** 792–3*
Belgium **13** 61
Britain **4** 778–80*; **32** 276
Burma **5** 226
Byzantine **4** 773–4*; **9** 524, 547, 553, *554*
Central Asia, Eastern **6** 295
Central Asia, Western **16** 160, 169, 199–200, 239
China **6** 645*, 686
Czech Republic **8** 376, 379
Denmark **4** *789*; **8** 721
Early Christian (*c*. AD 250-843) **9** 524, 553, *554*
England **4** *785*; **10** 229; **30** 365–6
France **4** 780*
Germany **4** 776–7*; **12** 362
Gothic **12** 362; **13** 61; **24** 347
Greece **9** 547
Indian subcontinent **3** 908; **4** 793–4*; **15** 263, 337, 351
Iran **4** 791; **16** 158, 160, *164*, 164–5, 199–200; **32** 320
Iran, ancient **15** 913
Iraq **16** 182
Islamic **4** 791–2*; **16** 140, 186, 268, 269
Islamic: Central Asia, Western **16** 169, 239
Islamic: Indian subcontinent **15** 337, 351
Islamic: Iran **16** 158, 160, *164*, 164–5, 199–200; **32** 320
Islamic: Iraq **16** 182
Islamic: Turkey **16** 207
Italy **4** 774–6*; **23** *621*; **31** 442
Korea **18** 264, 266
Netherlands, the **4** 777–8*, *778*
Ottoman **16** 207
Poland **4** *782*, 783; **24** 347, 698
Portugal **4** 784–5*
Rome, ancient **23** *621*; **26** *912*, *914*
Scandinavia **4** 780–81*
Spain **4** 784–5*; **13** 68
Sweden **30** 66
Syria **4** 791
Thailand **2** 884; **4** *795*
Turkey **16** 186, 207; **26** *912*, *914*
bronze **6** 645*
cast iron **3** 35; **10** 236; **11** 522; **12** 221; **16** 51–3*, 54*; **18** *582*; **20** 570; **26** 18; **30** 109, 284; **31** 592, *592*
cement **15** 169; **26** 879
chalk **29** 699
clay **1** 305; **15** 909; **16** 269
concrete **7** 690, 691–6*; **19** 41; **30** 27
Brazil **3** 66
Cambodia **5** 482
England **33** 204
France **7** 531, *694*; **11** 771
India, Republic of **15** 168
Islamic **16** 143
Japan **17** 86
Korea **18** 266
Mexico **7** *695*
Peru **24** 505
Poland **3** *768*
Rome, ancient **26** 879–80*, 881, 887
Vietnam **32** 477
copper **7** 813*
coral **1** 305; **16** 269; **20** 188
corrugated iron **26** 18; **32** 308
corrugated steel **29** 105
cypress **17** 45, 46
earth **6** 643–4*; **18** 264
fibreglass **25** 24
flint **26** 874
glass **12** 790–94*, *793*; **19** 320; **20** 560; **22** 365; **28** 65
Brazil **12** *794*

architecture
materials
glass—cont.
England **8** *279*
Germany **12** 374
Ireland **3** 536
Korea **18** 266
New Zealand **23** 56
Scotland **28** 231
United States of America **12** *794*
Venezuela **32** 171, *171*
granite **8** 376; **9** 773; **18** 264; **26** 874
grasses **1** 307
gypsum **16** 269
inscriptions **16** 134, 143, 165, 166, 169, 193, 250, 810
iron **3** 536; **9** 464; **12** 374; **16** 51–4*; **28** 228
laterite **29** 452
lead **20** 560
limestone **1** 305; **9** 538, 773; **10** 536; **21** 213; **26** 874, 875; **27** 470; **29** 701
locust-beans **1** 305
marble **16** 221, 239; **26** 854, 875*, 885, 889; **32** 477
masonry **5** 482
mastic **4** 787
metal **2** 194; **27** 879
mortars (building) **4** 767
mortars (vessels) **16** 268
mosaics **16** 216; **22** *164*
moss **32** 286
mouldings **16** 182
mud **1** 305; **15** 909; **25** 498, 499, 500
mud-bricks **4** 793; **6** 195, 199; **9** 775, 824–5, 850; **15** 169; **16** 140, 150, 199; **21** 283, 749; **30** *177*
nails **17** 45
oils **29** 712
palm **16** 269, 487; **29** 226
palm leaves **1** 305–7
paper **18** 264; **24** 51–2*
pisé de terre **19** 837; **32** 308
plaques **4** 794
plaster **1** 305; **4** 793; **8** 376, 379; **16** 165, 269
plaster of Paris **10** 683
plastics **25** 24*; **32** 171, *171*
poles **1** 306
poplar **6** 295; **16** 269
putty **4** 787
reeds **16** 269; **25** 500; **32** *314*
sandstone **1** 305; **8** 376; **9** 773; **15** 340; **16** 239; **26** 874; **29** 703
scoria **26** 916
slate **8** 376; **10** 236
staff **10** 683
steel **1** 743; **5** 562; **15** 169; **16** 51*, 54–6*, *55*, 143; **17** 86; **18** 266; **20** 570; **21** 631; **28** 228; **30** 27; **31** 596, *596*
stone **1** 305; **2** 362; **16** 150
Africa **1** 377
Bhutan **3** 913
Britain **32** 276
Burma **5** 226
Byzantine **9** 538
Central Asia, Western **16** 199
China **6** 644–5*
Czech Republic **8** 379
Denmark **8** 721
Early Christian (*c*. AD 250-843) **9** 538
Egypt **16** 176
Egypt, ancient **9** 779, 825; **25** 761; **27** 811
France **32** 278
Georgia **12** 318–19
Germany **32** 281
Greece, ancient **13** 386–9*
Indian subcontinent **4** 794; **16** 239
Iran **16** 199

architecture
materials
stone—cont.
Islamic **16** 141, 176, 182, 186, 199, 239, 266, 269
Korea **18** 264, 265, 266
Malta (Republic of) **20** 210–11
Micronesia, Federated States of **23** *716*
Ottoman **16** 266
Pacific Islands **23** 715, *716*
Prehistoric art **25** 498, 502–3*
Rome, ancient **26** 874–5*
Russia **27** 368
Scandinavia **31** 363
South America, Pre-Columbian **30** 240
Sweden **30** 66
Syria **16** 182
Syria-Palestine **30** 190
Tairona **30** 240
Turkey **16** 186, 266
Ukraine **31** 546
straw **25** 500
stucco **12** 372; **15** 338; **16** 133, 158, 160, 214, 217
studs **30** 896, *896*; **32** 276
tamarisk **6** 295
teak **16** 269
terracotta **16** 165, 169; **30** 501–7*; **32** *905*
tiles **16** 217, *236*, 269; **18** 264
tufa **4** 778; **16** 269; **26** 874
wood **1** 305–7; **20** 167, 560
Anglo-Saxon **2** 64
Belarus' **17** *546*
Cambodia **5** 482
Canada **5** 558
Central Asia, Eastern **6** 295
Central Asia, Western **16** 199
China **6** 637–43*, 650
Czech Republic **8** 376, 379
Egypt **16** 176
Egypt, ancient **9** 775, 824
England **23** 809
Finland **32** 286–7
Indian subcontinent **15** 721
Iran **16** 199
Islamic **16** 141, 176, 199, 269, 491–2, 494–5
Japan **17** 45
Jewish art **17** *546*
Korea **18** 264–5, *264*
Norway **23** 219, 220, 221; **32** 286–7
Pacific Islands **23** 715–18, *717*
Papua New Guinea **23** *717*
Prehistoric art **25** 499
Rome, ancient **26** 856
Russia **18** 104; **27** 368
Scandinavia **31** 363
South-east Asia **29** 226
Spain **16** 494–5
Sweden **32** 286–7
Thailand **30** 585–6, *586*
Ukraine **31** 546
wrought iron **10** 236; **16** 52, 53–4*
restoration **2** 318–25*, *321*; **7** 729
technical examination **30** 395, 409*
techniques
ā'inakārī **16** 257
anti-seismic **4** 789; **16** 239; **17** 88, 90; **32** 25
bricklaying *see* BRICKLAYING
brique et fer **4** 788
cavity-walling **4** 788, 789
coiling **1** 305
frame-and-mat **1** 306
joinery **17** 45, 50
Knitlock **13** 648
murus gallicus **21** 551
painting **6** 638; **15** 548, 806, *807*; **16** 160, 250*
pointing *see* POINTING (ii) (ARCHITECTURE)

architecture
techniques—cont.
polychromy **4** 769, 787–8; **13** 613; **25** 171–4*
Catalonia **25** II2
England **8** 48; **10** 238; **25** I2
Greece, ancient **25** I1
Mesoamerica, Pre-Columbian **21** 213
Mexico **25** II1
Rome, ancient **26** *877*, 878
Scandinavia **4** 781
post-and-lintel *see* trabeated construction
post-and-plank **15** 286, *286*
prefabrication **4** 771; **5** 173; **10** 681; **22** 719; **26** 17–20*; **29** 105; **31** 592, *592*
Ancient Near East **4** 771
Australia **26** 18
Bolivia **4** 260
Brazil **4** 709
Britain **12** 597; **26** 19
Denmark **31** 776
England **5** 14; **26** 17, *17*, *19*, 461
Germany **26** *18*
Japan **17** 50–51, 89
Romania **26** 709
Rome, ancient **21** 559; **26** 911
South Africa **26** 18; **29** 105
Sri Lanka **29** 453
United States of America **26** 19; **28** 488; **31** 592, *592*, 596
quincha **25** 822*; **32** 25
rationalized construction **26** 16*, 17–20*
sand-blasting **4** 789
stressed-skin construction **21** 407
swish **1** 305
systems building **8** 729; **26** 16*
taipa de pilão **2** 903
trabeated construction **1** 306; **6** 667, 689; **13** 390; **31** 269–70*, *269*
welding **1** 743
terminology **10** 204, 205, 206, 208–9, 211–12
theories *see under* THEORIES
types
additive **31** 776
community **6** 483; **14** 18
exhibition **10** 679, 681–5*
Australia **2** *739*
Austria **2** *788*
Brazil **4** *712*
England **10** *679*
Fascism **19** *305*
France **10** *416*, *682*; **15** *884*; **16** *55*
Germany **10** *685*; **21** *491*; **23** *394*; **30** *370*
Italy **19** *305*
United States of America **1** *9*; **5** *273*
folk *see* vernacular
landscape **12** 61, 104–6
China **12** 85–93
England **12** 126–31
Japan **12** 95–101, *96*, *97*, *99*, *100*, *101*
Korea **12** 93–5
Russia **27** 376–7
United States of America **9** 205; **24** 742
see also GARDEN DESIGN; HOUSES → types → country
megalithic **21** 39–45*, 134
Africa **21** 43*
Algeria **21** 43
Balearic Islands **21** 43
Britain **21** 43
Central African Republic **21** 43
China **21** 44
England **2** 851; **21** *41*
Eritrea **10** 577*

architecture
types
megalithic—cont.
Ethiopia **10** 577*; **21** 43
France **5** 780, *780*; **21** 43
Indian subcontinent **15** 192; **21** 43–4*
Indonesia **15** 754, 756; **21** 45
Japan **21** 45
Jordan **21** 43
Korea **21** 45
Madagascar **21** 43
Malaysia **21** 45
Malta (Republic of) **21** 43
Morocco **21** 43
Pakistan **21** 43
Prehistoric art **5** 780, *780*; **21** 40–43*, *41*; **25** 498, 504–6*
Sabah (Malaysia) **21** 45
Sarawak **21** 45
Sardinia **21** 43
Scandinavia **21** 43
Senegal **21** 43
Sri Lanka **29** 445
Taiwan **21** 44
Tibet **21** 44
Tunisia **21** 43
see also HENGES; MENHIRS; MONOLITHS; TRILITHONS
military **21** 545–50*, 551*, 561–4*, 565*, 571–2*, 576–81*, *579*, 592*, 597*
Africa **21** 596–7*
Anatolia, ancient **21** 552–3*
Ancient Near East **21** 552–4*
Arabia: Islamic **21** 588
Assyrian **21** 552
Aztec **21** 598, 599
Babylonian **21** 552
Britain **21** 568–9*, 573–5*
Britain: North America **21** 573–4
Byzantine **9** 553–6*, *554*, *555*; **21** 562
Canaanite **5** 557
Canada **21** 575*
Central Asia **21** 591*
Central Asia, Eastern **21** 592*
Central Asia, Western **21** 591–2*
Champa **6** 425–6*; **21** 595
Chimú **21** 599
China **21** 593–4*
Cyprus, ancient **21** 555
Denmark **21** 570
Early Christian (*c*. AD 250-843) **9** 553–5*, *554*
Egypt **21** 587–8
Egypt, ancient **9** 843–9*, *845*, *846*, *847*; **21** 554–5*
England **10** 359; **19** 60; **21** 549, 564
France **21** 549, 550, 567–8*, 573*
Germany **21** 571*
Greece, ancient **21** 551, 555–8*, *557*
Haiti **14** 57
Indian subcontinent **15** 541; **16** 239; **21** 574, 590–91*
Indonesia **21** 596, *596*
Iran **21** 588–9
Iran, ancient **21** 553–4*
Iraq **21** 588
Islamic **4** 464; **16** 186, 206, 239, 240; **21** 581–9*, *583*, *586*, *588*
Italy **3** *360*; **21** 565–7*
Japan **17** 83–6*; **21** 595*
Korea **21** 594*
Malta (Republic of) **21** 574, 580
Mauritius **21** 573, 574
Maya **21** 598, 599
Mesoamerica, Pre-Columbian **21** *598*, 598–9*
Mesopotamia **14** 21; **21** 552*
Morocco **16** 240; **21** 585

architecture
types
military—cont.
Mozambique **21** 572
Native North Americans **21** 597–8*
Netherlands, the **21** 569–70*, 572–3*
North America **21** 573–4, 575–6*
Nubia **21** 554–5
Ottoman **16** 206; **21** 585–7, *586*
Palestine **21** *588*
Philippines **21** 596
Portugal **21** 572*
Prehistoric art **21** 551–2*
Romania **26** 707
Rome, ancient **3** 329*; **21** 548, 558–61*
Russia **21** 561
Sarawak **21** 596
Sasanian **21** 554
Scandinavia **21** 570*
Scotland **21** 549
Sicily **21** 556, *557*
Singapore **21** 575
South America, Pre-Columbian **21** 599*
South-east Asia **21** 595–6*
Spain **21** 573*, 584–5
Sri Lanka **21** 572, 575
Sweden **21** 570
Syria **21** 582–3, *583*, 587–8
Syria-Palestine **21** 553; **30** 185
Thailand **21** 595
Tibet **21** 592–3*
Turkey **16** 186, 206; **21** 585–6, *586*
United States of America **21** 575–6*
Urartian **21** 553
Venetian Empire **21** 550
Vietnam **6** 425–6*; **21** 595, 596
see also CASTLES; FORTRESSES; FORTS; WAR CEMETERIES
organic *see* ORGANIC ARCHITECTURE
rock-cut
Byzantine **5** 673–5*
Cappadocia **5** 673–5*; **9** 543
Mesoamerica, Pre-Columbian **21** 208
see also TEMPLES → types → rock-cut
temporary **10** 681; **23** 767–9, 770–71
vernacular **2** 362; **32** 272–5*, 289–94*, 295–300*, 305–7*
Albania **32** 290, 293
Algeria **32** 309–11*
Australia **32** 307–9*
Azerbaijan **2** 893
Berber **32** 310
Bolivia **32** *305*
Bosnia **32** 293
Britain **32** 275–7*
Canada **32** 300–304*
Central Asia, Western **32** 320–22*
China **7** 143*
Corsica **32** 291
Crete **32** 294
Croatia **32** 293
Czech Republic **32** 296
Denmark **32** 285–6*
Egypt **32** 312–14*, *314*
England **8** *830*, 830; **30** *896*, *897*
Finland **32** 286–9*
France **32** 278–80*, 290
Germany **32** 281–3*
Greece **32** 289, 290, 293–4
Indian subcontinent **15** 235–6*; **32** 322–5*
Iran **32** 319–20*
Iraq **32** 314–15*
architecture
types
vernacular—cont.
Islamic **16** 123, 142; **32** 309–16*, *310*, *314*, 317–22*
Italy **32** 289, 290, 291–2*
Libya **19** 324
Mexico **32** 306, 307
Montenegro **32** 293
Morocco **32** 309–11*, *310*
Netherlands, the **32** 283–5*
New Zealand **32** 307–9*
Nigeria **1** *250*
Norway **32** 286–9*
Nubia **32** 314
Peru **32** *306*
Poland **32** 296
Russia **32** 295
Sardinia **32** 290, 291
Saudi Arabia **32** 315–16*
Scotland **28** 229
Serbia **32** 293, 294
Sicily **32** 292
Slovenia **32** 293
Spain **32** 290–91*
Sweden **32** 286–9*
Syria **30** *177*; **32** 314–15*
Tunisia **32** 311–12*
Turkey **32** 318–19*
United States of America **32** 300–304*
Yemen **32** 317–18*
wattle-and-daub **10** 587; **18** 277; **32** 921*
see also GEOMETRY (CONSTRUCTIVE); MANUALS → types → architecture; SETTING OUT; TREATISES → types → architecture
Architecture + Design **24** 436
Architecture, bâtiment, construction/ Architecture Concept **24** 430
Architecture: the AIA Journal **24** 433
Architecture Australia **24** 438
Architecture Bureau **30** 685
Architecture d'aujourd'hui **24** 442
architecture parlante **2** 363*
Architecture Vivante, L' **29** 661
Architecture Workshop Number 6 **18** 205
Architekt **20** 398; **24** 441; **29** 792
Architekt, Der **24** 427, 438; **28** 155
Architekten Groep de 8 **21** 782
Architektengruppe Kantonsspital Zürich **29** 603
Architektenteam **8** 631
Architekten- und Ingenieursverein für den Niederrhein und Westfalen **33** 173
Architekten-Verein zu Berlin **3** 799; **4** 504; **18** 160
Architektonische Rundschau **24** 444
Architektonisches Album **18** 161
Architektura **24** 441
Architektura i budownictwo **24** 441
Architektur des XX. Jahrhunderts: Zeitschrift für moderne Baukunst, Die **19** 327
Architekturforum Zürich **28** 190
architetto girovago, L' **24** 447
Architettura e arti decorative **12** 718; **24** 448, 693
Architettura italiana **24** 448
Architext **2** 363*; **17** 91
members **1** 477; **2** 909; **21** 742; **30** 50, 260
architrave icons *see under* ICONS → types
architraves **2** 363*; **23** 477, 478
Byzantine **9** *592*
Greece, ancient **13** 377, *378*, 379, 393
Turkey **9** *592*
Archive, The **24** 434
archives **2** 363–72*, 560; **4** 27
conservation **2** 366, 368*
archives—cont.
historical and regional traditions
Argentina **2** 369*
Australia **2** 369*
Austria **2** 370*
Belgium **2** 370*
Brazil **2** 369, 370*
Britain **2** 371*
Bulgaria **2** 369
Canada **2** 365, 367, 369, 370*
China **6** 764
Denmark **2** 369, 370*; **8** 724, 725
Egypt **2** 370*
Egypt, ancient **2** 364
England **2** 365, 372
Finland **2** 369
France **2** 365, 366, 369, 370*; **4** 332
Germany **2** 370*, 372
Greece **2** 370*
Iraq **2** 370*
Israel **2** 370*
Italy **2** 365, 370*; **32** 204
Japan **2** 369, 371*
Jewish art **2** 372
Mexico **2** 371*
Monaco **18** 573
Netherlands, the **2** 371*
New Zealand **2** 371*
Nigeria **2** 371*
Norway **2** 369
Peru **2** 369, 371*
Philippines **2** 369, 371*
Poland **2** 371*
Rome, ancient **2** 364
Russia **2** 369, 371*
Spain **2** 369, 371*
Sweden **2** 371*
Switzerland **2** 371*
United States of America **2** 365, 366, 367, 368, 369, 371–2*
see also COLLECTIONS → types → study; PHOTOARCHIVES
Archives, bibliothèques et musées de Belgique **24** 440
Archives and Manuscript Control *see* AMC
Archives Centrales Iconographiques d'Art National & Laboratoire Central des Musées de Belgique **3** 619
Archives de l'Art Français **2** 366; **6** 545; **11** 675
Archives de l'impressionnisme, Les **2** 366
archives education *see* EDUCATION (ART) → types
Archives marocaines **22** 129
Archives of American Art *see under* WASHINGTON (DC) → museums
Archives of American Art Journal **2** 368
Archives of Asian Art **24** 433
Archives of Contemporary Art **2** 364
Archives of the Chinese Art Society of America **24** 433
Archiv für christliche Kunst **2** 366; **24** 444
Archiv für die zeichnenden Künste mit besonderer Beziehung auf Kupferstecher- und Holzscheidekunst und ihre Geschichte **24** 444
Archiv für zeichende Künste **2** 366
Archivio storico dell'arte **12** 824; **24** 423, 448; **32** 233
Archivo español **24** 452
Archivo español de arqueología **24** 452
Archivo español de arte **24** 452
Archivo General de la Nación Departamento Documentos de Imagen y de Sonido **2** 369
archivolts **2** 292, *292*, 373*; **19** *405*
Archivum **2** 365
Archizoom (Associati) **2** 373*
Arch of Caracalla *see under* DJEMILA
Arch of Constantine *see under* ROME
Arch of Titus *see under* ROME → Forum Romanum
Arciero, Giovan Mattea **28** 388, 389
Arcimboldi, Giuseppe *see* ARCIMBOLDO, GIUSEPPE
Arcimboldi, Guidantonio, Archbishop of Milan **20** 618
Arcimboldi Missal, Master of the **20** 618*
Arcimboldi Missal *see under* MISSALS → individual manuscripts
Arcimboldo, Biagio **2** 373
Arcimboldo, Giuseppe **2** *373*, 373–4*; **25** 432; **32** 442
methods **28** 203
patrons and collectors **13** 908, 911, 912, 914; **29** 799
works **2** *374*; **5** 755; **16** 746, 757; **20** 280
Arciniega, Claudio de **2** 375*
works **21** 375, *376*, 401
Arciniega, Luis de **2** 375
Arcis, Marc **2** 375–6*
Arciszewski, Krzysztof **32** 7
Arciszewski, Samuel **25** 841
arc lamps *see under* LAMPS → types
Arco, Alonso del **2** 376*; **24** 392
Arco, Carlo D', Conte *see* D'ARCO, CARLO, Conte
Arco del Meloncello **16** 641
Arcon **23** 426
Arconati, Francesco **2** 376
Arconati, Galeazzo (Maria), Conte **2** 376*; **19** 197
Arconati-Visconti, Marquise **6** 482
Arconati-Visconti cabinet **27** 682
Arconati-Visconti Tondo **8** 798
Arcondo, Mabel **24** 99
Arconio, Mario **2** 376–7*; **4** 567; **27** 764
ARCOP (Architects in Cooperation) **22** 37
Arcop Associates **1** 184
Arcos, Duque de **5** 791; **31** 191
Arcos, Duquesa de **15** 889
Arcos, Los *see* LOS ARCOS
Arcos, Luis Antonio Navarro de los *see* NAVARRO DE LOS ARCOS, LUIS ANTONIO
Arcos, Pedro Laso de la Vega, 1st Conde de **23** 156
Arcos, René **1** 21; **8** 243
Arcos de Valdevez, Espírito Santo **25** 306
arcosolia **9** *593*, 598
arcs **2** 292, *292*
Arct, Eugeniusz **9** 473
Arctic **22** 668; **28** 302
Arcucci, Camillo **2** 377*
collaboration **6** 23
patrons and collectors **24** 833
works **4** 431; **27** 486
Arcucci, Giuseppe Brusati **2** 377
Arcuccio, Angiolillo **26** 1
Arcueil Aqueduct **2** 242
Arculf, Bishop **13** 808; **17** 489
Arc-voltaic **8** 436
Arcy, Robert d', 4th Earl of Holderness **19** 531
Arda, Orhan **23** 441; **31** 452
works **31** *452*
Ardabil **2** 377*; **15** 921; **16** *105*
Ardabil Shrine **16** 90, 528; **28** 634
Chinikhana **16** 230
collections **28** 635
Dar al-Huffaz **16** 230
porcelain **4** 172; **6** 916; **16** 393, 424
congregational mosque **16** 194
funerary complex of Shaykh Safi **16** 194
Jannat Saray **16** 230
tomb of Isma'il **16** 526
Uč Dukkan Bath **3** 378
Ardabil carpets **2** 377, 437; **12** 504; **16** 128, *467*, 474*, 482
Ardagger, St Margarete **29** 501, 510, 511
Ardagh Chalice **2** *378*; **15** 872
Ardagh Treasure **2** 377–8*
Ardalan, Nader **2** 378–9*; **15** 897; **30** 415
Ardanuch **30** 305
Ardashir I (*reg* 224-41) **11** 121; **18** 85
architecture **15** 912; **16** 801
armour **1** 887
coins **27** 855, *855*
fortifications **18** 85
towns **11** 121; **18** 483; **27** 855
Ardashir-Khurrah *see* FIRUZABAD (IRAN)
Ardea
basilica **3** 328, *328*
sculpture **27** 9
town walls **26** 887
wall paintings **10** 617
Ardelet **24** 266
Ard el-Na'am **14** 331
Ardemans, Teodoro **2** 379*; **29** 303
patrons and collectors **4** 558, 560
works **27** 752; **29** 270
Ardenicë Church **1** 539
Ardenne Cross **5** 807; **26** 144
Arden Quin, Carmelo **2** 525
Ardent Factory **19** 398
Ardenti, Alessandro **2** 379*
Arderne, John of *see* JOHN OF ARDERNE
Ardeshir, A. C. **15** 183, 742
ardhamaṇḍapa **15** 243*
ardhapadma **15** 243*
Ardilaun, Arthur Edward Guinness, 1st Lord, *see* GUINNESS, ARTHUR EDWARD, 1st Lord Ardilaun
Ardinghelli (family) **27** 750
Ardini *see* MUṢAṢIR
Ardistan **2** 380*; **16** *105*
congregational mosque **16** 159, 162, 165; **22** 194
mihrab **16** 165, 245
squinches **16** 164
stucco **23** 557; **29** 820
mosque of Imam Hasan **2** 380
Ardita **27** 838
Arditi, Andrea **2** 380*
Ardito, Giovanni Antonio **28** 388
Ardizzone, Edward (Irving Jeffrey) **2** 380*; **4** 367, 368
Ardizzoni da Reggio, Simone **20** 322; **33** 689
Ardkinglas House (Strathclyde) **29** 843
Ardmore Church (Co. Waterford) **26** 618
Ardobicum Curonium *see* LA CORUÑA
Ardon, Mordecai **2** 381*; **3** 902; **17** 579
pupils **1** 448
works **16** 567
Ardre **31** 748
Ardres, Lambert, Lord of **6** 53, 407; **9** 143
Ardres Château **9** 143
Ardrossan, St Peter in Chains **28** 243
Ards, Willem **13** 111
Ardsruni, Sadun, Prince of Vaspurakan *see* SADUN, Prince of Vaspurakan
Ardsruni, Thomas **2** 444
Arduini, Girolamo **27** 274
Arduino da Baisio **10** 519; **11** 4
Areaubert, Claude-Charles Gérault d' *see* GÉRAULT D'AREAUBERT, CLAUDE-CHARLES
Arechi II, Duke of Benevento *see* ARICHIS II, Duke of Benevento
Arecibo **25** *698*
Arecuna **13** 874, 875

Aref 'ev, Anatoliy Vasiliyevich 18 568
Aref 'yev 31 486
Aref 'yev, Aleksandr 27 581
Aref 'yev, Stefan 29 54
Arel, Ruhi 2 634
Arelate *see* ARLES
Arellano, Agnes 24 620
Arellano, Cristóbal Ramírez de *see* RAMÍREZ DE ARELLANO, CRISTÓBAL
Arellano, Francisco (Domínguez) Chávez y *see* CHÁVEZ Y ARELLANO, FRANCISCO (DOMÍNGUEZ)
Arellano, José de 2 381
Arellano, Juan (1881-1960) 20 274; 24 615
Arellano, Juan de (1614-76) 2 381*
 collaboration 23 201; 24 401
 patrons and collectors 4 565; 27 792
 pupils 24 400
 reproductive prints by others 32 557
 teachers 29 45
 works 11 227; 29 668
Arelliano, Juan (*fl* 1789) 29 315
Arellius 27 52
Aren, Peet 33 566
Arena, Giuseppe d' 2 381–2*; 20 213
Arena Chapel *see under* PADUA → churches
Arenal, El 21 216
Arenal, Luis 30 275
Arenas, Diego López de *see* LÓPEZ DE ARENAS, DIEGO
Arenas, Hernando de 29 339
Areñas, Rafael 6 73
Arenas, Reinaldo 5 449
Arenas Betancourt, Rodrigo 21 380
Arenberg (family) 3 599
Arenberg, Duchess of 11 595
Arenberg, Auguste-Marie-Raymond, 6th Duke of 2 382*; 30 283
Arenberg, Charles-Philip, Duke of 32 706
Arenberg, Engelbert-Auguste, 8th Duke of 2 382
Arenberg, Engelbert Charles, 10th Duke of 2 382*; 20 642
Arenberg, Engelbert-Marie, 9th Duke of 2 382*
Arenberg, Louis-Engelbert, 5th Duke of 2 382
Arenberg, Prosper-Louis, 7th Duke of, Duke of Arschot 2 382
Arenberg Album *see under* ALBUMS → individual manuscripts
Arenberg Basin, d' 16 366, 367, 381
Arenberg Gospels *see under* GOSPEL BOOKS → individual manuscripts
Arenberg *Lamentation* 13 111, *112*
Arendtz, Cornelius 2 382–3*; 11 94; 30 77
Arene Candide 25 473
Arenenberg, Napoleonmuseum 4 304
Arenenberg, Schloss *see* SCHLOSS ARENENBERG
Areni, Church of the Mother of God 2 434, 435
Arenillas de San Pelayo Church 26 609
Arenius, Olof 28 95
Arens, Johann August 2 383*; 33 37
Arensberg, Louise 2 383–4*; 8 708; 9 356, 357, 359; 24 600
Arensberg, Walter (Conrad) 2 383–4*; 9 359; 11 360; 23 48
 collections 9 356, 359; 24 600; 31 663, 665
 groups and movements 9 357; 23 701; 28 925
 paintings 8 708
 sculpture 1 438
Arensnuphis 23 283
Arentsz., Jan 22 835
Arentsz. Noorwits, Pieter 2 385–6*; 3 353; 14 39
Arentsz. van's Gravesande, Arent 2 385*, 856
 works 9 299; 14 39; 19 100; 26 392
Ärentuna
 brooches 32 516, *516*
 church 30 76
Ärentuna, Master of 20 159
Areobindus 9 648, *648*
Areopolis 9 542
Arequipa 2 386–7*; 24 *498*
 Banco Industrial 2 387; 24 503
 Casa del Moral *see* Banco Industrial
 Casa Gibbs-Ricketts 2 387; 24 503
 Casa Ugarteche *see* Casa Gibbs-Ricketts
 Casa Williams *see* Banco Industrial
 ecclesiastical buildings 24 503
  Cathedral 2 387; 24 503, 504
  Convent of S Catalina 2 387; 24 503
  La Compañía 2 386, *386*; 21 315; 24 503
  S Agustín 24 503
  S Domingo 2 386; 24 503
  S Juan Bautista 2 386
  S Miguel 24 503
  Villa Hermosa de la Asunción 24 500
 education (art) 24 517
 Hospital del Empleado 2 387
 houses 2 387
 Sackville Street 24 504
 Universidad Nacional de S Agustín 24 517
  museum 24 516
Arequipa Pottery 26 287
Arerys 29 330
Arese (family) 20 95
Arese, Francesco Teodoro, Conte 14 266
Aretas III (*reg* 87-62 BC) 8 477
Aretas IV (*reg* 9 BC-AD 40) 22 419; 24 556, 558
Aretin, Christoph, Baron von 19 482
Aretino 11 384
Aretino, Cione 2 380
Aretino, Leonardo *see* BRUNI, LEONARDO
Aretino, Pietro 2 387–8*; 16 665; 19 200; 31 16, 34
 collaboration 10 477
 dealing 11 661; 21 18; 31 849
 personal collection 2 98; 19 201; 25 281; 31 7
 productions 21 647
 works 9 74; 18 708; 31 16
Aretino, Spinello *see* SPINELLO ARETINO
Aretusi, Cesare 2 388–9*; 7 888
Arévalo
 La Lugareja 29 263
 S Martín 29 263
Arévalo, Antonio de 5 886; 7 604
Arévalo, Luis de 13 284; 15 34; 29 841
areytos 5 748
Arezzo 2 389–90*; 10 *583*, 585; 16 *620*
 art forms and materials
  coins 10 633
  furniture 16 723
  glass 16 740
Arezzo
 art forms and materials—cont.
  metalwork 10 624
  pottery 27 106, 107
  see also POTTERY → wares → Arretine ware
  sculpture 10 588, 605; 13 93; 16 *684*; 26 644
  stained glass 29 504
  terracotta 10 604, *604*
  vases 10 616
 ecclesiastical buildings
  Cathedral 1 709; 13 52; 26 644
  Pieve di S Maria 2 *389*
  SS Annunziata 13 124
  S Bernardo *see* Museo Archeologico Ciao Cilnia Mecanate
  S Domenico 1 696; 8 212
  S Francesco 16 659, 837
   frescoes 5 443; 9 262; 11 709, *710*; 24 760–63
   tomb of Francesco Rosselli 30 496
  S Maria Assunta 26 624
  S Maria della Pieve 16 625
 Galleria e Museo Medioevale e Moderno 2 389
 Museo Archeologico Ciao Cilnia Mecenate 2 390
 Museo Casa Vasari 1 662; 2 390, 550
  Camera della Fama 1 662; 32 13
  Camera di Fortuna 1 662
  frescoes 32 16
  interior decoration 32 12
  Sala della Fama *see* Camera della Fama
  Sala Grande 2 *548*
  sculpture 32 22
 Palazzo Bruni-Ciocchi *see* Galleria e Museo Medioevale e Moderno
 Palazzo Comunale 13 676
 Palazzo della Fraternità 27 181
 patronage 16 762
Arezzo, Domenico d' *see* DOMENICO D'AREZZO
Arezzo, Giovanni Antonio d' *see* GIOVANNI ANTONIO D'AREZZO
Arezzo, Margarito d' *see* MARGARITO D'AREZZO
Arezzo, Montano d' *see* MONTANO D'AREZZO
Arezzo *Chimaera* 10 636; 21 19
Arfe, Antonio de 2 390; 29 334; 31 824
Arfe, Enrique de 2 390*; 13 166
 works 7 345; 29 333, *333*; 31 89
Arfe, Juan de 2 390–91*
 works 10 502; 21 156; 26 148; 28 516; 29 334, 337, 339
 writings 23 487; 29 356
Arfe y Villafañe, Juan 31 297
Arfvidson, André-Louis 2 391*; 4 71
arg *see* CITADELS
Argan, Carlo 7 782
Argan, Giulio Carlo 2 391–2*; 24 449
Argand, Aimé 19 361, 364
Argand, Louis 31 619
Argand lamps *see under* LAMPS → types
Arge, Thomas 10 813
Argead dynasty 14 407
 see also:
  ALEXANDER THE GREAT, King of Macedonia
  PHILIP II, King of Macedonia
Argeiro, Ambrosio 12 826; 25 291
Argelander, Friedrich 23 340
Argendoña (family) 5 551
Argenson, Marc René d', Vicomte de Paulmy, Marquis de Voyer *see* VOYER, Marquis de
Argenson, René d' 4 588
Argenta (*d* 1573) 28 4
Argenta, Jacopo Filippo d' *see* JACOPO FILIPPO D'ARGENTA
Argenta, L' *see* ALEOTTI, GIOVANNI BATTISTA
Argenta, S Giorgio 26 621
Argentan 11 650; 18 589, 591
 St Thomas 26 597
Argent Archer Studios 17 445
Argentarius, Julianus 20 876; 26 33, 35
Argenteuil 15 153; 21 863
Argenteuil, Charles Marcotte d' *see* MARCOTTE D'ARGENTEUIL, CHARLES
Argenti, Giosuè 4 100; 16 706
Argentina 2 392–406*, *393*; 15 *161*; 29 127, 128, 189–91, 203
 architecture 1 743; 2 394–7*
 archives 2 369*
 banks 30 *525*
 body arts 29 204
 books 2 398
 brass 4 681
 collections 2 403–5*
 education (art) 2 405–6*; 7 848
  architecture 2 405
 engravings 2 398, 399
 exhibitions 2 404
 gold 2 401–2*
 gourds 13 229
 government buildings 2 *396*
 houses 33 *203*
 libraries 2 406*
 marks 2 402
 museums 2 403–5*; 7 *847*
 opera houses 5 *122*
 painting 2 398–9*, *399*, 400–401
  murals 22 335*
 patronage 2 403–5*
 periodicals 2 399
 ponchos 2 403, *403*
 porticos 2 *395*
 portraits 2 *398*
 pottery 29 *191*, *202*, 203
 pulpits 2 398
 retables 2 398
 rock art 29 203, 204
 sculpture 2 398–9*, *400*, 401; 29 *190*
 silver 2 401–2*
 steel 1 743
 stone 29 *190*
 textiles 2 402–3*
 topographical views 2 399
 trade 4 723
 universities 7 847
 urns 29 *191*
 welding 1 743
 wood-carvings 2 398–9
Argenton-Château 26 600
Argentorate *see* STRASBOURG
Argentoratensis, Jacobus 4 397
Argenville, A(ntoine)-N(icolas) Dezallier d' *see* DEZALLIER D'ARGENVILLE, A(NTOINE)-N(ICOLAS)
Argenville, Antoine-Joseph Dezallier d' *see* DEZALLIER D'ARGENVILLE, ANTOINE-JOSEPH
Arghezi, Tudor 3 88; 26 715
Arghun, Khan (*reg* 1284-91) (Ilkhanid) 29 919; 30 470
Arghun al-Kamili 1 602
Arghun ibn 'Abdallah al-Kamili (1300-52) 16 283
 works 16 *275*
Argile 20 75
argillaceous earth *see under* CLAY → types
Argilly Château 5 207
Argimon, Daniel 3 219
Argirov Triddon 5 153
Argishti I, King of Urartu (*reg c.* 786-764) 31 699, 700
Argive *see* ARGOLID; ARGOS
Argo (Sudan) 23 285
ARGO (group) 15 831
Argonaut krater 10 *616*
Argos 2 406–8*; 9 *511*; 13 *362*, *363*; 14 *332*; 26 *908*
 aqueducts 26 910
 Archaeological Museum 14 361
 architecture 26 909
 baths 26 909
 bronzes 13 572
 coins 13 587
 ex-votos 13 376
 figurines 13 578
 Heraion *see* Sanctuary of Hera
 houses 14 339
 ivory-carvings 14 354
 limestone 13 387
 nymphaeum 2 408
 odeion 23 350
 pottery 13 534
 Sanctuary of Hera 2 406, 407, *407*; 13 389, 418, 595; 27 713
  bronze 13 441, 571
  jewellery 13 600
  models 24 317
  pediment 24 319
  pins 13 *600*
  proportions 2 351
  Temple of Hera 1 128; 13 457, 460; 25 179
 Sanctuary of Pythian Apollo 2 407
 Temple of Serapis/Asklepios 2 408
 Theatre 2 407; 13 385; 26 910
 urban planning 13 419
 Villa of the Months 9 566
 wall paintings 14 348
Argos Painter 13 533
Argote de Molina, Gonzalo 2 408–9*
a.r. group 2 409*; 19 537; 25 108
 members 18 181; 25 423; 29 582, 795
Argüero 26 643
Arguilla, Lyd 20 274
Arguin Island Fort 1 318
Argungu 14 232
Argunov, Fyodor (Semyonovich) 18 536; 28 593
Argunov, Ivan (Petrovich) 2 409–10*; 19 704; 23 615; 26 550
 works 2 *410*
Argunov, Nikolay 2 410; 23 615
Argunov, Pavel 2 410; 23 615
Argunovkov, Ya. 23 615
Argustinsky-Dolgorukov, V. N. 27 439
Argyll, Archibald Campbell, 3rd Duke of *see* CAMPBELL, ARCHIBALD, 3rd Duke of Argyll
Argyll, John Campbell, 2nd Duke of *see* CAMPBELL, JOHN, 2nd Duke of Argyll
Argyll, John Campbell, 9th Duke of *see* CAMPBELL, JOHN, 9th Duke of Argyll
argyllite 29 155
Argyros, Romanos III, Emperor of Byzantium *see* ROMANOS III ARGYROS, Emperor of Byzantium
Argy-Rousseau, Gabriel 11 613; 12 783, 795
Arhuaco 7 602
Århus 8 *720*
 architecture 32 533
 Arkitektskolen 8 761
 Cathedral 4 781; 8 722, 723, 731, 758; 23 255
  altarpiece 8 738; 13 120
 church 8 721
 Jyske Asyl 4 69
 Jyske Kunstakademi 8 761
 Kunstmuseum 8 759; 21 821; 29 72
 Statsbiblioteket 8 761
 University 4 790; 8 728; 21 820–21; 29 601

Aria, Giovanni d' see GIOVANNI D'ARIA
Aria, Michele d' see MICHELE D'ARIA
Arian 1 886
Ariano, Ferrante Gonzaga, Principe di see GUASTALLA, FERRANTE GONZAGA, Duca da
Ariano Irpino 16 736
Ariantes 13 576
Arias, Francisco 2 394
Arias, José 21 110; 29 293
Arias, Lope 7 362
Arias, Pedro Fermín see FERMÍN ARIAS, PEDRO
Arias, Susie 23 905
Arias, Virginio 6 597; 26 560
Arias de Avila, Pedro see DAVILA, PEDRARIAS
Arias Fernández, Antonio 2 410*; 8 254; 26 436; 29 340
Arias Montano, Benito 2 411*; 10 502, 503; 25 17
assistants 27 754
Ariassos Bouleuterion 4 530
Arías Vera, Luis 24 510
Aribert of Antimiano, Archbishop of Milan 21 523; 23 649
Ariccia 32 398
Palazzo Chigi 6 585
paintings 20 375; 21 54
Sala dell'Ariosto 5 366, 366
viaduct 27 7
Ariccia, Mario Chigi, Duca di 6 584*; 11 275
Ariccio, Casino Stazi 18 524
Arichis II, Duke of Benevento (reg 758-88) 3 716; 27 613
Aridikes 13 549
Arieh, Judah 14 35
'Arif (fl 20th cent.) 14 217
Arif (Turkey) see ARYCANDA
Arif, Sirri 16 587
'Arifi 16 347
works 16 348
Arighini, Giuseppe 5 845; 6 138; 30 676; 33 53
Ariha see JERICO
Arık, Remzi Oğuz 1 520
Arikamedu 15 409, 697
Arikara 22 551, 584, 649
Arikha, Avigdor 2 411–12*
Arilje Church 28 441
Arima 17 419
Arimaddanapura see PAGAN
Arimaspian 28 320
Arimatsu 17 316, 355
Ariminium see RIMINI
Arimnestus 10 591, 625
Arinberd see EREVAN
Arinbjarnar, Snorri 2 412*; 15 70
Aringhieri, Alberto 24 831
Arinobu see TAKUMA EIGA
Arinori Mori see MORI ARINORI
Ariobarzanes 2 668
Ariosto, Ludovico 2 412*; 4 362; 16 614
illustrated works 9 184; 22 466; 32 199
patrons and collectors 24 833
productions 11 4; 21 16; 24 342
Arisbe 19 234, 234
Arishima, Ikuma 17 205; 31 74
Ari Singh, Rana of Mewar (reg 1761-73) (Rajput) 15 600
arista tiles see under TILES → types
Aristedes 27 46
Aristeias 27 77
Aristeides (fl early 4th cent. BC) 2 412–13*; 10 649; 13 551; 23 144
Aristeides (fl late 4th cent. BC) 2 412–13*; 10 197; 13 548, 555
Aristide style pottery see under POTTERY → wares
Aristiguieta, Miguel Aguirre see AGUIRRE ARISTIGUIETA, MIGUEL
Aristion of Paros 13 444, 447; 24 204
Aristocratic Psalters see under PSALTERS → types
Aristodikos Kouros 13 422; 18 410
Aristokles 17 757
Ariston 13 551
Aristonothos 6 353; 10 611; 22 410
Aristophanes 1 175; 13 524, 548; 27 868
Aristophon 13 548; 25 176
Aristotele da Bologna see FIORAVANTI, ARISTOTELE
Aristotele di Fieravante see FIORAVANTI, ARISTOTELE
Aristotle 2 413–14*; 5 519; 10 592; 13 403, 467; 14 867; 22 354
personal collection 19 312
works 13 545; 15 878; 31 298
illustrated 9 618
on art 1 172, 175; 2 518; 6 176; 11 315; 28 915
on colour 7 627; 28 203
on decorum 8 612
on form 11 313
on glazes 13 551
on light 19 355
on proportion 2 345; 13 412
on sculpture 13 433
translated 18 686
Aristratos 13 561; 23 144
Arisugawa, Prince 18 87
Arita 17 11, 241
Akachō (Enamelers' Ward) 17 264
Ceramic Museum 17 433
ceramics 17 256
porcelain 2 414*; 17 242, 255–6, 263–4, 264, 351–2, 733; 18 538; 22 880
see also PORCELAIN → wares → Imari
pottery 17 255
Tengudani kilns 17 263
Aritthagiri see RITIGALA
Arivonimamo 20 36
Ariz, Francisco de 2 645
Ariza (family) 29 342
Ariza, Gonzalo 7 609
Arjan 6 196
Arjan, Guru 1 798
Arjián, Antonio de 32 99
Arjona, Marta 8 236
Arjumand Banu Begum 1 459, 460
Arjun 15 631
Ark 24 429
ark 2 414*
Arkades Cemetery 8 154
Arkadia 2 414–15*; 25 92, 99, 842
bronzes 13 572
gardens 12 134
Temple of Diana 23 203; 25 121
Arkadi Monastery 8 156; 32 159
Arkadios, Emperor of Byzantium (reg 395-408) 9 595, 635; 26 752
Arkady 24 441
Arkalochori 2 415*; 13 362; 21 651
Árkay, Aladár 2 415–16*
Árkay, Bertalan 2 416*; 25 74
Arkazhi, Church of the Annunciation 27 382
Arkel, Gerrit van 2 416*; 10 163
Arkell, William, J. 10 81
Arkesilaos 2 416–17*; 25 45; 27 29
works 5 375; 25 44; 26 783; 27 29
Arkesilaos Painter 13 512; 32 32*
works 13 512
Arkesine 1 795
Arkesios 13 403, 408
Arkhanes see ARCHANES
Arkhangel'skoye 2 417*; 22 180; 27 363, 376, 404; 33 579
collections 27 438
gardens 12 134
paintings 26 449; 30 355
Arkhipov, Abram (Yefimovich) 2 417*
groups and movements 2 633; 22 178; 27 392; 31 582
pupils 12 339; 15 891; 18 444; 24 566
Arkitekt 31 452
Arkitekten 24 451
Arkitekttidningen 24 451
Arkitektur 2 612; 24 451
Arkitektur DK 24 451
Arkitektur og skipúlag 24 452
Arkiv for Dekorattiv Konst, Lund 2 371
Arkkitehti 24 452
Arkoun, Muhammed 16 100
arks 17 569–70
Ark Tepe 10 896; 32 320
Arkwright, Richard 10 748; 21 600; 28 228; 30 540
Arlaud, Jacques-Antoine 2 417–18*; 21 642; 23 515
Arlaud, Marc-Louis 5 319
arlecchini ware see under POTTERY → wares
Arles 2 418–20*; 11 505; 26 904; 31 709, 709
amphitheatre 1 797; 2 418; 7 342
Archaeological Museum 13 716
architecture 26 907
cemetery of Les Alyscamps 11 653
hypogea 15 52
Musée d'Archéologie 7 343
Musée Lapidaire d'Art Chrétien 2 419
Musée Lapidaire d'Art Païen 2 419
Musée Réattu 26 58
Ste Anne see Musée Lapidaire d'Art Païen
St Trophîme 2 419–20*; 10 742; 11 554; 26 182, 584
cloister 2 420; 7 454, 455
portal 7 383
sculpture 26 603
sculpture 11 553; 26 603
theatre 26 904
urban planning 27 3
Yellow House 2 552
Arles-sur-Tech, Ste Marie 26 609, 610
Arleux, Louis-Marie-Joseph Morel d' see MOREL D'ARLEUX, LOUIS-MARIE-JOSEPH
Arlington, Henry Bennet, 1st Earl of see BENNET, HENRY, 1st Earl of Arlington
ARLIS see ART LIBRARIES SOCIETIES
Ar Livre group 26 130
Arlon 3 539, 588, 590
Armada chest 16 59, 59
Armada fire-back 10 340, 340
Armada Jewel 9 244; 14 547; 17 522
Armada Portrait 10 246, 247; 31 415
Armada table 16 25
Armadillo ware see POTTERY → wares → Biscuit ware
Armagh
County Museum 16 42
court-house 16 9
crosses 15 876
metalwork 15 872
Armagnac, Bernard d', Comte de Pardiac see PARDIAC, BERNARD D'ARMAGNAC, Comte de
Armagnac, Bonne of see BONNE OF ARMAGNAC
Armagnac, Catherine d', Duchess of Bourbon see CATHERINE D'ARMAGNAC, Duchess of Bourbon
Armagnac, Jacques d', Duc de Nemours see NEMOURS, JACQUES D'ARMAGNAC, Duc de
Armajani, Siah 31 615
Armallones 29 331
Arman 2 420–21*; 11 551, 570
collaboration 30 924
dealers 7 421; 16 570
groups and movements 10 416; 23 260; 30 924
patrons and collectors 14 48; 29 420
works 2 421; 15 868; 22 381; 23 261, 334, 334; 26 51
Arman, Fernandez 11 55
Armancourt, Perrault d' see PERRAULT D'ARMANCOURT
Armand, Alfred 14 786; 24 396
Armand-Calliat, Thomas-Joseph 11 622; 13 208
Armand-Dumaresq, Edouard 14 486
Armando 2 422*
groups and movements 8 668; 22 852; 23 298; 28 159
Armanin see ROMANINO, GEROLAMO
Armano 14 877
Armant 2 422*; 9 774
mammisi 20 231
mummies 22 286
necropoleis 9 843
sacred lake 27 496
Temple of Montu and Rattawy 2 422; 9 874
Armas, Ricardo 2 422–3*
armatures 2 423*; 18 902; 29 813
modelli 21 769
stained glass 29 501
stucco 29 813, 845
Armavir 2 439, 440, 441
Armazi 12 318, 323
Armaziskhevi 12 328
arm-bands 6 312; 17 I; 22 651; 25 542
armchairs see under CHAIRS → types
Armellini, Francesco, Cardinal 5 448; 26 756
Armenia (Colombia) 7 601, 605
Museo Arqueológico del Quindio 7 612
Armenia (Europe) 2 423–45*, 423; 16 104, 105
alphabets 2 430
altar curtains 2 442
amber 1 762
architecture 2 425–8*
azurite 23 785
banners 2 443
bell-towers 14 36; 27 701
bookbindings 2 442
bronze 2 441
canon tables 5 624
carpets 2 437–9*
castles 2 427
cathedrals 2 97
ceramics 2 439–40*
churches 2 425–8, 429–30, 433–5; 7 261–2; 9 731; 30 360
basilicas 2 425–6
centrally planned 7 256
cruciform 9 731
decoration 7 274
Early Christian (c. AD 250-843) 9 731, 732
6th cent. AD 23 355
7th cent. AD 2 426
10th cent. AD 2 434
17th cent. 9 732
cochineal 2 438
coins 2 441
collections 2 444–5*
liturgical objects 2 444
manuscripts 2 444, 445; 10 450
copper 2 441
domes 33 741
dress 1 886
dyes 2 438; 9 492
education (architectural) 2 428
embroidery 2 442–3, 443
fortresses 2 427
garden cities 10 449
Armenia (Europe)—cont.
gavit' 2 426–7; 27 701
glass 9 646
gold 2 441–2; 27 15
Gospel books 2 430
guidebooks 13 811
jewellery 2 440–41*
khatchk'ars 2 426, 435, 435–6; 8 198–9*
lace 2 443
manuscript illumination 2 425, 430–31*, 431
metalwork 2 441–2*
monasteries 2 427; 12 235; 14 36; 30 360
mosaics 2 429
museums 2 444–5*
painting 2 429*, 431–3*
wall 1 452; 2 429, 429–30*
watercolours 2 432
20th cent. 2 432
patronage 2 424, 444*
pewter 2 441
pilgrim flasks 2 441
religion 9 515
rugs 2 437–9*, 438
sculpture 2 433*, 436–7*
architectural 2 433–5*; 7 274
monumental 2 436
relief 1 451; 2 433–6*, 434, 435
vishap 2 435
silk 2 443
silver 2 441–2
stage design 2 432
temples 12 154
textiles 2 442–3*
theatres 10 450
trade 16 750
treatises (manuscript illumination) 2 430
urban planning 2 428
vaults (ceiling) 14 36
wood-carvings 2 436
wool 2 437
Armenian bole see under GROUNDS → types
Armenian Rug Society (USA) 2 437
Armenians 7 818
Armenini, Giovanni Battista 2 445–6*
works 15 84; 16 614; 25 71–2, 378; 26 767; 31 299
Armenoi 21 661
Armenonville, Joseph-Jean Baptiste Fleuriau d' 25 872
Armentia, S Andrés 13 105; 26 609
Armento 13 526
armets see under HELMETS → types
Armfelt, Gustaf 10 726
Armfield, Maxwell 25 556
Armi, dell' 18 584
Armidale, City Art Gallery 2 769
armillary spheres 12 812–13*, 813; 28 209, 209
Armillas, Pedro 18 784; 30 483
Armina see ARMENIA (EUROPE)
Armitage, Edward 2 446*; 10 372; 14 587; 19 614
Armitage, G. Faulkner 24 185
Armitage, Kenneth 2 446*; 3 373; 10 268; 13 629
Armleder, John (M.) 2 446–7*; 30 135
armlets 1 292, 293, 351, 876; 16 797
armoires 8 271; 10 288; 11 589, 593; 20 VII
see also CUPBOARDS
armorial bearings 6 332; 14 404–7, 416–26, 422, 428
Armorial of Gelderland (Brussels, Bib. Royale Albert Ier, MSS 15652-6) 22 834
armorials see BOOKS OF ARMS; COATS OF ARMS; ROLLS

armory see ARMORIAL BEARINGS; HERALDRY
Armory Show, 1913 see under NEW YORK → exhibitions
Armos 19 727; 22 74
armour 2 447–51*, 468–74*
 collections see under COLLECTIONS → types
 display 9 31*
 forgeries see under FORGERIES → types
 historical and regional traditions
  Ancient Near East 1 887
  Assyrian 1 886
  Austria 2 821
  Azerbaijan 2 900*
  Aztec 21 244, 247
  Belgium 2 471, 473
  Central Asia, Eastern 6 305–6*
  Central Asia, Western 6 259–62*; 16 503
  China 7 13, 14, 54–8*, *55*, *57*
  Crete 13 584
  Cyprus, ancient 14 356
  Egypt, ancient 10 *40*, 41
  England 2 *471*, 472
  France 2 473
  Germany 2 469, 470–71, *470*, 472
  Greece, ancient 13 583–4*, *584*
  Helladic 14 356
  Inca 29 205
  Indian subcontinent 15 676–9*
  Islamic 16 503–10*, *504*, *506*
  Italy 2 469, 471, 472
  Japan 2 448, 449; 17 297, 300, 302, 355, 361–4*, *362*, 375
  Kiribati 3 332; 18 83; 23 735
  Korea 18 353–4*
  Maya 21 246, 247
  Mesoamerica, Pre-Columbian 21 244–7, *245*
  Mongolia 21 875*
  Mycenaean 4 *851*; 14 356
  Netherlands, the 2 473
  Ottoman 16 507–9*
  Pacific Islands 23 735
  Poland 25 128, 130
  Prehistoric art 25 541
  Rome, ancient 27 94–5*
  South America, Pre-Columbian 29 204*, 205–6*
  Spain 29 343
  Sri Lanka 29 468–9*
  Toltec 21 246
  Ukraine 31 563
 historiography see under HISTORIOGRAPHY → types
 materials
  basketwork 3 332
  bone 6 305
  brocades 7 58
  bronze 4 *851*; 13 583–4, *584*; 14 356; 16 503
  ceramics 2 474
  copper 2 448; 17 *362*
  gold 17 *362*
  inscriptions 16 509
  iron 2 448, 469; 16 503
  kevlar 2 474
  lacquer 6 306, 313; 7 13, 14, 54; 17 297, 300, 302, 376
  leather 2 469; 6 305; 7 54; 16 503; 17 362, *362*, 363, 376; 19 2
  metal 6 305
  screws 2 449
  silk 17 *362*
  skins 6 305; 21 246
  steel 2 448, *471*; 7 57
  textiles 16 503
  velvet 7 58
 techniques
  etching 2 449, 471
  gilding 2 *471*
 types
  banded 6 262
  chain-mail 2 448, 468; 6 261, 306
armour
 types—cont.
  double-faced 7 *55*, 57
  elephant 14 185, *186*
  horse 2 448; 6 261, 262; 16 507
  karacena 25 130, *130*
  laced plate see lamellar
  lamellar 2 448, 469; 6 261; 7 54
  mail-and-plate 6 262; 16 507
  plate 2 448, 469, 470; 16 507
  scale 2 448, 469
armourers' guilds see under GUILDS → types
Armour Foundation 21 492
armouries 21 559
armrests 7 33
arm rings 6 155, *157*, 158; 25 545, 546
arms see WEAPONS
Arms, Master at 21 338
Armson, William Barnett 2 474*; 7 210; 23 54, 66
Armstead, Henry Hugh 2 474*
 collaboration 24 605; 28 278
 works 10 266; 29 766; 31 131
Armstrong, Bruce 2 754
Armstrong, Elizabeth (Adela) see FORBES, ELIZABETH (ADELA) STANHOPE
Armstrong, Frederick William 29 116
Armstrong, Hilary 2 151
Armstrong, John 31 673; 33 446
Armstrong, M. J. 26 237
Armstrong, Robert Williams 3 641; 7 559
Armstrong, Thomas 2 474–5*; 33 137
 collaboration 5 421
 groups and movements 10 641
 works 9 290
Armstrong, W. G. 23 20
Armstrong, William 9 13, 59; 12 840
Armstrong-Jones, Anthony (Charles Robert), 1st Earl of Snowdon see SNOWDON
ARMU see ASSOCIATION OF REVOLUTIONARY ART OF UKRAINE
Arnafjord 9 156
Arnal, André-Pierre 11 552
Arnal, Enrique 2 475*; 4 264
Arnal, François 30 6
Arnal, Jean Henri 29 336
Arnal, Juan Pedro 32 564, 620
Arnal, Pedro 4 563; 16 547
Arnald, George 24 735
Arnaldi (family) 23 874
Arnaldi, Enea 32 410
Arnaldo de Barbazán, Bishop of Pamplona 13 105; 23 409
Arnaldo de Gurb 16 440
Arnaldus of Orléans 31 227
al-Arnaouti, Mahmoud 19 324
Arnas see BAĞLARBAŞI
Árnason, Jón Gunnar 2 475*; 15 71
Arnaud, Bishop of Le Mans 19 126
Arnaud, Camille d' 22 424
Arnaud, Edouard 14 388
Arnaud, François-Thomas de Baculard d' see BACULARD D'ARNAUD, FRANÇOIS-THOMAS DE
Arnaud, Jean 12 831
Arnaud, Luigi 22 481
Arnaud, Noël 30 22
Arnaud, Thomas 33 520
Arnaud de Montjoie 13 264
Arnaud de Via, Cardinal 13 174
Arnau de la Peña 2 476*; 20 767
Arnau de Perexens, Bishop of Urgel 26 43
Arnauld, Catherine-Agnès 6 *436*
Arnauld, Céline 8 438
Arnauld, Jacqueline Marie Angélique 17 1, 2
Arnauld, Simon, Marquis de Pomponne see POMPONNE, SIMON ARNAULD, Marquis de
Arnault, Antoine-Vincent 6 487
Arnau Pintor 20 757
Arnautkeuy see ANAPLUS
Arnautoff, Victor 25 653
Arnau y Mascort, Eusebio 12 148
Arnd, Samuel 27 584
Arndes, Stephan 20 719
Arndt, W. Leo 18 177
Arndt & Marcus 19 719
Arndt-Tschleplin, Ewald 18 177
Arne, Thomas 14 269
Arneberg, Arnstein (Rynning) 2 476*
 collaboration 23 232; 25 376–7; 26 553; 31 243
 works 23 222, 232, 602, *602*
Arnekhamani, King of Kush (*reg c.* 221 BC) 23 283, *284*
Arnéra, Hidalgo 24 726
Arneson, Robert 17 694; 22 690; 27 731, 872; 31 609, 615, 640
Arnfred, Tyge 8 729
Arnheim, Rudolf 2 476–7*; 24 383; 25 685; 28 207
Arnhem
 Akademie voor Beeldende Kunst 26 379
 Buitensociëteit see Gemeentemuseum
 ceramics 22 *881*
 faience (ii) (ceramics) 22 882
 Gemeentemuseum 10 496; 22 906; 23 671
 Martinikerk 13 114
 Provinciehuis 4 790
 Rijksmuseum voor Volkskunde Hel Nederlands Openluchtmuseum 3 825
 St Eusebiuskerk 22 821
 St Janskerk 22 818
Arnhemsche Fayencefabriek 22 883
Arnhold, Eduard 12 474
Arnhold, Johann Samuel 21 66
Arniko 2 477*; 6 661; 22 775, 789; 30 825
 pupils 30 831
 works 30 812
Arnim, Ferdinand (Heinrich Ludwig) von 2 478*
Arniston House (Lothian) 23 860; 25 843; 28 246
Arno, Peter 5 759
Arnodin, F. 16 587
Arnold (*fl* 13th cent.) 13 48
 works 13 *48*
Arnold, Bishop of St Andrews (*reg* 1160-62) 26 591; 27 529
Arnold, C. D.
 works 5 *273*
Arnold, Christian Friedrich 2 478*; 19 705
Arnold, Christoph 33 40
 works 33 *40*
Arnold, Dieter 14 251
Arnold, Eduard 31 401
Arnold, Eve 20 99
Arnold, Friedrich 1 844; 33 40
Arnold, George 4 600; 14 *638*
Arnold, Grant 20 604
Arnold, J. C. 32 815, 816
Arnold, Jean 8 883
Arnold, Josef (1788-1879) 2 478–9*
Arnold, Josef (1823-62) 2 479
Arnold, Thomas (Walker) 2 479*; 16 549
Arnold, Walter 9 240; 11 320; 19 112; 29 733
Arnold, William 23 687; 28 896
Arnold de Maeler 3 569
Arnoldi, Alberto 2 479*; 7 334, 336; 13 94
Arnoldi, Charles 21 897
Arnoldi, King 11 836
Arnoldi, Michael 5 585
Arnoldo 31 322
Arnold of Brescia 26 844
Arnold of Carinthia 19 260
Arnold of Nijmegen see ARNOULT DE NIMÈGUE
Arnold Print Works 31 260
Arnold & Tripp 14 189; 16 574
Arnold van Egmont, Count see EGMONT, ARNOLD VAN, Count
Arnold von Born 7 592
Arnold von Westfalen 2 479–80*; 33 112
 assistants 21 99; 25 567
 attributions 31 166
 works 12 366; 13 58, *58*; 21 62, 63; 29 *522*
Arnolet de Catz 9 81; 20 614
Arnolfini, Giovanni di Arrigo 10 *708*, 709
Arnolfo III, Archbishop of Milan 21 523
Arnolfo di Cambio 2 480–85*; 11 197; 13 145; 24 868, 871; 26 765
 architecture 13 63; 31 711
  cathedrals 11 176, 195; 13 53; 30 272
  chapels 26 833
  churches 11 205; 13 65; 16 627
  loggias 11 203
 attributions 11 203, 211; 16 627
 collaboration 13 96; 16 688; 24 783, 868, 870; 25 724
 patrons and collectors 3 228; 23 96
 sculpture 2 *483*; 11 183
  ciboria (ii) (structure) 2 *481*; 6 104; 7 303; 10 743; 13 97
  fountains 13 96; 24 519
  religious 2 *482*; 23 414; 28 679
  tombs 2 *480*; 4 279; 13 *97*; 32 627
 teachers 24 854
 workshop 7 920; 24 783
Arnoraja, Ruler (*reg c.* 1133-53) (Chanahama) 1 502
Arnoso, S Eulália 25 289
Arnošt of Pardubice, Archbishop of Prague 8 422; 24 108
Arnošt the elder 24 108
Arnota' 26 712
 Monastery 25 340
Arnott, Bruce 29 113
Arnoud-Gerkens, Johannes Christiaan d' 18 226
Arnoul, Bishop of Amiens 1 777
Arnould, Reynould 19 91
Arnould, Victor 20 862
Arnould du Vivier 4 547
Arnoul de Cats see ARNOLET DE CATZ
Arnoul Gréban 11 726
Arnoullet, B. 20 793
Arnoult 20 137
Arnoult de la Pointe see ARNOULT DE NIMÈGUE
Arnoult de Nimègue 2 485–6*; 27 247; 29 504
 attributions 20 751–2
 works 13 182
 workshop 33 64
Arnoult van der Spits see ARNOULT DE NIMÈGUE
Arnout, Jules 4 80
 reproductive prints by others 32 *698*
Arnoux, (Charles-) Albert d', Vicomte d'Arnoux, Comte de Limoges-Saint-Saens see BERTALL
Arnoux, (Joseph-François-) Léon 10 312; 21 697
Arnsburg Monastery 12 365
Arnstein (family) 2 829
Arnstein an der Lahn Abbey 26 702
 manuscripts 26 673
 stained glass 26 *701*, 702; 29 502, 509
Arnstein Bible see under BIBLES → individual manuscripts
Arnt, Master 2 486*; 13 114
 attributions 17 740
 works 17 696, 741
Arnthe Praxias 10 592, 615
Arnt van Kalkar 22 856
Arnt van Zwolle see ARNT VAN KALKAR
Arnt von Westerburg 20 758
Arntz, Gerd 13 727; 22 923
Arntz, W. 4 26
Arntzen, E. 4 24; 10 211
Arntzenius, Floris 2 487*; 14 47
Arnulf, Emperor of Carinthia (*reg* 887-99) 1 697; 5 808; 7 512; 26 86, 87
Arnulf Ciborium 5 808; 11 614
Arnulf de Binche 3 542
Arnulphy, Charles 2 487
Arnulphy, Claude 2 487*; 12 595
Aroch, Arie 2 487*; 17 577; 23 25
Arochukwu 15 111
Aroer 1 867
A Romain (ruby), L' 11 634
Arona 27 498
Arondel, Guillaume d' see GUILLAUME D'ARONDEL
Aronovici, Carol 23 10
Aronson, Boris 17 577
Aronson, Naum 6 525
Arorae 10 779
Arosenius, Ivar 30 81
Aróstegui, Alejandro 25 455
Arouca, José Pereira see PEREIRA AROUCA, JOSÉ
Arouca, Monastery of S Maria 25 296; 26 253
Aroztegui, Ernesto 31 757
Arp, Hans (Peter Wilhelm) 2 488–91*; 11 550, 569; 19 476; 24 428; 30 125, 139, 234
 collaboration 9 63; 10 137; 14 845; 19 476; 20 603; 30 234
 collages 7 557
 dealers 16 906; 19 537; 26 193
 frames 11 419
 glass 32 204
 groups and movements 1 75; 8 434, 438; 10 415; 20 97
  Abstraction-Création 1 76, 89
  a.r. group 2 409
  Art Concret 1 77
  Art informel 2 544
  Cabaret Voltaire (group) 3 113; 8 434
  Cercle et Carré 6 342
  Concrete art 1 75, 76
  Dada 1 73; 8 433, 434, 436, 437; 12 396; 24 405; 31 503
  Dada Weststupidia 3 3 4; 8 438
  Groupe des Artistes Radicaux 8 436
  Merz 8 437
  Moderner Bund 12 649
  Neue Leben 8 434, 436; 9 758; 22 921
  Salon des Réalités Nouvelles 8 838; 9 87
  Stijl, De 29 661
  Stupid group 8 438
  Surrealism 8 439; 30 18, 19
  theosophy 30 711
 objets trouvés 23 333
 patrons and collectors 2 409; 9 189; 12 15; 32 568; 33 45
 performance art 24 405
 pupils 11 807
 sculpture 2 *491*; 4 74; 5 692; 12 407
  fonts (baptismal) 11 256
  reliefs 2 *489*; 8 *434*; 30 138
 woodcuts 33 363
 writings 19 848; 21 176
Arp, Sophie Taeuber- see TAEUBER-ARP, SOPHIE
Arpachiyah 1 894; 2 491–2*, 639; 21 *267*
 amulets 1 *856*

Arpachiyah—cont.
copper **21** 270, 303
houses **21** 281
pottery **2** *492*; **21** 270, 305, *305*; **22** 510
Arpád, Andrew III, King of Hungary *see* ANDREW III, King of Hungary
Arpád, Geza, Prince **10** 544
Arpád, Geza II, King of Hungary *see* GEZA II, King of Hungary
Arpád, Gizella, Queen of Hungary *see* GIZELLA, Queen of Hungary
Arpád, Mary, Queen of Naples *see* MARY OF HUNGARY, Queen of Naples
Arpád, Stephen I, King of Hungary *see* STEPHEN, Saint, King of Hungary
Árpás Church **14** 900
Arpels, Pierre **16** 539
Arphe *see* ARFE
Arpino, S Carlo **3** 249
Arpino, Cavaliere d' **1** 594; **2** 492–4*; **11** 52; **16** 670; **26** 770
assistants **5** 704; **8** 783; **30** 356
collaboration **7** 509; **8** 182; **25** 227; **27** 122
decorative works **1** 595
drawings **9** 221
house **25** 227
mosaics **26** 809, *809*, 810
paintings **1** 596; **2** *494*; **8** 138; **11** 741; **22** 484; **26** 818, 833
patrons and collectors
Aldobrandini, Pietro (ii), Cardinal (1571-1621) **1** 595
Borghese, Scipione, Cardinal **4** 406
Bourbon del Monte, Francesco Maria, Cardinal **4** 567
Clement VIII, Pope (*reg* 1592-1605) **1** 595
Costa, Ottavio **8** 9
Créquy, Charles de Blanchefort de **19** 238
Doria, Gian Carlo, Prince **9** 174
Faesch, Johann Jakob **10** 753
Jabach, Everard **16** 815
Orsini, Corradino **23** 575
Patrizi, Costanzo **24** 267
Paul V, Pope (*reg* 1605-21) **4** 405
Richelieu, Armand-Jean Du Plessis, Cardinal de **26** 349
Sannesio, Giacomo, Cardinal **27** 764
pupils **1** 20, 665; **6** 346; **22** 81; **27** 487
reproductive prints by others **4** 96
workshop **3** 56
Arpinum **26** 887
Arpi Painter **13** 530
Arpo, Guariento di *see* GUARIENTO (DI ARPO)
Arqr, Juan de *see* JUAN DE ARQR
Arques-la-Bataille Castle **12** 173
Arquitectonica **2** 494–5*; **21** 422
arquitecto peruano, El **24** 505
Arquitectura **22** 104
Arquitectura México **24** 9
Arquitectura portuguesa **24** 453
Arrabona *see* GYŐR
Arraiolos **2** 495*; **25** *288*, 303, 316
Arraiolos carpets *see under* CARPETS → types
Arrais, Amador, Bishop of Coimbra **26** 516
Arrak, Jüri **10** 540
works **10** *540*
Arran (Azerbaijan) **2** *890*; **16** 313
Arran, Isle of **29** 703
Arrapkha *see* KIRKUK
Arrarás, José E. **25** 703
Arras **2** 495–7*; **11** *504*
Cathedral of St Vaast (destr. 1804) **2** 496–7*, *497*; **9** 672; **13** 38, 39
choir **13** 39
Cathedral of St Vaast (after 1833) **7** *774*
Hôtel de Ville **11** 511; **31** 238
houses **4** 785
lace **11** 650
Musée des Beaux-Arts **2** 495; **6** 518; **20** 894
reconstruction **2** 322
St Nicolas d'Arroux **2** 723
tapestries **2** 496*; **3** 606; **11** 637, 639; **13** 196; **16** 755; **29** 298; **30** 312, 313
hunting scenes **29** 423, *423*
religious **30** *313*
Arras, Jean d' *see* JEAN D'ARRAS
Arras, Mathias of *see* MATHIAS OF ARRAS
Arras hoard **21** 1, *2*
Arrau y Barba, José **2** 62
Arredondo, Isidoro **2** 497–8*; **7** 524; **26** 438
Arrendondo, Eliseo **24** 181
Arrente **1** 67
Arretche, Louis **27** 253
Arretine ware *see under* POTTERY → wares
Arretium *see* AREZZO
Arrian **15** 677
Arriba, Manuel Andrés de *see* ANDRÉS DE ARRIBA, MANUEL
Arribas, Antonio **19** 704
arriccio **2** 498*; **10** 740; **11** 762; **32** 802
arrière-cabinets *see under* CABINETS (i) (ROOMS) → types
Arrieta, (José) Agustín **2** 498*; **21** 385, 395; **25** 696
Arrieta, Pedro de **2** 498*; **9** 418; **21** 377, 401
Arrighi, Alessandro **30** 414
Arrighi, Ludovico **5** 448, 844; **28** 307
Arrigo, Giuliano d' *see* PESELLO
Arrigo di Brabante **10** 519
Arrigo di Niccolò **8** 535
Arrigoni, Attilio **21** 519
Arrigoni, Cardinal **7** 297
Arrigucci, Luigi **2** 498–9*; **3** 208; **6** 23; **26** 758
Arriguzzi, Arduino **4** 280
Arringatore **10** 588, 636; **21** 19; **27** 20, 46
Arringhi, Paolo **4** 457
arrises **13** 377, 389; **22** 214, 215
Arrius Secundus, L. **27** 28
Arrivabene, Bishop of Urbino **32** 629
Arro, Jaak **10** 540
Arrojo (Valdés), Felipe **13** 252
Arrona, Juan Martínez de *see* MARTÍNEZ DE ARRONA, JUAN
Arron Group **22** 719
Arrost, Jan *see* ROST, JAN
Arrotino **23** 352; **27** 46
arrowheads
historical and regional traditions
Central Asia, Western **6** 260, 261
Helladic **14** 356
Indian subcontinent **15** 677
Indus civilization **15** 677
Mesoamerica, Pre-Columbian **21** 192
Mycenaean **14** 356
materials
bronze **6** 260; **14** 356
iron **6** 261
obsidian **21** 192
arrows
historical and regional traditions
Central Asia, Eastern **6** 313
Central Asia, Western **6** 261
Egypt, ancient **10** 40
Japan **17** 361
arrows
historical and regional traditions—cont.
Mangbetu **1** 362
Maya **21** 246
Mesoamerica, Pre-Columbian **21** 245, 246
Papua New Guinea **24** *70*
Vanuatu **31** 893
materials
feathers **10** 848
lacquer **6** 313
arrow-shooters **21** 557
arrow-slits **12** 174
Arrowsmith, Charles **2** 499; **4** 66; **8** 450; **12** 740; **22** 243
Arrowsmith, John **2** 499*; **13** 228
collections **11** 663
paintings **7** 754; **8** 911
prints **28** 170
Arroyo, Antonio Vanegas *see* VANEGAS ARROYO, ANTONIO
Arroyo, Diego de **25** 700
Arroyo, Eduardo **2** 499–500*; **11** 552
groups and movements **10** 443; **27** 307
works **29** 286, *287*
Arroyo, Marcelino Pérez de *see* PÉREZ DE ARROYO, MARCELINO
Arroyo Pesquero **21** 250
Arroyo Seco **29** 203
Arruda, António de **2** 500
Arruda, Belchior de **2** 501
Arruda, Diogo de **2** 500*
collaboration **2** 500
patrons and collectors **2** 872; **31** 101
works **2** *500*; **20** 325; **25** 291
Arruda, Dionísio de **2** 500
Arruda, Francisco de **2** 500–501*
attributions **10** 165, *165*
collaboration **2** 501, 872
patrons and collectors **2** 872, 873
works **3** *534*, 535; **10** 164; **13** 71; **20** 326; **25** 291
Arruda, João de (i) (*d* ?1490) **2** 500
Arruda, João de (ii) (*fl* 1531-8) **2** 500
Arruda, João Dias de *see* DIAS DE ARRUDA, JOÃO
Arruda, Miguel de **2** 500, 501*
attributions **2** 873; **31** 179
patrons and collectors **2** 873, 875
pupils **17** 486
works **25** 291
Arruda, Miguel Fernandes de *see* FERNANDES DE ARRUDA, MIGUEL
Arruda, Pedro de **2** 500
Arruda Torralva, Francisco de **31** 178
ARS (Lithuania) **19** 499
Ars (Sweden) **33** 575
ars: Periodico d'arte contemporanea, D' **24** 449
Arsa *see* RAS
Arsacid **1** 887, 889
Ars acustica *see* SOUND AND ART
Arsago, Paolo **6** 139
ARS Alliance **18** 507
Ars Asiatique **24** 436
Arsenal 575, Master of **32** 728
Arsenalists (Arsenałowcy) **2** 502–3*; **25** 108; **33** 416
members **3** 766; **12** 602; **28** 402; **30** 342; **33** 416
arsenals **2** 501–2*; **12** *370*; **13** 381; **23** *328*; **32** *183*
Arseneault, Norman **4** 482
Arsène-Henry, Luc **2** 660; **11** 527; **19** 535
Arsène-Henry, Xavier **2** 660; **11** 527; **19** 535
arsenic **15** 918; **16** 394; **21** 304; **30** 559
arsenical copper *see under* COPPER → types
Arsenios (*fl* 1185-1206) **24** 263
Arsenios (*fl* 1587) **13** 355
Arsenius, J. **27** 162
Arsenović, Nikola **28** 458
Arses (*reg* 338-336 BC) **9** *778*
Arseven, Celal Esad **2** 503*
Arshad, Rashid Ahmed **16** 288; **23** 800
Arshakuni, Zaven (Petrosovich) **27** 581
Arsikere **15** 327
Arsinoe *see* MEDINET EL-FAIYUM
Arsinoe II, Queen of Egypt (*reg c.* 276-270 BC) **9** 893; **27** 691; **30** 737
Ars Islamica **16** 550
Arslan, Edoardo **21** 537
Arslankaya **24** 690
Arslan Khan Muhammad II, Ruler (*reg* 1102-29) (Qarakhanid) **5** 139
Arslan Tash **2** 503*, 640; **21** *267*; **30** *180*
architecture **2** 640; **21** 288
furniture **30** 187
House of Ivories **1** 889
ivory-carvings **1** 866, 867, 870; **24** 643
sculpture **2** 640
tombs **24** 690
wall paintings **21** 309
Arslantepe *see under* MALATYA
års män *see* YOUNG ONES
Arsoli, Palazzo Massimo **3** 714
Ars Orientalis **16** 550; **24** 436
Arsos **8** *325*, 352
sculpture **8** 342, *342*
Ars Typographica **13** 224
Arsukidsze **22** 251
art (applied) *see* APPLIED ART
art (bibliographies of) *see* BIBLIOGRAPHIES
art (classification of) **6** 633–4*; **8** 845; **22** 354, 360; **30** 382*
art (criticism of) *see* ART CRITICISM
art (dictionaries of) *see* DICTIONARIES OF ART
art (display of) *see* DISPLAY OF ART
art (education) *see* EDUCATION (ART)
art (encyclopedias of) *see* ENCYCLOPEDIAS OF ART
art (environmental) *see* ENVIRONMENTAL ART
art (illustrations of works of) **6** 76–8, 80, 81; **10** 209, 210, 211, 212
art (fine) *see* FINE ART
art (imitation of works of) **7** 830; **11** 305, 306; **15** 93–4
art (interpretation of works of) **1** 172; **7** 659–61; **8** 609–10; **11** 311; **14** 458, 459*; **15** 89, 878–80; **25** 681–4; **26** 221–5; **28** 396–7; **29** 787–8
art (literature of) *see* BIBLIOGRAPHIES
art (original works of) **2** 558; **9** 25; **14** 690; **20** 601, 605; **22** 358; **24** 675; **26** 227
see also ATTRIBUTIONS; AUTHENTICITY
art (prices of works of) **2** 835; **6** 76; **7** 561, 565; **10** 208; **11** 310
see also ART (VALUES OF WORKS OF)
art (psychedelic) *see* PSYCHEDELIC ART
art (psychotic) *see* PSYCHOTIC ART
art (reproduction of works of) **2** 364, 368, 534; **4** 27; **6** 78; **7** 830; **10** 675; **11** 305, 306; **24** 667; **25** 281, 597; **26** 227–37*, *236*
England **26** *231*, *232*, *234*, *235*
France **26** *233*, *234*
Germany **12** 442
art (reproduction of works of)—cont.
Italy **26** 230
Japan **17** 204
Rome, ancient **26** 230
see also CARBON PRINTS; CD-ROM; DIGITAL IMAGING; PHOTOGRAPHY; PRINTS; REPLICAS; REPRODUCTIONS; RUBBINGS; TRANSPARENCIES
art (sociology of) **2** 534; **28** 925–7*
art (terminology of) **6** 78; **10** 203, 204, 206, 207, 209, 211–12
art (theories of) *see* THEORIES (ART)
art (titles of works of art) *see* TITLES OF WORKS OF ART
art (thesaurus of) **6** 78
art (traditions of) **15** 91–2
art (unfinished works of) **1** 897
art (values of works of) **7** 560
see also ART (PRICES OF WORKS OF)
art (works of) **1** 105; **2** 505–8*, 557–61; **4** 20; **10** 690, 691; **15** 888; **22** 665, 674, 679; **23** 713; **25** 361–2
see also ART (ORIGINAL WORKS OF); ART (REPRODUCTION OF WORKS OF); AUTHENTICITY; COPIES
Art, L' (Belgium) **31** 874
Art, L' (France) **24** 423
Art, Raymond **20** 103
Arta (Greece) **2** 508–10*; **9** *511*, 515
Archaeological Collection **13** 534
architecture **9** 550–51
Hagia Theodora **2** 509; **20** 571
tomb of St Theodora of Arta **27** 828
Kato Panagia monastery **2** 509; **7** 253
mosaics **13** 560
Panagia Parigoritissa **2** 509, *509*; **9** 550, *551*, 584
Panagia Vlacherna **2** 509; **7** 253; **9** 550, 593
Arta (Romania) **5** 74; **13** 651; **16** 877; **24** 429; **32** 669
Artabanus V (*reg* 213-224) **24** 218
Artaber, Rudolf von **10** 703
Art Abstrait **1** 79; **2** 510*; **5** 286; **17** 518; **29** 369; **31** 879
members **5** 45
Art à la Rue **2** 510–11*; **14** 769
Art Amateur **24** 423
Art Amateur: Devoted to Art in the Household **24** 431
Artamonov, Mikhail (Illarionovich) **2** 511*
Artan (de Saint-Martin), Louis (Victor Antonio) **2** 511*; **5** 44; **28** 921; **32** 380
Art and Archaeology Technical Abstracts **7** 743, 744
Art and Architecture Thesaurus *see* AAT
Art and Australia **24** 437
Artan de Saint-Martin, Louis **7** 245
Art and Freedom **2** 511*; **9** 766; **27** 523
Art and Language **2** 512*; **7** 685, 686; **10** 258
art and music *see* MUSIC AND ART
Art and Progress *see* MAGAZINE OF ART
Arta Nouă *see* NEW ART
Artari, Adalberto **12** 595; **29** 835
Artari, Giovanni Battista **12** 595
Artari, Giuseppe **10** 278; **12** 595; **28** 878; **29** 835; **32** 824
works **29** *837*
Artaria, Carlo **2** 512*
Artaria, Domenico **2** 512*
Artaria, Francesco **2** 512*
Artaria, Giovanni Casimiro **2** 512*
Artaria, Giuseppe **5** 8

Artaria, Paul **2** 512–13*; **7** *294*
collaboration **22** 187
groups and movements **13** 726; **21** 783
works **30** 128, *128*
Artaria & Co. **2** 512*, 829; **4** 84; **10** 530
Artaria & Fontaine **2** 512*
Arta Română **16** 877; **21** 38; **28** 788
Artas **27** 73
Artashat **2** 425, 440
Artasia **24** 436
Art Association of Montreal **5** 589, 591, 592; **22** 38; **23** 257; **31** 880
Artau, Francesc **29** 332
Artaud, Antonin **2** 513–14*; **17** 726; **24** 406
groups and movements **11** 551; **30** 18
patrons and collectors **19** 537
productions **3** 127
works **2** *514*; **30** 687
illustrated **8** 775; **33** 305
Artaud, François **19** 847
Artaud de Montor, Jean-Alexis-François **2** 514*
art autre **2** 514–15*, 543; **10** 838; **11** 551; **33** 305, *305*
see also ART INFORMEL; TACHISM
Artaxerxes I (*reg* 465-424 BC) **1** *118*; **9** *777*; **15** 906; **24** 482; **30** 476
Artaxerxes II Memnon (*reg* 404-358 BC) **2** 213; **15** 912; **30** 29
Artaxerxes III Ochus (*reg* 358-338 BC) **9** *778*; **15** 912; **33** *707*
Art belle époque *see* ART NOUVEAU
Artbibliographies Modern **4** 26
art books **12** 873
Art Books **4** 23
Art brut **2** 515–16*; **11** 551; **24** 144; **25** 686
collections **2** 515
works **2** *515*; **5** 56; **22** 441; **23** 334
Art Bulletin **4** 24; **24** 423, 424, 432, 433; **29** 584
art cabinets *see* CABINETS (ii) (FURNITURE) → types → *kunstkasten*
Art Club (USA) **33** 43
Art-Club (Austria) **2** 804; **11** 812; **32** 447
Art concert **24** 442
Art Concret **5** 776; **7** 772; **14** 329
Art concret **1** 76; **9** 64; **29** 661
Art Contemporain **2** 516–17*; **3** 614; **21** 167; **28** 891
members **23** 399; **31** 502, 878
art criticism **2** 517–19*, 532, 534; **6** 175; **14** 868; **22** 686
Africa **2** 519
Britain **12** 30; **14** 697–8
China **2** 519; **6** 537, 821–5*
England **26** 271
Fang **2** 519
France **10** 677; **18** 630; **26** 411; **30** 756
Greece, ancient **13** 467–9*, 553–4*
Islamic **2** 519
Italy **4** 454; **18** 699; **32** 18, 20
Japan **7** 716; **17** 437, 439
Netherlands, the **13** 3
Russia **31** 416
Spain **21** 128
Tibet **30** 848
United States of America **24** 431
Yoruba **2** 519
20th cent. **7** 659; **15** 879–80; **25** 362
see also DECORUM
Art Culture Society *see* BIJUTSU BUNKA KYŌKAI
Art dans les deux mondes, L' **24** 426
Art dans tout, L' **6** 489
Art d'aujourd'hui **11** 569; **24** 144, 428, 442
Art Deco **2** 519–22*; **10** 98; **15** 883; **19** 897; **21** 776
art forms
architecture
Canada **19** 869
France **11** 526
Honduras **14** 714
Indonesia **15** 770
New Zealand **22** 467, *468*
United States of America **2** 643; **14** 658; **21** *421*; **28** *629*, *833*; **31** 596
ceramics **10** 313
furniture **2** *520*; **11** 601–2, *602*; **22** 875
glass **19** 12; **25** 124
interior decoration **2** 756
jewellery **2** *521*; **17** 529
ornament **23** 548
posters **7** 653
statuettes **29** 576
regional traditions
France **2** 519–22; **29** 900
United States of America **2** 522; **8** 809
Art décoratif, L' **2** 520; **24** 427
Art de France **24** 442
Art Dialogue **24** 429
Art Digest *see* ARTS MAGAZINE
Art Documentation **4** 28
Arte, De **24** 430
Arte (Italy) **24** 449
Arte (Spain) **24** 452
arte: Rivista di storia dell'arte, L' **24** 423, 448
Arteaga, Bartolomé **2** 522
Arteaga, Francisco de **2** 522
Arteaga, Jorge **6** 594; **18** 797
Arteaga, Sebastian López de *see* LÓPEZ DE ARTEAGA, SEBASTIAN
Arteaga y Alfaro, Matías de **2** 522–3*; **13** 880; **31** 810
Arte antica a moderna **24** 449
Artec Consultants Inc **1** 126
Arte Colta **16** 683
Artecrazia **24** 448
Arte cristiana **24** 448
arte decorativa moderna, L' **4** 100; **24** 448; **30** 767
arte della stampa, L' **24** 447
Arte Destructivo **2** 837
Arte di Calimala **11** 199
Arte e dossier **24** 449
Arte e Arqueologia **7** 894
Arte en Colombia **24** 435
arte en España, El (Madrid, 1862-73) **21** 81; **24** 423
Arte español (Madrid, 1912-69) **24** 452
Arte e storia **5** 791; **24** 448
Arte generativo **2** 401, 525*; **19** 890; **32** 419
arte industriale illustrata, L' **24** 448
arte in Italia, L' **24** 423, 448
arte italiana decorativa e industriale, L' **4** 247; **24** 427
Arte Joven (periodical) **24** 714
Arte Joven (style) *see* ART NOUVEAU
Artek **1** 9; **11** 104
Artěl **2** 571; **8** 411, 414, 416; **25** 433, 435, 437
Artel' Khudozhnikov *see* ARTISTS' COOPERATIVE SOCIETY
Arte lombarda **24** 448
Arte Madí **2** 400, 525*, 575, 604; **18** 397; **31** 755
works **2** *400*
Arte medievale **24** 449
Arte Metafisica **25** 6
Artemide **2** 727
Artemidorus **10** 13, *197*
Artemis **5** 884
Artemisia of Caria **14** 69, *70*; **20** 871
Artemision Bronzes **2** 525–6*; **13** *363*, 421, 422, 428, *429*, 450, 470; **23** 291
Artemis of Ephesos **26** 141
arte moderna, L' **24** 448
Artemon **13** 552
Artemuskin, Ivan **19** 883
art en Provence, L' **24** 421
Arte nucleare **2** 526*; **3** 80; **9** 201; **17** 658
Arte Nuevo **4** 141; **24** 98
Arte Nuova (gallery) **31** 446
Arte Nuova (style) *see* ART NOUVEAU
arte photográphica, A **24** 453
Arte portuguesa **24** 453
Arte Povera **1** 80; **2** 526–7*; **10** 416; **16** 682; **27** 658
members **2** 129; **18** 407; **21** 172; **24** 26, 222, 368; **33** 704
sculpture **23** 334; **26** 51
Bolivia **4** 264
Italy **2** *527*; **16** *708*, 709
Arte programmata **1** 79, 745; **2** 528*
Artes (Poland) **2** 528*; **25** 108; **33** 288
see also NEOARTES
Artes (Sweden) **24** 451
Artes de México y del mundo **24** 429, 435
artesonado *see under* CEILINGS → types
Arteta, Aurelio **29** 286
Art et Action **31** 832
Art et décoration **24** 427, 442
Art et l'Architecture aujourd'hui, L' **29** 661
art et l'industrie, L' **24** 448
Art et Technique **4** 217; **32** 380
Arte veneta **24** 448
Art Exhibition Catalogs Subject Index **4** 27
Arte y la Ciencia, El **20** 436; **21** 379
Art fin de siècle *see* ART NOUVEAU
Art flamand et hollandais, L' **24** 439
Art for Architecture **22** 334
Art for Art's Sake **1** 181; **2** 530*; **12** 207; **24** 257; **30** 122
see also AESTHETIC MOVEMENT
Art for the People (*minjung yesul*) **18** 301
Artforum **24** 433
Art Front **24** 433
Art Furnishers' Alliance **9** 295
Art Furniture Warehouse **10** 282
art galleries *see* GALLERIES (ART)
Art Glass Company **26** 227
Arthaber, Rudolf von **1** *774*; **2** 825
art history **2** 165, 365, 366, 517, 530–39*, 560; **5** 189–90*; **6** 75–6, 79; **11** 315; **12** 61; **14** 868; **17** 693; **20** 527–8; **22** 357, 360, 686; **24** 575, 668; **28** 916; **33** 242, 307–14*
Afghanistan **1** 210–11*
Africa **1** 436*; **2** 533
Austria **2** 833–4*; **28** 114; **33** 159
Belgium **3** 619–20*; **19** 548
Brazil **33** 316–17
Bulgaria **5** 163–4*
Byzantine **3** 424; **18** 215, 899; **26** 332
Cambodia **29** 241
Carolingian **18** 187
Central Asia, Eastern **6** 320*
China **2** 531, 539; **6** 821; **7** 160–61; **33** 317–22*
Czech Republic **8** 426*
Denmark **8** 761–2*
Egypt, ancient **10** 83–4*, 93
England **10** 376–8*; **32** 826
Finland **11** 113*
France **6** 502; **8** 900; **9** 453; **10** 867; **11** 674–6*; **22** 357; **28** 529
Germany **12** 482–3*; **20** 246
art history —cont.
Gothic **9** 453
Greece, ancient **2** 531; **22** 686
Hungary **14** 888
India, Republic of **2** 530
Indian subcontinent **4** 883; **7** 792–3; **15** 210–12*; **18** 458
Ireland **16** 38*
Islamic **16** 468–9, 546–50*; **26** 332
Italy **6** 101; **12** 165; **16** 780–82*; **20** 242; **21** 538
Renaissance **32** 18–22
15th cent. **12** 543
16th cent. **12** 244; **16** 766
19th cent. **32** 233
Japan **7** 160; **17** 345, 439; **33** 317–22*
Java **29** 241
Korea **18** 259*
Latin America **33** 316–17*
Mesoamerica, Pre-Columbian **2** 533; **21** 262–3*
Mexico **33** 316
Mongolia **21** 884–5*
Native North Americans **2** 533; **22** 674
Netherlands, the **20** 245–6, 437; **22** 909–11*; **30** 756
Nigeria **2** 530
Norway **23** 244–5*
Pacific Islands **2** 533; **23** 738–9*
Poland **25** 364
Portugal **25** 319–20*
Rome, ancient **25** 824
Russia **18** 215; **27** 443–4*
Scotland **9** 725
South America, Pre-Columbian **2** 533
South-east Asia **29** 241–3*
Spain **29** 358–9*
Sweden **30** 119–20*
Switzerland **30** 156–7*
Thailand **2** 530; **29** 241
Tibet **30** 848*
United States of America **2** 532; **4** 477; **22** 359, 674; **31** 669, 671–3*
18th cent. **18** 755
see also ART CRITICISM; BIBLIOGRAPHIES; HISTORIOGRAPHY; SOCIAL HISTORY OF ART; STYLE
Art History **24** 425, 446
Arthois, Jacques d' **2** 540*
attributions **31** 793
collaboration **2** 875; **4** 589; **21** 427
patrons and collectors **6** 30
pupils **15** 43
works **3** 560; **5** 43
Arthois, Jan Baptist d' **2** 540
Arthois, Nicolaes d' **2** 540
Art House **7** 379
Arthuna **24** 102
Arthur, King (*reg c.* 6th cent.) **11** 151; **14** 415
coats of arms **14** *414*
Arthur III, Duke of Brittany (*reg* 1457-8) **4** 827*
Arthur, Eric (Ross) **2** 540*
Arthur de Richemont, Constable of France **13** 254
Arti **2** 439
Arti, Le **24** 424
Artia **8** 424
Artibus Asiae **24** 436
Artibus et historiae **24** 449
Artico, Paolo **17** 442
articulation **26** 568
Art Idéaliste **11** 746
Arti di disegno **24** 447
Arti et Amicitiae **1** 808, *809*; **21** 851; **24** 450; **29** 433; **30** 16; **32** 708
Artificer's Guild, The **19** 596
artificial mountains **12** 88, 90
artificial stone **2** 540–41*, *541*; **6** 9; **7** 480; **19** *95*
see also COADE STONE; HADDON STONE; KEENES CEMENT; PULHAM STONE; RANSOME'S STONE
Artifort **22** 876, 877; **32** 756
Artiga, Francisco **2** 542*; **21** 380; **31** 674
Artigas, Joan Gardy **2** 542*; **21** 709
Artigas, João B(atista) Vilanova **2** 542–3*; **32** 855
works **2** *543*; **4** 713, 714; **27** 808
Artigas, Josep Llorens **2** 542*; **9** 373; **21** 705, 708, 709; **29** 329
arti grafiche, Le **24** 447
Artigues, Aimé-Gabriel D' *see* D'ARTIGUES, AIMÉ-GABRIEL
Art'ik **2** 439
Artimino **10** 613
Palace **12** 115
Art in America **24** 424, 432, 433
Art in Australia **2** 769; **24** 437
Art Index **2** 534; **4** 26
Art informel **1** 78; **2** 422, 515, 543–5*; **10** 838; **30** 231
Argentina **2** 401; **26** 475
Belgium **2** 545; **17** 518
Brazil **4** 719
Britain **2** 545
England **10** 258
France **1** 77; **2** *544*; **5** 66; **10** *838*; **11** 551; **20** 815; **21** 428; **22** 313; **24** 144; **33** 305
Germany **2** 545; **12** 397; **13** 217; **25** 786; **29** 65; **30** 731; **33** 635
Greece **2** 545
Iceland **8** 569
Italy **2** 545; **6** 582; **29** 55
Japan **13** 866; **15** 143; **17** 207
Korea **18** 326
Mexico **5** 881
Netherlands, the **2** 545; **4** 229; **8** 668; **23** 298; **28** 159
Spain **2** 545; **3** 219; **5** 622; **25** 851; **30** 335, *336*
United States of America **2** 545; **11** 706
Venezuela **14** 880
Ártinger, Imre Oltványi **13** 638; **15** 16
Art Interchange **24** 423, 431
Art International **24** 429
Artis, William **1** 443
Artisan Mannerism **2** 545*; **19** 509
artisans *see* CRAFTSMEN AND ARTISTS
'Art is Life' Union of Artists and Poets *see* MAKOVETS
Artist (USA) **24** 431
Artist, The (Britain & Ireland) **24** 422
artista, El **20** 59; **24** 422, 452
Artista moderno, L' **24** 448
Artistas Modernos de la Argentina **2** 401, 546*; **23** 343
members **2** 604; **10** 906; **13** 654; **20** 189
Artiste, L' **4** 655; **24** 421, 426, 442
Artistes Méridionaux **4** 167
Artistic Film, The **30** 704
Artistic Forum **2** 546*; **8** 393, 423; **22** 729
members **20** 252; **24** 825; **25** 742, 832; **28** 133; **33** 710
Artistic Japan **24** 446
Artistic Youth (Tinerimea Artistică) **5** 73, 74; **13** 651; **16** 49; **28** 352; **29** 638, 721
Artist Placement Group **18** 830
artists *see* CRAFTSMEN AND ARTISTS
artists, war *see* WAR ARTISTS
artists, women *see* WOMEN ARTISTS
Artists' Artel *see* WANDERERS
Artists' Association (Amman) **17** 655

Artists' Association of New Orleans **23** 32
Artists Association of Pest **2** 546–7*; **4** 838; **15** 14; **18** 128
members **14** 315; **18** 89
Artist's Benevolent Fund **19** 586
artists' biographies **4** 26; **6** 78; **10** 203, 204, 205–7, 208, 210, 212; **14** 868
Belgium **10** 208
Britain **10** 206
China **6** 821–3; **7** 62, 161; **33** 322
Czech Republic **9** 50
England **5** 78; **10** 377
France **10** 208, 210, 212; **11** 57; **19** 144, 216
17th cent. **8** 525; **13** 830
18th cent. **8** 846
19th cent. **28** 744
Germany **14** 314; **20** 483; **22** 920
Greece, ancient **8** 535
Indian subcontinent **15** 681
Italy **16** 780–81; **21** 909; **23** 507; **28** 35
Renaissance **32** 18–22
14th cent. **12** 684; **32** 561
15th cent. **20** 263
16th cent. **4** 64; **12** 719; **20** 84, 93; **26** 49
17th cent. **3** 97–8, 673–4; **8** 535; **24** 238
18th cent. **9** 120; **11** 875; **19** 636; **24** 225
Japan **17** 159–60
Latvia **18** 849
Netherlands, the **10** 208; **13** 2–3; **22** 910*
18th cent. **14** 794; **33** 131
19th cent. **32** 713
Poland **25** 143
Rome, ancient **8** 535
Spain **6** 124; **10** 208; **23** 896
Switzerland **30** 156
United States of America **9** 396
see also DICTIONARIES OF ART
artists' books **4** 20; **7** 685; **26** 235
see also LIVRES D'ARTISTES
artists' collections *see under* COLLECTIONS → types
artists' colonies **2** 552
Artists' Cooperative Society **32** 835
Artists Group **2** 546
Artists Hopid **17** 716; **22** 598
artists' houses **2** 391, *547*, 547–52*, *548*, *549*, *550*, *551*, *552*; **3** *550*; **6** *551*
see also ATELIERS; STUDIOS
Artists International Association (AIA) **2** 553*; **10** 258; **19** 492; **22** 332
members **21** 36; **24** 417
works **28** 919
artists' models *see under* MODELS → types
artists of Passy *see* PUTEAUX GROUP
Artists' Repository and Drawing Magazine Exhibiting the Principles of the Polite Arts in their Various Branches **24** 422, 446
artists' seals *see under* SEALS → types
Artists' Society, The **32** 903
Artists' Suffrage League **10** 878
artists' supplies *see* COLOURMEN
Artists' Union **23** 48
Artiture group **23** 67, 73
Artiz, Arcadio **21** 381
Art Journal (England) **10** 299; **14** 78; **19** 587; **24** 418, 422, 423, 446
Art Journal (USA) **24** 431, 433
art journals *see* PERIODICALS
Art-Language: The Journal of Conceptual Art **2** 512; **18** 400; **24** 429, 446
art legislation **2** 553–7*, 561; **11** 305
Africa **1** 251
Britain **2** 555, 557, 560; **10** 367
Byzantine **9** 654
China **2** 554
Early Christian (*c.* AD 250-843) **9** 654
England **10** 370, 373
France **2** 554, 560; **11** 667–8*
Greece **2** 561
India, Republic of **15** 183–4*
Italy **2** 561; **10** 821; **16** 765, 766, 768–9
Monaco **2** 560
Native North Americans **22** 667, 670
Norway **23** 243
Pakistan **23** 804–5*
Russia **2** 557
Switzerland **2** 561
United States of America **2** 556
see also ART POLICIES; CENSORSHIP
art libraries *see* LIBRARIES
Art Libraries Journal **4** 28
Art Libraries Societies (ARLIS) **2** 533; **4** 28
Art Libraries Society, Australia and New Zealand Branch (ARLIS/ANZ) **2** 773
Art Libraries Society of the United Kingdom & Eire **10** 376
Art libre (Belgium) **3** 562; **5** 44; **28** 921
Art libre, L' (France) **9** 325; **24** 427
Artlook **24** 429
Art Lover's House *see* ZEITSCHRIFT FÜR INNENDEKORATION → Haus eines Kunstfreundes
Art Manufactures Co. **13** 209
art market **2** 557–61*; **6** 76, 79–81; **7** 560, 561; **11** 305, 307, 310; **15** 888
Africa **1** 251, 252–3*
Britain **2** 560
England **2** 559, 560
France **2** 558–9
Germany **2** 560; **12** 473–4
Greece, ancient **9** 20
Italy **2** 558; **10** 676
Japan **2** 561
Native North Americans **22** 660–61, 665, 666–70*
Netherlands, the **2** 558; **29** 374–5
Rome, ancient **9** 20; **10** 675
Russia **2** 560
Scotland **28** 239
South Africa **29** 121
Switzerland **30** 153–4
United States of America **2** 560; **20** 609–10; **22** 660–61; **31** 665
19th cent. **28** 340
art mobilier **2** 561*
Art moderne, L' (Belgium) **2** 562; **3** 563, 572; **5** 44; **20** 862; **24** 426, 439; **32** 591
Art moderne, L' (France) **24** 426
Art moderne: La Wallonie, L' **24** 439
Art monthly see UMĚLECKÝ MĚSÍČNÍK
art movements **13** 518; **26** 735
Art Net **7** 788
ARTnews **14** 489; **24** 428, 432, 433; **25** 263
Art News and Review see ARTS REVIEW
Art New Zealand **24** 437
Art Nouveau **2** 510, 561–8*; **4** 70, 74; **18** 129; **21** 340, 776, 779; **26** 235
art forms
architecture **13** 832; **25** 173
Australia **14** 19
Austria **30** *885*
Art Nouveau
art forms
architecture—cont.
Belgium **3** 550; **4** 138; **5** *41*; **14** 769, *771*
Brazil **4** 712
Chile **6** 594
Denmark **8** 727
France **4** 332; **11** 525
Germany **2** *566*; **12** *377*
Honduras **14** 714
Portugal **23** 177; **30** 492
Russia **19** 332; **27** *377*, 377–8; **30** 202
Slovenia **28** 860
Spain **12** 179
Uruguay **31** 753
books **4** 364
ceramics **10** 313; **11** 83
drawings **3** *445*; **32** 109
frames **11** *437*, *464*, *475*
furniture **2** *564*; **3** *586*, 586–7; **8** 235; **11** 600, *600*
gesso **19** *876*
glass **2** *563*; **12** 788; **31** *645*
interior decoration **3** *579*
jewellery **2** *565*; **3** 605; **12** 868; **17** 528, II1; **23** 120
lithography **20** *602*
medals **8** 41
metalwork **3** 601–2; **24** 258; **27** 421
mosaics **20** 223
ornament **23** 547
painting **5** 44
pewter **24** 580
posters **25** 346
sculpture **3** *604*
stained glass **18** 627
staircases **14** *770*; **27** *404*
statuettes **29** 575
textiles **19** 12; **22** 899
collections **4** 71; **18** 466
exhibitions **14** 604
periodicals **24** 426–7
regional traditions
Austria *see* JUGENDSTIL
Belgium **2** 510; **14** 137, 138; **19** 137
Catalonia *see* MODERNISME
Czech Republic *see* JUGENDSTIL
England **19** 311
France **2** 13, 510
Germany **31** 876
Germany *see* JUGENDSTIL
Italy *see* STILE LIBERTY
Latvia *see* JUGENDSTIL
Norway **23** 221
Norway *see* JUGENDSTIL
Spain *see* MODERNISME; MODERNISMO
Art of the Young *see* IMO
Artois (House of) **11** 655; **14** 419
Artois, Charles de Bourbon, Comte d' *see* CHARLES X, King of France
Artois, Mahaut, Countess of (*reg* 1302-39) **5** 663, 666–7*
manuscripts **26** 563
paintings **13** 128, 147; **26** 453
sculpture **4** 608; **10** 665; **13** 76; **17** 457, 463
wall paintings **13** 142
Artois, Robert d' *see* ROBERT D'ARTOIS
Artoisenet, Jacques **3** 589; **5** 51
Artoisenet, Joseph-Philippe **3** 589
Artotype **7** 575
art policies
France **11** 667–8*; **24** 139
Nazism **2** 560; **10** 413
Netherlands, the **29** 862
see also ART LEGISLATION
Art Portfolio **33** 575
Art Press **24** 442
Art Properites Inc. **12** 504
Art Quarterly **24** 424, 433
Art-Research-Technology **20** 609
Arts (France) **33** 183
Arts, The (USA) **24** 432, 433
Art sacré, L' **24** 442
Artsagh **2** 426
Okht Drnevank' **2** 426
Art Sales Index **4** 23
Arts and Crafts, John Th. Uiterwijk, & Co. **2** 568*; **14** 44; **22** 875
Arts and Crafts Centre **8** 420
Arts and Crafts Club (New Orleans) **23** 32
Arts and Crafts Exhibition Society **2** 569, 575; **8** 707; **10** 298, 679
members **19** 875
Bell, Robert Anning **3** 630
Blomfield, Reginald (Theodore) **4** 157
Crane, Walter **8** 122
Day, Lewis Foreman **8** 583
Frampton, George (James) **11** 499
Gimson, Ernest (William) **12** 649
Heal, Ambrose **14** 277
Lethaby, W(illiam) R(ichard) **19** 253
Pollen, John Hungerford **25** 165
Pomeroy, Frederick William **25** 187
Sumner, (George) Heywood (Maunoir) **30** 1
Arts and Crafts Movement **2** 568–73*; **6** 322; **8** 802; **20** 594–5; **26** 743; **32** 415, 722
art forms
architecture **2** 571; **8** 613; **9** 739; **12** 177; **22** 743; **23** 498
Australia **7** 530; **14** 19; **23** 212
Belgium **2** 571
Britain **2** 569–71; **26** 316; **29** 695
Canada **5** 562
England **3** 74; **10** 239; **19** *253*; **25** *634*
Switzerland **3** *75*
United States of America **31** 595
books **2** 571
ceramics **8** 706; **30** 887
England **10** 312
Finland **11** 83
United States of America **30** 887
fonts (baptismal) **11** *256*
frames **31** 49
furniture **2** 571; **6** 391; **11** 850; **19** 689; **23** *547*; **28** 666; **33** 155
England **2** *572*; **10** 283, 298; **19** 311
South Africa **29** 120
United States of America **29** 653
glass **2** *570*
industrial design **15** 823
interior decoration **10** 280, 283; **30** 1; **31** 621
jewellery **2** 594, *595*; **10** 346; **12** 869; **17** 528–9
manuscript illumination **20** *335*
metalwork
Australia **2** 765–6
England **10** 336, 343
Ireland **16** 32
United States of America **31** 650
ornament **10** 347; **23** 546
painting **2** 571
textiles **9** IV2; **10** *182*; **31** 657
vernacular art **2** 571; **7** 792
art history **20** 26; **21** 779
design **14** 832
exhibitions **19** 253
regional traditions
Belgium **32** 591
Ireland **2** 569
Scotland **2** 569
United States of America **2** 571–3
Arts and Decoration **24** 362, 432
Arts and Humanities Citation Index see AHCI
Arts and Literature Club (Bahrain) **3** 68
Artscanada **24** 429, 430
arts centres **21** *76*
Artschlag, Jakub **8** 386
art schools **1** 107; **2** 369, 523–4; **7** 562
Britain **1** 107; **28** 274
China **7** 148–9; **28** 553
Cuba (Caribbean) **8** *232*
England **10** 266; **18** 146
Estonia **10** 539
Finland **31** 461
France **2** 366; **9** *312*; **11** 229; **24** *173*
Germany **1** 107–8; **12** *378*; **28** *100*
India, Republic of **15** 171, 179
Indian subcontinent **15** 656
Japan **21** 59
Norway **23** 603
Poland **25** 123
Russia **22** 177; **28** 596; **33** 740
Tunisia **31** 425
United States of America **21** *492*; **26** 466; **27** *314*; **33** 42
Artschwager, Richard **2** 574*; **9** 310; **25** 232
Arts Club of Chicago **6** 575
Arts Council of Finland **11** 112
Arts Council of Great Britain **4** 169; **7** 157; **10** 226, 362; **14** 155; **19** 590; **22** 333
Arts Council of Wales **32** 791
Arts d'Afrique Noire **24** 430
Arts et métiers graphiques **4** 369; **24** 442
Arts in Ireland **24** 429
Arts in New Zealand **24** 437
Arts Magazine **24** 429, 432
Artsn **2** 426
Arts of Mankind **4** 24
Arts Review **24** 429
Arts Students League of Old San Juan **25** 703, 704
Art Students League **31** 669
Art Studies **25** 262
Artstudio **24** 443
Artsvashen **2** 439
Arttzenius, Floris *see* ARNTZENIUS, FLORIS
Artù, Master of the **33** 188
Artuad, Abbot of Vézelay **32** 395
Artula von Villach, Thomas **2** 574*, 792; **8** 836; **15** 146
Artums, Ansis
Art Union **3** 646; **24** 446
see also ART JOURNAL (ENGLAND)
Art Union of London **10** 362; **29** 575
Artuq Arslan **16** 380
Artuqid **2** 574–5*
see also:
DA'UD, Ruler
NASR AL-DIN MAHMUD, Ruler
Arturo **2** 400, 525, 575*; **18** 397; **20** 189
Artus Castle **25** 122
Artusi, Domenico **3** 886
Artusi, Giovanni **26** 810
Artus van Ort de Nieumegue *see* ARNOULT DE NIMÈGUE
Art vivant, L' **5** 38; **20** 75; **24** 442
Artweek **24** 429, 433
Art Weekly **19** 589
Artwell, Albert **16** 881, 885
Art Workers' Coalition **18** 833
Art Workers' Guild **2** 575*; **10** 298, 373
members **32** 2569; **3** 110
Bates, Harry **3** 367
Belcher, John, jr (1841-1913) **3** 532
Bell, Robert Anning **3** 630

Art Workers' Guild
members—cont.
Benson, W(illiam) A(rthur) S(mith) **3** 741
Blomfield, Reginald (Theodore) **4** 157
Crane, Walter **8** 122
Day, Lewis Foreman **8** 583
Ford, Edward Onslow **11** 303
Frampton, George (James) **11** 499
Gimson, Ernest (William) **12** 649
Heal, Ambrose **14** 277
Holden, Charles (Henry) **14** 674
Image, Selwyn **15** 142
Lee, Thomas Stirling **19** 61
Lethaby, W(illiam) R(ichard) **19** 253
Lorimer, Robert S(toddart) **19** 689
MacLaren, James M(arjoribanks) **20** 27
Medd, Henry (Alexander Nesbitt) **21** 3
Pite, A(rthur) Beresford **24** 891
Pomeroy, Frederick William **25** 187
Richardson, Albert E(dward) **26** 337
Schultz, Robert Weir **28** 174
Sedding, J(ohn) D(ando) **28** 347
Sumner, (George) Heywood (Maunoir) **30** 1
Thornycroft, (William) Hamo **30** 762
Townsend, Charles Harrison **31** 249
Art Workers' Quarterly **24** 445
artysci rewolucyjni *see* A.R. GROUP
Artz, (David) Adolphe (Constant) **2** 575–6*; **14** 47; **16** 575; **20** 433
ARU (Association of Architect-Urban Planners) **18** 620
Aruã **20** 372
Aruacos *see* ARAWAK
Aruba **2** 144, 149; **5** 744, *745*
see also ANTILLES, LESSER
à rubans **26** 303
Aruch Church **2** 429
Arundel (W. Sussex)
Castle **3** 209; **6** 53, 54, 55, 56, 61, 407; **23** 210
gate-house **12** 173
paintings **28** 313
sculpture **8** 884
dairy **8** 461
St Nicholas
tomb of John Fitzalan **31** *124*, 125
tomb of William, 9th Earl of Arundel and his Wife Joan Nevill **12** 626; **25** 175, V2
Arundel, Aletheia Howard (i), Countess of *see* HOWARD (i), ALETHEIA, Countess of Arundel
Arundel, Henry Fitzalan, 12th Earl of *see* FITZALAN, HENRY, 12th Earl of Arundel
Arundel, Henry Frederick Howard, 3rd Earl of *see* HOWARD (i), HENRY FREDERICK, 3rd Earl of Arundel
Arundel, Thomas Howard, 2nd Earl of *see* HOWARD (ii), THOMAS, 2nd Earl of Arundel
Arundel Inscriptions **23** 690
Arundell, Henry, 8th Baron Arundell of Wardour **2** 576–7*; **5** 366; **16** 814; **25** 790
Arundell, Matthew **28** 894
Arundel Marbles **6** 446; **10** 370, 658; **14** 806, 807; **23** 22, 690
restorations **13** 782
Arundel Society **2** 576; **7** 647; **10** 252; **17** 731; **18** 897; **19** 485, 786; **26** 235
Arup, Ove (Nyquist) **2** 577–8*
collaboration **7** 696; **10** 241; **19** 747; **23** 635; **31** 776
competitions **7** 670
groups and movements **20** 475; **30** 411
works **2** 318; **16** 56; **19** 578; **20** 166; **32** 783
Arup Associates **4** 823
Arva *see* ORAVA
Arvad **1** 850
Arvalem **12** 826
Arvanitopoulos, A. **15** 891
Arvatov, Boris (Ignat'yevich) **2** 578*; **15** 857
Arverni **27** 28
Arvika **30** 110
Arvine, Alice **14** 296
Arvis **21** 881
Arwad **24** 641
harbour **24** 642
Arwad & Rossbach **19** 318
Arwidsson, Truls **23** 255
Aryaminci Upadhyaya **3** 34; **15** 526
Aryans *see* INDO-ARYANS
Āryapura *see* AIHOLE
Arya Samaj **14** 555
aryballoi **2** 578*; **13** *475*, 478, *499*, *500*, *590*; **15** 163; **29** *175*
Arycanda **19** 837
Arz(an) al-rum *see* ERZURUM
Arzamas **27** 430, 442
Arzberg **12** 437
Arzere Padovano, Gualtiero dall' *see* PADOVANO, GUALTIERO DALL'ARZERE
Arzhan **2** 101
Arziniega, Claudio de *see* ARCINIEGA, CLAUDIO DE
Arzt, L'ubomír **28** 856
Arzubide, Germán List *see* LIST ARZUBIDE, GERMÁN
Arzu-khatun Church **2** 895, 896
A.S., Master *see* BORSJÖ, MASTER OF
Asachi, Gheorghe **26** 713, 722, 725
Asada, Benji **17** 295
Asada, Takashi **21** 317; **23** 627
Asad al-Iskandarani **16** 415
Asadallah **16** 509
Asadi **33** 626
As'ad Pasha al-'Azam **14** 98
Asadullah al-Kirmani **1** 473
As'ad Yasārī *see* ESAD YESARI
Asaf al-Daula, Nawab of Avadh (*reg* 1775-97) **15** 376, 654; **19** 774
Asaf Jah I **2** 729
Asaf Khan **3** *92*; **12** 74; **15** 364; **18** 646
Asaga Ohafia Shrine **15** 114
Asah, Spencer **22** 595
Asahi Brewery *see under* TOKYO
Asahi camera **24** 437
Asai, Chū **2** 578–9*; **17** 203, 204, 294
Asaka
synagogue **17** 551
Tokyo Golf Club **17** 88
Asakawa, Hakkyō **21** 634
Asakawa, Noritaka *see* ASAKAWA, HAKKYŌ
Asakawa, Takumi **21** 634
Asakura, Fumio **17** 134, 433; **27** 872; **31** 81
Asam (family) **22** 299, 300; **23** 543; **30** 137
Asam, Cosmas Damian **2** 579, 580–84*; **15** 865; **22** 302
assistants **13** 852
collaboration **2** 581, 582
Gesamtkunstwerk **12** 372
groups and movements **26** 497
interior decoration **2** *584*; **20** 282; **26** 88; **28** 110; **30** 126
Asam, Cosmas Damian—cont.
paintings **15** 139
frescoes **2** 580, *580*, *583*; **4** 58; **10** 116; **12** 391; **15** 139; **19** 362, *364*; **33** 41
patrons and collectors **33** 277
pupils **27** 587
stucco **11** 124; **29** 838
Asam, Egid Quirin **2** 579, 581–4*; **15** 865; **22** 302
altarpieces **1** 712, *712*
architecture **10** 117; **12** 372
collaboration **2** 580, 581
frescoes **2** *584*; **15** 139
Gesamtkunstwerk **8** 216; **19** *364*
groups and movements **26** 497
interior decoration **2** *584*; **20** 282; **26** 88; **30** 126
sculpture **1** 699; **12** 405; **29** 838
stucco **10** 116
Asam, Franz Erasmus **2** 580
Asam, Hans Georg **2** 579–81*; **22** 302
assistants **2** 580, 581
collaboration **25** 672
pupils **25** 448
works **2** *579*
Asam, Maria Salome **2** 579, 580
Asam, Maria Theresia **2** 579, 580
Asan **18** 369
āsanapaṭṭa **15** 243*
Asante **1** 388–9, 392, 503; **2** 584–91*; **5** 753; **16** 880
aesthetics **1** 235, 238
body arts **1** 288, 344
bone **4** 314
brass **1** *363*; **2** *585*, 589*, *589*, 590*
ceramics **2** 589*
chairs **1** 366; **2** 586*
collections **2** 588
combs (hair) **2** 590*
cooking pots **1** 369
craftsmen and artists **1** 250
currency **1** 363
dress **1** *388*
drums (musical instruments) **2** 590*, *591*
fans **10** 779
figurines **1** 273
Akua'ba **2** 588*, *588*
forowa **2** 590*
gesture **1** 265, 266
glass **2** *585*, *588*
gold **1** 288, 352, 353, 354; **2** *585*, *586*, 587
gourds **1** 303
houses **1** 311, 313
iconography **1** 262
jewellery **1** 350
kuduo **2** 589*, *589*
leather **1** *349*
lost-wax casting **2** 589
palaces **1** 242
palanquins **2** 588*
patronage **1** 240, 241, 242
pipes (smoking) **1** 368; **2** 590*
regalia **1** 351, 352, 353; **2** 585–8*
religion **16** 880
rings **1** 351
sceptres **1** 388
sculpture **1** 322; **2** 589*
figure **2** 590
wood **2** 588, *588*
shirts **1** *349*
shrines (i) (cult) **1** 309; **2** 589*
spoons **1** 369
staffs **1** 354; **2** 587*
stools **1** 353, 388; **2** *585*, 585–6*
sword ornaments **2** *587*, 587
swords **1** 242, 354, 361; **2** *586*, 586–7*
terracottas **2** 589
textiles **1** 290, 294, 424
tourist art **1** 253
umbrellas **1** 354; **2** 587–8*
weaving **1** 294
weights **1** 240, *363*; **2** 590*
whisks **1** 354
Asante—cont.
wood **2** 588, *588*, 590, *591*
wood-carvers **1** 435
wood-carvings **2** 137, *591*
wraps **1** 348
Asaoka Okisada **14** 702; **17** 180, 416, 439, 797
Asaris, Gunar **26** 384
Asarlik **5** 741
Asarwa, Bai Harir Tomb **15** 349
Asasif *see under* THEBES (i) (EGYPT)
Asat **12** 328
Asawa, Ruth **4** 110
Asbaşin Kalesi *see* ÇAVUŞTEPE
Asbjørnsen, Peter Christien **22** 540; **33** 77
Asbrugg, Franciscus *see* ASPRUCK, FRANZ
Ascalon **17** 500
fort **16** 155
Shrine of Husayn **16** 490; **21** 629
Ascanio, Corradino d' **15** 826
Ascargorta, Martín de, Archbishop of Granada **26** 421
Ascensão, Bento da *see* BENTO DA ASCENSÃO
Ascension Island **21** 574
Ascensius, Jodocus Badius **4** 358; **30** 487
Aschaffenburg **2** 591–2*; **12** *361*
Pompeianum **25** 193; **32** 555
SS Peter and Alexander **2** 591; **17** 688–9
altars **17** *689*
Schloss Johannisburg **2** 591–2*; **12** 369; **17** 689; **26** 368
Chapel **17** *690*
gold **14** 649
manuscripts **14** 649
paintings **8** 116; **18** 174
Aschaffenburg Golden Gospels *see under* GOSPEL BOOKS → individual manuscripts
Ascham, Roger **13** 298
Aschan, Marit Guinness **10** 347
Aschenbach, Andreas **11** 787
Aschenbach, Oswald **11** 798
Aschenbrenner, Lennart **30** 82
Ascher **6** 383; **28** 299
Ascher (Oved), Daisy **2** 592*
Ascher, Felix **17** 548
Ascher, Lida **9** 293
Ascher, Zika **9** 293; **20** 831
Aschieri, Pietro **16** 649, 650; **24** 694
Aschlager, Walter W. **7** 327
Aschwanden & Speck **4** 61
Asciano Painter **10** 616
Ascoli, Jerome of *see* NICHOLAS IV, Pope
Ascoli Piceno **2** 592–4*; **16** *620*
Baptistery **16** 625
Cathedral of S Emidio **16** 723; **23** 461
altarpiece **8** *168*
Palazzo del Capitano del Popolo **2** *593*
Palazzo Vescovile **11** 236
Piazza del Popolo **2** *593*
Ascona **23** 120; **30** *124*
Casa Serodine **30** 136
ASCORAL (Assemblée des Constructeurs pour une Rénovation Architecturale) **2** 660; **19** 44
Ascot Cup **12** 163
Ascott (Bucks) **7** 552
Asculum Picenum *see* ASCOLI PICENO
Åse, Arne **23** 235
Asebeido, Martín de **21** 375
Aselli, Gaspare **21** 6
Asen, Michael **17** 838
Asenovgrad *see* STANIMAKA
Ase Puonchu **3** 147
Asfar, B. **16** 390
Asgill, Charles **30** 387
ash **33** 324
historical and regional traditions
Austria **2** *811*
England **10** 288, 293
Germany **8** *271*
Hungary **14** 905
Indian subcontinent **15** 720
Native North Americans **3** 331
types
qin **7** 92; **22** 376
uses
baskets **3** 331
chests **2** *811*
cupboards **8** *271*
furniture **10** 288, 293; **14** 905
Ash, Samuel **22** 598
Asha Bhil **1** 471
Ashanti *see* ASANTE
Ashar, Ishtar Temple
plaques **10** *473*
'Ashârah, Tell *see* TERQA
Ashaval *see* AHMADABAD
Ashayt **10** 12, 43
Ashbee, C(harles) R(obert) **2** 594–5*, 766; **10** 344; **19** 576, 594; **20** 437
architecture **17** 492
assistants **14** 673
glass **2** *570*
groups and movements **1** 171; **2** 562, 566, 569, 570, 571, 575
jewellery **2** *595*; **10** 346; **17** 528
mother-of-pearl **22** 205
patrons and collectors **10** 465; **14** 132
silver **10** 336; **27** 641
studio **29** 858
teachers **4** 215
Ashbery, John **26** 431
Ashbourne School (Derbys) **28** 156
Ashburnham, Bertram, 4th Earl of Ashburnham **2** 595–6*; **4** 209; **30** 749
Ashburnham, George, 3rd Earl of Ashburnham **2** 595
Ashburnham, John, 2nd Earl of Ashburnham **2** 595; **22** 115
Ashburnham, William **5** 293
Ashburnham Centrepiece **29** 432
Ashburnham I **19** 194
Ashburnham Pentateuch *see under* OLD TESTAMENTS → individual manuscripts
Ashburnham Place (E. Sussex)
Crimson State Bedroom **30** XVI
Ashburton (Devon), statue of John Grigg **23** 62
Ashburton, Alexander Baring, 1st Baron *see* BARING, ALEXANDER, 1st Baron Ashburton
Ashburton, Francis Baring, 3rd Baron *see* BARING, FRANCIS, 3rd Baron Ashburton
Ashby (Norfolk), St Mary Church **26** 613
Ashby, Henry **12** 639
Ashby, Thomas **2** 596*
Ashcan school **2** 596–7*; **23** 47; **31** 705
members **3** 681; **10** 108; **12** 769; **14** 393; **24** 600; **28** 843
works **2** *596*; **12** 296; **15** 828; **24** *601*; **28** 919; **31** 605
Ashcombe, Robert **23** 460
Ashdod **17** 553; **24** 634, 636
Ashdown, J. H. **32** 861
Ashdown House **30** 503
Ashendene Press **20** 335
Asher **10** 91
Asher, Jacob ben **17** 565
Asher, Michael **19** 702
ashes
historical and regional traditions
China **6** 873; **7** 14, 17, 19; **18** 601
Egypt, ancient **10** 55
Indian subcontinent **15** 667
Japan **17** 242, 250–51; **27** 699

ashes
historical and regional traditions—cont.
Korea **18** *335*, 340
uses
glass **10** 55
glazes **6** 329, 873; **10** 315; **17** 242, 250–51; **18** *335*, 340; **27** 699
grounds **13** 708
lacquer **7** 14, 17, 19; **18** 601
mordants (iii) (dyeing) **15** 667
polishing **1** 761
Asheville (NC), Biltmore House **15** 22, *22*; **23** 423
Ashfield, Edmund **2** 597*; **19** 818; **20** 141
Ashford, William **2** 597–8*; **16** 14
Ashford Castle (Co. Mayo) **16** 25
Ashford Co. **23** 74
Ashguzai **28** 320
Ashihara, Yoshinobu **2** 598*; **17** 90
Ashikaga (family) **2** 598–9*; **17** 22, 746, 749, 780
collections **17** 428, 437; **18** 562
lacquer **17** 300, 424
paintings **17** 161, 166, 171–2, 419, 423, 794; **23** 371; **28** 493; **30** 465
sculpture **31** 675
tea ceremonies **17** 334, 342
Ashikaga, Kurita Museum **17** 433
Ashikaga Motouji **17** 747
Ashikaga Takauji, Shogun (*reg* 1338-58) **17** 22, 748; **18** 550
Ashikaga Yoshiharu, Shogun (*reg* 1521-45) **17** 780; **31** 198
Ashikaga Yoshikane **17** 746
Ashikaga Yoshimasa, Shogun (*reg* 1443-74) **17** 22; **18** 550
architecture **2** 598; **17** 22, 76, 335; **18** 562; **22** 349
collections **17** 428
gardens **12** 98; **17** 423
interior decoration **17** 795
lacquer **17** 301, 304; **22** 339
paintings **1** 776; **2** 598; **17** 172, 780; **30** 465
scrolls **17** 166
tea ceremonies **17** 342; **22** 339
Ashikaga Yoshimitsu, Shogun (*reg* 1367-95) **2** 598; **17** 22; **22** 349
architecture **17** 172; **18** 550, 561
collections **17** 428
gardens **18** 561
paintings **2** 599; **17** 172
textiles **17** 423
theatre **17** 22
Ashikaga Yoshimochi, Shogun (*reg* 1395-1423) **2** 599*
paintings **2** 598; **17** 171, *171*; **30** 465
screens (ii) (furniture) **17** 663
scrolls **7** 624; **17** 167
Ashikaga Yoshinori, Shogun (*reg* 1428-41) **17** 76, 166, 172; **30** 465
Ashikaga Yoshitane, Shogun (*reg* 1493-1508) **17** 780
Ashikaga Yoshizumi **17** 780
Ashina Moriuji **28** 493
Ashington Group **20** 590
Ashir Palace **16** 170
Ashiru **1** 429
Ashiya **17** 322
Ashiya Camera Club *see* CAMERA CLUB (ASHIYA)
Ashken, Tanya **23** 71
Ashkhabad **2** 599*; **6** *182*; **31** 457*, *458*, 459
architecture **31** 458, 459
Avant-garde School of Arts of the East **31** 459
Institute of History of the Academy of Sciences **2** 599
Ashkhabad—cont.
museums **6** 282
Archaeological Museum of the Turkmenian Academy of Sciences **6** 284
Trans-Caspian Regional Museum *see* Turkmenistan United Museum of History and Ethnography
Turkmenistan History Museum **2** 599
Turkmenistan Museum of Fine Arts **2** 599; **6** 283
Turkmenistan United Museum of History and Ethnography **6** 283
rhyta **6** 270
textile factory **31** 459
Ashkizar Mosque **16** 199
ashlar masonry *see under* MASONRY → types
Ashley, Frederick M. **23** 342
Ashley, Laura **10** 285, 300
Ashlin, George C(oppinger) **2** 599–600*; **14** 46; **25** 717
Ashlin, Martin **2** 600
Ashmole, Bernard **2** 600*; **7** 712
Ashmole, Elias **2** 600–601*; **26** *393*
collaboration **31** 276
collections **10** 364, 368; **13** 605; **23** 690
plaquettes **25** 18
writings **33** *249*
illustrated **32** 85
Ashmolean Crucifixion, Master of the **3** 247
Ashmolean Master **8** 315
Ashmolean Museum *see under* OXFORD
el-Ashmunein *see* HERMOPOLIS MAGNA
Ashoka, Ruler (*reg c.* 269-232 BC) (Maurya) **5** 94; **15** 194, 202; **17** 759; **20** 862; **24** 251
architecture **15** 202, 341; **27** 708
capitals **15** 181
epigraphy **15** 198; **28** 535
inscriptions **1** 647; **3** 194; **8** 671, 848; **15** 197; **29** 863
sculpture **15** 213, 415, 422; **24** 264; **29** 439
sponsorship **5** 101
stupas **22** 758
temples **30** 437
Ashot Bagratuni, King of Armenia (*reg* 732-48) **2** 424
Ashot I, Prince (*reg* 780-830) **30** 305
Ashot III, King of Armenia (*reg* 952-77) **2** 97, 444
Ashot Koukhi, Archbishop **30** 306
Ashour, Jamal **17** 655
Ashover (Derbys), All Saints tomb of Thomas Babyngton **1** 519
Ash Poitras, Jane *see* POITRAS, JANE ASH
ʿAshqābād *see* ASHKHABAD
Ashraf (painter) **2** 896
Ashraf (decorative artist; *fl* 1735-80) *see* ʿALI ASHRAF
Ashraf (Iran) *see* BEHSHAHR
al-Ashraf Muzaffar, Sultan (*reg* Damascus 1229-37) (Ayyubid) **16** 180
al-Ashraf Nāsaīr al-Dīn Shaʿbān II *see* SHAʿBAN II
al-Ashraf Qānṣūh al-Ghawrī *see* QANSUH AL-GHAWRI
al-Ashraf Sayf al-Dīn Barsbay *see* BARSBAY
al-Ashraf Sayf al-Dīn Qāʾitbāy al-Ẓāhirī *see* QAʾITBAY
Ashridge Park (Herts) **12** 136; **29** 835; **33** 99
Chapel **29** 515
Ashtarak **2** *423*, 601*; **9** *512*
Basilica of Tsiranavor **2** 601
Ashtarak—cont.
Church of the Mother of God **2** 601
Karmravor *see* Church of the Mother of God
urban planning **2** 428
Ashtarjan Mosque **16** 193
Ashtishat **2** 425
Ashton, Evans and Brazier **27** 642
Ashton, James **14** 507
Ashton, Julian (Rossi) **2** 601–2*, 769, 771; **30** 160
pupils **3** 124; **4** 107; **9** 53; **13** 718; **14** 531; **18** 672
works **2** 746
Ashton, Samuel **20** 238
Ashton, Thomas **20** 238
ashtrays **3** *402*; **17** 399
Ashur *see* ASSUR
Ashurov, Abdullo **30** 253
Asi **20** 106
ASI *see* ARCHAEOLOGICAL SURVEY OF INDIA
Asia (Peru) **19** 385; **29** 158
architecture **29** 158
clubs (weapons) **29** 205
sculpture **29** 169
textiles **29** 159
Asia, Central *see* CENTRAL ASIA
Asiab **15** 903, 913
Asian Art **24** 436
Asiatic Researches **24** 436
Asiatic Society (Calcutta) **15** 184, 210, 741; **16** 553; **22** 795
Asiatisk Kompagni **8** 758
Asif, Mohammad **23** 800, 802
Asihene, E. V. **12** 508
Asika, Ukpabi **18** 640
Aşıklı **1** 838
Asilah **22** 129
Asillo **24** *498*
church **24** 502
Asín, Carlos Quispez *see* QUISPEZ ASÍN, CARLOS
Asine **2** 602*; **13** *363*; **14** *332*
bone **14** 353
bronzes **14** *356*
faience (i) (glass) **14** 358
granaries **14** 339
ivory-carvings **14** 353, 354
pottery **13** 495
sculpture **14** 352
wall paintings **14** 348
Asinou **2** 602*; **8** *325*; **9** *512*
chapel **8** 358
Panagia Phorbiotissa **8** 358, 359; **9** 580, 623, 626
Asís Cambó y Batlle, Francisco de *see* CAMBÓ Y BATLLE, FRANCISCO DE ASÍS
Asis Soler, Francisco de **24** 714
Askainen Church **11** 90
al-ʿAskar *see under* CAIRO
Askar-Saryj, Khas-Bulat **27** 433
Aske **30** 73
Aske, Lawrence Dundas of *see* DUNDAS, LAWRENCE, OF ASKE
Askeaton Chalice **19** 394
Askeaton Friary (Co. Limerick) **21** 841
Aske Hall (N. Yorks) **3** 382; **7** 172; **9** 392; **13** 302
Asker, Curt **30** 82
Askhabad *see* ASHKHABAD
Askitario **14** *332*, 335, 338
Asklepiades **2** 603*; **8** 691; **13** 557
works **13** 557, 558, 567
Asklepiades **13** 552
Asko **11** 104
askoi **2** 603*; **13** 519, 537; **14** *342*; **32** *563*
Askut **21** 554
fort **9** 844, 845
Aslaia **1** 868
Aslán, José **2** 397
Aslanian, Oxan **10** 86
Aslin, C. Herbert **15** 887; **26** 19; **28** 158
Aslin, George Coppinger **6** 164
Asmar, Tell **1** 508, *849*, 893; **9** 44–5*; **21** *267*
architecture **21** 274, 284, 285
chariot **6** 478
figurines **9** *45*
glass **1** 864
sculpture **21** 294, 295
statues **9** 44
see also DIYALA REGION
Asmat **23** 713, 735
Asmat Begum **1** 460
Asmund **26** 691
Asmus, Dieter **33** 627
Asmussen, Erik **2** 603*
Asnaf, Mosque of al-ʿAbbas **16** 177
Asnaq Mosque **16** 194
As Nieves **20** 412
Asnova **2** 603–4*; **18** 457; **22** 178; **27** 379; **32** 661
members **9** 73; **18** 620
Asō, Saburō **17** 207
Asociación Arte Concreto Invención **2** 400, 525, 546, 575, 604*; **18** 397; **24** 386
members **14** 596; **15** 891; **20** 189
Asociación Colombiana de Museos (ACOM) **7** 612
Asociación de Arte Constructivo **31** 758, 183
Asociación de Grabadores de Cuba **8** 233
Asociación Nacional de Escritores y Artistas (ANEA) **24** 515
Asociația Femeilor Pictore *see* Association of Women Painters
Asomatos Church **2** 305
Asorey, Francisco **29** 295
Asotsiatsiya Khudozhnykiv Chervonoï Ukraïny *see* ASSOCIATION OF ARTISTS OF RED UKRAINE
Asotsiatsiya Revolyutsiynoho Mystetstva Ukraïny *see* ASSOCIATION OF REVOLUTIONARY ART OF UKRAINE
Aspari, Domenico **21** 527
Aspden, David **2** 604–5*, 751
Aspdin, Joseph **7** 693
Aspekt **32** 679
Aspelin, Eliel **11** 113
Aspelin, Johan Reinhold **21** 885
Aspelta (*reg* 593-568 BC) **21** 160; **23** 282
aspen **33** 324
Aspendos **2** 605–6*; **26** *908*
aqueduct **26** 913; **27** 7
basilica **32** 89
stage buildings **13** 391
Theatre **2** 605, *605*; **26** 912
postscaenium **30** 652
scaena frons **26** 873, 883; **30** 652
stage buildings **1** 164; **23** 491
staircases **29** 521
Asper, Hans **2** 606*; **21** 406; **30** 131; **33** 736
Asper, Hans Konrad **2** 606; **22** 299; **27** 664
Asper, Hans Rudolf **2** 606
Asper, Rudolf **2** 606
Asperen, Jan Van *see* VAN ASPEREN, JAN
Asperen de Boer, J. R. J. van **31** 577
Asperg *see* KLEINASPERGLE
Aspero **29** 159, 829; **30** 447
temple **29** 165
Aspertini, Amico **2** 606–8*; **26** 768
attributions **4** 311
collaboration **4** 276, 280
patrons and collectors **3** 743; **11** 700
reproductive prints by others **22** 466
works **2** 162, *607*
Aspettati, Jacopo di Bonapreso *see* JACOPO DI BONAPRESO ASPETTATI
Aspetti, Tiziano **2** 162, 608–10*; **5** 532; **23** 754; **32** 192
groups and movements **16** 697
patrons and collectors **13** 659
pupils **23** 880
works **2** *609*, *610*; **23** 880; **29** 570
asphalt **2** 239; **10** 548, 560; **13** 706; **24** 792; **32** 3
asphodel paste **16** 356
Aspinall, William **19** 359*
Aspiotes, Nikolaos **9** 206
Asplund, (Erik) Gunnar **1** 470; **2** 611–12*; **13** 30; **30** 92, 96
collaboration **11** 139; **19** 283
groups and movements **13** 613; **15** 885; **21** 783
pupils **10** 462
teachers **3** 784
works **2** *611*; **7** 328; **13** 31; **29** 686; **30** 74, *74*, 91
Aspremont Lynden ewer **3** *597*
Asprey & Co. **10** 346, 347; **19** 594, 596
Asprucci, Antonio **2** 612–13*
assistants **23** 701
garden buildings **31** 679
patrons and collectors **9** 23; **26** 780
pupils **4** 333
works **4** 407; **16** 644, 727
Asprucci, Mario (*fl* 1720) **2** 612
Asprucci, Mario (1764-1804) **2** 613; **4** 407; **14** 485; **25** 266
Aspruck, Franz **2** 613*; **18** 42; **25** 731
Asram Maharosei **5** 464
Assad, A. **12** 43
Assad Effendi **17** 552
Assad Lara, Enrique **1** 115
Assagao Church **12** 827
Assalieh **17** 556
Assamani Gospels *see under* GOSPEL BOOKS → individual manuscripts
assay marks *see* MARKS → metalwork
Assche, Marquis d' **3** 88
Assche, Auguste Van *see* VAN ASSCHE, AUGUSTE
Assche, Henri van **2** 613*; **32** 241
Asse, (Louis-)Auguste **2** 613–14*
Asse, Eugène **2** 614
Asse, Geneviève **11** 420
Asseca, Visconde de **24** 811
Asselberghs, Jean-Paul **30** 332
Asselbergs, Alphonse **4** 529
Asselbergs, Gustave **22** 853
Asselijn, Abraham **2** 614
Asselijn, Jan **2** 614–15*
collaboration **25** 33; **33** 26
copies **4** 657
groups and movements **9** 462; **28** 92
patrons and collectors **7** 778
pupils **22** 208
reproductive prints by others **8** 542
works **2** *615*; **9** *463*; **18** 710; **20** 860; **22** 843
Asselin, Maurice **2** 615*; **22** 751
Asseline, Charles **16** 876
Asselt, Bernardino van **11** 194
Asselt, Jacopo Ebert van **11** 194
Asselt, Jan van der **3** 552; **19** 721
Asselt, Pietro van **11** 194
Asselyn, Jean *see* ASSELIJN, JAN
Assemblage: A Critical Journal of Architecture and Design Culture **24** 434
assemblages **2** 615–17*; **7** 557; **16** 57; **17** 694; **21** 903*; **23** 333
Germany **28** *197*
United States of America **2** *616*; **7** *874*; **31** 608, 614
see also COLLAGES; PHOTOMONTAGES
Assemblée des Constructeurs pour une Rénovation Architecturale *see* ASCORAL

assembly halls **13** 386; **31** 235
assembly houses **2** 618
assembly lines **15** 823; **20** 593
Assembly of the Seven Brothers *see* UNVANIEZ AR SEIZ BREUR
assembly rooms **2** 617–18*, *618*; **4** *613*; **8** 105
see also MEETING HOUSES; TOWN HALLS
Assemini, S Pietro **27** 836
Assen, Provinciaalmuseum van Drenthe **22** 906
Assenza, Francesco **20** 216
works **20** *217*
Asser, Eduard (Isaac) **2** 618–19*; **19** 481
Assereto, Gioacchino **2** 619–20*; **12** 283; **16** 675
pupils **18** 740
teachers **2** 127
works **2** *619*; **4** 491
Assereto, Giuseppe **2** 620
Assergi, S Maria **26** 625
Asser Rig **8** 758
Asset, Martin, Abbot of St Vaast **3** 642
Assézat, Jules **9** 425
Assigny, Marie d', Mme de Canaples *see* CANAPLES, MARIE D'ASSIGNY, Mme de
Assiniboin **17** 770; **22** 551, 649, 650
Assiniboine, Cyril **22** 598
Assiros **19** 880
Assisi **2** 620–28*; **16** *620*
Cathedral of S Rufino **1** 609; **16** 625; **26** 625
maiolica **16** 732
Rocca Maggiore **19** 896
S Chiara **11** 711
altarpiece **25** *229*, 230
S Francesco **2** 620–28*; **11** 711; **13** 51–2, 185; **16** 627, 762
Lower Church **2** *621*; **7** 316; **13** 138, 192; **19** 665; **20** 760–61; **29** 599
crypt **3** 644
frescoes **1** 653; **2** *622*, *626*, *627*; **4** 493; **9** 261; **11** 709, 712; **12** 287; **13** 145, 147; **19** *665*; **22** 521
Montefiore Chapel *see* S Martino Chapel
S Martino Chapel **12** 304; **13** 147, 192; **20** 505–6, *506*
stained glass **2** 632*; **11** 711; **29** 502
metalwork **11** 614; **13** 163, *163*, 775
sculpture **13** 97
stained glass **2** 631–2*; **11** 712; **13** 132, 142
textiles **16** 444
throne **30** 778
Treasury **2** 632*
Upper Church **7** 314–16; **13** 132, 135, 192; **16** 837; **20** 697–8, 712–13, *713*, 759–60, 761; **23** 96; **24** 343; **26** 182; **31** 192
frescoes **2** *338*, *623*, *624*; **4** 493; **5** 443; **7** *315*; **11** 709, 712; **12** 691–4, *693*; **13** 132, 144, 145, *145*, 673; **15** 135; **16** 655; **20** *697*; **25** 230; **27** 124
stained glass **2** *631*, 631–2*
S Maria degli Angeli **1** 609; **8** 212
Assisi, Andrea Alovigi d' *see* INGEGNO, L'
Assisi, Angelo di Pietro d' *see* ANGELO DI PIETRO D'ASSISI
Assisi, Tiberio (Ranieri di Diotallevi) d' **2** 632–3*
Assisi embroidery *see under* EMBROIDERY → types
Assisi Vaults, Master of the **1** 653; **2** 625
Assis Rodrigues, Francisco de **28** 748
ASSIST **31** 737
Assiut *see* ASYUT
assize courts *see* LAW COURTS
ASSO *see* ASSOZIATION REVOLUTIONÄRER BILDENDER KÜNSTLER DEUTSCHLANDS
Associação Industrial **25** 293
Associated Architects **14** 199; **23** 43
Associated Artists **33** 134
Associated Artists in Water-Colours **19** 586; **32** 903
Associated Artists of Pittsburgh **25** 5
Association de la Libre Esthétique *see* LIBRE ESTHÉTIQUE
Association des Ecrivains et Artistes Révolutionnaires **17** 669
Association des Plasticiens Ivoiriens **8** 23
Association for Japanese Archaeology *see* NIHON KŌKOGAKU KYŌKAI
Association for Preservation Technology (APT) **7** 744
Association for the Conservation of Cultural Patrimony of the Americas *see* APOYO
Association for the Promotion of the Fine Arts *see* GLASGOW ART UNION
Associationism **24** 742; **26** 737
Association of AKhRR Youth **2** 633
Association of American Etchers **25** 629
Association of American Painters and Sculptors **2** 447, 633*
Association of Architects (Czech Republic) **17** 698
Association of Architectural Draughtsmen **10** 374
Association of Architect-Urban Planners *see* ARU
Association of Artists of Bosnia and Herzegovina **4** 461
Association of Artists of Red Ukraine (AKhChU) **2** 634
Association of Artists of Revolutionary Russia (AKhRR) **2** 431, 633–4*; **22** 178; **25** 653; **27** 395, 434; **28** 669
members **11** 358; **31** 582
Cheptsov, Yefim (Mikhaylovich) **6** 548
Fonvizin, Artur (Vladimirovich) **11** 291
Gerasimov, Aleksandr (Mikhaylovich) **12** 339
Gintsburg, Il'ya (Yakovlevich) **12** 653
Grekov, Mitrofan (Borisovich) **13** 633
Ioganson, Boris (Vladimirovich) **15** 891
Kasatkin, Nikolay (Alekseyevich) **17** 827
Lentulov, Aristarkh (Vasil'yevich) **19** 166
Malyutin, Sergey (Vasil'yevich) **20** 223
Mashkov, Il'ya (Ivanovich) **20** 549
Merkurov, Sergey (Dmitriyevich) **21** 157
Osmyorkin, Aleksandr (Aleksandrovich) **23** 605
Ryangina, Serafima (Vasil'yevna) **27** 460
Sokolov-Skalya, Pavel (Petrovich) **29** 19
Association of Artists of the Revolution (AKhR) **2** 633
Association of Artists Studying Revolutionary Life **2** 633
Association of Basque Artists **27** 768
Association of Fine Artists **20** 252
Association of Independent Artists *see* NEATKARĪGO MĀKSLINIEKU VIENĪBA
Association of Independent Painters and Sculptors **31** 454
Association of Independent Ukranian Artists (ANUM) **20** 807
Association of Lebanese Artists, Painters and Sculptors **19** 8
Association of New Architects *see* ASNOVA
Association of New Artists **33** 530
Association of Ottoman Painters **2** 634*; **31** 454
Association of Realist Artists (OkhR) **22** 178
Association of Revolutionary Art of Ukraine (ARMU) **2** 634*; **4** 605
Association of the Second Period *see* DAINI KIKAI
Association of the Stiff-necked **8** 393
Association of Turkish Painters *see* ASSOCIATION OF OTTOMAN PAINTERS
Association of Women Painters (Asociaţia Femeilor Pictore) **3** 88
Association of Workers of IZO **31** 783
Association pour l'Art, L' **22** 136
Associazione Italiana Acquarellisti **32** 903
Associazione per l'Architettura Organica *see* APAO
Assomption **5** 588
Assonville, Melchior d' **12** 513
Assos **2** 634–6*, *635*; **13** *363*; **31** 354, 356
architecture **11** 231; **13** 405
measurements **13** 411, *411*
mosaics **13** 559, 560, 565
stoas **13** 406
Temple of Athena **2** 635–6; **13** 378, 427, 432
Assotsiatsiya Khodozhnikov Revolyutsionnoy Rosii (AKhRR) *see* ASSOCIATION OF ARTISTS OF REVOLUTIONARY RUSSIA
Assotsiatsiya Novykh Arkhitektorov *see* ASNOVA
Assoziation Revolutionärer Bildender Künstler Deutschlands (ASSO) **11** 776; **12** 396; **32** 678
Assteyn, Bartholomeus Abrahamsz. **11** 226
Assur **1** *849*, 892; **2** 636–41*, *637*; **15** *901*, 912; **21** *267*, 268, 273
altars **1** 690
architectural decorations **6** 206
architecture **2** 639, 640, 641; **21** 274, 275, 288; **24** 216
bit akitu **12** 66
caravanserai **1** 889
excavations **14** 487
faience (i) (glass) **1** 878
glass **1** 865, 866
iconography **24** 218
ivory-carvings **1** 869; **24** 643
iwans **16** 801; **21** 291
metalwork **1** 827
New Palace **2** 639
Old Palace **2** 639, 640, 641; **21** 285, 288; **23** 806
religion **21** 277
sculpture **21** 294, 295, 296, 300, 302; **24** 218
seals **1** 861, 862
stelae **1** 509
stucco **29** 814, 815
Assur—cont.
temples **21** 287
Anu-Adad Temple **1** 889; **2** 639, 640, 641; **21** 286, 298; **33** 675
Assur Temple **2** 639, 640, 641; **21** 290
Ishtar Temple **1** 892; **2** 636, 639; **21** 285, 304
Nabu Temple **2** 641; **21** 290
Sin-Shamash Temple **2** 640; **21** 286, 288
Temple of the New Year's Festival **2** 641; **21** 290, 301
Tomb 45 **21** 304
town walls **2** 639, 640
trade **1** 825
wall paintings **21** 309
ziggurat **21** 286; **33** 675
Assurbanipal (*reg* 668-627 BC) **1** 895; **21** 274
architecture **1** 892; **14** 129; **21** 290; **23** 151, 153
dress **1** 883, 886
inscriptions **23** 154
reliefs **2** 641, *641*; **10** 133; **21** 290, 300, 301–2*; **22** 510, 511; **23** 154
sculpture **23** 154; **30** 774
writing-tablets **19** 311
Assur-bel-kala (*reg* 1073-1056) **2** 637, 638, 639
Assur-etel-ilani (*reg* 626-? BC) **23** 151
Assur-nadin-ahhe II (*reg* 1400-1391 BC) **2** 639
Assurnasirpal I (*reg* 1049-1031) **2** 640; **21** 298
Assurnasirpal II (*reg* 883-859 BC) **2** 638; **21** 274, *297*
architecture **1** 891; **2** 638, 640; **21** 287–8; **23** 149–50
inscriptions **23** 149, 153
reliefs **21** 296–8; **23** 153, 888
Assur-nirari I (*reg c.* 1525 BC) **2** 637, 639
Assur-resh-ishi I (*reg* 1132-1115 BC) **2** 637, 639; **23** 153
Assursharrat **21** 302
Assur-uballit I (*reg* 1363-1328 BC) **2** 639; **23** 153
Assy **29** 508
parish church **11** 659
Assyrian **1** 115, 854; **2** 638–41*; **17** 826; **21** *267*; **23** 152; **30** 178
alabaster (gypsum) **2** *641*; **10** 742; **21** *297*
arches **2** 297*
architecture **18** 27; **21** 287–90, 552
armour **1** 886
basalt **14** *64*
bit hilani **21** 290
brass **4** 681
brick **2** 640
bronze **21** *276*, 304
chariots **6** *478*, 479–80
collections **21** 310
copper **2** 639; **7** *813*
cotton **8** 35
cuneiform **1** 854
domes **9** 85
doors **9** 150
dress **1** *884*, 885–6, 887
exhibitions **21** 310
façade decoration **10** 742
figureheads **28** 611
fortifications **21** 552
gardens **12** 65
gates **7** *813*
gold **1** 875
halls **30** 187
harnesses **14** 179*, *180*
hunting scenes **29** 423
ivory-carvings **1** 871, *871*
jewellery **1** 875
limestone **10** 742; **21** 287; **22** *511*; **29** *701*, XI
metalwork **15** 919
mosaics **1** 889–90*; **2** 640
Assyrian—cont.
narratives **22** *511*
palaces **23** 806
palmettes **23** 888, *888*
parks **24** 178
plaques **21** *276*
porticos **18** 28
pottery **21** 308
propaganda **25** 650
religion **21** 278
rock reliefs **3** 418; **21** *278*
sculpture **2** 639; **14** *64*; **21** 296*; **25** 650
architectural **10** 742
relief **1** 831, 833, 854; **2** 641, *641*; **6** *478*; **21** 296–302*, *297*, 553, 554; **22** *511*; **26** 134; **29** *701*, XI; **30** 187
seals **1** 850, 856, *861*, 861–2
ship-decoration **28** 611
standards (vexilloid) **11** 150
stelae **29** 614
temples **30** 432
thrones **30** 774
trade **1** 825
trappings **14** 179*
vaults (ceiling) **32** 86, 87
villages **2** 639
wall paintings **2** 640; **21** 309*, *309*
women **1** 886
writing **1** 828; **20** *326*
writing-tablets **1** 853; **2** 364; **20** *326*
ziggurats **21** 286; **33** 675
Assyrian Colony period *see under* ANATOLIA, ANCIENT → periods
Assyrian Revival **1** 895; **2** 642–3*; **18** 897; **21** 310
Assyrian Trading Colonies period *see under* ANATOLIA, ANCIENT → periods
Ast, Balthasar van der **2** 643–4*; **4** 466; **22** 839, 843
pupils **11** 227
teachers **4** 466
works **2** *644*; **11** 226; **29** 666; **31** 882
Ast, Johannes van der **2** 644; **4** 466
Astaf'yeva, O. **27** 425
Astana **2** 644–5*; **6** *288*, *614*; **28** *719*
busts **6** *316*
dress **6** 310
furniture **6** 311
lacquer **6** 313
necropolis **18** 26
pottery **6** 309
prints **6** 314
shrines (i) (cult) **28** 637
silk **6** 290; **28** 721
statuettes **6** 315
textiles **6** 317–18; **7** 48
Tomb 1 **7** 52
Tomb 18 **7** 48
Tomb 37 **7** 49
Tomb 39 **7** 48
Tomb 85 **7** 52
Tomb 108 **7** 49
Tomb 306 **7** 48
Tomb 337 **7** 48
vestments (ecclesiastical) **6** 314
Astarita Collection *see under* ROME, VATICAN → museums
Astarte **33** 307
Astbury, John **2** 645*; **10** 306; **29** 495; **33** 341
Astbury, Richard Meir **29** 495
Asteas **13** 532
works **13** *533*
Asterios of Amasia **10** 129
Astete y Concha, Adelina **24** 517
Astete y Concha, Luis **2** 645*
Asti **16** 758
Cathedral **13** 64
Seminary **1** 624
Asti, Niccolò d' **6** 140
Astigi *see* ECIJA
Astley (family) **14** 316

Astley, Edward **25** 631; **33** 380
Astley, Philip **29** 489
Astley Hall (Lancs) **10** 274
Asto, Simón de **24** 504
Astolfo, King of the Lombards *see* AISTULF, King of the Lombards
Astolfo, Master of **33** 188
Astor, Diego de (*c.* 1585/90-*c.* 1650) **2** 645–6*; **13** 344
Astor, Diego de (*fl* late 17th cent.) **2** 645
Astor, John Jacob **18** 161; **24** 691; **26** 537
Astor, William Waldorf, 1st Viscount Astor **2** 646*; **7** 436; **8** 106; **31** 151
Astorga
  Bishop's Palace *see* Museo de los Caminos
  Cathedral of S María
    retable **13** 69; **29** 290, *290*
    sculpture **26** 642
    silver **2** 654
    stained glass **13** 192
  Museo de los Caminos **20** 581
Astorga, Marchese d' **4** 400
Astori, Prudenza **24** 894
Astorri, Pier Enrico **9** 159
Astous, Roger D' *see* D'ASTOUS, ROGER
astragal mouldings *see under* MOULDINGS → types
Astrakhan' **18** 543
Astrapas **2** 646*; **9** 585; **28** 446
  attributions **13** 265
  works **23** 373, 374; **25** 639; **28** 448; **29** 551
Astrapas, John **30** 719
Astrapas, Michael **30** 718
Astretsi **8** 154
astrolabes **2** 646–8*, *647*, *648*; **16** 369, 386; **23** 339; **28** 203, 209, *210*; **30** 26
astrological manuscripts **2** 648–51*, *649*, *650*; **22** 412
astrology **2** 648; **14** 560; **16** 138; **21** 207; **22** 411–12
  see also ASTRONOMY
Åström, Paul **14** 64
astronomical instruments **25** 139
astronomical manuscripts **2** 648*; **26** 661
astronomy **24** 669; **28** 209–10
  Carolingian **5** 800, 801
  Egypt, ancient **9** 805*
  Maya **21** 215–16; **31** 778
  Mesoamerica, Pre-Columbian **31** 778
  see also ASTROLOGY
Astronomy and Geography Clock **11** 627
Astroŭski, Ja. **3** 530
Astruc, Jules(-Godefroy) **2** 651*
Astruc, Zacharie **2** 651–2*; **17** 440
Astrup, Nikolai **23** 227
Åstrup farmhouse **32** *285*
Astudillo, S Clara **13** 123; **29** 311
Asturias (Spain)
  architecture **2** *652*, 652–3*, *653*
  churches **29** 261
  jet **17** 514
  wall paintings **29** 275
Asturias (House of) **2** 653–4*
Asturias, Princess of **5** 380
Asturias, Alfonso II, King of *see* ALFONSO II, King of Asturias
Asturias, Alfonso III, King of *see* ALFONSO III, King of Asturias
Asturias, Carlos, Prince of *see* CHARLES IV, King of Spain
Asturias, Fruela I, King of *see* FRUELA I, King of Asturias
Asturias, Fruela II, King of *see* FRUELA II, King of Asturias
Asturias, Nunilo, Queen of *see* NUNILO, Queen of Asturias
Asturias, Ramiro I, King of *see* RAMIRO I, King of Asturias
Asturias, Urraca, Doña *see* URRACA, Doña
Astyll, Richard *see* ATSYLL, RICHARD
Astypalaia **18** 394
Asucha, Ignacio García de *see* GARCÍA DE ASUCHA, IGNACIO
Asuka **2** 655; **17** 21
  Ishibutai tomb **16** 82–3*; **17** *11*, 59
  Misemaruyama tomb **17** 57, 59
  Takamatsuzuka tomb **10** 776; **17** *11*, 139; **30** 257*; **32** 804
  tomb of Emperor Temmu and Empress Jitō **17** 58
Asukabe Tsunenori **17** 155
Asukadera **6** 667; **17** 65, 67, 107
  Daibutsu (Great Buddha) **17** 107
  Daibutsuden (Great Buddha Hall) **17** 323
Asuka-Hakuhō period *see under* JAPAN → periods
Asuka period *see under* JAPAN → periods
asunaro **17** 356
Asunción **24** *91*
  academies and art schools
    Centro de Estudios Brasileros Taller de Arte Moderno **24** 102
    Escolinha de Arte **24** 102
    Escuela de Bellas Artes **24** 102
    Instituto de Arte **24** 102
    Instituto para el Desarrollo Armónico de la Personalidad Taller de Expresión Infantil **24** 102
    Instituto Paraguayo **24** 102
  Aduana (Customs House) **24** 95
  architecture **24** 96–7
  Asociación Nacional Republicana headquarters **24** 96
  Biblioteca Americana y Museo de Bellas Artes *see* museums → Museo Nacional de Bellas Artes
  churches
    Cathedral **24** 93, 95
    La Encarnación **24** 96
    La Compañía **24** 95
    Oratorio de Nuestra Señora de la Asunción *see* Panteón Nacional de los Héroes
    La Santísima Trinidad **24** 95
  Club Nacional **24** 95
  commercial buildings
    Banco Central de Paraguay **24** 96
    Cervecería Paraguaya **24** 96
    Fotográfico Fratta **24** 96
    Lido Bar **24** 96
    Marsal Hermanos building **24** 96
    Parafina building **24** 96
    Urrutia Ugarte building **24** 96
  Fundación Manzana de la Rivera **24** 102
  government buildings
    Ministry of Health building **24** 96
    Ministry of Public Works **24** 96
    Ministry of the Interior **24** 95
    Palacio de Congreso *see* Ministry of the Interior
    Social Security building **24** 96
  Hotel Ambassador **24** 96
  Hotel Guaraní **24** 96
  Hotel Hispania **24** 96
  houses
    Benigno Lopéz house **24** 96
    Casa Loma Cabará **24** 96
    Casa Masi *see* hotels → Hotel Hispania
    Casa Mulder **24** 96
    Casa Paco **24** 96
    Casa Pedro Duarte **24** 96
    Las Escalinatas **24** 96
    Venancio López house **24** 96
    Villa Vargas **24** 96
Asunción—cont.
  museums
    Centro de Artes Visuales **24** 101
    Museo de Arte Indígena **24** 101
    Museo del Barro **24** 101
    Museo de Cerámica y Bellas Artes Julián de la Herrería **24** 101
    Museo Etnográfico Andrés Barbero **24** 101
    Museo Etnográfico y de Historia Natural *see* Museo Etnográfico Andrés Barbero
    Museo Monseñor Juan Sinforiano Bogarín **24** 101
    Museo Nacional de Bellas Artes **24** 101
    Museo Paraguayo de Arte Contemporáneo **24** 101, 102
    Museo del Tesoro de la Catedral **24** 101
  Palacio de Gobierno **24** 95
  Panteón Nacional de los Héroes **24** 95, *96*
  railway station **24** 95–6
  Seminario Metropolitano **24** 96
  Teatro de la Opera **24** 95
  Terrazas de Villa Marra **24** 97
  Town Hall **24** 95
  Universidad Nacional de Asunción **24** 96
Asunción, Jose Maria **24** 622
Asunción, Justiniano **20** 274; **24** 621, 622
Asuncion, Leoncio **24** 619
Asunción, Mariano **24** 622
Asúnsolo, Ignacio **2** 655*; **21** 389
  pupils **23** 392, 583
  works **21** 389
Asuza, Kita **19** 320
Aswad **30** 196
Aswan **2** 655–7*; **7** *819*; **9** 773, *774*, 850; **16** *104*; **23** *276*; **26** *876*, *921*
  architecture **9** 765; **16** 172
  Aswan Museum **2** 657
  church **23** 287
  dams **10** 81, 83; **23** 277
  Deir Anba Sama'an *see* Monastery of St Simeon
  Elephantine **9** *774*
  figurines **10** 47
  fortifications **21** 554
  granite **9** 813, 815; **20** 570; **25** 761, 762; **26** 876; **27** 14
  High Dam **1** 320
  houses **9** 852
  mausolea **16** 175, 176
  muqarnas (architecture) **22** 322
  Nilometer sacred lake **27** 496
  obelisks **9** 813, 815
  pottery **27** 104, *104*
  quartzite **30** 694
  reliefs **3** 523
  sculpture **9** 854
  shrine complex of Heqaib **2** 657; **9** 795; **10** 77, *77*
    sculpture **9** *876*
  statue of Inyotef II **9** 873
  statue of Mentuhotpe-aa **9** 873
  Temple of Satis **9** 828, 829
  tombs **9** 838, 899; **31** 112, *113*
    Harkhuf (A8) **2** 656
    Heqaib (A9) **2** 656
    Sabni **2** 656
    Sabni and Mekhu (A1) **2** 656; **9** 838
    Sarenput II (A3) **2** 657; **9** 838
    Sebekhotpe (12th Dynasty) **2** *656*, 657
  town walls **9** 844
  wall paintings **9** 811
  see also PHILAE
asylums **2** 657–9*, *658*
asymmetrical knots *see under* KNOTS
asymmetry **22** 562
Asyut **2** 659*; **9** *774*; **10** 77
  alabaster (limestone) **9** 813
Asyut—cont.
  dress **10** 45
  sculpture **2** *659*; **9** 873
  textiles **16** 431
  tomb chapel of Khety II **9** 874
  tomb of Hepdjefa **2** 659
  tomb of Mesehti **10** 16, *40*
  tombs **9** 779
'Ata Allah **15** 373
  works **15** *373*
Atabey, Ertokuş Madrasa **16** 184
Atacameño **29** 186–9, *187*, *188*, *189*
Atafu **31** 75
Atai **10** 486
Ataíde, Manoel da Costa **2** 659–60*; **4** 708, 725
  patrons and collectors **4** 727
  works **4** 716, *716*; **23** 669
Atami, MOA Museum of Art **6** 826; **7** 154; **15** 746; **17** 433
Atan (family) **9** 676
Atan, Carlos Huki *see* HUKI ATAN, CARLOS
Atan, Joel Huki *see* HUKI ATAN, JOEL
Atan, Pedro Huki *see* HUKI ATAN, PEDRO
Atanacković, Milenko **4** 461
Atanasio Primario **22** 484
Atar, Chaim **16** 571
Atarco style pottery *see under* POTTERY → wares
Atasoy, Nurhan **16** 550
Atatürk, Kemal **33** 723
Atax, Varro of *see* VARRO OF ATAX
ATBAT **2** 660*; **4** 214; **5** 609; **11** 527
  staff **5** 609; **7** 295
ATBAT-Afrique **2** 660
Atchana, Tell **1** 815, *821*, 839, *849*; **2** 660–61*; **15** 32; **30** *180*, 185
  architecture **1** 830; **30** 192
  excavations **33** 373
  fortifications **21** 553
  frescoes **30** 197
  glass **1** 865
  gold **1** 874
  orthostats **30** 186
  palace (level IV) **30** 186
  palace of Yarim-Lim **30** 185, 197; **32** 802
  palaces **1** 893; **21** 730
  pottery **30** 197, *197*
  sculpture **2** *661*; **30** 193
  seals **1** 862, *862*
Atchin Island **31** 891
Atchison, John **32** 861
Ateca, S María **22** 255
Ategua **25** 529
Ateius **27** 107
Atel Church **13** 189; **26** 718
Atelier **24** 436
Atelier, Experimental *see* EXAT-51
Atelier 17 **20** 604, 605; **25** 628
  drypoints **9** 310
  engravings **10** 397
  etchings **10** 560, 563
  printmakers **9** 204; **13** 891; **18** 805; **23** 12; **26** 68; **30** 730; **32** 423
Atelier 5 **2** 661–2*; **5** 56; **30** 128
Atelier 66 **2** 175
Atelier ASP **29** 52
Atelier Borgila **30** 108
Atelier Borsani **16** 731
Atelier d'Art Abstrait **8** 838
Atelier de Haute-Claire **25** 78
Atelier de la Trinité **11** 639
Atelier de Montrouge **20** 862; **26** 192
Atelier des Bâtisseurs *see* ATBAT
Atelier Desjobert **20** 603, 604
Atelier Français **2** 520; **11** 583, 601; **29** 899
Atelier Gaii **30** 392
Atelier Garuda **30** 392
Atelier Grenoblois de Tapisserie de Haute Lisse **11** 160
Atelier Group **22** 431
Atelier H **12** 822
Atelier Hoenkan **30** 392
Atelier Iruka **30** 392
Atelier Lyle **19** 842
Atelier Maîtrise **11** 583
Atelier Martine **2** 520; **11** 582, 601; **25** 78; **32** 817
Atelier Mobile **30** 392
Atelier Mourlot **20** 608
Atelier Pomone **11** 241, 601
Atelier Populaire **22** 333; **25** 354; **28** 300
Atelier Primavera, L' **11** 601
Atelier Redon *see under* PARIS
ateliers **1** 106–7; **21** 759; **32** 81
  see also STUDIOS
Ateliers d'Art Sacré **8** 715, 818
Ateliers du Marais **1** 598; **5** 45
Atelier Simultané **8** 658
Ateliers Modernes, Les **11** 601; **17** 668
Atelier U **33** 563
Atelier voor Architectuur, Kunstnijverheid en Versieringskunst **18** 878; **22** 874
Atelier Zo **30** 392*
Ateneo, El **2** 404
Ateneo Puertorriqueño **25** 703, 704
Ateni **2** 662*; **9** *512*; **12** *317*
  Cathedral of Sioni **2** 662*; **7** 256; **12** 319, 323, *323*
Ater Fort **15** 373
Atero, Miguel María **6** 592
'Atf (Hafsid) **14** 27; **16** 219; **31** 423
Atger, Xavier **22** 35
Atget, (Jean-)Eugène (-Auguste) **1** 23; **2** 662–3*; **24** 671
  patrons and collectors **1** 23
  works **2** *663*; **24** 675; **31** 157
Ath **3** 584, 598, 603, 606
  Chapel of Notre-Dame-de-Loreto **13** 113
Athaide, Manoel da Costa *see* ATAÍDE, MANOEL DA COSTA
Athanasi, Giovanni D' *see* D'ATHANASI, GIOVANNI
Athanasios, Abbot of Mt Athos **7** 229
Athanasios, Saint (*c.* 915-1002) **21** 344; **22** 225; **24** 23
Athanasius, Saint (*c.* 296-373) **18** 686
Athanasius the Librarian **6** 173
Athanodorus **13** 464
Athapaskan **22** 546, 668
Athapaskan (Slave) **22** 645
Athelney Abbey (Somerset) **2** 64
Athelstan, King of England (*reg* 925-39) **33** 90*
  architecture **10** 359
  embroidery **2** 74, 83
  manuscripts **2** 74
Athelstan Psalter *see under* PSALTERS → individual manuscripts
Athenaeus **13** 570
Athenaeus Mechanicus **21** 577
Athenagoras **13** 549; **18** 108
Athena of Arezzo **10** 588
Athena Painter **13** 511; **32** 32*
Athena Parthenos see under ATHENS → Acropolis → Parthenon
Athena Promachos see under ATHENS → Acropolis
Athena Velletri **13** 454
Athenion **2** 664*
Athenis **2** 308; **5** 185
Athenodoros **14** 33–4*; **29** 389
  attributions **13** 468
  collaboration **18** 756; **25** 45
  works **26** 292; **27** *8*

Athens **2** 664–89*, *668*, *669*, *671*; **9** *511*, *512*; **13** *362*, *363*, 369; **14** *332*; **26** *908*
academies
Academy of Athens **13** 886; **23** 508
Academy of Plato **10** 670; **13** 419
Hellenic Academy **13** 348, 359, 612
Acropolis **2** *664*, 665, 674–8*, *675*; **13** 368, 374, *375*, 393, 416, 419, 603; **18** 124; **27** 713
Acropolis Museum *see under* museums
Athena Promachos **13** 570, 573; **22** 42
bronze **13** 435
cauldrons **13** 575
Erechtheion **2** 677–8, *678*; **9** 151; **13** 379, 390, 392, *392*, 393, 394, 395, 400, 410, 415, 417, 418, 427, 430, 438, 439, 440, 470; **23** 481, 533; **30** 434, 435; **31** 269
anthemia **2** 134
Athena Polais **30** 434
caryatids **5** 904; **10** 741
coffering **7** 526
consoles **7** 746
friezes **13** 457; **23** 889
glass **13** 594
heroa **14** 467
mouldings **3** 439; **8** 324; **9** *757*
Porch of the Maidens **5** *904*
sculpture **2** 680–81
hestiatoria **13** 417
monopteros **21** 892
Odeion of Herodes Atticus **2** 670; **23** 350
Odeion of Pericles **13** 386, 407; **23** 349; **27** 712
Old Propylon **25** 657
Old Temple of Athena Polias **2** *678*; **13** 379, 400, 414, 448, 470
Parthenon **2** 670–71, *672*, 676, *676*, *677*; **7** 502; **8** *370*; **13** 369, 374, 379, 387, 393, 394, 395, *400*, 410, 411, 415, 417, 439; **15** 132; **23** 481, 484, 533; **24** 456; **27** 712, 713; **29** 702; **30** 405, 434, 435; **31** 269
acroteria **1** 128
architectural refinements **13** 414, 415
Athena Parthenos **2** 682; **8** 262; **9** 20; **13** 374, 435, 453, 456, 464, 596; **22** 42; **24** 593–4; **25** 576; **30** 435
doors **13** 391
Elgin Marbles *see* ELGIN MARBLES
entablatures **13** 392
entasis **10** 415
friezes **11** 791, *791*; **13** 370, 391, 426, 432, 436; **30** 775
gems **12** 247
metopes **21** 348
mosque of the Parthenon **2** *672*
pediment **13** 391, 400; **24** 317, 318
polychromy **25** 11
proportions **2** 351
refinements **13** 413
reliefs **13** 425, *425*, 431, 432; **26** 132
roof **30** 903
sculpture **2** 679–80; **5** 876; **13** 436, *455*, 455–6, 469, 592; **21** 768; **22** 411
staircase **29** 520
pediments **13** 425; **24** 318
pottery **13** 539; **32** 53
Athens
Acropolis—cont.
Propylaia **2** 677; **13** 391, 394, 415, 417, 554; **21** 744; **23** 481; **25** 177, 657
architectural refinements **13** 414
coffering **7** 526
entasis **10** 415
Pinacoteca **10** 675
restoration **2** 323
Sanctuary of Athena **13** 416, 417
sculpture **2** 678–82*, *679*; **13** 433, 445, 446, *446*, 447–8, 449, 454, 468, 484, 518; **29** 396
architectural **2** 679–81
bronze **13** 441, 442
korai **13** 429; **18** *244*, 245; **22** 700
relief **13** 428, *428*, 431
shrine **13** 418
Temple of Athena Nike **2** 678; **13** 394, 418, 432, 456, 457, 470; **23** 481, *482*; **27** 713
acroteria **1** 127
frieze **13** 426
Nike Balustrade **13** 457
pediment **24** 319
sculpture **2** 680, *680*
trophy **31** 369
Temple of Athena Parthenos *see* Parthenon
Theatre of Dionysos **2** 666; **13** 385, 403, 406, 592; **27** 712; **30** 650
tripods **10** 591
wall **21** 556
Agora **2** 665, 668, *668*, 683–5*, *683*, *684*; **13** 381, 419; **26** 909
Agora Museum *see under* museums
basilica **26** 910
bronze **4** 851
Enneakrounos **11** 339; **13** 382
gardens **12** 68
gymnasium **6** 76
ivory-carvings **14** 354
Law Courts **13** 394
library **19** 312
metalwork **21** 322
monopteros **21** *893*, 893
New Bouleuterion **2** 684; **4** 530; **13** 381, 407
Odeion of Agrippa **23** 350, *350*; **26** 910
Old Bouleuterion **2** 684; **4** 530; **13** 381
Painted Stoa **13** 393, 394, 402; **25** 176, 177; **29** 681
paintings **13** 545, 548; **22** 514; **23** 901
Palace of the Giants **9** 558
Prytanikon **25** 675
Sanctuary of Apollo **13** 548
sculpture **2** 685–6*, *686*
South-east fountain house **13** 382
South Stoa I **29** 681
South-west fountain house **13** 382
Stoa Basileios **13** 402, *402*, 432; **29** 681
acroteria **1** 128
Stoa of Attalos **2** 685; **13** 416; **20** 438; **23** 483; **29** *681*
Stoa of the Herms **29** 681
Stoa of Zeus **29** 681
paintings **13** 545, 548, 551
Stoa Poikile *see* Painted Stoa
Temple of Ares **1** 128; **24** 319; **26** 911
Temple of Hephaistos **2** 683–4; **13** *377*, 379, 388, 393, 394, 414, 418, *418*, 419, 432, 456, 603; **23** 481; **31** 269, *269*
entasis **10** 415
gardens **12** 68
Museum **2** 673
Athens
Agora
Temple of Hephaistos—cont.
pediment **24** 317, 319
roof **30** *902*
theatre **30** 650
Tholos **13** 390, 411; **27** 235; **30** 736
water-clock **13** 382
aqueducts **11** 339; **26** 910
Arch of Hadrian **2** 670; **26** 909; **31** 350
Areopagos **13** 383
arsenal **13** 381
art forms and materials
architecture **13** 349; **26** 908
armour **14** 356
bronzes **13** 571, 572
candelabra **5** 604
coins **13** 585, *585*, 586, 587, 588, 589
figurines **13** 578, 579, 580, 581; **14** *352*
glass **27** 78
houses **9** 561
ivory-carvings **13** 595; **27** 100
jewellery **13** 597
lamps **13** 602, *603*; **27** 104, *104*
marble **2** 665
metalwork **13** 568, 570
mosaics **9** 565; **13** 557, 559, 563, 565
painting **13** 546
vase **13** 583
pottery **8** 312; **9** 634; **13** 368, 476, 482, 484, 487, 498, 500–501, 505, 507, 535, 536, 539; **27** 108
protomes **13** 582
sculpture **13** 440, 447, 450, 455, 462, *462*, 464, 466, 598; **14** 352, 456; **24** 328; **26** 854; **27** 18
chryselephantine statues **13** 435
copies **2** 557
monumental **13** 459
relief **13** 427, 428, 582
silver **2** 665, 666; **13** 538
spolia **2** 671
stelae **13** 427; **29** *616*
swords **2** 451
terracottas **27** 111
vases **32** 33
water pipes **13** 419
well-heads **33** 56
baths **26** 910
burial chambers **13** 384, *384*
cemeteries **13** 445
Dipylon cemetery **13** 494
First Cemetery **13** 354
tomb of Michael Tositsas **13** 354
Kerameikos cemetery **2** 686–7*, *686*; **13** 368, 384, 485, 491, 493; **31** 108; **32** 38, 47
amphorae **13** *492*
sculpture **2** 687–8*; **13** 470
textiles **7** 51
tomb of Hermon **13** 546
Choregic Monument of Lysikrates **2** 666; **9** 85; **13** 401, 407, *609*; **23** 482, 534; **30** 737
frieze **13** 426
competitions **7** 664
Cynosarges **13** 886
Difros complex **13** 351
Dipylon (Gate) **6** 170; **7** 358; **13** 442
Doxiadis Associates headquarters **9** *207*
Doxiadis Centre of Ekistics **13** 361
ecclesiastical buildings **2** 670–72
Cathedral of Hagios Dionysios **13** 349
Hagioi Apostoloi **2** 688–9*; **7** 256
Hagioi Theodoroi **20** 571
Athens
ecclesiastical buildings—cont.
Omorphi Ekklisia **9** 584
Panagia Gorgoepikoös **2** 689*; **9** 593
frieze **2** 648; **5** 427
Panagia Lykodimou **9** 547
Petraki Monastery **25** 336
St Eleutherios *see* Panagia Gorgoepikoos
St John Mangoutis **9** 593
Small Metropolis *see* Panagia Gorgoepikoös
Ermoglypheion **13** 354
Eye Clinic **13** 349
First Cemetery *see under* cemeteries
fortifications **14** 340; **21** 557
see also Long Walls; walls
gymnasia **13** 386, 419
Hekatompedon **21** 46
Hellenic Literary and Historical Archives Society **13** 361
heroön of Harmodios and Aristogeiton **14** 466
heroön of Theseus **14** 466
Higher School of Fine Arts **13** 352, 354, 360
Horologion of Andronikos of Kyrrhos *see* Tower of the Winds
Hôtel Grande Bretagne **13** 348
houses **9** 560; **13** 383
Dimitriou House *see* Hôtel Grande Bretagne
Hatzimihali House **13** 349
Skouzes House **13** 349
Valsamakis house **31** 853
Wertheim House **13** 349
Ilissia *see* museums → Byzantine Museum
Kallirhoe **13** 490
Kallithea **13** 384
Kerameikos cemetery *see under* cemeteries
Kolonus Hippios **13** 419
Kynosarges **10** 670
A. G. Leventis Collection **13** 359
libraries
central library **13** 348, 359, 361, 612
Gennadius Library **13** 361
Library of Hadrian **19** 312; **26** 883, *909*
Metroon *see* Agora → Old Bouleuterion **2** 669
Long Walls **21** 556
see also fortifications; walls
Lykeion **10** 670; **13** 886
Market of Caesar and Augustus **26** 909, 910
measurements **13** 411
Metroon *see* Agora → Old Bouleuterion
museums **13** 360*
Acropolis Museum **13** 360, 469, 470, 606
Agora Museum **14** 361; **27** 46
Benaki Museum
archives **2** 370
collections **3** 699; **10** 90, 649; **13** 359, 360; **16** 556
library **13** 361
Byzantine Museum **13** 349, 360; **29** 87
Goulandris Museum of Cycladic and Ancient Greek Art **8** 323; **13** 359
Gounaropoulos Museum **13** 228
Jewish Museum **17** 582
Museum of Greek Folklore **13** 360
National Archaeological Museum
collections **8** 323, 712; **10** 435; **13** 360, 555, 606; **14** 360–61; **17** 733; **31** 355, 356
Greek collection **13** 470
sculpture **27** 46
Athens
museums
National Archaeological Museum—cont.
Stathatou collection **32** 33
National Gallery and Alexandros Soutzos Museum **13** 353, 359, 360, 361
National Historical Museum **13** 360
Tsarouhis Museum **31** 396
National Capodistrian University **13** 348, 359, 612
National Technical University **13** 349
Department of Architecture **13** 360
observatory **23** 340
Odeion of Herodes Atticus *see under* Acropolis
Odeion of Pericles *see under* Acropolis
Old Propylon *see under* Acropolis
Panathenaic Stadium **2** 667; **29** 488
Parliament Building *see* Royal Palace
Pefkakia school building **13** 349
Pnyx **2** 667; **29** 488
Pompeion **2** 687; **13** 547
Propylon (Old) *see* Acropolis → Old Propylon
Royal Palace **2** *674*; **12** 168; **13** 348, 359, 612
Sanctuary of the Dioscuri **25** 177
School of Fine Arts *see* Higher School of Fine Arts
stadia **29** 489
stelae **1** *111*
stoas **13** 406
Stoa of Eumenes **2** 667
Stoa of the Asklepieion **23** 483
see also under Agora
temples **13** 374
Hephaisteion *see* Agora → Temple of Hephaistos
Temple of Olympian Zeus **2** 688*, *688*; **8** 3; **13** 373, 380, 405; **23** 482; **26** 911; **28** 384
cult statues **8** 263
entasis **10** 415
sculpture **27** 14
Temple of Rome and Augustus **26** 911
see also under Acropolis; Agora
Theatre of Dionysos *see under* Acropolis
Theseion **33** 700
Tholos *see under* Agora
tomb of Antiochos Philopappos **2** 668–9
tombs **2** 687; **13** 566
Tower of the Winds **2** 26, *667*, 668; **13** 382, 391; **33** 8
trade
pottery **13** 525; **28** 654
urban planning **13** 419; **14** 564; **27** 3
Vakalo School **13** 361
walls **2** 670, 686–7; **21** 556; **30** 903
see also fortifications; Long Walls
Xanthou 21 **13** *350*
Zappeion **13** 359
Athens, Diodorus of *see* DIODORUS OF ATHENS
Athens 1472, Painter of **17** 911
Athens 894, Painter of **32** 32–3*
Athens Charter *see* CIAM
Atherington (Devon), St Mary **28** 293
screens (i) (architectural) **28** *293*
Atherton, James **8** 287
Athey, Clement Kofi **5** 731
Athfield, Ian (Charles) **2** 689*; **23** 56; **33** 58
Athias, Joseph **4** 18
Athinai *see* ATHENS

Athlan, Gräfin **20** 494
'Athlith, Château Pèlerin **17** 505; **18** 153
Athlone (Co. Westmeath) **15** 872
Atholl, James Murray, 2nd Duke of *see* MURRAY, JAMES, 2nd Duke of Atholl
Atholl, John Murray, 4th Duke of *see* MURRAY, JOHN, 4th Duke of Atholl
Athos, Mount *see* MT ATHOS
Athribis **2** 689–90*; **9** *774*; **29** 14; **30** 237
tomb of Pefteuawiamun Tjaiemhorimu **2** 690
tomb of Tadubaste **2** 690
Atienza **2** 462
ATIKA **8** 403
Atık Sinan **16** 604
Atıl, Esin **16** 549
Atiles y Pérez, Ramón **25** 701
Atiquipa, Mateo **24** 514
Atisha **30** 736, 824
Atiu **7** 790
Atkins, Anna **2** 690*; **24** 650, 654
Atkins, John **27** 244
Atkins, Roy *see* ROY, NAMBA
Atkinson, Ethel **2** 760
Atkinson, Fello **8** 248
Atkinson, Frank **8** 770
Atkinson, Isaac *see* ANDERSON, JAMES
Atkinson, John **23** 786
Atkinson, John Augustus **2** 690*
Atkinson, Kevin **29** 109, 110
Atkinson, Lawrence **2** 691*; **32** 701
Atkinson, Peter **5** 847
Atkinson, R. Frank **2** 691
Atkinson, Robert **2** 691*
collaboration **11** 808; **33** 382
staff **26** 99
works **10** 371; **25** 403
Atkinson, Robin **18** 639
Atkinson, Sarah **16** 38
Atkinson, Terry **2** 512; **7** 685; **21** 892
Atkinson, Thomas **7** 758
Atkinson, Thomas Lewis **2** 692*
Atkinson, William **2** 692*
collaboration **14** 745; **32** 554
groups and movements **28** 288
patrons and collectors **28** 287
pupils **8** 105
works **4** 170; **28** *286*
writings **4** 788
Atkyns, Robert **4** 80; **18** 73
Atl, Dr **2** 692–3*; **21** 387, 405; **23** 565
al-Atlāl **16** 550
Atlan, Jean-Michel **2** 693*; **11** 551
dealers **26** 193
groups and movements **2** 543, 544; **7** 489
works **19** 491; **20** 75
Atlanersa **23** 282
Atlanta (GA) **2** 693–4*; **31** *587*
artificial stone **30** 505
Emory University Museum of Art and Archaeology **2** 694
High Museum of Art **2** 694, *694*; **21** 56; **22** 367; **23** 177; **31** 598
Hyatt Regency Hotel **14** 788
Marriott Marquis Hotel **12** 794; **14** 788, *788*
Peachtree Center **25** 657
terracotta **30** 505
Atlantic Bank (Belize City) **3** 624
Atlantic City (NJ), Blenheim Hotel **14** 787
Atlantic Codex *see under* CODICES → individual manuscripts
Atlantic Richfield Company **3** 423
Atlantic Wall **21** 548
Atlántida Church **31** 754
atlantids **2** 695*, *695*; **8** *385*; **10** *426*; **13** 415; **23** 477
see also CARYATIDS
Atlas **24** 451
atlases **2** 695–6*; **4** 360; **20** 364
historical and regional traditions
Belgium **23** 579
Brazil **30** 417
Germany **2** *695*
Netherlands, the **2** 696
types
portolan **2** 696
see also CARTOGRAPHY; MAPS; TOPOGRAPHY
Atlas of Prince Eugene of Savoy *see* ATLAS VAN DER HEM
Atlas van der Hem **9** *149*, 150; **10** 514; **14** 375; **27** 518
atlatls **21** 245, 246
Atlingbo **26** 639
'Atlit **9** 634
Atlixco **25** 57
Atmos clocks *see under* CLOCKS → types
atmospheric perspective *see* PERSPECTIVE → types → aerial
'Atn Allah **2** 729
atomic absorption spectrometry (AAS) *see under* TECHNICAL EXAMINATION → types
Atoni **15** 775
Atoyan, Rafayel **2** 433
Atrani
S Salvatore **9** 154
S Sebastiano **9** 154
Atri
Cathedral of S Maria Assunta **13** 124
Museo dell'Opera del Duomo **16** 774
Atri, Andrea Matteo III Aquaviva d'Aragona, Duca d' **1** 127*; **20** 144; **24** 840; **26** 2
atria (i) (Roman) **2** 696*
see also COURTYARDS *and under* HOUSES → types
atria (ii) (churches) **2** 696*
atria (iii) (public buildings) **2** 696*; **12** 794; **14** 788, *788*
ATRIA (Ahmadabad Textiles Industries Research Association) **17** 803
Atria, Jean-Baptiste **2** 704
Atrib, Tell *see* ATHRIBIS
atrophied free cross churches *see under* CHURCHES → types
Atrosokes **1** 188
Atsalyan, Ruben **2** 433
Atsız Elti **17** 864
Atskuri Triptych **12** 329
Atsugewi **22** 549, 641, 659
Atsuko, Empress **17** 157
Atsuko Tanaka *see* TANAKA, ATSUKO
Atsumi **17** *241*, 260, 351; **33** 487
Atsumi ware *see under* POTTERY → wares
Atsyll, Richard **12** 260
Attaingnant, Pierre **22** 369
Attaleia *see* ANTALYA
Attalid **24** 414
Attalos I, King of Pergamon (*reg* 241-197 BC) **1** 498; **8** 694; **13** 469, 555; **24** 414
Attalos II, King of Pergamon (*reg* 160-37 BC) **2** 413, 667, 682, 685; **13** 406; **29** 681
Attanagalla **29** 450
'Attar **16** 287
At-Tar Caves **1** 881; **5** 833
Attardi, Ugo **9** 168; **11** 314; **26** 777
Attarge, Désiré **11** 622
Attavanti, Attavante (Vante di Gabriello di Vante Attavanti) **2** 697–8*
attributions **20** 689
collaboration **4** 197; **11** 687
works **2** *697*; **20** 847
Atteck, Sybil **31** 335, 340
works **31** *337*
Attems, Ernest **28** 863
Attems, Ignaz Maria, Graf **11** 230; **26** 151
Attemstätter, David **8** 413
Attenborough, David
works **31** *892*
Atterbom, Per Daniel Amadeus **30** 119
Atterbury, Grosvenor **2** 698*; **26** 18
Atterdag, Valdemar, King of Denmark *see* VALDEMAR IV, King of Denmark
Attersee, Christian Ludwig **2** 698*; **32** 447
Attersee, Haus Gamerith **2** 789
Attert **3** 590
Atti, Isotta degli **24** 247; **26** 398
Attic mouldings *see under* MOULDINGS → types
attics (i) (architectural order) **2** 698*; **26** 923
attics (ii) (house storey) **2** 698*
Atticus, Herodes *see* HERODES ATTICUS
Atticus Petricus Marsus, M. **27** 88
Atticus Priscus **27** 52
Attie **1** 392, 503
Attigiati **27** 757
Attigny, Hôtel de Ville **2** 642
Attingham Park (Salop) **2** 164; **9** 17; **14** 539; **23** 789
paintings **4** 154
Attirala, Agastyeshvara Temple **15** 537
Attiret, Claude-François **2** 698–9*
Attiret, Jean-Denis **2** 699; **6** 41, 539, 818; **7** 84, 87; **14** 366
Attitudes International **24** 442
Attock **15** 409
fort **15** 362
Attolini Lack, Antonio **21** 381, 382
Attree, Thomas **3** 281
attributions **2** 560; **6** 76, 81; **11** 306; **22** 102; **30** 382
Greece, ancient **32** 26–7*
Attu **22** 655
Attwell, Mabel Lucie **10** 314
works **10** *314*
Atwater Kent Museum *see under* PHILADELPHIA (PA) → museums
Atwood, Charles B(owler) **2** 699*; **5** 274
assistants **25** 152
groups and movements **6** 578
works **5** 274; **8** 278
Atwood, Thomas Warr **3** 370
Atye, Bartholomew **16** 892
Atyeo, Sam **2** 756
Atzcoalco, Church of Santiago **21** 374
A(telier d')U(rbanisme et d')A(rchitecture) **2** 699–700*; **6** 534; **7** 343
Aua (Papua New Guinea) **24** 82
Aub, Mariae Himmelfahrt **8** 215
Aubazine Church **11** 585
Aube, Sainte-Savine **11** 154, 155
Aubé, Jean-Paul **2** 700*
Aubeaux, Pierre des **1** 766; **27** 247, 251
Au bei Aibling, St Martin **32** 822
Aubenas, Pierre d' *see* PIERRE DE PAIX
Auberjonois, René **2** 700–701*; **18** 874; **30** 134
Aubersque, Henri d' *see* HENRI D'AUBERSQUE
Aubert (France) **29** 702
Aubert (*fl* 1830) **8** 545; **24** 605
Aubert, Bishop of Avranches **22** 39
Aubert, Andreas **11** 783; **22** 540
Aubert, Augustin **20** 473; **24** 58; **26** 315
Aubert, David **4** 921; **8** 208; **17** 455; **19** 251, 350; **20** 452
Aubert, Félix **6** 489; **25** 52; **28** 525
Aubert, Georges **27** 240
Aubert, Jean **2** 701*
restorations by others **12** 728
Aubert, Jean—cont.
works **6** 453, 509; **14** 789; **18** 815; **24** 120; **26** 493; **29** *485*, 486
Aubert, Jehan **3** 604; **13** 171
Aubert, Louis-François **11** 632
Aubert, Marcel **1** 154; **2** 701–2*
Aubert, Michel **4** 514
Aubertin, Granel and Mathon **1** 125
Aubervilliers *Madonna*, d' **1** 456
Aubespine-Villeroy, L' (family) **7** 464
Aubigné, Françoise d', Marquise de Maintenon *see* MAINTENON, FRANÇOISE D'AUBIGNÉ, Marquise de
Aubigny, d' (*d c.* 1747) **19** 205
Aubigny, d' (19th cent.) *see* DAUBIGNY
Aubin **11** 623
Aubin, William **8** 240
Aubin Manuscript 20 *see under* CODICES → individual manuscripts
Auböck, Carl **25** 864
Aubrey, John **10** 376, *757*; **12** 127; **21** 40; **29** 717
Aubry, Charles(-Hippolyte) **2** 702*
Aubry, Etienne **2** 702*; **18** 858; **28** 754
Aubry, Jean **4** 242
Aubry, Louis-François **8** 538
Aubry, Peter, II **29** 644; **30** 793
Aubry de Humbert **26** 114
Aubry-Lecomte, Hyacinthe (-Louis-Victor-Jean-Baptiste) **2** 702*; **12** 732; **26** 232
Auburndale **7** 448
Auburtin, Léon-Marcel **24** 129; **31** 575
Aubusson **2** 702–5*; **11** *505*
carpets **2** 704–5*; **11** 652
Sainte-Croix **26** 641
tapestries **2** 703–4*
Aubusson, François de la Feuillade, Duc de Roannez, Duc d' **13** 224
Aubusson Looms *see* HERTER LOOMS
Aubusson tapestry factory **5** 839; **11** 640, 642; **12** 830; **20** 133; **30** 322, 326, 327
carpets **11** *651*, 652
designers **11** 644; **30** 328, 329
Adam, Henri-Georges **1** 142
Alix, Yves **1** 645
Bezombes, Roger **3** 902
Casanova, Francesco **5** 908
Dufresne, Charles (Georges) **9** 371
Linnqvist, Hilding **19** 428
Lurçat, Jean **11** 644; **19** 808; **30** 329
Mercier, Pierre **12** 468
Singier, Gustave **28** 777
Staël, Nicolas de **29** 494
Sutherland, Graham (Vivian) **30** 329
looms **31** 659
production **2** *703*, 704; **5** 837; **11** 643; **30** 323, IV1
Aucaner **30** 13
Auch, Cathedral of Ste Marie **13** 211
Auchentaller, J. M. **28** 344
Auchi **23** *129*, 137
Auchiah, James **22** 595
Auchincloss, Louis **23** 32
Auchinleck manuscript (Edinburgh, N. Lib., Advocates' MS 19.2.1) **26** 564
Auchmuty, Richard Tylden **26** 214
Auckland **2** 705–6*; **23** 51, *52*
Aotea Centre **23** 63
Auckland Institute and Museum **23** 76
Bank of New Zealand **23** 54
Bledisloe Building **23** 56
Auckland—cont.
bridge **4** 803
City Art Gallery **23** 54, 58, 75
library **23** 76
Civic Cinema **7** 328
college of St John the Evangelist **23** 53
Custom House **23** 54
Elam School of Art **2** 706; **23** 75
library **23** 76
Experimental House **23** 56
furniture **23** 66
Government House **23** 54
Highwic **23** 64
Holy Sepulchre **23** 53
Institute and Museum **23** 67, 739
Karangahape Road Fountain **23** 63
St Mary's **23** 53
St Paul's **23** 53
silk **23** 74
statue of Queen Victoria **23** 62
Supreme Court **23** 54
University
Arts Building **2** *706*; **23** 55
library **23** 76
War Memorial Museum **2** 705
Auckland Glass Works **23** 70
Auckland Society of Arts **2** 706
Aucoc **11** 623
Aucoq, Louis **18** 659
auctioneers **10** 677
auction houses **2** 365, 369, 557; **4** 23–4; **10** 675; **15** 888
Austria **2** 829
Denmark **8** 759
England **2** 559, 560–61; **10** 366; **19** *585*
Finland **2** 369
France **2** 369; **24** 141
Japan **2** 561
Netherlands, the **7** 562
Switzerland **30** 153
United States of America **4** 24
auctions **2** 557, 706–7*; **7** 234
Belgium **2** 559
catalogues *see under* CATALOGUES → types
Denmark **8** 758
England **2** 559, 560–61, 706; **21** 614
France **2** 559, 707
Germany **2** 559, 707
Japan **2** 561; **17** 424
Netherlands, the **2** 558, 706
Rome, ancient **27** 29
Venezuela **32** 179
Auden, W(ystan) H(ugh) **7** 547; **21** 36
Audenarde *see* OUDENAARDE
Auderghem *see under* BRUSSELS
audience halls *see under* HALLS → types
Audigier, Raymond **19** 91
Audincourt **29** 508
Sacré-Coeur **11** 256
Audio art *see* SOUND AND ART
auditoria **1** 122, 123, 125; **13** 380, 385, *385*; **30** 650, 667
Audivert, Eduardo **2** 707*
Audivert, Pompeyo **2** 399, 707
Audley, Thomas **19** 568
Audley End (Essex) **8** 45; **10** 229, *230*; **16** 823; **25** 192
frames **11** 426
furniture **7** 486; **11** 119
interior decoration **29** 748
stucco **29** 813
Audran (family) **30** 344
Audran, Antoine **2** *708*
Audran, Benoît, I (1661-1721) **2** 707, *708*, 708–9*; **24** 712
Audran, Benoît, II (1698-1772) **2** 707, *708*; **8** 130
Audran, Charles **2** 707, *708*; **15** 31; **21** 89
Audran, Claude, I (1592/7-1677) **2** 707, 708, *708*

Audran, Claude, II (1639-84) 2 707–8*, 708
collaboration 4 126; 26 260
pupils 2 708
works 11 538
Audran, Claude, III (1658-1734) 2 707, 708, 708–9*
assistants 8 812; 32 913
collaboration 14 846; 28 776
patrons and collectors 4 553
pupils 30 343
works 2 709; 11 643; 12 829; 13 701; 23 540; 24 134; 28 776; 30 323
Audran, Germain 2 707, 708; 9 296; 30 344
Audran, Girard 2 707, 708, 708–9*; 10 391; 12 832; 25 626
patrons and collectors 31 56
pupils 2 708, 709; 6 548; 9 296; 12 285; 17 684
works 21 498; 26 229
writings 2 163, 169
Audran, Jean 2 707, 708, 709*
Audran, Jean-Joseph 2 708
Audran, Louis 2 708
Audran, Michel 2 708
Audran, Prosper-Gabriel 2 708
Audreau, Paul 22 49
Audriake Granary 19 840
Audsley, Berthold 2 709
Audsley, George Ashdown 2 709*
Audsley, Maurice Ashdown 2 709
Audsley, William James 2 709
Audubon, John James (Laforest) 2 709–11*; 23 32
collaboration 14 242, 243; 20 604
reproductive prints by others 19 515
works 2 106, 710; 4 364; 24 600
Audubon, John Woodhouse 2 710, 711
Audubon, Victor Gifford 2 710, 711
Auer, Alois 22 645; 25 611
works 25 611
Auer, Carl, Baron von Welsbach see WELSBACH, CARL AUER, Baron von
Auer, Fritz 3 510
Auer, Hans Wilhelm 2 711*; 3 824; 30 127
Auer, Jakob 2 711–12*; 18 668
Auer, Nicolaus 3 779; 14 694
Auerbach, Ellen 29 641
Auerbach, Frank 2 712*
dealers 19 246
groups and movements 10 258
patrons and collectors 28 273
portraits 2 712
teachers 4 294; 10 257
Auerbach Factory 27 410
Auersperg, Anton Jozef 28 863
Auerswald, Fabian von 8 120
Auffenwirth, Johann 14 235
Auffenwirth, Sabina 14 235
Aufhausen, Our Lady of the Snows 23 473
Aufidius Lurcone, M. 29 389
Aufklärung see ENLIGHTENMENT, THE
Aufschneiter, P. 30 847
Augarten 25 404, 674
Augbergh, Antonis van see OBBERGHEN, ANTONIS VAN
Auger, Hezekiah 2 721*
Augerius, Amalricus see AMALRICUS AUGERIUS
Augmented Roundels, Master of the 25 20
Au Grand Monarque see LA PAGODE
Augsburg 2 713, 713–21*; 12 361; 26 906
Altes Rathaus 10 738
Armoury see Zeughaus
art forms and materials
altarpieces 12 391
armour 2 470, 471
Augsburg
art forms and materials—cont.
book jackets 24 50
books 17 565
cabinets (ii) (furniture) 2 716; 12 421, 422, 422–3
chess sets 6 557
clocks 7 440; 12 III2
cupboards 12 422, 422
cups 12 445
damask 12 469
enamel 12 456
etchings 12 386
façade decoration 10 737
faience (ii) (ceramics) 14 235
frames 11 455
furniture 2 812; 5 350; 7 166; 12 422, 423, 448; 33 332
gables 11 876
gold 12 443, 444, 446, 447, 448; 14 235; 25 137; 30 112
hardstones 12 461
heraldry 14 409
intarsia 12 421
ivory-carvings 12 460
jewellery 12 455
marks 20 444
marquetry 20 467
medals 20 920, 923
metalwork 2 717–18*; 12 446
mirror frames 21 721
painting 2 716; 12 384, 386–7, 389–90, 391
fresco 12 391
glass 12 798
paper 24 55
pattern books 24 271, 272
pewter 12 452; 24 578
plaquettes 25 22
porcelain 14 235
printing 12 385; 17 521
prints 2 718–19*; 12 391
reliquaries 12 447
sculpture 12 399, 402, 403; 33 II1
shells 22 204
silk 12 463, 464
silver 2 717, 718, 819; 12 445, 447
snuff-boxes 12 457
stained glass 27 255, 255
statuettes 12 445
tables 12 423
textiles 12 469
woodcuts 2 719; 33 353, 359
Augustus fountain 2 714
craftsmen and artists 12 472
ecclesiastical buildings
Cathedral of St Maria 2 719*; 13 89
doors 9 153; 26 684
sculpture 2 719–20*; 3 515
stained glass 2 720, 720–21*; 13 187; 29 509
throne 30 778
tomb of Bishop Hartmann 16 434
tomb of Bishop Wolfhart von Roth 13 160; 31 122
convent of St Katharina 5 198
Dominikanerkirche see museums → Römisches Museum
St-Annen-Kirche
Fugger Chapel 11 817–18; 12 366; 23 501
St Georgskirche
Hörwarth Altar 14 450
St Peter am Perlach 2 714; 4 777
Perlachturm 2 714
SS Ulrich und Afra 32 90
altarpieces 8 626–7, 627
brasses 4 693
cloister 7 453
sculpture 12 403; 23 887
Simpertus arch 10 221
education (art) 12 478, 479
exhibitions 10 678
Augsburg—cont.
foundry 12 370
Goldenen Traube, Zur 14 695
Grammar School 12 370
guilds 2 715; 24 579
houses and palaces
Böckenstein house see museums → Maximilianmuseum
Fuggerhaus 8 881; 11 818, 819; 13 701
fountains 30 34
Rehlingerhaus 10 737, 737
Schaezlerpalais 13 803
see also museums → Deutsche Barockgalerie im Schaezlerpalais
Kunstakademie 20 894
Kunstkammern 9 14
libraries 19 314
Luginsland Tower 2 336
Meat Market 12 370
museums
Deutsche Barockgalerie im Schaezlerpalais 2 717; 19 707; 28 60
see also houses and palaces → Schaezlerpalais
Maximilianmuseum 2 713, 717
Römisches Museum 2 717; 4 838
Staatsgalerie für Altdeutsche Gemälde 2 717
Staatsgalerie für Moderne Kunst 2 717
patronage 12 471
Perlachplatz 2 714
Perlachturm see under ecclesiastical buildings → St Peter am Perlach
Rathaus 2 714; 12 370; 13 236; 14 679, 679; 18 225; 31 239
Goldener Saal 12 389
paintings 17 699
sawmills 12 419
Staats- und Stadtbibliothek 18 47
trade school 1 107
urban planning 14 679
Zeughaus 12 370, 370
sculpture 26 104
Augsburg, Michael von 25 111
Augsburg Clock 10 140
Augsburg Ecce Homo, Master of the 14 381
Augsburg-Freising Visitation, Master of the see FREISING VISITATION, MASTER OF THE
Augsburg Legend of St Benedict, Master of the see BURGKMAIR, THOMAN
Augsburg Legend of Ulrich, Master of the 20 619*
Augsburg Portraits of Painters, Master of the see BB, MONOGRAMMIST
Augsburg Visitation, Master of the see FREISING VISITATION, MASTER OF THE
Augst 1 771; 2 721*; 26 908; 30 124
basilica 3 328
forum 11 327; 26 866
Kaiseraugst 27 17
Roman capitolium 26 905
tripods 27 100
urban planning 27 3
Augur, Hezekiah 16 796
August, Jaroslav 28 853
Augusta, Empress of Germany (1811-90) 14 648, 649, 655*; 33 110
Augusta, Queen of Prussia see AUGUSTA, Empress of Germany
Augusta, Cristóbal de 29 326
Augusta, Emanuele d' 8 766
Augusta Bagiennorum Basilica 3 328
Augustae 9 553, 554
Augusta Emerita see under MÉRIDA
Augusta of Hohenzollern, Electress of Hesse-Kassel (1780-1841) 5 286
Augusta Perusia see PERUGIA
Augusta Praetoria see AOSTA
Augusta Raurica see AUGST
Augusta Suessionem see SOISSONS
Augusta Taurinorum see TURIN
Augusta Treverorum see TRIER
Augusta Vindelicorum see AUGSBURG
August Belmont Memorial Cup 30 867
Auguste, Henri 2 722*; 4 302; 11 620, 621; 23 354
Auguste, Jules-Robert 23 503; 26 500
Auguste, Robert-Joseph 2 722*; 10 764; 21 544
collaboration 21 800
patrons and collectors 8 161; 27 420; 30 107
works 11 620; 12 448; 24 147; 27 584
Augustenborg Castle 29 841
Augustenburg, Frederich Christian II, Duke of 14 153
Augustijn, Govert M. 22 883
Augustin 20 859
Augustin, E. 28 380
Augustin, Jean-Baptiste (-Jacques) 2 722–3*; 3 785; 4 836; 18 867; 21 643
Augustín, Joseph 4 258
Augštinčić, Antun 8 179; 9 672
Augustine, Saint 7 230; 19 355; 22 411, 749; 25 277
cathedrals 5 642
writings 1 652; 2 518; 6 175
Augustine of Hippo, Saint 2 723, 725; 8 259
Augustini, Jan 23 299
Augustinian Altar, Master of the 12 385; 20 619*
Augustinian Canons 2 723–5*; 19 566
architecture 2 724; 4 256; 21 375, 840
iconography 2 724–5*
patronage 2 724–5*
Augustinian hermits 2 725, 725–6*
Augustinian Polyptych 25 102
Augustino see CARLINI, AGOSTINO
Augustin of Bordeaux 15 723
Augusto, Genner 26 60
Augustobona see TROYES
Augustodunensis, Honorius see HONORIUS AUGUSTODUNENSIS
Augustodunum see under AUTUN
Augustomagus Sulbanectium see SENLIS
Auguston, Jakub (d 1701) 25 54
Auguston, Jakub (1670-1735) 8 379; 25 54
Augustus (fl late 16th cent.) 21 485
Augustus, Duke of Brunswick-Lüneburg 14 52
Augustus, Duke of Brunswick-Wolfenbüttel (reg 1635-66) 19 315; 33 51, 52–3*, 293
Augustus, Emperor of Rome (reg 30 BC-AD 14) 2 726–7*; 23 805; 26 764; 32 632
altars 26 890
architecture 2 668; 9 312; 11 327; 16 760; 24 606; 26 786, 853, 856, 889–91; 28 673
amphitheatres 1 797
bridges 29 420
cities 3 872; 5 375, 891; 16 623; 23 144, 146; 24 518; 26 750, 904, 921
fora 31 324
libraries 19 312
macella 19 888
mausoleum 20 864
Augustus, Emperor of Rome (reg 30 BC-AD 14)
architecture—cont.
obelisks 23 331
palaces 23 808
sanctuaries 30 691
temples 1 615; 23 145, 809; 26 782, 783, 786, 865; 27 714
theatres 26 889
towns 2 212; 19 516; 31 323
triumphal arches 26 891; 31 349
villas 5 684; 26 892
coins 4 687; 27 96
gems 12 250
marble 26 875, 876, 877, 885
milestones 27 6
paintings 9 13
ports 25 748; 26 31
sculpture 24 320; 25 45; 27 13, 15, 28, 30*; 29 560
Augustus I, Elector of Saxony (reg 1553-86) 2 454; 12 133, 402, 461, 467, 577; 17 887; 18 435; 19 843; 23 252; 33 110, 110, 113*
collections 12 475
metalwork 16 900
Augustus II, King of Poland (reg 1697-1706; 1709-33) 7 422; 9 235, 238; 11 626; 12 547; 13 746, 802; 14 815; 18 82, 122; 19 243; 25 98, 124, 135; 28 362; 33 110, 113–15*, 114, 721, 722
architecture 4 218; 5 348; 9 242; 10 109; 19 642; 25 240; 32 752, 869, 879; 33 110, 115
collections 12 473; 25 138
enamel 12 457
frames 25 664
furniture 10 96
gardens 9 242
jewellery 12 455
paintings 8 880; 9 18; 10 857; 20 350; 21 756; 24 341; 25 1, 2; 28 743; 31 248
porcelain 4 176; 6 924; 12 412; 17 768; 21 64; 25 240
sculpture 1 533; 3 197; 9 752; 17 768; 24 460; 32 580
swords 2 456
Augustus III, King of Poland (reg 1733-63) 9 234; 14 314; 20 351; 25 2, 38; 33 110, 115–16*
altarpieces 30 859
architecture 6 572; 9 238; 10 418; 11 739; 18 162; 21 158; 23 471; 32 869, 879
collections 9 236; 12 473, 475; 13 605; 16 767; 25 138; 33 110
drawings (pastel) 5 878
faience (ii) (ceramics) 9 241
frames 11 458, 459
furniture 18 853; 26 420
gold 9 240; 12 447
hardstones 12 458
metalwork 8 904
paintings 1 632, 633; 3 15, 924; 8 880; 11 4; 17 912; 21 130, 756; 23 175; 25 135; 31 164
flower 15 47
history 3 714; 24 706; 30 859
religious 8 146
vedute 3 676, 677; 32 112
porcelain 8 202; 9 29
prints 25 631
sculpture 7 881; 14 445; 15 38; 16 703; 19 89
stage design 12 24
Augustus the Strong, King of Poland see AUGUSTUS II, King of Poland
Augustus William, Duke of Brunswick (reg 1714-31) 33 51
Auhadi see KARIM AL-MULK AUHAD KHAN
Aukana 29 442, 458
sculpture 29 458
Aukena see GAMBIER ISLANDS

Aula Pública de Desenho e Figura (Rio de Janeiro) 4 727
Auldjo, John 2 727*
Auldjo Jug 27 76
Aulenti, Gai 2 727*; 11 528, 660; 24 131
groups and movements 22 747
Auler, Alvaro 4 721
Aulerici Cenomani 19 126
Aulestia, Salvador 29 322
Auliczek, Dominikus 23 325
Aulie, Reider 23 226, 227
works 23 226
Aulinger, B. 28 917
Aulis-Ata *see* DZHAMBUL
Aulnay, St Pierre 2 727–8*, 728; 3 443; 11 505, 554; 26 585, 600
Aulnay-aux-Planches 25 536
Aulne Abbey
manuscripts 7 348
Aulnoy, Marie-Catherine, Comtesse d' 29 301, 302
Aulps, Pierre-Louis-Jean Casimir Blacas d', Duc de *see* BLACAS D'AULPS, PIERRE-LOUIS-JEAN-CASIMIR
Ault, George 1 772; 25 461
Aul Tepe 32 320
Ault Pottery 9 295
Aumale, Counts of 14 425
Aumale, Charles de Lorraine, Duc d' 1 782; 21 822
Aumale, Henri-Eugène-Philippe-Louis de Bourbon, Duc d' 16 876; 23 511, 522–3*
architecture 6 453
manuscripts 31 308
paintings 3 396; 11 546; 15 842; 22 338
Aumale, William the Fat, Comte d', Earl of York 7 351
Aumonier, Frederic 33 372
Aumonier, Louise 33 372
Aumont, Antoine, 1st Duc d' 19 263
Aumont, Louis-Marie-Augustin Aumont, Duc d' 3 523; 5 380; 9 379; 13 234; 23 778
Auneuil Church
tiles 30 886
Aungier, Gerald 4 287
Aungulo, Manuel de Mollinedo y *see* MOLLINEDO Y AUNGULO, MANUEL DE
Aurangabad 2 728–9*; 15 257, 259, 276, 285, 637
caves 2 729*; 5 95
Cave 1 15 259, 277
Cave 3 15 253, 259, 259, 277
Cave 6 15 275, 277
Cave 7 15 275, 277, 466, 466
ikat 15 672
metalwork 15 714
paintings 15 643*
sculpture 15 465*
temples 15 275
textiles 15 665
tomb of Dilrus Banu Begum 15 373, 374, 384
Aurangzeb, Emperor (*reg* 1658-1707) (Mughal)
architecture 2 729; 19 774; 22 258–9
fortifications 8 680
mosques 15 367; 18 647; 25 587; 31 903
portraits 15 590
shields 18 613
Aurdal, Synnøve Anker 23 232, 239
Aurelian, Emperor of Rome (*reg* 270-75)
education (art) 2 312; 16 777
fortifications 7 358; 21 560; 26 853, 901–2, 902
portraits 27 42
Aurelio (family) 31 32
Aurelio, José 25 302
Aurelius Artemidoros 23 692
Aureller, Johan (Johansson) (i) (1626-96) 2 730*
Aureller, Johan (ii) (1657-1733) 2 730*
Aureo, John de Bado *see* JOHN DE BADO AUREO
aureoles 2 730*
aureolin *see* PIGMENTS → types → cobalt yellow
Aurevilly, Jules-Amadée Barbey d' *see* BARBEY D'AUREVILLY, JULES-AMADÉE
Aurhaym, Heinrich 2 792
Auria, Geronimo d' 2 731*; 10 799
Auria, Giovan Domenico d' 2 730–31*
collaboration 2 731; 5 358
works 2 731; 5 358
Auria, Giovan Tomasso d' 2 731*
Auria, Michele d' 3 742
Auric, Georges 8 438
Auricoste, Emmanuel 11 569
Auricular frames *see under* FRAMES → types
Auricular style 2 732*; 13 701; 23 540
Hungary 14 905
Netherlands, the 19 817; 22 887; 32 400
Aurier, (Georges-) Albert 2 732–3*; 3 813
collaboration 13 232
groups and movements 22 422; 30 168
works 12 189; 19 10; 30 174
Aurifaber, Petrus *see* PETRUS AURIFABER
Aurifarber, Nicolaus 28 696
Aurignacian period *see under* PREHISTORIC ART → periods
Aurillac 11 649, 650
Aurillac, Gerbert of *see* SYLVESTER II, Pope
Aurinx *see* JAÉN
Auriol 1 693, 696
altars 1 693
Auriol, (Jean-)George (-Hulot) 2 733*
illustrated writings 29 627
Auriol Labeur *see under* TYPE-FACES → forms
auripigmentum *see* ORPIMENT
Aurispa 23 86
Auriti, Giacinto 2 733–4*
Aurora 14 901
Aurora (IL), Old Second National Bank 3 177
Aurora Painter 7 366; 10 615
Aurukun 1 43, 61, 62
sculpture 1 44
wood-carvings 1 43
aurum musicum *see* MOSAIC GOLD
Ausglass *see* AUSTRALIAN ASSOCIATION OF GLASS ARTISTS
Auspitz, Stefan von 3 889
Ausstellungsverband für Raumkunst 28 126
Aust, Gottfried 2 734*; 31 634
Austalis *see* AOSTALLI
Austen, (Elizabeth) Alice 2 734*
Austen, William 10 260; 31 123
Austere style *see* SEVERE STYLE (SUROVYY STIL')
Austerlitz *see* SLAVKOV U BRNA
Austin (TX)
court-house 18 888
Laguna Gloria Art Museum 32 235
University of Texas 25 894
Humanities Research Centre 12 486; 24 683
Huntington Art Gallery 15 30
Austin, Henry 2 734–5*; 15 407; 31 592
Austin, John 2 764
Austin, John Corneby Wilson 19 700; 23 342
works 19 700
Austin, Nathaniel 31 651
Austin, Robert Sargent 10 397
Austin Canons *see* AUGUSTINIAN CANONS
Australasian Art Review 24 437
Austral group *see* GRUPO AUSTRAL
Australia 2 735–73*, 736; 23 711
adobe 32 308
architects 4 167
architecture 2 736–43*; 4 786, 788; 10 852
anti-seismic 4 789
cavity-walling 4 788, 789
exhibition 2 739
prefabrication 26 18
vernacular 32 307–9*
archives 2 369*
arts centres 21 76
barracks 13 622; 32 923
bonding 4 770
bowls 2 761
brick 4 167, 786, 789
bronze 2 752, 753
cathedrals 32 858
cedar 2 757, 758
ceilings 2 739; 11 756
ceramics 2 759–62*, 761, 762
chairs 2 758
churches 2 741
collections 1 66–7*; 2 769–71*; 4 882; 10 487; 22 360
concrete 2 740
corrugated iron 32 308
cotton 2 768
court-houses 2 742
cups 2 761, 765
dealers 1 66*
dealing 2 770*
diamonds 12 269
display of art 22 360
domes 2 740
earthenwares 2 759, 761
education (art) 2 769, 771–2*; 9 464
archaeology 2 772
architecture 2 741
glass 12 805
sculpture 2 772
embroidery 2 767
emu eggs 2 765
engravings 2 747
exhibitions 1 67; 2 369, 754, 767; 3 124
furniture 2 757–9*
galleries (iv) (art) 2 771
gardens 12 142
glass 2 762–4*; 21 801
gold 2 764
government buildings 2 737; 5 602
houses 32 307
incinerators 2 741
interior decoration 2 754–7*, 755
kangaroo skins 2 758
knitting 2 768
lace 2 768
law courts 18 887, 888
libraries 2 369, 772–3*
lithography 2 744
mahogany 2 758
marks 2 758, 766
metal 2 739
metalwork 2 764–6*
museums 2 369, 770–71*; 22 360
nephrite 16 861
nude figures 4 606
objects of vertu 2 764–6*
opals 12 269
opera houses 31 777
painting 2 743–52*
Abstract art 2 751
genre 19 874; 26 465
hard-edge 32 909
history 2 750; 9 464
landscape 2 745, 745–6, 746, 747–8, 748; 13 784; 23 183; 29 767
20th cent. 4 606
panoramas 3 427
patchwork 2 767
Australia—cont.
patronage 2 769–70*
periodicals 24 437–8*
periods
Prehistoric 25 468
photography 10 580
pisé de terre 32 308
polychromy 4 788
postage stamps 25 328
pots 2 762
pottery 2 760–62
printing 2 768
prints 2 749, 751
prizes (artists') 19 641
quilts 2 767
sapphires 12 269
screenprints 2 767, 768
scrimshaw 28 302
sculpture 2 752–4*, 753, 754
she-oak 2 757, 758
silver 2 764–6, 765; 28 737
skyscrapers 2 742; 28 375, 834
stained glass 2 763; 11 756
steel 2 740, 754
stonewares 2 762
synagogues 17 547
tapestries 2 767
teapots 2 761
textiles 2 766–9*
towns 23 679
upholstery 2 758
verandahs 2 737; 32 240
villas 32 555
weaving 2 767
women 2 752
wood 2 757
see also ABORIGINAL AUSTRALIA; TASMANIA
Australian Architecture 2 740
Australian Art 24 437
Australian Artist 24 438
Australian Association of Glass Artists (Ausglass) 2 763
Australian black-wood 29 116
Australian Glass Manufacturers Co. 23 70
Australian Institute for Conservation of Cultural Material 7 744
Australian Photographic Journal *see* HARRINGTON'S PHOTOGRAPHIC JOURNAL
Australia Studios 33 681
Austral Islands 2 773–4*; 23 711; 25 896
adzes 25 896
barkcloth 2 773
body ornaments 23 720
fortifications 25 896
jewellery 2 773
paddles 23 724
pounders 25 896, 896
sculpture 2 773
shells 2 773
wood 2 773
wood-carvings 2 774
Austråt 13 121
Austria 2 774–834*, 776; 12 361
altarpieces 2 799
Baroque 31 678
Gothic 11 806
polyptychs 23 709
Schnitzaltar 28 133
15th cent. 23 707, 708
altars 1 698; 27 661
antependia 2 823
apartments 30 885
arcades 2 778
architecture 2 776–89*; 4 777
Baroque 2 780–83*
Gothic 2 777–8; 13 56
Jesuit Order 2 781
Jugendstil 2 788
Renaissance 2 778–80*
20th cent. 24 327
archives 2 370*
armillary spheres 12 813
armour 2 821
Austria—cont.
art history 2 833–4*; 28 114; 33 159
ash 2 811
auction houses 2 829
banks 32 762
beds 2 812–13, 813; 3 484
bentwood 15 822; 18 192
body arts 10 483
book covers 4 351
book illustrations 4 366
boxes 2 823*
brass 12 811; 33 165
brick 4 777
bronze 2 802, 821–2; 10 908; 14 88
Neo-classicism 2 803
Prehistoric 25 541
Renaissance 2 800
20th cent. 10 894
busts
Baroque 29 789; 32 442
Baroque Revival 30 889
Neo-classicism 33 623
18th cent. 21 314
buttresses 19 377
cabinets (i) (rooms) 5 347–8
cabinets (ii) (furniture) 2 812
Baroque 2 812
clock-cabinets 2 812
Eger cabinets 2 812
tabernacle cabinets 2 812, 812
carnivals 5 786
carpets 2 825
cartoons (drawings) 18 130
cast iron 2 822
catafalques 6 72
catalogues 9 18
cathedrals 13 857; 32 451
ceilings 2 805–6
cemeteries 6 154; 14 87
centrepieces 2 817
ceramics 2 815–17*
chairs 2 811; 15 822; 30 754; 33 156
chasubles 2 824; 32 388, 391
chess sets 6 557
chests 2 811, 811
choirs 19 377
churches 2 776–7, 779–81, 784–5
Baroque 2 781, 782; 5 772; 11 133; 19 433; 25 448; 28 184
Gothic 2 777; 14 309
hall 32 450, 452
19th cent. 11 30
20th cent. 2 789; 25 37
clocks 2 812; 7 442, 446, 447, 448
coffeepots 2 821
coffee-services 32 450
coffering 2 805, 805–6
coins 7 539
collages 14 236
collections 2 828–9*, 830–31*; 22 356
armour 15 866–7
casts 29 789
royal 9 18
concrete 25 37
copper 21 13
cotton 2 826
cult wagons 25 541
cupboards 2 811, 812; 8 271
dealing 2 828–9*
department stores 19 652
design 8 802
desks 2 812
diplomatic gifts 29 788
display of art 9 14, 18, 19; 22 356
domes 9 84
doors 9 152
drawings 2 797; 31 357–8
architectural 2 328; 22 211
Baroque 2 795–6
Gothic 2 792
Renaissance 2 794
dress 2 825
dyeing 30 558

Austria—cont.
education (art) **2** 831–2*
embroidery **2** *823*, 823–5*, *824*
needle-painting **2** 824
enamel **2** *818*, 818, *820*, 823
engravings **2** *779*, 793; **31** 680; **32** *436*
erotic art **10** *481*, 483
façade decoration **10** 737, 741; **30** *885*
factories **23** 358
faience (ii) (ceramics) **2** 815, *815*
figurines **25** 489, *541*; **33** 197, *198*
fortifications **2** 780
furniture **2** 811–15*, *812*, *813*, *814*; **33** 156
galleries (iv) (art) **9** 19; **32** 446
garden cities **25** 864
gardens **12** 133–4*; **32** *461*
gates **2** *822*
gateways **2** *778*, *786*
gems **2** 824
glass **2** 817–19*, *818*; **19** *523*
glasses **2** *818*
globes **12** *811*
goblets **2** *820*
gold **2** 819–21*, *820*, 823*, *823*, *824*
graves **14** 87
guilds **32** 448
guns **2** 821
halls **15** 866
sale terrene **27** *611*
hangings **2** 825
Hausmalers **14** 235
historicism **14** 580
historiography **2** 833–4*
houses **13** *846*; **25** *37*
housing **32** *439*
illusionism **15** 139
interior decoration **2** 805–10*, *805*, *810*; **33** 48
Rococo **2** *806*, *807*
Rococo Revival **2** *809*
19th cent. **20** *146*
iron **2** 822
ivory **2** *801*
jugs **2** *815*
knitting **18** 158
Kunstkammern **2** 812; **9** 14
lace **18** 158
lead **21** *314*
leather **4** 351
libraries **2** 832–3*; **32** *457*
limestone **2** *799*, *804*; **33** *198*
linen **2** 823, *824*; **32** *388*, *391*
lithography **18** *491*; **32** *446*
loden **2** 823
manuscript illumination **2** 790–91*, 792*; **26** 674–5*
maps **14** 573
marble **5** *628*; **29** *789*; **30** *889*; **32** *442*; **33** *623*
marks **20** *444*
mausolea **2** 781; **13** *329*
metalwork **2** 819–22*
Celtic **27** 663
mezzotints **21** 414
miniatures (manuscript illumination) **2** *790*; **26** *676*
monasteries **2** *777*; **19** *377*; **21** *83*
monuments **2** *803*; **10** *908*; **13** 315; **20** *390*; **33** 624
mother-of-pearl **22** *204*
mouldings **22** 211, 217
museums **2** 826, 830–31*; **9** 19; **15** 867; **22** 356, *356*
decorative arts **32** 446
19th cent. **2** *786*
niello **21** I3
nude figures **10** *481*, *894*; **33** *198*
observatories **18** *447*
opera houses **15** 864
painting **2** 790–98*, 817
allegorical
Baroque **1** *659*; **5** *774*; **29** *790*
Expressionism **28** *90*
Jugendstil **18** *130*

Austria
painting
allegorical—cont.
18th cent. **25** *56*
Baroque **2** *794*, 794–6*, *795*
Biedermeier **8** 445
bird's-eye views **32** *435*
ceiling **25** *56*; **26** 24
display **9** 19; **14** *191*; **22** *356*
fresco **13** *278*; **27** *664*; **31** *357*
glass **12** 798
Gothic **2** 791–2*
hanging **9** 19
history **2** *796*; **20** *857*; **26** *559*; **32** *443*
Jugendstil **2** *797*; **32** 446
landscape **32** *445*, *776*
murals **2** *798*
mythological **29** *401*
panel **2** 792*; **13** 151
quadratura **1** *659*; **15** 139
religious
Baroque **1** *732*
Gothic **13** *151*
Renaissance **14** *836*
16th cent. **26** *106*
18th cent. **27** *234*
Renaissance **2** 793–4*
Romanesque **2** 790–91*
townscapes **18** *199*; **32** *433*
wall
Benedictine Order **3** *711*
Gothic **2** 791–2*, *791*; **7** *274*
Renaissance **2** 793, *793*
Romanesque **2** 790*; **3** *711*; **18** 668; **26** 650, *650*, 653
watercolours **1** *688*; **4** *40*
19th cent. **18** 419
20th cent. **25** *864*
palaces
Baroque **11** *132*, *135*; **14** *528*, *529*; **32** *459*, *461*
Renaissance **2** 779, *779*; **15** *867*
18th cent. **10** *530*
patronage **2** 827–8*
pattern books **2** 807
performance art **5** *31*
periodicals **24** 438–9*; **28** 801
pewter **2** 821
photoarchives **2** 833
plaster **29** 838–9*, 843
porcelain **2** 816–17*, *817*; **32** *450*
portraits **2** 799
Baroque **21** *642*
Expressionism **28** *89*
Renaissance **2** *800*; **14** *837*
Rococo **23** *854*
19th cent. **1** *774*; **8** *503*; **10** *703*
20th cent. **18** *197*
posters **19** 69, *485*; **25** 350; **32** *446*
pottery **2** 815–16*
prints **10** *481*
sanatoria **14** *628*
satin **2** *824*
scabbards **14** 88
schools **2** *788*; **13** *204*
sculpture **2** 798–804*
Baroque **2** 801–2*; **5** *264*; **9** *146*; **13** *799*
bronze **2** *800*, 802; **10** *894*
Gothic **2** 798–9*, *799*; **32** *441*
marble **5** *628*
monumental **2** 798
mythological **10** *894*
Neo-classicism **2** 802, *803*; **5** *628*
Romanesque **2** 798*; **26** *634*, 634–5*
stone **26** *634*, 634–5*
wood **13** *799*
18th cent. **27** *661*
20th cent. **2** 803–4*, *804*
settlements **25** 502
shawls **2** 825
shopping centres **32** 439
silk **2** 824, 825; **32** *389*, *391*
silver **2** 819–21*, *821*, *824*
silver-gilt **2** *820*

Austria—cont.
snuff-boxes **2** 823
sofas **2** *814*
spires **32** 450
squares (town) **27** *662*
stained glass **13** 151, 186, *188*; **29** IV
staircases **27** *661*
statuettes **2** *801*
stone **26** *634*, 634–5*
stoves **2** 815
stucco **29** 838–9*, 843
swimming pools **32** 439
tabernacles (ii) (receptacle) **22** *204*
tables **2** 811–12
tapestries **2** 823, 826
teapots **21** I3
tea-services **2** *820*
tenements **10** 98
textiles **2** 823–6*, *826*
theatres **10** 871; **30** 676
tiles **2** 815; **30** 884–5*, *885*
tin **21** *314*
tombs **5** *628*; **7** *554*
treatises
architecture **15** 166
military **13** 845
urban planning **28** 800–801
tympana **27** *663*
urban planning **2** 780; **28** 801; **32** 437, *761*
vases **33** *165*
velvet **2** 825
vestments (ecclesiastical) **2** 823; **32** 391
walnut **7** *447*
wicker **15** *822*; **33** 156, *156*
willow **33** 156
wood **9** *152*; **12** *813*; **13** *799*
woodcuts **2** 792; **27** *660*
wool **2** 825
wrought iron **2** 822, *822*
Wunderkammern **2** 812
Autere, Hannes **11** 100, 111
Autheil **26** 598
authenticity **2** 834–5*; **11** 305; **24** 258
commentaries **7** 714
Native North Americans **22** 667
15th cent. **14** 869
16th cent. **2** 558
18th cent. **2** 559
19th cent. **2** 560
20th cent. **7** 565
see also ART (ORIGINAL WORKS OF); COPIES; FORGERIES
author portraits *see under* PORTRAITS → types
Autillo, Ramón de **13** 760
autism **25** 685
Autissier, Jean **19** 144
Autissiodurum *see* AUXERRE
Autochrome *see under* PHOTOGRAPHIC PLATES → types; PHOTOGRAPHY → processes
Auto-destructive art **2** 837*
autograph etching *see* PHOTOGRAPHY → processes → *cliché-verre*
autographie photographique see PHOTOGRAPHY → processes → *cliché-verre*
automata **2** 837–8*; **22** 375; **29** 96
historical and regional traditions
Britain **7** 445
Byzantine **29** 96
Germany **2** *838*; **12** 445
Japan **17** 373
treatises *see under* TREATISES → types
uses
clocks **7** 438, 445
cups **12** 445
dolls **17** 373
grottoes **13** 704
see also TOYS
automatic writing **30** 18

automation **15** 826
automatism **2** 838–9*; **25** 584; **30** 17, 18, 19, 22, 23, 231
France **2** 543, *839*; **9** *105*; **30** 291
United States of America **1** 85
see also BLOT DRAWING; DECALCOMANIA (ii) (PRINTING); DOODLES; FROTTAGE
Automatistes, Les **2** 839–40*; **5** 568; **22** 39
members **4** 402; **7** 681; **19** 58; **26** 76, 414
Automobile Association (AA) **13** 811; **28** 488
Automobile Club of Southern California **19** 700
automobiles *see* CARS
Automóvil Club Argentina **32** 538
autoradiography *see under* TECHNICAL EXAMINATION → types
Autotype Company **24** 649
Autotype Mechanical Process *see* PRINTING → processes → collotype
Autremont, Louis F. d' **28** 299
Autrey, S. **21** 396
Autricum *see* CHARTRES
Autricus *see* AUXERRE
Autry, Marc d' **10** 398
Autun **2** 840–42*; **11** *504*, *505*; **26** *905*
Augustodunum **2** 840*
Cathedral of St Lazare **2** 840*, *841*, 841–2*, *842*; **11** *509*, 510, 554; **12** 745; **23** 485; **26** 556, 584
architecture **2** 840–41*
gargoyles **12** 150
reliefs **26** 133
roof **30** 907
sculpture **10** 742; **11** 554; **23** 291; **26** 595, 596, 602
gates **7** 358; **26** 905
Hôtel Rolin *see* Musée Rolin
Musée Rolin **2** 840; **26** 554
Notre-Dame du Châtel **3** 612
Roman theatre **2** 840
sculpture **26** 641
Temple of Janus **26** 866; **30** 436
Autun, Honorius of *see* HONORIUS OF AUTUN
Auvera *see* AUWERA
Auvernier **25** 528
Auvillar, St Germain
beakheads **3** *443*
Auvorstadt, Mariahilfkirche **13** 202; **23** 372
Auvray, Louis **2** 843*; **10** 210
Auw, Meinrad von **29** 399
Auwa, Kameshvara Temple **15** 270, 487
Auwera, Jakob von der **2** 843*
Auwera, Johann Michael Josef von der **2** 843
Auwera, Johann Wolfgang von der **2** 843–4*
assistants **30** 866; **32** 758
works **5** 349; **12** 412; **32** 120; **33** 432
Auwera, Lukas von der **2** 843; **32** 758
Auxerre **2** 844–7*; **11** *504*
Bishop's Palace **11** 654
Cathedral of St Etienne **2** 844–5*, *844*; **13** 41, 59; **22** 220
arches **23** 368
crypt **8** 224; **22** 215
metalwork **6** 76
roof **30** 907
sculpture **2** 845–6*; **13** 75
stained glass **2** 846*; **13** 179, 180, 181; **29** 501, 502, 510, *511*
Treasury **2** 846*
westwork **7** 265

Auxerre—cont.
St Germain **2** 847*; **11** 511; **19** 709
Baptistery **3** 191
crypt **7** 265; **8** 222; **11** 509, 529; **23** 485
mouldings **22** 219, 220, 222
outer crypt **5** 795
wall paintings **5** 798
Auxerre, Conrad, Comte d' **2** 847
Auxerre, Etienne d' *see* ETIENNE D'AUXERRE
Auxerre, Milet d' *see* MILET D'AUXERRE
Auxerre, Remigius of *see* REMIGIUS OF AUXERRE
Auxerre Goddess **13** 444, 470
Auxonne, Notre-Dame **13** 78
Aux Quatre Vents **14** 505
aux trois crayons *see under* DRAWINGS → forms
Auzelle, Robert **3** 226
Auzelles **9** 156
Auzon Church **26** 641
Auzou, Pauline **2** 847–8*; **31** 373
Auzoux, I.-T.-J. **1** 844
Ava **2** 848*; **5** *221*, 222; **29** *225*
architecture **5** 237
Bagaya-kyaung **5** 241
Maha-aung-mye-bonzan Monastery **2** 848
sculpture **5** 241
weights **5** 260
Avallon **26** 602
St Lazare **9** 84; **26** 596, 602
Avalos, Alfonso d' **21** 525
Avalos, Juan de **10** 822; **29** 295
Avalos de Aquino, Francisco, Viceroy of Sicily **31** 285
Avalouze, St Bonnet **11** 613
Avani
Bharateshvara Temple **15** 529
Lakshmaneshvara Temple **15** 529
sculpture **15** 529
temples **23** 182
Avanos **5** 673, 676
Avanscoperta **25** 447
avant-garde films *see* FILMS → experimental
Avanti Architects **7** 698
Avantikaksetra *see* AVANI
Avantipura **2** 848*; **15** *264*
sculpture **15** 482
Temple of Avantishvara **2** 848; **15** 265
Temple of Avantisvamin **15** 265
temples **15** 265
Avantivarman of Kashmir (*reg* AD 855-83) (Utpala) **2** 848; **15** 265
Avanzi, Jacopo **2** 848–9*
collaboration **1** 725, 726
patrons and collectors **4** 275
works **16** 657
Avanzi, Jacopo di Pietro **2** 848
Avanzi, Nicoló **12** 258
Avanzini, Aloisio *see* AVANZINI, BARTOLOMEO
Avanzini, Bartolomeo **2** 849*; **10** 526; **13** 748; **21** 771
Avanzini, Sante **2** 849
Avanzo, Dominik **14** 309; **19** 378
Avar **21** 500, 501; **27** 432
Avaria, Manuel Aldunate *see* ALDUNATE AVARIA, MANUEL
Avaricum *see* BOURGES
Avaris *see under* PIRAMESSE
Avataṁsaka Buddhism *see under* BUDDHISM → sects
Avaux, Claude d' **19** 145
Avaux, Jean-François Félibien des *see* FÉLIBIEN DES AVAUX, JEAN-FRANÇOIS
'Avaz Muhammad **6** 236
Avcılar, Durmuş Kilisesi **5** 675
Avdey **31** 547
Avdeyevo **27** 364
Avdou, Hagios Konstantinos **8** 156; **25** 334
Avdyshev, Aleksey **27** 434

Avebury (Wilts) 2 850, 850–51*; 10 225; 21 40, 41; 25 470, 504
Aved, Jacques (-André-Joseph) 2 851–2*; 11 663
  reproductive prints by others 18 858; 19 10
  works 2 851; 11 539; 23 468; 30 524
Aved-Dimitry, Prince 25 679
Avedon, Richard 2 852*; 24 683; 26 41
Aveiro 25 313
  Cathedral of S Domingos 25 306
  Museu Regional 25 318
Aveiro, José Mascarenhas, Duque de 8 68; 12 357
Avelar, Francisco Gomes do see GOMES DO AVELAR, FRANCISCO
Avelar Rebelo, José de 2 852–3*; 25 297
  attributions 25 297
  patrons and collectors 4 633
  works 19 464
Aveline, Pierre, the elder (1656-1722) 2 853*; 24 397
Aveline, Pierre (-Alexandre) (1702-60) 2 853*; 4 514; 19 144
Avellaneda y Haro see CARPIO, Marquéses de
Avellaneda y Haro, García, Conde de Castrillo see CASTRILLO, Conde de
Avelli, Francesco Xanto 2 853–4*; 16 733; 31 741
  works 30 887; 31 741
Avenant, Jean L' see L'AVENANT, JEAN
Avenant, William d' 24 752
Avenas, Notre-Dame 26 602
Avenches see AVENTICUM
Avenionsis see AVIGNON
Avennes, (A. C. T.) Emile Prisse d' see PRISSE D'AVENNES, (A. C. T.) EMILE
Avennio see AVIGNON
Aventicum 2 854*; 26 908; 30 124
  baths 3 375
  ivory-carvings 27 100
  sculpture 27 15
Aventinum 22 393
Aventius see THURMAYR, JOHANNES
aventurine glass see under GLASS → types
avenues 12 120, 128, 131, 132
  see also CAUSEWAYS; ROADS; STREETS
Averbeck & Averbeck 31 655
Averbeke, Emiel Van see VAN AVERBEKE, EMIEL
Averbeke, Ernest van 2 194
Averbode Abbey 3 546, 570, 609; 10 717–18
Averbode Gospels see under GOSPEL BOOKS → individual manuscripts
Averboden 20 331
Avercamp, Barent 2 856*
Avercamp, Hendrick (Barentsz.) 2 854–6*
  attributions 2 856
  patrons and collectors 5 679; 27 271; 28 271; 32 539, 707
  pupils 2 856
  teachers 16 63
  works 2 855, 856; 9 221; 18 710
Averechte, Jacques 4 925
Averlino, Antonio di Pietro see FILARETE
Avermaete, Roger 3 619
Averoff, Evangelos 13 359
Averoff Gallery see under METSOVO
Averoldi, Altobello 23 413
Averoldo (family) 27 890
Aversa, Cathedral of S Paolo 16 626; 26 580, 625
Avery, Henry Ogden 2 858
Avery, Milton 2 856–7*
  groups and movements 1 84
  patrons and collectors 1 71; 22 917
  works 2 857; 9 310; 21 897
Avery, Samuel P(utnam) (1822-1904) 2 858*; 6 925; 19 756; 31 664
Avery, Samuel P(utnam), jr (1847-1920) 2 858
aves e ramagens tiles see under TILES → types
Avesnelles Church 13 113
Avet, Louis 27 556
Avetisyan, Minas 2 858*
  works 2 432, 433
Avetisyan Museum see under DJADJUR
Avèze, Marquis d' 10 678
AV group 13 531
Avguštinčić, Antun 9 496
Aviano, Girolamo di Bartolomeo Strazzarolo da see GIROLAMO DI BARTOLOMEO STRAZZAROLO DA AVIANO
Avianus 10 723, 724
Avianus Evander, C. 27 28
Avianwu 9 735
Avibus, Gaspare de 13 912; 30 519
Avicenna 19 355; 21 5
Avida Dollars see DALÍ (DOMÈNECH), SALVADOR (FELIPE JACINT)
Avienus 2 649; 10 190
Avigad, N. 3 880
Avignon 2 858–63*; 11 505
  Archbishop's Palace see Musée du Petit Palais
  art forms and materials
    faience (ii) (ceramics) 11 604
    manuscript illumination 17 562
    painting 11 532; 13 149, 150*
      fresco 13 135
    sculpture 11 556; 13 79; 26 603
    silk 11 644
    silver 11 616; 27 83
    tombs 14 416
    woodcuts 33 360
  bridges 4 801
  Cathedral of Notre-Dame-des-Doms 2 861*; 26 584; 30 778
    sculpture 26 603
    tomb of John XXII 7 303
  Hôtel de Tonduti-Lescarène 21 496
  Musée Calvet 2 860, 861; 5 445
  Musée Lapidaire 2 860, 861
  Musée du Petit Palais 2 860
    collections 2 860; 4 307; 5 537; 11 668
  Palais des Papes 2 859, 861–3*; 3 707; 11 511, 665; 12 697; 13 150*; 17 610
    Chambre du Cerf 2 862, 863; 13 128, 150
    Chambre du Pape 2 863
    Chapel of St Martial 12 697
    gate-house 12 175
    Great Chapel 2 862
    machicolation 19 895
    Tour de la Garde Robe 18 704
  Pont St Bénézet 4 801
  Porte St-Lazare 3 209; 12 173
  St Didier 13 150
  St Martial 18 641
    tomb of Cardinal Guillaume II d'Aigrefeuille 13 79
    tomb of Cardinal Jean de la Grange 13 79
    tomb of Cardinal Nicolas de Brancas 13 79
  St Ruf 2 723
Avignon, Marguerite 1 145
Avignon, Paul 1 145
Avignon Clock 4 248; 13 234
Åvik Factory 11 106
Ávila 2 863–7*; 29 258
  Arenas de S Pedro 29 271
Ávila—cont.
  churches
    Cathedral of S Salvador 2 864–5*; 13 50; 29 263
      altarpiece 1 710
      ambulatory 2 864
      metalwork 29 337, 338
      monument to Bishop Alonso de Madrigal 29 290
      retable 11 483
      sculpture 2 865*; 13 104
      stained glass 13 192
    S Tomás 9 112; 20 493
      retable 11 483
      tomb of Prince John 1 517; 10 783, 783
    S Vicente 2 866*; 7 643; 26 582; 29 263
      metalwork 26 689
      sculpture 2 866, 866–7*; 26 605, 608, 609
      Shrine of SS Vincente, Sabina and Cristeta 2 867
  embroidery 29 350
  sculpture 26 605, 607
  town walls 8 138; 29 263
Ávila, Master of 20 619–20*, 763
Ávila, Diego de los Santos y see SANTOS Y ÁVILA, DIEGO DE LOS
Ávila, Hernando de 2 867–8*; 29 278
Ávila, Juan de 2 868
Ávila, Lorenzo de 2 867
Ávila, Pedro de 2 868*
Ávila, Velasco de 2 868
Aviler, Augustin-Charles d' 2 868–9*
  architecture 3 334; 14 789; 22 34; 23 474
  collaboration 20 296
  writings 11 574; 19 17; 20 416; 23 488; 29 637; 31 296
Aviler, Claude-Louis d' 2 869
Avilés, Celestino 25 703
Avilés, Pedro Menéndez de 27 531
Avis, Joseph 17 544
Avisart, Claude 4 544
Avisseau, Charles-Jean 2 869*; 11 581, 606
Avitabile, Gen. 24 540, 541
Avitacum, Villa of Sidonius Apollinaris 32 542
Aviz (House of) 2 869–70*
Aviz, Alfonso V, King of Portugal see ALFONSO V, King of Portugal
Aviz, Antonio, Prior of Crato 14 659, 661
Aviz, Catherine of Austria, Queen of Portugal see CATHERINE OF AUSTRIA, Queen of Portugal
Aviz, Edward, King of Portugal see EDWARD, King of Portugal
Aviz, Eleanor, Holy Roman Empress see ELEANOR OF PORTUGAL, Holy Roman Empress
Aviz, Eleanor of Viseu, Queen of Portugal see ELEANOR OF VISEU, Queen of Portugal
Aviz, Ferdinand, Duque de Guarda see GUARDA, FERDINAND AVIZ, Duque de
Aviz, Henry, Cardinal Archbishop of Lisbon see HENRY, King of Portugal
Aviz, Isabella, Duchess of Burgundy see ISABELLA OF PORTUGAL, Duchess of Burgundy
Aviz, Joanna of Austria, Princess of Portugal see HABSBURG II., JOANNA OF AUSTRIA, Princess of Portugal
Aviz, John I, King of Portugal see JOHN I, King of Portugal
Aviz, John II, King of Portugal see JOHN II, King of Portugal
Aviz, John III, King of Portugal see JOHN III, King of Portugal
Aviz, John Manuel, Infante of Portugal 14 2
Aviz, Luis, Duque de Beja see BEJA, LUIS AVIZ, Duque de
Aviz, Manuel I, King of Portugal see MANUEL I, King of Portugal
Aviz, Maria 2 869, 874–5*
Aviz, Sebastian, King of Portugal see SEBASTIAN, King of Portugal
Avnatamov see HOVNAT'ANIAN
Avni, Aharon 16 571
Avogadro (family) 6 351
Avogaro, Marco di Giovanni dell' 12 733
Avola 28 657; 31 717
Avon 11 604
Avon, Merwyn 2 151
Avondo, Vittorio 2 10; 28 318
Avont, Pieter van 2 875–6*; 4 915; 25 221; 33 388
Avostali see ASTALLI
Avra 15 695
Avramidis, Joannis 2 804, 876*
Avramov, Dimiter 5 163
Avramova, Borka 19 885
Avramović, Dimitrije 28 451
Avranches
  Cathedral 13 36
  Musée d'Archéologie 11 667
Avrange, Jean-Baptiste d' 2 784
Avrig
  Brukenthal house 26 708
  church 26 710
Avril, Auguste 4 588
Avril, Léon 4 588
Avrorin, Vasily (Mikhaylovich) 33 621
Avroult, François d', Abbot 5 49
Avvocato, Paolo di Jacopino see PAOLO DI JACOPINO AVVOCATO
A. W., Master 9 274; 20 790–91*
Aw, (Andreas) Meinrad von 2 876*
Awag Vank' Gospels see under GOSPEL BOOKS → individual manuscripts
Awang Damit 20 172
awards, military see MEDALS
Awarikus, King of Adana (reg c. 738-709 BC) 17 810
Awataguchi 18 67; 23 196; 30 255
Awata school see SHŌREN'IN
Awatobi 10 474
Awatovi (AZ) 2 876–7*
  kivas 22 590
  pottery 22 609
  wall paintings 2 876–7
Awa Tsireh see ROYBAL, ALFONSO
Awayli, Tell see 'OUEILI, TELL EL-
Awazu, Kiyoshi 2 877*; 21 317; 23 627
Awibre Hor 9 876; 10 80
Awka 1 286; 15 116
Awliya Ata see ZHAMBYL
awnings 15 288; 23 803
Awsan 2 268
Axelson, Victor 19 428
Axelsson, Svend 14 690
Axente Sever 26 707
Axentowicz, Teodor 18 398; 25 649; 29 641; 31 396
axes 2 448
  historical and regional traditions
    Aboriginal Australia 1 37
    Africa 1 361
    Central Asia, Eastern 6 305
    China 6 841, 848; 7 1, 2, 45, 97; 28 603
      Anyang period (c. 1300-c. 1050 BC) 28 603
      Western Zhou (c. 1050-771 BC) 6 848
    Cuba (Caribbean) 8 229
    Egypt, ancient 9 820–21; 10 40–41
axes
  historical and regional traditions—cont.
    Globular Amphora culture 25 516
    Indonesia 15 754, 756
    Iran 16 509
    Iran, ancient 7 187
    Islamic 16 504, 508, 509
    Luba 19 740*
    Maya 21 246
    Mesoamerica, Pre-Columbian 21 242, 246; 23 418
    New Caledonia 23 19
    Olmec 21 242; 23 418
    Ottoman 16 508
    Prehistoric art 25 494, 515–16, 530
    Russia 32 527
    Shona 1 361; 28 621
    Viking 32 527
  materials
    bronze 6 841, 848, 848; 7 97; 28 603
    gold leaf 32 527
    iron 7 97; 16 504; 32 527
    jade 7 1, 2
    silver 7 187; 32 527
axial mouldings see under MOULDINGS → types
Axis 24 428
Axminster (Devon) 2 877*; 5 839; 10 225
Axminster carpet factory 10 279, 358
Axminster carpets see under CARPETS → types
Axos 8 154
  temple 8 154
Axouch, Alexios 9 519
Axoum see AKSUM
Ay (reg c. 1323-c. 1319 BC) 9 777, 826, 840, 885; 10 61; 15 306; 30 697
'Ay see AI
aya see under TEXTILES → types
Ayaa 28 667–8
Ayacucho 24 498
  ecclesiastical buildings 24 501, 502
    Buena Muerte 24 502
    Cathedral 24 502, 511, 512
    La Compañía 24 501, 502
    La Merced 24 500
    Monastery of S Domingo 24 502
    S Clara 24 500
    S Cristóbal 24 500
    S Francisco de Paula 24 502
    S Loreto 24 501
    S Teresa 24 502
  education (art) 24 517
  furniture 24 514
  Jesuit college 24 501
  retables 24 499
  silver 24 512
Ayala, Bernabé 2 878
Ayala, Diego López de see LÓPEZ DE AYALA, DIEGO
Ayala, Felipe Guaman Poma de see POMA DE AYALA, FELIPE GUAMAN
Ayala (e Cabrera), Josefa de 2 877–8*
  works 2 878; 25 297; 29 668
Ayala, Juan de 29 333
Ayala, Juan Interián de see ITERIÁN DE AYALA, JUAN
Ayala, Roger 24 96
Ayapata 14 829
Ayas 9 565
  congregational mosque 16 497
  fortifications 2 427
Ayasuluk see SELÇUK
Ayaviri 24 498
  church 24 502
Aybak 16 201

Aybek, T., Museum of the History of the Peoples of Uzbekistan *see under* TASHKENT
Aycher, Josef **8** 413
Ayck, Barthélemy de *see* EYCK, BARTHÉLEMY D'
Aycock, Alice **2** 878–9*; **18** 695; **31** 615
Aydamur al-Ashrafi **16** 384
AYDE *see* STUDIO AYDE
'Aydhab **16** *104*, 519; **23** 289
Aydın *see* TRALLES
Aydughdi ibn 'Abdallah al-Badri **20** 229
Aye, Mansur **23** 800
Ayer, Edward E. **6** 575
Ayerbe, Manuel Arbós y *see* ARBÓS Y AYERBE, MANUEL
Ayers, Louis **32** 887
Ayers Rock **1** *37*, 41, 56
  Yulara Tourist Village **2** 743
Ayia **8** 155
Ayia Irini (Cyprus) **8** 337
  sanctuary **8** 334
Ayia Irini (Greece) **8** *304*, 309, 310, 313, 323; **17** 874; **21** 653
  fortifications **8** 310
  House A **8** 309
  temple **1** 691; **8** 309, 311
  tombs **8** 310
  urban planning **8** 310
  wall paintings **8** 307, 321
Ayia Kyriaki **19** 234
Ayia Marina ware *see under* POTTERY → wares
Ayia Paraskeve (Lesbos) **19** *234*, 880
Ayia Paraskevi (Macedonia (i) (Greece)) **19** 234
Ayia Photeia **21** 663
Ayia Thekla **8** *304*, 311
Ayia Triada **2** 879*; **8** 153, 156; **13** *362*; **21** *651*, 664
  alabaster (gypsum) **21** 662
  bronzes **21** 688
  ceramics **21** 663
  faience (i) (glass) **21** 683, 684
  frescoes **2** *879*
  ivory-carvings **21** 681
  paintings **21** 660, 673
  palace **2** 879
  pottery **21** *669*
  sarcophagi **6** 479; **21** 660–61
  stone vessels **21** 659, 689
  Tomb 5 **21** 687
  towns **21** 664
  vases **21** *689*
  villa **21** 664
  wall paintings **21** 659, 673, 675, 676–7
Ayia Trias
  Baptistery **3** 190
  Basilica **8** 357, 358
Ayii Deka **8** 156
Ayin-Dara *see* AIN DARA
Ayioi Anargyroi **8** *304*
  cemetery **8** 310; **22** 698
Ayios Ambrosios, Christ Antiphonitis **8** 358
Ayios Andreas **8** *304*, 311
Ayios Demetrios (Kythera) *see* PALAIOCHORA
Ayios Dimitrios (Cyprus) **8** 330, 336; **17** 736
Ayios Epikitos-Vrysi *see* VRYSI
Ayios Iakovos **8** 334
Ayios Kosmas **14** 338; **21** 46
Ayios Nikolaos **18** 571
  Archaeological Museum **8** 157; **21** 691
  Hagios Nikolaos **8** 155
Ayios Onouphrios **21** *651*, 666, 679
Ayios Onouphrios I ware *see under* POTTERY → wares
Ayios Onouphrios II ware *see under* POTTERY → wares
Ayios Philon Baptistery **3** 191, *191*
Ayios Sostis **8** 322
Ayios Sozomenos **8** 330
Ayios Stephanos **14** 343
Ayios Vasilios *see* ZYGOURIES
Ay-Khanum *see* AI KHANUM
Ay Khwaja **30** 352
Ayla **6** 330
Aylesford (Kent) **6** 162
  Carmelite monastery **5** 778
Aylesford (family) **14** 675
Aylesford, Heneage Finch, 4th Earl of *see* FINCH, HENEAGE, 4th Earl of Aylesford
Aymaní, Federico **31** 815
Aymara **4** 267
Aymar de Poitiers **14** 423; **20** 632
Aymat, Tomas **29** 309
Aymé, Marcel **32** 669
Aymeric, Pierre **7** 865, *866*
Aymeric Chrétien **13** 168
Aymonino, Carlo **2** 880*; **16** 650
  collaboration **25** 792; **27** 192
  groups and movements **25** 359
  works **16** 650, 651
Aymonino, Maurizio **2** 880
al-'Ayn **2** *246*
'Ayn al-Jarr *see* 'ANJAR (LEBANON)
Aynalov, Dmitry (Vlas'yevich) **2** 880*; **27** 443
'Ayn al-Sira Cemetery **16** 488
Aynard, Edouard **2** 880–81*
'Ayn Ghazāl *see* AIN GHAZAL
'Ayn Jawan **2** *246*, 249, 261, 263, 268
Ay-O **11** 232
Ayodhya **2** 881*; **15** *261*, 262, *360*, 409
  congregational mosque **15** 361
Ayón, Tomás **23** 85
Ayoresi **24** 93
'Ayoun Mousa **18** 823
Ayr **28** *222*, 251, 254, 265
Ayrarat **2** 426
Ayres, Gillian **1** 81; **2** 882*; **28** 804
Ayres, Harold **7** 648
Ayres, Pietro **31** 445
Ayrinschmalz, Konrad **20** 192
Ayrivank' **12** 234
Ayrtam **2** 882*; **6** *182*; **30** 440; **31** *781*
  architecture **6** 198
  reliefs **6** 194, 216–17, *217*
Ayrton, Edward **10** 80
Ayrton, Frederick **16** 554
Ayrton, Maxwell **29** 489; **33** 204
Ayrton, Michael **2** 882–3*; **18** 718; **21** 697
  groups and movements **22** 751
  writings **22** 751
Ayston Hall (Leics) **27** 466
Aytaç, Hamid **2** 883*; **14** 217; **31** 454
Aytbayev, S. **17** 867
Aytbayev, Salikhitdin **17** 867
Aytmish al-Bajasi **16** 357
Ayton, Richard **4** 362; **8** 505
Aytoun, William **9** 723, 728; **28** 225, 226; **32** 799
Ayub Khan **16** 93
Ayuso, Emilio Rodríguez *see* RODRÍGUEZ AYUSO, EMILIO
Ayutthaya **2** *883*, 883–7*, *884*; **29** *225*; **30** 571, *571*, 574
  architecture **2** 884–7*; **30** 591
  Chanthara Kasem National Museum **29** 240
  Chao Sam Praya National Museum **29** 240
  metalwork **30** 635
  niello **30** 635
  palaces **30** 588
  porcelain **30** 611
  royal palace *see* Wang Luang
  sculpture **30** 605
  urban planning **30** 592
  Wang Luang **2** 887; **30** 588
  Wang Na **30** 590
  Wat Borom Phuttharam **30** 636
  Wat Chai Wathanaram **2** 887; **30** 587
Ayutthaya—cont.
  Wat Mahathat **2** 885; **26** 151; **30** 587, 633
  Wat Na Phra Men **9** 163, *163*; **30** 594
  Wat Phra Ram **2** 885; **30** 587
  Wat Phra Si Sanphet **2** 886–7; **30** 587, *587*, *605*
  Wat Phu Khao Thong **30** 587
  Wat Phutthaisawan **2** 885; **30** 587, 616
  Wat Ratchaburana **2** 886, *886*; **29** 866; **30** 587, 616, 633
  reliquaries **26** 151
  Wat Suwandararam **30** 588
  Wat Thammikarat **2** 884–5
  Wat Yai Chaimongkhol **2** 885
Ayvalı Kilise **5** 674
Ayvalı Köy Church **5** 678
ayvan *see* IWANS
Ayvan-i Karkha **15** 922
Ayvazovsky, Ivan (Konstantinovich) **2** 887–8*
  collaboration **30** 915
  patrons and collectors **12** 332; **17** 718
  personal collection **31** 565
Ayyad, Raghib **5** 401; **9** 766; **22** 431
Ayyampet **15** 684
Ayyapa, Ruler (*reg* 895-923) (Nolamba) **23** 182
Ayyāvoḷe *see* AIHOLE
Ayyubid **2** 888–9*; **16** 114, 122
  architecture **4** 464; **16** 175; **21** 582; **33** 584
  see also:
  AL-'ADIL I, Sultan
  AL-ASHRAF MUZAFFAR, Sultan
  AL-'AZIZ, Sultan
  AL-KAMIL, Sultan
  AL-MU'AZZAM SHARAF AL-DIN, Sultan
  AL-SALIH NAJM AL-DIN, Sultan
  AL-SHAF'I, Imam
  AL-ZAHIR GHAZI, Sultan
  DAYFA KHATUN
  RABI'A KHATUN
  SALAH AL-DIN, Sultan
  SHAJARAT AL-DURR
Ayzac, Félicie d' **33** 309
Azabache Bustamante, Pedro **24** 511, 517
Azaceta, Luis Cruz *see* CRUZ AZACETA, LUIS
Azagury, Elie **1** 319
azaleas **17** 367
Azamgarh **15** 662, 664
A'zam Khan **15** 372
A'zam Shah, Emperor (*reg* 1707) (Mughal) **15** 373
  architecture **15** *373*
Azande *see* ZANDE
Azapa, Eladio Orco *see* ORCO AZAPA, ELADIO
Azara, José Nicolás de **2** 889*; **6** 97; **9** 23; **21** 134
al-Azar Mosque *see under* CAIRO → Islamic religious buildings
Azarnoush, Massoud **17** 773
Azarova, Lyudmila **27** 411
Azatiwatas **17** 810
Azatiwataya *see* KARATEPE
Azay-le-Rideau Château **2** 889*; **6** 504, 505; **11** *504*, 512, *512*, 571, 726; **29** 833
  roof **27** 130
  staircases **29** 522
Azaz, Nehemia **16** 568
Azbak al-Yusufi **5** 398
Ažbe, Anton **2** 889–90*; **28** 863
  pupils **28** 860
    Burlyuk, David (Davidovich) **5** 219
    Burlyuk, Vladimir (Davidovich) **5** 220
    Dobuzhinsky, Mstislav (Valerianovich) **9** 57
Ažbe, Anton
  pupils—cont.
    Grabar', Igor' (Emmanuilovich) **13** 263
    Grohar, Ivan **13** 680
    Hudeček, Antonín **14** 840
    Iser, Iosif **16** 72
    Jakopič, Rihard **16** 874
    Jawlensky, Alexei **17** 452
    Kandinsky, Vasily (Vasil'yevich) **17** 761
    Kardovsky, Dmitry (Nikolayevich) **17** 812
    Kuba, Ludvík **18** 489
    Makovskaya-Luksh, Yelena (Konstantinovna) **20** 152
    Petrović, Nadežda **24** 566
    Petrov-Vodkin, Kuz'ma (Sergeyevich) **24** 566
    Raud, Kristjan **26** 26
    Vukanović, Beta **32** 743
Azcapotzalco **21** 248, 255, 263
  ceramics **21** 374
  masks **21** 251
  metalwork **21** 374
Azcargorta, Martín de, Archbishop **9** 407
Azcona, Antonio Cellés y *see* CELLÉS Y AZCONA, ANTONIO
Azechi, Umetarō **17** 295
Azeglio, Massimo (Taparelli), Marchese D' *see* D'AZEGLIO, MASSIMO (TAPARELLI), Marchese
Azeglio, Robert Taparelli, Marchese D' *see* D'AZEGLIO, ROBERT TAPARELLI, Marchese
Azeitão, Quinta da Bacalhôa **12** 114; **20** 832; **30** 880
Azelin, Bishop of Hildesheim **14** 531; **26** 686
Azéma, Léon **4** 240; **10** 684
Azéma, Louis **5** 776
Azemmour **16** 448, 470
Azerbaijan **2** *890*, 891, 896, 898, 902*; **15** 902, 920; **16** *104*, *105*
  architecture **2** 891–4*
  armour **2** 900*
  bazaars **2** *894*
  bowls **2** *899*
  bronze **16** *506*
  carpets **2** *438*, 901–2; **16** 481, 483
  copper **2** *899*
  embroidery **2** 901*
  fortifications **2** 892
  furniture **2** 898
  glass **2** 898*
  guidebooks **13** 811
  guns **2** 900
  inlays **2** 902
  interior decoration **2** 898–9*
  jewellery **2** 899–900*
  kilims **2** *901*, 901–2
  manuscript illumination **2** *896*
  manuscripts **2** 895
  metal vessels **2** 899
  metalwork **2** 899–900*; **16** 378
  nude figures **2** 897
  painting **2** 895–7*
  portraits **2** 895–6, *897*
  pottery **2** 898*
  sculpture **2** 894–5*
  stage design **2** 897
  swords **2** 900; **16** *506*
  tents **16** 193; **30** 473
  textiles **2** 900–901*
  towers **2** *892*
  weapons **2** 900*
  wood-carvings **2** 902
  woodwork **2** 902*
  wool **2** *901*
Azerbaijan State Artistic Studio **2** 896
Azevedo, Arthur **33** 679
Azevedo, Bento da Fonseca *see* FONSECA AZEVEDO, BENTO DA
Azevedo, Damião Pereira da *see* PEREIRA DA AZEVEDO, DAMIÃO
Azevedo, Fernando de **2** 902–3*; **25** 300
Azevedo, Francisco de Paula Ramos de **2** 903*; **9** 335; **27** 808
Azevedo, Warren L. d' **1** 231
Azevedo Leão, Carlos
  assistants **23** 117
  collaboration **4** 712; **8** 7; **22** 95; **23** 117; **26** 109
  works **4** *712*
Azezo **1** *379*; **10** 566
Azgur, Zair *see* AZHUR, ZAIR
Azhar **16** 285, 864; **29** 919
Azhur, Zair **2** 903*; **3** 531; **21** 697
Azilian period *see under* PREHISTORIC ART → periods
Azim, Emperor (*reg* 1712) (Mughal) **24** 264
'Azimabad *see under* PATNA
'Azim al-Nisa Begum (Nawabs of Bengal) **15** 378
Azim Khan **29** 480
Azimut **6** 21; **20** 352
Azimzade, A. **2** 896
Azincourt, Barthélémy-Augustin Blondel d' **2** 904*; **4** 167
  collections **23** 778
  drawings **8** 703
  teachers **14** 799
Aziran Mosque **16** 194
Aziz (painter) **15** 631
al-'Aziz, Caliph (*reg* 975-96) (Fatimid) **5** 396, 402; **14** 170; **16** 174; **31** 22
  ewers **10** *832*
Aziz, Abdul **23** 804
al-'Aziz, Sultan (*reg* Aleppo 1216-37) (Ayyubid) **2** 888; **16** 182
Aziz Khan **23** 804
Aziz Kokaltash **15** 362
al-'Aziz Muhammad *see* AL-MALIK AL-'AZIZ, Sultan
'Aziz Rifa'i **16** 287
Azmar, Tell-al- **16** 59
Azmi, Musa *see* AYTAÇ, HAMID
Aznar, José Camón *see* CAMÓN AZNAR, JOSÉ
Aznar, Juan Manuel Figueroa *see* FIGUEROA AZNAR, JUAN MANUEL
Aznavurtepe **1** 839; **24** 266
  temple **1** 830
azo-dyes *see under* DYES → types
Azor **24** 635; **30** *180*, *197*
Azores **18** 158; **25** 287, 290, 292; **30** 879
Azov **27** 375
Azov-Don Bank **19** 332
al-Azraqi **13** 812; **27** 698
Aztatlán **2** 904–5*; **33** 101
Aztec **2** 905–8*; **21** 177, 181–2, 200, 202
  altars **1** 701
  amulets **1** 818
  archaeology **21** 211
  architecture **2** 905*; **21** 598, 599
  armour **21** 244, 247
  ballcourts **3** 118
  bamboo **10** *779*
  body ornaments **21** 248
  bone **4** 314
  bone-carvings **21** 248
  calendars **21** *224*, 234, 262, 265
  cane **21** 249
  causeways **6** 97
  chacmools **28** 640
  chalcedony **21** 243
  coatepantlis **7** 481–2
  collections **21** 265
  colour **7** 636; **21** 183
  copies **21** 266
  cotton **21** 249
  craftsmen and artists **21** 190, *190*, 191, 249
  diorite **21** 243
  dress **7** 636; **21** 262
  drums (musical instruments) **21** 257
  dyes **9** 492; **21** 249

Aztec—cont.
erotic art **10** 474
fans **10** 779, *779*
feathers **2** 908; **7** 636; **10** *779*, 848; **21** 249, *250*
figurines **21** 243
forgeries **21** 266
fortifications **21** 598, 599
gardens **12** 71, 136
garnets **22** 164
glues **21** 249
gold **21** 252
guilds **21** 249
hardstones **2** 908; **21** 243
helmets **22** 164
houses **21** 208
iconography **21** 186, 189
jade **16** 859; **21** 252
jadeite **16** 861; **21** 243
knife-handles **22** 164
limestone **21** *223*
maguey **21** 249
manuscript illumination **21** 182, 234–5; **22** *518*
manuscripts **20** 327; **21** 233, 234, 235
maps **20** 362
masks **21** 250, 251–2; **22** 164
metalwork **2** 908

Aztec—cont.
mirror frames **21** 719, *719*
mirrors **21** 719, *719*
mosaics **2** 908; **21** 244, 248, 255; **22** 164
mother-of-pearl **22** 164
musical instruments **21** 248
narratives **22** *518*, 519
obsidian **21** *719*; **22** 164
painting **2** 907*
palaces **23** 825
paper **21** 249, *250*
plaster **29** 828
porphyry **21** *244*
pottery **2** 907*; **21** 240, 266
pyramids **30** *453*
quetzal **21** 249
rediscovery **21** 262
reliefs **2** *907*
religion **21** 184, 187, 188, 189
rock crystal **21** 243; **26** 487
roofs **27** 128
scripts **21** 233
sculpture **2** 905–7*; **21** 217, 222, 223–5*, *244*, *400*; **29** 901
seals **21** 258
shells **21** 260
shields **14** 411; **21** *250*; **22** 164
shrines (i) (cult) **28** 640

Aztec—cont.
signatures **21** 249
skins **21** 252
skull racks **31** *506*
staircases **29** 527, *527*
standards (vexilloid) **11** 152, *152*
stelae **29** 620
stone **2** 906–7, *907*; **21** 218
stone-carvings **2** *906*; **21** *223*, *224*
stucco **29** 828
temples **7** 481; **30** 449, *453*
tombs **31** 118
turquoise **21** 251, 252; **22** 164
urban planning **21** 375
weapons **21** 244, 245, 246, 247
wood **2** 907; **21** 719, *719*
Aztec (NM), Great Kiva **18** 103
Aztec Pueblo **22** 566
Aztec ware *see under* POTTERY → wares
Azuchi **17** *11*, 84, 163
Castle **2** 908–9*; **17** 22, 84; **21** 595, 827, 828; **23** 347
paintings **17** 22, 40–41, 783–4, 794, 796; **23** 554
Jesuit church **17** 84
metalwork **17** 323

Azuchi-Momoyama period *see* JAPAN → periods → Momoyama
azulejos de xadrez tiles *see under* TILES → types
azulejos tiles *see under* TILES → types
Azuma, Takamitsu **2** 909*; **17** 91
groups and movements **2** 363; **17** 91; **30** 260
Azure **24** 431
azurite
historical and regional traditions
Armenia (Europe) **23** 785
Central Asia, Eastern **6** 302
China **7** 632; **18** 600
Japan **17** 277; **18** 600; **24** 790
Mesoamerica, Pre-Columbian **1** 713
Rome, ancient **23** 785
uses
lacquer **18** 600
pigments **6** 302; **7** 632; **11** 763; **17** 277; **23** 785; **24** 789, 790*
az(z)ur(r)o dell' Allemagna see under PIGMENTS → types
az(z)ur(r)o della magna see under PIGMENTS → types
Azzawi, Dia **16** 2

Azzi, Stefano degli **4** 274
Azzo(ne), Lord of Milan (*reg* 1328-39) **32** 609–10*
architecture **3** 770
paintings **12** 683; **13** 151; **21** 524
tombs **12** 709
Azzo I, Lord of Ferrara (*reg* 1209-12) **10** 517
Azzo II, Marchese of Ferrara (*reg* 1215-22; 1240-64) **11** 2
Azzo III, 2nd Marchese of Ferrara (*reg* 1293-1308) **10** 517
Azzolini **25** 501
Azzolini, Decio, Cardinal **2** 909–10*; **30** 118
Azzolini, Giacomo **25** 814; **26** 363
Azzolino, Giovanni Bernardino **2** 910*; **9** 174; **22** 478; **32** 8
Azzolino, Pompeo **2** 910
Azzo of Siena **27** 751
Azzurri, Francesco **26** 837
Azzurri, Giovanni **29** 640
azzurro oltramarino see PIGMENTS → types → ultramarine

B

B 18, Master of 4 274
Bâ, Amadou 28 405
Baader, Johannes 3 801; 8 436, 437; 24 405
Baalbek 3 *1*, 1–3*; 13 *362*; 16 *104*; 19 8; 26 *915*
  architecture 16 208; 26 882
  Islamic Towers 32 89
  masonry 26 916
  mouldings 9 757
  pediments 24 318
  Sanctuary of Jupiter Heliopolitanus 3 2; 27 1, 714
    propylaeum 26 *917*
    Temple of Jupiter 3 2; 13 405; 26 867, 881, 917; 30 436
      exedrae 9 85; 23 491
      frieze 26 916
      meander 20 *912*
      mouldings 3 439
  temenos 26 915
  temples 26 858
    Temple of Bacchus 3 2–3, *3*; 26 867, 917
      aediculae 1 164
      coffering 7 527
      orders (architecture) 23 491
    Temple of Jupiter *see under* Sanctuary of Jupiter Heliopolitanus
    Temple of Venus 3 3; 9 83, 85; 23 491; 26 *881*, 882; 27 235
  textiles 16 441
Baal of Thinissut 25 733
Baanders, Herman Ambrosius Jan 14 693
Baanders, Jan 14 693
Baanders Bros 4 484
Baar *see* PARRI
Baardt, Claes Fransen *see* BAERDT, CLAES FRANSEN
Baargeld, Johannes Theodor 3 3–4*; 8 437, 438; 10 467
Baarová, Lída 33 599
Baba, Corneliu 3 4–5*; 26 726
Baba Jan 3 5–6*; 15 *901*, 905
  fort 3 *5*; 19 811
  house 15 910, *911*; 19 811
  paintings 15 922
  sculpture 19 812
Babakhanov, Abdulla 31 782
Baba Khatim *see* KIM SANE
Baba Nakkaş ware *see under* POTTERY → wares
Babanki 3 148
Babanki-Tungo 3 147
Baba Nyonya 20 181
Babar, Emperor *see* BABUR, Emperor
Babar, Prince 30 917
Babar ʿAli 17 806
Babayev, Abdulhusein 2 902
Babayev, R. G. 2 897
Babb, Cook & Willard 3 6*; 5 562; 14 174
Babb, George Fletcher 3 6*; 7 876
Babbage, Charles 2 838
Babcock, Charles 31 691
Babel, Johann Baptist 3 6–7*; 10 117; 30 137
Babel, Joseph 31 510
Babel, Peter 11 430
Babel, Pierre-Edmé 7 185; 22 925
Babel, Tower of *see* BABYLON (MESOPOTAMIA) → Tower of Babylon
Babeldoab 23 832, 834
Babelsburg Schloss 12 376; 13 202
Babemo 19 74
Babenberg (family) 2 819; 14 308
Babenberg, Henry II Jasomirgott, Duke of Austria *see* HENRY II JASOMIRGOTT, Duke of Austria
Babenberg, Leopold I, Margrave of Austria *see* LEOPOLD I, Margrave of Austria
Babenberg, Leopold III, Margrave of Austria *see* LEOPOLD III, Margrave of Austria
Babenberg, Leopold VI, Duke of Austria *see* LEOPOLD VI, Duke of Austria
Babenburg, Leopold VI, Duke of Austria *see* LEOPOLD VI, Duke of Austria
Babenburg, Poppo von, Archbishop of Trier 12 471; 31 326
Babene
  figurines 19 *72*
Babenhausen, Fugger-Museum 11 818
Babia, Juan Rodríguez de 3 7*; 20 69; 29 334
Babić, Gordana 9 528
Babić, Ljubo 22 371
Babichev, Alexey 15 857
Babics, Zsigmond 11 31
Babikov, Stanislav Gennadyevich 31 459
Babil 21 298
Babin, J.-P. 13 608
Babineau, Joseph 1 786
Babiska 3 376
Babisqa 9 *513*, 540, 543
al-Bab Mosque 16 179
Babo, Joseph Marius 25 787
Baboccio da Piperno, Antonio 13 98; 27 615
Babor 5 500
Babou, Philibert, Sieur de la Bourdaisière *see* BOURDAISIÈRE, PHILIBERT BABOU, Sieur de la
Babrius 10 723
Babu, Lala 32 732
Babur, Emperor (*reg* 1526-30) (Mughal) 22 258
  architecture 2 881; 8 674; 10 826; 15 361–2
  fortifications 24 540
  gardens 1 458; 3 238; 12 73; 17 716
  jade 15 698; 16 528
  manuscripts 10 *816*; 15 577–8; 16 551
  tents 15 716
Babur, Prince (Timurid) and Emperor (Mughal) *see* BABUR, Emperor
Baburen, Dirck (Jaspersz.) van 3 7–8*; 12 290; 26 772
  forgeries by others 11 309; 21 39
  groups and movements 5 1; 22 843; 28 92; 30 456; 31 772
  patrons and collectors 32 262
  teachers 22 94
  works 3 *8*
Baburov, Viktor 32 695
baby-carriers 1 296; 3 442
baby houses *see* DOLLS' HOUSES
Babyington, Richard 7 236
Babylon (Egypt) *see under* CAIRO
Babylon (Mesopotamia) 1 *849*, 891, 892; 2 *246*; 3 *9*, 9–12*; 16 2; 20 361; 21 *267*, 268, 275, 291, 310; 28 382, *719*, 721
  architecture 4 771; 21 274, 275
  brick 4 *771*, 772
  bridge 4 800
  Etemenanki *see* Tower of Babylon
Babylon (Mesopotamia) —cont.
  faience (i) (glass) 1 879
  glass 1 868
  Hanging Gardens 3 10; 12 65, 66; 21 291
  inscriptions 1 895
  Ishtar Gate 1 879; 3 10; 4 769; 21 275, 310
    polychromy 25 171
  Merkes 3 9
  metalwork 21 304
  murals 15 922
  Northern Palace 21 291
  Palace of Tiglath-Pileser III 20 *326*
  Processional Way 1 879
  reliefs 1 117
  religion 21 278
  sculpture 21 295, 302
  Southern Palace 1 879; 3 *10*, 10–11*; 21 291; 23 806
    polychromy 25 171
  Summer Palace 21 291
  Temple of Marduk 3 11; 28 383
  textiles 1 880
  throne-room of Nebuchadnezzar 21 310
  Tower of Babel *see* Tower of Babylon
  Tower of Babylon 1 156; 3 11*; 21 284; 23 338; 33 675
  writing 20 *326*
  ziggurat 21 291; 28 383; 33 675
Babylonia 1 *849*; 21 *267*, 268, 274–5
Babylonian 1 854; 3 11–12*; 21 *267*; 30 178
  architecture 21 552
  bricklaying 3 *10*
  bronze 21 304
  censorship 6 174
  chalcedony 1 *858*
  dress 1 *884*, 885, 886, 887
  façade decoration 10 742
  faience (i) (glass) 21 308
  fortifications 21 552
  kudurrus 21 276
  languages 3 11–12
  marble 3 *12*
  mud-bricks 10 742
  palaces 21 *285*
  sculpture 10 742; 21 302*
  seals 1 856, 858, *858*, 861, 862
  stelae 3 *12*
  writing-tablets 1 853; 2 364
  ziggurats 21 286; 33 675
Babylonian period *see under* MESOPOTAMIA → periods
Babytinga 16 861
Bač, Cathedral of St Paul 28 444
Baca, Judy 18 831
Baca Flor, Carlos 3 12*; 30 216
Baçakale 27 13
Bacanović, Branko 4 462
Bacarisas, Gustavo 28 516
Bacavi 22 567
Baccani, Gaetano 3 12–13*
  works 11 *180*
Baccano 27 62
Baccarat 3 13*; 11 *504*, 613; 24 58
  crystal 5 583
  paperweights 24 57
  production 11 612
Baccarelli, Vicenzo 19 523
Bacchiacca 3 13–15*
  collaboration 24 525; 27 848
  patrons and collectors 3 15; 4 404; 13 281; 16 711; 23 855; 27 729
  works 3 *14*; 11 193
Bacchias Temple 10 759
Bacchus, George, & Co. 10 320; 24 57
Bacci (family) 4 32; 24 762
Bacci, Edmondo 13 801
Bacci, Orazio 6 148
Bacci, Peleo 24 872
Bacciarelli, Marcello 3 14–15*; 25 38, 105, 140, 141; 32 876
  house 17 756
  patrons and collectors 25 212; 33 115
  pupils 23 530; 27 446
  works 25 99; 32 876, 879
Baccin (family) 16 738
Baccin, Giovanni Maria 16 738; 23 263
Baccio, Paolo di *see* PAOLO DI BACCIO
Baccio, Tonio di *see* TONIO DI BACCIO
Baccio d'Agnolo (Bartolommeo d'Agnolo di Donato Baglione) 3 15–17*; 4 404; 11 705
  collaboration 8 187; 16 724; 21 451; 27 739
  patrons and collectors 16 711; 29 782; 30 231
  works 3 *16*; 4 404; 25 265; 27 740
Baccio d'Agnolo, Giuliano di *see* BAGLIONE, GIULIANO
Baccio del Bianco, Luigi 3 17*; 30 664
  collaboration 24 771
  works 11 194; 25 446
Bach, Elvira 3 17–18*
Bach, Jaume 29 428
Bach, J(ohann) C(hristian) 1 125; 7 687
Bach, J(ohann) S(ebastian) 1 123; 9 20; 22 380
Bach, Oscar 31 653
Bachaumont, Louis-Petit de 3 18*; 8 209
Bache, Charles 12 211
Bache, Jules Semon 3 18*; 9 467
Bache, Otto 23 162
Bache, Sarah Franklin 14 *754*
Bachegraig 32 782
Bachelard, Gaston 3 18*
Bachelder, Ernest 30 888
Bachelier, Antoine 3 20
Bachelier, Dominique 3 20
Bachelier, Géraud 3 20
Bachelier, Jean-Jacques 1 107; 2 524; 3 19*; 11 657, 669; 25 81; 28 521
  methods 10 198
  pupils 30 45
  works 15 140; 29 668; 32 582, 583
Bachelier, Nicolas 3 19–20*; 5 346; 31 206
Bachelin, (Rodolphe-) Auguste 3 20*
  teachers 12 810
Bachenheimer, Beth 27 872
Bacher, Gideon 3 20*, 870; 31 567
Bacher, Josef, & Sons 17 527; 26 191
Bacher, Otto 9 468; 21 896
Bacher, Rudolf 3 20–21*
Bacherelli 26 554
Bachet, Marcel 13 856
Bachhofer, Ludwig 7 160; 15 211
Bachiacca *see* BACCHIACCA
Bachkovo Monastery 3 21*; 5 *144*, 147, 154, 160; 9 *511*
  charnel-house 5 150; 9 576, 579, *579*
  Church of the Virgin 5 148, 154
Bachkovo Monastery—cont.
  collections 9 523
  icons 5 154; 9 625; 25 338
  manuscripts 5 152
Bachman, Gábor 14 891
Bachman, John (1790-1874) 2 711
Bachmann, John (*fl* 1849-99) 4 81
  works 24 *180*
Bachmann, Jürgen 17 547
Bachmann, Simon 30 136
Bachmann, Walter 3 418; 17 826
Bachmatavičius, Kazimieras 19 498; 27 446
Bachmayer, H. M. 29 435
Bachot (family) 13 79
Bachot, Jacques 3 21*; 31 382
Bachot, Marc 3 21
Bachot, Yvon 3 21, 22
Bachrach Studios 30 216
Bachué 7 609
Bachuys (family) 22 452
Bach-y-graig (Clwyd) 4 780
Baciccio, Il *see* GAULLI, GIOVANNI BATTISTA
BACIF 13 877
bacini 16 100, 395, 404, 411; 30 886
Baciocchi, Elisa, Grand Duchess of Tuscany *see* ELISA, Grand Duchess of Tuscany
Baciocchi, Felice 25 893
Bäck 26 646
Bäcka 30 113
Backer, Adriaen 19 749, 783
Backer, Cornelis 21 489; 25 756
Backer, Harriet 3 22*; 23 225, 244
  pupils 9 750; 29 15, 78
Backer, Jacob (Adriaensz.) 3 22–3*; 22 843
  patrons and collectors 13 266; 33 700
  pupils 3 42; 30 425
  teachers 11 169; 16 833
  works 3 *23*
Backer, Jacob de 3 23–4*, 558; 29 799
  works 3 *24*
Backer, Jan de 17 649
Backer, John James 18 146
Backer, Lars (Thalian) 3 24*; 23 222, 602
Backer, Nicolas de *see* BACKER, JOHN JAMES
Backereel, Gilles 15 43
Backereel, Jacob 12 285
Backereel, Peter 12 15
Backes, Heinrich 29 751
Backhausen, Johann, & Söhne 2 826; 22 187; 24 309
  works 2 *826*
Backhuysen, Ludolf *see* BAKHUIZEN, LUDOLF, the elder
backless towers *see under* TOWERS → types
Backman, Johan N. 11 95
Backoffen, Hans 12 401; 20 129
back-painted mirrors *see under* MIRRORS → types
Bäcksbacka, Leonard 11 112
backscratchers 7 102
Backsteingotik see under GOTHIC → styles
back stitch *see under* STITCHES
back stools *see under* CHAIRS → types
backstrap looms *see under* LOOMS → types
Bäckström, Monica 30 103
Bäckström, Sven 1 470; 3 25*
Backström & Reinius 3 25*; 30 75
Backwell, Edward 10 328

Backworth 27 103
Bacler d'Albe, Louis-Albert 4 300
Baco, Jaime *see* JACOMART
Bacolod 24 607
Bacon, Edmund 24 598; 29 718; 31 735
Bacon, Francis 3 26–9*
dealers 19 246; 20 75
patrons and collectors 7 797; 14 575; 24 278; 27 524
works 3 28, 29; 7 831; 10 258; 23 297; 31 345
Bacon, Francis, 1st Baron Verulam, Viscount St Albans 3 29–30*; 31 150
architecture 6 128; 9 55
works 2 162; 31 297
illustrated 6 129
Bacon, Francis Henry 3 30
Bacon, Henry 3 30–31*
collaboration 27 558
teachers 20 18
works 25 235; 32 887
Bacon, John (i) (1740-99) 3 25–6*; 8 587; 19 599, 606; 30 502
pointing (i) (sculpture) 10 265
pupils 3 26; 8 481
sculpture 7 480; 10 264, 265; 16 884; 19 599
monumental 3 26; 5 751; 7 340; 16 884, 889
mythological 2 541; 7 480
Bacon, John (ii) (1777-1859) 3 26*; 15 542; 19 599
Bacon, Nathaniel 3 31*
Bacon, Nicholas 8 273
Bacon, Peggy (Frances) 3 31*; 9 310
Bacon, Roger 5 519; 7 627; 19 356; 24 486, 487; 28 202
Bacon, Thomas 3 26*
Bacon Cup 14 418
Bacon's Castle (VA) 31 589
Bacor, Josse 11 642; 22 456
Bacot, Edmond 14 853
Bacot, Jacques 30 849, 850
al-Bacr 28 779
Bactra *see* BALKH
Bactria 1 186
architecture 6 196, 197–8*
bosses 6 237
capitals 6 217
clasps 30 891
clay 6 215, 216, 216
coins 1 204, 204
dress 1 886; 6 251
earrings 9 457
gold 9 457; 30 891
limestone 6 217
painting 6 216, 224–6*, 225, 226; 28 722
plaster 6 214–15
pottery 6 255
sculpture 6 214, 214–17*, 215, 216, 217; 9 34; 15 914
silver-gilt 6 237
stamps 6 214
statuettes 6 275
stone 6 216–17
temples 6 197–8
textiles 6 214
urban planning 6 209
see also AFGHANISTAN
Bactrian and Indo-Greek monarchies 3 31–2*
Baculard d'Arnaud, François-Thomas de 20 421
Bacza, Balduccio de *see* BALDUCCIO DE BACZA
Bada, José de 15 33; 20 157
Bada Bagh 15 389
badahanj *see* WIND CATCHERS
Badajoz 16 411; 29 702
Monastery of S María de Tentudía 29 325; 30 882
Badajoz, Juan de (i) (*d* 1522) 3 32*; 19 172
assistants 3 32
works 19 175; 23 682
Badajoz, Juan de (ii) (*c*. 1498-*c*. 1560) 3 32*; 5 883; 23 681; 29 267
groups and movements 25 30
works 19 171, 172; 29 289
Badajoz, Rodrigo de 13 69
Badakhshan 15 902; 24 790
lapis lazuli 24 XII1
Badalocchio, Sisto 3 32–3*
collaboration 5 864, 867; 18 730, 732; 26 196
patrons and collectors 24 267
works 1 596; 3 33
Badaloni, Paolo di Stefano *see* SCHIAVO, PAOLO
Badami 3 33–4*; 15 276, 294
Cave 2 15 298
Cave 3 15 277, 293, 295, 477, 543, 558, 558
reliefs 15 477, 677
reliefs 15 227, 677
rock reliefs 15 477
sculpture 15 416
temples 15 293, 526
Bhutanatha Temple 15 295
Jambulinga Temple 15 300
Lower Shivalaya Temple 15 526
Malegitti Shivalaya Temple 3 34; 15 295, 526
Upper Shivalaya Temple 15 295, 526
Vaishnava cave 6 404
wall paintings 15 548, 549
Badan Singh 15 612
Badan Singh Badoria 15 373
Badaon 15 340; 20 226
Badar, Françoise 31 816
Badaracco, Giovanni Raffaello 2 127; 3 34–5*
Badaracco, Giuseppe 3 34
el-Badari 3 35*; 9 773, 774; 10 59
ivory 10 60
Tomb 3802 9 824, 824
Badarian period *see under* EGYPT, ANCIENT → periods
Bada Shanren *see* ZHU DA
Bad Aussee Spitalkirche 2 793
Badawy, Alexander 9 825
Badbury Rings (Dorset) 18 584, 585
Bad Cannstatt 25 542
Bad Dürkheim 6 155
Badea, Costel 26 719
Badeley, Henry John Fanshawe 10 397
Baden, Charles-Frederick, Grand Duke of *see* CHARLES-FREDERICK, Grand Duke of Baden
Baden, Elizabeth of *see* ELIZABETH ALEKSEYEVNA, Empress of Russia
Baden, Frederick I, Grand Duke of *see* FREDERICK I, Grand Duke of Baden
Baden, Hans Jurriaensz. van 8 663
Baden, Leopold, Grand Duke of *see* LEOPOLD, Grand Duke of Baden
Baden-Baden
Badischer Hof 14 786
misericords 21 725
Neues Schloss
Fürstensaal 29 674
Neue Trinkhalle 13 218; 27 335
SS Peter und Paul 27 125
crucifix 12 343
sculpture 13 91
Staatliche Kunsthalle 4 64
Trinkhalle 14 840; 30 503
Baden-Baden, Frances Sibyl Augusta, Margravine of *see* FRANCES SIBYL AUGUSTA, Margravine of Baden-Baden
Baden-Baden, Philibert, Margrave of *see* PHILIBERT, Margrave of Baden-Baden
Baden-Baden, William, Margrave of *see* WILLIAM, Margrave of Baden-Baden
Baden-Baden, William VII, Margrave of *see* WILLIAM VII, Margrave of Baden-Baden
Baden culture 25 512
Baden-Durlach, Carolina Luise, Margravine of *see* CAROLINE LOUISE, Margravine of Baden-Durlach
Baden-Durlach, Ernest-Frederick, Margrave of *see* ERNEST-FREDERICK, Margrave of Baden-Durlach
Baden-Durlach, George-Frederick, Margrave of *see* GEORGE-FREDERICK, Margrave of Baden-Durlach
Baden-Durlach, Karl-Friedrich, Margrave of *see* CHARLES-FREDERICK, Grand Duke of Baden
Baden-Durlach, Karl Wilhelm, Margrave of *see* CHARLES III, Margrave of Baden-Durlach
Badeni, Marcin 18 490
Baden Railway Station 29 491
Badens, Frans 23 124; 33 253
Badenweiler 26 872
Bader, O. N. 17 805
Badeslade, Thomas 4 80
Badew, Richard 5 511
Badger, Daniel D. 3 35–6*; 12 221; 16 54
works 26 18; 31 592, 592
Badger, Joseph 3 36*; 4 477
badger-hair *see under* HAIR → types
badges 7 179; 14 404, 414, 419, 419, 428–9, III1; 15 149; 17 521; 29 346
see also IMPRESA
badgir *see* WIND CATCHERS
Bad Hersfeld Theatre 30 469
Bad Homburg, Erlöserkirche 19 815
Badia a Isola, Master of 9 349; 20 620*
Badia Altarpiece 11 380; 12 686
Badiali, Carla 16 681; 25 838; 26 289
Badiʿ al-Zaman, Sultan (*reg* 1506) (Timurid) 4 50; 16 326
Bad Iburg, St Klemens
tomb of Gottschalk von Diepholz 26 632
Badie al-Shaykh 3 69
Badii, Líbero 2 401; 3 36–7*
Badii, Museo *see under* BUENOS AIRES → museums
Badile, Angelo 3 37
Badile, Antonio, I (*d* before 1409) 3 37
Badile, Antonio, II (*fl* 1424-1507) 3 37
Badile, Antonio, III (*fl* 1492) 3 37
Badile, (Giovanni) Antonio, IV (1518-60) 3 37–8*
pupils 32 347; 33 631
teachers 5 816
Badile, Bartolomeo, I (*fl* 1445-51) 3 37
Badile, Bartolomeo, II (*fl* 1464-1544) 3 37
Badile, Francesco, I (*fl* 1476-1544) 3 37
Badile, Francesco, II (*fl* 1505-57) 3 37
Badile, Giovanni 3 37*; 32 343
Badile, Girolamo 3 37
Badile, Niccolò 3 37
Badile, Pietro Paolo 3 37
Badis, Ruler (*reg* 1038-73) (Zirid) 20 156
Badischer Architekten- und Ingenieursverein 3 410
Badischer Kunstverein, Karlsruhe 17 818
Badischer Techniker-Verein *see* BADISCHER ARCHITEKTEN- UND INGENIEURSVEREIN
Badjau 24 625
Badlam, Stephen (1721-58) 3 38
Badlam, Stephen (1748-1815) 3 38*; 28 525, 819; 31 628
Bad Mergentheim Castle 25 2
Badminton Cabinet 2 561; 7 234; 13 302
Badminton House (Glos) 8 46; 29 58
Chinese Bedroom 10 295
collections 2 561; 9 28; 33 375
frames 11 424
furniture 10 293, 294
gardens 12 127
paintings 5 598; 29 31; 33 176
Ragged Castle 11 242
Root House 8 30; 11 243
Swangrove 10 277; 23 789
Worcester Lodge 12 176, 176
Bado Aureo, John de *see* JOHN DE BADO AUREO
Badodi, Arnaldo 7 894
Badoer, Francesco 23 866
Badoh 3 38–9*; 15 285
Gadarmal 15 288
pillar 15 495
reliefs 15 468
sculpture 15 495, 496
Sola Khambi 3 38; 15 288
toraṇas 31 160
see also PATHARI
Badoli *see* BAROLI
Badour 3 591
Badovici, Jean 13 328
Badr al-Din Lu'lu' 3 39*
architecture 16 182
brass 23 563
glass 16 520
manuscripts 16 114, 300; 22 202
metalwork 16 379, 380, 380, 381, 382
Badr al-Din Muslih 18 234
Badr al-Din Ulugh Qaymaz 16 374
Badr al-Jamali 5 396; 16 173, 175, 490; 21 582, 629; 28 634
Badran, Rasim 3 39*; 16 243
Bad Reichenhall, St Zeno 26 634
Badr ibn Hasanwayh 16 160
Badrinas, Antoni 29 308, 309
Bad Schandau Church 12 461
Bad Segeberg, Marienkirche 1 724; 4 776
Badsha, Omar 9 427
Badui 1 706
Badulunuvara 29 450
Badura, Bernard 11 499
Bad Wildungen, Stadtkirche 12 383
Wildungen Altarpiece *see* NIEDERWILDUNGEN ALTARPIECE
Bad Wimpfen Church 32 90
Bad Windsheim 32 282
Baeck, Elias 29 748
Baeck, Johan 31 772
Baeck, Leo, Institute *see under* NEW YORK → Institutes
Baedeker, Karl 13 304, 810, 811
Ba'ef-ba 29 X1
Baegert, Derick 3 39–41*; 17 600
works 3 40
Baegert, Jan 3 41*
Baehr, Andrew Adam 30 212; 31 196
Baehr, Johann 18 851
Baehr, Ulrich 3 803; 31 532
Baekelmans, François 10 662
Baekelmans, Louis 10 662
Baellieur, Cornelis de, the elder (1607-71) 3 41–2*; 5 352
Baellieur, Cornelis de, the younger (1642-87) 3 41
Baemler, Johann *see* BÄMLER, JOHANNES
Baen, Jacobus de 3 42
Baen, Jan de 3 42*
Baena, Church of Le Madre de Dios 29 266
Baer, Hans 14 437
Baerdesen, Willem 1 801
Baerdt, Claes Fransen 3 42*; 22 888
Baeren, Jan van der 19 260
Baers, Jan 11 226
Baert (family) 23 665; 30 324
Baert, Jan 31 219
Baert, Nicolaas 3 600
Baertels, Joseph Anton
works 20 282
Bærtling, Olle (Bertil Georg) 3 42–3*; 30 81, 86
Baertsoen, Albert 3 43*
Baerum, Henie-Onstad Kunstsenter *see under* HØVIKKODEN
Baerwald, Alexander 3 43–4*
assistants 26 20
collaboration 26 20
staff 18 421
works 16 572
Baerze, Jacques de *see* JACQUES DE BAERZE
Baes, Charles 3 44
Baes, Henri 3 44
Baes, (Pierre-)Jean (-Baptiste) 3 44*, 549, 579
Baes, Pierre 3 44
Baessler, Arthur 29 221
Baev, Georgi 3 44*; 5 163
Baeyer, Adolf von 24 791
Báez, Gaspar 2 386
Báez, Myrna 3 44–5*; 14 697; 25 702
Baeza 3 45*; 29 258
Monastery of S Francisco 29 266
University 31 674
Baeza, Francisco de *see* FRANCISCO DE BAEZA
Baeza, Juan de 5 737
Bafas, Georgios 13 358; 26 149
bafen script *see under* SCRIPTS → types
Bafetin Church 9 591
Baffier, Jean 11 629
Baffier, Jules 11 629
Bafo 1 266
Bafoussam 3 148
Bafut (people) 1 307; 3 145, 147, 148
Bafut (place) 1 309
Baga 1 387, 391; 3 45–8*
divination instruments 1 356
drums (musical instruments) 3 47
headdresses 1 391; 3 47*, 47
iconography 1 262, 263
masks 1 256, 279, 391; 3 46–7*
sculpture 1 322; 3 46; 13 834
wood 1 391; 3 46, 47
Båga, Axel Hansson 11 107
Bagam 3 147
Bagamoyo 30 57
Baganda 1 309, 344, 348
Bagaran Church 2 425, 426; 7 256
Bagard, César 1 132; 3 48*
Bagard, Nicolas 3 48
Bagard, Toussaint 3 48
Bagaretto (family) 31 32
Bagarris 3 48*; 12 266
Bagas, Mira 15 607
Bagassi 5 328, 329
Bagastāna *see* BISITUN
Bagatti Valsecchi, Fausto 3 49–50*
works 3 50
Bagatti Valsecchi, Giuseppe 3 49–50*
works 3 50
Bagatti Valsecchi, Pietro 3 49*
Bagavan 2 425
church 2 425
el-Bagawat 7 822–3; 18 20
chapel 17 534
Bagay, Nicolas de la Cruz 24 621
Bağcılar *see* OPIZA
Bage, Charles 10 748; 16 52

Bâgé, Etienne de, Bishop of Autun 2 840
Bagelaar, Ernst Willem Jan 10 562
Bagerhat
  mausoleum of Khan-i Jahan Ulugh Khan 15 352
  Sath Gunbad Mosque 15 353
Bagetti, Giuseppe Pietro 4 300; 31 445
Bagford, John 10 421
Baggara 1 306
Baggio, Anselmo da *see* ALEXANDER II, Pope
Baggio, Istituto Marchiondi Spagliardi 5 57
Baggs, Arthur Eugene 3 50*; 4 73; 30 887; 31 640
Bagh 3 50–51*; 15 257, 259, *276*, *285*
  Cave 2 15 470
  Cave 9 15 470
  paintings 22 516
  pillars 15 277
  sculpture 15 470
  wall paintings 3 51; 15 543, 548
Baghdad 3 51–3*; 16 *104*, 122; 21 268; 28 *719*, 721
  art forms and materials
    architecture 16 1, 161, 193, 228; 32 315
    chess sets 6 556
    coins 16 511
    manuscripts 16 *275*, 296, 307, 309–10, 314, 317, 318, 319, 320, 328, 350; 24 48
    metalwork 16 373
    miniatures (manuscript illumination) 16 *309*, *320*
    paper 24 48
    pottery 16 397, 398
    printing 16 361
    scrolls 21 48
    textiles 16 433, 434
    tiles 16 398
  baths 3 375
  cantonments 16 151
  caravanserais 5 723
    Khan al-Mirjan 5 723; 16 193; 20 438
    Khan al-Urtma *see* Khan al-Mirjan
  central library 2 370
  coins 16 *512*
  forgeries 1 896
  fortifications 21 588
  gates
    Bab al-Wastani 21 588
    Talisman Gate 9 161; 16 246, *247*; 21 583
  guidebooks 13 812
  houses 16 1, *267*, *268*, 270, *270*
  Income Tax Building 16 1
  Institute of Applied Arts 16 2
  Islamic religious buildings
    Ahmadiyya Mosque 16 228
    congregational mosque *see* University mosque
    madrasas 16 180; 20 55
    mihrabs 21 505
    mosque of al-Mansur *see under* Round City
    Mustansiriyya Madrasa 3 *52*; 20 55
    Nizamiyya Madrasa 20 55
    shrine of Zumurrud Khatun 22 322
    State Mosque 16 243
    University mosque 16 242
  Martyrs' Monument 10 833; 16 2, *3*
  Monument of Liberty 16 2
  Monument to the Unknown Soldier 16 2
  Municipality Building 16 1
  musalla 22 354
  museums
    Arab Museum 3 53; 16 558
    Archaeological Museum (1923) 16 557
Baghdad
  museums—cont.
    Iraq Museum 16 3, 558
      collections 3 53; 21 310; 31 694
    Mada'in Museum 3 53
    Museum of Pioneer Artists 16 3
    National Museum of Modern Art 16 2, 3
  observatory 23 338
  palace of Adud al-Dawla 16 160
  palace of al-Nasir 16 182
  palaces 16 136; 23 814
  Round City 3 51; 16 150, *150*; 21 582
    mosque of al-Mansur 16 152
    palace of al-Mansur 23 815
  al-Rusafa 3 51
  Saddam Arts Centre 16 3
  Salaat al-Kabiri 17 550
  Shaheed *see* Martyrs' Monument
  tomb of Abu Hanifa 28 634
  tombs 16 159
  urban planning 16 241, 260, 261, 262
  Water Board Building 16 1
Baghdad Group of Modern Art 16 2
Baghdad Group textiles *see under* TEXTILES → types
al-Baghdadi, al-Khaṭīb 13 812
al-Baghdadi, Hashem Muhammad *see* HASHEM MUHAMMAD AL-BAGHDADI
Baghdasaryan, Sergey 2 437
Bagheria
  Villa Palagonia 16 640
  villas 16 640
  Villa Valguarnera 15 881
Bagh Gai 1 195, 196, 201
Baghouz 21 269; 30 196
Bagijn, Pieter Jansz. 7 866
Bagis 19 841
  Aktepe I 19 841
Bagis, Jean de 31 206
Bağlarbaşi, Mar Cyriacus 31 435
bag leather *see under* LEATHER → types
Bagley 10 321
Bagley, Robert 7 160
Bagli, Kalleshvara Temple 15 527
Baglieto, Santiago 30 417
Baglione, Cesare 8 280
Baglione, Giovanni 3 53–5*; 26 770; 27 621
  collaboration 28 529
  groups and movements 30 456
  patrons and collectors 1 595; 4 549, 567; 10 861; 12 763, 912, 913; 24 399; 26 306; 28 337
  works 3 *54*; 6 78; 26 833
  writings 10 204; 16 781
Baglione, Giuliano 3 16; 31 448
Baglioni (Perugian family) 4 406; 10 651; 25 899
Baglioni (Venetian family) 29 40
Baglioni, Alessandro 3 55
Baglioni, Atalanta di Galeotto 3 55
Baglioni, Cesare 29 251
Baglioni, Domenico di Francesco 3 55
Baglioni, Gentile 3 55
Baglioni, Maddalena 3 55
Baglioni, Margherita 3 55
Baglioni, Pantasilea di Rodolfo I 3 55
Baglioni, Pietro di Gottifredo 3 55
Baglioni, Troilo di Rodolfo I, Bishop of Perugia 3 55; 24 831
Bagna, George 21 348
Bagnacavallo (Italy)
  S Pietro della Pieve 1 695
  S Pietro in Silvis 16 625; 26 577
Bagnacavallo (1484-1542) 3 55–6*; 25 578, 736
Bagnacavallo, Bartolomeo Ramenghi, I, 4 311
Bagnadore, Pietro Maria 3 56*, 767; 22 107
Bagnaia 16 *620*
  Villa Lante 3 56–7*; 24 290
    gardens 3 56–7; 11 343; 12 *60*, 61, 116; 32 547
    paintings 18 661
    Palazzina Gambara 3 56; 30 428
    Palazzina Montalto 3 56, *57*; 30 356
    park 12 116
    stucco 29 830
Bagnano Master 21 82
Bagnara 31 717
Bagnara, Francesco 5 378
Bagnato, Franz (Ignaz) Anton 3 58*
Bagnato, Johann (Hans) Caspar 3 57–8*
  collaboration 28 775
  works 3 58; 12 372; 30 536; 32 822
Bagneux, St Hermeland 13 39
Bagno, Niccolo Guido di 4 128
Bagnoli di Sopra
  Palazzetto Widman 4 311; 25 1
  Villa Widmann *see* Palazetto Widman
Bagnolo, Villa Pisani 23 862–3
Bagnols-sur-Cèze, Musée Léon Alègre 2 12
Bagnovatoye 31 557, 558
Bagobo 24 628, 631
Bagolāngo *see* SURKH KOTAL
Bagong 33 538
Bagot, Walter 33 409
bagpipes 22 374
Bagrat III, King of Imereti (*reg* 1008-14) 12 331
Bagrat IV, King of Georgia (*reg* 1027-76) 9 548
bags
  historical and regional traditions
    Aboriginal Australia 1 52
    Central Asia 10 873
    Germany 3 442
    India, Republic of 15 175
    Iroquois 22 627
    Kyrgyzstan 18 *569*
    Native North Americans 22 627, *643*, 645–6, *646*, 648, 662
    Thailand 30 *626*
    Yoruba 33 556
  materials
    bark 22 662
    beadwork 3 441
    cotton 30 *626*
    felt 10 873
    string 1 52
  techniques
    twining 22 645–6
  types
    seal 14 425
Bagshaw, Cradoc 14 165
Bagshaw, William 32 327
  works 32 *326*
Bagshaws 2 151
Bagshot Park (Surrey) 15 407
Bagsværd Church 8 729
Baguereth, Gabriel 8 816
Baguio 12 103; 24 *607*, 617
Bagumbayan 24 616, 617
Bagutti, Domenico 12 125
Bagutti, Giovanni 6 65; 10 278; 12 595; 29 835; 31 858
Bagwan *see* BHAGWAN
Bah, Chernoh 28 692
  works 28 *692*
Baha al-Dawla, Amir (*reg* 998-1012) (Buyid) 16 435, 551
Baha' al-Din (*fl* 17th cent) 12 37
Baha al-Din Muhammad 6 247
Bahadur Khan 15 595
Bahadur Shah I, Emperor (*reg* 1707-12) (Mughal) 15 590
Bahadur Shah II, Emperor (*reg* 1837-58) (Mughal) 15 681
Bahadur Singh (*fl c.* 1760-90) 15 592
Bahadur Singh, Ruler (*reg c.* 1553) (Pahari) 15 396
Bahā'ī 30 450
bahāl 22 763, *763*, *764*
Bahamas, the 3 58–65*, *59*; 5 744, *745*, 746*
  architecture 3 60–61*
  carnivals 3 60; 5 788
  collections 3 63–4*
  costumes 3 *60*
  dealing 3 63–4*
  education (art) 3 61, 64–5*
  festivals 3 *60*
  furniture 3 63*
  houses 3 *61*
  interior decoration 3 63*
  museums 3 64*
  painting 3 61–2*, *62*
  patronage 3 63–4*
  pottery 3 59
  sculpture 3 62–3*
  slaves 3 60
  stools 3 59
Bahamas Woodwork Company 3 63
Bahamian Creative Artists United for Serious Expression *see* B.-C.A.U.S.E.
Bahariya Oasis 3 65*; 9 *774*
Baharuddin, Eriche 16 242
Bahawalpur 15 664; 23 803
Bahçelievler 24 690
Bahía (culture) 3 65*; 27 609; 29 155
Bahia (Brazil) *see* SALVADOR
Bahiana, Elisiário (Antonio da Cunha) 3 66*
bahīl 22 763
Bahima 1 311
Bahla 21 588; 23 436
  fort 23 436
Bahlsen 8 428; 14 622; 28 197
Bahmani 3 66*; 16 201
  see also:
    'ALA' AL-DIN AHMAD, Ruler
    'ALA' AL-DIN HASAN BAHMANI, Ruler
    GHIYATH AL-DIN, Ruler
    MUHAMMAD I, Ruler
    SHIHAB AL-DIN AHMAD, Ruler
    SHIHAB AL-DIN MAHMUD, Ruler
    TAJ AL-DIN FIRUZ, Ruler
Bahn, Stephen 7 715
Bahnar 32 480
el-Bahnasa
  bone-carvings 7 825
  glass 10 55
  monuments 7 820
  Oxyrhynchus 7 *819*, 821; 9 *774*, 852; 23 692–3*; 26 *921*
  papyri 13 369
  sculpture 7 821
  stelae 7 821
  textiles 16 431, 441
  villas 9 852
Bahr *see* PARRI
Bähr, George 3 66–7*
  patrons and collectors 33 115
  works 3 *67*; 9 241; 12 373; 18 162; 19 815; 25 240
Bahr, Hermann 3 67–8*; 18 131; 22 379
  collaboration 22 187
  groups and movements 28 343, 344
Bahrain 2 *246*; 3 68–9*; 16 *105*; 21 268
  architecture 3 68*
  Barbar Temple 2 251, *252*
  coins 2 261
  glass 2 263
  graves 2 249
  incense burners 2 269
  painting 3 68–9*
  pottery 2 267, 268
  seals 2 271
  stone vessels 2 272
Bahrain—cont.
  University 3 68
  see also ARABIA
Bahrain Art Society 3 68
Bahram Mirza (Safavid) 1 474; 7 717; 9 461; 16 122, 319, 552, 876; 17 687; 22 390
Bahramshah, Sultan (*reg* 1118-52) (Ghaznavid) 12 512; 16 166
Bahri *see* MAMLUK (EGYPT AND SYRIA)
Bahri, Deir el- *see under* THEBES (i) (EGYPT)
Bahria Oasis *see* BAHARIYA OASIS
al-Baḥriyya *see* BAHARIYA OASIS
Bahrmann 21 62
Bahu 15 620, 630
  painting 15 *630*
Bahua Temple 15 263
Bahuche, Marguerite 5 172
Bahulara, Siddheshvara Temple 15 321
Bahuriband 15 497
Bahybayt al-Hagar *see* BEHBEIT EL-HAGAR
Baiae 26 *886*
  baths 26 872, 891; 27 67
  Baths of Venus 27 69
  Caligula's villa 26 892
  casts 10 68
  mosaics 27 66
  sculpture 27 18, *18*, 19, *19*, 28
  Temple of Mercury 26 891
  Temple of Venus 26 897
Baia Mare 15 5
  Political-Administrative Centre 26 710
  see also NAGYBÁNYA COLONY
Baiardi (family) 2 162
Baiardi, Francesco 24 201
Baičeni 30 770, 771
Baier, Fred 10 300
Baier, Melchior 3 69–70*; 23 312
  collaboration 11 224; 18 574
  patrons and collectors 16 866
  works 12 443, 445; 18 *574*; 24 356; 25 126
Baiga 15 734, 735
Baigai Totoki *see* TOTOKI BAIGAI
Baignol, Etienne 19 397
Baignol porcelain factory 19 397
Baigram 15 475
Baiitsu Yamamoto *see* YAMAMOTO BAIITSU
Baij, Ramkinker 3 70*; 15 173, 657
  pupils 29 891
  works 15 171
Baijnath (India)
  Lakshmi-Narayana Temple 15 265
  Shiva Temple 15 309
Baijnath (*fl c.* 1825-40) 15 600
Bai Juyi 7 35; 12 87; 17 228; 25 785
Baikan Sugai *see* SUGAI BAIKAN
Bail 15 705
Bail, Franck 3 71
Bail, Jean Antoine 3 70–71*
Bail, Joseph 3 71*
Bailey, Abe 29 121
Bailey, Albert 31 333
Bailey, Alvin 31 333
Bailey, David (Royston) 3 71*
  works 9 *294*
Bailey, George 31 333
Bailey, Henry T. 31 669
Bailey, James 5 582
Bailey, Malcolm 1 445
Bailey, Nathan 29 8
Bailey, Oakley Hoopes 4 81
Bailey, William 31 653
Bailey, William Willis 26 489
baileys 3 209; 21 545
Bailey & Saunders 8 106
Baili, Johannes *see* BADILE, GIOVANNI
Baillairgé (family) 25 802
Baillairgé, Charles 3 72–3*
  pupils 30 230

Baillairgé, Charles—cont.
works 3 73
Baillairgé, François 3 71–2*; 5 564
collaboration 3 71
pupils 27 281
works 3 72; 5 560; 25 802
Baillairgé, Jean 3 71*
Baillairgé, Pierre-Florent 3 71
Baillairgé, Thomas 3 72*; 5 560
Baillairgé, William-Duval 3 73
Baillehache, Jehan de 5 370
Bailles, Juan de see JUAN DE BAILLES
Baillet, Jean, Bishop of Auxerre 11 639
Baillet de Saint Julien, Louis-Guillaume, Baron 3 73–4*
Bailleul, Nicolas de
books 4 353
Bailli de Breteuil 19 25; 32 685
Bailli de Noailles, Jacques 11 9
Baillie, David 3 280
Baillie, Thomas, 7th Earl of Haddington 25 882
Baillie, William 3 74*; 25 622; 29 796
Baillie Scott, M(ackay) H(ugh) 3 74–5*
competitions 7 668
groups and movements 2 562, 566, 569, 570; 10 239
patrons and collectors 10 465
works 3 75; 10 182, 182, 283, 284; 14 362; 22 373
Baillieu, Sunday see REED, SUNDAY
Baillif, Claude 3 76*
pupils 20 121
works 5 558; 25 801
Bailliu, Pieter de 30 788
Bailly, Alice 3 76*; 30 134
groups and movements 22 921
works 30 134
Bailly, Antoine-Nicolas-Louis 3 76–7*; 14 238
Bailly, David 3 77, 77–8*
reproductive prints by others 8 665
works 22 841; 29 667; 31 882
Bailly, Jean 6 414
Bailly, Léon 30 867
Bailov 2 895
Palace of Culture 2 893
Bails, Benito 29 637
Bailundo Church 2 86
Bai Luotian
works 17 222
Baily, Edward Hodges 3 78–9*; 5 751; 20 478; 27 336
assistants 9 451; 22 314; 32 911
competitions 7 673
monuments 7 673; 10 266, 266; 16 889; 22 47; 23 20
pupils 30 703
sculpture 3 78; 9 322; 19 600
teachers 11 164
tureens 10 335
Baily, John 29 835
Baima 7 66
Bain, Alexander 7 448
Bain, Donald 12 777; 28 240
Bain, J. S. 7 486
Bainbridge, Christopher, Cardinal 28 901
Bainbridge, David 2 512
Baines, Georges 3 79*
Baines, Henry 14 863
Baines, Robert 2 766
Baines, Thomas 29 108; 33 678
Baini 12 598
Baining 24 83
Baioken Eishun 17 177
Bairamashvili, R. 12 320
Bairat 15 609
shrine 15 250
Baird, John I (1798-1859) 12 774; 28 228; 30 750
Baird, John II (1816-93) 30 750
Baird, John, Ltd 28 259, 260
works 28 259
Bairei Kōno see KŌNO BAIREI
Bairin youqi 7 25
Bairi Singh, Maharawal of Jaisalmer 16 871
Baisaō see KŌ YŪGAI
Baisch, Hermann 18 32
bai sema see THAILAND → boundary stones
Baisha 6 655; 7 37
Baisio, Arduino da see ARDUINO DA BAISIO
Baitei Ki see KI BAITEI
Baixas, Isabel 6 600
Baj, Enrico 3 80*; 16 682
dealers 7 842
groups and movements 2 526; 9 201; 17 658
works 23 334
Baja 30 182
Bajalović, P. 28 838
Bajau 20 175, 176; 24 630
Bajaura 3 80*; 15 264, 483
Shiva Temple 15 265
Bajpai, Durga 15 168
Bak see BEK
Bak, Imre 14 902
Bakalli, Naxhi 1 540; 3 80–81*
Bakalowits, E. 14 25, 749; 25 674
Bakalowits, E., & Söhne 2 818; 19 719
Bakanov, Ivan Mikhailovich 23 837
Bakărdzhiev, Georgi 5 158, 159
Bakchios 13 484
Bakelite 11 310; 25 26, 27; 26 244
Bakema, Jacob B(erend) 31 867
collaboration 31 867, 868
groups and movements 7 294, 295, 296; 20 475; 22 832; 30 391; 31 867
pupils 23 426
works 13 685; 22 832
Bakema & Weeber 19 320
Baker, Arthur 3 81
Baker, Benjamin 4 802; 16 55
Baker, C(harles) H(enry) Collins 3 81*
Baker, Edward F., Associates 17 620; 21 650
Baker, G. P. & J. 14 53
Baker, Henry Aaron 3 81*; 5 337; 16 800; 22 147
Baker, Herbert 3 81–2*; 15 411; 20 547–8; 29 120; 32 773
architecture
banks 3 174; 30 386; 31 375
cemeteries 6 167
government buildings 4 155; 8 675, 676; 15 404; 17 906; 25 566; 29 106
houses 5 667; 17 602; 29 105; 32 325
assistants 19 113; 32 792
collaboration 19 821
furniture 29 116
groups and movements 3 269; 7 618
pupils 19 113
staff 17 897
teachers 12 316
Baker, James 17 641
Baker, Josephine 19 653
Baker, Laurence Wilfred 3 82*; 15 169
Baker, Olive 10 336
Baker, Samuel 2 559; 29 88
Baker, William 19 506
Baker Brothers Furniture Co. 31 632
Baker & Fleming 24 306
Baker & Kendall 17 897
Baker & Leigh 29 88
Baker & Masey 17 897, 898; 20 547
Bakewell, Benjamin 3 84; 31 642
Bakewell, John 3 83*
Bakewell, Robert 3 82–3*; 10 342; 28 295
Bakewell & Brown 3 83*; 27 730
Bakewell & Co. 3 84*; 10 852; 31 642
Bakh see GOLLERBAKH, ERIKH (FYODOROVICH)
Bakh, Nikolay (Ivanovich) 27 425
Bakh, Robert (Ivanovich) 27 425
Bakhat Singh, Maharaja of Marwar (reg 1752) (Rajput) 15 615
Bakhchisaray 3 84*; 9 507; 31 546
Garden Palace 3 84; 31 564
Bakhetiyev (family) 27 403, 416
Bakhlul-zade, S. 2 897
Bakhmatyuk, Aleksandr 31 563
Bakhmetiyev, Aleksey (Nikolaievich) 27 415, 416
Bakhmetiyev, Anna 27 416
Bakhor Stepwell 29 636
Bakhretdinova, Zulfiya 30 253
Bakhrushin, Aleksey (Aleksandrovich) 27 439, 440
Bakhrushin State Central Theatre Museum see under MOSCOW → museums
Bakhsh, Khuda 15 742
Bakhta 15 600
Bakhtiari 16 484; 18 49
Bakhtiari carpets see under CARPETS → types
Bakht III 9 823
Bakhuijzen, Hendrik van de Sande see SANDE BAKHUIJZEN, HENDRIK VAN DE
Bakhuizen, Ludolf, the elder (1630-1708) 3 84–6*
collaboration 14 374
patrons and collectors 10 753, 864; 25 815; 28 169
teachers 9 314; 10 660
works 3 85; 20 424; 22 843; 28 612
Bakhuizen, Ludolf, the younger (1717-82) 3 86
Bakhushinsky, Anatoly (Vasilevich) 27 444
Bakhuyzen, Hendrik van de Sande see SANDE BAKHUYZEN, HENDRIK VAN DE
Bakić, Vojin 3 86*; 8 179
Bakin Takizawa see TAKIZAWA BAKIN
Bakker, Cornelis 30 373
Bakker, Frans de 25 363; 30 297
Bakker, Gijs 22 877, 896
Bakker Korff, Alexander Hugo 3 86*; 18 481
Bakócz, Tamás, Archbishop 10 544, 546; 11 28; 14 885
Bakonat 6 379
Bakong see under ROLUOS
Bakonybél Abbey Church 14 900
Bakos 9 621
Bakr, Mahrus Abu 9 767
Bakradze, A. 12 322
Bakre, S. K. 4 290
Baksa-Soós, János 14 896
Baksei Chamkrong see under ANGKOR
Baksh, Muhammad 15 629
Baksheyev, Vasily (Nikolayevich) 27 395
Bakst, Léon 3 86–7*; 27 392
collaboration 27 283
groups and movements 3 119, 120; 8 849; 27 580; 31 582; 33 379, 740
patrons and collectors 27 224, 225
productions 8 850; 30 681, 686
pupils 6 384; 9 495; 13 862; 20 850; 28 820; 31 502
works 8 849; 9 291; 30 686; 33 379
Baktari 5 830
Baktimur al-Silahdar 20 228
Baku 2 425, 890; 3 87–8*; 16 105
Academy of Sciences of Azerbaijan 3 88
Historical Museum see under museums
Baku—cont.
apartment blocks
Azenergo building 2 894
Azneft'zavody building 2 894
Buzonyneft' building 2 894
art forms and materials
architecture 2 428, 894
carpets 2 901
embroidery 2 901
jewellery 2 900
pottery 2 898
sculpture 16 247
textiles 2 900
Azerneshr Palace of Printing 2 893
Bukhara Caravanserai 2 892
Castle 2 892
Demolished Fortress see mosques → Muhammad Mosque → Synyk-kala
Duma 2 893
fortifications 2 892; 21 584
Maiden's Tower 2 891, 892, 892
Shemakhin Gates 2 892
Government House 2 894
Gyulistan Palace of Ceremonies 2 894
Hotel Azerbaijan 2 894
Hotel Baku 2 894
Hotel Moskva 2 894
Indian Caravanserai see Multani Caravanserai
Ismailiya charitable society building 2 893
Lenin Palace of Culture 2 894
Ministry of the Food Industry 2 893
monuments and statues
monument to Lenin 2 895
monument to M. F. Akhuodov 2 895
monument to Nizami 2 895
statue of Khurshudbanu Natavan 2 895
mosques
Djuma mosque 2 892
Muhammad Mosque 2 891, 892; 22 321
Synyk-kala 2 892
Taza-Pir Mosque 2 893
Mukhtarov House 2 893
Multani Caravanserai 2 892
museums
Historical Museum of the Academy of Sciences of Azerbaijan 6 285
Museum of Carpets and Applied Art 3 88
Museum of Fine Art 3 88
Nizami Museum of Azerbaijani Literature 2 894, 898; 3 88
Rustam Mustavayev Art Museum 3 88
Nizami Cinema 2 893
Oriental Bazaar 2 894, 894
palace of Husayn Kuli khan 2 896
palace of the Sharvanshahs 2 892, 895; 23 816
Public Assembly building 2 893
Republic Statistical Administration Building 2 894
Sadykhov house 2 893
Shemakhin Gates see under fortifications
Synyk-kala see under mosques → Muhammad Mosque
Theatre of the Mailov Brothers 2 893
Bakumatsu no Sanpitsu 15 74; 17 237; 20 148; 23 298
Bakūn, Tall-i 15 920
Bakundu 1 266
Bakusen Tsuchida see TSUCHIDA, BAKUSEN
Bal 33 313
Bala (Zaire) 29 70
Bala (monk) 15 440; 27 844; 29 439
Bala, Iwan 32 786
Balaam, Master of the 20 620*
attributions 20 785
collaboration 33 71
works 33 71
Balaban, Ibrahim 31 454
Balabin, Al'bert (Grigor'yevich) 27 418
Bālacanda see BALCHAND
Baláččaw, Salamon 10 573
Bălăcescu, Lucia Dem. 3 88*
Balaclava, Cattle Wharf 24 665
Baladine see SPIRO, ELIZABETH
Balaguer 16 103; 31 750
Balaguer, Pedro 31 814
Balaguer Alcazaba 16 189–90
architectural decorations 16 189
Balaju 22 753, 759, 768
Balaka 18 216
Balakbal 5 411
Balakhna 27 430
Balakot 15 718
Balalyk Tepe 6 232, 248; 32 320
balance 14 869
balanced cantilever bridges see under BRIDGES → types
Balanchine, George 19 844; 30 390
Bălăneşti 25 340
Balangoda Points 29 445
Balanos, Nikolaos 23 508
Balans chairs see under CHAIRS → types
Balanta 13 835
bālapañjara 15 243*
Balasaghun (Kyrgyzstan) see BURANA
Balasaghun (Xinjiang Uygur Autonomous Region) see KASHGAR
Balassi, Mario 19 374
Balat 8 462; 16 418
Ilyas Bey Mosque 16 202
Balat, Alphonse (-Hubert-François) 3 88–9*, 547; 5 42
assistants 14 769
pupils 3 44, 550
works 3 549
Balatah, Tell see SHECHEM
Balatonboglár Church 14 890
Balawaste 18 29
wall paintings 6 293, 303
Balawat 1 892; 31 699
architecture 21 288
gates 1 831; 7 813, 813; 9 150; 11 792, 792; 21 274, 298, 304
Temple of Mamu 9 150
Balāynah, Tādda sa 10 577
Balaz, A. 28 451
Baláž, Jozef 28 854
Balažany Church 3 527
Balazote 15 59
Balbas, Alessandro 3 89*; 10 524; 11 3
Balbás, Isidoro Vicente de 3 89; 21 383
Balbás, Jerónimo de 3 89*
groups and movements 7 289
works 9 407; 21 377, 383, 393; 29 292
Balbás, L. Torres see TORRES BALBÁS, L.
Balbi (family)
architecture 12 281; 13 321
paintings 6 34; 31 293
sculpture 25 705
urban planning 3 922
Balbi, Marchesa 25 285
Balbi, Alessandro 20 94
Balbi, Antonio 3 90
Balbi, Bartolomeo 3 90
Balbi, Costantino, the elder (1676-1740) 3 90
Balbi, Costantino, the younger (fl 1818-25) 3 90
Balbi, Francesco Maria, the elder (1619-1704) 3 90; 15 148

Balbi, Francesco Maria, the younger (1669-1737) 3 90
Balbi, Giacomo 3 90, 922
Balbi, Giovanni Agostino 3 90, 922
Balbi, Giovanni Francesco, the elder (*d c.* 1593) 3 90
Balbi, Giovanni Francesco, the younger (*fl* early 17th cent.) 3 90
Balbi, Giovanni Girolamo 3 90
Balbi, Niccolò 3 90
Balbi, Pantaleo, the elder 3 90
Balbi, Pantaleo, the younger (1582-1644) 3 90, 922
Balbi, Paolo 3 90, 923
Balbi, Stefano 3 90
Balbín, Bohuslav 3 91*; 8 426
Balbo, Alessandro *see* BALBAS, ALESSANDRO
Balbo, Italo 11 843
Balboa, Cabello de 29 217
Balboa, Pedro de 8 232
Balboa, Vasco Núñez de *see* NÚÑEZ DE BALBOA, VASCO
Balbus, Johannes 13 867
Balbus, M. Nonius 14 441
Balcácer, Ada 9 117
Balcanquall, Walter 28 268; 32 799
Balcar, Jiří 8 394
Balcarres (Fife) 14 381
Balcarres, Alexander Lindsay, 8th Earl of *see* LINDSAY, ALEXANDER (WILLIAM CRAWFORD), 25th Earl of Crawford
Balcarres, David Alexander Edward Lindsay, 10th Earl of *see* LINDSAY, DAVID ALEXANDER EDWARD, 27th Earl of Crawford
Balcaskie House (Fife) 4 890; 28 246
Balcells (i Buigas), Eduard (Maria) 3 91*
Balcera 4 262
Balchand 3 91–2*; 15 588, 589; 24 295
works 3 *92*; 16 345
Balchik 5 145
Balčiūnas, Vytautas 6 134
Balckeneynde, Claes Dircksz. van 25 370
Balconete 11 713
balconies (houses) 5 649, 752; 15 288; 16 269
balconies (theatres) 30 670, 677
Baldac, Albukasem de *see* IBN BUTLAN
baldacchinos 1 698; 30 776, 779
see also CIBORIA (ii) (STRUCTURES)
Baldaccini, César *see* CÉSAR
Baldasare, Gheorghe Panaiteanu *see* PANAITEANU BALDASARE, GHEORGHE
Baldass, Ludwig von 2 834
Baldassare, Maestro 23 191
Baldassare da Reggio *see* BALDASSARE D'ESTE
Baldassare da Urbino *see* LANCI, BALDASSARE
Baldassare de Cadighis 18 747
Baldassare de Canevali 18 586
Baldassare del Milanese 16 766
Baldassare d'Este 3 92–3*; 10 520; 11 7; 31 430
Baldassini, Melchiorre 24 419; 27 741
Baldemor, Manuel 24 623
Balden, Samuell *see* BALDWIN, SAMUEL
Balden, Theo 3 93*
Balderich, Abbot of Salzburg 27 660
Balderic II, Prince-Bishop of Liège 19 345
Baldersby Park *see* NEWBY PARK (N. YORKS)
Baldese, Ambrogio di *see* AMBROGIO DI BALDESE
Baldessari, John 3 93*
groups and movements 7 685
pupils 4 168; 27 633
works 22 523; 24 408
Baldessari, Luciano 3 93–4*
collaboration 11 63, 282
groups and movements 26 15
works 16 649; 23 169; 26 *15*
Baldessin, George 1 147; 3 94*
Baldev Singh, Ruler (*reg* 1922-59) (Pahari) 15 629
Baldi, Accursio 28 683
Baldi, Bernardino 3 94*; 4 277
pupils 6 113
works 10 204; 11 343
Baldi, Lazzaro 3 95*
collaboration 9 376; 11 22; 26 246
pupils 31 370
teachers 7 913
works 3 *95*; 26 840
Baldie, Robert 28 289
Baldigara, Giulio 14 885
Baldigara, Ottavio 14 885
Baldinger Architectural Lighting 13 326
Baldini, Baccio 3 96*; 4 502; 10 383; 19 412
Baldini, Giovanni Antonio 15 740
Baldini, Giuseppe (Italy) 10 833
Baldini, Joseph (Guyana) 13 875
Baldini, Pietro Paolo 3 96–7*; 29 251
collaboration 21 25; 26 837; 29 388, 831
works 3 *97*; 26 837; 29 831
Baldino di Surso 16 725
Baldinucci, Filippo 3 97–8*; 5 685; 7 714; 9 229; 11 188; 21 28
dealing 25 59
personal collection 9 230; 22 236
works 5 760; 7 389; 9 7; 10 204; 12 497; 16 781
writings 2 531
Baldinucci, Francesco Saverio 3 98; 9 120
Baldishol Church 23 233, 238, 241
tapestries 23 *239*
Baldner, Oswald 3 98*; 18 430; 25 129
Baldomar, Francisc 7 679
Baldovinetti, Alesso 3 98–101*; 27 183
attributions 11 198
collaboration 11 86; 12 549; 16 691
mosaics 22 165
paintings 3 *99*; 6 14; 11 210; 16 659
frescoes 9 98; 11 204; 32 688
portraits 3 *100*
religious 16 659; 20 111
pupils 12 548; 27 174
stained glass 13 193
Baldoyle, St Laurence O'Toole 11 256
Baldrighi, Giuseppe 3 101*; 24 193
Balduc, Rocque 5 362
Balducci, Giovanni 3 101–2*; 19 139; 22 448
Balducci, Matteo 10 651; 24 831
Balduccio, Giovanni di *see* GIOVANNI DI BALDUCCIO
Balduccio de Bacza 22 484
Balduin, Archbishop of Trier 19 828
Balduino del Monte 11 268
Baldung, Hans 3 102–4*; 8 595; 23 310, 311
book illustrations 12 385
collaboration 9 440; 19 256; 33 32
drawings 3 *102*
engravings 12 386
methods 12 386
Baldung, Hans—cont.
paintings 1 658, 840; 3 *103*; 9 433; 10 476; 23 294
patrons and collectors 1 771; 10 752; 13 903, 922; 33 594
portraits 33 593
pupils 20 796
stained glass 11 752; 14 572; 23 308; 27 256; 29 504
teachers 9 433; 23 308
woodcuts 1 841; 4 358; 28 57; 31 287; 33 354, 366
Baldus, Edouard-Denis 3 104*; 7 421; 24 663
Balduugin Sharav 21 881
Baldwin (*fl* 1432) 30 366
Baldwin, Abbot of Bury St Edmunds (*reg* 1065-97) 5 287
Baldwin I, Count of Flanders (*reg* 862-79) 4 918; 12 516
Baldwin I, King of Jerusalem (*reg* 1100-18) 18 421; 24 558
Baldwin, Almon 33 152
Baldwin, Benjamin 33 29
Baldwin, Cyrus 28 830
Baldwin, Loammi 5 64
Baldwin, Michael 2 512; 7 685
Baldwin, Nigel 31 864
Baldwin, Philip 30 145
Baldwin, Samuel 3 104–5*; 10 262
Baldwin, Thomas 3 371; 5 66; 32 783
Baldwin and Weese 33 29
Baldwin Brown, Gerald 2 64; 9 725
Baldwin Iron-Arm *see* BALDWIN I, Count of Flanders
Baldwin of Luxembourg, Archbishop 31 326
Bâle *see* BASLE
Balea 26 710
Balearic Islands 3 105–6*; 29 *259*
architecture 3 *105*, 105–6; 21 43
castles 3 *106*
metalwork 29 332
talayots 25 522
Balechou, Jean-Joseph 3 107*; 9 370; 17 466
baleen 22 656; 23 *539*; 28 302, *302*
Baleison, Giovanni 3 107*; 5 601
Balen, Gaspard van 3 107
Balen, Hendrik van, I (*c.* 1574/5-1632) 3 107–8*
collaboration 4 913, 914, 915, 916, 917; 21 830; 27 228
patrons and collectors 5 9; 28 904
personal collection 4 917
pupils 9 476; 28 364, 901
reproductive prints by others 32 700
works 3 *108*, 559; 5 352; 22 *372*, 373
Balen, Hendrik van, II (1623-61) 3 107
Balen, Jan van 3 107; 32 724
Balen, Mathys 14 794
Balenciaga, Cristóbal 9 294
Balestra, Antonio 3 108–9*; 32 194, 196
patrons and collectors 5 178; 7 779
pupils 7 309; 19 634; 23 174; 25 1, 191; 27 213; 33 612
reproductive prints by others 8 267; 12 582
teachers 3 681
works 3 *109*
Balestra, Carlo Pio 26 842
Balestra, Giacomo 18 184
Balfour, A. J. 5 268
Balfour, Andrew 28 271
Balfour, Eustace (James Anthony) 3 110*
Balfour, J. Lawson 2 771
Balfour Ciborium 10 322, 346; 26 694; 31 499
Balfour & Turner 3 110*
Balgo 1 56, 64
Bali (China) 6 712
Bali (Indonesia) 10 580; 15 *751*, *754*, 755; 29 234, 235
architecture 15 772–3*, 775–6
bamboo 15 809
bark 15 806
baskets 15 809, 810
boats 15 810
brick 4 796
bronze 29 229
candi bentārs 15 *767*
carving 15 812
coconuts 15 810
coffins 15 *812*
coins 15 811
colour 15 800
cotton 15 793
craftsmen and artists 15 776; 29 236
cremation towers 15 812*
dance 15 802
dolls 31 260
doors 15 785
drawings 15 804, 806*, *806*, 807, 808–9*
dress 15 813*
drums (musical instruments) 15 783, 817
dyes 15 806
fiddles 15 *816*
glass 15 806
gold 15 793
gold leaf 15 806
gongs 15 816
houses 15 770, 772–3
ikat 15 793; 30 556
jewellery 15 814
keris 15 817; 29 239
litters 29 *237*
looms 15 793
manuscript illumination 15 804
masks 15 802–4*, *803*
mirrors 15 812
painting 15 804, 806*, 807, 808–9*, 810, 812, *812*
palm leaves 15 806; 31 260
paper 15 806
pottery 15 806
rafters 15 787
religion 14 560–62
roofs 15 773
sanctuaries 15 758, 767–8
sarcophagi 27 831
sarongs 15 793
sculpture 15 776, 783–7*
relief 15 *786*
wood 15 784, 785–7*, *786*
shadow-puppets 15 799–800*
silk 15 793
silver leaf 15 806
stupas 15 763
temples 3 *872*; 15 763–4, 785; 30 447
textiles 15 793*, 806
theatre 15 797, 802–4*
shadow 15 799–800*
tinsel 15 812
tombs 15 *763*
tourist art 15 806, 809; 29 238
tufa 15 *786*, 787; 27 831
villages 15 772
windows 15 785
wood 15 785–7*, *786*, 806, *812*
xylophones 15 817
Balia Maden 4 682
Baliaricus, (Quintus) Caecilius Metellus *see* METELLUS BALIARICUS, (QUINTUS) CAECILIUS
Balıkesir Mosque 16 498
Balin, Jakub 17 873; 19 750
Balin, Paul 3 110*; 32 812, 816
Balin, White Pagoda 6 656; 19 303
Bălinești 26 711
Bälinge Altarpiece 13 120
Balinghem, Field of the Cloth of Gold 2 *339*; 30 467
Balingsta Memorial Stone 32 522, *523*
Baliński, Stefan 7 837
Bálint, Endre 3 110–11*; 10 650; 14 902
Bálint, István 14 896
Bálint, Zoltán 14 890
Bali-Nyonga 3 147, 148
Balin youqi *see* BAIRIN YOUQI
Balis *see under* MASKANA
Baliyev, Nikita 2 24; 29 899
Baljeu, Joost 3 111*; 7 772; 22 861
Balk, Georg 20 792
Bałka, Mirosław 25 116
Balkanderesi, Church 1 5 676
Balkans *see* ALBANIA; BULGARIA; ROMANIA; YUGOSLAVIA
Balkanski, Nenko 5 154; 20 895
Balkar 27 432, 433
Balkay, Pál 2 546
Balke, Peder (Andersen) 3 111–12*
teachers 8 451; 23 225
works 3 *112*
Balke Church 13 119
Balke Master 13 119
Balkh 1 *186*, 207; 3 112–13*; 6 *182*, 186, *623*; 11 335; 16 *105*; 28 *719*, 721
coins 1 203; 16 512
fort 15 365
fortifications 6 196
Gunbad-i Kabudi 16 237
Islamic religious buildings
Abu Nasr Parsa complex 1 208; 16 236
congregational mosque 1 207; 29 819
madrasa of 'Abdallah Khan II 16 236
madrasa of Allah Yar 16 236
madrasa of Nadhr Muhammad 16 236
madrasa of Subhan Quli 16 236
Masjid-i Nuh Gumbad 16 154, 244; 29 825
mausoleum of 'Ali 16 237
palace 16 238
ramparts 6 211
red lead 16 393
tomb of 'Ali ibn Abi Talib 16 237
Balkhar 27 411
Balkhash 17 *865*, 866
Balkhu 22 759
Balkuwara Palace *see under* SAMARRA' → palaces
Ball, Alexander 20 217
Ball, Douglas 5 580
Ball, E. M. 13 297
Ball, Gordon 21 347
Ball, Hugo 3 113*; 24 427
groups and movements 8 433, 434; 31 503
works 24 405
Ball, Thomas 3 114*; 11 189; 31 611
pupils 5 444; 11 755
Balla, Giacomo 3 114–17*; 16 679; 24 448; 26 776
groups and movements
Aeropittura 1 166; 8 771; 11 867
Cubism 1 73
Divisionism 9 41
Futurism 1 166; 4 199; 8 770; 10 415; 11 863, 865, 867; 16 679; 20 426; 25 358; 27 445
patrons and collectors 33 254
pupils 4 199; 25 446; 28 507, 792
works 3 *116*; 9 292; 11 397, *864*; 16 731; 29 97
writings 16 707
Ballachulish 28 241
Balladur, Jean 11 528
Ballagh, Robert 3 117*; 16 18
Ballana 23 *276*, 286
silver 9 655
Tomb B80 23 *286*
Tumulus 3 23 286

Ballana period *see under* NUBIA → periods
Balland, Philibert **12** 832
ball-and-claw feet *see* CLAW-AND-BALL FEET
Ballantine & Allan **28** 248
Ballantyne (family) **24** 810
Ballantyne, C. H. **23** 327
Ballantyne, John **20** 34
Ballantyne, Robert **28** 268
Ballarat **2** *736*, 764
  Fine Art Gallery **2** 771
Ballard, Bernice C. **16** 555
Ballard, James F. **8** 899; **16** 554, 559
Ballard White, Nellie **16** 554
Ballarpur **15** 323
ball clays *see under* CLAY → types
ballcourts **3** 117–18*
  Aztec **3** 118
  Czech Republic **33** *303*
  Honduras **20** *883*
  Maya **3** 117, *118*; **6** 579; **20** *883*, 886; **30** 254
  Mesoamerica, Pre-Columbian **3** 117–18*, *118*; **5** 408; **6** 579; **20** *883*; **21** 187; **27** 756; **30** 254
  Olmec **3** 117; **23** 417; **27** 756
  Toltec **3** 118, *118*; **31** 99, 505
Balle **32** 525
Ballechouse, John **10** 271
Ballejo, Jerónimo Cosida y *see* COSIDA Y BALLEJO, JERÓNIMO
Ballén, Sixto Durán *see* DURÁN BALLÉN, SIXTO
Baller, Hinrich **18** 114
Balleroy
  Château **11** 516; **12** 120; **20** 289; **32** 551
    staircase **29** 523, *523*
  Musée des Ballons **11** 301
Ballester, Diógenes **18** 833
Ballester, Pedro Juán **3** 119*
Ballesteros, Hernando de (*fl* 1474–1516) **29** 333
Ballesteros, Hernando de (*d* 1579) **29** 334
Ballesteros, Hernando de, the younger (*d* 1613) **29** 334
Ballestrieri, Gabriele **10** 526
Ballet des Champs Elysées **27** 281
Ballet Rambert **30** 687
ballets **30** 659
Ballets Romantiques Russes **14** 776
Ballets Russes **2** 520; **3** 119–20*; **28** 808; **30** 686; **33** 379
  costumes **30** *686*
  designers **8** 849–50; **26** 41; **30** 681, 686
    Bakst, Léon **3** 86
    Benois, Alexandre **3** 734
    Braque, Georges **4** 676
    Depero, Fortunato **8** 771
    Goncharova, Natal'ya (Sergeyevna) **12** 892, 894
    Gris, Juan **13** 671
    Larionov, Mikhail (Fyodorovich) **18** 791
    Picasso, Pablo **8** 246; **24** 718
    Roerich, Nicholas **26** 530
    Sudeykin, Sergey (Yur'yevich) **29** 899
    Tchelitchew, Pavel **30** 390
    Valmier, Georges **31** 832
    Zack, Léon **33** 588
  directors **8** 849
  programmes **33** *379*
  stage design **3** *119*
Ballets Russes de Monte Carlo **3** 809
Ballets Suédois **3** 120*; **24** 406; **30** 686
  designers **7** 508; **8** 523, 605; **22** 350; **24** 710; **27** 281
Balletta, il *see* FRANCESCO D'ANTONIO (ZACCHI) DA VITERBO
Balley, Richard **4** 353
ballflower **3** 121*, *121*
Ballhause, Walter **3** 121–2*
Balligrama **15** 532
Ballikinrain, Central **28** 288
Ballin, Charles **12** 832
Ballin, Claude (i) (1615–78) **3** 122*, 868; **11** 588, 618; **19** 22
Ballin, Claude (ii) (1661–1754) **3** 122; **11** 619; **24** 147
Ballin, Geoffroi **13** 231
Ballin, Jacques **3** 122
Ballin, Michel **3** 122
Ballin, (Francesco) Mogens (Hendrik) **3** 122*
  groups and movements **22** 421; **25** 215
  staff **17** 479
  works **8** 752
Ballina, Jorge **21** 382
Ballinderry Crannog (Co. Offaly) **15** 872
Ballintober Abbey **26** 618
ballistae **2** 448
Ballmer, Karl **22** 807
Ballocco, Mario **5** 279, 671; **7** 555; **16** 681
Ballochyle Brooch **28** 263
balloon clocks *see under* CLOCKS → types
balloon frames *see under* TIMBER STRUCTURE → types
balloon views *see* BIRD'S-EYE VIEW
ballpoint pens *see under* PENS → types
balls, devil's work *see* DEVIL'S WORK BALLS
Ballsh Monastery **1** 544
Balls Park (Herts) **2** 545
Ballu, Théodore **3** 123*; **12** 10
  assistants **12** 155
  groups and movements **26** 704
  works **5** 824; **22** 270; **31** 241
Ballús, Lluis Clotet *see* CLOTET BALLÚS, LLUIS
Bally, Johannes **14** 131
Ballybogey Bog (Co. Antrim) **6** 161
Ballyedmonduff (Co. Dublin) **25** 508
Ballyfin (Co. Laois) **16** 9, 24
Ballyglass (Co. Mayo) **25** 503
Ballyhaise (Co. Cavan) **16** 23
Ballykinvarga (Co. Clare) **21** 551
Ballylongford (Co. Kerry) **13** 164, 165
Ballynagilly (Co. Tyrone) **25** 503
Ballyshannon Bay (Co. Donegal) **6** 159
Ballyvourney (Co. Cork) **15** 876
Ballywater (Co. Down) **16** 25
Balmain, Pierre **9** 293
Balmaseda, Juan de **3** 123*
Balmer, Joseph A. **8** 790
Balmer, Wilhelm **3** 824; **33** 66
Balmerino **28** 251
Balmes, José **3** 123*; **6** 598
Balmford, Mary *see* MARTIN (iii), MARY
Bal'mont, Konstantin **12** 870
Balmoral Castle (Grampian) **6** 62; **9** 727; **14** 149; **26** 18; **28** 288
  interior decoration **28** 248
  paintings **22** 531
  sculpture **30** 703
balneae **26** 872, 919
  see also BATHS; THERMAE
Balodis, Pēteris **12** 825
Balogun, Hameed **23** 135
Balomir, Ion **21** 811
Balossi, John **25** 703
Balotă, Ileana **26** 721
Balparda, Leandro Castellanos *see* CASTELLANOS BALPARDA, LEANDRO
Balş, Gheorghe **26** 723
Balş, Stefan (Lupu M.) **3** 123–4*
Balsane **15** 316
Balšánek, Antonín **8** 379; **18** 462; **24** 109; **25** 54, 151, 429
balsawood **24** 7
Balsemão, S Pedro **25** 288
Balser, Carlos **29** 220
Balsha II **1** 544
Balsham, Hugh de *see* HUGH DE BALSHAM
Balsimelli, Francesco **16** 747
Balsimelli, Giacomo **26** 810
Balson, Ralph **3** 124*
Balstad **23** *218*
Balta, José **24** 504
Baltard, Louis-Pierre **3** 124–5*
  pupils **3** 125
  teachers **32** 80
  works **11** 522; **18** 888; **19** 846; **24** 166
Baltard, Victor **3** 125–6*; **12** 10
  collaboration **14** 238; **24** 126
  groups and movements **26** 704; **28** 345
  pupils **18** 99; **19** 296
  works **3** 124*, *125*; **11** 143, 522, 524; **16** 54; **19** 250; **31** 276
Baltars **30** 36
Baltasar Maio da Vomio *see* MAGGI, BALDASSARE
Baltens, Peeter **3** 126*, 558; **4** 896; **32** 708
Bal'termants, Dmitry Nikolaevich **3** 126*
Baltgailis, Kārlis
Balthasar, Joseph Anton Felix **33** 291
Balthazarsz, Peeter *see* BALTENS, PEETER
Balthus **3** 127–8*; **11** 551; **18** 138
  collaboration **2** 513
  dealers **19** 537
  patrons and collectors **14** 575; **19** 282; **20** 832; **33** 150
  works **3** *127*; **10** 482
Balti, Giovanni Batta **3** 90
Baltimore (MD) **3** 128–9*; **31** *587*
  Cathedral of the Assumption **7** 258; **10** *850*, 850; **18** 845, *845*; **26** 14; **31** 591
  copper **31** 653
  Fort McHenry **21** 575, *575*
  frames **11** 498
  furniture **3** 129*; **31** 628
  Glen Ellen **31** 232
  Johns Hopkins Hospital **14** 783, 785
  Johns Hopkins University
    Fowler Architectural Collection **4** 21
  Maryland Historical Society **3** 129
  Maryland Institute College of Art **19** 756
  Metro stations **21** 350
  museums
    Baltimore Museum *see* Peale Museum
    Museum and Gallery of the Fine Arts *see* Peale Museum
    Museum of Art **11** 878
      collections **3** 128; **7** 702; **19** 756
      Oval Room **29** 842
    Peale Museum **3** 129; **19** 626; **24** 304; **31** 666
    Walters Art Gallery **8** 652; **31** 667; **33** 371
      catalogues **5** 293
      collections **3** 129; **4** 339; **7** 156; **10** 91, 94; **12** 266; **15** 742, 745; **30** 332; **32** 829
      Greek collection **13** 470
      sculpture **18** 820; **27** 46
  Peabody Library **19** 318
  Roman Catholic Cathedral *see* Cathedral of the Assumption
  Ross Winans House **3** *128*
  silver **31** 646, 649
  terracotta **30** 505
  Union Bank **25** 268
  Unitarian Church **10** 850; **12** 837
Baltimore (MD)—cont.
  Washington Monument **13** 611; **21** 616–17
Baltimore/Washington International Airport **1** 494
Baltimore Painter **13** 530; **32** 33*
Baltistan **15** 562
Balty, J. C. **3** 620
Baltz, Lewis **3** 129*; **23** 37
Balu **15** 609
Balu'a **9** 737
  stele **30** 194
Baluan **24** 82
baluards **3** 359
Baluch **1** 209; **30** 473
Baluchar **15** 662
  textiles **15** *663*
Baluch carpets *see under* CARPETS → types
Baluchistan **9** 786
Balugani, Luigi (Antonio Melchiorre) **3** 129*; **19** 117
Baluschek, Hans **15** 828; **33** 210
baluster-glasses *see under* GLASSES → types
baluster measures *see under* MEASURES
balustrades **5** 474, 475; **9** 21; **10** 275, *275*; **25** *131*
balustroids *see under* GLASSES → types
Baluyia **1** 228, 344, 346
Balvaird, David Murray, 2nd Lord *see* MURRAY, DAVID, 2nd Lord Balvaird
Balvay, Charles-Clément *see* BERVIC, CHARLES-CLÉMENT
Balwant Singh, Prince (1724–63) (Pahari) **15** *631*; **22** *438*
  paintings **15** 630, 631–2, 740; **22** 439
  portraits **15** 232
Balyan (family) **2** 428; **16** 590; **23** 639; **31** 452
Balyan, Agop Bey **3** 130
Balyan, Garabed (Karabet) Amira **3** 130*; **23** 816
  assistants **3** 130
  works **16** 586, *587*
Balyan, Krikor Amira **3** 130*; **23** 644
  works **16** 221, 227
Balyan, Levon **3** 130
Balyan, Nikoğos Bey **3** 130*
Balyan, Sarkis Bey **3** 130*; **16** 611
Balyan, Senekerim Amira **3** 130
Balyan, Simon Bey **3** 130
Bal'yer, August **21** 811
Balzac (family) **7** 597
Balzac, Edmé Pierre **11** 619
Balzac, Honoré de **3** 131*
  groups and movements **26** 54, 501
  illustrated works **3** 259, 849; **13** 306; **17** 605; **21** 889; **24** 721
Balze, Paul **15** 839, 841
Balze, Raymond **15** 839, 841
Balzer, Jan Jiří **8** 391; **13** 717
Balzico, Alfonso **3** 131*; **5** 413; **16** 706
Bam **3** 131*; **16** *105*, 269; **21** 588
Bamako **1** *381*; **20** 199
  Colonial Government Offices **20** 198
  commercial art **3** 137
  Institut National des Arts **20** 199
  Musée National du Mali **11** 827; **20** 199
  Red Market **20** 198
  sculpture **1** 427
  signs (markers) **20** *200*
Bamana **1** 315, 385; **3** 131–7*; **11** 827; **14** 55
  architecture **3** 136*
  blacksmiths **3** 132
  body arts **1** 255–6
  commercial art **3** 137
  craftsmen and artists **1** 246; **3** 132, 136
Bamana—cont.
  divination instruments **1** 356
  doors **9** 164
  dress **1** 256
  dyeing **3** 379
  horn **3** *135*
  iconography **1** 263, 280
  iron **3** 133–4
  leather **3** 136*
  locks **3** *132*
  masks **1** 256, 279, 301, 340, 341; **3** 134–6*, *135*, *136*
  mixed-media **1** 301
  mud **1** 285
  patronage **1** 240
  pots **1** 329
  puppets **1** 385
  quills **3** *135*
  scarification **1** 345
  sculpture **1** 278, 280, 323, *323*, 385; **3** 132–4*, *133*
  shrines (i) (cult) **1** 261
  slit-gongs **1** 360
  textiles **1** 285, 294; **3** 136–7; **20** 198, *199*
  wood **1** *323*; **3** *132*, 132–3, *133*, *135*; **9** 164
  wood-carvings **3** *132*, 132
Bamba **33** 598
Bambaia **3** 137–9*; **20** 789; **21** 533
  collaboration **19** 561
  methods **21** 765
  patrons and collectors **2** 376
  teachers **4** 817
  works **3** *138*; **16** 562
Bambama **30** 419
Bambarende **29** 461
  sculpture **29** *460*
Bambeeck, Nicolaes van **26** 163
Bamberg **3** 139–43*, *139*; **12** *361*
  book covers **4** IV2
  books **4** *357*
  Cathedral of St Peter and St Georg **3** 140–42*, *141*; **7** 192; **13** 48; **26** 575
    altarpiece **29** 729–30, *730*
    chapter house **6** 464
    choir **13** *47*
    manuscripts **2** 791; **23** 652; **28** 25
    Rider **9** 258; **13** 87; **22** 44
    sculpture **3** *142*, 142–3*; **12** 399, 404, 808; **13** 86, 87; **22** 270; **26** 182, 634
    textiles **12** 462; **16** 434, 437; **30** 312
    tomb of Clement II **31** 123
    tomb of Henry II and Kunigunde **13** 92
    tracery **31** 271
  Krankenspital **14** 782
  Monastery of St Michael **3** 139
  Neue Residenz **12** 363
  oliphants **23** 400
  painting **12** 385, 390, 391
  St Martin **32** 822
  sculpture **12** 399; **13** 85
  tapestries **12** 466
  witch-house **25** 636
Bamberg, Felix **5** 792
Bamberg Altar, Master of the **20** 620*, 696; **23** 308
Bamberg Apocalypse *see under* APOCALYPSES → individual manuscripts
Bamberg Cathedral Gospel book *see under* GOSPEL BOOKS → individual manuscripts
Bamberger, Sebald, Abbot of Heilsbronn **31** 287
Bamberg Master **20** 620–21*
Bambilla, F.
  reproductive prints by others **10** *504*
Bambini, Nicolò **32** 194, 196; **33** 612, 697
Bambino Vispo, Master of the **1** 587; **20** 621–2*; **29** 550
  works **6** 2; **16** 442

Bamboccianti **3** 143*; **4** 486; **9** 462; **26** 772
  members **4** 486; **6** 346; **18** 624; **21** 482
  works **6** *347*; **21** *483*; **26** *772*
bambocciate **12** 289; **14** 367; **18** 622, *624*, 624–5
bambochades **22** 85
bamboo **3** 143–5*
  historical and regional traditions
    Africa **1** 307, 310, *367*
    Aztec **10** *779*
    Bali (Indonesia) **15** 809
    Bamileke **1** 307
    Bhutan **3** 913, 916
    Brunei **5** *13*
    Burma **5** 257; **6** 557
    Cameroon **1** 307
    China **6** 736, 740, 877; **7** 31, 58–63*, *59*, *60*, 113, 115, 141, 145, *145*, 146, 147; **20** 326; **28** 310, 312
    Colombia **7** 605
    India, Republic of **15** 173, 174
    Indian subcontinent **15** 551
    Indonesia **3** 144; **15** 770, 807, 809, 817; **20** 327
    Japan **3** 144; **17** 46, 297, 314, *341*, 358*, 365*, 368, 387, 388, 398, 400, 407; **28** *413*
      Edo period (1600-1868) **17** 401
      Momoyama period (1568-1600) **17** 397
    Java **15** 772, 809
    Korea **18** 303, 379, 380
    Malaysia **20** 180
    Mesoamerica, Pre-Columbian **10** *779*; **21** 241
    South-east Asia **29** 226
    Sudan **1** *367*
    Thailand **30** *637*
    Uganda **1** 310
  techniques
    carving *see* BAMBOO-CARVINGS
  uses
    architecture **1** 307; **3** 913; **7** 605; **29** 226
    baskets **3** 144, 331, 916; **5** *13*; **15** 809; **17** 365
    birdcages **7** 146, 147
    bows **3** 144
    boxes **15** 174; **18** 380
    brushes **5** 33; **6** 736, 877; **15** 551; **17** 368
    brush handles **18** 303
    brushpots **3** 144; **7** 58, 59, *59*
    calligraphy **6** 736, 740
    chairs **7** *145*
    chess sets **6** 557
    chopsticks **18** 380
    containers **3** 144; **15** 807
    drills **16** 859
    dyeing **17** 314
    fans **10** *779*; **18** 380
    flutes (musical instruments) **7** 58; **30** *637*
    furniture **7** 31, 145, 146
    granaries **1** 310
    houses **3** 144; **5** 236; **15** 770
    inkstones **17** 387
    kites **7** 113, 147; **17** 388; **20** 180
    lacquer **17** 297; **18** 605
    ladles **7** 58
    manuscripts **7** 62–3; **20** 327, *327*
    mats **7** 146; **15** 809
    netsuke **17** 398, 400, 401
    organs **17** 397
    paper **7** 63, 115; **24** 40; **28** 312
    perfume containers **7** 58, *60*
    pipes (musical) **7** 147
    pipes (smoking) **1** *367*; **7** 147; **18** 380; **32** 481
    polishing **16** 859; **21** 241
    puppets **17** 407
    rattles **15** 817
    rolls **20** 326
    roofs **1** 307; **3** 913; **15** 772; **17** 46
bamboo
  uses—cont.
    sat panchee **5** 255
    scrolls **28** 310
    spearheads **7** 58
    tea ceremonies **17** 365
    toys **7** 147
    vases **28** *413*
    whisks **17** *341*
    wristrests **7** 58
    writing **7** 58, 62
bamboo-carvings
  China **7** 58–62*, *59*, *60*, *61*
  Japan **17** *45*
  Malaysia **20** 183
  Vietnam **32** 481
bamboo painting *see under* PAINTING → types
Bambury, Stephen **23** 61
Bamen **17** 364
Bamenda **1** *394*; **5** 525
Bamford, Rod **2** 762
Bamfylde, Copplestone Warre **29** 734
  works **29** *734*
Bamha **19** 470
Bamileke **3** 145–9*, 170
  architecture **3** 148
  bamboo **1** 307
  baskets **3** 149
  beads **1** 298; **3** 145, *149*
  beadwork **3** *147*, 148
  brass **3** 145, 148
  doorframes **3** 148
  figurines **1** *277*
  houses **1** 307
  iconography **3** 146–7
  ivory **3** 145
  kapok **3** 145
  leopard teeth **3** 145
  masks **1** 278, 298; **3** 148, *149*
  patronage **3** 147
  portraits **1** 269
  raffia **3** 149, *149*
  sculpture **1** 322; **3** *146*, 147
  skins **3** 145
  slit-gongs **1** 360
  stools **3** *147*, 147–8
  wood **1** *277*; **3** *147*
Bamiyan **1** *186*, 193; **3** 149–50*; **6** *182*
  Cave F **1** 203
  caves **1** 201, 202, 203
  ceilings **6** 200
  Museum **1** 211
  niches **1** 201, 202
  sculpture **1** 189, 193, 196, 198, *198*
  stucco **1** 198
  wall paintings **1** 200, 201–3; **24** 790
Bämler, Johannes **3** 150*, 879; **5** 197
Bämlermeister **3** 150
Bamoun *see* BAMUN
Bampi, Richard **12** 432
Bampton (Oxon), St Mary **6** 565
Bampur **3** 150*; **15** *901*, 902, 921
Bamum **3** 145, 151–4*
  architecture **3** 151–2*
  beads **3** *152*
  beds **3** 152
  collections **3** 151
  dress **3** 153*
  furniture **3** 152–3*
  human figures **3** *151*, 152
  jewellery **3** 153
  masks **1** 339, *339*; **3** 153*
  palaces **1** 242, 309; **3** *151*, 151–2
  patronage **1** 241, 242; **3** 151
  pillars **3** *151*, 152
  pipes (smoking) **3** 154
  regalia **1** *352*, 353
  shells **3** *152*
  statuettes **3** 154
  stools **3** 152
  tables **3** *153*
  textiles **3** 153
  thrones **1** *352*, 353; **3** 152, *152*
Bamum—cont.
  weapons **3** 153
  wood **1** 353
  wood-carvings **3** 151, *151*, *152*, *153*
Bamyili **1** 58
Ban **25** 339
Bana (*fl* 7th cent.) **15** 260, 478
Bana Cathedral (Georgia) **7** 256; **12** 319; **30** 306
Banak Cathedral **7** 261
Banaket **6** 379
banana fibres *see under* FIBRES → types
banana leaves **15** 812; **24** 40
Banaras *see* VARANASI
Banaras, Hindu University **15** 742
Banasa
  baths **27** 67
  forum **11** 328
Banassac **27** 107
Banasymeon **31** 434
Banavari **15** 594
Banavasi **15** 526
Ban Baranae **30** 610
Banbhore **3** 154*; **15** *264*, 680; **16** *105*; **23** *797*
  Archaeological Museum **23** 804
  congregational mosque **15** 307, *307*; **22** 192
Banbridge, Down Shoe Factory **16** 39
Banbryols **3** 155
Banbury (Oxon) **31** 710
Bance **11** 598
Banchi, Zecca **27** *744*
Ban Chiang **3** 154–5*; **29** *225*; **30** *571*, 571
  bronze **4** 849
  ceramics **3** 154; **23** 554; **30** 608
  excavations **30** 591
  glass **30** 633
  pottery **29** 227
  weapons **30** 638
Băncila, Dan **26** 719
Banck, Pieter van der **12** 170
Banckes, John **18** 144
Banckes, Matthew **16** 893; **29** 58
banco see BUILDING TECHNIQUES → coiling
Banco, Antonio di *see* ANTONIO DI BANCO
Banco, El
  jewellery **28** *781*
Banco, Maso di *see* MASO DI BANCO
Banco, Nanni di *see* NANNI DI BANCO
Banco Atlántida **14** 715
Banco Central (Dominican Republic) **9** 118
Banco Central de Bolivia **4** 268; **29** 894
Banco Central de Reserva del Perú **24** 516
Banco Consolidado **32** 179
Banco Continental **24** 515
Banco de Crédito del Perú **24** 515
Banco Mercantil **32** 179
Banco de Moçambique **22** 245
Banco Obrero **15** 886; **32** 567
Banco Popular (Dominican Republic) **9** 118
Banco Popular de Puerto Rico **25** 703
Banco da Portugal **3** 811
Banco Wiese **24** 515
Bancredito **9** 118
Bancroft, Bronwyn **1** 64
Bancroft, Joseph **21** 697
Bancroft, Samuel **22** 351
Band, Charles **5** 589
Banda **15** 321
Bandalasta **25** 26
Bandaneira, Fort Belgica **21** 596
Banda Nkwanta **1** *386*
  congregational mosque **1** 316
Ban Dan Kwian **30** 511
Bandar Abbas **4** 173; **15** 902; **16** 449
Bandar Bushire **2** 272
Bandar-e Abbās **10** 719
Bandar Seri Begawan **5** *10*, 11
Bandatandrapadu **15** 534
  Shiva Temple **15** 300
Bandau, Jan Jerzy **32** 878
band cups *see under* CUPS → types
bandeaux **17** 529
banded armour *see under* ARMOUR → types
Bandeira, Antonio **3** 155*; **4** 719
Bandel, (Josef) Ernst von **3** 155–6*
Bandel, Heinrich von **3** 156*
Bandel, H. J. **19** 773
Bandelier, Adolph **8** 282; **23** 703
Bandelier, Alfred **6** 441
Bande Noire **3** 156*; **8** 34
Bandera, Juan de Oviedo y de la *see* OVIEDO (Y DE LA BANDERA), JUAN DE
Banderas Vela, Diego **9** 711; **25** 829
  works **25** *828*
Banderoles, Master with the **12** 385; **20** 622*, 785
Bandinelli, Baccio **1** 102; **3** 156–61*; **9** 142; **11** 187; **12** 283; **16** 695; **26** 769
  academy **16** 778, *779*; **21** 759
  collaboration **19** 688; **27** 777
  drawings **3** *157*; **4** 856
  interior decoration **27** 203
  models **9** 706; **31** 320
  patrons and collectors **11** 170; **13** 906; **14** 252; **21** 17, 20; **23** 855; **27** 648; **31** 524
  pupils **1** 789; **3** 161; **5** 525; **19** 672; **24** 756; **27** 203, 648; **31** 53; **32** 10
  reproductive prints by others **3** 448; **5** 699, 906; **8** 765; **13** 625; **22** 369; **25** *859*, 860
  sculpture **5** 360; **19** *688*; **21** 16
    busts **5** 301
    mythological **1** 791; **3** *158*; **7** 672; **11** 197; **21** 17; **22** 44, 166
    portraits **22** 32
    reliefs **26** 137
    religious **3** *159*, 161; **11** 214
    statuettes **29** 569
    tombs **19** 551; **22** 15
  writings **16** 781
Bandinelli, Clemente **3** 160
Bandinelli, Ranuccio Bianchi **19** 637
Bandini, Alamanno **19** 672
Bandini, Francesco **24** 756
Bandini, Giovanni (di Benedetto) **3** 161–2*
  patrons and collectors **11** 893; **27** 274
  teachers **3** 160
  works **3** *162*; **11** 197; **19** 512; **21** 24; **29** 569
Bandjoun (people) **3** 148
Bandjoun (Cameroon)
  masks **1** *279*
band looms *see under* LOOMS → types
Bandmann, G **9** 528
Bandogarh **15** 288
Bandol, Johannes *see* BOUDOLF, JAN
Ban Don Ta Phet **29** *225*, 230; **30** 633
Bandora, Nagesh Temple **12** 827
bandstands **18** 73; **21** 893
Bandundu **1** *401*
Bandung
  Army Commandant's house **15** 770
  DENIS office **15** 770
  Hotel Savoy Homann **15** 770
Bandung—cont.
  Institute of Technology (ITB)
    Faculty of Fine Arts and Design **15** 818
  painting **15** 807, 808
Bandura, Cristoforo *see* BONADURA, CRISTOFORO
Bandurek, Wolf **3** 162–3*; **24** 98
band windows *see under* WINDOWS → types
Bandzeladze, A. **12** 327
Banepa **22** 759
Banerjee, Amitabha **5** 421
Banerjee, Rakhaldas **20** 478
Banerji, D. **14** 162
Banerji, Jitendra Nath **15** 211
Banerji, R. D. **3** 911; **21** 792
Banes **8** *228*
Baney, Ralph **31** 335, 339
Baney, Vera **31** 339
Banff, School of Fine Arts **5** 592
Banfi, Gian Luigi **3** 438; **26** 536
Bang, Hieronymus **25** 731
Bang, Jacob **8** 749
Bang, Michael **8** 750
Bang, Ove **3** 163*; **23** 222
Bangalore **3** 163–4*; **15** *294*
  Darya Daulat Bagh **15** 648
  Indian Institute of Management **15** 169
  Karnataka Government Museum and Venkatappa Art Gallery **3** 164; **15** 182
  Lalbagh Botanical Gardens **12** 76
  verandahs **32** *240*
  Vidhan Soudha Secretariat Building **15** 168
Bangka **15** 812
Bangkalan **15** 811
Bangkinang **15** 787
Bangkok **3** 164–5*; **7** 154; **29** *225*; **30** *571*, 589
  Anand Phiman throne hall **30** 590
  art forms and materials
    architecture **29** 238
    coins **30** 632
    enamel **30** 632
    metalwork **30** 635
    niello **30** 635
    sculpture **30** 574, 597, 606
    silver **30** 634
    spirit-houses **28** III1
  Bank of Asia building **30** 591
  Chakri Maha Prasat *see* palaces → Grand Palace
  Chulalongkorn Hospital **30** 590
  Commercial Bank of Siam **30** 590
  French Embassy **30** 590
  houses
    Ban Khamthieng **30** 591
    Government House **30** 590
    house of M. Achille Clarac **12** *103*
    Phitsanulok House **30** 590
    Ratchawithi Road residence **30** 590
    Jim Thompson House **30** 591
    Wang Lee House **30** 590
  Hua Lampong railway station **30** 590
  Main Post Office **30** 590
  Makawarn Rungsun bridge **30** 590
  Ministry of Defence **30** 590
  Ministry of Foreign Affairs **30** 590
  Monument to Democracy **30** 590, 608
  Monument to Victory **30** 608
  museums
    Archaeology Museum *see under* Silpakorn University
    Hill Tribes Museum **29** 240
    National Museum
      collections **3** 165; **29** 240; **30** 636
      Wat Phutthaisawan **30** 589, 602, 616, 618

Bangkok—cont.
National Stadium 30 590
palaces
Aphon Palace 30 590
Chitlada Palace
King's private railway station 30 590
Grand Palace 3 164; 12 103; 23 823, 824; 30 575, 589, 590
Amarin Winichai 30 589
Aphon Phimok Pavilion 30 *589*
Dushit Maha Prasat 30 589
monument to King Chulalongkorn 30 608
National Museum *see under* museums
Tamnak Daeng Pavilion 30 589
Wang Ban Mo 30 589
Wang Na *see* museums → National Museum
Wat Chetuphon *see* temples → Wat Pho
Wat Mahathat *see under* temples
Wat Pho *see under* temples
Wat Phra Kaeo *see under* temples
Wat Suthat *see under* temples
Saranrom Palace *see* Ministry of Foreign Affairs
Seri Manangasila 30 590
Suan Pakkad Palace 30 591, 636
Lacquer Pavilion 30 619
Wimanmek Palace 30 590
Phra Borom Maha Ratchawang *see* palaces → Grand Palace
Phu Khao Thong 29 866; 30 589
Poh Chang School *see* School of Arts and Crafts
Portuguese Embassy 30 589
Royal Mint 30 590
School of Arts and Crafts 30 640
School of Fine Arts *see* Silpakorn University
Silpa Bhirasri Institute 30 617
Silpakorn University 30 616, 640
Archaeology Museum 3 170
Department of Thai Art 30 617
temples
Shrine of the Emerald Buddha *see under* Wat Phra Kaeo
Temple of the Dawn *see* Wat Arun Ratchaworaram
Wat Arun Ratchaworaram 3 *164*, 165
Wat Benchamabophit 30 601, *602*, 616, 636
sculpture 30 607
Wat Bowon Niwet 30 590, 601, 602, 616
Wat Chaloem Phra Kiat 30 589
Wat Chetuphon *see* Wat Pho
Wat Mahathat 30 589
Wat Pho 29 827; 30 589, 602, 636
reliefs 30 607
sculpture 30 607
wall paintings 30 616
Wat Phra Kaeo 3 164; 30 575, 589, 593
Shrine of the Emerald Buddha 28 639, *640*; 30 604
wall paintings 30 591, 616
Wat Phutthaisawan *see under* museums → National Museum
Wat Rakhang 30 616
Wat Ratchabophit 30 590
Wat Ratchapradit 30 590, 608, 616
Wat Suthat 3 164; 30 589, 594, 602
sculpture 30 607
wall paintings 30 616
Wat Thep Thidaram 30 589
urban planning 30 592–3
Bangladesh 3 165–70*, *166*; 15 185
architecture 3 167–8*
collections 3 169–70*
cotton 3 168
dolls 3 169
education (art) 3 169*
embroidery 3 168*
figurines 15 *726*
gold 3 169
jewellery 3 169
jute 3 169
metalwork 3 169
museums 3 169–70*
painting 3 168*, *169*
floor 3 169
ink 3 *168*
scroll 3 169
parliament buildings 3 *167*
pearls (pink) 3 169
pith 3 169
plaques 3 169
pottery 3 169; 15 727
quilts 3 168
rickshaws 3 169, *169*
sculpture 3 169; 15 *502*
silver 3 169; 15 *502*
stone 15 *502*
teak 3 169
temples 15 279–81*
terracotta 3 169
textiles 3 168*
toys 15 *726*
weaving 3 168
see also INDIAN SUBCONTINENT
Bangladesh Lalit Kala 24 436
bangles 7 145; 10 29; 15 700; 16 797; 25 546
Bangli 15 806
Pura Dalem 15 *786*
Bangor (Co. Down), North Down Heritage Centre 16 42
Bangor (Gwynedd) 32 *780*
Cathedral 32 786
Bangor, Anne Ward, Viscountess *see* WARD, ANNE, Viscountess Bangor
Bangor, Bernard Ward, 1st Viscount *see* WARD, BERNARD, 1st Viscount Bangor
Bang Pa-In
architecture 30 590
Palace 23 823, 824
Wat Niwet Tham Prawat 30 590
Wehat Chamrun 30 590
Bangs, Lemuell W. 7 486
Bang Saphan 30 635
Ban Gu 8 475
Bangubangu 1 403; 14 376; 19 72
Bangui 1 *394*, *401*
Musée Barthélemy Boganda 6 179
Bangura, Hassan 28 691, 692, 693
Bangwa 3 170–72*; 10 122
burial practices 1 259*
drums (musical instruments) 10 124
fetishes 3 171
gesture 1 266
masks 1 324; 3 171–2*
portraits 1 269
sculpture
figure 1 323, 324; 3 170–71*, *171*
tourist art 3 170
wood-carvings 3 170
Bangwa-Fontem 3 145
Bangwa-Oriental 3 147
Bangwis, Waypanal 24 *67*
Banham, (Peter) Reyner 3 172*; 7 293; 8 247; 15 166
al-Bani, Ali 19 324
Banier, Antoine 22 415
Banī Ḥasan al-Shurrūq *see* BENI HASAN
Bani Jamra 3 69
Banja Luka 4 *459*, 462
Banjarmasin 15 810
Banjeli 1 *287*
Banjska Monastery
St Stephen 28 441, 453
Banjul 12 32
National Museum 12 32
Banjumas 15 792
Bank, Karl 17 527
Banka Maruyama *see* MARUYAMA, BANKA
Bankart, George 29 843
bank barrows *see under* BARROWS → types
banker-mark 3 178*
Bankes, H. 19 479
Bankes, Henry 3 178, 179*
Bankes, John 3 178*
Bankes, Ralph 3 178*
Bankes, William John 3 178, 179*; 10 82, 90
Bank Hall 2 475; 5 421
Ban Khok Mai Den 30 *571*, 576
Bankier, Channa 30 82
banknotes 1 121; 3 179–83*, *180*, *181*; 5 916; 7 115; 10 396; 23 735
Banko 17 263, 399
Banko, Ignaz 19 339
Bank of Asia 30 591
Bank of Cyprus Cultural Foundation 8 367
Ban Kruat 30 610
banks 3 173–7*
Argentina 30 *525*
Austria 32 *762*
Belgium 3 *549*
Britain 3 175
England 28 *906*
Fascism 10 *821*
Guatemala 13 *762*
Hong Kong 11 *333*
Hungary 14 *889*
Italy 10 *821*
Romania 26 *709*
Scotland 28 228
United States of America 3 174–5, *175*, *176*, 176–7; 17 *621*; 29 *916*
Banks, J. H. 4 81
Banks, Joseph 2 743; 3 183*; 10 90; 18 5
clay 33 22
drawings 24 188
paintings 23 57; 24 188
Banks, Robert Richard 30 503
Banks, Thomas 3 183–4*; 7 480; 10 264, 372; 25 374, 406
patrons and collectors 7 541; 13 637; 14 485; 28 908; 32 787
works 3 *184*; 9 706; 14 509; 19 599; 31 130; 33 373
Banks, Thomas Lewis 31 249
Banks & Barry 33 9
Banks Islands 31 891, 892, 893
Banks & Turner 29 419
Bankura 15 229, 664
Bann, Stephen 25 362
Ban Na Di 29 228
bannā'ī see under BRICKS → types
Ban Na Mun Si 30 621
Bannatyne (family) 28 263
Bannenberg, Peggy 22 897
Banner, Peter 4 472; 14 597; 33 195
banners 11 54, 144, 147, 148; 14 404, 408
historical and regional traditions
Akan 1 503
Armenia (Europe) 2 *443*
Buddhism 6 304, 314, 777, 779–81*; 7 *47*; 15 570; 18 308; 22 *782*; 30 612–13, *613*, 828
Central Asia, Eastern 6 304, 314
China 6 777, 779–81*; 7 *49*; 28 310
Denmark 14 408
England 11 *145*; 12 272
Holy Roman Empire (before 1648) 11 148–9
banners
historical and regional traditions—cont.
Indian subcontinent 15 563, 570, 647
Islamic 11 146; 14 427; 16 429
Italy 11 149
Japan 17 *321*, 363
Knights Templar 11 148
Korea 18 308
Mongolia 21 877
Native North Americans 22 655
Nepal 22 778, 780–83, *782*
Rome, ancient 14 407
Thailand 30 612–13, *613*
Tibet 30 828
Viking 11 147
materials
bronze 17 *321*
hemp 6 304
silk 6 304
techniques
gilding 17 *321*
painting 30 612–13, *613*
see also HANGINGS
banners of victory *see* GYELTSEN
Banneux, Shrine of the Virgin 28 632
Bänninger, Otto-Charles 22 274; 26 351; 30 138; 33 737
Bannister, Edward Mitchell 1 440, 441; 3 185*; 31 603
Bannock
dress 10 *578*
Bannockburn (Central) 28 266
bannock racks 28 261, *262*
Bannu 15 446
Bañolas, Master of *see* ANTIGÓ, JOAN
Baños de Cerrato, S Juan Bautista 29 261; 32 618–19
Banoštor 28 439
Ban Phak Top
terracotta 29 *228*
Banpo 3 185*; 6 *615*, 663; 15 51
architecture 6 684
bone 4 313
ceramics 3 185; 6 629, 773
houses 6 646, *685*
kilns 6 870
paintings 6 773
pottery 6 875, 876, *876*
Banpur 15 290
banquet cameras *see under* CAMERAS → types
banqueting houses 3 185–6*
Banquet Stele 21 298
Banqusa Church 9 591
Bansberia, Vasudeva Temple 15 395
Ban Sen, Ruler (*d* 1346) (Pahari) 15 310
Banshan 3 186*; 6 *615*
ceramics 6 629, *877*
houses 6 646
paintings 6 773
Banshan culture 6 876, 877
Banská Bystrica 28 *848*
architecture 14 885
metalwork 15 5, 7; 28 856
monument to the Slovak National Uprising 28 850
Museum of Central Slovakia 28 857
Parish Church 28 849, 850, 853
St Barbara 28 855
St Mary 14 884
sculpture 28 854
Thurzo House 28 851
Banská Bystrica, Jan of *see* JAN OF BANSKÁ BYSTRICA
Banská Štiavnica 14 894; 15 9; 28 *848*
architecture 28 849
Banské Museum 28 857
lace 15 12
metalwork 15 7; 28 856
panel paintings 14 899
sculpture 28 855
Banská Štiavnica—cont.
silver 15 5
Bansko 5 147, 156, 158
Bansko school 3 186*; 5 154
Banteay Chhmar 5 479, 480, 495, 496
Banteay Kdei *see under* ANGKOR
Banteay Prei Nokor 5 *458*
Prasat Preah Theat Toc 5 463
Banteay Srei *see under* ANGKOR
Banten 15 *753*
ceramics 15 811
coins 15 811
congregational mosque 15 768
Fort Speelwijk 15 769
Banti, Cristiano 16 678; 19 870; 20 483
Banting, Frederick G. 16 818
Banting, John 30 22
Bantu language 3 145
Bantu peoples 1 304, 393; 3 693–4; 7 195; 9 115; 11 879; 18 217; 20 149; 22 243; 28 620; 30 418; 32 154; 33 724
anklets 1 351
beads 1 350
beadwork 3 440
horn 1 367
jewellery 1 350, 351
masks 1 333
palaces 1 308
pipes (smoking) 1 368
sculpture 29 111
sinew 3 440
snuff-boxes 1 367
tin 1 368
wood 1 367, 368
zinc 1 368
Bantzer, Carl 10 868
Banū'l-Aḥmar *see* NASRID
Banu Nagrallah 12 80
Banū Naṣr *see* NASRID
Banvard, John 24 19
Banvari *see* BHANWARI
Banwari Kalan *see* BHANWARI
Banyankole 1 309
Banyoles, Master of *see* ANTIGÓ, JOAN
Ban Yong 15 681
Banyoro 1 309
Banza, Julien 5 285
Banz Abbey Church 8 875
Baode 7 21
Baoding 6 899, 900
Beiyang Normal School 7 149
Baofeng 6 885, 893
Ba Ohn 5 246
Baoji 3 187*; 6 *615*
bronzes 3 187; 6 844, 847, 848; 30 217
jade 7 4
see also BEISHOULING; RUJIZHUANG; ZHUYUANGOU
baoli see stepwells
Baoning Temple 6 780
Baoshan 7 60, *60*
Bao Shichen 3 187*; 6 765; 8 713
Baoxiangsi (Guangshan) 7 139
Bapatla 15 539
Ba Phnom 5 *458*
Baphuon *see under* ANGKOR
BAPS *see* BLOCK OF PROGRESSIVE ARCHITECTURAL GROUPS
Bapst, Alfred 17 527
Bapst, Germain 10 771
Bapteur, Jean 3 188*
collaboration 18 684
patrons and collectors 7 597; 28 4
works 3 *188*
baptismal basins *see under* BASINS → types
Baptista, João 7 613
Baptista, Leopaldi 19 468
Baptista, Marciano A. 14 721; 19 866
Baptista Subirana, Juan 3 217; 12 177; 28 483; 29 273, 321; 31 184

Baptista Veneziano *see* FRANCO, (GIOVANNI) BATTISTA
Baptistère de St Louis **14** 428; **16** 366, 382, 383–4, *384*; **23** 562
baptisteries **3** 189–92*; **7** 256
Byzantine **3** 191*; **8** 155; **9** 524, 541
Crete **8** 155
Cyprus **3** 190, *191*
Early Christian (*c.* AD 250-843) **3** 189–91*, *190*, *191*; **7** 254, 255; **9** 524, 529, 533, 535, 541; **26** *822*
England **3** 191
France **3** 191; **25** *86*
Germany **3** 192
Italy **3** *190*, *192*, 192; **11** *199*; **26** *822*
Merovingian **25** *86*
Mesopotamia **9** 541
North Africa **9** 535
Palestine **9** 541
Romanesque **3** *192*; **11** *199*
Rome, ancient **27** 60
Syria **9** 541
Baptists *see under* CHRISTIANITY → sects
Baptitore, Jean *see* BAPTEUR, JEAN
Bapuka **15** 739
Baqala, Tašoma **10** 574
Baqaq 2, Tell **10** 507
Baqir **3** 193*; **16** 515; **22** 260; **28** 27
Baqir, Taha **2** 236
Baqirha **9** 540
Baquet, Maurice **9** 71
Bar **22** *17*; **28** 440, 452
Bar, Jean de **7** 595
Bar, Renauld de **3** 193–4*; **26** 334
el-Bara (Syria) **9** 591
Bara (Madagascar) **1** 269; **20** 35, 37, 38, 39
Bara, Ali Hadi **3** 194*; **22** 342; **31** 454
Bara, Hadi **31** 454
Bara Arch (Italy) **31** 349
Barab *see* OTRAR
Barabar **3** 194–5*; **15** *279*
caves **15** 236, 737
Gopika Cave **15** 251
Lomas Rishi Cave **2** 297; **15** 236, 250, *250*, 251, 423; **30** 437
Sudama Cave **15** 250
Barabás, Miklós **2** 546; **14** 901
Barabás Miklós Céh **18** 395; **30** 641
Barabino, Carlo Francesco **3** 195–6*; **12** 59
works **3** *196*; **12** 282; **16** 648
Barabudur *see* BOROBUDUR
Baracchini Caputi, Adriano **28** 319
Baracco, Juvenal **24** 506
Baracoa **8** 228, *228*
Bar-Adon, Avraham **16** 390
Baradostian period *see under* IRAN, ANCIENT → periods
Baragaon Shiva Temple **15** 322, *323*
Baraguru **23** 182
Barai **13** 882
Baraize, Emile **10** 81
Barajas
Almeda de Osuna *see* El Capricho
El Capricho **19** 657; **23** 627
Palacio de Alameda *see* El Capricho
Barakar **15** 321
Temple 4 **15** 321
Barakhshah *see* VARAKHSHA
Barakov, Vasil **4** 603
Barakzay *see*:
'ABD AL-RAHMAN, King
AMAN ALLAH, King
HABIB ALLAH, King
Baramba
Jagannatha Temple **15** 395
Simhanatha Temple **15** 281
Baramula **15** 459
Bar'an
'Arsh Bilqis *see* Temple of Almaqah
Temple of Almaqah **2** 253
Baranagar **15** 396
Barañano, Luis **18** 781
Baranceanu, Belle **27** 721
Baranik, Rudolf **7** 686
Baranoff-Rossiné, Vladimir (Davidovich) **3** 196–7*; **22** 380, 508; **32** 661
Baranovsky, Gavriil (Vasil'yevich) **1** 148; **3** 197*; **27** 578
Baranów, Sandomierski Castle **12** 114; **25** *92*, 97
Baranówka **25** 123
Baranowsky (family) **11** 33
Baraqish **2** *246*, 247
temple **2** 253
town walls **2** 251
Barat, Jean-Claude **33** 61
Barata **4** 66
Barata Feyo, João Rafael de Basto d'Eça **4** 629
Baratekov, Yuldashbek **30** 253
Baratta, Andrea **3** 197
Baratta, Antonio *see* BARATTI, ANTONIO
Baratta, Fausto **21** 815
Baratta, Francesco (uncle) (*b c.* 1600-66) **1** 629; **3** 197*; **13** 814
patrons and collectors **23** 898
works **23** 900; **26** 810
Baratta, Francesco (nephew) (*d* 1731) **3** 197, 198
Baratta, Giovanni di Isidoro **3** 197, 198*; **8** 303
collaboration **8** 303
patrons and collectors **27** 878; **28** 14
works **17** 544
Baratta, Giovanni Maria **3** 197, 198*; **5** 376
collaboration **26** 810
works **4** 434
Baratta, Giuseppe **3** 838; **20** 86
Baratta, Isidoro **3** 197
Baratta, Jacopo **3** 197
Baratta, Pietro **3** 197, 198; **26** 441; **30** 348; **32** 195
Baratta di Leopoldo, Jacobo **25** 226
Baratti, Antonio **3** 199*
collaboration **32** 759
pupils **27** 719; **32** 689
works **32** 501
Baratzite group **4** 603
Baravelli, Luís Paulo **4** 728
Barba **3** 849
Barba, Alonso **31** 866
Barba, José Arrau y *see* ARRAU Y BARBA, JOSÉ
Barba, Ramón **3** 199*; **4** 566; **27** 646
Barbadian cellarets *see under* CELLARETS
Barbadori (family) **5** 16, 21
Barbadori, Bartolommeo di Gherardo **5** 16
Barbadori, Donato **22** 798
Barbadori, Gherardo di Bartolommeo **19** 440
Barbadori Altarpiece **19** 440, *441*; **27** 495
Barbados **2** 144, 149; **5** *745*
architecture **2** 148
ceramics **2** 146, 152
Codrington College **7** 567
craftsmen and artists **2** 153
education (art) **2** 154
engravings **5** *751*
exhibitions **5** 746
furniture **2** 150
galleries (iv) (art) **2** 153
houses **2** *147*
interior decoration **2** 150, 151
jewellery **2** 152
mahogany **2** 151
museums **2** 153
Barbados—cont.
patronage **2** 153
pottery **2** 152
silversmiths **2** 152
textiles **2** 151
see also ANTILLES, LESSER
Barbados Foundry **2** 152
Barbados Society of Arts **2** 151
Barbagelata, Giovanni di Nicolò (da) **3** 199–200*; **4** 729
Barbaix, René **17** 518
Barbalissos *see* MASKANA
Barbantini, Nino **16** 679; **28** 395
Barbany, Agapito Vallmitjana y *see* VALLMITJANA Y BARBANY, AGAPITO
Barbany, Venancio Vallmitjana y *see* VALLMITJANA Y BARBANY, VENANCIO
Barbar, Louis **9** 31
Barbar, Temple IIa **2** 265
Barbara, Queen of Hungary (?1390-1451) **13** 162
Bárbara, Ferdinand, King of Spain *see* FERDINAND VI, King of Spain
Bárbara, María, Queen of Spain *see* MARÍA BÁRBARA, Queen of Spain
Barbara Glassworks **25** 125
Barbarana, Pedro de **11** *489*
Barbara of Austria, Duchess of Ferrara (*d* 1572) **10** 524
Barbara of Brandenburg, Marchesa of Mantua (*d* 1481) **3** 531; **12** 733, 906; **33** 702
Barbarat, Jean **31** 382
Barbari, Jacopo de' **3** 200–201*; **10** 385
paintings **2** 102; **15** 140; **29** 665
patrons and collectors **13** 25, 905; **22** 901; **25** 454; **33** 112
prints **9** 308; **25** 605
engravings **3** *200*; **32** 192
woodcuts **4** 80; **7** 517; **25** 606; **31** 152, 154; **32** *181*, 184, 199, 216; **33** 356
pupils **18** 510
reproductive prints by others **10** 477, 487
writings **16** 614
barbarian coats *see under* COATS → types
Barbarigo (family) **11** 287; **20** 622; **26** 734
Barbarigo, Agostino, Doge of Venice (*reg* 1486-1501) **3** 201–2, *659*; **32** 193
Barbarigo, Andrea **3** 201
Barbarigo, Antonio **12** 115
Barbarigo, Ida **22** 371
Barbarigo, Marco, Doge of Venice (*reg* 1485-86) **3** 201
Barbarigo, Pierfrancesco **20** 350
Barbarigo Reliefs, Master of the **20** 622–3*
works **20** *622*
Barbaro, Antonio **3** 202
Barbaro, Carlo Antonio, Marquis **20** 219
Barbaro, Daniele **2** 167; **3** 202–3*, *202*; **23** 870; **24** 489; **32** *350*
architecture **3** 202, 203; **20** 545, 546; **23** 865
paintings **32** 348, 350
writings **2** 356; **30** 656, 657; **32** 199
collaboration **23** 862; **32** 641
illustrated **32** *642*
Barbaro, Ermolao, Patriarch of Aquileia **3** 202; **11** 721; **32** 639
Barbaro, Francesco **3** 202; **23** 111
Barbaro, Francesco di Candiano **3** 202
Barbaro, Giuseppe **16** 473
Barbaro, Giustiniani **32** *350*
Barbaro, Marc'Antonio **3** 203*; **32** *350*
architecture **3** 202, 203; **20** 545, 546; **23** 865
collaboration **29** 85
paintings **32** 350
sculpture **5** 532
Barbaro, Umberto **19** 637
Barbaro, Villa *see* MASER, VILLA BARBARO
Barbaro, Zuanne **3** 202
Barbarus, Hermolaus *see* HERMOLAUS BARBARUS
Barbar ware *see* POTTERY → wares
Barbastro **29** 335
Barbatelli, Bernardo *see* POCCETTI, BERNARDINO
Barbault, Jean **3** 203–4*; **18** 47
Barbavara, Giovanni Battista **33** 625
Barbazán, Arnaldo de *see* ARNALDO DE BARBAZÁN
Barbazán, Arnaldo de, Bishop of Pamplona *see* ARNALDO DE BARBAZÁN, Bishop of Pamplona
Barbazza, Andrea **29** *387*
Barbé, Jean-Baptist **12** 15; **17** 599; **33** 168
Barbeau, Marcel **2** 839; **5** 568
Barbé-Coquelin de Lisle, G. **31** 297
Barbedienne **11** 629
Barbedienne, Ferdinand **3** 204*; **11** 621, 631, 753; **29** 574
collaboration **1** 498; **11** 622; **28** 520
groups and movements **28** 346
works **7** 421; **9** 326; **11** 622; **21** 147
Barbella, Costantino **3** 204–5*
Barber, Abayomí **18** 640; **23** 139
Barber, Charles **20** 925
Barber, Donn **3** 176; **31** 855
works **3** *176*
Barber, George **32** 421
Barber, Joseph **4** 86; **8** 83; **25** 836
Barber, Miranda **28** 541
Barberi, Giuseppe **3** 195; **10** 488; **12** 583
Barberi, Jacopo dei **32** 658
Barberigo, Pietro **11** 395
Barberigo Reliefs, Master of the **3** 201
Barberini (family) (17th cent.) **24** 752; **25** 412
architecture **2** 498; **4** 428; **7** 780, 912; **26** 748
archives **2** 366
books **4** 21
collections **16** 764; **25** 664; **26** 229, 773; **32** 612
decorative works **3** 744
interior decoration **29** 80
oil sketches **23** 381
paintings **4** 538; **5** 454; **19** 816; **20** 375; **26** 566; **27** 487; **30** 61
frescoes **26** 197
mythological **19** 525
portraits **10** 530
religious **4** 540; **12** 648; **18** 733, 734; **29** 388; **30** 649, 795
sculpture **4** 886; **21** 754
tapestries **16** 714
wall decorations **5** 453
Barberini (family) (20th cent.) **12** 795
Barberini, Anna *see* COLONNA, ANNA
Barberini, Antonio, Cardinal **3** 205, 208*
etchings **3** *208*
paintings **12** 308; **27** 488
altarpieces **20** 623
frescoes **27** 491
religious **5** 690, 782; **18** 734; **20** 375, 623, 896; **24** 339
Barberini, Carlo, Cardinal **23** 644
Barberini, Francesco, Cardinal **3** 205, 207–8*; **7** 907; **26** 771; **31** 227
architecture **7** 911; **24** 371
gems **12** 260
groups and movements **6** 360
manuscripts **2** 376
metalwork **12** 309
paintings **4** 538
allegorical **3** 207
battle **25** 386
frescoes **7** 907
history **25** 386
mythological **7** 908
portraits **14** 105; **29** 803
religious **4** 667; **18** 734, 736; **25** 395; **27** 893; **28** 367
sculpture **9** 411; **23** 644
tapestries **16** 758; **26** 771, 778, 838; **30** 322
Barberini, Giambattista **5** 845; **12** 914; **18** 447
Barberini, Maffeo, Cardinal *see* URBAN VIII, Pope
Barberini, Taddeo **3** 205, 208*
architecture **20** 46; **26** 836
paintings **5** 454; **20** 374
Barberini Codex *see under* CODICES → individual manuscripts
Barberini Collection *see under* ROME → museums → Museo Nazionale di Villa Giulia
Barberini Faun *see* SLEEPING SATYR
Barberini Gospels *see under* GOSPEL BOOKS → individual manuscripts
Barberini Harp **22** 374
Barberini Ivory **9** 519, 647, 649; **18** 824; **24** 330
Barberini Mosaic *see* NILE MOSAIC
Barberini Panels, Master of the **2** 339; **20** 623*
Barberini Psalter *see under* PSALTERS → individual manuscripts
Barberini *Suppliant* **17** 736
Barberini Tapestry Factory *see* ARAZZERIA BARBERINI (ROME)
Barberini *Togatus* **5** 298; **27** 20, *21*
Barberini Vase *see* PORTLAND VASE
Barberini *Venus* **10** 365; **33** 19
Barberino, Francesco da *see* FRANCESCO DA BARBERINO
Barber Institute of Fine Arts *see under* BIRMINGHAM → museums
Barbet, Jean **11** 573; **26** 346
Barbette, Iosias **8** 752
barbettes **21** 545
Barbetti, Angiolo **11** 190; **16** 730
Barbetti, Rinaldo **16** 730; **25** 74
Barbey d'Aurevilly, Jules-Amédée **3** 564; **5** 131; **21** 628; **24** 333; **26** 6
Barbiano, Villa Guastavillani **20** 541
Barbicano, Lope el *see* LOPE EL BARBICANO
barbicans **3** 209*, *209*; **9** 554; **12** 174; **21** 545
see also CASTLES; FORTIFICATIONS
Barbier **8** 890
Barbier, Georges **10** 824; **29** 628
Barbier, Jean-Jacques-François Le *see* LEBARBIER, JEAN-JACQUES-FRANÇOIS
Barbier, Louis Le *see* LE BARBIER, LOUIS
Barbier, Nicolas-François **26** 257, 743; **27** 324
Barbier de la Rivière, Bishop of Langres **30** 354
Barbiere, Alessandro del *see* FEI, ALESSANDRO (DI VINCENZIO)

Barbiere, Domenico del 3 209–11*; 10 388; 11 532
collaboration 29 833
groups and movements 11 264
works 1 841; 3 *210*; 10 551
Barbieri, Domenico del 21 366
Barbieri, Filippo 3 211*
Barbieri, Giovanni Francesco *see* GUERCINO
Barbieri, Giuseppe 32 342
Barbieri, Leonardo 14 463
Barbieri, Paolo Antonio 3 211*; 13 784
Barbieri, Piero 12 282
Barbiers (family) 3 461
Barbiers, Anthonie 3 211
Barbiers, Balthazar 2 204; 3 211
Barbiers, Bartholomeus (Pietersz.), I (1740-1808) 3 212
Barbiers, Bartholomeus (Pietersz), II (1784-1816) 3 212
Barbiers, Maria Geertruida 3 212
Barbiers, Pieter (Anthoniesz.) (1717-80) 3 211–12*
Barbiers, Pieter (Bartholomeusz.) (1772-1837) 3 212
Barbiers, Pieter (Pietersz.), I (1749-1842) 3 212*
Barbiers, Pieter (Pietersz.), II (1798-1848) 3 212; 17 472
Barbin (*fl* 18th cent.) 24 148
Barbin (*fl* 1894) 21 869
Barbin, Claude 10 725
Barbin, François 11 608; 21 136–7
Barbin, Jean-Baptiste 11 608; 21 137
Barbioni, Nicola 31 31
Barbizon school 3 212–13*; 4 216; 15 20, 152; 18 680, 715; 19 355; 21 611, 613; 23 697; 25 38; 26 527, 741; 27 266
collections 9 425; 26 113; 28 271
Barnes, Albert C. 3 251
Bogolyubov, Aleksey (Petrovich) 4 232
Chauchard, Hippolyte-Alfred 6 516
Drummond, George A(lexander) (1827-1910) 9 305
Durand-Ruel, Paul (Marie Joseph) 2 559; 9 424
Faure, Jean-Baptiste 10 837
Huntington, Collis P(otter) 15 29
Knyff, Alfred (Edouard Hyacinthe) de 8 632
Kröller-Müller, Hélène 18 466
Laurent-Richard 18 869
Mesdag, H(endrik) W(illem) 14 47; 21 176
Morozov, Ivan (Abramovich) (1871-1921) 22 135
Palizzi, Giuseppe 23 852
Reid, Alex(ander) 26 107
Salting, George 27 641
Walker, (Byron) Edmund 32 794
Walters, William T(hompson) 19 755
dealers 31 664
members
Andreescu, Ioan 2 22
Daubigny, Charles-François 8 538
Dupré, Jules 5 343; 9 406
Grigorescu, Nicolae 13 651
Henriet, (Charles-)Frédéric 14 394
Hone, Nathaniel (ii) (1831-1917) 14 718
Jacque, Charles(-Emile) 16 850
Maris, Jacob(us Hendricus) 20 433
Paizs Goebel, Jenő 23 794
Rousseau, (Pierre-Etienne-)Théodore 27 265
works 3 *212*; 7 433; 15 *20*; 21 *611*, *612*; 27 *266*, *267*
Barbo, Marco, Cardinal 19 444; 21 694
Barbo, Pietro, Cardinal *see* PAUL II, Pope
Barbon, Nicholas 19 570; 23 212; 25 655
Barbone & Miller 30 266
Barbor Jewel 10 *345*
Barbosa, Duarte 15 682
Barbosa, Rui 4 728
barbotine 6 462
Barbotine ware *see under* POTTERY → wares
Barboza, Diego 3 213*
Bar Breviary *see under* BREVIARIES → individual manuscripts
Barbuda 2 144; 5 *745*
see also ANTILLES, LESSER; LEEWARD ISLANDS
Barbus, Les *see* PRIMITIFS, LES
Barbusse, Henri 17 669
Barc 26 641
Barca 25 *471*, 522
pottery 25 *528*
Barca, Giovanni Battista 11 42
Barca, Pietro Antonio 3 213*; 21 518
Barcala, Washington 3 214*; 10 509; 31 756
Barcalounger 30 870
Barcarena 13 781
Barc de Boutteville, Louis Le *see* LE BARC DE BOUTTEVILLE, LOUIS
Barcelo 9 118
Barcelo, Joan 27 836
Barceló, Miquel 3 214*
Barcelona (Spain) 3 214–22*, *216*; 14 784; 29 *259*
academies and art schools
Academia de la Lonja 3 218; 29 283, 293
Escola de Llotja 29 318
Escuela de Bellas Artes de la Lonja *see* Academia de la Lonja
Escuela de Maestros de Obras *see* Escuela Provincial de Arquitectura
Escuela de Nobles Artes *see* Academia de la Lonja
Escuela Provincial de Arquitectura 3 219
Ajuntament 13 68
Saló dels Cent 13 67; 29 306
Archivo Mas 29 358
Arco de Triunfo 29 272
art forms and materials
Bibles 17 562
coral 7 834, 835
embroidery 29 349, 350
furniture 29 319
glass 29 330
gold 3 220*; 13 165; 29 332, 337
guns 2 467
interior decoration 29 306
jewellery 17 521; 29 345, 346
lace 29 351
marks 3 220
metalwork 29 332, 335, 341
monstrances 29 *333*
painting 13 150; 29 276
porcelain 29 *330*
posters 25 348
pottery 29 323
silver 3 220*
textiles 29 350, 351
Ayuntamiento *see* Ajuntament
Bernat Metge Foundation 5 510
Bíblica Catalana 5 510
Café las Delicias 29 306
Calle Muntaner 29 273, *274*
Casa Amatller 29 273, 321
Casa Batlló 2 568; 12 181–2; 29 308, *308*, 321; 30 506
Casa Calvet 29 308, *320*, 321
Casa de la Ciutat *see* Ajuntament
Casa Desplá 29 265
Casa Gralla 29 265
Barcelona (Spain)—cont.
Casa Jover 29 306
Casa de la Llotja 10 667; 13 68; 29 271
Casa Lonja 29 20
Casa Martí 29 273
Casa Milà 2 216; 10 697; 12 *181*, 182; 21 779; 29 273, 321
Casa Planás 29 306
Casa Sangrá 29 308
Casa Thomas 29 273
Casa Vicens 29 273, 319; 30 506
Castell des Tres Dragons 29 308
cemeteries 31 131
Cine Coliseum 29 309
Colegio Jesus María 29 319
Colegio Teresiano 12 180
dealing 29 354
Diputació General de Catalunya *see* Palau de la Generalitat de Catalunya
Dispensario Antituberculoso 29 273
ecclesiastical buildings 13 50
Cathedral of S Eulalia 3 *220*, 220–21*; 7 *282*; 10 727; 13 67; 29 263
altars 1 695
chapel of St Mark 11 480
choir-stalls 13 106, 123; 23 494
misericords 21 725
mosaics 22 163
Reliquary of the Holy Thorn 29 332
sarcophagus of S Eulalia 13 105
stained glass 13 191, 192; 29 502
throne 30 779
tiles 29 325
tomb of Bishop Ramon d'Escales 13 106
Clarissan church *see* Monestir de Pedralbes
Convento de Pedralbes *see* Monestir de Pedralbes
Dominican church 13 67
early Christian basilica 29 274
Franciscan church 13 67
Monestir de Pedralbes 13 150
church 13 67, 68
wall paintings 3 *339*; 29 276
S Agata *see* Palau Reial Major → Chapel of S Agueda
S María del Mar 3 221–2*; 13 67, 192; 29 502
S Maria del Pi 3 222*; 13 67, 68
S Pau del Camp 2 296
S Pere de les Puelles 29 262
Templo Expiatorio de la Sagrada Familia 2 568; 7 277; 12 *182*, 182–3; 13 204; 22 *164*; 29 273; 30 506
Editorial Montaner y Simón 29 273
education (art) 29 357
Exchange *see* Casa de la Llotja
exhibitions
Exposició Internacional, 1929 3 216; 10 684; 15 883; 20 400; 29 355
German Pavilion 12 792; 21 491, *491*; 24 291; 29 273, 321
Pueblo Español 29 273
Exposició Internacional del Moble i Decoració d'Interiors, 1923 29 321
Exposició Universal, 1888 3 219; 29 272
fountains 29 294
Gracia Sports Centre 29 428
Grau Inglada pharmacy 29 321
Hospital de la Santa Creu 13 67
Hospital de Sant Pau 14 785
Mallá monument 15 60
Market Hall *see* Casa de la Llotja
Mataro Station 29 272
Monumenta Catalana 5 510
Barcelona (Spain)—cont.
museums
Fundació Joan Miró 21 710; 28 483; 29 355
Instituto Amatller de Arte Hispánico 29 358
Museu d'Arqueologia 29 355
Museu d'Art de Catalunya 29 355
collections 9 156; 26 649; 29 354
library 29 357
Museu Clarà 7 373
Museu Etnològic 29 241
Museu Frederic Marès 29 354
Museu d'Història de la Ciutat 29 345
Museu Municipal de les Belles Artes 5 509
Museu Picasso 27 478; 29 357
Myrurgia factory 29 309
Olympic Village 20 *516*
Palau de la Generalitat de Catalunya 1 610; 13 107; 23 492; 29 268
Chapel of S Jordi 3 *215*; 13 69; 29 349
Palau Güell 2 568; 12 180; 29 273, 319, 321
furniture 29 320
Palau de Justicia 29 309
Palau Reial Major
Chapel of S Agueda 11 483; 13 67
Saló del Tinell 13 67
parks and gardens
Montjuïc park 21 491; 24 181; 29 272, 273
German Pavilion 21 *491*
stadium 29 274, 490
see also exhibitions → Exposició Internacional, 1929
Park Güell 12 181; 23 333; 24 181; 29 273, 308
mosaics 21 IV2; 22 158, *158*
Parlamento Catalán 29 309
La Pedrera *see* Casa Milà
Els Quatre Gats 3 219
Real Colegio de Cirugía 26 *520*
Sants Square 29 274
Stock Exchange *see* Casa de la Llotja
theatres
Gran Teatre del Liceu 29 306, 308, 321
S Creu Theatre 30 663
Teatre Lirico 29 306
Teatre Poliorama 29 308
Town Hall *see* Ajuntament
Trade Office Building 7 *511*
University 31 829
Paraninfo Hall 29 306
urban planning 3 215–16, 217; 31 184, 724
Villa Roviralta 29 309
Barcelona (Venezuela) 32 *165*
Barcelona chairs *see under* CHAIRS → types
Barcelona school 20 517
Barcelos, Senhor da Cruz 25 292
Barcham, John 23 690
Barcheston (Warwicks) 10 349; 30 318
Barchin, (M.) G. 22 174; 30 684
Barcia y Pavón, Angel María de 3 222*
Barcin 25 109
Barclay, David 2 764
Barclay, Edgar 10 641
Barclay, H. & D. 12 775
Barclay, John 21 152
Barclay Curle & Co. 28 228
Barclay & Fry 25 594
Barco, Garcia de *see* GARCIA DE BARCO
Barco y Minusca, Gabriel del 3 222*; 24 394; 27 802; 30 881
Barcroft, Ambrose 32 903
Barcsay, Jenő 3 223*
groups and movements 10 650; 14 902; 30 207
works 30 207
Barczewo Church
tomb of Baltazar Batory 4 *147*
tomb of Cardinal Andrzej Batory, Bishop of Varmia 4 *147*
Barda 2 *890*; 3 223*; 16 *105*
congregational mosque 2 893
jewellery 2 900
textiles 2 900
tomb tower 2 892
Bardaxema *see* BHADRESHVAR
Barde, Chevalier de *see* LEROY DE BARDE, ALEXANDRE-ISIDORE
Bardejov 3 223–5*; 28 *848*
architecture 28 849
metalwork 28 856
paintings 14 899
St Aegidius 3 *224*
St Giles 14 893, 903, *903*
Šarišské Museum 3 *224*, 224; 28 849, 855, 857
sculpture 28 854
Town Hall *see* Šarišské Museum
Bardel, René 10 669
Bardellini (family) 28 32
Bardellino, Pietro 3 225*; 22 479, 481
Bardet, Gaston 3 225–6*; 18 810
Bardi (i) (family) 3 173; 11 183; 14 409
Bardi, Agnolo 2 186
Bardi, Agostino 29 2
Bardi, Alberto, Conte 11 56
Bardi (ii), Antonio Minello de' *see* MINELLO (DE BARDI), ANTONIO (DI GIOVANNI)
Bardi (i), Bartolomeo, Bishop of Spoleto 3 226*
Bardi, Bartolomeo di Betto 28 681
Bardi (i), Boniforte de 3 226*
Bardi (i), Donato de' 3 226–7*
works 3 *227*
Bardi, Donato di Niccolo di Betto *see* DONATELLO
Bardi (i), Giovanni Maria 3 226*
Bardi, Giuseppe 1 643; 4 842
Bardi, Ilarione de' 2 291; 4 30
Bardi, Lina 3 227–8*
works 4 721, *721*, 726; 22 366; 27 808, *808*
Bardi, Pietro Maria 3 227, 438; 4 726; 10 821; 21 422; 27 307
bardiglio *see under* MARBLE → types
Bardin, Jean 26 93
Bardinelli 16 750
Bardini, Stefano 3 228*; 4 209; 11 190; 23 126
Bard-i Nishandeh 1 *849*, 887; 10 171; 24 216, 217
Bardi St Francis, Master of the 20 623–4*
Bardo, Archbishop of Mainz 20 127
Bardon, Geoffrey 1 63; 19 258
Bardonecchia Church 16 722
Bardot, E. 7 304
Bardou, Emanuel 17 739
Barducci, Andrea di Oderigo 19 675
Barducci, Rosa 14 32
Bardwell, Robert 3 228
Bardwell, Thomas 3 228*
Bardwell, William 23 211
Barea, Q. Marcius 19 221
Bareh 15 449
Bareira, Natalio 24 96
Barelli, Agostino 3 228–9*; 33 276
works 3 *229*; 11 456; 12 371; 22 299, 308; 23 811; 33 276
Baren, Jan Anthonie van der 3 230*; 13 919
Barendsz., Dirck 3 230*
groups and movements 26 728
patrons and collectors 23 112

Barendsz., Dirck—cont.
reproductive prints by others 12 529
works 1 806; 3 230; 12 881
Barendsz., Frick 4 150
Barfoot, J. R. & J. W. 31 267
Barford, John 5 839; 33 226
Barga 21 870
Barga, Pietro Angeli da 3 231
Barga, Pietro (Simone) da 3 231*
Barga Cathedral 25 723
Bargaon 22 447
Bargas, A. F. 4 589
Bargellini (family) 5 852
Bargellini Madonna 5 852
Bargeroosterveld 25 523, 529; 30 434
barges
ceremonial 3 231–3*, 232, 233
festival 23 769
livery 3 233*, 234
state 5 254; 13 407; 30 639
Bargiella, Andrea di Bartolo di Simone di see CASTAGNO, ANDREA DEL
Barglum, Gutzon 23 392
Bargoan 15 495
Bargrave, John 13 299; 22 675
Bargrave, Robert 29 303
Bargués, Arnau 3 218, 221
Barham, R. H. 19 62
Bar Harbor (ME)
Charles J. Morrill Cottage see Redwoods
Redwoods 28 604
Barholme 13 211
Barhut 14 186
Bari (i) (Italy) 3 233–8*; 9 510; 16 621
Cathedral of S Sabino 3 234–5*; 16 626; 26 580, 626, 628
throne 16 688; 26 619
S Benedetto 26 627
S Maria Nea 9 581
S Nicola 3 235, 235–6*; 8 260; 16 626; 26 580, 627, 628
Bari Throne 3 237, 237–8*; 26 627; 30 777
icons 28 448
metalwork 13 163; 26 690; 28 455
sculpture 3 236, 236–7*
stadium 1 798; 29 489
Bari (ii) (India) 3 238*; 15 261, 279
hunting-lodge 15 373
Lal Mahal 3 238
Bari (Sudan) 1 410
Bari, Niccolò de see NICCOLÒ DELL'ARCA
Bariba 1 303
Barich, B. 1 370
Barid Shahi 3 238*
Barid Shahi, 'Ali Barid see 'ALI BARID, Ruler
Barier, François-Julien 12 262
Barigioni, Filippo 5 682; 20 392; 25 259; 31 894
Barile, Antonio 11 388, 389
works 11 386
Barile, Gian (fl before 1510) 27 846
Barile, Giovanni (fl 1514-29) 26 780
Barili, Antonio 16 724
Barillet-Deschamps, Jean-Pierre 1 685; 24 179
Barilli, Cecrope 7 339
Barın, Emin 23 391
Barincou, J. 14 58, 60
Baring, Alexander, 1st Baron Ashburton 3 239*; 4 304
Baring, Eugen Albert William 21 66
Baring, Francis (1740-1810) 3 239*
Baring, Francis, 1st Lord Northbrook (1796-1866) 3 239
Baring, Francis, 3rd Baron Ashburton (1800-68) 3 239
Baring, Henry 3 239
Baring, John 3 238
Baring, Thomas (i) (1772-1848) 3 239*; 14 146
Baring, Thomas (ii) (1799-1873) 3 239–40*
Baring, Thomas George, 1st Earl of Northbrook 3 240; 32 377
Barisanus of Trani 3 240*; 9 154; 31 279
Barisini, Tommaso da see TOMASO DA MODENA
Barisino Barisini 31 103
Bariş tepe 9 621
Mar Yaqub 31 434
Bäriswill 30 144
barium 7 81; 12 781
Barium see BARI (ii) (ITALY)
barium carbonate 4 767
barium chromate 24 799
barium hydroxide 28 339, 340; 32 809
barium oxide 29 813
barium sulphate 6 336; 24 797
Barjola, Fundación see under GIJÓN → Palacio de la Trinidad
Barjola, Juan 3 240*
bark
historical and regional traditions
Aboriginal Australia 1 52
Africa 1 293, 295, 306
Bali (Indonesia) 15 806
Central Asia, Western 6 261
China 7 43, 114
Inca 15 163
Indian subcontinent 15 551
Japan 17 47
Korea 18 278
Native North Americans 22 547, 648, 651, 656, 657, 663
Samoa 27 684
Tibet 30 844
Tonga (Pacific Islands) 31 143
types
aloe 15 548
betel-nut 7 115
birch 15 544, 549; 20 327; 22 655, 656; 31 260
cedar 3 331; 22 657
elm 1 493
lime-wood 1 493
mixiang 7 115
oak 6 253; 19 1
paperbark 1 49
Quillaia 12 628
sandalwood 28 312
stringybark 1 49, 50
uses
architecture 1 306
bags 22 662
barkcloth see BARKCLOTH
baskets 1 295; 3 331; 22 655, 656, 657, 662, 663
blankets 22 547
brushes 15 551
conservation 12 628
containers 1 52; 22 656
dolls 31 260
dyes 6 253; 15 163; 22 648
inks 15 850
manuscripts 15 544, 548, 549; 20 327; 21 233
mats 22 662
painting 15 806
paper 7 114, 115; 21 233; 28 312; 30 844
quivers 6 261
roofs 17 47; 18 278
rugs 27 316
shelters 1 49
solvents 7 92
string 1 52
tanning 19 1
textiles 1 493; 7 43; 31 143
trays 22 656
weaving 1 293; 22 620
bark
uses—cont.
writing 15 850
Barka see BORKA
Barkai 30 421
Barkan, M. 31 670
barkcloth
historical and regional traditions
Austral Islands 2 773
Cook Islands 7 790, 791
Easter Island 23 713
Fiji 11 69; 23 713, 735
Hawaii 14 249
Indonesia 15 807
New Guinea 23 713
Pacific Islands 23 713
Philippines 24 623
Polynesian outliers 25 182
Shona 28 621
Society Islands 28 922, 922
Tonga (Pacific Islands) 23 735
uses
bedding 14 249; 28 922
dress 7 791; 11 69; 14 249; 15 807; 25 182; 28 922, 922
staffs 7 790
Barker, Alexander 3 241–2*; 27 224
Barker, Alfred Charles 7 210
Barker, Benjamin, the elder (?1720-93) 3 241
Barker, Benjamin, the younger (1776-1838) 3 241*, 373
Barker, Benjamin (1817-89) 3 241
Barker, Cecil 7 798
Barker, Clive 10 268; 25 231
Barker, Henry Aston 24 18
Barker, J. 33 136
Barker, John Jesse 15 858
Barker, John Joseph 3 241
Barker, Joseph 3 241
Barker, Matthew Henry 8 218
Barker, Merete 8 736
Barker, Octavius William 3 241
Barker, Robert 24 17, 18; 25 726; 26 124
works 24 18
Barker, Thomas (1716-c. 1790) 29 495
Barker, Thomas Edward (fl 1803-07) 26 124
Barker, Thomas Jones (1813-82) 3 241*; 22 208
Barker, Tom (fl 1984) 14 521
Barker of Bath, Thomas (1769-1847) 3 241*, 373
pupils 3 241; 18 891
works 3 241; 19 483
Barkhin, B. G. 17 744
Barkhin, Georgy 25 170
Barkhin, Grigory 18 116; 23 590
Barking (Essex), Round House 25 689
Barklem, Jill 4 368
Barkly, Henry 13 783
Barkóczy, Ferenc, Count, Bishop of Eger 9 754; 10 546, 845; 12 356; 26 316
bark paintings see under PAINTING → forms
barkpaper see under PAPER → types
bark shrines see TEMPLES → types → peripteral
Barlacchi, Tommaso 3 448; 10 389; 32 412
Barlach, Ernst 3 242–3*; 5 924
figurines 12 437
groups and movements 10 694, 695, 696
lithographs 19 490
methods 6 471
monuments 14 102; 20 88; 22 48
prints 25 626; 27 871
reproductions in porcelain 12 437; 21 67
sculpture 3 243; 12 407; 20 396
woodcuts 33 363
Barlaeus, Caspar 4 868
Barlag, Isak Philip 28 770
Barlandus, Hadrianus 29 892
Barlaston (Staffs), Wedgwood Museum 33 23
Barlay, Olivier de see OLIVIER DE BARLAY
Bar-le-Duc, Jean Errard de see ERRARD DE BAR-LE-DUC, JEAN
Bar-le-Duc, St Etienne
tomb of René de Châlons, Prince of Orange 26 350
Barletta
Museo-Pinacoteca Comunale 8 719
sculpture 9 587; 16 686; 18 824, 824
S Maria Maggiore 26 627, 628, 690
Barli 15 808
Barlois & Dabot 23 510
Barlovento 32 167
Barlow, (James) Alan (Noel) 3 243–4*; 16 395, 555
Barlow, Arthur 10 312
Barlow, Florence 10 312
Barlow, Francis 3 244–5*
collaboration 12 221–2; 33 260
illustrated writings 10 757
patrons and collectors 20 141
reproductive prints by others 13 647; 18 73; 25 10
works 3 244, 245; 4 359; 10 725; 29 424
Barlow, Hannah 9 201; 10 312
Barlow, Montague 29 88
Barlow, Thomas Oldham 3 245*; 21 604; 29 634
Barlow, W(illiam) H(enry) 3 245–6*
works 16 54; 19 404, 575; 25 857; 30 27
Barlow, William 3 183
Barluzzi, Antonio 3 883
Barma 22 169, 184
works 22 184
Barna (da Siena) 3 246–7*; 13 149
attributions 16 657; 19 455
pupils 19 753
works 3 247; 27 751
Barnaart, Willem Philip 14 202
Barnaba da Modena 3 247–9*
patrons and collectors 28 656
works 2 16; 3 248
Barnabites 3 249–50*
architecture 3 249; 27 160
Barnack (Cambs) 10 227; 29 531
St John the Baptist 2 66, 66, 72; 26 614; 29 775, 776
Barna di Turino 31 450
Barnard, Bishop & Barnard 17 466
Barnard, Edward 10 334; 19 594
Barnard, George Grey 3 250*; 7 375; 26 487; 31 612
Barnard, George N. 3 250*; 24 666
Barnard, John 9 230; 18 895; 25 631; 30 451
Barnard, William, 7th Baron Barnard 25 401
Barnard Castle (Co. Durham)
Bowes Museum 4 600
collections 9 19; 18 69; 29 353; 33 345
carpets 10 358
Barnasconi, W. 31 576
Barnech, Marcelino 31 756
Barn Elms see under LONDON → houses
Barnenez 3 251*; 11 504; 25 470, 498, 508
Barnes, Albert C. 3 251–2*; 12 769; 13 826; 24 600; 25 553
collections 31 663, 665
paintings 8 708; 20 827, 829; 29 246
sculpture 1 438; 19 438
Barnes, Alfred 8 606
Barnes, Blakeslee 31 652
Barnes, Djuna 12 215
Barnes, Edward Larrabee 3 252*; 8 470; 21 650; 22 367
Barnes, Frederick 2 738; 26 74
works 2 739
Barnes, Hobbs & Co. 14 603
Barnes, James B. 14 603
Barnes, Joseph 23 690
Barnes Foundation see under MERION STATION (PA)
Barnet (Herts), Ravenscroft Secondary Modern School 28 158
Barnet, Bishop of Ely 10 167
Barnet, James 3 252*; 18 888; 23 36
works 2 739, 752, 770; 18 887; 30 158
Barnet, John 28 326
Barnet, Nahum 23 327
Barnet, Will 19 492
Barnett, Haynes & Barnett 27 565
Barnett, Henrietta 19 574, 576; 24 186
Barnett, John 33 550
Barnett, Samuel Augustus 19 574
Barnett-Aden Gallery see under WASHINGTON (DC) → museums
Barneville 26 598
Barney, W. Pope 17 838; 29 718
Barni, Roberto 16 683
Barnim IV, Duke of Pomerania (reg 1326-65) 24 331
Barnoldswick 7 351
Barnovschi, Miron, Prince 15 55
barns
Britain 32 277
England 13 331; 27 126
France 24 104, 105
Shakers 28 540
United States of America 28 540; 32 304
Barnsdall, Aline 23 10; 33 407
Barns-Graham, Wilhelmina 27 563
Barnsley, Ernest 2 569; 10 299; 12 650; 28 347
Barnsley, Sidney 9 527; 28 173
furniture 2 570; 10 299; 12 650; 19 253
workshop 2 569
Barnstaple (Devon) 10 297, 303, 305; 31 710
Barnstone & Aubry 14 803
Barnuevo, Herrera see HERRERA BARNUEVO
Barnum, P. T. 15 407
Barnum's American Museum see under NEW YORK → museums
Baró, José Tapiró see TAPIRÓ BARÓ, JOSÉ
Baró, Maria Fortuny i see FORTUNY I BARÓ, MARIA
barocchetto 3 253*
Barocci, Ambrogio (d'Antonio) 3 253*
assistants 12 582
attributions 31 743, 744
patrons and collectors 22 13
works 27 184; 31 746
Barocci, Federico 3 253–8*; 31 740
attributions 20 213
collaboration 8 268; 19 371
drawings 9 220, 221; 24 243
engravings 26 229
etchings 10 551; 25 618; 26 229
methods 5 614
oil sketches 13 676; 23 380
paintings
altarpieces 3 254, 256
ceiling 26 770
religious 3 255, 256; 11 78; 13 824
patrons and collectors
Anna Maria Luisa de' Medici, Electress Palatine (1667-1743) 21 31
Benavente, 8th Conde de (1575-1621) 3 700

Barocci, Federico
patrons and collectors—cont.
Borghese, Scipione, Cardinal **4** 406
Carpio, Luis Méndez de Haro y Guzmán, 6th Marqués del **5** 844
Clement VIII, Pope (*reg* 1592-1605) **1** 595
Crozat, Pierre **8** 209
Damery, Chevalier de **8** 481
Dezallier d'Argenville, Antoine-Joseph **8** 845
Francesco-Maria II, Duke of Urbino **27** 274
Guidobaldo II, 4th Duke of Urbino (*reg* 1538-74) **27** 274
Lely, Peter **19** 124
Medinaceli, Luís de la Cerda Fernández de Córdoba Folch de Cardona y Aragón, 9th Duque de (1660-1711) **21** 35
Pius IV, Pope (*reg* 1559-66) **25** 7
Watson, William F. (*fl* mid-19th cent.) **28** 271
pupils **23** 348; **32** 626, 658
reproductive prints by others
Bertelli, Orazio **3** 851
Carracci, Agostino **5** 856
Cort (van Hoorn), Cornelis **7** 899
Jode, Pieter de (ii) (1606-74) **17** 599
Lauwers, Nicolaes **18** 879
Le Blon, Jacob Christoph **19** 15
Sadeler, Aegidius, II (1570-1629) **27** 504
Sadeler, Jan, I (1550-1600) **27** 502
Thomassin, Philippe **30** 746
Villamena, Francesco **32** 560
restorations by others **20** 375
teachers **11** 720
Barocco, Giuseppe **31** 285
Baroda *see* VADODARA
Baroda School **18** 16
Baroffio, Eugenio P. **31** 758
Barois, François **3** 258*
Baroja, Gregorio **29** 334
Baroja y Nessi, Ricardo **3** 258*; **29** 286
Barokhera Shiva Temple **15** 323
Baroli **3** 258-9*; **15** *276*, *285*
Ghateshvara Mahadeva Temple **3** 258-9; **15** 488, *488*
Baron, Bernard **3** 259*
works **10** 392; **14** 642; **20** 910; **32** 917
Baron, Henri (Charles Antoine) **3** 259*
collaboration **11** 500
dealers **8** 618
teachers **12** 608
Baron, Jacques **30** 17, 20
Baron, Jean **26** 206
Baron, Théodore **3** 562; **7** 245
Baroncelli, Francesco **31** 189
Baroncelli, Gian Francesco **28** 14
Baroncelli, Giovanni **3** 260; **10** 520; **12** 163; **31** 189
Baroncelli, Niccolò **3** 259-61*
collaboration **11** 4
pupils **9** 97
works **1** 711; **3** *260*; **9** 97; **11** 2
Baroncelli Portraits, Master of the **3** 553; **20** 624*
Baronci, Tommaso **7** 333
Barone di Berlinghiero **3** 808*
Baroni, Eugenio **24** 509
Baroni, Giovanni **16** 738; **23** 263
Baroni, Giuseppe **24** 894
Baroni, N. **21** 471
Baronial Revival **28** *229*, 230, *230*, 248
Baronino, Bartolomeo **29** 250
Baronio, Cesare, Cardinal **26** 758; **31** 884; **32** 658
Baron Jenney, William Le *see* JENNEY, WILLIAM LE BARON
Baronscourt (Co. Tyrone) **16** 25
Baronzio (da Rimini), Giovanni **3** 261*; **6** 466; **12** 706
Baroque
aesthetics **1** 178-9*
art forms **3** 261-8*; **7** 383
allegories **1** 658-60*
altarpieces
Austria **31** *678*
Belgium **3** *263*; **27** *290*
Czech Republic **33** *212*
Germany **8** *627*
Hungary **14** *894*; **30** *206*
Italy **1** *711*; **9** *90*; **11** *681*; **13** *815*; **20** *904*; **22** *478*
Spain **11** *492*; **26** *251*; **29** 291; **31** 92
altars **1** 699, *699*; **5** *533*; **19** *374*; **27** *661*; **32** 195
anatomical studies **1** 842
arches **2** 292
architecture (general) **12** 497
Austria **2** 780-83*
Belgium **3** 545-6
Croatia **8** 175-6
England **8** 47; **13** 623
Germany **3** 791; **12** 370, 389
Guatemala **13** 761
Italy **16** 636-9*; **22** 484; **32** 217
Lithuania **19** 496-7
Malta (Republic of) **20** 212
Mexico **21** 376-7, 401
Poland **25** 97
Sicily **16** 640-41
Slovakia **28** 849-50
Slovenia **28** 859
Spain **29** 268-71*
Switzerland **3** 334
architecture (castles) **19** *780*
architecture (cathedrals)
England **19** *599*
Germany **12** *371*, *404*
Honduras **14** *713*
Italy **3** *836*
Mexico **21** *377*; **25** *696*
Portugal **22** *533*; **32** *616*
Russia **22** *182*; **26** *9*
Spain **5** *368*
architecture (châteaux) **32** *369*
architecture (churches)
Austria **2** *781*, *782*; **5** *772*; **11** *133*; **19** *433*; **25** *448*; **28** *184*
Belgium **3** *546*
Brazil **4** *710*
Croatia **33** *592*
Czech Republic **8** *378*, *874*, *876*; **18** *505*, *506*; **25** *428*
England **10** *232*; **12** *593*; **14** *256*; **33** *394*, *395*
France **20** *294*; **24** *164*
Germany **2** *584*; **8** *873*, *875*; **23** *473*; **24** *562*; **32** *822*
Guatemala **13** *761*
Italy **3** *249*, *355*; **4** *430*, *431*, *432*, *435*; **7** *912*, *913*; **9** *339*; **11** *275*; **13** *750*; **16** *638*, 638, *641*; **17** *707*, *708*; **19** *28*, *628*, *629*, *634*; **23** *331*; **25** *886*; **26** *318*, *758*, *759*, *760*, *807*, *823*; **28** *735*; **29** *80*; **31** *674*; **32** *644*
Lithuania **19** *496*
Poland **32** 895
Portugal **2** *189*; **13** *751*; **25** *292*; **28** *911*
Russia **27** *374*; **31** *318*
Sicily **16** *640*
Slovakia **28** *850*
Switzerland **19** 769; **30** *126*
Ukraine **31** *553*
wall-pillar **8** 874
architecture (cloisters) **22** *485*
architecture (colleges) **14** *887*; **26** *319*; **29** *269*
architecture (domes) **13** *749*; **15** V; **16** *642*; **26** *809*; **32** *645*
architecture (façades) **29** *80*
Baroque
art forms—cont.
architecture (galleries) **16** 771*
architecture (gateways) **25** *433*
architecture (government buildings) **26** *730*
architecture (halls) **19** *748*; **27** *611*
architecture (hospitals) **13** *624*; **24** *164*; **31** *544*; **33** *398*
architecture (houses)
Belgium **2** *549*
Czech Republic **8** *377*
England **2** *307*; **6** *515*; **14** *253*; **30** 278, *278*; **31** *858*, *859*, *860*, *861*
Germany **28** *106*
Scotland **28** *226*
architecture (libraries) **12** *594*; **19** *315*
architecture (loggias) **19** *634*
architecture (mausolea) **14** *258*
architecture (monasteries) **10** *116*; **21** *83*; **23** *5*
architecture (museums) **24** *163*; **25** *240*
architecture (observatories) **18** *447*
architecture (palaces) **23** 811-12*
Austria **11** *132*, *135*; **14** *528*, *529*; **32** *459*, *461*
Czech Republic **25** *427*
England **33** *397*
France **8** *33*
Germany **3** *266*; **9** *236*, *747*; **22** *309*; **23** *3*, *4*, *812*; **25** *367*; **28** *110*, *117*; **33** 429
Italy **1** *622*; **16** *562*; **20** *541*
Poland **12** *35*; **32** *870*
Portugal **28** *912*
Russia **25** *745*
Slovakia **4** *696*
Spain **8** *32*; **20** *72*; **29** *270*
architecture (palazzi) **13** *752*; **16** *644*, *764*; **17** *709*; **20** *44*, *45*; **27** *320*; **32** *187*
architecture (pavilions) **26** *8*
architecture (schools) **2** *784*
architecture (squares) **3** *836*
architecture (theatres) **1** *601*; **14** 469; **30** 665-6*
architecture (town halls) **4** *324*; **23** *317*; **25** *444*
cartoons (drawings) **26** *565*
cartouches **5** *899*
catafalques **11** *276*
cornices **23** *542*
crucifixes **5** *532*
doors **18** *783*
drawings
Austria **2** 795
Belgium **17** *651*; **21** *765*; **27** *299*
France **3** *632*; **21** *764*; **32** *716*
Italy **1** *842*; **2** *126*; **3** *54*; **5** *866*; **7** *913*; **8** *42*; **11** *10*; **13** *788*; **21** *766*; **24** *835*; **32** *884*
Netherlands, the **9** *222*; **24** *349*; **26** *162*
engravings
Belgium **4** *360*; **27** *503*
France **19** *33*, *34*
Italy **12** *23*; **23** *842*
erotic art **12** *764*
etchings **6** *34*; **16** *668*; **24** *272*; **26** *165*
fountains **11** 343-5*
France **11** *560*
Italy **11** *343*, *344*; **16** 698, *700*; **22** *45*; **27** *647*
frames **11** 373
England **11** 422-3*, *423*, 424-6*, *425*, 455-7*
Germany **11** *456*, *457*
Italy **11** *386*, 392-5*, *393*, *394*
Netherlands, the **23** *542*
Scandinavia **11** 468-9*
Baroque
art forms
frames—cont.
Spain **11** 487-92*, *488*, *489*, *492*
Sweden **11** *468*
frontispieces **25** *411*
furniture
Austria **2** 812, *813*
Germany **12** *422*, 422-3*
Hungary **14** 905-6
Mexico **21** *391*
Netherlands, the **29** 114
Nicaragua **23** 80
South Africa **29** 114
gardens **11** *740*, *741*; **27** *753*; **28** 110
Gesamtkunstwerk **12** 497
interior decoration **9** 336; **16** 712, 714; **31** *90*; **32** *371*
lace **16** 754, *754*
marks **20** *446*
metalwork **16** *901*; **27** 419-20
miniatures (paintings) **21** *640*
modelli **21** *770*
monotypes **6** *34*
monteiths **31** *647*
monuments **22** 44-5*
monuments (equestrian) **3** *798*; **10** 441-2*; **13** 315; **16** 700
monuments (funerary)
Finland **11** *99*
France **28** *846*
Ireland **16** *20*
Italy **27** *830*; **31** *127*
mouldings **23** *542*
nude figures **23** 294
Belgium **17** *650*; **25** *273*; **27** *288*, *292*, *293*
France **12** *725*; **25** *706*; **29** *572*
Germany **23** *309*
Italy **1** *535*, *536*; **3** *829*; **5** *406*, *860*, *863*, *866*; **11** *846*; **12** *764*; **20** *376*; **26** *201*, *321*; **27** *816*; **29** *563*
Netherlands, the **1** *657*; **26** *158*
Spain **32** *132*
oil sketches **8** *127*; **12** *201*; **13** *676*; **20** *856*; **22** *415*; **23** 381
ornament **23** 541-3*
painting (general) **7** 905
Austria **2** 794-6*
Belgium **27** 287
Croatia **8** 178
Germany **12** 389-90*
Italy **5** 860; **16** 668-76*
Lithuania **19** 496
Malta (Republic of) **20** 213
Poland **25** 105
Slovakia **28** 852-3
Slovenia **28** 860
Spain **29** 278-82*
Switzerland **30** 131*
painting (allegorical)
Austria **1** *659*; **5** *774*; **29** *790*
Belgium **17** *4*, *652*
England **26** *322*
France **4** *125*; **19** *23*
Italy **12** *764*; **24** *341*; **26** *321*; **28** *39*; **30** *860*
Netherlands, the **1** *657*, *658*; **11** *170*; **14** *617*; **33** *80*
Spain **24** *392*
Switzerland **24** *564*
painting (animal subjects) **4** *916*
painting (battle) **19** *20*, *22*, *309*
painting (*bodegones*) **32** *126*
painting (ceiling) **3** *97*; **26** *837*
painting (flower) **4** *915*
painting (fresco)
Austria **2** *794*, *795*; **31** *357*
England **18** 644, *644*; **30** *759*
Germany **2** *579*, *580*, *583*; **28** 109
Italy **5** *863*; **6** *28*; **7** *908*; **9** *92*; **11** *9*, *24*, *53*, *681*; **13** *786*; **16** *669*, *674*; **18** *733*, *735*; **27** *488*; **29** *40*; **30** *372*, *858*
Baroque
art forms—cont.
painting (genre)
Denmark **17** *880*
France **11** *535*; **19** *146*, *147*, *148*, *149*
Germany **12** *390*
Italy **5** *706*, *707*, *859*; **8** *143*; **12** *288*, *305*; **20** *264*, *640*; **21** *701*; **30** *863*
Netherlands, the **14** *91*; **26** *164*, *171*
painting (grisaille) **13** *676*
painting (history)
Austria **20** *857*
Belgium **3** *559*
France **14** *583*; **24** *212*
Italy **5** *383*, 861; **6** *27*; **7** *907*; **11** *15*, *287*; **20** *96*; **24** *340*
Netherlands, the **4** *250*; **21** *790*; **22** *842*
Spain **19** *179*; **26** *437*
painting (hunting scenes) **28** *903*
painting (landscape)
Belgium **27** *297*
France **24** *211*
Germany **28** *148*
Italy **5** *861*; **9** *91*; **18** *709*; **28** *220*
Netherlands, the **26** *159*
Spain **32** *131*
painting (literary themes) **6** *36*; **9** *479*
painting (military scenes) **32** *129*
painting (mythological) **22** 414*
Austria **29** *401*
Belgium **17** *650*; **25** *273*; **27** *292*, *293*
England **19** *120*
France **4** *535*, *537*; **17** *672*; **32** *717*
Germany **27** *228*; **28** *147*
Italy **1** *535*, *536*; **4** *54*; **5** *453*; **6** *126*; **7** *684*; **8** *141*, *144*; **11** *680*, *846*; **12** *661*; **16** *672*; **20** *265*, *376*, *496*; **26** *199*, *201*; **27** *817*; **30** *857*, *859*
Netherlands, the **26** *158*
Spain **32** *132*, *133*
painting (*pièta*s) **5** *860*
painting (*quadratura*)
Austria **1** *659*
Italy **5** *280*, *652*; **7** *909*; **9** *109*; **12** *199*, *663*; **22** *327*; **25** *415*; **27** *522*; **29** *38*
painting (religious)
Austria **1** *732*
Belgium **4** *914*; **8** *126*; **9** *478*, *488*; **19** *650*, *651*; **27** *288*, *295*, *296*
France **6** *434*; **8** *90*; **11** *534*; **17** *671*; **19** *24*; **25** *708*; **32** *715*, *718*
Germany **19** *706*; **27** *227*
Holy Roman Empire (before 1648) **13** *847*
Italy **1** *672*, *673*; **3** *33*, *95*, *353*, *381*, *713*, *737*, *834*; **4** *334*, *413*; **5** *405*, *406*, *442*, *694*, *695*, *704*, *709*, *710*, *713*, *714*, *715*, *718*, *862*; **6** *33*, *108*, *110*, *114*, *337*, *338*, *339*; **7** *312*, *313*, *683*, *903*; **8** *142*, *147*, *148*; **9** *76*, *77*, *89*; **10** *746*; **11** *678*; **12** *306*, *307*, *589*, *662*; **13** *754*, *785*, *787*; **16** *671*, *673*; **18** *731*, *732*; **19** *472*, *816*; **20** *266*, *377*, *598*; **21** *526*; **22** *530*; **24** *801*, *836*; **25** *562*, *564*, *643*; **26** *197*, *198*, *309*, *311*, *397*; **27** *489*, *490*, *816*, *864*; **28** *473*; **29** *37*, *252*, *544*, *545*; **30** *798*, *863*; **31** *791*

Baroque
art forms
painting (religious)—cont.
Netherlands, the 3 23; 4 52; 8 292; 11 169; 12 241; 19 347, 348; 23 II; 25 230; 26 154; 33 262
Portugal 32 424
Spain 5 526, 618, 619; 7 522; 11 710; 12 58; 20 617; 22 695; 26 435, 436; 29 280, 281, 282; 31 809; 32 127; 33 729, 731
painting (sacra conversazione) 23 447
painting (still-lifes) 3 322; 16 675; 28 902; 29 667; 33 730
painting (vanitas) 31 810
pattern books 24 272
pediments 24 317
portraits (drawings)
Belgium 9 481; 25 284
England 2 314
Italy 12 202
Netherlands, the 26 167
portraits (engravings) 25 411; 27 503
portraits (etchings) 3 560; 19 349; 26 160
portraits (miniatures) 21 641, 642
portraits (painting) 17 653
Belgium 9 277, 486; 17 653; 25 274, 284; 27 289, 298
Denmark 30 41
England 9 278, 281, 483; 19 120–23*, 121, 122, 123; 29 802
France 9 280; 11 537; 18 788, 789; 21 497, 498; 31 378
Italy 3 382, 383; 4 292; 9 477, 480; 12 308, 660; 20 378; 23 321; 25 285; 27 491; 29 42; 30 40
Netherlands, the 1 *658, 807; 4 251; 13 895; 14 92, 93; 23 I; 26 163, 169; 28 50
Spain 7 524; 11 489; 14 9, 793; 25 645; 32 128, 130, 131, 134
portraits (sculpture)
Austria 2 801–2*
Germany 13 679
Italy 11 189
portraits (self)
Belgium 9 486
Italy 12 308; 20 378
Netherlands, the 22 846; 26 160
portraits (silverpoints) 26 156
proportions (architecture) 5 17
pulpits 8 740
sarcophagi 27 830, 831
sculpture (general)
Czech Republic 8 385–6
Hungary 14 894
Italy 16 697–704*
Poland 25 114
Spain 29 291–3*
Switzerland 30 136–7
sculpture (allegorical)
Austria 9 146
France 25 706
Italy 4 621; 16 700; 33 726
sculpture (architectural) 8 385; 11 558; 28 116
sculpture (busts) 5 301–2*
Austria 29 789; 32 442
England 24 753
France 3 833
Holy Roman Empire (before 1648) 5 301
Italy 1 630; 4 406; 5 302; 20 902; 26 773
Netherlands, the 22 859
sculpture (monumental) 5 264

Baroque
art forms—cont.
sculpture (mythological)
France 1 133; 7 423; 12 725; 29 563
Italy 3 829; 29 563
sculpture (relief)
Italy 1 629; 5 377; 11 235; 13 815; 19 88; 22 478; 29 29
sculpture (religious) 7 276
Austria 13 799
Belgium 9 411; 25 811, 812
Brazil 19 461
Czech Republic 4 698, 844
Germany 9 752; 13 684, 777
Italy 1 711; 2 609; 3 262, 828, 832; 7 276; 9 410; 11 18, 280; 16 698; 20 47, 909; 31 790
Malta (Republic of) 20 214
Slovenia 28 862
Spain 29 292
sculpture (statuettes) 29 570*
Austria 2 801
France 29 572
Germany 23 309
Italy 2 610; 16 700
sculpture (tomb)
Belgium 3 417; 9 413
England 10 264
France 2 91; 12 726; 24 786; 28 846
Germany 32 833
Italy 1 627; 16 704; 27 347, 830
Spain 9 407
silver 2 820; 10 329; 27 584; 31 647, 647–8
stage design 25 414
stained glass 14 737
staircases
Germany 25 188
Italy 26 760, 814; 27 711, 729
stucco 1 626; 12 404; 16 704; 28 130, 477; 29 830, 832
tapestries 17 649; 27 294; 30 321
thrones 3 832
title-pages 4 360
tombs
Belgium 3 417
France 2 91; 12 726
Germany 26 25; 32 833
Italy 1 627; 4 621; 16 703; 27 347
trompe l'oeil 32 359
wood-carvings 32 536
woodcuts 5 294; 17 471
regional traditions
Argentina 2 394
Austria 2 775
Belgium 14 488
Bolivia 4 257, 258
Brazil 4 710, 716
Czech Republic 8 385–6
Hungary 14 894
England 10 231–3, 263
Germany 3 805; 33 276
Honduras 14 713
Hungary 10 529; 11 31
Ireland 26 475
Italy 3 828; 7 905; 10 744; 29 251; 30 667
Mexico 21 383–4
see also POBLANO
Moscow see NARYSHKIN BAROQUE
Naryshkin see NARYSHKIN BAROQUE
Ottoman see OTTOMAN BAROQUE
Panama 23 904
Poland 9 74; 17 615; 25 135
Russia 27 575
Spain 7 288; 31 134
treatises 29 269
Baroque Master 23 228, 600; 32 515, 525, 531
works 23 600

Baroque Revival 3 269*; 9 739; 14 580
Austria 30 889
England 10 239, 239, 266; 22 28
France 5 879; 28 346
Germany 3 498; 12 376, 406, 450
Hungary 32 775
New Zealand 5 541
Norway 11 474
South Africa 29 106
Barott, Blackader & Webster 3 270
Barott, Ernest I(sbell) 3 269–70*
Barov, Aleksandr 5 150
Barovier (family) 9 128; 32 200
Barovier, Angelo 3 270; 32 201
Barovier, Antonio 3 270
Barovier, Anzoleto 3 270
Barovier, Bartolomeo 3 270
Barovier, Benvenuto 3 270
Barovier, Ercole 3 270; 32 204
Barovier, Giovanni 3 270
Barovier, Giuseppe 3 270
Barovier, Iacobello 3 270
Barovier, Iacobo 3 270
Barovier, Maria 3 270
Barovier, Marino 3 270
Barovier, Viviano 3 270
Barovier Cup 12 VIII3
Barovier & Toso 3 270
Barozzi, Giacinto 25 259; 32 503
Barozzi, Giuseppe 27 402
Barozzi, Pietro, Bishop of Padua 2 186; 4 99; 16 836
Barozzi, Serafino 27 402
Barozzi Missal see under MISSALS → individual manuscripts
Barozzo (family) 4 76
Barquisimeto 32 167, 177
Barquq, Sultan (reg 1382-89) (Mamluk) 16 521; 20 229–30*; 21 587
architecture 16 211
Barr, Alfred H(amilton) 2 532; 3 270–71*; 4 74; 14 752; 17 620; 26 59, 489; 31 667, 672
groups and movements 2 596
works 17 613; 31 672
Barr, Ewen 7 327
Barr, Flight & Barr 33 378
Barr, Martin 33 378
Barr, Percy 29 768
Barra, Didier 3 271–2*; 11 534; 19 696; 23 191, 897
Barra, Joannes 29 649
Barraband, Jean, II 12 468
Barracco, Giovanni 3 272*; 18 184; 27 46
Barracco, Museo see under ROME → museums
Barrackpur 12 75; 15 402
barracks
Antilles, Lesser 2 148
Australia 13 622; 32 923
Grenada 2 148
Islamic 16 225
Ottoman 16 225
Rome, ancient 21 559
Russia 29 555
Turkey 16 225
Barradale, Isaac 12 649
Barradas, Antonio Pérez see PÉREZ BARRADAS, ANTONIO
Barradas, Jorge Nicholson Moore 19 468; 30 882
Barradas, Rafael (Pérez) 3 272*; 31 755, 757
Barra da Tijuca 8 8
Barragán, Luis 3 273*; 14 581; 22 21
architecture 21 381; 32 307
courtyards 8 65
housing 3 273; 13 731; 21 403
museums 21 396
collaboration 6 365; 12 844
gardens 12 143
groups and movements 2 400; 15 886; 21 783
Bar-Rakib 30 187; 33 684, 685

Barral, Vincent 24 353
Barranquilla 7 611
Barranquitas 25 698
Barrantes Monge, José María 8 16
Barratt, Thomas James 19 269
Barraud, C(harles) D(ecimus) 23 58
works 23 53
Barraud, Francis Phillip 18 882
Barraud, Maurice 12 277
Barrault, Alexis 10 682
Barrault, Jean-Louis 18 577; 20 591
Barre 24 491
Barré, Claude 18 782
Barre, Jean-Auguste 3 274*, 296; 11 564
Barré, Jean-Benoît-Vincent 3 274*, 547
collaboration 5 40
works 13 831, 832; 22 33
Barre, Jean de la 20 629
Barre, Jean-Jacques 3 274; 4 424; 20 925
Barre, Melchior-René 10 348
Barre, William Joseph 3 274*, 537
Barreau de Chefdeville, François (-Dominique) 3 275*
Barreau Taurel, André Benoît 3 870
Barrell, John 10 378
barrel vaults see under VAULTS (CEILING) → types
Barrera, Francisco de 3 275*
Barrès, (Auguste-) Maurice 3 275–6*; 17 593
Barreswil, Charles-Louis 25 618
Barret, George (1728/32-1784) 3 276–7*; 5 215
collaboration 12 647
groups and movements 32 903
patrons and collectors 7 552; 19 531; 24 18
pupils 10 378
works 3 276; 10 278; 16 14, 15; 23 782
Barret, George, jr (1767-1842) 3 277; 14 548; 30 384
Barret, James 3 277
Barret, Mary 3 277
Barret, Ranelagh 32 824
Barrett, Lawrence 20 604
Barrett, Nathan F. 25 722
Barretto, Carlos 24 615
Barrevau, Gilbert 4 546
Barri, Giacomo 13 809
Barriales, Valeriano Salvatierra y see SALVATIERRA Y BARRIALES, VALERIANO
Barrias, Félix (-Joseph) 3 277*; 13 828; 25 150
Barrias, Louis-Ernest 3 277–8*; 11 563, 565, 567
methods 12 626
patrons and collectors 23 794
pupils 7 373; 8 811; 28 366
teachers 17 667
works 11 566, 636; 29 575; 31 241
Barrie, Dennis 7 327
Barrie, J. M. 11 500
Barrientos, Simón de 2 386; 24 503
Barrier Canyon Style 13 332
Barrière, Dominique 3 278*; 20 495
Barriles 3 278–9*; 29 136, 219
sculpture 13 290; 29 143, 144
Barrington (Glos) 23 684
Barrington, Shute, Bishop of Salisbury 2 692; 27 626
Barrington Court (Somerset) 8 44
Barrio, Artur Alípio see ALÍPIO BARRIO, ARTUR
Barrio, Museo del see under NEW YORK → museums
Barrios, Alvaro 3 279*
Barrios, Armando 32 568

Barrios, César 3 279
Barrios, Gracia 3 123; 6 598
Barrios, Moisés 3 279*
Barrois, François see BAROIS, FRANÇOIS
Barrois, Jean-Baptiste-Joseph 2 595
Barron, Frank 25 685
Barron, Hugh 3 280*; 26 277
Barron, William 31 151
works 31 150
Barros, Angel Botello see BOTELLA BARROS, ANGELS
Barros, Geraldo de 4 719
Barros, Jerónimo de 26 554
Barros, João de 13 334
Barros, José António Benedito de 3 280*
Barros, Manuel Fernandes see FERNANDES BARROS, MANUEL
Barros Laborão, Joaquim José de see LABORÃO, JOAQUIM JOSÉ DE BARROS
Barroso, Miguel 10 503; 29 278
Barroso de la Escayola, Vicente 21 377
Barrott, Blackader and Webster 31 863
Barrow, Joseph Charles 11 703; 31 908
Barrow, Thomas 9 199; 33 545
Barrow Court (Avon) 9 305
Barrowfield Pottery 28 258
barrows
historical and regional traditions
Britain 25 507
Celtic 6 154
Funnel Beaker culture 25 507
Georgia 12 318
Germany 6 154; 25 507
Poland 25 506, 507
Prehistoric art 25 506, 506, 507, 518, 523
types
bank barrows 20 116
long barrows 25 506–7
round 25 507
see also TUMULI
Barrow Valley Crosses 8 196
Barr Smith (family) 2 756
Barry, Alfred 3 284
Barry, Charles (1795-1860) 3 280–84*; 8 48
architecture 10 236
belvederes 3 690
castles 3 283; 6 62
chapels 23 194
churches 4 809
clubs (meeting places) 3 282; 7 469, 470; 8 65; 20 237; 30 503
government buildings 10 237; 13 237, 238; 16 52; 19 613–14, 614, 618
hotels 30 503
houses 10 238
museums 10 369
prisons 10 236
restorations 19 609
schools 28 156
urban planning 19 574
villas 32 554
assistants 12 599; 25 712
collaboration 13 237; 22 808; 25 712, 714; 26 288; 31 241
competitions 7 667
drawings 2 333
garden design 12 139, 139
groups and movements 13 202; 26 190; 32 415
patrons and collectors 3 178, 179; 9 755; 24 571
pupils 3 284; 14 748
sculpture 30 742
Barry, Charles, the younger (1823-1900) 3 280
Barry, Comtesse Du see DU BARRY, (MARIE-JEANNE BÉCU), Comtesse

Barry, David F. 10 580
Barry, E(dward) M(iddleton) 3 280, 284*; 33 191
architecture
museums 3 325
palaces 3 282; 19 615
public buildings 6 408
railway stations 25 856
schools 3 281; 28 157
theatres 20 212; 30 677
town halls 3 283
collaboration 31 241
competitions 7 667
interior decoration 7 470
Barry, François 20 473
Barry, Helga 31 661
Barry, James (1741-1806; Ireland) 3 284–7*; 10 394; 14 585; 16 16; 19 588, 621; 31 524
groups and movements 13 297; 26 737; 29 891
sponsors 5 215
works 2 240; 3 *286*; 9 1; 10 250; 16 14; 19 158, 483
Barry, James (*fl* 1772-89; Scotland) 12 773
Barry, John Wolfe 4 799; 17 633
Barry, Patrick 33 134
Barry, Redmond 2 769
Barry, Robert 7 685; 24 24
Barry Gasson Architects 12 775
Barsanti, Anastasio 16 729
Barsbay, Sultan (*reg* 1422-37) (Mamluk) 16 211; 20 230*
Barsebäck 26 691
Barshch, Mikhail (Osipovich) 3 287*; 12 655; 22 174
Barsippa *see* BORSIPPA
Barsi-Talki, Kalikadevi Temple 15 316
Barsiyan Mosque 16 162
Barsky, Basil 18 640
Barstow, John 29 870
Bar-sur-Seine, St Etienne 13 60
Bart, Karl 7 870
Barta, Lajos 14 896
Barta, Sándor 24 440
Bartatua 28 322
Bartel, Bürgermeister 2 383
Bartelli, Liberato 24 830
Bartels, Hans von 3 287–8*
Bartels, Lulef 8 629
Bártfa *see* BARDEJOV
Bártfa Bookcase 14 903, *903*
Bartfeld *see* BARDEJOV
Barth, Carl 14 694
Barth, Ferdinand 8 885; 29 847
Barth, Franz Xaver 28 196
Barth, Gottlob Georg 29 874; 33 616
Barth, Johann August 25 623
Barth, Joseph 10 883
Barth, Julius Arthur 21 66
Barth, Karl 7 284
Barthe, Richmond 1 442
Barthel, Hieronymus 3 288
Barthel, Melchior 3 288*; 19 630; 32 195
Barthélemy, Jacques-Eugène 3 288*
groups and movements 13 203
works 13 *202*
Barthélemy, Jean 4 573
Barthélemy, Jean-Jacques, Abbé 3 288–9*
Barthélemy, Jean-Simon 4 554
Barthes, Roland 3 289*; 13 716; 25 361; 26 62
Bartholdi, Frédéric-Auguste 3 289–91*
collaboration 10 106
teachers 28 68
works 3 *290*; 11 346; 12 157; 15 23; 22 42, 47; 26 338
Bartholdy, (Jakob) Salomon 3 291*
collections 10 90
paintings 7 870; 22 704; 23 676
Bartholomae, Georg Ludwig 11 832
Bartholomäus von Hamm 24 190
Bartholomé, Albert 3 291*; 11 568
Bartholomeus Anglicus 10 202, 203; 21 5
Bartholomew, Harland 27 730
Bartholomew Master *see* ST BARTHOLOMEW ALTAR, MASTER OF THE
Bartholomew of Trent 16 837
Bartholotti von Barthenfeld, Freiherr 19 338
Bartlesville (OK), Harold Price Tower 28 834
Bartlett, Edwin 33 135
Bartlett, Jennifer (Losch) 3 291–2*; 22 523
Bartlett, Paul Wayland 31 612; 32 892
Bartlett, Roger 4 353
Bartlett, Scott 32 420
Bartlett, William Henry 3 292*
reproductive prints by others 8 66; 25 635, 837
works 5 564
Bartlett Head 13 459
Bartłomiejczyk, Edmund 32 877
Bartmann, Heinrich 8 631
Bartmann & Deilmann 8 631
Bartning, Otto 3 292–3*; 12 378; 14 571
collaboration 3 795; 11 299
groups and movements 2 288; 8 826; 10 697; 21 781; 26 405
staff 14 24
teachers 11 129
works 3 *292*; 7 582
Bartoccio di Paolo 11 118
Bartol'd, V. V. 6 278, 279
Bartoletti, Tino 21 533
Bartoli, Andrea de' 2 18*; 4 274, 275
collaboration 20 751
patrons and collectors 4 275; 32 610
works 2 627–8; 9 261
Bartoli, Bartolomeo de' 2 18; 4 274; 23 91
Bartoli, Carlo, Bishop of Siena 9 94
Bartoli, Cosimo 3 293*; 5 887; 15 87
collaboration 4 408; 32 14
personal collection 12 545
works 1 568; 32 14
Bartoli, Daniello 21 483
Bartoli, Domenico 7 758
Bartoli, Francesco 2 125; 5 697; 6 140; 17 521; 18 595; 21 17
Bartoli, Niccolò 11 194
Bartoli, Papirio 3 293*
Bartoli, Pietro Sante 3 294*
collaboration 3 674; 18 595
patrons and collectors 20 588; 26 280
works 2 163; 15 861; 19 732; 23 353; 26 230
Bartoli, Simone 3 293
Bartolin, Thomas 14 25
Bartolini (family) 3 16; 31 581
Bartolini, Dario 2 373
Bartolini, Giovanni 3 16; 27 770
works 3 *16*
Bartolini, Leonardo di Bartolommeo 19 443
Bartolini, Lorenzo 3 294–7*; 4 305, 457; 11 189
groups and movements 25 581, 741
methods 21 770
patrons and collectors 4 301, 305; 6 117; 25 143, 383
pupils 13 621; 26 539; 30 459
works 3 *295*, *296*; 8 19; 9 404; 15 839; 16 705, *706*; 24 855; 26 137
Bartolini, Lucia 2 373
Bartolini, Luigi 3 297–8*
Bartolini, Niccolò Enea 2 853
Bartolini Salimbeni Altarpiece 19 *681*, 681
Bartolino da Novara 3 298*; 21 531
patrons and collectors 10 517; 12 903; 20 318
Bartolo, Andrea di *see* CINI, ANDREA DI BARTOLO
Bartolo, Cino di *see* CINO DI BARTOLO
Bartolo, Domenico di *see* DOMENICO DI BARTOLO (GHEZZI)
Bartolo, Giovanni di *see* GIOVANNI DI BARTOLO (*fl* 1365-85)
Bartolo, Nanni di *see* NANNI DI BARTOLO
Bartolo, Taddeo di *see* TADDEO DI BARTOLO
Bartolo di Fredi *see* CINI, BARTOLO DI FREDI
Bartolo di Michele 12 537, 544; 16 741
Bartolo di Sasso Ferrato 14 406
Bartolomé de Solórzano 14 578
Bartolomej of Cinperk 8 415
Bartolomeo (*fl* 1426) 11 382
Bartolomeo, Giovanni di *see* GIOVANNI DI BARTOLOMEO
Bartolomeo, Martino di *see* MARTINO DI BARTOLOMEO
Bartolomeo, Master (*fl* 1493) 20 323
Bartolomeo, Michelozzo di *see* MICHELOZZO DI BARTOLOMEO
Bartolomeo, Niccolò di *see* NICCOLÒ PISANO
Bartolomeo, Peramore di *see* PERAMORE DI BARTOLOMEO
Bartolomeo Alfei, Francesco di *see* ALFEI, FRANCESCO DI BARTOLOMEO
Bartolomeo da Camogli 28 656
Bartolomeo da Foggia 23 107
Bartolomeo da Gadio 7 568; 28 530
Bartolomeo da Modena 4 274
Bartolomeo de Blavis 12 734
Bartolomeo della Fonte 12 552
Bartolomeo della Gatta 2 389; 3 298–9*; 5 451
collaboration 24 521; 28 700, 701
works 3 *299*; 27 739
Bartolomeo di Donato 24 754
Bartolomeo di Fruosino 3 299–300*
Bartolomeo di Giovanni 3 300–301*
patrons and collectors 29 361
works 6 4; 12 552; 31 173
Bartolomeo di Tommaso (da Foligno) 3 301*
Bartolomeo di Tommé *see* PIZZINO
Bartolomeo Mattioli di Torgiano 24 520
Bartolomeo Papini, Guasparri di *see* PAPINI, GUASPARRI DI BARTOLOMEO
Bartolomeo Veneto 3 301–2*
patrons and collectors 4 411; 29 763
teachers 3 667
works 3 *302*
Bartolommei (family) 30 229
Bartolommeo, Fra 3 302–7*; 16 663, 766; 26 769
altarpieces 3 *303*, *304*, *305*, 873; 11 186
assistants 24 27
collaboration 1 569, 570–71; 24 27
drawings 9 220
methods 18 898; 24 493
paintings 27 496
Bartolommeo, Fra—cont.
patrons and collectors 11 186
Alfonso I, 3rd Duke of Ferrara, Modena and Reggio (*reg* 1505-34) 10 522; 29 860
Billi, Antonio 4 64
Cowper, George Nassau Clavering, 3rd Earl 8 83
Dominican Order 9 112
Doni, Agnolo 9 142
Francis I, King of France (*reg* 1515-47) 31 849
Gabburri, Francesco Maria Niccolò 11 875
Gondi, Bartolomeo 12 897
Koenig, Fritz 9 229
Lely, Peter 19 124
Medici, Ferdinando de', Grand Prince of Tuscany (1663-1713) 21 30
Mond, Ludwig 21 849
Nelli, Plautilla 22 727
Paolino, Fra 24 27
Soderini, Piero (di Tommaso) 28 928
Udney, Robert 31 524
William II, King of the Netherlands (*reg* 1840-49) 23 469
pupils 12 556
reproductive prints by others 24 252
teachers 24 771; 27 176
Bartolommeo, Francesco di *see* FRANCESCO DI BARTOLOMMEO
Bartolommeo, Geri di *see* GERI DI BARTOLOMMEO
Bartolommeo, Maso di *see* MASO DI BARTOLOMMEO
Bartolommeo, Michele di *see* MICHELE DI BARTOLOMMEO
Bartolommeo (di Pietro) da Cortona 31 707
Bartolommeo de Lino 20 418
Bartolommeo di Francesco 8 797
Bartolommeo di Gregorio 20 307
Bartolotto, Filippo 4 442
Bartolozzi, Francesco 3 307–9*; 29 675
assistants 6 528; 18 149; 30 353
collaboration 1 135; 7 340; 8 131; 10 394; 13 220; 24 708; 29 675; 31 137; 32 759; 33 14
engravings 3 *308*; 4 373; 8 474; 13 789; 20 26; 24 894; 28 432; 29 675, 676; 33 714
etchings 19 620; 26 230
forgeries by others 4 331
patrons and collectors 8 864; 32 377
pupils
Bartolozzi, Gaetano (Stefano) 3 309
Bovi, Mariano 29 676
Cheesman, Thomas 6 528
Cromek, Robert Hartley 8 186
Marcuard, Robert Samuel 20 400
Martin (iii), Johann Fredric (1755-1816) 20 485
Ruotte, Louis Charles 29 676
Sherwin, John Keyse 28 597
Skorodumov, Gavnil (Ivanovich) 28 893
Tomkins, Peltro William 31 137
Vendramini, Giovanni 32 156
reproductions in beadwork 3 *440*
reproductive prints by others 12 582; 28 86; 32 501, 689
teachers 14 848
workshop 25 622
Bartolozzi, Gaetano (Stefano) 3 307, 309*
Bartoluccio *see* BARTOLO DI MICHELE
Bartomeu, Master 3 309*
works 12 739; 13 105; 29 288, 332; 30 347
Bartomeu of Girona 13 169
Barton, Benjamin Smith 3 310
Barton, Charles E. 4 481
Barton, Rose 16 17
Barton, Thomas 31 422
Barton, William 31 653
Barton-le-Street (N. Yorks), St Michael 26 614
Barton-upon-Humber (Humberside), St Peter's 2 66; 26 591
Bartorelli (family) 28 734
Bartoš, Antonín 8 406
Bartos, Armand 16 566; 18 34
Bartoszewicz, Kazimierz 19 537
bar tracery *see under* TRACERY → types
Bartram, John 3 310; 12 136, 137
Bartram, William 3 309–10*; 24 302
Bartsch, Adam von 3 310–11*; 11 262; 25 604
attributions 4 308
patrons and collectors 11 789
prints 25 619
writings 9 443; 10 208; 21 895; 25 631; 26 177
illustrated 6 78
Bartusz, Juraj 28 855
Barucci (family) 31 3
Baruffaldi, Giovanni Antonio 30 358
Baruffaldi, Girolamo 3 311*; 8 146
Baruffaldi, Nicolò 3 311
Barujird Mosque 16 162, 164
Barumini 3 311–12*; 16 *620*; 25 *470*, 522
Barungi 1 311
Barvitius, Antonín (Viktor) 3 312*; 8 379
Barvitius, Viktor 3 312*; 8 392
Barwa Sagar, Jarai Math 15 289, 496
Barwell, Frederick 23 249
Barwig, Franz 2 803; 32 446
Bary, Hendrick 4 96
Baryatinsky, Count 1 687
Barye, Antoine-Louis 3 312–16*; 11 564, 629; 29 343
assistants 23 633
collaboration 30 32
groups and movements 26 742; 28 345
methods 21 770
patrons and collectors 5 58; 6 548; 8 705; 19 755; 25 234
pupils 26 510
teachers 13 692
works 2 99, 106; 3 *313*, *315*; 19 487; 29 575; 33 3
Barye & Cie. 3 312
Barygaza *see* BHARUCH
Barysaŭ 3 525, *525*
Cathedral of St Aleksandr Nevsky 3 527
Baryshnikov, I. I. 17 870
Barzaghi, Francesco 16 707
Barzaghi-Cattaneo, Antonio 3 316*, 824
Barzizza, Gasparino 1 555
Barzizza, Guiniforte 20 783
Barzun, Henri-Martin 1 21; 8 243; 25 747
Bas, Le *see* LE BAS
Basa 1 399; 23 283
temple 23 283
Ba Sabrina 31 435
Basail 29 202
Basaiti, Marco 3 316–17*
attributions 32 658
patrons and collectors 7 775
works 3 *317*; 32 658
Basaldella, Afro *see* AFRO
Basaldella, Dino 1 446
Basaldella, Mirko *see* MIRKO
Basaldúa, Héctor 2 400; 3 318*; 26 475
basalt 29 698–9*
historical and regional traditions
Africa 1 292

basalt
historical and regional traditions—cont.
Anatolia, ancient 1 829
Assyrian 14 64
Byzantine 9 538
Early Christian (c. AD 250-843) 9 538
Egypt, ancient 9 813*, 814; 10 72; 25 762; 27 824, 825; 28 34
Gulf Coast, Mesoamerica 21 218
Indian subcontinent 15 328
Mesoamerica, Pre-Columbian 21 188, 218, 251; 23 417; 30 341
Mesopotamia 21 296
Mexico 21 218; 23 417; 30 341
Nabataea 22 419
Olmec 21 218; 23 417, 417
Pacific Islands 23 712
Palestine 9 538; 14 273
Phoenician 27 825
Prehistoric art 14 273; 25 493
Rome, ancient 26 880
Society Islands 23 712
Syria 26 916
Syria-Palestine 9 694; 14 64
Tarascan 30 341
uses
adzes 23 712
architecture 9 538; 26 880, 916
churches 9 538
colossal heads 23 417
figurines 21 218
masks 21 251
orthostats 33 685
pyramids 9 813; 25 762
reliefs 33 685
rock reliefs 1 829
sarcophagi 27 824, 825
scarabs 28 34
sculpture 4 265; 5 121; 14 64, 273; 21 188; 22 419; 23 417; 30 341
stelae 9 694; 21 296
temples 15 328
tools 25 493
vessels 10 72
Basan see SREI SANTHOR
Basan, Antoine-Simon-Ferdinand 3 319
Basan, Henry-Louis 3 319; 33 44
Basan, Pierre-François 3 318–19*; 9 395; 11 663
assistants 8 542
collaboration 19 268
dealing 11 663; 17 668; 24 137; 30 24
personal collection 3 310
pupils 12 178
works 6 78; 7 193; 8 542; 20 584; 26 229
writings 10 206
Basarab I, Voivode of Wallachia (reg c. 1310-52) 26 706
Basarab, Ioana 26 719
Basarab, Matei 26 712, 722; 31 23
Basarabi-Murfatlar 26 483
Basara group 26 550
Basarh 15 213; 31 798
Basavakkulam 29 459
Basawal 1 196
Cave 130 1 203
Basawan 3 319–20*; 15 577; 20 284
attributions 15 581
collaboration 8 847; 17 775; 30 338
works 3 320; 8 848; 15 546, 579, 581, 582; 17 512
Basbous, Alfred 19 8
Basbous, Joseph 19 8
Basbous, Michael 19 8
Bascapè, Carlo, Bishop of Novara 27 498; 31 898
Baschenis, Cristoforo 6 99
Baschenis, Evaristo 3 321–2*
works 3 322, 772; 16 674, 675; 29 667; 31 883
Baschet, Bernard 22 375; 29 97
Baschet, François 22 375; 29 97
Baschet, Marcel-André 18 803
Baschieri, Niccolò 20 320
Bascio, Matteo da 5 689
Bascourt, Joseph 3 322–3*, 550
bascule bridges see under BRIDGES → types
bas-de-page 3 323*, 323; 4 394; 21 638
Ba Sebrina see HABERLI
Basedow, Johann Bernhard 7 183
Basegio, Pietro 13 95
Basekpio 1 394, 401; 33 609
Basel see BASLE
Baselitz, Georg 3 323–4*; 17 818
exhibitions 3 803
groups and movements 1 81; 10 696; 25 360; 28 146
house 18 114
patrons and collectors 27 478
works 3 324; 9 310; 12 397, 408; 33 364
Base Ring I ware see under POTTERY → wares
Base Ring II ware see under POTTERY → wares
Baseroo, Andries van 3 494
bases 22 211; 23 477, 478, 482, 484
mouldings 22 213, 213, 214, 215, 216, 218–19, 221–2
Baset, Abdul 23 799
Basevi, (Elias) George 3 324–5*
competitions 10 370
patrons and collectors 13 696
works 5 512; 6 412; 8 248; 11 141; 22 362
BASF Lacke und Farben 7 585
Basgo 30 806
architecture 15 311
Maitreya Temple 15 311
Serzang Temple 15 397
stupas 30 817
wall paintings 30 833
Bashadar 24 297
Basharov, Kutluk 31 783
Bashindjaghyan, Gevorg 2 431
Bashir 6 254
Bashir, Murtaza 3 168; 23 799
Bashir, Tell 17 499
Bashir II Shihab 3 429
Bashkend see ARTSVASHEN
Bashkir 27 434
Bashkiria 27 434
Bashkirtseva, Mariya (Konstaninovna) 3 325–6*; 11 672; 33 313
Bashtak 20 228; 32 313
bāshūra 21 545
Basia 15 629
Basil (fl 963-89) 9 658, 661
Basil (fl 1169) 3 882; 17 504
works 17 504
Basil, Bishop of Caesarea (fl 330-79) 9 570
Basil II Bulgaroctonos, Emperor of Byzantium (reg 976-1025) 2 671; 9 614; 21 137; 22 520; 31 304
Basil II, Menologion of see MENOLOGION OF BASIL II
Basildon (Essex) 31 733
Basildon Park (Berks) 30 XVI
Basile, Ernesto 3 326–7*; 16 731
architecture 3 326, 327; 16 646; 23 842; 26 762; 28 657; 32 555
furniture 16 721, 731
Basile, Giovanni Battista 3 326*
works 16 646; 23 842; 28 657
Basilewski Situla 23 659; 28 805
Basil I, Emperor of Byzantium (reg 867-86) 9 522; 19 886–7*
architecture 9 558, 576; 16 582, 603, 607
coins 9 638
Basil I, Emperor of Byzantium (reg 867-86)—cont.
mosaics 22 156
Basilica of Maxentius see under ROME
Basilica of the Virgin of Guadelupe 28 632
basilicas (ecclesiastical) see under CHURCHES → types
basilicas (non-ecclesiastical) 3 327–9*; 18 886; 26 867–8, 868, 890; 31 235
Rome, ancient 7 917; 26 748, 797, 867, 888, 902, 905, 907, 910; 27 3; 31 324
Britain 3 328; 26 905
Germany 31 324
Italy 3 328; 7 917; 26 748, 797, 868, 888
Libya 3 328; 19 222
Basilier, J. 7 556
basilika see under COINS → types
Basilius (fl 540) 9 648
Basilius (fl 1135) 17 502; 21 83
Basilius Pictor see BASIL (fl 1169)
Basil the Great, Saint 7 212; 9 615; 15 75; 21 833
Basin, Pyotr 15 19; 18 203
basinets see under HELMETS → types
Basing, Adam of see ADAM OF BASING
Basini, Basinio de' 12 699
Basinio da Parma 2 649
basins 10 666*
historical and regional traditions
Buddhism 18 349
Central Asia, Western 6 286
China 10 III2
Egypt 16 384; 20 228
France 11 617
Germany 12 445; 17 888
Hungary 15 6
Islamic 6 IV1; 16 384, 397
Korea 18 349
Netherlands, the 22 881, 890
Spain 29 325
Sweden 30 111
Syria 16 384, 397; 20 228
Turkey 6 IV1
materials
brass 16 384; 20 228
bronze 6 286; 18 349
copper 30 111
enamel 10 III2; 15 6
inlays 16 384
pottery 6 IV1; 22 881
silver 22 890
silver-gilt 11 617; 15 6; 17 888
types
baptismal 28 261
piscine see PISCINE (ii) (BASINS)
see also PERIRRHANTERIA
Basire (family) 14 856
Basire, Isaac 3 329; 13 789
Basire, (John) James, I (1730-1802) 3 329*; 4 116; 10 394; 13 225; 24 50
Basire, James, II (1769-1822) 3 329, 646; 10 396
reproductive prints by others 23 688
Basire, James, III (1796-1869) 3 329
Basit, Abdul 22 489
Baskerville, John 3 330*; 24 43, 45, 61
works 4 8; 31 495
basket arches see under ARCHES → types
basket lids 22 657
Basketmaker culture 22 554, 661
basketry see BASKETWORK
baskets 3 330–32*
historical and regional traditions
Aboriginal Australia 1 52; 3 331, 332
Africa 1 296, 310–11, 424, 426; 3 331, 332
baskets
historical and regional traditions—cont.
Angola 1 296
Bali (Indonesia) 15 809, 810
Bamileke 3 149
Botswana 1 296
Brunei 5 13, 13
Burma 5 257
Chokwe 1 357
Colombia 7 602
Egypt, ancient 3 330, 332; 10 41, 41–2*
England 3 442
Ethiopia 1 295; 3 442
Fiji 3 330
Guyana 3 331
Hopi 3 332
Iceland 3 332
India, Republic of 15 173, 174
Indian subcontinent 3 331, 332; 15 727
Indonesia 3 331; 15 809–10*
Inuit 22 656
Jamaica 16 882
Japan 17 358, 365; 31 167
Java 15 809, 810
Kenya 1 295, 296
Malaysia 3 332; 4 I2; 20 182
Maori 3 331
Native North Americans 3 331, 332, 332; 8 537; 22 641, 652, 655–7*, 658–63*, 659, 660, 662, 663
Nigeria 1 296; 3 331
North Africa 3 331
Paraguay 24 92
Peru 3 330
Sarawak 3 332; 4 I2
Scandinavia 3 332
Songye 1 251
Spain 3 331
Sudan 1 295
Sumatra 15 810
Tasmania 1 52
Uganda 1 295
United States of America 1 426
Zaïre 1 296
Zambia 1 310
materials
ash 3 331
baleen 22 656
bamboo 3 144, 331, 916; 5 13; 15 809; 17 365
bark 1 295; 3 331; 22 655, 656, 657, 662, 663
beads 1 295; 3 331; 4 I2; 22 655, 656
beadwork 3 442
bird's feet 22 655
buttons 1 295
cane 3 331; 4 I2; 15 809; 17 365; 20 182; 22 662
cloves 3 331; 15 810
coconuts 15 810
cotton-wood 3 331
feathers 3 331; 10 848; 22 652
ferns 3 331
flax 3 331
fur 1 295; 22 656
gold leaf 3 331; 15 810
grasses 1 426; 3 331, 332; 15 809; 22 655, 656, 661, 662, 663
hazel 3 331
hemp 22 663
hickory 3 331
hides 1 295
ivory 22 656
lacquer 3 331; 5 257; 15 810
leather 1 295; 3 331; 17 365; 22 663
liana 3 331
maple 3 331
moose-hair 22 663
oak 3 331
osier 3 331
palm leaves 1 295, 296; 3 331; 15 809
baskets
materials—cont.
pandanus 1 52; 3 330, 331; 15 809
pine-needles 22 663
plastics 1 295
quills 22 663, 663
raffia 1 295; 3 149, 331
rice 3 331
roots 1 295; 3 331; 22 656, 657
rushes 3 331; 22 662
sedges 3 331
shells 1 295; 3 331; 4 I2
silver 22 890
sinew 1 295
sisal 1 296
skins 1 295
straw 17 358
sumac 3 331
vine 17 365
willow 3 331, 332; 22 662, 663
wire 3 331
wisteria 17 365
wood 1 295; 22 662, 663
yarn 22 655
yucca 3 331, 332; 22 661, 662
techniques
coiling 3 332; 22 655, 658
looping 3 332
painting 3 331
plaiting 3 332; 15 809; 22 655
stamping 22 662, 663
twining 3 332; 22 655, 658, 663
weaving 3 331, 332; 24 92
types
cake 22 890
layette 22 890
reliquary 18 402; 19 741*
Basket-weave bond see under BONDING
basketwork 33 155
historical and regional traditions
Africa 1 295–6*, 296; 3 332
Ancient Near East 1 879
Angola 1 296, 296
Bhutan 3 916
Cameroon 1 246
Carib 2 145
China 7 101
Dan (Africa) 8 489
Dominica 2 145
Fulani 23 127
Gabon 11 878
Guyana 13 874
Hausa 14 233; 23 127
Indonesia 15 809–10*
Inuit 22 656
Japan 17 358*, 359, 365*
Jukun 3 332; 17 680
Kenya 1 296
Kiribati 3 332
Liberia 1 296
Malaysia 20 183
Mali 1 296
Martinique 2 145
Native North Americans 22 655–7*, 657, 658–63*, 666, 668, 669
Ndebele 1 296
Nuba 23 275
Pakistan 23 802
Papua New Guinea 24 71
Philippines 24 628*, 628
Rome, ancient 3 332
Rwanda 1 296
Somalia 1 296
South America, Pre-Columbian 29 188, 194
Thailand 30 630*
Togo 31 73
Tonga (Pacific Islands) 31 143
Tuareg 31 407*
Uganda 1 296
Zaïre 1 295, 296, 296
Zambia 1 296
techniques
coiling 22 655, 659
twining 22 659

basketwork—cont.
types
woodsplint **22** 662–3
uses
armour **3** 332
baby-carriers **1** 296
beds **1** 296
bottles **22** 661
bowls **22** *659*
bracelets **1** 296
chairs **33** 155
dance-crests **31** 73
dress **3** 332
earplugs **1** 296
fibre art **11** 54
hats **1** 296; **22** *659*
houses **1** 295
masks **1** 296; **3** 332; **24** 71
mats **1** 296
quivers **3** 332
shields **1** 296; **3** 332
sledges **1** 296
teapots **7** 101
Baskin, Leonard **3** 333*; **17** 580; **33** 364
Basle **3** 333–7*, *334*; **25** *470*; **30** *124*
ART exhibition **3** 336
art forms and materials
antependia **11** 379
Bibles **4** 9
books **4** *358*
coins **6** 160
engravings **9** 190; **10** 381
gold **30** 145, 146
metalcuts **21** 337
metalwork **30** 147
mother-of-pearl **22** 203
objects of vertu **30** 148
painting **30** 125
pottery **25** 544
prints **30** 131
sculpture **30** 136
tapestries **12** 466; **13** 196; **30** 148–9, 311
Badischer Bahnhof **30** 127
carnivals **5** 787
civic buildings
Geltenzunft **30** 126
Rathaus **10** 738; **30** 126
Spiesshof **30** 126
ecclesiastical buildings
Allerheiligenkirche **11** 256
Barfüsserkirche *see* museums → Historisches Museum
Dreifaltigkeitskirche **7** 270
Franciscan church *see* museums → Historisches Museum
Leonhardskirche **30** 126; **33** 286–7
Minster **3** 336–7*; **9** 191; **30** 126, 136
gold **24** 36
liturgical furnishings **26** 620
organ shutters **23** 501
sculpture **3** 337*; **13** 87; **26** 635
Treasury *see* museums → Historisches Museum
St Alban monastery **3** 333
St Antoniuskirche **22** *186*; **30** 128
fountains **30** 136
Carnival Fountain **11** *346*, 347
houses **30** 126, 128
Blaues Haus **30** 127
Haus zum Tanz **10** 737, 739; **15** 137
Haus Zwinger **10** 739, *739*
Sandreuter House **29** 602
Weisses Haus **30** 127
housing **30** 127
Sierenzerstrasse Estate **3** 841
Kunstgewerbeschule **30** 156
Kunsthalle **3** 336; **4** 205
libraries
Bibliothek der Öffentlichen Kunstsammlung **30** 156
Universitätsbibliothek
collections **1** 771; **30** 154
Basle—cont.
Markgräfischer Hof **3** 334, 336
museums
Amerbach-Kabinett **1** 771
Antikenmuseum Basel und Sammlung Ludwig **19** 779
Gewerbemuseum Basel *see* Museum für Gestaltung Basel
Haus zur Mücke *see* Kunstmuseum
Historisches Museum **3** 333, 337*; **30** 146
collections **1** 771; **3** 337; **10** 752; **30** 154, 332
Jewish museum **17** 582
Kaiserstuhl, Zum *see* Amerbach-Kabinett
Kunstmuseum **3** 336; **4** 309; **30** 155
collections **1** 771; **4** 207; **5** 75; **9** 758; **10** 752; **30** 152, 154
engravings **4** 128
Mücke Haus, Zur *see* Amerbach-Kabinett
Museum an der Augustinergasse *see* Museum für Völkerkunde
Museum für Gegenwartskunst **30** 129
Museum für Gestaltung Basel **30** 155
Museum für Völkerkunde **3** 335, 336, 843; **30** 137, 154, 155
collections **15** 745; **21** 265; **29** 240
interior decotation **4** 205
Naturhistorisches Museum **1** 771; **30** 155
Spalentor **30** 126, 136
Stadt-Casino **7** 687
Swiss Bank Corporation **30** 152, 153
University **1** 771; **3** 336; **30** 154
Basle Mission houses *see under* HOUSES → types
Basler, Adolphe **17** 577
Baslini, Giuseppe **16** 769
Basmanov, Pavel (Ivanovich) **27** 581
Basohli **15** *619*
painting **7** VI1; **15** 618–19*, *620*, 630
Basoli, Antonio **4** 277; **16** 729; **20** 497; **22** 741; **23** 829
Bason **11** 438
Basotho **19** 241
Basov, Vyacheslav (Ivanovich) **27** 425
Basquiat, Jean-Michel **3** 338*; **7** 413; **14** 177; **32** 863
Basra **3** 338*; **6** *623*; **16** *104*; **21** 581
cantonments **16** 151
education (art) **16** 2
fortifications **21** 588
houses **16** 269, 270
maqṣūras **20** 368
metalwork **16** 369, *370*
mosque **16** 145; **22** 192
pottery **16** 398
rock crystal **16** 540; **26** 487
bas reliefs *see* RELIEF SCULPTURE
al-Basri, Abu Nasr *see* ABU NASR AL-BASRI
Bass, Alberto **9** 118
Bassa, Antonio **11** 324
Bassa, Arnau **3** 339–40*; **9** 262; **11** 480; **20** 767
Bassa, Ferrer **3** 218, 339–40*; **5** 911; **27** 818
collaboration **8** 817
works **3** *339*; **13** 150; **29** 275
Bassai **3** 340–42*; **13** *363*; **23** 490
architecture **3** 340–41*
reliefs **3** 341–2*
Temple of Apollo **3** 340–41; **7** 502; **13** 394, 400–401, *401*, 417, 457, 470; **15** 132; **30** *435*
capitals **1** 109
Bassai
Temple of Apollo—cont.
ceiling **13** 391
colonnade **13** 391
columns **13** 415; **24** 456
gardens **13** 418
orders (architecture) **23** 482
sculpture **3** 341–2; **11** 791; **13** 426, *426*, 432
tiles **13** 387; **30** 435
Bassallectus *see* VASSALLETTUS
Bassani, Giorgio **19** 637
Bassano (family) **3** 351*; **5** 431; **12** 340
Bassano, Annibale Magi da *see* MAGI DA BASSANO, ANNIBALE
Bassano, Francesco, il Giovane **3** 342, 348–51*; **23** 381; **32** 190
collaboration **3** 345, 346, 347; **32** 352
patrons and collectors **27** 723; **28** 5
works **3** *346*, 350; **12** 288
Bassano, Francesco da Ponte, il Vecchio **3** 342–3*, 351
patrons and collectors **13** 919
pupils **3** 343
Bassano, Gerolamo **3** 342, 347, 350–51*
Bassano, Giambattista (i) (uncle) **3** 342, 351
Bassano, Giambattista (ii) (nephew; 1553-1613) **3** 342, 346, 347, 350, 351
Bassano, Gianfrancesco **3** 351
Bassano, Jacopo **3** 342, 343–51*
assistants **3** 349
collaboration **3** 343, 348
copies **11** 722
drawings (pastel) **24** 243
methods **9** 216; **23** 377; **30** 456
paintings **2** 102; **3** 351; **9** 14
genre **11** 393; **12** 287, 288
landscape **18** 708
portraits **30** 358
religious **3** *344*, *345*, *346*; **16** 667; **32** 215
patrons and collectors **3** 351
Alcalá, 3rd Duque de (1583-1637) **26** 307
Carlo Borromeo, Saint **4** 424
Carol I, King of Romania (*reg* 1866-1914) **5** 792
Carr, Robert **5** 847
Charles-Emanuel I, 11th Duke of Savoy (*reg* 1580-1630) **28** 5
Contarini, Jacopo **7** 776
Contini Bonacossi, Alessandro, Conte **7** 782
Créquy, Charles de Blanchefort de **19** 238
Danvers, Henry, Earl of Danby **23** 326
Dezallier d'Argenville, Antoine-Joseph **8** 845
Fouquet, Nicolas **11** 356
Guzmán, Ambrosio Ignacio Spínola y, Archbishop of Seville **13** 880
Habsburg I., Leopold William, Archduke of Austria, Governor of the Netherlands **13** 919
Hesselin, Louis (-Cauchon) **14** 492
Howard (i), Aletheia, Countess of Arundel **14** 807
Jabach, Everard **16** 815
Lambert, Jean-Baptiste (1608-44) **18** 671
Lerma, Francisco Gómez de Sandoval y Rojas, Duque de **27** 723
Medinaceli, Luís de la Cerda Fernández de Córdoba Folch de Cardona y Aragón, 9th Duque de (1660-1711) **21** 35
Museu Nacional de Belas Artes (Rio de Janeiro) **4** 726
Bassano, Jacopo
patrons and collectors—cont.
National Gallery of Scotland **28** 272
Nicquet, Jan **23** 112
Nisbet, William Hamilton **28** 271
Royal Institution (Edinburgh) **28** 271
Ruffo, Tommaso, Cardinal, Archbishop of Ferrara **27** 316
Rushout, John, 2nd Baron Northwick **27** 350
Spencer, Robert, 2nd Earl of Sunderland (1641-1702) **29** 381
Tallard, Marie-Joseph d'Hostun, Duc de **30** 274
Villiers, George, 1st Duke of Buckingham (1592-1628) **32** 575
Wotton, Henry **33** 387
pupils **3** 348, 349
reproductive prints by others **17** 599; **18** 44; **25** 622; **27** 502, 503
teachers **24** 889
Bassano, Leandro **3** 342, 349–51*
collaboration **3** 346, 347
patrons and collectors **27** 723
pupils **30** 923
works **3** 349; **32** 215
Bassano del Grappa
Biblioteca Comunale **32** 690
maiolica **16** 735, 736
Museo Civico **26** 324
Bassano di Sutri, Palazzo Giustiniani **1** 534; **6** 26; **12** 764
Bassano Romano, Palazzo Odescalchi **15** 137
Bassante, Bartolomeo **3** 351–2*; **20** 617
Bassarguechar **2** 439
Bassari **1** 256, 287; **13** 835; **28** 405; **31** 73
Bassarini, Marco **3** 316
Bassein **5** *221*; **15** 401
Bassen, Bartholomeus Cornelisz. van **3** 352–3*; **14** 41; **22** 844
collaboration **2** 385; **11** 718; **25** 68; **32** 139
pupils **14** 795
works **2** 341, *341*; **9** 28; **11** 455; **14** 39, 795
Bassenheim, St Martin **13** 86
Rider **13** *86*; **20** 735
Bassermann, Otto **5** 290
Basset, André **15** 142
Basset, Francis (1690-1758) **31** 651
Basset, Francis (*fl* 1785) **10** 785
Basset, Fulk **14** 416
basse taille enamel *see under* ENAMEL → techniques
Basseterre, Clock-Tower **2** 148
Bassetki **1** 510
Bassetti, Marcantonio **3** 353–4*
collaboration **26** 840; **27** 817
teachers **5** 32
works **3** *353*
writings **23** 380
Bassett-Lowke (family) **21** 782
Bassett-Lowke & Co. **31** 257
Basse-Yutz **25** *470*
flagons **6** 155, *155*; **21** 324, 328; **25** 547
Bassi, Carlo **10** 218; **11** 91, 92; **30** 73, 284
Bassi, Francesco Maria **7** 779
Bassi, Girolamo de **32** 205
Bassi, Martino **3** 354–5*
patrons and collectors **4** 425
works **1** 608; **3** *355*, 384; **21** 518, 537; **30** 802; **31** 898
Bassia **15** 632
Bassias, Edouard **29** 843
bassinets **8** 107
Bassiti, Marco **3** 316
Basso, Ana M. **25** 702
Basso, Bartolommeo **2** 127
Basso, Girolamo, Cardinal **21** 97
Basso, Leo **31** 336
Bassompierre, Joseph **2** 391
Bassot, Jehan **4** 150
Bassum Collegiate Church **14** 81
Bassus, Franciscus **12** 814
Basta **5** 70
Basta, Tell *see* BUBASTIS
Båstad **30** 328
Bastalus *see* NASTALUS
Bastam (Azerbaijan) **3** 356*; **15** *901*; **31** 701
architecture **1** 831
fortress **15** 905; **31** 699
seals **17** 879
Bastam (Iran) **1** *821*; **6** *182*
Bastam (Khurasan) *see* BISTAM
Bastam (*fl* 6th cent.) **4** 99
Bastar **15** 175, 732
Bastard (family) **8** 47
Bastard, John **8** 533
Bastard d'Estang, Auguste de, Comte **14** 772; **26** 234
Bastar Muria **15** 735
Bastaro, il *see* PUGLIA, GIUSEPPE
Bastarolo, il *see* MAZZUOLI, GIUSEPPE (*c.*1536 -89)
ba statues *see under* SCULPTURE → types
bastejas **21** 545, *579*
Bastero, Luis de Durán y de *see* DURÁN Y DE BASTERO, LUIS DE
bast fibres *see under* FIBRES → types
Bastian, Adolf **10** 580; **29** 220
Bastiani, Lazzaro **3** 356*
collaboration **3** 656; **8** 855; **32** 657
patrons and collectors **22** 127
pupils **5** 818; **8** 855
works **3** 659; **32** 224
Bastianini, Giovanni **3** 357*; **11** 306
Bastiano **4** 197
Bastiano da Montecarlo **31** 53
Bastiano di Francesco d'Jacopo **18** 820
Bastida, Joaquín Sorolla y *see* SOROLLA Y BASTIDA, JOAQUÍN
Bastidas, Rodrigo de **23** 902
Bastien, Alfred **23** 398
Bastien-Lepage, Jules **3** 357–9*
groups and movements **15** 156
patrons and collectors **19** 875; **31** 312
pupils **3** 325
teachers **5** 342
works **3** *358*
Bastier, Charles Le *see* LE BASTIER, CHARLES
Bastiné, Johann Baptiste **26** 255
bastions **3** 359–60*; **21** 545, 561, 565*, 567, 579, *579*
historical and regional traditions
Britain **21** 568
France **3** 359; **21** 567–8, 581
Germany **21** 551
Greece, ancient **21** 551
Italy **3** 359, *360*; **21** 561, 566, *566*; **24** *532*; **28** 309
Prehistoric art **21** 551
Russia **27** *371*
Scotland **21** *550*
Spain **21** 551
types
angle **2** 501; **3** 359, 360; **21** 565
pentagonal beaked tower **21** 547
Bastion Ulmer **33** 349
Bastl, Vjekoslav **3** 360*; **14** 724
Basto, Ferreira Pinto, (family) *see* FERREIRA PINTO BASTO
Basto Furnace **31** 652
Bastone, Giovan Battista **16** 724
Bastos, José **28** 729
Bastos, Vítor **3** 360–61*; **8** 11; **25** 301; **28** 748
Bastrup Tower **8** 723
Basu, Nirmal Kumar **15** 212
Basufân Church **7** 259

basura houses *see* AFRICA → houses
Basutoland *see* LESOTHO
Bata **1** 241, 328; **6** 406
Bat'a, Tomáš **8** 423
Baťa Company **8** 425; **12** 834; **17** 813
Batadomba Cave **29** 445
Bataille, Colin *see* BATAILLE, NICOLAS
Bataille, Georges **10** 486; **11** 549; **17** 726; **20** 591; **24** 144; **30** 20, 21
Bataille, Jean **3** 361
Bataille, Laurent-Edme **3** 452
Bataille, Nicolas **3** 361–2*
  collaboration **19** 382
  dealing **3** 606; **4** 525; **30** 312, 313
  patrons and collectors **2** 112
  works **2** 49, *50*; **11** 637; **13** 195; **28** 1; **31** 841
Batailles, Martin des **3** 388
Batak **15** *752*, 753
  amulets **1** 817
  architecture **9** 164; **15** 771
  books **20** 327
  jewellery **15** 814
  masks **15** 804
  sarcophagi **27** 831, *831*
  sculpture **15** 788
  textiles **15** 794, 795
  weapons **24** 631
Batalha Priory **3** 362–3*; **10** 900; **13** 71; **14** 857; **25** 288, *288*, 289–90, 317
  architectural decorations **20** 325
  Capelas Imperfeitas **2** 296; **3** *362*, 363; **13** 71; **25** 290
  Founder's Chapel **2** 294; **3** 362–3; **20** 325
  sculpture **13** 101; **25** 300
  stained glass **13** 192; **25** 311
Batali **19** 74
Batammaliba **1** 261, 262
  architecture **1** 312; **3** 728; **31** 73
  dance-crests **31** 73
  sculpture **1** 265, 267
Batammbang, Musée Povéal **29** 239
Batanero, F. **25** 225
Batang **30** 808
Batán Grande **3** 363–5*; **28** 650; **29** *156*
  bottles **28** *650*
  Huaca del Pueblo furnaces **29** 211
  knives **29** 186
  tomb **31** 116
Batarda (Fernandes), Eduardo (Manuel) **3** 366*; **25** 300
Batashev (family) **27** 424
Batave, Godefroy le *see* GODEFROY LE BATAVE
Batavia *see* JAKARTA
Batchelder, Ernest **33** 344
Batchelor, John **17** 433
Bat Chum **5** 462
Bate, Francis **11** 363, 809; **19** 589
Bate, Inez **33** 142
Bate, Richard **26** 414
Bateau-Lavoir *see under* PARIS → studios
Bate-Dudley, Henry **3** 366*
Batéké
  masks **30** *420*
Batelli **4** 842
Bateman, Ann **3** 367
Bateman, Edward LaTrobe **26** 74
Bateman, Hester **3** 366–7*; **19** 593
Bateman, James **4** 36
Bateman, John (*c.* 1704-60) **3** 366
Bateman, Jonathan (1747-91) **3** 367
Bateman, Peter **3** 367
Bateman, Richard **22** 320
Bateman, Thomas **21** 7
Bateman, William, Bishop of Norwich **5** 511
Bateman, William (father) **3** 367; **27** 337
Bateman, William (son) **3** 367
Bateman & Bateman **25** 688
Batenin, Sergey **27** 412
Bates (family) **4** 597
Bates, Barrie *see* APPLE, BILLY
Bates, Edward A(rthur) **3** 368*
Bates, Harry **3** 367–8*
  groups and movements **3** 269; **23** 34
  works **3** *367*, 533; **10** 266, *267*
Bates, Sarah **28** 541
Batesar **15** 288
  Mahadeva Temple **15** 287
Bateson, Gregory **10** 580
Bates Smart & McCutcheon **2** 740, 742; **3** 368*; **15** 887; **26** 75
Bath (Avon) **2** 324; **3** 368–73*, *370*, *371*; **10** *225*; **26** *905*, *908*
  Abbey **6** 166; **20** 579
  American Museum **3** 373; **31** 616
  Aquae Sulis **3** 368–9*
  architecture **23** 860
  bath complex **3** 368–9, *369*; **26** 872
  Beazer Gardens **18** 585
  building regulations **2** 325
  Circus **2** 324
  Claverton Manor *see* American Museum
  Doric House **3** 241
  furniture **10** 297
  Guildhall **31** 235
  Holburne of Menstrie Museum **3** 371, 373
  houses **12** 332
  King's Circus **22** 741; **25** 655; **33** 341
  Lower Assembly Rooms **2** 617
  Museum of East Asian Art **7** 155
  Museum of English Naive Art **3** 373
  New Assembly Rooms *see* Upper Assembly Rooms
  Queen Square **25** 655
  Queen Victoria Art Gallery and Library **5** 66
  Royal Crescent **22** 741; **25** 655; **33** 341
  Sanctuary of Sulis Minerva **27** 1, *2*
  sculptors **10** 265
  stone **10** 236; **26** 875
  Sydney Hotel *see* Holburne of Menstrie Museum
  Upper Assembly Rooms **2** 617
  urban planning **10** 233; **31** 716
  Victoria Art Gallery **3** 373
Bath, John Alexander Thynne, 4th Marquess of *see* THYNNE, JOHN ALEXANDER, 4th Marquess of Bath
Bath, John Greville, Earl of *see* GREVILLE, JOHN, Earl of Bath
Bath, Thomas Thynne, 2nd Marquis of *see* THYNNE, THOMAS, 2nd Marquis of Bath
Bath, Youssouf **8** 22
Bathas, Markos Strelitzas **25** 333
Bathas, Thomas **25** 333
Bather, F. A. **2** 153
Batheur, Jean *see* BAPTEUR, JEAN
bath-gymnasia **13** 887; **15** 894; **23** 828; **26** 912, 914; **27** 837, *837*
  see also BATHS; GYMNASIA; PALAESTRA
Bathilde, Queen (*fl* 660) **10** 181; **11** 653
Bathori, Miklós, Bishop **31** 786
Báthory (family) **14** 904; **26** 722
Báthory, Julia **15** 5
Bathory, Stephen, King of Poland *see* STEPHEN BATHORY, King of Poland
baths **3** 374–8*
  Byzantine **9** 553, 560, 561
baths—cont.
  Early Christian (*c.* AD 250-843) **9** 553, 560
  Greece, ancient **3** 374–5*; **13** 386, 407, 556; **26** 909–10
  Indian subcontinent **15** 193, 382
  Indus civilization **15** 193, *246*
  Islamic **3** 375–8*; **16** 142, 252
    Central Asia, Western **6** 211
    Egypt **3** 376, 377
    Indian subcontinent **15** 382
    Iran **16** 193
    Jordan **3** 376
    Ottoman **16** 224
    Palestine **16** *149*
    Syria **3** 376, 377; **16** 148
    Turkey **3** 376, 377, *377*; **16** 204–5, 224
  Libya **19** *221*
  Mesoamerica, Pre-Columbian **3** 378*
  North Africa **26** 872
  Ottoman **16** 224
  Rome, ancient **3** 374–5*; **15** 51, *51*; **21** 559; **22** 161; **26** 863, 864, 868, 871–2*, *872*, 877, 902, 912, 924; **27** 48
    Germany **26** 907; **31** 323
    Greece **26** 909–10
    Italy **3** *374*; **26** 888
    Libya **19** *221*
    Tunisia **5** 891
    Turkey **26** *912*
    1st cent. BC **26** 891
    1st cent. AD **26** 892
    2nd cent. AD **26** 897
    3rd cent. AD **26** 901
    4th cent. AD **26** 903
  Turkey **16** 204–5, 224; **26** *912*
  see also BALNEAE; BATH-GYMNASIA; LIDOS; PALAESTRA; SWIMMING POOLS; THERMAE
Baths of Caracalla *see under* ROME → baths
Baths of Diocletian *see under* ROME → baths
Bath stone *see under* LIMESTONE → types
Bath stoves *see under* STOVES → types
bathtubs **21** 667
Bathurst **1** *37*; **2** *736*
  Cathedral **2** 738
  Gaol **2** 739
  gold **2** 764
  law courts **18** 888
Bathurst, Allen, 1st Earl Bathurst **13** 199; **27** 323; **30** 123
Bathykles of Magnesia **1** 692; **29** 367
Batigny **5** 825
batik **3** 378–9*; **30** 557, 558
  historical and regional traditions
    Aboriginal Australia **1** 64
    Antilles, Lesser **2** 151
    Burkina Faso **5** 217
    China **7** 45
    Egypt **3** 378
    Indian subcontinent **3** 378; **15** 670
    Indonesia **3** 379, *379*; **9** IV1; **15** 790–92, *791*, 796; **30** XI
    Java **3** *379*, 379; **9** IV1; **15** *791*; **30** XI
    Malaysia **3** 379; **20** 176
    Mesoamerica, Pre-Columbian **21** 261
    Netherlands, the **22** 900
    Uganda **31** 528
  materials
    cassava paste **3** 378
    cotton **3** 378
    rice paste **3** 378
    silk **3** 378
    waxes **3** 378
  uses
    paper **24** 56
    sarongs **30** XI
batik—cont.
  see also DYEING → types → resist-dyeing
Bâtiments du Roi *see under* MAISON DU ROI
bating **24** 106
Batissier, Louis **11** 521
Batista, Eugenio **8** 232
Batista, João Gomes *see* GOMES BATISTA, JOÃO
Batista, Simão **26** 554
Batista, Tomás **25** 702
Batiz **15** 2
Batley, Henry W. **28** 742; **30** 266
Batliwala, Soli **4** 291
Batlle, Berenguer **20** 749
Batlle, Francisco de Asís Cambó y *see* CAMBÓ Y BATLLE, FRANCISCO DE ASÍS
Batlle Planas, Juan **1** 499; **2** 400; **3** 380*
Batlló **26** 642; **27** 124
Batna, Medracen **23** 299
Batoni, Domenico **3** 383
Batoni, Felice **3** 383
Batoni, Pompeo (Girolamo) **3** 380–84*; **26** 774
  assistants **8** 493
  attributions **20** 456
  collaboration **3** 920; **4** 154; **19** 525; **20** 806
  copies **2** 576
  groups and movements **13** 297
  paintings **11** 394; **26** 840
    portraits **2** 164; **3** *381*, *382*; **11** 460, 494; **13** 303; **16** 677; **19** 64
    religious **3** *381*, *383*, 708; **26** 824
  patrons and collectors
    Bankes, Henry **3** 179
    Benedict XIV, Pope (*reg* 1740-58) **3** 707
    Brudenell, John, Marquess Monthermer and Baron Montagu **4** 894
    Caulfeild, James, 1st Earl of Charlemont **6** 93
    Clement XIII, Pope (*reg* 1758-69) **26** 286
    Clements, Robert, 1st Earl of Leitrim **16** 36
    Coke, Thomas William, 1st Earl of Leicester of the 2nd creation (1752-1842) **7** 541
    Fetherstonhaugh, Matthew **11** 39
    Garrick, David **12** 165
    Harrach (family) **2** 829
    Harrach, Ernst Guido, Graf von **14** 190
    Hervey, Frederick Augustus, 4th Earl of Bristol **14** 486
    Hoare (i), Henry the younger (1705-85) **14** 598
    Morice, Humphry **22** 115
    Ramsay, Allan (1713-84) **28** 271
    Smithson (Percy), Hugh, 1st Duke and 2nd Earl of Northumberland **1** 533
    Spencer, John, 1st Earl Spencer **29** 381
    Weddell, William **33** 20
    Williams-Wynn, Watkin, 4th Baronet, of Wynnstay (1749-89); **32** 790; **33** 208
  pupils **4** 727; **6** 111; **7** 176; **11** 118; **12** 583; **18** 697
  reproductive prints by others **11** 241; **33** 196
  teachers **7** 682; **15** 149; **20** 806
Batoni, Romualdo **3** 383
Baton Rouge (LA), Union Tank Car Company Repair Shop **11** 835; **29** 250
batons **25** 493
Batoufam **1** 309; **3** 147
  sculpture **3** *146*
Batoul, Ahmad **1** 317
Batowski, Aleksander **19** 752
Batres, Leopoldo **18** 784; **21** 227, 263; **30** 483; **33** 472
bats **6** 330
Batsalis, Angelous *see* NIOTIS
Batsamyan, Vahan **2** 444
Bätschmann, Oskar **15** 91; **30** 157
Batsford & Co. **28** 593
Battaggio, Antonio **3** 385
Battaggio, Gabriele **3** 385
Battaggio, Giacomino **3** 385
Battaggio, Giovanni di Domenico **3** 355, 384–5*
  collaboration **11** 248
  pupils **31** 277
  works **3** *385*; **8** 135; **21** 517
Battaglia, Alessandro **28** 381
Battaglioli, Francesco **3** 385–6*
  reproductive prints by others **31** 821; **33** 721
  works **4** 561
Battambang **5** *458*, 507; **29** *225*
  sculpture **5** 499
  Vat Kdol **5** 500, *500*
  Vat Samrong Khnong **5** 500
Battarbee, Rex **1** 63; **22** 449
Battel, Boudewijn van *see* BOUDEWIJN VAN BATTEL
Battem, Gerrit van **3** 386*; **11** 847
Batten, John Dickson **33** 361
battens **24** 5, *5*, 6–7
batter **21** 545
Battersea enamel factory **10** 192, 195; **14** 857; **19** 596
Batteux, Charles **1** 179; **3** 386*
Batthyány (family) **2** 782; **14** 893, 899; **15** 13
Batthyány, Count (*fl* 1640) **19** 770
Batthyány, Adam **14** 900
Batthyány, Géza **14** 239
Batthyány, Ignatius, Count of (*fl* 1794) **1** 531; **26** 724
Batthyány, Joseph, Cardinal Archbishop **14** 298
Batthyány, Lajos **15** 18
Batticaloa **29** *440*, 452
Battiss, Walter (Whall) **3** 386–7*; **25** 566; **29** 108, 110
Battista, Michele **2** 467
Battista Bossi **3** 783
Battista Clemente, Angelo di **32** 205
Battista da Fruosino **4** 749
Battista d'Antonio **12** 542
Battista di Niccolò da Padova **26** 325; **28** 687
Battistella **26** 358
Battistelli, Pier Francesco **3** 744
Battistello *see* CARACCIOLO, GIOVANNI BATTISTA
Battle, John of *see* JOHN OF BATTLE
Battle Abbey (E. Sussex) **5** 169; **13** 46; **26** 615; **30** 502; **31** 710; **33** 198
  gate-house **12** 175
Battlefield Palette **9** 868; **23** 848
battlements *see* CRENELLATIONS
battle paintings *see under* PAINTING → types
Bat Trang **32** *468*, 484, 486
Battuta, Ibn *see* IBN BATTUTA
Batuan **15** 809
Batubulan **15** 785
Batugajah **15** 787
Batumi **12** *317*, 320
  Revolutionary Museum **12** 320
Baturin Palace **31** 551, 564
Batusangkar **15** 788
Bat-Yam **17** 854
  Municipal Building **16** 566
Batzendorf, Johann Friedrich von **17** 816
Bätzner, Helmut **17** 817
Bau **14** 685
Bauausstellung **30** 128
Bauch, Jan **3** 391*; **8** 394
Bauch, Kurt **14** 635
Bauchant, André **3** 391*; **22** 440

Baucher, Alexandru 12 547
Bauchi 23 *129*
Friday Mosque 1 316
Bauchkannen see FLAGONS → types
Baud 8 51
Baud, Marcelle 10 83
Baud-Bovy, Auguste 3 391–2*; 8 57
Baude, Alphonse 11 637
Ba'udeh Church 9 591
Baudelaire, Charles (-Pierre) 3 392–3*; 8 58, 596; 18 716; 20 *829*; 22 379; 23 296
groups and movements 26 53; 30 168
personal collection 17 440
works 2 517; 11 545; 14 802; 21 776, 778
illustrated 4 588; 8 811; 20 830; 26 6, 481; 27 140
on caricatures 5 760
on colour 7 629
on dress 9 245
on photography 24 667
translated 11 697
Baudesson, Claude 12 725
Baudesson, Daniel 12 459
Baudesson, Nicolas 29 668
Baudet, Etienne 12 170
Baudet, Jehan 33 347
Baudewyns, Adriaen Frans see BOUDEWIJNS, ADRIAEN FRANS
Baudh 15 283
Baudichon, René 3 393*
Baudicour, Prosper de 10 210
Baudin, François 6 454
Baudin, Nicolas 2 744
Baudion, Mme 4 *331*
Baudisch, Gudrun 2 816; 3 393*; 12 822; 27 665
Baudizzone, Miguel 2 397
Baudo (da Novara), Luca 3 199, 393*
Baudoin, François 21 368
Baudois, Robbert de 14 709
Baudolf, Jan see BOUDOLF, JAN
Baudot, (Joseph-Eugène-) Anatole de 3 394–5*; 11 525
collaboration 8 30
pupils 14 386; 19 36
teachers 32 595, 598
works 7 693; 11 522
Baudot, Claude-Louis-Henri 3 394
Baudot, Félix 3 394
Baudot, Louis-Bénigne 3 394*
Baudouin, Claude 11 262; 29 747
Baudouin, Paul 25 751; 26 265
Baudouin, Pierre 11 644; 19 49; 30 329
Baudouin, Pierre-Antoine 3 395*
patrons and collectors 10 478
reproductive prints by others 6 563; 14 366; 16 905; 18 858; 20 585; 21 800; 28 754
Baudouin, Silvain-Raphaël 3 395*; 26 733
Baudouin, Simon-René see BAUDOUIN, SILVAIN-RAPHAËL
Baudouin de Bailleul see BAUDUIN DE BAILLEUL
Baudouin des Pacauds, Jean 3 395
Baudouine, Charles A. 3 395–6*, 685; 31 629
Baudous, Robert de 5 62; 32 140
Baudoyn, Jean 4 390
Baudri, Friedrich 26 102
Baudry, Etienne 9 447
Baudry, Léon-Georges 28 525
Baudry, (Jacques-Aimé-) Paul 1 69; 3 396*; 11 671; 15 49
collaboration 6 545; 8 659
groups and movements 2 530; 28 345, 346
patrons and collectors 23 794
prizes (artists') 24 171
pupils 28 171
reproductions in tapestry 12 830
teachers 9 300
Baudry, (Jacques-Aimé-) Paul—cont.
works 3 *396*; 7 832; 11 546; 22 330
Bauduin de Bailleul 3 397*
patrons and collectors 5 211
works 30 314; 31 218
Bauens, Antoon 29 591
Bäuer 21 81
Bauer, Adam 11 731; 19 781
Bauer, Augustus 1 158
Bauer, Catherine K. 20 890
Bauer, Conrad 4 208
Bauer, Erhard 6 526
Bauer, Ferdinand 2 743; 11 229
Bauer, Francis (1760-1826) 3 183; 11 229
Bauer, Frank (*b* 1942) 2 766
Bauer, G. H. (father) 3 397
Bauer, G. H. (son) 3 397
Bauer, Hermann (*fl c.* 1850) 22 891
Bauer, Hermann (*b* 1929) 2 834
Bauer, Johann Wilhelm see BAUR, JOHANN WILHELM
Bauer, Jörg 6 526
Bauer, Joseph 9 177
Bauer, Konštantín 28 853
Bauer, Leopold 3 398*; 28 344, 670; 30 755
Bauer, Marius (Alexander Jacques) 3 397–8*; 22 854
Bauer, Matheaus 12 457
Bauer, Mihály 14 895
Bauer, P. 6 526
Bauer, Rotraud 30 332
Bauer, Rudolf 13 800; 29 871, 872
Bauer, W(ilhelm) C(ornelis) 3 397*
Bauer & Hill 20 106
Bauermeister, Mary 29 97
Bauernfeind, Gustav 23 504
Bauersfeld, Walther 23 342
Bauert, Iohan Ephraim 8 753
Bauffe, Victor 33 47
Baugh, Benjamin 4 78
Baugh, Cecil 16 887; 31 339
works 16 *887*
Baugin, Lubin 3 399*; 4 521; 11 535
works 3 *399*; 29 668
Baugniet, Marcel-Louis 3 399*, 579, 587, 602
Baugut, František 8 385; 18 539
Baugy Château 7 595
Bauhaus 1 75, 76, 107–8; 2 288, 524; 3 399–403*; 7 771–2; 8 803; 11 360; 12 378–9, 396, 450, 480, 497; 15 824; 19 897; 24 676; 26 235
archives 2 370
art forms
architecture 5 523; 12 *378*; 17 421
ceramics 12 432, *432*, 437
costumes 28 *111*
furniture 6 391; 12 428, *428*
jewellery 12 456
lamps 32 756
lithography 19 491
masks 28 *111*
metalwork 1 738; 3 *402*; 8 803; 12 452
performance art 24 406
posters 25 349, 350
prints 12 894; 18 793
sculpture 12 407
stained glass 29 508
textiles 12 468, 470; 30 327
theatre 30 683, 686
typography 31 *497*
Bauhausbücher 30 8
curriculum 3 *400*
exhibitions 25 740; 28 920
locations
Berlin 3 403*; 17 765–6; 21 491; 33 304
Dessau 3 402–3*; 8 816; 13 687; 21 782
Bauhaus locations—cont.
Frankfurt am Main (structural engineering office) 21 407
Weimar 3 400–402*; 8 825; 10 698; 13 687; 21 407, 781
members 1 548; 7 293; 11 841
Ardon, Mordecai 2 381
Bjerke-Petersen, Vilhelm 4 104
Brandt, Marianne 4 671
Breuer, Marcel (Lajko) 4 761
Citroen, Paul 7 356
Feininger, Lyonel 10 862
Hirschfeld-Mack, Ludwig 14 570
Itten, Johannes 16 789
Klee, Paul 18 110, 111
Marcks, Gerhard 20 395
Meyer, Hannes 21 408
Moholy, Lucia 21 792
Moholy-Nagy, László 20 104; 21 793–4
Molnár, Farkas 21 824
Muche, Georg 22 253
Schlemmer, Oskar 28 111, 112
Wagenfeld, Wilhelm 32 756
publications 17 764
staff 11 299
studios 29 858
Bauhaus 24 428
Bauhütten see MASONS' LODGES
Bauhütte zum weissen Blatt 14 212
El Baúl 21 219; 27 780
Stele 1 29 620
Baule 1 235, 392, 503; 3 404–9*; 8 21
aesthetics 1 235, 238
body arts 1 344
collections 3 404; 8 23
divination instruments 1 356, 357
doors 1 314; 3 *408*
gesture 1 264, 265, 266
gold 3 408, *409*; 8 22
gold leaf 3 407
gong hammers 3 407
heddle pulleys 3 407
jewellery 1 350
masks 1 279, 324, 392; 3 405–6
mouse oracles 3 *407*, 407
patronage 1 243
pendants (jewellery) 3 *409*
portraits 1 269
sculpture 1 231, *233*, 322, 323, *324*, 392; 3 404–5, *405*; 8 22
slit-gongs 1 360
staffs 3 407
stools 3 407
textiles 1 294; 3 408; 8 22
tools 1 *364*
whisks 3 407
wood 1 *233*, *324*; 3 *405*, *407*, *408*
wood-carvings 3 406–8, *407*
Baullery, Jérôme 24 134
Baum, Don 6 577
Baum, M. 18 114
Baum, Martin 7 326
Baum, Otto 7 325
Baum, Paul 22 746, 921
Bauman, Elias see BOUMAN, ELIAS
Bauman, Frederic 18 693
Baumanis, Arturs 12 825; 18 852
Baumanis, Jānis Frīdrihs 3 409*; 18 850; 24 333; 26 383
Baumanis, Kārlis see ZEMDEGA, KĀRLIS
Baumann, Elisabeth see JERICHAU BAUMANN, ELISABETH
Baumann, Fritz 8 434, 436; 22 921
Baumann, Gustave 33 362
Baumann, Hans Felix Siegismund see MAN, FELIX H(ANS)
Baumann, Horst H. 18 809
Baumann, Johann 18 849
Baumann, Ludwig 2 787, 830; 23 813; 32 457
Baumann, Povl (Erik Raimond) 3 409–10*, 749; 29 77
collaboration 29 77
Baumann, Povl (Erik Raimond)—cont.
personal collection 18 136
works 8 728
Baumberger, Otto 25 351
Baumeister, August 10 211
Baumeister, Der 24 444
Baumeister, Reinhard 3 410*
Baumeister, Willi 3 411*; 11 550; 29 875
groups and movements 1 90; 2 545; 8 826; 12 397; 14 624; 21 407; 33 635
patrons and collectors 2 409; 9 121
personal collection 28 300
pupils 5 26; 18 421; 30 172
works 4 75; 19 491; 22 331
writings 33 635
Baume-Latrone, La see LA BAUME-LATRONE
Baume Le Blanc, Louis-César de la, Duc de La Vallière see LA VALLIÈRE, LOUIS-CÉSAR DE LA BAUME LE BLANC, Duc de
Baumgart, Emile 28 524
Baumgarten, Alexander Gottlieb 1 171, 179; 3 411–12*; 26 62
works 1 179; 26 736
Baumgarten, John Ernst 4 354
Baumgarten, Paul 5 76
Baumgarten, Sándor 3 412*
Baumgarten, William 10 351; 30 327; 31 621, 659
Baumgarten & Co. 30 327; 31 659
Baumgartl, Monika 24 408
Baumgartner, Andreas 32 449
Baumgartner, Bernát 3 412*; 14 906; 30 207
Baumgartner, Christoph 1 *763*
Baumgartner, Hans 1 764
Baumgartner, Johann Wolfgang 3 413–14*
reproductive prints by others 18 47
teachers 3 779
works 3 *413*; 12 391; 29 748
Baumgartner, Ulrich 12 422, 461; 14 51
Baumhauer, Gaspard 3 414
Baumhauer, Joseph 3 414*
patrons and collectors 20 897; 25 82
works 7 658; 11 596, 597
Baumhauer, Lienhardt 3 414–15*
Baumhauer, Veit 3 414, 415*
Bäuml (family) 23 325
Baungart, Emilio 3 66; 23 117
Baupaul 11 879
Bauqué, Armand 18 693
Baur, Alfred 7 156
Baur, Georg Frederich 14 152
Baur, Hans Jacob, I 11 714
Baur, Hermann 11 256, 304
Baur, Johann Ulrich 12 447
Baur, Johann Wilhelm 3 415–16*
patrons and collectors 8 845; 25 815
reproductive prints by others 18 535
teachers 4 747
works 3 *416*; 31 247
Baur, John I. H. 19 791
Baur, Matthias 2 127
Baur, Nicolaas 22 847
Baur, Tobias 12 445
Baurenfeind, Georg Wilhelm 23 114
Baurnadomeeny 25 508, 509
Baurscheit, Jan Pieter van (i) (1669-1728) 3 417*, 571
collaboration 3 417
works 3 *417*; 23 12
Baurscheit, Jan Pieter van (ii) (1699-1768) 3 417*, 571
collaboration 20 459
works 2 193; 3 546, 583; 14 39; 20 459; 22 826, *826*
Bausch, Pina 24 409
Bauschlott, Schloss see SCHLOSS BAUSCHLOTT
Bause, Johann Friedrich 13 269
Baussan, Georges 14 57
Baussan, Robert 14 57
Bausele, Rase van 4 591
Bausset, Marquis de 4 330
Bautista, Francisco 3 418*
collaboration 31 180
works 1 587; 23 489; 29 269; 31 88
Bautista, Manuel 29 342
Bau- und Wohnungskunst GmbH 32 756
Bauwelt 24 444
Bauwens, Gabriel 13 664
Bauwens, Lieven 12 518
Baux, Les see LES BAUX
Bauyn, Prosper 20 138
Bavai 27 85
Bavarese see OELEFE, FRANCESCO
Bavarese, Il see HELDMANN, IGNAZ
Bavarians 21 501
Bavay 27 100
forum 11 327
Baver, Johann Wilhelm see BAUR, JOHANN WILHELM
Bavera, Matteo 31 285
Bavian 3 418–19*; 21 *267*
canals 23 153
rock reliefs 2 640; 21 277, 300
Baviera 3 419*; 25 625
collaboration 25 859–60
works 27 208
Bavière, Anne de, Princesse de Condé see CONDÉ, ANNE DE BAVIÈRE, Princesse de
Bavinger, Eugene 12 855
Bavor of Nečtin, Abbot of Břevnov 8 412
Bavosi, Jacopino di Francesco see JACOPINO DI FRANCESCO BAVOSI
Bavosi, Pietro 2 18
Bawa, Geoffrey 3 419–20*; 7 613
works 29 *455*, 455–6
Bawa, Manjit 8 677
Bawden, Edward 3 420*; 4 366; 28 808
works 4 369; 25 628; 33 23
Bawdwin 5 259
Ba Weizu 7 130
Bawit 3 420–21*; 7 *819*; 9 *507*
Chapel 17 3 *420*
funerary monuments 7 820
Monastery of St Apollo 7 820, 821, 822; 9 574
mummy portraits 7 823
North Church 9 591
sculpture 7 822
South Church 7 822
walls 7 820
wood-carvings 7 828
Bawok 3 147
Baxaiti, Marco see BASAITI, MARCO
Baxandall, Michael 1 174; 28 917
Baxter, Geoffrey 10 321
Baxter, George 3 421*
methods 25 591
works 25 619, 621, 623, VII1; 33 360
Baxter, Iain 5 569
Baxter, John, the elder (*fl* 1730s-*c.* 1770) 7 418; 28 227
Baxter, John, the younger (*d* 1798) 7 418
Baxter, Richard 3 193
Baxter, Thomas 6 408; 10 309; 33 378
works 10 *309*
Bay, Carlo 6 572; 19 750; 25 98
Bay, J. B. J. de 27 282
Bay, Jean-Baptiste de 12 230
Baya 1 635; 3 421*
works 1 *635*
Bayamo 8 228, *228*
Bayamon 25 *698*
Museo Oller 25 704

Bayana
  architecture 15 344–6
  Ba'oli of Mutam Khan 15 346
  Bare Kamar 15 346
  'idgāhs 15 340
  Jhalar Ba'oli 15 345
  mihrabs 15 339
  Muftipara Mosque 15 345
  Pahar Mosque 15 346
  Talakini Mosque 15 345
  tomb of Auhad Khan 15 346
  Ukha Mandir 15 340, 344
  Ukha Mosque 15 344, *345*
Bayard, Hippolyte 3 421–2*; 24 646, 659
  collaboration 3 849
  works 24 663
Bayard, William 24 691
Bayardi, O. A. 14 445
Bayardo, Nelson 31 754
Bay Area figurative school 8 871; 23 406; 24 182
Bay Area style 33 428
Bayas Delgado, Francisco 25 815
al-Bayati, Basil 27 875
Bayazid Purani 5 140
Baybars I, Sultan (*reg* 1260-77) (Mamluk) 4 464; 14 427; 16 520; 20 227–8*; 22 323
  architecture 5 397; 16 208
  banners 11 146
  fortifications 5 403
  heraldry 16 247
  minbar 16 496
Baybars II, Sultan (*reg* 1309-1310) (Mamluk) 16 389; 20 229*
Baybars, al-Zahir 16 256; 20 56
Baybars al-Jashankir 16 284; 18 17, *18*
Bayburt 16 186; 21 583
al-Bayda 2 *246*
  Temple 2 253
Baye Château 13 180
Bayen, Francisco 20 73; 23 381
Bayenyeye, Léonidas 5 285
Bayer 19 808
Bayer, Adolf 19 535
Bayer, Herbert 3 422–3*; 7 654
  groups and movements 3 402, 403
  works 3 182; 7 654, 656; 24 686; 25 350
Bayer, Johann Cristoph 7 807
Bayer, Josef 33 197
Bayer, Pavel Ignác 6 526; 17 776
Bayer, Theophilus 1 210
Bayer, Wilhelm 33 623
Bayerische Hypotheken- und Wechselbank 12 472
Bayerische Motorwerke *see* BMW
Bayerle, Julius 3 423*
Bayes, Alfred Walter 3 423
Bayes, Gilbert 3 423*; 23 34, 35
Bayes, Jessie 3 423
Bayes, Walter 3 423; 4 293; 5 516; 17 631
Bayet, Charles 3 424*
Bayeu (y Subías), Francisco 3 424–6*; 4 564; 13 241, 242; 27 819
  assistants 3 426
  collaboration 20 77
  patrons and collectors 4 563, 565
  pupils 13 241; 26 308; 28 389
  works 3 *425*; 4 564; 24 108; 27 753; 29 283, 304, 350; 31 90
Bayeu (y Subías), Manuel 3 424, 425*; 29 304
Bayeu (y Subías), Ramón 3 424, 425–6*; 13 242
  reproductions in tapestry 10 504
  reproductive prints by others 32 99
  works 3 424; 13 241; 29 350
Bayeux 6 53
  Cathedral of Notre-Dame 3 443; 11 510, 654; 13 41
    capitals 26 598
    crypt 22 216
Bayeux
  Cathedral of Notre-Dame—cont.
    Labyrinth 18 584
    sculpture 26 597
    spires 29 413
    tapestries 3 426
    tracery 31 273
  great tower 6 52
  lace 11 650
Bayeux, Thomas of, Archbishop of York *see* THOMAS OF BAYEUX, Archbishop of York
Bayeux Tapestry 2 83; 3 426–7*, *427*; 9 *255*; 10 181, 353, 475; 11 647, 654; 22 520; 26 703; 30 553
  castles 6 53; 9 143; 33 198
  chairs 6 389; 30 780
  copies 29 733
  cult of carts 8 *258*
  dress 9 255
  fables 10 724
  flags 11 147
  halls 14 74
  oliphants 23 401
  photographed 26 233
  reproductive prints by others 3 329
  shields 14 405
  weathervanes 33 8
Bayev, N. G. 2 893; 3 88
Bayezid, Prince (Ottoman) 16 446
Bayezid I, Sultan (*reg* 1389-1402) (Ottoman) 5 282; 8 363; 9 86, 729; 16 206; 18 509; 21 585
Bayezid II, Sultan (*reg* 1481-1512) (Ottoman) 9 595; 16 346, 378; 23 638, 641*
  architecture 1 757; 9 729–30; 14 270; 16 222; 18 509
  bridges 9 730
  calligraphy 14 103
  ceramics 16 421, 422
  manuscripts 14 103; 16 285, 330, 552
Bayhaqi, Abu'l-Fadl *see* ABU'L-FADL BAYHAQI
Bayındır 1 836; 10 151
Bayinnaung I, King (*reg* 1581-99) (Toungoo) 5 238
Baylakan 2 *890*, 898
Bayle, Pierre 10 205
Bayleaf Farm (Kent) 10 271; 32 276
Bayley, Edgar 2 604; 18 397
Bayley, Nicola 4 368
Bayliss, Charles 2 745; 3 427*
Baymatov, Abdumumin 31 783
Baymursayev, O. 17 867
Baynard Press 7 652; 11 747; 19 485; 25 628
Bayne, Robert Turnill 14 281
Bayne, R. Roskell 1 648; 5 418
Bayon *see under* ANGKOR → Angkor Thom
bayonets 2 448
Bayonne
  Brethous house 26 493
  Cathedral 22 219
  Musée Bonnat 4 329
Bayr, Hans Jakob 25 22
Bayraklı Tepe *see* SMYRNA → Old Smyrna
Bayram-Ali 31 *458*, 459
Bayram ibn Derviş Şir 16 349
Bayramov, Durdy 31 459
Bayram Tahti 30 784
Bayreuth 3 428–9*; 12 *361*
  Altes Schloss Eremitage *see* Hermitage
  faience factory 3 429*; 12 430, 431; 14 235; 19 733
  Festspielhaus 1 125; 30 678, *678*, 682, 687
  Hermitage 3 428; 5 349; 12 134, 412; 14 460
  Iwalewa-Haus 1 439
  Markgräfliches Opernhaus 1 124
Bayreuth—cont.
  Neues Schloss 3 *429*; 5 349; 12 411
    paintings 4 914; 27 169
  Residenztheater 30 676
  Sanspareil *see* SANSPAREIL
Bayreuth, George William, Margrave of *see* GEORGE WILLIAM, Margrave of Bayreuth
Bayreuth, Wilhelmina, Margravine of *see* WILHELMINA, Margravine of Bayreuth
bays 17 65; 19 403; 26 569
Baysal, Haluk 16 588
Baysunghur (Timurid) 16 *122*; 30 917, 921*
  albums 1 583
  bookbindings 16 358
  calligraphy 7 717; 16 *276*, 285
  inscriptions 16 197
  manuscripts 16 283, 322, 323–4*, 325, 551; 28 616
    Herat scriptorium 1 208; 16 272, 285, 864; 30 917
    Ja'far (*fl* 1412-31) 16 285, 303, 545, 864
    Khwaja 'Ali 18 30
    Sa'di (*d* 1292) 16 301
  paintings 16 122
Baysunghuri, Ja'far *see* JA'FAR
Bayt al-Din Palace 3 429*; 16 *104*; 19 9
Bayt al-Faqih 33 520
Bayt Laḥm *see* BETHLEHEM
Baza, Dama de *see* DAMA DE BAZA
bazaar art *see* POPULAR ART
bazaars 2 *894*; 6 211; 16 205, 206
Bazaine, Jean (-René) 3 429–30*; 11 551
  groups and movements 2 543; 30 231
  works 11 256
Bazaklik *see* BEZELIK
Bazalgette, Joseph (William) 3 430*
  works 10 236; 19 575, *576*
Bazan 17 401
Bazán, Alvaro de, Marqués de Santa Cruz *see* SANTA CRUZ, ALVARO DE BAZÁN, Marqués de
Bażanka, Kasper 3 431*; 18 428; 25 98
Bazán y Guzmán, Alvaro de, 1st Marqués de Santa Cruz *see* SANTA CRUZ, ALVARO DE BAZÁN Y GUZMÁN, 1st Marqués de
Bazas, St Jean-Baptiste 13 75
Baz Bahadur 20 251
Bazel, K(arel) P(etrus) C(ornelis) de 3 431–2*; 17 910; 22 829, 830, 867, 874
  collaboration 33 676
  groups and movements 18 878; 22 875
  staff 8 206
  teachers 8 298
  works 1 803; 21 122; 22 860, 885
Bazel, Wissekerke Castle 3 578
Bazemont, Nicolas 4 391
Bazhbeuk-Melik'yan, Alek'sandr 2 433; 3 432*
Bazhenov, Vasily (Ivanovich) 3 432–3*; 27 375, 402, 442, 579; 28 646
  assistants 33 517
  patrons and collectors 26 731, 733; 27 438
  teachers 31 828; 32 766
  works 3 *433*; 17 869; 22 171; 27 *376*, 377
Bazhong 30 443
  Qianfo Cliff 6 715
  Wofo Temple 6 715
Bazidpur 15 456
Bazile 11 571
Bazile, Castera 3 433–4*; 14 58
Bazilewsky, A. P. 26 734
Bazille, (Jean-)Frédéric 3 434–5*
  groups and movements 15 151, 152, 153; 26 55
  patrons and collectors 22 35
  teachers 12 810
  works 3 *434*
Bazin, Thomas 11 614
Bazin de Champigny, Claude 19 247
Bazinière, Bertrand de La *see* LA BAZINIÈRE, BERTRAND DE
Baziotes, William 3 435–6*
  groups and movements 1 78; 13 214; 30 22; 31 607
  patrons and collectors 13 801
Bazna 26 718
Bazovsky, Miloš A. 28 853
Bazzacco, Giovanni Battista *see* PONCHINO, GIAMBATTISTA
Bazzani, Cesare 3 436*; 16 648; 26 776
Bazzani, Domenico Conti 31 135
Bazzani, Giovanni 3 436
Bazzani, Giuseppe 3 436–7*; 20 322
Bazzani, Luigi 3 436
Bazzaro, Ernesto 3 437; 16 706; 29 59
Bazzaro, Leonardo 3 437*
Bazzi, Giovanni Antonio *see* SODOMA
Bazzicaluva, Ercole 3 437*
Bazzuoli, Giuseppe *see* BEZZUOLI, GIUSEPPE
BB, Monogrammist 20 791*
BBC 7 652
BBPR Architectural Studio 3 438–9*; 6 409; 26 536
  collaboration 1 578; 11 63; 25 792
  groups and movements 15 887; 26 15
  staff 13 213
  works 3 *438*; 16 650, *651*, 775; 31 731
B.-C.A.U.S.E. 3 62, 64
Beach, James Malone 20 926
Beach, Macklin and Neesham 8 286
Beach, Thomas 3 373, 439*; 26 272, 277
beach-rock 2 248
bead and reel mouldings *see under* MOULDINGS → types
Beadle, John 3 62, 64
  works 3 *62*
Beadle, Paul 23 63, 72, 73
bead mouldings *see under* MOULDINGS → types
beads 3 440–42*
  historical and regional traditions
    Africa 1 295, 296–8*, *297*, *298*, *325*, 347, 349, *350*, 352, 353–4, *367*, *411*, *420*; 12 440
    Ancient Near East 1 864, 883
    Angola 7 *197*, *198*
    Bamileke 1 298; 3 145, *149*
    Bamum 3 *152*
    Bantu peoples 1 350
    Benin, Kingdom of 1 297, 354
    Cambodia 5 500
    Cameroon 1 298; 3 *152*
    China 7 80, 88, 89, 108, 110, 836
    Chokwe 7 *197*
    Cuba (Caribbean) 8 229
    Cyprus, ancient 8 352
    Czech Republic 3 145, 442
    Ecuador 29 155
    Egypt, ancient 1 864; 7 80; 9 815; 10 28, 47, 56
    England 25 *545*
    Germany 12 440, 462, 463
    Ghana 1 297
    Gothic 13 194
    Greece, ancient 13 393, *600*, 602
    Guyana 13 875
    Indian subcontinent 1 850
    Iran, ancient 4 172
beads
  historical and regional traditions—cont.
    Italy 16 744
    Japan 17 385–6; 26 487
    Kenya 1 *297*, *350*, *411*
    Korea 18 364
    Kuba (iii) (Zaïre) 1 298, 352; 18 *488*
    Luba 1 *325*
    Lwena 7 *198*
    Maasai 1 297
    Mauretania 1 297
    Maya 21 259
    Mesoamerica, Pre-Columbian 21 243, 259, 260
    Mesopotamia 1 850, 873, 877
    Native North Americans 3 331; 22 648, 654, 655, 656
    Ndebele 1 297, 298; 22 712, *713*
    Nok 1 297
    Paraguay 24 93
    Philippines 24 625
    Prehistoric art 3 440; 25 473, 545, *545*, 546–7
    Punic 25 734
    San 1 297
    Solomon Islands 29 *49*
    South Africa 22 *713*; 29 104
    South America, Pre-Columbian 29 155
    Sudan 1 *367*
    Sumerian 1 873
    Tairona 29 155
    Thailand 30 633
    Tibet 30 839
    Toltec 21 243
    Troadic 31 355
    Yoruba 1 298, *298*, 353–4; 33 557–8, *558*, 559
    Zaïre 18 *488*
    Zulu 1 297; 29 104; 33 723, 724–5
  materials
    agate 30 839
    amber 1 761, 762; 3 440, 441, 442; 7 110
    bone 1 296; 3 440
    bronze 13 *600*, 602
    clay 1 296; 25 546
    copper 1 296
    coral 1 297, 354; 3 440, 441, 442; 7 835, 836; 21 260
    cornelian 1 350; 3 440, 441; 7 89
    eggs 1 297
    faience (i) (glass) 1 877; 3 440; 10 47
    frit 10 47
    gems 3 440
    glass 3 440, 442; 25 546–7
      Africa 1 296, 297
      Cambodia 5 500
      Cameroon 3 145, *147*, *149*
      China 7 80, *81*
      Egypt, ancient 1 864; 10 56; 12 789
      Iran 4 172
      Italy 32 202
      Japan 17 385–6
      Kenya 1 *297*
      Korea 18 364
      Micronesia, Federated States of 21 *477*
      Punic 25 734
      Thailand 30 633
      Vietnam 23 344
    glazes 10 47
    gold 1 296; 3 440, 441; 14 *357*; 31 355
    iron 1 296, *297*
    ivory 3 440, 441; 25 473
    jade 3 441; 7 108; 21 260
    jet 3 441, 442
    lapis lazuli 3 441, 442
    nuts 1 296
    pearls 3 440, 442
    rock crystal 16 744; 26 487; 29 155
    seed pods 3 440

beads
materials—cont.
seeds 1 296
shells 1 296; 3 440, 441, 442; 21 259, 260
silver 3 440, 442
soapstone 10 47
stone 1 297; 3 441; 9 815; 30 633
teeth 1 296
terracotta 7 80
turquoise 3 441, 442; 7 88
wood 3 441
types
eyebeads 7 80–81, 81
relief 14 357, 357; 21 687
uses
aprons 1 297; 3 442; 13 875
baskets 1 295; 3 331; 4 I2; 22 655, 656
body arts 1 297
bracelets 25 545
crowns 1 298, 353; 17 386; 33 557–8, 558
currency 3 441; 12 440
dolls 1 420
dress 1 347; 22 712, 713; 25 546
dresses 4 II
embroidery 1 296; 3 442; 12 462, 463; 13 194; 22 648
figureheads 29 49
footwear 1 349
furniture 3 152
hats 1 296
headrests 1 411
inlays 5 500
jewellery 25 546
knitting 18 158
lace 18 588, 590
masks 1 298; 3 149; 7 198; 18 488
necklaces 1 350; 25 545
pipes (smoking) 1 367
polychromy 13 393
pottery 25 546
pouches 4 I1
regalia 1 352, 353–4
sashes 17 386; 21 477
sculpture 1 325; 4 I3; 7 197; 29 104
shoes 17 386
textiles 17 386; 25 546
beadwork 3 441–2*
conservation 7 729
historical and regional traditions 3 440–41*
Africa 1 349, 350, 410, 418–19*, 419; 4 I3
Anglo-Saxon 3 442
Bamileke 3 147, 148
Bantu peoples 3 440
Benin, Kingdom of 3 441
Borneo 3 441
Central Asia, Western 6 251
Chimú 3 442
Egypt, ancient 3 441
England 3 442
Eskimo 3 441
Ethiopia 3 442
France 3 440, 442; 4 II
Germany 3 442
Guyana 3 441
Indian subcontinent 15 676
Indonesia 15 814–15*
Indus civilization 3 442
Inuit 22 638*
Iroquois 22 643
Italy 3 442
Kenya 3 442
Kuba (iii) (Zaïre) 3 441
Maasai 3 442; 19 859, 859–60
Malaysia 3 442; 4 I2; 20 182
Mongolia 3 441
Native North Americans 3 440, 441, 442; 4 I1; 22 637–40*, 639, 640, 641–4*, 641, 642, 643, 655, 665
Ndebele 1 262, 418, 419; 3 442
Nigeria 4 I3
beadwork
historical and regional traditions—cont.
Poland 3 442
Romania 3 442
San 4 489
Sarawak 3 442; 4 I2
Shona 1 419
South Africa 1 262; 3 442
Tanzania 1 410; 3 442
Thailand 3 441
Tibet 3 442
United States of America 4 I1
Venda 1 419
Yoruba 3 442; 4 I3
Zaïre 3 440
Zulu 1 418, 419; 3 442
restoration 7 729
techniques
couching 3 440
crochet 3 440
knitting 3 440
weaving 3 440
types
sablé work 3 440, 440, 442
tambourwork 3 440
wampum 3 441
uses
aprons 1 419; 3 441, 442
baby-carriers 3 442
bags 3 441, 442
baskets 3 442
blankets 3 441
boxes 3 440, 442
caps 3 442
cloaks 3 441
coats 3 440, 441
collars 3 441
costumes 3 441
dolls 3 442
dress 1 349; 3 441; 6 251
fire-screens 3 442
gloves 3 442
gourds 3 442
headdresses 3 441
moccasins 3 441
necklaces 3 442
parasols 3 442
pectoral ornaments 3 442
perfume containers 3 442
pouches 3 442
purses 3 442
sashes 3 442
shrouds 3 442
skirts 1 410; 3 442
stools 3 147, 148
wall decorations 3 442
wreaths 3 442
Beafada-Nalu 13 835
Beaghmore 25 505
beaked half-roll mouldings see under MOULDINGS → types
beaked ogee keel mouldings see under MOULDINGS → types
beaked roll-and-fillet mouldings see under MOULDINGS → types
beaked roll mouldings see under MOULDINGS → types
beakers
historical and regional traditions
Ancient Near East 1 866
Byzantine 9 646
China 7 102
Czech Republic 8 407
Egypt, ancient 10 72
England 10 337; 14 763
Germany 12 439, 444; 14 425
Indian subcontinent 15 708
Iran, ancient 1 866; 14 211
Islamic 16 520, 521
Netherlands, the 22 884, 886, 890
Prehistoric art 6 327
Romania 30 771
Rome, ancient 27 79
Sweden 30 105
Syria 16 521
Thracian 30 771, 771
beakers
historical and regional traditions—cont.
United States of America 31 646
materials
glass 1 866; 16 521; 27 79
gold 14 211
horn 14 763, 763
ivory 7 102
pewter 24 580
pottery 6 327
silver 10 337; 15 708; 22 886, 890; 30 105, 771; 31 646
stone 10 72
types
Bell 25 514
Beakey, Patrick 16 28
beakheads 3 442–3*, 443; 10 259; 26 589, 612, 616; 28 612
beak mouldings see under MOULDINGS → types
Beale, Bartholomew 3 444
Beale, Charles (1631-1705) 3 444
Beale, Charles (1660-?1714) 3 444*
Beale, Mary 3 444*
assistants 3 444
reproductive prints by others 4 169; 33 147
teachers 19 123
Beall, Joanna 33 96
Beam, Carl 22 598
beam bridges see under BRIDGES → types
beams
historical and regional traditions
Belgium 3 576
China 6 684; 7 12
Vietnam 32 472
types
anchor 30 853
Laves 18 883
rainbow 17 72
Bean, Anne 33 223
Beard, Richard 24 660, 672
Beard, Thomas 16 15
Beard, William 24 754
Beard, William Holbrook 31 870
Bearded Sphinx Painter 10 613
Bearden, Charles 1 443
Bearden, Romare 1 443, 444; 25 654
Beardsley, Aubrey (Vincent) 3 444–6*; 8 596; 12 216
book covers 4 369; 20 22
book illustrations 4 363, 363; 10 480; 33 180
drawings 3 445; 9 225
ephemeral art 10 420
groups and movements 2 562
patrons and collectors 10 487, 655; 12 15; 14 163; 33 180
posters 25 347, 623
teachers 4 880
works 10 255
Beardsley, Monroe 1 173, 182; 10 691
Beardy, Jackson 22 597
Beare, George 3 446*
beargrass see under GRASSES → types
bearings, armorial see ARMORIAL BEARINGS
Béarn, René de, Comtesse 8 486
Bear Run (PA), Fallingwater 5 649; 7 695; 31 596
bear teeth see under TEETH → types
Bear Wood (Berks) 8 49, 49; 16 823
Bearzi, Bruno 2 484
Beasley, Harry G. 23 742
Beata Umiltà, Master of the 19 668
Beatia see BAEZA
beating 12 621, 621; 19 1
Beatis, Ambrogio de' 19 184
Beatis, Antonio de see ANTONIO DE BEATIS
Beatles 4 116
Beato, Antonio 3 446–7; 24 664; 26 468
Beato, Felice 3 446–7; 5 262; 24 664; 26 468
works 19 774
Beato, Pietro 3 351
Beato and Wirgman 3 447
Beato & Co. 3 447
Beaton, Cecil (Walter Hardy) 3 447–8*; 12 216; 30 687
productions 30 687
works 9 293, 293; 10 284; 28 808
Beaton, James, Archbishop of Glasgow (1517-1603) 14 424
Beaton, James, Archbishop of St Andrews (reg 1523-39) 27 530
Beaton, Penelope 9 725
Beaton Panels 28 241, 250
Beatrice d'Este, Duchess of Milan (1475-97) 10 518, 522*; 25 466
Beatrice of Aragon, Holy Roman Empress (1457-1508) 12 114; 14 903
Beatrix of Champagne, Duchess of Burgundy (c. 1270) 27 593
Beatrizet, Nicolas 3 448*
works 2 103; 7 623; 26 174; 27 606, 650
Beatson, Helena 26 50
Beattie, William 8 66
Beatty, (Alfred) Chester 3 448–9*; 15 743; 16 555, 560
Beatty, J. W. 1 496
Beatty Rosarium (Dublin, Chester Beatty Lib., MS. W.99) 3 727
Beatus Apocalypses see under APOCALYPSES → types
Beatus Commentary (Madrid, Bib. N., MS. Vit. 14-2) 19 178
Beatus of Liébana 20 341; 22 248
Beau see BAUD
Beau, John Anthony 31 649
Beaubec Abbey 7 353
Beaubrun, Charles 3 449*; 25 461; 28 11; 30 660
Beaubrun, Henri (i) (fl c. 1600) 3 449
Beaubrun, Henri (ii) (1603-77) 3 449*; 25 461; 28 11; 30 660
Beaubrun, Louis 3 449
Beaubrun, Mathieu (i) (c. 1529-97) 3 449
Beaubrun, Mathieu (ii) (d 1608) 3 449
Beaubrun, Michel 3 449
Beaucaire 6 55; 26 603
Beauce, Jehan de see JEHAN DE BEAUCE
Beauchamp, Abbé de 21 310
Beauchamp, Charles 10 483
Beauchamp, Richard, Bishop of Salisbury 27 625
Beauchamp, Thomas Proctor 32 835
Beauchemin, Micheline 5 573
Beauclair, Henri 19 535
Beauclerk, Charles, 1st Duke of St Albans 21 891
Beauclerk, Diana 3 449–50*; 6 528; 33 22
Beauclerk, William, 10th Duke of St Albans 30 533
Beaucourt, François Malepart 5 564; 22 37
Beaucourt, Laurens 3 600
Beaucourt, Paul 5 564
Beaucousin 9 683
Beaudin, André 3 450*; 17 726; 19 66; 28 820
Beaudouin, Eugène (Elie) 3 450–51*; 11 526
collaboration 4 57, 214; 19 535; 26 19; 28 809; 30 468
pupils 13 716; 29 420
staff 25 663
works 11 526; 23 122; 29 752
Beaufaux, Polydore 23 1
Beaufort, Charles Noel Somerset, 4th Duke of see SOMERSET, CHARLES NOEL, 4th Duke of Beaufort
Beaufort, Francis 28 664
Beaufort, Henry, Cardinal 5 638; 33 236
Beaufort, Henry Somerset, 10th Duke of see SOMERSET, HENRY, 10th Duke of Beaufort
Beaufort, Henry Somerset, 1st Duke of see SOMERSET, HENRY, 1st Duke of Beaufort(, 3rd Marquess of Worcester)
Beaufort, Henry Somerset, 3rd Duke of see SOMERSET, HENRY, 3rd Duke of Beaufort
Beaufort, Jacques-Antoine 3 451*; 14 586
Beaufort, Margaret, Countess of Richmond and Derby 3 451*; 5 511; 14 418
Beaufort, Pierre Roger de see CLEMENT VI, Pope
Beaufort-Beauchamp Hours see under BOOKS OF HOURS → individual manuscripts
Beaufort Saints, Master of the 3 555; 20 624*
Beaufort's Cup, Lady Margaret see LADY MARGARET BEAUFORT'S CUP
Beaufort-Spontini, Alfred, Duke 33 687
Beaugency Hôtel de Ville 31 238
Beau Geste Press/Libro Acción Libre 10 99
Beaugrant (family) 11 485
Beaugrant, Guyot de 3 451–2*, 569; 17 700; 29 289
Beaugrant, Juan de 3 452; 29 289
Beauharnais, Alexandre de 18 576
Beauharnais, Eugène de, Duc de Leuchtenberg see LEUCHTENBERG, EUGÈNE DE BEAUHARNAIS, Duc de
Beauharnais, Hortense de, Queen of Holland see HORTENSE DE BEAUHARNAIS, Queen of Holland
Beauharnais, Josephine, Empress of the French see JOSEPHINE, Empress of the French
Beauharnais, Maximilian de, Duc de Leuchtenberg see LEUCHTENBERG, MAXIMILIAN DE BEAUHARNAIS, Duc de
Beaujeu 6 488
Beaujeu, Anne of, Duchess of Bourbon see ANNE, Duchess of Boubon
Beaujeu, Peter of, Duke of Bourbon see PETER II, Duke of Bourbon
Beaujon, Nicolas 3 453*; 11 663; 12 724
Beaulieu (Co. Louth) 16 8, 22
Beaulieu, Peter 16 31
Beaulieu, Pierre-François Mathis de 11 633
Beaulieu Abbey (Hants) 7 350, 353; 22 220
Beaulieu-lès-Loches Abbey 26 586, 599
Beaulieu-sur-Dordogne Abbey 11 505; 26 602
church 3 453*; 26 585
Beaumarchais, Pierre Augustin Caron de 3 330; 8 867; 27 623; 31 373
Beaumaris (Gwynedd) 32 780
Castle 6 53, 56; 9 144; 16 895, 895; 21 564, 564; 32 781
gate-house 12 173, 174
St Mary 32 786
Beaume, Joseph 29 248
Beaumetiel, Henri de see HENRI DE BEAUMETIEL

Beaumetz, Jean de *see* JEAN DE BEAUMETZ
Beaumetz, Pierre de *see* PIERRE DE BEAUMETZ
Beau Monde 24 422
Beaumont (*fl* 1757) 11 408
Beaumont, 10th Lord (*fl* 1873-5) 25 717
Beaumont, Lady 5 71
Beaumont, Claudio Francesco 2 27; 3 453–4*
collaboration 31 446
dealing 28 18
patrons and collectors 28 18
pupils 3 824; 7 571
works 30 324; 31 444, 446
Beaumont, Etienne, Comte de 24 718
Beaumont, George (Howland) 3 454–5*; 19 599; 22 86
architecture 26 282
collections 10 369; 29 548
paintings 5 71; 7 572, 748; 8 97; 14 262; 18 689; 19 588; 32 856; 33 188
watercolours 12 742
panoramas 24 18
pupils 7 749
sculpture 12 597
sketches 8 95
sponsorship 16 819
Beaumont, Jean 28 525
Beaumont, J. T. 1 647
Beaumont, Pierre-François 21 800
Beaumont, T. W. 19 879
Beaumont & Collinot 24 148
Beaune
Hôtel-Dieu 11 511, *511*, 603; 30 331
altarpiece 1 710
Infirmary 14 780
interior decoration 26 *555*
paintings 3 612; 14 784
sculpture 13 111
Notre-Dame 11 639; 26 584; 30 331
Beaune, Jacques de 4 571
Beauneteaux, Felix 27 882
Beauneveu, André 3 455–6*, 553, 568*; 4 582; 11 555; 13 77, 78; 17 456; 20 742; 31 836
collaboration 16 852; 17 457
miniatures 13 133, 154
patrons and collectors 13 77, 153; 19 721; 31 835, 836, 839
portraits 31 120
sculpture 3 *456*, 567; 4 578, *583*, 583; 13 100; 17 457
tombs 13 76; 17 458; 24 132; 27 546
Beaupré, Augustin-Phidias Cadet de *see* CADET DE BEAUPRÉ, AUGUSTIN-PHIDIAS
Beaupré Antiphonal *see under* ANTIPHONALS → individual manuscripts
Beaupré Castle 32 782
Beauraing, Shrine of the Virgin 28 632
Beaurains 21 1
Beauregard, Lesourd de 11 228
Beauregard Château
Cabinet des Grelots 6 506
Beauregard *Madonna* 8 798
Beausire, Jean-Baptiste-Augustin 8 32; 22 93; 24 122
Beautiful Madonnas, Master of the 8 382; 31 196
Beautiful Style *see* GOTHIC → styles → *schöner Stil*
Beautility Furniture Ltd 10 299
beauty 1 176–7, 178–9, 180, 558, 559–60; 2 362; 10 691; 13 468; 14 877–8; 15 37; 19 356; 23 292; 24 741; 25 276, 285; 26 924; 29 889
see also AESTHETICS; NATURE, BEAUTY OF
Beauvais 3 456–62*; 11 *504*
Basse-Œuvre 4 780
Cathedral of St Pierre 3 457–9*; 6 414; 13 39, 40, 211; 14 519; 26 44, 45
apse 2 347
choir 3 *457*, *458*
façade 13 61
ivory-carvings 13 172
mouldings 22 220, 221
piers 13 40
plans 3 *457*
stained glass 3 *459*, 459–60*; 13 141, 181
tapestries 5 549; 11 639; 31 219
textiles 30 314, 331
tracery 11 155; 13 41
transept 6 *414*, 414; 11 154; 31 281
ivory-carvings 26 697
Musée Départemental de l'Oise 1 499
pottery 11 603, 606
St Etienne 11 154, 155; 13 36, 60, 181; 22 216, 218; 24 751
St Lucien 13 38
St Quentin 2 723
tapestries 3 460–62*
Beauvais, Jean 27 494
Beauvais, Nicolas-Dauphin de 19 216
Beauvais (St-James), René 25 817
Beauvais, Vincent of *see* VINCENT OF BEAUVAIS
Beauvais, Yann 10 689
Beauvais Tapestry Factory 3 456, 460–62*; 4 550; 11 641, 643; 12 829, 830; 20 133; 30 321, 326
carpets 11 652
collaboration 2 105; 30 326
collections 28 527
designers 4 514; 11 644; 23 381
Alix, Yves 1 645
Benedictus, Edouard 5 841
Boucher, François 3 841; 11 643; 14 422
Casanova, Francesco 5 908
Chabal-Dussurgey, Pierre-Adrien 6 376
Dufresne, Charles (Georges) 2 521
Dugourc, Jean-Démosthène 9 379
Lebarbier, Jean-Jacques-François 19 9
Le Prince, Jean-Baptiste 19 219
Matisse, Henri (Emile Benoît) 20 831; 30 329
Monnoyer, Jean-Baptiste 21 891
Natoire, Charles-Joseph 22 682
Oudry, Jean-Baptiste 11 643; 23 667
Singier, Gustave 28 777
directors 23 668
furniture 10 187; 30 327
production 30 323
tapestries 3 *462*; 7 167, *168*; 9 30; 11 576, 643; 25 193
Beauvallet, Pierre-Nicolas 3 463*; 23 209
Beauvarlet, Catherine-Françoise *see* DESCHAMPS, CATHERINE-FRANÇOISE
Beauvarlet, Jacques-Firmin 3 318, 463; 5 884; 19 261; 21 800; 32 719
Beauvarlet, Mathieu 11 726
Beauvau, Prince de 19 26
Beauvau, Louis de *see* LOUIS DE BEAUVAU
Beauvau-Craon, Prince de 4 225
Beauvillier, Paul-Hippolyte de, Duc de Saint-Aignan *see* SAINT-AIGNAN, PAUL-HIPPOLYTE DE BEAUVILLIER, Duc De
Beauvoir, Simone de 27 853
Beauwelz 3 593
Beaux, Cecilia 3 463–4*; 24 600
Beaux-Arts style 3 464–5*, *465*; 5 562; 31 612
Beaven, Peter (Jamieson) 3 465–6*; 7 210; 23 56
Beaver 22 546
Beaver, Fred 22 595
Beaver, J. A. 33 409
Beaver, Jan van 16 26
Beaver, William 22 677
Beaverbrook, William Maxwell Aitken, 1st Baron *see* AITKEN, WILLIAM MAXWELL, 1st Baron Beaverbrook
Beaverbrook Art Gallery *see under* FREDERICTON
Beaver Hall Hill Group 5 567; 14 676; 22 39
Beazley, Charles 2 306
Beazley, J(ohn) D(avidson) 3 466*; 22 102
attributions 32 27, 28, 45, 61, 64
works 13 542
Beazley, Samuel 5 309
Bebb, Charles H. 28 327
Bebenhausen Abbey 12 365; 13 57
dormitory 21 843, 844
Beblinger *see* BÖBLINGER
Beblo, Fritz 29 751
Bebo, Károly 14 894
bec, à see under TOWERS → types
Becaert, Adrian 7 368
Becán 21 246
Building I 21 207
fortifications 21 208, 599
Structure IV 21 214
stucco 29 829
Becanus, Guilielmus 22 717
Beccadelli, Antonio 3 466*
Beccafumi, Domenico (di Giacomo di Pace) 3 467–9*; 16 766; 20 796; 26 769; 28 677, 687
architectural decorations 10 739
attributions 4 30
collaboration 29 3
frames 11 388, 389
methods 30 427
mosaics 6 569
paintings 3 *468*; 16 667; 24 860
ceiling 15 86
frescoes 28 677, 688, *688*
panel 29 362
religious 28 683
patrons and collectors 3 228, 740; 4 599; 9 172; 20 482; 25 664; 29 799
pupils 24 827
reproductive prints by others 2 20
sculpture 3 *469*; 28 681, 687
woodcuts 33 357, 365, 366
Beccafumi, Lorenzo 3 467
Beccaloro 9 93
Beccari, Agostino 1 601
Beccari, Francesco 16 729
Beccari, Giuseppe 16 729
Beccaria, Antonio 18 686
Beccaria, Cesare 21 527
Beccaruzzi, Francesco 3 470*
Beccharia, Zaccarina 11 293
Becchetti Altarpiece 8 170
Beccles, Roos Hall 10 230
Bec Crespin, Antoine du *see* CRESPIN, ANTOINE DU BEC
Becerra, Alonso 3 470
Becerra, Domingo 3 470
Becerra, Francisco 3 470*; 21 375
cathedrals 6 520; 9 710; 19 385; 20 501; 24 501, *501*, *503*; 25 697; 32 239
churches 21 375
Becerra, Gaspar 3 470–71*; 8 504; 20 65; 29 278, 289, 290
assistants 1 847
patrons and collectors 13 922; 14 5
works 9 706; 20 67, 72; 24 107; 29 290, *290*
Becerra, Miguel Pou *see* POU BECERRA, MIGUEL
Becerra, Moisés 14 716
Becerril, Master of 29 277
Becerril, Cristóbal 3 471; 29 334
Becerril, Francisco 3 471*; 29 333
Bech, Henrik Lorentzen 23 235, 237
Bechade de Rochepine, Petr Filip 4 833; 23 424
Bechara, Tony 18 834
Becher, Bern(har)d 3 472; 23 37
Becher, Hans 19 815
Becher, Hilla 3 472; 23 37
Becher, Johannes R. 23 267
Becher, Johann Joachim 2 825
Bechert, Joseph 31 786
Bechler, Theobald 29 843
Béchot, Marc 21 538
Bechtejeff, Wladimir von 4 133
Bechteller, Kašpar 8 384
Bechtle, Robert 24 686, 687
Bechtler, Kašpar 8 396
Bechtold, Erwin 30 172*
Bechuanaland Protectorate *see* BOTSWANA
Bechyně 8 377, 404, 425
Ceramics School 8 406
Becić, Vladimir 8 181
Beck (ii), András 3 474
Beck, David 30 77
Beck (ii), Fülöp Ö(tvös) 3 474*; 14 896
Beck (i), Georg 3 472–3*
collaboration 3 473
works 3 *472*
Beck, Helena Maria Holstein, 4th Duquesa de Palmela *see* PALMELA, HELENA MARIA HOLSTEIN BECK, 4th Duquesa de
Beck, Henry C. 19 575
Beck (i), Leonhard 2 715, 716, 718; 3 473–4*
attributions 20 791
collaboration 3 472, 473; 28 58
patrons and collectors 13 903
pupils 1 763
teachers 14 665
works 3 *473*; 12 385, 387; 19 813; 28 58; 33 353
Beck (i), Sigmund 14 665
Beck (ii), Vilmos Fémes 3 474–5*; 10 108; 14 896
Becker, Adolf von 3 821; 12 19; 28 104
Becker, Benno 31 368
Becker, Felix 10 212; 12 483; 28 165; 30 731*
Becker, Friedrich 12 451, 456; 17 530
Becker, Gilbert 2 217; 30 684
Becker, Herman (*c.* 1617-78) 3 475*
Becker, Hermann (1817-85) 19 97
Becker, Howard 28 927
Becker, Jakob 11 802; 28 142
Becker, Ludwig 29 751
Becker, Ludwig Philipp Henrich 2 745; 3 475*
Becker, Peter 12 394
Becker, Philipp Christoph 12 262
Becker, Philipp Jakob 17 817
Becker, Wilhelm Gottlieb 14 570
Beckerath, Adolf von 28 165
Beckers, José 13 762
Beckert, Adolf 8 411; 19 719
Beckert, Hansgeorg 2 217; 30 684
Becker-Voigt 15 56
Becket, Thomas à *see* THOMAS BECKET, Saint
Beckett, Clarice 3 475–6*
Beckett, Francis 8 762
Beckett, Gilbert à 28 526
Beckett, Isaac 3 476*; 9 327; 21 416; 28 881
Beckett, Samuel 8 844; 14 271; 24 144; 31 375; 32 136
Beckett, Welton, & Associates
works 12 *794*
Beckford, William (1709-70) 5 907
Beckford, William (*d* 1799) 5 750; 16 889
Beckford, William (1760-1844) 2 560; 3 476–7*; 13 304; 16 554; 28 781
albums 1 583
architecture 2 337; 3 372; 10 235, 361; 13 200, 206
collections 2 559; 11 663; 14 107
decorative works 25 874
drawings 8 96
furniture 10 280
groups and movements 29 890
metalwork 2 722
paintings 5 907; 8 97, 98; 10 365, 753; 19 624; 28 430
sculpture 2 558
stained glass 29 515
teachers 8 95
weapons 9 31
Beckington Abbey (Somerset) 29 748
Beckius, Jean-Pierre 19 827
Beckley (E. Sussex), Woodgate House 26 130
Beckley, Bill 28 397
Beckmann, Max 3 477–81*, *479*; 9 *309*; 11 735; 12 395, 396; 24 427; 25 651; 28 920
groups and movements 10 695; 22 922, 923
paintings 3 *477*, *478*, *480*; 8 597; 22 416; 31 345
townscapes 11 *735*
urban life 31 705
patrons and collectors 11 729; 20 880; 23 7
prints 9 310; 19 491; 25 626; 33 363
propaganda 25 653
pupils 22 202; 23 406; 31 335
Beck's Journal of Decorative Art 24 431
Beckwith, Carl 10 580
Beckwith, James Carroll 24 362
Becontree (Essex) 31 730
Becq de Fouquières, Louise-Marie 8 616
Bécquer (family) 28 516
Bécquer, Joaquín (Domínguez) 3 482; 23 523
Bécquer, José (Domínguez) 3 482
Bécquer, Valeriano (Domínguez) 3 482*; 29 284
Bécu, Anne 9 313
Bécu, Marie-Jeanne, Comtesse Du Barry *see* DU BARRY, (MARIE-JEANNE BÉCU), Comtesse
Becuccio 27 849
bedcovers *see* COVERLETS
bedding 3 482; 14 249; 28 922
Bede 2 649; 8 259; 9 13; 12 255; 25 277; 31 499
Bédeilhac 25 476
Bedel, Jacques 2 401; 3 485*, 712; 13 725
Bedel and Benedit 30 525
Bedell, William, Bishop 17 564
Bedeloo, Frans 13 679
Bede Orosius 33 89
Bederski, Adam 26 266
Bedet, C. M. 29 748
Bedford 4 768
Bedford, Dukes of 7 479; 18 746
Bedford, Francis 3 486*; 24 657, 664
collaboration 33 545
groups and movements 23 504
patrons and collectors 14 148
works 19 *484*, 485; 24 664
Bedford, Francis Russell, 4th Earl of *see* RUSSELL, FRANCIS, 4th Earl of Bedford
Bedford, Francis Russell, 5th Duke of *see* RUSSELL, FRANCIS, 5th Duke of Bedford

Bedford, Jacob 9 727
Bedford, John, Duke of *see* PLANTAGENET, JOHN OF LANCASTER, Duke of Bedford
Bedford, John Russell, 4th Duke of *see* RUSSELL, JOHN, 4th Duke of Bedford
Bedford, John Russell, 6th Duke of Bedford *see* RUSSELL, JOHN, 6th Duke of Bedford
Bedford, Lucy Russell, Countess of *see* RUSSELL, LUCY, Countess of Bedford
Bedford, Master of the Breviary of the Duke of *see* BEDFORD MASTER
Bedford Breviary *see under* BREVIARIES → individual manuscripts → Salisbury Breviary
Bedford Hours *see under* BOOKS OF HOURS → individual manuscripts
Bedford Hours, Master of the *see* BEDFORD MASTER
Bedford Master 20 624–6*
  assistants 10 713
  collaboration 20 701
  patrons and collectors 5 208; 7 525; 17 669; 18 685; 31 842
  works 4 395; 12 107; 20 625, 626, 633
  workshop 6 503
Bedford Master, Chief Associate of the 20 625
Bedford Park *see under* LONDON
Bedia, José 8 229, 234
Bedia chalice 12 328
Bédiat, Roger 8 23
Bedini, Danielle 30 887
Bedjmes 9 866
Bednarski, Krzysztof 3 486*; 17 448; 25 116
Bednov, Viktor 27 434
Bedogni, Lorenzo 6 138; 33 53
Bedojev, Shalva 23 92
  works 27 433
Bedoli, Alessandro Mazzola 20 904
Bedoli, Girolamo Mazzola 3 486–7*; 12 561
  attributions 2 128
  teachers 20 904
  works 3 486; 24 193, 196, 197
Bedollière, Emile de La *see* LA BEDOLLIÈRE, EMILE DE
Bedón, Pedro 4 102; 7 607; 9 712, 714, 715
Bedouin 33 97
  carpets 5 830; 16 486
  dress 16 454
  looms 30 544
  tents 1 307; 30 471
Bedoukian, Paul Z. 2 444
Bedoya, Francisco 8 233
Bedre Byggeskik 8 728
Bedřich z Valdštejn, Jan, Archbishop of Prague 8 422; 25 426
Bedri Rahmi Eyüboğlu *see* EYÜBOĞLU, BEDRI RAHMI
bed rugs *see under* RUGS → types
beds 3 482–5*; 11 850; 14 425
  historical and regional traditions
   Africa 1 366
   Ancient Near East 1 890
   Austria 2 812–13, *813*; 3 484
   Bamum 3 152
   Belgium 3 581, 582, 584
   Byzantine 3 483
   Cameroon 1 366
   China 7 7, 34, 36, *38*, 38–9, 145
   Egypt, ancient 3 482*; 10 51, *51*, 53
   England 3 484, 485; 10 287, 291
   chinoiserie 7 *167*
   Renaissance 10 *289*
   18th cent. 10 *354*
beds
  historical and regional traditions—cont.
   France 3 484*; 11 *576*, 585, 593, 598; 31 *684*
   Germany 3 484; 12 420, 424, 426, *427*
   Greece, ancient 3 482–3*
   Hungary 14 905
   Italy 3 483, *483*, 484; 9 14; 16 722
   Korea 18 360
   Mangbetu 1 366
   Netherlands, the 3 484; 22 865, 870, 871
   Papua New Guinea 24 82
   Portugal 3 484
   Rome, ancient 3 483
   San 1 366
   Scandinavia 3 485
   Scotland 28 245
   Serbia 28 454
   Spain 3 483, 484; 29 310, 315*, 319
   Sudan 1 285
   Sweden 30 *93*
   United States of America 31 624, 627, 629, 631
   Zaïre 1 296
  materials
   basketwork 1 296
   beech 3 *484*; 11 *594*
   brass 3 485
   bronze 3 483
   damask 3 483
   ebony 3 482
   embroidery 10 *354*
   fringes 3 483
   gesso 3 482
   gold 10 51
   gold leaf 3 482
   huang huali 7 *38*
   iron 3 485
   ivory 3 482
   jade 7 7
   lacquer 7 *167*
   mahogany 3 485, *485*
   mud 1 285
   oak 10 *289*
   silver 3 483
   silver leaf 3 482
   upholstery 31 682–3*, *684*
   velvet 3 483
   walnut 3 *483*, 484, 582
  techniques
   gilding 3 482, 582; 10 *51*; 11 *594*
  types
   beds of state *see lits de parade*
   closs 28 252
   couch 3 581
   day-beds 29 8, 316; 31 623
   French 31 629
   lits à housse 3 484
   lits à la Duchesse 11 593
   lits à la polonaise 3 484, *484*; 11 593
   lits à la romaine see lits en chaire à prêcher
   lits à la turque 11 593, *594*
   lits de parade 11 588
   lits-en-bateau 3 485, *485*
   lits en chaire à prêcher 11 593
   lits en tombeau 11 593
   sleigh 31 629
Bedsa 3 487–8*; 5 94; 15 *276*, 435
  temple 15 252
Bedu 1 229
Bedulu 15 *754*
Beduzzi, Antonio (Maria Nicolao) 3 488*; 32 436
  collaboration 1 668; 27 196
  patrons and collectors 31 510
  works 2 794; 19 55; 21 84; 25 448; 32 454, 459
Beduzzi, Carl Joseph 3 488
Beduzzi, Wenzel 28 836
beech 33 324
  historical and regional traditions
   England 10 *290*, 293, *296*
   France 3 *484*; 11 589, *594*, 595
  uses
   beds 3 *484*; 11 *594*
   chairs 10 *290*, 293, *296*; 11 595
   panel paintings 24 3
   tables 11 589
Beech Aircraft Corporation 11 835
Beecham, Thomas 26 531
Beecher, Catherine (Esther) 3 488–9*
Beechey, Henry 3 179
Beechey, William 3 489–90*
  groups and movements 23 248
  patrons and collectors 14 144, 146; 19 271; 25 39
  pupils 15 32
  reproductive prints by others 32 856
  works 3 *489*; 10 249; 11 *431*
Beechworth, Burke Memorial Museum 1 66; 17 436
Beechy, George 15 655
Beechy, Richard 16 16
Beeck, Jan Simonsz. van der *see* TORRENTIUS, JOHANNES
Beeckestijn 12 132
Beeckmans, François 26 83; 30 451
beehive tombs *see* TOMBS → types → tholos
Beek, Jan Bontjes van *see* BONTJES VAN BEEK, JAN
Beekman, Chris 3 490*; 22 852
Beekum, Radboud van 22 877
beeldenkasten see under CUPBOARDS → types
Beenken, Hermann 14 580
beer 8 127; 29 813
Beer, Aert de 3 492
Beer, Alexander 17 548
Beer, Alois 18 490
Beer, Arnold de 19 547
Beer, Ellen 29 514
Beer, Franz (*fl* 1841) 14 889
Beer (von Bleichten), Franz, II (1660-1726) 3 490–91*; 23 636; 33 41
  attributions 28 130
  collaboration 12 371; 28 130; 30 790
  works 3 490, 491; 12 372; 28 130; 32 822
Beer, Frederike 25 282
Beer, Georg 3 491–2*
  assistants 28 87
  patrons and collectors 33 429
  works 12 368; 29 874
Beer, Hans 23 306
Beer, Jan de 2 204; 3 492–3*
  assistants 20 615
  pupils 19 547
  works 3 *492*
Beer, Johann Michael 3 490, 491*; 30 126
Beer, Joos de 4 150
Beer, Joseph 10 893
Beer, Julius 4 597
Beer, Michael 3 490*; 12 371; 30 790
Beer, Theodor 10 102
Beer, William 28 900
Beerblock, Johannes
  works 14 *785*
Beerbohm, (Henry) Max(imilian) 3 446, 493*; 5 758
Beerem, Provinciaal Museum van het Bulskampveld 3 616
Beerleire, C. Van *see* VAN BEERLEIRE, C.
Beers, De *see* DE BEERS
Beers, Jacob 17 549
Beers, Toegangspoort 4 785
Beersheba 16 566; 17 553; 30 192
  Negev Monument 16 567
  Soroka Health Centre 16 565
Beers Kempson, Julie Hart *see* KEMPSON, JULIE HART BEERS
Beer stone 29 699
Beerstraten, Abraham 3 493–4
Beerstraten, Anthonie 3 493–4
Beerstraten, Jan (Abrahamsz.) 3 493, 494*
Beert, Osias, I (*c.* 1580-1624) 3 494*
  pupils 25 221; 33 536
  works 3 561; 5 352; 11 227; 29 666; 31 882
Beert, Osias, II (1622-78) 3 494
Beervelde 19 756
  Castle 3 565
Beese, Lotte 29 531
Beest, Albert van 4 627
Beest, Jacoba Heemskerck van *see* HEEMSKERCK VAN BEEST, JACOBA
Beest, Jacob Eduard van Heemskerck van *see* HEEMSKERCK VAN BEEST, JACOB EDUARD VAN
Beest, Sybrand van 31 246
Beeston Castle (Ches) 12 173
beeswax *see under* WAXES → types
Beetle 25 26
beetles 15 618
Beeton, Isabella 30 219
Beffie, W. 28 864
Beffroi, Le 33 7
Bega, Abraham *see* BEGEYN, ABRAHAM (JANSZ.)
Bega, Cornelis (Pietersz.) 3 494–5*; 7 866
  attributions 3 762
  patrons and collectors 7 584; 9 456, 457; 33 700
  teachers 22 840; 23 609
  works 3 *495*; 10 553; 21 895
Begarawiya *see* MEROË
Begarelli, Antonio 3 495–6*
  patrons and collectors 10 523
  pupils 1 17; 3 496; 29 363
  works 3 *496*; 30 496, 498
Begarelli, Ludovico 3 496*
Begas, Adalbert 3 496, 497
Begas, Carl (Joseph) (i) (1794-1854) 3 496, 497*
  pupils 3 497; 29 600
  works 3 799; 11 *461*
Begas, Carl (ii) (1845-1916) 3 496, 497, 499*
Begas, Oskar 3 496, 497
Begas, Reinhold 3 496, 497–9*
  assistants 4 762; 12 196
  collaboration 3 499; 12 407
  pupils 3 497
   Begas, Carl (ii) (1845-1916) 3 499
   Cauer, Ludwig 6 93
   Felderhoff, Reinhold Karl 10 866
   Friedrich, Nikolaus 11 784
   Kraus, August 18 441
   Starck, Constantin Karl 29 546
   Tuaillon, Louis 12 407; 31 401
   Uphues, Joseph (Johann Ludwig) 31 688
  teachers 12 406
  works 3 *498*, 800
Begas, Werner 3 497
Begay, Apie 22 594
Begay, Harrison 3 499–500*; 22 595
  works 3 *500*
Begay, Kenneth 22 616
Begeer, Carel Joseph (1840-79) 10 119; 22 891, 892; 26 378; 33 163
Begeer, Carel Joseph Anton (1883-1956) 22 892
Begeer, Cornelis 22 892
Begeijn, Abraham *see* BEGEYN, ABRAHAM (JANSZ.)
Begeler, Johannes 26 718
Beger, Lorenz 12 266; 13 605; 14 651
  works 9 *27*
Beget, S Cristobál 26 642
Begeyn, Abraham (Jansz.) 3 500–501*; 14 650; 20 141
Begg, John 3 501*
  assistants 27 360; 33 283
  collaboration 33 283
  works 4 289
Beggarstaff Brothers 8 109; 23 102; 25 347, 674
Begheyn, Abraham *see* BEGEYN, ABRAHAM (JANSZ.)
Béghin (family) 3 599
Beghin, Antoine 31 220
Béghin, J. F. J. 3 599
Begijn, Pieter Jansz. 3 494
Beglyarov, Sergei Nickitovich 31 459
Bégon 25 281
Bégon III, Abbot of Conques (*reg* 1087-1107) 5 808; 26 681, 691
Bégouën (family) 31 360
Bégouën, Henri, Count 31 409
Begram 1 *186*, 191, 195, 211; 3 502*; 6 *182*, 187; 11 335
  architecture 6 296
  beakers 27 78
  coins 1 204, 211
  glass 27 78, 79
  ivory 15 695
  ivory-carvings 1 195; 3 *501*; 6 271
  jewellery 1 205
  metalwork 1 206
  sculpture 1 193, 196
  stucco 29 814, 824
Bègue, Jean Le *see* LE BÈGUE, JEAN
Béguier, Serge 20 913
Beguillet, M. 20 497
Beguines 3 502–4*
  painting 3 *503*, *504*
Béguins, Master of the 20 627*
Begur 15 529
  inscriptions 3 163
  reliefs 15 528
  sculpture 15 529
  temples 15 528
Behaeddin, Ahmet (Vural) 3 505*; 8 364
Behaegel, Philippe *see* BÉHAGLE, PHILIPPE
Behagel, Daniel 12 430; 14 131
Béhagle, Philippe 3 461; 11 642; 23 665; 30 320, 322
Béhague, Comtesse de 10 91; 11 664
Behaim, Bernhard 16 867
Behaim, Hans *see* BEHEIM, HANS, the elder
Behaim, Martin 12 813
Beham, Barthel (1502-40) 3 505, 506–7*; 10 385; 20 791; 22 302; 23 308
  collaboration 22 302
  groups and movements 19 501
  patrons and collectors 33 271
  pupils 3 505; 21 485
  works 3 *507*; 12 386; 19 813; 25 605; 33 354
Beham, Barthel (*fl* 1502-15) *see* BB, MONOGRAMMIST
Beham, Georg *see* PECHAM, GEORG
Beham, Hans *see* BEHEIM, HANS, the elder
Beham, Hans Sebald *see* BEHAM, SEBALD
Beham, Jan (*fl* 1517-33) 16 867; 25 129
Beham, Paul 22 918
Beham, Sebald 2 716; 3 505–6*; 10 385; 23 308
  groups and movements 12 386; 19 501

Beham, Sebald—cont.
prints 19 813; 25 605
engravings 2 224; 10 326; 23 294
etchings 3 506
woodcuts 12 815; 29 719; 33 354, 366
pupils 3 506
reproductive prints by others 5 63; 18 619
stained glass 14 572; 27 256
Behan, John 16 22
Behanzin Palace 3 728
Behar School of Athens see UNITED PATNA AND GAYA SOCIETY
Behayle, G. 3 752
Behbeit el-Hagar 3 508*; 9 774, 892
Behdet see EDFU
Beheading of St John the Baptist, Master of the 20 627–8*
Beheim, Hans, the elder (1455/60-1538) 3 508–9*; 18 430
patrons and collectors 15 144
works 23 306, 307, 317; 25 621; 31 567
Beheim, Hans, the younger (d 1535) 3 509
Beheim, Johann (fl c. 1760-70) 3 204
Beheim, Paulus 3 509; 15 144; 23 306
Behem, Baltazar 18 427; 25 117
Behistan see BISITUN
Behles, Edmond 29 61
Behling, Johan Erich 5 30
Behn, Andreas von 3 509*
Behna Shiva Temple 15 310, 310
Behne, Adolf 2 288; 3 801; 10 697; 12 378; 29 872
Behnes, William 3 509*; 32 911, 921; 33 24, 373
Behnisch, Günter 3 510*
collaboration 12 380; 23 635; 29 489; 30 469
groups and movements 23 500
works 28 159; 29 427; 30 469
Behnisch & Partner 3 510
Behr, Johann Friedrich 3 790
Behramkale see ASSOS
Behrend, J. L. 29 383
Behrendt, Walter Curt 26 405
Behrens, Alex 19 6
Behrens, Christian 3 510–11*; 19 54
Behrens, Peter 2 789; 3 511–14*; 12 472, 480; 14 31; 15 823, 824; 31 497
architecture 10 683; 14 142; 23 493; 25 173
factories 3 512, 795; 4 789; 10 749; 11 734; 12 378, 792; 16 55; 21 780; 27 131
garden cities 14 31
halls 3 513
house 12 417
houses 3 795; 8 531; 9 460; 10 241
office buildings 30 760; 32 759
restorations 14 724
synagogues 17 548
assistants 19 39; 22 725
carpets 12 468
collaboration 19 434
furniture 12 417, 428; 33 156
groups and movements
Art Nouveau 2 565, 566; 10 215
Darmstädter Künstler-Kolonie 8 531; 12 416; 24 591
Deutscher Werkbund 8 824, 825, 826; 21 490, 780
Expressionism 10 697
Greek Revival 13 613
Modern Movement 8 247; 21 782
Ring, Der 26 405
Vereinigte Werkstätte für Kunst und Handwerk 24 279
Behrens, Peter—cont.
industrial design 8 802
kettles 8 802; 15 823
posters 25 348
pupils 2 416; 22 725; 25 48
silver 12 450
staff 13 686; 21 407, 490; 25 48
stonewares 12 430
tiles 30 885
writings 29 872
Behr furniture factory 33 84
Behringer, Wolf see BERINGER, WOLF
Behrman, Beatrice 31 261
Behshahr
gardens 12 82
palace 16 254
Behshahr Industrial Group 15 900
Behyo Church 1 764; 9 540
Beian see ICHIKAWA BEIAN
Beich, Daniel 3 514
Beich, Franz Joachim 3 514*; 22 302
Beichel, Desiderius 13 721
Beichlingen, Adam von, Count 3 69
Beichlingen, Counts of 3 66
Beidar, Tell 4 641
Beidha 3 514–15*; 30 180, 182, 191, 198
Beier, Georgina 15 57
Beier, Ulli 1 429, 439; 15 57; 23 136
Beierlein, Hans, the elder (c. 1460-1508) 3 515*; 14 449, 450
Beierlein, Hans, the younger (d 1523/4) 3 515*
beige stone 1 857
Beigutai (Jingxing) 6 700
Beijer, Jan de 33 676
Beijing 3 515–20*; 6 614, 615; 23 821
altars 1 702–3, 705
Altar of Agriculture 6 666, 681
Altar of Earth 6 666
Altar of Heaven 1 702, 702; 3 518; 6 643, 660, 666, 681; 27 129
Altar of Silkworms 6 666
Altar of the Moon 6 666
Altar of the Sun 6 666
Altars of the Soil and Grain 6 660
art forms and materials
architecture 3 518–20; 4 795; 6 658, 659
book covers 30 836
carpets 7 51, 68
enamel 7 71
glass 7 83, 84
ivory-carvings 7 104
kites 7 113
lacquer 7 18
painting 3 516–17
porcelain 4 173
prints 7 119
puppets 7 122
sculpture 3 517*; 6 732, 733; 7 57; 22 775
shoes 7 145
shrines (i) (cult) 28 637
vases 6 900
Balizhuang Pagoda 6 668
Beihai Park 3 520
pailou 23 780
Round Fort 7 9
White Pagoda 6 661
Yongan Temple 23 773
Beiping Academy of Art 7 149
churches
East Cathedral 6 678
North Cathedral 6 678, 678
South Cathedral 6 677
West Cathedral 6 678
Coal Hill 6 666
collections 3 517
Dadu 3 516; 6 665; 21 875
Daming gong 6 658
Drum tower 3 519
Beijing—cont.
exhibitions 7 158
Forbidden City 3 519; 6 659, 665, 666, 680, 681–2, 688; 21 548; 23 821
Baohe dian (Hall of Preserving Harmony) 6 660, 666, 681
enamel 7 70, 71
gardens 12 89
gargoyles 12 150
glass 7 84
heating system 15 52
horn 7 126
jade 7 10
Jiaotai dian (Hall of Union) 6 682
kang 17 772
Kunning gong (Palace of Earthly Tranquillity) 6 682
library 19 317
Ningshou gong (Palace of Peaceful Longevity) 6 682; 7 136
Qianqing gong (Palace of Heavenly Purity) 6 682
Ruyi guan (Hall of Fulfilment of Wishes) 7 10
sculpture 6 732, 733
Taihe dian (Hall of Supreme Harmony) 6 638, 641, 660, 660, 666, 681, 682; 25 171
Taihe men (Gate of Supreme Harmony 6 681
towers 6 681
Zhonghe dian (Hall of Middle Harmony) 6 660, 666, 681; 23 821
gardens 12 89, 90
gates 7 361
Heyi men 6 658
Qian men 6 666; 7 361
Qianqing men (Gate of Heavenly Purity) 6 681
Shenwu men 6 666
Taihe men (Gate of Supreme Harmony) see under Forbidden City
Tianan men (Gate of Heavenly Peace) 6 666
Wu men (Meridian Gate) 6 666, 681
Xizhi men 6 687
Yongding men 6 666
see also town walls
Great Hall of the People 6 705
houses 6 688
Houyingfang 6 658; 7 15
Imperial Library 3 518
imperial workshops 2 477
Institute of Archaeology 7 159, 160
library 3 518
Longquanwu kilns 6 891
Lugou Bridge 4 800; 6 731
Mao Zedong Memorial Hall 14 826
Maxim's 31 905
museums
Historical Museum 7 53
Museum of the Dazhong Temple 7 100
Palace Museum
collections 6 772, 925; 7 26, 27, 54, 62, 68, 69, 71, 100, 154
exhibitions 7 157
observatory 23 339, 340
palaces 6 681
Kunning gong (Palace of Earthly Tranquillity) see under Forbidden City
New Summer Palace 6 662, 682–4, 683, 684
Baoyun ge (Precious Clouds Pavilion) 6 683
collections 22 127
Dehe yuan (Garden of Harmony and Virtue) 6 683; 7 136, 136
Beijing
palaces
New Summer Palace—cont.
Donggong men (East Palace Gate) 6 683
Foxiang ge (Buddha Fragrance Pagoda) 6 683
gardens 12 89, 90
Jingfu ge (Tower of Great Happiness) 6 684
kang 17 772
Kunming hu (Lake of Vast Brightness) 3 520
Longevity Hill 6 683
Long Gallery 6 683
pailou 23 780
Paiyun guan (Hall of Dispelling Clouds) 6 683
Renshou dian (Hall of Benevolence and Longevity) 6 683
Revolving Archive 6 683
sculpture 6 732, 733, 733
Xiequ yuan (Garden of Harmonious Pleasures) 6 684; 12 89
Yulan tang (Hall of Jade Billows) 6 683
Ningshou gong (Palace of Peaceful Longevity) see under Forbidden City
Old Summer Palace 6 41, 662, 682, 733; 7 53, 132; 11 338
fountain 3 517
glassworks 7 84
Qianqing gong (Palace of Heavenly Purity) see under Forbidden City
Qinian dian (Hall of Prayer for a Prosperous Year) 1 702; 3 518
temples 3 519–20
Baiyun guan (White Cloud Temple) 6 674, 724
Biyun Temple 6 722
Diamond Throne Pagoda 6 661
Guangji Temple 6 779, 782
Miaoying Temple 6 658; 33 570
White Pagoda 2 477; 6 658; 23 773, 774, 775; 29 868
Tianning Temple 6 656, 668; 23 773
Xihuang Temple 6 722
Yonghe gong (Lama Temple) 6 661, 671; 10 485; 23 773; 30 443
Wanfu Pavilion 6 671
Zhenjue Temple (Five Pagoda Temple) 6 661, 671
Tiananmen Square 6 666
tomb of Hua Feng 7 83
tomb of Li Wei 7 27
town walls 3 516; 6 661, 681
see also gates
urban planning 6 662, 666
Beikthano 5 221, 222, 223, 224
architecture 5 237
coins 5 255
Beilby (family) 10 318
Beilby, Mary 3 521; 10 318
Beilby, Ralph 3 521, 897
Beilby, William (1705-65) 3 521
Beilby, William, jr (1740-1819) 3 521; 10 318
works 10 318
Beiles, Eliahu 16 571
Beilter, Matthias 7 166
Beimiao 7 15
Beinaschi, Giovan Battista 3 521*; 22 479
Beinasco, Francesco Valeriano Dellala di see DELLALA DI BEINASCO, FRANCESCO VALERIANO
Beine, Karl 18 850
Being (Objective Reality Group) see BYTIYE
Beinhart, Jacob 14 160
Beipiao, Tomb of Feng Sufou 7 22, 83
Beiping see BEIJING
Beira, Museu Municipal 22 245
Beirlin see BEIERLEIN
Beirut 16 104; 17 500; 26 917
'A'isha Bakkar Mosque 16 242
American University 19 8
Archaeological Museum 19 9
architecture 19 7
Berytus 26 915
carpets 16 470
forgeries 1 896
Lebanese Academy of Fine Arts 19 8
Lebanese University, Fine Arts' Institute 19 8
Musée National 1 896; 5 331
National Archaeological Museum 19 9
Nicholas Ibrahim Sursock Museum 19 8, 8
printing 16 361
St George's Hotel 19 7
St John's 17 502, 506
Beisamun 30 181
Beisān see BETH SHAN
Beisanjin Okada see OKADA BEISANJIN
Beishouling (Baoji) 3 187; 6 685
Beisteguy y Benítez, Carlos de 3 522*; 11 584
Beit, Alfred 3 522; 4 209
Beit, Alfred Lane 3 522
Beit, Otto (John) 3 522*; 4 209
Beit ed Din see BAYT AL-DIN
Beit el-Wali
reliefs 9 886
temples 9 833; 23 280; 25 874; 29 386
Beith 28 249, 255, 256
Beit Khalaf, Tomb K1 9 838
Beit Mirsim, Tell 1 880
stele 29 613
textiles 1 881
Beixin culture 7 159
Bei Yiyuan 6 744
works 6 744
Beja (African people) 1 306
Beja (Portugal) 25 288, 313
Convento da Conceição 30 880
Museu Pacense 32 538
Museu Regional 25 318
S Maria 25 301
tiles 30 880
Beja, Luis Aviz, Duque de 2 501, 869, 873*; 14 659, 660, 661
Bejaïa 16 171
Palace 16 246
Béjar, Museo Municipal 14 463
Bejarano (family) 28 516
Bejarano, Antonio Cabral y Aguado see CABRAL Y AGUADO BEJARANO, ANTONIO
Bejarano, Sebastián 27 703
Béjart, Maurice 23 901
Bejbehara 15 459
Bejemark, Karl Göte 30 87
Béjot, Eugène 3 522–3*
Bejsce
Firlej Chapel 25 97, 129
tomb of Nicolaus and Elisabeth Firley 25 113
palace 29 839
Bek (fl c. 1340 BC) 3 523*; 9 883
works 9 790
Bek, Bishop of Durham (fl 1295-1311) 10 163
Bekabad Hoard 18 530
Beke, Joos van der see CLEVE (i), JOOS VAN
Bekenrenef 9 841, 891; 27 813
tomb 27 811
Bekensloer, János 9 754
Beketov, Aleksey 9 458
Bekhazi, Najib 19 7
bekhen stone 9 813, 881; 22 399; 27 14, 14
Bekhruz Kengerli 2 895

Bekhteyev, Vladimir **22** 921
Beklemishev, Vladimir A. **18** 234; **20** 152, 275; **28** 570
Bekmuradov, Kulnazar **31** 459
Beknazarov, Murirat Dambunyevich **30** 253
Beksiński, Sdzisław **32** 878
Bektaş, Cengis **16** 242; **31** 453
Bektashi Order **16** 461
Bekynton, Bishop **33** 59
Bel, Temple of *see under* PALMYRA
Béla **33** 596
Béla I, King of Hungary (*reg* 1060–63) **14** 883
Béla III, King of Hungary (*reg* 1172–96) **10** 545; **14** 903
Béla IV, King of Hungary (*reg* 1235–70) **14** 883; **26** 687; **32** 614
Beļacova, Aleksandra
Belaguntha, Jagannatha Temple **15** 541
Belanda **33** 609
Bélanger, François-Joseph **3** 523–4*; **4** 556; **10** 643; **11** 627
architecture **24** 120
châteaux **6** 509; **27** 559; **32** 553
domes **8** 65; **10** 669; **16** 53; **19** 85; **20** 438
garden buildings **12** 123
grottoes **13** 705
urban planning **31** 714
assistants **14** 592
collaboration **9** 379; **13** 234; **24** 123
gardens **21** 150
groups and movements **10** 96
interior decoration **11** 411, *579*
mouldings **11** *412*
patrons and collectors **4** 556; **18** 579; **20** 897; **24** 570; **25** 578
pupils **8** 133; **25** 873
stage design **30** 672
Bélanger, Louis **10** 754
Bélanger, Mme **3** 524
Bélapátfalva Abbey **3** 524*; **14** *881*
Belarus' **3** *525*, 525–31*
architecture **3** 525–7*; **4** 783; **17** *546*
brick **4** 783
churches **3** 526, *526*
education (art) **3** 528, 529; **32** 412
fortifications **3** 526
government buildings **21** *696*
houses **32** 298
icons **3** 527, 528, *530*; **25** 341*
lubki **3** 528
manuscript illumination **3** 527
painting **3** 527–30*, *529*
portraits **3** 528
reliefs **3** *530*
sculpture **3** 530–31*
slate **3** *530*
stone-carvings **3** 530
synagogues **17** *546*
wood **17** *546*
woodcuts **3** 528
Belas, Marquês de **18** 578, 579; **19** 894; **28** 430
Belasyse, John, 1st Baron Belasyse **10** *248*
Belasyse, Thomas, 4th Viscount Fauconberg **29** 31
Belau *see* PALAU
Belaúnde Terry, Fernando **19** 387; **24** 505, 517
Belaya Tserkov' *see* BILA TSERKV
Belbaşı **1** *821*, 823
Belbello, Luchino di Giovanni *see* BELBELLO DA PAVIA
Belbello da Pavia **3** 531–2*
collaboration **20** 783
patrons and collectors **10** 519; **32** 612
pupils **20** 631
works **3** *532*; **12** 733, 906; **20** 631
Belcamp, Jan van **9** 485
Belcastel Church
tomb of Alzias de Saunhac **13** 79
Belcayre **25** 485
Belchamp Hall (Essex) **2** 461
Belcher, George **32** 395
Belcher, John, sr (1817-90) **3** 532
Belcher, John, jr (1841-1913) **3** 532–3*
assistants **13** 615
collaboration **3** 368; **23** 34; **24** 891; **25** 187
competitions **7** 668
groups and movements **3** 269; **9** 739
pupils **26** 111
staff **2** 691; **33** 219
works **3** *533*; **10** 239, *239*
Belchier, John **10** 292
Belcobe, Heinrich **29** 334
Beļcova, Aleksandra **26** 384; **30** 36
Belcredi (family) **32** 157
Beldam Painter **32** 33*
Beldibi **1** *821*, 823
Beleau, Paul **8** 232
Belec **8** *174*
St Mary of the Snows **8** 178
Belém (i) (Portugal) **3** 534–5*; **25** *288*
Jerónimos Monastery *see* Monastery of S Maria de Belém
Monastery of S Maria de Belém **3** 534; **6** 451; **7** 703; **13** 71; **14** 516; **17** 486; **20** 325; **25** 290, 304, 317; **31** 179, *179*
bosses **4** 465
choir-stalls **27** 823
cloisters **25** *290*
metalwork **25** 312, 313
sculpture **6** *451*
south portal **25** 300
west portal **25** 300
palace **26** 363
Tower of Belém **3** *534*, 535; **13** 71; **20** 326; **25** 291, 317
Belém (ii) (Brazil) **3** 535*; **4** *705*
chapel of S João Batista **4** 711
college of S Alexandre **4** 709, 715
Compahia do Grão-ará headquarters **4** 711
governors' palace **4** 711
Museu Paraense Emílio Goeldi **3** 535; **4** 726
collections **4** 706, 708, 728
Nossa Senhora das Mercês **4** 711
S Francisco Xavier **4** 709, 715
Belém, Juan de **5** 410
Belém Monstrance **25** 312; **32** 406, *406*
Belén culture **29** 191
Beleuli **6** 222
Belevi **13** *363*; **31** 108
couches **13** 592
Heroön *see* Mausoleum
marble **27** 13
Mausoleum **3** 535–6*; **13** 407; **20** 863; **28** 383; **31** 109
drawings **13** *407*
roof **13** 384
sculpture **13** 384, 426
Belewale
spoons **8** *489*
Belfast **3** 536–7*; **16** *5*
Botanical Gardens
Palm House **3** 536
Botanic Primary School **16** 39
cemetery **31** 130
Cenotaph **6** 171
Central Reference Library **16** 42
Church of the Pentecost **16** 42
City Hall **3** 269; **7** 668; **9** 739; **16** 11
collections **16** 42
Clifton Burying-Ground **6** 166
Clifton House **3** *536*
College of Art **16** 42
Cregagh Estate **16** 40
Custom House **16** 11
glass **16** 29, 30
Grand Opera House **15** 408; **30** 678, *679*
Harbour Commissioners **16** 42
Belfast—cont.
Linen Hall Library **16** 42
Museum and Art Gallery *see* Ulster Museum
Natural History and Philosophical Society Museum **9** 369
painting **16** 16
Presbyterian College *see* Union Theological College
Queen's College **16** 11
Queen's University **16** 42; **24** 391
Sir William Whitla Hall **16** 39
Royal Courts of Justice **16** 39
Royal Ulster Academy of Arts **16** 42
Royal Victoria Hospital **3** 537
Strandtown Primary School **16** 39
Stranmillis College **16** 39
synagogue **17** 548
Ulster Museum **3** 537; **16** *39*, 40
collections **3** 537; **16** 42
Union Theological College **18** *753*
urban planning **16** 8
Belfast Banking Co. **18** 754
Belfiore Villa *see* FERRARA → Palazzo Belfiore
Belfort
Castle **17** 500
Lion of Belfort **22** 48
belfries *see* TOWERS → types → bell
Belgaum **15** 358, 664
Bel Geddes, Norman **3** 537–8*; **8** 802; **15** 824; **33** 410
collaboration **5** 7; **14** 399; **28** 835
patrons and collectors **20** 926
productions **30** 687
staff **13** 716; **27** 475
works **10** 684; **19** 897; **30** 684
Belgiojoso, Ludovico (Barbiano di) **3** 438; **26** 536
Belgium **3** 538–620*, *539*; **23** 678
academies **19** 547
allegories **30** *316*, II1
altarpieces
Baroque **3** *263*; **27** *290*
Early Netherlandish style **3** *641*, *739*; **4** *591*; **8** *551*; **10** *704*; **12** *845*, *847*; **17** *675*; **20** *667*, *668*; **21** *101*, *103*, *104*; **30** *165*; **31** *343*, *344*; **33** *119*, *122*
Gothic **4** *416*; **13** 110
Renaissance **5** *625*; **7** *424*; **8** *86*; **11** *441*; **21** *353*; **23** *525*
15th cent. **25** 183
altars **1** 698
amboyna **3** 584
animal subjects **32** 252
appliqué **3** 610
architectural history **28** 61
architecture **2** 194; **3** 540–51*; **4** 790
brick **13** 61
cavity-walling **4** 789
Gothic **3** 542–4; **13** 61–3*
Jesuit Order **17** 511
Romanesque **31** 220
archives **2** 370*
armour **2** 471, 473
art history **3** 619–20*; **19** 548
artists' biographies **10** 208
artists' houses **2** *549*; **3** *550*
atlases **23** 579
auctions **2** 559
banks **3** *549*
bas-de-page **21** *637*
beams **3** 576
beds **3** 581, 582, 584
benches **3** 581
Bibles **26** 666
blankets **3** 606
book illustrations **3** 555
Books of Hours **4** 372
borders (manuscript) **4** *396*
Belgium—cont.
brass **3** *566*, 582, 602–3, *603*; **4** 685, *685*; **5** *611*; **13** 159–60
brick **3** 575, 588; **4** 790; **13** 61
bronze **2** *237*; **3** *571*, *573*, 602; **13** 159–60; **21** *499*; **26** *145*
buffets **3** 581, 583
building regulations **5** 40
busts **3** *604*
cabinets (ii) (furniture) **3** *581*, 582–3, *583*, 585, 610
calamine **3** 602
candlesticks **5** *611*; **30** 732
cane **33** 157
canopies (i) (architecture) **5** *625*
canopies (ii) (textile coverings) **3** 581
caricatures **21** *356*
carnivals **5** 785
carpets **16** 466
cartoons (drawings) **3** 606, 607
caskets **3** 581
cast iron **3** 575, 585
castles **3** *541*
catafalques **6** 72
catalogues **9** 16; **14** 688; **33** 8
cathedrals **5** *52*; **31** *221*; **33** *568*
cedar **3** 585
ceilings **3** 576, 577
cemeteries **25** 539
ceramics **3** 575, 588–9*, 591–2*
chairs **3** 581–2, 583, 584
chandeliers **3** 602, *603*
chasubles **32** 392
chests **3** 580; **6** 560
chests-of-drawers **3** 583
choir-stalls **3** 581, 585
churches
Baroque **3** *546*
Carolingian **3** 541
Gothic **2** 191, *202*; **3** 542, *543*
Gothic Revival **3** *548*; **13** *208*
Romanesque **12** 520; **23** *164*
ciboria (ii) (structure) **7** 303
coats of arms **12** 272
cobalt **21** 137
coffee-urns **3** *600*
coffering **3** 576
coffers **3** *580*, 580
coins **14** *413*
collections **3** 611–15*
paintings **7** *563*
photographic **3** 619
columns **26** 905
commodes **3** 583
concrete **8** 633
confessionals **7** *703*, 703
connoisseurship **3** 615
conservatories **7** 745
containers **3** 592
copes **32** *389*
copper **3** *583*, 602
costumes **30** 665
cotton **3** *611*
crucifixes **3** 604
cupboards **8** 271
curtains **3** 576, 578, 582
cushion covers **3** 606
damask **3** 576; **19** *415*, 418
dealing **3** 615*
desks **3** 582, *586*
diamonds **3** *605*, 605
dictionaries of art **10** 208
display of art **9** 15–16, 22
doors **3** 575, 576, 578
dossals **3** *609*
drawings **12** 273
animal subjects **4** *222*
Baroque **17** *651*; **21** *765*; **27** *299*
chalk **4** *522*
Early Netherlandish style **10** *711*
intimisme **21** *87*
landscape **4** *522*; **7** *498*; **21** 360
Mannerism **29** *742*
Renaissance **4** *906*; **33** *170*
Symbolism (movement) **3** *564*
topographical **14** 618, *618*
Belgium
drawings—cont.
16th cent. **4** *839*; **32** *711*
dress **3** 609; **18** *591*
ebony **3** 582, 583, *583*, 585; **11** 445
education (art) **3** 617–18*
elm **3** 577
emblem books **32** 115
emblems **14** *619*
embroidery **3** 608–10*, *609*; **10** II2
enamel **3** 596; **5** *213*; **30** 408
champlevé **10** IV2; **26** 682, *693*
Romanesque **26** 692–3*, *693*
engraving **3** *594*
engravings **3** 558*, 561*; **10** 393
Baroque **4** *360*; **27** *503*
Renaissance **7** *556*
townscapes **32** *725*
16th cent. **12** *16*, *17*, *885*; **27** *502*; **29** *854*
17th cent. **2** 196, *196*
epitaphs **31** *126*
erotic art **10** 483
etchings **3** 561*; **12** *513*
Grotesque **13** *701*
Renaissance **4** *907*; **32** *152*
16th cent. **7** *499*
ewers **2** *237*; **3** *597*
exhibitions **33** 8
façade decoration **10** 745, *745*
faience (ii) (ceramics) **3** 588, 589–90, *590*
fireplaces **3** 575, 576, 578, 588
flagons **6** 155
floors **3** 575, 577, 578
flutes (glasses) **3** *594*
fonts (baptismal) **3** *566*
forgeries **3** 585
fortifications **25** 503
forts **21** *577*
fountains **2** 510
frames **11** 438–50*, *442*, *450*
frontispieces **12** *885*
funerary monuments **3** *571*
furnaces **4** *685*
furniture **3** 580–88*, *583*, *587*; **8** 633; **25** 303; **33** 157
gables **3** 544; **5** *40*; **11** 875–6
galleries (iv) (art) **7** *563*; **9** 15–16, 22
garden cities **4** 577; **8** 681; **9** 759; **11** 724; **25** 190; **31** 875; **32** 380
gems **3** 609; **26** *145*
gilding **3** 575, 576, 577, 582; **26** *145*
glacite **3** 576
glass **3** 575, 576, 583, 592–4*, 595–6*
glazes **3** *589*
gold **3** 596–602*, 606, *607*, 609, *609*; **5** *213*; **14** *413*; **18** *591*
government buildings **5** *42*
guidebooks **13** 808, 810
guildhalls **3** 544
guilds **3** 598, 605, 617; **5** 46
goldsmiths' **3** 596
painters' **2** 194
pewterers' **3** 603
tapestry-weavers' **12** 519
weavers **3** 606
harpsichords **22** *372*
headdresses **9** 271
heraldry **12** 273
heritage **16** 907
historiography **3** 619–20*
hospitals **14** *783*
houses **3** 575
Art Nouveau **5** *41*
Baroque **2** *549*
Gothic **4** *920*
Modern Movement **3** *550*
17th cent. **5** *40*
20th cent. **14** *629*
initials (manuscript) **7** *189*; **26** 666
interior decoration **3** 575–9*
Art Nouveau **3** *579*

Belgium
interior decoration—cont.
15th cent. **3** *576*
17th cent. **3** *577*
iron **3** 575, 580; **13** 160
ivory **3** 576, *602*, 603–4*, *604*; **29** 575
ivory-carvings **26** 695
jars **3** 588
jewellery **3** 604–5*, *605*
jugs **3** 588, 589, *589*
justice scenes **4** *592*; **17** *700*
knives **8** *283*
Kunstkammern **11** *718*
lace **3** 610–11*, *611*; **18** 589, *589*, 590, 591, *591*, *592*, 593; **31** 816
lacquer **3** 583, 585
leather **3** 575, 576, 577, 582, 583; **19** 4*
lecterns **13** 159
libraries **3** 618–19*
lighting **2** 510
limestone **26** 630; **29** 701
linen **3** *609*; **5** 654; **18** *589*, *592*; **19** 418
looms **3** 605
mansions **3** *547*
manuals (architecture) **26** 192
manuscript illumination **3** 552*, 555*
Cistercian Order **7** *348*
Early Netherlandish style **5** *429*; **9** *271*; **20** *682*, *725*; **31** *449*
Romanesque **26** 666–8*
14th cent. **9** *269*
manuscripts **12** 272
marble **3** *417*, *571*, 583; **9** *413*
marks **3** 596, 600–601, 603; **20** *443*, *444*; **30** 317
marquetry **3** 585; **20** 467
medals **20** 921
metal **3** 610
metalwork **3** 596–8*, 601–3*; **13** 159–60*; **26** 682–3*
miniatures (manuscript illumination)
Early Netherlandish style **3** *727*; **4** *370*; **5** *211*; **13** *660*; **14** *389*; **19** *252*, *340*; **20** *659*, *682*, *687*, *700*, *725*, *726*
Ottonian **3** *552*
Romanesque **26** *667*
15th cent. **21** *637*; **32** *729*
16th cent. **14** *760*
mirrors **3** 576, *576*
misericords **21** 725
mitres **32** *389*
modelli **21** *765*
models **3** 591
monstrances **3** 598, *599*
monuments **9** *413*
museums **3** 616–17*
nude figures **32** 151
Baroque **17** *650*; **25** *273*; **27** *288*, *292*, *293*
Early Netherlandish style **12** *847*
Mannerism **3** *24*
Renaissance **33** *170*
Surrealism **8** *700*
17th cent. **3** *108*; **33** *388*
oak **3** 575, 577, 578, *580*, 580, *581*, 582, 583, 585, *586*; **25** *727*
objects of vertu **3** 603*
office buildings **14** *771*
oil sketches **23** *381*
Baroque **8** *127*; **22** *415*
17th cent. **8** *878*, *879*; **32** *115*
19th cent. **32** *853*
olive-wood **3** 585
orders (architecture) **3** 544
pageant wagons **30** 665
painting **3** 551–65, 596–7
allegorical **1** 663
Baroque **17** *4*, *652*
Mannerism **21** *358*

Belgium
painting
allegorical—cont.
Renaissance **4** *898*, *899*, *901*, *902*, *903*, *906*, *907*; **11** *222*
16th cent. **11** 221; **25** *381*
17th cent. **4** *912*; **17** *919*; **32** *704*
animal subjects
Baroque **4** *916*
16th cent. **14** *619*
17th cent. **2** *104*; **17** *918*
architectural **2** 340–41*; **14** *785*; **32** *726*
battle **32** 722
cabinet pictures **5** 351–3; **9** 15–16
17th cent. **3** *108*; **5** *351*, *353*; **11** *442*, *718*; **30** *463*
conversation pieces **3** *561*; **22** *864*
display **9** 15–16, 22
Expressionism **24** *459*
flower **4** *915*; **28** *364*; **29** *665*
genre **3** 560, 562; **12** 290*, 296
Early Netherlandish style **9** *272*
Renaissance **4** *904*; **7** *428*; **21** *354*
16th cent. **3** *557*, *887*
17th cent. **4** *871*, *872*; **8** *108*; **26** *391*; **30** *461*, *462*; **32** *712*, *723*
19th cent. **8** *591*; **19** *291*; **21** *370*
glass **32** *151*
grisaille **13** 674–5, *675*
hanging **9** 15–16
history
Baroque **3** *559*
Neo-classicism **19** *166*
17th cent. **9** *197*
19th cent. **26** 740; **33** *171*
hunting scenes **28** *903*; **32** *706*; **33** *182*
landscape **3** 558, 562; **18** 711*
Baroque **27** *297*
Mannerism **31** *50*
Renaissance **4** *140*, *903*
16th cent. **7** *497*, *711*; **12** *171*; **18** *706*; **24** 259, *260*, 262, *262*, VIII2; **31** *804*
17th cent. **11** *357*; **21** *829*; **31** *523*; **33** *182*
18th cent. **23** *438*
literary themes **9** *479*
marine **9** 745; **24** *323*
Modernism **3** *563*
murals **3** 588
mythological
Baroque **17** *650*; **25** *273*; **27** *292*, *293*
Neo-classicism **26** *285*
16th cent. **11** 221
17th cent. **3** *108*; **25** *809*; **30** *788*; **33** *388*
panel **24** 3
pietàs **21** *102*
religious
Antwerp Mannerism **3** *492*
Baroque **4** *914*; **8** *126*; **9** *478*, *488*; **19** *650*, *651*; **27** *288*, *295*, *296*
Early Netherlandish style **3** *553*; **4** *593*, *594*, *595*; **8** *25*, *524*, *552*; **10** *706*, *709*, *710*; **11** *440*; **12** *848*, *849*; **15** *95*; **16** *70*; **20** *660*, *715*, *716*, *780*; **22** *863*; **25** *281*; **29** *692*; **33** *121*, *123*, *125*, *129*
Expressionism **3** *565*
Mannerism **3** *24*; **7** *414*; **17** *896*
Renaissance **2** *195*; **3** *554*; **7** *519*; **11** *221*; **12** *846*; **19** *548*; **20** *665*; **21** *357*; **25** *668*

Belgium
painting
religious—cont.
16th cent. **4** *911*; **23** *201*, *378*; **24** VIII2; **32** *114*, *710*
17th cent. **4** *219*; **11** *719*; **25** *810*; **32** *755*
19th cent. **22** *696*
sacra conversazione **4** *162*; **23** *447*
still-lifes **11** *871*; **28** *902*; **29** *665*; **33** *537*
Surrealism **8** *700*; **20** *101*, *102*; **31** *51*
Symbolism (movement) **11** *450*; **18** *24*
townscapes **16** *767*
vanitas **4** *917*
wall **3** 551–3*, 577
Romanesque **26** 648
Surrealism **5** *45*
14th cent. **3** *551*
watercolours **14** *619*
19th cent. **3** 562–4*; **10** *410*
panelling **3** 577
panels (wall) **3** 575, 576
parquetry **3** 578
patronage **3** 611–14*
pattern books
architecture **7** 480
furniture **3** 581, 582, 585
interior decoration **3** 579
pearls **3** 609, *609*; **10** II2
pendants (jewellery) **3** *605*
periodicals **24** 439–40*; **32** 380
pewter **3** 603
photoarchives **2** 370
pine **3** 585
plate **3** 596
playing cards **31** 266
porcelain **3** *590*, 590–91*
portraits **3** 559–60
double **17** *653*
drawings **8** *1*; **9** *481*; **25** *284*
engravings **10** 393
Baroque **27** *503*
Renaissance **33** *169*
17th cent. **14** *503*; **17** *598*
etchings **3** *560*
group **7** *833*; **23** 758; **27** *298*
miniatures (manuscript illumination) **3** *726*; **20** *724*
painting
Baroque **9** *277*, *486*; **17** *653*; **25** *274*, *284*; **27** *289*, *298*
Early Netherlandish style **3** *576*; **4** *593*, *921*, *922*; **10** *707*, *708*; **20** *670*, *676*; **21** *104*; **33** *124*
Renaissance **18** *6*; **21** *355*; **26** *185*
16th cent. **18** *6*; **25** *280*
17th cent. **7** *833*; **13** *920*; **30** *789*; **32** *703*
19th cent. **3** *614*
20th cent. **10** *411*
sculpture **21** *499*
self-portraits **3** *726*; **9** *486*; **20** *676*
posters **2** 510; **25** 347
pottery **3** 589–90*, 591; **21** 137
presses **25** *593*
print publishers **7** 499
prints **3** 555–6*
pulpits **25** 727, *727*
quarries **26** 630
railways **5** 41
reliquaries **3** 593; **5** *213*; **26** *145*, 683, *693*
Romanesque **10** IV2
romance manuscripts **26** 563*
roofs **12** 522, *522*
rose-wood **3** 585
samplers **27** 694
sandstone **29** *660*
sapphires **3** *609*
schnellen **3** 588
scissors **8** *286*

Belgium—cont.
sculpture **3** 566–74
Abstract art **3** *574*
architectural **10** 745, *745*; **31** *222*
bronze **3** *571*, *573*; **21** *499*
display **9** 15–16, 22
Gothic **13** 98–101*, 109–15*, *112*
Gothic: Late Gothic **8** 662
marble **3** *417*; **9** *413*
religious
Baroque **9** *411*; **25** *811*, *812*
Gothic **13** *99*, *100*, *111*
Romanesque **26** *645*
Romanesque **26** 630–31*, 644–5*
stone **13** 98–101*, *99*, *100*; **26** 630–31*
Surrealism **20** *102*
tomb **3** *417*, *571*; **9** *413*
wood **13** 109–15*, *111*, *112*; **26** 644–5*, *645*
19th cent. **3** *573*
20th cent. **4** *861*; **29** *660*
sheets **18** *591*
shields **2** *473*
shrines (i) (cult) **28** 630
shutters (window) **3** 575
sideboards **3** 585
signs (markers) **2** 510
silk **3** *607*, 609, *609*, 610; **4** *923*; **10** II2; **30** I2, II1; **31** *218*
silver **3** 596–601*, *602*, *604*, *605*, 606, *607*; **5** *213*; **13** 159; **22** 885; **26** *145*
17th cent. **3** *599*
18th cent. **3** *600*
silver-gilt **3** *597*
silver leaf **3** 575
spires **13** 62–3; **29** 414
springs **3** 585
stage design **30** *665*
stained glass **13** 181–3*, *182*, *909*; **26** *745*
staircases **14** *770*
stamps **3** 588
statuettes **29** 575
steel **3** 576
stitches **3** *609*, 610
stone **3** *568*, 575, 578; **13** 98–101*, *99*, *100*; **26** 630–31*
stonewares **3** 588, 589*, *592*
stools **3** 581
stoves **3** 575, 588
strapwork **29** *748*
streets **2** 510
stucco **3** 577, 578
studios **11** 220; **29** *854*
tabernacles (ii) (receptacle) **3** *568*
tablecloths **19** *415*
tables **3** 581, 582, 584
tapestries **2** *200*; **3** 576, 605–8*; **4** *923*, 923; **5** *47*, *48*, *50*; **30** 312–17*, 320, 324; **31** *218*, 219
Baroque **17** *649*; **27** *294*
millefleurs **14** III2
Renaissance **2** *198*; **3** *607*; **23** *527*
15th cent. **5** 43; **30** I2
16th cent. **30** *316*, II1
17th cent. **3** *608*
tea-services **3** *602*
terracotta **3** 588
textiles **3** 578, 605*; **26** 703
theatres **30** 665*
theories (urban planning) **5** 170
threads **3** 610; **10** II2; **14** III2
thuya **3** 585
tiles **3** 575, 576, 577, 588; **30** 878
tin **3** 602, 603
title-pages **4** *360*
tombs **3** *417*; **14** *421*
topaz **3** *609*
tortoiseshell **3** 583, 585
towers **13** 62–3
bell-towers **4** *924*

Belgium—cont.
town halls **2** *203*; **3** 543, *544*; **5** *53*; **12** *523*; **31** *238*
Gothic **4** *925*
trade
brass **3** 602
brick **3** 588
ceramics **3** 588
chairs **3** 582
copper **3** 602
damask **19** 418
furniture **3** 584, 585; **25** 303
glass **3** 592, 593
gold **3** 597
ivory **3** 604
lace **3** 610; **5** 51; **11** 649
manuscripts **4** 372
papier mâché **3** 578
plaster **3** 578
porcelain **3** 589; **11** 610
silk **28** 716
silver **3** 597
tapestries **3** 607; **5** 49
textiles **25** 315
tiles **3** 575
tin **3** 602
wallpaper **3** 578
wood **3** 584
wool **28** 716
transfer (printing) **3** 591
treatises **27** 300
architecture **3** 581; **23** 489
trompe l'oeil **11** 440
tureens **3** 589
underdrawings **31** *577*
varnishes **3** 575
veils **18** *592*
velvet **3** 582
veneers **3** *583*
vestments (ecclesiastical) **3** 609, 610; **32** *389*
wall coverings **3** 605
wallpaper **3** 576, 578
walls **3** 575–6, 577–8; **8** 681
walnut **3** 582, 583
war cemeteries **6** 166
wicker **33** 157
willow **33** 157
windows **3** 575, 576
wine-coolers **3** *590*
wood **3** 576, 578; **12** *522*; **13** 109–15*, *111*, *112*; **26** 644–5*, *645*
openwork **3** 585
woodcuts **2** *191*; **3** *556*; **17** *471*
wool , ; **3** *607*; **4** *923*; **30** I2, II1; **31** *218*
workshops **3** 585
wrought iron **3** 580
Belgorod **4** 110; **31** 545, *546*
architecture **31** 547, 548
fortress **31** *549*, 550
Belgrade **3** 620–21*; **25** *471*; **26** *906*; **28** *437*, 440, 444
central library **28** 445
Cooperative and Mortgage Bank **28** 444
Energoprojekt building **28** 445
Fairground **28** 445
Fiat Building **28** 444
Genex building **28** 445
museums
Archaeological Collection *see under* University
Aviation Museum **28** 445
Dositej Obradović Museum *see* Vuk and Dositej Museum
Ethnographical Museum **3** 621
Floegel Art Collection **28** 459
Fresco Gallery **3** 621; **28** 459
Jewish museum **17** 582
Museum of Applied Art **3** 621
Museum of Contemporary Art **28** 445, 459
Museum of the City of Belgrade **3** 621
Museum of the Serbian Orthodox Church **3** 621

Belgrade
museums—cont.
National Museum **3** 621; **13** 470; **28** 458, 459
Tašmadjan Museum **9** 54
Vuk and Dositej Museum **28** 458
National Assembly Building **28** 444
National Bank **28** 444
National Theatre **28** 444
New Belgrade **28** 444
painting **28** 451
palace *see* parliament praesidium
parliament praesidium **3** *620*; **28** 444
Post, Telegram and Telephone Head Office **28** 444
Sava Congress Centre **28** 445
Spasić Foundation **28** 444
Telephone Exchange **28** 444
University Collection **3** 621
University Hospital for Children **28** 444
Belgrano, Manuel **2** 405
Béliard **8** 545
Beli bi Ta **13** 861
Beli Cave *see under* KITULGALA
Bélidor, Bernard Forest de *see* FOREST DE BÉLIDOR, BERNARD
Bélier, Charles **14** 305
Beligala **29** 450
Beliliou **23** 832
Belin (de Fontenay), Jean-Baptiste (1653-1715) **3** 621*; **5** 837; **29** 668
collaboration **21** 891; **26** 386
patrons and collectors **18** 693; **31** 56
works **7** 167
Belin, Jean-Baptiste (1688-1730) **3** 621
Belin (of Modena), Nicholas *see* BELLIN (OF MODENA), NICHOLAS
Beling, Geoffrey **29** 468; **33** 74
Beling, J. E. **19** 497
Belin Segged **10** 570
works **10** *570*
Belisario, Isaac Mendes *see* MENDES BELISARIO, ISAAC
Belisırma
Açıkel Ağa Kilise **5** 674
Ala Kilise **5** 678
Balı Kilise **5** 677
Bezirhanı Kilisesi **5** 678
Direkli Kilise **5** 674, 676, 678
Kirk Dam Altı Kilise **5** 674
St George **5** 675, 676
Sümbüllü Kilisesi **5** 678
Belisle, Louis **3** 623
Belize **3** 621–5*, *622*; **21** 177
architecture **3** 622–3*
brick **3** 623
carnivals **5** 788
cathedrals **3** *623*
collections **3** 624–5*
exhibitions **3** 624
jade **23** 418
museums **3** 624–5*
painting **3** 623–4*
patronage **3** 624–5*
sculpture **3** 624*, *624*
trade
brick **3** 623
wood-carvings **3** 624
ziricote **3** *624*
Belize City **3** *622*
architecture **3** 622
Belisle Art Gallery **3** 624
Bliss National Gallery *see* Belisle Art Gallery
Cathedral of St John **3** 622, *623*
Court House **3** 623
Government House **3** 622
Beljon, Joop **22** 861
Belkahia, Farid **3** 625*; **22** 129
Belkein (family) **22** 205
Belkhodja, Najib **31** 426
Belkin, Anatoly **27** 581
Belkin, Arnold **3** 625*
Belkin, Veniyamin **18** 477; **27** 413
Belkovski, Stancho (Iliev) **3** 625*; **5** 149
Bell (family) **28** 224, 268; **31** 230
Bell, Adam Schall von *see* SCHALL VON BELL, ADAM
Bell, Alexander Graham **12** 311; **29** 250
Bell, Alfred **7** 410; **18** 882
Bell, Andrew **28** 156
Bell, Charles (*fl* 1800; sculptor) **22** 276
Bell, Charles (1774-1842; surgeon) **1** 844; **21** 6, 7
Bell, Charles (Davidson) (1813-82) **29** 108
Bell, Charles (1846-99) **17** 632
Bell, Charles L. **18** 629
Bell, (Arthur) Clive (Heward) **1** 181; **3** 628*, 631; **19** 591
groups and movements **4** 168; **10** 652
personal collection **10** 367
works **1** 172; **10** 652; **11** 315; **31** 300
Bell, Deborah **29** 109, 111
Bell, Denis **2** 152
Bell, Edward Ingress **33** 9
Bell, Mrs Fitzroy **9** *290*
Bell, George (Henry Frederick) **2** 772; **3** 628*
pupils **9** 310; **31** 410; **33** 203
works **4** 367
Bell, Gertrude Margaret Lowthian **3** 628–9*; **4** 67; **9** 527; **10** 874
Bell, (Frank) Graham **3** 629*
groups and movements **10** 375, 652; **20** 590; **23** 333
works **10** 652; **23** 333
Bell, H. C. P. **20** 188
Bell, Henry **7** 486
Bell, Ingress **4** 85
Bell, Isaac **20** 16
Bell, J. **28** 257
Bell, Jacob (*fl* 1858) **11** 796
Bell, James (*fl* 1835) **30** 162
Bell, John (*fl* 1476-1503) **5** 511
Bell, John (1721-64) **14** 642; **33** 359
Bell, John (*fl* 1776-97; writer) **8** 840; **22** 153
Bell, John (*fl* 1784; draughtsman) **1** 844
Bell, John (1811/12-95) **3** 629*; **7** 548; **10** 373; **15** 821
works **10** 311
Bell, Joseph **4** 826
Bell, Larry (Stuart) **3** 629–30*; **19** 702; **31** 609; **33** 45
Bell, Mildred Agnes *see* ARCHER, MILDRED (AGNES)
Bell, M. P. **28** 257
Bell, Reginald **33** 550
Bell, Robert Anning **3** 630*; **31** 250
Bell, Samuel **10** 306
Bell, Serafino **24** 533
Bell, Steve(n) **3** 630*
Bell, Trevor **27** 563
Bell, Vanessa **3** 628, 630–31*; **4** *169*; **13** 313, 314; **19** 591
collaboration **10** 284
exhibitions **10** 255
groups and movements **4** 168, 169; **10** 256; **11** 774; **19** 623; **23** 437, 438; **25** 356
house **2** 552
studio **29** 858
works **5** *840*; **7** 434; **22** 332; **28** 298, 299
Bell, William (*fl* 1826) **14** 863
Bell, William E. (*fl* 1858) **30** 898
Bella, Francesco della **3** 631
Bella, Stefano della **3** 631–4*; **16** 669; **20** 415
caricatures **5** 756
collaboration **3** 17
Bella, Stefano della—cont.
costumes **30** 660
drawings **3** *632*
etchings **2** 239; **3** *633*; **14** 394; **25** 605; **30** 229
glass **16** 740
patrons and collectors **4** 531; **10** 657; **14** 492; **20** 417; **21** 26, 27; **25** 815
pattern books **10** 333; **24** 273
reproductive prints by others **18** 534, 879; **21** 733
teachers **8** 497
Bella Bella **22** 547, 564, 580
Bellac Church **11** 614; **26** 691
Bella Coola *see* NUXALK
Bellaert, Jacob **20** 698, 773
Bellaert Master *see* JACOB BELLAERT, MASTER OF
Bellagha, ʿAli **31** 426
Bellagio
Frizzoni-Salis collection **11** 797
Villa Melzi **16** 719
Bellamont Forest (Co. Cavan) **16** 8; **23** 860; **24** *305*; **32** 553
Bellamy, John **28** 613
Bellan-bandi Palassa **29** 445
Bellange, Henri **3** 635
Bellangé, Henri-Horace **29** 668
Bellangé, (Joseph-Louis-)Hippolyte **3** 634*; **17** 453
Bellange, Jacques (Charles) (de) **3** 634–5*; **11** 533, 657; **19** 696; **22** 455
patrons and collectors **26** 470
pupils **8** 783; **18** 837
works **3** *635*; **10** 551–2; **25** 618
Bellano, Bartolomeo **3** 636–7*; **32** 192, 363
attributions **28** 509
collaboration **9** 130
competitions **7** 671, 672
patrons and collectors **9** 298; **28** 560
pupils **26** 326
teachers **16** 693
works **3** *637*, 860; **16** 691; **21** 632; **26** 326, 328; **29** 568
Bellanti, Francesco **12** 714
Bellanti di Terra d'Otranto, Giacomo *see* GIACOMO BELLANTI DI TERRA D'OTRANTO
Bellany, John **9** 725; **28** 240, 273
Bellapais Abbey **3** 637–9*; **8** *325*, 361, 362
church **3** 638
cloister **3** 639
refectory **3** *638*, 638
Bellarmato, Girolamo **19** 90
Bellarmine jugs *see under* JUGS → types
Bellati (family) **24** 703
Bellavite, Innocente **27** 324
Bellay, Charles **5** 921
Bellay, Du *see* DU BELLAY
Bell Beakers *see under* BEAKERS → types
Belle, Alexis-Simon **3** 639*
pupils **2** 851
reproductive prints by others **6** 549
teachers **31** 379
works **11** 406; **25** 635
Belle, Augustin-Louis **3** 639
Belle, Clément (-Louis-Marie-Anne) **3** 639*
Belle, Gaschon **4** 801
Belle, Jean **3** 639
Belle, Van, Triptych **25** 382
Belleardi, Giacomo **3** 496
Belle Assemblée **24** 422
Bellechose, Henri **3** 639–40*; **13** 156; **20** 207
attributions **11** 531
collaboration **20** 207
patrons and collectors **5** 209, 210, 895
works **3** *640*; **8** 890, 893
Belle Cordière, La **19** 848
Belle Croix **3** 21
Belleek Porcelain Factory **3** 641*; **6** 164; **13** 22; **16** *5*, 29, 41; **24** 149
works **16** *29*
Belleek Pottery Ltd **3** 641
Belleek Pottery Works Co. Ltd **3** 641
Bellefleur, Léon **25** 635
Bellefond, Maréchal de **20** 293
Bellefonds, Linant de **3** 179; **10** 82
Bellegambe, George **3** 641
Bellegambe, Jean **3** 641–2*
patrons and collectors **3** 394
teachers **25** 668
works **3** *641*
Belle Isle **25** 34, 266
Bellel, Jean-Joseph (-François) **1** 642; **6** 519
Bellelli (family) **8** *619*
Bellenger, Georges **19** 39
Bellermann, Ferdinand **5** 691; **32** 173
Belleroche, Albert (Gustavus) de, Count **3** 642*
Bellerophon Painter **13** 507
Bellers, William **6** 513
Bellerus, Joannes **25** 17
Bellery Desfontaines, H. J. F. **11** 600
Belles Heures *see under* BOOKS OF HOURS → individual manuscripts
Belleteste, Jean-Antoine **11** 637; **29** 574
Bellette, Jean **30** 160
Bellevaux **24** 148
Belleville (family) **25** 691
Belleville, Jeanne de **3** 642
Belleville Breviary *see under* BREVIARIES → individual manuscripts
Bellevois, Jacob (Adriensz.) **27** 230; **32** 673
Bellevue Château **6** 474; **11** 658
Chambre du Roi **18** 642
furniture **21** 817
interior decoration **32** 338
paintings **4** 517; **9** 208; **18** 655; **19** 646; **30** 343
sculpture **1** 133; **10** 764; **24** 785; **27** 659
Belle Vue Pottery **14** 863
Bellew, Henry **25** 891
Belleza, Norma **24** 622
bellflower *see* BALLFLOWER
Bellhouse, Edward T. **26** 18
Belli (i), Alessandro **3** 643
Belli (i), Andrea **3** 643
Belli (i), Antonio **3** 644
Belli, Bartolomeo **29** 832
Belli, Carlo **10** 822; **16** 681
Belli (i), Filippo **3** 644
Belli (i), Giacomino **3** 643
Belli (ii), Giovacchino **3** 644*; **26** 148
Belli (i), Giovanni di Ponteranica **3** 643
Belli (i), Giuseppe **3** 643, 644
Belli, Onorio **8** 155
Belli, Pasquale **3** 644–5*; **29** 640
assistants **25** 147
collaboration **7** 726
pupils **5** 552
teachers **5** 551
works **31** 801
Belli (ii), Pietro **3** 644
Belli, Valerio **3** 645*; **16** 742
patrons and collectors **31** 849
works **12** 258; **14** 171; **16** 745, *745*; **21** 16; **25** 21; **26** 486
Belli (ii), Vincenzo, I (1710-87) **3** 644*
Belli (ii), Vincenzo, II (*fl c.* 1820) **3** 644
Belliazzi, Raffaele **16** 707; **28** 317
Bellicard, Jérôme-Charles **2** 164; **3** 645–6*; **14** 445; **29** 94
Bellier, Catherine Henriette **19** 210
Bellier de La Chavignerie, Emile **2** 843; **10** 210
Bellière, Jean du Mas, Vicomte de La *see* LA BELLIÈRE, JEAN DU MAS, Vicomte de
Bellin (of Modena), Nicholas **3** 646*
collaboration **29** 833
patrons and collectors **31** 413
works **23** 198; **29** 835
Bellin, Samuel **3** 646*
Bellincioni, Bernardo **19** 182, 195
Belling, Rudolf **3** 646–7*, 802; **16** 591; **31** 454
collaboration **19** 773
exhibitions **12** 407
groups and movements **2** 288; **3** 801
pupils **12** 506
teachers **4** 762
works **3** 801; **12** 407
Bellinge **8** *720*
church **8** 730, 731, *731*
Bellingham, Daniel **3** 647*
Bellini (family) **16** 665; **23** 754; **32** 190, 191
works **32** 110
Bellini, Antonio **4** 635
Bellini, Carlos **31** 756
Bellini, Filippo **3** 670*
Bellini, Gentile **3** 647, 655–8*; **16** 254, 536, 660, 661, 662; **32** 225
attributions **8** 14; **21** 747; **31** 321
collaboration **3** 356, 653, 658; **26** 439
drawings **3** 651, 652
groups and movements **23** 503
methods **5** 657
paintings **16** 470; **23** 501; **32** 191
frescoes **16** 659
portraits **3** *657*, 876
religious **3** *656*; **32** 225
topographical views **31** 154, 703; **32** 212, 224
townscapes **8** 855; **32** 191, *225*
patrons and collectors **3** 201; **16** 659, 660; **23** 640; **27** 778
personal collection **3** 651
pulpits **32** 192
pupils **3** 301; **5** 818; **13** 834; **20** 300, 529; **27** 778; **31** 32
Bellini, Gian Antonio **12** 762
Bellini, Giovanni **3** 647, 651, 657–70*, 771; **4** 99; **16** 662, 665; **32** 190
assistants **18** 846; **20** 300, 398, 529; **27** 778; **32** 155
attributions **3** 657; **4** 336, 560; **14** 877; **28** 819
collaboration **3** 655, 656; **5** 818, 913; **8** 817; **18** 872; **32** 657
copies **20** 398; **22** 134
drawings **3** 651, 652, 653; **25** 557
groups and movements **26** 186, 187
methods **5** 657; **31** 578
paintings **32** 220
altarpieces **1** 711; **3** *663*; **11** 382, *382*, 383; **18** 872; **32** 190, 216, 217
landscape **18** 705, *705*; **32** 191
mythological **10** 443
portraits **3** *659*, *664*
religious **2** 3; **3** 657, *662*, *665*, *666*, 670; **9** 111; **11** 384; **24** 777; **31** 90; **32** 225, 226, 658
sacra conversazione **27** 495, *495*, 496
patrons and collectors **7** 775; **16** 769; **28** 271
Albarelli, Giovanni **5** 432
Alfonso I, 3rd Duke of Ferrara, Modena and Reggio (*reg* 1505-34) **10** 522; **11** 4; **14** 870; **29** 860
Bagatti Valsecchi family **3** 49

Bellini, Giovanni
patrons and collectors—cont.
Barbarigo, Agostino, Doge of Venice (*reg* 1486- 1501) 3 201
Bardini, Stefano 3 228
Barker, Alexander 3 241
Beckford, William (1760-1844) 3 477
Benson, R(obert) H(enry) 3 740
Bossi, Giuseppe 4 470
Buchanan, William 5 71
Burrell, William (1861-1958) 5 278; 28 273
Campbell, John, 1st Baron Cawdor (1755-1821) 5 541
Camuccini, Pietro 5 554
Caraman, Duc de 5 700
Catena, Vincenzo 6 86
Contarini, Taddeo 7 775; 12 675
Davenport Bromley, Walter 8 549
Eastlake, Charles Lock (1793-1865) 9 683
Frick, Henry Clay 9 200
Holloway, Thomas 14 688
Howard (ii), Frederick, 5th Earl of Carlisle 14 808
Hume, Abraham, 2nd Baronet 14 877
Isabella d'Este, Marchesa di Mantua (1474-1539) 2 558
Josephine, Empress of the French (1763-1814) 4 304
Leuchtenberg, Eugène de Beauharnais, Duc de 3 452
Leyland, F(rederick) R(ichard) 19 290
List, Herbert 19 478
Mond, Ludwig 21 849
Museu de Arte de São Paulo 4 726
Percy, Algernon, 4th Duke of Northumberland 10 367; 24 390
Pourtalès-Gorgier, James-Alexandre, Comte de 25 383
Reynolds, Joshua 26 279
Robien, Christophe-Paul Gautron, Marquis de 26 469
Solly, Edward 29 46
Tallard, Marie-Joseph d'Hostun, Duc de 30 274
Turner, Dawson 31 465
William II, King of the Netherlands (*reg* 1840-49) 23 469
personal collection 3 651
pupils
Belliniaro, Vittore 3 670
Carpaccio, Vittore 5 818
Cima da Conegliano, (Giovanni Battista) 7 320
Gambello, Vittore 12 31
Jacopo (di Paride Parisati) da Montagnana 16 836
Licinio, Bernardino 19 330
Montagna, Bartolomeo 21 904
Pennacchi, Pier Maria 24 363
Previtali, Andrea 25 570
Rondinelli, Niccolò 27 123
Sebastiano del Piombo 28 331
Titian 31 32
Vecellio, Francesco 32 106
reproductive prints by others 26 233
restorations by others 24 343; 27 321
workshop 3 655; 20 51
Bellini, Jacopo 3 647–55*; 11 3; 16 662; 32 189
assistants 3 658
attributions 9 244
collaboration 3 655, 658; 12 302
drawings 3 *651*; 9 220; 24 269; 25 557
metalpoints 3 *652*
methods 5 657
paintings
portraits 8 602
Bellini, Jacopo
paintings—cont.
religious 3 *650*, 655, 661; 32 224, 225
patrons and collectors 2 716; 3 655, 698; 10 519; 32 156
pupils 3 655, 670; 8 168
Bellini, Leonardo 3 647, 670*; 32 198
Bellini, Nicoletto 3 647
Belliniano, Vittore 3 667, 670*; 32 226
Bellini carpets *see under* CARPETS → types
Bellini de Pádua, João António *see* PÁDUA, JOÃO ANTÓNIO BELLINI DE
Bellinzona-Ravecchia, S Biagio 30 129
Bellio, Georges de 3 671*; 13 652; 24 883; 26 722
Bellis, Antonio de 3 671*
Bellis, Hubert 21 *499*
Belliu, Georges de *see* BELLIO, GEORGES DE
bell kraters *see under* KRATERS → types
Bellmann & Kober 20 253
Bellmer, Hans 3 672–3*; 11 568
dealers 7 842
exhibitions 7 842
groups and movements 24 144; 30 21
patrons and collectors 7 842
works 3 *672*; 10 482
bell metal *see* ALLOYS → types → speculum metal
Bello, Andrés 6 591
Bello, Arnulfo Domínguez *see* DOMÍNGUEZ BELLO, ARNULFO
Bello, José Luis 21 395
Bello, Marco 3 667
Bello, Nazario Quintana 9 741
Bello, Pedro 12 19
Bello, Robert de, Abbot of Canterbury *see* ROBERT DE BELLO, Abbot of Canterbury
Belloc, Jean-Hilaire 8 572; 11 563
Belloc, M.
works 19 *368*
Bellocq, Adolfo 2 399
Bellocq, E(rnest) J(ames) 3 673*; 11 777
Bellona 25 181, 182
Belloni 32 917
Belloni, Giorgio 21 896
Belloni, José 31 755
Belloni, Pietro 11 39; 19 64
Bellori, Giovanni Pietro 1 103, 659; 2 42–3, 162; 3 673–4*; 6 568; 9 92; 11 674; 32 8
interior decoration 1 728
patrons and collectors 14 651
personal collection 9 230; 13 541, 605; 26 245
works 3 *674*; 9 120; 16 781
illustrated 7 466
on antiquity 2 163, 170
on artists 6 78; 10 204
on beauty 1 179
on caricatures 5 760
on decorum 8 612
on degenerate art 10 413
on naturalism 22 686
on painting 13 296; 15 89; 16 672; 31 299
on sculpture 31 302
Bellosio, Carlo 10 644; 12 902; 16 720
Bellosio, Eugenio 3 675*
Bellot, Paul 3 675*
Bellotti, Józef Szymon 32 875
Bellotti, Pietro 8 427
Bellotto, Bernardo (Michiel) 3 675–9*; 16 676, 677; 31 155; 32 194, 195, 876
collaboration 5 600
copies 1 598
groups and movements 9 239
Bellotto, Bernardo (Michiel)—cont.
paintings 9 238; 31 248; 32 459
landscape 32 461, *461*
topographical views 31 155
townscapes 3 *677*, *679*; 25 105, 140; 31 704; 32 436, *436*
vedute 2 342; 10 *530*; 14 530; 32 112
patrons and collectors 7 437; 19 338; 25 212, 213; 28 18, 173; 31 445; 33 115
pupils 18 121
Bellotto, Lorenzo 3 678
Bellotto, Umberto 16 744
Bellovaci *see* BEAUVAIS
bellows (cameras) 11 361
bellows (furnaces) 1 287, 365; 9 817; 11 118, 119
Bellows, George (*fl* 1880s) 3 679
Bellows, George (Wesley) (1882-1925) 3 679–81*
collaboration 20 604
groups and movements 1 773; 2 597
methods 8 128
patrons and collectors 20 142; 33 151
pupils 3 31; 20 287; 29 382
teachers 21 606
works 3 *680*; 12 296; 15 828; 19 492; 29 426; 31 705
Bellpuig 13 150
Chapelle de la Trinité 26 641
Bell Rock Lighthouse 19 361
bells 3 625–8*; 22 372, 375, 376
historical and regional traditions
Ancient Near East 1 891
Benin, Kingdom of 3 627
Buddhism 7 98; 17 *322*, 397; 18 347–8
Burma 5 253*
China 3 626, *626*; 6 829, 834, 841, *846*, 849*, 855; 7 98, 100; 28 *626*
England 3 *627*
Japan 3 626; 17 100, 104, 321, *322*, 397; 27 599, 600
Java 22 376
Korea 3 626; 18 346, 347–8
Kuba (iii) (Zaïre) 1 360
Mesoamerica, Pre-Columbian 21 254, 256
Mexico 21 254
Niger 1 360
Ottonian 23 658
Poland 16 867
Romanesque 26 686*
Tibet 30 843
Vietnam 32 489
Zaïre 1 360
Zande 1 360
materials
bronze 3 627; 4 855
China 3 *626*; 6 829, 834, 841, *846*, 849*, 855; 28 *626*
Japan 17 100, *319*, 319–20, *322*, 397
Korea 18 346, 347–8
Ottonian 23 658
Romanesque 26 686*
cast iron 7 98
copper 21 256
glass 3 628
iron 3 627
porcelain 3 627
pottery 21 256
silver 3 627, *627*
types
dōtaku 17 30, *319*, 319–20
uses
clocks 7 438
Bell-Smith, Frederic Martlett 5 565; 32 414
Bell-Smith, John 22 38
bell-towers *see under* TOWERS → types
Bellucci, Antonio 2 795; 3 681*
patrons and collectors 5 65; 7 779; 33 280
pupils 1 784; 3 108
Bellucci, Elego *see* BELYUTIN, ELY (MIKHAILOVICH)
Bellucci, Giovan *see* BELLUZI, GIOVANNI BATTISTA
Bellucci, Giuseppe 5 310
Belluco 27 720
Belluno 32 *158*
Palazzo del Consiglio dei Nobili 1 750; 16 836
Palazzo Piloni 32 107
Palazzo dei Rettori 32 159
Belluš, Emil 3 682*; 28 850
Belluschi, Pietro 1 736; 3 682*; 14 200; 17 549; 31 596
Belluzzi, Giovanni Battista 3 682–3*; 21 579
Bellver, Francisco 3 683
Bellver, Joan Rubió i *see* RUBIÓ I BELLVER, JOAN
Bellver y Ramón, Ricardo 3 683–4*; 29 295
Bellville, University of the Western Cape
Mayibuye Centre for History and Culture in South Africa 29 122
Bell Works 26 362
Belly, Léon (-Adolphe-Auguste) 3 684*; 23 504
Belly, Vincenzo 12 4
belly amphorae *see under* AMPHORAE → types
belly-handled amphorae *see under* AMPHORAE → types
Bélmez, Juan 31 427
Belmont, Oliver, H. P. 15 22
Belmonte, Collegiate Church 13 123; 22 255
Belmonte, Léo 12 839; 21 4; 22 433
Belmopan 3 *622*, 623
Museum of Belize 3 624
Belmore, Armar Lowry-Corry, 1st Earl of *see* LOWRY-CORRY, ARMAR, 1st Earl of Belmore
Belmore, Armar Lowry-Corry, 2nd Earl of *see* LOWRY-CORRY, ARMAR, 2nd Earl of Belmore
Belo, Antônio Rodriques *see* RODRIQUES BELO, ANTÔNIO
Beloeil Château 2 125
Belogrud, Andrey (Yevgen'yevich) 3 684–5*; 11 245; 27 378; 31 371
Belo Horizonte 4 *705*, 722
Museu de Arte Moderna 4 727
St Francis Pampulha 7 696; 23 *118*
Belon, Pierre 10 78
Belopol'sky, Yakov (Borisovich) 3 685*
collaboration 32 685
works 27 381; 32 *685*, 737
Belorussia *see* BELARUS'
Belosel'sky, A. M. 27 438, 439
Belosel'sky-Belozersky (family) 28 642
Belov, Viktor 23 392
Belovo *see* ZEMEN
Belpaire (family) 14 838
Bel Pensiero *see* GIUSTINIANI (ii), NICOLA
Belper Mill (Derbys) 10 748; 16 52; 28 831
Belrespiro, Villa *see* ROME → villas → Villa Doria-Pamphili
Belsk 28 321
Bel'sky, Aleksey 24 546
Belsky, Franta 22 49
Bel'sky, Ivan 24 546
Belter, John Henry 3 685*; 31 630
works 6 391; 31 620, *620*, 629, *630*; 33 331
belthooks 3 685–6*, *686*; 6 832, 855, 859; 7 7, 74, 81, 88, 97, *98*, 107
bronze 3 685; 6 855, 859; 7 107
glass 7 81, 107
gold 7 *98*, 107
iron 7 97, *98*
jade 3 *686*; 7 7, 107
malachite 7 107
rock crystal 7 107
silver 7 *98*, 107
turquoise 7 88, 107
see also CLASPS
Belting, Hans 15 91
Belton House (Lincs) 10 274; 29 835
gems 20 389
paintings 14 877; 26 394; 30 892
silver 14 382
Beltramelli, Domenico 29 831
Beltrami, Giovanni 3 687*; 12 264
Beltrami, Luca 3 687–8*
assistants 21 139
collaboration 22 105
pupils 4 746
teachers 4 247
works 16 647; 20 321; 21 521
Beltrán, Alberto 3 688*; 21 388; 30 275
Beltrán, Alonso 24 501
Beltrán, Diego 32 116
Beltrano, Agostino 3 688*; 29 544
belts 14 418; 17 521
historical and regional traditions
Byzantine 9 653
Central Asia, Western 6 244*, 251, 252, 274
China 7 74, 76, 108, 109, 110, 111, 124
Early Christian (*c*. AD 250-843) 9 653
Egypt 16 530
Egypt, ancient 10 29
Iran 16 463
Islamic 16 462, 463, 530
Laos 18 *776*
Lengyel culture 25 517
Native North Americans 3 441; 22 *651*, 652, 653
North Africa 16 530
Ottoman 16 462
Prehistoric art 25 517; 28 806
Russia 32 528
Syria 9 653; 16 530
Turkey 16 462
Viking 32 528
materials
bronze 7 108, 109
feathers 22 652, 653
glass 7 109, 111
gold 7 109, 110, 111
horn 7 109, 124
ivory 16 799
jade 7 109, 111
metal 6 244
quills 22 *651*
shells 25 517
silver 7 108, 109, 111; 18 *776*
wampum 3 441
Belur 3 688–9*; 15 *294*
Chennakeshava Temple 15 327, 328, 533
reliefs 15 227
sculpture 15 517
temples 15 532
Virupaksa temple 14 186
Belus Na'aman 16 519
Belvedere (Kent) 12 601
Belvedere (periodical) 24 438, 484
Belvedere, Andrea 3 690*; 22 479
Belvedere di Cetona 25 523
belvederes 3 *689*, 689–90*; 12 222; 16 266
see also GAZEBOS; PAVILIONS (BUILDINGS)
Belvedere Torso 2 168, 559; 3 690*; 7 621; 13 303, 470; 26 767; 32 613
Belverte, Pietro 20 418

Belvoir Castle (Israel) 3 691, 691–2*; 17 504; 18 151, 152; 21 564
Belvoir Castle (Leics; UK) 4 600
dairy 8 461
Elizabeth Saloon 10 280; 33 447
paintings 10 146; 25 385, 388, 412
Belwa 15 453
Belwood, William 26 475; 33 20
Bely, Andrey 3 692*; 12 870
Belyakova, Nina (Yefimovna) 27 423
Belyunes 16 218
Belyutin, Ely (Mikhailovich) 3 692–3*
Belz, Walter 29 874
Belzer, Zacharias see PELTZER, ZACHARIAS
Belzile, Louis 5 568; 25 28
Belzoni, Giovanni Battista 3 721; 10 86, 90, 92, 94, 97; 14 863
Belzons, Jean 29 918
Bém, Rudolf 31 792
Beman, Solon S(pencer) 3 693*; 5 274
collaboration 4 475
works 6 573; 25 723
bemas see AMBOS; BIMAHS
Bemba 1 256–7, 261, 262, 289, 403, 409
Bembe 3 693–4*; 19 72, 74*
masks 1 256, 405; 19 74
megaphones 1 360
portraits 1 269
sculpture 1 403, 404, 418; 3 693–4, 694
wood 3 694
Bembel', Andrei 3 531; 21 697
Bembo (family) 8 135
Bembo see under TYPE-FACES
Bembo, Ambrosio 3 694, 695
Bembo, Andrea 3 694; 4 747
Bembo, Benedetto 3 694, 696–7*; 9 112
works 3 697
Bembo, Bernardo 27 806
Bembo, Bonifacio 3 694, 695–6*
attributions 33 626
collaboration 5 127; 11 293
patrons and collectors 9 112; 28 530, 531
works 3 696; 21 525
Bembo, Giovan Francesco 3 694, 697–8*; 4 195; 21 94
Bembo, Giovanni 3 694
Bembo, Lodovico 3 695
Bembo, Pietro, Cardinal 3 698*; 14 582, 869, 870; 20 350
collections 16 767; 22 696
medals 6 140
paintings 3 648, 649; 12 676; 16 835
personal collection 5 534
sculpture 3 698; 15 101
works 14 868; 20 350; 31 494
Bembridge, Ruskin Galleries 27 354
Bement, Alon 23 387
Bemer, Andreas 19 835
works 19 836
Bemler, Hans see BÄMLER, JOHANNES
Bemme, Johannes A. 18 739
Bemmel, Georg Christoph Gottfried von 18 115
Bemmel, Jan (Gerritsz.) van 27 518
Bemmel, Willem van 10 464; 12 390; 27 518
Ben 3 698–9*; 11 553
groups and movements 11 232
patrons and collectors 29 16, 420
works 24 407
Bena 1 381
Benabarre, Pedro García de see GARCÍA DE BENABARRE, PEDRO
Benaglio, Bernardino 32 199
Benaglio, Francesco 3 699*
Benaki, Anthony 3 699*; 10 90; 13 359, 360
Benalcázar, Sebastián de 9 708; 25 828
Benalio, Bernardino 3 699*; 5 843; 13 338; 33 356
Benamati, Stefano 20 385
Benameji (family) 9 699
Benanteur, Abdullah 1 635
Bénard 26 6
Bénard, Adrien 6 489
Bénard, Charles Joachim 20 472
Bénard, Henri-Jean-Emile 21 403
Benard, J. F. 12 119
Bénard, Philibert 23 508
Benares see VARANASI
Benasar Moner, Gaspar 23 881
Benavente, Condes de 29 353
Benavente, 8th Conde de (1575-1621) 3 700*
Benavente, 10th Conde de (1584-1653) 5 712
Benavente, Condesa de 32 566
Benavente, Alvaro de 17 692
Benavente, Juan de 29 334
Benavente, María Josefa, Condesa de see OSUNA, 9th Duquesa de
Benavente, Toribio de 25 696
Benavides, Julián González de see GONZÁLEZ DE BENAVIDES, JULIÁN
Benavides, Marco Mantova 3 700*; 5 535; 30 33
Benavides, Vicente 26 438
Benayoun, Robert 30 23
Benazech, Peter-Paul 13 220
Ben Bella, Mahjoub 1 636
Benbridge, Henry 3 700–701*; 28 882; 33 92
Bencharong ware see under POTTERY → wares
bench-ends 24 576, 577, 577
benches 24 575
historical and regional traditions
Belgium 3 581
Philippines 24 629, 630
Scandinavia 32 519
Spain 29 310, 310
Sweden 32 519
Viking 32 519
materials
pine 29 310
wood 24 630
types
syntroni 30 174*
wangenbankje see wing
wing 3 581
Benci (family) 19 443
Benci di Cione 11 203; 28 680
Bencivenni, Antonio (da Mercatello) 3 701*; 16 724
Bencivenni, Sebastiano 3 701
Bencivenni Pelli, Giuseppe 3 701*; 16 772
Benciviene di Pepo see CIMABUE
Benckert, Hermann 23 313
Benckgraff, Johann Kilian 11 851; 12 433; 14 606
Bencomo, Mario Díaz see DÍAZ BENCOMO, MARIO
Bencovich, Federico 3 702*; 8 178
pupils 5 877; 31 356
teachers 7 309
Benczúr, Gyula 3 702–3*; 5 85; 14 588, 901; 15 18; 20 875
pupils 1 611; 10 888; 17 736; 18 387
teachers 18 128
works 3 703; 14 580
Benda, Gustav 2 830; 3 703*
Benda, Julius 9 686–7*
Benda & Hipauf 31 262
Ben Day dots 3 703*
Benday prints see BEN DAY DOTS
Bende 15 111
Bendel, Ehregott Bernhard see BENDL, EHREGOTT BERNHARD
Bendelmeyer 8 401
Bendemann, Eduard (Julius Friedrich) 3 703*
collaboration 14 838
groups and movements 9 239; 12 394
teachers 14 838
works 17 575; 22 329
Bender, Albert 1 143
Bender, Ralf 16 889
Bendery 21 810
castle 21 810
monument to P. Tkachenko 21 812
Bendidio, Battista 8 14
Bendien, Jacob 3 704*; 21 775, 855; 22 852
Bendigo 2 736
court-house 18 888
gold 2 764
Town Hall 4 374
Bendigo Pottery 2 760
Bendixen, Siegfried 13 859; 22 112; 29 376
Bendl, Ehregott Bernhard 3 704–5*; 12 447
Bendl, Georg see BENDL, JIŘÍ
Bendl, Ignác 3 704*
Bendl, Jan Jiří 3 704*
works 8 384; 25 432; 28 855
Bendl, Jiří 3 704; 27 285
Bendl, Johann Christian 3 704
Bendl, Johann Georg see BENDL, JAN JIŘÍ
Bendones, S María 2 653
Bendorp, Johann Christiaan 18 739
Bendz, Wilhelm (Ferdinand) 3 705*
works 3 705
Bene, del (family) 11 221
Benech, Enrique 31 754
Benedetta see CAPPA, BENEDETTA
Benedetti, Cristoforo 15 864
Benedetti, Elpidio 3 706*; 4 765, 766; 11 662; 24 828
Benedetti, Giovanni Battista 3 706*; 24 489
Benedetti, Michele 6 92
Benedetto 2 31
Benedetto, Giachetto di see GIACHETTO DI BENEDETTO
Benedetto Aquilio, Antonio di see ANTONIAZZO ROMANO
Benedetto da Como, Giovanni di see GIOVANNI DI BENEDETTO DA COMO
Benedetto da Rovezzano 3 706*; 31 191
collaboration 3 742; 20 116; 22 166; 27 546; 32 603
patrons and collectors 4 404; 24 1; 27 831; 28 928
works 3 16; 10 260; 19 600; 20 116; 27 770
Benedetto di Bindo 3 707*
Benedetto di Domenico d'Andrea 22 800
Benedetto di Leonardo see MAIANO, BENEDETTO DA
Benedetto Padovano see BORDON, BENEDETTO
Benedict, Canon 26 755
Benedict, Master 25 96
Benedict III, Pope (reg 855-58) 9 657; 26 833
Benedict IX, Pope (reg 900-903) 7 676
Benedict XI, Pope (reg 1303-05) 7 50
Benedict XII, Pope (reg 1334-42) 3 707*
architecture 2 859, 861
paintings 2 863; 12 697
Benedict XIII, Pope (reg 1394-1423) 23 576–7*
architecture 2 862; 25 852–3, 854
collections 23 576
paintings 5 906; 12 534; 20 842
Benedict XIV, Pope (reg 1740-58) 3 707–8*
architecture 11 815; 13 626; 25 144; 26 761, 832, 840
catalogues 32 237
collections 16 768; 26 775
education (art) 26 842
gems 8 13
paintings 3 380; 8 145; 12 23; 13 330; 20 806; 24 833; 27 486; 29 888, 889
sculpture 31 826; 32 374
Benedict Biscop 2 68; 3 708*; 10 243; 15 871
architecture 3 708; 9 13; 21 835, 844
glass 10 315
paintings 2 72; 31 499
stained glass 2 83
Benedictine Order 3 708–11*; 4 715, 724; 7 230, 232
architecture 7 453; 21 835–6*, 844
Brazil 4 709, 728
England 3 708; 21 836, 839, 840
France 3 708; 4 869; 17 685; 21 836
Germany 3 709
Italy 21 898
iconography 3 709–11*
manuscripts 3 709, 710
painting 3 711; 28 702
patronage 3 709–11*; 7 218; 10 359; 16 762
pottery 28 256
sculpture 28 861
see also CISTERCIAN ORDER; CLUNIAC ORDER
Benedictionals 28 487
individual manuscripts
Benedictional of Archbishop Robert (Rouen, Bib. Mun., MS. Y.7) 2 75; 33 232
Benedictional of St Aethelwold (London, BL, Add. MS. 49598) 1 110, 111, 183; 2 73, 75, 75; 10 243; 20 330; 23 537; 28 487; 33 8, 232
Ramsey Benedictional (Paris, Bib. N., MS. lat. 987) 2 75; 33 232
Benedict of Aniane, Saint 5 794; 7 231; 12 363; 21 835
Benedict of Nursia, Saint 3 708; 7 230; 19 312; 21 833; 22 9
Benedictus, Edouard 5 841; 7 434
Benedikt 3 711*; 18 425; 25 111
patrons and collectors 16 867
works 18 431; 27 722
Benediktbeuern Abbey 2 579; 12 382; 33 681
Benedit, Luis 2 401; 3 485, 712*; 13 725
Bénédite, Georges 12 226
Bénédite, Léonce 1 634; 3 156, 712*; 20 834
Benedito, Manuel 4 127
Benefial, Marco 3 712–14*; 16 672; 26 774
assistants 24 366
collaboration 2 27
methods 21 766
pupils 3 15; 14 133; 18 420; 21 131; 26 263; 27 200
teachers 18 674
works 3 713
Beneman, Guillaume 3 714–15*; 11 597, 627; 29 683
collaboration 26 39
patrons and collectors 11 595
works 7 658; 11 593
Ben'en Enni see ENNI BEN'EN
Beneš, Vincenc 3 715*
groups and movements 8 249; 10 107; 13 711; 20 103
Benes, W. Dominick 7 429; 22 365
works 7 429
Benesch, Heinrich 3 715; 28 89
Benesch, Otto 3 715*; 28 89
Benešov 8 398
Benetton, Antonio 16 60
Benevagienna see AUGUSTA BAGIENNORUM
Benevente, Adelma 24 518
Benevento 3 715–17*; 16 621; 26 886
Arch of Trajan 3 715; 10 742; 26 791, 868, 896, 897; 27 45; 31 349
reliefs 27 35
Cathedral 9 154; 13 98
obelisk 23 330
sculpture 13 470; 27 28
S Sofia 3 716; 7 256; 16 625; 26 625
cloister 3 716; 7 455
wall paintings 16 654
Benevento, Arichis II, Duke of see ARICHIS II, Duke of Benevento
Benevento, Oderisius of see ODERISIUS OF BENEVENTO
Benevento, Perrinetto da see PERRINETTO DA BENEVENTO
Beneventum see BENEVENTO
Benevenuti, Benvenuto 28 319
Benevivere 5 882
Bénézit, Emmanuel 10 212
Benfica, S Domingos 25 301
Bengalis 3 165
Bengal School 5 420
Bengen, Harold 4 732
Benghazi, Garyounis University 8 248; 19 324
Bengkulu, Fort Marlborough 21 596
Benglis, Lynda 3 717*; 10 879
Beng Mealea 5 473, 474
gallery 5 474
gopura 5 474
lintels 5 475
reliefs 5 492
sculpture 5 493
Bengoechea, Zenón Somodevilla y see ENSENADA, Marqués de
Bengough, J. W. 5 566
Bengston, Billy Al 19 702; 25 232; 31 609
Bengtson, Hertha 30 99, 101
Bengtsson, Dick 30 82
Benguela 1 401
Cathedral 2 86
Nossa Senhora do Pópulo 2 86
Benguiat, Hadji Ephraim 17 581
Bengutas, Sabiha 31 454
Benhaud, Jean de see JEAN DE BENHAUD
Benia 29 615
Bénian see ALA MILIARA
Benicampi, Corintio 20 374
benie see under PRINTS → types → ukiyoe
Benig see BENING
Benigno 25 383
Beni-Gómez (family) 13 104
Beni Hasan 3 717–18*; 9 773, 774, 822
arches 2 295
drums (musical instruments) 10 64
paintings
tomb 31 703
wall 1 885; 9 808, 811, 844, 845
Speos Artemidos 9 833; 29 386
tombs 9 779, 824, 837, 838, 900
Ammenemes (BH 2) 9 820, 822, 823, 838, 900; 11 231
Bakht III (Tomb 15) 9 823
Kheti (Tomb 17) 9 823, 824
Khnumhotpe II (Tomb 13) 10 65
Khnumhotpe III (Tomb 3) 9 820, 821, 823, 900; 10 75; 23 532
Beni Mguild 16 486
Beni M'tir 16 486

Benin, Kingdom of 1 222, 436; 3 718–24*
altarpieces 3 *721*
altars 3 721, *721*
armlets 1 292, *293*
beads 1 297, 354
beadwork 3 441
bells 3 627
brass 1 250, 288; 3 *720*, *721*, 723, *723*, *724*; 6 9
bronze 6 9
casts 6 9
ceramics 1 329
copper 3 *722*
coral 1 297, 354; 3 721
craftsmen and artists 1 245; 3 722
dress 3 441
footwear 1 349
funerary objects 1 258
guilds 1 242; 3 722
historiography 3 723–4*
horns 1 328
ivory 1 *219*, 292, 293, *293*, 326, *327*, 327–8, 352; 3 *722*, 723
ivory-carvings 1 *293*; 3 719
masks 3 *722*
metalwork 23 131–2
mirrors 1 *219*
palaces 1 284
patronage 1 242; 3 721–2*
plaques 3 *720*, 722
portraits 1 268, 270, 354
pots 1 329
regalia 1 352, 354
salts 1 327, *327*
sculpture 1 *219*, 278, 280, 322, 329; 3 *723*, *724*
shrines (i) (cult) 1 289
spoons 1 328
swords 1 354, 361
trade 3 719
see also EDO (AFRICA); NIGERIA
Beninc *see* BENING
Benincasa, Bartolomeo, Conte 9 426
Benincasa, Lupardo de *see* LUPARDO DE BENINCASA
Benincasa, Manno di *see* MANNO DI BENINCASA
Benin City 1 *381*; 3 718–19, *719*; 23 *129*
furniture 33 III2
houses 1 305
ivory 1 *293*
jewellery 1 350
metalwork 4 855
National Museum 23 139
painting 23 136
palace 1 308, 314; 3 719
regalia 1 350
sculpture 4 854
tourist art 1 239
Bening, Alexander *see* BENING, SANDERS
Bening, Alexandrine 3 725
Bening, Levina *see* TEERLINC, LEVINA
Bening, Sanders 3 724, 725*; 12 519; 20 727, 737
collaboration 3 555
groups and movements 12 525
patrons and collectors 2 871
pupils 14 658
works 13 661
Bening, Simon 3 724–7*, *726*; 4 921
attributions 20 692
collaboration 3 555; 14 658
groups and movements 12 524
patrons and collectors 2 874; 3 612; 14 649
works 3 *727*; 13 24, 661; 14 659; 21 639; 27 159; 28 234
Beningborough Hall (N. Yorks) 10 276; 11 426; 14 500
Benini, Lorenzo 2 103
Benin Republic 1 *214*, 386; 3 727–9*; 5 753
altars 3 728
Benin Republic—cont.
architecture 1 261; 3 728*
body arts 1 288
collections 3 728–9*
fans 10 778, 779
figurines 1 271–2, *272*
houses 1 311, 312
iconography 1 282, 284
iron 3 728; 11 *246*
masks 1 *337*; 3 728
Musée d'Histoire de Ouidah 3 728
painting 3 *729*
patronage 3 728–9*
portraits 1 267
sculpture 11 *246*
textiles 1 349
wood 1 *272*
Benintendi, Cristoforo *see* CRISTOFORO DI JACOPO BIONDI DA BOLOGNA
Benintendi, Giovan Maria 3 13, 15; 27 849
Benintendi, Puccio di *see* PUCCIO DI BENINTENDI
Benintendo di Puccio 25 690
Benisti, Mirelle 15 211
Benitani, Kichinosuke 22 445
Benítez, Carlos de Beisteguy y *see* BEISTEGUY Y BENÍTEZ, CARLOS DE
Benítez, Francisco 9 712
Benítez, Isaac Leonardo 3 729*; 23 905
Benito, Eduardo Garcia *see* GARCIA BENITO, EDUARDO
Benivieni, Lippo di *see* LIPPO DI BENIVIENI
Benizi, Filippo *see* FILIPPO BENIZI, Saint
benizurie see under PRINTS → types → *ukiyoe*
Benjamin 19 623
Benjamin, Asher 3 729–30*; 10 850
collaboration 31 231
illustrated writings 24 275
staff 33 195
works 4 472; 14 786; 23 25; 31 591
Benjamin, Dionne 3 62
Benjamin, Karl 19 702
Benjamin, Samuel G(reen) W(heeler) 3 730*
Benjamin, Walter 1 183; 3 731*; 26 235; 28 917
works 20 527; 21 778; 28 926
Benjamin-Constant *see* CONSTANT, (JEAN-JOSEPH-) BENJAMIN
Benji Asada *see* ASADA, BENJI
Benjumeda, Tocuato José de 31 808
Benk, Johannes 3 731–2*
Benka, Martin 28 853
Benkai Museum *see under* ATHENS → museums
Benkeigaana Tomb 17 142, 143
Benkert, Johann Peter 12 405; 32 675
Benkhard, Agost 14 891
Benkó, István *see* MEDGYASZAY, ISTVÁN
Ben'kov, Pavel (Petrovich) 31 783
Benlafaremo, Bassiano 32 421
Benlliure, Mariano 1 529; 21 81; 31 816
Benlowe, Edward 3 244; 4 360
Benn, Ernest 13 811
Benna 2 73
Benneman, Guillaume *see* BENEMAN, GUILLAUME
Benner, Gerrit 3 732*; 22 852
Bennet, Dorothy 1 66
Bennet, Edward 31 727
Bennet, Henry, 1st Earl of Arlington 32 358
Bennett 11 139
Bennett, Albert A. 9 685
Bennett, Anna 31 661
Bennett, Dorothy 21 733
Bennett, Edward H. 5 275; 6 574; 7 357; 10 684; 32 887
works 31 *727*
Bennett, Gary Knox 31 634
Bennett, John (*fl* 1840-60) 28 772
Bennett, John (*fl* 1876-82) 30 887
Bennett, Paul 16 888
Bennett, Richard 22 111
Bennett, Wendell C. 6 523; 12 27
Bennett Steamship Co. 10 239
Bennewitz, Diederik Lodewijk 1 811; 22 891
Benney, Gerald 8 202; 10 337; 17 580
works 8 *202*
Bennier, Peter *see* BESNIER, PETER
Benninck, Carel 3 600
Benninck, Levina *see* TERRLINC, LEVINA
Benning (family) 25 129
Benningen 21 559
Benninghausen, St Martin 23 648; 26 646
Bennington (VT)
ceramics 31 *636*
Benno 3 732*; 12 471
Bennvik 11 105
Beno de Rapiza 26 656, 825
Benois, Albert 3 732
Benois, Alexandre 3 732, 734–5*; 27 392, 394, 441; 30 265
groups and movements 3 86, 119; 8 849; 12 870; 27 444, 580; 31 582; 33 379
patrons and collectors 22 135; 27 459
productions 8 849, 850; 30 681, 686; 33 608
sponsors 30 464
works 27 444
Benois, François 14 145
Benois, Leonty (Nikolayevich) 3 732, 733–4*; 27 580; 31 782
collaboration 24 400
pupils 3 684; 12 243; 15 132; 18 750; 19 332; 25 89; 27 313; 28 570, 571; 32 71
works 8 531
Benois, Louis 32 773
Benois, Nikolay (Leont'yevich) 3 732–3*; 17 859; 18 749; 27 377
collaboration 33 516
pupils 5 333
works 27 578
Benoist, Antoine (1632-1717) 3 735*; 13 228; 33 3
Benoist, Antoine (1721-70) 14 520
Benoist, Marie-Guillemine 3 735*
Benoist, Michel 6 41
Benoit 11 338
Benoît, Fernand 27 142
Benoit, Jean 7 842; 30 23
Benoit, Pierre (*fl c.* 1820s) 2 395
works 2 *395*
Benoît, Pierre (1886-1962) 1 646
Benoit, Pierre-Jacques 30 15
Benoit, Rigaud 3 735–6*; 14 58
works 14 *59*
Benoît de Montferrand 29 398
Benoît de Sainte-Maure 7 242; 22 412; 26 563
Benoît de Sainte-Paulle, F. 19 161
Benoît-Lévy, Georges 12 145; 31 728
Benood, William 10 351; 19 596; 22 154
Benouville, Jean-Achille 3 736*
Benouville, (François) Léon 3 736*; 19 153
Benouville Château 6 509
Benozzo di Lese *see* GOZZOLI, BENOZZO
Benrath 12 413
Benš, Adolf 3 736*; 25 430
Bens, José María 8 232
Bensberg Schloss 3 681; 24 341
Rathaus 12 380, *380*; 31 243
Benso, Giulio 3 736–7*
collaboration 5 770
pupils 21 145; 29 75
teachers 23 772
works 2 127; 3 *737*
Benson 7 652
Benson, Ambrosius 3 554, 738–40*; 4 921
attributions 7 865
collaboration 8 552, 553
works 3 *739*; 11 441; 20 667; 28 369
Benson, Eugene 10 641
Benson, Evelyn 3 740
Benson, Frank W(eston) 3 740*; 4 478
groups and movements 30 452
works 27 613
Benson, Jan 3 738
Benson, John Howard 28 307
Benson, Mary 3 737–8*; 22 660
Benson, Rex 14 511
Benson, R(obert) H(enry) 3 740*; 9 467
Benson, Robert, 1st Baron Bingley 33 340
Benson, W(illiam) A(rthur) S(mith) 3 741*; 19 594
groups and movements 2 570; 30 1
patrons and collectors 4 71
works 10 335, *343*, 344; 20 445
Benson, Willem (1521/2–74) 3 738
Benson, William (*fl* 1718) 5 539
Benson, William (1862-1937; basket-weaver) 3 737–8*; 22 660
Benson & Forsyth 28 273
Benson Master *see* BENSON, AMBROSIUS
Benson Tondo 11 388
Bensusan, Esther 4 366; 24 885
Bent *see* SCHILDERSBENT
Bent, James Theodore 13 334
Bent, J. S. 18 147
Bent, Julia T. 2 160; 8 324
Bentham, James 3 741*
Bentham, Jeremy 2 657; 11 334; 25 276, 636
Bentham, Samuel 25 636
Bentheim, Lüder von 3 741*; 4 743; 18 7; 22 823
Benti, Donato (di Battista di Matteo) 3 742*; 27 546; 29 496; 32 603
Bentinck, Henry, 1st Duke of Portland 21 348; 26 321
Bentinck, Margaret, 2nd Duchess of Portland 6 118*; 19 165
gardens 10 101
glass 5 337; 14 114
paintings 3 310
Bentivoglio (family)
architecture 1 601; 4 279
ceramics 4 278
coats of arms 32 *201*
glass 32 201, *201*
paintings 2 607; 11 700
Bentivoglio, Alessandro 19 784
Bentivoglio, Annibale 3 745; 31 432
Bentivoglio, Anton Galeazzo 11 700
Bentivoglio, Cornelio I, Marchese di Gualtieri *see* GUALTIERI, CORNELIO I BENTIVOGLIO, Marchese di
Bentivoglio, Cornelio II, Marchese di Gualtieri *see* GUALTIERI, CORNELIO II BENTIVOGLIO, Marchese di
Bentivoglio, Enzo, Marchese di Gualtieri *see* GUALTIERI, ENZO BENTIVOGLIO, Marchese di
Bentivoglio, G.
works 3 *208*
Bentivoglio, Ginevra Sforza *see* SFORZA, GINEVRA
Bentivoglio, Giovanni II, Lord of Bologna 3 743–4*
paintings 4 276; 8 3
paxes 11 699
Bentivoglio, Girolamo 15 60
Bentivoglio, Guido, Cardinal 3 743, 744–5*
paintings 11 845; 22 487
Bentivoglio, Ippolita Sforza *see* SFORZA, IPPOLITA
Bentivoglio, Ippolito, I 3 744
Bentivoglio, Maddalena 15 60
Bentivoglio, Sante, Lord of Bologna 3 743*
Bentley, Charles 3 745*; 11 60; 13 876
Bentley, John Francis 3 745–7*
groups and movements 5 340; 9 739
teachers 7 479
works 3 *746*; 4 788; 7 304; 17 877
Bentley, Richard 4 361; 7 290; 13 199; 32 825
reproductive prints by others 4 *362*
works 32 *826*
Bentley, Thomas 10 642; 33 20, 21
works 33 *21*
Bentley Wood (E. Sussex) 6 *551*
Bentmann, R. 28 917
bentō boxes *see under* BOXES → types
Bento da Ascensão 30 799
Benton, Fletcher 18 63
Benton, Linn Boyd 31 496
Benton, Park, Candreva 28 671
Benton, Thomas Hart 3 747–8*; 17 800; 31 606, 702
collaboration 20 604
groups and movements 1 773; 26 90; 30 173
patrons and collectors 25 629
pupils 25 165, 263
works 3 *748*; 12 296; 15 828; 19 492; 22 335; 23 48; 28 920
Bent Pyramid *see under* DAHSHUR → pyramids
Bentsen, Andreas 3 749
Bentsen, Ivar 3 749*; 17 480; 29 77
collaboration 3 410; 18 136; 23 116; 24 549; 29 77
Bentsoen, Ambrosius *see* BENSON, AMBROSIUS
Bentum, Christian Philipp 19 748
Bentveld, Theodorus Gerardus 22 891
bentwood 15 *822*; 18 192; 30 753, *755*
Benty Grange (Derbys) 14 412
Benty Grange Helmet 10 338
Bentz, Georg *see* PENCZ, GEORG
Bentzen, Edvard Harald 17 482
Bentzon, Martha Drachmann 8 762
Benua, Leontiy (Nikolayevich) *see* BENOIS, LEONTY (NIKOLAYEVICH)
Ben Uri Art Society 17 578
Benvegnudo, Pietro di 20 546
Benvenuti, Giovanni Battista *see* ORTOLANO
Benvenuti, Giuseppe 16 729
Benvenuti, Matteo 11 194
Benvenuti, Niccola 7 344
Benvenuti, Pietro 3 749–50*; 14 586; 16 677
assistants 30 418
collaboration 5 363
patrons and collectors 4 300, 305
pupils 3 903; 5 444; 7 344; 8 19; 22 383; 31 763; 33 42
works 11 189
Benvenuti, Pietro de *see* PIETRO DE BENVENUTI

Benvenuti da Bologna, Simone di Filippo see SIMONE DEI CROCEFISSI
Benvenuti dagli Ordini, Pietro 27 189
Benvenuti Situla 10 528; 28 807
Benvenuto, Girolamo di see GIROLAMO DI BENVENUTO
Benvenuto da Imola 12 683
Benvenuto di Giovanni (di Meo del Guasta) 3 750–51*
 attributions 32 103
 pupils 11 842
 works 3 751; 32 104
Benvoglienti, Leonardo 1 621
Benwell, Stephen 2 762
Benyon, Margaret 14 690
Benz 15 824
Benzi, Massimiliano Soldani see SOLDANI (BENZI), MASSIMILIANO
benzine 10 560
benzoin 18 610; 32 2
Benzone, Ambrogio see BENSON, AMBROSIUS
Benzoni, Girolamo 5 750
Beograd see BELGRADE
BEP + MAA Akitek Sdn 20 169
BEP Akitek Sdn Bhd 20 169
Bepshes 9 887
Beqiraj, Halim 3 751–2*
Ber, Jakob 11 229
Bér, Rudolf 14 902
Bérain (family) 26 420
Berain, Claude 2 463; 3 752
Berain, Jean (fl before 1640) 2 463; 3 752
Berain, Jean, I (1640-1711) 2 463; 3 752–3*; 18 591; 20 137, 139; 31 444
 cabinets (ii) (furniture) 12 423
 clocks 3 753
 coffers 6 560
 collaboration 11 626; 20 458; 21 891
 costumes 7 167; 30 671
 decorative works 18 854; 23 543; 28 776
 frames 11 374
 furniture 4 552; 11 589, 590; 26 83
 guns 2 463
 interior decoration 3 752
 marquetry 20 467
 mirrors 26 492
 pageants 4 550
 pattern books 24 271, 272
 prints 18 745
 reproductions in ceramics 20 474
 ship-decoration 28 612
 silver 11 618
 stage design 30 671–2
 stucco 13 701
 tapestries 11 576
 teachers 30 660
Berain, Jean, II (1678-1726) 3 752, 753; 11 626; 20 137; 30 672
Beraldi, Henri 3 753*; 10 210; 19 488
Beram, St Maria on Škrlinah 8 178
Beran, Gustav 22 892
Beranek, Jindra 19 523
Beránek, Jiří 8 388
Beránek-Jelínek, Bartolomej 6 363
Béranger, Pierre-Jean de 7 169
Bérard, Christian 3 753–4*
 collaboration 11 727
 groups and movements 22 752; 30 389
 patrons and collectors 16 892; 28 914
 productions 16 892
Bérard, Paul 26 209
Berardi, Fabio 5 599
Berardi, Giovanni 25 814
Berardi, P. N. 21 471
Berardus I, Abbot of Farfa 10 805
Berat 1 537, 538, 539
 architecture 1 538
Berat—cont.
 ceramics 1 543
 furniture 1 542
 guns 1 544
 Helveti hospice 1 539
 houses 1 539; 16 228
 King Mosque 1 538
 metalwork 1 543
 Museum of the National Liberation War 1 546
 painting 1 546
 St Mary of Vllaherna 1 540
 seraglio 1 539
Berat Textile Combine 1 545
Béraud, Jean 3 754*
Bérault de la Haye, Charlotte-Jeanne, Marquise de Montesson see ORLÉANS, CHARLOTTE-JEANNE DE BOURBON, Duchesse d'
Berbati 14 346
Berbena, Andrea 9 173
Berber 1 304, 377, 633; 3 754–6*; 16 107, 108; 19 323; 20 861; 23 290; 33 97
 architecture 1 305, 377; 3 754–5*; 20 861; 32 310
 carpets 16 486, 487
 chests 3 755
 dress 16 457
 fibulae 16 532
 goat-hair 1 307
 jewellery 3 756, 756
 pottery 3 755–6
 saddle-bags 3 755
 silver 3 756
 stone 1 305
 tattoos 1 346
 tents 1 307; 3 755; 30 473
 villages 3 754–5*
 weaving 1 294; 3 755, 756
 wool 3 755
 wraps 16 459
Berber, Mersad 4 461
Berbice 12 132
berbice chairs see CHAIRS → types → planter
Berbier Du Metz, Gédéon, 1st Comte de Rosnay see ROSNAY, GÉDÉON BERBIER DU METZ, 1st Comte de
Berbier Du Metz, Jean, 2nd Comte de Rosnay see ROSNAY, JEAN BERBIER DU METZ, 2nd Comte de
Berbiette, Pierre 18 745
Berce, Jacques 2 699; 7 343
berceaux 12 131
Berch, Gysbrecht van den 13 234
Berch, Hans van den 11 871
Berchem, Huis De Slag van Waterloo 4 788
Berchem, C. P. see BERCHEM, NICOLAES (PIETERSZ.)
Berchem, Max van 3 757*; 16 101, 559
 collaboration 27 846
 works 16 548
Berchem, Nicolaes (Pietersz.) (c. 1620-83) 3 757–60*; 7 370; 13 895; 19 858; 22 843
 attributions 3 501
 collaboration 14 15; 21 827; 22 208; 28 74
 groups and movements 9 462
 methods 6 470; 8 128; 9 216
 patrons and collectors 2 852; 3 178; 10 365, 864; 14 692; 18 796; 23 469; 25 815; 32 368, 377
 pupils 3 500; 9 380; 12 801; 14 732; 15 45; 23 344; 27 116; 32 270
 reproductive prints by others 7 466; 8 542; 12 515; 23 590
 teachers 13 257; 21 791; 33 26
 works 3 758, 759; 22 840
Berchem, Nicolaes (van) (c. 1649/50-72) 3 757
Berchère, Jean-Baptiste Legoux de la see LEGOUX DE LA BERCHÈRE, JEAN-BAPTISTE
Berchet, Federico 4 776
Berchigny, Col. de 21 428
Berchmans, Emile 25 347
Berchod, Pierre 4 870
Berchorius, Petrus see PETRUS BERCHORIUS
Berchtesgaden 31 255
 Gasthaus zum Hirschen 10 738
 SS Peter und Johannes 26 634
Berchtold, Leopold, Graf 13 809
Berchtold IV, Duke of Zähringen (reg 1152-86) 11 773
Berciu, Dumitru 6 344; 30 770
Berckel, Théodor Everard van 28 594
Berckel, Théodor Gaspar van 28 594
Berckel, Théodor Victor van 28 594
Berckenboom, Mattheus 30 568
Berckheyde, Gerrit (Adriaensz.) 3 495, 760, 761–2*; 13 895
 groups and movements 13 895
 patrons and collectors 9 457; 10 753; 33 700
 works 2 338, 342; 3 761; 22 840; 31 155, 246, 704
Berckheyde, Job (Adriaensz.) 3 760–61*; 13 895
 groups and movements 13 895
 reproductive prints by others 6 547
 works 2 342; 22 840; 31 246
Berckman, Hendrick 11 446; 33 391
Berckmans, Ferdinand 3 547, 762–3*; 28 41
Berckmüller, Joseph 17 817; 33 40
Berçot, Paul 29 108
Bercy Park 24 132
Berczy, William (von Moll) 3 763*; 5 564
Berda, Pedro see VERDA, PEDRO
Berdan, Michael 20 609
Berdecio, Roberto 6 365
Berdel, E. 23 120
Berdellé, Johann 24 825; 25 742
Berden, J. W. H. 22 265
Berdt, Johann Christian
 works 33 432
Berdyansk Art Museum 4 838
Berdyszak, Jan 3 763*; 25 116
Berdzenishvili, M. 12 322
 works 12 322
Berefelt, Gunnar 30 120
Berend 22 870
Berende 3 763*; 5 144; 9 511
 St Peter 3 763; 5 151
Berendrecht, Jan Pietersz. 19 348; 28 79
Berendrecht, Michiel de Bruyn van see BRUYN VAN BERENDRECHT, MICHIEL DE
Berengar, Master 20 128; 23 658
Berengaria of Castile, Queen of León (1181-1244) 16 440
Berengaudus 2 222; 20 341
Berengo Gardin, Gianni 3 764*
Berenguer (i Mestres), Francesc 3 764*; 12 182
Berenike II (reg 246-221 BC) 13 560, 566
Berenike IV (reg 58-55 BC) 9 778
Berenson (family) 16 777
Berenson, Bernard 3 764–5*; 11 190, 307; 20 679
 connoisseurship 2 532; 7 715; 22 102
 dealing 2 560; 4 477; 7 579, 782; 9 467; 14 764; 16 769; 18 448; 19 92
 personal collection 24 838
 staff 28 283
 works 8 595; 11 315; 19 715; 20 538; 24 448; 31 671; 32 356
 translated 6 125; 19 637
Berens River Reserve (Man.) 22 645
Berentz, Christian 23 874
Berény, Róbert 3 765–6*
 groups and movements 10 108; 13 638; 14 901
 works 10 109
Berepa 24 76
Bereś, Jerzy 3 766*; 9 394; 25 116
Beresford, A. Edgar 3 75
Beresford Hope, A. J. see HOPE, A(LEXANDER) J(AMES) B(ERESFORD)
Beresford Hope Cross 8 203, 203; 9 660
Beresin, Alexander von 18 527
Berestechko 31 553
Beresteyn, Arnold van 14 287
Beresteyn, Claes van 3 766*
Beresteyn, van (family)
 silver 22 886
Berestiv 18 35; 31 547
Berestya see BREST (BELARUS)
Bereterbide, Fermin 1 122
Beretta, A. 21 520
Beretta, Carlo 5 327
Beretta, Giulio 29 388
Beretta, Giuseppe 14 266
Beretta, Ludovico 3 766–7*
 works 3 767
Beretta, Milo 31 754
Beretti, Aleksandr V. 31 553
Beretti, Vikenty I. 18 36; 27 345; 31 551
 works 18 36
Berezhany Castle 31 550
Berezin, I. N. 6 281
Berezwecz, Basilians church 19 497; 26 498
Berg 2 790
Berg, Adam 29 44
Berg, Adolf I, Count of see ADOLF I, Count of Berg
Berg, Alban 25 354
Berg, Arja van den 14 43
Berg, Christian 30 86
Berg, Claus 3 768*; 8 731, 738; 12 401
 pupils 5 295
 works 13 120
Berg, Clive van den 29 110
Berg, Engelin, Maiser von see MAISER VON BERG, ENGELIN
Berg, Gerard van den 22 877
Berg, J. A. 30 118
Berg, Johann Petter
 works 30 95
Berg, L. 6 279
Berg, Magnus 23 238
 ivory-carvings 8 740, 753; 23 229, 229, 238
Berg, Max 3 768–9*
 assistants 25 69
 groups and movements 10 697
 teachers 28 46
 works 3 768; 7 694; 9 86; 33 417
Berg, Sigrun 23 232
Berg, Simon van den 3 769*; 4 59
Berg, Werner 2 797
Berg, William II, Duke of see WILLIAM II, Duke of Berg
Berga, S Quirze de Pedret 22 247; 26 650; 29 275
Berga i Boix, Josep 7 373; 32 98
Bergama see PERGAMON
Bergamaschi, i see BUON (ii)
Bergamasco, Bartolomeo di Francesco 32 192
Bergamasco, Guglielmo 31 316
Bergamasco, Il see CASTELLO (i), GIOVANNI BATTISTA
Bergamasco, Mauro 21 747
Bergamín, Rafael 21 783; 29 273
Berg am Laim
 St Michael 11 125; 26 498
 summer palace 18 140
Bergamo 3 769–73*, 771; 16 618
 Accademia Carrara di Belle Arti 3 772; 5 872; 8 912; 16 773
Bergamo—cont.
 Banca Bergamasca 10 820, 821
 Colleoni Chapel 3 772
  tomb of Bartolomeo Colleoni 1 746–7, 747; 27 830
 Galleria dell'Accademia Carrara 5 872
 Hospital 14 781
 Museo Archeologico 3 770
 Museo di Scienze Naturali 3 770
 Palazzo del Municipio 31 236
 Palazzo del Podestà 4 643; 10 737
 S Bernardino Altarpiece 19 711
 S Maria Maggiore 3 772–3*, 772; 20 467; 30 331
  Baptistery 13 94
  sculpture 13 94
 urban planning 3 770
 Villa Pizzigoni 16 649
Bergamo, Damiano Zambelli da see ZAMBELLI DA BERGAMO, DAMIANO
Bergamo, Martino da 25 889
Bergamo, Michele da
 works 5 690
Bergamo, Moretto da see CODUSSI, MAURO
Bergamo Sketchbook see under SKETCHBOOKS → individual manuscripts
Bergander, Rudolf 21 365
Bergant, Fortunat 3 773*; 28 860
Bergara, Francesco see VERGARA, FRANCISCO
Berg Arkitektkontor AB 14 227; 32 730
Bergaz, Alfonso 29 293
Berglau see under PIGMENTS → types
Berg & Clark 28 831
Bergdoll, Adam 11 730, 731; 12 433
Bergé, Henri 8 544
Bergé, Jacques 3 571, 773*; 5 43
Berge, Jan van den see JAN VAN DEN BERGE
Bergen (Belgium) see MONS
Bergen (Germany), Kloster- und Wallfahrskirche Heilige Kreuz 3 413
Bergen (Netherlands) 13 131; 19 768; 22 851
 Park Meerwijk 29 483
Bergen (Norway) 3 773–5*; 23 218, 219
 Billedgalleri 23 243
 Cathedral 26 593
 education (art) 23 244
 Exchange 23 226
 furniture 23 233
 Gamle Bergen 23 243
 gold 23 236
 Harmoniske akademis Tegneskole 23 244
 Historisk Museum 3 774; 23 243
 interior decoration 23 231
 King Haakon's Hall 3 774, 774–5*; 23 219, 232
 marks 20 444; 23 236
 New Church see Nykirke
 Nykirke 23 221
 Nyttige Selskaps Tegneskole 23 244
 paintings 23 223
 Rasmus Meyers Samlinger 23 243
 Rosenkrantz Tower 23 220
 St Mary 23 219
 sculpture 13 119
 silver 23 236
 Statens Høgskole for Kunsthåndverk og Design 23 244
  library 23 244
 Stiftelsen Stenersens Samling 23 243
 Stiftsgård 23 221
 Studieatelier 23 244

Bergen (Norway)—cont.
 Stundt's Department Store 23 222
 textiles 23 239
 Torvalmenningen 23 222
 trade 23 242
 Vestlandske Kunstindustrimuseum 23 239
  collections 3 774; 22 319, 320; 23 243
 Vestlands Kunstakademi 23 244
 walls 23 220
Bergen, Dirck van den 3 775*; 20 141
Bergen, Edgar de 14 120
Bergen, Oluf Jørgensen 23 236
Bergen-op-Zoom 21 570; 22 813
 ceramics 22 878
 earthenwares 22 877
 fortifications 21 570
 Markiezenhof 22 822
 St Gertrudiskerk 13 62, 63; 22 820
 silver 22 887
Bergen-op-Zoom, Marquis of 17 883
Bergen school 12 502; 19 65, 796
Berger, Albert 28 111
 works 19 485
Berger, Daniel 27 345; 29 676
Berger, Ernst 4 207
Berger, F. G. 14 18
Berger, François 19 142
Berger, Georg 23 424
Berger, Hans 30 134
Berger, Jacques see BERGÉ, JACQUES
Berger, Johann Wilhelm von 13 605
Berger, John 18 97–8; 20 528; 28 927
Berger, Julius Victor 17 897; 18 129
Berger, Lewis (fl 1760-1810) 23 786
Berger, Luis (fl 1636) 2 398
bergères see under CHAIRS → types
Bergeret, Gaston 29 58
Bergeret, Pierre-Nolasque 3 775*
 groups and movements 31 374
 patrons and collectors 4 301, 303
 works 12 898; 19 483
Bergeret de Frouville, J.-F. 4 517
Bergeret de Grancourt, (Pierre-) Jacques-Onésyme 3 775–6*; 4 517; 32 685
Bergerhöhe 2 809
Berges, Heinrich 33 392
Bergfried 6 57; 9 144; 21 546, 564
Berggren, Edward 26 508
Berggrun see MALACHITE
Bergh, (Johan) Edvard 3 776*; 14 537; 30 79
Bergh, Elis 30 102
Bergh, Fritz Mayer van den see MAYER VAN DEN BERGH, FRITZ
Bergh, Henriette Mayer van den see MAYER VAN DEN BERGH, HENRIETTE
Bergh, (Sven) Richard 3 776–7*; 30 80
 groups and movements 22 540; 23 206; 29 774
 pupils 10 399
Berghausen im Sauerland, St Cyriakus 26 654
Berghe, Christoffel van den 11 226
Berghe, Frits van den 3 564
Berghe, Hans van den see BERCH, HANS VAN DEN
Berghe, Jan van den (fl 1452; printmaker) 25 624
Berghe, Jan van den (1396-1486; architect) see JAN VAN RUYSBROECK
Bergheim Predella 28 149
Berghem, Nicolaes (Pietersz.) see BERCHEM, NICOLAES (PIETERSZ.)
Berghen, Dirck van see BERGEN, DIRCK VAN DEN
Berghes, Georges-Louis de 2 122
Berghoef, Johannes F. 3 777*; 13 898
 groups and movements 8 669, 670
 works 8 670
Bergholtzzell 26 634
Bergisch-Gladbach 8 824
Bergkvist, Knut 30 102
Bergl, Johann Wenzel 2 795; 3 777*; 5 84
 works 2 794; 14 900; 32 456, 460
Bergler, Ettore de Maria 28 657
Bergler, Josef, the elder (1718-88) 3 778
Bergler, Josef, the younger (1753-1829) 3 778*
 pupils 1 774; 14 364, 756; 20 875; 22 426; 31 64
 works 25 417
Bergman, Anna-Eva 3 778*; 14 205, 206
Bergman, Edwin A. 6 576
Bergman, Erasmus 15 7
Bergman, Folke 21 885
Bergmann, Althof 31 256
Bergmann, Hermann 3 779*
Bergmann-Michel, Ella 3 779*; 21 430
Bergmeister, Manfred 12 454
Bergmüller, Johann Georg 2 717, 719; 3 779–81*
 assistants 10 215
 collaboration 13 258; 24 370
 groups and movements 26 498
 pupils 14 695; 18 497
 reproductive prints by others 18 47
 works 3 780; 12 391; 15 139; 28 130
 writings 14 872
Bergner, Yosl (Vladimir Jossif) 2 749; 3 781–2*; 17 579
Bergognone (da Fossano), Ambrogio 16 663; 21 525
 assistants 27 194
 collaboration 9 75
 patrons and collectors 4 427; 25 144
 works 1 529; 21 534, 538
Bergolat, Pablo 8 236
Bergonone (da Fossano), Ambrogio (di Stefano) 3 782–3*
 works 3 782; 24 285
Bergonone, Bernardino 3 783
Bergonzi, Melchior 7 889
Bergonzo, Alziro 3 772
Bergonzoni, Giovan Battista 4 273
Bergöö, Karin 18 801
Bergs, Frantz 30 112
 works 30 112
Bergslien, Brynjulf Larsen 3 783*; 23 229; 26 5; 32 497
Bergslien, Knud 9 750; 10 457; 24 549; 33 76
Bergson, Henri 3 783–4*; 8 243
 works 1 182; 28 202
  translated 14 864
Bergsten, Carl (Gustav) 2 611; 3 784*; 13 31; 30 74
Bergström, Ingvar 30 120
Bergues, Alphonse, Archbishop of Mechelen 11 699
Berhampore 15 402, 693, 724
Berhampur 15 671
Berichte und Mitteilungen des Altertums-Vereines zu Wien 24 438
Beridze, Aleksandre 12 326
Berighem, Nicolaes (Pietersz.) see BERCHEM, NICOLAES (PIETERSZ.)
Berindey, D. 15 56
Beringar 5 804; 7 512
Beringer, Wolf 3 784–5*; 33 36, 430
Beringhen, Jacques-Louis, Marquis de Château-Neuf 3 785*; 18 692
Berini, Antonio 12 264
Berjon, Antoine 3 785*; 11 229
Berk, Nurullah 3 785–6*
 groups and movements 31 454
Berke, Hubert 31 328
Berkel, Sabri 3 786*; 31 454
Berkeley (Glos; UK)
 Castle 3 209; 6 55; 9 144
 St Mary 10 262
Berkeley (CA; USA)
 Holy Spirit Chapel 24 281
 Judah L. Magnes Museum 17 582
 University of California
  Phoebe A. Hearst Museum of Anthropology 10 94; 14 510; 27 47; 29 218, 221
  Robert H. Lowie Museum of Anthropology see Phoebe A. Hearst Museum of Anthropology
  University Art Museum 6 826; 22 367
Berkeley, Busby 30 687
Berkeley, Daniel 31 497
Berkeley, George (1685-1753) 3 786–7*; 13 303
Berkeley, George, Lord (1628-98) 23 199
Berkeley, Wayne 31 333
Berkeley, William 31 634
Berkemeyer see under GLASSES → types
Berkenkamp, Johann Christoph 6 92
Berkey & Gay 13 297; 26 190
Berkhamsted (Herts) 6 56
 school 28 156
Berkhout, Lijsbeth Teding van 20 926
Berkovich, Elmar 21 362
Berkowitz, Leon 32 890, 894
Berlage, H(endrik) P(etrus) 3 787–8*; 4 73; 7 669; 17 910; 22 895
 architecture
  exchanges 4 788; 10 668, 669; 16 55; 30 506
  museums 14 40, 43
  office buildings 3 787; 14 691; 21 122; 22 829–30, 830, 861; 33 692
  urban planning 1 803; 13 313; 14 40; 17 910; 18 126; 22 830
  villas 32 555
 collaboration 8 778; 10 418; 19 32; 22 860; 33 676
 glass 22 885
 groups and movements 1 814; 2 567; 13 204; 21 779; 22 875; 26 14
 interior decoration 22 867
 metalwork 1 810
 patrons and collectors 18 466
 pupils 29 482; 33 387
 staff 8 206; 10 163; 27 136; 32 696; 33 215, 743
Berlam, Ruggiero 4 247
Berlanga de Duero
 S Baudelio 22 246, 247; 26 655; 29 262, 275; 32 821
 S María del Mercado 29 265
Berlaymont (family) 20 452
Berlaymont, Philippe de 22 680
Berlewi, Henryk 3 788*; 4 148; 25 108
Berliawksy, Louise see NEVELSON, LOUISE
Berlin (Germany) 3 789–807*, 789; 12 360, 381; 13 717; 31 715, 731
 academies 12 478–9
  Akademie der Künste 1 105, 107; 2 365, 370; 3 798, 799, 800; 6 79; 9 465; 22 358; 28 343
   collections 4 136
Berlin (Germany)
 academies—cont.
  Bauakademie 3 792, 799; 4 787; 12 375; 25 173; 28 100, 101–2
  Geologische und Landwirtschaftliche Lehranstalt 3 794
  Hochschule für Bildende Künste 3 802
  Königliche Akademie der Künste see Akademie der Künste
  Preussische Akademie der Künste see Akademie der Künste
  Singakademie 3 792; 7 687
 AEG factory (Wedding) 3 512; 12 378; 23 493
 AEG Turbine Factory (Moabit) 3 795; 8 247; 10 697, 749; 12 792; 16 55; 21 780; 27 131
 Allgemeiner Deutscher Nachrichtendienst
  collections 12 482
 Alte Post see palaces → Palais Wartenburg
 art forms and materials
  architecture 12 374, 376; 18 114; 26 743
  beadwork 3 442
  dioramas 8 911
  faience (ii) (ceramics) 12 430
  furniture 12 424, 426
  glass 12 441
  hangings 12 413
  interior decoration 12 409
  iron 3 804*; 12 454
  jewellery 3 804*; 12 454, 454; 17 526
  lace 8 756
  lacquer 18 614
  metalwork 12 447
  painting 12 390, 391, 393, 394; 26 742
  porcelain 3 804–5*; 12 435, 437
  rugs 12 410
  samplers 27 694
  sculpture 12 404, 406
  silk 3 804; 12 464; 28 717
  silver 12 446, 449
  snuff-boxes 12 457, 459*, 459
  statuettes 29 576
  tankards 12 444
  tapestries 3 804; 12 468; 30 322, 324
  textiles 3 804*; 12 469
 art market 12 474
 Bauschule see academies → Bauakademie
 Börse 3 793; 12 376
 Brandenburg Gate 3 791, 792; 12 374; 13 608; 23 490
 cinemas
  Babylon Cinema 7 328
  Schaubühne 30 685
  UFA Cinema 7 328
  Universum/Luxor-Palast 7 328
  Universum-Kino see Schaubühne
 collections 12 474
 Collegienhaus 3 791
 Cygnet Fountain 12 196
 Deutsche Lebens-Rettungs-Gesellschaft (DLRG) building 19 168
 ecclesiastical buildings
  Cathedral (Protestant; before 1893) 7 277
  Cathedral (Protestant; after 1893) 12 376; 26 3
   monument to Frederick I, King of Prussia 28 117
   monument to Sophie Charlotte, Queen of Prussia 28 116
  Epiphanienkirche 3 795
  Friedrich-Werdersche-Kirche 3 792; 12 376; 13 202
  Helenakirche 14 82
Berlin (Germany)
 ecclesiastical buildings—cont.
  Kaiser-Wilhelm-Gedächtniskirche 12 380; 22 163
  Marienkirche 3 790, 792, 797; 11 253; 25 727
  Michaelkirche 3 794; 25 173
  Nazarethkirche 12 376
  Nikolaikirche 3 789
  Petrikirche 3 789
  St Hedwig's Roman Catholic Cathedral 7 258
  St Johanneskirche 12 376
  St Walpurgis 12 382
 education (art) 3 798
 exhibitions 12 380
  Deutsche Bau-Ausstellung, 1931 3 796
  Interbau, 1957 3 797
  Internationale Bau-Ausstellung, 1957 see Interbau, 1957
  Internationale Bau-Ausstellung, 1979 12 380
  Internationale Bau-Ausstellung, 1984 3 797
  Internationale Bau-Ausstellung, 1987 3 797
 film studios 18 193
 fortifications 14 650; 21 548
 Frankfurterallee 12 380
 Friedrich-Wilhelm University see Humboldt University
 Galerie Rosen 3 802
 Georgsspital 3 790
 Gertaudensspital 3 790
 Gewerbeinstitut 3 890
 Gewerbeverein 3 890
 Gewerkschule 1 107
 government buildings 31 241
  Justizamt 3 794
  Mint 12 310, 375; 23 490
  Neue Packhof 3 792; 12 375
  Reichskanzlei 12 379, 417–18; 13 238; 23 814; 25 268
  Reichstag 3 794; 7 668; 12 376, 377, 416; 13 237, 238; 32 801
   portico 25 268
  Senat 30 350
  Statistisches Amt 3 794
  Zeughaus 2 502; 3 790
   sculpture 14 651; 28 116, 116
 Haus Wiegand 3 795; 13 613
 Heiliggeistsspital 3 790
 Hochhaus Weberwiese 12 380
 Hohes Haus 3 790
 housing 30 371
  Hufeisensiedlung housing development 3 796
  Siemensstadt apartments 13 688; 30 458
  Villenkolonie Friedenau 32 555
 Humboldt University 13 802; 14 653
 Jewish Community Centre 17 549
 Köpenicker Tor 3 790
 Kreuzberg 13 207; 22 47
  cemetery 6 166
 Lebensrettungstation 19 168
 libraries 2 366
  Hochschule der Künste Library 12 481
  Kunstbibliothek 2 370; 24 846
  Kunstbibliothek Berlin mit Museum für Architektur, Modebild und Grafik-Design 9 703
  Old Royal Library 3 791
  Preussische Staatsbibliothek 3 795
  Staatsbibliothek Preussischer Kulturbesitz 12 482; 15 745
   Turfan collection 6 306
 Lietzenburg see palaces → Schloss Charlottenburg
 Lustgarten 3 790
 Märkisches Viertel 12 380
 Marschallbrücke 3 792

Berlin (Germany)—cont.
Metro stations **21** 350
Moderner Unterricht in Malerei-Institut *see* MUIM-Institut
monuments
Karl Liebknecht and Rosa Luxemburg Monument **4** 789
monument to Emperor William I **3** 498–9; **12** 406
monument to Frederick I, King of Prussia *see under* Cathedral (Protestant; after 1893)
monument to Frederick the Great **26** 23, *23*; **29** 566
monument to Frederick William, the Great Elector **3** *798*
monument to Johann Christoph Friedrich von Schiller **3** 497
monument to Sophie Charlotte, Queen of Prussia *see under* Cathedral (Protestant; after 1893)
Mühlendamm **3** 789
MUIM-Institut **18** 79; **24** 311
museums
Ägyptisches Museum **10** 93
Alte Nationalgalerie **3** 807; **14** 207; **29** 737, 863; **33** 295
collections **4** 205; **13** 605; **16** 556; **19** 112; **22** 253; **31** 397
directors **28** 342
portico **25** 268
Altes Museum **2** 359, 560; **3** 792, 799, 807; **9** 17, 18, 25; **12** 375, *375*, 476; **13** 610; **14** 575, 653; **18** 89; **22** 358, 362; **24** 805; **25** 172; **26** 735; **28** 98, 99–100; **30** 854; **32** 748; **33** 295
collections **3** 807; **4** 209; **10** 637; **29** 46
directors **4** 209
frames **11** 461
frescoes **7** 872
portico **25** 267
sculpture **33** 155
Antikenmuseum **3** 291; **13** 542; **27** 46
Antikensammlung *see under* Pergamonmuseum
Berlin Museum **10** 90, 93
Beuth-Schinkel Museum *see* Kunstgewerbemuseum (Tiergarten)
Bodemuseum **3** 794, 807; **14** 655; **15** 122
Ägyptisches Museum **10** 93; **13** 470
catalogues **28** 165
collections **9** 200; **10** 93; **16** 556; **27** 846
directors **32** 714
Gemäldegalerie **10** 366; **11** 777; **29** 46
Gemäldegalerie: directors **7** 561
Münzkabinett **10** 773; **11** 362
Museum für Ur- und Frühgeschichte **31** 356
Brücke-Museum **4** 893; **9** 465; **28** 126
Deutsches Historisches Museum *see* government buildings → Zeughaus
Gropiusbau
Bauhaus-Archiv **2** 370
see also Kunstgewerbemuseum (Prinz-Albrecht- Strasse)
Islamisches Museum *see under* Pergamonmuseum
Jüdisches Museum **17** 581, 582
Kaiser-Friedrich-Museum *see* Bodemuseum
Kolbe Museum **4** 181; **28** 71
Königliche National-Galerie *see* Alte Nationalgalerie
Berlin (Germany)
museums—cont.
Kunstbibliothek Berlin mit Museum für Architektur, Modebild und Grafik-Design *see under* libraries
Kunstgewerbemuseum *see* Gropiusbau; Kunstgewerbemuseum (variously in the Prinz-Albrechtstrasse, Königliches Schloss, Tiergarten, and Schloss Köpenick)
Kunstgewerbemuseum (Königliches Schloss) **3** 806
Kunstgewerbemuseum (Prinz-Albrechtstrasse) **9** 691; **12** 505; **13** 685, 717; **19** 244; **22** 363
collections **13** 677
Kunstgewerbemuseum (Schloss Köpenick) **12** 273; **14** 651
Kunstgewerbemuseum (Tiergarten)
collections **3** 890; **29** 516; **30** 332
exhibitions **16** 559
Kupferstichkabinett
collections **11** 777; **14** 651; **25** 631; **26** 177; **32** 622
Märkisches Museum **3** 795; **14** 632
Metzner Museum **21** 365
Münzkabinett *see under* Bodemuseum
Museum am Lustgarten *see* Altes Museum
Museum Dahlem **2** 275; **16** 556
Museum für Indische Kunst **1** 583; **6** 321; **15** 745; **19** 38; **22** 795; **29** 240
Museum für Ostasiatische Kunst **6** 735, 826; **7** 155
Museum für Völkerkunde **1** 437, 439; **6** 321; **9** 64; **10** 214; **21** 264, 265, 886; **23** 302; **24** 279; **27** 780; **29** 220–21, 240
Museum für Architektur, Modebild und Grafik- Design *see* libraries → Kunstbibliothek Berlin mit Museum für Architektur, Modebild und G.-D.
Museum für Deutsche Geschichte **12** 405
see also government buildings → Zeughaus
Museum für Indische Kunst *see under* Museum Dahlem
Museum für Naturkunde **3** 794
Museum für Ostasiatische Kunst *see under* Museum Dahlem
Museum für Ur-und Frühgeschichte *see under* Bodemuseum
Museum für Völkerkunde *see under* Museum Dahlem
Museuminsel **3** 807*; **12** 476, 477
Nationalgalerie (Tiergarten) *see* Neue Nationalgalerie
Neue Nationalgalerie **3** 797; **4** 61; **12** 380, 477; **21** 493; **22** 366
directors **33** 82
Neues Museum **3** 807; **9** 210; **12** 376; **14** 654; **22** 362; **29** 863
Otto-Nagel-Haus **22** 430
Pergamonmuseum **3** 795, 807; **14** 632; **21** 311
Antikensammlung **27** 46
collections **1** 855; **13** 470, 606; **16** 548, 556; **21** 310; **24** 415
Islamisches Museum **1** 583; **15** 741; **16** 556
Vorderasiatisches Museum **1** 839
Berlin (Germany)
museums—cont.
Schinkelmuseum *see* ecclesiastical buildings → Friedrich-Werdersche-Kirche
Staatliche Museen Preussischer Kulturbesitz **10** 447
library **12** 481
Verborgenes Museum **33** 310
Vorderasiatisches Museum *see under* Pergamonmuseum
Neptune Fountain **3** 498, *498*
Neues Tor **3** 792
Neue Wache **3** 792, *793*; **7** 360; **12** 375; **13** 610; **23** 490; **28** 98
observatories **23** 339
Royal Observatory **23** 340
Urania Public Observatory **23** 342
Oderberger Tor **3** 790
Operncafé *see* palaces → Prinzessinnenpalais
palaces
Altes Palais **3** 792
Jagdschloss Grunewald **9** 53
paintings **4** 152; **17** 5; **21** 510; **31** 780
sculpture **14** 650
Königliches Schloss **3** 790, 805–6*, *806*; **12** 373, 414; **18** 202; **23** 811; **28** 116, *117*; **30** 703
collections **9** *27*
Elisabethsaal **28** 116
frames **11** 458
interior decoration **12** 374
paintings **14** 650
Weisser Saal **19** 244
Niederländisches Palais **26** 506
Palais Borsig **3** 794
Palais Redfern **25** 193
Palais Wartenburg **28** 116
Prinzessinnenpalais **3** 792
Prinz-Heinrich-Palais *see* Humboldt University
Prinz-Karl-Palais **28** *101*
Schloss Charlottenburg **1** 133; **3** 790, 792, 806–7*; **11** 731; **12** 405, 413, 414, 424; **20** 868; **25** 193; **31** 328
Ägyptisches Museum *see under* museums
Antikenmuseum *see under* museums
Belvedere **3** 792
Bergsteinsaal **1** 762
drawings (pastel) **18** 160
frames **11** 458
frescoes **15** 139
furniture **12** *427*; **18** 614
gardens **12** 133
Gläsernes Schlafgemach **5** 349
Goldene Galerie **12** 412; **26** 496
interior decoration **12** 410; **22** 436
monument to Frederick William, the Great Elector *see under* monuments
Museum für Ur- und Frühgeschichte *see under* museums → Bodemuseum
paintings **2** 559; **4** *136*, 537; **11** 36; **12** 489; **14** 651, 652; **18** 160, 477, 693; **20** 415; **24** 542; **26** 94, 564; **33** 298
porcelain **12** 434
Porzellankabinett **5** 347, 349; **9** 29; **12** 412
Schinkel-Pavillon **18** 202; **24** 290, *290*
sculpture **9** 760, 761; **14** 650, 651
Winter Apartments **12** 413
Schloss Köpenick *see* museums → Kunstgewerbemuseum (Schloss Köpenick)
Schloss Monbijou **5** 348
Berlin (Germany)
palaces—cont.
Stadtschloss *see* Königliches Schloss
parks **24** 181
Pfaueninsel
dairy **8** 461
Schloss **11** 242; **12** 413
Philharmonie **1** 126; **7** 688; **12** 380; **28** 55, *56*
Postfuhramt **3** 794
Reichsbank **3** 794
Reimann-Schule **14** 176
Rotes Rathaus **3** 793; **4** 787; **12** 376; **30** 503
sculpture **12** 505
Royal Mint **3** 792
Schatzamt **3** 794
Schlossbrücke **3** 792
Schlösser *see* palaces
Seebad Rangsdorf **19** 332
shops
Havana Cigar Shop **2** 565; **31** *876*
Hermann Tietz **8** 770
Kaiser-Galerie **3** 794
Lindenhaus department store **27** 657
Wertheim **2** 565; **3** 795; **8** 770; **12** 376, *377*; **21** 311; **24** 549
Siegesallee **12** 407
Siemensstadt Siedlung **21** 782
apartments *see under* housing
Spandauer Tor **3** 790
sports centres
Deutsches Sportforum **20** 387
Horst Kober Sports Centre **29** 428
Olympic Stadium **1** 798; **29** 489
Sporthalle (Charlottenburg) **19** 168
squares
Mariannenplatz **3** 794
Schinkelplatz **18** *455*
Schlossplatz **11** 346
Wilhelmplatz **30** 353
Staaken **28** 126
Staatsoper **3** 791
Stadtschloss *see* palaces → Königliches Schloss
Stalin Allee *see* Frankfurterallee
stations
Alexanderplatz Bahnhof **25** 856
Anhalter Bahnhof **3** 795
Friedrichstrasse Bahnhof **25** 856
Hamburger Bahnhof **3** 794; **12** 477; **25** 856
Lehrter Bahnhof **3** 794
Metro stations **21** 349
Stettiner Bahnhof **25** 856
Stralauer Tor **3** 790
Sturm-Galerie **3** 801; **10** 695; **29** 871; **32** 775
synagogues
Heidereutergasse synagogue **17** 544
Kottbuser Ufer synagogue **17** 548
Oranienburgerstrasse synagogue **17** 547
Teltower Tor **3** 790
Tempelhof **1** 494
theatres
Anatomical Theatre **3** 792
Grosses Schauspielhaus **10** 417, 697, *697*; **19** 367; **30** 683
Schauspielhaus **3** 791; **12** 375; **13** 610; **18** 202; **26** 735; **28** 98–9, *99*; **30** 677
sculpture **30** 854
Schillertheater **30** 682
Staatsoper **30** 676
Theater unter den Linden **30** 679
Treptower Park **32** 737
University **26** 236
see also Humboldt University
Unter den Linden **3** 790, 792, *793*
Berlin (Germany)—cont.
urban planning **14** 300; **31** 715, 724, 729, 730
Versuchsanstalt für Wasserbau und Schiffahrt **19** 168
Viktoriapark **20** 1
Villa Ende **32** 555
Villa Gurlitt **18** 115
Villa Kamecke **3** 791
Villenkolonie Friedenau *see under* housing
Weissensee Jewish cemetery **17** 555
XIII Realschule **28** 158
Zoo **33** 698, 699
Elephant House **33** *699*
Berlin (CT; USA) **31** 652
Berlin, Eugenia **5** 571
Berlin, Joseph **3** 807*; **30** 421
Berlin, Leonid **27** 397
Berlin, Neue Gruppe *see* NEUE GRUPPE BERLIN
Berlin, Sven **27** 563
Berlin, Zeev **3** 807
Berlin 1686, Painter of **13** 509
Berlin A 34, Painter of **13** 506
Berlin Album *see under* ALBUMS → individual manuscripts
Berlin blue *see under* PIGMENTS → types
Berlin-Charlottenburg *see under* BERLIN
Berlin Critical Realists **9** 470; **24** 561
Berlin Dancing Girl, Painter of the **13** 526
Berliner, Emile **7** 375
Berliner Architekturwelt **21** 796
Berliner Eisengiesserei **17** 739
Berliner Kunstblatt **24** 421, 443
Berlin F2268, Painter of **13** 538
Berlin Foundry Cup **13** *437*, 439, 440
Berlinghieri (family) **16** 655
Berlinghieri, Berlinghiero **3** 808–9*
Berlinghieri, Bonaventura **3** 808–9*
patrons and collectors **7** 885
works **1** 708; **3** *808*; **12** 759; **13** 541; **18** 703; **25** 462
Berlinghiero, Barone di *see* BARONE DI BERLINGHIERO
Berlinghiero, Marco di *see* MARCO DI BERLINGHIERO
Berlin Green Head **10** 93
Berlin Hydria, Painter of the **13** 522
Berlinischer Künstler Verein *see* VEREIN BERLINISCHER KÜNSTLER
Berlin Kore **13** 602
Berlin-Kreuzberg *see under* BERLIN (GERMANY)
Berlin Painter **13** 511; **32** 33–5*
pupils **13** 521; **32** 28, 59, 62
works **13** *519*, 519–20; **32** *35*
Berlin Passion, Master of the **12** 385; **20** 628*, 915
Berlin St Jerome, Master of the **12** 171
Berlin Secession *see* SECESSION (BERLIN)
Berlin Sketchbook, Master of the **7** 869; **20** 628*
Berlin-Staaken *see under* BERLIN (GERMANY)
Berlin woolwork *see under* EMBROIDERY → types
Berlitz, Johann **17** 472; **18** 851
Berlyne, Daniel E. **25** 684
Berman, Eugene **3** 809*; **19** 702; **20** 609
groups and movements **3** 753; **22** 752; **30** 389
patrons and collectors **16** 892; **28** 914
Berman, Leonid **3** 809; **22** 752; **30** 389
Berman, Menachem **16** 568

Berman, Wallace 17 694; 19 702; 23 334; 31 608
Berman, Yevgeny (Gustavovich) see BERMAN, EUGENE
Bermano, Giovanni Siro Cattaneo da see GIOVANNI SIRO CATTANEO DA BERMANO
Bermejillo, Marquesa de 29 308
Bermejo, A. (*fl* 1882) 27 129
Bermejo, Antonio (*b* 1588) 4 261; 29 893
Bermejo, Bartolomé 3 809–11*
 collaboration 23 605
 patrons and collectors 2 278; 18 899
 pupils 27 818
 works 3 221, *810*; 11 483; 29 276
Bermondsey Dish 10 323
berms 21 546, 559
Bermuda 2 146; 4 786; 5 788
Bermudes, (Arnaldo Redondo) Adães 3 811*; 8 74; 28 781
Bermúdez 9 118
Bermúdez, Ceán 23 606
Bermúdez, Cundo 3 811–12*
Bermúdez, Guillermo 7 606
Bermúdez, Juan Agustín Ceán see CEÁN BERMÚDEZ, JUAN AGUSTÍN
Bermúdez, Ricardo de 14 714; 23 904
Berna (da Siena) see BARNA (DA SIENA)
Berna, Maria, Gräfin von Oriola see ORIOLA, MARIA BERNA, Gräfin von
Bernabé, Felix 3 812*; 12 262, 547
Bernabei, Domenico see DOMENICO DA CORTONA
Bernabò, Lord of Milan (*reg* 1354-85) 32 609, 610*
 architecture 3 770; 21 516; 24 193; 32 639
 manuscripts 20 688, 710
 sculpture 14 421
Bernacchino see MATTIA DI GIOVANNI
Bernadazzi, A. I. 7 174
Bernadet, F. 28 513
Bernadet, José Oriol y see ORIOL Y BERNADET, JOSÉ
Bernadino da Brescia 11 571, 585
Bernadoni, Giovanni Maria 3 526
Bernadotte, Eugen (Napoleon Nicolaus), Prince of Sweden (1865-1947) 10 648*; 30 79, 80, 91, 113
Bernadotte, Gustavus Adolphus, Prince of Sweden (1906-47) 30 108
Bernadotte, Gustav VI Adolf, King of Sweden see GUSTAV VI ADOLF, King of Sweden
Bernadotte, Karl XIV, King of Sweden see KARL XIV, King of Sweden
Bernadotte, Karl XV, King of Sweden see KARL XV, King of Sweden
Bernadotte, Sibylla, Princess of Sweden 30 108
Bernadotte, Sivgard 17 479
Bernadsky, Yevstafy 10 855
Bernaerts, Nicasius 8 811; 28 904; 29 668
Bernal, J. D. 30 411
Bernal, Ralph 3 812*; 10 367; 11 737
Bernaldo de Quirós, Cesáreo 2 404
Bernard (*fl* 1122) 27 794
Bernard, Charles 19 231; 24 821
 works 24 *821*
Bernard, Emile 3 812–13*; 12 187, 189; 19 10; 30 326
 exhibitions 28 171
 groups and movements 7 451, 452; 25 215, 358; 27 639; 30 169
Bernard, Emile—cont.
 patrons and collectors 12 191
 pupils 1 465
 works 11 648; 19 488; 30 174; 32 687; 33 361
Bernard, Henry 23 122; 24 130; 29 752
Bernard, Huet 14 846–7*
Bernard, Jacques-Samuel 3 813–14*; 9 379; 10 144
 pupils 10 909
Bernard, Jean, Archbishop of Tours 11 352
Bernard, Jean-Claude 11 527
Bernard, Joseph (-Antoine) 3 814*; 11 568
 groups and movements 2 521
 pupils 16 49
Bernard, Le Petit see SALOMON, BERNARD
Bernard, Manuel Ossorio y see OSSORIO Y BERNARD, MANUEL
Bernard, Noël 3 813
Bernard, Oliver (Percy) 3 814*; 10 98
Bernard, Paul 1 485
Bernard, Salomon
 works 11 *604*
Bernard, Samuel 24 136
Bernard, Simon 21 575
Bernard, Thomas 20 922
Bernardakis, Demetrios 13 606
Bernardatsi, A. I. 21 810
Bernard d'Abbeville, Bishop of Amiens 1 777, 781
Bernard de Castanet, Bishop of Albi 1 576, 577
Bernard de Palau 25 58
Bernard de Soissons 26 114, 115
Bernardelli, Félix 22 19
Bernardelli, Henrique 4 717, 726; 32 613
Bernardelli, Rodolfo 3 814*; 4 717
Bernardelli group 23 907
Bernardes, António de Oliveira 3 814–16*; 30 881
 collaboration 3 816
 pupils 3 816; 27 804
 works 3 *815*; 10 664
Bernardes, Inácio de Oliveira 3 816*; 25 814
Bernardes, Policarpo de Oliveira 3 815, 816*; 28 500; 30 881
Bernardes, Sérgio (Vladimir) 3 816–17*; 4 713, 714
Bernardi, Bernardo (1463-1553) 3 817
Bernardi, Bernardo (1912-1985) 10 667
Bernardi, Giovanni (Desiderio) 3 817–18*; 20 919
 collaboration 14 171
 patrons and collectors 10 810; 13 906; 16 745
 works 3 *817*; 10 751; 12 258, *259*; 25 21
Bernardi, Giuseppe 5 625; 31 187
Bernardi, Jacopo 2 232
Bernardi, Theodore C. 33 428
Bernardine Order 25 120
Bernardino da Milano 32 409
Bernardino da Modena 20 680
Bernardino d'Antonio see BERNARDINO DEL SIGNORACCIO
Bernardino da Parenzo 3 818*; 9 175
Bernardino da Venezia 26 457
Bernardino del Castelletto (di Massa) 3 818–19*; 6 14
Bernardino del Signoraccio 24 26
Bernardino di Lorenzo 11 118
Bernardis, Bernardo di 19 113
Bernardo 24 193
Bernardo, Constancio 24 623
Bernardo, Giovanni di see GIOVANNI DI BERNARDO
Bernardo, Giovan Simone di 7 332
Bernardo, Monsù see KEIL, BERNHARD
Bernardo da Campione 14 421
Bernardo da Gualdo 20 844
Bernardo da Venezia 3 298; 21 531, 533; 24 284; 31 431; 32 611
Bernardo delle Girandole see BUONTALENTI, BERNARDO
Bernardo di Francesco 6 11; 31 513
Bernardo di Matteo see ROSSELLINO, BERNARDO
Bernard of Clairvaux, Saint 3 709, 819*; 6 *463*; 7 231, 267, 346, 348, 371; 16 627; 26 380, 700
 architecture 7 371; 11 288; 21 836
 stained glass 29 500
 works 7 454; 8 612; 24 776
Bernardo Forno da Campione 11 897
Bernardone, Giovanni see FRANCIS OF ASSISI, Saint
Bernardoni, Francesco 7 901; 32 216
Bernardoni, Giovanni Maria 19 496, 750; 25 840
Bernardo Romano 2 184
Bernardozzi, Aleksandr (Osinovich) 23 354
Bernardsky, Yevstafy 27 390
Bernardt, Győző 5 83
Bernardt, Karl 28 228
Bernard the elder (*fl* 1075) 27 793
Bernardus Gelduinus 3 820*; 11 554; 26 602, 607
 works 7 719; 26 595; 31 208, *209*
Bernart, Martín 3 810; 33 469
Bernascone, Giuseppe 27 499, 500
Bernasconi (family; early 19th cent.) 29 835
Bernasconi (family; mid-20th cent.) 6 571
Bernasconi, Antonio 13 761, 770
Bernasconi, Bernato 29 835
Bernasconi, Francis (father) 29 835
Bernasconi, Francis (son) 29 835
Bernasconi, G. A. 1 736
Bernasconi, Giuseppe 29 830
Bernasconi, Laura 20 432
Bernasconi, Pietro 19 688
Bernat de Corbera 20 514
Bernat de Olivella 3 309
Bernáth, Aurél 3 820*; 13 638; 14 901
Bernatowicz, Bartholomeo 25 38, 114
Bernatzik, Hugo Adolf 10 580
Bernatzik, Wilhelm 3 821*
Bernay Abbey 3 709, 821*; 7 266; 11 *504*; 30 728
 capitals 26 596, 597
 church 26 586
 mouldings 22 215
Bernazzano, Cesare 6 356
Berndl, Richard 27 662
Berndt, Catherine H. 1 66, 68; 20 419; 21 482
Berndt, Ronald M. 1 66, 68; 20 419; 21 482
Berndtson, Gunnar (Fredrik) 3 821–2*; 30 715
Berne 3 822–4*; 20 *560*; 25 ; 30 *124*, 126
 architecture 30 140
 Bundeshaus 3 824*; 30 127
  Ständeratssaal 33 66
 Burgerspital 30 127
 ceramics 30 143, 144
 chronicles 7 244
 church 14 81
 Erlacherhof 3 *823*; 30 127
 fountains 30 136
 Franziskanerkirche 30 131
 Galerie Jürg Stuker 30 153
 Galerie Kornfeld 30 153
 glass 30 145
Berne—cont.
 Heiliggeistkirche 30 126
 Historisches Museum 14 281; 15 745; 29 516; 30 332
 houses 30 126, 127
 Kunstgewerbeschule 30 156
 Kunsthalle 3 824
 Kunstmuseum 2 116, 662; 3 824; 30 155
  collections 25 685; 27 343
  Paul Klee Stiftung 3 824; 11 309; 30 155
 libraries 19 314
 Lory-Spital 30 128
 masons' lodges 19 532
 Minster 10 407; 12 365; 18 518; 30 126
  sculpture 14 *318*; 30 136
  stained glass 13 188; 30 130
 Naturhistorisches Museum 30 155
 orphanage 30 127
 painting 30 135
 Rathaus 30 126
 St Christopher's Gate 30 136
 Sammlung für Angewandte Kunst im Kanton Bern und Gewerbebibliothek 30 155
 Swiss National Library 19 319
Bernea, Horia 3 824*
Berne Altarpiece of St John, Master of the 20 641
Berneç, Pere 12 739; 13 165, 169; 29 332
Berne Chronicle 30 130
Berneck 30 144
Bernecker, Jakob 28 51
Berne Convention 2 554
Berneker, Fran 28 862
Berneo 29 272
Berner, Bernd 30 172*
Berner, Dórte 33 245
Berner, Finn 23 222
Berner, Samuel 11 90; 31 461
Berner Arbeitsgemeinschaft 9 759
Bernerio, Girolamo, Cardinal of Ascoli 11 269
Berner Nelkenmeister see CARNATION MASTERS
Bernero, Giovanni Battista 3 824–5*; 28 19; 31 445
Bernero, Luigi 3 825
Bernero, Vittorio Amadeo 3 825
Berners, Gerald Hugh Tyrwhitt-Wilson, 14th Baron see TYRWHITT-WILSON, GERALD HUGH, 14th Baron Berners
Berners, Lord 18 793
Bernès, Pere see BERNEÇ, PERE
Bernet, G. T. Otto 24 183
Bernet Kempers, August Johan 3 825*
Berneuchen Church 1 711
Berneuil 11 623
Berneval, Alexandre de 1 519; 3 825*; 25 554; 27 254
Berneval, Colin de 3 825
Bernhard, Karl 3 512
Bernhard, Lucian 25 348
 works 25 *349*
Bernhard, Marko see PERNHART, MARKO
Bernhard, Rudolf 10 537; 30 277
Bernhard Goldschmied 33 608
Bernhard I, Bishop of Hildesheim 14 531
Bernhardt, Caspar 19 111
Bernhardt, Sarah 18 659; 25 346
 costumes 25 78
 jewellery 11 635
 posters 22 252, *252*; 25 345
 sculpture 21 830
 teachers 29 645
Bernhardt, Simon 13 852
Bernhard von Brehdenbach 12 385
Bernhard von Rohr, Archbishop of Salzburg 11 852
Bernhart, Jörg 32 771
Bernhaupt, Pankratz see SCHWENTER
Bernheim (family) 19 807; 26 209
Bernheim-Jeune (company) 3 826*; 8 622; 20 824; 24 883; 28 660; 32 740
 paintings 30 375
 prints 32 577
 staff 10 885
Bernheim-Jeune (family) 32 740
Bernheim-Jeune, Alexandre 3 826
Bernheim-Jeune, Gaston see VILLIERS, GASTON DE
Bernheim-Jeune, Joseph 3 826
Berni, Antonio 3 826*
Bernier, Claude-Louis 24 387, 389
Bernier, François 15 208, 701; 21 717
Bernier, Guillaume 31 834
Bernier, Jean 30 19
Bernier, Stanislas Louis 3 826–7*
Bernifal 25 479
Bernigeroth, Johann Martin 10 857
Bernigeroth, Martin 20 351
Bernik, Janez 3 827*; 28 861
Berninger, Jules 29 751
Berninghans, Oscar Edmund 33 185
Bernini, Domenico 3 827; 11 393
Bernini, Gianlorenzo 3 827, 828–40*; 6 584; 11 517; 16 670; 26 771, 842
 architecture 16 637
  baldacchinos 1 698; 6 485; 7 301; 14 416; 16 712; 23 489, 541; 28 632; 30 776, 781
  catafalques 6 72
  cathedrals 13 210; 26 807–8
  chapels 25 907; 29 251
  churches 4 434; 12 648; 15 121; 16 637, 638, *638*; 26 *758*, 759; 31 713
  loggias 26 840
  palaces 23 493; 24 162
  palazzi
   Collegio di Propaganda Fide 4 434
   Palazzo Barberini 4 428; 26 836
   Palazzo Capodiferro-Spada 29 250
   Palazzo Chigi-Odescalchi 6 585; 13 338; 23 493, *493*; 27 647; 31 894
   Palazzo Montecitorio 11 275; 23 492; 26 759
   Palazzo del Quirinale 26 840
  ruin buildings 27 323
  squares (town) 3 *836*; 26 759, 800
  staircases 26 760, *814*; 29 524
  turrets 26 794
 assistants 20 375
  Abbatini, Guido Ubaldo 1 20
  Anguier, Michel 2 92
  Baratta, Francesco (uncle) (*b c.* 1600-66) 3 197
  Baratta, Giovanni Maria 3 198
  Cortona, Pietro da 7 906
  Ferrata, Ercole 1 631
  Finelli, Giuliano 11 84
  Fontana (iv), Carlo (1638-1714) 11 275
  Gimignani, Giacinto 12 648
  Giosafatti, Giuseppe 12 680
  Mazzuoli, Giuseppe (1644-1725) 20 909
  Raggi, (Ercole) Antonio (1624-86) 1 631; 25 851
  Romanelli, Giovanni Francesco 26 565
  Rossi, Mattia de 6 585; 27 195
  Vanni, Raffaele 31 885
 attributions 3 828; 19 59
 book illustrations 3 205
 caricatures 5 755, 756, 760; 23 353
 cartouches 5 *899*

Bernini, Gianlorenzo—cont.
choir-stalls **26** 810
coats of arms **2** 105
collaboration **18** 76; **24** 339
Abbatini, Guido Ubaldo **1** 20
Bernini, Luigi **3** 840
Borromini, Francesco **4** 428
Carlone (i), Giovanni Andrea, II (1639-97) **26** 823
Castelli, Domenico **6** 23
Du Quesnoy, François (1597-1643) **9** 410
Fancelli, Cosimo **10** 782
Ferrata, Ercole **11** 17
Lucenti, Girolamo **19** 768
Maratti, Carlo **20** 375
Mochi, Francesco (1580-1654) **21** 754
Pellegrini, Carlo **22** 103
Raggi, (Ercole) Antonio (1624-86) **25** 851
Rainaldi, Carlo **25** 862
Schor, Johann Paul **28** 162
Urban VIII, Pope (*reg* 1623-44) **3** 205
competitions **7** 665, 913
copies **32** 395
decorative works **26** 771
drawings **9** 222; **14** 873; **24** 339
frames **11** 393
furniture **16** 727; **26** 780
Gesamtkunstwerk **12** 497
groups and movements **3** 261, 262, 263, 264
metalwork **16** 743; **20** 921; **21** 805
methods **19** 356; **21** 770
modelli **21** *770*
models **2** 336
musical instruments **22** 374
pageants **24** 404
paintings **1** 20; **3** *834*; **26** 818
patrons and collectors **16** 639
Alexander VII, Pope (*reg* 1655-67) **6** 584, 585; **8** 202; **16** 638, 763; **26** 810, 814; **28** 681
Alfonso IV, 9th Duke of Modena and Reggio (*reg* 1658-62) **10** 527
Altieri, Padrone, Cardinal **1** 728
Barberini (family) (17th cent.) **2** 499; **3** 205
Barberini, Antonio, Cardinal **3** 208
Borghese, Marcantonio IV, Prince **4** 407
Borghese, Scipione, Cardinal **4** 404, 406; **16** 670; **26** 773
Bracciano, Livio Odescalchi, Duca di **23** 353
Carmelite Order **5** 778
Charles I, King of England and Scotland (*reg* 1625-49) **29** 801
Christina, Queen of Sweden (*reg* 1632-54) **32** 8
Clement IX, Pope (*reg* 1667-70) **27** 172
Clement X, Pope (*reg* 1670-76) **1** 727
Coke, Thomas, 1st Earl of Leicester of the 1st creation (1697-1759) **7** 540
Contini Bonacossi, Alessandro, Conte **7** 782
Cornaro, Federigo, Cardinal **7** 861
Francesco I, 8th Duke of Modena and Reggio (*reg* 1629-58) **10** 526
Gregory XV, Pope (*reg* 1621-3) **19** 778
Henrietta Maria, Queen of England and Scotland (1609-69) **29** 803
Howard (ii), Henry, 4th Earl of Carlisle **14** 808
Innocent X, Pope (*reg* 1644-55) **23** 898, 899; **26** 810
Jesuit Order **16** 763; **17** 510
Bernini, Gianlorenzo
patrons and collectors—cont.
Lely, Peter **19** 124
Louis XIV, King of France (*reg* 1643-1715) **4** 551; **11** 744
Ludovisi, Ludovico, Cardinal **1** 626
Mazarin, Jules, Cardinal **20** 895
Medinaceli, Luís de la Cerda Fernández de Córdoba Folch de Cardona y Aragón, 9th Duque de (1660-1711) **21** 35
Paul V, Pope (*reg* 1605-21) **4** 405
Peretti (-Montalto), Alessandro, Cardinal **24** 399
Pio di Savoia, Carlo Francesco, Cardinal **24** 834
Pourtalès-Gorgier, James-Alexandre, Comte de **25** 383
Pozzo (Lumbroso), Cassiano dal **25** 412
Reynolds, Joshua **26** 280
Roscioli, Giovanni Maria **27** 160
Tarnowski, Jan Feliks, Count and Waleria **30** 345
Urban VIII, Pope (*reg* 1623-44) **2** 319; **3** 205, 206; **26** 809
Victoria and Albert Museum **20** 27
productions **30** 668
pupils
Antomaria Parodi, Domenico di **24** 203
Bernini, Luigi **3** 840
Bolgi, Andrea **4** 254
Chéron, Charles-Jean-François **6** 553
Contini, Giovanni Battista **7** 780
Delcour, Jean (1631-1707) **8** 661
Fancelli, Cosimo **10** 782
Lucenti, Girolamo **19** 768
Parodi, Filippo **16** 701
Pellegrini, Carlo **24** 339
reproductions in ceramics **8** 748
reproductive prints by others **17** 599; **21** 85; **25** 77; **29** 399
sculpture **1** 626; **2** 163; **4** 254; **7** 380, 382, 383; **9** 410; **10** 744; **16** 698; **19** 768; **23** 294; **26** 847; **28** 677
altarpieces **1** 627, 712
altars **27** 172
busts **3** *833*; **4** *406*; **5** 301, *302*; **9** 175; **32** 864
ciboria (ii) (structure) **1** 698; **7** 303
crucifixes **8** 216; **10** 501
equestrian monuments **10** 442; **11** 558; **12** 726
fountains **5** 826; **11** 343, *343*; **16** 638; **20** 840; **22** 44, *45*; **24** 572; **26** 758, 759; **31** 63
monumental **2** 849
mythological **2** 612; **3** *829*; **22** 414; **29** 562, 563, *563*
pedestals **24** 316
religious **3** *262*, *832*; **7** 226; **10** 478; **15** 138
sarcophagi **27** *830*, 831
statuettes **29** 570
tombs **6** 583; **20** 909; **26** 809; **29** 570; **31** 127, *127*
sponsorship **23** 899
stage design **30** 668
stucco **29** 830
studio **16** 697
workshop **20** 839; **26** 773
writings **3** 265; **16** 637
Bernini, Leonardo **11** 194
Bernini, Luigi **3** 827, 831, 838, 840*
Bernini, Paolo **3** 827, 838
Bernini, Pietro **3** 827–9*; **22** 477
attributions **3** 829
collaboration **3** 840; **4** 405; **22** 422; **25** 227
Bernini, Pietro—cont.
patrons and collectors **3** 205; **22** 486
pupils **3** 829, 840; **10** 801
restorations **4** 407
restorations by others **4** 406
works **3** *828*; **16** 703; **22** 484; **26** 847
Bernis, François-Joachim de Pierres, Cardinal **2** 27; **3** 840*; **24** 583; **30** 865
Bernl, Richard **24** 826
Bernolakov, Esterházy Palace **14** 886; **15** 13
Bernold, Bishop **22** 817; **31** 769
Bernouard, François **22** 92
Bernouin, Archbishop **3** 872
Bernoulli, Hans **2** 512; **3** 840–41*; **28** 122; **30** 127
Berns, Marla C.
works **1** *248*, *286*, *345*
Bernshtam, A. **1** 504
Bernshteyn, Mikhail D. **19** 13; **33** 522
Bernstein **14** 893
Bernstein, Carl **3** 800; **12** 474
Bernstein, Henry **32** 740
Bernstein, Morris Louis *see* LOUIS, MORRIS
Bernstorff, J(ohan) H(artvig) E(rnst) von, Graf **3** 841*; **8** 758; **17** 446
Bernt, Rudolf **18** 101
Bernts, Henrik **17** 741
Berntsen, Kåre **23** 243
Bernulphus Codex *see under* CODICES → individual manuscripts
Bernus, Jacques **3** 841–2*
Bernus, Noël **3** 841
Bernward, Saint, Bishop of Hildesheim **3** 842*; **12** 452, 471; **14** 531; **26** 572
architecture **14** 532
bronze **9** 153
manuscripts **4** 6; **14** 532; **23** 652, 654
metalwork **14** 532, 535; **23** 658, 659
monuments **22** 44
sculpture **7** 381; **14** 532; **23** 648
textiles **14** 532
Bernward Bible *see under* BIBLES → individual manuscripts
Bernward Cross *see under* HILDESHEIM → Cathedral of St Mariae
Beroaldo, Filippo, I **13** 314
Beroe-Augusta Trajana *see* STARA ZAGORA
Beroepsvereniging van Nederlandse Interieurarchitecten **22** 869
Beromünster **30** 144
Monastery **30** 146
St Michael **9** 668; **26** 635; **30** 150
Berquin, Jean **4** 391
Berquin, Pierre **4** 391
Berrecci, Bartolomeo **3** 842–3*; **18** 425, 427
architecture **25** 96
architectural decorations **25** 111
castles **3** 711; **11** 713; **18** 431
churches **18** 427, 432, *433*
assistants **33** 614
patrons and collectors **16** 866
sculpture **22** 167; **25** 111, 113, 135; **30** 345
tombs **18** 433
workshop **18** 433; **30** 345
Berrettini, Filippo **7** 906
Berrettini, Francesco **7** 905, 906
Berrettini, Giovanni **7** 905, 906
Berrettini da Cortona, Pietro *see* CORTONA, PIETRO DA
Berrettoni, Niccolò **6** 568
Berri, Melchior **3** 843*; **19** 769
teachers **33** 40
works **3** 335, 336; **30** 154
Berrighem, Nicolaes (Pietersz.) *see* BERCHEM, NICOLAES (PIETERSZ.)
Berrima Court House **18** 887
Berrington Hall (Hereford & Worcs) **8** 47, *48*
Berrio, Gaspar Miguel de **4** 261; **25** 365
works **25** *365*
Berrio, Marqués de Xaral de *see* XARAL DE BERRIO, Marqués de
Berritsgård **4** 781
Berrocal, Miguel **3** 843*; **29** 297
Berrojo de Isla, Felipe **29** 270; **31** 823
Berruecos, Diego Durán *see* DURÁN BERRUECOS, DIEGO
Berruer, Pierre-François **3** 843–4*; **7** 837; **28** 847
Berruguete, Alonso **3** 844, 845–7*; **27** 818; **29** 289, 290, 313; **32** 493
assistants **32** 576
choir-stalls **29** 290
collaboration **32** 493; **33** 622
paintings **29** 277
patrons and collectors **7** 488; **11** 250; **30** 374
pupils **12** 722
retables **29** 289
sculpture **3** *847*; **5** 362; **8** 79; **16** 695; **26** 250; **31** 89, 90, 92, 822
tombs **31** 87
wood-carvings **3** *846*; **29** 311
Berruguete, Inocencio **17** 656; **31** 89
Berruguete, Pedro **3** 844–5*; **7** 345; **29** 277
attributions **17** 702, 705; **31** 740
collaboration **11** 483
paintings **29** 276, *277*, 298, *298*
portraits **31** 744
retables **1** 710; **2** 865; **3** *845*; **9** 108; **11** 483
patrons and collectors **2** 278; **9** 112; **16** 659; **21** 125
pupils **3** 845
Berry, de **29** 668
Berry, Ducs de **11** 655
Berry, Caroline de Bourbon, Duchesse de **4** *543*, 556–7*, *557*
collections **4** 330
drawings **12** 154
paintings **2** 702; **8** 640; **9** 364; **14** 489; **31** 373
porcelain **13** 206
prints **28** 170
sculpture **19** 125
Berry, Charles (-Ferdinand) de Bourbon, Duc de (1778-1820) **4** 330, *543*, *557*; **8** 705; **11** 258; **12** 153; **18** 700; **24** 418
Berry, Charles de Valois, Duc de **17** 458; **20** 651; **31** *833*, 843–4*
architecture **5** 888
manuscripts **11** 355; **17** 458; **20** 646, *646*; **31** 832
paintings **32** 744
silver **9** 29
Berry, Christina **10** 483
Berry, James **1** 533
Berry, Jean I de Valois, Duc de **17** 456; **22** 901; **31** *833*, 834, 836–41*
altars **16** 854
architecture **4** 578, 582; **8** 484, 485; **11** 511; **13** 59; **14** 74; **25** 83; **27** 550
coats of arms **14** 413, 423
collections **6** 76; **7** 564; **11** 660; **18** 521; **19** 391
coral **7** 835
enamel **11** 615; **13** 170
gems **12** 257
gold **11** 738; **13** 159
hardstones **11** 635
ivory-carvings **13** 175, 176
jewellery **31** 834
Berry, Jean I de Valois, Duc de—cont.
manuscripts **13** 133, 153
manuscripts (religious) **2** 113; **11** 660; **17** 462; **25** 693; **31** 832
Belles Heures (New York, Cloisters) **4** 395; **6** 174; **16** 838; **19** 388, 389–90, *392*; **25** 692
Belleville Breviary (Paris, Bib. N., MSS lat. 10483-4) **3** 642
Berry Apocalypse (New York, Pierpont Morgan Lib., MS. M. 133) **2** 223; **20** 629
Bible historiale **4** 12; **20** 652
Books of Hours **31** 308–10
Grandes Heures (Paris, Bib. N., MS. lat. 919) **3** 642; **20** 633
Lectionary (Bourges, Bib. Mun., MSS 33-6) **20** 634
miniatures (manuscript illumination) **16** *852*
Petites Heures of Jean, Duc de Berry (Paris, Bib. N., MS. lat. 18014) **3** 642; **13** 672; **17** *462*, 462; **25** 691
Psalter of Jean, Duc de Berry (Paris, Bib. N., MS. fr. 13091) **4** 583; **6** 389; **13** 154
Très Belles Heures (Brussels, Bib. Royale Albert 1er, MSS 11060-1) **4** 395; **20** 634, 637
Très Belles Heures de Notre-Dame (Paris, Bib. N., MS. nouv. acq. lat. 3093; Paris, Louvre, R.F. 2022-4) **8** 469; **13** 154; **20** 742, 751
Très Riches Heures (Chantilly, Mus. Condé, MS. 65) **4** 371; **7** 597; **9** 13; **10** 475; **13** 155; **14** 74; **19** 388, *394*; **23** 523; **29** 414; **31** 50, 154, *838*
calendar **2** 649
calendar miniatures **5** 428; **19** *394*
Château **2** 339; **6** 58, 63; **21** 549, *549*
naturalism **11** 531; **12** 287; **18** 704
portraits **3** 596
Turin-Milan Hours (Turin, Mus. Civ. A. Ant., MS. 47) **31** 448
manuscripts (secular) **7** 234; **13** 826; **16** 854; **20** 719
Antiquités judaïques (Paris, B. Nat. MS. fr. 247) **7** 242; **11** 355
Des Cleres et nobles femmes (Paris, Bib. N. MS. fr. 598) **20** 629, 652
Fleur des histoires de la terre d'Orient **31** 290
Grandes Chroniques **20** 652
Le Brut d'Angleterre (Paris, Bib. N., MS. fr. 1454) **20** 629
Livre des merveilles (Paris, Bib. N., MS. fr. 2810) **5** 209; **20** 633; **31** 290
romances **26** 561
Térence des Ducs (Paris, Bib. Arsenal, MS. 664) **30** 487
Terence of Martin Gouge (Paris, Bib. N., MS. lat. 7907 A) **30** 487
medals **13** 155; **24** 864
metalwork **27** 550
paintings **10** 180; **11** 655; **13** 131; **17** 461
sculpture **3** 455; **13** 76, 77, 78; **17** 457
sponsorship **16** 851
tapestries **30** 313
Berry, Jean II de Valois, Duc de **17** 515
Berry, Jeanne de Valois, Duchesse de **10** 180
Berry, John L. **33** 224
Berry, Marie de Valois, Duchesse de **20** 719

Berry, Marie-Louise-Elisabeth de Bourbon, Duchesse de **11** 626
Berry, Maurice **8** 111
Berry, Melchior **29** 848
Berry Apocalypse, Master of the **6** 503; **20** 629*
Berry's Cleres Femmes, Master of **20** 629*
attributions **20** 652
works **20** *629*
Berselius **20** 852
Bersha, Deir el- **3** 848*; **9** 773, *774*
coffins **10** 10
tombs **9** 838
Ahanakht (Tomb 5) **3** 848
Djehutihotpe (Tomb 2) **3** 848; **9** 815, *816*, 823, 824
Djehutinakhte (Tomb 10) **3** 848
wall paintings **9** 811
Bersohn, Matthias **17** 581; **25** 138
Berssenbrugge, (Bernhard) Henri (Wilhelm) **3** 849*
Bersuire, Pierre **15** 83
Berswordt, Segebodo **7** 723; **20** 766
Berswordt Master **7** 724; **20** 630*
Bertalan, William **2** 152
Bertall **3** 422, 849*
Bertalozzo, Gabriele **20** 320
Bertani, Giovanni Battista **3** 849–50*
collaboration **8** 4
house **3** *850*
patrons and collectors **12** 909
reproductive prints by others **12** 558
works **2** 20; **12** 911; **20** 320, 322
Bertani, Giuseppe **9** 740
Bertarelli, Achille, collection *see under* MILAN → Castello Sforzesco
Bertaut, François **25** 278
Bertaux, Emile **3** 851*; **14** 578; **32** 233
Bertaux, Léon **14** 282
Bertea, Ernesto **28** 318
Bertelli, Ferdinando **3** 851
Bertelli, Luca **3** 851
Bertelli, Orazio **3** 851
Bertel's, Andrey **12** 856
Bertelsmann, Walter **33** 383
Bertem, Pieterskerk
sculpture **7** *739*
Bertemmes, Roger **19** 827
Bertessi, J. **31** 816
Berthault, Louis Marie **11** 579; **23** 259
Berthault, Louis-Martin **4** 303; **7** 677
Bertheau, Margarita **1** 783; **8** 17
Berthélemy, Jean-Simon **3** 851–2*
groups and movements **26** 737; **31** 373
reproductions in tapestry **12** 830
works **11** 261; **14** 586; **30** 672
Berthélmy, Jean-Simon
works **19** *723*
Berthelot, Gilles **2** 889
Berthelot, Guillaume **3** 852–3*; **4** 405
collaboration **13** 825
patrons and collectors **26** 348
works **26** 840
Berthenoux, La *see* LA BERTHENOUX
Berthet, Paul **30** 417
Berthevin, Pierre **30** 97, 99
Berthiau **25** 627
Berthier, Alexandre, Marshal (*fl* 1806) **18** 176
Berthier, Alexandre, Prince de Wagram (1883-1918) **11** 664; **26** 209
Berthier, Marc **11** 584, 602
Berthing, Otto **18** 849
Berthold (*fl* 1070) **26** 674
Berthold, Abbot of Weingarten (*fl* 1200-15) **26** 677
Berthold, Bishop of Hildesheim (*reg* 1119-30) **14** 531
Berthold III, Duke of Zähringen **11** 749
Berthold, Hans **3** 853*; **25** 111
Berthold, Karl **12** 450; **29** 120
Berthold-Mahn, Charles **1** 21
Bertholdus, Master **33** 458
Bertholle, Jean **4** 98; **8** 891
Bertholo, René (Augusto da Costa) **3** 853*; **6** 68; **8** 15; **25** 300
Berthon, George Theodore **3** 853–4*; **5** 564
Berthon, Paul **3** 854*
Berthon, René Théodore **3** 853
Berthoud **5** 380
Berthouville **26** 858, *859*, *905*; **27** 2, 82
Berthoz, Hippolyte de **12** 846
Berti, Pagno d'Antonio **27** 656
Bertie, Charlotte (Elizabeth) *see* SCHREIBER, CHARLOTTE (ELIZABETH) (1813-95)
Bertie, Robert, 4th Earl and 1st Marquess of Lindsey **30** 123
Bertiga, Jurubena **20** 166
Berti Gospels *see under* GOSPEL BOOKS → individual manuscripts
Bertin, Armand **22** 208
Bertin, Christophe **8** 883
Bertin, Edouard (-François) **3** 854*; **4** 36
Bertin, François **11** 894
Bertin, Henri **29** 92
Bertin, Jean-Victor **3** 854–5*
pupils **7** 877; **8** 538; **14** 489; **21** 424; **24** 892; **27** 265; **31** 571
works **18** 714
Bertin, Léger **3** 414
Bertin, Léonard-Jean-Baptiste-Henri **28** 521
Bertin, Nicolas **3** 855–6*
collaboration **8** 883
pupils **8** 792; **31** 69
reproductive prints by others **30** 344
teachers **4** 536; **31** 817
works **3** *855*
Bertin, Rose **4** 555
Bertinelli, Andrea **29** 839
Bertinetti, Francesco **3** 856*
Bertini, Brenta & Co. **3** 856, 857; **29** 507
Bertini, Domenico **7** 366
Bertini, Fratelli **3** 857
Bertini, Gianni **2** 526; **20** 913
Bertini, Giovanni **2** 110; **13** 98
Bertini, Giuseppe (*fl* 1839-45; father) **2** 632
Bertini, Giuseppe (1825-98; son) **3** 856–7*; **25** 143
personal collection **16** 774
pupils **3** 316, 437, 903, 919; **5** 726; **6** 115; **8** 135; **22** 83; **25** 894; **30** 277
works **3** *857*
Bertini, Lodovicha **27** 859
Bertini, Pacio **2** 110; **13** 98
Bertino di Piero **12** 710
Berto di Giovanni (di Marco) **3** 858*; **15** 60
Bertoia, Harry **3** 858*; **27** 474
works **3** 177; **29** 97; **31** 633
Bertoia, Jacopo **3** 858–9*; **26** 770
collaboration **33** 718
patrons and collectors **10** 810
works **3** *859*; **5** 684; **32** 506
Bertoia chairs *see under* CHAIRS → types
Bertolani, Gaetano **12** 584
Bertoldo di Giovanni **1** 102; **2** 523; **3** 859–61*; **11** 217; **16** 778; **27** 775
assistants **1** 161
attributions **1** 161; **11** 694
collaboration **1** 161; **3** 636
competitions **7** 672
Bertoldo di Giovanni—cont.
patrons and collectors **16** 689; **21** 14; **25** 76; **27** 863
pupils **13** 280; **16** 695; **21** 433; **31** 188
works **3** *860*, *861*; **11** 217; **13** 730; **16** 691; **20** 919; **29** 568
Bertolini (family) **32** 203
Bertolino da Novara *see* BARTOLINO DA NOVARA
Bertolino della Canonica **11** 294
Bertolli, Antonio **4** 493
Bertolotti, Antonino **3** 862*
Bertolotti, Davide **23** 829
Bertolucci, Attilio **19** 637
Bertolucci, Giuseppe **24** 535
Bertoncini, Mario **29** 99
Bertoni, Gabriele de *see* GABRIELE DE BERTONI
Bertoni, Wander **2** 804
Bertos, Francesco **3** 862*
Bertotti Scamozzi, Ottavio **3** 862–4*; **32** 410
works **3** *864*
Bertozzi, Bartolommeo **8** 535
Bertrade, Queen (*fl* 751-68) **27** 549
Bertram, Master **3** 864–6*; **13** 152, 153; **14** 101
altarpieces **1** 710; **3** *865*, *866*; **12** 382, *383*; **13** 116
paintings **12** 383, 469; **13** 151; **18** 157
Bertram of Minden *see* BERTRAM, MASTER
Bertrán, José **5** 509
Bertrand, Abbot of Cluny **7** 476
Bertrand, Claude-Joseph-Alexandre **3** 866–7*
Bertrand, David **3** 867
Bertrand, Gaston **3** 867*
groups and movements **3** 565; **5** 45; **17** 518
works **3** 565
Bertrand, James **3** 867*
Bertrand, Philippe **3** 867–8*; **4** 587; **11** 754
Bertrand, Pierre **18** 795
Bertrand de Deux, Cardinal **2** 18
Bertrand de Meynal **3** 868*; **23** 709
Bertrand de Montaigu, Abbot of Moissac **21** 798
Bertrés, Philippe **4** 259; **18** 777; **27** 702
Bertrix, Enrique **6** 597
Bertsch, Auguste **22** 424
Bertsch, Karl **11** 582; **14** 362
Bertubani Monastery *see under* DAVID GAREDZHI
Bertucci, Giovanni Battista, il vecchio (*fl* 1495-*d* 1516) **3** 868*, 916
Bertucci, Giovanni Battista, il giovane (*c.* 1540-1614) **3** 868
Bertucci, Girolamo **3** 868
Bertucci, Michele **3** 868
Bertucci, Nicola *see* BERTUZZI, NICOLA
Bertucci, Raffaelle **3** 868
Bertuch, Friedrich Justin **12** 413; **33** 37
Bertuchi, Mario **22** 129
Bertuzzi, Nicola **3** 869*; **11** 395; **20** 497
Beruete (y Moret), Aureliano (de) **3** 869*; **14** 26; **24** 829; **29** 284
Bérulle, Cardinal de **23** 472
Berullians *see* ORATORIANS
Bervic, Charles-Clément **3** 869–70*; **14** 394; **33** 196
Bervic, Jean-Guillaume *see* BERVIC, CHARLES-CLÉMENT
Berwart, Blasius, I (*d* 1590) **3** 870*
collaboration **3** 20, 870; **31** 311
works **12** 369, 370; **17** 740; **29** 875
Berwart, Blasius, II (*d* ?1610) **3** 870
Berwart, Georg **3** 20
Berwart, Martin **3** 870*; **12** 369
Berwart, Sylvester, I (*d* 1553) **3** 870
Berwart, Sylvester, II (*d* after 1565) **3** 870
Berwick, Carlos Miguel Fitz-James Stuart y Silva, 7th Duque de *see* ALBA, 14th Duque de
Berwick, James Fitz-James Stuart y Falco, 10th Duque de *see* ALBA, 17th Duque de
Berwick, Robert Alexander Dean **28** 557*; **31** 864
Berwick, Thomas Noel Hill, 2nd Baron *see* HILL, THOMAS NOEL, 2nd Baron Berwick
Berwick-upon-Tweed (Northumb.) **21** 569; **31** 711
fortifications **19** 60; **21** 548; **31** 710
beryl **22** 158
see also AQUAMARINES; EMERALDS
Bérythe, Monsignor de **2** 884
Berytus *see under* BEIRUT
Berzé-la-Ville, priory chapel of **3** 871*; **11** *505*; **13** 139; **22** 520
wall paintings **11** 530; **26** 651, *651*, 654, 655
Berzighelli, Camillo **23** 880
Bērziņš, Boriss **3** 871*
Bes **9** 859
Besakih **3** 871–2*, *872*; **15** *754*
Pura Penataran Agung **3** 871–2*
temples **15** 768
Besalú, S Vicenç **26** 610
Besamampy **1** *413*; **20** 40
Besançon **3** 867, 872–3*; **11** *504*
Bibliothèque Municipale **3** 873
cameo **27** 76
Cathedral **1** 695
fortress **21** 568
glass **11** 611
Hôtel de l'Intendance **4** 755
Monastery of St Vincent **11** 665
Musée des Beaux-Arts et d'Archéologie
collections **3** 873; **4** 755; **12** 567; **24** 177; **27** 571
directors **12** 568
silver **11** 617
theatre **23** 490; **30** *670*, 671
Besançon, Master of Jacques de *see* JACQUES DE BESANÇON, MASTER OF
Besançon Psalter *see under* PSALTERS → individual manuscripts
Besant, Annie **30** 710; **31** 903
Besarab, Matei, Prince **25** 340
Besarel **16** 731
Besawal **29** 824
Beschey, Balthazar **3** 873*; **14** 479; **19** 165; **32** 252
Beschi, Constanzo Giuseppe **17** 512
Beseler, B. **12** 168
Besford Court (Hereford & Worcs) **10** 272
wallpaper **32** *814*
Beshelmeyer, German **7** 527
Beshir
carpets **5** III
Mausoleum of Sayyid Ahmad **6** 277
Beshkov, Il'ya, Art Gallery *see under* PLEVEN
Beshmai, Tell **31** 435
church **9** 543
Besho, Mambo
works **1** *515*
Beşika Bay **31** 354, 356
Beşik-Sivritepe **31** 354
Beşik-Yassítepe **31** 354
Besisi *see* MAH MERI
Beskhov, Il'ya **3** 873–4*
Besler, Basilius **18** 44
Bešlić, Ana **28** 453
Besme, Victor **5** 41
Besnagar **3** 874*; **15** 245, *285*, 292
capitals **15** 430
inscription **15** 213
pillar **15** 215, 430
sculpture **15** 429–30, 494
stepwell **29** 635
stucco **29** 824
Vasudeva Temple **15** 251
yakṣa **15** *430*
Besnard, (Paul-) Albert **3** 874–5*; **11** 547, 548
collaboration **12** 13
patrons and collectors **19** 230; **23** 882; **24** 142
works **22** 330
Besnes y Irigoyen, Juan Manuel **31** 754
Besnier, Isaac **3** 875
Besnier, John **3** 875
Besnier, Nicolas **3** 461
Besnier, Peter **3** 875*; **10** 263
Besnier, Thomas **3** 875
Besnyő, Eva **3** 876*
Besoli, Carlo **8** 159
Besovy-Sledki **27** 365
Besozzi, Giovanni Ambrogio **5** 290
Besozzo, Leonardo (de' Molinari) da *see* LEONARDO (DE' MOLINARI) DA BESOZZO
Besozzo, Michelino (Molinari) da *see* MICHELINO (MOLINARI) DA BESOZZO
Bespalov, Ivan **27** 420
Bespalova-Mikhaleva, Tamara **27** 414
Beşparmak Daği **7** 228; **26** 483
Besprosvanni, Sam(uel) *see* VANNI, SAM(UEL)
Besro, Devi Marha **15** 323
Bessa, Pancrace **11** 228
bessales *see under* BRICK → types
Bessarabia *see* MOLDOVA
Bessarabova, Natalya **27** 411
Bessarion, Cardinal **3** 876*; **14** 869
architecture **32** 545
books **32** 222
manuscripts **20** 675
Bessborough, Frederick Ponsonby, 10th Earl of *see* PONSONBY, FREDERICK, 10th Earl of Bessborough
Bessborough, Mary Ponsonby, Countess of *see* PONSONBY, MARY, Countess of Bessborough
Bessborough, William Ponsonby, 2nd Earl of *see* PONSONBY, WILLIAM, 2nd Earl of Bessborough
Besse, Antonin **23** 684
Bessel, Abbot of Gottweig **2** 825
Bessel, Gottfried **3** 876–7*
Bessel, Johann Georg *see* BESSEL, GOTTFRIED
Bessemer, Henry **8** 285; **16** 51, 54
Bessemers, Anthoni **32** 252
Bessemers, Marie de *see* VERHULST, MAYKEN
Besser, Hans **3** 877*
Besserer, Heinrich **13** 187
Besserer, Johann Jakob **4** 747
Besseringen **6** 155
Bessho Onsen, Anrakuji **17** *72*, 73, 132
Bessi, Carlo Giuseppe **11** 458
Bessiere, Giovanni **20** 216
Bess of Hardwick *see* TALBOT, ELIZABETH, Countess of Hardwick
Besson, Faustin **3** 877*; **8** 618
Besson, Hyacinthe **9** 112
Besson, Jean-Séraphin-Désiré **3** 877
Besṭām *see* BISTAM
Bestard, Jaime **3** 877–8*; **24** 102
patrons and collectors **24** 101
pupils **17** 585
works **24** 98

Bestelmeier, Georg H. **31** 258
Bestelmeyer, German **3** 878*
  groups and movements **4** 143
  pupils **20** 387; **29** 377
  teachers **30** 733
  works **19** 111
Besterman, T. **4** 20
Bestiaries **2** 102; **3** 878–9*; **13** 130; **14** 406; **24** 577; **26** 661
Bestiarius **26** 639
Bestle, Georg **4** 69
Best Mangard, Adolfo *see* MANGARD, ADOLFO BEST
Best Products Co. Inc. **4** 790; **19** 286; **28** 798
Bestürling, Arnold von *see* ARNOLD VON WESTFALEN
Besuki **27** 831
Beswicke, John **23** 327
Besztercebánya *see* BANSKA BYSTRICA
Betancourt, A. **27** 576
Betancourt, Rodrigo Arenas *see* ARENAS BETANCOURT, RODRIGO
Betancourt, Walter **8** 233
Betania Church **12** 320, 323
Betanú **29** 217
Bēta Śellāsē, Mikā'ēl **10** 577
Betatakin **22** 566
Bete **1** 360, 391–2; **8** 21, 22; **13** 860
betel-nut *see under* BARK → types
betel sets
  historical and regional traditions
    Burma **5** 254*
    Cambodia **5** 508*, *508*
    Indian subcontinent **15** 727
    Indonesia **15** 810, 813
    Laos **18** 776*
    Malaysia **20** 175*
    Philippines **24** 627–8
    Thailand **30** 631*
  materials
    brass **20** 175
    bronze **20** 175
    enamel **18** 776
    gold **20** 175; **30** 631
    lacquer **5** 254; **30** 631
    silver **5** 254, *508*, 508; **18** 776; **20** 175; **30** 631
    teak **30** 631
Bête Noire, La **30** 488
Betew, Panton **11** 909
Beth Alpha **3** 880*; **16** *565*
  mosaics **9** 567; **17** 542
  synagogue **17** 542
    mosaics **17** 534, 557, 558
  wall paintings **17** 556
Bethel **1** 892
Bethel, Alfred **22** 329
Bethel, Carrie
  works **22** *660*
Bethencourt da Silva, Joaquín **13** 295
Bethersden **10** 227
Bethge, Hans **20** 380
Beth Guvrin **9** 568
Beth Hala **9** 620
Béthisy-Saint-Pierre **13** 211
Bethlehem (Israel) **3** 880–83*; **9** *513*; **16** *565*; **17** 500; **23** 847
  Cave of the Nativity **3** 882
  Church of the Nativity **3** 329, 880–83*, *881*, *882*; **7** 252, 254; **9** 523, 529, 539, 540, 549; **20** 519; **28** 629
    frescoes **17** 502
    mosaics **9** 567; **17** 504, *504*; **22** 157
    roof **30** 905
    sculpture **26** 629
  embroidery **16** 459
  Georgian church **12** 323
  hats **16** 459
  mosaics **3** 882
  sculpture **26** 629
Bethlehem (PA; USA) **22** 80; **31** 634
  Old Chapel **22** 80
Bethlen, Gabriel, Prince of Transylvania *see* GABRIEL BETHLEN, Prince of Transylvania
Bethlen, Katá, Princess of Transylvania *see* KATÁ BETHLEN, Princess of Transylvania
Beth Ris'yar Church **9** 543
Beth Shan **3** 883–4*; **9** *513*, 568; **16** *565*; **30** *180*
  coffins **24** 635
  glass **1** 865
  mosaics **9** 567, 568
  pottery **24** 634
  seals **1** 863; **30** 188
  synagogues **17** 558, 570
  temples **30** 188
  Tomb 66 **24** *635*
Beth Shearim **3** 884*; **16** *565*; **17** 534
  reliefs **17** *554*
  sarcophagi **17** 554
Béthune, Armanol de **31** 879
Béthune, François Gaston, Marquis de **32** 700
Bethune, Jean-Baptiste-Charles-François, Baron **3** 585, 884–5*; **32** 251
  collaboration **5** 828; **8** 191; **14** 167; **31** 855
  education (art) **3** 618; **12** 519
  groups and movements **13** 207, 208
  pupils **3** 548; **31** 855
  works **3** 548, 549, 578; **4** 922; **13** *208*; **25** 717
Béthune, Maximilien de, Baron de Rosny *see* SULLY, MAXIMILIEN DE BÉTHUNE, Duc de
Béthune, Maximilien-François de, Duc de Sully *see* SULLY, MAXIMILIEN-FRANÇOIS DE BÉTHUNE, Duc de
Béthune, Philippe de **4** 552; **7** 394
Beti **5** 523; **10** 787, 791
Betini, Giovanni **12** 668
Betjeman, John **3** 885*; **10** 377; **20** 475; **24** 839
Betlanovce Castle **28** 849
Betle, Georg *see* PETEL, GEORG
Betliar Castle **28** 850
béton brut **5** 55
Betondorp *see* AMSTERDAM → housing → Watergraafsmeer
Betsileo **20** 35, 36, 37, 38, 39
Betsimisaraka **20** 35, 39, 40
Betskoy, Ivan **27** 442, 579; **31** 486
Betten, Herman **10** 221
Betten, Michiel **10** 221
Better Building Practice *see* BEDRE BYGGESKIK
Betterton, Thomas **30** 674
Bettes, Edward **3** 886
Bettes, John (i) (*fl* 1545–*d*?1570) **3** 886*; **10** 246
Bettes, John (ii) (*d* 1616) **3** 886*; **19** 515
Betti, Antonio Giusto **1** 766
Betti, Betto di Francesco **25** 159
Betti, Sigismondo **31** 901
Bettignies, A. C. de (*b* 1736) **3** 599
Bettignies, Amélie de (*b* 1757) **3** 591; **31** 220
Bettignies, de (family) **3** 599
Bettinelli, Pecora **6** 91
Bettini, Constantino **11** 189
Bettini, Francesco di *see* FRANCESCO DI BETTINI
Bettini, Giovanni (Battista) **3** 886*
Bettini, Riccardo **4** 630
Bettino da Bologna **4** 275; **13** 96
Bettisi, Leonardo **5** 413; **10** 751
Bettkober, Christian Friedrich Heinrich Siegismund **30** 854
Betto, Giovanni **19** 696
Betto di Geri **19** 200
Bettoli, Luigi **3** 887
Bettoli, Nicola **3** 886–7*; **24** 193
Bettona, Crispolto di Polto da *see* CRISPOLTO DI POLTO DA BETTONA
Betton & Evans **29** 506
Betts, Georgina **23** 136
Betts, John **31** 265, 267
Bettystown (Co. Meath)
  brooches **15** *872*
Bétula **31** 509
Betussi, Giuseppe **5** 887; **15** 87; **23** 332
Betz **13** 200
Betz, Willem **3** 230
Beuckelaer, Joachim **3** 887–8*
  teachers **1** 168
  works **1** 658; **3** 558, *887*; **12** 288; **29** 666
Beudot, Augustin-Marie **24** 387
Beuerlein *see* BEIERLEIN
Beughen, Jan Carel van, II **32** 241
Beugniet, Adolphe **3** 888*
Beugniet, Georges-Albert-Félix **3** 888*
Beugnot **25** 383
Beulé, Ernest-Charles-Auguste **2** 670; **3** 888–9*; **25** 172
Beuningen, Daniel George van **3** 889*; **22** 905
Beuque, Jacques van de **4** 727
Beurdeley, (Louis-Auguste-) Alfred (1808–82) **3** 889; **11** 599; **28** 346
Beurdeley, (Emmanuel-) Alfred (1847–1919) **3** 889*
Beurdeley, Jean **3** 889
Beurer, Arnold **20** 804
Beurer, Wolfgang **20** 804
Beurlin *see* BEIERLEIN
Beurnonville, Etienne-Edmond Martin, Baron de **3** 890*
Beuron school **3** 890*
Beusecom, Frans van **5** 62; **32** 708
Beuth, Peter Christian Wilhelm **3** 890*; **28** 100
Beutlich, Tadek **30** 330
Beuys, Joseph **3** 890–93*; **19** 493; **23** 49; **24** 407; **25** 585; **28** 208
  collaboration **1** 34; **29** 492
  drawings **9** 213, 227
  groups and movements **1** 80; **10** 416; **11** 232; **24** 407; **28** 344
  installations **15** 869; **29** 13
  lithographs **3** *892*
  patrons and collectors **12** 474; **20** 524; **29** 420
  performance art **24** 408; **29** 98
  pupils **8** 736; **15** 146; **23** 846; **27** 452
  sculpture **3** *891*; **10** 875; **12** 408; **19** 396; **22** 381; **23** 334
Bevagna
  S Michele **26** 625
  S Silvestro **16** 625; **26** 625
Bevan, Charles **3** 893*; **10** 298
Bevan, E. J. **30** 542
Bevan, George Alfred **3** 893
Bevan, Robert (Polhill) **3** 893–4*
  groups and movements **5** 516, 517; **8** 264, 265; **10** 255; **25** 215
  works **10** *256*; **19** 492
Bevans, James (Santiago) **2** 395
Bevegom, Jan van **7** 833
Bevelled style **3** 894*; **9** 160; **16** 491, 540, *541*; **23** 556
  Central Asia, Western **16** 160
  Egypt **16** 488, 489
  Iran **16** 160, 244
  Iraq **16** 244, 488–9
  Syria **16** 489
  Turkey **16** 497
Bever, Louis Van *see* VAN BEVER, LOUIS
Beveren, Boudewijn van **17** 648; **31** 793
Beveren, Mattheus van **3** 570, 894*
  attributions **10** 717
  collaboration **10** 844
  teachers **32** 242
  works **3** 604; **8** 21
Beveren, van (family) **20** 915
Beverido **27** 756
Beverland, Adrian **9** 327
Beverley (Humberside) **10** *225*
  law courts **18** 886, 887
  Minster **3** 895*; **4** *141*; **9** 670; **13** 45, 54; **26** 382
    furniture **30** 776
    paintings **2** 73
    Percy tomb **8** 183
    piers (ii) (masonry) **24** 751
    screen **28** 295
    sculpture **3** 895–6*; **13** 82
    tracery **31** 271
    transept **31** 281
Beverley, Robert of *see* ROBERT OF BEVERLEY
Beverley, Samuel **32** 257
Beverley, William Roxby **27** 601; **30** 679, 681
Beverloo, Corneille Guillaume *see* CORNEILLE
Beverly Hills Civic Center (CA) **31** 598
Beverningk, Hieronymus van **20** 81
Beverwijck, Johan van **14** 738
Bevignate, Fra **23** 585; **24** 871
Bevilacqua (i) (family) **12** 474
Bevilacqua (ii) *see* SALIMBENI, VENTURA
Bevilacqua (i), Antonio **3** 896; **27** 759
Bevilacqua, Bonifazio, Cardinal **27** 620
Bevilacqua, Carlo **20** 91
Bevilacqua (i), Francesco **3** 896; **27** 759
Bevilacqua (i), Gregorio **3** 896; **27** 759
Bevilacqua (i), Lamberto, Duca **3** 896
Bevilacqua (i), Mario, Conte **3** 896; **32** 343
Bevilacqua (i), Onofrio **3** 896
Bevilacqua Cantelli, Camillo **3** 896
Bevilacqua-Lazise altarpiece **32** 343, 347, *347*, 354
Bew, John **32** 790
Bewcastle Cross (Cumbria) **2** 68, *69*; **8** 196; **23** 537; **28** 241
Bewdley (Hereford & Worcs) **10** 341
Bewe *see* WEILL, BRUNO
Beweging, De **24** 449
Bewick (Northumb.) **18** 584
Bewick, John **3** 897; **4** 362; **32** 502
Bewick, Thomas **3** 896–8*; **23** 21; **25** 628; **33** 359
  assistants **7** 413
  banknotes **3** 182
  book illustrations **4** 357; **24** 391
  engravings **3** *897*; **19** 233
  pupils **7** 413; **14** 208
  vignettes **32** *501*, 502
  wood-engravings **4** 361, 373; **25** 592, 598; **33** 368, *368*, 369
Bewick, William **14** 263
Bexhill-on-Sea (E. Sussex), De la Warr Pavilion **1** 738; **7** 670; **24** 291
Bexleyheath (Kent) **25** 804
  Red House **2** 365, 552; **4** 788; **10** 235, 320; **22** 142; **27** 131; **33** 12
Bey, Hakky **16** 554
Bey, Kemalettin *see* KEMALETTIN
Beyaert, Henri (-Joseph-François) **3** 578, 579, 898*
  collaboration **3** 548; **5** 24; **17** 8
  pupils **16** 906; **17** 450
  staff **14** 137
  works **2** 194; **3** 549, *549*, 613; **5** 41
Beyaert, Joes **19** 260
Beyalispati, Gangeshvari Temple **15** 319
Beyazit, Basilica A **7** 278
Beycesultan **1** *821*, *849*; **3** 898–9*, *899*
  architecture **1** 824, 826, 830
  figurines **1** 832
  metalwork **1** 824
  palace **1** 826, 893; **3** 899; **23** 806
    wall paintings **1** 839
  pottery **1** 837, *837*
  seals **1** 856
  shrines (i) (cult) **1** 828
Beyeler, Ernst **30** 153
Beyer, August von **31** 568
  works **31** *568*
Beyer, Christian Friedrich Wilhelm **3** 899–900*; **25** 34
  assistants **4** 375; **25** 648
  collaboration **14** 32
  pupils **29** 73
  works **2** 802; **19** 781; **32** 461
  workshop **32** 461
Beyer, Christoph **29** 547
Beyer, Hans **3** 604
Beyer, Heinrich **19** 111
Beyer, Jan de **3** 900*
  collaboration **19** 347
  reproductive prints by others **29** 402
  teachers **25** 649, 823
Beyer, Theo **30** 153
Beyeren, Abraham van **3** 900–901*; **14** 41
  teachers **32** 673
  works **11** 227; **20** 424; **22** 845; **29** 667, 669; **31** 882
Beyeren, Leendert Cornelisz. van **22** 843
Beyerlé, Jean-Louis de, Baron **11** 606, 609; **23** 113
Beykoz **16** 522
Beyla **1** *386*
  Regional Museum **13** 835
Beyle, Marie-Henri *see* STENDHAL
Beylerbeyi *see* ISTANBUL
Beylié, Gen. de **16** 550; **25** 771
Beylie, L. de **9** 528
Beylik **3** 901*; **16** 418
Beyşehir
  bazaars **16** 205
  carpets **16** 469
  Eşrefoğlu Hammam **16** 204
  Eşrefoğlu Mosque **16** 202; **22** 195
  tomb of Şeyh Süleyman **16** 204
Beywinkler, Joseph **2** 825
Beza, Theodore **31** 889
Bezalel Academy of Arts and Design *see under* JERUSALEM
Bezault wallpaper company **27** 719
Bezborodko, A. A. **25** 791; **27** 439
Bezděz Castle **8** 376
Bezeklik **3** 902*; **6** *288*, *614*; **28** *719*, 720
  Cave 20 **6** 293
  Cave 38 **30** 442
  Monastery **5** 102; **6** 294; **18** 26
  prints **6** 314
  temples **6** 289, 295; **30** 441
    Temple 9 **3** 902; **6** 295
      wall paintings **6** *304*, 310
    Temple 37 **6** 297
  wall paintings **6** 293, 304, 311
Bezem, Naftali **16** 567; **17** 579
Bézenval, Baronne de **26** 493
Béziers
  Cathedral of St Nazaire **7** 265; **8** 137; **13** 135, 147
  Musée d'Archéologie **11** 667
  Musée des Beaux-Arts **11** 667
Bezmin, I. A. **27** 442
Bezold, Andreas *see* PETZOLDT, ANDREAS
Bezold, Gustav von **8** 629
Bezombes, Roger **3** 902*; **20** 926
Bezperchy, Dmitry I. **31** 559
Bezunah, Alamāyyahu **10** 577
Bezzi, Bartolomeo **3** 903*
Bezzi, Cristoforo **21** 98
Bezzi, Giovanni Aubrey **2** 576
Bezzi, Giovanni Francesco **6** 361
Bezzola, Leonardo **19** 782

Bezzuoli, Giuseppe **3** 903–4*; **11** 189; **14** 586
pupils **1** 152; **7** 344; **8** 19; **10** 833; **19** 70; **22** 383; **29** 380; **31** 763
teachers **3** 750
works **3** *903*; **16** 677
B.F., Master **20** 791*
b ∝ 8, Master **20** 792*
B. G., Master (*fl* 15th cent.) **20** 792*
B. G., Master (*fl c.* 1589) **20** 792*
BHA (*Bibliography of the History of Art*) **2** 534; **4** 25, 26
Bhabha, Homi **4** 290
Bhaca **1** 417, 418, 419
Bhadgaon *see* BHAKTAPUR
bhadra **15** 243*
Bhadra *see* BHADRESHVAR
Bhadrabahu **29** 438
bhadraratha *see* BHADRA
Bhadravarman I, King of Champa (*reg c.* 377) **6** 418; **29** 231
Bhadravati **15** 327
Bhadreshvar **15** 241
architecture **15** 308–9
Chhoti Mosque **15** 308
inscriptions **15** 680
mihrabs **15** 309
Shrine of Ibrahim **15** 308, *308*
Solakhambi Mosque **15** 308
tombs **31** 114
Bhagat, Dhanraj **15** 172
Bhagwan **3** 904*; **15** 621
Bhairavakonda **3** 904–5*; **15** *294*, 534, 535
caves **15** 534, 535
rock reliefs **15** 534
shrines (i) (cult) **15** 534
temples **15** 301
Bhaja **3** 905*; **5** 94; **15** 194, *276*; **21** 847
arches **2** 297; **23** 368
Cave 12 **15** 433
Cave 19 **15** 433–4, *434*
halls **14** 77
reliefs **14** 186; **15** 416
sculpture **15** 216, 433–4*
temple **3** *905*, 905; **15** *251*, 252; **30** 437
wall paintings **15** 553
Bhakli, Devi Temple **15** 621
Bhaktapur **3** 905–6*; **22** *753*, 754–5
architecture **22** 759
Chaturbrahma-mahavihara **22** 763
Museum **22** 793
National Art Gallery **22** 796
Royal Palace **22** 775, 785
sculpture **22** *755*
temples **22** 761
Bhalla, Jai Rattan **9** 181
Bhanadas Chaudhari **15** 739
Bhanasara **15** *276*
temples **15** 266–7, *267*
Bhanwari **3** 906–7*; **22** 263
Bharany, C. L. **15** 632
Bharata **15** 230, 550
Bharatpur **15** 390, 449
Bharhut **15** 194, 221, *285*
iconography **15** 213
ivory **15** 695
reliefs **11** 151; **13** 3; **15** 248, 249, 250, *251*, *415*, 442, 677; **23** 817; **30** 438
sculpture **5** 94, 95; **15** 220, 229, 412, 422, 424–6*, *425*, 677, 700
stupas **3** 907*; **4** 794; **15** 303; **22** 516
toraṇa **31** 160
Bharmal, Rao of Kachchh (*reg* 1585-1631) (Rajput) **15** 617
Bharmaur *see* BRAHMAUR
Bhartrihari **15** 227
Bharuch **3** 907–8*; **15** 200, 347, 409, 697
congregational mosque **15** 347
Bhasa **15** 227
Bhaskaran, R. B. **20** 54
Bhatkal, Ketapai Narayana Temple **15** 336
Bhattacharya, Benoytosh **15** 211
Bhattacharya, Bikash **5** 421
Bhattacharya, Chittaprasad **5** 420
Bhattanarayana **15** 227
Bhattasali, Nalini **15** 211
Bhattiprolu **15** 438
Bhatti Shankar **15** 615
Bhavabhuti **15** 227
Bhavanasi Sangam **15** 301
Rupala Sangameshvara **15** 301
Bhavanidas **15** 739
Bhavani Das (*fl* before 1590) **13** 235
Bhavani Das (*fl c.* 1719-22) **15** 612
Bhavanipura, Naktimata Temple **15** 487
Bhavnani, Ashok M. **17** 605
Bhawalpur **15** 712
Bheraghat, Chausath Yogini Temple **15** 290, 497
Gauri-Shankara Temple **15** 290, 323
Bheta Temple **15** 264
Bhika, Rao of Bikaner (*reg c.* 1490) (Rajput) **4** 57
Bhik Chand **15** 612
Bhil **15** 174, 205, 732, 735, *735*
Bhima (*fl* 18th cent.) **15** 600
Bhima I, Ruler (*reg* 1022-64) (Solanki) **21** 785
Bhimbetka **15** 551, 552
Zoo Rock **15** *552*
Bhimsen **15** 606
Bhim Singh, Rana of Mewar (*reg* 1778-1828) (Rajput) **15** 600
Bhim Singh, Rao of Kota (*reg* 1707-20) (Rajput) **15** 390
Bhirasri, Silpa *see* FEROCI, CORRADO
Bhir Mound *see under* TAXILA
Bhita **15** 213
Bhitargaon **3** 908*; **15** *261*, *279*, *285*
arches **2** 297
plaques **30** 510
sculpture **15** 413
temple **15** 256, *256*
terracotta **15** 455
Bhitari, Vishnu Temple **15** 738
Bhoj, Rao of Bundi (*reg* 1585-1606) (Rajput) **15** 603
Bhoja, Ruler (*reg c.* 1000-55) (Paramara) **3** 908; **15** 550
Bhojpur **3** 908*; **15** *285*, 292
reliquaries **15** 698; **26** 150
Bhokardan **15** 450
Bhongapal **15** 467
Bhong Mosque **23** 799
Bhonsala, Kings of Nagpur **25** 886
Bhopal **3** 908*; **15** *285*
Archaeological Museum **3** 908
Bharat Bhavan Museum **3** 908
Birla Museum **3** 908; **15** 181
Madhya Pradesh Tribal Research and Development Institute Museum **3** 908
State Museum **15** 181
Vidhan Bhavan **15** 169
Bhrikuti **19** 293
Bhubaneshwar **3** 908–11*; **15** 195, *279*, 409, 503
Orissa State Museum **3** 909; **15** 182
reliefs **15** 227
sculpture **15** *503*, 503–4, *504*
temples **15** 229, 230, 309, 317
Ananta Vasudeva Temple **15** 319, 320
Brahmeshvara Temple **15** 317, 318
Chitrakarini Temple **15** 319
Dakrabhimeshvara Temple **15** 318
Ekambareshvara Temple **15** 318
Gauri Temple **15** 283, 318
Bhubaneshwar
temples—cont.
Indreshvara Temple *see* Rajarani Temple
Kapileshvara Temple **15** 320
Lingaraja Temple **3** 910–11*, *911*; **14** 77; **15** 318, 319, 320, 504
Parvati Temple **15** 319
Makareshvara Temple **15** 320
Markandeshvara Temple **15** 281
Megheshvara Temple **15** 317, 319
Mitreshvara Temple **15** 320
Mukteshvara Temple **3** 910*; **15** *282*, 283
Parashurameshvara Temple **3** 909*; **14** 77; **15** 281, 503
Rajarani Temple **3** 910*; **14** 77; **15** 318, *318*, 503
Sari Deul Temple **15** 319
Siddheshvara Temple **15** 318
Sisireshvara Temple **15** 281
Tribhuvaneshvara Temple *see* Lingaraja Temple
Vaital Deul Temple **3** 909–10*; **15** 282, 319
Vakeshvara Temple **15** 319, *320*
Varuneshvara Temple **15** 320
Yameshvara Temple **15** 319, 320
Bhuiya **15** 734, 735
Bhuj **15** 671
Bhumara **3** 911–12*; **15** *285*
sculpture **15** *471*
Shiva Temple **15** 255–6, 470–71
Bhumibol, King (Rama IX; *reg* 1964-) (chakri) **30** 617
bhūmija **15** 243*
bhūmyāmalaka *see* KARṆAṆḌAKA
Bhundana Shiva Temple **15** 487
Bhupatindra, King (*reg c.* 1696-1722) (Malla) **22** 754, *755*
Bhuri Singh, Ruler (*reg* 1904-19) (Pahari) **6** 405
Bhuri Singh Museum *see under* CHAMBA (INDIA)
Bhutan **3** *912*, 912–16*
appliqué **3** 915
architecture **3** 913*, *913*
bamboo **3** 913, 916
basketwork **3** 916
bowls **3** 916
boxes **3** 916
brocades **3** 915, *915*
brooches **3** 916
brushes **3** 914
chalk **3** 914
charcoal **3** 915
clay **3** 914
collections **3** 916*
containers **3** 916
copper **3** 914, *914*
coral **3** 914
cotton **3** 914, 915
dress **3** *915*
exhibitions **3** 916*
fortresses **3** 913, *913*
glues **3** 914
gold **3** 914
gum arabic **3** 914
hair **3** 914
yak-hair **3** 915
houses **3** 913
iconography **3** 914
inlays **3** 914
jewellery **3** 916
lacquer **3** 916
lime **3** 914
looms **3** 915
lost-wax casting **3** 914
mansions **3** 913
metalwork **3** *914*
monasteries **3** 913; **21** 848*
National Museum **3** 916
nettles **3** 915
painting **3** 914–15*
paints **3** 914
palaces **3** 913
Bhutan—cont.
patronage **3** 913
pine **3** 913
plaster **3** 914
postage stamps **25** 329
roofs **3** 913
sculpture **3** 913–14*, *914*
silk **3** 915, *915*
silver **3** 914, 916
silversmiths **3** 916
slate **3** 914
statuettes **3** 914
stone **3** 913
tangkas **28** 309
temples **3** 913, *913*
textiles **3** 914, 915–16*
treatises **3** 914
turquoise **3** 914
weaving **3** 915
willow **3** 913
wood **3** 914
woodblock printing **3** 914
woodwork **3** 913, 916
wool **3** 915
Bhutapura **15** 538
Bhutia **15** 733
Bhuvanadeva **15** 550
Bhuvanekabahu I, King of Sri Lanka (*reg* 1272-84) **29** 460, 479
Bhuvanekabahu IV, King of Sri Lanka (*reg* 1341-51) **29** 460
bi *see* CHINA → discs
Biada, Francesco di Pietro della *see* BENAGLIO, FRANCESCO
Biadaiolo Master **20** 630*, 658
Biadaiolo, Il (Florence, Bib. Medicea-Lorenziana, MS. Tempi 3) **20** 630
Biagetti, Biagio **26** 817
Biagi, G. **29** 742
Biagio, Antonio di *see* ANTONIO DI BIAGIO
Biagio, Raffaello di *see* RAFFAELLO DI BIAGIO
Biagio, Vincenzo di *see* CATENA, VINCENZO
Biagio d'Antonio (Tucci) **3** 916–17*; **29** 362
attributions **3** 868
patrons and collectors **29** 58, 782
works **3** *917*; **6** 4; **31** 173
Biagio di Giorgia de Traù **32** 160
Biagio di Goro Ghezzi **3** 917–18*
Biahmu **10** 759
Biała Podlaska **25** 122, 131, 132
Białogen **25** 130
Białostocki, Jan **3** 918*; **15** 91, 92; **25** 143
Biały, Jan **3** 918–19*; **25** 113
Biały, Piotr **3** 918
Bialynicki-Birula, Vitaly **3** 529
Białystok
palace **25** 115, 121, 135
St Roch **25** 100
Biamange **33** 609
Bian (family) **7** 118
Bianca, Matteo Galzetta *see* WITHOOS, MATTHIAS
Bianca de' Medici, Grand Duchess of Tuscany (*fl* late 16th cent.) **11** 180, 193
Bianca Maria Sforza, Holy Roman Empress (1472-1510) **13** 905; **25** 466; **33** 118
Bianca Maria Visconti, Duchess of Milan (1425-68) **28** 529, 531*
altarpieces **3** 695
architecture **8** 135
manuscripts **20** 697
paintings **28** 531
Bianchi, Andrea **2** 394; **3** 919*
attributions **7** 847
collaboration **17** 514; **25** 586
works **2** 395; **5** 122; **7** 847, *847*; **22** 313
Bianchi, Antonio **25** 212
Bianchi, Baldassare **7** 357; **10** 526, 527; **29** 775
Bianchi, Bernardo **19** 55
Bianchi, Bornio de' **8** 173
Bianchi, Brunone **6** 148
Bianchi, Carlo Antonio **12** 583
Bianchi, Clemente **6** 97
Bianchi, Ernestine **31** 661
Bianchi, Federico **12** 560
Bianchi, Francesco **16** 562; **24** 520; **28** 10
Bianchi, Gaetano **3** 919*; **11** 318
Bianchi, Giosuè **3** 919
Bianchi, Giovanni Andrea *see* ALBIO
Bianchi, Hernan **7** 847
Bianchi, Isidoro **28** 10; **29** 831; **31** 443
Bianchi, John **31** 680
Bianchi, Marco **16** 641
Bianchi, Mosè (di Giosuè) **3** 857, 919–20*; **21** 527
Bianchi, Pietro (i) (1694-1740) **3** 920*; **12** 533; **19** 817; **20** 125
Bianchi, Pietro (ii) (1787-1849) **3** 920–21*; **8** 807
collaboration **8** 12
works **16** 646; **18** 778; **22** 473, *473*
Bianchi, Pompeo **28** 10
Bianchi, Salvatore **3** 921*
Bianchi Ferrari, Francesco de' **7** 885
Bianchini **3** 108
Bianchini, Antonio **3** 921–2*; **5** 378; **25** 741; **26** 776
Bianchini, Bartolomeo **11** 699, *700*; **12** 559
Bianchini, Francesco **1** 532, 533; **2** 162, 164; **26** 785
Bianchini, G. **12** 666
Bianchini, Vincenzo **8** 705
Bianchini-Férier **9** 373; **11** 649
Bianco, Adalberto **32** 895
Bianco, Bartolomeo **3** 90, 922–3*; **12** 281; **13** 321
Bianco, Battista **3** 922
Bianco, Bernardo del **3** 304
Bianco, Cipriano **3** 922
Bianco, Giovanni Battista **11** 53
Bianco, Mario **24** 505
Bianco, Simone **3** 923–4*
patrons and collectors **23** 355
works **3** *924*
bianco di Spagna *see under* CHALK → types
Bianconi (family) **6** 357
Bianconi, Carlo **1** 633; **23** 497; **30** 520; **32** 689
Bianconi, Giovanni Lodovico **3** 924*; **5** 622
Biancori, A. M. **18** 680
bianco sangiovanni *see under* PIGMENTS → types
Biancour, Martin **5** 914; **11** 345
Biandrate, Cesare **5** 407
Biandrate, Giovanni Giacomo **1** 529
bian hu *see under* VESSELS → types
Bianliang *see* KAIFENG
Bian Luan **6** 799
Bian Shoumin **33** 497
Bian Wenjin **6** 801, 817; **19** 426
Bianya, Raimon de *see* RAIMON DE BIANYA
Bianzago, Bartolomeo **3** 699
Biard, Colin (de) **3** 924–5*
patrons and collectors **11** 904; **31** 844
works **4** 155; **31** *844*
Biard, François **23** 126
Biard, Nicolas *see* BIARD, COLIN (DE)
Biard, Noël **3** 925
Biard, Pierre (i) (1559-1609) **3** 925*; **20** 133
Biard, Pierre (ii) (1592-1661) **3** 925*
Biardeau, Pierre **4** 1*
Biardeau, René, the elder (*fl* 1614-34) **4** 1

Biardeau, René, the younger (fl 1633-8) 4 1
Biarelle, Johann Adolf 5 8
Biarelle, Paul Amadeus 26 257
Biaro Bahal I 15 767
Biaro Bahal II 15 767
Biaro Bahal III 15 767
Biaro Si Joreng Belangah 15 767
Biaro Si Pamutung 15 767
Biart (family) 23 508
Biart, Pierre 11 260; 23 508
Biascuccio, Giovanni 28 744
Biasi, Alberto 13 728
Biasi, Giuseppe 27 836
Biasi, Mario De see DE BIASI, MARIO
Biasino, Cipriano 2 780; 4 1–2*; 28 198; 29 371
Biasiny-Rivera, Charles 18 833
Biauneveu, Andrieu see BEAUNEVEU, ANDRÉ
Biazin, Clément-Marie 6 179
works 6 179
Bibān al-Ḥarim see THEBES (i) (EGYPT) → Valley of the Queens
Bibān al-Mulūk see THEBES (i) (EGYPT) → Valley of the Kings
Bibb, John 32 248, 249
Bibbiena, Bernardo, Cardinal 4 2*
architecture 26 813
decorative works 31 523
frescoes 10 477; 31 523
paintings 13 700; 24 365; 25 902; 30 281
productions 12 278; 21 16; 30 659
Bibby, Geoffrey 27 877
Biberach-an-der-Riss 30 907
Bibesco, Princess 20 120
Bibescu, Gheorghe, Prince of Wallachia (reg 1842-8) 30 202
Bibiena, SS Ippolito e Donato altarpiece 4 32
Bibiena, Ferdinando 27 483
Bibiena, Francesco 1 623; 22 456
Bibi-Eybat 2 893
bibila lace see under LACE → types
Bible (The) 2 300; 5 800
Bible, Jean de Sy, Master of the see BOQUETEAUX, MASTER OF THE
Bible Lands Museum see under JERUSALEM → museums
Bible of Charles the Bald, First see BIBLES → individual manuscripts → Vivian Bible
Bible of Jean de Sy, Master of the see BOQUETEAUX, MASTER OF THE
Bibles 4 2–20*; 5 624; 20 340–41
historical and regional traditions
Belgium 26 666
Byzantine 4 3–5*; 9 602, 606–8*, 620; 19 169; 20 340; 32 461
Carolingian 4 5; 5 803, 804
Early Christian (c. AD 250-843) 4 3–5*; 9 602, 606–8*, 612
England 4 6
France 13 140
Carolingian 5 804
Gothic 4 3, 7; 13 129, 130, 136, 140
Italy 4 6; 26 660, 666
Romanesque 4 6–7; 26 660, 666, 676
Spain 4 5, 14; 26 676
individual manuscripts
Admont Bible (Vienna, Österreich. Nbib., Cods s.n. 2701-2) 2 790, 791; 4 6; 14 898; 26 652, 660
Albergati Bible (New Haven, CT, Yale U., Bienecke Lib., MS 407) 12 666
Anjou Bible (Mechelen, Grand Séminaire, Bibliothèque, MS1) 23 506
Antwerp Bible (Antwerp, Mus. Plantin-Mortus) 33 71
Bibles
individual manuscripts—cont.
Arnstein Bible (London, BL, Harley MSS 2798-9) 4 6; 32 852
Ashburnham Pentateuch (Paris, Bib. N., MS. nuov. acq. lat. 2334) 2 595; 4 4; 9 602; 31 48
Bamberg Bible (Bamberg, Staatsbib., MS. Misc. class. Bibl. 1) 11 529
Bernward Bible (Hildesheim, Diözmus., Cod. 61) 14 532
Bible Historiaux (London, BL, Harley MSS 3481-2) 32 852
Bible of Borso d'Este (Modena, Bib. Estense, MS. V.G. 12-13, lat. 422-3) 4 7, 18–20*, 19; 8 172; 10 520; 11 4, 722; 12 666, 721, 733; 21 771
Bible of Charles the Bald (Rome, S Paolo fuori le Mura) see Bible of San Paolo
Bible of Charles the Bald, Second (Paris, Bib. N., MS. lat. 2) 5 804, 804; 23 537
Bible of Charles V see Giffard Bible
Bible of Clement VII (Paris, Bib. N., MS. lat. 18) 16 836
Bible of Clement VII (Rome, Vatican, Bib. Apostolica, MSS. lat. 50-51) 16 852
Bible of Evert Soudenbalch (Vienna, Österreich. Nbib., Cod. 2771) 20 662
Bible of Jean de Sy (Paris, Bib. N., MS. fr. 15397) 13 154; 31 834, 841
Bible of Niccolò III (Rome, Vatican, Bib. Apostolica, MS. Barb. lat. 613) 4 18
Bible of Niketas (Copenhagen, Kon. Bib. Cod. G.K.S.6; Florence, Bib. Medicea-Laurenziana, MS.5.9; Turin, Bib. N. U., Cod. B.I.2) 9 607, 613
Bible of Queen Christina of Sweden see Leo Bible
Bible of Robert of Taranto (Rome, Vatican, Bib. Apostolica , MS. Vat. lat. 14430) 23 505
Bible of San Callisto see Bible of San Paolo
Bible of San Juan de la Peña (Madrid, Bib. N.) 26 642
Bible of San Paolo (Rome, S Paolo fuori le Mura) 4 5, 20*; 5 803, 804; 9 155; 20 330
Bible of S Isidoro (León, Mus.-- Bib. Real Colegiata S Isidoro, MS. I.3) 26 676
Bible of S Maria ad Martyres see Pantheon Bible
Bible of Stephen Harding (Dijon, Bib. Mun., MSS 12-15 4 6; 7 352; 26 669
Bible of the Duke of Alba (Madrid, Pal. Liria, Fund. Casa de Alba) 9 264; 21 48
Bible of Van-des-Escoliers (Liège, Bibl. Grand Sémin., MS 1) 3 553
Bible of William of Devon (London, BL, Royal MS. 1.D.1) 4 7, 393, 393; 5 642; 10 245; 13 141
Biblia Hispalense (Madrid, Bib. N., Cod. Vit. 13-1) 16 307; 22 246
Bishop Gandulf's Bible (San Marino, CA, Huntington Lib., Phillips MS. 3504) 24 637
Book of Armagh (Dublin, Trinity Coll. Lib., MS 52) 16 13
Bibles
individual manuscripts—cont.
Bourges Bible (Bourges, Bib. Mun., MS. 3) 26 660, 677
Bury New Testament (Cambridge, Pembroke Coll., MS. 120) 26 671
Bury St Edmunds Bible (Cambridge, Corpus Christi Coll., MS. 2) 4 6; 5 288, 289*, 339; 10 244, 244; 20 331; 26 659, 660, 663, 672, 672
Byllyng Bible (Paris, Bib. N., MS. lat. 11935) 13 148; 25 691, 692, 692, 693, 694
Calci Bible (Certosa di Calci, MS. 1) 24 854
Carilef Bible (Durham, Cathedral Lib., MS. A.II.4) 26 669
Codex Amiatinus (Florence, Bib. Medicea- Laurenziana, MS. Amiatinus 1) 4 4; 5 923; 10 243; 15 874; 19 733; 20 330
Codex Sinaiticus (London, BL, Add. MS. 43725) 4 343, 343; 9 606; 15 847; 19 888
Cotton Genesis (London, BL, Cotton MS. Otho B. VI) 4 3; 7 220; 8 38*; 9 606, 611; 22 519
Dover Bible (Cambridge, Corpus Christi Coll., MSS 3-4 5 641; 26 659, 660, 671
Duke of Sussex Bible (London, BL, Add. MS. 15250) 17 561, 561
Duque de Alba Bible 17 536
Egerton Genesis (London, BL, Egerton MS. 1894) 13 152
Fiesole Bible (Florence, Bib. Medicea-Laurenziana, MS. Fiesole 1) 25 694
Floreffe Bible (London, BL, Add. MSS 17737-8) 3 552; 4 6; 26 662, 667
Foa Bible (Paris, Bib. Couvent Pères Sulpiciens Barcelone) 17 562
Frowinus Bible (Engelberg, Abbey) 11 806
Giffard Bible (Oxford, Bodleian Lib., MS. Laud. Misc. 752) 26 677
Girona Bible (Girona, Bib. Capitolare) 20 680
Hamilton Bible (Berlin, Kupferstichkab., MS. 78.E.3) 2 110
Holkham Bible Picture Book (London, BL, Add. MS. 47682) 4 7; 13 128
Kennicott Bible, First (Oxford, Bodleian Lib., Kenn. MS. 1) 16 307; 17 561, 562, 661
Koblenz Bible (Pommersfelden, Schloss Weissenstein, MSS 333-4) 26 660, 673, 673
Lambeth Bible (London, Lambeth Pal. Lib., MS. 3; Maidstone Mus. & A.G.) 4 6, 7; 5 641; 10 244; 18 674–5*; 26 659, 663, 664, 672; 27 528
Leo Bible (Rome, Vatican, Bib. Apostolica, MS. Reg. gr. 1) 4 4; 9 607, 613; 19 169*
León Bible (Lén, Mus.--Bib. Real Colegiata S Isidoro, MS. 2) 26 676
Lisbon Bible (Lisbon, Bib. N., MS. Il.72) 17 661
Lobbes Bible (Tournai, Bib. Sémin. Episc., MS. 1) 3 552; 4 6; 26 660
Lübeck Bible (Lübeck, St Annen-Kloster) 1 721, 721
Lyon Bible (Lyon, Bib. Mun., MSS 410-11) 26 677
Bibles
individual manuscripts—cont.
Maciejowski Bible (New York, Pierpont Morgan Lib., MS. M.638) 7 765; 13 129, 141
Malines Bible (Mechelen, Grand Sémin., Bib., MS. 1) 2 110
Manerius Bible (Paris, Bib. Ste-Geneviève, MSS 8-10) 26 677
Mazarin Bible (Paris, Bib. Mazarine) 13 866; 25 622
Milan Bible (Milan, Bib. Ambrosiana, MS. B 30-32 inf.) 17 563
Moutier-Grandval Bible (London, BL, Add. MS. 10546) 4 5, 5; 5 803; 11 529; 19 169; 31 226, 226
Palatine Bible (Rome, Vatican, Bib. Apostolica, MSS Vat. lat. 3-5) 26 666
Pantheon Bible (Rome, Vatican, Bib. Apostolica, MS. Vat. lat. 12958) 4 6; 16 655, 655; 26 666
Pommersfelden Bible see Koblenz Bible
Quedlinburg Itala (Berlin, Dt. Staatsbib., Cod. theol. lat., fol. 485) 4 3; 9 602
Rijm Bible (The Hague, Rijksmus. Meermanno-Westreenianum, MS. 10B21) 22 833
Ripoll Bible (Rome, Vatican, Bib. Apostolica, MS. lat. 5729) 4 5; 26 676
Roda Bible (Paris, Bib. N., MS. lat. 6) 4 5; 26 675
Royal Bible (London, BL, Royal MS. 1.E.VI) 15 875
Ste Marie du Parc Bible (London, BL, Add. MS. 14788-90) 26 667
St Petersburg Bible (St Petersburg, Saltykov-Shchedrin Pub. Lib., MS. B 19a) 17 560, 560
St Vaast Bible (Arras, Bib. Mun., MS. 559) 4 6; 26 663
S Cecilia Bible (Rome, Vatican Bib. Apostolica, MS. Barb. lat. 587) 26 666
S Maria ad Martyres Bible see Pantheon Bible
Souvigny Bible (Moulins, Bib. Mun., MS. 1) 4 6; 26 660, 677
Stavelot Bible (London, BL, Add. MSS 28106-7) 3 552, 552; 4 6; 26 660, 666
Syriac Bible (Paris, Bib. N., MS. syr. 341) 4 4
Urbino Bible (Rome, Vatican, Bib. Apostolica, MSS Urb. lat. 1-2) 11 686, 687; 32 384
Vatican Book of Kings (Rome, Vatican, Bib. Apostolica, MS. Vat. gr. 333) 9 612
Velislav Bible (Prague, Libs Facs & Insts Charles U., MS. XXIII. C.124) 13 151
Vienna Genesis (Vienna, Österreich. Nbib., Cod. theol. gr. 31) 4 4, 4; 7 246; 9 606, 612; 12 71; 15 135; 18 703; 22 520; 25 743; 27 174; 32 461–2*, 462; 33 159
Vivian Bible (Paris, Bib. N., MS. lat. 1) 4 5; 5 803; 6 174, 485; 7 512; 11 529; 26 79; 30 780; 31 226
Walther Bible (c. 1120-30; Michaelbeuren, Stiftsbib., MS. perg. 1) 4 6; 26 675
Wenceslas Bible (Vienna, Österreich. Nbib., MSS 2759-64) 4 7, 7; 19 830; 33 71, 71–2*
Bibles
individual manuscripts—cont.
Winchester Bible (Winchester, Cathedral Lib.) 4 7; 10 244; 13 140; 14 398, 423; 20 331, V1; 26 659, 660, 662, 672, 677; 31 284; 33 233, 239, 239–40*
Winchester Bible, 'second' (Oxford, Bodleian Lib., MSS Auct. E. inf. 1-2) 15 847; 26 660
Wrocław Bible (U. Wrocław Lib., MS. 1106) 17 563
types
Alcalá 25 17
Bible de Richelieu 26 349
Bible historiale 4 12–13*
Bible of Royaumont 4 9
Bibles moralisées 1 653; 4 3, 10–11*; 13 140, 140, 141, 179; 31 500
Biblia pauperum 4 3, 11–12*; 31 500
Biblia regia see Polyglot
Cologne Bible 2 223; 4 9
Complutensian Polyglot 4 8
Doves Press Bible 4 8
Great Bible of Mortier 19 832
Gutenberg Bible 4 8, 8; 25 589
Jenson Bible 4 8
Latin Bible 2 223
Malermi Bible 4 9
Oxford Lectern Bible 4 8
Polyglot 4 8; 25 17
Radziwiłł Lithuanian Brest Bible 19 496
Strasbourg Bible 2 223
Vulgate 7 214
Wittenberg Bible 2 224; 8 120
World Bible 4 8
see also APOCALYPSES; GOSPEL BOOKS; GOSPEL LECTIONARIES; LECTIONARIES; NEW TESTAMENTS; OLD TESTAMENTS; PSALTERS
Bibliothèque Nationale 178, Painter of the 10 614
bibliographies 4 20–28*
16th cent. 4 21
17th cent. 4 21
18th cent. 4 21; 10 207
19th cent. 4 21; 10 208, 209, 210, 211
20th cent. 2 534; 6 76, 81; 10 211, 212, 213
see also ART HISTORY
Bibliography of the History of Art see BHA
Biblioteca Capitolare 20 85
Biblioteca Corviniana 20 847
Biblioteca Mesa-Gisbert 4 270
Bibliothek der schönen Wissenschaften und freien Künste 23 108
Bibliothek der schönen Wissenschaften und der freyen Künste 24 443
Bibra, Lorenz von, Prince Bishop see LORENZ VON BIBRA, Prince Bishop
Bibury (Glos), St Mary 2 71
biccherne 4 29, 29–30*; 14 424
see also BOOK COVERS
Bicci, Lorenzo di see LORENZO DI BICCI
Bicci, Neri di see NERI DI BICCI
Bicci di Lorenzo 4 30–33*; 11 698; 22 797
assistants 28 69
attributions 19 674; 22 798
collaboration 8 683
works 4 31, 32; 11 197, 381; 20 748; 22 801
workshop 24 762
Bîchâpour see BISHAPUR
Bichi, Francesco 22 481

Bichitr 4 33*; 15 208, 587, 588, 589
attributions 24 295
works 12 74; 15 587, 587; 16 345; 30 785
Bichler, Heinrich 11 787
bichromated gelatin see GELATIN → uses → photography
bichromates 24 651
Bichrome Red ware see under POTTERY → wares
Bichrome ware see under POTTERY → wares
Bichrome Wheelmade ware see under POTTERY → wares
Bichvinta 4 34*; 12 317
Basilica 12 323
Cathedral 4 34; 12 319
Bichweiler, Herbert Robert 13 209
Bicini, Gregorio 10 569
Bick, G. Elayne 31 660
Bickel, Moidele 30 688
Bicker (family) 27 725
Bicker, J. 1 801
Bickford, George P. 15 743, 745
Bickford, P. 15 748
Bickford, Robert 10 342
works 10 342
Bickham, George, the elder (1684-1769) 4 34*; 22 370; 26 499
Bickham, George, the younger (d 1758) 4 34
Bickham, John 4 34
Bicknell, Albion Harris 21 895, 896
Bicknell, Elhanan 4 35*; 31 474
biconical urns see under URNS → types
Bicorp 29 364
Bida 23 302, 303
beads 1 297
gowns 23 302
pots 1 369
Bida, Alexandre 6 489; 7 304; 18 864
Bidar 4 35–6*; 15 294; 16 105
architecture 15 356–8; 16 201
calligraphy 15 681
Chaubara 15 357
congregational mosque 15 357
Diwan-i 'Am 15 356–7
fort 15 686
Gagan Mahal 15 356; 23 818
khanaqah of 'Ali Husayn Qutb-i Thani 15 357
khanaqah of Shah Abu'l Faid 15 357
khanaqah of Shah Wali'ullah Kirmani 15 357
La'l Bagh 15 356
madrasa of Mahmud Gawan 15 357, 357, 686
manuscript illumination 15 572
metalwork 4 687; 15 713, 714, 724; 21 330
Rangin Mahal 15 356
Solahkhamba Mosque 15 356
Takht Mahal 15 356, 357
Tarkash Mahal 15 356
tombs and mausolea 15 358, 383
mausoleum of 'Ala al-Din Ahmad Bahmani 29 825
mausoleum of 'Ali Barid Shah 15 383
mausoleum of Khan Jahad Barid 29 825
tomb of Ahmad Shah 15 358
tomb of 'Ala al-Din Bahmani 15 358
tomb of Khalil'ullah Kirmani 15 358
tomb of Multani Padshah 15 358
tomb of Qasim Barid II 15 383
Bidart, Andrés Etchebarne 12 916
Bidau, Nicolas 4 36*
Bidauld, Jean-Joseph-Xavier 4 36*
collaboration 19 255
groups and movements 24 387
Bidauld, Jean-Joseph-Xavier—cont.
pupils 3 854; 24 892
works 18 713, 714
Bidauld, Jean-Pierre-Xavier 4 36
Bidayuh 15 774; 20 164, 182, 183
Biddenden (Kent) 32 277
Biddle, George 25 653
Biddle, Nicholas 13 611; 24 597; 32 827, 828
Biddulph, John 8 834
Biddulph Grange (Staffs) 4 36–7*; 10 225
Bideford (Devon) 10 303
bidentalia see WELL-HEADS
Bidermanas, Izis see IZIS
Bidjar see BIJAR
Bidjogo see BIJOGO
Bidlake, George 4 37
Bidlake, William Henry 4 37*
Bidlake & Lovatt 31 240; 33 11
Bidleston (Suffolk)
ivory-carvings 16 798
Bidloo, Govert 1 842; 21 6
Bidó, Cándido 9 117, 119
Bidor 20 165
bidri see under ALLOYS → types
Bidri ware see under INDIAN SUBCONTINENT → metalwork
Biduini 24 858
Biduini Codex see under CODICES → individual manuscripts
Biduino 4 37*; 26 623
Bidwell, A. J. 28 772
Bidwell, R. A. J. 28 773
Bidya 2 248
Bidyogo see BIJOGO
Bid Zard 10 171
Bie, Adriaan de 4 38
Bie, Cornelis de 4 38*
pupils 27 134, 135
works 3 619; 22 910; 27 518
illustrated 25 221
Bie, de (family) 2 199
Bie, Jacobus de 12 885
Biebricher, August 31 368
Biebuyck, Daniel 2 137; 4 27
Bié Church 2 86
Biecz 25 119
Biederman, Charles (Karel Joseph) 1 79; 4 38*; 7 772
Biedermann, Irving 24 385
Biedermann, Johann Jakob 4 39*; 30 133
patrons and collectors 5 168
teachers 1 31
works 25 VII2
Biedermeier 4 39–40*
art forms
frames 11 461, 461–2, 472, 472–3
furniture 8 235; 14 907–8
interior decoration 2 808; 22 866, 866–7
painting 12 294; 26 740
Austria 2 796; 4 40; 8 445; 32 445
Denmark 18 178, 179
Germany 12 393, 414; 28 196
portraits 8 445
silver 2 821
regional traditions
Austria 2 785
Denmark 8 745
Germany 3 799; 12 414, 415, 426–7, 448
Biedermeier, Gottlieb 4 39
Biedermeier chairs see under CHAIRS → types
Biedma, Nicolás de see NICOLÁS DE BIEDMA
Bief: Jonction surréaliste 24 428; 30 23
Biefve, Edouard de 3 562
Biegas, Bolesław 4 41*; 25 115
Biehler, Tobias 12 266; 14 285
Bielby, Ralph 25 628
Biel Congress Hall 29 428
Bieleeld, Neustädter Marienkirche
tomb of Otto III of Ravensberg 33 28
Bielefeld
Ravensberg Spinning Mill 10 748
Städtische Kunsthalle 12 477
Bielefeld, Charles Frederick 24 62
Bielefeld Altarpiece 20 630
Bieler, Ted 5 571
Bielino 32 879
Bieliński, Franciszek, Count 21 70; 25 135; 26 493; 32 876
Bielke, Master of 20 630*
Bielke, Nils (1569-1639) 20 630
Bielke, Nils (1644-1716) 30 93
Bielke, Nils Adam, Count (1724-92) 30 89
Biella
Baptistery 16 625
Istituto Nazionale di Fotografia Alpina Vittorio Sella 16 777; 28 387
Bielorussia see BELARUS'
Bielus, Angela 2 397
Biemann, Dominik 4 41*; 8 410; 25 435
Biemann, Vincenz 4 41
Bienaimé, Luigi 4 41–2*; 30 766
Bienaimé, Pietro Antonio 4 42
Bienart, I. 21 854
Bienaymé, Pierre 11 637
Bieng 18 484
Bien Hoa 6 431
Bieniasz, Maciej 29 742, 743
Bieninc see BENING
Biennais, Martin-Guillaume 4 42*; 11 597, 629
groups and movements 10 186
patrons and collectors 4 302, 303
pupils 3 313
works 11 621
Bieraście see BLEZASCIE
Bierbauer, Virgil see BORBIRÓ, VIRGIL
Bierbaum, Otto Julius 4 42–3*; 25 350
Bierce, Ambrose 27 868
Biermann, Aenne 4 43*
Biermann, Peter see BIRMANN, PETER
Biermans, Hans 14 467
Bierpfaff, Jan Chrystian 4 43*; 25 127, 130; 31 196
Bierstadt, Albert 3 61; 4 43–5*; 31 603
groups and movements 14 843; 19 791; 31 602
patrons and collectors 17 823; 29 536
reproductive prints by others 19 485
sponsors 19 259
works 2 106; 4 44; 18 715, IV1; 33 185
Bierstadt, Charles 4 44
Bierstadt, Edward 4 44
Biertan 26 705
church 13 189; 26 707, 712
pews 26 718
Bieruma Oosting, Jeanne 22 854
Bierum Church 22 813, 819
Biesa see BAEZA
Biest, Hans van der 10 222; 12 467; 30 319
works 5 606
Biet, Georges 31 829
Bieterich, Juan 6 592
Biezus, Ladi 4 725
Biffi, Gian Andrea 4 45*, 426; 21 533
collaboration 16 562
patrons and collectors 21 533
Bifur 24 144
Bifur see under TYPE-FACES
Bigaglia, Nicola 4 45*
Bigaglia, Pietro 24 57; 32 204
Bigallo Crucifix 20 630
Bigallo Master 20 630–31*
Bigardi, Vittorio 4 277
works 4 277
Bigarelli, Guido di Bonagiunta see GUIDO DA COMO
Bigari, Gaspare 20 497
Bigari, Vittorio (Maria) 4 46*
patrons and collectors 1 597
pupils 3 869; 24 320
works 25 893
Bigarny, Felipe 8 79
Bigatti, Alfredo 2 400; 12 490
Bigaud, Wilson 4 46*; 14 58
Big Babanki 3 147
Bigbear, Frank, jr 22 665
Big Circle earthworks 18 7
Bigelow, Erastus Brigham 5 831–2, 840
Bigelow, Jacob 4 473
Bigelow, William Sturgis 17 431; 20 16; 26 467
Biger Monastery 5 156
Bigg, William Redmore 4 46–7*
reproductive prints by others 5 216; 12 187; 21 417; 29 675
teachers 24 367
works 10 786; 12 294
Bigge, John 31 673
Bigge, Thomas 27 337
Biggers, John 1 425; 14 803
Biggi, Francesco 11 10
Biggs, Thomas 1 483
Big-head Shāhnāma 16 328
Bighordi see GHIRLANDAIO
Bigio, Baccio 4 47
Bigio, Il 4 622
Bigio, Nanni di Baccio 4 47*
methods 21 766
patrons and collectors 11 740; 22 6; 25 7; 27 648
works 20 839; 26 822
Bigle, Jean 9 2
Bigne, Mme Valtesse de la see VALTESSE DE LA BIGNE, Mme
Bignon, François 14 313
Bignor Villa 26 907; 32 542
Bigo, Abraham 16 29
Bigordi see GHIRLANDAIO
Bigot, Alexandre 2 391; 4 47–8*; 7 694; 18 884
Bigot, Paul 24 129
Bigot, Trophime 4 48*; 11 534; 20 640
Biguerny, Felipe see VIGARNY, FELIPE
Bihać 4 459
church 4 460
Biharail 15 476
Biharea Fortress 26 706
Bihari, Sándor 30 211
bihārī script see under SCRIPTS → types
Bihar Sharif 15 369
Bihat 15 694
Bi hihyō 24 436
Bihzad 1 208; 4 49–50*; 15 578, 585; 16 127, 294, 326, 332; 27 512
attributions 7 717; 14 431; 16 294, 326; 20 VI
forgeries by others 16 545
patrons and collectors 1 645; 16 326, 553; 28 566
pupils 9 461; 22 390; 25 774; 27 513; 28 568
teachers 21 702
works 4 49; 15 578; 16 132, 286, 296; 26 434; 30 917
Bihzad, Husayn 15 898
Bijago see BIJOGO
Bijan Island 14 21
Bijapur 4 51–2*; 15 294, 637; 16 105
Archaeological Museum 4 52
Arquila 21 591
art forms and materials
architecture 15 382
calligraphy 15 681
domes 9 84
manuscripts 16 345
Bijapur
art forms and materials—cont.
painting 15 638–40*
portraits 15 638, 639, 639–40
textiles 15 664
Drum House see Archaeological Museum
fortifications 15 380–81
gardens 12 73
Islamic religious buildings
Athar Mahal 15 381
congregational mosque 15 382
Dad Mahal see Athar Mahal
Ibrahim Rauza complex 4 51; 15 383
Ikhlas Khan's Mosque 15 382
Malika Jahan's Mosque 9 84; 15 382
Yusuf's Old Jami' Mosque 15 382
Naqqar Khana see Archaeological Museum
palaces
Anand Mahal 15 381
Chini Mahal 15 381
Gagan Mahal 15 381; 23 818
Jal Mandir 15 381
Mihtar Mahal 15 382
Sat Manzil 15 381
tombs 15 383
Gol Gumbaz 4 52; 15 383, 383; 31 111
water supply 15 382
Bijar 15 897, 899
carpets 16 483
Bijaya see EL-'ANNĀBA
Bije, Marcus de 25 371
Bijelić, Jovan 4 461; 28 451
Bijelo Polje 22 17; 28 439
St Peter 28 446
Bijkerk, M. J. 30 15
Bijl, Guillaume 3 574
Bijl, van der 4 790
Bijlaer, G. van 20 923
Bijlert, Herman (Beerntsz.) van 4 52
Bijlert, Jan (Hermansz.) van 4 52–3*
attributions 14 729
groups and movements 22 843; 31 772
patrons and collectors 5 9; 14 190
pupils 33 194
teachers 4 153
works 4 52, 733
Bijlivert, Jacques 4 53*; 11 188; 22 887, 896
patrons and collectors 16 746; 21 25
works 16 747
Bijogo 4 55–6*; 13 835
architecture 4 55*
costumes 4 55
locks 4 55
masks 1 391; 4 55, 55–6*
sculpture 1 391; 4 56*
shrines (i) (cult) 4 55
wall paintings 4 55*
wood-carvings 4 56*
bijoux modelés 17 527
Bijutsu Bunka Kyōkai (Art Culture Society) 11 827; 17 206; 18 96
Bijutsu hihyō 24 437
Bijutsuin 17 138
Bijutsu kenkyū 24 437
Bijutsushi 24 425, 437
Bijutsu shinkō 24 437
Bijutsu shinpō 24 436
Bijutsu techō 24 437
Bijvoet, Bernard 4 56–7; 6 476; 12 792; 14 693
works 12 793
Bijvoet & Duiker 4 56–7*
competitions 7 669
staff 18 138, 212
works 4 57; 7 669
Bikaner 4 57–8*; 15 279, 597
dyeing 15 671

Bikaner—cont.
Ganga Golden Jubilee Museum **4** 58
halls **14** 77
paintings **15** 597, *608*, 608–9*
palaces **4** 57–8*; **15** 388, 390
Bikerts, Gunnar **14** 803
Bikkavolu **4** 58*; **15** *294*, 534, 535
Golingeshvara Temple **15** 536
Kanchan Gudi **15** 301, *301*
Rajarajeshvara Temple **15** 536
sculpture **15** 535–6, 537
temples **15** 301, 302
Virabhadra Temple **15** 536
reliefs **15** *536*
Bikov, Dragan **19** 885
Bílá Hora **4** 58*; **8** *374*
Villa **4** 58*
Bilalova, A. **2** 901
Bilaspur **15** *619*
paintings **15** *624*, 624*
Bila Tserkv Hotel **31** 551
Bilbao (Guatemala) *see* SANTA LUCÍA COTZUMALHUAPA
Bilbao (Spain) **29** 341
Bilcoq, L(ouis-)M(arc-)A(ntoine) **4** 59*
Bild, Atlanten zur Kunst, Das **14** 234
Bildarchitektur **20** 104
Bild Archiv Foto-Marburg *see under* MARBURG
Bildende Kunst **24** 429
bildende Kunst der Gegenwart, Die **14** 234
bildenden Künste, Die **24** 438
Bilders, (Albertus) Gerard(us) **4** 59*; **22** 849
Bilders, Johannes Warnardus **4** 59
Bildtidningen **24** 451
Bilecik **16** 445
Orkhan Gazi Mosque **16** 205
Bílek, František **4** 59–60*; **25** 433
works **8** 387, 401; **30** 221
Bileq **14** 34
Bileshvara Temple **15** 267
Bilger, Hans *see* HANS VON WORMS
Bilhamer, Joost Jansz. **1** 812
Bilhana **15** 228
Bilibili **24** 83
Bilibin, Ivan (Yakovlevich) **4** 60*; **27** 580
groups and movements **27** 392; **31** 582; **33** 379
productions **8** 849
teachers **30** 464
bilingual cups *see under* CUPS → types
bilingual vases *see under* VASES → types
Bilinski, Eleshnitski Monastery **25** 343
Bilivert, Giovanni **4** 53–4*; **16** 673
patrons and collectors **4** 549; **24** 1; **27** 205
pupils **3** 17; **6** 126; **11** 845
teachers **7** 311, 313
works **4** *54*; **24** 860
Bilivert, Jacopo *see* BYLIVERT, JACQUES
Biljan-Bilger, Maria **2** 804
Bilkahīyya, Farīd *see* BELKAHIA, FARID
Bilkis *see* ASPENDOS
Bill, Max **4** 60–62*; **12** 418; **30** 128, 139
dealers **26** 193
groups and movements **1** 76, 77, 666; **7** 546, 698, 772; **30** 135, 139; **33** 737
methods **28** 202
patrons and collectors **30** 153
works **4** *61*; **11** 734; **12** 480; **25** 351; **30** *138*
writings **1** 666; **17** 767; **28** 208
Billant, Pierre du *see* PIERRE DU BILLANT
Billard de Belisard, Claude **25** 578
Billarderie d'Angiviller, Comte de la *see* ANGIVILLER, CHARLES-CLAUDE DE FLAHAUT DE LA BILLARDERIE, Comte d'
billboards **15** 177; **25** 345
Bille, Ejler (Kristian Torbensen) **4** 62*; **8** 736; **22** 150
groups and movements **7** 488
works **8** 741
Billedkunstneren **24** 452
Biller (family) **2** 718; **12** 446
Biller, Albrecht **4** 62
Biller, Johannes **4** 62, 63; **12** 446
Biller, Johann Jacob **4** 62; **12** 423
Biller, Johann Ludwig, the elder (1656-1732) **4** 62
Biller, Johann Ludwig, the younger (1692-1746) **4** 62–3*; **14** 651
Biller, Johann Martin **4** 63
Biller, Lorenz (i) (*fl c.* 1664-85) **4** 62
Biller, Lorenz (ii) (1678-1726) **4** 62; **12** 446
Biller, Olive Allen **4** 63*
Billerey, Fernand **4** 172
Billeter, Maurice **22** 920
billets **4** 63*, *63*
Billfrith the Anchorite **19** 409; **29** 851
Billgren, Ola **30** 82
Billi, Antonio **4** 63–4*; **10** 730; **16** 781; **21** 469
Billiet, Joseph **11** 336
Billing, Hermann **4** 64–5*
pupils **14** 524; **29** 377
staff **30** 371
works **20** 282
Billing, John **33** 11
Billing, Rudolf **30** 371
Billings, Hammatt **14** 207
Billings, Joseph E. **14** 207
Billings, Robert **28** 248, 288
Billingsley, William (*d* 1770) **4** 65
Billingsley, William (1758-1828) **4** 65*; **8** 776; **32** 789
Billington, Dora **4** 444; **25** 39
Billmark, Carl Johan **30** 80
Billnäs **11** 104
Billo, Tiberio **22** 805
Billoin, Charles **14** 116
Billotey **10** 782
Bills, Thomas **23** 25
Billson, Edward (Fielder) **4** 65*
collaboration **2** 705; **19** 453
works **2** *706*, 741
Billyng, Robert de **25** 691
Bilokur, Kateryna **31** 564
Biloli Mosque **15** 373
Bilot **15** 266
Bilotti, Alfred **26** 290
Biloxi **22** 552
Bilsadh **15** 455
Bilston (Staffs) **10** 195, 346; **18** 615
Bilston and Battersea Enamels plc **10** 347
Bilyarsk
axes **32** *527*, 528
Bilzen, Château Oude Biezen **8** 482
Bilzingsleben **25** 491
Bima **15** 775, 812, 813; **29** 235
bimah **4** 65*
Bimann, Dominik *see* BIEMANN, DOMINIK
Bimaran
casket **1** 206, *206*, 211; **15** 706
reliquaries **15** 446; **26** 149
Stupa 2 **1** 188
Bimbi, Bartolomeo **4** 65–6*
collaboration **26** 242
patrons and collectors **2** 105; **21** 29, 31
works **9** 78; **29** 668
Bin, Emile **4** 124; **18** 904; **26** 432
Bin, Jean-Baptiste **28** 697
Bin, Prince **7** 152
Bíňa **28** *848*
St Mary **28** 849, 850, 854
Binagadi **2** 893
Binago, Lorenzo **3** 249, 250; **16** 641; **26** 317
Binant **4** 66*
Binasco, Francesco **20** 791
Binasco, Giovanni **14** 264
Binbirkilise **3** 628; **4** 66–7*; **9** *512*
Basilica **9** 536
Değler **4** *66*
Binche **5** 787
Château **3** 545, 613; **18** 691; **31** 39
paintings **17** 711; **33** 118
sculpture **13** 909
tapestries **7** 520; **13** 910
lace **3** 610
see also under LACE → types
St André **13** 100, 112, 113
tapestries **3** 606
Binche, Arnulf de, *see* ARNULF DE BINCHE
Binck, Jakob **4** 67–8*; **20** 799
groups and movements **19** 501
works **4** *67*; **8** 731, 732; **13** 26
Bindenschu, Ruppert **18** 848; **26** 383
Binder, Bastian **20** 87
Binder, Ludwig **8** 816
Binder, Zacharias **12** 405; **28** 75
binders **7** 92; **8** 127–8; **18** 118; **23** 782; **25** 477; **32** 118*
Bindesbøll, (Michael) Gottlieb (Birkner) **4** 68–9*; **8** 727; **25** 173
furniture **8** 746
groups and movements **13** 611, 612
interior decoration **8** 744; **18** 136
museums **4** *68*, 184; **7** 805; **8** 759; **22** 362; **30** 766
teachers **12** 178; **14** 497
wall paintings **25** 173
works **8** 727
Bindesbøll, Thorvald **4** 69*
collaboration **17** 720
pupils **14** 119
works **7** 805; **8** 727, 748; **11** 790
binding media *see* BINDERS
bindings *see* BOOKBINDINGS
Bindo, Ambrosio da *see* AMBROSIO DA BINDO
Bindo, Benedetto di *see* BENEDETTO DI BINDO
Bindon, Francis **4** 69–70*; **16** 8
Binduccio, Nerio di *see* NERIO DI BINDUCCIO
Bīne, Jēkabs
Binellus **4** 70*; **26** 523
Binet, Louis **10** 478
Binet, René **4** 48; **8** 626; **22** 271
Binford, Lewis **2** 300
Bing, Adolf **31** 256
Bing, Alexander **27** 216
Bing, Ignaz **31** 256
Bing, Ilse **4** 70*
Bing, Jacob H. **7** 807
Bing, Leo **27** 216
Bing, Marcel **4** 71
Bing, M. H. **7** 807
Bing, S(iegfried) **3** 741; **4** 70–71*, 672; **8** 787; **11** 582, 904; **17** 441; **22** 422; **24** 426
architecture **4** 332
ceramics **11** 83
collaboration **2** 391
collections **17** 430
furniture **11** 600
groups and movements **2** 562, 564; **22** 60
interior decoration **11** 47; **31** 876
lithographs **26** 419
prints **3** 522
staff **7** 623; **31** 888
stained glass **4** 325; **30** 869
writings **11** 600
Bing, Samuel *see* BING, S(IEGFRIED)
Bing, Valentijn **25** 269
bingata see RYŪKYŪ ISLANDS → dyeing
Bingebruck, Rupertsberg Abbey **1** 696; **10** 181
embroidery **10** *181*
Bingen, Hildegard of (1098-1179) *see* HILDEGARD OF BINGEN
Bingen, H. von (*fl* 1507-36) **11** 734
Bingen, Pfarrkirche **33** 629
Bingen am Rhein, St Martin
altarpiece **4** *149*
Bingerville **8** 23
Bing & Grøndahl **7** 807; **8** 748, 749; **33** 214
designers **8** 749; **11** 797; **24** 549; **27** 413, 643
stonewares **8** 748, 749
tea-services **7** 807
tiles **30** 884
Bingham, Edward (*fl* 1837-1872; father) **6** 64
Bingham, Edward (1829-*d c.* 1900; son) **6** 64; **10** 312
Bingham, Edward William **6** 65
Bingham, George Caleb **4** 71–3*; **17** 800; **31** 602
dealers **18** 161
works **4** 40, *72*; **12** 294; **31** 602
Bingham, Hiram **20** 3; **29** 219
Bingham, Lavinia, Countess Spencer **8** 461
Bingham, Richard, 2nd Earl of Lucan **24** 86
Bingham, Robert, Bishop of Salisbury **27** 625
Bingham, William **10** 850; **29** 805
Bingley, Robert Benson, 1st Baron *see* BENSON, ROBERT, 1st Baron Bingley
Bingling si **5** 107; **6** 708; **28** 720; **30** 443
Cave 169 **6** 776
Bingo **17** 354
Binh Dinh **6** *418*; **32** *469*
Binh Lam **6** 423
Binh Tri Thien *see* QUANG TRI
Bini **1** 273; **21** 597; **23** 134, 824
Bini, Bernardo **3** 16
Binja **19** 72, 74
Binji **1** 405; **18** 484
Binket *see* TASHKENT
Binkley, David A.
works **1** *336*, *338*
Binnenhuis, 't **1** 811; **4** 73*; **22** 875; **24** 351
Binney, Don **23** 61
Binney, Edward **22** 795
Binney, Edwin III **15** 743, 748; **16** 555
Binney, R. K. **2** 705; **23** 55
Binney Collection *see under* SAN DIEGO (CA) → Museum of Art
Binnink *see* BENING
Binns, The (Lothian) **28** 245
Binns, Charles Fergus **4** 73*; **31** 639
pupils **3** 50; **8** 82; **13** 699; **31** 640
Binns, Richard William **4** 73
Binns, Vivienne **2** 751; **10** 879
Binnya U, King of Pegu (*reg* 1353-85) **25** 889
Binoit, Peter **11** 227; **12** 389
Binon, J. B. **13** 621
Binondo **24** 616
Bin Tepe **19** 841
Tomb of Alyattes **31** 108
Binyang Cave *see under* LONGMEN
Binyinyiwuy **4** 73–4*
Binyon, (Robert) Laurence **4** 74*; **13** 838; **15** 742
collaboration **2** 479; **13** 327
Binyon & Fryer **32** 904
Biograd **8** *174*
Basilica **8** 175
biographies (artists) *see* ARTISTS' BIOGRAPHIES
biographies (saints) *see* SAINTS' LIVES
Biombo **1** 403; **18** 484, 488
biomorphism **2** 488, *489*, *491*; **4** 74–5*
Bion, Nicolas **12** 812, 814
Biondi, Giacomo **3** 436
Biondi, Jacopo **8** 164
Biondi, Luigi **5** 616
Biondi da Bologna, Cristoforo di Jacopo *see* CRISTOFORO DI JACOPO BIONDI DA BOLOGNA
Biondo, Flavio **2** 161; **4** 75*; **14** 867; **26** 767
works **26** 847–8; **32** 639
Biondo, Giovanni del *see* GIOVANNI DEL BIONDO
Biot **11** 613
Biot, Jean-Baptiste **24** 494
Bioulès, Vincent **11** 552, 553; **30** 6
Biow, Hermann **4** 75–6*; **24** 660; **29** 626
Biow, Raphael **4** 75
bipedales see under BRICK → types
Bipi **24** 82
Biraghi, Luigi **22** 70
Birago, Clemente **12** 260
Birago, Francesco Lodovico, Conte di Vische *see* VISCHE, FRANCESCO LODOVICO, Conte di
Birago, Giovanni Pietro **4** 76–7*
attributions **24** 271
patrons and collectors **14** 759; **28** 532, 533
reproductive prints by others **33** 689
teachers **25** 465
works **3** 201; **13** 700; **29** 747
Birago Hours *see under* BOOKS OF HOURS → individual manuscripts
Birago Hours, Master of the **20** 631*
Birague (family) **24** 813–14
Bir al-Aneziyya **16** 155
Birambad, 'Idgah Mosque **15** 345
Birbal **15** 629
Birbal's House *see under* FATEHPUR SIKRI
Birbhum **15** 229, 634
Birbir *see* BERBER
birch **6** 305; **33** 324
historical and regional traditions
Canada **5** *577*
Central Asia, Eastern **6** 305
Finland **8** *803*; **11** 98
Germany **12** 426
Russia **33** I1
Tibet **30** 845
uses
chairs **5** *577*
desks **33** I1
printing **30** 845
stools **8** *803*
veneers **12** 426
Birch, Børge **8** 759
Birch, Charles Bell **11** 239; **17** 610
Birch, Eugenius **4** 810; **24** 748
Birch, Lamorna **23** 26
Birch, Michael **17** 402
Birch, Thomas **4** 77–8*; **11** 906; **14** 795; **32** 378
Birch, William (1755-1834) **4** 77–8
Birch, William (*fl* 1840) **14** 523
Birch, William Russell **31** 601
works **24** *597*
birch bark *see under* BARK → types
Birche, Henry *see* EARLOM, RICHARD
Bircher, André **10** 90
Birchington-on-Sea (Kent) **5** 173; **28** 349
Birch-Lindgren, G. **10** 490
Birckenholtz (family) **11** 736
Bird, Edward **4** 78–9*; **7** 413
patrons and collectors **14** 147
pupils **24** 753; **26** 418
Bird, Edward Chapman **4** 79
Bird, Francis **4** 79*
assistants **10** 372

Bird, Francis—cont.
collaboration 5 827; 7 298; 8 698; 19 606
works 4 *79*; 10 263, 264; 12 595; 19 599, 606
Bird, Gail 22 616
Bird, Junius 29 158, 219
Bird, Nathaniel 18 64
Bird, Richard 33 152
Bird, Walter W. 30 469
Bird, William *see* BYRD, WILLIAM
bird-and-flower painting *see under* PAINTING → types
birdcages 7 146, 147
Bird cycle 10 614
Bird Painter 13 536
bird seal script *see under* SCRIPTS → types
bird's-eye views 4 80–82*; 28 206; 31 152
Austria 32 *435*
Belgium 2 *191*
Canada 4 81
Czech Republic 30 *221*
England 4 80, *81*
France 4 80; 25 *84*
Germany 17 *817*; 33 *431*
Italy 11 *178*; 19 *764*; 24 *535*; 31 *713*
Netherlands, the 1 *800*; 4 80
Scotland 9 *723*
United States of America 2 *121*; 4 81, *82*
birds' feet 22 655
birds of paradise feathers *see under* FEATHERS → types
Birdwood, George (Christopher Molesworth) 4 82–3*; 15 725, 747
Bir el-Abd 28 760, *760*
birettas 32 389*
Birge, M. H., & Sons Co. 5 188; 32 816
Birger, Boris 27 397
Birger (Petterson), Hugo 4 83*
Birger Jarl 30 64
Birgi 12 83; 16 266; 30 478
congregational mosque 16 497
Birgu *see* VITTORIOSA
Bir Hambir 4 93
Bir Hima 2 270
Birhor 15 205
Biringucci, Oreste Vannocci 4 83–4*
Biringucci, Paolo di Vannuccio 4 83
Biringucci, Vannuccio 4 83*, 683; 24 347; 31 302
Biris, Elias G. 33 635
Birka
brooches 32 515
crosses 32 523
dress 9 254, *254*
metalwork 32 524
textiles 7 52
Birkás, Ákos 4 84*
Birkat Habu *see* THEBES (i) (EGYPT) → Malqata
Birkedal Lorentzen, Vilhelm *see* LORENTZEN, VILHELM BIRKEDAL
Birkenbringhausen 26 646
Birkenfeld, Charles I, Count Palatine of 33 *272*
Birkenfeld, Christian, Count Palatine of *see* ZWEIBRÜCKEN, CHRISTIAN III, Duke of
Birkenfeld, Frederick Michael, Count Palatine of 33 *272*, *273*
Birkenhead (Merseyside) 12 635
People's Park 24 179, 293
Showboat Lido 19 332
Williamson Art Gallery 10 371
Birkerts, Gunnar 12 794; 21 650
Birket Foster, Myles *see* FOSTER, MYLES BIRKET
Birkhart, Anton 18 106
Birkhoff, G. D. 28 208
Birkidji 20 893
Birkin (N. Yorks), St Mary 26 614
Birklin 21 298
Birkmire, William H. 28 831
Birks, Henry 1 786; 5 589
Birks, Henry, & Sons 5 586
Birla (family) 3 908; 15 405, 742
Birla, Basant Kumar 15 183
Birla, Saraladevi 15 183
Birley, S. Patrick 32 414
Birmann (family) 3 336
Birmann, Dezső Bokros 10 446, 650; 14 896
Birmann, Peter 4 84–5*
patrons and collectors 33 116
pupils 4 85; 21 735
teachers 1 31
Birmann, Samuel 4 84, 85*; 30 133
Birmann, Wilhelm 4 84, 85
Birmingham (W. Midlands; UK) 4 85–8*, *86*; 10 *225*; 31 724
art forms and materials
armour 16 509
brass 4 688; 10 343, 344
Britannia metal 10 343
clocks 7 448
copper 10 344
enamel 10 346
furniture 10 297
glass 10 320
gold 10 335, 348
jewellery 10 345, 346; 17 526
lacquer 18 615
marks 20 444
medals 20 924
metalwork 4 87–8*
papier mâché 24 62
pens 24 350
silver 4 87; 10 331, 333, 335; 28 739
silverplate 28 576, 577
snuff-boxes 10 479
steel 10 342; 16 61, *61*
art schools 2 569; 10 373
School of Design 2 524; 4 87; 8 802
Barber Institute of Fine Arts 2 691; 4 87; 10 371; 32 906
Barton Arms 25 688
Black Horse 25 688
Cathedral of St Chad 28 296
Cathedral of St Philip 10 232
Centenary Square 4 790
Central Library *see* Reference Library
Council House 31 240
craftsmen and artists 10 265
exhibitions 10 678
Guild of Handicraft 4 87; 10 336
Ikon Gallery 4 87
International Convention Centre Concert Hall 1 126
King Edward VI's Grammar School 28 156
Methodist Central Hall *see* Mission
Mission 21 347
Museum and Art Gallery 2 275; 4 85, *86*; 9 19; 10 370
collections 4 87; 15 744; 22 351; 29 221; 31 305
Odeon Cinema 7 *328*
Reference Library 4 540; 19 320
Town Hall 10 235; 25 268; 31 240
Birmingham Group 4 87
Birmingham Museum of Art (AL; USA) 7 156
Bir Nasb 28 760, *760*
Birnau, Wallfahrtskirche 29 838; 30 *791*; 32 94
Birnbaum, Dara 32 421
Birnie, Frederick
works 24 *18*
Birnin Kebbi 23 *129*
Birnirk 22 574
Biró, Iván 14 896
Biró, László József 24 350
Biró, Márton 29 922
Biró de Stern, A. 29 202
Birolla, Gvidon 28 860
Birolli, Renato 4 88*
groups and movements 7 894; 11 802; 13 727, 872; 16 681; 32 403
Biron, Ernest-John, Duke of Kurland *see* ERNEST-JOHN, Duke of Kurland
Biron, Peter, Duke of Kurland *see* PETER, Duke of Kurland
biros *see under* PENS → types
Birot, P. Albert 25 447
birri 9 640
Birsel, Melih 16 588
Bir Singh Deo, Raja of Gwalior (*reg* 1398-1425) (Rajput) 15 373
Bir Singh Deo, Raja of Orchha (*reg* 1605-27) (Rajput) 4 93; 15 393
Birs Nimrud *see* BORSIPPA
Birth of Dionysos, Painter of the 13 528
Birth of Venus, Master of the 25 20
birth trays *see* TRAYS → types → *deschi da parto*
Birtingur 1 468
al-Biruni 15 308
writings 6 320; 15 202
on ceramics 16 398
on glass 6 268
on jewellery 6 273
on metallurgy 16 363
on mineralogy 16 527, 540
Birushana *see* DAIBUTSU
Biržai 19 *494*
Radziwiłł Palace 19 496
Bis, Nicolás 2 466, 467
Bisa 1 409
Bisacco, Giuseppe 17 443
Bisantius, Archbishop of Bari 3 234
Biscaino, Bartolomeo 4 89*; 6 29
works 4 *89*
Biscaino, Giovanni Andrea 4 89
Biscarra, Giovan Batista 12 901
Bischof, Peter 21 84
Bischof, Werner 4 90*; 20 99; 24 677
Bischoff, Elmer 8 871; 27 731; 31 608
Bischoff, Jakob Christoph 30 133
Bischoffheim, Marie-Laure *see* NOAILLES, MARIE-LAURE DE, Vicomtesse
Bischofsberger, Bruno 24 683
Bischofshofen Church 2 79
Biscia, Lelio, Cardinal 4 90*; 27 489
Biscop, Benedict *see* BENEDICT BISCOP
Biscop Baducing *see* BENEDICT BISCOP
biscuit 29 573
biscuit firing *see under* FIRING → types
Biscuit ware *see under* POTTERY → wares
Bisembaya Mausoleum 17 866
Bisenzio
bronzes 10 604, 625
pottery 10 610
terracotta 10 602
urns 10 595
vases 10 610, 611
Bishah 32 316
Bisham Abbey 4 439
Bishan Das 4 90–91*; 15 584, 586
works 4 *91*; 15 *586*, 587; 16 345
Bishapur 4 91–2*; 15 899, *901*, 906, 908, 912, 915
metalwork 15 920
palace of Shapur I 16 801; 27 65; 29 816
rock reliefs 15 *918*
sculpture 1 887
textiles 16 433
Bishkek 4 93*; 6 *182*; 18 *567*, 568; 31 542
architecture 18 568
Hospital 18 568
House of Radio 18 568
Kyrgyzstan State Historical Museum 4 93; 6 284
Kyrgyzstan State Museum of Fine Art 4 93; 6 284; 7 291; 18 568
Medical Institute 18 568
museums 6 282
Bishnupur 4 93*; 15 *279*
Keshta Raya Temple 15 396, *396*
Shyama Raya Temple 15 395
temples 15 395
Bishop, Cortland F. 24 183
Bishop, Isabel 1 773; 4 93*; 21 606
Bishop, Olive 2 762
Bishop Auckland (Co. Durham)
Bishop's Palace 6 61; 14 75
Newton Cap Bridge 4 801
Bishopdale (N. Yorks)
houses 32 *277*
Bishop Fox's Salt 10 325
Bishop Gandulf's Bible *see under* BIBLES → individual manuscripts
Bishop Mellitus 19 597
Bishop Museum *see under* HONOLULU
Bishopp, Hawley 26 37
Bishop's Hull (Somerset), SS Peter and Paul 24 577
Bishop's Lydeard (Somerset), St Mary's 24 577
Bishops of Paris, Missal of the *see under* MISSALS → individual manuscripts
Bishop's Rock Lighthouse 19 361
Bi Shou 7 116
Bishu *see* SAITO, KATSUTOSHI
Bisi, Giuseppe 3 856; 21 527
Bisi, Luigi 21 495
Bisi, Michele 2 232
Bisilliat, Maureen 4 94*
Bisingen, Schloss Hohenzollern 12 415
Bisitun 4 94; 15 *901*, 902, 906, 908; 21 167
dress 1 887
inscriptions 1 892; 4 94
rock reliefs 1 116, *116*, 886; 4 94*; 15 906, 916; 24 217; 29 614
Biskra, Mausoleum of Sidi 'Uqba 28 634
Biskupin 4 94–5*; 21 551; 25 *92*, *470*, *471*
body ornaments 25 518
fortifications 25 522
settlements 25 536
wood-carvings 25 545
Bismarck Archipelago 23 727, 728; 24 64, *64*, 83, 85
pottery 23 728
Bismaya 2 272
bismuth 24 578, 798
bismuth chromate 24 799
Bison, Giuseppe Bernardino 4 471
Bissau 1 *386*; 15 611
Museo Etnográfico Nacional 13 835
Bisschop (family) 22 893
Bisschop, Christoffel 4 159
Bisschop, Cornelis 5 440
Bisschop, Dirck Anthonie 18 738
Bisschop, Jan (1680-1771) 4 95*; 22 904
Bisschop, Jan de (1628-71) 4 95–6*
patrons and collectors 10 864; 27 271
reproductive prints by others 31 797
works 4 *96*; 5 *542*; 14 669
Bisschop, Pieter 4 95*; 22 904
Bisschop, Richard 26 468
Bisschop-Robertson, Suze *see* ROBERTSON, SUZE
Bissell, George 31 611
Bissell & Holman 5 732
Bissen, Christian Gottlieb Wilhelm 30 258
Bissen, Hermann Wilhelm 4 96–7*
assistants 17 720
patrons and collectors 16 829
pupils 3 783; 21 478, 815; 23 230; 27 337; 28 813; 30 258; 32 497
teachers 8 740
works 7 805; 8 741
Bissen, Wilhelm 8 741
Bisset, James, Prior 27 529
Bisseuil, Jean-Baptise Amelot, Vicomte de 26 91
Bissier, Julius 2 545; 4 97*; 33 635
Bissière, Mousse 4 98
Bissière, (Jean-Edouard-) Roger 4 98*, 391; 11 551
groups and movements 2 543
pupils 6 84; 12 546; 14 549; 20 512; 33 628
works 19 491
Bissing, Friedrich W(ilhelm) von 1 90; 10 80, 82, 84, 93
Bissinger, Georges 4 98–9*; 12 265
Bissolo, Francesco 4 99*; 15 831; 32 190
patrons and collectors 7 775
teachers 3 667
Bisson, Auguste-Rosalie 4 99*
Bisson, Louis-Auguste 4 99*
Bisson de la Roque, Fernand 10 81
Bissone, Elia de *see* GAGINI, ELIA
Bissone, Giambono da *see* GIAMBONO DA BISSONE
Bisson Frères 4 99; 24 660, 663; 28 346
Bissucio, Leonardo (de' Molinari) da *see* LEONARDO (DE' MOLINARI) DA BESOZZO
Bistam 4 99–100*; 16 *105*
minaret 16 164
shrine of Abu Yazid *see* shrine of Bayezid Bistami
shrine of Bayezid Bistami 4 99; 16 194, 374; 28 634
mosque 16 501
Bistega, Luca Antonio 4 320
Bisti, Dmitry (Spiridonovich) 4 100*
Bisticci, Vespasiano da *see* VESPASIANO DA BISTICCI
Bistolfi, Giovanni 4 100
Bistolfi, Leonardo 4 100–101*, 278
assistants 27 303
pupils 8 267
teachers 16 706; 30 215
works 4 *101*; 31 446
writings 5 413
Bistra Monastery 28 860
bistre 4 101*; 9 216; 15 852, 855; 24 792
Bistricius, Krzysztof *see* BYSTRZYCKI, KRZYSZTOF
Bistrița 26 *705*, 707, 722
metalwork 26 719
Monastery 25 340, 341; 26 719, 720
Bolnitsa Church 25 344; 26 718
reliquaries 26 149
Bistritz pax 22 203
Bīsutūn *see* BISITUN
Biswas, Sutapa 10 882
Bitar 14 21
bite 4 101*
Bithal Das 15 614
Bithia 25 733
bit hilani 1 831; 5 557; 21 290; 30 185, 186, 187, 191, *191*, 194
Bithna 2 248
Bithu, Mahadeva Temple 15 486
Bitik 1 522; 15 159; 22 511
Bitlis, Kızıl Mosque 16 202
Bitner, Albert 8 372

Bitola 1 544
  Hacı Mahmud Mosque 16 228
  Slepche Monastery 5 155
Bitolj 4 101–2*; 9 *511*; 19 *882*
  Archaeological Museum 19 886
  architecture 9 560
  Bezistan 19 882
  Hadji Kaddi Mosque 19 882
  mosaics 12 71
  Moša Pijade Art Gallery 19 886
Biton 13 412, 413; 21 577
Bitonto, Cathedral of S Valentino 16 626; 23 109; 25 165; 26 628
  pulpit 25 723
Bítov Castle 8 379; 24 462
bitta 15 243*
Bitte, il *see* CAPORALI, GIOVAN BATTISTA
Bittel, Kurt 1 893; 4 229; 14 498
Bitter, Karl 3 30; 15 23; 31 612
Bitter, Naomi 16 568
Bitti, Bernardo 4 102*, 264
  works 4 261; 8 302; 17 514; 24 506
Bittiga, Ruler (*reg c.* 1106-56) (Hoysala) 3 688; 14 816
Bittner, Lajos 15 8
bitumen 1 155; 4 102–3*
  historical and regional traditions
    Egypt, ancient 24 792
    Islamic 4 688; 16 269
    Mesopotamia 21 283
    Sumerian 22 159
  uses
    aquatints 2 239
    architecture 16 269
    etchings 10 558
    masonry 1 156
    metalwork 4 688
    paints 4 103
    photography 24 655
    pigments 24 792
Biuletyn historii sztuki 24 425, 441; 25 143
Biure, Abbot 16 436
BI-ware *see under* POTTERY → wares
Biyanayman
  ossuaries 6 193; 23 608, *608*
Bizariano *see* PIYI
bizarre silk *see under* SILK → types
Bizen 17 *11*, *241*
  Bizen Ceramics Museum 17 433
  kilns 17 255
  pottery 4 103*; 17 241, 242, 255, 256, 351, 399, 438
    stoneware 17 *255*, 259, 262, 267, 351
    see also under POTTERY → wares
Bizuti, Filippo *see* RUSUTI, FILIPPO
Bizzacheri, Carlo Francesco 1 532, 758; 4 104*; 31 854
Bizzelli, Giovanni 21 23
Bjaalid, Bjørn 23 242
Bjälbo 9 156
Bjäresjö Church 1 123; 30 75
Bjärka-Säby 30 89
Bjarnason, Sveinn Kristján *see* HOLGER, CAHILL
Bjerg, Johannes C. 3 749; 8 741
Bjerke, Arvid 9 685; 10 460; 13 31
Bjerke-Petersen, Vilhelm 4 104–5*; 8 736
  groups and movements 4 62; 30 22
  pupils 10 378
Bjernede Church 4 781; 8 723
Bjerreby, St Martin 13 190
Björck, (Gustaf) Oscar 4 105*; 16 67; 28 814
  works 11 473, *476*
Björk, Jacob 11 471
Björk, Karl Olov 30 86
Bjørnholm 8 724
Bjornson, Maria 30 687
Björquist, Karin 30 99, 101
Björsäter Church 30 76
Bjurström, Tor Sigurd 13 31; 33 566
BKI (Bond voor Kunst en Industrie) 22 876
bkra-shis lhun po *see* TASHILHUNPO
bkra-shis sgo-mang mchod-rten see under STUPAS → types
Blaas, Karl von 4 106*; 13 215, 702
Blaauw, C(ornelis) J(onke) 4 106*
Blacas, Pierre-Louis-Jean-Casimir de Blaces d'Aulps, Duc de 4 106–7*, 556
  collections 23 36
  gems 12 266
  paintings 12 738; 15 838
  sponsorship 20 901
Blacas Collection *see under* LONDON → museums → British Museum
Blacas Ewer 16 381, *381*
Blachernitissae see under COINS → types
black *see under* PIGMENTS → types
Black, Alexander 20 92
Black, Dorrit (Foster) 2 771; 4 107*; 30 160
Black, George Nixon 24 300
Black, James Wallace 24 669
Black, Mary 22 655
Black, Milton J. 18 73
Black, Misha 2 553; 20 475
Blackadder, Elizabeth 9 725; 28 240
Blackadder, Robert, Archbishop of Glasgow 12 778
Blackader, Gordon Home 3 269
Blackall, Clapp & Whittemore 4 475
Blackall, Clarence H. 4 474
Black American art *see* AFRICAN AMERICAN ART
Black-and-red-on-buff ware *see under* POTTERY → wares
Black-and-red style pottery *see under* POTTERY → wares
Black-and-Red ware *see under* POTTERY → wares
black-and-white granite *see under* GRANITE → types
Black and White style mosaics *see under* ROME, ANCIENT → mosaics
Black and White style pottery *see under* POTTERY → wares
Black Box Collotype 7 576
Blackburn, Amelia 24 57
Blackburn, James 2 738; 4 107*
  works 2 306, 738
Blackburn, Joseph 4 107–8*, 477
  attributions 20 7
  patrons and collectors 4 599
  works 31 600
Blackburn, Nicholas 33 543
Blackburn, Robert 19 492; 20 605, 606; 25 628
Blackburn, William 4 108*; 25 636
Blackburne, E. L. 5 314
Blackburn & Norburn 14 850
Black Carib 14 712
black chalk *see under* CHALK → types
Black Cloak 28 320
Black Decorated style pottery *see under* POTTERY → wares
Blackere, Gilles de *see* GILLES DE BLACKERE
Blacket, Arthur 4 108
Blacket, Cyril 4 108
Blacket, Edmund (Thomas) 4 108*; 23 36; 24 495
  assistants 15 24
  collaboration 30 158
  staff 3 252
  works 2 738
Blackett, Walter 23 20
Blackett & Forster 13 709
black exercise *see under* CALLIGRAPHY → types
Black Expressionism 1 443, 444–5; 25 654; 31 609
Black-figure pottery *see under* POTTERY → wares
Blackfoot 17 770; 22 551
  beadwork 22 *642*
  dress 22 636
  headdresses 22 653
  quillwork 22 650
  sculpture 22 584
Blackfriars *see* DOMINICAN ORDER
Blackfriars Glasshouse 10 316
Black Fury group 13 528
Black Glazed pottery *see under* POTTERY → wares
Black-glazed ware *see under* POTTERY → wares
Black Hours *see under* BOOKS OF HOURS → individual manuscripts
Black House of Art *see* WEUSI NYUMBA YA SANAA
Blackie, Walter 10 299; 20 24; 28 249, 270
blackjacks 4 109*
Black Jesus 19 242
black lead *see* GRAPHITE
Black Lustrous Wheelmade ware *see under* POTTERY → wares
Blackman, Aylward 10 81, 82; 21 61
Blackman, Charles 2 161, 750; 4 109*
Blackman, George 26 76
Blackmore 2 877; 5 840; 10 580; 33 226
Blackmore, Howard 2 451
Black Mountain College (NC) 3 403; 4 109–10*; 5 381; 8 270, 803; 24 406–7; 31 660
  pupils 6 408; 23 183, 184; 28 374, 899
  teachers
    Albers, Anni 1 549; 30 328
    Albers, Josef 1 548
    Bolotowsky, Ilya 4 282
    Feininger, Lyonel 10 863
    Fuller, R(ichard) Buckminster 11 835
    Rauschenberg, Robert 26 26
    Stamos, Theodoros 29 534
Black Mountain Review 4 109; 24 429
Black Neighborhood Mural Movement 1 445; 6 576; 31 609
Black Obelisk 1 892; 18 896; 21 298, 310; 23 150; 30 187
Black-on-red ware *see under* POTTERY → wares
Black Oribe ware *see under* POTTERY → wares
Black Polished ware *see under* POTTERY → wares
Blackpool (Lancs)
  Lido 19 332
  piers 24 748
Black Prince *see* PLANTAGENET, EDWARD, Prince of Wales
Black Prince's Ruby 12 270
Blackrock Convent (Co. Cork) 16 34
black rot 19 6
Black Sea Colonies 4 110–13*
  gold 1 118
  marble 4 *111*, *113*
  metalwork 4 111
  reliefs 4 *111*
  sculpture 4 111, *113*
  stelae 4 111
Black Seto ware *see under* POTTERY → wares
Blackshaw, Basil 16 41
Black-slip-and-combed ware *see under* POTTERY → wares
Black Slip ware *see under* POTTERY → wares
blacksmiths 3 132; 9 65; 20 218; 29 474
blackstone 1 *856*; 21 251
Black Tai *see* TAI DAM
Black-topped ware *see under* POTTERY → wares
black ware *see under* POTTERY → wares
Blackwell, Ursula 12 871
Blackwell & Craig 33 628
Black Western Painting Exhibition *see* KOKUSHOKU YÔGA TEN
black-wood 15 813
blackwork embroidery *see under* EMBROIDERY → types
Blacqueville, La Queue du Chien 32 *278*
bladder colours *see under* PAINTS → types
bladders 4 113; 23 787, *787*
Bladelin, Pierre 4 113*; 31 147; 33 120
Bladelin triptych 4 113; 13 675
Bladen, Ronald 4 114*
Bladen, Thomas 2 121
blades 1 361; 8 283, *283*; 25 494, 515
Blado, Antonio 27 606
Blaeser, Gustav (Hermann) 4 114–15*; 24 817; 33 392
  assistants 9 691; 14 482
  pupils 28 672
  teachers 26 23
Blaeu (family) 2 696; 20 364
Blaeu, Johannes 4 868; 12 811, 814; 14 375; 28 73
  works 24 *535*
Blaeu, Willem (Jansz.) 10 391; 12 812; 17 183; 32 588
Blagoevo 25 512
Blai, Pere 29 268
Blaikie, Thomas 3 524; 12 123, 134; 23 519
Blain, Jean-Baptiste *see* BELIN (DE FONTENAY), JEAN-BAPTISTE (1653-1715)
Blainville, Marquis de 19 33
Blair, Claude 2 450
Blair, David 23 75
Blair, Lee 19 701
Blair, Robert 8 186; 28 86
Blair Castle (Strathclyde) 5 169; 7 409; 17 623; 28 252
  collections 9 28
  paintings 21 34
Blairquhan (Strathclyde) 28 230
Blais, Jean-Charles 11 553
Blaise, Barthélemy 7 162
Blaise Hamlet (Avon) 8 30, 461
Blaj 26 708
Blak, Lyubov' 27 414
Blake 4 532
Blake, George Henry
  works 20 VIII1
Blake, John 7 420; 20 561
Blake, Peter 4 115–16*; 7 385; 19 590
  groups and movements 4 823; 25 231, 556
  methods 25 25
  works 1 130; 4 *115*; 29 426
Blake, Quentin 4 368
Blake, William 4 116–22*; 19 621; 23 884
  book illustrations 1 640; 4 362; 7 576; 8 186; 11 862; 18 714; 19 426; 20 335; 22 277; 25 72
  facsimiles 26 236
  groups and movements 1 897; 26 736, 737, 742
  methods 24 3
  patrons and collectors 1 154; 10 655; 15 29; 27 166; 28 276; 33 453
  prints 10 252; 25 592, 610, 621
    engravings 4 9; 8 264; 10 394, *395*
    etchings 4 *117*; 7 226, *227*; 10 555, 560–61, *561*
    lithographs 20 602
    monotypes 4 *118*, *119*; 21 896
    wood-engravings 33 368
Blake, William—cont.
  reproductive prints by others 19 483; 28 86; 31 909
  teachers 3 329
  watercolours 4 *121*
Blake and Whitman 33 491
Blakebrough, Les 2 761
Blakelock, Ralph Albert 4 123*; 16 884; 31 603
  patrons and collectors 18 672; 26 472
Blakeney, William, Baron Blakeney 17 622
Blaker 6 389; 23 233
Blaker, Hugh 32 791
Blakeway, Edward 6 93; 7 480
Blakstad, Gudolf 4 123
Blakstad & Munthe-Kaas 4 123*; 23 222, 602
Blamars, Loys 11 641
Blanc, (Auguste-Alexandre-Philippe-) Charles 4 123–4*; 11 667, 672; 22 329
  personal collection 7 831; 12 608; 13 829
  works 24 837
    on art 31 300
    on artists 11 674
    on chiaroscuro 6 570
    on colour 7 629
    on encaustic painting 10 199
Blanc, Hippolyte 3 501
Blanc, Honoré 31 175
Blanc, Horace Le *see* LE BLANC, HORACE
Blanc, (Paul) Joseph 4 124*; 25 552; 33 455
Blancard, Frans 22 826
blanc de chine see under PORCELAIN → types
Blanc de Dupain, J. 26 130
Blanc-Garin, Ernest 10 658
Blanch, Antoni Rigalt i *see* RIGALT I BLANCH, ANTONI
Blanchaert, Leonard 3 578, 585, 884
Blanchaert, Leopold 3 578, 884
Blanchard, Auguste (Thomas Marie), III 4 126*; 26 233
Blanchard, Auguste Jean-Baptiste Marie 4 126
Blanchard, Edouard Théophile 5 342
Blanchard, Gabriel 4 125, 126*; 11 536
  collaboration 2 707; 24 211
  dealing 11 662
  groups and movements 27 286
  patrons and collectors 4 808
  works 7 195
Blanchard, Jacques 4 124, 125–6*; 24 467
  attributions 7 863
  collaboration 4 126
  patrons and collectors 5 168; 30 274
  pupils 4 534
  reproductive prints by others 8 525; 20 415
  teachers 19 14
  works 4 *125*; 20 894
Blanchard, Jean 4 125, 126*
  collaboration 4 125; 20 860
  patrons and collectors 14 492
  pupils 4 126
Blanchard, Joshua 22 296; 24 300
Blanchard, María 4 126–7*; 29 285
  groups and movements 8 240
  teachers 2 62
  works 27 783
Blanchard, Mark 30 503
Blanchard, Porter 31 650
Blanche, Queen of Navarre and Aragon (*reg* 1425-41) 23 402; 31 832
Blanche, Jacques-Emile 4 127*; 11 547
  collaboration 26 191

Blanche, Jacques-Emile—cont.
groups and movements 3 156
pupils 12 878; 13 313; 18 667; 23 694; 26 255
teachers 12 496
Blancheau, Geneviève 27 789
Blanche Capet, Duchess of Austria (*d* 1305) 33 164
Blanchefort de Créquy, Charles de *see* CRÉQUY, CHARLES DE BLANCHEFORT DE
Blanchefosse Church 11 614; 13 158; 26 146
Blanche of Burgundy, Countess of Savoy (*d* 1348) 28 1
Blanche of Castile, Queen of France (before 1188-1252) 5 664–5*
architecture 2 48; 5 663, 665; 13 42; 27 541
manuscripts 2 222; 5 665; 11 530
stained glass 5 665
Blanche of England (*fl c.* 1380-90) 11 614
Blanche of France (*fl c.* 1320) 25 692
Blanche of Savoy, Duchess of Milan (*fl c.* 1378) 12 710
Blanchery, Vittorio 31 447
Blanchet 25 771
Blanchet, Alexandre 2 700
Blanchet, Félix 20 472
Blanchet, Louis-Gabriel 4 128*; 26 50
Blanchet, Thomas 4 128*
collaboration 8 158
reproductive prints by others 20 592; 30 793
works 4 36, *128*; 19 846; 32 574
blanching of paint 4 129*
Blanchon, Georges 17 463
Blanck, Jurian 31 647
Blanckerhoff, Jan Theunisz. 11 446
works 11 *447*
Blanco, Alberto Ríos *see* RÍOS BLANCO, ALBERTO
Blanco, Eloy 18 832
Blanco, José Miguel 6 597, 601
Blanco, Luis Amado *see* AMADO BLANCO, LUIS
Blanco, Rafael 8 233
Blanco, Sylvia 25 702
Blanco Soler, Luis 29 321
Blandon, Antonio Fernández 7 362
Blanes, Juan Luis 4 129; 31 754
Blanes, Juan Manuel 4 129*; 31 754, 757, 758
Blanes, Juan Manuel, Museo Municipal *see under* MONTEVIDEO → museums
Blanes, Nicanor 4 129
Blanes Viale, Pedro 4 129*; 31 754, 758
Blangstedgård *see under* ODENSE
Blank, Antoni 25 141; 29 86; 32 876
Blank, Karl (Ivanovich) 18 536; 22 171; 23 26; 27 374
Blankenberch Altarpiece 7 723
Blankenberg (Germany) 12 452
Blankenberg, J. F. L. 15 770
Blankenberge 17 699
Blankenberghe Pier 24 747
Blankenhain 30 793
Blankenstein, Hermann 3 794
blankets
historical and regional traditions
Belgium 3 606
Fulani 11 *829*, 829–30
Mali 11 *829*, 829–30
Native North Americans 22 *547*, *623*, 652, 669, 673
Navajo 22 624–5; 27 317
Ndebele 1 348
Thailand 30 *621*
materials
bark 22 *547*
blankets
materials—cont.
beadwork 3 441
cotton 11 830; 30 *621*
embroidery 22 *623*
feathers 22 652
tapestries 3 606
wool 11 *829*, 829–30; 22 *547*, *623*
types
arkilla 11 829, *829*
kaasa 11 829
kerka 11 829, *829*
blanket stitch *see under* STITCHES
Blano, Sylvia 25 703
Blanquart-Evrard, Louis-Désiré 4 129–30*; 20 523; 24 648, 659
staff 26 91
works 9 340
Blantyre 1 319, *407*
Mt Soche Hotel 20 161
Museum of Malawi 20 161
Blantyre Psalter *see under* PSALTERS → individual manuscripts
Blanuša, Milan 28 451
Blarenberghe, Henri-Désiré van 4 130
Blarenberghe, Henri-Joseph van 4 130; 21 643
Blarenberghe, Jacques-Wilhelm van 4 130
Blarenberghe, Louis-Nicolas van 4 130*; 11 633; 21 643
collaboration 7 193
works 7 *194*; 14 792
Blas 5 751
Blas, Camilo 24 509
Blas, Martín de 29 265
Blasco, Arcadio 29 330
Blasco, Eleuterio 29 296
Blasco, Miguel Angelo de 27 803
Bläser, Gustav (Hermann) *see* BLAESER, GUSTAV (HERMANN)
Blashfield, Edwin Howland 4 130*; 28 889; 30 62
Blashfield, James 4 769; 30 505
Blashfield, John Marriott 2 541; 30 503
Blasio, Nicola de 26 148
Blasius, Johann *see* SANTINI(-AICHEL), GIOVANNI
Blasius, Lennart 23 396
Blass, Bill 5 531
Blasse, Pierre 11 639
Blasset, Nicolas 4 131*
pupils 25 79
works 10 *436*, 437
Blasset, Philippe 4 131
Blasset, Pierre 4 131*
Blast: The Review of the Great English Vortex 9 9; 10 256, 547; 24 427; 25 380; 26 466; 32 700–701, 753
blast furnaces *see under* FURNACES → types
Blåtårn faience factory 8 748
Blathwayt, William 4 131*
Blatná
Castle 6 364; 8 377
church 32 88
Blatten, Wallfahrtskirche St Jost 30 136
Blattner, Andreas 24 309
Blau, Luigi 2 789, 810, 815
Blau, Tina 2 797
Blaubeuren Abbey Church 28 134; 32 821; 33 629
altarpiece 1 710; 12 401; 13 117; 25 464; 28 133, *133*
Blauen Vier *see* BLUE FOUR
Blaue Reiter 4 131–3*; 10 694–5, 696; 18 717; 22 304; 28 89; 29 871
collections 12 472; 18 187; 20 880
exhibitions 8 656; 17 764; 20 381; 22 318, 921; 23 569; 28 139; 29 871; 32 775
Blaue Reiter—cont.
members 1 74; 4 177; 12 395; 16 817; 20 12
Arp, Hans (Peter Wilhelm) 2 488
Campendonk, Heinrich 5 543
Feininger, Lyonel 10 862
Klee, Paul 18 109
Kubin, Alfred (Leopold Isidor) 18 491
Mendelsohn, Erich 10 697
Morgner, Wilhelm 22 114
Münter, Gabriele 22 318
works 4 *132*; 25 348; 32 902
Blaue Reiter Almanach 6 588; 17 764; 18 187; 19 751; 20 381; 24 427; 25 582
contributors 2 488; 5 219; 18 109; 20 12; 22 114
Blaumann, Johann Eberhard 7 471; 26 708
Blauw, Jacobus 8 *558*
Blauwe Schuit 33 81
Blavatsky, Helena (Petrovna) 30 710
Blavatsky, Vladimir (Dmitriyevich) 4 133–4*
Blavet, Raymond 15 41
Blavis, Bartolomeo de *see* BARTOLOMEO DE BLAVIS
Blay, Miguel 17 683; 29 295
Blay, Pedro 23 492
Blaye 21 568
Blaye, Jourdain de *see* JOURDAIN DE BLAYE
Blažek 18 539
Blažíček, Oldřich 4 134
Blažíček, Oldřich Jakub 4 134*; 8 426
blazons 12 272; 13 137, 583; 14 404–5, 408, 409, 423
see also COATS OF ARMS
Blázquez, Casiano Alguacil *see* ALGUACIL BLÁZQUEZ, CASIANO
Blažuj 4 *459*
Basilica 4 459
bleaching 6 335; 9 490; 24 649
Blechen, Karl 4 134–6*
groups and movements 26 742
works 4 *135*, *136*; 12 393; 15 828
Bleckner, Ross 1 81; 23 50
Bled Ecclesiastical Museum 28 863
Bledlow Cross 14 544
bleed (i) (printing) 4 136*
bleed (ii) (pigments) 4 136*
bleeding bowls *see under* BOWLS → types
Bleeker, Bernhard 33 228
Blegen, Carl (William) 2 406; 4 137*; 25 753
excavations 31 356, 375; 33 746
Blegvad, Jacob 8 729
Bleicherhof *see under* ZURICH
Bleijs, A. C. 29 876
Bleken, Håkon 13 726
Blekinge 30 76
Blendea, Maria 26 721
Blendeff, Martinus 19 260
blenders *see under* BRUSHES → types
Blenheim (New Zealand) 23 *52*
Blenheim Painter 32 59
Blenheim Palace (Oxon) 3 266; 4 137–8*, *138*; 7 286; 8 47; 10 *225*, 232, 274, 276, 292; 12 592; 23 806, 812, 857; 31 *859*, 859–60
collections 2 560; 10 364, 365, 367
frames 11 431
furniture 10 292
gardens 12 *63*, 128; 33 257
paintings 7 461; 15 44; 18 644; 19 384; 27 841
park 24 179
portico 25 266
sculpture 27 466, *467*
silver 8 149; 10 332; 18 677
staircases 29 524
Blenheim Palace (Oxon)—cont.
tapestries 30 331
Blénod, Barthélemy de 11 604
Blera 10 617
Blérancourt Château 4 865; 6 507, *507*; 11 515
Blérot, Ernest 3 550; 4 138–9*
Bléry, Eugène (-Stanislas-Alexandre) 4 139*; 21 170
Blerzy, Joseph-Etienne 11 630
Bles, David Joseph 4 139*; 18 481; 22 848
Bles, Herri met de 2 204; 3 554; 4 139–41*
attributions 20 750
patrons and collectors 12 897; 32 7
pupils 22 199
works 4 *140*; 18 706
Blesch, Otto 10 103–4
Blesendorf, Samuel 9 28; 12 457
works 9 *27*
Blesle, St Pierre 9 152; 26 641
Blessed Virgin Mary of Mt Carmel, Order of the *see* CARMELITE ORDER
Blessington, William Stewart, 1st Earl of *see* STEWART, WILLIAM, 1st Earl of Blessington
Bletkin, P. 12 327
Bleu 8 436; 24 428
bleu d'Allemagne see under PIGMENTS → type
bleu de Namur see under LIMESTONE → types
Bleuet, Florent 6 414; 31 384
Bleuland, Jan 18 176
Bleuler (family) 30 143
Bleuler, Johann Heinrich 28 120
Bleus de la G.G.G. 5 37
Bleyl, Fritz 4 891; 10 694; 14 284; 18 77
Blezascie 3 *525*, 527; 31 549
Blick, Thomas 23 73
Blicke, Maurits 2 510
Blickling Hall (Norfolk) 8 45; 16 823
collections 32 114
interior decoration 11 430; 29 748
Long Gallery 29 834
mausoleum 20 867, *867*; 25 766
Blidaru 27 843
Blieck, Daniël de 2 341; 8 663
Bligh, John, 3rd Earl of Darnley 4 845
Blijenberch, Abraham van *see* BLYENBERCH, ABRAHAM VAN
Blijk, J. F. van den 9 169
Blin, Jean-Baptiste *see* BELIN (DE FONTENAY), JEAN-BAPTISTE (1653-1715)
Blin, Louis 3 621
blind arcades *see under* ARCADES → types
blind arches *see under* ARCHES → types
blind-blocking *see* EMBOSSING
Blind Brook (NY), PepsiCo Sculpture Garden 28 315
Blinder, Olga 4 141–2*; 24 101, 102
groups and movements 22 743; 24 98, 99
patrons and collectors 24 101
works 24 99
Blind Man 24 428, 432
blinds 7 732; 9 12; 10 279
blind tracery *see under* TRACERY → types
Blinn, Henry Clay 28 540
Bliquey 27 85
Bliss, Douglas Percy 4 367
Bliss, Lillie P(lummer) 4 142*; 25 553
collections 8 571; 31 663, 667
Bliss, Mildred 4 142*; 32 890
Bliss, R., Manufacturing Co. 31 255, 263, 264
Bliss, Robert Woods 4 142*
Blissett, David 17 402
blistering 4 142*
Bloc, André 11 569; 24 111; 28 300
Bloch, Adolpho 4 726
Bloch, Albert 4 132
Bloch, Armand 8 77
Bloch, Carl (Heinrich) 4 142*; 8 735
Bloch, Ernst 8 826
Bloch, Jan Gotlib 20 152
Bloch, Jean Richard 19 81
Bloch, Martin 4 143*
Bloch-Bauer 2 829
Block 24 425, 446
Block (family) 25 136
Block, Agnes 27 518
Block, Benjamin von 14 899
Block, Der 4 143*, 309; 28 126
members 3 878; 12 379
Block, Eugène de 30 373
Block, Herbert 27 872
Block, Willem van den 18 435
block altars *see under* ALTARS → types
blockboard 24 3; 33 328
block-books 2 223; 4 143–6*, 345, *345*, 356, 357
China 4 143
Germany 4 143, 144, 146*, *357*; 12 385
Gothic 12 385
Netherlands, the 4 143, 144–6*, *144*, *145*
Blocke, Abraham van den 4 146, 147*; 12 224
works 12 224; 25 114
Blocke, Izaak van den 4 147–8*; 25 104
works 4 146, *148*; 21 820
Blocke, Servaes van den 33 88
Blocke, Willem van den 4 146–7*; 12 224
pupils 4 147
teachers 17 740
works 4 146, *147*; 12 224; 24 586; 25 113; 30 84, 345
Block group 4 148*; 25 108, 422
members 3 788; 7 772; 18 181; 29 582, 794; 30 199, 204
blocking 12 865; 24 55
Blocklandt, Anthonie 4 148–50*
groups and movements 26 728
patrons and collectors 4 150
pupils 12 888; 21 485
reproductive prints by others 3 558; 4 443; 18 629
works 3 230; 4 *149*; 12 881
Blockley Chapel (Glos) 23 194, *194*
Block of Progressive Architectural Groups (BAPS) 8 251
block-printing *see* PRINTING → processes → woodblock
block-resist dyeing *see under* DYEING → types
blocks 4 143*; 5 474
block statues *see under* SCULPTURE → types
block-thrones *see under* THRONES → types
Bloc of Professional Plastic Artists 10 872
Blocq, Jean Du *see* DU BLOCQ, JEAN
Blocq, Pierre-Balthasar de 11 723
Blodgett, Samuel 3 174
Blodworth, James *see* BLOODWORTH, JAMES
Bloem, Hans *see* BLUM, HANS
Bloemaert, Abraham 4 149, 150–53*; 12 233; 22 844; 31 771
groups and movements 22 843; 31 772
methods 24 493

Bloemaert, Abraham—cont.
patrons and collectors **5** 325; **14** 370, 692; **23** 465
pupils
Bijlert, Jan (Hermansz.) van **4** 52
Bloemaert, Adrian **4** 149
Bloemaert, Cornelis, II (1603-?84) **4** 149
Bloemaert, Frederick **4** 149
Bloemaert, Hendrick **4** 149
Both, Andries **4** 485
Brugghen, Hendrick (Jansz.) ter **5** 1, 6
Cuyp, Jacob (Gerritsz.) **8** 291
Geest, Wybrand (Symonsz.) de, I (1592-*c.* 1662) **12** 233
Honthorst, Gerrit (Hermansz.) van (1592-1656) **14** 728
Poelenburch, Cornelis van **25** 65
Weenix, Jan Baptist **33** 25
reproductive prints by others **4** 150, 282; **5** 63, 294; **10** 387; **12** 529; **20** 812; **22** 272; **25** 619; **30** 60; **31** 881; **33** 367
works **4** *151*, *152*; **11** *457*; **25** 68, 606; **33** 365
Bloemaert, Adrian **4** 150
Bloemaert, Cornelis, I (*c.* 1540-*d* 1593) **4** 149-50*
assistants **4** 150
engravings **7** 569
pupils **4** 150; **7** 466; **18** 8
Bloemaert, Cornelis, II (1603-?84) **4** 150-52*; **8** 139; **11** 53; **23** 347
pupils **6** 502
works **4** 152
Bloemaert, Frederick **4** 150, 152; **25** 619
Bloemaert, Hendrick **4** 149-50*, 153; **31** 772
works **11** *443*
Bloemandael, Jan *see* BLOMMANDAEL, JOHANNES
Bloemen, Jan Frans van **4** 153-4*; **26** 774, 841
attributions **5** 295; **9** 378
collaboration **8** 12; **18** 871
groups and movements **9** 462; **28** 92
patrons and collectors **3** 708; **4** 305; **22** 115; **23** 874; **27** 172
teachers **13** 222
works **4** *154*; **18** 710; **32** 112
Bloemen, Norbert van **4** 153
Bloemen, Pieter van **4** 153*
collaboration **30** 284
groups and movements **28** 92
Bloemfontein **4** 154-5*; **29** 103, *103*
A. C. White Gallery **4** 155
Law Courts **3** 269
Oliewenhuis Art Museum **4** 155; **29** 122
Opera House **29** 121
Raadzaal **29** 105
St Patrick's **29** 105
School of Art **29** 123
Bloemfontein Group **4** 155
Bloempot, De **30** 879
Bloemsteen, Nicolaas **33** 168
Blois **11** *504*
Cathedral of St Louis **13** 211
Château **4** 155-6*; **6** 504, 505, 507; **11** 512, 516, 656, 727; **20** 289-90, *290*
Cabinet of Catherine de' Medici **6** 506; **9** 12
Escalier François I **4** *156*; **29** 521
façade **4** 780
Francis I Wing **29** 833
gardens **12** 110, 112
gate-house **12** 175
hall **14** 74
park **24** 179
roof **30** 908
sculpture **13** 825; **20** 906
coins **7** 535
Blois—cont.
enamel **11** 629
Hôtel d'Alluye **11** 512
St Laumer *see* St Nicolas
St Nicolas **13** 40
watches **7** 441
Blois, Charles de **3** 609
Blois, Henry of *see* HENRY OF BLOIS
Blois, Louis II, Count of *see* LOUIS II, Count of Blois
Blois, Mlle de *see* CONTI, MARIE-ANNE DE BOURBON, Princesse de
Blois, William of, Bishop of Winchester *see* WILLIAM OF BLOIS, Bishop of Winchester
Blok **4** 148; **24** 441; **25** 100; **29** 794
Blok *see* BLOCK GROUP
Blok, Agnete **27** 271
Blok, Aleksandr (Aleksandrovich) **4** 156*
groups and movements **12** 870
illustrated works **2** 122; **18** 793; **33** 607
productions **21** 410; **27** 809
Blok, Diana **10** 483
Blokhin, Boris **5** 276
Blokhuis, Peter **14** 43
Blom *see* BLUME
Blom, Frans **7** 645; **18** 881; **31** 145
Blom, Fredrik **17** 814; **29** 686; **30** 73, 90
Blom, Piet(er) **4** 156-7*; **22** 832; **27** 230
Blomaert, Georges **11** 642
Blome, Richard **3** 244; **33** 177
Blomefield, Tom **33** 679
Blomerius, K. **27** 409, 410
Blomfield, Arthur C. **33** 204
Blomfield, Arthur William
collaboration **4** 884; **25** 187
patrons and collectors **7** 647; **12** 926; **25** 689; **29** 766
pupils **4** 157; **8** 528
works **5** 512
Blomfield, Austin **4** 158
Blomfield, Charles **23** 58
Blomfield, Reginald (Theodore) **4** 157-8*; **12** 105; **31** 151
collaboration **12** 650; **26** 316; **30** 743
groups and movements **22** 743
pupils **9** 741
works **4** *158*; **6** 167; **12** 222; **13** 875
writings **12** 141
Blommandael, François **4** 159
Blomme, Léonard **28** 41
Blommendael, Johannes **4** 158-9*; **14** 42; **19** 540; **22** 859
Blommér, Nils Jakob (Olsson) **4** 159*; **30** 79
Blommers, Bernard (Johannes) **4** 159-60*; **16** 575
collaboration **21** 175
groups and movements **14** 47
teachers **20** 434
works **11** 448; **14** 43
Blomqvist, C.W. **23** 243
Blomstedt, Aulis **4** 160-61*; **11** 92; **13** 843; **14** 372
Blomstedt, Juhana **11** 97*
Blomstedt, Märta **2** 317; **4** 160
Blomstedt, Pauli (Ernesti) **4** 160*; **30** 368
Blomstedt, Rafael **30** 368
Blon, Jacob Christoph Le *see* LE BLON, JACOB CHRISTOPH
Blon, Michel le *see* LE BLON, MICHEL
Blon, Nicolas Le *see* LE BLON, NICOLAS
Blond, Le *see* LE BLOND
Blond Boy **13** 449
Blonde, Gabriel de **6** 363; **27** 285
Blondeel, Lanceloot **3** 554; **4** 161-2*, 921
teachers **23** 526
works **3** 452; **4** *162*, 922, 923; **17** 699; **28** 219
Blondel, André *see* BLONDER, SASZA
Blondel, (Nicolas-)François **2** 358; **3** 360; **4** 165-6*; **11** 515, 670
groups and movements **24** 169, 170
works **5** 167; **7** 360; **8** 787; **16** 862; **24** 118, *170*; **30** 669; **31** 351
writings **5** 344; **11** 573; **23** 488; **31** 296
Blondel, Georges-François **4** 162; **21** 416
Blondel, Henri **14** 786
Blondel, Jacques-François **1** 106; **4** 162, 163-5*; **9** 12; **11** 670; **24** 821; **26** 13; **29** 751; **30** 71
architecture **4** *165*; **21** 362; **31** 713
assistants **19** 232
collaboration **9** 455; **11** 761; **31** 296
engravings **19** 231; **28** *486*; **29** *91*
groups and movements **24** 170, 174
interior decoration **4** *164*
pupils
Boullée, Etienne-Louis **4** 532
Brogniart, Alexandre-Théodore **4** 847
Cellerier, Jacques **6** 138
Chambers, William (1723-96) **6** 410
Cherpitel, Mathurin **6** 554
Couture, Guillaume-Martin **8** 75
Cuvilliés, (Jean) François Vincent Joseph de, I (1695-1768) **8** 288
Desprez, Louis-Jean **8** 815
Du Ry, Paul **9** 454; **12** 373
Gondoin, Jacques **12** 898
Gontard, Karl Philipp Christian von **12** 902
Gucewicz, Wawrzyniec **13** 775
Guimard, (Gilles) Barnabé **13** 831
La Guépière, Phillippe de **18** 643
Legrand, Jacques-Guillaume **19** 85
Lenoir, Samson-Nicolas **19** 161
Le Roy, Julien-David **19** 232
Leveilly, Michel **19** 268
Mique, Richard **21** 699
Molinos, Jacques **21** 817
Neufforge, Jean-François de **22** 925
Nicole, Nicolas **23** 110
Peyre, Marie-Joseph **24** 581
Rondelet, Jean-Baptiste **27** 123
Swart, Pieter de **30** 62
Vallen de la Motte, Jean-Baptiste-Michel **31** 827
Wailly, Charles de **32** 766
reproductive prints by others **17** 668
writings **2** 337; **8** 793; **10** 206; **20** 131; **23** 488; **26** 470, 494
illustrated **12** 357; **20** 457; **24** 268, 821
translated **26** 285
Blondel, Jean-Baptiste **4** 162; **19** 812
Blondel, Jean-François **4** 162-3*; **11** 171
collaboration **24** 821
works **4** 865; **12** 277; **13** 637; **20** 567
Blondel, Merry-Joseph **4** 166*
groups and movements **31** 374
patrons and collectors **8** 649
teachers **26** 93
Blondel, Paul **3** 811; **11** 143; **12** 159; **18** 884
blonde lace *see under* LACE → types
Blondel d'Azincourt, Barthélémy-Augustin *see* AZINCOURT, BARTHÉLÉMY-AUGUSTIN BLONDEL D'
Blondel de Gagny, Augustin **2** 904; **4** 166-7*; **11** 663
collections **2** 904; **3** 453
furniture **3** 414
Blondelu, Constance Marie *see* CHARPENTIER, CONSTANCE MARIE
Blonder, Sasza **4** 167*; **18** 433
Blondet, Carmen Inés **25** 702
Blondi, Onossorius de *see* ONOSSORIUS DE BLONDI
Blondus, Michael *see* LE BLON, MICHEL
blood **18** 601; **27** 471; **29** 813
blood jasper *see under* JASPER → types
bloodstone (chalcedony) **14** 167
historical and regional traditions
Byzantine **12** 254, *255*
Czech Republic **21** *726*
Holy Roman Empire (before 1648) **21** *726*
Mesoamerica, Pre-Columbian **21** 241
uses
amulets **1** 817
cameos **12** *255*
goblets **21** *726*
bloodstone (haematite) *see* HAEMATITE
Bloodworth, James **4** 167*; **30** 158
attributions **2** 737, *737*
works **2** 737; **30** 158
bloom **4** 167-8*
Bloom, Barbara **4** 168*
Bloom, Hyman **4** 168*, 478; **17** 580; **31** 606
pupils **24** 572
Bloom, Phil **28** 104
Bloome, Hans *see* BLUM, HANS
Bloomer, Amelia **9** 289-90
Bloomfield (CN), Conneticut General Life Insurance complex **5** 175
Bloomfield, Henry, & Sons **5** 572
Bloomfield, James **5** 572
Bloomfield, Marie **3** 466
Bloomfield, Tom **1** 429
Bloomfield Hills (MI), Cranbrook Academy of Art **27** 474; **31** 595, 640, 660
Bloomington (IN), Kinsey Institute for Sex Research **10** 487; **24** 683
Bloomsbury Group **4** 168-9*; **10** 256; **19** 591, 623; **23** 23
exhibitions **10** 255
members **3** 628, 631; **13** 313
works **4** *169*
Bloor, Joseph **8** 776
Bloor, Robert **8** 776
Bloor, William **31** 637
Bloore, Ronald (Langley) **4** 169*; **5** 569
Bloosaerken, Franciscus *see* NEVE, FRANS VAN DER
Bloot, Pieter de **14** 709; **27** 230, 518
Blooteling, Abraham **4** 169-70*; **10** 393; **31** 802
sponsorship **19** 540
works **3** 444, 500, 759; **21** 415; **22** 916; **23** 690
Blore, Edward **2** 738; **4** 170*; **21** 412
assistants **5** 193
collaboration **22** 808, 809
patrons and collectors **9** 31; **14** 148; **28** 287
pupils **7** 479; **20** 570; **24** 368
Blore, Edward—cont.
works **2** 692; **5** 512; **8** 249; **16** 10; **19** 287; **22** 527; **23** 250; **30** 533; **33** 9
Blore, Thomas **4** 170
Blossac, Comte de **25** 84
Blossfeldt, Karl **4** 170*
Blossius, C. **26** 885
Blot, Eugene **24** 143
blot drawings *see under* DRAWINGS → types
Blotnitzki, Léopold **12** 276
blotting papers *see under* PAPER → types
Blouet, Guillaume Abel **4** 171*; **7** 502; **11** 520, 522
collaboration **9** 312
patrons and collectors **6** 397
pupils **8** 544, 879; **14** 457; **18** 688; **25** 816; **32** 84
works **25** 637
Blouin, Blouin, Guité & Roy **22** 36
Blount, Godfrey **10** 354
Blouse, Blue, Group *see* BLUE BLOUSE GROUP
blouses **15** 795; **17** 375; **18** 772, 773
Blow, Detmar (Jellings) **4** 171-2*; **12** 650; **30** 464
Blow, Sandra **27** 563
blow guns **21** 245, 246
Bloye, William James **4** 87
Bluck, Judith **4** 789
blue *see under* PIGMENTS → types
Blue-and-green style painting *see under* CHINA → painting
blue-and-white ware *see under* PORCELAIN → wares; POTTERY → wares
blue bice *see under* PIGMENTS → types
Blue Blouse group **24** 405
Blue Eagle, Acee **22** 595
Bluefields **23** *79*
Blue Four **4** 177*; **28** 78-9
members **4** 133; **10** 862; **17** 453, 766; **18** 111
Blue Hmong **30** 624
Blue Koran **16** 279
Bluemner, Oscar **4** 177-8*; **29** 655; **31** 490
Blue painted ware *see under* POTTERY → wares
blueprints (architecture) **24** 650; **30** 430
see also PHOTOGRAPHIC PRINTS → types → blueprints
Blue Rider *see* BLAUE REITER
Blue Rose (Golubaya Roza) **4** 178*; **12** 870; **22** 178; **27** 392, 458
exhibitions **18** 542
members **27** 810, 855; **29** 899; **33** 486
Blue Vase **27** 76
blue verditer *see under* PIGMENTS → types
Bluget de Valdenuit, Thomas **27** 567
Bluhm, Ursula **28** 174
Blum, Benjamin **18** 852; **20** 440
Blum, Franz Friedrich **2** 803
Blum, Hans **4** 178-9*
works **2** 356; **12** 367; **24** 274, *274*
translated **30** 763
Blum, Johann **20** 923
Blum, Karl **22** 306
Blum, René **28** 347
Blum, Robert Frederick **4** 179*; **6** 500; **9** 468
Blumann, Elise **24** 496
Blumbergs, Ilmārs **4** 179-80*
Blume, Didrik **4** 180*
Blume, Henrik **4** 180*; **30** 70, 84
Blume, Peter **1** 772; **4** 180*; **20** 93; **23** 48; **25** 462
Blümel (family) **30** 311
Blumenau, Lili **31** 660

Blumenfeld, Erwin 4 180–81*; 24 657, 678
Blumenfeldt, Edmond-Arnold 10 542
Blumenschein, Ernest 33 185
Blumenthal, Florence 4 181
Blumenthal, George 4 181*
Blumenthal, Hermann 4 181*
Blumenthal, Mathias 23 224, 225, 231
Blumhardt, Doreen 23 69
Blumstead, Albert 20 3
Blundell (family) 12 639
Blundell, Charles 4 182
Blundell, Henry 4 181–2*; 6 97; 10 712; 13 303
Blundeville, Thomas 29 485
blungers 6 325
Blunt, Anne 22 743
Blunt, Anthony 4 182*; 19 590; 25 664, 665
 works 2 536; 20 769
Blunt, Wilfred Scawen 22 743
Bluntschli, Alfred Friedrich 4 182*
 collaboration 14 786; 17 853
 pupils 22 186; 27 214; 29 491
 works 28 46
Blurock 7 688
Bluskovtsi Basilica 5 155
Blutenburg Apostles, Master of the 22 301
Bluth, Manfred 13 729
Blyberg 30 113
Blyenberch, Abraham van 4 182*; 30 787
Blyenburgh, Adriaen van 14 739
Blyth (Notts)
 Priory 26 588
 SS Mary and Martin 26 655
Blyth, Benjamin 4 183*; 27 613
Blyth, John 5 828
Blyth, John Waldegrave 24 372; 28 273
Blyth, Samuel 4 183
Blythe, David Gilmour 4 183*; 17 823; 25 5
Blytt (family) 23 236
Blyudov, A. D., Count 26 734
B.M.F229, Painter of 13 532
BMN Painter 23 146
BMPT group 5 193
BMW (Bayerische Motorwerke) 12 472; 22 729; 28 187
Biniński, Piotr 25 134
Bo 1 341
Bo, Jørgen 4 183–4*; 8 729
Bo, Lina *see* BARDI, LINA BO
Boa 2 401
Boa 1 404
Boabdil *see* MUHAMMAD XI
Boaco Museum 29 222
Boada, Francisco Javier Parcerisa y *see* PARCERISA Y BOADA, FRANCISCO JAVIER
Boadilla del Monte, Palacio del Infante Don Luis 26 520; 29 271
Boai Hall 6 658
Boainai 23 *730*
 boarded seats *see under* CHAIRS → types
 Boardman (family) 31 652
 Board of Public Works (Ireland) 16 9–10, 11–12
 Board of the First Fruits of the Established Church 16 10, *10*
boards 4 184*; 30 5
 Academy Board 4 184
 cardboard *see* CARDBOARD
 hardboard 24 3
 matt board *see* mount board
 millboard 4 184; 24 3
 mount board 4 184
 museum board 4 184
 Board schools *see under* ENGLAND → schools
 Board school style 28 *157*, 158; 29 650
Boari (Dandini), Adamo 4 184–5*
 works 8 861; 20 460; 21 378, 379, *379*, 403
Boas, Franz 2 136, 534; 4 185*; 10 580
 pupils 22 673
 works 11 312; 22 559, 673, 674, 676
Boas, Franziska 2 840
Boat-Axe culture 25 514
boat chapels *see* TEMPLES → types → peripteral
boat coffins *see under* SARCOPHAGI → types
boats
 conservation 7 748
 historical and regional traditions
  Bali (Indonesia) 15 810
  Burma 5 254*
  China 3 *520*
  Egypt, ancient 9 *827*
  Indian subcontinent 15 721
  Indonesia 15 789, 810–11*
  Islamic 14 428
  Java 15 810
  Malaysia 20 179*
  Philippines 24 624–5*
  Thailand 30 631*
 materials
  marble 3 *520*
 techniques
  carving 24 625
  painting 15 810
 types
  funerary 10 17*; 25 760
  palace-boats 26 892
  state *see* BARGES → types → ceremonial
Bobadilla, Bernardino de 29 334
Bobadilla, Jerónimo de 4 185*
Bobadilla, Pedro Fernández de Cabrera y, Conde de Chinchón *see* CHINCHÓN, PEDRO FERNÁNDEZ DE CABRERA Y BOBADILLA
bobbin lace *see under* LACE → types
Bobbio 15 875; 19 549
 Monastery 19 549
Bobbio Missal *see under* MISSALS → individual manuscripts
Boberg, Anna 30 102
Boberg, (Gustaf) Ferdinand 4 185–6*; 30 96
 teachers 30 275
 works 30 74, 91, 102, 730
Bobić, Bernardo 4 186*
Bobillet, Etienne 17 457
Boblet, A. 21 909
Böblingen, Hans von, I (1435-82) 4 186–90*; 10 407
 collaboration 27 147
 pupils 4 188, 190
 works 4 186, *187*
Böblinger (family) 4 186, 191; 20 441
Böblinger, Dionysius 4 186, 190–91*
Böblinger, Hans, II (1459-1532) 4 186, 188*
Böblinger, Hans, III (*d* 1511) 4 186, 189, 191–2*
 works 4 *191*
Böblinger, Lux 4 186, 190*
Böblinger, Marx 4 186, 190*
Böblinger, Matthäus 4 186, 188–91*
 collaboration 4 190
 pupils 4 191
 works 4 186, *189*, *191*; 31 568, *568*
Böblinger, Nisi *see* BÖBLINGER, DIONYSIUS
Böblinger pillar 4 189
Bobo 4 192–4*; 5 216
 masks 1 279, 341; 4 192–4*, *193*; 5 217
 wood 4 192
Bobo Dioulasso 1 *381*
 congregational mosque 1 316
 Musée Provincial de Bobo 5 217
Bobo-Fing *see* BOBO
Bobo-Oulé *see* BWA
Bobosaidov, M. 30 252
Boboshevo
 Monastery of St Demetrius 5 153; 25 343
 St Theodor Tiron 5 151
Bobrinsky Bucket 1 208; 14 430; 16 366, *366*, 368, 373, 374, 375
Bobrowniki Church 25 105
Bobrun *see* BEAUBRUN
Bobuda Painter 10 614
Bobyshov, Mikhail 32 601
Bočan, Jan 29 438
Bocanegra, Pedro Atanasio 4 194*; 5 618
Bocarić, Anastas 22 17
Bocas, Las *see* LAS BOCAS
Boccacci, Vincenzo 7 313
Boccaccino, Boccaccio 4 194–5*; 8 135
 attributions 12 698
 patrons and collectors 28 533
 pupils 4 195; 12 161
 works 3 697; 4 *194*; 21 94
Boccaccino, Camillo 4 195*; 5 547; 32 407
Boccaccio, Giovanni 4 196*; 14 866; 16 780
 works 12 109, 683, 684, 695; 15 83, 87; 22 412; 31 681
  illustrated 3 259; 4 *196*, 357, 360; 13 833; 20 721
  translated 18 686
Boccaccio illustrations, Master of the 20 631*, 764
Boccador *see* DOMENICO DA CORTONA
Boccalini 19 688
Boccanegra, Giovanni 12 280
Boccara, Charles 1 320; 4 197*; 22 128
Boccardi, Francesco 30 514
Boccardi, Giovanni (di Giuliano) 2 697; 4 197*; 11 296; 20 847
Boccardino the Elder *see* BOCCARDI, GIOVANNI (DI GIULIANO)
Boccati (da Camerino), Giovanni (di Pier Matteo) 4 198*; 11 32; 12 737; 31 742
Bocchi, Achille 1 656; 4 309; 32 503
Bocchi, Francesco 4 198*; 11 216; 12 303; 16 781
Bocchini, Bartolommeo 3 437
Bocchoris 9 887
Bocchoris Painter 10 611
Bocchus I, King of Mauretania (*reg c.* 91 BC) 27 14
Boccia 12 30
Bocciardo, Pasquale 25 214; 31 292
Boccioni, Umberto 4 198–202*; 16 679; 24 448; 26 776
 collaboration 27 789
 collages 7 557
 exhibitions 32 774
 frames 11 397, 398
 groups and movements
  Divisionism 9 41
  Futurism 5 848; 11 863, 864, 865, 866, 867, 868; 16 679; 20 426; 21 527; 25 358; 27 445; 28 507
 methods 6 471
 paintings 4 *200*, *201*; 15 828; 16 679, 707; 31 706
 patrons and collectors 6 571; 16 906; 20 848; 33 254
 sculpture 11 *868*; 23 333; 29 576
 writings 11 868
Boch, Anna 11 83; 12 860; 19 792; 22 746; 32 591
Boch, François 32 574
Boch, Jean-François 32 574
Boch, William, & Bros 31 583, 637
Bocher, Emmanuel 13 325
Boch Frères 3 591, 592; 11 83; 30 886
Bochnak, Adam 25 143
Bochner, Mel 4 202*; 7 686
Bocholt, Franz von *see* FRANZ VON BOCHOLT
Bochoms, Léon 8 633
Bochum-Hiltrop 25 500
Bochum Museum 4 184
Bocion, François (-Louis-David) 4 202–3*; 8 57; 30 134
Bock, Alexander 1 148
Bock, Hans 3 336; 10 736, 739; 14 319; 30 131
 works 10 *739*
Bock, Jacobus de 2 200
Böck, Joseph, porcelain factory 22 187; 24 309
Bock, Richard W. 3 176
Bock, Théophile (-Emile-Achille) de 4 203*
 collaboration 21 175
 groups and movements 14 43; 31 147
 pupils 33 47
 works 14 43, *43*
Bock, Thomas 1 55; 32 769
Bock, Tobias *see* POCK, TOBIAS
Bock, William Rose 23 71
Bočkay, Milan 28 853
Bockberger 19 751
Bockemühl, Michael 26 62
Böckh, Josef 2 817; 32 450
Bockhorst, Johann *see* BOECKHORST, JAN
Böckler, Georg Andreas 4 203*; 31 298
Bockleton (Hereford & Worcs) 30 905
Böcklin, Arnold 4 203–7*; 11 190; 16 678; 17 886; 30 125, 133; 32 764; 33 38
 groups and movements 25 357; 29 600; 30 168; 33 379
 methods 10 191, 199
 patrons and collectors 19 151; 28 40; 31 397
 pupils 33 66
 teachers 28 104
 works 4 42, *204*, *206*; 11 462; 12 394; 18 716; 22 329, 416; 30 133
Böcklin, Carlo 4 207
Böckman, Edgar 30 99
Böckmann, Wilhelm 10 214*
Bocksberger, Hans, I (*b c.* 1510-*d* before 1569) 4 207–8*; 22 918; 33 278
 attributions 2 793
 patrons and collectors 19 815
 pupils 4 208
 works 2 794
Bocksberger, Hans, II (*fl* 1560-79) 1 788; 4 207; 28 188
Bocksberger, Johann Melchior *see* BOCKSBERGER, HANS, II
Bocksberger, Melchior 4 207, 208*; 10 737
 pupils 24 309
 works 10 737, 739; 33 271
Bocksberger, Ulrich 4 207*
Böckstiegel, Peter August 4 208*
Bockstorffer, Christoph 4 208*
Bocour Artists Colours Inc. 1 129
Bocskay, Georg 14 619, 620
Bocskay, Stephen 16 388; 21 50
Bocskay Schriftmusterbuch *see under* CODICES → individual manuscripts
Bod *see* TIBET
Boda Glasbruk 30 103
Bødalen Church 29 580
Boda Nova 30 101
Bodart (family) 22 452
Bodart, Pieter 14 621
Bodawpaya, King of Burma (*reg* 1781-1819) 1 753; 5 234, 253, 255
Bodbe Church 12 318
Boddason, Bragi 32 523
Boddien, A. v. 28 169
Bode, Arnold 5 306
Bode, Johann Elert 12 812
Bode, Wilhelm (von) 2 560; 3 522, 807; 4 208–9*; 7 561, 714; 12 474, 476, 483; 14 655; 16 470, 549, 556; 19 339; 22 112; 30 731
 architecture 22 250
 assistants 31 397, 819; 32 675
 collaboration 10 730; 27 846
 groups and movements 28 342
 paintings 9 200
 personal collection 2 365
 writings 28 165; 32 233
Bodecker, Johan Friedrich 3 42
Bodeghem, Loys van *see* LOYS VAN BODEGHEM
Bodekker, Bernard 18 848
Bodelsen, Merete 8 761, 762
Bodelwyddan (Clwyd), Marble Church 32 783
Bodemuseum *see under* BERLIN → museums
Bodendick, Jacob 4 212*; 10 328, 329
Bodenehr (family) 2 719
Bodenehr, Gabriel 3 620
 works 30 *221*
Bodenehr, Johann Gottfried 20 351
Bodenehr, M. 4 507
Bodenhausen, Eberhard von 22 291
Bodenheimer Adler, Jane *see* ADLER, JANE BODENHEIMER
Bodensee, Master of 11 452
Bodenstein von Karlstadt, Andreas Rudolf 7 215; 15 80
Bodhgaya 4 213*; 5 94; 15 220, *279*; 21 847
 Archaeological Museum 15 181
 jewellery 15 700
 Mahabodhi Temple 15 *280*, 280–81, 750; 32 89
 plaques 15 *221*; 30 510
 railings 15 749
 reliefs 15 248, 436–7*
 sculpture 15 216, 436, *437*, 454, 499
bodhighara *see* SHRINES (i) (CULT) → types → tree-shrines
Bodhnath 4 213*; 15 *261*; 22 *753*
 Little Bodhnath *see* CHA-BAHIL
 stupas 4 213*; 22 756
Bodiam Castle (E. Sussex) 6 53; 21 549
Bodiansky, Vladimir 2 660; 4 213–14*; 11 527
 collaboration 2 660; 3 450; 19 51, 535; 25 663; 28 809
 works 11 526
bodice ornaments 17 *523*, 524, *525*, 526
bodices 6 310
Bodin, Paul 30 27
Bodini, F. 17 622
Bodjani Monastery 28 444, 450
Bodkin, Thomas 16 38
bodkins 17 523
Bodleian Plate 33 206, *207*
Bodley, G(eorge) F(rederick) 4 214–15*
 collaboration 28 281; 29 537
 pupils 2 594; 7 663; 19 689; 30 743
 teachers 28 279
 works 4 *215*, 810; 5 512, 731; 13 198; 16 824; 20 238; 28 295; 32 887
Bodley, Thomas 19 313; 21 264; 23 686
Bodley & Garner 4 37; 29 695
Bodley's chest 16 60

Bodmer, Heinrich **5** 855
Bodmer, Johann Jacob **18** 880; **30** 132; **31** 764
Bodmer, Karl **4** 215–16*; **10** 561; **33** 184
  reproductive prints by others **22** *653*
Bodmer, Walter **1** 666; **4** 216*; **13** 726; **30** 139
Bodmin (Cornwall) **13** 822
  St Petroc **11** 252
Bodnant Garden **4** 216*; **32** *780*
Bodnarov, Stevan **28** 453
Bodny, F. **13** 702
Bodon, Alexander **4** 216–17*; **13** 679; **21** 362
Bodoni, Giambattista **4** 217*, 361; **20** 404
  works **16** 360; **31** 495; **32** 426
Bodrum *see* HALIKARNASSOS
Bodson (family) **22** 452
Bodson, Fernand (Lucien Emile Marie) **4** 217*
  collaboration **25** 190; **32** 380
  staff **11** 724
  teachers **14** 604
  writings **32** 380
Bodt, Jean de **4** 217–18*; **9** 236
  churches **3** 790
  collaboration **19** 642; **25** 240, 366
  government buildings **2** 502; **3** 790; **28** 116
  palaces **3** 791; **6** 490; **9** 235; **21** 64
  patrons and collectors **14** 651; **33** 114, 115
  pupils **18** 473
  teachers **4** 165
  works **12** 373; **14** 856
Body Art **10** 680
Body art *see* PERFORMANCE ART
body arts **24** 403
  historical and regional traditions
    Aboriginal Australia **1** 45–7*, *46*, 57, 59, *60*
    Africa **1** 254–6*, 285, 288–9, *289*, 297, 342–7*, *343*, *344*, 409, *409*
    Akan **1** 288, 342
    Ancient Near East **1** 855
    Argentina **29** 204
    Asante **1** 288, 344
    Austria **10** 483
    Bamana **1** 255–6
    Baule **1** 344
    Benin Republic **1** 288
    Brazil **4** 706–7
    Burkina Faso **1** 288
    Cameroon **1** 289
    Chile **29** 204
    Chokwe **1** 342
    Coptic **7** 829*
    Côte d'Ivoire **1** 288
    Dan (Africa) **1** 288, 344
    Easter Island **9** 676
    Egypt, ancient **10** 65–8*
    Ejagham **1** 342; **10** 124*
    Fulani **1** 288; **11** 830*
    Ghana **1** 288
    Guyana **13** 874
    Ibibio **1** 342, 344; **15** 65*
    Igbo **1** 288, *289*, 343, 344; **15** 115
    Indian subcontinent **15** 734
    Kenya **1** 288, 344
    Kuba (iii) (Zaïre) **1** 288
    Liberia **1** 289
    Lwena **1** 342
    Maasai **1** 254, 297, 344
    Madagascar **20** 38–9*
    Mangbetu **1** 342, *343*, 344
    Mende (Sierra Leone) **1** 342, 344
    Mesoamerica, Pre-Columbian **21** 258
    Native North Americans **22** 628*, 630, 631, 633, 635*, 636–7
    Ndebele **1** 285
    Niger **1** 288
body arts
  historical and regional traditions—cont.
    Nigeria **1** 288, *289*
    Nuba **1** 288, 344, *344*; **23** 274–5, *275*; **26** 221, 222; **29** 895
    Ovimbundu **1** 342
    Pacific Islands **23** 718–20*, 721–2*, *722*, 723*
    Pakistan **23** 803
    Papua New Guinea **23** 721–2*, *722*
    Paraguay **24** 93
    Samoa **27** *684*
    Songo **1** 342
    South America, Pre-Columbian **29** 204
    Sudan **1** 288, *344*
    Swahili **1** 409
    Tabwa **1** 344
    Vanuatu **31** 892*
    Yoruba **1** 342; **33** 559*
    Zaïre **1** 285, 288, *343*
  materials
    beads **1** 297
    kohl **1** 344
    mud **1** 285, 409
    paints **1** 288–9, *289*, 343–4, *344*; **10** 66; **13** 874
    seals **21** 258
  techniques
    gilding **30** 654
    painting **23** 721–2, *722*, 723
    tattooing *see* tattoos
  see also CICATRICES; SCARIFICATION; TATTOOS
bodycolour *see* PAINTS → types → gouache
body ornaments
  historical and regional traditions
    Aboriginal Australia **1** 52–3*
    Antilles, Lesser **5** 746, 747
    Austral Islands **23** 720
    Aztec **21** 248
    Britain **25** 518
    Chimú **29** 218
    Cook Islands **23** 720
    Easter Island **23** 720
    Ecuador **29** 155
    Fiji **11** 69
    Guadeloupe (country) **5** 747
    Hawaii **14** 249; **23** 720
    Kiribati **23** 735
    Maori **23** 720, 735
    Marquesas Islands **23** 720
    Martinique **5** 747
    Mesoamerica, Pre-Columbian **21** 248
    Moche (culture) **29** 218
    Native North Americans **22** 628*, 629*, 630, 632, 633, 635*, 636–7
    Pacific Islands **23** 719*, 723
    Palau **23** 723
    Papua New Guinea **23** 721, 735; **24** 75, *75*, 83, 84
    Philippines **24** 625–6*
    Poland **25** 127
    Polynesian outliers **25** 182
    Prehistoric art **25** 517–18*
    Santa Cruz Islands **27** 778, 779, *779*
    Solomon Islands **27** *779*; **29** 49, 51
    South America, Pre-Columbian **29** 155, 217–18
    Syria-Palestine **30** 182
    Vanuatu **31** 892
    Vietnam **32** 487*
  materials
    bone **21** 248; **25** 518
    feathers **23** 720
    jet **25** 518
    mother-of-pearl **23** 720
    seeds **1** 53
    shells **23** 721; **29** 217–18
    teeth **23** 720; **25** 518
Bodzentyn Church **25** 103
Boeblinger *see* BÖBLINGER
Boeck, Felix De **3** 564; **27** 392
Boeckel, Pieter van *see* BOUCLE, PIERRE
Boeckhorst, Jan (van) **4** 218–19*
  collaboration **9** 485; **28** 904; **33** 182
  teachers **5** 49
  works **3** 559, 560; **4** *219*
Boeckl, Herbert **2** 797, 831; **4** 219–20*; **32** 447
  works **2** *798*
Boecklin, Johann Christian **10** 857
Boeckmakere, Hennen **21** 352
Boecksent, Jan **25** 721
Boeckstuyns, Jan-Frans **3** 570; **4** 220*; **18** 742; **32** 251
Boegaert, Caspar **14** 542
Boeheim, Wendelin **2** 450
Boehlau Painter **10** 614
Boehm, Ernest **12** 468
Boehm, Joseph Daniel **4** 220; **20** 925
Boehm, Joseph Edgar **4** 220–21*; **10** 267
  assistants **9** 305; **18** 751
  groups and movements **23** 33
  patrons and collectors **14** 148
  pupils **12** 610
  works **9** 322
Boehm, Osvaldo **22** 702
Boehme, Johann **3** 288
Boeing **15** 824
Boeing 707 **30** 391
Boekele **7** 556
Boeken, Albert **4** 221*; **18** 212; **22** 831; **29** 484
Boekhoudt, Otto **22** 896
Boeksent, Jan **14** 326
Boel, Balthazar Lucas **4** 222
Boel, Cornelis **4** 221*; **19** 583
Boel, Jan **4** 221
Boel, Jan Baptist **4** 222
Boel, Pieter **4** 221–2*; **12** 832
  attributions **11** 872
  works **2** 200; **4** *222*
Boel, Quirin, I (uncle) **4** 221
Boel, Quirin, II (1620-40) (nephew) **4** 221; **11** 41
Boelema, Maerten **14** 287; **22** 840; **29** 666
Boels, Frans **4** 251
Boels, Gérard **27** 256
Boemke, Valentijn Casper **22** 890
Boendermaker, Piet **12** 502; **28** 864
Boer, Cornelis de **9** 62
Boer, J. R. J. van Asperen de *see* ASPEREN DE BOER, J. R. J. VAN
Boer, Piet de **4** 467
Boers **29** 103, 116, 120
Boese, Heinrich **4** 719
Boeswillwald, Emile **4** 222–3*
  collaboration **12** 312
  restorations **6** 494
  teachers **18** 581
  works **18** 758; **23** 510
Boë Sylvius, François de la **9** 194; **21** 488
Boethius **2** 354; **4** 358; **5** 666; **33** 89
Boethius BN fr. 809, Master of **20** 703
Boethos of Chalkedon **4** 223*; **20** 106
Boetti, Alighiero **4** 223*
Boetticher, Carl **14** 227
Boetticher, Friedrich von **10** 210
Boetto, Giovenale **28** 8, 11
Boeyens, Adriaan Florisz. *see* ADRIAN VI, Pope
Boeyermans, Theodor **4** 223–4*
Boezem, Marinus **18** 695
Bofa, Gus **10** 726
Boffiy, Guillermo **12** 739; **20** 566; **29** 263
Boffo, Franz Karlovich **21** 810; **23** 353
Boffrand, Germain **4** 224–6*; **33** 432
  architecture **11** 518; **12** 373; **19** 696, 800
    châteaux **4** *224*; **19** *800*
    churches **6** 417; **8** 31; **14** *82*; **22** 453, 455, 682
    hôtels particuliers **4** *225*; **14** 789; **19** 231; **22** 453; **24** 120; **26** 494
    houses **23** 514
    maisons de plaisance **20** 131
  attributions **19** 800
  collaboration **20** 296; **22** 682
  interior decoration **6** 508; **11** 578, *578*; **12** 410; **19** *722*; **26** 84, *494*
  patrons and collectors **16** 862; **19** 696; **32** 766; **33** 277
  pupils **3** 275; **7** 415; **9** 746; **24** 268, 820
  writings **31** 296
Boffrand, Jean **4** 224
Bofill, Guillem **5** 613
Bofill, Maria **29** 330
Bofill (Levi), Ricardo **4** 226–8*; **16** 101; **23** 490
  collaboration **6** 534
  groups and movements **25** 359
  works **2** 361; **3** 52, 217; **4** *228*; **11** 528; **14** 803; **22** 35; **29** 274
Bogaerd, Adriaan **30** 878
Bogaerde, Andries van den **13** 234
Bogaerts, Jan **2** 201; **3** 588; **30** 880
Bogarde, Hendrik van den *see* HENDRIK VAN DEN BOGARDE
Bogardus, James **3** 35; **4** 228–9*
  works **8** 278; **16** 54; **26** 18
Bogarín, Juan Sinforiano *see* SINFORIANO BOGARÍN, JUAN
Bogart, Adrian van den **13** 683
Bogart, Bram **3** 573; **4** 229*; **22** 852
  groups and movements **8** 668; **20** 846
Bogatyryov, Vasily **33** 601
Bogayevsky, Konstantin (Fyodorovich) **4** 229*; **27** 392
Boğazköy **1** *821*, 826, 839, 893; **4** 229–31*; **14** 591; **23** 806; **31** 456
  architecture **1** 826, 831, *831*
  Büyükkale *see* Royal Citadel
  cult statues **8** 261
  fortifications **4** 230; **21** 552–3
  glass **1** 865
  Great Temple **4** 230
  ivory-carvings **1** 870
  King's Gate **2** 296; **4** *231*
  palace **1** 826
  pins **13** 600
  pottery **1** 838; **15** 159
  reliefs **1** 833; **24** 690
  Royal Citadel **4** 230
  sculpture **1** 827, 833, *833*, 891; **29** 395
  seals **1** 856, 857, 863
  temple **1** 826, 829; **30** 432
  Temple 9 **1** 839
  vases **1** 833
  writing-tablets **4** 230
Bogdan **28** 447, 455
Bogdan, Catul **26** 719
Bogdanov, Aleksandr (Aleksandrovich) **4** 231–2*; **25** 649
Bogdanović, Bogdan **4** 462
Bogdanovka *see* NINOTSMINDA
Bogdan Piteşti, Alexandru **5** 73; **26** 245, 715, 723
Bogdány, Jakob **4** 232*; **28** 852
Bogdesko, Il'ya **21** 812
Bogdo Han **30** 476
Bogen, Carlos Gonzalez *see* GONZALEZ BOGEN, CARLOS
Bogenhausen Observatory **23** 340
Bogerts, Cornelis **3** 211
Bøggild, Mogens **8** 741, 749
Boggio, Emilio **4** 232*; **19** 659; **32** 175
Boggio, Gian Francesco di **20** 800
Boggs, S. H. **6** 394
Boghe, Jan **32** 712
Boghici, Jean **4** 725
Boghossian, Alexander **1** 433; **10** 573
Bogislav the Great, Duke of Pomerania-Stettin *see* BOGISLAV V, Duke of Pomerania-Stettin
Bogislav V, Duke of Pomerania-Stettin **13** 630; **30** 203
Bogler, Theodor **12** 432
bog oak **10** 346; **17** 527; **20** 466
Bog of Gight **31** 230
bogolanfini **20** 198, *199*
Bogolyubov, A. A. **16** 485
Bogolyubov, Aleksey (Petrovich) **4** 232*; **27** 440
Bogolyubov, Andrey **30** 915
Bogolyubovo **27** 369, 382
  Bogolyubsky Palace **27** 400
  see also VLADIMIR-SUZDAL
Bogolyubsky, Andrey **22** 168
Bogomazov, Alekseandr *see* BOHOMAZOV, OLEKSANDR (KONSTYANTYNOVYCH)
Bogomolov, Gleb **27** 581
Bogomolov, Ivan S. **28** 837, 838
Bogor **15** *753*
  botanic garden **12** 103
  Buitenzorg **15** 769, *769*
  puppets **15** 801
  sculpture **14** 561
Bogorodizk **31** 719
Bogorodskoye **31** 255
Bogorodsky, Fyodor (Semyonovich) **27** 395
Bogorosk **31** 719
Bogosian, Eric **24** 409
Bogoslovsky, N. V. **27** 409
Bogotá, Santa Fe de **4** 233–4*; **7** 600, *601*, 603; **31** 721
  art market **7** 611
  Capitolio Nacional **7** 605
  Cathedral **7** 605
    La Preciosa **7** 610
  Centro Antonio Nariño **7** 606
  Centro de las Américas **7** 606
  Ciudad Universitaria
    Faculty of Engineering **7** 606
  David Restrepo houses **7** 606
  Ecopetrol Centre **7** 606
  El Polo apartment building **7** 606
  Escuela de Conservación y Restauración de Cultura **7** 612
  Escuela Nacional de Bellas Artes **7** 609, 611, 612
  Escuela de la Sabana **4** 234; **7** 609
  Fiat Garages **7** 606
  Gobernación **7** 606
  Hipodromo Antiguo **7** 606
  houses **7** 604, 606
  metalwork **7** 610
  museums
    Museo Arqueológico **7** 612
    Museo Arqueológico del Banco Popular **4** 233
    Museo de Arte Colonial **4** 233, 234; **7** 611, 612
    Museo de Arte Moderno **4** 234; **7** 612
      library **7** 612
    Museo de Artes y Tradiciones Populares **7** 612; **24** 435
    Museo Nacional **4** 233, 234; **7** 611–12
      library **7** 612
    Museo del Oro **4** 234; **7** 612; **29** 221
  Panóptico *see* Museo Nacional
  observatory **7** 605; **23** 341
  painting **7** 607, 608
  Pubenza **7** 605
  Residencias El Parque **7** 606, *606*
  Santuario Monserrate **7** 607
  S Francisco **7** 604; **26** 252

Bogotá, Santa Fe de—cont.
S Ignacio **4** *233*; **7** 604, 610; **26** 252
Loreto Altar **26** 252
Teatro Colón **7** 605
Teatro Municipal **7** 605
Universidad Javeriana **7** 607
Bogra **3** *166*
Bogsha, Lazar' **18** 37
Bogstad Manor **23** 231
Bogucki, Peter **25** 516
Boguet, Nicolas-Didier (1755-1839; father) **4** 234*; **14** 486
Boguet, Nicolas-Didier (1802-after 1861; son) **4** 234
Boguslavskaya, Kseniya (Leonidovna) **30** 8; **32** 412
Bogusz, Marian **4** 234–5*
Boguszewski, Krzysztof **25** 104; **32** 6
works **25** *104*
bog yew **20** 466
Boh, Luis Alberto **24** 96, 99; **26** 76
Boháček, Karel **2** 546; **8** 393
Bohatsch, Erwin **32** 447
Bohdaneč, Sanatorium **8** 373, 380
Bohdziewicz, Emilia **11** 54
Bohemen, Kees van **2** 422; **8** 668; **22** 852; **23** 298; **28** 159
Bohemia *see* CZECH REPUBLIC
Bohemian Crown **8** 412
Bohemian jasper *see under* JASPER → types
Boher **26** 688
Shrine of St Manchan **32** 530
Bohier (family) **11** 656
Bohier, Antoine, Abbot of Rouen **27** 254; **32** 603
Bohier, Thomas **6** 545
works **6** *545*
Bohigas (Guardiola), Oriol **3** 217; **13** 725; **20** 516–17*; **29** 274, 309, 322
Bohle, Peter **5** 586
Böhler, Hans **23** 1; **33** 166
Böhm (i) *see* BEHAM
Böhm, Adolf **28** 344
Böhm, August **8** 410
Böhm (ii), Dominikus **4** 235*; **12** 378
groups and movements **13** 204
staff **26** 402
works **4** *235*; **11** 256
Böhm (ii), Gottfried **4** 235–6*; **12** 380; **28** 127
collaboration **4** 235
works **12** 380, *380*; **31** 243
Böhm, Johann Heinrich **12** 405
Böhm, Joseph Daniel **11** 33; **15** 15; **30** 888
Bohm, Max **9** 9
Böhm, Pál **23** 697
Böhme, Lothar **4** 236*
Böhme, Martin **28** 118
Bohnshtedt, Ludwig Franz Karl *see* BONSHTEDT, LYUDVIG (LYUDVIGOVICH)
Bohol **24** *607*
Bohomazov, Oleksandr (Konstyantynovych) **2** 634; **4** 236–7*; **31** 559
Bohon, St André **26** 598
Bohorquez, Ricardo, Museo *see under* POTOSÍ → Universidad Autónoma Tómas Frías
Bohosudov **8** 398
Bohrmann, Horst Paul Albert *see* HORST
Bohun (family) **4** 237–8*; **13** 153; **14** 423
Bohun, Eleanor de, Duchess of Gloucester *see* PLANTAGENET, ELEANOR, Duchess of Gloucester
Bohun, Elizabeth de, Countess of Northampton **4** 237
Bohun, Henry VII de, 7th Earl of Hereford and 6th Earl of Essex **4** 238
Bohun, Humphrey V de, 4th Earl of Hereford and 3rd Earl of Essex **4** 237
Bohun, Humphrey VI de, 6th Earl of Hereford and 5th Earl of Essex **4** 237; **25** 676
Bohun, Joan de, Countess of Hereford and Essex (*d* 1491) **4** 238
Bohun, Joanna de, Countess of Hereford and Essex (*d* 1283) **4** 237
Bohun, Mary de, Countess of Derby *see* MARY DE BOHUN, Queen of England
Bohúň, Peter Michal **28** 853
Bohun, Reginald de, Bishop of Wells **33** 59
Bohus, Zoltán **15** 5
Bohuslaw, Abbot **13** 173
Boí **26** 642
S Joan **26** 650
Boi, Pierron **4** 608
Boiadjieva, S. **8** 900
Boian **26** 712
Boiardo (family) **1** 17
Boicervoise (family) **11** 628
Boichot, Guillaume **4** 238*
Boides, Wilhelm **10** 523
Boiffard, Jacques-André **30** 20
Boii **6** 159
Boijen, Richard Bouwens van der *see* BOUWENS VAN DER BOIJEN, RICHARD
Boijen, William Bouwens van der *see* BOUWENS VAN DER BOIJEN, WILLIAM
Boijmans, F(rans) J(acob) O(tto) *see* BOYMANS, F(RANS) J(ACOB) O(TTO)
Boiken **24** 67, 68
Boiko, Juris **33** 378
Boileau **11** 663
Boileau, Etienne **4** 240*
works **11** 633, 636; **24** 132
on ivories **13** 171
on pottery **24** 148
on tapestries **11** 637
Boileau, Jacques-René **28** 521
Boileau, Jean Jacques **27** 336
Boileau, J. F. **7** 194
Boileau, Louis-Auguste **4** 239*; **8** 769
collaboration **4** 239; **11** 524
works **8** *769*; **11** 522; **16** 54; **19** 812
Boileau, Louis-Charles **4** 239*; **8** 769
collaboration **2** 700; **4** 239; **7** 530, 693
works **8** *769*
Boileau, Louis-Hippolyte **4** 239–40*; **5** 776; **10** 684
Boileau, Nicolas **4** 240–41*
Boileau, Peter **15** 652
boilers **7** 765
Boilly, Arnould **4** 241
Boilly, Louis-Léopold **4** 40, 241*
collaboration **4** 36; **8** 703
groups and movements **26** 740
lithographs **5** 757
paintings
genre **9** 285, 286, *286*; **11** 542; **12** 292
grisaille **15** 140
portraits **9** 244, 285, *285*
patrons and collectors **8** 868
reproductive prints by others **8** 595
Boilvin, Emile **4** 242*
Boim (family) **19** 835
Boime, A. **6** 176
Bōin *see* KUSUMI MORIKAGE
Boiotian Dancers group **13** 513, *513*
Bois, Edward Du *see* DU BOIS, EDWARD
Bois, Emile **4** 508
Bois, Guy Pène du *see* PÈNE DU BOIS, GUY
Bois, Hendrik Du *see* DU BOIS, HENDRIK
Bois, Horacio Caille *see* CAILLE BOIS, HORACIO
Bois, Jacob Du *see* DU BOIS, JACOB
Bois, Le **33** 361
Bois, Simon Du *see* DU BOIS, SIMON
Bois, Yve-Alain **24** 743; **25** 362
Boisbaudran, Horace Lecoq de *see* LECOQ DE BOISBAUDRAN, HORACE
Bois de Vroylande, Du *see* DU BOIS DE VROYLANDE
Boiserée, Sulpicius **25** 675
boiserie see PANELLING
Boisjermain, Luneau de *see* LUNEAU DE BOISJERMAIN
Bois-le-Duc *see* 'S HERTOGENBOSCH
Boislève, Claude **26** 91
Boisot, Jean-Baptiste **3** 873; **11** 664
Bois-Préau Château **4** 304
Boisrouvray, Guy de, Comte **25** 248
Boissard, Jean-Jacques **2** 162; **4** 242*; **5** 63; **26** 848
Boisseau, Jean **6** 503
Boisselier, Jean **2** 56; **5** 483; **29** 242
Boissens, Cornelius **10** 391
Boisserée, Melchior Hermann Josef Georg **4** 242–3*; **7** 584; **22** 303; **27** 231
collections **12** 474
lithographs **29** 776
paintings **17** 922; **32** 823
Boisserée, Sulpiz (Melchior Damiticus) **4** 242–3*; **7** 590; **21** 822; **22** 303; **27** 232; **33** 745
collections **7** 584; **12** 474
lithographs **29** 776
paintings **17** 922; **32** 823
writings **13** 204; **24** 443; **31** 284
Boisset, (Pierre-Louis-) Paul Randon de *see* RANDON DE BOISSET, (PIERRE-LOUIS-) PAUL
Boissière, Notre-Dame-du-Rosaire **26** 645
Boissieu, Jean-Jacques de **4** 243–4*; **8** 542
pupils **11** 301
works **4** *244*; **9** 308
Boit, Charles **4** 244–5*; **21** 641
pupils **33** 685
works **7** 814; **21** *642*
Boit, Edward Darley **27** 840; **29** 870
Boitac, Diogo **4** 245–6*
architectural decorations **20** 325
attributions **25** 300
churches **4** *245*; **13** 71
cloisters **25** *290*
monasteries **3** 534; **13** 71; **20** 325; **25** 290
patrons and collectors **2** 872; **28** 780
works **31** 179
Boitard, François **2** 851; **25** 627
Boitchuk, Mikhail *see* BOYCHUK, MIKHAIL
Boitel, Léon **19** 848
boîtes à portrait see under SNUFF-BOXES → types
Boito, Camillo **2** 321; **4** 246–8*; **16** 648, 721; **27** 788
pupils **3** 687; **4** 746, 842; **6** 352; **22** 105
works **4** *246*; **9** 159; **21** 521; **23** 753
Boitsov, G. P. **31** 551
Boitsov, Pyotr (Samoylovich) **27** 377
Boix, Josep Berga i *see* BERGA I BOIX, JOSEP
Boix, Manuel **31** 816
Boix Merino, Emilio **31** 188
Boizot, Antoine **4** 248; **5** 436
Boizot, Louis-Simon **4** 248–9*; **11** 627; **28** 521
collaboration **11** 305, 627; **13** 234; **22** 210; **24** 893
teachers **28** 847
works **11** 562, *626*, 627, *627*; **28** 522; **30** 747
Bojesen, Kay **8** 751
Bojnice **28** *848*
Castle **28** 850
museum **28** 857
Bojonegoro **15** *753*
Bo Juyi *see* BAI JUYI
Bokanić, Trifon **31** 359
Böke **31** 453
Bokelmann, Christian Ludwig **11** 463
Boké Museum **1** *386*; **13** 835
Boker, S'de **26** 20
Bokhara stitch *see under* STITCHES
Bokhoven Mausoleum **22** 859
Bokkei Hyōbu *see* HYŌBU BOKKEI
Boklund, Johan Kristoffer **18** 468
Bokros Birmann, Dezső *see* BIRMANN, DEZSŐ BOKROS
Boks, Joost Willem Cornelis **31** 867
Boksburg East Potteries **29** 117
Bokshaya, I. I. **31** 560
Boku Heii *see* KIYOEMON
Bokujinkai **17** 239
Boku Mokei **17** 414
Bokusai Shōtō *see* SHŌTŌ BOKUSAI
bokuseki see under CALLIGRAPHY → types
Bokyi **10** 122
Bol, Cornelis (i) (*c.* 1576-*c.* 1621) *see* BOEL, CORNELIS
Bol, Cornelis (ii) (*fl c.* 1636-66) **4** 249*
Bol, Ferdinand **4** 249–51*
attributions **10** 146
patrons and collectors **31** 342; **32** 377
pupils **18** 144
teachers **8** 291; **22** 843; **26** 163; **31** 341
works **1** 813; **4** *250*, *251*; **11** 170, 446; **14** 584; **22** 843; **26** 166
Bol, Hans **4** 251–2*; **20** 769; **22** 841
attributions **3** 126
copies **13** 664
patrons and collectors **13** 631
pupils **14** 618; **27** 884
reproductive prints by others **7** 499, 556; **9** 64; **12** 16; **14** 505, 709; **27** 502
works **3** 558; **4** 907
Bol, Jacob, I **4** 251
Bol, Jan **4** 251
Bolagno, Giuseppe di, Conte **5** 595
Bolander, Lars **14** 543
Bölcske
metalwork **6** *153*
Bold **21** 881
Boldewin **12** 467
Bold Hall (Lancs) **29** 835
Boldini, Antonio **4** 252
Boldini, Giovanni **4** 252–3*; **11** 4; **16** 678
collaboration **28** 706
groups and movements **20** 482
patrons and collectors **7** 377
works **4** *253*; **9** 310; **22** 22
Boldini, Museo *see under* FERRARA → Palazzo dei Diamanti
Boldogasszony *see* FRAUENKIRCHEN
Boldoni, Sigismondo **8** 149
Boldrini, Nicolò **4** 253–4*, 828
attributions **4** 828
collaboration **32** 199
works **31** 43; **33** 356, 367
Boldu, Giovanni **20** 918
Boldva Abbey **14** 883
Bole (people) **1** 366, 369
bole *see under* CLAY → types
Bolea, Buenaventura de Urrea Abarca de, 9th Conde de Aranda *see* ARANDA, BUENAVENTURA DE URREA ABARCA DE BOLEA, 9th Conde de
bole grounds *see under* GROUNDS → types
Bolehyde (Wilts) **12** 176
boleros **21** 878
Boleslas-Biegas *see* BIEGAS, BOLESŁAW
Boleslav I, Duke of Silesia (*reg* 1163-1201) **19** 748
Boleslav I, King of Poland (*reg* 992-1025) **12** 823; **25** 137
Boleslav II, Duke of Bohemia (*reg* 967-999) **8** 421
Bołeslav the Brave, King of Poland *see* BOLESLAV I, King of Poland
Bolesławice **25** 124
Boletim da Academia Nacional de Belas Artes **24** 424
Boletim do Museu Nacional de Belas Artes **24** 435
Boletín de la Comisión de monumentos históricos y artísticos de Navarra **24** 452
Boletín de la sociedad castellana de excursiones **24** 452
Boletín de la sociedad española de excursiones **24** 452
Boletín del Centro de Investigaciones Históricas y Estéticas **24** 435
Boletín del seminario de estudios d'arte y arqueología de Valladolid **24** 452
Boletín enciclopédico de nobles artes **24** 452
Boletín español de arquitectura **24** 452
Bolevár **15** 2
Bolfgangus of Crngrob **4** 254*
Bolgi, Andrea **4** 254*
collaboration **26** 810
works **3** 830, 838; **9** 410; **11** 81; **22** 477; **26** 809
Bolgié, Francesco **16** 719
Bolin **27** 429
Bolin, Henrik **30** 113
Bolin, Jonas **30** 110
Bolívar, Elsa **6** 598
Bolivar, Martín **13** 283
Bolívar, Simón **7** 611
Bolivia **4** 254–70*, *255*; **15** *161*; **29** 127
alpaca hair **4** *266*
andesite (volcanic) **30** *796*
architecture **4** 256–61*, *257*, *258*; **17** 513
prefabrication **4** 260
vernacular **32** *305*
bronze **4** 255
cathedrals **18** *778*
chapels **4** 256
Charcas **4** 254
churches **4** 256–7, 258–9
collections **4** 267–9*; **29** 894
copper **4** 255
dealing **4** 268*
dress **4** 266*
education (art) **4** 269–70*
architecture **32** 568
exhibitions **4** 263
fotoleos **4** 262
gold **4** 265–6*
graves **29** 133
guilds **4** 269
houses **4** *260*; **5** *887*
interior decoration **4** 262
libraries **4** 270
masonry **4** 256
murals **4** 263; **22** 335*
museums **4** 268–9*; **21** 147
painting **4** 261–4*, *262*, *263*
patronage **4** 267–8*

Bolivia—cont.
photoarchives **4** 269*
portals **4** *258*
pottery **31** *46*
pouches **4** *266*
prints **4** 261
retables **4** 264
sanctuaries **4** *257*
sculpture **4** 264–5*, *265*; **30** *796*
silver **4** 255, 256, 265–6*
textiles **4** 266–7*
tin **4** 256
towns **29** 893
urban planning **4** 256*
wood **4** 255
see also PERU
Böll, Heinrich **6** 477
Bolla, Abondio **25** 438
Bolla, Michael **31** 510
Bolla, Rocco **29** 830
Bollaert-Alardi (family) **10** 717
Bollé, Hermann **4** 270*; **8** 176; **18** 411; **33** 592, 593
Bolle, Leendert **22** 861; **23** 450
Bollemard, Michiel **10** 709
Bollery, Nicolas **4** 125, 126
Bolleshaus, Ignác Cyrani von **18** 467
Bolles-Wilson & Partner **22** 315
Bollettino della Società fotografica italiana **1** 643
Bollettino d'arte del Ministero della Pubblica Istruzione **24** 423, 448
Bollettino del Reale Istituto di archeologia e storia dell'arte in Roma **24** 448
Bollingen Foundation **18** 187
Bollstädt, Albert, Count of *see* ALBERTUS MAGNUS
Bolnisi **12** *317*
Church of Sioni **12** 318, 321
bolo clay *see under* CLAY → types
Bologna **4** 270–81*, *271*, *272*; **10** 638, 639; **16** *616*, *618*
academies
Accademia Clementina **4** 277; **7** 308; **8** 159; **21** 733; **31** 164; **33** 615
Accademia degli Desiderosi *see* Accademia degli Incamminati
Accademia degli Incamminati **1** 103; **5** 850; **16** 779; **23** 294
Carracci Academy *see* Accademia degli Incamminati
Ghisilieri academy **1** 104
Archiginnasio **30** 515; **31** 674
Biblioteca Comunale dell'Archiginnasio **8** 159
chapel of S Maria dei Bulgari **6** 361
collections **1** 597; **23** 829
Cubiculum Artistarum **20** 541
Arco del Meloncello **9** 190
art forms and materials
askoi **10** 610
books **13** 130
cassoni **6** 7
ceramics **4** 278*
decretals **8** 614
dress **9** 259
engravings **10** 383
façade decoration **10** 737
frames **11** 382, *385*, *386*, 387, 392, *393*, *394*
guns **2** 464
icons **19** 787
jewellery **10** 632
manuscripts **4** 273–5*, *274*, 395; **20** *331*, 332, 341; **26** 564
metalwork **28** 806, 807, *807*
mirrors **10** 589
niello **16** 750
painting **4** 275*; **12** 288, 292; **16** 661, 669–70
pottery **10** 610; **32** 563
prints **25** 614
sculpture **4** 275*; **13** 95, *96*; **16** 688, 691–2*, 699*
stained glass **13** 193
Bologna
art forms and materials—cont.
tapestries **16** 756
textiles **16** 714
tiles **30** 887
vases **10** 609
watermarks **32** 908
Benacci grave 525 **32** *563*
Casa Gennari **13** 789
cemeteries **32** 562
colleges **7** 566, 567
Collegio di Spagna **7** 566, *566*; **13** 65; **31** 674
Credito Romagnolo *see* palazzi → Palazzo Magnani-Salem
ecclesiastical buildings
Cathedral of S Pietro **30** 803
Garganelli Chapel **26** 457
convent of S Michele **5** 854
Corpus Domini
altarpiece **11** *681*
frescoes **11** 680, *681*
Monti Chapel **11** 680
Madonna del Monte **3** 876
Madonna di Galliera **16** 699
Madonna di S Luca **3** 876; **9** 190
S Bartolomeo **11** 680; **30** 649
S Cristina **5** 450; **16** 699
paintings **5** *855*
S Domenico **4** 278–9*; **9** 111
frescoes **9** 110
paintings **11** 384
sculpture **13** 96
shrine of St Dominic **4** 276, 278–9*; **5** 905; **9** *106*, 108, 109; **23** 89; **24** 868
textiles **23** 461
tomb of Alessandro Tartagni **11** *27*
S Francesco **13** 52; **32** 93
altarpiece **1** 709; **20** 543–4; **25** 183
sculpture **13** 96
tomb of Alexander V **30** 498
tomb of Bartoluzzo de' Preti **13** 95
tomb of Michele de Bertalia **13** 95
tombs of the Glossators **20** 865
S Giacomo Maggiore **3** 743
altarpiece **24** 31
frescoes **15** 137
Oratory of S Cecilia **2** *607*; **4** 276
paintings **6** *362*
S Giovanni in Monte
paintings **10** *746*
S Maria Maddalena **30** 496
S Maria dei Servi
tomb of Andrea Manfredi **13** 96
S Maria della Vita **30** 498
sculpture **18** 677; **23** 89, *90*
S Martino **4** 276; **28** 658
S Paolo Maggiore **1** 712; **3** 249, 250
altarpiece **1** *711*
S Petronio **4** *279*, 279–80*, 774, 775; **9** 680; **13** 66, 210; **16** 627; **30** 515–16
altarpiece **8** *4*
Bolognini Chapel **12** 703–4
façade **1** 490
gems **8** 13
models **20** 576
mouldings **22** 221
portal **16** *692*
Porta Magna **13** 96; **16** 692, 843, *844*
S Abbondio Chapel **12** *704*
sculpture **1** 490; **13** 96; **25** 175
tiles **30** *886*, 887
Vaselli Chapel **16** 733
vaults **32** 92
S Salvatore **16** 641; **20** 898
S Stefano **4** 280–81*, *281*; **28** 428–9
Chapel of S Sepolcro **28** *428*
Bologna—cont.
Facciata dei Banchi **32** *507*
Felsina **10** *583*, 585
Aureli II Tomb **10** 631
Foro dei Mercanti *see* Loggia dei Mercanti
Fountain of Neptune **11** *341*, 342; **12** 569; **16** 695, 696
guidebooks **18** 680
Libreria di S Marco **20** 586
Loggia dei Mercanti **10** 667; **13** 96
museums
Museo d'Arte Industriale e Galleria Davia-Bargellini **20** 158
Museo Civico **7** 782; **30** 515
collections **10** 91; **16** 776; **23** 829
Museo Civico Archeologico **13** 470
Museo della Civiltà Contadina **16** 775
Pinacoteca Nazionale **11** 387; **16** 773; **20** 158
observatory **23** 339
Ospedale della Morte *see* museums → Museo Civico
palazzi
Palazzo Aldini **12** 584
Palazzo Aldrovandini *see* Palazzo Montanari
Palazzo Bentivoglio **3** 743
Palazzo Bianconcini **12** 40; **20** 902; **29** 32
Palazzo Bovi-Silvestri **12** 38
Palazzo Brazzetti **11** 680
Palazzo Calzoni **12** 40
Palazzo della Cassa di Risparmio **26** 190
Palazzo Comunale **4** *272*; **8** 164
Camera degli Atti **16** 848
frescoes **4** *271*; **24** 321; **30** 802
paintings **12** 38
Sala Farnese **7** 308; **24** 227
Sala Urbana **15** 138
sculpture **19** 551; **30** 498
Palazzo Davia-Bargellini **11** 392, 394; **28** 753
Palazzo Fava
frescoes **4** 830; **5** 852, 857
friezes **5** 850
paintings **8** 159
Palazzo Fibbia **5** 651
Palazzo Ghisilieri **12** 559
Palazzo Gini-Veronese **12** 40
Palazzo di Giustizia *see* Palazzo Ranuzzi
Palazzo Grande *see* Palazzo Bentivoglio
Palazzo Guidotti-Senni **12** 40
Palazzo Hercolani **24** 321
Palazzo Lucchini **5** 853
Palazzo Magnani-Salem **30** 803
frescoes **5** 853, 857
friezes **5** 850, 860
paintings **5** 853
Palazzo Malvasia **12** 38
Palazzo Malvezzi **12** 38
Palazzo Marescalchi **12** 584
Palazzo Marescotti **5** 653
Palazzo Marescotti-Brazzetti **11** 679
Palazzo Masetti-Calzolari *see* Palazzo Fibbia
Palazzo Monari *see* Palazzo Calzoni
Palazzo Montanari **4** 46
frescoes **4** *277*
Palazzo del Monte Matrimonio **20** 497
Palazzo Monti *see* Palazzo Brazzetti
Palazzo Odorici *see* Palazzo Zani-Odorici
Palazzo Pepoli-Campogrande **5** 651–3; **8** 141, 159
frescoes **5** *652*
Palazzo Pini Alamandini **5** 281
Bologna
palazzi—cont.
Palazzo del Podestà **4** *272*
façade **11** 116
Salone **8** 601
sculpture **19** 551
Theatre **30** 666, *666*
Palazzo Poggi
frescoes **1** *17*, 18; **15** 137; **30** 800
Sala d'Ulisse **30** *800*
Palazzo Ranuzzi **4** 46; **11** 679; **14** 27
Palazzo Salina **20** 497
Palazzo Sampieri Talon **5** 850, 857; **27** 693
Palazzo Sanguinetti *see* Palazzo Viziani
Palazzo della Sapienza *see* Archiginnasio
Palazzo Scagliarini **12** 40
Palazzo Torfanini *see* Palazzo Zucchini-Solomei
Palazzo Viziani **18** 870; **30** 802
Palazzo Zani-Odorici **12** 40
Palazzo Zucchini-Solomei **1** 17
Passarotti Collection **24** 233
Stadio Littoriale **29** 489
Stazione Centrale **29** 833
Teatro Communale **30** 667
Tomb of the Gold Objects **10** *635*
Torre degli Asinelli **4** 776; **5** 648, 649; **16** 627
Torre Garisenda **4** 776; **5** 648, 649; **16** 627
Università degli Studi
Biblioteca Universitaria **30** 800
library of the Department of Visual Arts **16** 776
sculpture **12** 571
see also palazzi → Palazzo Poggi
Villa Boschi **3** 466
Villa La Sampiera **20** 497
Bologna, Andrea dei *see* ANDREA DEI BRUNI
Bologna, Aristotele da *see* FIORAVANTI, ARISTOTELE
Bologna, Bettino da *see* BETTINO DA BOLOGNA
Bologna, Carlo **27** 759
Bologna, Cristoforo di Jacopo Biondi da *see* CRISTOFORO DI JACOPO BIONDI DA BOLOGNA
Bologna, Francesco *see* FRANCESCO BOLOGNA
Bologna, Francesco Griffo da *see* FRANCESCO GRIFFO DA BOLOGNA
Bologna, Il *see* AIMO, DOMENICO
Bologna, Lorenzino da *see* SABATINI, LORENZO
Bologna, Lorenzo da *see* LORENZO DA BOLOGNA
Bologna, Maria di *see* MARIA DI BOLOGNA
Bologna, Matteo da *see* MATTEO DA BOLOGNA
Bologna, Niccolò di Giacomo da *see* NICCOLÒ DI GIACOMO DA BOLOGNA
Bologna, Simone da, Archbishop of Palermo *see* SIMONE DA BOLOGNA, Archbishop of Palermo
Bologna, Simone di Filippo Benvenuti da *see* SIMONE DEI CROCEFISSI
Bologna, Tommaso (di Andrea) il (*d* 1534/6) *see* VINCIDOR, TOMMASO (DI ANDREA)
Bologna, Vitale da *see* VITALE DA BOLOGNA
Bologna Cope **13** *194*, 196
Bolognese, Battista **16** 725
Bolognese, Franco *see* FRANCO BOLOGNESE
Bolognetti, Giorgio **4** 667
Bolognini, Augusto **3** 318
Bolognini, Bartolomeo **12** 703
Bolognini, Gino **22** 27
Bolognini, Giovan Battista **12** 559
Bolognini Amorini, Antonio, Marchese **4** 281–2*
Bolomey, Benjamin Samuel **14** 42; **23** 469
Bolonakis, Constantinos **8** 602
bolos **24** 631
Bolotov, Andrey (Timofeyevich) **12** 134; **21** 512; **29** 551
Bolotowsky, Ilya **4** 282*
groups and movements **1** 771; **4** 109; **13** 214; **27** 219
pupils **23** 183
Bolozhany *see* BALAŻANY
bolsal cups *see under* CUPS → types
bolsals **13** 536
Bölsche, Wilhelm **8** 824
Bolsena **10** *583*
mirrors **10** *595*
reliquaries **13** 169
S Cristina **7** 302; **26** 624
vases **10** 616
Bol'shaya Bliznitsa **4** 110, 111
Bol'shetarkhansky **27** 434
Bolshevism **27** 364
Bol'shiye Vyazemy, Church of the Holy Trinity **27** 371
Bolsover (Derbys) **6** 59–60
Castle **6** *60*; **10** 273
Little Castle **10** 272; **28** 896–7; **32** 551
Bolstad House **23** 231
Bolsterer, Hans **20** 920
Bolsward **22** 856, 881
silver **22** 890, *890*
Bolswert, Boetius (Adamsz.) (à) **3** 561; **4** 282*; **10** 391
collaboration **10** 391; **27** 299
pupils **4** 282
Bolswert, Schelte (Adamsz.) (à) **3** 561; **4** 282–3*; **10** 391
collaboration **9** 480; **10** 391; **18** 879; **27** 299
patrons and collectors **2** 725
works **18** 879
Bolt, Johann Friedrich **7** 870
Bolt, P. **14** 44
Boltanski, Christian **4** 283*; **11** 553, 571
Boltayev, Abdulla **29** 823
Bolten, Arent van **4** 379; **25** 22
Boltenstern, Erich **2** 789, 810, 815
Bolton (Lancs) **20** *589*
Bolton Hall **5** 169
cotton **8** 35
Hall i't'Wood **30** *897*
mills (industrial) **21** 601
Octagon Theatre **30** 684, 687
St Stephen **30** *502*, 503
Town Hall **10** 266; **31** 241
Bolton, Charles Paulet, 5th Duke of *see* PAULET, CHARLES, 5th Duke of Bolton
Bolton, John **5** 169
Bolton, Thomas **9** 320
Bolton, William Jay **18** 629
Bolton-in-Wensleydale (N. Yorks) **6** 53
Boltraffio, Giovanni Antonio **4** 283–5*; **19** 193; **21** 525
attributions **2** 376; **29** 26
collaboration **23** 368
patrons and collectors **4** 427; **8** 146; **25** 144
works **4** *284*; **19** 191
Boltschhauser, J. H. **5** 77
Boltz, Valentin **20** 109, 325
Bolu Mosque **16** 205
Bolure, Alebret de **19** 388
Boly, Merten **32** 709
Bolzani, Achille *see* BOCCHI, ACHILLE
Bolzano **16** *618*
Cathedral of the Assumption **4** 286*
Museo Civico **16** 776

Bom, Emmanuel de see DE BOM, EMMANUEL
Boma (Zaïre) 1 401; 18 218
Boma (people) 18 217; 30 418
Bomalino, Giovanni 33 36
Boman, Axel Enoch 23 235; 30 102
Boman, Nikolai 11 104
Bomarzo 16 620
Villa Orsini 20 280
gardens 12 63
Sacro Bosco 4 286–7*, 287; 12 116; 28 314
sculpture 16 696
Bomarzo, Pier Francesco Vicino Orsini, Duke of 4 286; 23 575; 32 627
Bombarda 20 920
Bombay 4 287–91*; 6 623; 15 276; 16 105
architecture 15 411
art school 15 542
Bombay Club 7 470
Crawford Markets 15 542
Ganapatya 15 217
Gateway of India 4 290; 7 361; 15 403
goldsmiths 15 723
Jamshetjee Jeejheebhoy School of Art 15 656, 657
Kanchunjunga Apartments 15 169
Law Courts 18 889
metalwork 15 714
Nehru Memorial Museum and Library 24 682
New Municipal Buildings 31 241
Prince of Wales Museum of Western India 4 289; 15 403; 22 364, 364
collections 15 182, 184, 742; 17 428
paintings 22 795
printing 15 679
prints 15 177
religion 15 204
sculpture 15 542
shrine of B. R. Ambedkar 28 635
silk 15 662
Tata Institute of Fundamental Research 4 290
textiles 15 671
Town Hall 15 403, 542; 31 241
University Hall 15 403
Victoria Terminus 4 289, 289; 15 403
Bombay Art Society 15 657
Bombay City and Suburbs Post-War Development Committee 4 289
Bombeck, Seger 12 467; 30 319
Bombelli, Pietro Leone 6 111
Bombelli, Sebastiano 4 291–2*; 16 676
assistants 12 559
patrons and collectors 7 780
pupils 24 203
works 4 292; 21 832
Bomberault, Benoît 4 292–3*; 7 407
Bomberault, Mathurin 4 293
Bomberg, Daniel 17 565
Bomberg, David 4 293–4*; 10 374; 17 578
groups and movements 10 256; 19 622; 32 701
patrons and collectors 20 476
pupils 2 712; 10 258; 18 399; 21 363
teachers 19 591
works 4 18, 293; 10 257; 19 492
Bomberg, Paul 4 844*
Bomberghen, Cornelis van 13 277; 25 17
Bombicci, Francesco 3 812
Bombois, Camille 4 294–5*; 22 440
Bominaco, S Maria 26 625
Bom Jesus do Monte 25 293, 301; 27 498, 500
Bomma, Chinna 32 153
Bömmels, Peter 9 72
Bommiers 26 599
Bompiani, Roberto 7 858
Bon (religion) 30 808, 810–11, 822
Bon see BUON (i) (FAMILY)
Bon, Antonio 3 595
Bon, Bartolomeo 1 456; 19 560
Bon, Christoph 6 409–10
Bon, Girolamo 10 529
Bon, Guido 3 595
Bon, Pietro 2 181
Bona, Giacomo Antonio see BONI, GIACOMO ANTONIO
Bona, Giovanni 15 866
Bonaccorsi, Raimondo see BUONACCORSI, RAIMONDO
Bonaccorso, Lapo di see LAPO DI BONACCORSO
Bonacina 29 90
Bonacina, Carlo Mauro 25 414
Bonacolsi (family) 20 318
Bonacolsi, Piero Jacopo Alari see ANTICO
Bonacossi, Alessandro Contini, Conte see CONTINI BONACOSSI, ALESSANDRO, Conte
Bonacossi, Ettore d'Antonio de' 11 8
Bonadura, Cristoforo, the elder (b c. 1582) 4 295*; 25 97, 408
Bonadura, Cristoforo, the younger (fl 1662-97) 4 295
Bonafè, Matís 3 221
Bonafous, Louis-Abbel, Abbé de Fontenai see FONTENAI, Abbé de
Bonagiunta da Como 13 817
Bonaguida, Pacino di see PACINO DI BONAGUIDA
Bonaguil 3 209; 6 56; 12 174; 21 564
Bonaire 2 144, 149; 5 745
see also ANTILLES, LESSER; ANTILLES, NETHERLANDS
Bonaiuti, Ernesto 7 344
Bonaiuti, Raffaello 32 108
Bonaiuto, Andrea di see ANDREA DA FIRENZE (i)
Bonaiuto, Paolo di see PAOLO DI BONAIUTO
Bonalino, Giovanni 3 139
Bonamico see BUFFALMACCO
Bonampak 4 295–7*; 20 882; 21 246, 372
stelae 4 296
Structure 1 4 295–6, 296
wall paintings 7 636, I1; 10 779; 20 883; 21 226, 231–2, 246, 256, 257, 259, 261; 22 518
B(u)onanni, Filippo 25 413; 32 237
Bonanni, Pietro 32 889
Bonanos, Georgios 4 297*; 13 354
Bonanus of Pisa 4 297*
attributions 24 857
works 9 154; 10 743; 16 688; 24 854, 858
Bonao 9 114
Escuela Cándida Bidó 9 119
Bonapaduli (family) 5 337
Bonaparte (family) 4 298*
cameos 22 103
furniture 33 48
paintings 11 32
sculpture 3 314
Bonaparte, Caroline, Queen of Naples see CAROLINE MURAT, Queen of Naples
Bonaparte, Charlotte 26 452
Bonaparte, Elisa, Grand Duchess of Tuscany see ELISA, Grand Duchess of Tuscany
Bonaparte, Eugène-Louis-Jean-Joseph, Prince 5 825
Bonaparte, Eugénie, Empress of the French see EUGÉNIE, Empress of the French
Bonaparte, Hortense, Queen of Holland see HORTENSE DE BEAUHARNAIS, Queen of Holland
Bonaparte, Jérôme, King of Westphalia see JÉRÔME BONAPARTE, King of Westphalia
Bonaparte, Joseph, King of Naples and Spain see JOSEPH BONAPARTE, King of Naples and Spain
Bonaparte, Josephine, Empress of the French see JOSEPHINE, Empress of the French
Bonaparte, Laetitia 30 267
Bonaparte, Louis, King of Holland see LOUIS, King of Holland
Bonaparte, Lucien, 1st Prince of Canino see CANINO, LUCIEN BONAPARTE, 1st Prince of
Bonaparte, Marie-Letizia 22 103
Bonaparte, Marie-Louise, Empress see MARIE-LOUISE, Empress of the French, Duchess of Parma
Bonaparte, Mathilde, Princess 4 299, 307–8*
busts 5 825
collections 4 298
paintings 27 265; 28 346
sculpture 9 326
Bonaparte, Napoléon (-Jérôme), Prince 4 299, 308*
architecture 22 744; 23 209; 25 193
interior decoration 11 580
paintings 9 424; 12 487; 15 843; 22 89
sculpture 4 298; 13 826
Bonaparte, Napoleon I, Emperor of the French see NAPOLEON I, Emperor of the French
Bonaparte, Napoleon II, King of Rome see REICHSTADT, NAPOLEON II BONAPARTE, Herzog von, King of Rome
Bonaparte, Napoleon III, Emperor of the French see NAPOLEON III, Emperor of the French
Bonaparte, Pauline, Princess Borghese 4 299, 306*; 19 67
architecture 4 298
paintings 17 731
silver 4 42
Bonaparte-Gabrielli, Charlotte, Princess 24 660
Bonapreso Aspettati, Jacopo di see JACOPO DI BONAPRESO ASPETTATI
Bonarelli, Matteo 26 810
Bona Sforza, Duchess of Milan (fl c. 1468-90) 4 76; 14 759; 16 751
Bona Sforza, Queen of Poland (1494-1557) 7 439; 16 867; 18 427; 22 167; 25 119, 134, 137
Bonasone, Giulio di Antonio 4 308–9*; 10 386
patrons and collectors 33 56
works 7 777; 11 391; 27 606; 31 43
Bonastri da Lucignano, Lattanzio 13 340
Bonati, Eduardo M. 6 598
Bonatti, Giovanni 24 833
Bonatz, Karl 3 797; 30 370
Bonatz, Paul (Michael Nikolaus) 4 309*; 11 129; 16 591
collaboration 10 134; 25 856
groups and movements 4 143; 28 126
pupils 9 59; 12 235; 22 186
teachers 30 733
works 3 336; 9 460; 12 379; 14 142; 19 332; 29 874
Bonaventura, Segna di see SEGNA DI BONAVENTURA
Bonaventure, Nicolas de see NICOLAS DE BONAVENTURE
Bonaventure, Saint 2 632; 11 709; 19 356; 24 776
Bonavera, Domenico 19 732
Bonaveri, Telesforo 27 407
Bonavia, Carlo 4 309–10*, 894; 14 190; 32 333
Bonavia, Giacomo 4 310*
pupils 12 923
works 2 284, 285; 29 271
Bonavía, Santiago 4 561; 10 806; 27 753; 29 271, 304
Bonay, Francisco 5 452
Bonazza (family) 32 195
Bonazza, Antonio 4 311*
collaboration 4 310*, 311
works 16 703
Bonazza, Francesco 4 310–11*
Bonazza, Giovanni 4 310–11*; 29 736
Bonazza, Michelangelo 4 311*
Bonazza, Tommaso 4 310–11*
Boncampagni Ludovisi, Ignazio see LUDOVISI, IGNAZIO BONCAMPAGNI
Boncampagni Ludovisi, Ugo, Prince of Piombino see PIOMBINO, UGO BONCAMPAGNI LUDOVISI, Prince of
Bonchev, Bozhidar 5 159
Boncompagni (family) 3 56; 21 804
Boncompagni, Cristoforo 4 311
Boncompagni, Francesco, Cardinal 4 311
Boncompagni, Giacomo, Cardinal 4 312
Boncompagni, Pietro 4 311
Boncompagni, Ugo see GREGORY XIII, Pope
Boncquet, Victor 17 700
Bond, Alan 2 561, 770
Bond, F. Bligh 14 156
Bond, Frances (Flora) see PALMER, FRANCES (FLORA)
Bond, Francis 9 70
works 24 749
Bond, J. L. 29 533
Bond, Richard (fl 1526) 5 514
Bond, Richard (fl 1820-50) 4 312*
Bonda, H. 1 803
Bondarenko, Il'ya (Yevgrafovich) 4 312–13*; 22 173; 27 377; 28 837
Bonde, Gustaf, Count see TROLLE-BONDE, GUSTAF, Count
Bonde, Peter 8 736
Bonde, Robert 15 149
bonding 4 769, 769–70*
Basket-weave bond 4 790
Colonial bond 4 770
see also English garden-wall bond
Cross bond 4 785, 787, 790
United States of America 4 786
English bond 4 769, 770, 779, 785, 786, 787
English garden-wall bond 4 769, 770
see also Colonial bond
Flemish bond 4 769, 770, 778, 781, 785, 787, 790
Flemish stretcher bond 4 769, 770
Gothic bond 4 782
header bond 4 770, 787, 790
Monk bond 4 769, 770, 781, 790
Monk stretcher bond 4 770
Polish see Gothic
Rat-trap bond 4 769, 769, 790
Stack bond 4 790
stretcher bond 4 770, 790
Sussex bond 4 769, 770
Sussex stretcher bond 4 770
tack bond 4 769
bonding—cont.
West bond 4 782
Bondington, William, Bishop of Glasgow 12 778
Bondolf, Jehan de see BOUDOLF, JAN
Bondoukou 1 386; 8 22
Museum 8 23
Bond van Nederlandsche Architecten 3 432
Bondy, Taillepied de see TAILLEPIED DE BONDY
bone 4 313–14*; 16 796
dating methods 2 304; 11 309
historical and regional traditions
Aboriginal Australia 4 314
Africa 1 296
Asante 4 314
Aztec 4 314
Britain 4 314
Buddhism 4 314
Byzantine 9 521, 651, 651
Canaanite 30 184
Central Asia 6 305
China 4 313; 6 736; 7 19, 106, 107, 109
Crete 8 153; 21 681
Cycladic 8 323*
Egypt 16 523
Egypt, ancient 4 313; 9 864; 10 59–60*, 65
Etruscan 10 635*
Fiji 4 314
France 11 637; 25 491
Germany 25 490
Greece, ancient 12 247; 13 595*; 14 353–4*; 21 712
Hawaii 4 314
Helladic 14 353–4*
Inca 15 163
Indian subcontinent 4 314
Islamic 16 487, 503, 523
Italy 10 179, 635*
Japan 4 314
Lebanon 30 181
Maori 4 314
Maya 4 314
Mesoamerica, Pre-Columbian 4 314; 21 256, 257
Mesopotamia 4 313
Minoan 21 681
Mixtec 21 737
Native North Americans 4 314; 22 668
Nepal 4 314
Papua New Guinea 4 314
Parthian 24 218
Prehistoric art 4 313; 16 615; 25 472, 473, 488, 490, 491, 491, 492–3*, 518
Rome, ancient 9 647; 27 101
Russia 2 101
Spain 6 558; 29 313
Syria-Palestine 30 181, 181, 184, 192
Tibet 4 314
Tonga (Pacific Islands) 4 314
patinas 19 73
technical examination 30 397, 410
techniques
carving see BONE-CARVINGS
engraving 25 491, 492–3*
painting 25 493
uses
altarpieces 10 179
amulets 10 60; 21 248
architecture 25 473
armour 6 305
batons 25 493
beads 1 296; 3 440
body ornaments 21 248; 25 518
calligraphy 6 736
candlesticks 5 611
caskets 9 521, 651
chess sets 6 555, 557, 558
combs (hair) 7 107, 109
contours découpés 25 493
crosses 8 203

bone
 uses—cont.
  drills 16 859
  figurines 21 247; 24 218; 25 488, 490
  flutes (musical instruments) 21 257
  glove stretchers 4 314
  hairbrushes 4 314
  harps 10 65
  ideograms 21 248
  inks 15 851
  inlays 4 313, 314; 16 487; 29 313
  jewellery 7 106, 107; 10 60
  knife-handles 4 314; 8 284, 285
  knucklebones 31 266
  lacquer 7 19
  marquetry 20 466
  masks 21 247
  mirror handles 21 712
  mosaics 16 487; 21 248
  musical instruments 21 247, 248, 256
  panel paintings 24 4
  pendants (jewellery) 21 247
  pens 4 314
  plaques 2 101
  pyxides (boxes) 9 651
  rondelles (sculpture) 25 493
  scrimshaw 28 302
  seals 12 247
  sickles 30 181
  spear-throwers 25 491
  spoons 8 283, 284
  tools 8 153; 16 615; 21 247; 25 472
  toys 31 254
  vomiting sticks 8 229
  weapons 16 503
Bône *see* HIPPO REGIUS
Bone, D. W. 4 315
Bone, H. A. 10 351
Bone, Henry 7 814
 works 7 814
Bone, James 4 315
Bone, (David) Muirhead 4 314–15*
 catalogues 9 61
 patrons and collectors 1 496
 works 9 309; 28 238
bone-ash 4 600; 6 326; 10 308
bone black 24 789
bone-carvings 28 302
 Aztec 21 248
 Castelluccio 28 653
 Chorrera culture 29 206
 Coptic 7 825*
 Crete 21 680*
 Cycladic 8 323*
 Dorset culture 22 575
 Egypt 7 825*
 France 25 491, 492
 Huastec 21 248
 Maya 21 247–8
 Mesoamerica, Pre-Columbian 21 247–8*
 Minoan 21 680*
 Mixtec 21 248
 Native North Americans 22 573, 575
 Prehistoric art 25 491, 492, 495
 Sicily 28 653
 South America, Pre-Columbian 29 206–7*
 Zapotec 21 248
 see also SCRIMSHAW
Bonechi, Lorenzo 7 385
Bonechi, Matteo 4 315*; 7 897; 11 194; 21 31
bone china 4 600; 6 326*; 10 309, 310; 30 100–101
Bonello, Vincenzo 20 219
Boner, Jan 16 866; 18 428, 511; 25 120
Boner, Seweryn 16 866
Boner, Ulrich 4 357; 10 724, 725
Bo'ness 28 252
Bonet, Antonio 2 397; 4 315–16*; 29 273, 321; 31 753
Bonet, José Esteve *see* ESTEVE BONET, JOSÉ
Bonet, Paul (1889-1971)
 works 4 IV3
Bonet Bertran, Josep 29 861
Bonet i Cari, Lluís 3 217
Bonetti, Baccio 7 906
Bonetti, Mattia 11 584
Bonevardi, Marcelo 4 316*
Bonfanti, Ezio 30 455
Bonfigli, Benedetto 4 316–17*; 24 520; 26 765
 collaboration 5 672
 patrons and collectors 3 55
 works 4 317
Bonfiglio *see* BONFILIUS
Bonfiglioli (family) 5 853
Bonfili 21 430
Bonfilius 24 858; 25 863
Bonfill, Pedro 31 814
Bonfils, Robert 5 841
Bonfin, François 4 389
bonfire kilns *see under* KILNS → types
Bonfol 30 144
Bonfratelli, Apollonio de' 4 317–18*
Bongard, Germaine 25 740
Bongarde, Armand 2 465
Bonge, Andries 22 873
Bonge, Filip 28 696
Bonger, André 26 72
Bongianni, Jacopo 19 677
Bongiovanni di Geminiano 9 97; 11 7
Bongo 1 360, 410; 29 895
Bongu
 sculpture 24 80
Bonhams 2 706
Bonheur, Isidore Jules 2 99
 works 2 100
Bonheur, Raymond 4 318; 11 672
Bonheur, (Marie-)Rosa 4 318*, 391; 12 215
 dealers 12 30; 31 664
 patrons and collectors 29 651; 32 708
 pupils 6 122
 reproductive prints by others 12 30; 19 285; 22 208
 teachers 11 672
 works 2 99, 106; 10 781; 19 487; 24 141, 141
Bonhomme (family) 3 593
Bonhommé, (Ignace-)François 4 319*; 15 828
Bonhomme, Jean (*fl* 1636; architect) 26 113
Bonhomme, Jean (1587-after 1638; glassmaker) 3 593
Bonhomme, Léon (-Félix-Georges) 4 319*
Bonhomme, Macé 26 261
Bonhomme, Nicolas 29 524
Boni (Mali)
 masks 5 328, 330
 sculpture 5 330
Boni (family) *see* BUONO
Boni, Giacomo 4 320*; 26 762, 830
Boni, Giacomo Antonio 4 320*; 11 679; 12 559
Boni, Giuseppe 27 788
Bonicelli 20 70
Bonichi, Gino *see* SCIPIONE
Bonici, Giuseppe 20 212
Boniface, Abbot of Conques 26 691
Boniface, Saint 2 775; 3 709; 5 779, 794
Boniface IV, Pope (*reg* 608-15) 25 265
Boniface VIII, Pope (*reg* 1294-1303) 12 256; 14 416; 16 759; 23 584
Boniface IX, Pope (*reg* 1389-1404) 26 811
Bonifacio, Martín Sanchez *see* SANCHEZ BONIFACIO, MARTÍN
Bonifacio, Pedro 13 191; 31 92
Bonifacio Frigimelica *see* FRIGIMELICA, BONIFACIO
Bonifacio Lupi di Soragno 1 725
Bonifacio monument 24 619
Bonifás, Luis (*d* 1697) 4 320
Bonifas, Paul 30 144
Bonifás y Masó, Francisco 4 320
Bonifás y Masó, Luis 4 320*; 29 294
Bonifás y Sastre, Luis 4 320
Bonifazio, Piero 30 672
Bonifini, Antonio 13 196
Bonilla Norat, Felix 18 832; 25 701, 702
Bonin, Alexandre 24 883
Bonincontri, Lorenzo 28 532
Bonington, Richard (1768-1835) 4 321; 11 309
Bonington, Richard Parkes (1802-28) 4 321–2*; 11 543; 23 258, 503; 25 628; 32 196
 attributions 10 152
 book illustrations 30 385
 dealers 4 66; 7 579; 26 107; 28 170; 29 248
 etchings 10 562
 groups and movements 26 500, 739; 31 373, 374
 lithographs 8 867; 14 861; 19 487; 25 626; 31 156
 paintings 9 286
  history 4 322
  watercolours 9 217; 11 309; 32 901
 patrons and collectors
  Combe, Thomas and Martha 7 647
  Coutan, Louis-Joseph-Auguste 8 73
  Demidov, Anatoly, Prince 8 705
  Hawkins, John Heywood (1803-77) 14 252
  Munro (of Novar), H(ugh) A(ndrew) J(ohnstone) 22 314
  Petty-Fitzmaurice, Henry, 3rd Marquess of Lansdowne 24 571
  Rushout, John, 2nd Baron Northwick 27 350
  Russell, John, 6th Duke of Bedford 27 358
  Seymour-Conway, Richard, 4th Marquess of Hertford 28 527
  Vernon, Robert 32 338
  Webb, Henry 28 170
  Windus, B(enjamin) G(odfrey) 33 251
 personal collection 4 615
 pupils 12 809; 18 678
 reproductive prints by others 3 745; 5 827; 6 519
 teachers 13 692
Bonini, Bonino de' 4 99
Bonino 29 419
Bonino da Campione 5 551*
 patrons and collectors 21 524; 32 343
 works 13 94; 16 688; 28 29; 32 345, 610
Boninsegna 24 871
Boninsegna, Giampaolo 16 741
Bonirote, Pierre 13 360
Bonis, Martino de 5 631
Bonis, Niccolo de' 4 322–3*
Bonis, Vincenzo De *see* DE BONIS, VINCENZO
Bonitate, Pietro de *see* PIETRO DE BONITATE
Bonito, Giuseppe 4 323*; 22 479
 collaboration 11 136
 patrons and collectors 4 562
 pupils 15 881
 tapestries 22 481
 works 5 914
Bonito, Nicolo 4 154
Bonkil, Edward 12 846; 28 268
Bonkotsu Igami *see* IGAMI, BONKOTSU
Bonn 4 323–4*; 8 824; 12 361
 collections 12 476, 481
 Kunsthistoriches Institut Library 12 481
 Kunst- und Ausstellungshalle der Bundesrepublik Deutschland 24 326
 Minster 12 364; 13 47
 museums
  Akademisches Kunstmuseum 4 324
  Bundeskunsthalle 4 324
  Frauen Museum 33 310
  Museum Vaterländischer Altentümer *see* Rheinisches Landesmuseum
  Rheinisches Landesmuseum 4 324; 12 476
  Städtisches Kunstmuseum 4 324
  Zoologisches Museum Alexander Koenig 4 324
 observatory 23 340
 Rathaus 4 324
 University 13 218
Bonn, Giulia 27 852
Bonnac, De 32 510
Bonnafé, A. A. 4 324–5*
Bonnar & Carfrae 28 250
Bonnard, Jacques-Charles 26 190
Bonnard, Paul 19 396
Bonnard, Pierre 4 325–7*; 11 667; 24 144
 book illustrations 12 601
 books 4 366
 collaboration 14 486; 20 603
 dealers 3 826; 9 425; 19 10; 32 686
 frames 11 419
 groups and movements 8 714; 15 156, 888; 22 421, 422; 28 344; 30 169
 lithographs 19 489, 490; 25 623
 livres d'artiste 19 513; 32 687
 methods 4 184; 7 631; 21 761
 nude figures 23 296
 paintings 11 549
  genre 4 326, 327
  landscape 18 717
  still-lifes 29 669
 patrons and collectors 4 71; 20 76; 22 135, 136, 538; 24 183; 26 472, 534, 723
 pottery 11 606
 prints 25 600, 626; 32 687
 productions 3 120; 17 449; 30 682, 685
 reproductive prints by others 32 577
 screens (ii) (furniture) 28 298
 stained glass 30 869
Bonnars, Roger 20 138
Bonnart, Jean-Baptiste 6 502
Bonnassieux, Jean-Marie-Bienaimé 4 328*
Bonnat, Léon (-Joseph-Florentin) 4 328–9*; 11 659, 672
 collaboration 6 545; 11 156
 patrons and collectors 29 536
 personal collection 25 750
 pupils
  Backer, Harriet 3 22
  Béraud, Jean 3 754
  Bernadotte, Eugen (Napoleon Nicolaus), Prince of Sweden (1865-1947) 10 648
  Bernatzik, Wilhelm 3 821
  Blashfield, Edwin Howland 4 130
  Braque, Georges 4 673
  Brožík, Václav 4 887
  Caillebotte, Gustave 5 389
  Cederström, Gustaf (Olof) 6 130
  Dufy, Raoul 9 372
  Eakins, Thomas (Cowperthwaite) 9 500
  Enneking, John Joseph 10 402
  Eysen, Louis 10 718
Bonnat, Léon(-Joseph-Florentin)
 pupils—cont.
  Forbes, Stanhope (Alexander) 11 299
  Forsberg, Nils (1842-1934) 11 318
  Friesz, (Emile) Othon 11 789
  Gay, Walter 12 212
  Harris, Robert 14 193
  Helsted, Axel (Theophilus) 14 374
  Heyerdahl, Hans (Olaf Halvor) 14 506
  Joy, George W(illiam) 17 673
  Kossak, Wojciech 18 398
  Krøyer, P(eder) S(everin) 18 470
  Lewis, Roberto (Gerónimo) 19 287
  Lindholm, Berndt (Adolf) 19 408
  Marchand, Jean (Hippolyte) 20 387
  Mehoffer, Józef 21 51
  Munch, Edvard 22 291
  Osbert, Alphonse 23 598
  Philipsen, Theodor (Esbern) 24 633
  Reis, Carlos 26 130
  Schjerfbeck, Helene (Sofia) 28 104
  Skovgaard, Joakim (Frederik) 28 824
  Skredsvig, Christian 28 825
  Suzor-Coté, Marc-Aurèle de Foy 30 50
  Toulouse-Lautrec (Montfa), Henri (Marie Raymond) de 31 213
  Tuxen, Laurits Regner 31 485
  Wentzel, (Nils) Gustav 33 76
  Werenskiold, Erik (Theodor) 33 78
 teachers 7 529
 works 4 329; 11 547
Bonn Diptych, Master of the 20 718
Bonne, François de, Duc de Lesdiguières *see* DE LESDIGUIÈRES, FRANÇOIS DE BONNE, Duc
Bonnecroy, Jan Baptist 31 523
Bonnefill, Lesmes Jiménez *see* JIMÉNEZ BONNEFILL, LESMES
Bonnefond, (Jean-)Claude 3 867; 7 679, 876
Bonnefons 10 657
Bonnefontaine 13 158
Bonnefoy, Antoine 11 606; 20 474
Bonnefoy, J. D. 29 676
Bonnefoy, Yves 20 75
Bonnejonne, Eloi 11 698
Bonnemaison, Ferréol de 4 329–30*; 33 55
Bonnemer, François 12 832; 22 191
Bonnemère 33 357
Bonnemers, François 32 659
Bonne of Armagnac 31 308
Bonne of Luxembourg, Queen of France (*fl c.* 1345-50) 17 463; 25 694
Bonner, George Wilmot 19 431
Bonnestrenne, Pierre-François 11 619; 21 70
Bonnet, Anne 3 565; 5 45; 17 518
Bonnet, Claude 17 911
Bonnet, F. E. *see* TOBEEN
Bonnet, Louis-Marin 4 330–31*; 10 391
 assistants 16 905
 engravings 8 130, 131; 13 220; 17 627
 prints 4 331, 517, 518; 13 220; 25 623
 reproductive prints by others 3 463
 teachers 11 723

Bonnet, Nicolas 11 627
Bonnet, Paul (fl 1854) 32 84
Bonnet, Rudolf 15 807, 809; 29 234, 238, 239
- works 29 *234*

bonnets 16 459
Bonneuf, Georges 7 528
Bonneuil, Etienne de *see* ETIENNE DE BONNEUIL
Bonneville Architects 27 642
Bonnier, Joseph 4 331*; 18 654; 22 34
Bonnier, Louis (-Bernard) 4 331–2*; 5 135; 24 127, 128
- collaboration 25 52
- patrons and collectors 8 257
- teachers 3 395
- works 4 71

Bonniér, Olle 7 699; 30 81
Bonnin, Gousse 4 332*
Bonnin & Morris 4 332*; 31 635
- works 31 *635*

Bonnivet Château 13 224
Bono *see* BUONO
Bono, Giacomo Antonio *see* BONI, GIACOMO ANTONIO
Bono, Marco *see* FRIAZIN, BON
Bono, Michele *see* GIAMBONO, MICHELE
Bono da Ferrara 4 332–3*; 20 305
Bonolis, Giuseppe 4 333*; 22 916; 23 851
Bonomi (family) 31 13
Bonomi, Ignatius 4 333; 24 307
Bonomi, Joseph, the elder (1739-1808) 4 333*; 10 82; 22 738
- collaboration 1 140; 11 83
- groups and movements 10 97, 644; 13 608
- patrons and collectors 24 570
- works 10 277; 20 867, *867*; 25 192, *193*, 766

Bonomi, Joseph, the younger (1796-1878) 4 333
Bonomi, Lorenzo 12 532
Bonomo, Jacobello di *see* JACOBELLO DI BONOMO
Bononcini, Giovanni 24 340
Bononi, Carlo 4 334–5*; 11 3
- works 4 *334*; 11 4; 28 38; 33 592

Bononia (Italy) *see* BOLOGNA
Bononia (Serbia) *see* BANOŠTOR
Bononia, Baveram de *see* BAVIERA
Bonorva, S Nicolo di Trullas 27 836
Bonoto, Pietro
- works 5 *628*

Bonoua Museum 8 23
Bonpland, Aimé-Jacques A. 4 303; 26 73
Bonpō Gyokuen *see* GYOKUEN BONPŌ
bonsai 17 365–8*, *366*
Bonset, I. K. *see* DOESBURG, THEO VAN
Bonshtedt, Lyudvig (Lyudvigovich) 3 409; 4 335*; 7 668
- collaboration 28 628
- pupils 28 628
- works 19 563; 27 578; 33 516, 517

Bonsignore, Ferdinando 5 615; 7 258; 31 442
Bonsignori, Albertus 4 335
Bonsignori, Bernardino 4 335
Bonsignori, Francesco 4 335–6*
- attributions 3 667; 12 908; 18 872
- collaboration 8 4
- works 4 *336*

Bonsignori, Giovanni di *see* GIOVANNI DI BONSIGNORI
Bonsignori, Girolamo 4 335
Bonsignori, Stefano 11 180
Bontecou, Lee 4 337*
- collaboration 20 606
- dealers 6 23
- groups and movements 17 694
- works 29 12

Bontempelli, Massimo 5 671; 8 605; 16 680; 23 264
Bontemps, Georges 7 195
Bontemps, Pierre 4 337–8*; 8 68
- assistants 24 812
- collaboration 11 557
- groups and movements 11 265
- works 4 *338*; 19 692; 27 547

Bontepaert, Dirck Pietersz. 27 805
Bontjes van Beek, Jan 12 432
Bontoc 24 607, 617, 624, 625, 626, 628
Bontour style pottery *see under* POTTERY → wares
Bontridder, Albert 3 551
Bonu Ighinu 27 834
Bonventura, Segna di *see* SEGNA DI BONVENTURA
Bonvicino, Alessandro (*d* before 1484) 22 106
Bonvicino, Alessandro (*c.* 1498-1554) *see* MORET MORETTO (DA BRESCIA)
Bonvicino, Ambrogio 4 404, 405; 29 559
Bonvicino, Pietro 22 106
Bonvin, François (Saint) 4 338–9*
- dealers 30 425
- groups and movements 26 54
- works 4 *339*; 5 364; 11 230; 12 294; 29 669

Bonvin, Léon 4 338, 339*
Bonvisi, Francesco 7 553
Bony, Jean 30 729
Bony, Jean-François 11 648; 19 850
Bony, Paul 20 831; 29 508
- works 29 *509*

Bonyhád Synagogue 17 544
Bonynge, Robert 4 481
Bonzagna, Gian Federigo 4 339–40*; 6 360
Bonzagna, Gian Giacomo 4 339
Bonzagni, Aroldo 4 340*; 16 680
Bonzagni, Gianfrancesco 29 409
Bonzanigo, Giuseppe Maria 4 340*
- works 5 192; 11 396; 16 719, 728; 28 298

Bonzi, Pietro Paolo 4 340*; 7 906
- collaboration 4 813
- patrons and collectors 20 841; 27 160
- works 29 667

Bo O 18 771
Boocke, Frederick 19 274
Boodt, Anselmus de 29 740
Boody, Henry 33 134
Boogaert, Jan 22 893
Boogaert, Thomas 1 811
Book, Max 30 82
bookbindings 4 346–56*; 14 424
- conservation 4 355–6*, *356*
- historical and regional traditions
  - Anglo-Saxon 4 347, 348
  - Armenia (Europe) 2 442
  - Buddhism 6 307; 7 64
  - Carolingian 4 346, 347, 348
  - Central Asia, Eastern 6 306, 307
  - China 7 63–4
  - England 4 347, 348, 349; 12 628; 24 51
  - France 4 347, 348, 349; 24 51
  - Germany 4 347, 348, 349; 17 566–7*; 24 51
  - Insular art 4 348
  - Iran 18 *609*
  - Islamic 1 682; 12 627; 16 271, 353, *355*, 355–9*, 533; 18 *609*
  - Italy 4 347, 348, 349; 12 628; 17 566*; 24 51
  - Japan 17 272, *272*
  - Jewish art 17 566–7*
  - Morocco 1 682; 12 628
  - Netherlands, the 4 348, 349; 24 51
  - Portugal 17 566*, 567
  - Romanesque 4 348
  - Scotland 4 349
  - Spain 4 347, 349; 12 628; 17 566*, 567
  - Tibet 30 836
  - United States of America 4 347
- materials
  - asphodel paste 16 356
  - canvas 4 347
  - clasps 4 350, 355; 24 107
  - glues 16 356; 24 107
  - gold 1 682; 24 107
  - gum arabic 16 356
  - hemp 7 63
  - lacquer 18 *609*
  - leather 4 347; 7 63; 17 566
  - linen 4 347; 16 356
  - paper 4 347; 16 353; 24 50–51*
  - papyrus 4 347
  - parchment 4 347; 24 106, 107
  - silk 7 63, 64
  - silver 2 442
  - tackets 24 107
  - threads 4 346
  - varnishes 16 533
  - wheat starch 16 356
  - wood 4 347; 24 107; 30 836
- techniques
  - gilding 12 623, 627–8*
  - sewing 4 346–7*; 16 356; 24 107
  - stamping 17 566
- types
  - accordion-folded *see under* BOOKS → forms → accordion-books
  - butterfly books *see under* BOOKS → forms
  - stitched-bound books *see under* BOOKS → forms

bookcases 9 29
- historical and regional traditions
  - England 23 *547*
  - Hungary 14 *903*
  - Ireland 16 *27*
  - Islamic 16 487
  - Korea 18 362
  - Malta (Republic of) 20 215
  - United States of America 31 626, *626*, *628*, 629
- materials
  - larch-wood 14 *903*
  - lime-wood 14 *903*
  - mahogany 31 *626*, *628*
  - satin-wood 31 *628*
  - walnut 16 *27*
  - wood 16 487

book covers 4 349–55*
- historical and regional traditions
  - Afghanistan 12 II1; 16 *358*
  - Austria 4 351
  - Buddhism 6 319; 15 570; 30 846
  - Burma 20 327
  - Byzantine 9 651, 656, 658; 16 798
  - Carolingian 4 IV2; 5 808, *809*, 809–11, *811*; 7 *513*; 22 *520*
  - Central Asia, Eastern 6 306, 319
  - China 1 580
  - Early Christian (*c.* AD 250-843) 9 656
  - Egypt 4 349; 16 357, *357*
  - England 4 *346*, 349, 350, *350*, 351, *351*, 352, 353–4, *353*; 12 628; 23 *539*
  - France 4 349, 350, 351, *351*, 352, *353*, 354, *354*, IV3; 5 *811*
  - Germany 4 349, 351, 352, 354, III, IV2; 5 *809*; 12 442; 22 *520*; 26 695
  - Indian subcontinent 4 IV1; 15 549, 563–4, 570; 16 359
  - Insular art 4 *346*, 349
  - Iran 16 358–9
  - Islamic 12 627, II1; 15 549; 16 355–9*, *357*, *358*
  - Italy 4 349, 350, 351, 352, *352*, 353, 354; 12 628
  - Jainism 15 563–4
  - Mongolia 21 876
  - Morocco 12 628
  - Netherlands, the 4 350, 352, 353, 354; 13 *159*
  - North Africa 16 357
  - Ottoman 16 359
  - Ottonian 4 III, IV2; 23 660
  - Poland 4 352
  - Romanesque 4 *350*, 351; 23 *539*; 26 695
  - Romania 26 720
  - Serbia 28 456
  - Spain 4 350, 351, 352, 353; 12 628; 16 357
  - Syria 16 357, *357*
  - Thailand 20 327
  - Tibet 30 836, 846, *846*
  - Turkey 16 359
  - Yemen 16 357
- materials
  - baleen 23 *539*
  - canvas 4 350
  - enamel 4 III, IV2
  - gems 4 III; 7 *513*; 13 *159*
  - gold 4 III, IV2; 7 *513*; 13 *159*
  - gold leaf 4 *351*, 352, *352*, *353*
  - horn 14 763
  - ivory 4 IV2; 5 *809*, 809–11; 9 651; 16 798; 22 *520*; 23 660; 26 695
  - lacquer 4 IV1
  - leather 4 *346*, 349, *350*, *351*, 351–4, *352*, *353*, *354*, IV3; 12 II1; 15 549; 16 356, *357*, *358*
  - metal 12 442
  - paper 4 349; 24 55
  - papier mâché 16 359
  - parchment 4 349; 24 106
  - pasteboard 16 356
  - pearls 7 *513*
  - silver 9 656, 658; 26 720
  - textiles 4 349, 350
  - varnishes 16 356
  - wood 6 306; 16 356; 20 327; 30 836, 846, *846*
- techniques
  - carving 30 836
  - embossing 4 354
  - embroidery 4 351
  - gilding 12 627–8*, II1; 13 *159*; 16 357, *357*; 30 836
  - painting 4 *353*; 15 563–4; 30 836
- *see also* BICCHERNE; BOOK JACKETS; MANUSCRIPT COVERS

book design 8 109, 779; 12 327; 31 496; 32 231
Booker, Francis 16 26
Booker, John (*fl c.* 1725) 16 26
Booker, John (*fl* mid-18th cent.) 16 26
book illustrations 1 580; 4 345, 356–68*; 14 424; 25 597
- historical and regional traditions
  - Austria 4 366
  - Belgium 3 555
  - Britain 4 362–4*, *363*
  - Buddhism 6 777; 21 876
  - Central Asia, Western 16 196
  - China 6 777, 782; 7 64–5, 120–21
  - Denmark 8 731
  - Egypt, ancient 4 345; 10 7
  - England 4 366, 367; 10 254, 255
    - 17th cent. 9 375
    - 18th cent. 4 *362*; 31 *869*
    - 19th cent. 4 *363*, *885*; 22 *146*
    - 20th cent. 4 *367*
  - France 4 356, 359, 360, 364*, 365–6
    - Rococo 4 *361*
    - 17th cent. 6 518
    - 20th cent. 7 *508*
  - Germany 4 365, 366; 14 869; 25 872
    - Gothic 12 385
    - Ottonian 12 382
    - Renaissance 9 *436*
    - 15th cent. 4 *357*
    - 19th cent. 5 *291*
  - Gothic 12 385
  - Hinduism 22 *786*
  - Indian subcontinent 15 207
  - Iran 16 196
  - Islamic 16 196
  - Italy 4 359; 14 424
    - 15th cent. 4 *196*; 11 685
    - 17th cent. 3 *674*
  - Japan 17 186, 270, *271*, 272, 273–4*, 280, 285, 419
    - Edo period (1600-1868) 23 *162*
  - Jewish art 17 565–6*
  - Moldova 21 812*
  - Mongolia 21 876
  - Nepal 22 *786*, 786–7, 795
  - Netherlands, the 4 359; 20 631
  - Ottonian 12 382
  - Romania 14 424
  - Rome, ancient 23 692
  - Russia 11 82, *82*
  - South Africa 29 121
  - South America, Pre-Columbian 29 *130*
  - Spain 4 365; 31 750
  - Switzerland 4 *358*
  - Tibet 30 835, 836
  - United States of America 4 364–5*, 366, 367, *368*; 24 672, 673, *673*
    - 19th cent. 4 *365*
- types
  - aquatints 2 241; 4 362
  - carbon prints 24 649
  - chemitypes 6 534
  - chromolithography 4 362
  - collotype 24 650
  - colour 4 357
  - colour-plates 2 240; 4 357, 362
  - engravings 4 345, 356, 357, 359; 10 380, 389; 20 631; 21 579; 26 742; 32 199
  - etchings 4 359, 362; 10 550
  - lithography 4 345, 357, 362, 364, 367
  - mezzotints 4 359
  - photography 9 340; 24 649, 658, 661, 662, 663, 671, 672; 30 269
  - photolithography 24 650
  - prints 4 356, 357
  - watercolours 4 *368*
  - woodcuts 4 *345*, 356, 357–9, 366; 7 413; 8 731; 12 385; 21 578; 32 198–9
  - wood-engravings 4 356, 363, 366, *367*
- *see also* MANUSCRIPT ILLUMINATION

book jackets 4 347, 368–9*; 24 50
- *see also* BOOK COVERS

book labels *see under* LABELS → types
Booklet Press 13 223
booklinings *see* DOUBLURES
Book of Armagh *see under* NEW TESTAMENTS → individual manuscripts
Book of Cerne (Cambridge, U. Lib., MS. L.I.1.10) 15 875
Book of Deer (Cambridge, U. Lib., MS. Ii.6.32) 15 875; 28 233
Book of Dimma *see under* GOSPEL BOOKS → individual manuscripts

Book of Durrow *see under* GOSPEL BOOKS → individual manuscripts
Book of Kells *see under* GOSPEL BOOKS → individual manuscripts
Book of Llandaff (Aberystwyth, N. Lib. Wales) **10** 338
Book of Mulling *see under* GOSPEL BOOKS → individual manuscripts
Book of Murrow *see under* GOSPEL BOOKS → individual manuscripts
Book of Nunnaminster (London, BL, Harley MS. 2965) **15** 875; **32** 852
Book of the Dead for Ani **9** 905; **10** 92
Book of the Dead for Hunefer **9** *904*, 905
Book of the Dead for Nakhte **9** 905
Book of the Dead for Nesitanebtasheru **9** *905*, 906
bookplates **4** 372–3*, *373*; **10** 7, 396; **14** 424
books **2** 365; **4** 20, 341–5*, *342*, *345*
  conservation **24** 107
  forms
    accordion books
      Buddhism **1** 580, *580*; **30** 613, *614*
      Central Asia, Eastern **6** 307, *307*
      China **1** 580, *580*; **7** 63
      Japan **1** 581; **17** 220, *272*
      Mongolia **21** 875
      Thailand **30** 613, *614*
    butterfly books **1** 580, 581
    chapbooks *see* CHAPBOOKS
    de luxe **4** 359, 365–6*; **10** 7; **17** 271
    double-leaf **21** 875
    jing zhe zhuang *see* accordion books
    notebooks **24** 107
    sagabon **14** 703; **30** 376
    stitched-bound **1** 582
  historical and regional traditions
    Argentina **2** 398
    Buddhism **5** 102
    Burma **5** 245*
    Central Asia **5** 102
    Central Asia, Eastern **6** 306–7*, 314
    China **6** 736, 740; **7** 7, 62–5*, *64*
    Christianity **4** 343
    Czech Republic **25** 54
    Egypt **16** 361
    Egypt, ancient **4** *341*, 343, *343*, *344*; **10** 3, 5, 6–7*
    Etruscan **10** 589, 590, 636
    France **19** 870
    Germany **10** 724; **12** 385; **13** 866
    Gothic **12** 385
    Indian subcontinent **15** 549, 679–80*
    Islamic **15** 549; **16** 360–62*, *361*
    Italy **10** 589, 590, 636; **15** 50; **32** 198
    Japan **17** 269–74*, *271*, *272*; **22** 432
    Jewish art **17** 537, 565–6*; **29** 62
    Korea **18** 354–6*
    Mongolia **21** 875–6*
    Netherlands, the **8** 666
    Ottoman **16** 360
    Rome, ancient **20** 327
    Sweden **30** 77
    Tibet **30** 835–6*
    Turkey **16** 360
  materials
    consolidants **7** 748
    jade **7** 7
    leather **10** 5
    linen **10** 589, 636; **20** 327
books
  materials—cont.
    palm leaves **21** 876
    paper **4** 342; **7** 64; **15** 549
    parchment **4** *343*; **24** 107
    silver **21** 876
  techniques
    printing **4** 342, 344; **7** 63–5*, 576; **8** 666; **13** 866; **16** 360–62, *361*; **18** 354–6; **19** 870
    varnishing **8** 447
  see also MANUSCRIPTS
books, artists' *see* ARTISTS' BOOKS
book script *see under* SCRIPTS → types
Books of Arms **12** 272
Books of Hours **2** 3; **3** 323; **4** 3, 358, 369–72*; **8** 835; **9** 13; **20** 332, 339; **25** 678
  historical and regional traditions
    Belgium **4** 372
    England **4** 369, 370; **13** *130*
    France **13** *148*; **20** *637*
    Gothic **13** 127, 129, 130, *130*, *148*; **20** *637*
    Italy **4** 370; **12** 710
    Netherlands, the **4** 370; **24** 809; **29** 666
  individual manuscripts
    Adimari Hours (Baltimore, MD, Walters A. G.) **29** 786
    Albani Hours (London, BL, Yates Thompson MS. 29) **2** 606
    Beaufort-Beauchamp Hours (London, BL, Royal MS. 2. A. XVIII) **13** 153; **20** 624; **28** 66, *66*
    Bedford Hours (London, BL, Add. MS. 18850) **2** 223; **4** 372; **12** 107; **18** 685; **20** 624, 625, *625*, 626; **28** 66
    Belles Heures (New York, Cloisters) **2** 113; **6** 174; **16** 838; **19** 388, 389–90, 391–2, *392*; **20** 755; **31** 837
    Birago Hours (Abbey Collection, MS. J.A. 6960) **20** 631
    Black Hours (Vienna, Österreich. Nbib., MS. 1856) **7** 246
    Book of Hours of King Het'um II (Erevan, Matenadaran Inst. Anc. Armen. MSS, MS. 979) **10** 450
    Borromeo Hours (Milan, Bib. Ambrosiana) **25** 465
    Boucicaut Hours (Paris, Mus. Jacquemart-André, MS. 2) **4** 370, 810; **13** *154*; **14** 423; **18** 704; **20** IV; **24** 492; **32** 572
    Bourbon-Vendôme Hours (Paris, Bib. Arsenal, MS. 417) **4** 569
    Brussels Hours *see* Très Belles Heures
    Coëtivy Hours (Dublin, Chester Beatty Lib., W. MS. 82) **20** 625, 626
    Crohin-de la Fontaine Hours (Malibu, CA, Getty Mus., MS. 23) **20** 659
    Dunois Hours (London, BL, MS. Yates Thompson 3) **10** 713; **20** 625
    Eales Hours (U. Reading Lib., MS. 2067) **20** 735
    Farnese Hours (New York, Pierpont Morgan Lib., MS. M. 69) **7** 468; **8** 178; **21** 640
    Giac Hours (Toronto, Royal Ont. Mus., Lee of Fareham Col.) **20** 756
    Golf Book (London, BL, Add. MS. 24098) **3** 727
Books of Hours
  individual manuscripts—cont.
    Grandes Heures (Paris, Bib. N., MS. lat. 919) **3** 642; **13** 154; **16** *852*; **20** 625, 751; **31** 837
    Grandes Heures de Rohan *see* Rohan Hours
    Grandes Heures of Anne of Brittany (Paris, Bib. N., MS. lat. 9474) **4** 570–71, *571*; **25** 405
    Grandes Heures of Philip the Bold, Duke of Burgundy (Brussels, Bib. Royale Albert 1er, MSS 10392 & 11035-7; Cambridge, Fitzwilliam, MS. 3-1954 **5** 208; **17** 454; **20** 631, 652
    Hague Hours (The Hague, Kon. Bib., MS. A A 178, Th. 87) **18** 662
    Hastings Hours (Madrid, Mus. Lázaro Galdiano, inv. 15503) **20** 727
    Heineman Hours (New York, Pierpont Morgan Lib., MS. H. 8) **25** 405, *405*
    Hennessy Hours (Brussels, Bib. Royale Albert 1er, MS. II, 158) **3** 727
    Homoet Hours (Cologne, Wallraf-Richartz-Mus., 1961/32) **20** 758
    Hours of Alfonso, Duca di Calabria (London, V&A, MS. 2397) **10** 868
    Hours of Alfonso I d'Este (Zagreb, Yug. Acad. Sci. & A.) **20** 844
    Hours of Anne, Duchess of Bourbon (New York, Pierpont Morgan Lib., MS. 677) **4** 547
    Hours of Anne of Brittany *see* Grandes Heures of Anne of Brittany
    Hours of Ascanio Sforza (Oxford, Bodleian Lib., MS. Douce 14) **20** 618
    Hours of Blanche of Savoy (Munich, Bayerstaatsbib., Clm. 23215) **12** 710
    Hours of Bonaparte Ghislieri (London, BL, Yates Thompson MS. 29) **20** 844
    Hours of Bona Sforza (London, BL, Add. MSS 34294, 45722 & 62997) **4** 76; **13** 905; **14** 759, *760*
    Hours of the Burggraf Willem van Montfort *see under* BOOKS OF HOURS → individual manuscripts → Montfort Hours
    Hours of Catherine of Cleves (New York, Pierpont Morgan Lib., MSS M. 917 & 945) **5** 443, *443*; **20** 616, 642–5, *643*, *644*, 667; **22** 835
    Hours of Charles de France (Paris, Bib. Mazarine, MS. 473; New York, Cloisters, 58.71 a-b) **11** 355; **20** 646, *646*; **31** 844
    Hours of Charles the Noble (Cleveland, OH, Mus. A., MS. 64.40) **20** 637
    Hours of Edward I of Portugal (Lisbon, Arquiv. N., MS. 140) **2** 871, 873; **20** 682
    Hours of Elizabeth the Queen (London, BL, Add. MS. 50001) **24** 478
    Hours of Engelbert of Nassau (Oxford, Bodleian Lib., MSS Douce 219-220) **11** 224; **20** 724, *725*, 726, 727; **29** 663
Books of Hours
  individual manuscripts—cont.
    Hours of Etienne Chevalier (Chantilly, Mus. Condé; London, BL; New York, Met.; Paris, Bib. N.; Mus. Marmottan; Upton House, Warwicks) **6** *463*, 562; **11** *353*, 353–4; **23** 523
    Hours of Folpard van Amerongen (Malibu, CA, Getty Mus., MS., Ludwig, IX 7) **31** 449
    Hours of Francesco Maria Sforza (London, BL, Add. MS. 63493) **4** 76
    Hours of Frederick III of Aragon (Paris, Bib. N., MS. lat. 10532) **4** 570
    Hours of Gijsbrecht van Brederode (U. Liège, Bib. Gén., MS. Wittert 13) **22** 836
    Hours of Henry VII **4** 569–70
    Hours of Isabella di Chiaromonte (Cambridge, MA, Harvard U., Houghton Lib., MS. Typ. 463) **10** 868
    Hours of Isabella Stuart, Duchess of Brittany (Cambridge, Fitzwilliam, MS. 62) **2** 113; **14** 423; **20** 756
    Hours of Isabella the Catholic (Madrid, Bib. Pal.) **20** 682; **32** 728
    Hours of Jacques de Langeac (Lyon, Bib. Mun., MS. 5154) **11** 726
    Hours of Jacques d'Estouteville (Turin, Bib. Reale, MS. Var. 88) **20** 757
    Hours of James IV and Margaret Tudor (Vienna, Österreich. Nbib., Cod. 1897) **20** 699–700, *700*; **28** 234, 268; **29** 798
    Hours of Jeanne de Savoie (Paris, Mus. Jacquemart-André, MS. 1) **25** 692, 694
    Hours of Jeanne d'Evreux (New York, Cloisters, MS. 54.1.2) **4** 370, 394; **5** 667; **11** 531; **13** 148, *148*, 673, *674*; **20** 742; **25** 692, 693, *693*; **31** 835
    Hours of Jean Robertet (New York, Pierpont Morgan Lib., MS. M. 834) **7** 596
    Hours of Joanna of Navarre (Paris, Bib. N., MS. nouv. acq. lat. 3145) **13** 149; **17** 463; **25** 694
    Hours of John the Fearless (Paris, Bib. N., MS. nouv. acq. lat. 3005) **20** 687
    Hours of Kaetzaert van Zaer (Leiden, Bib. Rijkskuniv., MS. B.P.L. 224) **20** 644
    Hours of Katharina von Lokhorst (Münster, Westfäl. Landesmus., MS. 530) **20** 644
    Hours of King Manuel (Lisbon, Mus. N. A. Ant.) **14** 658, 659
    Hours of Laudomia Medici (London, BL, Yates Thompson MS. 30) **2** 697
    Hours of Lorenzo the Magnificent and Clarice Orsini (Holkham Hall, Norfolk Lib., MS. 41) **11** 686
    Hours of Louis de Laval (Paris, Bib. N., MS. lat. 920) **4** 395, 547; **7** 597, *598*; **22** 30; **33** 28
    Hours of Maréchal de Boucicaut *see* Boucicaut Hours
    Hours of Margaret, Duchess of Clarence (sold London, Sotheby's, 19 June 1989, lot 3018) **4** *372*, 372
Books of Hours
  individual manuscripts—cont.
    Hours of Margaret of Cleves (Lisbon, Mus. Calouste Gulbenkian, MS. LA148) **22** *833*, 834, 835
    Hours of Marguerite of Foix (London, V&A, MS. Salting 1222) **4** 828
    Hours of Marguerite of Rohan (Princeton U., NJ., Lib., Garrett MS. 55) **20** 647
    Hours of Maria of Navarre (Venice, Bib. N. Marciana, MS. Lat. I, 104) **3** 339
    Hours of Mary of Burgundy (Vienna, Österreich. Nbib., Cod. 1857) **19** 350, *350*; **20** 723, 724, *724*, 726; **24** 605; **32** 729
    Hours of Mary Stuart (Paris, Bib. N., MS. lat. 1405) **20** 612
    Hours of Mary van Vronenstein (Brussels, Bib. Royale Albert 1er, MS. II. 7619) **20** 663; **22** 836
    Hours of Philippe de Commyne **11** 399
    Hours of Philippe of Cleves (Brussels, Bib. Royale Albert 1er, Ms. IV.40) **14** 618
    Hours of René II of Lorraine (Lisbon, Gulbenkian Mus., MS. L.A. 147) **11** 726
    Hours of René of Anjou (Paris, Bib. N., MS. lat. 1156A) **2** 113; **20** 756
    Hours of Saluces (London, BL, Add. MS. 27697) **20** 775
    Hours of Sophia von Bylant *see* Homoet Hours
    Hours of Thiebaut de Luxembourg (Brussels, Bib. Royale Albert 1er, MS. 9785) **1** 782
    Hours of Yolande de Soissons (New York, Pierpont Morgan Lib., MS. M. 72) **1** 782
    Hours of Yolande of Flanders (London, BL, Yates Thompson MS. 27) **17** 462; **25** 694
    Huth Hours (London, BL, Add. MS. 38126) **20** 452, 659
    Lamoignon Hours (Lisbon, Mus. Gulbenkian, MS. 237) **20** 625, 626
    La Rochefoucauld Hours (Brussels, Bib. Royale Albert 1er, MS. 15077) **30** 529
    Llanbeblig Hours (Aberystwyth, N. Lib. Wales) **32** 784
    Llangatock Hours (Malibu, CA, Getty Mus. Ludwig IX, 7) **20** 682
    Louthe Hours (Leuven, U. Catholique, Archv. MS. A. 2) **20** 659
    Milan Hours *see* Turin-Milan Hours
    Montfort Hours (Vienna, Österreich. Nbib., Cod. s.n. 12878) **20** 644, 682; **32** 728
    Murthly Hours (Edinburgh, N. Lib.) **28** 233
    Neville Hours (Berkeley Castle, Glos.) **28** 66
    Nuremberg Hours (Nuremberg, Stadtbib., MS. Solger 4 **13** 142
    Paris Rothschild Hours (Paris, Bib. N., MS. Rothschild 2534) **20** 735
    Petites Heures of Anne of Brittany (Paris, Bib. N., MS. nouv. acq. lat. 3027) **20** 744; **31** 846

Books of Hours
individual manuscripts—cont.
Petites Heures of Jean, Duc de Berry (Paris, Bib. N., MS. lat. 18014) 3 642; 13 154; 16 852; 17 *462*, 462, 463; 19 390; 20 751; 31 837
Pierpont Morgan Book of Hours (New York, Pierpont Morgan Lib., MS. M. 358) 20 708; 25 795
Rohan Hours (Paris, Bib. N., MS. lat. 9471) 2 113, 648; 4 11; 20 755–6*, *756*
Savoy Hours (New Haven, CT, Yale U., Beinecke Lib., MS. 390) 13 154; 28 1
Sforza Hours (London, BL, Add. MS. 34294) 20 700
Soane Hours (London, Soane Mus., MS. 4) 4 395, *396*
Sobieski Hours (Windsor Castle, Royal Lib.) 4 395; 20 625, 626, 735
Solger Hours (Nuremberg, Stadtbib., MS. Solger) 13 129
Spinola Hours (Malibu, CA, Getty Mus., MS. 83) 5 428, *429*; 14 760; 20 659, 700
Stuart de Rothesay Hours (London, BL, Add. MS. 20927) 7 467
Talbot Hours (Edinburgh, N. Lib.) 28 233, 268
Tilliot Hours (London, BL, Yates Thompson MS. 5) 25 405
Très Belles Heures (Brussels, Bib. Royale Albert 1er, MSS 11060-1) 4 395; 7 525; 13 154; 16 852; 19 390; 20 637; 31 837
Très Belles Heures de Notre-Dame (Paris, Bib. N., MS. nouv. acq. lat. 3093; Paris, Louvre, R.F. 2022-4) 8 469; 13 154; 17 461; 19 390; 20 742, 751; 31 837
Très Petites Heures (Paris, Bib. N. MS. nouv. acq. lat. 3120) 20 778; 31 846
Très Riches Heures (Chantilly, Mus. Condé, MS. 65) 9 453; 13 155; 19 392; 31 50, 308–10*
Adoration of the Magi 11 *530*
architectural paintings 2 339; 11 340; 12 175; 21 549; 29 414
assistants 20 635, 636
Aumale, Henri-Eugène-Philippe-Louis de Bourbon, Duc d' 23 523
Berry, Jean I de Valois, Duc de 31 837–9, *838*
borders (manuscript) 4 371, 395; 11 531
calendar 2 649; 5 428; 9 29; 13 155; 19 393, *394*
Charles I, 5th Duke of Savoy (*reg* 1482-90) 28 1
Château de Mehun-de-Yèvre 21 *549*
Château de Poitiers 25 83
Château de Saumur 2 111; 6 63
Colombe, Jean 7 597; 19 392
drawings 9 221
genre 3 596; 9 13; 12 287; 30 218, 313
hunting scenes 29 423
landscape paintings 6 58; 18 704; 31 154
Limbourg, de (family) 19 388, 390, 391
Margaret of Austria, Duchess of Parma and Regent of the Netherlands (1522-86) 13 905
Meeting of the Magi 19 *394*
Books of Hours
individual manuscripts
Très Riches Heures (Chantilly, Mus. Condé, MS. 65)—cont.
miniatures (manuscript illumination) 10 475; 19 391
Mont-Saint-Michel Abbey 22 41
Palais de la Cité 14 74
The Funeral of Raymond Diocrès 31 *309*
Turin-Milan Hours (Turin, Mus. Civ. A. Ant., MS. 47) 3 323, 555; 9 221, *269*, 453; 10 705, 712; 20 667; 21 *637*; 22 835; 23 671; 28 1; 31 448–9*, *449*
Vienna Hours (Vienna, Österreich. Nbib. Cod. 1855) 20 625, 626
Vienna Hours of Charles the Bold *see* Hours of Mary of Burgundy
Vienna Rothschild Hours (Vienna, Österreich. Nbib., Cod. s. n. 2844) 14 760; 20 737
Visconti Hours (Florence, Bib. N. Cent., MSS Banco Rari 397 and Landau Finlay 22) 3 531, *532*; 4 395; 13 149, 318; 32 611, 612
Voustre Demeure Hours (Madrid, Bib. N., MSS Vit. 25-5) 4 371; 20 659, 725, *725*, 726, *726*
Wharncliffe Hours (Melbourne, N. G. Victoria, MS. Felton 1; London, BL, Egerton MS. 2045; New York, Pierpont Morgan Lib., MS. M. 73) 11 726
Books of the Dead 10 3, 7
bookstands 17 301
Boom, M. 30 871
boomerangs 1 54; 10 40
booms 7 765, 766, 767
Boom style 4 373–4*; 21 75
Boon, Abraham *see* JANSSEN, ABRAHAM
Boon, Adrian 8 861; 33 358
Boonen, Arnold 4 374*
pupils 8 887; 20 850; 25 649, 822; 31 365
Boonzaaijer, Karel 22 877; 31 576
Boonzaier, Grégoire 29 108
Boorluut, Elisabeth 12 521
Boorne, W(illiam) Hanson 4 374*
Boorne and May 4 374
Boos, (Georg Christian) Carl 4 374–5*
Boos, Franz 32 461
Boos, Roman Anton 4 375–6*; 9 690; 22 302
assistants 28 186
collaboration 10 860
works 4 *376*
Booth 5 759
Booth, Enoch 10 306; 29 495
Booth, George (*fl* 1920s) 27 474
Booth, George, 2nd Earl of Warrington (1675-1758) 2 304; 26 558
Booth, Jessica 2 767
Booth, Peter 4 376*
Booth, T. Dwight 25 892
Booth, Wayne 1 174
Boothby Pagnell (Lincs) 14 75; 28 301; 29 22
Booth *Virgin and Child* 3 666
boots 6 251; 7 75, 76; 21 878; 32 491
Boots, Jan 9 745; 13 889
Boott, Elizabeth 9 468
Bopp, Sebald 4 376–7*
Boppard Altarpiece 12 626
Boppard am Rhein
Carmelite monastery 29 503
stained glass 29 III
St Severus 26 686; 27 125
Boqueirão do Sitio da Pedra Furada 29 195
Boquet, Josep 29 319
Boquet, Louis René 30 672
Boqueteaux, Master of the 20 631–2*, 652
patrons and collectors 5 208; 31 834, 835
works 4 525; 13 154, 826, 827
Bor (Czech Republic) *see* NOVÝ BOR
Bor (Turkey) 24 690
Bor, Paulus 4 377–8*
groups and movements 28 92; 31 772
works 4 *377*
Bor, Walter 19 519
Bora Bora 28 921
Borana 1 306; 17 906
Borassà, Francesc 4 423
Borassà, Guillem 4 423
Borassà, Lluís 3 218; 4 423–4*; 29 276
works 4 *423*
borax 4 684; 6 326; 12 866; 21 325; 29 498
Borbetomagus *see under* WORMS
Borbiró, Virgil 4 378*; 14 890
Borbjerg Church 1 518
Borbolla, Daniel Rubín de la *see* RUBÍN DE LA BORBOLLA, DANIEL
Bórbon *see* BOURBON II. (House of)
Borbón, Jorge 8 17
Borbón y Braganza, Sebastián Gabriel 4 378–9*; 12 925; 29 354
Borby 11 253
Borch, Anna ter 4 379
Borch, Frans van der 3 494
Borch, Gerard ter (i) (1582/3-1662) 4 379–80*
pupils 4 380
works 1 659; 4 *380*; 22 845
Borch, Gerard ter (ii) (1617-81) 4 379, 380–82*; 22 843
attributions 13 262
copies 4 657
forgeries by others 21 39
patrons and collectors
Beit, Otto (John) 3 522
Bisschop, Jan and Pieter 4 95
Boilly, Louis-Léopold 4 241
Boymans, F(rans) J(acob) O(tto) 4 614
Choiseul, Etienne-François, Duc de 7 194
Cosimo III, Grand Duke of Tuscany (*reg* 1670-1723) 21 29
Demidov, Anatoly, Prince 8 705
Frick, Henry Clay 11 774
La Caze, Louis 18 588
Marquand, Henry G(urdon) 20 461
Peel, Robert (1788-1850) 24 322
Peñeranda, Conde de 4 619
Ryerson, Martin A(ntoine) 27 463
Seymour-Conway, Richard, 4th Marquess of Hertford 28 527
Sparre, Gustaf Adolf 29 366
Steengracht van Oostkapelle, Johan 29 592
William V, Stadholder of the Netherlands, Prince of Orange (*reg* 1751-95) 23 469
pupils 2 124; 22 915
reproductive prints by others 8 481; 30 47
teachers 21 827
works 4 *381*, *382*; 7 784; 9 279; 11 444, 446; 12 290, 292; 13 255
Borch, Gesina ter 1 663; 4 379; 29 535
Borch, Harmen ter 4 379
Borch, Moses ter 4 379, 384*
Borchardt, Ludwig 1 755; 9 791; 10 78, 80, 84, 93; 30 794
Borchmans, Jan 22 856
Borcht, Hendrik van der 10 658; 21 711
Borcht, Joseph van der 3 600
Borcht, Pieter van der 1 686; 3 558; 4 384*; 19 64
reproductive prints by others 5 61
Borcht, Sebastian van der 28 294, 518
Borda, Arturo 4 262, 384*
patrons and collectors 4 267
works 4 262, *263*
Borda, José de la 9 418
Bordalo Pinheiro, Columbano 4 385–8*; 25 299
collaboration 27 141
groups and movements 25 299
sponsors 4 638
works 4 *386*, *387*; 25 299
Bordalo Pinheiro, Manuel Gustavo 4 385; 5 421
Bordalo Pinheiro, Manuel Maria 4 385
Bordalo Pinheiro, Rafael 4 385–6*; 5 421; 30 882
collaboration 27 141
groups and movements 4 386
works 25 299
Bordeau, Michel de 6 433
Bordeaux 4 388–92*, *388*, *390*; 9 596; 11 *505*; 26 *905*, *908*; 31 714
Académie des Arts 4 391; 11 705
Bourse 11 705
Burdigala 4 388
Cathedral of St André 4 392*; 13 42, 43
Royal Portal 4 392
sculpture 13 76
Ecole des Beaux-Arts 4 391
Ecole de Dessin 11 669
exchange 10 668
faience (ii) (ceramics) 4 391–2*
glass 11 612
Grand Théâtre 11 518; 19 725–6, *726*; 30 670, 674, 677
heraldry 14 413
Musée d'Aquitaine 4 389; 11 674
Musée des Arts Décoratifs 4 556
Musée des Beaux-Arts 11 665, 666; 22 357
Musée de Bordeaux 4 391
St Seurin 4 392*; 13 75; 30 779
university *see* Musée d'Aquitaine
Bordeaux Pilgrim 13 808
Borden, John 1 158
Border Limner *see* PHILLIPS, AMMI
borders (manuscript) 4 393–7*; 9 219; 15 848; 20 338–9
Anglo-Saxon 20 338
Belgium 4 *396*
Byzantine 20 338
England 4 *393*, 394, 395; 14 *424*
France 4 394, *394*, 395
Gothic 4 *393*, *394*; 14 *424*; 20 338–9
Italy 4 395
Netherlands, the 4 395
Ottonian 20 338
see also DROLLERIES
Borders Decorated with Fathers of the Church, Master of the 21 338
works 21 *339*
Bordesley (Hereford & Worcs) 7 353; 10 349
Bordet, Gaston 11 526
Bordiau, Gédéon 5 42; 6 415
Bordier, Etienne 28 4
Bordier, Jacqueline 9 176
Bordier, Jacques (1616-84) 6 508; 9 371; 19 262, 264; 21 641; 24 553
Bordji-i Kafariha *see* TEPE KALAN
Bordon, Benedetto 2 186; 4 397*
works 4 *397*; 32 198, 199
Bordone, Paris 2 716; 4 398–401*; 16 665; 31 316
patrons and collectors 4 427; 5 407; 9 112; 16 867; 28 4, 272
pupils 31 6
works 3 470; 4 *399*, *400*; 21 525; 23 877; 29 787; 31 316; 32 226
Bordoni, Francesco di Bartolomeo 4 401–2*; 11 503
Bordoni, Pierre 4 402
Borduas, Paul-Emile 4 402*
groups and movements 2 839; 5 568; 22 39; 26 76, 77, 414
works 5 568; 22 *38*
Boreads Painter 13 512; 32 36*, 66
Boreas-Florence group 13 523
Boreas Painter 13 523
Boreel, Jan 12 132
Borel, Antoine 13 871
Borel, Petrus 12 609
Borella, Carlo 32 410
Borella, Gotami Vihara 29 468
Borelli group 13 530
Borély, Louis 7 416
Borély, Musée *see under* MARSEILLE
Boreman, Zachariah 8 776
Borenius, (Carl) Tancred 4 402–3*; 29 88
Bores, Francisco 4 403*; 29 286
Boretsky, Andrey 25 170
Boretti 22 488
Borg, Elsi 2 317
Borg, Georg 4 403*; 20 214
Borgatti, Jean M.
works 1 *268*, *270*, *335*
Borges, Jacobo 4 403*; 32 175
Borges, Jorge Luis 2 400
Borges, Leonor Augusta da Rocha *see* ROCHA BORGES, LEONOR AUGUSTA DA
Borges, Max 8 232
Borges, Pedro Alexandrino 4 726; 30 348
Borgestuen 23 231
Borget, Auguste 14 721; 19 866
Borgherini (family) 3 16; 16 711, 766
Borgherini, Giovanni 4 404
Borgherini, Pierfrancesco 4 403–4*
furniture 16 766
interior decoration 3 15
paintings 3 13, 14; 13 281; 23 855; 25 222; 28 333, 334
Borgherini, Salvi di Francesco 4 404
Borghese (family)
architecture 26 748; 32 9
collections 16 764, 774; 27 114, 115
drawings 19 205
frescoes 26 196
interior decoration 29 79
paintings 7 916; 10 530; 13 655, 656; 19 205
sculpture 1 631; 2 168; 3 852; 4 407
Borghese, Camillo, Prince of Sulmona (1775-1832) 4 404, 406, 407; 16 768
Borghese, Francesco 4 407
Borghese, Giovanni 5 842; 25 736
Borghese, Giovanni Battista, Prince 9 377
Borghese, Giovanni Ventura 7 910
Borghese, Ippolito 11 114
Borghese, Marcantonio, Prince of Sulmona *see* SULMONA, MARCANTONIO BORGHESE, Prince of
Borghese, Marcantonio IV, Prince 4 404, 407*
architecture 2 612
frescoes 27 201
interior decoration 26 780
paintings 6 98; 7 684; 13 797; 14 109; 18 781; 30 865; 31 679
sculpture 9 23

Borghese, Michele *see* CIAMPANTI, MICHELE
Borghese, Paolo 20 904
Borghese, Pauline Bonaparte, Princess *see* BONAPARTE, PAULINE, Princess Borghese
Borghese, Scipione, Cardinal 4 404, 405–7*, *406*
architecture 7 312; 11 741; 29 80; 32 9
collections 3 744; 26 773
decorative works 30 355; 32 771
drawings 19 205
gardens 11 270
paintings 2 493; 3 744; 5 715; 10 525; 18 730
altarpieces 31 436
frescoes 4 813; 18 733; 24 239
mythological 1 535, 596; 9 89
religious 3 8; 5 711; 9 88
parks 12 117; 24 179
sculpture 3 829, 830; 4 407; 7 842; 11 895; 26 847; 27 46; 29 562
sponsorship 13 223
Borghese Altar 4 406; 32 771, *772*
Borghese *Ares* 13 454; 25 178
Borghese Gladiator 2 169; 4 406, 407–8*; 11 895; 13 466
Borghese *Hera* 25 179
Borghese *Hermaphrodite* 2 169; 3 830; 4 406, 407
Borghese *Hero* 23 441
Borghese Vase 2 169; 4 406
Borghese Warrior *see* BORGHESE GLADIATOR
Borghetti, Ranieri 26 396
Borghi, Achille 13 764
Borghi, Bartolommeo 32 353
paintings 32 *353*
Borghini, Inocencio 31 750
Borghini, Raffaele 4 408*
works 4 492; 16 614, 781; 24 91; 25 262
Borghini, Vincenzo (Maria) 1 102, 662; 4 408–9*; 9 14; 15 84
academies 11 216
collaboration 32 14, 16
methods 15 87
patrons and collectors 21 21; 25 77
personal collection 25 378
works 21 22; 23 769; 24 90
Borgholm Castle 30 *65*, 66, 68, 69
Borght, Jacob van der 5 50; 30 324
Borght, Jaspar van der 5 50
Borght, van der (family) 3 579, 587; 30 324
Borgia (family) 27 46
Borgia, Alfonso *see* CALIXTUS III, Pope
Borgia, Cesare, Duca di Valentino 4 409, 410–11*
architecture 19 183, 194; 21 578
leather 19 4
sculpture 10 521
weapons 2 453; 20 800
Borgia, Giovanni Battista, Prince of Squillace *see* SQUILLACE, GIOVANNI BATTISTA BORGIA, Prince of
Borgia, Lucrezia, Duchess of Ferrara *see* LUCREZIA BORGIA, Duchess of Ferrara
Borgia, Maria Enríquez *see* ENRÍQUEZ BORGIA, MARIA
Borgia, Rodrigo, Cardinal *see* ALEXANDER VI, Pope
Borgia, Stefano, Cardinal 4 409, 411–12*
Borgia Altar 4 410, 737
Borgia Group 21 233, 234–5, *234*, 737
Borgianni, Orazio 4 412–13*; 16 670; 29 280
attributions 5 693
groups and movements 30 456
patrons and collectors 5 427; 31 340
Borgianni, Orazio—cont.
works 4 *413*
Borgiotti, Mario 28 319
Borglum, Gutzon 15 47; 22 49; 23 175
Borglum, Solon 20 299
Børglum Cathedral 8 722
Borgnes, G. A. 10 488
Borgnis, Giovanni 4 413; 8 533
Borgnis, Giuseppe Mattia 4 413*
patrons and collectors 8 533; 10 278
pupils 17 682
Borgnis, Pietro Maria 4 413; 10 643
works 10 *643*
Borgo, Cristofano dal *see* GHERARDI, CRISTOFANO
Borgo, Francesco del *see* FRANCESCO DEL BORGO
Borgo, Giovan Paolo dal 28 730
Borgo, Lorenzo dal 1 673
Borgo, Luca di *see* PACIOLI, LUCA
Borgognio, Tommaso 28 10
Borgognone, Francesco *see* SIMONOT, FRANCESCO
Borgognoni, Annibale 10 524; 11 279
Borgoña, Felipe de *see* VIGARNY, FELIPE
Borgoña, Juan de (*fl* 1495–*d c.* 1535) 3 218; 4 414*; 29 277
altarpieces 1 710; 2 865; 3 845; 7 345; 11 484
carvings 3 221
collaboration 11 483
frescoes 7 345
metalwork 29 333
paintings 31 89
patrons and collectors 11 250
pupils 7 883
Borgoña, Juan de, II (*fl* 1533–*d* 1565) 4 414; 29 277
Borgoñón, Juan de Castro el *see* JUAN DE CASTRO EL BORGOÑÓN
Borgo Pinti, Grand Ducal studio and foundry 11 234
Borgo San Sepolcro 3 359
Oratory of the Compagnia del SS Crocifisso 1 551
Palazzo del Comune 1 551
Palazzo Rigi 1 551
Residenza 24 763
S Francesco 11 382
altar 1 696, *696*
altarpiece 11 709; 27 862
Borgovico Villa 12 720
Borgström, Carl Fredrik 11 108
Borgu 21 597
Borgund 23 *218*
St Andrew 23 219; 29 *579*, 580, *580*
sculpture 23 228
Stave church *see* St Andrew
Borheck, Georg 23 340
Bori 12 328, 330
Bori, Jenö 32 419
Boriani, Davide 13 728, 729
Borica, Mañuel Arana *see* ARANA BORICA, MAÑUEL
Borie, Charles 31 390
Boring, William A. 11 143
Borioni, Antonio 32 237
Boris I Michael, King of Bulgeria (*reg* 852–89) 25 559
Boris Godunov, Tsar of Russia (*reg* 1598–1605) 27 438; 30 784
Borisov *see* BARYSAŬ
Borisov, Leonid 27 581
Borisov-Musatov, Viktor (Yel'pidiforovich) 4 414–15*; 27 391
groups and movements 4 178; 27 392; 31 582; 33 379
patrons and collectors 27 458
Bořivoj I, Duke of Bohemia (*reg* 873–95) 25 437, 552
Borja, A. Jiménez *see* JIMÉNEZ BORJA, A.
Borja, Cardinal 25 *645*
Borja y Aragon, Francisco 4 409
Borje, Gideon 30 81
Börjesson, John 30 86
Borjomi 12 *317*, 320
Borka
sculpture 14 892, *892*
Borland, Kevin 2 742; 4 415*; 16 819; 20 8
Borland, Murphy & McIntyre 20 8
Borluut, Elisabeth 10 704
Borman (family) 4 417
Borman, Jan, I (*d* before 1498) 4 415
Borman, Jan, II (*fl c.* 1479–1520) 4 415; 30 732
altarpieces 3 569; 4 415–17, *416*; 5 43; 11 439; 13 112
assistants 4 417
collaboration 13 160
models 30 732
sculpture 13 112
Borman, Jan, III (*fl c.* 1499–1522) 4 417; 13 112
Borman, Passchier 4 415, 417; 7 712; 13 112; 30 732
Bormio 11 151
Born, Arnold von *see* ARNOLD VON BORN
Bornebusch, Gehrdt 4 417–18*; 18 799
Bornemann, Gerburg 4 418
Bornemann, Hans 4 418*; 11 843
Bornemann, Henrik 4 418*; 12 384
Bornemisza, Géza 13 638
Borneo
beadwork 3 *441*
caves 29 226
coats 3 440, *441*
interlace 15 882
sarcophagi 27 831
trade 6 622
Borneo, British North *see* SABAH
Börner, Emil Paul 21 67
Bornholm
church 8 722; 26 593
Hammershus 8 724
kaolin 7 806
Østerlars 7 257; 26 593
plaques 32 523
Borno, Maurice 14 58; 21 894
Bornschlegel, Johann Philipp 2 580
Bornu 1 305, *394*
Borobudur 4 *419*, 419–20*, *420*; 5 100; 15 *753*, 754, 758, 759–60, 778; 28 639; 29 237, 865, *866*; 30 446
reliefs 15 810, 816, 817; 23 556, 823; 30 785
sculpture 15 777, 779, 780
temple 15 757
Böröcz, András 10 447
Boroday, Vasily Z. 31 561; 33 518
Borody, V. Z. 18 38
Borofsky, Jonathan 4 420–21*; 30 153
Boroko 24 *64*
Papua New Guinea National Museum and Art Gallery 23 736; 24 65
Parliament Building 23 736, *736*
Borom Ratchathirat II, King of Ayutthaya (*reg* 1424–48) 2 885, 886
Borom Trailokanat, King of Ayutthaya (*reg* 1448–88) 2 886, 887; 30 588, 605
Boronat, José Camarón y *see* CAMARÓN Y BORONAT, JOSÉ
Bororo (Africa) 1 263; 11 827
Bororo (Brazil) 4 707, *707*
Borostyánkő *see* BERNSTEIN
Börö style 20 835
Boroszló 13 162
Boroughbridge (N. Yorks) 31 709
Boroughbridge Roll (London, BL, MS. Egerton 2850) 12 272
Borough Marsh 26 50
Borovany *Pietà* 8 383
Borovikovsky, Vladimir (Lukich) 4 421–2*; 27 388, 579; 31 559
patrons and collectors 31 312, 565
pupils 32 162
works 4 *421*
Borovitsky Hill 22 168
Borovo 13 569
Borovsky, David 27 397
Borowski, Elie 1 839, 896; 15 922; 16 571; 30 199
Borowski, Wacław 26 296
Borowski, Włodzimierz 4 422*
Borra, Giovanni Battista 4 422–3*
patrons and collectors 13 637; 29 736; 33 344
pupils 26 475
works 4 758
Borrani, Odoardo 16 678; 19 870, 871; 20 482; 28 705; 32 257
Borrassà (family) 2 142
Borrassà, Francesc, I 2 142
Borrassà, Lluís 13 150
patrons and collectors 2 276
works 3 221; 11 481; 30 664
Borre
grave 32 525
harness-mounts 32 *515*, 516
Borreby 8 724
manor house 4 781
Borrekens, Jean Baptist 4 917; 32 706
Borrekens, Mattheus 17 599; 22 717
Borrel, Alfred 4 424*
Borrel, Valentin Maurice 4 424*; 20 925
Borrello, Gennaro 11 136
Borreman *see* BORMAN
Borreman, Frans 13 909
Borremans, Guglielmo 23 843, 845
Borremans, Peter 13 277
Borrero Alvarez, Ricardo 7 609
Borre style *see under* VIKING → styles
Borromeo (family)
gardens 12 115
paintings 13 213; 16 710; 20 95
frescoes 21 463
Borromeo, Carlo II, Cardinal *see* CARLO BORROMEO, Saint
Borromeo, Carlo III, Count 16 562
Borromeo, Federico, Cardinal 4 424, 425–7*; 21 525, 532, 533; 26 770; 28 901
architecture 5 328; 19 313; 21 518; 26 317; 30 801, 803
art policies 1 103
books 6 381
collections 16 771
drawings 9 229
education (art) 16 779; 21 526
engravings 4 911
paintings 4 813, 913; 5 704; 12 720; 21 526; 27 227; 33 719
sacrimonti 27 498
sculpture 6 338
sponsorship 4 913, 915; 26 317
tapestries 20 323
writings 15 82
Borromeo, Francesco 25 465
Borromeo, Vitaliano (1451–95) 25 465
Borromeo, Vitaliano VI, Conte (1620–90) 4 424, 427*; 12 718; 16 562
Borromeo Hours *see under* BOOKS OF HOURS → individual manuscripts
Borromini, Francesco 2 377; 3 830, 838; 4 427–36*; 5 827; 16 637, 641
altars 7 912; 9 411
Borromini, Francesco—cont.
architecture 2 171
colonnades 20 521
ecclesiastical buildings 3 835; 7 276
Collegio di Propaganda Fide 4 434–5*; 23 493
Oratory of S Filippo Neri 4 *431*
S Agnese in Agone 7 *276*; 16 638, *638*; 25 861; 26 759
S Andrea delle Fratte 4 435*, 786
S Carlo alle Quattro Fontane 4 *429*, 429–31*, *430*, *431*; 6 23; 16 637
S Filippo Neri 4 431–2*; 20 521; 23 473, 492; 24 805; 29 251
S Giovanni in Laterano 4 432–3*; 24 861; 26 820; 27 346
S Ivo della Sapienza 4 432*, *432*; 9 84; 31 *674*
S Maria degli Angeli 29 251
S Maria dei Sette Dolori 13 292
libraries 19 314
palazzi 4 428*, 434*, *435*; 5 826; 23 836; 26 836; 29 250
screens (i) (architectural) 26 810
squares (town) 4 433–4*
villas 11 740
attributions 10 769; 11 741
collaboration 3 278, 830; 6 23; 13 321; 29 830
furniture 26 780
groups and movements 3 261, 262, 264, 267, 268
patrons and collectors
Alexander VII, Pope (*reg* 1655–67) 6 584; 16 763
Bufalo, Paolo del, Marchese 5 123
Clement XI, Pope (*reg* 1700–21) 21 889
Falconieri, Orazio 10 769
Falconieri, Paolo Francesco (1626–96) 10 769
Filomarino, Ascanio, Cardinal 11 81
Giustiniani (i), Orazio, Cardinal 20 495
Innocent X, Pope (*reg* 1644–55) 23 899; 26 821
Oratorians 23 473
Pamphili (family) 23 898
reproductive prints by others 20 495
restorations by others 29 251
teachers 20 43
writings 6 30; 20 495
Borroni, Giacomo 5 327
Borrowdale 13 315; 24 353
Borsa, Roger, Duke of Apulia *see* ROGER BORSA, Duke of Apulia
Borsato, Giuseppe 16 729
Borselaer, Pieter *see* BORSSELER, PIETER
Borselen, J. W. van 4 203
Borsetti, Bartolomeo 5 872
Borsieri, Girolamo 21 526
Borsippa 4 437*; 21 *267*
architecture 21 291
metalwork 21 304
ziggurat 33 675
Borsjö, Master of 20 632*
Borso, 1st Duke of Ferrara, Modena and Reggio (*reg* 1450–71) 10 517, *518*, 519–20*
architecture 11 2, 6; 27 189; 29 859
decorative works 31 429
heraldry 11 1
interior decoration 11 4; 16 711
jewellery 8 164
manuscripts 4 7, 18, *19*; 11 4; 12 665, *666*, 721
medals 29 386

Borso, 1st Duke of Ferrara, Modena and Reggio (*reg* 1450-71)—cont.
paintings **2** 42; **4** 332; **7** 925; **8** 173; **20** 308; **24** 16; **31** 429, 430
sculpture **3** 260
tapestries **11** 5; **31** 429
Borsook, Eve **13** 811
Borsos, József (i) (1821-83) **4** 438*; **14** 901
Borsos, József (ii) (1875-1952) **4** 438*
Borsos, Miklós **4** 438–9*; **14** 896; **30** 212
Borsseler, Pieter **4** 439*; **17** 599
Borssom, Anthonie van **4** 439–40*; **17** 920
works **4** *440*
Bort, Jaime **4** 440–41*; **29** 271
Bort, Vicente **4** 441
Borthagaray, Juan Manuel **2** 397; **31** 754
Borthwick **31** 230
Bortkevičius, L. **19** 497
Bortnyik, Sándor **4** 441*; **11** 299
collaboration **17** 833
groups and movements **1** 131; **14** 901; **20** 103, 104
Bortnyk, Alexander **32** 9
Bortoloni, Mattia **7** 861
Bortolotti, Timo **20** 522
Borujerd **16** 482
Borunda, Domingo **10** 532
Borutta, S Pietro di Sòrres **27** 836
Borzone, Carlo **4** 442
Borzone, Giovanni Battista **4** 442
Borzone, Luciano **4** 441–2*; **9** 174
patrons and collectors **4** 811
pupils **2** 619; **6** 581
Bos, A. W. **1** 804
Bos, Balthazar van den **4** 442*; **7** 499; **11** 222
Bos, Cornelis **3** 556, 597; **4** 442–3*; **10** 389; **22** 870
reproductive prints by others **29** 44
works **3** 576; **10** *477*; **14** 293; **17** 486; **23** 540; **25** 607; **29** 747, *748*
writings **3** 581
Bos, Hans **2** 199
Bos, Jacob(us) **4** 443*
Bos, Michel de **2** 198, 199
workshop **2** *198*
Bos, Paul de **33** 181
Bosa, Antonio **24** 496
Bōsai Kameda *see* KAMEDA BŌSAI
Bosanquet Painter **32** 48
Bosarte, Isidoro de **4** 443*
Bosarve Memorial Stone **32** 522
Bosboom, Johannes **4** 443–4*
groups and movements **14** 46
patrons and collectors **32** 708
teachers **14** 804; **23** 322
works **4** *444*; **22** 848, 849
Bosboom, Simon **1** 813; **13** 683
Bosc **5** 440
Bosc, Claude Du *see* DU BOSC, CLAUDE
Bosc, Ernest **10** 209
Boscaratti, Felice **8** 267
Bösch, August **30** 138
Bosch, Bernardus de **9** 298
Bosch, Cornelis (1510-66) *see* BOS, CORNELIS
Bosch, Cornelis van den (*fl* 1643) **7** 832
Bosch, Den *see* 'S HERTOGENBOSCH
Bosch, Esias **4** 444–5*; **25** 834; **29** 117
Bosch, Frederik David Kan **4** 445*; **29** 242
Bosch, Hieronymus **1** 654; **4** 445–53*; **25** 653; **28** 594
commentaries **31** 95
forgeries by others **11** 307
Bosch, Hieronymus—cont.
paintings **3** 554; **25** 650
allegorical **4** *446*, *450*, *451*; **27** 868
religious **4** *447*, *448*, *449*; **10** 713; **12** 287; **33** 87
patrons and collectors
Akademie der Bildenden Künste (Vienna) **2** 831
Beuningen, Daniel George van **3** 889
Coninxloo (i), Gillis van, III (1544-1607) **7** 711
Ferdinand II, King of Portugal (1816-89) **4** 638
Fernández de Velasco, Juan **10** 906
Figdor, Albert **11** 62
Grimani, Domenico, Cardinal, Patriarch of Aquilea **13** 657
Guevara, Felipe de **29** 352
Johnson, John G(raver) (1841-1917) **17** 619
Margaret of Austria, Duchess of Savoy and Regent of the Netherlands (1480-1530) **13** 905
Museu de Arte de São Paulo **4** 726
Nassau, Hendrik III, Count of **22** 535
Philip II, King of Spain (*reg* 1556-98) **10** 503; **13** 922; **29** 352
Philip of Burgundy, Bishop of Utrecht **5** 214; **22** 901
Pimentel, Francisco **3** 700
Rudolf II, Holy Roman Emperor (*reg* 1576- 1612) **30** 118
William the Silent, Stadholder of the Netherlands, Prince of Orange (*reg* 1572-84) **23** 464
reproductive prints by others **4** 442; **14** 505
Bosch, H. van den **2** 318
Bosch, Jacob van den **4** 73; **22** 867, 875, 895; **32** 779
Bosch, Jan de **6** 89
Bosch, Jeronimo de **26** 284
Bosch, Karl **15** 824
Bosch, Peter **29** 98
Bosch, Robert, Foundation **2** 369
Bosch, Theo **4** 454*; **10** 716
Bosche, Balthasar van den **5** 352
Bosche, Jacob van den **1** 810
Bosche, van den (family) **20** 915
Boscherati **24** 894
Boscherville, Abbey of St Martin **30** 907
St George **7** 454
Boschetto *see* BUSCHETTO
boschi **12** 114, 116, 119
Boschi (family) **3** 466
Boschi, Fabrizio **21** 25; **24** 801
Boschi, Valerio **3** 466
Boschini, Marco **4** 454–5*
dealing **21** 28
works **9** 7; **16** 767, 781; **19** 871; **24** 865; **30** 923; **31** 17; **32** 196, 355
Bosch Studio **29** 117
Bosco, Don **8** 23
Bosco, El *see* BOSCH, HIERONYMUS
Boscoli, Andrea **31** 55
Boscoli, Giovanni **22** 166
Boscoreale **26** *886*
bronzes **27** 87
gardens **12** 70
Villa no. 13 **26** 869
Villa of Publius Fannius Synistor **18** 701
megalographia **27** 54
wall paintings **13** 552; **26** 862, *862*; **27** 53, 58
wall paintings **15** 135; **27** 58
Boscoreale Treasure **27** 80, 81, 224
Boscotrecase, Villa of Agrippa Postumus **18** 702; **26** 861; **27** 54
Boscovich, Ruggero **21** 532
Boscry, Charles **4** 455; **19** 231
Boscry, Pierre **4** 455*; **24** 821
Bosdari, C. de **5** 661
Böse, Albert **9** 303
Bose, Atul **15** 657
Bose, Fanindranath **15** 657
Bose, Nandalal **4** 455–6*; **5** 420
collaboration **15** 657
patrons and collectors **15** 180
pupils **22** 267; **29** 891
works **15** *656*; **31** 794
Boselli, Clara **4** 456
Boselli, Ercole **2** 163
Boselli, Felice **4** 456*
Boselli, Giacomo **4** 456*; **16** 736, 739; **27** 893
Boselli, Orfeo **2** 163
Boselli, Pietro **26** 478
Bosello, Domenico **8** 101; **16** 738; **23** 263
Boseva, Lilyana **5** 158
Bosham (W. Sussex)
hall **14** 74
Holy Trinity Church **2** 67
Boshier, Derek **4** 456*; **19** 591; **25** 231
Bosin, Blackbear **22** 595
Bosio, Antonio **4** 457*
groups and movements **26** 742
works **4** 492; **15** 89; **19** 630; **26** 799, 848
illustrated **1** 551
Bosio, Astyanax-Scévola **4** 458
Bosio, François-Joseph **4** 457–8*
patrons and collectors **4** 301, 303
pupils **3** 313; **4** 765; **8** 510; **9** 447; **11** 234; **12** 228; **20** 454; **33** 154, 449
works **4** *458*; **11** 562, 563, 564; **19** 11
Bosio, Jean-Baptiste-François **4** 458
Bosio, Lanfranco **16** 737
Bosio, Pietro **25** 147; **29** 640
Boskam, Jan **20** 923
Boškov, Petar Hadji *see* HADJI BOŠKOV, PETAR
Boskovice Castle **8** 379, 384
Bosman, Richard **19** 430; **20** 609
works **20** *609*
Bosmans, Balthazar **2** 199
Bosmelet, Anne-Marie de, Duchesse de la Force *see* FORCE, ANNE-MARIE DE BOSMELET, Duchesse de la
Bosmont-sur-Serre Church **30** 907, 908
roof **30** *906*
Bosmun **24** 79
Boşnak Osman Efendi **27** 683
Bosnia **4** 458–63*, *459*; **16** *103*; **33** 571
architecture **4** 459–60*; **16** 228; **32** 293
collections **4** 462–3*
decorative arts **4** 462*
galleries (iv) (art) **4** 463
gravestones **4** 461, *461*
metalwork **4** 462
mosques **4** *460*
museums **4** 462–3*
painting **4** 460–62*
pins **13** 600
sculpture **4** 460–62*
silver **4** 462
stone-carvings **4** *461*
synagogues **17** 547; **27** *820*
textiles **4** 462
water supply **27** 819
Bosnia & Herzegovina *see* BOSNIA; HERZEGOVINA
Boso **33** 609
Boson, John **10** 294
El Bosque **21** 192
Bosquet, Alain **11** 728
bosquets **12** 105, 119, 121
Bosra **4** 463–4*; **9** *513*; **16** *104*; **26** *915*, 918; **30** *180*
congregational mosque **16** 148
al-Mabrak Madrasa **4** 464
madrasa of Kumushtakin **16** 180; **20** 56
museum **30** 178
SS Sergius, Bacchus and Leontius **9** 539, *540*
theatre **4** *463*, 464
trade **30** 179
Boss, Roman Anton **29** 761
Bossan, Pierre **4** 465–6*; **7** 304; **19** 847
Bossanyi, Ervin **5** 648; **33** 550
Bossard, Johann Karl **30** 147
Bosschaert, Abraham **4** 466, 467; **11** 226; **22** 839; **29** 666
Bosschaert, Ambrosius (i) (1573-1621) **2** 643; **4** 466–7*; **22** 843
pupils **2** 643, 644
works **4** 466, *467*; **11** 225–6, *226*; **15** 140; **22** 839; **29** 666; **31** 882
Bosschaert, Ambrosius (ii) (1609-45) **2** 643; **4** 466, 467*; **22** 839
works **11** 226; **29** 666
Bosschaert, Johannes **4** 466; **11** 226; **22** 839; **29** 666
Bosschaert, Thomas Willeboirts
collaboration **11** 872; **28** 364, 904; **31** 772; **32** 705, 706
painting **14** 46
works **2** 200; **28** *364*
Bossche, E. Vanden *see* VANDEN BOSSCHE, E.
Bossche, Gilles van den *see* GILLES VAN DEN BOSSCHE
Bossche, Jan van **11** 731
Bosscher, J. de **5** 61
Bossche school **28** 594
Bosse, Abraham **4** 467–9*; **10** 390; **19** 16; **25** 627; **31** 226
methods **9** 697; **24** 490
prints **11** 401, 535
engravings **8** 525; **9** 13, 14, 30, 388; **10** *780*; **11** 36, *573*, 587; **19** 255; **26** 452; **27** 562; **32** 510
etchings **4** *468*; **25** *612*, *613*
reproductions in tapestry **2** 703
reproductive prints by others **23** 191
writings **6** 570; **7** 714; **10** 551; **24** 493; **31** 300
on inks **25** 598
translated **10** 757
Bosse, Harald Julius **4** 469*
works **18** 851; **19** 563; **27** 578; **29** *771*
bossed brooches *see under* BROOCHES → types
Bosselt, Rudolf **4** 469*; **8** 531
Bossert, H. T. **17** 810
bosses **4** 464–5*; **32** 92
Bactria **6** *237*
Central Asia, Western **6** *237*
England **4** 465, *465*; **13** 83, *83*
France **4** 465
Germany **22** *693*
Gothic **13** 83, *83*; **22** *693*
Greece, ancient **13** 388, *388*
Romanesque **4** *465*
Bosset, de, Colonel **17** 909
Bosshardt, Johann Caspar **29** 600
Bosshardt & Cie **3** 824
Bossi (family) **6** 571; **12** 405
Bossi, Antonio **29** 838; **33** 432, 434
Bossi, Battista *see* BATTISTA BOSSI
Bossi, Benigno **4** 470*; **24** 553
Bossi, Domenico (*d*?1628) **4** 470*; **25** 426
Bossi, Domenico (1765-1853) **21** 644
Bossi, Erma **22** 921
Bossi, Giovanni Battista de **25** 426
Bossi, Giovanni Domenico **31** 362
Bossi, Giuseppe **2** 233; **4** 470–71*
patrons and collectors **6** 151
Bossi, Giuseppe—cont.
pupils **5** 444
works **19** 197; **21** 527
Bossi, Luigi **29** 73
Bossi, Materno **33** 672
Bossi, Pietro **16** 27
Bossi, Pietro Luigi **4** 470
Bossi, Santin Norbert de *see* BUSSI, SANTINO DE
Bosso, Renato Di *see* DI BOSSO, RENATO
Bossuet, François-Antoine **14** 116; **29** 781
Bossuet, Jacques-Bénigne **6** 91; **24** 707; **32** 501
Bossuit, Frans van **3** 604; **4** 471*; **22** 895; **26** 230
Bossut, Jean **19** 382
Boštík, Václav **2** 546; **8** 394
Bostock, Cecil **9** 397
Boston (Lincs; UK) **4** 692
St Botolph
tracery **31** *272*
tile-kiln **4** 779
Boston (MA; USA) **2** 325; **4** 471–83*; **31** *587*
Anthology Society **13** 606
Archaeological Institute of America **31** 356
Arnold Arboretum **17** 368
art forms and materials
ceramics **4** *482*, 482–3*
clocks **31** 624
copper **4** 481*
frames **11** 497, 498
furniture **2** 150; **31** 623, 624, 625, 626, 628, 629; **33** II2
glass **31** 642
interior decoration **31** 616
jewellery **31** 655
lacquer **18** 615
metalwork **4** 479–81*
pewter **4** 481*; **31** 651, 652
pottery **31** 634, 635
silver **4** 479–81*; **31** 616, 647, 648, 649
silver-gilt **4** *480*
wallpaper **32** 815
Arts Centre **30** 469
Athenaeum **4** 477; **13** 606; **31** 662, 666
Boston Art Club **25** 806
Boston Common **31** *612*
churches
Brattle Square Church **7** 668
King's Chapel **31** 590
New South Church **25** 266
Old South Church **31** 593
Trinity Church **7** 258, 668; **13** 204; **18** 627; **26** 338–9, *339*, 704; **31** 593
City Hall **13** 239; **31** 243
Eastern Exchange Hotel **14** 787
Emerald Necklace **23** 422, *422*
Exchange Coffee House **14** 786
Faneuil Hall **2** 324; **24** 209; **31** 653, *653*; **33** 8
Fenway Court *see* museums → Isabella Stewart Gardner Museum
Filene's **30** 507
First Town House **20** 438
Frederick L. Ames House **25** 806
furniture **4** 478–9*
Harrison Avenue **30** 458
interior decoration **31** 617
John Foster's House **4** 786
John Hancock Tower **12** 794; **28** 834
land use **10** 142
Massachusetts Historical Society **31** 666
Massachusetts State House **4** *473*; **31** 591
Metro stations **21** 349
museums
Columbia Museum **27** 882

Boston (MA; USA)
museums—cont.
Isabella Stewart Gardner Museum **2** 560; **8** 266; **12** 147; **29** 870; **31** 667, 668
collections **4** 477; **14** 807; **20** 679; **30** 332
courtyard **8** 65
sculpture **27** 46
Museum of Fine Arts (1870-79; destr.) **2** 560; **4** 474, 477; **22** 359; **24** 456; **25** 806; **29** 871; **30** 505; **31** 666, 670
ceramics **22** 148
collections **13** 606; **17** 431
Museum of Fine Arts (1906) **4** 475; **8** 111; **12** 101; **19** 733; **22** 365; **24** 326; **27** 840
Cesnola collection **13** 470; **26** 410; **27** 46
collections **5** 917; **6** 735, 826, 925; **7** 156; **10** 90, 94, 887; **12** 54, 266; **15** 742, 745; **16** 557; **17** 434, 436, 823; **18** 384; **28** 560; **29** 656; **30** 332
drawings **9** 231
Egyptian collection **10** 71
Etruscan collection **10** 640
exhibitions **10** 94; **15** 747; **16** 559; **27** 47
Greek collection **13** 470; **31** 356
Indian collection **7** 792
manuscripts **22** 795
paintings **15** 742
periodicals **24** 433
Ross Collection **7** 705
sculpture **22** 795
Old State House **5** 142; **29** 583
parks **31** 725
Proctor Building **30** 507
Public Library **4** *475*; **9** 84; **19** 318; **20** 17–18, *18*; **25** 750; **27** 840; **31** 594
murals **1** *22*, 23
Quincy Market **31** 591
Rowe's Wharf **9** 59
skyscrapers **28** 591
State House *see* Old State House
Suffolk County Court House **18** 887
Symphony Hall **1** 122; **7** 687
Tontine Crescent **4** 786; **31** 591
Tremont House **14** 786, *787*; **26** *537*
urban planning **31** 735
Boston, Florance George Henry Irby, Lord *see* IRBY, FLORANCE GEORGE HENRY, Lord Boston
Boston & Albany Railroad **26** 342
Boston Associates **31** 656
Boston Co-operative Building Company **30** 458
Boston Etching Club **25** 629
Boston Furniture Warehouse **28** 525
Boston Opera Company **31** 702
Boston Painter **13** 500
Boston Polyphemos Painter **22** 410
works **22** *410*
Boston & Sandwich Glass Co. **4** 483*; **13** 209; **22** 240; **24** 57; **31** 642
works **31** *643*
Boston Society of Arts and Crafts **2** 572
Boston Spa, Lending Division of the British Library **19** 320
Boston Terracotta Company **30** 505
Boston Throne **13** 451, 470; **19** 544
Bostra *see* BOSRA
Boswell, James **2** 553; **3** 700; **13** 303; **14** 109
Boswell, Jessie **31** 446
Boswell, Peyton, jr **26** 90
Boswell Psalter *see* PSALTERS → individual manuscripts → Kinloss Psalter
Bosworth Psalter *see under* PSALTERS → individual manuscripts
Bosznay, István **13** 333
Botana, Natalio **6** 10
botanical books **4** 358, 362; **17** 274; **28** 206
botanic gardens *see under* GARDENS → types
Botarelli, Carlo **2** 456
Bot Church **30** 83
Botelho, Carlos (António Teixeira Bastos Nunes) **4** 484*; **25** 299
Botelho, João Luís **26** 254
Botelho, José Rafael **19** 467; **25** 294
Botelho, Pedro **24** 395
Botelho de Almeida, João Anastacio **26** 52
Botelho Mourão, Antonio José **22** 534
Botelho Pereira, Diego **32** 99
Botello Barros, Angel **25** 701
Boten, Anton **28** 60
Botener, William *see* WORCESTRE, WILLIAM
Boterame, Rinaldo *see* WOUTERSZ., REINAUT
Boterenbrood, Jan **4** 484*; **14** 693
Botero, Alvaro **7** 607
Botero, Fernando **4** 484–5*; **7** 609, 612; **21** 4; **27** 872
Both, Andries **4** 485–6*; **26** 772
attributions **4** 486; **25** 797
collaboration **4** 486
groups and movements **3** 143; **28** 92
reproductive prints by others **19** 731
Both, Dirck **4** 485
Both, Jan **4** 485, 486–8*; **26** 772
collaboration **4** 485, 486; **25** 68
groups and movements **3** 143; **9** 462, 463; **28** 92
patrons and collectors **6** 30; **12** 680; **27** 160; **33** 700
pupils **14** 499
teachers **4** 153; **14** 731
works **4** 485, *487*, *488*; **10** 553; **18** 710; **22** 843, 844
Botha, Andries **29** 113
Both de Tauzia, Vicomte **28** 528
Bothenhampton (Dorset), Holy Trinity **9** 739
Bothwell (Strathclyde) **28** 242
Castle **28** 224
St Bride's **26** 617
Boti (son of Sabu) **13** 861
Botkin (family) **22** 178
Botkin, Dmitry **4** 489
Botkin, Mikhail **4** 489*; **12** 331
Botkin, Vasily **4** 489; **27** 440
Botkina, Aleksandra **31** 312
Botkina, Yekaterina **4** 489
Botkyrka altarpiece **13** 112
Botolf **26** 639
Botonti, Giovanni **28** 333, 334
Botoşani **2** 427
Botschlin, Hans Georg **12** 403
Botswana **1** *214*; **4** 489–90*
baskets **1** 296
fences **1** 311
houses **1** 320
linocuts **4** *490*
Bott, Thomas John **7** 481
Botta, Mario **4** 490–91*
collaboration **19** 48
groups and movements **25** 359; **26** 16
patrons and collectors **30** 153
works **11** 773; **19** 782; **27** 731; **30** 129
Botta, Paul Emile **1** 891, 895; **2** 642; **21** 299, 310
Bottaccio, Giovan Pietro **27** 482
Bottai, Giuseppe **16** 681
Bottalla, Giovanni Maria **2** 619; **4** 491*; **7** 913; **27** 486
Bottani, Giuseppe **4** 491*; **11** 118; **30** 451
Bottari, Giovanni **33** 15
Bottari, Giovanni Gaetano **2** 165; **4** 492*; **7** 897; **16** 781; **30** 852
patrons and collectors **7** 898
works **5** 872; **8** 146
bottege **4** 492*
see also STUDIOS; WORKSHOPS
Bottenbroich *see* GREFRATH
Bottengruber, Ignaz **14** 235
Bottesford (Leics), St Mary's **9** 269
tomb of the 3rd Earl of Rutland **1** 520
tomb of the 4th Earl of Rutland **1** 520
Böttger, Johann Friedrich **4** 493*; **6** 332, 924; **9** 241; **12** 433; **21** 63, 64
Böttgerporzellan see under POTTERY → wares
Botti, Carlos **4** 696
Botti, Francesco **4** 315; **24** 801
Botti, Guglielmo **4** 493*
Botti, Rinaldo **11** 20; **12** 528; **27** 522
Botticelli, Carlo **8** 522
Botticelli, Sandro **4** 493–503*; **11** 184; **12** 214; **14** 869; **15** 80; **16** 658, 660
attributions **14** 848; **16** 847; **19** 445; **23** 873; **31** 173
cartoons (drawings) **16** 755
collaboration **3** 300; **7** 676; **11** 384; **12** 551, 553; **24** 521, 523; **26** 186; **27** 175
commentaries **14** 764, 868
competitions **32** 364
copies **22** 351
decorative works **21** 14
drawings **9** 220
forgeries by others **11** 308, *308*, 309
frames **11** 384, 389, 392
groups and movements **26** 186, 187
methods **12** 625; **30** 427
paintings
allegorical **1** 655, 656; **4** *494*, *495*; **10** 476; **14** 870; **16** 660, 661; **22** 521; **25** 161; **29** *362*
frescoes **24** 521; **26** 815; **29** 859; **32** 386
history **1** 656; **10** 130; **14** *582*; **16** 660
literary themes **1** 640; **4** 196; **25** 71
mythological **4** *495*, *499*; **14** 868; **22** 412; **23** 292; **25** 151–2, 276; **32** 386
religious **4** *496*, *497*; **10** 713; **18** 677
spalliere **29** 361, 362
patrons and collectors
Altman, Benjamin **1** 731
Barker, Alexander **3** 242
Benson, R(obert) H(enry) **3** 740
Burton, Frederic William **3** 241
Butler, Charles (1822-1910) **5** 311
Cambó y Batlle, Francisco de Asís **5** 509
Campana (di Cavelli), Giampietro, Marchese **5** 537
Drury Lowe (Holden), William (1802-1877) **9** 306
Fesch, Joseph, Cardinal **11** 32
Ficino, Marsilio **11** 56
Gardner, Isabella Stewart **12** 147
Gonzaga, Francesco, Cardinal **12** 907
Hermitage Museum, St Petersburg **7** 579
His de La Salle, (Aimé-Charles-) Horace **14** 577
Botticelli, Sandro
patrons and collectors—cont.
Ionides, Constantine Alexander **15** 895
Isabella I, Queen of Castile-León (*reg* 1474-1504) **2** 278
Johnson, John G(raver) (1841-1917) **17** 619
Leyland, F(rederick) R(ichard) **19** 290
Lorenzo the Magnificent, Lord of Florence (*reg* 1469-92) **21** 14
Maitland, William Fuller **20** 142
Mellon, Andrew W(illiam) **21** 90
Mond, Ludwig **21** 849
Musée du Louvre (Paris) **10** 432
Ottley, William Young **10** 366; **23** 634
Poldi Pezzoli, Gian Giacomo **25** 144
Pucci, Antonio (1418-84) **25** 690
Raczyński, Atanazy, Count **25** 836
Robien, Christophe-Paul Gautron, Marquis de **26** 469
Sixtus IV, Pope (*reg* 1471-84) **7** 218; **16** 661; **24** 521; **27** 271
Solly, Edward **29** 46
Vespucci, Giorgio Antonio **32** 386
Vespucci, Guidantonio **32** 386
Wildenstein, Georges **33** 182
pupils **3** 916; **19** 445
reproductions in textiles **16** 759
reproductive prints by others **10** 383; **12** 505; **19** 412; **27** 176
sponsorship **21** 15
teachers **19** 444
workshop **21** 758
Bötticher, Karl (Gottlieb Wilhelm) **4** 504–5*; **13** 685; **28** 192
Botticini, Francesco **4** 505–6*
attributions **6** 14
collaboration **2** 632
teachers **22** 800, 801, 802
works **4** *506*; **11** 388; **24** *5*; **27** 184
Botticini, Raffaello **4** 505
Bottigella, Silvestro **11** 293
Bottiglieri, Matteo **22** 479, 485; **27** 756; **31** 789
Bottini, George (Alfred) **4** 507*
Bottini, Imperiale **11** 10
Bottisham, Holy Trinity **26** 613
bottles **23** 787
historical and regional traditions
Byzantine **9** 646
Central Asia, Western **6** *268*
China **6** 890, *896*; **7** 84
Czech Republic **8** *404*
Egypt, ancient **12** IV2
England **10** *301*, *304*
Germany **4** *176*; **12** *429*
Hungary **15** *4*
Japan **17** *256*, *258*, *264*, *265*, *303*
Korea
15th cent. **18** *341*
Native North Americans **22** 661
Netherlands, the **22** 884
Peru **28** *650*
San Pedro culture **29** *187*
Scotland **28** *257*, 259
Sicán culture **28** *650*
South America, Pre-Columbian **28** *650*; **29** *187*
materials
basketwork **22** 661
earthenwares **4** *176*; **28** *257*
glass **6** *268*; **9** 646; **10** *319*; **12** IV2; **15** *4*
lacquer **17** *303*
pewter **24** 580
porcelain **17** *264*, *265*
pottery **6** 890; **10** *301*; **29** *187*
stonewares **6** *896*; **10** *304*; **12** *429*; **17** *256*, *258*
bottles—cont.
types
feeding **24** 580
scent **10** *319*
snuff *see* SNUFF BOTTLES
Böttner, Wilhelm **14** 878
Bottoli, Oskar **2** 804
Bottomley, William Lawrence **26** 353
Bottoni, Piero **1** 578; **3** 438; **8** 600; **11** 62, 63; **21** 422
Bottschild, Andreas (*c.* 1590-1657) **4** 507
Bottschild, Johann Andreas **4** 507
Bottschild, Samuel **4** 507–8*; **10** 857; **12** 478; **29** 547
Botzheim, Johann von **14** 665
Bouabré, Frédéric Bruly **8** 22
Bouake Mosque **1** 317
Bouar **21** 43
Boubais, Jeanne de, Abbess of Flines **3** 641
Boubée, (Francesco Carlo) Paolo **8** 275; **22** 474; **26** 478
Bouch, Thomas **4** 802
Bouchard, Claude **19** 33
Bouchard, Henri **4** 508*; **5** 530; **11** 568, 569
assistants **1** 132
collaboration **18** 659
pupils **3** 194; **16** 877
works **5** *446*; **12** 276
Bouchard, Jean **8** 891
bouchardes **4** 508*
Bouchardon, Edme **4** 508–11*; **9** *302*; **11** 559; **24** 135; **25** 82
collaboration **4** 511; **32** 374
competitions **7** 672
patrons and collectors **7** 897; **14** 485; **19** 144; **20** 417; **23** 519; **25** 150; **30** 524
pupils **9** 388; **13** 805; **21** 146; **32** 76
reproductive prints by others **2** 853; **7** 495; **8** 703; **15** 31; **24** 480
sculpture **4** *510*; **7** 195; **11** 560–61; **32** 372; **33** 3
equestrian monuments **5** 889; **24** 122, 786
fountains **11** *560*, 657; **24** 123
portraits **9** 469
sponsors **6** 121
teachers **8** 72
tokens **4** *509*
Bouchardon, Jacques-Philippe **4** 508, 511*; **29** 689
patrons and collectors **30** 524
works **30** 85
Bouchardon, Jacquette **4** 508
Bouchardon, Jean-Baptiste **4** 508, 511
Bouché, Louis **5** 530
Bouché, Nicolas **4** 512
Boucher, Alfred **27** 307; **29** 858; **31** 382
Boucher, Claude **4** 389
Boucher, François **2** 853; **4** 511–19*; **11** 508; **24** 135, 136; **25** 286
attributions **31** 362; **33** 261
book illustrations **3** 318; **4** 360, *361*, 362
carpets **5** 837
cartoons (drawings) **23** 668
clocks **11** 627
collaboration **10** 764; **11** 368; **14** 846; **22** 88; **27** 169
decorative motifs **18** 614
exhibitions **10** 679
frames **11** 406, 407, 408, 411
gems **13** 771
interior decoration **8** 743; **10** 111; **11** 577; **14** 791; **19** 231; **21** 825; **22** 682
paintings **8** 733; **9** 283; **11** 539, *539*; **23** 680
ceiling **11** 261
fancy pictures **10** 785

Boucher, François
paintings—cont.
fêtes champêtres 11 36
genre 4 *514*; 23 788, *788*
history 14 584
landscape 14 791; 18 712
literary themes 30 358
mythological 4 *515*, *516*; 22 415
pastoral 2 105
portraits 4 *512*; 9 244, 283, *283*; 11 590; 18 591; 23 295; 24 242; 25 *275*, 276
patrons and collectors
Angran, Louis-Auguste, Vicomte de Fontpertuis 2 90
Azincourt, Barthélémy-Augustin Blondel d' 2 904
Barker, Alexander 3 241
Bergeret de Grancourt, (Pierre-) Jacques-Onésyme 3 776
Beurdeley, (Emmanuel-) Alfred (1847-1919) 3 889
Caffiéri, Philippe (ii) (1714-74) 5 380
Calonne, Charles-Alexandre de 5 439
Cognacq, (Théodore-) Ernest 7 528
Conti, Louis-François de Bourbon, Prince de (1717-76) 7 778
Creutz, Gustav Filip 8 161
David-Weill, David 8 569
Dezallier d'Argenville, A(ntoine)-N(icolas) 8 845
Groult, Camille 13 705
Guinness, Edward (Cecil), 1st Earl of Iveagh 13 836
Hohenzollern, Henry, Prince of Prussia 14 653
La Caze, Louis 18 588
Lancret, Nicolas 18 693
La Roque, Antoine de 18 796
Lempereur, Jean-Denis, II 19 144
Livois, Marquis de 19 510
Louis XV, King of France (*reg* 1715-74) 4 554; 10 478; 11 658; 14 585
Louisa Ulrica, Queen of Sweden (1720-82) 14 692
Mariette, Pierre-Jean 20 417
Marigny, Marquis de 25 81
Morny, Charles-Auguste, Duc de 22 127
Murray, Charles Fairfax 22 351
Paignon-Dijonval 23 777
Pâris, Pierre-Adrien 24 177
Pater, Jean-Baptiste 24 256
Péreire (family) 24 396
Pompadour, Jeanne-Antoinette Poisson, Marquise de 25 80
Randon de Boisset, (Pierre-Louis-)Paul 25 888
Rothschild, Salomon Albert Anselm de, Baron 27 223
Seymour-Conway, Richard, 4th Marquess of Hertford 28 527
Sireul, Jean-Claude Gaspard de 28 789, 790
Stanislav II Poniatowski, King of Poland (*reg* 1764-95) 25 212
Tessin, Carl Gustav, Count 30 118, 523, 524
Thiers, Louis-Antoine Crozat, Baron de 8 210
Trudaine de Montigny, Jean-Charles-Philibert 31 390
Vanloo, Carle 19 646
Wallace, Richard 28 528
Wildenstein, Nathan 33 182
Wille, Jean-Georges 33 196
Yusupov, Nikolay (Borisovich), Prince (1751- 1831) 2 417
personal collection 5 380; 9 229
porcelain 8 617; 11 609; 18 804
Boucher, François—cont.
prints
engravings 7 168; 24 271; 26 494
etchings 26 230
pupils
Baldrighi, Giuseppe 3 101
Baudouin, Pierre-Antoine 3 395
Brenet, Nicolas-Guy 4 743
Challe, (Charles-) Michel-Ange 6 401
Drouais, François-Hubert 9 301
Floding, Per Gustaf 11 173
Fragonard, Jean-Honoré 11 366
Gravelot 13 324
Guay, Jacques 13 771
Hilleström, Pehr 14 543
Jullienne, Jean de 17 684
Le Brun, Jean-Baptiste-Pierre 19 25
Lélu, Pierre 19 119
Le Mettay, Pierre-Charles 19 135
Le Prince, Jean-Baptiste 19 219
Mannlich, Johann Christian von 20 282
Ménageot, François-Guillaume 21 113
Pasch, Lorens (1733-1805) 24 222
Pompadour, Jeanne-Antoinette Poisson, Marquise de 25 80
Ravenet, Simon Francis, the younger (1748-1812) 26 31
reproductions in enamel 10 *347*
reproductions in porcelain 12 434, *434*; 16 738; 21 64; 30 100
reproductions in tapestry 11 643; 14 543; 22 726; 30 323, 324
reproductive prints by others 8 130, 131; 9 370
Aveline, Pierre (-Alexandre) (1702-60) 2 853
Beauvarlet, Jacques-Firmin 3 463
Bergeret de Grancourt, (Pierre-) Jacques-Onésyme 3 776
Bonnet, Louis-Marin 4 330, 331, *331*; 25 623
Cals, Adolphe-Félix 5 440
Cars, Laurent 5 884
Daullé, Jean 8 544
Demarteau, Gilles 8 703; 29 675
Flipart, Jean-Jacques 11 172
François, Jean-Charles 11 723
Gravelot 32 501
Hédouin, (Pierre-)Edmond (-Alexandre) 14 288
Hoüel, Jean-Pierre-Louis-Laurent 14 799
Huquier, Gabriel 15 31
Janinet, Jean-François 16 905
Joullain, François 17 668
Lebas, Jacques-Philippe 19 10
Lempereur, Louis-Simon 19 144
Lépicié, Renée-Elisabeth 19 216
Le Vasseur, Jean-Charles 19 261
Le Veau, Jean-Jacques (-André) 19 268
Moitte, Pierre-Etienne 21 800
Moles, Pedro Pascual 21 815
Moreau (i), Jean-Michel 22 88
Nilson, Johann Esaias 23 146
Papillon de La Ferté, Denis-Pierre-Jean 24 63
Perronneau, Jean-Baptiste 24 480
Pompadour, Jeanne-Antoinette Poisson, Marquise de 25 80
Saint-Aubin, Augustin de 27 531
Saint-Non, Richard de, Abbé 27 571
Salvador Carmona, Manuel 27 645
Voyez, François 32 720
stage design 30 672
Boucher, François—cont.
tapestries 3 461; 7 167; 11 643; 19 382; 23 381; 24 137; 29 92
Chinese Hangings 11 643
Fêtes Italiennes 3 *462*
Loves of the Gods 3 841; 12 830; 30 *323*; 33 19
Noble Pastorale 14 422
teachers 19 143
Boucher, Graeme J. 2 689
Boucher, Guillaume 9 37
Boucher, James 33 218
Boucher, Jean 4 125, 519–20*; 11 568; 21 497
Boucher, Jean-Marie 26 192
Boucher, Juste-François 4 513; 7 747
Boucher, Yves-Eloi 32 77
Boucherat, Charles, Abbot of Pontigny 25 220
Boucher de Perthes, James 2 299
Boucher-Desnoyers, Auguste-Gaspard-Louis 8 773; 26 232
Boucherle, Pierre 31 425
Boucheron 11 631, 635; 17 529; 18 659; 24 147; 28 741
rock crystal 26 486
Boucheron, Andrea 4 520; 16 742; 18 618
Boucheron, Frédéric 17 527
Boucheron, Giovan Battista 4 520; 16 742
works 16 *742*
Boucheron, Luc 26 206
Bouchier, Guillaume 28 723
Bouchon, Basile 16 850
Bouchot, Francois 8 40
Bouchot, Henri 4 520*; 11 675
Bouchot, Jacqueline 4 520
Bouchut, Louis 20 218
Boucicaut, Aristide 4 239; 8 769
Boucicaut, Jean II le Meingre de (1365-1421) 4 370; 7 178; 13 155; 14 423; 20 632
Boucicaut, Jean III le Meingre de (*fl c.* 1430) 20 632
Boucicaut Hours *see under* BOOKS OF HOURS → individual manuscripts
Boucicaut Master 7 525; 13 155; 20 632–5*
collaboration 20 635, 647, 689, 751
methods 24 492
patrons and collectors 5 208, 209; 7 525; 11 354; 31 842
works 4 370, 395; 6 562; 13 *154*; 18 704; 20 *633*, *634*, 664, 689; 31 290
workshop 20 682; 28 4
Boucken, Pieter van *see* BOUCLE, PIERRE
Bouckhorst, Jan van 13 895; 28 309
Boucle, Pierre 4 521*; 29 668
Bouclet, Guillaume 11 405
Boucry, Pierre *see* BOSCRY, PIERRE
Bouda, Cyril 30 162
Boudan, Louis 11 903
Boudard, Jean-Baptiste 4 521*
collaboration 24 193, 553
illustrated writings 4 470
Bouddé, Jean-François 27 584
Bouderelle, David 2 91
Boudewijns, Adriaen 4 522
Boudewijns, Adriaen Frans 4 521–2*
collaboration 4 589
works 4 *522*
Boudewijn van Battel 20 686
Boudewijn van der Wyct *see* BOUDEWIJN VAN BATTEL
Boudhors, P. Valentin 29 751
Boudin 17 666
Boudin, (Louis-)Eugène 4 522–4*
exhibitions 15 154
patrons and collectors 4 725, 726; 5 278; 7 528; 19 92; 28 272; 30 375
Boudin, (Louis-)Eugène—cont.
pupils 21 862
teachers 8 539
works 4 *523*; 20 426
Boudin, Guillaume 4 524
Boudin, Jacques 4 524
Boudin, Léonard 4 524*
Boudin, Robert 19 59
Boudin, Thomas (*c.* 1570-1637) 4 524*; 16 856
Boudin, Thomas (1610-*d* after 1660) 4 524
Boudník, Vladimír 8 394
Boudolf, Jan 2 49, 50, 51; 3 552, 553, 606; 4 524–6*; 20 632
collaboration 17 463
patrons and collectors 2 112; 31 835
works 2 *50*; 4 *525*; 13 154; 24 133; 30 312
Boudon, Philippe 27 838
Boudrillet, Jean 27 681
Boudrion, Lazarine 15 12
Bouet, Georges 12 484
Bouffioulx 3 *539*, 588, 589; 4 526*
Boufflers, Château de *see* CHÂTEAU DE BOUFFLERS
Bougainville 10 779; 24 64, *64*; 29 48
Bough, Sam(uel) 4 526*; 28 236
Boughton, George B. 8 121; 11 761
Boughton House (Northants) 12 127; 21 907
carpets 10 357
collections 9 31; 10 364
frames 11 426
furniture 10 291
paintings 6 554; 27 263
Bougie *see* BEJAÏA
Bougouni 1 *386*
Bouguer, Pierre 24 494
Bouguereau, William (-Adolphe) 4 526–8*; 11 545, 546, 659, 664, 672; 14 588; 23 295; 24 141, 142
collaboration 24 221
competitions 25 638
dealers 2 858; 9 424; 13 228; 31 664
groups and movements 2 530; 26 54; 28 345
patrons and collectors 7 377; 31 870; 32 708
prizes (artists') 24 171
pupils 22 421
Amiet, Cuno 1 782
Brymner, William 5 67
Chabas, Maurice 6 377
Chabas, Paul (-Emile-Joseph) 6 377
Chabaud, Auguste 6 378
Corinth, Lovis 7 855
Ferenczy, Károly 10 892
Luchian, Ştefan 19 770
Mašić, Nikola 20 549
Matisse, Henri (Emile Benoît) 20 821
Ménard, (Marie Auguste Emile) René 21 114
Petraşcu, Gheorghe 24 560
Popescu, Gabriel 25 237
Pryde, James (Ferrier) 25 674
Putz, Leo 25 748
Roussel, Ker-Xavier 27 269
Steer, Philip Wilson 29 594
Wentzel, (Nils) Gustav 33 76
teachers 24 737
works 4 *527*, *528*; 11 415; 14 588; 18 100; 24 396
Bouhot, Etienne 8 598
Bouilhet, Tony 25 218
Bouillac 28 631
Bouillon (family) 8 589
Bouillon, Cardinal de 19 88
Bouillon, Duc de 4 865; 19 300
Bouillon, Jean 6 433
Bouin-Luce, Jean 19 768
Boukhatim, Fares 1 635
Boukyovtsi 13 571
Boulanger, Gustave (-Clarence-Rodolphe) 4 528–9*; 11 672
collaboration 19 153
groups and movements 28 346
patrons and collectors 4 308; 12 186
pupils
Ahmet, Ali 1 475
Benson, Frank W(eston) 3 740
Boutet de Monvel, (Louis-) Maurice 4 589
Dewing, Thomas Wilmer 8 841
Hassam, (Frederick) Childe 14 219
Hitchcock, George 14 589
Khnopff, Fernand 18 23
Melchers, (Julius) Gari(baldi) 21 76
Metcalf, Willard Leroy 21 342
Moore, George (Augustus) (1852-1933) 22 54
Osman Hamdi 23 604
Rochegrosse, Georges (Antoine Marie) 26 481
Tarbell, Edmund C(harles) 30 343
Weir, Julian Alden 33 43
works 25 193
Boulanger, Jean 7 356; 10 526, 527; 18 745; 21 732; 28 506
Boulanger, Louis (-Candide) 4 529*; 14 853
collaboration 27 143
groups and movements 26 742
pupils 16 82
Boulanger, Louis Verceil 11 414
Boulaouane 16 240
Boularchos 4 529*; 13 545, 549
Boulard 9 379
Boulbon altarpiece 7 526
Boulderclough, Methodist Church 21 347
Boulen, de 11 606
Boulenger 30 886
works 30 *886*
Boulenger, Hippolyte 3 562; 4 529–30*; 5 44
bouleuteria 4 530*; 13 236, 380–81, *381*, 405, *405*, 407; 14 73; 23 349
Boulevard, Le 8 547
boulevards 3 359
Boulez, Pierre 7 688
Boulge, St Michael 26 613
Boulger, James 9 317
Boulin, Arnoul 7 190
boulingrins 12 122
Boulle, André-Charles 4 531–2*; 11 625, 626; 19 22; 20 139; 24 150; 33 333
assistants 12 832
collaboration 11 305
furniture 4 *531*; 11 577, 596; 17 684; 19 261; 23 458
armoires 11 593; 20 VII
bureaux plats 5 191; 11 593
cabinets 11 589
candelabra 11 626
chandeliers 11 626
coffre de toilette 11 593
commodes 7 657; 11 589, *589*, 626
cupboards 8 271
lighting 11 626
pedestals 24 316
groups and movements 19 724
interior decoration 13 701
patrons and collectors 4 552, 553; 5 439; 7 546; 9 467; 14 145; 17 684; 19 722; 27 223
pattern books 24 271
personal collection 4 568; 20 293, 417
techniques 11 588, 590; 16 748
marquetry 11 575, 589; 20 467; 23 543
veneers 11 576; 31 195

Boulle, André-Charles—cont.
workshop **1** 110; **11** 590
Boulleau, Claude **29** 93
Boullée, Etienne-Louis **4** 532–4*; **10** 83; **11** 519, 670; **13** 236; **26** 13
architecture **25** 267
cemeteries **6** 166
cenotaphs **4** *533*; **6** 171; **10** 401; **22** 42; **27** 237
chapels **20** 867
circuses **1** 798
government buildings **2** 172
hôtels particuliers **3** 453
law courts **18** 887
libraries **19** 316
military **4** 848
pyramids **25** 766
roofs **27** 131
theatres **30** 671
assistants **9** 420; **12** 724
capriccios **5** 688
drawings **6** 510
groups and movements **10** 96; **22** 738; **24** 173, 174; **26** 735, 743
pupils **4** 847; **6** 396; **8** 216; **9** 420; **12** 724, 729, 746
teachers **19** 76
writings **31** 297
Boullée, Louis-Claude **4** 532
Boullemier, Anton **10** 312
Boullet, Pierre **24** 148
boullework *see under* MARQUETRY → types
Boullogne, Bon **4** 534, 535–6*
collaboration **4** 536; **8** 91; **17** 670
patrons and collectors **23** 513; **31** 56
pupils **3** 855; **6** 121; **15** 38; **19** 34; **24** 211; **25** 895; **27** 789; **28** 743; **31** 223
reproductive prints by others **30** 746
works **4** *535*; **20** 894; **23** 512
Boullogne, Geneviève **4** 534; **7** 415
Boullogne, Louis (1609-74) **4** 534–6*
collaboration **19** 22
patrons and collectors **30** 727
pupils **4** 535, 536
reproductive prints by others **6** 548
Boullogne, Louis de (1654-1733) **4** 534, 536–7*
collaboration **4** 536; **8** 91; **31** 510
patrons and collectors **32** 368
pupils **12** 27, 356
works **4** *537*; **14** 784; **24** 470
Boullogne, Madeleine **4** 534
Boulnois, William Allen **12** 315
Boulogne, Jean de *see* JEAN DE BOULOGNE
Boulogne, Jeanne de *see* BERRY, JEANNE DE VALOIS, Duchesse de
Boulogne, Valentin de (*fl* 1590s) **4** 538
Boulogne, Valentin de (1591-1632) **4** 538–40*; **11** 533; **20** 267
attributions **26** 95
groups and movements **28** 92; **30** 456
patrons and collectors **7** 552; **10** 861; **11** 81; **25** 150, 364, 383; **27** 133; **30** 274
pupils **31** 223
reproductive prints by others **27** 269
works **4** *539*, *540*; **26** 810
Boulogne-Billancourt, Hôtel de Ville **24** 129; **31** 243
Boulogne-sur-Mer
Colonne de la Grande Armée **4** 458
Henin Liétard Abbey **26** 668
houses **11** 659
St François de Sales **11** 614
Boulou, Le *see* LE BOULOU
Boulsa **22** 198
Boulsover, Thomas **10** 331; **28** 577
Boultbee, John **20** 477
Boulton (family) **32** 170, 178
Boulton, Alfredo **32** 178
Boulton, Fundación *see under* CARACAS
Boulton, Matthew **2** 456; **4** 86, 540–41*; **10** 333, 335; **15** 820; **16** 61; **20** 925; **23** 544; **28** 739, 831; **33** 445
assistants **3** 25; **9** 303; **20** 924
collaboration **1** 140
works **2** 164; **4** 87–8; **10** 331, 333, *333*, 342, 345; **16** *61*; **19** 366; **20** *444*; **28** 577, 831
Boulton, Matthew, Plate Co. **4** 541
Boulton, Matthew Robinson **5** 169
Boulton & Fothergill **4** 540
works **21** II3
Boulton & Paul **13** 619
Bouman, Elias **1** 802, 813; **4** 541*; **17** 545
Boumann, Georg Friedrich **3** 791; **4** 541
Boumann, Johann **4** 541–2*
patrons and collectors **14** 651, 653
works **3** 791; **4** 786; **25** 366, 367; **28** 98
Boumann, Michael Daniel Philipp **4** 541; **12** 413
Boumeester, Cornelis **22** 881; **30** 878
boundary stones **30** 575
Boundiali **1** *386*
Museum **8** 23
bound-resist dyeing *see* DYEING → types → tie-dyeing
Bouqras *see* BUQRAS
Bouquel, Aníbal Alvarez *see* ALVAREZ BOUQUEL, ANÍBAL
Boura **1** *381*
Bourassa, Napoléon **4** 542*; **14** 103, 282
Bouray **6** 159
Bourbon Chappes (family) **22** 30
Bourbon-Condé, Louis de, Comte de Clermont *see* CLERMONT, LOUIS DE BOURBON-CONDÉ, Comte de
Bourbon-Condé, Louise-Bénédicte de, Duchesse du Maine *see* MAINE, LOUISE-BÉNÉDICTE DE BOURBON-CONDÉ, Duchesse du
Bourbon-Condé, Marie-Thérèse, Princesse de Conti *see* CONTI, MARIE-THÉRÈSE DE BOURBON-CONDÉ, Princesse de
Bourbon del Monte, Francesco Maria, Cardinal **4** 567*; **12** 214
architecture **2** 377
frescoes **27** 487
glass **32** 203
paintings **5** 705, 708; **11** 188; **27** 623
patronage **26** 773
Bourbon del Monte, Guidobaldo del **1** 113; **4** 567; **7** 650; **23** 348; **24** 489; **28** 202
works **24** *489*
Bourbon I. (French House of) **4** 542–3*, *543*; **11** 531, 655
architecture **20** 292
collections **4** 558
Bourbon I., Adelaïde de, Princesse **5** 767; **11** 882; **19** 261; **21** 699; **32** 240
Bourbon I., Anne, Duchess of *see* ANNE, Duchess of Bourbon
Bourbon I., Anne-Marie-Louise d'Orléans, Duchesse de Montpensier *see* MONTPENSIER, ANNE-MARIE-LOUISE DE BOURBON, Duchesse de
Bourbon I., Anthony, King of Navarre *see* ANTHONY, King of (Lower) Navarre
Bourbon I., Antoine d'Orléans *see* Orléans, Antoine de Bourbon
Bourbon I., Antoine-Marie-Philippe-Louis d' Orléans, Duc de Montpensier *see* MONTPENSIER, ANTOINE-MARIE-PHILIPPE-LOUIS DE BOURBON, Duc de
Bourbon I., Antoinette de, Duchesse de Guise *see* GUISE, ANTOINETTE DE BOURBON, Duchesse de
Bourbon I., Caroline, Duchesse de Berry *see* BERRY, CAROLINE DE BOURBON, Duchesse de
Bourbon I., Catherine d'Armagnac, Duchess of *see* CATHERINE D'ARMAGNAC, Duchess of Bourbon
Bourbon I., Catherine de, Duchess of Lorraine *see* CATHERINE DE BOURBON, Duchess of Lorraine
Bourbon I., Charles, Duc de Vendôme et de Bourbon **4** *543*
Bourbon I., Charles de, Cardinal-Archbishop of Lyon **4** 542, *543*, 544–5*; **20** *733*; **28** 418
gardens **11** 905
manuscripts **20** 699
paintings **20** 733
Bourbon I., Charles de Bourbon, Comte d'Artois *see* CHARLES X, King of France
Bourbon I., Charles X, King of France *see* CHARLES X, King of France
Bourbon I., Charlotte-Jeanne, Duchesse d'Orléans *see* ORLÉANS, CHARLOTTE-JEANNE DE BOURBON, Duchesse d'
Bourbon I., Christina, Duchess and Regent of Savoy *see* CHRISTINA, Duchess and Regent of Savoy
Bourbon I., Clémence, Princesse de Condé *see* CONDÉ, CLÉMENCE, Princesse de
Bourbon I., Elisabeth-Charlotte, Duchesse d'Orléans *see* ORLÉANS, ELISABETH-CHARLOTTE DE BOURBON, Duchesse d'
Bourbon I., Ferdinand-Philippe (-Louis-Charles-Henri), 7th Duc d'Orléans *see* ORLÉANS, FERDINAND-PHILIPPE(-L.-C.-H) DE BOURBON, 7th Duc d'
Bourbon I., (Jean-Baptiste) Gaston, Duc d'Orléans *see* ORLÉANS, (JEAN-BAPTISTE) GASTON, Duc d'
Bourbon I., Hélène-Louise-Elisabeth, Duchesse d'Orléans *see* ORLÉANS, HÉLÈNE-LOUISE-ELISABETH DE BOURBON, Duchesse d'
Bourbon I., Henrietta Anne, Duchesse d'Orléans *see* ORLÉANS, HENRIETTA ANNE DE BOURBON, Duchesse d'
Bourbon I., Henri-Eugène-Philippe-Louis Duc d'Aumale *see* AUMALE, HENRI-EUGÈNE-PHILIPPE-LOUIS DE BOURBON, Duc d'
Bourbon I., Henri II de, Prince de Condé *see* CONDÉ, HENRI II DE BOURBON, Prince de
Bourbon I., Henri-Jules de, Prince de Condé *see* CONDÉ, HENRI-JULES DE BOURBON, Prince de
Bourbon I., Henry IV, King of France *see* HENRY IV, King of France
Bourbon I., Isabel de **29** 336
Bourbon I., Jacques de **16** 854
Bourbon I., Jean-Philippe, Chevalier d'Orléans *see* ORLÉANS, JEAN-PHILIPPE DE BOURBON, Chevalier d'
Bourbon I., Joanna of France, Duchess of Bourbon *see* JOANNA OF FRANCE, Duchess of Bourbon
Bourbon I., John II, Duke of *see* JOHN II, Duke of Bourbon
Bourbon I., Louis, 3rd Duc d'Orléans *see* ORLÉANS, LOUIS DE BOURBON, 3rd Duc d'
Bourbon I., Louis, Duc de Nemours *see* NEMOURS, LOUIS DE BOURBON, Duc de
Bourbon I., Louis-Alexandre de, Comte de Toulouse *see* TOULOUSE, LOUIS-ALEXANDRE DE BOURBON, Comte de
Bourbon I., Louis Auguste de, Duc de Maine *see* MAINE, LOUIS AUGUSTE DE BOURBON, Duc de
Bourbon I., Louis de, Bâtard de Bourbon (*d* 1486) **7** 597; **20** 646
Bourbon I., Louis (-Antoine) de, Duc d'Angoulême *see* ANGOULÊME, LOUIS(-ANTOINE) DE BOURBON, Duc d'
Bourbon I., Louis de, Duc de Penthièvre *see* PENTHIÈVRE, LOUIS DE BOURBON, Duc de
Bourbon I., Louis de, le Dauphin (1729-65) **4** *543*; **8** 161; **12** 356; **23** 356, 668; **24** 786; **26** 420
interior decoration **32** 240
Bourbon I., Louis de, le Grand Dauphin (1661-1711) **4** *543*, 553*, *557*; **20** 295, 297
architecture **21** 366
bronze **11** 625, 626
collections **29** 352
furniture **29** 303
paintings **8** 91, 812; **9** 12
porcelain **9** 28
teachers **28** 742
Bourbon I., Louis de, le Petit Dauphin, Duc de Bourgogne (1682-1712) *see* BOURGOGNE, LOUIS DE BOURBON, Duc de, le Petit Dauphin
Bourbon I., Louis d'Orléans, Duc de Nemours *see* NEMOURS, LOUIS DE BOURBON, Duc de
Bourbon I., Louise de, Princesse **5** 767; **17** 666; **21** 699
Bourbon I., Louise-Françoise, Duchesse de **2** 701
Bourbon I., Louis-Henri de, Prince de Condé *see* CONDÉ, LOUIS-HENRI DE BOURBON, Prince de
Bourbon I., Louis I, Duke of *see* LOUIS I, Duke of Bourbon
Bourbon I., Louis I de, Comte de Montpensier *see* MONTPENSIER, LOUIS I DE BOURBON, Comte de
Bourbon I., Louis I de, Prince de Condé *see* CONDÉ, LOUIS I DE BOURBON, Prince de Condé
Bourbon I., Louis II, Duke of *see* LOUIS II, Duke of Bourbon
Bourbon I., Louis II de, Prince de Condé *see* CONDÉ, LOUIS II DE BOURBON, Prince de
Bourbon I., Louis-Joseph de, Prince de Condé *see* CONDÉ, LOUIS-JOSEPH DE BOURBON, Princede
Bourbon I., Louis-Philippe, 4th Duc d'Orléans *see* ORLÉANS, LOUIS-PHILIPPE DE BOURBON, 4th Duc d'
Bourbon I., Louis-Philippe, 6th Duc d'Orléans *see* LOUIS-PHILIPPE, King of the French
Bourbon I., Louis-Philippe-Albert, Comte de Paris *see* PARIS, LOUIS-PHILIPPE-ALBERT DE BOURBON, Comte de
Bourbon I., Louis-Philippe-Joseph, 5th Duc d'Orléans *see* ORLÉANS, LOUIS-PHILIPPE-JOSEPH DE BOURBON, 5th Duc d'
Bourbon I., Louis XIII, King of France *see* LOUIS XIII, King of France
Bourbon I., Louis XIV, King of France *see* LOUIS XIV, King of France
Bourbon I., Louis XV, King of France *see* LOUIS XV, King of France
Bourbon I., Louis XVI, King of France *see* LOUIS XVI, King of France
Bourbon I., Louis XVIII, King of France *see* LOUIS XVIII, King of France
Bourbon I., Marie (-Christine-Caroline-Adélaïde-Françoise-Léopoldine *see* ORLÉANS, MARIE(-C.-C.-A.-F.-L.), Princesse d'
Bourbon I., Marie-Adelaïde d'Orléans *see* ORLÉANS, MARIE-ADELAÏDE DE BOURBON, Abbess of Chelles
Bourbon I., Marie-Adelaïde of Savoy, Duchesse de Bourgogne *see* BOURGOGNE, MARIE-ADELAÏDE OF SAVOY, Duchesse de
Bourbon I., Marie-Antoinette, Queen of France *see* MARIE-ANTOINETTE, Queen of France
Bourbon I., Marie de' Medici, Queen of France *see* MARIE DE' MEDICI, Queen of France
Bourbon I., Marie Isabelle, Comtesse de Paris *see* PARIS, MARIE ISABELLE DE BOURBON, Comtesse de
Bourbon I., Marie Louise d'Orléans, Queen of Spain *see* MARIE-LOUISE D'ORLÉANS, Queen of Spain
Bourbon I., Orléans (House of) *see* ORLÉANS (BOURBON HOUSE OF)
Bourbon I., Peter II, Duke of Bourbon *see* PETER II, Duke of Bourbon
Bourbon I., Philippe I de, 1st Duc d'Orléans *see* ORLÉANS, PHILIPPE I DE BOURBON, 1st Ducd'
Bourbon I., Philippe II, 2nd Duc d' *see* ORLÉANS, PHILIPPE II DE BOURBON, 2nd Duc d'
Bourbon I., Robert-Philippe-Louis-Eugène-Ferdinand d'Orléans, Duc de Chartres *see* CHARTRES, ROBERT-PHILIPPE-LOUIS-E.-F., Duc de
Bourbon I., Victoire de, Princesse **5** 767; **19** 261; **21** 699
Bourbon II. (Spanish House of) **4** 556–7*, *557*
architecture **31** 93
furniture **16** 748
sculpture **27** 46; **29** 293
tortoiseshell **16** 748
Bourbon II., Alfonso XII, King of Spain *see* ALFONSO XII, King of Spain
Bourbon II., Alfonso XIII, King of Spain *see* ALFONSO XIII, King of Spain
Bourbon II., Charles III, King of Spain *see* CHARLES III, King of Spain

Bourbon II., Charles IV, King of Spain *see* CHARLES IV, King of Spain
Bourbon II., Charles VII, King of Naples *see* CHARLES III, King of Spain
Bourbon II., Elizabeth, Duchess of Parma *see* ELIZABETH DE BOURBON, Duchess of Parma
Bourbon II., Elizabeth, Queen of Spain *see* ELIZABETH FARNESE, Queen of Spain
Bourbon II., Ferdinand VI, King of Spain *see* FERDINAND VI, King of Spain
Bourbon II., Ferdinand VII, King of Spain *see* FERDINAND VII, King of Spain
Bourbon II., Gabriel, Infante of Spain **32** 564
Bourbon II., Isabella II, Queen of Spain *see* ISABELLA II, Queen of Spain
Bourbon II., Louise, Queen of Spain *see* LOUISE, Queen of Spain
Bourbon II., Louise Elizabeth, Duchess of Parma *see* LOUISE ELIZABETH, Duchess of Parma
Bourbon II., Louis I, King of Spain *see* LOUIS I, King of Spain
Bourbon II., Luisa Fernanda, Infanta of Spain *see* MONTPENSIER, LUISA FERNANDA DE BOURBON, Duchesse de
Bourbon II., Luis Antonio, Infante of Spain **4** *557*, 560, 564–5*
architecture **29** 271
Bourbon II., Maria Amalia, Queen of Naples *see* MARIA AMALIA, Queen of Spain
Bourbon II., Maria Amalia, Queen of Spain *see* MARIA AMALIA, Queen of Spain
Bourbon II., Maria Antonia, Infanta of Spain **4** *557*
Bourbon II., Maria Christina, Queen of Spain *see* MARIA CHRISTINA, Queen of Spain
Bourbon II., Marie Louise de, Queen of Spain *see* MARIE LOUISE D'ORLÉANS, Queen of Spain
Bourbon II., Philip, Duke of Parma *see* PHILIP, Duke of Parma
Bourbon II., Philip V, King of Spain *see* PHILIP V, King of Spain
Bourbon II., Victoria Eugenia, Queen of Spain *see* VICTORIA EUGENIA, Queen of Spain
Bourbon III. (Neapolitan House of) **4** *557*
Bourbon III., Caroline, Duchesse de Berry *see* BERRY, CAROLINE DE BOURBON, Duchesse de
Bourbon III., Ferdinand I, King of the Two Sicilies *see* FERDINAND I, King of the Two Sicilies
Bourbon III., Ferdinand II, King of the Two Sicilies *see* FERDINAND II, King of the Two Sicilies
Bourbon III., Francis I, King of the Two Sicilies *see* FRANCIS I, King of the Two Sicilies
Bourbon III., Leopold, Prince of Salerno **23** 523
Bourbon III., Maria Christina of Sicily, Queen of Spain *see* MARIA CHRISTINA OF SICILY, Queen of Spain
Bourbon-l'Archambault Sainte-Chapelle **27** 550
Bourbonnais Ferron, Monique **5** 582
Bourbons, Master of the *see* MOULINS, MASTER OF
Bourbon-Vendôme Hours *see under* BOOKS OF HOURS → individual manuscripts
Bourbourg, Charles Etienne Brasseur de *see* BRASSEUR DE BOURBOURG, CHARLES ETIENNE
Bourbourg Church **11** 623
Bourcier, Berthélemy **11** 605
Bourd, John **13** 85
Bourdais, Jules **8** 573; **10** 683; **22** 59
Bourdaisière, Philibert Babou, Sieur de la **11** 262; **20** 133; **31** 227
Bourdaloue, Claude de **4** 568*
Bourdelle, Antoine **14** 815
Bourdelle, Emile-Antoine **4** 568–9*; **5** 355; **11** 568, 569; **26** 514
assistants **7** 555; **26** 351
collaboration **20** 153
groups and movements **2** 521; **27** 639
pupils
Apartis, Thanassis **2** 215
Butler, Margaret **23** 62
Čelebonović, Marko **6** 136
Desnoyer, François **8** 810
Ferenczy, Béni **10** 893
Giacometti, Alberto **12** 563
Gutfreund, Otto **13** 867
Hjorth, Bror **14** 595
Lunde, Rolf **23** 230
Mukhina, Vera (Ignat'yevna) **22** 268
Nikoladze, Yakov **23** 143
Obreshkov, Bencho **23** 335
Parsons, Betty (Bierne) **24** 213
Pena, Antonio **31** 755
Petraşcu, Miliţa **26** 716
Robus, Hugo **26** 477
Shadr, Ivan (Dmitriyevich) **28** 534
Shervud, Leonid (Vladimirovich) **28** 597
Sochos, Antonēs **28** 915
Sveinsson, Ásmundur **30** 54
Ternovets, Boris (Nikolayevich) **30** 491
Vieira da Silva(, Marie-Helène) **32** 423
Vitullo, Sesostris **32** 651
Zaļkalns, Teodors **33** 601
works **4** *568*; **11** 568; **22** 331; **26** 723
Bourdery, Louis **11** 631
Bourdichon, Jean **4** 569–72*; **20** 334; **31** 226
assistants **3** 646
attributions **25** 405
patrons and collectors **4** 544; **25** 405; **31** 413, 832, 834, 843, 845, 846, 847
works **4** *571*, *572*; **11** 532; **25** 275
workshop **31** 845
Bourdieu, Pierre **28** 917, 926
Bourdin, Michel (*c.* 1580-1650) **4** 572–3*; **33** 3
Bourdin, Michel (1609-78) **4** 572, 573
Bourdon, A. **3** 885
Bourdon, Eugène **30** 241
Bourdon, Francisque *see* BORDONI, FRANCESCO DI BARTOLOMEO
Bourdon, Gaston **18** 888
Bourdon, Marin **4** 573
Bourdon, Sébastien **4** 573–5*; **11** 536; **26** 772; **30** 117
collaboration **6** 434
groups and movements **3** 143; **25** 398
patrons and collectors
Bankes (family) **3** 178
Bourdon, Sébastien
patrons and collectors—cont.
Beaumont, George (Howland) **3** 454
Boyle, Richard, 3rd Earl of Burlington and 4th Earl of Cork **4** 610
Bretonvilliers, Benigne de **4** 756
Christina, Queen of Sweden (*reg* 1632-54) **30** 77
Colebrooke, George **7** 552
Hesselin, Louis (-Cauchon) **14** 492
Jabach, Everard **16** 815
Orléans, Philippe I de Bourbon, 1st Duc d' (1640-1701) **23** 512
Papillon de La Ferté, Denis-Pierre-Jean **24** 63
Quentin de Lorangère **25** 815
Reynolds, Joshua **26** 277
Spencer, Robert, 2nd Earl of Sunderland (1641-1702) **29** 381
Tallard, Marie-Joseph d'Hostun, Duc de **30** 274
Temple, Richard, 1st Viscount Cobham **30** 451
Vassal de Saint-Hubert, Jean-Antoine-Hubert **32** 74
Wyndham, Charles, 2nd Earl of Egremont **33** 453
pupils **19** 542; **22** 190
reproductions in textiles **16** 760
reproductive prints by others **3** 813; **8** 773; **15** 31; **27** 269; **28** 756
works **4** *574*; **6** 435; **7** 394; **9** 278, 379; **11** 535, 641; **20** 894; **22** 34
Bourdon-De Bruynes **3** 601
Bourdonny, Francesco *see* BORDONI, FRANCESCO DI BARTOLOMEO
Bouré, Félix **12** 230
Bouré, Paul **12** 230; **28** 756
Boureima, Boubacar **23** 128
Bouret, Etienne-Michel **4** 575*
Bouret, Jean **14** 701
Bouret, Michel **19** 27
Bouret d'Aubusson **7** 508
Bourgas **5** *144*, 149, 156
Bourge, Romain de **11** 524
Bourgeau, Victor **4** 575–6*; **5** 561; **22** 36
Bourgeois (family) **25** 729
Bourgeois, Constant **18** 579
Bourgeois, Djo **21** 363
Bourgeois, Emile **28** 525
Bourgeois, Francis **8** 792
Bourgeois, Jean le **2** 460
Bourgeois, Louise **4** 576*; **31** 614
Bourgeois, Marin Le **2** 460; **4** 549; **30** 659
works **2** *460*
Bourgeois, Peter Francis **4** 576–7*; **10** 366; **25** 212
architecture **10** 234
collections **10** 369
paintings **19** 588; **28** 908
Bourgeois, Pierre (*fl* 1922-8) **3** 564; **5** 44
Bourgeois, Pierre le (*d* 1627) **2** 460
Bourgeois, Victor **3** 564; **4** 577*; **7** *294*
groups and movements **5** 44; **7** 293; **8** 826; **21** 782
pupils **30** 213
works **3** 551; **33** 246
Bourgery, Jean-Baptiste-Marc **1** 844; **21** 6
Bourges **4** 577–85*; **11** *504*; **26** *905*
Cathedral of St Etienne **4** 578–80*, *579*; **9** 672; **11** 510; **13** 39, 40; **14** 80, 518; **22** 218; **26** 44
ambulatory **1** 768
buttresses **5** 319
choir **4** *578*
Bourges
Cathedral of St Etienne—cont.
choir-screen **4** 581–2*; **28** 292
nave **13** *41*
portals **4** 580–81*, *581*
sculpture **4** 580*; **11** 555; **13** 72, 73, 75
stained glass **4** 582*, *582*; **7** 526; **13** 179, 180, *180*, 181; **29** 501, 506, 510, 511
tomb of Jean, Duc de Berry **13** 78; **17** 457
Hôtel Jacques-Coeur **3** 173; **4** *584*, 584–5*; **7** 526; **11** 511, 655; **14** 75; **29** 22
Chapel **6** 459
gate-house **12** 175
grilles **11** 624
sculpture **13** 79
Hôtel Lallemant **18** 662
painting **11** 531
Palais Jacques-Coeur *see* Hôtel Jacques-Coeur
Sainte-Chapelle **4** 582–3*; **27** 551
collections **31** 837, 839
pews **13** 125
sculpture **4** *583*; **13** 79
tomb of Jean, Duc de Berry *see under* Cathedral of St Etienne
St Ursin **4** 583–4*; **26** 599
sculpture **13** 78
stained glass **13** 179
Bourges, Fernand **4** 918
Bourges Bible *see under* BIBLES → individual manuscripts
Bourget, Paul **6** 377
Bourget, Pierre **8** 596
Bourgevin Vialart de, Charles Paul Jean-Baptiste de, Comte de Saint-Morys *see* SAINT-MORYS, CHARLES PAUL JEAN-BAPTISTE DE BOURGEVIN VIALART DE
Bourgevin Vialart, Charles Etienne, Comte de Saint-Morys *see* SAINT-MORYS, CHARLES ETIENNE,Comte de
Bourgiba, Habib **20** 450
Bourg-la-Reine **11** 608
Bourgneuf de Cucé, Charles de **33** 418
Bourgogne, Louis de Bourbon, Duc de, le Petit Dauphin **4** *543*; **19** 33
Bourgogne, Marie-Adelaïde de Savoy, Duchesse de **20** 612; **25** 71; **26** 492
Bourgoin, Jean-Baptiste-Alexis **26** 206
Bourgoin, Jules **16** 547
Bourgon, Désiré **22** 456
Bourgot **17** 462
Bourguignon, Antoine **6** 448
Bourguignon, Hubert-François *see* GRAVELOT
Bourguignon, Jacques **6** 448
Bourguinon, Jean le *see* CHANGENET, JEAN
Bouriant, Pierre **10** 86
Bourke, Brian **4** 585*; **16** 18
Bourke, Edmund **10** 530
Bourke, S. J. **12** 510
Bourke-White, Margaret **4** 586*; **24** 677
works **15** 831; **24** 676, *676*
Bourla, Dominique **26** 191
Bourla, Pierre (Bruno) **4** 586*
pupils **3** 762
teachers **26** 192
works **2** 194; **3** 547
Bourlet **11** 433
Bournazel, Château of **11** 514
Bourne, James **14** 813
Bourne, John Cooke **4** 586–7*
works **15** 830; **19** 484; **32** *399*
Bourne, Samuel (*c.* 1789-1865) **21** 697
Bourne, Samuel (1834-1912) **4** 587*; **10** 580
Bourne & Co. **10** 310
Bourne End (Bucks), Noah's House **7** 712
Bournemouth (Hants)
Pier **24** 748
Punshon Memorial **21** 347
Russell-Cotes Art Gallery and Museum **19** 625
Bourne & Shepherd **4** 587; **24** 664
Bournville (W. Midlands) **5** 365; **11** 785; **12** 144; **31** 725
Bouro, S Maria **25** 306
Bourouiba **25** 771
Bourseigne-Vieille **13** 99
Boursette, Vincent **30** 312; **32** 823
Boursier **12** 833
Boursse, Esaias **4** 587*
Bousch, Valentin **21** 362
Bousies (family) **3** 590
Bousmard, Henri Jean Baptiste de **21** 581
Bousquet, Jean-Baptiste **25** 822
Boussargues **25** 503
Bousseau, Jacques **4** 587–8*
teachers **8** 71
works **3** 867; **11** 754; **27** 754
Boussemart, Joseph-François **19** 382
Boussingault, Jean-Louis **4** 588*; **5** 530; **13** 790; **22** 751
Boussod, Etienne **4** 588; **13** 228
Boussod, Jean **4** 588
Boussod, Jean, Manzi, Joyant **20** 351
Boussod, Léon **4** 588; **13** 228
Boussod, Valadon & Cie **4** 588–9*; **8** 622; **21** 868; **24** 883; **25** 234; **26** 38; **31** 214; **33** 141
assistants **26** 107
directors **20** 351
Boussu-lez-Mons Château **3** 545; **13** 113
Boussy, Clement **33** 357
Bout, Pieter **4** 589*
Boutades **7** 853
Bouteas, Yiannis **13** 355
Boutelou (family) **12** 125
Boutelou, Etienne (*d* 1734) **2** 285; **27** 753
Boutelou, Etienne (*fl* 1735) **2** 285
Boutelou, Guillaume **7** 466
Bouteroue d'Aubigny, Jean **10** 842
Boutet, Nicolas Noël **2** 456, 467
Boutet de Monvel, Bernard **4** 364; **29** 899
Boutet de Monvel, (Louis-) Maurice **4** 368, 589–90*
Bouteux, Michel Le *see* LE BOUTEUX, MICHEL
Bouthillier, Claude **6** 434; **19** 145
Bouthillier, Léon *see* CHAVIGNY, LÉON BOUTHILLIER, Comte de
Bouthroton *see* BUTRINT
Boutilimit **20** 861
library **20** 862
Boutin, Charles-Robert **3** 275
Boutin, Rodrigue **9** 2
Boutin, Simon **3** 275
Bouton, Charles-Marie **8** 449, 450, 857, 910–11; **12** 740; **14** 396; **24** 18; **30** 679
Boutry **10** 781
Bouts, Albrecht **3** 553; **4** 590, 596*; **19** 260
attributions **4** 594, 595
works **4** *595*
Bouts, Dieric, I (*c.* 1415-75) **4** 590–95*, 752; **19** 260; **22** 836
assistants **17** 703
attributions **11** 308; **12** 846; **20** 715, 734, 743; **23** 673; **25** 675
copies **20** 660
methods **23** 376; **28** 813
paintings **3** 553; **4** 752
altarpieces **4** *591*; **17** 883; **26** 186; **30** 166
justice scenes **4** *592*; **9** 271; **17** 699, 700

Bouts, Dieric, I (*c.* 1415-75)
paintings—cont.
landscape **18** 704
portraits **4** *593*
religious **3** *553*; **4** *594, 595*; **15** 85
patrons and collectors **1** 154; **2** 278; **3** 612; **26** 541
pupils **20** 660, 772; **22** 835; **33** 629
teachers **5** 43
workshop **11** 149
Bouts, Dieric, II (*c.* 1448-91) **3** 553; **4** 590, 594; **20** 743; **23** 470
Bouts, Jan **4** 590
Bouttats, Frederick **31** 871
Bouttats, Gaspard-Martin **7** 466
Boutteville, Louis Le Barc de *see* LE BARC DE BOUTTEVILLE, LOUIS
Bouvard, (Joseph-) Antoine **4** 596*; **16** 587
Bouverie, Jacob de, 1st Viscount Folkestone **20** 911; **32** 540
Bouverie, John **4** 596–7*; **33** 344
drawings **9** 26; **25** 665
sponsorship **4** 422
Bouvet **30** 588
Bouvet, Henri **33** 175
Bouvet, Honoré **5** 208
Bouvier, Gilles **31** 843
Bouvier, Michel **10** 851
Bouvier, Pierre-Louis (1766-1836) **4** 303
Bouvier, Pietro **5** 918
Bouvignes **3** 603
Bouvrie, Jan des **22** 869, 877
Bouw **24** 450
Bouwens, Simon **2** 199
Bouw en sierkunst **24** 449
Bouwens partnership **3** 607
Bouwens van der Boijen, Richard **4** 597; **10** 689
Bouwens van der Boijen, William (Oscar) **4** 597*
Bouwkundig Weekblad **4** 221
Bouwkunst en Vriendschap **23** 450
Bouwmeester, Cornelis **27** 230
Bouwonderneming Jordaan **24** 332
Bouwploeg, N. V. de **15** 769
Bouwsma, O. K. **10** 691
Bouwwereld, De **19** 117
Bouxières-aux-Dames Abbey **11** 614
Bouys, André **31** 379
Bouzey, Pierre Woeiriot de *see* WOEIRIOT, PIERRE
Bouzianis, Giorgos **4** 598*; **13** 353
Bouzid, Mohammed **1** 635
Bouzonnet-Stella, Antoine **25** 398; **29** 624
Bouzonnet-Stella, Claudine **29** 623
Bouzonnet-Stella, François **29** 624
Bouzzonet-Stella, Antoinette **29** 624
Bova, Vincenzo Giovanni **4** 598
Bovallius, Carl **13** 311
Bove, Osip (Ivanovich) **4** 598–9*; **22** 181; **27** 404
groups and movements **13** 611
works **2** 417; **4** *598*; **21** 512; **22** 172; **27** 376
Bovi, Mariano **29** 676
Bovianum Vetus **26** *886*, 888
theatre **26** 873
Bovie, Felix de **30** 373
Bovie. J.-J. **2** 201
Bovio **29** 32
Bovy, Hughes **3** 76
Bovy, Jules **3** 391
Bovy, Maria **28** 482
bowcases **6** *259*, 261, 305; **16** 505; **21** 875, 878
Bowcher, Frank **4** 599*
Bowden, J. A. **32** 801
Bowden, Pamela **24** 321
Bowden, Ross **2** 137
Bowdich, Thomas **2** 585
Bowdoin, James, II (1726-90) **4** 599
Bowdoin, James, III (1752-1811) **4** 599*; **31** 664, 666
Bowdoin, Sarah **4** 599
Bowdoin College *see under* BRUNSWICK (ME)
Bowdoin Painter **13** 523; **32** 32
Bowen, Edward **31** 335
Bowen, George **23** 71
Bowen, John T. **2** 711; **24** 600
Bowen Cup **23** 71, *71*
bowenite **10** *721*; **16** 858
Bower, Edward **4** 599–600*; **10** 248
Bower, George **20** 923; **25** 759
bowers **6** 407; **12** 94
Bowers, Henry G. **31** 232
Bowes, Jerome **10** 316
Bowes, John **4** 600*; **18** 69; **29** 353; **33** 345
Bowes, Josephine **18** 69
Bowes-Lyon, Elizabeth, Queen of England *see* ELIZABETH BOWES-LYON, Queen of Great Britain
Bowes Museum *see under* BARNARD CASTLE (CO. DURHAM)
Bow Gamelan Ensemble **29** 99; **33** 223
Bowler, Henry Alexander **4** 600*
Bowler, Thomas (William) **29** 108, 121
Bowles, George Rushout, 3rd Baron Northwick **27** 350
Bowles, John **19** 595
Bowles, Oldfield **32** 902
Bowles, Thomas **32** 778
works **19** *570*
Bowles, Thomas Gibson **31** 29
Bowles & Carver **31** 265
Bowling, Frank **13** 876
Bowl of Sigismund III **25** *127*
bowls
historical and regional traditions
Africa **1** *356*
Ancient Near East **1** 867, 878
Australia **2** *761*
Azerbaijan **2** *899*
Bhutan **3** 916
Brazil **29** *193*
Byzantine **9** 634, *645*, 657
Central Asia, Western **6** *188*, *240, 241*, 245, *245, 257, 267*
China **6** *874*, 875, *875*, *884*, *885*, 893, *897*, 900, 902, 903, *917*, III3; **7** 14, *15*, 22, 23, *24, 26, 84*, 103, 143; **12** IV3
Coclé culture **29** *147*
Colombia **29** *150*
Cycladic **8** *312*
Cyprus, ancient **8** *347, 348*; **24** 644, *644*
Czech Republic **8** *410, 412*; **12** VI3; **14** II1
Egypt **16** *385*, 415, *518*
Egypt, ancient **9** *824*; **10** *25*, 48, 57, *67*
Elamite **10** 132
England **10** 301, *321*
Fiji **11** 68, *68*
Finland **11** *106*
Germany **27** *75*
Greece, ancient **10** 474; **13** 476, 490, 536, 594, *594*
Helladic **14** *342, 345, 347*
Inca **29** *186*
Indian subcontinent **15** *694*, *727*
Iran **6** IV3; **12** V2; **16** *123, 402*, 410, *410, 413, 426, 554*
Iran, ancient **33** *688*
Iraq **12** V2; **16** 398, *398*; **23** *558*
bowls
historical and regional traditions—cont.
Islamic **2** *899*; **6** IV3; **16** *123*, 365–6, *385*, 394, 398, *398*, *402*, 404, 410, *410, 413*, 415, 419, *421, 426, 518, 554*; **23** *558*
Italy **12** VIII2; **25** 543; **27** *107*
Japan **18** *555*
Korea **18** *255, 336, 340, 341, 342*, 351
Kyrgyzstan **6** *267*
Mesoamerica, Pre-Columbian **21** *240*
Mexico **21** *240*
Mixtec **21** *240*
Moche (culture) **29** *134*
Mycenaean **14** *345, 347*
Nabataea **22** *420*
Native North Americans **22** 586, *603, 604, 612*
Netherlands, the **22** 890
Nicaragua **23** *83*
Nigeria **1** *356*; **4** *854*
Ottoman **16** *421*
Panama **29** *147*
Papua New Guinea **24** 82
Phoenician **24** 644*, *644*; **30** 187
Poland **25** *127*
Prehistoric art **25** 543
Rome, ancient **6** *267*; **12** VIII2; **26** *859*; **27** *75, 77, 107*
Russia **27** *419*
Serbia **28** *455*
Sierra Leone **1** 241
Sogdiana **6** *240, 241*
Solomon Islands **29** 50, *50*
South America, Pre-Columbian **29** *134, 147, 150, 186, 193*
Spain **16** 404, 419
Switzerland **27** *77*
Syria-Palestine **30** 187, *197*
Thailand **30** *611*
Thracian **30** 769
Trinidad and Tobago **31** *338*
United States of America **4** *482*; **22** *603, 604*; **26** *262*
Uzbekistan **6** *188*
Venda **32** *154*, 154–5
Weeden Island culture **22** *612*
Yoruba **1** 329, *356*; **33** 559
materials
agate **14** II1
amber **1** 762
amethyst **14** *171*
basketwork **22** *659*
brass **16** *385*
bronze **4** *854*; **6** *245*; **24** 644
citrine **14** *171*
clay **7** 143; **29** *193*
copper **2** *899*
earthenwares **2** *761*; **6** *257*; **16** *398, 426*
enamel **8** *412*; **14** *171*; **27** *419*
faience (i) (glass) **1** 878; **10** 48, *67*
garnets **14** *171*
gems **12** V2; **27** *419*
glass
China **7** *84*; **12** IV3
Czech Republic **8** *410*; **12** VI3
Egypt, ancient **10** 57
England **10** *321*
Greece, ancient **13** 594, *594*
Indian subcontinent **15** *694*
Iran **12** V2
Iraq **12** V2
Islamic **16** *518*
Rome, ancient **6** *267*; **12** VIII2; **27** *75, 77*
gold **7** 22; **12** V2; **14** *171*; **18** 351; **22** *435*; **24** *644*; **27** *419*; **30** 769; **31** 531
hyacinth **14** *171*
inlays **16** *385*
inscriptions **16** *123*
ivory **7** 103
bowls
materials—cont.
lacquer **7** 14, *15*
lapis lazuli **33** *688*
metal **6** 245
pearls **27** *419*
pewter **24** 580
porcelain **6** 875, 902, 903; **11** *106, 608*
pottery
Byzantine **9** 634
China **6** *884, 885*, III3
Cyprus, ancient **8** *347, 348*
Egypt, ancient **9** *824*; **10** *25*
Greece, ancient **13** *540*; **14** *342, 345, 347*
Iran **6** IV3; **16** *123, 554*
Iraq **23** *558*
Mexico **21** *240*
Moche (culture) **29** *134*
Nicaragua **23** *83*
Ottoman **16** *421*
Rome, ancient **27** *107*
Syria-Palestine **30** *197*
Weeden Island culture **22** *612*
shells **29** *50*
silver **6** *188, 241*; **7** 23, *24, 26*; **9** 657; **16** 31; **18** 351; **24** 644; **26** *262, 859*; **28** *455*; **29** *119*
silver-gilt **6** *240*; **8** *412*
stone **29** *186*
stonewares **6** 893, *897, 917*; **18** *336, 555*; **30** *611*
wood **1** *356*; **11** 68, *68*; **22** 586; **29** *50*; **31** 305
types
bleeding **24** 580
carinated **30** 185, *197*
hanging **15** 871
Homeric **13** 539
kinrande **6** 332, 905
Long-petal bowls **13** 540
Megarian **13** 477, 491, 539, *540*
mush **22** *659*
offering bowls **6** 152
Shield bowls **13** 540
sugar **10** *314*; **11** *608*; **16** 31; **29** *119*
teabowls *see* TEABOWLS
totai **6** 905
Bowman, Alexander H. **33** 564
Bowman, James **29** 541
Bowman & Crowther **31** 584; **33** 385
Bowman's **10** 299
Bo & Wohlert **4** 183–4*
works **22** *366*, 367
Bowood House (Wilts) **3** 493; **20** 867; **21** 806
Bow Porcelain Factory **4** 600–601*; **8** 776; **9** 369; **10** 308; **19** 595
collections **28** 168
directors **11** 810
marks **20** 441
production **4** 177; **6** 326, 332; **9** 29; **10** 308; **30** *397*; **33** 380
bows **2** 448
historical and regional traditions
Central Asia, Eastern **6** 305
Central Asia, Western **6** 260, 261
Egypt, ancient **10** 39–40
Indian subcontinent **15** 676, *677*, 677
Islamic **16** 508
Japan **17** 361, 362; **31** 167*
Maya **21** 246
Mesoamerica, Pre-Columbian **21** 245, 246
Mongolia **21** 875
Ottoman **16** 508
Papua New Guinea **24** *70*
materials
bamboo **3** 144
ivory **6** 261
types
crossbows **2** 448
Bowser, David **1** 440
bow-string arch bridges *see* BRIDGES → types → tied arch
bow-string arches *see under* ARCHES → types
bow-string girder bridges *see under* BRIDGES → types
bowtell mouldings *see under* MOULDINGS → types
Bowyer, Robert **2** 11; **4** 601*; **19** 588, 728; **23** 452; **29** 491
book illustrations **33** 95
paintings **31** 308
printmakers **29** 732
works **14** 115; **23** 213; **25** 626
illustrated **7** 413; **18** 720; **28** 558
Box, John **25** 15
Box, Nicolaas **30** 16
Boxall, William **4** 602*; **6** 100; **22** 296
box altars *see under* ALTARS → types
Boxberger, Michiel **31** 238
box chariots *see under* CHARIOTS → types
Boxer, David **4** 602*; **16** 884
Boxer Codex *see under* CODICES → individual manuscripts
Boxer Rhyton **21** 654, 659, 689, *690*
boxes **6** 388; **9** 14
historical and regional traditions
Africa **1** 366
Ancient Near East **24** 336, *336*
Austria **2** 823*
Bhutan **3** 916
Burma **5** 254
Byzantine **9** 648, 651
Central Asia, Eastern **6** 303
China **7** 14, 15, 16, *16, 17, 18, 19, 20*, 96, 100, 133, 134, 141; **18** *601, 605, 612*; **31** *194*
Czech Republic **8** *405*
Denmark **8** 752
Early Christian (*c.* AD 250-843) **9** 648
Egypt, ancient **10** 51, *53*, 53–4
England **3** 442; **10** *347*, 347–8*; **14** *763*
France **3** *440*, 442; **4** *601*; **11** 630, 631–3*; **24** 147; **28** I2
Germany **24** 62
India, Republic of **15** 174, 175
Indian subcontinent **15** *696*
Islamic **16** 365
Jamaica **16** *889*
Japan **14** 429, *429*; **17** 297, 300, *301*, 302, *305*, 386; **18** *613*
Jordan **24** 336, *336*
Korea **18** 363, *370, 371*, 380, *602*; **33** IV1
Kuba (iii) (Zaïre) **18** 487
Madagascar **20** *39*
Netherlands, the **22** 897*
Peru **24** 512
Scotland **28** 264
Sri Lanka **29** 470
Sweden **30** *110*, 112*
Tibet **30** 847
Vietnam **32** 487, 488
materials
agate **10** 347
amboyna **33** IV1
baleen **28** 302
bamboo **15** 174; **18** 380
beadwork **3** *440*, 442
brass **10** *341*; **16** *383*; **21** I1; **22** *894*; **33** IV1
diamonds **10** IV3
ebony **10** 53
enamel **4** *601*; **10** *347*, IV3; **11** 630, 633; **30** 112
faience (i) (glass) **10** 51, 53
glass **17** 386
gold **2** 823*; **4** *601*, 601–2*; **7** *19, 20*; **8** 752; **10** 51, 347*, *347, 721*; **11** 631–3*; **21** I1; **22** 897*; **24** 147; **28** I2; **30** 112*
gourds **1** 367

boxes
materials—cont.
horn 14 763, *763*
inlays 16 *383*
ivory 9 648, 651; 10 51, 53; 15 *696*; 16 797, 798
lacquer 7 13, 14, 15, 16, *16*, *17*, *18*, *19*, *20*, 96, 100; 14 *429*, *704*; 17 297, 300, *301*, 302, *305*, *383*; 18 *370*, *371*, *601*, *602*, *604*, *605*, *612*, *613*
mother-of-pearl 4 *601*; 18 *602*; 28 I2
paulownia 18 363
pewter 7 100
pottery 6 257
rock crystal 11 633
silver 11 *108*; 16 32, *32*, *889*, *900*; 21 I1; 24 512; 30 *840*; 32 488
silver-gilt 30 *105*
soapstone 7 133, 134
steel 30 *110*
tortoiseshell 31 *194*
wood 7 141; 16 *383*, 487, 497; 30 847
zelkova 33 IV1
techniques
gilding 10 53; 20 *39*
types
account 17 358
amulet 21 878; 30 *840*
bentō 17 382, *383*
bible 5 918; 31 624
charm 30 840
cigarette 10 *721*, IV3
deed 32 814
see also freedom
etrog 17 572
freedom 16 32, *32*
see also deed
ice 7 *807*
jewellery 9 240
Koran 16 *383*, 487, 497
musical 22 375
paintboxes *see* PAINTBOXES
peepshow *see* PEEPSHOW BOXES
penboxes 6 257; 16 365, *376*; 21 I1
snuff-boxes *see* SNUFF-BOXES
sponge-boxes 30 *105*
sugar 11 *108*
tebako 17 300
theatre *see* THEATRE BOXES
tobacco-boxes
Africa 1 367*
England 10 340, *341*, 342
Germany 12 452
Netherlands, the 22 *894*
Sweden 30 111
toilet-boxes 7 13
work-boxes 28 264
writing-boxes 5 191; 14 *704*; 16 *900*; 18 *604*; 20 VIII3; 25 304
see also BOX LIDS; CASKETS
box frames *see* TIMBER STRUCTURES → types → wall frames
box girder *see under* BRIDGES → types
Bo xian, Xianping si 29 617
box looms *see under* LOOMS → types
box mirrors *see under* MIRRORS → types
box tiles *see under* TILES → types
box-wood
historical and regional traditions
Catalonia 29 *313*
China 7 141
England 33 I2
France 29 571
Germany 12 423, 426; 19 *108*; 29 *728*; 33 326
Gothic 29 *728*; 33 I2
Holy Roman Empire (before 1648) 29 570
Indian subcontinent 15 721
box-wood
historical and regional traditions—cont.
Japan 17 399
uses
brushpots 7 141
cupboards 12 423
desks 29 *313*
furniture 12 426
marquetry 12 423
mirror frames 21 720, 721
musical instruments 33 I2
netsuke 17 399
relief sculpture 19 *108*
sculpture 29 *728*
wood-engravings 33 367
Boy, Adolf 25 104; 32 875
Boy, Peter (1645-1727) 7 835; 12 457
Boy, Willem 4 602–3*
attributions 30 69
patrons and collectors 30 68; 32 5
works 11 466; 30 84, *84*
Boyadjiev, Zlatyu 4 603*
patrons and collectors 5 163
works 5 *154*, 155
Boyalikoy Hanikahi 16 185
Boyana 4 603*; 5 *144*; 9 *511*
Church of the Virgin 5 155
SS Nicholas and Panteleimon 4 603; 5 147, 162
wall paintings 5 150, *151*; 9 582
Boyar Pisanitsy 4 603*; 25 *471*; 27 *362*, 367
Boyce, Brown & Kemp 31 423
Boyce, George Price 4 604*; 25 555; 33 64
Boyce, Joanna Mary *see* WELLS, JOANNA MARY
Boyce, Sonia 4 604*
groups and movements 10 882
works 10 *882*
Boyceau (de la Barauderie), Jacques 4 604–5*
patrons and collectors 4 548, 549; 32 369, 371
works 12 120; 19 162
Boychuk, Mykhaylo 2 634; 4 605*; 31 559
Boyd, Alice 28 249, 276
Boyd, Andrew 29 454–5
Boyd, Arthur (Merric Bloomfield) 4 605, 606–7*
groups and movements 2 161, 750
patrons and collectors 4 882; 33 744
works 2 749, 750, 760–61, *761*, 767; 4 *606*
Boyd, Arthur Merric 4 605, 606
Boyd, Arthur Merric, Pottery 2 760–61; 4 606
works 2 *761*
Boyd, David 2 161, 761; 4 605
Boyd, Doris Lucy Eleanor 2 760; 4 605, 606
Boyd, George 23 68
Boyd, Guy 4 605
Boyd, Harriet (Ann) 4 607*; 13 233
Boyd, Hermia *see* LLOYD-JONES, HERMIA
Boyd, John 12 772
Boyd, Lucy 4 605
Boyd, Mary 4 605
Boyd, (William) Merric 2 760; 4 605, 606
Boyd, (Theodore) Penleigh 4 605; 29 243
Boyd, Robin (Gerald Penleigh) 2 772; 4 373, 605–6*
collaboration 4 415; 13 709; 26 744
groups and movements 2 756; 30 160
works 2 742; 21 76
Boyd, Spencer 28 249
Boydell, John 4 362, 607–8*; 10 393; 19 588; 24 820; 25 626; 26 230, 231
architecture 10 369, 677
book illustrations 33 95
drawings 10 806
painters
Barry, James (1741-1806; Ireland) 3 285
Downman, John 9 205
Edwards, Edward 9 740
Hamilton, William (ii) (1751-1801; painter) 14 115
Hodges, William 14 611
Ibbetson, Julius Caesar, the elder (1759-1817) 15 57
Kauffman, (Maria Anna) Angelica (Catharine) 17 852
Opie, John 23 452
Peters, Matthew William 24 548
Reynolds, Joshua 26 274, 275
Rigaud, John Francis 26 388
Smirke, Robert (i) (1753-1845) 28 871
Stothard, Thomas 29 732
Thomson, Henry 30 751
Tresham, Henry 31 308
Wheatley, Francis 33 133
Wright of Derby, Joseph 33 414
paintings 3 239; 10 250; 14 586; 26 737; 33 95
printmakers 29 676
Basire, (John) James, I (1730-1802) 3 329
Bromley, William 4 845
Browne, John 4 886
Burke, Thomas 5 216
Cheesman, Thomas 6 528
Cunego, Domenico 8 267
Earlom, Richard 9 506
Haid (i), Johann Gottfried 14 49; 21 416
Hall, John (1739-97) 14 79
Heath, James 14 280
Pether, William 24 551
Ravenet, Simon Francis, the elder (1706-74) 26 30
Sharp, William 28 558
Stadler, Joseph Constantine 29 491
Taylor, Isaac (1730-1807) 30 384
Walker, Anthony 32 793
Watson, Caroline 32 910
Watson, James 32 910
Webber, John 33 14
Woollett, William 10 393; 26 230; 33 372
prints 25 619; 26 231; 29 675, 676
Boydell, Josiah 2 690
Boyden, Elbridge 2 699
Boye, Pierre 4 608*; 5 666; 7 411
Boyens, Willem *see* BOY, WILLEM
Boyer 14 58
Boyer, Bob 22 598
Boyer, Christine 13 *691*
Boyer, Jean-Baptiste 18 626
Boyer d'Eguilles 4 48
Boyes, G. T. W. B. 25 662
Boyes, John 4 374
Bøyesen, Peter Rostrup *see* ROSTRUP BØYESEN, PETER
Boyle (family) 4 608; 25 210
Boyle, Charles, 4th Earl of Orrery 30 123
Boyle, Georgia 4 608
Boyle, John 21 697; 33 22
Boyle, Mark 4 608*
works 11 55, *55*; 25 26; 28 240; 29 97; 31 706
Boyle, Richard, 1st Earl of Cork 4 608–9*
architecture 6 96
paintings 16 13
reliefs 10 663
sculpture 16 20, 35
Boyle, Richard, 3rd Earl of Burlington and 4th Earl of Cork 4 609–13*, *611*; 11 172; 19 621; 25 233
architecture 2 314; 7 175; 10 233, 361; 12 332; 17 900; 19 157, 570; 23 858; 28 156
assembly rooms 2 617, *618*; 4 *613*; 33 543
country houses 4 *612*, 757; 7 174; 8 47; 10 294; 23 *856*, *859*; 25 266; 27 237; 32 411, 553
houses 5 539
town houses 7 666
collaboration 14 436; 17 903
collections 2 559; 10 276
drawings 17 638; 23 871
furniture 7 171
gardens 7 174; 12 129
groups and movements 12 333; 13 300, 608; 22 738; 23 856, 858, 859, 860
illustrated writings 32 859, 860
interior decoration 11 348
paintings 1 488; 10 364; 13 301; 18 672; 26 321; 27 465
sculpture 13 301, 782; 18 902; 27 466
Boyle, Robert 9 473; 19 354
Boyle, Sebastian 4 608
Boyle Abbey 16 19; 26 618
Boyleaux, Etienne *see* BOILEAU, ETIENNE
Boylen, James 1 496
Boymans, F(rans) J(acob) O(tto) 4 614*; 21 39; 22 905; 27 230
Boymans-van Beuningen Museum *see under* ROTTERDAM → museums
Boyne, John 14 278
Boynes, Robert 2 751
Boyo 1 403; 14 376
Boys, Thomas Shotter 4 614–15*, *615*
dealers 4 66
pupils 25 406
works 4 362; 19 *484*, 485; 20 602; 25 623, 626; 31 155
Boysen, Bill 2 763
Boytac, Diogo *see* BOITAC, DIOGO
Boyvin, André 13 700
Boyvin, René 4 615–16*; 11 532, 634
attributions 21 538
groups and movements 11 264
patrons and collectors 13 232
pupils 24 366
teachers 21 538
works 11 *264*, 616; 13 701; 21 538; 24 271; 27 210; 30 735
Boyvin, Robert 1 766
Boza, Cristián 6 594
Boze, Joseph(, Comte de) 4 616*; 5 733; 19 67
Bozen *see* BOLZANO
Božetěch 8 381
Bozhenitsa Church 5 156
Bozhkov, Atanass 5 163
Božicković, Vera 28 451
Božidarević, Nikola 8 178; 25 340
Bozidarović, Vicenzo 25 339
Boznańska, Olga 4 616–17*, *617*; 25 107
Bozo 1 385
Bozo, Dominique 4 617–18*
Bozoluk *see* LETOON
Božović, Milan 22 18
Bōzumachi kiln 17 811
Bozum Church 22 *813*, 819
vaults (ceiling) 22 *819*
Bozzalino da Campione 5 549
Bozzato, Giovanni Battista *see* PONCHINO, GIAMBATTISTA
bozzetti *see* MODELLI → types → sculpture; OIL SKETCHES
B⊥R, Master 20 792*
Brå (Denmark) 6 158
Bra (Italy)
S Chiara 7 258; 16 643; 32 644, *645*
Santa Trinità 29 831
Bra, Eustache-Marie-Joseph 4 618
Bra, Théophile-François-Marcel 4 618*
Braakman, Cees 22 876; 31 576
Braakman, Dirk Lubertus 31 576
Braam, J. A. van 16 873
Braamcamp, Gerrit 1 808; 4 618*; 22 902
collections 22 904
paintings 7 662; 18 186; 31 367
sculpture 8 150
Braat, F. W. 22 895
Brabant *see* BELGIUM
Brabant, Catherine de *see* CATHERINE DE BRABANT
Brabant, Henry I, Duke of *see* HENRY I, Duke of Brabant
Brabant, Jean de *see* JEAN DE BRABANT
Brabant, Louis de Mâle, Duke of *see* LOUIS II, Count of Flanders and Duke of Brabant
Brabant, Margaret of *see* MARGARET OF BRABANT, Countess of Flanders
Brabante, Arrigo di *see* ARRIGO DI BRABANTE
Brabant Fauvism 4 618–19*; 28 104; 30 726
see also FAUVISM → regional traditions → Belgium
Brabanti, Guillaume di *see* GUILLAUME DI BRABANTI
Brabazon, Hercules Brabazon 4 619*; 17 471
Brabazon, John, 10th Earl of Meath 16 24
Brabender, Franz 22 315
Brabender, Heinrich 22 316
Brabender, Johann 22 315, 316
bracae 9 251, 640
Bracamante, Gonzáles de Güemes *see* GÜEMES BRACAMANTE, GONZÁLES DE
Bracamonte y Guzmán, Gaspar de, 3rd Conde de Peñaranda *see* PEÑARANDA, GASPAR DE BRACAMONTE Y GUZMÁN, 3rd Conde de
Bracceschi, Giovanni Battista *see* BERTUCCI, GIOVANNI BATTISTA
Braccesco, Carlo 4 619–21*
attributions 4 *620*
Bracci, Antonio 11 503
Bracci, Giuseppe 14 131
Bracci, Mario 5 *843*
Bracci, Pietro 4 621–2*
collaboration 3 920; 20 125; 22 45; 25 322
patrons and collectors 3 708; 4 635; 23 577; 25 301
teachers 27 347
works 3 708; 4 *621*; 10 744; 11 345; 16 704; 26 810; 27 646
Bracciano (family) 23 353
Bracciano, Palazzo Orsini-Odescalchi 23 575, 576; 33 717
Bracciano, Livio Odescalchi, Duca di 23 352, 353*
collections 2 910; 32 8
paintings 7 394; 20 376, 378
sculpture 23 353
Bracciano, Paolo Giordano I Orsini, Duca di 23 576
Bracciano, Paolo Giordano II Orsini, Duca di 23 576*
collections 23 576
etchings 25 62
gardens 9 339
paintings 4 733; 32 715
Braccio da Pisa, Niccolò 28 85
Bracciolini, Francesco 7 908

Bracciolini, (Gian Francesco) Poggio **1** 101; **2** 161; **4** 622*; **9** 20; **11** 184; **14** 867; **16** 658; **26** 767; **27** 114; **32** 638
- collaboration **23** 86
- personal collection **23** 86
- works **26** 400, 847; **28** *307*

bracelets **17** 519, 520, 524, 526, 528; **26** 82
- historical and regional traditions
  - Africa **1** 292, 296, 350, 351
  - Ancient Near East **1** 875
  - Byzantine **9** 653
  - Central Asia, Eastern **6** 312
  - China **7** 109, 111
  - Early Christian (*c.* AD 250-843) **9** 653
  - Egypt, ancient **10** 29, *29*
  - England **17** *528*
  - France **17** III2
  - Germany **12** *454*
  - Greece, ancient **13** *600*, 601
  - Indonesia **15** 814
  - Iran **16** *530*
  - Islamic **16** *530*, 532
  - Italy **6** *20*; **16** *752*
  - Kenya **1** 362
  - Korea **18** 366, 367
  - Morocco **16** 532
  - Native North Americans **22** 613, 614, 651
  - Netherlands, the **22** *896*
  - Ottoman **16** 532
  - Prehistoric art **25** 545; **29** 228
  - Rome, ancient **27** 102, *102*
  - Senufo **1** 357
  - South-east Asia **29** 228
  - Sudan **1** 362
  - Troadic **31** 355
  - Uganda **1** 362
  - Vietnam **32** 487
  - Yemen **16** 532
- materials
  - aluminium **22** *896*
  - amethyst **17** *528*
  - basketwork **1** 296
  - beads **25** 545
  - bronze **7** 109; **13** *600*, 601; **29** 228
  - chrysolite **17** *528*
  - copper **22** 613
  - diamonds **17** III2
  - enamel **17** III2
  - glass **7** 109
  - gold **6** *20*; **7** 109, 111; **16** *530*, *752*; **17** *528*, III2; **31** 355
  - iron **12** *454*; **22** 613
  - ivory **1** 292, 351; **15** 814
  - jade **7** 109, 111
  - quills **22** 651
  - silver **7** 109; **10** *29*; **18** 366; **22** 614
  - stone **1** 350
  - turquoise **16** *530*

Bracelli, Giovanni Battista **4** 622–3*
Brach, Paul **28** 53
Brachelieu, Léandre **4** 310
Bracho, Carlos **21** 389
Bracht, Christian van **8** 742
Bracht, Eugen **28** 104
Bracht, Johan van **8** 742
bracing **28** 830
Brack, John **2** 750; **4** 623*
- groups and movements **2** 161, 750
- patrons and collectors **1** 147
- works **2** 752

Brackenware **29** 117
bracket clocks *see under* CLOCKS → types
brackets **4** 623–5*; **23** 480
- Buddhism **17** 66, 72
- Chile **6** 591
- China **4** 623*; **5** 649; **6** 640–41, *641*, *642*, *644*, 667, 686, 690; **7** 143; **30** 913
- Indian subcontinent **10** *827*; **15** *431*, *531*
- Japan **4** 623–5*, *624*; **17** 66, 72; **30** 913
- Korea **4** 623*; **18** *264*, 264–5, *265*; **30** 913
- Nepal **22** 774, 792–3, *793*
- Scotland **28** 245
- *see also* CONSOLES

Brackett, Edward **19** 286
Brackh, Antonis van **15** 866
Bracknell (Berks) **31** 733
Braco, William Duff, Lord of *see* DUFF, WILLIAM, 1st Earl of Fife
Braconnier, Stéphane **19** 848
Bracquemond, Félix (-Auguste-Joseph) **4** 625–7*; **6** 462; **11** 672; **14** 246
- collaboration **6** 489; **7** 880; **8** 607; **20** 603
- groups and movements **2** 565; **17** 440, 441
- patrons and collectors **5** 284
- pupils **4** 627
- teachers **13** 806
- works **4** *626*; **5** 364; **9** 204, 309, 310; **10** 556, 563; **11** 606; **12** 830; **19** 397; **21** 171; **24** 148, 552; **29** 58

Bracquemond, Marie **4** 626–7*; **11** 672
Bracquemond, Pierre **4** 627
bracteates *see under* COINS → types
Bractwo Świetgo Łukasza *see* FELLOWSHIP OF ST LUKE
Brad **3** 376
Bradaški, M. **13** 680
Bradburn, John **11** 431
Bradbury, R. E. **3** 723
Bradbury, Robert **10** 274; **29** 835
- works **10** *275*

Bradbury, Thomas, & Sons **28** 577
Braddan **32** 530
Braddock **29** 250
Braden, Norah **10** 315; **25** 39
Bradford (N. Yorks)
- Buttershaw School **28** 158
- Cartwright Hall **10** 370
- National Museum of Photography, Film and Television **24** 683
- Undercliffe School **28** 158
- Wool Exchange **10** 237, 669

Bradford, William **4** 627*; **31** 651
Bradford & Inskeep **19** 239
Bradford-on-Avon (Avon), St Lawrence **2** 67, 71; **5** 319; **10** 227; **27** 124
Bradley, B. Harley **33** 400
Bradley, Humphrey **30** 26
Bradley, R. J. **21** 160
Bradley, Thomas **2** 324
Bradley, William **20** 239; **25** 347
Bradley & Hubbard **31** 653
Bradshaw **19** 531
Bradshaw, Joseph **1** 57
Bradshaw, Lawrence **7** 420
Bradshaw, William **10** 351
Bradshawe, Edmund **10** 303
Bradshaw factory
- works **10** *352*

Bradshaw & Gass **23** 194
Bradt, Hilary
- works **20** *37*

Bradvicë **1** 543
Bradwell on Sea (Essex), St Peter by the Wall **2** 65
Bradwell Wood (Staffs)
- pottery **10** *304*

Brady, A. B. **3** 269
Brady, Josiah **8** 573
Brady, Mathew B. **4** 627–8*; **12** 146; **24** 660, 661, 666; **31** 602
- staff **3** 250; **23** 624
- works **24** 661

Bradzys, Antanas **19** 499
Braekeleer, De *see* DE BRAEKELEER
Braellier, Jean le *see* JEAN LE BRAELLIER
Braem, René **3** 551; **4** 628*; **19** 260
Braevius, Johannes Georgius **26** 849
Braga **4** 628–9*; **25** *288*
- Cathedral **13** 71; **25** 289; **26** 690
  - tomb of Archbishop Gonçalo Pereira **13** 102
  - wall paintings **25** 295
- metalwork **25** 313
- Misericórdia **25** 307
- Museu dos Biscainhos **25** 318
- Palácio do Raio **25** 293; **28** 911, *912*
- sanctuary of Bom Jesus do Monte **4** *629*
- Santa Cruz **26** 254
- S Maria Madalena **28** 910–11, *911*

Braga, Leandro **4** 629–30*; **25** 308
Braga, Martin of *see* MARTIN OF BRAGA
Braga, Teodoro **4** 722
Bragaglia, Anton Giulio **4** 630; **11** 865; **25** 447
Bragaglia, Arturo **4** 630
Bragaglia, Carlo Ludovico **4** 630
Bragança *see* BRAGANZA
Bragança Sousa Tavares Mascarenhos e Silva, Pedro Henrique de, Duque de Lafões *see* LAFÕES, PEDRO HENRIQUE, Duque de
Braganza (Portugal) **25** 315
Braganza (House of) **4** 630–32*, *631*
Braganza, Alfonso Aviz, Duque de **4** *631*
Braganza, Alfonso VI, King of Portugal *see* ALFONSO VI, King of Portugal
Braganza, Amalia, Queen of Portugal *see* AMALIA, Queen of Portugal
Braganza, Carlos da **28** 781
Braganza, Carlos I de *see* CHARLES, King of Portugal
Braganza, Carlota Joaquina **2** 41
Braganza, Catharine, Queen of England *see* CATHARINE OF BRAGANZA, Queen of England
Braganza, Gaspar de, Archbishop of Braga **1** 752; **28** 911
Braganza, Isabel of Savoy, Queen of Portugal *see* MARIA FRANCISCA ISABELLA, Queen of Portugal
Braganza, Jaime, 4th Duque de **4** *631*, 632*
- architecture **2** 500; **4** 630; **32** 539

Braganza, João I, 6th Duque de **4** 633
Braganza, John IV, King of Portugal *see* JOHN IV, King of Portugal
Braganza, John V, King of Portugal *see* JOHN V, King of Portugal
Braganza, John VI, King of Portugal *see* JOHN VI, King of Portugal
Braganza, José de, Archbishop of Braga **4** 629
Braganza, Joseph, King of Portugal *see* JOSEPH, King of Portugal
Braganza, Luís, King of Portugal *see* LUÍS, King of Portugal
Braganza, Maria Anna Josepha, Queen of Portugal *see* MARIA ANNA JOSEPHA, Queen of Portugal
Braganza, Maria Francisca of Savoy, Queen of Portugal *see* MARIA FRANCISCA ISABELLA, Queen of Portugal
Braganza, Maria I, Queen of Portugal *see* MARY I, Queen of Portugal
Braganza, Maria II, Queen of Portugal *see* MARIA II, Queen of Portugal
Braganza, María Isabel de, Queen of Spain *see* MARÍA ISABEL DE BRAGANZA, Queen of Spain
Braganza, Maria Pia, Queen of Portugal *see* MARIA PIA, Queen of Portugal
Braganza, Peter II, Emperor of Brazil *see* PETER II, Emperor of Brazil
Braganza, Peter II, King of Portugal *see* PETER II, King of Portugal
Braganza, Peter III, King of Portugal *see* PETER III, King of Portugal
Braganza, Peter IV, King of Portugal *see* PETER I, Emperor of Brazil
Braganza, Peter V, King of Portugal *see* PETER V, King of Portugal
Braganza, Sebastián Gabriel Bórbon y *see* BÓRBON Y BRAGANZA, SEBASTIÁN GABRIEL
Braganza, Teotónio of **4** 630, *631*, 632*
Braganza, Theodosius, 5th Duque de **4** *631*, 633
Bragg, Charles **27** 872
Bragge, Robert **32** 824
Braggernes **18** 614
Braghieri, Gianni **5** 123; **16** 651; **25** 359; **27** 192
Braghirolli, Wilhelmo **19** 834
Bragny-sur-Saone **25** 540, 547
Brahe, Knud **8** 725
Brahe, Per, Count **33** 81
Brahe, Tycho **4** 639–40*; **23** 339; **25** 432
- armillary spheres **28** *209*
- house **8** 725; **24** 237
- observatories **29** 593
- patrons and collectors **13** 914

Brahetrolleborg **17** 678
Brahim, Mubarak **22** 129
Brahm, Otto **8** 109; **30** 685
Brahmanabad *see* AL-MANSHURA
Brahmāpura *see* BRAHMAUR
Brahmapuri **15** 450
Brahmaur **4** 640*; **15** *264*, 483
- temples of Lakshanadevi **15** 264

Brahmeshvara Temple *see under* BHUBANESHWAR
Brahmipuri **21** 716
Brahmi script *see under* SCRIPTS → types
Braibant, Jacques de *see* JACQUES DE BRAIBANT
braided rugs *see under* RUGS → types
braiding **30** 550
braids **17** 308*, 313; **21** 876, 877; **24** 237; **30** 540, 542
- *see also* RIBBONS

Braidwood, R. J. **1** 815; **17** 447; **30** 196
Braila **26** 709
Brailes (Warwicks), St George **11** 253
Brailes, William de *see* WILLIAM DE BRAILES
Braillard, Maurice **12** 276
Braine, St Yved **13** 39, 179, 180; **22** 218
- altar **7** 263
- stained glass **29** 511

Braine-le-Conte **31** 187
brain tannage *see under* TANNING
Braisch, Aurelius, Abbot of Neresheim **22** 796
Braith, Anton **2** 106
Brajkov, Miho **9** 331
Brak, Tell **1** 508; **4** 640–42*; **21** *267*, 271; **30** 178, *180*, 184
- alabaster (gypsum) **1** 516
- architecture **21** 281
- Eye Temple **4** 640; **21** 282, 294; **30** 184
  - altar **1** 690
  - eye idols **4** *641*
- glass **1** 864
- ivory-carvings **1** 869
- Khabur **1** 856
- metalwork **12** 627
- palace **1** 893
- pottery **21** 270, 306; **30** 197
- sculpture **4** *641*
- seal amulets **1** *856*
- seals **21** *731*
- shrine **21** 286
- temples **21** 272
- trade **30** 179
- writing-tablets **21** 271

Brake, Brian **4** 642*
Brakenburg, Richard **13** 895
brakes **7** 765
Brakhage, Stan **7** 874; **10** 688
Brakspear, W. H. **3** 283
Bramante, Donato **4** 642–52*; **14** 869; **16** 661; **21** 532; **23** 539; **31** 740
- architecture **4** 643*; **7** 380, 383; **9** 181; **26** 768
  - cathedrals **13** 210; **24** 284
  - choirs **7** 527; **30** 656
  - churches **7** 257
    - St Peter's (Vatican, Rome) **4** 404; **7** 541; **23** 492; **26** 756, 804–5
    - S Ambrogio (Milan) **16** 633
    - S Maria di Canepanova (Pavia) **3** 249
    - S Maria della Consolazione (Todi) **16** *633*
    - S Maria delle Grazie (Milan) **9** 86; **21** *516*
    - S Maria di Loreto (Loreto) **19** 686
    - S Maria di Loreto (Rome) **9** 339
    - S Maria del Popolo (Rome) **27** 777
    - S Maria presso S Celso (Milan) **19** 561
    - S Maria presso S Satiro (Milan) **4** *644*; **15** 137; **16** 632; **21** 517; **30** 501
  - Tempietto (S Pietro in Montorio, Rome) **4** *648*; **8** 224; **23** 486; **26** 186; **27** 236
  - courtyards **4** *649*; **8** 65; **16** 770; **21** 535; **24** 399; **25** 7; **26** *813*; **28** 754; **32** 546
  - crypts **32** 94
  - exedrae **25** 7
  - façade decoration **10** 737
  - niches **9** 20
  - nymphaea **13** 703
  - orders (architecture) **23** 488
  - palazzi **3** 771; **19** *685*, 686, 688; **23** 492; **25** 907; **31** 742
  - piers (ii) (masonry) **7** 692; **24** 752
  - plans **26** *804*
  - shrines (i) (cult) **19** 686, *688*
  - squares (town) **5** 701
  - staircases **22** 6; **29** 522
- attributions **5** 698; **17** 705; **20** 623; **31** 744
- collaboration **9** 75; **11** 248; **26** 228; **27** 741, 776
- commentaries **1** 572
- drawings **2** 328; **26** 800
- friezes **14** 416; **21** 525
- paintings **4** 643*; **16** 662
- patrons and collectors
  - Carafa, Oliviero, Cardinal **5** 698
  - Dominican Order **9** 112
  - Julius II, Pope (*reg* 1503-13) **2** 168; **7** 218; **19** 687; **26** 186, 768, 800, 801, 811; **27** 272–3

Bramante, Donato
patrons and collectors—cont.
Ludovico (Maria), 7th Duke of Milan (*reg* 1494-99) 16 630; 28 532
Sforza, Ascanio Maria, Cardinal 28 532
pupils 6 357
restorations by others 3 688; 6 115
Bramantino 4 653*
patrons and collectors 18 897; 21 517, 525; 27 273
works 1 462; 4 *653*; 26 817, 818; 31 352, 842
Bramberger, Ferdinand 25 435
Brambilla, Ambrogio 4 654*
Brambilla, Francesco, the elder (*fl* 1560-*d* 1570) 4 654–5*
Brambilla, Francesco, the younger (*d* 1599) 4 654, 655*
patrons and collectors 32 612
pupils 25 642
works 11 280; 21 525, 533
Brame (family) 4 655
Brame, Emma 30 425
Brame, Hector (-Henri-Clément) 4 655–6*; 8 622; 9 424; 11 663; 30 425
paintings 8 647; 18 869; 27 267
Brame, Hector-Gustave 4 656
Brame, Paul-Louis 4 656
Brame, Philippe 4 656
Brameld, George Frederick 26 489
Brameld, John Wager 26 489
Brameld, Thomas 26 489
Bramer, Hans Georg 3 416
Bramer, Leonard 4 656–7*; 8 667
patrons and collectors 27 133
pupils 32 260
works 4 *657*; 22 844; 28 359
Bramhope (W. Yorks) 23 193
Bramley, Frank 4 657–8*
groups and movements 10 254; 23 26
works 10 *255*
Brampton, John 25 15
Bramsen, Alfred 28 814
Bramsen, Henrik 8 762
Braña, Marquesa de la 29 304
Branca, Alexander von 12 380, 477; 22 305
Branca, Antonio del *see* ANTONIO DEL BRANCA
Brancacci, Antonio 20 530
Brancacci, Felice (di Michele) 4 658*; 20 534, 554
Brancacci, Francesco Maria, Cardinal 27 150
Brancacci, Pietro 20 534
Brancacci Chapel *see under* FLORENCE → ecclesiastical buildings → S Maria del Carmine
Brancaccio, Francesco Maria, Cardinal 18 624
Brancadoro (family) 12 706
Brancaleone, Antonio II, Count 4 664
Brancaleone, Nicolò 10 569
Brancas, Comte de 1 665
Brancepeth (Durham), St Brandon 25 726
Branchi, Filippo 11 636; 12 830
Branchi, Pietro 31 826
Branchidai *see* DIDYMA
Branchini (family) 28 677
Branco, Cassiano 4 658*
works 25 294, *294*
Branco, Francisco 23 455
Branco & Preto 27 308
Brâncoveanu, Constantine, Prince 26 722; 31 23
academies 26 725
metalwork 14 138; 26 720
paintings 7 763; 31 23
textiles 5 72; 26 721
Brancusi, Constantin 2 52; 4 658–62*; 6 575; 11 568; 24 144; 25 582, 584; 26 715
assistants 7 555; 23 175
collaboration 9 70
drawings 26 716
exhibitions 31 490
groups and movements 1 76; 5 73; 9 705; 10 137
patrons and collectors 26 723, 725
Arensberg, Walter and Louise 2 384
Bogdan Pitești, Alexandru 26 723
Duchamp, (Henri-Robert-) Marcel 9 359
Guggenheim, Peggy (Marguerite) 13 801
Mallet-Stevens, Robert 20 203
Quinn, John 25 823
Schreiber, Taft and Rita 28 167
Simu, Anastase 26 723
Stieglitz, Alfred 29 655; 31 605
Winston, Harry Lewis and Lydia 33 254
pupils 7 645; 26 716
sculpture 4 *660*, *661*; 26 715; 28 314; 29 576
monumental 4 *662*; 26 716
wood-carvings 25 *584*
Brand, Christian Hilfgott 1 463; 2 795; 4 663*
Brand, Daniel 30 278
Brand, Donald 2 904
Brand, Friedrich August 25 358
Brand, Hans 12 824
Brand, Johann Christian 4 662, 663–4*; 5 9
reproductive prints by others 2 512
works 2 795; 4 *663*
Brand, Margarethe 30 149
Brand, Thomas (*fl* 1774) *see* HOLLIS, THOMAS BRAND
Brand, Thomas (*fl* 1802) 27 357
Branda, Castiglione, Cardinal 20 556, 557, 558; 26 766
Brandani, Federico 4 664*; 27 274
Brandard, John 4 87; 22 371
Brandard, Robert 10 396
Brändel, Friedrich, I *see* BRENTEL, FRIEDRICH, I
Brandel, Petr Jan *see* BRANDL, PETR JAN
Branden, J. F. Van den *see* VAN DEN BRANDEN, J. F.
Branden, Johann Matthäus van den 33 280
Brandenberg, Hildebrand *see* HILDEBRAND BRANDENBERG
Brandenberg, Johannes 30 132
Brandenbourgs 17 524
Brandenburg 4 665–6*; 12 *360*
Godehardskirche 13 160
Rathaus 30 501
St Katharinen 4 *665*; 5 27; 11 254; 13 56, 58; 30 501
stained glass 13 186
Brandenburg, Albrecht von, Cardinal 8 116; 12 471; 25 *274*
altarpieces 3 103
architecture 12 402
coats of arms 19 131
engravings 9 439
fountains 11 223
manuscripts 3 506, 725, 727; 12 816
metalwork 3 69
paintings 13 722
woodcuts 31 288
woodwork 26 127
Brandenburg, Barbara of, Marchioness of Mantua *see* BARBARA OF BRANDENBURG, Marchioness of Mantua
Brandenburg, Christian William, Archbishop of 12 494
Brandenburg, Frederick I, Elector of *see* FREDERICK I, Elector of Brandenburg
Brandenburg, Frederick II, Elector of *see* FREDERICK II, Elector of Brandenburg
Brandenburg, Frederick William, Elector of *see* FREDERICK WILLIAM, Elector of Brandenburg
Brandenburg, Joachim II, Elector of *see* JOACHIM II, Elector of Brandenburg
Brandenburg, Louisa Henrietta, Electress of *see* LOUISA HENRIETTA, Electress of Brandenburg
Brandenburg, Martin 1 549
Brandenburg-Ansbach, Frederick, Margrave of *see* FREDERICK, Margrave of Ansbach
Brandenburg-Ansbach, Sophie, Margravine of *see* SOPHIE, Margravine of Ansbach
Brandenburg-Bayreuth, Christian, Markgraf von 23 252
Brandenburger, Ernst 8 726; 25 29
Brandenburg Gate *see under* BERLIN (GERMANY)
Brandenburg glassworks 4 666*
Brandenburg-Kulmbach, Carl August, Markgraf zu 29 60
Brandenburg-Kulmbach, Kasimir, Markgraf zu 12 494
brander-back chairs *see under* CHAIRS → types
Brandes, Georg 28 814
Brandes, Jan Laurens Andries 4 666*
Brandesj, Alexander 8 400
Brandi, Domenico 14 191
Brandi, Giacinto 4 666–7*; 15 138; 26 771
attributions 3 521
collaboration 7 509; 18 871; 20 431
patrons and collectors 4 610; 13 880; 16 82; 28 367
pupils 26 424; 27 135
works 28 379
Brandimarte, Benedetto 9 173
Brandin, Philipp 4 667–8*
Branding, De 6 378; 22 852; 29 397
Brandini, Bartolomeo *see* BANDINELLI, BACCIO
Brandini, Michelangelo de' 6 139
Brandjes, Wed. N. S. A., & Co. 22 883
Brandl, D. 3 505
Brandl, Eva 5 572
Brandl, M.
works 1 *47*
Brandl, Petr 4 668–9*
patrons and collectors 29 422
works 8 391; 16 817; 18 506; 25 432, 443, *448*
Brando, Carlos 32 567
Brandoin, Charles 9 506; 10 677
Brandolese, Pietro 18 756
Brandon, Alexander Hamilton, 7th Duke of *see* HAMILTON, ALEXANDER, Duke of Hamilton and Brandon
Brandon, Charles, Duke of Suffolk 1 746
Brandon, David 7 470; 10 238; 33 263, 449
Brandon, Henry, 2nd Duke of Suffolk 14 *672*
Brandon, J. Arthur 11 836
Brandon, (John) Raphael 11 836
Brandon, Robert 14 545
Brandon Portrait, Master of the 14 759; 20 635*
Brands, Eugène 4 669*; 7 489
Brandt, Åsa 30 103
Brandt, Bill 4 669–70*; 24 674
works 4 *670*; 31 706
Brandt, C. M. 33 280
Brandt, Edgar 2 521; 11 601, 628; 16 60; 23 548
Brandt, Federico 4 670*; 32 175
Brandt, G. N. 29 76
Brandt, Hans 25 111
Brandt, Henri François 20 924
Brandt, Jan Baptist 23 665
Brandt, Józef 4 670–71*; 18 413; 25 107
Brandt, Marianne 4 671*
groups and movements 3 401, 402, *402*; 12 450
works 1 738; 8 803; 12 452
Brandt, Rex 19 701
Brandt, Reynier 1 811; 4 671*; 22 889
Brandt, Yefim von 27 430
Brandtner, Fritz (Wilhelm) 4 672*
Brand von Tzerstede 4 418
Brandy, Robert 19 827
Bran Fort 26 707
Brangwyn, Frank 4 672–3*; 20 834
groups and movements 23 504
pupils 18 901
works 3 579, 587; 7 434; 22 331
Brangwyn, William (Curtis) 3 610; 4 672
Brangwyn Museum *see* LONDON → museums → William Morris Gallery and Brangwyn Gift
Brangwynmuseum *see under* BRUGES → museums; ORANGE (FRANCE)
Brâni, Wolfgang *see* BRENY, WOLFGANG
Branicki (family) 3 431; 25 135
Branicki, Jan Klemens 25 121, 135
Branicki Painter 13 532
Braniff, Daniel 16 41
Branitz 12 134
Branković (family) 25 339; 28 440
Branković, George 28 450
Brankston, A(rchibald) D(ooley) 4 673*; 6 924; 17 594
Branlard, Pierre 24 148
Branly, Elizabeth 31 224
Branner, Robert 26 44
Branscombe (Devon), St Winifred 25 726
Bransford 29 220
Branson, Doug 7 482
Branston, Robert 33 368
Brant, Isabella 9 *277*
Brant, Sebastian 1 654, 656; 9 429; 14 *503*, 868, 869; 29 673
Branteghem, Willem van 33 268
Brantenberg, Tore 7 546
Brantford 5 581
Brantingham, Thomas of *see* THOMAS OF BRANTINGHAM
Brantwood (Cumbria) 27 354
Brantzky, F. 7 582
Branzi, Andrea 2 373
Braque, Georges 4 673–8*; 24 144, 716, 726; 30 328; 31 142; 32 327
assemblages 2 616
book illustrations 20 75; 33 362
catalogues 6 80
collaboration 2 542; 20 603; 21 312; 31 508
collages 4 *675*; 7 557; 23 333
commentaries 4 98; 20 75
dealers 17 725; 19 537; 20 75; 27 162, 163
exhibitions 2 447; 10 680; 13 711; 17 436
forgeries by others 11 307
frames 11 376
groups and movements
Blaue Reiter 4 132
Cercle d'Art Moderne 19 92
Cubism 1 73; 8 239, 240, 241, 242, 243, 245, 246
Fauvism 10 839, 842
Jack of Diamonds (Bubnovy Valet) 16 817
Junk art 17 694
Moderne Kunstkring 21 775
Braque, Georges
groups and movements—cont.
School of Ceret 30 3
house 2 552
jewellery 11 635; 17 529
lithographs 19 *491*
mosaics 22 163
paintings 4 *676*; 11 548; 15 140
landscape 18 717
still-lifes 4 *677*; 29 670, *670*
patrons and collectors
Arensberg, Walter and Louise 2 383
Cooper, Douglas 7 797
Dutilleul, Roger 9 465
Fénéon, Félix 10 885
Fondation Maeght (Saint-Paul-de-Vence) 28 314
Gallatin, A(lbert) E(ugene) 12 15
Heemskerck van Beest, Jacoba (Berendina) van 14 295
Kramář, Vincenc 18 435
Maitland, Ruth (Esther) 20 142
Marx, Sam and Florene 20 524
Mattioli, Gianni 20 848
Musée des Beaux Arts (Le Havre) 19 92
Ōhara, Sōichirō 23 371
Paul VI, Pope (*reg* 1963-78) 24 278
Reber, Gottlieb Friedrich 26 59
Rothschild, Elie de, Baronne (*b* 1916) 27 224
Rupf, Hermann and Margrit 27 343
Stein, Gertrude 11 659
Tetzen-Lund, Christian 30 532
Thompson, G(eorge) David 30 749
Vallenilla Echeverría, Pedro 32 178
personal collection 1 438
posters 25 350
prints 4 *676*; 19 491; 25 626
productions 3 120; 8 850
reproductive prints by others 32 577
stained glass 29 508
tapestries 2 704; 11 644
Braque, Jehan 33 121
Braque Triptych 31 881; 33 121
Brasanelli, Giuseppe 2 394
Brascassat, Jacques-Raymond 4 391, 678*
patrons and collectors 8 705
pupils 8 538
teachers 14 482
Brascha, Jacopo 17 585
Braschi, Giovanni Angelo, Cardinal *see* PIUS VI, Pope
Braschi-Onesti, Duca 10 849
Braschi-Onesti, Romualdo, Cardinal 6 111
Bras de Cheminée Duplessis 9 398
Brash, John 12 773
Brasília 4 679*, *705*, 706, 725; 7 670; 8 *7*, 8; 23 118–19
architecture 4 714
Cathedral 7 258; 12 793, *794*; 19 365
Congresso Nacional 4 714; 7 696; 9 83; 13 238; 15 886; 23 *119*
Fundação Pró-Memória 4 728
Ministry of Foreign Affairs *see* Palacio dos Arcos
Palácio dos Arcos 4 714
Banqueting Room 4 722
gardens 5 *218*
sculpture 4 *720*
sculpture 4 719
urban planning 7 295; 15 886
Brașov 4 679–80*; 26 *705*
Black Church 4 679–80; 26 707, 711
fortifications 26 707
metalwork 15 7; 26 719, *720*
Museum of History 4 680

Braşov—cont.
St Mary *see* Black Church
Braşov, Ulrich of *see* ULRICH OF BRAŞOV
Brasovan, Dragiša **4** 680*
brass **4** 680–89*, 848; **21** 319; **33** 684
historical and regional traditions
Afghanistan **16** *378*
Africa **1** *265*, 287, 350, 351, *363*; **4** 854
Akan **2** 590
Anatolia, ancient **1** 836
Ancient Near East **4** 681
Anglo-Saxon **4** 688
Argentina **4** 681
Asante **1** *363*; **2** *585*, 589*, *589*, 590*
Assyrian **4** 681
Austria **12** *811*; **33** *165*
Bamileke **3** 145, 148
Belgium **3** *566*, 582, 602–3, *603*; **4** 685, *685*; **5** *611*; **13** 159–60
Benin, Kingdom of **1** 250, 288; **3** *720*, *721*, 723, *723*, *724*; **6** 9
Brunei **5** 11, *12*
Buddhism **6** 706; **30** 822, *823*, *824*, *825*, *826*, *827*, *849*
Bulgaria **5** 160
Burkina Faso **5** 217, *217*
Cameroon **1** 368
Central Asia, Western **16** *378*
China **4** 681, *683*, 684, *684*, 688*; **6** 706, 830; **7** 79, 101; **30** *398*
Coptic **4** 688
Cyprus, ancient **4** 681
Denmark **8** 751–2, *752*
Egypt **16** *384*, *385*, *389*
England **4** 685, 688; **10** *268*, 339, 340*, *341*, *342*, 343, 344
France **11** 624
Germany **3** *402*; **4** 682, *689*; **12** 451–2*, *452*; **13** 160–61; **32** *604*, *605*, *606*
Gothic **13** 159–61; **32** *605*
Greece, ancient **4** 682, *686*
Holy Roman Empire (before 1648) **26** 684–6*
Ibibio **15** 65
Ife (kingdom of) **1** 250; **15** *106*
Igbo **15** 109
India, Republic of **15** 174
Indian subcontinent **4** *682*, 683–4, 687*, 853, 854; **15** *708*, 712, *714*, 733, 735, *735*
Iran **16** 373, *376*, *391*, *392*, 392–3, *506*; **32** *161*
Iraq **16** 379, *380*
Islamic **4** 688*; **16** *99*, 363, 373, *376*, 377, *378*, 379, *380*, *381*, *383*, *384*, *385*, *388*, *389*, *391*, *392*, 392–3, *506*, *543*; **21** I1; **32** *161*
Israel **16** *569*
Italy **16** 743, *744*
Japan **17** 276, 370
Jukun **1** 382
Khurasan **16** 377
Korea **18** *356*, 357, *363*, 378; **33** IV1
Kota (ii) (Gabon peoples) **18** *402*
Malaysia **20** 173, 174, 175
Mongolia **21** 882
Morocco **4** *687*
Mossi **5** 217, *217*; **22** 197
Nepal **4** 687; **22** 789
Netherlands, the **13** 159–60; **22** *894*, 894–5*
Nigeria **15** *106*
Nupe **23** *303*, 303*
Ottoman **16** *388*
Ottonian **23** 658
Philippines **24** *627*, 627–8
Phrygian **1** 836; **4** *686*
Portugal **25** 306
brass
historical and regional traditions—cont.
Romanesque **26** 684–6*
Rome, ancient **4** 687, 852
Sabah (Malaysia) **20** 173, 180
Sarawak **20** 173, 180
Scotland **2** 462
South America, Pre-Columbian **4** 681
Sweden **30** 111
Syria **16** *99*, 379, *384*
Tibet **4** 687; **30** 822, *823*, *824*, *825*, *826*, *827*, 839, 841, *849*
Turkey **16** *388*; **32** *161*
Ukraine **31** 562
United States of America **31** 653*
Yoruba **1** *265*; **15** *106*; **33** 558
Zulu **33** 723
technical examination **30** *398*, 408
techniques
cementation process **4** *681*, 682–3*
chasing **16** *388*
electroplating **10** 136
incising **16** *388*
lost-wax casting **15** 735
speltering **4** 683–5*
uses
altarpieces **3** *721*
anklets **1** 351
basins **16** *384*; **20** *228*
beds **3** 485
betel sets **20** 175
bowls **16** *385*
boxes **10** *341*; **16** *383*; **22** *894*; **33** IV1
buckets **4** *687*
buckles **10** 340
candlesticks **5** 611, *611*; **10** 343; **16** *376*, *388*
cannons (guns) **5** 11, *12*
canteens **16** *99*
caskets **10** *342*
casts **6** 9
chairs **3** 582; **16** *569*
chandeliers **3** 602, *603*; **9** 13
chests **18** *363*; **25** 306
clocks **7** 439
coins **4** *686*, 686–7, 688; **17** 370; **18** *356*, 357; **27** *96*
containers **24** *627*, 627–8
crosses **8** 200
enamel **7** 79
ewers **12** 452; **16** *378*, *381*; **23** *303*
fire-screens **10** 343
fonts (baptismal) **3** *566*; **32** *604*
furniture **25** 306
globes **12** *811*
gun stocks **2** 462
inlays **15** 712, *714*
jewellery **1** 350; **20** 180; **30** 839; **31** 562
keris **20** 174
kettles **5** 11
lamps **15** *708*
lampstands **16** *391*
lanterns (lights) **8** *752*
lecterns **4** 688
maces **16** *506*
marquetry **20** 466
medals **20** 917
musical instruments **22** 375
necklaces **1** 350
penboxes **16** *376*; **21** I1
pilgrim badges **24** 809
pipes (smoking) **1** 368
plaques **3** *720*
plaquettes **25** 19
printing plates **10** 548
prints **17** 276
reliefs **32** *606*
reliquaries **30** *849*
salvers **32** *161*
brass
uses—cont.
sculpture **3** *723*, *724*; **6** 706; **10** *268*; **15** *106*, *173*, 733, 735, *735*; **18** *402*; **30** *398*, 822, *823*, *824*, *825*, *826*, *827*; **32** *605*
seals **16** *543*; **21** 882
spoons **8** 284
staffs **1** *265*
stands **16** *389*
statuettes **4** 687
stools **2** *585*; **3** 148
sundials **28** *211*
tea-caddies **7** 101
thimbles **10** 340
trays **16** *380*
vases **33** *165*
veneers **31** 195
vessels **2** 589, *589*; **23** 303
weights **1** *363*; **2** 590
wire **10** 340
Brassaï **4** 689–91*; **24** 677
patrons and collectors **7** 842
works **4** *690*; **7** 434; **12** 215; **31** 706
Brassai, Daniel **15** 7
Brassempouy **25** 488
brasses (monumental) **4** 688, 691–3*; **31** 123
England **9** 268; **10** 260; **19** *580*
Germany **4** *693*; **32** 604
Gothic **4** *693*; **19** *580*
see also EFFIGIES; TOMBS
Brasseur de Bourbourg, Charles Etienne **21** 262
Brassington, J. W. **18** 889; **20** 53
works **20** *53*
Brassington, William **23** 62
Brassó *see* BRAŞOV
Bratby, John (Randall) **4** 693–4*
groups and movements **10** 258; **18** 97, 98; **28** 880
patrons and collectors **33** 744
Brateau, Jules **11** 622, 629
Brathwait, Richard **20** 478
Brătianu, Eliza **26** 723
Bratislava **4** 694–6*; **13** 162; **28** *848*
Appónyi Palace **28** 850
architecture **14** 885
Archive of the City of Bratislava **4** 696
Basilica **28** 850
Castle **4** *695*; **14** 884, 885, 886, 899; **28** 849, 852
chapel **14** 899
Central Archive of Slovakia **4** 696
churches **28** 850
Capuchin church **28** 849
Cathedral of St Martin **14** 884; **28** 849, 855
altarpiece **14** 893, 894
Elemosynarius Chapel **9** 146; **14** 887, 894
portal **14** 892
sculpture **28** *855*
Church of the Elizabethine Nuns **28** 852
Church of the Poor Clares *see* Municipal Gallery
Church of the Sisters of St Elizabeth **14** 894, 900; **28** 850, 855
Franciscan church **14** 883, 893; **28** 849
Jesuit church **14** 894; **28** 849
St John the Evangelist **14** 884
Trinitarian Church **14** 900; **28** 849, 852, 853
altarpiece **14** 894
Ursuline church **28** 849
copper **15** 9
crematorium **28** 850
episcopal palace *see* Palace of the Primates
Grassalkovich Palace **28** 850
Illésházy Palace **28** 850
Bratislava—cont.
Institute of the History of Art **28** 857
manuscripts **28** 851
metalwork **15** 7; **28** 856
Mirbach Palace **28** 850
Municipal Gallery **4** 696; **28** 853, 857
Municipal Museum **4** 696
painting **28** 852, 853
Palace of the Primates **4** *696*; **12** 369; **14** 888, 900; **28** 850
chapel **28** 852
pewter **28** 856
prints **28** 852
Reduta concert hall **28** 850
Roland Fountain **14** 893; **28** 855
Royal Chamber **28** 850
School of Fine Arts **28** 853, 857
sculpture **28** 855
Slovak National Gallery **4** 696; **28** 857
Slovak National Museum **4** 696; **28** 857
Soros Centre for Contemporary Art **28** 857
Bratke, Carlos **4** 696
Bratke, Oswaldo Arthur **4** 696–7*, 713; **27** 808
brattices **21** 546
Brattinga, Peter **25** 352
Bräuer, Albrecht **10** 463
Brauer, Arik **2** 797; **4** 697*; **24** 592; **32** 447
Brauer, Friedrich **18** 77
Brauer, Heinrich **5** 760; **33** 285
Braula Reis, João **24** 395
Braun, Adolphe **4** 697*; **24** 659, 663, 667; **26** 232
Braun, Anna Maria **4** 697*
Braun, Anthonín **4** 699
Braun, Artur **15** 826
Braun, Augustin **33** 274
Braun, Caspar **5** 290
Braun, Erwin **15** 826
Braun, Georg
atlases **2** 696; **4** 80; **14** 618, 644; **26** 533; **31** 71
engravings **24** *114*
maps **20** 364; **31** *713*
panoramas **21** 580; **31** 154
Braun, Herman **24** 511
Braun, Johann Bartholomäus **4** 697
Braun, Matyáš Bernard **4** 698–9*; **25** 432
collaboration **4** 668, 669; **17** 777
doors **25** 432, *433*
patrons and collectors **29** 422
sculpture **8** 385, 397
history **29** 789
religious **4** *698*; **18** 505, 506, *506*; **22** 45; **25** 432
workshop **28** 163
Braun, Maurice **27** 721
Braun, Peter Friedrich, Freiherr von **14** 645
Braun, Zdenka *see* BRAUNEROVÁ, ZDENKA
Braun AG **12** 480; **15** 826
Braunau am Inn
St Stephan **32** 90
Spitalkirche **14** 82
Braune, Heinz **31** 397
Braune Porcelain Fabrique **3** 429
Brauner, Victor **4** 699–700*; **26** 716
exhibitions **7** 842
groups and movements **2** 515, 544; **20** 877; **30** 21, 22, 23
works **4** *700*
Braunerová, Zdenka **4** 700*; **8** 393
Braunschweig *see* BRUNSWICK (GERMANY)
Braunschweig-Oels zu Oels, Erdmann , Herzog von **31** 28
Braunsdorf, Julius Eduard **21** 66
Braunstein, Johann Friedrich **12** 134; **24** 546; **25** 745; **27** 401
Braunton (Devon), St Brannock **24** 577
Brauntuch, Troy **25** 360
Braunweiler, Arnold von **5** *60*
Brauron **13** *363*; **14** *332*
graves **13** 383
houses **14** 339
reliefs **13** 582
Sanctuary of Artemis **4** 700–701*; **13** 370
stoa **29** 681
Brauweiler
chapter house **6** 466
SS Nikolaus und Medardus **23** 647; **26** 633, 646
altarpiece **1** 708
wall paintings **26** 648, 654
Bravães, S Salvador **25** 300; **26** 611
Bravmann, René A.
works **1** *341*
Bravo, A. García *see* GARCÍA BRAVO, A.
Bravo, Alvarez **30** 22
Bravo, Cecco *see* CECCO BRAVO
Bravo, Claudio **4** 701*
Bravo, González *see* GONZÁLEZ BRAVO
Bravo, Manuel Alvarez *see* ALVAREZ BRAVO, MANUEL
Bravo, Ricardo Larraín *see* LARRAÍN BRAVO, RICARDO
Bravo Jiménez, Jorge **24** 401
Brawer, Joan de **29** 337
Bray (Berks), Ockwells Manor **14** 422; **20** 571
Bray, Dirk de **4** 701; **33** 358
Bray, Francis de **8** 742
Bray, Jan de **4** 701, 702–4*; **13** 895; **19** 349; **22** 839
attributions **19** 293
patrons and collectors **28** 271
reproductive prints by others **18** 387
works **4** *703*; **7** 787; **11** 445
Bray, Joseph de **4** 701
Bray, Reginald **33** 248
Bray, Salomon de **4** 701–2*; **13** 895; **22** 839
collaboration **14** 46; **27** 508
groups and movements **10** 660; **13** 895
pupils **3** 766
works **4** *702*; **13** 896; **32** 865
writings **18** 9; **31** 298
Bray, Simon de **4** 701
Bray, Theodore **30** 15
Brayda, Boggio and Reycend **10** 886
Brayde, Riccardo **26** 389
Brayer, Yves **28** 750
brayers **4** 704*
Brayley, Edward Wedlake **4** 828
Brayton (N. Yorks)
St Mary **3** 443
St Wilfrid **26** 614
Braz, Osip **28** 459
Brazalieri, Francesco **16** 836
Brazdžius, Pranas **19** 498
Brazer, Abram **3** 531
braziers **10** 613; **17** 341; **25** 734; **29** 301, 302
Brazil **4** 704–29*, *705*; **29** 128, 195, 197–8
annatto **4** 724
architecture **3** 66; **4** 709–10*, 711–15*
Modernism **4** *712*, *713*
Neo-classicism **4** 710–11*
neo-colonial style **2** 903
prefabrication **4** 709
20th cent. **32** 855
archives **2** 369, 370*
art history **33** 316–17
atlases **30** 417
body arts **4** 706–7
bowls **29** *193*
caricatures **4** 717
carnivals **5** 787
cathedrals **12** *794*

Brazil—cont.
cedar **4** 721
ceramics **4** 722
chairs **4** *721*
chapels **4** *714*
churches **4** 707, *710*; **19** *460*; **23** *118*
cinemas **19** 271
clay **29** *193*
coins **7** 538
collections **4** 708, 724–7*
concrete **3** 66
cotton **4** 724
dealing **4** 724–6*
diamonds **12** 269
dyes **4** 724
education (art) **4** 725, 727–8*
architecture **4** 705
emblems **8** 231
ethnography **4** 708
exhibitions **4** 725, 727
faience (ii) (ceramics) **25** 310
feathers **4** 707, *707*
fibres **4** 724
furniture **4** 720*
gardens **5** *218*; **7** 884
gems **12** 268; **17** 525
glass **4** 722*; **12** *794*
gold **4** 723–4*
government buildings **23** *119*
headdresses **4** *707*
houses **13** *782*
housing **26** *110*
human figures **29** *194*
iconography **29** 134
incense boats **4** *723*
indigo **4** 724
jacaranda **4** 720, 721
jade *see* nephrite
jewellery **4** 723–4*
libraries **4** 728–9*
lithography **4** 717
looms **4** 724
mahogany **4** 721
marble **4** *720*
marks **4** 724
mulberry **4** 721
museums
Neo-classicism **13** *296*
19th cent. **4** 726
20th cent. **4** 719, 726–7*, 728; **27** *808*
necklaces **4** 707
nephrite **16** 861
towns **4** 715; **13** 781–2; **20** 269
painting **4** 715–16*, 717–20*
landscape **22** 840; **25** *326*; **26** *413*
Modernism **4** *718*
quadratura **4** *716*; **26** 412
20th cent. **30** *348*; **32** *690*
patronage **4** 718, 724–6*
photoarchives **4** 729*
photographic prints **24** *664*
photography **10** 580
plaiting **4** 706
pottery **4** 706, 722*; **29** *194*
retables **26** 254, *254*
rock art **29** 195–7*, *196*
sculpture **4** 715–16*, 717–20*, *720*
Baroque **19** *461*
marble **4** *720*
Pre-Columbian **29** *197*, 197–8*
wood **4** *708*
20th cent. **4** *720*
silver **4** *723*, 723–4*
skyscrapers **14** 295; **21** 631
slaves **4** 707–8
tangas **20** *372*
tapestries **4** 724
terracotta **20** *372*
textiles **4** 724*
tiles **4** 722
trade
furniture **4** 721
silver **4** 723
universities **2** *543*
urban planning **4** 704, 710

Brazil—cont.
urns **29** *194*
verandahs **32** 240
weaving **4** 706, 724
women artists **33** 316–17
wood **4** *708*
wood-engravings **4** 717
wool **4** 724
Brazil, Álvaro Vital *see* VITAL BRAZIL, ÁLVARO
brazilein *see under* PIGMENTS → types
Brazilian walnut *see* IMBUIA
brazil-wood **9** 491; **18** 655; **23** 786; **24** 796; **25** 315
brazing **12** 866; **21** 325
Brazzacco, Giovanni Battista *see* PONCHINO, GIAMBATTISTA
Brazzaville **1** *394*, *401*
Centre d'Art Africain **7** 708
Musée National de Brazzaville **7** 709
painting **7** 708
Poto-Poto art school **1** 432
Ste Anne du Congo **7** 709
Brazzi, Cristoforo *see* RUSTICI, CRISTOFORO
Brazzi, Cristoforo di Lorenzo **27** 447*
Brazzi, Francesco *see* RUSTICI, FRANCESCO
Brazzi, Lorenzo *see* RUSTICI, LORENZO
Brazzi, Vincenzo *see* RUSTICI, VINCENZO
Brdadzor Church **2** 435
Bréa, Louis **4** 729–30*
collaboration **3** 199; **11** 294
works **4** *730*; **9** 264; **21** 830
bread **28** 339
Breadalbane, John Campbell, 1st Marquess of *see* CAMPBELL, JOHN, 1st Marquess of Breadalbane
breakwaters *see* MOLES
Breamore (Hants), St Mary **2** 66
Brearley, Harry **8** 285
Breasted, James Henry **10** 81, 83, 90
breast-ornaments **17** 519; **30** *253*; **31** *459*
breastplates **2** 469, 472; **11** *69*; **28** 922
Brébiette, Pierre **4** 730*; **19** 16, 252
Brébion, Maximilien **24** 163, 166; **27** 123; **29** 94
brecciated marble *see under* MARBLE → types
Breccioli, Bartolomeo **20** 43
Breccioli, Filippo **20** 43
Breceris, Jokubas **19** 497
Brechbühl, Otto **27** 657
Brechbühler, Hans **2** 661
Brèche, Jean **25** 405
Brèche, La **30** 23
Brecheret, Victor **4** 717, 730–31*; **28** 394; **32** 855
Brechfeld, Jordan **33** 271
Brechin (Tayside) **26** 591; **28** *222*
Round Tower **28** 223
Brecht, Bertolt **16** 892; **30** 686, 687; **31** 421
Brecht, George **4** 731*; **11** 80
collaboration **27** 215
groups and movements **11** 232
patrons and collectors **14** 48
teachers **24** 407
works **24** 407
Brecht and McDiarmid Research Associates **4** 731
Brechtel, Hans **14** 42; **22** 888, 890
Breckenheijmer, Joannes Henricus Albertus Antonius **14** 804; **28** 72
Breckenridge, Hugh **2** 130; **8** 708; **20** 421
Breckerfeld, Janez Ziga **28** 863
Břeclav-Pohansko **8** 388

Brecon (Powys) **32** *780*
Cathedral of St John the Evangelist **26** 618
Maenddu well **32** 781
Brecquessent, Jean de *see* JEAN DE BRECQUESSENT
Breda **22** *813*
bronze **22** 894
Castle **4** 732*; **22** 535, 823
choir-stalls **22** 856
Grote Kerk **22** 837
mausoleum of Engelbert van Nassau **22** 857
Onze Lieve Vrouwekerk **8** 670; **13** 62, 114; **22** 820, 855
silver **22** 887
Breda, Carl Fredrik von **4** 731*; **11** 113; **30** 79; **31** 362
Breda, Willem of *see* KEY, WILLEM (ADRIAENSZ.)
Bredael, Jean Pierre van **10** 757
Brède, Charles-Louis Secondat, Baron de la et de Montesquieu **12** 122
Brède, La *see* LA BRÈDE
Bredekamp, H. **28** 917
Bredel **7** 490
Bredero, G. A. **32** 140, 588
Brederode, António Sampaio de Pina de *see* SAMPAIO DE PINA DE BREDERODE, ANTÓNIO
Brederode, Franziska van **22** *200*
Brederode, Gijsbrecht van *see* GIJSBRECHT VAN BREDERODE
Brederode, van (family) **21** 510
Brederode Castle **22** 822
Brede Værk **8** 751
Brēdikis, Vytautas **6** 134
Bredius, Abraham **4** 732*; **11** 306; **14** 635
personal collection **22** 905
works **22** 910; **30** 531
Bredons **26** 641
Bredow, Rudolf **4** 732*
Bredstedt **31** 718
Brée, Van *see* VAN BRÉE
breech-cloths **22** 654
Breedam, Camiel Van *see* VAN BREEDAM, CAMIEL
Breeding Desert **29** 896
Breedon-on-the-Hill (Leics), St Mary **2** 65; **15** 875
sculpture **2** 70, *70*
tomb **10** 261
Breen, Adam van **2** 856; **23** 224
Breen, Gillis van **12** *880*
Breenbergh, Bartholomeus **4** 733–5*; **26** 772
attributions **25** 66
collaboration **17** 881; **25** 369
groups and movements **9** 462; **28** 92
patrons and collectors **8** 845; **20** 142; **27** 271
reproductive prints by others **4** 96; **6** 527
works **4** *734*, *735*; **10** 161, 551; **18** 708; **22** 843
Breer, Robert **10** 688
Breeschoten, J. **28** 65
Breese im Bruch Church **19** 815
Brega, Giuseppe **32** 555
Brégeaut, L.-R. **14** 863
Bregenz
Martinskapelle
wall paintings **7** *274*
Vorarlberger Landesmuseum **2** 831
Breglia **1** 745
Bregman and Hamann **5** 573; **21** 492; **31** 176
Bregno (family) **11** 328; **32** 192
Bregno, Ambrogio **4** 735
Bregno, Andrea **4** 735, 736–7*; **26** 766
assistants **31** 188
attributions **26** 836
collaboration **12** 699; **21** 694; **26** 767

Bregno, Andrea—cont.
excavations **26** 767
patrons and collectors **4** 410; **24** 732
personal collection **3** 690
pupils **12** 582
works **4** *737*; **7** 526; **16** 691
Bregno, Antonio (di Giovanni), I (*fl* 1425-57) **4** 735, 736*
attributions **26** 439
works **4** *736*
Bregno, Antonio, II (*fl* 1470-80) **4** 735
Bregno, Antonio di Pietro **4** 736
Bregno, Cristoforo di Ambrogio **4** 736
Bregno, Domenico **4** 735
Bregno, Giovanni Antonio **4** 736
Bregno, Giovanni Battista (di Alberto) **4** 735, 736, 738–9*; **32** 192
assistants **4** 739
collaboration **27** 888; **33** 633
works **4** *738*; **31** 316
Bregno, Girolamo **4** 735
Bregno, Lorenzo (di Alberto) **4** 735, 739*; **32** 192
patrons and collectors **21** 632
works **4** 738, *739*; **11** 384; **31** 316
Bregno, Marcantonio **4** 735
Bregno, Paolo **4** 735, 736; **23** 92; **26** 439
works **4** *736*
Bregovac, Zdravko **10** 667
Bregues **29** 330
Bréguet, Abraham-Louis **4** 302; **7** 446, 447
works **26** *304*
Brehme, Hugo **4** 739–40*; **21** 398
Brehon, Collins **19** 394
Breidfjord, Leifur **15** 72, 74
Breikšs, Nīkolajs **25** 745
Brein, Ferenc **14** 889
Breisach Altar, Master of the *see* H.L., MASTER
Breisach Altarpiece **20** 796
altarpiece **12** 401, *401*; **28** 134
Breisgau, Ferdinand, Duke of *see* HABSBURG, FERDINAND, Archduke, Duke of Breisgau
Breit, Johannes *see* BRITTO, GIOVANNI
Breitenauer, Joseph Anton **22** 919
Breitenfelde Church **13** 185
Breitinger, Johann Jacob **30** 132
Breitkopf, Johan Gottlob Immanuel **22** 370
Breitkopf & Härtel **32** 686
Breitkreutz, Christian **18** 849
Breitner, George Hendrik **4** 740*; **19** 102; **22** 851
collaboration **2** 487; **21** 175
groups and movements **14** 47; **19** 654; **22** 850; **32** 392
pupils **20** 153; **32** 376
teachers **1** 650; **18** 188; **20** 435
works **11** 448; **14** 43, *43*; **22** 850, *850*
Breitner, Joseph **25** 403
Breitschneider, Volkmar **21** 67
Breivik, Bård **23** 231
Brekelenkam, Quiringh (Gerritsz.) van **4** 740–41*; **22** 841
Breker, Arno **4** 741*; **12** 408; **22** 711, 712
Breman, H. J. **2** 416
Breme, Ferdinando, Marchese di **11** 284
Bremen **4** 742–3*; **12** *360*
Cathedral of St Peter **11** 253; **16** 437; **26** 684
collections **12** 474, 476, 481
cupboards **12** 425, *426*
Gerhard Marcks Museum **20** 396
Grosssiedlung Neue Var **12** 380
Kunsthalle **9** 465; **12** 476
murals **22** 333
Paula-Modersohn-Becker-Haus **4** 789; **14** 622

Bremen—cont.
railway station **25** 856
Rathaus **3** 741; **4** 742; **17** 700
Güldenkammer **12** 410, *410*
stucco **29** 843
Roseliushaus **3** 41
Schütting **4** *742*
silver **12** *450*
textiles **12** 469
Unsere Liebe Frau **14** 80, 81
US Consulate **2** 216–17
Bremen blue *see under* PIGMENTS → types
Bremerhaven **31** 724
Bremmer, H(endricus) P(etrus) **4** 743*; **19** 31; **22** 746, 905
Brémond, Jean François **3** 874
Brenan, James **16** 34, 37
Brenchley, Julius **29** 48
Brend'Amour, Robert-François-Richard **33** 369
Brendekilde, H(ans) A(nderson) **4** 743*; **8** 749
Brendel **12** 413
Brendel, Albert Heinrich **7** 434
Brendel, Friedrich, I *see* BRENTEL, FRIEDRICH, I
Brendel, Johann Gottlieb **8** 461; **11** 242
Brener, Roland **5** 572
Brenet, André **28** 847
Brenet, Guy **4** 743
Brenet, Nicolas-Guy **4** 743–4*
patrons and collectors **11** 540; **30** 514
pupils **9** 302; **12** 334; **13** 791; **30** 343, 369
works **4** *744*; **20** 924
Brenet, Nicolas-Guy-Antoine **12** 177
Brenna, Vincenzo **4** 744–5*; **12** 134
assistants **27** 345
collaboration **27** 407; **32** 698
patrons and collectors **12** 173; **25** 364; **26** 733; **31** 244
pupils **27** 198
works **3** 433; **5** 521; **12** 173; **18** 693; **24** 292; **27** 403, 576
Brennan, Archie **23** 736; **28** 266; **30** 329, 330; **31** 660
Brennan, Cecily **16** 18
Brennan, Peter **16** 29
Brennand, Francisco **4** 719, 722, 745*
Brenner, Elias **21** 641; **28** 68
Brenner, Valentin **22** 918
Brenner, Victor D(avid) **4** 745–6*
Brenner Associates **23** 67
Brenno, Carlo Antonio **27** 664
Brenno, Carlo Enrico **8** 726, 742; **29** 840, 841
works **29** *840*
Brenno, Francesco **27** 664
Brent, Enrique Camino *see* CAMINO BRENT, ENRIQUE
Brentani, Charles **2** 764
Brentani, G. B. **17** 585
Brentano, Clemens **29** 611
Brentano, Giovanni **5** 817
Brentano, Giuseppe **4** 247, 746*; **21** 532
Brentel, Anna Maria **4** 747
Brentel, Friedrich, I **4** 746–7*; **5** 9
assistants **21** 151
pupils **3** 415; **29** 725
works **8** 882; **19** *697*; **21** 640; **29** 607
Brentel, Georg **4** 746; **20** 792
Brentel, Hans Friedrich **4** 747
Brentford (Middx)
Boston Manor **29** 834
Firestone Tyre Factory **10** 749
Brent Knoll (Somerset), St Michael **24** 577
Brentwood (CA), J. Paul Getty Arts Center **21** 57
Breny, Wolfgang **20** 803

Brequessant, Jean de *see* JEAN DE BREQUESSANT
Bréquin de Demange, Jean-Baptiste 32 461
Brera Altarpiece 1 711; 3 844; 22 13; 24 764; 27 495
Brereton, William 13 299
Breri 24 80
Brescia 4 747–8*; 16 *618*; 19 549; 26 *886*
books 17 565
Duomo Vecchio 4 *748*
façade decoration 10 737
forum 26 895
furniture 16 723
guns 2 464
Palazzo Broletto 6 351; 12 29; 26 690
Palazzo del Comune 31 237
Palazzo Gambara 29 832
Palazzo della Loggia 3 *767*; 5 545
Palazzo Martinengo-Cesaresco dell'Aquilone 3 767; 22 27
Palazzo Salvadego 22 109
reliefs 19 549
Roman capitolium 26 895
Rotonda *see* Duomo Vecchio
S Alessandro 3 649
SS Cosma e Damiano 16 701
S Maria della Pace 20 585
S Salvatore 5 796, 797; 16 625; 29 816
urban planning 27 3; 31 731
Villa Lechi *see under* MONTIRONE
Brescia, Antonio da *see* ANTONIO DA BRESCIA
Brescia, Bernardino da *see* BERNARDINO DA BRESCIA
Brescia, Giovanni Antonio da *see* GIOVANNI ANTONIO DA BRESCIA
Brescia, Jacopo da 25 907
Brescia, Jan Frans de 2 201; 3 588
Brescia, Leonardo da 10 523, 524; 11 5
Brescia, Prospero da *see* ANTICHI, PROSPERO
Brescia, Raffaello da *see* RAFFAELLO DA BRESCIA
Bresciani, Andrea 22 27
Bresciani, Carlos 6 594
Brescianino 4 749*; 19 190
Bresciano, Gerolamo Roberto *see* GEROLAMO ROBERTO BRESCIANO
Bresciano, il *see* ANTICHI, PROSPERO
Bresdin, Rodolphe 4 749–51*
pupils 26 71
works 4 *750*; 9 309; 10 555, 556; 19 488; 25 620
Bresilwood see under PIGMENTS → types
Breslau *see* WROCŁAW
Breslau, Louise C(atherine) 4 751*
Breslauer, Chrystian 12 490, 603; 30 207
Bresolin, Domenico 25 217
Bress, Johan 30 105
Bressani, Auguste 30 414
Bressers, A. 3 578, 884
Bressuire Castle 12 173
Brest (Belarus') *see* BIERAŚCIE
Brest (France) 28 612; 31 718
Brest, Jorge Romero *see* ROMERO BREST, JORGE
Bretagna, Giovanni Carlo di *see* GIOVANNI CARLO DI BRETAGNA
Bretagna, Rinaldo da *see* RINALDO DA BRETAGNA
Bretby 2 755
Bretcher, Claire 5 759
Breteuil, Louis-Auguste Le Tonnelier, Baron de 2 84; 18 879; 32 508
Bretherton, James 4 751*; 9 308; 28 25
Brethon, Jules Le *see* LEBRETHON, JULES
Brethous, Léon de 21 70; 26 493
Brethren of the Common Life 2 223; 4 751–2*
Breton, Adela 21 263
Breton, André 4 752–3*; 8 605; 9 196; 30 22–3; 31 607
collaboration 2 279; 30 23
dealers 20 75
exhibitions 7 842; 26 414
groups and movements 30 22–3
Art brut 2 515; 11 551
Dada 8 433, 438; 11 549; 24 405
Surrealism 2 839; 8 439; 24 405; 30 18, 22
personal collection 1 439; 15 53; 20 590; 23 742; 26 306; 30 19
writings 16 808; 20 336; 21 176; 25 686; 30 19, 22
catalogues 4 699
illustrated 8 775; 21 709
manifestos 11 549; 15 99; 24 428; 30 17
periodicals 8 438; 24 428, 720; 30 17, 19, 20; 31 503, 852
translated 30 262
Breton, Emil 4 755
Breton, Gilles Le *see* LE BRETON, GILLES
Breton, Jacqueline 30 21
Breton, Jean-François 11 630
works 11 *633*
Breton, Jules 4 754–5*
dealers 2 858
patrons and collectors 31 870
teachers 9 300
works 4 *754*; 12 294
Breton, Luc-François 3 873; 4 755*
Breton, Simone 30 17
Breton, Virginie 4 755
Bretonne, Nicolas E. Restif de La *see* RESTIF DE LA BRETONNE, NICOLAS E.
Bretonvilliers, Bénigne de 4 756
Bretonvilliers, Claude le Ragois de 4 755–6*
Bretschneider, Andreas, III 4 756*
Bretschneider, Johann 9 18
Brett, John 4 756–7*
groups and movements 10 253; 25 554
patrons and collectors 33 251
works 4 *757*; 20 424
Brett, John Watkins 6 79
Brett, Rosa 4 757
Brett and Hall 32 414
Brettingham, Matthew (i) (1699-1769) 4 757–8*
patrons and collectors 7 540; 8 281; 33 453
works 9 23
Brettingham, Matthew (ii) (1725-1803) 4 757, 758*; 7 540
dealing 1 533; 2 164; 19 157; 33 453
works 6 97; 10 293
Brettingham, Robert William Furze 3 178, 179
Bretton Hall (W. Yorks) 13 619
Bretzenheim
Hermitage 14 460
Breu, Anthoni Jörg 32 681
Breu, Georg 4 758
Breu, Jörg (i) (*c.* 1475/80-1537) 2 715, 716, 718; 4 758–60*
collaboration 22 302; 31 23
patrons and collectors 11 818; 13 903; 33 271
pupils 4 760
works 4 *759*; 10 738; 12 385; 13 188; 19 813; 21 83; 23 501; 25 605; 27 256
Breu, Jörg (ii) (*c.* 1510-1547) 2 718; 4 760–61*
collaboration 31 23
pupils 11 48
Breu, Jörg (ii) (*c.* 1510-1547)—cont.
reproductive prints by others 10 174
works 4 *760*; 22 918; 33 278, 354
Breu, Klaus 4 759
Breuer, Johan Georg 14 288; 29 690
works 30 *93*
Breuer, Marcel (Lajko) 4 761–2*; 7 482, 772; 8 803; 13 688; 24 815
architecture
museums 13 326; 22 366
office buildings 7 429; 32 888
schools 28 159
collaboration 2 578; 11 527; 13 689; 22 806; 24 130; 27 214; 33 552, 627
furniture 4 *761*; 6 391; 7 241; 12 417, 428, *428*; 30 218, *218*, 755
gardens 23 176
groups and movements 1 77; 3 402, 403; 7 772; 10 241; 15 885, 886
museums 23 43
pupils 3 252; 14 90; 17 620
staff 2 598; 17 605; 21 56; 23 273; 28 374
Breuer, Peter 3 646; 4 762*; 12 196
Breugel, Ambrosius *see* BREUGHEL, AMBROSIUS
Breugel, Jan *see* BREUGHEL, JAN
Breugel, Pieter, I *see* BRUEGEL, PIETER I
Breughel, Abraham 4 894, *895*, 917; 7 903; 23 701; 27 133
Breughel, Ambrosius 4 *895*, 917*
works 4 894, *917*
Breughel, Jan, I (1568-1625) 4 894, *895*, 913–15*; 11 227; 17 598; 26 770
attributions 11 227
collaboration 5 352; 7 414; 22 718; 32 251
Avont, Pieter van 2 875
Balen, Hendrik van, I (*c.* 1574/5-1632) 3 107
Hoecke, Jan van den 14 617
Kessel, Hieronymus van, II 17 918
Momper, Josse de, II (1564-1635) 21 830
Rottenhammer, Hans, I (156/5-1625) 27 227
Rubens, Peter Paul 11 487; 27 299
Steenwijk, Hendrick van (ii) (1580-1649) 29 592
Verhaecht, Tobias 31 882
Vrancx, Sebastiaen 32 724
copies 13 917
drawings 26 *900*
groups and movements 11 731
monotypes 21 895
musical instruments 22 *372*, 373
paintings 2 104; 7 814
allegorical 5 353; 13 917; 29 668
flower 3 561; 4 *915*; 11 225, 226–7; 29 666
landscape 3 560; 8 390; 11 455; 18 707
mythological 15 828
religious 4 *914*
patrons and collectors
Angran, Louis-Auguste, Vicomte de Fontpertuis 2 90
Borromeo, Federico, Cardinal 4 426; 16 771; 21 526
Bourbon II., Luis Antonio, Infante of Spain 4 565
Carol I, King of Romania (*reg* 1866-1914) 5 792
Dezallier d'Argenville, Antoine-Joseph 8 845
Duarte, Diego 9 311
Breughel, Jan, I (1568-1625)
patrons and collectors—cont.
Ferdinand II, King of Portugal (1816-89) 4 638
Francis-Joseph, Prince of Liechtenstein (*reg* 1772-81) 19 338
Frederick Henry, Stadholder of the Netherlands, Prince of Orange (*reg* 1625-47) 23 463, 465
Habsburg I., Ernest, Archduke of Austria 3 613
Hanover, Frederick (Louis), Prince of Wales (1707-51) 14 143
John II (Casmir), King of Poland (*reg* 1648-68) 32 7
Le Nôtre, André 19 164
Philip, Duke of Pomerania-Stettin (*reg* 1606-18) 13 631
Röver, Valerius 27 270
Ryerson, Martin A(ntoine) 27 463
Sigismund III, King of Poland (*reg* 1587- 1632) 32 6
Snyders, Frans 28 904
personal collection 4 911
pupils 4 915; 11 227, 357; 28 363; 32 754
reproductive prints by others 5 62; 6 527; 27 504; 29 648
teachers 4 910; 32 254
Breughel, Jan, II (1601-78) 4 *895*, 915–17*
collaboration 2 875–6; 3 108; 11 443; 17 6; 21 830; 27 288
patrons and collectors 9 453
pupils 4 917; 13 889; 17 919
works 4 894, *916*; 11 227
Breughel, Jan Baptist 4 894, *895*
Breughel, Jan Pieter 4 894, *895*
Breughel, Pieter, I *see* BRUEGEL, PIETER, I
Breughel, Pieter, III *see* BRUEGHEL, PIETER, III
Breuhaus, Fritz August 18 185; 24 826
Breuil, Henri 4 763*; 20 542; 25 481, 482, 484; 27 695
works 1 370, 373; 11 285; 19 236; 31 360
Breul, Nicolas de 10 157
Breuner, Friedrich Philipp, Graf, Bishop of Vienna 2 824; 31 585
Breunig, Johann Adam 14 306
Breunissen Troost, A. 24 547
Breviaries 4 763–4*; 13 130; 20 332; 25 676; 28 486, 487
individual manuscripts
Bar Breviary (London, BL, Yates Thompson MS. 8) 13 141, *142*
Bedford Breviary *see* Salisbury Breviary
Belleville Breviary (Paris, Bib. N., MSS lat. 10483-4) 3 323, *323*, 642–3*, *643*; 4 394, 764; 5 428; 13 148; 17 670; 18 703; 25 691, 692, 693, 694
Breviary of Blanche of France (Rome, Vatican, Bib. Apostolica, MS. Urb. lat. 603) 25 692
Breviary of Charles de Neufchâtel, Bishop of Besançon (Besançon, Bib. Mun., MS. 69) 20 757
Breviary of Charles the Bold (untraced) 20 451
Breviary of Charles V (Paris, Bib. N., MS. lat. 1052) 3 642; 4 764; 17 462; 28 *487*, 487; 31 835, *836*
Breviary of Ercole I d' Este (Modena, Bib. Estense, MS. VG. 11, lat. 424) 20 844
Breviaries
individual manuscripts—cont.
Breviary of Isabella the Catholic (London, BL, Add. MS. 18851) 20 659
Breviary of Jeanne d'Evreux (Chantilly, Mus. Condé, MS. 51) 4 764; 23 523; 25 692, 694
Breviary of Jean sans Peur (London, BL, Add. MS. 35311 & Harley MS. 2897) 4 *763*, 764; 19 393; 20 *340*
Breviary of King Martin (Paris, Bib. N., MS. Rothschild 2529) 4 764*; 8 140
Breviary of Martin of Aragon (Paris, Bib. N., MS. Rothschild 2529) 4 764
Breviary of Mary of Guelders (Berlin, Staatsbib. Preuss. Kultbes., MS. germ.qu.42) 20 740
Breviary of Matthias Corvinus (Rome, Vatican, Bib. Apostolica, MS. Urb. lat. 112) 4 764
Breviary of Mayer van den Bergh (Antwerp, Mus. Mayer van den Bergh, MS. lat. ix, 67) 3 555
Breviary of Oderisius (Paris, Bib. Mazarine, MS. 364) 4 763
Breviary of Philip the Fair (Paris, Bib. N., MS. lat. 1023) 8 857; 11 531; 13 142; 14 *725*, 726
Breviary of Philip the Good (Brussels, Bib. Royale Albert 1er, MSS 9026 & 9511) 4 764; 32 728
Breviary of Queen Dona Leonor (untraced) 14 658
Brukenthal Breviary (Sibiu, Brukenthal Mus.) 5 9
Egmond Breviary (New York, Pierpont Morgan Lib., MS. M. 87) 20 740, 786
Grimani Breviary (Venice, Bib. N. Marciana, MS. lat. I,99) 3 725; 4 764; 5 428; 12 524; 13 24, 657, 659–61*, *660*; 14 760; 20 700
Longleat Breviary (Longleat House, Wilts, MS. 10) 4 237
Moneypenny Breviary (untraced) 22 30
Salisbury Breviary (Paris, Bib. N., MS. lat. 17294) 4 764; 18 685, 880; 20 624, 625, 626, *626*
see also BOOKS OF HOURS; PSALTERS; SERVICE BOOKS
Breviary of Jean sans Peur, Master of the 19 391, 393; 20 635–6*; 31 309
Breviary of the Duke of Bedford, Master of the *see* BEDFORD MASTER
Brevier *see under* TYPE-FACES
Brevière, Louis Henri 33 369
Brevik 23 *218*
Brewer, Cecil Claude 14 277; 28 888*
Brewer, John Hart 31 637
Brewster, David 24 657; 33 134
Brewster, John 4 764*; 9 504
Brewton, Miles 32 303
Brey, Dietrich *see* BRY, THEODOR DE
Brey, Ricardo Rodríguez 8 229
Breydenbach, Bernhard von 4 358; 13 808; 26 259; 31 154
Breyer, Tadeusz 17 448; 31 106
Breysig, Kurt 10 215
Breytspraak, Carel 22 873
works 22 *874*
Brežanin, Marko 22 18

Breže, Andris
Brežice Castle 28 858, 859
Březnice
castle 8 395
church 8 378
Březnická Virgin and Child 19 830
Brezoski, Slavko 19 883
Březová 8 405
Brhaspati calendar see under INDIAN CONTINENT → calendars
al-Bria see MAGNA MAHUMERIA
Brialmont, Henri de 21 576, 581
works 21 577
Brian, Jean-Louis 4 765*
Brian, Joseph 4 765*
Brianchon 24 149
Brianchon, Maurice 4 765*; 21 628; 22 751
Briançon 21 568
Briand, Thomas 8 776; 10 308
Briani, Giovanni Battista (di Alberto) de' see BREGNO, GIOVANNI BATTISTA (DI ALBERTO)
Briano, Pedro Zonza 2 399
Briant, Jean 15 836
Briard, Gabriel 8 703; 32 494
Briard, Pierre 26 348, 350
Briare Aqueduct 2 242
Briati, Giuseppe Lorenzo 6 443; 12 789; 32 203–4
Bribir 8 174
Basilica 8 175
Bribri 29 214
Bricci, Basilio 3 706; 4 765
Bricci, Francesco 30 803
Bricci, Giovanni 4 765
Bricci, Plautilla 3 706; 4 765–6*; 26 841
Brice, Germain 4 766*; 24 119, 137
Brice, Roland 19 83
Brice, W. 14 192
Briceño, Pedro 21 376
Briceño, Trixie 4 766*; 23 905
Brichard, Eloy 28 520
Brichaut, Johannes Josephus 3 599
Bricher, Alfred Thompson 4 766–7*; 19 791
brick 4 767–97*, 771
conservation 4 797*
historical and regional traditions
Afghanistan 16 169
Africa 1 305, 315, 317, 377; 4 792–3*
Ancient Near East 1 879; 4 769, 771
Assyrian 2 640
Australia 4 167, 786, 789
Austria 4 777
Bali (Indonesia) 4 796
Belarus' 4 783
Belgium 3 575; 13 61
Belize 3 623
Britain 4 769, 770, 778–80*, 786–7, 788, 789; 32 276
Burma 4 796; 5 226
Byzantine 4 771, 773–4*; 9 524, 545, 547
Cambodia 5 474, 487
Central Asia, Eastern 4 794; 6 295
Central Asia, Western 6 201, 206, 206; 16 154, 159, 160, 169, 199–200, 239
Chad Republic 1 305
China 4 793, 794–5*; 6 645*, 648, 668, 686, 686, 696, 697, 698, 882, 887, 906; 7 143, 144
Cistercian Order 4 782
Czech Republic 4 782, 783; 8 376, 379
Denmark 4 789; 8 721
Dominican Order 4 782
Early Christian (c. AD 250-843) 9 524
Egypt 4 771–2; 16 270
Egypt, ancient 2 296; 23 807
brick
historical and regional traditions—cont.
England 4 770–71, 770, 779, 785, 785, 786; 10 229; 30 365–6
France 4 780*
Germany 4 776–7*, 777; 12 362; 31 195
Gothic 4 782; 12 362; 13 61, 64; 24 347
Greece 4 774; 9 547
Greece, ancient 13 404
Hinduism 5 487
India, Republic of 15 168
Indian subcontinent 4 793, 793–4*; 15 256–7*, 262, 263, 280, 328, 413
Islamic 15 337, 351
Uttar Pradesh 3 908
Indonesia 4 796
Indus civilization 4 772
Iran 4 791; 16 154, 158, 160, 164, 164–5, 199–200, 244; 32 320
Iran, ancient 15 912
Iraq 16 182
Islamic 4 791–2*; 16 140, 143, 268, 269; 20 166; 29 618; 32 320
Afghanistan 16 169
Africa 1 315, 317
Central Asia, Western 6 206; 16 154, 159, 160, 169, 199–200, 239
Egypt 16 270
Indian subcontinent 15 337, 351
Iran 16 154, 158, 160, 164, 164–5, 199–200, 244
Iraq 16 182
Ottoman 16 207
Turkey 16 186, 207
Italy 4 774–6*; 13 64; 23 621; 26 877, 878; 30 667; 31 442
Java 4 796
Khmer 4 795
Korea 4 795*; 18 264, 266, 271
Lithuania 4 782, 783
Malaysia 20 166
Maya 4 796; 7 645
Mesoamerica, Pre-Columbian 4 796*; 7 645
Mesopotamia 4 771, 771–2, 772
Mycenaean 4 772
Netherlands, the 4 777–8*, 778, 785–6; 8 299
Norway 4 781
Ottoman 16 207
Parthian
Peru 19 385
Poland 4 782, 782, 783; 24 347, 347, 698
Portugal 4 784–5*
Prehistoric art 4 771, 771
Romania 26 706
Rome, ancient 4 767, 769, 771, 772; 23 621; 26 864, 877, 877–9*, 878, 900, 903, 903, 911, 912, 914
Russia 4 783*
Scandinavia 4 780–81*
South America, Pre-Columbian 4 796*
South-east Asia 4 795–6*
Spain 4 784–5*; 13 68
Sudan 1 305
Sweden 30 66
Switzerland 4 777, 789
Syria 4 791
Syria-Palestine 4 771
Thailand 2 884; 4 795, 796
Turkey 4 771, 771; 9 545; 16 186, 207; 26 912, 914
United States of America 4 786, 789
Vietnam 4 795; 32 476
materials
barium carbonate 4 767
brick
materials—cont.
clay 2 362; 4 767, 771
concrete 4 767
faience (i) (glass) 1 879
glazes 4 769
lime 4 767
manganese dioxide 4 767
mud 2 362
oils 1 305
porcelain 6 906
salt 4 797
sand 4 767
straw 4 771
terracotta 4 768–9*
reuse 4 772
technical examination 30 409
techniques
carving 4 769, 793, 794
drying 4 768
extrusion see wirecutting
firing 4 767–8*, 768
gauging 4 786, 787
inscriptions 4 771
mass production 4 771, 793
moulding 4 767, 768, 771; 6 882
pressing 4 767–8
stamping 3 588; 4 771, 772; 26 750, 879
wirecutting 4 767, 787
types
adobe see ADOBE
bannā'ī 16 195, 199, 250, 259
bessales 26 877
bipedales 26 877
briques de foyer 3 588
calcium silicate 4 788
hollow 4 788, 790
mud-bricks see MUD-BRICKS
pisé see PISÉ
Riemchen 4 771
sesquipedales 26 877
uses
altars 1 698; 4 793
arches 2 296; 4 767, 769, 774, 787; 26 877
architectural decorations 1 317; 4 769, 771, 771, 774, 782; 15 262; 16 143, 165, 169, 195, 199, 239, 250
architecture 2 362; 4 767*, 769, 769–72*, 770, 771, 774*, 781–3*, 785–90*; 15 168; 16 154, 244; 26 911
Afghanistan 16 169
Africa 1 377; 4 792–3*
Belgium 13 61
Britain 4 778–80*; 32 276
Burma 5 226
Byzantine 4 773–4*; 9 524, 547
Central Asia, Eastern 6 295
Central Asia, Western 16 160, 169, 199–200, 239
China 6 645*, 686
Czech Republic 8 376, 379
Denmark 4 789; 8 721
Early Christian (c. AD 250-843) 9 524
England 4 785; 10 229; 30 365–6
France 4 780*
Germany 4 776–7*; 12 362
Gothic 12 362; 13 61; 24 347
Greece 9 547
Indian subcontinent 3 908; 4 793–4*; 15 263, 337, 351
Iran 4 791; 16 158, 160, 164, 164–5, 199–200; 32 320
Iraq 16 182
Islamic 4 791–2*; 16 140, 268, 269
Islamic: Afghanistan 16 169
Islamic: Central Asia, Western 16 239
Islamic: Indian subcontinent 15 337, 351
Islamic: Iran 16 158, 160, 164–5, 164, 199–200; 32 320
Islamic: Iraq 16 182
brick
uses
architecture—cont.
Islamic: Turkey 16 186, 207
Italy 4 774–6*; 23 621; 31 442
Korea 18 264, 266
Netherlands, the 4 777–8*, 778
Ottoman 16 207
Poland 4 782, 783; 24 347, 698
Portugal 4 784–5*
Rome, ancient 23 621; 26 912, 914
Scandinavia 4 780–81*
Spain 4 784–5*; 13 68
Sweden 30 66
Syria 4 791
Thailand 2 884; 4 795
Turkey 16 186, 207; 26 912, 914
bricklaying see BRICKLAYING
chimneys 4 769, 778, 779
churches 4 771, 774–5, 780–81; 26 706
cladding 4 767, 788
columns 4 769, 772; 26 877, 878
copings 4 769
domes 4 767, 774
entablatures 26 878
facings 26 900
fireplaces 3 588; 4 778
floors 3 575
fortifications 31 195
gables 4 785–6
gateways 4 777
houses 3 575; 4 780
inscriptions 4 774
masonry 16 160; 20 560, 573
mausolea 6 206
mosaics 2 640
mosques 20 166
mouldings 4 769
niches 4 769
pagodas 6 668
palaces 23 807
pediments 26 878
pilasters 4 769; 26 878
ribs 26 879, 903, 903
sculpture 4 789; 5 487
architectural 15 413
relief 4 769, 789–90
service stations 28 488
shuttering 4 767
stelae 29 618
stupas 4 794; 32 476
superstructures 4 794
temples 4 772, 793, 794; 15 256–7*, 280, 328
theatres 30 667
tombs 4 793; 6 648, 696, 697, 698; 18 271; 26 877
towers 4 779; 13 64, 68
tracery 4 769
vaults (ceiling) 4 767, 778, 779; 15 912; 16 140, 199, 270; 21 275; 24 347; 26 878, 878, 911
walls 4 767
Brickbuilder see Architectural Forum
Brickdale, (Mary) Eleanor Fortescue see FORTESCUE-BRICKDALE, (MARY) ELEANOR
brick dust 20 327; 28 339
Brickell, Barry 4 797–8*; 23 69
works 23 69
Brickfield Hill 4 167, 787
Brick Kiln 2 152
bricklaying 4 767, 769–71*, 790
historical and regional traditions
Babylonian 3 10
Byzantine 7 273, 273–4*
Greece 7 273
Iran 23 559
Islamic 23 559
Mesopotamia 3 10
Rome, ancient 26 878
types
bonding see BONDING
bricklaying
types—cont.
diapering 4 770–71*, 770, 779, 783
nogging 4 770*, 770; 16 269
Bridan, Charles-Antoine 4 798*
collaboration 19 233
patrons and collectors 11 561
pupils 4 798; 5 888; 7 915; 10 508
Bridan, Pierre-Charles 4 798*
collaboration 1 527
patrons and collectors 11 562
pupils 4 618; 7 915
Bridel, Dickes House 19 827
Bridell, Frederick (Lee) 4 798*
Bridford (Devon), St Thomas Becket 30 778
Bridge, James 15 741
Bridge, John 27 336; 29 723
Bridge, John Gawler 27 337
Bridge-building Relief 13 456, 457
Bridge Crystal Glass Co. 33 50
bridge design 22 532; 26 206; 28 868; 30 421–2; 32 465
Bridgeman, Charles 4 805–6*; 12 593, 594
patrons and collectors 14 178; 25 635; 29 735; 30 451
teachers 33 257
works 4 806; 7 374; 8 281; 12 128; 13 704; 18 5; 27 259
Bridgeman, George (1864-1943) 28 887
Bridgeman, George S. (1839-c. 1900) 20 809
Bridgeman, Sarah 4 806
Bridgen, Timothy 31 652
Bridgens, Richard (Hicks) 4 806–7*; 5 169; 10 298
bridges 4 798–804*
historical and regional traditions
Britain 4 801
Byzantine 9 560; 17 702
China 4 800
Czech Republic 25 425
Early Christian (c. AD 250-843) 9 560
England 4 802; 14 198; 16 52; 19 574; 27 715
France 4 801; 7 691; 12 206; 24 479
Iran 16 231, 232
Iran, ancient 4 800
Islamic 4 801; 16 141, 207, 217, 225, 231, 232
Italy 14 388; 32 186
Korea 18 280, 280–81*
Norway 4 804
Ottoman 4 801; 16 207, 225
Peru 19 385
Poland 24 698
Portugal 10 106; 25 293
Rome, ancient 4 800; 26 864; 27 7*
Russia 14 222; 27 376
Scotland 29 651; 30 422
Spain 16 217
Switzerland 14 388; 20 119
Turkey 16 207; 17 702
United States of America 9 499; 24 674; 27 565
materials
cast iron 4 802*; 14 222; 16 53
chains 4 803
chromium steel 9 499
concrete 4 803*, 804; 7 691; 14 388; 20 118
granite 18 280
iron 4 801
steel 4 802–3*; 27 565; 31 594
stone 4 802*; 18 281; 19 385; 26 749
wire 31 594
wood 4 802*; 14 198; 18 281
wrought iron 4 802*, 802; 30 422
techniques
centering 6 178

bridges—cont.
types
aqueducts see AQUEDUCTS
arch 4 799*, 799, 800; 20 118
balanced cantilever 4 799
bascule 4 799
beam 4 799
bow-string arch see tied arch
bow-string girder 4 799
box girder 4 799
bridges of boats 4 799
cable-stayed 4 799
cantilever 4 799; 5 648
drawbridges 4 799; 7 359; 8 902; 12 174
floating 4 799
girder 4 799
opening 4 799
open-spandrel arch 4 799; 29 905
pontlevis 12 174
pontoons 4 799; 18 281
suspension 4 799, 800, 803; 5 14; 23 42; 26 523, 523, 524; 30 467; 31 594
swing 4 799
tied arch 4 799; 22 532
transporter 4 800
truss 4 799, 801
turning-bridges 12 174
vertical lift 4 800
viaducts 32 398–9*
voussoir arch 4 799
Bridges, Henry 7 446
Bridges, James 4 821
Bridges, John 30 890
bridges of boats see under BRIDGES → types
Bridgetine Order see BRIGITTINE ORDER
Bridget of Sweden, Saint 4 810
Bridgetown
Garrison 2 148
Government House 2 148
St Mary 2 148
statue of Horatio Nelson 5 751
Bridgewater, Francis Egerton, 3rd Duke of see EGERTON, FRANCIS, 3rd Duke of Bridgewater
Bridgewater, Francis Henry Egerton, 8th Earl of see EGERTON, FRANCIS HENRY, 8th Earl of Bridgewater
Bridgewater, John William Egerton, 7th Earl of see EGERTON, JOHN WILLIAM, 7th Earl of Bridgewater
Bridgewater *Madonna and Child* 9 755
Bridgman, Frederick A. 31 603
Bridgwater, Henry (Scott) 4 807*
bridles 21 878
Bridlington Priory 7 455; 26 615
Bridport, Giles of, Bishop of Salisbury see GILES OF BRIDPORT, Bishop of Salisbury
Briefe, die neueste Literatur betreffdend 23 108
Brieg, Friedrich II, Duke of 24 207
Brieg, Georg II, Duke of 24 208
Brieg Castle 24 207–8
Brielle Church 22 820
Briem, Jóhann 4 807*; 8 569; 15 70
Brien (Desrochers), Urbain 25 817
Brienne, Louis-Henri, Comte de 4 807*; 24 258
Brienne-le-Château 11 154
reliquary of St John the Baptist 11 623
Brieno, il see BREGNO, DOMENICO
Brienz 17 526
Brière, Gaston 4 808*
Brierly, O. W. 31 185
Brierre, Murat 14 58
Briet, Peter 10 316
Brigada khudozhnikov 24 450
Brigade, Simon 3 547
Brigance, Tom 9 294
brigandines 2 472
Brigantium see LA CORUÑA
Brigden, Fred 7 648
Brigdon, Dennis 16 93
Brigg (Lincs) 31 709
Briggs, Frederico Guilherme 4 717
Briggs, Henry W. 19 806
Briggs, Raymond 4 368
Briggs, Robert Alexander 5 173
Briggs, W. R. 28 158
Brigham, Charles 4 475; 29 870
Brigham City Tabernacle (UT) 22 126
Bright, George 4 479
Bright, Henry 4 808*; 21 482
Bright, Richard 28 25
Bright, Tom 19 424
Brighthelmstone see BRIGHTON
Brightling (E. Sussex) 11 243
brightness 4 808*; 19 352
Brighton (E. Sussex) 4 808–10*; 10 225
architecture 4 787
Art Gallery and Museum 4 810; 10 370; 29 221
Chain Pier 24 747
Hippodrome 15 408
Palace Pier 24 748, 748
railway station 25 855
Royal Pavilion 4 809, 809; 7 168; 10 234, 279, 361; 14 145; 15 407; 22 59; 26 85
chandeliers 6 443
dome 9 84
furniture 10 297; 23 790
interior decoration 8 105, 106; 26 84
overdoors 23 678, 679
porcelain 9 29
The Dome 25 249
St Michael
stained glass 22 143
West Pier 24 748
brights see under BRUSHES → types
Brigid, Saint 18 42
Brigittine Order 4 810*; 8 723
architecture 21 840; 31 794, 794–5
textiles 11 109
Brigman, Anne 13 710
Brignano Gera d'Adda Castle 12 22
Brignolas, Michel 10 351
Brignole (family) 12 283
Brignole, Emanuele 4 811*; 25 705
Brignole, Giovanni Francesco 4 811; 9 479
Brignole-Sale (family) 12 281, 284
Brignole-Sale, Anton Giulio, Marchese di Groppoli see GROPPOLI, ANTON GIULIO BRIGNOLE-SALE, Marchese di
Brignole-Sale, Giovanni Francesco 4 811
Brignole-Sale, Maria see GALLIERA, MARIA DE FERRARI, Duchessa di
Brignole-Sale, Ridolfo Maria 4 811
Brignoni, Serge 30 135, 139
Brigode 5 52
Brigot, Ernest-Paul 8 57
Brigstocke, Thomas 32 786
Brik, Osip (Maksimovich) 4 811–12*
groups and movements 7 768; 15 857; 18 536; 22 508
Brikcí 18 539
Brikcí of Cinperk 8 415
Bril, Matthijs, the elder (*fl c.* 1550) 4 812
Bril, Matthijs, the younger (1550-1583) 4 812*
assistants 4 812
collaboration 25 185; 30 428
patrons and collectors 13 628; 30 274
Bril, Matthijs, the younger (1550-1583)—cont.
reproductive prints by others 11 794
Bril, Paul 4 812–14*; 9 462; 16 671; 26 772
attributions 4 812; 21 828
collaboration 9 90; 10 157; 26 196; 27 227; 28 529; 32 593
decorative works 22 372, 373
etchings 10 551
paintings 7 814; 18 708
altarpieces 22 393
frescoes 4 405; 18 707; 20 840, 841; 30 356
hunting scenes 4 813
patrons and collectors
Angran, Louis-Auguste, Vicomte de Fontpertuis 2 90
Borromeo, Federico, Cardinal 21 526
Bracciano, Paolo Giordano I Orsini, Duca di 23 576
Clement VIII, Pope (*reg* 1592-1605) 1 595; 26 818
Clement IX, Pope (*reg* 1667-70) 27 172
Coninxloo (i), Gillis van, III (1544-1607) 7 711
Conti, Louis-François de Bourbon, Prince de (1717-76) 7 778
Elizabeth Farnese, Queen of Spain (1692-1766) 4 559
Ferdinando, 6th Duke of Mantua (*reg* 1612-26) 12 912
Gregory XIII, Pope (*reg* 1572-85) 13 628
Hollar, Wenceslaus 14 682
La Roque, Antoine de 18 796
Le Nôtre, André 19 164
Peretti (-Montalto), Alessandro, Cardinal 26 836
Philip, Duke of Pomerania-Stettin (*reg* 1606-18) 13 631
Quentin de Lorangère 25 815
Roomer, Gaspar 27 133
Rosso, Andrea del (1570-1644) 27 133
Segers, Hercules (Pietersz.) 28 358
Verrue, Jeanne-Baptiste d'Albert de Luynes, Comtesse de 32 368
personal collection 4 812
pupils 23 124
reproductive prints by others 18 476; 24 236, 397; 27 503, 504
Brili Cross 12 328
Brilli, Giuseppe Antonio 5 8
brilliance see BRIGHTNESS
Brimbal, Scipion 7 466
Brinani, Giacomo 31 329
Brinay, St Aignan 26 650
Brinckmann, Albert 27 657
Brinckmann, Justus 9 703; 12 468
Brinckmann, Philipp Hieronymus 4 814*; 28 351
reproductive prints by others 20 914
Brindaban see VRINDAVAN
Brindisi
S Andrea dell'Isola 26 627
S Benedetto 26 627
S Giovanni al Sepolcro 26 627
Brink, J. van den 13 679
Brink Evers, J. see EVERS, J. BRINK
Brinkman, J(ohannes) A(ndreas) 4 814–16*; 15 885, 886; 19 861; 21 781; 29 489
collaboration 22 868; 31 867
works 4 815
Brinkman, M(ichiel) 4 814*; 27 230
collaboration 23 663
staff 28 122; 29 531
Brinkman, Paul Ehrenberg see EHRENBERG BRINKMAN, PAUL
Brinkman & Van den Broek 4 814
Brinkman & Van der Vlugt 4 814, 815; 10 749; 18 73; 22 830; 27 230
Brinnin, John Malcolm 29 534
Brinsop, St George 26 616
Brinton 17 640
Brioloto 4 816*; 26 621; 32 345
Brion, Edmond Charles 22 128
Brion, Gustave 4 816*
Brione-Verscio, S Maria Assunta 30 129
Brioni Cathedral 9 529
Brionne Tower 6 52
Briosco, Ambrogio di Cristoforo 26 326
Briosco, Andrea see RICCIO, ANDREA
Briosco, Antonio 10 743; 21 533
Briosco, Benedetto 4 816–17*; 21 533
collaboration 1 748; 6 123
pupils 3 137
works 12 582; 21 525; 24 286, 287
Briosco, Francesco 4 817; 11 897
Brioso, Manuel da Costa see COSTA BRIOSO, MANUEL DA
Briot, François 4 817–18*; 11 624
works 24 578, 579; 25 22
Briot, Isaac (1585-1670) 25 816, 833
Briot, Nicolas 4 818*
patrons and collectors 4 553
pupils 12 261; 26 40; 28 749
works 20 923; 27 562
Briots, C. D. 3 585
Brioude, St Julien 11 623; 26 601
Bri-Plax 31 259
brique et fer see under ARCHITECTURE → techniques
briques de foyer see under BRICK → types
Brisbane 1 37; 2 736; 4 818–19*, 819
architecture 2 737, 738, 739, 741
Brisbane Civic Art Gallery 4 819
ceramics 2 760
City Hall 2 741
Institute of Modern Art 4 819
parliament buildings 2 738
Queensland Art Gallery 2 770; 4 819
Queensland Museum 1 66; 2 739; 4 819
Queensland National Bank 2 739
Queensland State Library 2 772
St Andrew's 2 740, 741
Town Hall 2 738
Treasury Building 2 739
University of Queensland 2 772
Art Museum 4 819
War Memorial Shrine 2 741
Briscoe, Birdsall P. 14 803
Briseis Painter 13 521; 32 36
brises-soleil 4 819*; 10 417; 12 793; 26 462
Briseux, Charles-Etienne 4 819*; 30 71
collaboration 24 821
works 24 821
writings 2 358; 20 131; 23 488
Brisley, Stuart 4 820*
groups and movements 10 258
works 10 483; 24 407, 408
Brislington pottery 7 166; 10 304, 305
Brisman, Lars 14 79
Brison, Alessandro 28 340
Brissac, Charles de Cossé, Comte de 7 463
Brissac Château 11 515
Brissaud, Pierre 10 824
Brisseau de Mirbel, Charles-François 4 303; 7 744
Brisset, Pierre 12 496
Brisset press see under PRESSES → types
Brissonet, Guillaume 19 248
Brissot de Warville, Félix 20 484
bristle 5 33, 33, 34, 35; 6 736
Bristol (Avon) 4 820, 820–26*; 10 225; 11 243; 31 710
Arnolfini Gallery 4 823
art forms and materials
brass 4 685, 688, 824
ceramics 4 823–4*
dioramas 8 911
furniture 10 297
glass 4 824*; 10 318
metalwork 4 824*
mouldings 22 211
pewter 4 824; 10 341; 24 579
pottery 4 177; 10 304, 305, 306
sculptors 10 265
tiles 30 877
woodcuts 25 244
Bank of England 3 175
Blaise Castle House Museum 4 824
Brunel House 14 786
Cathedral of the Holy Trinity 4 824–5*; 18 827; 32 91, 92, 416
Berkeley Chapel 32 89
bosses 4 465
chapter house 6 466
choir 4 825; 8 611; 13 54; 22 220
Elder Lady Chapel 18 622
mouldings 22 220, 221, 222
pulpitum 28 294
sculpture 10 266; 26 616
stained glass 4 826*
churches 4 821
City of Bristol Museum and Art Gallery 4 821, 823
collections 6 925; 7 155
Clifton Suspension Bridge 5 14; 10 97; 30 467
Exchange 4 822
Exchange and Market 10 668
Eye Hospital 4 789
Goldney House 28 581
Great Western Station see Temple Meads Station
Market Cross 29 707
New Room 21 347
Prince Street Assembly Rooms 2 618
Royal Western Hotel see Brunel House
St Augustine's Abbey see Cathedral of the Holy Trinity
St Mary Redcliffe 4 821; 9 681; 13 54
Labyrinth 18 585
north porch 8 611
screen 28 295
sculpture 13 82, 83
vaults 32 90, 92, 93
Temple Meads Station 25 854
Theatre Royal 30 673
topography 33 378
town walls 31 710
Tramways and Carriages Co. power station 25 402
Bristol, Frederick Augustus Hervey, 4th Earl of see HERVEY, FREDERICK AUGUSTUS, 4th Earl Bristol
Bristol, John Hervey, 1st Earl of see HERVEY, JOHN, 1st Earl of Bristol
Bristol Bay 22 655
Bristol Brass Wire Co. 4 824
Bristol glaze see under GLAZES → types
Bristol porcelain factory 7 166; 33 377
Bristow Church 19 815
Brisville, Hugues 3 752
Brit, Johannes see BRITTO, GIOVANNI

Britain **32** 513
aesthetics **10** 101; **24** 740
airbrushes **1** 494
ambulatories **1** 768
animal subjects **2** 105–6
antefixes **26** 878
aquatints **2** 240
aqueducts **2** 242
architectural publications **12** 333
architecture **4** 786–7, 788, 789; **7** 693; **12** 791
brick **4** 778–80*; **32** 276
cavity-walling **4** 788
Indian subcontinent **15** 401
megalithic **21** 43
military **21** 568–9*, 573–5*
prefabrication **12** 597; **26** 19
Sri Lanka **29** 453–4
stone **32** 276
United States of America **31** 589–90
vernacular **32** 275–7*
Viking **32** 533
archives **2** 371*
art criticism **12** 30; **14** 697–8
artificial stone **2** 541
artists' biographies **10** 206
art legislation **2** 555, 557, 560; **10** 367
art market **2** 560
art schools **1** 107; **28** 274
assembly rooms **8** 105
automata **7** 445
balconies (theatres) **30** 677
bandstands **21** 893
banknotes **3** 180, 182
banks **3** 175
barns **32** 277
barrows **25** 507
basilicas (non-ecclesiastical) **3** 328; **26** 905
bastions **21** 568
beakheads **26** 612
body ornaments **25** 518
bonding **4** 770
bone **4** 314
book design **8** 109
book illustrations **2** 240; **4** 362–4*, *363*
bookplates **4** 373
botanical books **4** 362
brick **4** 769, 770, 778–80*, 786–7, 788, 789; **32** 276
calcium silicate **4** 788
bridges **4** 801
bronze **4** 849
camps (military) **26** 905
canals **2** 242
capitals **26** 611
cards
cartes-de-visite **24** 661
playing **31** 266
caricatures **2** 240; **10** 554; **26** 742
carpenters **20** 567
carpets **5** 839, 841*; **16** 466
cast iron **2** 242; **28** 874
castles **6** 62; **16** 896
catalogues **4** 22, 27; **6** 81; **10** 213
chairs **20** *595*; **29** 763
chalets **6** 395–6
chess sets **6** 557
children's books **4** 362, 363
chimneys **4** 778, 779
chromolithography **17** 639
clocks **7** 441–2*, *443*, 445–6*, *445*, 448
clubs (meeting places) **7** 469–70
coats of arms **14** 409
coins **7** 538, 539; **29** 469; **31** 527
collections **2** 561; **27** 114; **29** 426
painting **28** 273, 274
portraits **10** 213
royal **2** 559; **14** 767; **19** 197
columns **26** 905
commercial art **7** 651, 652, 653, 654, 655
competitions **7** 666, 667–8
concrete **7** 693
county halls **31** 242

Britain—cont.
craftsmen and artists **15** 401, 820; **32** 327
dealing **12** 30
department stores **29** *454*
design **8** 802*, 804*
dictionaries of art **10** 206, 213
drawings **7** 666; **10** *882*
dress **9** 290*
dyes **9** 492
ebony **7** 445
education (art) **2** 475; **9** 475; **15** 821
emblem books **10** 175
encyclopedias of art **10** 206
engravings **10** 393–4, 396, 397; **13** 220; **29** 675–7
erotic art **10** 482
etchings **10** 555, 562
exhibitions **4** 27; **15** 821; **29** 426
factory design **5** 271
feathers **10** 848
felt **10** 875
figureheads **28** 612, 613, *613*
fireplaces **4** 778
fireproofing **31** 240
follies **11** 242
fora **26** 905
fortifications **5** 417; **21** 568–9*, 573–5*, *574*; **26** 905
forts **1** 318; **21** 568, *574*; **26** 907
furniture **12** 333; **29** 471
garden design **24** 740
gardens **12** 70, 105
gay and lesbian art **10** 482
gilding **7** *444*, 445
girders (beams) **28** 874
glass **12** 791
gold **27** 15
greenhouses **13** 619
guidebooks **13** 809
henges **23** 808; **25** 505
heraldry **14** 408, 409*
heritage **14** 452–3
hill-figures **14** 544–5*, *544*
houses **32** 276–7
bungalows **5** 173–4
prefabricated **26** 18, 19
Prehistoric **25** 503*
South Africa **29** 105
United States of America **31** *590*
19th cent. **28** 874
human figures **14** *544*, 544
ice-houses **15** 67
industrial design **15** 820, 824*
industrial scenes **15** 829
iron **7** 445
jade **16** 861
jet **25** 518
jewellery **17** 526, 528
laburnum **7** 442
lacquer **18** 615
lakes **27** 715
landscape **14** 544, *544*
libraries **4** 22; **19** 318
lighthouses **19** *360*
lighting **24** 641
lithography **4** *363*; **19** *482*, 482–3*; **25** *353*
locks **20** 442
mahogany **7** 445
manuals **12** 333
manufacturing **15** 820–21*, 824*; **20** 593
manuscript illumination **26** *863*
marks **20** 442, 443, 445
mass production **20** 593, *595*
master printers **20** 607
medals **20** 923–4*, 925
meeting-houses **23** 193
mosaics **27** 62; **32** 542
museums **2** 601; **8** 802; **22** 364; **29** 426
music-halls **30** 679
natural history books **4** 363
nickel-brass **7** 539
nude figures **23** 295
observatories **21** 42

Britain—cont.
olive-wood **7** 442
orangeries **23** 470
ormolu **7** *445*
ornithological books **4** 362
painting
landscape **26** 740–41
murals **22** 330–31, 332, 333, *333*
wall **27** 56–7
watercolours **2** 240; **26** 740
papier mâché **18** 615
park design **24** 740
patchwork **24** 253
patronage **12** 30
pattern books **12** 333; **15** 820; **32** 553
periods
Celtic **6** 162
Iron Age **25** 533
pewter **24** 578
photography **24** 646, 658, 672; **29** 426
plaster **29** 829
polychromy **11** 499
porcelain **19** 595
postage stamps **25** 328, 329, *329*
posters **7** 652, *652*, 653; **25** 347, 351, *353*, 354
pottery **25** 513; **30** 875
power stations **25** 402, 403
print publishers **25** 626
prints **14** 638
animal subjects **4** *363*
monotypes **21** 896
tinsel **11** 173
public houses **25** 687–9*, *688*
rock art **25** 531, 532
rugs **27** 317*, *318*
sanctuaries **27** *2*
satin-wood **7** 445
schools **12** 597; **26** 19
scrimshaw **28** 302
scripts **28** 307
sculpture **2** 541; **15** 542–3; **26** 611–12*
service stations **28** 488
settlements **25** 504
shields **14** 409
ship-decoration **28** 612, 613, *613*
shrines (i) (cult) **27** *2*
silver **7** 442, 445
sporting scenes **29** 422, 426, *427*
sports centres **29** 427
stadia **29** 489
stage design **30** 687–8, *688*
stage scenery **30** 680–82
stanchions **28** 874
stone **26** 611–12*; **32** 276
stone-carvings **25** 513
stone circles **21** 41; **25** 522
straw **29** 763
studs **32** 276
surveyors **30** 26
swords **2** 452
tartans **9** 492
tattoos **30** 367
temples **26** 858; **30** 434
tenements **30** 457–8*
textiles **19** 418; **21** 600
theatres **30** 677
theories (art) **5** 215; **20** 527–8
tiles **30** 876–7*
timber structures **32** 276
tin **16** 393
topographical books **2** 240; **4** 362
topographical illustrations **2** 240
towers **21** 569
town halls **31** 239–41*
towns **31** 722
garden cities **12** 144–5, *145*; **31** 728
new **9** 741; **19** 519; **31** 732–3
tracery **31** 273
trade
brick **3** 623
dress **1** 347
figurines **27** 111
glass **7** 87
pigments **24** 799

Britain
trade—cont.
tin **16** 393
treatises **12** 595
urban planning **1** 29; **15** 411; **24** 185; **31** 723, 724, 725, 736–7, 738
vaults (ceiling) **4** 778, 779
verandahs **32** 240
villas **26** 906, *907*; **32** 542, 544, 553, 555
wall coverings **10** 848
wallpaper **32** 817
walnut **7** 442
war artists **24** 666
warehouses **32** 861
watches **7** 443, *443*, 447
water supply **2** 242
wood-engravings **33** 368–9
see also ENGLAND; SCOTLAND; WALES
Britain, Alice **16** 41
Britain's, William, Ltd **31** 256, 264
Britannia metal *see under* ALLOYS → types
Britannia Pottery **28** 258
Brite, James **3** 30
Brite & Bacon **3** 30
Britford (Wilts), St Peter **2** 65, *65*
Brithdir (Flints), St Mark's **32** 783
British Cast Plate Glass Company **21** 720
British Council **19** 590; **24** 515, 517
British East India Company **6** 622, 624; **10** 328; **15** 201; **16** 553
architecture **4** 287; **5** 416, 418; **14** 681; **15** 401, 405; **20** 52, 73; **21** 574
cane **5** 612
carpets **16** 482
ceramics **7** 165
collections **15** 741
dyes **15** 667
enamel **16** 516; **22** 261
fortifications **21** 596
metal **22** 789
paintings **2** 306; **15** 653; **16** 535
sculpture **3** 184; **28** 64
surveys **31** 342
swords **2** *457*
textiles **8** 35; **16** 449; **28** 564
wallpaper **10** 278; **32** 818
British Empire Exhibition, 1924 *see under* WEMBLEY
British Empire Marketing Board **7** 616
British Guiana *see* GUYANA
British Honduras *see* BELIZE
British Museum *see under* LONDON → museums
British North Borneo *see* SABAH
British North Borneo Company **20** 164
British Nyasaland *see* MALAWI
British Petroleum **17** 850; **19** 538
British Porcelain Works (Canada) **5** 581
British Railways Pension Fund **15** 888
British School **19** 586
British Silverware **10** 143
British Somaliland Protectorate *see* SOMALIA
British Surrealist Group **24** 369; **26** 335
Britius, Giuseppe *see* BRIZZI, GIUSEPPE
Brito, Francisco Xavier de **23** 669
Brito, Jorge de **25** 318
Brito, Júlio de **4** 658
Brito, Luis **4** 826*
Brito, Manuel de **27** 804
Brito (Avellana), María **4** 826*; **18** 835
Brito, Ramón Vásquez *see* VÁSQUEZ BRITO, RAMÓN
Britsyn **27** 584
Britsyn, Ivan **27** 422, 426

Brittain, Miller (Gore) **4** 826*; **5** 568
Brittany (France) **9** 80; **14** 412, 413
Brittany (House of) **4** 827*
Brittany, Anne, Duchess of *see* ANNE OF BRITTANY, Queen of France
Brittany, Arthur III, Duke of *see* ARTHUR III, Duke of Brittany
Brittany, Catherine, Duchess of *see* CATHERINE OF LUXEMBOURG
Brittany, Francis I, Duke of *see* FRANCIS I, Duke of Brittany
Brittany, Francis II, Duke of *see* FRANCIS II, Duke of Brittany
Brittany, Isabella, Duchess of *see* ISABELLA, Duchess of Brittany
Brittany, John IV of Montfort, Duke of *see* JOHN IV OF MONTFORT, Duke of Brittany
Brittany, Marguerite of Foix, Duchess of *see* MARGUERITE OF FOIX, Duchess of Brittany
Britten, Benjamin **24** 839
Brittle ware *see under* POTTERY → wares
Britto, Giovanni **4** 828*; **20** 799; **33** 356
Britton, Alison **4** 828*; **10** 315
Britton, John **1** 612; **4** 828–9*; **9** 70
collaboration **23** 214
personal collection **6** 90; **25** 661, 753
pupils **3** 292
works **8** *911*; **10** 208, 377; **13** 204
illustrated **4** 586; **10** 236; **12** 45; **14** 745; **33** *445*
Britton & Gilson **29** 507
Britz, Bannie **29** 107
Brive-la-Gaillarde **22** 160
St Martin **11** 623, 624
Brix, Alexander *see* MORETTO (DA BRESCIA)
Brix, Michal **8** 381
Brixen, Prince-Bishop of **28** 382
Brixen Globe **12** 813
Brixia *see* BRESCIA
Brixworth (Northants) **10** *225*
All Saints' **2** 65; **4** *829*, 829–30*; **32** 87
crypt **1** 767; **8** 222
piers (ii) (masonry) **24** 750
stained glass **2** 83
Brizguz y Bru, Athanasio Genaro **4** 830*
Brizi, Giuseppe **3** 644
Brizio, Francesco **4** 830*
collaboration **26** 196; **29** 251
patrons and collectors **27** 693
works **5** 854
Brizuela, Gabriel **24** 99
Brizuela, Pedro de **13** 764; **28** 369
Brizzi, Alfredo **8** 601
Brizzi, Ary **2** 401; **4** 831*
Brizzi, Giuseppe **31** 312; **32** 5
Brjakin, Ivan **17** 868
Brno **4** 831–3*, *832*; **8** *374*
architecture **8** 377, 380
Avion Hotel **8** 380
Bank of Moravia **8** 380
Cathedral **8** 379
Children's Teaching Hospital **8** 380
Dubsky palace **5** 348
Dubsky Zimmer **2** 816
education (art) **8** 425, 426
figurines **4** 313; **25** 488, 490
furniture **8** 398, 402
glass **8** 407
Klein Palace **8** 379
Mitrovský palace **8** 379
Moravian Diet building **8** 392
Moravian Gallery **8** 425
Moravian Museum **4** 833; **8** 424; **13** 662
Museum of Applied Art **8** 424
Old Town Hall **4** *833*
pewter **8** 415

Brno—cont.
pottery **8** 404
St James **8** 382, 383
St Thomas **8** 382
School of Arts and Crafts **8** 425
sculpture **8** 386
Špilberk Castle **4** 833
textiles **8** 419
Town Hall **24** 807
urban planning **13** 661
Villa Tugendhat **8** 380, *380*, 402; **15** 885; **25** 741
Broa
harness-mounts **14** 182; **32** *513*, 515, 521
Broach *see* BHARUCH
Broad, Rodney **2** 754
Broadacre City **31** 596; **33** 404
Broadhead, Caroline **4** 834*; **25** 27
Broadlands (Hants) **24** 213; **30** 451
Broadsheet **24** 438
broadsheets **25** 244; **33** 360
Broadside Map **14** 708
broadsides **4** 359, 834*; **27** 872
see also PRINTS → types → catchpenny; popular
Broad Street Glasshouse **10** 316
Broadwalk **22** 612
Broadway (Hereford & Worcs) **1** 22; **10** 224
Broadway Damask Company **14** 397
Broadwood, John, & Sons **5** 268; **22** 373; **28** 593
Broa style *see under* VIKING → styles
Brobo **3** 408
Broc, Jean **4** 834*; **11** 542; **25** 581
brocades **30** 553*
historical and regional traditions
Bhutan **3** 915, *915*
Buddhism **30** 846
China **7** 58; **30** 846
England **28** *717*; **30** X3
France **11** *645*, *646*
Indian subcontinent **15** 662–4*, *663*, *664*, 716
Japan **17** 371
Korea **18** 373, 380
Laos **18** 771
Mesoamerica, Pre-Columbian **21** 261
Spain **29** *348*
Tibet **30** 846
Vietnam **32** 490
uses
armour **7** 58
dolls **17** 371
fans **18** 380
scrolls **28** 310, 312
tents **15** 716; **30** 470, 476
Brocade style **1** 860
Brocandel, Hipólito Rovira y *see* ROVIRA Y BROCANDEL, HIPÓLITO
Brocas (family) **16** 16
Brocas, Henry, sr (1762-1837) **4** 834*; **16** 15
Brocas, Henry, jr (*c.* 1798-1873) **4** 835*; **5** 283
Brocas, James Henry **4** 835*; **5** 283
Brocas, John **31** 623
Brocas, Samuel Frederick **4** 835*; **5** 283
Brocas, William **4** 835*; **5** 283
Brocchi, Francesco de' **11** 898
Brocchi, Giovanni Battista **11** 188
Brocco, Antonio **4** 58
Brocco, Giovanni Antonio **2** 213
Brochado, José **29** 202
brochantite **24** 793
Brochard, George **19** 91
Brochier, F. **33** 283
Brochów Church **25** 96
brochs *see under* TOWERS → types
Bro Church **13** 118
Brock, Thomas **4** 835*
assistants **33** 343
Brock, Thomas—cont.
collaboration **10** 267; **27** 879
groups and movements **23** 34
teachers **11** 239
works **11** 238, 239; **19** 600; **29** 566, *566*
Brockbank, Alan **27** 642
Brockedon, W. **8** 66
Bröckelschen collection **1** 896
Brocket Hall (Herts) **7** 172; **22** 153
Brockhampton (Hereford & Worcs), All Saints **9** 739; **19** 253, *253*
Brockhorst, Arnold **9** 724; **28** 234
Brockhurst, Gerald Leslie **4** 87, 835*
Brocklesby Park (Lincs) **4** 157; **20** 868
collections **33** 385
gems **12** 266; **20** 389
mausoleum **33** *444*
paintings **3** 207; **7** 394, 775; **8** 297; **17** 674; **28** 803
Brockman (family) **14** 271
Brockunier, Charles W. **14** 603
Brocky, Károly **4** 836*
Brocos y Gomez, Modesto **4** 717
Brocquy, Louis Le *see* LE BROCQUY, LOUIS
Brod, Max **24** 427
Broddetorp **26** 691
Brodel, Giovanni Vittorio **16** 739
Brödel, Max **1** 845
Broderick, George, 3rd Viscount Midleton (*d* 1765) **6** 412
Broderick, George, 4th Viscount Midleton (*d* 1836) **6** 412
broderie anglaise *see under* EMBROIDERY → types
Brodick Castle (Strathclyde) **3** 476
Visitor Centre **28** 232
Brodie, Francis **9** 727; **28** 252
Brodie, J. A. **26** 18
Brodie, William **9** 727; **28** 243
Brodósqui, Casa-Mueu Portinari **4** 727
Brodovitch, Alexey **4** 836*; **7** 656; **11** 728
assistants **26** 41
pupils **2** 289, 852; **11** 87, 747; **22** 452; **24** 363; **33** 253
staff **11** 728; **14** 816
Brodowski, Antoni (Stanisław) **4** 836–7*; **25** 141; **32** 876
pupils **30** 359
works **25** 106
Brodowski, Józef **4** 837; **12** 821
Brodowski, Tadeusz **4** 837; **25** 106
Brodrick, Cuthbert **4** 837*
competitions **7** 667
works **10** 236, 669; **12** 792; **14** 863; **16** *54*; **18** 888; **30** 503; **31** 240
Brodrick, John **28** 299
Brodsky, Hopf & Adler **1** 495; **8** 470
Brodsky, Horace **25** 624
Brodsky, Isaak (Izrailevich) **4** 837–8*; **17** 577; **27** 443
groups and movements **2** 633; **27** 395; **31** 582
pupils **18** 657
teachers **26** 220
works **27** 581
Brodsworth (S. Yorks) **9** 25
Brodszky, Sándor **4** 838*
Brody **25** 133
Brody, Samuel **10** 685; **30** 469
Brodzki, Wiktor **25** 115
Broe, Pierre-Jean De *see* DE BROE, PIERRE-JEAN
Broebes, Jean Baptist **3** 790
Broeck, Barbara van den **4** 838
Broeck, Crispin van den **4** 838, 839*
groups and movements **26** 728
patrons and collectors **23** 112; **27** 501
Broeck, Crispin van den—cont.
reproductive prints by others **7** 555, 556; **17** 598; **27** 501; **33** 169, 170
works **4** *839*; **25** 619; **33** 365
Broeck, Hendrik van den **4** 838, 839–40*; **25** 185
collaboration **8** 706
patrons and collectors **4** 424; **10** 811
works **4** 316, *840*; **26** 817
Broeck, Jan van den **4** 838, 839
Broeck, Raphael van den **4** 838
Broeck, Willem van den **3** 569; **4** 838–9*
attributions **3** 545
works **2** 203, *203*; **29** 571
Broecke, Berent ten **22** 904
Broederlam, Melchior **3** 552; **4** 840–42*; **13** 133, 156
paintings **3** 552; **4** *841*; **13** 131
altarpieces **1** 710; **8** 892; **13** 109, 154; **16** 854
triptychs **11** 439
patrons and collectors **5** 207, 208, 895; **11** 438, 531; **19** 721
Broederschap der Schilderkunst **1** 806
Broederstroom **1** *413*, 414, 415
Broeghel, Ambrosius *see* BREUGHEL, AMBROSIUS
Broek, Jan van *see* JORISZ, DAVID
Broek, J. H. van den **4** 816; **22** 832; **31** 867, 868
collaboration **19** 861; **30** 871
groups and movements **31** 867
pupils **17** 472
staff **23** 426
works **22** 832; **27** 230
Broek, Van den, & Bakema *see* VAN DEN BROEK & BAKEMA
Broekmans, Marlo **10** 483
Broel-Plater, Władysław **25** 139
Broeucq, Jacques Du *see* DU BROEUCQ, JACQUES
Brogden, John **17** 527
Brøgger, Stig **8** 741
Broggi, Luigi **4** 247, 842*; **20** 908; **29** 59
Broggia, Ottaviano **8** 379
Brogi, Carlo **4** 843
Brogi, Giacomo **4** 842–3*; **16** 777
Brogi, Giacomo, photograph collection *see under* FLORENCE → museums → Alinari Museum
Brogi photographic studio **11** 190
Broglie, Prince de **15** 842; **27** 768
Broglio, Mario **8** 604; **16** 680; **21** 87; **26** 776; **31** 851
Brogniart, Alexandre-Théodore **19** 11
Brohier, John **5** 417; **20** 52; **21** 574
Brohn, Wolf Ernst **32** 833
Broighter **6** 161; **25** 542
Broighter Collar **12** 866, *867*
Brokar, A. A. **27** 439
broken ashlar *see under* MASONRY → types
broken kufic script *see* SCRIPTS → types → New Abbasid style
broken pediments *see under* PEDIMENTS → types
Broker, Nicholas **25** 16
Brokof (family) **14** 515
Brokof, Ferdinand Maximilián **4** 843–4*
works **4** *844*; **8** 385, *385*; **22** 45; **25** 432; **33** 417
Brokof, Jan **4** 843–4*
pupils **4** 843; **31** 739
works **4** 844; **8** 385
Brokof, Michal Jan Josef **4** 843
Bromander, Johan
works **11** *102*
Bromberg, Paul **4** 844
groups and movements **22** 868
works **21** 362; **23** 908; **32** 756
Brome, Richard **7** 431
Brome Lake County Building (Que.) **5** 560
bromelia *see under* FIBRES → types
Bromfield, Hugh **16** 889
bromide prints *see under* PHOTOGRAPHIC PRINTS → types
Bromig, Hans Leonhard **10** 445
Bromley, A. N. **23** 258
Bromley, Frederick **4** 845*
Bromley, James **4** 845*
Bromley, John Charles **4** 845*
Bromley, Valentine W. **2** 692
Bromley, Walter Davenport *see* DAVENPORT BROMLEY, WALTER
Bromley, William **4** 845*; **7** 413
Bromley Davenport, William **8** 549
Bromma Church **30** 66
bromochromotype *see under* PHOTOGRAPHY → processes
bromoil prints *see under* PHOTOGRAPHIC PRINTS → types
Brompton, Richard **4** 845*
Bromsgrove Guild **5** 66; **18** 903
Bromwich, Isherwood & Bradley **4** 845
Bromwich, Thomas K. **4** 845*; **10** 278; **31** 683
Bromwich & Isherwood **4** 845
Bronchorst, Gerrit (Jansz.) van **4** 846
Bronchorst, Jan (Gerritsz.) van **4** 846*; **22** 844
collaboration **4** 846
patrons and collectors **5** 9
pupils **10** 658
teachers **14** 731
works **25** 68
Bronchorst, Johannes (Jansz.) van **4** 846*; **31** 772
Bronckhorst, Arthur *see* BRONCKORST, ARNOLD
Bronckhorst-Bosschuysse (family) **4** 446
Bronckorst, Arnold (van) **4** 847*; **28** 268
Bronconi, Antonio **11** 194
Brøndum, Anna (Kirstine) *see* ANCHER, ANNA (KIRSTINE)
Broneer, Oscar **16** 612
Bronescomb, Bishop of Exeter **10** 672
Brong **1** 503
Brongniart, Alexandre (1770-1847) **6** 535; **10** 728; **28** 522, 523
Brongniart, Alexandre-Théodore (1739-1813) **4** 847–8*; **17** 445
teachers **4** 533
works **6** 166, *166*; **10** 669; **20** 868; **23** 518; **24** 120; **28** 523; **31** 714
Broniatowski, Karol **17** 448
Bronkhorst, Jan Gerritsz. van **31** 772
Bronner, Michael **3** 870
Brönnestad **30** 76
Bronnitsy **27** 414, 423
Bronocice **25** 504
Bronson, A. A. **12** 275
Bronstein, Lev (Davidovich) *see* TROTSKY, LEON
Bronstein, Max *see* ARDON, MORDECAI
bronze **4** 848–55*; **21** 319
dating methods **30** 404
historical and regional traditions
Aegean **8** 262
Afghanistan **1** 207; **16** *366*, *375*
Africa **1** 287, 350; **4** 854–5*
Akan **1** 288
Akkadian (people) **4** 850
Anatolia, ancient **1** *521*, 521–2, *825*, 834, *835*, 836
Ancient Near East **9** 150; **21** 711; **30** 774; **31** 530
bronze
historical and regional traditions—cont.
Anglo-Saxon **9** 253
Arabia **2** 258–9
Argentina **33** *569*
Armenia (Europe) **2** 441
Assyrian **21** *276*, 304
Australia **2** 752, *753*
Austria **2** *800*, 802, *803*, 821–2; **10** *894*, *908*; **14** 88
Prehistoric **25** *541*
Azerbaijan **16** *506*
Babylonian **21** 304
Bali (Indonesia) **29** 229
Belgium **2** *237*; **3** *571*, *573*, 602; **13** 159–60; **21** *499*; **26** *145*
Benin, Kingdom of **6** 9
Bolivia **4** 255
Britain **4** 849
Buddhism **5** *240*; **17** *375*
Afghanistan **1** 207
Cambodia **5** 485
Central Asia, Eastern **6** 298
China **6** 706, 707, *708*, *710*, 712, 718, *719*, *720*, 720–22, 835
Indian subcontinent **15** *223*, 476, *530*, 530–31; **22** 447; **26** *150*
Japan **17** *34*, *107*, *110*, 110–12, *111*, *112*, *113*, 120, 320, *322*, 397; **22** *497*
Korea **5** *114*; **18** *284*, *285*, *294*, 347–9*, *348*
Laos **18** 768, *768*
Sri Lanka **29** *460*, *479*
Thailand **30** 593–5*, 596–7, *597*, *598*, *601*, 601–2*, *602*, *605*, *607*
Tibet **30** 351, *841*
Burma **5** 239, *240*, 241, 256–7, 260, *260*
Byzantine **8** 199
Cambodia **5** 485, 494–5, 497–8*, 507
Carolingian **5** 805, 806, *806*; **9** 152
Celtic **6** 157–8, 159, 161; **14** 88
Czech Republic **6** *158*
England **6** *161*
France **6** *155*
Germany **18** 120
Central Asia, Eastern **6** 298, 315, *315*
Central Asia, Western **6** 242*, *243*, *245*, *246*, 260, 261, *263*, 274, *286*
Champa **6** 427, 432
Chile **6** *598*
China **3** 685; **4** 852–3*, 855; **6** 631, 635, 645*, 706, 707, 725, 726–7, 733, 735, 737, 738, *738*, 772, 773, 788, 826–34*, *827*, 835*, 857*, 860–66*, 868*; **7** 21, 22, 54, 68, *72*, 94, 101, 107, 108, 109, 128, 129, *129*, 130, *130*, 139; **17** 587, *587*; **23** 495, *495*, 496, *496*; **24** 258
Anyang period (*c.* 1300-*c.* 1050 BC) **6** 835, 836, 839, 840; **23** *155*; **28** 603
Buddhism **6** *719*, 835
Chu **7** 247
Daoism **6** *628*
Dian culture **8** 852–4, *853*, *854*
Erligang period (*c.* 15th-14th cent. BC) **6** 831, 835, 836, 838–9, 840
Erlitou period (first half 2nd millennium BC) **6** 831; **10** *464*
Han period (206 BC-AD 220) **6** 857–60*, *858*, *859*, *860*, *861*, 861–2*; **7** 95; **21** *715*
Ming period (1368-1644) **6** *720*, 720–22

bronze
historical and regional traditions
China—cont.
Northern and Southern Dynasties (AD 310-589) **6** *708*, *710*
Prehistoric **6** 835
Qijia culture **6** 835
Qing period (1644-1911) **6** *733*
Qin period (221-206 BC) **6** 727, 857*
Shang period (*c.* 1600-*c.* 1050 BC) **4** 849; **6** 8, 625, 736, 798, *831*, 835–41*, *836*, *837*, *838*, *839*; **7** 3–4, 55, 97, 107, 123; **13** *736*; **21** 714, I4; **23** 549–50; **24** *14*; **28** 603
Song period (AD 960-1279) **6** 718, *865*, *866*
Sui period (AD 581-618) **6** 712
Tang period (AD 618-907) **6** 730, *863*, 863–4*, *864*; **7** 14, 109
Western Zhou (*c.* 1050-771 BC) **6** *848*
Xin period (AD 9-23) **6** 860–61*
Zhou period (*c.* 1050-256 BC) **3** *626*; **6** *695*, 808, *833*, 841–9*, *842*, *843*, *844*, *845*, *846*, *847*, *849*, 850–56*, *850*, *851*, *852*, *853*, *854*, *855*, *856*; **7** *55*, 97, 107, 533; **28** *626*; **29** 229, *906*; **33** *471*
20th cent. **6** 767
Confucianism **7** 705
Crete **8** 154; **21** *679*, 680, *688*
Minoan **8** 153, 154; **21** 688*
Croatia **21** *316*
Cycladic **8** 322–3*
Cyprus, ancient **8** 339, 342, 349, 353, *354*; **10** *400*; **14** 356
Czech Republic **8** 416; **33** *435*
Daoism **6** *628*
Denmark **25** 526, *527*
Dian culture **6** 834; **8** 852–4, *853*, *854*
Dong Son **4** 852; **29** 230
Edo (Africa) **9** 736
Egypt **9** *160*; **16** *506*
Egypt, ancient **9** 817, 860; **10** 35–7, *36*; **21** 711
Late Period (664-332 BC) **5** *71*; **9** 855, *856*
New Kingdom (*c.* 1539-*c.* 1075 BC) **6** 559; **10** 54; **21** *712*
Roman **27** *89*
Third Intermediate Period (*c.* 1075-*c.* 656 BC) **9** *861*, 886
13th Dynasty (*c.* 1756-*c.* 1630 BC) **10** *36*
Ejagham **10** 124*
Elamite **15** *919*
England **10** 339–40; **25** *540*
Arts and Crafts Movement **11** *256*
Celtic **6** *161*, 161
Gothic **13** 164
Neo-classicism **3** *26*
New Sculpture **23** *34*; **30** *762*
New Sculpture (UK) **3** *367*; **11** *303*; **29** *575*
Romanesque **10** 322
1st cent. AD **27** *95*
17th cent. **10** *263*
18th cent. **27** *467*
19th cent. **10** *267*; **11** *238*; **19** *600*; **23** *172*
20th cent. **10** *438*; **11** *157*
Etruscan **6** 388; **10** 587, 588, *590*, *595*, 602, 604–6, *605*, 608, *608*, 624–30*, *625*, *626*, *627*, *628*, *629*, 633, *635*, 638; **16** *684*; **21** 712, *712*; **27** 85
Finland **11** *100*

bronze
historical and regional traditions—cont.
France **11** 623, 625–7*; **29** 571, *572*, 573, 574–5
Baroque **7** *423*; **24** *786*
Carolingian **5** *806*
Celtic **6** *155*
Cubism **9** *362*
Empire style **11** 629
Mannerism **11** *558*; **24** *814*
Migration period **21** *503*
Neo-classicism **14** *798*; **27** *311*
Roman **27** 89, 90
Romanesque **26** *682*
Romanticism **3** *313*, *315*; **8** *565*
15th cent. **11** 624
16th cent. **11** 624; **27** *548*
17th cent. **8** *94*; **27** *822*
18th cent. **5** *381*; **11** *589*, *626*, *627*; **26** *112*
19th cent. **2** *100*; **26** *510*, *511*
20th cent. **4** *661*; **12** *566*; **20** *825*, *828*; **26** *351*
Georgia **12** *322*
Germany **11** 253; **12** *399*, 451–2*; **28** IV2
Baroque **3** *798*; **23** *309*
Celtic **18** 120
Holy Roman Empire (before 1648) **13** *160*, 160–61
Mannerism **12** *346*, *347*; **26** *104*
Ottonian **7** *381*; **9** *153*; **23** *658*
Prehistoric **9** 689, *690*
Renaissance **11** *223*; **12** *402*
Rococo **12** 424, *425*
Roman **27** *86*, *88*
Romanesque **26** *146*, *535*
16th cent. **28** 492
20th cent. **20** *396*
Gothic **11** *200*; **13** 159–61, *160*, 164; **24** *874*; **28** IV2
Greece, ancient **1** 123; **2** 451; **3** 483; **4** 849, 850–52*; **8** *690*; **13** 390, 391, 422, 434–5*, 437–8*, 568, 571–7*, *572*, *574*, 583–4, *600*, 600–602*; **21** *712*; **24** 258; **25** *179*
Archaic **8** 262, 458; **13** 572–3*; **24** *328*; **30** *339*; **32** *660*
Archaic, Late **13** 448
Attica **13** 572
Boeotia **13** *601*
Classical **8** 262, *696*; **13** 573*
Classical, Early **1** 481; **13** 433, *573*; **25** 177, *178*; **29** 567, *567*
Classical, High **13** *429*, *453*; **26** *297*
Classical, Late **13** *460*
Dark Age (*c.* 1050-*c.* 750 BC) **13** 597
Geometric (*c.* 900-*c.* 700 BC) **13** 441, 572*
Hellenistic **13** 573–4*, 588, 589
Italy **30** 339
Proto-Daidalic **13** *443*
4th cent. BC **13** *577*
5th cent. BC **6** 9; **13** 438, 586; **23** 290
6th cent. BC **13** *575*, *576*
7th cent. BC **13** *584*; **21** 712
8th cent. BC **8** *262*
Helladic **14** 356*, *356*; **22** *397*
Hinduism **15** *219*, *516*, *517*, 523, *728*
Holy Roman Empire (before 1648) **5** *301*; **13** *160*; **26** 684–6*, *685*; **28** IV2
Hungary **14** *897*
Hurrian **15** *33*
India, Republic of **15** 175
Indian subcontinent **4** 853–4*, 855; **15** 414, 459, 730; **21** 716
Buddhism **15** *223*, 476; **22** 447; **26** *150*

bronze
historical and regional traditions
Indian subcontinent—cont.
Colonial period **15** *725*
Hinduism **14** *557*; **15** *219*, *728*
Indus civilization **15** *412*, 417–20*
Jainism **15** 453
Karnataka **15** *530*, 530–31
Kerala **15** 521, 522, *523*, 523, 524, *525*, 708–9
Tamil Nadu **4** *853*; **15** *516*, 516, *517*
Indonesia **15** 776, 777
Indus civilization **4** 853; **15** *412*, 417–20*
Insular art **15** *872*, *873*; **28** *630*
Iran **2** *648*; **16** 370, 373, *374*, *504*, *506*; **19** *810*, *811*
Iran, ancient **15** 902, 905, 918, *919*; **21** *712*
Iraq **2** *647*; **16** *370*, *538*
Ireland **15** *872*, *873*; **16** *21*; **28** *630*; **32** *530*
Islamic **2** *647*, *648*; **4** 855; **9** *160*; **16** *135*, 363, 364, 503, *504*; **21** 717
Afghanistan **16** *366*, *375*
Iran **16** 370, 373, *374*, *506*
Iraq **16** *370*, *538*
Khurasan **16** 370
Spain **16** *368*, 386, *387*; **20** 51
Syria **16** *511*
Transoxiana **16** 370
Italy **9** 152, 153–5, 158–9; **10** 587; **16** 689, 690, 743
Baroque **2** *609*, *610*; **5** *532*, *533*; **16** *700*; **27** *830*; **29** *29*
Etruscan **10** 587, 588, *590*, *595*, *605*, *608*, 624–30*, *625*, *626*, *627*, *628*, *629*, 633, *635*, 638; **16** *684*
Futurism **4** *201*
Gothic **11** *200*; **24** *874*
Greece, ancient **30** 339, *339*
Mannerism **1** *791*; **3** *162*, *469*; **6** *142*, *144*, *145*; **12** *572*, *573*; **29** *569*
Prehistoric **10** 527
Renaissance **1** *162*, *556*; **2** *140*, *141*; **3** 636, *637*, *860*, *861*; **8** *796*; **9** *127*, *130*, 156–7, *157*; **11** *71*, *693*; **12** *538*, 539, *539*, *540*, *541*; **16** *690*; **19** *202*, *208*; **20** *622*; **21** II4; **24** *863*; **25** *20*, *725*; **26** 327, *327*, *329*, *330*, *766*; **29** *408*, *561*; **32** *105*, *360*, *362*, *363*
Roman **14** *443*; **25** *202*; **27** *9*, *10*
Romanesque **26** 690; **32** *342*
16th cent. **5** *415*; **9** *340*
17th cent. **7** *842*; **24** *696*
19th cent. **32** *122*
20th cent. **9** *159*; **16** *707*; **20** *353*, *429*
Jainism **15** 453, 531
Japan **17** 21, 100–101*, *110*, 110–12, 120, 318, 319–20, *323*, *324*, 361, *370*, 396, 397, 409; **22** *497*
Asuka-Hakuhō period (AD *c.* 552-710) **17** *321*
Asuka period (AD *c.* 552-645) **17** *107*
Buddhism **17** *34*, *322*, *375*
Edo period (1600-1868) **17** 370
Hakuhō period (AD 645-710) **17** *111*, *112*
Kofun period (*c.* AD 300-710) **17** *320*; **21** 716
Nara period (AD 710-94) **17** *113*
Yayoi period (*c.* 300 BC-*c.* AD 300) **17** 319, *319*
Java **15** 777, 811; **29** 229

bronze
historical and regional traditions—cont.
Jewish art **17** 574
Khurasan **16** 370
Korea **18** 249, *287*, 302, 344–7*, *346*, 353, *356*, 378; **21** 715
Buddhism **18** 347–9*, *348*
Prehistoric **18** 297
6th cent. AD **18** *284*
7th cent. AD **5** *114*; **18** *285*
9th cent. AD **18** *364*
13th cent. **18** 349
14th cent. **18** *294*
20th cent. **18** 300, 301
Laos **18** *768*, 768
La Tène culture (*c.* 450-.*c* 50 BC) **6** *155*, *158*
Latvia
Majiayao culture **6** 835
Malaysia **20** 175
Mesoamerica, Pre-Columbian **21** 245
Mesopotamia **21** *276*, 296, 298, 303, 304; **30** *28*
Mexico **21** *384*
Minoan **2** 451; **4** 850; **8** 153; **21** *679*, 679–80, 688*, *688*
Mongolia **21** 882; **23** 495, *495*, 496, *496*
Animal style **21** 885
Mycenaean **2** 451; **4** 849, 850, *851*; **14** 356*, *356*; **22** *397*
Netherlands, the **13** 159–60; **22** 894–5*
New Zealand **23** 63, *63*, *67*, *72*; **33** *374*
Nigeria **4** 854, *854*; **15** 118, *118*, *119*
Norway **3** 783; **23** *230*; **32** *497*, *515*
Ottonian **7** *381*; **9** *153*; **12** *399*; **23** 657–9*, *658*
Pakistan **23** *802*
Parthian **24** *217*
Peru **24** *510*
Philistine **24** 635
Phoenician **24** *642*, 644
Phrygian **1** 836
Poland **25** *131*
Portugal **19** *893*
Prehistoric art **1** *825*; **8** 339; **25** 518, 526–7, 547; **27** *835*; **29** *229*, 230
Anatolia, ancient **1** *835*
Bronze Age **25** 518, 526
China **6** 835
Este art **10** 527
Germany **9** 689, *690*
Iron Age **25** 540, *540*, *541*, 541–2*, 546
Italy **10** 527
Punic **25** 734
Qijia culture **6** 835
Rhodes (island) **26** 292
Romanesque **26** *145*, *146*, 690
England **10** 322
France **26** *682*
Germany **26** *535*
Holy Roman Empire (before 1648) **26** 684–6*, *685*
Romania **30** 769
Rome, ancient **4** 852, 855; **8** 263; **20** 328; **21** 1; **25** 43; **27** 10–11, 12, 17, 85–92*, 105; **28** *383*; **29** *561*, *562*, 567
Augustan **27** 32
Egypt **27** *89*
Italy **2** 168
Late Antiquity **18** *824*
Republican **24** 258; **25** *202*; **27** 29, *30*
Switzerland **27** *91*
1st cent. BC **14** *443*; **21** 713
2nd cent. BC **8** 342
5th cent. BC **27** *9*
1st cent. AD **11** *151*; **27** *95*
2nd cent. AD **27** *86*

bronze
historical and regional traditions
Rome, ancient—cont.
3rd cent. AD **27** *88*
Sardinia **25** 734; **27** 835, *835*
Scandinavia **32** *513*, *515*, *516*
Scythian **6** 242; **28** 322
Seleucid **28** 384
Sicán culture **28** 651
Sicily **13** 572
Slovenia **28** *806*
South Africa **29** *112*
South America, Pre-Columbian **28** 651
South-east Asia **29** 228, *229*, 229–30
Spain **16** *368*, 386, *387*, *506*; **20** 51; **29** 339, 341, *343*
Sri Lanka **29** *460*, *461*, 474, 478, *479*
Sweden **30** 111; **32** *513*, *516*
Switzerland **25** 547; **27** *91*; **30** *138*, *146*
Syria **16** *511*
Syria-Palestine **15** *33*; **21** *331*; **30** 180, 193, 194, 195
Thailand **4** 855; **29** 228, 229; **30** 593–5*, 596–7, *597*, *598*, *601*, 601–2*, *602*, *605*, *607*, 633
Thracian **30** 769, 770
Tibet **30** 351, 839, 840–41, *841*
Transoxiana **16** 370
Turkey **16** *506*; **31** *700*
Ukraine **31** 562
United States of America **7** *875*; **18** *594*; **22** *426*; **27** *557*; **31** 611, *612*, *613*, 653*
Urartian **1** 836, *836*; **31** 158, *700*, 700–701
Vietnam **4** 852; **6** 427; **29** 228, 229; **32** 480, 487–8, *488*
Champa **6** 432
Viking **32** *512*, *515*, *516*, *530*
Yemen **2** *258*, *259*
patinas **4** 848, 852; **11** 309; **24** 258
technical examination **30** 408
techniques
casting **4** 853–4
Carolingian **5** 806
China **6** 725, 830–34*
Etruscan **10** 625
Greece, ancient **13** 435, *437*, 437–8*
Indian subcontinent **4** *853*; **15** 414
Islamic **16** 370
Vietnam **32** 480
gilding **4** 851
China **6** 707, *708*, *710*, *719*, *720*, 859, 866
Etruscan **10** 625
France **11** *589*, 625–7*, *626*, *627*; **23** 531; **29** *343*
Japan **17** 100, 101, 319
Rome, ancient **27** *10*
Viking **32** *530*
hammering **4** 851
hollow-casting **4** 850, 851
inlays **7** 107
laminating **10** 625
lost-wax casting **4** 850, 851, 852, 854
China **6** 833, 834, 855, 865; **8** 339
Greece, ancient **13** 575
Japan **17** 100–101, 320
Rome, ancient **27** 17
moulding **4** 852; **6** *833*, 838; **17** 101, 319
polychromy **4** 850, 851
raising **4** 850
repoussé **16** 364; **17** 320
riveting **21** 324
smelting **17** 318
smoking **24** 258

bronze
techniques—cont.
soldering **4** 850; **10** 625
sphyrelaton technique **8** 154; **10** 625; **13** 435
uses
altars **5** *533*; **6** *243*; **26** *535*
amphorae **6** 827
aquamanilia **2** 237
architecture **6** 645*
armour **4** *851*; **13** 583–4, *584*; **14** 356; **16** 503
arrowheads **6** 260; **14** 356
astrolabes **2** *647*, *648*
axes **6** 841, 848, *848*; **7** 97; **28** *603*
balustrades **25** *131*
banners **17** *321*
basins **6** *286*; **18** 349
beads **13** *600*, 602
beds **3** 483
bells **3** 627; **4** 855
China **3** *626*; **6** 829, 834, 841, *846*, 849*, 855; **28** *626*
Japan **17** 100, *319*, 319–20, *322*, 397
Korea **18** 346, 347–8
Ottonian **23** 658
Romanesque **26** 686*
belthooks **3** 685; **6** 855, 859; **7** 107
belts **7** 108, 109
betel sets **20** 175
bowls **4** *854*; **6** *245*; **24** 644
bracelets **7** 109; **13** *600*, 601; **29** 228
brooches **6** 158; **15** *872*; **32** *516*
buckets **16** *366*
buckles **6** 856; **10** *625*; **18** 347; **21** *503*
busts
England **10** *263*
Etruscan **10** 604
Finland **11** *100*
France **8** *565*
Holy Roman Empire (before 1648) **5** *301*; **21** II4
Italy **5** *415*; **6** *144*
Rome, ancient **27** *30*; **28** *383*
cabinets (ii) (furniture) **11** *627*
candelabra **5** 604; **26** 686*
candlesticks **26** *329*, *682*
caskets **5** 918
casts **6** 8, 9
cauldrons **7** 97; **8** 154, *354*; **13** 575, *575*
censers **6** 173, 859, 866
chairs **6** 388, 389
chandeliers **6** 442; **16** *387*
chariot fittings **6** 158, 848
chariots **6** 727
châtelaines **7** 109
chests **6** 559; **10** 54
cists **10** *629*
clocks **11** *626*
coins **6** *263*; **7** 539; **16** *511*
Cambodia **5** 507
China **7** *72*, 533
Cyprus, ancient **8** 349
Etruscan **10** 633
Greece, ancient **13** 586, 588, 589
Indonesia **15** 811
Japan **17** 370, *370*
Korea **18** *356*
Rome, ancient **11** *151*
commodes **12** *425*
conservation **6** 336
cooking pots **15** 708
couches **9** 689
crossbow-bolts **7** 97
crosses **8** 199, 200, 203
crowns **18** 349
crucifixes **5** *532*; **26** 684–5
cups **7** 123
cymbals **4** 855
daggers **16** *506*; **18** 345; **22** *397*; **23** 495
diadems **13** 601

bronze
uses—cont.
door fittings **10** 338
doors
Ancient Near East **9** 150
Carolingian **5** 806; **9** 152–5*
Egypt **9** *160*
France **26** *511*
Germany **9** *153*
Greece, ancient **13** 390, 391
Holy Roman Empire (before 1648) **26** 684*
Italy **9** 156–7, *157*, 158–60*, *159*; **11** *71*; **12** *538*, *540*; **32** *342*
Ottonian **23** 657, 658, *658*
drinking-horns **9** *690*
drums (musical instruments) **5** 256–7, 258; **8** 853, *853*; **29** *229*, 229
écorchés **9** 706
effigies **10** 338; **13** 164; **31** 122
enamel **7** 68
equestrian monuments **10** *442*
ewers **2** *237*; **6** *246*; **16** *370*, *375*; **21** *688*; **26** 685–6*
fibulae **8** 154; **13** *600*, 600–601, *601*; **30** *841*
figurines **21** *331*; **25** *541*
Anatolia, ancient **1** *825*
Ancient Near East **31** 530
China **6** *856*, *860*, *861*, 862; **17** *587*
Crete **8** 154
Etruscan **10** 604
Greece, ancient **13** 571–2*, 573*
Indian subcontinent **15** *412*, 417–20*
Sardinia **27** 835, *835*
Urartian **31** *700*
flagons **6** *155*
fonts (baptismal) **11** 253*, *256*; **26** 684*
fountains **12** *347*; **16** *368*; **33** *435*
fountain-spouts **20** 51
furniture **10** 633; **12** 424
gilding **12** 623, 627, 629
gongs **4** 855; **18** 348
hairpins **7** 109
halberds **6** 841, 848; **18** 345
harness-mounts **32** *513*, *515*
helmets **6** 261; **7** 55, *55*; **8** 154; **13** 583; **27** *95*
hydriai **13** *576*
incense burners **6** *859*; **16** *374*; **18** *348*, 348–9
inks **25** 598
inkstones **7** 94, 95
inlays **7** 107
inscriptions **6** 736
jewellery **1** 350; **6** 274; **7** 107; **13** 600–602; **15** *119*; **25** 547; **30** 633, 839; **31** 562
jingles **17** 396
jugs **10** 626; **14** *356*; **27** 86, *86*; **30** 770
knife-handles **27** 87
knives **23** 495, *495*
kraters **13** *577*; **32** *660*
kuṇḍikās **18** 349
lacquer **18** 605
ladles **6** *849*
lamps **6** 854, 856, 859; **15** 708–9; **27** 87*, 105; **29** *343*
lanterns (lights) **17** *323*
lustre **6** 336
maces **16** *504*
matrices **16** *506*
medallions **21** 1
medals **1** *556*; **7** *875*; **16** 690; **20** 917; **23** *72*; **24** *863*; **29** *387*, *408*, *409*
mirror frames **21** 720
mirror handles **10** 627
mirrors **21** 714
Celtic **6** 161

bronze
uses
mirrors—cont.
China **4** 855; **6** 854, 855, 858, 859–61, 862–4, *863*, *864*; **7** 14; **21** 714, *715*
Egypt, ancient **21** 711, *712*
England **6** 161
Etruscan **21** *712*
Greece, ancient **21** 712, *712*
Indian subcontinent **21** 716
Iran, ancient **21** *712*
Islamic **21** 717
Italy **10** *595*, *628*; **21** 712
Japan **17** 319, *320*, *324*; **21** 716
Korea **18** 345–6, *346*; **21** 715
Rome, ancient **21** *712*, 713
Tibet **30** *841*
models **10** *590*
monuments **10** *266*, 440; **23** *172*
Austria **10** *908*
England **3** *26*; **19** *600*; **27** *467*
France **26** *112*; **27** *822*
Germany **12** *399*
Italy **32** *363*
Italy: Mannerism **12** *573*; **30** *228*
Italy: 17th cent. **24** *696*
Rome, ancient **27** *10*
musical instruments **6** 829*
pateras **27** 86
pendants (jewellery) **10** *635*; **13** *600*, 601; **15** *118*; **25** 546
pins **13** 600, *600*
pipes (musical) **8** 853
plaques **6** *695*; **7** 108; **8** 854, *854*; **15** *873*; **21** *276*; **23** 496, *496*
plaquettes **25** 19, *20*
pulpits **25** *725*
rattles **18** 346, *346*
relief sculpture
Assyrian **21** 296
England **3** *367*
France **24** *814*
Germany **7** *381*
Gothic **24** *874*
Greece, ancient **8** *690*
Italy **3** *637*, *860*; **9** *130*; **10** 604; **11** *200*, *693*; **12** *540*, *541*; **19** *208*; **20** *622*; **24** *874*; **26** *327*, *766*; **29** *29*; **32** *122*
United States of America **27** *557*; **31** *612*
reliquaries **18** *364*; **26** *145*, *146*, *150*; **28** *630*
rings **13** 601; **17** 574
ritual objects **17** *322*; **18** *346*, 346–7
roofs **32** 487
sarcophagi **27** *830*
scabbards **6** 157; **14** 88
sculpture **4** 851, 855; **7** 670–72; **10** 702; **15** 175, 476; **19** *893*; **21** *709*; **25** *456*; **29** 559; **31** 611
Aegean **8** 262
Afghanistan **1** 207
Albania **1** *541*
Arabia **2** 258–9
Argentina **33** *569*
Australia **2** 752, *753*
Austria **2** *800*, 802, *803*; **10** *894*
Baroque **27** *830*
Belgium **3** *571*; **21** *499*
bronze **16** *135*
Buddhism **7** 68; **15** *223*; **17** *34*; **29** *479*
Buddhism: Afghanistan **1** 207
Buddhism: Burma **5** *240*, 241
Buddhism: Cambodia **5** 485
Buddhism: Central Asia, Eastern **6** 298
Buddhism: China **6** 706, 707, *708*, *710*, 712, 718, *719*, 720, *720*, 721, 835

bronze
uses
sculpture—cont.
Buddhism: Indian subcontinent **15** 476, *530*, 530–31
Buddhism: Japan **17** *107*, *110*, 110–12, *111*, *112*, *113*, 120, 320, *375*
Buddhism: Korea **5** *114*; **18** *284*, *285*, *287*, *294*
Buddhism: Laos **18** 768, *768*
Buddhism: Sri Lanka **29** *460*
Buddhism: Thailand **30** 593–5*, 596–7, *597*, *598*, *601*, 601–2*, *602*, *605*, *607*
Buddhism: Tibet **30** 351
Burma **5** 239, *240*, 241
Cambodia **5** 485, 497–8*
Central Asia, Eastern **6** 298
Chile **6** *598*
China **6** *628*, 706, 707, *708*, *710*, 721–2, 726–7, 733, 855–6; **7** 68; **24** 258; **29** *906*
China: Buddhism **6** *719*, *720*, 835
China: Han period (206 BC–AD 220) **8** *853*
China: Ming period (1368-1644) **6** 720–21
China: Qing period (1644-1911) **6** *733*
China: Qin period (221-210 BC) **6** 727
China: Shang period (*c.* 1600-*c.* 1050 BC) **7** 160; **13** *736*
China: Song period (AD 960-1279) **6** 718
China: Sui period (AD 581-618) **6** 712
China: Tang period (AD 618-907) **6** 730
Crete **8** 154; **21** *679*, 679–80
Croatia **21** *316*
Cyprus, ancient **8** 342
Czech Republic **8** *249*; **32** *731*; **33** *435*
Daoism **6** *628*
Dian culture **8** *853*
Edo (Africa) **9** 736
Egypt, ancient **5** *71*; **9** 855, *856*, 860, *861*, 886
Ejagham **10** 124*
Elamite **15** *919*
England: New Sculpture **23** *34*; **30** *762*
England: 19th cent. **11** *238*
England: 20th cent. **10** *438*; **11** *157*
Etruscan **10** 587, 602, 604–6, *605*, 608, *608*; **16** *684*
France: Baroque **7** *423*; **24** *786*
France: Mannerism **11** *558*
France: Neo-classicism **14** *798*; **27** *311*
France: Romanticism **3** *313*, *315*
France: 16th cent. **27** *548*
France: 17th cent. **8** *94*; **27** *822*
France: 19th cent. **26** *509*, *510*
France: 20th cent **4** *661*; **9** *362*; **12** *566*; **20** *825*, *828*; **26** *351*
Georgia **12** *322*
Germany: Baroque **3** *798*
Germany: Gothic **13** *160*
Germany: Mannerism **12** *346*, *347*; **18** *478*, *479*; **26** *104*
Germany: Renaissance **11** *223*; **12** *402*
Germany: 16th cent. **28** 492
Germany: 20th cent. **20** *396*
Gothic **13** *160*
Greece, ancient **1** 481; **6** 9; **8** 262; **13** 422, 433, 434–5*, 448; **24** 258, *328*; **26** *297*; **30** 339

bronze
uses
sculpture—cont.
Greece, ancient: 5th cent. BC **8** *696*; **13** 438; **23** 290; **25** 177, *178*, *179*
Greece, ancient: 6th cent. BC **8** 262, 458
Greece, ancient: 8th cent. BC **8** *262*
Greece, ancient: Classical, High **13** *429*, *453*
Greece, ancient: Classical, Late **13** *460*
Greece, ancient: Geometric **13** 441, *442*
Greece, ancient: Proto-Daidalic **13** *443*
Hinduism **15** *219*, *516*, *517*, 523, *728*
Holy Roman Empire (before 1648) **13** *160*; **26** 684–5*, *685*
Hungary **14** *897*
Hurrian **15** *33*
Indian subcontinent **15** 708, 730
Indian subcontinent: Buddhism **15** *223*
Indian subcontinent: Colonial period **15** *725*
Indian subcontinent: Hinduism **15** *219*
Indian subcontinent: Jainism **15** 453
Indian subcontinent: Karnataka **15** *530*, 530–31
Indian subcontinent: Kerala **15** 521, 522, 523, *523*, 524, *525*
Indian subcontinent: Madhya Pradesh **15** *728*
Indian subcontinent: Tamil Nadu **14** *557*; **15** *516*, 516, *517*
Indonesia **15** 776, 777
Iran, ancient **15** *919*
Ireland **16** *21*
Italy **12** 539; **30** 339
Italy: Baroque **2** *609*; **5** *533*; **27** *830*
Italy: Etruscan **10** 587, *605*, *608*; **16** *684*
Italy: Futurism **4** *201*; **11** *866*
Italy: Mannerism **1** *791*; **3** *162*, *469*; **6** *142*, *145*; **12** *572*
Italy: Renaissance **2** *140*, *141*; **9** *127*; **12** 539; **16** *690*; **19** *202*; **27** *448*; **29** *561*; **32** *105*, *360*, *362*
Italy: Roman **14** *443*; **27** *9*, *10*
Italy: 17th cent. **7** *842*
Italy: 20th cent. **16** *707*; **20** *353*, *429*
Jainism **15** 453, 531
Japan **17** 100–101*, 320
Japan: Asuka-Hakuhō period (*c.* 552-710) **17** *34*, *375*
Japan: Asuka period (AD *C.* 552-645) **17** *107*
Japan: Hakuhō period (AD 645-710) **17** 110–12, *111*, *112*
Japan: Heian period (AD 794-1185) **17** 120
Japan: Nara period (AD 710-94) **17** *113*; **22** *497*
Java **15** 777
Korea **5** *114*; **18** *284*, *285*, *287*, *294*, 297, 300, 301, 302
Laos **18** 768, *768*
Latvia
Mesopotamia **30** *28*
Mexico **21** *384*
Minoan **21** *679*, 679–80
New Zealand **23** 63, *63*; **33** *374*
Norway **3** 783; **23** *230*; **32** *497*
Pakistan **23** *802*

bronze
uses
sculpture—cont.
Parthian **24** *217*
Peru **24** *510*
Prehistoric art **25** *527*
Punic **25** 734
Rhodes (island) **26** 292
Romanesque **26** 684–5*, *685*
Rome, ancient **2** 168; **8** 263; **25** 43; **27** 10
Rome, ancient: Augustan **27** 10–11, 32, 85
Rome, ancient: Italy **14** *443*
Rome, ancient: Late Antiquity **18** *824*
Rome, ancient: Republican **24** 258; **27** *9*, 12, 29, 85; **29** *561*, *562*
Rome, ancient: 2nd cent. BC **8** 342
Sardinia **25** 734
Seleucid **28** 384
Slovakia **28** *855*
South Africa **29** *112*
Sri Lanka **29** *460*, *461*, 478, *479*
Switzerland **30** *138*
Syria-Palestine **15** *33*; **30** 193
Thailand **30** 593–5*, 596–7, *597*, *598*, *601*, 601–2*, *602*, *605*, *607*
Tibet **30** 351
Turkey **31** *700*
United States of America **18** *594*; **31** *613*
Urartian **31** *700*, 700
Vietnam **32** 480
Yemen **2** *258*, *259*
seals **6** 315, *315*; **7** 128, 129, *129*, 130, *130*; **17** 409; **21** 882
shields **6** *161*; **31** *159*
shrines (i) (cult) **28** *630*, IV2; **32** *530*
situlae **28** 806–7, *807*
spearheads **14** 356; **25** *540*
standards (vexilloid) **23** 496, *496*
stands **6** 827, *855*; **7** 139
statuettes **13** 571–2*
Carolingian **5** *806*
Celtic **6** 159
Cyprus, ancient **8** 339; **10** *400*
Egypt, ancient **9** 860; **10** 35–7, *36*
England **10** *267*; **11** *303*; **29** *575*
France **2** *100*; **5** *381*, *806*; **29** *572*
Germany **23** *309*
Greece, ancient **13** 571, *573*, 573*; **29** 567, *567*; **30** *339*
Indian subcontinent **15** 459
Italy **1** *162*; **2** *610*; **3** 636, *861*; **9** *340*; **16** 689, *700*; **25** *202*; **26** 327, *330*; **29** *569*; **30** *339*
Phoenician **24** *642*
Roman **27** *91*
Rome, ancient **27** 87–91, *88*, *89*
Vietnam **6** 427
stools **6** 388
swords **2** 451; **7** 56; **14** 356; **16** *506*; **18** 345
tables **23** *67*
tea-caddies **7** 101
thrones **30** 774
tombs **8** *94*; **26** 684*
tools **6** 841; **29** 228
toys **31** 255
trappings **25** 547–8
trays **6** *246*; **17** *322*
tripods **10** *626*, *627*
tureens **30** *146*
urns **8** *796*
bronze
uses—cont.
vessels **27** 85–7*
China **6** 625, 631, 635, 735, 737, 738, *738*, 767, 788, 798, 808, 826, 827–9*, *827*, 830–34, *831*, *833*, 835, 836–48*, *836*, *837*, *838*, *839*, *842*, *843*, *844*, *845*, *846*, *847*, *850*, 850–54*, *851*, *852*, *853*, 857–8, *858*, 859, 861, 864, 865, *865*, *866*, 866, 867, 868; **7** 12, 22, 88; **10** *464*; **21** 14; **23** *155*, 549–50; **24** *14*; **33** *471*
Greece, ancient **13** 574–7
wallpaper **32** 812
war hammers **16** *504*
weapons
Central Asia, Western **6** 260
China **6** 841, 848–9*; **7** 54, 55, 97
Cyprus, ancient **8** 353
Islamic **16** 503
Japan **17** 319, 361
Korea **18** 345, 353
weights **5** 260, *260*
wheel fittings **27** 91–2*
wheels **25** 547
writing-tablets **20** 328
Bronzet, Pierre **26** 315
Bronzino, Agnolo **4** 855–60*; **7** 560; **11** 216; **16** 766; **19** 92; **26** 769
assistants **7** 560
cartoons (drawings) **22** 727
collaboration **9** 185; **27** 273
groups and movements **20** 281
interior decoration **11** 211; **24** 536
musical instruments **22** 373
paintings **16** 663
allegorical **1** 657; **4** *857*; **20** 280; **23** 293
altarpieces **8** 274; **21** 22
frescoes **25** 224
mythological **10** 476
portraits **4** *858*; **5** 682; **9** 266; **11** 187, *187*, 390; **29** 348; **30** 358, 783
religious **4** *857*; **12** 711
patrons and collectors **11** 193
Butler, Charles (1822-1910) **5** 311
Canino, Lucien Bonaparte, Prince of (1775-1840) **4** 304
Caro, Annibal **5** 789
Carol I, King of Romania (*reg* 1866-1914) **5** 792
Cosimo I, Grand Duke of Tuscany (*reg* 1569- 74) **11** 193; **16** 664; **21** 22
Demidov, Anatoly, Prince **8** 705
Dennistoun, James **8** 763
Doria, Andrea, I (1466-1560) **9** 172
Doria-Pamphili (family) **9** 175
Eastlake, Charles Lock (1793-1865) **9** 683
Esterházy, Miklós II, Prince (1765-1833) **10** 530
Francis I, King of France (*reg* 1515-47) **10** 477; **31** 849
Guidobaldo II, 4th Duke of Urbino (*reg* 1538-74) **27** 274
Poniatowski, Stanisław, Prince **25** 213
Pourtalès-Gorgier, James-Alexandre, Comte de **25** 383
Rushout, John, 2nd Baron Northwick **27** 350
Salviati (family) **27** 648
pupils **1** 670, 730; **5** 182, 317; **31** 53
reproductive prints by others **7** 499
restorations by others **28** 340
tapestries **11** 193, 194; **25** 223; **27** 650; **30** *319*, 319
Bronzino, Agnolo—cont.
teachers **25** 224, 848
bronzo **4** 848
brooches **17** 519, 520, 524, 527, 529
historical and regional traditions
Anglo-Saxon **2** 79, 80, *80*; **9** 253; **10** 322
Bhutan **3** 916
Celtic **6** 156, 157, 158
England **2** *80*, *595*; **10** 322; **14** 418, *427*
Germany **14** 418
Korea **18** 367
Norway **32** *514*
Prehistoric art **25** 540, 541, 545–6
Russia **10** *721*; **27** *429*
Scandinavia **32** *514*, 515, *516*, 520, 524, 531
Sweden **32** *516*
Switzerland **6** 157; **17** *520*
United States of America **31** *655*
Viking **9** 254; **32** *514*, 515, *516*, 520, 524, 531
materials
amber **1** 761; **15** *872*
aquamarines **10** *721*
bronze **6** 158; **15** *872*; **32** *516*
cameos **17** 519, 520, *520*
copper **2** *595*
diamonds **27** *429*; **31** *655*
enamel **15** *872*
gold **14** *417*; **15** *872*; **17** *520*; **27** *429*; **31** *655*
niello **2** *80*
pearls **17** *520*; **31** *655*
platinum **10** *721*; **31** *655*
silver **2** *80*; **15** *872*; **32** *514*
types
bossed **15** 873
heart **28** 263–4
Johnny Faa **28** 264
kite **15** 873
Luckenbooth **28** 263
penannular **15** 871, 872, 873
pseudo-penannular **15** 872, *872*, 873
Queen Mary **28** 264
ring **28** 263
thistle **15** 873
Witches' **28** 264
see also FIBULAE
Broodhagen, Carl **31** 335, 340
Broodhagen, Marjorie **13** 877
Broodhagen, Samuel Horace **13** 876
Broodthaers, Marcel **3** 565; **4** 860–61*
groups and movements **5** 45
works **3** 574; **4** *861*; **5** 45
Brook, Alexander **1** 773; **3** 31
Brook, Peter **30** 687
Brooke (family) **20** 179; **21** 596
Brooke, Charles Greville, 7th Earl *see* GREVILLE, CHARLES, 7th Earl Brooke and 7th Earlof Warwick
Brooke, E. Alvano
works **12** *139*
Brooke, Francis Greville, 1st Earl *see* GREVILLE, FRANCIS, 1st Earl Brooke and 1st Earl of Warwick
Brooke, Francis Greville, 5th Earl *see* GREVILLE, FRANCIS, 5th Earl Brooke & 5th Earl of Warwick
Brooke, Frederick H. **4** 142
Brooke, George Greville, 2nd Earl *see* GREVILLE, GEORGE, 2nd Earl Brooke and 2nd Earl of Warwick
Brooker, Bertram (Richard) **4** 861*; **5** 567
Brookes, George
works **25** *627*
Brookgreen Gardens (SC) **15** 30
Brooking, Charles (*fl* 1729-36) **4** 861
Brooking, Charles (*c*. 1723-59) **4** 861–2*; **20** 424; **21** 91; **28** 481
Brookland (Kent), St Augustine **10** 339; **11** 253; **26** 688
Brooklyn-Budapest Painter **13** 525
Brooklyn Etchers Club **25** 629
Brooklyn Flint Glass Works **7** 875; **14** 252
Brooklyn Knife-handle **9** 865, *866*
Brooklyn Museum *see under* NEW YORK → museums
Brooklyn Scratches Club **25** 629
Brooklyn Society of Etchers *see* SOCIETY OF AMERICAN GRAPHIC ARTISTS
Brooks, E. S. **14** 219
Brooks, Geoffrey H. **30** 684
Brooks, Hope **16** 884
Brooks, James (i) (1825-1901) **4** 862*
groups and movements **10** 238
pupils **20** 26
works **28** 156
Brooks, James (ii) (1906-92) **4** 862–3*; **31** 607
Brooks, John **10** 346; **14** 803; **16** 15; **18** 829; **19** 867
Brooks, Peter **27** 137, 138
Brooks, Robinson & Co. **2** 763; **12** 805
Brooks, Romaine **4** 863*; **12** 215
Brooks, Ronald *see* KITAJ, R(ONALD) B(ROOKS)
Brooks, Shepherd **27** 137, 138
Brooks, William **14** 681
Brooks, W. McIntosh **5** 512
Brookshaw, George **7** 659
Brookshaw, Richard **18** 176
Broom **19** 476
Broome, Isaac **4** 863*; **30** 887
works **31** 637, *637*
Broome, Myrtle **10** 83
Broome Heath **25** 503
Broome Park **4** 786
Broomhall (Fife) **4** 549
brooms (flat) **28** 542
Broota, Rameshwar **8** 677
Brophy, A. F. **19** 359; **33** 372
Brosamer, Hans **4** 863–4*
reproductions in wall paintings **11** 94
works **2** 224; **4** *864*; **24** 271
Brosamer, Martin **4** 864
Brossa, Joan **8** 538
Brosse, Jean de **4** 864; **9** 352
Brosse, Paul de **4** 864; **9** 354
Brosse, Salomon de **4** 864–7*
architecture **6** 506; **11** 515
châteaux **4** 548; **6** *507*; **29** 918
churches **14** 855; **21** 346
hôtels particuliers **19** 133
law courts **4** *867*; **18** 886; **26** 204
palaces **4** *866*; **6** 397; **9** 352; **12** 120; **24** 165
attributions **11** 516, *516*
collaboration **3** 853; **9** 353, 454; **30** 735
patrons and collectors **4** 548; **5** 168; **11** 656; **19** 300; **29** 917; **30** 735
personal collection **9** 454
reproductive prints by others **20** *457*
Brosses, Charles de **4** 867*; **12** 118
Brosset, Marie-Félicité **6** 280; **12** 331
Brost and Grosser **9** 382
Brosterhuisen, Jan (van) **4** 868*
Brostoloni, Giambattista *see* BRUSTOLON, GIAMBATTISTA
Brotherhood of Painting *see* BROEDERSCHAP DER SCHILDERKUNST
Brotherhood of Ruralists **4** 116, 823; **25** 556
Brotherhood of St Luke *see* FELLOWSHIP OF ST LUKE
Brotherhood of the Holy Sacrament of the Church of St Peter (Leuven) **3** 606
Brotherhood of the Linked Ring *see* LINKED RING
Brothers, The **11** 703; **25** 264; **32** 903
Brothers Dalziel **4** 363, 868–9*; **14** 800; **32** 794
Brotonne Bridge **4** 804
Brotze, Johann **18** 849
Brou, Priory Church of St Nicholas of Tolentino **4** *869*, 869–70*; **11** 154, *504*; **13** 59
sculpture **13** 100
tiles **11** 604
tomb of Margaret of Austria **2** 296; **3** 569; **21** 72; **31** 125
tomb of Margaret of Bourbon **21** 72
tomb of Philibert II, Duke of Savoy **21** 72; **31** 125
Brouchy, Le *see* LE BROUCHY
Broude, Norma **31** 673; **33** 312
Brough, Robert **4** 870*
Broughton, Thomas Delves **33** 442
Broughton Castle (Oxon) **10** 269; **21** 549
Broughton Place (Borders) **28** 231
Broughty Ferry (Tayside), Orchar Collection **28** 273
Brouilla Church **26** 610
Brouke, Willem van den *see* BROECK, WILLEM VAN DEN
Broumov **8** 420
Monastery **8** 397, 399
Brounckhorst, Arthur van *see* BRONCKORST, ARNOLD **12** 224
Brousse *see* BURSA
Broutin, Ignace François **23** 31
Brouwer, Adriaen **4** 870–73*
attributions **19** 349; **30** 462
copies **4** 657
groups and movements **13** 895
patrons and collectors **2** 382; **3** 671; **19** 124
pupils **8** 108; **23** 609
reproductive prints by others **12** 851; **20** 812; **32** 700
teachers **14** 94, 95; **22** 840
works **3** 560; **4** *871*, *872*; **11** 445; **12** 290
Brouwer, Willem C(oenraad) **4** 873–4*; **22** 883
Brouwere, W. H. **30** 506
Brouwershaven Church **22** 819
Brovtsev, Sergey **23** 392
Brown (family) **12** 835
brown *see under* PIGMENTS → types
Brown, A. Page **7** 619; **20** 19; **25** 152; **28** 193, 604
Brown, Arthur **3** 83*; **18** 664; **27** 730
Brown, Barbara **1** 432, 738
Brown, Basil **30** 43
Brown, Benjamin **19** 701
Brown, Bernard **4** 415
Brown, Bolton **19** 492; **20** 604
Brown, (Lancelot) 'Capability' **4** 876*; **8** 48; **12** 63, 65, 129–30; **26** 743
collaboration **14** 681; **21** 607; **29** 736
furniture **10** 295
gardens **4** 806
Ashburnham Place (E. Sussex) **2** 595
Blenheim Palace (Oxon) **12** *63*; **24** 179
Cardiff Castle (S. Glams) **5** 194
Claremont (Surrey; UK) **7** 374, 437
Heveningham Hall (Suffolk) **4** *876*
Royal Botanical Gardens (Kew) **18** 5
Wimpole Hall (Cambs) **13** 645

Brown, (Lancelot) 'Capability' gardens—cont.
Wrest Park (Beds) **13** 645
groups and movements **24** 741
patrons and collectors
Arundell, Henry, 8th Baron Arundell of Wardour **2** 576
Cavendish, William, 4th Duke of Devonshire (1720-64) **6** 116, 515
Cecil, Brownlow, 9th Earl of Exeter (1725-93) **6** 117, 127
Churchill, John, 1st Duke of Marlborough **4** 137, 138
Clive, Robert, 1st Baron Clive **7** 374
Constable, William **7** 758
Dundas, Lawrence **9** 392
Garrick, David **12** 164
George III, King of Great Britain (*reg* 1760-1820) **14** 144
Greville, Francis, 1st Earl Brooke and 1st Earl of Warwick (1719-73) **13** 644
Harcourt, George Simon, 2nd Earl Harcourt **14** 163
Methuen, Paul (1723-94) **21** 348
Smithson (Percy), Hugh, 1st Duke and 2nd Earl of Northumberland **24** 390
Temple, Henry, 2nd Viscount Palmerston **30** 451
Temple, Richard, 1st Viscount Cobham **30** 452
Williams-Wynn, Watkin, 4th Baronet, of Wynnstay (1749-89) **33** 209
Wyndham, Charles, 2nd Earl of Egremont **33** 453
Brown, Catherine Madox **4** 879
Brown, Cecil **4** 82
Brown, Charles **4** 874; **12** 263
Brown, Clinton **4** 876*
Brown, David **22** 122
Brown, David James **29** 113
Brown, Deborah **4** 876*
Brown, Earle **5** 381
Brown, Eileen **20** 475
Brown, Eric **13** 712
Brown, Ernest (*fl c.* 1880) **33** 143
Brown, Ernesto (*fl* 1937) **23** 81, 85
Brown, Everald **4** 876*; **16** 885, 890
Brown, Ford Madox **4** 876–9*; **19** 507; **25** 398
collaboration **11** 433; **22** 142, 143; **28** 349
dealers **12** 30
frames **11** 432, 433, *433*
groups and movements **2** 642; **23** 504; **25** 554, 555, 556; **26** 56
paintings **10** 253; **20** 239
genre **4** *877*, *878*; **12** 295; **15** 829
murals **22** 331; **31** 241
patrons and collectors **10** 362; **18** 906; **20** 239; **22** 54; **25** 41; **33** 251
pupils **13** 1; **27** 185; **29** 369
works **11** 432
Brown, Frederick **4** 880*; **10** 374; **19** 589
groups and movements **19** 589; **23** 23
pupils **3** 630; **10** 255; **11** 363; **17** 608; **31** 146; **32** 794
Brown, G. Baldwin *see* BALDWIN BROWN, G.
Brown, George (*fl* 1485-1515) **28** 268
Brown, George (1811-85) **20** 869
Brown, George (*b* 1852) **31** 334
works **31** *334*
Brown, George Loring **4** 880*; **21** 342
Brown, George W. **31** 256, 264
Brown, Georgia **16** 889
Brown, Grafton Tyler **1** 440, 441; **31** 603
Brown, Henry Kirke **11** 833; **15** 19; **31** 611; **32** 857
Brown, Jenny **30** 153
Brown, Jim **31** 661
Brown, Joan **17** 694
Brown, John (i) (*d* 1532) **4** 880*; **28** 466
Brown, John (ii) (1749-1787) **4** 880–81*
pupils **23** 634
teachers **28** 274
works **28** 235
Brown, John (1805-76) **10** 236; **23** 247
Brown, John (1814-66) **5** 581
Brown, John (*fl* 1840-54) **2** 758
Brown, John George **4** 881*; **31** 603, 870
Brown, John-Lewis (*fl* 1820s) **4** 322
Brown, John-Lewis (1829-90) **4** 391, 881*; **19** 488
Brown, Joseph (i) (1733-85) **4** 881*; **25** 266
Brown, Joseph (ii) (*b* 1918) **2** 770; **4** 881–2*
Brown, Kathan **20** 609
Brown, Lucy Madox *see* ROSSETTI, LUCY MADOX
Brown, Lyde **20** 911
Brown, Mather **4** 882*
Brown, Mike (Gordon Challis) **2** 120, 751; **4** 882–3*; **18** 689
Brown, Milton **25** 462
Brown, M. S., & Co. **5** 586
Brown, Oliver Madox **4** 879
Brown, Percy **4** 883*; **15** 653
Brown, Ricardo (*fl* 1840; Chilean architect) **32** 651
Brown, Richard (*fl* 1804-45; English architect) **4** 883*; **24** 275
works **24** *275*
Brown, Robert (*d* 1753) **14** 269
Brown, Robert (*d* 1859) **33** 22
Brown, Robert Montgomery **14** 811
Brown, Roger **6** 577
Brown, Samuel **4** 803; **24** 747
Brown, Sidney **30** 153
Brown, Stanley **11** 232
Brown, Thomas (*fl* 1686) **5** 760
Brown, Thomas (*fl* 1840s) **23** 787
Brown, Trisha **24** 407
Brown, Vernon **4** 883*; **23** 56, 75
Brown, William **4** 874; **12** 263; **26** 499
Brown, William, Library and Museum *see under* LIVERPOOL
Brown, William Kellock **12** 780
Brown, William Theo **8** 871
Brown and red painted ware *see under* POTTERY → wares
Brown and Wardrop **28** 289
Browne (family) **29** 532
Browne, Alexander **3** 476; **4** 884*; **7** 639; **21** 416
writings **8** 128
Browne, George (*fl* early 19th cent.) **4** 884
Browne, George (1811-85) **4** 884*; **5** 560
Browne, George (*fl* 1875) **24** 894
Browne, George Washington **4** 884–5*; **24** 315; **33** 283
Browne, Hablot Knight **4** 885*
collaboration **8** 863
works **4** 362, *885*
Browne, Herbert **19** 500
Browne, Howe (Peter), 2nd Marquis of Sligo **23** 345
Browne, J. J. **23** 631
Browne, John **4** 886*
Browne, Lyde **4** 886*; **6** 97; **17** 475
Browne, Martha **7** 164
Browne, Robert **19** 734
Browne, Samuel **29** 58
Browne, Thomas **10** 304
brown earth *see under* PIGMENTS → types
Brownfield, William, & Sons **5** 878
brown haematite *see* LIMONITE
Brownie cameras *see under* CAMERAS → types
Browning, J. M. **31** 863
Brownlow (family) **33** 260
Brownlow, Adelbert Cust, 3rd Earl *see* CUST, ADELBERT, 3rd Earl Brownlow
Brownlow, Emma **4** 886–7*
Brownlow, John **29** 542, 835
brown ochre *see under* OCHRES → types
Brown-on-buff ware *see under* POTTERY → wares
Brózer, István **15** 7
Brožík, Václav **4** 887*; **8** 392; **14** 840; **25** 433
Brozzi, S Andrea **12** 548–9
Brskovo **28** 454
Bru **31** 261
Bru, Manuel **28** 389
Bruand, François **4** 887
Bruand, Jacques **4** 887*; **19** 145
Bruand, Libéral **4** 887*; **20** 294; **24** 164
collaboration **4** 887
groups and movements **24** 169
patrons and collectors **4** 551
works **14** 782; **19** 59; **24** 164, *164*
Bruand, Sébastien **4** 887
Bruandet, Lazare **4** 888*
Bruant *see* BRUAND
Bruant, Aristide **29** 612
Bruce, Edward (*fl* 1934-43) **31** 663
Bruce, Edward, Lord of Kinloss (1548-1610) **28** 225
Bruce, George (16th cent.) **28** 225
Bruce, George (19th cent.) **4** 228
Bruce, James **3** 129; **10** 79; **26** 774
Bruce, Murdoch **14** 721
Bruce, Patrick Henry **4** 888*; **23** 570
Bruce, Peter Henry **3** 60
Bruce, Thomas, 2nd Earl of Ailesbury **3** 773
Bruce, Thomas, 7th Earl of Elgin and 11th Earl of Kincardine **4** 889*; **10** 365; **12** 742; **13** 468, 469
architecture **29** 549
casts **29** 377
sculpture **2** 555; **5** 631; **9** 25; **10** 368; **12** 504; **13** 606; **14** 199
Bruce, William **4** 889–90*
collaboration **11** 836; **28** 226
house **28** 226
patrons and collectors **28** 269
staff **28** 880
works **9** 728, *728*; **28** 225, 226, 227, 234, 246
Bruce-Joy, Albert **11** 239
Bruch, St Anne **30** 311
Bruchsal **12** *361*
Residenz **12** 371
Schloss **4** 890–91*; **23** 3, *3*; **26** 495; **27** 611; **33** 671
staircases **29** 525
Watteau-Kabinett **33** 672
Bruck, Johannes à **10** 175
Bruck, Johannes von *see* JORISZ, DAVID
Bruck an der Mur **2** 822
Brücke, Die **3** 801; **4** 891–3*; **9** 234, 239; **10** 693, 694, 841; **18** 77–9; **23** 296; **25** 582
art forms
linocuts **19** 429
lithographs **10** 695
paintings **12** 395; **18** 717; **24** *311*; **28** *125*
posters **25** 348
sculpture **10** 695–6; **12** 407, *408*
woodcuts **4** *893*; **10** 695; **14** 580; **25** *582*; **33** 363
Brücke, Die—cont.
collections **20** 880
exhibitions **16** 817; **23** 7
members **29** 871
Amiet, Cuno **1** 783
Giacometti, Giovanni **12** 562
Heckel, Erich **14** 284
Kirchner, Ernst Ludwig **18** 77
Mueller, Otto **22** 257
Nolde, Emil **23** 185, 186
Pechstein, (Hermann) Max **24** 311
Schmidt-Rottluff, Karl **28** 124
studios **29** 858
Brücke-Museum *see under* BERLIN → museums
Brucker, Nikolaus *see* PRUGGER, NIKOLAUS
Bruckmann **13** 216
Bruckmann, Peter (1850-91) **20** 405
Bruckmann, Peter (*b* 1865) **8** 825, 826; **12** 450; **15** 824
Bruckmann & Söhne **1** 763
Brückwald, Otto **3** 428; **30** 678
works **30** *678*
Brudenell, George, 4th Earl of Cardigan and 1st Duke of Montagu **4** 893–4*
Brudenell, John, Marquess Monthermer and Baron Montagu **4** 894*; **17** 627
Brudenell, John Montagu, Lord *see* MONTAGU, JOHN, Marquess of Monthermer
Brudenell, Mary, Countess of Cardigan and Duchess of Montagu **4** 893–4*
Brüderle, Michal Jan **8** 385; **25** 443
Bruegel (family) **4** 559, *895*
Bruegel, Ambrosius *see* BREUGHEL, AMBROSIUS
Bruegel, Jan *see* BREUGHEL, JAN
Bruegel, Pieter, I (*c.* 1525/30-1569) **2** 194; **4** 894–908*, *895*; **22** 839; **25** 653
attributions **3** 126; **12** 912; **20** 769; **27** 884, 885
collaboration **3** 126
drawings **4** *906*
paintings **4** *898*, *899*; **31** 50, 255
allegorical **4** *901*, *903*; **20** 277, 280; **25** 651
genre **3** 556–7, *557*; **4** *903*, *904*, 912; **8** 284; **11** 456; **12** 288; **22** 521, 522
landscape **18** 706, 707, 708
marine **20** 424
mythological **31** *50*
religious **4** *902*, 911, 912
satirical **27** 868–9
topographical **31** 154
patrons and collectors
Bowdoin, James, III **4** 599
Christina, Queen of Sweden (*reg* 1632-54) **30** 118; **32** 7
Clovio, Giulio **7** 469
Coninxloo (i), Gillis van, III **7** 711
Créquy, Charles de Blanchefort de **19** 238
De la Gardie, Magnus Gabriel **30** 118
Duarte, Diego **9** 311
Geest, Cornelis van der **12** 233
Habsburg I., Ernest, Archduke of Austria **13** 916
Hollar, Wenceslaus **14** 682
Jabach, Everard **16** 815
Jonghelinck, Niclaes **3** 612, 615; **17** 643
Ortelius, Abraham **23** 579
Rockox, Nicolaas **26** 490
Rudolf II, Holy Roman Emperor (*reg* 1576- 1612) **13** 914
Ryabushinsky, Nikolay (Pavlovich) **27** 458
Bruegel, Pieter, I (*c.* 1525/30-1569)
patrons and collectors—cont.
Salamanca (y Mayol), José, Marqués de **27** 607
Savoy, Eugene of, Prince (1663-1736) **28** 15
Segers, Hercules (Pietersz.) **28** 358
Seilern, Antoine, Count **28** 377
Snyders, Frans **28** 904
prints **1** 654; **4** *907*; **25** 598, 605, 606; **33** 355
reproductive prints by others **4** 911, 912; **9** 64; **25** 596, 605
Cock, Hieronymus (Wellens) **7** 499
Galle, Philip **12** 15, *16*
Heyden, Pieter van der **14** 505
Hondius (ii), Hendrik, I (1573-1650) **14** 709
Huys, Frans **15** 43
Visscher, Claes Jansz. (1587-1652) **32** 622
teachers **5** 43; **7** 518
Bruegel, Pieter, II *see* BRUEGHEL, PIETER, II
Brueghel, Ambrosius *see* BREUGHEL, AMBROSIUS
Brueghel, Jan *see* BREUGHEL, JAN
Brueghel, Pieter, II (1564/5-1637/8) **4** 894, *895*, 910–12*
collaboration **29** 528
patrons and collectors **18** 467; **28** 358
pupils **7** 832; **28** 901
teachers **7** 710; **32** 254
works **3** 560; **4** *911*, *912*
Brueghel, Pieter, III (1589-*c.* 1640) **4** 894, *895*; **23** 409
Bruehl, Anton **4** 918*; **33** 146
Brüel, Max **4** 417; **18** 799
Bruen *see* BRUYN
Brueton, Bertrand **1** 29
Bruff (family) **7** 481
Brugada, Antonio **13** 249; **27** 781
Brugada Panizo, Ricard **25** 786
Brugal **9** 118
Bruges **3** *539*; **4** 918–25*, *919*
Academie **12** 147
Arentshuis *see* museums → Brangwynmuseum
art forms and materials
amber **1** 761
architecture **3** 541
armour **2** 471
cabinets (ii) (furniture) **3** 582
ceramics **3** 588
coats of arms **12** 273
embroidery **3** 609, 610
faience (ii) (ceramics) **3** 590
furniture **3** 585
gables **4** 786; **11** 875
gold **4** 924*
jewellery **3** 604
manuscripts **3** 552, 555; **4** 372, 921; **9** 219; **20** 333, 334; **26** 563
marks **3** 596, 601, 603
metalwork **3** 596, 597; **13** 159
painting **3** 553, 559; **4** 920–21, *921*, *922*; **17** 699
pewter **3** 603
sculpture **3** 567, 568, 570; **13** 113
seals **33** 5
silver **3** 598; **4** 924*
stained glass **27** 255
tapestries **3** 576, 606; **4** *923*, 923–4*; **30** 317
textiles **25** 315
Begijnhof **13** 110
Belfry **3** 542; **4** 924*, *924*; **31** 238
churches
Basilica of the Holy Blood **13** 182
Bloedkapel **3** 544, 598

Bruges
churches—cont.
Cathedral of St Salvator 3 581; 7 179
choir-stalls 3 568
sculpture 13 113
tapestries 5 50
textiles 3 609
wall paintings 2 726
Onze Lieve Vrouwekerk 3 552, 609
Madonna see BRUGES MADONNA
sculpture 16 695
tomb of Charles the Bold 14 420
tomb of Mary, Duchess of Burgundy 13 160; 14 420, 421
St Donatian 3 612; 7 179; 10 710; 13 38
St Gilliskerk 31 341
St Jacobskerk
brasses 4 693
epitaph to Soyer van Marle 10 436; 31 126, 127
wall paintings 3 552
St Walburgakerk 3 546; 25 727, 813
craftsmen and artists 13 133
De Potterie hospital chapel 13 99
education (art) 3 617
Gerechtshof see museums → Brugse Vrije Museum
Gruuthuse Hof see museums → Gruuthusemuseum
guilds 3 596, 603; 4 920–21
houses 4 785
markets 31 711
Markt 31 238
museums 3 616
Brangwynmuseum 4 673
Brugse Vrije Museum 4 922; 5 320
collections 4 161
Schepenzaal 3 452, 569
collections 33 8
Groeningemuseum 3 617; 4 922
Gruuthusemuseum 2 294; 3 617; 19 726
collections 4 922; 33 8
Memlingmuseum 4 922
see also St Janshospitaal
Museum voor Volkskunde 3 617
Stedelijke Musea 30 332
Oosterlingenhuis 4 920
Oude Griffie 3 544
patronage 4 921
Potterie 3 588
Prinsenhof Library 5 210
Rijksnormaalschool 3 549
St Janshospitaal 3 567; 4 919; 13 110, 113; 14 784
paintings 14 785
roof 30 908
sculpture 13 99
see also museums → Memlingmuseum
Stadhuis 3 542, 567; 4 465, 924–5*, 925; 17 460–61; 29 414; 32 94
paintings 8 551; 25 668
sculpture 13 100
stained glass 13 182
wall paintings 4 161
Steinmetzkabinet 8 764
warehouses 32 860
Zilverpand precinct 4 790
Bruges, F. of see F. OF BRUGES
Bruges, Jean de see BOUDOLF, JAN
Bruges, William 7 179
Bruges Madonna 1 711; 21 435
Bruges Master of 1473 see MASTER OF 1473
Bruges school see GHENT-BRUGES SCHOOL
Brugge see BRUGES
Brugge, Johannes von see JORISZ, DAVID
Brüggeman 27 756
Brüggemann, Hans 4 925*
Bruggen, Coosje van 23 398
Bruggen, Hans van der see BRUGGEN, LOUIS VAN DER
Bruggen, Jan van der 18 788; 21 416; 28 49
Bruggen, Louis van der 30 660
Brügger, Arnold 22 921
Brugghen, Hendrick (Jansz.) ter 5 1–6*, 9; 26 772; 30 456; 31 771
groups and movements 3 8; 9 462; 22 843; 31 772
teachers 4 153
works 5 2, 3, 4, 5; 12 290
Brugghen, Richard ter 4 38; 5 1
Brughi, Giovanni Battista 31 315
Brugh na Boinne 25 510, 511
Brugière de Barante, Baron 31 374
Brugis, Johannes de see BOUDOLF, JAN
Brugman, Til 15 36; 22 868
Brugnoli, Alvise (Luigi) 5 6*
Brugnoli, Bernardino 5 6*
Brugnoli, Francisco 6 598
Brugnoli, Paulina 6 600
Brugsal, Alexander van 20 803
Brugsch, Heinrich 10 82; 33 481
Bruguière, Francis 5 7*; 7 434; 8 270
Brühl, Gräfin von 13 802
Brühl, Heinrich, Graf von 5 7*; 14 314; 33 115
architecture 9 236; 18 162, 473
collections 12 473; 27 438
decorative works 30 885
engravings 21 800
paintings 3 318, 677; 8 880; 23 855; 26 732; 28 743; 32 706
porcelain 9 692; 17 769; 21 64, 65
Brühl, Johann Michael 22 437
Brühl, Schloss Augustusburg 5 7–8*; 12 361, 368, 413; 14 420; 26 495, 496
Falkenlust 5 348, 349; 26 497
Marble Room 23 789
sculpture 13 680
summer rooms 12 413
Brui i Salelles, Lluís 29 329
Bruin see BRUYN
Bruin, Cornelis de 6 280; 24 481
Bruisselles, Henry de see HENRY DE BRUISSELLES
Brukalska, Barbara 5 8*; 32 872
Brukalski (family) 25 100
Brukalski, Stanisław 5 8*; 25 55, 422; 32 872
Brukenthal, Samuel, Baron von 5 8–9*
architecture 26 708; 28 649
collections 26 722
paintings 26 724
Brukenthal Breviary see under BREVIARIES → individual manuscripts
Bruley, Samson 3 873
Brulle, Albert van der 32 215
Brulliot, Franz 10 208
Brullus, Jan Jiří 8 413
Brument (fl 1699) 27 248
Brument, Le (fl 1783) see LE BRUMENT
Brumidi, Constantino 5 9*
works 22 335; 32 892, 893
Brummell, Beau 9 286; 11 703
Brummell, George Bryan see BRUMMELL, BEAU
Brummer, Arttu 11 106
Brummer, Ernest 1 438; 10 91
Brummer, Eva 11 110
Brummer, Imre 10 91
Brummer, Joseph 1 438; 10 91
Brumwell, Alfred 7 668
Brumwell, Su see ROGERS, SU
Brun, Charles-Frédéric 5 9*
Brun, Donald 25 353
Brun, Franz (fl c. 1559-96) 5 9–10*
Brun, Franz (fl 1589-1652) 5 10
Brun, Friedrike 6 98
Brun, Jean-Baptiste Le see LE BRUN, JEAN-BAPTISTE
Brun, Jean Esprit 20 472
Brun, Joseph-Sylvestre 27 544
Brun, Louis-Auguste 5 10*
Brun, Róbert 28 854
Brun, Sigismund 29 332
Bruna, Francisco de 28 516
Brunache, Guy 5 609
Brunais, Augustin 1 140; 2 149, 151, 152, 153; 5 750
Brundage, Avery 7 156; 15 743; 27 731
Brun de Versoix see BRUN, LOUIS-AUGUSTE
Brune, A. 3 877
Brune, Johan de 31 881
Bruneau, Eugène 25 52
Bruneck, Hans Maler von see HANS MALER VON BRUNECK
Brunei 5 10, 10–13*
alloys 5 11
architecture 5 11*
bamboo 5 13
baskets 5 13, 13
brass 5 11, 12
cannons (guns) 5 11, 12
censers 5 11
ceramics 5 12*
coins 5 12*
kettles 5 11
mats 5 13
metalwork 5 11–12*
silver 5 11–12
trade 5 12*
weaving 5 13, 13
see also SOUTH-EAST ASIA
Brunel, Emil 30 216
Brunel, Isambard Kingdom 5 13–14*; 25 854
architecture
bridges 3 246; 4 802, 802, 823; 5 14
hospitals 26 18
railway stations 10 236; 25 854, 856
viaducts 32 398, 399
water towers 24 294
assistants 11 301
collaboration 12 791; 16 53; 19 575; 25 857
groups and movements 10 97
Brunel, Marc Isambard 5 13
Brunel, Raullin see BUNEL, RAULLIN
Brunelleschi, Filippo 2 161, 313; 5 14–23*, 128; 7 692; 14 869; 16 658, 741, 778; 21 11; 22 44
architecture 11 184; 16 628, 658; 23 835; 26 183
arcades 2 290
architectural decorations 23 539; 30 501
cathedrals 3 159; 5 128; 13 65
chapels 5 18, 19, 20; 7 257, 527; 11 206; 21 468; 25 171
churches 7 254
Cathedral of S Maria del Fiore (Florence) 11 178, 195; 21 468
S Lorenzo (Florence) 1 110; 5 16, 17; 11 178, 206; 21 466; 25 322
Santo Spirito (Florence) 20 112; 26 183; 27 655
domes 5 15; 9 82, 85, 86; 11 196; 16 628–9; 32 88
engineering (civil) 21 465
exedrae 5 21
hospitals 14 781, 784; 16 143; 32 94
lanterns (architecture) 5 21
monasteries 21 468, 842
Brunelleschi, Filippo
architecture—cont.
orders (architecture) 23 485, 486
palazzi 10 784
plans 16 628
urban planning 11 177, 178; 31 712
assistants 8 799; 12 710; 26 443
attributions 11 206, 213, 381; 14 158
collaboration 9 129; 11 196, 201; 12 542, 713; 20 263, 264, 533; 22 462; 26 442, 443
commentaries 20 263
competitions 7 664, 671; 12 537
crucifixes 11 209
frames 11 382
methods 24 486
models 2 336; 5 129; 11 202; 15 135; 16 629; 27 656
niello 16 750
patrons and collectors 5 450; 16 763; 20 159; 21 10; 24 299
perspective 28 202
pupils 11 895; 18 861; 27 180
sculpture 8 215, 215; 11 200
stage design 2 837; 30 657
teachers 31 200
Brunelleschi, Umberto 29 628
Brunelli, Gabriele 1 631
Brunet, Emile 29 18
Brunet, Joseph 5 570
Brunet, M. 33 345
Brunet-Debaines, Alfred-Louis 5 23–4*; 19 91
Brunet-Debaines, Charles-Louis-Fortuné 5 23
Brunet-Debaines, Claude François 6 602; 27 792; 32 652
collaboration 32 652
pupils 32 651
works 6 592, 593; 27 791
Brunet-Houard, Pierre-Auguste 6 130
Brunetti, Antonio Paolo 30 672
Brunetti, Gaetano 10 277; 11 427; 14 791; 22 682
Brunetti, Paolo Antonio 14 791; 22 682
Brunetto, Tomás 5 24*; 19 467; 25 310
works 19 468; 26 52
Brunfaut, Fernand 5 24*
Brunfaut, Gaston 5 24*
Brunfaut, Jules 5 24–5*
Brunfaut, Maxime 5 24*; 14 771
Brunfels, Otto 4 358; 14 433; 28 206; 33 33
works 33 32
Brunhoff, Jean de 4 368
Bruni, Andrea dei see ANDREA DEI BRUNI
Bruni, Anton (Osipovich) 5 25
Bruni, Domenico 19 308
Bruni, Fyodor (Antonovich) 5 25–6*; 27 389, 390
patrons and collectors 26 734
pupils 14 163
works 5 25; 27 579, 580
Bruni, Leonardo 5 26*; 14 867, 870; 15 85; 16 658
works 16 614; 18 686; 32 384
Bruni, Lev (Aleksandrovich) 5 26*; 22 178; 27 394, 396; 32 661
groups and movements 10 843; 11 358
pupils 3 692
Brunias, Agostino see BRUNAIS, AUGUSTIN
Brüning, Peter 5 26–7*; 13 727; 14 238
Bruniquel 25 493
Brunius, Carl Georg 30 73, 119
Brunius, Jacques 30 22
Brunlees, James 24 748
Brünn see BRNO
Brunn, Heinrich 11 854; 22 733
Brunn, I. 29 756
Brunner 2 711
Brunner, Arnold William 17 548
Brunner, Johann Michael see PRUNNER, JOHANN MICHAEL
Brunner, Karl 4 233; 27 792
Brunner, Kaspar 3 823
Brunner, Martin 20 923
Brunner, V. H. 13 711
Brünnow, Rudolph E. 22 419; 24 556, 557
Brunnsee, Schloss see SCHLOSS BRUNNSEE
Brunnurinn 24 452
Bruno 5 28
Bruno, Saint 5 893; 7 231
Bruno I, Archbishop of Cologne 7 580, 594; 29 4; 33 108
Bruno, Antonio 31 447
Bruno, Armando 17 655
Bruno, Charles 10 346
Bruno, Giordano 14 867
Bruno, Paulo J. V. 19 272
Bruno of Segni 29 500
Brunor, Martin 2 773
Brunov, N. I. 1 685
Brunovský, Albín 5 27*; 28 853, 854
Brunovský, Daniel 28 853
Brunoy, Marquis de 3 414; 24 787
Brunoy, Marquise de 5 767
Bruns see BRUYN
Brunsberg, Hinrich 5 27–8*
works 4 665, 665, 783; 5 28; 13 58
Brunschwig, Hieronymus von 21 6
Brunswick (Germany) 5 28–30*, 29; 12 360
brass 12 452
Cathedral of St Blasius 4 776; 5 29; 27 124
candelabrum 26 686
Imerward Cross 5 29
metalwork 26 685
sculpture 26 632, 646
wall paintings 26 653
collections 12 481
faience (ii) (ceramics) 5 30*; 12 430
fountain 13 161
Jüdisches Museum 17 582
metalwork 23 659; 26 683
painting 12 394
papier mâché 24 62
St Blasius 14 81
sculpture 26 685, 685
synagogue 17 580
Brunswick (ME; USA), Bowdoin College 31 666
collections 4 599; 27 46
Walker Art Building 32 109
Brunswick, Augustus William, Duke of see AUGUSTUS WILLIAM, Duke of Brunswick
Brunswick, Dukes of see WELF, HOUSE OF
Brunswick, Ernest Augustus III, Duke of see ERNEST AUGUSTUS III, Duke of Brunswick
Brunswick, Monogrammist of 32 254
Brunswick, Otto I, Duke of see OTTO I, Duke of Brunswick and Lüneberg
Brunswick-Bevern, Ferdinand Albert, Duke of 33 51
Brunswick-Calenberg, Erich I, Herzog von 20 683
Brunswick-Calenberg, Erich I, Herzog von see ERICH I, Herzog von Brunswick-Calenberg
Brunswick Diptych, Master of the 12 232; 20 636–7*; 22 199, 835
works 20 636
Brunswick green see PIGMENTS → types → emerald green

Brunswick-Grubenhagen, Albrecht, Herzog von *see* ALBRECHT, Herzog von Brunswick-Grubenhagen
Brunswick-Lüneburg, Augustus, Duke of *see* AUGUSTUS, Duke of Brunswick-Lüneburg
Brunswick-Lüneburg, Christian Ludwig, Duke of *see* CHRISTIAN LUDWIG, Duke of Brunswick-Lüneburg
Brunswick-Lüneburg, Ernest the Confessor, Duke of *see* ERNEST THE CONFESSOR, Duke of Brunswick-Lüneburg
Brunswick-Lüneburg, Ernst the Confessor, Duke of **6** 138
Brunswick-Lüneburg, William, Duke of *see* WILLIAM, Duke of Brunswick-Lüneburg
Brunswick-Lüneburg-Calenberg, George, Duke of *see* GEORGE, Duke of Brunswick-Lüneburg-Calenberg **14** 141
Brunswick Model Book (Brunswick, Herzog Anton Ulrich-Mus., Kupf. Inv. 63) **24** 269
Brunswick Monogrammist **1** 799; **14** 381; **20** 792–3*; **21** 167
Brunswick-Wolfenbüttel, Anna Amalia of, Duchess of Saxe-Weimar *see* ANNA AMALIA, Duchess of Saxe-Weimar
Brunswick-Wolfenbüttel, Anton Ulrich, Duke of *see* ANTON ULRICH, Duke of Brunswick-Wolfenbüttel
Brunswick-Wolfenbüttel, Augustus, Duke of *see* AUGUSTUS, Duke of Brunswick-Wolfenbüttel
Brunswick-Wolfenbüttel, Charles I, Duke of *see* CHARLES I, Duke of Brunswick-Wolfenbüttel
Brunswick-Wolfenbüttel, Charles III, Duke of *see* CHARLES III, Duke of Brunswick-Wolfenbüttel
Brunswick-Wolfenbüttel, Friedrich Ulrich, Duke FRIEDRICH ULRICH, Duke of Brunswick-Wolfenbüttel
Brunswick-Wolfenbüttel, Henry II, Duke of *see* HENRY II, Duke of Brunswick-Wolfenbüttel
Brunswick-Wolfenbüttel, Henry Julius *see* HENRY JULIUS, Duke of Brunswick-Wolfenbüttel
Brunswick-Wolfenbüttel, Julius, Duke of *see* JULIUS, Duke of Brunswick-Wolfenbüttel
Brunswik, Jan von *see* JAN VON BRUNSWIK
Brunt, Henry Van *see* VAN BRUNT, HENRY
Brunt, Van & Howe *see* VAN BRUNT & HOWE
Brunton, Guy **3** 35; **18** 647
Brunton, John **31** 375
Brunus **27** 561
Brus, Anni **1** 513; **5** 30
Brus, Günter **5** 30–31*
  collaboration **27** 216; **28** 192
  groups and movements **1** 513; **2** 798; **22** 256; **32** 447
  works **5** *31*; **10** 483
Brusasorci, Domenico **5** 31–2*; **32** 343
  collaboration **5** 617, 816
  patrons and collectors **10** 805; **12** 910; **32** 348
  pupils **5** 32
  teachers **5** 816
  works **27** 202
Brusasorci, Felice **5** 32*
  pupils **3** 353; **23** 633; **31** 436
Bruschi, Domenico **7** 339
Bruschi, Gasparo **9** 58
Bruse, Anders **11** 107
Bruselas **8** 15, *15*
Bruselas, Giralte de **3** 123
Bruselas, Hanequin de *see* HANEQUIN DE BRUSELAS
Brusell, J. G. **10** 754
Brush, George de Forest **5** 35*; **7** 875; **18** 161
Brush, Leif **29** 98
brush backs **14** 763
brushes **5** 32–6*, *34*, *36*; **24** 348
  historical and regional traditions
    Bhutan **3** 914
    China **5** 35; **6** 736–7, 877; **7** 62, 65–6*
    Egypt, ancient **5** 32; **9** 898, *898*
    Indian subcontinent **15** 551
    Japan **5** 35; **7** 66; **17** 208–9, 213*, 226, 227, 315, 368–9*, *369*, 399
      Edo period (1600-1868) **17** 235
    Korea **5** 35; **7** 66; **18** 303
    Prehistoric art **25** 477
    Vietnam **7** 66
  materials
    badger-hair **5** 32, 33, 34, *34*; **25** 477
    bamboo **5** 33; **6** 736, 877; **15** 551; **17** 368
    bark **15** 551
    bear-hair **5** 32
    bristle **5** 33, *33*, 34, 35; **6** 736
    camel hair **32** 899
    cannons (brushes) **5** 33
    cat-hair **17** 368
    containers **5** 34
    deer-hair **5** 32; **17** 209, 227
    dog-hair **17** 368
    ermine **5** 32
    feathers **5** 32; **7** 65
    ferrules **5** *32*, 33
    fibres **5** 32, 33; **17** 209
    fox-hair **5** 32
    goat-hair **5** 32; **17** 209
    grasses **15** 551
    hair **3** 914; **5** 33, 35; **6** 736, 877; **7** 65; **15** 551; **17** 368; **18** 303
    hemp **17** 209
    hog bristle **5** *34*
    hog-hair **17** 209
    horsehair **17** 368
    human hair **5** 32–3
    miniver **5** 32, 33; **30** 426
    mink **5** 32
    netsuke **17** 399
    nylon **5** 33
    oils **5** 34
    ox-hair **5** 32, *32*, 33, 34
    polecat-hair **5** 32
    polyester **5** 33, 34
    quills **5** *32*, 33
    rabbit-hair **17** 227, 368
    raccoon-hair **17** 368
    rats' whiskers **7** 66
    sable **5** 32, *32*, 33, 34; **30** 426; **32** 899
    silver **5** 33
    squirrel-hair **5** 32, 33, 34
    stoat-hair **5** 32
    tin **5** 33
    turpentine **5** 34
    vegetable fibres **25** 477
    washers (brush) **5** 34
    weasel-hair **5** 32
    white spirit **5** 35
    wolf-hair **5** 32; **17** 368
    wood **3** 914
    wool **17** 213; **18** 303
  types
    blenders **4** 137*
    brights **5** 33
    fan **5** 33, *33*, 34
    filbert **5** 33, *33*, 34
    fitched **5** 33, 34
    flat **5** 33, *33*, 34
    hairbrushes *see* HAIRBRUSHES
    pencils **5** 33
    pointed **5** 33, 34
brushes
  types—cont.
    riggers **5** 34
    round **5** 33, *33*, 34
    short **5** *32*, 34
    softeners **5** 34, *34*
    sweeteners **5** 34
  uses
    acrylic **5** 34
    aquatints **2** 239
    calligraphy **5** *32*; **6** 736–7; **17** 213, 226, 227, 235
    canvases **5** 34
    conservation **17** 208–9
    drawings **9** 216; **15** 849, 855; **24** 350
    dyeing **17** 315
    impasto **5** 34
    miniatures (paintings) **5** *32*, 34
    oil paintings **23** 376, 379
    paints **5** 33, 34
    panel paintings **5** 34
    photography **5** 34
    portraits **5** 34
    resins **5** 34
    rock art **25** 477
    tempera **5** 33; **30** 426
    varnishes **5** 33
    wall paintings **25** 477
    washes **5** 34
    watercolours **5** 32, *32*, 34; **32** 898
    writing **7** 62; **15** 849, 853; **17** 213
  see also AIRBRUSHES; PENCILS
brush handles **7** 102; **18** 303
brushline **5** 35–7*, *36*, *37*; **6** 800; **17** 226
brushpots
  historical and regional traditions
    China **7** 58, 59, *59*, 102, 134, *134*, 141, *141*
    Korea **4** *175*; **18** 362
  materials
    bamboo **3** 144; **7** 58, 59, *59*
    box-wood **7** 141
    porcelain **4** *175*
    soapstone **7** 134, *134*
    wood **7** 141, *141*
brush-rests **7** 102, 134, 141
Bruskin, Grigory **27** 398; **29** 89
Brussa (family) **32** 203
Brusse, David de **25** 436
Brusse, Jobst de **25** 436
Brussel, Alexander van **22** 896
Brussel, Jacob van *see* JACOB VAN BRUSSEL
Brussel, Jean van *see* ROOME, JAN VAN
Brusselmans, Jean **2** 516; **4** 619; **5** 37–8*, 44
Brussels **3** *539*; **5** 38–54*, *39*
  Académie Royale des Beaux-Arts **1** 105; **8** 701
    library **3** 619
  art forms and materials **3** 567
    architecture **2** 510
    armour **2** 471
    brass **3** 602, 603
    catafalques **6** 71
    ceramics **3** 591; **5** 50–51*
    dossals **3** *609*
    embroidery **3** 609, *609*; **10** 181, II2
    façade decoration **10** 745, *745*
    gables **5** *40*; **11** 876
    glass **3** 593, *594*
    gold **5** 51–2*
    jewellery **3** 605
    lace **3** 610, *611*; **5** 51*; **18** 589, *589*, 591, 593
    leather **19** 4
    marks **2** 198
      metalwork **3** 601, 603; **5** 51; **20** 444
      tapestries **5** 47
    metalwork **3** 596, 598, 599; **13** 159
    painting **3** 554–5, 559, 560
Brussels
  art forms and materials—cont.
    pewter **3** 603
    porcelain **3** 591
    pottery **3** 589–90, *590*
    sculpture **3** 569, 570, 572; **13** 100, *111*, 111–12, *112*
    silver **3** 598, 599, 600, *602*; **5** 51–2*
    stained glass **13** 182; **27** 255
    tapestries **3** 576, 606, *608*; **5** 45–50*, *47*, *48*, *50*; **10** 277; **25** 131, 137; **29** 301; **30** 314, 315, *316*, 317, 320, 326, II1; **31** 446
    textiles **13** 195
  art market **3** 615
  Atomium *see under* Exposition Universelle et Internationale, 1958
  Auderghem **8** 681
  Banque Nationale **3** 548
  Berlaymont **5** *42*
  Bourse **3** 549, 613
  Cité de L'Helmet **30** 458
  Cité de L'Olivier **30** 458
  Cité Moderne **3** 551; **4** 577; **7** 293; **33** 246
  Colonne du Congrès **3** 548
  ecclesiastical buildings
    Augustinian church **3** 545, *546*
    Cathedral of St Michel and Ste Gudule **3** 542, 570, 572; **5** 50, *52*, 52–3*; **10** 322; **13** 62; **31** 874
      cross **2** 80
      pulpit **25** 727, *727*
      stained glass **3** 554; **13** 182, *909*
      textiles **3** 609
      tomb of Pieter Ferdinand Roose, Baron von Boechout **3** *417*
    Discalced Carmelite church **3** 545
    Jesuit church **3** 545
    Notre-Dame du Sablon **13** 62
    Onze Lieve Vrouwekerk **3** 548
    Sacré Coeur basilica **7** 301, 304
    Ste Gudule *see* Cathedral of St Michel and Ste Gudule
    St Jacques-sur-Coudenberg **3** 547
    St Joseph **3** 547
    St Michel *see* Cathedral of St Michel and Ste Gudule
    SS Pierre et Guidon **13** 182
      funerary relief of Ditmar de Brême **13** 100
  education (art) **3** 617, 618
  exhibitions **3** 564, 565
  Expo '58 *see* Exposition Universelle et Internationale, 1958
  Exposition Internationale, 1897 **15** 883
  Expositions Générales des Beaux-Arts **7** 677
  Exposition Universelle et Internationale, 1910 **15** 883
  Exposition Universelle et Internationale, 1958
    architecture **3** 551
    Atomium **3** 565; **10** 684; **15** 883
    Czechoslovak Pavilion **8** 251
    Pan-American Airways Pavilion **30** 469
    Spanish Pavilion **29** 274
    US Pavilion **30** 468
  Floréal **9** 759; **11** 724; **31** 875
  Galerie Sélection **3** 564
  Galeries St-Hubert **3** 548
  guilds **5** 46, 51
  Hôtel Delhaye *see* houses → Van Eetvelde
  Hôtel de Nassau *see* libraries → Bibliothèque Royale Albert Ier
  Hôtel Solvay **3** 586
Brussels—cont.
  Hôtel Van Eetvelde *see* houses → Van Eetveld House
  Hôtel de Ville **3** 543, 546, 568; **5** *53*, 53–4*; **13** 62, 161; **17** 700; **29** 414; **31** 238
    Escalier d'Honneur **8** 651
    Golden Chamber *see* Salle des Mariages
    paintings **23** 528
    Salle des Mariages **33** 118
    Salle du Conseil Communal **17** 7
    sculpture **13** 100
  houses
    Bloemenwerf **2** 563
    De Beir House **3** 551
    Hôtel Tassel **3** 550, 586; **5** *41*; **11** 449; **14** 769–70; **16** 55; **21** 779; **25** 173; **29** 508
      staircase **14** *770*
    Lenglet House **25** 741
    Résidence Léopold **3** 551
    Van Eetvelde House **3** 586; **25** 173; **29** 525
    17th cent. **5** *40*
  institutes
    Hoger Instituut voor Sierkunsten **3** 618
    Institut des Sciences Naturelles *see under* museums
    Institut Royal du Patrimoine Artistique (IRPA) **3** 619
      library **3** 619
  Jardin Botanique Conservatory **3** 547
  Koninklijke Vlaamse Schouwburg **3** 549
  Laeken Palais Royal *see under* LAEKEN
  libraries and archives
    Archives d'Architecture Moderne **3** 619, 620
    Bibliothèque Africaine **1** 439
    Bibliothèque Royale Albert 1er **3** 618; **21** 499
      collections **2** 382; **7** 487
      textiles **3** 609
    Institut Supérieur d'Architecture de l'Etat Library **3** 619
    Sint-Lukasarchief **3** 619
    see also under institutes → Institut Royal du Patrimoine Artistique; museums → Musées Royaux d'A. et d'Hist.; Musées Royaux des Beaux-Arts
  Le Logis **9** 759; **11** 724; **31** 875
  Maison du Pain **3** 543, 546
  Maison du Peuple **3** 550; **14** 770, *771*; **25** 173
  Metro stations **21** 350
  Métro stations **21** 350
  Monplaisir factory **3** 591
  museums
    Institut des Sciences Naturelles **3** 616
    Koninklijk Museum van het Leger en van Krijgsgeschiedenis **3** 616
    Musée des Archives d'Architecture Moderne **8** 257
    Musée d'Art Ancien *see under* Musées Royaux des Beaux-Arts
    Musée d'Art Moderne *see under* Musées Royaux des Beaux-Arts
    Musée Constantin Meunier **21** 369
    Musée Horta **2** 369; **3** 586; **14** 770
    Musée Instrumental du Conservatoire Royale **22** 376
    Musée de la Porte **3** 898
    Musées Royaux d'Art et d'Histoire **2** 275; **3** 616
      Chinese collection **7** 155

Brussels
museums
Musées Royaux d'Art et d'Histoire—cont.
collections **3** 620
Egyptian collection **10** 94
Iranian collection **15** 922
Japanese collection **17** 434
library **3** 618
Nepalese collection **22** 795
South-east Asian collection **29** 240
stained glass **29** 516
tapestries **30** 332
Musées Royaux des Beaux-Arts **2** 125; **3** 547, 616; **8** 699, 831
collections **11** 371
library **3** 618
Musée d'Art Ancien **2** 382; **3** 89, 549, 616; **7** 490; **15** 42; **31** 874; **32** 590
Musée d'Art Moderne **3** 616
Musée d'Art Moderne: collections **17** 921; **26** 527
Musée Wiertz **33** 171
Palais des Beaux-Arts (1875-) *see* Musée Royaux des Beaux-Arts → Musée d'Art Ancien
Palais des Beaux-Arts (1919-) **14** 771
Vrije Museum **17** 700
Palace for the Council of Brabant *see* Palais de la Nation
Palace of Cardinal Granvelle **3** 545
Palace of Charles of Lorraine *see* museums → Musées Royaux des Beaux-Arts
Palace of the Prince of Orange *see* Palais des Académies
Palais des Académies **3** 547, 578
Palais des Beaux-Arts (1875-) *see* museums → Musées Royaux des Beaux-Arts → Musée d'Art Ancien
Palais des Beaux-Arts (1919-) *see under* museums
Palais des Congrès **8** 700
Palais Ducal *see* Palais des Académies
Palais de Justice **3** 549, 613; **18** 889; **23** 814; **25** 64–5
decorative works **8** 701
Palais de la Nation **3** 547
Palais Royal **28** 756
monument to Godefroid de Bouillon **5** 43
sculpture **4** 417
Palais Stoclet **2** 567, 809; **3** 550; **14** 628, *629*; **21** 779; **27** 129; **29** 693; **33** 166
dining-room **3** *579*
furniture **3** 587
interior decoration **3** 579; **12** 497; **18** 130–31
mosaics **22** 163
paintings **17** 692
sculpture **25** 404
Porte de Hal *see* museums → Musée de la Porte
Rue Josaphat school **16** 827
Senate
Salle des Séances **8** 651
Serres Royales **7** 745
squares
Grande Place **3** 546; **31** 238
Place des Martyrs **3** 547; **11** 137
Place Royale **3** 547; **13** 831–2
Place St Catherine **5** *40*
Stadhuis *see* Hôtel de Ville
tenements **30** 458
Uccle Observatory **23** 340
Université Catholique de Louvain Medical Faculty Building **18** 466; **23** 500
urban planning **5** 170; **30** 47
Van Neck clinic **25** 190
Woluwe-Saint-Pierre **8** 681
Brussels, Juan of *see* JUAN DE BRUXELAS
Brussels carpets *see under* CARPETS → types
Brussels Hours *see* BOOKS OF HOURS → individual manuscripts → Très Belles Heures
Brussels Initials, Master of the **4** 275; **20** 637–8*; **31** 837
works **20** *637*
Brustolon, Andrea **5** 54–5*
patrons and collectors **7** 775; **16** 728
pupils **20** 394
works **5** *54*; **23** 541; **26** 500; **32** 195
Brustolon, Giambattista **5** 55*, 599; **13** 744; **21** 747; **32** 195
Brustolon, Jacopo **5** 54
Brustolon, Paolo **5** 55
Brutalism **2** 362; **5** 55–7*; **10** 698; **15** 887
England **10** 242
Finland **18** 781
France **5** *56*; **19** *45*
United States of America **27** 313
Brutelle, Charles-Louis L'Héritier de *see* L'HÉRITIER DE BRUTELLE, CHARLES-LOUIS
Bruto, Giovanni Michele **25** 17
Brütt, Adolf (Carl Johannes) **5** 57*; **28** 52
Brütt, Barthold Friedrich **5** 57
Brütt, Ferdinand **3** 511
Brutus, Lucius Junius **27** *30*
Brutus' Boy **29** 781
Brutzkus, David Anatol **28** 557
Bruun, Edith Sonne **28** 22
Bruun, Hans Nicolai **23** 235
Bruun Neergaard, T. C. **9** 700
Bruxelas, Juan de *see* JUAN DE BRUXELAS
Bruxelles, Pierre de *see* PIERRE DE BRUXELLES
Bruyas, Alfred **5** 57–8*; **11** 659
collections **22** 35
paintings **5** 342; **8** 53; **12** 770
Bruycker, Joseph De *see* DE BRUYCKER, JOSEPH
Bruycker, Jules de **3** 564
Bruyenne, Justin **5** 58*; **31** 221
Bruyen van Berendrecht, Michiel de **32** 402
Bruyère, Elise **19** 9
Bruyère, Jean Baptiste François Graux de la *see* GRAUX DE LA BRUYÈRE, JEAN BAPTISTE FRANÇOIS
Bruyère, Louis **5** 58–9*; **24** 174
Bruyn, Abraham de **5** 61*; **19** 564
Bruyn, Arnt **5** 59, 61
Bruyn, Bartholomäus (i) (1493-1555) **5** 59–61*; **20** 765
collaboration **5** 61
pupils **5** 61
teachers **17** 601
works **5** *59*, *60*; **7** 583, 590; **11** 453–4; **31** 881; **33** 458
Bruyn, Bartholomäus (ii) (*c*. 1530-1607/10) **5** 59, 61*; **11** 454
Bruyn, Claes de *see* CLAES DE BRUYN
Bruyn, Michel de **22** 888
Bruyn, Nicolaes de **5** 62*; **27** 885; **32** 588
Bruyn, Peer de **22** 877
Bruyn, Willem de **7** 915; **8** 21
Bruyne, Pieter De *see* DE BRUYNE, PIETER
Bruyn van Berendrecht, Michiel de **5** 62*
Bruyn van Berendrecht, Nicolaes de **5** 62
Bruynyng, Robert, Abbot of Sherborne **17** 611
Bruynzeel Company **15** 36; **33** 743
works **22** *869*
Bry, Auguste **20** 602
Bry, de (family) **11** 735, 736; **17** 886
Bry, Dittert *see* BRY, THEODOR DE
Bry, Johann Israel de **5** 62, 63
Bry, Johann Theodor de **5** 62, 63*; **21** 151
pupils **19** 15
works **3** 604; **5** 750
Bry, Theodor de **5** 62–3*; **10** 326, 389
collaboration **4** 242
emblem books **10** 175
engravings **2** 103; **14** 855; **19** 143; **22** *555*, *637*; **33** 146, 252
pattern books **24** 271
pupils **19** 15
Bryan, Arthur **33** 23
Bryan, John Neely **8** 469
Bryan, Michael **5** 63*; **10** 366
patrons and collectors **8** 87
works **9** 755; **14** 808
writings **10** 208
Bryan, Philip **16** 888
Bryan, Thomas Jefferson **23** 46; **31** 662, 664, 666
Bryan Castle **16** 886
Bryan's **19** 587
Bryans, Lina **5** 63*
Bryant, Ann, Art Gallery *see under* EAST LONDON (SOUTH AFRICA)
Bryant, Antoine **31** 844
Bryant, Gridley J(ames) F(ox) **5** 63–4*
collaboration **12** 643; **29** 870
staff **8** 265
works **4** 473; **27** 613
Bryant, Joshua **13** 876
Bryant, William Cullen **14** 699, 843
Bryant, W. S. **23** 632
Bryant & Gilman **24** 299
Bryas Palace **9** 558
Bryaxis **5** 64–5*; **13** 459
collaboration **19** 170
copies **13** 463
works **1** 616; **2** 157; **13** 463; **14** 69; **18** 148; **26** 292; **28** 383
workshop **13** 460
Bryce **19** 388
Bryce, David **5** 65, 263; **24** 315; **28** 288
apprentices **2** 5; **26** 481; **29** 650
collaboration **28** 228, 230
patrons and collectors **30** 464
staff **31** 462
works **3** 175; **9** 724; **28** *230*, 288, 289, *289*
Bryce, Hugh **1** 746
Bryce, John **28** 228
Bryce, John Annan **12** 315
Bryce Salomons, Vera *see* SALOMONS, VERA BRYCE
Brychta, Jaroslav **33** 630
Brychtová, Jaroslava **8** 411; **33** 631
Bryde, H. C. **18** 896
Brydges, Anna Eliza **13** 637
Brydges, James, 1st Duke of Chandos **5** 65*; **10** 361
architecture **12** 6, 593
gardens **19** 622
miniatures **21** 642
paintings **3** 681; **7** 500; **11** 141; **14** 598; **17** 901; **30** 759
sculpture **5** 827
Brydon, J(ohn) M(cKean) **5** 65–6*
competitions **7** 668
groups and movements **3** 269; **9** 739
staff **31** 375
works **3** 373
Brydone, Patrick **13** 303
Bryen, Camille **5** 66*; **11** 551
dealers **19** 537
groups and movements **2** 543, 544; **3** 155
illustrated writings **31** 508
Bryer, Henry **27** 463, 716
Bryetes **24** 283
Bryggman, Erik (William) **5** 66–7*; **11** 92; **31** 461
collaboration **1** 8
groups and movements **15** 885
works **11** 92
Brygos **13** 520; **32** 36
Brygos Painter **13** 520, 535; **32** 36*
teachers **32** 61
works **9** 248; **12** 286; **13** *477*, 520, *520*
Bryk, Rut **11** 106
Brykalski, Przemysław **2** 502
Brykina, G. A. **6** 285
Brymner, William **5** 67*; **22** 38
groups and movements **5** 566, 593
pupils **11** 901; **14** 282, 499, 676
works **5** 566
Bryn Athyn (PA)
Glencairn Museum **24** 890; **29** 515
Swedenborgian Cathedral **24** 890
Bryndælaskald, Illuga **32** 523
Bryndreinog **32** 781
Brynmawr (Gwent; UK), Dunlop Rubber Factory **32** 783
Bryn Mawr College (PA; USA), Deanery **15** 408
Brynmawr Valley Industries **32** 789
Brynzey, B. **21** 812
Bryson, Norman **2** 538; **25** 362; **29** 664
Bryullov, Aleksandr (Pavlovich) **5** 67–8*; **23** 340; **27** 377
pupils **21** 887
works **27** 585; **31** 68
Bryullov, Ivan **14** 587
Bryullov, Karl (Pavlovich) **5** 67, 68–9*; **27** 389, 390, 579
groups and movements **26** 740
patrons and collectors **26** 734; **27** 438; **31** 312
pupils **11** 895; **12** 326; **28** 598, 672
works **5** *68*
Bryus, Ya. V. **27** 438
Bryusov, Valery (Yakovlevich) **5** 69*; **8** 596
Bryusova, Nadezhda **15** 857
Brzechff (family) **3** 431
Brzękowski, J. **2** 409; **29** 582
Brześć Kujawski **25** 500, 518
Brzeżany **25** 130
tomb of Nicolaus and Hieronimus Sieniawski **25** 113
Brzozowski, Tadeusz **5** 70*; **25** 108
bsam yas *see* SAMYE
Bshirri Museum **19** 9
Bteddin *see* BAYT AL-DIN
Bua, Mercurio **3** 138
Búadóttir, Asgerður **15** 73
Buafle, Master of **13** 861
Bual, Artur **25** 300
Buandi
masks **33** *484*
Buang **23** 729
Buba, Ovidiu **26** 719
Bubák, Alois **5** 70*; **14** 235
Bubaque **4** 56
Bubastis **5** 70–71*; **9** 773, *774*; **10** 80; **24** 840
cat statues **5** *71*
cult temple **9** 829, 830, 831; **30** 433
jewellery **10** 32
necropoleis **9** 843
palace of Ammenemes III **23** 807
sculpture **9** 879
silver **9** 655
Bubastos **9** 849
Bubb, James George **30** 503
bubby-pots **24** 37
Bubenheim, St Peter **12** 471
Bubenhoven, von (family) **29** 787
Buberl, Caspar **30** 505
Bubi **10** 440
Bubich, Bernardo *see* BOBIĆ, BERNARDO
Bubnoûski, V. **3** 530
Bubnovy Valet *see* JACK OF DIAMONDS
Bubyr', Aleksey (Fyodorovich) **15** 132; **27** 378; **30** 277; **32** 72
Buçaco de Coimbra **27** 498
Palace Hotel **25** 293
Bucareli, Viceroy **21** 265
Bucareli y Urzúa, Antonio María, Viceroy of New Spain **21** 402
Bucarelli, Palma **26** 777
Buccellati, Giorgio **30** 492
Bucchero pottery *see under* POTTERY → wares
Bucci, Anselmo **11** 843; **16** 680; **23** 263
Buccleuch, Anne Scott, Duchess of *see* SCOTT, ANNE, Duchess of Buccleuch
Buccleuch, Elizabeth Montagu, Duchess of *see* MONTAGU, ELIZABETH, Duchess of Buccleuch
Buccleuch, Francis Scott, 2nd Duke of Monmouth and *see* SCOTT, FRANCIS, 2nd Duke of Monmouth and Buccleuch
Buccleuch, James Scott, Duke of Monmouth and *see* SCOTT, JAMES, Duke of Monmouth and Buccleuch
Buccleuch, Walter Francis Montagu-Douglas-Scott, 5th Duke of *see* MONTAGU-DOUGLAS-SCOTT, WALTER FRANCIS, 5th Duke of Buccleuch
Buccleuch, Walter Scott, 9th Duke of *see* SCOTT, WALTER FRANCIS JOHN, 9th Duke of Buccleuch
Bucco Cross **26** 646
Bucelin, Gabriel **3** 737
Bucer, Martin **14** 868
Bucevschi, Epaminonda **26** 714
Buch, Carl Emil **23** 222
Buch, Christian von *see* CHRISTIAN VON BUCH
Buch, Mirta García *see* GARCÍA BUCH, MIRTA
Buchach, St Nicholas **31** 561
Buchan, Alexander **3** 183
Buchanan, Colin **31** 735
Buchanan, F. **15** 695
Buchanan, William **5** 71–2*; **10** 366; **22** 148
collections **14** 675
paintings **3** 239; **4** 304, 330; **6** 438; **24** 322; **25** 39; **28** 271; **33** 216
Buchanan & Cowper **2** 741
Buchanan-Hamilton, Francis **15** 741
Buchanan & Partners **18** 541
Buchan Pottery **28** 258
Bucharest **5** 72–4*; **26** *705*
academies and art schools
Academy of Art **26** 719, 721, 725; **30** 364
Academy of Decorative Arts **26** 719
Romanian Academy Library **26** 723, 725
School of Fine Arts *see* Academy of Art
architecture **26** 709
Architecture Institute **5** *73*; **26** 709
Aro block **26** 709
Buftea restaurant **26** 709
Curtea Veche **5** 72
Dinescu House **26** 709
ecclesiastical buildings
Cotroceni monastery **26** 708, 718
epitaphioi **26** 721
Doamnei church **26** 721

Bucharest
ecclesiastical buildings—cont.
Kretzulescu church **5** *72*; **26** 708
Lady Bălaşa Church **26** 709
Monastery of St George **26** 720
Pantelimon monastery **26** 708, 713
St Dumitru **26** 708
St Elefterie Vechi **26** 713
education (art) **26** 725, 726
fortifications **21** 577
History of Art Institute **26** 725
Hotel Bulevard **26** 709
houses **26** 708
Ion Mincu Institute of Architecture **26** 726
ketubbot **18** 3
Librecht House **26** 709
Ministry of Foreign Affairs **26** 709
museums **26** 724
Jewish museum **17** 582
Kalinderu Museum *see* National Museum of Art
Minovici Museum of Folk Art **6** 342
Museum of Art Collections *see under* National Museum of Art
Museum of Art of the RSR *see* National Museum of Art
Museum of National Art *see* Museum of the Romanian Peasant
Museum of the HIstory and Art of Bucharest
Storck Collection **29** 721
Museum of the Romanian Peasant **12** 547; **13** 204
National Gallery *see* National Museum of Art
National History Museum **5** 74
National Museum of Art **1** 751; **5** 73, 74; **26** 724; **29** 638
collections **5** 73, 792; **17** 873
Department of Medieval Romanian Art **26** 724
Museum of Art Collections **5** 74; **26** 723, 724
National Gallery **26** 724
Storck Museum *see* Museum of the History and Art of Bucharest → Storck Collection
Teodor Aman Museum **1** 751; **29** 638
Toma Stelian Museum *see* National Museum of Art
Village Museum and Museum of Popular Art **9** 70
Zambaccian Museum *see* National Museum of Art → Museum of Art Collections
Palace of the Savings and Deposit Bank **26** 709, *709*
Princely Palace **26** 707
St Sava College **26** 724, 725
Spark House **26** 709
Şutu Palace **26** 709
U. C. B. district **26** 709
University **26** 709; **29** 721
urban planning **5** 634; **26** 710
Buchau **23** 808; **25** *521*, 522
Buche, Paul de **32** 5
Bucheck, Berthold von, Bishop of Strasbourg **29** 755
Buchel, Aernout van
works **30** *662*
Buchell, Arnhout van **5** 74*; **24** 236
Buchen, Bill **22** 375
Buchen, Mary **22** 375
Bucher, Bruno **10** 209
Bucher, Hertha **18** 412
Bucher, Jeanne **3** 391; **20** 399
Bucher, Paul de **30** 114
Bücher, Wilhelm **1** 161
Bücherei Maiandros **24** 427
Bucheum **5** 74*; **9** 843; **27** 825
Buchheim, Ludwig **28** 169
Buchheister, Carl **5** 74–5*; **7** 771; **32** 695
Buchkala **15** 486–7
Vishnu Temple **15** 270
Buchlov Castle **8** 376
Buchlovice Castle **8** 378, 382
Buchman and Kahn **17** 722
Buchman & Fox **17** 722
Buchner, Christian **1** 6
Buchner, Ernst **8** 514
Buchner, Paul **18** 121; **33** 113
Buchon, Max **8** 51
Buchow-Karpzow **25** 507
Buchs, Herz-Jesu Kirche **30** 128
Buchser, Frank **5** 75*; **30** 134
Buchsteiner, Joh. **32** 757
Buck, Jonathan, II **19** 394
Buck, Nathaniel **5** 75–6*; **6** 513; **33** 545
Buck, Samuel **5** 75–6*; **6** 513; **23** 258; **33** 545
works **30** *365*
Buckden Palace **4** 770
Bückeburg **5** 76–7*; **12** *360*
Schloss **28** 60
Chapel **12** 405
Goldener Saal **12** 410; **27** 229
Stadtkirche **5** *76*; **10** 745; **12** 369; **14** 82
sculpture **12** 405
Buckeridge, Baynbrigg *see* BUCKRIDGE, BAINBRIGG
buckets **4** *687*; **10** 341; **13** 475; **16** *366*; **33** 724
see also SITULAE
bucket seat chairs *see under* CHAIRS → types
Buckett, Rowland **24** 752
Buckfast Abbey (Devon) **31** 348
Buckie Church (Grampian) **28** 288
Buckingham, Clarence **17** 431
Buckingham, David Austin **28** 540
Buckingham, Edward Stafford, 3rd Duke of *see* STAFFORD, EDWARD, 3rd Duke of Buckingham
Buckingham, George Temple-Nugent-Grenville, 1st Marquess of *see* TEMPLE-NUGENT-GRENVILLE, GEORGE, 1st Marquess of Buckingham
Buckingham, George Villiers, 1st Duke of *see* VILLIERS, GEORGE, 1st Duke of Buckingham
Buckingham, James Silk **31** 726
works **31** *726*
Buckingham, John Sheffield, 2nd Duke of *see* SHEFFIELD, JOHN, 2nd Duke of Buckingham
Buckingham, Thomas of Woodstock, Earl of *see* PLANTAGENET, THOMAS OF WOODSTOCK, Duke of Gloucester
Buckingham and Chandos, Richard, 1st Duke of *see* TEMPLE-NUGENT-BRYDGES-CHANDOS-GRENVILLE, RICHARD, 1st Duke of Buckingham and Chandos
Buckingham and Chandos, Richard, 2nd Duke of *see* PLANTAGENET-TEMPLE-NUGENT-BRYDGES-CHANDOS, RICHARD, 2nd Duke of Buckingham and Chandos
Buckingham and Chandos, Richard Grenville, 3rd Duke of *see* GRENVILLE, RICHARD, 3rd Duke of Buckingham and Chandos
Buckingham Palace *see under* LONDON → palaces
Buckingham Palace Madonna, Master of the **5** 537; **9** 96
Buckinghamshire, John Hobart, 2nd Earl of *see* HOBART, JOHN, 2nd Earl of Buckinghamshire
Buckland, James **5** 77
Buckland, William **2** 121; **5** 77*; **31** 590
Buckland House (Oxon) **7** 339
Buckland-Wright, John **4** 366; **10** 397, 561
Buckle, J. **7** 559
Bückle, Johann Martin **5** 77*
Buckler, John Chessell **19** 404; **23** 690; **27** 626; **32** 274
works **10** *280*
Bucklersbury Pavement **19** 579
buckles **17** 524, 525
historical and regional traditions
Anglo-Saxon **2** 79
China **6** 856; **7** 108, 145
England **10** 340; **21** II3
Etruscan **10** *625*
France **2** *565*; **21** *503*
Indonesia **15** 814
Italy **10** *625*
Korea **18** 347, 366
Malaysia **20** 180
Migration period **21** *503*
materials
brass **10** 340
bronze **6** 856; **10** *625*; **18** 347; **21** *503*
steel **21** II3
Buckley, Stephen **5** 77–8*
Buckley Potteries **32** 789
Bucklin, James C(hamplin) **5** 78*; **20** 438; **25** 666; **32** 866
Bückmann, Herman **30** 925
Buckminster Park (Lincs) **9** 14
Buck Mounds (FL) **22** 611
pottery **22** *611*, *612*
Bucknall, William **7** 663
Buckner, Richard **5** 78*
Bucknor, Kobina **12** 509
Buckridge, Bainbrigg **5** 78–9*; **7** 784; **10** 376
buckthorn berries **18** 656; **24** 794, 799
Bučovice **5** 79*; **8** *374*
palace **5** 79, *79*
Bucquet, Maurice **24** 738
bucrania **5** 79*; **13** 392
Bucur **5** 72
Buczacz **5** 79–80*; **25** 133
Buczkó, György **15** 5
Buda *see* BUDAPEST
Budagh Khan **15** 372
Budai, Isaiah **10** 472
Budapest **5** 80–87*, *83*; **14** *881*; **16** *103*
academies and art schools **5** 85
Academy of Fine Arts **15** 18; **17** 885
Academy of Music **14** 889; **18** 389
Atelier Studio School **15** 18
Design and Drawing Teachers' Institute *see* Academy of Fine Arts
Első Magyar Festészeti Akadémia **15** 18
Ferenc Liszt Academy of Music **15** 4
Hungarian National Academy of Sciences **26** 190; **30** 210
Art Historical Research Group **15** 19
library **15** 19
School of Decorative Arts *see* Academy of Fine Arts
School of Decorative Drawing **15** 18
Ungarische Akademia der Wissenschaften *see* Hungarian National Academy of Sciences
amphitheatre **26** 906
Aquincum **5** 80; **26** *906*, 907; **27** 72
Budapest—cont.
art forms and materials
architecture **14** 884, 888, 889
ceramics **5** 85–6*; **15** 2
furniture **14** *908*
metalwork **13** 162; **15** 5
silk **15** 11
textiles **15** 11
tiles **5** 85
Art Hall **14** 889
Atrium Cinema **14** 890
baths **14** 886; **16** 224
Császár Baths **15** 14
Bedő Building **32** 421–2
bridges
Chain Bridge **14** 888
Erzsébet Bridge **14** 891
Buda Castle **5** *82*, 86*; **14** 883, 893
gardens **12** 114
Hunyadi Hall **3** 702
sculpture **5** 86–7*, *86*
commercial buildings
Gresham Life Assurance Company Building **14** 889; **15** 4
Hungarotex office block **14** 891
MTI (Hungarian Mass Media) Headquarters **14** 891
Court of Justice *see* museums → Ethnographic Museum
Customs House **15** 9
Dohány Street synagogue **17** 547
Eastern Railway Station **15** 9; **25** 856
East-West Trade Centre **14** 891
ecclesiastical buildings
Basilica **15** 9
Church of Our Lady *see* Matthias Church
Cistercian monastery **14** 890
Dominican convent monument to Princess Margaret Árpád **14** 892
Hermina Chapel **14** 889
Matthias Church **14** 883, 884, 889; **28** 172
Óbuda Parish Church **13** 162; **14** 894
Pauline church *see* University Church
Pest parish church **14** 885
Reformed Church **2** 415
St Anthony **14** 890
SS Peter and Mary **14** 884
St Peter's priory church **14** 883, 892; **26** 638
St Stephen *see* Basilica
Trinitarian Monastery **5** 82
see also museums → Kiscelli Museum
University Church **14** 887, 894, 900
education (art) **15** 18
exhibitions **14** 908
Ferenciek Square fountain **14** 895
Fishermen's Bastion **14** 889
Heroes' Square **28** 87
Hilton Hotel **14** 788
Hotel Kempinszky **14** 891
Institute of Geology **14** 890
Institutum Geometricum *see* UNIVERSITIES → Technical University
Kazinczy Street synagogue **17** 547
Kerepesi cemetery **31** 131
libraries
library of the Paulist Fathers **14** 894, 907
National Monument Trust Library **15** 19
National Széchényi Library **15** 16, 19
University Library **14** 889
see also museums → Hungarian National Museum → Archaeological Library
Budapest—cont.
Magyar Tudományos Academia *see* academies → Hungarian National Academy of Sciences
Metro stations **21** 349
Ministry of the Interior **14** 891
monuments
Holy Trinity column **14** 894; **15** 13
István Széchenyi Monument **14** 896
József Eötvös Monument **14** 896
Lajos Kossuth Monument **15** 14
Millenary Monument **14** 896; **15** 14
St Stephen Monument **14** 896
mosque of Mustafa Pasha **14** 886
Municipal Council **14** 886
museums
Arts and Crafts Collection *see* Museum of Applied Art
Ethnographic Museum **14** 889; **15** 17; **20** 447; **29** 241
Ferenc Hopp Museum of Oriental Art **15** 17
collections **15** 742, 745; **29** 241
György Ráth Museum **15** 17
Historical Museum **5** 85, 86, 87; **15** 17
Hungarian Museum of Architecture **15** 19
Hungarian National Gallery **5** 85; **15** 17
collections **8** 780
Esterházy collection **25** 728
library **15** 19
periodicals **24** 441
Hungarian National Museum **5** 82; **14** 11, 889; **15** 14; **19** 31
Archaeological Library **15** 19
architectural sculpture **22** 28
collections **2** 547; **5** 84; **15** 16; **18** 419; **20** 400, 439
murals **30** 641
paintings **4** 838
Picture Gallery **15** 17
Hungarian Photographic Archives **24** 682
Kiscelli Museum *see* ecclesiastical buildings → Trinitarian Monastery
Lajos Kassák Memorial Museum **5** 82
Magyar Nemzeti Múzeum *see* Hungarian National Museum
Municipal Picture Gallery **15** 17
Museum of Applied Art **5** 85; **14** 890; **15** 17, 408; **19** 30
library **15** 19
Museum of Ethnography *see* Ethnographic Museum
Museum of Fine Arts **2** 416; **5** 83, 85; **14** 889; **28** 87
collections **10** 531; **14** 901; **15** 16
Esterházy collection **15** 15, 17
Ferenczy collection **10** 895
Graphic Art Research and Exhibitions Hall **30** 762
Greek collection **13** 470
library **15** 19
Pálffy collection **28** 856
sculpture **27** 46
National Jewish Museum **15** 17; **17** 581
observatory **23** 340
Opera House **14** 896; **15** 9; **25** 245
OTI apartment block **14** 890
Parisiana Bar **14** 890
Parliament Building **13** 203, 237, 238; **14** 580, *888*, 889; **15** 9; **23** 814; **27** 129; **29** 606
frescoes **18** 389
paintings **22** 311
Postal Savings Bank **14** *889*, 890; **19** 30
Révai Villa **16** 795

Budapest—cont.
Royal Palace **5** 86; **14** 883, 884, 887, 888, 889, 891
ceramics **15** 1
metalwork **15** 9
sculpture **10** 750; **20** 848
Rózsavölgyi Building **14** 890, 909
tomb of Gül Baba **14** 886
Unger House **14** 889
universities
Loránd Eötvös University **15** 19
Technical University **15** 17
'R' Building **14** 891
urban planning **31** 797
Vas Street School **14** 890
Vigadó Concert Hall **14** 889, 896; **15** 9; **30** 641
Zoo **33** 699
Budapest Secession *see* SECESSION (BUDAPEST)
Budaspay *see* BUDSLAŬ
Budayya **3** 69
Buddeus, Karl **10** 539
Buddhagupta **20** 170
Buddhamitra **15** 439, 440
Buddhism **5** 87–120*; **26** 140
art
aisles **17** 65
albums **1** 581–2
alloys **22** *787*
altars **1** 701
China **1** 703; **5** *112*
Japan **1** 703–4
Korea **1** 704
Lamaism **1** 704–5*
Mongolia **1** 705
portable **28** 638
Tibet **1** 704–5*
Vietnam **1** 706
amulets **1** 818; **30** 845
appliqué **30** 846
architectural decorations **18** 337, 766*; **30** 842
architecture
Afghanistan **1** 191–3*
Bactria **6** 198
Burma **5** 233*
Central Asia, Eastern **6** 296–7
Central Asia, Western **6** 198
Champa **6** 421–2*; **9** 133
China **6** 666–71*
Indian subcontinent **15** 311, 406
Indonesia **15** 758
Japan **14** 773; **17** 71–5*; **18** *561*
Korea **18** 261, 266–8*
Malaysia **20** 165*
Maldives, Republic of **20** 188
Sarawak **20** 165
Sri Lanka **29** 446–8*, 449
Thailand **30** 576–7
Tibet **30** 815–21
Vietnam **6** 421–2*; **9** 133
banners
Central Asia, Eastern **6** 304, 314
China **6** 777, 779–81*; **7** *47*
Indian subcontinent **15** 570
Korea **18** 308
Nepal **22** *782*
Thailand **30** 612–13, *613*
Tibet **30** 828
basins **18** 349
bays **17** 65
beams **17** 72
bells **7** 98; **17** *322*, 397; **18** 347–8
bone **4** 314
bookbindings **6** 307; **7** 64
book covers **6** 319; **15** 570; **30** 846
book illustrations **6** 777; **21** 876
books **1** 580, *580*; **5** 102; **30** 613, *614*
boundary stones **30** 575
brackets **17** 66, 72
brass **6** 706; **30** 822, *823*, *824*, *825*, *826*, *827*, *849*

Buddhism
art—cont.
brocades **30** 846
bronze **1** 207; **5** *114*, *240*, 241, 485; **6** 298; **15** *223*, *530*, 530–31; **17** 110–12, *111*, 120, 320, *375*, 397; **18** *284*, *285*, *294*; **22** 447; **30** 351, 593–5*, 596–7, *597*, *598*, *601*, 601–2*, *602*, *605*, *841*
Burma **5** 241
China **6** 706, 707, *708*, *710*, 712, 718, *719*, *720*, 720–22, 835
Indian subcontinent **15** 476; **26** *150*
Japan **17** *34*, *107*, *110*, *112*, *113*, *322*; **22** *497*
Korea **18** 347–9*, *348*
Laos **18** 768, *768*
Sri Lanka **29** *460*, *479*
Thailand **30** *607*
caityas **1** *500*
calligraphy **6** 748, 772; **30** 845
Chan **17** 229–31
China **6** 751–2*, *752*, 756
Japan **15** *130*, *131*, *833*; **17** 211, 217–21*, *218*, *220*
Japan: Ōbaku **17** 234–5
Japan: Zen **14** 61; **17** 229–31*, *230*
camphor-wood **17** *109*
capitals **27** *844*
caricatures **5** 761
cartouches **6** 777
caskets **18** 351, 352
casting **17** 320; **30** 842
cast iron **7** 98, 99
cave art **29** 462
caves
Central Asia, Eastern **18** 105; **30** 441–2
China **30** 442–3*
Indian subcontinent **5** 94; **15** *236*, 236, 252–3, 257–9, *258*
cement **18** 769
ceramics **5** *111*
certificates **17** 230
chapels **17** *422*
charms **6** 707
chortens *see* stupas
cinnabar **29** 462
clay **1** 197, 198, *199*, 202; **6** *194*, *216*, *221*, 221–2, 298, *299*, *300*, 706, 708, 717; **18** *292*, 295; **30** *220*, 596, 823
cloisters **17** 66
collections **17** 432
colophons **7** 624; **17** 230, *270*; **30** *836*
colour **18** 310–12
columns **6** *422*
conch shells **28** 582, *582*
copies **7** 114
copper **15** *223*; **22** *769*, *777*; **30** 822, *844*
coral **6** 706
cosmologies **5** 463
craftsmen and artists **6** 706; **17** 419
cupboards **6** *669*
dāgabas
see also stupas
doorways **5** *241*
dormitories **17** 68
dress
Central Asia, Eastern **6** *310*, 311
China **7** 78
Japan **17** 374
Mongolia **21** 877
dyes **29** 477
earthenwares **18** 337
education (art) **17** 419; **32** 492
embroidery **7** 45, *47*, *49*; **17** *306*; **21** 877; **30** 846
enamel **7** 68
entasis **17** 66

Buddhism
art—cont.
fans **10** 778
fibulae **30** *841*, 841–2
figurines **7** 104–5, *105*
flower arrangements **17** 379
frontispieces **17** *148*
ganjira **30** 842
gardens
dry-landscape **18** *563*, 564
Japan **12** 97
Japan: Zen **12** 85, *97*, 97–9, *101*; **18** *560*, *562*, *563*
Pure Land **12** 97
garnets **1** *206*
gates **18** 280
gesso **6** 717, 779
gilding **6** *300*, 706, 707, *710*, *719*, *720*, *722*; **15** *501*; **17** *34*, *107*, 110–12, *111*, *112*, *113*; **18** *285*, *287*, *294*, *295*, *296*, *607*; **22** *497*; **28** *582*; **29** *460*; **30** *844*
China **6** *708*
fire gilding **12** 626
glass **6** 717; **7** 82
glues **1** 202
gold **1** *206*; **7** 21, 23, 24, 25, 27; **18** 351–2; **30** 823, *836*
gold leaf **17** *116*
gongs **18** 348
grounds **29** 462
gypsum **1** 202
halls **14** 77; **17** *815*; **30** 575
hammering **17** 320
hardstones **7** 91; **22** *787*; **28** *582*
iconoclasm **15** 79–80
iconography **5** 87–8, *88*, 90–92*, 224, 462–3; **15** 779; **29** 458, 459
Afghanistan **1** 188–9, 198, 206
Burma **5** 237, 240
Cambodia **5** 495, 496, 499–500
Central Asia **5** 102
Central Asia, Eastern **6** 292–3*, 302, 303
Central Asia, Western **6** 194–5*
Champa **6** 427
China **5** 91; **6** 627–8*, 721, 799; **7** 34, 104–5, *105*
China: Lamaism **6** 627
China: Tantric **6** 627
Esoteric **5** 91, 92, 116; **7** 633
Indian subcontinent **3** 907; **5** *92*, 93, *96*; **7** 633; **15** 220–24*, 229, 416, 425, 428–9, 431–2, 446–8, 501
Indonesia **15** 757*, 777
Japan **5** 116, 118; **17** 33–9*, 107, 108, 109, 168
Japan: Esoteric **17** 37*, 146–7
Japan: Pure Land **17** 37–8*, 147–8
Japan: Zen **17** 38–9*
Java **15** 777
Korea **5** 91; **18** *254*, 254–5, 305–6, 307–9
Korea: Pure Land **18** 305–6
Lamaism **7** 104–5
Laos **18** 763
Mahayana **5** 91, 116
Mongolia **5** 91; **21** 872–3, 880
Nepal **5** 103; **22** 756–7*
Pure Land **5** 118
South-east Asia **5** 91
Sri Lanka **29** 442–4, *443*
Thailand **29** 826; **30** 573–4*, 594
Tibet **5** 91; **30** 809–11*, 813, 822, 825–6, 845
Vietnam **6** 427; **32** 470
image-houses **25** 169; **29** 443, *449*
incense burners **7** 68; **18** *348*, 348–9
inlays **18** *348*
inscriptions **6** 777; **17** 126; **30** 809
iron **6** 706, 721; **18** *290*, *291*

Buddhism
art—cont.
ivory **15** 695
ivory-carvings **7** 104–5, *105*
jewellery **6** 312*, *312*; **7** 108; **15** 700–701
kaolin **1** 202; **29** 462
kondō **17** 66
kuṇḍikās **18** 349
lacquer **7** 14; **17** *114*, 115–16, *116*, *130*; **18** 768
China **6** 706
dry **7** 14; **18** 606
Japan **17** 117, 118
Korea **18** 370
Nara period (AD 710-94) **17** *299*
urushi **18** *607*
Vietnam **32** 479, *479*, 482
libraries **19** 317
limestone **6** *217*; **19** *638*; **29** *457*; **30** *595*
lotus **19** 717; **23** 550
maṇḍalas **5** 90
Esoteric **5** 96
Indian subcontinent **5** 96; **26** *139*
Japan **5** 117, *117*, 119; **17** 37, 146
Pure Land **5** 119
Shingon **5** 117, *117*
Tibet **5** *104*, 104
manuals **6** 706
manuscript illumination
China **6** 782*
Indian subcontinent **5** *92*, 96, *96*; **15** 544, *545*, 549, 563, 570–71, 739
Korea **18** 304–5, *304*
Sri Lanka **29** 462
Thailand **30** 613–14, *614*
Tibet **30** 827, 828, 830, 836, *836*
manuscripts
Central Asia, Eastern **6** 303, 306
China **7** 114
Japan **17** 211, 217
Tibet **30** 836
marble **6** 706
masks **17** 394, 395
mass production **6** 314; **15** 448; **17** 320
metal **15** 499, *500*, *501*; **22** 768–9, 771, 773
metalwork **30** *849*
Afghanistan **1** 206
Central Asia, Eastern **6** 313
Mongolia **21** 878–9, *879*
Tibet **30** 841–3
monasteries **21** 846–8*
Bhutan **21** 848*
Cambodia **5** 481
Central Asia **5** 102
Central Asia, Eastern **6** 294, 296
China **7** 25
Gelugpa **5** 105
Indian subcontinent **1** 499; **21** 847*; **22** 447
Japan **5** 116, 120; **12** 97
Japan: Zen **17** 77, 231
Laos **18** 763, 764–6*, *765*
Mongolia **21** *874*, 875
Nepal **5** 103; **21** 847*; **22** 763, *763*, *764*, 765–6
Thailand **2** *886*; **29** *910*; **30** 574–5, 582, 585–6, *586*, 587–8, *588*
Tibet **5** 105; **21** 847–8*; **27** 695; **30** *351*, 808, *817*, 818, 828
Zen **5** 120
monuments **5** 234
moonstones **29** 443, *443*
moulds **1** 198; **6** 298, *298*
mounts (works on paper and scrolls) **22** *233*

Buddhism
art—cont.
musical instruments **17** 396; **21** 879; **30** 843
narratives
China **6** 788
Indian subcontinent **15** 442, 448; **22** 516*
Indonesia **15** 779
Japan **17** 149–50
Java **15** 779
necklaces **22** *787*
ornament **23** 550–51, 553, 555–6
orpiment **29** 462
pagodas **6** 666, 668; **18** *261*; **22** *499*; **23** 776
painting (general)
Japan: Ōbaku **17** 183–4*
painting (cultural and regional traditions)
Bhutan **3** 914–15*
Central Asia **5** 102
Central Asia, Eastern **6** 302
China **6** 776–85*, *780*, *781*
China: Chan **6** 782–5*
Indian subcontinent **15** 570, *570*
Japan **17** 144–50*, 156–7, 158–9, 166; **18** *223*
Japan: Asuka-Hakuhō period (*c*. 552-710) **17** *151*
Japan: Daigo **18** *557*
Japan: Heian period (AD 794-1185) **17** *147*, *148*
Japan: Nara period (AD 710-94) **17** *146*
Japan: Ōbaku **17** 189
Japan: Pure Land **5** *118*; **17** 38, 147–8
Japan: Zen **17** *193*, 194*
Korea **18** 303–12*, *310*, *374*
Mongolia **21** *873*, 880–81*
Nepal **22** *782*
Sri Lanka **29** 466
Thailand **30** 612–13*, *613*, *617*
Tibet **5** *104*; **21** 880–81; **30** *810*, 827–35*
Tibet: Sakyapa **30** 832
painting (flower) **6** 804
painting (fresco) **15** 570
painting (ink) **14** *62*; **17** 38–9; **18** **309*
Japan **17** 168–71
Japan: Zen **17** *169*
painting (landscape) **6** *784*; **17** *192*
painting (monochrome) **6** *785*
painting (panel) **6** 303
painting (screen) **17** 145
painting (scroll)
China **22** *325*
Japan **5** 119; **14** *62*; **17** *149*, *150*, *158*; **22** *233*
Korea **18** *305*
Mongolia **21** *880*
Nepal **22** *784*
Pure Land **5** 119
Tibet **30** *829*, *830*, *831*, *833*, *834*
painting (secco) **6** 301
painting (wall)
Afghanistan **1** 201–3*, *201*, *202*
Burma **5** 242*, *243*
Central Asia **5** *102*
Central Asia, Eastern **6** *292*, 294, *301*, 301–4*, *303*, *304*, *310*, *312*, 314; **32** 804
Central Asia, Western **6** 225–6*, *226*, 228, 232; **17** *734*
China **6** 776–9, *777*, *822*; **9** *393*; **32** 804
Indian subcontinent **1** 500; **15** *562*; **32** 804
Japan **17** 156
Laos **18** 770
Nepal **30** 833

Buddhism
art
painting (wall)—cont.
Sri Lanka **5** *97*; **25** 170; **29** 443, 462*
Thailand **30** *615*, 615–16*
Tibet **30** 827, 828, 829–30, 831–2, *832*, 833
palaces **30** *589*, *820*, 820
palmettes **23** 550
palm leaves **5** *96*; **15** 570; **30** 613
paper **30** 613
patronage
Central Asia, Eastern **6** 294–5*
Indian subcontinent **5** 95; **15** 737, 739
Japan **17** 421–3; **18** 213
Mahayana **5** 95
South-east Asia **29** 237
Tibet **5** 104; **30** 813–14*, 822, 828
paubhās **22** 781, *782*
pavilions (buildings) **18** *561*
pearls **6** 706
pedestals **15** 448
pigments **30** 835
pilgrimages **5** 97, *97*
pillars **15** *415*, 422–3; **17** 66; **27** 867
plaques **15** *221*
plaster **6** 706; **29** 823–4
polychromy **1** 198; **5** *100*; **6** *713*
ponds **12** 93
portraits **6** 718, 811, 812; **17** *130*, 130–32*, 184, 230; **18** 308–9; **30** *830*, 830–31
Japan **5** 120; **17** 36
Korea **18** 295
Zen **5** 120
pottery **6** 717; **17** 252
pouncing **30** 845
prayer flags **30** 845
prayer wheels **30** 842
printing
China **5** 110
Gelugpa **30** 845
woodblock **5** 115; **7** 624; **18** 354–6
prints
Central Asia, Eastern **6** 314
China **7** 117–18
Hossō **17** 270
Japan **17** 269, *270*
Tibet **5** 105
woodblock **7** 624; **17** 270, *270*; **30** 845
rafters **17** 66
reliquaries **26** 149–51*
Afghanistan **1** *206*
Central Asia, Eastern **6** 319
China **7** 24, 25, 82; **23** 776; **26** 150
Indian subcontinent **26** 149–50, *150*, *151*
Thailand **26** 151
Tibet **30** *849*
repoussé **17** 320
ritual objects **17** 320, 322, *322*
robes **18** *374*
rock art **30** 823
rock crystal **26** 487
rock reliefs **5** 107; **15** *464*, *466*
roof decorations **30** 842
roofs **17** 66, 72–3; **30** 842
rosaries **7** 90; **17** 386
sanctuaries **6** 296–7, *422*; **15** 759–62, *761*
sandstone **5** *100*, *462*, *498*; **15** *440*, *441*, *455*, *456*, *457*; **20** *819*; **27** *844*; **30** *600*, 606; **33** *574*
China **6** 706, *714*, *716*
schist **1** *197*; **15** *222*, 448
scripts **30** 832
scrolls **6** 779–81*; **22** 784, *784*; **28** 311; **30** 823
handscrolls **17** 145, 149–50

Buddhism
art
scrolls—cont.
hanging **6** 779, *784*; **7** *49*; **17** 145, *230*
tangkas **28** 309; **30** 827, 828, 830, 832–5, 845
sculptors **31** 676
sculpture (general) **5** 91; **9** 34; **17** 730; **18** 606; **28** *640*
conservation **17** 138
sculpture (cultural and regional traditions)
Afghanistan **1** *196*, 197–8*, *198*, *199*, 207; **3** 149
Burma **5** 239–42*, *240*, *241*; **18** *607*
Cambodia **5** *100*, *462*, 484, 485, 490, 494, *494*, 495–500*, *498*
Central Asia, Eastern **6** 294, 297–301*, *300*, 318–19, *319*; **29** *823*
Central Asia, Western **6** *194*, 215–17, *216*, *221*, 221–2*
Champa **6** 427–8*, *428*; **9** 133
China **6** 706–23*, 835; **7** 14, 68, 98, 99, 161; **19** 638–40, *639*
China: Han period (206 BC–AD 220) **12** 626
China: Lamaism **6** 722; **30** 443
China: Liao period (907-1125) **5** *111*
China: Ming period (1368-1644) **6** *719*, *720*
China: Northern and Southern Dynasties (AD 310- 589) **6** *708*, *710*; **12** 901; **19** *638*; **33** *574*
China: Northern Zhou period (AD 557-81) **23** 216
China: Qing period (1644-1911) **6** *722*
China: Song period (AD 960-1279) **6** *718*
China: Sui period (AD 581-618) **6** *713*
China: Tang period (AD 618-907) **6** *714*, *716*
China: Tantric **6** 719–20
Gelugpa **30** 822
Indian subcontinent **10** 484; **15** *222*, *223*, 415–16, *425*, *431*, 439–42*, *440*, *441*, 446–9, 451, 453–4*, *455*, *456*, *457*, *462*, *470*, 476, 499–502, *500*, *501*, 505, *505*, 521, *530*; **17** 857; **20** 818–19; **30** *220*
Indonesia **15** 776, *778*, 778–9, *782*
Japan **5** 120; **12** 626; **17** 97–8, 106*, *109*, *114*, *125*, 126–7*, *130*, 130–32*, 320; **22** *497*; **31** 167
Japan: Asuka-Hakuhō period (*c.* 552-710) **17** *375*
Japan: Asuka period (AD *c.* 552-645) **17** *34*, 106–9*, *107*
Japan: Edo period (1600-1868) **17** *126*
Japan: Esoteric **17** 118
Japan: Hakuhō period (AD 645-710) **17** *99*, *110*, 110–12*, *111*, *112*
Japan: Heian period (AD 794-1185) **17** *116*, 116–21*, *117*, *118*, *120*
Japan: Kamakura period (1185-1333) **17** 121–6*, *123*
Japan: Nara period (AD 710-94) **17** 113–16*, *113*, *299*
Java **15** 778, *778*, 779, *782*
Khmer **5** 100; **6** 430; **30** *600*
Korea **12** 626; **18** 282–96*
Korea: 6th cent. **18** *284*
Korea: 7th cent. **5** *114*; **18** *283*, *285*
Korea: 8th cent. **18** *287*, *288*

Buddhism
art
sculpture (cultural and regional traditions)—cont.
Korea: 9th cent. **18** *290*
Korea: 10th cent. **18** *288*, *291*, *292*
Korea: 14th cent. **18** *294*
Korea: 16th cent. **18** *295*
Laos **18** 763, 767, *768*, 770
Mahayana **6** 427
Maitreya **5** *114*
Malaysia **20** 170*
Mongolia **21** 880, 883*
Nepal **22** *758*, 758–9, 768–9, *769*, 770, *771*, 771, 773, *777*
South-east Asia **5** 100*; **29** 231
Sri Lanka **25** *170*; **29** 442, *457*, *458*, *460*, 461, *479*
Thailand **5** 100; **29** *911*; **30** 573–4, 593–5*, *594*, *595*, 596–7*, *597*, *598*, 599*, *600*, *601*, 601–4*, *602*, *605*, 605–6*, 607, *607*
Tibet **21** 880–81; **30** 351, 809, 821–7, *823*, *824*, *825*, *826*, *827*
Vietnam **5** *100*; **6** 427–8*; **9** 133; **32** 478, *478*, *479*, 479–80
Vietnam: Mahayana **6** *428*
sculpture (materials)
bronze **6** *719*; **17** *34*, 120, *375*
bronze: Afghanistan **1** 207
bronze: Burma **5** *240*, 241
bronze: Cambodia **5** 485
bronze: Central Asia, Eastern **6** 298
bronze: China **6** 706, 707, *708*, *710*, 712, 718, *720*, 720–22, 835; **7** 68
bronze: Indian subcontinent **15** *223*, 476, *530*, 530–31
bronze: Japan **17** *107*, *110*, 110–12, *111*, *113*, 320
bronze: Korea **5** *114*; **18** *284*, *285*
bronze: Laos **18** 768, *768*
bronze: Sri Lanka **29** *460*, *479*
bronze: Thailand **30** 593–5*, 596–7, *597*, *598*, *601*, 601–2*, *602*, *605*, *607*
bronze: Tibet **30** 351
Japan: Hakuhō period (AD 645-710) **17** *112*
stone **6** 221, *428*, 706, *713*, 718; **15** *500*, *501*, *505*, *778*, *782*; **18** 295; **22** *758*, 758–9, 770, *771*; **30** 593–5*, *594*, 823
wood **5** *100*; **6** 298, 300, 706, 717, 718, 721, *722*, 722; **17** *116*, 116–26*, *117*, *118*, *120*, *123*, *125*, *126*; **18** *292*, 295, *295*, 768; **30** 823; **32** 479, *479*
sculpture (relief) **5** *88*
Central Asia, Eastern **6** *299*
Central Asia, Western **6** *217*
China **6** 714
Indian subcontinent **5** *88*, *95*; **9** *35*; **15** *248*, *415*, 425–6, *429*, *435*, *437*, 442, 448, 453, *454*; **20** *819*
Indonesia **15** 779
Java **15** 779
Korea **18** *296*
Laos **18** 768–9
Thailand **30** *604*
shrines (i) (cult) **28** *636*
Central Asia, Eastern **28** *636*, 637
Indian subcontinent **28** 635
Japan **28** 639
Korea **28** 638
Sri Lanka **17** 769; **25** 169
Thailand **28** *640*
silk **18** *254*, 305, *374*

Buddhism
art—cont.
silver **15** *223*, *500*; **18** *348*; **22** *777*; **30** 823
China **7** 21, 23, 24, 25
Korea **18** 351–2
sites **4** 213; **15** 220; **29** 439, 442; **30** 53
soapstone **26** *151*
statuettes **6** 298
stelae **6** *711*; **15** 448; **29** 617
stencilling **30** 835
stone **6** 221, *428*; **15** *454*, *500*, *501*, *505*, *778*, *782*; **18** 295; **22** *758*, 758–9, 770, *771*; **30** 593–5*, *594*, 823
China **6** 706, *713*, 718–19
storehouses **22** *494*
straw **6** 706
stucco **1** 197–8; **30** 595*, 602–3*, *604*, 823
Central Asia, Eastern **6** 298; **29** *823*, 823–4
Indian subcontinent **15** 448; **29** 824
Thailand **29** 826
stupas **5** 88; **9** 86; **29** 863
Afghanistan **1** 191–2, *192*, 198; **3** 113
Burma **5** 224, *225*, *234*; **25** *890*; **29** 866, *866*
Cambodia **5** 481
Central Asia **5** 102; **29** 867*
Central Asia, Eastern **6** *297*, 297
China **29** 868*
Indian subcontinent **1** *500*, *754*; **5** 94, *95*; **15** 194, 220, 237, *262*, 431; **27** *709*; **29** 863–4*, *864*
Indonesia **29** 865, *866*
Japan **29** 869*
Korea **29** 868–9*
kumbum **13** *885*
Laos **18** 765*
Nepal **5** *103*; **29** 867–8*
pagoda-stupas **22** *459*
South-east Asia **5** 99; **29** 865–7*
Thailand **29** 866–7; **30** 576, *576*, *583*, 583–4, *584*, *586*, 586, *587*
Tibet **13** *885*; **29** 867–8*; **30** 842
see also chortens; *dāgabas*
sutras **5** 90; **17** 214
China **6** 781–2*; **7** *118*
Japan **7** 624; **17** 148, 211, 217–21, 270, 423
symbolism (critical term) **6** 632
tablets **17** 230; **30** 596, 606, 638*
tantras **5** 90
tea ceremonies **17** 336
tempera **1** 202; **29** 462
temples **30** 431
Bhutan **3** *913*
Burma **5** 233*; **23** *763*
Cambodia **5** 463*, *479*
Central Asia, Eastern **3** 902*; **6** 294, 319; **30** 441–2, *442*
Central Asia, Western **6** 200; **30** 440
China **5** 107; **6** 667–71, *670*; **9** 393–4; **30** 442–3*
China: Lamaism **30** 443
Ferghana **6** 200
Indian subcontinent **3** *905*; **15** *280*; **30** 437
Japan **5** *335*; **10** 404, *405*; **12** 97; **17** 46, 65–8*, *67*, *68*, *71*, *72*, *73*, *74*, 432, *748*; **20** *286*; **22** *490*, *503*; **30** *445*, 445–6*
Japan: Esoteric **18** 222
Japan: Pure Land **30** 445
Japan: Shingon **30** 445
Japan: Shōtoku **14** *774*
Japan: Tendai **30** 445
Japan: Zen **30** 446

Buddhism
art
temples—cont.
Java **30** 446
Khmer **30** *579*, 581
Korea **18** 260, 266–8*, *268*; **30** 444–5
Laos **18** 764–5*
Mongolia **30** *442*
rock-cut **6** 626; **15** 252–3, 464–5, 492; **22** 239; **30** 431, 437, 442–3*
Ryūkyū Islands **27** 470
Sri Lanka **29** *451*
Tendai **10** 404, *405*
Thailand **3** 164, *164*; **30** 446, *579*, 581, 589–90
Tibet **19** *294*; **30** *815*, 818–19, 842
Tokharistan **6** 200
Vietnam **30** 446; **32** 471–4*, *472*, *473*
terracotta **6** *298*; **15** *221*, *462*; **30** 595*
textiles **5** *104*; **6** 706; **18** 374
theories (art) **29** 462
thrones **30** 785
tower-sanctuaries **30** 575, 587
trays **17** *322*
trumpets **28** *582*; **30** *844*
turquoise **6** 706
type-faces **5** 112
varnishes **29** 462
wood **5** *100*; **6** 298, 300; **17** *116*, 116–26*, *117*, *118*, *120*, *123*, *125*, *126*; **18** *292*, 295, *295*, 768; **28** *636*; **30** 585–6, *586*, 823; **32** 479, *479*
China **6** 706, 717, 718, 721, 722, *722*
wood-carvings **6** 318–19*, *319*; **17** 100; **18** 295
writing **17** 229–31, *230*
branches
Esoteric **5** 87, 89, 90; **30** 809–11, *810*, 850
Bhutan **3** 912
China **5** 109, 110; **6** 626, 719–20, 777–8
iconography **15** 757
Indian subcontinent **5** 96; **10** 484–5
Indonesia **15** 757
Japan **5** 116–18*; **17** 270
Mongolia **5** 106
Tibet **5** 103–5; **30** 808
see also Lamaism
Greater Vehicle *see* Mahayana
Lamaism **6** 722; **7** 104–5; **30** 443
see also Esoteric
Lesser Vehicle *see* Theravada
Mahayana **5** 87, 89–90, 116, 473; **6** 746; **29** 442; **30** 809–11, *810*
Cambodia **5** 462, 476, 479
Central Asia **5** 101
Central Asia, Eastern **6** 303
Champa **6** 419
China **5** 107; **6** 626
Indian subcontinent **5** 95*, 96; **10** 147
Malaysia **20** 165
Vietnam **6** 419
Mantrayana *see* Esoteric
Tantrayana *see* Esoteric
Tantric *see* Esoteric
Theravada **5** 87, 89, 90, 462; **29** 442
Burma **5** 223; **29** 226
Cambodia **5** 462, 480; **29** 226
China **5** 107; **6** 626
Indian subcontinent **5** 93, 94
Laos **29** 226
Sri Lanka **5** 97; **29** 441
Thailand **29** 226
Vietnam **29** 226
Vajrayana *see* Esoteric
cultures and regions
Afghanistan **1** 188–9

Buddhism
cultures and regions—cont.
Burma **5** 99, 222, 223–4; **29** 231
Cambodia **5** 461, 462–3, 479, 480
Central Asia **5** 101–2*
Central Asia, Eastern **6** 290, 291*
Central Asia, Western **6** 194–5*
Champa **6** 420*, 421–2
China **5** 106–13*; **6** 618, 626*, 668, 740, 746, 748, 751–2, *752*, 756
Indian subcontinent **5** 93–7*; **6** 746; **15** 190, 202, 203–4
Indonesia **15** 756
Japan **2** 654; **5** 114, 115–16*, 120*; **6** 752; **12** 95, 97; **17** 21, 22, 215, 217–21; **28** 608
Java **5** 99
Korea **5** 113–15*; **18** 249, 252–3, 282
Laos **18** 763
Malaysia **20** 164
Mongolia **5** 106*; **21** 872*, 884
Nepal **5** 102–3*; **22** 755–6, 758
South-east Asia **5** 98–100*; **29** 234
Sri Lanka **5** 94, 97–8*; **29** 440, 441, 442–3, *443*, 462
Thailand **5** 99
Tibet **5** 103–5*; **19** 293; **27** 695; **30** 805–7, 808, 809–11, *810*, 813–14, 848, 850
Vietnam **6** 420*, 421–2
sects
Ambedkar **5** 93
Avataṁsaka **5** 115
Caodong **5** 109
see also Sōtō
Chan **5** 90, 109, 110; **6** 626, 748, 751–2, 784, *752*; **17** 215, 229–31
see also Ōbaku; Sŏn; Zen
Chogye **5** 115
Ch'ŏnt'ae **5** 115
Dharma Nature **5** 115
Drigungpa **30** 818
Faxiang **5** 109
Fayan **5** 109, 110
Gelugpa **5** 105; **30** 813, 819
Mongolia **5** 106
Tibet **21** 872, 880; **30** 807, 808
Guiyang **5** 109
Hossō **5** 116
Huayan **5** 109
Ji **5** 119
Jōdo **5** 119
Jōdo Shin **5** 119
Jōjitsu **5** 116
Kadampa **5** 105; **15** 397; **30** 808, 818, 819
Kagyupa **30** 813
Karmapa **5** 105; **30** 818
Kegon **5** 116
Kusha **5** 116
Kyo **5** 115
Linji **5** 109; **6** 752, *752*, 756
see also Rinzai
Madhyamika **5** 114
Mahasanghika **5** 93, 94
Maitreya **5** 114
Neo-Buddhism *see* Ambedkar
Nichiren **5** 119
Nirvana **5** 114, 115
Nyingmapa **27** 695; **30** 808
Ōbaku **5** 120; **17** 216; **20** 285, 286
Phagdupa **30** 818
Pŏpsang *see* Yogacara
Pŏpsŏng *see* Dharma Nature
Pure Land **5** 89, 90; **17** 68
China **5** 109, 110; **6** 626
Japan **5** 118–19*; **12** 97; **30** 445
Korea **5** 114, 115
Rinzai **5** 119; **6** 752; **14** 63
see also Linji
Ritsu **5** 116
Sakyapa **27** 600; **30** 808, 818

Buddhism
sects—cont.
Samnon *see* Madhyamika
Sanlun **5** 108
Sanron **5** 116
Sarvastivada **5** 94, 462
Shingi **5** 119
Shingon **5** 116; **14** 302; **17** 65, 68; **30** 445
Sōka Gakkai **5** 120; **17** 433
Sŏn **5** 115
see also Chan; Zen
Sōtō **5** 119
see also Caodong
Sthaviravada **5** 93
Tendai **5** 116; **10** 404; **14** 302; **17** 65, 68; **30** 445
Tiantai **5** 108, 114
Time *see* Ji
True Pure Land *see* Jōdo Shin
Vinaya **5** 109, 114, 115
Wŏnyung *see* Avatamsaka
Yangqi **6** 752, *752*
Yogacara **5** 115
Yŏlban *see* Nirvana
Yunmen **5** 109
Zen **5** 90, 119–20*; **6** 752; **7** 161; **12** *97*, 97–9; **14** 61; **17** 215, 270; **25** 891; **26** 140; **30** 446; **33** 635
see also Chan; Ōbaku; Sŏn
Buddhu **15** 633
Budé, Guillaume **14** 868, 869; **20** 334
works **20** *334*
Budé, Jean **20** 651; **21** 5
Budeč
architecture **8** 376
Budějovice, Václav of *see* VÁCLAV OF BUDĚJOVICE
Budeşti, Nicolae Ghika *see* GHIKA-BUDEŞTI, NICOLAE
Budge, E(rnest) A(lfred) T(hompson) Wallis **10** 91, 92
Budhanilkantha **5** 121*; **15** *261*; **22** *753*
sculpture **5** *121*; **22** 756, 767
Budhā Nilkaṇṭha *see* BUDHANILKANTHA
Budich, Bernardo *see* BOBIĆ, BERNARDO
Budini **28** 320
Budko, Joseph **17** 566
Búdrio **5** 796
Budslaŭ, Cathedral of the Assumption **3** 530
Buduruvagala **5** 98; **29** 442
Budva **22** *17*; **28** 452
St Mary **22** 19
Budzyniewicz, Wojciech **5** 121*; **25** 127
Budzyński, M. **25** 100
Buea **5** 525
Bueckelaer, Joachim *see* BEUCKELAER, JOACHIM
Bueil, Jacqueline Varde de, Comtesse de Moret *see* MORET, JACQUELINE VARDE DE BUEIL, Comtesse de
Buenaventura **7** *601*
Terminal de Ferrocarril **7** 606
Buenaventura, Teodoro **24** 622
Bueno, Alberto **6** 348
Bueno, Diego López *see* LÓPEZ BUENO, DIEGO
Bueno, León **10** 906
Bueno, Mauricio **5** 122*; **9** 713
Buenos Aires **2** 392, *393*, 394; **5** 122–3*; **31** 721
academies and art schools
Academia de Dibujo **2** 405
Academia Nacional de Bellas Artes **2** 405
Escuela Nacional de Bellas Artes 'Manuel Belgrano' **2** 405
Escuela Nacional de Bellas Artes 'Prilidiano Pueyrredón' **2** 399, 405, 406

Buenos Aires
academies and art schools—cont.
Escuela Superior de Bellas Artes 'Ernesto de la Cárcova' **2** 404, 405, 406; **5** 730
Instituto Torcuato di Tella **2** 394
Centro de Artes Visuales di Tella **2** 401
Instituto Vocacional de Arte (IVA) **2** 405
Alto Palermo shopping centre **2** 397
art forms and materials
architecture **2** 394
bronze **33** *569*
engravings **2** 398
painting **2** 398
sculpture **2** 398; **33** *569*
silver **2** 402; **4** 723
Banco Central de Argentina **2** 395
Belgrano Town Hall **2** 395
Biblioteca Nacional **2** 397, 404
Calle Chacabuco 78 **2** 396
Calle Rivadavia 2031 **2** 396
Casa de Bombas de la Recoleta *see* museums → Museo Nacional de Bellas Artes
Centro de Arte y Comunicación (CAYC) **2** 369, 401
churches
Cathedral of St John the Baptist (Anglican) **2** 395
Cathedral of the Immaculate Conception (Roman Catholic) **2** 394, 395, *395*, 398
silver **2** 402
La Compañía *see* S Ignacio
German Evangelical Church **2** 395
La Inmaculada Concepción **2** 395
La Merced **2** 394, 398
La Piedad **2** 395
El Pilar **2** 394
St Andrew **2** 395
S Felicitas **2** 396
S Francisco **2** 394, 402
S Ignacio **2** 394, 398, 402
S José de Flores **2** 395
cinemas and theatres
Gran Rex Cinema **2** 396
Teatro Colón **2** 396; **5** *122*
Teatro General San Martín **2** 397
City Hall **2** 395
commercial buildings
ATC headquarters **2** 397
Banco de Londres y América del Sur *see* Lloyds Bank
Casa Moussion *see* Fundación Banco Patricios
Club del Progreso **2** 395
Comega building **2** 397
Fundación Banco Patricios **2** 396
Galería Jardín **2** 397
Galerías Pacífico **2** 397; **6** 10
IBM offices **2** 397
Kavanagh building **2** 397
Lloyds Bank **2** 397; **30** 525
Paseo Alcorta shopping centre **2** 397
Prourban office tower **2** 397
Safico building **2** 397
Somisa Headquarters **1** 743
Stock Exchange **2** 396
Telephone building **2** 397
Escuela Carlos della Penna **2** 397
Estuario building **2** 397
Galería Witcomb **2** 404
government buildings
Casa de Gobierno **2** 396, *396*
Casa Rosada *see* Casa de Gobierno
Congreso Nacional **2** 396
Customs House **2** 395
Foreign Office **2** 396

Buenos Aires—cont.
25 de Mayo tower **2** 397
Metro stations **21** 349
Monastery of La Recoleta **2** 405
museums
Jewish museum **17** 582
Museo de Arte Colonial *see* Museo Saavedra
Museo de Arte Isaac Fernández Blanco **2** 396; **5** 123
Museo de Arte Moderno **2** 405
library **2** 406
Museo Badii **2** 401; **3** 37
Museo de Calcos y Escultura Comparada **2** 404; **5** 730
Museo Casa de Yrurtia **33** 570
Museo Municipal de Arte Colonial *see* Museo Saavedra
Museo Municipal de Artes Plásticas Eduardo Sívori **26** 385
Museo Nacional de Arte Decorativo **2** 405; **5** 123
library **2** 406
Museo Nacional de Bellas Artes **2** 399; **5** 123
collections **2** 404; **8** 273; **29** 641
library **2** 406
Museo Saavedra **2** 405
Old Stock Exchange *see* Banco Central de Argentina
Palacio Anchorena *see* government buildings → Foreign Office
Pirámide de Mayo **2** 395
residential buildings
Avenida del Libertador 3590 **2** 396
Calle M. T. de Alvear 534 **2** 397
Calle Salguero 2450 **2** 397
Calle Virrey del Pino 2446 **2** 397; **15** 886
Palermo de San Benito **2** 395
Le Parc apartment tower **2** 397
San Isidro
Casa Moores **2** 397
Museo General Juan Martín de Pueyrredón **2** 395
Sociedad Estímulo de Bellas Artes **2** 399
Buen Retiro porcelain factory *see* FÁBRICA DEL BUEN RETIRO
Bueras, Melchor de **3** 418
Bueren, Johann von **18** 497
Bueren, Nicolaus von **18** 497
Bufalini, Maria **24** 199
Bufalini, Niccolò di Manno **24** 830
Bufalo (family) **31** 825
Bufalo, Antonio da *see* ANTONIA DA BUFALO
Bufalo, Ottavio del, Marchese **5** 123*
Bufalo, Paolo del, Marchese **5** 123*
bufetes *see* SIDEBOARDS
Buffa, Frans & Zn **23** 1; **33** 47
Buffagnotti, Carl Antonio **4** 46
Buffalini, Andrea **9** 331
Buffalmacco **5** 123–4*; **20** 776
attributions **2** 625, 628; **20** 776
works **24** 860
Buffalo (NY) **5** 124*; **31** *587*
Albright-Knox Art Gallery **5** 124; **18** 170
Darwin D. Martin House **24** 291; **33** 246
Guaranty Building **19** 365; **23** 359; **29** *914*; **30** 505; **31** 594
Kleinhans Hall **7** 687
Larkin Building **4** 788; **10** 417; **21** 780; **23** 360; **31** 595, 633; **33** 401–2
Martin House **2** 360
Prudential Building *see* Guaranty Building
State University of New York Burchfield Art Center **5** 124

Buffalo, Charles O. *see* OHETTOINT
buffalo hide *see under* HIDES → types
Buffalo Meat **5** 124–5*
buffalo trappings *see under* TRAPPINGS → types
Buffavento Castle **8** 357, 361
Buffequin, Georges **30** 659, 660
Buffet, Bernard **5** 125*
groups and movements **14** 701; **27** 307
patrons and collectors **12** 724
works **11** 551
Buffet, John **24** 891
Buffet-Picabia, Gabrielle **23** 569
buffets
historical and regional traditions
Belgium **3** 581, 583
France **8** 271; **9** 30; **11** 586, *586*, 587, 589
materials
oak **11** 589
walnut **11** *586*, 587
see also CUPBOARDS
Buffi, Jean-Pierre **22** 49
Buffington, LeRoy Sunderland **5** 125–6*; **10** 146; **14** 317
Buffington Iron Building Company **5** 126
Buffon, Georges-Louis Leclerc, Comte de **4** 366
book illustrations **19** 144; **20** 497, *604*
engravings **3** 318, 591; **20** 604; **28** 522; **31** 220
Buffoni, Decio **27** 788
Bufford, John H. **14** 699; **17** 617
bugaku *see under* THEATRE→ types
Bugarama **5** 285
Bugarski, Aleksandar **28** 444
Bugatti, Carlo **5** 126–7*; **28** 354
assistants **25** 793
groups and movements **2** 567
works **11** 397; **16** 721, 731; **22** 60; **25** 767
Bugatti, Ettore **5** 126, 127
Bugatti, Giovanni Luigi **5** 126
Bugatti, Jean **5** 126
Bugatti, Rembrandt **2** 100; **5** 126, 127*; **11** 568
Bugatto, Zanetto **5** 127–8*; **7** 898; **28** 531
collaboration **3** 695; **11** 293
patrons and collectors **28** 531; **31** 843
teachers **28** 531; **33** 118, 126
works **5** *128*
Bugayev, Boris (Nikolayevich) *see* BELY, ANDREY
Buggiano **5** 128–9*
works **5** *128*; **11** 197, 198, 209; **21** 10; **27** 830
Bugiardini, Agostino **23** 264
Bugiardini, Giuliano (di Piero di Simone) **5** 129*
collaboration **1** 572
pupils **27** 648
works **3** 306; **11** *383*, 389; **26** 816; **28** 335
Buginese **15** 753, 796
Bugios **32** 539
Bugis **20** 174
Bugis *keris* *see under* KERIS → types
bugles **22** 375
Bugliaco, Villa Bettoni **16** 719
Buglioni, Benedetto **5** 130*; **19** 412
Buglioni, Francesco **5** 130
Buglioni, Santi (di Michele Viviano) **5** 130–31*; **21** 452
Bugnon Altar **11** 787
Bugthorpe **6** 161
Buguda, Viranchi Narayana Temple **15** 541, 636
buguru houses *see* AFRICA→ houses

Buhagiar, Emanuele **5** 131*; **20** 215
Buhagiar, Gian Nicola **5** 131*; **20** 213
buhardilla del arte, La **24** 452
Buhen **9** *774*, 851; **23** *276*, 278; **30** 237
carpets **7** 827
fort **9** 825, 844, 845, *845*, 846–7, *847*; **10** 81; **21** 554, 555
metalwork **9** 818
temples **23** 279
Temple of Amun **23** 281
Temple of Hatshepsut **10** 803
Temple of Isis **9** 832
Temple of Tuthmosis III **10** 803
Bühler, Denis **1** 685
Buhler, Gen.
Natakhamani, King of Kush (*reg c.* 1st cent. AD) **30** 414
Bühler, Hans **4** 747
Bühler, Wolfgang **20** 803
Bühler-Oppenheim, Alfred **29** 178
Bühler-Oppenheim, Kristin **29** 178
Buhlig, Richard **5** 381
Buhot, Félix (-Hilaire) **5** 131*; **9** 309; **10** 396
Bührle, Emil Georg **5** 131–2*
collections **30** 152, 153; **33** 737
Buić, Jagoda **11** 54; **30** 329, 330
Buijs, C. B. **21** 175
Buijs, J. **18** 879
Buijs, Jacobus **7** 662
Buijs, Jan (Willem Eduard) **5** 132*; **14** 295; **22** 831
Buijs and Lürsen **4** 216
Buijssens, Jan Baptist, I **32** 241
Builder **12** 841; **14** 156; **24** 446
Builder, The **2** 315, 333; **10** 235; **13** 204
builders **2** 362; **20** 559
Egypt, ancient **9** 826
Greece, ancient **13** 395
Islamic **16** 143
see also ARCHITECTS
Builders, Gerard **14** 42
Builder's Magazine or Monthly Companion for Architects, Carpenters, Masons, Bricklayers **24** 445
building **2** 361
see also ARCHITECTURE
building contractors **20** 559, 560
England **7** 420; **8** 248; **20** 561
Greece, ancient **13** 395
building machinery *see* CONSTRUCTION MACHINERY
Building News **24** 445
building regulations **5** 40, 132–7*, *133*, *134*; **7** 429; **13** 395; **26** 887, 891
see also ENVIRONMENTAL DESIGN
buildings **2** 362
building services **28** 831
building speculation *see* PROPERTY DEVELOPMENT
building techniques *see* ARCHITECTURE → techniques
Building World **28** 349
Buirette, Jacques **19** 242
Buisson, R. du Mesnil du **25** 777
Buitrago, Hospital de S Salvador **9** 264; **15** 834
Buitrago, Pedro de **29** 336
Buitre **29** 364
Buix, Domingo **24** 560
Buixadé, Carles **7** 884
Bui Xuan Phai **32** 483
works **32** *483*
Bujil, Master **13** 166
Bujumbura **1** *407*
Living Museum **5** 285
Bük, Nagy Mansion **14** 886
Buka **23** 728, 735
Bukhara **3** 168; **5** 137–41*; **6** *182*, 186, 201, 204–5, 210, 211; **16** *105*; **28** 721; **30** 253; **31** *781*, 781
art forms and materials
architecture **16** 196; **30** 252; **31** 782; **32** 309
carpets **6** 254; **16** 484
coins **6** 265, 266
dress **6** *252*
embroidery **6** 250; **31** 783
felt **10** 874
jewellery **6** 242, 274
manuscript illumination **6** *234*, 235, 236; **16** 332
manuscripts **5** *138*; **16** 326, 327, 342–3
metalwork **16** 370; **31** 783
pottery **6** 257, 258, 259
sculpture **6** 222
textiles **6** 250; **16** 451; **31** 783
tiles **6** 207
toys **6** 277
woodwork **16** 502
baths **6** 211
bazaars **6** 211
citadel **6** 210
fortifications **21** 584, 589, 592
Goldsmiths' Market *see* Taq-i Zargaran
Hatters' Market *see* Taq-i Tilpaq-furushan
houses **16** 269
Islamic religious buildings
Baha' al-Din *khānaqāh* **6** 205
Bala-khauz complex **31** 782
Balyand Mosque **29** 822
Char-minar Madrasa of Caliph Niyazkul **31** 782
congregational mosque **16** 163
Faizabad *khānaqāh* **6** 204
Farjak Madrasa **5** 137
Grand Mosque *see* Masjid-i Kalan
Kalan Mosque (1370) **5** 139–40*; **6** 203, 211
minaret **5** *140*; **6** 202, 206, 207
mosaics **6** 208
Kukeltash Madrasa **6** 278
Lab-i Hawz complex **6** 205; **16** 235, 236
Madar-i Khan Madrasa **6** 204
madrasa of ʿAbd al-ʿAziz **6** 205, 208
madrasa of ʿAbdallah Khan **6** 204, 208
madrasa of Nadr Bi Arlat **6** 208; **16** 239
madrasas **6** 211; **16** 235
Magoki Attari Mosque **5** 139*, *139*; **6** 202, 207
Magoki-Khurpa Mosque **6** 205
Masjid-i Boland **16** 237
Masjid-i Kalan **16** 236, 245
Masjid-i Zayn al-Din **16** 237
minarets **16** 160, 237
Mir-i ʿArab Madrasa **6** 204, *205*, 278; **16** 237
ivory-carvings **6** 272
mosaics **6** 208
Mokh Mosque *see* Magoki Attari Mosque
musalla **22** 354
Namzagah Mosque **6** 206
Qul Baba Kukaltash Madrasa **6** 204; **16** 235, 236, 237
shrine of Chashma-i Ayyub **16** 197
Ulughbeg Madrasa **6** 203; **16** 197
market of ʿAbdallah Khan **6** 204
markets **16** 238
Mausoleum of Buyan Quli Khan **5** 140–41*; **6** 207
Mausoleum of Sayf al-Din Bakharzi **5** 140–41*; **6** 277; **16** 91
Bukhara—cont.
Mausoleum of the Samanids **4** 791; **5** 137, 139*; **6** 201, 206, 277; **16** 159, *159*, 491
squinches **16** 161
Moneychangers' Market *see* Taq-i Sarrafan
Museum **6** 283
palace **16** 238; **23** 820
ramparts **6** 211
Registan **6** 211
Taq-i Sarrafan **6** 204
Taq-i Tilpaq-furushan **6** 204
Taq-i Zargaran **6** 204; **16** *237*
tomb of Baha' al-Din Naqshband **16** 237
tomb of Bulyan Quli Khan **16** 248
urban planning **6** *211*; **16** 264
warehouses **16** 238
Bukhari **16** 86
Bukharin, Nikolay (Ivanovich) **5** 141*
Bukhvostov, Yakov **5** 141*; **27** 372, 460
Bukidnon **24** 630
Bukov, Nikolay **5** 159
Bukovac, Vlaho **5** 141–2*; **8** 178; **18** 473; **22** 17; **33** 593
groups and movements **18** 411
patrons and collectors **8** 181; **22** 19
pupils **18** 230, 434; **25** 832
works **8** *179*
Bukovat Monastery **25** 344
Bukowski **8** 759; **30** 118
Bukowski, Jan **29** 791
Bülach **30** 145
Bulandibagh
figurines **15** 718; **24** 264; **30** *510*
glass **15** 694
Bulang **18** 484, 489
Bulaq Press **16** 361
Bulatov, Erik (Vladimirovich) **5** 142*; **27** 397; **29** 89
Bulatov, Mutkhat (Sagadatginovich) **31** 782
Bulatova, V. A. **18** 540
Bulawayo, Mzilikazi Art And Craft Centre **33** 680
Bulayiq **6** 307
library **6** 292
bulbous domes *see under* DOMES→ types
Bulckaert, L. **3** 884
Buldra, František **30** 221
Bulfin, Michael **16** 22
Bulfinch, Charles **4** 786; **5** 142–3*; **10** 850; **13** 237
architecture **31** 591
churches **5** *143*; **25** 266
civic buildings **4** 472
government buildings **3** 730; **4** *473*; **14** 202; **30** 761; **32** 892
hospitals **4** 472
law courts **18** 886, 887
urban planning **4** 472
collaboration **27** 613
models **33** 195
staff **33** 195
Bulgakov, Mikhail **31** 572
Bulgakova, Olga **27** 397
Bulgar (people) **27** 434
Bulgar (Tartarstan) **27** 434
Bulgaria **5** 143–64*, *144*
architecture **5** 145–50*
Byzantine **5** 147; **9** 551–2
archives **2** 369
art history **5** 163–4*
brass **5** 160
calendars **32** 149
carpets **5** 161
cathedrals **5** *149*
ceramics **5** 158–9*, *159*
churches **5** 145–7, 148–9
Byzantine **9** 551–2
Early Christian (*c.* AD 250-843) **5** *145*; **25** 559
rock **26** 483
Bulgaria—cont.
collections **5** 162–3*
photographs **5** 162–3*
prints **5** 163
copper **5** 160
education (art) **5** 163–4*
embroidery **5** 161
engravings **5** 154
fortifications **21** 551
furniture **5** 157–8*
galleries (iv) (art) **5** 150
glass **5** 159*
gold **5** 160; **25** *517*
Gospel books **5** 160, *160*
hangings **5** 161, *162*
historiography **5** 163–4*
houses **5** 147–8, 156
housing **5** 150
icons **5** 151–2*, *152*, 154; **9** 633; **25** 338–9*, 559
inns **5** *148*
interior decoration **5** 156–7*, *157*
iron **5** 160–61
jewellery **5** 160
kilims **5** 161
lace **5** 161
libraries **5** 162–3*
liturgical furnishings **7** 279
manuscript illumination **5** 152–3*
manuscripts **5** 152, 162
markets **5** 148
metalwork **5** 155, *160*, 160–61*
miniatures (manuscript illumination) **5** *153*
monasteries **5** 147
mosques **5** 148
museums **5** 162–3*
obelisks **5** 156
painting **5** 150–55*
Byzantine **5** 152
tomb **5** 150
wall **5** 150–51*, *151*, 153–4; **9** *579*, 582; **25** 342–3*; **30** *768*
20th cent. **5** *154*
panels (wall) **5** 159, *159*
patronage **5** 162*
periodicals **22** 539
pewter **5** 160
plaques **25** *517*
pottery **9** 633; **17** *808*
printing **5** 154
prints **5** 163
Psalters **9** 613
screens (i) (architectural) **5** 159
iconostases **5** 155
sculpture **5** 155–6*
settlements **25** 499
silver **5** 152, *160*, 160
synagogues **17** 545
textiles **5** 161*
theatres **5** 150
tiles **5** 159; **9** 633
tombs **5** 150, 155
trade **9** 515
wood **5** 155–6
wood-carvings **5** 155–6
Bulgarini (da Siena), Bartolommeo **5** 164–5*
attributions **4** 30
teachers **19** 668
works **4** 30; **5** *164*; **31** 57
Bulgarini, Bulgarino **12** 525
Buli **14** 377, 378
Bulič, Branko **28** 445
Bulić, Frane **27** 638
Buli Master **19** 744
Buljovčić, Mirko **4** 463
bulk elemental analysis *see under* TECHNICAL EXAMINATION→ types
Bulkington, St James **11** 255
Bull, Georg (Andreas) **5** 165*; **23** 602
Bull, Henrik **5** 165–6*
works **23** 221, *222*, 602
Bull, John **14** 675
Bull, Ole **23** 242
Bull, Randolf **7** 441
Bull, Thelma **14** 223; **32** 153
Bulla **13** 306
Bulla, G. B. **8** 386
bullae **10** 636; **21** 271; **28** 537
Bull and Jeffryes **18** 149
Bullant, Jean **5** 166*; **11** 513; **20** 133; **23** 492
attributions **19** 693
patrons and collectors **11** 656; **22** 31; **31** 850
works **6** 453, 506, *545*, 546; **9** 707; **11** 514; **25** 577
writings **2** 356; **31** 296
Bulla Regia **1** *376*; **23** 299
Basilica I **9** 570
Basilica II **9** 570
Baths of Julia Memmia **3** 374
House of the Hunt **26** 920
houses **1** 377
macellum **19** 889
mosaics **27** 63, 67
Bulle, H. **23** 476
Bullemont, A. de **5** 24
Bullet (de Chamblain), Jean-Baptiste **5** 167–8*
works **4** 578; **6** 508, 509, *509*
Bullet, Martin **5** 167
Bullet, Pierre **5** 167*
collaboration **5** 167
pupils **5** 167
teachers **4** 165
works **7** 360; **16** 814; **24** 118
writings **31** 296
Bulletí dels museus d'art de Barcelona **24** 452
Bulletin **24** 439
Bulletin, The **2** 769; **24** 437
Bulletin archéologique **24** 422
Bulletin D **3** 4
Bulletin de la classe des beaux-arts **24** 439
Bulletin de la Gilde de Saint-Thomas et de Saint-Luc **24** 439
Bulletin de la Société de l'histoire de l'art français **11** 675
Bulletin de la vie artistique **3** 826
Bulletin de l'école française d'extrême orient **24** 437
Bulletin des métiers d'art **24** 439
Bulletin du Musée d'Ethnographie du Trocadéro **24** 430
Bulletin du Musée hongrois des Beaux-Arts **24** 441
Bulletin du musée national de Varsovie **24** 441
Bulletin KNOB **24** 450
Bulletin monumental **6** 95; **24** 422
Bulletin of the Allen Memorial Art Museum **29** 584
Bulletin of the American Art-Union **24** 431
Bulletin of the Archives of American Art *see* JOURNAL OF THE ARCHIVES OF AMERICAN ART
Bulletin of the College Art Association *see Art Bulletin*
Bulletin of the Madras Government Museum **24** 436
Bulletin of the Metropolitan Museum of Art **24** 433
Bulletin of the Museum of Fine Arts Boston **24** 433
Bulletin of the Society for the Study of Architecture in Canada/Société pour l'étude de l'architecture au Canada **24** 430
Bullettino **24** 447
Bullettino delle arti del disegno e dei mecenati di quelle in Italia **24** 447
Bullettino di archeologia cristiana **8** 781
Bulleus, Hans **13** 646
Bullinger, Heinrich **33** 745
Bullinger, Johann Balthasar, I **5** 168*; **33** 736
patrons and collectors **33** 196
pupils **33** 424
works **10** 464; **30** 132

Bullinger, Johann Balthasar, II 5 168
Bullion, Claude de 4 125; 5 168*; 27 821; 32 718
Bull Mosaic 10 56
Bullock, Edwin 4 86
Bullock, George 5 168–9*; 19 507
groups and movements 26 85
patrons and collectors 28 287
works 4 806, 883; 10 297, 298; 11 119; 20 468; 23 545
Bullock, J. F. W. 22 810
Bullock, William (d c.1827) 5 169; 10 97; 21 265; 22 678; 23 740
works 21 265
Bullock, William (d 1867) 25 594
Bullock, Wynn 5 169–70*
Bullough, Edward 1 181
Bulloz, Jacques-Ernest 26 514
Bull Palette 9 868; 23 848
Bullrich, A. Cazzaniga de 30 525
Bullrich, F. 30 525
bull's eye windows see WINDOWS → types → oeil-de-boeuf
bullwheels 7 765
Bully 26 598
Bulmer, William 4 362; 25 164
Bulnes, Oscar 22 21
Bulnes Valero, Oscar 21 381
bulol see SCULPTURE → types bulul
Bulolengabip 24 73
Bulova 7 448
Bulovka Dermatology Unit 8 402
Bulow-Hube, Sigrun 5 573
Bülow-Hübe, Torun 30 113
Buls, Charles (François Gommaire) 5 170*; 31 727
works 3 620; 5 42; 14 386; 16 878
Bulsinck, Gert 13 161
Bulstrode Park (Bucks) 6 118
Bulthuis, Jan 23 299
Bultinc, Pieter 21 102
Bulu 10 787, 791
Buluggin, Ruler (reg 972-84) (Zirid) 33 686
bulul see under SCULPTURES→ types
Buluma, Mordechai Ochungo 31 528
Bulunbulum, Johny 1 67
Buluñits 3 45
bulwarks 3 359
Bulwer, Henry 9 451
Buma 1 403
Bumaldo, G. A. see MONTALBANI, OVIDIO
Bumilâtre, Alphonse Jean 4 390
Bumpstead, John 18 31
Bumstead, J. F., & Co. 32 815
Bumstead, Thomas 4 481
Bumthang 3 912
Tamshing 3 915
Bünau, Heinrich von see HEINRICH VON BÜNAU
Bünau, Heinrich von, Count 33 241
Bunbury, Henry William 5 171*
reproductive prints by others 4 751; 8 864; 17 630; 18 149; 27 278; 29 676
Bunce, William Gedney 27 557
Bunce Island 28 691
Bunchō Ippitsusai see IPPITSUSAI BUNCHŌ
Bunchō Kitsu see KITSU BUNCHŌ
Bunchō Tani see TANI BUNCHŌ
Bundala
dune 29 445
Iranamadu Formation 29 444
Bundarabad Mosque 16 199
Bundel, Willem van den 17 647; 22 844
Bundelkhand 6 444; 15 596, 602
Bundesamt für Kultur 30 152
Bundesverband der Bildarchive 2 370
Bundesverband der Deutschen Industrie (BDI) 12 472
Bund für Heimatschutz 2 571
Bundi (Papua New Guinea) 15 276; 24 75
Bundi (Rajasthan) 5 171*; 15 597
Badal Mahal 15 604, 605, 608
Chatar Mahal 15 605
Chitrashala 15 605
palace 15 388, 389
Bundikalam see BUNDI SCHOOL
Bundi school 15 603–7*
works 15 604, 606, 607
bundled pilasters see under PILASTERS→ types
Bundock, Mary 1 66
Bund Österreichischer Kunsterzieher 2 832
Bundt, Livinius van der 22 853
Bundura, Cristoforo see BONADURA, CRISTOFORO
Bundzhikat 5 171–2*; 6 182; 16 105; 30 252
jewellery 6 274
palace 32 321
wall paintings 5 172
Bunel, François, the elder (d 1580) 5 172
Bunel, François, the younger (1552-before 1599) 5 172; 30 746
Bunel, Jacob 5 172*; 24 134
collaboration 9 385
pupils 32 509
reproductive prints by others 4 547
works 29 917
Bunel, Marguerite see BAHUCHE, MARGUERITE
Bunel, Raullin 14 83
Bunendō 17 294
bungalows see under HOUSES→ types
Bungay, John 10 316
Bungay, Peter 10 316
Bunge, Ernesto 2 396
Bunge Church 13 120
Bunge Master 11 98; 13 120; 30 83
Bungorō III see YOSHIDA BUNGORŌ III
Buniatyan, Nikolay 13 653
Büning, Wilhelm 3 796
Buniyar, Vishnu Temple 15 266
Bunjinga see JAPAN → painting → Nanga
Bunkachō see CULTURAL AFFAIRS AGENCY
Bunkado see NISHIKAWA SUKENOBU
Bunker, Dennis Miller 5 174*
Bunkō Kitsu see KITSU BUNKŌ
Bunmei Oku see OKU BUNMEI
Bunnens, Guy 30 873
Bunnick, Jan van 27 518
Bunning, J. B. 10 669; 16 52
Bunning, W. R. 2 742
Bunning & Madden 5 602
Bunny, Rupert (Charles Wulsten) 5 174–5*
Bunpō Kawamura see KAWAMURA BUNPŌ
Bunpo Nakayama see NAKAYAMA, BUNPO
bunraku see under PUPPETS→ types; THEATRE → types
Bunrakuken Uemura see UEMURA BUNRAKUKEN
Bunraku no shibai see UEMURA BUNRAKUKEN II
Bunratty Castle (Co. Clare) 16 25
Bunrei Katō see KATŌ BUNREI
Bunriha kenchikukai see SECESSION (JAPAN)
Bunrin Shiokawa see SHIOKAWA BUNRIN
Bunsaburō Yoshida see YOSHIDA BUNSABURŌ
Bunsai Isono see ISONO BUNSAI
Bunsei 5 175*; 17 172; 18 314; 30 466
Bunshaft, Gordon 5 175–6*; 16 101; 28 818
collaboration 23 176
works 3 177; 14 200; 15 887; 23 43; 27 876; 28 818; 31 597; 32 888
Bunshōjo see SHIMIZU ONOE
Bunshō Jugaku see JUGAKU, BUNSHŌ
Bunshu Isshi see ISSHI BUNSHU
Bunt see REVOLT GROUP
Bunten (Ministry of Education Art Exhibition) 17 134, 201, 205, 424, 435
see also TEITEN
Buntingford, St Peter 4 786
Bunton, Sam, & Associates 28 231
Buñuel, Luis 8 465; 10 687; 23 169; 30 20, 21
works 10 687
Bunyan, John 3 193; 4 360
Bunzel, Ruth 22 673, 676
Bunzlau 12 428, 430, 431
Buon (i) (family) 32 190
Buon (i), Bartolomeo (c.1400-10-c.1464-7) 5 176–7*; 13 95; 16 692; 20 728
attributions 5 176
collaboration 12 666; 16 692; 32 189, 218
patrons and collectors 13 657, 658
teachers 5 176
works 5 176; 11 328; 13 95; 16 825; 32 215, 215
workshop 32 227, 228
Buon (ii), Bartolomeo (c. 1450-?1509) 5 177–8*; 32 227
Buon (i), Giovanni 5 176; 13 95; 20 728
collaboration 5 176; 16 692; 32 189, 218
patrons and collectors 11 328
pupils 12 666
works 16 692
Buon (ii), Pietro 5 177–8*; 32 227
assistants 13 649
attributions 13 649
collaboration 13 650
works 28 37, 37; 31 717
Buonaccorsi, Pietro see PERINO DEL VAGA
Buonaccorsi, Raimondo 3 109; 5 178*; 12 30; 29 33, 40
Buonaccorso, Niccolò di see NICCOLÒ DI BUONACCORSO
Buonaccorso di Pace 23 90
Buonafede, Leonardo di Giovanni 5 130, 131; 27 207
Buonaiuto di Giovanni 4 31, 32
Buonajuto, Raphael 33 515
Buonamici, Agostino see TASSI, AGOSTINO
Buonamico di Lapo Guidalotti see GUIDALOTTI, BUONAMICO DI LAPO
Buonamico di Martino see BUFFALMACCO
Buonanni 8 845
Buonarroti, Filippo 2 164; 8 708; 10 637, 642; 13 541
Buonarroti, Michelangelo (1475-1564) see MICHELANGELO (BUONARROTI)
Buonarroti, Michelangelo (1568-1646) 4 53; 5 178–9*; 7 908; 27 178
Buonauiti 11 362
Buoncompagni, Pietro 1 627
Buonconsiglio, Giovanni 5 179–80*
works 5 179
Buonconsiglio Castle see under TRENT
Buoncuore, Giovanni Battista 26 242
Buoncuore, Martino 12 657
Buondelmonte, Christopher 5 181*; 15 149
works 8 155; 16 584
Buoneri, Francesco 5 702
Buonfigli, Benedetto see BONFIGLI, BENEDETTO
buon fresco see FRESCOES
Buoni de Pellezuoli, Donato 3 544; 12 517
Buono, Carlo Antonio 5 182, 297
Buono, Giuseppe 5 182
Buono, Lippo di see LIPPO DI BUONO
Buono, Silvestro 15 147
Buono, Vincenzo del 3 869
Buono di Jacopo, Mariano del see MARIANO DEL BUONO DI JACOPO
Buono di Marco, Marco del see MARCO DEL BUONO DI MARCO
Buonsignori, Stefano 16 771; 20 365
Buontalenti, Bernardo 5 182–4*; 16 724; 21 23; 24 404, 853; 27 274
architecture
belvederes 11 180
casinos (i) (garden) 21 23
cathedrals 19 511; 21 24
fortresses 3 689; 21 24
galleries (iv) (art) 9 14; 11 215; 16 771
government buildings 32 15
grottoes 5 183; 11 214; 13 703; 16 696
palaces 5 361; 11 215; 21 23; 24 853; 28 734
palazzi 11 187
theatres 30 656
urban planning 19 511; 31 718
attributions 18 690
collaboration 4 83; 5 360; 19 709; 28 733
fountains 11 343
furniture 5 350
gardens 2 837; 11 187
objects of vertu 4 53; 16 747
patrons and collectors 3 226; 11 191; 16 746, 771; 21 22, 441; 25 452; 27 323
porcelain 7 165; 11 191
pupils 7 311, 492; 23 139; 24 112, 771
stage design 5 184; 30 656, 657, 667
Buonvicini, Nicola 4 407
Buonvisi (family) 20 709
Buonvisi, Girolamo 30 527
Buonvisi Painter 11 747
Buora, Andrea 32 214
Buora, Giovanni di Antonio 7 517; 19 554; 32 192, 214, 225
works 32 226
Bupalos 2 308; 5 185*
Bu Qianqiu 6 697
Bu Qi ding 6 848
Buqras 5 185–6*; 30 180
beads 30 182
figurines 5 186
frieze 30 182
plaster 30 196
pottery 30 196
sculpture 30 192
seals 1 856
wall paintings 30 197
Buquet de Montvallier, Jean-Baptiste Suzanne see MONTVALLIER, JEAN-BAPTISTE SUZANNE BUQUET DE
Buquoy (family) 23 264
Buquoy, Jiří, Count of 8 410; 23 264, 272
Burachek, Nikolay G. 31 559
Buraimoh, Jimoh 1 429; 15 57; 23 136
Burakuji 17 120
Burakumin 17 19
Burana 5 186*; 6 182; 16 105; 18 567, 568
State Reserve Museum 6 284
Burano 32 206
burato see under LACE → types
Buratti, Antonio 12 40
Buratti, Carlo 5 186*
Buratti, Girolamo 7 313
Buratti, Giulio 20 47
Buraydah 32 316
Burbank (CA), Lockheed aircraft plant 5 531
Burbera, La 12 718
Burbidge, Pauline 10 354
Burbure, Xavier de 3 615
Burch, Cornelius van der 31 647
works 31 646
Burch, Edward (1730-1814) 5 187*; 12 263; 20 389
Burch, Edward, jr (fl 1789-1804) 5 187
Burch, Hendrick van der 5 187*
Burch, Henry Jacob 5 187
Burch, Meinard 8 204
Burchard, Bishop of Worms 8 614; 33 381
Burchard, C. 23 253
Burchard, Ludwig 5 187*
Burchard, Pablo 5 187–8*; 6 598
Burchard, Teodoro 6 593
Burchard Aguayo, Pablo 5 188
Burchart, Jenny 32 414
Burchart, Robert 32 414
Burchartz, Max (1887-1961; graphic artist) 7 770; 24 686; 29 540
Burchell, William 26 414
Burchett, Arthur 19 424
Burchett, Josiah 31 871
Burchett, Percy 12 650
Burchfield, Charles (Ephraim) 5 188–9*; 31 606
groups and movements 1 772, 773
patrons and collectors 5 124; 25 629
works 5 188; 12 296; 15 828; 18 718
Burchi, Augusto 7 164; 19 682
Burch-Korrodi, Meinrad 30 147
works 30 147
Bürck, Hans 28 714
Bürck, Paul 8 531
Burckhard, Max (fl 1898; theatre director) 28 344
Burckhardt, Carl 28 77; 30 138
Burckhardt, Christopher von see MÜNNICH, CHRISTOPHER VON BURCKHARDT, Count
Burckhardt, Gedeon 31 342
Burckhardt, Jacob (Christoph) 2 532; 3 333; 5 189–90*; 10 737; 12 483; 29 848; 30 156
personal collection 22 329
pupils 33 297
works 10 730; 12 482, 873; 13 810, 811; 22 296; 28 916; 30 157
on the Baroque 3 262
Burckhardt, Jean-Louis 1 95; 5 190*; 10 90; 24 556
works 14 97; 17 655; 20 914; 21 33
Burckhardt, Lucius 11 304
Burckhardt, Rudolph 7 874; 8 634
Burdach 6 245, 246
Burdadzori 12 321
Burdalyk 6 254
Burde, Joseph 2 825
Burden, Chris 19 703; 24 407
Burdett, Basil 30 160
Burdett, Edward 28 302
works 28 302
Burdett, Peter Perez 2 240
Burdett Coutts 10 782
Burdett-Coutts, Angela Georgina, Baroness 30 457
Burdick, Charles, L. 1 494
Burdigala see BORDEAUX

Burdwan, tomb complex of Khwaja Anwar-i Shahid 15 370
Bure, Leon (Leonardovich) 31 783
Bureau (family) 7 597
Bureau, Gaspard 20 133; 21 567
Bureau, Jean 21 567
Bureau, T. 26 526
Bureau des Marchands-Drapiers see PARIS → museums → Musée Carnavalet
Bureau du Roi Louis XV 5 192, 192; 26 376
bureaux 5 191–3*; 18
  historical and regional traditions
    England 5 191, 192–3
    Finland 11 103
    France 5 191, 192, 192, 193; 11 589, 591
    Germany 5 191
    Indian subcontinent 15 693
    Ireland 16 27
    Netherlands, the 5 191
    Russia 27 583
    Sweden 5 191
    United States of America 5 192; 31 624, 626, 626, 628, 629
  materials
    ivory 5 192
    japanning 32 337
    mahogany 5 191, 192; 27 583; 31 626, 628
    maple 5 191
    marquetry 11 103
    oak 5 192
    rose-wood 5 192
    satin-wood 5 192; 31 628
    walnut 5 191, 191, 192; 16 27
  techniques
    japanning 5 191, 192
    marquetry 5 191, 192
  types
    bombé 20 215
    bombé chests 31 626
    bureaux à cylindre 5 192
    bureaux brisés 5 191
    bureaux-cabinets see under CABINETS (ii) (FURNITURE) → types
    bureaux plats 5 191; 11 589, 593, 597; 26 84; 32 338
    Carlton House 5 192
    jardinière 27 583
    Mazarin 5 191; 7 657; 11 589
    Schreibschränke 5 191, 191
  see also DAVENPORTS; DESKS; SECRETAIRES
Bureba, La see LA BUREBA
Büren 12 391
Buren, Alexander von see PASQUALINI, ALEXANDER (i)
Buren, Counts of 22 823
Buren, Daniel 5 193*; 11 552, 553; 24 145
  collaboration 31 869
  groups and movements 7 685, 686; 10 416
  works 10 416; 11 570; 24 145
Buren, Floris von Egmont, Count of 8 102; 24 230
Buren Castle 3 544; 11 876
Buret' 27 364, 365
Burford (Oxon) 23 684
Burford, James 28 798
Burford, John 24 18
Burford, Robert 24 18
Burg, Adriaen van der 9 169; 28 165
Burg, Doherty, Bryant & Partners 25 566
Burg, Lodge & Doherty 25 566
Burga, Teresa 24 510
Burgal Church 26 580
Burganov, Aleksandr 27 397
Burgdorf, Sammlung für Völkerkunde 29 240
Burgee, John (Henry) 17 620; 31 598
  banks 3 177
  cathedrals 12 794; 16 56; 19 365
Burgee, John (Henry)—cont.
  libraries 27 345
  office buildings 21 650; 25 5
  skyscrapers 7 385; 23 43; 25 359, 359; 28 835
Burgen, John S. van 6 578
Burgen und Schlösser 24 444
Burger, Anton 12 394
Burger, Fritz 12 483; 22 113
Bürger, Gottfried 20 28
Burger, John 30 853
Burger, Nikolaus see JUNG, MORIZ
Burger, Richard L. 6 523
Bürger, W(illem) see THORÉ, (ETIENNE-JOSEPH-)THÉOPHILE
Burges, Alfred 5 193
Burges, William 5 193–6*; 6 605; 8 48; 10 298; 20 446
  architecture 10 281
    castles 5 194, 731; 6 61, 61; 29 797; 32 784
    cathedrals 19 381
    churches 4 810; 13 645
    colleges 14 203
    country houses 5 195; 8 106
    law courts 7 665
  armour 2 450
  assistants 14 50; 25 406
  collaboration 7 479; 17 610
  competitions 7 664, 668
  exhibitions 2 450
  furniture 10 298; 23 547, 547; 28 666
  groups and movements 5 340; 13 203, 207, 209; 17 440; 32 415
  interior decoration 32 788
  metalwork 10 335
  patrons and collectors 14 132; 29 797
  personal collection 11 738
  polychromy 25 173
  pupils 10 185; 30 364
  staff 7 701
  typography 2 333
  wallpaper 17 469
Burgess, Adam 28 261
Burgess, Cefyn 32 790
Burgess, David Lowry 28 829
Burgess, Gregory 2 742; 5 196*
Burgess, Hugh 24 41
Burgess, James 1 483, 500, 753; 5 196*; 15 211
Burgess, M. 21 34
Burgess, William 10 238
Burgh, Adriaen van der 14 794
Burgh, Albertus van der 32 258
Burgh, Elizabeth de, Lady of Clare 5 511
Burgh, Hendrick van der see BURCH, HENDRICK VAN DER
Burgh, Thomas 5 197*
  works 9 316, 323; 16 8; 26 475
Burgh, Ulick John de, 14th Earl of Clanricarde 23 345
Burghausen, Hans von see HANS VON BURGHAUSEN
Burgh Castle (Norfolk) 21 548
Burghclere, Sandham Memorial Chapel 6 460; 29 384
Burghers, Michael 2 601; 23 690
Burghley, William Cecil, 1st Baron see CECIL, WILLIAM, 1st Baron Burghley
Burghley House (Cambs) 6 127, 128; 10 360
  Ballroom 18 644, 644
  chimney-piece 24 845
  collections 10 364
  floors 10 273
  frames 11 393
  frescoes 32 358
  furniture 15 165
  gardens 4 875
  Great Hall 6 604
  Heaven Room 10 274; 18 644; 32 359
  interior decoration 11 423
  metalwork 10 329, 342; 30 872
Burghley House (Cambs)—cont.
  miniatures 9 44; 23 407
  paintings 3 347; 5 414; 6 129; 8 186, 493; 9 77; 12 600; 29 732; 30 354, 355
  sconces (lighting) 28 215
  silver 14 161
  silver-gilt 33 158
  staircases 29 522
  tapestries 10 275
  wood-carvings 12 591
Burghley Nef 11 616, 616; 22 694, 722
Burgi, Jost 10 119; 13 914
Burgin, Victor 5 197*
  groups and movements 7 686; 10 879, 882
  works 24 679, 681
Burgio 16 736
Burgis, Livinus Gilii de see LIVINUS GILII DE BURGIS
Burgis, William 4 477; 23 46
Burgkmair, Hans, I (1473-1531) 2 715, 716, 718; 5 197, 198–200*; 12 385; 33 349
  altarpieces 5 200; 12 386
  book illustrations 4 358; 12 385; 28 58; 33 353
  collaboration 3 474; 6 165; 15 144; 22 302; 28 58; 33 353, 365
  drawings 1 719
  methods 6 470; 33 353
  paintings 5 198
  patrons and collectors 2 716
    Frederick III, Elector of Saxony (reg 1486- 1525) 33 112
    Fries, Moritz, Graf von 11 789
    Fugger, Jakob, II (1459-1525) 11 818
    Maximilian I, Duke of Bavaria (reg 1598- 1651) and Elector of Bavaria (reg 1623-51) 33 275
    Maximilian I, Holy Roman Emperor (reg 1493- 1519) 13 903, 903, 904; 33 365
    Reimer, Georg Andreas 26 112
    William IV, Duke of Bavaria (reg 1508-50) 33 271
  prints 9 436; 12 386; 25 605, 622
    etchings 10 549
    woodcuts 5 199; 14 182; 33 353
  pupils 32 680; 33 33, 673
  reproductive prints by others 22 723
  roundels 27 256
  teachers 28 149
Burgkmair, Hans, II (c. 1500-62) 5 197
Burgkmair, Thoman 5 197–8*; 11 818
Burg Meran 2 815
Burgo, Thomas de see THOMAS DE BURGO
Burgoa, Francisco de 21 733
El Burgo de Osma
  Cathedral (1232) 13 104; 16 436; 26 609, 642
  Church (1110) 16 436
Burgo de Osma, Master of 20 638*; 23 109
burgomaster chairs see under CHAIRS → types
burgomeister chairs see under CHAIRS → types
burgonet see under HELMETS → types
Burgon Sianas, Painter of the 32 37
Burgos 5 201–5*; 29 258
  Arco de S María see Puerta de S María
  art forms and materials
    crosses 13 165
    ivory-carvings 16 525
    metalwork 29 333
    sculpture 13 108
  Casa del Cordón 5 201
Burgos—cont.
  Casa de Miranda see museums → Museo Arqueológico Provincial
  ecclestiastical buildings
    Cartuja de Miraflores see collegiate church
    Cathedral of S María 5 202–4*, 203; 13 51, 69; 29 263, 265, 288, 289
      Capilla de la Visitación 13 69
      Capilla del Condestable 7 614; 8 183; 14 578; 17 515; 32 124
      chests 29 312
      crucifix 8 214
      Escalera Dorada 29 266
      metalwork 13 166; 29 333, 337, 338
      Puerta de la Pellejería 25 31; 29 265
      reliquaries 29 333
      retables 26 250, 250; 29 289
      sculpture 5 204, 204–5*; 13 103–4, 112
      spire 29 414
      stained glass 5 205*; 13 191
      textiles 30 331
      tympanum 13 109
      workshop 13 68
    collegiate church 29 298
      interior decoration 29 298
    convent of S Pablo 13 123
    Las Huelgas Abbey 5 205*; 7 350; 29 263
      Capilla de la Asunción 22 255
      doors 16 493
      metalwork 10 322
      Museo de Telas y Preseas see under museums
      sculpture 13 122
      textiles see under museums → Museo de Telas y Preseas
      tombs 29 350
      tomb of Doña Berenguela 29 288
      tomb of Eleanor of Castile 16 440
    S Nicolás 26 249
  Hospital del Rey 29 342
  museums
    Museo Arqueológico Provincial 5 201
    Museo de Telas y Preseas 16 439, 440
      cushions 18 157
  Puerta de S María 5 202
  statue of Charles III 29 293
Burgos, Alonso de, Bishop of Palencia 13 69; 14 578; 31 822
Burgos, Lucas de see LUCAS DE BURGOS
Burgos, Nicolás de 7 610
Burgos Mantilla, Francisco de 5 206*; 8 254; 32 135
Burg Ottenstein 2 790
Burg Rapottenstein 2 806
Burg Strechau Chapel 2 793
Burgun, Schwerer et Cie 12 18
Burgundian Prelates, Master of the 20 638*; 29 398
Burgundians 21 500, 501
  bronze 21 503
Burgundio di Tadio 24 872
Burgundy (House of) 3 555, 605; 5 206*; 11 655; 13 182; 22 901; 31 218
Burgundy, Adolphe of see ADOLPHE OF BURGUNDY
Burgundy, Alfonso I, King of Portugal see ALFONSO I, King of Portugal
Burgundy, Alfonso IV, King of Portugal see ALFONSO IV, King of Portugal
Burgundy, Antoine of see ANTOINE OF BURGUNDY
Burgundy, Beatrix of Champagne, Duchess of see BEATRIX OF CHAMPAGNE, Duchess of Burgundy
Burgundy, Blanche of, Countess of Savoy see BLANCHE OF BURGUNDY, Countess of Savoy
Burgundy, Charles the Bold, 4th Duke of see CHARLES THE BOLD, 4th Duke of Burgundy
Burgundy, Isabella of Portugal, Duchess of see ISABELLA OF PORTUGAL, Duchess of Burgundy
Burgundy, John the Fearless, 2nd Duke of see JOHN THE FEARLESS, 2nd Duke of Burgundy
Burgundy, Louis, Duke of, le Petit Dauphin see BOURGOGNE, LOUIS DE BOURBON, Duc de, le Petit Dauphin
Burgundy, Margaret of, Queen of France see MARGARET OF BURGUNDY, Queen of France
Burgundy, Margaret of Flanders, Duchess of see MARGARET OF FLANDERS, Duchess of Burgundy
Burgundy, Marie-Adelaïde of Savoy, Duchess of see BOURGOGNE, MARIE-ADELAÏDE OF SAVOY, Duchesse de
Burgundy, Mary, Duchess of see MARY OF BURGUNDY, Holy Roman Empress
Burgundy, Odo I, Duke of see ODO I, Duke of Burgundy
Burgundy, Philip II, Duke of see PHILIP THE BOLD, 1st Duke of Burgundy
Burgundy, Philip III, 3rd Duke of see PHILIP THE GOOD, 3rd Duke of Burgundy
Burgundy, Philip of, Bishop of Utrecht see PHILIP OF BURGUNDY, Bishop of Utrecht
Burgundy, Philip the Bold, 1st Duke of see PHILIP THE BOLD, 1st Duke of Burgundy
Burgundy, Philip the Fair, Duke of see PHILIP I, King of Castile
Burgundy, Philip the Good, 3rd Duke of see PHILIP THE GOOD, 3rd Duke of Burgundy
Burgundy, Sancho I, King of Portugal see SANCHO I, King of Portugal
Burgundy Goblet 13 159
Burgusio, Castel Appiano 26 653
Burgwart, Der see BURGEN UND SCHLÖSSER
Burhan, Sami 30 178
Burhanpur
  brocades 15 662
  congregational mosque 15 373
  dress 15 691
  gardens 15 373
  Jahangipura 15 373
  Lal Bagh 15 373
  palace 15 373
  textiles 15 669
Buri, Anna Rapp see RAPP BURI, ANNA
Buri, Max (Alfred) 5 215*; 30 134
Buri, Samuel 30 135
burial chambers 17 58, 58–9*, 59
burial grounds see CEMETERIES
burial jars see under JARS → types
burial mounds
  Celtic 32 773
  England 5 292
  Germany 9 689; 25 539; 32 773
  Greece, ancient 13 383, 384
  Japan 17 57–9; 18 190
  Korea 18 271
  Native North Americans 1 153; 22 570, 571–2, 571; 31 116*

burial mounds—cont.
Prehistoric art 5 292; 9 689; 25 523–4, 538*, 539
Sri Lanka 29 442
United States of America 22 570, 571–2, 571
see also TOMBS; TUMULI
Burial of St John, Master of the 33 629
burial practices 1 257–60*, 258, 260; 15 192; 17 104; 21 269
burials see GRAVES
burial suits 7 6; 20 236, 236; 22 466
Burić, Anka 22 18
Burin, de 29 376
Büring, Johann Gottfried 12 373; 14 652; 19 76; 25 366, 368
burins (flint tools) 25 494
burins (engraving) 5 215*; 10 379, 379; 25 612, 612
Buritaca-200 30 240
burj see ISLAMIC → towers
Burji see MAMLUK (EGYPT AND SYRIA)
Burke, Edmund (d 1920) 18 743
Burke, Edmund (1729-97) 5 215*
drawings 8 95
groups and movements 24 741; 29 889
sponsorship 3 285
writings 26 736
on aesthetics 8 613; 22 740
on nature 16 14
on the Sublime 1 180; 18 700, 713; 26 275; 31 300
Burke, Edmund (1850-1919) 5 562
Burke, Frances 2 756
Burke, Frances, Fabrics 2 767
Burke, Jackson 17 431
Burke, Mrs Jackson 17 431
Burke, John (fl early 19th cent.) 28 255
Burke, John (b 1946) 5 215–16*
Burke, P. 28 917
Burke, Robert O'Hara 2 745
Burke, Selma Hortense 1 442; 5 216*
Burke, Thomas 5 216*; 12 187; 29 675
Burke & Co. 7 559
Burkert, Nancy Ekholm 4 368
Burkhalter, Jean 21 363
Burkhard, Bishop of Fenis 3 333
Burkhardt, Ernst 6 409
Burkina Faso 1 214, 380; 5 216–17*, 217
batik 5 217
body arts 1 288
brass 5 217, 217
collections 5 217*
compounds 1 312
dolls 22 198
figurines 1 273
gesture 1 264
granaries 1 310
houses 1 311, 312; 21 597
iconography 1 280
masks 1 341, 342; 4 193; 5 217; 22 197
museums 5 217*
portraits 1 267
sculpture 22 197
shrines (i) (cult) 1 289; 19 522
tools 1 364
wood 22 197, 198
Bürklein, Friedrich 5 217–18*
pupils 11 34
staff 31 580
teachers 12 168
works 22 300; 25 856
Bürkli, Arnold 33 735
Burlamacchi, Michiel see BOLLEMARD, MICHIEL
burlap 27 317
Burlazzi, Francesco 31 901
Burleigh, Sydney Richmond 25 666
Burle Marx, Roberto 4 718; 5 218–19*
gardens 4 713, 714; 5 218; 12 143; 19 271; 26 462
parks 24 181; 26 109
pupils 7 376
works 4 679, 712; 23 117
Burlet, René 19 848
Burley Hill (Derbys) 10 302
Burley on the Hill (Leics)
Sanctuary of the Hermit Finch 11 243
stables 29 485
Burlima see PALERMO
Burling, Edward 1 158
Burling & Adler 1 158
Burlington (NJ)
ceramics 31 634
Riverside 23 256; 32 555
St Mary's 13 203
Burlington, Lady 17 902
Burlington, Richard Boyle, 3rd Earl of see BOYLE, RICHARD, 3rd Earl of Burlington
Burlington Glass Co. 5 583
Burlington House Cartoon 2 376; 19 185; 31 847
Burlington Magazine 10 377; 24 423, 424, 446; 25 665; 26 49, 235; 28 560
Burling & Whitehouse 5 274
Burlison, John 7 410
Burlison & Grylls 14 281
Burlyuk, David (Davidovich) 5 219*; 24 405; 27 434; 31 583
collaboration 18 507
groups and movements
Blaue Reiter 4 132
Cubism 8 250
Cubo-Futurism 8 250
Futurism 20 886–7
Hylaea 13 862; 18 22
Jack of Diamonds (Bubnovy Valet) 16 817
Miraiha Bijutsu Kyōkai (Futurist Art Society) 17 205
Neo-primitivism 22 750
Neue Künstlervereinigung München (NKVM) 22 921
Union of Youth 31 583
works 19 491
writings 21 645; 24 404
Burlyuk, Nikolay (Davidovich) 20 886
Burlyuk, Vladimir (Davidovich) 5 219, 220*
collaboration 18 507
groups and movements 4 132; 13 862; 16 817; 20 886; 22 921
patrons and collectors 8 10
works 19 491
Burma 5 220–63*, 221; 29 225
amber 1 761
appliqué 5 248*, 249
architecture 5 224–32*, 233*, 234–8*
brick 5 226
Buddhism 5 233*
stone 5 226
bamboo 5 257; 6 557
barges 5 254
baskets 5 257
bells 5 253*
betel sets 5 254*
boats 5 254*
book covers 20 327
books 5 245*
boxes 5 254
brick 4 796; 5 226
bronze 5 239, 240, 241, 256–7, 260, 260
ceramics 5 254–5*
chess sets 6 557
coins 5 255*, 259
costumes 5 251
cotton 5 247; 20 327
craftsmen and artists 5 261, 262*
cupolas 5 227
doors 9 163
Burma—cont.
doorways 5 241
dress 5 248, 249–50*, 249
drums (musical instruments) 5 256–7*, 258; 22 376
earplugs 5 250
earthenwares 5 255
education (art) 5 262*
embroidery 5 248*
ephemeral art 5 255–6*
exhibitions 5 246
gems 12 268
gilding 5 256, 261, 261; 12 626; 18 607
glass 5 256*; 18 604
gold 20 329
gong-chimes 5 258
hangings 5 248, 249
harps 5 259, 259
houses 5 236–7*
iconography 5 223–4*, 237, 240
ikat 5 248*; 30 554
iron 29 228
ivory 6 557
ivory-carvings 5 256*
jade 7 11; 16 858, 860–61
jewellery 5 250*
lacquer 5 257–8*, 257, 261; 18 600, 602, 604, 605, 606, 606, 607; 30 618
libraries 5 232
loom pulleys 5 258*
manuals 5 263
manuscript illumination 5 244–6*
manuscripts 5 251
marionettes 5 252–3*, 253
marks 5 259
Martaban jars 5 255*
masks 5 251*, 252
miniatures (manuscript illumination) 5 245, 246
monasteries 5 227, 232*, 232, 234–5*, 236
mother-of-pearl 20 327
musical instruments 5 253*, 256–7*, 258–9*, 259
opium weights see WEIGHTS
ordination halls 5 232
ornament 23 556
pagodas 23 772
painting 5 242*, 246–7*; 18 605
wall 5 242–4*, 243; 32 804
watercolours 5 247
palaces 5 235–6, 236
palm leaves 5 245*
pediments 5 230
periodicals 24 437
plaques 5 230, 231, 254–5*
pottery 5 255*
proportions (human) 5 224
religion 5 223–4*
roofs 5 261
sapphires 7 91
sat panchee 5 255–6*
sculpture 5 238–42*
bronze 5 239, 240, 241
Buddhism 5 239–42*, 240, 241; 18 607
Hinduism 5 240*
stone 5 239
shrines (i) (cult) 2 280–81, 282; 28 639, 640
silk 5 247, 248*
silver 5 259*
stone 5 226, 239
stucco 5 230, 231; 29 826
stupas 5 223, 224, 225, 227, 231, 231–2*, 234*, 234; 25 890; 29 866, 866
swords 5 259–60
tablets 5 240
tapestries 5 248*
tattoos 5 250–51*, 251; 30 366
temples 5 222, 227–30*, 227, 228, 229, 233*; 23 763
śikhara 5 229–30
terracotta 5 255; 30 511
textiles 5 247–9*, 248
lün taya 5 248, 248
Burma—cont.
theatre 5 251*
thrones 5 261; 30 785
tiles 5 254
tourist art 29 238
trade 6 557; 7 11, 91; 16 269
treatises 5 262
urban planning 5 237–8*
vaults (ceiling) 5 226–7
vernacular art 5 262*
weapons 5 259–60*
weaving 5 247–8*
weights 5 260*, 260
wood 20 327
wood-carvings 5 261, 261–2*; 12 626
wool 5 247, 249
writing 20 329
see also SOUTH-EAST ASIA
Burman 5 223, 237
Burman, Chila 10 882
Burman, Karl 10 537; 30 349
Burman, Paul 33 566
Burman, Thomas 5 263*, 293
Burmantofts Faience 10 312; 30 877
Burn, Currie & Co. 5 418
Burn, Ian 2 512
Burn, Robert 5 263
Burn, William 5 263–4*
architecture 16 10
churches 28 230
country houses 28 230; 29 835
government buildings 28 228
hospitals 28 229
porticos 2 618
schools 28 156, 273
assistants 17 894; 22 809
country houses 28 230
furniture 28 254
groups and movements 28 288
interior decoration 28 248
pupils 28 561
teachers 28 872
Burnaburiash II, King of Babylonia (reg c. 1375–c. 1347 BC) 1 869
Burnaby, Simon Fraser University 5 562
Burnacini, Giovanni 5 264; 13 919; 30 675
Burnacini, Lodovico Ottavio 5 264–5*
collaboration 11 130; 32 442
patrons and collectors 13 919
works 2 801; 5 264; 26 25; 30 676
Burnakov, Mikhail 27 436
Burnand, Eugène 3 392; 5 265*
Burnand, F. C. 17 877
Burnay, Conde de 25 318
Burne, William 15 149
Burne-Jones, Edward (Coley) 4 42, 87; 5 265–9*; 9 19; 10 282; 27 186; 29 368
assistants 22 351
book illustrations 4 364; 10 255; 22 146
collaboration 10 254; 20 335; 22 142, 143, 145; 30 680
dealers 1 453
drawings 9 217
exhibitions 19 588
frames 11 434
furniture 23 547
groups and movements 2 575; 8 6; 17 440; 19 588; 25 555, 556; 30 168
methods 21 765
mosaics 7 226; 26 776
musical instruments 22 373
paintings 5 267, 268; 8 121; 10 254; 22 416
patrons and collectors
Benson, R(obert) H(enry) 3 740
Foster, Myles Birket 11 331
Graham, William 13 273
Grosvenor, Hugh Lupus, 1st Duke of Westminster 13 697
Burne-Jones, Edward (Coley)
patrons and collectors—cont.
Handley-Read, Charles and Lavinia 14 132
Howard (ii), George James, 9th Earl of Carlisle 14 809
Ionides, Aleco 15 895
Leathart, James 18 907
Leyland, F(rederick) R(ichard) 19 290
McCulloch, George 19 875
Murray, Charles Fairfax 22 351
Plint, T(homas) E(dward) 25 41
Shchukin, Sergey (Ivanovich) 28 569
Wilde, Oscar (Fingal O'Flahertie Wills) 33 180
photographed works 14 688
reproductive prints by others 19 868
stained glass 6 66; 22 143; 23 690; 25 398; 28 348; 29 507, 513, 516, VI2
tapestries 10 352; 30 326, 326, III2
teachers 10 373
Burne-Jones, Philip 5 266
Burnell, Robert 5 270*
works 33 64, 64
Burnes, Alexander 1 210
Burnet, Gilbert 12 118
Burnet, James 5 271*
Burnet, J(ohn) J(ames) 5 270–71*
assistants 30 241
collaboration 10 173
groups and movements 3 465; 9 740; 10 98
staff 28 622
works 10 240; 12 775; 28 228
Burnet, John (1784-1868) 5 271*; 33 189
assistants 11 362
groups and movements 28 289
works 2 690; 28 237
Burnet, John (1814-1901) 5 270; 12 775; 25 267; 28 228
works 12 773
Burnet, John, Tait & Lorne 10 240; 28 231, 250
Burnet, Son & Campbell 12 775
Burnet, Tait & Lorne 4 810; 5 271
Burnet, Tate & Powell 4 823
Burnett, Alexander 28 268
Burnett, Micajah 28 539
Burnett, Thomas (fl 1619-53) 28 269
Burnett, Thomas (fl 1783) 7 857
Burney, Charles 5 337
Burney, Charles A. 14 28; 17 862; 33 498
Burney, Charles Parr 8 28
Burney, Edward Francesco 5 271–2*
works 5 272
Burney, Sidney 10 91
Burnham, Daniel H(udson) (1846-1912) 2 315; 5 272–6*; 7 326; 10 683; 13 271; 17 476; 20 16; 24 614; 25 152; 27 137
architecture 33 174
department stores 8 770; 19 576; 30 507
exhibition architecture 5 273; 31 727
railway stations 5 274
skyscrapers 8 821; 16 55; 27 730; 28 832; 31 594
urban planning 7 357; 20 274; 24 617; 27 730; 31 727, 729
collaboration 6 573, 574; 7 429; 28 830, 833; 30 505
groups and movements 6 577, 578; 7 357
restorations by others 33 29
staff 2 699; 13 271, 844
Burnham, Daniel Hudson (1886-1961) 5 274; 10 684; 13 271

Burnham, D. H., & Co 8 770; 13 271
Burnham, Franklin P. 2 693; 9 715
Burnham, Hubert 5 274; 13 271
Burnham, Wilbur 8 111
Burnham Brothers 13 271
Burnham & Co. 12 792; 28 833
Burnham Deepdale, St Mary 26 613
Burnham Library see under CHICAGO (IL) → museums → Art Institute of Chicago
Burnham Norton, St Margaret 25 723
Burnham-on-Crouch, Royal Corinthian Yacht Club 25 741
Burnham & Root 4 788; 5 273–4; 27 137–8, 216; 30 505; 31 595
works 27 138
Burningham, John 4 368
burnishers 5 276*; 10 379
burnishing
historical and regional traditions
Afghanistan 1 207
China 6 874, 876
Islamic 16 394
Japan 17 276
Prehistoric art 25 514
materials
agate 12 622
haematite 12 622
teeth 12 622
uses
ceramics 16 394
gold 12 622
paper 24 44
pottery 1 207; 6 874, 876; 25 514
prints 17 276
Burnitz, Heinrich 10 669
Burnitz, Karl-Peter 12 394
Burnley, William 31 339
Burns, A. J., & Co. 23 73
Burns, Cecil 15 657
Burns, Marla C.
works 1 255
Burns, Robert 5 271
Burns, Vivian 12 510
Burns, W. H. 4 597
Burns and Oates 22 117
Burnside, Jackson 3 62
works 3 62
Burnside, Stan(ley) 3 62, 65
works 3 62
Burnsides, John 5 276
Burnsides, Mabel 5 276
Burnsides, Tom 5 276*
Burntisland, St Columba 28 252
burnt jade see under JADE → types
burnt sienna see under SIENNA → types
Bürolandschaft 24 188
Burov, Andrey (Konstantinovich) 5 276–7*; 27 380
Burov, F. 24 566
Burr, Aaron 31 872
Burra, Edward 5 277–8*
groups and movements 31 673
works 5 277; 10 257
Burrell, Peter, 2nd Lord Gwydyr and 19th Lord Willoughby de Eresby 8 20
Burrell, William (fl 1780-91) 13 664
Burrell, William (1861-1958) 5 278*; 7 155
collections 12 777; 28 272, 273
paintings 8 125; 14 47
stained glass 29 515
Burrell Collection see under GLASGOW
Burrel Museum 18 459
Burri, Alberto 5 279*; 16 775; 17 694
dealers 16 820
groups and movements 2 526, 543, 545; 5 671; 7 555; 16 681; 26 777
works 5 279; 16 681; 28 657
Burri, Giacomo 19 732
Burri, René 5 279*; 20 846
Burri, Werner 30 144
Bürring, Johann Gottfried 7 168
Burrini, Barbara 5 281
Burrini, Gian Antonio 5 280–81*
collaboration 8 141; 14 27
patrons and collectors 12 559
teachers 24 227
works 5 280
Burrough, James 5 287, 512; 10 516
Burroughs, Alan 31 672
Burroughs, Betty 20 476
Burroughs, William S. 13 890
Burroughs Wellcome company 27 314
Burrowes, Edward Rupert 13 876, 878
Burrows, P. F. M. 33 58
Burrows, Stephen 3 62
burrs 5 277*
Burry, Davidt de 19 293
Bursa 5 281–2*; 16 104
Alâeddin Mosque 16 205
architecture 16 202
bazaar 16 206
Caravanserai 5 723
carpets 16 473
congregational mosque 9 83; 16 205
minbar 16 497
Emir Han 16 206
fortifications 21 585
Green Mosque see Yeşil Cami
Green Tomb see Yeşil Türbe
guilds 16 445
Hüdavendigar Mosque see MOSQUE OF MURAD I
Ipek Han 16 206
külliye 18 509
mosque of Murad I 16 205, 206; 18 509
Muradiye Cami 32 88
Museum of Turkish and Islamic Art 31 456
palaces 23 816
shadow-puppets 16 544
silk 16 428, 445
textiles 16 430, 444, 445, 447
tomb of Mehmed I see Yeşil Türbe
tomb of Şehzade Mustafa 16 206
Ulu Cami see congregational mosque
urban planning 16 266
Yeni Kaplica 16 224
Yeşil Cami 2 295; 5 282; 16 199, 257; 21 506; 22 195
loge 20 369
Yeşil complex 16 206, 249; 18 509
Yeşil Türbe 6 172; 16 206; 21 506; 31 112
Yildrim Bayezit Mosque 20 57
Bursa-type mosque see MOSQUES → types → T-plan
Burscheid Church 16 540
burse reliquaries see under RELIQUARIES→ type
Burslem (Staffs) 29 495
Wedgwood Institute 30 503
Burssens, Jan 2 510
Bursze, T. 28 839
Bursztyn, Felisa 7 610
Burt, Alexander 23 72
Burt, Benjamin 4 480; 31 649
Burt, Charles Thomas 4 86
Burt, Michel 24 99
Burt, Thomas 23 72
Burt'el 23 202
Burtius, Nicolaus 22 369
Burton, Alfred (Henry) 5 282*; 23 58
Burton, Charles 19 867
Burton, David 20 590
Burton, Decimus 5 282–3*
architecture 12 791
arches 22 47; 31 351
Burton, Decimus
architecture—cont.
clubs (meeting places) 7 469
greenhouses 12 137; 13 619; 18 4, 5
urban planning 4 809; 12 773
villas 28 527
zoos 33 698
collaboration 14 391; 16 52; 24 293
patrons and collectors 6 118
Burton, F. C. 23 692
Burton, Frederic William 3 241; 5 283*; 16 16, 33
Burton, Harry 10 81
Burton, James 5 282; 10 82, 92; 22 528
Burton, John 21 7; 29 807; 33 545
Burtón, Juan Alonso de 5 313*
Burton, Mildred 2 400; 5 283–4*
Burton, Richard 1 284, 476*; 13 812; 27 877
Burton, Scott 24 408
Burton, Walter 5 282
Burton, W. F. P. 19 739
Burton, William 15 150
Burton, William Shakespeare 5 284*
Burton Agnes Hall (N Yorks) 6 604; 28 895, 896
Burton Bros 5 282
Burton Constable (Humberside) 5 907; 7 172, 758; 19 644
Burton Hall (Lincs) 7 486
Burton-on-Trent (Staffs) 1 517, 518, 520
Burtsev, Eremey (Grigorievich) 30 253
Burty, Philippe 5 284*; 6 377; 8 647; 17 440
groups and movements 17 440
personal collection 16 559
works 5 364
Burueva, Roi Martínez de see MARTÍNEZ DE BURUEVA, ROI
Buruncuk 21 556
Burundi 1 214; 5 285*
Burushhanda 1 114
Burway Prints see BURKE, FRANCES, FABRICS
Burwell, Frederick 23 54
Burwell, Paul 33 223
Bury (France) 11 504
Château 5 285*; 6 504; 11 512, 571, 726
gardens 12 113, 113
staircase 29 522
Bury (Lancs; UK)
Art Gallery 10 370
manuscripts 26 661
monument to Sir Robert Peel 10 266
Bury, Charles William, Viscount Charleville 2 598
Bury, Claus 12 451, 456, 865
Bury, E. 14 243
Bury, Friedrich 5 286*; 12 273; 33 116
Bury, Jean Jacques 5 286
Bury, John 30 687
Bury, Maxwell 23 54
Bury, Pol 5 286*; 29 369
dealers 20 75; 26 193
groups and movements 2 510; 17 518; 18 62, 63; 20 913; 33 636
works 3 574; 10 135; 11 570
Bury, Richard de 6 547
Bury, Thomas Talbot 25 710
Burya, Mikhail 21 811
Buryakov, Yu. F. 17 776
Buryat 21 869, 870, 870
drawings 27 436
fretwork 27 436
jewellery 21 878
scripts 21 882
tunics 21 877
Buryat Autonomous Republic see MONGOLIA
Burylin, Sergey 27 431
works 27 431
Bury New Testament see under NEW TESTAMENTS → individual manuscripts
Bury St Edmunds (Suffolk) 5 286–8*; 10 225
Abbey 5 287; 7 419; 31 710
chapter house 6 466
crypt 18 621
doors 9 153; 26 688
Great Gate 2 295; 12 175
ivory-carvings 26 697, 697, 698
Lady Chapel 18 622
manuscripts 2 77; 5 288, 288; 10 244; 14 432; 26 672
Norman Gate see St James' Tower
St James' Tower 12 175; 26 613
sculpture 19 405
brasses 4 692
crucifixes 8 213
houses 5 287; 14 76
manuscripts 5 288*; 20 331; 26 661; 27 592
Moyse's Hall 26 613; 29 22
St Mary's 5 287; 32 89
Bury St Edmunds, Mabel of see MABEL OF BURY ST EDMUNDS
Bury St Edmunds Bible see under BIBLES → individual manuscripts
Bury St Edmunds Ivory Cross 14 854
Bury St Edmunds Psalter see under PSALTERS → individual manuscripts
Bus, Cornelis see BOS, CORNELIS
Busa 17 388
Busarello, Orlando 4 715
Busarello, Silva Cândida 4 715
Busati, Andrea 5 289*; 7 323
Busato 25 419
Busatti, Luigi 20 497
Busavisk 31 557
Busbecq, Ogier Ghislain de 12 76, 85; 16 254, 446
Busbee, Jacques 31 639
Busbee, Juliana 31 639
Busbequius see BUSBECQ, OGIER GHISLAIN DE
Busby, Charles Augustin 4 809
Busby, Peter 31 864
Busby, Richard 14 742
Busby, R. V. M. 19 359
Busca, Antonio 5 289–90*; 21 526
collaboration 12 560
pupils 18 755
works 5 297
Busca, Giovanni Battista 4 655
Buscaglia, José 25 702
Buscaglione, Giovanni 21 4
Busch, Andreas 12 811
Busch, Christian 32 449
Busch, John 5 520; 12 134, 173; 23 76
Busch, Wilhelm 5 290–91*; 33 369
works 5 291, 758; 7 648
Buschener, Johann de 4 742
Buscher, Frank 1 782
Buschetto 5 291–2*; 24 856, 857, 858
Buschiazzo, Giovanni Antonio 2 395, 396; 5 122
works 2 396
Buschor, E. 27 687
Buschow & Beck 31 262
Buschulte, Wilhelm 7 592; 29 508
Buscot Park 5 268; 10 785; 11 913; 12 141
Buseck, Amadeus von, Prince-Bishop of Fulda 11 832
Buseira 9 737; 30 197
Bušek, Dominik 8 400
Bušek, Konstantin 8 400
Bušek, Petr 8 400
Busenello, Giovanni Francesco 33 608
Bush, Fenner 16 799
Bush, Jack (Hamilton) 5 292*
groups and movements 5 568; 23 790, 791
works 5 569
Bush, Norton 23 904
Bushara, Mohamed Omer 1 433; 29 897
Bush Barrow 5 292*; 10 225; 25 470, 525, 531
Bush Creoles (Bush negroes) 30 13
Būshehr 10 719
Bushell, Stephen Wooton 5 293*; 7 161; 33 465
Bushell, Thomas 12 127
Bushey Park (Surrey), Diana Fountain 19 250
bush hammers see BOUCHARDES
bushidō 17 42*
Bushire 16 449
Bushmen see SAN
Bushnaq, Yusuf 5 405
Bushnell, Geoffrey H. S. 13 735
Bushnell, John 5 293*
works 10 263, 264; 19 606
Bushong 18 484, 488
Busi, Giovanni de' see CARIANI, GIOVANNI
Büsinck, Ludolph 5 294*
works 5 294; 18 663; 33 358, 366
Büsinck, Wilhelm 5 294
Busintsi 5 158
al-Busiri 16 453
Busiri, Giovanni Battista 5 294–5*; 8 12; 13 301; 32 111
Busiris see ABUSIR
Busiris Painter 13 514, 516
works 13 516
Busiri-Vici, Andrea 9 175
Busketus see BUSCHETTO
busks 28 302
Buslayev, Fedor (Ivanovich) 18 215; 27 443
Busler, Petrus see BORSSELER, PIETER
Busleyden, Gillis van 8 87
Busleyden, Jerome 12 845
Buson Yosa see YOSA BUSON
Busquets (family) 29 319
Busquets, Eusebi 29 320
Busquets, Jaume 29 309
Busquets i Jane, Joan 29 308, 321
Buṣrā see BOSRA
Bussa 21 597
Bussaert, Martin 4 781; 5 295*; 8 738
Bussat, Pierre 18 874
Bussell, Joshua H. 28 540–41
Busselle, Rebecca
works 1 237
Busshi Tori see TORI BUSSHI
Bussi, Carlo Antonio 30 454
Bussi, Giovanni Francesco 5 295
Bussi, Santino de 5 295–6*; 8 426; 28 836; 29 838; 31 510
works 32 459
Bussière, Gaston 5 296*
Bussière, Victor 5 296
Busso, Aurelio 6 24
Bussola, Cesare 5 296, 297*; 31 901
Bussola, Dionigi 5 296–7*; 21 526, 533; 27 499
collaboration 21 533
works 10 744; 16 701; 31 901
Bussola, La 6 103; 22 27
Bussoni, Bernardino 32 205
Bussy, Nicolás de 5 297*; 29 292
Bussy-Rabutin Château 2 699
Bust 18 810
Arch 2 294; 16 168
architecture 16 167–8, 168
coins 6 265
gravestones 16 168
manuscripts 1 208; 16 290, 290
mausoleum 16 166, 169
palace 16 167
Bustamante (Herrera), Bartolomé (de) 5 305*; 8 79; 30 374

Bustamante, Pedro Azabeche *see* AZABECHE BUSTAMANTE, PEDRO
Bustamante de Herrera, Jerónimo de **12** 920
Bustamente **11** 571
Bustamente, Bartolomé **31** 87
Bustamente, Jean Marc **11** 553
Bustelli, Franz Anton **5** 305–6*; **12** 434
groups and movements **26** 498
works **12** *433*; **23** 325; **33** 278
Busti, Agostino *see* BAMBAIA
Busti, Polidoro **3** 137
Bustillo, Alejandro **5** 123, 306*
Bustler, Petrus *see* BORSSELER, PIETER
Bu ston Rinpoche **30** 813
Bustos, Arturo García **31** 92
Bustos, Hermenegildo **5** 306*; **21** 385
busts **5** 297–304*; **19** 315
historical and regional traditions
Akkadian (people) **1** *510*
Austria
Baroque **29** *789*; **32** *442*
Baroque Revival **30** *889*
Neo-classicism **33** *623*
18th cent. **21** *314*
Belgium **3** *604*
Byzantine **5** 299–300*; **9** 587
Central Asia, Eastern **6** *316*
Champa **6** *429*
Crete **13** *443*
Czech Republic **24** *190*
Early Christian (*c.* AD 250-843) **5** 299–300*; **9** 587
Egypt, ancient **5** 298*; **22** *723*; **29** 814
England
Baroque **24** *753*
Rococo **27** *243*
17th cent. **10** *263*
19th cent. **6** *457*; **16** *799*; **23** *190*
Etruscan **10** 604
Finland **11** *100*
France **5** 304
Baroque **3** *833*
Gothic **17** *459*
Neo-classicism **14** *797*
Romanticism **8** *565*
18th cent. **19** *141*
19th cent. **5** *303*, *304*, *826*; **7** *163*
Germany **12** *406*
Gothic **17** *459*
Greece, ancient **5** 298–9*; **13** *443*, 583*
Hinduism **6** *429*
Holy Roman Empire (before 1648) **5** *301*; **21** II4
Italy **5** 300–302, 304; **9** 21, 23
Baroque **1** *630*; **4** *406*; **5** *302*; **20** *902*; **26** *773*
Mannerism **6** *144*
Neo-classicism **6** *129*
Renaissance **5** *300*; **9** *124*; **16** *691*; **21** 692, *693*, II4; **25** V1
Roman **27** *12*, *110*
15th cent. **18** *860*
16th cent. **3** *924*; **5** *415*; **32** *648*, *649*
Nabataea **24** *557*
Netherlands, the **22** *859*
Rome, ancient **5** 298*, 299*; **7** 642; **9** 246; **26** 861; **27** *30*
Antonine **5** *299*; **27** *15*
Hadrianic **27** *37*
Italy **27** *110*
Republican **27** *12*
Trajanic **27** 35
3rd cent. AD **27** *41*
Scotland **28** *243*
Seleucid **28** *383*
Spain **29** *328*
Sweden **5** *303*
Switzerland **27** *15*
busts
historical and regional traditions—cont.
Vietnam **6** *429*
materials
alabaster (gypsum) **17** *459*
bronze
England
Etruscan **10** 604
Finland **11** *100*
France **8** *565*
Holy Roman Empire (before 1648) **5** *301*; **21** II4
Italy **5** *415*; **6** *144*
Rome, ancient **27** *30*; **28** *383*
copper **1** *510*
earthenwares **29** *328*
gold **27** *15*
ivory **3** *604*; **16** *799*
lead **21** *314*
limestone **22** *723*
marble **5** 298
Austria **29** *789*; **30** *889*; **32** *442*; **33** *623*
England **6** *457*; **23** *190*; **24** *753*
France **3** *833*; **5** *304*, *826*; **7** *163*; **19** *141*
Italy **1** *630*; **3** *924*; **4** *406*; **5** *300*, *302*; **6** *129*; **20** *902*; **21** *692*; **26** *773*; **32** *648*
Rome, ancient **5** *299*; **27** *37*, *41*
Sweden **5** *303*
plaster **5** *303*; **12** *406*; **28** *243*
silver **3** *604*
stone **6** *429*; **24** *190*, *557*
stucco **29** 814
terracotta **30** 495
Central Asia, Eastern **6** *316*
England **27** *243*
France **14** *797*
Greece, ancient **13** *443*, 583*
Italy **9** *124*; **32** *649*
Rome, ancient **27** *110*
tin **21** *314*
waxes **5** 298
wood **6** *316*; **27** *12*
Busturia **29** 329
Busuttil, Michele **5** 306
Busuttil, Salvatore **5** 306*; **20** 213
busycon see under SHELLS → types
Buta **1** *401*
Butades **30** 496
butanol **29** 53
Butay, Boniface **30** 659
Butay, Robert **19** 20
Butchart, Mrs **20** 30
Butcher, Enid **10** 397
Bute (family) **28** 266; **32** 910
Bute, John Crichton-Stuart, 4th Marquess of *see* CRICHTON-STUART, JOHN, 4th Marquess of Bute
Bute, John Patrick Crichton-Stuart, 3rd Marquess of *see* CRICHTON-STUART, JOHN, PATRICK, 3rd Marquess of Bute
Bute, John Stuart, 3rd Earl of *see* STUART (ii), JOHN, 3rd Earl of Bute
Bute, John Stuart, 4th Earl & 1st Marquess of *see* STUART (ii), JOHN, 4th Earl & 1st Marquess of Bute
Bute, Mary Ellen **10** 688
Bute Mazer **28** 260
Butembo, Centre de Butembo **33** 598
Butera, Prince of (*c.* 1500–*c.* 1600) **31** 717
Buteux, François-Charles **11** 410
Buthaud, René **4** 391
Buthaul **30** 808
Buthe, Michael **5** 306*
Buthrotum *see* BUTRINT
Buti, Domenicho d'Antonio **11** 193
Buti, Ludovico **31** 55
Butinone, Bernardino **5** 307–8*
collaboration **21** 525; **33** 633
patrons and collectors **9** 112
restorations by others **21** 825
works **5** *307*; **11** 294
Butinone, Jacopo **5** 307
Butkara **5** 308–9*; **15** *264*; **23** *797*
Butkara I **5** 308–9; **15** 445
Butkara III **5** 309
reliefs **5** *308*, 309, *309*; **15** 446
Butler (family) **31** 652
Butler, Charles (1822-1910) **5** 311*
Butler, Charles (1870-1953) **17** 547
Butler, Cotterell *see* BUTLER, REG(INALD COTTERELL)
Butler, Edmund **2** 570
Butler, Guillermo **7** 847; **9** 113
Butler, Horacio **2** 400; **5** 311*; **23** 174; **27** 460
Butler, Howard Crosby **5** 311*; **9** 527, 528
Butler, James **14** 281
Butler, James, 19th Earl of Ormonde *see* BUTLER, JAMES, 1st Marquess of Ormonde
Butler, James, 1st Duke of Ormonde (1610-88) **5** 312*; **16** 6; **26** 475
architecture **9** 315; **16** 22, 35
paintings **16** 13; **31** 779
sculpture **3** 875
Butler, James, 1st Marquess of Ormonde (*d* 1838) **29** 723
Butler, James (John) Sterling **5** 310*
Butler, Lady **5** 310*
groups and movements **10** 878
patrons and collectors **14** 148
reproductive prints by others **6** 451; **8** 549; **29** 486
works **3** 390, *390*; **10** 254
Butler, Lawrence **2** 757
Butler, Margaret **23** 62
Butler, Michael **16** 28
Butler, Mildred Anne **16** 17
Butler, Pierce, 8th Earl of Ormonde **5** 835
Butler, Reg(inald Cotterell) **5** 312*
patrons and collectors **13** 629
pupils **8** 282; **32** 423
works **10** 268; **19** 492
Butler, R. M. **16** 11
Butler, Samuel (1613-80) **4** 361; **14** 637
Butler, Samuel (*fl c.* 1760s) **10** 295
Butler, Theodore Earl **21** 868
Butler, Thomas **19** 592
Butler, Thomas, 10th Earl of Ormonde **16** 22
Butler, Walter Richmond **31** 763
Butler, William Deane **5** 309–10*; **22** 282
Butler-Bowden Cope **23** 461
Butler *Madonna and Child* **20** 309
Butler Manufacturing Company **11** 835
Butler Museum *see under* HARROW SCHOOL (MIDDX)
Butley Priory (Suffolk) **14** 420; **20** 571
gate-house **14** *420*
Butlins **6** 396
Butmir **4** *459*; **5** 313*; **25** *470*, *471*
Buto *see* FARAIN, TELL EL-
Butoh **24** 409
Buton Rinpoche **5** 105; **28** 543
Butor **14** 910
Butor, Michel **29** 606
Butrint **1** *537*, 538; **5** 313*; **26** *906*
Archaeological Museum **1** 546
shrine of Asklepios **26** 907
Butrón castle **29** 272
Butrymowicz, Zofia **30** 330
Butsel, Andries van **2** 199
Butsel, Joost van **2** 199
Butt, Fuad 'Ali **23** 799
Butt, Khalid Saeed **23** 800
Butt, Rashid **23** 800
butter **8** 128
Butterfield, Lindsay **10** 356
Butterfield, William **5** 313–16*; **10** 335
architecture **4** 787
cathedrals **1** 151; **4** 65; **26** 74; **28** 296
chapels **10** 238
churches **5** *314*, 561, 731; **10** 237; **25** 173; **28** 295; **30** 503; **32** 783
colleges **4** 769; **5** *316*; **7** 647; **23** 688; **27** 626
houses **13** *203*
restorations **9** 203
schools **25** I2; **28** 156
collaboration **5** 640; **14** 746; **33** 213
groups and movements **10** 237, 238, 281; **13** 203, 207, 209; **32** 415
methods **25** 172
butterfly books *see under* BOOKS → forms
Butteri, Cresci **5** 317
Butteri, Giovanni Maria **4** 859; **5** 317*; **21** 22
Buttet, David **18** 873
But Thap Temple **32** 473–4, 476
Lotus Tower **32** *473*
sculpture **5** *100*; **32** *479*, 479–80
Butti, Enrico **16** 707; **21** 533
Buttigli, Marcello **20** 94
Büttikofer, J. **14** 817
Buttle Church **26** 647
Büttner, Gottlob **2** 127
Button, John **12** 218
button rugs *see under* RUGS → types
buttons **1** 295; **9** 259; **10** 136; **17** 524, 525
materials
horn **14** 763
ivory **16** 799
papier mâché **24** 61
uses
baskets **1** 295
buttresses **5** 317–19*; **28** 498
angle **5** 317–19*, *318*
clasping **5** *318*, 319*
diagonal **5** *318*, 319*
flying **5** *318*, 319*; **20** 574, *574*, 575, 581–2, 583; **24** 825–6
Austria **19** 377
England **33** 209
France **6** 493; **13** 39; **20** *581*, *582*, 583
Gothic **5** 319; **9** 672; **13** 35, 39; **14** 519
internal **5** 319*
setback **5** *318*, 319*
wall **5** 317–19*, *318*
Butts, Alfred **31** 266
Butts, John **3** 284
Butts, Thomas **4** 119, 120
Butucheny Church **21** 810
Buty, Laurent, Bishop of Carpentras **3** 841
Butzbach, Georg **12** 906; **20** 322
Butzbach, Hesse Schloss **31** 526
Butzbach, Paul **12** 906; **20** 322
Buu Chi **32** 483
Buvelot, Abram-Louis **2** 745, 746; **4** 717; **5** 319–20*
Buvina, Andrija **8** 177, 180
Buwayhid *see* BUYID
Bux, Allah **5** 320*; **23** 799, 804
Buxadera & Compañía **3** 826
Buxar **15** 453
Buxbom, Hanns *see* PUCHSPAUM, HANS
Büxel, Winfried **3** 510
Buxheim Abbey **5** 895; **21** 841
Abbey Church **29** 838
bookplates **4** 372, *373*
woodcuts **33** 348
Buxtehude *Madonna* **12** 469
Buxton, 5th Baronet **30** 533
Buxton, Lady **30** 533
Buyck, Pierre François **3** 548; **5** 320*
Buyck, René **5** 320
Buyid **5** 321–2*; **16** 113
architecture **16** 76
woodwork **16** 492
see also:
'ADUD AL-DAWLA, Amir
BAHA AL-DAWLA, Amir
FAKHR AL-DAWLA, Amir
'IZZ AL-DAWLA, Amir
RUKN AL-DAWLA, Amir
SAMSAM AL-DAWLA, Amir
Buynaksk **27** 433
Buys, Cornelis (1745-1826) **5** 322
Buys, Cornelis, I (*fl* 1490-1524) **7** 868; **16** 831; **20** 615; **22** 836; **28** 215
Buys, Cornelis, II (*c.* 1500-45/6) **7** 868; **16** 831; **22** 71
Buys, Cornelis Bernudes **16** 573
Buys, Jacobus **1** 808; **5** 322*; **22** 907
teachers **25** 649; **31** 365
Buys, Jan *see* BUIJS, JAN (WILLEM EDUARD)
Buysse, Georges **19** 792
Buyst, Edward **24** 259
Buyster, Philippe de **3** 570; **5** 322–3*
collaboration **20** 291; **26** 91; **27** 821
patrons and collectors **5** 168; **18** 885
pupils **20** 480
works **11** 559; **19** 76
Buyten, Hendrick van **32** 267
Buytewech, Willem (Pietersz.) **5** 323–6*; **13** 895; **27** 230
collaboration **14** 94
drawings **22** 840
pupils **29** 79
reproductive prints by others **28** 79; **32** 140, 621
works **1** 659; **5** *324*, *325*; **10** 553; **12** 290; **18** 710; **25** 606
Buytewech, Willem Willemsz. **5** 323
Büyükada, Şakir Pasha Mansion **12** 85
Büyük Arslan Taş *see* ARSLANTAŞ
Buyukijskii, Dimitar **5** 326*
Büyük Kapıkaya **24** 690
Büyük Kasislik Church **9** 543
Buza, Abdurrahim **1** 546; **5** 326*
works **1** 540, *540*
Buzas, Stefan **8** 248
Buzău, Dumbrava cemetery **26** 715
Bu Zhongqian **7** 60
Buzio, Ippolito **4** 405; **29** 559
Buzun, Imamzada Karrar **16** 165
Buzzacarina, Fina *see* FINA BUZZACARINA OF PADUA
Buzzi, Carlo **5** 327*; **21** 518, 532
Buzzi, Elia Vincenzo **5** 326, 327*; **21** 533
works **16** 701, 704
Buzzi, Giovanni Antonio **25** 7
Buzzi, Giuseppe **5** 326, 327*; **23** 701
Buzzi, Giuseppe Maria **5** 326, 327
Buzzi, Ippolito **2** 163
Buzzi, Lelio **4** 426; **5** 327–8*
works **4** *426*
Buzzichelli, Giovanni **9** 95
Buzzini, Giacopo Antonio **8** 429
Bwa **5** 216, 328–30*
divination instruments **5** 330*
leaves **1** *384*
masks **1** 290, *384*; **5** 217, 328–30*, *330*
sculpture **5** 330*
Bwaka **1** 366
Bwende **1** 259, 269, 403
burial practices **1** *260*
By, John **23** 630
Byala **5** 156
By altarpiece **13** 120

Byalynitsky-Birulya, Vitol'd **27** 395
Byam Shaw *see* SHAW, BYAM
Byars, James Lee **4** 168
Byart *see* BIARD
Byart, Colin (de) *see* BIART, COLIN (DE)
Bya-rung-kha-shor *see* BODHNATH
Byblos **5** 331; **9** 786
Byblos *see under* GIBELET
Bybrook Plantation, Great House **16** 885
Bycullah, Victoria and Albert Museum **4** 289
Byde Mill **2** 148
Bydgoszcz **25** 120
Bye, Johan de **9** 194; **19** 102
Byelorussia *see* BELARUS'
Byer, Pat **16** 889
works **16** *889*
Byer-Dunphy, Patricia **2** 152
Byerley, Tom **33** 22
Byfield (MA), Dummer Academy **28** 156
Byfield, George **5** 640; **32** 243
Bygdö, Norsk Folkemuseum **29** 541
Bygdøy **23** *218*
Museum **32** 274
Oscarshall **23** 221, 232, 233; **30** 852
Byggekunst **24** 452
Byggeriets Studiearkiv **8** 761
Byker **23** 20
Bykov, Gennady (Vasil'yevich) **27** 426
Bykov, N. D. **27** 439
Bykovsky, Konstantin (Mikhaylovich) **5** 333–4*; **25** 187
Bykovsky, Mikhail (Dorimedontovich) **5** 332–3*; **27** 377, 578
Byland Abbey (N. Yorks) **7** 353; **12** 5–6; **13** 44; **21** 838; **22** 217; **26** 381; **32** 94
ambulatory **1** 768
tiles **7** 275; **30** 877
Bylany **25** 498, 500
Bylert, Jan van *see* BIJLERT, JAN (HERMANSZ) VAN
Bylica, Martin **12** 812
Byllyng Bible *see under* BIBLES → individual manuscripts
Byloye **27** 580
Byneset **23** 224
Byng (family) **21** 832
Byng, Edward **18** 146
Byng, George **29** 808
Byōdōin *see under* UJI
Byram House **10** 643
Byrd **32** 784
Byrd, J. **24** 407
Byrd, William (1543-1623) **14** 675
Byrd, William (1624-90?) **5** 336*; **23** 688, 691
Byrd, William (1674-1744) **13** 619
Byrdcliffe Colony **2** 572
Byres, James **2** 559; **5** 336–7*; **10** 637, 642; **13** 303
dealing **2** 559; **10** 366; **31** 244
pupils **13** 644
works **14** 114; **24** 845
Byrne, (Francis) Barry **5** 337*; **25** 446
Byrne, Patrick **5** 337–8*
Byrne, William **14** 279; **18** 720; **33** 14
Byron, George Gordon, 6th Baron Byron **2** 555; **3** *295*; **9** 286; **31** 471; **32** 496
screens (ii) (furniture) **28** 298
writings **2** 642; **8** 639; **13** 304; **32** 196
Byron, Richard **9** 308
Byron, Robert **5** 338*
Byron, William, 4th Lord Byron **30** 890
Byss, Johann Joseph **5** 338
Byss, Johann Rudolf **5** 338–9*; **8** 391; **25** 188; **33** 432
Bysta, Master of **2** 383
Byström, Johan Niklas **5** 339*; **30** 86
assistants **21** 471
patrons and collectors **31** 362
pupils **29** 1
works **30** 109
Bystrzycki, Krzysztof **33** 606
Bytča Castle **28** 849, 852
Bytiye **22** 178; **29** 19
Bytová kultura **24** 440
Bytown *see* OTTAWA
Bytyń **25** 512
Byzantine **9** 506–669*, *507*, *510*, *511*, *512*, *513*
acanthus **1** 109, *110*, *111*
aesthetics **9** 622
alabaster (gypsum) **9** 657
albs **9** 642
allegories **9** 519–20*
altarpieces **5** 300; **9** 623
altars **1** 694*; **9** 656
alum **9** 665
ambos **1** 764; **9** 590
amices **9** 642
amphorae **9** 632
aprons **9** 643
aquamarines **9** *653*
aqueducts **2** 242; **9** 560
arcades **9** 524, 549
arches **4** 774
architectural decorations **6** 564; **9** 527, 543, 547
architecture **9** 523–8*, 542*, 543–7*, 549*, 550–53*, 556–9*, 560–61*
brick **4** 773–4*; **9** 524, 547, 553, *554*
Bulgaria **5** 147; **9** 551–2
Cappadocia **5** 673*
Crete **8** 155
Georgia **9** 548–9
Greece **7** 170; **9** 545–7*, 550–51*
Macedonia (ii) (former Yugoslavia) **19** 882
Mesopotamia **9** 538–41*, 542–3*
military **9** 553–6*, *554*, *555*; **21** 562
Palestine **9** 538–41*, 542–3*, 547–9*
Portugal **18** 390
Rhodes (island) **26** 293*
rock-cut **5** 673–5*
Serbia **9** 552–3
stone **9** 538
Syria **9** 538–41*, 542–3*, 547–9*
Turkey **9** 536–7*, 542*, 543–5*, 549–50*
Ukraine **31** 546
architraves **9** *592*
arcosolia **9** *593*, 598
art history **3** 424; **18** 215, 899; **26** 332
art legislation **9** 654
audience halls **9** 557
automata **29** 96
baptisteries **3** 191*; **8** 155; **9** 524, 541
barbicans **9** 554
basalt **9** 538
baths **9** 553, 560, 561
beakers **9** 646
beds **3** 483
belts **9** 653
Bibles **4** 3–5*; **9** 602, 606–8*, 620; **19** 169; **20** 340; **32** 461
birri **9** 640
bloodstone (chalcedony) **12** 254, *255*
bone **9** *521*, *651*, 651
book covers **9** 651, 656, 658; **16** 798
borders (manuscript) **20** 338
bottles **9** 646
bowls **9** 634, *645*, 657
boxes **9** 648, 651
Byzantine—cont.
bracae **9** 640
bracelets **9** 653
brick **4** *771*, 773–4*; **9** 524, 545, 547
bricklaying **4** 770; **7** *273*, 273–4*
bridges **9** 560; **17** *702*
bronze **8** 199
busts **5** 299–300*; **9** 587
cage-cups **9** 645
calendars **9** 603, 610, 616; **21** 138
cameos **12** 254–5, *255*
campagi **9** 641, 642
camps (military) **9** 553
canon tables **5** 624; **9** 608, 620
capitals **1** *110*; **5** *670*; **9** 589, *589*, 592
carpets **9** 666
caskets **5** 917; **9** *521*, *651*
catacombs **9** 570
cathedrals
Croatia **25** *252*
Italy **31** *162*
Macedonia (ii) (former Yugoslavia) **23** *373*
Mesopotamia **9** 539
Palestine **9** 539
Syria **9** 539
Turkey **16** *592*
Ukraine **18** *38*
ceilings **9** 654
censers **6** 173–4; **9** 632, 656
chalcedony **12** 254
chalices **9** 656, 657, 661
chapels **9** 544
see also parekklesia
chasubles **9** 642, 643
chess sets **6** 557
chlamydes **9** 251
chronicles **7** 244
chronologies **1** *852*
churches **7** 260–62*; **9** 85, 522, 523–4, 526, 527, 528, *529*, 536–7, 542*, 543–7*, 549, 550–53, 588
basilicas **7** 252–3*; **8** 155; **9** 525, 528, 535*, 536–7, *537*, 542, 544, 547
Bulgaria **9** 551–2
Cappadocia **7** 261; **9** 536
centrally planned **7** 255–6*; **16** 602–3
compact-domed basilicas **7** 252; **9** 542
cross-domed **7** 256; **9** 542
cross-in-square **7** 256, 260; **9** *545*, 545–7, *546*
decoration **7** 272*; **9** 518, 576
bricklaying **7** *273*, 273–4*
mosaics **7** 272–3*
sculpture **7** 273–4*
wall paintings **7** 272*
domed basilicas **9** 537
domed octagon **7** 170; **9** 547
Georgia **7** 262; **9** 548–9; **30** *305*, *306*
Greece **7** *260*; **9** 542*, 545–7*, *546*, *547*, 550–51, *551*, *552*; **14** *776*; **17** *839*; **18** 571; **21** *860*; **30** *725*
Greek-cross octagon **9** *547*; **14** 776
Mesopotamia **9** 538–41*, 542–3*
Palestine **9** 538–41*, *541*, 542–3*, 547–9*, *548*
rock **5** *674*, 674–5*; **26** 483
Russia **7** 261
Serbia **9** 552–3; **13** *264*
Sicily **23** *846*
Syria **7** 261; **9** 538–41*, *539*, *540*, 542–3*, 547–9*
Turkey **4** *771*; **8** *777*; **9** 536–7, 543–5*, *545*, 549–50
Ukraine **31** *547*, *548*
ciboria (i) (vessels) **9** 656
ciboria (ii) (structure) **7** 301–2*
cingula **9** 642, 643
circuses **9** 556, 560
cisterns **7** *354*; **9** 560
Byzantine—cont.
citadels **9** 554
Classicism **7** 382
cloaks **9** 639
coats **9** 643
cochineal **9** 665
coins **7** 533; **9** 635–9*, *636*; **14** 408
collections **32** 212
icons **9** 623
sculpture **7** 562
textiles **9** 664
colophons **9** 605
combs (liturgical) **9** 648
consular diptychs **9** *251*, 647, *648*, 648–9, 650
copper **9** 652, 659, 663
cosmologies **9** 616
cotton **9** *640*, 664, *665*
craftsmen and artists **9** 509
crenellations **9** 553
crosses **8** *199*, 199–200*, 202–3*, *203*; **9** 656, 658, *659*
cross feet **8** 205
crowns **9** 653; **26** 79
crucifixes **8** 210
dalmatics **9** 640, 642
damask **9** 665
dictionaries of art **10** 209, 213
dies (ii) (stamps) **9** 635
diplomatic gifts **9** 509, 657
domes **4** 774; **9** 85, 525, 544
Crete **8** 155
semi-dome **9** 84
Turkey **19** *363*
donjons **9** *555*, 555–6
doors **9** 599–600, *600*
dosserets **2** 292
drawings **9** 615
dress **9** 252*, 639–44*, *644*
dyes **9** 612, 664–5
earrings **9** 653
embroidery **9** *668*, 668–9
enamel **9** 623, *633*, *645*, 659–63*; **12** V2; **15** I; **32** *212*
champlevé **9** 659, 661, 663
cloisonné **4** IV2; **8** *203*; **9** 653, 657, *658*, 659–63, *660*, *662*, *663*; **10** 193
filigree **9** 659, *659*
Italy **16** 750
Senkschmelz **9** 660–63
Vollschmelz **9** 660, 663
enceintes **9** 553–5, *554*
enchiria **9** 643
encolpia **8** 203
encyclopedias of art **10** 213
epigonatia **9** 643, *643*
epimanikia **9** 642, *643*
epitaphioi **9** *668*; **10** 437
epitrachelia **9** 642, *643*
erotic art **10** 475
Evangeliaries **9** 608, 610–11, 616
fans **9** 656
fibres **9** 664*
fibulae **9** 653
firing **9** 633
fonts (baptismal) **9** *591*
fora **9** 560
fortifications **9** 524, 553–6*, *554*, 558*; **21** 562, *563*
fortresses **9** 553, 554, 555–6*
forts **9** 554, 555; **21** *563*
frames **9** 658; **11** 374
friezes **29** *817*
frontispieces **9** 608, 610, 611, 613, 615, 616, 617
fucus **9** 665
galleries (ii) (corridors) **9** 555
gardens **12** 71–2*
gates **27** *344*
gem-engraving **12** *254*, 254–5*, *255*
gems **9** 657, *660*, *662*; **32** *212*
gilding **9** *645*, 654
glass **9** 562, 644–6*, *645*, 657; **12** 788
glazes **9** 633
goblets **9** *634*
Byzantine—cont.
gold **6** 173; **7** *763*; **8** *203*; **9** 606, 611, 618, 623, *636*, 652–3, *653*, 654*, 657*, *658*, 659, *659*, *660*, *662*, *663*, 668; **15** I; **19** 351; **22** 162; **32** 212, *212*
gold glasses **9** 645
gold leaf **9** 617, 623, 645; **19** 356
Gospel books **7** 222; **9** 608–10, 620, 651; **13** 21
guidebooks **13** 808
hardstones **8** *199*; **9** 623, 657; **14** 170; **15** I
harnesses **14** 183*
hats **9** 644
headpieces (manuscripts) **9** 609, 610, 618
headscarves **9** 643
historiography **2** 880; **8** 872; **9** 527–8
hoods **9** 643, *644*
hospitals **9** 561
houses **9** 560, 561
human figures **9** 622
iconoclasm **6** 175; **9** 514; **12** 71; **15** 75, 80
iconography **7** 220–22*; **9** 516*, 517–18*, 519–21*, *520*, *521*, 572, 573, 575, 576, 583, 595, 596, 609–10, 616, 617, 622, 623, 625–6, 629, 635; **10** 209, 437; **12** 71–2; **15** 76; **19** 169; **22** 162; **23** 374
icons **2** 3; **7** *221*, 222, 230; **9** 517, 518, 597–8, 601*, 621–30*, 632, 658; **10** 197; **13** 131; **15** 75*, 76, *76*, I, II3, III; **24** 3; **26** 332; **31** 343
architrave **9** 622, 625, 628, 629
Bulgaria **5** 151–2, *152*; **9** 633
calendar **25** 183
Crete **9** 622
Cyprus **9** 627
double-sided **9** 622
Egypt **9** *624*, *625*, *626*; **28** *762*, *763*
Greece **9** *630*; **15** II1
Italy **32** *212*
Jerusalem, Latin Kingdom of **9** 627
Macedonia (ii) (former Yugoslavia) **9** *628*
Palestine **9** 627
relief **9** 597–8, *601*
Russia **9** 629; **15** *76*, II2; **27** *305*, *383*, *384*; **30** V3
Syria **9** 627
Ukraine **26** *141*; **31** *555*
indigo **9** 665
initials (manuscript) **9** 609, 618
inkwells **9** 657
inscriptions **4** 774; **9** 576, 660
insignia **9** 603
ivory **5** 917; **9** *251*, *514*, *521*, *600*
ivory-carvings **9** *521*, *647*, 647–52*, *648*, *650*; **16** 798; **18** 676; **23** 660
jasper **12** 254, *255*
jewellery **9** 652–4*, 657; **17** 519
kaftans **9** *641*
kermes **9** 665
kilns **9** 633
Lamentation groups **18** 676
lamps **9** *520*, 656, 657
lapis lazuli **9** 623; **12** 254
lead **9** *637*
Lectionaries **9** 611, 620–21, *621*
limestone **9** 538, 590–91, *591*
linen **9** 664, 668
liturgical furnishings **7** 278–9*
liturgical objects **9** 656; **10** 437
machicolation **9** 554, 556
madder **9** 665
maniples **9** 642
mantles **9** 639, 643
manuals **12** 71

Byzantine—cont.
manuscript illumination **9** 602–3*, 604–18*, 619–21*, 622; **17** 664; **19** 356; **20** 340; **21** *138*; **22** 519; **24** 177, *178*
Egypt **9** 619
England **9** *603*
Greece **9** *607*, *609*, *611*, *614*, *615*; **28** *764*
Lebanon **9** 619
Mesopotamia **9** 619
Syria **9** 619
Turkey **9** *621*
9th cent. AD **7** *181*
manuscripts **9** 602–3*, 604–18*, 619–21*; **17** 664
France **9** 603
North Africa **9** 603
Spain **9** 603
mappae **9** 641, 642
marble **7** *221*; **9** 587, *587*, 588, *592*, *593*, *595*, *598*; **27** 827
Crete **8** 155
Prokonnesian **9** *589*, *593*
marks **9** 654; **20** 443
martyria **8** 155; **9** 528
masonry **9** 553
cloisonné **4** 773; **9** 547, *551*; **20** 571
herringbone **20** 571
opus mixtum **4** 773
spolia **4** 773
mausolea **9** 556–7
medallions **7** *763*; **21** 2
metal **9** 668
metalwork **9** 539, 654*
miniatures (manuscript illumination) **4** *4*; **9** *605*, *620*; **20** I
Greece **9** *607*, *609*, *611*, *614*, *615*
Turkey **7** *228*; **9** *621*
Ukraine **31** *556*, *558*
6th cent. AD **27** *174*; **32** *462*
mitres **9** 643
monasteries **7** 227–30*; **9** 514, 522, 524, 561, 576; **21** 834
Cappadocia **5** *675*
Egypt **28** 761
Greece **22** *226*, *227*
Ukraine **18** *40*
monuments **22** 43*
mortars (building) **4** 773
mosaics **9** 526, 561–2*, 563–4*, 570–81*, 582–6*, 623, 627, 630, 645; **12** 71; **15** II3; **19** 351, 356; **22** 161–2, 163, 165
Byzantine
mosaics—cont.
Crete **8** 155
Cyprus **9** 566–7*, 580
Egypt **28** *763*
Greece **7** 170; **9** 565–6*, *572*, 577–9, *585*, *630*; **22** *162*; **30** *721*, *723*
Italy **9** *573*, 581; **22** *161*; **26** 652–3
North Africa **9** 569–70*
Palestine **9** 567–8*, *574*
Sicily **9** 581
Syria **9** *567*, 567–8*
Turkey **2** *158*; **7** *220*; **9** *564*, 564–5*, *577*, *583*; **16** *594*, *598*, *601*, *809*; **21** III2; **22** *157*
Ukraine **18** *37*, 38–9; **31** *554*
mounts (icons) **9** 622, 625
narratives **9** 609–10; **22** 519–20*
naturalism **9** 520–21*
necklaces **9** 653, *653*
New Testaments **9** 608–11*; **27** 173
niello **10** 381
ochre **9** 623
Old Testaments **9** 611–14*
omophoria **9** 642, 643, *643*
opus interrasile **9** 652, 653; **21** 327
opus sectile **16** *596*
orbs **26** 81
ornament **9** 618, 619, 620, 621
outworks **9** 555
painting **9** 561*, 621–30; **19** 351, 356
encaustic **9** 623; **10** 197
fresco **8** 155; **9** 562, 576; **18** 417
landscape **18** 703*
panel **19** 356; **24** 3
secco **9** 562
still-lifes **29** 665
wall **9** 526, 561–2*, 570–81*, 582–6*; **26** 332; **32** 804*
Bulgaria **9** *579*
Cappadocia **5** 675–6*, *676*, *677*, 677–8*
Crete **8** 155; **18** 460–61
Cyprus **7** *229*; **9** 580; **17** 743
Greece **9** 577–9, *578*, *584*, 585; **17** *839*; **22** *406*, *407*, *409*
Italy **9** 581
Macedonia (ii) (former Yugoslavia) **23** 373, *374*
Byzantine
painting
wall—cont.
Nubia **10** 803
Serbia **28** *445*, 445–7, *446*
Turkey **9** *581*; **32** II1
Ukraine **18** 39
palaces **9** 524, 553, 556–8*
block **9** 558–9*, *559*
Croatia **9** *558*
fortified **9** 557–8*
Turkey **9** *559*
pallia (ecclesiastical) **9** 641, 642
parekklesia **9** 544–5, 547; **24** 110*, *110*
pastophoria **8** 155
patens **9** 656, 657
patronage **7** 217; **9** 519, 521–3*, 539, 623
pattern books **9** 623; **24** 269
pavements **8** 155
pearls **9** 653, *653*, 657, *660*, *662*, 668
pendants (jewellery) **9** 645, *659*, *663*
perfume burners **9** *520*
peristyle courtyards **9** 557
personifications **9** 519–20*
phelonia **9** 643, *643*
pigments **9** 612, 623, 664
plaques **9** *514*, 590, 593, 646, 647, *650*, 650, 651, 658, 661
plaster **9** 562; **29** 816–17*, *817*
plates **9** 655, *655*, 656, 657
poetry **25** 72
polykandela **9** 656, *656*
polystauria **9** 643
porphyry **27** 827
portraits **9** 622, 628
author portraits **2** 836; **9** *605*, 609, 610; **20** I
coins **9** *636*
painting **9** 580, 609, 611, 616, 617
sculpture **9** 587, *587*
seals **9** *637*
pottery **9** 631–4*, *633*, *634*
proportions (human) **14** 871
Psalters **7** 222; **9** 604, 611, 613–14, 620
purple codices **27** *174*; **32** *462*
pyxides (boxes) **9** 648, 651; **16** 798
religion **21** 138
reliquaries **5** 300; **9** *647*, 657, 658, *658*, 659–60, *663*; **26** 143–4*
Byzantine
reliquaries—cont.
Italy **9** *520*
staurothèques **9** 650; **26** 143
representation **9** 622
revetments **9** 656, 658; **16** 599
rings **9** 653
rock crystal **26** 485
romance manuscripts **9** 519
roofs **9** 539
rotondas **8** 155
roundels **9** *645*
saints' lives **9** 616; **21** 138
sakkoi **9** 643
sapphires **12** 254
sarcophagi **9** 596–7; **27** 827–8*
sardonyx **12** 254
scapulars **9** 644, *644*
scarves **9** 643
sceptres **26** 80
screens (i) (architectural) **9** 600–601*; **28** 291*
iconostases **7** 279, *279*; **9** 622–3, 625, 627; **28** 291
templa **28** 291, *291*
scriptoria **9** 604
scripts **9** 514, 604, 610, 612
sculpture **9** 587–8*
architectural **7** 273–4*; **9** 588, 589*, 599*
marble **9** 587, *587*
reliefs **7** *221*; **9** 594–9*, *595*, *598*; **26** 135–6*
stone **9** 589*, 594–9*
wood **9** 599–602*
seals **9** 635–8*, *637*; **33** 5
sewing **9** 640
shields **14** 408
shirts **9** 252
shrines (i) (cult) **9** 656
shrouds **9** *666*
silk **9** 520, *640*, *641*, 663–4, *664*, *665*, 665–9, *666*, *668*; **16** 429; **28** 715; **30** 552
silver **8** 199; **9** *520*, 612, 623, 652, 654–6*, *655*, *656*, 657–8*; **32** 212
silver-gilt **8** *199*; **9** *520*, 623, 657, *658*, *660*
skaramangia **9** 252, 641
soapstone **9** 647, 651
spoons **9** 654, 656
stamps **9** 655
sticharia **9** 642, *643*
stoles (ecclesiastical) **9** 642–3
stone **1** 694; **9** 538, 562, 589*, 594–9*; **27** 827
Byzantine—cont.
stucco **29** 816–17*, *817*
symbolism (critical term) **9** 519–20*
tables **9** 656
tapestries **9** 666
textiles **9** 663–9*
theatres **9** 553, 560
theories (art) **15** 75
threads **9** 668
thrones **9** 656
tie-bars **9** 599
tiles **9** 632, 633, *633*
togas **9** 639–40
towers **9** 549, 553, 554, 555–6, *555*
trade **9** 515
craftsmen and artists **16** 146
glass **3** 593
paper **16** 351
pottery **16** 416
silk **28** 721
trappings **14** 183*
treatises **9** 603
tripods **9** 633
trousers **9** 640
tunics **9** *252*, 639, 640, *640*, 641, 643, *644*
vases **14** 170
vaults (ceiling) **9** 524, 526; **32** 89
veils **9** 644
vestments (ecclesiastical) **9** 641–3*, *643*
villas **8** 155; **9** 553
voussoirs **4** 774
walls **9** 553–4, *554*, 557–8
waxes **33** 5
weaving **9** 665–6; **30** 552
weights **9** 645
woad **9** 665
women **23** 830
wood **1** 694; **9** *521*, 539, 599–602*, *600*
wool **9** 664
zonaria **9** 643, *644*
see also POST-BYZANTINE
Byzantine blossom **5** 339*
Byzantine Institute of America **16** 595
Byzantine Revival **3** *746*; **4** 787; **5** 339–40*; **14** 580
Byzantion *see under* ISTANBUL
Byzantios **26** 639
Byzantios, Pericles **13** 353
Byzes of Naxos **13** 387
Bzummar, Armenian Monastery **2** 443

C

C, Master **5** 803
C. A., Master **20** 793*
Caaba *see* MECCA → Ka'ba
Ça Anglada, Pere **3** 218; **5** 341*
assistants **13** 106
pupils **5** 613; **23** 415
works **3** 221; **13** 106, 123
Caba, Antonio **32** 97
Cabaleto, Giovanni Battista de *see* CAVALLETTO, GIOVANNI BATTISTA
Caballero, José **5** 341*; **29** 286
Caballero, Juan **5** 368
Caballero, Luis **5** 341*; **7** 610
Caballero, Martín Polo *see* POLO CABALLERO, MARTÍN
Caballero y Góngora, Antonio, Bishop of Córdoba **1** 741
Caballero y Llanes, R. **31** 718
Caballettus, Giovanni Battista *see* CAVALLETTO, GIOVANNI BATTISTA
Caballito Pintado **21** 230–31
Caballo Muerto **21** 718; **29** 160
sculpture **29** 170
temple **29** 165
Cabaña, La *see* LA CABAÑA
Cabanel, Alexandre **5** 341–2*; **11** 544, 546, 664; **14** 588; **24** 141
competitions **25** 638
dealers **9** 424
groups and movements **2** 530; **24** 171; **28** 345
patrons and collectors **5** 57; **22** 35
prizes (artists') **24** 171
pupils
Almeida Júnior, José Ferraz de **1** 681
Bastien-Lepage, Jules **3** 357
Besnard, (Paul-)Albert **3** 874
Blanc, (Paul) Joseph **4** 124
Boutet de Monvel, (Louis-)Maurice **4** 589
Bukovac, Vlaho **5** 141
Bussière, Gaston **5** 296
Carrière, Eugène **5** 880
Constant, (Jean-Joseph-)Benjamin **7** 759
Cormon, Fernand **7** 859
Cox, Kenyon **8** 85
Dagnan-Bouveret, P(ascal)-A(dolphe)-J(ean) **8** 447
Debat-Ponsan, Edouard-Bernard **8** 589
Flameng, François **11** 156
Gervex, Henri (Alexandre) **12** 496
Josselin de Jong, Pieter de **17** 664
Kossak, Wojciech **18** 398
Léandre, Charles-Lucien **18** 904
Lepic, Ludovic (-Napoléon) **19** 215
Le Sidaner, Henri (Eugène Augustin) **19** 239
Lévy, Henri Léopold **19** 282
Loureiro, Artur José de Sousa **19** 728
Maillol, Aristide (-Joseph-Bonaventure) **20** 120
Marques de Oliveira, João **20** 463
Moore, George (Augustus) (1852-1933) **22** 54
Pousão, Henrique **25** 384
Ramalho, António **25** 870
Regnault, (Alexandre-Georges-)Henri **26** 92
Salgado, José Veloso **27** 615
Cabanel, Alexandre
pupils—cont.
Seyyit, Süleyman **28** 528
Silva Porto, António (Carvalho da) **28** 735
Sousa-Pinto, José Júlio de **29** 101
Steer, Philip Wilson **29** 594
Willette, (Léon) Adolphe **33** 198
teachers **24** 737
works **5** *342*; **10** 480; **11** 545, *545*, 546; **14** 588; **23** 295; **24** 396
Cabañeras, José **5** 544
cabaret **24** 409
Cabaret Lagarene, Michael *see* LAGARENE, MICHAEL CABARET
Cabaret Pantagruel *see under* ZURICH
Cabaret Voltaire (group) **3** 113; **8** 434; **14** 845; **16** 903; **22** 279; **24** 405; **26** 75; **28** 352
Cabaret Voltaire (periodical) **8** 434; **24** 427
Cabat, (Nicolas-)Louis **5** 342–3*; **8** 281; **11** 800; **23** 522
Caba y Casamitjana, Antonio **29** 306
Cabbaye, Michiel **7** 466
Cabe **10** 568
Cabeceiras de Basto, Refóios de Basto monastery **26** 254
Cabel *see* ARENTSZ., ARENT
Cabel, Adriaen van der **5** 343*; **12** 801; **13** 257
Cabellero, Rodrigo **7** 288
Cabello, Francisco Gutiérrez *see* GUTIÉRREZ CABELLO, FRANCISCO
Cabello, Luis **4** 258; **15** 34; **25** 365
Cabestany, Notre-Dame-des-Anges **26** 610
Cabestany, Master of **20** 638–9*; **26** 610
works **20** *639*; **27** 805
Cabeza Larga cemetery **24** 89; **29** 158
Cabezalero, Juan Martín **5** 343*, 874; **29** 282
Cabezas, Francisco **27** 481
Cabianca, Francesco **5** 343–4*; **7** 901
Cabianca, Vincenzo **8** 6; **16** 678; **19** 870; **20** 482; **32** 108
Cabinda **1** *214*
cabinet cards *see under* CARDS → types
cabinet-cupboards *see under* CUPBOARDS → types
Cabinet de l'amateur **24** 838
Cabinet de l'amateur et de l'antiquaire, Le **24** 442, 837
Cabinet des modes, Les *see* JOURNAL DE LA MODE ET DU GOÛT, LE
Cabinet Industries **10** 299
cabinetmaking **11** 595–7, 850; **28** 252, 253–5; **31** 623, 625, 628
cabinet pictures *see under* PAINTING → types
cabinet portraits *see under* PORTRAITS → types
cabinets (i) (rooms) **5** 344–9*; **9** 27, 28; **22** 355, 361
historical and regional traditions
England **10** 368; **22** 356
France **5** 344, *345*; **9** 11
Germany **21** 64
materials
lacquer **5** 349
cabinets (i) (rooms)
materials—cont.
wood **5** 346
techniques
painting **5** 346
types
arrière-cabinets **5** 344
cabinets de jardin **5** 344
cabinets des glaces *see* mirror
cabinets de tableaux *see* painting
cabinets de toilette **5** 344
cabinets de treillage **5** 344
cabinets de verdure **5** 344
Chinese **5** 347; **12** 412
chinoiserie *see* porcelain
grands cabinets **5** 344, 346
mirror **5** 347, *348*, 349*; **12** 412
painting **5** 345
porcelain **5** 347–8*, *348*; **7** 166; **12** 412
see also KUNSTKAMMERN; STUDIOLI; WUNDERKAMMERN
cabinets (ii) (furniture) **5** 350*; **8** 271; **9** 27, 29
historical and regional traditions
Austria **2** 812, *812*
Belgium **3** *581*, 582, 583, 585
China **7** 41
Denmark **8** 739
Egypt, ancient **33** III1
England **9** 27; **10** *298*; **20** *468*
France **9** *28*; **11** 587, 589, *627*; **12** *831*; **24** *150*
Louis XIII style **11** *587*
Louis XIV style **11** *588*
19th cent. **5** *350*; **11** *599*
Germany **12** 421–2, 461
17th cent. **2** *45*, *716*; **12** *422*, *456*, *460*
Gothic **3** *581*
Indian subcontinent **20** VIII2
Italy **5** 191, 350; **16** *728*
Japan **5** 350; **18** II2
Netherlands, the **20** *467*; **22** 873, *873*; **33** IV2
Portugal **25** *306*
Spain **5** 191, 350
Sri Lanka **29** 470, 471
United States of America **31** 631, *631*
materials
acacia **33** IV2
amber **1** 762
bronze **11** *627*
cedar **3** 585; **11** *599*; **25** *305*; **33** III1
ebony **3** 582, 583; **5** 350; **9** 687; **11** 587, *587*, 589; **12** 421, *422*
enamel **12** *456*
glass **3** 583
hardstones **12** 421, 461
ivory **2** *45*; **11** *588*; **12** 421, *460*, 461; **29** 471
lacquer **3** 583; **7** 166; **12** 421; **18** II2
mahogany **30** *95*
marble **12** 423
mother-of-pearl **16** *728*
oak **3** *581*; **22** *873*; **33** IV2
olive-wood **3** 585; **33** IV2
pietra paesina **12** 461
rose-wood **25** *306*; **31** *631*
satin-wood **29** *115*
silver **29** *115*
stink-wood **29** *115*
thuya **3** 585
tortoiseshell **3** 583; **12** 421, 423
veneers **11** *588*, 589
walnut **3** 582; **5** *350*
wood **2** *45*
cabinets (ii) (furniture)—cont.
techniques
carving **11** *587*
gilding **16** *728*
marquetry **11** *588*, 589; **20** *467*, *468*, VIII2
polychromy **11** 589
types
bureaux-cabinets **5** 191, 192
cabinets d'Alemagne **5** 350
cantoor **3** *583*, 583
Cantourgen **12** 424
chiffoniers **30** *95*
clock-cabinets **2** 812
Eger cabinets **2** 812
kunstkasten **3** 582–3, 610
Kunstschränke **18** 522
scriptors **25** *305*
tabernacle cabinets **2** 812, *812*
two-stage **29** *115*, 115
cabins, log *see* LOG CABINS
cable mouldings *see* ROPEWORK
cables **7** 765, 766, 767; **13** 411; **29** 489, *490*; **30** 468
cable-stayed bridges *see under* BRIDGES → types
Cabo Frio **4** *705*
S Mateus **4** 709
Caboolture, Abbey Museum of the Orthodox Church of Christ the King **29** 516
Cabot, Edward Clarke **4** 473; **8** 843; **12** 643; **15** 24; **32** 859
Cabot, Francesc Sans i *see* SANS I CABOT, FRANCESC
Cabot, Lila *see* PERRY, LILA CABOT
Caboud **6** 453
Cabral, Bartolomeu Costa *see* COSTA CABRAL, BARTOLOMEU
Cabral, Francisco **10** 812
Cabral, Lucas **4** 258
Cabral, Manuel **17** 586
Cabral, William Reid *see* REID CABRAL, WILLIAM
Cabral y Aguado Bejarano, Antonio **23** 523
Cabré, Manuel **5** 354*; **21** 902; **32** 175
Cabrera, Daniel **21** 386
Cabrera, Enríquez de *see* CASTILLA, ALMIRANTES DE
Cabrera, Francisco **5** 354–5*; **12** 53, 57; **13** 764
Cabrera, Geles **5** 355*; **28** 330
Cabrera, Germán **5** 355*; **31** 756
Cabrera, Jerónimo de **24** 23
Cabrera, Jerónimo Luis **7** 847
Cabrera, Miguel **5** 355*; **21** 384, 397, 404
pupils **31** 307
works **13** 730
Cabrera, Roberto **5** 356*; **13** 765; **25** 826; **26** 549
Cabrera Moreno, Servando **8** 234
Cabrera y Bobadilla, Pedro Fernández de, Conde de Chinchón *see* CHINCHÓN, PEDRO FERNÁNDEZ DE CABRERA Y BOBADILLA, Conde de
Cabrero (*fl* 1770) **21** 393
Cabrero, Francisco **29** 273
Cabrini, Domenico **7** 925
Cabrini, Jacopo **7** 925
cabriole legs **5** 356*; **10** 292
Cabrita Reis, Pedro **25** 302
Cabrol, Fernand **10** 213; **15** 89
Cabyle **30** 772
Cacahuatenco **14** 829
Cacala, Vladimir **23** 67
Cacault, François **5** 356*; **11** 663
Cacault, Pierre **5** 356
Cacaxtla **5** 356–8*; **21** 185, *193*, 203, 211, *372*
architecture **21** 211
Battle Mural **5** *357*; **21** 229
Building A **5** 357; **21** 229
Building B **5** 357
fortifications **21** 599
Portico Mural *see* Building A
religion **21** 186
wall paintings **5** 356–8*; **7** 636; **21** 226, 229, *229*, 231, 246, 251
Caccavello, Annibale **2** 731; **5** 358*
Caccavello, Desiato **5** 358
Caccavello, Salvatore **2** 731; **5** 358
Caccia, Guglielmo *see* MONCALVO, IL
Caccia, Matteo **3** 96
Caccia, Orsola Maddalena **21** 849
Caccianiga, Francesco **4** 407; **5** 358–9*
Caccianiga, Paolo **2** 395
Cacciatore, Benedetto (1618-54) **26** 148
Cacciatori, Benedetto (1794-1871) **5** 385; **16** 705; **30** 215; **32** 121
Caccini, Giovanni Battista **5** 359–61*
assistants **28** 733
collaboration **3** 827; **21** 755
patrons and collectors **25** 690
works **3** 159; **5** *359*, *361*; **11** 204; **22** 484; **27** 850; **28** 733
Caccini, Giulio **7** 311
Cáceda, Romano Espinoza *see* ESPINOZA CÁCEDA, ROMANO
Cáceres **5** 362*; **26** *908*; **29** *258*, 289, 350
Palacio Episcopal **5** *362*
Cáceres, Alfred **30** 275
Cáceres, Esther **30** 275
Cachan-sur-Seine **4** 788
Cachemaille-Day, N. **3** 110
Cachet, C(arel) A(dolph) Lion *see* LION CACHET, C(AREL) A(DOLPH)
Cacheux, François-Joseph-Emile **5** 362–3*
Cachiopin, Jacomo de **9** 481, *481*
Cachmaille-Day, N. F. **10** 240
Cacho, Raúl **2** 280; **24** 402; **33** 493
Cachoeira do Campo Church **4** 716
Cacialli, Giuseppe **3** 12; **5** 363*; **10** 760; **16** 646
Caconda Church **2** 86
Cacoub, Olivier-Clement **1** 320
CAD (Computer-Aided Design) **2** 334
CADA *see* COLECTIVO ACCIONES DE ARTE
Cadafalch, Josep Puig i *see* PUIG I CADAFALCH, JOSEP
Cadalso de los Vidrios **29** 331
Cadalus, Peter, Count-Bishop of Parma *see* HONORIUS II, Pope
Cadard, Jean **25** 794
Cadard, Pierre **32** 571
Cadart (*fl* 1674) **14** 469
Cadart, Alfred **2** 232; **5** 363–4*; **19** 90; **20** 256
printmakers **20** 603
works **6** 582
Cadart, Alphonse **19** 487
Cadart, Célonie-Sophie **5** 364
Cadart, Léon **5** 364
Cadaval, Jaime de Melo, 3rd Duque de **5** 364–5*
Cadaval, Nuno Alvares Pereira de Melo, 1st Duque de **5** 364*

Cadbury, George **5** 365*; **12** 144
  architecture **4** 85; **11** 785; **31** 725
  ceramics **10** 313
Cadbury, Richard **31** 725
Caddick, Richard **19** 507
caddies, tea *see* TEA CADDIES
caddinets **5** 365*
Caddo **22** 552; **29** 415
Caddy, A. E. **19** 690
Cadell, F. C. B. **15** 892; **24** 372; **28** 238, 270, 289, 290
Cadell, Robert **22** 278
Cadell & Davies **29** 677
Cadena, Luis **5** 365*; **9** 715
Cades (family) **12** 264
Cades, Alessandro **12** 263; **28** 790
Cades, Giuseppe **5** 365–7*
  collaboration **7** 493; **31** 679
  methods **10** 199
  patrons and collectors **2** 577; **4** 471
  personal collection **24** 734
  teachers **7** 916
  works **5** *366*
Cades, Tommaso **3** 812; **14** 285; **28** 790
Cadet, Auguste-Alexandre **22** 128
Cadet de Beaupré, Augustin-Phidias **5** 812; **12** 206
Cadham, J. H. **32** 861
Cadien, Philip **16** 889
Cadighis, Baldassare de *see* BALDASSARE DE CADIGHIS
Cádijsdu'axtc
  works **22** *580*
Cadillac (France) **5** 367*; **11** *505*
Cadillac, Antoine Laumet de La Mothe *see* LA MOTHE CADILLAC, ANTOINE LAUMET DE
Cadillacs *see under* CARS → models
Cadilla de Martínez, María **25** 701
Cadioli, Giovanni **20** 322
caditoia tombs *see under* TOMBS → types
Cádiz **5** 367–8*; **9** 58; **29** *258*
  furniture **29** 316
  Hospital de Mujeres **30** 883
  metalwork **25** 734
  Museo Provincial **5** 368
  New Cathedral **5** *368*; **29** 336
  Nuestra Señora del Rosario **31** 808
cadmium **24** 799*
cadmium chromate **24** 799
cadmium red *see under* PIGMENTS → types
cadmium sulphides **12** 782
cadmium yellow *see under* PIGMENTS → types
cadmopone *see* PIGMENTS → types → cadmium lithopone
Cadmus, Paul **5** 368*; **12** 216; **27** 872
Cadogan (family) **25** 805
Cadogan, George Henry, 5th Earl of Cadogan **33** 565
Cadogan, Gerald **22** 402
Cadogan, William, 1st Earl Cadogan **21** 348; **24** 341
Cadomus *see* CAEN
Cadorin, Guido **22** 371
Cadouin Abbey **5** 369*, *369*; **11** *505*
  cloister **7** 453, 455; **11** 155, 511
Caduveo **29** 202
Cadwalader, John **24** 602
Cady, J. C. **7** 708
Caedmon **17** 693, 694; **33** 8
Caedmon Manuscript *see* JUNIUS MANUSCRIPT
Cael *see* KAYALPATNAM
Caelaverock Castle (Dumfries & Galloway) **28** 224
caementa **26** 879
Caen **5** 369–73*; **11** *504*
  Château **6** 52, 53, 54
  damask **19** 418
  Hôtel d'Escoville **11** 513
  lace **11** 650
Caen—cont.
  La Trinité **3** 443, 709; **5** 372–3*; **26** 589; **30** 729; **33** 198
   capitals **5** *372*; **26** 597, 598
   piers (ii) (masonry) **24** 750
   sculpture **26** 598
   vaults **32** 93
  Musée des Beaux-Arts **11** 665, 666; **22** 357
  Ste Paix **26** 598
  St Etienne **1** 723; **3** 709; **5** *370*, 370–72*, *371*; **11** 509; **13** 41; **26** 586; **30** 728–9; **33** 198
   buttresses **5** *318*
   capitals **26** 598
   mouldings **22** 215
   piers (ii) (masonry) **24** 750
   spires **29** 413
   vaults **32** 89, 93
  St Jean
   tracery **31** *272*
  St Nicolas **26** 598
  St Pierre **11** 512; **13** 60
  stone **10** 227
Caen, Paul of *see* PAUL OF CAEN
Caerdydd *see* CARDIFF
Caere *see* CERVETERI
Caere Novum *see* CERI
Caerffili Castle (Mid Glam.) **6** 51, 53, *56*, 56; **8** 278; **10** 227; **32** 781
  gate-house **12** 173
Caerleon (Gwent) **3** 375; **32** 780
Caernarfon (Gwynedd) **31** 711, *711*
  art school **32** 792
  Castle **5** *373*, 373–5*, *374*; **6** 49, 50, 53, 56; **8** 278; **9** 144; **16** 895; **22** 211; **32** *780*, 781
   King's Gate **12** 174
   mouldings **22** 220
  Castle Square **32** 787
  Gwynedd County Council offices **32** 784
Caerphilly Castle *see* CAERFFILI CASTLE
caeruleum *see under* PIGMENTS → types
Caesar, Julius, Dictator (*reg* 49-44 BC) **5** 375*; **6** 152; **7** 852
  architecture **7** 851; **11** 174; **26** 764, 916
   agorai **2** 668
   basilicas **26** 782, 890
   cities **2** 418; **3** 872
   fora **11** 327; **26** 749, 783, 865, 889
   military **2** 1; **21** 559; **29** 16; **32** 632
   porticos **25** 265
   tabularia **26** 856
   temples **26** 856; **27** 714
   urban planning **26** 904
  coins **25** 650; **27** 96
  gems **12** 265
  marble **27** 13
  paintings **25** 44; **30** 916
  sculpture **7** 561; **27** 29, 30, 31
  writings **4** 804; **27** 89
Caesar, Julius (*b* 1910) **22** 616
Caesaraugusta *see* SARAGOSSA
Caesarea (Algeria) *see* CHERCHEL
Caesarea (Cappadocia) **5** 673; **16** 406; **21** 2
Caesarea (Israel) **9** *513*; **14** 465; **17** 500, 505, 556; **26** *915*
  aqueduct **26** 916
  Cathedral **9** 539
  jewellery **16** 529
  theatre **26** 916; **27** 47
Caesarea, Procopius of *see* PROCOPIUS OF CAESAREA
Caesarodunum *see* TOURS
Caesaromagus *see* BEAUVAIS
Caesar's Palace **18** 822
Caetani (family) **24** 854
Caetani, Camillo **28** 657
Caetani, Enrico **32** 692
Caetani, Michelangelo, Duca di Sermoneta *see* SERMONETA, MICHELANGELO CAETANI, Duca di
Caetani, Nicola, Cardinal **32** 692
Caetano, Inácio **4** 629
Caetano, Manuel **25** 293
Caetano de Carvalho, José **25** 313
Caetano de Sousa, Manuel **5** 375–6*
  works **8** 9; **10** 728; **25** 814; **29** 101
Caetano Rivara, João **1** 466
Cafà, Melchiorre *see* CAFFA, MELCHIORRE
Cafaggiolo Ceramic Factory **5** 376*; **16** 734; **21** 15; **22** 14; **28** 81
Café Gresham group *see* GRESHAM GROUP
Cafer **4** 771
Ca'fer Efendi **2** 316; **16** 221
cafés **17** *443*; **24** *553*
Caffa, Lorenzo **5** 376, 377
Caffa, Melchiorre **5** 376–7*; **20** 214; **26** 773
  assistants **20** 909
  collaboration **3** 198; **29** 830
  teachers **1** 630, 631; **11** 18
  works **5** *377*; **16** 699
Caffagiolo, Villa Medici **3** 99, 173; **32** 545
Caffarelli (family) **27** 172
Caffarelli, Scipione *see* BORGHESE, SCIPIONE, Cardinal
Caffarelli Pamphili, Olimpia, Princess **13** 277
Caffarini, Tommaso d'Antonio **7** 330
Cafferata, Francisco **2** 399; **5** 378*
Caffi, Francesco **5** 378
Caffi, Ippolito **5** 378*; **16** 836; **17** 443; **32** 197
Caffi, Lodovico *see* CAFFI, FRANCESCO
Caffi, Margherita **5** 378*
Caffiéri (family) **14** 145; **25** 138; **28** 527
Caffiéri, Charles-Marie **5** 379
Caffiéri, Charles-Philippe **5** 379
Caffiéri, Daniel **5** 379
Caffiéri, François-Charles **5** 379
Caffiéri, Jacques **5** 379–80*; **11** 625, 626
  attributions **7** 194
  collaboration **7** 657
  groups and movements **26** 494
  patrons and collectors **4** 554; **27** 223
  pupils **5** 380
  works **1** 110; **7** *658*; **11** 119, 577, 626
Caffiéri, Jean-Jacques **5** 379, 380–81*; **11** 335, 561, 626; **29** 573
  patrons and collectors **7** 194; **11** 561; **24** 418
  teachers **19** 142
  works **5** *381*
Caffiéri, Philippe (i) (1634-1716) **5** 379*; **28** 612
  pupils **6** 518
  works **11** 119, 575; **12** 832
Caffiéri, Philippe (ii) (1714-74) **5** 379, 380*; **11** 625
  collaboration **25** 577
  patrons and collectors **13** 665
  works **11** 626, 627; **23** 518; **25** 118
Caffin, Charles H. **7** 551; **24** 739; **29** 655
Cafoglio **14** 425
Cagaan-gol **21** 882
Cagayan de Oro, Xavier Kolklife Museum **29** 240
Cage, John **5** 381–2*; **22** 381; **23** 48; **26** 27
  collaboration **8** 270; **23** 176
Cage, John—cont.
  groups and movements **4** 109, 110; **11** 232
  productions **24** 407
  pupils **4** 731; **17** 805; **24** 407
  works **7** 699; **29** 97
  writings **24** 407
cage-cups *see under* CUPS → types
Caggiano, Emanuele **12** 267
Çağıltemeller **19** 838
Cagli, Corrado **5** 382–3*; **11** 191; **26** 777
  groups and movements **5** 671; **16** 680; **21** 87; **26** 777; **28** 319
  works **16** 758
  writings **10** 821
Cagli, Ridolfo Capoferro da *see* CAPOFERRO DA CAGLI, RIDOLFO
Cagliari
  Cathedral of S Maria **16** 625; **26** 623; **27** 836
   pulpit **13** 804; **25** 723
   sculpture **26** 619
  S Saturno **27** 836
Cagli Bastion **3** 359
Caglieri, Liborio **32** 424
Cagnacci, Guido **5** 383–4*
  patrons and collectors **13** 920; **31** 306
  works **5** *383*
Cagnola, Giovan Antonio **12** 285
Cagnola, Luigi **5** 384–7*
  collaboration **20** 390
  groups and movements **22** 741
  illustrated writings **1** 575
  patrons and collectors **16** 705
  pupils **3** 920
  reproductive prints by others **1** 575
  works **5** *387*, 622; **16** 647; **19** 561; **21** 520, *520*; **32** 457
Cagnola Triptych **16** 838
Caguana **29** 201
  stone-carvings **29** *199*
Caguanas **25** 699
Cahen, Albert, Count of Antwerp *see* ANTWERP, ALBERT CAHEN, Count of
Cahen, J. P. **18** 874
Cahén, Oscar **5** 568; **23** 790
Cahier, Charles **29** 514
Cahier, Jean-Charles **4** 42; **11** 621
Cahiers Archéologiques **13** 263
Cahiers d'art **24** 144, 428, 442
Cahiers du Musée National d'Art Moderne **24** 443
Cahiers Henry Van de Velde **24** 439
Cahill, Holger **2** 596; **5** 386*; **31** 663, 672
Cahill, James **7** 161
Cahir **8** 30; **21** 564
Cahn, Miriam **5** 386*; **30** 135
Cahokia (IL; USA) **5** 386–7*, *387*; **22** *544*; **30** 449; **31** 116
  burial mounds **5** 386–7
  church **32** 273
Cahokia (MS; USA) **22** 572
Cahors **5** 387–8*; **11** *505*
  Cathedral of St Stephen **5** 388*; **11** 510; **26** 570, 584, *584*, 602
  Pont Valentré **4** 801; **5** 388*; **19** 895
Cahrs, Paul *see* CASSIRER, PAUL
Cahuachi **5** 388–9*; **22** 706; **29** *156*
  masks **29** 208, *209*
  pyramid **29** 160
Cahuilla **22** 550, 634
Cahyup **25** 765
Cai, Zhao, Marquis of **6** 851; **7** 21, 247
Çaias, Diego de **2** 455
Caiger-Smith, Alan **5** 389*; **10** 314
Cai Jing **5** 389*
Caillé, Joseph-Michel **25** 207
Caille, Pierre **3** 573, 592
Cailleau, Hubert
  works **30** *653*
Caille Bois, Horacio **2** 404
Caillebotte, Gustave **5** 389–91*
  groups and movements **15** 151, 153, 154, 155; **26** 55
  patrons and collectors **30** 375
  personal collection **3** 712; **15** 154; **24** 142, 883
  teachers **4** 329
  works **5** *391*; **26** 207; **31** 704
Cailler, Pierre **8** 775; **28** 820
Caillet (*fl* 19th cent.) **3** 591
Caillet, G. (*fl* 1659) **32** 706
Cailleteau *see* LASSURANCE
Cailleux, (Achille-Alexandre) Alphonse de **5** 392*; **11** 302
  collaboration **8** 867; **11** 521; **30** 385
  illustrated works **7** 304; **32** 594
Caillot, Claude-Augustin *see* CAYOT, CLAUDE-AUGUSTIN
Cai Lun **7** 62, 114; **20** 329; **24** 46
Caimi, Bernardino **1** 608; **27** 497; **31** 897
Cain, Auguste-Nicolas **2** 99; **5** 392*; **21** 127; **23** 794
Cain, Errol le **4** 368
Cain, Rhys **32** 784
Cainberg, Erik **11** 99
cain chairs *see under* CHAIRS → types
Caipler, Jan *see* CEYPLER, JAN
Caiquetios *see* CAQUETIOS
Caire, Nicholas (John) **5** 392–3*
  works **32** *307*
Cairness House (Grampian) **10** 96; **28** 227
Cairney, Robb & Ray **9** 727
Cairnpapple Hill (Lothian) **28** 223
cairns **21** 44; **25** 538; **28** 640
Cairns (Australia) **1** *37*, 61, 62
Cairo **1** *376*; **5** 393–405*, *394*; **10** 832; **16** *104*
  academies and art schools
   Atelier of Fine Arts **9** 768
   College of Fine Arts **9** 766, 768
   Higher Institute for Art Teachers **9** 768
   Leonardo da Vinci School of Arts **9** 768
   School of Applied Arts **9** 768
   School of Fine Arts *see* College of Fine Arts
   School of Irrigation and Architecture **9** 768
  Amnis Trajani **5** *394*
  art forms and materials
   architectural decorations **16** 244
   architecture **2** 428; **9** 768; **16** 142, 143, 149, 172, 207, 208–13, 229; **20** 227, 228, 231
   books **5** 400
   carpets **5** 400, 833; **16** 469, *472*, 473
   ceramics **9** 767
   coins **16** 512, *512*, *513*
   domes **16** 210, 211, 496
   doors **16** 384
   furniture **5** 400
   glass **9** 767; **16** 517, 518, 519
   ivory-carvings **16** 523
   jewellery **16** 529
   kilims **18** 49
   manuscripts **4** *14*; **16** *129*, *275*, 304, 305, *306*, 312, *312*, 350, 356
   masonry **16** 180
   metalwork **16** 382, *385*, 385, 389
   minbars **21** 630
   muqarnas (architecture) **22** 322
   paper **24** 40
   porcelain **9** 767
   pottery **6** 330, 915; **7** 826; **16** 398, 404, 405, 416, 420; **28** 723; **29** 324
   printing **16** 359, 361
   rock crystal **16** 121, 540

Cairo
art forms and materials—cont.
silver 16 505
tapestries 9 767
tents 30 478
textiles 3 378; 5 400; 9 767; 15 658; 16 431, 432, 441; 31 20, 21
tracery 31 273
wall paintings 16 252
windows 16 257
art galleries
Atelier 9 768
Hanagir Arts Centre 9 768
Nile Exhibition Hall 9 768
Opera House Art Gallery 9 768
al-'Askar 5 394, 395
al-Azbakiyya 16 213
Bab al-Nasr 5 396
Babylon 5 393, 394; 9 849
baths 3 375
bath of Abu'l-Su'ud 22 322
Hammam al-Sukkariyya 3 376
caravanserais 5 723; 16 262
cemeteries
Qarafa al-Kubra (east cemetery) 5 394; 16 175, 211; 18 71
mosque 16 253
al-Sultaniyya 16 211
Qarafa al-Sughra (south cemetery) 5 394; 28 634; 31 113
craftsmen and artists 5 401
Cultural and Educational Complex 9 765
Cultural Park for Children 9 765
ecclesiastical buildings 5 398
Abu Sarga see St Sergius
Amir Tadrus 7 821
Convent of St George 7 829; 9 600; 16 489, 490
Deir Mari Girgis see Convent of St George
Hanging Church 7 820, 828, 829; 9 600
Sanctuary of St Takla Hamanout 9 600
St Barbara 7 820
doors 7 828
screens (i) (architectural) 7 829
wood-carvings 7 829; 9 599; 16 489
St Sergius 7 820, 829; 9 600
Theodore the Commander see Amir Tadrus
excavations 16 550
façades 16 142
factories 16 441
fortifications 10 832; 16 173; 21 582, 587
Bab al-Futuh 21 582
Bab al-Nasr 2 294, 295; 21 582
Bab Zuwayla 21 582
Burj Muqattam 21 588
Burj al-Turfa 21 583
Citadel 5 394, 397, 402–3*; 21 583
al-Ablaq Palace see under palaces
Mosque of al-Nasir Muhammad see under Islamic religious buildings
Mosque of Süleyman Pasha see under Islamic religious buildings
Fortress of Ahmad ibn Tulun 5 394
Fustat 5 393–5, 394, 395; 9 768; 10 833
gardens 12 82
Geniza documents see GENIZA DOCUMENTS
Heliopolis Palace Hotel 9 764
House of Arts and Crafts 9 766
houses 1 315; 5 397; 16 263, 270; 32 312
Bayt al-Razzaz 16 257
Bayt al-Suhami 16 257
Cairo—cont.
Islamic religious buildings
Aqmar Mosque 16 100, 138, 174, 174–5, 176, 489; 22 323
inscriptions 16 258
al-Azhar Mosque 4 791; 5 394, 402*; 15 351; 16 173–4, 213; 20 230
arches 2 295
doors 16 489
grilles 16 257
inscriptions 16 244
maqṣūra 20 368
mihrab 21 506
squinches 16 176
stucco 29 820
Blue Mosque 16 210, 229
Complex of Azbak al-Yusufi 16 213
Complex of Barquq 16 211, 496
Madrasa 16 245, 385, 389; 20 230
Mosque 9 84; 16 257, 384
Complex of Faraj 16 211; 20 56
Khanaqah 20 230
Mosque 20 230
Complex of Mahmud al-Kurdi
Tomb of Mahmud al-Kurdi 16 244
Complex of al-Mu'ayyad Shaykh 9 160, 160; 16 211; 20 229
Mosque 16 257, 385; 20 230; 21 630
Complex of al-Nasir Muhammad 16 209; 20 228
Madrasa 9 161; 16 244; 29 820
Complex of Qa'itbay 5 394, 404–5*; 9 84; 16 212, 213; 20 56, 230
Mausoleum of Qa'itbay 16 244; 23 561
Mosque 16 257
muqarnas (architecture) 22 323, 324
Complex of Qajmas al-Ishaqi 16 213
Complex of Qala'un 5 394, 397, 403–4*; 7 527; 16 91, 208–9, 209, 490; 20 228
Hospital 12 78; 16 173
Mausoleum of Qala'un 9 160; 16 208–9, 257, 384, 496, 496; 23 559; 31 20
Complex of Qansuh al-Ghawri 16 213
Complex of al-Salih Najm al-Din Ayyub
Madrasa 16 176
Tomb of al-Salih Najm al-Din Ayyub 22 323
Complex of Shaykhu 16 250
Complex of Sultan Barsbay 16 211, 497; 20 230
Mosque 20 230
Complex of Sultan Baybars II 20 229
Complex of Sultan Hasan 5 394, 397, 404*; 16 210–11; 18 507; 20 229
doors 9 160; 16 92, 384
Madrasa 20 56
Mausoleum of Sultan Hasan 16 496
metalwork 16 385
minbar 21 630
Mosque 5 404; 16 210
muqarnas (architecture) 22 323
Complex of Sultan Sha'ban 20 229
Complex of Zayn al-Din Yusuf
Tomb of Zayn al-Din Yusuf 31 111
Fakahani Mosque 16 490
al-Ghamri Mosque 16 497
Khānaqāh of Bektimur al-Saqi 16 91
khānaqāhs 16 210; 18 17, 18
Madrasa of Abu Bakr ibn Muzhir 16 497
Cairo
Islamic religious buildings—cont.
Madrasa of Baybars I see Zahiriyya Madrasa
Madrasa al-Ghannamiyya 16 250
Madrasa of Khushqadam al-Ahmadi 16 250
Madrasa of Khwand Baraka 16 497
madrasas 20 55
Madrasa of Sultan Barsbay 16 385
Madrasa of Umm al-Sultan Sha'ban 20 229
maqṣūras 20 368
Mashhad of Badr al-Jamali see Mashhad of al-Juyushi
Mashhad of al-Juyushi 16 175, 176, 244; 22 321; 28 634; 29 820
inscriptions 16 258
Mashhad of Sayyida Ruqayya 16 175, 176; 21 504, 505
Mashhad of Sharif Tabataba 16 175
mihrabs 21 504
minarets 16 175
Mosque of Abu'l-'Ila 16 497
Mosque of al-Nasir Muhammad 16 209
Mosque of Altinbugha al-Maridani 16 209–10
Mosque of 'Amr 4 791; 5 394, 401–2*; 16 155, 174
Mosque of Aqsunqur see Blue Mosque
Mosque of Aslam al-Silahdar 16 210
Mosque of Baybars I 5 394, 403*; 16 208, 496; 20 227
Mosque of al-Hakim 4 791; 5 394, 402*; 16 173, 174, 244; 21 626; 22 194; 23 557; 29 820
inscriptions 16 258, 259
Mosque of Ibn Tulun 3 894; 4 791; 5 394, 402*; 16 155; 22 194; 31 421
arches 2 295, 298
architectural decorations 16 174
grilles 16 257
metalwork 16 382
mihrab 2 294
minaret 21 626
minbar 16 496
piers (ii) (masonry) 16 155
stucco 16 244; 29 819
woodwork 16 488, 496; 18 242
Mosque of al-Juyushi see Mashhad of al-Juyushi
Mosque of Malika Safiya 16 221, 229
Mosque of Muhammad 'Ali 5 394, 404, 405*; 16 229
Mosque of al-Salih Tala'i' 16 175, 384; 21 630
Mosque of Sayyidna Husayn 16 241
Mosque of Süleyman Pasha 16 221
Mosque al-Rifa'i 9 764; 16 241
mosques 16 145, 173–5, 209, 222; 22 193, 354
sabīl-kuttāb of Ruqayya Dudu 16 229
Sayyidna Husayn Mosque 28 633
Shrine of Husayn 16 175
shrine of Sayyida Nafisa 16 490
Zahiriyya Madrasa 16 208; 20 56, 227
Khalij Misri see Amnis Trajani
kiosks 18 70
Library (Fatimid) 19 316
Library (Khedival) 16 557
Cairo—cont.
markets 5 397; 16 261, 262; 20 438
see also wakalas
mausolea see tombs and mausolea
Metro stations 21 350
Ministry of Waqfs building 9 764
al-Mu'allaqa see ecclesiastical buildings → Hanging Church
museums
Arab Museum see Museum of Islamic Art
Coptic Museum 5 401; 9 768
archives 2 370
collections 5 393
Egyptian Museum 9 768; 10 80; 20 418
archives 2 370
catalogues 10 84
collections 5 401; 9 768; 10 71, 90, 91, 92, 93
jewellery 1 469
Khalil Museum 5 401
Mahmud Mukhtar Sculpture Museum 9 765, 768; 22 269
Modern Art Museum 5 401
Muhammad Naghi Museum 22 431
Museum of Arab Art see Museum of Islamic Art
Museum of Islamic Art 5 400, 402
collections 5 401; 9 768; 16 389, 553, 557
Museum of Modern Egyptian Art 9 768
National Cultural Centre see Cultural and Educational Complex
Nilometer 5 394
observatory 23 338
Old Cairo see Babylon; Fustat; al-Qahira
Opera House 9 765
palaces
al-Ablaq Palace 20 228
Alin Aq Palace 16 257
Amir Taz Palace 7 527
Bashtak Palace 7 527; 16 257; 32 314
Eastern Palace 16 173
Gazira Palace 9 764
Lesser Palace 16 173, 490, 496, 524
Musafirkhana Palace 16 257
Qa'itbay Palace 16 257
al-Qata'i' 5 394, 395; 16 155; 31 421
Striped Palace see al-Ablaq Palace
Western Palace see Lesser Palace
Yashbak Palace 16 257; 20 230; 22 323
al-Qahira 5 394; 7 819; 16 261
Qal'at al-Kabsh 16 209, 213; 20 230
Qasr al-Sham see Babylon
sabīl-kuttāb of 'Abd al-Rahman Katkuda 5 399; 16 229
schools 16 229
shops 16 175
synagogues
Ben Ezra synagogue 17 550, 551
Capusi synagogue 17 551
tombs and mausolea 16 175, 208; 31 111
mausoleum of Ibrahim Ağa Müstahfizan 16 210
mausoleum of Muzaffar 'Alam al-Din Sanjar 16 210
mausoleum of Qala'un see under CAIRO → Islamic religious buildings → Complex of Qala'un
mausoleum of Sa'd Zaghlul 9 764, 765
Cairo
tombs and mausolea—cont.
mausoleum of Sultan Hasan see under CAIRO → Islamic religious buildings → Complex of Sultan Hasan
mausoleum of Yunus al-Dawadar 16 211
tomb of Amir Sarghatmish 16 211
tomb of al-Salih Najm al-Din Ayyub see under CAIRO → Islamic religious buildings → Tomb of al-Salih Najm al-Din
tomb of al-Shafi'i 5 394, 403*, 403; 16 122, 175, 176, 213; 28 634; 31 111
ceiling 7 527
muqarnas (architecture) 22 323
woodwork 16 490–91
tomb of Shajarat al-Durr 16 256
tomb of Zayn al-Din Yusuf see under CAIRO → Islamic religious buildings → Complex of Zayn al-Din Yusuf
University 9 766, 766
urban planning 9 765; 16 241, 260, 261, 262, 262, 263, 264
wakalas
Wakala of Qa'itbay 20 438
Wakala of Qansuh al-Ghawri 20 438
see also markets
Cairo, Francesco 5 405–7*; 28 11
attributions 20 738
patrons and collectors 28 8
pupils 8 563
reproductive prints by others 28 479
works 5 405, 406; 16 673, 674
Cairo, Giovanni Battista del 7 307
Caiselli, Giovan Battista, Conte 5 782
Caiselli, Leonardo, Conte 5 782
Caisra see CERVETERI
Caisses de St Jean, Les see LES CAISSES DE ST JEAN
caissons 28 830
Caister Castle (Norfolk) 4 779; 10 270, 287; 19 896
Caithness, William Sinclair, 1st Earl of see SINCLAIR, WILLIAM, 3rd Earl of Orkney
Caithness Glass Ltd 28 260
caityagṛha 15 243*
caityas 1 500; 10 147; 15 237, 249; 17 815; 22 760; 29 867
see also STUPAS
Caius, John 5 511
Caius Servius Lupus 18 598
Caivano 27 48
Caivano Painter 13 531
Cai Xiang 5 407–8*; 6 748, 749; 14 825
caixilho tiles see under TILES → types
Cai Yong 6 769–70, 816
Cai Yu 6 759
Cai Yuanpei 7 149
Caizhuang (Hanjiang) 7 141
Cajabamba-Cicalpa 9 709
Museum 9 714
caja-espiga see under JOINERY → types
Cajahuaringa, José Milner 5 408*; 24 510
Cajal, Santiago Ramón y see RAMÓN Y CAJAL, SANTIAGO
Cajamarca 5 408–10*; 15 161; 24 498; 29 127, 156
Cathedral 24 503
churches 24 503
clay 29 175
education (art) 24 517
El Belén 24 503
Museo de Arte Colonial 24 516
sculpture 6 520

Cajamarca—cont.
S Francisco **24** 503
Cajamarca culture **5** 408–10*
Cajamarquilla **29** 162
Cajés, Eugenio **5** 411*; **19** 178; **29** 280
methods **21** 766
patrons and collectors **14** 6; **21** 73; **31** 89; **32** 129
pupils **8** 268; **10** 905; **18** 689; **25** 297; **31** 853
works **13** 732; **27** 724
Cajés, Patricio **5** 411*; **12** 916; **14** 6
Cajetan, Saint **22** 680
Cajetan, Pierre de *see* PIERRE DE CAJETAN
Cajigas, Zoilo **25** 703
Čajniče **28** 449
Cakaudrove **11** 69
Cakchiquel **16** 803; **20** 885, 886
cake baskets *see under* BASKETS → types
Čakelja, Miko **19** 883
cakes **17** 382–3
cakonian droop cups *see under* CUPS → types
Čakovec
garden **14** 886
palace **14** 899; **15** 15
Calabar **1** *386*; **8** 231; **15** 61; **23** *129*
houses **1** 318
University **23** 135
calabashes **1** 302; **30** 13; **31** 73
Calabazar *see* HAVANA
Calabre, Jean de *see* JEAN DE CALABRE
Calabre Pérau, Gabriel-Louis **4** 766
Calabrese, Il *see* PRETI, GREGORIO
Calabrese, Il Cavalier *see* PRETI, MATTIA
Calabria, Reggio di *see* RHEGION
Calacura, Pariso **20** 215
Calacura, Pietro Antonio **20** 215
Calado, Rafael Salinas *see* SALINAS CALADO, RAFAEL
Calado da Fonseca, José **10** 729
Calagrani, Gerolamo **3** 782
Calah *see* NIMRUD
Calahorra (La Rioja) **29** 333
Calahorra, La (Granada) *see* LA CALAHORRA
Calais
Dessin's Hotel **14** 786
theatre **30** 660
Calakmul **5** 411–12*; **20** *882*; **21** *372*
calamander **10** 279; **29** 470
Calamarca, Master of **4** 261
Calamarca Church **4** 261, 266
Calamatta, Luigi **4** 123; **5** 412*
works **10** 781; **13** 228; **15** 839, 843
Calame, Alexandre **5** 412*; **12** 277
pupils **4** 204; **6** 15; **7** 896; **8** 632; **33** 727
teachers **8** 864
works **30** 134
Calamech, Andrea **28** 657
Calamelli, Virgiliotto **5** 413*; **10** 751
calamine **3** 602; **4** 682, 688; **12** 88
Calamine, La *see* KELMIS
Calandra, Davide **4** 100; **5** 413*; **16** 706; **30** 215
Calandra, Giovan Battista **6** 343; **9** 411; **26** 810
Calandrelli, Alexander (Emil Lodovico) **4** 115; **5** 413*; **12** 196; **19** 54
Calandrelli, Giovanni **12** 264
Calandrucci, Giacinto **5** 413–14*
Calangute Church **12** 827
Calanova **26** 689
Calaqot, Sellasé Church **10** 572
Calarcá **7** *601*, 605
Calatayud
armour **2** 472
S Domingo **13** 68
S María **22** 255
Calatrava, Santiago **5** 414*; **29** 274
collaboration **26** 106
works **19** 847; **33** 736
Calau, Benjamin **10** 199
Calcagni, Antonio (di Bernardino) **5** 414–15*
assistants **32** 249
collaboration **9** 158; **19** 560; **21** 455
patrons and collectors **5** 789
pupils **16** 835
works **5** *415*; **19** 687
Calcagni, Tiberio **21** 440
Calcagnini, Teofilo **8** 172; **31** 429
Calca Palace **29** 164
Calcaprina, Cino **26** 364
Calcar *see* KALKAR
Calcar, Jan Joest von *see* JOEST (VON KALCAR), JAN
Calcar, Jan Steven van **5** 415–16*
works **4** 358, *358*; **32** 199, 381
Calcethorpe (Lincs) **6** 407
Calci, Silvio **1** 627
calcified jade *see under* JADE → types
Calcina, Michele da *see* MICHELE DI MATTEO DA BOLOGNA
calcined jade *see under* JADE → types
calcite **6** 400; **14** 167
calcite alabaster *see* ALABASTER (LIMESTONE)
calcium carbonate **6** 400; **7** 740, 834; **10** 380; **18** 656; **22** 203
see also CHALK; LIME
calcium chromate **24** 799
calcium hydroxide *see* LIMEWATER
calcium phosphate *see* BONE-ASH
calcium silicate bricks *see under* BRICK → types
calcium sulphate **7** 740; **12** 501; **25** 174
Calcografia Camerale **7** 897, 898; **8** 867
Calcographic Society **25** 629
Calcographie des Piransi Frères **24** 846
Calcott, Maria Dundas Graham, Lady *see* GRAHAM, MARIA DUNDAS, Lady Calcott
Calcut China Manufactory **7** 480
Calcutta **5** 416–21*; **15** *279*, 401
Academy of Fine Arts **5** 421; **15** 657
art forms and materials
architecture **2** 428; **15** 411
chromolithography **15** 635
painting **5** *420*; **15** 230, 634, 653*, *654*
printing **15** 679
prints **15** 635
sculpture **15** 542
silver **15** 707
Asutosh Museum of Indian Art **3** 170; **15** 181, 184
Bat-tala **5** 419
Bengal Club **7** 470
Birla Academy of Art and Culture **15** 181, 183, 742
botanic garden **12** 76
Dakshineshwar Temple **15** 405
Edward VII Memorial Arch **5** *419*
Esplanade **5** *417*
fortifications **21** 591
Fort William **5** 417; **15** 401, 411; **21** 574, *574*
St Peter **15** 403
Gaganendra Shilpa Pradarshanshala **5** 421
Government House **12** 75; **15** 402, 693; **23** 819
Gurushaday Museum **3** 170
Hamilton's **15** 723
High Court **18** 889, *889*
Calcutta—cont.
Indian Museum **3** 170; **5** 418, 419
collections **1** 211; **15** 181, 184, 741; **16** 557; **22** 795
Kalighat **5** 419; **15** 405; **22** 517
paintings **15** 177, 634
Lalit Kala Akademi **5** 421
National Library of India **15** 184
Rohilla Monument **15** 402
St Andrew **15** 402
St John **15** 402
St Paul's Cathedral **15** 403
School of Art **5** 419, 420; **15** 542, 656
School of Industrial Art *see* School of Art
Silver Mint **15** 403
Society of Contemporary Artists **5** 421
South Park Street Cemetery **6** 165; **15** 542
Town Hall **15** 402; **31** 241
United Services Club **7** 470
Victoria Memorial **3** 269; **5** 417, 418, *419*; **10** 185; **15** 404, 542
Victoria Memorial Hall **15** 181, 184
Zimindari Mullick's Marble Palace **23** 820
Calcutta Art Studio **15** 635
Calcutta Group **5** 420
Caldani, L. M. A. **1** 845
Caldara, Emilio **21** 521
Caldara, Polidoro *see* POLIDORO DA CARAVAGGIO
Caldara, Simone **16** 742
caldaria **13** 386; **26** 919
Căldăruşani **26** 708, 725
Museum **26** 724
Caldas, José Zanine *see* ZANINE CALDAS, JOSÉ
Caldas da Rainha **4** 385; **5** 421*; **25** *288*, 310
Museu de José Malhoa **25** 318
Nossa Senhora do Pópulo **25** 290
Caldas Júnior, Waltércio **4** 720
Caldecott, Randolph **2** 475; **4** 363; **5** 421–2*; **20** 239
Caldecott, (Harry) Strat(ford) **29** 108
Calden, Schloss Wilhelmstal **8** 150; **26** 496
Calder, Alexander **4** 75; **5** 422–4*; **19** 491; **24** 144; **27** 854; **28** 299; **31** 660
collaboration **10** 417; **20** 603, 605
dealers **18** 162; **20** 75; **26** 193
groups and movements **1** 90; **18** 62, 63
jewellery **17** 529; **31** 655
mobiles **2** 554, 838; **5** *423*; **21** 745, 746, *746*
patrons and collectors **2** 409; **9** 189; **19** 439; **20** 832; **23** 7; **28** 167, 314, 315; **32** 567
sculpture **5** 692; **6** 577; **16** 58; **31** 613
tapestries **11** 644; **12** 830
Calder, Alexander Milne **5** 422*
Calder, Alexander Stirling **5** 422*
Calder, William **31** 652
Caldera, Adolfo León *see* LEÓN CALDERA, ADOLFO
Calderari, Conte (*fl* 1719) **5** 358
Calderari, Ottone Maria(, Conte; 1730-1803) **5** 424–5*; **32** 410
Calderini, Guglielmo **5** 425*
assistants **27** 492
works **3** 644; **16** 645; **18** 889; **24** 520; **25** 147; **26** 762
Calderini, Marco **5** 425–6*
Calderon **9** 710
Calderón, Coqui **5** 426*; **23** 905
Calderón, José Antonio **21** 262
Calderón, Juan Carlos **4** 260, 261; **5** 426*; **18** 778
Calderon, Philip Hermogenes **5** 175, 426*; **27** 564
Calderón, Rodrigo **5** 426–7*
Calderón de la Barca, Pedro **3** 17; **19** 710; **30** 664
Calderoni **20** 908
Calderón Zilveti, Luis **4** 264
Calderwood, James **28** 245
Calderwood, Robert **5** 611; **9** 320; **16** 31
works **16** *31*
Caldor, Louis J. **22** 189
Caldrini, Senator **24** 226
Caldwell, Alfred **14** 524; **21** 493
Caldwell, Erskine **4** 586
Caldwell, James **20** 53
Caldwell, Victor **17** 364
Caledon, James Alexander, 1st Earl of *see* ALEXANDER, JAMES, 1st Earl of Caledon
Caledonia Cabinet and Chair Works **28** 255, 256
Caledonian Co. **23** 71
Caledonian Pottery **28** 257, 258
Caledon Jade Green *see under* PIGMENTS → types
Calegari, Antonio **16** 701
Calenberg Altar **20** 683
Calenberg and Celle, Eleonore, Duchess of *see* ELEONORE, Duchess of Calenberg and Celle
Calenberg and Celle, George William, Duke of *see* GEORGE WILLIAM, Duke of Calenberg and Celle
calendar icons *see under* ICONS → types
Calendario, Filippo **5** 429–30*; **13** 95
works **5** *430*
Calendar of AD 354 (Rome, Vatican, Bib. Apostolica, MS. Barb. lat. 2154) **5** 427; **9** 603; **15** *91*; **31** 48
Calendar of Filocalus *see* CALENDAR OF AD 354
calendars **2** 648; **4** 371; **5** 427–9*; **15** 827; **23** 338–9; **25** 676
Aztec **21** *224*, 234, 262, 265
Bulgaria **32** 149
Byzantine **9** 603, 610, 616; **21** 138
Carolingian **5** 427
Christianity **21** 138
Early Christian (*c.* AD 250-843) **9** 603, 610, 616
France **20** *612*
Gothic **13** 137
Greece, ancient **2** 648
India, Republic of **15** 178
Indian subcontinent **15** 199*
Islamic **23** 338
Maya **1** 14; **6** 579; **9** 498; **20** 883, 885; **21** 234; **22** 444; **27** 786; **31** 778
Mesoamerica, Pre-Columbian **1** 14; **6** 579; **9** 498; **21** *224*, 234, 265; **22** 444; **23** 338; **27** 786; **31** 778
Mixtec **21** 234, 253, *253*
Rome, ancient **9** 603
Calendar Stone **2** 907
Calendra, Davide **27** 303
Calenian ware *see under* POTTERY → wares
Calera, La *see* LA CALERA
Calera de Tango **6** 592, 599, 601
Caleruega, Dominican Chapel **9** 113
Caletti, Giuseppe **5** 430*
calfskin *see under* LEATHER → types
Calgary (Alberta) **5** *559*, 561
Calgary Group **19** 878
Calhau, Fernando **25** 300
Cali **7** *601*, 603, 606, 611
Museo Arqueológico La Merced **7** 612
Museo de Arte Moderno La Tertulia **7** 612
library **7** 612
Museo Manuel María Buenaventura **7** 612
Cali—cont.
Palacio de Justicia **7** 606
S Francisco **7** 605
Cali, Antonio **5** 430; **16** 705; **22** 480
Cali, Beniamino **5** 430
Cali, Gennaro **16** 705; **22** 480
Calí, Giuseppe **5** 430–31*; **20** 213
Cali, Ramiro Raffaele **5** 431
Caliari, Benedetto **5** 431*; **28** 5; **32** 354
attributions **32** 349, 352
collaboration **32** 77, 352
Caliari, Carlo **5** 431*; **32** 354
Caliari, Gabriele **5** 431; **32** 354
Caliari, Giovanni **5** 432
Caliari, Paolo (i) (1528-88) *see* VERONESE, PAOLO
Caliari, Paolo (ii) (1763-1835) **5** 432*
calices *see* CHALICES
calico **8** 35; **28** 266; **30** 470
Calicut **5** 432*; **6** *623*; **15** 200, *294*
Allahrapalli Mosque **15** 358
architecture **15** 410
congregational mosque **15** 358
Idrispalli Mosque **15** 358
Mithqalpalli Mosque **15** 358, *359*
mosques **15** 358
Muchandipalli Mosque **15** 358
Nakhuda Mithqal Mosque *see* Mithqalpalli Mosque
Pazhassiraja Museum **5** 432
trade **8** 35
V. K. Krishna Menon Museum **5** 432
California Aerospace Museum *see under* LOS ANGELES (CA)
California Architect and Building News **24** 432
California Architect and Building Review **24** 432
California Society of Etchers **25** 629
Caligula, Emperor of Rome (*reg* AD 37-41) **27** 32, 34
amphitheatres **1** 797
coins **27** 96
gates **18** 238
obelisks **23** 330
portraits **27** 33
statues **27** 15, 34
temples **23** 809; **26** 786, 892
villas **13** 555; **26** 892
Çalik, Şadi **31** 454
Calima **29** 209
Calimaya, Condes de Santiago de *see* SANTIAGO DE CALIMAYA, Condes de
Călineşti, Gheorghe Iliescu *see* ILIESCU-CĂLINEŞTI, GHEORGHE
Calini (family) **31** 747
Caliste, Canute **2** 149
works **2** *150*
Calisto, Tomaso di *see* TOMASO DI CALISTO
Calixtlahuaca **5** 433*; **21** *193*, *372*
Altar of Skulls **31** 506
pyramids **25** 764
sculpture **21** 223
skull racks **31** 506
Temple of Quetzlcóatl-Éhecatl **5** 433
Calixtus I, Pope (*reg* AD 217-222) **26** 833
Calixtus II, Pope (*reg* 1119-24) **16** 762
Calixtus III, Pope (*reg* 1168-78) **4** 409*
architecture **31** 815
decorative works **11** 684
paintings **26** 267
tapestries **26** 778
Calkin & Holden **30** 390
Call, Jan van **30** 568
Calla, Christophe **18** 582
Callahan, Harry **5** 434*; **6** 577
groups and movements **1** 86; **4** 109

Callahan, Harry—cont.
pupils **13** 240; **16** 84
Callahan, Kenneth **28** 328
Callahuaya **4** 266
Callandar House (Central) Forbes Mausoleum **20** 868
Callani, Gaetano **8** 912
Callanish (Western Isles) **21** 42
stone circle **28** 223
Callao **24** *498*, 504
Museo Histórico Militar del Perú **24** 501
Real Filipe Fort *see* Museo Histórico Militar del Perú
Callapa Church **4** 261
Callaú, Marcelo **4** 265
Callaway, Joseph **1** 476
Callcott, Augustus Wall **5** 434–5*
groups and movements **32** 903
patrons and collectors **4** 35; **24** 571; **28** 908; **32** 338
pupils **27** 778
reproductive prints by others **5** 435
Callcott, Maria, Lady **5** 434, 435*
Calle, Benjamín de la **5** 435*; **7** 612
Calle, Sophie **5** 435*; **11** 553
Callegari (family) **16** 736
Callegari, Filippo Antonio **24** 535
Calleja, Andrés de la **5** 435–6*; **10** 406
collaboration **6** 47
works **5** 902; **27** 710
Callejas, Manuel López *see* LÓPEZ CALLEJAS, MANUEL
Callejo, Andrés Hernández *see* HERNÁNDEZ CALLEJO, ANDRÉS
Callenberghe, Cornelis van **16** 69
Callery, Mary **4** 109
Callet, Antoine-François **3** 870; **5** 436*; **12** 830; **25** 404
Callet, Charles-François **24** 387
Callet, Félix-Emmanuel **3** 125
Calleva Atrebatum **5** 436*; **10** *225*; **26** 875, *905*
amphitheatre **26** 905
forum **11** 328
urban planning **27** 3
Callewaert, Albert **8** 633
Çallı, Ibrahim **5** 437*; **31** 454
groups and movements **2** 634
pupils **16** 805
Callicrates *see* KALLIKRATES
calligraphers
Indian subcontinent **15** 207, 546
Iran **16** 232
Islamic **16** 232, 273, 276–7*, 283, 285
Japan **17** 214, 227, 236*
Korea **18** 258
Ottoman **16** 285
Turkey **16** 285
Calligraphic Movement **23** 800
calligraphy **4** 344; **5** 437*
collections *see under* COLLECTIONS → types
conservation **1** 580; **15** 856
display **1** 580–82; **17** 215, *236*
education *see under* EDUCATION (ART) → types
exhibitions *see under* EXHIBITIONS → types
historical and regional traditions
Afghanistan **16** *276*, *354*
Algeria **1** *636*
Buddhism **6** 748, 772; **30** 845
Chan **17** 231
China **6** 751–2*, *752*, 756
Japan **15** *130*, *131*, *833*; **17** 211, 217–21*, *218*, *220*, 231
Japan: Ōbaku **17** 234–5
Japan: Zen **14** 61; **17** 229–31*, *230*
Central Asia, Eastern **6** 307–8*, 314
Central Asia, Western **6** 257
calligraphy
historical and regional traditions—cont.
China **1** 580–81; **4** 344; **5** 36; **6** 612, 735–61*, *736*, *744*, *747*, 762–8*, 769–71*, 772*, 818; **7** 129, 146, 148, 161; **15** 853, 854; **17** 211, 215, 227; **25** 72; **29** 617
Buddhism **6** 751–2, *752*, 756
Chan **17** 231
Five Dynasties (AD 907-60) **6** 748*
Han period (206 BC-AD 220) **6** 633–4, 636, *740*, 740–41*
Jin period (AD 1115-1234) **6** 750–51*, 753
literati **17** 234–8*
Ming period (1368-1644) **6** 756–61*, *757*, *758*, *759*, *762*
Northern and Southern Dynasties (AD 310-589) **6** *743*, 743–4*
Qing period (1644-1911) **6** 762–6*, *763*, *765*
Qin period (221-206 BC) **6** *739*, 740*
Shang period (*c.* 1600-*c.* 1050 BC) **6** 737–8*, *738*
Song period (AD 960-1279) **6** 748–52*, *749*, *750*, *751*, *752*, 753; **7** 161
Sui period (AD 581-618) **6** 744–5*
Tang period (AD 618-907) **6** 745–8*, *746*
Three Kingdoms (AD 220-80) **6** 741–2*
Western and Eastern Jin period (AD 265-420) **6** 742–3*, *742*, *747*; **32** 836
Yuan period (1279-1368) **6** 752*, *753*, *754*
Zhou period (*c.* 1050-256 BC) **6** 738–9*, *740*
4th cent. AD **30** 251
18th cent. **7** *624*
20th cent. **6** 766–8*, *768*
Confucianism **17** 236
Egypt **16** *275*; **18** *241*
Egypt, ancient **10** 6*
Hausa **14** 233
Hong Kong **6** 772
Indian subcontinent **15** 199, 338, 354, 497, 680–81*, *680*, 727
Mughal **15** 680–81
Indonesia **15** 757
Iran **16** 232, *286*
Iraq **16** 1, *283*
Islamic **4** 344; **14** 217; **16** 124, 126, 134, 273–9*, *275*, 280–84*, *284*, 285–8*, 354; **18** *240*
Abbasid **16** *279*, *280*
Afghanistan **16** *276*, *354*
Egypt **16** *275*; **18** *241*
Indian subcontinent **15** 338, 354, 497, *680*, 680–81*, 727
Indonesia **15** 757
Iran **16** 232, *286*
Iraq **16** *283*
North Africa **16** *281*
Ottoman **14** 27; **22** *235*
Spain **16** 215
Syria **16** *275*
Japan **6** 772; **11** 822; **17** 210–17*, *213*, 221–31*, *223*, 232–40*, *235*, *236*, *237*, 341, 342–4*, *343*; **23** *445*
Buddhism **15** *130*, *131*, *833*; **17** 217–21*, *218*, *220*
Buddhism: Zen **6** 752; **17** 229–31*, *230*
Confucianism **17** 236
Edo period (1600-1868) **17** *216*, *233*; **27** *465*
Gokyōgoku **17** 224
calligraphy
historical and regional traditions
Japan—cont.
Heian period (AD 794-1185) **1** 581–2; **17** *212*, *222*; **23** 445
Hosshōji **11** 822, 824; **17** 224
Meiji period (1868-1912) **33** 495
Sesonji **11** 822, 823; **17** 215, 223–4, 226
Shōren'in **17** 225, *227*, *228*
Shōwa period (1926-89) **17** *239*, *240*
Zenga **14** 61; **28** 408
Jewish art **21** *476*
Korea **18** 327–32*, *330*
Neo-Confucianism **17** 234
North Africa **16** *281*
Ottoman **14** 27; **22** *235*
Pakistan **23** 800, *801*
Scythian **6** 307
Singapore **6** 772
Spain **16** 215
Sudan **29** *896*
Syria **16** *275*
Taiwan **6** 772; **30** 246
Tibet **30** 845
United States of America **6** 772
materials
aluminium **17** 213
bamboo **6** 736, 740
bone **6** 736
brushes **5** *32*; **6** 736–7; **17** 213, 226, 227, 235
gold **17** 219, 220, *228*
gums **6** 736
inks **6** 736; **15** 853–4*; **17** 212–13; **23** *801*
inksticks **6** 736; **17** 227
inkstones **6** 736
lacquer **17** 213, 227
lampblack **6** 736; **17** 213
mounts (works on paper and scrolls) **1** 580
paper **6** 736, 740; **17** 213–14, 219, 220, 223, 227; **24** 55
pens **24** 348, 349
resins **17** 213
silk **6** 736
silver **17** 219, 220, *228*
soot **6** 736; **17** 213
styluses **6** 736
types
black exercise **16** 287
bokuseki **6** 752, *752*; **17** 342–4, *343*
zoomorphic **16** 287, *288*
uses
architectural decorations **15** 338, 354, 680
design **17** 217
mats **15** 727
pottery **6** 257
screens (ii) (furniture) **17** 215
tea ceremonies **17** 341, 342–4*, *343*
textiles **17** 235
wood-carvings **17** 215
see also CARMINA FIGURATA; SCRIPTS; WRITINGS
Çallı group **5** 437; **13** 856; **31** 454
Callinicum **9** 543
Calliope Painter **13** 523; **32** 40
Calliopius **30** 486
callipers **5** 437*; **13** 438; **26** 861
Callisto da Lodi *see* PIAZZA, CALLISTO
Callisto de Toccagni *see* PIAZZA, CALLISTO
Callistratus **2** 517
Calloigne, Jan-Robert **8** 831; **30** 46
Callot, Claude **17** 615; **25** 105; **32** 881
Callot, Jacques **5** 437–9*; **10** 390, 551; **11** 188, 657; **14** 394; **19** 696; **22** 455; **26** 772; **30** 746
collaboration **18** 811; **22** 487
Callot, Jacques—cont.
frames **11** 401
methods **9** 697
patrons and collectors
Arenberg, Englebert-Marie, 9th Duke of **2** 382
Cavendish, William Spencer, 6th Duke of Devonshire (1790–1858) **25** 665
Mariette, Jean **20** 416
Mariette, Pierre-Jean **20** 417
Medici, Leopoldo de', Cardinal **21** 28
Paignon-Dijonval **23** 777
Quentin de Lorangère **25** 815
Tessin, Carl Gustav, Count **30** 524
Thibaudeau, Narcisse-Adolphe, Comte de **30** 727
Worlidge, Thomas **33** 380
Zanetti, Anton Maria (Girolamo) (i), Conte (1680-1767) **33** 613
prints **3** 388; **4** 359; **7** 648; **11** 534; **12** 304; **31** 156
emblem books **10** 175
engravings **5** 786: **11** 269
etchings **5** *437*, *438*; **10** 551; **12** 289; **25** 605
pupils **7** 569
reproductions in ceramics **21** 137
reproductive prints by others **18** 535; **28** 79
Callot, Jean **29** 399
Callot Soeurs **9** 291
works **4** II
Callow, John **5** 439
Callow, William **4** 66; **5** 439*; **11** 60
Calman, Mel **12** 152
Calmann, Michel **6** 925; **7** 155
Calmels, Célestin-Anatole **4** 629; **25** 301
Calmo, Andrea **31** 17
Calmon, Franciso Goés *see* GOÉS CALMON, FRANCISCO
Calne (Wilts) **13** 211
hall **14** 73
Caló, Giovanni Battista **8** 716, 717
Calonne, Alexandre de **19** 57
Calonne, Charles-Alexandre de **5** 439–40*; **19** 587; **26** 280
Calonne, Charles-Antoine de **8** 792
Calos, Nino **18** 63
calotte domes *see under* DOMES → types
calotype process *see under* PHOTOGRAPHY → processes
calotypes *see under* PHOTOGRAPHIC PRINTS → types
Calpe *see* GIBRALTAR
Calperós, Joan **3** 221
Calpurnius Fabatus **25** 47
Calraet, Abraham (Pietersz.) van **5** 440*; **8** 298
Calraet, Barent (Pietersz.) van **5** 440; **8** 298
Calraet, Pieter Jansz. van **5** 440
Cals, Adolphe-Félix **5** 440–41*
works **5** *441*
Calsat, François **5** 609
Caltagirone **16** 736; **30** 887
Calthorpe, Frederick Gough, 5th Baron *see* GOUGH, FREDERICK, 5th Baron Calthorpe
Calthrop, Gladys **30** 687
Călugăreanu, Stefan **20** 400
Căluiu **25** 344; **26** 712
Caļukyas, Early *see* CHALUKYAS OF BADAMI
Calumbo Fortress **2** 86
Calusa **11** 321; **18** 7
Calvaert, Denys **4** 277; **5** 441–2*
collaboration **27** 480; **32** 17
pupils **1** 533; **9** 88; **12** 499; **26** 196; **27** 893; **28** 395
Calvaert, Denys—cont.
reproductive prints by others **5** 856; **27** 504
works **5** *442*
Calvary **5** 442–3*; **8** 195; **17** 497, *498*
Calventi, Raphael **9** 116
Calverley, Amice M(ary) **10** 83
Calvert (family) **3** 128
Calvert, Albert F. **18** 868
Calvert, Edward **1** 897; **5** 444*; **10** 394; **23** 884
Calvert, Frank **31** 375
Calvert Collection *see under* LONDON → museums → British Museum
Calvet, Esprit-Claude-François **4** 241; **5** 445; **18** 573
Calvet, Musée *see under* AVIGNON
Calvi (family) **16** 725
Calvi, Girolamo-Luigi **5** 444*
Calvi, Jacopo Alessandro **5** 444*; **10** 446
Calvi, Lazzaro **9** 173
Calvi, Marcantonio **9** 173
Calvi, Pompeo **21** 495
Calvi Cathedral **16** 686; **30** 777
Calvière, Charles-François, Marquis de **5** 445*
Calvillo, Fernando Pérez *see* PÉREZ CALVILLO, FERNANDO
Calvillo, Pedro Pérez *see* PÉREZ CALVILLO, PEDRO
Calvin, Jean **5** 445–6, *446*, 447; **14** 868; **15** 80
academy **12** 276
writings **6** 175; **7** 215, 258, 269, 277; **10** 534; **11** 255
Calvinism *see under* CHRISTIANITY → sects
Calvit, Mario **5** 447*; **23** 905
Calvizzano, S Maria delle Grazie **26** 500
Calvo, Bishop of Naples **22** 469
Calvo, Agustín **31** 159
Calvo, Javier **31** 816
Calvo, Juan **32** 568
Calvo, Marco Fabio **2** 161; **5** 448*; **32** 641
Calvo, Marta **2** 405
Calvo, Reinaldo **8** 236
Calvo, Santiago Agurto *see* AGURTO CALVO, SANTIAGO
Calvo de la Puerta, Martín **8** 231
Calw, Adalbert II, Count of **14** 569
Calydon *see* KALYDON
calyx kraters *see under* KRATERS → types
Calzada, Humberto **5** 448*
works **18** *834*, 835
Calzetta, Domenico **28** 509
Calzetta, Francesco **28** 509
Calzetta, Pietro **28** 509
Calzetti, Matteo *see* WITHOOS, MATTHIAS
Calzolari, Francesco **16** 770
Cam, John de La *see* LA CAM, JOHN DE
Camac, Kyan & Camac **22** 199
Camacho, Alvaro Sáenz *see* SÁENZ CAMACHO, ALVARO
Camacho, Jorge **5** 448–9*; **30** 23
Camacho, Paul **14** 464
Camagüey **5** 449*; **8** *228*, 236
Museum **8** 239
camaieu painting *see under* PAINTING → types
Camaino, Primo da *see* PRIMO DA CAMAINO
Camaino, Tino di *see* TINO DI CAMAINO
Camaino di Crescentino **28** 679; **31** 2
Camaldolese, Simon *see* SIMONE CAMALDOLESE
Camaldolese Order **3** 709; **5** 449–51*
architecture **25** 135
iconography **5** 450*

Camaldolese Order—cont.
painting **5** *450*
patronage **5** 450–51*
Camaldolese Triptych **3** 868
Camaldoli **5** 449; **7** 231
Romitorio **24** 240
SS Donato ed Ilariano **5** 451
paintings **32** *12*
Camanyes, Aloi **29** 335
Câmara Filho, João **4** 719; **23** 400
Cámara Santa, Master of the **29** 288
Camarena, Jorge González **5** 451*; **23** 335
Camargo, Fernando **3** 811
Camargo, Gabriel Serrano *see* SERRANO CAMARGO, GABRIEL
Camargo, Iberê **4** 719; **5** 451*; **12** 29; **25** 880
Camargo, Sérgio de **4** 719; **5** 451–2*
camarín **5** 452*; **21** 859
Camaro, Alexander **3** 803; **5** 452*
Camarón (Meliá), José **5** 452–3*; **32** 248
Camarón, Nicolás **5** 452
Camarón y Boronat, José **5** 452*; **21** 815; **31** 808
Camarotti, Antonio **26** 400
Camars *see* CHIUSI
Camassei, Andrea **5** 453–4*; **9** 92
patrons and collectors **3** 206, 208, 744; **27** 160
works **5** *453*; **26** 837
Camastra, Giuseppe Lanza, Duca di **23** 257; **31** 717
Cambambe Fortress **2** 86
Cambay *see* KHAMBHAT
Çambel, Halet **1** 894; **17** 810
Cambellotti, Duilio **16** 679, 731; **25** 446
Camberlain, Joseph **17** 920
Camberley (Surrey) **7** 679
compound **7** *679*
Camberlin, Joseph **27** 575
Camberwell School of Art *see under* LONDON → academies and art schools
Cambi, Andrea *see* BOMBARDA
Cambi, Iacobo **16** 759
Cambi, Piero (*fl* 1510) **3** 304
Cambi, Pietro (*fl* 1807) **5** 454
Cambi, Tommaso di **12** 719
Cambi, Ulisse **5** 454*; **16** 705
Cambiaso, Giovanni **5** 454, 455
Cambiaso, Luca **5** 454–7*; **20** 66; **29** 280
attributions **2** 94; **14** 114
collaboration **6** 24
paintings **9** 173; **12** 283; **28** 709
altarpieces **10** 502, 503
frescoes **5** *455*, *456*; **10** 502, 503, *504*; **12** 662; **21** 830; **22** 484
wall **10** 503
patrons and collectors **3** 700; **9** 172, 174; **12** 763; **13** 922; **15** 147; **29** 411; **30** 373
pupils **30** 372
reproductive prints by others **31** 347; **33** 357
Cambiaso, Michelangelo, Marchese **31** 292
Cambiaso, Orazio **2** 125; **5** 457; **6** 25; **13** 307
Cambio, Arnolfo di *see* ARNOLFO DI CAMBIO
Cambitoglou, A. **33** 591
Cambó, Francesc **29** 321
Cambodia **5** 457–509*, *458*; **29** *225*
architectural decorations **5** 464, 475–6*
architecture **5** 463–83
art history **29** 241
balustrades **5** 474, 475
beads **5** 500
betel sets **5** *508*, 508*
blocks **5** 474
Cambodia—cont.
brick **5** 474, *487*
bronze **5** 485, 497–8*, 507
causeways **5** 474, *478*
cement **5** 500, *500*
ceramics **5** 506–7*
clay **5** 474
coins **5** 507*
colonnettes **5** 475
concrete **5** 482
copper **5** 507
cosmologies **5** 463*, 467–8, 474
costumes **5** 504*, *504*
cotton **5** 501, 502
doorways **5** 475
dress **5** 502, 503*
drums (musical instruments) **5** 508, 509
earthenwares **5** 506
fiddles **5** 508
filigree **5** 500
forecourts **5** 474
Funan **5** 460, 462; **6** 420; **14** 560
funerary monuments **5** 461
gables **5** 476
galleries (ii) (corridors) **5** 468, 474, 475, *475*
garden design **12** 102
gardens **12** 102–4*
gateways **2** *60*
gopuras **5** 474
glass **5** 500
glazes **5** 506
gold **5** 507
gold leaf **5** 501
gong-chimes **5** 508
halls **5** *482*
harps **5** 508
headdresses **5** *504*
hides **5** 505
hospitals **5** 479
houses **5** 483*, *483*
human figures **5** 484
hydraulic works **5** 459
iconography **5** 461–3, 467, 495, 496, 499–500, 501–2
ikat **5** 502, *502*, 503
inlays **5** 500
inscriptions **5** 463, 464, 491
jewellery **5** 504, 508
lacquer **5** 500
leather **5** *505*
lintels **5** 475
manuscript illumination **5** 501
marks **5** 506
masks **5** 504, *504*
masonry **5** 482
metalwork **5** 507*, 508*
monasteries **5** 462, 481, 501
musical instruments **5** 508–9*
narratives **5** 487, 490–92, *492*, 495–6
painting **5** 501–2*, *501*
landscape **5** 502
wall **5** 501, *501*
pantaloons **5** 502
paper **5** 501
pavements **5** 475
pavilions (buildings) **5** 474
pavilions (crematory) **5** 507*
pearls **5** 500
pedestals **5** 496
pediments **5** 470, 476
pegs **5** 474
pillars **5** 474
plaster **5** 501
platforms **5** *473*
porches **5** 474
portraits **5** 496, *497*
pots **5** *506*
puppets **5** 504–5*, *505*
pyramids **2** 56, *56*; **5** *473*
regalia **5** 508
relief sculpture **5** *492*
religion **5** 461–3*; **14** 561
rest-houses **5** 479
roofs **5** *475*
sanctuaries **5** 467, 468–9*, *473*, 475, 477, 496
Cambodia—cont.
sandstone **5** *100*, 459, *462*, 474, *485*, *488*, *489*, *492*, *493*, *494*, *498*
sculpture **5** 483–501*
bronze **5** 485, 497–8*
Buddhism **5** *100*, *462*, 484, 485, 490, *494*, 494, 495–8*, *498*, 499–500
cement **5** 500
early Angkor period **5** 486–90*
Hinduism **5** 484–5, *485*, 486–90, *489*
Khmer **5** 499
liṅga **14** 561
reliefs **5** *487*, 487–9, *488*, 490–93, *493*, 495–6, *496*, 499, 500, *500*
wood **5** 499
shrines (i) (cult) **2** 57; **5** 474
silk **5** 501, 502, *502*
silver **5** 507, *508*, 508
stonewares **5** 506*, *506*
stucco **29** 826
stupas **5** 481
temple-mountains **2** 56, *56*; **5** 461, 467–72*, 473, *473*, 474
Hinduism **5** 464, 466, *466*, *469*, *471*
Khmer **5** 479
temples **2** 55; **5** 461, 467–72*, *473*, 473–80*, *475*; **30** 446
Buddhism **5** *479*
Hinduism **5** 463–7*, *465*, *469*, *470*, *471*, 473
Khmer **2** *58*; **5** *477*, *478*
rock-cut **2** 57
terraces **5** 474
textiles **5** 502–3*; **6** 432
theatres **5** 503–5*, *505*
thrones **30** 785
towers **5** 474, 477
tower-sanctuaries **5** 465, *466*, *473*, 474
trumpets **5** 509
tympana **5** 476
wall decorations **5** 476
water supply **5** 459
weaving **5** 502
wood **5** 482, 499
wood-carvings **5** 509*
xylophones **5** 508
zithers **5** 509
see also SOUTH-EAST ASIA
Cambo-les-Bains **32** 280
Cambon, Armand **15** 839, 843
Cambon, Charles Antoine **19** 89; **29** 306
Cambó y Batlle, Francisco de Asís **5** 509–10*; **29** 308, 354
Cambrai
Cathedral **9** 672; **13** 38, 39
choir **13** 42
epitaph to Guillaume Dufay **13** 79
transept **31** 281
St Aubert **2** 723
woodcuts **33** 360
Cambrai, Jean de *see* JEAN DE CAMBRAI
Cambrai, Nicolas de *see* GUILLAIN, NICOLAS DE
Cambray-Digny, Luigi De *see* DE CAMBRAY-DIGNY, LUIGI
Cambrian Pottery **32** 789
cambric **12** 463
Cambridge (UK) **5** 510–15*; **10** *225*; **31** 710
art forms and materials
architecture **4** 779
bookbindings **4** 351, 353
coats of arms **14** 420
churches
Church of the Holy Sepulchre **7** 257
King's College Chapel *see under* colleges → King's College
Memorial Church **31** 584
Cambridge (UK)
churches—cont.
Round Church *see* Church of the Holy Sepulchre
St Bene't **2** 67
St Botolph **11** 255
St Mary Magdalene **26** 613
St Mary the Great **25** 726; **29** 513
St Peter **26** 613
colleges **7** 565, 566, 567; **10** 230; **14** 418
Christ's College **3** 451
collections **10** 324, 325; **14** 418
Master's Lodgings **10** 272
wallpaper **32** 814
Churchill College **5** *513*
Clare College **14** 76
Corpus Christi College **24** 184
collections **10** 323, 325
Darwin College **4** 790
Downing College **7** 567; **10** 235; **13** 609
Howard Building **10** 242
Master's Lodge **33** *192*
pilasters **24** 805
portico **25** 267
Girton College **4** 787
Godshouse *see* Christ's College
Gonville and Caius College **5** *512*; **14** 245
Jesus College
Chapel **29** 507
King's College **18** 687
Chapel **5** 513–14*, *514*; **6** 459; **7** 419; **13** 55; **24** 465, 466; **26** 89; **32** 895
Chapel: bosses **4** 464
Chapel: pulpitum **28** 293
Chapel: stained glass **5** 514–15*, *515*; **12** 790; **13** 185; **29** 504, 512
Chapel: tracery **31** *272*
Chapel: vaults **13** 55; **20** 579; **32** 88
Fellows Building **10** 233
manuscripts **18** 686
model **2** 336
King's Hall *see* Trinity College
Magdalene College
Pepys Library **10** 421; **24** 373
Michaelhouse *see* Trinity College
Newnham College **4** 788; **25** 804; **30** 504, 749
Pembroke College **2** 336; **24** 348
Peterhouse College
Chapel **29** 505, 506
stained glass **29** *513*
William Stone Building **4** 789
Queens' College **5** *511*; **12** 175; **28** 302
gate-house **12** *175*
St John's College **3** 451; **14** 420
gate-house **10** 744; **12** 175
library **4** 785, *785*; **13** 210
Merton Hall **29** 22
Sidney Sussex College
Blundell Court **4** 790
Trinity College **7** 566
Chapel **11** 424
collections **27** 225
gate-house **12** 175
metalwork **30** 872
Wren Library **7** 339; **10** 341; **19** 314, *315*; **29** 506; **33** 395
Trinity Hall **7** 837
library **4** 786
libraries **19** 313, 314
Pepys Library *see under* colleges → Magdalene College
University Library **10** 241; **19** 319; **22** 795
museums
Fitzwilliam Museum **3** 325; **5** 512; **7** 640; **9** 19; **22** 362
ceramics **6** 925
Chinese collection **7** 155
collections **13** 718
Cycladic collection **8** 324
Cambridge (UK)
museums
Fitzwilliam Museum—cont.
directors **16** 893
Egyptian collection **10** 90, 92
Fitzwilliam collection **10** 369–70; **11** 141
Indian collection **15** 744
Islamic collection **3** 244
Korean collection **18** 383
manuscripts **30** 749
Messel Collection **10** 782
paintings **22** 351
Ricketts collection **26** 360
sculpture **9** 25; **27** 46
staircase **3** 284
Kettle's Yard Art Gallery **9** 716
University Museum of Archaeology and Anthropology **1** 66; **21** 265; **29** 240
collections **3** 916; **23** 741; **28** 581; **29** 48, 221
St John's Hospital *see* colleges → St John's College
Schlumberger Laboratories **14** 521
university buildings
History Faculty building **12** 793; **29** 677
Mond Laboratory **4** 789
observatory **23** 340
Old Schools **31** 674
Senate House **10** 232, 342
University Centre **14** 812
University Library *see under* libraries
University Museum of Archaeology and Anthropology *see under* MUSEUMS
Cambridge (MA; USA)
Carpenter Center for the Visual Arts *see under* Harvard University
Harvard Square **6** 176
Harvard University **31** 669
Arthur M. Sackler Museum **22** 367; **29** 678
collections **6** 735, 826, 868; **16** 555, 557; **17** 434; **18** 384
Austin Hall **4** *474*
Carpenter Center for the Visual Arts **19** 47
ceramics **21** 709
collections **2** 382; **27** 493; **31** 666
Fine Arts Library **4** 23; **31** 670
Fogg Art Museum **15** 23; **27** 493
collections **7** 156; **9** 231; **11** 307; **14** 624; **15** 745; **16** 557; **19** 538; **29** 241
drawings **9** 231
Greek collection **13** 470
Sackler Collection **30** 496
sculpture **27** 46
Graduate School of Design **8** 803; **24** 300
Harvard Hall **7** 619
Hemenway Gymnasium **25** 806
Holyoke Center **27** 222
Houghton Library **14** 624
Lamont Library **19** 320
library **4** 23, 24
Loeb Drama Center **30** 684
Memorial Hall **4** 788; **31** 593
observatory **23** 341
Peabody Museum of Archaeology and Ethnology **1** 437
collections **1** 439; **22** 675; **29** 221, 222; **32** 238
Mesoamerican collection **21** 265
Widener Memorial Library **19** 319
Loeb Drama Center *see under* Harvard University

Cambridge (MA; USA)—cont.
Massachusetts Institute of Technology **2** 315
chapel **4** 790
Kresge Auditorium **31** 597
M. F. Stoughton House **28** 604
Mt Auburn Cemetery **6** 166; **10** 97; **20** 869; **31** 131
Chapel **31** 131
University Library **10** 376
Cambridge (Ont; Canada), Galt War Memorial **5** 570
Cambridge Camden Society *see* ECCLESIOLOGICAL SOCIETY
Cambridge Seven **23** 593
Cambridge University Press **31** 498
Cambron-Casteau **29** 700
Abbey Church **13** 99
Camden, William **2** 162; **5** 515–16*; **13** 225; **14** 408
decorative works **32** 814
pupils **5** 764; **8** 38
works **2** 162; **15** 150
illustrated **18** 73
Camden Park House **2** 738
Camden Society *see* ECCLESIOLOGICAL SOCIETY
Camden Town Group **5** 516–17*; **8** 265; **10** 256; **19** 591, 622
exhibitions **10** 255
members
Bevan, Robert (Polhill) **3** 894
Gilman, Harold **12** 644
Ginner, Charles (Isaac) **12** 652
Gore, Spencer (Frederick) **13** 9
Grant, Duncan (James Corrowr) **13** 313
Lamb, Henry **18** 668
Lightfoot, Maxwell Gordon **19** 359
Pissarro, Lucien **24** 884
Ratcliffe, William (Whitehead) **26** 10
Sickert, Walter Richard **28** 661
paintings **5** *517*; **10** *256*; **12** 296; **23** 297; **31** 706
Camelford, Thomas Pitt, 1st Baron *see* PITT, THOMAS, 1st Baron Camelford
camel hair *see under* HAIR → types
camel harnesses *see under* HARNESSES → types
Camelio, Vittore *see* GAMBELLO, VITTORE
Camélique Factory **30** 144
Camelli, Francesco **21** 27
camellia **17** 399
Camelot *see under* TYPE-FACES
Camelot (1702-66) *see* AVED, JACQUES (-ANDRÉ-JOSEPH)
Camelot, Robert **33** 627
Camelot Press **13** 223
camel trappings *see under* TRAPPINGS → types
Camelus, Vittore *see* GAMBELLO, VITTORE
Camenisch, Paul **13** 726; **18** 81; **27** 213*; **30** 135
Cameo Doll Co. **31** 261
cameo glass *see under* GLASS → types
Cameo Gonzaga **12** 265
cameos **5** 518*; **12** 256, 262, 264–5; **17** 520; **26** 132
historical and regional traditions
Byzantine **12** 254–5, *255*
England **10** *345*; **21** II3
France **12** 259, *262*, *264*
Germany **21** *162*
Greece, ancient **12** 248
Indian subcontinent **15** 723
Italy **12** *256*, *258*, 258–9; **16** 690, 746, *746*
19th cent. **17** *527*
Merovingian **21** *162*
Poland **25** 128
Rome, ancient **1** *652*; **12** 250; **14** II2; **21** *162*; **27** 34
cameos
historical and regional traditions—cont.
Scotland **28** *263*
Switzerland **17** *520*
materials
bloodstone (chalcedony) **12** *255*
coral **7** 834, 836; **12** 264; **25** 128
glass paste **17** *525*
jasper **12** *255*
Jasper ware **21** II3
onyx **12** *256*, *258*, *262*; **14** II2; **16** *746*; **17** *520*
sardonyx **1** *652*; **12** 248, *264*; **15** *702*
shells **12** 264
uses
brooches **17** 519, 520, *520*
earrings **17** *527*
fibulae **21** *162*
jewellery **17** 525; **28** *263*
medals **16** 690
necklaces **17** *527*
pendants (jewellery) **10** *345*
portraits *see under* PORTRAITS → media
Camera **24** 438
Camera Austria **24** 439
camera bellows *see* BELLOWS (CAMERA)
Camera Club (Ashiya) **22** 445
Camera Club (London) **10** 184; **24** 739
Camera Club (New York) **29** 655, 744
cameraless images *see* PHOTOGRAMS
camera lucida **5** *518*, 518–19*; **14** 481; **24** 378, 659; **25** 281; **28** 203
Camera Notes **24** 432; **29** 655
camera obscura (instrument) **2** 342; **5** 519*, *519*; **24** 378, 658; **28** 203; **32** 110, 266
Camera oscura (periodical) **24** 447
Camerarius, Joachim **10** 174
cameras (i) (rooms) **5** 518*
cameras (ii) (photography) **14** 540; **24** 646, 647, 648, 658, 660, 669–70, 671; **25** 354
types
35mm **24** 677, 678
Al Vista **24** 654
banquet **28** 779
Brownie **9** 685
cinematography **17** 732
Cirkut **24** 654
daguerreotype **24** 653, 659
electric photographic guns **20** 406
Ermanox **24** 677
Johnson's Pantascopic **24** 654
Kodak **9** 685; **24** 670
Kodak Baby Brownie **30** 390
Kodak Bantam Special **15** 825; **30** 390
Kodak Vanity **15** 825
Leica **24** 677
Linhof **24** 677
Megaskop-Kamera **20** 483
miniature **24** 651, 670
panorama **24** 653
Panorama-Kamera *see* Megaskop-Kamera
Panoram Kodak **24** 654
Polaroid **24** 655
roll film **20** 406; **24** 654, 656
Speed Graphic **24** 677
Stirn Secret **24** 670
Sutton's Panoramic **24** 654
twin lens **24** 657
see also CAMERA LUCIDA; CAMERA OBSCURA; FILM; SHUTTERS
cameras, multiple *see under* PHOTOGRAPHY → processes
Camerata, Giuseppe, I (*d* 1762) **10** 770
Camerata, Giuseppe, II (1718-1803) **20** 415
Camera Work **10** 655; **24** 432, 434, 688, 739; **29** 655, 656, 744; **31** 605; **33** 146
Camerino, Palazzo Ducale **31** 904
Camerino, Arcangelo di Cola da *see* ARCANGELO DI COLA DA CAMERINO
Camerino, Francesco da *see* FRANCESCO DA CAMERINO
Camerino, Giovanni Angelo di Antonio da *see* GIOVANNI ANGELO DI ANTONIO DA CAMERINO
Camerino, Girolamo di Giovanni da *see* GIROLAMO DI GIOVANNI DA CAMERINO
Camerino, Piergentile da **27** 273
Camerlo, Humbert **26** 333
Cameron, Charles **5** 520–21*
architecture
baths **1** 111; **25** 193
bridges **23** 76
palaces **5** *520*; **24** 291–2, *292*; **25** 746; **27** 376
pavilions (buildings) **12** 134; **23** 545
assistants **4** 745; **14** 221
furniture **27** 407, *408*, 582, 583
gardens **12** *134*; **24** 292; **25** 746
interior decoration **5** 349; **27** 403; **29** 839, *839*
patrons and collectors **4** 745; **12** 134; **27** 438
restorations by others **27** *403*
writings **25** 192
Cameron, Chisholm & Nicol **17** 898; **19** 320
Cameron, D(avid) Y(oung) **5** 521*; **15** 892
works **9** 309; **11** 436, *437*; **28** 238
Cameron, Henry Hay **19** 424
Cameron, James **14** 173
Cameron, Julia Margaret **5** 522–3*; **10** 254; **24** 662; **29** 58, 368; **33** 308, 310
groups and movements **24** 738
patrons and collectors **12** 486
works **5** *522*; **24** 668
Cameron, Walter **5** 520
Cameroon **1** *214*, 393; **5** 523–5*
architecture **1** 307, 312; **5** 523*
bamboo **1** 307
basketwork **1** 246
beads **1** 298; **3** *152*
beds **1** 366
body arts **1** 289
brass **1** 368
burial practices **1** 259*
ceramics **1** 329
collections **5** 525
craftsmen and artists **1** 396
cult houses **1** 395
dyeing **11** 828
figurines **1** 273, *277*
gesture **1** 265, 266
gourds **1** 303; **11** 828
granaries **1** 310, *310*
houses **1** 307
human figures **3** *151*
iconography **1** 263, 276
iron **1** 287
looms **1** 294
masks **1** 259*, *279*, *339*, 399; **6** *406*
metalwork **1** 400
painting **5** 523–4*
palaces **1** 309; **3** *151*
photography **10** 580
pillars **3** *151*
pipes (smoking) **1** 368
portraits **1** 269
prints **5** *524*
regalia **1** 242, 352
sculpture **1** 278, 396; **3** *171*; **5** 523–4*
shells **3** *152*
slit-gongs **1** 360
Cameroon—cont.
stools **1** 365
tables **3** *153*
textiles **1** 400
thrones **3** *152*
tourist art **3** 170
women **1** 259*
wood **1** *277*
wood-carvings **1** 242; **3** *151*, *152*, *153*
woodcuts **5** *524*
Camesina, Alberto **27** 216
Cametti, Bernardino **5** 525*
patrons and collectors **28** 16
teachers **23** 645
works **16** 702
cami *see* MOSQUES
Camicia, Chimenti di Leonardo **5** 81, 86; **14** 884, 904; **20** 847
Camilliani (family) **7** 682
Camilliani, Camillo **5** 525–6*; **11** 342; **22** 422; **28** 656
Camilliani, Francesco **5** 525; **11** 342; **13** 773; **22** 422; **29** 289
Camillo, Giulio **1** 178; **5** 526*; **18** 522
Camilo, Francisco **5** 526–7*
collaboration **2** 381
pupils **27** 331; **31** 907
teachers **8** 254
works **5** *526*
Čamilov, Rumen **19** 885
Caminha, Pero Vaz de **4** 706
Camini, Aldo *see* DOESBURG, THEO VAN
Camino Brent, Enrique **5** 527*; **24** 509, 515
Camirus **12** 868
camlet *see* HAIR → types → camel hair
Cammarano, Antonio **5** 527
Cammarano, Giuseppe **5** 527
Cammarano, Michele **5** 527–8*; **22** 480; **32** 257
Cammas, Guillaume **5** 528
Cammas, Lambert-François-Thérèse **4** 329; **5** 528*
Cammen, Jan van der **10** 222
Cammen, Philips van der **10** 222
Cammerlander **33** 18
Camnitzer, Luis **29** 26; **31** 756
Camogli, Bartolomeo da *see* BARTOLOMEO DA CAMOGLI
Camogli, Stefano **24** 835, 836
Camoin, Charles **5** 528–9*
groups and movements **10** 839, 840, 841
works **5** *529*
Camoletti, John **12** 276
Camoletti, Mark **12** 276
Camollano, Fernando **25** 826
Camón Aznar, José **5** 529*
Camondo, Isaac de, Comte **5** 530*; **11** 417; **20** 351
Camondo, Moïse de, Comte **5** 530*
Camondo collection *see under* PARIS → museums → Musée d'Orsay
Ca' Morosini Polyptych **32** 656, *656*
Camot, André **3** 752
camouflage **5** 530–31*, *531*
Camp (*fl* 1854) **13** 821
Camp, Joseph Rodefer De *see* DE CAMP, JOSEPH RODEFER
Camp, Maxime Du *see* DU CAMP, MAXIME
Camp, Peter van **2** 199
Camp, Sokari Douglas **1** 247, 438; **15** 123; **23** 138
works **1** *247*
Camp, William **3** 129; **10** 852
campagi **9** 641, 642
Campagna, Girolamo **5** 531–3*; **23** 754; **31** 740; **32** 192, 193, 195
collaboration **2** 608; **19** 627
patrons and collectors **11** 818; **27** 274
Campagna, Girolamo—cont.
personal collection **30** 496
teachers **6** 90
works **2** 608; **5** *532*, *533*; **6** 90; **11** 711; **16** 697; **29** 570; **32** 193, 215, 223
Campagna, Giuseppe **5** 531, 532
Campagnola, Domenico **3** 700; **5** 534, 535*; **10** 385; **32** 192
attributions **26** 170
collaboration **32** 199
patrons and collectors **3** 700; **25** 630
reproductive prints by others **11** 270
works **5** 535; **8** 130; **9** 308; **18** 708; **25** 606; **33** 356
Campagnola, Girolamo **5** 534
Campagnola, Giulio **5** 534–5*; **10** 385; **32** 192
collaboration **20** 314
patrons and collectors **3** 698; **25** 630
pupils **5** 535
reproductive prints by others **22** 369
works **5** *534*; **8** 130; **12** 677; **25** 618, *619*; **26** 229; **29** 675; **32** 199; **33** 356
Campaña, Antoni **5** 535*
Campana, Giacinto **20** 221
Campana (di Cavelli), Giampietro, Marchese **5** 536–7*
collections **2** 861; **4** 307; **10** 637; **11** 667; **12** 608; **26** 473, 734; **27** 579
forgeries **10** 639
jewellery **6** 20
paintings **27** 58
pottery **13** 542
terracottas **26** 878
Campaña, Joaquin **29** 309
Campana, Musée *see* PARIS → museums → Musée du Louvre → Galerie Campana
Campaña, Pedro de *see* KEMPENEER, PEETER DE
Campana Collection (France) *see* PARIS → museums → Musée du Louvre → Galerie Campana
Campana Collection (Russia) *see under* ST PETERSBURG → museums → Hermitage Museum
Campana C ware *see under* POTTERY → wares
Campana group pottery *see under* POTTERY → wares
Campanari (family) **10** 637, 640; **13** 542
Campanato, Alvise **5** 537
Campanato, Pietro di Giovanni Battista **5** 537*; **27** 888
Campane, Pietro delle *see* CAMPANATO, PIETRO DI GIOVANNI BATTISTA
Campane, Pietro di Giovanni Battista delle *see* CAMPANATO, PIETRO DI GIOVANNI BATTISTA
Campanhã, Francisco Pereira *see* PEREIRA CAMPANHÃ, FRANCISCO
Campanhã, Palacio do Freixo **22** 534
Campani (family) **16** 726
Campani, Tommaso **26** 780
campanili *see* TOWERS → types → bell
Campanizing group **10** 615
Campano, Andrea **16** 725
Campanus, J. J.
works **11** *853*
Campari **23** 169
Campbell, Archibald, 3rd Duke of Argyll **13** 200; **22** 138; **25** 882

Campbell, Colen (1676-1729) **5** 537–40*; **10** 276; **12** 593; **13** 301; **19** 570
architecture
country houses **4** *138*; **5** *538*, *539*; **8** 47; **12** 176; **14** 597; **19** 157, 204; **23** *858*; **25** 266; **29** 861; **32** 553
town houses **4** *610*; **12** 772; **14** 436
assistants **10** 278
collaboration **22** 138; **29** 835
drawings **6** *65*; **10** 233; **13** *624*; **32** 824
groups and movements **23** 856, 857, 858, 859
patrons and collectors **3** 173; **4** 610; **29** 733
personal collection **28** 226, 881
writings **2** 314; **4** 612; **10** 233; **19** 599; **23** 857; **31** 298; **32** *552*
Campbell, Colin (*fl* 1970s) **5** 569; **28** 269
Campbell, Colin, 8th Laird of Glenorchy (*fl* 1630s) **16** 897
Campbell, Colin Minton **21** 697
Campbell, Elizabeth **16** 42
Campbell, Elmer Simms **1** 443
Campbell, George **5** 540*
Campbell, Ian **16** 40
Campbell, Joan **2** 761
Campbell, John (1857-1942) **5** 540–41*; **23** 55; **33** 58
Campbell, John, 1st Baron Cawdor (1755-1821) **4** 181; **5** 541*; **17** 475
Campbell, John, 1st Marquess of Breadalbane **10** 145
Campbell, John, 2nd Duke of Argyll (*d* 1743) **1** 488; **12** 593, 594; **25** 882
Campbell, John, 5th Duke of Argyll (*fl* 1770s) **9** 302; **28** 227
Campbell, John, 9th Duke of Argyll (1845-1914) **5** 590; **32** 911
Campbell, John Archibald (1859-1909) **5** 270; **12** 775
Campbell, Laurence **16** 21
Campbell, Nick **13** 225
Campbell, Noel **16** 40
Campbell, Patricia **30** 330
Campbell, Ralph **5** 541*; **16** 884
Campbell, Robert (*fl* 1747) **15** 820
Campbell, Robert, jr (1822-88) **13** 622
Campbell, Robert, jr (1944-93) **1** 65
Campbell, Sophia **2** 744
Campbell, Steven **2** 561; **12** 777; **28** 240
Campbell, Thomas **28** 242; **31** 471
Campbell, Walford **16** 888
Campbell, Wallace **16** 890
Campbell Collections *see under* DURBAN → University of Natal
Campbell Douglas & Sellars **31** 375
Campbell-Thompson, Reginald **10** 460
Campe, Friedrich **9** 444
Campeche **21** 391
Museo Arqueológico Etnográfico e Histórico del Estado **21** 396
Campeche, Ignacio de Rivafrecha y *see* RIVAFRECHA Y CAMPECHE, IGNACIO DE
Campeche, José de Rivafrecha y *see* RIVAFRECHA Y CAMPECHE, JOSÉ DE
Campeche, Manuel de Rivafrecha y *see* RIVAFRECHA Y CAMPECHE, MANUEL DE
Campeggia, Lorenzo, Cardinal **1** 605; **7** 467
Campello (family) **29** 422
Campello sul Clitunno, Tempietto del Clitunno **16** 624
Campelo, António **5** 541–2*; **25** 296
Campen, Herman van **22** 870
Campen, Jacob van **4** 868; **5** 542–3*; **22** 840, 871, 902
architecture **1** 801; **2** 358; **22** 824–5
churches **13** 893; **18** 7
country houses **25** 324
houses **1** 802; **14** 39; **23** 492
palaces **4** 786; **5** *542*; **9** 299; **14** *38*, 39; **22** 536, 825, 842; **32** 551
theatres **30** 665; **33** 268
tombs **32** 255
town halls **1** 802, 813; **8** 496; **18** 11; **22** 858; **25** 812; **31** 239, *239*; **32** 589
assistants **4** 377; **8** 126; **29** 530
attributions **4** 377
collaboration **4** 378; **10** 659; **14** 46, 635; **15** 40; **18** 11; **25** 324; **27** 508
paintings **14** 139, 584, 730; **23** 465
patrons and collectors **13** 266
personal collection **4** 378
pupils **33** 264
Campen, Laurens van **26** 284
Campen, Pieter van **13** 893
Campendonk, Heinrich **5** 543–4*; **29** 872
exhibitions **32** 774
groups and movements **4** 132; **8** 434; **10** 695; **12** 395
works **29** 871; **33** 363
Campenhout, Jan Jacob van **3** 600
Campenon-Bernard **11** 771
Campeny y Estrany, Damián **3** 219; **5** 544*
collaboration **21** 815
pupils **1** 610; **31** 829; **32** 538
works **29** 294
Camper, Pieter **24** 494
Camperdown, Purumbete **33** 264
Camperdown House (Tayside) **5** 263; **28** 230
Campero, Juan **27** 605; **28** 369
camphor **7** 91; **15** 850; **25** 309
camphor-wood
historical and regional traditions
Buddhism **17** *109*
China **7** 31
Japan **17** *99*, *109*, 390, 399; **33** 325
uses
furniture **7** 31
sculpture **17** *99*, *109*
Camphuys, Johannes
works **6** *921*
Camphuyzen, Govert (Dircksz.) **5** 544–5*; **30** 78
Camphuyzen, Jochem (Govertsz.) **22** 719
Camphuyzen, Rafael (Govertsz.) **22** 719
Campi (family) **8** 135; **22** 26; **30** 456
Campi, Andrea **5** 547
Campi, Antonio **5** 545–7*; **21** 525
collaboration **5** 545, 547
patrons and collectors **4** 424; **28** 479
works **5** 545, *546*, 856; **33** 366
Campi, Bernardino **5** 547*
attributions **27** 483
collaboration **31** 746
commentaries **18** 679
patrons and collectors **12** 910; **16** 562
pupils **2** 92, 93; **31** 372
reproductive prints by others **2** 88
teachers **8** 4
works **2** 93; **29** 26
Campi, Claudio **5** 545
Campi, Francesco **22** 481
Campi, Galeazzo **5** 545
Campi, Giovanni da *see* GIOVANNI DA CAMPO
Campi, Giulio **5** 545–7*
attributions **31** 32
collaboration **5** 545
patrons and collectors **4** 424
pupils **5** 545, 547; **12** 29; **32** 403
Campi, Pietro **5** 547
Campi, Pietro Paolo **5** 547*
Campi, Ristoro de' **9** 111
Campi, Sebastiano **5** 545
Campi, Vincenzo **5** 545, 546–7*; **21** 525
collaboration **5** 546
patrons and collectors **11** 819
works **5** 546; **12** 288, *288*; **16** 674; **29** 666
Campi Bisenzio, S Giovanni Battista **16** 650
Campidoglio, Michele Pace del *see* PACE DEL CAMPIDOGLIO, MICHELE
Campigli, Massimo **5** 547–8*; **11** 843
exhibitions **10** 822
groups and movements **5** 849; **10** 821; **16** 680
works **12** 601; **16** 681; **19** 491; **23** 754
Campiglia **4** 492
Campiglia Marittima **10** 624
Campilo, J. **6** 67
Campin, Robert **3** 553; **5** 548–9*; **20** 666; **31** 218; **33** 119
attributions **20** *667*, *668*, *670*; **30** *165*, 166
groups and movements **26** 184
methods **12** 501, 803
patrons and collectors **27** 642
pupils **8** 524; **33** 117
works **3** 568, 597; **8** 662; **12** 287; **19** 356; **20** 671; **29** 665
Câmpineanu, Ion **26** 723
Câmpineanu, Irina **26** 723
Campion Cup **10** 325
Campione, S Maria dei Ghirli **30** 129; **32** 256
Campione (family) *see* CAMPIONESI (FAMILY)
Campione, Alberto da *see* ALBERTO DA CAMPIONE
Campione, Anselmo da *see* ANSELMO DA CAMPIONE
Campione, Bernardo da *see* BERNARDO DA CAMPIONE
Campione, Bernardo Forno da *see* BERNARDO FORNO DA CAMPIONE
Campione, Bonino da *see* BONINO DA CAMPIONE
Campione, Bozzalino da *see* BOZZALINO DA CAMPIONE
Campione, Egidio da *see* EGIDIO DA CAMPIONE
Campione, Enrico da *see* ENRICO DA CAMPIONE
Campione, Enrico di Ottavio *see* ENRICO DI OTTAVIO CAMPIONE
Campione, Giacomo da *see* GIACOMO DA CAMPIONE
Campione, Giambono da *see* GIAMBONO DA CAMPIONE
Campione, Giovanni da *see* GIOVANNI DA CAMPIONE
Campione, Jacopo da *see* JACOPO DA CAMPIONE
Campione, Matteo da *see* MATTEO DA CAMPIONE
Campione, Nicolino di Giovanni da *see* NICOLINO DI GIOVANNI DA CAMPIONE
Campione, Ottavio da *see* OTTAVIO DA CAMPIONE
Campione, Ubaldino da *see* UBALDINO DA CAMPIONE
Campione, Ugo da *see* UGO DA CAMPIONE
Campione, Zeno da *see* ZENO DA CAMPIONE
Campionesi (family) **2** 129; **5** 549–51*; **26** 620, 621; **33** 187
works **3** 771; **5** *550*; **7** 251; **21** 772, 773–4; **26** 619
Campioni, Santino **12** 633; **23** 531
Campis, Joannes de *see* DESCHAMPS, JEAN (*fl* 1248)
Campo, Apolinar del **29** 338
Campo, G. **11** 490
Campo, Giovanni del **18** 622
Campo, Pedro Fernández del *see* MEJORADA, Marqués de
Campo, Rafael López del *see* LÓPEZ DEL CAMPO, RAFAEL
Campo, Santiago del **13** 5
Campo Alegre **32** 170
Campobasso **16** 651
Campolargo, Pedro **19** 664
Campondonica, Rodolfo **22** 335
Camponeschi, Angelo María **2** 398
works **2** *398*
Camponeschi, Maria Pereira **28** 745
Camponeschi Carafa, Vittoria **16** 751
Camponovo, Antonio **5** 551*
works **4** 259, 260; **18** 777, *778*; **27** 702; **29** 894
Camponovo, Miguel **5** 551
Camporese (family) **26** 814
Camporese, Francesco **13** 653
Camporese, Giulio **5** 551, 552*
Camporese, Giuseppe **5** 551, 552*
collaboration **5** 552; **9** 12
patrons and collectors **16** 772
pupils **25** 147
works **16** *773*; **22** *361*, 362; **28** 755
Camporese, Pietro (i) (1726-81) **5** 551–2*
collaboration **9** 12; **28** 755
pupils **3** 644; **5** 551, 552
reproductive prints by others **13** *669*
Camporese, Pietro (ii) (1792-1873) **5** 551, 552–3*; **25** 147
Camporesi, Francesco **4** 598; **23** 615
Camporesi, Giulio **7** 726
Campori, Giuseppe, Marchese **5** 553*; **28** 479
Campos, Augusto de **7** 698
Campos, Haroldo de **7** 698
Campos, João da Costa *see* COSTA CAMPOS, JOÃO DA
Campos, Miguel **5** 188
Campos de Fonollosa Church **13** 122
Campos Guevara, Andrés de **29** 336
Campovecchio, Giovanni **10** 199; **31** 679
Campo Villar, Marqués de **32** 564
Camprena, Convento di S Anna **29** 1
Camprobín (Passano), Pedro de **5** 553*; **29** 668; **31** 347
camps (causewayed) **25** 504
camps (holiday) **6** 395–6
camps (military) **21** 545
Britain **26** 905
Byzantine **9** 553
Denmark **8** 721
Early Christian (*c.* AD 250-843) **9** 553
Germany **26** 905, 907
Rome, ancient **6** 68–9*; **25** 423; **26** 905, 907; **27** 4
Viking **8** 721
Campsall (S. Yorks), St Mary Magdalene **26** 614
Campton (Beds), All Saints **28** 294
Campus, Bertrandus de *see* DESCHAMPS, BERTRAND
Campuzano, Jorge **21** 380; **22** 314, 366; **25** 878
works **21** *380*
Camp Verde Visitor Center (AZ) **22** 671
Camuccini, Pietro **5** 553–4*; **24** 390
Camuccini, Vincenzo **5** 554–6*
collaboration **23** 829; **29** 639
patrons and collectors **4** 471; **5** 554
personal collection **10** 367; **24** 390
pupils **4** 333; **5** 9, 444; **7** 528; **8** 5, 912; **11** 249; **23** 829; **25** 62
restorations by others **20** 901
teachers **7** 916
works **5** *555*, *556*; **16** 677, *677*
Camulodunum *see* COLCHESTER
Camus, C. E. D. **24** 268
Camus, Louis-Denis Le *see* LE CAMUS, LOUIS-DENIS
Camus, Paul Duval Le *see* DUVAL LE CAMUS, PAUL
Camus, Pierre Duval Le *see* DUVAL LE CAMUS, PIERRE
Camus, Renato **1** 578
Camus de Mézières, Nicolas Le *see* LE CAMUS DE MÉZIÈRES, NICOLAS
Camuzi, Vincenzo **30** 418
camwood **9** 491
Canaam, Lazzaro **32** 205
Canaan **9** 786, 787
Canaanite **5** 556–7*; **30** 179, 185
alphabets **5** 556
architecture **5** 557*; **30** 184
bit hilani **5** 557
bone **30** 184
cult statues **8** 261
curtain walls **5** 557
dyes **5** 556
fortifications **30** 185
gold **1** 874
houses **5** 557; **30** 185
ivory-carvings **5** 557, *557*; **30** 186
jars **30** 185
languages **5** 556
orthostats **30** 186
pendants (jewellery) **30** 186
pottery **5** 557; **30** 184, 185
ramparts **30** 185
seals **30** 184, 186
statuettes **30** 186
temples **5** 557; **30** 184, 185
trade **1** 880; **10** 590
Canaanites group **17** 579
Canabas (Gegenbach, Joseph) **11** 591
Canada **5** 558–93*, *559*
apartments **5** *563*
architecture **5** 558–63*, 572–4*
military **21** 575*
Native North Americans **22** 563–5*
vernacular **32** 300–304*
wood **5** 558
20th cent. **22** *37*
archives **2** 365, 367, 369, 370*
balloon frames **5** 562
birch **5** *577*
bird's-eye views **4** 81
canoes **22** 563
carpets **5** 587–8
carving **22** 574–5
catalogne **5** 587
catalogues **4** 22
cathedrals **5** *560*
ceramics **5** 580–82*
chairs **5** 577, *577*, 578
chalices **5** *585*
churches **3** *73*
ciboria (i) (vessels) **5** *585*
coins **7** 539
collections **5** 588–91*; **17** 434; **25** 803; **31** 177, 880
Impressionism **5** 589
commodes **5** 577
coverlets **5** 587, *587*
dealing **5** 589–90*
drawings **5** 566*
dress **22** 630
earthenwares **5** 580–81, *581*
education (art) **5** 591–2*; **31** 177

Canada—cont.
exhibitions 22 598, 670
fortifications 21 575
forts 21 575
furniture 5 576–80*; 11 850
galleries (iv) (art) 5 590
gardens 12 136
gay and lesbian art 12 *219*
glass 5 582–4*, *583*
glazes 5 581, *581*, *582*
gold 5 584–6*, *585*
government buildings 11 *837*
hemlock 22 563
heritage 32 414
historiography 32 304*
houses 5 173, *573*; 22 563–5, *564*
installations 12 *219*
interior decoration 5 572–6*, *573*, *575*
jade 16 859, 861
jars 5 *581*
libraries 2 367; 4 22; 5 592–3*; 19 *320*, 321
mahogany 5 578, *578*
masks 20 *492*
metro stations 31 176
Milchschranken 5 579
models 7 *858*
monstrances 5 *585*
museums 5 590–91*; 10 *459*; 31 177
painting 5 564–9*
animal subjects 7 *644*
genre 18 *454*
landscape 5 564; 14 *195*; 30 *754*; 33 *14*
murals 22 335
Native North Americans 22 597–8*, *666*
townscapes 31 *175*
19th cent. 5 *575*
20th cent. 5 *567*, *568*, *569*, *846*; 13 *712*; 22 *38*
patchwork 5 587
patronage 5 588–9*
periodicals 22 39; 24 430–31*
photoarchives 5 592*
plaster 5 572
plates 5 *583*
poles 22 *564*
porcelain 5 *582*
portraits 5 *565*
pottery 5 582
prints 5 566*; 25 *802*
quilts 5 587
red (*Thuja plicata*) 22 563
red-wood 22 563
ritual objects 22 575
rock art 22 575
rugs 5 588; 27 317–18*
rushes 5 *577*
sashes 5 588
sculpture 5 570–72*, *571*; 14 282; 22 574–5
silver 5 584–6*; 28 737
spruce 22 563
steel 5 562
stonewares 5 581
tabernacles (ii) (receptacle) 19 261
tables 5 *578*
tapis à languette 5 588
teapots 5 584
textiles 5 586–8*
tin 5 *571*
town halls 31 *176*
towns 20 890
trade
fur 22 546
travel books 23 336
treatises (fortifications) 6 518
universities 7 *858*
vases 5 *582*
warehouses 32 861
weaving 5 586, 587, *587*
wood 5 558, 578, 579
wood-carvings 5 570; 22 *564*
see also NATIVE NORTH AMERICANS; NORTH AMERICA
Canada balsam 26 243
Canada Council 5 588–9, 590, 591
Canada Glass Works 5 583
Canada Steamship Lines Ltd 2 308; 5 589; 8 81
Canadian Architect 24 430
Canadian Architect and Builder 24 430
Canadian Art see ARTSCANADA
Canadian Art Club 5 566, 570, 592, 593*; 8 256; 32 796
Canadian Artists Representation (CAR) 6 410; 8 274
Canadian Group of Painters 5 567; 11 141; 13 711; 14 499, 676
Canadian Guild of Potters 5 582
Canadian Handicrafts Guild 5 582; 22 575, 670
Canadian Indian Affairs Branch 22 670
Canadian Inventory of Historic Building 5 593
Canadian National Railways 2 308
Canadian Northern Railroad 32 866
Canadian Pacific Railway (C. P. R.) 5 589; 6 513; 31 863
Canadian Society of Painters in Watercolour 32 903
Canadian Society of Tapestry Designers and Weavers 30 331
Çanakkale
Archaeological Museum 31 356
fortifications 21 586
pottery 16 423
Canal 24 442
Canal (family) 5 594
Canal, Bernardo 5 593, 600
Canal, Cristoforo 5 593
Canal, Fabio 27 864; 29 736
Canal, Francesco 32 689
Canal, Giambattista 16 719
Canal, Giovanni Antonio *see* CANALETTO
Canal, Ramón Alva de la *see* ALVA DE LA CANAL RAMÓN
Canal du Berry 2 242
Canal du Midi 2 242
Canale, Giuseppe 2 395
Canale, Luigi Malabila, Conte di 13 802
Canale, Mario 2 399
Canale, Nicolá 2 395
Canales, Alejandro 5 593*; 22 335; 23 84
Canales, Alvaro 14 716
Canaletto 5 593–600*; 12 477; 14 687; 16 677; 31 155; 32 194, 195
attributions 3 676; 13 743; 20 449
collaboration 8 159; 13 743; 24 704; 32 615
copies 1 598
drawings 9 223
etchings 10 554; 25 607; 29 556
methods 5 519; 28 203
paintings 5 *596*; 16 767
barges 3 231
capriccios 5 686; 31 155; 32 *112*
townscapes 5 *595*, *597*; 10 251, *677*; 16 676; 19 619; 31 248, *248*, 704; 32 195
vedute 2 342, *343*; 5 *599*; 31 155; 32 111, 194
patrons and collectors 2 559; 4 725; 32 111
Algarotti, Francesco 1 633
Bergeret de Grancourt, (Pierre-) Jacques-Onésyme 3 776
Caraman, Duc de 5 700
Cognacq, (Théodore-) Ernest 7 528
Conti, Stefano 7 780; 20 391
Crespi, Cristoforo Benigno 8 146
George III, King of Great Britain (*reg* 1760-1820) 8 474; 14 144
Canaletto
patrons and collectors—cont.
Gerini, Andrea, Marchese 12 355
Gibbs, James 12 594
Greville, Francis, 1st Earl Brooke and 1st Earl of Warwick (1719-73) 13 644
Hoare (i), Henry the younger (1705-85) 14 598
Howard (ii), Henry, 4th Earl of Carlisle 14 808
Lennox, Charles, 2nd Duke of Richmond and Lennox 19 157
Long, Charles, 1st Baron Farnborough 19 624
Ludwig I, King of Bavaria (*reg* 1825-48) 12 476
McSwiny, Owen 5 686
Mead, Richard 10 364; 20 910
Montagu-Douglas-Scott, Walter Francis, 5th Duke of Buccleuch, 7th Duke of Queensberry 21 908
Morice, Humphry 22 115
Napoleon III, Emperor of France (*reg* 1852-70) 4 306
Poniatowski, Stanisław, Prince 25 213
Russell, Francis, 5th Duke of Bedford 27 357
Russell, John, 4th Duke of Bedford 13 301
Sagredo, Zaccaria 27 521
Schulenburg, Johann Matthias, Graf von der 28 173
Scott, Samuel 28 285
Smith, Joseph, Consul (*c.* 1674-1770) 10 366; 28 884
Soane, John 28 908
Strange, John 29 746
(Joseph-)Wenceslas (-Lorenz), Prince of Liechtenstein (*reg* 1748-72) 19 338
pupils 3 676
reproductive prints by others
Brunet-Debaines, Alfred-Louis 5 24
Brustolon, Giambattista 5 55; 13 744; 21 747; 32 195
Giampiccoli, Marco Sebastiano 12 582
Sandi, Antonio 27 720
Visentini, Antonio 24 705; 32 111–12, 195, 615
Wagner, Joseph (1706-1780) 32 759
Canaletto, Bernardo (Michiel) *see* BELLOTTO, BERNARDO (MICHIEL)
Canaletto frames *see under* FRAMES → types
canal-ponds 27 496
canals
Britain 2 242
France 2 242
Indian subcontinent 15 192
Ireland 9 341
Maya 9 741
Mesoamerica, Pre-Columbian 9 741
Netherlands, the 12 132; 31 *770*
Nineveh 3 418
United States of America 2 242
Urartian 31 700
Canals, Esteve 29 306
Canal Stelae 1 886
canapés 29 8
Canaples, Marie d'Assigny, Mme de 7 *462*
Canapost, Master of 20 639–40*
Canapote 29 138
canards see BROADSIDES
Cañari 15 832; 29 145
Canarin, François de 11 604
Canary Islands
masonry 20 571
Canary Islands—cont.
periodicals 11 886
Canas 24 514
Cañas, Benjamín 10 154
Cañas, María Eugenia 6 600
Cañas, María Martínez *see* MARTÍNEZ CAÑAS, MARÍA
Canavesi, Hieronimo 25 113
Canavesio, Giovanni 3 107; 5 601*
Canberra 1 *37*; 2 *736*, 740; 5 601–2*; 31 728
Academy of Science Building 2 742
Australian National Gallery *see* National Gallery of Australia
Australian National University 2 770
Australian War Memorial 2 763, 771
Canberra Contemporary Art Space 5 602
Canberra School of Art 21 801
Canberra School of Art Gallery 5 602
High Court of Australia 2 *742*, 743, 763; 18 890
Italian Embassy 26 779
Melbourne Building 2 741
Museum of Australia 1 66; 5 602
National Ethnographic Collection 1 67
National Gallery of Australia 2 743, 770; 5 602
archives 2 369
collections 1 67; 2 770; 3 87; 24 682; 29 241; 33 534
library 2 773
National Library of Australia 2 771; 29 509
collections 2 369, 772; 15 742
paintings 15 746
Nolan Gallery 5 602
Parliament House 2 743, 767, 770; 5 602, *602*; 7 670; 30 331
School of Art 2 764
sculpture 2 *754*
urban planning 13 *647*, 648
cancelleria corsiva script *see* SCRIPTS → types → chancery cursive
cancelli see under SCREENS (i) (ARCHITECTURAL) → types
Cancellieri, Bartolomeo 7 623
Cancor, Graf 19 697
Cancrin, Franz Ludwig 8 530
Cancún, Camino Real Hotel 14 788
Candamo de los Tablos, Juan de 23 681
Can Daoren *see* KUNCAN
Candavène, Enguerrand, Count of St Pol *see* ST POL, ENGUERRAND, Count of
Candavène, Hugues, Count of St Pol *see* ST POL, HUGUES CANDAVÈNE, Count of
Candāyana 15 576–7
manuscripts 15 *576*
Candedy, Grace 12 644
Candela, Antonio 5 602
Candela (Outeriño), Félix 5 602–3*; 7 696; 21 404; 29 273
collaboration 7 696; 22 69
works 5 *603*; 7 *695*, 696; 21 380; 28 583
Candela, José Maria Galván *see* GALVÁN CANDELA, JOSÉ MARIA
candelabra 5 604*; 28 215
historical and regional traditions
China 7 80
Etruscan 10 627
Greece, ancient 5 *604*
Italy 5 604; 10 627
Ottonian 23 659
Romanesque 26 686*
Rome, ancient 5 *604*
materials
bronze 5 604; 26 686*
enamel 7 80
marble 5 604, *604*
candelabra—cont.
types
epheboi lychnophoroi 5 604
Candelaria culture 29 190
Candeli, Romualdo di *see* ROMUALDO DI CANDELI
candelilla wax *see under* WAXES → types
Candelot, Pierrette *see* PERRIN, LA VEUVE
Candelottaro *see* CERRUTI, MICHELANGELO
Candi, Francesco dei 13 292
Candi, Giovanni 32 159
Candia *see under* HERAKLEION
Cândia, Salvador 8 181
Candiana ware *see under* POTTERY → wares
Candiani 7 913
Candiano 4 400
Candi Arjuna 8 873; 15 759
Candi Asu 15 777
Candi Badut 15 *753*, 759, 762
Candi Bajangratu 15 765
Candi Banon 15 778
*candi bentār*s *see under* GATEWAYS → types
Candi Bima 8 873; 15 759, 760
sanctuary 15 *759*
sculpture 15 777
Candi Borobudur *see* BOROBUDUR
Candi Brahu 15 765
Candi Bukit Batu Pahat 20 164, 165
Candice Baskets 29 117
Candi Ceto 1 706; 15 781; 30 10
Candid, Peter 5 605–7*; 22 302; 27 504; 30 319
assistants 13 633; 32 403
collaboration 19 705; 33 81, 274
patrons and collectors 11 819; 12 387; 33 275
pupils 19 705
reproductive prints by others 1 787; 27 503, 504
works 5 *606*, *607*; 12 389, 467; 22 305; 28 109; 30 35
Candid, Wilhelm 5 605
Candida 32 450
Candida, Giovanni (di Salvatore Filangieri) 5 607–8*; 27 272
patrons and collectors 5 213
works 5 214; 20 918
Candido, Elia 5 605
Candidus 10 109
Candi Gatokaca 8 873
Candi Gunung Wukir 15 *753*, 758, 759, 762
Candi Ijo *see under* YOGYAKARTA
Candi Jabung 15 *753*, 765–6, 783
Candi Jago 15 *753*, 764–5
Candi Jawi 15 *753*, 757, 764
reliefs 15 783
sculpture 15 781
Candi Jedong 15 765
Candi Kalasan 15 *753*, 757, 760–61; 29 231
sanctuary 15 *761*
sculpture 15 777, 779
Candi Kedaton 15 783
Candi Kidal 15 *753*, 760, 764
sculpture 14 561, *561*
Candilis, Georges 2 378, 660; 4 214; 5 608–10*; 7 295; 11 527; 30 391
Candilis-Josic-Woods 5 608–10*
works 5 *610*
Candi Loro Jonggrang *see* LORO JONGGRANG
Candi Mahligai 15 766
Candi Mendut 15 *753*, 760
reliefs 15 814
sculpture 15 757, 777, *778*
Candi Ngawèn 15 *753*, 760
Candi Panataran *see* PANATARAN
Candi Pawon 15 760, 814
Candi Plaosan 15 *753*, 779
Candi Plaosan Kidul 15 762
Candi Plaosan Lor 15 757, 762

Candi Plumbangan 15 766
Candi Puntadewa 8 873; 15 760
Candi Sari 15 753, 761, 779
Candi Semar 8 873
Candi Sewu 15 753, 757, 761–2, 765
  sculpture 15 777, 778
Candi Singasari 15 753, 757, 764
  sculpture 15 780, 781
Candi Srikandi 8 873; 15 759, 777
Candi Sukuh 1 706; 15 766, 766
  reliefs 15 783
  sculpture 15 781, 782; 30 10
Candi Sumberjati 15 780
Candi Surawa 15 783
Candi Tigawangi 15 783
Candi Tikus 15 765
Candi Wringin Lawang 15 765
candle holders 11 383; 18 777; 28 215; 29 338
  see also SNUFFERS
Candlelight Master 20 640–41*
  attributions 4 48
  works 20 640
candles 5 610–12; 6 71; 9 13; 17 341; 19 364; 33 1, 2
candle stands 29 115
candlesticks 1 697; 5 610–12*; 14 419
  historical and regional traditions
    Belgium 5 611; 30 732
    China 7 86, 86
    England 10 304, 332, 341, 343, 344; 26 688
    France 14 419; 26 493, 493, 682
    Germany 12 452, 453, 454
    Iran 16 375, 376
    Ireland 16 31, 31, 32
    Islamic 16 364, 375, 376, 388
    Italy 16 541, 742; 26 329
    Japan 17 399
    Jewish art 5 612
    Korea 18 363
    Ottoman 16 388
    Romanesque 26 682, 688
    Russia 10 721; 27 424
    South Africa 28 121
    Turkey 16 388
    United States of America 24 581
  materials
    amber 1 762
    baitong 5 612; 10 341
    bone 5 611
    brass 5 611, 611; 10 343; 16 376, 388
    bronze 26 329, 682
    ceramics 5 611
    copper 12 452
    earthenwares 10 304
    glass 7 86, 86
    iron 5 611; 12 454
    marble 7 919
    nephrite 10 721
    netsuke 17 399
    ormolu 27 424
    pewter 5 611; 12 453; 24 580, 581, 581
    rock crystal 16 541
    Sheffield plate 5 612
    silver 5 611, 612; 10 332; 16 31, 31, 32
    silver-gilt 16 541, 742
    steel 27 424
    wood 5 611
  techniques
    casting 5 611
  types
    paschal 7 919; 26 328–30, 329, 624
    pricket 5 611
Candolle, Augustin-Pyramus de 26 73
Candounis, Nikolaos *see* KANTOUNIS, NIKOLAOS
candraśālā 15 243*
Candrātreya *see* CHANDELLA
Candrella *see* CHANDELLA
cane 5 612*; 33 157
  historical and regional traditions
    Africa 1 311; 3 331
    Aztec 21 249
    Belgium 33 157
    Caribbean Islands 5 752
    China 7 113, 114
    England 5 612; 10 291; 33 157
    France 33 157
    Germany 33 156
    Indian subcontinent 15 693
    Indonesia 15 809
    Japan 17 365, 401; 21 716
    Malaysia 4 I2; 20 182
    Mesoamerica, Pre-Columbian 21 249
    Native North Americans 22 662
    Sarawak 4 I2
    Scotland 28 252
    Sri Lanka 29 470, 471
    Sumatra 15 810
    Switzerland 33 157
    United States of America 33 156
  uses
    baskets 3 331; 4 I2; 15 809; 17 365; 20 182; 22 662
    chairs 5 612; 10 291; 19 592; 28 252; 29 470; 33 155, 156
    furniture 5 612, 752; 15 693; 29 471; 33 155, 156, 157
    granaries 1 311
    kites 7 113
    mats 15 809; 20 182
    mirror handles 21 716
    netsuke 17 401
    paper 7 114
    wicker 33 155
Cane, Louis 5 612*; 11 552, 553; 30 6
Cane, Peter Du *see* DU CANE, PETER
Cane, Thomas 23 54
Canea, La *see* CHANIA
Canécaude 25 493
Caneja, Juan Manuel 5 613*
Canella, Giuseppe 31 156
Canella, Guido 16 651; 22 747
Caner, Henry 23 25
Caneri, Anselmo *see* CANNERI, ANSELMO
canes 1 423; 28 302
Canesse 24 96
Canet, Antoni 3 221; 5 613*; 12 739; 13 106
Canete, Mencía de Mendoza, Marquesa de *see* NASSAU, MENCÍA DE MENDOZA, Countess of
Canevale, Antonio 4 1
Canevale, Carlo Antonio 5 613; 32 442
Canevale, Christoph 2 779
Canevale, Elia 4 832
Canevale, Giovanni 5 613
Canevale, Isidore 5 613–14*
  patrons and collectors 14 11; 31 786
  works 2 784, 785; 10 546; 14 887, 888; 19 55; 31 787; 32 436
Canevale, Marcantonio 5 613*; 25 427; 32 822
Canevale de Moneto, Domenico 25 446
Canevali, Baldassare de *see* BALDASSARE DE CANEVALI
Canevari, Antonio 5 614*
  collaboration 4 562; 11 277
  patrons and collectors 1 532, 680; 4 635
  pupils 27 646
  works 7 781; 20 109; 22 473; 25 292; 29 374; 32 422
Canevari, Giovanni Battista 5 78
Canevari, Raffaele 26 762; 28 19
cangianti 5 614*; 6 569; 19 352
Cangiullo, Francesco 11 865
Cang Jie 6 735, 769
Cangrande I, Lord of Verona (*reg* 1311-29) 16 443; 28 28*, 791; 32 341, 345
Cangrande II, Lord of Verona (*reg* 1351-9) 19 683; 28 29; 32 341
Cāṅgū Nārāyaṇa *see* CHANGU NARAYAN
Cangzhou 6 731
  sculpture 7 99, 99
Canhabaque 4 56
Can Hasan 1 821, 849; 5 615*, 615
  architecture 1 824, 830
  copper 1 824
  figurines 1 832, 883
  pottery 1 824, 837
  wall paintings 1 838
Caniana, Giovanni Battista 10 798
Canidae Palette 23 847, 848
Canifrú, Víctor 23 84
Canillac, Abbé de *see* MONTBOISSIER, FRANÇOIS-CLAUDE DE
Canina, Luigi 5 615–16*; 10 620, 637; 24 390
  works 5 616
Canini, Giovan Antonio 6 585
Canini, Giovanni Angelo 3 673; 24 238
Canino, Lucien Bonaparte, Prince of (1775-1840) 4 299, 304*; 19 254
  ceramics 25 383
  collections 4 298; 10 637
  paintings 15 836; 19 399
  pottery 13 541
  works 3 461
Canisius, Peter 17 511; 29 674
Cañizares, Miguel Navarro y *see* NAVARRO Y CAÑIZARES, MIGUEL
Çankırı Mosque 16 205
Canlassi, Guido Baldo *see* CAGNACCI, GUIDO
Canlers 32 279
Çanlı Kilise 4 773; 9 544
Canneel, Thomas 8 831
cannel coal 17 514
cannellé see under WEAVING → types
Canneri, Anselmo 5 617*, 816; 32 348; 33 631
cannetillé see WEAVING → types → *cannellé*
Cannicci, Niccolò 7 344
Canning, F. Lennox *see* LENNOX CANNING, F.
Canning, George 12 640
Canning, Hubert de Burgh, 2nd Marquis of Clanricade 29 380
Canning and Goad 29 105
Cannon, Henry W. 26 358
Cannon, T. C. 22 597
cannons (brushes) 5 33
cannons (guns) 5 11, 12
Cannons (Middx) 5 65
Cano, Alonso 5 617–21*; 28 515; 29 281
  collaboration 21 109; 26 436
  groups and movements 7 289, 290
  patrons and collectors 3 179; 4 378, 565; 5 792, 871; 10 530; 12 839; 17 673; 18 811; 23 404, 437; 27 607; 29 96
  pupils 14 478; 22 69; 23 157; 26 421
  reproductive prints by others 10 906
  teachers 32 125
  works 5 618, 619; 13 284; 20 71, 157; 28 515; 29 269, 292; 33 732
Caño, El 5 621*; 7 507; 29 136, 145
Cano, Francisco Antonio 31 69
Cano, Miguel 5 618
Cano de la Peña, Eduardo 5 621–2*; 17 586; 20 67; 29 284
Caño del Oso 29 128
canoe-houses *see under* HOUSES → types
canoes 28 611
  historical and regional traditions
    Canada 22 563
    Fiji 11 68; 23 725; 27 234
    Guyana 13 874
    Hawaii 23 724, 737
    Indonesia 15 810; 23 724
    Irian Jaya 16 43, 44
    Kiribati 18 83; 23 726
    Maori 10 848; 20 356–7; 23 724–5, 725; 28 611
    Marquesas Islands 23 725
    Marshall Islands 20 479; 23 726
    Native North Americans 22 563
    New Caledonia 23 725
    New Guinea 23 724, 725
    Pacific Islands 23 723–6*, 725, 726
    Palau 23 726
    Papua New Guinea 23 725–6; 24 81, 83
    Philippines 23 724
    Samoa 27 683
    Santa Cruz Islands 27 779
    Society Islands 28 923, 923
    Solomon Islands 23 724, 725, 726; 29 49
    Tokelau 31 75, 75
    Tonga (Pacific Islands) 23 725
    Torres Strait Islands 23 725; 31 185
    Tuvalu 31 484
    United States of America 22 563
    Vanuatu 23 725; 31 893*
  materials
    feathers 10 848
    mother-of-pearl 28 611
    shells 28 611
  types
    double-hull 23 724
    outrigger 15 810; 23 725
Canogar, Rafael 5 622*; 29 286
Canon, Hans 17 818
Canon, Thomas 19 609; 25 17
Cañón de la Mano 21 251, 254
Canongate 4 369
Canonica, Bertolino della *see* BERTOLINO DELLA CANONICA
Canonica, Luigi 5 622*
  groups and movements 22 741
  teachers 30 215
  works 1 798; 8 135; 16 647, 729; 21 520
Canonica, Pietro 5 623*; 16 706
Canonici, Matteo Luigi 5 623–4*; 31 432
canons 20 600
Canons Ashby (Northants) 10 277
  Painted Parlour 23 789
Canons Regular *see* AUGUSTINIAN CANONS
canon tables 5 624*, 624; 6 564; 9 608, 620; 20 339
canopic chests 10 15–16*, 20
canopic jars 5 298; 10 14–15*, 15, 28; 22 283; 30 408
canopies (i) (architecture) 5 625*, 625, 649
canopies (ii) (textile coverings) 5 625*; 14 425; 26 82; 30 774; 31 682
  historical and regional traditions
    Africa 1 354
    Belgium 3 581
    Denmark 8 754
    Egypt, ancient 10 51, 51
    England 30 778
    Islamic 16 429
  materials
    copper 10 51
    gold 10 51
    silver 10 51
    tapestries 8 754
  uses
    thrones 30 778, 778
Canops, José 29 304, 316
Canosa, Minarro da *see* MINARRO DA CANOSA
Canosa di Puglia 13 362
  Cathedral of S Sabino 1 112; 26 619, 626; 27 120
    mausoleum of Bohemond I 9 153
    throne 30 777, 777
  fans 10 776
  figurines 13 581
  glass 13 594
  helmets 6 157
  pottery 13 482, 526, 530, 539
  S Leucio 9 533
  tombs 32 38
  urns 13 582
Canosa Group 13 594
Canossa, Galeazzo 12 912
Canossa, Girolamo 32 343
Canossa, Ludovico, Bishop of Bayeux 27 758, 759
Canossa, Matilda of, Countess of Tuscany *see* MATILDA OF CANOSSA, Countess of Tuscany
Canova, Antonio 2 165; 3 645, 750; 5 625–32*; 7 726; 9 13, 25; 14 635; 16 705, 768; 25 418; 26 842; 31 316
  assistants 8 709; 14 265; 15 837; 30 233
  attributions 1 466
  collaboration 13 31; 25 147; 29 639
  dealing 3 454; 30 345
  groups and movements 22 734, 741; 26 742, 774, 776
  methods 21 770
  patrons and collectors
    Alexander I, Emperor of Russia (*reg* 1801-25) 26 733
    Blundell, Henry 4 181
    Bonaparte, Pauline, Princess Borghese 4 306
    Bossi, Giuseppe 4 471
    Campbell, John (1857-1942) 5 541
    Cavendish, William Spencer, 6th Duke of Devonshire (1790-1858) 6 117
    Consalvi, Ercole, Cardinal 7 726
    Demidov, Anatoly, Prince 8 705
    Elisa, Grand Duchess of Tuscany (*reg* 1809-14) 4 305
    Esterházy, Miklós II, Prince (1765-1833) 10 530
    Farsetti, Filippo 10 818
    Fesch, Joseph, Cardinal 11 32
    Fries, Moritz, Graf von 11 789
    Hervey, Frederick Augustus, 4th Earl of Bristol 14 485
    Hope, Thomas 14 744
    Joachim Murat, King of Naples (*reg* 1808-15) 22 338
    Josephine, Empress of the French (1763-1814) 4 303
    Ludwig I, King of Bavaria (*reg* 1825-48) 12 476
    Napoleon I, Emperor of the French (*reg* 1804-14) 4 300, 301; 11 562
    Pisani, Pietro Vettor 24 865
    Pius VI, Pope (*reg* 1775-80) 25 8
    Rezzonico (family) 26 286
    Russell, John, 6th Duke of Bedford 10 365; 27 357
    Simonetti, Michelangelo 28 755
    Sommariva, Giovanni Battista 29 59
    Stanislav II Poniatowski, King of Poland (*reg* 1764–95) 25 212
    Tarnowski, Jan Feliks, Count and Waleria 30 345
    Torlonia (family) 31 172
    Wellesley, Arthur, 1st Duke of Wellington 33 55
    Yusupov, Nikolay (Borisovich), Prince (1751- 1831) 33 579
    Zamoyski, Stanisław 33 607

Canova, Antonio—cont.
pupils
Aguiar, João José de 1 466
Campeny y Estrany, Damián 5 544
Eberhard, Konrad 9 690
Gandolfi, Democrito 12 38
Gibson, John (i) (1790-1866) 12 597
Marchesi, Pompeo 20 390
Salvatierra y Barriales, Valeriano 27 646
Wyatt, Richard James 33 449
reproductive prints by others 26 230, 231, *232*; 28 474
sculpture 16 705; 17 850; 29 562; 31 610
allegorical 4 *301*
funerary monuments 5 *628*; 22 *736*
monuments 11 206; 26 810; 27 831
mythological 5 *627*, *629*; 10 479; 11 189; 16 *705*; 22 415; 23 295; 32 195, 437
portraits 21 106; 23 295; 25 115
relief 26 137; 31 130
tombs 2 802; 5 *628*; 29 100; 31 130; 33 28
studio 29 855
Canova, Pasino 5 625
Canova, Pietro 5 625
Canovas, Manuel 11 584
Cánovas del Castillo, Antonio *see* KAULAK
Canozi (family) 16 723
Canozzi da Lendinara (family) 16 724
Canozzi da Lendinara, Cristoforo 10 519; 11 4
Canozzi da Lendinara, Lorenzo 10 519; 11 4
Cansahcab 6 97
Cansever, Turgut 5 633*; 31 452
works 31 *453*
Cansignorio, Lord of Verona (*reg* 1351-75) 4 776; 28 29; 32 341, 345–6
Cant, James 2 749
Cantacuzino (family) 26 708, 712, 722
Cantacuzino, Constantin 26 722
Cantacuzino, G(eorge) M(atei) 5 634*; 9 70; 26 709
Cantacuzino, Ion 26 723
Cantacuzino, Mihai 26 708, 713, 722
Cantacuzino, Şerban, Prince 5 72; 26 721
Cantagalli, Ulysse 22 59
Cantagallina, Remigio 3 631; 5 634*
Cantagalli pottery 8 707
Cantalamessa, Giulio 4 493; 16 774
Cantanhede, 3rd Conde de *see* MARIALVA, 1st Marquês de
Cantarelli, Gino 8 436
Cantarini, Simone 5 634–5*
pupils 24 226; 31 187
works 5 *635*
canteens 16 *99*, *542*
Cantel 13 *758*, 766
Cantelli, Camillo Bevilacqua *see* BEVILACQUA CANTELLI, CAMILLO
Cantelmo (family) 10 442
Cantemir, Demetrius, Prince of Moldavia (*reg c.* 1700) 19 280
Canter, Bernard 6 378; 29 397
Canterbury (Kent; UK) 5 636–48* 1065-97) 5 *636*, *637*, 640; 10 *225*; 26 *905*
Archbishop's Palace 14 75; 29 22
art forms and materials
bookbindings 4 351
embroidery 10 181
ivory-carvings 23 *539*; 26 698
limestone 26 875
Canterbury (Kent; UK)
art forms and materials—cont.
manuscripts 3 *710*; 5 428, *428*, 640–42*, *641*; 9 219; 13 140; 15 875; 20 330; 26 661, 671, 677; 32 637
pilgrim badges 24 808, 809, *809*
sculpture 26 615
silk 10 356
silver 16 30
Castle 10 359; 14 75; 33 199
Cheker of the Hope Inn 5 *639*
Cogan House 14 76
Eastbridge Hospital 14 76
ecclesiastical buildings
Christ Church Cathedral 1 723; 3 191; 5 638, *642*, 642–5*, *645*; 7 231, 254; 9 672; 10 227, 228, 359; 13 43, 44–5, 55; 21 836, 839; 23 462; 26 587, 588, 659; 31 284; 33 201, 209
altarpieces 11 420
ambulatory 1 768
apse 2 347
arches 2 295, 296
Bell Harry tower 13 55; 32 89, 895
bosses 4 465; 29 659
buttresses 5 319
capitals 5 646; 26 611, 615, 616
Chapter House 27 131
choir 5 643*, *644*; 7 664; 9 669; 13 40, *44*; 22 211; 26 589
choir-screens 13 164
choir-stalls 7 191
cloister 7 456; 19 312
Court Gate 12 175
crypt 8 222, 224; 13 139; 18 621; 23 538; 26 67
dogtooth 9 70
Gospel books 9 499
ironwork 10 339
ivory-carvings 26 697
Lady Chapel 18 621, 622
manuscripts 2 76; 5 641–2, *641*; 7 246; 10 243; 14 432; 26 660, *670*, 671; 31 773
mouldings 22 217, 218, 220
nave 24 465
piers (ii) (masonry) 24 751
pilgrim badges 24 808, *809*
pulpitum 13 85
Reculver shaft 2 70
rood 27 124
St Anselm's Chapel 31 273
St Augustine's chair 30 778
St Gabriel's Chapel 3 710; 10 244; 26 652, 654, 657
sculpture 5 645–7*, *646*; 10 261; 13 84; 26 616; 31 284
Shrine of St Thomas Becket 10 141; 22 44; 29 500
south porch 24 466
spire 29 413
stained glass 3 710; 5 *647*, 647–8*, *648*; 13 140, 179, 183; 26 702; 29 422, 501, 509, 511; 31 499
tapestries 10 348
throne 30 781
tomb of Archbishop Simon of Sudbury 24 465
tomb of Edward the Black Prince 2 449; 6 458; 10 338; 13 152; 15 149
tomb of Henry IV and Joan of Navarre 13 84
tombs 5 646–7; 31 131
towers 24 466
transept 31 281
Treasury 9 84
Trinity Chapel 2 294; 3 710; 5 644; 8 261; 13 45, 135, *135*; 18 621; 28 630
vaults (ceiling) 20 578; 32 93, 94
Canterbury (Kent; UK)
ecclesiastical buildings
Christ Church Cathedral—cont.
wall paintings 10 244; 26 652
St Augustine's Abbey 2 65, 66, 67; 5 *638*; 10 227; 26 587; 27 236
candelabrum 26 686
capitals 26 615
crypt 18 621
Great Gateway 12 175
manuscripts 5 641; 9 602; 18 674; 26 661, 662, 671; 27 532, *591*, 592; 32 637
orders (architecture) 23 491
St Martin 2 65; 10 227; 11 252
St Pancras 2 65
hill-figures 14 545
houses 14 76
King's School 28 156
pilgrim badges 24 809
Poor Priest's Hospital 14 76
town walls 31 710
University of Kent Sports Hall 29 427
Water Tower 9 70
Westgate 20 571
Canterbury (NH; USA) 28 542
Shaker buildings 28 539, 540
Canterbury, Michael of *see* MICHAEL OF CANTERBURY
Canterbury, Thomas of *see* THOMAS OF CANTERBURY
Canterbury Censer Cover 10 338
Canterbury Codex Aureus *see* GOSPEL BOOKS → individual manuscripts → Stockholm Codex Aureus
Canterbury Inventory (untraced) 16 443
Cantero, Antonio Fernández *see* FERNÁNDEZ CANTERO, ANTONIO
Cantero, Justo 18 781
Canti, Giovanni 3 436
Cantiers, Guillaume de, Bishop of Evreux *see* GUILLAUME DE CANTIERS, Bishop of Evreux
cantilever bridges *see under* BRIDGES → types
cantilevers 4 623; 5 648–9*, *649*; 6 *652*
Cantilupe, Walter de, Bishop of Winchester 23 461
Cantimpré, Thomas 31 289
Cantini, Pietro 4 233; 7 605
Canton (China) *see* GUANGZHOU
Canton (OH; USA) 20 870
Cantón, Francisco Javier Sánchez *see* SÁNCHEZ CANTÓN, FRANCISCO JAVIER
Canton balls *see* DEVIL'S WORK BALLS
Cantone, Bernardino 1 607; 5 650*; 6 24; 29 411
Cantone, Giovanni Battista 9 173
Cantone, Pier Francesco 3 90; 12 282
Canton enamel *see under* ENAMEL → types
Cantoni, Arrigo 27 788
Cantoni, Carlo 31 524
Cantoni, Simone 5 650–51*; 16 646
patrons and collectors 29 411
works 16 647, *647*
cantonments 16 151; 21 546
Canton ware *see under* PORCELAIN → wares
cantoor see CABINETS (ii) (FURNITURE) → types → *kunstkasten*
Cantor, B. Gerald 26 511
Cantourgen see under CABINETS (ii) (FURNITURE) → types
Cantré, Jan 20 547
Cantré, Jozef 3 573; 5 651*; 33 363
Cantrill, Arthur 10 688
Cantrill, Corinne 10 688
Cantu 18 593
Cantú, Federico 1 783; 5 651*
Cantwell, John 25 399
Canuck Pottery Ltd 33 146
Canudo, Riciotto 3 120
Canusium *see* CANOSA DI PUGLIA
Canuti, Domenico Maria 5 651–3*; 16 670
collaboration 14 26, 27
pupils 5 280; 8 140; 14 27; 20 902; 29 32
works 5 *652*
Canuti, Giuseppe Maria 15 138
canvas 5 653–8*
conservation 5 657–8*
historical and regional traditions
England 10 353
Ireland 16 33
materials
consolidants 7 747
cotton 5 654–5
fibres 5 655
flax 5 654
grounds 5 654; 13 706
hemp 5 653, 654
hessian 5 655
jute 5 655
linen 5 654
size 5 654; 13 706
techniques
brushwork 5 34
stretching 5 654; 28 559
types
cotton duck 5 654
uses
altarpieces 24 3
bookbindings 4 347
book covers 4 350
carpets 5 830, 831
catafalques 6 71
chairs 6 388
conservation 24 7
embroidery 10 353
mounts (works on paper and scrolls) 22 236
oil paintings 23 376
paintings 5 653, 655–7*
panel paintings 24 7
roofs 13 619
supports 24 3; 30 5
tents 30 470, 474
upholstery 31 682
Canyes, Marc 29 332
Canyon de Chelly (AZ) 5 658*; 22 *544*
Canzio, Michele 16 720
Canzler, Joseph Friedrich 13 852; 22 305
Canzoli, Benedetto 33 634
Cao Ba 14 135
Cao Buxing 6 635
Cao Cao 23 821
Cao dai 32 471
Caodong Buddhism *see under* BUDDHISM → sects
Caojiagang (Dangyang) 7 139
Cao Lao Ha 6 426
Caoxieshan 19 302
Cao Yuanzhong 7 118
Cao Zaikui 6 867
Cao Zhao 6 635, 637; 7 14, 82, 83, 90, 141, 716
Cao Zhibai 5 659*; 7 151
Cap, Le *see* LE CAP
Capa, Cornell 20 99; 24 677
Capa, Robert 5 659–60*, 897; 24 677
groups and movements 6 603; 20 99
Capablanca, Aquiles 8 232
Capacha-Opeño 5 660–61*; 21 *193*
pottery 5 660, *660*; 33 101, 102
see also EL OPEÑO; COLIMA; JALISCO
CA Painter 13 532
Capalatitis, Giovanni Battista de *see* CAVALLETTO, GIOVANNI BATTISTA
Capalti, Alessandro 9 175; 31 172
Capanna, Aristide 26 779
Capanna, Puccio 2 625, 626, 627; 5 661*; 12 681, 693
Caparn, Rhys 18 301
Caparó, José Lucas 24 516
Caparra 25 698, 700
Caparra, Niccolò 16 743
Capart, Jean 3 620; 10 84
Capauli, G. de 30 221
Cap Blanc 25 477, 487
Cap d'Antibes 10 592
Capdevila, Bartomeu 20 757
Capdevila, Francisco Moreno *see* MORENO CAPDEVILA, FRANCISCO
Capdevilla, Joaquim 29 346
Capdevilla, Manuel 29 346
Cape Artemision *see* ARTEMISION BRONZES
Capeau, Barthélémy 19 341
Capece, Oscar 6 600
Capecelatro, Antonio, Duca di Siano *see* SIANO, ANTONIO CAPECELATRO, Duca di
Cape Coast Fort 1 318
Cape Cormorin *see* KANYAKUMARI
Cape Denbigh 22 655
Cape Dutch style 5 661–2*, *662*; 29 105, 111, 113; 33 678
Cape Gelidonya 4 850; 14 333; 30 180
Čapek, Josef 5 662–3*
groups and movements 2 546; 8 250, 393; 13 711; 33 710
works 8 249, 393
Čapek, Karel 5 662; 8 250; 13 711
Capel, Arthur, 1st Earl of Essex 20 880
Capel, Henry 7 744
Capel-Cure, Francis 6 537
Capell, William, 3rd Earl of Essex 27 360
Capell, William Anne, 4th Earl of Essex 31 467
Capella, Alessandro 3 860
Capella, Martianus Mineus Felix *see* MARTIANUS MINEUS FELIX CAPELLA
capella ardente 6 72
Capellades, Pere 29 332
Capellán, Tony 9 118
Capellaro, Charles Romain 5 824
Capelli, Camillo 13 658; 24 536; 27 273
Capelli, Pasquino 24 779
Capellitti, Fedeli 16 736
Capello, Bianca 5 182
Capena 7 366
Capen & Molineaux 31 652
Cape of Good Hope 1 *413*
Caper, Thomas 25 726
Capernaum 5 663*; 9 *513*; 16 *565*
St Peter 7 254; 20 520
synagogue 5 663; 17 541, *541*, 542
capes *see* CLOAKS
Cape Spada *see* DIKTYNNAION
Capesthorne 26 346
Capestrano, S Pietro ad Oratorium 26 625
Capet, Mme 18 *576*
Capet (House of) 5 663–4*; 26 571
Capet, Blanche, Duchess of Austria *see* BLANCHE CAPET, Duchess of Austria
Capet, Blanche of Castille, Queen of France *see* BLANCHE OF CASTILE, Queen of France
Capet, Henry, Archbishop of Reims 7 352
Capet, Isabella 5 665

Capet, Isabella, Queen of England *see* ISABELLA, Queen of England
Capet, Joanna of Evreux, Queen of France *see* JOANNA OF EVREUX, Queen of France
Capet, Louis VI, King of France *see* LOUIS VI, King of France
Capet, Louis IX, King of France *see* LOUIS IX, King of France
Capet, Mahaut, Comtesse d'Artois *see* ARTOIS, MAHAUT, Comtesse de
Capet, Marie **17** *459*
Capet, Philip III, King of France *see* PHILIP III, King of France
Capet, Philip IV, King of France *see* PHILIP IV, King of France
Capet, Robert, Comte de Clermont *see* CLERMONT, ROBERT CAPET, Comte de
Capet, Robert the Pious, King of France *see* ROBERT II, King of France
Cape Tainaron **27** 13
Cape Town **5** 667–8*, *668*; **29** 102, *103*, 104
- BP Centre **29** 106
- Burgher' Watch House *see* Old Town House
- Cape Town School of Arts **5** 668; **29** 122
- Castle of Good Hope **29** 104, 122
  - William Fehr Collection **29** 114
- Community Arts Project **29** 123
- Groot Constantia **5** 662, *662*; **29** 105, 122
- Groote Kerk **29** 119
- Groote Schuur **12** 142; **29** 105, 116
- Irma Stern Museum **29** 122, 641
- Jewish Museum **17** 582
- Judge Clothing Factory **29** 106
- Koopmans de Wet House **29** 122
- Lutheran church **29** 111
- Masonic Lodge of Good Hope **29** 105
- Michaelis School of Fine Art **29** 123
- Old Town Hall *see* Old Town House
- Old Town House
  - Michaelis Collection **5** 668; **29** 121, 122
- pottery **29** 116
- Rhodes Memorial **29** 105
- Roeland Street Art School *see* Cape Town School of Arts
- Rust en Vreugd **29** 122
- South African Association of Arts **29** 121
- South African Astronomical Observatory **23** 340
- South African Cultural History Museum **29** 114, 122; **30** 728
- South African Library **29** 121
- South African Museum **29** 121
- South African National Gallery **5** 668; **29** 121
- Stellenberg House **5** 662
- Strandfontein Beach Pavilion **29** 107
- Supreme Court **18** 887
- Town Hall *see* Old Town House
- Truworth Factory **29** 106
- University **29** 105, 107
- William Fehr Collection **29** 104, 122
Cape Verde Islands **1** *214*, 424
Cape Vrysa **19** 234
Capey, Reco **10** 375
Capezzuoli, G. B. **33** 226, 227
Capgrave, John **5** 668–9*; **18** 686
Cap-Haïtien **14** *54*, 57
Capheaton **27** 83
Capiatá **24** *91*
- Franciscan church **24** 94
Capiello, Leonetto **5** 669*
- works **3** 462; **11** 644; **12** 830; **25** 348, *348*
Capio, Marchese del **24** 731
Capists *see* KAPISTS
Capitalist Realism **12** 397; **25** 153
capitals **5** 669–71*; **22** 216; **23** 477
- historical and regional traditions
  - Bactria **6** 217
  - Britain **26** 611
  - Buddhism **27** *844*
  - Byzantine **1** *110*; **5** *670*; **9** 589, 592
  - Carolingian **5** 796
  - Catalonia **26** *610*; **27** *568*
  - Central Asia, Western **6** 217; **29** *822*
  - Early Christian (*c.* AD 250-843) **5** *670*; **9** 589
  - Egypt, ancient **1** *615*; **5** *670*; **9** 834
  - England **26** 615–16; **29** *659*
  - France
    - Merovingian **17** *665*
    - Romanesque **5** *372*; **7** *232*, *477*; **17** *686*; **19** *224*; **22** *115*; **25** *88*; **26** 596, 597–9, *598*, *601*, 601–2, *610*; **27** *534*, 534, *552*; **31** *211*, 225
  - Gothic **5** *670*
  - Greece, ancient **5** *670*; **10** 742; **13** 376, 377, 387, 391, *392*, 393, 399, 401, 405, *413*, 415
  - Indian subcontinent **5** *669*; **15** *259*, 430; **27** *844*
    - Maurya **15** *413*, 415, 750
    - 1st cent. BC **15** *428*
  - Ireland **16** 19
  - Islamic **5** *669*; **16** 188, 191, 243
  - Jerusalem, Latin Kingdom of **22** *705*
  - Merovingian **17** *665*
  - Morocco **16** 191
  - Nabataea **22** 419
  - Netherlands, the **19** *863*
  - Norway **31** *750*
  - Romanesque **5** *670*; **26** 569
    - Britain **26** 611
    - Catalonia **26** *610*; **27** *568*
    - England **26** 615–16
    - France **5** *372*; **7** *232*, *477*; **17** *686*; **19** *224*; **22** *115*; **25** *88*; **26** 596, 597–9, *598*, *599*, *601*, 601–2, *610*; **27** 534, *534*, *552*; **31** *211*, 225
    - Germany **26** *573*
    - Netherlands, the **19** *863*
    - Sicily **21** *900*
    - Spain **19** *177*; **26** *605*, 606–7
  - Rome, ancient **5** *670*; **26** 875, 877
  - Sicily **21** *900*
  - Spain **16** 188; **19** *177*; **26** *605*, 606–7; **28** *727*
  - Tajikistan **29** *822*
- materials
  - limestone **7** *477*; **28** *727*; **31** *211*
  - marble **9** *589*; **17** *665*; **21** *900*; **26** *876*, 877
  - mouldings **22** *213*, 215, 216, 218–19, 221–2
  - sandstone **15** *413*; **22** *705*; **27** *844*
  - stucco **29** *822*
  - wood **31** *750*
- types
  - Aiolic **5** *670*; **15** 893
  - basket **9** 589
  - Composite **1** 109; **5** *670*; **23** 480
  - Composite-Ionic **9** 589
  - Corinthian **1** 109; **3** 341; **5** *670*; **9** 589, *589*; **17** 742; **23** 480, 482; **26** *876*
  - crocket **5** *670*; **8** 183; **13** 35
  - cubic **23** 228
  - cushion **5** *669*, *670*; **26** 573, *573*, 587
  - Doric **23** 478; **32** *502*
  - historiated **27** *534*
  - Ionic **5** *670*; **9** 589; **23** 478; **24** *274*
  - *muqarnas* (architecture) **5** *669*
  - Persian **16** 145
  - Tuscan **5** *670*
  - volute **10** 168, *169*
Capital style **27** 587
Capitanata **26** 628
Capitani, Giulio De *see* DE CAPITANI, GIULIO
Capitelli, Bernardino **25** 413
Capitino, Giunta di *see* GIUNTA PISANO
capitolia **26** 905; **27** 3
Capitolias **27** 57
Capitoline *Antinous* **2** 169
Capitoline *Flora* **2** 169
Capitoline *Lucius Junius Brutus* **10** 608
Capitoline Obelisk **20** 840
Capitoline *Venus* **3** 707; **23** 291; **27** 46
capitols **31** *232*, 236
Caplan, H. H. **10** 212
Capocorp Vell **3** 105
Capodimonte **16** *620*
- Museo e Gallerie Nazionali di Capodimonte **2** 462; **10** 487, 808; **16** 774
- observatory **23** 340
- Palazzo Reale di Capodimonte **8** 716; **11** 136
Capodimonte Porcelain Factory **4** 562; **5** 671*; **7** 166; **16** 737
- designers **13** 646; **16** 738
- production
  - chandeliers **6** 443
  - cribs **22** 680
  - figurines **16** *737*
  - porcelain cabinets **5** 348; **9** 29; **16** 717, *718*
  - tiles **30** 887
Capoferri di Lovere, Gianfrancesco **3** 643, 773
Capoferro da Cagli, Ridolfo **28** 80
Capo Graziano **25** *521*, 522
Capogrossi, Giuseppe **5** 671*
- groups and movements **5** 279; **7** 555; **16** 681; **20** 93; **21** 87; **26** 777; **28** 319
- works **19** 491
Capon, Kenneth **2** 318; **10** 242
Capon, William **30** 675, 680
Caponi (family) *see* COVONI-DANEO (FAMILY)
Caponi, Ferrante **20** 376
caponiers **21** 546, 571, *571*, 576
Caponigro, Paul **5** 671–2*
Caporale, Francesco **20** 47
Caporali, Bartolomeo (di Segnolo) **5** 672*; **24** 520
- attributions **11** 118
- collaboration **4** 317
- pupils **24** 829
- works **24** 781
Caporali, Giapeco **5** 672
Caporali, Giovan Battista **5** 672*; **10** 651
- collaboration **24** 525, 832
- pupils **1** 605
- writings **6** 359
Caporali, Giulio **5** 672
Capote, Luís Pereira *see* PEREIRA CAPOTE, LUÍS
Cappa, Benedetta **1** 166; **8** 771; **11** 867
Cappadocia **1** *821*; **5** 673–8*, *674*, *675*; **9** *512*; **26** *852*
- architecture **5** 673–5*; **9** 543
- churches **5** *674*, 674–5*, 676–8*; **7** 261; **9** 536; **26** 483
- dress **1** 886
- hermitages **5** 675
- liturgical furnishings **7** 279
- monasteries **5** 675*, *675*
- narratives **22** 520
- painting **5** 675–8*, *676*, *677*; **9** 580–81
- patronage **5** 674
- pigeon houses **5** 673
- portraits **9** 580
- *see also* ANATOLIA, ANCIENT; TURKEY
Cappadocian ware *see under* POTTERY → wares
cappae magnae **32** 389*
Capparoni, Gaspare **5** 678–9*; **12** 262, 264
Cappelen, (Herman) August **5** 679*; **13** 776; **23** 225
Cappella, Francesca **24** 707
Cappella, Gennaro **22** 482
Cappella degli Scrovegni *see* PADUA → churches → Arena Chapel
Cappella del Santissimo **11** 711
Cappella Medici Polyptych, Master of the **20** 641*
Cappellari, Bartolommeo Alberto, Cardinal *see* GREGORY XVI, Pope
Cappelle, Jan van de **5** 679–82*
- attributions **13** 257
- patrons and collectors **9** 392
- personal collection **5** 325; **25** 248; **28** 362; **32** 673
- works **5** *680*, *681*; **13** 223; **20** 424; **22** 843
Cappelle, Louis van de **5** 679
Cappellemans (family) **3** 591
Cappellemans, Jean-Baptiste, the elder **3** 591, 595; **5** 51
Cappelletti (family) **6** 21
Cappelletti, Giovanni Vincenzo **17** 198; **21** 59
Cappellino, Giovanni Domenico **24** 835
Cappello, Bianca, Grand Duchess of Tuscany *see* BIANCA DE' MEDICI, Grand Duchess of Tuscany
Cappello, Gabriele *see* MONCALVO
Cappello, Guido *see* MONCALVO, GUIDO
Cappello, Luigi **19** 59
Cappenberg, Master of *see* BAEGERT, JAN
Cappenberg, Otto, Graf von **14** 646; **26** 685
Cappenburg, St Johannes **26** 685
Capper, Daniel **30** 533
Capperello, Benedetto **12** 734
Cappini, Janez Andrej **28** 863
Capponi (family) **3** 708; **4** 21, 209, 546; **5** 16
Capponi, Alessandro Gregorio, Marchese **5** 682; **6** 97; **24** 834
Capponi, Giuseppe **16** 649, 650; **24** 694
Capponi, Ludovico (*d* 1534) **5** 682
Capponi, Ludovico (1534-1614) **4** *858*
Capponi, Maria Teresa **27** 205
Capponi, Raffaelle de' *see* RAFFAELLINO DEL GARBO
Cappucci **18** 791
Cappuccino, Il *see* STROZZI, BERNARDO
Capra, Girolamo **23** 877
Capra, Lorenzo Alvarez *see* ALVAREZ CAPRA, LORENZO
Capra, Mario, Marchese **3** 862
Capralos, Christos **5** 683*; **13** 355
Capranesi, Giovanni **13** 816
Capranica, S Francesco
- tomb of Francesco Anguillara and Nicolò Anguillara **13** 97
Caprara **29** 32
Caprara, Counts of **30** 118
Caprarola **16** *620*
- Villa Farnese **5** 683–4*, *683*; **6** 59; **10** 810; **15** 87; **16** 633; **23** 489; **32** 506, 546–7; **33** 718
  - frescoes **3** *859*; **5** 684*; **29** 428; **32** 101
  - gardens **5** 684*
  - paintings **5** 887
  - Sala degli Angeli **3** 858
  - Sala dei Guidizi **3** 858
  - Sala dei Sogni **3** 858
  - Sala della Penitenza **3** 858
  - Sala del Mappamondo **20** 365, *366*
  - Sala d'Ercole **3** 858
  - staircase **29** 523
  - Stanza dell'Aurora **15** 87
Caprarola, Cola (di Matteuccio) da *see* COLA (DI MATTEUCCIO) DA CAPRAROLA
Capreae **5** 684–5*; **16** *621*; **26** *886*
- Damecuta Villa **26** 869
- Tiberius' Palace **27** 58, 66
- Villa Jovis **5** 684–5, *685*; **26** 892
- well-heads **33** 56
Capri *see* CAPREAE
Capri, Ugo da *see* UGO DA CAPRI
Capriani, Francesco *see* VOLTERRA, FRANCESCO DA
capriccios **5** 685–8*, *686*, *687*; **18** 700, 711
- France **18** *654*; **26** *450*
- Italy **20** *414*
- *see also* PAINTING → types → *vedute ideate*
Capriles, Miguel Angel **32** 179
Caprinis, Adriano de **4** 650
Caprino, Meo da *see* MEO DA CAPRINO
Caprinozzi, Marco **2** 40
Caprioli, Aliprando **24** 239
Capriolo, Domenico (di Bernardino) **5** 688*
Capronnier **29** 507
Capronnier, Jean-Baptiste **2** 485; **28** 595
Caprotti, Gian Giacomo **5** 688–9*; **23** 368
- collaboration **19** 184
- personal collection **19** 187
- works **19** 191
Cap Rouge Pottery **5** 581
caps
- historical and regional traditions
  - China **7** 76
  - England **9** 271; **18** 157
  - France **9** 271; **18** 157
  - Germany **3** 442; **18** 157
  - Iran **16** 454
  - Islamic **16** 454, 457, 459, 462
  - Korea **18** 351
  - Native North Americans **22** 658
  - Netherlands, the **9** 271
  - North Africa **16** 459
  - Ottoman **16** 462
  - Spain **18** 157
  - Turkey **16** 462
- materials
  - beadwork **3** 442
  - gold **18** 351
- techniques
  - knitting **18** 157
Capsella Africana **26** 143
Capsia, Margareta **11** 95
capstans **7** 764
Captain chairs *see under* CHAIRS → types
Capua **5** 689*; **10** *583*, 585, 638; **16** *621*; **26** *886*
- amphitheatre **1** 797; **26** 874, 892
- bronze **27** 85
- Capua Gate **5** 689; **7** 383; **14** 647, *647*; **22** 44; **26** 182
  - sculpture **13** 98
- Cathedral of SS Stefano e Agata **26** 625, 626
- inscriptions **10** 589
- Museo Campano **5** 689
- pottery **13** 531, *537*

Capua—cont.
S Giovanni delle Monache **9** 154; **26** 625
tower tomb **26** 883
Capua, Janne Maria de **2** 201; **3** 588
Capua, Jordan I, Prince of **26** 333
Capua, Richard I, Prince of **26** 333*
Capua Painter **13** 531
Capua Tile **10** 638
Capuchins **5** 689–91*; **11** 708
architecture **5** *690*; **25** 135
capucine chairs *see under* CHAIRS → types
Capugnano, Girolamo de **7** 917
Capulí **29** 217
Capurro, Juan Alberto **31** 753
Capus, Jean *see* Chapus, Jean
Caputi, Adriano Baracchini *see* BARACCHINI CAPUTI, ADRIANO
caput mortuum *see under* PIGMENTS → types
Capuz, Francisco **29** 345
Capuz, José **29** 295
Capuz, Raimondo **29** 345
caqueteuse chairs *see under* CHAIRS → types
Caquetios **2** 145, 149
caquetoires see under CHAIRS → types
Caquiaviri Church **4** 256
Carabajal, Luis de **30** 803
Carabin, (François-) Rupert **5** 691*; **11** 600
Carabuco Church **4** 261
Caraca, César **23** 84
Caracalla, Emperor of Rome (*reg* AD 211-17) **8** 477; **9** 895, *895*; **26** 795
temples **26** 866, 900; **30** 436
triumphal arches **31** 350
Caracas **5** 691–2*; **31** 721; **32** *165*
23 de Enero complex **32** 171
Academia de Bellas Artes *see* Escuela de Artes Visuales Cristóbal Rojas
Academia de Dibujo y Pintura *see* Escuela de Artes Visuales Cristóbal Rojas
Academia Militar **32** 170
architecture **32** 170–71
Archivo General de la Nación **32** 170
Arco de la Federación **32** 170
Ateneo **32** 171
Banco Central de Venezuela **32** 171, 179
Banco Metropolitano **32** 171
Biblioteca Nacional
Archivo Audiovisual de Venezuela **32** 181
Casa Amarilla de la Cancillería **32** 170
Centro Simón Bolívar **32** 171
Cerro Piloto **32** 171
churches
Cathedral **32** 168, *168*, 176
Las Mercedes **32** 168
Nuestra Señora de Altagracia **32** 168, 176
Santa Capilla **32** 170
Santísima Trinidad *see* Panteón Nacional
S Francisco **32** 167–8, 176, 177
S Teresa **5** *692*; **32** 170, 176
Ciudad Universitaria *see* Universidad Central de Venezuela
Colegio de Ingenieros **32** 169
Corporación Venezolana de Guayana building **32** 171
craftsmen and artists **32** 172
Edificio Polar **32** 171
Escuela de Artes Plásticas y Aplicadas *see* Escuela de Artes Visuales Cristóbal Rojas
Caracas—cont.
Escuela de Artes Plásticas y Artes Aplicadas Cristobal Rojas *see* Escuela de Artes Visuales Cristobal Rojas
Escuela de Artes Visuales Cristóbal Rojas **32** 173, 175, 179, 180
Escuela Gran Colombia **32** 170
Escuela Normal de Dibujo **32** 180
Fundación Boulton **19** 768; **32** 181
Fundación Eugenio Mendoza **32** 179
Galería Adler-Castillo **32** 179
Galería Clara Sujo **32** 179
Hijos de Dios cemetery **32** 169
Hospital Vargas **32** 170
Hotel Jardín **32** 170
houses **32** 169, 170
Instituto Provincial de Bellas Artes **32** 180
Instituto Universitario de Estudios Superiores de Artes Plásticas Armando Reverón **32** 180
La Florida **32** 170
linen **32** 178
Ministry of Education
División de Tecnología Educativa **32** 181
museums
Galería de Arte Nacional **22** 524; **32** 179, 567, 568
Centro de Información y Documentación Nacional de las Artes Plásticas (CINAP) **32** 181
Museo de Arte Colonial **32** 179
Biblioteca Carlos Manuel Muller **32** 181
Museo de Arte Contemporáneo **32** 179
Biblioteca Pública de Arte Sofía Imber **32** 181
Museo Audiovisual **32** 181
Museo de Bellas Artes **32** 170, 178, 179
collections **24** 682; **32** 178, 179
Library **32** 180
Museo Bolivariano **32** 170, 180
Museo de Ciencias Naturales **22** 523; **32** 170, 567
Museo Cuadra de Bolívar **32** 180
Museo de Los Caobos **32** 567
Museo Nacional *see* Museo de Bellas Artes
Palacio Federal **32** 169, *169*
Salón Elíptico **32** 173
Palacio de la Gobernación y de Justicia **32** 170
Palacio Legislativo **32** 169
Palacio de Miraflores **32** 170
Panteón Nacional **32** 168
Parque de El Calvario **32** 170
Plaza Bolívar **32** 170
rugs **32** 177
S Jacinto market **32** 169
Teatro Nacional **32** 170
Teatro Teresa Carreño **32** 171, *171*
textiles **32** 178
Torre Europa **32** 171
Universidad Central de Venezuela **32** 169, 170, 171, 178, 567–8
architecture faculty **32** 181
Aula Magna **10** 417; **32** 171 *567*
Housing Centre **32** 10
Universidad Simón Bolívar
Artevisión **32** 181
Urbanización General Rafael Urdaneta **32** 171
Villa Zoila **32** 170
Caracca, Giovanni **28** 4, 5
Caraccetto, Il *see* LAPIS, GAETANO
Caraccio, Kathleen **20** 609
Caracciolo, Giovanni Battista **5** 692–6*; **11** 188; **16** 673; **22** 478
attributions **28** 389
groups and movements **30** 456
patrons and collectors **4** 567; **9** 174; **19** 139; **21** 25; **22** 486
pupils **23** 897; **29** 543
teachers **7** 848
works **5** *694*, *695*; **11** 114; **22** 484, 486; **24** 782; **28** 389
Caracciolo, Pompeo **5** 695
Caraciolo, Giovanni Battista **27** 133
Caracol *see under* CHICHÉN ITZÁ
Carada, Eugeniu **26** 723
Caradosso **5** 696–7*; **16** 742
patrons and collectors **1** 767; **27** 272
works **4** 649; **16** 750; **20** 848; **21** 16; **25** 20
Caraduje, Antonio **2** 604
Carafa, Diomede (1406-87) **5** 698; **26** 2
Carafa, Diomede, Duca di Maddaloni (*fl* 1655) *see* MADDALONI, DIOMEDE CARAFA, Duca di
Carafa, Gian Pietro *see* PAUL IV, Pope
Carafa, Gregorio **20** 216
Carafa, Oliviero, Cardinal **5** 698*
architecture **4** 646; **16** 632; **26** 766
collections **26** 767
paintings **6** 355; **19** 447; **24** 526
Carafa, Vittoria Camponeschi *see* CAMPONESCHI CARAFA, VITTORIA
Caraffa, Emilio **7** 847
Caraglio, Giovanni Jacopo **5** 699*; **10** 386; **16** 867
collaboration **3** 419; **24** 199
reproductions in ceramics **31** *742*
teachers **25** 860
works **24** 419; **27** 208; **31** 43
Caraíba **4** 715; **13** 781–2
Carajía **6** 380
Caraman, Comte de **32** 374
Caraman, Duc de **5** 699–700*
Caraman, Anthony de *see* ANTHONY DE CARAMAN
Caraman, Peter de *see* PETER DE CARAMAN
Caramuel de Lobkowitz, Juan **5** 700–701*
works **5** *700*; **31** 297
Caran d'Ache **5** 701*, 758
Carapeguá **24** *91*, 100
Carare **7** 602
Carastu, Antonio **20** 215
Carata, Francesco *see* CARATTI, FRANCESCO
carats **12** 864
Caratti (family) **28** 372
Caratti, Francesco **5** 701–2*
patrons and collectors **8** 426, 427
works **8** 378, 396; **12** 370; **19** 55, 259; **25** 258, 427
Carattoli, Pietro **24** 520
Carau, Marguerite **30** 330
Caravacque, Louis **27** 388, 401, 442
Caravaggi, Giovan Antonio **5** *743*
Caravaggio, Cecco del **5** 702*, 719; **9** 363
Caravaggio, Francesco Sforza, Marchese di **5** 703
Caravaggio, Giovanni Paolo Sforza da *see* SFORZA DA CARAVAGGIO, GIOVANNI PAOLO
Caravaggio, Michelangelo Merisi da **1** 179; **3** 862; **5** 702–20*; **12** 214, 304; **16** 665, 669, 670, 672; **20** 265; **21** 525; **22** 477, 478; **26** 770, 773; **27** 621
assistants **20** 265
Caravaggio, Michelangelo Merisi da—cont.
attributions **5** 693; **8** 139; **18** 840; **20** 267; **29** 252
collaboration **13** 275
copies **21** 650; **26** 306
groups and movements **3** 261, 263, 265; **30** 456
methods **6** 570; **7** 783; **19** 354, 356; **21** 759; **31** 578
paintings **5** 883; **20** 213; **26** 307; **31** 142
allegorical **10** 476; **12** *764*; **23** 294
altarpieces **1** 712; **8** 138, 613; **16** 670
genre **5** *706*, *707*; **12** 288
mythological **12** 706
religious **5** *704*, *709*, *710*, *713*, *714*, *715*, *718*; **9** 110; **11** 78; **15** 138; **22** 521, 686; **28** 657
still-lifes **29** 667, *667*
patrons and collectors **13** 824; **19** 92
Alcalá, 3rd Duque de (1583-1637) **26** 307
Alexander I, Emperor of Russia (*reg* 1801-25) **26** 733
Arpiro, Cavaliere d' **2** 493
Balbi, Francesco Maria, the elder (1619–1704) **3** 90
Benavente, 8th Conde de (1575-1621) **3** 700
Borghese, Scipione, Cardinal **4** 404, 406; **26** 773
Borromeo, Federico, Cardinal **4** 425, 426; **16** 771
Bourbon del Monte, Francesco Maria, Cardinal **4** 567
Cesare, 6th Duke of Modena and Reggio (*reg* 1597-1628) **10** 525
Charles I, King of England and Scotland (*reg* 1625-49) **2** 558; **10** 363; **29** 800
Costa, Ottavio **8** 9
Créquy, Charles de Blanchefort de **19** 238
Doria, Marcantonio **9** 174
Ferdinando I, Grand Duke of Tuscany (*reg* 1587-1609) **11** 188
Filomarino, Ascanio, Cardinal **11** 81
Finson, Louis **11** 115
Frederick William III, King of Prussia (*reg* 1797-1840) **14** 653
Giustiniani (i) (family) **12** 763
Giustiniani (i), Benedetto, Cardinal **12** 763
Giustiniani (i), Vincenzo, Marchese **12** 764
Jabach, Everard **16** 814
Lambertini (family) **12** 53
Lastanosa, Vicencio Juan de **18** 816
Lemos, Conde de **19** 139
Liancourt, Duc de **19** 300
Methuen, Paul (1672-1757) **21** 348
Nisbet, William Hamilton **25** 664
Odescalchi (family) **23** 352
Pamphili, Camillo, Prince **9** 175
Patrizi, Costanzo **24** 267
Pio di Savoia, Carlo Francesco, Cardinal **24** 833
Rocca Sinibaldi, Asdrubale Mattei, Duca di **20** 841
Rocca Sinibaldi, Ciriaco Mattei, Duca di **20** 840
Ruffo, Tommaso, Cardinal, Archbishop of Ferrara **27** 316
Sandoval y Rojas, Bernardo de, Cardinal Archbishop of Toledo **27** 724
Sannesio, Giacomo, Cardinal **27** 764
Caravaggio, Michelangelo Merisi da
patrons and collectors—cont.
Santiago, Francisco Esteban Rodríguez de los Ríos, 1st Marqués de **27** 792
Serra, Giovan Francesco, Marqués di Cassano **28** 479
Thyssen-Bornemisza, Heinrich, Baron von **30** 795
Urban VIII, Pope (*reg* 1623-44) **3** 205
Vincenzo I, 4th Duke of Mantua (*reg* 1587- 1612) **12** 912
pupils **5** 693; **11** 115
reproductive prints by others **27** 502; **30** 47; **32** 689
restorations by others **27** 321
sponsors **26** 773
Caravaggio, Polidoro da *see* POLIDORO DA CARAVAGGIO
Caravaggio, Violante Sforza da *see* SFORZA DA CARAVAGGIO, VIOLANTE
Caravaggisti, Flemish *see* FLEMISH CARAVAGGISTI
Caravaggisti, Utrecht *see* UTRECHT CARAVAGGISTI
caravanserais **5** 722–4*; **16** 141, 193, 198, 205, 238, 246, 266
Arabia **21** 548
Central Asia **16** 163
Central Asia, Western **6** 201, *202*; **16** 154, 238; **26** 302
Indian subcontinent **15** 202, 364
Iran **16** 154, 193, 198, 232
Ottoman **16** 206, 224, 228, 266
Syria **16** 148, 228
Turkey **5** *723*; **16** 141, 186, 205, 206, 224, 266
see also RIBĀTS
Caravaque, Louis **24** 820; **26** 729; **27** 420; **32** 617
Caravita, Giuseppe, Prince of Sirignano *see* SIRIGNANO, GIUSEPPE CARAVITA, Prince of
Carbajal Sebastián, Enrique *see* SEBASTIÁN, ENRIQUE CARBAJAL
Carballo, Amelia **8** 237
Carballo, Marcelín **10** 154
carbon **21** 319
carbon-14 **30** 403
carbon blacks **15** 849, 850, 851, 853; **18** 608; **19** 480; **23** 376; **24** 647, 649, 651, 789–90*
Carbondir *see under* PHOTOGRAPHIC PRINTS → types
Carbone, G. **16** 706
Carbone, Giovanni Bernardo **5** 724*; **16** 674
Carbonel, Alonso de **5** 724–5*
patrons and collectors **23** 404
works **10** 501; **20** 70, 71; **29** 269
Carbonel, Antonio **29** 267
Carbonell, Guillem **3** 218
Carbonero, José Moreno *see* MORENO CARBONERO, JOSÉ
Carbonet, Charles **12** 723; **22** 309
carbon papers *see under* PAPER → types
carbon prints *see under* PHOTOGRAPHIC PRINTS → types
carborundum **7** 11; **29** 706
carborundum prints *see under* PRINTS → types
Çarça, Diogo de *see* SARÇA, DIOGO DE
Carcani, Filippo **12** 649
Carcano, Filippo **5** 726*; **24** 206; **28** 34
Carcassonne **5** 726–8*, *727*; **11** *505*
Castle **7** 358
Cathedral *see* St Nazaire
Château Comtal **3** 209; **5** 727; **6** *49*, 49, 56, 61

Carcassonne—cont.
Porte Narbonnaise 3 209; 5 727; 12 173, 174; 19 895
St Nazaire 5 727–8, 728; 13 43; 26 46, 585
sculpture 5 727–8; 13 76
stained glass 5 728
vaults 32 90
Tour l'Evêque 8 277
town walls 5 726–7; 11 511
Carcassonne Codex see under CODICES → individual manuscripts
Carchemish 1 821, 829, 839, 893; 5 728–9*; 14 592; 21 267; 30 180, 187, 194; 31 456
architecture 1 831
dress 1 885
excavations 33 373
figurines 1 833
ivory-carvings 1 870
metalwork 1 827
reliefs 5 729; 24 690; 30 190
sculpture 1 833; 30 187, 189
seals 1 862, 863
stelae 29 616
trade 30 179
wall paintings 1 839
Carchera, Nicolas see KARCHER, NICOLAS
Carco, Francis 2 615; 19 86
Carcopino, François see CARCO, FRANCIS
Cárcova, Ernesto de la 2 399, 404; 5 730*; 32 415
Cardal 6 523
Cardamatis, Wolfgang 30 160
cardboard 4 184; 24 52; 31 258
collagraphs 7 558
dolls' houses 31 262, 263
game-boards 31 265
mounts (works on paper and scrolls) 22 233, 236
papier mâché 24 61
puzzles 31 267
toys 31 258
Cardeilhac, Ernest 11 622
Cardelli 24 846
Carden, Jerome 2 354
Cardena, Michael 22 853
Cardenal, Ernesto 23 86; 29 34
Cárdenas 8 238
Cárdenas, Agustín 5 730*; 8 229, 233; 30 23
Cárdenas, Bartolomé de see BERMEJO, BARTOLOMÉ
Cárdenas, Carlos R. 8 234
Cárdenas, Garci López de see LÓPEZ DE CÁRDENAS, GARCI
Cárdenas, Rafael de 8 232
Cárdenas, Santiago 7 610
Cardenio see RUHL, LUDWIG, SIGISMUND
Cardenosa, Bartolomé 17 514
Carder, Frederick 5 730*; 14 252; 29 644; 31 644
Carderera y Solano, Valentín 20 59; 31 827
Cardew, Michael 2 761; 5 730–31*; 25 834
assistants 4 445
collaboration 18 543
groups and movements 2 571; 10 314
pupils 4 444
teachers 18 901
works 10 314
Cardew, Peter 31 864
Cardi, Beatrice de 3 150
Cardi, Lodovico see CIGOLI, LODOVICO
Cardi, Sebastiano 7 313
Cardial-impressed ware see POTTERY → wares → Impressed ware
Cardiff (S. Glams) 5 731–2*; 32 780
architecture 32 783
art school 32 792
Cardiff (S. Glams)—cont.
Castle 5 194, 194; 6 61; 22 59; 32 784, 788
Chapel 5 340
interior decoration 13 209
City Hall 3 269; 5 731; 7 668; 32 784
sculpture 32 788
Civic Centre 32 784
Law Courts 5 731; 7 668; 18 890; 32 784
National Museum of Wales 5 732; 28 888; 32 784
collections 5 732; 32 791
directors 33 135
sculpture 32 787
Welsh School of Architecture 32 792
Cardigan, George Brudenell, 4th Earl of see BRUDENELL, GEORGE, 4th Earl of Cardigan and 1st Duke of Montagu
Cardigan, Mary Brudenell, Countess of see BRUDENELL, MARY, Countess of Cardigan and Duchess of Montagu
Cardim, Fernão 4 715
Cardin, Pierre 9 294; 31 905
Cardinal, Douglas (Joseph) 5 563, 591, 732*; 23 632
Cardini, Antonio di Berto 22 800
Cardini, Santi 23 845
Cardino of Paris 3 188
Cardito, Prince of 6 109
card looms see under LOOMS → types
cardo 5 733*; 10 602
Cardon, Anthony 5 733–4*; 29 677
collaboration 28 86
works 7 579; 19 66
Cardon, Antoine Alexandre Joseph 5 733
Cardon, Forci 5 733
Cardon, Jan (i) (b c. 1605) 5 733
Cardon, Jan (ii) (1614-56) see CARDON, JOANNES
Cardon, Joannes 5 733*
Cardon, Servaes 5 733*
Cardona 29 259
S Vicente 5 319, 734, 734–5*; 26 568–9, 569, 571, 580; 29 262
Cardona, Bremon, Vizconde de 5 734
Cardona, Duque de Segorbe y see SEGORBE Y CARDONA, Duque de
Cardona, Duquesa de 21 35
Cardona, Jésus 25 702
Cardoso (family) 28 812
Cardoso, Amadeo de Sousa see AMADEO (DE SOUZA-CARDOSO)
Cardoso, Diego 22 23
Cardoso, Edgar 23 454
Cardoso, Joaquim 23 117
Cardoso de Saldanha, Manuel 4 710; 27 644
Cardoze, Maurice 2 148
cards
types
cabinet 24 648*, 649
cartes-de-visite 9 6; 24 648, 649*, 660, 661
Christmas 7 548
credit 14 690
greeting 24 56
pattern 8 37
playing 15 730; 20 746; 21 881; 31 265, 266*
postcards 11 795; 17 915; 26 236
punch-cards 16 849
trade 10 419, 420, 421
valentines 24 56
visiting see cartes-de-visite
uses
jewellery 17 530
Cards, Master of the Playing see PLAYING CARDS, MASTER OF THE
Cardston, Alberta Temple 22 126; 30 450
card-tables see under TABLES → types
Carducci, Achille 19 28
Carducci, Filippo 6 13
Carducho, Bartolomé 5 735–6*; 29 280
collaboration 5 411, 736; 33 719
patrons and collectors 14 6; 26 307; 27 723
pupils 5 736
works 1 586; 5 736; 10 503
Carducho, Vicente 5 735, 736–9*; 20 66; 29 279, 280
attributions 19 179
collaboration 5 411, 735; 6 25
methods 21 764
patrons and collectors 13 869; 14 6, 7; 27 723; 31 89; 32 128
pupils 6 25; 7 558; 19 178; 26 434, 435; 32 557
works 5 737, 738; 13 732; 20 71, 72; 24 391; 27 724
writings 4 212; 20 66; 29 353, 354, 357, 358
Careaga, Enrique 5 739–40*; 24 99, 101
Carée 11 426
Careggi, Villa Medici 12 110; 21 468; 32 545
sculpture 16 694; 30 497; 32 361
Carelli, Consalvo 22 480; 28 317
Carelli, Giuseppe 22 480
Carême, Jacques-Philippe see CARESME, JACQUES-PHILIPPE
Carena, Felice 5 671, 740*; 16 680
Carennac, St Pierre 26 602
Caresale, Angelo 30 667
Caresme, Claude-François 5 740
Caresme, Jacques-Philippe 5 740*
Carette, Georges, & Cie 31 256
Caretti, Giovanni Battista 31 172
Carew (Dyfed) 32 780
High Cross 32 786, 787
Carew, John Edward 5 740–41*; 33 453
Carewe, Sylvia 31 660
Carey, Arthur Astor 31 650
Carey, Evelyn 15 830
Carey, F. S. 10 373
Carey, William (fl 1790s) 15 679
Carey, William Paulet (1759-1839) 5 741*; 16 15, 38
Carfaro, Donato Antonio 28 367
Cargaleiro, Manuel Alves see ALVES CARGALEIRO, MANUEL
Caria 1 821; 5 741–3*; 13 363; 14 68; 26 852
dress 1 887
friezes 14 69
pottery 13 497, 504
sculpture 13 459; 14 70
tombs 14 71; 31 108
see also ANATOLIA, ANCIENT; TURKEY
Cariani, Giovanni 3 771; 5 743–4*; 32 190
attributions 31 32
collaboration 28 467
patrons and collectors 23 355; 26 284; 32 155
works 5 743; 11 387; 12 288
Carib 2 144–5; 3 622; 5 744–7*, 754; 7 602; 9 113; 13 874; 25 698; 29 132, 191; 30 12; 31 330, 331; 32 166
basketwork 2 145
dress 29 194; 30 13
houses 30 13
pots 30 13
pottery 13 874; 30 13
textiles 29 194
Caribbean Islands 2 144; 5 744–55*, 745; 8 227; 29 123, 128
architecture 5 749–50*
areytos 5 748
balconies (houses) 5 752
cane 5 752
carnivals 5 753
cars 5 754
concrete 5 753, 755
copper 5 747
decorative arts 5 752*
dress 5 748
exhibitions 5 745–6*
furniture 5 752
gold 5 747
gold leaf 5 747
guanin 5 747
houses 5 749
interior decoration 5 755
mahogany 5 752
masks 5 748
metalwork 5 752
mortars (vessels) 29 133
mosques 5 755
mud 5 755
necklaces 5 748
painting 5 750–52*
paper 5 755
pendants (jewellery) 5 748
pottery 5 747
prints 5 750
rice 5 755
scientific books 5 750
sculpture 5 750–52*, 753
figure 5 747–8, 748
santos 5 750
shells 5 747
slaves 5 753
stone 5 748
stone-carvings 5 748
stools 5 748
temples 5 755
tourist art 5 754
trade
furniture 5 752
iron 5 752
wood 5 748, 748, 755
see also ANTILLES, GREATER; ANTILLES, LESSER
Caribé 26 60
Caribelle Batiks 2 151
Caricature, La 5 757; 8 545–6; 12 210; 13 306; 20 602; 24 605; 27 871; 31 293
caricatures 5 755–61*; 7 648; 10 554; 25 243, 283, 284
historical and regional traditions 5 755*, 761*; 10 554; 26 742
Africa 5 761*
Belgium 21 356
Brazil 4 717
Britain 2 240; 10 554; 26 742
Buddhism 5 761
Egypt, ancient 9 904
England 5 756–7*, 757, 758–9*; 7 648; 9 225; 10 252; 27 869
18th cent. 12 639, 640
19th cent. 10 251
France 5 756, 757–8*; 8 510; 27 871
19th cent. 5 303; 27 870
Germany 5 758*
Igbo 5 761
Iran 5 761
Islamic 5 761*
Italy 5 755–6*, 756; 9 222; 12 535
17th cent. 5 866
18th cent. 13 300
Makonde (Mozambique) 5 761
Mesoamerica, Pre-Columbian 5 761*
Moche (culture) 5 761
Netherlands, the 5 756
Olmec 5 761
Russia 5 759*
South America, Pre-Columbian 5 761*
caricatures
historical and regional traditions—cont.
Spain 5 757
Switzerland 30 133
United States of America 5 758, 759*, 759; 25 651
Yoruba 5 761
historiography see under HISTORIOGRAPHY → types
see also SATIRES
Caričin Grad 5 762*; 9 511, 554; 28 437, 439
aqueduct 9 560
architecture 9 524
Bishop's Palace 9 557, 558
churches 9 538
mosaics 9 566
Cariès, Jean (-Joseph-Marie) see CARRIÈS, JEAN(-JOSEPH-MARIE)
Carignan 7 778
Carignano
Cathedral 3 825
S Giovanni Battista 26 500
SS Remigio e Giovanni 1 623–4
Carignano, Emanuel-Philibert of Savoy, Prince of 13 750; 16 643; 28 2
Carignano, Eugene, Prince of 12 163
Carignano, Filiberto di, Prince 5 281
Carignano, Ludovico di, Prince of 4 423
Carignano, Princess of 32 368
Carignano, Thomas of Savoy, Prince of 28 2, 220
Carignano, Victor Amadeus I, Prince of (d 1741) 4 42; 12 601; 27 587; 30 274
Carignano, Victor Amadeus II, Prince of (1666-1732) see VICTOR-AMADEUS II, 15th Duke of Savoy; King of Sicily and Sardinia
Carignano, Victor Amadeus II, Prince of (1743-80) 5 432
Çarıklı Kilise Monastery 5 675
Carilef Bible see under BIBLES → individual manuscripts
Carillo, Alfonso, Archbishop 1 586; 3 119; 28 368
Carillo, Lilia 21 406
Carillo Polychrome ware see under POTTERY → wares
Carin, Dräxler von 11 33
carinated bowls see under BOWLS → types
Carings, Alexander see KEIRINCKX, ALEXANDER
Carini-Motta, Fabrizio 1 124; 5 762*; 30 667
Carinola Cathedral 16 626
Carinthia, Arnold of see ARNOLD OF CARINTHIA
Cario 24 93
Carisbrooke Castle (Hants) 21 568
Caristie, Auguste-Nicolas 24 387
works 30 652
Carito, Raffaele 7 850
Carjat, Etienne 5 762–3*; 8 547
works 24 661, 661
Carl (fl 12th cent.) 26 639
Carl, Hans Johann 5 763*
Carl, Peter 5 763*; 33 294
Carlandi, Onorato 8 6, 786
Carlberg, Bengt Wilhelm 13 30
Carlberg, Carl Wilhelm 13 30
Carlberg, Johan Eberhard 13 30; 23 890; 29 685; 30 72
Carlborg, Carl Anton 11 108
works 11 108
Carlerio, Anselmo see CANNERI, ANSELMO
Carles, Arthur B(eecher) 5 763*; 24 600
exhibitions 2 447; 31 490
patrons and collectors 3 251

Carleton, Dudley, 1st Viscount Dorchester 5 764*; 10 363; 21 486; 29 800
collections 5 847
paintings 9 476; 14 806; 21 486; 23 326; 26 158; 27 300; 29 799
Carletti, G.
works 26 788
Carletti, Nicola 26 780
Carlevaris, Luca 5 764–5*; 16 676; 31 155; 32 194
assistants 5 594
methods 5 519
patrons and collectors 7 779; 21 908; 28 173
works 5 765; 31 248; 32 111
Carlhian, Jean-Paul 22 368; 32 889, 890
works 32 889
Carli, Carlo de 30 684
Carli, Giuseppe 22 481
Carli, Raffaelle de' see RAFFAELLINO DEL GARBO
Carlier, Emile 19 75
Carlier, François Antoine 4 561; 5 766*; 29 271
Carlier, Jean-Guillaume 5 766*; 11 166; 19 344
Carlier, René 5 766*; 20 71
fireplaces 29 303
gardens 12 125; 27 753
interior decoration 20 72; 29 303
sculpture 4 558
Carlin, Martin 5 767*; 7 658; 11 627; 20 388; 26 375
patrons and collectors 5 530; 11 593; 14 145; 20 897; 27 223
works 6 I3; 11 593, 595; 12 831; 30 885
Carlín, Master 28 518
Carline, Hilda 29 385
Carline, Richard 2 553
Carlini, A. 20 503
Carlini, Agostino 5 767*; 10 264
assistants 6 323
collaboration 6 323
works 9 706
Carlini, L.
works 4 272
Carlisle (Cumbria; UK) 10 302; 27 103
Cathedral of the Holy Trinity 28 294
County Courts 18 887
Carlisle (PA; USA), Indian School 22 594
Carlisle, Charles Howard, 3rd Earl of see HOWARD (ii), CHARLES, 3rd Earl of Carlisle
Carlisle, Frederick Howard, 5th Earl of see HOWARD (ii), FREDERICK, 5th Earl of Carlisle
Carlisle, George James Howard, 9th Earl of see HOWARD (ii), GEORGE JAMES, 9th Earl of Carlisle
Carlisle, Henry Howard, 4th Earl of see HOWARD (ii), HENRY, 4th Earl of Carlisle
Carlisle, Joan 5 766*
Carllyle, Archibald 15 551
Carlo I, 8th Duke of Mantua (reg 1627-37) 12 904, 913*
architecture 21 346; 31 719
medals 21 805
paintings 25 833
sculpture 12 902
tapestries 26 113
Carlo II, 9th Duke of Mantua (reg 1637-65) 12 904, 913–14*
paintings 5 635; 6 35; 9 489
sculpture 25 705
Carlo, Adolfo De see DE CARLO, ADOLFO
Carlo, Ferrante 5 767–8*; 10 909
Carlo, Giancarlo De see DE CARLO, GIANCARLO
Carlo Borromeo, Saint 4 424–5*; 7 276; 16 637, 700; 21 525, 533
architecture 21 517–18
churches 21 532, 533
sacrimonti 27 498
tapestries 2 373
writings 7 215; 11 255; 23 576; 26 317
Carlo da Milano see BRACCESCO, CARLO
Carlo di Cesari del Palagio 5 768–9*
collaboration 8 881; 11 819; 12 345, 346, 403
works 23 252
Carlo di Monlione 24 248
Carlo Emanuele III, King of Italy (reg 1730-73) 1 623
Carlone (ii) (family) 12 370; 29 838
Carlone (ii), Bartolomeo 5 773*; 27 553
Carlone (i), Battista 9 173
Carlone (ii), Carlo Antonio (b ?1635) 5 771–2*
architecture 2 781
churches 5 772; 18 447; 27 553
gates 18 447
monasteries 2 781; 12 371; 25 449
collaboration 5 771
frescoes 5 8
Carlone (ii), Carlo Innocenzo (1685-1775) 2 795; 5 771, 774–5*; 19 780
collaboration 5 773
works 5 774; 10 117; 15 139; 32 459; 33 417
Carlone (ii), Carlo Martino 2 782; 10 529; 14 886; 29 839; 32 442
Carlone (ii), Diego Francesco 1 667; 5 771, 773–5*; 19 780
collaboration 1 667; 5 774, 775
patrons and collectors 27 878
works 10 117; 12 404; 27 553; 28 79; 29 838
Carlone (i), Francesco 3 6; 5 769
Carlone (ii), Franz Isidor 5 773
Carlone, Gioannetto 19 806
Carlone (i), Giovanni (fl 1570) 5 769
Carlone (i), Giovanni (Andrea), I (1584-1630) 5 769–70*; 16 675
Carlone (i), Giovanni Andrea, II (1639-97) 5 769, 770*
collaboration 14 27; 26 823
patrons and collectors 4 811
Carlone (i), Giovanni Battista (1603-84) 5 770; 16 675
Carlone (ii), Giovanni Battista, I (1580/90-1645) 5 769, 770–71*
assistants 5 769
collaboration 11 53
patrons and collectors 3 90
pupils 5 770
works 2 127; 5 769; 11 53; 14 886; 19 55
Carlone (ii), Giovanni Battista, II (c. 1650-1707) 5 771, 772–3*
collaboration 11 42, 43
pupils 1 667; 5 773
works 2 781; 12 404, 404; 14 887; 27 553; 29 838
Carlone (i), Giuseppe 5 769; 9 173
Carlone (ii), Johann Joachim 2 783; 5 773*; 13 330
Carlone, Michele 18 586; 21 124; 29 265
Carlone (i), Niccolò 5 769, 770
Carlone (ii), Peter Franz 5 771*
collaboration 5 771
works 2 781; 19 433
Carlone (i), Pietro 5 769
Carlone, Sebastian 29 27
Carlone (i), Simon 5 769
Carlone (i), Taddeo 5 769; 9 173
Carlone, Tomasso 29 831
Carloni, Tita 4 491
Carlos 9 712
Carlos, Frei (fl 1517-29) 2 872; 5 775–6*; 20 719; 25 295
Carlos I de Bragança see CHARLES, King of Portugal
Carlos III, King of Spain see CHARLES III, King of Spain
Carlos IV, King of Spain see CHARLES IV, King Spain
Carlotta, Villa see VILLA CARLOTTA
Carlotto see LOTH, JOHANN CARL
Carlow (Co. Carlow)
Castle 16 7
court-house 16 9
Carlow, John Dawson, 2nd Viscount see DAWSON, JOHN, 2nd Viscount Carlow
Carlsbad see KARLOVY VARY
Carlsberg 4 69
Carlsberg Foundation see NY CARLSBERGFOND
Carlsen, Emil 11 230; 26 477
Carlsen, Frederik Wilhelm (Christian) see FREDDIE, WILHELM
Carlson, Chester F. 24 654; 25 592
Carlsruhe Painter 13 523, 538
Carlsruhe Paris, Painter of the 13 524
Carlstedt, Birger 31 886
Carlsten Lighthouse 19 361
Carlsund, Otto G(ustaf) 5 776*
groups and movements 7 698, 772; 11 550; 14 329
teachers 19 83
works 30 81
Carl Theodor, Elector Palatine and Elector of Bavaria see CHARLES THEODORE, Elector Palatine and Elector of Bavaria
Carlton Studio 19 877
Carlu, Jacques 4 240; 5 776–7*; 8 573; 10 684
Carlu, Jean 7 653; 25 350, 352
Carl Wilhelm Ferdinand, Duke of Brunswick see CHARLES II, Duke of Brunswick-Wolfenbüttel
Carlyle, Thomas 5 777*; 28 916
Carman, Albert 19 492
Carmarthen (Dyfed) 32 780
Town Hall 32 782
Carmelite Order 5 777–8*
architecture 19 566
frescoes 5 778
iconography 5 778*
patronage 5 778*
Carmichael, Frank 13 711
Carmichael, Peter 7 505
Carmichael, Thomas 10 91
Carmichael, W. H. 32 414
Carmichael Smyth, James see SMYTH, JAMES CARMICHAEL
Carmina Burana manuscript (Munich, Cod. Lat. 4660) 12 382
carmina figurata 4 345; 5 779*, 779; 7 246
see also CALLIGRAPHY; MICROGRAPHY
Carminati, Antonio 30 684
carmine see under PIGMENTS → types
Carmo, tomb of Postumius 27 52
Carmona 25 734; 29 334
Carmona, José Salvador see SALVADOR CARMONA, JOSÉ
Carmona, Juan Antonio Salvador see SALVADOR CARMONA, JUAN ANTONIO
Carmona, Luis Salvador see SALVADOR CARMONA, LUIS
Carmona, Manuel Salvador see SALVADOR CARMONA, MANUEL
Carmontelle 12 105
Carmontelle, Louis de 5 779–80*; 6 171; 11 541; 23 519, 523
Carmoy, Etienne 13 227
Carmoy, François 27 547
Carmuel de Lobkowitz, Juan 23 489
Carmyan, Ellys 20 116
Carnac 5 780–81*; 11 504; 21 40, 43; 25 470
megalithic architecture 5 780, 780
Ménec alignments 25 505
menhirs 25 505
passage tombs 5 780–81
stone circles 25 505
Tables des Marchands 25 511
Carnage Painter 10 614
Carnarvon, George Herbert, 5th Earl of see HERBERT, GEORGE, 5th Earl of Carnarvon
Carnarvon, Henry John George Herbert, 3rd Earl of see HERBERT, HENRY JOHN GEORGE, 3rd Earl of Carnarvon
Carnarvon Knife-handle 9 865
Carnation Masters 12 384; 20 641*; 30 130; 33 736
carnauba wax see under WAXES → types
Carnavalet, Musée see under PARIS → museums
Carnegie, Andrew 5 781*; 11 774; 14 40; 25 5
architecture 14 174; 19 319; 25 5
Carnegie, David 25 35
Carnegie, Margaret 1 66
Carnegie, Roderick 1 66
Carnegie Phipps & Co. 16 54
Carneiro, Alberto 25 302
Carneiro, António Teixeira 5 781–2*; 25 299
Carneiro, Fernando Alvarez see ALVAREZ CARNEIRO, FERNANDO
Carneiro Adão, Manuel 26 253
carnelian see CORNELIAN
Carnelutti, Gjuro 18 411
Carneo, Antonio 5 782*
Carnet des Artistes, Le 32 96
Carnevale, Carlo 2 781
Carnevale, Fra 5 782*; 31 742
attributions 20 623
pupils 4 642
teachers 19 445
works 31 739
Carnevali, Domenico 26 769, 817, 818
Carnevali, Giovanni 5 782–3*; 16 678
groups and movements 28 34
works 5 783
Carnicero (family) 5 783–4*
Carnicero, Alejandro 5 783, 784*; 27 603
Carnicero, Antonio 5 784*; 29 283
patrons and collectors 23 626
reproductive prints by others 10 906
teachers 13 252
works 4 362; 5 452
Carnicero, Gregorio 5 783
Carnicero, Isidro 5 784
Carnide, Nossa Senhora da Luz 26 253
Carniello, Antonio see CARNEO, ANTONIO
Carnieri, Paolo 1 631; 8 202
Carniola Construction Society 28 859
Carniolian Institute for Weaving (Ljubljana) 28 863
Carnivalism 27 397
carnivals 1 423*; 2 146–7, 153; 3 60; 5 753, 784*, 785, 786, 786, 787, 788, 788; 16 881, 881; 31 332, 332
see also FESTIVALS; MARDI GRAS
Carno 32 790
Carnot, Lazare-Nicolas Marguerite, Comte 21 581
Carnot Wall 21 581
Carnovale, Fra see CARNEVALE, FRA
Carnuntum 12 70; 26 906; 30 903
amphitheatre 26 906
carnyxes 22 371, 372
Caro (family) 5 415
Caro, Annibal 5 415, 684, 789*; 10 810; 15 84; 33 718
collaboration 24 24
works 1 734; 5 887; 11 740, 741; 15 87
Caro, Anthony 5 789–90*; 10 375; 19 591
collaboration 22 58
groups and movements 1 80; 28 805
patrons and collectors 18 170
pupils 20 27; 28 285
works 5 790; 10 268; 16 58
Caro, Francisco López see LÓPEZ CARO, FRANCISCO
Caro, Julio Martín 20 513
Caro, Lorenzo de 5 790*; 22 479
Caro, Rodrigo 5 791*; 12 80; 28 515
Caro Alvarez, José Antonio 9 116
works 9 117
carob-beans see LOCUST-BEANS
Carocci, Baverio de see BAVIERA
Carocci, Guido 5 791*; 24 448
Caroë, Alban 27 538
Caroë, Martin 27 538
Caroë, William Douglas 5 732; 12 631; 24 308; 27 538
Caro Ginebra, Danilo 9 116
works 9 117
Caro Ginebra, José A. 9 116
works 9 117
Caro Idogro, Pedro 2 284
Carol I, King of Romania (reg 1866-1914) 5 791–2*
architecture 26 718
collections 26 722, 725
paintings 30 202
Carolina, La see LA CAROLINA
Caroline Augusta, Empress of Austria (1792-1873) 27 665
Caroline Islands 21 476; 23 711, 832; 25 181
sculpture 25 182
weapons 23 735
see also POLYNESIAN OUTLIERS
Caroline Louise, Margravine of Baden-Durlach (1723-83) 17 817; 26 110; 33 593, 594*
Caroline Mathilda, Queen of Denmark and Norway (1751-75) 8 753; 14 382
Caroline Murat, Queen of Naples (1782-1839) 4 299, 305; 13 308; 15 838; 16 747; 20 90; 22 338
Caroline of Brandenburg-Ansbach, Queen of England (1683-1737) 1 488; 4 875; 9 26; 11 243; 13 782; 14 460; 17 905; 18 5; 21 640
Carolingian 5 792–812*
acanthus 1 110
altars 5 807, 807, 808; 7 263–4
amulets 5 807
arches 2 294
architecture 5 793–6*; 6 482
France 11 509*; 12 485; 27 539
Germany 12 362–3*; 26 100
Switzerland 27 554
art history 18 187
astronomy 5 800, 801
author portraits 5 801, 802
Bibles 4 5; 5 803, 804
bookbindings 4 346, 347, 348
book covers 4 IV2; 5 808, 809, 809–11, 811; 7 513; 22 520
bronze 5 805, 806, 806; 9 152
calendars 5 427
canon tables 5 624, 624; 6 564
capitals 5 796
casting 5 806
churches 5 793; 7 263–5*
Belgium 3 541
centrally planned 7 256
France 12 484

Carolingian
churches—cont.
Germany **5** *793*; **26** *100*, *101*
ciboria (ii) (structure) **5** 796, 808
cloisters **5** 795; **7** 452, 453
codices **5** 801
purple codices **25** *743*
coins **7** 534, *534*
columns **5** 794
copies **5** 802
crosses **5** 796, 807
cross feet **8** 205
crowns **5** 807
crucifixes **5** 807; **8** 213
crypts **7** 265
France **13** *636*
hall **27** 554
outer **5** 795, *795*; **8** 222
diptychs **9** 3
domes **9** 84
doors **5** 806; **9** 152
drawings **5** 794–5
dress **9** 253–4*
enamel **5** 806
Evangeliaries **5** 800
exempla **5** 800
frames **11** 374
frontispieces **30** *487*
gem-engraving **5** 811–12; **12** *256*
gems **5** *808*; **7** *513*
gold **5** *808*; **7** *513*
Gospel books **5** 800, 801, 802; **13** 20, *20*
hardstones **14** 170
herbals **14** 432
initials (manuscript) **5** 801, *804*; **15** 848; **21** *729*; **31** *226*
ivory **9** 3; **22** *520*
ivory-carvings **4** IV2; **5** 809–11*, *809*, *810*, *811*; **11** 636
jewellery **17** 519
leather **5** 807
manuals **5** 800, 801
manuscript illumination **5** 800–805*; **6** 564; **13** *20*; **19** 827; **20** *337*; **31** 773, *773*
commentaries **18** 187
France **9** 686; **31** *226*
Germany **12** *381*, 382
manuscripts **5** 800–805*; **20** 330; **28** *303*
marble **5** 794, *796*
metalwork **5** 805–9*; **23** *538*
miniatures (manuscript illumination) **2** *221*; **4** *5*; **5** *801*, *804*; **9** *253*; **11** *151*; **21** 637; **30** *166*
monasteries **5** 794–5, 800; **19** *698*
mosaics **5** 799*; **12** 485
narratives **22** *520*
ornament **23** 537
painting **5** 797*; **12** 381–2
wall **5** 796, 797–8*
Germany **5** *799*
Italy **5** *798*
Switzerland **22** 385
patronage **12** 471
pearls **7** *513*
pilasters **5** 796
plaques **5** *811*
portraits
author portraits **2** *836*; **30** *166*, *487*
medallion **30** *487*
painting **5** 798
Prayerbooks **5** 804
Psalters **5** 800, 803
quartz **5** 811
reliquaries **5** 806, 807–8, *808*; **10** *115*; **26** 144–5*
revetments **5** 794
rock crystal **5** 811–12*; **12** *257*; **26** 485
Sacramentaries **5** 800
scriptoria **5** 800
scripts **6** 483; **28** *303*, 305
sculpture **5** 796–7*
Germany **12** 398
relief **5** *796*, 796–7
Carolingian—cont.
shrines (i) (cult) **5** 807
silver **5** 806; **7** *534*; **10** *115*
silver-gilt **5** *807*
spolia **5** 794
statuettes **5** *806*
stucco **5** 796
thrones **30** 776
title-pages **31** 48
westworks **5** 795, *795*; **7** 264–5; **12** 363; **33** *107*
see also:
CHARLEMAGNE, Holy Roman Emperor
CHARLES THE BALD, Emperor
IRMINGARD, Empress
LOTHAIR I, Emperor
LOTHAIR II, King Lotharingia
LOUIS THE PIOUS, Emperor
PEPIN THE SHORT, King
Carolingian *renovatio see* RENOVATIO
Carolis, Adolfo De *see* DE CAROLIS, ADOLFO
Carolis, Livio de, Marchese **5** 812*
Carolsfeld, Johann Veit Schnorr von *see* SCHNORR VON CAROLSFELD, JOHANN VEIT
Carolsfeld, Julius (Veit Hans) Schnorr von *see* SCHNORR VON CAROLSFELD, JULIUS (VEIT HANS)
Carolsfeld, Ludwig Ferdinand Schnorr von *see* SCHNORR VON CAROLSFELD, LUDWIG FERDINAND
Carolus-Duran **5** 812–13*; **11** 547, 672; **16** 17; **19** 767
dealers **30** 425
groups and movements **26** 55
patrons and collectors **4** 656; **29** 536
pupils
Belleroche, Albert (Gustavus) de, Count **3** 642
Boutet de Monvel, (Louis-) Maurice **4** 589
Casas (i Carbó), Ramon **5** 909
Cox, Kenyon **8** 85
Farquharson, Joseph **10** 813
Fujishima, Takeji **11** 821
Garstin, Norman **12** 166
Maro, Henri and Jules **14** 188
Mann, Alexander **20** 276
O'Conor, Roderic (Anthony) **23** 346
O'Meara, Frank **23** 437
Robinson, Theodore **26** 474
Sargent, John Singer **27** 839
Schuffenecker, (Claude-) Emile **28** 171
Stanisławski, Jan (Grzegorz) **29** 539
Van de Velde, Henry **31** 875
studio **29** 856
works **5** *813*; **19** 381, *381*
Caron, Adolphe-Alexandre-Joseph **3** 870
Caron, Antoine **5** 813–14*; **11** 533; **19** 257
collaboration **30** 659
groups and movements **11** 262, 266
patrons and collectors **31** 850
works **5** *814*; **10** 130; **13** 878; **16** 856; **24** 133
Caron, Martin **2** 91; **25** 79
Carona, Marco da *see* MARCO DA CARONA
Carondelet, Ferry, Abbot of Montbenoît **1** 571; **3** 305, 873
Carondelet, Jean **26** 745
Carondelet Diptych **11** 440
Caronesi **6** 18; **31** 440
Caroni, Ambrogio **11** 191; **14** 171; **21** 22, 529
Caroni, Stefano **11** 191; **14** 171; **21** 22, 529
Caronia, G. **11** 63
Carora **32** 167
Caroselli, Angelo **5** 815*
attributions **5** 695
pupils **18** 870; **24** 26
Caroselli, Carlo **5** 815
Carosio, Giovanni Battista **28** 219
Carothers, W. H. **30** 542
Caroto, Gian Francesco **5** 815–16*; **32** 343
attributions **5** 815, 816
collaboration **5** 816
pupils **3** 37; **5** 31, 816; **15** 167
works **5** 815
Caroto, Giovanni (Battista) **5** 816*; **27** 820
attributions **5** 815
collaboration **5** 816
pupils **5** 617; **32** 347
works **5** 815, *816*; **27** 820
Carouge **30** 144
Carove, Carlo **5** 817*; **29** 690
patrons and collectors **14** 288
works **29** 840; **30** 85, *93*
Carove, Giovanni **5** 817; **29** 690, 840
Carpaccio, Benedetto **5** 817, 823*; **8** 855; **29** 46
Carpaccio, Pietro **5** 817
Carpaccio, Vittore **5** 817–23*; **16** 662, 665; **32** 191
architecture **32** 191
attributions **22** *237*
collaboration **3** 656
copies **22** 351
drawings **5** 823; **26** 363
frames **11** 377, 382
interior decoration **16** 659; **32** 220
paintings **16** 711; **32** 160
architectural **2** 340; **23** 486
portraits **5** *820*
religious **3** 876; **5** *818*, *819*, *820*; **7** 564, *564*; **9** 21, 263; **16** 659, 660; **20** 424; **24** 638; **30** 780, *781*; **31** 703
friezes **26** 222; **29** 859; **32** 224
plaquettes **25** 18
topographical **31** 154
vedute **32** 110
patrons and collectors **3** 670; **14** 869
Campana (di Cavelli), Giampietro, Marchese **5** 536
Celotti, Luigi, Abbot **6** 151
Contarini, Antonio **7** 775
Correr, Teodoro **7** 895
Scuola di S Orsola (Venice) **13** 824
Thyssen-Bornemisza, Heinrich, Baron von **30** 795
Vendramin, Andrea **32** 155
pupils **21** 904
restorations by others **24** 343
teachers **3** 356
workshop **32** 160
Carpeaux, Jean-Baptiste **4** 306; **5** 824–6*; **11** 563, 659; **29** 343
assistants **32** 865
collaboration **2** 843; **30** 32
groups and movements **26** 500; **28** 345, 346
methods **30** 499
prizes (artists') **24** 171
pupils **11** 297
sculpture **11** 563, 565; **24** 141
busts **5** 304, *826*
reliefs **5** *825*; **10** 745; **26** 137
statuettes **29** 574
teachers **9** 447
Carpegna, Ambrogio, Conte **4** 434; **5** 826–7*; **25** 383
Carpegna, Guido Orazio Gabrielli di, Conte di Falconieri *see* FALCONIERI, GUIDO ORAZIO GABRIELLI DI CARPEGNA, Conte di
Carpegna, Nolfo di **2** 451
Carpegna, Ulderico, Cardinal **4** 434; **5** 827
Carpenter, Andrew **5** 827*; **18** 902; **23** 253; **29** 862
Carpenter, Arthur **31** 634
Carpenter, Charles E. **25** 666
Carpenter, Frederick **4** 482
Carpenter, George W. **17** 626
Carpenter, James **5** 827
Carpenter, Jane Henrietta **5** 827
Carpenter, Margaret Sarah **5** 827*; **12** 33
Carpenter, R(ichard) C(romwell) **5** 828*
pupils **22** 230; **33** 134
works **4** 808, 810; **14** 746
Carpenter, Richard Herbert **5** 828
Carpenter, William **5** 751, 827
Carpenter, William Hookham **5** 827
Carpenter Center for the Visual Arts *see under* CAMBRIDGE (MA; USA) → Harvard University
carpenters **20** 560
Anglo-Saxon **2** 64
Britain **20** 567
Egypt, ancient **9** 820, *820*, *821*
Fiji **11** 67
Germany **12** 420
Greece, ancient **13** 394
Japan **17** *49*, 51–2
Spain **29** 312
Carpenters' Company **19** 592
carpenters' guilds *see under* GUILDS → types
Carpenters Mountains
sculpture **16** *879*
Carpentier, Alejo **8** 233
Carpentier, Antoine-Mathieu Le *see* LE CARPENTIER, ANTOINE-MATHIEU
Carpentier, Eugène **3** 549; **5** 828*
Carpentier, Marie Charles Edouard **8** 618
Carpentier, Mathieu Le *see* LE CARPENTIER, MATHIEU
Carpentière, Andries *see* CARPENTER, ANDREW
Carpentras
Arc de Triomphe **31** 369
Bibliothèque Inguimbertine **11** 673
Cathedral of St Siffrein **3** 841; **26** 603
Hôtel Dieu **9** 399
synagogue **17** 545
carpentry **28** 498
see also WOODWORK
Carpentry and Building **24** 432
carpets **5** 828–42*; **6** 388; **14** 425
display **9** 30–31*
historical and regional traditions
Afghanistan **1** 209*; **16** 466
Albania **1** 544–5, *545*
Algeria **16** 486
Anatolia, ancient **2** 437
Armenia (Europe) **2** 437–9*
Austria **2** 825
Azerbaijan **2** *438*, 901–2; **16** 481, 483
Belgium **16** 466
Berber **16** 486, *487*
Britain **5** 839, 841*; **16** 466
Bulgaria **5** 161
Byzantine **9** 666
Canada **5** 587–8
Central Asia **16** 468
Central Asia, Western **6** 186, 248, 252–4*; **24** 298, *298*
Islamic **16** 466, 469, 484–5*
Turkmenistan **6** *253*, 254
China **7** 51, *67*, 67–8*; **16** 466
Coptic **5** 834; **7** 827
Early Christian (*c*. AD 250-843) **9** 666
Egypt **9** 666; **16** 466, 468, *472*; **28** 716
England **5** *836*, 837–9*, *838*, *839*, *840*, 840–41*, *841*; **10** 273, 276, 279, 357–8*, *358*; **16** 472
carpets
historical and regional traditions—cont.
France **5** 835–7*, *837*, 839–40*, 841*; **11** 651*; **27** 894–6
Islamic **16** 466
17th cent. **5** I; **27** *895*
19th cent. **11** *651*
Germany **12** 468–9*; **14** 65
Indian subcontinent **5** 829; **15** 681–4*
Deccan **15** 684
Gujarat **15** 682
Islamic **16** 466, 476*, 485*
Kashmir **15** 681
Mughal **5** 833; **15** 682–4*, *683*
Punjab **15** 684
Rajasthan **15** 684
Sind **15** 681
Iran **5** 829, 830, IV; **9** 492; **15** 899; **16** 466, *467*, 469, 474–5*, *475*, 476, *482*, 482–4*
Safavid **16** 474
Timurid **16** 474
16th cent. **5** 833
Iraq **16** 468
Ireland **5** 841
Islamic **16** 123, 124, 428, 429, 466–70*, 472–3*, 476*, 480–81*, *480*
Afghanistan **16** 466
Algeria **16** 486
Azerbaijan **16** 483
Belgium **16** 466
Berber **16** 486
Britain **16** 466
Central Asia **16** 468
Central Asia, Western **16** 466, 469, 484–5*
China **16** 466
commentaries **16** 468
Egypt **16** 466, 468, *472*
England **16** 472
France **16** 466
Indian subcontinent **16** 466, 476*, 485*
Iran **5** IV; **16** 466, *467*, 469, 474–5*, *475*, 476, *482*, 482–4*
Iraq **16** 468
Kurdistan **16** 483–4
Morocco **16** 486, *487*
North Africa **16** 473, 485–7*
Ottoman **5** II; **16** 470–72*, *471*, 476–9*
Romania **16** 466
Spain **16** 430, 466, 468, 471
Syria **16** 466
Tajikistan **16** 466
Tunisia **16** 486
Turkey **5** II; **16** 430, 466, 469, *470*, 470–72*, *471*, 476–9*
Turkmenistan **16** 466
United States of America **16** 466
Uzbekistan **16** 466
Kazakhstan **17** 867–8
Kurdistan **16** 483–4
Kyrgyzstan **18** 569
Morocco **16** 486, *487*
Nepal **22** 791
Netherlands, the **22** 900*
North Africa **16** 473, 485–7*
Ottoman **5** II; **16** 470–72*, *471*, 476–9*; **28** 716
Pakistan **23** 802*
Peru **5** 829
Poland **25** 131, *132*
Portugal **25** 316
Romanesque **14** 65
Romania **16** 466
Rome, ancient **26** 855
Sasanian **16** 469
Scotland **5** 830, 839; **28** 248, 252
Siberia **16** 467
Spain **5** 833–5*, *834*, *835*; **8** 252; **29** 297, 298, 347–8*
Islamic **16** 430, 466, 468, 471

carpets
historical and regional traditions
Spain—cont.
15th cent. **29** *347*
Syria **16** 466; **28** 716
Tajikistan **16** 466
Tibet **30** 836–7*
Tunisia **16** 486
Turkey **2** 439; **5** 829; **18** 234; **31** 455
Islamic **16** 430, 466, 469, *470*, 470–72*, *471*, 476–9*
Ottoman **16** 470–72*, *471*, 476–9*
Turkmenistan **6** *253*, 254; **16** 466; **31** 459–60*
Ukraine **31** 564
United States of America **5** 832, 839; **16** 466
Uzbekistan **16** 466
Yuncu **16** 478
materials
canvas **5** 830, 831
cotton **5** 829, 830; **6** 253; **15** *683*; **16** 466, 473
dyes **5** 834
felt **10** 874; **16** 466
fibres **5** 832
gold **5** 836
hair **5** 830; **16** 466
inscriptions **16** 467
jute **5** 829, 830, 840
linen **5** 831
mosaics **16** 466
silk **5** 829, 831; **6** 253; **7** *67*, 68; **16** 466, 473, 474, *475*; **28** 716
silver **5** 836
wool **5** 829, 830, 831; **9** 490
Central Asia, Western **6** 248, 253, *253*; **24** *298*
China **7** 68
Finland **11** *109*
France **5** 836, I; **27** *895*
Indian subcontinent **15** *683*
Iran **5** IV
Islamic **16** 466, *467*, *470*, *471*, *472*, *478*
Nepal **22** 791
Poland **25** *132*
Spain **29** *347*
Turkey **5** II; **16** *478*
Turkmenistan **5** III
techniques
appliqué **16** 466
dyeing **5** 832
embroidery **5** 830–31*; **10** 358
knotting **5** 828–9, *829*, 831, 832; **10** 357–8, *358*; **14** 65; **24** *298*
mechanical tufting **5** 832
needlework **5** 830–31*
printing **5** 832
warp-printed **5** *839*
weaving **5** *829*, 829–30, *830*, 831–2, *831*, *832*; **10** 358; **16** 466, 476–7, 478–9
types
Afshar **16** 484
animal **16** 470, *470*
Arraiolos **2** 495
Axminster **5** *832*, 832; **10** 358
Bakhtiari **16** 484
Baluch **16** 484
Bellini **16** 471
Brussels **5** 831, *831*, 839, 840; **10** 358
Chenille **5** 831
Chichaoua **16** 486
Compartment **16** 473
Crivelli **16** 471
Deventer **22** 900
Dragon **2** 437–8; **16** 479–80, *480*
Faraghan **16** *483*, 484
flijs **16** 486
Gandja/Karabagh **16** 481
Garden **12** 77, *77*; **16** 475
Gördes **16** 478, *478*
carpets
types—cont.
Gripper Axminster *see* Jacquard Axminster
Heriz **16** 483
Holbein **5** 834
Imperial Axminster **5** 832
Ingrain **5** 830; **28** 266
Jacquard Axminster **5** 832
Kazakh/Borchaly **16** *481*, 481
Kidderminster **5** 830, 839; **10** 358
kilims *see* KILIMS
Kirakos **2** 438
Kirşehir **16** 478
Konya **16** 469
Kuba **16** 481
Lâdik **16** 478
Large-pattern Holbein **16** 471
Lilihan **16** 484
list **5** 830
Lotto **16** 471, *471*
Mamluk **5** 401; **16** *472*, 472–3, 486
Memling **16** 471
Milâs **16** 478
millefleurs **15** 684
moquette *see* Brussels
Mucur **16** 478
Ottoman Court **16** 473
Para-Mamluk **16** 473
Patent Axminster *see* Chenille
picture-format **15** 682
Polonaise **16** 475; **25** 131
prayer rugs **5** III; **15** 683, 684; **16** 467, *478*
Qashqa'i **16** 484
qtifs **16** 486
row *see ṣaff*
Royal Axminster **5** 832
ryers **5** 829
ryijys **5** 829, 841; **11** 109, *109*, 110–11; **27** 316
ṣaff **16** 467
Sanguszko **16** 475
Scotch **5** 830; **28** 266
Scotch *see* Kidderminster
Serabi **16** 483
Shemakha *see* Kuba
Small-pattern Holbein **16** 471
Smyrna **22** 900
Spool Gripper Axminster **5** 832
Sultanabad **16** 483
table **14** 425
tanchras **16** 486
tapestry *see* Venetian
tile pattern **15** 684
Transylvanian **16** 472
Turkoman **16** *484*, 484–5
Union **5** 830
Ushak **5** II; **10** 357; **16** 471–2
Vase **16** 475
Venetian **5** 830; **10** 358
warp-printed **5** 832*, *839*
Wheel **5** 834
Wilton (Wilts) **5** 831, *831*, 839, 840; **10** 358
Ziegler **16** 483
see also MATS; RUGS
Carpi
Cathedral of S Pietro **24** 531
S Maria
Chapel of S Martino **1** *554*
Carpi, Aldo **5** 842*; **8** 161; **9** 201
Carpi, Anton Maria da *see* ANTON MARIA DA CARPI
Carpi, Berangario da **1** 841
Carpi, Carlo Giuseppe **12** 559
Carpi, Francisco Scibec de *see* SCIBEC DE CARPI, FRANCISCO
Carpi, Giovanni Francesco Donella da **1** 765
Carpi, Girolamo da **3** 89; **5** 842–3*; **11** 4; **25** 736; **26** 769, 770
collaboration **11** 76; **12** 162; **25** 736
copies **28** 38
Carpi, Girolamo da—cont.
patrons and collectors **10** 523, 524; **11** 5; **22** 6; **24** 833; **26** 813
pupils **11** 76
works **4** 311; **5** *843*; **11** 4
Carpi, Riccardo da **1** 767
Carpi, Rodolfo Pio da, Cardinal **13** 541; **26** 768
Carpi, Scibec de **11** 400; **19** 692
works **19** *692*
Carpi, Tommaso da **5** 842; **10** 523
Carpi, Ugo da **5** 843–4*
collaboration **24** 199
works **6** 569; **25** 622, VI; **26** 229, 809; **31** 43; **32** 199; **33** 366, 367
Carpignano, SS Cristina and Marina **9** 581; **26** 484
Carpineta, S Maria **24** 32
Carpini, Piano **30** 476
Carpinoni, Domenico **29** 410
Carpio (family) **1** 528; **22** 21
Carpio, Diego del **4** 262; **18** 777
Carpio, García Avellaneda y Haro, Garcia, Conde de Castrillo *see* CASTRILLO, GARCÍA AVELLANEDA Y HARO, Conde de
Carpio, Gaspar de Haro y Guzmán, 7th Marqués del **2** 170; **5** 844–5*; **32** 706
collections **22** 472; **25** 664; **26** 245
medals **11** 130
paintings **29** 353; **32** 131
Carpio, Luis Méndez de Haro y Guzmán, 6th Marqués del **5** 844*; **11** 872; **14** 8; **32** 706
Carpio, Mario del **4** 260
Carpioni, Giulio **5** 845–6*; **16** 675
Carpoli, C. **2** 853
Carpy, Francisque de **32** 582
Carr, Alwyn Charles Ellison **10** 336; **25** 885
Carr, (M.) Emily **5** 846*
groups and movements **5** 567; **32** 414
works **5** *846*
Carr, Emily, Art Gallery *see under* VICTORIA (CANADA)
Carr, Francis **28** 300
Carr, Henry **12** 837
Carr, John **5** 846–7*
architecture
country houses **10** 233, 279
hospitals **23** 453; **25** 293
law courts **18** 887; **33** 543
mausolea **20** 868
stables **6** 66; **14** 808
town halls **2** 617
patrons and collectors **1** 675; **7** 758; **9** 392
Carr, Robert **1** 648; **5** 847
Carr, Robert, 1st Earl of Somerset **5** 847*
collections **10** 363
paintings **14** 806; **23** 326
sculpture **5** 764
Carr, Thomas **23** 333
Carr, William Holwell **5** 71, 847–8*; **10** 369; **19** 588
Carrà, Carlo (Dalmazzo) **5** 848–9*; **8** 604; **11** 843; **16** 680; **24** 448
collaboration **7** 557
groups and movements **25** 6, 358
Divisionism **9** 41; **16** 679
Futurism **4** 199; **11** 863–5, 866; **20** 426; **21** 527; **25** 5; **27** 445
Pittura Metafisica **31** 852
Razionalismo **10** 821
Valori Plastici **31** 852
patrons and collectors **7** 782; **20** 97, 848
pupils **8** 161; **9** 201
works **5** *848*; **7** 557; **16** 681; **22** 332; **28** 793; **29** 670
Carracci (family) **5** 849–51*; **21** 759
attributions **6** 114; **7** 312
collections **25** 384
Carracci (family)—cont.
copies **21** 609
drawings **9** 92
methods **24** 493
patrons and collectors **2** 51; **4** 304; **5** 311; **9** 755; **14** 144; **19** 124; **23** 777; **26** 280; **31** 306, 525; **33** 345
pupils **9** 88; **10** 746
reproductive prints by others **2** 709; **3** 294, 309; **8** 763; **25** 77; **32** 689
works **9** 706; **20** *446*
Carracci, Agostino **1** 103; **4** 277; **5** 849, 850, 856–8*, 866; **9** 7; **16** 667, 669, 779; **26** 770
attributions **26** 839
collaboration **5** 852, 853
copies **21** 497
engravings **6** 114; **10** 390
etchings **26** 229
patrons and collectors **4** 567; **5** 850; **8** 481; **10** 525, 811; **11** 739; **26** 838; **27** 693
pupils **3** 32; **18** 730; **26** 196
reproductive prints by others **3** 851; **10** 487; **21** 496; **30** 804; **31** 268
works **4** 309; **5** 442, 755, 850, *857*; **6** 25; **7** 308; **9** 222; **10** 477; **11** 52; **16** 714; **30** 668; **32** 356
writings **1** 178
Carracci, Annibale **1** 103; **4** 277; **5** 755, 849, 850, 858–69*; **9** 7, 88; **16** 665, 667, 669, 671, 779; **25** 284; **26** 770, 773
assistants **1** 534; **9** 88; **30** 230
attributions **5** 857; **6** 488; **21** 830
collaboration **5** 852, 853, 857, 858; **7** 312; **16** 670
copies **10** 818; **11** 744; **21** 497
drawings **5** 755, *866*; **9** 222; **16** 669
engravings **10** 390
frames **11** 404
methods **5** 898
paintings
allegorical **1** 659
altarpieces **16** 669; **27** 496
frescoes **5** *863*; **7** 383; **13** 676; **15** 87, 137; **16** *669*, 670, 714; **22** 414; **23** 294, 577, 680
genre **5** *859*; **12** 288, 289; **22** 686
history **14** 583
landscape **5** *861*; **18** 708, *709*
literary themes **30** 358
mythological **22** 414; **26** 839
pietàs **5** *860*
religious **1** 596; **5** *862*; **11** 387; **24** 777; **25** 640
patrons and collectors **10** 365
Alfonso IV, 9th Duke of Modena and Reggio (*reg* 1658-62) **10** 527
Angeloni, Francesco **2** 42; **3** 673
Aumale, Henri-Eugène-Philippe-Louis de Bourbon, Duc d' **23** 523
Bellori, Giovanni Pietro **3** 673
Borromeo (family) **16** 562
Bourbon del Monte, Francesco Maria, Cardinal **4** 567
Boyle, Richard, 3rd Earl of Burlington and 4th Earl of Cork **4** 610
Brienne, Louis-Henri, Comte de **4** 807
Brydges, James, 1st Duke of Chandos **5** 65
Carr, William Holwell **5** 848
Cesare, 6th Duke of Modena and Reggio (*reg* 1597-1628) **10** 525
Créquy, Charles de Blanchefort de **19** 238
Crozat, Pierre **8** 209
Damery, Chevalier de **8** 481
Carracci, Annibale
patrons and collectors—cont.
Egerton, Francis, 3rd Duke of Bridgewater **9** 755
Einden, van den (family) **10** 115
Esterházy, Miklós, Prince (1817-94) **10** 531
Everdingen, Allart van **10** 660
Faesch, Johann Jakob **10** 753
Farnese, Odoardo, Cardinal **5** 850; **10** 811; **26** 838–9
Filomarino, Ascanio, Cardinal **11** 81
Guise, John **10** 365; **13** 837
Herrera, Giovanni Enriquez de **8** 9
Howard (ii), Frederick, 5th Earl of Carlisle **14** 808, 809
Howard (i), Thomas, 2nd Earl of Arundel **14** 806
Joachim Murat, King of Naples (*reg* 1808-15) **22** 338
Lancellotti, Orazio, Cardinal **18** 689
Louis XIV, King of France (*reg* 1643-1715) **4** 552
Lubomirski, Henryk **19** 752
Mariette, Pierre-Jean **20** 417
Meynier, Charles **21** 412
Orléans, Philippe II de Bourbon, 2nd Duc d' (1674-1723) **23** 515
Petty, William **24** 572
Poniatowski, Stanisław, Prince **25** 213
Resta, Sebastiano **26** 245
Richelieu, Louis-François Armand-Jean Vignerod du Plessis, Duc de (1629-1715) **26** 349
Rogers, Samuel **26** 541
Ruffo, Tommaso, Cardinal, Archbishop of Ferrara **27** 316
Sampieri (family) **27** 693
Sannesio, Giacomo, Cardinal **27** 764
Seignelay, Jean-Baptiste (-Antoine) Colbert, Marquis de **7** 546
Serra, Giovan Francesco, Marqués di Cassano **28** 479
Simonelli, Niccolò **28** 754
Skippe, John **28** 819
Suttermans, Giusto **30** 41
Tallard, Marie-Joseph d'Hostun, Duc de **30** 274
Tarnowski, Jan Feliks, Count and Waleria **30** 345
Waldegrave, William, 1st Baron Radstock **32** 774
Weddell, William **33** 20
pupils **3** 32; **6** 113; **18** 730; **28** 61
reproductive prints by others **25** 210
Bartolozzi, Francesco **3** 308
Bartolozzi, Gaetano (Stefano) **3** 309
Beinaschi, Giovan Battista **3** 521
Bisschop, Jan de (1628-71) **4** 96
Cesi, Carlo **6** 362
Chasteau, Guillaume **6** 502
Couvay, Jean **8** 77
Goltzius, Hendrick **12** 881
Guillain, Simon, II (1618-54) **1** 465
Jode, Pieter de (i) (1570-1634) **17** 599
Lombart, Pierre **19** 562
Mattioli, Lodovico **20** 849
Mignard, Nicolas **21** 496
Neeffs, Jacob **22** 717
Panneels, Joannes **24** 15
Pò, Pietro del **25** 55
Pond, Arthur **13** 300
Rousseau, Jacques (1630-93) **27** 264
Sadeler, Jan, I (1550-1600) **27** 502

Carracci, Annibale
reproductive prints by others—cont.
Sadeler, Raphael, I (1560/61-d c. 1628/32) 27 503
Siegen, Ludwig von 28 671
Simon, Pierre (c. 1650-1710) 28 751
Traballesi, Giuliano 31 268
Vispré, François-Xavier 32 621
restorations by others 20 375
sponsorship 26 773
Carracci, Antonio 5 849, 870*
collaboration 5 864, 867; 26 196
patrons and collectors 24 399; 25 872
pupils 31 885
works 26 840
Carracci, Francesco 5 849
Carracci, Giovanni Antonio 5 849
Carracci, Gobbo dei see BONZI, PIETRO PAOLO
Carracci, Ludovico 1 103; 5 849, 851–8*; 16 667, 669, 779; 21 526; 26 770
assistants 4 830; 6 114
attributions 12 53; 31 884
collaboration 5 857; 6 361; 28 38
patrons and collectors 5 850; 9 755; 10 525; 11 739; 14 877; 19 238; 27 316, 693; 31 322
pupils 1 533, 626; 5 858; 12 53; 20 597; 26 196; 27 893
reproductive prints by others 5 444
restorations by others 29 892
works 5 852, 853, 855; 9 222; 11 393; 16 669; 27 160; 30 358
Carracci, Paolo 5 849
Carracci Academy see BOLOGNA → academies → Accademia degli Incamminati
Caracciolo, Luciano 30 176
Carraciolo, Pietro 30 649
carracks 28 611
Carradori, Francesco 6 8; 16 705
works 29 705
carragheen 24 55
Carrand, Jean-Baptiste 5 870; 16 774
Carrand, Louis 5 870–71*; 12 712; 16 774
Carrand Diptych 11 398
Carrand Triptych, Master of the see GIOVANNI DI FRANCESCO (DEL CERVELLIERA) (i)
Carranza, Antonio José 31 229; 32 173, 180
Carraquiri, Nazario 5 871*
Carrara 26 876
marble 26 865, 876, 876, 889; 29 702
see also under MARBLE → types
S Maria Nova 16 747
Carrara, Alberto Maffiolo da see ALBERTO MAFFIOLO DA CARRARA
Carrara, da (family) 7 243; 13 747; 23 752
Carrara, Fina see FINA BUZZACARINA, Lady of Padua
Carrara, Francesco, Cardinal 5 872
Carrara, Francesco I da, Lord of Padua see FRANCESCO I, Lord of Padua
Carrara, Francesco II da, Lord of Padua see FRANCESCO II, Lord of Padua
Carrara, Giacomo, Conte 3 772; 5 872*; 16 773
Carrara, Giacomo II, Lord of Padua see GIACOMO II, Lord of Padua
Carrara, Ubertino da, Lord of Padua see UBERTINO, Lord of Padua
Carraresi see CARRARA, DA
Carraresi, Eugenio 28 319
Carrarino, Il see BOLGI, ANDREA
Carrasco, Ted 4 265; 5 872–3*
Carrasquila, Isabel de 31 808
Carré, Charles 7 605; 21 4
Carré, J. B. L. 2 450
Carré, Jean 10 316
Carré, José P. 31 758
Carré, Louis 1 10, 438
Carreaud de Rosemond, Mme 18 576
Carré de Montgeron, Louis-Basile 26 248
Carrée, Antoine 16 906
Carrenhof, Jacobus 1 811; 22 891
Carreño, Andrés 5 873
Carreño, Fernando 4 784; 7 492; 18 681
Carreño, Mario 5 873*; 6 598; 18 834; 27 155
Carreño, Omar 5 873*
Carreño de Miranda, Juan (fl before 1614) 5 873
Carreño de Miranda, Juan (1614-85) 5 873–5*; 9 5; 20 66; 29 281
collaboration 11 491; 26 436–8; 31 89
patrons and collectors 4 378; 10 530; 14 10, 190; 17 673; 21 125; 27 607
pupils 5 343; 6 343; 17 586; 27 331
teachers 8 254; 26 560
works 5 874, 875; 13 732; 21 125
Carrera, Augusto Font y see FONT Y CARRERA, AUGUSTO
Carrera, Francesc, the elder (1797-1862) 29 338
Carrera, Francesc, the younger (1832-81) 29 338
Carrera, José Antonio Jimeno y see JIMENO Y CARRERA, JOSÉ ANTONIO
Carrera, Josep 29 338
Carrera, Laureano Jimeno y see JIMENO Y CARRERA, LAUREANO
Carrera, Manuel José 8 232
Carrera, Vicente Jimeno y see JIMENO Y CARRERA, VICENTE
Carrera, Vito 23 265
Carrera Ceiling Co. 23 64
Carreras 10 98
Carreras (family) 33 358
Carreras, Augusto Font i see FONT I CARRERAS, AUGUSTO
Carreras, Mariano 29 306
Carreras, Rafael 29 322
Carrère, John Merven 5 875–6*; 20 19
Carrère & Hastings 5 875–6*; 26 111
assistants 8 652
collaboration 29 648
staff 11 807; 20 889; 27 173; 28 628
works 11 774; 14 787; 19 319; 23 40, 41, 41; 27 532; 32 892
Carrest, Simon du 31 147
Carretto, Cardinal 29 25
Carrey, Georges 2 510
Carrey, Jacques 5 876*
groups and movements 13 608
patrons and collectors 23 178
works 2 680; 13 455
Carrhae see HARRAN
Carriacou Museum 2 153
carriage clocks see under CLOCKS → types
Carrick, Alexander 28 243
Carrick, William 5 876–7*; 24 672
Carrickfergus (Co. Antrim)
Castle 16 7
St Nicholas 16 20
Carrick Fox, Ethel see FOX, ETHEL CARRICK
Carrickmacross (Co. Monaghan) 16 34; 18 590, 593
Carrick-on-Suir (Co. Tipperary), Manor House 16 22
Carrier 22 546, 656
Carrier, A. see CARRIER-BELLEUSE, ALBERT-ERNEST
Carrier, David 4 24; 25 362
Carrier, Willis 28 831
Carriera, Angela 16 780
Carriera, Giovanna 16 780
Carriera, Rosalba 5 877–8*; 22 86; 24 340; 26 841; 32 194, 195; 33 308
patrons and collectors 13 301
Augustus III, King of Poland (reg 1733-63) 1 633
Boyle, Richard, 3rd Earl of Burlington and 4th Earl of Cork 4 610; 13 301
Conti, Stefano 7 780
Dezallier d'Argenville, Antoine-Joseph 8 845
Mariette, Pierre-Jean 20 417
Medici, Ferdinando de', Grand Prince of Tuscany (1663-1713) 21 30
Piot, Eugène 24 838
Poniatowski, Stanisław, Prince 25 213
Strange, John 29 746
Tallard, Marie-Joseph d'Hostun, Duc de 30 274
Vassal de Saint-Hubert, Jean-Antoine-Hubert 32 75
Walpole, Robert, 1st Earl of Orford (1676-1745) 32 824
Watelet, Claude-Henri 32 898
Zanetti, Anton Maria (Girolamo) (i), Conte (1680-1767) 33 613
pupils 16 780; 19 796
reproductive prints by others 3 309; 10 770; 19 216
works 5 878; 9 216, 224; 11 460; 16 676; 21 642; 24 242, IV
Carrier-Belleuse, Albert-Ernest 5 878–80*; 21 697
assistants 8 896; 10 770; 26 509; 27 636
collaboration 10 771; 11 622
furniture 11 599
groups and movements 26 191, 500; 28 345
jewellery 17 III2
patrons and collectors 23 794
pupils 6 550; 19 271
sculpture 11 565
architectural 3 76
group 30 496
monuments 8 599
mythological 5 879; 30 500
porcelain 10 311; 19 398; 28 524
portraits 30 495
statuettes 29 574, 575; 30 499
Carrière, Ernest 5 880
Carrière, Eugène 5 880–81*; 19 489
collaboration 20 603
groups and movements 28 341; 33 379
pupils 14 294; 17 826; 22 136; 25 752; 28 597
works 5 880; 19 490
Carriès, Jean (-Joseph-Marie) 5 881*; 11 567
Carrigaline Pottery 16 29
Carrig-Rohane Shop 11 498
Carrillo, Alfonso, Cardinal and Archbishop of Toledo 5 882; 7 345
Carrillo, Lilia 5 881*; 10 866
Carrillo de López, Graciela 18 832
Carrillo Gil, Alvar 21 395
Carrillo y Salsedo, Stefano 1 731
Carrington, Dora (de Houghton) 5 881*
Carrington, Fitzroy 18 161
Carrington, Leonora 5 882*; 10 469; 21 388
groups and movements 30 22
patrons and collectors 16 892; 20 832
Carrington, Robert John, 2nd Lord see JOHN, ROBERT, 2nd Lord Carrington
Carrión, Bartolomé 3 470; 7 604; 24 501; 31 427
works 7 604
Carrión, Jesús Martínez see MARTÍNEZ CARRIÓN, JESÚS
Carrión, Juan de 5 882*; 28 368
Carrión, Pedro de 5 882
Carrión de los Condes 5 882–3*; 29 258
Church of Santiago 5 883*
sculpture 26 608, 608
S María del Camino 5 883*; 26 607
S Zoilo 26 607
tomb of Alvar Fernández Podestat 13 104
Carritt, (Hugh) David (Graham) 5 883–4*
Carr Lynch Associates 19 843
Carrogis, Louis see CARMONTELLE, LOUIS DE
Carroll, Kevin 1 228, 431
Carroll, Lawrence 23 50
Carroll, Lewis 5 884*
illustrated works 4 363; 14 677; 18 863; 30 465
patrons and collectors 12 486
Carroll's Cigarette Factory see under DUNDALK
Carrolup 1 63
Carron Iron Co. 3 741; 11 119; 16 60; 28 255, 263
Carrouges, Jacques le Veneur, Comte de 1 535
Carrthach, Cormac mac, King of Desmond see MAC CARRTHACH, CORMAC, King of Desmond
cars 1 494; 10 136; 20 594
historical and regional traditions
Caribbean Islands 5 754
Germany 15 824
United States of America 10 136; 15 822–3, 824–5; 20 593, 594
models
Cadillacs 15 824; 20 594
Fiat Ritmo 15 826
Model T Ford 8 802; 15 822; 20 593, 594
Oldsmobile (1926) 10 136, 136
Volkswagen Beetle 15 824, 825; 20 594
Cars, Jean-François 4 512, 514; 5 884
Cars, Laurent 5 884*
assistants 19 144; 25 549
pupils 3 463; 6 527; 11 171, 173; 12 634; 24 480
teachers 30 344
works 3 639; 17 668; 25 895
Carsalade du Pont, de, Bishop of Perpignan 27 566
Carse, Alexander 5 884–5*
Carshore, Andrew Nayfield 7 666
Carsoli, S Maria in Cellis 9 152
Carson, Roberto Dávila see DÁVILA CARSON, ROBERTO
Carstairs, Carroll 18 161
Carstairs, Charles 18 161
Carstens, Asmus Jakob 5 885–6*; 12 479
groups and movements 26 735
pupils 12 310; 18 201
works 5 886; 12 392
Carstensen, Claus 8 736
Carswell, John 16 550; 20 188
Carta, Natale 5 555; 7 528, 841; 30 364
Cartagena (de Indias) (Colombia) 5 886–7*; 7 601, 603; 21 573
Calle de la Factoria 7 604
Casa de Huéspedes Ilustres 7 607
Casa del Marqués de Valdehoyos 7 604
Church of the Third Order 7 604
houses 5 887
Cartagena (de Indias) (Colombia)—cont.
La Tenaza 7 604
museums
Museo Antropológico 5 887
Museo de Arte Moderno 5 887
Museo de Arte Religioso 5 887
Museo Colonial 5 887
Museo Histórico 5 887; 7 612
Museo Naval del Caribe 5 887
Museo del Oro y Arqueológico 5 887
Palacio de la Inquisición 7 604
S Pedro Claver 7 604
stadium 7 606
Cartagena (Spain) 29 329
Cartagena, Alonso de, Bishop of Burgos see ALONSO DE CARTAGENA, Bishop of Burgos
Cartagena Portalatín, Aida 9 119
Cartago 7 601, 603; 8 15, 15, 16
Basílica Nuestra Señora de Los Angeles 8 16
Church of Guadalupe 7 605; 8 16
Nuestra Señora del Carmen 8 16
Cartari, Giulio 3 838
Cartari, Mario
works 26 823
Cartari, Vincenzo 1 656; 5 887–8*
works 15 83, 87; 22 414
Cartaro, Mario 5 888*
Cartaud, Jean-Silvain 5 888*
collaboration 7 773
patrons and collectors 8 208, 210
works 19 213; 23 514, 516
Carte Géométrique de la France 30 26
cartel clocks see under CLOCKS → types
Cartellier, Pierre 5 888–9*; 11 671, 885
collaboration 27 547
patrons and collectors 4 303; 11 562
pupils 8 770; 16 877; 19 125; 22 465; 24 554; 27 309; 28 506
works 6 516, 517; 8 764; 11 562; 21 411; 24 554; 26 112, 113
cartellini 5 889*; 19 440
Cartellino Painter 32 39
Carter, Amon, Museum see under FORT WORTH (TX)
Carter, Amy 5 889
Carter, Asher 27 137; 33 174
Carter, Benjamin 33 226
Carter, Drake & Wight 5 273
Carter, Edward 24 390
Carter, Howard 2 300; 5 889–90*; 10 80, 82; 20 118
excavations 1 770; 10 81, 98; 30 693
Carter, John (fl c. 1770) 10 333
Carter, John (1748-1817) 5 890*
groups and movements 23 210
patrons and collectors 21 620
reproductive prints by others 3 329
works 2 319; 10 673; 22 211; 25 766; 27 628
Carter, John (fl 1850s) 17 516
Carter, John Coates 28 349
Carter, Morris 12 147
Carter, Norman 32 770
Carter, Owen 29 764
Carter, Samuel John 5 889
Carter, Sibyl 31 661
Carter, Sidney (1880-1956; Canada) 24 739
Carter, Stabler & Adam see POOLE POTTERY LTD
Carter, Sydney (1874-1945; South Africa) 4 155
Carter, Thomas (d 1757) 27 242
Carter, Thomas (d 1795) 2 541; 8 587
Carter, Tony 21 621
Carter, William 5 889
Carteret, John, Baron 31 871

cartes-de-visite see under CARDS → types
Cartesianism *see* DESCARTES, RENÉ
Carthage 1 *376*, 377; 5 890–93*, *891*; 9 *507*, *510*; 24 641; 25 732; 31 427
amulets 25 734
Antonine Baths 5 891; 7 354; 26 872, 919, 921
mosaics 27 67
aqueducts 26 919
architecture 9 560; 25 732; 26 921; 31 426
Baptistery 9 572
Basilica Dermech I 9 570
Basilica Dermech II 9 570
Bir al-Knissia 7 301
Borj Jedid 7 354
circus 5 891
coins 27 97
copper 25 734
Damous al-Karita 7 255; 9 535, 597; 20 520
Douimes 7 301
eggs 25 735
faience (i) (glass) 1 879; 24 645
figurines 24 643; 25 733
Gens Augusta altar 27 31
glass 9 645; 25 734
ivory-carvings 24 643; 25 734
jewellery 25 735
kilns 25 733
limestone 25 *733*
masks 25 733
mosaics 5 427; 9 *569*, 570; 27 63
moulds 25 734
odeion 23 350
pendants (jewellery) 25 *735*
razors 25 734
rock crystal 26 485
Ste Monique 25 733
sarcophagi 10 592
seals 24 645; 25 734
stamps 9 655
stelae 5 *892*; 25 733, *733*; 29 613
stucco 27 72
terracottas 25 733
trade 10 592
tusks 25 734
villa of Dominus Julius 9 570
Carthage Treasure 9 655; 27 84
Carthusian Order 3 709; 5 893–5*; 7 231
architecture 5 894*, *894*; 7 453; 21 840–41*, *841*
iconography 5 895*
patronage 5 895*
sculpture 28 861
Cartier 10 346; 15 702; 17 529
designers 14 697; 18 659
exhibitions 11 635
production 17 113; 28 741
Cartier, George-Etienne 5 586
Cartier, Louis 2 521
Cartier-Bresson, Henri 5 896–7*
groups and movements 5 659; 6 603; 20 99
works 5 *897*; 24 677; 30 488; 31 706
Cartlidge, Charles, & Co. 31 637
cartography 20 361–7
China 20 361
Italy 18 635
Japan 20 361–2
Mesoamerica, Pre-Columbian 21 235
Portugal 26 125; 32 98
see also ATLASES; MAPS; TOPOGRAPHY
Carton 29 835
Carton, Enguerrand *see* QUARTON, ENGUERRAND
cartonboard *see under* PAPER → types
Carton House (Co. Kildare) 12 127
interior decoration 16 23
Saloon 18 634
Carton House (Co. Kildare)—cont.
stone-carvings 16 26
cartonnage 10 10, 12, 13–14*; 22 *284*
carton-pierre 24 61
cartoons (drawings) 5 898–9*
historical and regional traditions
Austria 18 *130*
Belgium 3 606, 607
Etruscan 10 617
France 6 *536*
Germany 23 *315*
Greece, ancient 13 556
Italy 5 *898*; 9 102–3; 10 617; 16 757; 25 *902*; 26 *565*
types
petit patron 24 554*
uses
façade decoration 10 740
frescoes 11 763
mosaics 13 556; 22 156, 163
painting 5 898
stained glass 23 *315*; 29 498
tapestries 30 310
wall paintings 32 805
cartoons (comic strips) 5 758; 25 653; 26 222, 742
see also COMIC-STRIP ART
cartoons (satirical) 19 62; 27 871, 872
cartouches 5 899*; 20 364–5, *365*
Buddhism 6 777
China 6 777
Egypt, ancient 5 899
Germany 18 43
Islamic 16 215, 216, 260
Italy 5 *899*
Japan 17 220
Spain 16 215, 216
carts 21 691
carts, cult of *see* CULT OF CARTS
Cartuja de las Cuevas 29 329
Cartwright, Francis 27 626
Cartwright, John Solomon 4 884
Cartwright, Julia 5 899–900*
Cartwright, Richard *see* ROYLEY, RICHARD
Cartwright, Thomas 10 263; 13 614
Cartwright, William 5 900*; 13 618
Caruana, Pietro Paolo 5 900*; 20 213
Caruana, Raffaele 5 900
Caruaru 4 *705*
Carucci, Jacopo *see* PONTORMO, JACOPO DA
Caruelle, Jean-Baptiste 1 641
Caruelle d'Aligny, Théodore *see* ALIGNY, THÉODORE CARUELLE D'
Carus, Carl Gustav 5 901*
collaboration 12 393
groups and movements 9 239
patrons and collectors 12 853
works 5 *901*; 11 462
Carvajal, Cardinal (*fl* 1502) 4 647
Carvajal, Alberto de 32 100
Carvajal, Bernardino, Cardinal (*fl* 1512) 19 785
Carvajal, Francisco de 5 362
Carvajal, Gaspar de 29 192, 193
Carvajal, Girón de 25 23
Carvajal, Gutierre de Vargas, Bishop of Plasencia 12 722
Carvajal, Jacinto de 29 194
Carvajal, Javier 29 322
Carvajal, Luis de 5 902*; 21 858; 29 280
collaboration 5 735; 10 503; 29 278
works 10 502; 22 695; 31 89
Carvajal, Manuel Dositeo *see* DOSITEO CARVAJAL, MANUEL
Carvajal y Lancaster, José 5 902*; 23 413
Carvalheira, Rosendo (Garcia de Aráujo) 5 902*; 19 892; 25 294
Carvalho, Eugenio dos Santo e *see* SANTOS E CARVALHO, EUGENIO DOS
Carvalho, Flavio de (Resende) 4 718; 5 902–3*
Carvalho, Genaro de 4 724
Carvalho, José Caetano de *see* CAETANO DE CARVALHO, JOSÉ
Carvalho, José Leandro de 26 413
Carvalho, Léon 4 655
Carvalho, Pedro Alexandrino 4 637; 5 903*; 19 464; 25 297
Carvalho, Zulmiro de Neves *see* NEVES CARVALHO, ZULMIRO DE
Carvalho e Melo, Sebastião José de, 1st Marquês de Pombal *see* POMBAL, SEBASTIÃO JOSÉ DE CARVALHO E MELO, 1st Marquês de
Carvalho Franco, Luiz Roberto 19 271
Carvalho Mange, Ernest Robert de *see* MANGE, ERNEST (ROBERT DE CARVALHO)
Carvalho Monteiro, António Augosto de 20 275
Carvallo, Cota 24 509
Carvallo, Feliciano 5 904*
Carvallo, Joachim 32 561
Carvallo, Teresa 24 509
Carvão, Aluísio 4 719
Carver, Martin 30 43
Carver, Robert 16 14
carving
historical and regional traditions
Africa 1 303, 428
Alaska 22 573–4, 575–6
Bali (Indonesia) 15 812
Canada 22 574–5
Central Asia, Eastern 6 313
Central Asia, Western 16 248
China 7 16–17, 18–19, 58, *85*; 18 601
Dorset culture 22 575
Eskimo 22 573, 575
France 11 587, *587*, 589, 595
Indian subcontinent 4 *793*, 794
Islamic 16 248, 395
Japan 17 298, *301*; 18 601
Makonde (Mozambique) 1 428
Maori 20 355–6
Marquesas Islands 20 463
Mongolia 21 878, 879–80
Native North Americans 22 573–82*, 585–6*
Prehistoric art 25 544–5*; 27 365
Russia 27 365
Ryūkyū Islands 18 601
Scythian 6 212
Spain 29 *317*
Vietnam 32 480
Yoruba 1 239
materials
alabaster *see* ALABASTER-CARVINGS
bamboo *see* BAMBOO-CARVINGS
bone *see* BONE-CARVINGS
glass 7 *85*
gourds 7 141; 29 159
horn *see* HORN-CARVINGS
ivory *see* IVORY-CARVINGS
jade *see* JADE-CARVINGS
lacquer 7 16–17, 18–19
lapis lazuli 7 91
malachite 7 91
peach stones 7 141
rock *see under* ROCK ART → techniques
roots 7 142
shells 28 581
steel 21 878
stone *see* STONE-CARVINGS
turquoise 7 91
walnuts 7 141
wood *see* WOOD-CARVINGS
types
chip 21 326; 32 618
carving
types—cont.
intaglio 15 878*; 26 132
rilievo schiacciato 9 128; 26 136
uses
boats 24 625
book covers 30 836
brick 4 769, *793*, 794
cabinets (ii) (furniture) 11 *587*
canoes 28 611
cassoni 6 6–7*, *7*
chairs 11 587
chess sets 6 557
frames 11 374
furniture 11 589, 595
glass 7 84–6
gold 12 869
gourds 1 303
hardstones 14 168–9*
lacquer 6 313; 17 298, *301*; 18 601–3*
metalwork 21 326*
mother-of-pearl 22 203–4
pottery 16 395
sculpture 26 595
ships 28 611–14
see also SHIP-DECORATION
tables 29 *317*
tiles 16 248
towers 15 812
woodwork 16 500
Carwick Painter 13 734
Cary, F. S. 8 706; 20 493; 29 47; 32 800
Cary, Guy Fairfax 25 235
Cary, Henry 31 590
Cary, Lewis 4 480
Cary, William 12 815
Caryanda, Scylax of *see* SCYLAX OF CARYANDA
caryatids 5 904–6*; 10 741
England 5 *905*
France 11 *558*; 13 *227*
Greece, ancient 5 904*, *904*; 13 415; 23 477
Rome, ancient 5 904*; 27 29, 30, 31, 39
see also ATLANTIDS
Caryll, 3rd Viscount Molyneux of Maryborough 16 *14*
Carysfort, John Proby, 1st Earl of *see* PROBY, JOHN, 1st Earl of Carysfort
Carzoni, Giovanna 26 307
Casa, Antonio dalla *see* ANTONIO DALLA CASA
Casa, Giovanni della 8 504
Casa, Nicolò della 5 906*
Casabella 16 649, 650; 24 448; 26 15
contributors 24 484
staff 2 727; 20 189; 23 764; 26 536; 27 192
Casablanca
Bank of Morocco building 22 128
Dar Lamane Complex 22 128
Ecole des Beaux-Arts 22 129
fortifications 21 585
Gardens of Résidence Moulay Youssef 22 129
Great Mosque of Hassan II 22 128, *128*
Law Courts 22 128
New Medina 22 128
Post Office 22 128
Sijelmassi House 22 128
Casablanca Group 3 625; 22 129
Casa Candina 25 703, 704
Casada, Giovanni 23 843
Casa de la Caridad 29 348
Casa de las Américas 24 435
Casademunt Torrens, José 21 815; 26 533
Casado del Alisal, José María 5 906*; 23 440; 29 284
Casa Gardé e Guyeté 25 308
Casa Grande (AZ) 22 566
Casagrande, Marco 9 754; 10 546; 14 895
Casal, Conde de 29 308
Casala *see* K'ASAGH
Casale, Villa Imperiale 22 160
Casale, Francesco 22 384
Casale, Giovanni Vincenzo 4 633; 30 518
Casa Leiria e Nascimento 25 318
Casale Monferrato
Cathedral of S Evasio 26 690
Santuario di Crea
altarpiece 1 *530*
Theatre
paintings 12 *22*
Casali (family) 16 736
Casali, Andrea 5 906–7*; 31 341
Casali, Antonio 24 535
Casali, Giovanni Vincenzo 7 332; 18 820
Casali, Governatore of Lorento (*fl* 16th cent.) 5 414
Casalini, Lucia 31 164
Casalvecchio Siculo, SS Pietro e Paolo d'Agrò 28 655
Casamari Abbey 13 51; 16 627
paintings 28 *473*
sculpture 13 98
Casamitjana, Antonio Caba y *see* CABA Y CASAMITJANA, ANTONIO
Casanova, Antonio 3 896; 23 756
Casanova, Francesco 5 907–8*
attributions 18 804
patrons and collectors 8 481
personal collection 5 908
pupils 14 799; 19 728; 23 202; 30 369
works 3 461; 5 907
Casanova, Giovanni Battista 5 908*
pupils 11 241; 26 98
reproductive prints by others 11 241
works 5 907
Casanova, Giovanni Giacomo 5 907
Casanova, Henrique 4 639; 28 781
Casanova, Juan de, Cardinal *see* JUAN DE CASANOVA, Cardinal
Casanovas i Roy, Enric 29 329, 886
Casanova y Ramos, Vicente 3 272
Casante (family) 4 21
casapanca 29 8
Casa Piola 24 835, 836
Casaranello, S Maria della Croce 3 190
Casares
houses 32 *291*
Casari (family) 22 107
Casaril, Wanda 16 758; 32 205
Casarín, Alejandro 32 571
Casario, Lazzaro 4 280
Casarriera, Marqués de 29 306
Casas, Francesc Xavier Nogués i *see* NOGUÉS I CASAS, FRANCESC XAVIER
Casas, José Planas *see* PLANAS CASAS, JOSÉ
Casas, Mariano Ignacio de las 25 815
Casas (i Carbó), Ramon 3 219; 5 509, 909*; 25 348
interior decoration 29 308
works 5 *909*; 29 285
Casas Grandes 5 909–10*; 22 *544*
pottery 22 603, *603*, 604
Casas i Bardés
works 29 *320*
Casasola, Agustín Víctor 5 910*
Casasola, Gustavo 5 910
Casa Sonia 8 658
Casasopra, Paolo 25 212
Casas y Nóvoa, Fernando 5 911*; 29 341
groups and movements 7 289
works 18 598; 26 251; 27 *794*, 794; 29 271

Casaubon *see* KERSEBOOM
Casbert, John **10** 291; **19** 592
Cascading Coiffure, Master of the **19** 744
 works **1** *325*
Cascais, Nossa Senhora da Assunção **25** 297
Cascalls (family) **3** 309
Cascalls, Jaume **5** 911*; **13** 106; **29** 289; **30** 347
Cascella, Andrea **5** 912; **21** 528
Cascella, Maria Cesarini *see* SFORZA, MARIA CESARINI
Cascella, Pietro **5** 911–12*; **21** 528
Cascella, Tommaso **5** 911; **21** 528
Cascina, S Cassiano in Settimo **26** 623
Câscioarele **30** 434
Casdin-Silver, Harriet **14** 690; **28** 204, 829
Čaše, Ivan *see* ZASCHE, IVAN
case, lower *see* LOWER CASE
Case, Nicolas La *see* CASA, NICOLÒ DELLA
Casé, Paulo Hamilton **5** 912*
case, upper *see* UPPER CASE
casein **1** 155; **5** 912*; **25** 23, 27
 consolidants **7** 747
 encaustic paintings **10** 196
 fixatives **11** 142
 painting **22** *63*
 paints **5** 912; **9** 39; **32** 898
 panel paintings **24** 4
 plywood **1** 156
 sealants **25** 174
 secco paintings **28** 338
 stucco **29** 813
case leather *see* LEATHER → types → bag
Casella, Alessandro **29** 831; **31** 443
Casella, Alfredo **21** 471
Casella, Battista **27** 648
Casella, Francesco **10** 524; **31** 443
Casella, Giovanni Battista **27** 878
Casella, Pierleone **26** 416
Casella, Pompeo **31** 443
Caselli (da Parma), Cristoforo **5** 913*; **24** 193
 teachers **3** 667
 works **5** *913*
Caselli, Giovanni **5** 671
casemates *see under* WALLS → types
Casembrood, Agnes **21** 102
Casembrot, Abraham **4** 249
casement mouldings *see under* MOULDINGS → types
Casentino, Jacopo del *see* JACOPO DEL CASENTINO
Caserta **16** *621*
 gardens **12** 115, 119
 maiolica **4** 562
 Palazzo Reale **5** 914*, *914*; **16** 645; **31** 894–5
  Castelluccio Reale **29** 832
  fountains **11** 345
  frescoes **11** 136; **21** 850; **27** 201
  furniture **16** 730
  interior decoration **16** 717
  models **3** 921
  paintings **4** 323; **11** 817
  Sala di Astrea **16** 645
  Sala di Marte **16** 645, 719, *720*; **23** 678
  staircases **29** 525; **31** *895*
  tapestries **11** 136; **22** 481
  Throne Room **16** 645
 Reggia *see* Palazzo Reale
Caserta Vecchia, Cathedral of S Michele **16** 626; **26** 626
cases (bags) **14** 426; **21** 878
Casey, Edward Pearce **28** 889
Casey, J. & D. **9** 321
Casey, Thomas L. **28** 889
Cashel (Co. Tipperary) **5** 914–16*; **16** *5*
 Cathedral **5** *915*, 916
Cashel (Co. Tipperary)—cont.
 Cormac's Chapel **5** 915–16; **16** 7; **26** 592, *592*, 618
  sarcophagus **16** 19
  wall paintings **16** 13; **26** 652
 High Cross **26** 618
 Round Tower **5** *915*
 sculpture **5** 916*
cashels *see* IRELAND → forts
cashmere **16** 430; **30** 539*
Casier Archéologique et Artistique de Paris **4** 332
Casigliani **32** 501
Casildo España, José **12** 57
Casilear, George **5** 916
Casilear, John William **5** 916–17*
Casillas, Andrés **21** 381
Casillas, Martín **13** 730
Casillis, David Kennedy, 10th Earl of *see* KENNEDY, DAVID, 10th Earl of Casillis
Casimir *see* KARPFF, JEAN-JACQUES
Casimir III, King of Poland *see* KASIMIR III, King of Poland
Casin d'Utrecht **31** 844
Casini, Antonio, Cardinal **9** 94; **16** 844; **20** 536; **28** 677, 681
Casino, Dyraaba **32** 308
casinos (i) (garden) **5** 917*; **19** *371*
casinos **5** 917*; **18** *821*
Casio, Gerolamo **3** 303; **4** 284; **20** 905
Casipoora Creek **30** 14
caskets **5** 917–18*; **6** 559; **14** 426
 historical and regional traditions
  Anglo-Saxon **2** *81*
  Belgium **3** 581
  Buddhism **18** 351, 352
  Byzantine **5** 917; **9** *521*, *651*
  Early Christian (*c*. AD 250–843) **5** 917, *917*
  Egypt, ancient **10** 52
  England **2** *81*; **5** 918; **10** *342*
  Etruscan **10** 635
  France **5** 917, 918
  Indian subcontinent **15** 696
  Islamic **16** 365, 524, 525, *525*
  Italy **5** *917*; **10** 635; **14** *170*; **16** *746*; **24** *249*
  Korea **18** 351, 352
  Maya **21** 259
  Mesoamerica, Pre-Columbian **21** 259
  Netherlands, the **22** 890, *890*
  Rome, ancient **5** *917*
  Sicily **16** 525
  Spain **16** 524, *525*; **17** 516; **29** 302
  Sri Lanka **29** 471, *472*, 479
  Sweden **30** *108*
 materials
  alder **24** 248
  amber **1** 762; **29** 302
  bone **9** *521*, *651*
  brass **10** *342*
  bronze **5** 918
  coral **7** 835
  cornelian **10** 52
  ebony **14** *170*
  enamel **16** *745*
  faience (i) (glass) **10** 52
  faience (ii) (ceramics) **5** 918
  gold **10** 52; **18** 351, 352
  hardstones **14** *170*
  ivory **2** *81*; **5** 917; **9** *521*; **10** 52; **15** 696; **16** 524, 525, *525*, 799; **29** 471, *472*
  jet **17** 516
  leather **5** 918
  pastiglia **24** 248, *249*
  porcelain **5** 918
  rock crystal **16** *746*
  shells **21** 259
  silver **5** *917*; **22** *890*
  silver-gilt **16** *745*; **30** *108*
  steel **10** *342*
  wood **9** *521*
caskets—cont.
 types
  kaptorgas **25** 125
 see also BOXES
Caskey, J. **2** 406; **17** 874
Caskey, John L. **19** 227
casks **17** *357*
Caslav, Prince **28** 436
Caslon, William, IV **16** 360; **31** 497
Casma, Museo Regional de Casma Max Uhle **6** 348
Casnedi (family) **20** 95
Casnedi, Raffaele **5** 918*; **22** 83; **30** 277
Caso, Alejandro **21** 381
Caso, Alfonso **21** 253, 263, 737; **30** 452; **33** 618, 619
Caso, Margarita **21** 381
Casolani, Alessandro **2** 20; **4** 53; **27** 620
Casolani, Antonio **27** 447
Casolis, Pietro de *see* PIETRO DE CASOLIS
Casone, Antonio **3** 206; **26** 758
 works **5** *690*
Casone, Felice Antonio **2** 376; **27** 160
Casone, Giovanni Battista **11** 53
Casorati, Felice **5** 918–19*; **16** 680; **24** 448
 collaboration **27** 853
 groups and movements **25** 6
 works **5** *919*; **16** 758; **31** *445*, 446
Casotti, Antonio **29** 363
Caspar **1** 810
Caspar, Carl **30** 730
Caspari, W. H. **20** 400
Caspe Collegiate Church, tomb of Juan Fernández de Heredia **13** 106
Caspicara **5** 920*; **9** 712
casque **16** 797
Cass, Christopher **10** 263
Cass, Gilbert **12** 613–15*
 works **12** *614*
Cassadio, Luigi **2** 10
Cassagne, A. **2** 530
Cassai, Tommaso di Ser Giovanni di Mone *see* MASACCIO
Cassala *see* KASSEL
Cassana, Giovanni Agostino **7** 779
Cassana, Giovanni Francesco **5** 920; **18** 740
Cassana, Niccolò **5** 920*; **21** 30
Cassandra Painter **13** 531; **32** 37
Cassandre **5** 920–21*
 works **7** 653; **25** 349, *350*
Cassano, Cristoforo da *see* CRISTOFORO DA CASSANO
Cassano, Francesco **2** 731
Cassano, Giovan Francesco Serra, Marqués di *see* SERRA, GIOVAN FRANCESCO, Marqués di Cassano
Cassano Giustiniani, Andrea di *see* GIUSTINIANI (i), ANDREA DI
Cassar, Gerolamo **20** 211
Cassarino **20** 213
cassaro **6** 57
Cassas, Louis-François **5** 921*; **8** 542
Cassatt, Mary (Stevenson) **5** 921–3*; **17** 293; **25** 5; **31** 603, 664
 collaboration **20** 603
 frames **11** 417
 groups and movements **15** 151, 154, 155
 paintings **15** VIII
 pastels **5** *922*
 patrons and collectors **14** 244; **19** 756; **20** 142; **23** 882
 prints **2** 241; **9** 309; **20** *603*; **25** 607, 624
cassava paste **3** 378
Cassel *see* KASSEL
Cassel, Richard *see* CASTLE, RICHARD
Cassel earth *see under* PIGMENTS → types
Cassell, John **4** 9
Cassell and Co. **4** 366; **8** 864
Cassel Painter **13** 538
Cassel's (publishers)
 works **10** *135*
Casserio, Giulio **1** 842; **21** 6
cassetta frames *see under* FRAMES → types
Cassetti, Giacomo **20** 422
Cassian, John **7** 230; **9** 643; **20** 475
Cassie, James **1** 30
Cassignola, Giacomo **19** 372
Cassigoli, Pia **11** 194
Cassinari, Bruno **5** 923*; **7** 894; **11** 802; **21** 528
Cassington (Oxon), St Peter's **24** 577
Cassini, Giovanni **4** 53
Cassini de Thury, César François **30** 26
Cassini de Thury, Jacques **30** 26
Cassiobury Park (Herts) **10** 275
Cassiodorus, Flavius Magnus Aurelius **2** 319; **5** 923–4*; **20** 329
 works **2** 313; **10** 201
Cassioli, Amos **22** 384; **25** 567
Cassioli, Giuseppe **9** 159; **10** 893
Cassirer, Bruno **3** 800; **4** 366; **24** 444; **28** 342, 840
Cassirer, Ernst **28** 23
Cassirer, Paul **3** 801; **5** 924*; **6** 371, 384; **10** 102; **12** 472, 474; **18** 198; **20** 382; **21** 67; **25** 626
 groups and movements **28** 342, 343
 sponsorship **3** 242
 staff **26** 405
 works **7** 856; **12** 197, 805; **19** 490; **24** 223; **28** 840, 841
Cassirer Collection *see under* STANFORD (CA) → Stanford University
Cassis shells *see under* SHELLS → types
Cassiterides Islands **10** 624
Cassius **31** 58
cassocks **32** 387*
Cassola, Jacopo di *see* JACOPO DI CASSOLA
Casson, A. J. **5** 567; **13** 711
Casson, Conder & Partners **5** 513; **20** 238
Casson, Hugh (Maxwell) **5** 924–5*
cassoni **6** 1–7*, *1*, *2*, *3*, *4*, *7*, 560; **9** 14; **14** 426; **16** 722, *722*, *724*, 726; **22** 413
 materials
  pastiglia **6** 5–6*, *6*
  stucco **16** *722*
  walnut **6** 7, *7*; **16** *722*, *724*
 techniques
  carving **6** 6–7*, *7*
  gilding **6** 7, *7*
  painting **6** 1–5*, *1*, *2*, *3*, *4*
 see also CHESTS; SPALLIERE
Cassou, Jean **30** 262
Castagnary, Jules-Antoine **6** 9–10*; **15** 151, 157
 groups and movements **26** 53, 55
 works **6** 80; **22** 685, 687
Castagné, Jean **3** 20; **11** 514; **31** 206
Castagneto, João Batista **4** 717; **6** 10*; **13** 662
Castagnini, Bernardo **30** 649
Castagnino, Juan Carlos **6** 10*
Castagno, Andrea del **2** 17; **6** 10–15*; **9** 98; **16** 661; **26** 765
 assistants **20** 704
 collaboration **3** 99, 649; **4** 32; **9** 103; **12** 713
 methods **11** 184
 mosaics **12** 580; **22** 163; **32** 212
Castagno, Andrea del—cont.
 paintings
  frescoes **26** 184
   Cathedral of S Maria del Fiore (Florence) **6** *13*; **11** 198; **13** 676; **16** 659: **29** 565
   SS Annunziata (Florence) **6** *13*; **11** 204; **32** *805*
   S Apollonia (Florence) **5** 443; **15** 135; **16** 659, 660; **26** *184*
   S Egidio (Florence) **3** 99; **9** 98
   S Zaccaria (Venice) **32** 653
   Villa Carducci (Florence) **6** *12*; **16** 660
  panel **6** *12*
 patrons and collectors **6** 601; **7** 782; **9** 306; **14** 869; **21** 11; **24** 1
 personal collection **31** 516
 pupils **12** 713; **16** 847; **25** 160
 restorations by others **19** 677
 stained glass **11** 198; **29** 504; **31** 513
Castagnola, Villa Favorita **19** 782; **30** 795
Castagnoli, Ubaldo **13** 728
Castaigne, Guillaume **31** 834
Castaing, Madeleine **11** 584; **29** 246
Castaing, Marcel **29** 246
Castaldi, Giacomo **17** 598
Castaldo, Giovanni **1** 531
Castan, Gustave (Eugène) **6** 15*; **7** 434
Castañeda (family) **13** 104
Castañeda (*fl* 1815) **2** 405
Castañeda, Abdón **6** 29; **26** 302
Castañeda, Alonso Pérez de **27** 763
Castañeda, Consuelo **8** 234
Castañeda, José Luciano **21** 262, 384
Castanet, Bernard de, Bishop of Albi *see* BERNARD DE CASTANET, Bishop of Albi
Castanier, François **30** 298
Castañón, Joaquín **4** 262
Castayls, Jaime *see* CASCALLS, JAUME
cast collections *see under* COLLECTIONS → types
Casteelen, D. Van de *see* VAN DE CASTEELEN, D.
Casteels (family) **11** 227
Casteels, Peter **30** 890
Castel, (Louis) Bertrand **22** 380; **28** 203
Castel, Gaston **20** 472
Castel, Jeanne **10** 838; **27** 888
Castel, Jehan **12** 257
Castel, Moshe **17** 577, 579
Castelao, Alfonso Daniel **6** 16*; **29** 286
Castelar, Emilio **31** 827
Castelazzo, Villa Arconati **12** 119
 garden **12** *118*
Castelbarco, Guglielmo **28** 28; **32** 341
Castel Bolognese, Giovanni da *see* BERNARDI, GIOVANNI (DESIDERIO)
Castel d'Asso **10** 598
Castel del Monte **6** 16–17*, *17*, 57; **7** 383; **16** *621*
 architecture **16** 627
Castel Durante **14** 425; **16** *620*
 maiolica **6** 17–18*; **16** 733
Casteldurante, Giovanni Maria di **4** 664
Casteleijn, Pieter **25** 230
Castelfranco **31** 711
Castelfranco, Pietro Damini da *see* DAMINI, PIETRO
Castelfranco, Zorzi da *see* GIORGIONE
Castelfranco Altarpiece **12** 671, 672–3, *673*, 674, 676, 677; **26** 364; **27** 496

Castelfranco Veneto
Cathedral of S Liberale **25** 561
Palazzo Piacentini **25** 209
Palazzo Soranzo **25** 209
S Maria in Pieve **16** 705
Villa Soranzo **5** 617; **33** 631
Castel Fusano, Villa Chigi **7** 907; **27** 643
Castelgandolfo
Domitian's Villa **27** 72
Papal Palace **12** 533, 534
sculpture **27** 22
S Tommaso da Villanova **29** 830
Castelijn **22** 877
Castell, Robert **23** 860; **32** 553
Castellaccio, Santi **29** 830
Castellammare, Villa San Marco **26** 869
Castellamonte, Amedeo di **6** 19*
assistants **12** 163
collaboration **6** 18
patrons and collectors **6** 18; **28** 5, 10, 11, 13
works **12** 163; **17** 708; **31** 440; **32** 631
writings **28** 12
Castellamonte, Carlo di **6** 18–19*
assistants **6** 19
collaboration **6** 18
patrons and collectors **6** 18; **10** 526; **28** 5, 6, 7, 9, 10
works **6** *18*, 19; **13** 748, 749; **17** 707; **31** 440
Castellani (family) **6** 19–20*
works **10** 639; **12** 265, 867; **17** 527
Castellani, Alessandro **6** 19, 20*
personal collection **13** 542
works **6** *20*
Castellani, Alfredo **6** 20, 21
Castellani, Augusto **6** 19, 20–21*; **16** 752
personal collection **13** 542
Castellani, Enrico **6** 21*; **16** 682
collaboration **20** 352
groups and movements **10** 416; **26** 778
Castellani, Fortunato Pio **6** 19, 20*; **10** 639; **16** 752
works **16** *752*
Castellani, Giovanni Maria **7** 906
Castellani, Ludovico de *see* LUDOVICO DE CASTELLANI
Castellani Brooch **6** 20
Castellani Collection *see under* ROME → museums → Museo Nazionale di Villa Giulia
Castellani Painter **10** 614; **13** 508
Castellano, Giuseppe **3** 521; **23** 577
Castellano, Michele **28** 657
Castellanos, Carlos Alberto **31** 755
Castellanos, Juan de **7** 607, 611
Castellanos, Julio **6** 21*; **21** 388
Castellanos Balparda, Leandro **31** 755
Castellar, Jean Paul Lascaris de *see* LASCARIS CASTELLAR, JEAN PAUL
Castellare Crucifix Master **10** 403
castella urbana **27** 6
Castellazzo, Villa Arconati **2** 376; **32** 548
Castellazzo di Bollate, Villa Crivelli **12** 22
Castell Coch (S. Glams) **6** 61, *61*, 62; **13** 203; **32** 784, 788
Castellesi da Corneto, Adriano **1** 572; **31** 188
Castelletto (di Massa), Bernardino del *see* BERNARDINO DEL CASTELLETTO (DI MASSA)
Castelli (i) (Italy) **6** 21–2*; **16** *621*, 735
S Donato **16** 735
Castelli (ii) (family) **6** 22; **28** 733; **30** 887
Castelli, Alessandro **8** 6
Castelli, Andrea **6** 22
Castelli, Antonio **6** 22; **22** 918; **33** 279
Castelli, Bernardo **4** 430, 436
Castelli, Carlo **19** 269
Castelli (da Parma), Cristoforo *see* CASELLI (DA PARMA), CRISTOFORO
Castelli, Domenico **3** 97; **6** 22–3*; **19** 269
Castelli, Francesco (1599-1667) *see* BORROMINI, FRANCESCO
Castelli, Francesco (1655-92) **16** 562
Castelli, Johann-Jacob **5** 296
Castelli, Leo **6** 23*; **31** 665
Castelli, Matteo **3** 205; **6** 22*; **25** 97; **31** 312; **32** 879
Castelli, Michele **22** 918; **33** 279
Castelli, Pietro **22** 918
Castelli, Quirico **18** 467
Castelli, Toiny **6** 23
Castelli Graphics **6** 23; **12** 599
Castellin, Nicolas **24** 478; **33** 357
Castellini, Giovanni Zaratino **26** 416
Castello
Palazzo Isnardi
Mirror Salon **5** 349
Villa del Pozzino **12** 707
Villa di Castello **12** 116
fountains **11** 342; **31** *321*
garden **16** 696
Grotta degli Animali **13** 703; **16** 696
La Topaia **21** 29
paintings **11** 678
sculpture **1** 791; **12** 572; **18** 820
castello **6** 57
Castello (ii), Bernardo **5** 769; **6** 25–6*
assistants **5** 769
patrons and collectors **1** 595; **12** 763; **15** 147, 148; **28** 9; **29** 411
pupils **11** 14
reproductive prints by others **5** 857
works **5** 769; **30** 358
Castello, Elia **2** 781, 800; **27** 664
Castello (i), Fabrizio **6** 24–5*
collaboration **5** 411, 457; **13** 307; **30** 372
patrons and collectors **6** 23; **13** 922
teachers **13** 307
works **10** 503; **29** 339; **32** 620
Castello (i), Félix **6** 24, 25*; **29** 280; **32** 129
Castello, Filippo **18** 729
Castello, Giacomo da **6** 29*; **11** 871
Castello, Gian Antonio **30** 136
Castello (i), Giovanni Battista (*d* 1569) **6** 23, 24*
collaboration **5** 455, 457, 650; **8** 80; **29** 411
patrons and collectors **9** 172; **13** 922; **15** 147
pupils **13** 307
works **10** 499; **12** 281; **19** 806; **20** 72; **23** 539; **24** 107; **32** 620
Castello (ii), Giovanni Battista (1547-1637) **6** 25
Castello (i), Giovanni Maria **6** 24
Castello, Matteo (da) **13** 628; **24** 398; **32** 5
Castello, Michael **33** 275
Castello (i), Niccolò **32** 620
Castello (ii), Pietro (*fl* 1582-92) **6** 25
Castello, Pietro (*fl* 1606-26) **30** 136
Castello (ii), Valerio **6** 25, 26–9*; **15** 138
assistants **4** 89
collaboration **24** 835
patrons and collectors **3** 90; **23** 873
pupils **20** 94; **21** 145; **31** 293
Castello (ii), Valerio—cont.
teachers **11** 14, 53
works **6** *27*, *28*
Casteló, Vicente **6** 29–30*; **26** 299, 301, 302
Castello Coira *see* SCHLOSS CHURBURG
Castello della Manta **14** 422
Sala Baronale **16** 710, *710*
Castelló d'Empúries, Master of *see* AMPURIAS, MASTER OF
Castello di Belcaro **24** 533
Castello Italico de Mediolano, Franciscus de *see* FRANCISCUS DE CASTELLO ITALICO DE MEDIOLANO
Castellón **29** 364
Castellón, Federico **19** 491
Castello Nativity, Master of the **12** 711; **20** 642*, 704
Castello Reale di Racconigi **10** 644
Castello Sforzesco Plaque **28** 806
Castello Trebbio **24** 299
Castells, Esteban Rodríguez *see* RODRÍGUEZ CASTELLS, ESTEBAN
Castelluccio **6** 30*; **16** *621*; **25** *470*, 530
bone-carvings **28** 653
Castellum Tingitanum *see* CHLEFF
Castell y Bere **32** 781, 786
Castelnuovo, Giovanni **28** 683
Castelnuovo Berardenga Church
altarpiece **12** *714*
Castelo, Felix **26** 436
Castelo Branco, Museu de Francisco Tavares Proença **25** 318
Castel Porziano **27** 46
Castel Rodrigo, Manuel de Moura y Corte Real, 2nd Marqués de **4** 486; **6** 30–31*; **7** 394
Castel Roncolo **16** 710
Castel San Mariano **10** 626
Castel Sant' Angelo *see under* ROME
Castel Sant' Elia Abbey Church **1** 764; **26** 651, 657
Castelsardo, Master of **27** 836
Castelseprio **6** 31–2*; **9** *510*; **16** *618*
S Giovanni Evangelista **6** 31
S Maria Foris Portas **6** 31–2; **16** 654
wall paintings **6** *32*; **9** 575; **19** 549
Castelvetro, Giacomo **15** 87
Casterné de Noals **26** 642
casters (furniture) **31** 684
casters (vessels) **6** 32*; **8** 217; **10** 419; **29** *335*
see also CRUETS; SALTS
Casteyne, O. Van de *see* VAN DE CASTEYNE, O.
Castiel, Juan Pérez *see* PÉREZ CASTIEL, JUAN
Castiglioncello **10** 586
Castiglione, Baldassare **6** 38–9*; **11** *401*; **12** 278; **14** 867, 869; **25** *905*; **31** 742
patrons and collectors **7** 540; **19** 144
personal collection **14** 869; **25** 282; **31** 413
reproductive prints by others **3** 308; **19** 144
works **6** 569; **24** 90; **31** 740
on beauty **1** 178
translated **13** 298
Castiglione (Olona), Branda di, Cardinal **26** 827; **32** 103, 639
Castiglione, Camillo **2** 829
Castiglione, Cristoforo **12** 714
Castiglione, Franceschino **12** 714
Castiglione, Giovanni Benedetto **1** 659; **6** 32–7*; **16** 669
assistants **6** 37
attributions **4** 222
drawings **9** 215, 222
Castiglione, Giovanni Benedetto—cont.
etchings **10** 551; **16** *668*, 672
paintings **6** *33*, *34*, *36*; **11** 393; **16** 675; **24** 50
patrons and collectors **3** 90; **12** 913; **27** 521; **29** 411; **33** 613
prints **21** 895, *895*; **25** 616
pupils **6** 37
reproductive prints by others **33** 613, 697
teachers **11** 14; **23** 772
Castiglione, Giovanni Francesco **6** 32, 37–8*
works **6** *38*
Castiglione, Giuseppe (1688-1766) **3** 517; **6** 39–41*; **7** 120, 151; **17** 512, 513; **25** 783
collaboration **6** 818
patrons and collectors **25** 779
teachers **25** 416
works **6** *40*, 538, 811
Castiglione, Giuseppe (*fl* 1865)
works **22** *358*
Castiglione, Nicolaus **18** 431
Castiglione, Piero d'Albino da *see* PIERO D'ALBINO DA CASTIGLIONE
Castiglione, Sabba da **6** 41*
Castiglione, Salvatore **6** 32, 35, 36–7*
dealing **12** 913
works **6** *37*
Castiglione Colonna, Adèle d'Affry, Duchessa di *see* MARCELLO
Castiglione Olona
Baptistery **16** 659
frescoes **20** 557–8, *558*
Collegiata **20** 557
Castiglion Fiorentino **13** 163
Collegiata di S Giuliano
altarpiece **28** 365–6, *366*
Castiglioni (family) **16** 732
Castiglioni, Achille **6** 42*
Castiglioni, Enrico **6** 42*
Castiglioni, Giacomo **6** 42
Castiglioni, Giannino **6** 42*; **21** 533
Castiglioni, Livio **6** 42*; **25** 26
Castiglioni, Pier Giacomo **6** 42*; **25** 26
Castiglioni Monstrance **21** 529
Castile, Blanche of, Queen of France *see* BLANCHE OF CASTILE, Queen of France
Castile, Estefanìa, Countess of *see* ESTEFANÌA, Countess of Castile
Castile, Garcia III, Count of *see* GARCIA III, Count of Castile
Castilho, Diogo de **6** 42, 44*
assistants **6** 451
works **7** 531, *531*; **19** 139
Castilho, João de **6** 42, 43–4*
attributions **25** 300; **31** 179
patrons and collectors **2** 872
pupils **6** 44
works **3** 363, 534; **6** *43*; **25** 290, *290*, 291; **31** 101, 102, *102*, 178, 179
Castilho, Salomon del **30** 16
Castiliscar **26** 643
church **9** 596
Castilla (family) **29** 347
Castilla, Diego de **6** 44*
Castilla, Juan Alfonso Enríquez de Cabrera 9th Almirante de **29** 353
Castilla, Luís de **6** 44–5*; **14** 474
Castille, Janin de **4** 534
Castillo *see under* CHICHÉN ITZÁ
Castillo, Agustín del **6** 45
Castillo, Andrés **10** 154
Castillo, Antonio Cánovas del *see* KAULAK
Castillo (y Saavedra), Antonio del **6** 45–6*
pupils **1** 621; **31** 808
works **6** *46*; **11** 488, *488*
Castillo, Consuelo Méndez *see* MÉNDEZ CASTILLO, CONSUELO
Castillo, El **6** 46–7*; **25** *470*, 484, 487; **27** 780; **29** *258*
Castillo, Francisco de (*fl* 1621; Venezuela) **32** 178
Castillo, Francisco del (*fl* 1578; Spain) **13** 284; **29** 268
Castillo, Jorge **6** 47*
Castillo, José del **6** 47–8*; **29** 283
collaboration **12** 587
patrons and collectors **5** 871; **11** 218
reproductions in tapestry **10** 504
sponsors **5** 902
works **4** 362, 564
Castillo, Juan del **5** 619; **6** 48*; **22** 342
Castillo, Luis de **3** 471
Castillo, Marcos **6** 48*; **32** 175
Castillo, María Luisa Penne de *see* PENNE DE CASTILLO, MARÍA LUISA
Castillo, Mario **14** 716
Castillo, Monte *see* MONTE CASTILLO
Castillo (Guash), Teófilo **6** 48–9*; **24** 509, 517
Castillo, Tomás del **9** 712
Castillo de Garcimuñoz **8** 15
Castillo de Teayo **21** 200
Castillo Velasco, Fernando **6** 594
casting
historical and regional traditions
Buddhism **17** 320
Carolingian **5** 806
Central Asia, Eastern **6** 313
Central Asia, Western **6** 274; **16** 370
China **6** 725, 830–34*; **7** 98
Cyprus, ancient **8** 340
Egypt, ancient **12** 782
Germany **12** 454
Greece, ancient **13** *437*, 437–8*, *594*, 594–5
Indian subcontinent **4** *853*; **15** 414
Iran **16** 370
Islamic **16** 363, 370
Italy **27** *18*
Japan **17** 320, 321
Khurasan **16** 370
Mesopotamia **12** 782
Prehistoric art **25** 524
Rome, ancient **27** 17–18*, *18*
South America, Pre-Columbian **29** 211–12
Vietnam **32** 480
types
core-casting **5** 612
electrotype **10** 137*; **22** 28
hollow-casting **4** 850, 851; **10** 587; **17** 99, 101
lost-wax casting *see* LOST-WAX CASTING
open-mould **1** 288
sand **21** 322*; **28** 739; **30** 842
uses
bronze **4** 850, 851, 853–4
Carolingian **5** 806
China **6** 725, 830–34*
Greece, ancient **13** 435, *437*, 437–8*
Indian subcontinent **4** *853*; **15** 414
Islamic **16** 370
Vietnam **32** 480
candlesticks **5** 611
ceramics **6** 327, *327*
glass **12** 782–3*; **13** *594*, 594–5
gold **12** 865; **29** *211*
inscriptions **17** 321
iron **6** 725; **7** 98; **12** 454
jewellery **6** 274
medals **20** 917, 921
metal **21** 320–22*; **29** 211–12
metalwork **16** 363
sculpture **27** 17–18*, *18*
silver **28** 739

casting
uses—cont.
swords 2 452
waxes 33 2
Castings, Arthur 8 831
cast iron 16 50–54*; 21 319
historical and regional traditions
Austria 2 822
Belgium 3 575, 585
Britain 2 242; 28 874
Buddhism 7 98, 99
China 7 97, 98, 99–100; 16 50; 21 320
Buddhism 7 98, 99
Five Dynasties (AD 907-60) 7 99, *99*
Han period (206 BC-AD 220) 7 98
Northern and Southern Dynasties (AD 310-589) 21 715
Song period (AD 960-1279) 7 *100*
Zhou period (*c.* 1050-256 BC) 7 96, 97
Czech Republic 8 *386*, 416
England 10 236, 297, 748; 11 *119*; 16 52, *53*
Finland 30 284
France 3 524; 9 86; 11 522; 18 *582*; 30 671
Germany 3 793; 12 426
Hungary 15 9
Iran 16 *504*
Islamic 16 *504*
Netherlands, the 22 *860*, 894
Russia 14 222
Scotland 28 255, 263
Slovenia 28 863
Sweden 30 109, 110
United States of America 3 35; 12 221; 16 54; 31 257, *258*, 592, *592*; 32 *893*
uses
aqueducts 2 242
arches 3 793
architecture 3 35; 10 236; 11 522; 12 221; 16 51–3*, 54*; 18 *582*; 20 570; 26 18; 30 109, 284; 31 592, *592*
bells 7 98, 100
bridges 4 802*; 14 222; 16 *52*
columns 7 98
dolls' furniture 31 264
domes 3 524; 9 86; 32 *893*
façades 23 *39*
factories 10 748
furniture 3 585; 10 297; 12 426; 28 255
girders (beams) 28 874
maces 16 *504*
mills (industrial) 16 52
mirrors 21 715
monuments 22 *860*
moulds 7 97; 21 320
pagodas 7 98, 99
piers (i) (seaside) 24 747
ribs 3 524
roofs 10 236; 30 671
sculpture 7 98, 99–100, *99*, *100*; 8 *386*
stanchions 28 874
stoves 3 575
theatres 30 650
toys 31 257*, *258*
vaults (ceiling) 3 793
weapons 7 97
Castle, Len 6 63*; 23 69
Castle, Richard 6 63–4*
architecture 9 316–17; 16 8, 23
assembly rooms 2 617
colleges 9 323
country houses 3 276; 16 23; 19 63; 23 *861*; 25 402
follies 11 242
town houses 6 *64*
collaboration 4 70
groups and movements 23 860
teachers 24 305
Castle, Wendell 31 634; 33 328
Castle Acre Priory (Norfolk) 1 723; 2 292; 21 838
Castle Ashby (Northants) 8 45; 13 541; 23 295
Castle Balfour (Co. Fermanagh) 16 8
Castle Butte (MT) 22 592
Castle Campbell (Central) 31 230
Castle Coole (Co. Fermanagh) 16 8
furniture 16 27
interior decoration 16 24, *24*
Castle Cornet (Guernsey) 21 568
Castledermot (Co. Kildare) 16 19
Castle Drogo (Devon) 2 337; 6 62, *62*; 19 820
Castle Espie (Co. Down) 16 28
Castle Frome (Hereford & Worcs), St Michael 26 616
Castle Hedingham (Essex) 6 54, 64–5*; 10 *225*
keep 6 603
pottery 10 312
St Nicholas 9 155
Castle Howard (N. Yorks) 6 *65*, 65–6*; 8 47; 10 96, *225*, 232; 14 807–8; 23 812, 857; 30 361; 31 *858*, 858–9
Belvedere Temple *see* Temple of the Four Winds
gardens 5 827; 12 128; 19 622; 23 253
interior decoration 10 274
Mausoleum 14 257, *258*; 20 866; 25 766
metalwork 10 334
paintings 7 900; 10 785; 11 912; 13 301; 24 340; 29 803
sculpture 18 902
stucco 29 835
Temple of the Four Winds 24 290
Wray Wood 12 128
Castlemaine 2 *736*
Castlemaine, Richard Childe, Viscount *see* CHILDE, RICHARD, Viscount Castlemaine
Castlemaine, Richard Tylney, Viscount *see* TYLNEY, RICHARD, Viscount Castlemaine
Castlemaine, Roger Palmer, Earl of *see* PALMER, ROGER, Earl of Castlemaine
Castlemilk (Strathclyde) 28 230, *230*
Castlereagh, Robert Stewart, Viscount *see* STEWART, ROBERT, 2nd Marquess of Londonderry
Castlerigg (Cumbria) 25 *470*
stone circle 25 *505*
Castle Rising (Norfolk) 6 54
Castle 26 613
St Lawrence 26 613
Castle Rodengo 16 711
castles 6 49–63*; 21 545, 548, 561, 562–4; 23 806; 31 708, 710
historical and regional traditions
Armenia (Europe) 2 427
Balearic Islands 3 *106*
Belgium 3 *541*
Britain 6 62; 16 896
Central Asia, Western 6 199–200, 206
Islamic 32 *321*
Khwarazm 6 199
Sogdiana 6 200
Tokharistan 6 199, 200
Crusaders 6 58*; 18 421, *422*; 21 563–4
Cyprus 8 361
Czech Republic 8 *376*; 24 *463*; 25 *437*
Denmark 8 723–4, *724*; 14 *370*
England 6 *51*, *52*, *55*, 60–61; 10 226, 359; 21 561, 563, 564, *569*; 33 *249*, *250*
Gothic Revival 5 *194*
Romanesque 9 *203*; 10 227
castles
historical and regional traditions
England—cont.
15th cent. 30 *365*
17th cent. 6 *60*
18th cent. 12 *7*
19th cent. 27 *656*
20th cent. 6 *62*
France 6 *49*, *50*, *54*, 504; 21 *549*, 561, 563, 564
12th cent. 6 *512*
13th cent. 2 *49*; 8 40
15th cent. 31 *844*
Germany 6 57*; 33 88
Baroque 19 *780*
Renaissance 12 *367*
Romanesque 32 *883*
16th cent. 22 *918*
17th cent. 2 591
19th cent. 6 *62*
Gothic 13 53
Balearic Islands 3 *106*
Czech Republic 8 *376*
Italy 6 *17*; 13 64
Poland 20 *185*
Romania 14 *880*
Slovakia 4 *695*
Sweden 14 *368*
Hungary 5 *82*; 10 *544*
Ireland 6 61; 16 7–8; 21 564
Islamic 32 *321*
Italy 6 57*, 59; 21 564, *566*
Gothic 6 *17*; 13 64
14th cent. 11 *2*; 21 *515*
Japan 14 551; 17 22, 45, 46, 71, 83–6*, 95–6*, *95*, *96*; 21 595
Edo period (1600-1868) 14 *552*; 17 *86*; 22 *432*
Momoyama period (1568-1600) 21 828; 23 592
Khwarazm 6 199
Knights Hospitaller 3 *691*, 691–2; 6 *52*, 58; 18 421, *422*
Knights Templar 6 58
Lithuania 19 495
Luxembourg (country) 19 *826*
Netherlands, the 17 *884*; 22 822
Palestine 3 *691*
Poland 18 *431*; 20 *185*, 185–6; 25 96
Portugal 28 *499*
Romanesque 9 *203*; 10 227; 26 569–70; 32 *883*
Romania 14 *880*
Ryūkyū Islands 27 470
Scotland 6 60; 28 224, *230*; 29 *679*
Slovakia 4 *695*
Sogdiana 6 200
Spain 6 *58*, 58*
Mudéjar 7 *491*
14th cent. 23 *403*
15th cent. 18 *681*; 31 *181*
Sweden 14 *368*; 30 67, *67*, *68*
Switzerland 6 *602*
Syria 6 *52*; 18 421, *422*
Teutonic Order 20 *185*, 185–6; 30 535
Tokharistan 6 199, 200
Wales 6 *56*, 61; 21 564
Gothic 16 *896*
Norman Revival 23 *210*
13th cent. 5 *374*
19th cent. 6 *61*
restoration 27 656
types
concentric 6 56*; 8 277; 18 422, *422*; 19 616; 21 *564*
mock 6 58, 59
motte-and-bailey 6 52–3; 9 143–4
ring-works 6 53*; 21 547, 562
see also ARCHITECTURE → types → military; BARBICANS; CHÂTEAUX; DONJONS; FORTRESSES; TOWERS
castles, ships' *see* SHIPS' CASTLES
Castleton China Co. 31 639
Castletown House (Co. Kildare) 12 6, 127; 13 301; 16 14
architecture 16 8
furniture 16 26
interior decoration 11 430; 16 23, 24
Obelisk 11 242
stucco 18 634; 29 835
Castle Ward (Co. Down) 16 24
Castor (Cambs) 26 *905*
pottery 27 108, *108*
St Kyneburg 2 70; 26 613
Castorlo di Nanni 16 845
Castoro Francesco 6 139
castor oil *see under* OILS → types
castra *see* ROME, ANCIENT → forts
Castrén, Heikki 26 261
Castres, Edouard 6 66*; 24 19
Castri, John Di *see* DI CASTRI, JOHN
Castries Cathedral 2 148
Castril de la Peña 29 331
Castrillo, Conde de 5 844*; 29 303
Castrillo, Eduardo 24 620
Castriota, Giacomo 21 578
castro 25 536
Castro, Amílcar de 4 719; 6 66–7*
Castro, Angelo di 17 548
Castro, Antonio de 23 83
Castro, António Vaz de *see* VAZ DE CASTRO, ANTÓNIO
Castro, Casimiro 6 67*; 21 385
works 21 *402*
Castro, Constantino de 29 347
Castro, Damián de 6 67*; 7 846; 29 337
Castro, Felipe de 5 902; 6 67–8*
collaboration 29 293
pupils 20 77; 29 294
works 5 902
Castro, Fernando (Alvaro) de 6 68*
Castro, Fernando de, Casa Museu *see under* LISBON → museums
Castro, Fidel 18 243
Castro, Francisco de 8 268; 28 780
Castro, Francisco López de *see* LÓPEZ DE CASTRO, FRANCISCO
Castro, Guiomar de 6 452
Castro, João de 2 501; 9 40; 14 661; 28 780
Castro, João de Almeida e Mello e *see* ALMEIDA E MELLO E CASTRO, JOÃO DE
Castro, Joaquim Machado de *see* MACHADO DE CASTRO, JOAQUIM
Castro, José Damián Ortiz de *see* ORTIZ DE CASTRO, JOSÉ DAMIÁN
Castro (y Morales), José Gil de 6 68*, 596
works 6 *596*; 24 508
Castro, José María Fernández de *see* FERNÁNDEZ DE CASTRO, JOSÉ MARÍA
Castro, L. A. 5 900
Castro, Lorraine de 25 703
Castro, (Maria de) Lourdes (Bettencourt) 3 853; 6 68*; 8 15
Castro, Noé 19 84
Castro, Rodrigo de, Bishop of Cuenca 6 44
Castro, Tomás 11 493
Castro, V. de 12 43
Castro, Willys de 4 719
Castro Andrade y Portugal, Pedro Fernández de, Conde de Lemos *see* LEMOS, Conde de
Castro el Borgoñón, Juan de *see* JUAN DE CASTRO EL BORGOÑÓN
Castro e Osório (family) 18 676
Castro e Vasconcelos, Félix Machado da Silva *see* MACHADO DA SILVA CASTRO E VASCONCELOS, FÉLIX
Castrojeriz
S Esteban 13 104
Castrojeriz—cont.
S Juan 14 82
Castro Lucas, Diogo 31 102
Castro Maya, Raymundo Ottoni de *see* OTTONI DE CASTRO MAYA, RAYMUNDO
Castromediano, Sigismondo, Duke 16 774
Castro Mello, Icaro de 4 713
Castromocho Church 21 393
Castro Neto, Vicente Ferreira de *see* FERREIRA DE CASTRO NETO, VICENTE
Castro Pacheco, Fernando 21 155
Castro Quesada, Angela 8 18
Castro Tartas, David de 4 18
Castro-Urdiales, S María 13 68
Castroverde, Juan de Uceda *see* UCEDA CASTROVERDE, JUAN DE
Castrucci (family) 8 395, 418
Castrucci, Cosimo (*fl* 1596-1600) 8 418; 13 914; 25 436
works 8 *417*
Castrucci, Cosimo, the younger 8 418
Castrucci, Giovanni 8 418; 13 914; 25 436
castrum 6 57
castrum doloris 6 72
casts 2 169–70; 6 7–9*, *8*; 11 306; 26 226
collections *see under* COLLECTIONS → types
historical and regional traditions
Benin, Kingdom of 6 9
China 6 8, 9
Egypt, ancient 6 9; 10 68–9
England 6 9
Greece, ancient 6 9; 7 562; 27 30
Italy 27 *18*, *19*
Poland 25 140
Rome, ancient 6 9; 7 562; 27 18, *18*, *19*, 30
Sumerian 6 9
materials
artificial stone 6 9
brass 6 9
bronze 6 8, 9
clay 6 7; 23 115
concrete 6 7, 9
fibreglass 6 7
lampblack 23 115
plaster 6 7, 9; 10 68; 27 18, *18*, *19*; 28 *243*; 29 812
plaster of Paris 6 7
sulphur 23 115
terracotta 6 9
waxes 6 7
uses
prints 23 115
Cástulo 15 59
Castulo cups *see under* CUPS → types
casuarina 32 488
Casuccini Collection 10 640
Catacomb culture 27 366
catacomb graves *see under* GRAVES → types
catacombs 6 69–71*, 165
Byzantine 9 570
Early Christian (*c.* AD 250-843) 6 *70*; 9 562, 570; 26 798–9; 28 629
Italy 6 *70*
Malta (Republic of) 6 70
Rome, ancient 9 562; 26 798–9; 31 110
see also CEMETERIES; MAUSOLEA; TOMBS
catafalques 6 *71*, 71–2*, *72*; 11 *276*
Cataio 23 332–3
Catalán, Pau Gargallo i *see* GARGALLO I CATALÁN, PAU
Catalan Atlas 20 363
Catalan hearth *see under* FURNACES → types

Catalan Machzor *see under* MACHZORS → individual manuscripts
Catalano, Francesco **30** 61
Catalano, Giovanni Domenico **7** 818
Catalano, Westman and Associated Architects **3** 682
Català Pic, Pere **6** 73*
Català Roca, Francesc **6** 73*
Catalayúd **29** 323, 335
S Pedro Mártir **29** 323
Çatalca, Damad Ferhad Pasha Mosque **16** 222
Cataldino, José **24** 94
Çatal Hüyük **1** *821*, *849*, 894; **6** 73–5*; **31** 456; **33** 245
architecture **1** 830; **6** 73
figurines **1** 832, 883; **10** 473; **30** 774
interior decoration **1** 823
market **20** 438
metalwork **1** 824
mirrors **21** 711
painting **1** 839, 881, 883; **6** 73–5, *74*; **10** 873; **23** 532; **32** 802
pottery **1** 837
sanctuaries **30** 431
sculpture **6** 75
shrines (i) (cult) **1** 828
textiles **1** 880, 881, 883; **9** 490
trade **1** 823
Catalin **25** 27
catalogne **5** 587
catalogues **2** 534, 559; **6** 75–81*; **7** 714; **10** 210; **11** 309; **25** 664
historical and regional traditions
China **6** 800; **7** 158, 161
England **10** 377; **31** 276
France **2** 559; **6** 545; **28** 221
Germany **12** 475, 482; **23** 108
Italy **32** 237
Japan **7** 161; **17** 428–9, 437–8
Mesoamerica, Pre-Columbian **21** 265
Mexico **21** 265
Native North Americans **22** 679
Netherlands, the **28** 882
types
archive *see* collection
auction **4** 21, 23–4*; **6** 76, 80–81*
Britain **6** 81
England **2** 559
France **6** 80; **11** 662; **19** 25; **20** 416
Netherlands, the **6** 80; **14** 622
United States of America **4** 24
bronzes **6** 843
calligraphy **17** 230
catalogues raisonnés **2** 534; **4** 26*; **6** 75, 76, 78–9*; **31** 671
see also oeuvre
CD-ROM **31** 671
ceramics **7** 161
collection **2** 163, 364, 365, 367, 368; **6** 75, 76–8*; **10** 210
Austria **9** 18
Belgium **9** 16; **33** 8
China **6** 745, 764, 800, 804, 822
England **2** 600; **6** 77; **32** 825
France **6** 77; **8** 209; **17** 667; **19** 216, 782
Germany **5** 338; **9** 18
Italy **16** 767; **27** 114
Syria-Palestine **30** 199
computer **2** 367; **4** 23*, 25–6*; **6** 78, 81
engravings **3** 311; **10** 212
exhibitions **4** 22, 27*; **6** 75, 76, 79–80*; **10** 681; **22** 360; **26** 235
Britain **4** 27
Denmark **8** 761
England **10** 299, 677; **21** 265
Italy **6** 80; **10** 676
Mesoamerica, Pre-Columbian **21** 265
Mexico **21** 265
catalogues
types
exhibitions—cont.
United States of America **4** 23, 27; **24** 820
inks **7** 94
library **4** 21, 22–4, 26
metalwork **6** 865, 867
museum **3** 712; **6** 75, 77–8; **29** 592
national **4** 23
oeuvre **10** 208, 210, 212
see also catalogues raisonnés
optical discs **31** 671
painting **6** 773
portraits **10** 207, 211, 213
prints **4** 27; **6** 78, 80; **10** 208, 211, 212; **25** 599, 631
Belgium **14** 688
Germany **14** 688
Italy **18** 635
Netherlands, the **14** 688
print-sellers' **18** 635
sales *see* auction
sculpture **21** 423
seals **29** 85
stock **6** 80
stone **12** 88
union **4** 23*, 24
video discs **31** 671
see also COLLECTIONS
Catalonia **29** *259*
altarpieces **14** *858*; **20** *515*, *516*
architecture **5** 734
box-wood **29** *313*
capitals **26** *610*; **27** *568*
cathedrals **7** *282*
chairs **29** *320*
churches **5** *734*; **12** *182*
coffers **29** 310
earthenwares **29** 328
furniture **29** 319–21
glass **29** 330–31, *331*
guns **2** 467
housing **12** *181*
interior decoration **29** 305, *308*
manuscript illumination **4** 764
marquetry **29** 320–21
mosaics **21** IV2; **22** *158*, *164*
oak **29** *320*
office buildings **7** *511*
painting **3** *339*; **5** *909*
polychromy **25** II2
pommels (guns) **2** 464
pottery **29** 323, 329
retables **13** 106; **26** 249, 251
sculpture **20** *639*; **26** 605, 609–10*
stone **26** 609–10*
stone-carvings **26** 595
tiles **29** 328, 329
velvet **29** *313*
villas **25** II2
walnut **29** *313*
writing-desks **29** *313*, 313
see also SPAIN
Catamarca **2** *393*, 403; **29** 206
S Pedro de Fiambalá **2** 394
Catana *see* CATANIA
Catanach, Archibald **33** 246
Cataneo, Girolamo **21** 579
Cataneo, Pietro **6** 82*; **26** 516
collaboration **24** 533
works **31** 712
writings **21** 578; **31** 295
Catani, Stefano **22** 308
Catania **6** 83–4*; **16** *621*; **26** *886*; **31** 717
architecture **16** 640
Castello Ursino **6** *83*, 83–4*; **16** 172; **28** 656
coins **13** 587
figurines **13** 579, 580
furniture **20** 215
gold **16** 742
Museo Civico **6** 83
Teatro Bellini **28** 213
Catanio, Francesco Costanzo **24** 833
Cataño, Church of Beato Martin de Porres **25** 701
Cataño, Quirio **10** 154; **13** 761, 764
catapults **2** 448; **21** 557
Catargi, Henri **6** 84*; **26** 716
Catawba **22** 552, 670
catchpenny prints *see under* PRINTS → types
Cate, Asuncion Aguilar **22** 607
Cate, Herman Gerrit ten **17** 825; **29** 432
Cateau **29** 508
Cateau van Roosvelt, J. F. A. **30** 16
catechisms **21** 233
Catel, Franz Ludwig **6** 84–5*; **7** 896; **12** 414
Catel, Louis *see* CATEL, LUDWIG FRIEDRICH
Catel, Ludwig Friedrich **12** 414; **32** 243
Catelin, Prosper **2** 395
works **2** *395*
Catell, Arnau **26** 610
Catena, Vincenzo **6** 85–6*
patrons and collectors **14** 877; **21** 849; **23** 355; **28** 479; **32** 155
teachers **3** 667
works **3** 876; **6** *86*
Catenacci, Jan **11** 17
catenary arches *see under* ARCHES → types
Catenazzi, Giorgio **4** 295; **25** 408
Catenazzi, Giovanni **25** 408; **32** 895
Cateni, Giovanni Camillo **6** 86–7*
collaboration **11** 23; **24** 696
patrons and collectors **21** 29
Caterina Cornaro, Queen of Cyprus (?1454-1510) **3** *657*; **7** 861, 862*; **32** 545
Caterina dei Franceschi **1** 725
Catesby, Mark **6** 87*
Cathach of St Columba *see under* PSALTERS → individual manuscripts
Il Cathaio **15** 87
cat-hair *see under* HAIR → types
Cathcart, Charles (*d* 1788) **15** 57
Cathcart, Charles, 9th Baron Cathcart (1721-76) **1** 649
Cathcart, Holmwood Villa **28** 248, *249*
Cathcart, W. D'Arcy **33** 678
cathedrae *see* THRONES
cathedrals **7** 764; **31** 710
historical and regional traditions
Anglo-Saxon **33** *234*
Armenia (Europe) **2** *97*
Australia **32** *858*
Austria **13** *857*; **32** *451*
Belgium **5** *52*; **31** *221*; **33** *568*
Belize **3** *623*
Benedictine Order **21** *898*
Bolivia **18** *778*
Brazil **12** *794*
Bulgaria **5** *149*
Byzantine
Croatia **25** *252*
Italy **31** *162*
Macedonia (ii) (former Yugoslavia) **23** *373*
Mesopotamia **9** 539
Palestine **9** 539
Syria **9** 539
Turkey **16** *592*
Ukraine **18** *38*
Canada **5** *560*
Catalonia **7** *282*
Colombia **7** *604*
Croatia **12** *667*; **25** *252*
Cuba (Caribbean) **8** 231
Cyprus **10** *774*; **23** *112*
Czech Republic **25** *440*
Denmark **27** *167*
Dominican Republic **9** *116*
Early Christian (*c.* AD 250-843) **9** 529, *531*, 539
Ecuador **9** *711*
cathedrals
historical and regional traditions—cont.
England **2** *322*; **10** 359
Anglo-Saxon **33** *234*
Baroque **19** *599*
Byzantine Revival **3** *746*
eclecticism **9** *704*
Gothic **4** *825*; **5** *644*, *645*; **10** *167*, *673*; **13** *44*, *45*, *54*; **19** *402*, *403*, *597*; **24** *545*; **27** *627*, *628*; **33** *59*, *60*, *61*, *236*, *237*, *548*
Gothic: Decorated style **8** *611*
Gothic: Early English style **9** *669*
Gothic: Early Gothic **33** *62*
Romanesque **9** *449*, *450*; **10** *166*; **12** *5*; **23** *250*, 250; **26** *588*, *589*; **27** *526*; **33** *235*
17th cent. **19** *597*
20th cent. **12** *591*
Finland **14** *371*
France
Gothic **1** *577*, *778*; **2** *46*, *497*; **4** *578*, 579, *579*; **6** *494*, *495*; **8** *74*; **13** *36*, *37*, *40*, *41*; **18** *757*, *758*, *759*; **19** *127*; **20** *582*; **22** *505*; **24** *152*, *153*, *154*; **26** *115*, *116*; **27** *250*, *254*; **28** *414*, *415*; **29** *753*, *754*, *881*; **31** *383*
Gothic: Flamboyant style **6** *414*
Gothic: High Gothic **2** *844*; **3** *457*, *458*; **29** *17*
Gothic: Rayonnant style **11** *510*; **26** *45*
Romanesque **2** *321*; **5** 388; **11** *509*; **26** *584*
18th cent. **4** *165*
19th cent. **32** *83*
Georgia **12** *319*
Germany **3** *141*
Baroque **12** *371*
Gothic **4** *189*; **7** *587*, *588*; **10** *451*; **12** *492*; **13** *47*, *48*; **20** *87*; **28** *182*; **31** *569*
Gothic: Transitional style **31** *284*
Rococo **12** *404*
Romanesque **12** *364*; **20** *128*; **26** *575*; **29** *392*; **31** *326*
Gothic **12** 497; **20** 573, 574, 575, 582*
Austria **32** *451*
Belgium **5** *52*; **31** *221*; **33** *568*
Catalonia **7** *282*
Cyprus **10** *774*; **23** *112*
Czech Republic **25** *440*
Denmark **27** *167*
England **4** *825*; **5** *644*, *645*; **10** *167*, *673*; **13** *44*, *45*, *54*; **19** *402*, *403*, *597*; **24** *545*; **27** *627*, *628*; **33** *59*, *60*, *61*, *236*, *548*
England: Early English style **9** *669*
England: Early Gothic **33** *62*
France **1** *577*, *778*; **2** *46*, *497*; **4** *578*, 579, *579*; **6** *494*, *495*; **8** *74*; **13** *36*, *37*, *40*, *41*; **18** *757*, *758*, *759*; **19** *127*; **20** *582*; **22** *505*; **24** *152*, *153*, *154*; **26** *115*, *116*; **27** *250*, *254*; **28** *414*, *415*; **29** *753*, *754*, *881*; **31** *383*
France: Flamboyant style **6** *414*
France: High Gothic **2** *844*; **3** *457*, *458*; **29** *17*
France: Rayonnant style **11** *510*; **26** *45*; **31** *385*
Germany **4** *189*; **7** *587*, *588*; **10** *451*; **12** *492*; **13** *47*, *48*; **20** *87*; **28** *182*; **31** *569*
Germany: Transitional style **31** *284*
Greece **2** 11
cathedrals
historical and regional traditions
Gothic—cont.
Ireland **5** *915*, 916; **9** *321*
Italy **8** *134*; **13** 63, *66*; **16** 627; **18** *785*; **21** *530*, *531*; **25** *451*; **28** *678*, *679*; **31** *329*
Netherlands, the **13** *62*; **28** *595*
Poland **12** *823*; **18** 431
Scotland **12** *778*
Spain **2** *864*; **5** *203*; **13** *67*, 68, *69*; **19** *172*; **23** *881*; **27** *605*, *606*; **28** *708*; **31** *91*, *814*; **33** *604*
Sweden **31** *693*
Switzerland **12** *276*; **14** *518*
Greece **2** 11
Guatemala **2** *143*
Guyana **13** *876*
Honduras **14** *713*
Hungary **10** *545*; **14** *890*
Ireland **5** *915*, 916; **9** *321*
Italy **9** 529
Baroque **3** *836*
Byzantine **31** *162*
Early Christian (*c.* AD 250-843) **9** *531*
Gothic **8** *134*; **13** 63, *66*; **16** 627; **18** *785*; **21** *530*, *531*; **25** *451*; **28** *678*, *679*; **31** *329*
Renaissance **11** *196*; **20** *112*; **24** *747*; **31** *447*
Romanesque **12** *280*; **19** *766*; **21** *772*; **23** *585*; **24** *193*, *288*, *855*, *857*, *858*; **26** *576*; **32** *185*, *206*
Macedonia (ii) (former Yugoslavia) **23** *373*
Mexico **21** 375–6, *376*, *377*; **25** *696*
Montenegro **22** *18*
Netherlands, the **13** *62*; **28** *595*
Nicaragua **23** 80, *81*
Panama **23** *903*
Peru **24** *501*, *503*
Poland **12** *823*; **18** *431*, 431
Portugal **19** *462*; **22** *533*; **32** *616*
Romanesque **26** 570
Austria **13** *857*
Belgium **31** *221*
England **9** *449*, *450*; **10** *166*; **12** *5*; **23** *250*, 250; **26** *588*, *589*; **27** *526*; **33** *235*
France **2** *321*; **5** 388; **11** *509*; **26** *584*
Germany **12** *364*; **20** *128*; **26** *575*; **29** *392*; **31** *326*
Italy **12** *280*; **19** *766*; **21** *772*; **23** *585*; **24** *193*, *288*; **26** *576*; **32** *185*
Montenegro **22** *18*
Poland **18** 431
Portugal **19** *462*
Romania **26** 706
Russia **26** *594*
Sicily **21** *898*; **23** *843*; **27** *614*
Spain **26** *581*
Sweden **19** *795*
Wales **27** *537*
Romania **26** 706
Russia
Baroque **22** *182*; **26** *9*
Byzantine **29** *54*
Neo-classicism **27** *577*; **29** *552*; **32** *698*
Post-Byzantine **22** *184*
Romanesque **26** *594*
11th cent. **23** *270*
12th cent. **23** *268*; **32** *664*
13th cent. **27** *369*
14th cent. **33** *741*
15th cent. **11** *116*; **22** *183*
Scotland **12** *778*; **28** 224
Sicily **21** *898*; **23** *843*; **27** *614*
Spain
Baroque **5** *368*

cathedrals
historical and regional traditions
Spain—cont.
Churrigueresque **27** *794*
Gothic **2** *864*; **5** *203*; **13** *67*, *68*, *69*; **19** *172*; **23** *881*; **27** *605*, *606*; **31** *91*, *814*; **33** *604*
Gothic: Early Gothic **28** *708*
Plateresque style **8** *253*
Renaissance **14** *475*
Romanesque **26** *581*
16th cent. **16** *863*; **28** *369*
18th cent. **26** *521*
Sweden **19** *795*; **31** *693*
Switzerland **12** *276*; **14** *518*
Turkey **16** *592*
Ukraine **18** *38*; **31** 547
United States of America **16** *56*
Federal style **10** *850*
Gothic Revival **17** 877; **26** *214*
19th cent. **4** 215
Venezuela **32** *168*
Wales **27** *537*
restoration **33** 445–6
types
double **9** 529, 534; **26** 908
Cathelin, Louis-Jacques **9** 365; **19** 11
Cathels, Sydney **14** 397
Catherine, Queen of Sweden (1526-83) **11** 108
Catherine I, Empress of Russia (*reg* 1725-27) **6** 571
Catherine II, Empress of Russia (*reg* 1762-96) **26** 731–3*; **27** *579*; **28** 465; **33** 579
architecture **17** 871; **18** 196; **25** 193; **27** 438; **31** 486
baths **5** 520
churches **26** 383
monasteries **3** 432
palaces **3** 433; **14** 221; **19** 563; **25** 746; **26** 403; **32** 767
pavilions **23** 861
theatres **26** *732*
urban planning **31** 719
bridges **4** 801
ceramics **30** 884; **33** 20, 22
collections **2** 559; **8** 867; **10** 368; **11** 663; **17** 475; **26** 729; **27** 115; **33** 579
decorative works **30** 356
drawings **7** 416; **14** 799
enamel **15** 710
engravings **5** 780; **28** 823
furniture **7** 172; **9** 379; **10** 199; **26** 530
gardens **12** 134
gems **4** 874; **5** 337; **8** 209; **12** 263, 266; **24** 298
glass **27** 415
gold **27** 420
hardstones **14** 172; **27** 427
interior decoration **25** 791; **26** 449; **27** 402
jewellery **7** 112; **27** 429
medals **23** 520
metalwork **11** 620; **26** 532; **27** 424
miniatures **21** 644
paintings **1** 598; **3** 395; **4** 618; **8** 208, 210; **9** 398; **10** 367; **11** 287, 663; **13** 841; **14** 833; **19** 25; **23** 874; **27** 438, 440, 579; **31** 362, 363; **32** 706, 824
genre **12** 312; **13** 642; **18** 186; **25** 888
history **2** 690; **3** 382; **5** 908
landscape **19** 399
mythological **5** 366; **13** 740; **19** 645; **26** 275, 277
portraits **4** 845; **10** 461; **18** 683; **30** 714
religious **11** 902
porcelain **7** 807; **21** 65; **27** 412; **28** 521
pottery **10** 307, *307*
Catherine II, Empress of Russia (*reg* 1762-96)—cont.
sculpture **3** 184; **4** 886; **6** 97; **7** 575; **10** 442, 764; **14** 797, 798; **26** 389; **28** 646
silk **19** 850
silver **5** 530; **27** 584
stucco **29** 839
textiles **18** 805
urban planning **31** 486
Catherine d'Armagnac, Duchess of Bourbon (*d* 1487) **4** 544
Catherine de Bourbon, Duchess of Lorraine (1559-1604) **3** 634; **21** 345
Catherine de Brabant (*fl c.* 1452) **33** 121
Catherine de' Medici, Queen of France (1519-89) **21** 7, *8*; **26** 779; **31** *833*, 850–51*
architecture **5** 166; **6** 506, 545, 546; **11** 260, 513, 656; **14** 855; **19** 692, 693; **20** 865; **24** 117, 161; **25** 580; **31** 834
collections **9** 12, 387; **11** 400
decorative works **3** 645
drawings **7** 462, 464; **14** 848; **23** 523
furniture **11** 586
gardens **6** 546; **23** 850
gems **12** 259
glass **11** 611
hardstones **21** 725
lace **11** 649
leather **19** 3
metalwork **11** 617
paintings **5** 813; **9** 387
pottery **11** 604
sculpture **10** 441; **24** 812, 813; **25** 577; **26** 447; **27** 547; **30** 498
tapestries **14** 296; **23** 464
Catherine Howard, Queen of England (1522-42) **31** 415
Catherine of Aragon, Queen of England (1485-1536) **31** 751
Catherine of Austria, Queen of Portugal (1507-78) **2** 869, 874*; **13** *900*; **14** 661; **17** 486
furniture **22** 71; **27** 823
manuscripts **14** 659
paintings **22** 64
Catherine of Braganza, Queen of England (1638-85) **2** 190; **4** *631*; **10** 291; **12** 279; **15** 43, 44; **29** 719
Catherine of Cleves, Duchess of Gelders (*fl c.* 1450) **5** 443; **20** 616, 642, 643, 667; **22** 835, 901
Catherine of Cleves, Master of **20** 642–5*; **22** 835
attributions **20** 786
collaboration **32** 728
works **5** *443*; **20** *643*, *644*
Catherine of Luxembourg **4** 827
Catherine of Sainte-Suzanne Champaione **6** *436*
Catherine Parr, Queen of England (1512-48) **3** 886
Catherine the Great, Empress of Russia *see* CATHERINE II, Empress of Russia
Catherwood, Frederick **6** 87*; **21** 262, 263, 385
works **7** 800; **31** 420
writings **13** 811
Catholicism *see* CHRISTIANITY → branches → Roman Catholicism
Catholic Kings, the *see* FERDINAND II, King of Aragon and Sicily; ISABELLA, Queen of Castile-León
Catholicos Mashtots **12** 155
Catholme **2** 65
Cati, Pasquale **19** 632; **26** 834
Catina *see* CATANIA
Catino, Gregorio di *see* GREGORIO DI CATINO
Catio **7** 602
Cation, David **28** 242
Catlett, Elizabeth **1** 443
Catlin, George **6** 87–8*; **23** 32
patrons and collectors **12** 618
personal collection **22** 678
works **2** 106; **22** 584
Catling, H. **29** 367
catlinite **22** 584, *585*
Catnach, James **6** 84; **24** 391; **25** 244
Cato **3** 327; **12** 68, 110; **26** 884; **32** 550
Caton-Thompson, Gertrude **3** 35; **13** 335
Catroux, François **11** 584
cats **11** 120
Cats, Arnoul de *see* ARNOLET DE CATZ
Cats, Jacob (i) (1577-1660) **6** 88*; **22** 842
architecture **14** 39
writings **1** 659; **10** 174, 175, *175*, 176; **31** 881
illustrated **17** 599; **32** 231
Cats, Jacob (ii) (1741-99) **1** 807, 808; **6** 88–9*
Cats, Johannes **6** 88
cat's-eye **7** 91; **12** 252
cat statues *see under* SCULPTURE → types
Cat Stele **1** 481
Cattaneo, Alberto **4** 76
Cattaneo, Cesare **16** 650; **25** 838; **26** 16
Cattaneo, Danese **5** 533; **6** 89–90*; **32** 192
attributions **13** 658
collaboration **10** 799; **19** 560; **21** 647; **27** 637
groups and movements **16** 697
patrons and collectors **5** 531; **30** 496
pupils **5** 531
teachers **27** 772
works **5** 302, 531; **6** *90*; **31** *125*, 127; **32** 222
Cattaneo, Elena Grimaldi, Marchesa **9** *477*
Cattaneo, Francisco **5** 49; **27** 291
Cattaneo, Gerolamo **27** 482
Cattaneo, Giuseppe **29** 109, 110
Cattaneo, R. **9** 527
Cattani, Alberto de' **7** 927
Cattani, Emmanuel **23** 262; **27** 853
Catteau, Charles **3** 592
Cattel, Pieter **19** 102
Cattermole, George **6** 90–91*
collaboration **4** 885; **8** 863
reproductive prints by others **33** *445*
Cattermole, Richard **6** 90
Catterson Smith, Stephen *see* SMITH, STEPHEN CATTERSON
Cattini, Giovanni **6** 91*
works **24** 707; **30** 923; **32** 501; **33** 613
Catton, Charles **23** 683
Cat Tuong **32** 486
Catulus, (Quintus) Lucius **26** 867
Catumagos *see* CAEN
Catuogno, Domenico **31** 789
Catz, Arnolet de *see* ARNOLET DE CATZ
Causí, Gregorio **25** 233
Cauchie, Paul **3** 550; **6** 91*
Caucig, Francesco **6** 91–2*; **10** 702; **11** 161; **24** 586
Caudebec-en-Caux, Notre-Dame **11** 154; **13** 60; **22** 219, 221
Caudí, Josep **30** 664
Caudill, Rowlett and Scott **6** 92
Caudill, William W(ayne) **6** 92*; **7** 688
Cauer, Carl **6** 92–3*
Cauer, Emil, the elder (1800-67) **6** 92; **12** 407
Cauer, Emil, the younger (1867-1946) **6** 93
Cauer, Friedrich **6** 93
Cauer, Hanna **6** 93
Cauer, Hans **6** 93
Cauer, Hugo **6** 93
Cauer, Ludwig **6** 93
Cauer, Robert, the elder (1831-93) **6** 92
Cauer, Robert, the younger (1863-1947) **6** 93
Cauer, Stanislaus **6** 93
Caughley Porcelain Factory **6** 93*, 408; **7** 480; **10** 309; **21** 697
collections **28** 168
Cauja, José Antonio **9** 714
Caula, Sigismondo **22** 26
Cauldon Place **26** 362
Cauldon Potteries Ltd **7** 481; **13** 22
cauldrons
historical and regional traditions
Celtic **6** 159
China **7** 97
Crete **8** 154
Cyprus, ancient **8** *354*
Denmark **6** 159; **13** *849*
Greece, ancient **13** 371, 492, 575–6, *575*
Thracian **13** *849*
materials
bronze **8** 154, *354*; **13** 575, *575*
silver **13** *849*
caulecole **6** 93*
Caulery, Louis de **11** 36
Caulfeild, James, 1st Earl of Charlemont **6** 93–4*; **16** 35
architecture **6** 412; **16** 8; **22** 320
education (art) **19** 585
interior decoration **16** 24
paintings **3** 383; **14** 640; **16** 36; **27** 356
sculpture **16** 21
Caulfield, Patrick **6** 94–5*; **19** 591
collaboration **10** 258
groups and movements **25** 231
works **6** *94*; **18** 631; **25** 25; **28** 300
Caulibus, Joannes de *see* JOANNES DE CAULIBUS
Caulkin, Horace J. **8** 821
Caumont, Arcisse de **2** 319; **6** 95*; **11** 521; **26** 568; **31** 283
architecture **13** 210
writings **11** 521; **13** 34
Caumont, Jan de **19** 260
Caumont, Joseph de Seytres, Marquis de **32** 331
Cauquil-Prince, Yvette **11** 644
Caurapañcāśikā **15** 574–6*
manuscripts **15** *575*
Caus, Isaac de **6** 96*; **11** 243; **23** 492
patrons and collectors **17** 635; **29** 803
works **10** 231; **12** 127; **14** 435, 855; **27** 356; **33** *224*, 225
Caus, Salomon de **6** 95–6*
collaboration **7** 487
patrons and collectors **12** 126, 133; **29** 798, 799
works **11** 242, 343; **13** 704; **14** 306, 855; **17** 633
writings **2** 837; **23** 470
Causeus *see* LA CHAUSSE, MICHEL-ANGE
causeuses **29** 8
causewayed camps *see* CAMPS (CAUSEWAYED)
causeways
Aztec **6** 97
Cambodia **5** 474, *478*
Egypt, ancient **25** 760, 762
England **23** 685
Khmer **5** *478*
Maya **6** 97, *97*; **21** 213
Mesoamerica, Pre-Columbian **6** 96*, *97*
Mexico **6** *97*
see also AVENUES; ROADS; STREETS
Causí, Gregorio **7** 605
Causici, Enrico **21** 616
Caussade **4** 780
Caussy, Pierre-Clément **25** 822
caustic soda **18** 590; **24** 41
Causton, Joseph, Ltd **26** 466
Cautheren, Jan van der *see* JAN VAN DER CAUTHEREN
Cauvet, Gilles-Paul **11** 627
Cauvin, Jacques **22** 341
Cava, Onofrio di Giordano della *see* ONOFRIO DI GIORDANO DELLA CAVA
Cavaceppi, Bartolomeo **6** 97–8*; **11** 306; **13** 303
assistants **23** 189
collaboration **24** 846
dealing **13** 665; **19** 531; **33** 19
illustrated writings **6** *98*
patrons and collectors **24** 570; **25** 8
personal collection **4** 886; **24** 757
studio **6** *98*
works **2** 164; **4** 181
Cavael, Rolf **33** 635
Cavagna, Giovanni Battista **6** 98–9*
pupils **6** 343
works **2** 594; **3** 771; **12** 680
Cavagna, Giovan Paolo **6** 99*
Cavagna, Giuseppe **29** 832
Cavaillon
Cathedral of St Véran **26** 603
synagogue **17** 545
cavalarizzo *see* RIDING HOUSES
Cavalcabò, Giovanna **3** 695
Cavalcanti, Andrea di Lazzaro *see* BUGGIANO
Cavalcanti, Emiliano (de Albuquerque e Mello) di **4** 717, 718; **6** 99*
exhibitions **28** 394
groups and movements **4** 719
patrons and collectors **4** 727
works **32** 855
Cavalcanti, Giovanni **31** 189
Cavalcanti, Viscondessa de **4** 725
Cavalcaselle, Giovanni Battista **2** 560; **6** 100–101*; **16** 769, 774
collaboration **4** 493; **8** 206; **16** 782
works **9** 200; **16** 769
Cavalier, Jean **6** 101*; **11** 637; **30** 417
Cavaliere d'Arpino *see* ARPINO, CAVALIERE D'
Cavalieri, Giovanni Battista de' **6** 102*
patrons and collectors **33** 606
works **4** 860; **9** 181; **17** 910; **26** 230
writings **2** 161, 162, 169
Cavalieri, Marcello **23** 577
Cavalieri, Tiberio de' **26** 397
Cavalieri, Tommaso de' **21** 450; **25** 558; **32** 237
cavaliers **21** 546
Cavallari, Javier **21** 378
Cavallari, Saverio **28** 175
Cavalleri, Giovanni Battista de' *see* CAVALIERI, GIOVANNI BATTISTA DE'
Cavallerino della Mirandola, Niccolò **13** 658
Cavalletto, Giovanni Battista **6** 102*
Cavalletto, Scipione **6** 102
Cavalli (family) **1** 726
architecture **1** *727*
Cavalli, Alberto **12** 910; **27** 483
Cavalli, Emanuele **5** 671; **28** 319
Cavalli, Gian Marco **6** 102–3*; **12** 908; **20** 322
Cavalli, Giuseppe **6** 103*; **22** 27
Cavalli, Nicolò **32** 689
Cavallier, Barthélémy **6** 103*
Cavallini, Francesco **10** 782; **29** 830, 831

Cavallini, Pietro 2 481; 6 103–7*; 13 135, 145; 16 655; 22 476
attributions 2 627; 20 697
frescoes 2 109; 6 103, 104; 16 657; 20 697; 29 596
methods 6 569; 12 695; 13 138
mosaics 6 105; 13 145; 19 353; 22 163; 26 834; 29 597
patrons and collectors 13 146, 150; 17 610; 23 96, 575; 26 765
workshop 13 132
Cavallino, Bernardo 6 107–10*; 22 479
patrons and collectors 14 191; 28 367
teachers 29 544
works 6 108, 110; 31 791
Cavallo, Domenico del see DOMENICO DI PARIS
Cavallo, Niccolò del see BARONCELLI, NICCOLÒ
Cavallon, Giorgio 6 110–11*
Cavallón, Juan de 8 15
Cavalls, Els see ELS CAVALLS
Cavallucci, Antonio 6 111*; 28 429
Cavalori, Mirabello (d'Antonio di Pacino) 6 111–12*; 16 664; 19 872
Cavanilles, Antonii Joséphi 12 33; 19 659
Cavanna, Angelo 29 832
Cavanna, Giovanni Nicolo 29 75
Cavanna, Michelangelo 22 481
Cavaquinho 25 310
Cavaro (family) 27 836
Cavarozzi, Bartolomeo 6 112*; 29 280
Cavazza, Pier Francesco 32 402
Cavazzo, Carlos Gómez see GÓMEZ CAVAZZO, CARLOS
Cavazzola, Paolo 6 112–13*; 10 765; 22 131
Cavazzolo, Pietro 33 585
Cavazzoni, Francesco 6 113*
Cave, S Carlo 26 624
Cave, Henry 33 545
Cave, Henry William 6 113*
caveae (i) (seating) 6 113*; 26 873; 30 651–2
caveae (ii) (cells) 6 113*
cave art 25 474–7*, 483
see also ROCK ART
Cave Creek (AZ), Dome House 29 35
Cavedone, Giacomo 6 113–15*
collaboration 26 196
pupils 20 221
teachers 5 851
works 6 114
Cavedone, Pellegrino 6 113
Cavedoni, Giacomo 31 187
Caveiro, Miguel Ferro see FERRO CAVEIRO, MIGUEL
Cavelier, Adrien 6 115
Cavelier, Milet le see MILET LE CAVELIER
Cavelier, Pierre-Jules 3 250; 6 115*
groups and movements 28 345
pupils
Barrias, Louis-Ernest 3 277
Charlier, Guillaume (-Joseph) 6 487
Coutan, Jules-Félix 8 72
Desbois, Jules 8 787
Gilbert, Alfred 12 610
Lantéri, Edouard 18 751
Lee, Thomas Stirling 19 60
Segoffin, Victor 28 366
Teixeira Lopes, António 30 417
Vallgren, Ville 31 828
Vinçotte, Thomas 32 590
works 24 396
Cavelli, Giampietro Campana, Marchese di see CAMPANA (DI CAVELLI), GIAMPIETRO
Cavenaghi, Luigi 3 49; 6 115*; 22 102
Cavendish (family) 6 116; 9 506; 10 364; 20 446
Cavendish, Charles 6 59; 28 896
Cavendish, James, Lord 25 664
Cavendish, William (1505-57) 6 115, 515
Cavendish, William (fl 1658) 8 877
Cavendish, William, 1st Duke of Devonshire (1640-1707) 6 116*
architecture 6 115, 515, 515; 10 361; 14 856; 30 278
decorative works 18 644; 25 29
metalwork 33 195
paintings 4 232
sculpture 7 298; 23 253
Cavendish, William, 1st Earl of Devonshire (1552-1626) 19 531; 29 834
Cavendish, William, 2nd Duke of Devonshire (1671-1729) 6 116–17*
drawings 9 230; 11 170; 25 664
gems 12 266
paintings 6 115; 10 365; 14 810; 21 368
Cavendish, William, 3rd Duke of Devonshire (1698-1755) 6 116, 117*
Cavendish, William, 3rd Earl of Devonshire (1617-84) 6 115
Cavendish, William, 4th Duke of Devonshire (1720-64) 6 117*
architecture 6 116, 515
furniture 32 540
Cavendish, William, 4th Earl of Devonshire see CAVENDISH, WILLIAM, 1st Duke of Devonshire
Cavendish, William, 5th Duke of Devonshire (d 1811) 6 515
Cavendish, William, 7th Duke of Devonshire (1808-91) 26 337
Cavendish, William, Duke of Newcastle (1592-1676) 23 258; 28 896, 897; 29 424
Cavendish, William Spencer, 6th Duke of Devonshire (1790-1858) 6 117–18*; 33 447
architecture 6 116, 515; 24 295
gardens 24 293
houses 8 106
interior decoration 8 106; 33 145
paintings 7 572; 9 682; 19 508
prints 25 665
sculpture 3 296; 4 42; 10 365; 12 597; 13 213; 17 921; 30 459; 33 449
Cavendish-Bentinck, William, 4th Duke of Portland (d 1854) 29 723
Cavendish-Bentinck, William Henry, 3rd Duke of Portland (1738-1809) 3 276; 6 118*; 26 237
Cavendish-Bentinck (-Scott), William John, 5th Duke of Portland (1800-79) 6 118–19*; 22 351
Cavengahi, Luigi 16 774
Cave of Letters 1 881; 27 86, 87, 105, 112, 113
Cavera, Anselmo 32 411
Caveri, Claudio 2 397
Cavernas 29 180
Cavernas cemetery 24 89
Caversham Press 29 111
caves
Africa 1 304
Borneo 29 226
Buddhism
Central Asia, Eastern 30 441–2
China 30 442–3*
Indian subcontinent 5 94; 15 236, 236, 252–3, 257–9, 258
Central Asia, Eastern 18 105; 30 441–2
China 6 691, 691, 692; 30 442–3*
Crete 8 153
Greece, ancient 15 98
caves—cont.
Indian subcontinent 3 194; 15 194, 236, 250, 275–9, 279, 302–4; 18 18; 24 887–8
Buddhism 5 94; 15 236, 236, 252–3, 257–9, 258
Java 29 226
Mesoamerica, Pre-Columbian 22 443
Minoan 8 153
Namibia 1 304
Prehistoric art 29 226–7
South-east Asia 29 226–7
Spain 1 688–9, 689
Tanzania 1 304
Thailand 29 226
Tibet 30 817, 818
Timor 29 226, 227
Zambia 1 304
Cave Taillebourg see under ANGLES-SUR-L'ANGLIN
cavetto cornices 10 51, 52
cavetto mouldings see under MOULDINGS → types
Caviglia, Giovanni Battista 12 767
Cavina, Virgilio, Conte 21 623
Cavino, Giovanni da 3 700; 6 119*; 13 658; 20 919
cavity-walling see under ARCHITECTURE → techniques
Cavos, Al'bert see KAVOS, AL'BERT
Cavrioli, Francesco 19 630
Cavtat 8 181
Çavüşin 5 673
architecture 5 673
Pigeon House Church 5 674; 7 221
wall paintings 5 676, 678; 9 580
St John the Baptist 5 674, 676
Çavuştepe 1 821, 894; 6 119–20*
architecture 1 831
wall paintings 1 839
Caway 11 759
Cawdor, John Campbell, 1st Baron see CAMPBELL, JOHN, 1st Baron Cawdor
Cawdor vase see LANTE VASE
Cawek 20 886
Cawén, Alvar 23 266
Cawnpore see KANPUR
Cawood Castle (N. Yorks) 26 615
Cawse, John 32 855
Cawston (Norfolk), St Agnes 24 577
Caxeri see CAJÉS
Caxés see CAJÉS
Caxés, Eugenio see CAJÉS, EUGENIO
Caxete see CAJÉS
Caxton, William 6 120*, 557; 19 727
patrons and collectors 5 214; 20 142; 22 111; 24 637; 33 94
teachers 4 921
works 10 247; 25 345; 27 592
writings 10 725
Çay, Taş Madrasa 16 184
Caye Caulker Academy of Arts 3 625
Cayenne 11 756, 757, 760
architecture 11 758
Céprou fort 11 757
Musée de Cayenne 11 759
Cayes, Les see LES CAYES
Cayetana y Silva y Alvárez y Toledo, Maria Teresa see ALBA, MARIA TERESA CAYETANA Y SILVA Y ALVÁREZ Y TOLEDO, 13th Duqesa de
Cayetano, Pen 3 624
Cayeux, Philippe 11 404
Cayey 25 698
Museo Frade 25 704
Cayla, Mme de 14 482
Cayla de Mailhac 21 551
Caylus, Comte de 6 120–21*; 10 642; 11 662, 675; 13 468; 19 11; 22 415; 24 136
collaboration 19 232
Caylus, Comte de—cont.
collections 10 83; 14 687
drawings 14 162
encaustic paintings 10 198
engravings 4 509; 11 579; 19 117
etchings 2 239; 11 541; 20 416
patrons and collectors 29 487
prints 25 622
sculpture 11 561
woodcuts 33 365
writings
illustrated 4 330; 22 88; 24 552
on antiquity 1 898; 2 164, 559; 10 78, 96; 11 674; 14 445; 15 89; 22 415
on encaustic painting 10 199
Cayman Gallery see NEW YORK → museums → Muse of Contemporary Hispanic Art
Cayman Islands 5 745
Çayönü 1 821; 21 280
architecture 1 823, 830
copper 1 824, 834; 21 269
reliefs 1 832
Cayot, Claude-Augustin 6 121*
Cayuga 16 61; 22 552, 612
Cazabon, Michel Jean 31 335, 339, 340
Cazalis, Henri 22 421
Caze, Louis La see LA CAZE, LOUIS
Cazeaux, Euryale 6 491
Cazes, Jacques-Nicolas 6 122
Cazes, Pierre-Jacques 6 121–2*
collaboration 10 842
pupils 6 471; 19 796; 26 448, 452
reproductive prints by others 19 144
teachers 4 536
Cazes, Pierre-Michel 6 122
Cazin, (Stanislas-Henri-) Jean Charles 6 122*
patrons and collectors 7 832; 23 882
teachers 8 539; 19 39
Cazin, Marie 6 122–3*
Cazin, Michel 6 122
Cazneau, Pierce Mott 6 123
Cazneaux, Harold (Pierce) 2 747; 6 123*
groups and movements 24 739
Cazzaniga, Francesco 4 816, 817; 6 123*; 9 112
Cazzaniga, Tommaso 4 817; 6 123; 9 112; 24 286; 27 830
CB, Master see BAUER, CONRAD
C.C., Master 20 793*
CCBE Co. 3 816
CCS-school voor Beeldende Kunsten 30 16
CD-ROM 2 534; 26 236; 31 671
Ceán Bermúdez, Juan Agustín 6 123–4*; 17 673
collections 29 353
prints 14 196
writings 6 365; 10 208; 13 242; 29 358
Ceauşescu (family) 26 724
Ceauşescu, Nicolae 26 706
Ceballos, Gregorio Vázquez de Arce y see VÁZQUEZ DE ARCE Y CEBALLOS, GREGORIO
Ceballos, Jerónimo 2 28
Ceballos, Pedro Vicente Gómez see GÓMEZ CEBALLOS, PEDRO VICENTE
Cebes 10 129; 15 84
Cebrolu, Bhimeshvara Temple 15 301
Cebu City 24 607, 616, 617
Basilica of the Santo Niño see S Agustín
Fort San Pedro 21 596
S Agustín 24 611–12*
wood-carvings 24 630
St Theresa's College Museum 29 240
Cecca, Francesco d'Angelo 27 733
Cecca, La 11 705
Ceccarella, Olivuccio di see OLIVUCCIO DI CECCARELLA
Ceccarini, Giuseppe 6 125
Ceccarini, Sebastiano 6 124–5*
collaboration 13 277
works 6 125
Cecce di Saracino 5 661
Cecchi, Emilio 6 125*; 19 637
Cecchino del Frate 3 307
Cecco, Giovanni di see GIOVANNI DI CECCO
Cecco (di Luca), Gregorio see GREGORIO DI CECCO (DI LUCA)
Ceccobelli, Bruno 16 683
Cecco Bravo 6 125–6*; 16 673
collaboration 21 26
patrons and collectors 3 97
personal collection 11 875
works 6 126; 30 41
Cecco d'Ascoli 12 681
Cecco del Caravaggio see CARAVAGGIO, CECCO DEL
Cecco di Pietro 6 127*; 17 644
Ceccoli, Raffaello 13 360
Cechpauer, Jan Pavel 8 386
Cecil (family) 8 165
Cecil, Brownlow, 2nd Marquess of Exeter (fl c. 1825-50) 33 145
Cecil, Brownlow, 9th Earl of Exeter (1725-93) 6 127
Cecil, Edward, Viscount Wimbledon 21 486
Cecil, Hugh 19 867
Cecil, James, 5th Earl of Salisbury 10 291
Cecil, John, 5th Earl of Exeter 6 127, 128–9*
interior decoration 32 358
paintings 6 29; 10 364; 13 299; 20 411; 33 260
sculpture 21 890; 30 267
Cecil, Robert, 1st Earl of Salisbury 6 127, 128*; 17 633
architecture 8 45
gardens 31 276
paintings 33 387
sculpture 7 236, 641
stage design 17 637
Cecil, Thomas, 1st Earl of Exeter 6 127
Cecil, William, 1st Baron Burghley (1520-98) 6 127–8*
architecture 10 226, 287, 360; 24 237; 28 526
porcelain 4 177
sculpture 8 273
Cecil, William, 2nd Earl of Salisbury (1591-1668) 19 120; 24 390; 33 387
Cecilia 22 801
Cecilia Gallerani 19 183
Cecioni, Adriano 6 129–30*
groups and movements 16 678; 19 871; 28 317, 318
teachers 16 706
works 32 257
Cecotto, Leonor 24 98, 99
CEDAE see CENTRE D'ETUDES ET DE DOCUMENTATION SUR L'ANCIENNE EGYPTE
cedar 33 326
historical and regional traditions
Africa 1 307
Belgium 3 585
Brazil 4 721
Egypt, ancient 6 559; 10 54; 33 III1
England 10 277, 288
France 11 599
Indian subcontinent 15 721; 21 717
Kenya 1 307
Lebanon 30 179
Native North Americans 9 165
Peru 24 515
Portugal 25 304, 305
Surinam 30 16
Syria-Palestine 30 179

cedar—cont.
types
red (*Thuja plicata*) **2** 757, *758*; **22** 563
sugi (Japanese cedar) **17** 47, 356
uses
boats **15** 721
cabinets (ii) (furniture) **3** 585; **11** *599*; **25** *305*; **33** III1
chairs **2** *758*
chests **6** 559; **10** 54, 288; **25** 304
desks **25** 304
doors **9** 165; **17** 47
furniture **2** 757; **4** 721
lintels **17** 47
mirror frames **21** 717
Cedar Tree Associates **22** 671
CEDDCI *see* MARSEILLE → Centre d'Etude et de Documentation sur l'Image
Cedeño, Juan Manuel **4** 766; **6** 130*; **23** 905; **33** 588
Cederboom *see* QUELLINUS, JAN-ERASMUS
Cedergren, P. W. **18** 800
Cederström, Gustaf (Olof) **3** 193; **6** 130*; **16** 67
Cédille Qui Sourit, La **4** 731; **11** 80
CEDLA *see* SANTIAGO (DE CHILE) (CHILE) → Centro de Estudios de la Arquitectura
Cedrini, Marino (di Marco) **6** 130–31*; **19** 686
Cedrosan Saladoid culture **29** 198–200*
Cedrosan style pottery *see under* POTTERY → wares
Ceesay, Momodou **12** 32
Cefalà Diama **16** 171
Cefalù **6** 131–4*; **16** *103*, *621*
Cathedral of Salvatore and SS Pietro e Paolo **4** 141; **6** 131–2*; **16** 171, 627; **23** 211; **26** 579, 628; **28** 655
mosaics **6** 132–4*, *133*; **9** 581, 645; **14** 240; **22** 162; **26** 680
paintings **16** 306
tombs (royal) **26** 628
Cathedral of S Maria Nuova **16** 762
throne **30** 779
Cefalù Painter **13** 531
Cefn-coed-y-cymmer **32** 787
CEGRA *see* CENTRO DE ENSEÑANZA GRÁFICA
Cehtzuc **31** 778
ceiling decorations **29** 812
ceiling paintings *see under* PAINTING → forms
ceilings **14** 420; **22** 211
historical and regional traditions
Australia **2** 739; **11** 756
Austria **2** 805–6
Belgium **3** 576, 577
Byzantine **9** 654
China **6** 643
Early Christian (*c*. AD 250-843) **9** 654
England **10** 271
France **11** 574
Greece, ancient **13** 390, 392
Indian subcontinent **15** 313, *313*, 325
Islamic **16** 216, 494–5, *495*
Italy **30** *357*; **32** *404*
Korea **18** 265
Romanesque **26** 569
Rome, ancient **27** 47, 51, 55
Scotland **28** 245, 246, *247*
Spain **16** 216, *495*; **19** 658
materials
gold **9** 654
metal **2** 739
plaster **28** 245, 246
stucco **3** 577; **28** 246, *247*
wood **2** *529*; **13** 390; **16** 216, 494–5, *495*; **30** *357*
Mudéjar **19** 658
ceilings—cont.
types
artesonado **2** 528–9*, *529*
Ceineray, Jean-Baptiste **8** 216
Céitinn, Seān *see* KEATING, JOHN
Čekanāuskas, Vytautas **6** 134*
Çekirge *see* BURSA
celadons *see under* POTTERY → wares
Celandro, Sante di Apollonio del *see* SANTE DI APOLLONIO DEL CELANDRO
Celano, Tommaso de *see* TOMMASO DE CELANO
Celanova Monastery **6** 134–5*; **29** *258*, 269
S Miguel **6** 135
chapel of S Miguel **6** 135, *135*; **22** 247; **29** 262
Celant, Germano **2** 526; **16** 682
Cela Velha, Monument to Humberto Delgado **25** 302
Cele **33** 725
Celebes **16** 861
Çelebi, Ali (Avni) **6** 135*; **31** 454
Čelebi, Evliya **4** 460; **22** 446; **30** 479
Çelebi, Hasan **31** 454
Çelebi, Süleyman **9** 729
Çelebi Arif *see* ARIFI
Čelebonović, Marko **6** 136*; **28** 451
Celebrano, Francesco **22** 482
Celega, Jacopo **32** 216
Celega, Pietro Paolo **32** 216
Celej, Bartłomiej **17** 873
Celentano, Bernardo **6** 136–7*
works **6** *136*
Celer **16** 623; **26** 884, 892; **28** 510*
patrons and collectors **22** 804
works **26** 788
Celesti, Andrea **6** 137*; **32** 194
patrons and collectors **8** 427
pupils **33** 721
teachers **25** 227
Celestine Order **3** 709
Čelic, Stojan **28** 451
Céline, Louis Ferdinand **27** 868
Céline Dangotte **31** 880
Celio, Gaspare **26** 823; **31** 820
Celje **28** *858*
Abbey Church **28** 858
parish church **28** 860
Regional Museum **28** 863
cellae **6** 138*; **8** 154; **13** 376, *376*, 377, 405, 415
cellarets **2** 151, *151*; **28** 666
cellophane **7** 432
cellos **22** 374
cellular vaults *see under* VAULTS (CEILING) → types
celluloid **16** 797; **24** 669; **25** 23, 26, 27; **26** 244; **31** 195
historical and regional traditions
Japan **31** 259
Russia **25** *25*
uses
collagraphs **7** 558
sculpture **25** 25, *25*
toys **31** 259
cellulose **7** 747, 748; **18** 612
cellulose acetate **25** 23, 27*; **26** 244; **30** 542
cellulose ethers **7** 747
cellulose fibres *see under* FIBRES → types
cellulose nitrate **25** 23, 27*; **26** 244; **30** 542; **32** 3
Celmins, Vija **6** 150*; **19** 703; **20** 606
Celnikier, Izaak **2** 502
Celoistre, Claux *see* SLUTER, CLAUS
Celón, S María **26** 642
Celotti, Luigi, Abbot **4** 471; **6** 151*
Cels, Cornelis **6** 151*; **12** 12
Celsi (family) **20** 846
Celsing, Peter **6** 151–2*; **30** 75
Celsus (Polemaeanus), C(aius) Iulius **26** 913
architecture **26** *914*
Cellini, Benvenuto—cont.
drawings **6** *141*
groups and movements **11** 263; **20** 281
metalwork **11** 556
coins **7** 537
gold **6** 9, *143*; **12** 865; **15** 867; **20** 280; **23** 540; **27** 640
jewellery **17** 521
medals **6** *140*
niello **16** 750
patrons and collectors
Altoviti, Bindo **1** 734
Clement VII, Pope (*reg* 1523-34) **21** 17
Cosimo I, Grand Duke of Tuscany (*reg* 1569- 74) **3** 160; **21** 21
Diane de Poitiers, Duchesse de Valentinois **8** 856
Ercloe II, 4th Duke of Ferrara, Medena and Reggio (*reg* 1534–59) **10** 523
Ferdinand, Archduke of Austria, Count of Tyrol (*reg* 1564-95) **6** 76
Francis I, King of France (*reg* 1515-47) **16** 695; **18** 662; **30** 219; **31** 848, 849
Gonzaga, Ercole, Cardinal **12** 910
Philip II, King of Spain (*reg* 1556-98) **13** 922
Salviati, Giovanni, Cardinal **27** 648
pupils **12** 3; **30** 357
sculpture
busts **5** 301; **6** *144*
crucifixes **10** 503
fountains **11** 342
lunettes **10** 745
mythological **6** *142*, *145*; **22** 44; **29** 561, *562*
nude figures **23** 293
plaquettes **25** 18
reliefs **2** 28; **16** 695; **20** 278
statuettes **29** 571
teachers **3** 156
writings **16** 781; **24** 90
on jewellery **17** 520
on sculpture **31** 302
Cellini, Giovanni **6** 139
Cellini, Giuseppe **26** 776
Cellini Madonna, Master of the **3** 352
Cellonite *see under* IVORY → types
Celle **6** 138*; **12** *360*
exhibitions **16** 560
Rathaus **33** 88
Schloss **6** 138*
synagogue **6** 138
theatre **30** 676
Celle, La *see* LA CELLE
Celle, Pierre de *see* PIERRE DE CELLE
Celle di Pistoia, Gori collection **16** 775
Cellerier, Jacques **6** 138–9*; **25** 873
assistants **1** 527
works **27** 539, 543
Celles-le-Dinant, St Hadelin **26** 574; **31** 281; **33** 108
Celles-sur-Belle Church **13** *211*, 211
Cellés y Azcona, Antonio **21** 315
Cellini, Andrea **6** 139
Cellini, Baccio **14** 904
Cellini, Benvenuto **6** 139–49*; **9** 13, 21; **11** 187, 634, 656; **12** 214; **14** 869; **16** 689, 695, 742, 751; **21** 255; **24** 146; **26** 769; **29** 569
assistants **12** 4; **18** 820; **30** 530
attributions **4** 53; **10** 751; **20** 277; **21** 804
bookbindings **26** 42
competitions **7** 672
Çeltek Church **5** 675
Celtic **6** 152–62*; **8** 527
amber **1** 761
arm rings **6** 155, *157*, 158
barrows **6** 154
bowls **6** 152
bronze **6** 157–8, 159, 161; **14** 88
Czech Republic **6** *158*
England **6** *161*
France **6** *155*
Germany **18** 120
brooches **6** 156, 157, 158
burial mounds **32** 773
carnyxes **22** *371*, 372
cauldrons **6** 159
cemeteries **6** 154; **14** 87
chariot fittings **6** 155, 158
chariots **6** 481*
chronologies **16** 830
coins **6** 159–60; **25** 542; **31** 527
compasses **6** 154, 155, 161
coral **6** *155*, *161*; **7** 834
crosses **32** 786, *787*
cups **6** 161
doorways **27** *142*
dress **9** 252–3*
enamel **6** 155, *155*
erotic art **10** 473
flagons **6** *155*, 155–6
foot rings **6** 158
glass **6** 159
gold **6** 155, *157*, 158; **12** *867*; **18** 120; **25** 542
graves **14** 87
chariot **6** 155
harnesses **14** 181*
helmets **6** 157
human figures **6** 159
Ireland **6** 161
iron **6** 157
jewellery **25** 546
metalwork **6** *153*, 155–6, 157–8, 159–60; **27** 663
openwork **6** *158*
mirrors **6** *153*, 161
neck rings **6** 155, 157, *157*, 158, 161; **12** *867*
periods and styles
Continuous Vegetal Style *see* Waldalgesheim Style
Early Style (*c*. 450-*c*. 350 BC) **6** *153*, 154–6*, *155*, *156*
Mirror style **6** *153*
oppida (*c*. 125-*c*. 50 BC) **6** 159–60*
Plastic style (*c*. 350-*c*. 125 BC) **6** 158–9*
Strict Style *see* Early Style
Sword style (*c*. 350-*c*. 125 BC) **6** *153*, 157*
Ultimate La Tène **15** 871, 872
Waldalgesheim style (*c*. 350-*c*. 250 BC) **6** *153*, 156–7*, *157*
see also HALLSTATT CULTURE; LA TÈNE CULTURE
pillars **6** *156*; **27** *142*
portraits **6** *158*
pottery **6** 156, 159, 161; **25** *543*, 544
ragstone **6** *158*
sanctuaries **27** 142
scabbards **6** 157, 160; **14** 88; **18** 828
sculpture **6** 152, 156, *158*, 158–9; **28** 241
shields **6** *161*
silver **6** 159; **22** *371*
standards (vexilloid) **11** 151
statuettes **6** 159
stone **6** *156*
stone-carvings **6** *156*, *158*
swords **6** 157, 159; **18** 828; **25** 540
temples **26** 905
trappings **6** 155, 161; **14** 181*
vases **25** *543*
wood-carvings **6** 152, 159
Celtic Revival **6** 164*; **24** 391
Ireland **14** 580; **16** 28, 36
Celtic Revival—cont.
Scotland **12** 780
Celtis, Konrad **6** 164–5*; **14** 868; **18** 705; **24** 573
patrons and collectors **13** 903
works **9** 442; **12** 386; **15** 85
illustrated **9** 433; **18** 512
celts **18** *881*; **21** 242, 266
CEMA *see* COMMITTEE FOR THE ENCOURAGEMENT OF MUSIC AND ARTS
C.E.M.A. Bulletin **24** 446
Cemal Tollu *see* TOLLU, CEMAL
Cemelenum **3** 375
cement
historical and regional traditions
Africa **1** 331–2*, *332*
Buddhism **18** 769
Cambodia **5** 500, *500*
Côte d'Ivoire **1** 331
Ejagham **10** 124
Ghana **1** 331, *332*
Greece, ancient **13** 404
Ibibio **1** 331, 332
Igbo **1** 331
India, Republic of **15** 169
Kenya **1** 331
Kongo **1** 331
Laos **18** 769
Madagascar **1** 331
Nigeria **1** 331; **23** 137–8
Rome, ancient **26** 879
Togo **31** *74*
Yoruba **1** 331, 332
Zaïre **1** 331
technical examination **30** 409
types
Portland **7** 693; **29** 701
reinforced **22** 805
Roman **2** 692; **7** 693
uses
architecture **15** 169; **26** 879
houses **1** 331
plaster **29** 813
reliefs **5** *500*
sculpture **1** 331–2, *332*; **10** 124; **18** 769; **23** 137–8; **31** *74*
shrines (i) (cult) **1** 331, *332*
stucco **29** 813
cementarius **20** 559
cementation process **4** *681*, 682–3*
Čemerski, Gligor **19** 884
cemeteries **6** 165–7*; **20** 869; **31** 130–31
Aegean **2** 304–5
Anglo-Saxon **30** 43
Austria **6** 154; **14** 87
Belgium **25** 539
Celtic **6** 154; **14** 87
China **6** 685, 694
Crete **8** 153
Czech Republic **6** 154
Dawenkou culture **6** 694
Egypt **16** 175
England **25** 539
Etruscan **10** 586
France **6** 154, *166*; **20** 868; **25** 539
Greece, ancient **13** 396
Helladic **23** 476
Indian subcontinent **6** 165
Ireland **19** 720
Islamic **16** 175
Italy **10** 586; **28** *36*; **32** 562–3
Minoan **2** 304–5; **8** 153
Prehistoric art **6** 694; **19** 720; **25** 467, 538–9
Rome, ancient **14** 515
Switzerland **6** 157
Tibet **30** 815
Turkey **14** 515
United States of America **20** 869
Villanovan culture **32** 562–3
see also CATACOMBS; HYPOGEA; MAUSOLEA; NECROPOLEIS; TOMBS
cemeteries, war *see* WAR CEMETERIES

Cemfiglia, Pietro **4** 413
Cempoala **21** 200, 240, 598
Cenáculo, Manuel do *see* VILAS BOAS, MANUEL CENÁCULO
Cenad Cathedral **26** 706
Cenami, Giovanna **10** *708*
Cenci (family) **26** 755
Cencio, Mastro *see* ANDREOLI, VINCENZO
Cencio Savelli *see* HONORIUS III, Pope
Cendrars, Blaise **6** 167*, 384; **16** 808
- collaboration **8** 658; **19** 79
- groups and movements **8** 245; **27** 307
- illustrated works **9** 71; **19** 78; **21** 629; **30** 348
- productions **3** 120

Cendrier, François-Alexis **19** 847
Cenete, Rodrigo Diaz de Vivar y Mendoza, 1st Marqués del *see* ZENETE, RODRIGO DIAZ DE VIVAR Y MENDOZA, 1st Marqués del
Ceng Xi **33** 640
Ceng Yi **33** 640
Cenni di Francesco di ser Cenni **6** 168*; **19** 674
Cenni di Pepo *see* CIMABUE
Cennini, Andrea **6** 168
Cennini, Bernardo **32** 384
Cennini, Cennino (d'Andrea) **6** 168–9*
- studio **29** 854
- works **7** 627; **13** 133, 144; **20** 324; **31** 299
  - on art training **2** 523
  - on brushes **5** 33
  - on cartoons **5** 898
  - on chalk **6** 399
  - on charcoal **6** 469
  - on chiaroscuro **6** 569
  - on drawing **9** 219
  - on glazes **12** 803
  - on glues **5** 912
  - on gold **12** 621
  - on grounds **13** 708
  - on light **19** 353
  - on modelling **19** 352
  - on models **21** 757
  - on paintboxes **23** 788
  - on painting **13** 135, 138; **32** 805
  - on panel painting **24** 4, 5
  - on paper **24** 50
  - on pens **24** 349
  - on perspective **24** 492
  - on pigments **23** 785; **28** 338, 778
  - on pouncing **25** 378
  - on punching **25** 730
  - on sculpture **31** 302
  - on size **28** 812
  - on squaring up **29** 437
  - on styluses **29** 883
  - on tempera **30** 425
  - on textile painting **5** 656
  - on underdrawings **31** 578
  - on varnishes **32** 3
  - on workshops **11** 185
  - translated **21** 165; **22** 207; **33** 309

Cennini, Jacopo **11** *704*
Cennini, Pietro Paolo **1** 796
cenobitic cells **7** 819–20*
cenobrium *see under* PIGMENTS → types
cenotaphs **6** 170–72*
- Central Asia, Western **6** *207*
- Early Christian (*c.* AD 250-843) **6** 170
- Egypt **6** 171
- Egypt, ancient **6** 170
- France **4** *533*
- Germany **13** *610*
- Greece, ancient **6** 170
- Indian subcontinent **15** 389
- Iran **6** 172, *172*; **16** 249
- Islamic **6** 171–2*, *172*, *207*; **16** 249, *500*, 500–501
- Madagascar **20** 36, 37–8
- Mycenaean **6** 170
- Rome, ancient **6** 170
- Syria **6** 171
- Turkey **6** 172
- Yemen **16** *500*, 500–501

Cens, Anciau de *see* ANCIAU DE CENS
Censerie, Louis Dela *see* DELA CENSERIE, LOUIS
censers
- historical and regional traditions **6** 173–4*
  - Brunei **5** 11
  - Byzantine **6** 173–4; **9** 632, 656
  - China **6** 859, 866, 883
  - Christianity **6** 173
  - Early Christian (*c.* AD 250-843) **9** 632, 656
  - England **13** *164*
  - Germany **6** 173, *174*
  - Gothic **13** *164*
  - Greece, ancient **6** 173
  - Romanesque **6** 173, *174*
  - Rome, ancient **6** 173
  - Syria **6** 174
- materials
  - bronze **6** 173, 859, 866
  - copper **6** 173
  - gold **6** 173
  - pottery **6** 883; **9** 632
  - silver **6** 173, *174*; **9** 656
  - silver-gilt **13** *164*

Censore, Clemente **29** 341
censorship **6** 174–7*
see also ART LEGISLATION
Centaure, Le **5** 44; **8** 809; **17** 508; **31** 502
Centaure, Le **24** 439
Centcelles Mausoleum **6** 177*; **9** *510*, 570; **26** *904*; **29** *259*, 261, 274
- mosaics **27** 68

Centelles, Augustí **6** 177–8*
Centen, Dirck Hendricksz. *see* HENDRICKSZ. (CENTEN), DIRCK
Centen, Giovan Luca **14** 386
Centenar de la Pluma, Master of the **11** 481
- works **11** *481*

Center: A Journal for Architecture in America **24** 434
Centerfold *see* FUSE
Center for Creative Photography *see* ARCHIVE, THE
Center for Environmental Structure **1** 610
Center for Tapestry Arts **31** 661
centering **6** 178*, *178*; **20** 573; **32** 90
Centocelle, tomb of the Haterii **20** 864; **27** 36
centone, Il **7** 779
Central African Republic **1** *214*, 393; **6** 178–9*; **11** 880
- containers **1** 369
- megalithic architecture **21** 43
- painting **6** *179*

Central America *see* LATIN AMERICA
Central America, Pre-Columbian *see* MESOAMERICA , PRE-COLUMBIAN; SOUTH AMERICA, PRE-COLUMBIAN
Central Asia **6** 179–322*
- architecture **21** 591*
- bags **10** 873
- bone **6** 305
- books **5** 102
- caravanserais **16** 163
- carpets **16** 468
- cotton **6** 249
- felt **10** 872, 873–5
- fortifications **21** 591*
- harnesses **10** 873; **14** 180*
- iconography **5** 102
- inks **15** 850
- jade **7** 1
- leather **6** 305; **20** 327
- mantles **10** 873
- mats **10** 873
- metal **6** 305
- monasteries **5** 102
- mosques **22** 354
- painting **5** 102, *102*
- plaster **29** 821*
- rugs **10** 873
- saddlery **10** 873
- sculpture **6** 220; **9** 34
- shrines (i) (cult) **28** 635*
- stucco **29** 821*
- stupas **5** 102; **29** 867*
- temples **30** 440*
- tents **10** 873; **30** 473–6*
- terracotta **30** 510*
- trade **6** 621
  - fur **16** 456
  - jade **28** 718
  - pottery **6** 333, 888
- trappings **14** 180*; **16** 429

Central Asia, Eastern **6** 287–322*, *288*
- anklets **6** 312
- architectural decorations **6** 319
- architecture **6** 295–7*; **21** 592*
- arm-bands **6** 312
- armour **6** 305–6*
- arrows **6** 313
- art history **6** 320*
- axes **6** 305
- azurite **6** 302
- banners **6** 304, 314
- birch **6** 305
- bodices **6** 310
- bookbindings **6** 306, 307
- book covers **6** 306, 319
- books **6** 306–7*, *307*, 314
- bowcases **6** 305
- bows **6** 305
- boxes **6** 303
- bracelets **6** 312
- brick **4** 794; **6** 295
- bronze **6** 298, 315, *315*
- busts **6** *316*
- calligraphy **6** 307–8*, 314
- camel hair **6** 299, 301
- carving **6** 313
- casting **6** 313
- caves **18** 105; **30** 441–2
- ceramics **6** 308–9*; **33** 563
- charcoal **6** 302
- clay **6** 298, 299, *299*, *300*, 301
- clubs (weapons) **6** 305
- coats **6** 310
- coins **6** 309*
- collections **6** 320–21*
- containers **6** 313
- copper **6** 309, 313, 315
- cosmetics **6** 310
- craftsmen and artists **6** 294
- cuirasses **6** 306, 313
- cupolas **6** 295–6
- diadems **6** 312
- dress **6** 309–11*, *310*
- earrings **6** 310, 312
- exhibitions **6** 321–2*
- figurines **6** 298, 315–16
- flails **6** 305
- fortifications **6** 296; **21** 592*
- frontispieces **6** 307
- funerary equipment **6** 289
- furniture **6** 311–12*, 313
- gilding **6** *300*
- grounds **6** 301
- gypsum **6** 301
- hairstyles **6** 310
- headdresses **6** 310, 311
- helmets **6** 306
- hemp **6** 304, 314
- historiography **6** 320*
- iconography **6** 292–3*, 302, 303
- iron **6** 313; **7** 97
- jade **16** 858, 860
- jewellery **6** 312*, *312*
- lacquer **6** 306, 313*
- lances **6** 305
- lapis lazuli **6** 302
- leather **6** 313
- lost-wax casting **6** 313
- malachite **24** 793
- manuscripts **6** 303, 305, 306*, 314
- mass production **6** 314
- metalwork **6** 313–14*
- monasteries **6** 294, 296
- moulds **6** 298, *298*
- museums **6** 320–21*
- necklaces **6** 312
- painting **6** 301–5*, 314
  - miniatures **6** 305
  - panel **6** 303
  - scroll **6** 306
  - secco **6** 301
  - wall **6** 289, *292*, 294, *301*, 301–4*, *303*, *304*, *310*, *312*, 314; **32** 804
- paper **6** 314*
- paper mulberry **6** 314
- paratacamite **24** 793
- pasteboard **6** 306
- patronage **6** 294–5*
- pennons **6** 305
- pens **6** 307
- periods
  - Bronze Age **6** 289
  - Neolithic **6** 289
  - Palaeolithic **6** 289
- pigments **6** 302
- pillars **6** 319
- plaster **29** 823–4*
- platforms **6** 311
- poplar **6** 295
- portraits **6** 304
- pots **6** *308*
- potter's wheels **6** 309
- printing **6** 307, 314
- prints **6** *307*, 314*
- reeds **6** 295, 306
- religion **6** 291–2*, 303
- reliquaries **6** 319, *321*
- robes **6** 310
- roofs **6** *295*, 295–6
- sanctuaries **6** 296–7
- sand **6** 301
- scabbards **6** 305
- scripts **6** 307, 308
- scrolls **6** 306
- sculpture **6** 294, 297–301*, *299*, *300*, 308–19, *319*; **29** *823*
- seals **6** 314–15*, *315*
- shields **6** 306
- shirts **6** 309
- shrines (i) (cult) **28** *636*, 637*
- silk **6** 304, 309, 316
- silver **6** 305, 306, 309
- skins **6** 305
- statuettes **6** 298
- stencilling **6** 302
- stone **6** 315
- straw **6** 301
- stucco **6** 298; **29** *823*, 823–4*
- stupas **6** 297, *297*
- supports **6** 303, 314
- swords **6** 305
- tamarisk **6** 295, 296
- teapots **6** 313
- temples **3** 902*; **6** 294, 319; **30** 441–2*, *442*
- terracotta **6** *298*, *308*, 315–16*, *316*
- textiles **6** 303, 316–18*, *317*
- thrones **6** 311
- trade **6** 290–91*
- vestments (ecclesiastical) **6** 314
- walls **6** 295
- watch-towers **28** *720*
- weapons **6** 305–6*
- wicker **6** 311
- windsocks **6** 305
- wood **6** 295, 298, 300, 303, 306, 315, *316*; **28** *636*
- wood-carvings **6** 318–19*, *319*
- workshops **6** 298
- *see also* CHINA

Central Asia, Western **6** 181–287*, *182*; **16** *105*
- altars **6** *243*
- amphorae **6** *256*
- appliqué **6** 250, 251
- arches **16** 167, 168
- architectural decorations **6** 205–8*; **16** 169, 239, 245
- architecture **6** 195–205*
  - anti-seismic **16** 239
  - Bactria **6** 196, 197–8*
  - brick **16** 154, *159*, 160, 169, 199–200, 239
  - Buddhism **6** 198
  - Ghurid **16** 169
  - Islamic **6** 201–3*, 204–5*; **16** 142, 153–4*, 158–61*, 166–9*, 195–200*, 235–9*, *236*, 264
  - Khwarazm **6** 199*
  - Khwarazmshah **16** 158
  - military **21** 591–2*
  - Naqshbandiyya **16** 235
  - Parthian **6** *198*, 198–9*
  - Qarakhanid **16** 158, 258
  - Samanid **16** 158
  - Shaybanid **16** 220, 235
  - Sogdiana **6** 200, 201
  - stone **16** 199
  - Timurid **6** 202; **16** 195–8
  - vernacular **32** 320–22*
  - wood **16** 199
- armour **6** 259–62*; **16** 503
- arrowheads **6** 260, 261
- arrows **6** 261
- bark **6** 253, 261
- basins **6** *286*
- baths **6** 211
- bazaars **6** 211
- beadwork **6** 251
- belts **6** 244*, 251, 252, 274
- book illustrations **16** 196
- boots **6** 251
- bosses **6** *237*
- bottles **6** *268*
- bowcases **6** *259*, 261
- bowls **6** *188*, *240*, *241*, 245, *245*, *257*, *267*
- bows **6** 260, 261
- brass **16** *378*
- brick **6** 201, *206*, 207; **16** 154, *159*, 160, 169, 199–200, 239
  - *bannā'ī* **16** 199
- bronze **6** 242*, *243*, *245*, *246*, 260, 261, *263*, 274, *286*
- calligraphy **6** 257
- capitals **6** 217; **29** *822*
- caravanserais **6** 201, *202*; **16** 154, 238; **26** 302
- carpets **6** 186, 248, 252–4*; **24** 298, *298*
  - Islamic **16** 466, 469, 484–5*
  - Turkmenistan **6** *253*, 254
  - Turkoman **16** *484*, 484–5
- carving **16** 248
- casting **6** 274; **16** 370
- castles **6** 199–200, 206; **32** *321*
- cenotaphs **6** *207*
- ceramics **6** 224
- chalcedony **6** 261
- chalk **6** 224
- chariots **6** 260
- chasing **6** 274
- churches **6** 200
- citadels **6** 200, 210
- clasps **6** *273*; **30** *891*
- clay **6** *187*, *194*, *214*, *215*, 216, *216*, 217, 218, *218*, *219*, 219–20, *221*, 221–2
- cobalt **6** 258
- cochineal **6** 253
- coins **6** 262–6*, *263*, *265*
- collections **6** 282–5*
- columns **6** 200; **16** 168, 502
- copper **6** *243*, 260, 274
- cornelian **6** 274

Central Asia, Western—cont.
cotton **6** 248, 249–50*, *250*, 253; **8** 34
courtyards **16** *238*
cuirasses **6** 262
daggers **6** 260, 261
diadems **6** 274
diplomatic gifts **16** 413
domes **6** 199; **16** 161, 164, *237*, 238
doors **16** 492, 501–2
dress **6** 250–52*
dyes **6** 249, 253, 254; **16** 485
earrings **9** *457*
earthenwares **6** *257*, 258; **16** 413
eggs **6** 227
embroidery **6** 248, 250–51*, 252; **16** 451
enamel **6** 258
epigraphy **16** 166, 169
ewers **6** *239*, 245, *246*; **16** *378*
exhibitions **6** 285–7*
felt **6** 248, 251; **10** *874*; **16** 485
figurines **6** 276
filigree **6** 274, *274*
fortifications **6** 197, 199; **21** 591–2*
friezes **6** *230*, *231*
frit **6** 258
gardens **12** 81–3*; **16** 197–8, 238
gems **6** 250, 273
gilding **6** 269, 274
glass **6** 267–9*, *267*, *268*
glazes **6** 207, 257, 258; **16** 239, 248
goblets **6** 268
gold **6** 236–42*, 250, *259*, *260*, 261, 273, *273*, 274, *274*; **9** *457*; **27** *599*; **30** *891*
grounds **6** 224
gums **6** 227
hardstones **6** 273
hats **6** 252
hauberks **6** 261
helmets **6** 261, 262
hemp **6** 251
historiography **6** 278–81*
hospices **16** 237
houses **6** 200, *200*, 229–30; **16** 154
hunting-lodges **16** 238
iconography **6** 192–3*, *193*, 194–5*
ikat **16** 451
impressing **6** 275
indigo **6** 253
inkwells **6** 269
inlays **16** *378*
inscriptions **6** 208, 274; **16** 166, 169, 248, 378, 492
interior decoration **16** 200
iron **6** *260*, 261
ivory **6** 261, *270*, 270–71, *271*
ivory-carvings **6** 269–72*, *270*, *271*; **16** 526*; **23** *160*; **30** *262*
iwans **6** *205*; **16** 167
jade **6** 272*
jewellery **6** 238*, 272–4*; **16** 530–31*
*khānaqāh*s **6** 211
Koran stands **16** *501*
lamps **6** 257
languages **6** 184–5*
lead **6** 257
leather **6** 251, 261, 262; **16** 503
limestone **6** *217*
looms **6** 248, 253
maces **6** 261
madder **6** 253; **16** 485
madrasas **5** 137; **6** 201, *205*, 211; **16** 237
maiolica **6** 207
manganese **6** 207
manuscript illumination **6** 233*, *234*, 234–5*, *235*, 236*; **16** 252, 321–7*, 342–3*; **30** *922*
manuscripts **6** *189*; **16** 321, 342
markets **16** *237*, 238
masonry **16** 160

Central Asia, Western—cont.
mausolea **5** 137, 139
Islamic **6** 201, *206*; **16** *140*, *159*, 159–60, 166, 197
Samanid **16** *159*, 159
Turkmenistan **21** *169*
metalwork **6** 236–47*
Islamic **16** 370*, 377
Timurid **16** 377
mihrabs **16** 161, 245, *492*, 492
minarets **6** 201; **16** 160, 166, 237; **18** 22
miniatures (manuscript illumination) **16** *343*
mosaic **16** 199
mosaics **6** 208; **16** 248
mosques **6** 202, 211; **16** 153–4, 159, 166, 236–7
congregational **6** 201
courtyard **16** 153–4
four-iwan **16** 162–3
hypostyle **16** 159
*musalla*s **16** 163
Timurid **30** *918*
moulds **6** 218, 275
mud-bricks **6** 195, 199; **16** 168, 199–200
muqarnas (architecture) **6** 202; **16** 161, 169
museums **6** 282–5*
nails **6** 217
niches **16** 161
niello **6** 274
observatories **16** 198
ochre **16** 248
ossuaries **6** 193, *213*, 233, 276; **23** 606–9*, *608*
painting **6** 222–36*
Bactria **6** 216
Islamic **16** 160
Sogdiana **6** 230
vase **6** 233
wall **6** 223*, 224*, 228–33*
Bactria **6** 224–6*, *225*, *226*
Buddhism **6** 225–6*, *226*, 228, 232; **17** *734*
Islamic **6** 202; **16** 169, 200, 252, 253
Khwarazm **6** 223*, *227*, 227–8*, *228*, 233*
Kyrgyzstan **6** 232
Sogdiana **6** 228–32*
Tajikistan **17** *734*
Tokharistan **6** *232*, 232–3*
Turkmenistan **6** 223–4*
watercolours **16** *132*
paints **6** 222
palaces **16** 160; **23** 815, 820*
garden **23** 820
Islamic **6** *203*; **16** 167, *238*
Timurid **6** *203*; **23** 820
paper **27** 673
patronage **16** 235*
pavilions (buildings) **16** 197
pearls **6** 251
penboxes **6** 257
pendants (jewellery) **6** *274*
pigments **6** 253; **16** 248, 485
pīshṭāq **16** 160, 164
plans **16** 196
plaques **27** *599*
plaster **6** 214–15, *220*; **16** 200; **29** 821–3*
polychromy **6** 206, *219*, 221
portals **6** *203*
pots **6** *243*
pottery **6** *213*, 254–9*, *256*; **31** 701
Bactria **6** 255
Barbotine ware **6** 257
blue-and-white ware **6** 258; **16** 413
Chach **6** 256, 257
Islamic **16** 123, 400–402*, 407–10*, 412–14*
Khwarazm **6** 255, 257, 258, 259
lājvardīna ware **16** 413
lustreware **6** 258; **16** 413
Prehistoric **6** 255*

Central Asia, Western
pottery—cont.
Sogdiana **6** 255, 256, 257, 258
Tajikistan **6** 259
Timurid **16** 413–14
Turkmenistan **6** 255
printing **6** 249, *250*; **16** 451
quivers **6** 261, 262
religion **6** 192–3*, 194–5*
revetments **16** 199
rhyta **6** *256*, 270–71, *271*; **23** *160*
*ribāṭ*s **16** 154
ribs **16** 164
robes **6** 251, *252*
rock art **6** 222–3*; **10** 896
rock crystal **6** *274*
rugs **10** *874*
sabres **6** 261
sand **6** 224
scabbards **6** *270*
scripts **6** 202; **16** 166, 169, 378
sculpture **6** *187*, *194*, 211–22*, *214*, *215*, *216*, *217*, *218*, *219*, *220*, *221*, 275–6; **16** 239; **23** *608*
relief **6** *276*; **18** *16*
seals **23** 159
sgraffito **16** 407–8*
sheepskin **6** 251
shields **6** 261, 262
shrines (i) (cult) **28** 635–6*
silk **6** 248–9*, *248*, 250, 251, *252*, 253; **28** 715
Islamic **16** 435
Sogdiana **6** 285; **28** *722*
Timurid **16** 430
silver **6** *188*, *193*, 236–42*, *239*, *241*, 250, 262, *263*, 274; **16** *378*; **28** *723*
silver-gilt **6** *237*, *240*
slip **6** 255, 257, *257*; **16** 408*
squinches **6** 199; **16** 161, 168–9
stamping **6** 274, 275
stamps **6** 214, 249
statuettes **6** 275
steel **6** 261
stelae **29** 618, 619
stitches **6** 250
stone **6** 216–17, 220, 221, 224, 260; **16** 199
strapwork **31** 784
stucco **16** 160; **29** 821–3*, *822*
sword grips **6** *260*
swords **6** 260, 261, 262
*talar*s **16** 238, *238*
temples **6** 197–8, 200; **30** 440–41*
tents **16** 197, 485; **23** 820
terracotta **6** 206–7, 274*, 275–7*, *276*; **16** 166, 169, 245
textiles **6** 247–8*, 249
Bactria **6** 214
Islamic **16** 435, 443, 451*
zandanījī **16** 435
threads **6** 250
tiles **6** 202, 204, 206, 207–8*, *207*; **16** *140*, 169, 199, *236*, 239, 248
cuerda seca **16** 239
lājvardīna **16** 249
tin **6** 257
tombs **6** 196; **16** 159–60, 164, 197, 237, 492
towers **16** 159–60
toys **6** 276
trade **6** 185*
books **16** 343
cotton **6** 249
glass **6** 267, 268
manuscripts **16** 342, 346
porcelain **16** 412
pottery **16** 402, 413
silk **6** 248; **16** 430
stone **16** 199
textiles **16** 444
trays **6** 245, *246*
turquoise **6** 261, 262
urban planning **6** 208–11*, *210*, *211*; **16** 264
vambraces **6** 262
vaults (ceiling) **6** 202; **16** 199

Central Asia, Western—cont.
velvet **6** 250
vine leaves **6** 253
walls **6** 211
war hammers **6** 261
weapons **6** 259–62*
weaving **6** 249; **16** 443
wicker **6** 261, 262
windows **6** 269
women **30** 917
wood **6** 220; **16** 199
wood-carvings **6** 277–8*; **16** 492
woodwork **16** 491–2*, *492*, *501*, 501–2*
wool **6** 248, 251, 253, *253*; **24** *298*
see also AFGHANISTAN; KAZAKHSTAN; KYRGYZSTAN; TAJIKISTAN; TURKMENISTAN; UZBEKISTAN
Central Bank of the Bahamas **3** 64
Central Bank of Trinidad and Tobago **31** 339
Centralblatt der Bauverwaltung see ZENTRALBLATT
Central Board of National Antiquities and National Historical Museums (Sweden) **8** 649
central heating *see under* HEATING SYSTEMS → types
centrally planned churches *see under* CHURCHES → types
Central Photographic Services **14** 173
Central Public Works Department, India **15** 168
Central Rectangle Binder **4** 353
centre, geometrical *see* GEOMETRICAL CENTRE
Centre 5 **2** 753; **18** 65
Centre de Rénovation de la Tapisserie **30** 328
Centre des Métiers du Verre du Québec **5** 583, 592
Centre d'Etudes et de Documentation sur l'Ancienne Egypte (CEDAE) **10** 83
Centre International des Civilizations Bantu *see* CICIBA
Centre of People's Power **29** 907
centrepieces
historical and regional traditions
Austria **2** *817*
Germany **12** *450*; **16** *899*
Italy **32** 203–4
Portugal **25** *313*
materials
porcelain **2** *817*
silver-gilt **16** *899*; **25** *313*
Centro Artístico, Olot **29** 284; **32** 97
Centro Bohemio **13** 796
Centro Cultural Peruano Japonés **24** 515
Centro de Artes Visuales di Tella **2** 405
Centro de Enseñanza Gráfica (CEGRA) **10** 511; **32** 176, 180
Centro de Tapicería Uruguaya **31** 757
centrolobian **24** 515
Centula *see* SAINT-RIQUIER-ABBEY
Centurión, Emilio **2** 400; **6** 322*
Centurión, Manuel **21** 389
Centuripe **13** *362*
figurines **13** 581
pottery **13** 539, *539*; **28** 655
Century Association *see* CENTURY CLUB
Century Club **9** 733; **15** 30, 834; **17** 899; **29** 870; **33** 152
Century Guild Hobby Horse, The see HOBBY HORSE, THE
Century Guild of Artists **6** 322*; **10** 298; **14** 281
members **14** 764; **15** 142; **20** 26
Century Home **5** 576
Century Magazine **7** 551

Cenwalh, King of Wessex (*reg* 643–72) **33** 229
Ceolfrith **15** 874
Ceos *see* KEA
Ceparelli, Silvio di fu Giovanni di Neri de' *see* COSINI, SILVIO
Cepelia Folk Art Trade Cooperative **25** 122, 133
Cepero, Carlos Celis **32** 567
Cepero, Manuel López *see* LÓPEZ CEPERO, MANUEL
Cepha **31** 434
Cephalonia *see* KEPHALLINIA
Cepka, Anton **28** 856
Ceppas, Antonio **22** 95
Ceppi, Carlo **6** 322–3*
collaboration **25** 856
pupils **10** 886
works **13** 752; **31** 442
Cera **9** 709
Ceracchi, Giuseppe **6** 323–4*; **8** 481; **16** 705; **32** 101
Ceraiolo, Antonio del *see* CERAIUOLO, ANTONIO DEL
Ceraiuolo, Antonio del **25** 721; **31** 205
Ceraiuolo, Orsino **16** 749
Ceramex Mandini **29** 117
ceramic, reinforced *see* REINFORCED CERAMIC
Ceramica Ibis **28** 176
Ceramic Art Co. *see* LENOX CHINA CO.
ceramic marks *see under* MARKS
ceramic models *see under* MODELS → types
Ceramic Neolithic period *see under* ANATOLIA, ANCIENT; SYRIA-PALESTINE → periods
ceramics **6** 324–36*; **14** 424–5
cleaning **6** 334–5*
collections *see under* COLLECTIONS → types
conservation **6** 334–6*; **7** 727–8, 729
dating methods **2** 304; **11** 309; **30** 404, *404*
display **9** 28–9*
England **9** 29; **29** *221*
France **9** *28*
Moche (culture) **29** *221*
South America, Pre-Columbian **29** *221*
historical and regional traditions
Aboriginal Australia **1** 44
Africa **1** 285–6*, 328–30*, *329*, *330*, 378
Akan **1** 392
Albania **1** 543*
Ancient Near East **1** 877
Antigua (island) **2** 146, 152
Antilles, Lesser **2** 144, 146, 152*
Armenia (Europe) **2** 439–40*
Asante **2** 589*
Australia **2** 759–62*, *761*, *762*
Austria **2** 815–17*
Barbados **2** 146, 152
Belgium **3** 575, 588–9*, 591–2*
Benin, Kingdom of **1** 329
Brunei **5** 12*
Buddhism **5** *111*
Bulgaria **5** 158–9*, *159*
Burma **5** 254–5*
Cambodia **5** 506–7*
Cameroon **1** 329
Canada **5** 580–82*
Central Asia, Eastern **6** 308–9*; **33** 563–4
Central Asia, Western **6** 224
Chad Republic **1** *330*
Champa **6** 432*
Chile **6** 600*
China **6** 772, 868–9*, 870–73*, 874–5*, *875*, 889*, 913–18*; **7** 94, 106, 143–4, 157; **9** 34; **16** 398
Buddhism **5** *111*
commentaries **5** 293; **14** 604; **17** 481

ceramics
historical and regional traditions
China—cont.
Qing period (1644-1911) **14** 425
Song period (AD 960-1279) **6** 891–2*, 894–5*
Tang period (AD 618-907) **30** 288
Yuan period (1279-1368) **6** 896–901*
Zhou period (*c.* 1050-256 BC) **33** 660
20th cent. **6** 911–13*
Coptic **7** 826*
Crete **13** 358
Croatia **8** 180
Cuba (Caribbean) **8** 229, 234, *236*, 236–7*
Cycladic **8** 308, 309
Cyprus **8** 363
Czech Republic **8** 403–6*; **9** 80
Denmark **8** 747–9*
Dominica **2** 152
Dominican Republic **9** 114
Ecuador **9** 709
Egypt **7** 826*; **9** 767
England **6** 329, 558; **10** 281, 300*, 305–15*
Finland **11** 105–6*
Fon **1** 329
France **11** 603*; **14** 425
Germany **12** 428*
Ghana **1** 330
Greece **13** 358*
Hausa **14** 232*
Hungary **15** 1–3*
Iceland **15** 72*
Igbo **1** 329, 330
Indian subcontinent **15** 685*
Indonesia **15** 811*
Iran **9** 34; **16** 419, 423*, 515; **29** 618
Safavid **16** 423–5
Iran, ancient **15** 903, 904, 905, 920–21*, *921*
Iraq **9** 34
Ireland **16** 28–9*
Islamic **14** 427; **16** 393–6*, 419–23*, 515
Iran **16** 419
Israel **16** 568*
Italy **16** 732*
Jamaica **16** 887–8*
Japan **4** 70; **17** 240–44*, *241*, 252*, 256–8*, 265–8*, 297, 350, *352*, 398, 399; **18** 601; **21** 650; **23** 365; **28** 495
Edo period (1600-1868) **14** 704
Heian period (AD 794-1185) **17** *244*
Meiji period (1868-1912) **17** 378
Nara period (AD 710-94) **17** 387
Java **15** 811
Kenya **17** 906
Knights Hospitaller **20** 215
Korea **17** 351, 352; **18** 257, 332*, 337*, *338*, 340*, 344*
Laos **18** 775*
Malaysia **20** 179*
Malta (Republic of) **20** 215*
Mangbetu **1** *329*
Maya **1** 706; **20** 884, 886
Mesoamerica, Pre-Columbian **1** 706; **21** 181, 195, 266, 737
West Mexico **33** 102, *102*
Mongol **6** 331
Mumuye **22** 287*
Nabataea **22** 420*, *420*
Native North Americans **22** 562, 563
Netherlands, the **3** 589; **22** 865, 877–84*
Nevis **2** 152
New Zealand **23** 68–70*

ceramics
historical and regional traditions—cont.
Niger **1** 330
Nigeria **1** 328
Norway **23** 234–5*
Nubia **23** 284–5, 289
Ottoman **16** 419–23*
Pakistan **23** 802–3
Paraguay **24** 97
Peru **24** 514*
Philippines **24** 626*
Poland **25** 122–4*, *123*
Portugal **25** 308–11*
Prehistoric art **6** 772; **9** 80
Rhodes (island) **1** 877; **13** 358
Romania **26** 718–19*
Russia **27** 410*
Scotland **28** 256*, 257–8*
Serbia **28** 454*
Slovenia **28** 862
South Africa **29** 116–17*
South America, Pre-Columbian **30** 282
South-east Asia **29** 231–2
Spain **29** 322*, 327–30*
Sumatra **15** 811
Sweden **30** 97*
Switzerland **30** 143–4*
Thailand **5** 12; **29** 232; **30** 608–9*, 611–12*
Toltec **31** 99
Trinidad and Tobago **31** 338–9*
Tunisia **31** 426
Turkmenistan **6** 224
Ukraine **31** 563
United States of America **10** 852; **31** 634–40*
Venezuela **32** 166
Vietnam **5** 12; **6** 432*; **29** 232; **32** 481, 484–6*
Wales **32** 789–90*
West Mexico **33** 102, *102*
Zaïre **1** 328, *329*
historiography *see under* HISTORIOGRAPHY → types
materials
adhesives **6** 335–6
bronze **6** 336
china stone **16** 393
clay **6** 324–5*; **16** 393; **17** 240–41
consolidants **6** 335
copper oxides **6** 330
earthenware **2** *761*
enamel **6** 328; **10** 199; **16** 515; **17** 242, 256, 378; **30** 611
flint **6** 330
frit **17** 242
glazes **4** 172; **6** 324, 328, 329*, 869, 872–3*; **11** 794; **16** 393–4; **17** 242, 266; **28** 495
gold **6** 328, 329
gold leaf **6** 328
incising **16** 425
inscriptions **16** 395, 425
iron oxide **6** 330
lacquer **17** 297
lithography **6** 328
monograms **16** 425
oils **6** 329
plaster **6** 335
platinum **6** 329
resins **6** 335–6
saggars **27** 520
sand **6** 328, 330
silver **6** 329
slip **6** 327, 328; **28** 842
restoration **7** 729
technical examination **6** 334*; **30** 393, 395, 397, *397*, 400, 406–7*
techniques
acid-gold process **21** 697
casting **6** 327, *327*
coiling **6** *326*; **16** 394
drying **6** 330
fettling **6** 327

ceramics
techniques—cont.
gilding **6** 328–9, 336
impressing **6** 327
jiggering **6** 327
moulding **6** 327–8, *327*, 336
overglaze decoration **6** 328, 334; **16** 423, 425, 426; **17** 242; **18** *554*
painting **6** 772, 773
printing **6** 328; **10** 311
riveting **6** 335
rouletting **6** 327
sgraffito **6** 328; **28** 534
sprigging **6** 327, *328*
throwing **6** *326*; **16** 394
transfer (printing) **3** 591; **4** 177; **6** 328; **10** 281, 306; **25** 310; **28** 257–8; **30** 97
turning **6** 327, *328*
underglaze decoration **6** 328; **10** 310; **16** 248–9, 419, 420, 421, 423, 426; **17** 242, 254
see also FIRING
uses
architecture **22** 270
armour **2** 474
candlesticks **5** 611
chess sets **6** 555
figurines **1** *330*
finials (architectural) **1** 328
grounds **6** 224
incense burners **20** 884
inkstones **7** 94; **17** 387
jewellery **7** 106; **17** 530
lacquer **18** 601, 615
mosaics **32** 481
murals **16** 568
netsuke **17** 398, 399
panels (wall) **5** 159, *159*
pots **1** *329*
screens (i) (architectural) **5** 159
sculpture **1** 44, 328*; **11** 106; **17** 267
stelae **29** 618
stoves **3** 575, 588; **11** 105
tea ceremonies **17** 341
see also EARTHENWARES; PORCELAIN; POTTERY; STONEWARES; TERRACOTTA
Ceramic Studio **29** 116
Cerano **6** 337–40*; **16** 674
assistants **4** 45
collaboration **22** 82; **25** 643, 644; **26** 318
patrons and collectors **4** 425; **16** 562; **21** 526; **22** 26; **28** 496
pupils **23** 320
works **6** *337*, *338*, *339*; **10** 744, 763; **16** 701; **21** 529, 534; **31** 883; **32** 620
Cerasi, Tiberio **22** 521
Cerato, Domenico **5** 424; **6** 340–41*; **21** 106; **23** 752
cerba, La **24** 448
Cerbaia, Casa Bandinelli Gradi **4** 32
Cerbara, Giovanni Battista **6** 341; **12** 262
Cerbara, Giuseppe **6** 341*; **12** 262, 738
Cerbara, Nicola **6** 341*; **12** 738
Cerbellón, Conde de **19** 657
Cerberus Painter *see* PASEAS
Cerceau, Du *see* DU CERCEAU
Cercel, Petru, Prince **31** 23
Cerchez, Cristofi **6** 342*; **26** 709
Cerchez, Grigore **5** 72; **26** 709, 718
works **5** *73*
Cercina, S Andrea **12** 549
Cercle Artistic Industrial **29** 306
Cercle Artistique (Antwerp) **18** 680
Cercle Artistique (et Littéraire Volney) **31** 214
Cercle d'Art Moderne **19** 92
Cercle d'Art Photographique **24** 738

Cercle d'Elèves et Anciens Elèves des Académies des Beaux-Arts *see* ESSOR, L'
Cercle et Carré **1** 76, 89; **6** 342*; **7** 772; **25** 108; **28** 198; **32** 696
collections **2** 409
members
Arp, Hans (Peter Wilhelm) **2** 490
Foltýn, František **8** 393
Gorin, (Albert) Jean **13** 10
Henri, Florence **14** 393
Martyn, Ferenc **20** 518
Mondrian, Piet(er Cornelis) **21** 854
Pevsner, Antoine **24** 574
Prampolini, Enrico **25** 447
Rees, Otto van **26** 75
Sartoris, Alberto **27** 853
Seuphor, Michel **22** 749
Stażewski, Henryk **29** 582
Täuber-Arp, Sophie **30** 234
Torres García, Joaquín **31** 183
Vantongerloo, Georges **31** 890
Cercle et Carré **24** 428, 442; **29** 661
Cercle Sébastien Gryphe **19** 848
Cercueil, Joseph **11** 404
Cerda, Ferdinando de la *see* FERDINANDO DE LA CERDA
Cerda, Fernando de la **12** 920
Cerdá, Francisco **3** 219
Cerdà, Ildefonso **6** 342*
works **3** 215, *216*; **27** 276; **29** 272; **31** 724
Cerda, Joseph de la **33** 728
Cerda, Juan II de la, Duque de Medinaceli *see* MEDINACELI, JUAN II DE LA CERDA, Duque de
Cerda, Luis de la, Duque de Medinaceli *see* MEDINACELI, LUIS DE LA CERDA, Duque de
Cerdagne, Guibert, Comte de **27** 566
Cerda y Mendoza, Luis de la, Conde de Medinaceli *see* MEDINACELLI, LUIS DE LA CERDA Y MENDOZA, Conde de
Cerdeña, Pedro de **29** 340
Cerdo, M. Cossutius *see* COSSUTIUS CERDO, M.
ceremonial barges *see under* BARGES → types
ceremonial objects **22** 668, 669
ceremonial palettes *see under* PALETTES → types
ceremonial wagons *see under* WAGONS → types
Ceresa, Antonio **6** 343
Ceresa, Carlo **6** 343*
Ceresa, Giuseppe **6** 343
Ceresara, Paride (da) **10** 520; **14** 582, 870; **15** 86; **20** 312; **25** 249; **29** 860
ceresin *see under* WAXES → types
Ceresola (il Vannone), Andrea **9** 173
Ceresola, Venerio **5** 81
Céret Bridge **4** 801
Cerezo, Mateo (*fl* 1610-40) **6** 343
Cerezo, Mateo (1637-66) **6** 343–4*; **29** 282
attributions **5** 343; **25** 168
teachers **5** 874
Cerezo de Salamanca **21** 596
Cergy-Pontoise **4** 227; **18** 809; **24** 131; **32** 26
Ceri **6** 354; **10** 606
S Maria Immacolata **26** 649, 655
Ceri, Andrea de' **24** 419
Ceri, Lorenzo di **31** 316
Cerialis Caesius Rufus, Quintus Petillius **33** 541
Cerigo *see* KYTHERA
Ceriset, François **13** 234
Cerisy-la-Forêt, St Vigor **26** 598; **30** 729; **32** 89
piers (ii) (masonry) **24** 750
Cerknica Church **28** 858

Čermák, Jaroslav **6** 344*; **8** 392; **22** 17; **25** 433
Cermenate, Ambrogio da *see* AMBROGIO DA CERMENATE
Čermínová, Marie *see* TOYEN
Cernavoda **6** 344–5*; **25** *471*; **26** *705*
figurines **6** 344–5; **25** 512
Cerne Abbas Giant (Dorset) **10** 473, *473*; **14** 544; **25** *470*
Černé Údolí **23** 264
Cerni, Vicente Aguilera *see* AGUILERA CERNI, VICENTE
Cernica **25** 516
Černigoj, Avgust **28** 860
Černik, Artus **8** 437
Cernil, St Basil **5** 677
Černín *see* CZERNIN
Černín von Chudenitz, Humprecht Jan, Count *see* CZERNIN VON CHUDENITZ, HUMPRECHT JAN, Count
Cerno, Barbara **22** 608
Cerno, Joe **22** 608
Černohorský z Boskovice, Jan Šembera **5** 79; **29** 738
Cernuschi, Henri **4** 597; **6** 345*, 868; **7** 155
Cernuschi, Musée *see under* PARIS → museums
Černý, František M(aria) **6** 345*
Černý, Karel **20** 254
Černý, Stanislav **28** 853
cerography *see* ENCAUSTIC PAINTINGS
Ceroli, Mario **6** 345–6*; **26** 778
Ceron, Antonio **29** 350
Ceroni, Juan Antonio **29** 341
Ceroni, Karol **18** 440
Cerqueira Cesar, Roberto **19** 271
Cerquozzi, Michelangelo **6** 346–7*
collaboration **2** 43; **7** 509; **27** 643
groups and movements **3** 143
patrons and collectors **6** 585
works **6** *347*; **12** 289
Cerrato, Leonel **23** 84
Cerretani, Agostino **12** 7
Cerreto Sannita **16** 736
Cerri, Pierluigi **13** 629
Cerrig-y-Drudion **6** 160
Cerrini, Giovanni Domenico **6** 347–8*
patrons and collectors **21** 27
reproductive prints by others **3** 521
works **26** 771
Cerrini, Lorenzo **1** 673
Cerro Blanco **6** 522, 523; **29** 167
Cerro de Hojas **20** 316
chairs **20** *317*
Cerro del Huistle **33** 101
Cerro de los Mesas **21** 197
Cerro de los Santos **15** 58, 60
Cerro de Moctezuma **1** 713
Cerro Jaboncillo **20** 316; **29** 145
Cerro la China **29** 203
Cerro Mangote **7** 506
Cerro Ñañañique **6** 523
Cerro Nestepe **21** 219; **31** 311
Cerroni, P. **8** 426
Cerros **20** 881, 882, *882*; **21** 196
pyramids **20** 881
stucco **29** 828
Cerro Sechín **6** 348–50*, 521; **29** 131, *156*, 160
adobe **29** 162
architecture **29** 159, 160
monoliths **29** 167
sculpture **29** 169
stone-carvings **6** *349*, *350*
temples **29** 165; **30** 447
Cerroti, Violante **8** 20
Cerro Trinidad **6** 440; **29** *156*, 173
Cerro Zapotecas **7** 202
Cerruti, Michelangelo **6** 350*
certificates **17** 230
Certosa **25** *470*
Certosa da Galuzzo **20** 280
Certosa Situla **28** 806, *807*

certosina 6 351*; 20 467
cerulean blue see under PIGMENTS → types
ceruse see under PIGMENTS → types
Ceruti, Fabio 1 463
Ceruti, Giacomo 6 351–2*
works 4 748; 6 351; 12 292
Ceruti, Giovanni 6 352*; 31 898
Cerutti 9 331
Cerutti, Col. 14 527
Cerva, Giovanni Battista della 18 747; 19 545
Cervantes Saavedra, Miguel 4 364, 365; 8 218; 14 868; 21 704; 30 664
Cervara, S Maria 29 332
Cerveira, Lima da Villa Norvada see LIMA DA VILLA NORVADA CERVEIRA
Cervelli, Federico 26 320
Cervelló 29 330
Červen 24 440
Cervenbreg 9 655
Červenka 8 401
Červený Kameň 28 848
Castle 14 886; 28 849, 852
collections 28 857
paintings 14 899
sculpture 14 893
Cervera
manuscripts 4 16
S Tecla 29 263
University 31 674
Cerveteri 6 352–4*; 10 583, 585, 601, 637, 638, 640; 16 620; 26 886
Banditaccia Necropolis 6 353; 10 597; 22 716
bronzes 10 626
fibulae 10 630; 12 868
gold 10 631
holmoi 10 610
hydriai 13 516
jewellery 10 632
Museo Nazionale Cerite 6 354; 10 640
paintings
vase 10 613, 614, 615, 635
wall 10 587, 617, 620; 16 652
Palazzo Ruspoli see Museo Nazionale Cerite
plaques 10 620
pottery 10 591, 610; 13 486, 516, 542; 32 57
sarcophagi 10 588, 636
sculpture 10 591, 603, 608; 27 31
Throne of Claudius 27 32
tiles 6 388
tombs 10 591, 592
Regolini-Galassi Tomb 6 353; 10 587, 591, 597, 626, 631, 640; 31 109
Tomba degli Scudi e Sedie 10 598, 599
Tomba dei Capitelli 10 599
Tomba dei Letti e Sarcophagi 10 598
Tomb of the Five Chairs 10 603, 634
Tomb of the Greek Vases 10 598
Tomb of the Painted Animals 10 620
Tomb of the Painted Lions 10 612, 620
Tomb of the Painted Reliefs 10 597, 599, 633; 29 814; 31 109
Tomb of the Sarcophagi 10 607, 607–8
Tomb of the Ship I 10 620
trade 10 584, 591, 592
urns 10 593, 603
vases 10 595, 610, 611, 612, 613, 615, 616
Cerveto, Ramón 25 816
Cervetto, Giovanni Paolo 6 29
Cervi, Giuseppe 14 106
Cervicornus, Eucharius 33 289
Cervini, Marcello, Cardinal see MARCELLUS II, Pope
Cervoni Gely, Fran 25 701
Césaire, Aimé 30 22
César 6 354–5*; 11 569, 570
groups and movements 17 694; 23 261; 30 924
methods 19 395
patrons and collectors 7 797, 842; 14 48; 27 224; 29 420
works 6 354; 16 58
Cesar, Josef 18 517
César, Julio de 24 95
Cesar, Miguel 22 245
Cesare, 6th Duke of Modena and Reggio (reg 1597-1628) 3 744; 5 857; 10 518, 525*; 11 4
Cesare, Carlo di 12 575
Cesare, Francesco De see DE CESARE, FRANCESCO
Cesare da Santo 25 144
Cesare da Sesto 6 355–6*; 21 525; 28 656
patrons and collectors 24 526; 25 639; 28 479
works 4 285; 6 356; 19 191
Cesareo, Marc'Antonio 27 634
Cesare of Reggio see CESARIANO, CESARE
Cesari, Bernardino 2 492, 493; 22 484; 24 267
Cesari, Carlo de see CARLO DI CESARI DEL PALAGIO
Cesari, Giovanni 10 810
Cesari, Giuseppe see ARPINO, CAVALIERE D'
Cesari, Muzio 2 492
Cesariano, Cesare 6 356–9*
collaboration 12 719
works 6 358; 21 534; 26 432
writings 4 653; 5 905; 23 486; 26 432; 31 295; 32 635, 640
Cesarini, Giuliano 7 332
Cesariny (de Vasconcelos), Mário 6 359*; 8 221; 25 300
Cesarotti, Melchior 5 628
Cesati, Alessandro 6 360*; 20 919
collaboration 4 339, 340
patrons and collectors 10 810; 28 4
works 12 258
Cesena
Biblioteca Malatestiana 19 313
palace 15 150
Cesena, Nicolò da see NICOLÒ DA CESENA
Cesena, Peregrino da see PEREGRINO DA CESENA
Cesena, Teofilo di Jacopo see TEOFILO DI JACOPO CESENA
Cesena treasure 23 624
Cesi (family) 26 768, 846; 27 203
Cesi, Angelo 23 473; 24 199
Cesi, Bartolomeo 4 276; 6 361–2*
personal collection 25 412
pupils 30 798
restorations by others 29 892
works 6 362
Cesi, Carlo 6 362*; 26 840
Cesi, Emilio, Cardinal 26 845
garden 26 845
Cesi, Federico, Cardinal 2 162; 4 340; 6 360*; 11 721; 13 813
Cesi, Federico, Duca d'Acquasparta see ACQUASPARTA, FEDERICO CESI, Duca d'
Cesi, Giovanni Federico, Duca 6 360
Cesi, Ludovico 23 473
Cesi, Paolo Emilio, Cardinal 6 360
Cesi, Pier Donato, Cardinal 6 360*; 23 473
Cesières, Pierre de, Abbot of Souillac 29 94
Cesi Juno 1 533
Cesi Master 20 645*
Cesio, Carlo see CESI, CARLO
Cēsis 18 847, 847
Castle 18 847; 30 534
St John 18 848
Česká grafika 25 548
Česká Lípa 8 415
České Budějovice 8 376, 379, 415, 425, 426
Museum of Applied Art 8 424
Československá fotografie 24 440
Český Krumlov 6 363, 363–4*; 8 374
Castle 6 363–4; 8 377
Orangery 27 285
theatre 30 677
education (art) 8 425
façade decoration 10 741
Oberburg 26 496
Regional Museum 6 363
St Vitus' Cathedral 6 363; 8 376
sculpture 8 382, 383; 13 90
Český Krumlov Madonna, Master of the 8 382
Český Rudolec 8 377; 31 898
Český Šternberk Castle 6 364*; 8 374
Cesnola, Luigi Palma di see PALMA DI CESNOLA, LUIGI
Cesnola collection see under BOSTON (MA; USA) → museums → Museum of Fine Arts (1906)
Cesnola Painter 13 496
works 13 497
Céspedes, Domingo de 29 339; 31 89
Céspedes, Pablo de 6 364–5*; 26 307; 29 278
works 6 365
Cessac, Léon de 22 676
Cestaro, Jacopo 22 479
Cestero, José 9 118
Cesti, Pietro Antonio 5 264
cestri see STYLUSES
Cesura, Pompeo 27 711
Cetatea Alba 26 719
fortress 26 707
Cetăteni 26 710
Cetinje 22 17
Crna Gora Art Gallery 22 19
Ethnographical Museum 22 19
Njegoš Museum 22 19
Orthodox Church Museum 22 19
State Museum 22 19
Cetto, Max (L.) 3 273; 6 365*; 21 381
Cettomai, Felice 26 778
Ceulen, Cornelis Jonson van see JONSON VAN CEULEN, CORNELIS, I
Ceuli (family) 4 406
Ceuli, Curzio 26 396
Ceuninc, Jacob 21 102
Ceuta 16 298, 307
Ceva, Marchesi di 16 795
Cevizliköy see TBETI
Ceylon see SRI LANKA
Ceypler, Jan 6 365–6*
works 25 127, 128
Ceypler, Józef 6 366
Cézanne, Paul 3 813; 6 366–75*; 7 674; 11 508, 547, 667; 13 830; 20 473
collaboration 20 603
commentaries 14 594
dealers 19 10; 26 107; 32 686
drawings 9 226; 24 382
exhibitions 2 447; 10 680; 13 711; 24 142; 31 490
groups and movements 25 355
Aktion, Die 24 585
Golden Fleece (Zolotoye Runo) 12 870
Impressionism 15 151, 152, 153, 155
Moderne Kunstkring 21 775
Post-Impressionism 25 356
Secession (Berlin) 28 343
Secession (Vienna) 28 344
Cézanne, Paul
groups and movements—cont.
Société Anonyme Coopérative à Capital Variable des Artistes, Peintres, Sculpteurs, Graveurs etc. 8 621; 15 154
XX, Les 5 44; 32 591
lithographs 19 489
methods 7 630; 9 673; 23 379; 28 813
paintings 8 596
fêtes champêtres 11 39; 23 296
genre 6 370; 12 296
landscape 1 498; 6 368; 18 716, 717; 25 357
literary themes 22 379
portraits 6 367, 370; 24 382
still-lifes 6 369, 588; 11 418; 29 669, 669
watercolours 6 373; 32 902
patrons and collectors
Alexandre, Arsène 1 614
Arensberg, Walter and Louise 2 383
Barnes, Albert C. 3 251; 12 769
Beuningen, Daniel George van 3 889
Bliss, Lillie P(lummer) 4 142
Bührle, Emil Georg 5 132
Burrell, William (1861-1958) 5 278
Caillebotte, Gustave 5 391; 24 142
Camondo, Isaac de, Comte 5 530
Clark, Stephen 7 377
Cone family 7 702
Courtauld, Samuel (1876-1947) 8 62
Doucet, Jacques (-Antoine) 9 196
Duret, (Jules-Emmanuel) Théodore 9 448
Fåhreu, Klas 30 118
Gachet, Paul (-Ferdinand) (1828-1909) 11 887
Gauguin, Paul 12 188
Havemeyer, Louisine (Waldron) 14 244
Lehman, Robert 19 92
Liebermann, Max 19 334
Loeser, Charles Alexander 19 538; 29 604
Maitland, Ruth (Esther) 20 142
Matisse, Henri (Emile Benoît) 10 842; 20 822
MOMA (Museum of Modern Art) 2 447; 4 142
Morozov, Ivan (Abramovich) (1871-1921) 22 136; 30 361
Pellerin, Auguste 22 55
Phillips, Duncan 24 638
Quinn, John 25 823
Reber, Gottlieb Friedrich 26 59
Robinson, Edward G(oldenberg) 26 472
Rockefeller, Abby Aldrich 26 488
Sadler, Michael 22 55
Schreiber, Taft and Rita Bloch 28 167
Schuffenecker, (Claude-) Emile 28 172
Seilern, Antoine, Count 28 377
Shchukin, Sergey (Ivanovich) 28 569
Stein, Leo 29 604
Stein, Michael 29 604
Stieglitz, Alfred 29 655; 31 605
Tanguy, Julien-François 30 290
Tavernier, Adolphe-Eugène 30 375
Tetzen-Lund, Christian 30 532
Van Horne, William (Cornelius) 31 880
Vollard, Ambroise 24 143; 32 687
Cézanne, Paul
patrons and collectors—cont.
Walter-Guillaume Collection 13 826
Whitney, John Hay 33 150
Wildenstein, Georges 33 183
Zambaccian, K. H. 26 723
reproductive prints by others 32 577
Cezerla see CHEZARLA
C-group culture 23 278
Chaalis Abbey 7 303; 21 843
Chab, Víctor 2 400; 6 376*
Chabacier, José see LEONARDO, JUSEPE
Cha-bahil 22 758
stupa 4 213
Chabal-Dussurgey, Pierre-Adrien 3 461; 6 376–7*; 12 830
Cha Ban
citadel 6 426
Copper Tower 6 423, 426
Chabanais, Ademar of see ADEMAR OF CHABANAIS
Chabas, Maurice 6 377*; 27 639
Chabas, Paul (-Emile-Joseph) 6 377*
Chabat, Pierre 6 377–8*
Chabaud, Auguste 6 378*
Chabe 10 576
Chabet, Roberto 24 623
Chablis, St Martin 9 156; 13 39
Chabot, Hendrik 6 378–9*; 22 852, 861
Chabot, Léonor, Comte de Charny see CHARNY, LÉONOR CHABOT, Comte de
Chabris 30 905
Chabrol, Christophe-André-Jean, Comte de 11 543; 24 124
Chabrun, Jean-François 30 22
Chabry, Jean-Baptiste 6 379
Chabry, Marc 6 379*; 25 709
Chacalal 21 231
Chacao 32 178
Chach 6 182, 379*; 16 105
cotton 6 249
fortifications 6 199; 21 592
pottery 6 256, 257
Chachapoyas 6 380*; 15 161; 27 833
Chachba, Prince see SHERVASHIDZE, ALEKSANDR
Chachet 24 83
Chachoengsao 30 590
chacmools 28 640
Chacmultún 21 231
Chaco Canyon (NM) 1 820; 6 380–81*; 20 571; 22 544, 566
Pueblo Bonito 22 566
kivas 6 381
Chaco culture 6 380; 22 602; 24 92–3; 29 125
pottery 22 602
Chacón, Alonso 6 381–2*
Chacón, Ignacio 33 617
Chacón, Luis 25 824
Chacula style sculpture see under MAYA → sculpture
Chadderton, Hawthorne Mill 10 748
Chaddesley Corbett (Hereford & Worcs), St Cassian 11 252
Chadenac Church 26 600
Chad Gospels see GOSPEL BOOKS → individual manuscripts → Lichfield Gospels
Chadimba, Reinata 22 244
Chadirji, Rifat (Kamil) 6 382*; 16 1, 241
Chad Republic 1 214; 6 382*
brick 1 305
ceramics 1 330
currency 1 363
figurines 1 330
lip-discs 1 351
Chadwick, Edwin 31 723
Chadwick, Gordon 22 728

Chadwick, Lynn **6** 383*; **10** 268; **13** 629; **21** 746
Chadwick, W. **33** 310, 311
Chadwyck-Healy **2** 369
chādya **15** 243*
Chadyr-Lunga **21** 812
Chaffers, Richard, & Co. **19** 508
Chagall, Marc **4** 196; **6** 383–6*, *384*; **9** 747; **17** 577, 580; **19** 474; **25** 626; **27** 394; **31** 607; **32** 412
 book covers **16** 808
 book illustrations **4** 366; **10** 726; **30** 488
 collaboration **2** 542; **20** 603, 605; **29** 508
 dealers **20** 75
 exhibitions **3** 801; **32** 775
 furniture **28** 298
 groups and movements **8** 240, 244; **9** 144, 705; **11** 550; **22** 750; **27** 307, 392; **33** 380
 mosaics **17** 493; **22** 163
 musical instruments **22** 373
 paintings **2** 107; **3** 529; **6** *385*; **20** 208; **22** 331
 patrons and collectors **28** 314
  Abrams, Harry N(athan) **1** 71
  Arensberg, Walter and Louise **9** 383
  Brodsky, Isaak (Izrailevich) **4** 838
  Coquiot, Gustave **7** 834
  Costakis, George **8** 10
  Guggenheim, Solomon R(obert) **13** 800
  Hussey, Walter **15** 36
  Maitland, Ruth (Esther) **20** 142
  Masson, André **11** 659
  Matisse, Pierre **20** 832
  Morozov, Ivan (Abramovich) (1871-1921) **22** 135
  Musée National Marc Chagall **2** 370
  Nierendorf, Karl **23** 121
  Rothschild, Elie Robert de, Baron (*b* 1917) **27** 224
 periodicals **29** 871
 prints **25** 626
  drypoints **9** 310
  lithographs **19** 491, 492
  monotypes **21** 897
  posters **25** 350
  woodcuts **33** 362
 pupils **20** 194
 reproductive prints by others **25** 628
 sculpture **6** 577
 stained glass **14** 785; **17** 493; **21** 362; **26** 113
 studio **29** 858
 tapestries **17** 493
 teachers **3** 86; **24** 350; **33** 740
Chagall, Marc, Musée National *see under* NICE
Chagang Island **18** 334
Chagar Bazar **1** 862, 864; **6** 386–7*; **30** *180*
Chagas, Francisco das **4** 708
Chagga **30** 300
Chago *see* YU T'OK-CHANG
Chahamana **6** 387*
Chahamana *see*:
 ARNORAJA, Ruler
 PRITHVIRAJ III, Ruler
Chahar **21** 870, 878, 879
Chahar Aymaq **30** 476
Chahar Bagh *see under* ISFAHAN
chahār ṭāq *see under* TEMPLES → types
Chahine, Edgar **20** 603
Chah-i Torogh **1** 194
Chaiaese, Leonardo **22** 486
Chaïbia **22** 129
Chaikin, Benjamin **6** 387*
Chaillot **11** 652
Chainat **30** 632
Chainaye, Achille **32** 591
chain-mail armour *see under* ARMOUR → types
Chain-ridged ware *see under* POTTERY → wares
chains **17** 520, 524, 526
 historical and regional traditions
  China **7** *107*, 108, 145
  Germany **12** 450
  Greece, ancient **13** 411
  Islamic **16** 532
  Ottoman **16** 532
 materials
  gold **7** *107*, 108; **16** 532
  mother-of-pearl **12** 450
  quartz **12** 450
 uses
  bridges **4** 803
  display of art **9** 14
chains, watch *see* WATCH CHAINS
chain stitch *see under* STITCHES
Chair, René **21** 709
Chairestratos **9** 249; **13** 462
 works **9** *248*
Chaironea **14** 361
chairs **6** 387–92*
 historical and regional traditions
  Africa **1** 366
  Akan **1** 291
  Ancient Near East **1** 890; **30** 774
  Antilles, Lesser **2** 151
  Asante **1** 366; **2** 586*
  Australia **2** *758*
  Austria **2** 811; **15** *822*; **33** *156*
  Belgium **3** 581–2, 584
  Brazil **4** *721*
  Britain **20** *595*; **29** 763
  Catalonia **29** *320*
  China **6** 390*; **7** 32, 34, 35, 36, 39–40, 145, *145*
  Chokwe **1** 291, 366
  Czech Republic **8** 398, *400*, *402*
  Ecuador **20** *317*
  Egypt, ancient **6** 388; **10** 50, *51*, 52, *52*, 53
  England **5** 612; **6** 390; **10** 291, 292, *296*; **14** 522–3; **19** 592; **30** 783; **31** 682, 684–5
   Arts and Crafts Movement **2** *572*
   Roman **6** 388
   18th cent. **10** *295*; **31** *685*
   19th cent. **22** *143*
   20th cent. **10** *300*
  Etruscan **6** 388
  France **6** 390; **11** 585, 586, 587, 589, 594–5, 597, 598, 599; **30** 783; **31** 684, 685
   Art Nouveau **11** *600*
   Roman **6** 388
   19th cent. **30** XV
  Germany **12** 419, 426, 428, 461
   Bauhaus **12** *428*
   Roman **6** 388
  Greece, ancient **6** 388; **13** 591*
  Guro **13** 861
  Hungary **14** 903, 904, *908*
  Iceland **15** *72*
  Indian subcontinent **15** *697*
  Indonesia **15** 813
  Israel **16** *569*
  Italy **6** 390; **16** 722; **19** 5
   Etruscan **6** 388
   16th cent. **6** 725
   18th cent. **5** *54*
  Japan **17** 384
  Korea **18** 361
  Kuba (iii) (Zaïre) **1** 366
  Malta (Republic of) **20** 215
  Manteño culture **20** 316–17, *317*; **29** 145
  Netherlands, the **22** 870, *875*; **29** 763
   Sri Lanka **29** *471*
   20th cent. **22** *868*; **26** *378*
  Norway **6** 389; **23** 234
  Pende **1** 366
  Peru **24** 514
  Poland **25** 120
  Portugal **25** 304, 305, 306, 307, *307*
chairs
 historical and regional traditions—cont.
  Romania **26** 717–18
  Rome, ancient **6** 388
  Russia **7** 769; **27** *408*
  Scotland **6** *391*; **11** *850*; **28** 251, 253, 256
  South Africa **29** 115–16
  South America, Pre-Columbian **20** *317*; **29** 145
  Spain **19** 5; **29** 297, 301, 309–10, 314*, 315–16, *316*, 318, 319
   Gothic Revival **29** *318*
  Sri Lanka **25** 305; **29** 470
  Swahili **30** 57
  United States of America **4** *761*; **15** *825*; **31** 623, 625, *625*, 628, 630–31, *632*, *633*; **33** 156
  Wales **32** 788
  Zaïre **1** 366
 materials
  amaranth **11** 595
  bamboo **7** *145*
  basketwork **33** 155
  beech **10** *290*, 293, *296*; **11** 595
  bentwood **15** *822*; **30** *755*
  birch **5** *577*
  brass **3** 582; **16** *569*
  bronze **6** 388, 389
  cane **5** 612; **10** 291; **19** 592; **28** 252; **29** 470; **33** 155, 156
  canvas **6** 388
  carpets **28** 252
  cedar **2** *758*
  cherry-wood **8** *747*
  chromium steel **22** *875*
  copper **10** 50
  damask **11** 589
  ebony **10** 52
  faience (i) (glass) **10** 50, 52
  fibreglass **6** 392; **15** *825*
  glass **10** 52
  gold **6** 388; **10** 50, 52
  gold leaf **10** 52
  huang huali **7** *39*
  inlays **10** 52
  iron **6** 388, 389
  ivory **6** 388, 389; **10** 52; **15** *697*
  kumbuk **29** *471*
  laminates **6** 391
  leather **3** 582, 583; **6** 388; **19** 5; **25** 306; **28** 252
  mahogany **2** *758*; **6** 390; **11** 595; **28** *253*
  maple **28** *542*
  oak **6** *391*; **8** *400*; **11** *850*; **29** *320*
  papier mâché **24** 62
  pear-wood **29** *318*
  pine **6** *389*; **29** *318*
  plastics **6** 392; **22** 876
  plywood **10** *300*
  rose-wood **25** *307*
  rushes **5** *577*; **6** 388, *391*
  satin-wood **11** 595
  shells **25** 306
  she-oak **2** *758*
  silk **11** 589
  silver **29** 301
  steel **4** *761*
  stone **6** 388; **20** *317*
  straw **29** 763
  tapestries **9** 30; **11** 589
  tubular steel **3** 402; **6** 391; **12** *428*
  tusks **6** 389
  upholstery **11** 587; **31** 682, 684–5*, 686–7*
  velvet **3** 582
  walnut **8** *402*; **11** 589, *600*; **16** *569*, *725*; **25** 306; **29** *314*; **31** *625*
  wicker **15** *822*; **31** 684; **33** *156*
  wood **1** 291; **2** *572*; **5** *54*; **6** 388, 389; **15** *72*
 techniques
  carving **11** 587
chairs
 techniques—cont.
  gilding **8** *746*; **10** 50, *51*, *52*; **12** *626*
  mass production **20** *595*
 types
  Ant **16** 829
  armchairs
   China **7** *39*
   Denmark **8** *747*
   Egypt, ancient **10** 50–51
   England **12** *626*
   France **11** 598, *600*
   Sweden **30** *96*
   see also fauteuils
  back stools **6** 390
  Balans **23** 234
  balloon-back **24** 62
  banister-back **31** 623
  Barcelona chairs **30** 784
  bergères **6** 390; **11** 589
  Bertoia **3** 858
  Biedermeier **30** 753
  boarded seats **6** 389–90
  brander-back **28** 252, *253*
  bucket seat **22** 876
  burgomaster chairs **29** 470, *471*
  burgomeister **15** 813
  cain **28** 252
  Captain **31** 625
  capucine **5** 577, *577*
  caqueteuse **28** 251
  caquetoire **3** 582; **6** 390
  chairs of state **30** 782
  chaise au vertugadin **6** 390
  church-chairs **29** 470
  confidant **6** 391
  conversation **29** 8
  Cromwell **31** 623
  diphros **6** 388; **8** 746; **13** 591
  diphros okladias **13** 591
  double **29** 8
  duchesse brisée **19** 723; **26** 84
  Eames **31** 633
  easing-chairs **10** 53
  easy-chairs **6** 390; **12** 427; **31** 623, 684
   see also fauteuils de commodité
  Egg **16** 829
  ergonomic **6** 392; **23** *233*
  faldstools *see* X-frame
  fauteuils **6** 390; **11** 587, 589, 594–5
  fauteuils de commodité **6** 390; **31** 684
   see also easy-chairs
  folding **27** *409*; **29** 310; **31** 631
  friary **21** *391*
  gondole **31** 628
  Hitchcock **14** 590
  indiscret **6** 391
  invalid **6** 390; **31** 684
  klismos **6** 388, *388*; **13** 591; **33** 330
  Klismos **6** 390; **8** 745, *746*; **31** 628
  kubbstol **6** 389
  loungers **31** *632*, 633
  Martha Washington **31** 628
  Morris **2** 151; **22** 143; **31** 630
  Nasrid **29** 314, *314*
  Paimio Sanatorium **1** 8
  peinetas **29** 316
  planter **2** 151
  Polyprop **8** 583
  post seats **6** 389, *389*
  Raffles **15** 813
  rocking
   Austria **30** 754
   Shakers **28** *542*
   United States of America **28** 542, *542*; **31** 631; **33** 156
  sella curulis *see* X-frame
  sgabello **6** 390
  sièges courants **6** 390
  sièges meublants **6** 390
  sillas de cadera **29** 311
  sleeping-chairs **6** 390; **10** 291, *291*; **31** 684
chairs
 types—cont.
  Spanish **3** 582, 583; **22** 870
  stick-back **28** 251
  Sussex **6** 391; **22** 143, *143*
  Swan **16** 829
  thrones *see* THRONES
  thronos **6** 388; **13** 591
   see also GREECE, ANCIENT → thrones
  Trafalgar **27** 139, *139*
  tub **2** 151
  turned **31** 623
  wainscot **31** 623
  Windsor
   Canada **5** 578
   England **10** 293; **14** 522
   Scotland **28** 252
   United States of America **31** 625
  X-frame **6** 388–9; **10** 288, *290*; **13** 591; **30** 783
chairs of state *see under* CHAIRS → types
chaise au vertugadin see under CHAIRS → types
Chaise-Dieu Abbey, La *see* LA CHAISE-DIEU ABBEY
chaises longues **11** 594; **29** 8
Chaissac, Gaston **6** 392–3*; **7** 421; **11** 551
Chaitanya, Krishna **8** 677
Chaitu *see* CHETU
Chaix & Compagnie **7** 652
Chaiya **30** *571*
 sculpture **30** 606
 Wat Kaeo **30** 578
 Wat Long **30** 578
 Wat Phra Boromathat **30** 578
Chajang **5** 114; **18** 295
Chajul **13** *758*, 759
Chakanyuka, Chrispen **33** 679
Chakipampa style pottery *see under* POTTERY → wares
Chakkraphat, King of Ayutthaya (*reg* 1548-69) **30** 631
Chakma **3** 165
Chakparor, Darkembaj **17** 868
Chakpori **21** 846
Chakravarti, Ajit **15** 173
Chakravarti Paloja **15** 532
Chakravarty, Kalyan Kumar **30** 264
Chakri *see*:
 BHUMIBOL (Rama IX), King
 CHULALONGKORN (Rama V), King
 MONGKUT (Rama IV), King
 RAJANUBHAD DAMRONG, Prince
 RAMA I, king
 RAMA III, King
 RAMA VI
Chala, Bakalo Tower **21** 593
Chalandarjo, Filippo *see* CALENDARIO, FILIPPO
Chalandon, Albin **6** 393
Chalandon, Elisabeth **6** 393
Chalandon, Emmanuel **6** 393
Chalandon, Georges (*fl* 1890s) **6** 393*
Chalandon, Georges (*fl c.* 1970s) **6** 393
Chalandon, Henri **6** 393
Chalandon, Xavier **6** 393
Chalandriani **8** *304*, 315, 322
 cemetery **8** 323
Chalcatzingo **6** 393–4*; **21** *193*, 196, *372*
 architecture **21** 209*
 mirrors **21** 718
 Monument 1 **6** *393*, *394*
 reliefs **30** 786
 sculpture **21** 219, 246; **23** 416
chalcedony **14** 167; **16** 859; **17** 514
 historical and regional traditions
  Ancient Near East **1** *858*
  Aztec **21** 243
  Babylonian **1** *858*
  Byzantine **12** 254

chalcedony
historical and regional traditions—cont.
Central Asia, Western 6 261
China 7 132, *132*
Greece, ancient 12 247, 248
Italy 14 I1
Mesoamerica, Pre-Columbian 21 192, 241, 243
Sasanian 1 *858*
techniques
staining 12 270
uses
arrowheads 21 192
daggers 6 261
jewellery 17 519
pietre dure 14 I1
seals 1 *858*; 12 247, 248
snuff bottles 7 132, *132*
spearheads 21 192
swords 6 261
see also AGATE; BLOODSTONE (CHALCEDONY); CHRYSOPHRASE; CORNELIAN; JASPER; ONYX; PRASE; SARD; SARDONYX
chalcedony glass *see under* GLASS → types
Chalchihuites 33 101
Chalchuapa 6 394–5*; 10 *153*; 20 *882*
hardstones 29 153
sculpture 23 416
Structure E3-1 6 *394*
Chaldaea *see* MESOPOTAMIA
Chaldaean 3 12
Chalee, Pop *see* LUJAN, MARINA
Chalepas, Yannoulis *see* HALEPAS, YANNOULIS
chalets 6 395–6*, *395*
Chalette, Jean 6 396*; 31 207, 382
patrons and collectors 24 330
pupils 23 748
Chaley, Joseph 11 773
Chalgrin, Jean-François-Thérèse 6 396–7*
architecture
churches 6 *397*; 11 520; 24 120; 28 486
colleges 19 251
palaces 24 165
triumphal arches 10 745; 11 523; 12 616; 22 47; 24 124, *124*; 31 351
assistants 24 387
collaboration 3 852; 5 889
patrons and collectors 4 555; 13 665; 17 467; 20 897
pupils 12 746; 32 427; 33 599
reproductive prints by others 30 343
teachers 4 534
Chaliang 28 794
sanctuary 30 582
Wat Phra Si Ratana Mahathat 28 794; 29 826
Chaliapin, Fyodor 32 72
Chalice of St Lebuinus 23 537
Chalice of Theseus 27 607
chalices 1 697, 707; 6 398–9*
conservation 7 *728*
historical and regional traditions
Byzantine 9 656, 657, 661
Canada 5 *585*
Crete 21 *665*
Early Christian (*c.* AD 250-843) 9 656
Egypt, ancient 10 48
England 10 322, 325
France 11 616; 21 *163*
Germany 12 442
Gothic 10 322; 13 161–2, *162*, *163*, 169, 170
Holy Roman Empire (before 1648) 6 *398*
Hungary 13 161–2, *162*, 170
Insular art 2 377–8*, *378*; 8 *782*
Ireland 2 377–8*, *378*; 8 *782*, 782–3; 16 30
chalices
historical and regional traditions—cont.
Italy 13 *163*, 169
Merovingian 21 *163*
Mexico 21 *393*
Minoan 21 *665*
Poland 13 170; 25 125
Romanesque 6 *398*
Spain 13 169
materials
enamel 2 *378*; 13 *163*, 169, 170
faience (i) (glass) 10 48
gold 2 *378*; 5 *585*; 13 *162*; 21 *163*
hardstones 2 *378*
pewter 24 580
pottery 21 *665*
sardonyx 9 661
silver 2 *378*; 6 398; 8 *782*; 9 656, 657
silver-gilt 6 *398*; 13 *163*; 21 *393*
wood 31 305
techniques
gilding 2 *378*; 6 398
Chaligny, Antoine de 22 455
Chaligny, David de 22 455
chalk 6 399–400*; 8 127; 29 699*, 701
historical and regional traditions
Bhutan 3 914
Central Asia, Western 6 224
England 14 544; 29 699; 31 *527*
France 29 699
Gothic 13 135
Indonesia 15 807
Turkmenistan 6 224
types
bianco di Spagna 28 338
black 6 399–400; 8 127; 24 790
red 6 400; 8 127
sanguine *see* red
white *see* CALCITE; CALCIUM CARBONATE; SOAPSTONE
uses
architecture 29 699
conservation 7 737
crayons 8 128
drawings *see under* DRAWINGS → forms
etchings 10 548
gesso 12 501
glass 12 439
glazes 12 803
grounds 6 224; 13 135, 706*; 24 798; 25 174; 30 426
paints 3 914
panel paintings 13 135
polishing 1 761
scroll paintings 3 914
size 28 310
wallpaper 32 815
writing-tablets 4 342
Chalk, Warren 2 308
Chalkedon, Boethos of *see* BOETHOS OF CHALKEDON
Chalkedon, Hagia Euphemia 9 536
Chalki, Virgin Prothronos 9 575, 578; 22 700
Chalkios, Hagios Ioannes Prodromos 9 550
Chalkis 13 *363*
armour 2 449
collections 14 361
gems 12 248
mosaics 13 560, 565
pottery 13 486
Chalky Mount 2 152
Challant (family) 16 725
Challant, Bianca Maria di 24 248
Challe, (Charles-)Michel-Ange 6 401*; 20 137; 23 544
assistants 3 523
groups and movements 22 734
patrons and collectors 5 380
reproductive prints by others 20 497
works 2 332; 20 867; 30 672
Challe, Simon 4 238; 6 401–2*
Chalmers, Alexander 28 268
Chalmers, George Paul 28 238, 269
Chalmers, P. MacGregor 15 892
Chalmers, Roderick 9 724
works 9 *725*
Chalmers, R. P. 26 108
Chalon, Alfred Edward 6 402*; 32 903
Chalon, H(enry) B(ernard) 6 402*; 14 146
Chalon, Jan 6 402
Chalon, John James 6 402*; 32 903
Chalon, Maria A. 6 402
Châlons, Simon de *see* MAILLY, SIMON DE
Châlons-sur-Marne 11 *504*
Abbey Church 8 258
Cathedral of St Etienne 26 702; 31 499
chariot 6 481
Notre-Dame-en-Vaux 6 402–3*; 13 38, 39
cloister 7 454, 455
roof 30 907
sculpture 6 *403*; 13 72, 73
Chalon-sur-Saône
Hôtel Virey 12 309
St Vincent 13 78
tomb of S Marcellus 7 302
Chalopin, Jean 3 64
Chalov, Igor K. 19 13
Chal-Tarqan/Eshqabad 29 818
Chalukyas of Badami 6 404*; 24 267
see also:
LOKA MAHADEVI, Queen
MANGALESHA, Ruler
PULAKESIN II, Ruler
TRAILOKYA MAHADEVI, Queen
VIJAYADITYA, Ruler
VIKRAMADITYA, Ruler
Chalukyas of Gujarat *see* SOLANKI
Chalukyas of Kalyana 6 404*
Chalukyas of Kalyana, Someshvara III *see* SOMESHVARA III, Ruler
Chalvet, Henri-Auguste de 4 329
Chalvet, Maxence de, Marquis de Rochemonteix *see* ROCHEMONTEIX, MAXENCE DE CHALVET, Marquis de
Cham (Africa) 1 328, 381
Cham (South-east Asia) 1 706; 5 459, 503; 29 826; 32 468, 490
brick 4 795
temples 30 446
Cham (1819-79) 5 758; 6 404*
Chamacoco 24 92, 93
Chamalières (Auvergne) 6 159; 27 52
Chamalières-sur-Loire 13 140; 22 270
St Gilles 9 152; 26 641
Chaman-i-Hazuri 1 204
Chamarro 20 411
Chamaryŏ 18 304
Chamba (i) (India) 6 404–5*; 15 *264*, *619*
Bhuri Singh Museum
collections 6 405; 15 180
embroidery 15 675
paintings 15 625–7*, *626*
Rang Mahal 15 627
Chamba (ii) (Africa) 6 405–7*; 17 680; 31 73
masks 1 382; 6 405–6, *406*; 22 287
sculpture 1 382; 6 406; 22 287
Chamba, La *see* LA CHAMBA
Chambard, La 20 602
Chambas, Jean-Paul 27 307
Chambellan, François 5 584
Chambellan, Richard 20 638
chambered tombs *see under* TOMBS → types
Chamberlain (family) 6 408
Chamberlain, Brenda 32 786
Chamberlain, Henry 26 414
Chamberlain, Humphrey (1762-1841) 6 93, 408
Chamberlain, Humphrey, jr (1791-1824) 6 408
Chamberlain, J(ohn) H(enry) 4 85; 6 408*
Chamberlain, John A(ngus) 6 408*; 31 614
dealers 6 23; 16 820
groups and movements 4 110; 17 694
works 16 58; 29 13; 31 614
Chamberlain, Joseph 4 85
Chamberlain, Robert 6 93, 408; 10 309; 33 377
works 10 *309*
Chamberlain, William 10 310
Chamberlain & Co. 6 408; 10 310, 311; 33 378
Chamberlaine, John (1745-1812) 6 528
Chamberlayne, John (1666-1723) 29 676
Chamberlin, M. 4 24
Chamberlin, Mason, the elder (1727-87) 6 409*
Chamberlin, Mason, the younger (*fl* 1786-1826) 6 409
Chamberlin, Peter 6 409–10
Chamberlin, Powell & Bon 6 409–10*
staff 16 819; 33 373
works 5 513; 6 *409*; 19 578
Chamberlin & Austin 13 617
Chamberlin & Whidden 3 30
chamber pots 10 316
chambers 6 407*, *407*
see also SOLARS
chambers (council) *see* COUNCIL CHAMBERS
chambers (underground) *see* HYPOGEA
Chambers, Campbell, Isaacson and Chaplin 22 568
Chambers, Ephraim 10 205
Chambers, Jack 5 569; 6 410*; 8 274
Chambers, Thomas 12 54
Chambers, Walter B. 11 143
Chambers, William (1723-96) 6 410–13*; 8 48; 10 293; 12 130; 13 301; 14 856; 19 620; 23 362; 28 348
architecture 7 339
colleges 9 323
country houses 32 553; 33 225
garden buildings 18 5; 21 893; 22 59; 27 237
government buildings 10 233, 677; 19 621
houses 6 *411*; 7 437; 16 8, 21, 24; 28 227, 247; 31 906
mausolea 2 *331*; 20 867
monasteries 31 906
orangeries 23 470
orders (architecture) 23 488
pagodas 7 168; 10 233; 23 776
palaces 4 138
porticos 25 266
pyramids 25 766
ruin buildings 27 324
stables 6 66; 19 158
staircases 6 *412*
assistants 11 431
collaboration 1 647; 17 851; 33 226
drawings 2 332
furniture 6 390; 10 293, *293*, 295, 296; 14 230
groups and movements 12 332; 22 739; 23 860
interior decoration 16 24
lighting 9 12
patrons and collectors 6 94; 9 392; 10 361; 14 144, 145; 27 356; 28 908
pupils 12 43; 14 144, 172; 24 838
sculpture 10 265; 33 227
Chambers, William (1723-96)—cont.
silver 4 540; 10 332, 333
sponsors 1 533
teachers 7 415
writings 12 131; 18 72; 23 489; 31 298
illustrated 7 340
on proportion 2 358
Chambers, William (*fl* 1903) 4 289
Chambert, Julien 4 755
chamber tombs *see under* TOMBS → types
Chambéry 23 769
Sainte-Chapelle 27 551
Chambi, Martín 6 413*; 10 580; 24 518
Chambi, Victor 6 413
Chambiges (family) 11 511; 24 116
Chambiges, Martin 6 413–14*; 22 220
architecture 3 456; 13 61
cathedrals 11 154; 31 281
Beauvais 3 457, 458; 6 *414*; 22 221
Sens 28 415
Troyes 31 384
churches 13 60
assistants 6 414; 8 288
Chambiges, Pierre 6 413, 414–15*
collaboration 6 414; 9 48–9
patrons and collectors 22 31
works 6 453; 13 61; 27 558; 28 409
Chamblain, Jean-Baptiste Bullet de *see* BULLET (DE CHAMBLAIN), JEAN-BAPTISTE
Chambon, Alban 6 415*; 9 759; 14 106
Chambon, Alfred 3 587; 6 415
Chambon, Fernand 6 415
Chambon, Gaston 6 415
Chambord 11 *504*
Château 6 59, 415–17*, *416*, 504, 505, *505*; 11 512, 727; 21 550; 23 810; 24 290; 30 II2; 32 551
architecture 11 656
gardens 12 120
gate-house 12 175
models 2 336
park 24 179
roof 27 129
staircases 29 522, 523
Chambray, Roland Fréart, Sieur de *see* FRÉART, ROLAND
Chambré, Anne de 19 247
works 19 *247*
Chambrette, Jacques 11 606; 19 800, 801
Chambure, Auguste de 11 319
Chamdo 30 *806*, 814
Chameroi, Nicolàs 20 501; 29 337
Chametla 2 904; 21 203
chamfered mitre mouldings *see under* MOULDINGS → types
chamfer mouldings *see under* MOULDINGS → types
chamfers 22 213, *213*, 214, *214*, 216, 220, 222
Chami 7 602
Chamisso, Adelbert von 21 140
Chamois, Charles 6 417*; 8 31; 11 61
chamoising *see under* TANNING
Champa 6 417–33*, *418*; 29 *225*
architecture 6 420–25*
Buddhism 9 133
military 6 425–6*; 21 595
bronze 6 427, 432; 29 230
busts 6 *429*
ceramics 6 432*
citadels 6 425–6*
colonettes 6 421
columns 6 422, *422*
façades 6 *423*
fortifications 21 595
gold 6 432
iconography 6 419–20*, 427
inscriptions 6 418, 420

Champa—cont.
lost-wax casting 6 428
metalwork 6 432*
periods 6 420
Prehistoric 29 230
pilasters 6 421
regalia 6 432
religion 6 419–20*
sanctuaries 6 420, 421
sandstone 29 IX2
sculpture 6 426–7*, 429–31*
architectural 6 428
Buddhism 6 427–8*, 428; 9 133
Hinduism 6 427, 428–9*, 430
relief 6 426, 429; 29 IX2
stone 6 428
shrines (i) (cult) 28 639
statuettes 6 427
stelae 6 420
funerary 6 420, 431
stone 6 428, 429
temples 6 420, 421, 421, 424
terracotta 6 426
textiles 6 432–3*
tiles 6 432
wall paintings 6 432*
Champagnat 26 691
enamel 26 692
Champagne, Mary, Countess of see MARY, Countess of Champagne
Champaigne, Jean-Baptiste de 6 433, 437*
collaboration 6 435
groups and movements 25 398
reproductive prints by others 24 890
teachers 6 436
works 17 1–2
Champaigne, Philippe de 4 549; 6 433–7*; 11 533, 587; 22 85
assistants 21 891
cartoons 11 641; 26 113
collaboration 6 437; 9 363, 718; 18 662; 32 718
groups and movements 25 398
paintings 11 534; 29 667; 31 883; 32 582
portraits 6 435, 443; 26 349
religious 6 434, 436; 11 403; 17 1–2; 32 573
sporting scenes 29 424
patrons and collectors
Aumale, Henri-Eugène-Philippe-Louis de Bourbon, Duc d' 23 523
Henry, Bon-Thomas 14 395
La Caze, Louis 18 588
Lancret, Nicolas 18 693
Louis XIII, King of France (reg 1610-43) 4 549
Maugis, Claude, Abbé 20 855
Orléans, Philippe I de Bourbon, 1st Duc d' (1640-1701) 23 512
Périer, Casimir 24 418
Pourtalès-Gorgier, James-Alexandre, Comte de 25 383
Richelieu, Armand-Jean Du Plessis, Cardinal de 11 662; 26 348
Seymour-Conway, Richard, 4th Marquess of Hertford 28 527
Trolle-Bonde, Gustaf, Count 31 362
pupils 6 437; 10 757
reproductive prints by others 3 813; 13 898; 15 31; 18 45, 46, 812; 19 562; 20 855; 22 116; 24 890; 25 77; 28 178; 30 746
teachers 11 358
Champallement, Geoffroy de, Bishop of Auxerre 29 501
Champanagar 15 695
Champaner 6 437–8*; 15 276, 348
Bohra Mosque 15 348
congregational mosque 15 348
Jaipur Mosque 15 348
Mandavi 15 348
Champaner—cont.
Nagina Mosque 15 348
Shahr Masjid see Bohra Mosque
Champeaux, Guillaume of see GUILLAUME OF CHAMPEAUX
Champeaux, St Martin 13 39
Champeaux, William of see WILLIAM OF CHAMPEAUX
Champenois 22 253
Champernowne, Arthur 5 71; 6 438*
Champeverne, Florimond de 20 133
Champfleury 6 438–9*; 11 675
collections 17 440
groups and movements 26 54
sponsorship 7 169
works 5 760
illustrated 20 257; 25 346
Champigny-sur-Veude, Sainte-Chapelle 27 551
Champion, Richard 4 824; 7 791; 10 309; 29 495
Champion, William 4 685; 11 242
Champion des Dames, Master of the 20 785
Champlâtreux Château 6 508
champlevé enamel see under ENAMEL → techniques
champlevé ware see under POTTERY → wares
Champlieu 26 872
Champlin, John Denison 10 210
Champlin, Samuel de 25 801
Champlin, William Christopher 18 66
Champlin de la Blancherie, Pahin 24 136
Champmartin, Charles-Emile de 23 503
Champmol Charterhouse see DIJON → Charterhouse
Champneys, Basil 6 439*
groups and movements 25 804
pupils 3 110, 741; 26 316
works 4 788; 5 513; 20 238; 30 504
Champoiseau, Charles 23 141
Champollion, Jean-François 9 830; 10 93; 17 713; 20 231
dealing 10 90
epigraphy 2 299; 10 97
excavations 27 593
pupils 20 418
surveys 10 78, 82, 83
writings 4 107
Champollion-Figeac, Jacques Joseph 10 93
Champ-près-Froges 26 702
Champs, des see DESCHAMPS
Champs Château 6 508, 509, 509; 7 168; 11 658
Chamu 4 846
Chamundaraya 15 528; 29 438
Chamuneshvari Hill 15 533
Chan (family) 20 156
Chan, Luis 6 439–40*; 14 721
Chan, Román Piña see PIÑA CHAN, ROMÁN
Chaná 29 203
Chanáe 31 752
Chanaux, Adolphe 11 727
Chan Bahlúm 23 838
Chan Buddhism see under BUDDHISM → sects
Chancay 6 440*
cuchimilcos 6 440
dress 29 183
fans 10 780
jars 6 440
chinas 6 440, 440
pottery 6 440
textiles 6 440; 29 181
tombs 31 118
Chance, Ivan 2 560
Chance, William 4 824
Chance Bros 24 293
chance in art 2 488; 5 381; 13 890
Chancelade 25 492
Chancellor, William David 6 440
Chancellor & Patrick 2 742; 6 440*
chancels 6 440*; 12 363
chancery cursive script see under SCRIPTS → types
Chan Chan 6 441–2*; 23 826; 29 130, 132, 156, 161, 218
architecture 29 161, 163, 166
Ciudad Velarde 6 441
craftsmen and artists 6 606
fans 10 780
fortifications 21 599
friezes 6 606, 607
gardens 12 71
masonry 29 162
plaster 29 829
reliefs 6 607
sculpture 29 168
temples 29 165; 30 447
Chan Cheng Siew 20 181
Chan Ching-feng see ZHAN JINGFENG
Chand, Gopal 15 654
Chand, Lal 15 654
Chand, Nek 6 446
Chandaman 21 882
Chandan Shahid Hill 27 857
Chandanu 15 633
Chandasiri, Queen (c. 4th-3rd cent. BC) (Ikshvaku) 15 453
Chandelier, Guillaume 13 78
works 13 78
chandeliers 6 442–3*
historical and regional traditions
Belgium 3 602, 603
Denmark 31 481
England 6 443; 10 319
France 6 443; 9 13; 29 573
Germany 6 443; 12 452, 454
Ireland 6 443, 443
Islamic 16 365, 386–7, 387
Italy 6 443; 32 204
Morocco 16 386–7
Netherlands, the 6 443; 9 13
Ottonian 23 659
Portugal 25 303
Spain 16 387
Sweden 30 111
materials
amber 31 481
brass 3 602, 603; 9 13
bronze 6 442; 16 387
copper 12 452
glass 6 443, 443; 9 13; 12 789
gold 9 13
inscriptions 16 387
iron 12 454
rock crystal 6 443
silver 6 443; 9 13
see also LAMPS
Chandella 6 444*
see also:
DHANGA, Ruler
VIDYADHARA, Ruler
YASHOVARMAN, Ruler
Chanderi 6 444*; 15 285
architecture 15 354, 355*
Badal Mahal 15 355
congregational mosque 15 355
house of Kamal Singh 15 355
Kushk Mahal 15 355; 23 818
Raj Mahal 15 355
Shahzadi-ka Rauza 15 355
Chandigarh 6 445, 445–6*; 9 297; 15 168, 264; 19 46–7; 20 890
architecture 7 695
Capitol 13 238; 31 236
Courts of Justice 18 890
Government Museum and Art Gallery 6 446; 15 180; 22 365
Palace of Assembly 19 47
Punjab University Museum 6 446
rose garden 12 76
urban planning 6 445–6; 23 273
Chandler, Dona 1 445
Chandler, Richard 2 164; 6 446*; 22 736
Chandler, Theophilus Parsons 6 446*
Chandler, Winthrop 6 446–7*; 12 54
Chandos, James Brydges, 1st Duke of see BRYDGES, JAMES, 1st Duke of Chandos
Chandos, John 14 407
Chandpur 15 323
Chandra 5 255
Chandra, Moti 6 447*
Chandra, Pramod 15 212, 748
Chandragiri 15 540; 31 24*
palace 23 817
Chandragupta, Ruler (reg c. 321-297 BC) (Maurya) 15 194; 21 590; 24 264; 29 438
Chandragupta II, Ruler (reg c. 380-415) (Gupta) 15 231, 738
Chandrajeewa, Sarath 29 462
Chandraketugarh 15 227, 452, 453, 718
Chandrasekaran 28 774
Chandravati
sculpture 15 225
Chandrehi 15 497
Shiva Temple 15 290
Chanduketugarh 30 510
Chanel, (Gabrielle) Coco 8 850; 9 292; 18 864; 24 718; 30 25
Chang, K. C. 7 160
Chang, Peter 25 27
Chang'an see under XI'AN
Chang Ch'eng see ZHANG CHENG
Chang Chi-chih see ZHANG JIZHI
Chang Ch'ien see ZHANG QIAN
Chang Chih see ZHANG ZHI
Ch'ang ch'u see CHO SOK
Changchub Ö 30 219, 831
Chang Dai Chien see ZHANG DAQIAN
Changdeva 15 316
Changenet, Jean 6 447–8*; 19 341; 29 638
Chang Feng see ZHANG FENG
Changgŏk Temple
sculpture 18 291, 294, 294
Changhang Temple 18 288
Chang Han-jong 18 52
Ch'ang Hsieh see CHANG XIE
Chang Hsi-huang see ZHANG XIHUANG
Chang Hsü see ZHANG XU
Chang Hsüan see ZHANG XUAN
Chang-hua 6 674
Chang-huai, Prince see ZHANGHUAI, Prince
Chang Huai-kuan see ZHANG HUAIGUAN
Chang Hung see ZHANG HONG
Changhung, Porim Temple
sculpture 18 289–90, 290
Chang I see CHEUNG YEE
Chang Jan see ZHANG RAN
Chang Jui-t'u see ZHANG RUITU
Ch'ang Kang see CHO SOK
Chang Keng see ZHANG GENG
Chang Ki-nam 18 300
Chang Lien see ZHANG LIAN
Changlu (China) 7 10
Chang Lu (c. 1468/95–1538/70) see ZHANG LU
Changma 30 443
Chang Ming-ch'i see ZHANG MINGQI
Changnak Pagoda 23 775
Changping 7 111
Ming Tombs 6 659, 701, 703
Chang ling 6 696, 701, 702, 703, 732
Hall of Heavenly Favours 6 659, 659, 703
Ling'en dian see Hall of Heavenly Favours
Ding ling 6 659, 703, 703; 7 10, 153; 33 465
metalwork 7 26
sculpture 7 57, 57
Shisan ling see Ming Tombs
Changping—cont.
see also BAIFU
Chang Seng-yu see ZHANG SENGYOU
Changsha 7 139, 140, 247
brushes 7 66
kilns 6 871
lacquer 7 12
mirrors 21 714
models 6 686
paintings 6 799, 808
pottery 6 637; 20 302
textiles 7 46, 51
Tomb 1 7 140
see also SHAZITANG; WAZHAPING
Chang Shan-tzu see ZHANG SHANZI
Chang Sheng see ZHANG SHENG
Chang Sheng-wen see ZHANG SHENGWEN
Chang Shih-ch'eng see ZHANG SHICHENG
Changsu, King (reg 413-91) 18 327, 328
Chang Sŭng-ŏp 1 847; 6 448*; 18 315
Chang Ta-ch'ien see ZHANG DAQIAN
Changtaiguan (Xinyang) 6 853; 33 471
Chang Tan-yol 18 328
Chang Tao-chün see ZHANG DAOJUN
Chang Tao-ling see ZHANG DAOLING
Ch'ang Tsao see CHANG ZAO
Chang Tse-tuan see ZHANG ZEDUAN
Chang-tsung, Emperor (Chin; reg 1190-1234) see ZHANGZONG, Emperor
Chang T'ung-chih see ZHANG TONGZHI
Chang Tzu see ZHANG ZI
Chang Tzu-wan see ZHANG ZIWAN
Changu Narayan 6 448–9*; 22 753
pillar 22 754
sculpture 6 449; 22 756, 759, 768, 770, 770, 771, 772
temples 22 761; 23 907
Chang Un-sang 18 326
Chang U-song 18 60
Chang Wan-fu see ZHANG WANFU
Chang Wu see ZHANG WU
Changye 28 720
Chang Yen-yüan see ZHANG YANYUAN
Chang Yin-wen see ZHANG YINWEN
Chang You-sheng see ZHANG YOUSHENG
Chang Yü see ZHANG YU
Chang Yü-kuang see ZHANG YUGUANG
Chang Zao 30 49
Changzhi (city) 6 855; 7 33, 140
Changzhi (c.960-d after 1016) see ZHAO CHANG
Changzhou 7 37, 58
Ch'anha see YUN CHE-HONG
Chanh Lo 6 423, 429
Chanhu-daro 6 449*; 15 246, 264, 279; 23 797, 798
figurines 15 421
gems 12 252
Chani, Miguel 24 518
Chania 6 450*; 8 153, 156; 13 362; 21 651
Archaeological Museum 8 156, 157; 21 691
Mitsotakis Collection 21 692
Franciscan Church see Archaeological Museum
Hagios Nikolaos 8 156, 157
Historical Museum and Archive 8 157

Chania—cont.
  Kydonia 6 450*
  mosaics 8 155
  Naval Museum 8 157
  palace 21 657, 658, 663; 23 808
  pottery 13 497
  seals 21 654
Chanin, Irwin 23 43
Chanjenko, Bohdan see KHANENKO, BOHDAN
Chanka 31 118
Chankanai 16 864
Chankuna 15 265, 482
Chanlatte, Nicolaus, Abbot of Pontigny 25 220
Channel Islands 18 157, 158
channelled roll mouldings see under MOULDINGS → types
Channel style see under GOTHIC → styles
Channing, William 31 249
Channon, John 6 450–51*; 7 171; 10 294; 19 592
Channon, Otho 6 450; 7 172
chanoyu see TEA CEREMONIES
Chansen 30 592
Chant, James (John) 6 451*
Chantarene, Nicolau 2 501
Chantelou, Paul Fréart, Sieur de see FRÉART (DE CHANTELOU), PAUL
Chanteloup 7 194, 194; 12 123
  pagoda 23 776
Chantereine, Camille de 11 228
Chanterene, Nicolau 6 451–3*
  patrons and collectors 2 872, 873
  works 3 534; 6 44, 451, 452; 7 531, 531; 25 300–301; 28 780
Chanteuges 26 601
Chanthaburi 30 635
Chantilly (France) 6 453–5*; 11 504
  Château 6 453*, 506, 509, 510; 7 168; 11 656; 14 174; 26 493
    Chinese kiosk 18 73
    furniture 11 626
    gardens 6 453–4*, 454; 8 794; 12 122, 123; 19 163–4, 164
    sculpture 11 754
    Hameau 8 461
    interior decoration 3 396; 14 846
    Musée Condé 6 453
      collections 5 780; 7 462; 9 707; 11 396, 415; 14 848; 22 338; 23 522, 523
    paintings 10 884; 11 546; 12 285; 28 776, 776
    Petit Hameau 8 30
    sculpture 6 468
    stables 29 485, 486
  craftsmen and artists 3 590
  lace 6 455*; 11 650; 18 593
  lacquer 18 614
  pottery 11 606
Chantilly (VA; USA), Washington Dulles International Airport 27 477, 477
Chantilly porcelain factory 6 332, 454–5*; 11 608
  works 11 608
Chantoforo, Pedro 13 695
Chantre, Ernest 1 520
Chantrell, R. D. 5 320
Chantrey, Francis (Legatt) 6 455–8*; 20 478; 23 690
  assistants 14 686; 32 911; 33 24
  groups and movements 26 742
  patrons and collectors 7 541; 27 357; 28 908; 32 787
  personal collection 29 548
  staff 8 269
  works 5 751; 6 456, 457; 10 265; 19 599, 606; 31 130, 610
Chantrey Bequest 6 457; 18 830; 19 590, 872; 30 761
  paintings 4 658; 7 407, 548; 13 30; 21 165; 23 26; 26 108; 27 840; 30 359; 31 418
Chantrey Bequest—cont.
  sculpture 11 303; 12 617
chantry chapels see under CHAPELS → types
Chan Tzu-ch'ien see ZHAN ZIQUAN
Chao Anu, King of Vientiane (reg 1805-28) 32 465
Chao Ch'ang see ZHAO CHANG
Chao Chao see ZHAO ZHAO
Chao Chih-ch'en see ZHAO ZHICHEN
Chao Chih-ch'ien see ZHAO ZHIQIAN
Chao Chih-feng see ZHAO ZHIFENG
Chao Chung see ZHAO ZHONG
Chaodaogou 23 495
Chao Hsi-ku see ZHAO XIGU
Chao Hung see ZHAO HONG
Chao I see ZHAO YI
Chao Kan see ZHAO GAN
Chao Krom On 30 618
Chao Lan-po see ZHAO LANBO
Chao Ling-jang see ZHAO LINGRANG
Chao Meng-chien see ZHAO MENGJIAN
Chao Meng-fu see ZHAO MENGFU
Chao Ping-wen see ZHAO BINGWEN
Chao Po-chü see ZHAO BOJU
Chao Po-su see ZHAO BOSU
Chao Shao-ang see ZHAO SHAOANG
Chao Shugong 7 93
Ch'ao Shu-kung see CHAO SHUGONG
Chao Ta-nien see ZHAO LINGRANG
Chao Tso see ZHAO ZUO
Chao Tsung see ZHAO ZONG
Chaouèn 16 103, 448; 32 309
  embroidery 16 448
Chaource, Master of 20 645*
Chaourse Treasure 27 82, 82
Chao Wu-chi see ZAO WOU-KI
Chaoyang Pagoda 6 656
Chao Yen see ZHAO YAN
Chao Yüan see ZHAO YUAN
Chao Yung see ZHAO YONG
Chaozhou 6 906; 7 122, 142
Chapallaz, Edouard 30 144
Chapara 15 286
Chapard, Gilbert 1 765
Chaparro, Julio Cesar Cubillos see CUBILLOS CHAPARRO, JULIO CESAR
chapbooks 4 359; 6 458*
Chapcha Dzong
  sculpture 3 914
Chapeaurouge, Donat de 15 93
Chapelain, Jean 25 461
Chapelle, Jacques 11 606
Chapelle, J.-O. Pauvert de La see PAUVERT DE LA CHAPELLE, J.-O.
Chapelle, Pierre 27 249
Chapelle Cardon 25 183
chapels 6 458–61*
  historical and regional traditions
    Bolivia 4 256
    Brazil 4 714
    Byzantine see PAREKKLESIA
    Cyprus 8 358
    Czech Republic 33 742
    Egypt, ancient 9 831
    England 6 459; 33 542
      Gothic 5 514
      Nonconformist 23 193–4*, 194
      Protestantism 7 283
    France 2 862; 6 460; 19 46, 368, 691; 20 297
    Germany 1 3; 26 574
    Gothic 2 862; 5 514; 13 127; 33 742
    Holy Roman Empire (before 1648) 1 3
    Hungary 10 544
chapels
  historical and regional traditions—cont.
    Ireland 26 592
    Italy 31 674
      Baroque 12 526
      Renaissance 1 563; 5 18, 19, 20; 11 186
      14th cent. 23 756
    Japan 2 7
    Mexico 21 376
    New Zealand 23 56
    Poland 18 433; 25 135
    Portugal 3 362; 6 43
    Romanesque 19 177; 26 569, 574, 592; 33 542
    Spain 6 135; 19 177
    Sweden 19 284
    Ukraine 19 836
    Wales 32 783
  types
    absidiole 1 72*
    boat see TEMPLES → types → peripteral
    chantry 6 458*; 7 267, 282; 10 260; 13 84
    disc 18 70
    double 29 392
    funerary
      Byzantine 9 544
      France 20 865
      Portugal 3 362
      Spain 17 693
      Turkey 9 544
      see also MAUSOLEA
    Lady 6 458; 7 265; 12 799; 13 54, 55; 18 621, 621–2*
    peripeteral see KIOSKS
    pyramid 9 839
    Saintes-Chapelles 27 550*, 550
    tomb 9 833, 836, 839–41, 882
    two-storey 5 371
  see also CHURCHES
chapel tombs see under TOMBS → types
Chaperon, Nicolas 6 461*
  works 11 402
Chapillon, Jean 7 595
Chapin, Eliphalet 31 625
Chapingo
  Escuela Nacional de Agricultura see Universidad Autónoma
  Universidad Autónoma
    murals 21 387; 26 428, 428–9*
Chapin Mesa 21 174
Chaplain, Jules-Clément 6 461–2*; 20 925; 22 125; 32 338
Chaplet, Ernest 2 700; 6 462*
  collaboration 12 189
  works 11 606; 19 397; 24 148
chaplets 17 519
Chaplin 3 239
Chaplin, Charles 5 921; 6 462*; 12 915; 25 145
Chaplin, Elisabeth 11 397
Chapman, Christopher 4 353
Chapman, Conrad Wise 6 463
Chapman, George 10 248; 14 675
Chapman, John 9 367
Chapman, John Gadsby 4 364; 6 462–3*; 12 645; 18 64
Chapman, John Linton 6 463
Chapman, Kenneth 22 594
Chapman and Snape 10 173
Chapman & Hall 28 526
Chapman-Taylor, J. W. 23 67
Chapman-Taylor, Rex 23 67
Chaponnière, Jean-Etienne 6 463*
Chappel, T. J. H.
  works 1 255
Chappell, Warren 4 367
Chappey, Marcel 31 224
Chappuzeau 20 137
Chapron, Nicolas see CHAPERON, NICOLAS
Chaptal, Jean-Antoine 11 667
chapter houses 6 463–7*, 464, 465, 467; 20 859; 21 839; 26 382
  see also MONASTERIES
Chapu, Henri (-Michel-Antoine) 6 467–8*; 11 563, 672; 20 925
  collaboration 24 221; 28 349
  pupils 8 818; 23 114
    Puech, Denys(-Pierre) 25 697
  teachers 9 447
  works 6 468; 11 563; 26 92
Chapu, Henri, Musée see under LE MÉE-SUR-SEINE
Chapuis, J. 3 578, 584
Chapus, Jean 6 469*; 9 82; 20 614
Chapuy, Jean-Baptiste 16 906; 25 619
Chapuy, Nicolas-Marie-Joseph 19 160
Chaqalaq Tepe 1 186, 196
Char, René 10 838; 29 494; 30 20; 32 423
Characene 1 889
Charachel see CHERCHEL
characters (writing)
  China 6 735–6, 736, 737–9, 739, 740, 740, 741, 742, 742, 743, 743, 744, 744, 745, 746, 746–7, 747, 749, 749, 750, 751, 752, 752, 753, 754, 755, 756, 757, 758, 759, 759, 760, 761, 762, 763, 763, 765, 766, 768, 768; 7 128, 129, 143; 17 21, 211, 230, 231, 234
  Japan 17 21, 211, 212, 219, 220, 226, 230, 234
Charaf, Rafic 19 8
Charaf ed Din 21 5
Charai, Abderahim 22 128
Charalambous, Andreas 8 365
Charan, Baghwan 20 54
Charat Singh, Ruler (reg 1808-44) (Pahari) 6 405
Charax 4 111
  fortress 4 110
Char Bakr 6 204; 16 236; 28 636
Charbonnier, Martin 12 133; 14 469
Charbonnier, Philippe 10 145
Charbonnier, Pierre 3 120
Charbonnier and Elliott 10 145
Charcas see BOLIVIA
Charchera, Nicolas see KARCHER, NICOLAS
Charchoune, Serge (Ivanovich) 2 409; 6 469*; 8 436, 438
charcoal 6 469–71*, 470; 8 127, 128, 128
  conservation 8 129
  historical and regional traditions
    Antilles, Lesser 5 746
    Bhutan 3 915
    Central Asia, Eastern 6 302
    China 7 98
    Japan 17 297, 310
    Prehistoric art 25 477, 484
  uses
    arriccio 10 740
    drawings see under DRAWINGS → forms
    dyeing 17 310
    etchings 10 549
    grounds 25 174
    inks 15 851
    lacquer 17 297; 18 604
    painting
      frescoes 11 762
      scroll 3 915
      wall 6 302
    paints 5 746
    pigments 6 469; 24 789; 25 477, 484
    rock art 25 477, 484
    smelting 21 319
    stucco 29 813
Charcot, Jean-Martin 21 7; 28 206
Chardin, Jean-Baptiste-Siméon see CHARDIN, JEAN-SIMÉON
Chardin, Jean-Pierre 6 475
Chardin, Jean-Siméon 6 471–6*; 10 676; 24 135, 136, 167, 168, 243
  attributions 2 852; 9 398; 33 44
  collaboration 2 851
  dealers 17 668
  exhibitions 10 677, 679
  methods 24 242, 494
  paintings 11 578; 15 888
    allegorical 11 407
    fire-screens 15 140
    flower 11 229, 229
    genre 6 473, 474; 12 292; 29 668, 669
    portraits 24 243
    still-lifes 2 105; 6 472, 475; 11 408, 410, 539
  patrons and collectors
    Beuningen, Daniel George van 3 889
    Beurnonville, Etienne-Edmond Martin, Baron de 3 890
    Caffiéri, Philippe (ii) (1714-74) 5 380
    Caroline Louise, Margravine of Baden-Durlach (1723-83) 33 594
    Catherine II, Empress of Russia (reg 1762- 96) 26 732
    Cognacq, (Théodore-) Ernest 7 528
    Conti, Louis-François de Bourbon, Prince de (1717-76) 7 778
    Desfriches, Aignan-Thomas 8 793
    Didot, Saint Marc 8 868
    Doucet, Jacques (-Antoine) 9 196
    Duglére, Adolphe 9 378
    Frederick II, King of Prussia (reg 1740-86) 12 473
    Gigoux, Jean(-François) 12 609
    Hall, Peter Adolf 14 80
    Hohenzollern, Henry, Prince of Prussia 14 653
    Houssaye, (François-) Arsène 14 802
    Hunter, William (1718-83) 15 29
    La Caze, Louis 18 588
    La Live de Jully, Ange-Laurent de 18 660
    Lancret, Nicolas 18 693
    Laperlier, Laurent 4 339
    La Roque, Antoine de 18 796
    Laurent-Richard 18 869
    Livois, Marquis de 19 510
    Louisa Ulrica, Queen of Sweden (1720-82) 14 692; 30 118
    Morny, Charles-Auguste, Duc de 22 127
    Phillips, Duncan 24 638
    Sparre, Gustaf Adolf 29 366; 30 118
    Tessin, Carl Gustav, Count 14 692; 30 118, 523
    Thiers, Louis-Antoine Crozat, Baron de 8 210
    (Joseph-)Wenceslas (-Lorenz), Prince of Liechtenstein (reg 1748-72) 19 337
    Whitney, John Hay 33 150
  pupils 11 366; 14 543
  reproductive prints by others 5 884; 6 563; 7 495; 11 81; 12 208; 19 10, 216; 30 24
  studio 29 855
  teachers 6 122
Chardin, John 11 634; 16 463, 539, 542; 30 541
Chardin, Sébastien 28 847
Chardonnet, Hilaire de, Comte 30 542
Chardzhou 31 458, 459
  Regional History Museum 6 284
Chareau, Dolly 32 423

Chareau, Pierre **6** 476*; **7** *294*; **11** 584
collaboration **4** 57; **12** 792
groups and movements **11** 526, 602
patrons and collectors **23** 169
works **11** 526, 584, 602; **12** *793*
Charenton
Asile des Aliénés **11** 521; **12** 616, *616*
Temple **14** 855
Chares of Lindos **6** 476*; **13** 462, 504; **26** 292
Chargaon **15** 444
Chargate *see* CLAREMONT
chargers **6** 476*; **16** *418*
charges **12** 272; **14** 405, 406–10*, 416
Charges, Cornelis de Montigny de *see* MONTIGNY DE CHARGES, CORNELIS DE
Chargesheimer **6** 476–7*
Charifker, Guita **23** 400
Charing, Archbishop's Palace **12** 175
chariot fittings **6** 155, 158, 848
chariot graves *see under* GRAVES → types
chariots **6** 477–82*
historical and regional traditions
Anatolia, ancient **6** 478
Ancient Near East **6** 479–80*
Assyrian **6** *478*, 479–80
Celtic **6** 481*
Central Asia, Western **6** 260
China **6** 481–2*, 727; **7** 55; **28** *549*
Cyprus **6** 480*
Egypt, ancient **6** *477*, 478–9; **9** 822; **10** 61
Etruscan **6** 480*, *481*
Greece, ancient **6** 480*
Indian subcontinent **6** 479, 481*; **15** 193
Iran, ancient **6** 480
Italy **6** 480*, *481*
Mesopotamia **6** 478
Prehistoric art **6** 479; **25** 547–8
Rome, ancient **6** 480*
Syria-Palestine **6** 478
Thailand **30** 639
Urartian **6** 480
materials
bronze **6** 727
leather **10** 61
wood **30** 639
types
box **6** 479
dual **6** 479
rail **6** 479
Charité-sur-Loire, La *see* LA CHARITÉ-SUR-LOIRE
Charivari, Le **5** 757; **8** 545; **12** 210; **13** 306; **20** 602; **22** 424; **24** 605; **27** 871; **31** 293
Charkh-i Lugar, Mosque of Shah Muhyi'l-Din **16** 168, 492
Charklik **28** *719*, 720
Charle, Albert Joseph *see* CHARLE-ALBERT
Charle, Gabriel **8** 633
Charle-Albert **6** 482*
house **3** 579, 585
pupils **3** 44; **11** 746
works **31** 896
Charlecote Park (Warwicks) **10** 142; **13** 541; **18** 795
furniture **28** 666
paintings **7** 814
Charlemagne, Court School of *see* COURT SCHOOL OF CHARLEMAGNE
Charlemagne, Holy Roman Emperor (*reg* 768-814) **1** 1, 4, 5; **5** 792, 794, *806*; **6** 482–3*; **8** 260; **11** 653; **23** *306*; **27** 588; **28** 417
architecture **1** 1; **6** 459; **7** 251, 382; **11** 507; **12** 363; **14** 73; **23** 485; **31** 57; **32** 432
art policies **2** 319
astronomy **5** 800
banners **14** 408
books **10** 115
bronze **9** 152, 153
chess sets **6** 557
coats of arms **14** *414*, 415
coins **7** 534, *534*
collections **12** 473
furniture **30** 779
ivory **15** 695
manuscripts **5** 800, 801; **7** 246; **12** 837; **20** 330; **25** 743
metalwork **5** 806, 807; **26** 681; **33** 8
mosaics **9** 569; **22** 165
oliphants **23** 401
paintings **11** 529
palaces **23** 748
sculpture **1** 4; **22** 43
statuettes **5** *806*
sword **26** 82
tents **30** 476
Charlemagne, Jean-Baptiste **27** 407
works **27** *408*
Charlemagne, Joseph **4** 469
Charlemagne Ludwig (Ivanovich) **21** 127; **27** 377
Charlemont, James Caulfeild, 1st Earl of *see* CAULFEILD, JAMES, 1st Earl of Charlemont
Charleroi **3** *539*; **31** 718
glass **3** 593, 594, 595
Musée Archéologique **3** 617
Musée Communal des Beaux-Arts **3** 617
Musée de la Photographie **3** 617
Musée de Verre Art et Technique **3** 617
museums **3** 616
Charles, Archduke of Austria, Duke of Styria (*reg* 1564-90) **10** 889; **12** 558; **13** 329, *900*
Charles, Archduke of Austria, Prince-Bishop of Breslau (*reg* 1590-1624) **29** 777
Charles, Duke of Orléans (*reg* 1407-65) **31** 832, *833*, 834, 842*
architecture **4** 155
manuscripts **21** 5; **28** 66
Charles, Duke of Teschen (*reg* 1771-1847) **2** 813; **8** 502; **14** 11
Charles, Elector of Bavaria *see* CHARLES VII, Holy Roman Emperor
Charles, Elector Palatine (*reg* 1680-85) **23** 513; **29** 60
Charles, Emperor of Austria (*reg* 1916-18) **4** 20
Charles, King of Portugal (*reg* 1889-1908) **4** 629, *631*, 639*
Charles, Landgrave of Hesse-Kassel (*reg* 1670-1730) **14** 491*
amber **9** 52
architecture **9** 454; **17** 834, 835; **18** 634
ceramics **17** 835
engines (steam) **11** 134
glass **12** 440, 897
hardstones **12** 462
paintings **8** 887
sculpture **21** 889
urban planning **17** 834
Charles I, 5th Duke of Savoy (*reg* 1482-90) **3** 188; **7** 596, 597; **28** 1; **31** 308
collections **25** 664
Charles I, Duke of Brunswick-Wolfenbüttel (*reg* 1735-80) **33** 54*
architecture **12** 26
collections **19** 245; **33** 51
paintings **33** 49
porcelain **11** 851; **33** 49
Charles I, King of England and Scotland (*reg* 1625-49) **4** *543*; **6** 96; **9** *483*; **10** *263*, 360; **11** 845; **12** 306; **15** 158; **18** 747; **29** 800–802*, *802*
architecture **17** 636; **18** 8; **21** 569; **33** 10
coins **7** 537
collections **2** 558; **7** 560; **8** 166; **9** 167; **11** 661, 895; **13** 919; **14** 8; **15** 38; **16** 767, 814; **19** 63, 124, 582, 833; **20** 318; **29** 352
decorative works **32** 402
drawings **2** 558; **9** 229, 230; **14** 435, 684; **16** 815
engravings **32** 699
furniture **8** 107
gardens **21** 822; **31** 276
gold **7** 565
heraldry **23** 208
jewellery **17** 523
metalwork **3** 598
paintings **2** 558; **3** 613; **5** 764, 766, 844; **7** 832; **10** 363; **12** 913; **19** 617; **25** 65; **30** 463
architectural **17** 880
ceiling **33** 388
collections **2** 560, 829; **5** 764; **12** 913; **18** 580; **20** 312; **23** 326; **27** 802; **29** 797, 799; **32** 133, 379, 797
decorative **8** 166
diptychs **23** 883
genre **18** 580; **19** 348
miniatures **10** 666; **13** 309; **14** 855; **21** 640; **23** 407, 409; **24** 553
mythological **9** 479; **14** 730; **17** 648; **20** 896; **23** 208
Old Masters **9** 16
portraits **4** 847; **8** 428; **9** 480, 482, 483; **14** 730; **19** 644; **25** 263, 362; **29** 799; **33** 387
pretentious **29** 798
religious **3** 179; **9** 480; **13** 919
restorations **9** 481
still-lifes **14** 755; **28** 364
porcelain **9** 28
prints **18** 745
sculpture **2** 163, 558; **3** 875; **4** 408; **9** 21, 23; **10** 786; **12** 577; **13** 920; **19** 249, 250; **27** 723; **32** 236, 575
silver **7** 565
sponsorship **21** 509
stage design **17** 637
tapestries **10** 349; **22** 153
Charles I, King of Naples and Sicily (*reg* 1266-85) **2** 109, 481, *483*; **7** 536; **22** 470, 486; **31** 385
architecture **24** 774
manuscripts **12** 704
sculpture **24** 393; **31** 121
Charles I, King of Spain *see* CHARLES V, Holy Roman Emperor
Charles I, Prince of Liechtenstein (*reg* 1608-27) **19** 336*
architecture **11** 77
hardstones **8** 418
paintings **29** 649
sculpture **32** 731
Charles II, Count of Maine *see* CHARLES III, Count of Provence
Charles II, Duke of Brunswick (*reg* 1780-1806) **5** 30; **33** 51
Charles II, Emperor *see* CHARLES THE BALD, Emperor
Charles II, King of England and Scotland (*reg* 1660-85) **29** 797, 804*
architecture **9** 728; **10** 232, 360; **13** 623; **14** 126; **20** 880; **23** 210; **31** 716; **33** 231, 249
art legislation **30** 673, 674
books **4** *353*
coins **7** 538; **26** 532; **28** 749
collections **15** 38; **22** 904
costumes **30** 675
decorative works **12** 591
drawings **7** 794
Dutch Gift collection **9** 194; **10** 363; **26** 283; **32** 155
furniture **10** 291; **30** 783
gardens **21** 822
gold **25** 759; **32** 402
interior decoration **32** 358; **33** 409
manuscript illumination **15** 805
medals **20** 923; **26** 532
metalwork **10** 328; **14** 814
paintings **29** 767; **32** 141, 700
history **32** 358
landscape **8** 495
marine **32** 143
portraits **7** 794; **9** 44; **12** 600; **13** 310; **18** 144; **19** 63, 122
still-lifes **26** 532
seals **28** 750; **33** 6
silver **10** 328
tapestries **10** 350
upholstery **31** 681
Charles II, King of Naples and Jerusalem (*reg* 1285-1304) **2** 109*; **6** 105; **13** 146, 163; **22** 470, 479, 483
Charles II, King of Navarre (*reg* 1349-87) **23** 402; **29** 333
Charles II, King of Spain (*reg* 1665-1700) **5** *875*; **7** *524*; **14** *2*, 10–11*
architecture **14** 478; **21** 149; **27** 819
chandeliers **29** 303
frescoes **12** 662; **23** 895
furniture **29** 303
jewellery **17** 523
metalwork **29** 341
paintings **7** 523; **14** 472, 478; **20** 375; **22** 313, 720; **23** 301; **27** 331, 802; **29** 352
sculpture **7** 287; **8** 663; **13** 725; **22** 69; **26** 553
silk **29** 348
Charles III, Count of Anjou (*reg* 1290-1325) **26** 453
Charles III, Count of Provence (*reg* 1480-1) **11** 724
Charles III, Duke of Brunswick-Wolfenbüttel (*reg* 1815-30) **33** 54–5*
Charles III, Duke of Lorraine (*reg* 1545-1608) **3** 634; **7** 842; **8** 783; **11** 656; **19** 696; **26** 350; **31** 719
Charles III, Duke of Savoy (*reg* 1504-53) **28** *2*
Charles III, King of Naples (*reg* 1382-86) **22** 486
Charles III, King of Navarre (*reg* 1387-1425) **13** 68; **23** 402
Charles III, King of Spain (*reg* 1759-88) **4** 556, *557*, 562–4*, *563*; **10** 808; **17** 626; **20** 69, 70; **23** 350; **24** 351; **25** 191; **32** 247, 413
architecture **5** 614; **11** 815; **22** 472, 473; **27** 480; **31** 72
churches **27** 481; **28** 369, 518
government buildings **27** 481
museums **20** 67
palaces **2** 284; **5** 914; **16** 645; **20** 67; **24** 108; **29** 271; **31** 894
urban planning **31** 718
barges **3** 233
book illustrations **5** 908
cameos **12** 547
Charles III, King of Spain (*reg* 1759-88)—cont.
ceramics **29** 220
collections **2** 164; **4** 560; **13** 605; **29** 354
excavations **25** 206
furniture **29** 316
gardens **2** 285; **12** 115, 119, 125
guns **2** 467
hardstones **14** 171; **16** 747; **22** 481
interior decoration **2** 285; **29** 304; **30** 860
ivory-carvings **29** 345
paintings **10** 406, 509; **12** 587; **17** 892; **20** 73; **22** 479; **28** 62
altarpieces **3** 424
battle **29** 40
frescoes **3** 425; **20** 77; **21** 133
landscape **24** 111
marine **27** 710
still-lifes **21** 80
wall **27** 58
porcelain **5** 671; **9** 29; **16** 737; **22** 482; **29** 329
sculpture **14** 445; **21** 111; **22** 680; **27** 46
tapestries **16** 758; **22** 481; **30** 324
tiles **30** 887
Charles III, Margrave of Baden-Durlach (*reg* 1709-38) **17** 816; **33** 593, 594*
Charles IV, Duke of Lorraine (*reg* 1661-70) **2** 465; **3** 48; **21** 427
Charles IV, Holy Roman Emperor (*reg* 1346-78) **8** 421; **19** 828–9*
architecture **12** 471; **13** 57; **25** 425, 445
castles **17** 818; **25** 437
cathedrals **13** 89; **20** 814; **24** 189; **25** 439, 440
churches **23** 305; **25** 431
towers **19** *829*
towns **8** 375, 376
coats of arms **14** 420
collections **8** 423; **16** 908
embroidery **25** 431
glass **8** 407
guilds **25** 431
hardstones **25** 431, 435
liturgical objects **1** 5
metalwork **8** 412
mosaics **13** 134; **25** 442
paintings **8** 389; **13** 128, 152; **17** 819; **20** 774; **23** 627; **25** 275; **30** 705; **31** 104
frescoes **33** 428
regalia **26** 80
sculpture **25** 441
Charles IV, King of France (*reg* 1322-28) **5** 667; **25** 691
Charles IV, King of Spain (*reg* 1788-1808) **4** 556, *557*, 565–6*; **21** 262, 265; **29** 337
architecture **2** 285; **24** 108; **27** 480; **29** 272; **32** 564
collections **2** 889
decorative works **9** 379; **20** 70
frames **11** 494
furniture **29** 315
interior decoration **29** 305
paintings **8** 558; **10** 406, 509, 534; **12** 925; **20** 9, 58; **26** 738; **29** 352
pottery **29** 342
sculpture **1** 149, 462, 742; **9** 23; **10** 532; **12** 651; **29** 293
silk **11** 646
sponsorship **1** 742
tapestries **13** 241; **29** 350
Charles V, Holy Roman Emperor (*reg* 1519-58) **4** 896; **7** 519; **10** 498; **13** 899, *900*, 905–10*; **14** *2*; **19** *202*; **20** 73; **21** 19, 264; **28** *377*; **31** 181; **32** 271; **33** *290*, 577
amber **1** 761

Charles V, Holy Roman Emperor (reg 1519-58)—cont.
architecture 2 175, 375; 20 71; 32 116
castles 9 330; 22 822; 31 770
cathedrals 2 202; 12 521
chapels 28 518
châteaux 13 909
hospitals 13 283
military 12 517; 14 661; 30 176; 31 93
palaces 8 79; 10 904; 13 283, 285, 288; 20 62; 32 116, 117
armour 15 866
astronomy 5 700
books 10 445
cartoons (drawings) 5 49
catafalques 6 71
coats of arms 14 422
collections 21 264, 395; 29 351
drawings 13 137, 137
furniture 3 580
gardens 12 114
glass 3 593
gold 29 333
guns 2 458, 458
heraldry 14 405
interior decoration 29 299
liturgical objects 1 5
manuscripts 4 764; 6 140; 7 243, 468; 13 903; 17 462; 20 690; 26 42; 28 487
medals 3 817; 20 921; 22 923
metalwork 16 899
monuments 10 502
mosaics 21 256
paintings 3 846; 13 25; 23 524; 31 37, 38–9
battle 3 612
mythological 7 891
religious 2 388; 8 87; 27 726
portraits 2 827; 14 658; 22 64; 24 200
prints 25 631
sculpture 3 158; 10 784; 13 77, 910; 16 697; 19 200, 201; 21 857
sponsorship 9 438
stained glass 26 744
swords 16 899
tapestries 13 907, 909; 14 422; 24 15; 29 350; 30 317; 32 272
woodcuts 33 289
Charles V, King of France (reg 1364-80) 2 49; 24 116; 31 833, 834, 835–40*, 836
architecture 8 484; 11 655; 20 133; 24 115; 26 42; 27 254, 550, 558; 31 832, 840; 32 573, 581
fortifications 31 832
military 7 359; 24 161
cameos 11 634
collections 11 660; 13 158; 18 521; 31 839
decorative works 30 780
enamel 11 629
gems 12 257, 265
gold 13 158; 27 550
hardstones 11 635
ivory 11 637
ivory-carvings 13 175
leather 19 2
manuscripts 11 531; 13 154; 25 691
Apocalypses 2 112
Bibles 4 7, 525; 20 631, 652, 680
Breviaries 3 642; 14 725; 17 462
chronicles 7 243
encyclopedias 10 202
Parement de Narbonne 18 686; 31 837
Psalters 27 565
romances 26 561
treatises 8 139
maps 20 363
metalwork 2 112; 11 614; 13 158; 31 840
Charles V, King of France (reg 1364-80)—cont.
paintings 4 524, 525; 12 723; 13 150, 153
sculpture 3 455; 13 76; 17 458, 459, 461; 19 721; 21 525
tapestries 14 75; 30 312
textiles 20 742
Charles V, Master of the Coronation Book of see CORONATION BOOK OF CHARLES V, MASTER OF THE
Charles V's Grandes Chroniques de France, Master of 13 827; 20 451
Charles VI, Holy Roman Emperor (reg 1711-40) 1 531; 12 262; 13 899, 901, 921–2*; 29 42
architecture 1 724; 2 827; 12 24; 23 606; 32 453, 456
art policies 2 828
ceramics 6 332
collections 2 830; 32 444
enamel 13 170
furniture 2 812
gold 2 819
interior decoration 2 806
paintings 8 762; 9 18; 14 111; 17 8; 26 151
prints 2 830
sculpture 13 725
Charles VI, King of France (reg 1380-1422) 11 654; 13 76; 31 833, 839–41*; 33 272
architecture 26 42; 27 254; 31 832, 841
art policies 11 655
collections 11 660
decorative works 7 544
enamel 11 615
gold 11 738; 13 158
manuscripts 18 686; 20 633; 26 561; 31 841
metalwork 31 841
paintings 17 461
pottery 11 603
sculpture 17 457, 461
tapestries 3 362; 11 638; 30 313
Charles VII, Holy Roman Emperor (reg 1742-5) 1 579; 8 809; 9 145; 12 410, 424; 22 307; 26 495; 33 273, 682
architecture 8 288, 289
decorative works 29 811
interior decoration 11 458
paintings 14 757
Charles VII, King of France (reg 1422-61) 31 833, 842–3*
architecture 13 59; 25 83; 27 736
interior decoration 11 571
manuscripts 2 113; 11 354; 20 722; 32 744
paintings 4 546; 7 544; 11 350; 31 832
sculpture 17 457
tapestries 11 639
Charles VII, King of Naples see CHARLES III, King of Spain
Charles VIII, King of France (reg 1483-98) 8 664; 31 833, 844–6*
architecture 6 59, 504; 12 656; 20 133; 23 809; 31 832, 844
books 26 556
gardens 12 110, 112
manuscripts 4 76; 20 699, 732; 25 405
paintings 4 569; 23 355; 24 471; 31 846
sculpture 11 556; 20 906; 23 709; 30 498
stained glass 24 157
tapestries 4 545; 13 634
Charles VIII, King of Naples see CHARLES III, King of Spain
Charles VIII, Master of see PERRÉAL, JEAN
Charles IX, King of France (reg 1560-74) 2 846; 31 833
architecture 9 352
Charles IX, King of France (reg 1560-74)—cont.
gem-engravings 12 259
medals 20 920
paintings 9 466
salts 6 142
sculpture 25 577
tapestries 11 572
vases 11 635
Charles X, King of France (reg 1824-30) 4 542, 543, 556*; 11 591, 658; 13 234; 19 261, 397; 31 480
architecture 3 523–4; 27 559
collections 10 90; 11 258
decorative works 26 182
furniture 16 822; 19 130
glass 3 13
interior decoration 24 163
medals 12 221
paintings 8 445; 9 209; 13 791; 14 482; 19 25, 699; 22 87; 26 449
miniatures 21 644
prints 8 867
sculpture 11 564
sponsorship 11 658
Charles X, King of Sweden see KARL X, GUSTAV, King of Sweden
Charles XII, King of Sweden see KARL XII, King of Sweden
Charles, Claude 13 805; 22 456
Charles, D. (fl 19th cent.) 13 328
Charles, Dudley (b 1945) 13 877
Charles, Nicholas 14 420
Charles, Nicolas-Toussaint 8 595
Charles, Normil 14 60
Charles, Richard 6 484*
Charles, William 10 562
Charles-Albert, Duke of Savoy and King of Sardinia (reg 1831-49) 28 2
furniture 16 730
interior decoration 10 644; 16 720; 23 829
paintings 5 555; 14 267; 25 62
sculpture 16 706
Charles Albert, Elector of Bavaria see CHARLES VII, Holy Roman Emperor
Charles Alexander, Duke of Württemberg (reg 1736-7) 5 775
Charles Alexander, Grand Duke of Saxe-Weimar (reg 1853-1901) 25 550; 28 195; 32 882
Charles Augustus, Grand Duke of Saxe-Weimar (reg 1775-1828) 33 110, 116–17*
architecture 8 41
collections 33 110
gardens 33 37
paintings 28 376
sculpture 18 107
sponsorship 28 376
staff 12 851
Charles Borromeo, Saint, Archbishop of Milan see CARLO BORROMEO, Saint
Charles City Court House (VA) 18 887
Charles d'Angoulême, Master of see TASTARD, ROBINET
Charles de Neufchâtel, Bishop of Besançon 20 757
Charles-Emanuel I, 11th Duke of Savoy (reg 1580-1630) 20 430; 28 2, 5–7*
architecture 6 18; 11 65; 16 771; 31 440; 32 631
military 32 631
coins 7 537
gardens 12 115
medals 21 804
paintings 2 379; 4 125; 11 754; 12 306; 21 849; 22 82; 28 220; 31 443
sacrimonti 27 498
Charles-Emanuel I, 11th Duke of Savoy (reg 1580-1630)—cont.
urban planning 6 18; 31 440
Charles-Emanuel I, King of Sardinia see CHARLES-EMANUEL III, Duke of Savoy and King of Sardinia
Charles-Emanuel II, 14th Duke of Savoy (reg 1638-75) 5 406; 28 2, 11–13*
architecture 6 19; 12 163; 13 749; 18 728
paintings 21 482; 25 644
prints 30 793
urban planning 6 19
Charles-Emanuel III, Duke of Savoy and King of Sardinia (reg 1730-73) 28 2, 17–18*; 31 446
collections 2 27
medals 14 106; 18 885
metalwork 4 520
paintings 5 359; 7 309; 8 145; 28 15; 31 445; 32 243
frescoes 19 646; 27 200
sculpture 7 571; 23 412
sponsorship 3 824; 32 643
tapestries 16 758
Charles-Emanuel IV, Duke of Savoy and King of Sardinia (reg 1796-1802) 28 2
Charles-Eugene, Duke of Württemberg (reg 1737-93) 13 805; 19 780; 33 429–30*
architecture 18 643; 19 780; 29 875
art policies 29 875
collections 33 429
paintings 13 852, 853; 30 713
sculpture 3 899; 8 508
stucco 29 73
Charles-Eusebius, Prince of Liechtenstein (reg 1627-84) 19 336–7*
architecture 2 828; 5 701, 771; 19 55
collections 32 444
ivory-carvings 19 153
paintings 15 158; 20 788; 24 227; 27 452
Charles-Felix, Duke of Savoy and King of Sardinia (reg 1821-31) 10 90; 21 74; 28 2, 3; 31 447
Charles-Frederick, Grand Duke of Baden (reg 1806-11) 12 456; 17 816, 817; 18 523, 643; 33 196
Charles Frederick, Grand Duke of Saxe-Weimar (reg 1828-53) 28 376; 33 110
Charles le Hardi, Duke of Burgundy see CHARLES THE BOLD, Duke of Burgundy
Charles-Leopold, Duke of Meckleburg-Schwerin (1678 - 1747) 19 772
Charles le Téméraire, Duke of Burgundy see CHARLES THE BOLD, Duke of Burgundy
Charles Ludwig, Elector Palatine (reg 1649-80) 3 760; 12 266; 20 281; 24 588; 27 134; 33 272
Charles of France (1446-72) see BERRY, CHARLES DE VALOIS, Duc de
Charles of France, Duke of Lower Lorraine (reg 978-91) 5 38
Charles of France, Master of 17 458; 20 646–7*
patrons and collectors 31 844
works 20 646
Charles of Lorraine, Prince see HABSBURG-LORRAINE, CHARLES ALEXANDER, Prince, Governor of the Netherlands
Charles Philip, Elector Palatine (reg 1716-42) 9 752; 12 23; 20 281; 24 342; 33 278, 280
Charles Robert of Anjou, King of Hungary (reg 1308-42) 7 177; 13 161; 14 411; 32 614
Charles the Bald, Emperor (reg 840-77) 5 803, 804, 811; 6 484–5*
altars 1 697
furniture 30 776
ivory-carvings 5 810; 31 773
manuscripts 5 800, 803; 20 330; 31 227
Bibles 4 20; 26 79
Codex Aureus of St Emmeram (Munich, Bayer. Staatsbib., Clm. 14000) 7 512; 23 654; 25 743
Psalters 26 81
metalwork 5 808; 27 549
textiles 18 621; 20 762
Charles the Bold, 4th Duke of Burgundy (reg 1467-77) 5 206, 212–14*
architecture 17 10
coats of arms 14 389, 422, III2
decorative works 8 524
flags 11 149
gold 3 596; 19 736
hardstones 11 635
jewellery 11 634, 818
manuscripts 3 555; 12 524; 14 389; 19 341, 350; 20 450, 451
Books of Hours 7 246; 24 605; 32 729
metalwork 5 213; 13 159
paintings 8 69
reliquaries 26 147
swords 2 452
tapestries 13 634; 14 422; 20 651; 31 219
textiles 13 197
Charles the Great, Holy Roman Emperor see CHARLEMAGNE, Holy Roman Emperor
Charles the Lame, King of Naples and Jerusalem see CHARLES II, King of Naples and Jerusalem
Charles Theodore, Elector Palatine (reg 1742-99) and Elector of Bavaria (reg 1777-99) 11 730; 32 375; 33 272, 278, 280–81*
architecture 9 459; 12 23; 20 281, 282; 24 784; 25 787
catalogues 6 77
education (art) 9 460
engravings 13 614
frescoes 18 140
gardens 8 897; 28 194, 213
paintings 18 173, 175, 420; 22 271; 23 146; 30 713
patronage 18 173
sculpture 6 98; 9 752
Charles the Simple, King of France (reg 898-922) 31 216
Charles the Victorious see CHARLES VII, King of France
Charles the Wise, King of France see CHARLES V, King of France
Charleston (E. Sussex; UK) 2 552
Charleston (SC; USA) 6 485–6*; 31 587
architecture 1 422
bridges 4 803
Charleston Hotel 25 268
Drayton Hall 4 787; 29 842; 31 590
Fireproof Building 6 486
furniture 31 626
Gibbes Art Gallery 17 626
houses 6 486
Library Society 31 666
metalwork 11 119
Miles Brewton House 32 303
St John's 31 652
St Michael 31 652
St Philip 4 786; 31 590
silver 31 647, 649
theatre 30 677

Charlestown (MA; USA) **4** 482; **31** 634
Charlesworth, Sarah **6** 486–7*
Charlet, Frantz **10** 517; **32** 591
Charlet, Nicolas-Toussaint **6** 487*
dealers **9** 423
patrons and collectors **8** 72; **14** 577
pupils **6** 404; **21** 426; **25** 849
works **11** *413*; **19** 486, 488
Charleton, William **10** 364
Charleval Château **6** 506; **11** 514; **12** 120; **23** 492
Charleville (France) **11** 640; **12** 913; **21** 346; **31** 719
Charleville, Antoine Raucourt de *see* RAUCOURT DE CHARLEVILLE, ANTOINE
Charleville, Charles William Bury, Viscount *see* BURY, CHARLES WILLIAM, Viscount Charleville
Charleville Forest (Co. Offaly) **16** 10, 24
Charlevoix **5** 587
Charlier, Guillaume (-Joseph) **6** 487*; **31** 874
groups and movements **32** 591
teachers **28** 756
works **31** 218
Charlier, Jacques **11** 633; **21** 643
Charlier, Marcelin **11** 645
Charlier studios **19** 260
Charlieu Priory **4** 63; **6** 487–8*; **11** *505*; **26** 601, 602
chapter house **6** 464
sculpture **26** 601, 602
wall paintings **26** 654
Charlot, Jackson **14** 59
Charlot, Jean **6** 488*; **21** 388, 405
collaboration **20** 605
groups and movements **10** 543; **30** 275
works **19** 492; **22** 334
Charlotte, Queen of Belgium (1796-1817) **4** 78; **6** 408; **7** 490; **14** 270, 391; **24** 86; **25** 630
Charlotte, Queen of Denmark and Norway (1650-1714) **8** 755
Charlotte, Queen of France (1445-83) **31** 832, 843
Charlotte, Queen of Great Britain (1744-1818) **7** *814*; **10** 306; **18** *891*; **31** 137; **33** *693*
architecture **8** 30; **23** 398; **33** 446
ceramics **33** 20
engravings **29** 675; **32** 910
furniture **9** 28; **24** 62; **32** 540
interior decoration **22** 185
paintings **3** 489; **4** 601; **14** 144; **21** 409; **26** 50; **33** 694
portraits **25** 281
sculpture **2** 11
silver **29** 723
Charlotte Amalie **2** 148
Fort Christian **2** 148
Charlotte Bay **1** 44
Charlottenhof *see under* POTSDAM
Charlottenlund, Ordrupgaardsamlingen **8** 759
Charlotte of Savoy, Queen of France (1443-83) **4** 569; **7** 599
Charlottesville (VA), University of Virginia **4** 787; **10** 850; **17** 468–9; **26** 735
Library **25** 266; **31** 591
Rotunda **17** *468*
Charlottetown **5** *559*
Province House **5** 560
Charmantides **10** 649
charm boxes *see under* BOXES → types
Charmois, Martin de **6** 488–9*; **24** 167
charms
Buddhism **6** 707
China **6** 707
Madagascar **20** 38–9
Native North Americans **22** 652
charms—cont.
Prehistoric art **25** 489
Charmy, Emilie **33** 36
Charnay, (Claude-Joseph-) Désiré **6** 489*; **7** 645; **21** 263, 264
excavations **33** 510
works **24** 664
Charney Bassett (Berks)
manor house **29** 22
St Peter's **26** 616
Charnley, James **33** 400
Charnock, Job **5** 416, 417
Charny, Léonor Chabot, Comte de **27** 682
Charoenwongsa, Pisit **3** 154
Charolais, Charles, Comte de *see* CHARLES THE BOLD, Duke of Burgundy
Charonton, Enguerrand *see* QUARTON, ENGUERRAND
Charopinos **13** 439
Charost, Duc de **24** 268
Charoux, Lothar **4** 719
Charoux, Siegfried **2** 803
Charpentier, A. D. **9** 113
Charpentier, Alexandre (-Louis-Marie) **6** 489*; **11** 600; **20** 925; **27** 879
assistants **9** 370
collaboration **25** 52; **27** 879
pupils **18** 682; **33** 285
reproductions in ceramics **22** 270
teachers **25** 214
works **10** 178; **22** 373
Charpentier, Constance Marie **6** 490*
Charpentier, François-Philippe **2** 239–40
Charpentier, Georges **6** 489*
Charpentier, Gervais **6** 489*
Charpentier, René **6** 490*
collaboration **9** 390
reproductive prints by others **12** 727
works **9** 22
Charpignon, Claude **15** 31
Charrat, Janine **3** 430
Charraton, Enguerrand *see* QUARTON, ENGUERRAND
Charron, Amable **25** 817
Charroux Abbey **26** 600
Charrúa **31** 752
Chars, St Sulpice **4** 465; **13** 38
Chars, Christoph **30** 115
Charsadda **5** 94; **6** 490*; **15** *264*; **23** *797*
Charter, R., & Co. **18** 896
Charterhouse of Champmol *see* DIJON → Charterhouse
charters **14** 423; **20** 328, *328*
Charters de Almeida e Silva, João **19** 468
Chartham (Kent), St Mary **31** 273
tracery **31** *272*
Chartier, Emile-Auguste *see* ALAIN
Chartier, Jean **6** 491*
Charton, Edouard-Thomas **6** 491*
Charton de Tréville, Ernest **6** 596; **9** 715; **23** 904
Chartoryysk **31** 549
Chartran, Théobald **22** 329
Chartrand, Esteban **6** 491–2*
Chartrand, Philippe **6** 491
Chartres **2** 324; **6** 492–9*; **11** *504*
Cathedral of Notre-Dame **6** 492*, *493*, *494*; **7** 266; **8** 257; **9** 671, 672; **11** 510, 521, 654; **13** 37, 39–40, 41, 42; **14** 518, 519; **16** 837; **20** 566; **26** 44, 570, 585; **29** 881, *881*; **31** 710
architecture **6** 492–5*
buttresses **5** 319
cloister **7** 454
collections **18** 621
commentaries **4** 21
crypt **11** 509
Labyrinth **7** 275; **18** 584, *585*
Chartres
Cathedral of Notre-Dame—cont.
manuscripts **26** 660
mouldings **22** 216, 217, 218
nave **13** *40*
pier **24** 751
repair **20** 566
rood screen **7** 267
roof **16** 53; **30** 902
rose window **31** *270*
Royal Portal **6** *495*, 495–6; **7** *224*; **9** 256, *257*; **11** 554, 555, 792; **13** 73; **31** 284
sculpture **1** 653; **6** 495–7*, *497*; **7** 643; **13** 72, 73, 74, *74*
spire **29** 412, 414
stained glass **6** 497–9*, *498*; **12** 790; **13** 127, 132, 136, 179, 180, 181, 672, 824; **15** 827; **16** *837*; **26** 701, 702; **29** 501, 509, 510, 517; **33** 246
tracery **31** 271
vaults **32** 87, 92, 93
wall paintings **7** 275; **13** 132
Centre International du Vitrail **29** 516
coins **7** 535
St Pierre **13** 42, 142, 179, 181
stained glass **26** 702
woodcuts **33** 360
Chartres, Clement of *see* CLEMENT OF CHARTRES
Chartres, François de *see* LANGLOIS, FRANÇOIS
Chartres, Headmaster of **6** 496; **27** 561
Chartres, Jacques de *see* JACQUES DE CHARTRES
Chartres, Jean (Guillaumet) de *see* JEAN (GUILLAUMET) DE CHARTRES
Chartres, Robert-Philippe-Louis-Eugène-Ferdinand, Duc de **23** 522
Chartreuse, La Grande *see* LA GRANDE CHARTREUSE
Charumati **22** 758
Charushin, Yevgeny (Ivanovich) **6** 499*; **27** 396
Charvet, Jean-Gabriel **9** 370
Charvet, Jules **20** 461
Charyyev, Ruzy **31** 783
Charzidakis, Nicolas **2** 660
Chase, Arlen F. **27** 786; **30** 383
Chase, Barbara *see* CHASE-RIBOUD, BARBARA
Chase, Beatriz **24** 96
Chase, Diane **27** 786
Chase, Louisa **20** 609
Chase, William Merritt **4** 179; **6** 499–500*; **23** 47; **24** 600; **31** 603
dealers **18** 161
groups and movements **25** 629; **30** 452; **31** 603
pupils
Bruce, Patrick Henry **4** 888
Bunker, Dennis Miller **5** 174
Demuth, Charles (Henry Buckius) **8** 708
Dickinson, Edwin (Walter) **8** 863
Forbes, Elizabeth (Adela) Stanhope **11** 300
Frost, A(rthur) B(urdett) (1851-1928) **11** 804
Hartley, Marsden **14** 203
Hopper, Edward **14** 751
Kent, Rockwell **17** 899
Li Tiefu **14** 721
O'Keeffe, Georgia **23** 387
Pach, Walter **23** 701
Pène du Bois, Guy **24** 362
Schamberg, Morton Livingston **28** 51
Sheeler, Charles (Rettew) **28** 574
works **6** *499*; **11** 230; **12** 296; **21** 896
Chase Brass & Copper Co. **31** 653
Chaseling, Wilbur **1** 66; **20** 419; **33** 573
Chase-Riboud, Barbara **1** 444; **6** 500*
Chase Village **31** *330*, 339
Cha Shih-piao *see* ZHA SHIBIAO
Chashnik, Il'ya **1** 75; **8** 10; **27** 413; **30** 8; **31** 677
chasing **31** 147
historical and regional traditions
Central Asia, Western **6** 274
China **7** 109
Egypt, ancient **9** 818
Indian subcontinent **15** *708*
Islamic **16** 364, *388*
Ottoman **16** *388*
Turkey **16** *388*
uses
brass **16** *388*
gold **12** 868–9
jewellery **6** 274
metalwork **21** 326
silver **15** *708*; **28** 740
swords **2** 452
see also INCISING
Chassaignon, Antoine **25** 244
Chasse, Michel-Ange de La *see* LA CHASSE, MICHEL-ANGE DE
Chasse à la Licorne, Le Maître de la *see* UNICORN HUNT, MASTER OF THE
Chasseloup-Laubat, François-Charles-Louis, Marquis de **21** 581
châsse reliquaries *see under* RELIQUARIES → types
Chassériau, Théodore **6** 500–501*; **11** 544, 659; **23** 503
groups and movements **23** 504; **26** 740
works **6** *501*; **19** 487; **22** 329
Chassevent, Gustave Adolphe **21** 166
Chassey culture **25** 502
Chassinat, Emile Gaston **2** 659; **9** 721; **10** 82
Chasteau, Guillaume **6** 502*; **25** 70; **28** 756
Chastel, André (-Adrien) **6** 502*; **11** 676
Chastel, Roger **8** 63; **20** 75; **27** 238
Chastel, Tanneguy de, 1st Vicomte de La Bellière and Baron de Durval *see* TANNEGUY DE CHASTEL, 1st Vicomte de La Bellière
Chastel Blanc *see* SAFITA
Chastellain, Georges **14** 389
Chastillon, Claude **6** 503*
patrons and collectors **7** 194
reproductive prints by others **24** *117*
works **29** 917, 918
Chastillon, Jean de *see* JEAN DE CHASTILLON
Chastleton House (Oxon) **10** 271; **28** 896
chasubles **14** 425; **32** 388–92*
historical and regional traditions
Austria **2** *824*; **32** *388*, *391*
Belgium **32** 392
Byzantine **9** 642, 643
Early Christian (*c.* AD 250-843) **9** 642, 643
England **14** *426*; **23** *461*; **32** 392
Germany **12** *463*, *464*, 469; **32** 392
Gothic **13** *197*; **32** *388*
Hungary **15** 11
Italy **13** *197*; **32** 392
Netherlands, the **32** 392
Rome, ancient **9** 251
materials
linen **12** *464*; **32** *388*, *391*
satin **2** *824*
silk **12** *464*; **13** *197*; **32** *389*, *391*
see also PHELONIA
Châtaigneraie, Denis Marin de la **19** 145
Chataing, Alejandro **5** 692; **32** 170
Chāta-pabbata *see* DAMBULLA
Chatar Muni **15** *582*
works **15** *546*
Chatarsal, Rao of Bundi (*reg* 1631-58) (Rajput) **5** 171
Chatberdi **30** 307
Chateaubriand, Assis **4** 726
Chateaubriand, François-René, Vicomte de **6** 510–11*
groups and movements **13** 201
sculpture **20** 422
writings **11** 521; **26** 738
illustrated **4** 238; **17** 605; **27** 531; **30** 353
Chateaubriand, Gilberto **4** 725; **26** 414
Château de Boufflers **12** 726
Château de Chilly **32** 718
Château de Cirey **32** 337
Château de Commarque **6** 55
Château de La Bâtie d'Urfé **11** 604
Château de Maisons-Laffitte **11** 574; **19** 642
Oval Cabinet des Glaces **5** 349
Château de Malmaison *see under* MALMAISON
Château de Vauvert **5** 894
Château du Fayel *see under* PARIS → châteaux
Château du Marais **3** 274
Châteaudun **6** 54; **31** 717
Sainte-Chapelle **27** 551
Château-Gaillard **6** 51, 55, 56, 511–12*, *512*; **8** 278; **9** 144; **11** *504*
donjon **8** 278; **19** 895
fortifications **21** 548
Château Gontier **26** 657
Chateauneuf, Alexis de **12** 414; **14** 140; **27** 334, 335; **33** 40
Chateau-Neuf, Jacques-Louis Beringhen, Marquis de *see* BERINGHEN, JACQUES-LOUIS, Marquis de Chateau-Neuf
Châteauneuf-sur-Charente Church **26** 600
Château Pèlerin **21** 564
Château style **6** 513*
Château-sur-Epte **6** 53, 55, 56
Château-Thierry **11** 650
Musée Jean de La Fontaine **14** 394
châteaux **4** 865; **6** 51, 59, 503–10*; **20** 131; **23** 806, 809; **32** 369
Baroque **32** *369*
Neo-classicism **4** *224*; **11** *257*, *883*; **19** *800*; **32** *767*
Renaissance **2** *27*; **6** *505*, *545*; **9** *351*, *352*; **11** *512*, *905*
Rococo **11** *884*; **32** *373*
16th cent. **6** *416*; **9** 706, *707*; **11** *261*; **27** *559*; **28** *467*
17th cent. **6** *507*; **11** 356; **19** *266*; **20** 288, *290*, *291*, *449*, *457*; **29** *917*
18th cent. **6** *509*
see also FRANCE → castles; villas
Châtel, Louis-François Crozat, Marquis de **8** 209
Chatel, Marie du **22** 720
Chatelain, Jean-Baptiste-Claude **5** 76; **6** 513*; **14** 856
Châtelain, Léo **22** 920
châtelaines **7** 109; **10** 342; **16** *61*; **17** 524, 527
Châtelet **3** 588, 589
Châtelet, Jean Du III, Baron des Thons *see* THONS, JEAN DU CHÂTELET III, Baron des
Châtelet, Marie-Florent, Comte du **6** 554
Chatelet, Mme de **32** 337
Châtelier, Jacques du *see* JACQUES DU CHÂTELIER
Châtellerault, Pont Henri IV **4** 801, 803

Châtenay-Malabry 2 391; 24 129
housing 24 129
Chatham 21 569
Chatham Islands 6 513–14*; 23 52, 711
rock art 6 514, 514
tree-carvings 6 514
Chatillon, André-Marie 9 336
Chatillon, Henri-Guillaume 12 732
Châtillon, Louis de (1639-1734) 9 379; 20 586
Châtillon, Louis de, Count of Blois (reg 1342-46) see LOUIS II, Count of Blois
Chatillon, Pauline 12 186
Chat noir, Le 5 758; 20 602
Chatou Nymphaeum 13 705
Châtre, Le Dreux de la see LE DREUX DE LA CHÂTRE
chatrī see INDIAN SUBCONTINENT → pavilions (buildings)
Chatrousse, Emile (-François) 6 514–15*
Chatsa 15 488
Chatsworth (Derbys) 3 690; 4 81; 6 116, 117–18, 515, 515–16*; 8 47; 10 225, 275, 276, 361; 14 452; 30 278
catalogues 25 238
collections 10 364
conservatory see Great Stove
drawings 2 170; 4 896; 5 454, 853, 866; 12 910; 19 124; 20 308; 24 757; 25 388; 26 175, 176, 177
animal subjects 9 484
architectural 2 329; 17 634, 638; 33 10, 11
books 9 230, 476
Flinck Collection 11 170
hunting scenes 19 707
landscape 26 167
portraits 5 200; 9 78; 25 557
Resta Collection 26 246
topographical 14 683
embroidery 15 150
frames 11 426
furniture 10 294, 296; 30 783
gardens 6 515–16; 12 127, 128; 19 622; 24 293; 33 199
gems 12 250, 260, 261, 266
gold 10 330
Great Stairs 11 422
Great Stove 7 744, 745; 12 791, 791; 13 619; 24 293
interior decoration 10 274; 13 702
Japan Closet 7 167
leather 19 5
library 10 376
metalwork 10 329; 20 444; 30 871
paintings 6 117; 24 637
flower 4 232
frescoes 15 139; 18 644
history 33 176
landscape 9 719; 23 874
mythological 4 807; 9 377; 25 386
portraits 2 123; 17 645; 19 121; 21 509; 24 553; 27 841
religious 13 301; 20 374
still-lifes 18 787
Palm House 12 137
plaster 29 834
sculpture 1 742; 7 298; 10 365; 12 597; 13 213; 17 921; 22 705; 24 757
silver 11 618; 22 728; 30 299
State Dining Room 6 604
Chatsworth Head 8 341
Chatsworth Relief 27 38
Chattankulangara 15 721
Chattel, Du see DU CHATTEL
chattel houses see under HOUSES → types
chattering see under POTTERY → techniques
Chatto & Windus 21 32
Chatwin, Julius Alfred 4 85
Chatzikyriakos-Ghikas, Nicos see GHIKA, NICO
Chau, de La see LA CHAU, DE
Chau Can 29 230
Chaucer, Geoffrey 4 364; 12 107
Chauchard, Hippolyte-Alfred 6 516*; 21 612
Chaudanpur, Mukteshvara Temple 15 325
Chaudet, Antoine-Denis 6 516–17*
groups and movements 26 742
patrons and collectors 4 301, 303; 11 562
pupils 12 17
works 5 889; 6 517; 8 764, 867; 11 562; 20 924; 22 47
Chaudet, Jeanne-Elisabeth 6 517–18*; 11 542
patrons and collectors 4 303
teachers 6 516
Chaudfontaine, Casino 8 700
Chaudhuri, Sankho 15 172, 173
Chaudor see CHODOR
Chaudron, Simon 10 851
Chauhan see CHAHAMANA
Chauhan, Prithviraj see PRITHVIRAJ
Chaukandi 23 803
Chaule, Pierre de see PIERRE DE CHAULE
Chauliac, Guy de see GUY DE CHAULIAC
Chaulnes, Joseph d'Albert d'Ailly, Duc de 10 79; 19 115; 20 295
Chaume 24 267
Chaume, Nicolas de see NICOLAS DE CHAUME
Chaumont, Chevalier du 30 670
Chaumont Château 6 504; 11 511
Chaumont-sur-Loire 11 612
Chauncey, Florence Nupok 22 596
Chaundler, Thomas 6 518*
Chaurand-Naurac, Jean Raoul 27 307
Chaurasi 15 504
Varahi Temple 15 283, 318, 319
Chausa 15 453
Chau Srei Vibol 5 472
Chaussard, Jean-Baptiste 6 563
Chaussard, Pierre 11 674
Chaussée-Notre-Dame-Louvignies Church 30 907
Chaussée-Tirancourt, La see LA CHAUSSÉE-TIRANCOURT
Chaussegros de Lery, Gaspard-Joseph 6 518*; 20 121
chausses 2 468, 469
Chausson, Ernest 18 25; 19 230; 32 591
Chauveau, Bernard 29 840
Chauveau, Charles 6 518
Chauveau, Evrard 6 518; 29 690
Chauveau, François 6 518*
pupils 18 632
works 9 22; 10 725; 18 745; 19 247; 20 896; 24 258; 25 461; 30 659
Chauveau, Louis 6 518
Chauveau, René 6 518–19*; 8 190
collaboration 30 523
works 11 336; 29 689; 30 85
Chauvel, Théophile-Narcisse 1 642; 6 519*
Chauvet, Louise 7 596; 11 355
Chauvigny, St Pierre 26 585, 600
Chauvin, Charles 4 308
Chauvin, Pierre-Athanase 6 519*; 31 817
Cháva 15 2
Chavaletto, Giovanni Battista see CAVALLETTO, GIOVANNI BATTISTA
Chavalliaud, Léon Joseph 23 30
Chavannes, Edouard Puvis de see PUVIS DE CHAVANNES, EDOUARD
Chavannes, Pierre (-Cécile) Puvis de see PUVIS DE CHAVANNES, PIERRE(-CÉCILE)
Chavarria, Felipe 4 258
Chaves, J. Ferreira see FERREIRA CHAVES, J.
Chaves, Pedro Gomes see GOMES CHAVES, PEDRO
Chaves Pinheiro, Francisco Manuel 4 717
Chávez see ECHAVE
Chávez, Diego de 21 375
Chávez, Gerardo 6 519*; 24 511
Chávez, Ignacio 32 558
Chavez, Pedro Gomez see GOMEZ CHAVEZ, PEDRO
Chávez Morado, José 6 519–20*; 8 8; 21 388
collaboration 24 402; 25 878; 33 493
pupils 10 99; 31 415
works 21 380
Chávez y Arellano, Francisco (Domínguez) 6 520*; 24 501
Chavigny 19 145
Chavigny, Léon Bouthillier, Comte de 19 145; 20 290
Chavín culture 6 520–23*; 29 127, 160
architecture 6 522–3*
chronologies 6 520–21
crowns 29 214
gold 29 214
granite 29 167
hardstones 29 185
iconography 6 521–2*; 29 133, 134
metalwork 29 214–15
mortars (vessels) 29 133
pottery 6 522*; 29 177–8
repoussé 29 214
sculpture 6 521–2*; 29 167, 167, 169–70
stone-carvings 6 521
textiles 29 180
Chavín de Huántar 6 520–25*, 524; 29 96, 127, 156, 160, 215, 219
altars 1 701
architecture 29 135
Black and White Portal 9 166; 29 170
Great Image 6 521; 29 169, 169, 620
hardstones 29 185
joinery 5 408
Lanzón Stone see Great Image
masonry 29 162
Raimondi Stele 6 522, 523, 524; 29 167, 170, 620
sculpture 29 167, 167, 169–70, 217
stele 29 130
Tello Obelisk 6 523, 524; 29 131, 131, 169, 620
temples 29 165; 30 447
tombs 31 118
Chavrak, Dagmar 8 181
Chawand 15 598
Chawner, William 7 30
Chawuhugou 6 308
Chaykov, Iosif (Moiseyevich) 6 525*; 17 577; 27 396, 443
works 27 411
Chazal, André 12 187
Chazhashi 12 330
Cheadle (Staffs), St Giles 11 256
Cheadle Hulme Methodist Church (Ches) 23 194
Cheah Sequah see HILL, JOAN
Cheal, Joseph 31 151
Cheapside Hoard 10 345; 17 523, 524
Cheb 6 525–6*; 8 374
Gallery of Fine Arts 6 526
glass 8 407
Monastery 8 382
Museum 6 526
pewter 8 415
Cheb—cont.
St Clare 8 378
woodwork 8 396
Cheb, Master of 6 526
Chebaa, Mohamed 3 625; 22 129
Chébab, Maurice 31 501
Cheban Bridge see SALKOJIDARI BRIDGE
Chebo'er 7 110
Cheboksary 27 434
Chebotaryov, Konstantin 27 434
Chebrolu 15 537, 538
Chéchaouen see CHAOUEN
Chechen 27 433
Chechenya 27 363, 432, 433
Chechulin, Dmitry (Nikolayevich) 6 526*
collaboration 12 879; 25 323
works 22 174, 175; 27 381
Chęciny 25 114, 118
Checkley, George 6 527*; 10 241
Chedanne, Georges(-Paul) 6 527*
works 8 770; 26 793
Cheddar (Somerset) 2 66, 67; 14 73, 75
Chedel, Pierre-Quentin 6 527*
Chédeville, Joseph 12 467, 468; 30 326
chedi see THAILAND → stupas
Chedi Ngam 30 578
Chedis see HAIHAYA
Chedi Si Yang 30 578
Chedworth Villa (Glos) 26 905, 907, 907; 32 544
Chedziel, Jan 3 526
Cheek, C. D. 17 753
Cheere, Henry 6 528*
assistants 10 264; 27 242
attributions 10 265
collaboration 28 64
personal collection 4 79
pupils 30 386
works 19 606, 606; 31 128
Cheere, John 4 758; 6 528*; 8 587
patrons and collectors 7 758; 29 734
works 5 751; 10 264; 18 902; 25 814
Cheers, Henry 29 105
Cheesman, Thomas 6 528*
Cheesman, Wendy Ann see FOSTER, WENDY ANN
Chefdeville, François (-Dominique) Barreau de see BARREAU DE CHEFDEVILLE, FRANÇOIS(-DOMINIQUE)
Chegodayev, Andrey (Dimitriyevich) 6 529*
Che-i see ZHEYI
Cheirosophos 8 458
Cheit Singh, Maharaja (reg 19th cent.) 31 903
Cheju Island 18 248, 250, 300
Chekanāuskas, Vitautas see ČEKANĀUSKAS, VYTAUTAS
Chekhonin, Sergey (Vasil'yevich) 6 529*; 27 394, 413
groups and movements 1 453; 22 508
teachers 30 464
Chekmasov, Valentin 27 434
Chekrygin, Vasily (Nikolayevich) 6 530*; 20 151; 27 394
Chelichev, Pavel see TCHELITCHEW, PAVEL
Chelidone, Cornelia 27 86
Chelis 32 60
Chella 25 832
congregational mosque 16 218
fortifications 21 584
funerary complex of Abu'l-Hasan 16 218
tombs 31 112
Chellaston 1 517, 518; 13 84
Chelles 5 800, 809; 9 668; 10 181
Chelles, Jean de 6 530*; 24 154, 156, 774
groups and movements 26 45
works 24 115, 152
Chelles, Pierre de 6 530–31*; 24 152
Chelli, D. 31 818
Chelli, Eusebio 6 593
Chellini, Dr 9 128
Chellini, Antonio 9 131; 12 705; 31 707
Chellini Madonna 32 912
Chellino, Antonio 11 895
Chełmno 6 531–2*; 25 92
Cathedral 25 128
St Mary's 6 531, 531–2; 13 187, 189
Chełmoński, Józef 6 532–3*; 25 107; 29 539; 32 876
Chełmża Cathedral 25 114
Chelsea Keramic Art Works 4 482; 26 467; 30 887; 31 638
Chelsea Porcelain Factory 6 533*; 10 308; 14 857; 19 595; 27 242; 29 432
collections 28 168
designers 10 308
directors 8 776; 9 368
production 4 177; 6 332; 9 29; 10 308, 308; 19 596
Chelsea Pottery (Bahamas) 3 64, 65
Chelsum, Dr 8 96
Cheltenham (Glos)
Everyman Theatre 30 678
Queen's Hotel 14 786; 25 268
Thirlestane House 27 350
Cheltout, Khelifa 31 426
Chely, Christoph Rudolf 5 30
Chely, Rudolf Anton 5 30
Chemchemi 1 429, 433
Chemehuevi 22 549, 661
Chemesov, Yevgraf 27 389
Chemetov, Alexandre 6 534
Chemetov, Paul 6 534*
collaboration 23 119; 24 132
groups and movements 2 699, 700
works 6 534
Chemiakin, Mihail see SHEMYAKIN, MIKHAIL (MIKHAYLOVICH)
chemical lace see under LACE → types
chemical printing see LITHOGRAPHY
Cheminais, Bertie 29 116
chemin-de-ronde 21 546
chemitypes 6 534–5*; 25 611
Chemmis see AKHMIM
Chemnitz 12 469
Schocken Store 15 886; 21 120, 782
Chemtou see SIMITTHUS
Chemyrev 13 372, 538, 570, 571
Chen, Colvin 31 335
Chen, Georgette 28 774
Chen, Margaret 16 885
Chenantais, Joseph-Fleury 28 372
Chénard, Simon 9 285
Chenavard, (Claude-) Aimé 6 535*; 10 559; 11 598; 28 523
Chenavard, Antoine-Marie 6 535*; 7 170; 19 846
Chenavard, Paul (-Marc-Joseph) 3 461; 6 535–7*; 14 587
groups and movements 2 643
teachers 14 482; 15 839; 19 847
works 6 536
Chencha 1 308
Ch'en Chi see CHEN JI
Ch'en Chieh-ch'i see CHEN JIEQI
Ch'en Chi-ju see CHEN JIRU
Ch'en Ch'i-k'uan 30 249
Ch'en Chin 30 247
Chen Chong Swee 28 774
Ch'en Chuan see CHEN ZHUAN
Chenda, Il see RIVAROLA, ALFONSO
Chen Dengbo see CH'EN TENG-PO

Chen Dewang *see* CH'EN TE-WANG
Chendey Monastery **15** 397
Chenes style *see under* RÍO BEC STYLE
Chenet, Jean **26** 478
Chenevière, Cecile **10** 782
Chenevière, Pierre **27** 682
Cheney, Edward **6** 537*
Chen Fushan *see* CHAN, LUIS
Cheng, King (2nd millennium BC) **6** 663
Cheng, King (Ch'in) *see* QIN SHI HUANGDI
Cheng, Madam *see* ZHENG, MADAM
Chengam, Venugopala Parthasarathi Temple **15** 646
Chengannur, Narasimha Temple **15** 524
Ch'eng Cheng-k'uei *see* CHENG ZHENGKUI
Cheng Ch'eng-kung Zheng Chenggong
Cheng Chen-to *see* ZHENG ZHENDUO
Cheng-chou *see* ZHENGZHOU
Ch'eng Chün-fang *see* CHENG JUNFANG
Cheng Chung *see* ZHENG ZHONG
Cheng Dayue **7** 119, 120; **10** 379
Chengde **6** 537–9*, *614*; **30** 443
architecture **5** 113
Bishu shanzhuang **6** 537–8*, 661, 684; **12** 89
Wenjin Pavilion **24** 289
Eight Outer Temples *see* Wai ba miao
gardens **12** 89
Mountain Village for Escaping the Heat *see* Bishu shanzhuang
sculpture **6** 733
Wai ba miao **6** 538, 661
Putuo zongsheng miao **6** *538*
Chengdu **6** 539–40*, *615*
Bureau of Fine Textiles **7** 49
houses **6** 689, 692
jade **7** 7
lacquer **7** 16
mosques **6** 677
prints **7** 118
reliefs **6** 648
Temple of the Military Marquis *see* Wuhou si
tiles **6** 788, *788*, 808
tomb of Wang Jian **6** 539, 730; **27** 832
urban planning **6** 664
Wanfo Temple **6** 711
Wuhou si **6** 539, 724
Yong ling **6** 653; **7** 71
Chenge brothers **33** 596
Cheng Fu se ZHENG FU
Cheng Ho *see* ZHENG HE
Cheng Hsieh *see* ZHENG XIE
Chenghua emperor (Ming) **6** 817, 866; **33** 437
Cheng Jiasu **19** 378
Cheng Junfang **7** 93, *93*, 94
Cheng Min *see* ZHENG MIN
Cheng Pan-ch'iao *see* ZHENG XIE
Cheng P'ei *see* ZHENG PEI
Cheng Shan-hsi **30** 249
Cheng Shifa **6** 540*; **28** 555
Cheng Ssu-hsiao *see* ZHENG SIXIAO
Cheng Sui **2** 96; **7** 130; **33** 496
works **2** *96*
Cheng Tao-chao *see* ZHENG DAOZHAO
Ch'eng Ta-yüeh *see* CHENG DAYUE
Ch'eng-te *see* CHENGDE
Chen Guan **25** 784
Cheng Wei Kwok **14** 722
Cheng Wen-lin *see* ZHENG WENLIN
Cheng Wuyong **14** 823
Cheng Zhengkui **6** 541*; **22** 460
works **18** *517*
Chengzhou *see* LUOYANG
Chengziyai (Licheng) **6** 663; **21** 593
Chen Heqing **17** 122
Ch'en Ho-ch'ing *see* CHEN HEQING
Chen Hongshou **6** 541–3*, 813
groups and movements **7** 130
works **6** *543*, 781, 810, *810*; **7** 83, 119
Ch'en Hsien *see* CHEN XIAN
Ch'en Hsien-hang *see* CHEN XIANHANG
Chen Huan **33** 422
Ch'en Hung-shou *see* CHEN HONGSHOU
Chénier, M.-J. **31** 373
Chenies (Bucks), St Michael **10** 265
Ch'en I-hsi *see* CHEN YIXI
chenille **30** 552
Chenille carpets *see under* CARPETS → types
chenille rugs *see* RUGS → types → shirred
Chenillion, Jean-Louis **10** 770
Chen Ji **6** 547; **19** 858; **28** 589
Chen Jieqi **6** 867; **33** 422
Chen Jin *see* CH'EN CHIN
Chen Jiru **6** 544*, 820; **7** 151; **23** 215; **29** 243
Ch'en Jung *see* CHEN RONG
Ch'en Jung-chang *see* CHEN RONGZHANG
Ch'en Ju-yen *see* CHEN RUYAN
Chen-k'o *see* ZHENKE
Chen Kuan **6** 547; **28** 589
Ch'en Kuan *see* CHEN GUAN
Chen Lin **6** 800; **17** 881; **28** 586
Chen Mei **6** 818
Chen Nanpin *see* SHEN NANPIN
Chennevières (-Pointel), Charles-Philippe, Marquis de Falaise **6** 544–5*; **11** 675; **12** 13; **22** 330
Chenonceaux **11** *504*
Château **6** 59, 504, *545*, 545–6*; **9** 158; **11** 512, 571, 656, 726
gardens **12** 120
Chen period *see under* CHINA → periods
Chen Qikuan *see* CH'EN CH'I-K'UAN
Chen Qing gui **6** 844
Chenqqiao (Luhe) **7** 97
Chen Rong **6** 546*
Chen Rongzhang **7** 132
Chen Ruyan **6** 546–7*; **32** 846
Chen Shu **33** 321
Ch'en Shu-jen *see* CHEN SHUREN
Chen Shun **6** 547*, 759, 806; **33** 436
Chen Shuren **7** 149; **12** 49; **19** 421, 422
Chen Si **6** 769
Ch'en Ssu *see* CHEN SI
Chensuntang *see* LUO ZHENYU
Ch'en Teng-po **30** 247
Ch'en Te-wang **30** 248
Ch'en Tzu-ho *see* CHEN ZIHE
Chenu, Peter Francis **3** 509; **31** 477
Chenu, Pierre **6** 547*; **19** 879
Chenu, Thérèse **6** 547
Chenu, Victoire **6** 547
Chen Voon Fee *see* VOON FEE, CHEN
Chen Wen Hsi **28** 774
Chen Xian **20** 286; **33** 659
Chen Xianhang **6** 757–8
Chen Yixi **6** 764
Chen Yuanpin *see* ZHEN YUANYUN
Ch'en Yü-chung *see* CHEN YUZHONG
Chen Yuzhong **7** 130
Chen Zhuan **33** 497
Chen Zihe **33** 657
Cheo Chai Hiang **28** 775
Cheong Laitong **20** 172
Cheong Soo Pieng **28** 774
Cheops (*reg c.* 2551–*c.* 2528 BC) **9** *776*; **31** 107
funerary objects **9** 819, 822, 870; **10** 60, 81
pyramids **9** 779, 813; **20** 863; **25** 761, *761*, 762
sarcophagi **27** 824
Chephren (*reg c.* 2520–*c.* 2494 BC) **9** *776*, 869
pyramids **20** 863; **25** 762
sculpture **9** 870; **10** 50
seated figures **9** 856, 869, *869*
sphinxes **9** 870
temples **9** 825; **27** 127
Ch'e-po-erh *see* CHEBO'ER
Chepstow (Gwent)
bridge **4** 802
Castle **6** 54; **12** 174
keep **26** 617
Marten's Tower **8** 278
sculpture **26** 612
wall paintings **26** 655
St Mary's **26** 590
Cheptsov, Yefim (Mikhaylovich) **6** 547–8*; **25** 653
Chequer Painter **13** 530; **28** 655; **30** 175
Chequers Court (Bucks) **4** 157
Chera *see* KULASHEKHARA
Chéramy, Paul-Arthur **6** 548*
Cheramyes **15** 893
Cheramyes Kore **13** 470; **15** 893; **27** 688, *689*
Cherasco, S Maria del Popolo **29** 831
Cherauz, Henri de *see* HENRI DE CHERAUZ
Cherbourg, Musée Thomas-Henry **14** 396
Cherchel **1** 634; **6** 548*; **9** *510*
aqueducts **2** 242; **26** 919
gold **2** 442
metalwork **2** 441
mosaics **9** 570; **27** 63, *63*, 67
sculpture **27** 31
theatre **26** 921
Cherchi, Sandro **7** 894
Chéréac **11** 527
Chéreau, François, I (1680-1729) **2** 708; **6** 548–9*
printmakers **4** 513, 514; **33** 44
reproductive prints by others **9** 296
works **3** 639
Chéreau, François, II (1717-55) **6** 549; **18** 804
Chéreau, Jacques **6** 549; **15** 31
Chéreau, Marguerite **6** 527
Cheremi **12** *317*
church **12** 318
palace **12** 319
Cheremnykh, Mikhail (Mikhaylovich) **6** 549*; **27** 394
Cheremule, Tomba Branca **27** 835
Cheret, Gustave-Joseph **6** 550; **11** 599
Chéret, Jean Baptiste François **11** 620
Chéret, Jules **5** 880; **6** 549–50*
collaboration **4** 626; **6** 489
groups and movements **2** 510
posters **6** *550*; **7** 652; **19** 485, 490; **25** 345, 346, *346*, 601, 615, 623
tapestries **12** 830
Cherico, Francesco di Antonio del *see* FRANCESCO DI ANTONIO DEL CHIERICO
Cherikover, L. Z. **22** 174; **27** 409
Chérin, Jean **11** 404
Cherkaoui, Ahmed **6** 550–51*; **22** 129
Cherkasov, Pavel **25** 145
Cherkassky, Abram **17** 867
Cherkos Church **1** 315
Chermayeff, Serge (Ivan) **6** 551–2*
assistants **10** 284; **23** 679
collaboration **1** 610; **19** 891; **21** 120
competitions **7** 670
house **6** *551*
pupils **23** 385
works **1** 738; **10** 284
Chermside, Mabel *see* MORRISON, MABEL
Chernigov *see* CHERNIHIV
Chernihiv **6** 552*; **9** *507*; **31** 545, *546*, 551
architecture **31** 546, 551
Black Tomb **31** 562
Borisoglebsky Collegium **31** 551
carpets **31** 564
ceramics **31** 563
ecclesiastical buildings **27** 368
Cathedral of SS Boris and Gleb **27** 369; **31** 548, *548*, 554, 561
Cathedral of the Transfiguration **27** 368; **31** 547, 554
St Paraskeva Pyatnitsa **27** 369; **31** 548, 554
Trinity Monastery **31** 551
Church of the Prophet Elijah **31** 548, 552
Yeletsky Monastery
Cathedral of the Dormition **31** 547, 554, 561
glass **31** 563
Historical Museum **6** 552
jewellery **31** 562
metalwork **31** 562, 563
reliefs **31** 561
Ya. Lizogub house **31** 551
Chernikov, Yakov (Georgievich) **3** 734; **6** 552–3*; **27** 379
Chernole culture **31** 545
Chernovtsy, Metropolitan's House **31** 553
Chernyshevsky, Nikolay M. **7** 150
Chernyshov, Nikolai M. **20** 151
Chernyshov, Sergey **22** 174; **27** 379
Cherokee (people) **22** 552, 662, 663, 670, 673
Cherokee (NC) **22** 671
Chéron **17** 577
Chéron, Anne **3** 639
Chéron, Charles-Jean-François **6** 553*; **10** 773
Chéron, Elisabeth-Sophie **6** 553–4*; **22** 85
personal collection **33** 726
pupils **8** 24
reproductive prints by others **28** 756
Chéron, Fanny **10** 797
Chéron, Henri **6** 553*
Chéron, Jean-Charles **6** 553
Chéron, Louis **6** 553, 554*; **10** 372; **14** 637; **19** 584
collaboration **21** 907; **30** 759
patrons and collectors **6** 116
pupils **8** 501; **14** 641; **18** 142; **31** 871
reproductive prints by others **9** 407
works **6** 515; **10** 274; **14** 856; **21** 907
Chéron, Marie-Anne **6** 553*
Cheronnet, Louis **11** 526
Cherpitel, Mathurin **6** 554*; **24** 120
Cherqos Church **10** 565, 568
Cherry, D. **33** 314
Cherry, Kathryn **27** 565
cherry gum *see under* GUMS → types
cherry-wood **33** 324
historical and regional traditions
Denmark **8** *747*
France **2** 459, *460*; **11** 596
Germany **2** *458*; **12** 425, 426
Hungary **14** 907
Japan **17** 399
types
sakura *(Japanese cherry)* **17** 47
cherry-wood—cont.
uses
chairs **8** *747*
furniture **12** 425; **14** 907
gun stocks **2** *458*, 459, *460*, 465
netsuke **17** 399
panel paintings **24** 3
veneers **11** 596; **12** 426
Chersiphron of Ephesos **2** 312; **10** 430, 431; **13** 394, 408
Chersonesos (Ukraine) **4** 110; **6** 554–5*; **9** *507*, *512*; **26** 483; **31** *546*
architecture **4** 110; **9** 523
icons **9** 627; **31** 554
mosaics **4** 110; **13** 560, 565
pottery **9** 631, 632, 633, 634
sculpture **4** 111
silk **9** 668
Chersonisos (Crete)
basilica **8** 155
fountain **8** 155
chert **29** 699
historical and regional traditions
Mesoamerica, Pre-Columbian **1** 713; **21** 192, 246
Prehistoric art **25** 493
South America, Pre-Columbian **29** 155
uses
arrowheads **21** 192
spearheads **21** 192
tools **25** 493
see also FLINT
Chertomlyk **4** 111, 112; **28** 324
Chertomlyk Amphora **28** 323, *324*
Chertsey Abbey (Surrey) **14** 424
Cherubini, Laerzio **12** 763
Chéruit, Madeleine **10** 824; **25** 78
Cherven **5** *144*, 147
Cherven Bryag **5** 158
Cherves Tabernacle **13** 167, *168*
Cherzi, Mongush **27** 436
Cheselden, William **1** 844; **14** 519; **21** 6; **31** 871
Cheshmeh Ali ware *see under* POTTERY → wares
Cheshunt (Herts), Burleigh Infants School **28** 158
Chesneau, Ernest **6** 555*; **26** 53
Chessa, Gigi **31** 446
Chessa, Luigi **3** 438
chess sets **6** 555–8*, *556*, *558*; **7** 103; **16** 523, *798*
Chessy Château **11** 574
Chester (Ches) **2** 324; **6** 560–61*; **10** *225*; **26** *905*
architecture **2** 67
Castle **10** 235; **13** 609; **14** 198–9; **18** 887
wall paintings **26** 653
Cathedral of Christ and the Blessed Virgin **6** 561; **22** 221
choir-stalls **7** 191, 192
misericords **21** 725
shrine **13** 82
Grosvenor Bridge **4** 802; **14** 198
Grosvenor Museum **6** 561
guilds **24** 579
railway station **25** 855
stage design **30** 653
stage machinery **30** 653
The Rows **2** 324; **6** *561*
urban planning **10** 226
Chester, Greville **12** 266
Chester, Hugh I, Earl of *see* HUGH I, Earl of Chester
Chester, John **4** 806; **17** 900
Chester Beatty, (Alfred) *see* BEATTY, (ALFRED) CHESTER
Chester Beatty Library and Gallery of Oriental Art *see under* DUBLIN → museums
Chesterfield, Philip Stanhope, 4th Earl of *see* STANHOPE, PHILIP DORMER, 4th Earl of Chesterfield
Chesterfield (Derbys), Saltergate **21** 347

chesterfields **29** 8
Chesterton, G. K. **7** 769; **32** 382
Chesterton, Maurice **28** 283
Chesterton House **7** 297
chestnut **17** 46; **24** 3; **25** 303
Chestnut Hill (PA; USA) **25** 656
Chestnut Hill (MD; USA), Venturi house **32** 235
Chest of Kypselos **13** 592; **15** 85
Chestret, R. F. de **19** 161
chests **5** 350; **6** 388, 558–60*; **19** 312
historical and regional traditions
Africa **1** 366; **33** III2
Austria **2** 811
Belgium **3** 580; **6** 560
Berber **3** 755
China **7** 41, 145
Cuba (Caribbean) **8** 235
Czech Republic **8** *396*
Egypt **18** *139*
Egypt, ancient **6** 558–9; **10** 54
England **6** 560; **10** *286*, 286–7, 288
France **6** 559, 560; **11** 585
Germany **6** *559*, 560; **12** 419, 420–21, 454; **16** *59*
Gothic **6** 559, *559*
Greece, ancient **13** 592*
Hungary **14** 903, 905, *905*
Islamic **16** *499*, 517; **18** *139*
Japan **17** *302*, 357–8
Korea **18** 362–3, *363*
Malta (Republic of) **20** 215
Montenegro **22** 19
Netherlands, the **6** 560; **22** 870
Nigeria **33** III2
Ottoman **16** *499*
Portugal **25** 303, 304, 306
Rome, ancient **27** 100
Spain **29** 310, 312*
Sri Lanka **29** 470
Thailand **30** 618
United States of America **31** 623
materials
acacia **6** 559
alabaster (gypsum) **10** 54
ash **2** *811*
brass **18** *363*; **25** 306
bronze **6** 559; **10** 54
cedar **6** 559; **10** 54, 288; **25** 304
cypress **10** 288
deal (wood) **20** *215*
ebony **6** 559; **10** 54
enamel **7** *70*
faience (i) (glass) **6** 559
gesso **6** 560
iroko-wood **33** III2
iron **6** 560; **12** 454; **16** 59, *59*
ivory **6** 559; **18** *139*
juniper **25** 304
lacquer **6** 560; **17** *302*; **30** 618
leather **6** 560; **29** 312
oak **6** *559*; **10** *286*
sycamore **6** 559
walnut **16** *499*
zelkova **18** *363*
techniques
gilding **6** 559, 560
intarsia **8** *396*
types
bombé **20** *215*
canopic *see* CANOPIC CHESTS
cassoni *see* CASSONI
hutch **6** 559
ice-chests **7** *70*
lum **28** 255
Nonsuch **6** 560; **10** 288
ship's chests **17** 358
tilting **6** 559
tomb-chests *see under* TOMBS → types
travelling *see* TRUNKS
Tugendenkasten **2** *811*, 811
wheeled **17** 357
see also COFFERS
chests-of-drawers
historical and regional traditions
Belgium **3** 583
chests-of-drawers
historical and regional traditions—cont.
Cuba (Caribbean) **8** 235
Czech Republic **8** 398
England **8** *804*; **10** 288
France **20** *469*
Italy **16** *732*
Japan **17** 357, 358
Sweden **30** 94, 95
materials
iron **17** 358
mahogany **31** *627*
oak **3** 583
walnut **3** 583
techniques
marquetry **20** *469*
types
commodes *see* COMMODES
highboys *see* tallboys
tallboys **31** 624, 626, *627*
Cheticamp **27** 317
Chetiyagiri *see* MIHINTALE
Chetro, Jean de *see* JEAN DE CHETRO
Chetsada, Luang Vichit **30** 616
Che-tsung, Emperor (Sung; *reg* 1086-1101) *see* ZHEZONG EMPEROR (SONG)
Chetu **15** 628
Chetyapabbata *see* MIHINTALE
Cheung Yee **6** 562*; **14** 722
Chevakinsky, Savva (Ivanovich) **6** 562*
collaboration **18** 543
groups and movements **28** 837
pupils **3** 432; **23** 76; **29** 551
works **25** 745; **27** 374, 407, 575; **31** 828
Cheval, Le Facteur (Ferdinand) **2** 516
Chevalier, Charles **19** 279
Chevalier, Claire **4** 520
Chevalier, Etienne **6** 562*; **11** 531
manuscripts **11** *353*, 353–4; **20** 635; **23** 523
paintings **11** 352
Chevalier, Félix **5** 364
Chevalier, Jean *see* CAVALIER, JEAN
Chevalier, Nicholas **2** 745; **4** 882; **6** 563*; **28** 868
Chevallier **24** 148
Chevallier, Adrien **19** 282
Chevallier, Etienne Le *see* LE CHEVALLIER, ETIENNE
Chevallier, Nicolas **9** 22; **12** 727
chevaux-de-frise **9** 391; **21** 546, 551; **25** 536
Cheverney Château **6** 506
Cheverton, Benjamin **10** 311
Cheverton, James **16** 799
chevets (beds) **3** 484
chevets (chapels) **6** 563*; **25** *439*; **26** 572
Chevignerie, Emile Bellier de La *see* BELLIER DE LA CHEVIGNERIE, EMILE
Chevillet, Juste **6** 563*
Chevotet, Jean-Michel **6** 508, 563*; **24** 120
Chevrette Château **4** 125
Chevreul, Michel-Eugène **6** 564*; **19** 355; **30** 325
groups and movements **9** 40
works **1** 74; **7** 629, 637; **22** 745
Chevreuse **11** 611
Chevreuse, Jacquesson de La *see* LA CHEVREUSE, LOUIS-MARIE-FRANÇOIS JACQUESSON DE
Chevreuse, Marie Charles Louis d'Albert Luynes, Duc de **20** 295; **32** 511
Chevrier (family) **7** 597
Chevrier, J. **25** 691
chevrons **6** 564–5*, *565*; **10** 259
Chevrot, Jean, Bishop of Tournai **6** 565*; **20** 749; **33** 120
Chew (family) **1** 184
Chewa **1** 256, 296, 375, 409; **20** 161; **33** 602
Chew & Percival **8** 177
Cheyenne **14** 814; **22** 551, 669
dolls **31** 260
drawings **14** *814*
harnesses **14** 185
jewellery **22** 629
moccasins **22** 616
quillwork **22** 649, 650
weapons **22** *654*
Chezarla **6** 565–6*; **15** 257, 259–60, *276*, *294*
Kapoteshvara Temple **15** 252
temples **15** 295
Chez Francis Jourdain **17** 668
Chhaganlal **15** 601
Chhajju **15** 615, 626
Chhatradi **6** 566*; **15** *264*
sculpture **15** 483
temple of Shaktidevi **6** 566*; **15** 264
Chhimka **15** 322
Chhota Pandua
Bari Mosque **15** 352
Minar **15** 352
Chhoti Deori **15** 495
Chhusya Bahal **21** 847
Chia, Sandro **2** 561; **6** 566*; **16** 682; **25** 360
Chia-ch'ing emperor (Ch'ing; *reg* 1796-1820) *see* JIAQING EMPEROR
Chiaiese, Leonardo **16** 735
Chiang Chao-shen **30** 249
works **30** *249*
Chiang Ch'en-ying *see* JIANG CHENYING
Chiang Chia-chou *see* JIANG JIAZHOU
Chiang Chia-p'u *see* JIANG JIAPU
Chiang Jen *see* JIANG REN
Chiang Jung *see* JIANG RONG
Chiang Kai-shek **6** 772
Chiang Khan, Wat Nantaram **30** 586
Chiang K'uei *see* JIANG KUI
Chiang-ling *see* JIANGLING
Chiang Mai **6** 566–8*, *567*; **29** *225*; **30** 571, *571*, 604, 617
architecture **30** 590
ceramics **30** 608
coins **30** 632
fortifications **21** 595
metalwork **30** 635
National Museum **29** 240
silver **30** 634
stupas **30** 584
textiles **30** 620, 623
Wat Chedi Chet Yot **29** 826; **30** 586, 604, *604*
Wat Ku Tao **30** 586
Wat Lok **30** 586
Wat Pan Tao **12** II2
Wat Phra Sing Luang **30** 585, *586*, 604, 636
Wat Phra That Chae Haeng **30** 585
Wat Saen Fang **29** 827, *827*
Wihan Lai Kham **30** 585, *586*, 606
wood-carvings **30** 639
Chiang Rai **30** 632
Chiang Saen
Wat Chedi Luang **30** 586
Wat Pa Sak **29** 866; **30** 586, 604
Chiang Sung *see* JIANG SONG
Chiang Tung **30** 623
Chiang Yen-yang *see* JIANG YANYANG
Chiao Ping-chen *see* JIAO BINGZHEN
Chiapa **6** 592
Chiapa de Corzo
bone-carvings **21** 247
Stele 1 **29** 620
Chiapa de Corzo—cont.
Stele 2 **21** 219; **29** 620
Tomb 1 **21** 247
Chiapanec Maya **20** 885
Chiapas **21** 599
Museo de Tuxtla Gutiérrez **21** 397
Chiaradia, Enrico **27** 492
Chiaramella, Francesco **33** 50
works **33** *50*
Chiaramonte (family) **23** 841
Chiaramonti, Scipione **30** 657; **33** 587
Chiaravalle Milanese Abbey **13** 51, 64; **16** 627
Chiari, Giuseppe **4** 611; **24** 407
Chiari, Giuseppe Bartolomeo **6** 568*; **16** 672; **26** 774
attributions **25** 644
collaboration **19** 816; **20** 377
patrons and collectors **1** 532; **5** 812; **10** 364; **27** 172
pupils **2** 26; **4** 621; **17** 900
works **6** *568*; **26** 827
Chiari, Tommaso **6** 568
Chiarimalla, Francesco **33** 292
Chiarini, Marcantonio
paintings
ceiling **12** 30; **29** 32
frescoes **5** 774; **8** 141, 159; **32** 458
friezes **5** 281
wall **5** 281
stage design **30** 668
Chiaristi **21** 528; **24** 255
Chiaromonte, Isabella di *see* ISABELLA DI CHIAROMONTE
chiaroscuro **2** 227; **6** 569–70*, *570*; **7** 783; **13** 472; **16** 820; **17** 186; **19** 352; **24** *376*, 377, *377*, 492–3; **30** 456; **33** 640
chiaroscuro woodcuts *see under* WOODCUTS → types
Chia Ssu-hsieh *see* JIA SIXIE
Chia Ssu-tao *see* JIA SIDAO
Chiattone, Mario **6** 571*
groups and movements **11** 843, 868, 869; **21** 781; **27** 788
staff **27** 788
works **16** 648; **28** 833
Chiaureli, Mikhail **17** 732
Chiavacci **12** 630
Chiavelli, Chiavello **12** 299
Chiaveri, Gaetano **6** 571–2*; **25** 98, 135
patrons and collectors **33** 115
pupils **22** 202
works **9** 236, *237*; **18** 162; **20** 839; **25** 98, 322; **27** 574; **33** 115
Chiavistelli, Jacopo **11** 214
Chia-yü-kuan *see* JIAYUGUAN
Chibana **17** 262
Chiba Prefectural Library **17** 90
Chiba Ryuboku **17** 381
Chibcha **7** 602; **22** 519
Chibusan Tomb **17** 143
Chibwe, David **33** 602
Chicago (IL) **6** 572–8*; **12** 144; **31** *587*, 722, 724, *727*
apartment buildings
Commonwealth Promenade Apartments **1** 736
900 Esplanade Apartments **1** 736
Lake Shore Drive Apartments **12** 792; **15** 887; **28** 834; **31** 597, *597*
Auditorium Building **1** 111, 158, *158*; **6** 578; **14** 787; **29** 845, 913; **30** 678
building regulations **2** 325
Burnham Library *see under* museums → Art Institute of Chicago
Carl Schurz High School **6** 578
Chicago Theater **31** 596
City Hall **31** 242
Chicago (IL)—cont.
Civic Center *see* Richard J. Daly Center
Criminal Courts Building **18** 888
expositions
Century of Progress Exposition, 1933-4 **10** 684; **15** 883
World's Columbian Exposition, 1893 **5** *273*, 273–4; **10** 683; **15** 883; **27** 138; **31** 725, 727
Administration Building **15** 23
architecture **7** 485; **31** 594
ethnographic art **22** 673, 679; **29** 222
glass **19** 304
model tenement **25** 371
objects of vertu **27** 421
paintings **8** 85
photography **16** 821
sculpture **11** 755, 784
Street of Cairo **16** 389
stucco **29** 845
Transportation Building **6** 578; **29** 915
travolator **14** 384; **28** 728
Federal Center **13** 238
Fine Arts Building *see* museums → Museum of Science and Industry
furniture **31** 629, 631
Graceland Cemetery
Getty Tomb **1** 111; **20** 869
Hull House **2** 572
Illinois Institute of Technology (IIT) **21** 492
College of Architecture, Planning and Design *see* Crown Hall
Crown Hall **2** 360; **16** 55; **21** *492*
jewellery **31** 655
Lake View Presbyterian Church **28** 604
Lincoln Park **31** 725
Madlener House **6** 578
Masonic Temple **28** 833
Metro stations **21** 349
Midwest Interlibrary Center **19** 320
museums
Academy of Fine Arts *see* Art Institute of Chicago
Art Institute of Chicago **2** 560; **6** 575; **22** 359; **27** 138; **31** 666
Burnham Library **31** 670
collections **1** 437; **6** 735, 826; **7** 53, 156; **9** 231, 716; **15** 746, 750; **20** 524; **23** 882; **27** 463; **29** 222, 657; **30** 332
directors **18** 498
exhibitions **27** 47
Greek collection **13** 470
Helen Birch Bartlett Memorial Collection **6** 575
Ryerson Collection **27** 463
Ryerson Library **31** 670
sculpture **27** 46
Du Sable Museum **6** 576
Field Museum of Natural History **1** 437; **33** 29
collections **1** 439; **6** 772; **15** 687; **22** 675; **23** 739; **29** 241
Fuller Collection **23** 737
Maurice Spertus Museum **17** 582
Museum of Contemporary Art **6** 577
Museum of Science and Industry **2** 699
Oriental Institute Museum *see under* University of Chicago
O'Hare International Airport **1** 494, 495
Richard J. Daly Center **13** 238; **31** 242
Ryerson Library *see under* museums → Art Institute

Chicago (IL)—cont.
Schiller Theater *see* skyscrapers → Schiller Building
skyscrapers **28** 831
Chicago Tribune *Tower* **7** 669, *669*; **13** 204; **28** 833; **31** 595
Equitable Life Assurance Society Building **28** 831
Gage Building **30** 505
Home Insurance Building **6** *573*, 577, 578; **16** 55; **28** 830, 831; **31** 594
John Hancock Center **28** 834; **31** 597
Kendall Building **28** 831
Mile-High Skyscraper **28** 834
Monadnock Building **4** 788; **6** 578; **28** 833
Northwestern Terminal **28** 835
Old Colony Building **28** 833
Rand McNally Building **6** 577; **28** 830
Reliance Building **8** 278; **12** 792; **28** *832*, 833; **30** 505
Republic Building **31** 595
Rookery Building **27** 138, *138*; **30** 505
Schiller Building **6** 578; **28** 833
Sears Tower **5** 649; **28** 834, *834*; **31** 597
1 South Wacker Drive **6** *574*; **28** 835
Wrigley Building **30** 505
stores
Carson Pirie Scott & Co. Store **2** 568; **8** 770; **12** 792; **29** *915*; **33** 246
Marshall Field Wholesale Store **6** 578; **8** 770; **20** 572; **26** 343, *343*, 704; **30** 507; **31** 594; **32** 861
roof **27** 129
Schlesinger & Mayer Store *see* Carson Pirie Scott & Co. Store
Schlessinger & Mayer Store **21** 780
Temple Isaiah **17** 547
tomb of Martin A. Ryerson **25** 766
Unity Temple **7** 259; **31** 595; **33** 402
University of Chicago
Oriental Institute Museum **1** 839; **10** 81, 83; **15** 922; **21** 48
collections **10** 90, 94; **21** 310
Rockefeller Chapel **6** 459
urban planning **5** 275; **6** 574; **7** 357; **31** 725
Wall of Respect and Community as One **1** 445
warehouses **32** 861
Walker Warehouse **32** 861
Water Tower Place **28** 623
Chicago, Judy **6** 577*; **28** 53; **31** 609, 661; **33** 311
groups and movements **10** 878, 879, 880, 882
works **10** 483, *879*; **12** 217; **19** 492
Chicago construction *see* TIMBER STRUCTURE → types → balloon frames
Chicago Imagist group **22** 441; **24** 223
Chicago Mural Group **6** 577
Chicago Painter **13** 523; **32** 37–8*
Chicago school **6** 573, 577–9*; **16** 55; **31** 594–5
members **3** 693; **25** 446; **29** 915–16
works **19** 453; **28** 833; **31** *595*
Chicago Society of Arts and Crafts **2** 572; **6** 575
Chicago Society of Etchers **25** 629
Chicago Terra Cotta Company **30** 505
Chicama, Sala de Cultura del Banco Wiese **24** 517
Chicaneau (family) **24** 148
Chicaneau, Jean **27** 536
Chicaneau, Louis-Dominique François **27** 537
Chicaneau, Pierre (*d* 1677) **11** 607; **27** 536
Chicaneau, Pierre (1661-1710) **27** 536
Chicanná **9** 165; **21** 206; **26** 412; **29** 829
Chicano **18** 830
architecture **18** 832
craftsmen and artists **18** 831–2
fibreglass **18** *831*
iconography **18** 831–2
nude figures **18** *831*
Chican-Taíno culture **29** 200–201
pottery **29** *199*, 200
stone-carvings **29** *199*, 200
wood-carvings **29** 200
Chichagov, Dmitry **22** 173; **28** 837
Chichaoua **16** 190
Chichaoua carpets *see under* CARPETS → types
Chichele, Henry, Archbishop of Canterbury **7** 350; **23** 686; **28** 66
Chi Ch'eng *see* JI CHENG
Chichén Itzá **6** 579–80*; **20** *882*, 884; **21** 190, *193*, 200, 202–3, 262, *372*; **31** 98; **32** 88
architecture **20** 884; **21** 216
Ballcourt **3** 118, *118*
beads **29** 154
Caracol **3** 622, *622*; **5** 696*; **6** 579; **20** *882*, 884; **23** 338
Castillo **6** 579; **20** 884; **21** 213, 248; **25** 765; **30** 449, *449*
throne **30** 786
chacmools **21** *223*; **28** 640
church **20** 884
gold **21** *253*
Great Ballcourt **6** 579; **20** 884; **21** 187
lintels **9** 166
metalwork **21** 252, 254
mosaics **21** 255; **22** 164
reliefs **21** 188, 251
religion **21** 186
Sacred Cenote **21** 243, 248, 260, 263
Sacred Well **21** *253*
sculpture **21** 222, 225
skull racks **21** 188; **31** 505
Structure 3E5 **3** 378
talud-tablero **30** 280
Temple of the Chacmool **21** 214, 263
throne **30** 786
wall paintings **21** 259
Temple of the Jaguars **21** 232, 247
Temple of Kukulcán **21** 247
Temple of the Warriors **6** *580*, 580; **20** 884; **21** 214, 232, 247
wall paintings **21** 226, 232, 263
Chicherin, Denis **27** 420
Chichester (W. Sussex) **2** 324
Bishop's Palace **12** 175
Bishop Storey's Cross **21** 893
Cathedral of the Holy Trinity **12** 6; **20** 576
ironwork **10** 339
jet **17** 516
pulpit **25** 728
roof **30** 908
sculpture **10** 476; **26** 612, 616, 643
spire **29** 413
stained glass **29** 508
tapestries **10** 352
Festival Theatre **30** 684, 687
kilns **10** 301
Chichester, Arthur, 5th Earl of Donegal (*fl* 1757) **3** 536
Chichester, Arthur, Lord Deputy of Ireland (1563-1625) **3** 536
Chichester, Henry of *see* HENRY OF CHICHESTER
Chichester, John **27** 729
Chichester-Constable Chasuble **13** 196; **23** 461
Chichi, Antonio **10** 818
Chichicastenago, Museo Regional **13** 769
Chichimec **21** 201
Chichimecs **30** 452
Chi-chou *see* JIZHOU
Chichow *see* JIZHOU
Chickasaw **22** 552, 667
chicken-bone-white jade *see under* JADE → types
Chiclayo **29** 217
Chicomoztoc *see* LA QUEMADA
Chiconcuac **21** 394
Chidambaram **6** 580–81*; **15** 79, *294*
architecture **15** 333
gopuras **13** 4
Nataraja Temple **15** 335, 412
sculpture **15** 414
Shivakamasundari Temple **15** 646
Chiddingstone (Kent) **20** 866
Chief Associate of Maître François *see* JACQUES DE BESANÇON, MASTER OF
Chief Directorate for Cottage Industry *see* GLAVKUSTPROM
Chieftain Cup **21** 659, 689
Ch'ien Ch'en-ch'ün *see* QIAN CHENQUN
Chien Dang **6** 423, 430
Chieng Mai *see* CHIANG MAI
Ch'ien hsien *see* QIAN XIAN
Ch'ien Hsüan *see* QIAN XUAN
Ch'ien Ku *see* QIAN GU
Ch'ien Kung *see* QIAN GONG
Ch'ien-lung emperor (Ch'ing; 1736-96) *see* QIANLONG EMPEROR
Ch'ien Shun-chü *see* QIAN SHUNJU
Ch'ien Sung *see* QIAN SONG
Ch'ien Tien *see* QIAN DIAN
Chiera, E. **23** 322
Chieri, S Bernardino **32** 644–5
Chierico, Francesco di Antonio del *see* FRANCESCO DI ANTONIO DEL CHIERICO
Chiesa, Achillito **7** 782
Chiesa, Francesco della *see* FRANCESCO DELLA CHIESA
Chiesa, Giorgio della *see* GIORGIO DELLA CHIESA
Chiesa, Innocenzo **2** 808
Chiesa, Luis Quero *see* QUERO CHIESA, LUIS
Chiesa, Pompeo della **2** 472
Chiesa, Silvestro (della) **6** 581*
Chieti Students' Residences **16** 651; **30** 455
Chièvres, St Martin **13** 113
Chiewitz, Georg Theodor Policron **6** 581–2*
Chifeng *see* DAYINGZI (CHIFENG)
Chifflart, François (-Nicolas) **5** 363; **6** 582*; **14** 853
Chifflot brothers **23** 177
Chiggio, Ennio **13** 728
Chighine, Alfredo **6** 582*
Chigi (family) **28** 677
architecture **26** 748, 756; **32** 627
books **4** 21
collections **16** 764, 769; **26** 773
paintings **20** 375; **28** 335; **30** 121
sculpture **20** 745
Chigi, Agostino (i) (1466-1520) **6** 583*; **26** 759
architecture **16** 633; **20** 865; **24** 530; **25** 907; **26** 769; **27** 486; **32** 545
paintings **12** 278; **22** 412; **24** 525; **25** 905; **28** 332, 333, 335; **29** 2; **31** 523
sculpture **19** 710
Chigi, Agostino (ii) (1634-1705) **6** 585–6*; **21** 808; **27** 152
Chigi, Fabio, Cardinal *see* ALEXANDER VII, Pope
Chigi, Flavio, Cardinal **6** 585*
architecture **11** 275
collections **16** 771
interior decoration **26** 780
paintings **14** 367; **23** 701; **27** 152
allegorical **18** 871; **20** 431; **21** 54
flower **20** 431
genre **31** 313
mythological **18** 779
vedute **7** 509
sculpture **5** 377; **6** 585; **20** 909; **25** 852
Chigi, Mario, Duca di Ariccia *see* ARICCIA, MARIO CHIGI, Duca di
Chigi, Prince **5** 623; **13** 605
Chigi, Sigismondo **5** 366; **24** 529; **29** 2; **31** 714
Chigi, Sulpizia **6** 139
Chigi Painter *see* MACMILLAN PAINTER
Chigi Vase **10** 591; **13** 485, 488, *488*, 549
Chigi-Zondadari, Anton Felice, Cardinal **7** 682
Chigi Zondadari, Cardinal **8** 12
Chignal Smealy, St Nicholas **11** 252
Chigwell (Essex), St Mary's **4** 693
Chihil Sutun Palace *see under* ISFAHAN
Chih Lou-chia-ch'an *see* ZHI LOUJIACHAN
Chih-sheng *see* YOU KAN
Chih Tz'u-an *see* ZHI CIAN
Chihuahua
Cathedral **21** 377
Museo de Ciudad Júarez **25** 878
Museo Regional **5** 910
Chihuata **24** *498*
Espíritu Santo **24** 503
Chihuly, Dale **21** 801
Chihuzan Takada *see* TAKADA, CHIHUZAN
Ch'ihwa-ssi *see* SIN YUN-BOK
Chih-yung *see* ZHIYONG
Chikamatsu Monzaemon **9** 738; **17** 350, 357, 406
Chikamichi, Ōe no *see* ŌE NO CHIKAMICHI
Chikamori **6** 586*; **17** *11*
Chikanobu Hashimoto *see* HASHIMOTO CHIKANOBU
Chikanobu Yōshū *see* YŌSHŪ, CHIKANOBU
Chikashi Hata *see* HATA CHIKASHI
Chikiti, Chaitanya Temple **15** 636
Chikji Temple **18** 308
Chikkei Nakabayashi *see* NAKABAYASHI CHIKKEI
Chikkyō Ono *see* ONO, CHIKKYŌ
Chikovani, Simon **8** 437
Chikuden Tanomura *see* TANOMURA CHIKUDEN
Chikudō Kishi *see* KISHI CHIKUDŌ
Ch'i Kung *see* QI GONG
Chikusan Takada *see* TAKADA, CHIKUSAN
Chikusei Mimura *see* MIMURA, CHIKUSEI
Chikushun Kawase *see* KAWASE, CHIKUSHUN
Chikutō Nakabayashi *see* NAKABAYASHI CHIKUTŌ
Chikuyuki Sayama *see* SAYAMA CHIKUYUKI
Chikuzen **30** 258
Chilamkuru **15** 534
Agastyeshvara Temple **15** 537
Ch'ilbul Hermitage **18** 288
Chilca **19** 385; **29** 158
Chilcotin **22** 546, 656
Child, Abigail **10** 689
Child, Alfred E. **7** 378; **29** 507; **31** 229
Child, Richard, 1st Earl of Tilney **23** 189
Child, Robert **1** 139; **3** 173; **10** 643; **14** 230; **19** 426
Child, Thomas **4** 476
child art **6** 586–9*, *587*; **24** 696; **25** 685; **31** 490
Childe, (V.) Gordon **2** 300; **20** 81; **25** 503; **28** 815
Childe, Henry Langdon **20** 92
Childe, Richard, Viscount Castlemain **17** 901
Childebert of Paris (*reg* 511-58) **24** 115, 159
child jade *see* JADE → types → river
Children, Anna *see* ATKINS, ANNA
Children's Aid Society **32** 95
children's books **4** 357, 360, 362, 363, 364, 368; **8** 121–2; **10** 176
Childs, Cephas G. **15** 857
Childs, Lucinda **24** 407, 409
Childs & Inman **15** 857
Chile **6** 589–602*, *590*; **15** *161*; **29** 127
architecture **6** 591–5*
body arts **29** 204
brackets **6** 591
bronze **6** *598*
ceramics **6** 600*
collections **6** 600–601*
dolls' houses **31** 264
education (art) **6** 601–2*
escalators **18** 797
ewers **6** 599
gold **6** 599*
government buildings **6** *593*
heritage **6** 601
iconography **6** 596
ikat **6** *599*
jade **16** 861
jewellery **6** 599*
kettles **6** 599
libraries **6** 600–601*
museums **6** 600–601*
office buildings **6** *595*
painting **5** 188; **6** 595–9*
landscape **6** *597*
murals **22** 335*
patronage **6** 600–601*
pins **6** 599
ponchos **6** *599*
portraits **6** *596*
prints **6** 598
sculpture **6** 595–9*, *598*
silver **6** 599*
spurs **6** 599
textiles **6** 599–600*
trade **6** 591
universities **27** *792*
vaults (ceiling) **6** 592
wool **6** *599*
Chilek
silver **6** *188*
Ch'ilgok, Songrim Temple **18** 364; **26** 151
reliquaries **18** *364*
Chili **24** 514
Chili, Manuel *see* CASPICARA
Chiliktin **2** 101
Chilkhudzhra **32** 320
Chillán **6** *590*
Museo de Bellas Artes **6** 601
Chillenden **5** 638, 645
Chillida, Eduardo **6** 602*; **22** 315
dealers **20** 75
works **16** 58; **27** 768; **29** 296, *296*
Chillon Castle **6** *602*, 602–3*; **19** 895; **30** *124*
Burgkapelle **30** 129
Chilmark **10** 227
Chiloé **6** *590*, 592
Chilperic I of Soissons (*reg* 561-84) **11** 653
Chilvers Coton *see under* NUNEATON
Chim **5** 659, 897; **6** 603*; **20** 99
Chimaera of Arezzo *see* AREZZO CHIMAERA
Chimaera Painter **32** 58

Chimalistac **10** 505
Chimay **3** 590
Chimay, Anna, Princesse de **8** 208
Chimay, Charles, Prince de **8** 208
Chimay, Charles III de Cröy, Prince de **3** 614; **8** 208
Chimay, Charlotte de Saint-Simon, Princesse de **13** 701; **28** 776
Chimay, Jean, Comte de **8** 208
Chimay, Philippe, Comte de **8** 208
Chimay, Philippe II de Cröy, Prince de **3** 612; **8** 208
Chimayo (NM) **22** 626
Chimbong **18** 342
Chimei Hamada *see* HAMADA, CHIMEI
Chimenti, Jacopo *see* EMPOLI, JACOPO DA
Chimento di Piero **4** 505
Chimera **24** 441
Chimère, La **9** 766; **22** 268, 431; **27** 523
chimeres **32** 389*
Chimid, B. **21** 874
Chimishliya **21** 812
Chimkent **16** 530; **17** *865*, 866
chimney-boards **11** 119
chimney-breasts **14** 420
chimney furniture **11** 119
chimney-pieces **6** 603–5*; **11** 119
historical and regional traditions
England **6** 604, *604*, 605; **10** 276; **29** *647*
France **6** *604*, 605
Ireland **16** *23*
Netherlands, the **23** *188*
Scotland **28** 246, 247
materials
marble **29** *647*
plaster **16** *23*
sandstone **23** *188*
tiles **30** 874
chimneys **4** 769, 778, 779; **13** 390
Chimpa Sonambum **30** 831
Chim Son **6** 423
Chimú **6** 440, 441, 605–7*; **15** 163; **29** 127, 161
adobe **29** *168*
altars **1** 701
architectural decorations **6** *441*
architecture **21** 599
beadwork **3** 442
body ornaments **29** 218
dress **29** 183
feathers **29** 207
fortifications **21** 599
friezes **6** *441*, *607*
hardstones **29** 186
iconography **29** 133
masks **29** 209
metalwork **6** 606–7*
mud **6** *607*
musical instruments **29** 216
palaces **23** 826
pectoral ornaments **3** 442
pottery **6** 606*; **29** 177
relief sculpture **6** *607*; **29** *168*
religion **29** 130–31
shells **29** 218
stirrup jars **29** 176
textiles **6** 606*; **29** 181, 207
tombs **31** 118
wood-carvings **6** 607*
Chimu *see* XIAO YUNCONG
Chin **5** 220, 248
Chin (family) *see* JIN (FAMILY)
Chin, Benjamin **5** 671
China **6** 607–925*, *614*, *615*; **7** 1–161*
academies **7** 148, 151
acorns **7** 45
adobe **6** 691
aesthetics **6** 769, 795–8
agate **7** 4, 90, 91, 109, 111, *111*
albums **1** *580*, 580–81; **6** 762, 791; **22** 234
alizarin **7** 45
alloys **6** 829–30*
altars **1** 701–3*, *702*; **6** *704*
Buddhism **1** 703; **5** *112*

China
altars—cont.
Confucianism **1** 703
Daoism **1** 703; **6** 786
altar sets **7** 86, *86*, 101
alum **7** 632
aluminium **7** 115
aluminium oxides **6** 897
aluminium salts **7** 45
amateurs **6** 771
amber **1** 761; **7** 89, 90, 91, 110, 111, *111*
amethyst **7** 91
amphorae **6** 827, 875, *876*, 888
amulets **1** 818; **7** 6, 107, 145
animal subjects **6** 798–9
appliqué **7** 14, 19, 144
apprentices **7** 147
aprons **7** 76, 145
archaeology **1** 150; **7** 157–60*
marine **7** 160
archaism **6** 865, 866
architects **2** 317*
architectural decorations **7** 143
architecture **6** 631, 637–45*, 646–66*, *647*, 679–92*, 693–6*; **12** 313; **19** 865; **25** 171
brick **6** 645*, 686
Buddhism **6** 666–71*, *670*
Christianity **6** 677–8*
Confucianism **6** 674–6*
Daoism **6** 671–4*, *672*
Islamic **6** 676–7*
landscape **12** 85–93
megalithic **21** 44
military **21** 593–4*
Prehistoric **6** 684–5
Qing period (1644-1911) **3** 516
stone **6** 644–5*
trabeated construction **6** 667, 689; **31** 269
vernacular **7** 143*
wood **6** 637–43*, 650
20th cent. **28** *551*
archives **6** 764
armour **7** 13, 14, 54–8*, *55*, *57*
armrests **7** 33
art (classification of) **6** 633–4*
art (imitation of works of) **11** 306
art criticism **2** 519; **6** 537, 821–5*
art history **2** 531, 539; **6** 821; **7** 160–61; **33** 317–22*
artificial mountains **12** 88, 90
artists' biographies **6** 821–3; **7** 62, 161; **33** 322
art legislation **2** 554
art schools **7** 148–9; **28** 553
ashes **6** 873; **7** 14, 17, 19; **18** 601
axes **6** 841, 848; **7** 1, 2, *45*, 97; **28** *603*
Anyang period (*c.* 1300-*c.* 1050 BC) **28** *603*
Western Zhou (*c.* 1050-771 BC) **6** *848*
azurite **7** 632; **18** 600
backscratchers **7** 102
bamboo **6** 736, 740; **7** 31, 58–62*, 115, 141, 145, *145*, 146, 147; **20** 326; **28** 310, 312
Han period (206 BC-AD 220) **7** 62–3
Prehistoric **6** 877
Qing period (1644-1911) **7** *59*, *60*
Song period (AD 960-1279) **7** 141
Zhou period (*c.* 1050-256 BC) **7** 62
20th cent. **7** 113
bamboo-carvings **7** 58–62*, *59*, *60*, *61*
bangles **7** 145
banknotes **3** 180, 182; **7** 115
banners **6** 777, 779–81*; **7** *49*; **28** 310
barium **7** 81
bark **7** 43, 114
betel-nut **7** 115

China
bark—cont.
mixiang **7** 115
sandalwood **28** 312
basins **10** III2
basketwork **7** 101
batik **7** 45
beads **7** 80, 88, 89, 108, 110, 836
eyebeads **7** 80–81, *81*
beakers **7** 102
beams **6** *684*; **7** 12
beds **7** 7, 34, 36, *38*, 38–9, 145
bells **3** 626, *626*; **6** 829, 834, 841, *846*, 849*, 855; **7** 100; **28** *626*
Buddhism **7** 98
belthooks **3** 685–6*, *686*; **6** 832, 855, 859; **7** 7, 74, 81, 88, 97, *98*, 107
belts **7** 74, 76, 108, 109, 110, 111, 124
binders **7** 92
birdcages **7** 146, 147
bi see discs
block-books **4** 143
boats **3** *520*
bone **4** 313; **6** 736; **7** 19, 106, 107, 109
bookbindings **7** 63–4
book covers **1** 580
book illustrations **6** 777, 782; **7** 64–5, 120–21
books **6** 736, 740; **7** 7, 62–5*, *64*
accordion books **1** 580, *580*; **7** 63
butterfly books **1** 580
boots **7** 75, 76
bottles **6** 890, *896*; **7** 84
bowls **6** *874*, *875*, 893, III3; **7** 22, 23, 143; **12** IV3
kinrande **6** 905
Ming period (1368-1644) **6** 875, 902, 903
Qing period (1644-1911) **7** *84*, 103
Song period (AD 960-1279) **6** *897*; **7** *15*, *26*
Tang period (AD 618-907) **6** *885*, *917*; **7** 14, *24*
totai **6** 905
Western and Eastern Jin period (AD 265-420) **6** *884*
Yuan period (1279-1368) **6** 900
boxes **7** 96, 134; **18** *601*, *605*; **31** *194*
Han period (206 BC-AD 220) **7** 133
Ming period (1368-1644) **7** *17*, *18*, 100
Qing period (1644-1911) **7** *19*, *20*; **18** *612*
Song period (AD 960-1279) **7** 14, 15, 141
toilet-boxes **7** 13
Yuan period (1279-1368) **7** 15, 16, *16*
box-wood **7** 141
bracelets **7** 109, 111
brackets **4** 623*; **5** 649; **6** 640–41, *641*, *644*, 667, 686, 690; **7** 143; **30** 913
brass **4** 681, *683*, 684, *684*, 688*; **6** 706, 830; **7** 79, 101; **30** *398*
brick **4** 794–5*, *794*; **6** 645*, 648, 668, 686, *686*, 696, 697, 698, 882, 887, 906; **7** 143, 144
bridges **4** 800, *800*; **29** 905
bristle **6** 736
brocades **7** 58; **30** 846
bronze **3** 685; **4** 852–3*, 855; **6** 631, 635, 645*, 706, 707, 725, 726–7, 733, 735, 737, 738, *738*, 772, 773, 788, 826–34*, *827*, 835*, 857*, 860–66*, 868*; **7** 21, 22, 54, 68, *72*, 94, 101, 107, 108, 109, 128, 129, *129*, 130, *130*, 139; **17** 587, *587*; **23** 495, *495*, 496, *496*; **24** 258

China
bronze—cont.
Anyang period (*c.* 1300-*c.* 1050 BC) **6** 835, 836, 839, 840; **23** *155*; **28** 603
Buddhism **6** *719*, 835
Chu **7** 247
Daoism **6** *628*
Dian culture **8** 852–4, *853*, *854*
Erligang period (*c.* 15th-14th cent. BC) **6** 831, 835, 836, 838–9, 840
Erlitou period (first half 2nd millennium BC) **6** 831; **10** *464*
Han period (206 BC-AD 220) **6** 857–60*, *858*, *859*, *860*, *861*, 861–2*; **7** 95; **21** *715*
Majiayao culture **6** 835
Ming period (1368-1644) **6** *720*, 720–22
Northern and Southern Dynasties (AD 310-589) **6** *708*, *710*
Qijia culture **6** 835
Qing period (1644-1911) **6** *733*
Qin period (221-206 BC) **6** 727, 857*
Shang period (*c.* 1600-*c.* 1050 BC) **4** 849; **6** 8, 625, 736, 798, *831*, 835–41*, *836*, *837*, *838*, *839*; **7** 3–4, 55, 97, 107, 123; **13** *736*; **21** 714, I4; **23** 549–50; **24** *14*; **28** 603
Song period (AD 960-1279) **6** 718, *865*, *866*
Sui period (AD 581-618) **6** 712
Tang period (AD 618-907) **6** 730, *863*, 863–4*, *864*; **7** 14, 109
Western Zhou (*c.* 1050-771 BC) **6** *848*
Xin period (AD 9-23) **6** 860–61*
Zhou period (*c.* 1050-256 BC) **3** *626*; **6** *695*, 808, *833*, 841–9*, *842*, *843*, *844*, *845*, *846*, *847*, *849*, 850–56*, *850*, *851*, *852*, *853*, *854*, *855*, *856*; **7** *55*, 97, 107, 533; **28** *626*; **29** 229, *906*; **33** *471*
20th cent. **6** 767
brushes **5** 35; **6** 736–7, 877; **7** 62, 65–6*
brush handles **7** 102
brushline **5** 35, 36; **6** 800
brushpots **7** 58, 59, *59*, 102, 134, *134*, 141, *141*
brush-rests **7** 102, 134, 141
buckles **6** 856; **7** 108, 145
building regulations **5** 135
burial suits **7** 6; **20** 236, *236*; **22** 466
burnishing **6** 874, 876
cabinets (ii) (furniture) **7** 41
calamine **12** 88
calligraphy **1** 580–81; **4** 344; **5** 36; **6** 612, 735–61*, *736*, 762–8*, 769–71, 772*, 818; **7** 129, 146, 148, 161, *624*; **15** 853, 854; **17** 211, 215, 227, 234–8*; **25** 72; **29** 617
bokuseki **6** 752, *752*
Buddhism **6** 751–2, *752*, 756
Chan **17** 229–31
display **1** 580–81
Five Dynasties (AD 907-60) **6** 748*
Han period (206 BC-AD 220) **6** 633–4, 636, *740*, 740–41*
Jin period (AD 1115-1234) **6** 750–51*, 753
Ming period (1368-1644) **6** 756–61*, *757*, *758*, *759*, *762*
Northern and Southern Dynasties (AD 310-589) **6** *743*, 743–4*, *744*; **30** 251
Qing period (1644-1911) **6** 762–6*, *763*, *765*

China
calligraphy—cont.
Qin period (221-206 BC) **6** *739*, 740*
Shang period (*c.* 1600-*c.* 1050 BC) **6** 737–8*, *738*
Song period (AD 960-1279) **6** 748–52*, *749*, *750*, *751*, *752*, 753; **7** 161
Sui period (AD 581-618) **6** 744–5*
Tang period (AD 618-907) **6** 745–8*, *746*, *747*
Three Kingdoms (AD 220-80) **6** 741–2*
Western and Eastern Jin period (AD 265-420) **6** 742–3*, *742*, *747*; **32** 836
Yuan period (1279-1368) **6** 752–6*, *753*, *754*
Zhou period (*c.* 1050-256 BC) **6** *738*, 738–9*
20th cent. **6** 766–8*, *768*
camphor **7** 91
camphor-wood **7** 31
candelabra **7** 80
candlesticks **7** 86, *86*
cane **7** 113, 114
cantilevers **4** 623; **5** 649; **6** *652*
caps **7** 76
carpets **7** 51, *67*, 67–8*; **16** 466
cartography **20** 361
cartouches **6** 777
carving **7** 16–17, 18–19, 58, *85*; **18** 601
casting **6** 725, 830–34*; **7** 98
cast iron **7** 97, 98, 99–100; **16** 50; **21** 320
Buddhism **7** 98, 99
Five Dynasties (AD 907-60) **7** 99, *99*
Han period (206 BC-AD 220) **7** 98
Northern and Southern Dynasties (AD 310-589) **21** 715
Song period (AD 960-1279) **7** *100*
Zhou period (*c.* 1050-256 BC) **7** 96, 97
casts **6** 8, 9
catalogues **7** 158, 161
bronzes **6** 843
calligraphy **17** 230
collections **6** 745, 764, 804
inks **7** 94
metalwork **6** 865, 867
painting **6** 773
stone **12** 88
cat's-eye **7** 91
cauldrons **7** 97
caves **6** 691, *691*, *692*; **30** 442–3*
ceilings **6** 643
cemeteries **6** 685, 694
censers **6** 859, 866, 883
censorship **6** 176
ceramics **6** 772, 868–9*, 870–73*, 874–5*, *875*, 889*, 913–18*; **7** 94, 106, 143–4, 157; **9** 34; **16** 398
Buddhism **5** *111*
commentaries **5** 293; **14** 604; **17** 481
conservation **7** 729
Qing period (1644-1911) **14** 425
restoration **7** 729
Song period (AD 960-1279) **6** 891–2*, 894–5*
Tang period (AD 618-907) **29** 232; **30** 288
Yuan period (1279-1368) **6** 896–901*
Zhou period (*c.* 1050-256 BC) **33** 660
20th cent. **6** 911–13*
chains **7** *107*, 108, 145
chairs **6** 390*; **7** 32, 34, 35, 36, 39–40, 145, *145*
armchairs **7** *39*

China—cont.
  chalcedony **7** 132, *132*
  characters (writing) **6** 735–6, *736*, 737, 741; **7** 128, 143; **17** 21, 211, 230, 231, 234
    Han period (206 BC-AD 220) **6** *740*
    Ming period (1368-1644) **6** 756, *757*, *758*, 759, *759*, 760, 761, *762*
    Northern and Southern Dynasties (AD 310-589) **6** *743*, 744, *744*
    Qing period (1644-1911) **6** 763, *763*, *765*, 766
    Qin period (221-206 BC) **6** *739*, 740
    Shang period (*c.* 1600-*c.* 1050 BC) **6** 737–8
    Song period (AD 960-1279) **6** 749, *749*, *750*, *751*, 752, *752*
    Sui period (AD 581-618) **6** 745
    Tang period (AD 618-907) **6** *746*, 746–7, *747*
    Western and Eastern Jin period (AD 265-420) **6** 742, *742*, 743, *747*
    Yuan period (1279-1368) **6** *753*, *754*, 755; **7** 129
    Zhou period (*c.* 1050-256 BC) **6** 738–9
    20th cent. **6** 766, 768, *768*
  charcoal **7** 98
  chariot fittings **6** 848
  chariots **6** 481–2*, 727; **7** 55; **28** *549*
  charms **6** 707
  chasing **7** 109
  châtelaines **7** 109
  chess sets **6** 555, 557; **7** 103
  chests **7** 41, 145
    ice-chests **7** *70*
  china stone **6** 869, 897
  chronologies **6** *617*; **30** 848
  churches **6** 677–8*, *678*
  cinnabar **7** 631–2
  clay **6** 706, 832, 869; **7** 98, 101, 128, 141, 143, 147; **18** 601; **31** 255
    Northern and Southern Dynasties (AD 310-589) **6** 708
    Song period (AD 960-1279) **6** 706, 717
    Tang period (AD 618-907) **7** 95
    Zhou period (*c.* 1050-256 BC) **6** 832–3, *833*
    20th cent. **6** *734*
  cliff inscriptions **6** 741, 744
  clocks **7** 438
  coal **7** 98
  coal tar **7** 53
  coats **7** 74, 75, 76, *76*, 77
  cobalt **6** 869, 872, 888, 901, 902, 903, 906, 909; **16** 394
  cobalt oxides **6** 904
  cobble **7** 95
  coconuts **7** 101
  cocoons **7** 113
  codices **7** 63
  coffers **7** 41
  coffins **7** 13
  coins **4** 688; **7** *72*, 72–4*, 533; **15** 811, 812
  collars **7** 78
  collections **2** 558; **6** 764; **7** 53, 151–6*, 158; **17** 237; **30** 850
    bamboo **7** 62
    bronzes **6** 868*
    calligraphy **6** 772*; **7** 129; **17** 229, 230, 232
    ceramics **6** 331, 898, 925*; **7** 161
    erotic art **10** 487
    furniture **1** 150
    impressions **7** 129
    inks **7** 93–4
    inkstones **17** 388
    inscriptions **23** 673
    jade **7** 8
China
  collections—cont.
    metalwork **6** 867
    painting **6** 826; **7** 129, 161; **17** 229
    porcelain **1** 150; **16** 393, 424
    royal **6** 744, 745, 753, 764, 772, 822, 826, 867; **7** 150–51*; **14** 604
    rubbings **17** 237
    sculpture **6** 734–5*; **24** 258
    seals **7** 129, 130
    textiles **7** 53–4*
  colophons **6** 750, 751, *751*, 755, 760, 761, 823, 824; **7** 623–4*, *624*
  colour **7** 631–2*
  columns **6** 640; **7** 98
  combs (hair) **7** 7, *7*, 102, 107, 109, 110
  Comic-strip art **6** 775
  cong **7** *1*, 1–2
  connoisseurship **6** 637, 770, 823, 824, 866, 886; **7** 715–16*; **11** 307, 309; **17** 230
  conservation **1** 580; **7** 729–30; **28** 312
  copies **2** 558; **11** 310; **26** 226
  copper **6** 829–30*, 869; **7** 79, 101
    Dian culture **8** 852
    Ming period (1368-1644) **6** 873, 901, 905
    Qing period (1644-1911) **6** 910; **7** *70*, *79*, 84, 112, 132
    Song period (AD 960-1279) **6** 895
    Tang period (AD 618-907) **7** 92
    Zhou period (*c.* 1050-256 BC) **6** 832, 853; **7** 80, 88; **21** 714
  copper oxides **6** 872, 885, 895, 899
  copybooks **6** 761, 762, 764
  coral **6** 706; **7** 18, 19, 89, 91, 111, *111*, 836
  cornelian **7** 89
  correspondence **6** 741, 742
  cosmetics **7** 137–8
  costumes **7** 137, *137*
  cotton **7** 43, 51, *52*, 113, *144*, *145*; **8** 34
  courtyards **6** 674, 687–8, *689*, 691, 692
  coverlets **7** *53*, *144*
  craftsmen and artists **6** 635–7*, 770, 771; **7** 9; **16** *859*
    Buddhism **6** 706
  crossbow-bolts **7** 97
  crowns **7** 25, *25*, 75, 76, 108, 110–12, *111*
  cuirasses **7** *55*
  cupboards **6** *669*
  cups **7** *23*, 81, 123, *126*; **16** III1
    Han period (206 BC-AD 220) **7** 6, 13
    Ming period (1368-1644) **7** 124–5
    Qing period (1644-1911) **7** *85*, 100, 103, 126, *127*, 128
    stem **6** 875, *875*
    Sui period (AD 581-618) **7** 82
    Tang period (AD 618-907) **7** 82, 123–4; **23** *551*
    two-handled **7** *9*
    Zhou period (*c.* 1050-256 BC) **16** *857*
  curtains **7** 51, *51*, 145
  dāgabas **6** 658
  daggers **23** 495
  damask **7** 49; **30** 551
  darning **7** 45
  devil's work balls **7** 103, *104*
  diadems **7** 108, 110
  diamonds **7** 88
  dictionaries **6** 764, 769; **9** 311
  dies (ii) (stamps) **7** 128
  diplomatic gifts **16** 413
  discs **7** 2, 81, 102
  dolls **31** 259, 261
China—cont.
  doors **6** 643; **9** 162*
  drawings **6** 811
  dress **7** 74–9*, 144, 632
    Han period (206 BC-AD 220) **7** *75*
    Qing period (1644-1911) **7** *78*
    Song period (AD 960-1279) **7** *76*
    Yuan period (1279-1368) **7** 50
  dresses **7** 78
  drums (musical instruments) **8** 853, *853*; **29** 229
  dyeing **7** 45
    paste resist **30** 558
    resist **7** 45, 52, *144*; **30** 560
    stitching **30** 556
    tie-dyeing **7** 144; **30** 556
    wax resist **7** 144, 145; **30** 558
  dyes **7** 45, 53, 115, 116, 123, 126; **30** 561
  dynasties *see* periods
  earpicks **7** 102
  earrings **7** 111
  earth **6** 643–4*
  earthenwares **6** 868, 869, 872, 874, 885; **7** 101
    Han period (206 BC-AD 220) **6** *686*, 874, 882, *883*
    Liao period (AD 907-1125) **6** *890*, *891*
    Northern and Southern Dynasties (AD 310-589) **6** 886
    Prehistoric **6** 868
    Qing period (1644-1911) **7** 101, *101*
    Qin period (221-206 BC) **6** 881–2
    Shang period (*c.* 1600-*c.* 1050 BC) **6** 870, 875, 879, 880, *880*
    Tang period (AD 618-907) **4** 172; **6** *887*, 888, *888*, *889*
  education (art) **6** 775, 811; **7** 147–50*; **28** 553
    archaeology **7** 160
    calligraphy **6** 745
  embossing **7** 116
  embroidery **7** 144, 145
    Buddhism **7** 45, *49*
    count-stitch **7** 45
    Ming period (1368-1644) **7** *50*, *53*
    petit point **7** 45
    Qing period (1644-1911) **7** *51*, 78, *78*; **10** 11
    Shang period (*c.* 1600-*c.* 1050 BC) **7** 44–5
    Song period (AD 960-1279) **7** 49
    whitework **7** 53
    Yuan period (1279-1368) **7** 50–51
  enamel **6** 557; **7** 79–80*, 109, 146; **17** 513
    Buddhism **7** 68
    Canton enamel **7** 80
    champlevé **7** *27*, 68; **10** 193
    cloisonné **7** 68–71*, *69*, *70*, 112; **10** 193, III2
    Jesuit Order **7** 79
    Ming period (1368-1644) **6** 872, 905, 907; **7** 111
    painted **10** 195
    plique à jour **10** 195
    Qing period (1644-1911) **6** 907, 909, 910, 911; **7** *79*, 86, 112, 132, *133*
    Song period (AD 960-1279) **6** 872
  encyclopedias **7** 65
  engravings **10** 379
  entasis **6** 640
  epigraphy **6** 762, 764–8; **23** 673; **33** 422
  epitaphs **6** 741
  erotic art **6** 633; **10** 485*
  ewers **6** *875*, *878*, 888, *888*, *892*, *918*; **7** 23
  exhibitions **7** 131, 157–8*; **30** 850
  expression **10** 692–3*
China—cont.
  fans **6** 791; **7** 103; **10** 776–7, *776*; **11** 152; **22** 234; **28** *554*
  feathers **7** 65, 113
    kingfisher **7** 108, 110, 111, *111*, 112; **10** 848
  felt **10** 873–4; **30** *475*
  festivals **7** 143
  fibres **7** 43
  figurines **6** *856*, *860*, *861*, 862, 883, *887*, 887–8, 889, *889*, *898*, 907, 910; **7** *55*, 104–6, *105*, *106*, 125, *126*, 140, 141, 143, 247; **28** *618*
  filigree **7** 68, *107*, 108, 109, 110, 111, 112, *112*
  finials (architectural) **6** 668, 686, 691; **7** 143
  flags **11** 145*
  flasks **6** *890*, *910*; **7** *69*; **23** *553*
  flour **7** 116
  flutes (musical instruments) **7** 58
  forgeries **2** 558; **11** 307
  fortifications **21** 593–4*
  foundations **6** 640, 690
  foundries **6** 830*, 865
  fountains **3** *517*; **11** 338
  frit **6** 888
  funerary monuments **6** 725–33*
  furnaces **7** 97, 98
  furniture **7** 30–42*, *32*, *34*, *35*, *36*, 145–6; **25** 303
  gables **6** 692
  garden design **12** 85–93, *91*, *92*
  gardens **6** 631, 632, 682–4, 692, 795; **11** 338; **12** 63, 85–93*, *88*, *89*, *90*, *91*, *92*; **30** 49
  gargoyles **12** 150
  gates **7** 361*
  gateways **6** 675
  gauze **7** 46; **30** 551
  ge see halberds
  gems **7** 90, 95
  geomancy **6** 667, 675, 690, 696, 698, 699; **12** 313*, *313*; **23** 773
  gesso **6** 717, 725, 779
  gilding **6** 706, *708*, *710*, *719*, *720*, 832, 866, 874; **7** *24*; **18** 607
    fire gilding **12** 624, 626
    Han period (206 BC-AD 220) **6** 859
    Liao period (AD 907-1125) **7** *25*
    Ming period (1368-1644) **6** 905
    Northern and Southern Dynasties (AD 310-589) **6** 707
    Qing period (1644-1911) **6** *722*
    Song period (AD 960-1279) **6** 706; **7** *26*
    Tang period (AD 618-907) **6** 863; **12** 623
    Zhou period (*c.* 1050-256 BC) **7** 22; **12** 625
  glass **7** 80–87*, *81*, 109, 111; **12** 789
    aventurine **7** 84
    Buddhism **7** 82
    cameo **12** 787
    export **7** 86–7*, *87*
    glassblowing **7** 82–3
    Ming period (1368-1644) **7** 18, 110, 111
    Qing period (1644-1911) **7** 19, *84*, *85*, *86*, 132, *133*; **12** IV3
    Song period (AD 960-1279) **6** 717
    Sui period (AD 581-618) **7** *82*, *109*
    Zhou period (*c.* 1050-256 BC) **7** *81*, 107; **21** 714
  glazes **6** 869, 872–3*, 879, 881, 882, 885, 886, 887, 888, 893, 894, 895
    liuli **6** 890
    oil spot **6** 896
    temmoku **6** 873, 896
  globes **12** 812
  glues **7** 92
  goblets **7** 12
China—cont.
  gold **6** *632*; **7** *20*, 21–7*, 45, 68, 79, 106, *107*, 108, 109, 111, 116, 128, 632; **21** 715
    Buddhism **7** 21, 23, 24, 25, 27
    Han period (206 BC-AD 220) **7** 108
    Liao period (AD 907-1125) **7** 110
    Ming period (1368-1644) **7** 17, *27*, 50, *50*, *53*, 110, 111, *111*
    Northern and Southern Dynasties (AD 310-589) **21** 715
    Qing period (1644-1911) **7** 19, *19*, 20, 51, *51*, 111, 112
    Shang period (*c.* 1600-*c.* 1050 BC) **7** 106, 107
    Song period (AD 960-1279) **6** 895; **7** 15, 110
    Sui period (AD 581-618) **7** *107*
    Tang period (AD 618-907) **7** 14, *14*, 109
    Yuan period (1279-1368) **7** 50
    Zhou period (*c.* 1050-256 BC) **6** 853, 855; **7** *22*, 88, *98*, 107, *107*, 108; **21** 714
    20th cent. **7** *112*
  gold dust **7** 20
  gold leaf **7** 15, 92
  gourds **7** 113, 141, 147; **13** 229*
  graphite **7** 92, 632
  grasses **7** 115
  graves
    chariot **28** *549*
  gromwell **7** 45
  guidebooks **13** 812
  guilds **6** 690, 787; **7** 147
  gums **6** 736
  hair **6** 877; **7** 65
  hair ornaments **7** 108, 112, *112*, 836
  hairpins **7** 102, 109, 110, 111, 145
  hairstyles **7** 74
  halberds **6** 841, 848; **7** 3
  halls **3** *518*; **6** *639*, *649*, *651*, *653*, 656–8, *657*, *659*, *660*, *682*; **14** 78*
  hammering **6** 830
  hardstones **6** *632*; **7** *27*, 88–91*, 107, 112
  harnesses **14** 181*, 184*
  hats **7** 145
  headdresses **7** 2, 109, 110; **10** 848
  heating systems **15** 51, *52*
  helmets **7** 55, *55*
  hemp **7** 43, 45, 63, 64, 114; **17** 101; **18** 601
  heritage **14** 452
  hides **7** 92
  historiography **7** 160–61*
    bronzes **6** 867–8*; **7** 160
    ceramics **7** 161
    painting **7** 161
    sculpture **7** 160, 161
    terracottas **7** 160
  hong wood **7** 31
  horn **1** 760
    buffalo **7** 126
    deer **7** 92
    rhinoceros **7** 102, 103, 109, 123–8*, *125*, *126*, *127*, 130
  horn-carvings **7** 125, *125*, *126*, *127*
  houses **6** *647*, 661, 684–92*, *685*, *686*, *689*, *693*; **7** 143
    courtyard **6** 648, 661, *686*, *688*, *689*, 690, *692*
  huali **7** 31
  huang huali **7** 31, *38*, *39*, *40*, 141, *141*
  huaru **7** 130
  human figures **7** 3, 104–6
  hypocausts **15** 51–2*, *52*
  iconoclasm **15** 78
  iconography **6** 627–8*, 629–33*; **7** 75, 76
    Buddhism **5** 91; **6** 627–8*, 721, 799; **7** 34, 104–5, *105*

China
iconography—cont.
Buddhism: Lamaism **6** 627
Buddhism: Tantric **6** 627
Confucianism **6** 628*
Daoism **5** 107; **6** 628*; **7** 61, 105–6, *106*; **10** 485
ideograms **17** 211
ikat **7** 144
impressing **6** 874, 876, *876*, 882, *884*, 888, *891*, 892
incense burners **6** 795, *859*, *875*, *882*, 900; **7** 86, *86*, 110
Buddhism **7** 68
Daoism **6** 785
incense smoke **7** 102
incising **6** 874, 882, *890*, 892, 901, 905
indigo **7** 45; **18** 600; **30** 561
indigot **7** 45
inks **6** 736; **7** 50, 62, 91–4*, *93*; **15** 852; **24** 790; **29** 617
stone **7** 92
insticks **6** 736; **7** 91–4*, *93*, 95
inkstones **6** 736; **7** 92, *94*, 94–6*, *96*, 134–5
inlays **6** 808, 832; **7** 88, 101; **18** 603, *612*
Ming period (1368-1644) **7** 17–18
Qing period (1644-1911) **7** 19–20, 91
Shang period (*c.* 1600-*c.* 1050 BC) **6** 841; **7** 12, 88, 107
Song period (AD 960-1279) **6** *865*, *866*
Tang period (AD 618-907) **6** 863; **7** 14
Yuan period (1279-1368) **7** 15–16
Zhou period (*c.* 1050-256 BC) **6** 853–4, 855; **7** 22, 81, 107
inscriptions **6** 735–9, *736*, *738*, *739*, *740*, *743*, *744*, 745, 750, *753*, 755, 762–8, *763*, *765*, 772, 774, 777, 805, 823, 826, 836, 840*, 842, 857, 863, 865, 900, 903; **7** 65, 96, 124, 128, 130, 152; **29** 617
insect repellants **7** 115
inventories **17** 229
iron **6** 706, 721, *724*, 725, 730, 731, 869, 905; **7** 56, 80, 94, 96–100*, *98*, *99*, *100*, 107, 146
pig **7** 98
iron oxide **6** 872, 873, 881, 885, 899, 909
iron salts **7** 45
ivory **6** 557; **7** 18, 19, 107, 128, 130, 132; **10** 777
elephant **7** 102, 103
mammoth **7** 102
ivory-carvings **7** 101–6*, *103*, *104*; **16** 797
Buddhism **7** 104–5, *105*
Daoism **7** 105, *106*
export **7** 103–4
jackets **7** 77, 144
jade **1** 818; **7** 1*, 21, 76, 88, 90, 94, 106, *107*, 109, 111, 128, 129, 130; **16** 857, 858–9, 860; **22** 466
Han period (206 BC-AD 220) **7** 81; **20** 236, *236*
jadeite **7** 1, 11, 132; **16** 860
Ming period (1368-1644) **7** 10, *111*
mountain **7** 10
nephrite **7** 1, *7*, 106; **16** 857, 858, 860, 861
Prehistoric **7** 1, *2*, 2, 106, 107
Qing period (1644-1911) **7** 11, 20, 101, *101*, 112, 132
river **7** 10
Shang period (*c.* 1600-*c.* 1050 BC) **7** 107
Song period (AD 960-1279) **7** *8*, 110; **16** 858
Tang period (AD 618-907) **7** 109

China
jade—cont.
Zhou period (*c.* 1050-256 BC) **3** *686*; **7** *5*, 56, 106, 107, 108; **16** *857*; **21** 714
20th cent. **7** 112
jade-carvers **7** 9
jade-carvings **7** 3–11*
Han period (206 BC-AD 220) **7** *6*
Ming period (1368-1644) **7** *9*; **16** III1
Prehistoric **6** 636; **7** *1*, 1–3*
Qing period (1644-1911) **7** *11*, 91; **16** I, II2, IV
Shang period (*c.* 1600-*c.* 1050 BC) **7** *4*
Tang period (AD 618-907) **7** *7*
Zhou period (*c.* 1050-256 BC) **7** 4
jars **6** *886*, 888, *888*, *899*, 901, *906*; **7** 69, *69*, *82*, 144
guan **6** *875*
kendi **6** 875, *875*
leys **6** *875*
jasmine **7** 45
jewellery **7** 26, 106–12*, *111*, *112*, 145, 836
Buddhism **7** 108
jichi **7** 31
joinery **7** 31–2, *32*, 138, 139–40
jute **7** 114
kang **6** 691; **7** 36, 67, 143, 145; **17** 772*
kaolin **6** 869, 876, 880, 895, 897
kilns **6** 685, 870–72*, 879, 886
dragon **6** 870, 871*, *871*
long see climbing
mantou **6** 870*, *870*, 892
Prehistoric **6** 875, 877
step **6** 871*
up-draught **6** 870, 873, 876
Yangshao culture **6** 870, *870*
zhenyao **6** *871*, 871–2*
kiosks **18** 72*
kites **7** 113*, 114, 147; **17** 388
whistling **7** 113
knitting **7** 53; **18** 157
knives **7** 1; **23** 495, *495*
lacquer **6** 706, 725, 773; **7** 12–20*, 31, 54, 92, 94, 114, 138, 140; **17** 101, 254; **18** *612*
Coromandel **7** 19
dry **7** 13, 14; **18** 606
filled-in *urushi* **7** 15, 17, 19; **18** 602
gilt-engraved *urushi* **7** 15, 16, 17, 19; **18** 602
guri **7** 15, 16; **18** 601
Han period (206 BC-AD 220) **7** *13*, 95
imitation carved *urushi* **18** 601
kingindeigawa **18** 606
marbled *urushi* **18** 602
Ming period (1368-1644) **7** *17*, *18*, 100; **18** II1
Prehistoric **7** 12; **14** 384
qiangjin see gilt-engraved *urushi*
Qing period (1644-1911) **7** *19*, *20*, 96
Song period (AD 960-1279) **6** 706; **7** *15*, 25
sprinkled **18** 604
Tang period (AD 618-907) **7** *14*; **12** 623
tianqi see filled-in *urushi*
urushi **7** 14; **18** 599, 600, 601, *601*, 603, 605, *605*, 606, 607
wet inlay **18** 605
Yuan period (1279-1368) **7** *16*
Zhou period (*c.* 1050-256 BC) **7** 107, *139*
lacquer-tree **7** 12, 45
ladles **6** *849*; **7** 58
lakes **12** 85
lampblack **6** 736; **7** 91, 92; **24** 790
lamps **6** 854, 856, 859
languages **6** 737, 764
lanterns (lights) **7** 114, 143; **16** II2

China—cont.
lapis lazuli **7** 89, 90, 91; **14** I2
lead **6** 872, 882, 886, 888; **7** 81, 100, 632
lead oxides **6** 872
leather **7** 50, 54, 63, 122, 147
leaves **6** 874
letters **6** 740, 742, *742*, 750, 755
libraries **19** 317*
lime **6** 873, 881; **7** 114
limestone **12** 88; **19** *638*
literati **1** 581; **6** 619, 630, 631–2, 636, 637, 787, 823–5
lithography **7** 120
lodestone **7** 133
looms **7** 43–4
card **7** 43
draw **7** *44*, 44, 52; **30** 547
Jacquard **7** 53
lost-wax casting **6** 833, 834, 855, 865; **7** 99; **8** 853
lotus **19** 717, *717*; **23** 550
lutes **6** 788; **7** *14*; **17** 396; **22** 376
magnesium **7** 80, 82
malachite **6** 830; **7** 88, 91, 107, 632; **21** 714; **23** *495*
manganese **6** 869
manganese oxide **6** 872
manuals
architecture **4** 623; **6** 638, 640, 643
calligraphy **6** 767; **32** 839
connoisseurship **7** 715
fortifications **21** 594
jade collecting **7** 8
painting **6** 803, 806, 824; **7** 120, 148; **15** 854; **17** 189; **19** 478; **22** 461; **32** 839
papers **7** *116*, 117
sculpture **6** 706
seals **33** 663
manuscript illumination **6** 782*
manuscripts **6** 740, 741; **7** 62–3*, 114
Mao suits **7** 78
maps **31** 152, 153, *153*
marble **1** *702*; **3** *520*; **6** 706; **7** *57*
marbling **7** 14, 18, 20; **24** 55
marks
ceramics **6** *922*, 922–3*, *923*; **20** 441
enamel **7** 69; **12** 152
glass **7** *84*, 86
metalwork **20** 444
porcelain **6** 903, 909
silver **7** 30
mats **7** 146
mausolea **6** 697, 698, 699
merchants **6** 620
metal **6** 726; **7** 31
metalwork **7** *107*, 108, 109
mica **7** 116
minarets **6** *677*
mirrors **6** 862–3, *863*; **21** 714–15*
back-painted **7** 87, *87*
Han period (206 BC-AD 220) **6** 858, 859–60
Liao period (AD 907-1125) **6** 864
Shang period (*c.* 1600-*c.* 1050 BC) **4** 855
Song period (AD 960-1279) **6** 864
Tang period (AD 618-907) **6** 863–4, *864*; **7** 14
TLV mirrors **6** 860–61, 862; **21** 714, *715*
Zhou period (*c.* 1050-256 BC) **6** 854, 855
models **6** *883*, 883–4, 889; **7** 103
architectural **6** 648, 686, *686*; **23** 821
artists' **7** 149
monasteries **7** 25
mortars (vessels) **7** 103
mosques **6** 676–7*
mother-of-pearl **7** 14, 15–16, *16*, 17–18, 19–20, 101; **18** *601*, 603, *612*; **21** 715

China—cont.
moulding **6** 882, 883, 888, 893
piece moulding **21** 321
moulds **6** 830–32, *831*, *833*, 838–9, 874, 887, 889, *895*, 895, 899; **7** 92, 97, 98; **14** *800*; **21** 320
mounts (works on paper and scrolls) **1** 580; **22** 233–4*
mugs **6** *920*; **7** 29, *29*
mulberry **7** 64, 114–15
museums **6** 772; **7** 154–6*
musical instruments **6** 829*; **7** 14; **22** 376
musk **7** 91
nan wood **7** 31
narratives **6** 777, 779
Buddhism **6** 788
necklaces **7** 4, *107*, 109, 111
netsuke see toggles
nuts **7** 113
oak **7** 45, 115
observatories **23** 338
ochre **6** 874; **7** 632
oinochoai **6** 875
onyx **7** *89*, 90
opals **7** *109*
oracle bones **4** *313*; **6** 625, 735, 737–8, *738*, 767, 836; **19** 804
Shang period (*c.* 1600-*c.* 1050 BC) **2** *208*
ornament **23** 549–52*
orpiment **7** 632
orthodoxy in art **23** 581–2*
pagodas **6** 668; **7** 98, 99; **23** 772–5*
close-eave **23** 773, *774*
flower **23** 773
Liao period (AD 907-1125) **6** 656; **19** 303
Northern and Southern Dynasties (AD 310-589) **6** 649, *650*, 666
pavilion **23** 773, *774*
Song period (AD 960-1279) **6** *645*, 654
storeyed pavilion **23** 773, *774*
Yuan period (1279-1368) **6** *658*
pagoda tree **7** 45
pailou **23** 779–80*, *780*
painting **1** 580–81; **6** 638, 725, 735, 772*, 773–82*, 785–92*, 795–814*, 821–5*, 826*; **7** 157, 158, 632; **10** 777; **25** 72; **30** 559; **33** 496–8*
Anhui school **2** 95–6*
animal subjects **6** *800*, *802*; **19** *370*; **26** *211*
architectural **6** 687
bamboo **6** 802, 803–4, 805, 806, 807, *807*, 818, *820*, 823, *823*; **33** 75, 653, *654*
bird-and-flower **6** 798, 799, *801*, 802, 803, 804
Blue-and-green style **6** 789
boundary **32** 851
Buddhism **6** 776–85*, *780*, *781*; **9** *393*
Communism **6** *774*, 774–5, 811
Confucianism **6** 803, 807, 808; **7** 632
court **6** 635–6, 789, 790, 797, 799, 800, 801, 803, 810, 814–18*, *815*
Daoism **6** 785–7*, *786*, 823, 824
display **1** 580–81
export **6** 624
finger **12** 50, *51*
floor **14** *826*
flower **6** 631, 803, 805, 806, 807, 818
Buddhism **6** 804
Daoism **6** 804
Ming period (1368-1644) **12** *49*; **33** *320*
Qing period (1644-1911) **28** *759*; **33** *576*
Yuan period (1279-1368) **6** *806*

China
painting
flower—cont.
20th cent. **14** *821*
fresco **6** 776
Han period (206 BC-AD 220) **6** 633–4, 636; **7** 13
history **33** *474*, *499*
iconography **6** 803
ink **15** 853, 854, *854*; **17** 168
Ming period (1368-1644) **15** *854*; **19** *514*, *833*; **28** *587*; **30** *294*; **33** *478*
Song period (AD 960-1279) **20** *107*; **33** *651*
20th cent. **14** *821*, *826*
landscape **6** 632, 773, 787–92*, 795–8*; **7** 150; **19** *325*; **28** 311
Buddhism **6** *784*
Confucianism **7** *706*
Daoism **6** 785–6
Five Dynasties (AD 907-60) **17** *591*
Ming period (1368-1644) **6** *791*, *825*; **8** *459*; **9** *137*, *138*; **11** *855*; **15** *854*; **19** *514*, *833*; **25** *785*; **28** *587*; **30** *48*; **33** *68*, *69*, *70*, 642, *650*, *656*
Northern Song period (AD 960-1127) **19** *479*
Qingbai ware **18** *752*
Qing period (1644-1911) **2** *96*; **7** *624*; **8** *518*, *520*; **12** *90*; **14** *723*, *825*, *831*; **18** *517*; **28** *590*; **32** *838*, *839*, *844*; **33** *426*
Song period (AD 960-1279) **9** 139; **10** *795*; **13** *855*; **17** *697*; **19** *504*; **33** *476*
Southern school (China) **21** *419*
Southern Song period (1127-1279) **19** 478
Tang period (AD 618-907) **19** 298, *299*
Yuan period (1279-1368) **6** *790*, *797*, *819*; **7** IV1; **32** *846*; **33** *440*
16th cent. **18** *51*
literati **6** 631, 783, 788, 789, 790, 795, 797, 798, 818–20*, 824; **7** 147
Ming period (1368-1644) **6** 806, *820*; **7** 148
Qing period (1644-1911) **6** 818
Song period (AD 960-1279) **6** 636, 773–4, 783, 804, 812, 823; **30** *30*
Yuan period (1279-1368) **6** 805, *819*
20th cent. **25** *781*
Ming period (1368-1644) **6** *802*, *810*; **19** 857; **33** *420*
monochrome **6** 784, 789, 796, 801, 802, 803, 804–6, *805*, *806*, *807*, 818
Buddhism **6** *785*
Northern and Southern Dynasties (AD 310-589) **6** 887
Northern school **19** 299
plum blossom **6** 802, 803, 804–5, *805*, 806, 807, 818
Song period (AD 960-1279) **33** 493
Yuan period (1279-1368) **32** 847
Prehistoric **6** 773, 876
Qing period (1644-1911) **6** *40*; **18** 605; **28** *554*; **33** *497*
screen **28** 296, 311
scroll **6** *800*, *813*, *820*, *825*; **7** *48*, *49*; **10** *795*; **32** *838*; **33** *68*, *69*, *70*, *436*, *641*, *654*, *666*
Buddhism: Song period (AD 960-1279) **22** *325*
Confucianism **7** *705*

China
  painting
    scroll—cont.
      Ming period (1368-1644) **6** *807*; **9** *137, 381*; **11** *855*; **15** *854*; **25** *785*; **32** *841*; **33** *438, 659*
      Nanjing school **12** *900*
      Northern Song period (AD 960-1127) **33** *650*
      Qing period (1644-1911) **2** *96*; **6** *543, 621*; **7** *624*; **8** *518, 520*; **12** *90*; **14** *723, 825*; **17** *592*; **18** *752*; **19** *469, 802*; **21** *802, 803*; **22** *460*; **23** *580*; **25** *73*; **28** *590*; **32** *844, 845*; **33** *643*
      Song period (AD 960-1279) **6** *784*; **17** *697*; **19** *301, 331, 370, 504*; **20** *107*; **33** *319, 501, 647, 651*
      Southern school (China) **9** *141*; **13** *738*; **21** *419*
      Tang period (AD 618-907) **13** *838*; **14** *136*; **19** *299*; **32** *849*; **33** *499, 662*
      Yuan period (1279-1368) **6** *805, 806*; **7** IV1; **14** *822, 823*; **23** *166, 167*; **26** *211*; **32** *846*; **33** *440*
      11th cent. **12** *87*
      20th cent. **25** *781*
    secco **6** 776
    Song period (AD 960-1279) **1** 580; **6** 631, *800*; **7** *36*; **10** 776; **19** 857, *857, 858*
    Southern school (China) **7** 632
    Tang period (AD 618-907) **6** *809*, 888; **30** 288
    wall **6** 698, 700–701, 773, 776, 808
      Buddhism **6** 776–9*, *777, 822*; **32** 804
      Daoism **6** *787*
    watercolours **7** *122*
    20th cent. **6** *775*; **19** *422*; **33** *641*
  palaces **6** 663, 679–84*, *680, 683*; **23** 820–21*
  palmettes **23** 550
  paper **6** 725, 874, *874*; **7** 114–17*, 146–7; **22** 234; **24** 44, 46–7*, 51, 55; **25** 597; **28** 312; **31** 258
    Han period (206 BC-AD 220) **6** 736; **7** 62, 63; **20** 329; **28** 310
    Ming period (1368-1644) **7** *116*
    Northern and Southern Dynasties (AD 310-589) **6** 740
    powdered **7** 116
    Song period (AD 960-1279) **6** 776; **7** 64, *117*
    Xuan **7** 115, *115*
    Zhou period (*c*. 1050-256 BC) **7** 114
    20th cent. **7** 113
  papercuts **6** 691; **7** 114, 122, 144, 146; **24** 56, 57
  paper mulberry **7** 114; **30** 560
  paperweights **7** 91
  papier mâché **7** 114; **24** 61
  parasols **11** 152
  parchment **7** 122
  parks **12** 85, 86, *87*; **24** 178
  partitions **24** 51
  patronage **6** 631, 743; **7** 148, 150*, 151–2*; **33** 318
    royal **7** 143, 150–51*
  pavilions (buildings) **6** *655*, 675; **24** 289*; **28** *552*
  peach stones **7** 141
  pearls **6** 706; **7** 109, *109*, 110, 111, *111*, 112, *112*
  pectoral ornaments **7** *107*
  pendants (jewellery) **7** 2, *2, 5*, 76, 103, *104, 107*, 111
  pepper **7** 115
  perfume containers **7** 58, *60*
  periodicals **19** 831; **24** 435–6*

China—cont.
  periods
    Chen period (AD 557-89) **6** 537*, *617*
    Ch'ing period *see* Qing period
    Chin period (1115-1234) *see* Jin period
    Ch'in period *see* Qin period
    Chin period (AD 265-420) *see* Western and Eastern Jin period
    Chou period *see* Zhou period
    Eastern Han (AD 25-220) **6** *617*
    Eastern Zhou (771-256 BC) **6** *617*
    Five Dynasties (AD 907-60) **6** *617*
    Han period (206 BC-AD 220) **6** *617*; **14** 133–4*
    Hsia *see* Xia
    Jin period (AD 1115-1234) **5** 112; **6** *617*
    Jin period (AD 265-420) *see* Western and Eastern Jin period
    Liang period (AD 502-57) **6** *617*
    Liao period (AD 907-1125) **6** *617*; **19** 303*
    Liu Song period (AD 420-70) **6** *617*
    Ming period (1368-1644) **6** *617*; **21** 633*
    Neolithic **6** *617*
    Northern and Southern Dynasties (AD 310-589) **6** *617*
    Northern Ch'i period *see* Northern Qi period
    Northern Chou period *see* Northern Zhou period
    Northern Qi period (AD 550-77) **6** *617*; **23** 214–15*
    Northern Song period (AD 960-1127) **6** *617*; **29** 67*
    Northern Zhou period (AD 557-81) **6** *617*; **23** 216*
    Qing period (1644-1911) **6** *617*; **25** 783*; **33** 465
    Qin period (221-206 BC) **6** *617*; **25** 782–3*
    Shang period (*c*. 1600-*c*. 1050 BC) **6** *617*; **7** 159; **24** 14; **28** 550*
    Shu Han period (AD 221-63) **6** *617*
    Six Dynasties (AD 222-589) **6** *617*
    Sixteen Kingdoms (AD 310-439) **6** *617*
    Song period (AD 960-1279) **6** *617*; **29** 67*
    Southern Qi period (AD 479-502) **6** *617*
    Southern Song period (1127-1279) **6** *617*; **29** 67–8*
    Sui period (AD 581-618) **6** *617*; **29** 905–6*
    Tang period (AD 618-907) **6** *617*; **30** 287–8*
    T'ang period *see* Tang period
    Three Kingdoms (AD 220-80) **6** *617*
    Wei period (AD 220-65) **33** 34*
    Wei period, Eastern (AD 534-50) **6** *617*; **33** 35*
    Wei period, Northern (AD 386-534) **6** *617*; **33** 34–5*
    Wei period, Western (AD 535-56) **6** *617*; **33** 35*
    Western and Eastern Jin period (AD 265-420) **6** *617*; **17** 588–9*
    Western Han (206 BC-AD 220) **6** *617*
    Western Zhou (*c*. 1050-771 BC) **6** *617*
    Wu period (AD 222-80) **6** *617*
    Xia period (before *c*. 1600 BC) **7** 159; **33** 462*
    Xin period (AD 9-23) **6** *617*

China
  periods—cont.
    Yuan period (1279-1368) **6** *617*; **33** 570*
    Zhou period (*c*. 1050-256 BC) **6** *617*; **7** 159, 160; **33** 660–61*
  perspective **24** 486, 492
  pewter **7** *16*, 96*, 100–101*, *101*; **24** 580
  pictographs **6** 738
  pigments **6** 775; **7** 631–2
    black **7** 632
    blue **7** 632
    minium **7** 95, 632
    red **7** 631, 632
    ultramarine **24** 790
    vermilion **7** 632
    white **7** 632
    yellow **7** 632
  pilgrim flasks **6** 875, *875*, 887, 890
  pillows **6** *895*; **7** 145
  pins **7** 107
  pipes (musical) **7** 147; **8** 853
  pipes (smoking) **7** 147
  pisé de terre **6** 696, 697; **7** 143
  plans **6** 663, *663*
  plaques **6** *632, 695*; **7** *27, 107*, 108, 124, 140; **23** 496, *496*
    Dian culture **8** 854, *854*
  plaster **6** 706
  plates **6** *902, 914, 921*, II3; **23** *552*
  platforms **6** 640*, 689; **7** 33
  poetry **6** 633, 636, 735, 820, 823; **25** 72–3, *73*
  polychromy **6** *713*; **25** 171, 175
  ponds **12** 85
  popular art **7** 142–7*, *144, 145, 146*
  porcelain **6** 325, 331, 868, 875, 918–21*, 923–5*; **7** 94; **9** 28; **17** 589; **25** 303, 309
    blanc de chine **6** 332, 871, 907, 911; **7** 126; **16** 425
    blue-and-white ware **4** 172, 173–4*; **6** *916*; **7** 144, 165
      Ming period (1368-1644) **4** *174*; **6** 875, *901*, 902, *902, 903, 906*, 907, *918*; **23** *553*
      Qing period (1644-1911) **6** 624, *908*, 909; **25** 309
      Yuan period (1279-1368) **6** 896, 898–9, *898*
    chine de commande **6** 918, 919, 921, *921*
    clair de lune **6** 909
    Dehua wares **6** 907
    Ding ware **6** 870, 885, 895*, 913, 922; **7** 25; **23** 551
    doucai **6** 905, 910
    eggshell **6** 912
    encre de Chine **6** 920
    export **6** 904, 908
    fahua **6** 332, *906*
    famille jaune **6** 332, 910
    famille noire **6** 332, 910
    famille rose **6** 332, 872, *908*, 910, *910*
    famille verte **6** 332, 910, 919
    Five Dynasties (AD 907-60) **7** 25
    guyue xuan **6** 910; **7** 86
    Imari **4** 174; **6** 920
    Kraak ware **4** 173; **6** 331, 904, 918, *919*; **16** 424
    marks **6** 903
      Ming period (1368-1644) **4** 173, *174*; **5** 12; **6** 872, *901*, 901–7*, *902, 903, 906, 914*; **7** 125; **17** *589*
      Northern and Southern Dynasties (AD 310-589) **6** 885
      Qingbai ware **6** 331, 894–5*, 897, 898; **23** 551
      Qing period (1644-1911) **6** 907–11*, *908, 909, 910, 911*; **7** 79, 100, 131, 132; **25** 309; **29** 113
    Shonzui **6** 904

China
  porcelain—cont.
    Song period (AD 960-1279) **6** 869, 895*, *895*
    Swatow ware **6** 906–7
    Tang period (AD 618-907) **4** 172; **7** 95
    Tenkei **6** 904
    Transitional ware **6** 331, 904, 919, *920*
    whiteware **6** 897–8
    wucai **6** 906, 910
    Xing ware **6** 870–71
    Yingqing ware **6** 894
    Yuan period (1279-1368) **6** 874, 897, *898, 899*
    yuebai **6** 909
    Zheijang greenware **6** *916*
    20th cent. **6** *912*, 912–13
  portraits **6** 718, 811–14*, *812, 813*, 824; **26** *216*
  postage stamps **25** 329
  potassium **7** 82
  potassium oxide **6** 872, 873
  potters **6** 637
  potter's wheels **6** 877, 879, 880
  pottery **6** *686*, 868, 869, 879–89*; **7** 94, 95, 107, 144
    Banshan culture **6** 876, 877
    black ware **6** 896*, *896, 897*
    Buddhism **6** 717
    celadon **6** 328, 331, 873, 892–3, *893*, 899–900, *900*, 910, *916*; **7** 95
      see also Longquan ware
    Cizhou ware **6** 870, 872, 874, 885, 892, 895*, *895*, 900–901*, 913, 922; **23** 551
    coiling **6** 879
    Ding ware **6** 874, 886
    Ge ware **6** 894*
    greenware *see* celadon
    Guan ware **6** 875, 892, 894*, *894*, 909
    Jian ware **6** 873, 896, 901*, III3
    Jizhou ware **6** 874, *874*, 896, 901*
    Jun ware **6** 870, 895*, 900*, 909, II3
    lead-glazed ware **6** 889
    Liao period (AD 907-1125) **6** 889*, *890, 891*
    Linru ware **6** 870, 892–3*
    Longquan ware **6** 869, 893*, *893*, 899–900*, *900*, 915, 916
      see also celadon
    Machang culture **6** 876, 877
    Majiayao culture **6** 876; **20** *143*
    Nanking wares **29** 114
    Prehistoric **6** 629, 772, 773, 798, 875*, 876, 877–9*, *879*; **7** 128
      Dawenkou culture **6** 877–8
      Daxi culture **6** 878–9
      Hemudu culture **6** 877, 878
      Longshan culture **6** 869, 877, *878*, 878
      Majiabang culture **6** 877, 878
      Qinlongquan culture **6** 879
      Qujialing culture **6** 879
      Songze culture **6** 877, 878
    Qijia culture **6** 877
    Ru ware **6** 870, 892, 893–4*, *894*, 909
    sancai **6** 872, 886, 888, *888, 889*, 889, *891*, III3; **23** 389
    Shajing culture **6** 877
    Shang period (*c*. 1600-*c*. 1050 BC) **6** *880*
    Song period (AD 960-1279) **6** 892–4*, *894*, 895*, 896*
    Tang period (AD 618-907) **6** *885*
    Xindian culture **6** 877
    Yangshao culture **6** 875–7*, *876, 877*; **7** 159
    Yaozhou ware **6** 870, 885, *892*, 892–3*, 913
    Yixing ware **7** 101; **33** *535*, 535–6

China
  pottery—cont.
    Yuan period (1279-1368) **23** *552*
    Yue ware **6** 869, 873, 881, 884–5, *884*, 886, 892*; **7** 25
    Zhou period (*c*. 1050-256 BC) **6** *881*
  pouncing **25** 378
  printing **7** 63–5*, 117, 144; **25** 588
    Buddhism **5** 110
    colour **7** 64–5, 119–20; **15** 852
    woodblock **7** 62, 63, 114, 117; **25** 597
  prints **7** 117–21*, 143, 146, *146*
    Buddhism **7** 117–18
    woodblock **4** 143; **7** *44*, 59, *118, 119, 121*; **17** 270
  pudding-stone **7** 133
  puppets **7** 122–3*, *122*, 147; **31** 258
  qin **7** 92
  quartz **6** 872
  quilts **7** 145
  radiocarbon dating **7** 160
  railings **6** 675; **7** 136
  rami (fibre) **7** 43, 45
  rats' whiskers **7** 66
  realgar **7** 632; **12** 88
  red lead **24** 796
  religion **6** 625–7*
  reliquaries **7** 24, 25, 82; **23** 776; **26** 150
  resins **7** 116
  restoration **7** 729–30
  rhyta **7** *89*
  ringmatting **7** 109
  rings **7** 109, 111
  robes **7** *50*, 75, *75*, 77, 78, *78*; **10** I1; **30** VI1
    court **7** 77, *78*
    dragon **7** 77
  rock art **6** 743
  rock crystal **7** 89, 111; **26** 486
    Qing period (1644-1911) **7** 91, 132
    Tang period (AD 618-907) **7** 90, 109
    Yuan period (1279-1368) **7** 130
    Zhou period (*c*. 1050-256 BC) **7** 4, 107
    20th cent. **26** 484
  rockeries **12** 85–90
  rock reliefs **5** 107
  rocks **12** 87–8
  rolls **6** 736; **7** 63; **20** 326
  roof decorations **7** 143
  roofs **5** 649; **6** 641–3*, 658, 668, 691; **27** 127; **30** 912–14*, *913*
  roots **7** 142
  rosaries **7** 90
  rose quartz **7** 91, 111
  rouletting **6** 874
  rubbings **29** 617
  rubies **7** 91, 111, 112
  safflower **7** 45
  saggars **6** 869, 895
  saltpetre **6** 872
  sandalwood **7** 115
  sandstone **6** 706, *714, 716, 718*; **33** *574*
  sappan-wood **7** 45
  sapphires **7** 91, *107*
  sarcophagi **27** 832*
  sashes **7** 75
  satin **7** 49, *51*
  sceptres **7** 141
    zhang **7** 3
  scholars' tables **28** 141*
  schools **6** 676
  screens (ii) (furniture) **6** 773; **7** 33, 140; **28** 296–7
    table-screens **7** 102; **18** *601*
  scripts **4** 344; **6** 737–9, *740*
    bafen **6** 741–2
    bafen *see also* clerical
    bird seal *see* seal, bird

China
scripts—cont.
clerical **6** 739, 740, *740*, 742, 743, 755, 758, 763, *763*, 764–5, 767, 770; **7** 63; **29** 617
clerical *see also* bafen
clerical, cursive **6** 764
correct *see* regular
cursive **6** 735, 737, 741, 742–3, 745, *747*, 749, 754, *754*, 756, 757, *757*, 758, 759, 760, 761, 763, 765, 767, 769, 770; **14** 820; **33** 581
cursive, draft **6** 739, 741, 743, 754–5, 756, 757, 760, 767, 769
cursive, large **6** 762
cursive, modern **6** 739, 741, 742, 743, 754
cursive, running **6** *750*, 755, 758, 759, 761, *762*
cursive, small **6** 755
cursive, wild **6** *747*, 747–8, 749, *749*, 756, 758, *758*, 760, 771
cursive clerical *see* clerical, cursive
draft **6** 735
draft cursive *see* cursive, draft
grass *see* cursive
jiudie wen **7** 129, 130
large regular *see* regular, large
large running *see* running, large
large seal *see* seal, large
modern cursive *see* cursive, modern
oracle bone **6** 737–8, *740*, 767
regular **6** 737, 739, 741, 742, 743–4, *744*, 745, 746, *746*, 748, 749, 751, 753, *753*, 755, 757, 758, 760, 763, 765, 766, 767, 768, 770, 771; **23** 166; **29** 617
regular, large **6** 754, 761
regular, running **6** 758
regular, small **6** 756, 757, 758, 759, 764
running **6** 736, 737, 739, 741, 742–3, *742*, 745, 747, 748, 749, *751*, *752*, 759, *759*, 760, 761, 763, 764, 766, 767, 768
running, large **6** 763, 766
running, small **6** 757, 759
running cursive *see* cursive, running
running regular *see* regular, running
seal **5** 36; **6** 758, 760, 764, *765*, 765, 766, 768, *768*, 770; **7** 130; **29** 617
seal, bird **6** 739
seal, large **6** 737, 738–9, *738*, 741, 766, 767
seal, small **6** 738, 739, *739*, 740, 741, 767, 769; **7** 63, 129
semi-cursive **6** 736, 745, 747, 759, 760
Shang period (*c*. 1600–*c*. 1050 BC) **2** 208, *208*; **6** *739*
small regular *see* regular, small
small running *see* running, small
small seal *see* seal, small
standard *see* regular
true *see* regular
wild cursive *see* cursive, wild
scroll cases **28** 312
scrolls **6** 761, 776; **7** 63; **17** 158; **22** 233; **28** 309, 310–11, 312
Buddhism **6** 779–81*
conservation **7** 729–30
handscrolls **6** 740, 773; **7** *34*, *35*; **28** 311
Ming period (1368-1644) **6** *810*
Qing period (1644-1911) **32** *839*
Song period (AD 960-1279) **6** *823*; **33** *463*

China
scrolls
handscrolls—cont.
Tang period (AD 618-907) **6** *809*; **19** *299*
Yuan period (1279-1368) **6** *812*
hanging **6** 779; **7** 729–30; **13** *855*; **21** *802*, *803*
Ming period (1368-1644) **6** *820*; **33** *68*, *69*, *70*
Qing period (1644-1911) **6** *813*, *825*; **32** *838*; **33** *654*
Song period (AD 960-1279) **6** *800*; **7** *48*; **10** *795*; **13** *855*
Yuan period (1279-1368) **7** *49*
20th cent. **33** *641*
restoration **7** 729–30
sculptors **6** 705
sculpture **6** 705*, 725–33*, 882; **7** 98, 99–100, 135, 143, 160
bronze **6** 706, 707, *708*, *710*, 712, 718, *719*, *720*, 720–22, 726–7, 730, 733, 835, 855–6; **7** 68, 160; **24** 258; **29** *906*
Daoism **6** *628*
Han period (206 BC-AD 220) **8** *853*
Qing period (1644-1911) **6** *733*
Shang period (*c*. 1600-*c*. 1050 BC) **13** *736*
Buddhism **6** 706–23*, 835; **7** 68, 98, 99, 161; **19** 638–40
Han period (206 BC-AD 220) **12** 626
Lamaism **6** 722; **30** 443
Liao period (AD 907-1125) **5** *111*
Ming period (1368-1644) **6** *719*, *720*
Northern and Southern Dynasties (AD 310-589) **6** *708*, *710*; **12** 901; **19** *638*; **33** *574*
Northern Zhou period (AD 557-81) **23** 216
Qing period (1644-1911) **6** *722*
Song period (AD 960-1279) **6** *718*
Sui period (AD 581-618) **6** *713*
Tang period (AD 618-907) **6** *714*, *716*; **7** 14; **19** *639*
Tantric **6** 719–20
Daoism **6** *628*, 723–5*, *724*
Dian culture **8** *853*
Five Dynasties (AD 907-60) **7** 99, *99*
Han period (206 BC-AD 220) **6** *727*, *728*
Liao period (AD 907-1125) **6** *891*
Ming period (1368-1644) **6** 701; **7** *57*; **30** *398*
monumental **6** 725, 727, 730
Northern and Southern Dynasties (AD 310-589) **6** *729*
Qing period (1644-1911) **7** *134*
Qin period (221-206 BC) **19** *432*; **30** *509*
relief **6** 714, 730, *732*
Song period (AD 960-1279) **6** *731*; **7** *100*
stone **6** 706, 718, 725, 726, 727, 730
Sui period (AD 581-618) **6** *713*
Tang period (AD 618-907) **6** *730*; **25** 175
wood **6** 706, 717, 718, 721, 722; **7** 138, 140, 141
Qing period (1644-1911) **6** *722*
Zhou period (*c*. 1050-256 BC) **12** 625
20th cent. **6** *734*
seal impressions **7** 128

China—cont.
seals **7** 102, 128–31*, *129*, *130*, *131*, 134, 135; **15** 851; **17** 408
artists' **7** 129
collectors' **7** 129
Han period (206 BC-AD 220) **7** 117
Qing period (1644-1911) **7** 65; **8** 713; **17** *411*
serpentine **7** 1, 3
sgraffito **6** 895
shale **7** 95
shells **7** 14, 106, 107, 138; **21** 715
clam **7** 632
nautilus **7** 14
shields **7** 12–13
ship-decoration **28** 611
shoes **7** 145, *145*
shrines (i) (cult) **28** *637*, 637–8*
shuttlecocks **7** 147
signatures **7** 15, 64, 129; **17** 229
silica **6** 873; **7** 80
silk **6** 773, 776; **7** 43, 45, *49*, 74, 140; **10** 776; **16** 428; **18** 601; **30** 551, VI1
Han period (206 BC-AD 220) **6** 736; **7** *46*, 63; **28** 310; **31** *153*
Ming period (1368-1644) **7** 50, *50*, 64
Northern and Southern Dynasties (AD 310-589) **20** 327
Prehistoric **7** 45–8; **28** 715
Qing period (1644-1911) **7** 19, 51, *51*, *67*, 68, *78*; **10** I1; **28** 312
Shang period (*c*. 1600-*c*. 1050 BC) **7** 44
Song period (AD 960-1279) **7** 49, 76; **19** *857*, *858*
Tang period (AD 618-907) **7** *45*, *49*, 77
Yuan period (1279-1368) **7** 50
Zhou period (*c*. 1050-256 BC) **7** 51–2, 62
20th cent. **7** 51, 113; **22** 233; **28** 718
silver **7** 21–7*, *26*, *72*, 79, 106, 108, 109, 116, 128, 632; **21** 715
Buddhism **7** 21, 23, 24, 25
export **7** *28*, 28–30*, *29*
Liao period (AD 907-1125) **7** *25*
Ming period (1368-1644) **7** 111
Qing period (1644-1911) **7** *27*, 111, 112
Shang period (*c*. 1600-*c*. 1050 BC) **7** 106, 107
Song period (AD 960-1279) **6** 895; **7** 110
Tang period (AD 618-907) **7** 14, *14*, *23*, *24*, 82, 109; **23** 551, *551*
Yuan period (1279-1368) **7** 124
Zhou period (*c*. 1050-256 BC) **6** 853, 855; **7** *98*, 107; **21** 714
silver-gilt **7** 108, 109, 110, 112
silver leaf **7** 13
skirts **7** 76, 77, 78
slate **7** 94
slip **6** 874, 876, 882, 886, 895
smelting **7** 98
smoky quartz **7** *90*
snuff bottles **7** 86, 91, 103, 131–3*, *132*, *133*; **16** IV; **26** 484
soapstone **7** 133–5*, *134*; **18** *601*
soda-lime **7** 82
solders **7** 100
soot **6** 736; **7** 91, 92, *93*
spearheads **7** 58
spinning-wheels **7** 43
sponsorship **5** 113
squeezes **7** 65, 117
stages **7** 135–6
stage scenery **7** 138
stamping **6** 881, 882
standards (vexilloid) **11** 152; **23** 496, *496*

China—cont.
stands **6** 827; **7** 139
cup **6** 875, *875*
drum **6** *855*
ring-stands **7** 125
steel **7** 57, 96–7*, 98, 100
stelae **6** 740, 741, *743*, 744, *744*, 745, 764; **8** 713; **29** 617*; **33** 464
Buddhism **6** *711*
commemorative **29** 617*
funerary **29** 617
Nestorianism **22** *812*
votive **29** 617
wanfo bei **29** 617
stencilling **7** 48, 118; **29** 627; **30** 560, 561
stitches **7** 44, *47*, 50
stone **6** 644–5*, 706, 725, 726; **7** 94, 128, 130
Han period (206 BC-AD 220) **6** *697*, 697, *727*, 727–30, *728*
Ming period (1368-1644) **7** 18
Northern and Southern Dynasties (AD 310-589) **6** *729*
Qing period (1644-1911) **6** *704*; **7** 19
Shang period (*c*. 1600-*c*. 1050 BC) **6** 726
Song period (AD 960-1279) **6** 718–19, *731*
Sui period (AD 581-618) **6** *713*
Tang period (AD 618-907) **6** *730*
Yuan period (1279-1368) **7** 130
stonewares **6** 868, 869, 870, 871, 872, 873, 875, 879, 880, 881, 884, 885, 886, *886*, 892, *892*, *893*, 895, *895*, *900*, *917*; **7** *94*; **17** *595*; **28** *618*
stools **7** 34, 39, 145
straw **6** 706
streams **12** 85
stupas **29** 868*
pagoda-stupas **22** *459*; **23** 773, *774*; **29** 868
pillar-stupas **29** 868
votive **29** 867
styluses **6** 736
sumac **7** 45
supports **28** 312
sutras **6** 782*; **7** *118*
sword fittings **7** 81
swords **7** 7, *22*, 56, 97
symbolism (critical term) **6** 630–33*, 726
synagogues **17** 551
tables **7** 34–5, 37, *40*, 40–41, *41*; **30** 217
tablets **7** 4, 102
talc **7** 133
tankards **6** 902
tapestries **7** 48, *48*, 49, 51, *51*, *67*
teabowls **6** 896; **17** *595*
tea-caddies **7** 101
tea-grinders **7** *24*
teapots **7** 101, *101*; **24** 580; **33** *535*
tea-services **7** *28*, 101
teeth **7** 106
whale **7** 102
temples **6** *538*, *652*, *654*, 662; **30** 442*, 443–4*
Buddhism **5** 107; **6** 667–71; **9** 393–4; **30** 442–3*
Confucianism **6** 674–5*, *676*; **30** 443
Daoism **6** 671; **30** 443, *444*
rock-cut **6** 626, 650; **22** 239; **30** 442–3*
tents **30** *475*
terracotta **6** 9; **7** *55*, 80; **30** 509*, *509*
textiles **1** 881; **6** 706; **7** 43–53*, *51*, 114, 117, 144–5; **29** 627; **30** 559, 560, 561
thatch **6** 692

China—cont.
theatre **7** 122, 136–8*
shadow **7** 122
theatres **7** 135–6*, *136*
theories
art **2** 531; **6** 769
Confucianism **6** 631, 634, 637
Daoism **6** 634
Song period (AD 960-1279) **21** 418
calligraphy **6** 769–71*; **8** 519
painting **6** 795–8, 814, 818, 821–5*; **7** 147; **25** 72
Qing period (1644-1911) **8** 519*
11th cent. **6** 789
poetry **25** 72
threads **7** 45, 50, *50*, 51, *51*, *53*
thrones **7** 40; **30** 785*
tieli **7** 31
tiles **6** 643, 685, 686, 691, 772, *788*, 882, 906; **7** 94, 143, 144
timber structures **6** 640; **22** 240
tin **7** 97, 100; **8** 852; **15** 812
titanium oxide **6** 873
titles of works of art **31** 52–3*
tobacco juice **7** 102
toggles **17** 398
tombs **4** *793*; **6** 631, 693–9*, 700–705*; **7** 73, 133; **31** 115
Han period (206 BC-AD 220) **6** 648, *697*; **33** 532–3
Ming period (1368-1644) **6** *701*, *702*, *703*
Qing period (1644-1911) **6** *704*
shaft **2** 209
Shang period (*c*. 1600-*c*. 1050 BC) **6** *694*
Song period (AD 960-1279) **6** *699*, *700*
Tang period (AD 618-907) **6** *651*, *698*
Zhou period (*c*. 1050-256 BC) **6** *695*, *696*
tools **6** 841; **7** 97
topographical illustrations **1** 612
tortoiseshell **6** 737, *739*; **31** *194*
towers **3** *519*
Islamic **6** *677*
que **6** 648, 697; **23** 773; **25** 800–801*, *800*
toys **7** 143, 147; **31** 255, 258
tracing **7** 109
trade **6** 618, 619–24*, *623*; **10** 278; **13** 737; **16** 403; **17** 23–4; **18** 251–2; **26** 855
bronze **29** 230
ceramics **5** 12; **6** 330, 891, 913–18*; **7** 165–6; **11** 605; **15** 811; **16** 393, 398; **17** 22, 248, 259; **18** 251, 281; **20** 179; **24** 626; **28** 723; **29** 114; **30** 611–12
chess sets **6** 557
cobalt **6** 622; **16** 394; **18** 343
coins **15** 811; **17** 24
dolls **31** 259, 261
fans **10** 777–8
fur **16** 456
furniture **7** 166; **25** 303
glass **7** 83, 86–7*; **17** 385, 386; **28** 718
ivory-carvings **7** 103–4
jade **7** 10, 11; **16** 527; **28** 718
lacquer **17** 298; **18** 612–13*; **27** 471
mirrors **7** 87; **17** 319, 320, 322; **21** 716; **24** 298
painting **17** 162
porcelain **4** 174; **6** 330–32*, 333, 918–21*; **16** 124, 425; **22** 879; **25** 309–10
Ming period (1368-1644) **4** 174, 175, 177; **6** 333, 622, 904; **16** 420, 424; **22** 878; **25** 303

China
trade
porcelain—cont.
Qing period (1644-1911) **3** 589; **6** 259, 624, 908; **11** 607; **16** 425; **17** 263; **22** 879, 880
Song period (AD 960-1279) **6** 258
Yuan period (1279-1368) **6** 622; **16** 393, 412
pottery **6** 256, 330–32*, 622, 888; **16** 401, 412; **17** 253, 263
scrolls **28** 311
silk **6** 621, 624; **7** 51–2; **16** 428; **20** 302; **28** 715, 716, 718, 721
silver **7** 28–30*
smalt **6** 869
tea-services **7** 29
textiles **3** 378; **6** 624; **7** 51–3; **16** 438; **17** 311, 313; **18** 374; **29** 231; **30** 622
wallpaper **7** 168; **32** 818–19*
trappings **14** 181*, 184*
trays **6** 888, 890
treatises **7** 123; **17** 229
aesthetics **2** 519
architecture **2** 317; **6** 653, 661
calligraphy
Han period (206 BC-AD 220) **6** 769
Ming period (1368-1644) **6** 760
Qing period (1644-1911) **6** 764, 765, 766; **17** 775; **27** 286
Tang period (AD 618-907) **30** 2
Three Kingdoms (AD 220-80) **6** 769–71
20th cent. **6** 766, 767, 768
gardens **12** 64, 88
looms **7** 44
painting **6** 754, 784, 785, 804, 824; **7** 148; **14** 820
landscape **9** 141; **17** 590
Qing period (1644-1911) **6** 39, 814
Song period (AD 960-1279) **6** 804
Tang period (AD 618-907) **6** 799
Yuan period (1279-1368) **6** 814, 824; **14** 823
perspective **6** 40
seals **7** 130
tripods **7** 86
trousers **7** 74, 144
tumuli **6** 696, 698
Tung oil **7** 92
tureens **6** *921*
turntables **6** 879
turquoise **7** 88, 108
Ming period (1368-1644) **7** 111, *111*
Qing period (1644-1911) **6** 706; **7** 91
Shang period (*c.* 1600-*c.* 1050 BC) **6** 832, 841; **7** 107
Tang period (AD 618-907) **7** 109
Yuan period (1279-1368) **7** 89
Zhou period (*c.* 1050-256 BC) **7** 107; **21** 714
tusks **7** 102
type-faces **5** 112; **25** 588
urban planning **6** 662–6*, *663*, *664*, *665*
urns **6** *877*
vases **6** 890, *890*, *891*, *894*, *898*, 903, *903*, *908*, *909*, *911*; **7** *27*, *79*, *85*, *90*, 103; **16** I; **26** 487
arrow **6** *875*
baluster **6** *875*, III3
mallet **6** *875*, 893
meiping **6** 875, *875*, 893, *902*
rouleau **6** *875*
suantou hu **6** *875*
yuhuchun **6** *875*, 893
velvet **7** *50*, *53*, 58
vessels
bian hu **6** *853*

China
vessels—cont.
bronze **6** 631, 635, 738, 788, 826, *827*, 827–9*, 830–34, 836–48*, 850–54*, 867, 868; **7** 22, 88; **10** *464*; **21** I4
Han period (206 BC-AD 220) **6** 857–8, *858*, 859, 861
Ming period (1368-1644) **6** 866
Qin period (221-206 BC) **6** 857
Shang period (*c.* 1600-*c.* 1050 BC) **6** 625, 735, 737, 767, 798, *831*, 835, *836*, *837*, *838*, *839*; **7** 12; **23** *155*, 549–50; **24** *14*
Song period (AD 960-1279) **6** 864, 865, *865*, *866*
Zhou period (*c.* 1050-256 BC) **6** *738*, 808, *833*, *842*, *843*, *844*, *845*, *846*, *847*, *850*, *851*, *852*, *853*; **7** 88; **33** *471*
copper **7** 88
ding **6** *827*, 828, *831*, *833*
dou **6** *827*, 828, *846*
dui **6** *827*
fang ding **6** *827*, 836
fang hu **33** *471*
fang yi **6** *827*, 836, *837*, *844*
fou **6** *827*
fu **6** *827*, 828
gold **7** 88
gong **6** *827*
gu **6** *827*, 828; **7** *27*
gui **6** *827*, 828, *842*, *843*, 844, *845*, *846*, 851, *851*
he **6** *827*, *836*, *837*
hu **6** *827*, 828, *839*, 845, *846*, *847*, *850*, 853, *853*; **21** I4
jade **7** 3, 6, 9
jia **6** *827*, *838*
jian **6** *827*, 829, *833*
jiao **6** *827*
jue **6** 827, *827*, *838*, *846*; **10** *464*
lacquer **7** 12
lei **6** *827*
li **6** *827*, *846*
malachite **7** 88
pan **6** *827*, *846*
pou **6** *827*
turquoise **7** 88
xu **6** *827*
yan **6** *827*
yi **6** *827*, 828
you **6** *827*, 845
yu **6** *827*
zhan **6** *852*
zhi **6** *827*
zun **6** *827*, 828, 845, 851
vinegar **7** 95
wallpaper **10** *278*; **32** 815, 818–19*, 820, VI
Qing period (1644-1911) **32** *819*
walls **7** 98
defensive **13** 333–4
town **6** 661, 662; **21** 593, *594*; **22** 458
walnuts **7** 141
watermarks **7** 116, *117*
waxes **7** 114, 116
weapons **6** 841, 848–9*; **7** 54–8*, 97
weaving **7** 43–4, 48
compound tabby **30** 552
compound twill **30** 552
lampas **7** 50
windows **6** *689*, 690, *690*; **7** 114; **12** 92
wire **7** *107*, 110, 111, 122
women artists **33** 317–22*
wood **6** 637–43*, 706; **7** 30–31, 94, 109, 122, 126, 128, 138, 143, 145; **20** 326; **28** 310
Han period (206 BC-AD 220) **7** 62–3
Liao period (AD 907-1125) **19** 303
Ming period (1368-1644) **6** 721

China
wood—cont.
Qing period (1644-1911) **6** 722, *722*
Shang period (*c.* 1600-*c.* 1050 BC) **7** 107
Song period (AD 960-1279) **6** 717, 718
Tang period (AD 618-907) **6** 650; **7** 92, 109
Zhou period (*c.* 1050-256 BC) **6** *696*; **7** 62, 97
20th cent. **31** 259
wood-carvings **7** 138–42*, *139*, *141*, 143; **33** *423*
woodcuts **7** 146
woodwork **7** 140
wool **7** 43, 68
workshops **6** 787; **7** 147, 150
wristrests **7** 58, 102, *103*
writing **2** 209; **6** 612, *736*, *738*, *739*, *740*, *742*, *743*, *744*, *746*, *747*, *749*, *750*, *751*, *752*, *753*, *754*, *757*, *758*, *759*, *762*, *763*, *765*; **7** 58, 62, 92, 114, 128; **17** 211, 215, 234–8; **20** 328; **25** 468
20th cent. **6** *768*
writing-tablets **6** 740, 767; **20** 327
wrought iron **7** 96, 97, 98; **16** 59
yokes (dress) **7** 77
yurts **7** 143
zelkova **7** 31
zitan **7** 30, *41*, 141
see also CENTRAL ASIA, EASTERN; TAIWAN
china *see* BONE CHINA
China, Great Wall of *see* GREAT WALL OF CHINA
China, People's Republic of *see* CENTRAL ASIA, EASTERN; CHINA; MONGOLIA; TIBET
China, Republic of *see* TAIWAN
chinaberry **32** 488
china clay *see* KAOLIN
Chinandega **23** *79*
Nuestra Señora de la Concepción del Viejo **23** 80
Chinantec **21** 736, 738
Chinard, Joseph **7** 162–3*; **19** 847
groups and movements **26** 742
patrons and collectors **4** 301, 303
pupils **11** 364
works **7** *163*; **11** 563
chinas *see under* JARS → types
china stone **6** 325, 326, 329, 869, 897; **16** 393
Chinautla **13** *758*, 768
Chinaz **6** 274
Chincha **6** 520; **29** 127
Chin Ch'eng *see* JIN CHENG
Chinchero **7** 163*; **23** 826; **29** *156*, 167; **30** 447
architecture **29** 166
palace of Topa Inca **29** 164
sculpture **29** 172
Chinchilla de Monte Aragón **5** 833; **25** 409
S María **29** 266
Chinchón, Pedro Fernández de Cabrera y Bobadilla, 2nd Conde de **10** 498
Chindŏk, Queen (*reg* 647-54) **18** 275, 298
chine de commande see under PORCELAIN → wares
Chinese **5** 459
Chinese blue *see under* PIGMENTS → types
Chinese cabinets *see under* CABINETS (i) (ROOMS) → types
Chinese ink *see under* INKS → types
Chinese insect wax *see under* WAXES → types
Chinese Turkestan *see* CENTRAL ASIA, EASTERN
Chinese weave *see under* TEXTILES → types

Chinese white *see* PIGMENTS → types → zinc white
Ching, Prince *see* JING, Prince
Ching Chün *see* JING JUN
Chin Genpin *see* ZHEN YUANYUN
Chinggis Khan *see* GENGHIS KHAN
Ching Hao *see* JING HAO
Ch'ing-lien-kang *see* QINGLIAN'GANG
Ch'ing period *see under* CHINA → periods
Ching-te-chen *see* JINGDEZHEN
Ching-ti, Emperor (Han; *reg* 157-141 BC) *see* JINGDI, Emperor
Chinguetti **1** *376*; **20** 861
congregational mosque **1** 316
library **20** 862
chin'gyŏng sansu school **7** 203; **18** 52
works **7** *203*
Chinhŭng, King (*reg* 540-76) **18** 328
Chini, Galileo **7** 164*; **11** 190; **16** 679; **20** 428
Chiniot **23** 803
Chinish, John **3** 164
Chinjae *see* KIM (ii) YUN-GYŎM
Chinjŏn Temple **29** 869
Chin Jōtoku **20** 286
Chinju **18** 341
Ch'oksŏng-ru Pavilion **12** 95
Museum **18** 383
Chinkinbori see LACQUER → types → gilt-engraved *urushi*
Chinle (AZ) **22** 626
Chin Nakei *see* CHEN HEQING
Chin Nanpin *see* SHEN NANPIN
Chinnen Ōnishi *see* ŌNISHI CHINNEN
Chinnery, George **7** 164–5*; **19** 866; **21** 644
assistants **13** 734
works **7** *165*; **14** 721, *721*; **19** *866*; **21** 896
Chinnery, William (father) **7** 164
Chinnery, William (son) **7** 164
Chin Nung *see* JIN NONG
chinoiserie **7** 165–8*, 615; **32** 818
art forms
architecture **7** 168*
book illustrations **4** 361
ceramics **7** 165–6*; **22** 880
furniture **7** *167*
gardens **12** 123, 131
interior decoration **7** 168; **8** 742; **31** 617
lacquer **7** 166–7*
leather **19** 5
metalwork **7** 167*
pottery **7** *166*
textiles **7** 53, 167*, *168*
commentaries **6** 410
regional traditions
England **6** 412; **7** 166, 167, 168; **10** 276, 329; **12** 131
France **7** 166, 167, 168, *168*
Germany **7** 167; **33** 276
Italy **7** 165, 167
Netherlands, the **7** 166
Poland **25** 122
Sweden **1** 152
United States of America **7** 168
Chinon
Château **6** 56
St Mexme **26** 599
Chinooka **22** 548, 565, 668
Ch'inpa, Tomb 1 **18** 313, 349
Ch'in period (221-206 BC) *see under* CHINA → periods
Chin period (AD 265-420) *see under* CHINA → periods
Chin Shao-fang *see* JIN SHAOFANG
Chin Shao-t'ang *see* JIN SHAOTANG
Ch'in Shih-an *see* QIN SHIAN
Chin Shih-ch'üan *see* JIN SHIQUAN

Ch'in Shih Huang-ti (Ch'in emperor; *reg* 221-210 BC) *see* QIN SHI HUANGDI
Chin T'ing-piao *see* JIN TINGBIAO
Chintreuil, Antoine **7** 169*; **8** 539
Chin-ts'un *see* JINCUN
chintz **10** 276; **15** 717; **22** 899; **30** 559, VI2; **32** 815
Chinul **5** 115
Chin Ying *see* JIN YING
Chin Yüan-yü *see* JIN YUANYU
Chinzan Ōnuma *see* ŌNUMA CHINZAN
Chinzan Tsubaki *see* TSUBAKI CHINZAN
Chiodera, Alfred **29** 491
Chiodo (family) **1** 578
Chiodo, Domenico **18** 812
Chioggia **32** 182
Chiona, Giovanni Antonio **19** 560
Chionites *see* HUNS
Chios (island) **7** 169–70*; **9** *512*; **13** *363*; **15** 893
architecture **32** 294
ceramics **13** 358
churches **9** 550
coins **7** 535
heraldry **14** 411
korai **18** *244*, 245
Nea Moni **2** 426; **9** 522, 576; **22** 162
katholikon **7** 170; **9** 546, 547
mosaics **7** 170; **9** 578
sculpture **9** 593
Panagia Sikelia **9** 550
pottery **13** 497, 502, 504; **28** 893
Chios (town)
Adamantios Korais Library **7** 169; **13** 361
Archaeological Museum **2** 175; **7** 169
Ethnological and Folklore Museum **7** 169
Chios, Archermos of *see* ARCHERMOS OF CHIOS
Chiossone, Edoardo **17** 203
Chiostro degli Aranci, Master of the *see* GIOVANNI DI CONSALVO
Chios turpentine *see* RESINS → types → terebinth resin
Chiozzi, Luigi **8** 912
Chiozzotto, Il *see* MARINETTI, ANTONIO
Ch'i Pai-shih *see* QI BAISHI
Chiparus, Demeter **11** 629, 637; **29** 576
Chipault, Jean **23** 850
Chipaya **32** 305
houses **32** *305*
chipboard **7** 558; **31** 283
chip carving *see under* CARVING → types
Chipewyan **22** 546
Chipiez, Charles (-Jérôme) **7** 170–71*; **10** 84
Chipman, K. **4** 27
Chippendale (family) **12** 333
Chippendale, John **7** 171
Chippendale, Thomas (i) (1709-79) **7** 171–2*; **9** 727; **15** 820; **19** 592; **20** 593; **23** 544; **31** 683
carpets **5** 839
chairs **6** 390; **26** 303
clocks **7** 445
collaboration **10** 278, 294
fireplace furnishings **11** 119
frames **11** 431
furniture **5** 356; **7** 659; **9** 29; **10** 295, *295*; **28** 665, *665*
interior decoration **10** 276; **11** 430; **24** 317
methods **18** 614
mirrors **21** 721
musical instruments **22** 374
patrons and collectors **7** 659, 758; **9** 392; **24** 390
pattern books **7** *171*; **24** 273
style **26** 499

Chippendale, Thomas (i) (1709-79)—cont.
tables 7 746
writings 3 485; 4 361; 7 167; 10 276, 279, 294, 295; 24 316; 25 307
illustrated 8 528
Chippendale, Thomas (ii) (1749-1822) 7 172*
groups and movements 26 85
methods 20 468
patrons and collectors 14 598
Chippendale style 31 618, 625
Chippewa 22 627, 665
Chipping Campden (Glos) 10 224
houses 32 *276*
St James 5 319
Chipping Ongar (Essex) 30 906
Chiprovtsi 5 160, 161
Chipurik 6 380
Chiquinquirá 7 *601*
Cathedral 7 605, 607
Chiquitos 4 *255*
SS Michael and Raphael 4 261
Chiragan Villa 32 542, 544
Chirala 15 672
Chirawa 15 611
Chirchik Museum 6 283
Chircot 9 678, 679
Chirico, Andrea De *see* SAVINIO, ALBERTO
Chirico, Giorgio De *see* DE CHIRICO, GIORGIO
Chirigano 24 93
Chirin, Prokopy (Ivanov) 7 172–3*; 25 338; 27 386
groups and movements 29 779
works 29 54
Chirino, Martín 7 173*; 29 296
Chiripá 24 93
sculpture 24 *93*
Chiripa 9 166; 29 829; 31 45
Chiriquí *see* GRAN CHIRIQUÍ
Chirk (Clwyd)
aqueduct 2 242
Castle 9 31; 32 788, 789
Chirkov, Mikhail (Pavlovich) 27 422
Chirnside, Thomas 2 755
Chiromo, Kay 20 161
Chiron Press 20 609
Chirorro, Robert 22 245
Chirrambalam *see* CHIDAMBARAM
Chirtani, Luigi 28 393
Chiruo Yamanaka *see* YAMANAKA, CHIRUO
Chirwa, David 33 603
Chisan 18 339
chiselling 2 454, 455, 456; 31 147
chisel-nosed mouldings *see under* MOULDINGS → types
chisels 9 814, 815, 821; 13 436; 17 48; 27 16; 29 704; 30 366; 33 334
Egypt, ancient 9 815
Greece, ancient 13 436
Chishin *see* HATA CHITEI
Chisholm, Robert Fellowes 7 173*; 15 393
works 15 403; 20 53, 73; 31 793
Chisht 16 166, 169
Chişinău 7 173–4*; 21 *810*, 811
architecture 21 810
carpets 21 812
Cathedral of the Nativity 21 810
City Drawing School *see* College of Art
College of Art 21 811
monument to the Heroic Komsomol 21 812
Museum of Fine Art 7 174
Regional Museum 7 174
sculpture 21 812
Triumphal Arch 21 810
Chişinau-Criş 26 719
Chislehurst (Kent) 23 398
Bullers Wood 23 36
Chislett, John 25 4
Chissano 22 244, 245
Chistyakov, Pavel (Petrovich) 27 442
assistants 22 811
pupils 4 414; 17 812; 18 399; 24 350; 25 145; 27 685; 28 474; 30 10; 31 459; 32 735; 33 740
Chistyakova, Taisiya (Fyodorovna) 27 423
Chiswick House (Middx) 4 *612*; 7 *174*, 174–5*; 8 47; 10 233, 294; 12 129; 23 858, 859; 27 237; 32 553
Blue Velvet Room 4 609
furniture 10 294
gardens 7 174–5
paintings 9 17
portico 25 266
sculpture 18 902; 27 466
Summer Parlour 17 902
Chiswick Press 33 152
Chit'am
earthenwares 18 *333*
Chitarman 15 590, 591
Chitei Hata *see* HATA CHITEI
Chitimacha 22 662
chitones 9 246, 249
Chitorgarh *see* CHITTAURGARH
Chitral 23 798
Chitré 23 *902*
Chi-tsang *see* JIZANG
Chittagong University
Department of Fine Arts 3 169
Chittaurgarh 7 175*; 15 *276*, 598
Adbhutnath Temple 15 491
fortifications 21 590, *590*
halls 14 77
Kalika Mata Temple 15 270, 486, 750
Kirtistambha 15 491
Kshemankari Temple 15 *270*, 487
Kumbhashyama Temple 15 486
Manastambha 15 491
manuscript illumination 15 *227*
palace of Rana Kumbha 15 386, *386*; 23 818
palace of Rana Ratan Singh 15 386
temples 15 270, 314, 750
Chittick, Neville 1 512
Chittussi, Antonín 4 700; 7 175–6*; 8 392; 25 433
Chitty, Anthony 30 411
Ch'iu (?Chu) *see* QIU (?ZHU)
Chiu-ch'üan *see* JIUQUAN
Chiujae *see* CHŎNG SU-YŎNG
Chiulinovich, Juraj *see* SCHIAVONE, GIORGIO (DI TOMMASO)
Chi Un-su 18 61
Chiusi 7 176*; 10 *583*, 585, 602, 637, 639, 640, 642; 16 *620*; 26 *886*
bronze 10 626, 627
coins 10 633
collections 10 637
ex-votos 10 600
forgeries 11 306
gold 10 631
ivory-carvings 10 595, 635
limestone 10 602
mirrors 10 629
Museo Archeologico Nazionale 10 640
pottery 10 613, 639; 13 541
reliefs 10 596
sarcophagus of Seianti Thanunia Tlesnasa 10 588
sculpture 10 591, 607
S Vittore 16 625
tombs 10 607, 620
Pania Tomb 10 634, *634*
Poggio al Moro Tomb 10 619
Tomb of the Hill 10 622
Tomb of the Monkey 10 617, 622, 634
trade 10 592
Chiusi—cont.
urns 7 *176*; 10 593, *593*, 602, 607, 608
funerary 10 588
vase paintings 10 588, 592, 615
vases 10 612, 613
wall paintings 10 617
Chiusi Cup 13 550
Chiusole, Adamo, Conte 7 176–7*
Chiusuri, Francesco 11 20
Ch'iu Ying *see* QIU YING
chivalry, orders of *see* ORDERS (CHIVALRY)
Chivateros 29 168
Chixab 20 885
Chizhov, Matvey (Afanas'yevich) 18 236; 27 390, 578; 33 601
Chkhari Cross 12 329
Chkhenkeli, I. 12 320
Chladek, Anton 26 725
chlamydes 9 251
Chlanda, Marek 25 116
Chlef *see* ECH CHELIFF
Chlemoutsi Castle 7 180*
chlorine 18 590; 24 42; 33 1
chlorite 15 *504*, 902, 904, 913, 914; 21 *656*
chloromelanite *see under* JADE → types
chlorophyll 24 794
chloroprene 1 155
Chludov, Nikolay 17 867
Chludov Psalter *see under* PSALTERS → individual manuscripts
Chlum
metalwork 6 *153*
Chlumec nad Cidlinou Castle 8 378
Chlupáč, Miloš 8 388
Chmel, Viliam 28 853
Chmielewski, Jan 30 199
Chmielowski, Adam 7 181*; 25 107
Chmutina, N. B. 33 518
Chnab, Michael *see* MICHAEL OF WIENER NEUSTADT
Choate, Chris 20 878
Chobari, Chaumukhi Vav 29 635
Chōbunsai Eishi 17 797
Chocano, José Santo *see* SANTO CHOCANO, JOSÉ
Chocarne, Geoffroy-Alphonse 22 119
Cho Chi-on 7 207; 18 317
Chochol, Josef 7 182*; 8 401
groups and movements 8 373; 12 834; 13 711; 16 902; 21 781
works 8 380; 25 429, *430*
Chochola, Václav 7 182*
Chochołów
houses 32 *299*
Cho Chŏng-gyu 18 321
Chocho-Popoloca 21 736, 738
Cho Chung-du 18 60
Chocim Castle 4 783
Chocolate-on-White ware *see under* POTTERY → wares
Chocquet, Jean 6 453
Chocquet, Victor 6 371, 375; 26 207; 30 290
Choctaw 22 552
Chōdensu Minchō 7 182–3*; 17 29, 784, 789; 18 552, 559
Chodkiewicz, Aleksander 25 136
Chodor 16 485
Chodowiecki, Daniel Nikolaus 3 799; 7 183–4*; 18 201; 25 106
assistants 30 353
book illustrations 12 853; 18 880
caricatures 5 758
drawings 25 118
paintings 12 *411*, 457, 459
patrons and collectors 19 327; 21 643
personal collection 12 474
prints 5 353; 7 *183*; 9 308; 12 392; 25 *599*, 600
pupils 12 641; 18 202
Chodowiecki, Gottfried (1698-1740) 7 183
Chodowiecki, Gottfried (1728-87) 7 184
Chodowiecki, (?Ludwig) Wilhelm 7 184
Ch'oe An-do 18 351
Ch'oe Cha 18 324
Ch'oe Ch'i-wŏn 7 184*; 18 328
Ch'oe Ip 33 525
Ch'oe Ki-wŏn 18 301
Ch'oe Kyŏng 7 184*
Ch'oe Man-rin 18 301
Chōen 10 192
Ch'oe Puk 7 184–5*; 18 317
choes 13 *475*, 476, 479
Cho'e Suk-ch'ang 18 314
Ch'oe Sun-u 18 259
Choffard, Pierre-Philippe 7 185*; 11 57; 19 641
pupils 21 411
works 32 502
Chofwe 29 71
Chōgen 17 71, 122, 729; 22 496, 499
Chō Gesshō 17 273; 33 489
Chogha Mami 1 894; 7 185–6*; 21 *267*, 269
figurines 7 *186*; 21 269, 270, 293
flax 1 879
houses 21 280, 281
pottery 21 269, 270, 306, *306*
seals 22 510
Chogha Mish 7 186*; 15 *901*, 904, 909
houses 21 280
mud-bricks 21 270
Chogha Sefid 15 913, 918; 21 270
Chogha Zanbil 1 894; 7 186–7*; 10 132; 15 *901*, 905, 907
architecture 15 909–10
axes 7 *187*
faience (i) (glass) 1 878
fortifications 21 554
ivory-carvings 1 869
seals 1 864
temple 7 187; 30 432
ziggurat 1 866, 879; 15 *910*; 33 675
Chogye Buddhism *see under* BUDDHISM → sects
Chögyi Gyaltsen 30 830
Choh 22 594
Cho Hŭi-ryong 7 187–8*; 18 315, 325, 331
Cho Ik 7 207
Cho In-gyu 18 339
Choinier, E. C. 4 155
Choir-books 7 188–9*
see also ANTIPHONALS; GRADUALS
choirs 7 188*; 8 224; 19 377; 28 140
Choirs, Master of the 25 102
choir-screens *see under* SCREENS (i) (ARCHITECTURAL) → types
choir-stalls 7 189–92*, 281
Belgium 3 581, 585
Denmark 8 738
England 7 *190*
France 7 *191*; 13 126
Germany 13 *118*
Gothic 7 *190*, *191*; 13 *118*, 123, 126
Holy Roman Empire (before 1648) 13 *118*
Hungary 14 903, 904
Italy 16 722
Portugal 25 305
Romanesque 7 190
sculpture 13 *118*
Spain 7 *192*; 13 123; 28 *689*, 689–90; 29 311
Choiseul 29 49
Choiseul, Etienne-François, Duc de 7 193–4*; 8 542; 26 448
architecture 19 26; 23 776
collections 8 867
Choiseul, Etienne-François, Duc de—cont.
furniture 5 379; 12 159; 14 230; 23 356
paintings 3 319; 4 130; 5 354, 686; 7 778; 8 705; 13 638; 14 799; 26 448
prints 9 395
sculpture 13 805
snuff-boxes 7 *194*
sponsorship 4 130
Choiseul, Louise-Honorine, Duchesse de 8 209
Choiseul Box 4 130; 7 193
Choiseul-(Beaupré-) Gouffier, Marie-Gabriel (-Florent-Auguste), Comte de 5 921; 7 193*
architecture 19 11
engravings 14 366
illustrated writings 8 772
sponsorship 31 478
Choiseul-Praslin (family) 8 653
Choisy, (François-) Auguste 7 195*; 9 825
groups and movements 26 14
works 2 360; 9 528
Choisy, Hirel de 26 206
Choisy-le-Roi 7 195*
Château 4 517; 6 474; 7 195; 11 658; 18 804
carpets 5 837
furniture 11 593
paintings 4 554; 11 540; 14 84, 585; 18 642; 32 429
sculpture 1 133; 2 699; 4 510; 10 764
glassworks 11 613
Cho Jik 7 207
Chōjirō Tanaka *see* TANAKA CHŌJIRŌ
Chojna, St Mary's 4 783; 5 28
Chōka Adachi *see* ADACHI, CHŌKA
Chōkai 17 124, 131
Chō Kenkō 27 470
Chok Gargyar *see* KOH KER
Chokha 15 600–601
Chokichi Suzuki *see* SUZUKI, CHOKICHI
Chōki Eishōsai *see* EISHŌSAI CHŌKI
Chōki Miyagawa *see* MIYAGAWA CHŌKI
Chōkō Kameda *see* KAMEDA BŌSAI
Chokolov, Sergey 21 812
Chokonyū Tanomura *see* TANOMURA CHOKONYŪ
Chō Kōran 33 322
Chōkōsai Eisho 17 285, 287
Chōkōtei 27 470
Choksy, Pheroze 29 456
Chokuan Soga *see* SOGA CHOKUAN
Cho Kwang-jin 18 331
Chokwe 1 241, 252; 2 86; 7 195–8*; 33 602
aesthetics 1 236
architecture 1 406
baskets 1 357
beads 7 *197*
body arts 1 342
canes 1 423
chairs 1 291, 366
divination instruments 1 357
gesture 1 265, 266
hair 1 *404*; 7 *197*
iconography 1 261
masks 1 256, 405; 2 85; 7 196, 197*
mixed-media 1 301
patronage 1 241, 243
pots 1 328
sculpture 1 322, 359, 403, *404*; 7 196–7*, *197*
wire 7 *197*
wood 1 291, *404*; 7 *197*
wood-carvings 1 252, 406; 7 196

Cho Kyu-bong **18** 300
Chola **7** 200*; **12** 651; **29** 448–9, 459
  see also:
    ADITYA I, Ruler
    GANDARADITYA, Ruler
    KULOTTUNGA I, Ruler
    PARANTAKA I, Ruler
    RAJARAJA I, Ruler
    RAJENDRA I, Ruler
    SHEMBIYAN MAHADEVI
Cholamandal **15** 179; **20** 54; **24** 9
Chollerton **11** 252
Chollot, Edmé **11** 404
Cholmondeley (family) **14** 419
  coats of arms **14** *419*
Cholmondeley, Hugh, 1st Earl of Cholmondeley **3** 83
Cholmondeley Castle (Ches) **5** 169
Cholon **32** 469
Cholula **7** 201–2*; **21** *193*, 200, 202, 264, *372*
  Great Pyramid **7** 201, *201*; **21** 210; **25** 764; **28** 640
  Nuestra Señora de los Remedios **7** *201*; **21** 373
  Patio of Altars **7** *201*, 202
  pottery **21** 239
  S Francisco Acatepec **25** 57, II1; **30** 502
  skull racks **31** 506
  S Maria Tonantzintla **25** 57; **30** 502
  stucco **29** 829
  wall paintings **21** 228–9
Cholulteca **21** 186, 239, 738
Choluteca **14** *711*, 712
Chomedey, Paul de, Sieur de Maisonneuve *see* MAISONNEUVE, PAUL DE CHOMEDEY, Sieur de
Chōmeiji **17** 124
Chompré, Pierre **15** 84
Cho Mun-su **18** 329
Chŏn *see* KONGMIN
Chon, Atsidi **22** 614
Chonburi, Wat Yai Intharam **30** 616
Ch'ŏngam **18** 349; **23** 775
  Temple **18** 266
Chŏng Ch'ang-sŏp *see* CHUNG CHANG SUP
Chŏng Ch'an-sŭng **18** 301
Chong Fah Chong **28** 774
Chŏng Hak-gyo **7** 204; **18** 331
Ch'onghanja *see* KIM SI-SŬP
Chŏng Hwang **7** 203
Chong-hyŏn **33** 535
Ch-ŏngji *see* YI YŎNG
Chŏngjo, King **7** 202*, 208; **18** 52, 281
Ch'ŏngjŏn *see* YI SANG-BŎM
Ch'ŏngju
  Ch'ungbuk University **18** 381
  Museum **18** 383
  Posal Temple **18** 308, 310, 311
Chŏng Kang-ja **18** 301
Chong Neto, Manuel **7** 202–3*; **23** 905
Chongok **18** 382
Chongoyape **8** 272; **29** *156*, 214
  crowns **29** *214*
Chongqing Temple *see under* ZHANGZI
Ch'ongryong Temple **29** 869
Ch'ongsa *see* HAN HO
Chŏng Sŏn **7** 203–4*
  pupils **18** 52; **28** 758, 759
  works **7** *203*; **18** 257, 314–15, *315*, 317, 319
Chŏngsŏn Temple **18** 348
Chŏng Su-yŏng **7** 203, 204*; **18** 315
Chŏng Tae-yu **7** 204*; **18** 331
Chŏngt'o Buddhism *see* BUDDHISM → sects → Pure Land
Chongt'o Temple **29** 869
Ch'ŏngun bridge **18** 280
Chŏng Yag-yong **33** 572, 573*
Chon'gye **1** 448
Chongye **7** 205*; **30** *806*, 815
  tomb of Songtsen Gampo **7** 205
  tombs **30** 847
Chon'gye **1** 448
Chong-yong *see* KO UN
Choniates, Michael *see* MICHAEL CHONIATES
Choniates, Nicetas *see* NICETAS CHONIATES
Chŏnju
  City Hall **18** 264
  Wibong Temple **18** 307
Chŏn Ki **7** 205*; **18** 315, 331
Chono **29** 128
Ch'ŏnsimchukche *see* MIN YŎNG-IK
Ch'ŏnt'ae Buddhism *see under* BUDDHISM → sects
Chontal **21** 250
Chontales, Museo Juigalpa **23** 85
Chontal Maya **6** 579; **20** 884
Ch'ŏnyŏ *see* KIM MYŎNG-GUK
Choong Kam Kow **20** 172
Chōōrō *see* UTAGAWA KUNIYOSHI
Chopi **1** 416
Chopin, Fryderyk **21** 135
Chopin, Fryderyk, Museum *see under* ŻELAZOWA WOLA
Chopinot **4** 566
Chopli Tepe **6** 275
Choppin de Janvry, Olivier **26** 258
chopsticks **17** 399; **18** 380
Choquepuquiu **29** 164
Choquet, Victor **15** 154
Choquet collection **24** 552
Chora Museum (Amorgos) **1** 795
Chora (Kythera) **14** 361; **18** 570, 571
Chorasmian **1** 886
Chorazim **17** 556
Chordeleg **9** 710
chords **7** 205*
Choricius of Gaza **10** 129
Chorin Abbey **7** 205–6*, *206*; **12** *360*; **13** 49
chorizo **24** 96
Chorku **6** 222, 277
Chorley Hall (Ches) **14** 75
Chorleywood (Herts), The Orchard **10** 284; **21** 779
Chornancap **29** 174
Chorny, Andrey **27** 412
Chorny, Daniil *see* DANIIL CHORNY
Chorny, Ivan **27** 412
Choros-Gurkin, Grigory **27** 436
Chorotegas **14** 711
Chorrera culture **7** 206–7*; **27** 609
  bone-carvings **29** 206
  figurines **30** *512*
  pottery **7** 206–7; **29** 134, 151
  terracotta **30** *512*
Chortakia
  Hagios Giorgios **8** 358
  Hagios Theodoros **8** 358
chortens **29** 868; **30** 815–16, 817, 818, 819
  see also STUPAS
Chortkov, Church of the Ascension **31** 552
Cho Sang-u **7** 207
Chose, Geoffroi **31** 841
Chōsei **10** 192; **17** 119
Chō Shūkoku *see* ZHANG KUN
Chōshun Miyagawa *see* MIYAGAWA CHŌSHUN
Cho Sŏk **1** 847; **7** 207*
  works **18** 317, *317*, 325
Cho Sŏk-chin **7** 207*; **25** 760; **33** 534
  groups and movements **18** 57
  pupils **18** 59, 193
Ch'osŏn *see* HŎ P'IL
Chosŏn dynasty *see*:
  CHŎNGJO, King
  KOJONG, Emperor
Chosŏn dynasty—cont.
  see: KWANGHAE-GUN, King
  SEJO, King
  T'AEJO, King
Chosŏn kogo yŏnju **18** 382
Chosroes I (*reg* 531-79) **18** 483; **21** 275, 292
Chosroes II Parviz (*reg* 590-628) **15** 907; **21** 292
Chōsui Miyagawa *see* MIYAGAWA CHŌSUI
Chot'ap-dong Pagoda **4** 795
Chotek (family) **2** 305
Chotek, Karel **8** 422
Chō Tōsai **17** 237, 411
Chotuna **28** 651
Chou, Irene **7** 208–9*; **14** 722
Chou ch'en *see* ZHOU CHEN
Chou Chi-ch'ang ZHOU JICHANG
Chōudō *see* KUWAYAMA GYOKOSHŪ
Chou Fang *see* ZHOU FANG
Chou Feng-lai *see* ZHOU FENGLAI
Chou Hao *see* ZHOU HAO
Chou Hsi *see* ZHOU XI
Chou Hu *see* ZHOU HU
Ch'oŭi Sŏnsa **14** 817
Choukhaeff, Vasily *see* SHUKAYEV, VASILY
Chou K'ou-jen *see* ZHOU KOUREN
Choul, Guillaume Du *see* DU CHOUL, GUILLAUME
Chou Li *see* ZHOU LI
Chou Liang-kung *see* ZHOU LIANGGONG
Chou Li-ching *see* ZHOU LIJING
Chou Lu-yün *see* CHOU, IRENE
Choumara, Pierre-Marie-Théodore **21** 581
Choumeriakos **21** 683
Chou Mi *see* ZHOU MI
Chōun Yamazaki *see* YAMAZAKI, CHŌUN
Chou period *see under* CHINA → periods
Chou Pin *see* ZHOU BIN
Chources, Antoine de **7** 526
Chou Shang-chün *see* ZHOU BIN
Chou Shu-jen *see* LU XUN
Chou Ta-kuan *see* ZHOU DAGUAN
Chou Wen-ching *see* ZHOU WENJING
Chou Wen-chü *see* ZHOU WENJU
Chou Wen-shu *see* ZHOU WENSHU
Chou Yü *see* ZHOU YU
Chou Yüeh *see* ZHOU YUE
Chowdhury, Eulie **7** 209*
Chowdhury, Rashid **3** 168
Chowne, Gerard **19** 359
Ch'owŏn *see* KIM (iii) SŎK-SIN
Choy, José Antonio **8** 233
Choyang **18** 334
Chōyōdō *see* KAIGETSUDŌ ANVHI
Cho Yŏng-sŏk **7** 209*; **18** 319, 325
Cho Yu-su **7** 207
Chōzan Satō *see* SATŌ, CHŌZAN
Chrétien, Aymeric *see* AYMERIC CHRÉTIEN
Chrétien, Gilles-Louis **24** 692
Chrétien de Troyes **12** 109; **26** 561, 655
Chřibská **7** 209–10*; **8** *374*, 407, 408
Chriechpavm *see* KRIECHBAUM
Christ, John Friedrich **10** 205
Christchurch (Hants; UK) **14** 75; **22** 216; **28** 301
Christchurch (New Zealand) **7** 210–11*; **23** 51, *52*
  Anglican Cathedral **23** 54; **28** 296
  architecture **23** 64
  Bishopscourt Park Terrace **23** 55
  Canterbury College
    Clock-Tower **23** 54
    School of Art **23** 75
  Canterbury Museum **22** 230; **23** 54
Christchurch (New Zealand)—cont.
  Canterbury Provincial Council Buildings **23** 54
    Council Chamber **22** 230
  Chateau Regency Hotel **23** 56
  Chief Post Office **23** 54
  Daresbury **23** 54
  Dorset Street Flats **23** 56
  furniture **23** 66
  Great Hall **23** 54
  Methodist Church, Durham Street **23** 54
  Municipal Offices **23** 54
  Robert McDougall Art Gallery **7** 211
  St Michael and All Angels **23** 53
  silk **23** 74
  statue of Queen Victoria **23** 62
  Town Hall **1** 126; **23** 56
  United Bank Building **23** 56
Christel, Christian **19** 397
Christen, Jakob Lorenz **7** 211
Christen, Joseph Anton Maria **7** 211*; **30** 137
Christen, Raphael **3** 824
Christensen, C. C. A. **21** 815
Christensen, Christen **22** 126
Christensen, Erwin **31** 672
Christensen, Hans **31** 650
Christensen, Sigrid Flamand **8** 762
Christensen collection **1** 66
Christesen, Vilhelm **8** 751
Christian (*fl* 1430–40s) **30** 366
Christian I, Elector of Saxony (*reg* 1586-91) **5** 768; **12** 577; **17** 887; **18** 461; **23** 252; **32** 832; **33** *110*
Christian I, King of Denmark (*reg* 1448-81) **27** 168
Christian II, Elector of Saxony (*reg* 1591-1611) **8** 407; **13** 915; **17** 887; **19** 93; **32** 731; **33** *110*, 631
Christian II, King of Denmark and Norway (*reg* 1513-23) **5** 295; **8** 758; **9** 427; **13** 26, *27*; **23** 395
Christian III, King of Denmark, Norway and Sweden (*reg* 1534-59) **4** *67*; **8** 732, 752; **20** 206
Christian IV, King of Denmark and Norway (*reg* 1588-1648) **23** 395, 396*; **30** 734; **33** *421*
  architecture **7** 802; **8** 725; **14** 369, 542; **17** 633; **23** 601; **27** 168; **29** 593; **31** 715, 718
    chapels **29** 593
  drawings **24** 236
  engravings **33** 421
  interior decoration **8** 742; **23** 635
  paintings **7** 431; **8** 732, 733, 758; **16** 63; **23** 124, 224; **28** 362; **31** 807
    ceiling **14** 730
    history **21** 789
    miniatures **21** 641
    religious **18** 818
  patronage **23** 224
  porcelain **9** 28
  prints **24** 236
  sculpture **22** 857; **26** 105; **29** 594; **31** 139
  silk **8** 755
  sponsorship **20** 249
  tapestries **8** 754; **20** 244; **22** 897
Christian IV Altar **32** 772
Christian V, King of Denmark and Norway (*reg* 1670-99) **14** 245; **25** 29
  architecture **23** 217
  crowns **8** 752
  interior decoration **14** 543
  medals **21** 406
  paintings **1** 449; **8** 733
  silk **8** 755
  tapestries **8** 754; **30** 322
Christian VI, King of Denmark and Norway (*reg* 1730-46)
  architecture **8** 726; **10** 110
Christian VI, King of Denmark and Norway (*reg* 1730-46)—cont.
  art policies **8** 760
  glass **23** 235
  paintings **8** 733; **29** 386; **32** 765
  silk **8** 755
  sponsorship **10** 109
Christian VII, King of Denmark (*reg* 1766-1808) **3** 600; **7** 806; **8** 726; **14** 815; **24** 811; **32** 583
Christian VIII, King of Denmark (*reg* 1839-48) **17** 478
Christian IX, King of Denmark (*reg* 1863-1906) **17** 8
Christian, Ewan **10** 371; **14** 50
Christian, Franz Joseph **7** 212
Christian, Hans **8** 419
Christian, Johann Joseph **7** 211–12*
  collaboration **10** 859
  groups and movements **26** 498
  works **10** 859; **11** 125; **12** 405; **23** 636
Christian, Malcolm **29** 111
Christian Academy **8** 423
Christian-Albert, Duke of Holstein-Gottorp (fl c. *1663*) **23** 675
Christian Ernest, Margrave of Bayreuth (*d* 1712) **25** 257
Christiania *see* OSLO
Christiani & Nielsen **2** 577
Christianity **7** 212–32*; **26** 140
  art
    allegories **1** 653; **25** 650
    altars **1** 693, 698–9*, *699*, 700*
    ambos **1** 764*
    amulets **1** 818
    arches **2** 297*
    architecture **6** 677–8*; **26** 907, 923
    baptisteries **3** 189
    Bibles **4** 3*
    books **4** 343
    calendars **21** 138
    carnivals **5** 784, 785
    censers **6** 173
    censorship
      Protestantism **6** 175
      Roman Catholicism **6** 175
    churches **7** 251
      Anglicanism **25** 266
      China **6** *678*
      decoration **7** 276–7*
      Germany **12** 373
      Ireland **16** 11
      Lutheranism **19** 815
      Malaysia **20** 155
      Methodism **21** *347*
      Protestantism **7** 254, 258–9*, 269–70*, *270*; **12** 373; **30** 431; **31** 166; **33** 278
      Roman Catholicism **7** 257–8*, 262–9*; **16** 11; **20** 155
    Classicism **7** 381
    collections **7** 564
    combs (liturgical) **7** 646
    confessionals **7** 703
    crosses **8** 195
    devotional images **8** 835–6*
    devotional objects **8** 835–6*
    dictionaries of religious art **10** 209, 213
    domes **9** 84
    dress **16** 453
    education (art) **17** 419
    emblem books **10** 175
    embroidery **16** 760
    erotic art **10** 475
    ex-votos **8** 835, 836; **10** 701
    furniture **31** 625
    heraldry **14** 415
    iconography **1** 652; **2** 2, *3*, 237; **5** 443, 807; **6** 293; **7** 219*, 220*, 223–5*, 273, 627; **8** 210–11, 835; **11** 340; **12** 108; **13** 775; **14** 660; **15** 89; **16** 837; **18** 676–7;

Christianity
art
iconography—cont.
19 788, 788; 20 251; 22 411, 412; 24 775; 25 650; 26 329; 27 158–60, 494–6; 28 915–16; 30 707; 32 86
Byzantine 5 677; 7 220–22*; 9 595, 596, 609–10, 616, 622, 623, 624, 625–6, 629, 635; 23 374
Calvinism 5 447
commentaries 16 897
Early Christian (c. AD 250-843) 5 676; 7 219*; 9 595, 596, 609–10, 616, 622, 623, 624, 635; 24 336; 33 215
France 13 179
Germany 2 3; 26 654
Gothic 7 224; 13 73, 127, 128–9*, 129, 131, 179
Lutheranism 19 815
Philippines 24 610*
Post-Byzantine 7 222–3*
Protestantism 7 226–7*
Renaissance 7 225
Roman Catholicism 6 596; 7 225–6*
Romanesque 7 224; 26 605, 616, 651, 654–5*, 702
Spain 26 605
Vietnam 32 470–71
writings 15 881; 26 58
14th cent. 25 679
15th cent. 19 813
18th cent. 8 910
icons 19 788, 788–9
light 28 203; 29 500
liturgical furnishings
Methodism 7 284
Presbyterianism 7 283
Protestantism 7 283–4*
Roman Catholicism 7 280–82*
manuals 15 82*
manuscript illumination 16 455
martyria 20 518
monasteries 7 227–32*
narratives 2 3; 13 129
nude figures 23 291
painting
Eritrea 10 568–73*
Ethiopia 10 568–73*
palladia 19 788
patens 24 255
patronage 7 217*, 218*
plate 10 325
portraits 25 650
prints 5 447; 17 271
propaganda 25 650–51
reliquaries 26 142*
representation 13 128–9, 129
sanctuaries 27 714*
sarcophagi 9 596–7; 27 827
sculpture (general)
Germany 12 403
Lutheranism 12 403
Protestantism 12 402, 403
Roman Catholicism 12 402–3
sculpture (relief)
Byzantine 9 596–7*
Early Christian (c. AD 250-843) 9 596–7*
Germany 12 405
Protestantism 12 402, 405
shrines (i) (cult) 28 629
stelae 22 812
tea ceremonies 17 341
temples 22 126; 30 450
treatises 10 211
vaults (ceiling) 32 86
woodcuts 19 814
branches
Nestorianism 2 252, 273, 273; 6 291–2*, 627; 7 213; 22 811–12*
Orthodox 7 213–14*
Protestantism 7 215, 216*; 10 325; 12 401–3; 23 193–4
Christianity
branches—cont.
Roman Catholicism 6 175; 7 214–16*
cultures and regions
Africa 1 227–8*, 230
Byzantine 9 509
China 6 627
Early Christian (c. AD 250-843) 7 212*; 9 509
England 10 224
Indian subcontinent 14 555; 15 202, 204
Indonesia 15 756
Kongo 1 227
Korea 18 253
Malaysia 20 165
Native North Americans 22 559
Nigeria 1 230
Rome, ancient 26 854, 859, 867
South-east Asia 29 226
Sri Lanka 29 442
Zaïre 1 230
Zambia 1 230
sects
Anglicanism 7 215
Baptists 3 192–3*; 23 193
Calvinism 5 445–7*; 28 915
Christian Scientists 23 194
Church of Jesus Christ of the Latter-Day Saints see Mormons
Congregationalists 3 192–3*; 23 194
Friends, Religious Society of 11 785–6*; 23 193
Herrnhuters see Moravian Brethren
Independents 23 193
Jacobite 9 515
Jansenism 17 1–2*
Lutheranism 19 814–15*; 30 326
Maronite 9 515
Methodism 21 346–7*; 23 193
Monophysitism 7 213
Moravian Brethren 22 80*; 26 529
Mormons 22 125–6*; 30 431, 450
Presbyterianism 5 445; 23 193
Puritans 5 445; 23 193
Quakers see Friends, Religious Society of
Reformed Church 5 445
Renewed Church of the Brethren see Moravian Brethren
Shakers see SHAKERS
Unitarianism 23 194; 31 583–4*
Unitats Fratrum see Moravian Brethren
Christian Ludwig, Duke of Brunswick-Lüneburg (fl c. 1662) 7 538; 33 426
Christian-Ludwig II, Duke of Mecklenburg-Schwerin (reg 1747-56) 8 762; 19 773
Christianou, Hagios Sotirios 9 547
Christiansand 23 220
Christian Scientists see under CHRISTIANITY → sects
Christiansen, Hans 2 566; 8 531; 12 416, 468
Christiansen, Henning 29 98
Christiansen, Ole Kirk 31 259
Christiansen, Poul S(imon) 7 233*
Christiansen, Ursula Reuter see REUTER CHRISTIANSEN, URSULA
Christianshavn 8 725
Vor Frelser 8 725, 726, 739
Christiansson, H. 32 534
Christian von Buch, Provost 19 863
Christie, Adam 'The Highlander' 25 685
Christie, George Henry 7 233
Christie, Harold 3 63, 65
Christie, James, the elder (1730-1803) 2 559; 7 233, 234; 10 366; 19 587; 23 520
Christie, James, the younger (1773-1831) 7 233
Christie, James (fl 1889) 7 233
Christie, James-Cope 33 678
Christie, Manson & Woods 2 559; 5 311; 7 233; 25 213; 32 890
Christie, Sharp & Harper 7 233
Christie & Ansell 7 233
Christie & Manson 7 233; 25 213; 29 88
Christie Painter 13 522
Christie's 2 365, 559, 560–61, 706; 6 81; 7 233–4*; 9 725
catalogues 4 23
Denmark 8 759
England 5 884; 10 677; 15 888
Spain 29 354
Switzerland 30 153
Christie's Pictorial Archive 2 367
Christie-Tyler Ltd 32 789
(Mary) Christina, Duchess and Regent of Savoy (1606-63) 4 543; 28 2, 9–11*
architecture 31 440, 441
paintings 5 406; 9 482
Christina, Queen of Sweden (reg 1632-54) 3 294; 4 574; 7 795; 8 453; 26 771; 30 64, 117; 31 321, 824; 32 7–8*
architecture 8 660; 11 275; 14 388; 15 862; 30 675
books 3 98
collections 2 418, 559; 3 674; 4 538; 9 16; 11 662; 15 148; 19 817; 23 353, 516; 26 773, 774; 27 171; 30 118, 463
drawings 9 229; 20 417
engravings 10 761
gardens 12 135; 21 822
gems 12 266
interior decoration 1 898
manuscripts 19 169
medals 2 43; 20 921, 922; 28 749; 29 29
metalwork 11 714; 16 742
paintings 9 194; 14 381; 21 808; 29 352
flower 28 364
miniatures 7 794; 21 640, 641
mythological 22 312
portraits 33 421
sculpture 2 285; 4 558, 560; 25 645, 812; 29 352; 30 85
silver 9 234
sponsorship 30 522
throne 30 782
Christina of Denmark, Duchess of Milan (fl 1538) 25 280
Christina of Markyate (fl 1120-30) 26 671
Christina of Saxony, Queen of Denmark (1461-1521) 3 768
Christine, Master of 7 235
Christine de Pizan 7 234–6*; 21 578
metalwork 31 841
patrons and collectors 5 208
works 1 654; 7 235; 8 208; 23 679
illustrated 20 647, 647
Christinek, Karl Ludwig 19 563
Christine of Lorraine, Grand Duchess of Tuscany 7 311; 16 745; 25 280
Christ-Janer, Victor 5 531
Christler, Hanns Jacob see KRISTLER, HANS JACOB
Christliche Kunstblätter see KUNST UND KIRCHE
Christmas (family) 10 262
Christmas, Gerard 7 236
Christmas, John 7 236
Christmas, Matthias 7 236
Christmas cards see under CARDS → types
Christo and Jeanne-Claude 7 236–8*; 11 570; 31 615
groups and movements 10 416; 23 261; 28 344
patrons and collectors 14 48; 32 623
works 6 576, 577; 7 237; 18 694, 695; 19 492; 25 619; 28 829; 29 12
Christodoulos 24 263
Christofle 11 622; 24 147; 25 218
collaboration 8 72
groups and movements 11 622, 623
works 5 392; 10 135, 143; 11 621, 622; 28 739
Christofle, Charles 4 308; 11 621, 622, 631; 28 346
Christofle, Paul 11 599
Christol, Frédéric 19 242
Christoph, J. 25 426
Christophe, Ernest-Louis-Aquilas 3 393; 6 121; 7 238*; 10 842
Christophe, Henri, King of Northern Haiti see HENRI CHRISTOPHE, King of Northern Haiti
Christophe, Joseph 5 884
Christopher, Duke of Bavaria (d 1493) 2 452; 5 198
sword 2 453
Christopher, Duke of Württemberg (reg 1550-68) 29 875; 31 311; 33 429
Christopher I, Margrave of Baden (reg 1475-1527) 4 188
Christophersen, Alejandro 2 396; 7 238*
Christophoros, Governor of Longobardia 9 577; 30 724
Christophstal 11 766
Christoph und Unmack 32 750
Christov, Panayot Todorov see SKITNIK, SYRAK
Christow 13 211
Christus, Petrus 3 553; 7 238–40*
attributions 4 590
patrons and collectors 1 154; 19 92; 29 46
pupils 2 178
works 2 339; 3 596; 4 920; 7 239; 11 439, 440
Christy, Henry 11 738; 21 264
Christy, Howard Chandler 25 349, 652
Chrodegang, Saint 21 361
chromatography see under TECHNICAL EXAMINATION → types
chrome orange see under PIGMENTS → types
chrome red see under PIGMENTS → types
chrome yellow see under PIGMENTS → types
chromite 7 241
chromium 7 241*; 31 654
dyeing 9 493
dyes 9 490
electroplating 7 241; 10 135, 136–7*
furniture 7 241
glass 12 782
jewellery 7 241
pigments 24 794*, 799*
chromium oxide green see under PIGMENTS → types
chromium steel 7 241; 9 499; 22 875
bridges 9 499
chairs 22 875
printing plates 10 548
toys 31 257
chromolithography 19 480, 484; 20 603; 25 623; 26 234
historical and regional traditions
Britain 17 639
France 25 620
Germany 19 15
chromolithography
historical and regional traditions—cont.
United States of America 25 449
uses
book illustrations 4 362
dolls 31 259
Chromo-Luminarism 19 355; 25 78
Chromonastiri 8 155
Chromranice 25 102
Chromy, Bronisław 18 429
chronicles 4 358; 7 241–4*, 242, 243; 12 272; 13 130; 21 235; 26 662
individual manuscripts
Alexandrian World Chronicle (Moscow, Pushkin Mus. F.A., MSS 310/7 & 310/8) 7 824
Chronica Hungarorum (Budapest, Szechenyi Lib., Cod. lat. 404) 2 110; 14 898
Chronicle of Manasses (Rome, Vatican, Bib. Apostolica, MS. Slav. 2) 32 149
Skylitzes Chronicle (Madrid, Bib. N., MSS Vitr. 26-7) 7 220
see also HISTORIES
Chroniques de l'art vivant 24 442
Chronograph of 354 see CALENDAR OF AD 354
chronologies 2 299; 30 382
Aegean 25 472
Anatolia, ancient 1 852, 853
Ancient Near East 1 851–3*, 852; 14 335
Celtic 16 830
Chavín culture 6 520–21
China 6 617; 30 848
Crete 14 334; 21 655*, 655
Cycladic 8 307; 14 334
Egypt, ancient 2 300; 9 775, 776; 10 80; 14 335; 25 472
France 25 486
Greece, ancient 13 367
Helladic 14 334, 334–5*, 337*
Indian subcontinent 15 199*
Iran, ancient 1 852, 853
Japan 17 426–7
Mali 21 480
Maya 21 191; 31 507
Mesoamerica, Pre-Columbian 21 191, 191–2*, 262, 263; 31 507
Mesopotamia 1 852, 853; 21 272, 275; 25 472
Middle Niger cultures 21 480*
Minoan 21 655*, 655
Mycenaean 14 334, 334–5*
Native North Americans 22 672
Prehistoric art 2 299; 4 763; 16 830; 25 469–72*, 485, 486
South America, Pre-Columbian 6 520–21; 29 126
South-east Asia 29 231, 241
Syria-Palestine 1 852, 853; 30 181*
United States of America 22 672
chronophotography see under PHOTOGRAPHY → processes
Chrucki, Jan 3 528; 7 244–5*
works 3 529
Chrudim
Museum of Applied Art 8 424
Museum of Puppetry 8 424
Chrysalide, La 7 245*; 8 628; 10 517; 31 884; 32 679
chrysaliform figures see under SCULPTURE → types
Chrysalis 10 878
chryselephantine statues see under SCULPTURE → types
Chrysippus (280-207 BC) 29 694
Chrysippus (fl 1st cent. BC) 26 885
Chrysler, Walter P(ercy) 7 245*
Chrysler Art Museum see under PROVINCETOWN (MA)

Chrysler Building *see under* NEW YORK → skyscrapers
Chrysler Corporation **17** 722
Chrysler Museum *see under* NORFOLK (VA)
chrysoberyl **17** 524
chrysocolla **24** 793
chrysography **7** 245–6*, *246*; **12** 625; **20** 328–9, 367; **25** 742
Chrysolakkos **21** 680, 681, 687
chrysolite **17** *528*
Chrysoloras, Georgios **25** 334
Chrysoloras, Manuel *see* MANUEL CHRYSOLORAS
chrysoprase **16** 857; **17** 524
Chrysostomos Master **18** 411
Chryssa **7** 247*; **13** 355; **22** 748
Chščanovič, Kazimier **3** 527
Chu **7** 247–8*
Chuah Thean Teng **20** 172
Chuang Che **30** 249
Chuang-pai *see* ZHUANGBAI
Chuang Su *see* ZHUANG SU
Chuang-tzu *see* ZHUANGZI
Chūan Shinkō **17** 898
Chū Asai *see* ASAI, CHŪ
Chubb, George **9** 295
Chubbard, Thomas **19** 507
Chubei Tanida *see* TANIDA CHUBEI
Chubotsky, Albert **11** 105
Chubotsky, Fredrik **11** 105
Chubotsky, Nicolaus **11** 105
Chü Ch'ao *see* JU CHAO
Chu Ch'i-chan *see* ZHU QIZHAN
Chu Chien *see* ZHU JIAN
Chu Chih-cheng *see* ZHU ZHIZHENG
Chu Ching-hsüan *see* ZHU JINGXUAN
Chūchū Shūjin *see* ZŌROKU V
Chucuito **24** *498*; **29** 166
La Asunción **24** 500
Chucynski, Varlaam **3** 527
Chudenitz, Humprecht Jan Czernin von, Count *see* CZERNIN VON CHUDENITZ, HUMPRECHT JAN, Count
Chue-cheng, Yang *see* YANG CHUE-CHENG
ch'üeh *see* QUE
Chüeh-hsüeh *see* JUEXUE
Chüeh-lang *see* JUELANG
Chuera, Tell **7** 248*; **30** *180*
temple **30** 191, 432
Chu Foon, Pat **31** 335–6
Ch'ü-fu *see* QUFU
Chufutkale **7** 248–9*; **31** *546*
Chughā Mīsh *see* CHOGHA MISH
Chughā Zanbīl *see* CHOGHA ZANBIL
Chughtai, Abdur Rahman **7** 249*; **23** 799, 804
Chūgūji *see under* IKARUGA
Chu Hao-ku *see* ZHU HAOGU
Chu Ho *see* ZHU HE
Chu Hsi *see* ZHU XI
Chu Hsiao-sung *see* ZHU YING
Chu-hung *see* ZHUHONG
Chūichi Miyake *see* MIYAKE, CHŪICHI
Chuikov, S. A. **18** 568
Chui Tze-hung **14** 722
Chü-jan *see* JURAN
Chūji Hoshiyama *see* HOSHIYAMA CHŪJI
Chu Jui *see* ZHU RUI
Chukchi **27** 436
Chukotka **27** 367
Chukovsky, Korney **8** 250; **18** 474
Chuksŏ *see* KIM (i) SIK
Chu Kui *see* ZHU GUI
Chukuli Church **12** 322
Chukwa *see* YI (i) U
Chulalongkorn, King (Rama V; *reg* 1868–1910) (chakri) **16** 874; **30** 590, 593, 607, 608, 616, 622, 632
Chulatus **22** 589
Chü Lien *see* JU LIAN
Chulkov, Pyotr (Ivanovich) **27** 425
chullpas **31** 47, *47*
Chulmun ware *see under* POTTERY → wares
Chuluut **21** 882
Chumash **22** 550, 652, 655, 659; **27** 727
Chu Ming **7** 249*
Chunar
fort **15** 368
painting **15** 603
portal **15** 369
sandstone **15** 414
tomb of Iftikhar Khan **15** 369
Chungal 3 **1** *371*, *375*
Chungchong, Independence Hall **18** 264
Chung-feng Ming-pen *see* ZHONGFENG MINGBEN
Chunghu *see* KIM (i) SIK
Ch'unghyo-dong **18** 273, 342
sculpture **18** *298*
Chung-jen *see* ZHONGREN
Chungjong, King (*reg* 1506–44) **18** 300
Ch'ungju
Taewon Temple **18** 291
Tanho Temple **18** 291
Chung Li *see* ZHONG LI
Ch'un'gok *see* KO HŬI-DONG
Ch'ung-sŏn, King (*reg* 1308–18) **18** 324
Chung-ting *see* ZHONGDING
Chungwŏn **18** 327
Chung-yen *see* ZHONGYAN
Ch'ungyŏl, King (*reg* 1257–1308) **18** 339
Chung Yu *see* ZHONG YOU
Chunhua **7** 21
Chunnakam **16** 864
Chūō bijutsu **24** 436
Chu Pang *see* ZHU BANG
Chupícuaro **7** 250*; **21** *193*, 250, *372*
ceramics **33** 101, 102
figurines **33** *102*
pottery **7** 250
Chu Pi-shan *see* ZHU BISHAN
Chü Po-ya *see* JU BOYA
chuppah **17** 575*
Chuprasov, A. **27** 425
Chuquisaca *see* SUCRE
Chur **7** 250–51*; **26** *905*; **30** *124*
Cathedral of St Lucius **7** 251*; **26** 575; **30** 126
liturgical furnishings **26** 620
sculpture **26** 635
textiles **18** 157
pewter **30** 147
sculpture **30** 136
silk **9** 663
Churajón **31** 47
Churberg, Fanny (Maria) **7** 251*; **11** 95
Churburg, Schloss *see* SCHLOSS CHURBURG
Churbury, Edward Herbert, 1st Baron of *see* HERBERT, EDWARD, 1st Baron of Churbury
Church, Barbara **19** 41
Church, Frederick Edwin **7** 284–6*; **16** 884; **19** 889; **29** 671; **31** 603
dealers **18** 161
groups and movements **14** 843; **23** 504; **25** 629; **31** 602
patrons and collectors **29** 651, 870; **32** 753, 829
teachers **7** 549
works **7** *285*; **18** 715; **20** 425; **23** 46; **31** *602*
Church, Henry **19** 41
Church, John **15** 57
Church, Thomas D(olliver) **7** 286*; **12** 143; **14** 90
church-chairs *see under* CHAIRS → types
churches **6** 165; **7** 251–77*; **9** 12; **20** 559; **31** 710
acoustics **1** 122, 123*
decoration **7** 270*, 274–5*, 276–7*
decoration (art forms)
bricklaying **7** 273–4*, *273*
mosaics **7** 272*, 273*, 275*
Byzantine **7** 272–3*
Early Christian (*c.* AD 250–843) **7** 271, 272
Italy **7** 275
painting **7** 272*, 273*, 275*; **9** 13–20
Austria **7** *274*
Byzantine **7** 272–3*
Cappadocia **5** 676–8*
Denmark **8** 729–30
Georgia **12** 323–4
Gothic **7** *274*
Italy **7** 275
Poland **8** *590*
Romania **26** 710, 712
Sweden **30** 75–7
sculpture **7** 275*
Armenia (Europe) **7** 274
Byzantine **7** 273–4*
Georgia **7** 274; **12** 321–2
Italy **7** *276*
Romania **26** 711–12
Russia **7** 274
Ukraine **7** 274
stained glass **7** 275*; **29** 500
tiles **7** 275*
decoration (cultures and regions)
Byzantine **7** 272*; **9** 518, 576
Early Christian (*c.* AD 250–843) **7** 270–72*; **9** 518
Georgia **7** 273
Iceland **32** 517
Russia **7** 273
Scandinavia **32** 517
Viking **32** 517
historical and regional traditions
Africa **1** *314*, 314–15
Albania **1** 538, 541–2
Anglo-Saxon **2** 65–7, *65*, *66*, *67*; **10** 227; **21** *887*
Antilles, Lesser **2** 148
Arabia **2** 252*
Armenia (Europe) **2** 425–8, 429–30, 433–5; **7** 261–2; **9** 731; **30** 360
Early Christian (*c.* AD 250–843) **9** *731*, *732*
6th cent. AD **23** *355*
7th cent. AD **2** *426*
10th cent. AD **2** *434*
17th cent. **9** 732
Australia **2** *741*
Austria **2** 776–7, 779–81, 784–5
Baroque **2** *781*, *782*; **5** *772*; **11** *133*; **19** *433*; **25** *448*; **28** *184*
Gothic **2** *777*; **14** *309*
19th cent. **11** *30*
20th cent. **2** *789*; **25** 37
Barnabites **3** *249*
Belarus' **3** 526, *526*
Belgium
Baroque **3** *546*
Carolingian **3** 541
Gothic **2** 191, *202*; **3** 542, *543*
Gothic Revival **3** *548*; **13** *208*
Romanesque **12** 520; **23** *164*
Benedictine Order **4** *869*; **17** *685*
Bolivia **4** 256–7, 258–9
Brazil **4** 707, *710*; **19** *460*; **23** *118*
Brigittine Order **31** *794*, 794–5
Bulgaria **5** *145*, 145–7, 148–9; **9** 551–2; **25** 559
Byzantine **7** 260–62*; **9** 85, 522, 523–4, 526, 527, 528, *529*, 536–7, 542*, 543–7*, 549, 550–53, 588
Bulgaria **9** 551–2
Cappadocia **7** 261; **9** 536
churches
historical and regional traditions
Byzantine—cont.
Georgia **7** 262; **9** 548–9; **30** *305*, *306*
Greece **7** *260*; **9** 542*, 545–7*, *546*, *547*, 550–51, *551*, *552*; **14** *776*; **17** *839*; **18** 571; **21** *860*; **30** *725*
Mesopotamia **9** 538–41*, 542–3*
Palestine **9** 538–41*, *541*, 542–3*, 547–9*, *548*
Russia **7** 261
Serbia **9** 552–3; **13** *264*
Sicily **23** *846*
Syria **7** 261; **9** 538–41*, *539*, *540*, 542–3*, 547–9*
Turkey **4** *771*; **8** *777*; **9** 536–7, 543–5*, *545*, 549–50
Ukraine **31** *547*, *548*
Canada **3** *73*
Cappadocia **5** 675*, 676; **7** 261; **9** 536
Capuchins **5** *690*
Carolingian **3** 541; **7** 263–5*
France **12** *484*
Germany **5** *795*; **26** *100*, *101*
Catalonia **5** *734*; **12** *182*
Central Asia, Western **6** 200
China **6** 677–8*, *678*
Cistercian Order **4** *778*; **7** *347*, 371; **18** 621
Colombia **4** *233*; **7** 604
Coptic **7** 262*, *820*, 820–21*
Costa Rica **8** 16
Crete **8** 156–7
Croatia **8** 175, *176*; **33** *592*
Cyprus **8** *357*, 357–8, 361–3*, *362*
Czech Republic
Baroque **8** *378*, *874*, *876*; **18** *505*, *506*; **25** *428*
Gothic **17** *585*; **18** *539*
14th cent. **24** *190*
18th cent. **27** *798*
Denmark **8** 719, 721–3, *726*; **27** 167
Neo-classicism **14** *153*
Rococo **10** *111*
Romanesque **8** *722*; **26** *593*
20th cent. **4** *789*
Early Christian (*c.* AD 250–843) **7** *259*, 259–60*; **9** 522, 523–4, 528–35*, *529*, 536–7, 538*, 542*, 588
Armenia (Europe) **9** *731*, *732*
Bulgaria **5** *145*; **25** 559
Cappadocia **9** 536
Greece **9** 538*, 542*, *542*
Italy **9** 528–34*, *530*, *532*, *533*; **13** *266*; **16** *624*; **21** *537*; **26** *829*, *835*; **29** *421*
Mesopotamia **9** 538–41*, 542–3*; **31** *435*
Palestine **3** *882*; **9** 538–41*, *541*, 542–3*
Roman **26** 859
Syria **7** 259, 260; **9** 538–41*, *539*, *540*, 542–3*
Turkey **9** *525*, 536–7; **31** *435*
Egypt **7** *820*, 820–21*
El Salvador **10** *154*
England **2** 372; **5** 890; **10** 224, 226, 229, 232, 359; **18** 621; **23** 194; **30** 654
Anglicanism **25** 266
Anglo-Saxon **2** *65*, 65–7, *66*, *67*; **10** 227; **21** *887*
Arts and Crafts Movement **19** *253*
Baroque **10** *232*; **12** *593*; **14** *256*; **33** *394*, *395*
Gothic **5** *287*; **12** *800*; **13** *46*, *55*, 55–6; **23** *685*
Gothic: Late Gothic **12** *818*, *819*
churches
historical and regional traditions
England—cont.
Gothic: Perpendicular style **10** *229*
Gothic Revival **4** *215*; **5** *314*; **24** *307*; **25** *714*; **29** *765*; **30** *533*
Methodism **21** *347*
Neo-classicism **8** *493*
Romanesque **10** 227–9, *228*; **12** 818; **19** *601*, *617*; **23** *685*; **26** *589*
17th cent. **17** *636*
19th cent. **30** *502*
Eritrea **10** 565–6
Estonia **30** *276*
Ethiopia **1** *314*, 314–15; **10** 565–6
Finland **11** *88*, 89–90*, 91*
France **3** 125; **7** 693
Baroque **20** *294*; **24** *164*
Benedictine Order **4** *869*; **17** *685*
Carolingian **12** *484*
Gothic **5** *728*; **7** *578*; **13** *38*, *42*, *60*, 178; **24** *156*; **25** *220*; **26** *121*; **27** *253*, *541*, *542*; **31** *206*
Gothic: Early Gothic **27** *533*
Gothic: Flamboyant style **13** *59*
Gothic: Rayonnant style **31** *385*
Gothic Revival **13** *202*
Gothic survival **13** *211*
Knights Templar **18** *154*
Neo-classicism **6** *397*; **26** *13*; **29** *93*
Protestantism **30** 431
Romanesque **5** *370*, *371*; **7** *232*; **11** *529*; **17** *685*; **19** *527*; **23** *14*; **24** *103*; **25** *87*; **26** *122*; **31** *207*, *209*, 224; **32** *396*, *464*
17th cent. **11** *516*; **19** *135*; **20** *289*
18th cent. **7** 840; **28** *486*
19th cent. **11** 520, *525*; **14** *593*; **32** *84*
Franciscan Order **11** 711–12; **13** 51; **24** *94*
Georgia **12** 318–20
Byzantine **7** 262; **9** 548–9; **30** *305*, *306*
6th cent. AD **12** *318*; **22** *251*
10th cent. AD **4** *34*
12th cent. **31** *907*
13th cent. **18** *69*; **30** *388*
Germany **4** 776–7; **8** *531*; **11** *45*; **12** 370, 371–2; **14** *101*, *569*
Baroque **2** *584*; **8** *873*, *875*; **23** *473*; **24** *562*; **32** *822*
Carolingian **5** *795*; **26** *100*, *101*
Gothic **4** *191*; **8** *906*; **10** *408*, *451*, *515*; **11** *733*; **13** *49*, *57*; **18** *724*; **19** *745*; **20** *379*; **23** *314*, *316*; **31** *327*, *567*; **33** *457*
Gothic: Late Gothic **18** *828*; **23** *205*
Gothic Revival **13** *200*
Greek Revival **25** *366*
Modernism **3** *292*
Neo-classicism **16** *804*; **33** *39*
Oratorians **23** *473*
Protestantism **12** 373; **31** 166; **33** 278
Rococo **12** *372*; **26** *497*, 497–8; **32** *467*; **33** *683*
Roman **12** 362
Romanesque **1** *723*; **7** *591*, *594*; **9** *688*; **14** *533*, *534*; **17** *483*; **26** *572*, *573*
17th cent. **3** *67*, *229*; **28** *88*
18th cent. **4** *235*; **11** *125*, *126*; **30** *791*

churches
historical and regional traditions—cont.
Gothic **1** 123; **7** 267–8*; **13** 53, 132, 210; **29** 902
Austria **2** *777*; **14** *309*
Belgium **2** 191, *202*; **3** 542, *543*
Czech Republic **17** *585*; **18** *539*
England **5** *287*; **12** *800*; **13** *46*, *55*, 55–6; **23** *685*
England: Late Gothic **12** *818*, *819*
England: Perpendicular style **10** *229*
France **5** *728*; **7** *578*; **13** *38*, *42*, *60*, 178; **24** *156*; **25** *220*; **26** *121*; **27** *253*, *541*, *542*; **31** *206*
France: Early Gothic **27** *533*
France: Flamboyant style **13** *59*
Germany **4** *191*; **8** *906*; **10** *408*, *451*, *515*; **11** *733*; **13** *49*, *57*; **18** *724*; **19** *745*; **20** *379*; **23** *314*, *316*; **31** *327*, *567*; **33** *457*
Germany: Late Gothic **18** *828*; **23** *205*
Hungary **14** *886*; **29** *75*
Italy **4** *279*; **7** *347*; **13** *52*; **22** *483*; **32** *215*
Lithuania **19** *495*
Netherlands, the **1** *812*; **13** *61*; **19** *100*; **22** *820*
Poland **5** *28*; **6** *531*; **8** *590*
Portugal **25** *290*; **31** *102*
Slovakia **3** *224*
Slovenia **28** *859*
Spain **3** *215*; **12** 619–20; **13** *70*
Greece **2** 509; **9** 542*
Byzantine **7** *260*; **9** 542*, 545–7*, *546*, *547*, 550–51, *551*, *552*; **14** *776*; **17** *839*; **18** 571; **21** *860*; **30** *725*
Early Christian (*c.* AD 250-843) **9** 538*, *542*, 542*
Guatemala **13** *761*
Hungary **14** *886*; **16** *872*; **29** *75*
Indian subcontinent **7** 494; **15** 524
Ireland **2** 72; **16** 7, 10–11
Gothic Revival **16** *10*
Roman Catholicism **16** 11
Romanesque **12** *807*
20th cent. **7** *269*
Italy **2** 365; **4** 774–5; **8** *188*
Barnabites **3** *249*
Baroque **3** *249*, *355*; **4** *430*, *431*, *432*, *435*; **7** *912*; **9** *339*; **11** *275*; **13** *750*; **16** 638, *638*, *641*; **17** *707*, *708*; **19** *28*, *628*, *629*, *634*; **20** *44*; **23** *331*; **25** *886*; **26** *318*, *758*, *759*, *760*, *807*, *823*; **28** *735*; **29** *80*; **31** *674*; **32** *644*
Capuchins **5** *690*
Cistercian Order **7** *347*
Early Christian (*c.* AD 250-843) **9** 529–34*, *530*, *532*, *533*; **13** *266*; **16** *624*; **21** *537*; **26** *829*, *835*; **29** *421*
Gothic **4** *279*; **7** *347*; **11** *205*; **13** *52*; **22** *483*; **32** *215*
Lazio **7** 918
Mannerism **16** *636*; **23** *869*; **30** *802*; **32** *214*
Neo-classicism **31** *800*
Palladianism **30** *424*
Post-modernism **25** *272*
Renaissance **1** *564*, *566*, *567*, *606*; **3** *385*, *772*; **4** *644*, 652; **7** *516*; **11** *202*, *207*, *209*, *689*, *690*; **21** *470*, *516*; **24** *196*; **27** *734*, *735*, *739*, *743*; **31** *278*; **32** *630*

churches
historical and regional traditions
Italy—cont.
Renaissance: Early Renaissance **5** *16*, *17*; **16** *631*; **26** *183*
Renaissance: High Renaissance **16** *633*
Romanesque **2** *389*; **3** *235*; **4** *281*, *748*; **11** *210*; **16** *626*; **21** *535*; **26** *577*, *833*; **31** *316*
6th cent. AD **26** *34*, *35*, *36*
13th cent. **23** *755*
15th cent. **19** *554*; **27** *191*
16th cent. **25** *260*; **26** *806*; **32** *503*, *631*
17th cent. **7** *781*; **10** *801*; **25** *861*, *862*
18th cent. **11** *815*; **12** *8*
19th cent. **22** *473*
Knights Templar **18** *154*
Lithuania **19** 495, *495*, *496*
Lutheranism **19** 815
Macedonia (ii) (former Yugoslavia) **19** *883*
Malaysia **20** 155
Mesopotamia **9** 538–41*, 542–3*; **31** *435*
Mexico **5** *603*; **25** II1; **31** *65*
Native North Americans **22** 567
Netherlands, the **2** *192*
Cistercian Order **4** *778*
Gothic **1** *812*; **13** *61*; **19** *100*; **22** *820*
Gothic Revival **8** *299*
Romanesque **19** 862; **22** *816*, *818*
New Zealand **23** 53, *53*
North Africa **9** 535*
Norway **23** 219, 220; **32** 532
Nubia **23** 287–8
Oratorians **23** *473*
Ottonian **14** *533*, *534*
Palestine **3** *882*; **9** 538–41*, *541*, 542–3*, 547–9*, *548*; **17** *499*
Paraguay **24** *94*, 94–5, *96*
Paulist Fathers **24** *281*
Peru **2** *386*; **24** 500–504
Philippines **24** 611, *612*, *613*
Poland **25** 94–5, 96, 98, 128
Baroque **32** 895
Gothic **5** *28*; **6** *531*; **8** *590*
Romanesque **29** *793*
14th cent. **4** *782*
16th cent. **25** *96*
Portugal
Baroque **2** *189*; **13** *751*; **25** *292*; **28** *911*
China **19** *866*
Gothic **25** *290*; **31** *102*
Mannerism **10** *664*
Manueline style **4** *245*
Neo-classicism **4** *629*
Romanesque **25** 289
16th cent. **2** *500*; **30** *518*; **31** 179
17th cent. **1** *740*
Post-Byzantine **18** *207*
Protestantism **7** *270*; **31** 166
Roman Catholicism **16** 11
Romanesque **7** 265–6*
Belgium **12** 520; **23** *164*
Catalonia **5** *734*
Denmark **8** *722*; **26** *593*
England **10** 227–9, *228*; **12** 818; **19** *601*, *617*; **23** *685*; **26** *589*
France **5** *370*, *371*; **7** *232*; **11** *529*; **17** *685*; **19** *527*; **23** *14*; **24** *103*; **25** *87*; **26** *122*; **31** *208*, *209*, *224*, 224; **32** *396*, *464*
Germany **1** *723*; **7** *591*, *594*; **9** *688*; **14** *533*, *534*; **17** *483*; **26** *572*, *573*
Hungary **16** *872*
Ireland **12** *807*

churches
historical and regional traditions
Romanesque—cont.
Italy **2** *389*; **3** *235*; **4** *281*, *748*; **11** *210*; **16** *626*; **21** *535*; **26** *577*, *833*; **31** *316*
Netherlands, the **19** 862; **22** *816*, *818*
Palestine **17** *499*
Poland **29** *793*
Portugal **25** 289
Scotland **27** *529*; **28** *223*
Spain **19** *175*, *520*
Romania **5** *72*; **8** 279; **26** 706, *706*, 707, 708
17th cent. **26** *708*
Rome, ancient **12** 362; **26** 859; **27** 60
Russia **27** 368–73, 374
Baroque **27** *374*; **31** *318*
Byzantine **7** 261; **25** *680*
Post-Byzantine **18** *207*
Slav Revival **28** *837*
12th cent. **32** *663*
14th cent. **23** *269*; **27** *370*
16th cent. **22** *170*
17th cent. **33** *507*
Sardinia **27** 836
Scandinavia **4** 780–81; **32** 532
Scotland **27** *171*, *529*; **28** *223*, 223–4, 227, 230–31; **30** *751*
Serbia **9** 552–3; **13** *264*; **28** 440–42, *441*, *442*
Sicily **16** *640*; **23** *846*
Slovakia **3** *224*; **28** 848, 849, *850*; **31** *353*
Slovenia **28** *859*
Spain **29** 261, 311
Gothic **3** *215*; **12** 619–20; **13** *70*
Plateresque style **14** 662
Renaissance **14** *473*; **23** *625*; **29** *266*, *268*
Romanesque **19** *175*, *520*
United States of America **31** *589*
Visigothic **29** 261
9th cent. AD **2** *652*, *653*; **29** *262*
10th cent. AD **27** *763*
16th cent. **10** *502*; **31** *93*, *865*
18th cent. **7** *288*
Sweden **30** 66–7, *71*; **31** *794*
Switzerland **22** 186, *186*; **30** *126*
Syria **7** 259, 260, 261; **9** 538–41*, *539*, *540*, 542–3*, 547–9*
Turkey **4** *771*; **8** *777*; **9** *525*, 536–7; **31** *435*
Byzantine **9** 543–5*, *545*, 549–50
Ukraine **18** *36*; **31** 547, *547*, 548, *548*, 550, *552*, 552–4*, *553*
United States of America **31** 588, 589, 592
Colonial period **31** *589*
Gothic Revival **8** *110*; **12** *927*; **24** *281*; **31** *690*
Greek Revival **21** *617*
Native North Americans **22** 567
Neo-classicism **5** *143*; **24** *209*
Paulist Fathers **24** *281*
Rundbogenstil **31** *691*
19th cent. **18** *845*; **26** *339*
20th cent. **33** *402*, *403*
Venetian Empire **8** 156–7
Venezuela **5** *692*; **32** 167–8
Vietnam **32** 476, *476*
Viking **8** 721; **32** 532
Visigothic **29** 261
lighting **19** 362, *363*, *364*, 365, *368*
materials
basalt **9** 538
brick **4** *771*, 774–5, 780–81; **26** 706

churches
materials—cont.
concrete **7** 693; **22** 186; **25** 37
granite **11** *88*
iron **3** 125
limestone **9** 538
marble **9** 588; **13** 44
stone **4** 776; **9** 538; **27** 167; **31** 547
terracotta **30** *502*
wood **2** 67; **12** 362; **23** *53*; **25** *96*; **26** 706; **29** 579
types
ambulatory basilicas **9** 530, *530*
atrophied free cross **9** 544
basilicas **3** 329*; **7** 252*, 253–4*
Armenia (Europe) **2** 425–6
Byzantine **7** 252–3*; **8** 155; **9** 525, 528, 535*, 536–7, *537*, 542, 544, 547
Crete **8** 155
Cyprus **8** *357*, 357–8
Denmark **8** 723
Early Christian (*c.* AD 250-843) **7** 252*, *252*, 325; **9** 525, 527, 528, 529–32*, *533*, 533–4*, 536–7, *537*, 538*, 542, *542*; **26** 569, 798
England **33** 230
France **7** *253*
Georgia **12** *318*, 318
Gothic **19** *686*
Greece **3** 329; **9** 538*, *542*, 547
Italy **7** *252*, 325; **9** 529–32*, *533*, 533–4*; **19** *686*
North Africa **9** 533, 535*
Poland **25** 95
Portugal **20** *85*
Rhodes (island) **26** 293
Romanesque **7** *253*
Romania **26** 706
Syria **3** 329
Turkey **9** 536–7, *537*, 542, 544
centrally planned **7** 254*, 256–7*; **26** 752
Armenia (Europe) **7** 256
Byzantine **7** 255–6*; **16** 602–3
Carolingian **7** 256
Denmark **7** 257
Early Christian (*c.* AD 250-843) **7** 254–5*, *255*
Georgia **7** 256
Italy **7** *255*, 257; **16** 629, 632, 637
Knights Templar **7** 257, *257*
Portugal **7** *257*
Protestantism **7** 258–9*
Roman Catholicism **7** 257–8*
Romanesque **7** 257
Russia **7** 256
Switzerland **3** 886
Syria **7** 255
see also ROTUNDAS
circular **26** 752
compact-domed basilicas **7** 252; **9** 542
cross-domed **7** 256; **9** 542, *542*, 544
cross-in-square **7** 256, 260; **9** 543–4, 545–6
Greece **9** 545–6, *546*
Turkey **9** *545*
cross-vaulted **7** 253
cruciform **9** 731; **26** 212
domed **12** 319
domed basilicas **9** 537, 544
domed octagon **7** 170; **9** 547
domus ecclesiae **9** 416; **26** 752
eight-on-four **22** 170
fortified **26** 707
Greek-cross octagon **9** 546–7, *547*; **14** 776
hall **7** 254; **14** 80–82*; **20** 565–6; **29** 65; **32** 90
Austria **32** 450, 452
Denmark **8** 723; **13** 50
France **14** 80, *82*; **26** 585

churches
types
hall—cont.
Germany **2** *118*; **4** *665*; **5** *76*; **13** 49, *49*, 58; **14** 80, 81, *81*, 157; **19** 29; **23** *205*; **28** 497; **29** *5*
Gothic **13** 49, *49*, 50, *52*, 58; **23** *205*; **29** *5*
Italy **13** *52*
Poland **25** 96, 134
Romanesque **26** 585
Romania **26** 707
house *see* domus ecclesiae
pilgrimage **13** *761*; **27** 794
quatrefoil *see* tetraconch
rock **26** 483–4*
Bulgaria **26** 483
Byzantine **5** *674*, 674–5*; **26** 483
Cappadocia **5** *674*, 674–5*, 676; **26** 483
Early Christian (*c.* AD 250-843) **26** 483
Ethiopia **10** 565–6, *566*; **26** 484
Greece **26** 483
Italy **26** 483
Jordan **26** 483
Romania **26** 483
Turkey **26** *484*
Saalkirchen **29** 579
sepulchre **28** *427*, 427–9*, *428*
Staffelkirche *see* hall
stave **23** 217, 219, 228; **29** 579–81*, *579*, *580*; **30** 894
Stufenhalle *see* hall
tetraconch **7** 255; **22** 170
tituli **9** 529–30; **26** 752
transept basilicas **9** 538; **31** 281
trefoil *see* triconch
triconch **7** 255
wall-pillar **32** 821–3*, *822*
see also CHAPELS; CHAPTERHOUSES; GALILEES; MONASTERIES; WESTWORKS
Churchill (Australia) **23** 679
Churchill (family) **4** 209
Churchill, George **4** 232
Churchill, Henrietta, Duchess of Marlborough **25** 277
Churchill, Jennie, Lady **30** 367
Churchill, J. F. **29** 454
Churchill, John, 1st Duke of Marlborough **7** 286–7*; **27** *467*
architecture **4** 137; **31** 859
decorative works **18** 644
paintings **10** 364; **24** 633; **30** 759
sculpture **29** 30; **32** 236
Churchill, Louis **19** 6
Churchill, Mary **7** 290
Churchill, Sarah, Duchess of Marlborough **4** 138; **14** 257; **29** 381
architecture **7** 287; **14** 436
furniture **10** 292
gardens **4** 805
paintings **18** 146, 644; **29** 381
Churchill, Sidney **16** 554
Churchill, Winston **23** 102
Churchill Album *see under* ALBUMS → individual manuscripts
church interiors *see* LITURGICAL FURNISHINGS
church labyrinths *see under* LABYRINTHS → types
Church of Abba Antonios **10** 572
Church of Abreha Asbeha **10** 565, 573
Church of Debre Berhan Sellasé **10** 572
Church of Genneta Maryam **10** 568
Church of Jesus Christ of the Latter-Day Saints *see* CHRISTIANITY → sects → Mormons
Church of Kidane Mehret **10** 572, *573*

Church of Medhane 'Alem **10** 565
Church of Mika'el Ambo **10** 565
Church of the Virgin (Panagia) of Kera **8** 156
Church of World Messianity **17** 430, 433
Church of Yemrehenna Krestos **10** 565
church plate *see* PLATE (CHURCH)
Church Sermon, Master of the **1** 167
Churchyard Pottery **33** 20
churchyards *see* CEMETERIES
Churlyonis, Mykolas K(onstantinas) *see* ČIURLIONIS, M(IKALOJUS) K(ONSTANTINAS)
Churriguera (family) **7** 289, 290; **29** 292, 317
Churriguera, Alberto de **7** 287, 288–9*
works **7** 287; **12** 56; **14** 475; **27** 603, 605, 606; **29** 270; **31** 823
Churriguera, Jerónimo **7** 287
Churriguera, Joaquín de **7** 287, 288*
works **7** 288; **27** 603, 605, 606; **28** 689
Churriguera, José Benito de **7** 287–90*; **21** 377
architecture **6** *71*, 72; **7** *288*; **29** 270; **32** 564
collaboration **11** 491
groups and movements **7** 290
patrons and collectors **9** 112
pupils **7** 288
retables **7** 524; **11** *492*; **20** 67; **26** 250, *251*; **27** 603; **29** 292, 841
Churriguera, José de Larra *see* LARRA CHURRIGUERA, JOSÉ DE
Churriguera, José Simón de **7** 287
Churriguera, Manuel de Larra *see* LARRA CHURRIGUERA, MANUEL DE
Churriguera, Nicolás **7** 287
Churrigueresque **7** 287, 289–90*; **9** 711; **21** 377; **29** 292
architecture **7** *289*; **27** *794*
Churubusco, Museo Histórico **21** 396
Chūryō Satō *see* SATŌ, CHŪRYŌ
Ch'usa *see* KIM CHŎNG-HŬI
Chu San-sung *see* ZHU ZHIZHENG
Chūshin Zekkai *see* ZEKKAI CHŪSHIN
Chu Shou-ch'eng *see* ZHU SHOUCHENG
Chusini, Silvio *see* COSINI, SILVIO
Chūsonji *see under* HIRAIZUMI
Chu Suiliang **6** 745–6, 767; **7** 290*; **30** 251
patrons and collectors **32** 836
Chu Ta *see* ZHU DA
Chūta Itō *see* ITŌ, CHŪTA
Chu T'an *see* ZHU TAN
Chute, Chaloner **33** 10
Chute, Charles Leonard **7** 291
Chute, Desmond Macready **12** 631; **17** 631
Chute, John **7** 290–91*
architecture **32** 824, 825, *826*
collaboration **21** 607
glass **13** 302
groups and movements **13** 199
Chu Te-jun *see* ZHU DERUN
Chu Tuan *see* ZHU DUAN
Chu Tz'u-ch'i *see* ZHU CIQI
Chu'ü-chia-ling *see* QUJIALING CULTURE
Chuuk **21** 476, 477; **23** *711*, 723, 726
Chuva, Ângelo **10** 729
Chuvanov, Mikhail **27** 440, 441
Chuvash **27** 434
Chuvash Republic **27** *363*, 434
Chu Wang zhan **6** 852, *852*
Chu Wei-pi *see* ZHU WEIBI
Chu Yen *see* ZHU YAN
Chuyet Cong **32** 479
Chu Ying *see* ZHU YING
Chuykov, Ivan **27** 397
Chuykov, Semyon (Afanas'yevich) **7** 291*
Ch'ü Yüan *see* QU YUAN
Chu Yüan-chang *see* HONGWU EMPEROR
Chu Yün-ming *see* ZHU YUNMING
Chuzhak, Nikolay (Fyodorovich) **7** 291*
Chwala **25** 674
Chwast, Seymour **4** 369; **7** 292*; **12** 772; **25** 354
Chwátal, Martin Ferdinand *see* QUADAL, MARTIN FERDINAND
Ch'wi ch'u *see* CHO SOK
Ch'wimyŏn *see* KIM (I) CHE
Ch'wi Ong *see* CHO SOK
Chwistek, Leon **7** 292*; **11** 317; **18** 434; **25** 108
Chytil, K. **8** 426
Chytraeus, David **2** 793
Chyutin, Bracha **10** 719
Chzheshi *see* CHACH
Ciaccheri, Antonio Manetti **21** 468
Ciacchi, Jacopo **16** 729
Ciaccono, Alfonso *see* CHACÓN, ALONSO
Ciaffaroni **8** 267
Ciai (family) **11** 206
CIAM **2** 318; **4** 577; **6** 445; **7** 292–6*, *294*, *295*; **11** 526; **12** 601; **14** 24, 890; **15** 885; **20** 437; **21** 782; **28** 889; **29** 531; **30** 199, 391; **31** 730
Austria **2** 789
Belgium **4** 577, 628; **8** 633
Brazil **19** 272; **32** 624, 855
Britain **20** 475
Croatia **15** 66
Czechoslovakia **3** 736; **7** 182; **11** 812; **18** 445; **27** 283
England **28** 548; **33** 552
Finland **1** 8
France **4** 214; **5** 609; **12** 871; **13** 798; **19** 809; **22** 110
Germany **7** 344; **9** 60; **14** 176
Greece **8** 815; **17** 808
Hungary **8** 562; **11** 128; **20** 143; **21** 824
Italy **3** 438; **8** 600; **11** 62; **12** 59; **16** 649; **27** 853
Mexico **6** 365
Netherlands, the **4** 216; **9** 746; **10** 715; **19** 540; **21** 156; **26** 379; **31** 867
Norway **10** 857; **18** 390
Poland **30** 199
Russia **18** 205
South Africa **20** 484
Spain **12** 58, 177; **28** 483; **31** 184
Switzerland **2** 513; **4** 60; **7** 343; **21** 408; **22** 187; **27** 214; **29** 603; **30** 128
United States of America **14** 194
CIAM IV **15** 886
Ciambella, Giovanni di Francesco **10** 651; **24** 831
Ciamberlano, Luca **1** 842; **7** 906
Ciaminghi, Francesco **6** 86; **11** 23; **12** 547; **24** 696
CIAM-Ost **7** 294; **21** 824
Ciampanti, Ansano di Michele **7** 296*; **20** 771
Ciampanti, Michele **6** 5; **7** 296*; **20** 770
Ciampelli, Agostino **7** 297*; **31** 55
collaboration **3** 101; **7** 906; **26** 823
patrons and collectors **1** 595; **26** 834
Ciampi, Mario **22** 367; **24** 281
Ciampini, Giovanni **22** 161; **26** 830, 849
Cianfanini, Benedetto **3** 307
Ciani, Zanobio **22** 481
Ciani brothers **32** 121
Ciano profumiere *see* BASTIANO DI FRANCESCO D'JACOPO
Ciaran, Saint **7** 458
Ciardi, Guglielmo **32** 197
Ciarpi, Baccio **7** 906
Ciartres, François *see* LANGLOIS, FRANÇOIS
Cibachrome *see under* PHOTOGRAPHY → processes
Cibber, Caius Gabriel **7** 297–9*
assistants **4** 79
patrons and collectors **6** 116, 515
reproductive prints by others **18** 73
works **2** 657; **10** 263, 264; **14** 784
Cibei, Giovanni Antonio *see* CYBEI, GIOVANNI ANTONIO
Cibic, Aldo **29** 90
Cibiniensis, Vincentius *see* VINCENTIUS CIBINIENSIS
Cibo (family) **19** 430
Cibo,Giovanni Battista *see* INNOCENT VIII, Pope
Cibo, Innocenzo **6** 139
Cibodas **12** 103
Ciboney
Antilles, Lesser **2** 145
Cuba (Caribbean) **8** 228
rock art **8** *229*
Dominican Republic **9** 113
Haiti **14** 54
ciboria (i) (vessels) **7** 299–301*
historical and regional traditions
Byzantine **9** 656
Canada **5** *585*
Early Christian (*c.* AD 250-843) **9** 656
Germany **12** 442
Gothic **7** *300*
Netherlands, the **7** 300
Russia **7** 301
materials
gold **5** *585*
silver **9** 656
silver-gilt **7** *300*
ciboria (ii) (structure) **1** 695, 698, 707; **7** 301–4*
Belgium **7** 303
Byzantine **7** 301–2*
Carolingian **5** 796, 808
Early Christian (*c.* AD 250-843) **7** *278*, 301–2*, *302*; **28** 630
Germany **7** 303
Greece **7** *278*
Italy **1** *695*; **7** *302*, *303*
see also BALDACCHINOS
Cibot, (François-Barthélemy-Michel-)Edouard **7** 304*
Cibulka **8** 379
Cibulka, Heinz **1** 513; **28** 192
Cicala, Nicola **5** 650
Cicarelli, Alessandro **6** 596; **27** 792
cicatrices **1** 45, 344–5, 346, *346*
see also SCARIFICATION
Ciccani, Marco **27** 430
Cicchi, Biagio **24** 240
Ciccione, Andrea **2** 17
Ciceri, Eugène **7** 304*; **8** 616; **20** 420
Ciceri, Pierre-Luc-Charles **7** 304; **8** 449; **12** 13; **30** 679
Cicero(, Marcus Tullius) **2** 649; **7** 305*; **12** 62; **13** 468; **14** 867; **26** 864, 884, 885
house **10** 670
personal collection **9** 20; **26** 857; **27** 28
works **1** 652
on decorum **8** 612
on porticos **25** 265
on sculpture **22** 402
on villas **32** 541
Cicerone, Der *see* PANTHEON
Ciché, Francesco **32** 70
Cichiecki, Branislaŭ **3** 527
Cichocki, Edward **9** 498
CICIBA **11** 880
Cicignon, Caspar von **31** 363
Cicogna, Cavaliere **12** 761
Cicogna, Emmanuele Antonio **7** 305*
Cicogna, Pasquale, Doge of Venice (*reg* 1585-95) **23** *879*
Cicognara **25** 383
Cicognara, Antonio **7** 305–6*; **10** 520; **11** 8
Cicognara, (Francesco) Leopoldo, Conte **2** 125; **4** 22; **7** 306*; **32** 196
paintings **14** 264
writings **4** 21; **16** 782; **26** *232*; **31** 302
illustrated **14** 265
Cicognini, Jacopo **19** 709
Cid, El **29** 297
Cidambara *see* CHIDAMBARAM
Cid dos Santos, Bartolomeu *see* SANTOS, BARTOLOMEU (CID) DOS
Cie Anonyme des Verreries Namuroises **3** 595
Ciechanoŭski, M. **3** 531
Ciechanów Church **25** 126
Ciecierski, Tomasz **7** 307*; **25** 108
Cieco da Gambassi *see* GONNELLI, GIOVANNI FRANCESCO
Cielava, Jānis **26** 384
Ciempozuelos **29** 336
Ciénaga culture **29** 190
Cieplice **8** 409
Cierings, Alexander *see* KEIRINCKX, ALEXANDER
Ciermans, Jan **22** 717
Cieslewicz, Roman **25** 354
Cietario, Jacopino **20** 675
Cieza, José de **7** 307*
Cieza, Miguel Jerónimo **7** 307; **12** 889
Cieza de León, Pedro de **14** 827; **29** 134, 135, 140
Cifer, Ferdinand of *see* FERDINAND OF CIFER
CIFESA **29** 884
Cifka, Venceslas **19** 468
Çiftlik Han **16** 186
Cifuentes, Ferdinando da Silva, Conde de **28** 335
cigarette boxes *see under* BOXES → types
Cigler, Václav **8** 411
Cignani, Carlo, Conte **4** 277; **7** 307–9*
assistants **3** 702; **11** 679; **20** 391; **27** 521
patrons and collectors **21** 35; **23** 516; **27** 316; **31** 307
pupils
Boni, Giacomo Antonio **4** 320
Caccianiga, Francesco **5** 358
Crespi (ii), Giuseppe Maria **8** 140
Franceschini, Marcantonio **11** 679
Galli-Bibiena, Ferdinando **12** 23
Galli-Bibiena, Francesco **12** 24
Galli-Bibiena, Maria Oriana **12** 23
Lamberti, Bonaventura **3** 712; **18** 674
Mancini, Francesco **20** 241
Mazza, Giuseppe **20** 902
Rivalz, Antoine **26** 424
Stern, Ignaz **29** 639
Taruffi, Emilio **30** 349
reproductive prints by others **19** 437
teachers **1** 535
works **7** *308*; **18** 871
Cignani, Felice **7** 308
Cignaroli, Angelo Antonio **28** 19
Cignaroli, Diomiro **7** 309
Cignaroli, Felice *see* CIGNAROLI, GIUSEPPE
Cignaroli, Gaetano **7** 309
Cignaroli, Giambettino **7** 309–10*
pupils **5** 432; **31** 679
teachers **3** 109
Cignaroli, Giambettino—cont.
works **7** *310*
Cignaroli, Gian Domenico **7** 309
Cignaroli, Giuseppe **7** 309
Cignaroli, Vittorio Amedeo **16** 719; **28** 19; **31** 446
Cignoli, Ludovico **2** 493
Cigogne, Armand **23** 523
Cigoli, Lodovico **7** 310–13*; **16** 673, 749; **30** 355
assistants **1** 671; **4** 53
collaboration **9** 182; **11** 51; **21** 25
patrons and collectors **1** 595; **3** 97; **5** 735; **7** 492; **13** 880; **21** 28, 30
pupils **7** 492; **11** 39, 51; **22** 190
reproductions in hardstones **11** 191
works **2** 610; **4** 405; **7** *312*, *313*; **9** 706; **11** 194, 214; **24** 488; **26** 833; **27** 172; **30** 358; **31** 885
Cigri Dag **29** 700
Čikoš-Sesija, Bela **8** 173
cilery **7** 314*
Cilewent Farmhouse *see* ST FAGANS (S. Glam) → Welsh Folk Museum
Cili, Adriano di Pietro *see* FIAMMINGO, ADRIANO
Ciliberti, Franco **25** 838
Cilicia **9** *512*, 565, 567; **21** 564; **26** *852*
Cilindrismo **22** 78
Çilingiroğlu, Günay **31** 452, 453
Cima, Gaetano **27** 836
Cimabue **7** 314–19*; **13** 135, 145; **14** 868
attributions **2** 622; **9** 342, 343, 345, 349; **20** 697
collaboration **9** 341
methods **6** 569; **24** 486
mosaics **7** *318*; **13** 804; **24** 854
paintings **16** 655
altarpieces **1** 708; **11** 379; **25** 462
crucifixes **2** 389; **7** *317*, IX; **8** 212
frescoes **2** 622–3, *623*; **7** *315*; **15** 135; **16** 837
religious **2** 625, 627; **5** 443; **11** 183; **13** 144, 146; **20** 698
patrons and collectors **14** 485
pupils **6** 603; **9** 341; **12** 694
teachers **7** 817
workshop **13** 132
Cima da Conegliano (, Giovanni Battista) **7** 319–24*; **18** 846; **24** 231; **32** 190
assistants **27** 778
patrons and collectors **5** 432; **14** 147, 877; **20** 875; **29** 46
restorations by others **31** 283
teachers **3** 667
works **7** *320*, *321*, *322*, *738*; **18** 705; **32** 191, 658
workshop **5** 289
Cima Fiorentino **22** 12
Cimaise: Art et architecture actuels **24** 144, 428, 429, 442
Cimaroli, Giovanni Battista **5** 594; **24** 704
cimarres *see under* TANKARDS → types
Cimba, Maria **10** 93
Cimbalo, Jan Ignác **18** 505
Cimbri **6** 159; **13** 849
Ciminello, Antonio **31** 285
Cimiotti, Emil **7** 325*
Cimiterio, Giacomo *see* CASTELOO, GIACOMO DA
Cimitile-Nola **7** 325*; **9** *510*; **16** *621*
Baptistery **3** 190
Basilica Nova **7** 272, 325; **9** 535; **16** 624
Cinatti, Giuseppe **7** 326*; **19** 468; **25** 293; **29** 101
Cincinato, Diego de Romulo **24** 107; **26** 307; **30** 803
Cincinato, Romulo **5** 411

Cincinnati (OH) 2 572; 7 326–7*; 31 587
Art Museum 6 826; 15 746; 27 46
Belmont see Taft Museum
Hebrew Union College Museum see under LOS ANGELES → Hebrew Union College Skirball Museum
Ingalls Building 7 326; 28 833
Museum of Natural History 2 710; 7 327
Plum Street Temple 17 547
Taft Museum 1 440; 7 326, 327; 9 391
Terrace Hilton Hotel 21 708
Western Museum see Museum of Natural History
Cincinnato, Diego de Romulo see ROMULO CINCINNATO, DIEGO DE
cinctures (columns) 7 327*
cinctures (vestments) 32 387*
Cincu 26 718
Cînde (family) 26 710
cinema cameras see CAMERAS → types cinematography
cinemas 7 327–8*; 12 497; 16 143; 24 19
Brazil 19 271
England 7 328
France 19 368
lighting 19 368
Scotland 28 250
United States of America 31 596
cinerary urns see URNS → types → funerary
Cines 4 630
Cines Company 17 855
cinétisme 18 62
Cinganelli, Michelangelo 11 194; 21 25; 24 860
Cingle 29 365
cingula 9 642, 643
see also ZONARIA
Cini 11 384
Cini, Andrea di Bartolo 7 328, 330–31*
attributions 2 21
collaboration 7 329; 19 754
patrons and collectors 6 393
works 28 687
Cini, Ansano di Andrea di Bartolo 7 328
Cini, Bartolo di Fredi 7 328–30*; 13 149; 28 684
attributions 3 917
collaboration 19 754
pupils 7 330
works 3 246; 7 329; 8 836; 12 109; 27 751; 28 686, 687
Cini, Giorgio di Andrea di Bartolo 7 328
Cini, Giovan Battista 33 615
architecture 19 496; 25 96; 32 578; 33 615
sculpture 25 111, 113
writings 32 20
Cini, Vittorio, Conte 7 331*; 32 214
Çinici, Altuğ 31 452
Çinici, Behruz 31 452
Cinisello Balsamo, Villa Ghirlanda Silva 16 719
cinnabar
historical and regional traditions
Buddhism 29 462
China 7 631–2
Daoism 7 631
Greece, ancient 13 535, 536
Japan 17 246
Maya 21 259
Mesoamerica, Pre-Columbian 1 713; 21 250, 259
Rome, ancient 23 785; 27 51
Spain 23 785
Sri Lanka 29 462
uses
lacquer 18 600
cinnabar
uses—cont.
pigments 7 631–2; 11 763; 13 535, 536; 23 785; 24 795; 27 51; 29 462
pottery 17 246
cinnabar green see PIGMENTS → types → chrome green
cinnabaris see under PIGMENTS → types
Cinnamus of Lezoux 27 107
Cino, Giuseppe 19 27, 28
Cino di Bartolo 16 845
Cinperk, Bartolomej of see BARTOLOMEJ OF CINPERK
Cinperk, Brikcí of see BRIKCÍ OF CINPERK
Cinughi, Giovanni, Bishop of Pienza 28 677
Cioffi, Pasquale 23 87
Cioflec, Virgil 26 723, 724
Ciołek, Erazm see WITELO
Cioli, Andrea 22 423
Cioli, Simone (di Michele) 7 331–2*
Cioli, Valerio (di Simone) 7 331–2*; 12 607; 29 569
Ciolli, Giacomo 27 834
Ciolli, Simone (di Michele) see CIOLI, SIMONE (DI MICHELE)
Ciolli, Valerio (di Simone) see CIOLI, VALERIO (DI SIMONE)
Cione, Andrea di 7 332–8*; 13 133
architecture 23 585
assistants 2 15; 7 337
attributions 8 443; 13 124; 20 776
collaboration 7 336; 30 273
competitions 7 664
methods 25 379
paintings 7 338; 16 655
altarpieces 7 333, 335; 11 184, 209, 380; 13 149
frescoes 15 82
patrons and collectors 1 611; 2 514; 5 311
pupils 12 708
sculpture 7 334; 11 203; 13 94
Cione, Benci di see BENCI DI CIONE
Cione, Cione di Jacopo di 7 332
Cione, Jacopo di (1320/30–1398/1400) 7 332, 337–8*
collaboration 19 673; 23 94–5
methods 24 8
patrons and collectors 8 535
works 7 337; 11 660; 13 149
Cione, Jacopo di (fl 1386–1421) see CIONE, CIONE DI JACOPO DI
Cione, Matteo di 7 332, 334, 337*
Cione, Nardo di 7 332, 336*; 11 209; 20 432
collaboration 7 333
patrons and collectors 2 514
pupils 12 708
works 1 640; 7 333, 333; 13 149; 24 XII4; 30 V4
Cioni, Andrea di Michele di Francesco see VERROCCHIO, ANDREA DEL
Cioni, Michele di Francesco 32 360
Čipan, B. 19 883
Cipolla, Antonio 7 339*; 8 483
Cipollara 10 636
cipollino see under MARBLE → types
Cipper, Giacomo Francesco 30 451
cippi 7 339*; 27 6, 33
see also POSTS
Cipriani, Bartolomeo 19 531
Cipriani, Giovanni Battista 7 339–40*; 10 372; 19 157, 585
collaboration 3 277, 308; 26 335; 33 226
patrons and collectors 14 145
pupils 9 505; 13 650
Cipriani, Giovanni Battista—cont.
reproductions in stained glass 29 506
reproductive prints by others 3 308, 308; 29 675
sponsors 14 687
teachers 14 848
works 3 25, 26; 4 886; 7 340
Cipriani, Henry 7 340
Cipriani, Sebastiano 7 782
Cipriano, João 8 268
Cipriano da Cruz 7 340–41*; 25 301; 30 799
Cipriano Gomes, Manuel see GOMES, MANUEL CIPRIANO
Cirachi, Giuseppe see CERACCHI, GIUSEPPE
Çiralı see OLYMPOS
Ciraqui 29 335
Circa 16 42
Circassian 27 432
Circeii 26 887
Circignani, Antonio 20 841
Circignani, Niccolò see POMARANCIO, NICCOLÒ
Circle: International Survey of Constructive Art 20 491; 21 855; 22 749
Circle Art Group 14 722
Circle of Artists (Krug Khudoshnikov) 7 341*; 27 394
circlets 17 519
Circolo Artistico 8 463
circuits 21 555, 556
circular houses see under HOUSES → types
Círculo de Amigos del Arte 8 17, 18; 12 919; 17 586; 25 826
Círculo de Bellas Artes (Nicaragua) 23 81, 85
Círculo de Bellas Artes (Uruguay) 31 754, 758, 759
Círculo de Bellas Artes (Venezuela) 5 354; 21 902; 26 263; 32 175, 180
Circulo e cuadrado 31 183
circumcision sets 17 574
circuses 7 341–2*; 27 712
Byzantine 9 556, 560
Early Christian (c. AD 250–843) 9 556, 560
Egypt, ancient 7 342
Italy 7 342
Rome, ancient 5 891; 7 342; 26 864, 873
Spain 7 342
Tunisia 5 891
see also STADIA
Cirebon 15 783, 798, 811
Cirencester (Glos)
Abbey 2 65; 10 227
Cirencester Park 12 128; 28 874
Alfred's Hall 13 199; 27 323
mosaics 27 63; 32 542
St John the Baptist 10 262; 20 581
cire perdue see LOST-WAX PROCESS
Cirga 26 143
Ciriaco d'Ancona see CYRIAC OF ANCONA
Ciriaco di Filippo de' Pizzicolli see CYRIAC OF ANCONA
Ciriani, Henri 2 699, 700; 6 534; 7 343*; 19 387
Cirici Alomar, Cristian 29 861
Cirici Pellicer, Alexandre 8 538; 29 309, 322
Cirilli, Guido 27 492
Cirillo, Bernardo 4 47
Cirkel, De 18 435; 22 876
Cirkut see under CAMERAS → types
Cirligi 25 341
Cirlot, Juan Eduardo 8 538
CIRMA see ANTIGUA → Centro de Investigaciones de Mesoamérica
Cîrna 7 343*; 25 471, 528; 26 705
figurines 7 343; 25 528
vases 7 343
Cirou, Ciquaire 6 454; 11 608
CIRPAC 7 293, 343–4*; 12 58, 177; 27 853
Cirrus Editions, Ltd 19 492, 702; 20 609
Cirşana Valley 4 783
Cirta see CONSTANTINE (ALGERIA)
Cîrta Church 26 706, 710
Cīrulis, Ansis
Ciseri, Antonio 7 344*
pupils 4 129; 8 682; 19 70; 22 803
Ciseriano, Cesare see CESARIANO, CESARE
Cisheng, Empress (1546–1614) 33 318
Cismar Abbey Altarpiece 1 709, 709; 13 116; 25 183
Cisnădie Basilica 26 706
Cisneros, Francisco Jiménez de, Cardinal 7 344–5*; 14 868
alabaster-carvings 32 493
architecture 1 586; 2 529; 13 844
books 4 8
metalwork 2 390
paintings 4 414; 11 484
sculpture 31 92
Cisneros, Francisco W. 10 154
Cisneros, Gustavo 32 179
Cisneros, Patricia 32 179
Cisneros, Pedro de 4 414
Cisneros, Villa see DAKHLA
Cissarz, Johann Vincenz 7 346*
Cissarz Latin see under TYPE-FACES
Cisteaux Abbey see CÎTEAUX ABBEY
Cistercian Order 3 709; 7 214, 231, 232, 346–53*; 26 380
arches 2 298
architectural decorations 4 782
architecture 4 778; 6 464; 7 347, 350–51*, 371, 453, 455; 18 621; 21 836–9*, 844; 26 381, 382
Austria 2 777
Czech Republic 32 746
Denmark 8 722
England 10 227; 11 349, 350; 13 43–4; 21 833; 26 380, 590
France 13 37–8; 21 837, 838
Germany 4 776; 12 471; 13 47–8, 57
Gothic 11 349, 350; 13 35, 37–8, 43–4, 47–8, 50, 51, 57; 26 380; 32 746
Ireland 16 7, 7; 21 87, 88
Italy 13 51; 16 627
Netherlands, the 4 777
Poland 25 95
Portugal 1 590; 25 289
Romanesque 21 88; 26 590, 592
Sardinia 27 836
Scandinavia 13 50
Spain 13 50; 29 263
brick 4 782
iconoclasm 15 80
liturgical furnishings 7 280
manuscript illumination 7 348, 351–2*
metalwork 7 353
mouldings 22 214, 216, 217, 218, 220, 222
painting 7 352; 25 104; 26 702
patronage 7 350–53*; 16 762
pottery 28 256
sculpture 13 97–8
stained glass 7 353; 13 136; 26 702; 29 502
tiles 7 353
vaults (ceiling) 32 88
see also BENEDICTINE ORDER; ORDER OF STRICT OBSERVANCE; TRAPPISTS
Cistercian ware see under POTTERY → wares
cisterns 7 353–4*
Byzantine 7 354; 9 560
Early Christian (c. AD 250–843) 9 560
England 12 126
Greece, ancient 7 354; 13 381, 383, 391
Iran 16 232
Islamic 16 217, 232
Rome, ancient 7 353, 354; 26 864
Spain 16 217
Turkey 7 354
see also RESERVOIRS
cists
Etruscan 10 629, 630*
Helladic 14 339
Indian subcontinent 21 43–4
Italy 10 629, 630*
Prehistoric art 25 506
cist tombs see under TOMBS → types
citadels 21 546
Ancient Near East 24 482
Byzantine 9 554
Central Asia, Western 6 200, 210
Champa 6 425–6*
Early Christian (c. AD 250–843) 9 554
Helladic 14 340
Inca 20 3
Iran 16 264
Iran, ancient 24 482
Islamic 6 210; 16 130, 141, 215–16, 264, 266
Mycenaean 14 340
Ottoman 16 266
Peru 20 3
Siberia 31 68
South America, Pre-Columbian 20 3
Spain 16 215–16
Turkey 16 266
Vietnam 6 425–6*
Citania de Briteiros 25 536
Cité, La 24 439; 31 874; 32 380
Cîteaux Abbey 7 231, 346, 351, 354–6*, 355; 11 504; 13 38; 21 836
church 7 355
manuscripts 4 6; 7 352; 11 530; 15 848; 26 669
tomb of Philippe Pot 13 78, 78
Cité des Dames, Master of the 20 647–8*
patrons and collectors 7 525; 31 837, 841
works 7 235; 20 647
Cité industrielle 12 159–60, 160
cities 1 251; 14 12; 23 300; 26 570, 853, 854
see also TOWNS
cities, garden see under TOWNS → types
Cito, Claus 20 11
Citoni, Jeronimo 22 453
Citov, St Leonard 26 637
citrakāra 22 781
Citrakuta see CHITTAURGARH
Citrangad Maurya 7 175
citric acid 30 559
citrine 12 270, I; 14 171
Citroen, Paul 7 356*; 14 43; 22 852, 908
Citroën-Cévennes Park 24 132
Città, La 8 617
Cittadella-Vigodarzere (family) 28 392
Città di Castello
Palazzo Comunale 2 41–2
Palazzo del Podestà 2 42
Palazzo Vitelli a Sant'Egidio 27 667
S Domenico 16 723
Città di Castello, Master of 9 349; 20 648*
Città di Castello, Matteo da 11 78
Cittadini, Giacomo 3 868
Cittadini, Pier Francesco 7 356–7*; 30 41

Cittadini, Tito 2 62
città nuova, La 24 448
citterns 22 374
City and Country Home 5 576
City and Suburban Homes Company 30 458
City Beautiful Movement 7 357*; 14 115; 31 725, 727
- Canada 19 842
- United States of America 3 465; 19 700, *700*; 20 16; 31 594

City Corporation, London 19 572
city halls 19 *700*; 31 236, 242
- *see also* COUNTY HALLS; TOWN HALLS

City of Milan Improvement Co. Ltd. 21 130
city planning *see* URBAN PLANNING
cityscapes *see* TOWNSCAPES
Ciucurencu, Alexandru 7 361–2*; 23 699; 26 716, 726
Ciudad Bolívar, Fundación Museo de Arte Moderno Jesús Soto 32 180, 568
Ciudad del Este 24 *91*
Ciudad del Lodo *see* CARTAGO
Ciudad de los Reyes 8 15, *15*
Ciudad de Nuestra Señora de la Asunción *see* ASUNCIÓN
Ciudadela (Menorca) 3 105
- architecture (temples) 3 *105*
- Cathedral of S María 3 106
- Palacio Saura 3 106

Ciudad Real (Guatemala) 13 766
Ciudad Real (Spain), Palace of El Viso del Marqués 29 267
Ciudad Rodrigo 7 362–3*; 29 *258*
- Cathedral of S María 7 362–3*; 13 50
  - choir-stalls 13 123
  - sculpture 13 103; 26 609; 29 288
- Cerralbo Chapel 29 268

Ciuffagni, Bernardo (di Piero di Bartol) 7 363*
- collaboration 12 544; 24 232
- works 11 197, 198, 201; 22 462

Ciuli, Simone (di Michele) *see* CIOLI, SIMONE (DI MICHELE)
Ciuli, Valerio (di Simone) *see* CIOLI, VALERIO (DI SIMONE)
Ciumeşti 30 773
Ciurini, Bernardino 24 24
Čiurlionis, M(ikalojus) K(onstantinas) 7 363*; 22 380; 26 403
- exhibitions 19 498
- patrons and collectors 17 856
- works 19 *498*

Čiurlionis, M. K., State Art Museum *see under* KAUNAS
Ciutadilla, Marquesa de 29 344
Ciutadilla, Marqués de 29 344
Ciutat de Mallorca *see* PALMA DE MALLORCA
Ciuti, Goro di Guccio *see* GORO DI GUCCIO CIUTI
Civate, S Pietro al Monte 7 363–5*; 16 *618*, 625
- wall paintings 7 *364*; 16 655; 26 650

Civerchio, Vincenzo 7 365*
Civetta *see* BLES, HERRI MET DE
Civezzano 9 154
civic centres 16 *564*; 31 242, 243
Cividale 19 549
- Cathedral
  - Sigwald Altar Frontal 16 687
- reliefs 19 549
- S Maria in Valle 16 625; 29 817
  - choir-stalls 16 723
  - sculpture 16 687; 19 550; 26 622
  - wall paintings 5 797
- Tempietto Longobardo *see* S Maria in Valle

Civil Engineer and Architect's Journal 24 446
civil engineering *see* ENGINEERING (CIVIL)
Cività Alba 24 319
Cività Castellana 7 366*; 10 *583*; 16 *620*
- altars 1 692
- bronze 10 627
- Cathedral of S Maria 7 366, 919, 920, 922
- arch 7 *920*
- mosaics 26 680
- sculpture 26 624
- Lo Scasato temple 10 593, 604
- plaques 30 *494*
- vase paintings 10 615
- vases 10 616
- viaduct 32 398

Civitali, Bartolomeo 7 367
Civitali, Masseo di Bartolomeo 7 367
Civitali, Matteo (di Giovanni) 7 366–7*
- attributions 11 696
- collaboration 7 296
- pupils 29 496
- works 7 *367*; 19 766

Civitali, Nicolao 3 742; 7 367
Civitali, Vincenzo di Bartolomeo 7 367
Civitali, Vincenzo di Nicolao 7 367
Civitas Andecavorum *see* ANGERS
Civitas Vangionum *see under* WORMS
Civitavecchia
- bastion 3 359
- harbour 26 896
- Palazzo Comunale 1 795
- Trajan's Villa 26 897
- vases 10 609

Civoli, Giuseppe 3 129
Civray, St Nicolas 24 826; 26 600
Civrieux, Marc de 29 132
Ci xian *see* CIZHOU
Cixi empress 6 662, 682, 704; 7 71, 136; 25 783
Ciyun Pavilion 24 289
Cižek, Franz 2 524, 832; 6 588, 589; 7 368*; 19 429
Čížek, J. 30 221
Çizenel, Emin 8 365
Cizhou 6 637, 885, 886, 895, 896
Cizhou ware *see under* POTTERY → wares
Cizre
- bridge 4 801; 16 246, 247
- Great Mosque 9 160; 16 381

Clack, Rod 32 414
Clacton Pier (Essex) 24 748
cladding 1 307; 4 767, 788; 14 200
Cladel, Judith(-Jeanne) 7 368*
Claeissens, Antheunis 7 368, 369*; 22 886; 25 381
Claeissins, Gillis 7 368*; 25 585
Claeissins, Pieter (i) (1499/1500-1576) 7 368*
- works 11 *442*

Claeissins, Pieter (ii) (before 1536-1605) 7 368–9*
Claes de Bruyn 13 10
Claesen, Charles 2 468
Claessone, Moryn 26 269
Claessoon, Marinus 26 270
Claesz., Aernt *see* AERTGEN VAN LEYDEN
Claesz., Allaert 7 369*; 19 501
Claesz., Anthony, II 11 226
Claesz., Pieter 3 757; 7 369–70*; 13 894
- pupils 3 757
- works 7 *370*; 22 840, 887; 29 666; 31 882

Claeszon, Aris 7 370*; 30 84
Claesz. van Emden, Leendert *see* EMDEN, LEENDERT CLAESZ. VAN
Claeuw, Jacques de 13 255
Clagny, Seigneur de *see* LESCOT, PIERRE
Clagny Château 6 508
Clague, Richard 23 32
Clair, Jean 20 75
Clair, René 3 120; 8 439; 10 687; 24 406, 710
Clairambault, Pierre de 11 903
Claire, Godefroid de *see* GODEFROID OF HUY
Claire, June *see* WAYNE, JUNE (CLAIRE)
Clairin, (Jules-)Georges (-Victor) 7 371*
Clairin, Pierre Eugène 25 215
Clairmarais 13 158
Clairmont 11 33
Clairmont, Philip 23 61
clair obscur *see* CHIAROSCURO; WOODCUTS → types → chiaroscuro
Clairon, Mlle 30 672
Clairvaux, Drogo of, Abbot of Byloke *see* DROGO OF CLAIRVAUX, Abbot of Byloke
Clairvaux Abbey 7 346, 351, 371–2*, *372*; 11 *504*; 13 38; 21 836, 837, *837*, 838, 839; 26 380
- Haut Clairvaux 13 38
- manuscripts 7 352
- refectory 21 844

Clais, Master 20 764
Clallam 17 770
Clamart, Fondation Arp 2 490
clamp kilns *see under* KILNS → types
clamps 13 388, *388*, *389*, 391; 22 156, 165
clam shells *see under* SHELLS → types
Clandon Park (Surrey) 3 244; 4 787; 27 466
- interior decoration 29 *837*

Clanner, Augustin 27 664
Clanricarde, Ulick John de Burgh, 14th Earl of *see* BURGH, ULICK JOHN DE, 14th Earl of Clanricarde
Clap, Thomas 23 25
Claperós, Antoni (i) (*fl* 1414-61) 3 221; 7 373; 20 514
Claperós, Antoni (ii) (1438-after 1460) 7 373
Claperós, Francesc 7 373
Claperós, Joan 7 373
Clapes, Alexis 12 182; 13 782; 29 321
Clapham, Alfred 2 64; 26 589
Clapham, F. Dare 22 230
Clapis, von (family) 5 59
clappers 22 372
Clara, August 28 408
Clarà, Joan 7 373
Clarà (i Ayats), Josep 7 373*; 23 260; 29 295
Clarà, Museu *see under* BARCELONA (SPAIN) → museums
Clarac, Charles-Othon (-Frédéric-Jean-Baptiste), Comte de 2 165; 7 374*
Claravaux, Michel de 12 468
Clare (family) 6 56; 12 272; 14 425; 23 461
- chasubles 23 *461*

Clare, Saint 25 229
Clare, Gilbert de, Earl of Gloucester (*d* 1307) 14 422, *422*
Clare, Gilbert de, Earl of Hertford (*d* 1152) 14 408
Clare, Rohaise de, Countess of Lincoln 14 408
Clare, Thomas Pelham-Holles, Marquess of *see* PELHAM-HOLLES, THOMAS, Marquess of Clare
Clarello 11 712
Claremont (Surrey; UK) 7 374–5*, *375*; 10 *225*
- Belvedere 3 689, *689*; 11 242

Claremont (CA; USA), Pomona College
- mural 23 *566*

Clarence, Margaret Plantagenet, Duchess of *see* PLANTAGENET, MARGARET, Duchess of Clarence
Clarence, William, Duke of *see* WILLIAM IV, King of England
Clarendon, Edward Hyde, 1st Earl of *see* HYDE, EDWARD, 1st Earl of Clarendon
Clarendon, Frederick Villiers 16 11
Clarendon, Henry Hyde, 2nd Earl of *see* HYDE, HENRY, 2nd Earl of Clarendon
Clarendon Palace (Oxon) 6 407; 10 269; 13 80; 14 75
Claressans 19 566
Clari, Enrique 24 96
Clarines 32 *165*
Clarissan Order *see* POOR CLARES, ORDER OF
Clarisse, Louis 27 291
Clarisse, Rogier 27 291
Clark (family) 23 68
Clark, Adam 5 82; 14 888
Clark, Alfred 3 250; 7 157, 375*
Clark, Alson 19 701
Clark, Edward S. 14 164
Clark, George H. 26 471
Clark, Grahame 2 300
Clark, Harry 16 18
Clark, Henry Paston 33 136
Clark, Hillary 23 69
Clark, J. D. 1 373
Clark, J. J. 2 738, 739; 4 818; 21 75
Clark, John 1 736
Clark, J. W. 2 735
Clark, Kenneth (MacKenzie) 7 375–6*; 22 751; 23 182
- sponsorship 2 560; 7 547; 10 362; 24 228
- works 10 486; 18 701; 26 735

Clark, Larry 7 376*
Clark, Lygia 4 719; 7 376*; 26 414; 33 317
Clark, Lyonel 19 424
Clark, Matthew 16 53
Clark, M. E. 29 554, 555
Clark, Ossie 9 294
Clark, Paraskeva (Avdyevna) 7 376–7*
Clark, Robert *see* INDIANA, ROBERT
Clark, Robert Sterling 7 377*
Clark, Russell 23 63
Clark, Stephen 7 377
Clark, Thomas 29 835
Clark, T. J. 2 537, 538; 20 528; 31 673
Clark, William 4 477; 22 592
Clarke 15 57
Clarke, Brian 16 32
Clarke, Carey 16 18
Clarke, Caspar Purdon 15 741, 747
Clarke, C. H. *see* ADELER, MAX
Clarke, David 28 815
Clarke, Edward Daniel 7 378*
Clarke, Geoffrey 25 728
Clarke, George 7 378–9*; 23 688
- collaboration 31 234
- personal collection 17 507
- works 14 254; 23 690; 31 234

Clarke, George Somers 3 283; 4 810; 28 279
Clarke, Harry (Patrick) 7 377–8*; 9 321; 16 37
- pupils 19 891
- works 29 508, VII

Clarke, John 20 477
Clarke, John Clem 19 493
Clarke, Joseph (1819-88; England) 30 385
Clarke, Joseph (*fl* 1878; Australia) 2 755
Clarke, Joshua 7 378; 9 321
Clarke, LeRoy 31 336
Clarke, Margaret 7 377*; 16 17
Clarke, Simon 5 63
Clarke, T. Chatfield 20 26
Clarke, Thomas B(enedict) 7 379*
- collections 31 662
- paintings 8 608; 15 859; 27 462

Clarke, William 21 832
Clarté 30 19
Clason, Isak Gustaf 7 379–80*; 32 765
- assistants 23 615
- patrons and collectors 14 88
- pupils 32 765
- staff 30 2
- works 29 686; 30 73

CLASP (Consortium of Local Authorities Special Programme) 10 241; 12 597; 28 158
clasping buttresses *see under* BUTTRESSES
clasps 14 419; 17 519
- historical and regional traditions
  - Anglo-Saxon 10 322; 30 *44*
  - Bactria 30 *891*
  - Central Asia, Western 6 *273*; 30 *891*
  - England 4 350; 10 322
  - France 4 350; 14 418
  - Germany 4 350, 355; 23 *658*
  - Italy 4 350
  - Mongolia 21 877, 878
  - Netherlands, the 4 350, 355; 22 896
  - Ottonian 23 *658*
- materials
  - enamel 30 *44*
  - garnets 30 *44*
  - gold 6 *273*; 23 *658*; 30 *44*, *891*
- uses
  - bookbindings 4 350, 355; 24 107
- *see also* BELTHOOKS

Classical Designer 32 198–9
Classical Master 4 582
Classical Syrian style 1 862
Classicism 7 380–83*; 8 788; 19 246
classification of art *see* ART (CLASSIFICATION OF)
classification systems 15 96–7; 22 356–7, 358–9; 24 453–5; 30 381
classified collections *see under* COLLECTIONS → types
Classius, Peter 27 466
Claude, Georges 22 747
Claude, Piètre 4 544
Claude de France, Master of 20 790
Claude de Seyssel 31 846
Claude glasses 7 387*; 24 742
Claudel, Camille 7 387–8*; 26 514, 515; 31 382; 33 310
Claudel, Charles-Auguste 31 829
Claudel, Nicolas 3 590
Claudel, Paul (-Louis-Charles-Marie) 7 387, 388*; 20 387; 31 832; 33 486
Claude (le) Lorrain (1604/5-82) 6 78; 7 389–401*; 11 534, 587; 16 668; 19 696; 26 772
- attributions 11 358
- collaboration 4 486; 8 783
- commentaries 27 726
- drawings 9 222, 223; 25 558; 32 899
  - landscape 7 *391*; 9 *223*
- etchings 10 551, *552*, 552–3; 25 606
- frames 11 *403*, 404, 408
- groups and movements 3 267
- methods 19 353; 24 493, 793, 799
- paintings
  - landscape 7 *390*, *395*, *396*, *398*; 11 536; 14 583; 16 671–2; 18 708, 709, 712; 22 414; 26 772
  - marine 7 *392*; 20 426
  - wall 22 455
  - watercolours 32 900

Claude (le) Lorrain (1604/5-82)—cont.
patrons and collectors **10** 361
Alexander VII, Pope (*reg* 1655-67) **6** 584
Altieri (family) **1** 727; **13** 650
Angerstein, John Julius **2** 51
Angran, Louis-Auguste, Vicomte de Fontpertuis **2** 90
Aved, Jacques (-André-Joseph) **2** 852
Baring, Thomas (ii) (1799-1873) **3** 239
Beaumont, George (Howland) **3** 454; **7** 748
Beckford, William (1760-1844) **3** 477; **10** 753
Bentivoglio, Guido, Cardinal **3** 745
Bracciano, Livio Odescalchi, Duca di **23** 353
Bracciano, Paolo Giordano II Orsini, Duca di **23** 576
British Museum **9** 230
Bryan, Michael **5** 63
Calonne, Charles-Alexandre de **5** 439
Camuccini, Pietro **5** 554
Caraman, Duc de **5** 700
Carr, William Holwell **5** 848
Castel Rodrigo, Manuel de Moura y Corte Real, 2nd Marqés de **6** 30
Catherine II, Empress of Russia (*reg* 1762- 96) **26** 733
Cavendish, William, 2nd Duke of Devonshire (1671-1729) **6** 116
Chigi, Agostino (ii) (1634-1705) **6** 586; **27** 152
Choiseul, Etienne-François, Duc de **7** 194
Christina, Queen of Sweden (*reg* 1632-54) **32** 8
Clark, Robert Sterling **7** 377
Clement IX, Pope (*reg* 1667-70) **27** 172
Clive, Robert, 1st Baron Clive **7** 437
Coke, Thomas, 1st Earl of Leicester of the 1st creation (1697-1759) **10** 365
Colebrooke, George **7** 552
Conti, Louis-François de Bourbon, Prince de (1717-76) **7** 778
Crescenzi, Francesco **8** 139
Crescenzi, Pietro Paolo, Cardinal **8** 138
Dezallier d'Argenville, Antoine-Joseph **8** 845
Ellis, Welbore Agar **10** 146
Esdaile, William **10** 505; **33** 345
Esterházy, Miklós II, Prince (1765-1833) **10** 530, 531
Falconieri, Paolo Francesco (1626-96) **10** 769
George IV, King of Great Britain (*reg* 1820-30) **14** 146
Giori, Angelo, Cardinal **12** 680
Giustiniani (i), Vincenzo, Marchese **12** 764
Graham, William **13** 273
Grey (family) **13** 645
Grosvenor, Robert, 2nd Earl of Grosvenor and 1st Marquess of Westminster **13** 696
Hanover, Frederick (Louis), Prince of Wales (1707-51) **14** 143
Harcourt, Simon, 1st Earl Harcourt of Stanton Harcourt and 2nd Earl Nuneham **14** 163
Herbert, Thomas, 8th Earl of Pembroke **14** 435
Hesselin, Louis (-Cauchon) **14** 492

Claude (le) Lorrain (1604/5-82)
patrons and collectors—cont.
Hoare (i), Henry the younger (1705-85) **14** 598
Jabach, Everard **16** 814
John V, King of Portugal (*reg* 1706-50) **4** 636
Josephine, Empress of the French (1763-1814) **4** 303
Knight, Richard Payne **18** 150
La Live de Jully, Ange-Laurent de **18** 660
Lely, Peter **19** 124
Lempereur, Jean-Denis, II **19** 144
Le Nôtre, André **19** 164
Liancourt, Duc de **19** 300
Locke, William (1732-1810) **19** 531
Long, Charles, 1st Baron Farnborough **19** 624
Louis XIII, King of France (*reg* 1610-43) **11** 661
Lowther, William, 3rd Baronet of Marske **19** 735
Loyd, Samuel Jones, 1st Baron Overstone **19** 736
Mariette, Pierre-Jean **20** 417
Massimo, Camillo (Carlo), Cardinal **20** 588; **26** 773
Mead, Richard **20** 910
Medici, Leopoldo de', Cardinal **21** 28
Miles, Philip John **21** 541
Montagu-Douglas-Scott, Walter Francis, 5th Duke of Buccleuch, 7th Duke of Queensberry **21** 908
Morice, Humphry **22** 115
Morrison, James **22** 148
Munro (of Novar), H(ugh) A(ndrew) J(ohnstone) **22** 314
Paliano and Castiglione, Lorenzo Onofrio Colonna, Duke of **7** 620, 622
Pamphili (family) **23** 898
Pamphili, Camillo, Prince **9** 175; **23** 899
Périer, Casimir **24** 418
Piles, Roger de **24** 805
Reynolds, Joshua **26** 279
Richelieu, Armand-Jean Du Plessis, Cardinal de **26** 348
Richelieu, Louis-François Armand-Jean Vignerod du Plessis, Duc de (1629-1715) **26** 349
Rogers, Samuel **26** 541
Saint-Morys, Charles Paul Jean-Baptiste de Bourgevin Vialart de **27** 568
Sanford, John **27** 729
Seymour-Conway, Richard, 4th Marquess of Hertford **28** 527
Temple, Richard, 1st Viscount Cobham **30** 451
Tessin, Carl Gustav, Count **30** 524
Urban VIII, Pope (*reg* 1623-44) **3** 207
Vassal de Saint-Hubert, Jean-Antoine-Hubert **32** 74
Verrue, Jeanne-Baptiste d'Albert de Luynes, Comtesse de **32** 368
Verstolk van Soelen, Jan Gijsbert, Baron **32** 377
Vos (ii) Jbzn, Jacob de (1803-82) **32** 708
Wellesley, Henry **33** 56
Wilson, Andrew **33** 216
Yusupov, Nikolay (Borisovich), Prince (1751- 1831) **33** 579
personal collection **3** 278
pupils **2** 43; **8** 796
reproductions on porcelain **14** 323

Claude (le) Lorrain (1604/5-82)—cont.
reproductive prints by others **4** 607
Browne, John **4** 886
Daubigny, Charles-François **8** 539
Earlom, Richard **9** 506; **21** 417; **25** 619
Frenzel, Johann Gottfried Abraham **11** 760
Pond, Arthur **25** 210
Pye, John **25** 753
Vivares, Franćois **32** 652
Volpato, Giovanni **32** 689
Voogd, Hendrik **32** 693
Woollett, William **4** 607
teachers **30** 356; **32** 826
Claudet, Antoine (François Jean) **7** 403*; **24** 660; **30** 269; **33** 134
Claudia de' Medici, Countess of Tyrol (1604-48) **13** 845; **19** 452
Claudia Felicitas, Empress of Austria **30** 455
Claudius, Emperor of Rome (*reg* 41-54) **7** 404*; **14**
architecture **18** 238; **19** 360; **23** 619; **26** 891, *892*
bridges **31** 323
coins **27** 96
gems **12** 251
paintings **2** 726
sculpture **27** 32, 33, 34
Claudius Gothicus, Emperor of Rome (*reg* AD 268-70) **27** 42
Claudius Ptolemaeus *see* PTOLEMY
Claudius Pulcher, Appius **5** 904; **7** 404*
Claudot, Jean-Baptiste-Charles **2** 722; **16** 64
Clauet *see* CLOUET
Claus, Carlfriedrich **7** 404*
Claus, Emile **3** 564; **7** 404–5*
groups and movements **2** 197; **14** 507; **19** 791, 792
pupils **19** 792
works **3** 563
Claus, Nicolaus *see* NICOLAUS CLAUS
Claus, W. A. G. **30** 343
Claus de Haine **5** 207
Claus de Werve **7** 405*; **11** 555
attributions **26** 554
patrons and collectors **5** 209; **33** 28
works **8** 890, 893; **13** 77–8; **17** 460, 676; **20** 207; **28** 866; **33** *28*
Clausell, Joaquín **7** 405*; **23** 370
Clausen, Benedykt **28** 105
Clausen, Franciska **7** 405–6*; **8** 736
Clausen, George **7** 406–7*; **10** 254; **23** 22; **28** 341
Clausen, Nicholas **27** 586
Clausen, Rosemarie **7** 407*
Clausholm Castle **8** 726, 742; **29** 841
interior decoration **29** *840*
Claussé, Côme **19** 18
Claussin **32** 377
Claustre, Martin **4** 292; **7** 407*
Claus von Lore **29** 754
Claux de Fribourg **2** 112
Clavé, Antoni **5** 726; **7** 407–8*; **19** 491; **25** 620
Clavé, Josep Torres *see* TORRES CLAVÉ, JOSEP
Clavé (y Roqué), Pelegrín **7** 408*; **21** 385, 397, 404; **29** 283; **32** 538
pupils **13** 868, 869; **24** 206; **26** 60; **32** 123
Clavel, Gilbert **8** 771
Clavell, Chiara **26** 459
Clavering, Cecil
works **7** *328*
Clavet *see* CLOUET
Clavijero, Francisco Xavier **21** 262

Clavijo, Ruy Gonzalez de
on gardens **12** 82
on glass **6** 258, 269
on monasteries **19** 888
on palaces **21** 885; **23** 820; **30** 476
on Samarkand **6** 203; **27** 673
on textiles **16** 443
on Timurid court **16** 196
Clavina, Torcato José
works **3** *233*
Clavizo Castle **8** 138
Claw, Silas **22** 605
claw-beakers *see under* GLASSES → types
clay
historical and regional traditions
Afghanistan **1** 193, 196, 197, *197*, 198, *199*, 202
Africa **1** 285, 296, *367*, 418; **29** 827
Ancient Near East **4** 771; **20** 326
Bactria **6** *215*, 216, *216*
Bhutan **3** 914
Brazil **29** *193*
Buddhism **1** 197, 198, *199*, 202; **6** *194*, *216*, *221*, 221–2, 298, *299*, *300*; **18** *292*, 295; **30** *220*, 596, 823
China **6** 706, 708, 717
Central Asia, Eastern **6** 298, 299, *299*, *300*, 301
Central Asia, Western **6** *187*, *194*, *214*, 219–20, *221*
Bactria **6** *215*, 216, *216*
Khwarazm **6** 218, *218*, *219*
Parthian **6** 217
Tokharistan **6** 221–2
China **6** 706, 708, 717, *734*, 832–3, *833*, 869; **7** 95, 98, 101, 128, 141, 143, 147; **18** 601; **31** 255
Cyprus, ancient **8** 338
Egypt **16** 405
Egypt, ancient **10** 21–2*
Etruscan **10** 609, 612
France **25** 476–7
Greece, ancient **13** *436*, 436–7*, 479, 515, 535, *550*; **22** 160; **29** 814
India, Republic of **15** 174
Indian subcontinent **15** 192; **30** *220*
Iran **16** 393, 408
Iraq **16** 398
Islamic **6** 556; **16** 269, 393, 398, 405, 408
Italy **10** 609, 612
Japan **17** 98–9*, 240–41*, 371, *372*, 390
Hakuhō period (AD 645-710) **23** 822
Kamakura period (1185-1333) **17** 242
Kofun period (*c*. AD 300-710) **17** *31*
Prehistoric **17** 373, 390
Khwarazm **6** 218, *218*, *219*
Korea **18** *292*, 295
Mesoamerica, Pre-Columbian **21** *194*, 250; **26** *181*; **33** 617, *619*
Mesopotamia **1** 853; **20** 326
Mexico **21** *193*; **26** *181*; **33** 617, *619*
Netherlands, the **22** 877
North Africa **1** 368
Parthian **6** 217
Philistine **24** *635*
Prehistoric art **25** *464*, *476*, 476–7, 487, 488, 502, 512, 544, 546; **32** *581*
Remojadas **26** *181*
Rome, ancient **26** 877, 879; **27** 17, *104*
Serbia **25** *464*; **32** *581*
Sogdiana **6** 219–20
South America, Pre-Columbian **29** 175, *193*

clay
historical and regional traditions—cont.
Sri Lanka **29** 475
Sudan **1** *367*
Syria **16** 393
Syria-Palestine **27** 825; **30** 182
Thailand **30** 596
Tibet **30** 823
Togo **1** 305
Tokharistan **6** *221*, 221–2
Tula (Nigeria) **1** 381
Uzbekistan **6** *187*
Vinča culture **25** *464*; **32** *581*
West Mexico **33** *102*
Zapotec **33** *619*
types
argillaceous earth **27** 51
ball **6** 325
bole (red) **4** 254*; **12** 622, 626; **24** 248
bole (white) *see* KAOLIN
bolo **7** 607
china clay *see* KAOLIN
earthenware **30** 493
fire-clays **6** 328, 330
see also stoneware
kaolin *see* KAOLIN
laterite **1** 305; **5** 474; **29** 452, 827
marl clay **10** 21–2, 26, 28
Nile clay **10** 21, 25
pipe **6** 325; **12** 629
raslin *see* KAOLIN
red **6** 325
slip casting **6** 325
stoneware **6** 325; **23** *365*
see also fire-clays
white **13** 479
uses
architecture **1** 305; **15** 909; **16** 269
beads **1** 296; **25** 546
bowls **7** 143; **29** *193*
brick **2** 362; **4** 767, 771
casts **6** 7; **23** 115
ceramics **6** 324–5*; **16** 393; **17** 240–41
chess sets **6** 556
coffins **24** *635*
conservation **12** 629
crayons **8** 128
dolls **17** 371, *372*, 373
dyeing **30** 557, 558
earthenwares **6** 325
figurines
China **7** 141
Cyprus **8** 338
Mexico **21** *194*
Prehistoric art **25** 488, 512
United States of America **22** *669*
Vinča culture **32** *581*
West Mexico **33** *102*
Zapotec **33** *619*
floors **25** 502
frames **4** 254
game-pieces **31** 266
gilding **4** 254
glazes **17** 242
grounds **6** 301; **13** 708; **25** 174
hollow-casting **17** 99
impressions **7** 128
inkstones **7** 95
lacquer **18** 601
masks **17** 390; **21** 250; **29** *209*
modelli **21** 768
moulds **6** 7, 327, 832–3, *833*; **7** 98; **21** 320; **27** 17
panel paintings **4** 254
pendants (jewellery) **25** 546
pigments **27** 51
pipes (smoking) **1** *367*, 368
pisé **4** 771
plaques **13** *550*
plaster **11** 762; **15** 174; **29** 814
pots **1** 381
pottery **1** 285; **6** 869; **13** 535; **16** 398, 408
relief sculpture **6** *187*, *218*, *299*

clay
uses—cont.
rock art 25 487
sarcophagi 13 515; 27 825
sculpture 6 219; 7 607; 10 702
Afghanistan 1 193, 196, 197, 197, 198, 199
Africa 1 418
Bhutan 3 914
Central Asia, Eastern 6 298, 299, 300
Central Asia, Western 6 194, 214, 215, 216, 216, 217, 218, 219–20, 221, 221–2
China 6 706, 708, 717, 734
Greece, ancient 13 436–7*
India, Republic of 15 174
Indian subcontinent 30 220
Japan 17 31, 98–9
Korea 18 292, 295
Mesoamerica, Pre-Columbian 26 181; 33 617
Nubia 23 278
Serbia 25 464
seals 1 856; 15 192
spoons 8 283
statuettes 6 298
stucco 29 827
tablets 30 596
teapots 7 101
tiles 23 822; 30 874
tokens 1 853
toys 7 143, 147; 31 254, 255
wall paintings 1 202; 32 802
walls 1 305
writing-tablets 1 853; 20 326
see also CERAMICS
Clay, Charles 1 784; 7 446
Clay, Henry 24 61, 62
Clay & Co. 24 62
Claydon House (Bucks) 9 485; 10 276, 279; 20 415; 29 835
Claypoole, James (1720-c. 1784) 7 408*; 14 493; 25 452
Claypoole, James, jr (c. 1743-1800) 7 408
Claypotts Castle (Tayside) 28 224
Clays, Paul-Jean 7 408–9*
Clayton, Benjamin 16 15
Clayton, Ellen (Creathorne) 7 409*; 33 309
Clayton, Emilius 31 158
Clayton, John Richard 5 828; 7 410; 28 278
works 29 507
Clayton, Nicholas J(oseph) 7 409*
Clayton (Sussex), St John the Baptist 2 74; 26 650, 657
Clayton, Samuel 2 764
Clayton, Thomas 7 409*; 29 835; 30 675, 759
Clayton, Thomas Varsallis 7 409
Clayton, William Henry 7 409–10*; 23 54
Clayton & Bell 5 828; 7 410*; 19 406; 29 507; 30 533
collaboration 14 281; 28 278, 279
designers 20 446
staff 8 583; 12 493
works 5 514; 29 507, 766
cleaning 7 727*
ceramics 6 334–5*
drawings 9 232
glass 12 797*
metalwork 21 334–6*
paintings 7 727; 29 53; 32 4
silver 7 727
stained glass 29 518*
stone 29 712–13, 713
textiles 30 566*
wood 33 339–40
Cleanthes of Corinth see KLEANTHES OF CORINTH
Clear, Madeline 1 64
Cleare, Campbell 3 64
clear script see under SCRIPTS → types
Clearwell Castle (Glos) 23 209
cleavage see BLISTERING
Cleavin, Barry 7 211
Cleef, Jan van 8 127; 25 585
Cleer (family) 2 336
Cleethorpes Pier 24 748
Cleeve, Alexander 4 353
Cleeve Abbey (Somerset) 30 877
Clegg, John 1 68
Clein, Frantz see CLEYN, FRANCIS (1582-1658)
Cleland, Jack, Paterson & Co. 28 254
works 28 254
Clémansin du Maine, Georges 25 751
Clemen, Paul 18 187
Clemenceau, Georges 4 364
Clémence de La Haye 7 865
Clemens, Fenella Mary Anne see DIXON, FENELLA MARY ANNE
Clemens, Johan Frederik 7 410*; 17 678
collaboration 9 700
works 1 32; 8 734
Clemens, Marie-Jeanne 7 410
Clemens, Samuel 4 364; 30 868
Clemens Franz, Duke of Bavaria (d 1770) 11 124
Clemens Wenceslaus, Elector of Trier 12 167
Clemenswerth Hunting-Lodge 19 269
Clement V, Pope (reg 1305-16) 7 410–11*; 23 461
Clement VI, Pope (reg 1342-52) 7 411*; 11 654
architecture 2 859, 861, 862; 11 208
frescoes 12 697
paintings 2 862; 12 697; 13 150
Clement VII, (Anti-) Pope (reg 1378-94) 2 862; 22 95
Clement VII, Pope (reg 1523-34) 6 140; 19 184; 21 7, 8, 16, 17–18*; 26 769
altarpieces 10 675
architecture 11 208; 12 751; 16 633; 19 313; 21 451, 452; 23 584; 24 754; 25 907; 26 756; 27 742; 30 231; 31 713
fortifications 18 572
military 19 159
coins 6 140
collections 21 264
decorative works 3 645; 25 21
education (art) 16 778
gems 3 817; 12 258
hardstones 14 171
jewellery 5 697; 6 141; 17 521
medals 6 147
models 32 689
paintings 3 257; 24 198; 25 903; 28 333, 335; 31 523, 524
frescoes 25 77; 26 816, 818
rock crystal 16 745
sculpture 3 157, 158; 22 12; 27 448; 31 320
restoration 22 32
tapestries 26 779
Clement VIII, Pope (reg 1592-1605) 1 594–5*
architecture 11 270; 18 699; 30 344
books 23 898
drawings 26 802
gold 30 387
intarsia 26 779
medals 4 323
mosaics 26 809
paintings 1 553; 2 493; 4 813; 13 795; 18 870; 24 239; 26 809; 27 122
frescoes 1 551; 26 818
prints 1 551
sculpture 7 842; 20 412; 26 846
Clement IX, Pope (reg 1667-70) 20 378; 26 771; 27 171–2*
collections 27 172
drawings 3 834
Clement IX, Pope (reg 1667-70)—cont.
paintings 7 394; 25 563
sculpture 3 833; 25 851
sponsorship 12 649
stucco 29 830
Clement X, Pope (reg 1670-76) 1 727; 3 674; 20 921; 31 289
architecture 26 831
frescoes 1 728; 20 375
mosaics 26 810
Clement XI, Pope (reg 1700-21) 1 532–3*; 12 533; 14 106; 16 758; 20 921
architecture 25 636; 26 760, 826; 29 373
books 25 411
collections 26 775
competitions 26 842
decorative works 26 834
drawings 1 533
mosaics 11 682
paintings 6 568; 8 159; 19 816; 25 388, 690; 26 827, 836
frescoes 7 682; 26 817
sculpture 5 525; 16 764; 21 889; 26 774; 30 704
tapestries 25 644; 26 778
Clement XII, Pope (reg 1730-40) 7 896, 897–8*
architecture 2 1; 11 814; 12 8, 9; 16 764; 22 5; 26 761, 820
collections 13 605; 26 775
paintings 12 534
prints 4 492; 7 898
sculpture 2 169; 4 621; 7 860; 9 23; 16 771; 27 45, 46, 115; 31 826
allegorical 27 646
fountains 7 672
religious 1 132
restorations 1 533; 6 97; 26 798
Clement XIII, Pope (reg 1758-69) 3 707; 24 240; 26 286–7*; 33 242
architecture 24 844
furniture 24 844
prints 24 843
Clement XIV, Pope (reg 1769-75) 7 411–12*
architecture 14 198; 28 754
collections 13 605; 27 115; 33 385
sculpture 27 46
Clément, Adolphe 18 462
Clement, Augustine 20 678
Clément, Charles 7 412*; 11 674
Clement, Clara 33 308, 309
Clement, Paul 16 612
Clement, Richard 2 764
Clement, Saint 23 373
Clement, Samuel 20 678
Clément de Ris, (Athanase-)Louis (-Torterat) 7 412*
Clemente, Angelo di Battista see BATTISTA CLEMENTE, ANGELO DI
Clemente, Francesco 7 412–13*; 16 682
collaboration 32 863
groups and movements 25 360
patrons and collectors 2 561
works 16 683; 21 897; 32 902; 33 364
Clemente, Il see SPANI, PROSPERO
Clemente, José 23 445
Clementi, Maria Giovanni 28 18
Clementia of Hungary, Queen of France (d 1328) 13 158
Clementina, La see CLEMENTI, MARIA GIOVANNI
Clement of Chartres 27 252
Clements, Nathaniel 16 8; 23 860
Clements, Robert, 1st Earl of Leitrim 16 36
Clementsz., Jacob 19 101; 22 835
Clemmensen, Andreas 27 168
Clemmensen, Ebbe 4 184
Clemmensen, Karen 4 184
Clendenning, Max 8 804
Clennell, Luke 3 898; 7 413*
Cleomenes 1 614
Cleopatra III (reg 116-88 BC) 9 778, 893
Cleopatra VII (reg 51-30 BC) 1 615; 2 422; 9 778, 893
Cleopatra Berenike (reg 81-80 BC) 9 778
Cleopatra Tryphaena (reg 58-55 BC) 9 778
Cleopatra's Needle see under LONDON → monuments and memorials; NEW YORK → parks and gardens → Central Park
clepsydrae see CLOCKS → types → water-clocks
Clerc, Guillaume le see GUILLAUME LE CLERC
Clerck, Hans 30 104
works 30 104
Clerck, Hendrik de 3 613; 7 413–14*
collaboration 4 915, 916
patrons and collectors 3 613; 13 916
works 1 686; 7 414
Clerck, Jacob de 7 414
Clerck, Jakob Friedrich 21 417
Clerck, Nicolaus de 19 564
Clerck, Pieter de 10 725; 12 514
Clerc & Margeridon 8 792
Clercq, Jean du see JEAN DU CLERCQ
Clere, Frederick de Jersey 7 415*; 23 54
Clère, Pierre-Thomas Le see LE CLÈRE, PIERRE-THOMAS
clerestories 6 493; 7 415*; 13 40, 132
clerestory windows see under WINDOWS → types
Clérian, Louis-Mathurin 7 762
clerical script see under SCRIPTS → types
Clerichetti, Luigi 19 782
Clerici, Felice 16 736; 21 529
Clérion, Jean-Jacques 4 534; 7 415*
Clérisseau, Charles-Louis 7 415–17*; 11 627
collaboration 1 135; 2 337; 10 850; 17 467; 18 879; 26 352; 31 591
groups and movements 10 643; 22 734, 738
patrons and collectors 2 245; 28 908
pupils 1 135; 4 333; 10 447; 17 850
reproductive prints by others 8 267; 33 721
works 2 245, 332; 7 384, 416; 16 717; 18 886; 19 85; 24 583; 25 192; 26 352; 31 591
Clérisseau, Jacques Louis 23 544
Clérissy (family) 20 474
Clérissy, Antoine 11 605; 24 148
Clérissy, Joseph 11 605; 20 474
Clérissy, Pierre 4 177; 11 605; 22 242
Clerk, George 4 288
Clerk, James 28 235
Clerk, James, 3rd Baronet of Penicuik (1709-82) 7 417, 418*; 27 333; 28 227, 269
Clerk, John (i) (1611-74) 7 417–18*; 28 270
Clerk, John (ii) (1728-1812) 7 417, 418–19*; 32 799
Clerk, John, 1st Baron Eldin (1757-1832) 7 417, 419*
Clerk, John, 1st Baronet of Penicuik (1649-1722) 7 417
Clerk, John, 2nd Baronet of Penicuik (1679-1755) 7 417, 418*; 28 236
architecture 1 134; 28 227, 269
Clerk, John, 2nd Baronet of Penicuik (1679-1755)—cont.
gardens 12 129
paintings 28 271
Clerk, Simon 5 514; 7 419*
clerks of works 7 420*; 20 560, 561
Clermont, Andien de 10 278; 28 776; 33 225
Clermont, Beraud III, Comte de 20 634
Clermont, Louis, Comte de (fl 1326) 17 463
Clermont, Louis de Bourbon-Condé, Comte de (fl 1736) 2 701
Clermont, Robert Capet, Comte de 4 543
Clermont-Ferrand
Cathedral of Notre-Dame 1 765; 7 254; 8 224; 13 42; 26 46, 585
ambulatory 1 767
restoration 2 320
sculpture 26 601, 641
stained glass 26 702
tracing floor 31 275
vaults 32 87
figurines 27 110
Notre-Dame-du-Port 26 585
arches 2 294
capitals 26 601
sculpture 26 601
Clermont-Tonnerre, Antoine de, Comte 28 468
Clermont-Tonnerre, Charles-Henry de 25 790
Clert, Iris 7 421*, 685; 14 52
Clerville, Louis Nicolas, Chevalier de 20 472
Cléry-Saint-André, Notre-Dame 11 154, 511; 13 59, 59, 60
clock-cabinets see under CABINETS (ii) (FURNITURE) → types 22 220
Cles, Bernhard von, Cardinal, Prince-Bishop of Trent 5 180; 9 185; 11 236; 12 736; 13 293; 24 248
architecture 5 181
coats of arms 24 249
metalwork 3 69
Clésinger, (Jean-Baptiste-) Auguste 7 421*; 8 792
works 11 567
Clésinger, Georges Philippe 7 421
Clés pour les arts 24 429
Cless, Jean-Henri 8 561
Cletcher, Daniel 9 470
Cletcher, Thomas, the elder (fl c. 1612) 21 509
Cletcher, Thomas, the younger (fl 1643) 21 509
Cletos Noa, Amalia 25 701
Cletos Noa, Asunción 25 701
Cletos Noa, Juan 25 701
Cletos Noa, Magdalena 25 701
Cletus, Bishop of Eger 3 524
Cletzer, Thomas 30 118
Cleve 7 422*; 12 360
Franciscan church 13 114
Lustgarden 9 760
St Mariä Himmelfahrt 8 216
sculpture 13 91
Städtisches Museum Haus Koekkoek 18 188
Clève, Corneille van (1646-1732) 3 122; 7 422–3*; 8 71
collaboration 8 71; 12 727
reproductions in ceramics 8 748
works 7 423; 24 165
Cleve, Heinrich von, Abbot of Liesborn see HEINRICH VON CLEVE, Abbot of Liesborn
Cleve, Herman van 2 452
Cleve (i), Cornelis van (1520-70) 7 423, 424, 426–7*
Cleve (i), Joos van 2 206; 7 423–6*
collaboration 24 261

- Cleve (i), Joos van—cont.
  - patrons and collectors **4** 243; **21** 485; **26** 112; **28** 904
  - pupils **7** 426
  - teachers **17** 601
  - works **7** 423, *424*, *426*; **9** 274; **11** 459; **27** 693; **31** 882; **32** 874
- Cleve (ii), Gillis van, I (*fl c.* 1600) **7** 427
- Cleve (ii), Gillis van, II (1557-97) **7** 427, 428
- Cleve (ii), Hans van **7** 427
- Cleve (ii), Hendrik van, I (before 1489-after 1520) **7** 427
- Cleve (ii), Hendrik van, II (*fl* 1489-1520) **7** 427
- Cleve (ii), Hendrik van, III (1525-1590/5) **7** 427–8*
  - collaboration **7** 427, 428
  - pupils **14** 379
  - works **7** 427; **18** 706
- Cleve (ii), Hendrik van, IV (*c.* 1598-1649) **7** 427
- Cleve (ii), Joris van **7** 427, 428
- Cleve (ii), Marten van, I (1527-1581) **7** 427–8*
  - collaboration **7** 427; **23** 112; **32** 726
  - reproductive prints by others **4** 442
  - works **3** 558; **7** 427, *428*
- Cleve (ii), Marten van, II (before 1598-1649) **7** 427, 428
- Cleve (ii), Nicolaas van **7** 427, 428
- Cleve (ii), Willem van, I (*fl* 1518-43) **7** 427; **21** 368
- Cleve (ii), Willem van (1530/35-before 1560) **7** 427
- Clevedon Court (Somerset) **26** 419
- Clevedon Pier (Avon) **24** 748
- Cleveland (OH) **7** 428–9*; **31** *587*
  - Billingham Forum **29** 428
  - collections **17** 434
  - Museum of Art **7** 429, *429*; **10** 84; **14** 281; **16** 557; **22** 359, 365; **31** 667
    - collections **6** 735, 826; **7** 156; **10** 94; **11** 308; **14** 139; **15** 743, 745; **30** 332
    - drawings **9** 231
    - exhibitions **7** 157, 158
    - Greek collection **13** 470
    - manuscripts **22** 795
    - sculpture **22** 795; **27** 46
  - Park Synagogue **17** 549, *549*
  - Shaker Heights **7** 429
  - Trinity Cathedral **29** 515
- Cleveland, Barry **8** 528
- Cleveland, Frank **8** 111
- Cleveland, Grover **14** 252
- Cleveland, Horace William Shaler **7** 429–30*; **21** 649; **25** 666
- Cleveland Bridge and Engineering Ltd **4** 800
- Cleveley, John, sr (*c.* 1712-77) **7** 430–31*; **20** 424
- Cleveley, John, jr (1747-86) **7** 430*
- Cleveley, Robert **7** 430*
- Clevenberghe, Antoon **19** 260
- Cleves *see* CLEVE
- Cleves, Anne of, House Museum *see under* LEWES (E. SUSSEX)
- Cleves, John I, Duke of *see* JOHN I, Duke of Cleves
- Cleves, Margaret, Countess of *see* MARGARET, Countess of Cleves
- Cleves, Philip of *see* PHILIP OF CLEVES
- Clewell, Charles Walter **31** 639
- Clewell Metal Art **31** 639
- Cleyn, Francis (1582-1658) **7** 431*; **19** 592; **22** 153
  - patrons and collectors **3** 178
  - pupils **9** 56; **12** 600
  - reproductive prints by others **19** 562
  - works **6** 390; **10** 349, 725
- Cleyn, Francis, the younger (1625-50) **7** 431
- Cleyn, John **7** 431
- Cleyn, Penelope **7** 431
- *cliché photographique sur verre see* PHOTOGRAPHY → processes → cliché-verre
- *cliché-verre see under* PHOTOGRAPHY → processes
- Clichy **11** 613; **15** *829*; **24** 57
  - Maison du Peuple **11** 526
- Cliff, Clarice **7** 434*; **10** 313
- cliff inscriptions **6** 741, 744
- Clifford, Anne *see* SACKVILLE, ANNE, Countess of Dorset
- Clifford, Bede **3** 63
- Clifford, Charles **7** 435*; **24** 664
- Clifford, George, 3rd Earl of Cumberland **14** *546*
- Clifford, Henry E. **12** 775
- Clifford, Thomas **4** 79
- Clifford of Chudleigh, Baron **26** 532
- Clifton (NJ), Holy Face Shrine **28** 632
- Clifton, Arthur **5** 516, 517
- Clifton, Marshall (Waller Gervase) **2** 741; **7** 435*
- Clifton Art Pottery **31** 639
- Clifton Hall **2** 148
- climbing kilns *see under* KILNS → types
- Climent, Enrique **12** 59
- Climent, Josep **29** 306, 319
- Climping (W. Sussex), St Mary's **10** 286
  - chest **10** *286*
- Cline Town, Fourah Bay College **28** 691
- Clinic Painter **13** 523; **32** 55
- Clint, Alfred **7** 436
- Clint, George **7** 435–6*; **19** 806
- Clinton, Alan **10** 421
- Clinton, Charles William **7** 436*; **25** 371
- Clinton, De Witt **10** 851; **24** 691
- Clinton, Edward Fiennes de **7** 436*; **14** 296
- Clinton, Fiennes Henry, 9th Earl of Lincoln **8** 474; **13** 302
- Clinton, Margery **28** 258
- Clinton, Paul **19** 492
- Clinton & Russell **7** 436*; **31** 855
- Clio Painter **32** 28
- clipei (i) (medallions) **7** 436*
- clipei (ii) (baths) **7** 436*
- clippy rugs *see under* RUGS → types
- clips **17** 529
- Clipsham (Western Isles) **29** 531
- Clipstone Street Academy *see* ARTISTS' SOCIETY, THE
- Clique, the **7** 436–7*; **8** 152; **9** 756; **10** 254
  - members **11** 795; **23** 442; **24** 636
- Clisset, Philip **12** 649
- Clisson **5** 356; **12** 174
- Clite, Lieven van der *see* LIEVEN VAN DER CLITE
- Clitunno *see* CAMPELLO SUL CLITUNNO
- Clive, Edward, 2nd Baron Clive **12** 75; **20** 53
- Clive, Robert, 1st Baron Clive **7** 437*
  - architecture **7** 374; **14** 681; **20** 53
  - armour **14** 185
  - chess sets **15** 724
  - collections **15** 741, 744; **17** 475
  - drawings **13** 650
  - enamel **15** 712
  - interior decoration **4** 875
  - silver **15** 707
- Cliveden (Bucks) **8** 794; **24** 821; **28** 648
  - dovecot **9** 202
  - gardens **32** 552
  - paintings **14** 143; **21** 148
  - sculpture **2** 646; **6** 121; **29** 724
- Clive Museum *see under* POWIS CASTLE (POWYS)
- Clive of India *see* CLIVE, ROBERT, 1st Baron Clive
- cloak pins *see under* PINS → types
- cloaks
  - historical and regional traditions **9** 257–8
    - Aboriginal Australia **1** 56*
    - Africa **1** *424*
    - Byzantine **9** 639
    - Early Christian (*c.* AD 250-843) **9** 639
    - England **9** 274
    - Fulani **1** 348
    - Greenland **3** 441
    - Hawaii **14** 248–9, *249*
    - Indian subcontinent **15** 736, *736*
    - Maori **20** *357*, *358*
    - Native North Americans **22** 652
    - Netherlands, the **9** 274
    - Rome, ancient **9** 251
    - South Africa **10** 848
    - Surinam **1** *424*
    - Tarascan **30** 342
    - 11th cent. **9** 255
  - materials
    - beadwork **3** 441
    - cotton **1** *424*
    - embroidery **15** 736, *736*
    - feathers **10** 848; **14** 248–9, *249*; **22** 652; **30** 342
    - flax **20** *358*
    - skins **1** 56*; **20** *358*
- clochans *see under* HUTS → types
- Clochar, Pierre **20** 869; **31** 130
- Cloche, Antonin, Master General of the Dominican Order **19** 816
- Cloche, Jean de la *see* JEAN DE LA CLOCHE
- clocher-porche *see* WESTWORKS
- Clock, Hendrick **13** 255
- clock-cabinets *see under* CABINETS (ii) (FURNITURE) → types
- clocks **7** 437–48*
  - conservation **7** 729
  - historical and regional traditions
    - Austria **7** 442, 446, 448
    - Britain **7** 441–2*, *443*, 445–6*, 448
    - China **7** 438
    - Egypt, ancient **7** 437
    - England **7** 438, 439; **10** 291
    - France **3** *753*; **7** *438*, 439, 442, 446, 447; **11** *626*; **29** 573
    - Germany **7** 439, 442, 447; **12** III2
    - Ireland **16** 26
    - Islamic **7** *437*, 438
    - Italy **7** 439; **16** 726
    - Japan **7** 442*, 447
    - Malta (Republic of) **20** 215
    - Netherlands, the **7** 441, 442, 446
    - Poland **25** 129
    - Spain **7** 438
    - Switzerland **10** 135
    - United States of America **7** 446*; **20** 593; **31** 624, 629
  - materials
    - automata **7** 438, 445
    - bells **7** 438
    - brass **7** 439
    - bronze **11** *626*
    - ebony **7** 445
    - enamel **12** III2
    - gilding **7** 445
    - glass **7** 439
    - iron **7** 445
    - laburnum **7** 442
    - mahogany **7** 445
    - olive-wood **7** 442
    - ormolu **7** *445*
    - paper **7** 448
    - papier mâché **24** 63
    - rock crystal **7** 439
    - satin-wood **7** 445
    - silver **7** 439, *440*, 442, 445
    - springs **7** 439
    - steel **7** 439
- clocks
  - materials—cont.
    - velvet **7** 442
    - walnut **7** 442, *447*
    - weights **7** 438
  - restoration **7** 729
  - techniques
    - gilding **7** *440*; **8** *397*; **12** III2
    - intarsia **8** *397*
    - mass production **7** 447
  - types
    - 400-day **7** 448
    - alarm **7** 439
    - Atmos **7** 448
    - balloon **7** 445
    - bracket **7** 441, 445
    - carriage **7** 446, 447
    - cartel **7** 446; **26** 303, *304*
    - clepsydrae *see* water-clocks
    - cuckoo **7** 447
    - electric **7** 448
    - Eureka **7** 448
    - Gothic **7** 439
    - grandfather *see* longcase
    - lantern **7** 441
    - longcase **7** 441, 445; **8** *397*
    - lyre **7** 446
    - musical **22** 375
    - observatory **7** 446
    - organ **7** *445*, 446
    - pendulum **7** 441, 442
    - pillar **7** 439
    - portico **7** 446
    - quartz crystal **7** 448
    - Religieuse **7** 442
    - Roxbury **31** 629
    - shelf **7** 446
    - ship-clocks **7** 439, *440*
    - skeleton **7** 448
    - sundials *see* SUNDIALS
    - tabernacle **2** 812; **7** 439
    - table **7** 439
    - tavern **7** 446
    - Vienna Regulator **7** 446, *447*
    - wall **7** 442, 446
    - water-clocks **7** 437; **13** 382
    - zappler **7** 446
- clock towers *see under* TOWERS → types
- Clocociov **26** 712
- Clodion **1** 132; **7** 449–51*; **22** 456; **23** 796
  - attributions **11** 336
  - competitions **7** 673
  - patrons and collectors **5** 439; **11** 561; **13** 665; **27** 223
  - pupils **20** 422
  - reproductive prints by others **27** 571
  - sculpture **30** 496, *501*; **33** 3
    - history **2** 53; **7** *450*
    - monumental **21** 411
    - mythological **1** 133; **11** 562; **23** 295; **29** 573, *573*
    - reliefs **30** 495
    - statuettes **30** 499
- Clodion, Nicholas Michel **7** 450
- Clodion, Pierre-Joseph Michel **7** 450
- Clodion, Sigisbert-Francois Michel **7** 450
- Clodion, Sigisbert-Martial Michel **7** 450
- Cloes (family) **22** 452
- Cloete, Shirley **29** 118
- Cloetinge, Pieter Hugenz. van **20** 802
- cloisonné enamel *see under* ENAMEL → techniques
- cloisonné masonry *see under* MASONRY → types
- cloisonné paint *see under* PAINT → types
- Cloisonnism **2** 124; **3** 813; **7** 451–2*; **12** 189; **25** 215
- cloister gardens *see under* GARDEN → types
- Cloister Press **22** 117
- cloisters **6** 165; **7** 452–8*
  - Benedictine Order **7** 453
  - Buddhism **17** 66
  - Carolingian **5** 795; **7** 452, 453
  - Carthusian Order **7** 453
  - Cistercian Order **7** 453, 455
  - England **7** 452, 453, 455, 456, *456*; **12** 799
  - France **5** *369*; **7** 454, *455*, 455–6; **26** *604*
  - Gothic **5** *369*; **7** 455–6*, *456*
  - Islamic **16** 184, 204
  - Italy **3** *716*; **7** 455, *457*, 457–8, *920*; **22** *485*
  - Japan **17** 66
  - Peru **24** 502
  - Portugal **25** *290*; **31** *178*
  - Romanesque **3** 333, *716*; **7** 454–5*, *455*; **21** *899*; **26** *604*
  - Sicily **21** *899*
  - Spain **7** 455; **31** *87*
  - Switzerland **3** 333
  - Syria **7** 453
  - Turkey **16** 184, 204
- Cloisters Cross **8** 201; **26** *697*, 698
- Cloister Unicorn, Master of the *see* UNICORN HUNT, MASTER OF THE
- cloister vaults *see under* VAULTS (CEILING) → types
- Cloître, Martin *see* CLAUSTRE, MARTIN
- Clokey & Co. **16** 41
- Clones (Co. Monaghan) **16** 34
- Clonfert, Cathedral of St Brendan (Co. Galway) **3** 443; **7** 458*; **16** *5*; **26** 592, 618, *618*
  - sculpture **16** 19
- Clonmacnois Monastery (Co. Offaly) **7** 458–60*; **16** *5*; **21** 834
  - crosses **15** 876
  - Cross of the Scriptures **7** 459, *460*; **16** 19
  - Nuns' Church **16** 19
  - sculpture **7** 459–60*; **15** 877; **26** 618
  - Temple Fingin **26** 592
- Clonmel, Mechanics Institute **16** 37
- Clonney, James Goodwyn **7** 460*; **17** 823
- Cloquet, Jules **1** 845
- Cloquet, Louis **7** 460–61*
  - education (art) **3** 618
  - teachers **3** 885
  - works **3** 550; **12** 518
- Clore, Charles **8** 569
- Clos **29** 376
- Close, Chuck **7** 461*; **13** 677; **24** 686, 687; **31** 609
- close-eave pagodas *see under* PAGODA → types
- closets **9** 11, 14
  - lady's closets **28** 252
- Closs, Lambert **5** 574
- closs beds *see under* BEDS → types
- Closterman, John **7** 461–2*
  - collaboration **26** 394
  - patrons and collectors **7** 796
  - works **7** *796*; **11** *423*
- Closterman, John Baptist **7** 461
- Clot, Auguste **19** 489, 490; **20** 603
  - works **19** *489*, *490*
- Clot-Bey, Antoine Barthélmi **10** 94
- Clotet, Lluis **3** 217; **29** 274
- Clotet Ballús, Lluis **29** 861
- cloth *see* TEXTILES
- clothes *see* DRESS
- clothes-presses **12** 426
- Clothilde, Queen (*fl* 481-511) **2** 847
- Clothmakers' Altarpiece **14** 293
- Cloths of Aresta **16** 440
- Clotz, Valentin *see* KLOTZ, VALENTIJN
- Clouet, Albert *see* CLOUWET, ALBERT

Clouet, David *see* CLOUWET, DAVID
Clouet, François **7** 462, 464–6*; **11** 656
  attributions **7** 463
  patrons and collectors **19** 752; **23** 523; **31** 849
  portraits **11** 400, 532
    death-masks **25** 276
    miniatures (paintings) **21** 639
    paintings **7** *465*; **9** 274, 275; **11** 400, 634; **31** *849*, 851
Clouet, Genet *see* CLOUET, JEAN
Clouet, Jean **7** 462–6*; **11** 656; **20** 664
  patrons and collectors **21** 639; **31** 849
  pupils **7** 464, 466
  works **7** *462*, *463*; **9** 274; **11** 532; **21** 638; **24** 133
Clouet, Michiel **7** 462
Clouet, Pieter *see* CLOUWET, PIETER
Clouet, Polet **7** 462
Clough, A. H. **13** 810
Clough, Richard **32** 782, 784
cloutie rugs *see* RUGS → types → proggy
Cloutt, Thomas *see* RUSSELL, THOMAS CLOUTT
Clouwet, Albert **7** 466*
Clouwet, David, I (*d* 1668/9) **7** 466
Clouwet, David, II (*b* 1655) **7** 466
Clouwet, Pieter **7** 466*
cloves **3** 331; **15** 810
Clovio, Giulio **5** 182; **7** 467–9*; **25** 296; **32** 160
  collaboration **4** 896
  patrons and collectors **5** 789; **10** 810; **13** 658; **14** 5, 806
  pupils **4** 317; **14** 661
  reproductive prints by others **7** 899
  teachers **19** 323
  works **7** *467*, *468*; **8** 178; **21** 639; **33** 592
Clovis I, King of France (*reg* 481-511) **24** 115, 165
Clow, Alexander **28** 243
Clow, William **28** 243
Club Dada **8** 436
Club des Hydropathes **33** 198
Club dos Artistas Modernos **4** 718
Club du Livre **33** 634
Clube de Gravure **4** 719
Club Motonautico A.M.I.L.A. **19** 421
Club of Croatian Architects **18** 412
Club of the seven *see* SIEBENERKLUB
Club of Young Artists and Scientists **4** 234; **9** 50; **29** 582
clubs (meeting places) **3** *282*; **7** *469*, 469–70*, *470*; **12** *877*; **21** *93*; **27** *720*; **29** *370*, *770*; **31** *334*
clubs (weapons)
  historical and regional traditions
    Aboriginal Australia **1** 55
    Angola **7** *198*
    Central Asia, Eastern **6** 305
    Egypt, ancient **10** 40
    Fiji **11** 69; **27** 234
    Inca **29** 205
    Maori **23** *734*
    Maya **21** 246
    Mesoamerica, Pre-Columbian **21** 245, 246
    Native North Americans **22** 586
    Pacific Islands **23** *734*
    Papua New Guinea **23** 734
    Solomon Islands **29** 49
    Songo **7** *198*
    South America, Pre-Columbian **29** 205
    Sri Lanka **29** 469
    Zulu **1** 362
clubs (weapons)—cont.
  materials
    greenstone **23** *734*
    wood **7** *198*; **22** 586
Clugny, Ferry de, Cardinal *see* FERRY DE CLUGNY, Cardinal
Cluj, Thomas of *see* THOMAS OF CLUJ
Cluj-Napoca **7** 471–2*; **26** *705*, *906*
  architecture **14** 884, 885
  Bánffy Palace *see* Museum of Art
  Bontida Palace **26** 709
  churches
    Franciscan church **17** 601; **26** 708
    Jesuit church **26** 713
    Minorite house *see* Franciscan church
    Protestant church **15** 7
    St Michael **14** 884; **26** 711, 713, 718
  education (art) **26** 726
  enamel **13** 162
  Ethnographical Museum of Transylvania **7** 472
  Historical Museum of Transylvania **7** 471
  houses **26** 707, 712
  Institute of Fine Arts **26** 721
  iron **15** 9
  Jesuit college **26** 708
  jewellery **15** 10
  metalwork **15** 5; **26** 719
  monument to Matthias Corvinus **14** 896
  Museum of Art **7** 472; **26** 708, 713, 724
    collections **26** 717
  sculpture **14** 893
  Teleky Palace **26** 708
  Town Hall **26** 709
  University collection **26** 723
Clun **6** 55
clunch **29** 699
Cluniac Order **3** 709; **7** 231, 472–3*
  monasteries **7** *476*
  patronage **7** 473*
  sculpture **26** 596
  vaults (ceiling) **32** 88
  see also BENEDICTINE ORDER
Cluny (France)
  Abbey **3** 709; **7** 231, 472–3, 474*, 476*; **11** *505*, 554, 653; **21** *836*, 838
    arches **2** 295, 298
    chapter house **6** 464
    Cluny I **7** 474
    Cluny II **7** 266, 474; **11** 509; **12** 5; **13** 36; **21** 836; **26** 583
      refectory **21** 845
      westwork **33** 109
    Cluny III **7** 266, 473, 474–6*, *474*, *476*, 478–9; **11** 510; **12** 5; **14** 508; **21** 840; **26** *583*, 583–4; **32** 397
      capitals **7** 476–8, *477*; **26** 599, 601, 602
      sculpture **26** 602
      transept **31** 281
      Virgin chapel **18** 621
      West Portal **7** 478, *478*
    gate-house **12** 175
    Infirmary **14** 780
    manuscripts **11** 653; **26** 669; **32** 637
    sculpture **7** 476*, 478–9*; **11** 554
      capitals **7** 476–8*
      West Portal **7** 478*
    spires **29** 413
    vaults **32** 88
    wall paintings **26** 654
    workshops **29** 851
  houses **32** 280
  Maison Du Pontet **30** 904
Cluny Castle **22** 531
Cluny Lectionary *see under* LECTIONARIES → individual manuscripts
Cluny Master **7** 477
Clupea *see* KELIBIA
Clusium *see* CHIUSI
Clusium group **10** 616
Clusius, Carolus **12** 131, 133; **19** 64
clustered piers *see under* PIERS (ii) (MASONRY) → types
Clutterbuck, Jock **2** 754
Clutton, Henry (1814-95; surveyor) **7** 479
Clutton, Henry (1819-93; architect) **7** 479*
  assistants **3** 745; **5** 193
  collaboration **3** 745
  competitions **7** 668
  patrons and collectors **3** 746
  works **19** 381
Cluysenaar, Alfred **7** 480
Cluysenaar, Jean-Pierre **7** 479–80*; **27** 551
  assistants **31** 896
  works **3** 548; **5** 41
Cluzel **11** 417
Clydach Valley Industries **32** 789
Clyde Pottery **28** 257
Clynnog Fawr, St Beuno's **32** 782
clysters **24** 580
clyster tubes **29** 133
Clytha Castle (Gwent) **6** 61; **11** 242
C Magazine **24** 430
Ćmielów **25** 123
Cmolas **25** 121
C&N Buttons & Jewellery Production **4** 834
Cnidus *see* KNIDOS
Cnoop, Jacob **8** 551
Cnottaert, Hans **32** 709
Cnottaert, Jan Adriansen **32** 709
Cnudde, Louis **14** 326
Coabey **25** *698*
coach watches *see under* WATCHES → types
Coad, Richard **20** 27
Coade, Eleanor **2** 541; **7** 480*; **28** 242; **30** 502
  designers **10** 265
  works **6** 9
Coade and Sealy **7** 480
Coade Artificial Stone Manufactory **2** 541; **3** 25; **7** 480; **27** 197
Coade stone **2** 541, *541*; **7** 480; **30** 502–3
coal
  historical and regional traditions
    China **7** 98
    England **10** 297
    Japan **17** 388
    Scotland **28** 255
  uses
    arriccio **10** 740
    crayons **8** 128
    furniture **10** 297; **28** 255
    inksticks **17** 388
Coalbrookdale *see* IRONBRIDGE AND COALBROOKDALE (SALOP)
Coalbrookdale Iron Co. **3** 629, 741; **9** 295; **11** 119; **15** 821; **16** 60; **33** 343
Coalisland Pottery **16** 28, 29
Coalpit Heath Vicarage (Glos) **13** 203, *203*
Coalport China Co. **7** 481
Coalport porcelain factory **4** 65; **6** 93; **7** 480–81*; **10** 309, 310, 311, 312
  marks **20** 441
Coalport Pottery **7** 480
coal-scuttles **11** 119
coal tar **7** 53; **24** 790
Coandă, D. **26** 720
Coane, Robert **18** 834
coastal forts *see under* FORTS → types
coat-armour *see* SURCOATS
coatepantlis **7** 481–2*, *481*
Coates, Joshua **4** 479
Coates, Nigel **7** 482*
Coates, Wells (Wintemute) **7** 482–3*
  assistants **23** 679
  collaboration **2** 578; **19** 891; **22** 719
  groups and movements **10** 241; **20** 475; **31** 673
  pupils **18** 807
  works **2** 216; **4** 810; **7** *483*; **10** 284
coats
  historical and regional traditions
    Borneo **3** 440, *441*
    Byzantine **9** 643
    Central Asia, Eastern **6** 310
    China **7** 74, 76, *76*, 77
    Early Christian (*c.* AD 250-843) **9** 643
    Iran **16** 464, 465
    Islamic **16** 457, 462, 464, 465
    Mongolia **21** 876
    Native North Americans **22** 651
    Ottoman **16** 462
    Turkey **16** 462
  materials
    beadwork **3** 440, *441*
  types
    barbarian *see* short
    frock-coats **9** 284
    short **7** 74, 76
    spiral **7** 75
Coats, Alice Margaret **4** 87
Coats, W. A. **28** 272
coats of arms , ; **6** 332; **10** 328; **12** 271, 272–3; **14** *404*, 404–7, *408*, 408–28*, *412*, *413*, *414*, *415*, *416*, *417*, *418*, *420*, *421*, *422*, *424*, *426*, III1, IV; **25** 285, 328
  see also BLAZONS
Cobá **7** 483–4*; **20** *882*; **21** *372*
  causeway **6** 97
Cobaert, Jacob Cornelisz. **3** 604; **7** 484–5*
Coba Höyük *see under* SAKÇA GÖZÜ
cobalt
  historical and regional traditions
    Belgium **21** 137
    Central Asia, Western **6** 258
    China **6** 869, 872, 888, 901, 902, 903, 906, 909; **16** 394
    Egypt, ancient **10** 55
    Iran **16** 414
    Islamic **16** 248, 394, 414
    Korea **18** 343
  uses
    glass **10** 55; **30** 407
    glazes **6** 869, 872, 888, 902, 906, 909; **16** 248, 394, 407, 414
    pigments **23** 786
    porcelain **6** 901
    pottery **6** 258; **21** 137
cobalt blue *see under* PIGMENTS → types
cobalt oxides **4** 172, 173; **6** 328, 904; **10** 192; **12** 781; **24** 791
cobalt violet *see under* PIGMENTS → types
cobalt yellow *see under* PIGMENTS → types
Cobán **13** *758*
  Museo Regional Verapacense **13** 769
Cobar **1** 55
Cobb, Albert Winslow **29** 648
Cobb, Francis **19** 424
Cobb, Henry Ives **5** 274; **7** 485*
  assistants **22** 275
  collaboration **19** 158
  staff **25** 737
  works **5** 274; **6** 573; **22** 275; **23** 341, *341*; **27** 642
Cobb, Henry Nichols **22** 367; **24** 325, 326
Cobb, John **7** 485–6*; **19** 592; **32** 540
  collaboration **10** 295
  patrons and collectors **7** 659
  works **7** 659; **20** 468
Cobb, Ron **27** 872
Cobb, William R. **7** 745
Cobban Lironi Ltd **28** 231
Cobb & Frost **7** 485
cobble **7** 95
Cobbold, Lady **23** 692
Cobden-Sanderson, T(homas) J(ames) **2** 569, 571; **4** 348, 354; **7** 486–7*
Cobenzl, Charles, Comte de **3** 414; **19** 165
Cobenzl, Ludwig, Graf von **26** 732–3
Cobenzl, Philipp, Graf **6** 92
Cober, Marcin *see* KOBER, MARCIN
Cobergher, Wenceslas **7** 487*; **11** 501; **32** 709
  collaboration **7** 413; **19** 650
  patrons and collectors **13** 917
  works **3** 545, 613
Cobham (Kent)
  Hall **4** 845; **10** 270; **20** 868; **33** 99
  St Mary Magdalene **10** 261
Cobham, John Oldcastle, Lord *see* OLDCASTLE, JOHN, Lord Cobham
Cobham, Richard Temple, 1st Viscount *see* TEMPLE, RICHARD, 1st Viscount Cobham
Cobham, Thomas de, Bishop of Worcester **23** 685
Cobham Portrait **31** 415
Coblenz, Charles, Comte de **5** 43
Cobo, Bernabé **29** 207, 209
Cobo, Jesús **9** 714
Cobos, Diego de los **31** 866
Cobos, Francisco de los **7** 488*; **31** 509
  architecture **31** 865; **32** 116
  metalwork **32** 559
  paintings **12** 910
  sculpture **16** 898
Cobos, Francisco Vela de los **31** 866
Cobra **1** 77, 78, 810; **6** 588; **7** 488–90*, 805; **8** 736; **9** 188; **10** 715; **13** 780; **16** 829, 830; **22** 851, 852; **23** 392; **24** 144; **28** 240
  collections **8** 759; **9** 189; **19** 537; **22** 906; **33** 254
  exhibitions **2** 544; **14** 297
  members
    Alechinsky, Pierre **1** 598; **5** 45
    Appel, (Christiaan) Karel **2** 230
    Atlan, Jean-Michel **2** 693
    Bille, Ejler (Kristian Torbensen) **4** 62
    Brands, Eugène **4** 669
    Constant **7** 758
    Corneille **7** 864
    Ferlov Mancoba, Sonja **10** 899
    Götz, Karl-Otto **13** 217
    Jorn, Asger **17** 658
    Lucebert **19** 768
    Mancoba, Ernest (Methuen Ngungunyana) **20** 243; **29** 112
    Pedersen, Carl-Henning **24** 316
    Rooskens, (Joseph) Anton **27** 137
    Tajiri, Shinkichi **30** 255
  works **7** *489*
Cobra: Revue internationale de l'art expérimental **11** 551
Coburg, Veste Coburg **12** 410; **16** 898
Coburg (House of) **7** 490*
Coburg, Elizabeth, Queen of Belgium *see* ELIZABETH, Queen of Belgium

Coburg, Leopold I, King of Belgium *see* LEOPOLD I, King of Belgium
Coburg, Leopold II, King of Belgium *see* LEOPOLD II, King of Belgium
Coburg Roundels, Master of the **20** 648*
Coburn, Alvin Langdon **7** 491*; **8** 583
collaboration **25** 380
groups and movements **24** 688, 739; **32** 700, 702
works **24** *674*, 675
writings **29** 655
Coca **19** 896; **29** *258*
Castle **4** 784; **6** 58; **7** *491*, 491–2*
Coca, Luís García de *see* GARCÍA DE COCA, LUÍS
Cocama **24** 514; **29** 194
Coccapani, Regolo **7** 492
Coccapani, Sigismondo **7** 313, 492*; **11** 194; **21** 27
Cocceius Auctus, L. **25** 748
Coccetti, Liborio **7** 492–3*
Cocchi, Antonio **6** 148
Cocchi, Mario **28** 319
Cocchi, Raimondo **14** 12
Cocchia, Carlo **22** 474
Coccinà (family) **10** 526
Cochabamba **4** 255, *255*; **7** 493*
art school **4** 270
painting **4** 262, 264; **23** 174
Pinacoteca de Arte Colonial **4** 269; **7** 493
pouches **4** *266*
S Teresa **4** 259, 267
textiles **4** 267
Cochas Grande **13** 229
Coche **21** 292
Cocheco Print Works
works **31** *657*
Cochereau, Leon-Matthieu **8** 561
Cochet, Gustavo **2** 399; **26** 216
Cochetti, Luigi **7** 528; **26** 834
Cochin (i) (India) **6** *623*; **7** 493–4*; **15** *294*, 358, 401
architecture **15** 410
ceramics **6** 918
Mattancheri Palace **7** 494*, *494*; **15** 649
wall paintings **7** 494; **15** 543, *544*
St Francis **7** 494
Cochin (ii), Charles **7** 495
Cochin (ii), Charles-Nicolas, I (1688-1754) **7** 494, 495*; **11** 541, 561
works **2** 699; **10** 391; **31** 175
Cochin (ii), Charles-Nicolas, II (1715-90) **7** 494, 495–6*; **8** 72, 131; **19** 641; **20** 136; **24** 135; **25** 81
collaboration **2** 164; **3** 645; **11** 761; **14** 445; **19** 10
groups and movements **19** 724; **22** 738
patrons and collectors **30** 727
personal collection **19** 217
pupils **11** 173; **21** 815; **25** 80
reproductive prints by others **7** 185, 495; **8** 130, 703; **9** 365; **11** 171, 173; **19** 136; **27** 531; **32** 501
works **1** 104, *105*; **4** 518; **6** 473; **7** *496*; **18** 642; **23** 458; **24** 137, 773
writings **11** 578; **26** 495; **30** 670
Cochin, Denys (-Pierre-Augustin-Marie), Baron **7** 496*; **8** 715
Cochin, Louise-Magdeleine *see* HORTEMELS, LOUISE-MAGDELEINE
Cochin, Nicolas **7** 494*; **19** 144; **28** 742; **30** 659; **32** 356
Cochin, Noël **7** 494
cochineal
historical and regional traditions
Armenia (Europe) **2** 438
Byzantine **9** 665
Central Asia, Western **6** 253
Colombia **7** 607
Early Christian (*c.* AD 250-843) **9** 665
Inca **15** 163
Iran **16** 449
Islamic **16** 449, 468
uses
dyes **2** 438; **6** 253; **9** 491, 492, 665; **10** 872; **15** 163; **16** 449, 468
pigments **18** 655, 656; **23** 786; **24** 796
cochineal, Polish *see* POLISH COCHINEAL
Cóchiti (NM) **22** 607, 668
figurines **22** *669*
Cochläus, Johann **7** 441; **9** 442
Cochran, Charles Blake **21** 312; **30** 687
Cochran Shāhnāma **22** 266
Cochwillan house (Caerns) **32** 782
Cock, César De *see* DE COCK, CÉSAR
Cock, Christopher **7** 500*; **10** 366; **18** 146; **19** 584
dealing **14** 259
Cock, Enrique **29** 301
Cock, Hieronymus (Wellens) **2** 195; **3** 556, 558; **4** 906; **7** 496, 499–500*; **9** 64; **10** 389; **11** 307; **19** 548; **25** 625; **26** 229
collaboration **32** 725
printmakers **15** 42
Bol, Hans **4** 251, 907
Bos, Balthazar van den **4** 442
Bosch, Hieronymus **4** 448
Bruegel, Pieter, I (*c.* 1525/30-1569) **4** 894, 896, 905, 906, 908
Collaert, Hans, I (*c.* 1530-81) **7** 555
Cort (van Hoorn), Cornelis **7** 899
Floris, Cornelis, II (1513-75) **11** 220
Floris, Frans **11** 222
Gassel, Lucas **12** 172
Ghisi, Giorgio **12** 558
Heemskerck, Maarten van **14** 294; **31** 825
Heyden, Pieter van der **14** 505
Hogenberg, Franz **4** 898; **14** 643
Huys, Frans **15** 43
Visscher, Claes Jansz. (1587-1652) **32** 621
pupils **9** 64; **12** 15, 513
reproductive prints by others **14** 5
works **4** 860; **6** 596; **7** *499*; **18** 706; **20** 769; **25** 606; **26** *768*; **29** *748*; **31** 154
Cock, Jan Claudius de (1667-1735) **3** 571; **7** 500*; **32** 251
Cock, Jan de (*fl* 1506-29) **4** 443
Cock, Jan Wellens de (1480-1526) **2** 204; **3** 554; **7** 496, 497*; **25** 17; **33** 355
pupils **18** 5
works **7** *497*; **11** 441
Cock, John **7** 500
Cock, Lucas Cornelisz. de **10** 216
Cock, Maerten de **7** 501*
Cock, Matthijs **7** 496, 498–9*
assistants **13** 664
reproductive prints by others **7** 499
works **7** *498*; **18** 706
Cock, Xavier De *see* DE COCK, XAVIER
Cockburn, James Pattison **7** 501*; **22** 37
patrons and collectors **8** 81
teachers **30** 735
works **5** 564
Cockburnspath (Scotland) **18** 717
Cocke, Peter (*fl* 17th cent.) **10** 745
Cocke, Peter (*b* 1917) **2** 318
Cocker, George **21** 697
Cockerell, Charles **7** 502; **8** 505; **15** 406
Cockerell, Christabel *see* FRAMPTON, CHRISTABEL
Cockerell, C(harles) R(obert) **7** 502–4*; **10** 236
architecture **16** 10
banks **3** 175
chapels **6** 565
churches **4** 822
law courts **2** 171; **19** 505
libraries **5** 512
monuments **13** 201
museums **2** 601; **3** 325; **7** *504*; **10** 370; **22** 362; **23** 689; **25** 267
office buildings **7** *503*; **10** 235; **19** 506, 573
town halls **10** 236
collaboration **9** 723; **10** 152; **12** 167; **25** 35
competitions **7** 667
excavations **13** 612; **23** 490
groups and movements **13** 607, 610, 612–13
metalwork **10** 334
patrons and collectors **3** 239; **24** 571
teachers **7** 502; **28** 872
Cockerell, Samuel Pepys **7** 501–2*; **8** 266; **10** 374
collaboration **20** 490
pupils **30** 361
staff **18** 843, 844
teachers **30** 386
works **8** 461; **15** 406, *407*
Cockerell, Sydney (1906-87) **24** 55
Cockerell, Sydney Carlyle (1867-1962) **7** 505*; **30** 749
Cock Group **13** 510
Cockington (Devon), SS George and Mary **25** 725
Cockleshell Pottery **2** 152
Cockpit Glasshouse **19** 595
Cockpit Hill Pottery **8** 776
Cocks, Gonzales *see* COQUES, GONZALES
Cocks, Robin **7** 505
Cocks and Carmichael **2** 742; **7** 505*
Cockus, John *see* COOQUS, JEAN GÉRARD
Coclé culture **7** 505–7*; **23** *902*; **28** 799; **29** 140, 220
bowls **29** *147*
gold **7** 507; **29** *151*
hardstones **29** 153, 154
pendants (jewellery) **29** *151*
pottery **7** *506*, 506–7*; **29** 147
trade **32** 238
trays **7** *506*
tumbaga **7** 507
Coclers, Jean-Baptiste (1698-1772) **8** 618; **10** 825
Coclers, Jean Baptiste Bernard (1741-1817) **9** 308
Coclers, Louis Bernard **10** 559
Coclers, Marie Lambertine **10** 559
cocoa butter **8** 128
cocobola **24** 515
Cocoglia, Tripo *see* KOKOLJA, TRIPO
Cocom Itzá **21** 244
Cocom Maya **21** 248
Coconuco **7** 602
coconuts **7** 101; **15** 807, 810; **28** *922*
cocoons **7** 113
Cocquele, Guillaume **14** 727
Cocsell, Michal Josef **8** 413
Cocteau, (Clément-Eugène-)Jean (-Maurice) **7** 507–9*; **12** 216; **16** 808
collaboration **3** 754
Cocteau, (Clément-Eugène-)Jean (-Maurice)—cont.
groups and movements **8** 246; **24** 405; **30** 18; **31** 852
patrons and collectors **7** 797; **27** 225
productions **3** 119, 120; **8** 850; **9** 373; **24** 405, 718; **26** 357
textiles **9** 293
writings **6** 460; **7** *508*; **12** 795; **25** 79; **32** 578
illustrated **8** 606; **13** 694; **19** 297
Codallo, Alfred **31** 335
Codazzi, Agustín **7** 609
Codazzi, Viviano **7** 509*
collaboration **6** 35, 346, 347; **21** 483; **29** 253, 544; **30** 122
works **7** *509*
Codde, Pieter **7** 510–11*
pupils **9** 470
works **7** *510*; **11** *443*; **12** 290
Code of Gortyn **8** 154
Code of Hammurabi **1** 892; **3** 9; **5** 134, *134*; **21** 273, 295, *296*; **29** 614; **30** 28
Coderch (y de Sentmenat), José Antonio **7** 511–12*; **29** 274; **30** 391
groups and movements **3** 217
staff **7** 884
works **7** *511*
Codesido, Julia **14** 875; **24** 509
Codex Amiatinus *see under* BIBLES → individual manuscripts
codex aureus *see under* CODICES → types
Codex Aureus (London, BL, MS. Harley 2788) *see under* GOSPEL BOOKS → individual manuscripts
Codex Aureus of Echternach *see under* GOSPEL BOOKS → individual manuscripts
Codex Aureus of St Emmeram *see under* GOSPEL BOOKS → individual manuscripts
Codex Caesarius Upsaliensis *see under* GOSPEL BOOKS → individual manuscripts
Codex Coburgensis, Master of the **20** 649*
Codex Escorial *see under* GOSPEL BOOKS → individual manuscripts
Codex Huygens *see under* CODICES → individual manuscripts
Codex of Vlorë *see under* CODICES → individual manuscripts
Codex Resta *see under* CODICES → individual manuscripts
Codex Sinaiticus *see under* BIBLES → individual manuscripts
Codex style pottery *see under* POTTERY → wares
Codford St Peter (Wilts) stone-carvings **2** 71, *71*
Còdice di Bologna *see* CODICES → individual manuscripts → Codex Cospi
codices **4** 342–4, 346
historical and regional traditions
Carolingian **5** 801
China **7** 63
Egypt, ancient **4** *343*; **24** 88
Greece, ancient **20** 327
Islamic **16** 271
Jewish art **27** 226
Mixteca-Puebla **21** *739*
Rome, ancient **4** 342; **20** 327, 329
individual manuscripts
Anales de Tula (Mexico City, Bib. N. Antropol. & Hist., MSS 35-9) **21** 235
codices
individual manuscripts—cont.
Anonimo Magliabechiano Codex *see* Codex Magliabechiano
Atlantic Codex (Milan, Bib. Ambrosiana) **19** 203; **23** 744
Aubin Manuscript 20 (Paris, Bib. N., MS. Mexicain 20) **21** 202, 233, 235
Barberini Codex (untraced) **27** 733
Bernulphus Codex (Utrecht, Catharijneconvent) **23** 655
Biduini Codex (Koblenz, Landeshauptarchv) **7** 244
Bocskay Schriftmusterbuch *(Vienna, Kunsthistoriches Museum, Bocskay Codex)* **13** *913*
Boxer Codex (untraced) **5** 12
Carcassonne Codex (untraced) **9** 109
Codex Alexandrinus (London, BL, Royal MS. 1.D. V-VIII) **4** 343; **15** 847
Codex Arcerianus (untraced) **5** 448
Codex Aubin (London, BM, Add. MS. 312) **21** 235; **30** 786
Codex B (Paris, Inst. France) **19** 194
Codex Balduini (Koblenz, Landeshauptarchv, Iventory IC, no. 1) **19** 828
Codex Bambergensis (Bamberg, Staatsbib., Ms. Class. 42) **25** 43
Codex Becker 1 (Vienna, Mus. Vlkerknd., MS. 60306) **21** 233, 235
Codex Bodley (Oxford, Bodleian Lib., MS. Mex. d.1) **21** 202, 233, 235, 264; **30** 786
Codex Borbonicus (Paris, Bib. Assemblée N., Y. 120) **2** 907; **21** 234, 235, 256, 257; **30** 786
Codex Borgia (Rome, Vatican, Bib. Apostolica, MS. Borg. Mess. 1) **21** 183, 186, 202, 233, 235, 264, *739*; **33** 617
Codex Boturini (Mexico City, Bib. N. Antropol. & Hist., MSS 35-38) **21** 235; **22** *518*
Codex Calixtinus (Santiago de Compostela, Archvs Catedral, Cod. Calixt. Libert 5) **13** 808
Codex Clementino *see* Vienna Codex
Codex Colombino (Mexico City, Bib. N. Anthropol. & Hist., MS. 35-30) **21** 202, 233, 235
Codex Coner (London, Soane Mus.) **4** 648, 652; **30** 655
Codex Cospi (Bologna, Bib. U., MS. CC 4093) **21** 202, 233, 234
Codex Dioskurides (Vienna, Österreich. Nbib., Cod. med. gr. 1) **2** 98
Codex Dorenberg *see* Codex Colombino
Codex Dresdensis *see* Dresden Codex
Codex Egberti (Trier, Stadtsbib., MS. 24) **9** 750; **12** 382; **20** 330, 754; **23** 653; **26** 101; **31** 325
Codex Fejérváry-Mayer (Liverpool Mus., M 12014) **21** 183, 202, 233, *234*, 235
Codex Franz Josefino *see* Codex Becker 1
Codex Geymüller (Florence, Uffizi, MSS 7792-7907 A **27** 740
Codex Gigas (Uppsala, Ubib.) **13** 914

codices
individual manuscripts—cont.
Codex Hammer **7** 540; **13** 301; **14** 117
Codex Hieroglyphicorum Indiae Meridionales *see* Vienna Codex
Codex Huygens (New York, Pierpont Morgan Lib., MS. M. A. 1139) **14** 874
Varnav, Scarlat **31** 746
Codex Ixtlilxochitl (Paris, Bib. N.) **21** *261*
Codex Kreichgauer *see* Vienna Codex
Codex Laud (Oxford, Bodleian Lib., MS. 54b, Misc. 678) **21** 202, 233, 235, 264; **33** 617
Codex Leicester (Holkam Hall, Norfolk Lib.) **8** 563
Codex Leopoldino *see* Vienna Codex
Codex Magliabechiano (Florence, Bib. N. Cent., MS. Magl. XVII, 17) **4** 64; **11** 73, 691; **14** *873*; **20** 93; **21** 233; **33** 617
Codex Maimuni *(Budapest, Lib. Hung. Acad. Sci., MS. A77/I-IV)* **20** 122, *122*
Codex Mayer *see* Codex Fejéváry-Mayer
Codex Mendoza (Oxford, Bodleian Lib., MS. 3134, Arch. Selden A.1) **10** 779; **11** *152*; **21** 190, *190*, 233, 251, 255, 264; **23** 825
Codex Mexicana (Paris, Bib. N., MSS Mexicain 23-4) **21** 235
Codex Nuttall (London, BM, MS. 19023-8.1) **10** 779; **21** 184, 202, 233, 235, *738*; **30** 786
Codex of S Marta (Naples, Stato, MS. 99. C.I.) **10** 868
Codex of Vlorë (Tiranë, State Archvs) **1** 540
Codex Palatinus Graecus (Rome, Vatican, Bib. Apostolica, Cod. P. Gr. 367) **8** 363
Codex Peresianus *see* Paris Codex
Codex Pérez *see* Paris Codex
Codex Pesth *see* Codex Fejérváry-Mayer
Codex Petrei (Florence, Bib. N. Cent., MS. Magl. XIII, 89) **4** 64; **10** 730; **20** 94
Codex Pighianus (untraced) **2** 161
Codex Porfirio Díaz Reverse (untraced) **21** 235
Codex Purpureus (untraced) **25** 743
Codex Purpureus Petropolitanus (London, BL, Cotton MS. lib. C. IV) **25** 743
Codex Resta (Milan, Bib. Ambrosiana) **6** 146
Codex Riccardianus (Florence, Bib. Riccardiana, MS. 488) **25** 43
Codex Ríos (Rome, Vatican, Bib. Apostolica, MS. 3738) **21** 183, 184, 235
Codex Saussure *see* Codex Becker 1
Codex Sinopensis *see* GOSPEL BOOKS → individual manuscripts → Sinope Gospels
Codex Strozziano (Florence, Bib. N. Cent., MS. Magl. XXV, 636) **4** 64; **10** 730; **20** 94
Codex Telleriano-Remensis (Paris, Bib. N., MS. Mexicain 385) **21** 233, 235

codices
individual manuscripts—cont.
Codex Trivulziano (Milan, Castello Sforzesco) **19** 182
Codex Troana-Cortesianus *see* Madrid Codex
Codex Tro-Cortesianus *see* Madrid Codex
Codex Tudela (Madrid, Mus. América) **21** 183
Codex Tzapotèque *see* Codex Becker 1
Codex Usserianus Primus (Dublin, Trinity Coll. Lib., MS. 55) **15** 873; **16** 12
Codex Vallardi (Paris, Louvre) **24** 862
Codex Vaticanus 3773 *see* Codex Vaticanus B
Codex Vaticanus A *see* Codex Ríos
Codex Vaticanus B (Rome, Vatican, Bib. Apostolica, MS. 3773) **21** 183, 202, 233, 234, 235
Codex Vienna *see* Vienna Codex
Codex Vindobonensis *see* Vienna Codex
Codex Wittekindeus (Berlin, Staatsbib., MS. theol. lat. fol. 1) **23** 653
Codex Xolotl (Paris, Bib. N., MSS Mexicain 1-12 & 373) **21** 235
Codex Zouche *see* Codex Nuttall
Códice Bodleiano *see* Codex Bodley
Códice Borgiano *see* Codex Borgia
Códice Cospiano *see* Codex Cospi
Códice de Bolonia *see* Codex Cospi
Códice del culto a Tonatiuh *see* Aubin Manuscript 20
Códice de Teozoneas *see* Aubin Manuscript 20
Códice di Bologna *see* Codex Cospi
Códice Fábrega *see* Codex Vaticanus B
Codices of Berat (Tiranë, Cent. Archvs) **1** 539, 540
Codice Vaticano Rituale *see* Codex Vaticanus B
Dresden Codex (Dresden, Sächs. Landesbib., MS. R.310) **10** 474; **21** 184, 233, 234, 256, 257, 264
Egbert Codex *see* Codex Egberti
Florentine Codex (Florence, Bib. Medicea-Laurenziana, MS. Palat. 218-220) **21** 191
Fonds Mexicains 20 *see* Aubin Manuscript 20
Fulda Codex (Hannover, Niedersächs. Landesbib., Res. I. 189) **23** 652
Gero Codex (Darmstadt, Hess. Landes- & Hochschbib., Cod. 1948) **23** 653
Glazier Codex (New York, Pierpoint Morgan Lib., MS. G.67) **7** 824
Grolier Codex (Mexico City, Bib. N., Antropol. & Hist.) **21** 233, 234
Hidta Codex (Darmstadt, Hess. Landes- & Hochschbib., Cod. 1640) **7** 583
Hippiatrika Codex (Berlin, Staatsbib. Preuss. Kultbes. Cod. Phillipps 1538) **5** 339
Jordánsky Codex (untraced) **14** 899

codices
individual manuscripts—cont.
Justinian Codex (Turin, Bib. N. U., MS. E.1.8) **4** 395
Laurenziano Codex (Florence, Bib. Medicea- Laurenziana, MS. Ashburnham 361) **11** 692
Le Culte rendu au soleil *see* Aubin Manuscript 2
Liber Hieroglyphoricum Aegyptorum *see* Codex Laud
Libro della China *see* Codex Cospi
Liuthar Codex (Aachen, Domschatzkam.) **20** 330; **23** 654; **28** 24
Lorsch Codex Aureus (Alba Iulia, Batthyaneum Lib; Rome, Vatican, Bib. Apostolica, MS. Pal. lat. 50) **5** 801
Madrid Codex (Madrid, Mus. América, Inventory no. 70300) **21** 183, 184, *184*, 233, 234, 257
Madrid Codex (Dominican) **9** 109
Manasse Codex (Heidelberg, Ubib., MS. Pal. germ. 848) **2** 836; **12** 382; **13** 151; **30** 130; **33** 736
Manuscrit de Veletri *see* Codex Borgia
Manuscrit du cacique *see* Codex Becker 1
Mexicanus I *see* Vienna Codex
Nag Hammadi Codices (Cairo, Coptic Mus.) **7** 824
Paris Codex (Paris, Bib. N., MS. Mexicain 386) **21** 233, 234
St George Codex (Rome, Vatican, Bib. Apostolica, Archv Capitolare S Pietro, MS. C. 129) **20** 649, *650*; **29** 597
Saluzziano Codex (Turin, Bib. Reale, MS. Saluzziano 148) **11** 691
Siena Codex (Siena, Bib. Com. Intronati, MS. S. IV.4) **11** 692
Stockholm Codex Aureus (Stockholm, Kun. Bib., MS. A. 135) **15** 875
Tira de Tepechpan (Paris, Bib. N., MSS Mexicain 13-14) **21** 235
Tonalamatl Aubin (Paris, N. Bib., MS. Mexicain 18- 19) **21** 235
Vienna Codex (Vienna, Österreich. Nbib., Cod. Mexicanus 1) **21** 184, 202, 233, 235
Virgil Codex (Florence, Bib. Riccardiana, MS. 492) **2** 228
Vyšehrad Codex (Prague, Libs Facs & Inst Charles U., MS. XIV. A.13) **8** 388, 421; **25** 552
Weissenau Codex (Schloss Zeil) **14** 50
Wolfegg Codex (Schloss Wolfegg, Fürstl. Samml.) **2** 607
materials
dyes **25** 742–3, *743*
papyrus **24** 88
parchment **4** 342; **20** 329; **24** 107
types
codex aureus **7** 246
Psalmorum Codex *see* PSALTERS → types → Mainz Psalter
purple codices **25** 742–3*, *743*; **27** *174*; **32** *462*
see also BOOKS; MANUSCRIPTS; TABLETS

codicology **7** 513–14*; **28** 303
Codinus, Georgius *see* GEORGIUS CODINUS
Codman, Henry Sargent **5** 274; **6** 573; **23** 422
Codman, Ogden **7** 514–15*; **27** 216; **29** 870; **33** 132
Codman, William Christmas **31** 650
Codrington, Christopher (1668-1710) **14** 255
Codrington, Christopher (Bethell) (*fl* early 19th cent.) **33** 446
Codrington, Kenneth de Burgh **7** 515*
Codrus Painter **13** 523
Codussi, Mauro **7** 515–18*; **16** 630; **24** 25
architecture **32** 184
churches **7** *518*; **12** 31; **16** 631, *631*; **19** 556; **28** 293; **32** 185
palazzi **7** *516*; **13** 649; **16** 631
scuole **19** 554; **32** 185, 224, 225, *226*
towers **5** 177
attributions **19** 554
patrons and collectors **3** 201; **19** 663
pupils **5** 177
Coe, Benjamin Hutchins **7** 284
Coe, Ernest F. **17** 368
Coe, Michael D. **27** 756
Coe, R. T. **22** 679
Coe, Sue **31** 609
Coeberger, Wenceslas *see* COBERGHER, WENCESLAS
Coecke, Maria **4** 905
Coecke, Pieter van, II **7** 518
Coecke van Aelst, Paul **32** 254
Coecke van Aelst, Pieter **1** 799; **2** 195, 206; **4** *895*, 897; **7** 518–20*; **13** 909
assistants **32** 724
collaboration **1** 799; **16** 831; **24** 15
groups and movements **26** 728
paintings **7** *519*
patrons and collectors **13** 909
publications **3** 544, 554; **4** 442; **22** 823
pupils **4** 896; **7** 710; **18** 5; **22** 924
sculpture **3** 569
stained glass **27** 256
tapestries **2** 198; **5** *47*, 47–9; **30** 315; **33** 355
teachers **5** 43; **21** 167; **23** 526; **32** 254
writings **2** 194; **3** 576; **28** 471
Coedès, George **2** 56; **7** 520*; **29** 241
works **9** 401
Coëffier, Antoine, Marquis d'Effiat *see* EFFIAT, ANTOINE COËFFIER, Marquis d'
Coehoorn, Menno van, Baron **7** 520–21*; **21** 570, 580
attributions **7** 613
works **20** 281; **21** *570*
Coelemans, Jacobus **4** 48; **11** 305; **20** 220; **24** 828
Cöeler, Georg *see* KELLER, GEORG
Coelfrith, Abbot of Jarrow **10** 243; **20** 330
Coelho, Ambrósio **7** 521*; **26** 253
Coelho, Caetano de Costa *see* COSTA COELHO, CAETANO DE
Coelho, Domingos **7** 521
Coelho, Duarte **6** 43; **20** 155
Coelho, Francisco (*fl* 1740) **4** 715
Coelho, Francisco Manuel **28** 513
Coelho, Gaspar **7** 521; **26** 253
Coelho, Manuel **10** 729
Coelho da Silveira, Bento **4** 635; **7** 521–2*; **8** 221; **25** 317
Coelho Pó, João **10** 729
Coelho Sampaio, João (1710/20-84) **7** 522*

Coelho Sampaio, José (1750-1810) **7** 522
Coello, Alonso Sánchez *see* SÁNCHEZ COELLO, ALONSO
Coello, Claudio **7** 522–4*; **20** 66; **29** 282
assistants **22** 313
attributions **31** 183
collaboration **6** 343; **11** 491; **17** 586; **31** 183
paintings **26** 438; **31** 89
frescoes **23** 895; **29** 280
portraits **7** *524*
religious **7** *522*; **9** 108, 110; **23** 419; **27** 802
retables **11** 491, *492*; **26** 250
patrons and collectors **9** 112; **10** 406; **14** 11
pupils **2** 379; **32** 557
reproductive prints by others **32** 557
teachers **26** 438
works **10** 504
Coello, Francisco (*b* 1935) **9** 113
Coen, Arnaldo **7** 524–5*
Coene, De, brothers *see* DE COENE BROTHERS
Coene, Jacques **3** 552; **5** 208; **7** 525*; **20** 567
Coene, Jan **4** 925; **17** 699
Coene, Jozef De *see* DE COENE, JOZEF
Coene, Konrad *see* KUENE VON DER HALLEN, KONRAD
Coenens, J. **22** 906
Coenraets, Claes **25** 230
Coesfeld, Jesuit church **14** 82
Coester, Otto **14** 620
Coesvelt, Jan Hartman van *see* HARTMAN VAN COESVELT, JAN
Coëtivy, Alain de, Cardinal-Bishop of Avignon **2** 860; **7** 525–6*
Coëtivy, Katherine de **7** 526; **11** 726
Coëtivy, Master of **17** 458; **20** 650–52*; **32** 744
attributions **30** 314
patrons and collectors **7** 526; **31** 844
pupils **20** 778
works **11** 726; **20** *651*
Coëtivy, Olivier de **7** 526
Coëtivy, Prigent de **7** 525*; **20** 626, 634, 722
Coëtivy Hours *see under* BOOKS OF HOURS → individual manuscripts
Coetzee, Christo **29** 109
Coetzee, Neels **29** 112, 113
Coeur, Jacques **7** 526*; **11** 531, 655; **22** 34
architecture **3** 173; **4** 578, 584
house **29** 22
metalwork **11** 615
paintings **11** 352; **20** 623
sculpture **13** 79
stained glass **13** 181
Coeur, Jean, Archbishop of Bourges **7** 596
Coeuvres, Marquise de **7** 394
Cofà, Melchiorre *see* CAFFA, MELCHIORRE
coffeepots **6** *327*
historical and regional traditions
Austria **2** *821*
France **24** *147*
Germany **12** 446, *447*, 447, *451*
Malta (Republic of) **20** 217
Netherlands, the **22** *891*
Sweden **30** 106
materials
pewter **24** 580
silver **2** *821*; **12** *451*; **20** 217; **22** *891*; **24** *147*; **30** 106
coffee-services **12** *432*; **21** *65*; **32** *450*
coffee-urns **3** *600*
coffering **7** 526–7*; **23** 480
Austria **2** *805*, 805–6

coffering—cont.
Belgium **3** 576
Germany **8** *881*
Greece, ancient **7** *526*, 526–7*; **13** 390, 392
Islamic **7** 527*
Italy **16** 712
Poland **25** *117*
Rome, ancient **7** 526–7*
Coffermans, Marcellus **20** 665
works **11** *422*
coffers **6** 558
historical and regional traditions
Belgium **3** *580*, 580
Catalonia **29** 310
China **7** 41
Gothic **3** *580*
Japan **17** 301
Malta (Republic of) **20** 215
Spain **29** 310
materials
iron **3** 580
lacquer **17** 301
oak **3** *580*
see also CHESTS; SPALLIERE
Coffetier, Nicolas **4** 582; **6** 497; **29** 610
Coffin, José **16** 806
Coffin-Chevalier, Josephine **4** 600
coffins **6** 71; **27** 828–9
historical and regional traditions
Bali (Indonesia) **15** *812*
China **7** 13
Egypt, ancient **3** 848; **10** 1, 8–12*, *9*; **33** *580*
Ghana **12** *509*
Indian subcontinent **15** 192
Indonesia **15** 812, *812*
Japan **17** 58, *58*, *426*
Korea **18** 271
Mesopotamia **21** 304
Philistine **24** 635, *635*
Poland **25** 129
Punic **25** 733
Thailand **30** 639
materials
cartonnage **10** 10
clay **24** *635*
gilding **33** *580*
inscriptions **10** 10
lacquer **7** 13
terracotta **24** 218
wood **10** 8, 10; **15** *812*; **30** 639; **33** *580*
types
boat *see under* SARCOPHAGI → types
Philistine *see under* SARCOPHAGI → types
slipper **24** 218
see also SARCOPHAGI
Coffin Texts **10** 10
Coffre, Benoît Le *see* LE COFFRE BENOÎT
Coffre, Claude Le *see* LE COFFRE, CLAUDE
coffrets **11** *622*
Cofradía de las Ánimas **23** 905
Cofradía del Rosario **9** 712, 714
Cofradía del Santísimo **9** 710
cofre de Valencia **5** 350
Cogels, John **3** 322
Cogford, Samuel **4** 86
Coggeshall Abbey (Essex) **4** 778
Coghetti, Francesco **7** 528*; **8** 5; **24** 418
Coghill, Marmaduke **12** 6
Cogidubnus, Tiberius Claudius **11** 138
Cogliolo, Luis **24** 99
Cognacq, (Théodore-) Ernest **7** 528*; **17** 668
Cognacq-Jay, Musée *see under* PARIS → museums
Cogniet, Léon **7** 528–9*; **11** 671
assistants **5** 440
collaboration **8** 40
pupils
Barrias, Félix(-Joseph) **3** 277
Cogniet, Léon
pupils—cont.
Barrias, Louis-Ernest **3** 277
Blommér, Nils Jakob (Olsson) **4** 159
Brandt, Józef **4** 670
Chapu, Henri (-Michel-Antoine) **6** 468
Chifflart, François (-Nicolas) **6** 582
Cogniet, Marie-Amélie **11** 672
Dedreux, Alfred **8** 616
Dehodencq, (Edmé-Alexis-) Alfred **8** 629
Feyen-Perrin, (François-Nicolas) Auguste **11** 48
Gautier, Amand (-Désiré) **12** 206
Gerson, Wojciech **12** 490
Giraud, Louise Emilie **19** 115
Hervier, (Louis-Henri-Victor-Jules-François) Adolphe **14** 486
Jacquemart, Nélie **16** 851
Laurens, Jean-Paul **18** 864
Lefebvre, Jules(-Joseph) **19** 65
Madarász, Viktor **20** 41
Madrazo Garreta, Raimundo **20** 60
Martial Potémont, Adolphe (-Théodore-Jules) **20** 484
Meissonier, (Jean-Louis-) Ernest **21** 68
Merritt, Anna Lea **21** 165
Papety, Dominique (-Louis-Féréol) **24** 58
Ricard, (Louis) Gustave **26** 315
Robert-Fleury, Tony **26** 455
Rodakowski, Henryk **26** 502
Sellier, Charles-François **28** 388
Tovar y Tovar, Martín **31** 229; **32** 173
teachers **4** 328; **12** 732; **13** 794
Cogniet, Marie-Amélie **7** 529; **11** 672
Cogolludo, Palacio Medinaceli **29** 264, *264*
Cogswell, James **28** 525
Cogswell, John **4** 479; **5** 192
Coguin, Charles, Abbot of Anchin **3** 641, 642
Cogul **29** 365
Cohasset (MA), Dr John Bryan House **26** 341
Cohen, Bernard **7** 529*; **19** 591; **28** 804
Cohen, Elsbeth **16** 568
Cohen, Eustace Gresley **2** 741; **7** 529–30*
Cohen, Francis *see* PALGRAVE, FRANCIS
Cohen, Harold **7** 680; **19** 591; **28** 804
works **7** *680*
Cohen, Lewis I. **31** 266
Cohen, Monique **15** 748
Cohen, Moses ben Jekutiel ha- **27** 226
Cohen, Sorel **22** 39
Cohen Gan, Pinchas **7** 530*; **16** 568
Cohl, Emile **10** 686
Cohn, Abe **8** 537; **22** 660
Cohn, Amy **8** 537; **22** 660
Cohn, Norman **5** 569
Cohn, Ola **2** 753; **29** 633
Cohn, Susan **2** 766
Cohoon, Hannah **28** 541
Cohr, Carl M. **8** 752
Coia, Jack **7** 530*; **28** 231
coifs (armour) **2** 468, 469
coifs (dress) **12** 469; **17** 519
Coignet, Edmond **7** 530–31*, 693
Coignet, François **4** 239; **7** 530*, 693; **11** 359
works **7** *690*
Coignet, Gillis *see* CONGNET, GILLIS
Coignet, Jules **3** 855; **4** 66; **22** 243; **26** 38
Coigrich **28** 260
Coil *see* KAYALPATNAM
coiling *see under* ARCHITECTURE; BASKETWORK; CERAMICS; POTTERY → techniques
Coimbra **7** 531–2*; **25** *288*
art forms and materials
architecture **25** 289, 291
faience (ii) (ceramics) **25** 309
gold **25** 312
metalwork **25** 313
painting **25** 295
pottery **25** 308
sculpture **13** 101; **26** 611
textiles **25** 315
tiles **30** 879, 880
ecclesiastical buildings
Carmo church **25** 297
Cathedral **23** 414; **25** 289
Convent of S Clara **25** 292, 301
Convent of the Discalced Carmelites **27** 498
monastery of Celas **13** 102
New Cathedral *see* Sé Nova
Nossa Senhora de Graça **25** 297
Old Cathedral *see* Sé Velha
Santa Cruz **6** 451–2; **7** *531*; **25** 295, 297, 301, 304, 305, 308, 317; **26** 690
choir-stalls **13** 125
sculpture **13** 125
Santo Antonio do Olivas **27** 498
S Clara-a-Velha **9** 104; **25** 289
tomb of St Isabel **13** 102
Sé Nova **22** 680; **25** 291, 306, 724
Sé Velha **1** 679; **25** 289; **30** 880
retable **13** 125
tomb of Bishop Egas Fafes **13** 101
tomb of Bishop Tiburcio **13** 101
tomb of Vetaça **13** 102
S Marcos de Tentúgal **6** 452
S Miguel de Mirleus **26** 611
gardens **12** 125, *125*
Jesuit College *see* ecclesiastical buildings → Sé Nova
museums
Museu Nacional de Machado de Castro **7** 893; **19** 892; **25** 318; **26** 479
Natural History Museum *see under* University
University **7** 531; **10** 155–6; **11** 18
chapel **11** 19; **20** 326; **25** 313; **26** 253
Estudos Gerais **18** *783*
Hospital **6** 39
library **17** 595; **19** 316; **25** 306
Natural History Museum **10** 155
Coin, Robert **9** 60
Coinquilino del Saraceni *see* PENSIONANTE DEL SARACENI
coins **7** 532–9*; **14** 408, 419
display **9** 27
forgeries **12** 627
historical and regional traditions
Achaemenid **1** 116, 117, 203, 888*; **13** 586
Afghanistan **1** 203–5*; **15** 687
Africa **1** 362
Ancient Near East **1** 888–9*
Anglo-Saxon **4** 688; **7** 533, 534
Arabia **2** 260–63*, *262*
Armenia (Europe) **2** 441
Austria **7** 539
Bactria **1** 204
Bactrian and Indo-Greek monarchies **3** 32
Bahrain **2** 261
Bali (Indonesia) **15** 811
Belgium **14** *413*
Brazil **7** 538
Britain **7** 538, 539; **29** 469; **31** 527
Brunei **5** 12*
coins
historical and regional traditions—cont.
Burma **5** 255*, 259
Byzantine **7** 533; **9** 635–9*, *636*; **14** 408
Cambodia **5** 507*
Canada **7** 539
Carolingian **7** 534, *534*
Celtic **6** 159–60; **25** 542; **31** 527
Central Asia, Eastern **6** 309*
Central Asia, Western **6** 262–6*, *263*, *265*
China **4** 688; **7** *72*, 72–4*, 533; **15** 811, 812
Crete **8** 154
Cyprus **7** 535; **13** 585
Cyprus, ancient **8** 332, 349*
Czech Republic **7** 535
Denmark **7** 537; **14** 408
Early Christian (*c.* AD 250-843) **9** 635–7*
Egypt **16** 510, 512, *512*, 513, *513*, 514
Egypt, ancient **13** 588
England **7** 533, 534, 535, 536, 537, 538; **14** 419, *419*; **19** *581*
Ethiopia **1** 362
Etruscan **10** 586, 632–3*; **25** 245
Finland **7** 539
France **7** 533, 534, 535, 536, 537, 538, 539; **14** 419
Germany **7** 537, 538, *538*, 539; **12** 444, 447; **14** 419
Greece **7** 532, 539
Greece, ancient **1** 203; **4** *686*; **5** 298; **13** 585*; **14** 407; **21** 1
Archaic **13** 585–6*, *585*
Classical **13** 586–8*, *587*
Hellenistic **13** 588–9*, *588*
Italy **13** 586
Sicily **13** *587*
Haiti **7** 539
Hungary **7** 535; **14** 411; **15** 6
India, Republic of **15** 689
Indian subcontinent **7** 532, 533; **8** 269; **15** 193, 194, 200, 213, 219, 231, 687–9*, *688*; **16** 513; **23** 772; **29** 469
Mughal **15** 689; **16** 514
Indonesia **15** 811–12*, 814
Iran **16** 510, *511*, *512*, 513, *513*, 514
Iran, ancient **27** *855*
Iraq **16** 510, *512*
Ireland **7** 538
Islamic **7** 533; **14** 428; **15** 689; **16** 130, 510–14*; **21** 504
Central Asia, Western **6** 264–6*, *265*
Egypt **16** 510, 512, *512*, 513, *513*, 514
Indian subcontinent **16** 513
Iran **16** 510, *511*, *512*, 513, *513*
Iraq **16** 510, *512*
Malaysia **20** 179
Ottoman **16** *513*, 514
Pakistan **16** *513*
Saudi Arabia **16** 514
Spain **7** 534; **16** *513*
Sumatra **15** 811
Syria **16** 510, *511*
Tunisia **16** *512*
Turkey **16** *513*, 514
Umayyad (Syria) **21** *505*
Italy **7** 533, 534, 535, 536, 537, 538, 539
Etruscan **10** 586, 632–3*; **25** 245
Greece, ancient **13** 586
Japan **7** 533; **17** 24, 318, 369–71*, *370*
Java **15** 811
Jewish art **1** 889
Knights Hospitaller **18** 152
Korea **7** 533; **18** *356*, 356–7*
Laos **18** 774, 775*
Lombard art **7** 533
coins
historical and regional traditions—cont.
Lydia **1** 888; **7** 532; **19** 841
Madagascar **20** 39
Malaysia **20** 179–80*
Malta (Republic of) **18** 152
Merovingian **7** 533; **21** 162
Mexico **7** 537
Nabataea **1** 889; **2** 261; **22** 420
Netherlands, the **7** 536, 537, 538, 539; **29** 469
North Africa **7** 532; **16** 512, 513
Norway **7** 537
Ostrogothic **7** 533
Ottoman **16** *513*, 514
Pakistan **16** *513*
Parthian **1** 887, *888*, 888–9*; **24** 215, 217
Peru **7** 537
Philippines **24** 626*
Phoenician **5** *332*; **30** 187
Phrygian **4** *686*
Poland **7** 538, 539; **25** 127
Portugal **7** 537, 538; **29** 469
Rhodes (island) **7** 535; **13** 587, 588; **18** 152
Rome, ancient **4** 687; **7** 533; **11** *151*; **15** 200; **21** 1, 162; **25** 650; **26** 860; **27** 29, 31, 32, 39, 95–8*, *96*, *98*
Etruscan **10** 586
Phoenician **5** *332*
Russia **7** 538, 539
Sasanian **1** 204, *888*, 889*; **6** 264; **7** 82; **27** *855*
Saudi Arabia **16** 514
Scandinavia **7** 538
Seleucid **13** 588, 589; **28** 383, 384
Serbia **14** 411; **28** 454–5
Sicily **7** 536; **13** 586, *587*, 587; **28** 654
South Africa **29** 120
Spain **7** 532, 534, 536, 537, 538; **16** 513, *513*
Sri Lanka **29** 469*
Sumatra **15** 811, 812
Sweden **7** 538, 539
Switzerland **7** 537, 538, 539
Syria **13** 588, 589; **16** 510, *511*, 512, 538
Syria-Palestine **30** 187, 196
Taiwan **7** 73
Thailand **30** 631–2*
Tibet **30** 837*
Tunisia **16** *512*
Turkey **7** 535; **16** *513*, 514
United States of America **7** 538
Vietnam **7** 72, 533; **32** 486*
Viking **7** 534
Visigothic **7** 533
materials
aluminium **7** 539
brass **4** *686*, 686–7, 688; **17** 370; **18** *356*, 357; **27** *96*
bronze **6** *263*; **7** *72*, 539; **16** *511*
Cambodia **5** 507
China **7** 533
Cyprus, ancient **8** 349
Etruscan **10** 633
Greece, ancient **13** 586, 588, 589
Indonesia **15** 811
Japan **17** 370, *370*
Korea **18** *356*
Roman **11** *151*
copper **5** 507; **6** 309; **7** 537–9; **14** 419, 428; **15** 687, 811, 812; **17** 369, 370; **18** 356; **32** 486
cupro-nickel **7** 539
dies (ii) (stamps) **7** 532; **16** 510
electrum **13** 585; **15** 811
gold **7** 533, 534, 536, 537; **12** 866; **14** 419
Afghanistan **1** 204
Belgium **14** *413*
Byzantine **9** *636*
Cyprus, ancient **8** 349

coins
materials
gold—cont.
England 14 419; 19 581
Etruscan 10 632
Indian subcontinent 15 688
Indonesia 15 811, 812
Islamic 16 511, 512, 513
Italy 7 536
Japan 17 318, 370, 370
Malaysia 20 179
inscriptions 15 688, 688; 16 510–14; 17 369; 18 356, 356
iron 17 370
lead 17 370
nickel 7 539
nickel-brass 7 539
silver 7 534–7
Afghanistan 1 204, 204
Arabia 2 262
Carolingian 7 534
Celtic 6 159
Central Asia, Eastern 6 309
Central Asia, Western 6 263
China 7 72
Cyprus, ancient 8 349
England 7 535, 536, 537; 14 419
Etruscan 10 632, 632
Germany 7 535, 538
Greece, ancient 13 585, 585, 587, 588, 588, 589
Indian subcontinent 15 687, 688
Islamic 16 510, 511, 512, 513; 21 505
Japan 17 318, 369, 370, 370
Korea 18 356, 357
Malaysia 20 180
Parthian 1 888
Sasanian 27 855
Sumatra 15 812
stainless steel 7 539
steel 7 539
tin 15 811, 812; 20 179, 180
zinc 32 486
techniques
gilding 12 627
incuse method 13 586
moulding 32 486
types
basilika 9 639
Blachernitissae 9 638
bracteates 7 535, 535
colts 13 585
Croeseids 1 888
darics 1 888
didrachm 10 632
ducats 7 536
florins 7 536, 536
gigliati 7 535
groschen 7 535
grossi 7 535
gros tournois 7 535
hyperpyra 9 636, 638
miliaresoi 9 637
nomismates 9 636, 637
owls 13 585
pennies 7 535
piloncitos 24 626
siglos 1 888, 888
solidi 9 636, 636
testoni 7 537
testoons 7 537
tetradrachms 1 204; 13 585, 588, 589
thrymsas 7 533
tornesi 9 639
tremisses 7 533; 9 635
turtles 13 585
uses
beadwork 3 442
costumes 30 654
cups 15 6
jewellery 15 814
portraits see under PORTRAITS → media
tankards 12 444, 447
coins—cont.
see also MEDALLIONS; MEDALS
Cointre 11 637
Cointrel, Matthieu see CONTARELLI, MATTEO
Coiny, Joseph 3 870
Coira see CHUR
Coira, Castello see SCHLOSS CHURBURG
Coit, Job 31 626
Coixtlahuaca 21 202; 31 118
Cojes-Schade van Westrum, Josina 30 789
coke 10 740; 16 50; 21 319, 320
Coke, John 4 65
Coke, Thomas 14 805; 23 253
Coke, Thomas, 1st Earl of Leicester of the 1st creation (1697-1759) 2 163; 3 83; 7 540*; 8 708; 10 642; 13 300
architecture 4 757, 787; 10 361; 13 301; 17 900, 903; 23 856, 859; 33 442
books 10 636
collections 10 364; 17 900; 20 911; 32 112
drawings 9 230
groups and movements 22 738
paintings 3 382; 5 907; 9 18; 10 365; 13 301
sculpture 1 533; 4 758; 18 902
Coke, Thomas William, 1st Earl of Leicester of the 2nd creation (1752-1842) 7 540–41*
paintings 27 161
sculpture 6 97
Coke, Van Deren 20 912
Çoker, Adnan 31 454
Coker, Peter 33 744
Coker Court 6 407
chamber 6 407
Cokorda Gedé Soekawati 15 809
Cokorda Raka 15 809
Cola see CHOLA
Cola, Santi di 6 139
CoLab 26 382
Colaço, José 30 882
Colaço, Madeleine 4 724
Cola da Camerino, Arcangelo di see ARCANGELO DI COLA DA CAMERINO
Cola (di Matteuccio) da Caprarola 7 541*
attributions 16 633
works 16 633
Cola dell'Amatrice 2 593, 594; 7 541–2*; 18 785
Cola di Rienzo 26 755
Cola di Spinello 29 407
Colahan, Colin 3 475
Colantonio, Niccolò (Antonio) 7 542–4*; 22 477
attributions 20 614
pupils 2 178
works 7 543; 10 713
Cola Rapicano see RAPICANO, COLA
Colard de Douai 23 165
Colard le Voleur 5 210; 8 69
Colarossi, Filippo 18 749; 29 61; 33 740
Colart de Laon 7 544*; 31 842
patrons and collectors 31 840
works 31 841
Colas (family) 13 79
Colas, Alphonse 8 204
Colas, Anthoine 10 836; 31 384
Colás, Guillén 29 265
Colas, Pierre Michel 2 823
Colasson, Pierre 4 238
Colbert, de, Monseigneur 2 869
Colbert, Edouard, Marquis de Villacerf see VILLACERF, EDOUARD COLBERT, Marquis de
Colbert, Jacques-Nicolas, Archbishop of Rouen 7 546; 11 905
Colbert, Jean-Baptiste (1619-83) 2 558; 4 535, 550; 6 435; 7 544–6*; 11 662; 12 827; 20 132, 134, 135, 139; 22 465; 24 167, 467; 31 321
archaeology 13 608
architecture 19 268
châteaux 6 417, 508; 19 268; 20 896; 24 468; 32 582
orders (architecture) 23 489
palaces 3 835; 7 665; 11 657; 19 267, 268; 24 162, 468
art policies 2 314; 11 517, 536, 657; 24 169, 170
books 31 322
carpets 11 652
competitions 25 637
education (art) 2 170; 26 842
furniture 11 576, 588
glass 11 612
interior decoration 24 162
lace 11 649
manuscripts 16 553
mirrors 11 589; 32 203
paintings 11 357; 19 19
pottery 11 605
prints 20 455; 25 631
sculpture 11 559; 24 118; 25 705; 31 408, 409; 32 372
silk 28 716
tapestries 2 703; 3 460; 11 641, 642; 30 321
works 11 588
Colbert, Jean-Baptiste (-Antoine) (1651-90) see SEIGNELAY, JEAN-BAPTISTE (-ANTOINE) COLBERT, Marquis de
Colbert, Louvois 21 368
Colbert de Torcy, Jean-Baptiste 11 903
Colboc, P. 11 528; 24 131
Colchester (Essex) 26 905
Balkerne Gate 21 548
Castle 2 72; 6 603; 10 227; 14 75
keep 10 359; 33 198
Colchester and Essex Museum 6 65
great tower 6 52; 21 563
hill-fort 25 536
houses 6 407
Moot Hall 7 643
pottery 27 107, 108
St Botolph's Priory 2 294, 723; 4 787
shrine 27 2
Temple of the Deified Claudius 26 858
Town Hall 7 668; 10 239, 239
urban planning 27 4
Colchis 9 85; 12 316, 318; 27 15
Cold, Birgit 7 546*
Cold art 1 79; 7 546–7*
cold-gilt see under GILDING → types
Colding, T. Holck 8 762
Cold Mackeprang, Carl Mouritz see MACKEPRANG, CARL MOURITZ COLD
Coldoré, Olivier 12 259
Coldspot refrigerator 15 825; 20 594
Coldstream, William (Menzies) 3 629; 7 547–8*; 10 375; 19 591; 21 761
groups and movements 10 257, 375, 652, 653; 20 590; 23 333; 24 228
patrons and collectors 7 376
pupils 2 23
works 10 652; 23 333
Cole, Benjamin 7 758
Cole, Charles 12 270
Cole, E. K. 7 483
Cole, George (fl 1747-74) 17 623
Cole, George (1810-83) 7 548
Cole, George (1866-1913) 3 64
Cole, George Vicat 7 548*
Cole, Henry 2 524; 7 548–9*; 10 335, 370; 15 821; 17 639; 19 594; 23 248; 28 399
architecture 11 360
designers 22 278; 26 69
porcelain 3 629; 10 311
publications 24 422
writings 10 373
Cole, Henry Hardy 7 549
Cole, Henry Walter 7 549
Cole, Herbert M.
works 1 278; 15 112, 114
Cole, James 5 578
Cole, Peter 2 754
Cole, Rex Vicat 7 548; 10 373; 28 559
Cole, Thomas 7 549–51*
groups and movements 14 843; 26 742
patrons and collectors 7 840; 12 645; 14 203, 718; 17 823; 26 75; 29 870; 32 753
pupils 7 284
works 7 550; 18 715; 31 602
Cole, (Walter Sylvanus) Timothy 7 551*; 33 369
works 26 234, 234
Cole, William 3 741; 10 516
Colebrookdale Co. 30 266
Colebrooke, George 7 551–2*
Colebrookedale Furnace 31 652
Coleburne, William 28 242
Coleby Hall (Lincs), Temple of Romulus and Remus 6 412
Colechurch, Peter of see PETER OF COLECHURCH
Colectivo Acciones de Arte (CADA) 6 598; 22 335
Colefax, Sybil, Lady 10 284
Colegio del Arte Mayor de la Seda see REAL FÁBRICA DE SEDA (MADRID)
Coleing, Tony 2 754
works 2 754
Coleman, Edward 4 86
Coleman, Enrico 8 6
Coleman, G. D. 28 771, 772, 773
Coleman, Glenn O. 2 597
Coleman, James 7 552*; 16 22
Coleman, Thomas Aloysius 2 600
Coleman Smith, Pamela 31 490
Colen, Gisbert van 32 706; 33 276
Colen, Rothger Michelszoon van see SAVOYE, RUTGER
Colenbrander, T(heodoor) C(hristiaan) A(driaan) 7 552–3*; 22 883, 884, 900
Cöler, Georg see KELLER, GEORG
Coleraine (Co. Londonderry), St Malachy's 16 39
Coleridge, Samuel Taylor 1 180; 24 742; 28 276
Colerne (Wilts), St John the Baptist 2 71
Coles, George 7 327
Coleshill (Warwicks), SS Peter and Paul 26 613
Coleshill House (Berks) 8 45, 46; 10 231, 275, 360; 25 454
plaster 29 835
Colet, John 14 868; 28 156
Colette(, Sidonie-Gabrielle) 13 790; 14 457; 22 92
Coleyn, Evert Pietersz. see COLLIER, EDWART
Coli, Giovanni 7 553*; 15 138
collaboration 12 527; 13 292; 32 215
patrons and collectors 7 622
teachers 7 913
works 16 671, 714; 26 320
Colibert 7 783
Colibrant Triptych 33 128
Colijns, David 18 227
Colijn Willems van Camerick see NOLE, COLIJN DE
Colima 21 250, 265
figurines 21 196, 236; 33 101, 103
Colima—cont.
mirrors 21 719
pottery 5 660, 660
seals 21 258
statuettes 10 474
tombs 21 197
see also CAPACHA-OPEÑO
Colin, Abraham 7 554
Colin, Alexander 7 553–4*; 14 305; 15 865
assistants 11 502
dealers 22 243
patrons and collectors 8 384; 11 818, 819; 13 904, 908, 910; 29 738
works 2 800, 800; 6 171; 7 554; 9 340; 10 745; 15 866; 28 170; 33 278
Colin, Alexandre Marie 12 732; 16 875, 904
Colin, Gustave 7 554–5*; 11 156; 14 457
Colin, Jacques Antoine 25 814
Colin, Paul 25 350, 352
Colin, Paul Emile 25 215
Colin d'Amiens see DIPRE, NICOLAS (fl 1464)
Colin de Berneval 27 254
Colineaux, Firmin 3 728
Colines, Simon de 10 534; 31 196, 495
Colinet (family) 3 593
Colinet, Armand 3 593
Colinet, Claire Jeanne Roberte 11 637
Colinet, Emmanuel Constant Edouard 33 676
Colinet de Marties 31 842
Colin-Thiébault, Gérard 11 553
Colka, Maurice 10 577
Colla 15 163; 31 46
Colla, Briseide 7 889
Colla, Ettore 7 555*
groups and movements 5 279, 671; 16 681; 17 694
pupils 6 345
works 16 709
collaboration 7 830; 20 601–10
Colla del Safra 21 699
Collaert (family) 12 15
Collaert, Adriaen 2 455; 7 556–7*; 12 15
collaboration 7 556; 12 16
copies 13 664; 25 827
printmakers 32 708
reproductive prints by others 10 130; 27 504
works 7 556; 10 326; 13 664; 17 599; 27 502; 29 740, 748; 32 711
Collaert, Hans, I (c. 1530-81) 2 201; 7 555, 556; 11 634; 32 251
Collaert, Hans, II (1566-1628) 2 473; 3 604; 7 555; 11 717; 32 711
Collaert, Jan, I (c. 1470-c. 1524) 2 198; 7 555
Collaert, Jan Baptist, I see COLLAERT, HANS II
Collaert, Jan Baptist, II (c. 1590-1627) 7 557*
collage intaglio see COLLAGRAPHS
collages 2 615–16; 7 432, 557–8*; 10 470; 24 595, 654, 676, 679; 26 51
Austria 14 236
Cubism 8 241–2; 24 717, 725
Dada 7 557
Ecuador 9 712
England 14 112
France 4 675; 8 242; 10 468; 23 260; 24 726
Germany 7 558; 10 466; 14 605
Islamic 16 354
Japan 17 223
United States of America 26 357

collages—cont.
see also ASSEMBLAGES; PAPIER COLLÉ; PHOTOMONTAGES; MERZ
collagraphs 7 558*
Collalto, Gian Battista di 4 340
Collalto, Rombaldo, Conte 5 771; 24 772
Collantes, Francisco 7 558–9*; 20 66
patrons and collectors 17 673; 21 73
works 7 *559*
Collantes de Téran, F. 28 511
Collao pottery see under POTTERY → wares
collar and rafter roofs see under ROOFS → types
Collaro, Viera 8 736
collars 9 287; 17 520
historical and regional traditions
China 7 78
Egypt, ancient 3 441; 17 IV2
South America, Pre-Columbian 29 217
Vietnam 32 486
types
livery 7 177, 178, 179
see also NECK RINGS
Collas, Achille 3 204; 19 395; 26 514
Collas & Barbedienne 3 204
Collas Machine 19 395
collation 7 514
Collazo, Guillermo (Enrique) 7 559*; 8 233
Collcutt, T(homas) E(dward) 7 559*
assistants 29 695
collaboration 11 499
groups and movements 3 269
patrons and collectors 14 786
staff 28 557
works 10 298, *298*
Colle (family) 28 372
Collé, C. 31 373
Colle, Raffaello (di Michelangelo di Luca) dal 7 559–60*
collaboration 4 856, 859; 6 583; 9 185; 12 527; 27 273; 32 12
pupils 1 551; 12 527
works 24 536
Collectif de l'art sociologique, Le 24 145
Collection Coutan see under PARIS → Louvre (Musée du Louvre, 1793-)
collections 2 299, 364, 369, 557, 558–61; 4 23–4; 6 75–6, 80; 7 560–65*; 10 675–81; 15 888
catalogues see under CATALOGUES → types
historical and regional traditions
Aboriginal Australia 1 66*; 33 534
Afghanistan 1 211–12*
Africa 1 438–9*
Albania 1 545–6*
Algeria 1 636
Anatolia, ancient 1 839*
Ancient Near East 1 895–6*
Antilles, Lesser 2 144, 153–4*
Argentina 2 403–5*
Armenia (Europe) 2 444–5*
Asante 2 588
Assyrian 21 310
Australia 1 66–7*; 2 769–71*; 4 882; 22 360
Austria 2 828–9*, 830–31*; 22 356
Aztec 21 265
Bahamas, the 3 63–4*
Bamum 3 151
Bangladesh 3 169–70*
Baule 3 404; 8 23
Belgium 3 611–15*
Belize 3 624–5*
Benin Republic 3 728–9*
Bhutan 3 916*
collections
historical and regional traditions—cont.
Bolivia 4 267–9*; 29 894
Bosnia 4 462–3*
Brazil 4 708, 724–7*
Britain 2 561; 27 114; 29 426
Buddhism 17 432
Bulgaria 5 162–3*
Burkina Faso 5 217*
Byzantine 32 212
Cameroon 5 525
Canada 5 588–91*; 17 434; 25 803; 31 177, 880
Central Asia, Eastern 6 320–21*
Central Asia, Western 6 282–5*
Chile 6 600–601*
China 2 558; 6 764; 7 151–6*, 158; 17 237; 30 850
Christianity 7 564
Colombia 7 609, 611–12*
Côte d'Ivoire 8 23
Crete 21 691–2*
Croatia 8 180–81*
Cuba (Caribbean) 8 238–9*
Cycladic 8 314, 323–4*
Cyprus 8 366–7*
Cyprus, ancient 14 361
Czech Republic 8 421–4*
Denmark 8 757–60*, 761*
Dogon 9 64
Dominican Republic 9 118*, 119*
Ecuador 9 714
Egypt, ancient 2 558; 5 401; 10 6–7, 83, 87, 89–91*, 92–4*; 11 302
England 2 559, 560; 9 17; 10 226, 362–71*; 11 140; 18 383; 19 582; 22 356
19th cent. 32 748
Eritrea 10 577–8*
Estonia 10 540*
Ethiopia 10 577–8*
Etruscan 10 637–40*
Finland 11 111–12*
France 2 558–9; 7 561; 11 660–68*; 17 430; 22 359; 24 138, 163; 26 230
Gothic 13 153
Gabon 11 880*
Georgia 12 331*, 332*
Germany 2 367, 560; 12 446, 473–4*, 475–7; 17 434
18th cent. 21 64
19th cent. 33 282
Gothic 13 153, 155
Greece 13 359–60*
Greece, ancient 7 561; 13 424, 604–6*; 14 867
Guatemala 13 768–70*
Haiti 14 60
Helladic 14 360–61*
Herzegovina 4 462–3*
Honduras 14 716–17*
Hong Kong 7 154
Hungary 10 530; 15 15–17*
India, Republic of 15 178–9*, 180–83*
Indian subcontinent 15 211, 594, 618, 634, 737, 739–46*; 16 552
Iran 1 896; 15 900, 922*; 16 551–2
Iraq 16 3
Ireland 16 24, 36–7*
Islamic 8 759; 16 551–8*
Israel 16 570*, 571*; 17 582*
Italy 2 558; 4 408; 14 867; 16 760–69*, 770–76*; 22 356; 27 114–15; 32 106, 212
Etruscan 10 637–40*
Renaissance 16 770–71
15th cent. 13 469
Jamaica 16 889–90*
Japan 7 160; 17 421–4*, 425, 427–35*, *430*, *431*; 18 383; 22 359
Buddhism 17 432
collections
historical and regional traditions
Japan—cont.
Edo period (1600-1868) 17 237
Shinto 17 432
Zen 7 161
20th cent. 1 896; 2 561
Jewish art 8 424; 16 571; 17 580–82*
Kazakhstan 6 284*
Korea 18 382–4*
Kyrgyzstan 6 284*
Lebanon 1 896
Lithuania 19 497, 498
Lobi 19 521
Macedonia (ii) (former Yugoslavia) 19 886*
Mali 21 478
Maori 23 75
Mesoamerica, Pre-Columbian 21 262*, 264–5*, *265*, 266; 26 426
Aztec 21 265
Mesopotamia 21 310*; 31 827
Mexico 21 264, 265, 394–7*
Middle Niger cultures 21 478
Minoan 21 691–2*
Monaco 15 888
Mongolia 21 886*
Montenegro 22 19*
Mozambique 22 245*
Native North Americans 22 360, 562, 565, 648, 660, 667, 668, 669, 673, 675–8*
Nepal 22 795*, 796*
Netherlands, the 4 743; 6 77; 7 561; 22 904–7*
Newar 22 795
New Zealand 23 74–5*
Nicaragua 23 84–5*
Nigeria 23 139*
Nok 23 180
Northern Ireland 16 42*
Norway 23 242–3*
Nubia 10 93; 29 898
Ottoman 16 552
Pacific Islands 23 739–40*, 741–2*
Pakistan 23 804*
Paraguay 24 100–102*
Peru 24 515–17*
Poland 25 94, 136, 137–8*, 139–40*
Portugal 25 317–19*
Puerto Rico 25 703–4*
Romania 26 722–3*, 724–5*
Rome, ancient 2 558; 10 675; 13 469, 555; 14 867; 16 765; 26 782, 861; 27 29, 31, 114–16*
Russia 2 560; 6 284–5; 27 438–41*, 580
Saudi Arabia 1 896
Scotland 28 267–74*
Senegal 28 406
Serbia 28 458–9*
Shinto 17 432
Sierra Leone 28 692–3*
Singapore 7 154
Slovakia 28 856–7*
Slovenia 28 863*
South Africa 29 121–2*
South America, Pre-Columbian 7 609; 29 218–21*, 222*; 30 282; 31 758
South-east Asia 7 154; 29 239–41*
Spain 5 509; 29 351–5*
Sri Lanka 29 473, 478–9*
Surinam 30 17
Sweden 11 851; 30 118–19*
Switzerland 15 888; 17 886; 30 152–5*
Syria-Palestine 30 198–9*
Taiwan 7 154
Tajikistan 6 283*
Tanzania 30 302*
collections
historical and regional traditions—cont.
Tibet 30 813–14*, 848, 849*, 850
Trinidad and Tobago 31 339–40*
Troadic 31 355–6*
Tuareg 31 404
Turkey 1 839; 16 552
Turkmenistan 6 283–4*
Ukraine 19 789; 31 564–5*
Union of Soviet Socialist Republics 17 581
United States of America 1 896; 2 369, 560; 4 23, 24; 13 606; 15 745–6; 17 430–31, *431*; 18 384; 22 359, 360, 426; 27 224; 31 662, 663, 664–6*, 667–9; 32 889
19th cent. 7 840
Uruguay 31 757–8*
Uzbekistan 6 283*
Venezuela 32 175, 178–80*
Wales 32 790–91*
Yemen 1 896; 33 520
Yoruba 33 553
Zambia 33 603
illustrated see ART (ILLUSTRATIONS OF WORKS OF)
treatises see under TREATISES → types
types
Africana 29 121, 122
armour 2 449–50*; 7 565; 15 866–7
bamboo 7 62
books 7 564; 22 354, 356
bronzes 6 868*
calligraphy
China 6 772*; 7 129; 17 229, 230, 232
Hong Kong 6 772
Islamic 16 551–2
Japan 6 752, 772; 17 215, 229, 230, 232
Singapore 6 772
Taiwan 6 772
United States of America 6 772
carpets 16 554–5
cartes-de-visite 24 649, 661
casts 2 169–70; 7 562, 831; 22 358
Argentina 2 404
Austria 29 789
Italy 7 562
United States of America 22 359
ceramics
China 6 331, 898, 925*; 7 161
England 16 395
Islamic 16 395–6*
Japan 17 433
Scotland 28 273
classified 9 18–19; 22 356–7, 358–9
copies 22 355, 358
costumes 17 328, 433
curiosities 7 562, 565; 11 661; 17 425; 22 355
see also KUNSTKAMMERN; WUNDERKAMMERN
drawings 7 562; 9 223, 229–31*; 10 212; 19 143, 782; 20 445
England 9 230
France 19 143
Scotland 28 273
United States of America 9 231
see also MARKS → collectors'
dress 16 445; 17 317
engravings 19 111; 26 229
ephemeral art 10 420–22*
erotic art 10 487*
ethnographic art 22 666
folk art 17 344
furniture 7 565; 20 595; 22 355
China 1 150
France 7 565
collections
types
furniture—cont.
Scotland 28 273
gem-engraving 12 265–7*
gem impressions 19 439
glass 7 565; 8 424; 32 204
gold 7 565, 612
icons 9 623; 18 385
imprese 15 150
impressions 7 129
inks 7 93–4
inkstones 17 388
inscriptions 23 673
jade 7 8
jewellery 7 565
Kunstkammern see KUNSTKAMMERN
lacquer 17 342
liturgical objects 2 444
manuscripts 2 367; 7 564
Armenia (Europe) 2 444, 445; 10 450
Czech Republic 8 422
France 5 210
Islamic 16 551–2
Italy 6 151
Mauritania 20 862
Nepal 22 795
medals 3 288; 9 298
meibutsu 17 428–9
metalwork 6 867
microfiches 31 671
modern art 7 561
musical instruments 17 396; 22 376–7
natural history 7 564; 22 354, 355
objets de luxe 22 359
Old Masters 22 359
paintings 7 562–3*; 22 300, 355, 359
Belgium 7 *563*
Britain 28 273, 274
China 6 826; 7 129, 161; 17 229
England 3 178; 28 273
France 7 563; 28 273
Greece, ancient 7 562; 13 554–5*
Indian subcontinent 15 610, 611, 740
Italy 22 357
Japan 6 783, 826; 7 161; 17 229
Nepal 22 795
Netherlands, the 7 562, 563
Romania 5 73
Rome, ancient 7 562; 13 555; 27 58*
Russia 31 312
Scotland 28 272, 273
Sweden 29 366
United States of America 7 563
period rooms 22 359, 363
photographs 2 560; 24 675, 682–3*
Belgium 3 619
Bulgaria 5 162–3*
Colombia 7 612
England 10 376*
Guatemala 13 769*
Italy 16 777
Peru 24 518*
Poland 25 142*
Scotland 28 272, 275
South Africa 29 122
United States of America 24 682–3; 29 656
see also PHOTOARCHIVES
plaquettes 9 298
porcelain 5 347–8*; 7 166, 565
China 1 150; 16 393, 424
England 10 276, 371
Germany 5 *348*; 12 412
Iran 16 230, 424
Islamic 16 122, 230, 393, 424
Japan 4 174
Ottoman 16 122

collections
types—cont.
portraits 14 869; 22 355
Britain 10 213
Germany 10 213
Italy 7 726; 9 15
Scotland 28 272
postage stamps 25 328, 329
pottery 7 612; 13 540–42*, 555; 18 340
primitive art 22 359
prints 6 78; 7 563; 10 212; 19 782; 25 630–32*
Bulgaria 5 163
Germany 33 280
Indian subcontinent 15 617
Italy 16 777
Netherlands, the 14 563
Scotland 28 273
public 2 557, 559–60; 7 561, 563; 22 356–8*; 27 114
England 13 605; 20 911; 22 362
France 13 605; 22 357–8
Germany 12 476
Italy 13 605
Poland 2 409
Rome, ancient 25 43
Switzerland 1 771; 3 336; 30 154
United States of America 22 359
replicas 7 562
reproductions 22 359; 26 226
rocks 17 425
royal 2 558; 7 560, 562
Austria 9 18
Britain 2 559; 19 197
China 6 744, 745, 753, 764, 772, 822, 826, 867; 7 150–51*
Denmark 8 759
Egypt, ancient 7 563
England 7 579; 19 582; 31 220; 33 306
France 3 304; 7 561; 9 418; 19 216; 20 133; 24 138
Germany 22 358
Netherlands, the 9 27
Rome, ancient 26 784
Spain 9 18
rubbings 17 237
scientific instruments 7 564
sculpture 2 162; 7 561–2*; 22 355, 359
Africa 7 562; 13 826; 22 360
bronze 7 564
Byzantine 7 562
China 6 734–5*; 24 258
England 9 23–5; 13 299
France 7 562
Greece, ancient 7 561–2, 564; 9 23; 13 469–71*; 27 10, 45
India, Republic of 15 180
Italy 2 168–9; 7 562; 13 470; 26 768
Pacific Islands 7 562
Rome, ancient 7 561–2, 564; 9 23; 26 856; 27 34, 45–7*
United States of America 9 298; 13 469, 470
seals 7 129, 130; 17 413–14
silver 7 565; 28 273
slides 26 236
stained glass 28 273; 29 514–16*
state 7 561
study 7 831
tapestries 28 273; 30 331–2
textiles
Algeria 16 448
Byzantine 9 664
China 7 53–4*
Early Christian (c. AD 250-843) 9 664
Islamic 16 448
Morocco 16 448
United States of America 22 400
vernacular art 5 386; 17 433
collections
types—cont.
weapons 2 449–50*; 7 565
see also MUSEUMS
collectors' marks see under MARKS
collectors' seals see under SEALS → types
Collège Albert Museum 33 598
College Art Association 2 533
College Art Journal see ART JOURNAL (USA)
Collège des Ecossais see MONTPELLIER COLLÈGE DES ECOSSAIS
College of Antiquities (Sweden) see CENTRAL BOARD OF NATIONAL ANTIQUITIES AND NATIONAL HISTORICAL MUSEUMS (SWEDEN)
colleges 7 565–7*; 12 175; 31 674
England 7 566
Gothic 5 511; 7 566; 12 175
Gothick 14 255
Gothic Revival 5 317
Greek Revival 33 192
Mannerism 5 512
15th cent. 33 545
17th cent. 4 785; 23 686, 687
20th cent. 5 513
France 2 724; 19 265
Gothic 5 511; 7 566; 12 175
Hungary 14 887
Indian subcontinent 15 404
Ireland 9 323; 18 753
Italy 7 566, 566; 26 319
Jesuit Order 7 566–7
Mexico 21 381
Pakistan 24 540
Scotland 25 36
Spain 29 269; 31 823
see also SCHOOLS; UNIVERSITIES
Collelungo, Clemente Sannesio, Marchese di 18 730; 27 764
Cöllen, Henrik 7 567–8*
patrons and collectors 13 668
works 30 68, 68
Collen, Henry 30 269; 33 134
Colleoni, Bartolomeo 3 770; 7 568*; 32 363
Cöllertail, Herman see KOLERTAL, HERMAN
Collet, Jacques-Marie-Michel 3 233
Collet, John 18 672
Collett, William 11 431
Colleville-sur-Mer 26 598
Colleye 4 529
Colleyweston see under LIMESTONE → types
Collicola (family) 29 422
Collie, George 7 574; 16 18
Colliehole (Devon) 32 277
Collier, Edwart 7 568*; 31 883
Collier, John 7 569*; 22 677
Collier, Richard 31 653
Collier, Thomas 7 569*
Collignon, François 7 569*; 19 696; 20 415
collaboration 28 742
works 3 208, 208; 14 394; 18 745; 30 529
Collignon, Gaspard 8 93
Collignon, George 2 510
Collin, Antoine 4 637; 19 524
Collin, Marcus 23 266
Collin, Raphaël 11 851; 12 878; 17 204; 18 531; 28 104
Collin, Rémy 11 260, 515
Collin de Vermont, Hyacinthe 7 569–70*; 8 794; 27 530, 645
Colling, James Kellaway 8 576; 22 809; 28 279; 29 870
Collings, Charles John 32 414
Collingwood, R(obin) G(eorge) 2 508; 7 570–71*
works 1 172, 174, 181; 10 690
Collingwood, W(illiam) G(ershom) 7 570*
works 27 453; 32 529
Collingwood, William 7 570
Collini see COLLINO
Collino, Filippo 4 520; 7 571; 28 18, 19; 31 445
Collino, Ignazio (Secondo) 3 825; 4 520; 7 571; 28 18, 19; 31 445
Collins 13 811
Collins, Cecil 7 573*; 29 628
Collins, Charles Allston 7 571, 572–3*
collaboration 8 863
patrons and collectors 33 251
works 11 434
Collins, Hannah 7 573*
Collins, Jess see JESS (COLLINS)
Collins, Patrick 7 573–4*; 16 18
Collins, Polly 28 541
Collins, Richard 21 409
Collins, Samuel 14 879
Collins, Wilkie 25 347
Collins, William (d 1812) 7 571
Collins, William (1748-1847) 7 571–2*; 20 489
dealers 1 453
patrons and collectors 14 147; 24 322; 28 576
reproductive prints by others 25 837
works 7 572, 789
Collins Cleartype Press 20 404
Collinson, James 7 574*; 25 554
Collinson, Peter 3 310
Collinson & Lock 7 559; 26 190; 28 881
works 10 298
Collins & Parri 10 98
Collivadino, Pío 2 399, 406
Cölln see BERLIN (GERMANY)
Collodi, Villa Garzoni 12 118; 32 549, 550
garden 12 117
collodion 7 432; 24 649
collodion positives see under PHOTOGRAPHIC PLATES → types
collodion process see under PHOTOGRAPHY → processes
collograph see under PRINTING → processes
colloidal soldering see METALWORK → techniques → granulation
Collombe, de la 2 466, 467
Collonges-la-Rouge 26 602
Colloredo, Gerolamo, Conte 20 95
Colloredo-Mansfeld (family) 14 756
Colloredo-Waldsee, Anton Theodor, Archbishop 18 467
Colloredo Waldsee, Conte 5 594
Collot, Marie-Anne 7 574–5*; 10 765; 33 308
Collot, Pierre 11 573
collotype see under PRINTING → processes
Collyer, Joseph 10 378; 14 280
Collyweston (Northants) 29 531
Colman (family) 23 249; 31 647
Colman, George 7 340
Colman, Jeremiah James 23 249
Colman, John 7 702
Colman, Koloman 9 436
Colman, P. 3 620
Colman, Russell James 23 249
Colman, Samuel (i) (1780-1845) 7 577*
Colman, Samuel (ii) (1832-1920) 7 577*; 15 408; 30 868
patrons and collectors 31 870
works 14 244
Colmar 11 504
Dominican church 13 57
engravings 10 381
St Martin 7 578, 578–9*; 16 71–2
Colmar Painter 13 521
Colmenares, Diego de 2 645
Colmjon, G. 28 65
Cöln, Hanss (moler) von (fl 1501-60) 20 797, 798
Colnaghi, Dominic 7 579*; 11 60; 29 634
Colnaghi, Martin 18 727
Colnaghi, Paul 5 733; 7 579*; 29 634
Colnaghi's 5 522; 6 80; 7 377, 579*; 10 366, 679; 25 626; 29 676
staff 28 560
works 28 86
Co Loa 21 595
Co Loa Drum 29 230
Cologna, Zuan de see ZUAN DE COLOGNA
Cologne 7 579–95*, 581, 584; 9 510; 12 360, 361, 379, 382; 26 905; 33 458
art forms and materials
altarpieces 9 4; 12 400
architecture 26 905
bowls 27 75
brasses 4 692
ceramics 7 586*
ciboria (i) (vessels) 7 300
coins 7 534, 585*; 14 419
dioramas 8 911
embroidery 12 462
enamel 13 169; 26 693
engravings 9 190
faience (ii) (ceramics) 7 586
figurines 27 111
glass 7 586–7*; 12 441; 26 855; 27 74, 75, 76
gold 12 442; 26 683
intarsia 12 421
ivory 23 660; 29 571
ivory-carvings 26 695, 696
jewellery 17 519
manuscripts 12 382; 20 330; 23 651, 652, 654, 655; 26 661, 673
marks 7 586
metalwork 7 585*, 586*; 12 452; 26 683
monstrances 12 442
mosaics 27 62
painting 12 383, 384; 13 151, 156; 17 699
panel 13 131
wall 27 56
paper 10 381
pigments 24 792
pilgrim badges 12 455; 24 808, 809
pottery 7 586*; 27 108
printing 12 385
ribbons 26 703
sculpture 12 400; 13 85, 88, 91, 116; 26 632, 646
Romanesque 26 632
silk 9 664, 668; 12 464, 464
silver 12 446, 449
stained glass 27 255; 29 504
stonewares 12 428, 429, 429; 22 877
tapestries 12 465, 467; 30 319
terracottas 27 110
textiles 7 587*
tiles 30 340
wool 12 469
art market 12 474
churches
Cathedral of SS Peter and Maria 4 243; 5 794; 7 587, 587–9*, 588; 12 345, 362, 365; 13 48–9, 56, 201; 14 80; 20 573; 23 462; 26 45
altarpiece 19 528, 528–9*
altarpieces 11 452
ambulatory 7 267
Bible Window 29 510
choir-stalls 7 191
completion 2 321
Gero Crucifix 7 583, 589; 8 213, 213; 12 399; 23 646, 647; 26 145, 632
Klaren Altar 13 151, 152
Milanese Madonna 13 116
misericords 21 725
Cologne
churches
Cathedral of SS Peter and Maria—cont.
mouldings 22 219, 220
nave 13 48
paintings 13 151
piers 24 751
plans 2 326, 327, 327
restoration 26 102; 32 682–3; 33 745
rock crystal 16 540
sculpture 7 275, 589, 589–90*; 12 400, 400; 13 87, 88, 89
shrine of the Three Kings 12 265; 22 270; 28 630, 631
spire 20 581; 29 414
stained glass 7 590, 590–91*; 13 186; 29 512; 31 499
textiles 30 331
Three Kings Chapel 8 856; 13 186; 23 99–100; 26 146
tomb of Archbishop Walrams von Jülich 13 99
tomb of Archbishop Wilhelm von Gennep 13 99
tomb of Friedrich of Saarwerden 13 160
Treasury 7 585, 591*
Dominican church 29 510
Franciscan church 22 221
Gross St Martin 12 364; 26 673, 695
Jabachscher Hof Chapel 9 433
Jesuit church 12 369; 32 821
Mariä Himmelfahrt 12 238, 368; 13 211
Neu St Heribert (Deutz) 26 661, 673, 694
reliquaries 26 146
shrine of St Heribert 28 630
Pfarrkirche 20 717
Pressa Steel church see Stahlkirche
St Cäcilien 13 134; 26 633; 29 503
St Georg 12 364; 26 633, 646, 673
St Gereon 7 255, 591–2*, 591; 9 534; 12 364; 13 48, 186; 22 217; 26 681
manuscripts 23 652
textiles 7 587; 12 465; 26 703; 30 310
Treasury 7 585, 592*
wall paintings 12 382; 26 651, 659
St Johann 7 300
St Kunibert 12 364, 462; 13 185
ciborium 7 299
stained glass 13 185; 29 510
St Maria ad Gradus 26 633
St Mariä Empfängnis see St Maria im Kapitol
St Maria im Kapitol 1 768; 7 592–3*; 9 151; 12 363; 26 74, 574; 31 281
crucifix 8 214
doors 12 399; 23 648; 26 646
sculpture 13 91, 116; 26 633
tomb of Plectrudis 26 633
St Maria Lyskirchen 31 499
St Pantaleon 7 594*; 12 363; 13 18; 26 574
buttresses 5 319
manuscripts 26 673
metalwork 26 683
sculpture 23 646; 26 633
shrine of St Albinius 28 630
shrine of St Maurinus 26 683
stripwork 29 776
Treasury 7 585, 594–5*
westwork 7 265, 594; 33 107–8, 108
St Ursula 7 593*; 13 177
Stahlkirche 3 292, 293
collections 12 476
Colonia Agrippinensium 7 579–80*

Cologne—cont.
Dance Pavilion **30** 468
Eifel channel **27** 7
Glashaus **10** 683
guilds **12** 420
Hansahochhaus **28** 834
Hansasaal **13** 187
Hauptbahnhof **25** 856, 857
Heinrich-Böll-Platz **7** *585*
houses **32** 281
Kunst- und Museumsbibliothek und Rheinisches Bildarchiv **2** 370
library **2** 366
masons' lodges **19** 532
Müngersdorf **26** 870
museums
Erzbischöfliches Diözesan-Museum **7** 584
Historisches Museum *see* Kölnisches Stadtmuseum
Jüdisches Museum **17** 582
Kölnisches Stadtmuseum **7** 584; **27** 718
Kunstgewerbemuseum **7** 582, 584; **30** 332
Pallenberg-Saal **12** 497
Kunst- und Museumsbibliothek und Rheinisches Bildarchiv **2** 370; **12** 481
Lackmuseum **7** 585
Museum für Ostasiatische Kunst der Stadt Köln **7** 584; **20** 77
collections **6** 826; **7** 155; **18** 383
exhibitions **18** 384
Museum Ludwig **7** *585*; **22** 360
collections **7** 585; **19** 779; **24** 682
Rautenstrauch-Joest-Museum **7** 584; **19** 779; **29** 240
Römisch-Germanisches-Museum **7** 585; **27** 115
Schnütgen-Museum **7** 584; **29** 516
Wallraf-Richartz-Museum **7** 584, *585*; **12** 476; **26** 3, 346; **28** 191; **29** 611; **31** 579
collections **7** 585; **17** 887; **32** 823
palace **25** 423
Rathaus **7** 593*; **12** 367; **17** 700; **26** 190
Doxal **32** 339
reconstruction **2** 323
Schauspielhaus **7** *582*
synagogue **17** 544, 547
tombs **21** 162
trade **24** 48
urban planning **7** 581–2
Werkbundausstellung, 1914 **2** 814; **10** 683
Glashaus **12** 792; **21** 781; **25** 173; **30** 370, *370*
Werkbund Theater **10** 697; **31** *877*
Zoo **33** 698
Cologne, Clemens August, Prince-Bishop of *see* WITTELSBACH, CLEMENS AUGUST, Bishop of Regensburg, Münster and Paderborn, Archbishop of Cologne
Cologne, Conrad of *see* CONRAD OF COLOGNE
Cologne, Eilbertus of *see* EILBERTUS OF COLOGNE
Cologne, Gusmin of *see* GUSMIN OF COLOGNE
Cologne, Hans of *see* BESSER, HANS
Cologne/Bonn Airport **1** 495
Cologne Bible *see under* BIBLES → types
Cologne Diptych **11** 451, *451*
Cologne earth *see under* PIGMENTS → types
Cologne Town Hall Prophets, Master of the **7** 593
Colohete **14** *711*
S Manuel **14** 713
Colomb, Charles-Auguste **11** 518
Colomba, Christoph **2** 781
Colomba, Luca Antonio **19** 780
Colombe, François **7** 595, 599*
works **7** *599*
Colombe, Jean **7** 595, 596–9*
attributions **33** 28
collaboration **21** 72; **22** 30
patrons and collectors **3** 188; **4** 545, 547; **11** 355; **26** 454; **28** 1; **31** 308, 832, 843
works **7** *598*; **11** 340; **18** 662; **19** 392; **31** 309, *309*
Colombe, Michel **7** 595–6*; **11** 556; **13** 79; **24** 472
assistants **7** 599
attributions **17** 486
collaboration **11** 355; **23** 709
patrons and collectors **4** 544, 545; **11** 399, 556; **13** 905; **31** 843
pupils **4** 546
sculpture
altarpieces **3** 868
funerary monuments **7** *596*; **22** 464
reliefs **1** 766; **11** *557*
tomb **4** 828, 870; **11** 555; **17** 485; **23** 709
workshop **31** 846
Colombe, Philibert **7** 595, 597, 599
Colombe, Philippe **7** 595
Colombel, Nicolas **7** 600*; **25** 398; **31** 56
Colombes Château **9** 175
Colombia **7** 600–612*, *601*; **29** 125
apartments **7** *606*
architecture **7** 603–7*, *604*
bamboo **7** 605
baskets **7** 602
bolo **7** 607
bowls **29** *150*
cathedrals **7** *604*
churches **4** *233*; **7** 604
cochineal **7** 607
collections **7** 609, 611–12*
copper **30** 240, *240*
crypts **27** 700
daguerreotypes **7** 608, 612
dealing **7** 611*
domes **7** 604
drawings **7** 609, 610
dress **7** 602; **21** 804
education (art) **7** 612*
emeralds **7** 600, 610; **12** 269; **29** 155
ethnography **7** 609
exhibitions **7** 609
ferrotypes **7** 612
figurines **22** 266
flasks **29** *212*
gold **7** 600, 610–11*; **28** *781*; **29** 135, 152, *211*; **30** 240, *240*
iconography **29** 134
jade **16** 861
libraries **7** 612
mantles **29** 152
maps **7** 609
masks **7** 603
molas **21** 804
monstrances **7** 610
museums **7** 611–12*
painting **7** 607*, 608–10*, *610*
botanical **7** 601, 608
watercolours **7** 609
palm leaves **7** 603
patronage **7** 611*
pendants (jewellery) **28** *781*; **30** *240*
photographic plates **7** 612
photography **7** 609, 612
pigments **7** 607
pottery **7** 603; **29** 150
prints **7** 610
quilting **7** 607
Colombia—cont.
reeds **7** 603
retables **26** 252
roofs **7** 603
sarcophagi **27** 833
satires **27** 872
sculpture **7** 607–8*, *608*, 609*; **27** 700, *700*, 701; **29** 145–6
stone **27** *700*
sgraffito **7** 607
shells **29** 217
silver **7** 600, 610–11*
slaves **7** 603
statuettes **29** *143*
stone **27** *700*; **29** *143*
stone-carvings **29** 155
stools **7** *603*
textiles **7** 602; **29** 152
topography **7** 609
trade **5** 747
tumbaga **29** *212*
varnishes **7** 603, *603*
walls **7** 603
wood-carvings **7** 602, *608*
see also PANAMA
Colombino, Carlos **7** 612–13*; **24** 101
groups and movements **22** 743; **24** 99
patrons and collectors **24** 101
personal collection **24** 101
works **24** 96, 99, *99*
Colombo **7** 613*; **29** *440*
architecture **29** 452–3
Cargills, Messrs, department store **29** *454*, 454
Clock-Tower **29** 454
Customs Complex **29** 454
Dutch Period Museum **29** 478
Eye Hospital **29** 454
Flag Museum **29** 478
fortress **29** 452
furniture **29** 470
Galle Face Hotel **29** 461
gardens **29** 452
General Post Office **29** 454
Grand Oriental Hotel **29** 454
Karagampitiya Subodharama **29** 466
Law Courts **29** 453
Lionel Wendt Centre **33** 74
monument to D. S. Senanayake **29** 461
National Museum **7** 613; **29** 453, 478
Natural History Museum **29** 478
New Municipal Town Hall **29** 453, 454
painting **29** 466
Public Works Department offices **29** 454
Queen's House **29** 453
religion **29** 444
Secretariat **29** 454
Wesleyan Mission **29** 453
Wolvendaal Church **29** 452
Colombo, Bartolomeo **26** 840
Colombo, Carlos **24** 98
Colombo, Gian Carlo **8** 267
Colombo, Gianni **2** 528; **10** 416; **13** 728
Colombo, Giovanni **22** 703, 704
Colombo, Giovanni Bartolomeo **25** 443
Colombo, Giovanni Battista **18** 447
Colombo, Juan **24** 96
Colombo, Luigi *see* FILLIA
Colombo, Realdo **21** 449
Colombus Circle **23** 273
Colomer, Narciso Pascual y *see* PASCUAL Y COLOMER, NARCISO
Colón **23** *902*, 903
railway station **23** 904
Colón, Diego **9** 116
Colón Delgado, Oscar **25** 701
Colone, Adam de **7** 613–14*; **28** 268; **31** 889
colonettes **6** 421
Colonia, de (family) **13** 108; **29** 289
Colonia, Francisco de **7** 614*
collaboration **26** 299
groups and movements **25** 31
works **5** 201, 203; **25** 23; **26** 249; **29** 265
Colonia, Juan de **7** 614*; **13** 107; **14** 578
patrons and collectors **1** 684
works **5** 201, 203; **13** 69; **29** 263, 414
Colonia, Simón de **7** 614*; **13** 108
assistants **5** 204
attributions **13** 69
collaboration **7** 614
patrons and collectors **2** 278; **21** 124
works **5** 201, 203; **13** 69; **14** 578, *579*; **28** 518; **29** 263; **31** 822; **32** 124
Colonia Agrippinensium *see under* COLOGNE
Colonia Caesaria *see* ANTIOCH (ii)
Colonia del Sacramento **7** 614–15*; **31** 751, *751*, 752
church **31** 753
Colonia Genetiva Julia *see* OSUNA
Colonia Julia Augusta Felix Heliopolitana *see* BAALBEK
Colonial bond *see under* BONDING
colonialism **7** 615–18*, *616*
Colonial Revival **7** 618–20*; **22** 743
Australia **7** 619*; **33** 224
United States of America **7** 618–19*, *619*; **20** 568; **24** 300; **25** 806; **31** 594, 622, 657, 690
Colonial Williamsburg *see under* WILLIAMSBURG (VA)
Colonia Parmensis *see under* PARMA
Colonia Ulpia Traiana *see* XANTEN
colonies, artists' *see* ARTISTS' COLONIES
Colón Morales, Rafael **18** 833
Colonna (family) **26** 320, 765
architecture **13** 292; **25** 322; **26** 747
collections **2** 27; **16** 762; **26** 773; **27** 172
jewellery **16** 752
paintings **3** 758; **9** 375; **14** 367; **19** 525, 816; **21** 808; **23** 873; **25** 729
prints **24** 240
sculpture **29** 519
stage design **11** 277
Colonna, Prince (*fl* 1679-80) **29** 519
Colonna, Prince (fl c. *1730)* **31** 854
Colonna, Angelo Michele **7** 622*; **8** 280
assistants **5** 873
collaboration **4** 277; **21** 26, 732
patrons and collectors **3** 90; **10** 526; **23** 87; **32** 131
works **2** 849; **11** 214; **15** 138; **16** 714, *715*; **20** 66, 72, 94; **21** 26
Colonna, Anna **12** 169; **26** 837
Colonna, Ascanio (*fl* 1516) **27** 742
Colonna, Ascanio, Cardinal (*fl* 1592-4) **4** 913; **31** 536
Colonna, Edouard **4** 71; **7** 622–3*
collaboration **11** 904
groups and movements **2** 564
works **11** 582, 600
Colonna, Fabrizio **3** 920
Colonna, Filippo, I (1597-1639) **7** 620; **9** 409
Colonna, Filippo, II **7** 620
Colonna, Francesco **20** 865; **31** 150
works **1** 655; **5** 685; **11** 342; **15** 50; **22** 377; **32** 198
Colonna, Giovanna *see* DORIA, GIOVANNA
Colonna, Girolamo, Cardinal (1604-66) **7** 620, 621–2*
interior decoration **25** 411
paintings **7** 622
Colonna, Girolamo (*c.* 1688-*c.* 1766) *see* MENGOZZI, GIROLAMO
Colonna, Guido da
Colonna, Iacopo, Cardinal (*fl* 1288-97) **26** 832; **27** 450
Colonna, Jacopo (*d* 1524) *see* FANTONI, GIACOMO
Colonna, Lorenzo Onofrio, Duke of Paliano and Castiglione *see* PALIANO AND CASTIGLIONE, LORENZO ONOFRIO COLONNA, Duke of
Colonna, Oddone *see* MARTIN V, Pope
Colonna, Pietro, Cardinal **26** 832; **27** 450
Colonna, Pompeo, Cardinal **4** 651
Colonna, Prospero, Cardinal **7** 620, 621*
architecture **1** 555
sculpture **3** 690; **26** 767
Colonna, Stefano **6** 144
Colonna, Vittoria **7** 623*; **25** 296; **26** 769
personal collection **21** 450; **25** 558
colonnaded halls *see* STOAS
colonnades **7** 623*
England **19** *573*
Greece, ancient **13** 379, 381, 391, 397, *397*, 415, 417
Indian subcontinent **15** 399, *400*
Italy **26** *34*
Rome, ancient **26** 858, 863, *918*, 922
Syria **23** *892*; **26** *918*
see also ARCADES; PERISTYLES
Colonna di Sciarra, Giulio Cesare *see* SCIARRA, GIULIO CESARE COLONNA DI
Colonnes d'Hercules **18** 745; **25** 626
colonnettes *see under* COLUMNS → types
Colonnetti, Gustavo **22** 77
Colón y Mendoza, María **7** 883
Colón y Mendoza, Teresa **7** 883
colophons **7** 623–6*; **28** 310
Buddhism **7** 624; **17** 230, *270*; **30** *836*
Byzantine **9** 605
China **6** 750, 751, *751*, 755, 760, 761, 823, 824; **7** 623–4*, *624*
Early Christian (*c.* AD 250-843) **9** 605
Germany **7** *625*, 625
Islamic **7** 625–6*, *626*
Italy **32** 384
Japan **7** 624–5*; **17** 230, *270*
Malaysia **20** *171*
Tibet **30** *836*
Turkey **7** *626*
colophony *see* ROSIN
Colóquio artes **24** 453
Colorado Springs (CO), Pikes Peake Center **1** 126
Color and Rhyme **5** 219
Colorno
gardens **12** 115
Palazzo Ducale **24** 552
Color Print Society **25** 629
colossal heads *see under* SCULPTURE → types
colossal order *see* ORDERS (ARCHITECTURAL) → types → giant
colossal statues *see under* SCULPTURE → types

colossal temples *see under* TEMPLES → types
Colosseum *see under* ROME
Colossi of Memnon *see under* THEBES (i) (EGYPT)
Colossus of Rhodes **13** 462; **26** 290, 292
colour **7** 626–36*; **9** 490; **19** 351–3; **24** 375–7; **28** 203
historical and regional traditions
Africa **7** 635*
Aztec **7** 636; **21** 183
Bali (Indonesia) **15** 800
Buddhism **18** 310–12
China **7** 631–2*
Confucianism **7** 632
Egypt, ancient **10** 1
Gothic **13** 135–7
Greece, ancient **2** 227
Ibibio **7** 635
Igbo **7** 635
Indian subcontinent **7** 633–4*; **15** 228
Indonesia **15** 806
Iran **7** 634
Islamic **7** 634–5*; **16** 457
Italy **7** 627
Japan **7** 632–3*
Korea **7** 632; **18** 310–12
Maasai **19** 860
Maya **7** 635, 636; **21** 183
Mesoamerica, Pre-Columbian **7** 635–6*; **21** 183
Mixteca-Puebla **21** 183
Native North Americans **22** 561
Prehistoric art **25** 477, 480
South America, Pre-Columbian **7** 635–6*
Toltec **21** 183
Yoruba **7** 635
Zulu **7** 635
uses
cosmologies **21** 183
glass **12** 781–2*, 787*
heraldry **13** 137; **14** 406
lithography **20** 603
manuscript illumination **13** 138–9
music and art **22** 380, *380*
photography **24** 647–8*, 649, 650, 653, 656, 668, 670, 678, 679
see also PIGMENTS; POLYCHROMY
Colour **24** 427
colour-etchings *see under* ETCHINGS → types
colour field painting *see under* PAINTING → types
colour interaction **7** 637–8*, *638*, VII, VIII; **19** 353
Colourism **24** 13
Colourists **32** 877
colourmen **7** 638–9*; **23** 378, 786
colour perspective *see under* PERSPECTIVE → types
colour photography *see under* PHOTOGRAPHIC PRINTS → types; PHOTOGRAPHY → processes
colour-plates *see under* BOOK ILLUSTRATIONS → types
colour printing *see under* PRINTING → processes
colours *see under* FLAGS → types
Colours, Master of *see* BELLEGAMBE, JEAN
colour theories *see under* THEORIES
Colozier **30** 886
Colquhoun, Alan **7** 639–40*
Colquhoun, Archibald **21** 78
Colquhoun, Ithel **30** 22
Colquhoun, Patrick **28** 259
Colquhoun, Robert **7** 639*; **19** 868
groups and movements **22** 751; **32** 912
works **19** 492; **21** 897; **25** 616, VIII; **28** 240
Colquhoun & Miller **7** 639–40
Colsón, Jaime **9** 117
Colson, Jean-Baptiste **7** 640
Colson, Jean-François **3** 463; **7** 640*; **8** 891; **9** 407
Colsoul, C. Charles **22** 896
Colt (family) **10** 261
Colt, John (*d* 1637) **7** 641
Colt, John (*fl* 1660) **7** 641
Colt, Maximilian **7** 641*; **10** 261, 262, 270; **19** 605
Colt, Samuel **15** 822
Coltellini, Alessandro dei **7** 642
Coltellini, Baldassarre dei **7** 642
Coltellini, Galasso dei **7** 642
Coltellini, Michele di Luca dei **7** 641–2*; **11** 4
Colter, Mary **22** 568
Colt Hoare, Richard **9** 18; **13** 744; **18** 584
Coluccini, Giovanni Battista **4** 233; **7** 604
works **4** *233*
Columba, Saint **15** 892
Columban **19** 549
Columbanus, Saint **11** 529
columbaria *see under* TOMBS → types
Columba Triptych **19** 530; **33** 122, *122*, 124, 125, 127
Columbia (MO)
Missouri State House **31** 659
University of Missouri, Museum of Art and Archaeology **15** 746; **29** 241
Columbia Broadcasting System **19** 235
Columbian Academy of Painting *see under* NEW YORK → academies and art schools
Columbian Gallery *see under* PHILADELPHIA (PA)
Columbian press *see under* PRESSES → types
Columbianum *see under* PHILADELPHIA (PA) → museums
Columbia University *see under* NEW YORK
Columbus First Baptist Church (IN; USA) **4** 790
Columbus (OH)
First Christian Church **7** 259
Ohio State Capitol **13** 237
Ohio Theater **22** 325
Wexner Center for the Arts **10** 120–21
Columbus, Bartolomé **9** 116
Columbus, Christopher
First Voyage (1492-3) **2** 144; **8** 228; **9** 113; **14** 53, 57; **16** 879
Fourth Voyage (1502-4) **8** 15; **14** 711; **23** 79
writings **29** 133
Columbus Lighthouse **9** 117
Colum Cille *see* COLUMBA, Saint
Columella, Lucius Iunius Moderatus **12** 64, 68, 110; **26** 884
column chromatography *see under* TECHNICAL EXAMINATION → types
columned halls *see under* HALLS → types
column kraters *see under* KRATERS → types
Column of Marcus Aurelius *see under* ROME
columns **23** 477, 482
historical and regional traditions
Afghanistan **16** 168
Belgium **26** 905
Britain **26** 905
Buddhism **6** *422*
Carolingian **5** 794
Central Asia, Western **6** 200; **16** 168, 502
Champa **6** 422, *422*
China **6** 640; **7** 98
columns
historical and regional traditions—cont.
Egypt, ancient **9** 830, 831; **23** 477; **30** 432
Ejagham **1** 263
Ethiopia **10** 473
Germany **26** 905
Greece, ancient **10** *431*; **13** 376–7, *376*, 379, 388, 389, 391, 392, 393, 398, 399, 410, 412, 415–16; **26** *909*
Helladic **14** 340
Indian subcontinent **15** 330, *335*, 336, 386, 393, 448, 737
Iran **16** *502*
Islamic **16** 168, 188, 502, *502*
Italy **27** *40*
Khwarazm **6** 200
Latin America
see also ESTÍPITES
Lebanon **3** 2
Minoan **23** 477
Mycenaean **14** 340
Nigeria **1** 261
Poland **29** *793*
Romanesque **21** *900*; **26** 569; **29** *793*
Rome, ancient **4** 769, 772; **26** 135, 863, 874, 875, 876, 877, 878, 882–3, *892*, 905, 922, 923, *923*, 924, 925; **27** 39, 40
Belgium **26** 905
Britain **26** 905
Germany **26** 905
Greece **26** *909*
Italy **27** *40*
Sicily **21** *900*
Spain **16** 188
see also ESTÍPITES
Syria-Palestine **30** 191
Turkey **10** *431*; **26** *923*
Venezuela **32** 168
Vietnam **6** 422, *422*
materials
brick **4** 769, 772; **26** 877, 878
cast iron **7** 98
marble **21** *900*; **26** 877, 925
porphyry **26** 902
wood **16** 502, *502*
techniques
in antis **13** 376
types
Attic **23** 487
colonnettes **5** 475; **7** 623*; **16** 142
Corinthian **2** 666; **11** 231, *231*; **13** 379, 380, 401, 405, 415; **23** 392, 478; **26** 865
Doric **11** 231, *231*; **13** 398
engaged **7** 642*; **13** 401; **26** 874
half **15** 393; **22** 215; **26** 595; **32** 472
historiated **23** 487; **26** 791
Ionic **11** 231, *231*; **13** 377, 379, 398, 399, 401
Solomonic **21** 377; **23** 487
Tuscan **23** 480
see also PILASTERS
column statues *see under* SCULPTURE → types
Co Luy **6** 426
Colvalenza, Santuario dell'Amore Misericordioso **4** 790
Colville (family) **24** 149
Colville, (David) Alex(ander) **7** 643–4*
works **5** 569; **7** *644*; **28** 300
Colvin, Brenda **7** 644*; **8** 207
Colvin, Howard Montagu **10** 212, 377
Colvin, Marta **6** 598; **7** 645*
pupils **31** 812
works **6** *598*
Colvin, Sidney **14** 554
Colwell, David **6** 392; **32** 789
Colyear, David, 1st Earl of Portmore **30** 278
Colyer, Edwart *see* COLLIER, EDWART
Colyn, Michiel **4** 282
Colyn, Thomas **13** 84
Colyn & Meiring **5** 668
Colyns, Symon **7** 553
Colzi, Giuseppe **16** 719, 729
Coma, Pedro de *see* PEDRO DE COMA
Comacio, Tomaso di **12** 371
Comalapa **13** *758*, 765
Comalcalco **7** 645*; **20** *882*; **21** *372*
brick **4** 796
Platform VI **29** 829
sarcophagus **27** 832
stucco **29** 829
walls **21** 205
Coman, Dragoş *see* DRAGOŞ
Comanche **22** 551, 616, 629
Comandè, Giovanni Simone **26** 517
Comanducci, Agostino Mario **10** 212
Comane, Juan Bautista **10** 502; **11** 486; **20** 67; **26** 250
Comanini, Gregorio **1** 179; **7** 646*; **13** 914; **21** 525
Comans, Marc de **1** 782; **11** 640; **23** 665; **30** 321; **31** 227
Comayagua **14** *711*, 712
Cathedral **14** 713, 714
retables **26** 251
Caxa Real **14** 713
La Caridad **14** 713
La Merced **14** 712
Museo Arqueológico y Histórico de Comayagua **14** 716
Museo de Arte Religioso **14** 716
S Francisco **14** 714
Comayagüela **14** 714
Banco Nacional de Fomento **14** 714
Casa de los Muñecos **14** 714
Cementerio **14** 713
Instituto Hibueras **14** 714
Combarelles, Les *see* LES COMBARELLES
Combas, Robert **7** 647*; **11** 553
works **11** *552*
Combaz, Gisbert **19** 321; **20** 100; **32** 253
Combe (Oxon), St Laurence **25** 724; **28** 292
Combe, Etienne **16** 549
Combe, Joseph **19** 849
Combe, Martha **7** 647
Combe, Taylor **2** 165
Combe, Thomas **7** 647*; **23** 690
paintings **7** 573; **15** 26; **21** 603
Combe, William **1** 121; **4** 607; **29** 491
Combed ware *see under* POTTERY → wares
Combel, Le *see* LE COMBEL
Combes, Charles Alphonse **8** 22
combination prints *see under* PHOTOGRAPHIC PRINTS → types
combing **12** 785*
Combrinck, Johannes **29** 120
combs (hair) **7** 646
historical and regional traditions
Africa **1** *423*
Akan **2** 590*
Alaska **22** *574*
Asante **2** 590*
China **7** 7, *7*, 102, 107, 109, 110
Crete **21** 682
Greece, ancient **13** 595
Indian subcontinent **15** 726, 734
Japan **17** 386
Korea **18** 367
Minoan **21** 682
Native North Americans **22** 574, *574*
Punic **25** 734
Spain **25** 734
Sri Lanka **29** 471
combs (hair)
historical and regional traditions—cont.
Surinam **1** *423*
materials
bone **7** 107, 109
enamel **7** 109
glass **17** 386
gold **7** 109
horn **14** 763
ivory **7** 102; **13** 595; **16** 798, 799; **22** *574*; **25** 734; **29** 471
jade **7** 7, *7*, 109
silver **7** 110
silver-gilt **7** 109
wood **1** *423*; **2** 590; **7** 107, 109
combs (liturgical) **7** 646*, *646*; **9** 648; **32** 389
combs (mouldings) *see* MOULDINGS COMBS
Comédie-Française **20** 137; **30** 669, 671, 672; **32** 768
Comédie Italienne **20** 137
Comella, Esteban **12** 180
Comenico, Zanobi di *see* ZANOBI DI COMENICO
Comenius, Jan Amos **4** 360; **10** 175; **33** 637, 638
Comerford, John **9** 209
Comerio, Agostino **8** 522
Comes, Francesc **23** 881
Comes, Natalis *see* CONTI, NATALE
Comestor, Peter **4** 12; **15** 82
Cometa, Domenic Benedette **6** 363
Cometa, Giovanni Bartolomeo **8** 385; **25** 443
Cometta, Antonio **17** 588; **20** 90
Cometta, Domenico **27** 285
Comewijne **30** *12*, 15
Comfort, Charles (Fraser) **5** 567; **7** 648*
Comfort, Elijah **5** 731
Com-Fut **20** 887
Comic-strip art **6** 775; **7** 648–9*, *649*; **31** 149
see also CARTOONS (COMIC STRIPS)
Comillas
Casa El Capricho **25** II2
church **21** 393
Villa Ocejo **11** 494
Comillas, Marqués de **12** 179, 180
Comin (family) **32** 195
Comin, Andrea **7** 650
Comin, Francesco **7** 650
Comin, Giovanni **7** 650*
Comin, Leonardo **7** 650
Cominetti, María Rosa **6** 600
Comini, Alessandra **22** 523
Comino, Giovanni *see* COMIN, GIOVANNI
Comino da Pontevico **7** 439
Comisión Corográfica **7** 609
Comisión Nacional de Bellas Artes (Uruguay) **31** 759
Comité de Conservation des Monuments de l'Art Arabe (Cairo) **5** 401; **16** 550
Comité International pour la Réalisation des Problèmes Architecturaux Contemporains *see* CIRPAC
comitia **26** 867
Commagene **1** 828; **22** 731
sculpture **13** 466; **22** *731*; **24** 217
Commaille, Jean **2** 56, 57
Commandini, Federigo **7** 650*; **24** 489; **28** 202; **31** 740
commedia dell'arte **5** 787; **30** 657, 659, 669
Commei, Domenico dei **12** 257; **16** 746
commemorative arches *see under* ARCHES → types
commemorative cups *see under* CUPS → types

commemorative stelae *see under* STELAE → types
Commentari: Rivista di critica e storia dell'arte 24 449
commercial art 3 137; 7 650–56*; 15 180
see also POSTERS; TOURIST ART
Commercial Art 7 653
Comminelles, Hughes de *see* HUGHES DE COMMINELLES
Commission de l'Inventaire des Richesses Artistiques de la France 17 667
Commission des Monuments Historiques (France) 2 319; 13 810
Mission Héliographique 3 422; 19 86, 239; 24 662
Commission for Construction (Russia) 22 171, 172, 181
Committee for the Encouragement of Music and Arts (CEMA) 10 362
Committee of 100 21 363
Committee of Taste 19 599
commodes 5 192; 7 657–9*; 8 271
France 7 *658*
historical and regional traditions
Belgium 3 583
Canada 5 577
England 7 657, 659
France 6 I3; 7 657–8, *658*; 11 589, 591–3; 26 84, *84*
Louis XIV style 11 *589*
18th cent. 11 *592*
Germany 7 658; 12 424, *425*
Italy 7 659
Netherlands, the 22 *873*, *874*
Portugal 25 306–7
Sweden 7 659; 30 *94*
materials
bronze 12 *425*
ebony 11 *589*
gilding 7 *658*
mahogany 7 658
marble 7 657, *658*; 11 592
mother-of-pearl 12 424, *425*
mounts (furniture) 11 *589*
porcelain 6 I3
satin-wood 11 *592*
tortoiseshell 12 424, *425*
techniques
gilding 7 *658*; 11 *592*; 30 *94*
marquetry 11 *589*
types
à encoignures 11 593
à la Grecque 11 592
Commodi, Andrea 7 906; 11 39
Commodus, Emperor of Rome (*reg* 180-92) 27 39, 40, 97, *98*
Commodus as Hercules 27 46
Commonarts 22 *336*
common-tie-beam roofs *see under* ROOFS → types
Commune des Arts 24 137
communication theory 7 659–61*; 19 275
communion-cups *see under* CUPS → types
Communism 6 627, 636, *774*, 774–5, 811; 25 652–3
community architecture *see under* ARCHITECTURE → types
community gardens *see under* GARDENS → types
Commynes, Philippe de 11 355, 399, 726
Comnenos *see* KOMNENOS
Comnos, Spiridon 13 359
Como
Broletto 20 438
Casa del Fascio *see* Casa del Popolo
Casa del Popolo 7 695; 15 886; 16 *649*, 650; 26 15; 30 513
Cathedral of S Maria Maggiore 16 757; 26 502–3; 30 331
Civico Museo Archeologico 16 770
Como—cont.
Comum 27 3
Hospital 14 781
mills (industrial) 21 600
Novocomum apartment building 16 649; 21 783; 26 15; 30 513
Palazzo Broletto 31 236, *237*
S Abbondio 16 625; 23 491; 26 577, 635
nave 26 *577*
sculpture 26 619, 620
S Fedele 16 625; 26 620
silk 16 753
Villa Amalia 4 470
Villa Bagatti Valsecchi 3 49
Villa di Inverigo 16 647
Villa Olmo 16 647, *647*, 719
Como, Antonio de Rigezzo da *see* RIGEZZO DA COMO, ANTONIO DE
Como, Bonagiunta da *see* BONAGIUNTA DA COMO
Como, Giovanni da *see* GIOVANNI DA MILANO
Como, Giovanni di Benedetto da *see* GIOVANNI DI BENEDETTO DA COMO
Como, Giroldo da *see* GIROLDO (DI JACOPO) DA COMO
Como, Guido da *see* GUIDO DA COMO
Como, Manfredino da *see* MANFREDINO DA COMO
Comolera, Paul 10 312
Comolli, Angelo 4 21
Comolli, Giovanni Battista 7 662*; 16 705
Comontes, Antonio de 4 414; 29 277
Comontes, Francisco de 29 278; 31 89
Comoro Islands 1 *214*; 11 880
compact-domed basilicas *see under* CHURCHES → types
Compagni, Domenico (*d* 1508) *see* COMMEI, DOMENICO DEI
Compagni, Domenico (*fl c.* 1550-86) 12 258
Compagni, Scipione 7 662*; 22 478
Compagnia delle Quattro Arti 24 232
Compagnia di S Benedetto Bianco 27 179
Compagnie de l'Art Brut 2 515; 11 551
Compagnie des Arts Français 2 521; 11 601, 644; 29 899
Compagnie des Bronzes 3 572
Compagnie des Cristalleries de Baccarat 3 13
Compagnie des Grands Hôtels Européens 31 888
Compagnie des Verreries et Cristalleries de Saint-Louis 9 171; 11 612, 613; 24 57, 58
Compagnie Française de Cristal Daum 8 544; 11 613
Compagno di Pesellino *see* APOLLONIO DI GIOVANNI (DI TOMASO)
Compagnons de l'Art 5 38, 44
Compaire, René 21 126
Companhia das Fábricas Cerâmicas Lusitania 23 455
Companhia Fabril de Louça *see* FÁBRICA DE CERÂMICA CONSTÂNCIA
Compañon, Baltasar Jaime Martínez *see* MARTÍNEZ COMPAÑON, BALTASAR JAIME
Company of Goldsmiths of Dublin 9 320; 16 31
Company painting *see under* INDIAN SUBCONTINENT → painting
Comparetti, Piotr Innocenty 32 876
compartiments à l'anglaise 12 122
Compartment carpets *see under* CARPETS → types
compasses 11 763
Celtic 6 154, 155, 161
Greece, ancient 13 411
Ireland 6 161
Japan 17 399
Russia 22 182
Compe, Jan ten 7 662*; 14 42; 22 847
compendario *ware see under* POTTERY → wares
compendia *see* ENCYCLOPEDIAS
Comper, (John) Ninian 7 663*
teachers 4 215
works 5 731; 27 125; 28 295, *295*, 296
Comperis, Jacques 3 888
competitions 7 663–77*; 24 90
historical and regional traditions
France 24 138; 25 637
Germany 12 853
Greece, ancient 10 675
Japan 17 334
types
architecture 1 106; 7 664–70*, *665*, *668*, *669*; 13 394; 15 169; 16 639; 24 170
painting 1 106–7; 7 673–7*; 10 675; 13 375; 19 161
sculpture 3 783; 7 670–73*, *671*; 10 265
Compi, Bartolomeo 2 192
Compiègne 11 *504*; 25 193
carpets 27 896
Château 4 306, 307; 6 509; 7 677–8*; 12 769; 28 346; 29 834
furniture 12 831; 28 298
gardens 7 677–8
interior decoration 3 621; 4 301, 303; 10 187
paintings 5 281; 18 643
restorations 7 677
Salle des Gardes 3 463
tapestries 3 461; 31 379
textiles 21 368
Hôtel de Ville 11 511; 31 238
Complejo de El Tisure 27 703
Complutensian Polyglot Bible *see under* BIBLES → types
comports 16 *29*
Composite capitals *see under* CAPITALS → types
composite grounds *see under* GROUNDS → types
Composite order *see under* ORDERS (ARCHITECTURAL) → types
composite statues *see under* SCULPTURE → types
composition 24 61, 62
Compositiones variae 7 678*; 20 367; 24 795
Compostela 25 702
compound piers *see under* PIERS (ii) (MASONRY) → types
compounds 1 311–12; 7 678–9*, *679*; 29 166
see also PRISONS; SETTLEMENTS; VILLAGES
compound tabby *see under* WEAVING → types
compound twill *see under* WEAVING → types
compound warp-faced textiles *see under* TEXTILES → types
Compoy 14 714
compression 20 573
Compte, Pere 7 679*
works 29 263; 31 814, *815*
Compte-Calix, François Claudius 7 679–80*; 8 618
Comptoir National du Logement 25 375
Compton, Watts Gallery 30 506; 32 923
Compton, Charles, 7th Earl of Northampton 3 382, *383*; 4 845
Compton, Henry, Bishop of London 19 622; 23 467
Compton, Spencer, Earl of Wilmington 29 540
Compton, Spencer Joshua Alwyne, 2nd Marquess of Northampton 13 541
Compton, William (*c.* 1482-1528) 8 44
Compton, William, 1st Earl of Northampton (*fl c.* 1614) 10 290
Compton Place (E. Sussex) 29 540, 835
Compton Pottery 6 164
Compton Wynyates (Warwicks) 8 *43*, 44; 22 64
Council Chamber 10 272
Computer-Aided Design *see* CAD
computer art 7 *680*, 680–81*; 14 690; 28 202, 204, *204*
computer catalogues *see under* CATALOGUES → types
computers 2 367; 11 55; 26 236; 31 498
Comstock, Nelson 27 720
Comte, Adolf de 8 667
Comte, A. Le *see* LE COMTE, A.
Comte, Pierre-Charles 27 636
Comte, Pierre le 13 910
Comtois, Ulysse 7 681*
Comum *see under* COMO
Comyns-Carr, J. 19 413
Cona, Jacobo *see* COENE, JACQUES
Conagui 1 308
Conakry 1 *386*
Musée National de Sandervalia 13 835
Conal, Robbie 27 872
Conan Doyle, Arthur 11 310
Conant, Kenneth 7 478
works 22 *10*
Conant Ball Co. 31 632; 33 410
Conara, Wanstead 32 308
Conat, Abraham *see* ABRAHAM CONAT
Conca, Francesco 7 684
Conca, Giovanni 7 684; 18 780
Conca, Prince 12 912
Conca, Sebastiano 7 681–4*; 16 672; 22 479; 23 637; 26 774, 842; 31 444
attributions 26 477
collaboration 3 920; 8 12; 19 816; 20 903
patrons and collectors 4 560; 5 812; 14 190; 26 827; 27 316; 28 16, 18
pupils 2 26; 5 906; 12 762; 13 802; 18 780; 25 460; 27 200; 33 629
works 7 *683*, *684*; 20 213; 26 827; 28 683
Conca, Tommaso 7 684; 25 8; 28 755
Concanen, Albert 19 484
Concanen, Alfred 22 371
Concarneau 25 215
concave mouldings *see under* MOULDINGS → types
Conceição, Domingos da 26 412
concentric castles *see under* CASTLES → types
Concepción 6 *590*, 591; 24 *91*
Cathedral 6 592
Museo de Arte Sacro 24 102
Pinacoteca 6 601
Universidad de Concepción 6 601
Concepción, Antonio de la 28 516
Concepción, Carlos de la 24 502
Concepción, Juan de la 29 341
Concepción del Bermejo 2 394
Concepción del Uruguay Church 2 396
Concepción de Moxos 4 269
S Javier 4 259
S Rafael 4 259
Concepción ware *see under* POTTERY → wares
conceptual art 1 80; 5 197; 6 23; 7 684–7*; 9 360; 15 868, 869; 18 400; 21 646; 24 24, 403, 408, 679; 26 51, 235
Bolivia 4 264
Brazil 4 720
England 10 258, 269
Germany 7 *686*
Italy 20 352, *352*; 21 172
Poland 17 448
Russia 27 *398*
United States of America 31 *609*
Concerned Photographers 23 698
concert halls 7 687–8*
acoustics 1 122, 123, 124, 126*
England 19 *577*; 31 240
Germany 28 *56*
United States of America 7 *688*
see also ODEIA; OPERA HOUSES; THEATRES
concertina books *see* BOOKS → types → accordion books
Conçesti 9 655
Concha, Andrés de la 7 688–9*; 21 383
Concha, Ernesto 6 597
Concha, Luis Astete y *see* ASTETE Y CONCHA, LUIS
Conche, Jacques 10 562
Conches-en-Ouche, St Foy 13 181
Conchillos, Juan 7 689*
Conchillos, Juan Antonio 7 689
Conchopata style pottery *see under* POTTERY → wares
Conchort, P. 8 386
conch shells *see under* SHELLS → types
Conchy, Gérard de *see* GÉRARD DE CONCHY
Conconi, Luigi 7 689–90*
groups and movements 21 527; 25 567; 28 34
pupils 3 687
Conconi, Mauro 3 49; 7 689
concordances 6 76
Concordia 9 *510*, 533
Concordia Sagittaria Baptistery 26 650
Concord Meeting House (MA) 31 652
Concorezzo, Giovanni Boniforte da *see* GIOVANNI BONIFORTE DA CONCOREZZO
concrete 7 690–98*
conservation 7 697–8*
historical and regional traditions
Britain 7 693
Cambodia 5 482
Caribbean Islands 5 *753*, 755
Crete 8 155
England 2 600; 7 *712*; 10 241; 28 874
Finland 19 411
France 7 693, *694*, *697*; 11 771
India, Republic of 15 168
Italy 7 692*; 26 887
Korea 18 266
Mexico 7 *695*
Nigeria 1 319; 23 *138*
Norway 4 *804*
Peru 24 505
Rome, ancient 2 297; 6 9; 7 691–2; 20 572; 25 748; 26 864, 871, 874, 877, 879–80*, 881, 889, 893, 904
Crete 8 155
Italy 26 887
Switzerland 20 118; 22 186
United States of America 22 336; 27 *128*
Vietnam 32 477
technical examination 30 409
techniques
shuttering 7 690, *690*; 28 645*
types
ferro-concrete *see* reinforced fibrous 11 834

concrete
types—cont.
mass **7** 691
precast **7** 691
prestressed **7** 691, *691*, 694; **11** 771
reinforced **7** 691, 693–6*; **16** 55; **19** 41; **21** 4; **30** 677
Australia **2** 740
Austria **25** 37
Belgium **8** 633
Brazil **3** 66
England **7** 712; **33** 204–5, *205*
France **7** 531, 693; **14** 388; **24** 128, *128*, 472, *473*
Germany **19** 502
Islamic **16** 143, 241
Italy **14** 388; **22** *806*
Japan **17** 90
Mexico **4** 185
Poland **3** *768*
Romania **26** 709
Switzerland **31** 465
United States of America **7** 326; **25** 892; **31** 464, 465
uses
arches **2** 297
architecture **7** 690, 691–6*; **19** 41; **30** 27
Brazil **3** 66
Cambodia **5** 482
England **33** 204
France **7** 531, *694*; **11** 771
India, Republic of **15** 168
Islamic **16** 143
Japan **17** 86
Korea **18** 266
Mexico **7** *695*
Peru **24** 505
Poland **3** *768*
Rome, ancient **26** 879–80*, 881
Vietnam **32** 477
brick **4** 767
bridges **4** 803*, *804*; **7** *691*; **14** 388; **20** 118
casts **6** 7, 9
churches **7** 693; **22** 186; **25** 37
domes **2** 740; **22** *806*
factories **33** *205*
foundations **28** 874
houses **2** 600; **7** 712, *712*; **26** 18
insulae **26** 887
mosques **5** 755
murals **22** 336
office buildings **14** 388
roofs **26** 880; **27** *128*
sculpture **5** *753*; **7** 691*, 696–7*, *697*; **23** *138*
skyscrapers **7** 326
stressed-skin construction **21** 407
temples **5** 755
theatres **30** 677
thermae **26** 871
vaults (ceiling) **26** 864
Concrete art **1** 75, 76; **2** 490; **7** 698*; **11** 550; **17** 767
Brazil **4** 719; **28** 476; **32** 690
Denmark **1** 7
Switzerland **4** 60; **7** 546; **13** 267; **30** *138*
Concrete Art Association *see* GUTAI
Concreteness Art Society *see* GUTAI
Concrete poetry **7** 698–9*
Concretists, The **7** 699*; **30** 81
Condé (House of) **7** 699*; **10** 884; **14** 174; **19** 95
Condé, Anne de Bavière, Princesse de **4** 225
Condé, Clémence, Princesse de **12** 285
Conde, Domingo **20** 501; **29** 337
Conde, Francisco **22** 245
Condé, Grand *see* CONDÉ, LOUIS II DE BOURBON, Prince de
Condé, Henri-Jules de Bourbon, Prince de **4** 537, *543*, 572; **8** 776; **12** 747
Condé, Henry I de Bourbon, Prince de (1552-88) **4** *543*
Condé, Henry II de Bourbon, Prince de (1588-1646) **4** *543*, 578; **7** 699*; **24** 467; **25** 790
Condé, Jean **7** 699–700*; **29** 675
Condé, Louise de Bourbon, Princesse de **4** 848
Condé, Louis-Henri de Bourbon, Prince de **2** 701; **4** *543*; **6** 453, 454*; **8** 68, 813; **11** 608
Condé, Louis I de Bourbon, Prince de (1503-69) **4** *543*
Condé, Louis II de Bourbon, Prince de (1621-86) **4** *543*; **6** 453; **11** 637; **12** 747, 833; **19** 163
Condé, Louis-Joseph de Bourbon, Prince de **4** *543*, 847, 848; **5** 908; **6** 454; **7** 900; **8** 523, 791, 890; **13** 864; **14** 230; **18** 805; **24** 581; **25** 786
Conde, Luis **29** 337
Condé, Peter **7** 700
Condeixa *see under* CONIMBRIGA
Condé Nast **4** 918; **14** 816; **29** 602; **31** 138
Conder, Charles (Edward) **2** 601; **7** 700–701*; **21** 76
groups and movements **2** 746; **14** 306–7; **23** 22
patrons and collectors **22** 54
works **7** *700*; **10** 781
Conder, Josiah **7** 701*; **17** 52, 86
pupils **30** 364
teachers **17** 862
works **17** *86*, 381; **31** 79
writings **17** 417
Conder, Neville **5** 925
Conder, W. J. **7** 700
Condes, Marqués del **31** 96
Condesa de Reunión **8** 231
Condeso-Brokopp **20** 609
Condino Cathedral
paintings **9** *48*
Condivi, Ascanio **7** 701–2*; **16** 781; **21** 459
Condoré, Olivier **11** 635
Condorhuasi culture **29** 190
Condrus, Nora *see* STERIADI, NORA
Condulig Ua hInmainen
works **32** *530*
Cone (family) **31** 664
Cone, Claribel **7** 702
Cone, Etta **7** 702
Conegiano **24** 894
Conegliano, Scuola dei Battuti **31** 71
Conegliano, (Giovanni Battista,) Cima da *see* CIMA DA CONEGLIANO(, GIOVANNI BATTISTA)
Conegliano, Sebastiano di Giacomo di Bologna da *see* FLORIGERIO, SEBASTIANO
Coner Sketchbook *see under* SKETCHBOOKS → individual manuscripts
cones **6** 330
cones, pyrometric *see* PYROMETRIC CONES
Coney, John **4** 479; **7** 702*; **31** 647, 648
works **22** 14; **31** 647, *647*
Confalonieri, Giuseppe **21** 529
Confesseur, Jacques **11** 626
confessio **8** 222
confessionals **7** 282, 703–4*, *703*
confessios *see under* TOMBS → types
confidant *chairs see under* CHAIRS → types
confidantes **29** 8
Conflans Castle **13** 128, 134
Conforto, Giovanni Giacomo di **7** 704*
assistants **10** 799
works **9** 182; **22** 472, 484
confraternities *see* GUILDS
Confraternity of Servants of St Mary *see* SERVITES
Confucianism **7** 704–7*
art
altars **1** 703, 704
architecture **6** 674–6*; **18** 266, 269–71*
bronze **7** 705
calligraphy **17** 236
colour **7** 632
courtyards **6** 674
craftsmen and artists **18** 258
gardens **12** 93
gates **18** 280
gateways **6** 675
iconography
China **6** 628*
Japan **17** 40–42*
Korea **18** 256
Vietnam **32** 470
painting **6** 803, 807, 808; **7** 632, *705*, *706*
poetry **25** 73
railings **6** 675
schools **6** 676; **18** 269–71, *270*, *271*
shrines (i) (cult) **18** 269; **28** 638
temples
China **6** 674–5*, *676*; **30** 443
Korea **30** 445
Vietnam **32** *474*, 474–5*
theories (art) **6** 631, 634, 637; **7** 704–7*
regional traditions
China **6** 625; **17** 215
Japan **17** 215, 236
Korea **18** 250, 252, 253
Confucius **6** 625, 634; **7** 704; **33** 660
cong **7** *1*, 1–2
Cong Abbey (Co. Mayo) **16** 19
Congdon, Henry Martyn **7** 708*
Congdon, Herbert Wheaton **7** 708
Congdon, William **24** 213
Congiusto, Bernardo **27** 342
Congleton (Ches)
Town Hall **31** 241
Wagg Street Church **21** 347
conglomerate glass *see under* GLASS → types
Congnet, Gillis (*fl* 1530) **7** 708
Congnet, Gillis (*c.* 1538-99) **3** 865; **7** 708*, 866
Congo, French *see* GABON
Congo, Republic of **1** *214*, 393; **7** 708–9*; **11** 880
burial practices **1** 259*, *260*
figurines **1** *275*; **3** *694*
masks **1** *399*
megaphones **1** 360
niombos **1** 259, *260*
trade **1** 250
wood **1** *275*, *399*; **3** *694*
Congonhas do Campo **27** 499, 500
Bom Jesus de Matozinhos **4** 710, 716; **19** 461, *461*
Congo-Tervuren **24** 430
Congregationalists *see under* CHRISTIANITY → sects
Congregation of St Paul *see* PAULIST FATHERS
Congregation of the Oratory *see* ORATORIANS
Congregation of the Regular Clerks of St Paul *see* BARNABITES
Congregazione di S Giuseppe di Terra Santa alla Rotonda **26** 769
Congrès Internationaux de l'Architecture Moderne *see* CIAM
Congresso Nacional Complex *see* Congresso Nacional
Congreve, William **25** 277
Coniagui **13** 835
Conibo **24** 514
conical roofs *see under* ROOFS → types
Conick **23** 242
Conimbriga **26** *908*
basilica **3** 328
baths **3** 375; **26** 872
Condeixa **30** 879
gardens **12** 70
House of the Jets of Water **12** 70
houses **26** 904
mosaics **27** 63
museum **25** 318
Coninck, Aert de **18** 227, 228
Coninck, David de **4** 222; **11** 872
Coninck, Isaac de **14** 737
Coninck, Juan Ramón **7** 709*
Coninck, Kerstiaen de *see* KEUNINCK, KERSTIAEN DE
Coning, Jacob **23** 224
Coningham, William **7** 709*
Coningsby, George, 5th Earl of Essex **30** 278
Coninxloo (ii), Cornelis van, I (*d* 1527) **7** 712
Coninxloo (ii), Cornelis van, II (*fl* 1529-59) **7** 710, 712*
Coninxloo (i), Gillis van, I (*fl* 1539-43) **7** 710
Coninxloo (i), Gillis van, II (*fl* 1599) **7** 710
Coninxloo (i), Gillis van, III (1544-1607) **4** 910; **7** 709, 710–11*; **21** 167; **22** 841
collaboration **7** 428; **20** 248
groups and movements **11** 731; **18** 707
patrons and collectors **28** 904
pupils **28** 165, 358; **32** 137
reproductive prints by others **4** 282; **5** 62
works **3** 558; **7** *711*; **11** 487; **23** 112; **25** 606
Coninxloo (i), Gillis van, IV (1581-1619/20) **7** 709
Coninxloo (i), Hans van, I (*b* 1595) **7** 709
Coninxloo (i), Hans van, II (1565-*c.* 1620) **7** 709
Coninxloo (i), Hans van, III (*b c.* 1589) **7** 710
Coninxloo (i), Hans van, IV (*b* 1623) **7** 710
Coninxloo (i), Isaak van **7** 709
Coninxloo (i), Jan van, I (*fl* 1490) **7** 709; **20** 747; **32** 924
Coninxloo (i), Jan van, II (1489-1552) **7** 709, 710*
Coninxloo (i), Jan van (*fl* 1599) **7** 710
Coninxloo (i), Pieter van (*fl* 1470s-1513) **3** 554; **7** 710; **13** 905; **20** 716, 747
Coninxloo (i), Pieter van, I (*fl* 1544) **7** 709
Coninxloo (i), Pieter van, II (1604-48) **7** 710
Coninxloo, van (i) (family) **23** 526
Conisbrough Castle (S. Yorks) **10** 227
Conjeevaram *see* KANCHIPURAM
Conn (family) **31** 230
Connaissances des Arts **24** 442
Connal, William **22** 51
Connell, Amyas Douglas **2** 600; **7** 712–13; **10** 241; **21** 783; **23** 56
works **7** *712*
Connell, Neville **2** 154
Connell, Ward & Lucas **7** 712–13*; **13** 798; **20** 475
Connelly, Pierce Francis **23** 62
Connemara **29** 702
Conner, Bruce **17** 694; **19** 702; **31** 608
Conner, Robert **13** 208
Connestabile (family) **16** 769
Connestabile Madonna **26** 734
Connick, Charles **8** 111; **29** 508
Connoisseur, The **24** 423, 446
connoisseurs **7** 561
connoisseurship **2** 532, 558, 559, 560; **7** 713–17*; **11** 306–10; **20** 242; **22** 360; **25** 630–32
Belgium **3** 615
China **6** 637, 770, 823, 824, 866, 886; **7** 715–16*; **11** 307, 309; **17** 230
Germany **17** 818; **26** 358
Indian subcontinent **7** 717*; **15** 740
Islamic **7** 716–17*
Italy **21** 28; **22** 102
Japan **7** 716*; **17** 215, 230, 334, 343, 413–14, 423, 427, 437–40*
United States of America **31** 671
Connolly, John **2** 658
Connolly, Joseph **7** 717–18*
Connolly, Speaker William **3** 786
Connor, Jerome **16** 21
Connor, William *see* CONOR, WILLIAM
Conolly, Louisa **16** 24; **18** 746
Conolly, Tom **14** 278
Conolly, Mrs William **11** 242
Conolly, William **12** 6; **16** 23; **24** 305
conopas **24** 500
Conor, William **3** 537; **16** 40, 42
Conover, Allan D. **33** 400
Conques **11** *505*
enamel **7** 720
metalwork **7** 720
Ste Foy **7** 718–19*; **26** 585; **32** 89
altars **1** 697
ambulatory **1** 767, *767*, 768
enamel **26** 691
gems **12** 255
metalwork **11** 614
plaques **7** *718*
Reliquary of St Faith **11** 614; **22** 43, *43*; **26** 145
sculpture **7** 719–20*; **11** 554; **26** 596
Treasury **5** 806, 808, 811; **7** 720*; **26** 681
tympanum **7** *719*
Conquette **25** 503
Conrad (metalworker) (*fl* 1302) **31** 122
Conrad, Bishop of Canterbury (*fl* 1114-26) **5** 643; **28** 428
Conrad II, Holy Roman Emperor (*reg* 1024-39) **13** 19; **14** 81; **19** 394; **23** 656; **26** 573; **27** 616; **29** 390; **32** 458
Conrad III, Holy Roman Emperor (*reg* 1138-52) **23** 305
Conrad V, Duke of Franconia *see* CONRAD II, Holy Roman Emperor
Conrad, F. W. **23** 670
Conrad, Paul **27** 872
Conrad, William H. **7** 429
Conrad de Scharfeneck, Bishop of Metz **21** 361
Conrade, Augustin **11** 604; **23** 13
Conrade, Baptiste **11** 604
Conrade, Dominique **11** 604
Conrad of Cologne **31** 843
Conradsen, H. **17** 481
Conradsminde Glasværker **8** 749
Conradus **7** 205
Conradus Pictor **11** 98
Conrad von Einbeck **7** 721*; **13** 90
Conrad von Soest **7** 721–5*
assistants **20** 765
attributions **20** 630, 765
pupils **20** 681
works **7** *722*, *723*, *724*; **12** 383; **19** 528; **29** 4
Conran, Terence **7** 725*; **8** 804; **10** 285, 300; **20** 595
Conran Design Group **7** 725
Conran Foundation **7** 725; **8** 805
Conrath, Jean Geoffroy **29** 751
Conrat Swopp **28** 694

Conrat von Sinssheim see SIFER, CONRAT
Conrat von Sünnesheim see SIFER, CONRAT
Conrau, Gustav 3 170, 171
Conreshem, Christian 20 765
Conroy, Stephen 28 273
Consagra, Pietro 7 725*
groups and movements 7 782; 9 168; 11 314; 16 681, 709; 26 777
works 28 657
Consalvi, Ercole, Cardinal 3 644; 6 341; 7 726*
Consalvo, Giovanni di see GIOVANNI DI CONSALVO
Consejo Nacional para la Restauración y Conservación de Monumentos Históricos(Peru) 24 505
conservation 7 726–44*
education see under EDUCATION (ART) → types
historical and regional traditions
China 1 580; 7 729–30; 28 312
England 17 209; 23 248
Italy 7 738–9
Japan 7 729–30; 17 138–9*, 208–10*, 209; 18 617; 28 312
United States of America 30 564
materials
abrasives 6 334
acrylic 6 336; 28 339
adhesives 1 157*; 6 335–6; 7 730, 737; 17 209; 24 7
air-conditioning 7 734, 735, 736*
alkyds 6 336
alkyl alkoxy silanes 4 797
aluminium 24 7
ammonia 12 628
balsawood 24 7
barium hydroxide 28 339, 340; 32 809
barium sulphate 6 336
bark 12 628
blotting papers 6 335
bread 28 339
bronze 6 336
brushes 17 208–9
calcium carbonate 7 740
calcium sulphate 7 740
canvas 24 7
chalk 7 737
clamps 22 165
clay 12 629
consolidants 6 335; 7 747; 17 210; 24 7
dehumidifiers 7 735
detergents 6 334
eggs 28 340
fibreglass 24 7
fixatives 17 210
glues 17 138; 28 312
gypsum 7 737
heating systems 7 734
humidifiers 7 734
humidistats 7 734
hydrogen peroxide 6 335
hydrogen plasma 7 730
hygrometers 7 734
Japanese paper 17 209; 28 339
kaki juice 17 210
kaolin 7 740
lasers 7 730
magnesium silicate 6 335
methylene chloride 12 629
microscopes 24 569
moulds 6 336
nails 22 165
paper 7 730; 17 210; 28 312
Paraloid B67 10 195
Paraloid B72 7 737; 12 629; 28 340
plaster 6 335, 336
plaster of Paris 7 729
polyeurathanes 6 336
Primal AC33 28 340
psychrometers 7 734
conservation
materials—cont.
putties 6 335; 28 339
PVA 7 737; 25 27
resins 6 335–6; 10 195; 17 138; 28 339
epoxy 7 730
rubber 6 334
silica 6 336
silica gel 7 736
silicone resins 4 797
siloxanes 4 797
starch 17 209
talc 6 336
thermohygrographs 7 734
thermometers 7 734
toluene 12 629
ureaformaldehydes 6 336
varnishes 32 3–4*
vinegar 28 340
wood-pulp 28 339
techniques
bleaching 6 335
cleaning 7 727*
freeze-drying 7 730
repair 7 728*
riveting 6 335
soldering 7 730
stabilization 7 727–8*
transfer 29 892
uses
altarpieces 24 7
architecture 2 318–25*; 7 729; 29 713
archives 2 365, 366, 368*
beadwork 7 729
boats 7 748
bookbindings 4 355–6*, 356
brick 4 797*
calligraphy 1 580; 15 856
canvas 5 657–8*
ceramics 6 334–6*; 7 727–8, 729
chalices 7 728
charcoal 8 129
clocks 7 729
concrete 7 697–8*
crayons 8 128–9*
drawings 8 128–9; 9 231–3*; 15 856, 856
chalk 6 400–401*
pastel 6 400–401*
enamel 10 195–6*
furniture 7 727–8, 729
gilding 12 628–9*, 629
glass 12 796*, 796
glazes 6 334
inks 15 855–6*, 856
iron 7 748
ivory 16 799–800*
lacquer 18 615–17*, 616
leather 7 747; 19 6*
limestone 7 747
lustre 6 336
manuscript illumination 20 349*
masonry 4 797
metalpoints 21 340*
metalwork 21 333–6*, 334
mosaics 22 165*
overglaze decoration 6 334
painting 1 580; 5 657–8*; 7 727, 737–9*, 738; 17 208–10, 209; 24 569
encaustic 10 199*
fresco 19 395; 29 892
panel 7 IX, X; 24 6–8*, 7, 8
screen 17 210
scroll 15 856; 17 209
secco 28 339, 339–40*
tomb 10 618
wall 10 618; 32 807, 807–10*, 809, 810
watercolours 28 340
paper 15 850; 24 52–5*; 25 632–3; 32 819
parchment 24 107*
photography 2 365, 366; 24 683–4*
plaster 29 845–6*
plastics 2 366; 25 27–8*
conservation
uses—cont.
porcelain 6 334–6*
posters 2 366
pottery 6 334–6*; 7 XI1, 2
predellas 24 7
prints 15 856; 25 632–3*
sandstone 7 747
scabbards 7 727
scrolls 7 729–30; 28 312*
sculpture 7 729, 739, 739–40*, XII
silver 7 727
stained glass 29 517, 517–19*
stone 7 747; 29 707–13*, 708
stucco 29 845–6*, 846
supports 24 6–8
tapestries 30 332–5*, 333, 334
tempera 30 427–8*
terracotta 30 512*
textiles 30 563, 563–7*, 564, 567
upholstery 31 687–8*
wallpaper 32 819–20*
watches 7 729
waxes 10 199; 33 6*
wood 7 747, 748; 33 336–40*
writing 15 856
see also RESTORATION; TECHNICAL EXAMINATION
conservatories 7 744–5*; 23 471
Belgium 7 745
England 5 283; 7 744, 745; 12 137, 791; 24 294
France 7 744
Germany 12 415
United States of America 7 745
see also GARDENS → types → winter; GREENHOUSES; ORANGERIES
Consett, Matthew 3 897
Consetti, Antonio 29 33
Considérant, Victor 11 523
consistories 7 745*
consoles 7 746*; 16 142, 202; 29 315
see also BRACKETS
console tables see under TABLES → types
Consolí Blanc 13 169
consolidants 1 155; 7 747–8*; 11 141; 17 210
books 7 748
canvases 7 747
ceramics 6 335
conservation 6 335; 17 210
paintings 7 747; 24 7
fresco 7 747
wall 7 747
paints 7 747
paper 7 747–8
wood 33 339
see also ADHESIVES; CONSERVATION; FIXATIVES
Consolidated Glass Works Ltd 29 118
Consol Ltd see CONSOLIDATED GLASS WORKS LTD
Consoni, Nicola 31 172
Consorti, Vico 26 810; 28 681
Consortium of Local Authorities' Special Programme see CLASP
Constable (publishers) 4 367
works 4 367
Constable, John 7 748–57*; 14 452; 27 626; 29 877
collaboration 21 417
commentaries 19 241
dealers 2 499; 7 579; 26 107
drawings 9 225
groups and movements 24 742; 26 736, 739, 741
methods 13 708; 19 355; 24 3, 495
mezzotints 21 417
paintings
landscape 7 749, 752, 755, 756; 9 1; 10 252; 11 430, 431; 18 714, 715; 26 221
Constable, John
paintings—cont.
marine 4 810
oil sketches 10 251; 23 381
sketches 33 453
watercolours 9 217
patrons and collectors
Chéramy, Paul-Arthur 6 548
Forbes, James Staats 11 301
Holloway, Thomas 14 688
Lázaro Galdiano, José 18 900
Lever, William Hesketh, 1st Viscount Leverhulme 19 270
Mellon, Paul 21 91
Morrison, James 22 147
Munro (of Novar), H(ugh) A(ndrew) J(ohnstone) 22 314
Neeld, Joseph 22 719
Proby, William, 5th Earl of Carysfort 25 639
Schroth, Claude 28 170
Sheepshanks, John 28 576
Tennant, Charles 30 464
Thyssen-Bornemisza, Hans Heinrich, Baron von 30 795
Vernon, Robert 32 338
personal collection 8 99
reproductive prints by others 5 24; 25 596; 26 232
teachers 11 860
writings 18 701; 22 686
Constable, Lionel 7 757
Constable, William 7 757–8*
Constable & Co. 1 649
Constance see KONSTANZ
Constance, Queen of Bohemia (fl c. 1220s) 31 28
Constance, Queen of France (d 1032) 11 653
Constância, Companhia see FÁBRICA DE CERÂMICA CONSTÂNCIA
Constant 7 758–9*; 22 854
groups and movements 2 230; 7 488, 489; 9 188; 17 658; 22 852; 27 137
works 7 489
Constant, (Jean-Joseph-) Benjamin 7 759–60*
groups and movements 23 504
patrons and collectors 9 305
pupils 5 781
Baca Flor, Carlos 3 12
Blanes Viale, Pedro 4 129
Brough, Robert 4 870
Czajkowski, Józef 8 370
Peel, Paul 24 322
Prendergast, Maurice (Brazil) 25 552
Putz, Leo 25 748
Reid, George A(gnew) 26 108
Salgado, José Veloso 27 615
Sousa, Aurélia de 29 100
Tanner, Henry Ossawa 30 297
works 7 760
Constanța 4 110; 7 760–61*; 9 568; 26 705, 906
Archaeological Museum of Dobruja 7 761
Museum of Art 7 761
warehouses 26 907
Constant-Dufeux, Simon-Claude 7 761*
pupils 7 170; 27 343
works 2 320; 24 166; 25 173
Constantia see SALAMIS
Constantiacum see KONSTANZ
Constantiana see CONSTANȚA
Constantin, Abraham 29 629
Constantin, Amédée 7 762
Constantin, Guillaume 7 762*
Constantin, Jean-Antoine 7 762*; 20 473
pupils 1 497; 11 301; 13 308
Constantina 9 543; 26 752, 829; 31 434
Constantina Castra see LE HAVRE
Constantine (Algeria) 1 315, 376; 21 629; 25 733
Museum 1 636
Constantine (fl 720) 9 637
Constantine (fl 14th cent.) 23 374
Constantine I, Emperor of Rome see CONSTANTINE THE GREAT, Emperor of Rome
Constantine I, Katholikos (reg 1226-69) 31 177
Constantine II, Emperor of Rome (reg 337-40) 9 655
Constantine IV, Emperor of Byzantium (reg 668-85) 9 637
Constantine V Kopronymos, Emperor of Byzantium (reg 741-75) 9 514, 632, 637; 15 80
Constantine VI, Emperor of Byzantium (reg AD 780-97) 9 637
Constantine VII Porphyrogenitos, Emperor of Byzantium (reg 912-59) 9 514, 522; 19 887–8*
art policies 9 625
coins 9 636, 638
gold 9 657
iconography 9 520
manuscripts 14 432
writings 30 709
Constantine IX Monomachos, Emperor of Byzantium (reg 1448-53) 9 522, 577; 19 888*
architecture 7 170; 9 522, 558; 16 582, 608
crowns 9 653
gold 9 657
mosaics 9 578
Constantine X Dukas, Emperor of Byzantium (reg 1059-67) 9 519
Constantine Dukas (fl 1070s) 9 662
Constantine Lips 16 582
Constantine Manasses 7 241
Constantine of Trebizond 13 358
Constantine Palaiologos, Prince 23 830
Constantinescu, Mac 26 720
Constantinescu, Ștefan 26 716
Constantine the Great, Emperor of Rome (reg 306-37) 7 762–3*, 763; 9 509, 522; 16 578; 20 865; 27 56
architecture 9 522, 528, 536, 560; 16 761; 26 752; 31 324
baptisteries 3 189
basilicas 7 217; 26 782, 820, 902–3, 903
cathedrals 2 155, 158; 9 539
churches 3 880; 5 442; 7 252; 9 529–31*, 539, 654; 16 603, 623; 17 489; 22 43; 26 752
crypts 8 222
fortresses 7 580
martyria 20 519; 26 800; 27 235
mausolea 9 557
palaces 9 557; 16 606–7
towns 7 760
triumphal arches 31 350
art policies 2 312; 25 650
coins 9 635; 27 97; 28 791
crosses 8 195
devices 14 407
flags 11 146
gold 6 173; 9 654
manuscripts 7 246
metalwork 7 301; 26 820
obelisks 23 330
porphyry 26 876
regalia 26 79, 80
sculpture 1 694; 3 189; 18 825; 27 43–5*, 44
silver 9 656
Constantinople see under ISTANBUL
Constantinos of Tîrgoviște 7 763–4*; 25 340; 26 712, 725
works 31 23

Constantius II, Emperor of Rome (*reg* 337-61)
architecture 2 158; 9 536; 16 580, 603
coins 5 299–300; 9 635
obelisks 23 330
Constantius Africanus 8 800
Constantius Chlorus, Emperor of Rome (*reg* 305-6) 21 *2*; 27 *43*; 31 324
Constantius Rhodius 10 129
Constanza, Queen of Mallorca (*fl* *c.* 1346) 3 339
Constanzó, Miguel 21 396
Constitutions of Masonry 20 562–3*
Construção moderna 24 453
Construction 24 430
construction *see* BUILDING
Construction and architecture of Moscow see STROITEL'STVO I ARKHITEKTURA MOSKVY
construction machinery 7 764–7*
Greece, ancient 7 764; 13 387, *388*, 400
Rome, ancient 26 864
United States of America 7 *766*, 766
construction materials *see under* ARCHITECTURE → materials
Construction Moderne 8 476
constructive geometry *see* GEOMETRY (CONSTRUCTIVE)
Constructivism 1 75, 77, 79, 90; 2 488; 5 75; 7 767–72*; 8 437; 11 360; 26 235
art forms
architecture
Belarus' 12 653
Brazil 5 451
Japan 30 296
Poland 25 100
Russia 12 *654*, 877, *877*; 21 782; 22 *174*; 27 378–9, *379*
Ukraine 31 552
books 30 204
mobiles 11 *877*
painting 10 *257*; 29 *794*
posters 25 349
sculpture 1 147; 22 78
Argentina 2 *400*
Britain 20 486
France 24 *574*
Poland 7 *771*
Russia 7 *768*; 25 *25*
collections 26 193
exhibitions 23 262; 26 194; 28 920; 31 183
periodicals 24 428
regional traditions
Argentina 2 400, 525; 24 386
assemblages 2 616
Belgium 3 399; 24 324
Brazil 4 719
Britain 7 772; 30 748–9
Czech Republic 7 772; 18 445
Denmark 28 183
England 10 258
France 7 772; 24 574
Germany 5 75; 7 767, 770–72; 28 197
Hungary 1 132; 3 223; 20 104
Netherlands, the 1 79; 7 655, 772
Poland 3 788; 7 772; 25 108, 422; 29 582, 794
Romania 26 716
see also INTEGRALISM
Russia 1 76; 7 767–70*; 12 35; 15 99, 857; 18 141; 19 476; 20 192; 21 38, 735, 776; 24 405; 25 239; 26 503, 504; 27 394, 396; 29 626; 30 363; 32 381, 661
see also PRODUCTIVISM
Switzerland 7 546; 19 542
Uruguay 31 755, 758
consular diptychs 16 798
historical and regional traditions 7 772*; 9 3; 18 823; 25 183
Byzantine 9 *251*, 647, *648*, 648–9, 650
Early Christian (*c.* AD 250-843) 9 647, *648*, 648–9
Rome, ancient 26 862
materials
enamel 9 3
gold 9 3
ivory 9 3, *251*, *648*, 650; 18 *826*
metal 9 3
wood 9 3
techniques
painting 9 3–5
Consulate style 4 302; 7 772–3*
contact prints *see under* PHOTOGRAPHIC PRINTS → types
Contades, Maréchal de 3 274; 12 159
Container Corporation of America 3 423; 7 654
containers
historical and regional traditions
Aboriginal Australia 1 52
Ancient Near East 1 878
Belgium 3 592
Bhutan 3 916
Central African Republic 1 369
Central Asia, Eastern 6 313
Germany 15 *825*
Korea 18 362–3
Native North Americans 22 651, 654
Philippines 24 626–8*, *627*
San Pedro culture 29 *189*
South America, Pre-Columbian 29 *189*
materials
bamboo 3 144; 15 807
bark 1 52; 22 656
brass 24 *627*, 627–8
calabashes 31 73
coconuts 15 807
faience (i) (glass) 1 878
glass 3 592; 15 *825*
lacquer 3 916
quills 22 651
rawhide 22 654
silver 3 916
wood 24 626–7*; 29 *189*
uses
brushes 5 34
food 3 916
paints *see* PAINT CONTAINERS
containing arches *see under* ARCHES → types
Contaldino di Meuccio, Giovanni di *see* GIOVANNI DI CONTALDINO DI MEUCCIO
Contamin, Pierron & Charton
works 16 *55*
Contamin, Victor 9 464; 10 683; 14 384
Contant d'Ivry, Pierre 2 495; 7 773–4*
assistants 8 75, 617
collaboration 23 517
pupils 3 523
teachers 9 383
works 2 337; 7 *774*; 11 738; 23 517
Contarelli, Francesco 8 138
Contarelli, Matteo 5 709; 8 138
Contarini (family) 11 871; 19 627
Contarini, Alessandro 7 775*
Contarini, Alvise II 7 775
Contarini, Angelo 7 775
Contarini, Antonio 7 775
Contarini, Bertucci 7 775
Contarini, Camillo 8 851
Contarini, Caterina 7 775
Contarini, Domenico, Doge of Venice (*reg* 1659-75) 32 206
Contarini, Federico 7 775, 776*
Contarini, Giacomo 2 162
Contarini, Giovanni 23 113; 27 655; 30 923
Contarini, Girolamo 7 775
Contarini, Giulio 32 647
Contarini, Jacopo 7 775–6*
Contarini, Marin 5 176; 7 774; 26 37
Contarini, Michele 16 835
Contarini, Pietro 7 775; 19 627; 27 890
Contarini, Taddeo 7 775*; 12 675, 676; 22 696
Contarini, Tommaso 7 775; 31 13
Contarini dagli Scrigni, Giorgio 11 41
Contat, Mlle 16 *905*
conté *see under* CRAYONS
Conte, Ephrem *see* CONTE, MEIFFREN
Conte, Giovanni del, Archbishop of Nicosia 23 112
Conte, Jacob le *see* JACOB LE CONTE
Conte, Jacopino del 7 776–7*; 26 770, 809
pupils 25 729
teachers 27 851
works 7 *776*; 15 121; 27 648
Conte, Jehannin le *see* JEHANNIN LE CONTE
Conte, Le *see* LE CONTE
Conte, Meiffren 29 668
Conté, Nicolas-Jacques 8 128; 9 217; 24 353
Conte di Rinfredo 28 683
Conteh, D. L. 28 692
Contemporánea 24 453
Contemporaneo, Il 27 192
Contemporáneos, Los 6 21; 21 406; 26 521
Contemporary, The *see* CONTIMPORANUL
Contemporary Art Group 9 766; 12 222
contemporary art museums *see* MUSEUMS → types → modern art
Contemporary Art Society (Belfast) 16 42
Contemporary Art Society (London) 4 168; 10 362; 19 590
Contemporary Art Society for Wales 32 791
Contemporary Arts Society (Melbourne) 2 769; 3 628
Contemporary Arts Society (Montreal) 5 568; 19 843; 22 39
Contemporary Group 8 2
Contemporary Jamaican Artists' Association 32 910
Contemporary Lithographs 11 748
Contenau, G. 12 765
Contenebra 27 752
Contenson, H. de 5 185
Conte Polychrome pottery *see under* POTTERY → wares
Conti (House of) 7 778*
Conti, Angelo 7 778*; 8 509
Conti, Baldassare de' 7 778
Conti, Bernardino de' 7 778–9*; 20 741
Conti, Carlo 28 10
Conti, Carlo, Cardinal 18 669
Conti, Domenico 27 850
Conti, Francesco 21 31; 31 268
Conti, Inocenc de 25 426
Conti, Louis-François de Bourbon, Prince de (1717-76) 4 *543*; 7 778*; 11 663; 19 115; 20 417; 23 416; 33 4
collections 3 453
furniture 11 305
Conti, Louis-François-Joseph de Bourbon, Prince de (1734-1814) 11 257
Conti, Manfredino de 21 113
Conti, Marie-Anne de Bourbon, Princesse de (1666-1739) 3 752; 4 516
Conti, Marie-Thérèse de Bourbon-Condé, Princesse de (1666-1732) 8 32
Conti, Michelangelo, Cardinal *see* INNOCENT XIII, Pope
Conti, Natale 1 656; 15 83; 22 414
Conti, Pietro Antonio 10 528; 14 894; 29 76; 31 353
Conti, (Umberto) Primo 7 779*, 782; 16 680
Conti, Sigismondo de' 25 903
Conti, Stefano 3 109; 5 594; 7 779–80*; 20 391
Conti, Torquato de' 9 181
Conti di Segni, Lothario dei *see* INNOCENT III, Pope
Contieri, Jacopo 19 516
Conti Ferniani Factory 10 751
Contile, Luca 7 780*
Contimporanul 8 436; 16 903; 20 877; 25 237; 26 716
Contin, Francesco 19 629
Contin, Tommaso 19 629
Continental China 29 117
Contini, Edgardo 9 503
Contini, Francesco (Gaetano) 7 780*
collaboration 6 23
excavations 31 62
patrons and collectors 21 747
pupils 7 780
works 1 531
Contini, Giovanni Battista 7 780–82*
patrons and collectors 1 532; 5 178
works 5 614; 7 *781*; 18 785
Contini, Maffeo 7 780
Contini, Pietro 7 780
Contini, Tommaso 1 531
Contini Bonacossi, Alessandro, Conte 7 782*; 18 448
Contino, Bernardino di Francesco 7 861; 32 160
Continuità 7 782–3*
members 1 112; 7 725; 25 189; 31 436
Continuous Vegetal Style *see* CELTIC → periods → Waldalgesheim Style
contouring (holographic) *see under* TECHNICAL EXAMINATION → types
contour lines 21 568
contours découpés 16 615; 25 488, 493
Contra 30 58
Contractor, Hafeez 4 291
contractors *see* BUILDING CONTRACTORS
contracts 2 366; 10 4; 13 133; 22 157; 25 794
contrapposto 7 783*; 13 422, 453; 23 292
contrast 24 *376*, 376–7
contre-jour 7 783*
contre preuve see COUNTERPROOFS
Contreras (family) 13 285
Contreras, Francisco 32 173
Contreras, Jesús F(ructuoso) 7 783–4*; 21 386; 23 207
Contreras, José Melendez *see* MELENDEZ CONTRERAS, JOSÉ
Contreras, J. P. 7 484
Contreras, Rey Paz *see* PAZ CONTRERAS, REY
Contreras, Wenceslao Rivas *see* RIVAS CONTRERAS, WENCESLAO
Contri, Silvio 7 784*; 21 378, 396, 403
Controspazio 25 738
Contucci, Raffaello 24 240
Contugi, Matteo 13 833
Contugi, Pier Antonio 11 740
Conus *shells see under* SHELLS → types
Convalle, Master of 2 19
Conventi, Giulio Cesare 1 625
Convention Centre Partnership 4 86
conventions of representation *see* REPRESENTATION
Conventuals 11 707
Conversano
Castle 11 114
S Benedetto 16 626; 26 627
Conversano, Giangirolamo II Acquaviva d'Aragona, Conte di 11 114
conversation chairs *see under* CHAIRS → types
conversation pieces *see under* PAINTING → types
Converse, Morton E., Co. 31 263
convex lip mouldings *see under* MOULDINGS → types
Conway, Edward, Lord Conway 7 794; 8 46
Conway, Patricia 18 193
Conwy (Gwynedd) 31 711; 32 *780*
Castle 6 49, 50, 53, 56; 9 144; 16 895, *895*; 32 781
gate-house 12 174
machicolation 12 174
Plas Mawr 32 782, *782*, 788
railway bridge 4 799, 802
Conybeare, Henry 4 288
Con-Zinc Rio Tinto Australia 33 203
Coofa 18 484
Cooghen, Leendert van der 3 495; 7 787*
Cook (family) 10 367
Cook, Alfred 2 94
Cook, Andrea Theodore 28 206
Cook, Clarence 9 205; 25 805
Cook, Francis(, 1st Baronet) 7 787–8*
architecture 18 168; 28 781
collections 26 473
gems 12 266
Cook, George 4 627
Cook, Henry 14 807
Cook, James (1728-79)
collections 1 66; 14 248; 22 675; 31 143
voyages 2 743; 23 710
Endeavour (1768-71) 23 57; 28 921
Resolution (1772-5) 11 319; 14 610; 20 462; 23 163; 31 890
Resolution (1776-9) 16 859; 33 14
Cook, James (*fl* 1880-83) 29 118
Cook, J. M. 28 893
Cook, Lia 11 54, 55
Cook, Michael 23 70
Cook, Moses 6 128
Cook, Olive 28 878
Cook, Peter (Frederick Chester) 2 308, 309; 7 788*; 31 734
Cook, Richard 10 378
Cook, Rita *see* ANGUS, RITA (CATHARINE)
Cook, Thomas 13 304, 811; 29 118
Cook, T. & J., & Co. 29 118
Cook, Walter 3 6*
Cook, Walter William Spencer 7 789*; 31 672
Cook, Wilbur D. 19 700
Cook, William E. 19 41; 24 815
Cooke, Barrie 16 18
Cooke, Bernard 10 825; 20 484; 29 106
Cooke, E(dward) W(illiam) 4 36; 7 789*
works 3 233, *234*; 20 424; 28 561
Cooke, George 4 614; 7 789*; 31 469, 470
Cooke, Nathaniel 6 558
Cooke, Robert 33 42
Cooke, T. & H. 23 66
Cooke, William Bernard 7 789; 10 396; 31 469, 470

Cooke MS (London, BL, Add MS. 23198) 19 532; 20 562
Cooke's Ordinary 12 272
Cooke-Yarborough, Michael 2 318
Cookhorne, Robert 16 885
Cookingham, L.P. 17 799
cooking pots *see under* POTS → types
Cook Islands 7 790–91*; 23 *711*
  adzes 23 735
  banknotes 23 735
  barkcloth 7 *790*, 791
  body ornaments 23 720
  craftsmen and artists 7 790
  dress 7 791
  fans 7 791; 10 779
  feathers 23 720
  headdresses 23 720
  paper mulberry 7 791
  sculpture 7 790–91*
  staffs 7 *790*
  trade 23 735
  weapons 23 734
  wood 7 *790*
  wood-carvings 7 790–91*
Cook Tondo 19 442
Cooktown 1 61
Cookworthy, William 4 824; 7 791*; 10 309
Coolberger, Antonius 12 851
Coole (Co. Meath), Larch Hill House 11 243
Cooley, Thomas 7 791*; 16 24
  competitions 7 666
  pupils 17 625
  works 9 317; 10 669; 12 44
Coolgardie 2 740
Coolidge, Charles Allerton 26 343; 28 591; 29 536
Coolidge, Shepley, Bulfinch & Abbott 4 475; 19 320; 28 591
Coomans, Jules 4 920; 8 637
Coomaraswamy, Ananda Kentish 5 420; 7 360, 792–3*; 15 183, 206, 211; 29 454; 30 848
  collections 15 610, 742, 745, 747
  writings 2 539
Coombe, William 27 279
Coombes (W. Sussex), St John the Baptist 26 657
Cooney, John D. 10 84
Coonley, Avery 33 401
Cooper, Abraham 20 477
Cooper, Alexander 7 793, 795*; 14 777, 778; 21 640
  patrons and collectors 21 640
  pupils 21 641
Cooper, Anthony Ashley, 1st Earl of Shaftesbury (1621-83) 6 485; 13 646; 23 857
Cooper, Anthony Ashley, 3rd Earl of Shaftesbury (1670/1-1713) 7 713, 795–6*, *796*; 8 612
  gardens 12 128
  paintings 7 461; 20 842
  writings 1 180
Cooper, Douglas 7 797*; 8 240; 31 673
Cooper, Edward 3 476; 21 416; 28 881; 31 786
Cooper, (Thomas) Edwin 7 797*; 14 863
Cooper, F. A. 25 753
Cooper, James Fenimore 3 849; 8 528; 13 621; 14 843
Cooper, John Paul 2 570; 10 336
Cooper, Richard 28 236, 274; 29 746
Cooper, Samuel 7 793–5*; 14 777
  attributions 26 279
  patrons and collectors 8 186; 14 687; 21 908; 24 373
  reproductive prints by others 4 751
  teachers 14 778
  works 7 *794*; 10 248; 21 640
Cooper, Susie (Vera) 7 798*; 10 313
Cooper, Theodore 4 803
Cooper, Thomas Sidney 7 798*; 12 638
Coopérative des Malassis 11 552; 24 145
Cooperative Mural Workshops (New York) 9 233
Cooperative Preservation of Architectural Records *see* COPAR
Cooper Eckstut Associates 23 44
Cooper-Hewitt Museum *see under* NEW YORK → museums
Cooperstown (NY), Museum of New York State Historical Association 19 439
Co-op Himmelblau 2 789, 810; 7 798–9*
  works 32 440
Cooqus, Jean Gérard 10 328; 32 402
Coornhert, Dirck Volkertsz. 7 799*; 10 386, 389; 14 293
  collaboration 14 294
  pupils 12 15, 879
  works 11 222
Coornhuuse, Jacob van den
  works 11 *442*
Coorte, Adriaen 7 799–800*
  works 7 *800*
Coosemans, Alexander 14 289
Coosemans, Joseph 3 562; 4 529
Coosemans, Joseph Théodore 11 448
Coote, Algernon, 6th Earl of Mountrath 18 677
Coote, Charles 16 24
Coote, Jeremy
  works 1 *238*
Copacabana 4 *255*, 264
  architecture 31 47
  sanctuary 4 256, *257*
  sculpture 4 264
Copado, Bartolomeo 7 488
Copado, Manuel 8 232
copal 1 760; 18 609, 610, 611; 26 243
  glass 12 803
  paints 23 784
  varnishes 32 1
Copán 6 87; 7 800–801*; 14 *711*; 20 *882*; 21 190, *193*, 199, 246, 262; 23 826
  altars 1 700
  Ballcourt 20 *883*
  bone-carvings 21 247
  caskets 21 259
  Council House Throne 30 786
  Hieroglyphic Stairway 7 801
  inscriptions 20 883
  sculpture 7 800–801*; 21 221, 256
  shells 21 259
  stairs 21 206
  stelae 7 800–801*; 29 620
  Stele C 7 *801*
  stucco 29 829
  Temple 22 9 165
  Temple of Meditation *see* Temple 22
  tombs 31 116, 118
Copán Ruinas, Museo Regional de Arqueología 14 716
COPAR (Cooperative Preservation of Architectural Records) 2 369
Copcutt, Geoffrey 31 733
  works 31 *733*
Cope, Arthur Stockdale 3 631; 7 802
Cope, Charles 7 801
Cope, Charles West 7 801–2*
  patrons and collectors 28 576
  reproductive prints by others 28 283
  works 9 1; 19 *589*, 614
Cope, James 32 786
Cope, Paul 32 234
Cope, Walter 7 619, 808; 10 718
Copeau, Jacques 13 313; 30 682, 686
Copeland, Elizabeth E. 31 651
Copeland, Joseph 31 651
Copeland, Robert Morris 7 430
Copeland, William 29 419; 30 505
Copeland, William Taylor 3 629; 29 419
Copeland, W. T., and Sons Ltd 10 310, 311, 312; 13 22; 29 496; 30 703
Copeland and Day 8 582
Copeland and Dole 31 855
Copeland & Garrett 29 419
Copelands Statuary Porcelain 9 451; 22 28
Copen, Samuel 5 750
  works 5 *751*
Copenhagen 7 802–7*, *803*; 8 *720*
  Abel Catrine Foundation 8 727
  academies and art schools 1 105
    Eckersberg School 8 758
    Kongelige Danske Akademi for de Skønne Kunster 13 620
    Kongelige Danske Kunstakademi 7 804; 8 726, 727, 734, 758, 760
      collections 8 759; 14 151
      library 2 370; 8 761
      periodicals 24 451
      professorial residence (Freund's decorations) 8 740, 744, *744*, 746
      see also palaces → Charlottenborg
    Royal Academy *see* Kongelige Danske Kunstakademi
  Amalienborg Square 8 740
  art forms and materials
    embroidery 8 755
    jewellery 23 238
    lace 8 756
    lacquer 18 614
    marks 20 *444*
    metalwork 8 750
    necklaces 8 *753*
    pewter 8 751
    porcelain 7 806–7*, *807*
    silk 8 755
    silver 8 750
    tapestries 8 754; 30 322, 332
  auctions 8 758
  Bellahøj 8 729
  Carlsberg Brewery 4 790
  Castle 8 723, 725, 726, 738
    collections 8 759
    interior decoration 8 733
    Kunstkammer 8 759
    library 8 759
  churches
    Cathedral of Our Lady *see* Vor Frue Kirke
    Frederikskirke 8 726, 727; 10 *111*; 17 446
    Grundtvig Church 4 788, *789*; 8 728; 27 131
    Vor Frue Kirke 8 723, 726, 727, 739; 13 56; 14 153, *153*
  citadel 8 725; 18 *178*
  Dehn's steam laundry 14 392
  docks 2 324
  Eastern High Court *see* Østre Landsret
  education (art) 8 760
  Eremitage 30 883
  Erichsen Mansion 8 744; 25 874
  exchange 10 668
  Fælledpark 8 727
  fortifications 8 725; 21 570
  Frederiksberg Castle *see under* palaces
  Frederiks Hospital *see* museums → Danske Kunstindustrimuseum
  Frederiksstad 8 726, 734
    urban planning 10 111
  French Embassy 8 725
  Galleri Asbæk 8 759
  Gaol *see* Law Courts
Copenhagen—cont.
  Institute for the Blind 8 727
  Københavns Handelsbank *see* Erichsen Mansion
  Kongelige Bibliotek 22 795
  Kongens Nytorv 8 739
  Liberty Memorial 1 32–3
  Meat Market 8 728
  Ministry of Education 8 726
  Moltke House *see under* palaces → Amalienborg Palace
  monument to Frederick V 27 659
  museums
    Danish Museum of Decorative Art *see* Danske Kunstindustrimuseum
    Danske Kunstindustrimuseum 10 112; 18 136; 21 791
      collections 8 760
      furniture 4 71
      library 8 761
    Danske Samlinger 8 759
      see also Nationalmuseum
    Davids Samling 8 759; 16 556
    Etnografisk Museum 8 759
      see also Nationalmuseum
    Hirschsprungske Samling 7 806; 8 758, 759; 14 572
    Kongelige Billedgalleri 8 759
      see also Statens Museum for Kunst
    Kongelige Danske Kunstkammer *see* Statens Museum for Kunst
    Kongelige Kobberstiksamling 8 759
      see also Statens Museum for Kunst
    Nationalmuseum 8 759; 10 110
      Ålborg Room 8 742
      collections 2 299; 7 156; 8 725; 14 369; 15 744; 19 5; 21 886; 29 240
      see also Danske Samlinger; Etnografisk Museum; Oldnordisk Museum
    Nyborg Slot 4 781; 28 847
    Ny Carlsberg Glyptotek 7 804, 805; 8 727; 17 756
      collections 8 759; 10 91, 94, 639; 16 829; 22 731; 25 376
      directors 25 376
      Etruscan collection 10 640
      Greek collection 13 470
      Roman collection 27 115
      sculpture 27 46
    Oldnordisk Museum 8 759
      see also Nationalmuseum
    Orlogsmuseum 28 612
    Statens Museum for Kunst 7 803; 8 759
      collections 7 805; 8 759; 27 333; 30 533
      library 8 761
      paintings 8 758
      Prentenkabinet 24 237
      see also Kongelige Billedgalleri; Kongelige Kobberstiksamling
    Thorvaldsens Museum 4 68, *68*, 184; 7 805; 8 727, 745, 746; 13 612; 18 136; 22 362; 25 173; 27 643; 29 72, 541; 30 763, 766
      collections 8 758, 759
      library 8 761
    Zoological Museum 14 149
  Østre Landsret 8 726
  Palace Hotel 8 727
  palaces
    Amalienborg Palace 8 727, 740; 10 *110*, 111; 23 813; 30 763
      furniture 11 627
      interior decoration 1 33–4; 8 734; 11 473
      Moltke Mansion 8 742–3, *743*
      paintings 20 249
      sculpture 8 758
      stucco 29 841
    Bernsdorf Palace 11 626
Copenhagen
  palaces—cont.
    Charlottenborg 4 781; 8 725
      see also academies → Kongelige Danske Kunstakademi
    Christiansborg Palace 4 97; 8 723, 726, 727, 740, 751, 759; 10 110; 11 768; 14 153; 17 481
      banqueting hall 8 740
      interior decoration 8 733, 742, 744
      paintings 8 734
      Ragnarok frieze 8 740
      sculpture 30 764, 766
      stucco 29 841
      tapestries 8 754, 755
    Frederiksberg Castle 8 726, 733
      gardens 12 135
      interior decoration 23 789
      paintings 19 36
    Levetzau palace *see* Amalienborg Palace
    Prinsens Palais *see* museums → Nationalmuseum
    Rosenborg Palace 8 732, 742
      altars 17 887
      amber 31 481
      Banqueting Hall *see* Great Hall
      chandeliers 31 *481*
      Chronological Collections of the Danish Kings 8 759
      collections 23 235
      Dutch Kitchen 30 883
      gold 10 348
      Great Hall 8 733; 16 63
      Green Cabinet 23 238
      interior decoration 7 431; 8 733, 742; 23 789
      ivory-carvings 23 229
      mirrors 21 721
      paintings 19 36
      porcelain 9 28
      sculpture 3 198
      silver 11 618
      tapestries 8 754
      Throne Room 30 782, *782*
  Paustian Mobilhus 8 729
  Police Headquarters 8 728; 25 850
  Rådhus *see* Town Hall
  Rigshospital 14 783
  Round Tower 23 339, 340
  SAS Royal Hotel 16 829
  Staldmestergården *see* Ministry of Education
  synagogue 8 727; 17 547
  theatres
    Kongelige Teater 8 727
    Opera House *see* Østre Landsret
    Pantomimeteater 8 727
  Town Hall 7 *804*; 8 727, 745; 23 325; 31 242
  town hall, courthouse and gaol complex 8 726; 14 *152*, 153; 18 887
  trade school 1 107
  Tramway Waiting-room (Trianglen) 8 727
  University 8 727; 14 154
    library 8 727; 19 318
  urban planning 31 715, 735
  Valdemar Kleis Gallery 11 790
  Vesterport building 8 728
  Vestersøhus 8 728, *728*
  2 Vodroffsvej 8 728
  Zoo 33 699
Copenhagen 4223, Painter of 13 529, 530
Copenhagen Ewer 11 614
Copenhagen Gospels *see under* GOSPEL BOOKS → individual manuscripts
Copenhagen Master 8 315
Copenhagen Painter 13 520
Copenhagen Psalter *see under* PSALTERS → individual manuscripts

Cope of King Robert 16 437
Cope of the Seven Sacraments 3 609
Coper, Hans 4 828; 7 808*; 10 314; 11 797; 26 365
Copernicus, Nicolaus 28 210
Copers, Leo 3 574
copes 13 194; 14 425; 30 541; 32 389*, 389
Cope & Stewardson 7 808*; 24 598
Copford (Essex), St Mary the Virgin 26 654
Copia, Jacques-Louis 25 671; 29 676
Copiapo 6 590
Museo de la Catedral 6 601
Copier, A(ndries) D(irk) 7 808*; 22 885
copies 2 365, 835; 6 76, 77; 7 675, 830–31*; 11 305, 308; 14 690; 25 281; 26 226, 235; 27 114
historical and regional traditions
Aztec 21 266
Buddhism 7 114
Carolingian 5 802
China 2 558; 11 310; 26 226
Egypt, ancient 10 7
Etruscan 10 588
France 26 514
Greece, ancient 2 557; 13 423
Indian subcontinent 15 749–50*
Islamic 15 750
Italy 10 588; 14 867
Japan 17 217
Mesoamerica, Pre-Columbian 21 266
Rome, ancient 2 557; 13 423; 26 861; 27 104, 105
processes
electrography 24 654
electrostatic 24 654
photographic 24 650, 654*
types
busts 28 383
coins 13 587
engravings 14 638
mouldings 33 211
sculpture 9 22; 24 347; 30 495
Egypt, ancient 13 465
Greece, ancient 2 558; 7 561; 13 422, 423, 438–9*, 450, 454, 462, 463, 465, 469; 16 685; 18 148; 19 853; 23 291; 24 416, 593; 26 854; 27 10, 30, 39, 40
Italy 16 685
Renaissance 11 72
Rome, ancient 2 156; 7 561, 830; 13 450, 462, 464, 469; 15 92; 19 853; 23 291; 26 226, 854; 27 10, 30, 39, 40
see also Art (reproduction of works of); Photocopies; Photographic prints; Replicas
Copilco 31 117
Copín, Diego 7 345; 19 173; 26 249; 31 92
Copin de Gant 23 402
copings 4 769
Copland, F.
works 2 550
Copland, Henry 19 531
Coplans, John 28 300
Copley, John Singleton 4 477; 7 808–11*; 10 361; 13 303
patrons and collectors 7 379; 17 823
pupils 27 839
reproductive prints by others 3 309; 4 607; 10 394; 14 280; 28 558
works 7 787, 809, 811; 9 1; 11 496, 497, 497; 19 586; 24 335; 31 600, 600
Copley, William Nelson 7 812*
Copp, H. 28 557
Coppedè, Gino 2 567; 16 648, 720
Coppenolle, Daniël van 12 519, 520
Coppens, Augustin 5 43; 23 528
Coppens, Herman 3 599
copper 4 849; 7 812–14*; 21 319
alloys
calamine 4 682, 688
gold 5 747; 12 865; 17 318; 29 211; 30 240, 240; 32 238
lead 4 681, 849, 852; 17 318
silver 9 657; 17 318; 21 319; 29 211
sphalerite 4 684
tin 4 848, 849, 855; 12 621; 17 318; 21 319; 24 578
see also Bronze
zinc 4 680, 681; 12 621; 21 319; 24 61
see also Cupro-nickel
historical and regional traditions
Afghanistan 16 366
Africa 1 286, 287, 288, 296, 350, 411
Akkadian (people) 1 510; 2 639
Algeria 16 394
Anatolia, ancient 1 822, 834
Anglo-Saxon 10 338, 338
Arabia 2 264–5
Armenia (Europe) 2 441
Assyrian 2 639; 7 813
Austria 21 I3
Azerbaijan 2 899
Belgium 3 583, 602
Benin, Kingdom of 3 722
Bhutan 3 914, 914
Bolivia 4 255
Buddhism 15 223; 22 769, 777; 30 822, 844
Bulgaria 5 160
Byzantine 9 652, 659, 663
Cambodia 5 507
Caribbean Islands 5 747
Central Asia, Eastern 6 309, 313, 315
Central Asia, Western 6 243, 260, 274
China 6 829–30*, 869; 7 79, 101
Dian culture 8 852
Ming period (1368-1644) 6 873, 901, 905
Qing period (1644-1911) 6 910; 7 70, 79, 84, 112, 132
Song period (AD 960-1279) 6 895
Tang period (AD 618-907) 7 92
Zhou period (c. 1050-256 BC) 6 832, 853; 7 80, 88; 21 714
Colombia 30 240, 240
Côte d'Ivoire 8 22
Cucuteni culture 25 516
Cyprus 8 352, 365
Cyprus, ancient 8 352, 353
Denmark 8 751–2
Dian culture 8 852
Early Christian (c. AD 250-843) 9 652
Egypt 16 404
Egypt, ancient 7 813; 9 817; 10 29, 35, 35, 50, 51
England 2 595; 10 322, 338*, 338, 339, 341, 343
Etruscan 10 624
France 11 628, 629; 13 167; 20 922, VII
Germany 12 451–2*; 13 161
Gothic 13 161, 166, 167, 170
Greece 13 359
Greece, ancient 13 573; 21 712
Gumelnița culture 25 516
Hinduism 22 772
Holy Roman Empire (before 1648) 26 686*
Hungary 15 9
Ife (kingdom of) 15 104, 105
Indian subcontinent 4 853; 15 223, 336, 420, 687, 712*; 20 328, 328
copper
historical and regional traditions—cont.
Indonesia 15 812
Indus civilization 15 420
Iran 16 375, 394
Iran, ancient 15 902, 918
Islamic 14 428; 16 363, 364, 381, 394; 21 717
Afghanistan 16 366
Egypt 16 404
Iran 16 375
Italy 10 624; 16 743
Japan 7 813; 17 47, 276, 277, 318, 362, 369, 370, 401
Java 15 811
Kenya 1 411
Korea 18 356
Kota (ii) (Gabon peoples) 18 402
Lengyel culture 25 516
Mesoamerica, Pre-Columbian 21 245, 253, 256, 259
Mesopotamia 21 270, 303–4
Mexico 21 254
Mongolia 21 878
Native North Americans 14 746; 22 612, 613, 613, 617, 617–18*; 29 415
Nepal 22 769, 772, 774, 774, 775, 776, 777, 778, 789
Netherlands, the 14 293; 22 894–5*
Nigeria 1 287; 15 104, 105, 117–18, 119; 23 131
Peru 28 651
Polgár culture 25 516, 517
Portugal 13 166
Prehistoric art 25 516–17, 518
Punic 25 734
Romanesque 10 322; 26 686*
Romania 26 714
Rome, ancient 8 354
Russia 7 813
Sardinia 16 743; 25 734
Scythian 6 243
Sicán culture 28 651
South America, Pre-Columbian 28 651; 29 211; 30 240, 240
Spain 16 394; 29 339, 340, 342
Sri Lanka 29 474
Sumatra 15 812
Sumerian 22 159
Sweden 30 111, 111
Syria-Palestine 30 179, 183, 194–5
Tairona 30 240, 240
Tajikistan 6 243
Tibet 30 822, 841, 844
Tisza culture 25 516, 517
Transoxiana 16 394
Tripol'ye culture 25 516
Ukraine 31 562
United States of America 7 812; 14 746; 31 653*, 653
Vietnam 32 486
Vinča culture 25 516
Yoruba 15 104
patinas 21 329–30*; 24 258
technical examination 30 400, 408
techniques
electroplating 10 135, 136
gilding 7 813; 12 624; 17 319
inverse segregation 1 834
repoussé 22 755; 29 415
undercutting 21 878
types
arsenical 4 849; 8 353
Anatolia, ancient 1 834
Iran, ancient 15 918
Mesopotamia 21 304
South America, Pre-Columbian 29 211
Syria-Palestine 30 195
uses
aquamanilia 12 452
architecture 7 813*
armour 2 448; 17 362
copper
uses—cont.
basins 30 111
beads 1 296
bells 21 256
bowls 2 899
bracelets 22 613
brooches 2 595
buckets 10 341
busts 1 510
candlesticks 12 452
canopies (ii) (textile coverings) 10 51
censers 6 173
chairs 10 50
chandeliers 12 452
charters 20 328, 328
coins 5 507; 6 309; 7 537–9; 14 419, 428; 15 687, 811, 812; 17 369, 370; 18 356; 32 486
cooking 12 452
crosses 8 200
crucifixes 10 338
doors 7 813; 12 452
electroplating 10 135
enamel 6 905; 7 70, 79, 79, 812; 9 659, 663; 10 192; 13 167, 170; 15 712*
engravings 14 293
etchings 10 562
ewers 30 111
exchange 5 255
fan-holders 15 119
fonts (baptismal) 12 452
game-boards 31 265
gates 7 813
gilding 24 55
glass 7 80, 84; 10 55; 30 407
glazes 6 869, 873, 905, 910; 10 302
headdresses 28 651
headrests 1 411
helmets 10 338; 14 746
inks 15 852
inlays 6 832, 853; 7 101; 13 573; 16 364, 366, 375, 381; 21 329
jewellery 1 350; 6 274; 7 112; 9 652; 10 29; 21 253; 31 562
jugs 12 452
kettles 10 341
lecterns 12 452
manuscripts 22 778
marquetry 20 VII
masks 3 722; 15 104
medallions 26 714
medals 20 922
mirrors 21 712, 714, 717
monuments 3 290
mortars (vessels) 12 452
mosaics 22 159
moulds 7 92
necklaces 22 613
netsuke 17 401
obelisks 7 813
painting 7 814*
papier mâché 24 61
photographic plates 24 658
photography 24 646, 650, 655
pigments 24 793–4*
plaques 29 415
porcelain 6 895, 901
pots 6 243; 10 343
pottery 16 404
printing plates 7 814*; 10 379, 548, 549, 562; 25 612
prints 17 276, 277
razors 25 734
roofs 7 813; 15 336; 17 47
sculpture 15 223; 22 772
Assyrian 2 639
Bhutan 3 914, 914
Egypt, ancient 10 35, 35
Ife (kingdom of) 15 105
India, Republic of 15 173
Kota (ii) (Gabon peoples) 18 402
Nepal 22 755, 769, 776, 777
Tibet 30 822
seals 6 315; 15 420
copper
uses—cont.
silverplate 28 576
soldering 21 325
statuettes 22 774; 29 572
supports 30 5
teapots 21 I3
tea-urns 10 341
threads 30 540, 542
tobacco-boxes 12 452
tools 25 517
trumpets 30 844
vessels 7 88
weapons 6 260
weathervanes 31 653
writing 20 328
copperas 21 261; 25 315
copper hydroxide chloride 13 536
Coppermine (NWT)
dress 22 630
copper oxides 6 328; 10 192
historical and regional traditions
China 6 872, 885, 895, 899
Egypt, ancient 10 55
Islamic 16 394, 518
Korea 18 339, 340, 343–4
uses
ceramics 6 330
glass 10 55; 12 781; 16 518
glazes 6 872, 885, 895, 899; 16 394, 426
pigments 24 790*
Copper-plate Magazine, or Monthly Treasure for the Admirers of the Imitative Arts 24 445
copperplate script see under Scripts → types
copper resinate 24 793–4
copper sulphate 30 558
Copper Tower see under Cha ban
Coppi, Giacomo 7 815*; 32 17
Coppi, Stefano 31 188
Coppin, Daniel 29 542
Coppin, Emily 29 542
Coppini, Francesco 11 799
Coppino di Giovanni di Bramante 16 759
Coppit, Oopjen 26 157
Coppo di Marcovaldo 7 815–17*
attributions 13 124
collaboration 20 623
works 1 708; 7 815, 816; 8 212, 212; 11 183, 379; 16 655; 25 462
Coppo di Marcovaldo, Salerno di see Salerno di Coppo di Marcovaldo
Coppola (family) 23 350
Coppola, Carlo 3 388; 10 762
Coppola, Giovanni Andrea 7 818*
Coppola, Horacio 7 818*; 29 641
Coppolani, Xavier 20 861
Coptic 7 818–29*, 819
alphabets 10 1
altars 1 694
amulets 1 818
architecture 7 819*
body arts 7 829*
bone-carvings 7 825*
brass 4 688
carpets 5 834; 7 827
cenobitic cells 7 819–20*
ceramics 7 826*
churches 7 262*, 820, 820–21*
dress 9 639; 16 431
dyes 7 826
hermitages 7 820
icons 7 823*
ivory-carvings 7 825, 825–6*
languages 10 1
limestone 7 822
linen 7 826; 16 431; 30 IV2
liturgical furnishings 7 280*
manuscript illumination 7 823–4*, 824
monasteries 7 820; 27 813
monuments 7 820*

Coptic—cont.
painting 7 822*, 823–4*
wall 3 420; 7 822–3*, 823
religion 9 515
robes 16 431
scripts 10 1
sculpture 7 821–2*
stelae 7 822
tapestries 7 826, 827, 828; 16 431; 30 IV2
tattoos 7 829*; 10 68; 30 367
textiles 7 826–8*; 9 492, 664; 16 431
wood-carvings 7 829
woodwork 7 828–9*
wool 30 IV2
see also EARLY CHRISTIAN; EGYPT, ANCIENT
Coptos see KOPTOS
copy art see PRINTING → processes → electrography
copybooks 6 761, 762, 764; 17 237
Copybook school 6 764
copyists 7 830
Copyn 28 260
copyright 2 553–4; 13 133; 25 601; 26 230
England 14 638
Native North Americans 22 666
Coq, Albert von Le see LE COQ, ALBERT VON
coq-de-perle 17 524
Coquart, Georges-Ernest 7 831–2*; 24 221
Coquelet, Dieudonné 22 456
Coquelin, Ernest 7 832*
Coques, Gonzales 7 832–3*
collaboration 8 878; 14 46; 22 718; 28 364
patrons and collectors 25 810; 33 323
reproductive prints by others 25 221
teachers 26 390
works 3 560; 5 352; 7 784, 833; 9 28; 22 863, 864
Coquet, Jacques 19 145
Coquet Castle see BELVOIR CASTLE (ISRAEL)
Coquilhatville see MBANDAKA
coquillages 7 833*
Coquin, Louis see COSSIN, LOUIS
Coquiot, Gustave 4 507; 7 834*
Coradino 23 325
Corajoud, Michel 2 699, 700; 7 343
coral 7 834–6*; 12 268; 28 580
historical and regional traditions
Africa 1 305, 350
Algeria 7 834
Ancient Near East 1 876
Benin, Kingdom of 1 297, 354; 3 721
Bhutan 3 914
Buddhism 6 706
Celtic 6 155, 161; 7 834
China 6 706; 7 18, 19, 89, 91, 111, 111, 836
Corsica 7 834, 835
England 6 161
Fiji 7 834
France 6 155; 7 835
Germany 12 462; 18 522
Hungary 10 II1; 15 11
Indian subcontinent 12 252
Islamic 16 269
Italy 3 442; 7 834, 835; 16 750*
Japan 7 834; 17 398
Maldives, Republic of 20 188
Mesoamerica, Pre-Columbian 21 251, 260
Mongolia 3 441; 7 836, 836; 21 877
Morocco 7 834
Poland 3 442
Portugal 25 312
Prehistoric art 25 546
Romania 3 442
Rome, ancient 7 834; 16 750
coral
historical and regional traditions—cont.
Sardinia 7 834, 835
Sicily 7 834; 16 750; 31 285
Thailand 3 441
Tibet 7 836; 30 839
Tunisia 7 834
types
black 7 836; 17 398
uses
amulets 1 817; 7 834, 835
architecture 1 305; 16 269; 20 188
beads 1 297, 354; 3 440, 441, 442; 7 835, 836; 21 260
cameos 7 834, 836; 12 264; 25 128
caskets 7 835
coral 1 350
credenze 7 835
crowns 7 111, 111
cutlery 7 835
devotional objects 8 835
dresses 10 II1
embroidery 12 462; 15 11
flagons 6 155
frames 7 835
hair ornaments 7 836
headdresses 7 836
inlays 3 914; 7 835
jewellery 7 111, 836; 17 529; 21 877; 30 839
lacquer 7 18, 19
masks 21 251
monstrances 7 835
necklaces 3 442
netsuke 7 836; 17 398
paternoster beads 7 835; 17 520
rattles 7 835
salts 7 835
sculpture 6 706
shields 6 161
stoups 7 835
sword hilts 7 835
talismans 7 834
toys 7 835
writing sets 18 522
Coralli, Francesco 21 28
coral red see under PIGMENTS → types
Coral-Rémusat, Gilberte de 5 483; 29 242
coral-wood 15 721
Coram, Thomas (1668-1751) 11 907
Coram, Thomas (1757-1811) 11 742
Coray, Hans 1 738
Corazzi, Antoni 7 836–7*
collaboration 4 837; 12 212
groups and movements 13 611
pupils 15 104
works 25 99; 32 871, 871
Corazzi, Antonio 25 55
Corazzini, Francesco 1 551
Corbarelli (family) 16 747
Corbarelli, Antonio 16 747
Corbarelli, Benedetto 16 747
Corbarelli, Francesco 16 747
Corbarelli, Pietro Paolo 16 747
Corbarieu Church 7 693
Corbaz, Aloïse 25 685, 686
Corbechon, Jean 10 202; 12 107
Corbeil 11 649
corbelled arches see under ARCHES → types
corbelled domes see under DOMES → types
corbelled vaults see under VAULTS (CEILING) → types
Corbellini, Sebastiano 11 23
corbels 7 837*; 32 88
England 8 836
Gothic 8 836
Greece, ancient 7 837; 13 396
Indian subcontinent 10 828; 15 338
Iran 16 164
corbels—cont.
Ireland 12 14
Islamic 15 338; 16 164
Prehistoric art 25 508
Rome, ancient 7 837
corbel tombs see under TOMBS → types
Corberó, Xavier 3 220
Corbet, Charles-Louis 7 837–8*; 22 47
Corbet, Corbet 10 753
Corbet, Edith 10 641
Corbet, Matthew Ridley 10 641; 14 809
Corbett, Harrison & MacMurray 7 838; 14 199; 23 426
works 26 488
Corbett, Harvey Wiley 7 838–9*; 11 869; 31 729
collaboration 11 25
pupils 14 199
staff 29 718
works 31 728
Corbett & MacMurray 7 838
Corbie Abbey 13 199, 211
manuscripts 5 800; 7 512; 11 529; 15 848; 26 659, 669; 30 486
workshops 29 851
Corbie Psalter see under PSALTERS → individual manuscripts
Corbin, Raymond 7 839*
Corbinelli (family) 27 776
Corbinière, Jean de Fourcy, Sieur de 20 134; 21 346
Corbino, Jon 26 426
Corbould, Edward Henry 6 451; 7 839–40*
Corbould, George 4 845; 7 839*
Corbould, Henry 7 839*
Corbould, Richard 7 839*
Corbridge Lanx 18 825; 27 83, 84
Corbusier, Le see LE CORBUSIER
Corby 14 676
Corby, John see HOWARD, JOHN G(EORGE)
Corchin, Rolet 4 546
Corcomroe Abbey (Co. Clare) 16 19
Corcoran, William Wilson 7 840*; 31 667
Corcoran Gallery of Art see under WASHINGTON (DC) → museums
Corded ware see under POTTERY → wares
Cordeiro, Waldemar 4 719
Cordeliaghi, Andrea see PREVITALI, ANDREA
Cordemoy, Jean-Louis de, Abbé 7 840*; 11 515
groups and movements 22 734
works 2 724; 10 205; 23 489; 26 12; 31 296
Cordero, Helen 22 607
Cordero, Juan 7 841*; 21 405; 22 334
Cordes 32 280
cordia 16 500
Cordiani, Antonio see SANGALLO, ANTONIO DA (ii)
Cordier, Charles (-Henri-Joseph) 7 841*
groups and movements 23 503
works 11 567, 636; 21 403; 29 574
Cordier, Daniel 7 841–2*
Cordier, Henri 7 841
Cordier, Nicolas 2 163; 7 842–3*
collaboration 4 405
patrons and collectors 1 595
works 7 842
Córdoba (i) (Spain) 7 843–7*; 9 507, 510; 16 103, 158; 26 904; 29 258
boxes 7 844–5
caskets 16 545
Cathedral see under Mezquita
Córdoba (i) (Spain)—cont.
Corredera 31 718
factories 16 436
furniture 29 310, 311
gardens 12 79
gold 7 846–7*
Great Mosque see Mezquita
Hayr al-Zajjali 12 79
ivory-carvings 16 121, 524, 525, 525
leather 19 3; 21 391; 29 301, 311
manuscripts 20 330
marks 7 847; 20 444
metalwork 16 368, 369; 29 334, 336, 337
Mezquita 4 784; 7 844, 845–6*, 845; 9 84, 86; 16 157, 157–8, 188–9, 188, 243, 244, 493; 19 717; 22 156, 193, 246, 255; 29 261
arches 2 294, 296, 298; 4 791
Bab al-Wuzara' see Puerta de S Estebán
Cathedral 6 364, 365; 7 846*; 29 291
ceiling 2 528
coffering 7 527
columns 5 893
doors 16 494
grilles 16 257
maqṣūra 20 368
mihrab 2 244; 9 561, 645; 16 188; 21 505; 23 485
minaret 21 626
minbar 21 629; 23 560
mosaics 9 38, 633; 16 137, 256; 22 162
Patio de los Naranjos 8 64
Puerta de S Estebán 16 157, 493
reliefs 29 288
stone-carvings 2 245
minbars 16 493; 21 629
Museo Arqueológico 29 358
painting 29 280
pottery 16 404; 29 323
silver 7 846–7*
S Miguel 29 264
S Pablo 29 264
Synagogue 7 846*; 17 544; 22 254
urban planning 7 844
woodwork 16 492, 493, 494
Córdoba (ii) (Argentina) 2 392, 393, 394; 7 847–8*
Academia de Bellas Artes 7 847
architecture 2 394, 395
Cabildo see Museo Histórico
Casa del Virrey see Museo Histórico Provincial
Cathedral 2 394, 402
Convento de S Francisco 2 402
football stadium 2 397
Jesuit church 2 394
La Compañía 2 394, 398
La Merced 2 398
Museo Histórico 7 847
Museo Histórico Provincial 7 847, 847
Nuevocentro shopping centre 2 397
Office Centre 2 397
painting 2 398
Paseo Azul 2 397
sculpture 2 398
textiles 2 403
Town Hall 2 397
Universidad Nacional de Córdoba 7 847
Córdoba (fl 1971) 19 388
Córdoba, Alfonso Fernández de see FERNÁNDEZ DE CÓRDOBA, ALFONSO
Córdoba, Francisco Fernández de see FERNÁNDEZ DE CÓRDOBA, FRANCISCO
Córdoba, Inés 15 144
Cordonnier, Louis Marie 19 381; 30 506; 33 177
Cordouan Lighthouse 19 360, 361
Córdova, Francisco de see FRANCISCO DE CÓRDOVA
cords 9 14; 10 61; 23 712–13
corduroy 8 35, 35; 30 553
Cord van Soest 20 681
Cordys, Jan 17 648
Core, Philip 10 483; 12 218
core-casting see under CASTING → types
Corelli, Arcangelo 23 637
Corelli, G. 7 418
Corelli, Marie 25 282
Corenzio, Belisario 7 848*; 22 478
assistants 5 693
collaboration 5 693; 23 191
patrons and collectors 19 139
pupils 5 693; 19 434; 29 543
works 22 484
Corfe (Dorset) 10 260
Corfe, Adam of see ADAM OF CORFE
Corfey, Lambrecht-Friedrich von 28 105
Corfinio, S Pelino 26 625
Corfu (island) 7 848–50*; 13 363; 32 158
Antivouniotissa Monastery 25 333, 334
cenotaph of Menekrates 13 384
collections 13 359
fortifications 21 574
forts 21 574
icons 25 334
ivory-carvings 13 596
ketubbot 18 3
military architecture 21 574
silver 13 359
temple 13 398
Corfu (town) 7 849–50*
Archaeological Museum 13 470
coins 13 586
Reading Society 13 361
Temple of Artemis 7 849–50*; 13 393, 424, 432, 445–6, 470; 23 481; 24 317
pediment 24 318
sculpture 7 849
Corfu, Nicolo Rugina Greco da see NICOLO RUGINA GRECO DA CORFU
Corgi 31 257
Corgna, Ascanio della, Marchese 32 505
Corhampton Church (Hants) 26 655
Cori
Temple of the Dioscuri 23 482
Temple of Hercules 23 485; 26 865
Cori, Agnolo de' 20 263
Cori, Domenico di Niccolò di see DOMENICO DI NICCOLÒ
Cori, S Maria della Pietà 26 624
Coriate, Thomas see CORYATE, THOMAS
Corice 17 499
SS Cosmas and Damian 9 540
Corinaldo 3 359
Corinium see CIRENCESTER (GLOS)
Corinne, Tee 10 483; 12 219
Corinth 7 851–4*, 852; 9 511; 13 362, 363; 14 332; 26 908
Acrocorinth 7 851
amphitheatre 26 910
aqueducts 26 910
Archaeological Museum 7 851, 852, 853; 13 470; 14 361
architects 13 395
art forms and materials
arches 26 909
architecture 9 524; 13 381; 26 908
bronzes 13 572
clay 13 479
coins 13 585, 586
dolls 31 259
dromos 29 487
figurines 13 578, 580, 581, 582

Corinth
art forms and materials—cont.
glass 9 646
helmets 13 583
jewellery 13 597; 14 357
lamps 27 104
masonry 13 396
mosaics 13 556, 562, 563
painting 13 547, 549, 555
vase 10 613
pediments 24 318
pendants (jewellery) 13 602
pins 13 600
poros 13 387
pottery 9 631, 633, 634; 13 368, 472, 476, 483, *483*, 484, 486, 488, 498, 499–500, 536, 540, 549; 27 107
protomes 13 582
sculpture 7 853–4*, *854*; 13 433; 14 351; 27 29
bronze 13 442
Daidalic 13 443
relief 13 *371*, 582; 18 701
tiles 13 390
vases 13 487
basilicas (non-ecclesiastical) 26 910
baths 26 909
Baths of Eurykles 26 910
collections 13 359
forum 7 *852*
Fountain of Glauke 13 381
Fountain of Lower Peirene 11 339; 26 910
Fountain of the Lamps 26 910
Fountain of Upper Peirene 13 404
graves 14 339
houses 9 561
Isthmus 9 554
Laus Julia Corinthiensis 7 851
macella 26 910
monument of Cnaeus Babbius Philinus 21 892; 26 911
Pente Skouphia cave 13 370
Sanctuary of Apollo 7 851
Temple of Apollo 7 *852*; 13 376, 378, 400, 414; 23 481; 26 911
Sanctuary of Asklepios 13 603
Temple of Asklepios 13 418
Sanctuary of Demeter 13 416
South Stoa 7 852; 13 406, 414; 26 910
synagogue 17 543
temples 26 866
Temple of Aphrodite 26 911
Temple of Apollo *see under* Sanctuary of Apollo
Temple E 26 911
Temple F 26 911
Temple G 26 911
Temple H 26 911
Temple J 26 911
Temple of Asklepios *see under* Sanctuary of Asklepios
Temple of Venus 23 484
theatre 26 910
trade
pottery 7 851; 10 611; 13 525; 28 654
water supply 7 852
Corinth, Eumelos of *see* EUMELOS OF CORINTH
Corinth, Glaukion of *see* GLAUKION OF CORINTH
Corinth, Lovis 4 366; 7 854–6*; 12 395
dealers 5 924
groups and movements 3 511; 8 432; 10 694; 24 591; 25 357; 28 341, 342
prints 25 626
pupils 4 143; 20 11, 807; 21 819; 28 354; 29 609; 33 607
works 9 310; 19 490
Corinthian bronze *see under* ALLOYS → types
Corinthian capitals *see under* CAPITALS → types
Corinthian columns *see under* COLUMNS → types
Corinthian helmets *see under* HELMETS → types
Corinthian houses *see under* HOUSES → types
Corinthian kraters *see under* KRATERS → types
Corinthian order *see under* ORDERS (ARCHITECTURE) → types
Corinthian temples *see under* TEMPLES → types
Corinth-Lechaion 21 556
Corio, Bernardino 28 532
Corio, Francesco 1 748
Coriolano, Bartolomeo 7 857; 33 367
Coriolano, Cristoforo 2 103; 7 857
Coriolano, Giovanni Battista 7 857; 33 358
Coriolano, Teresa Maria 7 857
Coriolanus Inkstand 25 18
Coriolanus Legend, Master of the 25 18
Cork 7 857–8*; 16 *5*; 21 569
art school 16 37
Cathedral of St Finbar 13 203
Crawford Municipal Art Gallery 16 36
furniture 16 25
glass 7 857*; 16 30
gold 7 857–8*
mahogany 2 150
Nelson's Pillar 16 21
pottery 16 28
Queen's College 16 11
Royal Cork Institution 16 37
School of Art 16 22, 36
silver 7 857–8*; 16 31, *32*
urban planning 16 8
Cork Glass Co. 7 857
Cork Society for the Promotion of the Fine Arts 16 37
Corleone Polyptych, Master of the 28 656
Çorlu, Süleymaniye Mosque 16 222
Corm, Daoud 7 858*; 19 7
Cormac mac Carrthach, King of Desmond and Bishop of Cashel (*d* 1138) 5 916; 16 35
Cormac's Psalter *see under* PSALTERS → individual manuscripts
Cormantaigne, Louis de 21 581
Cormatin Château 6 506
Corme-Royal Church 26 600
Cormery Abbey 26 599
Cormier, Bruno 2 840; 26 77
Cormier, Ernest 5 573; 7 858–9*
house 5 562
works 5 *573*; 7 *858*; 22 36
Cormon, Fernand 7 859*; 11 672
pupils
Asselin, Maurice 2 615
Bernard, Emile 3 812
Borisov-Musatov, Viktor (Yel'pidiforovich) 4 414
Bottini, George (Alfred) 4 507
Burlyuk, David (Davidovich) 5 219
Çallı, Ibrahim 5 437
Chabaud, Auguste 6 378
Erichsen, Thorvald 10 457
Fujishima, Takeji 11 821
Galanis, Demetrios 12 2
Gallen-Kallela, Akseli (Valdemar) 12 19
Gogh, Vincent (Willem) van (1853-90) 12 859
Güran, Nazmi Ziya 13 856
Hébert (ii), Adrien 14 282
Longstaff, John (Campbell) 19 641
Mané-Katz 20 252
Cormon, Fernand
pupils—cont.
Nibbrig, F(erdinand) Hart 23 78, 598
Pallady, Theodor 23 872
Point, Armand 25 78
Roerich, Nicholas 26 530
Sandoz, Edouard-Marcel 27 724
Soutine, Chaïm 29 245
Toulouse-Lautrec (Montfa), Henri (Marie Raymond) de 31 213
Cormont, Jean de *see* JEAN DE CORMONT
Cormont, Regnault de 1 777; 7 859, 860*; 26 453
Cormont, Thomas de 7 859–60*; 24 156; 26 453
assistants 7 860
attributions 1 779
works 1 777
corn 31 260
Cornacchini, Agostino 7 860–61*
patrons and collectors 1 532; 7 897; 11 874; 23 577
pupils 8 303
teachers 16 700
works 16 699, 702; 29 572; 30 5
Cornaro (family) 8 483; 16 767; 21 463
Cornaro, Alvise (1484-1566) 7 862–3*
architecture 10 767; 23 862; 31 824; 32 547
paintings 10 767
sculpture 10 799
stucco 21 647
writings 31 296
Cornaro, Alvise, Cardinal (1517-84) 7 861
Cornaro, Andrea 13 658; 25 332
Cornaro, Andrea Antonio Giuseppe 7 861
Cornaro, Caterina, Queen of Cyprus *see* CATERINA CORNARO, Queen of Cyprus
Cornaro, Federigo, Cardinal 3 831; 7 861; 28 32
Cornaro, Federigo Prospero 7 861
Cornaro, Francesco, Cardinal 6 139; 7 861; 11 721; 20 313; 25 209
Cornaro, Giorgio 7 861
Cornaro, Giovanni 27 759
Cornaro, Girolamo (*d* 1551) 7 861; 19 628; 27 760
Cornaro, Girolamo Marco (1562-1634) 7 861
Cornaro, Marco, Doge of Venice (*reg* 1365-8) 7 861–2*; 13 747
Cornault, Etienne 22 456
Corneilla-de-Conflent, Ste Marie 9 156; 26 610
Corneille 7 864–5*; 22 854
groups and movements 2 230; 7 489, 758; 9 188; 17 658; 22 852; 27 137
works 19 491
Corneille, Barthélemy 3 294
Corneille, Jean-Baptiste 7 863, 864*
attributions 7 863
patrons and collectors 16 814
pupils 12 637; 20 416; 27 845
reproductive prints by others 20 416; 21 800
works 7 864, *864*
Corneille, Michel (i) (1601/3-64) 7 863–4*; 12 832
patrons and collectors 16 814
pupils 7 863, 864
works 11 641
Corneille, Michel (ii) (1642-1708) 7 863–4*
attributions 7 863
collaboration 31 510
works 4 575; 14 784; 24 470
Corneille, Pierre 4 360; 11 57; 13 325; 25 80; 30 658, 659; 31 165
Corneille, Thomas 5 344; 10 205
Corneille de La Haye (1500/10-75) *see* CORNEILLE DE LYON
Corneille de La Haye (*b* 1543) 7 865
Corneille de Lyon 7 865–6*; 11 656; 14 41; 20 793; 25 279
collaboration 29 740
works 7 *866*; 11 400, *400*, 532, *532*
Corneille des Gobelins *see* CORNEILLE, MICHEL (i)
Cornejo, Juan 4 566
Cornejo, Pedro Duque *see* DUQUE CORNEJO, PEDRO
Cornel, Theodor 26 715
cornelian 14 167
historical and regional traditions
Africa 1 350
Ancient Near East 1 *873*, 873
Central Asia, Western 6 274
China 7 89
Egypt, ancient 10 29, 38, 52; 12 246
England 20 *389*
Etruscan 12 249, *249*
Greece, ancient 12 247; 13 *599*
Iran, ancient 15 902
Islamic 12 253; 16 543, *543*
Italy 12 *257*
Rome, ancient 12 *250*, 251
Turkmenistan 31 *459*
uses
amulets 1 817; 10 38; 12 251
beads 1 350; 3 440, 441; 7 89
breast-ornaments 31 *459*
caskets 10 52
diadems 13 *599*
headdresses 1 *873*
jewellery 1 *873*; 6 274; 10 29; 17 525, 529
necklaces 20 *389*
scarabs 12 249, *249*
seals 12 247; 16 543, *543*
Cornelio de Flandria 33 350
Cornelis, Aelbrecht 4 921; 8 552; 33 8
Cornelis, Pieter, Baron van Leyden *see* LEYDEN, CORNELIS, PIETER, Baron van
Cornelissen, Jan Frans 2 199
Cornelis van Nerven 5 54
Cornelisz., Claes 22 823
works 22 *824*
Cornelisz., Lucas 10 523
Cornelisz., Pieter *see* KUNST, PIETER CORNELISZ.
Cornelisz. van Haarlem, Cornelis 1 104; 4 701; 7 866–8*; 12 881, 883; 20 244; 22 272, 839; 25 625; 26 728; 27 507
collections 3 494
groups and movements 13 895
patrons and collectors 5 9
pupils 24 777
teachers 7 708
works 7 *867*, *868*; 13 893, 895; 22 839
Cornelisz. van Oostsanen, Jacob 7 868–70*; 12 233; 20 615, 628; 28 215; 32 271; 33 354
attributions 20 656
pupils 16 831; 22 837
teachers 20 666
works 1 806; 7 *869*; 11 *443*; 17 699; 22 836; 27 256
Cornelius 23 431
Cornelius, Aloys 7 870
Cornelius, Peter (Joseph von) 7 870–73*; 9 444; 14 766; 26 776; 33 282
assistants 13 218
collaboration 8 40; 12 168; 23 676; 28 46
groups and movements 12 393; 22 703, 704; 26 740
Cornelius, Peter (Joseph von)—cont.
patrons and collectors 3 291; 14 586; 20 588; 22 303, 328; 26 111; 30 766
pupils
Deschwanden, Melchior Paul von 8 790
Foltz, Philipp von 11 244
Kaulbach, (Bernhard) Wilhelm (Eliodorus) 12 394; 17 855
Neureuther, Eugen (Napoleon) 23 9
Oldach, Julius 23 394
Schwind, Moritz (Ludwig) von 28 195
Seitz, Alexander Maximilian 28 380
Sonderland, Johann Baptist 29 66
Speckter, Erwin 29 376
Spence, William Blundell 29 380
Winterhalter, Franz Xaver 33 256
Ziegler, Jules-Claude 33 673
reproductive prints by others 27 346
works 7 *871*, *872*; 12 853; 18 123; 22 328; 25 172; 32 823; 33 282
Cornelius Pinus 27 52
Cornell, Elias 30 120
Cornell, Henrik 30 120
Cornell, Joseph 7 873–4*
groups and movements 30 22
patrons and collectors 7 812
works 2 616; 7 557, *874*; 10 688; 23 334; 31 614
Cornell, Thomas 28 25
Cornellà del Conflent, S María 13 106
Corner (family) 32 217
Corner, Luigi *see* CORNARO, ALVISE (*1484-1566*)
Corner, Philip 24 407
Cornet, Paul 11 569
Cornet, Ramón Gómez *see* GÓMEZ CORNET, RAMÓN
Corneto *see* TARQUINIA
Corneto, Adriano Castellesi da *see* CASTELLESI DA CORNETO, ADRIANO
Corneweyle, Robert 21 580
cornflour 24 56
cornhusks 22 647, 663
Cornia, Antonio della 28 8
cornices 7 874*; 23 477, 478, 480, 481, 482
Egypt 16 176
France 11 *412*
Greece, ancient 13 377, 392, 393, *393*
Indian subcontinent 15 258
Islamic 16 142, 176
Netherlands, the 23 *542*
Corning Museum of Glass (NY) 7 875; 12 794; 17 385; 27 115
Corning Ewer 16 519
Corning Glass Works 5 730; 7 874–5*; 14 252; 29 644; 31 *587*, 644
designers 19 501; 30 390
Corniole, Giovanni delle *see* GIOVANNI DELLE OPERE
Cornish (ME; USA) 31 *587*
Cornish (NH; USA) 7 875–6*; 25 32
medals 7 *875*
Cornish-to-Windsor Bridge 4 802
Cornman, Philip 27 336
corn-mummies 10 20*
see also MUMMIES
Cornu, Jean (1650-1710) 7 876*
Cornu, Jean-Jean (1819-76) 8 57
Cornu, Sébastien (Melchior) 7 876*
patrons and collectors 4 308
pupils 4 215; 13 651
teachers 15 839

Cornu, Sébastien (Melchior)—cont.
works **11** 159
Cornu, Willem **4** 161
Cornwall (family) **27** 601
Cornwall (CT), Frank House **10** *120*
Cornwall, Richard, Earl of, King of the Romans *see* PLANTAGENET, RICHARD, Earl of Cornwall, King of the Romans
Cornwall Clay Works **16** 887
Corny, Emmanuel Héré de *see* HÉRÉ, EMMANUEL
Coro **32** *165*
Cathedral **32** 167
houses **32** 169
textiles **32** 166
coromandel **29** 115
Coromandel lacquer *see under* LACQUER → types
Coromandel Peninsula **23** 70
Coromina, Josep Planella *see* PLANELLE COROMINA, JOSEP
Corona (NY) **31** 644
Corona, Leonardo **7** 877*; **31** 15
Corona, Michele **7** 877
Coronado, Juan Vásquez de *see* VÁSQUEZ DE CORONADO, JUAN
coronals **17** 520
Corona Nuñez, José **18** 784
coronas **7** 877*
Coronation Book of Charles V, Master of the **13** 827; **20** 632, 652*
patrons and collectors **5** 208; **31** 836
Coronation Cup **25** 712; **27** 336
Coronation Gospels *see under* GOSPEL BOOKS → individual manuscripts
Coronation Gospels of Charlemagne *see under* GOSPEL BOOKS → individual manuscripts
Coronation Master **20** 652
Coronation Missal of Gian Galeazzo Visconti *see under* MISSALS → individual manuscripts
Coronation of the Virgin, Master of the **5** 208; **20** 652*
coronation robes *see under* ROBES → types
Coronel, Pedro **7** 877*; **21** 395, 406
Coronel, Rafael **7** 877*; **21** 395; **33** 585
Coronelli, Vincenzo **12** 811, 812, 814; **23** 113; **31** 56
works **12** *814*
Coronel Oviedo **24** *91*
coronets **14** 404
Corot, (Jean-Baptiste-)Camille **7** 674, 877–80*; **11** 546, 659; **12** 277; **16** 678; **21** 425
cliché-verre **7** 433, *433*, 434
dealers **4** 589, 655; **30** 425
etchings **10** 556; **25** 607
forgeries by others **11** 309
groups and movements **3** 213; **26** 54, 741; **28** 921
methods **7** 387; **19** 355; **24** 668
paintings
architectural **2** 342; **31** 156
fans **10** 781
landscape **7** *878*, *879*; **18** 715
patrons and collectors **26** 113; **28** 271, 272
Aumale, Henri-Eugène-Philippe-Louis de Bourbon, Duc d' **23** 523
Bogolyubov, Aleksey (Petrovich) **4** 232
Boussod, Valadon & Cie **4** 589
Bruyas, Alfred **5** 57
Cadart, Alfred **5** 364
Corot, (Jean-Baptiste-)Camille patrons and collectors—cont.
Camondo, Isaac de, Comte **5** 530
Chauchard, Hippolyte-Alfred **6** 516
Cone, Claribel and Etta **7** 702
Drummond, George A(lexander) (1827-1910) **9** 305
Durand-Ruel, Paul (Marie Joseph) **28** 744
Forbes, James Staats **11** 301
Hammer, Armand **14** 117
Havemeyer, Louisine (Waldron) **14** 244
Laurent-Richard **18** 869
Lerolle, Henry **19** 230
Loyd-Lindsay, Robert, 1st Baron Wantage **19** 736
Lucas, George A(loysius) **19** 755
Moreau-Nélaton, Etienne **22** 93
Orléans, Ferdinand-Philippe (-Louis-Charles- Henri) de Bourbon, 7th Duc d' (1810-42) **23** 522
Robinson, Edward G(oldenberg) **26** 472
Rouart, Henri(-Stanislas) **27** 238
Salting, George **27** 641
Tavernier, Adolphe-Eugène **30** 375
Tret'yakov, Sergey (Mikhaylovich) **31** 312
Vever, Henri **32** 394
Whitney, John Hay **33** 150
personal collection **14** 189
pupils **7** 169; **19** 218; **22** 119
reproductive prints by others **4** 625; **5** 24; **6** 519; **11** 500; **18** 658
teachers **3** 855
Corović, Mile **4** 461
corozo nuts *see under* NUTS → types
Corpici, Pierre **20** 614, 708
Corpora, Antonio **7** 881*; **21** 528
groups and movements **2** 545; **11** 802; **13** 727; **16** 681
works **16** 758
Corporación Nacional de Turismo (Peru) **5** 527
Corporación Venezolana de Guayana **32** 171
corps de logis **7** 881*
Corps des Ponts et Chaussées (Paris) **11** 670; **24** 174*
Corpus-Lambeth cycle **2** 223
Corpus Vitrearum Medii Aevi **29** 514
Corque Church **4** 256
Corra, Bruno **10** 686
Corradi, Giovanni **20** 323
Corradi, Girolamo di Giovanni dei *see* GIROLAMO DA CREMONA
Corradi, Pietro Antonio **3** 90, 922
Corradini, Antonio **7** 881–2*; **32** 195
patrons and collectors **11** 395
works **13** 888; **16** 702, 703, *703*; **27** 757
Corradini, Bartolomeo di Giovanni *see* CARNEVALE, FRA
Corrado (family) **1** 578
Corral, Jerónimo del **29** 267
Corral, Juan del **24** 514; **29** 267
Corral, Rui Díaz del *see* DÍAZ DEL CORRAL, RUI
Corral del Villalpando, Jerónimo del **32** 559
Corral del Villalpando, Juan del **32** 559
Corral de Saus **15** 59
Corrales, José Antonio **29** 274
Corrales, Raúl **7** 882*
Correa, Carlos **22** 727
Correa, Charles (Mark) **4** 291; **7** 882–3*; **15** 242
works **3** 163; **4** 289; **7** *882*; **15** 169
Correa, Diego, the elder **7** 883
Correa, Diego, the younger **7** 883
Correa, Federico **7** 884*
Correa, José **7** 883
Correa, Juan **7** 883*; **21** 383; **24** 501
pupils **5** 355
works **21** 404; **32** 239
Correa, Manuel **24** 395
Correa, Martín **6** 594
Correa, Miguel, the elder **7** 883
Correa, Miguel, the younger **7** 883
Correa de Vivar, Juan **7** 883–4*; **29** 278; **31** 89
Corrêa Lima, Attilio **2** 190; **4** 713; **7** 884*
Corrêa Lima, José Octávio **7** 884
Correa & Milà **7** 884*
Correa Morales, Lucio **2** 399; **33** 569
Correas, Pedro de **28** 690
correct script *see* SCRIPTS → types → regular
Corredor, Juan Fernández *see* FERNÁNDEZ CORREDOR, JUAN
Correggio (Italy) **16** 755, 757
Correggio (*d* 1534) **7** 885–93*; **9** 7; **16** 766
assistants **24** 198
attributions **8** 149; **11** 304; **14** 114; **28** 5
copies **1** 671; **22** 26; **23** 409; **26** 564
drawings **9** 221
methods **6** 570; **18** 898; **30** 456
paintings **32** 612
allegorical **1** 657
ceiling **15** 137; **16** 667; **20** 279; **29** 788
frescoes **3** 487; **24** 193, 195
mythological **7** *891*; **10** 476; **23** 680; **25** 152
religious **7** *885*, *886*, *887*, *888*, *890*; **27** 496
patrons and collectors **10** 365; **11** 665
Alba, Duques de **1** 528
Albarelli, Giovanni **5** 432
Angerstein, John Julius **2** 51
Augustus III, King of Poland (*reg* 1733-63) **13** 746
Benson, R(obert) H(enry) **3** 740
Bonnemaison, Ferréol de **4** 330
Borromeo, Federico, Cardinal **4** 426
Canonici, Matteo Luigi **5** 623
Caraman, Duc de **5** 700
Caroline Murat, Queen of Naples (1782-1839) **22** 338
Carpio, Gaspar de Haro y Guzmán, 7th Marqués del **5** 845
Carpio, Luis Méndez de Haro y Guzmán, 6th Marqués del **5** 844
Charles I, King of England and Scotland (*reg* 1625-49) **10** 363; **29** 800
Charles V, Holy Roman Emperor (*reg* 1519-58) **13** 906
Christina, Queen of Sweden (*reg* 1632-54) **32** 8
Crespi, Cristoforo Benigno **8** 147
Duveen, Joseph, 1st Baron Duveen of Millbank **9** 467
Elizabeth Farnese, Queen of Spain (1692-1766) **4** 559
Ercolani, Vincenzo, Conte **10** 446
Este (i) (family) **21** 771
Esterházy, Miklós II, Prince (1765-1833) **10** 530
Correggio (*d* 1534) patrons and collectors—cont.
Federico II, 5th Marchese and 1st Duke of Mantua (*reg* 1519-40) **12** 909; **22** 413
Francesco I, 8th Duke of Modena and Reggio (*reg* 1629-58) **10** 526
Francis-Joseph, Prince of Liechtenstein (*reg* 1772-81) **19** 338
Godoy (y Alvárez de Faria), Manuel, Príncipe de la Paz **12** 839
Herbert, Philip, 4th Earl of Pembroke and 1st Earl of Montgomery **14** 435
Isabella d'Este, Marchesa di Mantua (1474-1539) **10** 521; **29** 860
Jabach, Everard **16** 814
Joachim Murat, King of Naples (*reg* 1808-15) **22** 338
Joseph Bonaparte, King of Naples and Spain (*reg* 1806-8) **4** 304
Josephine, Empress of the French (1763-1814) **4** 304
Leemput, Remi van **19** 63
Lely, Peter **19** 124
Leoni, Leone **19** 203
Mazarin, Jules, Cardinal **20** 896
Medici, Giovanni Carlo de', Cardinal (1611-63) **21** 27
Mond, Ludwig **21** 849
Musée des Beaux Arts (Le Havre) **19** 92
National Gallery (London) **8** 582
Pérez, Antonio (?1540-1611) **24** 400
Piles, Roger de **24** 805
Reynolds, Joshua **26** 280
Rudolf II, Holy Roman Emperor (*reg* 1576- 1612) **13** 914; **18** 522
Ruffo, Tommaso, Cardinal, Archbishop of Ferrara **27** 316
Salamanca (y Mayol), José, Marqués de **27** 607
Salviati (family) **27** 648
Serra, Giovan Francesco, Marqués di Cassano **28** 479
Sheremet'yev, Pyotr (Borisovich), Count **28** 593
Udney, John **31** 525
Udney, Robert **31** 524
Urban VIII, Pope (*reg* 1623-44) **3** 205
Vassal de Saint-Hubert, Jean-Antoine-Hubert **32** 75
Villiers, George, 1st Duke of Buckingham (1592-1628) **32** 575
Waldegrave, William, 1st Baron Radstock **32** 774
Wellesley, Arthur, 1st Duke of Wellington **33** 55
Wright, John Michael **33** 409
pupils **27** 122
reproductive prints by others
Badalocchio, Sisto **3** 33
Carracci, Agostino **5** 857
Cort (van Hoorn), Cornelis **7** 899
Duchange, Gaspard **9** 362
Gautier-Dagoty, Edouard **12** 209
Gregori, Carlo **13** 625
Henriquel-Dupont **26** 233
Jode, Arnold de **17** 599
Kilian, Philipp Andreas (1628-93) **18** 45
Le Blon, Jacob Christoph **19** 15
Moitte, Pierre-Etienne **21** 800
Ravenet, Simon Francis, the younger (1748-1812) **26** 31
Strange, Robert **26** 230
Toschi, Paolo **26** 232
Correggio (*d* 1534) reproductive prints by others—cont.
Volpato, Giovanni **32** 689
Correia, João **4** 715
Correia, João António **20** 463; **28** 735; **29** 101
Correia, Martins **25** 302
Correia, Natália **8** 221
Correia, Stephanie **13** 877
Correia, Vergílio **7** 893–4*; **25** 320
Correia Vale, António da Cunha *see* VALE, ANTÓNIO DA CUNHA CORREIA
Correia Vale, José da Cunha *see* VALE, JOSÉ DA CUNHA CORREIA
Correia Vale, Manuel da Cunha *see* VALE, MANUEL DA CUNHA CORREIA
Correira, José Honorato
works **2** *189*
Correllea, Ernest **25** 215
Corrente **7** 894*; **10** 822; **11** 281; **21** 528
members **4** 88; **13** 872; **16** 681; **21** 704; **22** 125; **24** 841; **32** 109
Correr (family) **5** 54, 55; **24** 865; **31** 747
Correr, Gregorio, Abbot of Verona **7** 894*; **20** 308
Correr, Isabella **24** 865
Correr, Museo *see under* VENICE → museums
Correr, Teodoro **7** 894–5*
collections **32** 196
furniture **7** 775
paintings **13** 745
plaquettes **25** 18
Correspondance **30** 20
Correspondance littéraire, philosophique et critique **13** 663
correspondence **2** 366, 367, 369; **6** 741, 742
correspondence art **7** 895*; **17** 621
Corretti, Gilberto **2** 373
corridor houses *see under* HOUSES → types
Corrie, L. G. **23** 212
Corrientes **2** *393*, 394
Cathedral **2** 396
Corrigan, Peter (Russell) **2** 742; **5** 602; **7** 895–6*
Corripus **9** 655
Corrodi, Arnold **7** 896*
Corrodi, Heinrich **33** 736
Corrodi, Hermann **7** 896
Corrodi, Salomon **7** 896*
corrosion *see* PATINAS
Corroyer, Edouard Jules **7** 896*; **22** 40
Corrozet, Gilles **10** 174, 725
corrugated iron **26** 18; **32** 308
corrugated steel **29** 105
Corselius (family) **8** 184
Corsen and Aitken **31** 763
Corsetti **17** 682
Corsham Court (Wilts) **7** 659; **21** 348; **27** 729
frames **11** 426
furniture **7** 486; **17** 623
paintings **9** 77, 78; **19** 778; **21** 348
Corsi, A. **17** 809
Corsi, Francesco **26** 779
Corsi, Nera **31** 124
Corsi, Simone **20** 530
Corsica **26** *886*
architecture **32** 291
coral **7** 834, 835
fortifications **21** 551
menhirs **11** 78
nuraghi **21** 551
sculpture **11** 78
stone-carvings **11** 78
torre **25** 522
Corsignano *see* PIENZA
Corsini (family) **12** 7, 8; **27** 178; **28** 735
Corsini, Agostino **7** 898*

Corsini, Bartolomeo 7 311, 897
Corsini, Filippo 7 896–7*; 28 735
Corsini, Lorenzo see CLEMENT XII, Pope
Corsini, Neri, Cardinal 7 896, 897–8*; 11 815
architecture 7 897; 12 8, 9
drawings 4 492
paintings 7 682; 13 802, 803; 24 212
sculpture 16 703
Corsini, Pietro (fl 19th cent.) 16 729
Corsini, Pietro, Cardinal (fl 1422) 20 621
Corsini, Tommaso, Prince 7 896
Corsini Throne 10 634
corslets 2 472
Corso, Giacomo di see GIACOMO DI CORSO
Corso, Lapo di see LAPO DI CORSO
Corso, Lippo di see LIPPO DI CORSO
Corso, Nicolò (di Lombarduccio) 7 898–9*; 20 901
Corson, Helen 14 804
Cort (van Hoorn), Cornelis 2 194; 7 899–900*; 10 389; 25 625
attributions 20 769; 30 803
collaboration 10 389
prints 1 840; 7 469
reproductive prints after
Floris, Frans 2 199; 11 221, 222; 17 643
Giulio Romano 17 183
Heemskerck, Maarten van 14 294
Muziano, Girolamo 18 708; 22 392
Passeri, Bernardino 24 239
Sabatini, Lorenzo 27 480
Speeckaert, Jan 29 377
Titian 7 899; 26 229; 31 43
Zuccaro, Federico 1 662; 33 253
pupils 1 551; 24 475; 32 560
reproductive prints by others 5 856; 27 212, 502
works 32 772
Cort, Hendrik (Josef) Frans de 7 900*; 14 178
Cort, Juste see CORTE, JOSSE DE
Cortale 31 717
Cortalim Church 12 827
Cortázar, Antonio de 27 767
Corte, Antonius da 8 754
Corte, Cesare 4 442; 29 783
Corte, Jean de 19 343
Corte, Josse de 7 900–901*
assistants 19 630
collaboration 19 630
patrons and collectors 7 861
pupils 20 422; 29 788
works 5 293; 16 702; 19 630; 23 754; 32 195, 195, 217
Corte, Juan de la 7 901*
Corte, Luigi Della see DELLA CORTE, LUIGI
Corte, Niccolò da 7 901*; 13 906; 25 255
Corté, St Jean 3 192
Corte, Valerio 5 456
Cortelazzo, Antonio 18 897
Corte Lepia, Master of 20 767
Cortellieri, Tebaldo de' 21 111
Cortello, Villa Caselli 16 719
Cor-Ten steel see under STEEL → types
Corte Real, Manuel de Moura y see CASTEL RODRIGO, MANUEL, 2nd Marqués de
Cortés, Hernán 12 71; 21 250, 255, 256, 264, 395; 31 721; 32 305
Cortés, Javier 18 812; 24 517
Cortés, José 9 714
Cortés, Martín, Marqués del Valle de Oaxaca see VALLE DE OAXACA, MARTÍN CORTÉS, Marqués del
Cortese, Cristoforo 7 903–4*; 32 198
Cortese, Federico 28 317
Cortese, Giacomo see COURTOIS, JACQUES
Cortese, Giovanni 10 278
Cortese, Giuseppe 29 835
Cortese, Guglielmo 7 902–3*
collaboration 7 902; 9 376; 11 22
reproductive prints by others 3 278
teachers 7 913
works 1 712; 7 903
Cortese, Paolo 19 451
cortile 7 904*
Cortina, Bosco Gutiérrez see GUTIÉRREZ CORTINA, BOSCO
Cortissoz, Royal 16 82
Cortona 7 904–5*; 10 583, 585, 602, 637; 16 620
Accademia Etrusca 2 164; 10 637, 642
bronzes 10 626
Cathedral 29 504
stained glass 29 504
coins 10 633
collections 10 637
Palazzo Mancini-Sernini 7 905
sculpture 13 93
S Domenico 11 185; 22 521
S Maria del Calcinaio 11 690, 690
S Maria Nuova
paintings 18 732
stained glass 29 504
Cortona, Bartolommeo (di Pietro) da see BARTOLOMMEO (DI PIETRO) DA CORTONA
Cortona, Domenico da see DOMENICO DA CORTONA
Cortona, Pietro da 7 905–14*; 16 670, 673; 25 851; 26 773; 27 489
architecture 26 758, 759, 837; 28 734
chapels 10 769; 26 810
churches 7 912, 913; 16 637–8, 638; 26 841
façades 7 905
temporary architecture 26 771
assistants 26 565
Allegrini, Francesco 1 665
Baldini, Pietro Paolo 26 837
Bottalla, Giovanni Maria 4 491
Camassei, Andrea 5 453
Cortese, Guglielmo 7 902
Dandini, Vincenzo (1609-75) 8 497
Gimignani, Giacinto 12 648
Lauri, Filippo 18 871
Mehus, Livio 21 53
Romanelli, Giovanni Francesco 26 837
Testa, Pietro 30 527
Vanni, Raffaelle 31 885
attributions 3 97
book illustrations 18 735
collaboration 4 428; 26 823
Bernini, Gianlorenzo 1 20
Bonzi, Pietro Paolo 4 341
Camassei, Andrea 5 454
Fancelli, Cosimo 10 782
Fontana (iv), Carlo (1638-1714) 11 274
Maratti, Carlo 20 374
Ottonelli, Giovanni Domenico 15 82
Rosa, Salvator 27 150
Sacchi, Andrea 27 487
Salucci, Alessandro 27 643
Schor, Egid 28 162
Schor, Johann Paul 28 162
copies 16 82
drawings 1 842; 7 911; 25 412
cartoons 11 23; 26 778, 810, 838
engravings 2 105
Cortona, Pietro da—cont.
interior decoration 11 214; 16 713, 713
mosaics 1 21
paintings 16 670
door hangings 4 766
frescoes
Chiesa Nuova (Rome) 7 909; 23 472
Palazzo Barberini (Rome) 14 583; 15 138; 16 670, 714; 26 837, 837; 27 488; 29 830
Palazzo Pamphili (Rome) 4 433
Palazzo Pitti (Florence) 7 908; 22 414
Palazzo del Quirinale (Rome) 26 840
S Bibiana (Rome) 3 830
oil
allegorical 1 658, 659
altarpieces 16 676; 26 809; 27 172
battle 3 388
literary themes 30 358
mythological 7 907
religious 29 683
patrons and collectors
Alexander VII, Pope (reg 1655-67) 6 584, 585
Barberini, Antonio, Cardinal 3 208
Barberini, Francesco, Cardinal 3 207; 9 411
Barnabites 3 250
Benedict XIV, Pope (reg 1740-58) 27 486
Boyle, Richard, 3rd Earl of Burlington and 4th Earl of Cork 4 610; 13 301
Capuchins 5 691
Cavendish, William, 2nd Duke of Devonshire (1671–1729) 6 116
Coke, Thomas, 1st Earl of Leicester of the 1st creation (1697-1759) 7 540
Ferdinando II, Grand Duke of Tuscany (reg 1621-70) 11 188; 21 26
Filomarino, Ascanio, Cardinal 11 81
Innocent X, Pope (reg 1644-55) 23 898, 899
Isham, Thomas 13 300
Jabach, Everard 11 662
La Vrillière, Louis Phélypeaux de 18 885
Lempereur, Jean-Denis, II 19 144
Medici, Giovanni Carlo de', Cardinal (1611-63) 21 27
Medici, Leopoldo de', Cardinal 21 28
Methuen, Paul (1672-1757) 21 348
Oratorians 16 763; 23 473
Pozzo (Lumbroso), Cassiano dal 26 773
Rocca Sinibaldi, Asdrubale Mattei, Duca di 20 841
Rosso, Andrea and Lorenzo del 27 133
Sacchetti (family) 27 486
Sacchetti, Alessandro 27 486
Sacchetti, Marcello 25 386
Urban VIII, Pope (reg 1623-44) 3 206, 207
Vassal de Saint-Hubert, Jean-Antoine-Hubert 32 75
pupils 23 381
Baldi, Lazzaro 3 95
Bottalla, Giovanni Maria 4 491
Cesi, Carlo 6 362
Coli, Giovanni 7 553
Ferri, Ciro 11 22
Fontana (iv), Carlo (1638-1714) 11 274
Gherardi, Antonio 12 525
Cortona, Pietro da
pupils—cont.
Gherardi, Filippo 12 527
Gimignani, Giacinto 12 648
Gismondi, Paolo 12 746
Langetti, Giovanni Battista 18 740
Mehus, Livio 21 53
Romanelli, Giovanni Francesco 26 565
reproductive prints by others 3 308; 7 466, 569; 29 399
Aquila, Pietro 10 140
Audran, Girard 2 708
Audran, Jean 2 709
Cesi, Carlo 6 362
Chasteau, Guillaume 6 502
Ciamberlano, Luca 1 842
Lempereur, Jean-Denis, II 19 144
Mellan, Claude 21 85
tapestries 30 322
Cortona, Urbano (di Pietro) da see URBANO (DI PIETRO) DA CORTONA
Cortor, Eldzier 1 443
Cortot, Jean-Pierre 7 915*
collaboration 5 889; 27 311
pupils 3 274; 11 42; 28 746
works 11 563, 564; 19 11; 27 547
Cortvriendt, Jan 7 915*
Corullõn 26 642
Coruña, La see LA CORUÑA
corundum 14 167
Corvalán, Juan Loperráez see LOPERRÁEZ CORVALÁN, JUAN
Corvey Abbey 3 709; 5 795, 795; 12 471; 13 18
crypt 7 265
manuscripts 5 805; 23 653; 26 675
outer crypt 5 795
paintings 12 382
piers (ii) (masonry) 24 750
wall paintings 5 797, 798
westwork 5 795; 7 265; 12 363; 26 569; 33 107, 107
Corvi, Domenico 7 915–16*
pupils 2 40; 5 365, 553; 8 554; 18 697; 24 733; 28 429; 32 425
works 18 733
Corvi-Morra, Camillo 20 352
Corvinus, Johann August 18 120
Corvinus, Matthias, King of Hungary see MATTHIAS CORVINUS, King of Hungary
Corvinus Goblet 2 819, 820
Corvisart, Charles Louis Scipion de see SCIPION DE CORVISART, CHARLES LOUIS
Corvus, Joannes see RAV, JAN
Corwin, Charles 20 106
Corwin, Jonathan 27 613
Coryate, Thomas 7 916–17*; 13 298; 14 675
Corydon see CABEL, ADRIAEN VAN DER
Corzas, Francisco 7 917*
Corzo, El see RUIZ, ANTONIO
Cosa 7 917*; 10 586; 16 620; 26 886
arches 2 297; 7 917
basilica 3 328; 7 917
comitium 26 867
curia 26 867
gardens 12 70
Roman capitolium 24 318; 26 865, 887
sculpture 27 9
stucco 27 69
tombs 10 620
town walls 26 874
Cosa, Juan de la see JUAN DE LA COSA
Cosanti Foundation 29 35
Cosci, il see BALDUCCI, GIOVANNI
Coscia, Nicola, Archbishop of Benevento 14 106
Cos Cob 14 220
Cosenza, Luigi 16 650; 22 474; 26 16
Čosevski, Vlado 19 883
Cosida y Ballejo, Jerónimo 13 862
Cosijn, Jan see COSYNS, JAN
Cosijn, Lies 22 884
Cosimo, Lord of Florence (reg 1434-64) 11 178, 185; 21 7, 8, 10–12*, 11
altarpieces 9 98
architecture 2 34; 3 173; 5 128; 11 178, 206, 207; 19 313; 21 464, 465, 466, 468; 23 835; 29 859; 32 545
books 14 867; 21 19; 32 384
gardens 12 110
hardstones 12 543
intarsia 26 779
manuscripts 11 686; 16 658; 21 468; 23 86
models 5 22
paintings 2 39; 11 799; 24 539; 25 8
sculpture 9 128, 131; 12 542; 16 689, 690; 20 552
sponsorship 11 56
Cosimo I, Grand Duke of Tuscany (reg 1569-74) 11 187; 12 573; 16 746; 21 7, 8, 19–22*, 20; 32 14
academies 11 216
architecture 7 560; 11 179, 206, 213, 215; 16 763; 21 22, 452; 22 355; 27 750; 32 15
fortifications 2 390
military 3 683; 18 690–91; 28 676
art policies 1 102; 11 187; 24 91
carpets 5 605
cartoons (drawings) 30 34
collections 3 293; 6 139; 11 187; 16 763, 771; 21 264
drawings 32 15
education (art) 16 778
engravings 32 412
fountains 1 791; 3 160; 7 672
gardens 11 214; 12 115; 31 320
gems 12 257, 258, 265; 31 318
gold 25 75
hardstones 21 725
heraldry 10 636
maps 8 513; 20 365
medals 12 4; 25 76; 32 393
metalwork 18 820; 25 76
paintings 4 840, 855, 856–8; 16 664; 27 851
allegorical 11 721
altarpieces 1 712; 4 859
ceiling 4 408
frescoes 21 22; 27 650
portraits 1 730; 11 721; 12 720
religious 7 468; 10 738; 19 190; 25 224
porcelain 9 28
porphyry 11 29
sculpture 3 160; 6 143–5; 7 331, 332; 12 576; 13 910; 16 696, 746; 19 672; 29 561; 31 320
allegorical 3 161
bronze 30 531
busts 3 160; 6 149
mythological 2 389; 7 332; 19 672; 22 32; 27 203; 31 851
religious 6 146; 9 124
seals 16 746
silver 25 75
tapestries 7 560; 11 192–3, 193; 16 757; 17 812; 27 210; 29 740, 741
Cosimo II, Grand Duke of Tuscany (reg 1609-21) 8 707; 21 9, 25*; 29 229
art history 10 636
gold 16 742
paintings 26 310, 746
allegorical 12 308; 14 729
frescoes 12 706
landscape 11 188; 25 65
portraits 14 806

Cosimo II, Grand Duke of Tuscany (*reg* 1609-21)
paintings—cont.
religious **4** 53; **7** 311; **10** 158; **11** 39; **13** 785; **14** 728; **29** 623
sculpture **22** 423; **23** 880; **30** 227
teachers **24** 112
Cosimo III, Grand Duke of Tuscany (*reg* 1670-1723) **10** 769; **11** 347; **21** *9*, 29*; **26** 771
architecture **11** 23, 181
art policies **11** 188; **16** 699
cameos **12** 547; **31** 187
collections **11** 348
drawings **3** 633
medals **20** 922; **29** 29; **33** 15
metalwork **26** 148
paintings **4** 65; **11** 23, 743; **19** 817; **21** 488; **22** 841; **26** 70; **28** 787
allegorical **12** 662
portraits **4** 383; **7** 308, 902; **11** 874; **18** 230; **22** 721; **25** 416; **26** 386; **33** 409
religious **5** 694; **11** 874; **22** 529
still-lifes **22** 288
pastels **5** 877
reliquaries **31** 187
sculpture
busts **20** 385
reliefs **6** 86; **11** 23; **12** 591; **24** 696
Roman **23** 352
tomb **12** 826
wax models **16** 749; **33** 725
sponsorship **11** 234; **26** 69; **29** 683
Cosimo, Andrea di *see* FELTRINI, ANDREA (DI GIOVANNI DI LORENZO)
Cosimo, Piero di *see* PIERO DI COSIMO
Cosimo il Vecchio *see* COSIMO, Lord of Florence
Cosin, John, Bishop of Durham **28** 295
Cosindas, Marie **7** 917–18*
Cosini, Silvio **7** 918*; **9** 142; **24** 419
collaboration **21** 647
patrons and collectors **9** 172
teachers **11** 28
works **20** 84; **21** 441; **27** 304; **31** 320
Cosini, Vincenzo **7** 918
Cosinius Primus, L. **9** 49
Cosio, Alan **24** 620
Coşkuntepe **31** 354
Cosma, Master **26** 718
Cosma di Iacopo **1** 819
Cosmander **10** 165
Cosmas **24** 23
Cosmas Indicopleustes **1** 362; **9** 616; **20** 302
Cosmas of Crete **28** 762
Cosmate Romano, Giacomo di *see* GIACOMO DI COSMATE ROMANO
cosmatesque art *see* COSMATI
Cosmati **7** 918–22*; **9** 304; **18** 868; **26** 619, 624, 680
members **24** 783
works **7** 275, 366, 455, *919*, *920*; **13** 145; **16** 762; **22** 163; **26** 624; **29** XII
Cosmati, Deodatus **7** 923*; **13** 97
Cosmati, Jacobus **7** 923*
Cosmati, Johannes **7** 920, 923*; **13** 97
Cosmati, Lucas *see* LAURENTII, LUCAS
Cosmati, Petrus **7** 923*
Cosmatus (family) **7** 918, 922, 923
Cosmes, Antonio **20** 502
cosmetic palettes *see under* PALETTES → types
cosmetics
Central Asia, Eastern **6** 310
China **7** 137–8
Egypt, ancient **10** 65–8, *66*
Indonesia **15** 802
Iran **16** 465, 466
Islamic **16** 465, 466
Japan **17** 332–3*
cosmetics containers **4** 314; **16** 797
cosmologies
Buddhism **5** 463
Byzantine **9** 616
Cambodia **5** 463*, 467–8, 474
Early Christian (*c*. AD 250-843) **9** 616
Hinduism **5** 463, 467–8, 474
Indian subcontinent **15** 703
Maya **21** *184*, 215, *215*
Mesoamerica, Pre-Columbian **21** 183–4*, *184*, 209
Native North Americans **22** 556–7
Yoruba **33** 554
Cosmopolitan Art Journal **24** 431
cosmoramas **7** 923–4*, *924*
Cospi, Ferdinando **21** 28
Cospicua, St Joseph **20** 213
Cossa, Antonio del **7** 924
Cossa, Baldassare *see* JOHN XXIII, Pope
Cossa, Cristoforo del **7** 924
Cossa, Francesco del **4** 276; **7** 924–7*; **11** 3; **14** 868; **16** 663
assistants **26** 456
paintings
allegorical **1** 655; **11** 4, 7; **16** 659; **22** 412
frescoes **32** 549
religious **7** *925*, *926*; **26** 457
patrons and collectors **8** 146; **10** 520
Bentivoglio, Giovanni II, Lord of Bologna **3** 743
works **12** 623
allegorical **11** *7*
Cossa, Gilberto **22** 245
Cossa, Luigi **15** 819
Cossa, Sansão **22** 245
Cossé, Charles de, Comte de Brissac *see* BRISSAC, CHARLES DE COSSÉ, Comte de
Cossé-Brissac, Catherine-Françoise-Charlotte Duchesse de Noailles *see* NOAILLES, CATHERINE-FRANÇOISE-CHARLOTTE, Duchesse de
Cosset (family) **2** 496
Cosset, Jean **5** 207; **30** 313
Cossiers, Anton **8** 1
Cossiers, Guilliellemus **8** *1*
Cossiers, Jan **8** 1–2*
patrons and collectors **24** 330
reproductive prints by others **18** 879
teachers **32** 705
works **8** *1*
Cossin, Louis **14** 83
Cossington Smith, Grace **2** 748, 749; **8** 2*
Cossio, Pancho Gutiérrez **8** 2*; **27** 783
Cossio del Pomar, Felipe **24** 509
Cosso, Marcos Antonio **29** 341
Cosson, C. A., Baron de **2** 450
Cossutii (family) **27** 28
Cossutius(, Decimus) **2** 688; **8** 3*; **28** 384
Cossutius Cerdo, M. **8** 3
Cossutius Menelaos, M. **27** 30
Costa, Agustín de **2** 386
Costa, Antonio (*fl* early 19th cent.) **16** 739
Costa, António (*fl* 1930) **30** 882
Costa, António da (*d* 1623) **8** 858; **30** 416
Costa, António José da (*b* 1840) **20** 463; **25** 384
Costa, Bartolomeu da **19** 893; **25** 310
Costa, Faria da **19** 467; **25** 294
Costa, Francesco **11** 9, 10
works **9** *12*
Costa, Francisco Jorge da **25** 814; **30** 881
Costa, G. A. (*fl* 1654) **24** 741
Costa, Giovann Battista **3** 130; **8** 3; **16** 557, 586, 591, 611
Costa, Giovanni **8** 5–6*, 701; **16** 678; **26** 776; **32** 108
groups and movements **10** 641; **14** 809; **16** 678; **19** 870
pupils **10** 834; **14** 808
teachers **7** 528
works **8** *5*
Costa, Giovanni Antonio (*b* 1935) **13** 728
Costa, Ippolito **5** 547; **8** 3, 4*
Costa, J. C. Ferreira da *see* FERREIRA DA COSTA, J. C.
Costa, Jerónimo **6** 597
Costa, Joachim **11** 568
Costa, Jorge Guerreiro da *see* GUERREIRO DA COSTA, JORGE
Costa, José da **28** 731
Costa, Joseph Mendes da *see* MENDES DA COSTA, JOSEPH
Costa, Lorenzo (di Ottavio) (i) (*c*. 1460-1535) **4** 276; **8** 3–4*; **11** 3
assistants **19** 200
collaboration **2** 607; **4** 276
patrons and collectors
Anne of Brittany, Queen of France (1477-1514) **31** 846
Bentivoglio, Giovanni II, Lord of Bologna **3** 743; **11** 700
Isabella d'Este, Marchesa di Mantua (1474-1539) **7** 891; **10** 521; **16** 770; **26** 349; **29** 860
Robertet, Florimond de **26** 454
pupils **12** 561; **20** 904, 905
restorations by others **6** 115
works **8** *4*; **13** 294
Costa, Lorenzo (ii) (1537-83) **3** 850; **8** 3, 4–5*; **20** 321
collaboration **12** 558
Costa, Lorenzo (*fl* 17th cent.) **24** 837
Costa, Lorenzo della **20** 767
Costa, Lúcio **4** 728; **8** 6–8*; **32** 855
assistants **22** 95
collaboration **4** 712, 713; **5** 218; **12** 793; **19** 44; **23** 117; **26** 109, 414; **31** 398
competitions **7** 670
groups and movements **7** 618; **15** 886; **21** 783
pupils **23** 117
works **4** 679, 712, *712*, *713*, 714, 721; **7** 695; **8** *7*
Costa, Luis da **8** 11
Costa, Luís Pereira da *see* PEREIRA DA COSTA, LUÍS
Costa, Marcela **2** 87
works **2** *87*
Costa, Margaret Della *see* DELLA COSTA, MARGARET
Costa, Michael **25** 712
Costa, Nino *see* COSTA, GIOVANNI
Costa, Olga **6** 520; **8** 8*; **33** 316
Costa, Olga, -José Chávez Morado, Museo-Casa *see under* GUANAJUATO
Costa, Ottavio **5** 708; **8** 8–9*
Costa, Pablo **26** 251
Costa, Pedro **12** 739
Costa, Tomás **25** 302
Costa Andrade, Manuel **8** 9*; **26** 253; **28** 732
Costa a S Giorgi, Nannocio della **30** 659
Costa Ataíde, Manoel da *see* ATAÍDE, MANOEL DA COSTA
Costabili, Giovanni Battista, Marchese **11** 4
Costa Brioso, Manuel da **25** 310
Costa Cabral, Bartolomeu **24** 395; **25** 294
Costa Campos, João da **4** 723
Costa Coelho, Caetano de **4** 716; **26** 412
Costa di Ottavio, Lorenzo **9** 184
Costa e Silva, José da **8** 9–10*
collaboration **5** 376; **10** 728
patrons and collectors **4** 637
works **1** 753; **25** 293
Costa e Silva, Raimundo **26** 413
Costa Faro, António da *see* FARO, ANTÓNIO DA COSTA
Costa Gomez, Henry da **2** 148
Costaguta, Andrea **28** 10
Costaguti (family) **24** 238
Costaguti, Giovanni Battista **10** 909
Costakis, George **8** 10–11*; **13** 359; **27** 439
Costa Lamego, António da **19** 467
Costa Lima, Caetano da **29** 100
Costa Lima Sampaio, Joaquim da **23** 453; **25** 293; **33** 149
Costa Meesen, Félix da **8** 11*; **25** 319
Costa Mesa (CA), Orange County Center for the Performing Arts **7** 688
Costa Mora **25** 302
Costa Mota, António Augusto da (1862-1930) **8** 11*
Costa Mota, António Augusto da (1877-1956) **8** 11
Costa Negreiros, José Manuel da **27** 801
Costa Negreiros, Manuel da **23** 405; **27** 800
Costanoan **22** 549, 641, 652
baskets **22** *641*
Costa Noronha, Manuel Pereira da *see* PEREIRA DA COSTA NORONHA
Costantini, Ermenegildo **4** 407
Costantino **26** 690
Costantino, Domenico **31** 307
Costanzi, Carlo **8** 12, 13–14*; **12** 261, 262
Costanzi, Giovanni **8** 12*; **12** 261, 262
Costanzi, Placido **8** 12–13*
collaboration **3** 920; **4** 154
patrons and collectors **1** 533; **3** 708; **14** 190
pupils **26** 21; **30** 429
teachers **19** 817
works **8** *13*
Costanzi, Tommaso **8** 12
Costanzo, Marco (di) **8** 14*; **27** 658
Costanzó, Miguel **21** 378
Costanzo, Tuzio **4** 398; **12** 676
works **12** *673*
Costanzo da Ello **25** 466
Costanzo da Ferrara **8** 14*; **16** 348
Costanzo de Moysis *see* COSTANZO DA FERRARA
Costanzo Lombardo *see* COSTANZO DA FERRARA
Costaperaria, Josip **28** 860
Costa Pinheiro(, António Agostinho) **8** 15*; **25** 300
Costa Pinto, Cândido **25** 300
Costa Pinto, Carlos **4** 725
Costa Pinto, Carlos, Museu da Fundação *see under* SALVADOR → museums
Costa Rebocho, Joaquim da **19** 468
Costa Rica **8** *15*, 15–18*; **9** 677–80*; **21** 177; **29** 123
architecture **8** 16–17*
celts **21** 242
churches **8** 16
education (art) **8** 18*
engravings **8** 18
exhibitions **8** 17
figurines **9** 677; **29** *143*
gravestones **9** *679*
Costa Rica—cont.
hardstones **9** 679–80; **29** 153–4
jade **29** *154*
metalwork **9** 679–80
metates **9** *678*, 678–9; **29** 142, *142*, *144*
painting **8** *17*, 17–18*
patronage **8** 18*
pendants (jewellery) **29** 154, *154*
pottery **9** 677
prints **8** 18
sculpture **8** 17–18*; **9** 677–9, *678*, *679*; **29** 143, 145
serpentine **29** 153
stone **9** 677–9, *678*, *679*; **29** *143*
stools **9** 679
trade **19** 385
metates **32** 239
Costa Sequeira, José da *see* SEQUEIRA, JOSÉ DA COSTA
Coste, Andreas de la **20** 766
Coste, Jean de *see* JEAN DE COSTE
Coste, Pascal (-Xavier) **5** 405; **8** 18–19*; **27** 854
gardens **12** 82; **20** 473; **25** 172
teachers **24** 353
writings **16** 547
Coster, Charles de **8** 628
Coster, Hendrik **22** 915
Coster, Laurens **22** 909
Coster, Samuel **21** 789
Coster, Vincent Jacobsz. **22** *859*
Costere, Balten Jansz. de **3** 126
Costerel, Henri **3** 21
Coster of Haarlem **25** 588
Costessey Hall Chapel (Norfolk) **29** 515
Coşteşti **27** 843
fortress **26** 906
Costigliolo, José P. **31** 755
Costinescu, Alexandru **26** 709, 725
Costner, Girolamo **11** 194
Costoli, Aristodemo **6** 129; **8** 19*
costume books **9** 245; **10** 822–3*; **32** 107
costume collections *see under* COLLECTIONS → types
costumes **30** 654, 666, 686
historical and regional traditions
Africa **1** *268*, *270*, 418–19*
Antilles, Lesser **2** *146*
Bahamas, the **3** *60*
Belgium **30** 665
Bijogo **4** *55*
Burma **5** 251–2
Cambodia **5** 504*, *504*
China **7** 137, *137*
England **9** 245; **30** 654, 662*, 663*, 674–5*, 680
France **30** 659*, 660*, *660*, *671*, 671–2*
Germany **28** *111*
Greece, ancient **9** 248; **30** 650
Hopi **22** *583*
Idoma **1** 270
Igalu **1** 270
Igbo **1** 270; **15** *111*
India, Republic of **15** 175–6
Indonesia **15** 802
Italy **30** 657*, 669*
Jamaica **16** *881*
Japan **17** *314*, 326–8*, 332*, 333–4
Kenya **1** 255
Kuba (iii) (Zaïre) **3** 441
Laos **18** 774
Malaysia **20** 177*
Native North Americans **22** *583*
Netherlands, the **30** 665
Nevis **2** *146*
Nigeria **1** *268*, 269–70, *270*; **15** *111*
Russia **30** *686*
St Kitts **2** *146*
Spain **30** 664*
Thailand **30** 629
Trinidad and Tobago **31** *332*, 332–3

costumes
  historical and regional traditions—cont.
    Vietnam **32** 491
    Yoruba **1** 270
  materials
    beadwork **3** 441
    coins **30** 654
    feathers **30** 654
    gold leaf **17** *314*
    leather **30** 654
    papier mâché **28** *111*
    shells **3** 441
    silk **32** 491
    skins **1** 418
    wire **31** 333
    wood **28** *111*
  see also DRESS
Cosuin, Gérard **29** 668
Cosway, Maria (Louisa Caterina Cecilia) **8** 19, 20–21*
Cosway, Richard **8** 19, 20–21*; **21** 644
  patrons and collectors **14** 146; **15** 29
  personal collection **19** 531; **21** 770; **25** 665
  reproductive prints by others **3** 309; **7** 700; **8** 21
  sponsors **8** 372
  teachers **19** 157
  works **8** *20*; **9** 1; **29** 675
Cosyns **4** 79
Cosyns, Jan **8** 21*; **32** 694
Cot, Pierre-Auguste **12** 316
Cotán, Juan Sánchez *see* SÁNCHEZ COTÁN, JUAN
Cotchett, Thomas **21** 600
Coté, Paul Marie **5** 563
Coteau **24** 148
Côte de Bretagne ruby **11** 634
Côte d'Ivoire **1** *214*, 386; **8** 21–3*
  architecture **8** 22
  body arts **1** 288
  cement **1** 331
  collections **8** 23
  compounds **1** 312
  copper **8** 22
  cotton **8** 22
  currency **1** 363
  dealing **8** 23
  divination instruments **1** 357
  doors **9** 164
  drums (musical instruments) **1** 360
  education (art) **8** 23
  exhibitions **8** 23
  figurines **1** 273, *281*
  gesture **1** 264, 265
  gold **8** 22
  gongs **1** 360
  ikat **8** 22
  iron **8** 22, *23*
  ivory-carvings **8** 22
  masks **1** 229, 256, 339; **13** *860*
  meeting-houses **1** 310
  metalwork **8** 22
  monuments **1** 331
  museums **8** 23
  painting **1** 313; **8** 22
  patronage **8** 23
  photography **10** 580
  portraits **1** *226*, 267
  pottery **8** 22
  raffia **8** 22
  sculpture **1** 514, *515*; **8** 22–3, *23*
  staffs **1** 263
  string **8** *23*
  textiles **1** 290; **8** 22
  tools **1** *364*, 370
  tourist art **1** 252
  weights **1** 277–8, 363
  wood **1** *281*; **9** 164; **13** *860*
  wood-carvings **8** 22
Cotehele House (Cornwall) **9** 29
Cotelle, Jean, I (1607-76) **8** 24; **11** 641
Cotelle, Jean, II (1642-1708) **8** 24*
  collaboration **1** 664; **20** 860
Cotelle, Jean, II (1642-1708)—cont.
  patrons and collectors **23** 513; **32** 372
  teachers **13** 878
  writings **11** 573
Cotelle, Père **20** 603
  works **20** *602*
Coter, Colijn de **3** 554; **8** 24–5*
  attributions **20** 702
  pupils **10** 216
  works **8** *25*
Cotes, Francis **8** 26*
  assistants **31** 139
  methods **9** 212
  patrons and collectors **14** 144, 597
  pupils **27** 359
  reproductive prints by others **21** 416
  works **8** *26*; **11** *428*, *429*
Cotes, Samuel **8** 26; **21** 643
Côtes-d'Armor **32** 280
Cothart, François **31** 227
Cothay Manor (Somerset) **29** 22
  solar **29** *22*
Cothem, Jacob van **8** 26–7*
Coti **29** 135
Cotignola, Francesco da *see* ZAGANELLI, FRANCESCO (DI BOSIO)
Cotman, Ann **8** 28
Cotman, Frederic George **8** 28
Cotman, John Joseph **8** 28; **23** 249
Cotman, John Sell **8** 27–9*; **23** 248; **30** 735; **33** 545
  assistants **8** 185
  groups and movements **10** 374; **23** 248; **25** 264; **26** 740; **32** 903
  patrons and collectors **3** 740; **21** 901
  pupils **5** 193; **8** 830; **31** 465
  works **8** *27*, *29*, 185; **10** 252; **18** 715; **31** 155, 465; **32** 901
Cotman, Miles Edmund **8** 28
Cotmeana Monastery **26** 718
Cotnari **26** 719
Coto, Luis **21** 385
Coţofeneşti **30** 770, 771, 772
Coţofenii-din-Dos **30** 772
Cotogno, Ottavio **13** 809
Cotoli, Manuel Piqueras *see* PIQUERAS COTOLI, MANUEL
Cotón, Gómez **17** 515
Cotoner, Nicholas **25** 564
Cotonou
  Centre de Promotion de l'Artisanat et d'Art **3** 728, 729
  Notre-Dame **3** 728
Cotswold Collotype **7** 576
Cotta, Giacomo **12** 559
Cotta, Johann Friedrich **27** 346
cottage orné see under HOUSES → types
Cottancin, Paul **3** 394; **7** 693; **8** 30*
Cottart, Pierre **8** 31*
Cottavoz, André **19** 848
Cotte, Jules Robert de **12** 134; **24** 164
Cotte, Robert de **5** 7; **8** 31–4*; **11** 518; **12** 373, 829; **20** 134; **29** 303; **33** 432
  altars **7** 422
  architecture
    cathedrals **23** 510; **31** 372
    châteaux **7** 194; **10** 842
    hôtels particuliers **1** 497; **4** 331; **14** 789; **24** 120, 221
    palaces **4** 324; **8** *32*, *33*; **20** 71; **26** 113; **29** 750, *751*; **33** 277
    restorations **26** 84
    urban planning **24** 121
  assistants **6** 121; **7** 423; **20** 489; **29** 303; **32** 510; **33** 691
  collaboration **6** 490; **14** 227; **19** 118; **20** 296, 298; **23** 458, 474
  interior decoration **5** 349; **6** 509; **11** 405; **20** 72
Cotte, Robert de—cont.
  patrons and collectors **2** 701; **28** 15; **32** 370; **33** 277
  personal collection **12** 831; **20** 293
  pupils **5** 766; **11** 134; **19** 268
Cotterell, Charles **9** 57
Cotterill, Edmund **12** 163
Cottesbrooke Hall (Northants) **28** 64
Cottet, Charles **8** 34*; **11** 547
  collaboration **28** 750
  groups and movements **3** 156
  pupils **23** 693, 694
Cotthem, Frans van **17** 648
Cottier, Daniel **2** 755; **5** 65; **19** 109; **25** 805; **27** 461; **28** 270; **31** 880
Cottin, Sophie **12** 154
Cottingham, Lewis Nockalls **8** 34*; **13** 206; **18** 667; **32** 95
Cottingham, Nockalls Johnson **8** 34
Cottingham, Robert **19** 702; **24** 686
Cottingley fairy photographs **11** 310, *311*
Cottington, Francis, Baron **10** 363
Cottis Grave, Master of the de **21** 523
cotton **7** 735; **8** 34–7*
  historical and regional traditions
    Africa **1** *218*, *229*, 251, 293, *424*, *425*; **9** III2; **30** VIII1
    Ancient Near East **1** 880
    Angola **2** *87*
    Antilles, Lesser **2** 144, 151; **5** 747
    Assyrian **8** 35
    Australia **2** *768*
    Austria **2** *826*
    Aztec **21** 249
    Bali (Indonesia) **15** 793
    Bangladesh **3** 168
    Belgium **3** *611*
    Bhutan **3** 914, 915
    Brazil **4** 724
    Burma **5** 247; **20** 327
    Byzantine **9** *640*, 664, *665*
    Cambodia **5** 501, 502
    Central Asia, Western **6** 248, 249–50*, *250*, 253; **8** 34
    Chach **6** 249
    China **7** 43, 51, *52*, 113, *144*, *145*; **8** 34
    Côte d'Ivoire **8** 22
    Cyprus **16** 445
    Czech Republic **8** 37, 419
    Early Christian (*c.* AD 250-843) **9** *640*, 664, *665*
    Egypt **8** 34; **9** *640*, *665*; **16** 428, 442; **31** 21
    Egypt, ancient **9** 823
    England **8** 35–6, *35*, *36*; **9** IV2; **10** *182*, 356*; **21** 600
    Ethiopia **8** 34
    Ferghana **6** 249, 250
    France **8** 36–7; **11** 649*; **23** 331, *545*; **30** X1
    Fulani **11** 830
    Germany **8** 37; **12** 463
    Ghana **30** VIII1
    Guatemala **13** 766
    Hausa **1** *218*
    Hinduism **15** *673*
    Hungary **15** 11
    Inca **30** IX
    India, Republic of **15** *176*
    Indian subcontinent **5** 829; **8** 34, 36; **10** I2; **15** 660–61*, 664–5*, 667, 668–70, *669*, *673*, 674, *675*, *683*, *691*; **20** 327; **31** 21
    Indonesia **9** III1, IV1; **15** 790, *791*, 792, 793, 794, *794*, *795*; **30** XI
    Iran **5** 829; **16** 449, 450; **18** 48; **31** 21
    Iraq **16** 434; **31** 21
cotton
  historical and regional traditions—cont.
    Ireland **16** 33, *34*
    Islamic **16** 428, 434, *438*, 438–9, 442, 449, 450, 462, 466, 473; **31** 21
    Cyprus **16** 445
    Italy **8** 37, *37*
    Japan **17** 305, *310*, 316–17*, *317*, 354, *354*, 355, *356*; **30** VII2
    Java **9** IV1; **15** 790, *791*, 792; **30** XI
    Khurasan **16** 428
    Khwarazm **6** 249, 250
    Korea **18** 358, 374, 375
    Malaysia **20** *175*
    Mali **11** 830; **20** *199*
    Malta (Republic of) **20** 218
    Maya **21** 246
    Mesoamerica, Pre-Columbian **21** 234, 246, 249, 261
    Mesopotamia **16** 428
    Native North Americans **22** 622–3
    Nepal **22** *791*, 791
    Netherlands, the **8** 36
    Niger **23** *128*
    Nigeria **1** *218*, *229*; **9** III2
    North Africa **8** 35
    Ottoman **16** 445, 462
    Paraguay **24** 100
    Peru **30** IX
    Philippines **24** *629*
    Russia **27** *431*
    Scotland **8** 37; **28** 266
    South America, Pre-Columbian **29** 178; **30** IX
    South-east Asia **29** 232
    Spain **8** 35
    Sudan **8** 34
    Sumatra **15** *794*
    Surinam **1** *424*
    Switzerland **8** 37
    Syria **16** 428
    Thailand **30** *621*, *626*
    Transoxiana **16** 428
    Tunisia **18** 48
    Turkey **16** 462
    United States of America **1** *425*; **8** 34, 35, 36; **10** 356; **30** VI3; **31** 656, *656*, *657*
    Uzbekistan **31** *783*
    Venezuela **32** 177, 178
    Vietnam **32** 489, 490
    Yemen **16** *438*, 438–9; **31** 21
  techniques
    dyeing **9** 490, 491; **15** 667, 668, 790, *791*, 792
    mercerization **28** 717; **30** 538
    painting **15** *673*, 674
    printing **6** 249, *250*; **7** *52*; **8** *35*, *36*, 36–7*, *37*; **10** 356*; **11** 649*; **15** 668–70, *669*; **23** 331; **28** 266; **30** 561, X1; **31** *657*
  uses
    bags **30** *626*
    batik **3** 378
    blankets **11** 830; **30** *621*
    canvas **5** 654–5
    carpets **5** 829, 830; **6** 253; **15** *683*; **16** 466, 473
    chintz **32** 815
    cloaks **1** *424*
    corduroy **8** 35, *35*
    coverlets **7** *144*; **31** *656*
    cushion covers **1** *218*
    dress **16** 462; **18** 358; **22** 622–3; **24** *629*; **28** 717; **31** *783*
    embroidery **6** 250; **10** *182*; **12** 463; **17** 355
    etchings **10** 561
    fibre art **11** 54
    flags **11** 145
    handkerchiefs **8** *35*, 36
    hangings **2** *87*; **15** *176*, *675*, *794*
    headcloths **15** 792; **20** *175*
cotton
  uses—cont.
    kilims **18** 48
    kites **7** 113
    knitting **18** 158
    lace **3** *611*; **18** 588, 590, 593
    mantles **15** *795*
    manuscripts **21** 234
    molas **21** *804*
    painting **5** 501
    paper **24** 40
    passementerie **24** 237
    patchwork **24** 253
    quilts **1** *425*; **30** VI3
    robes **15** *691*; **17** *356*
    sashes **15** 792
    satin **30** 551
    scroll paintings **3** 914
    shawls **8** 36, 37, *37*
    shoes **7** *145*
    skirts **30** *626*
    tapestries **30** 308
    threads **3** 440; **30** 538*, 541
    tiraz **31** 21
    tunics **1** *229*; **9** *640*; **30** *626*, IX
    turbans **30** *626*
    velveteen **8** 35; **30** 553
    waistcoats **8** 36
    wallpaper **32** 813
    weaving **1** 293
    wicks **5** 610
    wraps **15** 792
    writing **20** 327
Cotton, Clinton Neal **22** 676
Cotton, John
  works **2** *755*
Cotton, Peter **32** 414
Cotton, Robert Bruce **2** 162; **5** 515; **8** 38*
  manuscripts **10** 368; **19** 409; **28** 844; **31** 773
Cotton collection *see under* LONDON → British Library
cotton duck *see under* CANVAS → types
Cotton Genesis *see under* BIBLES → individual manuscripts
cotton twists *see under* GLASS → techniques
cotton-wood **3** 331; **22** 583, *583*
Cottrell, J. **1** 433
Coty, François **18** 659
Cotzumalhuapa *see* SANTA LUCÍA COTZUMALHUAPA
Cotzumalhuapa style **27** 780
Couberon, Marquis de **21** 902
Coubillier, Frédéric **8** 39*; **17** 3
Coubillier, Joseph **8** 39
Coubine, Othon *see* KUBÍN, OTOKAR
couch beds *see under* BEDS → types
Couché, Jacques **8** 772; **18** 858; **23** 520
Coucher Book of the Duchy of Lancaster, Great *see* GREAT COUCHER BOOK OF THE DUCHY OF LANCASTER
couches **11** 850; **29** 8
  Antilles, Lesser **2** 151
  Egypt, ancient **29** 8
  Etruscan **10** *633*
  France **11** 589, 593–4
  Germany **9** 689
  Greece, ancient **13** 383, 386, 591*, *591*, 596–7
  Italy **10** *633*
  Prehistoric art **9** 689
  Rome, ancient **3** 483; **27** 99–100; **29** 8
  United States of America **31** 623, 628
couching *see under* BEADWORK → techniques; EMBROIDERY → types
Couchman, Henry **23** 21
Coucy, Enguerrand, Lord of *see* ENGUERRAND, Lord of Coucy

Coucy-le-Château 6 56; 8 *39*, 39–40*; 11 *504*; 19 895
Porte de Laon 3 209; 7 358; 12 174
Couder, (Louis-Charles-) Auguste 8 40*; 11 415; 23 521
Couderc 3 461; 12 830
Coudray, Berthe 11 607; 27 536
Coudray, Clemens Wenzeslaus 8 40–41*; 33 37
Coudray, François 32 580
Coudray, Marie-Alexandre-Lucien 8 41*; 20 925
Coudray-Saint-Omer, Le *see* LE COUDRAY-SAINT-OMER
Coudres, Ludwig Des *see* DES COUDRES, LUDWIG
Coué 17 739
Coughtry, Graham 5 569; 8 41*
Cougnac 25 477, 484, 487
couleur *see under* PIGMENTS → types
coulisses 8 41*
see also REPOUSSOIRS
Coulommiers Château 4 865; 6 506; 11 515; 20 *457*
Coulon 19 540
Coulson, I. W. W., linen manufactory 19 418
Coulte, Maximilian *see* COLT, MAXIMILIAN
council chambers 31 235
see also BOULEUTERIA; CITY HALLS; TOWN HALLS
Council for Artistic Affairs (St Petersburg) 27 442
Council for the Encouragement of the Arts and Music 19 590
Council of Industrial Design 8 804; 10 299
Counihan, (Jack) Noel 2 749, 750; 8 41*
Counis, Salomon-Guillaume 4 305
counterfeits *see* FORGERIES; POSTICHES
counterproofs 8 41–2*, *42*; 21 895
Counter-Reformation 7 215
counters *see under* TABLES → types
counterscarp 21 546
Countess of Warwick, Master of the 9 275
country estates *see* ARCHITECTURE → types → landscape; GARDEN DESIGN
country houses *see under* HOUSES → types
Country Life Illustrated 10 284, 377; 24 425, 445
Counts Palatinate and Margraves, Master of the *see* BESSER, HANS
count-stitch embroidery *see under* EMBROIDERY → types
county halls 18 886; 31 236, 242
see also CITY HALLS; TOWN HALLS
coupé plates *see under* PLATES → types
Couper, James 28 259
Couper, James, & Sons 9 295; 10 320; 28 259
Couper, James H. 27 884
Couperin, François 23 500
Coupin de la Couperie, Marie-Philippe 4 303; 31 374
Cour, Jean del *see* DELCOUR, JEAN(-GILLES)
Cour, Nicholas de La *see* LA COUR, NICHOLAS DE
Cour, William de la *see* DELACOUR, WILLIAM
Courajod, Louis (-Charles-Léon) 8 50*; 11 675, 676; 32 643
Courajod Christ 8 50; 26 641
Couran, Ignatius 33 226
Courbes, Jean 8 50*
Courbet (family) 8 58
Courbet, (Jean-Désiré-) Gustave 7 674; 8 50–60*; 9 245; 11 545, 659, 735; 15 154; 21 776; 24 140, *661*; 25 659–60; 28 919, 921
attributions 23 697
catalogues 6 80
commentaries 3 392; 6 438–9
dealers 8 820; 30 425
exhibitions 10 679; 24 140
frames 11 *415*
groups and movements 22 687; 26 53, 54–5, 743
methods 9 673; 24 495, 667
paintings 8 *51*; 12 215; 21 761; 25 651
allegorical 1 661, 664; 8 *53*
genre 8 *52*, *54*, *56*; 11 545; 12 294, *295*; 26 *54*
history 14 588
hunting scenes 2 107; 11 415; 29 425
landscape 18 715
marine 20 426
nude figures 10 480; 23 295
portraits 8 *55*; 33 138
still-lifes 29 669
patrons and collectors 11 659
Barnes, Albert C. 3 251
Bowes, John 4 600
Bruyas, Alfred 5 57–8
Burrell, William (1861-1958) 5 278
Cognacq, (Théodore-) Ernest 7 528
Havemeyer, Louisine (Waldron) 14 244
Houssaye, (François-) Arsène 14 802
Hunt, William Morris 15 20
Ionides, Constantine Alexander 15 895
Kröller-Müller, Hélène 18 466
Silvestre (ii), (Paul-) Armand 28 744
Tret'yakov (family) 31 312
Tschudi, Hugo von 31 397
Whitney, John Hay 33 150
pupils 10 796; 14 396; 16 63; 23 225
reproductive prints by others 4 242, 807
studio 29 856
writings 22 687; 31 300
Courbevoie, Musée Roybet-Fould 27 281
Courcelles, Pauline Rifer de *see* RIFER DE COURCELLES, PAULINE
Courcy, Jean de *see* JEAN DE COURCY
Courcy, Simon de *see* SIMON DE COURCY
Courde de Montaiglon, Anatole de, Comte *see* MONTAIGLON, ANATOLE DE COURDE, Comte de
Courdijn, Jean 31 793
Courdouan, Vincent 13 791; 21 170
Courdrieu 11 650
Couronni, Nicolao 21 61
Courrèges, André 9 294
Courret, Eugenio 8 61*; 24 518
Courrier Artistique, Le 20 498
Courrières, E. de 22 92
Courrier Français, Le 20 602
Courselles-Dumont, Henri 8 659
Courson Château 23 704
Court, Abraham del 14 *374*
Court, Claude-Auguste 14 19
Court, Jean (b c. *1545) see* VIGIER, JEAN
Court, Jean de (*fl* 1541-64) 8 62; 19 396
Court, Jean le (*fl* 17th cent.) 7 900
Court, Joseph-Désiré 8 61*
Court, Juste le *see* CORTE, JOSSE DE
Court, Suzanne de 8 62*; 19 396
works 19 *397*
Courtauld, Augustine 8 62
Courtauld, George (*b* 1761) 8 62
Courtauld, George (1802-61) 8 62
Courtauld, Louisa Perina 3 627; 7 167; 8 62
works 3 *627*
Courtauld, Pierre 8 62
Courtauld, Samuel (1876-1947) 8 62*; 10 357
collections 10 367; 19 590
Courtauld, Samuel, I (1720-65) 8 62
Courtauld, Samuel, II (1752-1821) 8 62
Courtauld Institute of Art *see under* LONDON
Court Bureau (Pridvornaya Kontora) 27 584
court cupboards *see under* CUPBOARDS → types
Court de Gébelin, Antoine 12 208
Courtecuisse, Jean de *see* JEAN DE COURTECUISSE
Courteille, Jean-Dominique de 28 521
Courten, Juan Amador 32 169
Courten, William 28 844
Courtenay, Hercules 25 888
Courtenay, William, Earl of Devon (*d* 1512)
coats of arms 11 *145*
Courtenay, William, Earl of Devon (18th cent.) 14 419
Courtenay Bay Pottery 33 146
Courtens, Alfred 8 62
Courtens, Antoine 8 62, 63*
Courtens, Claude 3 604
Courtens, Franz 8 62–3*
groups and movements 3 562; 14 507
pupils 8 785
Courtens, Herman 8 62
Courtenvaux, Jacques Souvré de *see* SOUVRÉ DE COURTENVAUX, JACQUES
Courteys, Pierre 19 396
court-houses 31 235
Australia 2 *742*
England 31 239
France 27 *246*
Jamaica 16 *883*
United States of America 26 *342*; 31 591
see also LAW COURTS
Courtin, Pierre (-Louis-Maurice) 8 63*; 12 830
Courtivron, I. de 33 311
Courtney Devonish Pottery 2 152
Courtois 24 797
Courtois, Giuseppe 17 512
Courtois, Guillaume *see* CORTESE, GUGLIELMO
Courtois, Gustave-Claude-Etienne 10 507; 25 552; 28 104; 33 455
Courtois, Jacques 3 388; 7 902–3*; 11 535
assistants 19 137
collaboration 7 903
copies 26 242
patrons and collectors 17 512; 21 27; 25 815
pupils 24 210; 26 242
works 25 414
Courtois, Jean-Pierre 7 902
Courtois, Marie *see* NATTIER, MARIE
Courtois, Pierre 24 146
Courtois, Ulric 23 341
Courtonne, Jean 8 63–4*; 11 518
patrons and collectors 7 778
works 11 577; 14 789
Courtonne, Jean-Baptiste 8 64
court painting *see under* PAINTING → types
courtrooms 31 235
courts 13 383
Court School of Charlemagne 5 624, 800, 801, 809; 6 483; 11 636; 12 838; 13 20; 20 330
Court School of Charles the Bald 5 804, 808, 809, 810, 811; 7 512; 20 330; 23 653
Court style *see under* GOTHIC → styles
court tombs *see under* TOMBS → types
Court van der Voort, Pieter de la 12 132; 21 489
courtyard gardens *see under* GARDENS → types
courtyards 8 64–5*
Central Asia, Western 16 *238*
China 6 674, 687–8, *689*, 691, 692
Confucianism 6 674
Egypt 16 *210*
England 8 65
France 8 65; 19 *237*
Germany 18 *455*
Greece, ancient 8 64; 13 382
Iran 16 142, 264
Iraq 16 152
Islamic 8 64; 16 142, 260, 263
Central Asia, Western 16 *238*
Egypt 16 *210*
Iran 16 142, *154*, 264
Iraq 16 152
Morocco 16 *218*
Ottoman 16 221
Spain 8 *65*; 13 *288*
Syria 16 *148*, *181*
Tunisia 16 *156*
Turkey 16 142, 183, 186, 221
Italy 8 65; 11 *180*; 23 810
Renaissance 16 *631*, *632*; 21 *519*; 22 *132*; 27 *741*
Mesopotamia 8 64
Mexico 21 *401*
Morocco 16 *218*
Ottoman 16 221
Rome, ancient 8 64
Scotland 28 225
Spain 8 *65*; 13 *288*, *731*
Syria 16 *148*
Tunisia 16 *156*
Turkey 16 142, 183, 186, 221
courtyards, peristyle *see* PERISTYLE COURTYARDS
Courvoisier, Pierre
works 6 *166*
Courvoisier & Cie 30 148
Cousen, Charles 8 66*
Cousen, John 8 65–6*; 10 396
Cousens, Henry 1 483; 15 212
Cousin (family) 20 674
Cousin, Auguste 24 828
Cousin, David 28 289
Cousin, Jean (*d* 1549) 8 66
Cousin, Jean (i) (*c.* 1500–*c.* 1560) 8 66, 67–8*; 11 266, 532, 637
collaboration 9 176; 13 226; 20 488
methods 24 488, *488*
patrons and collectors 30 727
pupils 8 68
works 4 338; 8 *67*; 11 265, 639; 28 417
Cousin, Jean (ii) (*c.* 1525–*c.* 1595) 8 66, 68*; 11 533
works 4 338
Cousin, Louis *see* PRIMO, LUIGI
Cousin, René 33 249
Cousin, Victor 2 530; 9 704; 26 739
Cousinet, Ambroise-Nicolas 8 68; 11 619
Cousinet, Henri-Nicolas 8 68
Cousinet, Jean-François 8 68; 11 618; 29 689; 30 105
Cousinet, Nicolas-Ambroise 8 68; 11 618
Cousinet, René 8 68; 11 588, 618; 12 832
Cousins, Leonore 1 687
Cousins, Peter 11 426
Cousins, René 11 426
Cousins, Samuel 8 69*; 21 604; 25 627
collaboration 2 692
pupils 2 692
teachers 26 282
works 21 418; 25 619
Coussin, Jean-Antoine 8 69*
Coussmaker, George 26 *276*
Coustain, Pierre 8 69*
collaboration 5 213
patrons and collectors 5 210
works 5 214
workshop 11 149
Coustou, Charles Pierre 8 70
Coustou, François 8 69
Coustou, Guillaume (i) (1677-1746) 8 70, 71–2*; 11 559; 19 847
collaboration 6 379
pupils 4 508; 11 704; 15 39
works 5 889; 8 *71*; 11 560; 19 213; 20 450; 29 *563*, 564, 571, 572
Coustou, Guillaume (ii) (1716-77) 4 391; 8 70, 72*; 11 561
assistants 33 161
pupils 8 631, 834; 17 683; 25 374, 798; 29 540, 733
teachers 8 72
Coustou, Jean 10 726
Coustou, Nicolas 8 70–72*; 11 559, 704; 19 847
assistants 3 773
collaboration 6 379; 8 71; 12 727
pupils 4 587; 10 264; 27 242; 30 733
works 8 *70*, 71, 72; 11 560; 19 213; 24 165; 29 571
Coustouges Church 26 610
Coutan, Jules-Félix 8 72*; 33 569
Coutan, Louis-Joseph-Auguste 8 72–3*
Coutances 11 *504*
aqueduct 2 242
Cathedral of Notre-Dame 8 73–4*; 11 654; 13 41
choir 8 74, *74*
mouldings 22 218
nave 8 73
spires 29 413
Coutaud, Lucien 11 644
Coûteaux, Gustave 3 615; 8 592; 18 680
Coutereau (family) 4 391
couters 2 469
Coutin, Loys 31 92
Coutinho, António Mendes *see* MENDES COUTINHO, ANTÓNIO
Coutinho, Pedro José de, 4th Marquês de Marialva *see* MARIALVA, PEDRO JOSÉ DE COUTINHO, 4th Marquês de
Couto, António 8 74*
Couto, Diogo do 2 56, 61
Couto, Mateus do 4 634
Couto, Ribeiro 6 99; 8 433
Couto dos Santos Leal, José do 8 74–5*
Couto e Azevedo, Francisco do 8 9
Coutonne, Jean-Baptiste 4 331
Coutourier, Marie-Alain 5 568
Coutouzis, Nicholas *see* KOUTOUZIS, NICHOLAS
Coutts and Co 3 64
Couture, Guillaume-Martin 8 75*; 19 27
Couture, Thomas 2 524; 8 75–6*; 11 544, 545, 659, 672; 16 16; 19 285
assistants 20 206
dealers 8 618; 9 424
groups and movements 22 742; 26 500, 740; 28 346
patrons and collectors 5 57; 8 618; 31 870

Couture, Thomas—cont.
pupils
Bachelin, (Rodolphe-) Auguste 3 20
Cassatt, Mary (Stevenson) 5 921
Colin, Gustave 7 554
Desboutin, Marcellin (-Gilbert) 8 787
Dubois, Louis (Jean-Baptiste) (1830-80) 9 325
Dutuit, (Philippe-)Auguste (-Jean-Baptiste) 9 466
Ehninger, John W(hetten) 10 99
Frølich, Lorenz 11 798
Hamman, Edouard (-Jean-Conrad) 14 116
Hicks, Thomas 14 510
Hone, Nathaniel (ii) (1831-1917) 14 717
Hunt, William Morris 15 19
Isaachsen, Olaf 16 63; 23 225
Jernberg, August 17 485
Johnson, (Jonathan) Eastman 17 617
La Farge, John 18 627
Manet, Edouard 15 152; 20 254
Newman, Robert Loftin 23 31
Nordenberg, Bengt 23 204
Oller (y Cestero), Francisco 23 415
Piette, Ludovic 24 784
Pinkas, (Hippolyt) Soběslav 24 825
Purkyně, Karel 25 742
Puvis de Chavannes, Pierre (-Cécile) 25 749
Sickert, Walter Richard 28 659
Wells, Joanna Mary 33 64
teachers 8 654; 13 692
works 8 *76*, 596, 792; 11 95; 14 588
writings 6 570; 31 300
Couturier, Marie-Alain 11 659; 21 134
Couturier, Pierre 9 112; 22 35
Couturier, Robert 8 77*; 12 630
couturiers 9 291
Couvay, Jean 8 77*; 15 31; 18 745; 32 510
Couve de Murville, Maurice, Archbishop of Birmingham
coats of arms 14 *416*
Couven, Jakob 8 77
Couven, Johann Joseph 8 77*; 9 460; 24 784
Couvertoirade, La *see* LA COUVERTOIRADE
Couvillon, Louis (-Amable) *see* QUÉVILLON, LOUIS(-AMABLE)
Couvrechef, Louis 9 420
Couwenberg, Christiaen van 4 377; 22 844
Couwenhorn, Pieter 9 192; 28 309
Couzijn, Wessel 8 77–8*; 22 861
Cova, Jacobus *see* COENE, JACQUES
Covadonga
collegiate church 29 272
Nuestra Señora de las Batallas 26 520–21
Covalanas 25 478
Covarrubias 29 333
Covarrubias, Alonso de 8 78–80*; 9 748
architecture 28 726; 29 267; 32 559
cathedrals 25 23; 28 518, 709; 31 91
façades 8 *80*; 14 474; 31 87
hospitals 5 305; 8 *79*
orders (architecture) 10 534
palaces 1 587; 20 71
staircases 29 523
assistants 32 117
attributions 8 253; 32 620
collaboration 9 748; 16 898; 27 603; 29 266; 32 117
groups and movements 25 30, 31
Covarrubias, Alonso de—cont.
patrons and collectors 11 250; 13 922; 30 374
pupils 12 920
retables 28 709
sculpture 31 90, 92
Covarrubias, Ignacio 6 594; 18 797
Covarrubias, Miguel 8 81*; 15 807
collaboration 27 331
excavations 31 66
works 5 759; 21 396
Covarrubias Horozco, Sebastián de 4 209
Cove 28 230
coved vaults *see* VAULTS (CEILING) → types → cloister
Covel, John 30 479
Covens 12 814
Coventry (W. Midlands)
brasses 4 692
Cathedral of St Michael 2 *322*, 323; 7 254, 670; 10 242, 745; 29 379
Chapel of Christ in Gethsemane 6 459
Chapel of Unity 6 459
choir-stalls 7 192
font 11 256
spire 29 *413*, 413
stained glass 29 508
tapestries 30 329, 332
tapestry 30 38
St Mary's 23 491
St Mary's Guildhall 6 389
silk 10 357
urban planning 12 597
Coventry (family) 33 375
Coventry, Chandler 2 770
Coventry, George William, 6th Earl of 4 875; 7 486; 10 295; 15 165
Coventry, Maria Gunning, Countess of *see* GUNNING, MARIA, Countess of Coventry
Coverdale, Miles 4 9
Coverdale, William Hugh 8 81*
coverlets 5 587, *587*; 7 *53*, *144*; 23 240; 30 VI2; 31 656, *656*
Coverley, R. de, and Sons 1 23
Coverly, Roger de 7 486
Covert, John R. 2 384
Covijn, Reinier 20 81
Covilhã 25 315
Covington Church (Cambs) 26 613
Covo 25 311
Covo, Battista da 8 81–2*
Covocle *see* PAPHOS, OLD
Covoni-Daneo (family) 28 734
Cowan, Charles 24 810
Cowan, John 24 810
Cowan, R(eginald) Guy 3 50; 4 73; 8 82*; 31 639
Cowan Pottery Studio 3 50; 8 82; 31 639
Coward, Noël 30 687
Cowdell, Harry 28 808
Cowdery's Down 2 64
Cowell, Henry 5 381
Cowell, W. S. 19 481
Cowern, Jenny 10 875
works 10 *875*
Cowern, Raymond Teague 4 87
Cow Gum 24 53
Cowiconsult 3 68; 20 833
Cowie, E. 33 313
Cowie, James 1 30; 8 82*; 28 239
Cowin, Douglass M(aurice) 8 82*; 17 603; 29 106
Cowin, Norris Tynwald 8 82
Cowin, Powers & Ellis 8 82
Cowin & Ellis 8 82; 14 157
Cowles, George 7 167; 8 62
Cowleshow, W. F. 31 652
Cowlishaw, Nichol & Co. 30 266
Cowper, Edward Spencer 33 444
Cowper, George Nassau Clavering, 3rd Earl 8 83*; 23 87
Cowper, Hannah, Lady 14 110
Cowper, John 30 366
Cowper, Thomas 4 288; 15 403; 31 241
Cowper, William 1 842
Cowper *Madonna*, Large *see* NICCOLINI MADONNA
Cowthorpe (N. Yorks), St Michael 9 681
Cox, Anthony 2 318
Cox, David, the elder (1783-1859) 7 548; 8 83–5*; 18 906
groups and movements 32 903
illustrated writings 26 75
patrons and collectors 7 647
pupils 15 164
reproductive prints by others 25 837
teachers 4 86; 31 909
works 8 *84*; 10 252; 32 785, 901
Cox, David, the younger (1809-85) 8 85
Cox, E. B. 5 571
Cox, F. E. 2 760
Cox, G. A. 28 228
Cox, George 10 314
Cox, Gonzales *see* COQUES, GONZALES
Cox, James 6 533; 19 596; 29 432
Cox, Jan 3 565; 17 518
Cox, Kathleen 16 29
Cox, Kenyon 7 875; 8 85*; 19 66
Cox, Michael 13 876
Cox, Philip (Sutton) 5 602; 8 85–6*
groups and movements 30 161
works 2 743; 30 160
Cox Brothers 28 228
Coxcatlán Cave 21 261
Coxcie, Michiel, the elder (1499-1592) 8 86–7*
attributions 21 533
collaboration 32 726
groups and movements 26 728
patrons and collectors 13 906, 909, 922; 16 867; 27 501; 33 578
reproductive prints by others 9 79
tapestries 13 910
teachers 5 43; 23 526
works 3 558, 609; 5 49; 8 *86*; 14 5; 17 700; 28 334; 30 315
Coxcie, Michiel, the younger (1569-1616) 8 87
Coxcie, Raphaël 8 125; 17 643
Cox & Co. 10 299
Coxcyen, Michiel *see* COXCIE, MICHIEL
Coxe, Burrell & Foster 8 87
Coxe, Daniel 8 88; 31 634
Coxe, Peter 8 87*; 10 366
Coxed, John and G., and T. Woster 10 292
Coxe-DeWilde Pottery 8 88*; 31 634
Coxhead, Almeric 8 88
Coxhead, Ernest (Albert) 8 88*; 27 730; 28 604
Coxie, Anthonie 3 806
Coxie, Raphael 3 613; 14 502
Cox & Sons 30 266
Coyet, Gillis 30 112
Coymans (family) 14 94
Coymans, Balthasar 5 542
Coymans, Isabella 24 *357*
Coymans, Johan 5 542
Coyocán 10 505
Coyolapán 21 737
Coyotlatelco ware *see under* POTTERY → wares
Coypel (family) 30 118
Coypel, Antoine 8 88, 89–91*; 9 8; 11 537, 662; 23 515; 24 135
cartoons 12 832; 20 135
collaboration 3 621; 4 536, 537; 17 670, 671; 18 633; 31 510
groups and movements 27 286
paintings 7 195; 23 512, 514, 515
allegorical 11 *493*
Coypel, Antoine
paintings—cont.
ceiling 23 514
history 11 *403*, 538; 14 584
religious 8 *90*
patrons and collectors
Beurnonville, Etienne-Edmond Martin, Baron de 3 890
Bourbon I., Louis de, le Grand Dauphin (1661-1711) 4 553
Dezallier d'Argenville, Antoine-Joseph 8 845
Kelly, Florencio 17 893
Orléans, Philippe I de Bourbon, 1st Duc d' (1640-1701) 23 513
Orléans, Philippe II de Bourbon, 2nd Duc d' (1674-1723) 23 514, 516
Piles, Roger de 24 805
Tessin, Carl Gustav, Count 30 524
personal collection 30 274
pupils 23 514
reproductions in medals 20 854
reproductions in tapestry 11 642
reproductive prints by others 2 709; 7 495; 9 362; 20 497; 24 470; 28 756; 30 344
writings 1 898; 22 378
Coypel, Charles-Antoine 8 88, 92–3*; 11 670; 19 161, 216; 20 416; 23 516; 24 135
assistants 22 725
collaboration 6 121; 10 842
patrons and collectors 32 719
pupils 5 740; 6 120; 25 81; 31 799
reproductions in sculpture 10 764
reproductions in tapestry 19 382
reproductive prints by others 17 667; 19 216; 24 712; 30 24
tapestries 22 481
works 11 643; 12 830; 30 323
Coypel, Noël 8 88–91*; 12 832; 23 512
assistants 2 707
collaboration 6 502; 10 489; 19 22; 30 660
groups and movements 25 398
patrons and collectors 4 553, 808; 23 513
pupils 8 89, 91; 25 70; 28 756
reproductive prints by others 2 709; 6 502
works 12 829; 26 204
Coypel, Noël-Nicolas 8 88, 91–2*
pupils 6 471
reproductive prints by others 19 10; 30 24
works 11 575; 24 165
Coyzevox, Antoine 8 93–4*; 11 559; 12 832; 19 847; 31 409
assistants 8 71
collaboration 4 587; 8 70, 71; 19 96; 31 408
patrons and collectors 4 551; 7 546; 25 150, 635
pupils 8 70, 71; 11 754; 19 33, 140; 30 733; 32 580
sculpture 22 44; 31 408; 32 372
busts 5 301; 11 559; 27 466
equestrian monuments 8 72, 776; 10 442; 11 559, 560; 20 450
reliefs 24 165; 32 *371*
tombs 8 *94*
Coyzevox, Pierre 8 93
Cozad, Robert Henry *see* HENRI, ROBERT
Cozens, Alexander 8 94, 95–6*; 13 301
attributions 8 96
patrons and collectors 14 764
pupils 3 454; 8 96
works 8 *95*; 32 900
writings 4 171
Cozens, John Robert 8 94, 96–9*; 10 807; 13 304
patrons and collectors 12 741; 14 598, 764; 18 149; 21 901
works 8 *97*, *98*; 10 251; 18 712, 713; 32 900
Cozens, Richard 8 95
Cozette (family) 24 63
Cozia monastery church 25 344; 26 706, 707, 710, 712, 721
Cozins 4 79
Cozumel 20 884; 21 259
Cozza, Francesco 8 99–100*
patrons and collectors 23 898; 30 451
works 8 *99*; 15 138
Cozzarelli, Battista 8 100
Cozzarelli, Giacomo 8 100–101*
attributions 24 533
collaboration 11 691
teachers 11 694
works 8 *101*; 24 567; 28 675
Cozzarelli, Guidoccio (di Giovanni) 6 5; 8 100*
Cozzi, Geminiano 8 101; 16 737; 32 200
Cozzi, Giuseppe 3 903
Cozzi, Marco 32 217
Cozzi, Vincenzo 8 101
Cozzi Porcelain Factory 8 101–2*; 16 738; 32 200
C Painter 13 508; 32 37*
C. P. R. *see* CANADIAN PACIFIC RAILWAY
Crabbe (van Espleghem), Frans 3 556; 7 369; 8 102*; 14 643; 33 355
Crabbe, Jan, Abbot of Ten Duinen (*fl* 1500) 20 659, 749
Crabbe, Jan, III (*fl* 1587-1617) 3 598
Crabbet Park (W. Sussex) 22 743
Crabeels, Florent 3 562
Crabeth, Adriaen (Pietersz.) 8 102; 30 61
Crabeth, Dirck (Pietersz.) 8 102–3*
assistants 8 103
attributions 14 44
works 8 *103*; 13 222; 27 256, 258; 29 505
Crabeth, Wouter (Pietersz.) (i) (*fl* 1559–89) 8 102, 103*; 13 222; 29 505
Crabeth, Wouter (Pietersz.) (ii) (1594-1644) 8 102, 103–5*
works 8 *104*
Crabtree, William 26 111
Crac de Montréal *see* KRAK DE MONREAL
Crace (family) 13 702; 14 145
Crace, Alfred 8 105
Crace, Edward 8 105*
Crace, Frederick 4 809; 8 105–6*; 22 527
Crace, Frederick & Son 8 105, 106
Crace, Henry 8 105
Crace, John (i) (1754-1819) 4 809; 8 105*; 28 906
Crace, John (ii) (*fl* 1780) 8 105
Crace, John, & Co. 8 105*
Crace, John, & Sons 8 105
Crace, John Dibblee 4 809; 5 195; 8 105, 106*; 25 193; 31 241
Crace, John Gregory 8 105, 106*
collaboration 25 714, 715, 716
groups and movements 10 142; 13 207
patrons and collectors 6 118
wallpaper 2 755; 10 281; 19 614; 25 716; 33 372
Crace, Thomas 8 105
Cracherode, Clayton Mordaunt 12 266; 20 389
crachis 17 276
Crăciun, Stefan 26 719
cracking 7 747; 20 574, *574*, 575–6*, 579, 583, *583*, 584
Cracow *see* KRAKÓW

cradles (i) (cots) 8 106–7*, *107*; 22 651; 24 *389*
cradles (ii) (support) 8 107*; 24 6–7, *7*
Cradock, John 3 444
Cradock, Luke *see* CRADOCK, MARMADUKE
Cradock, Marmaduke 8 107*
Cradock, Mary *see* BEALE, MARY
Craesbeeck, Joos van 8 108*
works 3 560; 8 *108*
Craeyvanger, Gijsbertus 23 1
crafts *see* FOLK ART; TOURIST ART; VERNACULAR ART; VILLAGE ART
Crafts and Trades Schools (Brazil) 4 721
crafts education *see under* EDUCATION (ART) → types
Craftsman *(Canada)* 24 431
Craftsman *(USA)* 2 572; 10 147; 24 432; 29 653; 31 621
Craftsman House Building Company 29 653
Craftsman Workshops 31 631, 653
craftsmen and artists 1 102; 2 369, 557, 558; 7 830; 14 868; 15 99, 879; 20 560, 595
Aboriginal Australia 1 38–9*
Africa 1 242, 243–5*, *243*, *244*, 251, *286*, *300*, *303*, 312, *338*
Western Equatoria 1 396
Akkadian (people) 1 508
Ancient Near East 1 859
Asante 1 250
Aztec 21 190, *190*, 191, 249
Bali (Indonesia) 29 236
Bamana 1 246; 3 132, 136
Barbados 2 153
Benin, Kingdom of 1 245; 3 722
Britain 15 401, 820; 32 327
Buddhism 6 706; 17 419
Burma 5 261, 262*
Byzantine 9 509
Cameroon 1 396
Central Asia, Eastern 6 294
Chicano 18 831–2
China 6 635–7*, 706, 770, 771; 7 9; 16 *859*
Confucianism 18 258
Cook Islands 7 790
Cuba (Caribbean) 8 235, 237; 18 834–5*
Dacian 30 770
Dan (Africa) 8 488, 490*
Dogon 9 65
Early Christian (*c.* AD 250-843) 9 509
Egypt, ancient 9 789–91*, *814*, *816*, *817*, *818*, *823*, 897, *898*; 10 35, 61–2, *62*
England 10 249, 289, 312; 14 636, 855–7
Etruscan 10 587, 596
Fang 1 244
France 4 240; 14 855; 19 3; 24 139
Fulani 1 246
Germany 3 400
Gothic 13 132–3*; 20 332–3
Greece, ancient 10 587; 13 371, 375, 394–5*, 433, 439*, 440*, 444, 467, 468, *481*, *483*, 484–6*, *485*
Guro 13 861*
Hausa 1 246, 251
Helladic 14 335, 341
Holy Roman Empire (before 1648) 29 570
Ibibio 15 61*
Igbo 1 244
Inca 15 163; 29 134*
Indian subcontinent 15 207–8*, 209, 245, 401; 30 812
Chamba (i) (India) 15 626
Islamic 15 347
Mughal 15 546
16th cent. 15 608
Indonesia 15 791; 29 236
craftsmen and artists—cont.
Iran 16 232*, 331
Ireland 16 25; 32 529
Islamic 16 126–7*, 262
Indian subcontinent 15 347
Iran 16 232*, 331
Ottoman 16 346, 387
Syria 16 146
Turkey 16 346, 387
Israelite 16 573
Italy 10 596; 13 *823*; 16 660–61*; 32 189–90
Japan 17 27–30*, 51–3*, *309*, 318, 346, 356, 358, *403*, 418–19
Java 15 791
Judah 16 573
Korea 18 257–8*, 304
Kuba (iii) (Zaïre) 1 *338*; 18 485
Latin America 18 830–31*
Lega 1 244
Mali 1 *300*
Malta (Republic of) 20 216*
Maya 21 190
Mesoamerica, Pre-Columbian 21 *190*, 190–91*, 195, 198, 236, 238, 249
Mexico 18 831–2*
Moche (culture) 29 *134*
Mongolia 21 878–9
Native North Americans 22 561, 562, 563, 661, 665, 666, 667
Nepal 22 789, *790*, *794*, 794–5
Netherlands, the 10 245; 14 855
Nigeria 1 *243*, *244*, *286*, *303*
Nuba 1 245
Nupe 23 302
Olmec 21 190
Ottoman 16 346, 387
Pacific Islands 23 718, 724
Papua New Guinea 24 86
Prehistoric art 25 494, 519, 524, 535, 545
Puerto Rico 18 832–4*
Romanesque 26 594
Rome, ancient 9 647; 13 468; 27 52–3*, *93*
Samoa 23 718
Scotland 28 235, 250, 252
South America, Pre-Columbian 29 134–5*, *134*
South-east Asia 29 235–6*
Spain 29 315; 32 180
Syria 16 146
Syria-Palestine 30 180
Thracian 30 770
Tibet 13 885; 30 809, 811–13*
Tokelau 31 *75*
Tonga (Pacific Islands) 23 718
Tuareg 1 246
Turkey 16 346, 387
United States of America 18 830–35*
Venezuela 32 172–3, 180
Viking 32 529
Zaïre 1 *338*
Cragg, Tony 8 109*; 10 269; 23 335; 26 51
Cragnier, Jean 25 814
Cragsmoor colony 14 397
Craig, Edward Gordon 8 109*; 30 682, 686
pupils 30 715
works 4 366; 30 682, 685; 33 361
Craig, James 9 723; 12 773; 28 227; 31 716
Craig, James Humbert 16 17
Craig, John 33 158
Craig, Tom 23 736
Craig, William 32 903
Craig, William Marshall 20 239
Craig, Zeidler & Strong 5 563; 30 468; 33 628
Craigends (Strathclyde) 23 546; 28 288, *289*
Craigievar Castle (Grampian) 6 59; 13 211; 28 *222*, 224, 268; 31 230, *231*
Great Hall 28 245, *245*
Craig-Martin, Michael 8 110*; 19 591; 21 621
Craigmiller 31 230
Craignethan (Strathclyde) 21 564
Craik, D. M. 28 772
Crailsheim 12 430, 431
Craiova 26 *705*, 710, 725
metalwork 30 770
Museum of Art 26 725
St Dumitru 26 712, 718
Craiovescu (family) 26 722
Craiovești (family) 26 719
Crali, Tullio 1 166; 16 680
Cram, Goodhue & Ferguson 8 110; 12 926; 14 734
Cram, Ralph Adams 4 475; 8 110–11*
collaboration 12 926–7; 14 68
groups and movements 5 340; 31 595
works 4 475; 8 *110*, 184; 14 802
Cram, Wentworth & Goodhue 8 110; 12 926
Cramer, Daniel 21 406
Cramer, Gerald 25 626
Cramer, J. 14 45
Cram & Ferguson 8 111
Cram & Goodhue 31 595
Cramillion, Bartholomew 8 111*; 9 317; 16 24; 29 837
Crampton, Charles 33 157
Crams, Ralph Adams 14 317
Cram & Wentworth 8 110; 12 926
Cranach, Augustin 8 112
Cranach, Hans 8 112, 119*
Cranach, Lucas, I (1472-1553) 2 716; 3 387; 8 111, 112–20*, 595; 12 471; 20 801; 25 103, 138, 653; 31 166
assistants 21 71
attributions 4 863; 8 112, 120
book illustrations 4 9; 12 385; 19 813
bookplates 4 373
collaboration 8 119
drawings 12 385
groups and movements 2 792; 8 513, 514; 12 387; 18 705; 26 188
methods 8 816; 10 198
paintings 11 455
allegorical 1 657, 658; 8 *117*; 31 501
altarpieces 7 226; 8 *116*; 14 140; 33 36
genre 12 288
hunting scenes 29 423
mythological 22 414; 23 293
portraits 8 120; 11 *454*, 455; 25 274, *274*, 275, 279; 32 442
religious 7 226; 8 *113*; 9 273; 10 476; 11 455, 456; 19 813; 21 84
patrons and collectors 6 76; 7 215; 30 118
Boisserée, Melchior and Sulpiz 4 243
Burrell, William (1861-1958) 5 278
Carol I, King of Romania (*reg* 1866-1914) 5 792
Christina, Queen of Sweden (*reg* 1632-54) 32 7
Diocesan Museum (Sandomierz) 27 723
Ferrand de Monthelon, Antoine 26 113
Frances Sibyl Augusta, Margravine of Baden-Baden (*reg* 1675-1737) 33 594
Francis-Joseph, Prince of Liechtenstein (*reg* 1772-81) 19 338
Frederick III, Elector of Saxony (*reg* 1486- 1525) 33 110, 112, 365
Goering, Hermann (Wilhelm) 12 843
Cranach, Lucas, I (1472-1553) patrons and collectors—cont.
Henry, Duke of Saxony (*reg* 1539-41) 33 113
Hirsch, Robert von 14 570
Hohenzollern, Albert of Brandenburg, Cardinal, Elector-Archbishop of Mainz (*reg* 1514-45) 14 647, 649
Houssaye, (François-) Arsène 14 802
Howard (i), Aletheia, Countess of Arundel 14 807
Imhoff, Willibald 15 145
Joachim II, Elector of Brandenburg (*reg* 1535-71) 14 650
Loyd, Samuel Jones, 1st Baron Overstone 19 736
Maximilian I, Duke of Bavaria (*reg* 1598- 1651) and Elector of Bavaria (*reg* 1623-51) 33 275
Maximilian I, Holy Roman Emperor (*reg* 1493- 1519) 13 903
Mond, Ludwig 21 849
Morgan, J(ohn) Pierpont (1837-1913) 22 111
Rushout, John, 2nd Baron Northwick 27 350
Ryabushinsky, Nikolay (Pavlovich) 27 458
Simon, Norton 28 751
Thurzo, Stanislav 30 794
prints 8 838; 25 604, 622
engravings 8 *114*
woodcuts 4 358; 6 569; 12 386, 387; 25 650; 33 353, 366
pupils 8 119, 120
reproductive prints by others 2 224; 27 501; 31 371
sgraffito 9 238
studio 29 853
writings 33 112
Cranach, Lucas, II (1515-86) 3 387; 8 120*; 25 103
collaboration 8 119
patrons and collectors 14 148; 26 113
personal collection 3 200
works 1 711; 8 112; 25 651
workshop 16 867
Cranach, Lucas, IV (1586-1645) 8 112
Cranach, Wilhelm Lucas von 12 449
Cranach-Presse 4 366; 8 109; 17 625; 33 38
Cranborne Chase 2 300
Cranbrook (Kent) 32 277
Cranbrook Academy of Art *see under* BLOOMFIELD HILLS (MI)
Cranbrook Colony 8 121*; 10 254; 14 768; 33 16
members 22 278; 23 442
Crandall, Charles M. 31 267
Crane, Aimee 3 63
Crane, Arnold 24 683
Crane, Bruce 31 141
Crane, Francis 10 349; 19 596; 22 153; 30 322
Crane, John 8 901
Crane, Richard 10 349; 22 153
Crane, Thomas 8 121
Crane, Walter 8 121–2*; 25 165
book covers 33 180
book illustrations 4 363; 10 654
collaboration 23 192
groups and movements 2 562, 571, 575; 10 373, 641; 19 588; 25 555, 556; 32 591
interior decoration 1 *171*; 15 895
paintings 8 *122*
patrons and collectors 14 809
prints 10 420; 25 245
pupils 8 570; 26 10
stained glass 14 863
Crane, Walter—cont.
textiles 10 283; 19 417
wallpaper 17 469; 23 547; 32 817, V1
cranes 7 764, *765*, 766–7; 13 400
Cranes Painter 10 611
Cranfield, Richard 16 21, 26
Cranfield Sackville, Lionel *see* SACKVILLE, LIONEL CRANFIELD, 1st Duke of Dorset
Cranganur 15 358
Cheraman Mosque 15 358
Cranham, Gerry 29 426
Cranke, James 8 122–3*
Cranmer, Thomas 7 215; 19 792
Cranston, Catherine 20 22–3, 24; 28 255; 32 834
furniture 6 *391*
Cranston, Kate 28 270
Craon-Beavau, Prince of 26 449
craquelure 5 654; 8 123*; 30 393
Craskell, Henry 16 882
Crasna Monastry 26 712, 718
Craterographia of 1551, Master of the *see* ZÜNDT, MATTHIAS
craters *see* CHALICES
Crathes Castle (Grampian) 13 211; 28 234
Crato, Order of *see* ORDER OF CRATO
Crauk, Charles-Alexandre 8 123*
Crauk, Gustave-Adolphe-Désiré 8 123*; 12 650
Cravan, Arthur 8 435, 436; 24 427
Craven, Arthur *see* CRAVAN, ARTHUR
Craven, George Grimston, 3rd Earl of Craven 22 809
Craven, Hawes 30 679, 681
Craven, William, 1st Earl of Craven 12 341; 29 800; 33 244
Craver, Margret 4 480
Cravo, Mario 26 60
Cravo Neto, Mario 8 123–4*
Cravotto, Mauricio 31 753, 758
Crawford, Alexander (William Crawford) Lindsay, 25th Earl of *see* LINDSAY, ALEXANDER (WILLIAM CRAWFORD), 25th Earl of Crawford
Crawford, David Alexander Edward Lindsay, 27th Earl of *see* LINDSAY, DAVID ALEXANDER EDWARD, 27th Earl of Crawford and 10th Earl of Balcarres
Crawford, Flora 29 602
Crawford, H. R. 2 740
Crawford, James Ludovic Lindsay, Earl of *see* LINDSAY, JAMES LUDOVIC, 26th Earl of Crawford
Crawford, Mary Lindsay 14 108
Crawford, Ralston 8 124*; 19 491; 25 462
Crawford, Thomas 8 124*; 31 610, 662
assistants 4 863
patrons and collectors 24 456
works 26 353, 539; 32 892
Crawford, W. S., and Son 7 652, 653
Crawhall, Joseph 8 125*
dealers 26 107
groups and movements 12 779; 19 891
works 4 364; 33 361
Crawshay, William 32 784
Craxton, John 8 125*; 22 751; 32 912
Cray, John 3 167; 25 637
Crayer, Gaspar de 8 125–7*
collaboration 4 222
patrons and collectors 25 221
pupils 28 364
works 3 559; 5 43; 8 *126*, *127*; 23 381

Crayfish, Master of the see CRABBE (VAN ESPLEGHEM), FRANS
Crayon: A Journal Devoted to the Graphic Arts 24 431
crayon d'Angleterre see PENCILS
crayon manner see under ENGRAVINGS → types
crayons 8 127–9*, 128; 25 477; 33 1
 conté 8 127, 128, 128, 129
 crayons de couleur 8 127
 lithograph 8 127, 128
 oil 8 127, 128
 trempé 8 128
 tusche 8 128
 wax 8 128, 129
 wood-encased see crayons de couleur
 see also CHALK; CHARCOAL; CONTÉ; CRAYONS DE COULEUR; PASTELS; PENCILS
Crea 27 498, 500
Creamer, Norman 11 808
cream-jugs see under JUGS → types
cream stone 1 856
creamware see under POTTERY → wares
Creangă, Horia 5 72; 8 131*; 26 709
Creara, Sante 5 32
Crease, Josephine 8 131–2*
Creation 33 575
Creative Colour 9 494
Creative Print movement 17 279, 295
Creative work see TVORCHESTVO
Creatura di Baciccio, Il see BIANCHI, PIETRO (ii)
Creccolini, Giovanni Antonio 8 132*
Crécy Château 11 658
 dairy 1 665; 32 76
 paintings 4 517
 sculpture 4 517; 10 764
credenze 7 835; 9 30
 see also SIDEBOARDS
credit cards see under CARDS → types
Credo Altarpiece 3 641, 641
Cree (Canada) 22 546, 670
 beadwork 22 639
 dress 22 636, 645
 embroidery 22 639, 645, 648
 painting 17 770; 22 597
 pouches 22 649
 quillwork 22 648, 650, 651
Cree (Plains) 22 551, 584
Creed, Cary 14 436
Creeft, José de 5 651; 8 132*; 21 389
Creek 22 552, 558
 beadwork 4 I1
Creeley, Robert 4 109
Cree-Metis 22 645
Creevykeel 25 508
Cregan, Martin 8 132–3*
Creighton, Henry 15 352
Creil 11 606
 St Evremont
 buttresses 5 318
Creixell, José 21 382
Crema
 Cathedral 13 64; 30 501
 S Maria della Croce 3 385, 385
Crema, Giovanni da see FONDULI, GIOVANNI PAULO
Crema, Giovanni Fonduli da see FONDULI DA CREMA, GIOVANNI
cremation towers see under TOWERS → types
cremation urns see URNS → types → funerary
crematory pavilions see under PAVILIONS (CREMATORY)
Cremer, Engelbert 7 586
Cremer, Ferdinand Robert 8 133
Cremer, Friedrich Albert 8 133
Cremer, Fritz 8 134*; 11 320; 13 729
Cremer, Jan 22 852
Cremer, Johann Baptist 8 133
Cremer, Johann Peter 8 133*
Cremer, Markus 8 133
Cremna Basilica 3 328
Cremnitz white see under PIGMENTS → types
Cremona 8 134–5*; 16 618
 Baptistery 3 192
 Cathedral of S Maria Assunta 4 775; 8 134, 134; 13 64; 16 625; 21 94; 30 501
 frescoes 4 194; 25 250
 sculpture 26 621
 Torrazzo 13 65
 woodwork 16 725
 Museo Civico Ala Ponzone 8 135, 537
 paintings 8 135; 12 288; 29 666
 Palazzo Affaitai see Museo Civico Ala Ponzone
 Palazzo Comunale 8 135
 Palazzo Stanga 30 501
 Palazzo Ugolani Dati see Museo Civico Ala Ponzone
 S Domenico 23 320
Cremona, Emmanuel 25 329
Cremona, Francesco da 28 730; 32 616
Cremona, Gerard of see GERARD OF CREMONA
Cremona, Giovanni da see FONDULI, GIOVANNI PAULO
Cremona, Girolamo da see GIROLAMO DA CREMONA
Cremona, Maffiolo da see MAFFIOLO DA CREMONA
Cremona, Nebridio da see NEBRIDIO DA CREMONA
Cremona, Tranquillo 8 135–7*
 dealers 13 714
 groups and movements 16 678; 21 527; 28 34
 teachers 3 857
 works 8 136, 137
Cremonese, Giuseppe 25 8
Cremonese, il see CALETTI, GIUSEPPE
Cremonini, Giovanni Battista 11 51; 12 499; 27 893
crenellations 8 137–8*; 9 553; 12 175; 21 550
crenels 21 546
Creo, Cristoforo 18 780
Creole 3 621; 7 601; 8 138*, 228; 11 757, 760; 27 809; 28 691
 architecture 13 878
 houses 11 757, 758
 jewellery 2 152; 11 759
Creole Colonial style 3 622; 13 875; 31 337, 337
crêpe 17 313
Crepel Pier see PIETER DIRCKSZ.
Crépin, Louis-Philippe 11 413
Crépu, Larice see LARICE CRÉPU
Créqui, Duc de 20 293
Créqui, Jean de 19 251
Créquy, Charles de Blanchefort de 6 36; 11 661; 19 238*; 28 8
Cres 8 174, 175
Crescens, C. Julius 9 49
Crescent Head, Marie I. Short farmhouse 2 743
Crescentino, Camaino di see CAMAINO DI CRESCENTINO
Crescent Potteries 29 117
Crescenzi (family) 26 397; 30 649
Crescenzi, Bartolomeo del see CAVAROZZI, BARTOLOMEO
Crescenzi, Crescentio 8 139
Crescenzi, Francesco 8 138, 139*
Crescenzi, Giacomo 8 138
Crescenzi, Giovanni Battista 8 138–9*; 20 741
 dealing 18 580
 pupils 6 112
Crescenzi, Giovanni Battista—cont.
 works 4 405; 5 725; 10 501; 20 70, 72; 22 68; 29 269, 340, 667
Crescenzi, Marcello, Bishop 26 397
Crescenzi, Piero de see PIERO DE CRESCENZI
Crescenzi, Pietro Paolo, Cardinal 8 138*
Crescenzi, Virgilio 8 138
Crescenzio, Pietro 8 139*; 12 107, 109
Cresci, Giovanfrancesco 28 307
Crescione see CRISCUOLO
Cresconius (family) 5 892
Crespel, James 10 333
Crespel, Sebastian 10 333
Crespi (i) (family) 8 140
Crespi (ii), Antonio 8 140, 145
Crespi, Camilla 6 340
Crespi, Cristoforo Benigno 8 146–7*
Crespi, Daniele 8 147–9*; 21 526
 attributions 20 738
 patrons and collectors 4 427; 8 146; 22 26; 28 479
 pupils 6 343; 7 356
 reproductive prints by others 19 636
 teachers 21 849
 works 8 147, 148; 21 526
Crespi (i), Domingo 8 139, 140
Crespi, Giovanni Battista see CERANO
Crespi (ii), Giuseppe Maria 4 277; 5 653; 8 140–45*; 11 188; 12 658; 16 670
 frames 11 393, 394
 patrons and collectors
 Benedict XIV, Pope (reg 1740–58) 3 707
 Buonacorsi, Raimondo 5 178
 Charles-Emanuel III, Duke of Savoy and King of Sardinia (reg 1730–73) 28 18
 Conti, Stefano 7 780
 Ghisilieri, Francesco 12 559
 Medici, Ferdinando de', Grand Prince of Tuscany (1663–1713) 21 30
 Ottoboni, Pietro, Cardinal (1667–1740) 23 637
 Ruffo, Tommaso, Cardinal, Archbishop of Ferrara 27 316
 Sagredo, Zaccaria 27 521
 Savoy, Eugene of, Prince (1663–1736) 28 15
 Tessin, Carl Gustav, Count 30 523
 pupils 12 658; 13 746; 19 634; 20 848
 reproductive prints by others 20 849
 teachers 7 309
 works 8 141, 142, 143, 144; 12 292; 29 669; 32 459
Crespi, il see CERANO
Crespi (i), Lleonard 8 140
Crespi (ii), Luigi 7 715; 8 140, 146*; 19 117
 patrons and collectors 8 146
 personal collection 2 125
 teachers 8 145
 works 4 492
Crespi (i), Miguel 8 140
Crespi, Ortensio 6 340
Crespi (i), Pedro 8 140
Crespi (i), Pere 8 140
Crespi, Raffaele 6 337
Crespi d'Adda 24 851
Crespin, Adolphe 10 658; 14 138; 28 899
Crespin, Antoine du Bec 17 685
Crespin, Paul 8 149*; 10 332; 19 593; 29 432
 patrons and collectors 27 641
 works 10 330, 332; 14 857
Crespista style 32 170
Crespo, Cirilo Almeida see ALMEIDA CRESPO, CIRILO
Crespo, Joaquín 32 170
Crespo, Luis García see GARCÍA CRESPO, LUIS
Crespo, Luis Pecul y see PECUL Y CRESPO, LUIS
Crespo, Manuel García see GARCÍA CRESPO, MANUEL
Crespo, Ricard 29 309
Cressac Chapel 18 154
Cressant, Jacob 8 149–50*; 22 859; 32 798
Cressant, Jacob Matheus 8 150; 22 859
Cressbrook Mill (Derbys) 10 748
Cresselly (Dyfed) 32 788
Cressent, Charles 8 150*; 11 577, 626; 20 468; 23 516
 groups and movements 19 723; 26 494
 patrons and collectors 11 631; 23 517; 27 223; 28 527
 works 7 657; 11 592, 593, 595, 596; 23 458, 514; 24 149; 26 84, 84
Cressent, François 8 150
Cresset Press 4 366; 17 850
Cressey, Hugh 10 303
Cressing Temple Barley Barn (Essex) 27 126, 129; 30 908; 32 275
Cresswell, John 26 489
Cresta Silks 7 483; 14 465
Cresti, Domenico see PASSIGNANO, DOMENICO
crests 12 272; 14 404, 409, 412–13, 412, 413, 414, 421; 17 302
Creswell, H(arold) B(ulkeley) 8 151*; 32 783
Creswell, K(eppel) A(rchibald) C(ameron) 8 151*; 9 768; 16 101, 548, 550
Creswick, Thomas 4 86; 8 152*
 collaboration 2 128; 7 798
 groups and movements 7 436
Cret, Paul (Philippe) 8 152–3*
 collaboration 13 337
 pupils 17 723
 staff 17 723
 works 8 470, 470, 821, 821; 10 684; 24 598
Cretan, Theophanes the see THEOPHANES THE CRETAN
creta viridis see PIGMENTS → types → green earth
Crete 8 153–7*; 9 511; 13 362; 16 103; 21 651, 651; 26 852, 908, 919
 agorai 8 154
 archaeology 4 607; 14 275
 architecture 8 154
 Byzantine 8 155
 Minoan 8 153; 18 210; 21 658–9, 661–5*
 Roman 8 154–5
 Venetian 8 156
 vernacular 32 294
 armour 13 584
 baptisteries 8 155
 bathtubs 21 667
 beads 21 687
 bone 8 153; 21 681
 bone-carvings 21 680*
 bronze 8 154; 21 679, 679–80, 688
 Minoan 8 153, 154; 21 688*
 busts 13 443
 cauldrons 8 154
 caves 8 153
 cellae 8 154
 cemeteries 8 153
 ceramics 13 358
 chalices 21 665
 chlorite 21 656
 chronologies 14 334; 21 655*, 655
 churches 8 155, 156–7
Crete—cont.
 coins 8 154
 collections 21 691–2*
 combs (hair) 21 682
 concrete 8 155
 cups 21 688
 diadems 21 686
 domes 8 155
 ewers 21 688
 ex-votos 2 415
 faience (i) (glass) 8 153; 21 658, 682*, 683–4*, 683
 fibulae 8 154; 13 601
 figurines 8 154; 13 578; 21 656, 657–8, 678–80, 679, 680, 681*, 683*, 683
 filigree 21 687
 flasks 21 670
 forgeries 21 690–91*
 fortifications 32 159
 fortresses 8 156
 forts 8 154
 friezes 21 675*
 furniture 13 357
 goblets 21 669, 671
 gold 8 153; 21 686–7*, 686, 687, 688*, 688
 harbours 8 154
 helmets 8 154
 houses 13 396; 21 655–6
 country 8 153; 21 664*
 town 21 662, 664*
 iconography 21 677
 icons 7 850
 Byzantine 9 622
 Post-Byzantine 8 157; 25 331–2*, 332, 333, 333–4*
 Venetian Empire 8 157, 157
 inlays 21 682*, 684*
 inscriptions 8 154
 iron 8 154
 ivory-carvings
 Archaic 8 154
 Minoan 8 153; 21 680–82*, 681
 Orientalizing style 8 154
 jars
 bridge-spouted 21 668
 burial 21 657
 Minoan 21 665, 668, 669, 670
 jasper 21 685
 jewellery
 Minoan 8 153; 21 657, 658, 682, 683–4*, 686–7*
 Orientalizing style 8 154
 jugs 21 665, 666, 756
 kantharoi 21 658
 kraters 21 672
 lathes 21 689
 limestone 2 879
 Madonneri 25 331
 marble 8 155
 martyria 8 155
 metalwork 8 154; 21 652, 658, 659–60, 686–7*, 688*
 mosaics 8 155
 museums 8 157; 21 691–2*
 obsidian 21 689
 opisthodomoi 8 154
 painting 8 156; 25 330
 floor 21 660
 religious 20 51, 51
 sarcophagi 2 879
 vase 8 154
 wall 21 676
 Byzantine 8 155; 18 460–61
 Minoan 8 153; 21 657, 659, 660, 660, 672–7*, 674, 676, 677
 Post-Byzantine 25 334
 Venetian Empire 8 156–7
 palaces 8 153; 21 651, 657, 661, 663–4*; 23 808
 pastophoria 8 155
 pavements 8 154, 155
 pendants (jewellery) 21 687, 687
 periods
 Byzantine 8 155*
 Early Minoan (c. 3500/3000–c. 2050 BC) 21 655, 655–7*

Crete
  periods—cont.
    Final Neolithic (*c.* 3800-*c.* 3500/3000 BC) 21 *655*
    Late Minoan (*c.* 1600-*c.* 1050 BC) 21 *655*, 658–61*
    Late Neolithic (*c.* 4500-*c.* 3800 BC) 21 *655*
    Middle Minoan (*c.* 2050-*c.* 1600 BC) 21 *655*, 657–8*
    Neolithic 8 153*
    Roman 8 154–5*
    Sub-Minoan (*c.* 1050-*c.* 1000 BC) 21 *655*
    Venetian 8 155–7*
  pithoi 8 154; 18 *167*; 21 671
  plaques 21 *681*
  polychromy 8 154
  potter's wheels 21 667
  pottery 13 540, 542; 21 *756*
    Abstract style 21 670
    Alternating style 21 671
    Ayios Onouphrios I ware 21 666
    Ayios Onouphrios II ware 21 666, *666*
    Barbotine ware 21 667
    Byzantine 9 631
    Close style 21 *669*, 672
    Early Christian (*c.* AD 250-843) 9 631
    Fine Grey ware 21 666
    Floral style 21 *669*, 670
    Geometric (*c.* 900-*c.* 700 BC) 8 154; 13 497; 21 670
    Hellenistic 13 539
    Kamares ware 17 751; 21 657, *665*, 668, *668*
    Koumasa ware 21 *665*, 666
    Lebena ware 21 666
    Marine style 21 *669*, 670, *670*
    Minoan 8 153; 21 657, 661, 665–72*, *665*, *666*, *668*, *669*, *670*, *672*; 24 *591*
    Open style 21 672
    Orientalizing style 8 154; 13 498, 502
    Palace style 21 *669*, 671
    Plain style 21 672
    Post-Kamares ware 21 668
    Prehistoric 8 153
    Proto-Corinthian 8 154
    Protogeometric 8 154; 13 493
    Pyrgos ware 21 *665*, 666
    Red-figure 13 534
    Scored ware 21 666
    Special Palatial tradition 21 *669*, *670*, 670–71
    Tortoiseshell Ripple ware 21 668
    Vasiliki ware 21 666–7
    West Slope ware 13 539
    White-on-dark ware 21 *665*, 667
    Wild Goat style 8 154
  pronaoi 8 154
  protomes 8 154
  prytaneia 8 154
  pyxides (vases) 21 *656*
  reliefs 13 582
  rhyta 21 668, *669*
  rings 21 *685*, *686*
  ritual objects 8 153
  rock crystal 26 484–5
  rotondas 8 155
  sanctuaries 8 153; 18 164
  sarcophagi 2 *879*; 8 155; 21 657; 26 855; 27 825
  scripts 8 153
  sculpture
    bronze 8 154; 21 *679*, 679–80
    cult statues 8 154, 155
    Daidalic 13 443
    Minoan 8 153; 21 656, 657–8, 659, *663*, 678–80*, *679*
    Roman 8 155
  seals
    Minoan 8 153; 21 656–7, 658, 682, 684–6*
    Orientalizing style 8 154
Crete
  seals—cont.
    Popular group 21 686
    ring 21 *685*, *686*
    stamp 21 684
    Talismanic group 21 686
  serpentine 21 *690*
  shrines (i) (cult) 21 *663*, 663–4*
  silver 21 *658*, 686–7*, 688*
  soapstone 18 *168*
  staircases 29 *521*
  stelae 8 155
  stoas 8 154
  stone 8 154; 21 656, 659, 689–90
  stone-carvings 8 153
  stone vessels 21 656, 659, 689–90*
  stucco 13 603; 29 814
  temples
    Archaic 8 154
    Greece, ancient 18 *210*, 210–11
    Hellenistic 8 154
    7th cent. BC 8 154
  terracotta 8 154; 13 *443*, 582; 21 *680*; 27 825
  theatres 8 155
  tombs
    chamber 13 396; 21 659
    Minoan 18 164; 21 656, 657, 659, 664–5*; 31 107
    tholos 21 656; 30 738
  tools 8 153, 154
  towns 21 664*
  trade 21 652–3*
    obsidian 8 306
    pottery 8 309
    vases 8 313
  urban planning 8 154
  urns 8 154
  vases 8 154; 18 *168*; 21 *689*, *690*
  villas 8 155
  volutes 8 154
  walls 8 154; 21 662
  weapons 8 153, 154; 21 688*
  writing 8 153; 18 167
  see also MINOAN
Créteil, Abbaye de *see* ABBAYE DE CRÉTEIL
Cretensis, Dictys *see* DICTYS CRETENSIS
Cretey, Pierre-Louis 8 157–8*
Creti, Donato 4 277; 8 158–60*
  patrons and collectors 4 560; 27 316
  pupils 4 320; 13 330; 23 497
  reproductive prints by others 20 849
  teachers 24 227
  works 8 *158*, *160*; 31 357
Creti, Gioseffo 8 158
Crétien, Felix 8 907
Cretté, Louis 3 591; 5 51; 11 610
Creusa Painter 13 525
Creussen 8 160–61*; 12 *361*, 428, 429
Creutz (family) 11 111
Creutz, Daniel 19 93
Creutz, Gustav Filip 2 722; 8 161*; 30 107
Creuznach, Conrad Faber 11 453
Crevalcore, Antonio da *see* ANTONIO (LEONELLI) DA CREVALCORE
Creve, Jean 10 707
Crevel, René 8 439; 21 709; 30 17, 18, 20
Crevillente 15 59
Crévoisier, Marie-Jeanne *see* CLEMENS, MARIE-JEANNE
Crevole Madonna 9 341
Crewe, Bertie 23 122
Crewe, Emma 33 22
crewelwork *see under* EMBROIDERY → types
Crewenna Pottery 23 69
Criard, Mathieu 8 161*; 11 590; 17 666
cribs 8 107
crib tables *see under* TABLES → types
Criccieth Castle (Gwynedd) 32 781
Crichton, Alexander 22 531
Crichton, J. (*fl* 1883-4) 28 262
Crichton, John (*b* 1917) 23 67
Crichton Castle (Lothian) 31 230
Crichton Royal (Dumfires & Galloway) 28 228
Crichton-Stuart, John, 4th Marquess of Bute 28 266; 30 327
Crichton-Stuart, John Patrick, 3rd Marquess of Bute 29 796–7*
  architecture 2 5; 5 194, 340; 6 61; 13 203; 17 610; 28 174, 230; 32 784
  sculpture 17 610
Crick-Kuntziger, M. 3 619
Crickley Hill (Glos) 21 551; 25 535
Crickmay, G. R. 27 626
Crico, Lorenzo 10 853
Cricolini, Giovanni Antonio *see* CRECCOLINI, GIOVANNI ANTONIO
Cricoli Villa 32 547
Cricot 17 446
Crighton, Matthew 28 264
Crilley, Margaret *see* CLARKE, MARGARET
Crimca, Anastasie 8 161*; 26 708, 712
Crimpen, Adriaen Dircksz. van 8 102; 27 256
crimson *see under* PIGMENTS → types
Crimson Rose (*Alaya roza*) 4 178; 27 809, 855
Crippa, Roberto 8 161–2*; 16 681
Criscior Church 26 711
Criscuolo, Giovan Angelo 8 162*
Criscuolo, Giovan Filippo 8 162*; 27 479
Criscuolo, Mariangela 8 162
Criseby factory 8 748
Crisp, Frank 23 340
Crisp, Henry 12 840; 28 349
Crisp, Quentin 21 761
Crisp, William FitzJohn 23 53
Crispe, Nicholas 3 25
Crispi, Tiberio 10 809; 22 16
Crispijn, John 22 896
Crispo, Tiberio, Cardinal 1 605
Crispolto di Polto da Bettona 3 701
Crispus 9 655
Criss, Francis 26 126
Crissé, Lancelot-Théodore Turpin de *see* TURPIN DE CRISSÉ, LANCELOT-THÉODORE
Cristal da Badalona 29 330
Cristall, Joshua 8 163*; 32 903
Cristalleries de Vonêche 3 594
Cristalleries du Val-Saint-Lambert 5 583; 24 57
cristallo *see under* GLASS → types
Cristi, Ximena 6 598
Cristiani, Fabrizio 26 148
Cristina, Regent 6 19
Cristino da Silva, João 8 163*; 25 298; 28 781
  works 2 207
Cristino da Silva, João Ribeiro 8 163
Cristino da Silva, Luís (Ribeiro Carvalhosa) 8 163–4*
  works 19 467; 25 294
Cristofali, Adriano 27 759; 31 821; 32 342
Cristofani, M. 25 245
Cristofano, Giovanni di *see* GIOVANNI DI CRISTOFANO
Cristofano, Maso di *see* MASO DI CRISTOFANO
Cristofano dal Borgo *see* GHERARDI, CRISTOFANO
Cristofano (di Papi) dell'Altissimo *see* ALTISSIMO, CRISTOFANO (DI PAPI) DELL'
Cristofano di Michele Martini *see* ROBETTA
Cristofari, Fabio 26 810
Cristofari, Pietro Paolo 5 815; 26 810
Cristofol, Leandro 29 286
Cristofori, Bartolomeo 22 372
Cristoforo, Giovanni di *see* GIOVANNI DI CRISTOFORO
Cristoforo da Cassano 20 783
Cristoforo di Bindoccio 28 687
Cristoforo di Geremia 8 164*; 19 854
  patrons and collectors 20 322
  works 20 918; 25 19
Cristoforo di Jacopo Biondi da Bologna 8 164–5*; 32 626
Cristoforo di Michele Martini *see* ROBETTA
Crişul Alb, Mihu de la *see* MIHU DE LA CRIŞUL ALB
Critchlow, Keith 2 361
Crit Church 13 189
Criterion 16 877
Critica, La 24 427
Critica d'Arte 19 637; 24 448
Critical Realism 23 16; 24 464, *464*; 32 836
criticism of architecture *see under* ARCHITECTURE
criticism of art *see* ART CRITICISM
Critopol, Antim, Metropolitan of Wallachia 26 720
Critz, Emanuel de 8 166
Critz, John de (i) (*c.* 1551/2-1642) 8 165; 12 514; 14 297; 16 823; 28 466, 666; 33 387
  works 8 *165*
Critz, John de (ii) (*c.* 1591-*c.* 1642) 8 165; 24 752
Critz, Thomas de 8 166
Crivelli 27 445
Crivelli, Andrea 2 780; 15 866
Crivelli, Angelo 12 118; 16 562
Crivelli, Carlo (Giovanni) 8 166–72*; 16 661, 662; 32 159
  collaboration 8 171
  methods 30 427
  patrons and collectors 3 740; 4 602; 13 272; 19 290; 21 849; 29 46; 31 905
  pupils 1 600
  works 2 2, 594; 8 *167*, *168*, *169*, *170*; 15 137; 16 470, 773
Crivelli, Giacomo 8 166, 171
Crivelli, Giuseppe Dioigio 14 190
Crivelli, Jacopo 8 166
Crivelli, Protasio 23 368
Crivelli, Ridolfo 8 166
Crivelli, Taddeo 8 172–3*
  assistants 16 848
  patrons and collectors 4 18; 7 782; 11 4; 12 666
  works 4 *19*; 8 *173*
Crivelli, Vittore 8 166, 171–2*
  works 29 27
Crivelli carpets *see under* CARPETS → types
crizzling *see under* GLASS → techniques
Crna Gora *see* MONTENEGRO
Crnčić, Menci Clement 8 173*
Crngrob, Bolfgangus of *see* BOLFGANGUS OF CRNGROB
Crngrob Church 28 *858*, 860, 862
Crnković, I. 8 177
Crnojević 22 *17*
Croanjingalong
  house 32 *307*
Croat 8 174
Croatia 8 *174*, 174–81*; 33 571
  architecture 8 175–7*; 26 594; 32 293
  bronze 21 *316*
  cathedrals 12 *667*; 25 *252*
  ceramics 8 180
Croatia—cont.
  churches 8 175, *176*; 33 *592*
  collections 8 180–81*
  decorative arts 8 180*
  education (art) 8 181
  embroidery 8 180
  fortifications 32 *159*
  glass 8 180
  gold 8 180
  guilds 8 180
  houses 8 175
  jewellery 8 180
  lace 8 180
  manuscript illumination 8 177
  marble 23 *93*
  museums 8 180–81*
  painting 8 177–9*, *179*; 22 *441*
  palaces 8 176; 9 *330*, *558*; 29 *417*
  portraits 21 *316*
  rock art 25 475
  sculpture 8 177–9*
    bronze 21 *316*
    marble 23 *93*
    relief 8 *177*
    Renaissance 23 *93*
    Romanesque 8 177
  stone 8 *177*
  urban planning 8 175
  vaults (ceiling) 23 93
Croce, Aflalo and Gasperini 4 715; 8 181*
Croce, Baldassarre 8 181–2*
  collaboration 1 552
  works 1 *552*; 8 *182*; 33 587
Croce, Benedetto 1 179; 2 508; 8 182–3*; 24 448
  works 1 181; 2 517; 10 690; 16 782
  on art 1 172, 174; 28 114
Croce, Fernando della 19 497
Croce, Francesco 21 159, 519, 532, 534
Croce, Giulio Cesare 20 849
Croce, Plínio 8 181*
Crocefissi, Simone dei *see* SIMONE DEI CROCEFISSI
Crocetti, Venanzio 17 622; 24 278; 26 810
crochet 3 440; 16 34; 18 593; 27 318; 30 549, *549*, 550, 563
crochet hooks 4 314
Croci, Antonio 26 106
Crocifissaio, Girolamo del *see* MACCHIETTI, GIROLAMO (DI FRANCESCO DI MARIOTTO)
Crocifisso dei Bianchi, Master of the 20 653*, 709
Crocino 7 311
Crocke, R. 10 674
Crocker, Edward 19 611
Crocker, Templeton 11 727
crocket capitals *see under* CAPITAL → types
crockets 8 183–4*, *183*
Crocodilopolis *see* MEDINET EL-FAIYUM
crocoite 24 799
Crocq, Domange 5 437
Crocq, Jan 22 455
Croes, Jan van 11 221
Croeseids *see under* COINS → types
Croesus, King of Lydia (*reg* 560-47 BC) 1 888; 10 430; 13 372, 575; 15 893; 19 841; 26 296
Croft (Leics), St Michael 2 71
Croft, José Pedro 25 302
Croft Cups 25 759
Croft-Murray, E. 10 377
Crofton & Benjamin 9 427; 29 106
Croggan, Thomas John 7 480
Croggon, William 2 541; 7 480
Crogi, Pietro di Achille 28 682
Crohin-de la Fontaine Hours *see under* BOOKS OF HOURS → individual manuscripts
Croisant, Jacob *see* CRESSANT, JACOB
Croix, Camille de la 25 89

Croix, Pierre Frédéric de La *see* LA CROIX, PIERRE FRÉDÉRIC DE
Croix, Susanna de La *see* LA CROIX, SUSANNA DE
Croizette, Pauline-Marie-Charlotte 5 812
Croizette, Sophie 5 *813*
Croker, John 8 184*; 20 923
Crolius, William 8 184*; 31 635
Crolius and Remmey 8 184*; 31 635
Crollius, Johan Willem *see* CROLIUS, WILLIAM
Crom, Matthias 33 268
Crô Magnon 25 472
Cromarty Court House (Highlands) 31 239
Crome, Emily 8 185
Crome, Frederick James 8 185
Crome, John 8 184–5*
groups and movements 10 374; 23 248
patrons and collectors 31 465
personal collection 33 178
pupils 29 548; 31 465; 32 585
works 8 *185*; 10 555; 18 715; 23 *249*
Crome, John Berney 4 808; 8 185; 23 248
Crome, William Henry 8 185
Cromek, Robert Hartley 4 120; 8 186*; 28 86
Cromford (Derbys) 21 600
Cromford Mill 10 748
Masson Mill 10 748
cromlechs 8 186*
Crommelin, Louis 16 33; 19 418
Crommelynck, Albert-Jean 10 557
Crommelynck, Aldo 20 604; 24 726
Crommelynck, Fernand 7 769; 21 410
Crommelynck, Piero 24 726
Crommelynck, Robert-Hubert 10 557
Crompton, Dennis 2 308
Crompton, Rebecca 10 354
Crompton, Samuel 30 540
Cromwell (family) 8 186
Cromwell, Oliver 8 186*
medals 20 923
paintings 7 794; 29 801; 32 797
sculpture 33 412
Cromwell, Ralph, 3rd Baron Cromwell 6 603; 8 43; 30 365, 366
Cromwell, Thomas, Earl of Essex 8 187*; 14 670
Cromwell chairs *see under* CHAIRS → types
Cronaca 8 187–8*
collaboration 3 15; 27 739
patrons and collectors 29 782
works 2 295; 8 *188*; 11 178, 211, 705; 16 *629*, 635; 23 809; 27 656, 735; 31 237; 32 14
Cronaca bizantina 26 776
Cronache d'arte 20 158
Crone, Peter 2 742; 8 189*
Crone, Robert 16 14
Cronenburgh, Adriaen von 32 784
Cronenwett, Joal 25 218
Crónica de la Realidad 10 443
Cronin, Vincent 13 811
Cronjević, Djordje *see* GEORGE III, Prince of Montenegro
Cronkhill (Salop) 10 234; 22 *526*, 740; 32 554
Cronqvist, Lena 8 189*; 30 82
Cronstedt, Carl Johan 8 189–90*; 30 88
works 11 91; 29 689; 30 89, 97
Cronström, Daniel 3 752; 8 68, 190*; 30 105
Croock, Hubert de 3 556
Crookshank, Anne 16 38
Croom d'Abitot (Hereford & Worcs), St Mary Magdalene 11 255
Croome, George 4 479
Croome Court (Hereford & Worcs) 4 875; 23 859; 32 540
frames 11 431
furniture 7 486; 10 295; 11 119; 15 165
sculpture 6 528
tapestries 4 515; 10 277
Croos, Anthonie Jansz. van 23 788
cropmarks 2 *300*
Cropsey, Jasper F(rancis) 8 190–91*
groups and movements 14 843; 31 602
patrons and collectors 17 823; 31 870
pupils 17 616
works 8 *191*
Cropthorne (Hereford & Worcs), St Michael 2 70
Croquison, Arthur 8 191
Croquison, Pierre-Nicolas 3 548; 8 191*; 26 526
Cros, Charles 20 257
Cros, Georges 30 422
Cros, (César-Isidore-) Henri 8 191–2*, 204; 10 199; 11 613
Cros, Jean du 2 872
Crosato, Giovanni Battista 8 192–3*; 31 444
patrons and collectors 28 18
works 8 *192*; 16 719; 29 736
Crosby, Sumner McKnight 27 539
Crosby Brown, Mary 22 376
Crosby Brown Collection *see under* NEW YORK → museums → Metropolitan Museum of Art
Crosby & Morse 4 480
Croscombe (Somerset), St Mary 28 294
Crose, Francis 16 16
crosiers 8 193–4*; 14 404, 413; 32 389*
historical and regional traditions
England 8 *194*; 10 322
Gothic 10 322; 13 176
Hungary 26 *687*
Insular art 15 873
Ireland 15 873
Italy 13 176
Romanesque 8 *194*; 26 *687*
materials
ivory 8 *194*; 13 176
Cross, Arthur 19 431
Cross, C. F. 30 542
Cross, Henri Edmond 8 204*
dealers 19 10
groups and movements 22 745, 746
patrons and collectors 10 885
works 11 418; 13 323
Cross, John 26 107
Cross, Lowell 18 809; 29 97
Cross, Michael 14 755; 29 800
Cross, Peter 8 205*; 21 640, 641
Cross bond *see under* BONDING
crossbow-bolts 7 97
crossbows *see under* BOWS → types
cross-domed churches *see under* CHURCHES → types
Crosse, Richard 21 644
crossed looping textiles *see under* TEXTILES → techniques
crosses 8 195–204*
historical and regional traditions
Anglo-Saxon 2 68–9, *69*, 70; 10 322
Byzantine 8 *199*; 9 658
Carolingian 5 796, 807
Celtic 32 786, *787*
Czech Republic 8 *414*
Early Christian (*c.* AD 250-843) 8 195
crosses
historical and regional traditions—cont.
England 2 *69*; 10 322, 343; 26 *697*
Germany 12 442
Gothic 13 165
Ireland 1 468; 15 876–8*, *877*
Isle of Man 32 516
Pictish art 24 737, *737*
Romanesque 26 *697*
Scotland 24 *737*
Spain 13 165; 17 515; 29 332
Wales 32 786, *787*
materials
bone 8 203
brass 8 200
bronze 8 199, 200, 203
copper 8 200
enamel 8 *201*, *203*, *414*
garnets 8 *414*
gems 8 201
gold 8 201, 203, *203*, 204; 9 *659*
hardstones 8 *199*, *201*
ivory 26 *697*
jet 17 514, 515
leather 5 807
pearls 8 201
porcelain 8 202
rock crystal 8 *414*
schist 15 *892*
silver 8 199, 201, 203, 204; 9 656, 658; 29 *334*
silver-gilt 8 *199*, *200*, *201*, 201, *414*
stone 1 468; 7 *460*; 24 *737*; 32 *787*
wood 8 203
types
altar 8 199–201*, *200*, *201*, 202*, *202*
Anjou *see* Papal
arbor vitae 8 195
archiepiscopal 8 204
crux ansata 8 195
crux commissa *see* tau
crux gammata *see* SWASTIKAS
disc *see* Scheibenkreuz
Eleanor 2 295; 8 197–8*, *198*, 611; 13 53, 81; 22 44; 23 368; 25 14
Greek 8 195
High 8 195*
Anglo-Saxon 2 71; 27 *453*
England 8 195–6*; 10 259; 32 *529*
Insular art 7 *460*; 15 *877*; 17 *889*
Ireland 7 *460*; 8 *196*, 196–7*; 15 *877*; 16 18–19; 17 888–9*, *889*; 26 618; 31 402
Romanesque 26 618
Scotland 15 *892*; 27 *453*
Viking 2 71; 32 *529*
Wales 32 *787*
jewellery 17 518, 520, 524, 526, 527
Byzantine 9 *659*
Early Christian (*c.* AD 250-843) 9 *659*
khatchk'ars 2 426, *435*, 435–6; 8 198–9*
Latin 8 195
Living 8 195
Lorraine *see* Papal
Maltese 8 195
market 21 893
montjoie 8 197*
monumental 8 195*
Papal 8 195
Patriarchal 8 195
pectoral 8 202–4*, *203*
portable 8 199*
processional 8 199–201*, 202*
Byzantine 8 199–200*; 9 656
Early Christian (*c.* AD 250-843) 9 656
Gothic 13 *165*
crosses
types
processional—cont.
Ireland 8 *202*
Spain 13 *165*; 29 *334*
see also RELIQUARIES → types → cross
ring-headed *see* High
Russian Orthodox 8 195
St Andrew's 8 195
St Anthony's *see* tau
Scheibenkreuz 28 71*
swastikas *see* SWASTIKAS
tau 8 195
triumphal *see* ROODS
Y-shaped 8 195
cross feet 8 205*
cross frames *see under* TIMBER STRUCTURES → types
crosshatching *see* HATCHING
crossing piers *see under* PIERS (ii) (MASONRY) → types
crossing towers *see under* TOWERS → types
cross-in-square churches *see under* CHURCHES → types
Crossland, W. H. 14 688; 28 279
Crossley, J., & Sons 5 832; 9 295; 10 358; 14 67; 28 248
Crossley, John 5 831
Crossley Gallery 1 147
Crossley Print Workshop 1 147
cross-line screen printing *see under* PRINTING → processes
Crossman, Babbit 31 652
Crossman, West & Leonard 31 652
Cross of Abbess Mathilde and Duke Otto 8 201, *201*; 26 145
Cross of Abbess Theophanu 9 661
Cross of Charlemagne 26 144
Cross of Cong 20 77; 24 562; 26 592, 688; 32 530
Cross of Desiderius 26 143
Cross of Justin II 8 *199*
Cross of Paschal I 9 660; 26 144, *144*
Cross of Philip II Augustus 13 168
Cross of St Eligius 11 613; 20 762
Cross of the Monk Raphail 26 392
Cross of the Oath of the Order of the Golden Fleece 13 158
cross reliquaries *see under* RELIQUARIES → types
Cross River bronzes 10 124
Cross River monoliths 10 123, *123*
cross stitch *see under* STITCHES
cross-vaulted churches *see under* CHURCHES → types
cross-vaults *see* VAULTS (CEILING) → types → groin
Crothall, Ross 2 120, 751; 4 882; 18 689
Crotti, Jean 8 205–6*; 31 503
groups and movements 8 435, 438; 9 354
reproductive prints by others 32 577
Crouch, Butler and Savage 12 590
Crouch, Dora 1 13
Crouch, Joseph 2 570
Crouch, Nathaniel 10 176
Croucher, John 23 70
Crouch & Wilson 23 54
Crousaz, Abraham de 18 873
Crousaz, Rodolphe de 18 873
Crousse 19 388
Crousse & Paez 7 343
Crouwel, Joseph 8 206*
Crow 22 551, 584, 636, 673
dress 22 649
guilds 22 650
knives 22 616
regalia 22 635
ritual objects 22 *557*
shields 22 *562*
shirts 22 636
trade 22 649
Crow, Gonzalo Endara *see* ENDARA CROW, GONZALO
Crow Belt 22 653
Crowcombe Court 10 279
Crowe, Eyre 8 206*
Crowe, J(oseph) A(rthur) 2 560; 8 206–7*
collaboration 6 100, 101; 16 782
works 9 200
Crowe, Sylvia 8 207*
Crowe, Victoria 9 725
Crowe Corselet 13 584, *584*
Crowfoot, J. W. 27 669
Crowl, Robert 10 483
Crowland Abbey (Lincs) 2 77; 7 453
Crowland Psalter *see under* PSALTERS → individual manuscripts
Crowle (Hereford & Worcs), St John the Baptist 26 613
Crowley, Grace 2 748, 771; 3 124
Crowley, Nicholas Joseph 8 207*; 16 16
Crown Derby Porcelain Co. *see* ROYAL CROWN PORCELAIN CO.
crown glass *see under* GLASS → types
Crown House Ltd 9 726; 33 13
Crowninshield, Frank 1 438, 439
Crowninshield, Frederick 3 740
Crown Lynn Factory 23 68, 69
works 23 *68*
Crown of St Wenceslas 8 412; 26 80
Crown of Thorns 5 664
Crown Point Airport 31 335
Crown Point Press 5 382; 20 609
crowns 14 404, 413; 26 79–80*
historical and regional traditions
Africa 1 *298*, *353*
Byzantine 9 653; 26 79
Carolingian 5 807
Chavín culture 29 *214*
China 7 25, *25*, 75, 76, 108, 110–12, *111*
Early Christian (*c.* AD 250-843) 9 653
England 12 *866*
Guyana 13 875
Indian subcontinent 15 730
Iraq 16 *538*
Islamic 16 537–9*, *538*
Japan 17 386
Korea 18 349, *350*, 350–51
Nigeria 1 *353*
Nubia 23 286, *286*
Ottonian 23 656
Peru 29 *214*
Sasanian 1 888
South America, Pre-Columbian 29 *214*
Spain 29 345; 32 *617*
Syria-Palestine 30 183
Visigothic 29 345; 32 *617*, 618*
Yoruba 1 *298*, *353*, 353–4; 33 557–8, *558*
materials
agate 7 111, *111*
amber 7 110, 111, *111*
beads 1 *298*, 353; 17 386; 33 557–8, *558*
bronze 18 349
coral 7 111, *111*
feathers 7 110, 111, *111*, 112; 13 875
gems 32 *617*
glass 7 110
gold 7 110, *111*; 12 *866*; 18 *350*, 350–51; 23 656; 29 *214*; 32 *617*
hardstones 23 *286*
jade 7 111, *111*; 18 *350*
pearls 7 110, 111, *111*, 112
reeds 15 730
rubies 7 112
silver 7 25, *25*; 23 *286*
silver-gilt 7 110
turquoise 7 111, *111*

crowns
materials—cont.
wire **7** 110
see also PAPAL TIARAS
Crown Toy Co. **31** 261
Crown Works, Burslem **7** 798
Crowther, John **4** 600, 601
Croxhall, Samuel **31** 871
Croxton, John **19** 566
works **19** *567*
Cröy (family) **7** 773; **13** 905; **26** 744
Cröy, Charles III de *see* CHIMAY, CHARLES III DE CRÖY, Prince de
Cröy, Philippe de *see* CHIMAY, PHILIPPE II DE CRÖY, Prince de
Croydon (Kent)
airport **1** 494
Waddon Marsh power station **25** 403
Croyland Abbey *see* CROWLAND ABBEY (LINCS)
Croys, Louis **28** 388
Crozat (family) **10** 753; **25** 395; **32** 74
Crozat, Antoine **8** 208; **32** 511
Crozat, Mme Antoine **2** *851*
Crozat, Joseph-Antoine, Marquis de Tugny *see* TUGNY, JOSEPH-ANTOINE CROZAT, Marquis de
Crozat, Louis-Antoine, Baron de Thiers *see* THIERS, LOUIS-ANTOINE CROZAT, Baron de
Crozat, Louis-François, Marquis de Châtel *see* CHÂTEL, LOUIS-FRANÇOIS CROZAT, Marquis de
Crozat, Pierre **3** 18; **8** 208–9*; **24** 805
architecture **5** 888; **11** 657; **23** 458
catalogues **2** 239; **7** 714
collaboration **31** 69
collections **11** 662, 663; **17** 684; **19** 369; **20** 416; **25** 664; **26** 732; **27** 438; **30** 727
dealing **11** 662; **23** 516
decorative works **19** 89
drawings **5** 866; **9** 229; **16** 815; **18** 626; **19** 89; **20** 417; **24** 834; **26** 469; **30** 524; **32** 8
engravings **19** 10; **26** 70
gems **12** 266; **13** 771
mounts (works on paper and scrolls) **22** 236
paintings **18** 633; **22** 684; **26** 452, 732; **30** 344; **32** 916
prints **25** 631
sculpture **19** 89, 118
Crozat de Thiers **8** 867; **31** 363
Croze-Magnan, Simon-Célestin **3** 870; **8** 542, 773; **20** 585
Crozet **11** 413
Crozet, René **8** 210*
Crozier, Robert **20** 239
Crozier, William **12** 637
croziers *see* CROSIERS
CRS Inc. **6** 92
CRS Sirrine **6** 92
Crucifix Altar, Master of the *see* ST BARTHOLOMEW ALTAR, Master of the
crucifixes **8** 195, 210–16*
historical and regional traditions **1** 697
Africa **1** *228*, 406
Belgium **3** 604
Byzantine **8** 210
Carolingian **5** 807; **8** 213
Denmark **13** *171*
England **10** 338
Germany **8** 216; **24** *544*
Gothic **7** 593; **8** *214*; **12** *343*
Ottonian **7** 590; **8** *213*; **12** 399
Gothic
Denmark **13** *171*
Germany **7** 593; **8** *214*; **12** *343*
Italy **8** *212*; **13** 123–4, *124*, *176*; **28** *753*
Spain **13** 122, *122*
crucifixes
historical and regional traditions—cont.
Holy Roman Empire (before 1648) **26** 684–5
Hungary **15** *1*
Italy **8** 210, 211–12, 216
Baroque **5** *532*
Gothic **8** *212*; **13** 123–4, *124*, *176*; **28** *753*
Renaissance **8** *215*
Romanesque **8** *211*
13th cent. **7** *317*, IX; **8** *767*; **12** III1; **20** *761*; **24** *854*
14th cent. **7** 317; **12** *694*; **13** *747*
Kongo **1** *228*, 406
Ottonian **7** 590; **8** *213*; **12** 399; **23** 647–8, 659
Romanesque
England **10** 338
Holy Roman Empire (before 1648) **26** 684–5
Italy **8** *211*
Spain **26** *643*, 698
Sweden **26** *647*; **30** 83
Rome, ancient **9** 518
Spain **8** 213, 216
Gothic **13** 122, *122*
Romanesque **26** *643*, 698
11th cent. **29** *288*
17th cent. **22** *2*
Sweden **26** *647*; **30** 83
Zaïre **1** *228*
materials
bronze **5** *532*; **26** 684–5
ivory **3** 604; **13** *171*, *176*; **24** *544*; **26** 698; **29** *288*
polychromy **26** *647*
sandstone **12** *343*
wood **8** *215*; **13** *122*, 122, 123, *124*; **22** 2; **23** 647–8; **26** *643*, *647*
techniques
painting **8** 211–12*
polychromy **13** *122*, *124*
sculpture **8** 213–16*
see also ROODS
Crucifixion, Master of the **24** 860
Crucifix of St John Gualberto **11** 210
cruciform piers *see under* PIERS (ii) → (MASONRY) → types
cruck roofs *see under* ROOFS → types
Crucy, Felix **8** 217
Crucy, Jean **8** 217
Crucy, Louis **8** 217
Crucy, Mathurin **8** 216–17*; **22** 464
Crue, Silvanus **32** 789
Cruesen, Andreas, Archbishop **10** 844
cruets **1** 762; **6** 32; **8** 217*; **10** 419
Crüger, Dietrich *see* KRÜGER, DIETRICH
Cruickshank, Robert (1767-1809) **5** 584, 585
Cruickshank, Ronald **30** 329; **31** 660
Cruikshank, Eliza (Margaret) **8** 217
Cruikshank, George **2** 727; **5** 756; **8** 217–18*; **11** 173
collaboration **8** 217, 863
patrons and collectors **14** 148
pupils **30** 569
works **4** 362; **7** 433; **8** 217; **10** *251*, 252; **27** 870
Cruikshank, Isaac **5** 756; **8** 217*; **20** 912
Cruikshank, Mrs James **25** *845*
Cruikshank, (Isaac) Robert (1789-1856) **8** 217*; **20** 912
Crum, Alexander
works **28** *242*
Crumbo, Woody **22** 595
Crummock Park Cabinet Works **28** 255
Crundale **2** 81
Crunden, John **7** 469
Crupi, Giovanni **12** 817
Crusaders **17** 501–7
castles **6** 58*; **18** 421, 422, *422*; **21** 563–4
diptychs **9** 4
flags **11** 147
fortifications **18** 422
manuscript illumination **21** 83
paintings **17** 501
Crusader States *see* JERUSALEM, LATIN KINGDOM OF
Crusades **8** 218–19*
Cruse, Thomas **30** 531
Crutched Friars **19** 566
Crutched Friars glasshouse **10** 316
works **10** *315*
Crutcher, Michael **8** 220
Crutcher, Richard **8** 220*; **24** 754
Crutz, Gustav Philip, Comte de *see* CREUTZ, GUSTAV FILIP
crux ansata *see under* CROSSES → types
crux commissa *see* CROSSES → types → tau
Crux de Dames, Henriette de, Abbess **8** 12
crux gammata *see* SWASTIKAS
Crux Vaticana **26** 143
Cruycen, Louis van der **3** 605
Cruyl, Lieven **8** 220*; **26** 771; **31** 247
Cruys, Peter van de **2** 875
Cruz, André Monteiro da *see* MONTEIRO DA CRUZ, ANDRÉ
Cruz, Basilio Santa *see* SANTA CRUZ, BASILIO
Cruz, Cipriano da *see* CIPRIANO DA CRUZ
Cruz, Diego de la *see* DIEGO DE LA CRUZ
Cruz, Diego de la Santa *see* SANTA CRUZ, DIEGO DE LA
Cruz, Eugenio de la **29** 341
Cruz, Gaspar Mario **9** 117
Cruz, Hernando de la **9** 712
Cruz, Jaime **6** 598
Cruz, Juan de la (*fl* 1765) **4** 264
Cruz, Juan Pantoja de la (1553-1608) *see* PANTOJA DE LA CRUZ, JUAN
Cruz, Luis Hernández *see* HERNÁNDEZ CRUZ, LUIS
Cruz, Manuel de la **5** 452
Cruz, Marcos da **3** 814; **8** 220–21*; **25** 297
Cruz, Pablo de la **7** 606
Cruz, Sebastián de la **4** 258; **25** 365
Cruz a El Viso, Marqués di Santa *see* SANTA CRUZ A EL VISO, Marqués di
Cruz Azaceta, Luis **8** 221*; **18** 835; **25** 209
Cruz Bagay, Nicolas de la *see* BAGAY, NICOLAS DE LA CRUZ
Cruz-Diez, Carlos **8** 221*; **23** 448, 449; **26** 193; **32** 176
Cruzeiro Seixas(, Artur Manuel Rodrigues do) **8** 221*; **25** 299, 300
Cruz González, Manuel de la *see* GONZÁLEZ, MANUEL DE LA CRUZ
Cruz Mitima, Jorge de la *see* MITIMA, JORGE DE LA CRUZ
Cruz Montoya, Geronimo **22** 595
Cruz Montt, Alberto **6** 594
Cruz y Ríos, Luis de la **14** 25
cryptography **10** 1
cryptoportici **8** 225*
crypts **8** 222–5*
historical and regional traditions
Carolingian **7** 265; **13** *636*
Colombia **27** 700
Egypt, ancient **9** 834
England **10** 227; **14** *501*
France **13** *636*
Maya **23** 838
crypts
historical and regional traditions—cont.
Mesoamerica, Pre-Columbian **23** 838
Romanesque **8** 223–4; **14** *501*
San Agustín culture **27** 700
South America, Pre-Columbian **27** 700
types
annular **8** 222, *223*
hall **8** 224
Carolingian **27** 554
Germany **8** *224*, 224; **29** 391
Romanesque **8** 224, *224*; **29** 391
Switzerland **27** 554
lower **8** 222–3
outer
Carolingian **5** 795, *795*; **8** 222–3
Germany **26** 572
Romanesque **7** 265; **26** 569, 572
raised **8** 224
ring *see* annular
upper **8** 222–3
Crystal (NM) **22** 626
crystal (glass) *see under* GLASS → types
crystal (quartz) *see* ROCK CRYSTAL
Crystal Glassworks **25** 124
Crystallo Engraving **10** 319, *319*
Crystal Palace *see under* LONDON → exhibitions → Great Exhibition, 1851
Crystal Palace Company **22** 28
crystal vaults *see* VAULTS (CEILING) → types → cellular
Csaba, Vilmos Perlrott *see* PERLROTT CSABA, VILMOS
Csáktornya *see* ČAKOVEC
Csákvár, Esterházy Palace **14** 888
Csáky (family) **14** 899; **15** 13
Csáky, Count, Prince-Archbishop of Esztergom **26** 316
Csáky, Albin, Count **25** 728
Csáky, Joseph **8** 225*
groups and movements **8** 240; **11** 568
patrons and collectors **9** 196
works **26** 486
Császka, Bishop **30** 210
Csatár Abbey **14** 898
Cseklész *see* BERNOLAKOV
Csernus, Tibor **14** 902
Csete, György **14** 891
Csikász, Imre **17** 876
CSL Associates **20** 169
Csók, István **8** 225*; **14** 901
groups and movements **22** 434
pupils **31** 798
teachers **14** 687
Csoma de Koros, A. **30** 848, 850
Csomas **21** 882
Csontváry (Kosztka), Tivadar **8** 226–7*; **14** 901; **24** 313
works **8** *226*
Csürtörtökhely *see* SPIŠSKÝ ŠTVRTOK
Ctesibius **21** 577
Ctesiphon *see* KTESIPHON
Cuadra, Juan Bautista **23** 81
Cuadra, Pedro de la **26** 404
Cuadra de León, Rubén **23** 81, 85
Cuadros, Miguel Angel **24** 510, 511
Cuala Press **16** 18
Cualladó, Gabriel **8** 227*
Cuart **29** 324
Cuatro Mosqueteros **9** 713; **16** 806, 834
cuatros **32** *166*
Cuauhitlan **21** 374
Cuba (Azerbaijan) *see* QUBA (i)
Cuba (Caribbean) **2** 144; **5** 744, *745*; **8** 227–39*, *228*
altarpieces **8** 233
Cuba (Caribbean)—cont.
altars **8** 230
architecture **8** 231–3*
art schools **8** *232*
axes **8** 229
beads **8** 229
carnivals **5** 788
cathedrals **8** 231
ceramics **8** 229, 234, *236*, 236–7*
chests **8** 235
chests-of-drawers **8** 235
collections **8** 238–9*
craftsmen and artists **8** 235, 237; **18** 834–5*
drawings **8** 234
drums (musical instruments) **8** 230
earthenwares **8** 236
education (art) **8** 238*
emblems **8** 231
exhibitions **5** 746
fortifications **8** 231
furniture **8** 234–6*, *235*
galleries (iv) (art) **8** 238
gold **8** 237
gravestones **8** 233
guilds **8** 237
interior decoration **8** *235*
Isla de la Juventud **8** 227
jars **8** 236
kilns **8** 236
lithography **8** 233, 234
maces **8** 237, *237*
metalwork **8** 237–8*
museums **8** 238–9*
painting **8** 229, 233–4*, *234*; **18** *665*, *834*
patronage **8** 238*
photography **8** 234
porrón **8** *236*, 236
posters **25** 354
religion **8** 229–31
ritual objects **8** 230
rock art **8** 229, *229*
sculpture **8** 229, *230*, 233–4*
figure **8** 231
silver **8** 237, *237*
towers **8** 231
urban planning **14** *241*
vomiting sticks **8** 229
wall paintings **8** 230
wood-carvings **8** 229
writing **8** 231
Cubagua **32** *165*, 167
Church of Santiago **32** 167
Cubanacán Ceramic Workshop **8** 236
Cubas **14** 714
Cubas y González-Montes, Francisco **8** 239*; **29** 272
Cube, Johann Wonnecken von *see* JOHANN WONNECKEN VON CUBE
Cubels, Miguel **29** 336
Cubeo **7** 602
Cubero, Gonzala **8** 16
Cubero, José Alvarez *see* ALVAREZ CUBERO, JOSÉ
Cuberó, Valeri **29** 309
Cubex **3** 587
cubic capitals *see under* CAPITALS → types
cubicula (i) (bedroom) **8** 239*
cubicula (ii) (burial chamber) **8** 239*
see also BURIAL CHAMBERS
Cubillas, García de **28** 369
Cubillos Chaparro, Julio Cesar **29** 146
Cubism **1** 73; **6** 570, 588; **8** 239–47*; **11** 360; **18** 717; **19** 65; **21** 340, 781; **24** 490, 717; **26** 51, 224; **28** 202; **31** 52, 503
art forms
architecture **8** 247*; **11** *525*, 526
assemblages **2** 616
collages **4** *675*; **7** 557; **8** 241–2, *242*
etchings **4** *676*

Cubism
art forms—cont.
industrial scenes 15 828
nude figures 9 355; 23 296
painting 29 669, 670
Argentina 2 399
Czechoslovakia 11 79
England 23 104
France 4 676, 677; 8 244; 9 355; 12 806; 13 670; 18 636; 19 77, 297; 21 364; 24 719; 29 670
Jordan 9 452
Netherlands, the 21 853
Russia 27 581
Spain 14 588
United States of America 14 204; 31 605
papier collé 8 242; 13 669
ready-mades 8 245
sculpture
France 2 311; 9 362; 18 863; 24 716; 33 590
Spain 12 919; 16 57
United States of America 19 437
collections 2 383; 9 465; 12 724; 17 725; 18 435, 466; 21 135; 23 7; 27 162; 29 642; 33 36
England 7 797
commentaries 25 739; 26 261
exhibitions 1 809; 8 246; 10 680; 16 817; 28 920; 31 605
Netherlands, the 21 852
periodicals 24 427
regional traditions
Argentina 2 400; 24 570
Czechoslovakia 8 379, 393; 18 435, 492
see also CZECH CUBISM
England 23 104
France 1 90, 650; 2 225, 310; 4 673, 678; 8 225, 250; 9 362; 12 806; 13 668–71; 17 725; 18 636; 19 78; 21 363, 776; 23 569; 24 143, 712, 714, 716, 717, 725, 726; 25 747; 26 255; 30 3; 32 576
see also PUTEAUX GROUP
Netherlands, the 21 775
Poland 25 108
Romania 20 877
Russia 8 250; 10 699; 30 361
United States of America 29 670
Uruguay 31 755
types
Analytical 4 674–5; 8 241, 242–3; 12 11; 16 906; 18 435, 24 595, 716
Hermetic 8 241, 244; 24 716
Orphic see ORPHISM
Physical 19 64
Rondocubism 8 373, 380; 12 834; 16 902
Synthetic 8 243; 10 869; 11 79, 360; 13 670, 670; 24 595, 717
see also CUBO-FUTURISM; UNANISM
Cubist Centre see REBEL ART CENTRE
Cubist-Realism see PRECISIONSIM
Cubitt, James (William Archibald) 8 248*; 23 134
staff 23 212
works 1 319; 12 508; 19 324
Cubitt, James, and Partners 2 308; 7 788; 23 135
Cubitt, Lewis 4 787; 8 248; 25 856
Cubitt, Thomas 8 248–9*; 19 574
patrons and collectors 3 689; 13 696; 14 149
works 4 809; 19 574
Cubitt, William 8 248
Cubo-Expressionism 8 249, 249–50*
Cubo-Futurism 8 250–51*; 11 867; 15 828; 18 474; 27 394
painting 20 193
see also CUBISM; FUTURISM
Cubr, František 8 251*
Cucchi, Enzo 8 251*; 16 682; 25 360
Cucci, Domenico 2 91; 8 251–2*; 11 625, 626; 16 727; 20 139
patrons and collectors 4 552, 553
pupils 5 379
works 11 575, 588, 589, 626; 12 828, 831, 831, 832; 19 722
Cuccomos, Filippo 16 737
Čučera, St Nikita 9 585; 25 343
Cuchet, Francisque 8 7; 21 90
Cuchimachay 29 158
cuchimilcos see under FIGURINES → types
Cucinello and Bianchi 12 606
Cuciulat 25 477
cuckoo clocks see under CLOCKS → types
Cucuteni 8 252*; 25 471; 26 705
pottery 25 514
Cucuteni culture 25 501–2*, 512, 516
pottery 8 252; 25 514, 514
Cueillette, Jean 14 502; 20 733, 734
Cuelape 29 156, 162
masonry 29 162
Cuéllar, Monastery of S María de la Armedilla 29 265
Cuéllar, Hanequín de see HANEQUÍN DE CUÉLLAR
Cuéllar, José Tomás de 32 571
Cuéllar Tamayo, Camilo 7 606
Cuello 20 881; 21 208; 30 448
Cueman, Egas see EGAS CUEMAN
Cuenca (Ecuador) 9 709
Academia de Bellas Artes 'Remigio Crespo Toral' 9 715
Cathedral 9 711
Escuela de Pintura 9 715
jewellery 9 710
Las Monjas 9 710
Museo de Artesanís 9 714
Museo del Monasterio de la Concepción 9 714
Museo Municipal 9 714
pediments 9 710
wood-carvings 9 710
Cuenca (Spain) 8 252–4*; 16 103; 29 259
carpets 5 833, 835; 29 301, 347
Cathedral 8 252–4*, 253; 22 216; 29 263, 339, 341
choir-stalls 13 123
Transparente 26 251
ivory-carvings 16 524
Museo de Arte Abstracto Español 29 354, 357; 31 174; 33 690
Cuenca, Arturo 8 234
cuenca tiles see under TILES → types
Cuer, Cornelius see CURE, CORNELIUS
Cuer, William see CURE, WILLIAM
Cuera see CHUR
Cuerbo, Juan Antonio 2 864
cuerda seca tiles see under TILES → types
cuerda seca ware see under POTTERY → wares
Cuernavaca
Centro de Meditación 21 381
Franciscan Monastery 21 373
Museo Regional de Cuernavaca 21 396
Palacio de Cortés 21 376
Cueto, Germán 8 254*; 21 389, 390
groups and movements 10 543
pupils 10 497; 13 863
Cueur d'amour espris, Master of see KING RENÉ OF ANJOU, MASTER OF
Cueva 8 303
Cueva, Gaspar de la 4 264
Cueva, Juan 15 832
Cueva Blanca 21 192
Cueva de Civil
rock art 29 365
Cueva de las Manos 29 204
Cueva Grande del Arroyo Feo 29 204
Cuevas, Alonso 9 118
Cuevas, Eugenio de las 8 254
Cuevas, Francisco de la 1 599; 9 748
Cuevas, José Luis 8 254*; 19 492; 21 389
Cuevas, Pedro de las 8 254*
pupils 2 410; 5 206, 526, 873; 19 178; 24 391
Cuevas de Bonbón 9 114
Cuffle, Pierre de La see MILAN, PIERRE
cufflinks 10 721
Cugnoli, S Stefano 26 625
Cugnot, L. 24 509
Cuiba 7 602
Cui Bo 6 817; 8 255*
pupils 14 859
works 6 800, 800
Cuicatec 21 736, 738
Cuicuilco 8 255*; 21 193, 198
altars 1 700
architecture 21 209
fortifications 21 598
pyramid 8 255; 21 227; 25 764
Cuicul see under DJEMILA
Cuijp see CUYP
Cuijter, Job 20 80
Cuilapa see COYOLAPÁN
Cuílles 26 642
Cuinxae 4 489
Cuipers see CUYPERS
cuirasses 6 262, 306, 313; 7 55; 17 362
cuir-bouilli see under LEATHER → types
Cuiry-les-Chaudardes 25 500
Cuismancu 29 127
cuisses 2 469
Cuitt, George 23 634
Cuixart, Modest 2 545; 3 219; 8 255–6*, 538; 29 286
Cui Yanshen 19 326
Cui Yuan 6 770
Cularo see GRENOBLE
Culemborg, Zweder van see ZWEDER VAN CULEMBORG
Culemborg Town Hall 25 190
Culhuacán 21 248
Culiacán 2 904
Culin, Stewart 7 156; 22 676
Ćulinović, Juraj see SCHIAVONE, GIORGIO (DI TOMMASO)
Cullberg, Erland 30 82
Cullen, Abraham 10 304
Cullen, Francis Grant, Lord, of Monymusk see GRANT, FRANCIS, Lord Cullen of Monymusk
Cullen, (Thomas) Gordon 8 256*; 31 735, 736
works 31 737
Cullen, Maurice 8 256*; 22 38
groups and movements 5 566, 593
patrons and collectors 1 496
Cullinan, Edward 8 256*
Cullinan, Roland 29 116
Cullinan, Thomas 29 116
Cullinan Diamond 12 269
Cullinan Refractories 29 116
Cullompton (Devon) 13 211
Culmer, H. L. A. 27 642
Culot, Maurice 3 620; 8 257*; 18 456
Culpeper, Edmund 28 210
Culpin, Clifford 4 788
Culpin, E., & Sons 31 243
Culross (Fife) 2 325; 28 222
Abbey 28 251
Abbey House 28 225
manuscript illumination 28 234
Palace 28 225
culs-de-sac 16 261, 264
cult houses 1 395; 24 66–8, 67, 73
see also SHRINES (i) (CULT)
cult objects see RITUAL OBJECTS
cult of carts 6 492; 8 257–8*, 258; 20 559
cult of relics 7 262–3; 8 222, 259–61*
cult statues see under SCULPTURE → types
cult temples see under TEMPLES → types
Cultura 24 435
Cultural Affairs Agency (Bunkachō) 17 427
cult wagons see under WAGONS → types
Culzean Castle (Strathclyde) 6 60; 22 740; 23 210; 28 227, 269, 288
dining-room 28 247
paintings 22 190
Round Drawing Room 28 247
Stairhall 28 247
Cumae 8 263–4*; 10 583, 585; 13 362; 16 621
oinochoai 13 499
pottery 10 610; 13 531, 532
sculpture 27 32, 32
Cumaná 32 165
Cumberland, Ernest Augustus, Duke of see ERNEST AUGUSTUS, King of Hannover
Cumberland, Frederic W(illiam) 5 561; 8 264*
collaboration 11 836
works 5 572; 23 632; 31 176
Cumberland, George 8 264*; 10 560
Cumberland, George Clifford, 3rd Earl of see CLIFFORD, GEORGE, 3rd Earl of Cumberland
Cumberland, Henry Frederick, Duke of see HANOVER, HENRY FREDERICK, Duke of Cumberland
Cumberland, William Augustus, Duke of see HANOVER, WILLIAM AUGUSTUS, Duke of Cumberland
Cumberland Market Group 3 894; 8 264–5*; 12 652; 22 525
Cumbernauld (Strathclyde) 31 733, 733
Cumella, Antoni 29 329
Cuming, William 8 265*
Cumming, C. F. Gordon 23 737
Cumming, Robert 8 265*; 21 897
Cumming, Skeoch 28 266
Cummings, Byron 8 255
Cummings, Charles A. 8 265
Cummings, Nathan 29 221
Cummings, Thomas Seir 15 857
Cummings & Sears 4 474; 8 265–6*; 29 870; 31 593
Cummins, Nina see DAVIES, NINA
Cummyng, James 22 531
Cumont, Franz (Valéry Marie) 8 266*
Cumshing 7 30
Cun, Hans see KUN, HANS
Cun, Kaspar see KUN, KASPAR
Cunald 32 432
Cunani 4 705, 706, 722
Cunard 21 371
Cunda collection see under KINGSTON (JAMAICA) → National Gallery of Jamaica
Cundall, Charles 29 426
Cundall, Howlett & Co. 14 813
Cundall, Howlett & Downes 14 813
Cundall, Joseph 7 433; 8 652; 14 813; 31 496
Cundy, James 8 266
Cundy, Joseph 8 266
Cundy, Thomas (i) (1765-1825) 8 266*; 13 696
Cundy, Thomas (ii) (1790-1867) 8 266*; 13 696
Cundy, Thomas (iii) (1820-95) 8 266–7*
Cunego, Domenico 8 267*
works 14 108, 109; 28 332; 33 20
Cunego, Giuseppe 8 267
Cunego, Luigi 8 267
cuneiform see under SCRIPTS → types
Cunelachi, Nicolas see KOUNELAKIS, NICOLAS
Cuneo, Santa Croce 29 831
Cuneo, Gaspare 24 208, 462
Cúneo (Perinetti), José 8 267–8*; 31 755, 757, 758
Cúneo, José 10 509
Cuneo, Terence 29 426
Cungi, Giovanni Battista 8 268; 32 11, 12
Cungi, Leonardo 8 268*
Cungius, Cornelius 3 737
Cunha, António Alvares da see ALVARES DA CUNHA, ANTÓNIO
Cunha, Domingos da 8 268*; 25 297
Cunha, Félix Adaústo 8 268*
Cunha, George da 23 41
Cunha, J. A. da 10 580
Cunha, Luís 25 294
Cunha, Manuel da, Bishop of Elvas 8 268; 26 413
Cunha, Nuno da 9 40
Cunha, Simão da 26 412
Cunha Correia Vale, António da see VALE, ANTÓNIO DA CUNHA CORREIA
Cunha Correia Vale, José da see VALE, JOSÉ DA CUNHA CORREIA
Cunha Correia Vale, Manuel da see VALE, MANUEL DA CUNHA CORREIA
Cunha Menezes, Luiz da 4 710
Cunill, Josep Gudiol i see GUDIOL I CUNILL, JOSEP
Cuningham, Hamilton, Quiter 22 671
Cuningham, Vera 28 884
Cunliffe, B. W. 3 368; 11 137
Cunningham, Alexander 3 907; 8 269*; 15 211; 16 890; 23 692; 25 891; 28 535
excavations 1 469; 14 162
works 27 708; 31 520
Cunningham, Allan 6 457; 8 269*; 10 377
Cunningham, E. F. 7 410
Cunningham, Imogen 8 270*; 13 710; 24 676; 33 310
Cunningham, John 25 268
Cunningham, Merce 5 381; 8 270*; 18 688; 24 407; 26 28
collaboration 17 613; 23 176
groups and movements 4 109, 110
productions 24 407; 29 621; 30 688
Cunningham, Patrick 9 322; 16 21
Cunninghame, William 14 108
Cunnington, William 5 292
Cuno, Theodore 20 604
Cunu 33 725
Cupae see GOLUBAC
cupboards 8 270–71*; 19 312; 28 665
historical and regional traditions
Austria 2 811, 812; 8 271
Belgium 8 271
Buddhism 6 669
China 6 669
England 8 271; 10 288
France 8 271; 11 587; 27 682
Germany 8 271; 12 420, 420, 421, 421, 422, 422, 423, 425, 426
Hungary 14 906
Italy 8 271; 16 730
Korea 18 362
Laos 18 777

cupboards
historical and regional traditions—cont.
Netherlands, the **8** 271; **22** 871, 872, *872*
Norway **11** *240*
Poland **25** 120
Portugal **25** 304, 305
Scotland **28** *251*
South Africa **29** 115
Spain **29** 312*
Switzerland **30** *142*
Thailand **30** 618
United States of America **31** 624, *624*
materials
ash **8** *271*
box-wood **12** 423
ebony **22** *872*
iron **8** 270
ivory **12** 423
lacquer **30** 618
marquetry **8** 271
oak **8** 271; **22** *872*; **28** *251*; **31** *624*
pewter **12** 423
pine **12** *422*
veneers **8** 271; **12** *421*; **30** *142*
walnut **8** 271; **16** *730*; **27** *682*
wood **12** *420*; **18** 777
types
beeldenkasten **22** 871
cabinet-cupboards **12** 422–3
corner **11** 593
court **8** 270, 271; **28** 245
kussenkasten **22** *872*
library **11** 590
livery **8** 271
sacristy **12** 423
two-tiered **8** 271, *271*; **12** 421
vitrine **12** 423
see also ARMOIRES; BUFFETS; WARDROBES
Cupisnique **8** 271–2*
gold **8** 272
hardstones **29** 185
pottery **8** *272*, 272; **29** 177
sculpture **6** 522
stirrup jars **29** *177*
Cup of St Agnes *see* ROYAL GOLD CUP
Cup of Solomon **16** 540; **26** 485
cupolas **5** 227; **6** 295–6; **9** 82; **10** 500
cupro-nickel **7** 539
cups
historical and regional traditions
Australia **2** *761*, *765*
Baden culture **25** 512
Celtic **6** 161
China **7** *23*, 81, 123, *126*; **16** III1
Han period (206 BC–AD 220) **7** 6, 13
Ming period (1368-1644) **7** 124–5
Qing period (1644-1911) **7** *85*, 100, 103, 126, *127*, 128
Sui period (AD 581-618) **7** 82
Tang period (AD 618-907) **7** 82, 123–4; **23** *551*
Zhou period (*c.* 1050-256 BC) **16** *857*
Crete **21** *688*
Cyprus, ancient **21** *334*
Denmark **32** *516*
England **10** *323*, 325, *326*
France **10** III1; **13** 170; **28** *522*
Germany **12** 443, 444, 445, 447; **14** 418
Baroque **16** *901*
16th cent. **12** *444*
19th cent. **12** *449*
Gothic **10** *323*, III1; **13** 170
Greece, ancient **10** 474; **13** 476–7, 478, 510, *535*, 539–40, *570*
Attica **13** 518–19, 520, *520*, 523, *537*
cups
historical and regional traditions
Greece, ancient—cont.
Italy **13** *437*
Lakonia **13** *512*, 512
Protogeometric **13** 492
Helladic **14** *344*, 355
Hungary **15** 6
Inca **15** 163
Indian subcontinent **15** *699*
Ireland **6** 161
Islamic **16** 365–6
Italy **13** *437*; **27** *76*
Japan **17** *266*, 399
Korea **18** *364*
Kuba (iii) (Zaïre) **18** 487, *488*
Laos **18** 776
Luba **19** 741*
Mycenaean **14** 355
Netherlands, the **22** *889*
New Zealand **23** *71*
Prehistoric **25** 512
Rome, ancient **23** *535*; **27** *76*, 80
Scandinavia **32** *516*
Scotland **25** 789; **28** 261
Thracian **30** 769
Troadic **31** *355*
Viking **32** *516*
Yoruba **33** 558
Zaïre **18** *488*
materials
automata **12** 445
bronze **7** 123
coins **15** 6
earthenware **2** *761*
electrum **31** *355*
enamel **4** *480*; **10** *323*, III1; **13** 170
glass **7** 81, 82, *85*; **18** *364*; **27** *76*
gold **10** III1; **21** *688*; **22** *889*; **30** 769; **32** *516*
horn **7** 123–5, 126, *126*, *127*, 128; **14** 763
ivory **10** *326*
jade **7** 6, *9*; **15** *699*; **16** *857*, III1
lacquer **7** 13
netsuke **17** 399
niello **32** *516*
pewter **7** 100; **24** 580
porcelain **7** 100; **28** *522*; **30** *99*
pottery **13** *437*, *512*, *520*, *535*, *537*; **14** *343*; **17** *266*; **27** *108*
shells **22** 694
silver
Australia **2** *765*
China **7** *23*, 82; **23** *551*
Cyprus, ancient **21** *334*
Denmark **32** *516*
England **28** *740*
Germany **12** *444*
Greece, ancient **13** *570*
Hungary **15** 6
Ireland **16** 31
Laos **18** 776
Netherlands, the **22** 886, *886*, 889
New Zealand **23** *71*
Rome, ancient **23** *535*; **27** 80
Troadic **31** *355*
silver-gilt **4** *480*; **10** *323*, *326*, *334*; **12** *449*; **16** *901*
wood **18** *488*; **31** 305
types
band **13** *475*, 476
bilingual **13** 518
cage-cups **9** 645; **27** 73*, 76*, 78*
Castulo **13** 538
commemorative **22** 886
communion-cups **10** 325; **12** 444; **28** 261
diatreta *see* cage-cups
dippers *see* DIPPERS
eye **13** 476
Type A **13** *475*, 476; **32** 43
Type B **13** *475*, 476
Type C **13** *475*, 476
cups
types—cont.
finger **12** 785
grape **24** 573
hunt **27** *108*
ice cream **30** *99*
Ionian Little Masters **13** 515
komast **13** *475*, 476, 507
Lakonian **32** 36, 57
Lakonian droop **32** 47
lip **13** *475*, 476; **32** 37
Little Master **13** 490, 510
loving-cups **4** *480*; **24** 580
mastos **13** 477
Merrythought **32** 37
nautilus **22** 694*, 887
one-handler **13** 536
quaich **25** 789*; **28** 261, *261*
Rheneia **13** 536
Siana **13** *475*, 476, 508; **32** 37
standing **22** *886*
stem **6** 875, *875*
thistle **28** 261
trophies **10** *334*
two-handled **7** *9*; **16** 31; **28** *740*
Vapheio **14** 337, 344, *344*; **21** 659, *688*; **26** 134
windmill **22** 889
see also GLASSES; GOBLETS
cup-skyphoi **13** *475*, *476*, 477
cup stands *see under* STANDS → types
Curaçao **2** 144, 149; **5** *745*
architecture **2** 147
Brievengat Land House **5** 749
houses **2** 148
Jewish cemetery **17** 555
Mikve Israel synagogue **17** 545
see also ANTILLES, LESSER; ANTILLES, NETHERLANDS
Curahuara de Carangas **4** *255*
church **4** 261
Curatella Manes, Pablo **2** 399; **8** 272–3*
curd **29** 813
Cure (family) **4** 693; **10** 261
Curé, Claude **2** 843; **32** 758
Cure, Cornelius **8** 273*; **10** 262; **19** 605
Cure, William (i) (1514-79) **8** 273*
Cure, William (ii) (*fl* 1605-32) **8** 273*; **10** 262; **19** 605
curfews **11** 118, 119
curiae **26** 867; **27** 3
Ćurić, Alojz **4** 462
Curio **1** 797
curiosities *see under* COLLECTIONS → types
Curitiba **4** *705*, 715; **19** 228
Legislative Assembly **4** 715
Museu de Arte Contemporânea **4** 727
Curjel, Robert **3** 175; **22** 186
Curjel & Moser **3** 823; **22** 186*
Curmer **8** 546
Curmer, Léon **4** 364
Curnoe, Greg **5** 569; **8** 273*
Curr, Edward **1** 67
Curradi, Francesco **8** 274–5*, 497; **22** 448
works **8** *274*
Curradi, Raffaello **21** 26
Curradi, Taddeo **8** 274*
Curraghmore House **16** 14
Curran, Sarah **16** 33
Curre **29** 148
currency **1** 362–3*; **3** 441; **12** 440
see also BANKNOTES; COINS
Currey, Henry **10** 236; **14** 783
Curri, Antonio **8** 275*; **26** 478
Curridabat ware *see under* POTTERY → wares
Currie, B. W. **8** 830
Currie, Donald **20** 27
Currie, John **11** 774
Currie, Ken **12** 777; **28** 240
Currie, William **12** 266
Currier, Edward West **8** 276
Currier, J(oseph) Frank **8** 275*; **11** 300
Currier, Nathaniel T. **8** 276; **19** 485; **23** 883
Currier & Ives **8** 276*; **20** 604; **29** 536; **30** 241
staff **23** 883
works **8** *276*; **9** 453; **22** 371; **31** 602
Curry, John Steuart **8** 277*
collaboration **20** 604
groups and movements **1** 773; **26** 90
works **1** *773*; **12** 296; **19** 492
Curry, William **19** 235
cursive clerical script *see under* SCRIPTS → types
cursive script *see under* SCRIPTS → types
Curstgen *see* KNÜTGEN
curtain arches *see under* ARCHES → types
curtains **3** 483; **9** 12, 26; **31** 683–4*
historical and regional traditions
Algeria **16** 448
Belgium **3** 576, 578, 582
China **7** 51, *51*, 145
Czech Republic **17** 570
England **10** 275, 279
France **3** 484
Germany **12** 413; **17** 570
Islamic **16** 448; **30** VII1
Italy **17** 571
Japan **14** 429
Jewish art **17** 570
Spain **29** 298; **30** VII1
types
altar **2** 442
festoon **31** 683
fire **30** 650
curtain walls *see under* WALLS → types
Curtat, Louis **18** 873
Curtatone, Sanctuary of S Madonna della Grazie **2** 449
Curte, Louis De *see* DE CURTE, LOUIS
Curtea de Argeş **8** 279–80*; **9** *511*; **26** *705*, 706
Church of the Assumption of the Virgin **8** 279–80; **26** 707
frescoes **26** 710
Monastery **25** 340, 344; **26** 712
St Nicholas **4** 783; **25** 340; **26** 706, *706*, 710
tomb of Vladislav I **26** 719
sculpture **26** 710
Curtea Veche *see under* BUCHAREST
Curti, Girolamo **8** 280*; **16** 670, 714; **29** 251
collaboration **20** 586; **21** 732
patrons and collectors **10** 526
pupils **7** 622; **21** 732
works **15** 138
Curti, Pietro Leopoldo **3** 864
Curtilles Church **30** 129
Curtis, Edward S(heriff) **8** 280*; **10** 580
works **8** 270, 537, *537*; **24** 666
Curtis, William **10** 356
curtis beguinages **3** 502
Curtis & Davis **23** 32
Curtis Publishing Co. **30** 869
Curtiss, Louis **17** 799
Curtius, Ernst **1** 159; **2** 602; **14** 655, 864
Curtius, Jean de **3** 617
Curtius, Philippe **33** 4
Curtius, Quintus **9** 271
Curtius Auspicatus **2** 605
Curtius Crispinus **2** 605
Curtoni, Domenico **27** 762; **32** 341
Curtoni, G. Pietro **32** 343
Curtun *see* CORTONA
Curuchich, Andres **13** 760, 765
Curunas (family) **10** 623
curvature (architectural) **13** 414–15
curved weft weaving *see under* WEAVING → types
curvilinear perspective *see under* PERSPECTIVE → types
curvilinear tracery *see under* TRACERY → types → bar
curvilinear vaults *see* VAULTS (CEILING) → types → rib: curving
Curwen, Harold **29** 628
Curwen Chilford Prints **20** 607; **25** 628
Curwen Press **19** 485; **20** 607
production **4** 366; **11** 747; **19** 492; **20** 609; **24** 55; **25** 628; **26** 39
staff **3** 420
Curwen Studio *see* CURWEN CHILFORD PRINTS
Curzon, (Paul-)Alfred de **8** 281*; **11** 799; **12** 830
Curzon, Assheton **17** 476
Curzon, George Nathaniel, 1st Marquess Curzon of Kedleston **5** 418; **8** 676; **30** 365
Curzon, Nathaniel, 1st Baron Scarsdale **4** 758; **8** 281*; **16** 389
architecture **33** 442
furniture **10** 295; **19** 426
interior decoration **29** 806
sculpture **4** 758
Curzon, Richard, 1st Earl Howe **29** 723
Curzon, Robert, 14th Baron of Harringworth **2** 450
Cusa, Nicholas of *see* NICHOLAS OF CUSA
Cusae *see* MEIR
Cusanus, Nikolaus, Cardinal **20** 718
Cushing, Charles **4** 481
Cushing, Frank Hamilton **8** 282*; **22** 676
Cushing, Harry **4** 481
Cushing, Leonard Wareham **4** 481
Cushing, L. W., & Sons **4** 481; **31** 653
Cushing, Val **31** 640
cushion capitals *see under* CAPITALS → types
cushion covers **1** *218*; **3** 606; **12** 467; **14** 425
cushions **6** 388; **16** 429; **18** *157*; **29** 297
Cushman, Charlotte **14** 778; **29** 583
Cusichaca
pottery **29** *175*
Cusi Guzmán, Diego **24** 506
cusped arches *see under* ARCHES → types
cusped frames *see under* FRAMES → types
cusps **8** 282*
Cusse, Michael **33** 592
Cust, Adelbert, 3rd Earl Brownlow **14** 877
Custine, Adam-Philippe, Comte de **11** 609; **23** 113
Custiniani (family) **29** 376
custodia **29** *333*
Custodis, Hieronimos **8** 282*; **10** 344
Custodis, Peeter *see* BALTENS, PEETER
customization **20** 594
Custos (family) **12** 390
Custos, Berthold **23** 655
Custos, Dominicus **2** 718; **3** 126; **18** 42, 44, 177
Cutbercht Gospels *see under* GOSPEL BOOKS → individual manuscripts
Cutbush, Edward **27** 349
Cutbush, H. J. **31** 151
cut glass *see under* GLASS → techniques

Cuthbert, Archbishop of Canterbury (*reg* 740-60) **3** 191; **5** 643
Cuthbert, Saint, Bishop of Lindisfarne (*d* 687) **10** 181, 353; **19** 409
Cutileiro, João **8** 282–3*
works **25** 302, *302*
Cutler, Nancy Youngblood **22** 606
Cutler and Girard **16** 731
cutlery **1** 326; **8** 283–7*
coral **7** 835
horn **14** 763
ivory **1** 326; **16** 799
Cutlumus Monastery **26** 721
cut-off domes *see under* DOMES → types
cutouts **18** 49
Cutsem, Henri Van *see* VAN CUTSEM, HENRI
Cutshing **7** 30
works **7** *28*
cut-steel work **2** 456
Cuttack **15** 174, 672, 707
cutter's donkey *see* FRENCH HORSE
cutting **27** 75–6*
diamonds **12** 269–70
gems **8** 417; **12** *269*, 269–70*; **17** 522
glass **6** 269, 443; **8** 407–8, *408*, 409, *410*; **10** 318–19, *319*, 321; **12** 787*; **16** 30, *30*, 518; **17** *387*; **27** 75–6*, *416*
gold **12** 866*
hardstones **14** *168*, 168–9*
leather **19** *1*, 1–2
marquetry **20** 466
paper **24** 56
rock crystal **26** 485
rubies **12** 269
sapphires **12** 269
stained glass **29** 498*
Cutting, Sybil **28** 283
cuttle fish **15** 852
Cuttoli, Marie **9** 374; **11** 644; **19** 808
cutwork **11** 649; **18** 588, 590
Cutzescu-Storck, Cecilia **29** 721
Cuvelier, Eugène **7** 434
Cuvelier, Hugues **6** 413; **8** 288*
Cuvier, Georges **22** 101
Cuvilliés, François de, II (1731-77) **7** 746; **8** 289; **10** 464; **12** 372; **13** 852; **29** 761; **30** 213
Cuvilliés, (Jean) François Vincent Joseph de, I (1695-1768) **8** 288–90*; **9** 746; **12** 372, 410, 424; **13** 701; **22** 299; **30** 213; **33** 277
architecture **8** *289*; **12** 371, 412; **17** 835; **19** 268; **22** 299, 300, 307, 309; **32** 822; **33** 278
assistants **29** 838
collaboration **4** 375; **8** 880; **33** 682
frames **11** 458
furniture **6** 390; **7** 746; **12** 424
groups and movements **26** 496, 497
interior decoration **3** 229; **5** 7–8, 349; **8** *290*; **10** 859, 860; **28** 110; **29** 760; **30** 676; **31** 511; **33** 277, 278
parks **12** 723
patrons and collectors **14** 492; **22** 309
pattern books **24** 271; **26** 494
reproductive prints by others **14** 49
Cuvillon, Louis (-Amable) *see* QUÉVILLON, LOUIS(-AMABLE)
Cuxa, St Michel *see* SAINT-MICHEL-DE-CUXA
Cuyas, Ramon Puig *see* PUIG CUYAS, RAMON
Cuyk, Michel van **14** 116
Cuyp, Aelbert **8** 291, 293–8*; **22** 845
collaboration **8** 291
forgeries by others **29** 774
patrons and collectors
Altman, Benjamin **1** 731
Angerstein, John Julius **2** 51
Butler, Charles (1822-1910) **5** 311
Calraet, Abraham (Pietersz.) van **5** 440
Christie, James, the elder (1730-1803) **7** 233
Colebrooke, George **7** 552
Curzon, Nathaniel, 1st Baron Scarsdale **8** 281
Demidov, Anatoly, Prince **8** 705
Dordrechts Museum **22** 906
Dundas, Lawrence **9** 392
Frick, Henry Clay **11** 774
George IV, King of Great Britain (*reg* 1820-30) **14** 146
Gillott, Joseph **12** 638
Goll van Franckenstein, Pieter Hendrik **12** 876
Guinness, Edward (Cecil), 1st Earl of Iveagh **13** 836
Harvey, Thomas **8** 184
Holford, Robert Stayner **14** 675
Hope, John, 4th Earl of Hopetoun (1765-1823) **33** 216
Hume, Abraham, 2nd Baronet **14** 877
Johnson, John G(raver) (1841-1917) **17** 619
Mellon, Andrew W(illiam) **21** 90
Peel, Robert (1788-1850) **24** 322
Seymour-Conway, Francis Charles, 3rd Marquess of Hertford **28** 527
Stuart, John, 3rd Earl of Bute (1713-92) **29** 796
Trip, Hendrick and Louys **31** 342
Verstolk van Soelen, Jan Gijsbert, Baron **32** 377
Vos (ii) Jbzn, Jacob de (1803-82) **32** 707
pupils **5** 440
teachers **8** 291
works **8** *294*, *295*, *296*, *297*; **9** 169; **18** 710; **20** 424
Cuyp, Benjamin (Gerritz.) **8** 291, 292–3*
works **8** *292*
Cuyp, Gerrit (Gerritsz.), the elder (1565-1644) **9** 169
Cuyp, Gerrit (Gerritsz.), the younger (1603-51) **8** 291
Cuyp, Jacob (Gerritsz.) **8** 291–4*; **22** 845
collaboration **8** 294, 297
patrons and collectors **31** 342; **33** 453
pupils **4** 249; **8** 292, 293
teachers **4** 153
works **9** 169
Cuypens, Edward **33** 538
Cuyper, Olivier de **21** 359
Cuypers, Eduard (Gerard Hendrik Hubert) **8** 298, 299*
assistants **18** 125
pupils **1** 814; **4** 217
staff **13** 632; **18** 436, 617; **21** 58
works **15** 770
Cuypers, Joseph (Theodorus Johannes) **8** 298, 300*
collaboration **29** 876
pupils **23** 662; **29** 483
staff **13** 679
Cuypers, Pierre **8** 298
Cuypers, P(etrus) J(osephus) H(ubertus) **1** 547; **8** 298–300*; **21** 818; **22** 898
assistants **3** 431; **18** 878; **24** 547; **29** 876; **32** 778
collaboration **12** 271; **13** 798
groups and movements **13** 203
Cuypers, P(etrus) J(osephus) H(ubertus)—cont.
pupils **8** 299; **18** 878; **22** 874; **33** 177
restorations **14** 44
staff **8** 300
teachers **3** 763
works **1** 803; **8** *299*; **14** 45; **22** 265, 364, 828–9, *829*, 860; **29** 862; **30** 504; **33** 157
Cuypers & Co. **8** 298
Cuypers & Stolzenberg **8** 298; **24** 547; **29** 876
Cuzco **8** 300–303*; **15** 160, *161*; **23** 826; **24** *498*; **29** 155, *156*
Academia de Bellas Artes **24** 517
architecture **15** 162; **29** 163, 166; **32** 306, *306*
Casa del Almirante **24** 501, 514
Casa de los Cuatro Bustos *see* Liberatador Mariott Hotel
Casa Garcilaso de la Vega **24** 502
Casa Peralta **24** 502
Centro de Estudios Regionales Andinos Bartolomé de las Casas **24** 518
Coricancha **8** 301*; **15** 162; **29** 129, 167; **30** 447; **31** 119
ecclesiastical buildings **8** 302; **24** 502
Cathedral **3** 470; **24** 501; **32** 239
chapel of the Sagrada Familia **24** 502
El Triunfo **24** 502
paintings **24** 507
El Belén **24** 502
La Compañía **17** 513; **24** 502
chapel of Nuestra Señora de Loreto **24** 506
La Merced **24** 502
Soledad Altar **26** 252
S Catalina **24** 502
S Clara **24** 511; **26** 252
S Domingo **24** 501, 502, 514
S Francisco **24** 501, 502
S Jerónimo **24** 506
S Pedro **24** 502; **26** 252
S Teresa **24** 502, 512
education (art) **24** 517
Escuela Regional de Bellas Artes Diego Quispe Tito **24** 517
furniture **24** 514
gardens **12** 71
ikat **24** 513
Instituto Audio Visual Inka **24** 518
Liberatador-Marriott Hotel **24** 501
masonry **29** 163–4
museums
Museo de Arqueología *see* Museo de la Universidad
Museo de Arte Popular del Instituto Americano de Arte **24** 517
Museo de Arte Religioso **8** 302; **24** 516; **29** 164, *164*
Museo Histórico Regional **24** 516
Museo de la Universidad **8** 302; **24** 516
painting **6** 596; **8** 302–3
queros **24** *498*
religion **29** 130
retables **26** 252
sculpture **24** 499
silver **6** 599
Talleres de Fotografía Social (TAFOS) **24** 518
Temple of the Sun *see* Coricancha
Throne of the Inca **1** 701
Cuzco school **2** 398; **4** 261; **8** 302–3*; **24** 499, 506–7; **33** 617
Cuzi (family) **17** 565
Cuzin, Robert **25** 355
Cuzner, Bernard **6** 164; **10** 336
Cvijeta Zuzorić group **4** 461
Čvirka, Vitali **3** 530
Cwa **18** 484, 487
Cwenarski, Waldemar **2** 502; **8** 303*; **25** 108
Cwmbran (Gwent) **31** 733
cyan *see under* PIGMENTS → types
cyanine dyes *see under* DYES → types
cyanotype process *see under* PHOTOGRAPHY → processes
Cybei, Giovanni Antonio **3** 198; **8** 303–4*
Cybińska, Krystyna **25** 123
Cybis, Bolesław **10** 871
Cybis, Jan **4** 234; **17** 804; **32** 877
Cybo (family) **20** 375
Cybo, Alderano, Cardinal **20** 377
Cybulski, Stefan **25** 841
Cyclades **13** *363*; **32** *158*
obsidian **8** 305
trade **21** 652
Cycladic **8** *304*, 304–24*
architecture **8** 309, 310–11*, *310*
bone **8** 323*
bone-carvings **8** 323*
bowls **8** *312*
bronze **8** 322–3*
ceramics **8** 308, 309
chronologies **8** *307*; **14** 334
collections **8** 314, 323–4*
diadems **8** *322*
ewers **8** *314*
figurines **1** 795; **8** 308, 314–15*, *315*, *316*, 316*
forgeries **8** 314, 316*
fortifications **8** 310, 311
goblets **8** *313*
gold **8** 322*
human figures **8** 315
iconography **8** 306–7*
ivory **8** 323*
ivory-carvings **8** 323*
jars **8** *312*, *314*
jugs **8** *312*, *313*
marble **8** *315*, *316*, 317*, *317*; **29** 701
measurements **13** 411
metalwork **8** 307–8, 321–3*
museums **8** 323–4*
obsidian **21** 94
painting
vase **8** 309; **30** *712*
wall **8** 309, 318–21*, *318*, *320*; **30** *713*
periods
Early Cycladic (*c.* 3500/3000-*c.* 2000 BC) **8** *307*, 307–8*
Early Cycladic I (*c.* 3500/3000-*c.* 2800/2600 BC) **8** *307*
Early Cycladic II (*c.* 2800/2600-*c.* 2300 BC) **8** *307*
Early Cycladic IIIA (*c.* 2300-*c.* 2150 BC) **8** *307*
Early Cycladic IIIB (*c.* 2150-*c.* 2000 BC) **8** *307*
Final Neolithic (*c.* 4000-*c.* 3500/3000 BC) **8** *307*
Late Cycladic (*c.* 1600-*c.* 1050 BC) **8** *307*, 309–10*
Late Cycladic I (*c.* 1600-*c.* 1500 BC) **8** *307*
Late Cycladic II (*c.* 1500-*c.* 1390 BC) **8** *307*
Late Cycladic IIIA (*c.* 1390-*c.* 1335 BC) **8** *307*
Late Cycladic IIIB (*c.* 1335-*c.* 1190 BC) **8** *307*
Late Cycladic IIIC (*c.* 1190-*c.* 1050 BC) **8** *307*
Middle Cycladic period (*c.* 2000-*c.* 1600 BC) **8** *307*, 309*
pins **8** *322*
pottery **8** 309, 311*; **13** 492, 498; **14** 342
Black-and-red style **8** 309, *314*; **21** 95
Cycladic White ceramic ware **8** 313, *313*; **21** 95
Cycladic
pottery—cont.
Dark Burnished **8** 312–13, *313*
Early Cycladic (*c.* 3500/3000-*c.* 2000 BC) **8** 311–12*, *312*
Geometric (*c.* 900-*c.* 700 BC) **13** 496, 497
Late Cycladic (*c.* 1600-*c.* 1050 BC) **8** 313*, *314*; **30** *712*
Middle Cycladic period (*c.* 2000-*c.* 1600 BC) **8** 312–13*, *313*
Orientalizing style **13** 498, 502
Sub-Protogeometric **13** 492
pyxides (vases) **8** *312*
reliefs **22** 698
religion **8** 306–7*
sauceboats **8** 311
silver **8** 322*, *322*
stone vessels **8** 308, 317*, *317*
tankards **8** *312*
terracotta **8** 309
tombs **8** 310
trade **8** 305–6*
obsidian **8** 305
pottery **8** 309
stone vessels **8** 317
cyclohexanone resin *see under* RESINS → types
Cyclopean masonry *see under* MASONRY → types
cycloramas **8** 324*
cycloramic scenery *see under* STAGE SCENERY → types
Cyclostyle **28** 299
Cydias **13** 555
Cyfarthfa ironworks *see under* MERTHYR TYDFIL
Cyfflé, Paul-Louis **3** 590; **13** 805; **19** 801; **22** 456; **29** 537
Cyfrewas, John de *see* JOHN DE SIFERWAS
Cygnaeus, F. **11** 111
cylikes *see* KYLIKES
cylinder presses *see under* PRESSES → types
cylinders, photographic *see* PHOTOGRAPHIC CYLINDERS
cylinder seals *see under* SEALS → types
cylindrical piers *see under* PIERS (ii) (MASONRY) → types
cymagraphs **33** 211
cyma mouldings *see under* MOULDINGS → types
cyma recta *see under* MOULDINGS → types
cyma reversa *see under* MOULDINGS → types
cymbals **4** 855; **30** 769
Cymmrodorion Society **32** 790
Cymric style **10** 336
silver **19** 311
Cymru *see* WALES
Cynk, Florent **31** 396
Cypierre, Marquis de **11** 663
Cypraea shells *see under* SHELLS → types
cypress **10** 288, 776; **13** 390; **17** 399
types
hinoki (Japanese cypress) **17** 45, 46, 100, 350, 356, 372, 390, 392, 393, *394*, *395*; **23** 598; **33** 325
uses
architecture **17** 45, 46
chests **10** 288
dolls **17** 372
fans **10** 776
masks **17** 390, 392, 393, *394*, *395*
netsuke **17** 399
roofs **23** 598
sculpture **17** 100
Cypresses, Master of the **20** 653*
Cyprian of Toulon **6** 173
Cypriote glass *see under* GLASS → types

Cypro-Bucchero ware see under POTTERY → wares
Cypros 17 556
Cyprus 1 821; 8 324–7*, 325, 360–61*, 363*, 364*; 9 512; 13 362; 26 852, 908; 32 158
architecture 8 357–8*, 361–3*, 364–5*
baptisteries 3 190, 191
castles 8 361
cathedrals 10 774; 23 112
ceramics 8 363
chapels 8 358
chariots 6 480*
churches 8 357, 357–8, 361–3*, 362
coats of arms 14 411
coins 7 535; 13 585
collections 8 366–7*
copper 8 352, 365
cotton 16 445
doors 9 151
embroidery 8 366
fortifications 32 159
friezes 29 817
furniture 8 365*
goblets 9 634
gold 8 360*
heraldry 14 411
iconography 8 326–7*
icons 8 359; 9 623, 624, 626, 627
interior decoration 8 365*
lamps 13 603
lefkarítka 8 366
manuscripts 8 363; 9 605
metalwork 8 363, 365*; 13 359
monasteries 3 638
mosaics
Byzantine 9 566–7*, 580
Early Christian (c. AD 250-843) 8 358–9*; 9 566–7*
6th cent. AD 8 359
museums 8 366–7*
painting 8 364–5*; 25 330
wall 7 229; 8 358–9*, 360; 9 580; 17 743
pavements 8 359
periods
Early Christian (c. AD 250-843) 8 356–7*
phythiotika 8 366
pigments
green earth 24 793
plaster 29 816, 817
pottery 9 631, 634, 634
Psalters 9 613
religion 8 326–7*
sculpture 8 363, 364–5*
silk 8 356
silver 8 360*, 365
stucco 29 816
textiles 8 363, 366*
trade 8 326*; 21 652
copper 8 326
pottery 8 326; 16 415
terracottas 25 733
Cyprus, ancient 8 325, 327–56*
alabastra 1 868
amphorae 8 348
architecture 8 333–7*; 21 555
armour 14 356
beads 8 352
bowls 8 347, 348; 24 644, 644
brass 4 681
bronze 8 339, 342, 349, 353, 354; 10 400; 14 356
casting 8 340
cauldrons 8 354
clay 8 338
coins 8 332, 349*
collections 14 361
copper 8 352, 353
cups 21 334
diadems 8 352
earrings 8 352
enamel 8 352, 352
faience (i) (glass) 8 349–50*; 18 98
fibulae 8 352
Cyprus, ancient—cont.
figurines 8 329, 337–40*, 338, 339, 342; 19 131
flasks 8 343
fortifications 21 555
forts 8 334
funerary stelae 8 342
gold 8 349, 351, 352, 352, 353; 24 644
gravestones 8 341
hair ornaments 8 352
harnesses 14 179*
houses 8 333, 333–4
iconography 8 327*
iron 8 353, 354
ivory 8 350; 14 353
ivory-carvings 8 323, 350, 350–51*; 24 643; 27 608
jewellery 8 351–2*; 10 31
jugs 8 344, 348, 348
limestone 8 338, 340, 342
lost-wax casting 8 339, 353
marble 8 340, 342; 27 609
metalwork 8 352–4*, 354
mirrors 8 350
models 8 307
mosaics 8 333, 354–5*, 355; 27 63
Roman 8 333; 24 60
moulds 8 340
mouthpieces 8 352
necklaces 8 338
painting
vase 8 343–9*, 343, 344, 345, 347, 348
wall 8 356*
palaces 8 335–6, 336
pendants (jewellery) 8 328, 338, 352
periods 8 328
Aceramic Neolithic 8 328
Archaic 8 328, 331–2*
Bronze Age 8 329*
Chalcolithic 8 328*
Classical 8 328, 332*
Cypro-Geometric (c. 1050-c. 750 BC) 8 331*
Early Chalcolithic 8 328
Early Cypriot 8 328, 329–30*
ECyp see Early Cypriot
Geometric (c. 900-c. 700 BC) 8 328
Hellenistic 8 328, 332–3*
Late Chalcolithic 8 328
Late Cypriot 8 328, 330–31*
Late Neolithic (c. 4500-c. 3800 BC) 8 328
LCyp see Late Cypriot
MCyp see Middle Cypriot
Middle Chalcolithic 8 328
Middle Cypriot period 8 328, 330*
Neolithic 8 328–9*
Neolithic I see Aceramic Neolithic
Neolithic II see Late Neolithic
Prehistoric 8 328, 329*
Roman 8 328, 333*
picrolite 8 328, 337, 338; 19 131
pilasters 8 341
pins 8 352
pithoi 19 131
portraits 8 342, 342
pottery 8 331, 343–9*, 345, 347; 13 542
Base Ring wares 8 330
Base Ring I ware 8 345, 345
Base Ring II ware 8 345, 346
Bichrome Red ware 8 347
Bichrome ware 8 330, 346, 347, 348
Bichrome Wheelmade ware 8 345, 345
Black Lustrous Wheelmade ware 8 345
Black-on-red ware 8 346, 347
Black Polished ware 8 345
Black-slip-and-combed ware 8 343
Cyprus, ancient
pottery—cont.
Black Slip ware 8 345
Combed ware 8 328, 343
Cypro-Bucchero ware 8 346
Dark-faced Burnished ware 8 343
Drab Polished Blue Core ware 8 345
Fine-line style 8 343, 343
Free Field style 8 332, 348, 348
Geometric see Cypro-Geometric
Monochrome ware 8 345, 346
Northern Painted ware see Red-on-white ware
Panel style 8 344
Pastoral style 8 330, 346; 14 346
Plain White Wheelmade ware 8 346
Prehistoric 8 343
Proto-Base Ring ware 8 345
Proto-Monochrome ware 8 345
Proto-White Painted ware 8 346
Proto-White Slip ware 8 345
Red Lustrous Wheelmade ware 8 346
Red-on-black ware 8 344, 345
Red-on-white ware 8 328, 329, 338, 343, 343, 345
Red Polished ware 8 307, 329, 338, 339, 339, 344, 345
Red Polished III ware 8 344
Red Polished IV ware 8 344
Red Polished V ware 8 345
Southern Monochrome ware see Combed ware
White Painted ware 8 338, 346, 347, 347
White Painted I ware 8 329, 345
White Painted II ware 8 330, 345
White Painted IV ware 8 345, 345
White Painted Wheelmade ware 8 345
White Shaved ware 8 346
White Slip ware 8 330
White Slip I ware 8 345, 345, 346
White Slip II ware 8 345, 346
religion 8 326*, 327*
rhyta 18 98
rings 8 352, 352, 355
sanctuaries 8 307, 334, 341
sarcophagi 27 825
scripts 1 855
sculpture 8 333, 337*, 338–41*; 27 609
Archaic 24 61
bronze 8 342
cult statues 8 338
Hellenistic 8 342*
marble 8 340, 342
monumental 8 332
Prehistoric 8 337–8*
relief 8 339
Roman 8 342*
6th cent. BC 8 340
seals 8 355–6*; 19 131; 24 645
silver 8 349, 353; 21 334
stands 8 353, 354
statuettes 8 339, 353; 10 400
stone 27 825
tattoos 8 338
temples 8 335, 336
terracotta 8 338–9, 340, 342
tin 8 353
tombs 8 333, 335, 337
trade
copper 9 786; 13 372
pottery 8 345; 13 486
tin 8 353
trappings 14 179*
urban planning 8 336
vases 8 339, 343, 346
weapons 8 353
weights 8 353
writing 8 331
Cyprus Treasure 9 655, 655
Cyprus turpentine 18 611
Cyrén, Gunnar 30 109
Cyrenaica see LIBYA
Cyrene 8 367–9*; 9 507; 13 362; 26 919
amphitheatre 26 920
architecture 8 368–9*; 26 920
baths 26 920
Caesareum 3 328; 8 368; 26 920
Cathedral 9 570
coins 13 538
figurines 13 579
gems 12 250
heroön of Battos 14 466
metopes 13 544
Museum of Antiquities 13 470
pottery 13 512
Sanctuary of Apollo
baths 3 374
sculpture 8 369*
Temple of Zeus 8 367
terracottas 13 582
Cyriac of Ancona 2 161; 8 369–70*; 14 867; 26 767
works 8 370
Cyriades 2 312
Cyril 18 83
Cyrillus 10 724
Cyrrhus see CORICE
Cyrus (fl 1st cent. BC) 26 885
Cyrus I (reg 640-600 BC) 18 530; 31 701
Cyrus II see CYRUS THE GREAT
Cyrus the Great (reg 559-530 BC) 1 115, 116, 117; 12 66; 15 906, 911; 24 220; 33 706
Cysat, Renward 30 665
Cythera see KYTHERA
Cythera, Maximos of see MAXIMOS OF CYTHERA
Cyzicus, Iaia of see IAIA OF CYZICUS
Cyzicus, Temple of Zeus 26 925
Czajkowski, Józef 8 370–71*; 18 429
groups and movements 28 838
works 25 119, 122; 29 791
Czaky, Jozseph 20 203
Czapski, Józef 8 371*; 17 804; 32 877
Czarnków 25 129
tomb of the Czarnkowski family 25 113, 129
Czarny, Marcin 25 103
Czartoryska, Isabella, Princess (1746-1835) 8 371–2*; 18 428; 25 136
books 25 142
collections 25 138, 139
gardens 2 414; 12 134; 23 202; 25 99
interior decoration 18 693
Czartoryska, Iza(bella) (1830-99) see DZIAŁYŃSKA, IZA, Countess
Czartoryski (family) 1 482
carpets 16 475
collections 2 829
drawings 28 219
paintings 25 106, 138
Czartoryski, Adam Casimir, Prince 8 371*; 23 202; 25 136
collections 25 139
paintings 1 27
Czartoryski, Adam Jerzy 8 372
Czartoryski, August Aleksander 25 135
Czartoryski, Józef 25 123
Czartoryski, Władysław, Prince 8 372*; 18 428; 25 136, 138
Czartoryski Collection see under KRAKÓW
Czauczik, Josef 19 281; 28 853
Czech, Hermann 2 789, 810, 815; 8 372–3*
Czech Cubism 8 373*, 387; 12 834; 16 902; 21 781; 25 430
see also CUBISM → regional traditions → Czechoslovakia
Czech Fine Arts Fund 8 420
Czechoslovakia see CZECH REPUBLIC; SLOVAKIA
Czechowicz, Szymon 8 374*; 18 428
pupils 25 38; 28 892
works 25 105; 32 876
Czech Photographic Society 29 898
Czech Republic 8 374–426*, 374
agate 14 II1
altarpieces 33 212
architecture 4 782, 783; 8 375–81*; 24 109
brick 8 376, 379
Gothic 8 376–7; 13 56, 57
Romanesque 8 376; 26 594
stone 8 379
vernacular 32 296
wood 8 376, 379
18th cent. 23 425
art history 8 426*
artists' biographies 9 50
ballcourts 33 303
beads 3 145, 442
beakers 8 407
bloodstone (chalcedony) 21 726
books 25 54
bottles 8 404
bowls 8 410, 412; 12 VI3; 14 II1
boxes 8 405
brick 4 782, 783; 8 376, 379
bridges 25 425
bronze 8 416; 33 435
busts 24 190
cast iron 8 386, 416
castles 8 376; 24 463; 25 437
cathedrals 25 440
cemeteries 6 154
ceramics 8 403–6*; 9 80
chairs 8 398, 400, 402
chapels 33 742
chests 8 396
chests-of-drawers 8 398
chevets (chapels) 25 439
churches
Baroque 8 378, 874, 876; 18 505, 506; 25 428
Gothic 17 585; 18 539
14th cent. 24 190
18th cent. 27 798
clocks 8 397
coins 7 535
collections 8 421–4*
glass 8 424
manuscripts 8 422
cooking pots 8 404
cotton 8 37, 419
crosses 8 414
curtains 17 570
dealing 8 423–4*
display of art 9 14
earthenwares 8 404–5
education (art) 8 425–6*
embroidery 8 420–21*
enamel 8 407, 407, 409, 410, 412, 414; 12 VI1
engraving 8 408
engravings 14 683; 25 432
epitaphs 8 390
escritoires 8 398
etchings 30 221
ewers 32 401
exhibitions 17 581
façade decoration 10 737, 741
faience (ii) (ceramics) 8 404, 404
felt 10 875
figurines 9 80; 25 488
fonts (baptismal) 8 415, 415
fortifications 21 551
fountains 33 435
furniture 8 394–5*, 397–400*, 401–3*
gables 11 876
garden cities 18 405
gardens 12 133–4*
garnets 8 414, 416–17*
gateways 25 433
gilding 8 397

Czech Republic—cont.
glass **8** 406–11*, *407*, *408*, *410*; **12** 788, VI1, VI2, VI3; **21** 721
Reichsadlerhumpen **12** VI1
Waldglas **8** 407
goblets **8** 404, *408*; **21** *726*
gold **8** 411–14*
granite **8** 376
halls **23** 809; **26** *367*
hardstones **8** *417*, 417–18*
historiography **8** 426*
houses **8** *377*, *380*; **25** *430*
housing **25** 143
initials (manuscript) **4** *7*
intarsia **8** 395, *396*, *397*
interior decoration **8** 394–5*, 397–400*, 401–3*
iron **8** *388*, 415–16*
kilns **9** 80
Kunstkammern **9** 14
lace **8** 421*; **18** 593
libraries **8** 425*
limestone **13** *90*
linen **8** 418
lithography **19** 894
mahogany **8** 399
manuscript illumination **13** 137, 151; **31** *290*
marks **8** 414, 415
mass production **20** 593
metalwork **6** *158*; **8** 411*, 415–16*; **13** 161
miniatures (manuscript illumination) **33** *71*
mirror frames **21** 721
monasteries **27** *797*; **32** *746*
monuments **22** 403; **25** *434*
mouldings **22** 216, 217, 219, 220, 221, 222
museums **8** 424*
nude figures **1** *5*; **33** *435*
oak **8** 399, *400*

Czech Republic—cont.
objects of vertu **8** 416*
oil sketches **20** *856*
opera houses **29** 422
orangeries **27** 285
painting **8** 388–94*
allegorical **1** *6*; **29** *429*
cabinet pictures **5** 352
fresco **17** *820*
Futurism **18** *493*
genre **29** *649*
Gothic **13** *134*, 151–2*; **30** 706
mythological **1** *5*; **29** *429*
Orphism **23** *569*
Realism (style) **8** *392*
religious
Gothic **13** *152*; **17** *819*; **25** *431*; **30** *706*
Mannerism **29** *430*
14th cent. **20** *774*
18th cent. **25** *448*
Romanesque **8** 388
still-lifes **11** *79*
Surrealism **8** *393*
wall **8** *389*; **13** *134*, 151
watercolours **17** *544*
palaces **5** *79*, 702; **25** *427*
paperweights **24** 57
pastiglia **13** 152
patronage **8** 421–3*
pattern books **24** 269
periodicals **20** 254; **24** 440*
pewter **8** 415*, *415*
photoarchives **8** 425
photography **24** *678*
photolithography **9** 303
plaster **8** 376, 379, *387*
porcelain **8** 405–6*
portraits
engravings **25** *432*
group **28** *827*
painting **8** *391*; **28** *827*

Czech Republic
portraits—cont.
sculpture **6** *158*; **9** 81
self-portraits **24** *190*
woodcuts **13** *913*
pottery **8** 403–5*, *405*
printing **8** 37
ragstone **6** *158*
restoration **8** 425
rock crystal **8** *414*; **25** *436*
rose-wood **8** 399
sandstone **8** 376
sculpture **8** 381*, 385–6; **22** 403
atlantids **8** *385*
Baroque **4** *698*, *844*
bronze **32** *731*; **33** *435*
Celtic **6** *158*
Cubo-Expressionism **8** *249*
Gothic **13** *90*
limestone **13** *90*
Mannerism **32** *731*
pietàs **8** *383*
relief **8** *382*, *383*
Renaissance **33** *435*
Romanesque **26** 637–8*
stone **4** *698*, *844*; **26** 637–8*
wood **8** 383, *383*
14th cent. **25** *442*
19th cent. **8** *386*
20th cent. **8** *387*, *388*; **22** *404*
silk **8** 419
silver **7** 535; **8** 411–14*
silver-gilt **8** *412*, *414*
slate **8** 376
spires **25** 54
stained glass **8** 407; **13** 187, 189
stone **4** *698*, *844*; **8** 379, *382*; **24** *190*; **26** 637–8*
synagogues **17** 544, *544*, 547; **25** *444*
tables **8** 398
tapestries **8** *420*

Czech Republic—cont.
textiles **8** 418–21*
theatres **25** *429*; **30** 677
tiles **8** 403–4
tin **8** 415
tools **24** 332
topographical views **14** *683*; **23** *425*
towers **19** *829*; **24** 462; **26** *366*
town halls **4** *833*; **25** *444*
trade
garnets **8** 416
glass **8** 408; **16** 522
tin **3** 602
travel books **31** *290*
treatises **8** 416
tubular steel **8** 402
vases **12** VI2
vaults (ceiling) **25** 440, *441*; **26** 366; **32** 90, 92, 747
villas **20** *814*
walnut **8** *398*, 399, *402*
wardrobes **8** *398*
weaving **8** 418
wood **8** 376, 379, 383, *383*, *388*
woodcuts **33** 348
writing-desks **8** 399
Czech Society of Photography **11** 844
Czech Werkbund **12** 834; **33** 599
Czechy Glassworks **25** 124
Czernin (family) **18** 191; **19** 807; **32** 447
Czernin, Adalbert von, Graf **8** 840
Czernin, Eugen, Count **33** 687
Czernin, František Josef, Count **8** 427
Czernin, Heřman Jakub, Count **1** 669; **3** 488; **5** 338; **8** 426; **27** 195, 196

Czernin, Jan Rudolf, Count **8** 427–8*
collections **2** 829; **8** 427
paintings **31** 64; **32** 706
Czernin, Prokop Adalbert (Vojtěch), Count **8** 427; **25** 33
Czernin, Thomas Zacharias, Count **27** 195
Czernin von Chudenitz, Humprecht Jan, Count **8** 422, 426, 427*
architecture **5** 701, 702; **19** 807
collections **8** 423
paintings **11** 297
Czersk **25** 131
Czerwiensk **26** 687
church **4** 782; **25** 101, 129; **26** 636
portal **25** 109
Czeschka, Carl Otto **2** 826; **8** 428–9*; **17** 528
groups and movements **33** 166
pupils **17** 691
Częstochowa **8** 429*; **25** *92*, 126
Jasna Góra monastery **8** 429; **13** 162; **25** 114
Częstochowa Madonna **8** 429, *430*; **25** 126
Czetter, Sámuel **14** 901
Czigány, Dezső **8** 429–31*; **10** 108, 109
Czóbel, Béla **8** 431*
groups and movements **10** 108, 650; **13** 638; **14** 901; **22** 434; **30** 207
works **30** 207
CZWG **13** 225
Czyżewski, Tytus **8** 431*; **25** 108
groups and movements **11** 317; **25** 649
Czyzny Bridge **24** 698

D

D., Adam **20** 800
Ɒ, Master **24** 246
D, Monogrammist **21** 337, 338
Da, Popovi **22** 595
Dab'a, Tell el- *see* PIRAMESSE
Daba church **12** 320
Dabarski, St Nicholas **25** 343
dabbers **8** 432*
see also PADS
Däbeler, Michael *see* DÖBEL, MICHAEL
Dabenarti **21** 554
Dabhoi **7** 360; **8** 432*; **15** *276*
Dabica fortress **26** 706
Dabil *see* DVIN
Dabinovic, Gaido and Rossi **30** 525
Dabnarti **9** 846
Dabona **8** 852, 853
Dabruski **6** 249
Dabychos **30** 285
Dacca *see* DHAKA
dachas **27** 377
Dachau **12** *361*
Schloss **9** 133; **33** 271
Dachau colony **8** 432*
Dachau school, New *see* NEW DACHAU SCHOOL
Dacheröden, Caroline von *see* HUMBOLDT, CAROLINE VON
Dacian **25** 533; **26** *852*; **30** 767, 768, 770, 772–3*
Dacien si **21** 846
Dacosta, António **8** 433*; **24** 321; **25** 300
Dacosta, Mílton (Rodrigues) **4** 718, 719; **8** 433*
Dacre, Mary Fiennes, Lady *see* FIENNES, MARY, Lady Dacre
Dacre, Thomas Barrett Lennard, 17th Baron *see* LENNARD, THOMAS BARRETT, 17th Baron Dacre
Dacre, Winifred *see* NICHOLSON, WINIFRED
Dacre, Holy Trinity Church **2** 71
Dacron **30** 543
Dada **1** 73, 75; **2** 225; **8** 433–9*; **11** 360; **17** 694; **20** 287; **21** 176, 745; **26** 51, 235, 356; **31** 504
art forms **22** 279
assemblages **2** 616; **28** *197*
collages **7** 557; **10** *466*; **14** *236*
collections **16** 906; **23** 7
films **10** 687
objets trouvés **23** 333
painting **24** *709*, *710*
paintings **8** *434*, *435*; **11** *544*, 549*; **12** 395; **13** 698
photomontages **24** 685, *686*
sculpture **29** 12
commentaries **4** 753; **14** 852
exhibitions **28** 920
periodicals **24** 427–8
regional traditions **2** 488; **3** 113; **7** 685; **9** 62; **10** 467; **25** 380; **28** 113; **31** 503
Australia **4** 882
Brazil **4** 719
Czech Republic **8** 437*
France **8** 205, 438–9*, 657; **24** 143, 405, 708, 710; **26** 306; **30** 17
Germany **2** 489; **3** 4, 801; **7** 356; **8** 436*; **14** 236, 280, 845; **21** 776; **24** 404, 405; **25** 837; **28** 196; **29** 869
Spain **8** 435–6*
Dada
regional traditions—cont.
Switzerland **2** 488; **3** 76; **8** 433–4*, 436*; **9** 758; **14** 845; **25** 447, 585; **26** 75; **28** 40; **30** 125; **31** 396
United States of America **2** 383; **8** 435*; **9** 358; **29** 656
Dada **24** 427, 442
Dada, Der **24** 428
Dada, Nayyar 'Ali **23** 798
Dadashev, Sadykh A. **2** 893, 898, 899; **12** 37; **31** 761
Dada Weststupidia **3** **3** 4; **8** 438
Dadd, Richard **8** 440–41*; **25** 686
groups and movements **7** 436; **9** 756; **10** 254
works **8** *440*; **14** 785
D'Adda, Crespi *see* CRESPI D'ADDA
Dadda, Francesco del *see* FERRUCCI, FRANCESCO (DI GIOVANNI)
Daddi **20** 658
Daddi, Bernardo **8** 441–4*; **11** 183; **13** 149
attributions **12** 332
patrons and collectors **5** 356; **9** 306; **11** 32; **12** 32; **14** 147; **28** 377
reproductive prints by others **12** 203
teachers **12** 686
works **7** 333; **8** *442*, *443*; **9** 4; **11** 197, 203, 206; **16** 655; **25** 679; **30** 129
workshop **5** 537; **16** 759
Daddi, Cosimo **11** 678
Dädesjö church **30** 75
Dadizele, Pilgrimage Church **3** 549
Dadler, Samuel **25** 127
Dadler, Sebastian **8** 444*; **20** 923
Dado **8** 444*
dealers **7** 842
patrons and collectors **7** 842
works **22** 18, *19*
dados **16** 216; **22** 219; **32** 817
Dadswell, Lyndon (Raymond) **2** 753; **8** 444–5*; **18** 137
Dadu *see under* BEIJING
Dadyan, Khatchik **9** 471
Daean, tomb of Tŏkhŭng **18** 313
Daedalus *see* DAIDALOS
Daegong
rattles **18** *346*
Dael, Jan van *see* DALEM, JAN VAN
Dael, Jean-François van **4** 303; **8** 445*; **11** 228, 229; **29** 668
Daems, Alexander **32** 705
Daendels, Herman Willem **16** 873
Daenens, L. **3** 620
Dafana, Tell **9** 817, 849
Da Feng *gui* **6** 844
Daffinger, Johann **8** 445; **33** 737
Daffinger, Moritz Michael **2** 796; **8** 445–6*; **21** 643
Dafni **8** 446–7*; **9** *511*; **21** 834
katholikon **7** 221; **8** 446; **9** 526, 546, *547*, 576, 645; **22** 162
mosaics **9** 578; **19** 356; **22** *162*
Dafni Master **9** 578
Daga (person) **9** 824
Daga (Ethiopia), St Stephen **10** 570
*dāgaba*s **5** 98; **6** 658; **29** 864–5*
see also STUPAS
Dageraad, De **1** 815
housing **1** *814*
Dagestan **27** *363*, 423, 432, 433, 437
daggers **2** 448, 451, 452, 453
historical and regional traditions
Central Asia, Western **6** 260, 261
China **23** 495
Denmark **25** *516*
Egypt, ancient **10** 41
Germany **1** *593*
Helladic **14** 355; **22** *397*
Iran **16** *516*
Islamic **16** 504, *506*, 509, *516*
Korea **18** 345
Mongolia **23** 495
Mycenaean **14** 355; **22** *397*
Native North Americans **22** 613
Ottoman **16** 509
Prehistoric art **25** *516*, 540
Switzerland **30** 146
materials
bone **4** 314
bronze **16** *506*; **18** 345; **22** *397*; **23** 495
chalcedony **6** 261
enamel **16** *516*
flint **25** *516*
gold **6** 261; **16** *516*
ivory **16** *506*
steel **16** *516*
turquoise **6** 261
wood **16** *506*
techniques
damascening **16** *516*
inlays **22** *397*
types
ear **2** 452
Holbein **2** 455
parrying-daggers *see* poignards
poignards **2** 454
see also KERIS
Daggett, Alfred **17** 899
Daglish, Eric Fitch **4** 367
Dagly, Gerhard **8** 447*; **18** 614
Dagly, Jacques **8** 447; **18** 614
Dagmar Cross **9** 663
Dagnan-Bouveret, P(ascal)-A(dolphe)-J(ean) **8** 447–8*; **11** 156, 499; **23** 882
works **8** *448*
Dagnia (family) **4** 824; **10** 317
Dagnia-Williams glasshouse **3** 521; **10** 318
Dagobert, King of Austrasia and Neustria (*reg* 623-39) **20** 762; **27** 549
Dagomba **9** 164
Dagomer, Charles **14** 846
Dagon *see* RANGOON
D'Agostino, Gaetano **10** 512
Dagoty **24** 149
Dagpazarı **9** 537, 565
Daguerre, Dominique **2** 559; **8** 448*; **11** 593; **20** 388; **21** 817
designers **33** 48
patrons and collectors **11** 595
pupils **29** 626
works **5** 767; **7** 658; **19** 261; **26** 182
Daguerre, Louis (Jacques Mandé) **3** 421; **8** 448–50*; **10** 83; **23** 121; **24** 646, 650, 658; **28** 203
dealers **12** 740
pupils **4** 99; **7** 403
works **7** 327; **8** *449*, 857, 867, 910–11; **24** 18, 659; **30** 679
daguerreotype process *see under* PHOTOGRAPHY → processes
daguerreotypes *see under* PHOTOGRAPHIC PRINTS → types
Daguerrian Journal *see* HUMPHREY'S JOURNAL
Daguet, France **9** 425
D'Aguilar, Vincent **3** 64
Dagulf Psalter *see under* PSALTERS → individual manuscripts
Dahak, Ibrahim **31** 426
Dahe cun (Zhengzhou) **6** 875
Dahinden, Justus **30** 128
Dahistan **6** 266
mosque **16** 163
Dahl, Emil Ferdinand **8** 753
Dahl, George L. **8** 470
works **8** *470*
Dahl, J(ohan) C(hristian Clausen) **8** 450–53*; **16** 678
groups and movements **22** 540; **23** 602; **26** 742
patrons and collectors **30** 766
personal collection **23** 243
pupils **10** 846; **12** 634; **18** 77; **23** 225
works **8** *451*, *452*, 735; **11** *472*; **12** 393; **23** 225; **31** 750
Dahl, Michael, the elder (?1659-1743) **8** 453–5*; **30** 78
collaboration **18** 145; **33** 377
patrons and collectors **4** 131; **14** 178; **25** 634
pupils **15** 53
reproductive prints by others **33** 147
works **8** *454*; **10** 249
Dahl, Michael, the younger (*d* 1741) **8** 454
Dahl, Peter **30** 82
Dahl, Roald **4** 368
Dahl, Siegwald **8** 453; **33** 411
Dahlbergh, Erik **8** 455*; **13** 30; **21** 570; **30** 70
collaboration **19** 137; **29** 399
reproductive prints by others **29** *685*
works **24** 21; **30** 70, 78; **31** 693
Dahle, Lillian **23** 234
Dahlem **12** 477
Haus Sommerfeld **3** 401
Islamic Museum **11** 455
Dahlerup, Jens Vilhelm **7** 803, 804; **8** 727; **16** 829; **18** 237; **23** 325; **27** 161
Dahlgren, Gustav **30** 113
Dahlin, Dorthe **8** 736
Dahlin, Niels **18** 614
Dähling, Heinrich Anton **12** 393
Dahls Tapetfabrik **32** 817
Dahlström, Ernst **11** 111
Dahlström, Magnus **11** 111
Dahl-Wolfe, Louise **8** 455*
Dahm, Helen **33** 737
Dahmen, Karl Fred **2** 545; **13** 727
Dahn, Walter **9** 72; **12** 397; **31** 356
Dahomey *see* BENIN, REPUBLIC OF
Dahomian Rada **31** 332
Dahpid **16** 235
Dahshur **8** 456*, *456*; **9** *774*; **10** 90
funerary boats of Sesostris III **8** 456; **9** 819
pyramids **9** 838
Ammenemes II **10** 80
Ammenemes III **1** 793; **10** 80
Bent Pyramid **2** 296; **8** 456; **9** 812; **10** 81; **20** 863; **25** *761*, 762
reliefs **9** 871
Black Pyramid **8** 456
Red Pyramid **8** 456; **25** 762
Rhomboidal Pyramid *see* Bent Pyramid
Sesostris III **8** 456; **10** 80; **28** 491
Dahshur
pyramids—cont.
Sneferu (*reg c.* 2575–*c.* 2551 BC) **9** 779, 850
White Pyramid **8** 456
reliefs **9** 871, 877
sculpture **9** 863
tombs **9** 839
Awibre Hor **10** 80
Khnumet **10** 30, 56
Mereret **10** 30
Siese **9** 877, *878*
Sithathoriunet **22** 284
Dahuting *see* MI XIAN
Dai, Marchioness of **6** 834; **7** 13, 33, 34, 46, 75
Dai Benxiao **2** 96; **8** 456–7*
Daibutsu style **17** 48, *71*, 71–2*
Daidalos **2** 312; **8** 457–8*; **13** 439, 442, 444; **25** 179
attributions **25** 180
works **4** 851
Daidalos of Sikyon **22** 690
Daido Moriyama *see* MORIYAMA, DAIDO
Daig, Sebastian **28** 57, 58
Daigaku Shūsū **2** 599; **17** 171, 663
Daigo, Emperor (*reg* 897-930) **17** 221, 222; **23** 445
Daigu Ryōkan **17** 231
Dai Huu **6** 422, 431
Daijiji **17** 749
Dai Jin **6** 781, 817; **8** 458–9*; **21** 633
groups and movements **23** 215; **33** 656
works **6** 790; **7** 675; **8** *459*; **33** *656*, 657
Daijo Tokiwa *see* TOKIWA, DAIJO
Daikaku *see* RANKEI DŌRYŪ
Daikikuya **17** 287
Dai Kui **6** 707
Dai La **32** 484
Dailaman **1** 786
Dai Libri, Girolamo *see* LIBRI, GIROLAMO DAI
Daily, Gardner **27** 730
Daily, Leo A., & Associates **10** 131
Daily Telegraph **12** 152
Daima **23** *129*, 130
Daimabad **6** 479
figurines **4** 853
metalwork **15** 706
sculpture **15** 415, 422
seals **15** 421
Dai Mangong *see* DOKURYŪ SHŌEKI
Daimler **8** 825
Daini Kikai (Association of the Second Period) **17** 135
Daintree, Richard **2** 745; **8** 460*
Dainzú **8** 460–61*; **21** *193*, *372*
pottery **33** 619
reliefs **8** *460*; **21** 219
see also MACUILXÓCHITL
dairies **8** 461*; **30** 876
Dairsie **13** 211
Dairval, Charles-César Baudelot de **23** 513
dais **23** 768
Daisenberger, Matthias **9** 183
Daisenberger, Thomas **9** 183
Daishi Rigen *see* SHŌBŌ
Daishi school **17** 233, 236
Daishitsu Sōseki **28** 493
Daishōji **18** 537
Daitō Kokushi **8** 461–2*; **17** 343; **18** 559
Daiu Maruyama *see* MARUYAMA, DAIU

Daiwaille, Jean Augustin 18 187, 188, 480
Daja, Besim 1 539
Daji, Bhau 1 483
Dajon, Nicolai 1 33
Dajosa of Balligrame 3 689
Dakakari 1 246; 30 509
Dakar 1 386
Académie Africaine des Arts Plastiques 1 432
architecture 1 319; 28 405
Ecole Nationale des Beaux-Arts 28 406
Galerie Nationale d'Art 28 406
Musée d'Art Africain 28 406
Musée Dynamique 28 406
School of Arts and Letters 1 432
sculpture 1 427
Da Ke ding 6 868
Dakhfandun see VARAKHSHA
Dakhla, Ad 33 98
Dakhla Oasis 7 819; 8 462*; 9 765, 774
frescoes 8 462
Monastery of St Thecla 7 821
Dakin, Charles Bingley 8 462; 12 26; 14 786
Dakin, James H(arrison) 8 462*
collaboration 31 232
staff 12 26
teachers 8 574
works 18 629
Dakin & Dakin 12 26
Dakoji, Devraj 8 677
Dakota 22 627
Dal 13 120
Dal', Lev 27 580
Dalai Choinkor 21 878
Dalai Lama 30 813
Dalai Lama, 5th (reg 1617-82) 5 105; 19 294; 30 812, 836, 842
Dalai Lama, 6th (1683-1706) 30 351
Dalai Lama, 14th (reg 1935-59) 30 843, 845, 850
Dalavanur cave temple 15 507
Dalberg, Karl Theodor von, Archbishop 2 591
Dalberg, Karl von, Prince 7 870
Dalbergh, Erik 20 866
Dalbesio, Adolfo 28 318
Dălboki 13 372, 373, 571
tomb 30 770
Dalbono, Carlo Tito 8 462
Dalbono, Eduardo 8 462–3*; 22 480; 28 317
Dal-Bovo Altarpiece 4 335
Dalby
Cathedral 26 592, 593
Helligkorskirken 8 721; 9 680
Dalchand (fl c. 1720-30; Jodhpur) 15 614–15
Dalchand (fl 1726; Kishgarh) 15 612
Dale, Chester 8 463*; 24 362
Dale, Cornelis van see DALEM, CORNELIS VAN, I
Dale, David 28 228, 266
Dalem, Cornelis van, I (1530-73) 4 169; 8 104, 463–4*; 10 393; 20 769
collaboration 22 201
pupils 29 428
works 3 558
Dalem, Jan van 8 464*
Dalemir 31 394
Dalen, Cornelis van see DALEM, CORNELIS VAN, I
Dalen, Jacobus van 13 607
Dalen, Lanselot van 32 705
Dalena, Danilo 24 622
Dalens, Dirk, I (d 1676) 31 780
Dalens, Dirk, III (1688-1753) 7 662; 10 864
Dales, George F. 14 162; 21 792
Daley, Henry 16 884
Daley, Leonard 16 885
Dalgıç Ahmed Ağa 16 499
Dalham (Suffolk; UK) 13 210
Dalheim (Luxembourg) 19 826
Dalhem (Sweden) 30 115
church 13 190
Dalhoff, Jørgen Balthasar 8 751
Dalhousie, George Ramsay, 4th Earl of see RAMSAY, GEORGE, 4th Earl of Dalhousie
Dalhousie, George Ramsay, 9th Earl of see RAMSAY, GEORGE, 9th Earl of Dalhousie
Dalhousie, James Andrew Ramsay, 10th Earl of see RAMSAY, JAMES ANDREW, 10th Earl of Dalhousie
Dali (China) 6 780; 7 16
pagoda 23 774
Dali (Cyprus) see IDALION
Dalí (Doménech), Salvador (Felip Jacint) 2 560; 3 219; 8 464–8*, 613; 11 550, 568; 18 100; 24 144; 29 286, 295
book illustrations 4 3; 10 726; 28 819, 820
collaboration 10 687; 11 727; 20 605
decorative works 8 544
exhibitions 7 842; 33 744
films 10 687
groups and movements 11 549; 20 591; 21 341; 24 144; 25 6; 29 670; 30 20, 21
holograms 14 690
jewellery 17 529; 31 655
multimedia 22 279
paintings 8 466, 467; 9 293; 10 482; 15 140; 25 686; 29 12; 31 52
patrons and collectors 1 496; 2 384; 8 463; 16 892; 20 142; 23 169; 24 369; 27 225; 28 273; 32 912
productions 16 892; 19 660
stage design 29 286
textiles 9 293
writings 30 262
Dalidet 2 660
Dalivala 29 475
Daliwe, Jacques 8 468–9*; 24 269
Dalkeith (Lothian)
Dalkeith Palace 10 292; 28 246
James Calderwood's house 28 245
Dall, Nicholas Thomas 26 335
Dall'Abacco, Antonio see LABACCO, ANTONIO
Dall'Acqua, Cristoforo see ACQUA, CRISTOFORO DALL'
Dallaire, Jean (Philippe) 8 469*
Dallas (TX) 8 469–70*; 31 587
Allied Bank Plaza see First Interstate Bank Tower
Brook Hollow 10 749
First Interstate Bank Tower 10 417; 11 347; 12 794; 28 834
Fountain Place 11 347
Hall of State 8 470
Kalita Humphreys Theater 30 684
Morton H. Myerson Symphony Center
Eugene McDermott Concert Hall 1 126; 7 688
Museum of Fine Arts 8 470; 22 367
collections 3 363; 11 378
exhibitions 1 446; 27 47
Nieman-Marcus 8 770
Reunion Hotel 12 794
Southern Methodist University
Elizabeth Meadows Sculpture Garden 28 315
Meadows Museum 20 911
Dallas/Fort Worth Airport 1 495
Dallaway, James 8 470–71*; 31 283
translated works 21 614
D'Allemagne, Claude 18 572
dalles de verre see under GLASS → types
Dallin, Cyrus 31 612; 33 184
Dallinger von Dalling, Johann 19 338
Dallwitz porcelain factory 2 817
Dalma 15 903, 920
Dalmasio, Lippo di see LIPPO DI DALMASIO
Dalmasio (di Jacopo) Scannabecchi 4 276; 8 471*; 19 453; 28 753
Dalmata, Giovanni see GIOVANNI DALMATA
Dalmatic of Charlemagne 9 643, 668
dalmatics 9 251, 640, 642; 16 444; 32 388*
Dalmaticus, Georgius Matthei see GIORGIO DA SEBENICO
Dalmatie, Duc de see SOULT, (JEAN DE DIEU), Maréchal
Dalmatinac, Juraj Matejev see GIORGIO DA SEBENICO
Dalmatino, il see BENCOVICH, FEDERICO
Dalmau, Josep 8 436
Dalmau, José Ratés see RATÉS DALMAU, JOSÉ
Dalmau, Lluís (fl 1431) 3 218; 8 471–2*
works 3 218, 218; 29 276
Dalmau, Lluís (fl 1910-20) 21 705
Dalmau ces Planes 8 817
Dalmau de Mur, Archbishop 12 650
Dalmeny (Lothian)
Dalmeny House 6 94; 22 532; 26 617; 30 502; 31 472, 473
St Cuthbert 26 614
Dalokay, Vedat 16 94, 242
Dalou, Jules 5 879; 8 472–3*; 10 266; 11 564, 566, 567, 659
assistants 9 305
collaboration 30 32
groups and movements 23 33; 26 56
patrons and collectors 15 895; 23 794
pupils 3 367; 5 421; 17 610; 25 187
teachers 9 447; 19 39
works 8 473; 11 565, 566, 599; 22 48; 29 565, 566, 574; 30 499
Dalovice 8 405, 406
Dal Pozzo, Cassiano see POZZO, CASSIANO DAL
Dalrymple (family of Newhailes) 25 882
Dalrymple, Hew 28 235
Dalsace, Jean 6 476
Dalsgaard, Christen 8 735; 14 572
Dalsgaard, Sven 8 473*
Dalswinton 22 531
Dalton, John 2 743
Dalton, Ormonde Maddock 8 474*; 9 528
Dalton, Richard 8 474–5*; 9 230; 13 696; 25 631
dealing 14 144; 29 796
groups and movements 13 608
paintings 13 789
works 13 789
Dalton Plan 17 420
Dalu 15 606
Dal'verzin see DILBERDJIN
Dalverzin Tepe 6 182, 192, 196; 8 475*
architecture 6 198
House DT-5 6 224
ivory-carvings 6 271
jewellery 6 238, 273
Sanctuary DT-1 6 215–16
Sanctuary DT-9 6 215
wall paintings 6 225
sculpture 6 215, 216
Temple DT-7 see Temple of the Great Bactrian Goddess
Temple of the Great Bactrian Goddess
sculpture 6 215
wall paintings 6 224–5, 225
Dalverzin Tepe—cont.
wall paintings 6 224–5
Dalvui 12 142
Dalwood, Hubert 24 820
Daly, César-Denis 8 476*; 11 359, 522
collaboration 11 521
groups and movements 9 705
restorations 1 577
staff 6 581
teachers 9 312
works 25 807; 32 555
writings 26 13
Daly, Dominick 4 884
Daly, Greg 2 762
Daly, Marcel 8 476
Dalziel, Edward 33 369
book illustrations 4 868; 11 331; 24 832; 25 406
Dalziel, George 4 868; 11 331
book illustrations 24 832; 25 406
Dalziel, John 4 868
Dalziel, Margaret 4 868
Dalziel, Thomas 4 868
Dalziel Brothers see BROTHERS DALZIEL
Dam, Wouter 28 165
Dama de Baza 15 59
Damad Ibrahim Pasha 16 226
Daman 15 401; 21 591
Daman Amalan 15 233, 233
damar 18 611
Damar congregational mosque 16 177
damascene (i) (metalwork) see DAMASCENING
damascene (ii) (textiles) 8 476*
Damasceni, Alessandro see PERETTI(-MONTALTO), ALESSANDRO, Cardinal
Damasceni, Alessandro see PERETTI-MONTALTO, ALESSANDRO, Cardinal
damascening 2 454–5, 472; 8 476*; 15 712, 713*; 16 516; 21 327
see also INLAYS → uses → metalwork
Damascus 1 851; 8 476–80*; 9 513; 13 362; 16 104; 26 915; 30 180
art forms and materials
architecture 16 207, 211; 20 227; 30 177; 32 314
beakers 27 79
carpets 16 473
coins 11 146; 16 510, 511
glass 16 518, 519
manuscripts 16 311
masonry 16 180
metalwork 14 427; 16 379, 381, 382, 384, 389–90; 30 178
paper 24 48
pottery 8 479; 16 413, 415, 416, 416, 420
printing 16 361
silk 16 445
textiles 1 880; 16 430, 441
tiles 16 413, 422
baths 3 376
Hammam al-Bazuriyya 3 376
Hammam al-Mawsili 3 376
Hammam al-Safi 3 376
Hammam al-Silsila 3 376
Hammam al-Tayruzi 3 376
caravanserais 5 723
cenotaph of Salah al-Din 16 491
Dar al-'Aqiqi see Islamic religious buildings → Zahiriyya Madrasa
factories 16 441
fortifications 21 582; 33 614
Bab Sharqi 21 582
citadel 21 583
hospital of Nur al-Din 8 478; 12 78; 16 181, 381; 22 322
houses 16 263, 269
house of Nur al-Din 16 499
Damascus—cont.
Islamic religious buildings 16 180; 20 56
'Adiliyya Madrasa 16 180
congregational mosques 16 179
Great Mosque 8 479–80*, 480; 15 351; 16 136, 146, 147–8, 148, 208; 20 227; 22 192–3
dome 9 84
grilles 16 257
inscriptions 16 146
maqṣūras 20 368
minaret 21 627
mosaics 9 38; 12 71; 16 128, 255–6, 255; 18 70; 22 162
shrine of John the Baptist 22 192
towers 21 625
al-Hanabila Mosque 16 179
Jaqmaqiyya Madrasa 16 211
Madrasa of Baybars I see Zahiriyya Madrasa
mihrabs 21 504
Musalla 22 354
Nuriyya Madrasa 16 180
Tomb of Nur al-Din 31 112
Sabuniyya Mosque 16 211
Sulaymaniyya complex 16 228, 228
Mosque 16 221
al-Tawba Mosque 16 180
al-Tawrizi complex 16 249
Mosque of Ghars al-Din al-Tawrizi 16 417
Qubbat al-Tawrizi 31 112
Tomb of Ghars al-Din al-Tawrizi 23 557
Umayyad Mosque see Great Mosque
'Uthman Mosque 16 241
Zahiriyya Madrasa 20 227; 22 323
Tomb of Baybars I 16 256
maqṣūras 20 368
markets 16 262
metalwork 16 382
museums 30 178
Musée des Arts Populaires et Traditions 8 478; 16 228
see also palaces → 'Azm Palace
Musée National de Damas see National Museum of Damascus
Museum of Popular Arts and Traditions see Musée des Arts Populaires et Traditions
National Museum of Damascus 16 557; 30 178
collections 8 478; 9 414; 21 310; 30 199
palaces 23 815
'Azm Palace 30 177
see also museums → Musée des Arts Populaires et Traditions
Qasr al-Ablaq 20 227
Qubbat al-Khaḍra' 23 815
Striped Palace see Qasr al-Ablaq
Temple of Jupiter Damascena 26 915, 916, 917
tombs and mausolea 16 181; 31 111, 112
Rukniya Turba 31 111
Tomb of Baybars I see under Islamic religious buildings → Zahiriyya Madrasa
Tomb of Nur al-Din see under Islamic religious buildings → Nuriyya Madrasa
trade 30 179
University 30 177
urban planning 16 260, 261, 262, 263
Damascus, Apollodoros of see APOLLODOROS OF DAMASCUS
Damascus ware see under POTTERY → wares

damask 16 430; 19 415–19*; 30 551*
historical and regional traditions
Ancient Near East 30 551
Belgium 3 576; 19 415, 418
Byzantine 9 665
China 7 49; 30 551
Denmark 8 757
Early Christian (c. AD 250-843) 9 665
England 10 274; 19 415
France 11 589, 645
Germany 12 464, 469; 19 418
Iran 16 441
Ireland 19 419
Japan 17 311, 313, 315
Netherlands, the 19 416, 416; 22 899, 900
Poland 19 416
Russia 19 418
Scotland 28 265–6
Sweden 19 418; 30 115*
United States of America 19 419
uses
beds 3 483
chairs 11 589
hangings 10 274
interior decoration 3 576; 9 15
napkins 19 416, 416
tablecloths 19 415, 416
towels 19 416, 416
see also LINEN
Damaskenos, Michael 8 157; 24 263; 25 333
works 8 157; 25 333
Damast, Quirijn Jansz. 22 899
Dambadeniya 29 440, 450
Dambal, Dodda Basappa 15 324, 326
Damborg, P. C.
works 11 475
Dambrowsky, Ivan see GRAHAM, JOHN (1881-1961)
Dambulla 5 98; 8 481*; 29 440
monasteries 29 446
sculpture 29 461
textiles 29 476
wall paintings 29 462, 465
DAM DAN 16 84
Damel', Jan 19 498
Damer, Anne Seymour 6 323; 8 481*; 17 851; 33 308
Damer, Henrik 8 481*
Damer, Joseph, 1st Earl of Dorchester 31 906
Damery, Chevalier de 8 481–2*
Damery, Walthère 8 482*
Damgaard, Aage 8 758; 29 77
Damghan 8 482*; 15 901; 16 105
architecture 16 160
Chihil Dukhtaran 4 791
gardens 12 83
Immazada Ja'far 23 557
murals 15 922
Pir-i 'Alamdar 4 791; 16 250; 22 321
Tarik-Khana Mosque 4 791; 16 153, 154, 160; 22 194
Damhouder, De, Triptych 25 382
Dami, Benci di Cione 30 273
Damian, Ascanio 26 710
Damian, Horia 8 482–3*
Damiani, Antonio 26 478
Damiani Almeyda, Giuseppe 8 483*
Damiano 6 41; 16 725
Damiano, Giacomo da see GIACOMO DA DAMIANO
Damians, J. 29 344
Damietta 16 104
textiles 16 431, 432; 31 21, 21
Damini, Damina 8 483
Damini, Giorgio 8 483
Damini, Pietro 8 483*
Damini, Vincenzo 8 484*
Damisch, Hubert 29 788
Damishliyya 30 196
Damitz, Ernst 22 441
Damjanov, Andreja 8 484*; 19 883
Damjanović-Damjan, Radomir 28 451
Damjanovski, Bozidar 28 451
Damm, Johannes von 7 584
Dammam museum 2 275
Dammann 10 580
dammar 1 155, 760; 8 484*; 26 142, 243; 32 2
encaustic paintings 10 196
fixatives 11 142
glazes 12 803
varnishes 32 4
waxes 33 2
Dammartin, Drouet de 4 578; 8 484–5*, 891; 17 460; 24 132; 26 43
Dammartin, Guillaume de see GUILLAUME DE DAMMARTIN
Dammartin, Guy de 4 582; 8 484–5*; 13 59; 24 132; 26 43; 31 836, 839
collaboration 8 484
works 4 578; 8 485
Dammartin, Jean de 8 485; 19 128
Dammartin, Simon de 2 112
Dammazedi Ramadhipati, King of Burma (reg 1472-92) 5 241
Damme
Onze Lieve Vrouwekerk 13 61, 110
Stadhuis 3 543
Damme, Antonius van 3 727
Damme, E. Van see VAN DAMME, E.
Dammouse, Albert-Louis 12 783; 13 318; 19 397; 24 148
Damm Pottery, Aschaffenburg 14 606
Damoa 1 485
Damodarpur 15 475
Damon, Isaac 31 231
Damophilos 10 617; 26 764
Damophon 8 485*; 13 464; 21 46
Damotte, Jean 27 681
Damour, Alexis 16 860
Damour, Pierre 26 113
Dampier, Thomas, Bishop of Ely 6 117
Dampierre, Gwijde van see GWIJDE VAN DAMPIERRE
Dampierre Château 6 377, 508; 11 159, 567, 659; 15 842; 28 746
gardens 12 122
Dampt, Jean (-Auguste) 8 485–6*; 11 567
collaboration 25 52
groups and movements 6 489
pupils 29 397
Damrong Rajanubhab 8 486*; 29 241
Damsa Köyü, palace of Taşkin Pasha 16 204
Damscène-Morgand 9 466
Damsgård summer-house 23 220, 221
Damyanov, Krum 5 156, 162
Dan (Africa) 8 21, 486–90*
aesthetics 1 236
basketwork 8 489
body arts 1 288, 344
craftsmen and artists 8 488, 490*
gongs 1 360
houses 8 489–90*
ladles 8 489*
masks 1 236, 243, 333, 338, 339, 340, 390; 8 486–8*, 487, 488; 19 310
painting 8 22
patronage 1 241, 243
portraits 1 267
pottery 8 489
sculpture 8 22, 488–9*
spoons 1 291, 368, 368; 8 489*, 489
stelae 8 489
textiles 8 490
wood 1 291, 368
wood-carvings 8 487, 488, 489, 490
Dan (Israel) 1 862; 17 539; 30 185
fortifications 17 553
Dana 15 615
Danaid group 13 532
Danaid Painter 13 532
Danakil 1 306
Danakos, Hagios Ioannis Theolos 9 575
Dan Alexander of Kirkstall 7 351
Danang (Tibet) 6 623; 30 806, 818
Danang (Vietnam) 6 418; 32 468
National Museum of Cham Sculpture 29 240
Danauskas, Jonas 19 498
Danay, Richard Glazer 22 665
Danbolt, Gunnar 23 245
Danby, Francis 4 78; 8 491–2*; 16 16
commentaries 10 377
groups and movements 4 823; 26 741; 29 891
patrons and collectors 12 638
works 8 491
Danby, Henry Danvers, Earl of see DANVERS, HENRY, Earl of Danby
Danby, James Francis 8 492
Danby, Thomas 8 492; 12 638
Dancart, Pieter 13 123; 26 249; 28 518; 29 290
works 28 517
dance
Bali (Indonesia) 15 802
Indonesia 15 802*
Japan 17 333–4
Java 15 802*
Laos 18 774–5
Sumatra 15 802
Venezuela 32 167
Dance, Charles 8 495
Dance, George (i) (1695-1768) 8 492–3*
assistants 8 493
competitions 7 666
pupils 8 493
works 10 233; 19 571; 31 235
Dance, George (ii) (1741-1825) 8 492, 493–5*; 15 406
competitions 7 666
patrons and collectors 3 239, 454; 24 570; 28 908
pupils 28 872, 905
reproductive prints by others 8 505
restorations 19 566
works 2 595, 658; 8 493, 494; 10 233, 369; 19 571; 20 867; 24 641; 25 267
Dance, Suzanne 8 495*
Dance, Thomas 8 64
dance-crests 31 73
Dance-Holland, Nathaniel 8 492, 493–4*; 14 585; 26 774
artists' houses 8 494
patrons and collectors 14 144; 26 475; 33 20, 209
reproductive prints by others 14 49
works 7 340; 13 303
dancette see CHEVRONS
dancewands 33 555, 556
Dan Chand, Prince 15 624
Danchov, Ivan 3 625
Dancing Satyrs, Painter of the 10 615
Danckerts (family) 2 696
Danckerts see DANCKERTS DE RIJ
Danckerts, Cornelis 8 496
Danckerts, Dancker 28 74
Danckerts, Hendrick 7 785; 8 495*; 24 373; 32 784
Danckerts, Johannes (1615-c. 1681/7) 8 495
Danckerts de Rij, Cornelis (1561-1634) 8 496*; 18 8, 9
Danckerts de Rij, Cornelis (fl 1637-84) 8 496
Danckerts de Rij, Hendrick 8 496
Danckerts de Rij, Pieter 8 496; 19 496; 25 104; 32 7, 875
Danckerts I van Seevenhoven, Cornelis 8 496
D'Ancona, Paolo 8 496*
D'Ancona, Vito 16 678; 19 870
Danda, J. 25 430
Dandani see:
FIRUZ, Khan
MUJAHID, Khan
SHAMS KHAN DANDANI, Khan
Dandan-oilik 6 288, 614; 8 496–7*; 18 29; 28 719, 720
Monastery 6 296
paintings 6 292, 311
Sanctuary D.II 6 296
sculpture 6 300
stucco 29 823
wall paintings 6 303
Dandanqan see DASH-RABAT
Dandan-uilik see DANDAN-OILIK
Dandenong 2 736
Danderyd 30 83
church 26 646
Dandin 15 512
Dandini, Cesare 8 497–8*; 16 673
collaboration 8 498; 12 528
patrons and collectors 21 26
pupils 3 631; 8 497, 498; 12 527
teachers 1 673
works 8 498
Dandini, Ottavio 8 497
Dandini, Pietro 8 497, 498*
collaboration 21 30
pupils 11 743; 25 718, 890; 26 242
teachers 8 498
Dandini, Vincenzo (1609-75) 8 497–8*
patrons and collectors 7 897
pupils 11 873
works 11 194
Dandini, Vincenzo (1686-1734) 8 497
Dandolo, Andrea, Doge of Venice (reg 1343-54) 8 499*; 32 189, 198, 207, 212
Dandolo, Anne, Queen of Serbia see ANNE, Queen of Serbia
Dandoy, Jan 4 871
D'Andrade, Alfredo (Cesare Reis Freire) see ANDRADE, ALFREDO (CESARE REIS FREIRE) DE
Dandré-Bardon, Michel-François 8 499–500*
collaboration 11 761
pupils 17 681
reproductive prints by others 3 107
teachers 32 670
works 8 500, 612
Dandridge, Bartholomew 1 504; 8 501*; 31 871
Danebury (Hants) 6 160; 25 470, 536
hill-fort 25 537
Danedi, Giovanni Antonio see MONTALTO
Danedi, Giuseppe 31 901
Daneel de Rijcke 8 501*
Danel & Cie 31 261
Daneri, Carlo 16 650
Danestama 16 166–7
Danet, Louis 8 549
Danferganket 6 379
Danforth (family) 31 652
Danforth, Thomas (fl 1733-86) 31 651
Danforth, Thomas, II (b 1756) 31 651
Dangar, Ann 2 760
Dangel, Miguel von 8 501–2*
Dangelo, Sergio 2 526; 9 201
Danger see PUKAPUKA
Dangeville 24 893
Danglus, Jacques 3 634
Dangolsheim Madonna, Master of the 12 342; 20 653*, 736
Dangon, Claude 11 645; 19 849
Dangotte, Céline 3 579
Dangriga 3 622, 622
Dang Shiva Temple 15 288, 495
Dangu, François Sublet Des Noyers, Baron de see DES NOYERS, FRANÇOIS SUBLET, Baron de Dangu
Danguin, J.-B. 28 423
Dangulf Psalter see under PSALTERS → individual manuscripts
Dangyang, Yuquan Temple 7 99; 23 773
Danhauer, Gottfried 27 388
Danhauser, Josef David 8 502
Danhauser, Josef Franz 2 796, 808; 8 502–3*; 32 444
pupils 17 731; 26 501
teachers 18 419
works 2 546; 4 39, 40; 8 502, 503
Danhauser, Josef Ulrich 2 813; 8 502*; 32 448
pupils 8 502
works 2 814
Danicel 9 118
Daniel, Abraham 14 202
Daniel, Charles 4 180
Daniel, Ghandi 14 59
Daniel, Henry 29 419
Daniel, Juan Bautista 2 398; 7 847
Daniel, Mann, Johnson and Mendenhall 24 342
Daniel, Père 4 512
Daniel, Peter Clarke 29 120
Daniel, Pierre 24 146
Daniel, T. B. 2 764
Daniel-Dupuis, Jean-Baptiste 8 503*; 25 214
Daniele da Volterra 8 503–5*; 16 665, 766; 32 691
assistants 3 471
attributions 24 533
collaboration 24 827; 29 740
paintings 5 789; 8 504; 21 450; 24 419; 25 411; 26 817; 30 800
patrons and collectors
Bracciano, Paolo Giordano II Orsini, Duca di 23 576
Farnese, Alessandro, Cardinal (1520-89) 26 838
Filacciano, Elena Orsini, Baroness of 23 575
Gondi, Benedetto 12 897
Julius III, Pope (reg 1550–55) 22 6
Massimo, Pietro (d 1544) 20 587
Orléans, Philippe I de Bourbon, 1st Duc d' (1640-1701) 4 756
Orsini, Fulvio 23 577
Paul IV, Pope (reg 1555-59) 6 175; 26 769
Piot, Eugène 24 838
Pius V, Pope (reg 1566-72) 26 769
Richelieu, Armand-Jean Du Plessis, Cardinal de 26 348
pupils 25 185
sculpture 3 925; 5 789, 905; 10 441
stucco 26 818; 27 653
Danieletti, Daniele 17 442
Danieletti, Pietro-Antonio 6 341
Danieli, Bartolomeo 18 590
Danieli, Teramo 16 742
Daniell, Edward Thomas 8 505–6*; 9 309
Daniell, Samuel 8 505
Daniell, Thomas 8 505; 15 406
aquatints 1 648; 15 679
architectural decorations 7 502; 20 490
drawings 15 210; 19 774
engravings 5 419
prints 1 648
Daniell, William 4 362; 8 505; 15 406, 892
works 1 648; 5 419; 15 210, 679; 28 908
Danielová, Marie 8 421

Daniels, H. 18 887
Daniels, Mark 27 730
Daniëls, René 8 506*; 22 853
Daniels, William 33 251
Daniel Zifroni, Israel ben see ZIFRONI, ISRAEL BEN DANIEL
Danielzyck, Jörg 21 67
Daniil Chorny 8 506*; 27 304, 384
works 22 176; 27 304; 28 464; 32 665
Danil, Konstantin 28 450
Danill, Chorney see DANIIL CHORNY
Daniłłowicz (family) 25 135
Danilo 25 330, 340
Danilo II, Archbishop 8 599; 24 308; 28 446, 448
Danilov, V. V. 10 889
Danilovich, Vasily 23 269
Danilovka 32 527
Daniłowicz, Mikołaj 32 869
Danish Asiatic Company 7 80
Danish Cooperative Wholesale Society see FÆLLESFORENINGEN FOR DANMARKS BRUGSFORENINGER
Danish East India Company 6 332; 27 659
Danish Handicrafts Guild 8 756
Danishmendid, Malik Muhammad see MALIK MUHAMMAD, Ruler
Danišovce 28 854
Danjoy, Jean-Charles-León 7 170
Danjūrō I see ICHIKAWA DANJŪRŌ I
Dankers de Ryj see DANCKERTS DE RIJ
Dankertsz., Cornelis 1 801
Dan'ko, Nataliya (Yakovlevna) 8 506–7*; 27 413
Danko, Yelena 27 413
Dankward 5 28
Dankwart, Karl 8 429; 25 105
Danleng, Mt Zheng 6 715
Danlí 14 *711*
aqueduct 14 713
church 14 713
Museo del Cabildo 14 716
Danloux, Henri-Pierre 8 507*; 19 217
works 8 *507*
Dannatt, Trevor 8 508*; 20 491
writings 9 297
Dannecker, Johann Heinrich (von) 8 508–9*; 9 39; 29 875
patrons and collectors 12 406
pupils 14 307; 15 144; 28 86; 30 137
teachers 29 73
works 8 *509*; 12 406, *406*; 19 781; 28 45
Danneels, Justus 7 832
Danner, Countess 16 863
Danneskiold-Samsøe, Henriette, Countess 8 749
Dannevirke 8 721
D'Annunzio, Gabriele 8 509*, 596; 11 190; 26 776
collaboration 8 601
productions 21 473
works 8 702; 16 721; 20 404
Danran Zhai 33 536
Danske museer 24 451
Dansk kunsthåndværk 24 451
Dansk tidsskrift for museumsformidling 24 451
Dantan, Antoine-Laurent 2 700; 8 510*
Dantan, Jean-Pierre 5 303; 8 510*; 10 435; 11 564; 29 574; 30 32
works 5 *303*
Dante Alighieri see ALIGHIERI, DANTE
Dan Temple 30 446
Danthe 28 178
Danti, Antonio 13 628
Danti, Gerolamo 8 510
Danti, Giulio 8 510, 511
Danti, Ignazio 8 510, 513*; 12 814; 26 416
assistants 1 552; 19 806
patrons and collectors 13 628; 20 365, 366
works 4 812; 16 771; 24 489; 28 203; 32 508
Danti, Theodora 8 510
Danti, Vincenzio 8 510, 511–12*; 24 520; 26 770
attributions 1 789
collaboration 18 820; 29 403
competitions 7 672
works 1 609; 8 *511*; 10 499; 16 695; 29 569
writings 1 178; 31 302
Dantidurga, Ruler (*reg c.* 752-8) (Rashtrakuta) 10 147; 15 279
Danto, Arthur C. 1 183; 10 692; 25 362; 28 927
Danton 2 47
Dantyu, Mikhail Le see LE DANTYU, MIKHAIL
Danube school 2 792, 800; 8 513–15*; 12 386; 18 705–6; 25 606; 26 188; 32 441, 442
members 1 714; 4 758; 8 112; 12 387; 14 835; 20 801
works 8 *514*; 12 *387*
Danusso, Luigi 3 438; 11 63
Danuzio, Salvatore 2 396
Danvers (MA) 31 634
Danvers, Henry, Earl of Danby 5 764; 23 326; 29 714
Danvers, John 12 127
Danyang 6 698, 845
sculpture 6 729, *729*
Danzig see GDAŃSK
Danziger, (Max Wilhelm) Itzhak 8 515*; 16 567
patrons and collectors 16 570
pupils 28 187
works 17 579, *579*
Daochos of Pharsalos 8 697
Daochus 19 852
Daoguang emperor (Qing)
tomb 6 *704*
Daoism 8 515–17*; 12 62
art
altars 1 703; 6 786
architecture 6 671–4*, *672*
bronze 6 *628*
cinnabar 7 631
dress 7 78
figurines 7 105–6, *106*
iconography 8 516–17
China 5 107; 6 628*; 7 61, 105–6, *106*; 10 485
Japan 17 39–40*
Korea 18 255
Vietnam 32 470
incense burners 6 785
ivory-carvings 7 105–6, *106*
painting 6 785–7*, *786*, *787*, 804, 823, 824
sculpture 6 *628*, 723–5*, *724*; 8 *516*, *517*
stelae 29 617
symbolism (critical term) 6 632
temples 6 671; 30 443, *444*
theories (art) 6 634
regional traditions
China 6 625, 626*; 7 61; 10 485; 12 88
Japan 12 95
Korea 18 252
sects
Lingbao 6 626
Maoshan 6 626
Quanzhen 5 112; 6 626
Tianshhi dao see Way of the Heavenly Masters
True Unity see Way of the Heavenly Masters
Way of the Heavenly Masters 6 626
Zhengyi see Way of the Heavenly Masters
Daoji 6 762, 774, 781, 791, 818; 8 517–20*; 22 460
attributions 33 496
collaboration 21 60; 32 840
groups and movements 33 496, 497
works 5 35; 6 762–3, *763*, 785, 791–2, 801, 813; 8 *518*, *520*
writings 6 798, 825
Daoust, Sylvia 5 570
Daoxuan 5 109
Daphnae see DAFANA, TELL
Daphne 12 68; 13 419; 31 703
Temple of Apollo and Artemis 28 383
Daphne Ewer 27 79
Daphnis of Miletos 8 869
Daplyn, Alfred James 2 602
Dapolin 21 431
Dapper, Musée see under PARIS → museums
Dapperen, C. E. van 18 481
Daqian, Zhang 10 794
Dara 9 *513*, 543; 24 215; 31 434
Darab (Kazakhstan) see OTRAR
Darab (Iran) 16 802
Darab 'Ali Khan 15 380
Daragnès, Jean-Gabriel 3 786; 18 631
Dar al-Khilafa see under SAMARRA' → palaces
Daraniyagala, Justin Pieris 8 520*; 29 468
Darapgird
coins 16 *511*
Dararasami, Princess 30 623
Daras, Henry 25 751
Dărăscu, Nicolae 8 521*; 26 723
Dara Shikoh, Mughal prince 1 582; 15 367, 590, 678, 713; 18 646
weapons 15 *678*
Darasuram 8 521*; 15 *294*, 333
Airavateshvara 15 518
Darband-i Gaur 21 295
Darbishire, Henry 30 457
Darbourne, John 8 521
Darbourne & Darke 8 521*; 19 578
Darboven, Hanne 8 521–2*; 19 493
Darby, Abraham, II (1711-56) 16 50
Darby, Abraham, III (1750-91) 8 285; 16 52
works 16 *53*
Darby, William 4 623
Darb Zubayda 16 151
D'Arcangelo, Allan 8 522*; 18 719; 20 607; 25 232
Darcel, Alfred 8 522*
Dar Chaabane 31 426
D'Arco, Carlo, Conte 8 522–3*
Darcy 11 905
D'Arcy, William Knox 10 352
Darda 8 *174*
Esterházy Palace 8 176
Dardani, Antonio 5 178
Dardé (family) 29 319
Dardel, Nils 3 120; 8 523*; 30 81; 33 566
Dardel, Robert-Guillaume 8 523–4*
Dardón 14 714
Daremberg 10 211
Dares Phrygius 7 242
Dar es Salaam 1 *407*; 20 149
House of Arts see Nyumba ya Sanaa
King George V Memorial Museum see National Museum of Tanzania
Msasani Workshop 30 301
National Archives 30 302
National Arts of Tanzania Gallery 1 433; 30 302
National Museum of Tanzania 30 302
Nyumba ya Sanaa 30 300
Dar es Salaam—cont.
University 30 301
Village Museum 30 302
wood-carvings 1 253
Daret, Daniel 5 210; 8 524
Daret, Jacques 8 524–5*; 11 639; 31 218
collaboration 3 397; 8 501; 11 799
patrons and collectors 5 211, 212; 29 46
teachers 5 548; 20 671
works 8 *524*; 13 195; 20 670, 671; 30 732
Daret, Jean 1 497; 8 525*; 24 828
Daret, Pierre 4 125; 8 525*
assistants 25 77
works 19 247; 32 718
Darfur 29 895
Dargan, William 33 566
Darger, Henry 22 442
Dargie, William 25 710
Dargin 27 432
Darhan 21 *870*
darics see under COINS → types
Dariganga 21 878
Darilek, Henrik 15 2; 33 710
Darin 2 256, 273
Bayt 'Abd al-Wahhab 32 316
Dario, Giovanni Antonio 8 526*; 27 661; 29 27
Dario da Pordenone see DARIO (DI GIOVANNI) DA TREVISO
Dario (di Giovanni) da Treviso 8 526*; 24 638; 29 436
Darion 25 500, 503
Darius I (*reg* 521-486 BC) 1 115, 116–18; 9 *777*, 888, 892; 15 906; 24 481
architecture 2 213; 3 11; 15 912; 30 27, 29
palaces 1 876; 24 482; 26 134
inscriptions 1 872, 892
rock relief 1 *116*
rock reliefs 4 94
tomb 15 912
Darius II (*reg* 423-405 BC) 2 213; 9 *777*
Darius III Codoman (*reg* 335-332 BC) 9 *778*
Darius, Gary 14 58
Darius Painter 13 529; 32 38*
works 13 *528*
Darius the Great see DARIUS I
Darjeeling 8 526–7*; 15 *279*
botanic garden 12 76
Natural History Museum 8 526
Dark, Philip J. C. 3 723
works 3 *721*
Dark Age (i) (*c.* 1050-*c.* 750 BC; Greece) 8 527*
Dark Age (ii) (*c.* 5th-8th cent. AD; Western Europe) 8 527*
see also BYZANTINE; CELTIC; EARLY CHRISTIAN; GERMANIC ART; INSULAR ART; OSTROGOTHIC; VIKING; VISIGOTHIC
Darke, Geoffrey 8 521
Darkennes, Jan 28 595
Dark-faced Burnished ware see under POTTERY → wares
Dark-on-light style pottery see under POTTERY → wares
Darley (family) 9 317
Darley, Felix Octavius Carr 8 528*; 24 600; 33 369
patrons and collectors 2 858
works 4 364
Darley, Frederick 9 323
Darley, Henry 9 322; 28 894
Darley, Hugh 9 323
Darley, Mary 8 529
Darling, Frank 8 528*; 23 170
Darling, Governor 2 738
Darling & Curry 29 435
Darlinghurst Court House 18 887
Darling & Pearson 8 528*; 23 170
works 5 562; 22 36; 31 176, 863
Darlington, Henry Vane, 2nd Earl of see VANE, HENRY, 2nd Earl of Darlington
Darlington, Robert 13 298
Darly, Matthias 8 528–9*; 20 350
pupils 7 171
works 4 361; 7 172; 15 164
writings 10 295
Darmstadt 8 529–31*; 12 *361*, 456
Behrens House 12 *417*
Ernst Ludwig Haus 23 393
Haus Habrich 30 885
Hessisches Landesmuseum 21 311; 29 516
Hochzeitsturm 10 697; 21 779; 23 *394*; 30 885
Kunsthalle 27 131
Ludwigskirche 8 *531*
painting 12 394
Schloss 8 530, *530*
Schlossmuseum 8 530
synagogue 17 549
urban planning 21 821
Weltausstellung, 1901 10 683
Darmstädter Künstler-Kolonie 2 566; 3 511; 8 531*; 10 465, 683; 12 416, 428, 449; 22 541; 23 393; 24 591
members 4 469; 14 622; 19 707
Darmstadt Machzor see under MACHZORS → indvidual manuscripts
Darmstadt Madonna 8 530
Darmstadt Passion, Master of the 20 654–5*
works 12 384; 20 *654*
Darna, Jean 27 493
Darnault, Charles 3 414; 5 767; 19 261
Darnaway Castle 9 727
Darne, Macé 2 111
darning 7 45
Darnley, John Bligh, 3rd Earl of see BLIGH, JOHN, 3rd Earl of Darnley
Darnstedt, Johann Adolph 11 760
Daroca
Church of Santiago 22 255
collegiate church of S María 29 332
gold 13 165
metalwork 29 332, 335
S Domingo de Silos 3 810; 22 255
retable 3 *810*
S María 26 251
D'Aronco, Raimondo 8 531–2*; 16 590, 721
assistants 27 853
collaboration 26 389
groups and movements 2 567; 21 779
works 16 647, 648; 27 303; 29 843
Dar Qita 9 541
church 9 591
Darra temple 15 254
Darra-yi Shakh mosque 16 166
Darsan see TOK-KALA
Dar Si Sa'id 20 470
Darte 11 610; 24 149
Dartein, Fernand de 8 532*
D'Artigues, Aimé-Gabriel 3 13, 594, 595
Dartington Glass 10 321
Dartington Hall (Devon) 19 235
Dartington Hall Trust 8 810
Dartington Pottery 30 389
Dartmouth, William Legge, 2nd Earl of see LEGGE, WILLIAM, 2nd Earl of Dartmouth
Dartois, Jean-Melchior 3 600
Darton, William 31 267
Dart Pottery 10 315
darts 21 245, 246
daruma see under DOLLS → types
Darval 28 266

Darvish Muhammad 8 533*; 28 811
attributions 16 328
collaboration 28 567
patrons and collectors 16 328
works 28 811
Darwin 1 37, 51; 2 736
Northern Territory Museum 1 66, 67
Darwin, Charles 2 299; 11 840; 20 483; 26 131; 28 916
Darwin, Robin 10 375
Darwish, Ali Hussein 30 301
Darwish, Nabil 9 767
Darwood, John 25 889
Dary, Robert 3 397; 31 218
Daryl Jackson Evan Walker Architects 5 196
Darzin 16 154; 21 582
Das, Amar (1552-74) 1 798
Das, Amar (fl c. 1820-50) 15 615
Das, Bhawani 15 653
Das, Bulaki 15 615
Das, E. C. 15 653
Das, Jairam 15 653
Das, Keshav see KESHAV DAS
Das, Madho 15 603
Das, Ram (1574-81) 1 798
Das, Ram (fl 1777-82) 15 653
Das, Shiv 15 615
Dasa, Kanha 15 434
Dasaratha, Ruler (reg c. 232-25 BC) (Maurya) 3 194
Dasavanta see DASWANTH
Dasburg, Andrew 3 251; 30 173
Dasgupta, Pradosh 5 420; 15 172
Dashal, Gaurishankara Shrine 15 309
Dashchoelling temple 21 875
Dashdamirova, B. 2 896
Dashkesan 2 890, 894
Dashli 1 186; 6 196
Dashli 3 1 189, 190; 30 440
Dashlut 7 819, 821
Dashlydzhi Tepe 6 275
Dash-Rabat Mosque 29 822
Dashti Mosque 16 194
Dasht-i-Nawar 1 187
Dashwood, Francis, 15th Baron Le Despenser 4 413; 8 533*; 10 277; 26 263
Dasio, Maximilian 8 533*
Dasji, Charan
works 15 679
Daskalio 17 913
Dasnoy, Albert 3 565
Dasoja 15 528; 29 438
Dasoku Soga see SOGA JASOKU
Da Sonneville, Jacques see DASSONVILLE, JACQUES
Dassel, Rainald von, Archbishop of Cologne see RAINALD VON DASSEL, Archbishop of Cologne
Dassier, Antoine 8 534
Dassier, Domaine 8 533
Dassier, Jacques-Antoine 8 534*
Dassier, Jean 8 533–4*
Dassier, Paul 8 534
Dasson, Henri 5 193
Dasson, J. see DASSONVILLE, JACQUES
Dassonville, Jacques 8 534*
Dassoucy, Charles 31 165
D'Assunção, Manuel 25 300
Dassypris, Manolis 13 339
Dastagerd 21 292
Dastani
works 20 150
D'Astous, Roger 5 563
Daswanth 8 534–5*; 30 338
collaboration 3 904; 17 775
teachers 1 26
works 3 320; 8 534; 15 579, 581
Dasypodius, Konrad 29 673
Daszewski, Władysław 28 402
Dat, Simone 27 307
databases 2 364; 4 25–6*
Date (family) 17 429
Date Masamune 14 566; 17 363
Dathan, Johann Georg 4 814
works 11 460
D'Athanasi, Giovanni 10 90, 92
Dati, Carlo (Roberto) 3 701; 8 535*; 11 188; 25 411
Datia 15 373
Govinda Mandir 15 392, 393; 23 818, 818
dating methods 2 300; 11 309; 22 673; 30 403–5*
historical and regional traditions
Aboriginal Australia 1 40
Ancient Near East 1 851–3*
Egypt, ancient 2 300
Indian subcontinent 15 199*
Iraq 16 399*
Mali 21 479–80
Mesoamerica, Pre-Columbian 21 266
Middle Niger cultures 21 479–80*
Native North Americans 22 672
Palestine 2 300
Prehistoric art 25 469–72, 484–5*
South-east Asia 29 241
types
dendrochronology 2 302–3, 304; 11 309; 30 403, 404*, 405
fission-track dating 2 304
potassium-argon dating 2 304
pottery 1 851
radiocarbon dating 2 300, 302, 303–4; 7 160; 11 309; 22 673; 25 472; 30 403*, 403
sequence dating 8 912; 10 80; 24 561
thermoluminescence dating 2 304; 11 309; 21 479–80; 30 403–4*, 404
uranium-series dating 2 304
uses
archaeology 2 301–4*, 302; 24 561
architecture 21 40; 22 212
bone 2 304; 11 309
bronze 30 404
carpets 16 477
ceramics 2 304; 11 309; 30 404, 404
forgeries 30 404, 404
ivory 11 309
leather 11 309
panel paintings 11 309
paper 11 309
parchment 11 309
patinas 25 484
pottery 2 304; 16 399; 30 403–4
rock art 2 269, 270; 25 484–5*; 27 696
rocks 2 304
shells 2 304
terracotta 21 479–80
textiles 9 492; 11 309
wood 11 309; 30 403, 404, 405
see also TECHNICAL EXAMINATION
Datini, Francesco di Marco 8 535–6*; 25 450
architecture 3 173
ceramics 14 425
dealing 11 660
paintings 7 338; 11 892; 23 95
Datong 6 615; 8 536*
architecture 6 655
Good Transformations Temple see Shanhua Temple
Huayan Temple 6 656, 667, 717; 8 536; 23 773
library 19 303
sūtra cupboard 6 669, 669; 14 78
kang 7 145
lacquer 7 13
Nine Dragon screen 6 906
painting 19 298
paper 7 146
Shanhua Temple 6 719; 8 536; 24 289
Datong—cont.
silver 7 23
tomb of Feng Hetu 7 23
tomb of Sima Jinlong 6 808; 7 34
tomb of Ye Deyuan 7 36, 37
urban planning 6 662
Dat So La Lee 8 536–7*, 537
patrons and collectors 22 660
works 8 537
Dattari, Giovanni 10 91
Dattari, Giuseppe 12 911
Dattaro (family) 8 135
Dattaro, Francesco 8 134, 537
Dattaro, Giuseppe 8 135, 537
Dattel, Heinrich see TADDEL, HEINRICH
Dattilo Rubbo, Anthony 32 770
Dattoli, Vincenzo 8 716
Datuk Baharuddin bin Abu Kasim 20 166
Dau al Set 8 538*
members 3 219; 8 255; 29 286; 30 335, 644
Dau al Set 24 452
Daubenny, Giles, 1st Baron, Lord Chamberlain 14 126
Daubenton, Guillaume 7 287
Daubigny, Amélie 8 538
Daubigny, Charles-François 8 538–9*; 11 543, 546
dealers 4 589; 8 820; 30 425
groups and movements 3 212; 8 538; 28 921
patrons and collectors 4 124, 232; 6 516; 9 305; 11 301; 19 239; 21 176
pupils 8 538, 539; 10 402; 26 558; 28 735
reproductive prints by others 3 463
works 7 433, 434, 879; 8 539; 9 423; 10 562; 20 426; 25 607
Daubigny, Charles-Pierre see DAUBIGNY, KARL
Daubigny, Edmond-François 8 538*
Daubigny, Karl 8 539–40*
teachers 8 538, 539
works 11 415, 415
Daubigny, Philippe Cordier 2 461
Daubigny, Pierre 8 538
Daucher, Abraham 8 541
Daucher, Adolf (c 1460-1523/4) 2 715; 8 540–41*; 12 401
collaboration 8 541; 10 456; 14 663
works 2 118
Daucher, Adolf, the younger (1485-1557) 8 540
works 28 183
Daucher, Hans 2 715, 718; 8 540–41*; 10 457; 12 401; 14 663
collaboration 8 540
patrons and collectors 11 818
works 8 541; 10 455; 12 402; 20 920, 920; 33 II1
workshop 8 384
Dauchez, André 3 156; 14 486; 28 750
Dauchot, Fernard 25 215
Da'ud, Ruler (reg 1109-44) (Artuqid) 2 575; 16 515, 538
metalwork 16 538
Da'ud (fl mid-late 14th cent.) 15 228
Da'ud (fl late 16th-early 17th cent.) 8 542
Daudelin, Charles 5 571
Daudet, Alphonse 4 366; 5 131, 265; 7 690; 10 508
Daudet, Jean-Louis 8 542
Daudet, Robert (fl 1728-33) 8 542
Daudet, Robert (1737-1824) 8 542*; 33 196
Da'ud ibn Muhammad ibn Mahmud 15 573
Da'ud Khan Qurayshi 15 370
Daudnagar caravanserais 15 370
Daugavpils 18 847, 849
Daugel, V. G. 11 245
Daugherty, James 4 367
Daugirdas, Tadas 19 498
Daugny, Sieur 4 819
Daugulis, Augusts 18 851
Dauher see DAUCHER
Dauher, Bartholomäus 8 540*
Daujon 19 159
Daulat 8 542–3*, 543; 15 584, 586
patrons and collectors 15 745
works 16 345; 20 284
Daulatabad 8 543–4*, 673; 15 195, 276, 341; 16 105
architecture 15 355
Chand Minar 15 358
citadel 15 373
congregational mosque 15 355
fortifications 21 590
Daulby, Daniel 25 280; 27 161
Daullé, Jean 3 318; 8 544*, 772; 19 261
Daum (family) 11 582, 613; 12 795
Daum, Antonin 2 564; 8 544
Daum, Auguste 2 564; 8 544; 12 19; 22 456
Daum, Henri 8 544
Daum, Jacques 8 544
Daum, Jean 8 544
Daum, Michel 8 544
Daum, O. 10 83
Daum, Paul 8 544
Daumal, René 28 745
Daumas, F. 10 82
Daumenglas see CUPS → types → finger
Daumet, (Pierre-Gérôme-) Honoré 8 544–5*
pupils 3 826; 12 728; 29 491
works 1 14; 6 453; 9 337; 12 728
Daumier, Honoré 6 175; 8 545–7*; 11 567; 20 473; 24 605; 28 919; 31 704
busts 5 303
cartoons (satirical) 7 674; 12 294; 27 871
groups and movements 24 585; 26 54, 742
lithographs 5 757; 8 545; 19 484; 20 602; 25 345, 607, 651; 27 870
paintings 8 547; 22 416
patrons and collectors 5 163, 732
Burrell, William (1861-1958) 5 278
Camondo, Isaac de, Comte 5 530
Hammer, Armand 14 117
Havemeyer, Louisine (Waldron) 14 244
Lévy, Pierre and Denise 19 282
Liebermann, Max 19 335
Lucas, George A(loysius) 19 755
Tavernier, Adolphe-Eugène 30 375
Van Horne, William (Cornelius) 31 880
statuettes 29 574
Daun (family) 3 488
Daun, Alfred 4 41; 9 394; 30 204
Daun, W. Philipp Lorenz, Count of see LORENZ, W. PHILIPP, Count of Daun
Daunton, Thomas 19 594
Dauphin, Charles 28 10, 11, 12; 30 793
Dauphin, le (1396-1415) see GUYENNE, LOUIS, Duc de
Dauphin, le (1729-65) see BOURBON I., LOUIS LE DAUPHIN
Dauphin, Le Grand (1661-1711) see BOURBON I., LOUIS, Le Grand Dauphin
Dauphin, le Petit (1682-1712) see BOURGOGNE, LOUIS DE BOURBON, Duc de, le Petit Dauphin
Dauphin's Treasure 29 303, 352
Daura, Emir's Palace 1 315
Daurat, Maurice 11 629
Daurbekov, Gazi-Mahomed 27 433
D'Aurevilly, Jules-Amadée Barbey see BARBEY D'AUREVILLY, JULES-AMADÉE
Dausset, Nina 24 144
Dau Temple 32 471–2
Dauthe, Johann Friedrich Carl 1 125; 2 240; 7 687; 19 110
Dautry, Raoul 23 747; 24 129, 130
Dauzats, Adrien 4 391; 8 548*; 9 766; 23 504
Davad, Ankol Mata Vav 29 635, 636
Dávalos, Angel 4 262
Dávalos, Jaime 9 711
Davanne, Louis-Alphonse 25 618
Davanzati, Giuliano 10 180
Davanzo, Pietro 32 205
Daven, Lion see DAVENT, LÉON
Davenant, Henry 5 65
Davenant, William 30 673, 674
Davenport, A. H., Co. 4 479
Davenport, John (fl 1643) 23 25
Davenport, John (d 1848) 10 309; 14 682
Davenport Bromley, Walter 8 549*; 11 32; 12 32; 24 390
Davenport & Co. 10 307, 310, 311
Davenport House (Salop) 10 277
Davenport (IA) Municipal Art Gallery 14 60
Davenports 5 192; 10 297
Davent, Léon 8 549*; 11 532
groups and movements 11 264
works 10 551; 24 365; 30 735
Daverio, Pietro Antonio 21 533
Davesne, P. 32 494
Davey, William Turner 8 549*
Davia-Bargellini, Museo d'Arte Industriale e Galleria see under BOLOGNA → museums
David (Panama) 23 902
David, Abbot of Bristol 4 825
David, Master 26 712
David, Saint 27 537
David I, King of Scotland (reg 1124-53) 7 350; 8 549–50*; 26 591; 28 267
David II, King of Georgia (reg 990-1000) 12 331; 30 306, 307
David II, King of Scotland (reg 1329-32; 1334-71) 28 267
David III, King of Georgia (reg 1089-1125) 12 239, 331
David, Adolphe 12 265
David, Alexander 17 580
David, Antonio 30 267
David, C. L. 8 759; 16 556; 18 136; 24 549
David, Claude 8 550*; 25 833; 27 878; 28 79
David, Colin 23 800
Dávid, Ferenc 14 890
David, Fernand 11 568
David, Gerard 3 553, 554; 4 918; 8 550–53*; 20 616; 22 836; 33 8
assistants 3 738; 16 69; 24 259
attributions 20 663
drawings 9 221
frames 11 440
paintings 4 920
altarpieces 8 551
justice scenes 3 612; 17 700, 700
religious 4 925; 8 552; 9 271, 274; 18 704; 31 577; 32 389
patrons and collectors 25 729
Aders, Carl 1 154
Durrieu, Paul 9 453
Ertborn, Florent (Joseph) van 10 491
Frick, Henry Clay 9 200
Loyd-Lindsay, Robert, 1st Baron Wantage 19 736
Philip II, King of Spain (reg 1556-98) 13 922

David, Gerard
patrons and collectors—cont.
Richard van der Capelle, Canon 3 612
Ryerson, Martin A(ntoine) 27 463
pupils 3 738; 13 22
David, Giovanni 8 554*; 10 199
works 2 240
David, Jacques-Louis 5 43; 8 554–62*, 649; 11 541, 544, 659, 666, 670, 671; 16 677; 24 140, 168; 26 774; 29 878; 31 390; 32 259
assistants 3 294; 9 302; 11 738; 12 334; 26 264
attributions 6 490
book illustrations 8 867
caricatures 5 757
collaboration 8 867; 21 412
competitions 25 638
dress 9 244
festivals 23 766
frames 11 409, 410, 411, 412, 412
furniture 16 822
groups and movements 13 297; 22 734, 736, 741; 24 171; 26 735, 737, 738
methods 6 570; 21 759; 24 381
pageants 11 658; 31 703
paintings 9 244
history 11 543; 24 136; 25 651; 26 53
contemporary themes 11 508, 541, 541; 12 214; 24 138, 139
Greek themes 11 542; 21 761
Roman themes 2 53; 7 384; 8 555; 11 540, 658; 14 586; 20 135; 22 522, 735; 23 295; 24 139, 168, 380, 381
mythological 22 416
portraits 2 105; 8 558; 9 284, 285, 286; 25 193
patrons and collectors
Beisteguy y Benítez, Carlos de 3 522
Bonaparte, Laetitia 30 267
Bonnemaison, Ferréol de 4 330
Canino, Lucien Bonaparte, Prince of (1775-1840) 4 304
Charles X, King of France (reg 1824-30) 4 556
Chéramy, Paul-Arthur 6 548
Coutan, Louis-Joseph-Auguste 8 72, 73
Delafontaine, Pierre-Maximilien 8 649
Denon, (Dominique-) Vivant 8 763
Didot, Saint Marc 8 868
Forbin, (Louis Nicolas Philippe) Auguste, Comte de 11 302
Gigoux, Jean(-François) 12 609
Hamilton, Alexander, 10th Duke of Hamilton and 7th Duke of Brandon 14 107
Henry, Bon-Thomas 14 396
Louis XVI, King of France (reg 1774-92) 4 554
Napoléon, Musée see under PARIS → museums 4 300
Napoleon I, Emperor of the French (reg 1804-14) 4 300
Potocki, Stanisław Kostka 25 364
Pourtalès-Gorgier, James-Alexandre, Comte de 25 383
Sommariva, Giovanni Battista 29 59
Talbot, John, 16th Earl of Shrewsbury (1791- 1853) 30 267
Tret'yakov, Pavel (Mikhaylovich) 31 312
Trudaine frères 31 390
Vaudreuil Château 32 85
David, Jacques-Louis
patrons and collectors—cont.
Yusupov, Nikolay (Borisovich), Prince (1751-1831) 33 579
pupils 8 238; 25 581
Abel de Pujol, Alexandre (1785-1861) 1 28
Agasse, Jacques-Laurent 1 449
Aparicio Inglada, José 2 215
Aubert, Augustin 26 315
Audubon, John James (Laforest) 2 709
Auzou, Pauline 2 847
Benoist, Marie-Guillemine 3 735
Bergeret, Pierre-Nolasque 3 775
Berthon, René Théodore 3 854
Broc, Jean 4 834
Brodowski, Antoni (Stanisław) 4 836
Charpentier, Constance Marie 6 490
Couder, (Louis-Charles-) Auguste 8 40
Delafontaine, Pierre-Maximilien 8 648
Delaroche, Jules-Hippolyte 8 653
Drolling, Michel-Martin 9 300
Drouais, Jean-Germain 9 301, 302
Dubufe, Claude-Marie 9 331
Ducis, (Jean-)Louis 9 363
Duval Le Camus, Pierre 9 466
Eckersberg, C(hristoffer) W(ilhelm) 9 700
Fabre, François-Xavier, Baron 10 726
Flageoulot, Charles-Antoine 8 51
Forbin, (Louis Nicolas Philippe) Auguste, Comte de 11 301
Fragonard, Alexandre-Evariste 11 370
Franque, Jean-Pierre 11 738
Frémiet, Sophie 27 309
Garneray, Jean-François 12 153
Gautherot, Pierre 12 205
Gérard, François (-Pascal-Simon) 12 334
Girodet (de Roussy-Trioson), Anne-Louis 12 729, 730; 26 735
Giroux, François-Simon-Alphonse 12 740
Granet, François-Marius 13 308
Gros, Antoine-Jean 13 689
Harriet, Fulchran-Jean 14 192
Hennequin, Philippe-Auguste 14 389
Hervier, Marie-Antoine 14 486
Hetsch, Philipp Friedrich von 28 86
Huyot, Jean-Nicolas 15 42
Ingres, Jean-Auguste-Dominique 15 836
Isabey, Jean-Baptiste 16 64
Karpff, Jean-Jacques 17 824
Krafft, (Johann) Peter 18 418
Kruseman, Jan Adam 18 481
Laneuville, Jean-Louis 18 728
Liénard, Edouard 22 207
Louis-Philippe, King of the French (reg 1830-48) 23 520
Madrazo y Agudo, José de 20 57
Mayer, (Marie-Françoise-) Constance 20 890
Michallon, Achille (Etna) 21 424
Navez, François-Joseph 22 696
Odevaere, Joseph-Denis 23 354
Paelinck, Joseph 23 758
Paillot de Montabert, Jacques-Nicolas 23 779
Phélippes, Charles-François 21 170
Picot, François-Edouard 24 736
Pingret, Edouard (Henri Théophile) 24 823
David, Jacques-Louis
pupils—cont.
Ramboux, Johann Anton 25 872
Ribera y Fernández, Juan Antonio 26 308
Richard, Fleury (-François) 26 333
Riesener, Henri-François 8 638
Robert, (Louis) Léopold 26 450
Schnetz, (Jean) Victor 28 132
Tieck, (Christian) Friedrich 30 854
Wagner, (Johann) Martin von (1777-1858) 32 759
Waldeck, Johann Friedrich (Maximilian), Graf von 32 774
Wicar, Jean-Baptiste (-Joseph) 33 153
Wichmann, Ludwig (Wilhelm) 33 154
reproductions in tapestry 12 830
reproductive prints by others 1 645; 8 763; 17 453
studio 1 106; 2 524; 29 856
tapestries 11 643
teachers 32 427
David, Jan (fl 1601-17) 1 658
David, Jean (fl 20th cent.) 16 568
David, Jean-Louis 8 564; 19 140
David, Jérôme 18 745
David, Joe 8 562*; 22 581, 589
Dávid, Károly 8 562–3*; 14 890
David, Ludovico 8 563–4*
David, Michael 18 162
David, Neil, sr 22 598
David, Percival 5 293; 8 564*
collections 6 925; 7 155, 157; 10 367; 14 604
David, Percival, Foundation of Chinese Art see under LONDON → University of London
David, Pierre-Jean see DAVID D'ANGERS
David and St John Statuettes, Master of the 20 655*; 22 15; 30 497; 31 189
David ben Salomon ben David Gedaliah Ibn Yahya 20 122
David & Carvalho 22 245
David d'Angers 2 46; 8 564–7*; 11 563, 564, 565, 671; 24 353
collaboration 32 82
commentaries 17 667
groups and movements 26 742; 28 345
patrons and collectors 17 667
prizes (artists') 24 171
pupils
Auvray, Louis 2 843
Brian, Jean-Louis 4 765
Cavelier, Pierre-Jules 6 115
Geoffroy-Dechaume, Adolphe-Victor 12 312
Graillon, Pierre-Adrien 13 274
Hébert, (Antoine-Auguste-) Ernest 14 283
Maindron, Etienne-Hippolyte 20 124
Millet, Aimé 21 608
Ottin, Auguste-Louis-Marie 23 633
Préault, Auguste 25 458
Rochet, Louis 26 481
Schoenewerk, Pierre-Alexandre 28 139
Steinheil, Louis-Charles-Auguste 29 609
sculpture
architectural 8 566; 11 564; 29 93
busts 5 303; 8 565
fountains 1 497, 498
medals 20 925
portraits 11 566; 19 91
reliefs 26 137
statuettes 29 574
teachers 26 552
David da Staglieno 7 899
David Garedzhi 8 567–8*; 12 317; 26 483
Bertubani Monastery 12 323
wall paintings 8 567
Dodos-Rka 12 323
monasteries 12 319
wall paintings 12 323
David Leipnik, Joseph ben see LEIPNIK, JOSEPH BEN DAVID
David of Burgundy, Bishop of Utrecht 20 451; 22 901; 33 87
Davidovitch, David 17 583
David Scenes in the Grimani Breviary, Master of the 13 661
Davidson, Barbara 28 258
Davidson, Bruce 8 568*; 20 99
Davidson, Daniel Sutherland 1 68
Davidson, Florence 8 568
Davidson, Henry William 28 426
Davidson, Jeremiah 28 269
Davidson, Jim 1 66; 21 733; 33 573
Davidson, J(ulius) R(alph) 8 568*; 20 142
Davidson, Reg 8 569
Davidson, Robert 8 568–9*; 22 581, 589, 674
Davidson, Thomas 14 540
Davidson, William 20 23; 28 270
Davids Samling see under COPENHAGEN → museums
Davíðsson, Kristján 4 807; 8 569*; 15 71
Davidt see DAVID
David the Builder, King of Georgia see DAVID III, King of Georgia
David Vases 4 173; 6 898, 898
David-Weill, David 1 896; 7 155; 8 569*
David-Weill, Flora 8 569
Davie, Alan 8 569–70*; 9 725; 25 628
groups and movements 2 545; 27 563
works 19 492; 28 240, 300
Davierwalla, A. M. 15 172
Davies, Arthur B(owen) 2 447; 8 571*; 23 47, 701; 31 660, 663
collaboration 20 604
groups and movements 2 633; 10 108; 23 47; 31 605
patrons and collectors 4 142; 8 463; 24 638
works 10 563
Davies, David (b 1837) 32 787
Davies, David (1864-1939) 8 571*
Davies, Gwendoline 32 791
Davies, James Hey 20 239
Davies, John (d 1755) 32 789, 790
Davies, John (b 1946) 27 524
Davies, John Scarlett see DAVIS, JOHN SCARLETT
Davies, Margaret 32 791
Davies, Martin 8 571–2*
Davies, Nina 8 570*; 10 82
Davies, Norman de Garis 8 570*; 10 82
Davies, Robert 28 295; 32 789, 790
Davies, Thomas 5 564; 8 572*
Davies, William 32 787
D'Avignon, François 24 661
Dávila, Alberto 24 510
Davila, Juan 2 751; 8 572*; 12 218
Davila, Pedrarias 23 903
Davila, Pedro 29 220
Dávila Carson, Roberto 6 594
Daviler, Augustin-Charles see AVILER, AUGUSTIN-CHARLES D'
Davioud, Gabriel (-Jean-Antoine) 5 825; 8 572–3*
collaboration 25 301
works 4 240; 5 776; 10 683; 22 59
Davis, Alexander Jackson 2 734; 8 573–6*; 23 39
assistants 32 866
Davis, Alexander Jackson—cont.
collaboration 21 618; 25 267; 31 232, 233; 32 753
groups and movements 13 208
staff 8 462
works 7 745; 8 574, 575; 31 232, 592, 620
Davis, Alfred 27 224
Davis, Arthur Joseph 14 203; 21 371*; 31 392
Davis, Brody and Wisniewski 21 56
Davis, Charles (architect; 1827-1902) 3 74, 372; 29 647
Davis, Charles (dealer) 27 224
Davis, E. 14 53
Davis, Edward 32 787
Davis, Erwin 33 43
Davis, Gene 32 890, 894
Davis, Harry 23 69
Davis, Hart 10 365
Davis, Henry E. 19 424
Davis, James 4 481
Davis, John (b 1936) 2 754
Davis, John Scarlett 8 576*; 9 27
Davis, Lewis 10 685; 30 469
Davis, Lucien 8 579
Davis, Nike Olaniyi 1 247
Davis, Owen William 8 576–7*
Davis, Richard Hart 21 541
Davis, Robert 4 478
Davis, Ron(ald) 8 577*
Davis, Samuel 8 505
Davis, Stuart 1 772; 8 577–8*; 31 605, 607
collaboration 20 604
groups and movements 1 773; 8 246
patrons and collectors 18 498
works 8 578; 9 213; 19 492; 22 335; 23 48; 29 670; 31 705
Davis, Theodore M. 10 80, 81, 90
Davis, Thomas 16 38
Davis, Valentine 8 579
Davis, William (fl 1692) 6 515; 11 424
Davis, William (fl 18th cent.) 33 377
Davis, William (1812-73) 8 578–9*; 25 554
Davis, William, Photographic Agency 14 173
Davis, William Paul 8 579
Davis Album see under ALBUMS → individual manuscripts
Davis Comb 9 865
Davis & Flight 33 377
Davison, George 8 579*; 32 834
groups and movements 19 424; 24 738, 739
Davison, Nathaniel 10 79
Davis Virgin and Child 3 661
Davit see DAVID
Davud Ağa 1 474; 8 579*; 9 730; 22 384
Davud Pasha 12 85
Davutov, Zieratsho 30 253
Davy, Humphry 5 519
Davydova, Natal'ya 33 487
Dawadorj 21 879
Dawadzong 30 819
Dawahuu 21 881
Dawber, (Edward) Guy 7 529; 8 580*; 12 316
Dawe, George 7 244; 8 580*; 26 733
Dawe, Philip 8 580
Dawenkou 6 615; 8 580–81*
ceramics 8 580–81
jade 7 2
pottery 6 877
Dawenkou culture 6 694, 877–8; 7 159
Dawes, William 30 158
Dawit III, Emperor of Ethiopia (reg 1716-21) 10 566
Dawkins, Henry 26 263
Dawkins, James 8 581*; 22 736; 23 891; 33 344

Dawkins, Richard MacGillivray 17 751
Dawkins Pennant, G. H. see PENNANT, G. H. DAWKINS
Dawlatabad, minaret 16 166, 259
Dawlat al-Bahrayn see BAHRAIN
Dawnay, William, 7th Viscount Downe 5 315
Dawski, Stanisław 8 303; 25 125
Dawson, A. 24 748
Dawson, Archibald 28 243
Dawson, Dorothy 16 41
Dawson, Henry 23 259
Dawson, J. A. 24 748
Dawson, John, 2nd Viscount Carlow 12 44
Dawson, Margaret 7 211
Dawson, Montague 20 425
Dawson, Neil 7 211; 8 581*; 23 63
Dawson, Nelson 10 336; 20 437
Dawson, William 5 590
Dawud Agha 5 398
Dax 8 581–2*; 11 *505*
 Cathedral 8 581–2; 13 75
Dax, Adrien 30 23
Dax, Paul 15 865
Daxi 6 *615*; 8 582
Daxi culture 6 878–9; 8 582*
Daxing see XI'AN
Day, Alexander 8 582*; 25 665
Day, Alfred 1 491
Day, B. & Company 10 343
Day, Benjamin (1836-1916) 3 703; 19 480
Day, E. A. 5 612
Day, F(red) Holland 7 491; 8 582–3*; 12 214; 24 674; 33 146
 groups and movements 24 739
 works 12 215
Day, Francis 20 52
Day, Frank Miles 10 718; 24 598
Day, John 4 589
Day, Keith 33 23
Day, Kenneth 17 723
Day, Kent C. 23 897
Day, Lewis Foreman 1 171; 2 575; 8 583*; 10 354, 356
Day, Lucienne 8 583; 19 415
 works 32 V3
Day, R. (*fl* 1824) 20 868
Day, Robin (*b* 1915) 8 583*; 10 299; 21 363
 exhibitions 8 804
 works 6 391; 10 299, *300*; 20 595, *595*
Day, Thomas 32 303
Day, William
 works 13 *635*
Dayak 15 753, 789; 20 163, 182
 amulets 1 817
 boats 15 810
 houses 15 773–4
 jewellery 15 814
 metalwork 20 173
 musical instruments 15 817
 painting 15 807
 sarcophagi 27 831
Dayakhatyn 16 164
 caravanserai 16 163
Dayal, Lala Deen see DEEN DAYAL, LALA
Dayan, Ruth 16 569
Dayananda, Swami 14 555
Dayangzhou (Xin'gan) 7 159
day-beds see under BEDS → types
Daybul see BANBHORE
Dayes, Edward 8 584*; 12 741; 24 551; 27 626; 32 900
Dayez, Barré 29 628
Dayez, Georges 17 894
Dayfa Khatun (Ayyubid) 1 602; 2 888; 16 180
Dayfield body shield 2 474
dayflower 17 277
day-glo see under PAINTS → types
Daygurrgurr Gupapuyungu
 sculpture 1 *45*
Day & Haghe 15 165
Dayi
 sculpture 6 733, *734*
Dayingzi, tomb of Fuma Zeng 7 25
Dayr al-Barshā see DEIR EL-BERSHA
Dayr al-Gabrawi see DEIR EL-GEBRAWI
Day & Son 25 *590*, 628
 works 19 *484*
Dayton (OH)
 court-house 18 887
 Federal building 22 748
Dayun Temple 26 150
Daza, Ignacio 27 532; 31 588
 works 27 *532*
Dazaifu 17 19
Dazaincourt, Barthélémy-Augustin Blondel see AZINCOURT, BARTHÉLÉMY-AUGUSTIN BLONDEL D'
DAZ Consulting Architects 8 861
D'Azeglio, Massimo (Taparelli), Marchese 8 584*; 31 445
D'Azeglio, Robert Taparelli, Marchese 8 584
Dazzi, Arturo 4 730
dazzle painting 5 530–31, *531*
DDS see DEWEY DECIMAL SYSTEM
De 19 309
Deacon, Richard 8 584*
 works 10 *268*, 269
dead colouring see under PAINTING → techniques
Dead Sea Scrolls 24 107; 26 557
Deaf Adder Gorge
 rock art 1 *42*
Deák-Ébner, Lajos 8 585*; 14 901; 30 210
Deal (Kent) 21 568
 grave 112 6 160
 Pier 24 747, 748
deal (wood) 10 277; 18 610; 20 *215*; 21 721
Deal, Joe 23 37
De Albertis, Sebastiano 8 585*; 12 863
dealers 6 78, 79–80; 7 561; 10 675
 Australia 1 66*
 England 10 677, 679
 Germany 12 472
 Hungary 15 16
 Italy 16 766
 Netherlands, the 2 558; 7 562
 Portugal 25 317–18*
 United States of America 31 664–5*
dealers' exhibitions see under EXHIBITIONS → types
dealing 2 365, 557–61
 Africa 1 438–9*
 Ancient Near East 1 895–6*
 Australia 2 770*
 Austria 2 828–9*
 Bahamas, the 3 63–4*
 Belgium 3 615*
 Bolivia 4 268*
 Brazil 4 724–6*
 Britain 12 30
 Canada 5 589–90*
 Colombia 7 611*
 Côte d'Ivoire 8 23
 Czech Republic 8 423–4*
 Denmark 8 758–9*
 Egypt, ancient 10 89*, 91–2*
 England 2 559, 560; 10 362–8*
 Finland 11 111–12*
 France 2 558–9; 11 660–64*; 23 778
 Germany 2 560
 Greece 13 360*
 Guatemala 13 768–9*
 Ireland 16 36*
 Israel 16 570*
 Italy 16 765–9*
 Jamaica 16 889–90*
 Japan 2 561; 17 424
 Mexico 21 394–6*
dealing—cont.
 Netherlands, the 22 904–6*
 Nicaragua 23 84–5*
 Northern Ireland 16 42*
 Norway 23 242–3*
 Pacific Islands 23 741–2*
 Paraguay 24 100–101*
 Poland 25 137–8*
 Russia 2 560; 27 438–40*
 Scotland 28 270–72*
 South Africa 29 121*
 Spain 29 354*
 Sweden 30 118*
 Switzerland 30 153–4*
 Trinidad and Tobago 31 339
 United States of America 2 560
 Venezuela 32 178–9*
 Wales 32 790–91*
Dealu Church 26 707
Dealul Frumos 26 712
Dean, Bashford 2 450, 474
Dean, Beryl 10 354; 17 580
Dean, Flora Maitland 20 142
Dean, George 25 402
Dean, George Robinson 6 578; 25 446
Dean, Hugh Primrose 8 83; 16 14; 30 451
Dean, John 21 416
Dean, Laura 24 407
De Andrea, John (Louis) 8 585*; 10 482; 24 686, 687, 688
Deane, Alexander Sharpe 8 586
Deane, Harold A. 28 535, 712
Deane, Kearns 8 586
Deane, Son & Woodward see DEANE & WOODWARD
Deane, Thomas 8 585–6*; 14 635
 collaboration 16 11
 staff 8 580
 works 16 11
Deane, Thomas Manly 8 587; 9 317, 319; 16 11
Deane, Thomas Newenham 8 586–7; 16 11; 23 600
Deane & Woodward 8 585, 586–7*; 9 323; 23 600
 works 9 317, 323; 10 370; 16 54; 22 363; 27 351
Dean's Rag Co. 31 260
Dearborn (MI), Ford Motor Company River Rouge plant 11 835
Deare, John 8 587–8*; 13 650; 14 486; 24 86
 works 8 *587*
Deare, Joseph 8 588
De Arendshoeve (family) 15 36
Dearle, John Henry 10 352, 354
 works 30 III2
Dearn, Thomas Downes Wilmot 4 788
De arte illuminandi 8 588*; 13 136; 20 324–5; 31 299
Deas, Charles 8 588*; 12 294; 17 823
death-masks 6 9; 25 275, 281, 282; 31 840
Death of the Virgin, Master of the 7 424; 20 655*
De åtta see EIGHT, THE (iv)
Debabov, Dimitri (Georgyevich) 8 588–9*
Debach, Hugo 12 441
Debal see under BANBHORE
Debăr 19 *882*
 furniture 5 157
 icons 19 884; 25 340
 monastery of St John Bigorski 19 882
 sculpture 5 156
Debassige, Blake 22 598
Debat-Ponsan, Edouard-Bernard 5 342; 8 589*; 23 504
Debat-Ponsan, Jacques 8 589*; 12 161; 29 420; 31 243
Debay, J.-B. 17 667
Debbech, Amara 31 425
Débêche, Gérard 11 632
De Beer (family) 23 75
De Beer's 20 547
De Beer's Centenary Art Gallery see under ALICE → University of Fort Hare
Debeira 23 289
Debel 11 643
Debenham, Ernest 26 316
Debias-Aubry, François 2 216; 8 589*
De Biasi, Mario 8 590*
Dębniki
 majolica 18 822; 25 123, 213
 marble 25 114, 118
Dębno Church 8 590–91*; 25 *92*, 101
 painting 8 *590*
De Boeck, Felix see BOECK, FELIX DE
De Bois, J. H. 22 905
De Bom, Emmanuel 2 516
De Bonis, Vincenzo 25 164
Debonnaire, Girard 12 832
de Borchgrave-d'Alténa, J. 3 619
Debord, Guy-Ernest 10 688
De Braekeleer, Ferdinand, the elder (1792-1883) 8 591–2*; 31 857
 pupils 8 592; 19 291
 works 3 562; 8 *591*
De Braekeleer, Ferdinand, the younger (1828-57) 8 591
De Braekeleer, Henri (-Jean-Augustin) 2 197; 3 562, 615; 8 591, 592*
Debraux d'Anglure 21 426
Debrecen 13 333; 14 *881*
 collections 15 17
 Déri Museum 13 889; 14 60, 890
 Medgyessy Memorial Museum 21 5
 metalwork 15 6, 7
 St Andrew 14 884
 St Anne 14 887
Debre Damo 1 *379*
 monastery church 1 315, 379; 10 565, 568, 576
Debre Libanos 1 *314*, *379*
Debre Markos church 10 573
Debre Seyon, Church of Kidana Mehret 10 568
Debret, François 8 592–3*
 collaboration 19 11
 pupils 3 76; 12 178; 14 756; 19 160
 works 18 581; 27 539, 543, 544, 547
Debret, Jean-Baptiste 4 716, 727; 8 593*; 13 295; 26 413
 collaboration 9 312
 patrons and collectors 4 727
 works 4 706, 708, 717
De Broe, Pierre-Jean 8 593–4*
De Bruycker, Joseph 3 587
De Bruyne, Pieter 3 579, 587
De Bry Head 28 821
Debschitz, Wilhelm von 8 594*; 18 77; 22 304; 23 337; 28 126
Debucourt, Philibert-Louis 8 594–5*; 13 220; 23 203
 methods 13 220
 pupils 12 153; 17 453
 works 2 239; 5 757; 13 *221*; 25 619, 622
De Burgo-O'Malley chalice 16 30
Debussy, Claude 8 715; 32 591
Debuyl, André 29 764
decadence and decline 8 595–7*; 10 480
Decaisne, Henri 29 609
decalcomania (i) (papercuts) 8 597*
 see also DÉCOLLAGE
decalcomania (ii) (printing) 8 597*; 9 104, *105*; 10 *469*, 470; 14 852; 30 21
 see also AUTOMATISM; BLOT DRAWING
De Cambray-Digny, Luigi 8 597*; 19 512; 25 451
De Camp, Joseph Rodefer 8 598*; 9 468; 30 452
Decamps 23 515
Decamps, Alexandre-Gabriel 8 598–9*; 16 536
 dealers 9 423
 groups and movements 23 503, 504; 26 739
 paintings 7 879
 patrons and collectors 2 499; 8 664; 23 522; 24 396; 28 527, 705; 31 880
 pupils 3 877
 teachers 1 28
 works 8 *599*
Decamps, Maurice-Alexandre 8 598
Dečani Monastery 8 599–600*; 9 *511*, 561; 28 *437*, 440
 Church of Christ Pantokrator 28 441, *441*, 453
  wall paintings 28 446
 collections 28 459
 icons 9 629; 25 339, *339*; 28 448, *448*
 lectern 9 601
 manuscript illumination 28 449
 metalwork 28 456
 paintings 28 450
 tomb of Stephen Uroš IV Dušan 9 602
 wall paintings 12 71; 28 *446*, 447
decanters 2 *570*; 10 318; 16 *30*; 17 *387*; 27 *416*
Décap, Edouard 24 883
De Capitani, Giulio 29 486
De Capitani d'Arzago, A. 21 537
Decapitation of St John, Master of the 21 157
DeCarava, Roy 24 679
 works 24 *680*
De Carlo, Adolfo 3 439; 25 792
De Carlo, Giancarlo 8 600–601*
 collaboration 1 578
 groups and movements 12 59; 30 391
 works 11 689; 16 650; 31 740
De Carolis, Adolfo 4 278; 8 601*; 16 678
decastyle 8 601*
 see also PORTICOS; STOAS
Decatur (TX), Wise County Court House 18 888
Deccan 15 *191*, 681, 684
Decembrio, Angelo 8 601–2*; 13 754
Decembrio, Pietro Candido 12 558; 18 686
Decembristerne 7 805; 14 228, 297
Decentius, Emperor of Rome (*reg* 350) 9 635
De Cesare, Francesco 22 473
Dechaineux, Lucien 2 771; 14 397
Dechales, Claude François Milliet 29 637
Dechaume, Geoffrey 11 565
Dechazaux, Jean, I (*d* 1728) 12 468
Dechazaux, Jean, II (*d* 1779) 12 468
Dechencholing 3 916
Dechev, Danail 5 155
De Chirico, Andrea see SAVINIO, ALBERTO
De Chirico, Giorgio 4 196; 7 385; 8 602–7*; 24 448; 26 776; 27 888; 31 852
 copies 27 280
 dealers 13 826; 19 537; 27 163
 exhibitions 7 842; 10 822; 33 744
 groups and movements 3 120
  Artistic Forum 2 546
  Dada 8 434
  Italiani di Parigi 16 680
  Pittura Metafisica 5 849; 16 680; 18 717; 20 93; 25 5–6; 29 670
  Surrealism 30 19, 23
  Valori Plastici 31 852

De Chirico, Giorgio—cont.
methods **24** 490
pageants **11** 190
paintings **8** *603, 604, 605*
murals **16** 681; **28** 793
patrons and collectors **10** 164; **20** 142, 848; **21** 135; **24** 369; **32** 912; **33** 744
productions **3** 120
pupils **5** 451
statuettes **29** 576
writings **27** 163
Decimal Index of the Art of the Low Countries *see* D.I.A.L.
Decius, Emperor of Rome (*reg* 249-51) **27** 41, *41*
Decius Julius Brutus **31** 813
Decjusz, Justus Ludwik **18** 425; **25** 135; **33** 615
Deck, Joseph-Théodore **2** 116; **8** 607–8*; **28** 524
collaboration **14** 363
pupils **4** 625
works **11** 606; **22** 59; **24** 148
Decker, Cornelis **23** 611; **27** 329
works **17** *884*
Decker, Evert **33** 389
Decker, Francis *see* DUVENECK, FRANK
Decker, František **25** 648
Decker, Joseph **8** 608*
Decker, Matthew **11** 141, 348
Decker, Paul
teachers **28** 118
works **4** 362; **5** 347, 349; **9** 28; **24** 271, 275; **31** 298
deckle edge **8** 608*
Declercq brothers **3** 585
De Clercq collection **1** 895
Declerq **3** 591
De Cock, César **8** 608*
De Cock, Xavier **8** 608; **18** 680
De Coene, Jozef **3** 587
De Coene brothers **3** 579, 587
Decoeur, Emile **28** 525
Decol, Roland **10** 483
décollage **7** 557; **8** 608–9*; **23** *260*; **27** 214; **32** 714
see also DECALCOMANIA (i) (PAPERCUTS)
Décollage: Bulletin aktueller Ideen **8** 609
De coloribus et artibus Romanorum **8** 609*; **20** 324
Deconchy, Jean **4** 331
Deconstruction **2** 533; **8** 609–10*, 781; **14** 459; **15** 100; **25** 361
decor **26** 925
Decorata *see under* TYPE-FACES
Decorated ware *see under* POTTERY → wares
Décoration Intérieure Moderne (DIM) **11** 601
decorations, architectural *see* ARCHITECTURAL DECORATIONS
decorations, ceiling *see* CEILING DECORATIONS
decorations, façade *see* FAÇADE DECORATION
decorations, floor *see* FLOOR DECORATIONS
decorations, military *see* MEDALS
decorations, roof *see* ROOF DECORATIONS
decorations, wall *see* WALL DECORATIONS
decorative arts **30** 382
Antilles, Lesser **2** 150–52*
Bosnia **4** 462*
Caribbean Islands **5** 752*
Croatia **8** 180*
Denmark **32** 517
Georgia **12** 328–31*
Herzegovina **4** 462*
Indian subcontinent **15** 722–5*
Isle of Man **32** 530*
Kazakhstan **17** 867–8*
Kuba (iii) (Zaïre) **18** 487–8*
decorative arts—cont.
Kyrgyzstan **18** 569*
Macedonia (ii) (former Yugoslavia) **19** 885–6*
Montenegro **22** 18–19*
Northern Ireland **16** 41–2*
Puerto Rico **25** 702–3*
Shakers **28** 542*
Slovakia **28** 855–6*
Slovenia **28** 862–3*
Surinam **30** 16*
Tajikistan **30** 253–4*
Turkmenistan **31** 459–60*
Ukraine **31** 562*, 563–4*
Uzbekistan **31** 783–4*
Viking **32** 514*, 517*, 519–24*, 525*, 526–8*, 530*, 531–2*
Borre style **32** 515–16*
Britain **32** 528*
England **32** 528–9*
Ireland **32** 529–30*
Isle of Man **32** 530*
Jelling style **32** 516–17*
Mammen style **32** 517*
Oseberg style **32** 515*
Ringerike style **32** 517*
Scandinavia **32** 514–17*, 518–24*, 525*, 526–7*, 531–2*
Scotland **32** 530*
Style III:E **32** 514–15*
Style III:F **32** 515*
Urnes-Romanesque **32** 519*
Urnes style **32** 518–19*
see also CERAMICS; FURNITURE; GLASS; INTERIOR DECORATION; OBJECTS OF VERTU; METALWORK; TEXTILES
decorative paper *see under* PAPER → types
decorators **13** 395
Décorchement, François-Emile **12** 783, 795
Décorchemont, François Emile **11** 613
decorum **8** 612–13*; **9** 796–8*; **23** 533
see also ART CRITICISM
de Cottis Grave, Master of the *see* COTTIS GRAVE, MASTER OF THE DE
découpages **16** 354
Decourt, Jean **7** 464; **31** 851
Decraene, Alexandre-Auguste-François **26** 192
decretals **8** 614–15*
Decrolin **30** 559
decumanus **8** 615*; **10** 602
De Curte, Louis **3** 549; **5** 53; **8** 615*
Dedalo: Rassegna d'arte **24** 448
Dedan **2** *246*, 247, 249
pottery **2** 268
statues **2** 256–7
tombs **2** 255
Dedan Namgyel, Ruler of Basgo (*reg c.* 1642–75) **15** 397
Deddington **13** 211
Dedeček, Vladimir **28** 850
Dedeke, Wilm **4** 418; **8** 615*
Dedeline (family) **4** 692
Dedham (Essex), Sir Alfred Munnings Art Museum **22** 312; **29** 426
Dedham Pottery **4** 482; **26** 467; **31** 638, 639
Dedigama **29** 459
Kotavehara **29** 475
Dediot, Eugenio **8** 232
De Domenicis, Gino **8** 615–16*; **16** 682
De Dragon, Vittore Grubicy *see* GRUBICY (DE DRAGON), VITTORE
Dedreux, Alfred **4** 306; **7** 304; **8** 616*
Dedreux, Pierre-Anne **8** 616
Dedreux-Dorcy, Pierre-Joseph **8** 616
deed boxes *see under* BOXES → types
Deegan, Denby **22** 671
Deen Dayal, Lala **15** 184; **24** 664
Deen Dayal & Sons **10** 580
Deene, Jan van **3** 704
Deene Park (Northants) **5** 293
Deepadih **8** 616*; **15** *279, 285*
Deepdene (Surrey) **9** 24, 29; **10** 279; **14** 745; **32** 554
Deerbon, Una **2** 760
Deere and Co. **32** 861
Deerfield (MA), Ebenezer Wells House **32** *301*, 302
Deerfield Blue and White Society **31** 658
deer-hair *see under* HAIR → types
Deerham, George William Coventry, Lord *see* COVENTRY, GEORGE WILLIAM, 6th Earl of
Deerhurst (Glos)
Odda's Chapel **30** 905
St Mary's Priory **2** 65; **11** 252; **26** 618; **33** 108
deerskin *see under* LEATHER → types
De Fabris, Emilio **8** 616–17*; **11** 182, 196, 197; **16** 646, 774
de faldriquera **29** *331*
De Fazio, Guiliano **22** 474
defensive walls *see under* WALLS → types
Defeo, Jay **17** 694
Defer de Maisonneuve **20** 421
Defernex, Jean-Baptiste **1** 665; **8** 617*; **9** 416; **23** 517
Deferrari, Defendente *see* FERRARI, DEFENDENTE
De Feure, Georges *see* FEURE, GEORGES DE
Deffand, Marie Anne de Vichy-Chamrond, Marquise du **7** 495
De Finetti, Giuseppe **8** 617*
collaboration **23** 263
works **10** 820; **16** 649; **21** 521
Defoe, Daniel **8** 218; **27** 868
Deforge, Armand Auguste **8** 618*
Deforge et Carpentier **8** 618
Defossé, Jules **8** 792
Defrance, Jean-Pierre **27** 246
Defrance, Léonard **8** 618*; **10** 825; **19** 344
Dèfraoui, Chèrif **30** 156
Dèfraoui, Silvie **30** 156
Defrasse, A.
works **13** *379*
Defregger, Franz von **8** 618*; **22** 304
house **14** 227
pupils **7** 855
teachers **24** 815
works **12** 394; **22** *304*
Defroche **19** 27
Degaldoruva **29** 465
Deganello, Paolo **2** 373
Degannwy **32** 786
Degant, Joseph **5** 578
Degas, (Hilaire-Germain-) Edgar **8** 596, 619–25*; **11** 567, 667; **15** 211; **19** 589; **24** 552, 883; **27** 238
assemblages **2** 616
collaboration **5** 922; **24** 880
dealers **3** 888; **4** 589; **9** 424; **26** 107; **32** 686
drawings **8** *624*; **9** 217, 226; **31** 801
pastel **9** 216; **15** VI1; **23** 296, *296*; **24** III
frames **11** 416–17, *416*
groups and movements **11** 190; **15** 151, 152, 153, 154, 155; **22** 687; **26** 56; **28** 344; **33** 379
methods **6** 471; **21** 761, 769, 771; **24** 241, 667; **28** 813; **29** 863
modelli **21** *771*
models **29** 426
Degas, (Hilaire-Germain-) Edgar—cont.
paintings **5** 391; **8** 123, 596; **11** 417; **21** 761; **24** 50; **31** 282, 704
genre **8** *622*; **12** 295
portraits **8** *619*; **18** 899
sporting scenes **8** *620*; **29** 426
patrons and collectors
Barnes, Albert C. **3** 251; **12** 769
Bliss, Lillie P(lummer) **4** 142
Bührle, Emil Georg **5** 132
Burrell, William (1861-1958) **5** 278; **28** 273
Caillebotte, Gustave **5** 391
Camondo, Isaac de, Comte **5** 530
Clark, Robert Sterling **7** 377
Cochin, Denys (-Pierre-Augustin-Marie), Baron **7** 496
Cone, Claribel and Etta **7** 702
Coquelin, Ernest **7** 832
Courtauld, Samuel (1876-1947) **8** 62
Drummond, George A(lexander) (1827-1910) **9** 305
Durand-Ruel, Paul (Marie Joseph) **28** 744
Duret, (Jules-Emmanuel) Théodore **9** 448
Faure, Jean-Baptiste **10** 837
FitzGerald, Desmond **11** 141
Frick, Henry Clay **11** 774
Hanna, Leonard C(olton) **14** 139
Havemeyer, Louisine (Waldron) **14** 244
Ionides, Constantine Alexander **15** 895
Kay, Arthur **26** 107
Khalil, Muhammad Mahmoud **5** 401
Lehman, Robert **19** 92
Lerolle, Henry **19** 230
Lévy, Pierre and Denise **19** 282
Liebermann, Max **19** 334, 335
May, Ernest (1845-1925) **20** 878
Moore, George (Augustus) (1852-1933) **22** 54
Morozov, Ivan (Abramovich) (1871-1921) **22** 135, 136
Museu de Arte de São Paulo **4** 726
National Museum (Belgrade) **28** 459
Palmer, Bertha Honoré **23** 882
Pope, Alfred Atmore **25** 234
Robinson, Edward G(oldenberg) **26** 472
Ryabushinsky, Nikolay (Pavlovich) **27** 459
Sainsbury, Robert and Lisa **27** 524
Shchukin, Sergey (Ivanovich) **28** 569
Simon, Norton **28** 751
Tavernier, Adolphe-Eugène **30** 375
Whitney, John Hay **33** 150
personal collection **17** 440; **24** 883
photographs **2** 107; **24** 671
prints **25** 596, 599, 601, 621, 624; **29** 556, 557
aquatints **2** 240
drypoints **9** 309
etchings **10** 556, 563; **19** 215; **25** 607, *607*
lithographs **19** 488; **25** 607, 628
monotypes **10** 480; **21** 895, 896, *896*; **25** 616; **31** *705*
reproductive prints by others **19** 489; **20** 351
sculpture **11** 567
teachers **15** 152
De Gaulle, Charles **11** 660
De Geer-Bergenstrahle, Marie-Louise **30** 82
degenerate art *see* ENTARTETE KUNST
Degenhardt, Henry **31** 652
Degeorges, Charles-Jean-Marie **5** 304
Deger, Ernst **29** 66
works **11** *463*
Değirmentepe **1** 839, 856
Deglane, Henri-Adolphe-Auguste **2** 14; **8** 626*; **10** 683; **11** 524; **12** 728
Değler **4** 66, 67
Church No. 32 **4** 67
Degler, Andreas **8** 626
Degler, David **8** 626
Degler, Hans **2** 44; **8** 626–7*
works **8** *627*; **12** 403, 404; **13** 633; **24** 331
Degler, Johann **14** 65
Degottex, Jean **2** 545; **8** 627–8*; **11** 551; **30** 23
Degotti, Ignace-Eugène-Marie **8** 448, 559
Degoullons, Jules *see* DU GOULON, JULES
Degouve de Nuncques, William **3** 564; **5** 44; **8** 628*; **19** 792
De Grada, Raffaele **7** 894
Degrave, Jules-Alexandre Patrouillard **23** 693
De Gregorio, Marco **6** 129; **8** 716; **16** 678; **22** 480; **28** 317, 318
De Groot, Guillaume **30** 47
De Groux, Charles (-Auguste-Corneille) **3** 562; **8** 628*
groups and movements **28** 921
De Groux, Henry (-Jules-Charles) **8** 628–9*; **10** 517; **32** 591
Deguilleville, Guillaume de *see* GUILLAUME DE DEGUILLEVILLE
Degussa AG **12** 472
D'Egville, James **4** 619
Dehaye, Lucas **31** 223
Dehes **9** 540, 543
Dehio, Georg Gottfried **8** 629*; **11** 122; **13** 810
Dehmel, Richard **20** 380; **22** 291
Deh Morasi **1** 185
Dehn, Adolf **19** 492; **20** 603, 604
Dehn, Christian **29** 724
Dehne, Christoph **8** 629*; **12** 405; **20** 88
Dehner, Dorothy **28** 875
Dehodencq, (Edmé-Alexis-) Alfred **8** 629–30*; **23** 523; **26** 481
Dehoy, Charles **4** 618; **8** 630*
Dehra Dun **4** 794
Dehtice church **28** 849
Dehua
ceramics **6** 332, 624, 912, 917; **21** 633; **25** 783
kilns **6** 871
porcelain **6** 871, 907, 910–11, *911*, 913
see also under PORCELAIN → wares
DeHuff, Elizabeth **14** 477; **17** 716; **22** 594
dehumidifiers **7** 735
Dei (family) **8** 188
Dei, Antonio de Giovanni **32** 360
Dei, Benedetto **8** 630*; **11** 179
Dei, Pietro di Antonio *see* BARTOLOMEO DELLA GATTA
Deibel, Jan Zygmunt *see* DEYBEL, JAN ZYGMUNT
Deichmann, Erica **5** 582
Deichmann, F. W. **9** 528
Deichmann, Kjeld **5** 582
Deichsler (family) **18** 511
Deichsler Altarpiece, Master of the **20** 620, 696

Deick, Barthélemy see EYCK, BARTHÉLEMY D'
Deighton, Robert see DIGHTON, ROBERT (i)
Deiker, Carl Friedrich 19 379
Deilmann, Harald 8 631*; 22 315
Deincourt 4 63
Deineka, Alexander see DEYNEKA, ALEKSANDR
Deininger, Wunibald 27 662
deinoi see DINOI
Deinokrates of Rhodes 1 613
Deinomenes 2 682
Deipara Virgo, Master of the 3 738
Deira, Ernesto 2 401; 8 631*; 19 872
Deir Abu Ghanima 18 20
Deir Abu Hinnis see MONASTERY OF ST JOHN
Deir Abu Maqar see ST MACARIUS MONASTERY
Deir al-Abyad 9 *507*, 535
Deir al-Adas 9 543
Deir al-Anba Antunyus see MONASTERY OF ST ANTHONY
Deir Da'il 9 543
Deir el-Azab 10 758, 759
Deir el-Bahri see under THEBES (i) (EGYPT)
Deir el-Balah 1 880
Deir el-Ballas 9 851, 861; 10 80
Deir el-Gebrawi 9 *774*; 12 227–8*
 tombs 9 773, 822, 891, 899
Deir el-Malak 10 758, 759
Deir el-Medina see under THEBES (i) (EGYPT)
Deir el-Shelwit see under THEBES (i) (EGYPT)
Deir Mateina 31 434
Deir Rifa 9 840
Deir Saliba 31 434
Deir Sim'an 9 *513*, 540, 541; 25 772
 North Church 9 538, *539*, 540
Deir Solaib 9 543
Deir Tasa 10 59
Deir Zafaran 31 434
 manuscripts 31 436
 Mar Hananiya 31 435
 monastery church 31 *434*
Deir Zarafan 31 436
Deisslingen
 jewellery 21 *502*
Dejante, P. B. 25 308
Dejima see NAGASAKI
Dejoie, Thimoleon 14 58
Dejoux, Claude 1 742; 8 631–2*; 11 336; 19 140; 29 565
Dejuinne, François-Louis 17 628
Dejvice 8 380
Dékáni, Árpád 15 12
De Kat, Anne-Pierre 4 619
De Kat earthenware factory 22 883
De Kay, James E. 14 536
Dekeleia 21 556
De Kerckhove De Denterghem, Graaf 19 756
Dekert, Siri 30 81
De Keyser, Nicaise 8 632*; 31 857
 pupils 1 676; 7 404; 14 116; 18 670; 19 347; 31 873; 32 253
 works 2 197; 3 562
Dekkers, Ad(riaan) 8 632*; 22 852
De Knyff, Alfred see KNYFF, ALFRED DE
De Koninck, Louis Herman 3 579; 8 633*
 groups and movements 25 741
 house 3 551
 pupils 30 213
 works 3 551, *587*, 587
De Kooning, Elaine 8 633, 634, 636*
De Kooning, Willem 8 633–6*; 22 852; 31 607
 collaboration 20 605
 dealers 16 570, 820, 906; 18 161
De Kooning, Willem—cont.
 frames 11 499
 groups and movements 7 685; 31 607
  Abstract Expressionism 1 78, 83, 84, 87, 131; 2 839; 4 75; 23 48
  American Abstract Artists 1 771
  Art informel 2 544
  Black Mountain College (NC) 4 109
  Irascibles 29 534
 patrons and collectors 9 189; 14 575; 25 400; 26 489; 28 314; 33 45
 studio 29 858
 teachers 13 12
 works 1 *87*; 8 *634*, *635*; 18 132; 19 492; 22 335; 26 27; 31 705
Dekorative Kunst 2 562, 565; 21 57; 24 427, 444
Dekorativnoye iskusstvo SSSR 24 451; 27 444
De kroniek van kunst en kultuur 33 162
Delabal, Charlotte 26 *275*
Delabarre, Pierre 11 636
 works 11 *636*
Delaborde, Henri, Comte 8 637*; 13 871
Delabrière, Alexandre-Louis 14 681
Dela Censerie, Louis 2 194; 3 549, 550; 4 920, 922; 8 637*
Delacour, William 9 724; 24 188, 273; 28 246, 252, 274; 32 652
Delacroix, Charles 7 162
Delacroix, (Ferdinand-)Eugène (-Victor) 1 634; 7 385; 8 637–48*, *646*; 11 659; 14 188; 22 59; 24 140; 25 651; 26 376; 27 248
 book illustrations 12 853
 cliché-verre 7 433, 434
 collaboration 13 806
 commentaries 3 392; 16 875
 dealers 3 888; 9 425; 14 188
 drawings 13 252; 24 243
  facsimiles 19 484
 exhibitions 20 498; 24 140
 frames 11 413, *413*, 414, *414*
 groups and movements 20 498; 24 585; 28 345; 29 891
  Orientalism 23 503, 504
  Rococo Revival 26 500
  Romanticism 24 140; 26 736, 737, 739, 742; 28 345
  Troubadour style 31 373, 374
 interior decoration 15 88, *88*
 methods 6 570; 9 673; 10 199; 21 761; 23 788; 24 667
 paintings 8 *639*; 11 580; 24 777; 26 *739*
  allegorical 1 660, *660*; 11 542
  genre 7 II2
  history 8 *643*; 10 479; 12 187; 14 587
  hunting scenes 2 106, *107*
  literary themes 1 640; 11 543; 23 295; 30 358
  murals 17 629; 22 329
  mythological 8 *642*; 22 416
  oil sketches 23 381
  portraits 30 358
  religious 18 677
  still-lifes 29 669
  watercolours 8 *641*; 9 225; 32 900, 901, VII2
 patrons and collectors 11 544, 663
  Aumale, Henri-Eugène-Philippe-Louis de Bourbon, Duc d' 23 523
  Aynard, Edouard 2 881
  Bellio, Georges de 3 671
  Berry, Caroline de Bourbon, Duchesse de 4 556
  Beurnonville, Etienne-Edmond Martin, Baron de 3 890
Delacroix, (Ferdinand-)Eugène (-Victor)
 patrons and collectors—cont.
  Blacas, Pierre-Louis-Jean-Casimir de Blaces d'Aulps, Duc de 4 106
  Bruyas, Alfred 5 57; 11 659
  Burrell, William (1861-1958) 5 278
  Camondo, Isaac de, Comte 5 530
  Chéramy, Paul-Arthur 6 548
  Cochin, Denys (-Pierre-Augustin-Marie), Baron 7 496
  Demidov, Anatoly, Prince 8 705
  Dugléré, Adolphe 9 378
  Dumas, Alexandre, père (1802-70) 30 32
  Durand-Ruel, Paul (Marie Joseph) 28 744
  Gaugain, (Armand-Pierre-) Henri 12 186
  Haro, Etienne-François 14 188
  Houssaye, (François-) Arsène 14 802
  Ionides, Constantine Alexander 15 895
  Leopold I, King of Belgium (*reg* 1831-65) 7 490
  Leopold II, King of Belgium (*reg* 1865-1909) 7 490
  Lucas, George A(loysius) 19 756
  Moreau, Adolphe 22 93
  Moreau-Nélaton, Etienne 22 93
  Orléans, Ferdinand-Philippe (-Louis-Charles- Henri) de Bourbon, 7th Duc d' (1810-42) 23 522
  Paillet, Charles 23 778
  Péreire (family) 24 396
  Péreire, Jacob-Emile 14 188
  Petit, Francis 24 551
  Ricourt, Achille 4 655
  Roger-Marx, Claude 26 534
  Tavernier, Adolphe-Eugène 30 375
  Tschudi, Hugo von 31 397
  Vos (ii) Jbzn, Jacob de (1803-82) 32 708
 prints
  aquatints 2 240
  lithographs 4 364; 8 *640*; 19 486, 487; 20 602; 25 607, 628
 pupils 6 535; 14 188; 24 838; 28 196
 reproductions on banknotes 3 182
 reproductive prints by others 4 625; 26 234
 restorations by others 24 838
 stained glass 29 506
 studio 29 856, *857*
 teachers 13 794
 writings 7 629; 9 9; 22 379
Delacroix, Henri-Edmond-Joseph see CROSS, HENRI EDMOND
De Laet, S. 3 619
Delafleur, Nicolas Guillaume 26 772
Delafons, Pierre-François
 works 7 *194*
Delafontaine, Augustin-Maximilien 8 648
Delafontaine, Pierre-Maximilien 8 648–9*; 9 447
Delafont de Juis, Jean-Marie 7 162
Delafosse, Jean-Baptiste 8 130
Delafosse, Jean-Charles 8 649*; 9 8; 11 593
 patrons and collectors 30 524; 31 56
 works 7 747; 24 273
Delagardette, Claude Mathieu 11 521; 12 835; 17 629
De la Gardie (family) 8 481; 14 281
De la Gardie, Jakob 4 180; 18 459
De la Gardie, Magnus Gabriel 8 649–50*
 architecture 30 117
 interior decoration 1 899; 30 88
 paintings 2 730; 5 544; 10 133; 22 311; 30 77, 118; 31 824
 sculpture 18 682; 33 81
Delagrange, Guillaume 18 873
Delagrive, Abbé
 works 12 *61*
Delahante, Alexis 4 329, 330; 10 366; 31 465
Delahaut, Jo 2 510; 3 565; 5 45; 17 518; 29 369
Delaherche, Auguste 24 148
Delai, Giuseppe 4 286; 5 775
Delaissé, L(eon) M. J. 8 650*
Delaistre, François-Nicolas 8 650*; 11 627; 13 665; 32 77
De Lalaing, Jacques, Comte 8 650–51*
Delamain, Henry 16 28, 36
Delamain, Mary 16 28
Delamain, William 16 28
Delamair, Antoine 8 651
Delamair, Pierre-Alexis 8 651–2*
Delamarches, Charles-François 12 814
Delamarre, Victor 19 17
Delamayne, John see MAIANO, GIOVANNI DA, II
Delamere Station see LIGHTNING BROTHERS
Delamonce, Jean-Baptiste (1635-1708) 22 302; 33 276
De Lamonica, Roberto 29 26
Delamotte, Clement 31 189
Delamotte, George O. 8 652
Delamotte, P(hilip) H(enry) 8 652*
 pupils 8 125
 works 20 *239*; 24 665
Delamotte, William (Alfred) (1775-1863) 8 652*; 23 690
 pupils 31 477
 works 10 251
Delamotte, William Alfred (1825-55) 8 652
Delane, Solomon 16 14
Delaney, Edward 16 22
Delaney, Mary 16 23
Delanney, Marcel 24 128
Delano, William A(dams) 8 652–3*; 23 43
Delano & Aldrich 7 326, 470; 8 652–3*; 23 40; 32 829
Delanof, Alexandru 2 52
Delanois, Louis 9 313; 13 665; 25 118
Delanoy, Abraham 33 92
Delany, Mary 24 57; 29 31
Delapierre, Michel, II 11 619
Delaplaine, Joseph 23 629
Delaplanche, Eugène 8 653*
 assistants 12 316
 patrons and collectors 16 829; 23 794
 pupils 18 786
 works 29 843
De la Poer, Louisa Anne, Marchioness of Waterford 32 904*
Delaporte, L. 18 769; 19 737
Delaporte, Pacifique 1 895
Delaquis, Ato 12 509
Delaram, Francis 14 547; 28 357
De La Rive, Pierre-Louis see LA RIVE, PIERRE-LOUIS DE
Delaroche, Gregoire-Hippolyte 8 653*; 28 170
Delaroche, Jules-Hippolyte 8 653
Delaroche, Paul (Hippolyte) 1 106; 8 653–5*; 11 543, 544, 659, 663, 671
 assistants 7 169; 21 156; 24 312; 25 261; 26 308; 33 581
 groups and movements 26 740; 28 345; 31 374
Delaroche, Paul (Hippolyte)—cont.
 patrons and collectors 11 544
  Arrowsmith, John 2 499
  Aumale, Henri-Eugène-Philippe-Louis de Bourbon, Duc d' 23 523
  Coutan, Louis-Joseph-Auguste 8 72
  Demidov, Anatoly, Prince 8 705
  Louis-Philippe, King of the French (*reg* 1830-48) 23 521
  Orléans, Ferdinand-Philippe (-Louis-Charles- Henri) de Bourbon, 7th Duc d' (1810-42) 15 841; 23 522
  Péreire, Jacob-Emile and Isaac 24 396
  Pourtalès-Gorgier, James-Alexandre, Comte de 25 383
  Seymour-Conway, Richard, 4th Marquess of Hertford 28 527
  Walters, William T(hompson) 19 755
 pupils
  Antigna, (Jean-Pierre-) Alexandre 2 142
  Armitage, Edward 2 446
  Bonhommé, (Ignace-) François 4 319
  Boulanger, Gustave (-Clarence-Rodolphe) 4 528
  Cavelier, Pierre-Jules 6 115
  Cazabon, Michel Jean 31 335
  Cham (1819-79) 6 404
  Couture, Thomas 8 75
  Crowe, Eyre 8 206
  Delaborde, Henri, Comte 8 637
  Dubufe, (Louis-)Edouard 9 332
  Duval Le Camus, Jules 9 467
  Ekman, Robert Wilhelm 10 127
  Fenton, Roger 10 887
  Frère, (Pierre) Edouard 11 760
  Gallait, Louis(-Joseph) 12 12
  Gendron, (Etienne-) Auguste 12 270
  Gérôme, Jean-Léon 12 486
  Gignoux, Régis-François 12 608
  Hamon, Jean-Louis 14 120
  Hébert, (Antoine-Auguste-) Ernest 14 283
  Hédouin, (Pierre-)Edmond (-Alexandre) 14 288
  Israëls, Jozef 16 573
  Jalabert, Charles (-François) 16 875
  Jobbé-Duval, Félix (Armand Marie) 17 597
  Landelle, Charles (-Zacharie) 18 696
  Laso (de la Vega de los Ríos), Francisco 18 812
  Le Gray, (Jean-Baptiste-) Gustave 19 86
  Le Secq (des Tournelles), Henri (1818-82) 19 239
  Lucy, Charles 19 775
  Millet, Jean-François (1814-75) 21 610
  Monticelli, Adolphe (-Joseph-Thomas) 22 28
  Nègre, Charles 22 723
  Robert-Fleury, Tony 26 455
  Wappers, (Egidius Karel) Gustaf, Baron 32 852
 reproductive prints by others 2 499; 12 724; 13 228; 14 394; 26 232
 teachers 13 692
 works 8 *654*; 11 544; 14 587; 21 761; 22 329; 28 170
De La Roche, Pierre see LA ROCHE, PIERRE DE
De la Rue 17 640
Delarue, Louis-Félix 18 804*; 27 558
Delasensy, Wilhelm 25 127
Delatouche 20 137
Delatour, Alexandre 2 723

Delatour, Maurice-Quentin see LA TOUR, MAURICE-QUENTIN DE
Delâtre, Auguste 8 655*; 17 440; 20 603; 25 627; 33 137
Delâtre, Eugène 9 309; 20 603; 24 726
Delattre, Jean-Marie 29 676
Delaunay, (Jules-) Elie 8 659*; 11 546; 25 751
collaboration 28 349
pupils 8 818; 20 876; 26 191; 27 239, 615
works 11 546
Delaunay, Nicolas see LAUNAY, NICOLAS DE
Delaunay, Pierre 11 405
Delaunay, Robert (1749-1814) see LAUNAY, ROBERT DE
Delaunay (ii), Robert (1885-1941) 8 655–8*; 11 547, 548; 15 828
collaboration 4 98
dealers 16 906
exhibitions 32 775
groups and movements 1 74
Abstraction-Création 1 76, 90
Blaue Reiter 4 132; 23 569
Cubism 8 240; 12 805; 19 78; 25 747; 27 307; 31 705
Futurism 8 436
Jack of Diamonds (Bubnovy Valet) 16 817
Orphism 2 225; 8 240; 23 569, 570
Pointillism 22 747
Synchromism 30 173
lithographs 19 491
methods 7 630
paintings 1 74; 8 244, 245, 657; 9 292; 19 80; 23 570
murals 15 884
patrons and collectors 2 383; 13 800; 18 187; 32 178
productions 3 120
writings 8 245; 18 109
Delaunay (ii), Sonia 8 658–9*
collaboration 8 658
designers 13 798
groups and movements 1 90; 3 120; 8 436, 439, 838; 20 97; 23 570; 30 173
works 3 462; 6 167; 8 659; 9 245, 292, 292; 11 548, 647, 649
Delaune, Etienne 2 455, 718; 8 68, 660*; 10 387
patrons and collectors 30 727
reproductions in hardstones 12 259
works 2 455; 5 814; 12 455; 14 855; 17 521; 24 365; 25 22
writings 13 701
Delaune, Jean 8 660; 17 521
Delauney, Pierre-François 8 660*
Delaunois, Alfred N. 19 260
Delaval (family) 25 210
De la Vallée, Jean 8 660–61*
architecture
castles 30 69, 70
churches 1 152; 11 90; 19 815; 29 685; 30 70
government buildings 8 660; 29 685; 30 70
houses 29 685
palaces 8 650
attributions 30 69, 70
De la Vallée, Simon 8 660*
assistants 30 522
patrons and collectors 30 70
pupils 8 660
teachers 9 296
works 26 392; 29 685; 30 69, 70
Delavauld, Hans 12 514
Delavoy, Robert Leon 3 565
Delaware 22 628
Delbene 19 497
Delbosc 18 626
Delboy brothers 30 925
Delbridge, W. J. 26 107
Del Conte, Jacopino see Conte, Jacopino del
Delcour, Jean (1631-1707) 1 631; 8 661*
Delcour, Jean (-Gilles) (1632-95) 3 570; 8 661; 19 344
teachers 11 166; 14 393
works 3 571
Delécluse, Auguste 18 672
Delécluze, Etienne-Jean 6 570; 8 661–2*
Delécluze, Jean-Baptiste 8 661
De Leeuw, Bert 3 565; 20 846
Délégation à la création aux métiers artistiques et aux manufactures (DCMAM) 11 659
Délégation Archéologique Française en Afghanistan 1 211
Delektorskaya, Lidiya 27 440
Delemer, Jean 8 662*; 13 111, 113
collaboration 20 671
patrons and collectors 5 210
works 3 568; 5 549; 12 354; 13 100
Delémont 30 136
DeLemos & Cordes 8 770
De Lempicka, Tamara 8 662*; 10 483
Delen, Adriaan 3 615
Delen, Dirck (Christiaensz.) van 8 662–3*; 25 68
collaboration 14 96; 23 832
teachers 14 95; 22 840
works 2 341; 14 795
Delen, Jan van 3 570; 8 663*
Delen, Theodor van 4 224
De Léon, Omar 25 455
De Lera (family) 8 135
De Lera, Bernardino 8 134, 135; 25 857
De Lera, Guglielmo 8 135; 25 857
De Lescluze, Jean Baptiste 10 91, 93
Delespine, Nicolas-Pierre-Jules 4 171; 17 629; 24 387
Delespine, Pierre-Jules-Nicolas see DELESPINE, NICOLAS-PIERRE-JULES
Delessert, Benjamin (b 1692) 8 663
Delessert, (Jules-Paul-)Benjamin (1773–1847) 8 663–4*
Delessert, Benjamin (1817–68) 8 664*
Delessert, Etienne 15 842
Delessert, François-Marie 8 664*
Delevoy, Robert L. 3 620; 17 518
Delezenne, Ignace-François 5 584; 25 894
Delf, Coppin 2 114; 8 664*; 20 703
Delff, Jacob (Willemsz.) (1550–1601) 8 664
Delff, Jacob (Willemsz.) (1619–61) 8 665; 21 486
Delff, Willem Jacobsz. 8 664–5*; 9 470; 10 393; 21 486; 32 231
Delfín, Víctor 24 511
Delfini, Gentile 23 577
Delft 8 665–9*; 22 813
art forms and materials
brick 4 778
ceramics 6 332; 8 668–9*, 668; 22 878, 878, 880, 881, 882–3
faience (ii) (ceramics) 22 372, 879–80
glass 22 884
gold 22 889
painting 12 290; 22 835, 844
pewter 22 893
pottery 4 176; 30 875
silver 22 885, 887
tapestries 8 754; 22 897; 30 318, 320
tiles 3 576; 30 878
Museum Huis Lambert van Meerten 22 906
Nieuwe Doelen 22 844
Delft—cont.
Nieuwe Kerk 13 62; 22 820, 894
monument to William the Silent 18 8, 8–9; 22 858
Oude Kerk 22 820; 25 725; 30 531; 33 267
altar 22 857
pulpit 22 857
tomb of Admiral Maarten Harpertsz. Tromp 22 858
tomb of Piet Heyn 22 858
Polytechnische School see TECHNISCHE HOGESCHOOL
Stadhuis 18 9
Technische Hogeschool 22 908
Technische Universiteit 22 909
Volkenkundig Museum Nusantara 29 240
Delft, Jan Lucas van 22 837
Delft, Master of 8 666; 20 655–7*, 718
works 20 656
Delftfield Pottery 28 257; 30 877
works 28 257
Delft School (i) (17th cent.) 8 669*; 14 733
Delft School (ii) (20th cent.) 8 669–70*; 22 831
members 3 777; 11 776; 13 312; 23 450
works 8 670
Delftware see under POTTERY → wares
Delgado, Blas Antonio 16 863
Delgado, Cardinal 6 67; 29 337
Delgado, Francisco Bayas see BAYAS DELGADO, FRANCISCO
Delgado, Gaspar Núñez see NÚÑEZ DELGADO, GASPAR
Delgado, Jerónimo 24 500
Delgado, Juan 12 56
Delgado, Manuel 24 395
Delgado, Mauricio García y see GARCÍA Y DELGADO, MAURICIO
Delgado, Oscar Colón see COLÓN DELGADO, OSCAR
Delgado, Osiris 18 832; 25 701, 702
Delgado Rodas, Modesto 24 98
Del Giudice, Francesco Maria 23 88
Delheid 3 602
Delhez, Víctor 2 399
Delhi 8 670–81*, 671; 15 195, 245, 261, 264, 360, 409; 16 105
academies and art schools
College of Art 8 677
Lalit Kala Akademi 8 677; 15 179; 20 54
collections 15 180, 184
exhibitions 15 748
Sangeet Natak Academy 15 714
Sarada Ukil School of Art 8 677
'Adilabad 8 672; 15 340
art forms and materials
architecture 15 338, 340; 20 226
enamel 16 515
manuscript illumination 15 564, 566–7, 574; 16 326
mihrabs 15 339
painting 15 655*
miniatures 15 724
wall 15 544
watercolours 15 655
porcelain 6 918
prints 15 177
silver 15 707
textiles 15 664
tiles 15 686
Ashoka Hotel 15 168
Asian Games Village 15 169
Barakhamba 32 324
Bijai Mandal 15 341
Buddha Jayanti Park 12 76
canals 8 675
Chandni Chauk 8 675
craftsmen and artists 15 208
Dinpanah 8 674–5
citadel see Purana Qil'a
Delhi—cont.
façades 15 242
Firuzabad 8 673–4, 675; 12 73; 15 341
citadel see Firuz Shah Kotla
Firuz Shah Kotla 8 673; 15 341
Golden Minar 15 341
palace 29 816
Flagstaff House see MUSEUMS → Nehru Memorial Museum
French Embassy staff quarters 15 169
Gandhi Darsan Complex 29 891
gardens 12 73
Garhi Studios 15 179, 180
halls 14 77
'idgāhs 15 343; 22 354
India International Centre 15 169
Indian Statistical Institute 15 169
Islamic religious buildngs
Bara Gunbad complex
Bara Gunbad 15 343
congregational mosque 15 342
Begumpuri Mosque 15 341
Chawnsath Khamba Mosque 15 342
congregational mosque see Jami Mosque
Haud-i Khass congregational mosque 15 342
Jama'at Khana Mosque 8 672; 15 340
Jami' Mosque 8 680–81*; 15 341, 366; 16 239; 29 526, 527
Kalan Mosque (1387) 8 673; 15 342
Kali Masjid see Kalan Mosque
Kali Mosque see Sanjar Mosque
Kalu Sarai Mosque 15 342
Khirki Mosque 15 341
madrasa of Firuz Shah 15 341, 342
mosque of Adham Khan 15 342
Moth ki Mosque 15 342
Muhammadiwali Mosque 15 342
Nili Mosque 15 342
Qil'a-i Kuhna Mosque 8 678–9, 679; 15 362
Qudsiya Bagh Mosque 15 367
Quwwat al-Islam Mosque complex 8 672, 677–8*; 15 207, 339, 339, 340; 16 168, 201; 20 226
'Ala'i Darvaza 8 672, 677–8; 15 340; 16 201
'Ala'i Minar 15 340
arcades 15 261, 263, 338, 481–2
arches 2 294; 23 368
inscriptions 8 671; 15 241, 680
Iron Pillar 8 677; 15 454, 706, 738
Qutb Minar 8 672, 672, 677, 678; 15 339–40, 339, 680; 16 166, 201; 21 627
tomb of 'Ala' al-Din 'Alam Shah 15 343
tomb of Sultan Iltutmish 8 677, 678; 15 340, 680, 680; 20 226
Sanjar Mosque 15 342
shrine of Nizam al-Din 'Auliya 8 672
Jahanpanah 8 673
palace of Muhammad ibn Tughluq see under palaces
Jantar Mantar 8 675
Kilokari 8 672; 12 73; 20 226
Lakshmi-Narayana Temple 15 405, 405
Lal Kot 8 671
see also Qil'a Rai Pithaura
Lal Qil'a 8 675, 676, 680*; 15 365, 366, 410, 717; 16 239
Divan-i 'Am 8 680
Divan-i-Khas 2 294
gardens 12 74
Imtiaz Mahal see RANG MAHAL
Delhi
Lal Qil'a—cont.
Lahore Gate 7 360
Mumtaz Mahal see museums → Archaeological Museum
Rang Mahal 8 680
throne 30 785
Lodi Gardens 8 673, 674
tomb of Muhammad Shah Sayyid see under TOMBS
Mehrauli 8 671, 672
Quwwat al-Islam Mosque complex see under Islamic religious buildings
sculpture 15 426
Sultan Ghari see under tombs
tomb of Sultan Balban see under tombs
Mubarakabad 8 673
museums 15 180
Archaeological Museum 8 680
Central Asian Antiquities Museum see National Museum
Crafts Museum 8 677; 15 173, 180
Indira Gandhi National Centre for the Arts 15 184
National Gallery of Modern Art 3 170; 8 677; 15 179, 180, 184
National Museum 22 795
collections 6 321; 7 54; 14 296; 15 180, 183, 681, 747
exhibitions 15 748
Library 15 184
Stein Collection 15 180
Treasuryvala Collection 15 742
Nehru Memorial Museum and Library 27 360
Rabindra Bhavan Art Gallery 15 180
Tibet House Museum 30 849, 850
National Institute of Immunology 15 169
New Delhi 5 173; 8 676, 677; 9 35; 15 404, 411, 542; 19 821–2, 822
New Delhi Civic Centre 15 169
observatory see Jantar Mantar
Old Fort see Purana Qil'a
palaces
Kushk-i Lal 8 672
palace of 'Ala-al-din Khalji 23 817
palace of Firuz Shah Tughluq 15 543; 23 817
palace of Muhammad ibn Tughluq 15 341; 23 817
Qasr-i Safid 8 672
patronage 15 208
Polytechnic Institute 3 170
President's House see RASHTRAPATI BHAVAN
Purana Qil'a 8 670–71, 678–9*; 15 362; 22 258
Qil'a-i Kuhna Mosque see under Islamic religious buildings
Sher Mandal 8 679; 15 362
Qil'a Rai Pithaura 8 671, 673
see also Lal Kot
Rashtrapati Bhavan 8 676; 10 240; 15 404, 694; 19 821–2; 23 814, 820; 29 527
Durbar Hall 14 77
gardens 12 75, 76
paintings 8 833
portico 25 268
thrones 30 784
Red Fort see Lal Qil'a
Sahitya Kala Parishad 8 677
Sanskriti Pratishthan 8 677
Sat Pal 15 341
Shahjahanabad 8 675, 676, 680; 15 196, 366, 410; 22 258
citadel see Lal Quil'a
maps 15 705

Delhi—cont.
shrine of Mahatma Gandhi **28** 635
shrine of Nizam al-Din 'Auliya *see under* Islamic religious buildings
Siri **8** 672, 673; **15** 340
stepwells
Rajun ki Ba'in **15** 343
Ugar Sans Ba'oli **15** 343
Supreme Court **15** 168
temples **15** 406
Tijara
architecture **15** 343
La'l Mosque **15** 343
tomb complex of Hasan Khan **15** 343
tombs **8** 673, 675; **15** 343; **31** 114, 115
Bagh-i 'Alam ka Gumbaz **8** *674*
Chote Khan ka Gumbaz **29** 825
Dadi ka Gumbaz **15** 343
Shish Gumbaz **15** 343
Sultan Ghari **8** 672; **15** 340
tomb complex of Hasan Khan *see under* TIJARA
tomb of Adham Khan **15** 362
tomb of Ataga Khan **15** 362
tomb of Bare Khan **15** 343
tomb of Bhure Khan **15** 343
tomb of Chhote Khan **15** 343
tomb of Emperor Humayun **8** 675, *679*, 679–80*; **15** 362, 750
Barber's Tomb **15** 750
gardens **12** 73
tomb of Firuz Shah **15** 342
tomb of Ghiyath al-Din Tughluq **8** 678*; **16** 201
tomb of Jahan Ara **31** 114
tomb of Khan-i Jahan Maqbul Tilangani **8** 673; **15** 342; **29** 825
tomb of Maulana Jamali **15** 686
tomb of Mubarak Shah Sayyid **8** 674; **15** 343
tomb of Muhammad Shah Sayyid **8** 674, *674*; **15** 343
tomb of Safdar Jang **8** 675; **15** 367, 376–8, 750
tomb of Shahab al-Din Taj Khan **15** 343
tomb of Shaykh Salah al-Din Darwish **15** 342
tomb of Sikandar Shah Lodi **8** 674; **15** 343
tomb of Sultan Balban **15** 340
tomb of Taj Khan *see* Bagh-i 'Alam ka Gumbaz
tomb of Yusuf Qattal **15** 343
tomb of Zafar Khan **8** 673
Tughluqabad **8** 672–3; **15** 340
Viceroy's residence *see* Rashtrapati Bhavan
YMCA staff quarters **15** 169
Delhi Silpi Chakra **8** 677
Delhomme, Léon **8** 789
Deli, Antal **30** 207
Delidoushka Church **5** 146
Déligand, Louis Auguste **8** 653
De Ligne, Jean **8** 681*; **30** 213
Delille, Jacques **12** 124
Delineavit et sculpsit **24** 450
Delisi, Benedetto **31** 307
Delisle, Guillaume **12** 814
Delisle, Léopold(-Victor) **8** 681*
Delitala, Mario **27** 836
Delitio, Andrea **8** 682*
Delitzsch, Friedrich **14** 487
Delius, Baurat **25** 409
Dell, Christian **12** 450
Dell, Edwin La *see* LA DELL, EDWIN
Dell, Peter (i) (*c*. 1490-1552) **8** 682*; **12** 402; **33** 113
Dell, Peter (ii) (*d* 1600) **8** 682
Della Corte, Luigi **1** 745
Della Costa, Margaret **31** 339
Dellala di Beinasco, Francesco Valeriano **18** 729
Della Paolera, Carlos Maria **8** 682*
Della Porta, Giacomo *see* GIACOMO DELLA PORTA
Della Ragione, Alberto **16** 775
Della Robbia pottery **26** 12
Della Scala *see* SCALA, DELLA
Dellaurana, Luciano *see* LAURANA, LUCIANO
Della Valle, Angel **2** 399; **8** 682–3*; **10** 744; **32** 415
Delleani, Lorenzo **8** 683*
Delli, Dello (di Niccolò) **8** 683*; **11** 482; **21** 10
Delli, Niccolò **1** 710; **8** 683; **27** 604; **29** 276
Dellit, (Cedric) Bruce **2** 741, 753; **8** 684*; **14** 625
Delmaet, Clémence **9** 422
Delmarcel, Guy **30** 332
Del Marle, Félix **33** 627
Delmas, Baron **8** 816
Delmé, Elizabeth **26** *274*
Delmenhorst, Anton II, Count of **22** 317
Delmet, Paul **29** 612
Del Monte, Guidobaldo *see* MONTE, GUIDOBALDO DEL
Del Moro, Luigi **8** 616, 617
Delobel, Simon **11** 648; **31** 683
Deloose **17** 666
Delord, Taxile **13** 306
Delorme **11** 662; **12** 177; **20** 455
Delorme, Adrien Faizelot **7** 658; **8** 684*; **11** 596
Delorme, Alexis Faizelot **8** 684
Delorme, François Faizelot **8** 684
Delorme, Jean-Louis Faizelot **8** 684
Delorme, Philibert *see* L'ORME, PHILIBERT DE
Delorme, Pierre **8** 684*; **11** 905; **12** 732
Delorme, Toussaint **8** 684
Delos **8** *304*, 684–91*; **13** *363*; **26** *908*
Archaeological Museum **13** 470
Archegeseion **14** 466
art forms and materials
architecture **8** 685–8*
capitals **13** 391
doors **9** 151
glass **13** 594
ivory-carvings **8** 350; **14** 354
jewellery **13** 599
marble **13** 434
mosaics **8** 691*, *691*; **13** 556, 557, 559, 560, 561, 567; **22** 160
mud-bricks **13** 389
sculpture **8** 688–91*, *688*; **13** 371, 373, 429, 430, 434, 439, 445, 465; **26** 292; **27** 20, 27
bronze **13** 441
colossal statue **18** 409
korai **13** 445; **18** *244*
kouroi **13** 445; **22** 700
marble **25** *179*
relief **8** *690*
statuettes **29** 567
wall paintings **13** 394, 547
well-heads **33** 56
bouleuterion **4** 530; **14** 73
carpenters **13** 394
cisterns **7** 354; **8** 687–8; **13** 407
exedra **10** 671
gardens **12** 68
Granite Building **13** 407
Granite Palaestra **10** 670; **23** 828
gymnasium **10** *670*; **13** 406, 886
hestiatoria **13** 417
House IIIN **8** *691*
House of Hermes **13** 407
House of the Comedians **13** 407
House of the Dolphins **2** 603
House of the Masks **13** 407, 559, 567
Delos—cont.
houses **8** *687*; **13** 382, *382*, 383, 389, 603; **24** 456
Hypostyle Hall **3** 327; **13** 407; **14** 73
Karystos Treasury **31** 294
measurements **13** 411
Mykonos Treasury **31** 294
Neorion **13** 390
Oikos of the Naxians **8** *685*; **24** 456
prytaneion **13** 411, 568; **25** 675
Pythion **30** 435
Sanctuary of Apollo **13** 416; **22** 699
Temple of Apollo **9** 151; **13** 394, 426; **30** 435
Sanctuary of Artemis **8** 310, 323; **13** 416; **29** 396
Sanctuary of the Syrian gods **13** 558; **27** *712*, 713
Stoa of Philip V **8** *686*; **13** 388
stoas **29** 681
synagogue **17** 540, 543
temples **13** 390
Temple of Apollo *see under* Sanctuary of Apollo
Temple of the Athenians **1** 128; **13** 391
sculpture **8** *689*
Temple of Dionysos **10** 474
Temple of Leto **22** 700
Tholos of Hermes and Maia **30** 737
treasuries **31** 294
Delougaz, Pinhas P. **7** 186; **9** 45; **31** 509
Delouvrier, Paul **24** 130
Deloye, Gustave **20** 925
Delpech, François-Séraphin **20** 602
works **19** *486*
Delphi **8** 691–7*; **9** *511*; **13** *362*, *363*; **25** *471*; **26** *908*
Aemilius Paulus monument **13** 432
Altar of the Chians **13** 393
Apollo tripod **10** 585
Archaeological Museum **13** 470, 606
architects **13** 394
art forms and materials
architecture **8** 692–4*; **13** 374
bronzes **13** 571, 572, 573
cauldrons **13** 576
inscriptions **19** 841
ivory-carvings **13** 595
jewellery **13** 600
limestone **13** 387
metalwork **10** 591
pins **13** 600
sculpture **8** 695–7*, *695*, *696*, *697*; **13** 430, 445, 447, 448, 459; **26** 292; **28** 654; **29** 396
bronze **13** 441, 444, 445
chryselephantine statues **13** 435, 596
silver **13** 445
stone **13** 387
Basilica **9** 566
baths **13** 386
bouleuterion **4** 530
excavations **13** 606
exedra **10** 671
gymnasium **10** 670; **13** 406, 886, *887*; **23** 828
heroön of Neoptolemos **14** 466
Kastalian Spring **11** 339
Knidian Treasury **5** 904
Lesche of the Knidians **13** 394, 553; **25** 176–7
masons **13** 389
Monument of Daochos II **13** *459*
Naxian column **11** 231; **13** 398, 429
Sanctuary of Artemis **13** 416
Sanctuary of Athena Pronaia *see* Tholos of Athena Pronaia
Delphi—cont.
Sanctuary of Apollo **8** *692*, *693*; **13** 416, 419; **27** 1, 713
Temple of Apollo **8** 692; **13** 373, 374, 387, 388, 389, 391, 395, *395*, 417, 418, 449; **21** 46; **30** 434, 435
acroteria **1** 128
hypogea **15** 52
korai **18** 245
pediments **13** 425; **24** 318, 319
sculpture **8** 697; **18** 409
tholos **30** 435, 736
Treasury **6** 353
workshop **13** 371
sphinx **22** 700
stadium **13** 418; **29** 488
stoa **13** 402
Stoa of Attalos **10** 670; **31** 294
Temple of Athena Pronaia **13** 377, 390
tholoi **30** 736
Tholos of Athena Pronaia **8** 694, *694*, 696; **13** 387, 388, 390, 460; **27** 235; **30** 737
treasuries **27** 712; **31** 294
Athenian Treasury **13** 387, 414, 415, 418, 425, 448, 470; **31** 294, *294*
Corinthian Treasury **31** 294
Cyrene Treasury **31** 294
Sikyonian Treasury **13** 398, 415, 425, 432, 446; **21** 892; **31** 294
Siphnian Treasury **13** 373, 380, 398, 399, *399*, 400, 415, 427, 432, 448, 470; **31** 294
acroteria **1** 128
caryatids **5** 904
frieze **8** 695–6; **11** 791; **22** 513; **26** 134; **30** 775
reliefs **13** *447*
sculpture **13** 592
Theban Treasury **31** 294
Delpier, François **3** 773
Delpire, Robert **11** 728
Del Prete, Juan **2** 400; **8** 697–8*
Delpy, Adrien **25** 190
Delsaux, J. C. **3** 578
Delsenbach, Johann Adam **23** 308; **32** 606
Delteil, Loys-Henri **8** 698*; **10** 210; **19** 490
Deltombes, P. **11** 602
Delton, Louis-Jean **8** 698*
De Luca, Giulio **22** 474
Deluse, Jacques **2** 46
de luxe books *see under* BOOKS → forms
Delvada **15** 564
Delvaux, E. **2** 511
Delvaux, Laurent **3** 571, 613; **8** 698–9*
assistants **29** 540
collaboration **10** 264; **19** 606; **25** 53; **28** 63
pupils **2** 125; **12** 835; **19** 233; **30** 283; **33** 226
teachers **14** 326; **25** 53
works **5** 43; **28** *64*
Delvaux, Paul **3** 565; **8** 699–700*
groups and movements **25** 6; **30** 21
patrons and collectors **16** 892
works **5** 44, *45*; **8** *700*; **10** 482
Del Vecchio, James **16** 27
Delvenne, René **3** 595
Delvieux, Mlle *see* BÉLANGER, MME
Delvigne, Jean-Josèphe **13** 676
Delville, *ferme ornée* **12** 129
Delville, Jean **8** 700–701*
groups and movements **10** 735; **22** 1; **27** 639; **30** 169
pupils **3** 399; **5** 37
works **3** 564
Delvin, Jean **3** 43; **5** 651; **24** 458; **32** 591
Delvoye, C. **3** 620
Delyen, Jacques-François **18** 790
Dema **13** 536
Demachy, Pierre-Antoine **4** 59; **30** 672
Demachy, Robert **8** 701*; **24** 651, 674
groups and movements **24** 688, 738
Demak Mosque **15** 768
Deman, Edmond **29** 401
Demange, Jean-Baptiste Bréquin de *see* BRÉQUIN DE DEMANGE, JEAN-BAPTISTE
Demarco, Hugo Rodolfo **18** 63; **19** 209
De Maria, Mario **8** 509, 701–2*
De Maria, Nicola **8** 702*; **16** 682
De Maria, Walter **8** 702*
collaboration **22** 140
groups and movements **10** 416
works **15** 869; **18** 694
Demarne, Jean-Louis **8** 702–4*
collaboration **4** 888; **21** 429
groups and movements **31** 373
patrons and collectors **8** 704, 868; **14** 396
pupils **9** 406; **11** 301
works **24** 148
Demarteau, Gilles **8** 703*; **10** 391; **11** 368
collaboration **11** 723
house **14** 791
interior decoration **14** 846
reproductive prints by others **4** 330
works **4** 517, 518; **8** 130–31, *130*; **14** 846; **29** 675
Demarteau, Gilles-Antoine **8** 703
Demartini, Hugo **8** 388
De Matteis factory **11** 190
Demayanns, John *see* MAIANO, GIOVANNI DA, II
Demchinskaya, I. **30** 352
Deme (family) **17** 400
Demée, Luís **19** 866
Deme Jōman **17** 400, 401
Demel', Jan **3** 528
De Menil *see* MENIL, DE
Demereto, Lorenzo *see* SENES, LORENZO
De Merode, Saverio **26** 761
Demers, Jérôme **3** 72
Demertsov, Fedor I. **29** 554
Deme Saman **17** 400, 401
Demestri, Pedro Florentín *see* FLORENTÍN DEMESTRI, PEDRO
Dēmētriadēs, Kostas **2** 218; **8** 703*; **13** 354
Demetrias (Greece) *see* SIKYON
Demetrias (Syria) *see* DAMASCUS
Demetrios (*fl c*. 350-300 BC) **10** 431
Demetrios (*fl* mid 2nd cent. BC) **1** 618; **2** 682; **8** 704*; **13** 547, 549
Demetrios (*fl* 13th cent.) **18** 571
Demetrios I Poliorketes, King of Macedon (*reg* 306-285 BC) **13** 551, 588; **21** 557; **23** 141; **24** 374; **28** 712
Demetrios of Alopeke **8** 704*
Demetrios of Phaleron **13** 561
Demetrios Palaiologos, Despot of Thessaloniki **9** 616
Demeuldre-Coché (family) **3** 591; **5** 51
Deme Uman **17** 400, 401
De Meyer, C. **3** 587
Deme Yūkan Mitsuyasu **17** 393
Deme Zekan Yoshimitsu **17** 393
Demi, Emilio **16** 706
Demian, Anastase **26** 716
Demidoff, Nicolas **8** 704–5
Demidoff Altarpiece **8** 172
Demidov (family) **9** 78; **11** 189; **17** 870; **20** 809; **23** 355; **24** 396
Demidov, Anatoly, Prince **4** 307; **8** 705*
architecture **20** 809
collections **8** 704, 705

Demidov, Anatoly, Prince—cont.
gems **22** 103
paintings **5** 69; **7** 879; **8** 172; **23** 522; **27** 463; **28** 705
sculpture **3** 296
Demidov, I. I. **17** 870
Demidov, Nikita (Akinfiyevich) **8** 704
Demidov, Nikolay (Nikitich), Count *see* DEMIDOFF, NICOLAS
Demidov, Paul (Nikolayevich), Prince **8** 705
Demidov, Pavel (Pavlovich), Prince **8** 705; **11** 800; **26** 315
Demignot, Antonio **31** 446
Demignot, Francesco **3** 454; **31** 446, 447
Demignot, Giuseppe **31** 446
Demignot, Michele Antonio **31** 446
Demignot, Vittorio **11** 194; **16** 758; **30** 324; **31** 446
Demikovsky, Jules *see* OLITSKI JULES
De Mille, Cecil B. **8** 568
demi-lunes *see* RAVELINS
Demin, Giovanni **17** 443; **28** 391
Demio, Giovanni **8** 705–6*
Démir, Nihat **3** 596
Demircihöyük **1** 832
Demirci Hüyük **1** 824
Demmler, Georg Adolph **6** 62; **8** 706*; **23** 813; **26** 190
Demnig, Günter **29** 98
Democratic Art Society *see* DEMOKURĀTO BIJUTSUKA KYŌKAI
Demokritos **13** 553
Demokurāto Bijutsuka Kyōkai (Democratic Art Society) **10** 102; **15** 128
Demonstrationen **24** 403
De Mont, Pol **2** 516; **9** 196
De Monte Triptych **20** 718
Demophilos of Himera **33** 639
De Morgan, Evelyn **8** 707*
groups and movements **25** 555
works **11** 397, 436; **25** 688
De Morgan, William (Frend) **8** 706–7*; **9** 767; **25** 398; **26** 316
collaboration **8** 707
groups and movements **1** 171; **2** 570
patrons and collectors **12** 838; **14** 132
works **10** 312; **22** 59; **23** 547; **30** 507
Demosthenes **13** 548
demotic scripts *see under* SCRIPTS → types
Demotte, Georges (J.) **8** 707*; **15** 742
Demotte, Lucien **8** 707
Demotte *Shāhnāma* *see* GREAT MONGOL SHĀHNĀMA
Demoulin, Bertrand **8** 891
Demoulin, Jean **8** 891
Demoulin, Jean-Baptiste **8** 891
Demoulins, Francis *see* DU MOULIN, FRANCIS
Dempster, Thomas **2** 163; **8** 707–8*; **10** 636, 642; **13** 541
Demre *see* MYRA
Demuel, Mignolin **13** 851
Demus, Otto **2** 833, 834; **8** 708*; **29** 795
Demuth, Charles (Henry Buckius) **8** 708–9*; **12** 216; **23** 48; **24** 600; **31** 605, 606
groups and movements **23** 48; **25** 461
patrons and collectors **2** 384; **3** 251; **26** 488
teachers **6** 500
works **8** *709*; **15** 828
Demut-Malinovsky, Vasily (Ivanovich) **8** 709–10*; **18** 138; **27** 390; **30** 349; **33** 600
collaboration **18** 38; **24** 817, 818
Demut-Malinovsky, Vasily (Ivanovich)—cont.
pupils **3** 530; **30** 486
works **10** 539; **27** 579; **31** 561
Demyans, John *see* MAIANO, GIOVANNI DA, II
Den (*reg c.* 2850 BC) **9** *776*
De Napoli, Michele **22** 916
Denbies (Surrey) **27** 242
Denbigh **32** *780*
Denbigh, Countess of **33** 387
Denbigh, William Feilding, 1st Earl of *see* FEILDING, WILLIAM, 1st Earl of Denbigh
Den Bosch *see* 'S HERTOGENBOSCH
Denby, Elizabeth **11** 808
Denby, Jillian **10** 484
Denby Pottery **10** 313, 314
Denchū Hiragushi *see* HIRAGUSHI, DENCHŪ
Dendara **8** 710–12*; **9** *774*, 892, 896; **26** *921*
arches **2** 296
Circular Zodiac **10** 90
hypostyle hall **9** 896
inscriptions **10** 82
mammisi **9** 897; **20** 231, 232
necropoleis **9** 843
reliefs **9** 876, *896*
sacred lake **27** 496, 497
sculpture **9** 802, 873
Temple of Hathor **7** 820; **8** *710*, 711*, *711*; **9** 825, 832, 834, 835; **10** 64, 68; **18** 70; **33** 245
tomb of Meriri **9** 874
wall paintings **9** 805
Dendermonde **3** *539*, 617; **26** 630
Onze Lieve Vrouwekerk **3** 567
Dendra **8** 712*; **13** *363*; **14** *332*
armour **4** *851*; **14** 356
bronzes **14** 356
Chamber Tomb 2 **6** 170
Chamber Tomb 9 **14** 359
faience (i) (glass) **14** 358, 359
gold **14** 355
metalwork **14** 355
sculpture **4** 851
Tomb 8 **14** 356; **31** 108
tombs **30** 738
dendrochronology *see under* DATING METHODS → types
dendroglyphs *see* TREE-CARVINGS
Dendur, Temple of Peteese and Pihor **10** 94
Den Duyts, Gustave **3** 43
Dene, Edewaerd de **12** 514
Denecker, Jost de *see* NEGKER, JOST DE
Deneken, Friedrich **9** 703
Denes, Agnes **8** 712*
Dénes, Valéria *see* GALIMBERTI, VALÉRIA
Denes group **13** 263
Denev, Boris **5** 155
Deng Chun **6** 784, 817, 822; **33** 501
Dengfeng **6** *615*; **8** 712–13*
Cejing tai **6** 658; **23** 339
observatory *see* Cejing tai
que **25** 800
see also MT SONG
Deng Shi **14** 820
Deng Shiru **8** 713–14*
patrons and collectors **6** 767
Stele studies school **6** 765
works **6** *765*; **7** 131
writings **6** 867
Deng Wenyuan **6** 754
Deng xian **6** 788, 808, 887
Dengyō Daishi *see* SAICHŌ
Denham, John **23** 362
Denham, John Charles **25** 264
Den Helder, Minder Marinepersoneel building **10** 698
Denhoff, Maria Zofia **8** 843
Deni, Viktor **27** 394
Denia **8** *325*, 344
Tomb 1
figurines **8** *339*
Denia, Marqués de *see* LERMA, FRANCISCO GÓMEZ DE SANDOVAL Y ROJAS, Duque de
Denifle, Johann Peter **15** 865
De Nigris, Giuseppe **22** 480
Denike, B. P. **30** 261, 489
Deniliquin law courts **18** 888
denim **9** 491
Denis, Manuel **14** 660
Denis, Maurice **8** 714–15*; **11** 190, 667; **22** 379; **25** 893
collaboration **14** 486; **18** 867; **20** 603; **23** 192
dealers **19** 10; **32** 686
groups and movements **8** 818; **10** 821; **12** 870; **22** 421, 422; **25** 356, 358; **30** 169
patrons and collectors **7** 496; **8** 715; **12** 600; **22** 135, 136
productions **30** 685; **32** 258
pupils **2** 122; **3** 88, 753, 809; **6** 84; **8** 662; **17** 206; **18** 636
works **4** 364; **8** *714*; **11** 419; **12** 601; **19** 489, 490; **25** 626; **29** 508; **30** 869
writings **1** 73; **7** 630; **30** 170, 174, 231
Denis, Mme **14** 798; **32** 767
Denis, Pierre **6** 151
Denis, Simon **14** 486
Denis du Moulin **20** 626
Denison, Arthur R. **29** 435
Denisov-Ural'sky, Alexei (Kuzmich) **27** 428
De Nittis, Giuseppe **8** 715–19*; **16** 678; **20** 60; **22** 480; **24** 708
groups and movements **6** 129; **16** 678; **28** 317, 318
works **8** *716*, *718*; **28** 318
Denjirō Kiyokawa *see* KATSUKAWA SHUNKŌ
Denkendorf Church **9** 680; **17** 502
crosses **17** *502*
Denkmalpflege, Die **24** 444
Denman, Thomas **21** 7
Denmark **8** 719–62*, *720*; **32** 512, 517
alabaster (gypsum) **11** *219*
altarpieces **8** 730–31, 732, 735, 738; **11** *467*
amber **8** 752, *753*; **31** *481*
apartments **8** *728*
architectural history **8** 820
architecture **8** 721–9*
brick **8** 721
Gothic **13** 50, 56; **26** 304
military **21** 570
prefabrication **31** 776
Romanesque **26** 304, 592–3*
stone **8** 721
vernacular **32** 285–6*
Viking **32** *533*
archives **2** 369, 370*; **8** 724, 725
art history **8** 761–2*
auction houses **8** 759
auctions **8** 758
banners **14** 408
book illustrations **8** 731
boxes **7** *807*; **8** 752
brass **8** 751–2, *752*
brick **4** *789*; **8** 721
bronze **25** 526, *527*
cabinets (ii) (furniture) **5** 192; **8** 739
camps (military) **8** 721
canopies (ii) (textile coverings) **8** *754*
castles **8** 723–4, *724*; **14** *370*
catalogues **8** 761
cathedrals **27** *167*
cauldrons **6** 159; **13** *849*
ceramics **8** 747–9*
chairs **8** 745–6, *746*, *747*
chandeliers **31** *481*
cherry-wood **8** *747*
choir-stalls **8** 738
Denmark—cont.
churches **8** 719, 721–3, *726*; **27** 167
basilicas **8** 723
brick **4** *789*
centrally planned **7** 257
decoration **8** 729–30
hall **8** 723; **13** 50
Neo-classicism **14** *153*
Rococo **10** *111*
Romanesque **8** *722*; **26** *593*
coins **7** 537; **14** 408
collections **8** 757–60*, 761*
copper **8** 751–2
crucifixes **13** *171*
cups **32** *516*
daggers **25** *516*
damask **8** 757
dealing **8** 758–9*
drawings **8** *724*
earthenwares **8** 747
education (art) **8** 760–61*
embroidery **8** 753, 755–6*
enamel **8** 752; **26** 694*
engravings **19** *662*
erotic art **10** 482
etchings **8** 731
exhibitions **2** 370; **8** 729, 760
factories **16** *828*
faience (ii) (ceramics) **8** *747*, 747–8; **30** 883
figureheads **28** 612
flint **25** 515, *516*
fortifications **8** 721, 724; **21** 570
frames **11** *469*, 472, *472*, 473, *475*, *476*, *478*
furniture **8** 745–7*
gables **11** 876
gardens **12** 135; **16** 863
gasometers **23** 325
gilding **8** *746*
glass **4** 743; **8** 749–50*, *750*
gold **8** 750–51*, 752; **32** *516*
government buildings **14** *152*
gravestones **8** 738
heraldry **14** 408
historiography **8** 761–2*
horns **22** 372; **25** 526, *526*
hôtels particuliers **10** 110
houses **8** 725, 727; **10** 110; **32** 285, *285*, 286
iconography **8** 757*
interior decoration **8** 742–5*, *743*, *744*, 757*, 759
iron **8** 752
ivory-carvings **8** 752, 753; **13** *171*
jewellery **8** 753
knitting **8** 753
lace **8** 756*
lanterns (lights) **8** *752*
leather **19** 5*
libraries **8** 761*
linocuts **8** 736
lithography **8** 736
marble **11** *219*
marks **8** 750, 751
memorial stones **17** *474*; **32** 517, *517*
metalwork **8** 750–52*; **13** 167; **32** 515
monasteries **8** 721
monuments **10** *110*; **18** 682
museums **4** *68*; **8** 746, 759–60*, 761; **22** *366*
narwhal tusks **8** 752
necklaces **8** *753*
new towns **8** 729
niello **32** *516*
nude figures **1** *32*; **29** *541*
20th cent. **8** *736*
oak **11** *467*
objects of vertu **8** 752–3*
orders (chivalry) **7** *178*
paddles **31** 491
painting **8** 729–31*, 732–7*
architectural **27** *144*
fresco **8** 730, 732
genre
Baroque **17** *880*
Denmark
painting
genre—cont.
Biedermeier **18** *178*
Romanticism **3** *705*
19th cent. **8** *734*; **17** *606*; **18** *471*, *472*; **26** *407*
history **8** 734
landscape **18** *179*, 715; **26** 742; **28** *824*
literary themes **1** *33*
marine **9** *701*
mythological **1** *32*
panel **8** 730
secco **8** 730
sporting scenes **12** *602*
Symbolism (movement) **33** *214*
wall **8** 729–30, *730*, *731*; **26** 648
19th cent. **26** *525*
20th cent. **8** *736*; **17** *659*; **22** *151*; **24** *316*
palaces **10** *110*
paper **24** 48
patronage **8** 757–8*
periodicals **24** 451*
pewter **8** 751, 752
photoarchives **8** 761*
plaster **29** *541*, 840–41*
porcelain **7** *807*; **8** 748
portals **8** *737*
portraits
engravings **4** *67*; **8** *732*
group **14** *119*
painting **1** *846*; **8** 731, 732, 733; **17** *678*; **30** *41*
17th cent. **33** *421*
19th cent. **17** *478*
20th cent. **14** *119*
self-portraits **17** *678*
pottery **8** 747
prints **8** 731, 733, 735, 736
pulpits **8** *740*
repoussé **13** *849*
roods **8** 738
runes **32** 517
sandstone **8** *741*
screenprints **8** 736
sculpture **8** 737–8*, 739–40*, 741–2*
allegorical **29** *541*
Gothic **13** 118; **26** 304
marble **11** *219*; **30** *764*, *765*
Neo-classicism **30** *764*, *765*
relief **26** *305*
Renaissance **11** *219*
Romanesque **8** 737–8; **26** 304, 640*
stone **8** 737; **26** 640*
wood **8** 738
20th cent. **8** *741*
settlements **25** 504
ship-decoration **28** 612
silk **8** *754*, 755*
silver **8** 750–51*, *751*, 752, *753*; **13** *849*; **32** *516*
Celtic **22** *371*
sprang **8** 753
stained glass **13** 190
stainless steel **8** 752
stone **8** 721, 737; **26** 640*; **27** 167
stone-carvings **17** *474*; **32** *517*
stonewares **8** 748
stucco **29** *840*, 840–41*
synagogues **17** 547
tablets **8** 732
tapestries **8** *754*, 754–5*; **30** 320
textiles **8** 753–6*
thrones **8** 745; **30** *782*
tiles **8** 747; **30** 883–4*
timber structures **32** 285
tombs **11** *219*
tools **25** 515
towers **8** 723
town halls **7** *804*
trade **6** 332, 624
tympana **26** *305*
urban planning **8** 725, 727; **31** 738
vases **8** *750*

Denmark—cont.
vernacular art 8 756–7*
villas 8 727
walls 8 729
women artists 8 760
wood 8 738; 31 491
wood-carvings 25 495, *496*
woodcuts 8 731
wool 8 *754*
see also SCANDINAVIA; VIKING
Denn, Adolph 1 772
Denner, Balthasar 8 762*; 12 391; 22 127
Dennet and Ingle 31 240
Denniée 16 65
Denning, Stephen Poyntz 11 362
Dennis, George 8 762*; 10 637; 13 542
Dennis, John 29 889
Dennis glassworks 33 13
Dennison, Aaron L. 15 822
Dennistoun, James 8 762–3*
Denny, Anthony 14 671
Denny, Robin 19 591; 28 804
Denokrates 1 614
Denon, (Dominique-) Vivant 4 300; 8 763–4*, *764*; 9 18, 303; 10 93; 11 663, 666; 28 521, 523
collaboration 12 17; 22 47
dealing 27 439
engravings 2 *422*; 14 *461*; 26 129
etchings 33 345
furniture 10 97
groups and movements 7 773; 26 500
lithographs 19 483
medals 12 177; 20 924
paintings 12 731; 14 390
patrons and collectors 4 300, 303; 14 395
personal collection 2 25; 25 383
portraits 2 25
writings 8 867; 10 79, 97; 22 741; 23 545; 25 766; 27 571
De Noter, Jean-Baptiste 8 764
De Noter, Pierre François, the elder (1747-1830) 8 764–5*; 14 479
De Noter, Pierre François, the younger (1786-1855) 8 764
De Noyette, Ferdinand 8 765
De Noyette, Modeste 8 765*
Denpasar 15 *754*
Academy of Fine Arts 15 819
Bali Museum 15 809; 29 238, 239
Denqez 10 566
Dens, P. 3 763
Den Salm *see* SALM, DEN
Densus church 26 706
Dent, Frodsham & McCabe 7 448
Dent, J. M. 3 445
Dent, William 5 756
Dentalium shells *see under* SHELLS → types
Dente, Marco 3 157; 8 765*; 10 385; 25 860
Dent Hardware Co. 31 257
Denti, Girolamo 8 765–6*; 32 107, 229
dentils 8 766*; 11 791; 13 377; 23 478, 481
dentine 16 796
Denton Corker Marshall 2 743; 21 76
Dentone *see* CURTI, GIROLAMO
Dentone, Il *see* RUBINO, GIOVANNI
D'Entrecasteaux Islands 23 726; 24 64, *64*, 81
Dentz van Schaick, G. T. 23 125
Denucé, Jan (Baptist Ferdinand) 8 766*
Denuelle 25 796
Denuelle, Alexandre-Dominique 9 312
Denune, William 7 418
Denver (CO)
Art Museum 7 156; 22 677, 679, 795; 25 218
Jan and Frederick R. Mayer Collection 29 222
Broadway Theatre 15 408
Brown Palace Hotel 14 787
Den'yer, Andrey (Genrikh Ivanovich) 8 766*
Denys Godefroy 11 352
Denzaburō Fujita *see* FUJITA, DENZABURŌ
Denzler, Juraj 8 177, 766–7*
Deo, Domenico di *see* Domenico di Deo
Deo Barnarak 15 321
Surya Temple 15 321
deodar 15 310, 720
Deodato (di) Orlandi 8 767*
works 7 319; 8 212, *767*; 24 854, 860
Deogarh 8 767–8*; 15 *261*, *285*, 290
Dashavatara Temple 15 215, *255*, 256; 29 526
sculpture 8 767–8, *768*; 15 471–2, *472*
manuscript illumination 15 *227*
Nagarghati 15 494
painting 7 VI2; 15 600
pillar 15 495
reliefs 15 227, 690
sculpture 15 494, 495
temples 15 195, 323
Varaha Temple 15 494, 750
sculpture 15 *495*
Vishnu Temple *see* Dashavatara Temple
Deogracias Magdalena workshop 29 321
Deoguna 15 323
Déols
Abbey 26 599
St Etienne crypt 8 222
Deo Markandeya 15 322
Déon, Simon Horsin 28 340
Deopatan 22 771, 796
Deoria 15 424, 427
Deori Kalan 8 768–9*; 15 *285*, 473
Vamana Temple 15 255, 473
Deotalao 15 322, 323
Bhairava Temple 15 323
Somanatha Temple 15 323
Deotisalvi 24 857
Dep 10 802
Depaka 25 887
department stores 8 769–70*
Austria 19 *652*
England 19 *576*
France 4 239; 8 *769*
Germany 12 *377*; 21 *120*
Netherlands, the 18 *437*
Sri Lanka 29 *454*
United States of America 17 891; 26 *343*; 28 900; 29 *915*
see also SHOPPING CENTRES; SHOPS
Depaulis, Alexis-Joseph 8 770*
De Pauw, R. 3 885
Depay, Hans 24 295
Depay, Johann *see* PAY, JOHANN DE
depe 1 851
Depeaux, Félix François 24 883; 28 795
Depero, Fortunato 8 770–71*; 24 448; 26 776
collaboration 20 905
groups and movements 1 166; 11 866, 867, 869; 16 648, 680
works 16 707, 731; 29 97
writings 16 707
Depero, Rosetta 8 771
Deperthes, Jean-Baptiste 8 771*; 31 300, 817
Deperthes, Pierre-Joseph-Edouard 3 123
Depestre, Julien G. 8 840
Depey, Johann *see* PAY, JOHANN DE
De Peyster Limner 20 679
Dephot 5 659; 10 863
DePienne, Antonio 24 836, 837
DePillars, Murry 1 445
De Pisis, Bona 8 772
De Pisis, (Luigi) Filippo (Tibertelli) 8 772*; 16 680; 25 6, 447
De Ploeg 22 906
Depondt, Paul 19 535
Deppe, Gustav 12 397
depressed arches *see* ARCHES → types → basket
De Prey, Juan 18 832
Deptford culture 22 570
De Putti, Angelo 20 422
Deqing 6 885
De Quesnoy *see* DU QUESNOY
Dequevauviller, (Nicolas-Barthélemy-) François 8 772–3*; 11 579
works 14 *791*
Dequevauviller, François Jacques 8 773
Der, Tell ed- 21 552
Dera'a Great Mosque 2 295
Derain, André 7 385; 8 773–5*; 11 548, 568; 23 *379*; 27 240; 29 878
books 28 820
collaboration 19 808; 20 603, 822
dealers 11 165; 13 826; 17 725; 32 686
exhibitions 13 711; 28 808
groups and movements 9 705; 10 839, 840–41, 842; 16 817; 22 747; 25 356; 32 668
methods 7 630
paintings 8 596, *774*; 18 717
patrons and collectors
Fénéon, Félix 10 885
Kramář, Vincenc 18 435
Lévy, Pierre and Denise 19 282
Quinn, John 25 823
Rump, Johannes 27 333
Rupf, Hermann and Margrit 27 343
Russev, Svetlin 5 163
Shchukin, Sergey (Ivanovich) 28 569
Soby, James Thrall 28 914
Tetzen-Lund, Christian 30 532
Walter-Guillaume Collection 13 826
Zambaccian, K. H. 26 723
personal collection 30 420
pottery 11 606
productions 3 120
reproductive prints by others 32 577
sculpture 8 *773*
studio 29 858
textiles 9 293
woodcuts 2 225; 17 725; 33 362
Derand, François 8 775*
assistants 31 462
patrons and collectors 17 511
pupils 31 462
works 20 482; 26 348
writings 29 637
Deraniyagala, Justin Pieris 33 74
Deraniyagala, Ranil 29 468
Deranton, Jacques 21 643
Derbais, François 4 513, 514
Derbais, Jérôme 4 513; 8 776*
Derbecq, Germaine 2 525
Derbent 27 432
Derbet 21 878
Derby 10 *225*
Arboretum 12 137; 19 720; 24 179
Cathedral of All Saints 28 295
clocks 7 448
Derbyshire General Infirmary 28 831
mills (industrial) 21 600
railway station 25 855
Derby—cont.
silk mill 10 748
textiles 21 600
Derby, Anstiss 3 38
Derby, Edward Geoffrey Stanley, 14th Earl of *see* STANLEY, EDWARD GEOFFREY, 14th Earl of Derby
Derby, Edward Stanley, 11th Earl of *see* STANLEY, EDWARD, 11th Earl of Derby
Derby, Elias Hasket 3 38; 10 852; 20 7; 28 818
Derby, Elizabeth 28 525
Derby, Elizabeth Stanley, Countess of Derby *see* STANLEY, ELIZABETH, Countess of Derby
Derby, Henry Plantagenet, Earl of *see* HENRY IV, King of England
Derby, Mary de Bohun, Countess of *see* MARY DE BOHUN, Queen of England
Derby Crown Porcelain Co. *see* ROYAL CROWN DERBY PORCELAIN CO.
Derby House *see under* LONDON → houses
Derby porcelain factory 4 601; 6 533; 8 776*; 10 310; 14 857
painters 4 65
porcelain 10 308, 309
staff 21 697
Derbyshire, Andrew 26 461
Dereağzı 8 776–7*; 9 *512*
Abbey Church 7 252; 8 776–7, *777*; 9 525, 542
brick 4 773
fortifications 9 555
De Regis, Francesco 21 532
Dereham, Elias of *see* ELIAS OF DEREHAM
Deren, Maya 10 688
Derennes, Michel 26 206
De Renzi, Mario 19 304; 27 686
Derge 30 808, 841, 845
Derham, Frances 2 772
Der Husterknupp *see* HUSTERKNUPP, DER
De Ridder, André 3 564
Dering, Edward 9 374
Deriset, Antoine 25 790
De Rivera, José 8 777–8*
Derizet, Antoine 8 778*
Derkinderen, Antoon (Johannes) 8 778–9*; 14 691; 19 654; 22 851, 908; 28 595
collaboration 21 122
groups and movements 33 266
pupils 23 140
works 32 393
Derkovits, Gyula 8 779–80*; 14 901
patrons and collectors 30 212
works 8 *780*
Derkzen van Angeren, Antoon 6 378; 8 781*; 22 854
Derman' Monastery 31 550
Dermée, Paul 8 438; 11 525; 19 40; 30 18
Dermée, Pierre 13 671; 25 740
Dermer, John 2 762
Dermyans, John *see* MAIANO, GIOVANNI DA, II
Derneburg 20 869
Déroche, François 16 549
Deroche, Jean 2 699; 6 534; 23 119
Deroche, Jean and Maria (practice) 2 700
Deroche, Maria 2 699
Deroko, A. 9 528
Derome 4 354
Derosiers, Madeleine 19 136
De Rossi, Alessandro 2 880
De Rossi, Baldo 2 880
De Rossi, Giovanni Battista 8 781*; 26 799; 32 385
Derozhinskaya, Aleksandra 28 580
Derpt *see* TARTU
Der Querschnitt 11 165
el-Derr 9 833; 23 280; 25 874; 29 386
Derré Dawa 1 *379*; 10 568
Derrick, Ken 2 152
derricks 7 764, 765, *765*, 766; 13 387
Derrida, Jacques 8 781–2*; 26 62
collaboration 10 121
groups and movements 29 891
works 1 182; 8 609–10; 25 361
Derrière le Miroir 20 75
Derrière l'Etoile 19 492
Derrydale Press 11 804
Derrykeighan 6 161
Derrynaflan Chalice 8 *782*, 782–3; 15 873
Derrynaflan Paten 15 872
Derrynaflan Treasure 8 782–3*
Derschau, von, Col. 3 791
De Rudder, Hélène 3 610
De Rudder, Isidore 3 591, 601, 610, 611; 28 756
Déruet, Charles 8 783; 25 461
Déruet, Claude 8 783–5*; 19 696; 22 455; 26 772
assistants 7 389
collaboration 3 48; 5 438
patrons and collectors 11 534
pupils 3 635; 29 399
teachers 3 634
works 8 *784*
Deruta 16 *620*
maiolica 8 785*; 14 425; 16 734, *734*; 30 886
S Francesco 11 711
Derval, Tanneguy du Chastel, Baron de *see* TANNEGUY DU CHASTEL, 1st Vicomte De La Bellière and Baron de Derval
Derveni 13 *363*
Derveni Krater 13 476, 576–7, *577*
Derventum baths 3 375
Dervieux(, Mlle) 11 579
Derwent Wood, Francis *see* WOOD, FRANCIS DERWENT
Derzhavin, Gavrila (Romanovich) 19 837
Desa, Župan of Serbia 28 447, 455
De Saedeleer, K. 3 579
De Saedeleer, Valerius 3 564; 8 785–6*; 18 626; 21 648
Desai, Madhuri 4 291; 15 742
Desaint & Saillant 10 725
Desale, Jean Baptiste 33 638
Desalji, Rao of Kachchh (*reg* 1718–41) (Rajput) 15 617
Desana 4 706; 7 602; 29 210
De Sanctis, Francesco *see* SANCTIS, FRANCESCO DE
De Sanctis, Guglielmo 8 786*
Desanges, Louis William 8 786*
Desangles, Jesús 9 118
Desargues, Gérard 8 786–7*; 28 202
competitions 7 665
pupils 11 771
works 29 523
writings 24 490; 29 637
Desavary, Charles 7 434
Desbarats, Guy 23 632
Desboeufs, Antoine 28 746
Desbois, Jules 8 787*; 11 567, 629
Desbois, Martial 11 10
Desbordes, Constant-Joseph 8 653
Desbordes-Valmore, Marceline 3 785
Desborough 6 161
Desboutin, Marcellin (-Gilbert) 8 787*; 9 309; 19 870; 24 552
Descalzi (family) 16 730
Descalzi, Gaetano 19 656
Descalzi, Ricardo 9 714
Descalzo, Martín 6 67
Descamps, Alexandre-Gabriel 8 705; 22 93

Descamps, Guillaume 19 254
Descamps, Jean-Baptiste 8 787–8*; 27 248
patrons and collectors 8 705
pupils 8 794; 14 799; 18 879; 19 268; 29 747; 30 865
works 11 57
Descar see BELI BI TA
Descartes, René 2 837; 8 788*; 10 690; 14 94; 28 206
Deschamps, Bertrand 8 789
Deschamps, Catherine-Françoise 3 463
Deschamps, Claude 4 389, 390
Deschamps, Gérard 23 261; 29 12
Deschamps, H. 20 603
works 19 491
Deschamps, Jean (fl 1248) 8 789
Deschamps, Jean (fl 1286) 8 789; 22 505
Deschamps, Joseph 5 888; 27 536; 32 374
Deschamps, Léon (Julien) 8 789*; 24 426
Deschamps, Paul 18 421
Deschamps, Pierre 8 789
deschi da parto see under trays → types
Deschinger 9 86
Deschler, Joachim 8 790*; 12 402; 20 920; 23 309
De Schulthess Painter 13 529
Deschwanden, Louis Viktor von 8 790
Deschwanden, Melchior Paul von 8 790*; 22 328; 26 423
Deschwanden, Theodor von 8 790
Desclée 3 885; 7 460
D'Escoto, Miguel 23 85, 86
Des Coudres, Ludwig 33 82
Descourtis, Charles-Melchior 8 790–91*; 13 220; 16 906; 28 50
Deseine, Claude-André 8 791*
Deseine, Louis-Etienne 8 791
Deseine, Louis-Pierre 8 791*; 21 411; 32 582
Deseine, Madeleine-Anne 8 791
Desenfans, Noël Joseph 4 576; 8 792*; 10 365; 19 587; 25 212
collections 10 366; 19 588; 31 871
Desenne, Alexandre 14 394
Désert de Retz see RETZ, DÉSERT DE
Déserteur, Le see BRUN, CHARLES-FRÉDÉRIC
Desfontaine, René-Louiche 26 73
Desfontaines, J. H. F. Bellery see BELLERY DESFONTAINES, J. H. F.
Desfontaines, Pierre-François-Guyot 11 761
Desfossé & Karth 3 110; 8 792*; 9 370; 32 816
Desfour (family) 8 423
Desfriches, Aignan-Thomas 8 792–3*; 24 480
Desgodets, Antoine 2 168; 5 616; 8 793*; 10 205; 23 488
works 2 167
Desgoffe, Alexandre 8 794
Desgoffe, Blaise (Alexandre) 8 794*
Desgots, Claude 6 453; 8 794; 12 122; 19 164; 23 517; 33 277
Desgots, Jean 8 794
Desgots, Pierre 6 453; 8 794*
Deshayes, Jean-Baptiste (-Henri) see DESHAYS, JEAN-BAPTISTE(-HENRI)
Deshayes, Philippe 4 391
Deshays, Jean-Baptiste (-Henri) 8 794–6*
pupils 12 33; 19 25; 21 113
works 3 461; 8 795
Deshays, Jean-Dominique 8 794
Deshays de Colleville see DESHAYS, JEAN BAPTISTE (-HENRI)
Deshima see under NAGASAKI
Deshon, George 24 281
Desiderii, Gian Domenico 7 399; 8 796*
Desiderio, Monsù 3 271; 23 191
Desiderio da Firenze 8 796*; 29 569
collaboration 21 647
works 8 796; 21 784; 29 568
Desiderio da Settignano 8 797–9*; 26 136
collaboration 22 801; 32 360
groups and movements 26 186
patrons and collectors 3 703; 20 27; 21 11, 13
pupils 16 694; 21 692
works 5 129; 8 797, 798; 11 206; 16 690, 691; 20 113; 22 15; 27 830
Desiderius, Abbot of Montecassino 8 800–801*; 19 207; 22 9, 12; 26 625
architecture 16 626, 762; 22 10, 10; 26 333
frescoes 26 650, 656; 27 784, 784
manuscripts 16 654; 22 11; 26 665
metalwork 22 12
mosaics 26 679
opus sectile 7 920
Desiderius, King (reg 756-74) 7 363; 32 627
Design 8 804; 26 471
design 1 107; 6 42; 8 801–5*; 30 382
design, books see BOOK DESIGN
design, education see under EDUCATION (ART) → types
design, environmental see ENVIRONMENTAL DESIGN
design, garden see GARDEN DESIGN
design, industrial see INDUSTRIAL DESIGN
design, park see PARK DESIGN
design, stage see STAGE DESIGN
design, typographical see TYPOGRAPHICAL DESIGN
design amulets see SEALS → types → seal amulets
Design and Industries Association (DIA) 2 571; 3 741; 8 802; 10 336; 14 277, 674; 15 142, 824; 19 253, 689; 20 595; 29 484
Design Annual 24 451
Design DK 24 451
designers 2 362; 10 239; 15 823, 824
Design Group 15 56; 18 639
design museums see under MUSEUMS → types
Design Partnership 19 384
Design Quarterley 24 434
Design Research 30 227
Design Research Unit 11 878
Design System 28 376
Dési Huber, István 8 805–6*; 14 901
works 8 806
De Simone, Alfredo 8 806*; 31 756, 758
De Simone, Antonio 8 806–7*; 16 645
De Simone, Francesco 8 807*; 22 474
Desing, Anselm 2 783; 18 447; 23 339
works 18 447
Désiré, Raymond 11 759
Desislava 9 583
Desjardins, Louis-Joseph 5 589; 19 75
Desjardins, Martin 3 570; 5 380; 8 807–8*; 26 385
collaboration 12 726
patrons and collectors 4 551; 13 665; 19 731
works 6 379; 8 71; 10 442; 19 846; 32 372
DesJarlait, Patrick 22 596
Desjobert 20 605; 33 427
Desjobert, Eugène (1817-63) 1 642
Deskey, Donald 8 808–9*; 15 824
works 1 738; 2 522; 31 632
Deskey-Vollmer Inc. 8 809
Deskford 6 162
Dešković, Branislav 8 178
desks
historical and regional traditions
Belgium 3 582, 586
France 11 598
Japan 17 300
South Africa 29 115
United States of America 31 624, 629, 631; 33 II2
materials
birch 33 I1
box-wood 29 313
cedar 25 304
inlays 29 313, 313
juniper 25 304
lacquer 5 192; 17 300
mahogany 11 597, 598; 29 313, 314; 33 II2
oak 3 586
satin-wood 5 192
sycamore 11 591
tortoiseshell 29 314
velvet 29 313
walnut 29 313
techniques
gilding 11 591, 598
marquetry 5 192
secrétaires à abattant 33 I1
verre églomisé 5 192
types
escritoires 2 812; 8 398; 31 629
lectern 19 313
roll-top 12 425
secrétaires à abattant 5 192; 12 426; 31 629
secrétaires à cylindre 11 591
secrétaires en pente 5 192
writing-desks 5 350
Austria 2 812
Catalonia 29 313, 313
Czech Republic 8 399
Germany 12 423
Portugal 25 304
Spain 5 350; 29 312–14*, 313
see also BOXES → types → writing-boxes
see also BUREAUX; DAVENPORTS; SCHOLAR'S TABLES; SECRETAIRES
De Smaele see SMAELE, DE
Desmaisons, Louis Saint-Ange 3 461
Desmaisons, Pierre 4 517
Desmarais, Jean-Baptiste 3 903; 4 305; 31 73
Desmarais, Paul 32 739
Desmarées, Georges 8 809*; 11 459; 12 391; 22 302; 33 277, 278
Desmarests, Jean 31 266
Desmarets de Saint-Sorlin, Jean 3 632; 25 461; 30 659
Desmarquet(s), Pauline see AUZOU, PAULINE
Desmarz, Nicolaus 5 666
Desmay, M. L. S. 13 898
De Smet, Gustave 3 564, 614; 8 809–10*
groups and movements 2 516; 10 696; 18 626
works 11 450
De Smet, Jules 8 809
De Smet, Léon 8 809
De Smet, Lucie 32 852
Des Moines (IA), Arts Center 22 367
Desmoulins, Auguste 19 215
Desmoulins, Jean-Baptiste see MAILLOU, JEAN-BAPTISTE
Desneux de la Noue see LA NOUE, Abbé de
Desnos, Louis-Charles 12 814
Desnos, Robert 18 577; 21 709; 24 726; 30 17, 18, 19, 20, 22
Desnoues, Guillaume 33 726
Desnoyer, François 8 810*
Desnoyer, François-et-Souza, Musée Fondation see under SAINT-CYPRIEN
Desnoyer, Souza 8 810
Desnoyers, Fernand 26 53
Des Noyers, François Sublet, Baron de Dangu 11 743; 20 134; 26 348; 29 886*
architecture 6 507
paintings 6 461; 25 391
Desoches 11 852
De Soissons, Louis (Emmanuel Jean Guy de Savoie-Carignan), Vicomte d'Ostel, Baron Longroy 8 810–11*
assistants 28 283
collaboration 33 382
teachers 29 695
works 12 145; 31 584
De Soissons partnership 17 593
Desoye, Madame 17 440
Desparges workshop 24 148
Despax, Jean-Baptiste 26 423; 31 816
Despenser, Francis Dashwood, 15th Baron Le see DASHWOOD, FRANCIS, 15th Baron Le Despenser
Desperet, Auguste 13 306
Desperrois, Martin 27 253
Despiau, Charles 8 811*; 11 568, 569
pupils 3 194; 9 199; 23 143; 27 882; 30 54; 31 94; 32 423
Despierre, Jacques 11 302, 644
Despinis, G. 26 287
Desplá, Lluís, Canon 3 811
Desplaces, Louis 14 83
Desplechin, Edouard 28 399
Despo, Jan see DESPOTOPOULOS, IOANNIS
Despoineta 13 355
Desportes, Claude-François 8 811, 814*
Desportes, (Alexandre-) François 8 811–14*; 12 832
assistants 8 814
collaboration 26 386
paintings 2 105; 9 30; 11 539
flower 11 228
hunting scenes 29 424
still-lifes 8 812, 813; 11 537; 12 357; 29 668
patrons and collectors 4 554; 17 615; 30 523
tapestries 11 643
Desportes, Nicolas 8 814
despotic icons see under ICONS → types
Despotikon 2 160
Despotopoulos, Ioannis 8 814–15*; 13 349
Desprès, Jean 11 629; 17 529
Despret, Georges 11 613; 12 795
Desprez, Barthélemy 10 319; 12 789; 24 57
Desprez, François 33 357
Desprez, Louis-Jean 8 815*; 30 89, 95
aquatints 2 240
architecture 2 332; 11 91, 242; 30 72–3
collaboration 6 511; 30 72; 31 693
groups and movements 10 96; 13 864
interior decoration 30 90
patrons and collectors 14 692; 30 79, 524
stage design 29 691
Despuig, Cardinal 22 318
Desrais, Claude-Louis 10 823
Desroches, Numa 14 58
Desroches-Noblecourt, Christiane 10 83
Dessailliant de Richeterre, Michel 5 564
Dessarteaux, Jacques 2 704
Dessau 8 815–16*; 12 360
Bauhaus building 3 402; 12 378; 27 129
Park Georgium 27 324
Residenzschloss 12 413
Schlosskirche 1 711
Schloss Mosigkau 23 465
tenements 30 458
Dessau Chalkographische Gesellschaft 2 95
Dessauvage, M. 19 260
Desseine, F. 8 220
Dessert, Fritz 23 312
Dessert, Oskar 23 312
Dessert, Wilhelm 23 312
dessert stands 10 419
dessin héliographique see PHOTOGRAPHY → processes → cliché-verre
dessin sur verre bichromaté see PHOTOGRAPHY → processes → cliché-verre
Dessislava 5 162; 32 643
Dessy, Stanislao 27 836
Desta 30 755
Desta, Gebre Krestos see KRESTOS DESTA, GEBRE
Destach, John 10 328
DeStaebler, Stephen 6 460
Destailleur, François-Hippolyte 8 816; 11 524; 19 251; 32 613
Destailleur, Hippolyte (-Alexandre-Gabriel-Walter) 3 174; 8 816–17; 27 223
Destailleur, Walter-André 8 817
De' Stauris, Rinaldo see STAURIS, RINALDO DE'
De Stefani 28 213
Desterro 30 881
De Stijl see STIJL, DE
Destorrents, Rafael 8 817*; 28 478
Destorrents, Ramón 3 221; 8 817*; 9 262; 23 881
Destouches, Paul-Emile 2 614; 17 453; 24 166
Destré, Julien 19 380
Destre, Vincenzo dalle 3 667; 8 817*
Destrée, J. 3 620; 12 523
Destrez, Jean, Abbé 8 818*
Desvallières, Georges-Olivier 3 156; 8 715, 818*; 22 92
Desvergnes, Charles-Jean-Cléophas 8 818–19*
Desvignes, Peter Hubert 2 808; 19 113, 339; 30 754
works 2 809
Desvoges, Anatole 8 835
Desvres 30 885
De Taeye, Lodewijk Jan 8 831
Detaille, (Jean-Baptiste-) Edouard 3 389; 8 819*; 21 69; 23 11
detergents 6 334
determinatives 10 2
Detgiz Publishing House 19 13
Dethier, Philipp Anton 16 591
De Thurah, Laurids (Lauridsen) 8 726, 742, 819–20*
works 8 726, 740; 10 112; 27 167
De Tivoli, Serafino 16 678; 19 870; 28 318
Detmold
Hermann Monument 3 155–6
Residenzschloss 33 88
De Tolnay see TOLNAY, CHARLES ERICH DE
Detoni, Marijan 9 672
De Tonnancour, Jacques (Godefroy) see TONNANCOUR, JACQUES (GODEFROY) DE
Detournelle
works 11 579
Detra 28 856

Detrimont, Alexis-Eugène 8 820*
Detroit (MI) 8 820–21*; 31 *587*
Alex and Marie Manoogian Treasury Museum 2 445
Cathedral of St Paul 29 515
Dodge Half-Ton Truck factory 10 749; 12 792; 31 596, *596*
factories 31 596
Ford Rouge Plant 17 722, *722*
Historical Museum 8 821
Institute of Arts 2 368; 8 152, 821, *821*; 15 830; 31 667
archives 2 366
collections 5 917; 10 94; 15 746; 30 332
Greek collection 13 470
murals 26 427, *427*
periodicals 24 433
sculpture 27 47
Lafayette Park 21 493
Museum of Art 31 665
Museum of Arts *see* Institute of Arts
Northland Shopping Center 28 623; 31 735
Packard Motor Company Factory 10 749
Pewabic Pottery Museum 8 821
Philip A. Hart Plaza 11 347
Detroit Painter 13 505
Dettelbach Pilgrimage Church 12 368; 13 210
Dettlof, Szczęsny 25 143
Dettmann, Ludwig 8 821*
De Turris, Nicola 16 748
Detva 28 853
Deu, Jordi de *see* JORDI DE DEU
Deubler, Jan Zygmunt *see* DEYBEL, JAN ZYGMUNT
Deubler, Leonard 9 711
Deuchar, David 28 236
Deuchler, Dr 27 214
Deuil, Otto of, Abbot of Saint-Denis *see* OTTO OF DEUIL, Abbot of Saint-Denis
De Unga *see* YOUNG ONES
Deurasne-Pletinckx Co. 18 877
Deuren, Matthias J. van 3 600
Deuren, van (family) 3 600
Deurle, Gemeentelijk Museum Gustav de Smet 8 810
Deusdona 8 260
Deus Sepúlveda, João de *see* SEPÚLVEDA, JOSÉ DE DEUS
Deustamben, Petrus 19 175
Deutch, Oscar 7 328
Deutenhofer 12 770
Deutsch, Hans Rudolf Manuel 8 822, 823*
Deutsch, Julije 14 724*
Deutsch, Ludwig 23 504
Deutsch, Matthias 2 471
Deutsch, Niklaus Manuel, I (1484-1530) 3 387, 823; 8 821, 822–3*; 30 131
patrons and collectors 1 771; 10 752
reproductive prints by others 8 823
works 8 *822*, *823*; 23 294, 788; 30 131; 33 354
Deutsch, Niklaus Manuel, II (1528-88) 8 822
Deutsche, Der see NEUE TEUTSCHE, DER
Deutsche Bank AG 11 734; 12 472
Deutsche Bau-Ausstellung, 1931 *see under* BERLIN → exhibitions
Deutsche Bauhütte 24 444
Deutsche Bauzeitung 24 444
Deutsche Forschungsgemeinschaft (DFG) 12 481
Deutsche Gartenstadtgesellschaft 8 824*; 12 145; 30 370, 520
Deutsche Kunst 12 416
Deutsche Kunst und Dekoration 2 565; 24 427, 444
Deutsche Monatshefte 24 444
Deutsche Orient-Gesellschaft 10 82
Deutscher Künstlerbund 14 238; 17 736; 19 335; 30 730
Deutscher Künstlerverein (Rome) 31 401
Deutscher Museumsbund 12 477
Deutscher Photodienst *see* DEPHOT
Deutscher Verlag 13 811
Deutscher Volkskalender 13 773
Deutscher Werkbund 2 321; 8 802, 824–7*; 12 378, 418, 450, 480; 15 823; 20 593, 595; 21 780–81, 782; 22 304, 386; 23 548; 26 14; 29 874
art forms
architecture 8 *826*; 21 *780*, *783*; 31 *877*
ceramics 12 432, 437
furniture 6 391
interior decoration 12 416; 14 24
exhibitions 4 143, 722; 10 683; 12 379; 13 798; 21 782; 24 677; 28 126; 30 371; 31 876; 33 105
members
Bosselt, Rudolf 4 469
Döcker, Richard 9 60
Fischer, Theodor (1862-1938) 11 129
Frank, Josef 11 727
Gropius, Walter (Adolf Georg) 13 687
Kesting, Edmund 17 921
Mies van der Rohe, Ludwig 21 490
Migge, Leberecht 21 494
Olbrich, Joseph Maria 2 567
Pankok, Bernhard 24 13
Paul, Bruno 24 279
Poelzig, Hans 21 782
Powolny, Michael 25 404
Rading, Adolf 25 839
Riemerschmid, Richard 26 374
Schmidt, Karl (1873-1954) 14 362
Schumacher, Fritz (Wilhelm) 28 177
Schwarz, Rudolf 28 191
Tessenow, Heinrich 30 520
Thorn Prikker, Johan 30 760
Wendland, Winfried 33 73
Model Factory 12 792; 13 *686*
writings 26 405
Deutsches Archäologisches Institut 17 922
Deutsches Kunstblatt 24 444
Deutsches Museum see NEUES DEUTSCHES MUSEUM
Deutsche Werkstätten für Handwerkskunst G.m.b.H. Dresden und München 8 824; 12 428; 14 25, 362; 25 674
Deutsch-Gabel *see* JABLONNÉ V PODEŠTĚDÍ
Deutschkranz palace 2 779
Deutschmann, A. 19 54
Deutschmann, Josef 33 623
Deutz, Jozeph 32 589
Deux, Bertrand de, Cardinal *see* BERTRAND DE DEUX, Cardinal
Deux Piliers d'Ors, Les 6 548
Deva *see* CHESTER
Deva, Krishna 15 212
Deva, Rao of Bundi (*reg c.* 1240) (Rajput) 5 171
Devachandra, King of Arakan (*reg* 5th cent.) 5 255
Devade, Marc 11 552, 553; 30 6
Devagaḍh *see* MEWAR
Devagiri *see* DAULATABAD
Devakul, Trisuk 17 686; 30 591
devakulikā 15 243*
Devanampiya Tissa 5 97
Devaranne, Siméon Pierre 3 804
Deva Raya I, Ruler (*reg* 1422-48) (Vijayanagara) 15 329
Devas, Anthony 10 652
Devastich 17 735; 24 361
Devaye, Marguerite *see* MAEGHT, MARGUERITE
De Vecchi 5 127
De Vecchi, Gabriele 13 728
Deve Hüyük 1 858
Devekuyusu church 19 840
Develly, Jean-Charles 28 523
Developed Stamford ware *see under* POTTERY → wares
developing-out processes *see under* PHOTOGRAPHY → processes
Devenish, John 8 827*
Deventer 22 *813*
Bergkerk 22 818, 820, 834
bronze 22 894
Grote Kerk *see* St Lebuïnus
painting 22 835
patronage 22 886
pewter 22 893; 24 580
St Lebuïnus 22 817, 818; 26 574
crypt 8 223; 22 *818*
silver 22 886, 887
Stadhuis 5 3; 22 *825*, 826
Deventer, Jacob van 1 775
Deventer carpets *see under* CARPETS → types
Dévényi, Sandor 14 891
Dever 22 822
De Vere (family) 24 576
Deverell, Walter Howell 8 827–8*; 25 554; 26 56; 28 664
Devereux, Robert, 2nd Earl of Essex 8 828*; 10 360; 23 407
Devéria, Achille (-Jacques-Jean-Marie) 8 828–9*
collaboration 27 143; 32 597
groups and movements 26 500
pupils 12 769
reproductive prints by others 5 440; 11 319; 14 394
teachers 12 732
works 8 *828*, 829; 19 487
Devéria, Eugène (-François-Marie-Joseph) 8 829*; 11 543; 14 587
dealers 4 66
groups and movements 26 500, 739; 31 374
patrons and collectors 12 186
pupils 12 769
teachers 12 732
works 12 187
Devers, Giuseppe 28 68
Devers, Joseph 24 148
De Vestel, Lucien 5 42
works 5 *42*
Deveti Septemvri Factory 5 159
Devětsil - Svaz moderní kultury 7 293, 772; 8 829–30*; 25 433; 28 745
Linhart, Evžen 19 423
members 30 22
Černík, Artus 8 437
Černý, František M(aria) 6 345
Chochol, Josef 7 182
Feuerstein, Bedřich 11 47
Fragner, Jaroslav 11 365
Havlíček, Josef 14 247
Honzík, Karel 14 732
Krejcar, Jaromír 18 445
Muzika, František 22 393
Rössler, Jaroslav 27 205
Štyrský, Jindřich 29 884
Teige, Karel 30 416
Toyen 31 250
periodicals 24 440
Devey, George 8 830–31*; 23 398; 32 277, 720
works 8 *830*
Devi, Ganga 15 174
devices 7 177, *177*, 178, 179; 15 149
Devic Monastery, St Ioannikia 25 343
Devidas 15 619
De Vigne, Edmond 8 831
De Vigne, Edouard 8 831; 31 887
De Vigne, Emma 8 831
De Vigne, Félix 4 754; 8 608, 831, 841
De Vigne, Ignace 8 831
De Vigne, Louise 8 831
De Vigne, Malvina 8 831
De Vigne, Paul 3 572; 5 44; 8 831–2*
De Vigne, Pierre 8 831*
Devignes, Peter Hubert 2 813
Devi Kund 15 389
De Vilbiss, Alan 1 494
Devillard 2 660
Devillers, Christian 2 699, 700
Devillers, Marina 8 832
Devillers and Perot 8 832*
devil's work balls 7 103, *104*
Devín 28 *848*
Castle Church 28 850
De Vinck, Antoine 3 592
works 3 *592*
Devinuvara 29 448
Devi-ri-kothi, Chamunda-Devi Temple 15 627
Devis, Anthony (Thomas) 8 832, 833*
Devis, Arthur (1712-87) 8 832–3*
methods 18 898
patrons and collectors 11 39; 21 91; 30 890
reproductive prints by others 28 25
works 7 785, *786*; 8 *833*; 9 283; 10 *277*
Devis, Arthur William (1762-1822) 2 690; 4 845; 8 832, 833–4*
Devis, Thomas Anthony 8 832, 833*
Devisme, Gerard 28 781
De Vivo, Tommaso 22 916
Devizes (Wilts) 31 710
Castle 26 616
Dev Kala 6 206
Devliegher, L. 3 620
Devlin, Stuart 2 766; 8 834*
Devni Mori
Monastery 28 544
sculpture 15 450, 461–2, *462*, 463, 719
Devnja 5 145
Devon (South Africa) 1 *413*
Devon, William Courtenay, Earl of *see* COURTENAY, WILLIAM, Earl of Devon
Devon, William of *see* WILLIAM OF DEVON
Devonport Library 10 97
Devonshire, William Cavendish, 2nd Duke of *see* CAVENDISH, WILLIAM, 2nd Duke of Devonshire
Devonshire, William Cavendish, 4th Duke of *see* CAVENDISH, WILLIAM, 4th Duke of Devonshire
Devonshire, William Cavendish, 6th Duke of *see* CAVENDISH, WILLIAM SPENCER, 6th Duke of Devonshire
Devonshire Hunting Tapestries 32 823
De Voorst 8 834*; 12 132; 22 *813*
DeVore, Richard 31 640
Devosge, Claude-François, II (1697-1777) 14 657
Devosges, Anatole 27 312
Devosges, (Claude-) François, III (1732-1811) 8 834–5*, 890; 11 667, 669
collections 11 665
pupils 11 899; 25 876
works 8 889
Devosse, Cornelius *see* VOS, CORNELIUS DES
Devotio moderna 4 751
devotional images 8 835–6*
England 8 836, *836*
Gothic 8 *836*; 13 129
Romanesque 8 835
devotional objects 8 835–6*; 13 129
see also EX-VOTOS
devotional prints *see under* PRINTS → types
Devoto, John 18 749; 30 675
Devoty, Jan 8 397
Devoty, Karel Antonín 8 397
Devoyes, François 11 596
Devoyes, Toussaint 11 596
De Vriendt, Albert 23 459
De Vriendt, Cornelius *see* VRIENDT, CORNELIUS DE
De Vriendt, Juliaan 23 459
Dew, John 23 688
Dewan Bahasa 29 238
Dewandre, François-Joseph 28 756
Dewantoro, Ki Hadjar 15 807, 808, 818
Dewa Nyoman Batuan 15 809
Dewarlez, Benjamin 3 578; 32 259
De Wasme 11 359
Dewasne, Jean 8 838–9*; 19 381
assistants 12 613
dealers 7 842; 26 193
patrons and collectors 7 842
pupils 7 842
De Weert, Anna 19 792
Deweirdt, F.-C. 32 380
Dewey, John 1 179, 182; 2 517; 8 839*; 10 691
Dewey, Melvil 4 22
Dewey Decimal System (DDS) 4 22
Dewez, Laurent Benoît 2 125; 8 839–40*
assistants 2 125
collaboration 1 140
patrons and collectors 3 613
works 2 122; 3 547; 5 53; 19 260
Dewez, Michel-Paul-Joseph 3 599
Dewez, Pierre, Canon of Cambrai Cathedral 20 451
Dewhurst Haslam Partnership 14 521
DeWilde, John 8 88; 31 634
De Wilde, Samuel 8 840–41*
Dewin, Jean-Baptiste 8 633; 9 759
Dewing, Maria Oakey 7 875; 8 841
Dewing, Thomas 7 875; 30 452
Dewing, Thomas Wilmer 4 478; 8 841*; 31 141
groups and movements 7 875
patrons and collectors 11 748
works 31 141
De Winne, Liévin 8 841–2*; 11 448
De Wint, Peter 8 842–3*
reproductive prints by others 25 837
teachers 31 909
works 7 789; 8 *842*; 10 252; 32 901
De Witte, Adrien 26 6
DeWitt Wallace Decorative Arts Gallery *see under* WILLIAMSBURG (VA)
Dewrich 15 149
Dexamenos of Chios 12 248
works 12 *248*
Dexileos Stele 13 384, 431, 457, *457*; 31 108
Dexter, F. G. 8 843
Dexter, George Minot 8 843*
Dexter, Walter 5 582
Dextra, Zacharias 22 881
dextrin 29 813; 32 898
Deyan, Despot 33 632
Deyang 7 26
Deybel, Jan Zygmunt 8 843–4*; 25 98; 30 212; 32 870
Deyck, Barthélemy *see* EYCK, BARTHÉLEMY D'
Deyhle, Rolf 12 474

Deyneka, Aleksandr (Aleksandrovich) 8 844*; 15 830; 22 178; 27 395; 32 661
  groups and movements 27 394; 28 924
  works 14 589; 28 918
De Young, M. H. *see* YOUNG, M. H. DE
Deyrolle, Jean 8 844*; 26 193
Deyster, Lodewijk de 3 559
Dezaigre 8 776
Dezain 24 437
Dezallier, Antoine 8 844
Dezallier d'Argenville, A(ntoine)-N(icolas) 7 714; 8 845–6*; 24 137
Dezallier d'Argenville, Antoine-Joseph 8 844–6*; 12 64, 118, 127; 16 893; 31 151
  garden design 12 122
  writings 5 346; 19 17; 32 268
    artists' biographies 8 846; 10 205; 11 674
    on gardens 12 122, 132
Dezaunay, Emile-Alfred 25 751
Dezest, Raimond de *see* RAIMOND DE DEZEST
Dezeuze, Daniel 11 552; 22 35; 30 6
Dezon, François 24 148
Dezong, Emperor (Tang; *reg* 780-805) 33 661
dga 'Idan *see* GANDEN
D Group 3 785; 10 719; 22 342; 31 94, 454; 33 595, 628
Dhahran 2 *246*
  Air Terminal 27 876
  coins 2 261
  glass 2 263
  graves 2 249
  jewellery 2 264
  King Fahd University of Petroleum and Minerals 27 876
  pottery 2 268
Dhaka 3 *166*; 8 846–7*; 15 *279*
  Art School 3 168
  Bangla Academy 3 170
  Bangladesh College of Arts and Crafts *see* Institute of Fine Arts
  Bara Katra 15 370
  Institute of Fine Arts 1 27; 3 169
    Department of Graphic Art 3 169
  Lalbagh Fort 8 847; 15 370
  mosque of Khwaja Shahbaz 15 370
  muslin 15 660–61, 723
  National Art Gallery 3 170
  National Museum 3 170; 8 847
  Shaheed Minar 3 167
  Sher-e-Bangla Nagar 13 239
    Parliament Building 3 167, *167*
  silver 15 707
  textiles 15 665, 723
  weaving 3 168
dhaka cloth *see under* TEXTILES → types
Dhaky, M. A. 15 212, 266, 268, 271, 272
Dhamabhaga 3 905
Dhamar Mosque 16 245
Dhamnar 15 265
Dhanabhati 15 425
Dhananjaya 15 636
Dhanens, E. 3 619
Dhanga, Ruler (*reg c.* 954-1002) (Chandella) 15 290; 18 13
Dhank temple 15 267
Dhannavati 2 280, *281*; 5 225, 239
Dhannu 8 847*
Dhano 15 607
Dhanyavishnu, Ruler (*reg c.* 500) (Huna) 15 473
Dhar 15 354
  architecture 16 201
  Kamal Maulana Mosque 15 354
  Lat ki Mosque 15 354
  tomb of Shaykh Kamal al-Din Malwi 15 354
Dharakot, Jagannatha Temple 15 636
Dharamdas *see* Dharm Das
Dharanaka 25 887
Dharbhavati *see* DAHOI
Dharkar, Imtiaz 4 291
Dharmadatta 15 739
Dharma Nature Buddhism *see under* BUDDHISM → sects
Dharmapala, Ruler (*reg c.* 781-812) (Pala) 2 139; 15 281; 23 776
Dharmapuri 15 529; 23 182
Dharmarajika *see under* TAXILA
dharmaśālās 22 760, 792
Dharmasthala 29 438
Dharm Das 8 847–8*
D'Hastrel, Alphonse 31 754
Dhat Ras 26 *915*
  temple 26 917
Dhaulgiri *see* DAULATABAD
Dhauli 8 848*; 15 *279*, 423
Dhavalakkaka *see* DHOLKA
Dhaya 2 248
Dhelomme, Anny 19 397
Dhendrá *see* DENDRA
Dhenukakata 17 695
Dherbécourt, Amédée 27 880
Dheulland, Guillaume 7 185
Dhiban (Jordan) 17 655
Dhibin (Yemen) 16 215
Dhidhimotikhon 9 555
Ḍhilli *see* DELHI
Ḍhillikā *see* DELHI
Dhimíni *see* DIMINI
Dhlo Dhlo 1 305, *413*, 414, 418
Dhlomo, Bongiwe 29 110
Dhobini Shiva Temple 15 284
dhokra see under METALWORK → techniques
Dholavira 15 246
Dholba 15 483
Dholka 8 848–9*; 15 *276*, 347
  Hilal Khan Qadi Mosque 8 848; 15 347
  Taka Mosque 15 347
  Tanka Masjid *see* TAKA MOSQUE
Dholpur 12 73; 15 361
D'Hoym, Comte 18 880
Dhrami, Muntaz 1 541; 8 849*; 14 20; 25 869
Dhu'l-Jibla Mosque 16 500
Dhummun 15 629; 25 741
Dhumvarahi 8 849*; 15 *261*, *264*
Dhungri, Hirmadevi Temple 15 310, 396
Dhuwa 1 60
dhvaja 15 243*
DIA *see* DESIGN AND INDUSTRIES ASSOCIATION
Diabete, Ismael 20 199
diacetone alcohol 29 53
diadems 17 527
  historical and regional traditions
    Central Asia, Eastern 6 312
    Central Asia, Western 6 274
    China 7 108, 110
    Crete 21 686
    Cycladic 8 *322*
    Cyprus, ancient 8 352
    Egypt, ancient 10 29
    Greece, ancient 13 599, *599*, 601
    Minoan 21 686
    Russia 28 *325*
    Sarmatian 28 *325*
    Sasanian 1 888
  materials
    bronze 13 601
    cornelian 13 *599*
    enamel 13 *599*
    gold 13 *599*, 599; 28 *325*
    silver 8 *322*
Diaghilev, Serge (de) 3 86, 734; 8 849–50*; 12 892, 893, 894; 18 793, 863; 24 718; 26 41; 27 392; 28 596, 808; 30 686; 33 486
  collaboration 7 508
Diaghilev, Serge (de)—cont.
  groups and movements 3 86, 119, 120; 27 443, 580; 33 379
  productions 2 108; 12 878; 18 791, 864; 30 681, 686
    Apollon musagète 3 391
    Boris Godunov 33 577
    Boutique fantastique 8 775
    Cléopâtre 9 291
    La Chatte 11 877; 24 574
    La Tragédie de Salomé 29 899
    L'Enfant prodigue 27 241
    Le Rossignol 8 771; 20 828
    Les Tentations de la bergère 13 671
    Mavra 30 25
    Parade 12 497
    Romeo and Juliet 10 467; 33 342
    Schéhérazade 28 475
    Zéphyre et Flore 21 312
  sponsors 26 530; 30 464
Diago, Roberto 8 229
diagonal buttresses *see under* BUTTRESSES
Diaguita 2 392
Diakovce church 4 782; 28 849
D.I.A.L. 15 97
Dial, The 18 594; 24 426
Diallo, Alpha Woualid 28 405
Diamant Bleu *see* HOPE DIAMOND
Diamante (di Feo), Fra 8 850*; 19 443, 445; 24 538
Diamant fort 11 757
Diamantini, Giuseppe 5 877; 8 427, 851*
Diamantis, Adamantios 8 364, 851*
Diamantopoulos, Diamantis 8 851–2*
Diamatani, Bouriema 5 217
Diametrius, Daniel 10 195
Diamond *see under* TYPE-FACES
Diamond, A. J. 31 176
Diamond, Hugh Welch 8 852*; 21 7
Diamond, Katherine 28 671*
Diamond, Myers & Wilkin 5 563
Diamond Monstrance 25 443
Diamond Point masonry *see under* MASONRY → types
diamonds 12 268, 270, I; 14 167; 17 *525*
  historical and regional traditions
    Australia 12 269
    Belgium 3 *605*, 605
    Brazil 12 269
    China 7 88
    England 10 *345*
    France 11 634, *634*; 17 II3, III2
    Germany 12 *459*
    Indian subcontinent 12 252
    Portugal 25 314
    Russia 10 IV3; 12 269; 27 429, *429*
    South Africa 12 269; 29 103
    Spain 17 *523*
    Sri Lanka 20 302
    United States of America 31 654, *655*
  techniques
    cutting 12 269–70
  uses
    abrasives 16 859; 29 706
    amulets 1 818
    boxes 10 IV3
    drilling 7 11
    jewellery 10 136; 17 519, 522, *523*, 524, 526, 529
      Belgium 3 *605*, 605
      England 10 *345*
      France 11 *634*, 634; 17 II3, III2
      Russia 27 *429*
      United States of America 31 654, *655*
    sawing 7 11
    snuff-boxes 12 *459*
    tools 20 302
Diana, Benedetto 3 656; 8 855*; 32 224
Diana, Giacinto 8 856*; 22 479
Diana bracelet 17 III2
Dian culture 8 852–4*; 29 230
  bronze 6 834; 8 852–4, *853*, *854*
  copper 8 852
  drums (musical instruments) 8 853, *853*
  lost-wax casting 8 853
  mirrors 21 714
  pipes (musical) 8 853
  plaques 8 854, *854*
  sculpture 8 *853*
  tin 8 852
Diane Bracelet 17 III2; 26 191
Diane de Gabies 4 407
Diane de Poitiers, Duchesse de Valentinois 8 856*
  architecture 2 27; 4 780; 6 545; 11 514, 572; 19 691, 692
  books 14 616
  gardens 6 546
  patronage 11 656
  sculpture 11 265
Dianga, John 17 908
Diano, Giacinto *see* DIANA, GIACINTO
Diao Guan 6 799
diaper 8 856–7*, *857*
diapering *see under* BRICKLAYING → types
diaphanorama 8 857*, 910
diaphanous domes *see under* DOMES → types
diaphragm arches *see under* ARCHES → types
Diario de Costa Rica 8 18
Dias, Antonio 4 719; 8 857*
Dias, B. H. *see* POUND, EZRA (LOOMIS)
Dias, Carlos 4 658
Dias, Cícero 4 718, 719; 8 857*
Dias, Francisco 4 709; 17 513; 23 400; 27 644
Dias, Gaspar 8 857–8*; 19 464; 25 296
Dias, Luís 4 709
Dias, Manuel (*d* 1754) 8 858*
Dias, Manuel (1574-1659) 12 814
Dias da Silva, Antonio José 25 293
Dias de Arruda, João 2 500
Dias de Oliveira, Manuel 4 727
Diatessaron of Princess Marina 31 748
diatreta see under CUPS → types → cage-cups
Diaz 10 781
Diaz, Al 3 338
Díaz, Bernal 21 264
Díaz, Celedonio 29 342
Díaz, Daniel Vázquez *see* VÁZQUEZ DÍAZ, DANIEL
Díaz, Diego Valentín 8 858*; 19 303; 31 823
Díaz, Francisco 8 858
Diaz, Juan 28 520
Díaz, Juan Luis 28 330
Díaz, Lope Max 14 464
Díaz, Luis 8 858–9*
Díaz, Marcelo Martínez 8 858
Diaz (de la Peña), (Virgilio) Narcisse 4 391; 8 859–60*; 11 545
  dealers 4 655; 8 618; 30 32
  groups and movements 3 212; 31 374
  patrons and collectors 5 57; 9 378; 18 869; 23 882
  reproductive prints by others 6 519; 11 500
  works 8 *859*; 11 37; 18 715
Díaz, Porfirio 7 784
Díaz, Sanchez 7 345
Díaz Bencomo, Mario 8 860*; 18 835
Díaz Caneja, Juan Manuel *see* CANEJA, JUAN MANUEL
Díaz del Corral, Rui 29 339; 32 559
Díaz de León, Francisco 1 739; 10 906; 16 48
Díaz del Valle, Lázaro 8 860*
Díaz de Maldonado, Juan 8 237
  works 8 *237*
Díaz de Oviedo, Pedro 8 861*; 11 483; 20 620
Díaz de Palacios, Pedro 29 268
Díaz de Villanueva, Pedro 33 728
Díaz de Vivar, Rodrigo *see* CID, EL
Díaz de Vivar, Rodrigo, Duque de Mendoza-Infantado *see* MENDOZA-INFANTADO, RODRIGO, Duque de
Díaz Gamones, José 27 754
Díaz Infante, Juan José 21 381
Díaz MacKenna, Fernando 25 701
Díaz Minaya, Pedro 8 858
Diaz Morales, Ignacio 8 861*
Diaz Morante, Pedro 8 861*; 33 358
diazo *see under* PRINTING → processes
Díaz Valdéz, Wifredo 31 756
Díaz Vargas, Miguel 7 609
Díaz Yepes, Eduardo 31 756
Dib, Kenaan 19 7
Dib, Moussa 19 7
Diba, Kamran (Tabatabai) 8 861–2*; 15 897
  collaboration 15 897
  personal collection 15 900
  works 15 897; 30 415
Dibb, Barry 29 117
Dibbets, Jan 8 862*; 19 756
  groups and movements 1 80; 7 685
  works 18 695; 22 853, 862
Dibden, Marian Alice 22 26
Dibdin, Charles 7 340
Dibdin, Thomas Frognall 25 264
Dibër 1 542, 543, 546
Dibi 27 593
Dibon 9 737
Di Bosso, Renato 1 166
Dibra, Jakup (Isuf) 1 544; 8 862*
Dibra, Osman Ali 1 544
Dibsi Faraj 9 567
  church 9 539, 541
Di Castri, John 32 414
Di Cavalcanti, Emiliano *see* CAVALCANTI, EMILIANO (DE ALBUQUERQUE E MELLO) DI
Diccini, Lyddia 3 419
dice 28 621; 31 265
Dick, A. B. (*fl* 1930-39) 30 391
Dick, A. B. & Co. 28 299
Dick, Alexander (1791/1800-1843) 2 764; 8 862–3*
Dick, Cecil 22 595
Dick, Charlotte 8 863
Dick, Karl 17 741
Dick, Lexi 10 337
Dick, Norman Aitken 5 271
Dick, Peddie + McKay 24 315
Dickens, Charles (John Huffam) 8 863*
  patrons and collectors 22 111
  personal collection 26 463; 33 16
  works 27 868; 28 526
    illustrated 4 362, 885, *885*; 6 91; 8 218; 11 74; 19 62; 20 28; 29 536, 716
Dickerson, Bob 2 161
Dickie, George 28 927
Dickinson, Edwin (Walter) 8 863*
Dickinson, Eric 15 611, 612
Dickinson, John 24 44
Dickinson, Preston 25 461; 31 606
Dickinson, Sidney 23 403
Dickinson, William 5 216; 8 863–4*; 21 416; 29 675, 676; 33 398
  works 18 149; 24 391
Dicksee, Frank (Bernard) 8 864*; 21 606; 25 556
Dicksee, Herbert Thomas 8 864

Dicksee, John Robert 8 864
Dicksee, Margaret Isabel 8 864
Dicksee, Thomas Francis 8 864
Dickson, Ian 2 689
Dickson, Richard 8 461
Dickson, Walter 33 263
Dickson, William 7 327
dictionaries 6 764, 769; 9 311; 10 203, 204, 212
dictionaries of architecture 6 378; 10 206; 24 87; 32 598
dictionaries of art 2 534; 4 21, 26; 10 203–13*
Belgium 10 208
Britain 10 206, 213
Byzantine 10 209, 213
France 2 869; 10 206, 208, 209–10, 212; 11 288
Germany 30 731
Italy 3 98; 16 781
Netherlands, the 10 208
Spain 10 206, 208
Switzerland 30 156
see also ARTISTS' BIOGRAPHIES
dictionaries of religious art 10 209, 213; 25 714
Dictynnaeum 8 155
Dictys Cretensis 7 242
Dida 8 21, 22
Didarganj
sculpture 15 415, 423, 423, 453, 726
Diday, François 5 412; 8 864*; 12 277; 30 125, 134; 33 727
Diderichsen, Julius 8 753
Diderot, Denis 7 384; 8 864–7*, 866; 9 704; 10 401, 677; 11 540, 663; 24 63, 136, 137; 25 287; 26 62, 63, 182
collaboration 10 401
dealing 8 210; 26 731, 732; 27 438
personal collection 24 418
sculpture 24 787
works 10 206, 207; 21 778; 22 357
illustrated 7 496; 11 541; 20 108; 21 59; 22 88; 24 268; 32 767
on aesthetics 1 180
on architecture 4 163
on art 2 518
on brass 4 683
on caricatures 5 760
on chiaroscuro 6 570
on decorum 8 613
on display of art 5 346
on engraving 10 391, 392
on exhibitions 13 663; 28 528
on furniture 11 595
on leather 19 1
on painting 10 198
on paper 24 38
on passementerie 24 237
on perspective 24 494
on squaring up 29 437
on the Baroque 3 262
on weaving 30 309, 547
Didi, Mestre see SANTOS, DEOSCÓREDES MAXIMILIANO DOS
Didier, R. 3 619
Didier-Petit 27 563
Didim see DIDYMA
Didioni, Franceso 5 918
didjeridu 1 53*
Dido see ELISSA, Princess
Dido Master see APOLLONIO DI GIOVANNI (DI TOMASO)
Didot, Denis 8 867
Didot, Firmin 2 25; 8 867
Didot, François 8 867
Didot, François-Ambroise 7 762; 8 867; 31 495
Didot, Pierre 4 361; 8 867*; 24 387
works 6 516; 11 369; 12 334; 30 369
Didot, Pierre-François 8 867
Didot, Saint Marc 8 867, 868*
Didrikur of Karastovu 10 813
Didron, Adolphe-Napoléon 8 868*; 11 521, 565; 29 506
works 11 521; 15 89
Didwana
Delhi Darwaza 15 350
Qila' Mosque 15 350
Didyma 8 868–70*; 13 363
architecture 15 894
church 9 590
measurements 13 411
Sanctuary of Apollo 13 416, 417
dromos 29 487
Temple I 8 869; 15 893
Temple II 8 869
Temple of Apollo (Temple III) 8 869, 869; 13 389, 405, 406, 410, 412; 28 383; 30 25, 435
Sanctuary of Artemis 8 869
Sanctuary of Apollo
Temple of Apollo (Temple III)
arches 2 295, 297
architectural refinements 13 414
entasis 10 415
gardens 13 418
mouldings 13 392
palmettes 23 889
peristyle 24 456
sculpture 13 427
vaults (ceiling) 32 87
sculpture 8 870; 13 592; 15 893
korai 18 245
Didžiokas, Vladas 19 498
Die, Master of the 10 385; 20 658*; 27 606; 32 586
Diebel, Joseph 11 459, 460
Diebenkorn, Richard (Clifford) 8 870–71*; 19 702; 27 731
dealers 18 162
groups and movements 31 608
works 8 871; 19 492; 21 897; 29 670
Diébolt, Jean-Michel 9 406
Diedo, Antonio 7 306; 28 390
Dieffenbach, Karl 24 215
Diego, Demetrio 24 622
Diego de la Cruz 8 872*
collaboration 5 204; 26 249; 28 724
works 8 872
Diego del Aguila 8 861
Diego de la Santa Cruz 1 710; 2 865; 4 414; 11 483
Diéguez, José Sabogal see SABOGAL (DIÉGUEZ), JOSÉ
Diehl, (Michel-) Charles 8 872*; 9 527, 528; 31 532; 33 479
Diehl, Charles Guillaume 11 599
works 11 599
Diehl, Hans-Jürgen 3 803
Diekirch 19 826
St Laurentius 19 826
Dielen, Frans 32 121
Diemud of Wessobrun 33 308
Dienecker, Jost de see NEGKER, JOST DE
Diener see APPRENTICES
Diener, Roger 30 129
Dieng Plateau 8 873*; 15 753
sanctuaries 15 758–9
temples 15 756
Dientzenhofer (family) 25 98
Dientzenhofer, Christoph 6 526; 8 873–7*
architecture 12 372
chapels 6 526; 25 443
churches 8 378, 378, 873, 874, 877; 25 427; 32 822
monasteries 16 817
collaboration 8 397
groups and movements 26 498
patrons and collectors 17 511
teachers 19 259
works 8 397
Dientzenhofer, Georg 8 873*; 19 259; 23 6; 32 822
works 8 873
Dientzenhofer, Johann 3 140; 8 873, 875*; 33 431
architecture 27 611
churches 11 832; 12 372; 32 822
monasteries 3 140
palaces 3 266; 14 529; 25 188; 29 525; 33 432
collaboration 29 630
groups and movements 3 266; 26 495
patrons and collectors 25 188; 28 146
Dientzenhofer, Kilian Ignaz 8 873, 875–7*; 25 427; 32 554
architecture 8 379
churches 8 875, 876; 9 754; 12 356; 25 427, 443; 32 823
monasteries 18 539
palaces 19 807
summer-houses 28 163
assistants 8 398
collaboration 8 397, 398, 413; 14 515
Dientzenhofer, Leonhard 3 140; 8 873, 875; 28 146
Dientzenhofer, Wolfgang 8 873
Diepenbeeck, Abraham (Jansz.) van 7 466; 8 877–9*; 32 700
assistants 28 904
attributions 10 717
collaboration 4 222; 7 832
reproductive prints by others 4 283; 17 599; 18 879; 22 717; 24 890; 25 221
works 2 200; 3 559, 560; 8 878, 879; 17 471; 29 424
Diepenbeeck, Jan (Roelofsz.) van 8 877
Diependale, Hendrik van 26 744
Diependale, Hendrik van see HENDRIK VAN DIEPENDALE
Dieppe 6 558; 11 637
Dier, Jon 10 316
Dier, Jone 10 316
Diercks 32 879
Diercx, Volcxken 7 500
Dieric van Haarlem 22 835
dies (i) (pedestals) 8 870*
dies (ii) (stamps) 8 870*
historical and regional traditions 7 533
Byzantine 9 635
China 7 128
Early Christian (c. AD 250-843) 9 635
Greece, ancient 13 585
Islamic 16 510
Lydia 7 532
uses
ceramics 7 128
coins 7 532; 13 585; 16 510
dies (iii) (moulds) 8 870*
Dies, Albert Christoph 26 128
Diesbach, František Kryštof 8 413
Diesbach, Ghislain 23 786; 24 791
Diessen am Ammersee
Augustinian monastery 11 124
Klosterkirche St Maria 12 372; 25 728; 26 498
paintings 3 780
Diest
Begijnhof 3 503
St Sulpitius 3 543, 569; 13 62, 183
Stadhuis 3 546
Diest, Gillis Coppens van 12 885
Diest, Hieronymus van 32 230
Diest, Jan Baptiste van 3 372
Diest, Willem van 32 673
Dieste, Eladio 8 879*
works 31 754
Diet, Arthur-Stanislas 8 879–80*; 25 749
collaboration 12 617
pupils 27 768
works 12 617
Diéterle, Jules Pierre Michel 3 461; 12 830; 24 396; 28 399, 524
Dietisalvi 28 684
Dietisalvi, Bindo 28 684
Dietler, Johann Friedrich 29 848
Dietmann, Erik 14 48
Dietmayr, Berthold, Abbot of Melk 21 83; 25 448
Dietramszell, St Leonhard
frescoes 12 391
Dietrich II, Bishop 22 692
Dietrich, Adolf 22 441
Dietrich, Christian Wilhelm Ernst 8 880*
patrons and collectors 2 382
personal collection 10 896
pupils 5 908; 18 121
reproductive prints by others 13 871; 18 858; 33 196
works 12 390
Dietrich, Friedrich Christoph 25 143
Dietrich, Jakob 8 881; 11 819
Dietrich, (Johann) Joachim 8 289, 290, 880–81*; 11 458; 12 411
Dietrich, Johann Georg 8 880
Dietrich, Maria Dorothea 8 880
Dietrich, Rahel Rosina 8 880
Dietrich, Wendel 8 881*
patrons and collectors 11 819
works 8 881; 9 750; 12 403
Dietrichson, Lorentz 23 244–5
Dietrichstein (family) 3 488; 19 807
Dietrichstein, Count 5 702
Dietrichstein, Gundakar von 25 257
Dietrichstein foundry 8 416
Dietrich zur Wayge 20 768
Dietrick, Louise G. 31 650
Dietricy see DIETRICH, CHRISTIAN WILHELM ERNST
Dietsche warande, De 24 449
Dietterlin, Bartholomäus 8 882; 20 705
Dietterlin, Wendel 8 881–2*
collaboration 33 711
groups and movements 13 701
works 8 882; 12 386; 24 271; 29 376, 747
writings 1 110; 12 368, 369, 409; 13 210; 23 489; 24 274
Dietz, Diana 21 409
Dietz, Feodor 8 883*
Dietz, (Adam) Ferdinand see TIETZ, (ADAM) FERDINAND
Dietz, Ludwig 1 720
Dietz, Theodor see DIETZ, FEODOR
Dietz, Wilhelm von 20 380; 29 578
Dietze, Marcus Conrad 25 240
Dietzsch, Johann Christoph 10 464
Dieu, Antoine 8 883*
reproductive prints by others 2 709; 19 562; 28 756
works 8 883; 12 489
Dieu, Jean 8 883
Dieulafoy, Marcel Auguste 13 812; 30 27
Dieulefit Centre 11 613
Dieu Soult, Jean de see SOULT(, JEAN DE DIEU), Maréchal
Dieussart, François 8 884–5*; 10 263; 29 801, 803; 30 495
patrons and collectors 14 650
works 8 739; 22 858
Dieussart, Jean Baptiste 18 682; 30 85
Die Wies Church 29 838
Diez, Ernst 8 885*; 16 549
Diez, Heinrich Friedrich von 16 315, 319, 554
Diez, Julius 5 901; 8 885*
Díez, Pedro Ducete see DUCETE DÍEZ, PEDRO
Diez, Robert 3 242; 9 239
Diez, Wilhelm von 22 304
pupils 6 499; 14 694; 17 736; 18 473; 19 69; 24 279; 26 419; 29 638; 31 389
Diez Albums see under ALBUMS → individual manuscripts
Diez de Armendariz, Lorenzo María Muntaner y see MUNTANER Y DIEZ DE ARMENDARIZ, LORENZO MARÍA
Diéz de Liatzasolo, Martín 3 218
Díez del Valle, Lázaro see DÍAZ DEL VALLE, LÁZARO
Díez Navarro, Luis 8 885–6*; 12 28
works 2 143; 13 761
differential thermal analysis see under TECHNICAL EXAMINATION → types
Diffrient, Niels 31 633
diffusion see DISSEMINATION
Difnico, Domenico 3 681
Dig 12 75
palace 15 390
Dig, Hans 14 439
Digambara see under JAINISM → sects
Digby, Kenelm 9 478
Digby, Spencer 4 642
Digenis, Xenos 25 334
Digerud, Jan 23 222
Digges, Dudley 29 714
Digges, Leonard 30 26
Diggs, William 31 651
Dighton, Denis 8 886*
Dighton, John 8 886
Dighton, Joshua (1831-1908) 8 886
Dighton, Joshua (fl late 19th cent.) 8 886
Dighton, Richard (i) (1795-1880) 8 886
Dighton, Richard (ii) (1823-1900) 8 886
Dighton, Robert (i) (1752-1814) 8 886*
Dighton, Robert (ii) (1786-1865) 8 886*
Dighton, W. E. 22 275
digital imaging 2 534
Digneffe, Bartholomé 3 546; 8 886–7*
Digoin, Canal du Centre 2 242
Digswell viaduct 4 787
Digues de la Touche, David 16 34
Dihl
works 24 149
Dihl et Guerhard porcelain factory 4 166; 11 610; 24 148
works 24 149
Dihlī see DELHI
Dijck, Abraham van 8 887*
Dijck, Albert van 3 565
Dijk, Floris (Claesz.) van see DYCK, FLORIS (CLAESZ.) VAN
Dijk, Philip van 8 887–8*; 14 42
pupils 25 363
reproductive prints by others 14 795
teachers 4 374; 33 80
Dijk, Philip van der Linden van see LINDEN VAN DIJK, PHILIP VAN DER
Dijon 8 888, 888–94*; 11 504
academy 1 105
art school 11 665
Bibliothèque Municipale 8 891
Charterhouse 5 895; 8 891–2*; 10 743; 11 654, 660; 13 77
altarpieces 1 710; 10 179; 13 109, 109, 110, 155
choir-stalls 13 126
paintings 3 552; 5 209; 8 892–3*; 17 456
sculpture 5 209; 8 892*, 892; 13 77; 19 137–8; 28 865
stained glass 13 182
tomb of Philip the Bold 31 122

Dijon
Charterhouse—cont.
Well of Moses 11 555, *555*; 26 *185*; 28 865–6, *866*
Château de Montmusard 32 *768*
Ecole de Dessin 8 890; 11 669, 671
furniture 8 891*
Maison Milsand 11 514
metalwork 3 596
monument to Louis XIV 10 442
Musée des Beaux-Arts 8 891; 11 665, 666
collections 2 232; 8 891; 11 753; 14 577; 25 207; 30 332
directors 14 657; 27 567
see also Palais des Etats de Bourgogne
Musée Magnin 8 835, 891
Notre-Dame 7 438; 11 510; 13 41
painting 8 *890*
Palais des Etats de Bourgogne
Salle des Antiques 2 699
Salon Condé 11 901
see also Musée des Beaux-Arts
Palais de Justice Doors 27 *681*
pigments 24 797
Place Royale 8 *889*
St Bénigne 7 257; 8 893*; 26 595, 601, 602
capitals 26 596
crypt 23 485
sculpture 8 894*
throne 30 781
Sainte-Chapelle 27 550
St Michel 11 513
sculpture 13 77
urban planning 8 889
Dijon, Drot de *see* DUVEY, LOYS
Dijsselhof, Gerrit Willem 8 894*; 22 898, 908
collaboration 23 125
groups and movements 2 567; 21 122; 22 875
works 22 *874*, 875; 33 260
Dikaios, Charilaos 8 364, 894–5*
Dikaios, P. 18 21; 27 608
Dikaios Painter 13 518
Dike, Phil 19 701
Dikidiki 1 403
Dikmen Church 19 840
Dikshit, Rao Bahadur K. N. 1 469; 15 419
Dilao *see* PACO
Dilavar Khan Husayn, Sultan of Malwa (*reg* 1401-5) (Ghuri) 6 444; 15 354; 20 250; 31 542
Dilbat 1 874
Dilberdjin 1 *186*; 6 *182*, 197; 8 895*; 31 *781*
citadel 1 190
fortifications 1 190
sculpture 1 196; 6 219
stucco 29 824
Temple of the Dioscuri 1 200, 201
wall paintings 1 201, *201*
Dilettanti, Society of *see* SOCIETY OF DILETTANTI
Dilherr, Johann Michaël 29 762; 31 371
Dilherr Goblet 29 762
Dilich, Crato 8 895
Dilich, Johann 8 895
Dilich, Johann Wilhelm 8 895; 29 577
Dilich, Wilhelm 8 895; 21 580
Dilijian 2 439
Dilip Singh, Ruler (*reg* 1695-1741) (Pahari) 15 629
Dilke, Lady 8 895–6*; 33 309
Dill, Guy 19 703
Dill, Ludwig 14 694; 28 341
Dille, Frans 2 197
Dillen, Johan van 26 379
Dillens, Adolphe-Alexandre 8 896*
Dillens, Albert 8 896
Dillens, Henrik 8 896
Dillens, Julien 5 44; 8 896*
groups and movements 10 517
pupils 17 669
teachers 28 756
works 3 572, 604
Diller, Burgoyne 1 772; 8 896–7*; 22 749; 31 607
Dilling, Johannes 21 66
Dillingen, Hartmann I von, *see* HARTMANN I VON DILLINGEN
Dillingen, Jesuit Church of the Ascension 12 370; 32 821
Dillis, (Johann) Cantius 8 898–9*
Dillis, Ignaz 8 898*
Dillis, (Maximilian) Johann Georg von 8 897–9*; 22 303
attributions 8 898, 899
collaboration 8 898
pupils 8 898
works 8 *898*; 12 393
Dillon, Gerald 16 40
works 16 *40*
Dillon, Harold Arthur, 17th Viscount 2 450
Dillon, Henri-Patrice 19 488
Dillon, Pierre 13 295
Dillon, Richard, 9th Viscount Dillon 5 827
Dillwyn, L. W. 4 65
Dillwyn Llewelyn, John *see* LLEWELYN, JOHN DILLWYN
Dilly, H. 4 25
Dilmun *see* BAHRAIN; FAYLAKA ISLAND
dilrubā 22 376
Dilthey, Wilhelm 8 899*; 14 458
Di Luan
houses 32 *477*
diluents *see* SOLVENTS
Dilwara *see under* MT ABU
DIM *see* DÉCORATION INTÉRIEURE MODERNE
Dimai *see* SOKNOPAIOU NESOS
Dimakopoulos, Dimitri 23 632
Dimand, Maurice S(ven) 8 899*; 16 549, 557
DiMare, Dominic 11 54
Dimas, Marcos 18 833, 834
Dimbulagala
Maravidiya Cave 29 464
Pulligoda Cave 25 170; 29 464, 476
Dimchev, Emil, I 5 158; 8 900*
Dimech, Ferdinando 8 900
Dimech, Vincenzo 8 900*; 20 214
Di Meghio 20 105
dimensions *see* MEASUREMENTS
Dimes, Marin 19 885
Dimier, Louis 8 900*; 11 547, 676
Dimini 8 900–901*; 13 *363*; 21 46, 551; 25 500, 503
Dimini period *see under* GREECE, ANCIENT → periods
Dimitrescu, Ştefan 26 716; 28 788
Dimitrescu-Mirea, George 5 73; 26 714
Dimitriadis, Constantin 23 747
Dimitrijević, Braco 4 461; 8 179, 901*
Dimitrijević, Vojo 4 461
Dimitriyev, Vladimir 28 757
Dimitroff, Vladimir *see* DIMITROV-MAISTORA, VLADIMIR
Dimitrov, Ivan 5 154
Dimitrov, Khristo 5 154; 27 685; 33 695
Dimitrov, Lyouben 3 625; 32 78
Dimitrov, Stefan 5 158
Dimitrov-Maistora, Vladimir 8 901*
works 5 155
Dimitrov-Maistora Museum *see under* KYUSTENDIL
Dimitsana, Philosophos Monastery 25 336
Dimmert, Egor I. 29 555
Dimova, Irena 5 159
Dimowa, Louis 20 161
Dimsdale, Thomas 8 901*; 23 777; 33 154, 345
Dinan Castle 8 901–2*, *902*; 11 *504*
Dinant 3 *539*; 13 159
brass 3 602, 603; 4 688
marks 3 601
metalwork 3 602; 22 894
Notre-Dame 13 98, 99
sculpture 13 114
Dinant, Herry de *see* BLES, HERRI MET DE
Dinara
kiosks 18 *72*
Dinckmut, Konrad 30 487
Dine, Jim 8 902–4*; 31 608
collaboration 11 777; 20 605, 607
etchings 10 563
groups and movements 10 416; 25 231, 232
Happenings 24 407
installations 15 868
lithographs 19 493
methods 9 310
objets trouvés 8 *903*; 23 334
paintings 10 482
prints 5 726; 21 897; 25 621
woodcuts 33 364
Di Negro (family) 12 284
Dinet, Alphonse-Etienne 1 634; 28 597
ding *see under* VESSELS → types
Ding Daohu 6 745
Ding Gao 6 814
Ding Jieyin 6 733
Ding Jing 7 130
Dingley, Robert 10 329
Dinglinger, Georg-Christoph 8 904
Dinglinger, Georg-Friedrich 8 904; 9 240; 12 457
Dinglinger, Johann Frederich 8 416
Dinglinger, Johann Melchior 8 904*
collaboration 24 460
patrons and collectors 9 238; 33 114, *114*
works 2 456; 9 240; 10 96; 12 447, 455, 457, 461
Dingli parish church 20 214
Dingmaoqiao (Dantu) 7 23, 24
Ding Nanyu *see* DING YUNPENG
Ding ware *see under* PORCELAIN → wares
Ding xian
glass 7 82, 83
Jingzhi Temple 6 778
Jingzhong Monastery 6 776, 778
kilns 6 896
porcelain 6 895; 7 25
reliquaries 26 150
Ding Yanyong 14 722
Ding Yunpeng 2 95; 7 119; 8 905*; 20 286
Dinham, John, Lord 13 196
Dinh Bo Lang 32 486
Dini, Antonio 31 446, 447; 32 205
Dini, Gerozzo 3 303
Dini, Giovanni 27 650
Dini, Giuseppa 32 205
Dini, Lucia 32 205
Dini, Pietro 27 650
dining halls *see under* HALLS → types
dining-rooms 25 304
dining-tables *see under* TABLES → types
Diniz, King of Portugal (*reg* 1279-1325) 1 590; 9 104; 31 101; 32 539
Di Nizzoli, Giuseppe 10 91
Dinka 1 237, 409, 411
aesthetics 1 *238*
architecture 1 307, 311
beads 1 297
jewellery 1 351
Dinkeloo, John 22 366; 26 480
Dinkelsbühl 8 905–6*; 12 *361*
St Georg 8 905–6*, *906*; 12 365; 13 161; 14 80; 32 90
Spitalkirche 1 711
Dinklage, August Georg 13 677
Dinky Toys 31 257
Din Llugwy 32 780
Dinna 18 536
Dinnyawadi *see* DHANNAVATI
Dino, Abidin 31 454
Dinocrates 9 852
Dinogetia church 26 706
dinoi 8 906*; 10 *614*; 13 *507*, *509*
Dinorwig 32 783
Dinos Painter 13 522, 524; 32 48, 65, 68
Dinpanah *see under* DELHI
Dinsmoor, Samuel Perry 22 441
Dinsmoor, William Bell 8 906–7*
Dinsmore, James 17 468
Dinteville (family) 11 532
Dinteville, François, Bishop of Auxerre 3 209; 8 907*
Dinteville, Jean de, Seigneur de Polisy *see* POLISY, JEAN DE DINTEVILLE, Seigneur de
Dintr-un Lemn Monastery 26 720
Dinzenhofer, Wolfgang 32 822
Diocaesarea *see* OLBA
Dio Cassius 6 72
Diocletian, Emperor of Rome (*reg* 284-305) 8 907*; 26 902; 27 *43*, 52
architecture
curiae 26 867
fora 26 783
mausoleum 20 864
military 9 849; 23 891; 27 343
palaces 2 156; 8 175; 23 809; 26 870, 907; 29 417
triumphal arches 31 350
writings 26 876
coins 27 *96*
ivory 9 647
sculpture 27 43
Diocletianopolis *see* HISSAR
Diodone, Niklaas 23 460
Diodoros 18 460
Diodorus Siculus 10 618, 624, 632; 13 807
Diogenes 9 636, *637*
Diogenes of Athens 27 30, 31
Diogg, Felix Maria 8 907–8*; 30 133
Diogo, Mestre 1 590
Diogo Cão 2 85
Diogo de Castilho 14 609; 17 596
Diola 1 256; 13 835
Diomede, Miguel 2 400; 8 908*
Diomedes 9 636, *637*
Diomed Painter 13 571
Dion (Greece) 13 384; 19 880
Basilica A 9 565
Dion (family)
works 5 581, *581*
Dion, Antoine (1825-1902) 8 908
Dion, Antoine, jr (1846-1915) 8 908
Dion, Henri de 10 683
Dion, Jean-Baptiste 8 908
Dion, Joseph 8 908
Dioneo, Doriclo *see* ERCOLANI, FILIPPO, Marchese
Dionigi d'Andrea di Bernardo di Lottino 22 800
Dionisio, Fra 1 588
Dionisio Fiammingo *see* CALVAERT, DENYS
Dionisy 8 908–9*; 10 889; 15 895; 22 176; 27 384
collaboration 10 890
works 8 *909*; 22 182; 25 337, 342; 27 400
workshop 10 890
Dionyse, Carmen 3 573, 592
Dionysianopolis *see* BALCHIK
Dionysias 10 758
fortress 9 849
temple 10 759
Dionysios 8 909–10*; 13 549, 551; 27 27; 30 915
works 13 547; 24 227
Dionysios I (*reg* 405-367 BC) 21 556, 557
Dionysios of Argos 1 481
Dionysios of Furna 8 910*; 22 228
works 7 223; 15 82; 32 804
writings 25 331
Dionysius *see* DIONISY
Dionysodoros *see* DIODOROS
Diop, Sheikh Marône 28 406
diopside-jadeite *see under* JADE → types
dioptra 13 412
Dior, Christian 9 293
dioramas 7 327; 8 910–11*, *911*; 24 18; 28 206; 31 155
dioramascopio 25 217
diorite 29 699
historical and regional traditions
Aztec 21 243
Egypt, ancient 9 *869*; 29 700
Maya 21 *251*
Mesoamerica, Pre-Columbian 21 243, *251*
Mesopotamia 21 294; 29 X2; 30 *423*
Sumerian 29 X2
Syria 2 *661*
uses
mummy cases 28 *667*
sculpture 2 *661*; 9 *869*; 21 294; 29 X2; 30 *423*
Dios, Alberto de la Madre de *see* MADRE DE DIOS, ALBERTO DE LA
Dioscorides, Pedanius 4 682
Diósgyőr 14 *881*
Castle 14 883, 904
Dioskourides (*fl* 1st cent. BC; gem-engraver) 6 117; 12 250
works 12 *250*
Dioskourides of Samos (*fl* 1st cent. BC; mosaicist) 13 552, 557; 25 205
Dioskuren, Die 24 444; 28 56
Dioskuri 9 20
Dioskurides (*fl* 1st cent. AD; author) 9 520, 617; 12 72, 108, 287; 14 432; 21 5
Diosphos Painter 13 511
Diospolis *see under* LOD
Diospolis Parva 8 911–12*; 9 *774*
Diotimos 1 618
Diotisalvi 8 912*; 24 868
Diotti, Giuseppe 5 783; 7 528; 8 912*
Dip Chand, Ruler (*reg* 1650-67) (Pahari) 15 593, 624
Diphilos (*fl* 1st cent. BC; sculptor) 27 111
Diphilus (*fl* 1st cent. AD; architect) 26 884
diphros *see under* CHAIRS → types
diphros okladias *see under* CHAIRS → types
dipinto parolibero 7 557
diplomatic gifts 7 562; 9 509, 657; 10 324; 14 323; 16 413, 429, 445; 29 788
Diploma works 9 1–2*
Dipoinos 8 457; 13 439, 596; 25 44
dippers 9 2*
Dipre, Antoine 9 2
Dipre, Nicolas, the elder (*fl* 1464-*d* before 1508) 9 2; 20 703
Dipre, Nicolas (*fl* 1492-*d* 1532) 9 2–3*; 29 638; 31 843
dipteral temples *see under* TEMPLES → types
diptych of Boethius 16 686
diptychs (altarpieces) *see under* ALTARPIECES → types
diptychs (consular) *see* CONSULAR DIPTYCHS
Diputación Provincial de Caracas 32 180

Dipylon Head **13** 470
Dipylon Kouros **2** 687
Dipylon Master **32** 38–9*
works **2** 687; **13** 494, *494*
Di Qiong **28** 589
Diquís **13** 290, 291
Diraz temple **2** 251
Dirce Painter **13** 530; **28** 655; **30** 175
Dirc Jansz. **20** 781
Dircksen, Ernst **25** 856
Dircksz., Barend **3** 230
Dirc van Delft, Master of **22** 835
direct dyes *see under* DYES → types
Directoire style **9** 5*
frames **11** 411–13, *412*
see also ARABESQUE STYLE
directories **2** 364, 367
direct positive photography *see under* PHOTOGRAPHY → types
Diren, Sadi **31** 455
Diriamba **23** *79*
parish church **23** 84
Diricksen, Felipe **9** 5*; **14** 6
Diriditis *see* BASRA
Dirijiu church **26** 711
Dir'iyah **32** 316
Dirks, Rudolph **7** 648
Dirksen, Onnen **22** 317
Dirk van Staren *see* VELLERT, DIRK (JACOBSZ.)
Dirlos **26** 712
Dirmil **5** 741
Di Rosa, Hervé **11** 553
Dirr, Alois **9** 6
Dirr, Franz Anton **9** 5–6*; **11** 44; **27** 555
Dirr, Johann Georg **9** 5–6*; **11** 44; **12** 405; **27** 555; **33** 163
Dirr, Johann Sebastian **9** 6
Dirr, Martin **9** 6; **28** 118
Discalced Carmelites *see* CARMELITE ORDER
disc chapels *see under* CHAPELS → types
disc crosses *see* CROSSES → types → *Scheibenkreuz*
discharge dyeing *see under* DYEING → types
Discher, (Carl) Marcus *see* TUSCHER, MARCUS
discourses on art **1** 102
discs **7** 2, 81, 102; **29** 191, 218
discs, compact *see* CD-ROM
discs, optical *see* OPTICAL DISCS
discs, video *see* VIDEO DISCS
Disdéri, André Adolphe Eugène **9** 6*; **24** 649, 661
pupils **24** 552
works **24** *660*
disegno **1** 102, 557–8; **6** 14; **13** 133; **24** 91; **32** 19, 21
disegno e colore **3** 265; **7** 628; **9** 6–9*, *8*, 74–5; **24** 827–8
England **9** 8*
France **9** 8–9*; **19** 22; **25** 398
Italy **9** 6–8*; **31** 44
Disentis **30** 126
Disform **29** 547
Dishasha **10** 44, 45, 76
tomb of Shedu **9** 822
Dish Painter **13** 538
dish rings **16** 32
Disidentes, Los **5** 873; **12** 920; **23** 629; **24** 401; **32** 176
Disieult, Jean *see* DIZIEULT, JEAN
Disk **24** 440
Diskobolos **6** 9; **13** *422*; **22** 690; **23** 291; **27** 46; **31** 49
Diskow, Hans von **14** 369
Disler, Martin **30** 135, 140
Disloias **13** 570
Dismorr, Jessica **9** 9*; **13** 712; **32** 701; **33** 703
Disnematin-Dorat, Jean-Baptiste **26** 39
Disney, Walt(er Elias) **8** 468; **9** 10*
Disney, Walt, Studio **5** 531; **8** 124; **30** 729
Disney Painter **32** 40
D'Isola, Aimaro *see* ISOLA, AIMARO D'
di sotto in sù **9** 11*; **14** *729*; **15** *136*, 136
see also PAINTING → types → *quadratura*; TROMPE L'OEIL
display cases **7** 736*; **9** 11
display of art **2** 299, 552, 560; **7** 560, 565, 736*; **8** 911; **9** 11–31*; **10** 675
Australia **22** 360
Austria **9** 14, 18, 19; **22** *356*
Belgium **9** 15–16, 22
Czech Republic **9** 14
England **9** 11, 14, 16–17, *17*, 18–19, 22, 23–5, *26*; **10** 371
France **7** 561; **9** 11, 14, 18, 22, 23, 25, *28*; **22** 357–8, *358*, 359; **24** *138*, 139
Germany **9** 14, 18, *27*; **12** 475; **22** 358
Greece, ancient **9** 13, 20; **13** 604*
Italy **9** 11, *11*, *12*, 14–15, *15*, 18, 20–22, *22*, 23; **14** 867; **26** *837*
Japan **1** 777; **17** 76, 335, 342, 367, 423
see also TOKONOMA
Jewish art **17** *581*
Native North Americans **22** 360
Netherlands, the **1** *809*; **9** 15, 22
Rome, ancient **9** 13, 20
Russia **9** 18
Spain **9** 15, 18
Sweden **9** 23, 26, *26*
United States of America **2** 710; **22** 359, 360, 673, 678; **23** *47*, *49*
see also COLLECTIONS; EXHIBITIONS; FRAMES; LIGHTING; MOUNTS
displuviate houses *see under* HOUSES → types
Disraeli, Benjamin **3** 241; **18** 667
Dissanayake, Sumana **29** 468
Dissard, Paul **19** 848
Dissel, J. P. F. van **22** 899
dissemination **9** 33–8*; **15** 94
Dissertation Abstracts International **4** 26
dissertations **4** 26–7*
Dissing, Hans **8** 729; **16** 828
Dissius, Jacob (Abrahamsz.) **32** 263, 267
Distances **5** 44
Di Stasio, Stefano **16** 683
Distéfano, Juan Carlos **2** 401; **5** 123; **9** 38–9*
Distel, De **22** 883; **23** 120, 125
Distelbarth, Friedrich **9** 39*
Disteli, Martin **9** 39*; **30** 133
distemper paint *see under* PAINTS → types
distortion **24** 379–80, *380*, 651
distyle **9** 39*
distyle *in antis* **9** 39; **13** 376
distyle temples *see under* TEMPLES → types
Di Suvero, Mark **9** 39–40*; **31** 614
Ditcheat (Somerset), St Mary Magdalene **7** 837
ditches **12** 174, 176; **21** 546, 558, 559, 565, 567
ha has *see* HA HAS
Ditchley Park (Oxon) **10** 278; **26** 499
furniture **10** 294
interior decoration **11** 427
paintings **12** 514
sculpture **5** 827
stucco **29** 835
Ditchley Portrait **31** 415
Ditchling **14** 544; **17** 631
Diterrot *see* ROTH, DIETER
Ditherington (Salop)
Marshall, Benyon & Bage Flour Mill **10** 748; **16** 52
Ditlevsen, Eva *see* KOPPEL, EVA
Ditmar, Jean **19** 257
Dittborn, Eugenio **6** 598; **9** 40*
Ditterich, Bernard **23** 252
Dittman, Reinhard **17** 826
Dittmann, Christian **23** 195
Dittmar, Heinrich **14** 25
Dityat'yev, Nikolay (Gordivich) **27** 425
Ditzel, Nanna **8** 753; **17** 529
Ditzinger, Gustav Adolf **13** 864; **14** 230; **30** 95
Diu **9** 40*; **15** *276*, 401
Diulgheroff, Nicolay **11** 80
Divākara **5** 493
Divambika (Nolamba) **15** 529; **23** 182
Divan Club **2** 164
dīvānī script *see under* SCRIPTS → types
Diviaky church **28** 849
divination instruments **1** 355–8*, *356*; **5** 330*; **19** *742*, 742–3*
Divino, El *see* MORALES, LUIS DE
Divisionism **9** 40–41*; **22** 745; **24** 375; **25** 78; **28** 697, 698
commentaries **25** 568
exhibitions **28** 319
regional traditions
France **28** 500, 501, *698*
Italy **5** 918; **13** 714; **22** 84; **25** 567, *567*
Netherlands, the **28** 864
see also NEO-IMPRESSIONISM; POINTILLISM
Divodurum *see* METZ
Divorne, Daniel **16** 68
Divriği **9** 41*; **16** *104*
fortifications **16** 186
Great Mosque **16** 183, 245, 497
hospital of Turan Melik **16** 184, 245
Kale Mosque **16** 183
Divy, Jean **13** 277
Dix, Gerald **1** 29
Dix, (Wilhelm Heinrich) Otto **9** 41–3*; **12** 395; **25** 651
groups and movements **3** 802; **9** 239; **10** 695; **12** 396; **22** 922, 923; **23** 267
patrons and collectors **28** 273; **29** 875
pupils **26** 357
works **8** 597; **9** *42*, 292; **12** 396; **22** *922*; **23** 297; **28** 920; **31** 345; **33** 363
Dixcove **1** 318
Dixon, Alice **21** 263
Dixon, Anne **2** 690
Dixon, Arthur **10** 336, 344
Dixon, Cornelius **3** 179
Dixon, Fenella Mary Anne **9** 43; **31** 242
Dixon, Henry **23** 688
Dixon, James, & Sons **9** 295; **10** 343; **28** 576
Dixon, Jeremy **9** 43*; **28** 232; **31** 242
Dixon, John **5** 216; **9** 43*; **21** 416
Dixon, L. Murray **21** 421
Dixon, Nicholas **9** 44*; **21** 640
Dixon, Peter **9** 55
Dixon, Samuel **16** 33
Dixon, William **20** 52
Dixon & Ross **25** 627
Dixons & Sons **28** 577
Dixson, William **2** 771
D.I.Y. **10** 285
Diyala region **1** *849*; **9** 44–6*; **11** 732; **21** *267*
brick **4** *771*
bronze **4** 850
cities **1** 893
figurines **9** *45*
fortifications **21** 552
pottery **21** 306
sculpture **21** 294
seals **1** 860
Diyarbakır **9** 46–7*; **16** *104*, 379
Behram Pasha Mosque **16** 221, 222
Büyük Mehmed **9** 47
ceramics **16** 413
Church of Mar Yakub **9** 620, 621
congregational mosque **16** 179, *179*
Fatıh Pasha *see* Büyük Mehmed
houses **16** 270
Ibrahim Bey Mosque **16** 202
manuscripts **16** 308, 327
Mesudiye Madrasa **16** 180
metalwork **16** 364
palace **12** 78; **16** 182, 363
pottery **16** 420
sculpture **16** 247
Şeyh Matar Mosque **16** 202
tiles **16** 422
town walls **21** 583
Zinciriye Madrasa **16** 180
Díz, Antonio **2** 397
Díz de Vivar y Mendoza, Rodrigo, Marqués del Zenete *see* ZENETE, RODRIGO DÍZ DE VIVAR Y MENDOZA, Marqués del
Dizengoff, Meir **16** 571
Diziani, Antonio **9** 48
Diziani, Gaspare **9** 47–8*
pupils **9** 740
reproductive prints by others **21** 831
teachers **18** 901
works **9** *48*; **31** 316
Diziani, Giuseppe **9** 48, 740
Dizieult, Jean **9** 48–9*; **28** 409
Djabrail **2** *890*, 901
Djadjur, Avetisyan Museum **2** 858
Djaja, Agus **15** 807, 808, 818
Djaja, Otto **15** 807
Djak, Zivko **28** 452
Djakarta *see* JAKARTA
Djakovia, Hadim Mosque **28** 444
Djakovica **28** 444, 454
Djalilov, K. **29** 823
Djalmulchanov, Garif **17** 868
Djandjiberd fortress **2** 427
Djane *see* TANIS
Djanenjebu **27** 813
(Motta e Silva,) Djanira (da) **4** 719; **9** 49*
Djar **9** 900
Djau **12** 227, 228
Djaul **24** 85
Djauty *see* ASYUT
Djeba *see* EDFU
Djebel Amour **16** 486
Djebjerg **6** 159
Djedbastetefankh **10** *15*
Djed-djehutiiwefankh **24** 555
Djedkare (*reg c.* 2388–*c.* 2356 BC) **9** *776*
Djedmaatiusankh **9** 905
Djehutihotpe **3** 848; **9** 815, 823, 824
costumes **10** *43*
tombs **9** *816*
Djehutinakhte **3** 848
Djehutinefer **9** 808
Djeitun *see* DZHEYTUN
El Djem *see* THYSDRUS
Djemila **3** 191; **9** 49–50*; **23** 300
Arch of Caracalla **26** 868, 920, 922; **31** 350
baths **26** 919
Cuicul **1** 634; **9** *510*; **27** 72
double basilica **9** 535
forum **26** 921
houses **26** 920
markets **19** 888; **26** 871, 919
monopteros **21** 893
mosaics **27** 63
Museum **1** 636
North Church **9** 570
temple of the Severan family **2** 297; **26** *866*, 867, 919, 922
urban planning **27** 4
Djenné **1** 224, *381*
architecture **1** 315; **20** 198
fortifications **21** 597
Friday Mosque **1** *316*, 317; **4** 793; **20** 198
sculpture **1** 280
textiles **20** 198
Djer **9** *776*; **10** 29, 50; **27** 810
Djerba
jewellery **16** 532
Khara-Kbira **17** 551
Khara-Zrira **17** 551
Djerma **23** 127, *128*
Djeserkareseneb **10** 65
Djeserkheprure *see* HOREMHEB
Djibuti (country) **1** *214*, 378; **9** 50*
Djibuti (town) **1** *379*
Djilgu **10** 474
Djiwal, Jack *see* WUNUWUN, JACK
Djo-Bourgeois, Georges **23** 169
Djogdjakarta *see* YOGYAKARTA
Djola **1** 392
Djordjević, Miodrag **28** 452
Djoser (*reg c.* 2630–*c.* 2611 BC) **9** *776*, 789; **10** 47; **25** 761
architecture **9** 819, 833; **11** 231; **20** 863; **25** *761*; **27** 810, *810*, 811; **31** 107
ceramics **10** *47*
reliefs **9** 868, 891; **20** 571
sculpture **9** 867; **29** 615
Djoser, funerary complex of *see under* SAQQARA
Djoser, mortuary temple of *see* SAQQARA → pyramids → Step Pyramid
Djrvezh basilica **2** 425
Djuka
combs (hair) **1** *423*
Djukulul, Dorothy **21** 621
Djuric, Miodrag *see* DADO
Djuričić, Jakov **22** 18
Djurković, Pavel **28** 450
Djursholm, Villa Snellman **2** *611*
D'Kar **4** 489
Dlabač, Jan Bohumír **8** 426; **9** 50*
Dlouha Ves **8** 382
Dłubak, Zbigniew **4** 234; **9** 50–51*
Długosz, Jan **11** 149; **25** 95, 134; **33** 259
Dmachauskas, Vincentas *see* DMACHOŬSKI, VIKENCY
Dmachoŭski, T. **3** 530
Dmachoŭski, Vikency **3** 529; **19** 497
Dmanisi **12** 330
Dmitreyev-Mamonov, A. I. **27** 438
Dmitri IV Donskoy, Prince of Moscow (*reg* 1359–89) **32** 664
Dmitriyev, Aleksandr **12** 856
Dmitriyev, G. **27** 401
Dmitriyev, Maksim (Petrovich) **9** 51*; **24** 672; **28** 919
Dmitriyev, Sevast'yan **33** 507
Dmitriyev-Kavkazky, Lev Ye. **11** 82; **17** 732; **18** 528
Dmitrov **9** 51–2*; **27** *363*
Cathedral of the Dormition **30** 884
icons **25** 338; **27** 382; **31** 555
Dmitrov, Yury Ivanovich, Prince of **9** 51
Dmitrov Factory **27** 414
see also GARDNER PORCELAIN FACTORY
Dmitry **31** 557
DMKh *see* SOCIETY OF MOSCOW ARTISTS
Dmochowski, Z. R. **23** 135
Dmoelenyser **2** 201
Dmund, Hans **26** 249
Dneprgas **31** 552
Dnipropetrovs'k, Cathedral of the Transfiguration **31** 553
Do, Giovanni **9** 52*; **20** 617
Doane, George Washington, Bishop **31** 689, 691

Doat, Taxile 26 471; 27 565; 28 524
DOBAG cooperatives 16 479
Dobal, Narciso 25 701
Do Baradar 16 167
Dobbeleer, Claas de 10 222
Dobbelman, Theo 22 884
Dobbermann, Jacob 9 52–3*; 14 491
Döbel, Johann Christoph 9 53
Döbel, Johann Michael 9 53
Döbel, Michael 9 53*; 14 650
Döbeler, Michael see DÖBEL, MICHAEL
Dobell, William 2 750, 767, 770; 9 53–4*
Doberan Abbey 4 777; 12 400; 13 56; 27 125
Dobi, Eqerem 1 539
Dobie, James 9 54*
Dobie & Son 28 250
Dobkins, Walter 33 602
Döbler, Georg 8 405
Döblin, Alfred 29 872
Dobner, Jan Ignác 8 397, 398
Dobó, István 9 754
Dobolii-de-Jos 30 769
Dobova
 metalwork 6 153
Dobreisho Gospels see under GOSPEL BOOKS → individual manuscripts
Dobričević, Lovro 8 178; 25 340
Dobrinovich, P. 8 900
Dobříš, Mansfeld palace 8 379; 12 134; 25 33
Dobromilov Gospels see under GOSPEL BOOKS → individual manuscripts
Dobromir of Tîrgovişte 8 280; 25 344; 26 712
Dobrov, Matvey 18 477
Dobrova 28 859
 church 28 859
Dobrović, Nikola 9 54*; 28 445
Dobrović, Péter 1 131; 19 324; 20 103; 28 451
Dobrovo Gospels see under GOSPEL BOOKS → individual manuscripts
Dobrovol's'ky, Anatoli (Volodymyrovych) 9 54*; 33 518
Dobrowolski, Tadeusz 25 143
Dobrzyńska, Jadwiga 25 409
Dobson, Alexander 9 55
Dobson, Edward R. 30 504
Dobson, Frank (Owen) 9 54–5*
 groups and movements 13 712; 19 623
 works 10 267, 268; 28 299; 29 576; 30 500
Dobson, John 9 55*; 29 651
 groups and movements 32 415
 pupils 26 476
 works 23 20
Dobson, William (fl early 16th cent.; father) 3 30; 9 55
Dobson, William (1611-46; son) 9 55–7*
 patrons and collectors 5 311
 pupils 25 406
 reproductive prints by others 10 757
 teachers 7 431
 works 9 56; 10 248; 23 690
Dobursko 5 144
 SS Theodor Tyron and Theodor Stratilat 5 148, 156
Dobuzhinsky, Mstislav (Valerianovich) 9 57*; 32 412
 collaboration 32 724
 groups and movements 12 870; 27 580; 33 379, 740
 patrons and collectors 12 875
 pupils 1 507; 6 384; 9 495; 13 862; 20 850; 32 247
 works 27 413
Dobyrsko 25 339
Doccia 9 57–8*; 16 618, 620
Doccia porcelain factory 9 57–8*; 16 737, 739; 29 572
 designers 24 460; 29 30; 33 15
 works 16 737
Doceno, Il see GHERARDI, CRISTOFANO
Docharty, James 19 891
Dōchin Kitamuki see KITAMUKI DŌCHIN
Docimian marble see under MARBLE → types
Docimium see DOKIMEION
Döcker, Richard 9 59–60*
 groups and movements 8 826; 26 405
 pupils 8 631
 works 29 874
Docker River 1 43
Docket, Andrew 5 511
docks 9 58–9*, 59
Dockstader, Frederick J. 3 738
Doctor 15 168
Doctor, Albert 4 438
Doctor, Siegmund 14 320; 22 918
documentary photography see under PHOTOGRAPHY → uses
Documents 24 144; 30 20; 33 183
Dóczy, Orbán, Bishop 9 754; 13 888
Dodantale, Danagirigala Monastery 29 461
Dodart, Denis 26 452
Dodd, Margaret 2 762
Dodd, Ralph 9 60
Dodd, Robert 9 60*
Dodda Devaraja, Raja (reg 1659-72) (Wodeyar) 22 404
Dodda Gaddavalli, Lakshmidevi Temple 15 328, 532
Doddington Hall (Cheshire) 11 430; 33 443
Dodds, Margaret see WEST, MARGARET
Dodé 24 149
Dodeigne, Eugène 9 60*; 11 569; 19 381
Dodeka, Ta 22 714
Dodens, Rembert 14 433
Doderer, Wilhem von 5 792; 26 718
Dodeweerd, H. D. van see ARMANDO
Dodge, Mabel 29 643
Dodge, Nehemiah 13 9
Dodgson, Campbell 9 60–61*
Dodgson, Charles L(utwidge) see CARROLL, LEWIS
Dodington, Bubb 1 533
Dodington, George Bubb, 1st Baron Melcombe 4 805
Dodington Park 8 48; 10 235
Dodo (Australia) 1 44
Dodo (Burkina Faso) 1 342
 masks 1 341
Dodoma 1 407
Dodona 9 61*; 13 363, 418
 Basilica 9 538
 bronzes 13 572
 helmets 10 585
 metalwork 10 591
 Theatre 13 406, 418
Dodonaeus, R. 19 64
Dodong sŏwŏn 18 270
Dodos-Rka see under DAVID GAREDZHI
Dodrell, John 4 78
Dods, Espie 2 743
Dods, Robin 2 741; 4 818; 7 619; 9 61–2*
Dods, R(obert) S(mith) see DODS, ROBIN
Dodsley, Robert 3 330; 10 364
Dodson, Betty 10 483
Dodson, Richard 8 776
Dodwell, Edward 2 667; 10 91; 32 385
Dodwell Painter 13 505
Doell, Frederick Wilhelm Eugen 28 45
Dōen 17 228
Doerner, Max 2 381; 10 191
Doerpfeld, W. 19 258
Does, A. van der 7 556
Does, Jacob van der 21 791
Does, Simon van der 13 2
Doesburg, St Maartenskerk 22 821
Doesburg, Nelly van 1 77; 29 661
Doesburg, Theo van 3 111, 564; 9 62–4*; 11 550; 19 476; 21 853; 22 852; 23 663; 24 428
 collaboration 2 490; 9 745; 23 663; 26 410; 28 197; 30 234; 33 215
 groups and movements 1 76; 22 852; 31 852
  Abstract art 1 73, 75
  Abstraction-Création 1 90
  Art Concret 1 76; 5 776; 7 772; 14 329
  Bauhaus 3 401; 12 407; 21 782
  Concrete art 7 698
  Constructivism 7 770; 8 437
  Dada 8 437
  Elementarism 10 137–8
  environmental art 10 415
  Moderne Kunstkring 29 660
  Sphinx, De 29 397
  Stijl, De 1 75, 76, 90, 815; 7 770; 22 868, 875; 29 660, 661; 33 154
  theosophy 30 711
 methods 7 630; 28 202
 patrons and collectors 2 409
 works 2 337; 9 63; 11 360; 32 902
 writings 11 525; 17 833; 27 163
Doetechum, Baptist van 9 64; 10 550; 25 625
Doetechum, Jan van (fl 1554-95) 7 499; 9 64*; 10 389; 14 5; 17 598; 20 769
Doetechum, Jan van (d 1630) 9 64; 10 550; 25 246, 625
Doetechum, Lucas van 7 499; 9 64*; 10 389; 14 5; 17 598; 20 769
Doeve, Jan de 10 222
Dofigso
 masks 4 193
Doğançay, Burham 31 454
Dōgen 5 119; 10 112; 17 215
Doge's Palace see under VENICE → palazzi
dog-hair see under HAIR → types
Dogon 1 384–5; 9 64–9*; 22 196
 architecture 1 260, 312; 9 68–9*
 blacksmiths 9 65
 collections 9 64
 craftsmen and artists 9 65
 doors 1 314; 9 164
 erotic art 10 473
 figurines 1 273
 gesture 1 264, 265, 266
 granaries 1 263; 9 68
 iconography 1 261, 263, 275, 280
 iron 9 69
 leather 1 322
 masks 1 290, 339, 342; 9 67–8*, 68
 meeting-houses 1 309, 310, 314
 metal 1 322
 metalwork 9 69*
 musical instruments 1 358
 nude figures 9 66, 67
 sculpture 1 231, 262, 280, 322, 322; 9 66, 66–7*, 67
 shutters (window) 9 69
 villages 21 597
 wood 1 262, 322; 9 66, 67, 68, 69, 164
 wood-carvings 9 66, 69, 69
Dog Palette 9 868
Dogrib 22 546, 645
dogtooth 9 70*
dogū see under FIGURINES → types
Dogues, Les see LES DOGUES
Doha
 House of Muhammad Nasrullah 25 776
 museums 2 275
 National Museum 25 776, 777
 Sheraton Hotel 25 776
 University of Qatar Library 19 321
 'Uthman ibn 'Affan Mosque 16 242, 243
Dōhachi Nin'ami (1740-1804) see NIN'AMI DŌHACHI
Dōhachi Nin'ami (1783-1855) see TAKAHASHI DŌHACHI
Dōhachi Takahashi see TAKAHASHI DŌHACHI
Dohan Kaigetsudō see KAIGETSUDŌ DOHAN
Dohasan III, Chief 28 741
Doheny, Estelle 20 790
Doheny Master 20 789, 790
Dohme, Robert 15 122
Dohna (family) 21 510
Dohrn, Anton 20 405
Dohrn, Wolf 8 825; 14 362; 30 520
Dohuk 21 303
Doi (family) 17 811
Doicescu, Octav 9 70*; 26 709
Doiceşti church 26 713
Dòid Mhàiri 32 530
Doiger, Marx 33 31
Doirat, Etienne 9 71*
 attributions 11 592
Doire na bhFlann 8 782
Doisneau, Robert 6 167; 9 71*; 24 678; 31 706
Do-It-Yourself see D.I.Y.
Dōjin Fūgai see FŪGAI EKUN
Dōjin Nishimura see NISHIMURA DŌJIN
Dokathismata 1 795; 8 304, 315
Dŏkhŭng 18 328
Dokimasia Painter 13 521; 32 36
Dokimeion 9 72*; 13 362; 26 908
 marble 26 854, 855, 875, 876, 911; 27 826, 827; 29 702
  see also under MARBLE → types
 sculpture 27 28
Dokkum, Gerardus Wilhelmus van 22 891
Dokoupil, Jiří Georg 9 72*; 12 397; 31 356
Dokra 15 175
Doksany convent 8 376, 398; 26 637
Dokuchayev, Nikolay (Vasil'yevich) 9 73*; 32 661
 assistants 28 747
 collaboration 18 457
 groups and movements 2 603; 18 620
Dokumenta Archiv für die Kunst des 20 Jahrhunderts see under KASSEL → Neue Galerie
Dokumentum 17 833; 24 441
Dokuritsu Bijutsu Kyōkai (Independent Art Society) 17 206; 18 194; 29 894
Dokuritsu shojindan 17 239
Dokuryū Shōeki 9 73–4*; 17 234, 235, 409
Dokutan 20 286
Dolabella, Tommaso 9 74*; 18 428
 patrons and collectors 19 498; 32 6, 7
 works 18 431; 25 104; 32 874
Dolādri see CHANGU NARAYAN
Dolagiri see CHANGU NARAYAN
Dolāśikhara see CHANGU NARAYAN
Dölauer Heide 25 504
Dolbadarn Castle (Caerns) 32 781
Dolbeare, Edmund 4 481; 31 651
Dolbeare, John 4 481
Dolce, Ludovico 9 74–5*; 10 739
 works 9 7; 10 739; 15 82; 16 614, 665; 21 459; 23 680; 24 90; 29 400; 31 768
 on beauty 1 178
 on disegno e colore 7 628
 on painting 24 90
 on poesie 25 71
 translated 32 670
Dolcebuono, Giovanni Giacomo 9 75*
 attributions 21 517
 collaboration 4 645; 11 691; 21 532
 patrons and collectors 28 532
 works 3 385; 4 645; 6 357; 16 630; 29 23
Dolcet, Manuel 27 304
dolcezza see SWEETNESS
Dolci, Agnese 9 79
Dolci, Carlo 9 76–9*; 13 300
 patrons and collectors
  Caraman, Duc de 5 700
  Cecil, John, 5th Earl of Exeter 6 128; 10 364; 13 299
  Cosimo III, Grand Duke of Tuscany (reg 1670-1723) 21 29
  Medici, Lorenzo de' (1599–1648) 21 26
  Methuen, Paul (1672-1757) 21 348
  Poniatowski, Stanisław, Prince 25 213
  Souza, Madame de 22 126
  Yusupov, Nikolay (Borisovich), Prince (1751- 1831) 33 579
 reproductive prints by others 18 45
 teachers 32 500
 works 9 76, 77; 11 459; 16 673
Dolci, Giovanni de' 26 815
Dolcibene 33 385
Dol-de-Bretagne, St Samson 13 179
Dolder, Andreas 30 144
Dole 19 538
Dolema, César 27 639
Dolendo, Bartholomeus (Willemsz.) 9 79*, 192
Dolendo, Zacharias 9 79*; 10 387; 12 532; 20 247
Dolenja Vas Church 28 860
dolerite 9 814
Dolfin (family) 5 532
Dolfin', Cardinal 29 252
Dolfin, Dionisio 30 856
Dolfin, Jakob 13 191
Dolfin, Juan 31 92
Dolfus, Nicolas, & Cie 33 711
Dolgellau, St Mary 32 786
Dolgelley Chalice 10 322
Dolgelley Paten 10 322
Dölger, Franz Joseph 18 107
Doliana 29 702
Dolin, Anton 3 119
Dolin, Nicolas 11 618
Dolina 31 557
Dolinar, Lojze 13 263; 28 862
Dolinsek, Rafael 8 181
Dolishhan Church 11 451; 30 306
Dolla, Noël 11 552; 30 6
dollar rugs see under RUGS → types
Dollars, Avida see DALÍ (DOMÉNECH), SALVADOR (FELIPE JACINT)
Dolley House 3 63
Dollfus, Jean 17 619; 26 207
Döllgast, Hans 12 379, 477
Dollmann, Georg von 9 80*; 29 843
 collaboration 12 376
 patrons and collectors 12 376
 works 23 813, 814; 33 283
Dollmann, J. C. 1 146
Dollmayr, Hermann 28 344

dolls **31** 259–62*
historical and regional traditions
Africa **1** 419; **31** 261
Alaska **31** 259, 260
Bali (Indonesia) **31** 260
Bangladesh **3** 169
Burkina Faso **22** *198*
China **31** 259, 261
Egypt **31** 260
Egypt, ancient **31** 259, 261
England **31** 259, 260, *262*
France **31** 262
Germany **31** 259, 261, *261*, 262
Greece, ancient **31** 259
Guatemala **31** 261
Indian subcontinent **15** 731; **31** 259
Inuit **31** 259, 260
Japan **17** 262, 371–3*; **31** 259, 261
Mexico **31** 259, 261
Montenegro **31** 260
Mossi **22** 198*, *198*; **31** 259
Native North Americans **22** 574, 669; **31** 260
Ndebele **1** 419
Netherlands, the **31** 259
Peru **31** 259, 260, 261
Poland **31** 259
Portugal **31** 261
Rome, ancient **31** 259
Siberia **31** 260
South America, Pre-Columbian **31** 261
Spain **31** 261
Sweden **31** 260
United States of America **31** 260, 261
Zulu **1** 419
materials
automata **17** 373
bark **31** 260
beads **1** *420*
beadwork **3** 442
brocades **17** 371
clay **17** 371, *372*, 373
corn **31** 260
cotton-wood **22** 583, *583*
deerskin **31** 260
earthenwares **17** 262
feathers **22** *583*; **31** 260
felt **31** 260
gesso **31** 259
glass **17** 371, *373*
glues **31** 261
gold **17** 372
grasses **31** 260
hinoki (Japanese cypress) **17** 372
horsehair **31** 260
human hair **17** 371, *373*; **31** 260, 261
ivory **17** 371; **31** 259
kid-skin **31** 260, 262
leather **31** 260
linen **31** 259
lithographs **31** 262
mica **17** 371
mohair **31** 261
palm leaves **31** 260
paper **17** 371; **31** 258, 259–60*
papier mâché **17** 373; **24** 62; **31** 262
papyrus **31** 259
paulownia **17** 371
porcelain **31** 260–61*, *261*
pottery **31** 261*
rags **31** 259, 260
rubber **31** 260
sawdust **31** 260, 261
silk **17** 371
straw **17** 371, 373
sugar **31** 260
terracotta **31** 259
textiles **31** 260*
tin **31** 262*
waxes **31** 262*, *262*
willow **17** 372
wire **31** 260
dolls
materials—cont.
wood **17** 371, 372; **22** 198, *198*; **31** 259*, 262
techniques
chromolithography **31** 259
stencilling **31** 259
types
daruma **17** 373
dressing **31** 259
fertility **1** *420*
gosho **17** 371*, *372*
hina **17** 371*; **31** 260
Ichimatsu **17** 372–3*, *373*
kachina **22** 582–4, *583*; **31** 259
Kamo **17** 372*
kimekomi **17** 372*
kokeshi **17** 372*
Matryoshka **20** 222; **31** 259
Nara **17** 372*
peg **31** 259
rag **31** 260
Saga **17** 372*
tsuchibina **17** 373*
see also TEDDY BEARS
dolls' furniture **31** 264–5*, *264*
dolls' houses **31** 262–4*, *263*
Dolmabahçe *see* ISTANBUL
Dolmen, Andrzej **25** 119
Dolmen Press **1** 147; **16** 18
dolmens *see under* TOMBS → types
dolmens à couloir see under TOMBS → types
Dolna Kamenica Church **5** 151
Dolná Krupá Castle **28** 850
Dolní Kounice Cathedral **8** 376
Dolní Věstonice **8** *374*; **9** 80–81*; **25** *470*, *471*, 492
figurines **25** 488
Dolný Kubín, Orava Gallery **28** 857
dolomite **25** 174
Dolon Painter **13** 525
Dolores Hidalgo **21** 392
Dolphin Chandelier **11** 626
Dolphin Group **13** 510
Dolsk church **25** 96
Dolst, Christian Gottlieb **11** 760
Dolwyddelan Castle (Caerns) **32** 781
Dom, osiedle, mieszkanie **24** 441
Doma **15** 101
Domanek, Anton Matthias **2** 820
works **2** *820*
Domanovszky, Endre **9** 81*; **14** 902
Domány, Ferenc **14** 634
Domaszewski, Alfred von **22** 419; **24** 556, 557
Domat-Ems **30** 145
Dombay, Guillaume *see* DOMBET, GUILLAUME
Domberger, Luitpold **20** 607; **28** 299
Dombet, Aubry **7** 525; **9** 81, 82; **13** 264
Dombet, Guillaume **6** 469; **7** 525; **9** 81–2*; **13** 264; **20** 614
Dombet, Jacques **9** 81, 82
Dombet, Jean **9** 81
Dombó **14** 891
Dombrena Painter **13** 534
Domburg **14** 295; **21** 851, 852, 853
domed basilicas *see under* CHURCHES → types
domed octagon churches *see under* CHURCHES → types
dome huts *see under* HUTS → types
Domela (-Nieuwenhuis), César **9** 86–7*; **24** 686
groups and movements **1** 76; **7** 771; **10** 137; **11** 551; **28** 197; **32** 695
works **17** 767; **22** 749
Domenchin de Chavannes, Pierre-Salomon **9** 87*
Domenech, Franciso **9** 108; **26** 250
Doménech i Montaner, Luís **9** 87–8*; **12** 148; **14** 785; **29** 308, 329
assistants **2** 396
groups and movements **3** 216, 219
works **3** 216; **23** 881; **29** 273, 319
Domenge, Jeane **17** 551
Domenichino **1** 103; **9** 8, 88–93*; **16** 669, 671, 672; **22** 478; **26** 770, 773
architecture **3** *249*; **26** 833
assistants **27** 821; **30** 526
attributions **19** 238
book illustrations **18** 735
caricatures **5** 756
collaboration **1** 465, 626; **5** 864, 867; **13** 321; **26** 196, 771; **28** 364; **30** 356; **32** 593
copies **11** 744
drawings **9** 222
frames **11** 403
methods **5** 654; **6** 570; **19** 353
paintings **7** 814; **20** 841
altarpieces **9** *90*
frescoes **9** *92*; **11** 741; **16** 670; **18** 733; **26** 834
landscape **9** *91*; **18** 709
literary themes **30** 358
mythological **26** 839; **32** 550
religious **4** 406; **9** *89*; **10** 476; **15** 137; **26** 810, 834
patrons and collectors **10** 365
Aldobrandini, Pietro (ii), Cardinal (1571-1621) **1** 596
Anna Maria Luisa de' Medici, Electress Palatine (1667-1743) **21** 31
Aved, Jacques (-André-Joseph) **2** 852
Barnabites **3** 250
Borghese, Scipione, Cardinal **4** 406
Boyle, Richard, 3rd Earl of Burlington and 4th Earl of Cork **4** 610; **13** 301
Brienne, Louis-Henri, Comte de **4** 807
Caroline Murat, Queen of Naples (1782-1839) **22** 338
Carr, William Holwell **5** 848
Cavendish, William, 2nd Duke of Devonshire (1671-1729) **6** 116
Champernowne, Arthur **6** 438
Davis, Richard Hart **21** 541
Farnese, Odoardo, Cardinal **10** 811
Filomarino, Ascanio, Cardinal **11** 81
George III, King of Great Britain (*reg* 1760-1820) **14** 144
Giustiniani (i), Vincenzo, Marchese **12** 764
Gregory XV, Pope (*reg* 1621-3) **19** 778
Hieronymites **14** 517
Jabach, Everard **11** 662; **16** 814
John William, Elector Palatine (*reg* 1690-1716) **12** 473
Lancellotti, Orazio, Cardinal **18** 689
Le Nôtre, André **19** 164
Ludovisi, Ludovico, Cardinal **17** 510; **19** 779
Medinaceli, Luís de la Cerda Fernández de Córdoba Folch de Cardona y Aragón, 9th Duque de (1660-1711) **21** 35
Monterrey, Manuel de Acevedo y Zúñiga, 6th Conde de **22** 21
Orléans, Philippe II de Bourbon, 2nd Duc d' (1674-1723) **23** 515
Patrizi, Costanzo **24** 267
Domenichino
patrons and collectors—cont.
Peretti (-Montalto), Alessandro, Cardinal **24** 399
Poniatowski, Stanisław, Prince **25** 213
Pourtalès-Gorgier, James-Alexandre, Comte de **25** 383
Reynolds, Joshua **26** 280
Savoy, Maurice of, Cardinal **28** 9
Seignelay, Jean-Baptiste (-Antoine) Colbert, Marquis de **7** 546
Skippe, John **28** 819
Somerset, Henry, 3rd Duke of Beaufort (1707- 49) **13** 301
Tallard, Marie-Joseph d'Hostun, Duc de **30** 274
Temple-Nugent-Brydges-Chandos-Grenville, Richard, 1st Duke of Buckingham and Chandos **13** 637
Theatine Order **30** 648, 649
Udney, John **31** 525
Uffelen, Lucas van **31** 526
Waldegrave, William, 1st Baron Radstock **32** 774
Yusupov, Nikolay (Borisovich), Prince (1751- 1831) **33** 579
pupils **5** 453; **8** 99; **24** 238; **26** 565; **27** 864
reproductive prints by others
Audran, Girard **2** 708
Barrière, Dominique **3** 278
Bartolozzi, Francesco **3** 308
Bisschop, Jan de (1628-71) **4** 96
Blanchard, Auguste (Thomas Marie), III **4** 126
Chéreau, François, I (1680-1729) **6** 548
Cunego, Domenico **8** 267
Dorigny, Nicolas **9** 176
Mariette, Jean **20** 416
Picart, Etienne **24** 712
Pò, Pietro del **25** 55
Ruscheweyh, Ferdinand **27** 346
Testa, Pietro **30** 529
Vuibert, Rémy **32** 738
restorations by others **4** 106; **20** 901; **29** 892
teachers **5** 442, 851, 869
writings **1** 465
Domenichino, Girolamo **4** 252
Domenici, Carlo **28** 319
Domenicis, Gino De *see* DE DOMENICIS, GINO
Domenico *see* PALADINO, MIMMO
Domenico, Alunno di *see* BARTOLOMEO DI GIOVANNI
Domenico, Antonio di *see* ANTONIO DI DOMENICO
Domenico, Francesco di Giovanni di *see* BOTTICINI, FRANCESCO
Domenico, Giovanni di Andrea di *see* GIOVANNI DI ANDREA DI DOMENICO
Domenico, Maestro **16** 735; **32** 200
Domenico da Cortona **4** 155; **9** 93–4*; **11** 585
attributions **11** 512
works **2** 336; **3** 123; **6** 415, 416, 504, *505*; **11** 571; **24** 116, 133
Domenico d'Agostino **1** 457; **28** 679
Domenico d'Andrea, Benedetto di *see* BENEDETTO DI DOMENICO D'ANDREA
Domenico da Piacenza **16** 723, 726
Domenico d'Arezzo **2** 650
Domenico da Venezia **11** 316
Domenico dei cammei *see* COMPAGNI, DOMENICO
Domenico di Antonio da Fiesole **27** 181
Domenico di Bartolo (Ghezzi) **9** 94–5*
works **6** 4; **9** *95*, 262; **14** 784; **16** 470, 662; **28** *682*, 683, 686
Domenico di Deo **8** 630
Domenico di Francesco *see* DOMENICO DI MICHELINO
Domenico di Michelino **9** 95–6*
attributions **6** 3, *3*; **20** 743
collaboration **3** 100
works **9** *96*; **11** 197
Domenico di Niccolò **9** 96–7*; **28** 681, 687
Domenico di Paris **3** 260; **9** 97*
collaboration **11** 4; **20** 905
works **3** 260; **11** 7
Domenico di Piero **7** 517
Domenico di Polo **1** 454; **12** 258; **16** 746; **21** 19
Domenico Fiorentino **8** 907
Domenico Veneziano (*fl* 1438-61) **2** 389; **9** 97–103*; **16** 662; **20** 748
attributions **3** 188; **20** 743
collaboration **4** 32; **6** 14; **12** 302; **20** 557; **24** 759
methods **7** 628; **11** 184; **21** 758; **24** 487; **25** 379
paintings
altarpieces **1** 711; **9** *99*, *100*, *101*, *102*; **16** 661, *662*; **26** 184; **27** 495
frescoes **3** 99; **6** 13; **24** 520
religious **11** 709; **31** 142
patrons and collectors **3** 55; **5** 792; **6** 3; **19** 412; **21** 13
pupils **3** 99
Domenico Veneziano (*fl* 1548) **16** 867
Domenig, Günter **2** 552; **30** 214
Domergue, Jean-Gabriel **20** 75
domes **9** 82–6*; **32** 94
historical and regional traditions
Aboriginal Australia **1** 49–50
Algeria **16** 190
Armenia (Europe) **33** 741
Assyrian **9** 85
Australia **2** 740
Byzantine **4** 774; **8** 155; **9** 85, 525, 544; **19** *363*
Central Asia, Western **6** 199; **16** 161, 164, *237*, 238
Colombia **7** 604
Crete **8** 155
Early Christian (*c*. AD 250-843) **9** 85, 525
Egypt **16** 176, 244, 496
England **10** 232; **15** V
France **3** 524; **9** 86; **26** 584–5
Germany **9** 86; **30** 734
Gothic **13** 65; **33** *604*
Greece **2** 510
Greece, ancient **9** 85
Indian subcontinent **4** 52; **15** 359; **16** 201
Indonesia **9** 86
Iran **16** 161–2, *164*, 164, 193, 199, 270
Iraq **16** 182
Islamic **9** 86; **16** 130, 137, 142, 182; **28** 634
Algeria **16** 190
Central Asia, Western **16** 161, 164, *237*, 238
Egypt **16** 176, 210, 244, 496
Indian subcontinent **15** 359; **16** 201
Iran **16** 161–2, 164, 193–4, 199, 270
Iraq **16** 182
Morocco **16** 190
Ottoman **16** 205, 221, 222–3
Palestine **16** *147*
Syria **16** 182, 270
Turkey **16** 141, 205, 222–3
Yemen **16** 214–15
Italy **26** *903*
Baroque **13** *749*; **16** *642*; **26** *809*; **32** *645*

domes
historical and regional traditions
Italy—cont.
Gothic **13** 65
Neo-classicism **2** *177*
Renaissance **5** *15*; **27** *761*
Roman **26** *793*
5th cent. AD **26** *32*
Jainism **9** 86
Malaysia **9** 86
Morocco **16** 190
Ottoman **16** 205, 221, 222–3
Palestine **16** *147*
Portugal **20** *85*
Romanesque **9** 85; **26** 584
Rome, ancient **9** 11, 85; **26** *793*, 879, 880, 903, *903*, 923
Spain **33** *604*
Sri Lanka **9** 86
Syria **16** 182, 270
Turkey **16** 141, 205, 221, 222–3; **19** *363*
United States of America **13** 757; **22** 30; **32** *893*
Yemen **16** 214–15
materials
amphorae **26** 903
brick **4** 767, 774
cast iron **3** 524; **9** 86; **32** *893*
concrete **2** 740; **22** *806*
iron **3** 524
masonry **20** *579*, 579–80*
pots **9** 82
ribs **16** 164
steel **30** 734
wood **16** 496
wrought iron **3** 524
techniques
centering **6** 178
types
bulbous **9** 83*, *83*; **16** 211, 239
calotte **9** 83*
corbelled **9** 85
cut-off **9** 83*, *83*
diaphanous **9** 83*, *83*
false **9** 84*
fluted **9** *83*, 84*
geodesic **11** 834, 835; **12** 311*, *311*; **29** 250
hemispherical **23** 340
melon **9** *83*, 84*
muqarnas (architecture) **22** 322
onion **9** 82, *83*, 84*
pumpkin **9** *83*, 84*
revolving **23** 340
ribbed **9** *83*, 84*, 85
saucer *see* VAULTS (CEILING) → types → sail
segmental **9** *83*, 84*, 86
semi-dome **9** 84*, 85; **16** 176; **23** 641; **26** 923
sky-domes **30** 685
uses
houses **16** 270
markets **16** *237*, 238
mosques **16** 130, 141, 161–2, 221, 222–3
observatories **23** 340
shrines (i) (cult) **28** 634
tombs **16** 214–15
see also SHELL STRUCTURES
domical vaults *see* VAULTS (CEILING) → types → cloister; sail
Domien de Waghemakere **17** 883, 884
architecture **2** 192; **3** 543
chapels **2** 202
exchanges **3** 548; **10** 668
town halls **2** 203; **3** 543; **12** 523, *523*
collaboration **17** 885
Domin, André **11** 601
Dominé, Jacques **8** 792
Domingo, Damián **20** 274; **24** 621, 632
Domingo, Sebastiano **31** 285
Domingo de Guzmán *see* DOMINIC, Saint
Domingo Genevoix **4** 546
Domingos de Conceicão **4** 715
Domingo y Marqués, Francisco **9** 104*; **24** 829; **29** 284; **31** 816
Domingues, Afonso **3** 362; **14** 857; **25** 289
Domingues, Domingos **1** 590; **7** 531; **9** 104*; **25** 289
Domínguez, Alejandro **21** 382
Domínguez, Asdrúbal **9** 118
Domínguez, Cipriano **32** 171
Domínguez, J., Abbot of Valladolid **31** 822
Dominguéz, Juan **11** 65
Dominguéz, Juan Antonio **29** 337, 341; **31** 90
Domínguez, Lorenzo **6** 598
Domínguez, Martin **25** 823
Domínguez, Oscar **9** 104–5*; **11** 886
groups and movements **20** 591; **30** 21, 22
methods **8** 597
works **8** 606; **9** *105*
Domínguez Bécquer, Valeriano *see* BÉCQUER, VALERIANO (DOMINGUEZ)
Domínguez Bello, Arnulfo **23** 392
Domínguez de Obelar, Pedro **24** 94
Domínguez Neyra, Pedro **18** 415
Dominic, Saint **7** 231; **9** 105–7
Dominica **2** 144; **5** *745*
architecture **2** 148
basketwork **2** 145
ceramics **2** 152
Government Headquarters **2** 149
museums **2** 153, 154
painting **2** 149
see also ANTILLES, LESSER; WINDWARD ISLANDS
Dominican Effigies, Master of the **20** 641, 658*; **23** 744
attributions **20** 630
Dominican Order **7** 214, 231; **9** 105–13*; **15** 860
altarpieces **25** 463
architecture **4** 782; **19** 566; **21** 841–2*
Denmark **8** 723
England **21** *842*
Germany **13** 57
Gothic **13** 52, 57
Ireland **16** 7
Italy **13** 52
Mexico **21** 375
Poland **25** 95
brick **4** 782
iconography **9** 107–11*; **13** 127
manuscripts **9** 109*
marble **9** *106*
paintings **9** *107*, *109*; **26** 24
patronage **9** 111–13*
sculpture **9** *106*, *110*
wood **9** *110*
Dominican Polyptych **24** 33
Dominican Republic **2** 144; **5** 744, *745*; **9** 113–19*, *114*
amber **1** 761
architecture **9** 116–17*
carnivals **5** 788
cathedrals **9** *116*
ceramics **9** 114
collections **9** 118*, 119*
education (art) **9** 119*
exhibitions **5** 745, 746
houses **5** 749; **9** 116
jewellery **5** 752
masks **2** 146
museums **9** *117*, 119*
painting **9** *115*, 117–18*, *118*
patronage **9** 118*
prints **9** 118
religion **9** 114, 115, *115*
rock art **5** 748; **9** 114
sculpture **9** 117–18*
slaves **9** 115
Dominican Republic—cont.
stone-carvings **29** *199*
trigonolites **9** 114, *114*
wood-carvings **9** 117
see also HISPANIOLA (ISLAND)
Dominican Telephone Company **9** 118
Dominici, Antonio **22** 481
Dominici, Bernardo de **9** 119–20*; **13** 347; **29** 544
Dominici, Giovanni *see* GIOVANNI DOMINICI
Dominici, Paolo **19** 835
Dominici, Raimondo de **9** 119
Dominicus de Vivaldis **10** 725
Dominioni, Luigi Caccia **6** 42
Dominique de Faveran **22** 505
Dominique Florentin *see* BARBIERE, DOMENICO DEL
Dom-Ino **21** 781
dominoes **31** 265, 266
dominotiers **32** 814
Dominquiz, Micael **27** 604
Dominy, Felix **31** 625
Dominy, Nathanial (1737-1812) **31** 625
Dominy, Nathanial (1770-1852) **31** 625
Domitian, Emperor of Rome (*reg* 81-96) **9** 120–21*
architecture **26** 893–5; **31** 57
amphitheatres **26** 789; **32** 384
domes **9** 84, 85
fora **26** 784
fortifications **3** 620
odeia **23** 349
palaces **14** 73; **23** 808; **26** 751, 785, 853, *895*, 895–6, 923
stadia **26** 873, 895
temples **2** 656; **26** 866, 870; **31** 56
terraces **26** 787
villas **26** 895; **27** 72
coins **27** 96
sculpture **27** 15, 34
towns **23** 619
Domizlaff, Hildegard **8** 204; **26** 148
Domjian, Joseph **31** 660
Domme **25** 485
Dommer, George **22** 882
Dommer, Gijsbert **9** 179
Dommey, Théodore **9** 337
Dom Milley **7** 371
Domnick, Greta **9** 121
Domnick, Ottomar **9** 121*
Domodossola **27** 498
Domogatsky, Vladimir (Nikolayevich) **9** 121*; **27** 392
Domoko **28** 720
Domon, Ken **9** 121–2*; **17** 433
Dömös, St Margaret **14** 883
Dompé, Hernán **2** 401; **5** 123; **9** 122*
Domsaitas, Pransas **29** 109
domus *see* ROME, ANCIENT → houses
Domus **30** 92
Domus **16** 721; **24** 448; **25** 218; **26** 536
Domus Aurea *see under* ROME
Domus Nova **25** 218
Domuztepe **17** 811
Dona, Counts van **22** 720
Donà, Francesco, Doge of Venice (*reg* 1545-53) **27** 654
Dona, Iosif N. **26** 723
Donà, Leonardo, Doge of Venice (*reg* 1606-12) **32** 108
Donà, Lucia, Abbess **7** 516
Donadieu de Puychauric **2** 49
Donadoni, F. **22** 467
Donald, James **12** 777
Donald, John **10** 346; **17** 530; **30** 241
Donaldson, Anthony **25** 231
Donaldson, David **28** 239
Donaldson, James **9** 122; **19** 270
Donaldson, Jeff **1** 445
Donaldson, T(homas) L(everton) **7** 502; **9** 122*; **19** 270; **28** 349
Donas, Marthe **3** 564
Donat, Claude Joseph **32** 502
Donát, János **14** 901
Donatello **2** 161; **3** 226; **7** 383; **9** 122–32*; **10** 853; **12** 214; **14** 869; **16** 688, 689, 741; **18** 676; **26** 766; **28** 676
assistants **2** 17; **8** 180; **12** 705; **23** 772; **25** 9; **29** 568; **31** 707
attributions **8** 799; **20** 277
collaboration
Desiderio da Settignano **8** 797
Ghiberti, Lorenzo (di Cione) **12** 544
Giovanni Miniato **11** 295
Isaia da Pisa **16** 66
Maso di Bartolommeo **20** 552
Michelozzo di Bartolomeo **11** 185; **21** 465, 467; **22** 476; **25** 450; **27** 830
Nanni di Banco **22** 462
Nanni di Bartolo **11** 201; **22** 462
Robbia, Luca (di Simone) della (1399/1400-82) **11** 202
copies **11** 661
groups and movements **26** 183
methods **21** 768; **24** 487, 492; **26** 133, 136
patrons and collectors
Bardini, Stefano **3** 228
Camondo, Isaac de, Comte **5** 530
Castiglione, Sabba da **6** 41
Cosimo, Lord of Florence (*reg* 1434-64) **16** 689–90; **21** 11
Doni, Agnolo **9** 142
Gondi, Bartolomeo **12** 897
Gondi, Benedetto **12** 897
Medici (family) **16** 689, 763
Medici, Giovanni (di Cosimo) de' (1421-63) **21** 13
Museo Nazionale del Bargello **16** 774
Nieuwerkerke(, Alfred-Emilien O'Hara), Comte de **23** 126
Pourtalès-Gorgier, James-Alexandre, Comte de **25** 383
Robinson, John Charles **26** 473
Salviati (family) **27** 648
Shaw, Quincy Adams **28** 560
Watson-Wentworth, Charles, 2nd Marquess of Rockingham **32** 912
Widener, Joseph E. **33** 159
personal collection **27** 45
pupils **3** 636, 743, 859; **16** 693; **23** 92; **27** 180
sculpture **7** 380; **16** 658, 690
altarpieces **1** 711
architectural **10** 743; **11** 184, 197, 201, *201*, 204; **16** 689; **18** 673; **22** 44, 461, 462; **30** 497
bronze **21** 10; **26** 185
busts **9** *124*; **16** 690; **30** 495
crucifixes **8** 215
doors **9** 156, 157; **21** 10
effigies **31** 122
equestrian monuments **9** *127*; **10** 440; **14** 869; **22** 44; **23** 754; **29** 565
fonts (baptismal) **11** 254; **16** 692, 842, 843; **28** 681
plaquettes **25** 19
pulpits **11** 208; **18** 725; **21** 10; **25** 724, *725*
reliefs **3** 303; **9** *125*; **16** 689, 691; **18** 676; **24** 90; **31** 142
Baptistery (Siena) **16** 692
Cathedral of S Maria del Fiore (Florence) **11** 197; **16** 774
Medici Crucifixion **9** *130*
Orsanmichele (Florence) **11** 204; **26** 183
Il Santo (Padua) **5** 532; **11** 711; **23** 756
Santa Croce (Florence) **11** 206
Donatello
sculpture—cont.
religious **9** 21; **11** *203*; **16** 614, *690*, 692; **23** 292; **29** 560, *561*; **30** 496
Cathedral of S Maria del Fiore (Florence) **9** *123*; **11** 197
Cathedral of the Assumption (Siena) **28** 681
Orsanmichele (Florence) **1** 110; **26** 183
S Maria Gloriosa dei Frari (Venice) **32** 217
tombs **16** 690
wood **9** *129*
sponsors **21** 10
stained glass **6** 11; **11** 198; **29** 504; **31** 513
studio **29** 853
teachers **16** 689
workshop **27** 829
Donati, Enrico **9** 132*; **30** 22
Donati, Giovanni Ambrogio **16** 725; **33** 633
Donati, Giovanni Pietro **16** 725; **33** 633
Donati, Jacopo **30** 429
Donati, Lorenzo di Girolamo **11** 389
Donati, Nicolò **20** 898
Donati, Vitaliano **10** 91
Donato (family) **14** 420
Donato (*fl* late 13th cent) **2** 481; **24** 870
Donato, Alessandro **26** 849
Donato, Bartolomeo di *see* BARTOLOMEO DI DONATO
Donato, Carlota de Santamarco y, Duquesa de Nájera *see* NÁJERA, CARLOTA DE SANTAMARCO Y DONATO, Duquesa de
Donato, Girolamo **26** 328
Donato, Pier Francesco di Bartolomeo di *see* PIER FRANCESCO FIORENTINO
Donato, Pietro **18** 684; **32** 384
Donato di Niccolo di Betto Bardi *see* DONATELLO
Donato Martini **3** 247; **19** 454
Donauer, Georg **9** 133
Donauer, Hans, I (*c*. 1540-before 1596) **9** 133*
patrons and collectors **30** 34; **33** 271
pupils **27** 227
works **12** 811
Donauer, Hans, II (1569-1644) **9** 133
Donauer, Wilhelm **9** 133
Donaustauf
Castle **14** 81
Walhalla **6** 171; **10** 745; **12** 375, 406; **13** 201, 610, *610*; **15** 144; **18** 124; **22** 42, 738; **28** 44; **33** 282
portico **25** 268
sculpture **7** 211; **30** 854
Donauwörth, Schloss Fugger **12** 409
Don Bullebulle **24** 733
Doncaster (S. Yorks) **10** 302
Doncaster Gold Cup **10** 334; **12** 163
Doncel, Guillermo **29** 289
Donchenko, Aleksandr **12** 856
Donchō *see* Tam Chi
Donck, Jacob Frans van der **3** 613
Doncre, Dominique **4** 241
Dondé, Emilio **21** 378
Dondermonde, Onze Lieve Vrouwekerk **11** 253
Dondi, Giovanni de' **7** 438
Dondo **1** 360
dondoma houses *see* AFRICA → houses
Donducci, Giovanni Andrea *see* MASTELLETTA
Donegal **16** 34
Glebe Gallery **16** 36

Donegal, Arthur Chichester, 5th Earl of *see* CHICHESTER, ARTHUR, 5th Earl of Donegal
Donegal Carpets **5** 841
Donella **16** 780
Donella, Giovanni Francesco **1** 577
Dönertas *see* NAKRASON
Donets'k **31** 552
Don Fadrique, Villa de *see* VILLA DE DON FADRIQUE
Donga **6** 405, 406; **17** 680; **23** *129*
Dong An **8** 536
Dong Bai **33** 320
Dong Bangda **6** 818
Dong Chan **7** 99
Dong Dau **29** 230
Dong Duong **6** 418, *418*, 420; **9** 133*; **29** *225*; **32** *468*
  architecture **6** 420, 421–2*, *422*
  sculpture **6** 427–8*, *428*
Dongen, (Cornelis Theodorus Maria) Kees van **3** 366; **9** 134–5*; **22** 851; **30** 247
  collaboration **20** 603
  dealers **17** 725
  exhibitions **3** 826
  groups and movements **4** 892; **10** 694, 839, 841; **16** 817; **21** 775; **24** 311
  patrons and collectors **10** 885
  pupils **4** 127; **8** 267; **13** 695, 836; **28** 642
  studio **29** 858
  works **9** *134*, 292; **22** 851, *851*
Donghi, Antonio **9** 135*; **16** 680; **26** 776
Dong Ho
  prints **32** 481, *482*
Dong Hoi fortifications **21** 595
Dongjia cun (Qishan)
  bronzes **6** 847
Dongola (kingdom) **23** 287
Dongola (city) **23** *276*, 287
Dong Qichang **6** 760, 761, 764, 774, 787, 791, 820; **7** 147, 148, 151, 158, 707; **9** 135–9*; **11** 307; **19** 298, 857; **28** 588; **33** 466
  commentaries **18** 542
  groups and movements **6** 764; **23** 215, 579–80; **29** 243; **33** 652
  personal collection **18** 752
  pupils **6** 541; **32** 837; **33** 466
  studio **6** 544
  works **1** 581; **6** *825*; **7** 148; **9** *137*, *138*; **14** 823
  writings **6** 798, 824; **7** 675; **17** 188; **19** 299; **23** 581
Dong Sanqiao **17** 410
Dongshan **6** 714
Dong Shou *see* TONGSU
Dong Son **9** 139*; **15** 756; **23** 554; **29** *225*; **32** *468*
  bronze **4** 852; **29** 230; **32** 487, *488*
  drums (musical instruments) **4** 795; **15** 810; **23** 555; **29** 229; **32** 487, 489
  houses **32** 471
  sculpture **32** 478
Dongyang, Dongyue miao **6** 672
Dong You **6** 823
Dong Yuan **6** 773, 790, 798, 820, 824; **9** 139–42*; **23** 582; **29** 67
  groups and movements **29** 244
  works **6** 760, 789; **9** *141*
Dong Zuobin **7** 159
Doni, Agnolo **3** 306; **9** 142*; **11** 388
Doni, Antonio Francesco **9** 142–3*; **24** 90; **26** 564
Doni, Dono **12** 527
Doñihue **6** 600
Dōnin *see* HIRATA HIKOSHIRO
Doninelli, Antonio **33** 518
Donini, Tommaso **27** 893
Doni Tondo **9** 142; **11** 388; **21** 435, 442–3
Donje Butorke **9** 554
donjons **6** 50, 53–5*; **9** 143–4*; **21** 546, 550, 562, 571, 581
  historical and regional traditions
    Byzantine **9** *555*, 555–6
    England **9** 143, *144*; **10** 227, 359; **33** 198
    France **8** 902, *902*
    Japan **17** 83, *85*; **20** 835, *835*
    Poland **21** 571
    Romanesque **10** 227
    Spain **6** 50; **9** 144
  types
    donjons doubles **6** 53
    donjons jumeaux **6** 53
    shell **6** 55*; **9** 143
    tower **6** 53–5*; **9** 143, 144
  see also CASTLES
Donk, Jacob Frans van der **3** 599
Donkers, F. **27** 282
donkeys *see* HOISTS → types → steam-powered
Donkey's Tail **9** 144–5*; **22** 178, 750; **31** 583
  members **12** 893; **16** 817; **18** 792; **20** 193; **24** 850; **30** 361
Donnan, Christopher **27** 621; **29** 223
Donnat, Jacques **12** 721
Donnay, August **25** 347
Donnaz **27** 6
Donndorf, (Karl) Adolf (von) **9** 145*; **26** 378; **29** 546
Donndorf Museum *see under* WEIMAR
Donné, Alfred **24** 655
Donne, John **15** 40; **21** 102; **29** 714
Donner, Georg Raphael **8** 385; **9** 145–7*, 238; **15** 13; **27** 665
  architecture **4** 695; **14** 887
  groups and movements **26** 498
  patrons and collectors **10** 531; **14** 894; **28** 857
  pupils **23** 359; **24** 585; **25** 33
  sculpture **2** 801; **14** 530; **27** 661, *661*; **28** *855*, 855
    fountains **9** *146*; **32** 444
  teachers **12** 748
Donner, Matthäus **9** 145, 147–8*, 171
Donnerstagsgesellschaft **31** 328
Donnett, Cornelius Andreas **11** 735
Donnini, Emilio **28** 318
Donnini, Gaspare **16** 747; **22** 481
Donnino, Agnolo di Domenico di *see* AGNOLO DI DOMENICO DI DONNINO
Donohue, Dan
  works **31** *737*
Donop de Monchy, Victorine **3** 671
Donore (Co. Meath) **9** 153; **15** 872
Donoso, José Jiménez *see* JIMÉNEZ DONOSO, JOSÉ
Donostia *see* SAN SEBASTIÁN
Donough O'Carroll, King of Uriel (*reg c.* 1135) **21** 87
Donovan, Alan **17** 908
Donovan, Peter **16** 32
Donowell, John **8** 533
Dontas **8** 458
Dony, Jean-Jacques Daniel **4** 685
Dony, Paul **5** 609
Donyatt (Somerset) **10** 303
Dōnyū Tanaka *see* TANAKA DŌNYŪ
Donzel (family) **10** 781
Donzell, Guillelmus **19** 171
Donzello, Ippolito del **9** 148*
Donzello, Pietro del **9** 148*; **31** 173
Doo, George Thomas **9** 148*; **10** 396; **26** 233
doodles **9** 148*
  see also AUTOMATISM; DRAWINGS; SKETCHES
Doogallook Station **2** *736*
  interior decoration **2** *755*
Doogood, Henry **29** 843
Dōoku Kōnoike *see* KŌNOIKE DŌOKE
Doolaard, Cornelis **10** 483
Doolittle, Amos **9** 148*, 504
Doomer, Harmen **9** 149
Doomer, Lambert (Harmensz.) **9** 149–50*; **27** 887
  patrons and collectors **14** 375; **32** 377
  personal collection **25** 277
  teachers **22** 843
  works **2** 696; **9** *149*
Doones, Gaspard **7** 708
doophek see under PULPITS → types
Door, Master of the **3** 742
Doordt, Jacob van (der) *see* DOORT, JACOB VAN (DER)
door fittings **10** 338, 339; **16** 366; **26** 691
doorframes **3** 148; **25** 536; **30** 846
doorjambs **9** 161; **16** *885*
Doornenburg Castle **5** 122; **22** 822
Doornik *see* TOURNAI
Door of Hope Mission **31** 259
doors **9** 150–66*
  historical and regional traditions
    Africa **1** 314, *383*, *427*; **9** 164–5*
    Ancient Near East **9** 150*
    Assyrian **9** 150
    Austria **9** *152*
    Bali (Indonesia) **15** 785
    Bamana **9** 164
    Baule **1** 314; **3** *408*
    Belgium **3** 575, 576, 578
    Burma **9** 163
    Byzantine **9** 599–600, *600*
    Carolingian **5** 806; **9** 152
    Central Asia, Western **16** 492, 501–2
    China **6** 643; **9** 162*
    Côte d'Ivoire **9** 164
    Cyprus **9** 151
    Dogon **1** 314; **9** 164
    Early Christian (*c.* AD 250-843) **9** 151–2, 599–600
    Egypt **9** 160, *160*; **16** 384, *490*
    Egypt, ancient **9** 150*
    England **9** 155–6; **10** *169*; **14** 681
    France **9** 152, 156, 158; **26** *511*, 641; **27** *544*, *681*
    Germany **9** *153*; **12** 452, 454; **23** *658*
    Ghana **9** 164
    Gothic **27** *544*
    Greece **9** 151, *600*
    Greece, ancient **9** 150–51*, *151*; **13** 390, 391, 415
    Hausa **9** 164
    Holy Roman Empire (before 1648) **26** 684*
    Igalu **1** 383
    Igbo **9** 164
    Inca **9** 166
    Indian subcontinent **9** *161*, 161–2*
    Indonesia **15** 785
    Iran **9** 160
    Iraq **16** *489*
    Islamic **9** 160–61*
      Central Asia, Western **16** 492, 501–2
      Egypt **9** 160, *160*; **16** 384, *490*
      Iran **9** 160
      Iraq **16** *489*
      Ottoman **9** 160
      Spain **16** 495
      Turkey **9** 160
      Yemen **16** 500
    Italy **9** 152, 153–5, 158–9
      Early Christian (*c.* AD 250-843) **9** 151–2
      Neo-classicism **1** *574*
      Renaissance **9** 156–8*, *157*; **11** *71*; **12** *538*, *540*
      Romanesque **16** 687; **32** *342*
doors
  historical and regional traditions
    Italy—cont.
      20th cent. **9** *159*
    Japan **9** 162–3*; **17** 47, 155
    Java **9** 163
    Khmer **9** 163
    Korea **9** 162*; **18** 276
    Laos **9** 163
    Malaysia **9** 164
    Mali **9** 164
    Maya **9** 165–6, *166*
    Mesoamerica, Pre-Columbian **9** 165–6*, *166*
    Mesopotamia **21** 296
    Mexico **9** *166*
    Mongolia **21** 883
    Native North Americans **9** 165*
    Nigeria **1** *427*; **9** 164, *164*
    Norway **9** 156
    Nupe **1** 383, *383*; **9** 164; **23** 303
    Ottoman **9** 160
    Ottonian **9** *153*; **23** 657, 658, *658*
    Portugal **18** *783*
    Romanesque **9** *152*, *155*; **10** *169*; **16** 687; **26** 641, 684*; **32** *342*
    Romania **26** 718
    Rome, ancient **9** 150–51*
    Senufo **1** 314; **9** 164
    South America, Pre-Columbian **9** 166*
    South-east Asia **9** 163–4*
    Spain **16** 495
    Sri Lanka **29** 471
    Swahili **9** 165; **30** *57*
    Sweden **9** *155*, 156
    Tanzania **9** 165; **30** *57*, 300
    Thailand **9** 163, *163*
    Turkey **9** 160
    Venda **32** 154
    Vietnam **9** 163
    Yemen **16** 500
    Yoruba **1** 280, 314; **9** 164, *164*; **33** 554
  materials
    acacia **16** 500
    bronze
      Ancient Near East **9** 150
      Carolingian **5** 806; **9** 152–5*
      Egypt **9** *160*
      France **26** *511*
      Germany **9** *153*
      Greece, ancient **13** 390, 391
      Holy Roman Empire (before 1648) **26** 684*
      Italy **9** 156–7, *157*, 158–60*, *159*; **11** *71*; **12** *538*, *540*; **32** *342*
      Ottonian **23** 657, 658, *658*
    cedar **9** 165; **17** 47
    copper **7** 813; **12** 452
    cordia **16** 500
    earth **9** 164
    felt **10** 874
    glass **3** 575
    gold **13** 390, 391
    iron **3** 575; **9** 154*, *155*; **12** 454
    ivory **9** *600*; **13** 390; **29** 471
    metal **9** 160
    mother-of-pearl **9** 160
    mud **9** 164
    nails **9** 151
    oak **3** 575; **9** 157
    paper **18** 276
    silver **13** 390, 391
    stone **9** 150
    teak **16** *489*, *490*
    terracotta **9** 150
    walnut **9** 157
    wood
      Africa **9** 164, *164*
      Austria **9** *152*
      Baule **3** *408*
      Byzantine **9** *600*
      Early Christian (*c.* AD 250-843) **9** 151–2*, 599–600
doors
  materials
    wood—cont.
      France **26** 641
      Islamic **9** 160; **16** 492, 495, 501–2
      Nigeria **1** *427*
      Nupe **1** *383*
      Rome, ancient **9** 151
      Tanzania **30** *57*
  techniques
    gilding **12** *538*, *540*
    marquetry **9** 160
    painting **17** 155
  types
    sliding **11** 862
Doort, Abraham van der **9** 167*; **29** 801
Doort, H. van **12** 15
Doort, Isaak van der **9** 167
Doort, Jacob van (der) **8** 733; **9** 167*; **21** 641; **23** 396
Doort, Peter van (der) **9** 167
doorways
  Buddhism **5** *241*
  Burma **5** *241*
  Cambodia **5** 475
  Celtic **27** *142*
  England **7** *456*; **10** *169*; **18** *50*
  France **27** *142*
  Gothic **7** *456*
  Greece, ancient **13** 387
  Helladic **14** 340
  Indian subcontinent **15** 272; **31** 520
  Laos **18** *766*
  Mycenaean **14** 340
  Romanesque **10** *169*; **18** *50*
  see also GATES; PORTALS; PORTES COCHÈRE
Doorwerth Castle **22** 822
Dopmeyer, Carl **28** 164
Doppelkapelle **26** 574
Doppelmayr, Johann Gabriel **9** 167*; **12** 811, 812, 814
Dorado (family) **29** 331
Doraha caravanserai **15** 374
Doran, John **8** 111
Dōrasamudra *see* HALEBID
Dorat, Claude-Joseph **10** 118; **20** 421
  works **10** *118*
Dorat, Jean **5** 813
Doravaka-kanda **29** 445
Dorazio, Piero **9** 168*
  groups and movements **7** 782; **11** 314; **16** 681; **26** 777, 778
Dorchester Law Courts (Dorset) **18** 886
Dorchester (Oxon), Abbey of SS Peter and Paul **10** 260, 338
Dorchester, Dudley Carleton, 1st Viscount *see* CARLETON, DUDLEY, 1st Viscount Dorchester
Dorchester, Joseph Damer, 1st Earl of *see* DAMER, JOSEPH, 1st Earl of Dorchester
Dorchester Pottery **4** 482
Dorchi **19** 835
Dordabis farm **29** 577
Dórdio Gomes(, Simão César) **9** 168*; **26** 243
Dordrecht **9** 168–9*; **22** *813*
  academy **22** 907
  Ary Scheffer Museum *see* Dordrechts Museum
  Dordrechts Museum **22** 906; **28** 68; **29** 773
  furniture **22** 871
  glass **22** 884, 885
  Grote Kerk *see* Onze Lieve Vrouwekerk
  Museum Mr Simon van Gijn **22** 906
  Onze Lieve Vrouwekerk **13** 62; **22** 820, 857
  pewter **22** 893
  silver **22** 887

Doré, Gustave (-Paul) 9 169–71*; 24 605; 33 369
book illustrations 1 640; 4 2, 9, 364; 6 489; 10 726
caricatures 5 758
drawings 2 412; 31 704
groups and movements 2 643
lithographs 22 371
sculpture 21 830
wood-engravings 9 170
Dorer, Bartholeme see DAUHER, BARTHOLOMÄUS
Dorer, Robert 30 137
Dorez, Barthélémy 19 382
Dorffmeister, István 14 900; 30 212
Dorfles, Gillo 16 681; 22 242
Dorflinger, Christian 9 171*
Dorflinger & Sons 5 583
Dorfmeister, Johann Georg 9 171–2*; 19 337
Dorginarti 21 554
Dori, Alessandro 7 411; 9 12; 22 362; 28 754
works 22 361
Doria (family) 6 34; 12 280, 283; 24 552; 32 715
Doria, Agostino 9 173*
Doria, Andrea, Comte (fl 1860s) 7 555
Doria, Andrea, I (1466-1560) 9 172*; 19 201; 28 334
architecture 9 172; 12 281
furniture 16 725
gardens 12 115
painting 12 283
paintings 3 469; 24 419
woodwork 30 357
Doria, Andrea, II (1570-1612) 9 172, 173*
Doria, Armand, Comte 5 441
Doria, Brigida Spinola 27 289
Doria, Cardinal 13 650
Doria, Carlo, Duca di Tursi see TURSI, CARLO DORIA, Duca di
Doria, Filippo 7 901
Doria, Giacomo 9 173*
Doria, Gian Carlo, Prince 9 174*
art policies 1 104
collections 9 173
paintings 4 442; 12 283
sponsorship 4 441
Doria, Gian Luca 9 174
Doria, Giovanna 9 173
Doria, Giovanni Andrea, I (1539/40-1606) 9 172–3*; 19 806; 25 226
Doria, Giovanni Andrea, II (1607-40) 9 172
Doria, Lamba 9 173*
Doria, Marcantonio 9 174*
collections 9 173, 174
paintings 2 910; 5 694, 715; 29 783
Doria, Nicolò 9 172
Doria, Zenobia del Caretto 9 172
Doriac, Frank 11 759
Dorians 26 290
Doria-Pamphili (family) 9 174–5*; 10 530; 23 898; 30 331
Doria-Pamphili, Alfonso, Prince 9 175
Doria-Pamphili, Giuseppe, Cardinal 16 768
Doric capitals see under CAPITALS → types
Doric column see under COLUMNS → types
Dorichus, Valerius 5 448
Dorici, Claude, I 4 896; 32 725
Dorico brothers 27 606
Doric order see under ORDERS (ARCHITECTURAL) → types
Doric temples see under TEMPLES → types
Dorieu, Jean 22 466
Dorigny, Charles 9 176–7*; 11 265, 532
Dorigny, Jacqueline see BORDIER, JACQUELINE
Dorigny, Louis 9 175, 176*; 22 387; 32 194, 411
Dorigny, Michel 9 175–6*; 24 134
patrons and collectors 14 492; 30 727
pupils 9 176
teachers 18 662
works 9 175; 14 313; 19 247; 27 821; 29 803; 32 582, 718
Dorigny, Nicolas 9 175, 176*; 13 646
patrons and collectors 6 117
works 2 170, 170; 9 706; 11 24
Doring see DORCHI
Döring, Christian 8 115
Döring, Hans 8 118; 19 111
Döring, Julius 18 849; 31 854
dorings see under PILLARS → types
Dorion 14 339
Dorizy, Claude see DORICI, CLAUDE, I
Dorjsuren 21 885
Dorla 15 734
Dorla, Johannes Orthonis 10 453
Dorland International 3 423; 7 652
Dorland's Wax Medium see under WAXES → types
Dormal, Jules 2 396; 5 123
works 5 122
Dormer, James 27 259
dormer windows see under WINDOWS → types
Dormington (Hereford & Worcs), St Peter 10 338
dormitories 17 68; 21 843, 843–4*
Dorn, B. 6 280
Dorn, Hans 12 812
Dorn, Marion 5 841
Dornach
Goetheanum (1913-20) 10 698; 29 607, 607–8
Goetheanum (1924-8) 10 698
Dornava Mansion 28 859
Dornburg
earthenwares 12 432
Dorndorf Church 1 700
Dörner, Friedrich-Karl 22 731
Dorner, Johann Jakob, I (1741-1813) 8 897; 9 177*; 18 140; 22 303; 29 776
Dorner, Johann Jakob, II (1775-1852) 9 177
Dornicke, Jan van see MERTENS, JAN (1470-1518)
Dorokhoi, St Nicholas 25 344
Dorosiev, Aleksandăr 5 158
Dorostorum see SILISTRA
Dorotej, Abbot 28 449
Dorothy, James 19 242
Dorp, Arend van der 14 39
Dorpat see TARTU
Dörpfeld, Wilhelm 1 892; 13 410; 17 733; 23 508; 28 114; 29 99; 31 25, 356, 375
Dorsch, (Johann) Christoph 9 177*; 12 260; 25 549
Dorsch, Erhard 9 177
Dörsch, Ferdinand 10 868
Dorsch, Franz Ignaz 12 411; 29 403
Dorsch, Paul Christoph 9 177
Dorsch, Susanna Maria 9 177; 12 262
Dorset, Anne Sackville, Countess of see SACKVILLE, ANNE, Countess of Dorset
Dorset, Charles Sackville, 2nd Duke of see CHARLES SACKVILLE, 2nd Duke of Dorset
Dorset, Charles Sackville, 6th Earl of see SACKVILLE, CHARLES, 6th Earl of Dorset
Dorset, Edward Sackville, 4th Earl of see SACKVILLE, EDWARD, 4th Earl of Dorset
Dorset, John Frederick Sackville, 3rd Duke of see SACKVILLE, JOHN FREDERICK, 3rd Duke of Dorset
Dorset, Lionel Cranfield Sackville, 1st Duke of see SACKVILLE, LIONEL CRANFIELD, 1st
Dorset, Richard Sackville, 3rd Earl of see SACKVILLE, RICHARD, 3rd Earl of Dorset
Dorset culture 13 620; 22 546, 575
Dorsey, George 10 580
Dorsey, The 22 694
D'Orsi, Achille 9 177–9*; 22 480
works 9 178
Dorsman, Adriaen 1 801, 802; 9 179*; 22 418
Dorsman, Cornelis 29 79
Dorsten, J. van 22 843
Dort, Jacob van (der) see DOORT, JACOB VAN (DER)
dorters see DORMITORIES
Dört Kilise see OCKTHA-ECKLESIA
Dortmund
Dortsfeld West 10 749
Propsteikirche 3 40–41
St Reinhold 13 111; 20 688
Dortmund Altarpiece 7 723–4, 724; 19 528, 529
Dortsman, Adriaen see DORSMAN, ADRIAEN
Dortu, Frédéric 16 739
Dortu, Johann Jakob 30 100, 144
Dortu Richard et Cie 16 739
Dortzal, Jeanne 22 92
Dorykleides 8 458
Doryphoros 13 605; 23 291; 27 46
Dōryū Rankei see RANKEI DŌRYŪ
Dorze 10 566
Dosekun, Olusoji (Omoshola) 9 179–80*
Dōsen see ASHIKAGA YOSHIMOCHI
Doshi, Balkrishna V(ithaldas) 9 180–81*; 15 242
collaboration 19 47
studio 9 180
works 15 168, 169
Doshin Kaigetsudō see KAIGETSUDŌ DOSHIN
Doshū Kaigetsudō see KAIGETSUDŌ DOSHŪ
Dosio, Giovanni Antonio 9 181–2*
assistants 5 359
collaboration 5 360; 7 312
patrons and collectors 11 893; 23 87; 25 7
pupils 5 359
works 2 161; 5 789; 6 102; 18 900; 22 484, 485; 26 848
Dositeo Carvajal, Manuel 7 612
Dospevski (family) 27 685
Dospevski, Stanislav 26 392; 27 686
Dos Pilas 20 885
dossals 1 708; 3 609; 9 182*; 30 779
Dossari, Mojab 18 541
Dossena, Alceo 9 182*; 10 640; 11 306
Dossenberger, Hans Adam 9 183*
Dossenberger, Joseph (1694-1754) 9 183
Dossenberger, Joseph (1721-85) 9 183*; 28 49
dosserets 2 292
Dossi 5 328, 329
Dossi, Alberto Pisani 8 136
Dossi, Battista 9 183, 187*; 11 4; 25 736
collaboration 9 185; 12 162; 26 727; 27 273
patrons and collectors 10 522, 523; 11 5
pupils 11 76
tapestries 11 5; 17 812
works 2 412; 5 180; 10 130; 24 536; 30 319
Dossi, Carlo 7 690; 9 187–8*
Dossi, Dosso 7 560; 9 183, 184–7*; 11 4; 16 667
collaboration 5 843; 9 187; 12 162; 26 727; 27 273
paintings 5 180
allegorical 9 184; 11 392
frescoes 24 536
landscape 11 35, 36; 18 707, 708; 32 550
mythological 9 186; 10 443
portraits 26 459
religious 11 392, 392; 20 241
patrons and collectors
Alfonso I, 3rd Duke of Ferrara, Modena and Reggio (reg 1505-34) 10 522
Borghese, Scipione, Cardinal 4 406
Cesare, 6th Duke of Modena and Reggio (reg 1597-1628) 10 525
Créquy, Charles de Blanchefort de 19 238
Ercole II, 4th Duke of Ferrara, Modena and Reggio (reg 1534-59) 11 5
Este (i) (family) 21 771
Gualtieri, Enzo Bentivoglio, Marchese di 3 744
Mond, Ludwig 21 849
Phillips, Claude 24 638
Pio di Savoia, Carlo Francesco, Cardinal 24 833
stage design 2 412; 11 4
tapestries 17 812
Dossi, Guido Pisani 7 689, 690
Dossie, Robert 8 128; 25 621
Dossier, Michel 9 296
Dosso, Giovanni 11 236
Dost Muhammad Khan 3 908
Dostoyevsky, Fyodor (Mikhaylovich) 9 188*; 12 804
dōtaku see under BELLS → types
Döteber, Christian Julius 9 188*; 30 69, 84
Do Thi Ninh 32 483
Dotremont, Christian 3 565; 9 188, 189*
collaboration 1 598
groups and movements 5 45; 7 488, 489; 17 658; 30 23
Dotremont, Philippe 9 189*
Dotres, Amalia de Llano y, Condesa de Vilches see VILCHES, AMALIA DE LLANO Y DOTRES, Condesa de
Dot-rosette group 10 613
dotted prints see under ENGRAVINGS → types
Dotti, Carlo Francesco 9 190*
collaboration 24 834
works 4 271, 273, 278, 280, 312; 16 641; 23 339; 31 181
Dotti, Giovanni Giacomo 9 190
Dotti, Giovanni Paolo (fl 1659) 9 190
Dotti, Giovanni Paolo (1707-55) 9 190
Dotto, Diamante 1 725
Dotto, Vincenzo 32 594
Dottori, Gerardo 9 191*
groups and movements 1 166; 8 771; 11 867; 16 680
Dotzinger, Jodok 9 191–2*; 14 117; 29 757
works 9 191
Dotzinger, Johann 9 191*
dou see under VESSELS → types
Dou, Gerrit 9 192–5*, 193; 22 843; 29 375
attributions 4 304; 17 666
collaboration 3 757; 26 153
groups and movements 12 290; 19 102; 21 486; 22 841
methods 24 792
patrons and collectors 22 841
Angran, Louis-Auguste, Vicomte de Fontpertuis 2 90
Dou, Gerrit
patrons and collectors—cont.
Aved, Jacques (-André-Joseph) 2 852
Beckford, William (1760-1844) 3 476
Braamcamp, Gerrit 4 618
Brydges, James, 1st Duke of Chandos 5 65
Choiseul, Etienne-François, Duc de 7 193
Conti, Louis-François de Bourbon, Prince de (1717-76) 7 778
Cosimo III, Grand Duke of Tuscany (reg 1670-1723) 21 29
Fitzwilliam, Richard, 7th Viscount Fitzwilliam 11 141
George IV, King of Great Britain (reg 1820-30) 14 146
Gildemeester, Jan (Jansz.) (1744-99) 12 620
John William, Elector Palatine (reg 1690-1716) 12 473
Peel, Robert (1788-1850) 24 322
William IV, Stadholder of the Netherlands, Prince of Orange (reg 1747-51) 23 468
pupils 4 740; 21 487; 22 50, 442; 28 49, 842; 32 244
reproductive prints by others 21 800; 33 196
teachers 9 79; 19 101; 22 843
works 1 659; 9 192; 31 365
Douai 11 606
Hôtel de Ville 17 700
Douaihy, Saliba 9 195*; 19 8
Douala 1 394; 5 523, 525; 11 880
Post Office 5 523
Douanier (Le) see ROUSSEAU, HENRI
Doubios see DVIN
double ambulatories see under AMBULATORIES → types
double cathedrals see under CATHEDRALS → types
double chairs see under CHAIRS → types
double cloth weaving see under WEAVING → types
double courtyard villas see under VILLAS → types
double-faced armour see under ARMOUR → types
double gongs see under GONGS → types
double-hull canoes see under CANOES → types
double-leaf books see under BOOKS → forms
double ogee mouldings see under MOULDINGS → types
Double-palmette Painter 32 37
double-sided icons see under ICONS → types
Doublet, Philips 14 39
doublets 9 261, 265
double walls see THICK-WALL STRUCTURES
doublures 4 349; 9 195*; 16 356
Doubravník
church 8 377
Monastery 24 462
doucai see under PORCELAIN → wares
Douce, Francis 9 195*
Douce Apocalypse see under APOCALYPSES → individual manuscripts
Douce France 3 814; 11 568
Doucet, Henri 23 437
Doucet, Jacques (-Antoine) 9 195–6*, 291; 10 824; 11 551; 16 554
collections 11 664, 673; 18 864
dress 25 78
furniture 13 328; 19 85
groups and movements 7 489

Doucet, Jacques(-Antoine)—cont.
interior decoration 11 582
manuscripts 19 85
paintings 24 715
Douch 9 850
Douchez, Jacques 4 724
Douda, J. 30 221
Doudelet, Charles 9 196*
Doudelet, Charles, Cabinet see under GHENT → Museum Arnold Vander Haeghen
Doudijns, Willem 30 517; 33 260
Doué-la-Fontaine Castle 6 50, 50, 52, 54; 9 144
Douffet, Gérard 9 196–8*; 19 344; 20 704
pupils 11 166
works 9 197
Dougga 9 198*, 510
architecture 26 921; 31 427
baths 26 919
forum 10 415
macellum 19 889
mosaics 1 377
Roman capitolium 26 919
Temple of Caelestis 26 919
theatre 26 919
tower tomb 23 299
Dougherty, Paul 21 897
Doughty, Charles 27 877
Doughty, Dorothy 33 378
Doughty, Thomas 9 199*
patrons and collectors 7 840; 12 645; 14 718; 26 75
works 31 601
Doughty, William 9 199*; 26 277
Douglas (fl 1990) 20 54
Douglas, Aaron 1 442; 9 199–200*
Douglas, Archibald 31 230
Douglas, Campbell 5 65; 12 775; 29 650; 30 266
works 12 773
Douglas, David 12 137
Douglas, David, 12th Marquess of Queensberry 10 321
Douglas, Frederic 3 738; 22 674, 677, 679
Douglas, Gavin 28 264
Douglas, John 6 561; 9 200*
Douglas, Mollie 2 761
Douglas, Neil 2 760–61
Douglas, Robert Langton 9 200*; 10 367
Douglas (Strathclyde), St Bride's 26 617
Douglas, William 28 225
Douglas, William, 3rd Duke of Hamilton 28 252
Douglas, William Fettes 28 238
Douglas fir 33 324
Douglas-Hamilton, Alexander, 10th Duke of Hamilton see HAMILTON, ALEXANDER, Duke of Hamilton and Brandon
Douglas-Hamilton, James, 1st Duke of Hamilton 27 291
Douglas-Hamilton, James, 5th Duke of Hamilton 23 208
Douglas-Hamilton, James, 6th Duke of Hamilton 7 409
Douglas-Hamilton, William Alexander, 11th Duke of Hamilton 5 78
Douglass, A. E. 2 302; 22 672
Douglass, James 19 361
Douglass, Robert 1 440
Douglass, William Tregarthen 19 361
Douglas-Scott, Walter Francis Montagu-, 5th Duke of Buccleuch see MONTAGU-DOUGLAS-SCOTT, WALTER FRANCIS, 5th Duke of Buccleuch
Douglas & Sellars 4 884
Doukaina, Anna 16 601
Doukas, Isaak 28 448
Doullens, Musée Lombart 3 71
Doulting 10 227
Doulton, Henry 9 200; 10 312; 25 187
Doulton, John 2 541; 9 200
Doulton Ceramic Factory 6 558; 9 200–201*; 10 312, 313; 29 496; 30 506
designers 3 423; 23 34
pupils 2 760
production 2 755; 3 893; 14 771; 30 877
Doulton & Co. 3 746; 9 201; 19 595
Doulton & Watts 9 200
Douma, Nellie 22 452, 609
Doumas, Christos 22 698; 30 711
Dourdan 6 54
Dourdin, Jacques 3 362; 5 208; 11 637; 30 313
Dourge, Léon 2 396
Dourgnon, Marcel 5 401
Douris (c. 500-460 BC) 13 520, 523; 32 39*
patrons and collectors 4 308; 23 829
pupils 13 490
works 12 286; 13 489, 489, 490, 520; 22 411
Douris of Samos (340-260 BC) 13 561; 25 45
Dournanez 25 215
Dousiko, Great Gates Monastery 25 335
Doust, Len 24 495
Douvanli 9 201*; 25 471
furniture 13 592
Koukouva Mogila 30 772
metalwork 30 770
pottery 13 538
silver 13 373, 568, 570, 571
vases 13 551
Douven, Bartholomeus 33 80
Douven, Jan Frans van 9 460; 12 473; 33 279
Douvermann, Henrik 12 401; 17 741; 22 856; 31 322; 33 458
Douw, Simon van 4 153
Dou Wan, Princess 6 648, 727, 858, 859; 7 6, 81
dress 20 236
Doux, Jean Picart le see PICART LE DOUX, JEAN
Dova, Gianni 2 526; 9 201*; 11 844; 16 681
Dove, Arthur (Garfield) 9 202*; 23 47, 48; 31 605
exhibitions 31 490
groups and movements 8 435; 30 711
patrons and collectors 24 638; 29 655, 657
works 18 718
Dove, Heinrich-Wilhelm 22 745
dovecots 9 202–3*
Iran 9 203
Scotland 9 202
Dovecot Studios see EDINBURGH TAPESTRY COMPANY
Dover (Kent; UK) 10 225
Castle 3 209; 6 51, 51, 54, 55, 56; 8 278; 9 203, 203–4*; 21 549, 563
Constable's Gate 12 173
gate-house 12 173
King's Gate 12 173
Palace Gate 12 173
restoration 2 321
St Mary in Castro 2 66, 67
lighthouse 19 360
priory 26 660
Western Heights complex 21 548
Dover (NH; USA)
textiles 31 657
Dover, George Agar-Ellis, Baron see AGAR-ELLIS, GEORGE, 1st Baron Dover
Dover Bible see under BIBLES → individual manuscripts
Doveri, Lorenzo 24 218
Dover Pictorial Archives 2 364
Doves Press 2 570; 7 486, 487; 20 335; 24 107
Doves Press Bible see under BIBLES → types
Dove Stele 13 455
Doveston, Bird & Hull 30 266
Dovizi da Bibbiena, Bernardo see BIBBIENA, BERNARDO, Cardinal
Dow, Arthur Wesley 17 420; 23 387, 669; 31 670; 33 15, 362
Dow, John Wheeler 7 619
Dow, Thomas Millie 12 779; 20 276
Dowbiggin, Thomas 14 682
Dowdeswell, Frank 28 772
Dowdeswell, Walter 9 204
Dowdeswell, (C.) William 9 204*; 29 723
Dowdeswell's 33 140
dowels 13 388, 391
Dowgate Hill Brooch 19 579
down-draught kilns see under KILNS → types
Downe, William Dawnay, 7th Viscount see DAWNAY, WILLIAM, 7th Viscount Downe
Downey, Juan 9 204*
Downhill Castle (Co. Londonderry) 14 485
Downing, A(ndrew) J(ackson) 8 575; 9 204–5*; 24 179; 33 263
collaboration 32 95
groups and movements 13 209; 24 742
works 7 840; 29 653; 31 592; 32 886
writings 32 555; 33 134
Downing, Charles 9 204
Downing, George 5 512
Downing, George T. 3 185
Downing, Thomas 32 890, 894
Downing & Vaux 9 205
Downman, John 9 205*; 29 675
Downpatrick, Down County Museum 16 42
Downs, George 20 590
Downs/Archambault 31 864
Downshire Pottery 16 28
Downton Castle (Herford & Worcs) 6 61; 12 131; 18 150
dowries 15 175, 730; 17 302, 304, 385; 29 236
Dowshantepe palace 15 897
Dowson, Philip 5 513
Dowspuda, English Castle 25 99
Dowst Manufacturing Co. 31 264
Doxaras, Nikolaos 9 206*; 13 352; 18 410
Doxaras, Panagiotes 9 205–6*
Doxiadis, Constantinos A(postolos) 9 206–7*; 13 350
collaboration 8 862
works 9 207; 16 93; 23 799
Doxiadis Associates 9 206–7; 16 93
Doyen, Albert 1 21
Doyen, Gabriel-François 9 208–9*; 19 159
patrons and collectors 4 745; 24 63
pupils 3 854; 12 158; 18 74; 19 119, 159, 254; 24 477; 31 816
reproductive prints by others 27 571
teachers 19 646
works 3 203; 9 208
Doyen, Louis Marie 2 642
Doyère, Emile 6 594
Doyle, A. E., Associates 3 682; 31 596
Doyle, Dicky see DOYLE, RICHARD
Doyle, Henry E. 9 319
Doyle, J. Francis (1840-1913) 19 506
Doyle, John (1797-1868) 9 209*; 19 484
Doyle, Richard 9 209*; 30 569
Doyle, Roger 7 552
D'Oyly, Charles 5 419; 7 164; 15 653; 32 903
D'Oyly Carte, Richard 7 559; 14 786
Doynel, Eduardo 4 260
Dōzen Eiraku see EIRAKU SOSABURŌ
Dozza, Francesco Fucci di 11 116
Dra Abu el-Naga see under THEBES (i) (EGYPT)
Drab Polished Blue Core ware see under POTTERY → wares
Drachev, Nikolay 5 159
Drachmann, Holger 14 595; 28 814
Drachmann Bentzon, Martha see BENTZON, MARTHA DRACHMANN
Draeger Frères 4 364; 26 236
draft cursive script see under SCRIPTS → types
draft script see under SCRIPTS → types
Dragalevtsi Monastery 5 144, 147; 9 210*, 511
Church of the Virgin 5 148, 153; 25 343
Dragan, Giorgio 29 23
Dragendorff, H. 27 107
dragging up see PRINTS → techniques → retroussage
Draghi, Giovanni Battista 24 836
Drăgoescu, Şerbana 26 722
Dragojlović, Stjepan 4 461
Dragomanni (family) 27 178
Dragomirna Monastery 8 161
church 26 708, 712
Dragomirna school 8 161
Dragon, Master of the 28 509
Dragon, Vittore Grubicy De see GRUBICY (DE DRAGON), VITTORE
Dragon carpets see under CARPETS → types
dragon kilns see KILNS → types → climbing
Dragon Pond Society see RYŪCHIKAI
dragon robes see under ROBES → types
dragon's-blood 12 623, 803; 18 611; 24 795, 797
Dragon style 22 319; 23 236
Dragoş (Coman) 9 210*
Dragoslav, Jovan 28 446
Dragsholm Castle 8 723
Dragulj, Emir 4 462
Drahobejl, Krocín of 8 422
Drahoňovský, Josef 8 411; 13 867; 23 272; 25 435
Drahounet 11 448
Draibel, Henri see BERALDI, HENRI
drainage systems 10 236
drains 23 417
Drais, Pierre-François 11 633
Drake, Daniel 7 327
Drake, Francis 33 545
works 33 546
Drake, Frederick (fl 1884-96) 10 675
Drake, (Johann) Friedrich (1805-1882) 9 210–11*
house 14 594
pupils 5 413; 28 94
teachers 12 406; 26 23
Drake, Heinrich 13 729
Drake, Lindsay 11 808; 18 808; 23 134; 30 411
Drake, Nathan 9 211*; 33 545
Drake, William H. 27 137; 33 174
Drake & Lasdun 30 411
Drakelow Hall (Derby.) 27 717
Drakensberg 1 376
Drakos see PHILIA-DRAKOS
Drakpa Gyaltsen 30 831
Draksarama 15 537, 539
Bhimeshvara Temple 15 537
Drama 29 702
Dramatic Style 16 691*
Drammartin, Drouet de see DROUET DE DRAMMARTIN
Drammen 23 218, 235, 237
Drancy, Cité de la Muette 24 129
Dranger, Jan 6 392
Drangianan 1 886
Drapa Ngonshey 30 818, 830
Draper, John William 22 150
draperie mouillée 9 211*
drapery 9 246; 13 422, 423; 21 294; 22 269–70
drapery painters see under PAINTERS → types
drapery paintings see under PAINTING → types
Drapery Studies, Master of the see COBURG ROUNDELS, MASTER OF THE
Drasche, Heinrich 32 437
Drasche Brickworks 5 85
Drathang 30 830
draughtsmanship see DRAWINGS
Drausch, Valentin 12 260; 19 93; 25 436
Draveil 12 145; 24 128; 31 728
Dravidians 15 192; 29 440
Drawbridge, John 4 642; 9 212*
drawbridges see under BRIDGES → types
drawers, secretary see ESCRITOIRES
drawing, industrial, education see under EDUCATION (ART) → types
drawing-frames 29 437
drawings 1 102, 107; 2 239; 9 212–33*; 14 406
cleaning 9 232
conservation 6 400–401*; 8 128–9; 9 231–3*; 15 856, 856; 21 340*
display 1 582; 9 11, 26–7*
education see under EDUCATION (ART) → types
forms
aux trois crayons 2 847*; 9 I2
chalk 9 216
Belgium 4 522; 27 299
England 11 858
France: Baroque 32 716
France: Mannerism 5 814
France: Rococo 32 918
France: 17th cent. 21 85
France: 18th cent. 4 509; 6 400
France: 19th cent. 25 671
Germany 13 723
Indonesia 15 807
Italy: Baroque 3 54; 5 866; 7 911; 8 42
Italy: Mannerism 6 141
Italy: Renaissance 9 I1; 19 186, 193; 21 758; 25 558, 909; 29 883
Italy: 16th cent. 5 855
Italy: 17th cent. 21 807
Italy: 18th cent. 5 886
Netherlands, the: Baroque 26 162
Netherlands, the: Romanticism 32 694
Netherlands, the: Symbolism 31 148
Netherlands, the: 16th cent. 28 218
Netherlands, the: 17th cent. 9 456; 26 194
charcoal 9 216; 28 338
Belgium 3 564
Germany 7 872
Italy 24 706
Portugal 28 432
crayon 8 128; 10 882; 28 503; 29 109
graphite 26 513
ground 14 56, 56

drawings
forms—cont.
ink 9 216*; 15 849–52*, 853, 855*; 24 350
Africa 1 431
Belgium: Early Netherlandish style 10 711
Belgium: Mannerism 29 742
Belgium: Renaissance 4 906; 33 170
Belgium: 16th cent. 4 839; 32 711
England: Art Nouveau 3 445
England: Neo-classicism 7 340
England: Neo-Romanticism 22 752
England: Romanticism 22 152
England: 17th cent. 3 244, 245
England: 19th cent. 4 87
France: Art informel 2 544
France: Baroque 3 632
France: Gothic 13 137; 20 742
France: 17th cent. 8 883
France: 18th cent. 2 709; 12 596; 22 87; 27 531
France: 19th cent. 13 879
Germany: Gothic 12 385, 387
Germany: Renaissance 3 102; 4 760
Germany: 16th cent. 33 130; 24 355
Germany: 19th cent. 7 871
Gothic 12 385, 387; 13 137
Italy: Baroque 2 126; 13 788; 21 766; 24 836
Italy: Mannerism 19 545; 23 575; 24 199
Italy: Neo-Classicism 12 585
Italy: Renaissance 3 157; 9 220; 14 871; 19 184, 192; 22 237; 24 861; 32 13
Italy: 15th cent. 29 407
Italy: 16th cent. 1 103, 663
Italy: 17th cent. 6 37
Italy: 19th cent. 2 320
Mongolia 21 881
Native North Americans 14 814
Netherlands, the: Baroque 9 222; 24 349
Netherlands, the: Mannerism 22 840
Netherlands, the: 15th cent. 20 694
Netherlands, the: 16th cent. 20 247, 248; 30 62; 33 252
Netherlands, the: 17th cent. 4 96; 5 324; 12 531; 23 612
Portugal 32 157
South Africa 1 431
Spain 6 46; 9 II1
Sudan 29 896
Switzerland 1 788; 8 822; 13 268; 19 257, 414; 29 673
Tunisia 31 425
United States of America 28 541
20th cent. 2 839
leadpoints 21 339; 32 570
metalpoints 3 652; 9 216–17; 21 339–40*
oil transfer 18 110, 111
pastel 9 216; 23 784; 24 242–4*
England 14 549; 19 818
France 5 922; 8 624; 15 VI1; 23 296; 24 III; 31 705
Germany 18 80; 24 245, VI
Italy 5 878; 24 IV
Switzerland 30 132
pencil 9 226, 758
sand 1 56
silverpoints 9 217; 19 191, 192; 21 340, 340; 27 147
trois crayons, aux see aux trois crayons
wash 9 216*
Belgium 17 651
France 4 244; 32 334
Germany 9 214; 11 752
drawings
forms
wash—cont.
Italy 26 770; 32 17, 884
historical and regional traditions
Austria 2 792, 794, 795–6, 797; 31 357–8
Bali (Indonesia) 15 804, 806*, 806, 807, 808–9*
Belgium 12 273; 21 87, 765
Byzantine 9 615
Canada 5 566*
Colombia 7 609, 610
Cuba (Caribbean) 8 234
Early Christian (c. AD 250-843) 9 615
Egypt, ancient 9 897–8*, 903, 903–4*, 906
England 9 225
Gothic 13 136
Modernism 22 56
17th cent. 19 540
19th cent. 10 479
20th cent. 9 II2
France 9 222, 225; 12 273
Germany 9 225, 440; 12 386
Gothic 2 792; 13 133, 136, 138
Greece, ancient 18 108
Guyana 13 876
Indian subcontinent 8 534; 15 210, 626
Mughal 3 320
Indonesia 15 804–9*, 806
Italy 9 26, 222, 223
Baroque 1 842
Mannerism 32 354
Renaissance 1 841; 9 220–21; 12 554
16th cent. 25 221; 26 845
17th cent. 7 911
18th cent. 24 846
Java 15 804, 805–6*, 807–8*
Mexico 21 384
Native North Americans 22 593
Netherlands, the 2 856; 9 221; 16 770; 26 900
Panama 23 904
Paraguay 24 99
Poland 23 203
Prehistoric art 25 478, 484
Romania 26 715, 716
Russia 27 389, 390
St Vincent 2 149
South Africa 29 108, 109
Surinam 30 15, 15
Switzerland 25 686
Venezuela 32 172–6*
lighting 7 732; 9 232
materials
brushes 9 216; 15 849, 855; 24 350
chalk see under forms
charcoal see under forms
crayons 8 127, 128
fixatives 6 470
frames 8 129
glazes 11 407
gold leaf 15 806
graphite 2 330; 9 217; 19 540
inks see DRAWINGS, INKS
mounts 9 232–3; 22 236
palm leaves 15 806
paper 9 215; 15 850; 24 49–50*
papyrus 9 215
parchment 9 215; 31 425
pencils 9 217
pens 9 216; 15 855; 24 348, 349, 350
port crayons see PORT CRAYONS
pottery 15 806
silk 15 850
silver leaf 15 806
size 15 850
styluses 29 884
varnishes 32 3
verdaccio 28 338
techniques
reproduction 24 655
skiagraphia 13 549
drawings
techniques—cont.
transfers, oil 18 110
types
allegorical
France 8 883
Netherlands, the 31 148
Switzerland 19 414
architectural 1 106; 2 325–7*, 328–34*, 366; 7 666, 685; 20 560; 24 654; 28 497, 498; 30 430; 31 274–5
Austria 2 328; 22 211
Britain 7 666
Carolingian 5 794–5
Denmark 8 724
England 12 131; 22 211
England: Romanticism 23 886
England: 16th cent. 30 763
England: 17th cent. 25 10
England: 18th cent. 2 331
England: 19th cent. 7 668; 27 353
France 7 666; 21 568; 22 211
France: Gothic 2 326; 13 142; 31 275; 32 569
France: Rococo 4 164
France: 13th cent. 32 569
France: 16th cent. 19 694
France: 18th cent. 4 532; 24 582;
France: 19th cent. 2 332
Germany 19 532; 22 211
Germany: Gothic 2 327; 4 189, 191
Germany: 15th cent. 28 497
Germany: 18th cent. 33 40
Gothic 2 347; 28 497
Gothic: Austria 2 328
Gothic: France 2 326; 13 142; 31 275; 32 569
Gothic: Germany 2 327; 4 189, 191
Greece, ancient 13 395, 409–10*, 412
Italy 2 328–30
Italy: Futurism 27 788
Italy: Renaissance 2 329, 330; 5 15
Italy: 16th cent. 2 330; 14 659; 26 801
Netherlands, the 12 132
Netherlands, the: 17th cent. 4 440; 27 509
Portugal 27 803
Romanesque 28 497
United States of America 2 333, 367; 13 326; 17 468; 23 361
see also CAPRICCIOS
blot 4 171*
see also AUTOMATISM; DECALCOMANIA
elevation 10 140*
figure 13 472, 535
genre 6 46; 9 226; 13 257
landscape 9 221
Belgium 4 522; 7 498; 21 360
England 8 95, 95, 96; 9 487; 29 877
Germany 8 514
Italy 7 391; 9 218, 223; 13 656
Netherlands, the: Mannerism 4 152; 14 292
Netherlands, the: 17th cent. 3 759; 4 734; 10 514; 15 41; 27 518; 31 806; 32 140, 622, 900
Switzerland 19 257
life-drawings 1 101, 102, 105; 9 222; 19 620; 23 292
China 6 811
England 19 620
Germany 9 430
Italy 21 758
see also ACADEMY FIGURES; SUR LE MOTIF
literary themes 31 869
marine 29 720; 32 141, 734
drawings
types—cont.
mythological
France 18 626; 21 764
Germany 24 355
Italy 5 866; 6 141; 11 10; 12 214, 755; 27 209
Netherlands, the 20 248
presentation 2 334; 9 215; 19 449; 25 557–8*, 558; 30 506
religious
Italy 3 651; 19 449; 21 763; 24 835; 26 770
Portugal 14 661
section 28 346*, 347
topographical
Belgium 14 618, 618
England 9 149; 22 211
France 2 27; 11 259; 21 568
Netherlands, the 5 542; 9 149; 16 585; 28 74
Shakers 28 540–41
uses
coats of arms 12 273
medical books 21 6
rock art 25 478
secco paintings 28 338
topography 12 273
transfer (printing) 9 218
see also DOODLES; SKETCHES; STUDIES; UNDERDRAWINGS; PENSIERO, PRIMO
draw looms see under LOOMS → types
drawn-thread work 18 588
draw tables see under TABLES → types
Drax, Thomas Shettenden 2 148
Drax Hall (Barbados) see under ST GEORGE (BARBADOS)
Drax Hall (Jamaica) 16 882
Drayton, Michael 14 675
Drayton House (Northants) 10 275, 276; 30 278
collections 9 28
King's Dining-room 10 275
metalwork 30 872
Drayton Lodge (Norfolk) 4 779
Drazark Monastery 2 430
Drazdovič, Ja. 3 529, 530
Dražice, John IV of see JOHN IV OF DRAŽICE
Dražovce church 28 849
Drebbel, Cornelius 32 575
Dreber, (Karl) Heinrich 9 233*
Drechsler, Johann Baptist 11 229
Drefach Felindre, Capel Penrhiw see ST FAGANS → Welsh Folk Museum
Dreger, Fritz 22 671
Dreger, Moritz 2 834
Dreghorn, Allan 12 773; 25 266; 28 227
Dregt, Johannes van 2 25
Dreher (fl c. 1728-32) 22 449; 25 124
Dreher, Peter (b 1932) 18 31
Drei, Ercole 4 278
Dreiband, Laurence 19 702
Dreier, Katherine S(ophie) 9 233*, 359; 20 287; 23 48; 31 605
collections 8 435; 31 663, 665
groups and movements 9 358; 28 920–21, 925
paintings 9 358; 18 111
personal collection 2 384
sculpture 11 877; 24 574
Drelling see DROLLING
Drenča 22 79
Drenckwaert (family) 14 293
Drentwett (family) 2 718; 12 446
Drentwett, Abraham, I (1614-66) 9 234*; 10 529; 30 783
Drentwett, Abraham, II (1647-1729) 9 234*; 12 446; 24 271
Drentwett, Balduin 2 718; 9 233
Drentwett, Elias, I 9 233
Drentwett, Johann 18 46
Drentwett, Jonas 10 529; 27 611
Drentwett, Philipp Jacob, I (c. 1583-1652) 9 233; 10 529
Drentwett, Philipp Jacob VI (1686-1754) 9 234*
Drepung 21 848; 30 806, 819, 820, 846
Dreros 8 154
agora 13 380
cult statue 4 851; 8 262, 262
sculpture 13 442
statuettes 29 567
temple 8 154; 13 376
Dresco, Arturo 28 647
Dresden 3 677; 9 234, 234–42*; 12 360, 361, 471; 25 93; 29 547
academies
Akademie der Bildenden Künste see HOCHSCHULE FÜR BILDENDEN KÜNSTE
Akademie der Künste und Hochschule für Werkkunst 12 480
Hochschule für Bildende Künste 1 105, 107
see also libraries and archives → Bibliothek der Hochschule für Bildende Künste
Armoury 9 31
art forms and materials
faience (ii) (ceramics) 9 241*
furniture 25 121
glass 12 440
hardstones 12 461
interior decoration 12 416
jewellery 9 240
lacquer 18 614
marks 9 240
metalwork 9 240*; 12 447
mirror frames 21 721
objects of vertu 9 240*
painting 12 389, 390, 391, 392, 393; 26 738, 742
porcelain 6 333
sculpture 8 384; 12 402, 406; 26 378
silver 12 446
snuff-boxes 12 457–9*, 458
tapestries 30 324
textiles 9 241*
Diana Fountain 23 252
Dynamo Stadium 29 489
ecclesiastical buildings
Cathedral 6 572; 9 237
Pietà 9 239
pulpit 25 727
sculpture 24 461
Frauenkirche 3 67, 67; 7 258; 9 241–2*; 12 373; 19 815
Hofkirche see Cathedral
Konkathedrale see Cathedral
Kreuzkirche 12 461
Sophienkirche
tomb of Giovanni Maria Nosseni 32 833
education (art) 12 478, 479
exhibitions 10 678
Gesamtministerium 13 238
Hellerau see HELLERAU
Internationale Kunstausstellung, 1926 19 477
International Hygiene Fair, 1930 27 409
libraries and archives
Bibliothek der Hochschule für Bildende Künste
collections 12 481
see also academies → Hochschule für Bildende Künste
Deutsche Fototek 2 370
Sächsische Landesbibliothek 12 481, 482
Zentrale Kunstbibliothek 2 370; 12 481
Lusthaus 8 882
Marktplatz 12 380

Dresden—cont.
museums
Albertinum
Egyptian collection **10** 91
Gemäldegalerie Neue Meister **28** 840
Greek collection **13** 470
Skulpturensammlung **28** 175
see also Grünes Gewölbe
Deutsches Hygiene-Museum **9** 237
Gemäldegalerie Alte Meister **9** 12, 237; **14** 48; **22** 363; **28** 94, 399
collections **3** 924; **9** 18, 239
directors **32** 714
frames **11** 459, 460
Gewehrgalerie **9** 238
Grünes Gewölbe **9** 238; **19** 642
altars **17** 887
collections **12** 457; **17** 888; **33** 115
ivory **24** 460
metalwork **17** 887, 888
sculpture **24** 460
see also Schloss → *Kunstkammer*
Historisches Museum **2** 454; **9** 238; **17** 888
Johanneum **3** 511; **9** 238; **10** 738; **12** 475; **29** 485; **32** 832
collections **33** 115
Kupferstichkabinett **9** 238
collections **11** 760; **26** 177
directors **14** 314; **33** 115
silver **17** 888
Museum der Photographie **24** 682
Museum für Geschichte der Stadt Dresden **9** 236
Royal Gallery **24** 706; **26** 232
Schilling-Museum **28** 95
Semper-Galerie **26** 378
Staatliche Kunstsammlungen **19** 705; **27** 46
Zwinger **9** *236*, 238, 242*; **12** 373, 791; **23** 471, 812; **25** 240
metalwork **11** 626
Porzellansammlung **9** 238
sculpture **12** 405; **24** 460
Wallpavillon **25** *240*
see also Gemäldegalerie Alte Meister; Historisches Museum
palaces
Holländisches Palais *see* Japanisches Palais
Japanisches Palais **9** 235–6; **19** 642; **21** 64
collections **5** 348; **9** 29, 238; **12** 412; **33** 115
porcelain **33** 114
sculpture **18** 82
Neues Palais **25** 240
Palais im Grossen Garten **12** 373; **29** 547
Pirnaisches Tor **32** 832
railway station **25** 856
Sächsischer Kunstverein **25** 789
Schloss **10** 738, 741; **11** 626; **12** 369; **32** 681, 832
Georgentor **12** 366; **32** 831
Kunstkammer **9** 238; **33** 110, 113
see also Museums → Albertinum → Grünes Gewölbe
Langer Gang
Furstenzug **30** 506
Schloss Brühl **30** 885
Schloss Pillnitz **12** 373
Banqueting Hall **32** 676
Stallhof *see* Johanneum
Synagogue **12** 376; **17** 547, *548*; **22** 60
theatres
Burgtheater **30** 676
Dresden
theatres—cont.
Hoftheater (1719-1849) **30** 676
Hoftheater (1838-69) **12** 376; **26** 190; **28** *398*; **30** 677
sculpture **14** 48
Hoftheater (1871-) *see* Semperoper
Komödienhaus **30** 676
Semperoper (1871-) **26** 190; **30** 506, 677
sculpture **3** 511
Villa Rosa **32** 554
Der Weg (Schule für Gestaltung) **17** 921
Dresden/Wrocław Machzor *see under* MACHZORS → individual manuscripts
Dresden *Boy* **25** 179
Dresdener Werkstätten für Handwerkskunst **2** 571; **26** 374
Dresden Prayerbook, Master of the **3** 555; **19** 727; **20** 658–9*
collaboration **20** 452
groups and movements **12** 525
pupils **20** 749
works **20** 631, *659*, 725
Dresden Secession *see* SECESSION (DRESDEN)
Dresden Sketchbook *see under* SKETCHBOOKS → individual manuscripts
Dresden work *see* EMBROIDERY → types → *point de Saxe*
Dresdner Neustadt **19** 642
dress **9** 243–95*; **14** 425
collections *see under* COLLECTIONS → types
historical and regional traditions **9** 253
Achaemenid **1** *884*, 886–7*
Afghanistan **1** 208
Africa **1** 295, 347–9*, *348*, *388*
Ainu **1** 493, *493*; **30** VII2
Algeria **16** 458
Ancient Near East **1** 883–8*, *884*
Anglo-Saxon **9** 253, *253*
Antilles, Lesser **5** 747
Arabia **1** 887
Armenia (Europe) **1** 886
Asante **1** *388*
Assyrian **1** *884*, 885–6, 887
Austria **2** 825
Aztec **7** 636; **21** 262
Babylonian **1** *884*, 885, 886, 887
Bactria **1** 886; **6** 251
Bali (Indonesia) **15** 813*
Bamana **1** 256
Bamum **3** 153*
Belgium **3** 609; **18** *591*
Benin, Kingdom of **3** 441
Berber **16** 457
Bhutan **3** *915*
Bolivia **4** 266*
Britain **9** 290*
Buddhism **6** *310*, 311; **7** 78; **17** 374; **21** 877
Burma **5** *248*, 249–50*, *249*
Byzantine **9** 252*, 639–44*, *644*
Cambodia **5** 502, 503*
Canada **22** 630
Cappadocia **1** 886
Caria **1** 887
Carib **29** 194; **30** 13
Caribbean Islands **5** 748
Carolingian **9** 253–4*
Celtic **9** 252–3*
Central Asia, Eastern **6** 309–11*, *310*
Central Asia, Western **6** 250–52*
Chancay **29** 183
Chimú **29** 183
China **7** 74–9*, 144, 632
Han period (206 BC-AD 220) **7** *75*
Qing period (1644-1911) **7** *78*
Song period (AD 960-1279) **7** *76*
dress
historical and regional traditions
China—cont.
Yuan period (1279-1368) **7** 50
Christianity **16** 453
Colombia **7** 602; **21** 804
Cook Islands **7** 791
Coptic **9** 639; **16** 431
Daoism **7** 78
Early Christian (*c.* AD 250-843) **9** 251*, 639–44*, *644*
Egypt **1** 348; **16** 431, 452, 453, 456–7, 458
Ayyubid **16** 452
Early Christian (*c.* AD 250-843) **9** 643–4
Mamluk **16** 452, 454
Egypt, ancient **1** 887; **3** 441; **10** 42–6*, *43*, 61
Elamite **1** 885, 886
England **9** 244, 269
Anglo-Saxon **9** *253*
16th cent. **9** 271
17th cent. **9** 278–9*
18th cent. **9** 282*, *282*, 283–4*, *284*
19th cent. **9** 286, 288–9
Etruscan **10** 635–6*
France **9** 244, 269, 279–81*; **30** 672
8th cent. AD **9** *281*
17th cent. **9** 277, 278*
18th cent. **9** 281–5*, *283*, *285*
Gabon **11** 879
Germany **9** 269, 273, 279, 288
Greece, ancient **1** 887; **9** 245–9*
Guatemala **13** 760
Haida **22** 632
Hausa **1** 249; **14** *231*
Hawaii **14** 249
Hittite **1** *884*, 885
Hungary **16** 463
Igbo **15** 115
Inca **15** 162, 163–4; **29** *183*, 183–4
Indian subcontinent **15** 689–92*, *690*, 733, 734
Indonesia **15** 792, 794, *796*, 807, 812–13*
Indus civilization **15** 689
Inuit **22** 629, 630
Iran **16** 452, 453, 454, 457, 458, 463–6*
Iran, ancient **1** 883, *884*, 886
Iraq **16** 455–6
Islamic **16** 429, 452–8*, 459
Algeria **16** 458
Berber **16** 457
Egypt **16** 453, 456–7
Hungary **16** 463
Indian subcontinent **15** 692
Iran **16** 453, 458, 463*
Iraq **16** 455–6
North Africa **16** 456–7, 458–60*
Ottoman **16** 454, 458, 460–63*, *462*
Spain **16** 457
Tunisia **16** 458
Turkey **16** 453, 458, 460–62*, *462*
Italy **9** 259, 260–61*, 262–7*; **10** 635–6*; **16** 760
Japan **7** 632; **14** 429; **17** 314, 332, 353–7, 359, 373–7*
Buddhism **17** 374
Shinto **17** 374
Shugendō **17** *43*
Java **15** 792, 812–13*
Jewish art **16** 453
Kassite **1** 885
Kenya **1** 255, *256*
Khmer **30** 623
Khwarazm **6** 251
Korea **18** 357–9*, *358*
Laos **18** 770–74*
Libya **1** 887
Lydia **1** 887
dress
historical and regional traditions—cont.
Malaysia **20** 180*
Manichaeism **6** 311
Medes **1** 886
Merovingian **9** 252–3*
Mesoamerica, Pre-Columbian **21** *261*, 261–2*
Mesopotamia **1** 883–4, *884*
Mexico **21** 394
Micronesia, Federated States of **23** 723
Mitannian **1** 885
Mongol **7** 77
Mongolia **21** 876–7*
Nabataea **16** 454
Native North Americans **3** 441; **22** 623, 628–31*, 632*, *632*, 633*, 634*, *635*, 635–7*, *637*, *640*, *642*, 648, 649, 650; **28** *546*
Navajo **22** 634, *635*
Nazca **29** 182
Ndebele **22** 712, *713*; **29** 104
Nepal **22** 787*
Netherlands, the **9** 269, 277*, 278–9*
Nigeria **1** *348*; **14** *231*
North Africa **16** 456–7, 458–60*
Nubia **1** 887
Ottoman **16** 454, 458, 460–63*, *462*
Pacific Islands **23** 723
Panama **21** 804, *804*
Paracas culture **29** 182
Parthian **1** *884*, 886, 887*; **6** 251
Persian **1** 886; **16** 456
Philippines **24** 628*, *629*
Poland **25** 132–3; **27** 843
Prehistoric art **25** 473
Rome, ancient **9** 245–6*, 249–50*, 251*; **27** 112, *113*, 113–14
Sasanian **1** *884*, 887–8*
Scandinavia **9** 254*
Scythian **1** 886; **6** 251
Serbia **28** 456–7, 458
Shinto **17** 374
Shugendō **17** *43*
Siberia **28** *546*
Sierra Leone **1** 347
Society Islands **28** *922*, 922–3
Sogdiana **1** 886; **6** 251
South Africa **22** *713*; **29** 104
South America, Pre-Columbian **29** 151–2*, 181–4, 188–9, 194*
Inca **29** *183*, 183–4
Nazca **29** 182
Paracas culture **29** 182
Spain
Islamic **16** 457, 458
13th cent. **9** 259–60
14th cent. **9** 261–2*
15th cent. **9** 264*
16th cent. **9** 267–8*
17th cent. **9** 277
Sri Lanka **29** 470*
Sumatra **15** 794, 813*
Sumerian **1** 881
Surinam **30** 13
Syria **9** 644; **16** 452, 454, 455, 457
Syria-Palestine **1** *884*, 885; **30** 181
Tarascan **30** 342
Thailand **30** 619*, 622–8*, *625*
Tibet **30** 807, 837–9*, *838*
Tuareg **16** 457
Tunisia **16** 458
Turkey **16** 453, 458, 460–62*, *462*
United States of America **9** 289–90*
Uzbekistan **31** *783*
Vietnam **32** 486–7*, *487*, 490
Viking **9** 254*, *254*
Yoruba **1** 348, 349
Zoroastrianism **16** 453
dress
historical and regional traditions—cont.
Zulu **33** 724–5, *725*
11th cent. **9** 255–6*
12th cent. **9** 256–7*
13th cent. **9** 257–60*
14th cent. **9** 269–70*
15th cent. **9** 270–71*
16th cent. **9** 271–6*
17th cent. **9** 277–8*
18th cent. **9** 281*
19th cent. **9** 285–90*
20th cent. **9** *291*, 291–5*, *292*, *293*, *294*
materials
appliqué **6** 251
barkcloth **7** 791; **11** 69; **14** 249; **15** 807; **25** 182; **28** 922, *922*
basketwork **3** 332
beads **1** 347; **22** 712, *713*; **25** 546
beadwork **1** 349; **3** 441; **6** 251
coconuts **28** *922*
cotton **16** 462; **18** 358; **24** *629*; **28** 717; **31** *783*
embroidery
Africa **1** 295, 349
Central Asia, Western **6** 250–51, 252
China **7** 50, 78, *78*
Islamic **16** 459–60
Italy **16** 760
Japan **17** 314
ermine **9** 255
feathers **7** 636; **15** 163; **28** *922*
felt **6** 251
fur **16** 456
glass **25** 546
gold leaf **17** *309*, 314
hemp **6** 251
lace **18** *591*, 591
leather **6** 251; **10** 61; **19** 2
linen **9** 246, 247; **28** 717
miniver **9** 255
paper **17** 359
pearls **6** 251
quills **22** 648, 649, 650
quilting **25** 820, 821
rami (fibre) **17** 354; **18** 358
shells **28** 922, *922*
silk **3** *915*; **5** *248*; **6** 251, *252*, 309; **7** 76, 77, *78*; **9** 251; **16** 462, 465; **18** 357, 358; **27** *113*; **28** 715, 717; **31** *783*
silver leaf **17** 314
skins **6** 251
wool **6** 251; **9** 246; **16** 455
dressed masonry *see under* MASONRY → types
Dressel, Cuno & Otto **31** 262
Dressel, Kistler & Co, Passau **14** 606
Dresser, Christopher **1** 111; **9** 295*; **10** 283; **15** 821; **19** 594
ceramics **10** 312
collaboration **19** 415
furniture **16** 60
glass **10** 320, *335*; **28** 260
groups and movements **10** 98; **17** 440; **32** 415
metalwork **4** 88; **10** 344
patrons and collectors **14** 132
staff **28** 881
teachers **10** 373
wallpaper **19** 359; **25** 373
writings **10** 335
Dresser & Holme **9** 295
dressers **22** 870, *870*; **28** 666; **32** 788–9
dresses
historical and regional traditions
China **7** 78
England **10** *357*; **25** *821*
France **4** II
Hungary **10** II1; **15** *11*
Islamic **16** *460*, 461, 462
Jordan **16** *460*
Native North Americans **22** 655

dresses
historical and regional traditions—cont.
Ottoman 16 460, 461, 462
Turkey 16 461, 462
materials
beads 4 II
coral 10 II1
embroidery 10 II1; 15 11; 16 460
leather 22 655
quilting 25 821
sequins 4 II
silk 10 357
velvet 10 II1; 15 11
dressing dolls see under DOLLS → types
dressing-tables see under TABLES → types
dressoirs see BUFFETS
Dreutzler, Hannelore 30 103
Dreux, St Louis Chapel 20 868; 31 131
Dreux (family) 14 412
Dreux, Pierre Mauclerc, Comte de 6 498
Dreux de la Châtre, Le see LE DREUX DE LA CHÂTRE
Dreven, Maarten van 14 43
Drevet, Claude 9 296; 26 229
Drevet, Pierre 9 296*; 10 393; 24 805; 26 229, 388
Drevet, Pierre-Imbert 9 296; 10 393; 26 229
Drevin, Aleksandr (Davidovich) 9 296*; 27 395; 31 520; 32 661
groups and movements 26 384
pupils 28 394
Drevinishch, Rudolph Aleksandr see DREVIN, ALEKSANDR (DAVIDOVICH)
Drew, Edward 29 117
Drew, Jane B(everley) 9 296–7*; 23 134
collaboration 11 808; 17 463; 19 46; 23 134
staff 8 508
works 1 319; 6 445, 445; 15 168
Drew, Thomas 3 537; 9 297*, 322; 19 845*
Drewal, Henry John
works 1 239, 241
Drewe, Julius 6 62; 19 820
Drewitz 4 666
Drexel, Friedrich 13 848
Drexhage, Sterkenburg, Bodon and Venstra 4 217
Drexler, Arthur 3 465
Dreyer, Benedikt 12 401; 13 120
Dreyer, Carl 18 577
Dreyer, Dankvart (Christian Magnus) 8 735; 9 297–8*; 14 572
Dreyfus, Gustave 9 298*, 467; 19 188; 25 19
Dreyfus-Koch, Martha 14 570
Dreyfuss, Henry 3 538; 8 802; 15 824, 825
Dreyfuss & Blackford 1 495
Driade 29 547
Driel, G. van 17 466
Drielst, Egbert van 9 298*; 12 620; 19 116; 22 847
Drielst, Jan Vuuring van 9 298
Drière, de La (family) see LA DRIÈRE, DE (FAMILY)
Dries, Jan 3 574
Driessche, Gummarus van den 33 170
Driffield, Peter
works 24 579
Driggs, Elsie 25 461
Drigung 30 818
Drijfhout, Bartholomeus (Fransz.) 2 385; 9 179, 299*
Drijfhout, Laureys 9 299
Drillenburg, Willem van 14 794
drilling 29 705–6*
drills 9 821; 13 436; 16 859; 21 241; 27 16, 17; 29 705–6
Drinker, Catherine Ann 3 463
drinking fountains see under FOUNTAINS → types
drinking-horns 9 690; 14 763, 763; 30 110
Drinkwater, Peter 12 639
Drinov, Marin 5 163
Drion, Prosper 21 499
drip painting see under PAINTING → types
Drissi, Moulay Ahmed 22 129
Driver, James 14 207
Drivier, L.-E. 11 568, 569
Drizzan, Antonio 14 817, 818
Drljača, Lazar 4 461
Drnkov, Blagoja 19 884
Drnková-Zarecká, Věra 8 420
Dro 8 490
Drobeta-Turnu Severin fortress 26 706
Drobil, Michael 33 284
Drobin parish church 25 113
Drobník, Antonín 33 630
Drobný, Zdeněk 25 446
Droeshout, John 9 299
Droeshout, Martin (i) (1560s-c. 1642) 9 299*
Droeshout, Martin (ii) (b 1601) 9 299
Droeshout, Michael 9 299
Droeshout, Susanna 21 509
Drogheda, Charles Moore, Marquess of see MOORE, CHARLES, Marquess of Drogheda
Drogobych 31 546, 549, 550
Church of the Exaltation of the Cross 31 552, 552
St George 31 552
Drogo of Clairvaux, Abbot of Byloke 12 522
Drogo of Metz, Archbishop 5 800, 803, 810; 20 330; 21 729
Drogo Sacramentary see under SACRAMENTARIES → individual manuscripts
Droguet, Nicolas 2 115
drolleries 9 299*
see also BORDERS (MANUSCRIPT); MINIATURES (MANUSCRIPT ILLUMINATION)
Drolling, Louise-Adéone 9 299
Drolling, Martin 9 299–300*
pupils 9 300, 467; 11 48
reproductive prints by others 8 595
works 11 542; 24 148
Drolling, Michel-Martin 1 106; 9 299, 300*; 11 544, 671
assistants 27 165
pupils
Aman, Theodor 1 750
Baudry, (Jacques-Aimé-)Paul 3 396
Bertall 3 849
Breton, Jules 4 754
Curzon, (Paul-)Alfred de 8 281
Galland, P(ierre) V(ictor) 12 13
Henner, Jean-Jacques 14 390
Nègre, Charles 22 723
Robinson, John Charles 26 472
Strutt, William (1825-1915) 29 790
reproductive prints by others 4 126
works 28 170
Drollinger, Eugen 33 283
Drôme, Palais Idéal 23 334
dromoi 13 886; 14 340; 29 487
Dromore Castle (Co. Limerick) 12 840; 16 25
Dromton 5 105
Dronten, De Meerpaal Hall 29 428
Droochsloot, Joost Cornelisz. 9 364
drop arches see ARCHES → types → basket
drop black see BONE BLACK
drop ornaments see PENDANTS (i) (ROOFS)
Dropsy, Henry 7 839
Drossis, Leonidas 13 354
Drost, Erika 25 125
Drost, Jan 25 125
Drost, Willem 9 300–301*; 22 843
works 9 300
Drot de Dijon see DUVEY, LOYS
Drouais (family) 13 228
Drouais, François-Hubert 9 301–2*; 13 301
collaboration 11 368
patrons and collectors 3 890; 9 313; 12 312
pupils 9 302
reproductive prints by others 3 463; 30 24
works 9 302; 11 410, 493; 24 135
Drouais, Hubert 9 301*
pupils 9 301
reproductive prints by others 12 179; 24 480
teachers 31 379
works 21 643
Drouais, Jean-Germain 9 301, 302–3*
collaboration 8 561
competitions 25 638
pupils 12 186
teachers 8 556, 557
Drouet de Drammartin 5 206, 207
Drouillard 2 651
Drouin, Florent 3 635; 22 455
Drouin, René 6 23; 19 17
Drouot's 4 23; 10 91
Drouville, Gaspar 23 530
Drouyn, Leo 4 391
Drovetti, Bernardino 10 90, 93; 28 3
Drowne, Shem 4 481; 31 652, 653; 33 8
works 31 653
Droz, Jean see DUVET, JEAN (fl 1540-56)
Droz, Jean-Pierre 4 540; 9 303*
Drozhdin, Pyotr 19 279
D'rrbach, Jacqueline 11 644
Drtikol, František 9 303*; 25 433; 27 205
Drubbeck 23 647
al-Drubi, Hafid 16 2
Drucker, Philip 16 806; 18 881; 27 756; 31 140, 310
Drudus (family) 7 921, 922
Drudus de Trivio 9 304*; 18 869; 26 624; 32 75
Druet, Antoine 12 649; 22 136
Drugulin, Wilhelm Eduard 10 211
Druitgen von Andernach 20 758
Drukpa 3 912
Drukyul see BHUTAN
Drum, William 5 575; 25 803
Drum Castle (Grampian) 28 224; 31 230
Drumcondra printworks 10 356
Drumlanrig Castle (Dumfries & Galloway) 28 225
Drummond, Andrew 9 304*
Drummond, George (1687-1766) 9 723; 28 269
Drummond, George A(lexander) (1827-1910) 5 589; 9 305*; 22 38
Drummond, Henry 3 174; 13 610
Drummond, Huntly Redpath 9 305
Drummond, James 13 868; 24 569
Drummond, John, Duke of Melfort 4 610
Drummond, Malcolm 5 516, 517
works 5 517
Drummond, Robert Hay, Archbishop of York 33 91
Drummond, Samuel 14 178; 17 673
Drummond, William E(ugene) 6 578; 9 305*; 25 446
Drummonds 2 765
Drumont, Edouard 33 198
drum piers see under PIERS (ii) (MASONRY) → types
drums (architecture) 9 304*
drums (musical instruments) 22 375
historical and regional traditions
Ancient Near East 1 891
Asante 2 590*, 591
Aztec 21 257
Baga 3 47
Bali (Indonesia) 15 783, 817
Bangwa 10 124
Burma 5 256–7*, 258; 22 376
Burundi 5 285
Cambodia 5 508, 509
China 8 853, 853
Côte d'Ivoire 1 360
Cuba (Caribbean) 8 230
Dian culture 8 853, 853
Dong Son 4 795
Fiji 11 68
Ibibio 15 65*
Igbo 1 243; 10 124
Indian subcontinent 22 376
Indonesia 15 754, 756, 783, 787, 817
Japan 17 248, 333
Java 15 817
Kuba (iii) (Zaïre) 1 355
Laos 22 376
Luba 19 741*
Maya 21 257
Mesoamerica, Pre-Columbian 21 256–7*
Mongolia 21 879
Papua New Guinea 24 65
Prehistoric art 29 229
South-east Asia 29 229
Sumatra 15 787
Thailand 22 376; 30 637, 637
Tibet 30 844
Venda 32 154
Vietnam 32 489
Zaïre 1 360
materials
bronze 5 256–7, 258; 8 853, 853; 29 229, 229
parchment 24 106
skins 24 69
wood 2 591; 24 69; 30 637
types
Dong Son 15 816; 29 229
hand-drums 24 69, 74*, 75
Heger I 15 816
Heger III 5 256–7
military 22 375
Pejeng 15 816; 29 229, 229
slit-drums 1 357; 21 256, 257; 22 375, 375, 377; 24 68–9, 69; 31 892, 892–3
Drury, Alfred 9 305–6*
collaboration 4 221
groups and movements 23 34
patrons and collectors 14 132
Drury Lowe (Holden), William (1802-1877) 9 306*
Drury-Lowe, William (1877-1916) 9 306
Drusián, Bethlen 15 3
works 15 3
Druzba 5 150
Druzhinin, Pyotr 27 415
Dry, Camille N. 4 81
Dryad 33 157
works 33 157
Dryander 1 841
Dryburgh Abbey (Borders) 28 233
Dryden, John 9 306*
productions 29 767; 30 674
works 9 372; 13 646; 31 768
Dryffhout, Bartholomeus (Franz.) see DRIJFHOUT, BARTHOLOMEUS (FRANZ.)
drying
brick 4 768
ceramics 6 330
leather 19 1
drying—cont.
parchment 24 106
wood 33 327
drying kilns see under KILNS → types
drying oils see under OILS → types
dry lacquer see under LACQUER → types
dry-landscape gardens see under GARDENS → types
dry plates see PHOTOGRAPHY → processes → gelatin dry plates
drypoints 9 307–10*, 307, 308; 20 693, 693; 25 597, 605, 614; 26 230; 28 361
Drysdale, George 29 695
Drysdale, Russell 2 750, 767; 4 882; 9 310–11*
dry-stone masonry see under MASONRY → types
DS, Master 20 793–4*
Dschang 5 525
Du 24 429, 453
dual chariots see under CHARIOTS → types
Duane, G. W., Bishop 32 555
Duane Street Group 26 382
Duanfang (1861-1911) 6 867; 9 311*
Duan Fang altar table 7 32
Duanqi see DUANZHOU
Duany, Andres 2 494; 18 456
Duan Yucai 9 311*
Duanzhou 7 94, 135
Duart, José Piquer y see PIQUER Y DUART, JOSÉ
Duarte, António 25 302
Duarte, Carlos 19 467; 25 294
Duarte, Diego 9 311*
collections 3 615; 27 301
paintings 8 464; 32 268
Duarte, Gaspar 9 311
Duarte, Helio Queiroz see QUEIROZ DUARTE, HELIO
Duarte, Homero 24 96
Duarte Barbosa 15 698
Duarte da Silva, Manuel 23 454
Dubai
architecture 31 584
al-Fahidi Fort see Museum
houses 16 270
Jumayra 2 246, 250, 251, 273
Jumayra Mosque 31 584
Museum 2 275; 31 584, 585
palace of Shaykh Sa'id 31 584
see also UNITED ARAB EMIRATES
Dubai, J. 19 883
Dubain, Alain 11 631; 19 397
Duban, (Jacques-)Félix 9 312–13*; 11 520, 521, 671; 24 157
collaboration 9 338; 12 155; 18 581, 816; 28 746; 31 346
groups and movements 24 173; 26 190; 28 345
patrons and collectors 11 659
pupils 3 76; 8 476, 879; 25 816
restorations 4 156
works 3 422, 826; 8 593; 9 312; 11 521, 523, 905; 24 173; 25 172
Dubarry, Albert 32 96
Du Barry, (Marie-Jeanne Bécu,) Comtesse 9 313–14*
architecture 6 509; 11 883; 19 56; 20 131; 24 290
collections 27 224
furniture 5 767; 8 448; 19 115; 31 870
metalwork 13 234
paintings 10 478; 11 368; 22 111; 32 429
sculpture 1 665; 4 248; 5 380; 32 76
tapestries 19 649
Dubay, Orest 28 853, 854
Dubbels, Hendrik (Jakobsz.) 3 84; 9 314*; 20 424
Dube, Tubayi 33 603

Dube, Wolf-Dieter **12** 477
Du Bellay, Guillaume **19** 690
Du Bellay, Jean, Cardinal **11** 513; **19** 690
Düben, C. W. von **14** 692
Dubeneckis, V. **19** 499
Dubicki, Ignacy **25** 124
Dubicki, Jan **22** 449; **25** 124
Dubicki, Mikołaj **22** 449
Du Billant, Pierre *see* PIERRE DU BILLANT
Dubiner, Sam **16** 570
Dubino, SS Pietro e Andrea **30** 132
Dubinovsky, Lazar' **21** 811, 812
Dubkund, Jaina temple **15** 292
Dublin **9** *314*, 314–23*; **16** *5*, 6; **32** 528, 529
academies and art schools
College of Marketing and Design **16** 37
Metropolitan School of Art *see* National College of Art and Design
National College of Art and Design **16** 18, 37, 38
Royal Hibernian Academy **16** 16, 17, 37
Royal Irish Academy **16** 11; **24** 562
Airport, Terminal building **16** *11*, 12
art forms and materials
amber **1** 761
architecture **12** 45; **16** 9; **23** 860; **32** 534
bookbindings **4** 354; **12** 628
clocks **16** 26
dioramas **8** 911
forks **8** *284*
furniture **16** 25, 26, 27
glass **9** 320*; **16** 29, 30
gold **9** 320*; **16** 31
marks **9** 320
metalwork **15** 873
painting **9** *319*
pottery **16** 28
silver **9** 320*; **16** *31*
stained glass **9** 321*
tables **16** *27*
textiles **16** 34, *34*
Arts and Commerce Building **16** 12
banks
Allied Irish Bank **16** 35, 36
Bank of Ireland **9** 316, *316*; **13** 237; **14** 31; **16** 8, 12; **24** 305
collections **16** 35, 36
interior decoration **16** 23
portico **25** 268
Central Bank **16** 12
Bewley's Oriental Café **7** 378
Bluecoat School **16** 8
Bord na Móna Building **16** 12
Bus Station **16** 12
Castle **8** 133; **16** 9, 14
cemeteries
Glasnevin Cemetery **6** 164
Mt Jerome Cemetery **6** 164
City Hall **2** 452; **23** 253
collections **9** 318–19
craftsmen and artists **16** 25
Custom House **12** 44; **16** 9, 21
Dail Eireann Building *see* houses → Leinster House
ecclesiastical buildings
Cathedral of the Holy Trinity *see* Christ Church Cathedral
Christ Church Cathedral **9** *321*, 321–2*; **13** 45; **16** 7; **22** 217
St Mary's Chapel of Ease **16** 10, *10*
St Mary's Pro-Cathedral **16** 11
memorial to Archbishop Murray **16** 21
memorial to Cardinal Cullen **16** 21
Dublin
ecclesiastical buildings—cont.
St Patrick's Cathedral **9** 322*; **13** 45; **16** 7
monument to Archbishop Thomas Jones **16** 20
monument to Richard Boyle, 1st Earl of Cork **16** 20
St Thomas's Abbey **32** 416
University Church **5** 340
exhibitions **9** 318, 319
Great Industrial Exhibition, 1853 **15** 883
Four Courts **9** 83; **12** *44*, 44–5; **16** 9, 21; **18** 887
portico **25** 268
General Post Office **16** 9; **25** 268
Government Building and College of Science **16** 11, 28
guilds **9** 318, 320; **16** 25
House of Lords *see* banks → Bank of Ireland
houses **16** 8, 12
Charlemont House *see* museums → Municipal Gallery of Modern Art
9 Henrietta Street
interior decoration **16** 23, *23*
Leinster House **6** 63, *64*; **16** 24; **18** 634
20 Lower Dominick Street **16** 24
Mansion House **7** 377
St Patrick's Deanery **16** 26
80 St Stephen's Green **16** 23
85 St Stephen's Green **16** 23; **18** 634
Tyrone House **18** 634
Irish Management Institute Training Centre **16** 12
Kilmainham Hospital *see* Royal Hospital
King's Inns **16** 9, 21
libraries and archives
Central Library **16** 11
College of Technology Library **16** 38
Irish Architectural Archive **16** 38
National Library of Ireland **16** 38
see also under museums → National Gallery of Ireland; Trinity College; University College
monuments
Irish National War Memorial **16** 12
Thomas Davis Monument **16** 22
Wolfe Tone Monument **16** 22
Municipal Technical School **16** 37
museums **9** 318–19
Chester Beatty Library and Gallery of Oriental Art **3** 449
collections **15** 743, 744; **16** 36, 38; **17** 434
Douglas Hyde Gallery *see under* Trinity College
Guinness Museum **16** 37
Hugh Lane Gallery *see* Municipal Gallery of Modern Art
Irish Museum of Modern Art **16** 36
Municipal Gallery of Modern Art **6** 94; **9** 319; **16** 8, 36; **18** 727
collections **18** 727
National Gallery of Ireland **9** 319; **11** 360; **16** 16, 36
collections **3** 449, 522; **16** 36; **18** 727; **24** 562
directors **9** 200; **28** 886
library **16** 38
Milltown collection **19** 64
National Museum of Ireland **1** 66; **15** 744; **16** 11, 36
Dublin
museums—cont.
National Museum of Science and Art **9** 319
Natural History Museum **16** 11
see also academies → Royal Irish Academy
see also Trinity College
O'Connell Street **9** *315*
Old Parliament House *see* banks → Bank of Ireland
parks and gardens
Garden of Remembrance **16** 22
New Gardens **23** 254
Phoenix Park **12** 138
Parliament Building *see* houses → Leinster House
Radio Telefís Eireann Broadcasting Centre **16** 12; **28** 284
Rotunda Assembly Rooms **2** 617
Rotunda Hospital **8** 111; **16** 24; **29** 837
Royal Exchange **7** 666; **10** 669
Royal Hospital **16** 8, 20, 25, 35; **26** 475
interior decoration **16** 22
see also museums → Irish Museum of Modern Art
Royal Institute of Architects of Ireland **16** 37
Sackville Street *see* O'Connell Street
Smock Alley Playhouse **16** 14
Trinity College **9** 322–3*, *323*; **16** 12, 37
collections **16** 36
Douglas Hyde Gallery **16** 37
furniture **16** 28
library **5** 197; **16** 38; **19** 314
monument to Dr Richard Baldwin **14** *500*
Museum Building **8** 586; **16** *10*, 11, 21; **23** 600
Provost's House **16** 24; **23** 860
Richard Baldwin Monument **14** 500
sculpture **16** 21
University College **16** 11, 12, 37
library **16** 38
Sports Building **16** 12
urban planning **12** 229
Dublin Art Club **23** 599
Dublin Art Foundry **16** 22
Dubliner, Sam **30** 421
Dublin Painters **14** 397
Dublin Pottery **16** 29
Dublin Society **9** 318; **16** 14, 15, 21, 25, 33, 34, 37
Du Blocq, Jean **19** 826
Dubnica, SS Peter and Paul **25** 343
Dubno **31** 557
Church of the Transfiguration **31** 563
Dubois (family) **4** 391
Dubois, Abraham **31** 649
Dubois, (Louis-Auguste-) Albert **9** 323–4*; **22** 745, 746
Dubois, Alphée **25** 669
Dubois, Ambroise **9** 328, 385; **11** 260, 262, 267, 533, 656, 755; **24** 134; **30** 358
Dubois, Fernand **3** 605
Dubois, Gilles **6** 454; **11** 608
Dubois, Guillam (*c*. 1610-80) **21** 800
Dubois, Guillaume (1654-1740) **9** 325
Dubois, Guillaume, Cardinal (1656-1722) **11** 662; **23** 516
Du Bois, Guy Pène *see* Pène du Bois, Guy
Du Bois, Hendrik **9** 327
Du Bois, Jacob (*fl* 1710) **33** 280
Dubois, Jacques (1694-1763) **9** 324*; **11** 591, 596; **17** 666
Dubois, J. B. **22** 827
works **22** *827*
Dubois, Jean **9** 325*
pupils **21** 889
works **8** 890
Dubois, Louis (Jean-Baptiste) (1830-80) **9** 325–6*
groups and movements **2** 511; **3** 562; **5** 44; **28** 921; **32** 380
Dubois, Louis (1867-1916) **2** 396
Dubois, Max **19** 40
Dubois, Nicholas **12** 6
Dubois, Paul (i) (1829-1905) **9** 326*; **11** 566; **31** 382
groups and movements **11** 565; **28** 345
pupils **20** 839; **33** 601
works **6** 453
Dubois, Paul (-Maurice) (ii) (1859-1938) **9** 326–7*; **31** 874
groups and movements **19** 321; **32** 591
pupils **8** 485
teachers **28** 756
Dubois, René **7** 658; **9** 324; **11** 596
works **32** *337*
Dubois, Robert **6** 454; **11** 608
Du Bois, Simon **3** 759; **9** 327*
Dubois, Victor **6** 454
Dubois de la Vrillièrea **26** 206
Dubois de Montpéreaux **6** 280
Du Bois de Vroylande (family) **3** 418
Dubois-Drahonet, Alexandre-Jean **4** 556
Dubois-Pillet, (Louis-Auguste-) Albert *see* DUBOIS, (LOUIS-AUGUSTE-)ALBERT
DuBois Plumb partnership **25** 52
Dubos, Jean-Baptiste **1** 898; **7** 714; **9** 327*; **11** 578; **31** 768
Dubosc, Claude **3** 259; **6** 117; **9** 379; **13** 324; **19** 216
Dubosc, Pierre **27** 248
Dubourg **11** 417
Dubourg, (Marie-Louise-) Victoria *see* FANTIN-LATOUR, (MARIE-LOUISE-)VICTORIA
Dubout, Maurice **11** 640
Dubov, Yegor **23** 837
Dubovskoy, Nikolay (Nikanorovich) **9** 328*
Dubovsky, Valentin (Yevgen'yevich) **27** 378
Duboys, Jehan **7** 425
Dúbrava **28** 851
Dubreuil, Adolfo **24** 518
Dubreuil, Jean **6** 570
Dubreuil, Paul **10** 397
Dubreuil, Pierre **11** 644; **12** 830; **19** 808; **24** 739; **30** 328
Dubreuil, Toussaint **9** 328–9*; **24** 134; **31** 305
assistants **9** 385
collaboration **5** 172
groups and movements **11** 260, 262, 266, 656
works **9** *328*; **11** 533, *533*, 641
Du Broeucq, Jacques **3** 569; **9** 329–30*
attributions **3** 569
collaboration **18** 691
patrons and collectors **3** 613; **13** 906, 909
pupils **12** 568
works **3** 545
Dubrovčanin, Antun **9** 331
Dubrovitsy, Church of the Virgin of the Sign **27** 373
Dubrovnik **8** *174*; **9** 330–31*; **32** *158*
Archaeological Museum **8** 180
architecture **8** 175
Art Gallery **8** 181
Cathedral **8** 180
Church of Comolac **25** 332
Fort Bokar **8** 175
fountain **8** 175
glass **8** 180
jewellery **17** 519
Dubrovnik—cont.
ketubbot **18** 3
lace **8** 180
Old Town **9** 330
Rector's Palace **8** 175; **9** *330*
St Ignatius **8** 176
sculpture **28** 452
Sponza Palace **8** 175
urban planning **8** 175
Dubsky, Mario **10** 483; **12** 218
Dubufe, Claude-Marie **9** 331–2*
Dubufe, (Louis-) Edouard **4** 306; **9** 331, 332*; **23** 126
Dubufe, (Edouard Marie) Guillaume **9** 332
Dubuffet, Jean (-Philippe-Arthur) **6** 576; **9** 332–5*; **11** 569; **25** 584
collaboration **20** 608
dealers **7** 842
groups and movements **1** 78; **2** 515–16, 543; **5** 56; **11** 551; **20** 846; **24** 144
patrons and collectors **28** 315
Cordier, Daniel **7** 842
Dotremont, Philippe **9** 189
Hirshhorn, Joseph H(erman) **14** 575
Matisse, Pierre **20** 832
Musée des Beaux Arts (Le Havre) **19** 92
Neumann, Morton G. **23** 7
Power, E(dward) J(oseph) **25** 400
Thompson, G(eorge) David **30** 749
personal collection **23** 334; **25** 686
works **2** 616; **6** 577; **7** 557; **9** *334*, *335*; **19** 491; **21** 896; **28** *315*; **29** 97
Dubugras, Victor **4** 712; **9** 335*; **27** 808
Dubuisson, Jean-Baptiste **29** 669
Dubuisson, Louis **11** 527
Dubut, Charles-Claude **9** 336*; **22** 302, 309; **28** 110
Dubut, Jean-François **11** 596
Dubut, Louis-Ambroise **9** 336*
Dubuysson, Jules **14** 769
Duc, Gabriel Le *see* LE DUC, GABRIEL
Duc, (Joseph-) Louis **9** 336–8*; **11** 521
assistants **7** 832; **8** 544
collaboration **9** 312; **14** 238
groups and movements **28** 345
works **1** 527; **2** *332*; **9** *337*; **11** 324, 521, 522, 523; **18** 888
Duca, Antonio del **21** 456
Duca, Gheorghe, Prince **15** 55
Duca, Giacomo del **9** 338–40*
attributions **5** 123
collaboration **9** 340; **20** 840
patrons and collectors **7** 861; **10** 810; **20** 840; **23** 575, 576
works **5** 525, 683, 684; **9** *339*
Duca, Lodovico del **9** 339–40*
works **9** 339, *340*
Du Camp, Maxime **9** 340–41*; **23** 504
works **4** 130; **24** 663, *663*
Du Cane, Peter **30** 387
Ducare, Andrew **11** 521
Ducart, Davis **9** 341*; **16** 8
ducats *see under* COINS → types
Ducci, Virgilio **31** 31
Duccio (di Buoninsegna) **9** 341–9*; **13** 146; **14** 868; **28** 676, 677
altarpieces
Maestà altarpiece **1** 709; **4** 30; **7** X; **9** *344*, *345*; **10** 675; **13** *129*, 130; **24** 567; **25** 183, 462, 463; **28** 684
Rucellai *Madonna* **1** 708; **7** 314; **8** 857; **9** *342*; **11** 183, 379
triptych **9** *347*

Duccio (di Buoninsegna)—cont.
attributions 7 319; 11 380; 13 192; 20 620
book covers 13 146
collaboration 7 318
methods 9 348–9*; 12 625; 13 133; 24 4; 25 730
paintings 15 *94*
patrons and collectors 7 782, 905; 12 477; 14 148; 27 306; 28 676
pupils 20 504; 31 532
stained glass 13 *193*
Duccio, Agostino di *see* AGOSTINO (DI ANTONIO) DI DUCCIO
Duccio, Antonio di *see* ANTONIO DI DUCCIO
Duccio, Ottaviano di *see* OTTAVIANO DI DUCCIO
Du Cerceau, Baptiste Androuet 9 353*; 20 133
attributions 23 509
patrons and collectors 9 350; 31 851
works 7 665; 11 514; 12 120; 23 492; 24 161
Du Cerceau, Gabriel-Guillaume 9 350
Du Cerceau, Jacques Androuet (i) (*c.* 1515-85) 6 506; 9 350–53*; 11 634; 20 281
architecture 14 460; 23 492; 29 917
attributions 2 459; 11 905; 23 508
drawings 2 *27*; 6 453; 11 *259*; 19 691, 692, 693, *694*; 25 254
engravings 4 80; 5 166, 285; 9 *351*, *352*, *707*; 11 341, 514, 897, *905*; 25 607; 26 454; 31 *844*
furniture 3 484; 23 541
gardens 12 *113*, 120
illustrations 11 586; 19 693
metalwork 11 617, *617*
patrons and collectors 4 548; 11 656
plans 6 *505*; 19 692
publications 11 572; 14 855; 30 735
reproductive prints by others 29 44
tapestries 11 639
works 6 415; 30 68
writings 2 330; 6 390, 546; 11 514, 586; 13 700; 14 789; 31 296
on models 2 336
translated 30 763
Du Cerceau, Jacques Androuet (ii) (1550-1614) 9 353*
assistants 4 864
collaboration 21 345
patrons and collectors 9 350
pupils 4 864; 12 309
works 4 801; 8 271; 11 514; 12 120; 24 161, 271
Du Cerceau, Jean Androuet 9 353–4*
patrons and collectors 4 755; 28 370
works 8 65; 9 350; 11 260, *261*; 29 *524*
Du Cerceau, Paul Androuet 9 350; 18 745; 19 417
Ducete, Sebastián 9 354*; 27 314; 29 291
Ducete Díez, Pedro 9 354
Duchamp, Gaston *see* VILLON, JACQUES
Duchamp, (Henri-Robert-) Marcel 2 383; 8 435; 9 233, 354–61*; 11 360, 568; 13 800; 23 48; 24 428; 28 397; 31 605; 32 576
assemblages 2 616; 33 246
book covers 14 852
collaboration 10 687
Duchamp, (Henri-Robert-) Marcel—cont.
dealers 20 75; 26 193
dealing 2 384
exhibitions 2 447; 7 842; 10 680; 28 920
films 10 687
groups and movements
correspondence art 7 895
Cubism 8 240, 244, 245; 28 347
Dada 7 685; 8 433, 435, 438, 439
environmental art 10 416
Junk art 17 694
kinetic art 2 838; 18 62
Orphism 1 74; 2 225; 8 245
Puteaux group 8 240; 12 806; 25 747; 28 347
Société Anonyme 28 920
Society of Independent Artists (USA) 23 701; 28 925
Surrealism 26 414; 30 19, 21
installations 30 22
mixed-media 9 *357*, *359*
mobiles 21 745
multimedia 22 279
musical compositions 29 97
paintings 8 438; 9 *355*; 11 582; 23 296; 31 605
patrons and collectors 2 384; 7 842; 24 600; 31 503
posters 25 350
productions 26 357
ready-mades 1 174; 8 438; 9 *356*; 11 549; 24 405; 26 51, *51*; 29 12, 656; 31 613
reproductive prints by others 32 577
writings 20 287
translated 30 262
Duchamp, Suzanne 8 438; 9 354; 32 576, 577
Duchamp-Villon, (Pierre-Maurice-) Raymond 9 354, 360–62*; 32 576
collaboration 11 525, 582; 19 78
groups and movements 8 240; 12 806; 18 636; 20 431; 23 569; 25 747; 28 347; 32 576
patrons and collectors 25 823
works 9 *362*; 11 569
Duchan *see* DOKUTAN
Duchanee, Thawan 30 617
Duchange, Gaspard 9 362*, 407; 19 216; 22 684; 26 388
Ducharmé, Pier 29 303
Duchartre, P. L. 26 96
Duchâteau 11 33
Duchâtel, Edouard 19 489; 20 603
Duchatel, François 21 34; 22 720
Du Châtelet, Jean III, Baron des Thons *see* THONS, JEAN DU CHÂTELET III, Baron des
Du Châtelier, Jacques *see* JACQUES DU CHÂTELIER
Du Chattel 15 818
Duché, Andrew 9 362*; 11 810; 31 635
Duché, Anthony 9 362; 31 635
Duchemin, Catherine 12 726
Duchemin, Isaac 22 857; 30 531
Duchemin, Nicolas 19 90
Duchêne, Louis, & Fils 30 148
Duchesne, Achille 2 405; 5 123
Duchesne, Antoine-Nicolas 12 124
Duchesne, Jean 9 362–3*
Duchesne, L. 3 424
Duchesne, Nicolas 9 363*; 26 348
duchesse brisée *see under* CHAIRS → types
Duchesse lace *see under* LACE → types
Duchet, Claude 18 635; 30 746
Duchet, Etienne 18 635
Du Choul, Guillaume 15 83, 87; 26 261
Duchow, Achim 25 154
Ducie, Henry Moreton, 2nd Earl of *see* MORETON, HENRY, 2nd Earl of Ducie
Ducis, (Jean-) Louis 4 305; 9 363–4*; 31 374
Duck, Jacob 9 364*; 25 362
Dücker, Eugen 9 364*; 10 539, 855; 14 480; 33 95
duck feathers *see under* FEATHERS → types
Duckworth, Ruth 10 314
Duclaux, Jean-Antoine 11 158, 159
Du Clercq, Jean *see* JEAN DU CLERCQ
Duclere, Teodoro 8 716; 22 480; 28 317
Duclos, Antoine-Jean 9 364–5*; 27 531
Duclos, François 2 460
Duco *see under* PAINTS → types
Ducorron, Julien-Joseph 23 439
Ducq, Jan le 9 364
Ducq, Jean-François 30 46
Ducrest Saint-Aubin, Félicité, Comtesse de Genlis *see* GENLIS, FÉLICITÉ, Comtesse de
Ducreux, Joseph 9 365*, *365*; 12 206
works 4 555
Ducrollay, Jean 11 630, 632
Ducros, (Abraham-)Louis (-Rodolphe) 9 365–6*; 30 125
assistants 4 84; 17 731
collaboration 27 484
patrons and collectors 5 541; 13 304; 14 598
works 30 133; 32 901
Ducrot, Golia 16 731
Ducrot, Vittorio 3 327; 16 721
Ducruet, Pauline 2 723
Ducuing (family) 4 391
Dudas Kuypers Rowan Ltd 5 573
Duddingston House (Lothian) *see under* EDINBURGH → houses and mansions
Dudensing, Valentine 20 832
Duderstat, Henricus 20 683
Dudevant, Maurice 21 135
Dudgeon, Philip Maurice 9 366*, 426; 24 777; 29 105
Dudhai 15 290
temple 15 290
Dudin, Ivan 33 577
Dudin, S. M. 6 279
Düdingen, Jetschwill Manor House 30 *141*
Dudley, Henry 33 212, 213
Dudley, Herman Dudley 11 498
Dudley, John, 1st Duke of Northumberland 9 366–7*; 13 298
Dudley, John William Ward, 1st Earl of *see* WARD, JOHN WILLIAM, 1st Earl of Dudley
Dudley, Robert (1573-1649) 4 360; 19 772
Dudley, Robert, 1st Earl of Leicester (*c.* 1532-88) 9 367*; 10 360
gardens 12 126, *126*
jewellery 7 179
miniatures (paintings) 14 545
paintings 10 363
tapestries 10 349
Dudley, William 30 687
Dudley, William Ward, 2nd Earl of *see* WARD, WILLIAM, 2nd Earl of Dudley
Dudley Binder 4 352
Dudley *Madonna* 8 798
Dudley Zoo 33 700
Dudok, W(illem) M(arinus) 9 367–8*; 19 332; 27 230
architecture 4 790; 10 240
department stores 8 770
town halls 4 788; 9 *368*; 22 831; 31 243
urban planning 14 40
Dudok, W(illem) M(arinus) architecture—cont.
villas 33 387
collaboration 23 663
staff 18 138
Dudolov, Atanas 5 156
Dudreville, Leonardo 11 843; 16 680; 23 263; 27 788
Dudzele, Jossine van 14 784
Dueil, Gervaisot de *see* GERVAISOT DE DUEIL
Duékoué Museum 8 23
Duemichen, Johannes 10 82
Dueñas
Palace 29 299
S Pedro 26 607
Dueñas, Francisco Espinoza *see* ESPINOZA DUEÑAS, FRANCISCO
Duesbury, William (1725-86) 4 601; 6 533; 8 776; 9 368–9*; 10 308
assistants 3 25
pupils 4 65
works 10 308
Duesbury, William, II (*d* 1797) 8 776
Duesbury, William, III (*fl* 1811) 8 776
Duèse, Jacques *see* JOHN XXII, Pope
Duetecum, van *see* DOETECHEM, VAN
Duez, Ernest-Ange 9 369*
Dueze, Jacques *see* JOHN XXII, Pope
Dufaycolor *see under* PHOTOGRAPHY → processes
Dufeux, Constant 4 596
Duff 25 181, 182, 183; 27 778
Duff, Alison 23 62, 63
Duff, Thomas (J.) 3 274; 9 369*; 19 870
Duff, William, 1st Earl of Fife 1 134
Duffaut, Préfète 9 369*
Duffield, William 18 689
Duffour, Joseph 11 428
Duffy, Rita 16 41
Dufief, Canon 10 891
Duflaud *see* DUFLOS
Duflos, Augustin 24 111
Duflos, Claude-Augustin (1700-86) 9 370*; 14 85
Duflos, Philothée-François 3 645; 9 370
Duflos, Simon-Nicolas 9 370*
Du Ford, Grimod 22 682
Dufour, Alexandre 11 258; 24 387
Dufour, Guillaume-Henri 12 276; 21 568, 581
Dufour, Joseph, & Cie 9 370*; 32 816
works 32 III
Dufour, Joseph, & Leroy 9 370
Dufour, Lorenzo 28 12
Dufour, Pierre 9 370
Dufour, Pierre Charles Nicolas 7 662
Dufour, Pietro 28 12
Dufour Frères 9 370
Dufournet, Paul 3 226
Dufours, Jean, & Frères 3 601
Dufrêne, François 7 557; 8 609; 11 551; 23 260
Dufrêne, Maurice 11 583, 600, 601; 24 475
Dufrenne, Mikel 1 182; 10 686
Dufresne, Augustine 13 692
Dufresne, Charles (Georges) 5 530; 9 370–71*
groups and movements 2 521; 22 751
pupils 13 714
works 3 462
Du Fresne, Raphaël Trichet *see* TRICHET DU FRESNE, RAPHAËL
Dufresne de Saint-Léon, Arthur 21 150
Dufresnet, Mathieu 21 368
Du Fresnoy, Charles-Alphonse 9 371–2*
methods 18 898
works 1 179; 11 536; 31 300, 768
on chiaroscuro 6 569
translated 2 125; 9 8, 306; 13 646; 20 569; 24 494, 805
Dufresny, Charles Rivières *see* RIVIÈRES DUFRESNY, CHARLES
Du Fu 6 823; 25 72
Dufva, A. G. 30 108
Dufy, Jean 19 398
Dufy, Raoul 9 372–4*; 24 144
book illustrations 4 366; 25 79
collaboration 2 542; 12 497; 19 808; 20 603; 25 78, 79; 29 329
dealers 33 36
exhibitions 3 826; 28 808
forgeries by others 11 307, 310
groups and movements 2 522; 10 839, 840, 841; 23 569; 24 585
lithographs 19 491
paintings 9 *373*
patrons and collectors 19 92; 24 183; 27 277
prints 11 649
pupils 4 673
reproductive prints by others 32 577
stage design 7 508
tapestries 3 462; 11 644, *644*
teachers 4 329
textiles 9 291; 11 548; 23 548
watercolours 32 902
woodcuts 2 225; 33 362
Dugahiti 27 755
Dugardin, Camus 19 382
Dugardin, Pierre 19 382
Dugarov, Dashi-Nima 27 436
Dugdale, Michael 30 411
Dugdale, William 1 612; 9 374–5*; 12 273; 14 684; 19 597
works 12 *126*
Dughet, Gaspard 9 375–8*; 11 536; 26 773
attributions 20 769
collaboration 8 100; 13 656; 18 871; 20 374; 21 483; 23 874
methods 24 793
patrons and collectors
Beckford, William (1760-1844) 3 476
Boyle, Richard, 3rd Earl of Burlington and 4th Earl of Cork 4 609
Carmelite Order 5 778
Carolis, Livio de, Marchese 5 812
Carr, William Holwell 5 848
Castel Rodrigo, Manuel de Moura y Corte Real, 2nd Marqués de 6 30
Day, Alexander 8 582
Hoare (i), Henry the younger (1705-85) 14 598
Long, Charles, 1st Baron Farnborough 19 624
Miles, Philip John 21 541
Morice, Humphry 22 115
Paliano and Castiglione, Lorenzo Onofrio Colonna, Duke of 7 620, 622
Pamphili, Camillo, Prince 23 899
pupils 23 444
reproductive prints by others 12 802; 22 209; 25 210; 32 652, 693
works 7 621; 9 *376*, *377*; 18 709, 710, 712; 26 840
Dugléré, Adolphe 9 378*
Dugonjić, Tomislav 4 461
Du Goulon, Jules 2 701; 11 405; 32 240

Dugourc, Jean-Démosthène **9** 378–9*; **10** 643; **11** 627, 648
patrons and collectors **4** 555, 556, 565, 566
works **3** 461; **11** 646; **29** 305, 315, 691
Du Guernier, Alexandre **3** 813; **9** 379
Du Guernier, Louis, I (1614-1659) **9** 379; **21** 641
Du Guernier, Louis, II (1658-1716) **9** 379
Du Guernier, Pierre **9** 379
Duhameel, Alart *see* ALART DU HAMEEL
Duhamel, Georges **1** 21; **8** 243
Duhamel, Marcel **30** 18, 291
Duhamel du Monceau, H. L. **4** 683
Duhan, E. J. **1** 319
Duhart (Harosteguy), Emilio **6** 594; **7** 695; **18** 797
works **6** *595*
Duhem, Henri **3** 156
Duhring, Okie & Ziegler **7** 619
Du Huan **6** 330
dui see under VESSELS → types
Duia, Pietro **3** 667
Duiker, Johannes **1** 804; **4** 56–7; **21** 156; **22** 830, 831
groups and movements **11** 841
works **11** *840*
Duin, Jan van **17** 549
Duin, Johannes van **22** 881
Duintjer, M. F. **22** 832
Duisberg, Carl **18** 128
Duisbergh, Conradt **12** 239
Duisburg
exhibitions **21** 692
Volkschule **28** 159
Wilhelm-Lehmbruck-Museum **7** 818; **17** 517
Duits, Antoneim **24** 55
Duivenvoorde, Hendrick Adolf Steengracht van *see* STEENGRACHT VAN DUIVENVOORDE, HENDRICK ADOLF
Dujardin, Bénigne **11** 171
Dujardin, Edouard **2** 124; **3** 813; **7** 451
Dujardin, François **31** 851
Dujardin, Guilliam **27** 134
Dujardin, J. **3** 619
Du Jardin, Karel **9** 379–81*; **26** 772
copies **4** 657; **21** 170
groups and movements **3** 143; **9** 462; **28** 92
patrons and collectors **3** 239; **7** 778; **14** 692; **23** 469; **26** 284; **29** 366
pupils **28** 73
reproductive prints by others **6** 527, 547; **8** 542
teachers **3** 759; **22** 843
works **9** *380*; **22** 844
Dujardin, Paul **20** 138
Du Jin **9** 381–2*
works **9** *381*
Dujoirdin, Auguste **30** 644
Dujon, Jean **20** 138
Dujovne, Berardo **2** 397
Dukaginzade Gazi Mehmed Pasha **16** 222
Duke, Doris **23** 33
Duke of York Islands **24** 84
Dukes, Ashley **30** 687
Dukes, Bagrat, Duke of **30** 306
Duke's Company **30** 674
Dukhanino **22** 180; **27** 414
Dukla Church **25** 115
Duknović, Ivan *see* GIOVANNI DALMATA
Dukwa **33** 609
Dulac, Antoine **20** 388; **25** 82
Dulac, Charles-Marie **9** 382*; **19** 490
Dulac, Edmund **4** 367
Dulac, Germaine **10** 687
Dulaim **1** 868
Du Lau, Marquis **18** 869
Duldur-aqur **6** *288*, 300, 302, 304; **18** 494
Monastery **6** 294, 296, 315
Dule Temple **6** 667
Dulevsky factory **32** 661
Dülfer, Martin **9** 237, 382–3*; **28** 341; **31** 367
Dulière, C. **3** 620
Dulin, Nicolas **7** 773; **9** 362, 383*
Dulin, Pierre **18** 692
Duli Xingyi *see* DOKURYŪ SHŌEKI
Düll, Heinrich **22** 301
Dullaert, H. **22** 843
Dullin, Charles **18** 900
Dulong, R. **28** 482
Dulongpré, Louis **5** 564; **22** 37
Dulyovo Porcelain Factory *see* PRAVDA PORCELAIN FACTORY
Dum *see* THUMB
Du Maine, Georges Clémansin *see* CLÉMANSIN DU MAINE, GEORGES
Dumandré, Antoine **4** 558, 588
Dumandré, Hubert **4** 558, 560, 588; **11** 754; **27** 753
Dumandré, Joaquín **2** 285; **4** 588
Dumarçay, Jacques **29** 243
Dumarecq **10** 781
Dumaresq, James (Charles Philip) **9** 383*; **14** 68
Dumaresq, Sydney Perry **9** 383
Dumaresq & Stimson **9** 383
Dumas, Alexandre, fils (1824-95) **4** 364
Dumas, Alexandre, père (1802-70) **4** 319; **8** 548; **17** 605; **30** 32, 353, 682
Dumas, Alphonse **32** 686
Dumas, Fernand **11** 773
Dumas, Marlene **9** 384*; **22** 853
Dumas, Michel **19** 847
Du Maurier, George (Louis Palmella Busson) **9** 384*; **10** 254; **33** 137
groups and movements **27** 564
patrons and collectors **15** 894
works **4** 868
writings **2** 475; **21** 761
Dumba (family) **2** 829
Dumba, Nikolaus **20** 145
Dumbarton (Strathclyde)
Alcuit *see* Castle Rock
Castle Rock **21** 562
glass **28** 259
Dumbarton Oaks *see under* WASHINGTON (DC) → museums
Dumbrell, Lesley **2** 751; **9** 384–5*
Dumée, Guillaume **9** 329, 385*
Dumée, Toussaint **9** 385
Dumeel, Alart *see* ALART DU HAMEEL
Du Mège, Alexandre-Louis-Charles-André **31** 207, 211
Du Metz, Gédéon Berbier, Comte de Rosnay *see* ROSNAY, GÉDÉON BERBIER DU METZ, 1st Comte de
Du Metz, Jean Berbier, 2nd Comte de Rosnay *see* ROSNAY, JEAN BERBIER DU METZ, 2nd Comte de
Dumfries House (Strathclyde) **28** 227
furniture **7** 172; **9** 727; **28** 252
manuscripts **27** 506
Dumfries Law Courts (Dumfries & Galloway) **28** 288
Dumile (Feni) **1** 433; **9** 385*; **29** 109
Dumitrescu, Sorin **9** 386*
Dummer, Jeremiah **4** 479; **7** 702; **31** 647, 648
Dümmler, F. **1** 795
Du Molinet, R. P. Claude **5** 346; **19** 632; **22** 675
works **5** *345*
Dumon, F. **3** 585
Du Mond, Frank Vincent **14** 751
Du Mons, Jean Joseph **2** 704; **11** 643
Dumons de Tulle, Jean-Joseph **4** 514
Dumonstier (family) **9** *386*; **31** 850
Dumonstier, Cardin **9** 386
Dumonstier, Charles **9** 386
Dumonstier, Cosme, I (*d* 1552) **9** 386
Dumonstier, Cosme, II (*c.* 1545/50-*d* 1605) **9** 386
Dumonstier, Daniel **9** 386, *386*, 387–8*
collections **20** 455
reproductive prints by others **18** 812
works **9** *387*
Dumonstier, Etienne, I (*fl c.* 1501) **9** 386
Dumonstier, Etienne, II (1540-1603) **9** 386, *386*, 387–8*; **11** 533
collaboration **9** 387
patrons and collectors **9** 388
Dumonstier, Etienne, III (*b* 1606) **9** 386, *386*, 388
Dumonstier, Geoffroy **9** 386, *386*, 387*; **11** 264
Dumonstier, Jean **9** 386, *386*
Dumonstier, Louis **9** *386*, 387
Dumonstier, Meston **9** 386, *386*
Dumonstier, Nicolas **9** 386, *386*, 388; **30** 660
Dumonstier, Pierre (i) (*c.* 1545-1625) **9** 386, *386*, 387*; **11** 533; **31** 851
Dumonstier, Pierre (ii) (*c.* 1585-1656) **9** 386, *386*, 388*
Dumont, Albert **6** 415
Dumont, Alexis **29** 602
Dumont, Augustin-Alexandre **8** 41; **9** 388, 389*
pupils
Aizelin, Eugène-Antoine **1** 498
Bonnassieux, Jean-Marie-Bienaimé **4** 328
Carriès, Jean (-Joseph-Marie) **5** 881
Deschamps, Léon (Julien) **8** 789
Eakins, Thomas (Cowperthwaite) **9** 500
Georgescu, Ion **12** 316
Injalbert, (Jean-)Antoine **15** 849
Moreau, Mathurin **22** 92
Perraud, Jean-Joseph **24** 467
Ponscarme, (François-Joseph-) Hubert **25** 214
Roty, (Louis-)Oscar **27** 237
Thomas, Gabriel-Jules **30** 743
DuMont, Christine **23** 13
Dumont, Edme **9** 388–9*
Dumont, François (*c.* 1687/8-1726) **1** 132; **9** 388*; **13** 805; **16** 64
Dumont, François (1751-1831) **21** 643
Dumont, J. **11** 593
Dumont, Jacques (1715-79) **19** 117; **30** 499; **32** 920
Dumont, Jacques-Edme (1761-1844) **9** 388, 389*
Dumont, Joseph Jonas **3** 547; **9** 389*
pupils **5** 828; **16** 878
restorations **33** 567
works **3** 585
Du Mont, Louis **4** 537
Dumont, Marcus **23** 13
Dumont, Maurice **10** 178; **19** 490
Dumont, Pierre (*d* ?1737) **9** 388
Dumont, Pierre (*fl* 1907) **25** 747
Dumont, (Gabriel-) Pierre-Martin **9** 389–90*; **22** 734; **29** 91, 94
Dumont, Thomas **11** 410
Dumontier *see* DUMONSTIER
Dumontier, Alessandro (*fl* 18th cent.) **30** 176
DuMont Schauberg **23** 13
Dumouchel, Albert **9** 390*; **22** 39
groups and movements **25** 635
pupils **12** 179; **28** 23
works **5** 569
Du Mouchel, Bon **21** 610
Du Moulin, Denis *see* DENIS DU MOULIN
Dumoulins, François **12** 837; **30** 530
Dumoustier *see* DUMONSTIER
Dumrath, J. H. **30** 95
Du Mu **9** 390*
Dumvarahi **22** *753*, 790
Dun Aengus (Co. Galway) **9** 390–91*; **16** *5*; **21** 551; **25** *470*, 536
Dunaiszky, László **14** 896
Dunaiszky, Lőrinc **14** 895
Dunand, Jean **9** 391*; **11** 628, 629; **18** 615
collaboration **10** 689; **11** 727; **27** 322
groups and movements **2** 521
works **11** 583, 601, *629*; **28** 298
Dunand, Maurice **1** 889; **5** 331
Dunaújváros **14** 890
Dunaysir *see* KIZILTEPE
Dunbar, F. A. T. **5** 570
Dunbar, William Nugent *see* ANDERSON, JAMES
Dunbar Furniture Co. **31** 633
Dunbar Hay **26** 39
Dunblane (Central)
Bishop Leighton's Library **28** 252
Cathedral **28** 224, 250
Duncan, C. **33** 312
Duncan, Douglas M. **5** 589
Duncan, Edward **14** 849
Duncan, Isadora **30** 686
Duncan, James **8** 81; **22** 37
Duncan, John (1866-1945) **22** 331; **28** 238, 239
Duncan, John H. (1855-1929) **20** 869
works **20** *869*
Duncan, Jonathan (*fl* 1791) **31** 903
Duncan, Perry **28** 231; **29** 379
Duncan, Robert **4** 109
Duncan, Thomas **23** 106; **28** 238
Duncanson, Robert S(cott) **1** 440; **7** 327; **9** 391–2*; **31** 603
Duncker, Balthasar Anton **20** 915
Duncombe, Charles William Reginald, 2nd Earl of Feversham **33** 565
Duncombe Park **12** 128; **19** 531; **29** 835
Dundalk, Carroll's Cigarette Factory **16** 12; **28** 284
Dundas, Henry, 1st Viscount Melville **25** 35
Dundas, Lawrence **9** 392*
architecture **7** 409
furniture **7** 172; **10** 295, *295*; **32** 540
paintings **9** 17; **13** 624
sponsorship **14** 198
Dundas, Maria *see* CALCOTT, MARIA
Dundas, Thomas, 1st Baron Dundas **3** 382; **9** 392
Dundee (Tayside) **28** *222*
cabinetmaking **28** 254
Duncan of Jordanstone College of Art **28** 275
glass **28** 259
Greywalls **28** 231
McManus Galleries **28** 273
Orchar Collection **28** 273
mills (industrial) **28** 228
museums **28** 273
Nunnery Chapel **28** 250
pottery **28** 258
Town House **28** 227
University Chapel **28** 244
Dundlod **15** 611
Dunedin **23** 51, *52*
Bank of New Zealand **23** 54, 66
First Church **23** 54
furniture **23** 66
Knox Church **23** 54
Municipal Chambers **23** 54
New Zealand Express Company Building **23** 55
Olveston House **23** 64, *64*
Otago Boys' High School **23** 54
Otago Museum **24** 891
Otago School of Art **23** 75
Police Station **23** 54
Post Office **23** 54
railway station **23** 55, *55*
St Dominic's Priory **23** 54
St Joseph's Cathedral **23** 54
statue of Dr D. M. Stuart **23** 62
statue of Queen Victoria **23** 62
University of Otago **23** 54
Hocken Library **23** 76
Dunelmum *see* DURHAM
Dúnem, Francisco D. Van *see* VAN-DÚNEM, FRANCISCO D.
Dun Emer Guild **16** 34
Dun Emer Press **16** 18
Dune Treasure **10** 322
Dunfermline (Fife) **28** *222*
Abbey **6** 565; **13** 211; **26** 591, 617; **28** 223, *223*, 267
art schools **28** 274
Carnegie Centre **19** 319
damask **19** 419
Town Hall **28** 288
Dunfermline, Alexander Seton, 1st Earl of *see* SETON, ALEXANDER, 1st Earl of Dunfermline
dung **15** 174, 548; **29** 827; **30** 558
brass **4** 684
lacquer **18** 601
masks **29** *209*
plaster **15** 174
secco paintings **15** 548
stucco **29** 813, 827
Dungannon Council Offices (Co. Tyrone) **16** 40
Dungarpur **15** 460
Dunger **9** 237
Dungert, Max **31** 361
Dunguaire, Tower House **16** 8
Dungur **1** 513
architecture **1** *513*
Dunham, Rufus **31** 652
Dunham Massey (Ches) **13** 301; **24** 252; **26** 558
Dunhuang **5** 102; **6** *288*, *614*; **7** 151; **9** 392–4*; **21** *870*; **28** *719*, 720; **30** *806*
fortifications **21** 592
Mogao Caves **6** 650, 708–9, 712, 713, 715, 777, *777*, 778, 779, *822*; **7** 34; **23** 550; **25** 378; **30** 442, 831
altars **1** 703
banners **28** 310; **30** 828
books **5** 101; **7** 63, 64
inscriptions **6** 379
manuscripts **6** 306; **30** 805, 808, 828, 848
paintings **6** 305, 776, 788, 789; **7** 34; **9** *393*; **30** 807
paper **6** 314; **7** 114, 146; **24** 47
pillar-stupas **29** 868
prints **7** 118
rolls **7** 117
sculpture **6** 713, 716
silk **6** 248
squeezes **7** 117
stencilling **7** 118; **29** 627
sutras **6** 781–2
tangkas **28** 311
temples **9** 393–4*
textiles **6** *317*, 318; **7** *47*
Thousand Buddhas Caves **23** 216
tomb paintings **7** 57
wall paintings **6** 779, 826; **7** 108; **30** 831, 837, 848; **33** 35

Dunhuang
Mogao Caves—cont.
woodblock 6 314
writing-tablets 6 740, 741, 767, 772
Dunhuang xue jikan 24 436
Dunhuang yanjiu 24 436
Duni 5 150
Dunikowski, Ksawery 9 394*; 32 877
pupils 3 766; 17 446
works 25 115, *115*, 116
Dunin, L. F. 12 43
Dunkarton, Robert 22 152
Dunkeld (Tayside)
Cathedral 28 268
House 17 623
Dunker, Balthazar Anton 3 823; 9 395*; 18 224; 33 195
Dunker, E. D. 32 736
Dunker, Jens 4 123
Dunker, Philip Heinrich 9 395; 18 115
Dunkharjab 21 881
Dunkirk
Musée d'Art Contemporain 28 315
Musée des Beaux-Arts 8 788
Dunk Island Resort 2 743
Dunkley, John 9 395*; 16 884, 886
Dun Laoghaire School of Art (Co. Dublin) 16 37
Dunlap, John 31 625
Dunlap, Samuel 31 625
Dunlap, William 7 787; 9 395–6*; 14 718; 31 671; 33 92
Dunlop, Alexander F. 20 877
Dunlop, James 14 108
Dunlop Rubber Company 20 156
Dunluce Castle (Co. Londonderry) 6 59; 16 22
Dunmore Pottery 28 258
Dunmore Town 3 60
Dunn, Alfred 31 763
Dunn, Archibald Matthew 14 156
Dunn, David 16 888
Dunn, Dorothy 3 499; 14 801; 22 591, 595, 677; 30 238; 32 122
Dunn, Geoffrey 10 299
Dunn, Harvey 8 277
Dunn, Henry (*fl* 1766) 5 577
Dunn, Henry Treffry (1838-99) 27 188
Dunn, James 1 496
Dunn, Nathan 23 256
Dunn, Peter 10 879
Dunn, Richard 2 752
Dunn, Thomas 10 263
Dunn & Hansom 5 513
Dunn & Watson 9 61; 13 615; 20 27
Dunnett, Frank 24 802
Dunnill, Craven 10 311
Dunning, W. H. 23 212
Dunn's 10 299
Dunois, Jean, Comte de, Bâtard d'Orléans 13 254; 20 626
Dunois Hours *see under* BOOKS OF HOURS → individual manuscripts
Dunouy, Alexandre-Hyacinthe 8 703
Dunoyer de Segonzac, André (Albert Maris) 5 530; 9 396*, 705
assistants 9 370
groups and movements 10 696; 22 751; 28 347; 29 899
pupils 9 9; 31 519
teachers 13 790
works 4 366; 9 310; 11 548
Dunphail (Grampian) 28 230
Dunrobin Castle (Highland) 6 62; 32 910
Dunscombe, Clement 30 458
Dunsfold (Surrey), St Mary and All Saints 24 576
Dunsink observatory 23 340
Dunsmuir, Robert 20 30
Dunsoghley 16 22
Duns Scotus (1262-1308) 19 356
Dunstable (Beds) 23 491
priory 7 438; 26 616; 31 710
sculpture 26 614
Dunstable Downs (Beds) 14 545
Dunstable Swan Jewel 10 *193*, 194, 323, 344; 13 170
Dunstan, Helen *see* MARTIN, HELEN
Dunstan, Saint, Archbishop of Canterbury 9 396–7*; 29 851
architecture 2 66; 12 799; 21 836
manuscripts 2 74–5
Dunster Castle (Somerset) 10 275
interior decoration 4 845
leather 19 *5*, 5
paintings 4 599
wallpaper 32 818
Dunsterfield, George 4 890; 9 729; 28 246
Dunston power station (Lincs) 25 403
Dunthorne, John 7 754
Duntocher 28 241
Dünz, Hans Jakob, II 9 397
Dünz, Jakob, I 9 397
Dünz, Johannes 9 397*
Duodi 24 387
Duodo, Alvise 19 628
Duong Bich Lien 32 482, 483
Duong Long 6 432
Duonu, Master of 13 860
Duoré, Guillaume 11 635
Duo You *ding* 6 848
Dupain, J. Blanc de *see* BLANC DE DUPAIN, J.
Dupain, Max(well Spencer) 2 749; 6 570; 9 397*; 22 53
Dupaix, Guillaume 21 262, 265
Du Pan, Barthélémy 9 397–8*
Du Paquier, Claudius Innocentius 2 816; 12 433; 32 449
Duparc, Antoine 9 398; 20 472
Duparc, Françoise (-Marie-Thérèse) 9 398*; 20 472
Duparc, Josèphe-Antonia 9 398
Dupas, Jean 2 521; 10 689; 25 350
Dupaty, Charles 10 563; 28 746
Dupaty, Louis (-Marie-Charles) 5 889; 6 516; 27 547
works 6 *517*
Dupax 24 624
Dupchur, Brigad 27 436
works 27 *437*
Dupérac, Etienne 9 398*; 12 115; 26 770
collaboration 21 822
works 4 80; 12 120; 18 635; 21 453; 26 805, *806*; 31 *64*; 32 112
Duperly, Adolph 5 751
Du Perreux, Alexandre Millin *see* MILLIN DU PERREUX, ALEXANDRE
DuPeyrou, Pierre-Alexandre 22 920
Dupin, Jacques 20 75; 21 709
Duplan, J.-L. 4 588
Duplant de Laval, Pierre 15 650
Dupleix, Joseph-François 15 401; 25 211
Du Plessis, Armand-Jean, Cardinal de Richelieu *see* RICHELIEU, ARMAND-JEAN DU PLESSIS, Cardinal de
Duplessis, Georges 26 453
Duplessis, Jean-Claude Chambellan (*c.* 1690-1774) 6 533; 9 398; 29 432
metalwork 11 305, 626; 26 376
porcelain 11 609; 28 521; 30 219; 32 582
portraits 22 273
Duplessis, Jean-Claude-Thomas (Chambellan) (*c.* 1730-83) 9 399; 11 627; 30 747
Duplessis, Joseph-Siffred 9 399–400*
assistants 33 522
patrons and collectors 4 555
works 2 53; 9 *400*
Duplessis, Michel H. 30 63
Duplessis-Bertaux, Jean 14 366
Duplessis fils *see* DUPLESSIS, JEAN-CLAUDE THOMAS (CHAMBELLAN)
Du Plessis-Guénégaud, Henri *see* GUÉNÉGAUD, HENRI DE
Du Plessis-Liancourt, Roger, Duc de La Roche-Guyun *see* LIANCOURT, Duc de
Duplessis père *see* DUPLESSIS, JEAN-CLAUDE CHAMBELLAN
Duplessy, Michel 4 389
Dupljaja 25 *471*, 528–9
figurines 25 *528*
Dupon (*fl* 18th cent.) 21 430
Dupon, Josuë (*c.* 1864-1933) 20 926
Duponche, Edmond 28 746
Duponchel, Charles Eugène 9 365
Dupont, Gainsborough 9 400–401*; 11 911
Dupont, Gaspar 3 600
Du Pont, H(enry) F(rancis) 6 446; 9 401*; 12 143
Dupont, H. F., Winterthur Museum *see under* WINTERTHUR (DE)
Dupont, Paul *see* PONTIUS, PAULUS
Dupont, Pierre (1577-1640) 5 483, 836; 11 651, 652; 12 143; 27 894
Dupont, Pierre (1908-55) 9 401*
Dupont, Pieter (1870-1911) 9 401–2*; 19 259; 22 854
Du Pont Co. 30 391, 542, 543
Dupont-Zipcy, Emile 8 204
Dupouch, Claude 18 841
Duprà, (Giorgio) Domenico 9 402*
attributions 17 595
patrons and collectors 4 635; 5 364
works 7 532
Dupra, Giuseppe 3 714; 9 402
Duprat, Antoine, Cardinal 11 268
Duprat, Jean 10 665
Dupré, Abraham 9 406; 28 11
Dupré, Amalia 11 197
Dupré, Augustin 9 402–3*; 12 17; 20 922
Dupré, François 9 406
Dupré, Georges 9 403*; 20 925
Dupré, Giovanni 9 403–5*; 11 189; 28 677
pupils 26 423
works 3 296; 9 *403*, *404*; 11 197; 16 706; 24 855; 31 131
Dupré, Guillaume 9 405–6*
collaboration 25 577
works 4 818; 12 259; 20 922, *922*
Dupré, Jules 9 406*; 11 543
dealers 4 589, 655; 29 248
groups and movements 3 212, 213
patrons and collectors 6 516; 11 301; 18 869
pupils 31 853
works 3 *212*; 19 487
Dupré, Louis 4 305
Dupré, Museo *see under* FIESOLE
Dupuis, Charles 3 463; 9 407; 10 393; 20 497
works 20 *473*
Dupuis, Daniel 20 925
Dupuis, Jacques 3 551
Dupuis, Jean-Baptiste-Michel 11 410
Dupuis, Joseph 2 585
Dupuis, M. 9 169
Dupuis, Nicolas-Gabriel 9 407*; 10 393; 20 497
pupils 21 815; 27 645
works 7 640
Dupuytren, Musée *see under* PARIS → museums
Duque, Rodrigo *see* ALEMÁN, RODRIGO
Duque Cornejo, Pedro 9 407–8*; 26 552; 28 516
collaboration 29 292
pupils 6 67
works 7 846; 9 *407*
Duque Gómez, Luis 29 146
Duquesne, Eugène 27 270
Duquesney, François (1790-1849) 11 524; 25 856
works 25 *855*
Du Quesnoy, François (1597-1643) 2 163; 3 570; 9 408–12*
assistants 25 811
attributions 1 629
collaboration 9 408, 412; 22 103
groups and movements 3 266
ivory-carvings 3 604; 8 216
patrons and collectors
Castel Rodrigo, Manuel de Moura y Corte Real, 2nd Marqés de 6 31
Colonna, Filippo, I (1597-1639) 7 620
Crozat, Pierre 8 209
Delvaux, Laurent 8 698
Du Quesnoy, Jérôme (ii) (1602-54) 9 412
Girardon, François 12 727
Giustiniani (i), Vincenzo, Marchese 12 764
Hope, Henry 26 389
Nollekens, Joseph 30 496
Quellinus, Erasmus (ii) (1607-78) 25 811
Savoy, Maurice of, Cardinal 28 9
Uffelen, Lucas van 31 526
Vassal de Saint-Hubert, Jean-Antoine-Hubert 32 75
pupils 19 58
reliquaries 26 148
reproductive prints by others 32 738
sculpture 3 830; 4 254; 9 *410*, *411*; 16 698; 26 809
reliefs 11 81
teachers 9 408
Du Quesnoy, Jérôme (i) (*c.* 1570-1641) 3 570; 9 408–9*, 412
pupils 9 408, 409, 412
works 5 43
Du Quesnoy, Jérôme (ii) (1602-54) 3 570; 9 408, 411, 412–13*
collaboration 9 408
works 3 604; 9 *413*; 29 345
Duqueylar, Paul 25 581
al-Dur 2 *246*, 248, 249, 269
coins 2 261
figurines 2 260, *260*
fortress 2 251
glass 2 263
jewellery 2 264
pottery 2 267, 268
sculpture 2 257
temple 2 252
vessels 2 273
wine sets 2 265
Dur, shrine of Imam Dur 22 322
Du Raeumur, René 6 924
Dura Europos 1 *849*; 9 413–16*, *513*; 13 *362*; 15 *901*; 21 *267*; 24 215; 26 *915*; 30 178, *180*
agora 24 216
architecture 24 217; 26 918; 28 383
basilica 3 329
baths 3 376
domus ecclesiae 7 259, 260, 278; 9 416, 523
Baptistery 3 189; 9 541, 562; 22 519
ciborium 7 302
font 11 251
wall paintings 7 270; 9 416
doors 9 151
fortifications 21 559
Dura Europos—cont.
halls 16 800
jewellery 27 103
knitting 18 157
leather 27 105
Mithraeum 1 887; 9 562
murals 15 922
reliefs 9 *414*
sculpture 24 218
shields 27 52
stucco 29 814
synagogue 1 887; 9 414–15*, 562; 17 543; 18 826; 27 48
wall paintings 9 414–15, *415*, 562; 17 534, 535, 536, 556–7*, *557*
Temple of Bel 1 887; 9 562
Temple of Zeus 9 562
textiles 1 880, 881, 887; 7 52; 27 112
tombs 31 109, 110
urban planning 13 419, 420, *420*
wall paintings 9 517; 24 218; 27 57
weapons 16 505
Duramano 32 398
Durameau, Louis (-Jean)-Jacques 9 416–18*; 20 137
patrons and collectors 11 540; 32 719
pupils 12 158, 203; 24 477; 32 920
reproductions in tapestry 12 830
works 9 *417*
Durán 11 483
Durán, Diego 7 481; 30 786; 31 505
Duran, Feyhaman 2 634; 31 454
Durán, José 9 418*; 21 377
Durán, José María 10 154
Durán, Miguel Custodio 9 418*; 21 377, 401
Duran, Pedro 29 338
Durán Ballén, Sixto 9 711
Durán Berruecos, Diego 9 418*
Durand, Alexandre 8 705; 13 275
Durand, Alphonse 20 317
Durand, Amédée Pierre 8 770
Durand, André
works 31 *318*
Durand, Antoine 31 378
Durand, Antoine-Sébastien 11 619
Durand, Asher B(rown) 9 418–19*
collaboration 20 873
groups and movements 14 843; 26 742
patrons and collectors 17 823; 26 75; 29 870; 32 829
pupils 5 916; 7 577; 18 748
works 9 *419*; 14 166; 31 601, 602, 872
Durand, Charles-Emile-Auguste *see* CAROLUS-DURAN
Durand, Claude-Pierre 6 535
Durand, E. L. (*fl* 1859) 3 69
Durand, Etienne-Louis (*fl* 1793) 12 374
Durand, Georges 2 344
Durand, Hippolyte-Louis 9 420*
Durand, Jean-François 18 867
Durand, Jean-Nicolas-Louis 9 420–21*; 11 520; 13 236
groups and movements 9 704; 26 189
pupils 8 40, 133; 12 615; 19 35, 156
reproductive prints by others 6 *397*; 16 905
teachers 4 534
works 2 359; 18 888
writings 11 520; 22 362; 23 871; 26 13; 28 371
Durand, John 9 422*; 24 431
Durand, Madeleine-Cécile 13 689
Durand, Victor 31 644
works 31 *645*
Durand-Brager, (Jean-Baptiste-) Henri 9 422*

Durandelle, Louis-Emile 9 422*
Durandi, Christol 9 423
Durandi, Jacques 9 423*
Durand-Ruel (family) 5 589; 11 417; 20 603
Durand-Ruel, Charles 9 423, 425
Durand-Ruel, Georges 9 423, 425
Durand-Ruel, Jean Marie Fortuné 9 423*; 20 497
Durand-Ruel, Joseph 9 423, 425
Durand-Ruel, Paul (Marie Joseph) 9 423–5*; 19 544, 589; 21 426; 24 141, 143; 31 664
catalogues 6 80; 28 744
collections 19 37
drawings 19 295; 23 195
exhibitions 8 621; 10 680; 24 142; 27 639; 28 660
forgeries 27 563
monotypes 8 623
paintings 3 826; 4 523, 655, 656; 6 371, 375; 7 377; 8 647; 10 837; 18 869; 20 257, 854; 22 119; 24 883; 25 234; 26 207; 30 375
Barbizon school 2 559
genre 23 882; 27 238
Impressionism 8 622; 11 547, 663, 664; 15 154, 155; 21 863, 868; 31 880
landscape 11 663
sketches 27 266
periodicals 24 426
writings 19 37
Durand-Ruel Godfroy, Caroline 9 423, 425
Durandus (master mason; fl 1232) 27 249
Durandus of Mende (writer; c. 1220-96) 29 500
Durango Cathedral 21 377
Durant, Jean 27 682
Durant, M. 6 535
Duranti, Giovanni 22 481
Duranti, Pietro 22 481
Durantino, Francesco 6 358; 9 425*; 16 733; 31 741
Durantino, Guido see FONTANA (v), GUIDO
Duranty, Louis (-Emile)-Edmond 9 425–6*; 15 153, 157
groups and movements 26 53
works 22 687; 31 704
Durán y de Bastero, Luis de 15 881
Duras, Duc de 13 234
Durasov (family) 33 517
Durassier, Marcel 20 604
Durazno 31 751
Durazzo (family) 6 34; 11 9; 22 27; 24 203
Durazzo, Andrea di Niccolò da see ALESSI, ANDREA
Durazzo, Battina 3 90
Durazzo, Giuseppe M. 4 811
Durazzo, Jacopo, Conte 9 426*; 33 116
Durazzo, Marchese 29 32
Durazzo collection 20 453
Durban 9 426–7*; 29 103, 103
architecture 1 319; 29 105
Clarence Road Apartments 29 106
Colonial Mutual Building 29 106
Mangosuthu Technikon 29 107
Museum and Art Gallery 29 121
Post Office 9 366; 29 105; 31 241
pottery 29 116
School of Art 29 123
Southern Life Building 29 106
Technikon Natal 29 106
Town Hall see Post Office
University of Natal
Campbell Collections 29 122
Centre for Oral Studies 29 122
Westpoint 29 106
Durbon 5 894
Durbuto, Antoine 8 482
Durbuy 3 588
Durch 24 439
Durchner, Matthias 31 356
Durdans Palace 23 198, 199
Durell 2 4
Durello, S. 24 203
Düren, Adam van 8 738; 9 427*; 30 83
attributions 14 369
restorations 19 795
works 5 295; 13 103; 19 425; 30 67
Düren, St Anna 11 256
Dürer, Agnes 25 625
Dürer, Albrecht (1427-1502) 9 427, 428, 429
reproductions in tapestry 13 277
Dürer, Albrecht (1471-1528) 1 657; 2 716; 3 201, 335, 387; 8 595; 9 427–46*, 429, 431; 10 384; 13 905; 14 869, 872; 18 705; 19 501; 20 804; 22 836; 23 307, 308; 25 276, 284; 26 184; 29 878; 32 190, 274; 33 18
architecture 23 317
assistants 24 355; 28 57, 58; 31 287
attributions 5 541; 12 366; 13 160; 18 510, 512; 32 156; 33 703
book illustrations 9 436; 12 385; 21 579; 30 487
bookplates 4 373; 14 424
catalogues 9 60
collaboration 6 165; 18 474; 22 920; 23 311; 28 58, 143; 29 433; 31 287
copies 9 446; 11 734; 17 711
drawings 2 149; 9 216, 221, 273; 10 130; 17 520; 18 898; 29 776
ink 23 315
mythological 22 413
portraits 9 428; 12 838
silverpoints 21 340, 340
townscapes 31 154
wash 9 214
forgeries by others 9 445; 14 626
frames 11 377, 455
furniture 12 420
globes 12 810
groups and movements 26 188
house 23 307
metalwork 23 311
brasses 4 693
jewellery 12 455, 455
medals 14 419
methods 5 656; 14 873; 21 759; 24 488, 488; 28 203, 206
drawing 29 437, 884; 31 578
printing 25 590, 598
paintings 10 130; 17 700, 711
altarpieces 26 188, 349
portraits 9 244, 273, 439; 14 869; 23 305, 306; 30 167
religious 5 883; 9 108, 432; 16 772; 25 274, 275
topographical 2 339
wall 33 130
watercolours 2 102; 9 430, 433; 13 219; 22 686; 32 899
architectural 5 180; 13 904
landscape 9 217; 18 705
patrons and collectors 14 682; 25 631
Alcalá, 3rd Duque de (1583-1637) 26 307
Amerbach, Johannes 1 771
Arenberg, Engelbert-Marie, 9th Duke of 2 382
Becker, Herman (c. 1617-78) 3 475
Boisserée, Melchior and Sulpiz 4 243
Bracciano, Paolo Giordano II Orsini, Duca di 23 576
Butler, Charles (1822-1910) 5 311
Dürer, Albrecht (1471-1528) patrons and collectors—cont.
Carpio, Luis Méndez de Haro y Guzmán, 6th Marqués del 5 844
Charles I, King of England and Scotland (reg 1625-49) 29 800
Christina, Queen of Sweden (reg 1632-54) 30 118; 32 7
Clark, Robert Sterling 7 377
Crozat, Pierre 8 209
Czernin, Jan Rudolf, Count 8 428
Damery, Chevalier de 8 481
Douce, Francis 9 195
Faesch, Remigius (ii) (1596–1667) 10 752
Ferdinand, Archduke of Austria, Count of Tyrol (reg 1564-95) 6 76
Ferdinand VII, King of Spain (reg 1808; 1814-33) 4 566
Fitzalan, Henry, 12th Earl of Arundel 11 140
Francesco I, 8th Duke of Modena and Reggio (reg 1629-58) 10 526
Frederick III, Elector of Saxony (reg 1486- 1525) 33 112
Fries, Moritz, Graf von 11 789
Fugger, Jakob, II (1459-1525) 11 818
Germanisches Nationalmuseum (Nuremberg) 2 365
Gigoux, Jean(-François) 12 609
Grimani, Domenico, Cardinal, Patriarch of Aquilea 13 657
Grosvenor, Hugh Lupus, 1st Duke of Westminster 13 697
Hawkins, John Heywood (1803-77) 14 252
Heinecken, Karl Heinrich von 14 314
Heller, Jakob 13 720
Hervey, Frederick Augustus, 4th Earl of Bristol 14 485
Hoffmann, Lorenz 6 76
Hohenzollern, Albert of Brandenburg, Cardinal, Elector-Archbishop of Mainz (reg 1514-45) 14 647, 649
Howard, Hugh 14 810
Howard (i), Thomas, 2nd Earl of Arundel 14 806
Imhoff, Willibald 14 626
Imstenraedt, Franz Gerhard von 15 158
Jabach, Everard 16 814, 815
Jonghelinck, Niclaes 3 615; 17 643
Jullienne, Jean de 17 684
Kaiserliche Akademie 2 831
Lastanosa, Vicencio Juan de 18 816
Ligne, Charles-Joseph-Emmanuel de, Prince (1759-92) 19 369
Lindsay, Alexander (William Crawford), 25th Earl of Crawford and 8th Earl of Balcarres 19 412
Lubomirski, Henryk 19 752
Mariette, Jean 20 416
Mariette, Pierre-Jean 20 417
Maugis, Claude, Abbé 20 855
Maximilian I, Duke of Bavaria (reg 1598- 1651) and Elector of Bavaria (reg 1623-51) 9 446; 33 275
Maximilian I, Holy Roman Emperor (reg 1493- 1519) 13 902, 903, 904; 31 821
Medici, Ferdinando de', Grand Prince of Tuscany (1663-1713) 21 30
Meynier, Charles 21 412
Murray, Charles Fairfax 22 351
Nys, Daniel 23 326
Dürer, Albrecht (1471-1528) patrons and collectors—cont.
Paggi, Giovanni Battista 28 219
Papillon de La Ferté, Denis-Pierre-Jean 24 63
Passeri, Cinzio, Cardinal 1 594
Philip IV, King of Spain (reg 1621-65) 29 352
Pirckheimer, Willibald 15 145; 24 848
Potocki, Stanisław Kostka 25 364
Praun, Paulus 25 454
Puccini, Tommaso 25 691
Rosenwald, Lessing J(ulius) 27 166
Röver, Valerius 27 270
Rudolf II, Holy Roman Emperor (reg 1576- 1612) 11 803; 13 914; 18 522
Rushout, John, 2nd Baron Northwick 27 350
Sachs, Paul J(oseph) 27 493
Saint-Morys, Charles Paul Jean-Baptiste de Bourgevin Vialart de 27 568
Saxe-Teschen, Albert (Casimir) Wettin, Herzog von, Governor General of the Netherlands (1780-92) 33 116
Scott (i), William Bell 28 276
Tessin, Carl Gustav, Count 30 524
Thyssen-Bornemisza, Heinrich, Baron von 30 795
Verstolk van Soelen, Jan Gijsbert, Baron 32 377
Verdramin, Gabriele 25 630
Walker, (Byron) Edmund 32 794
Wawra, C. J. 25 729
Wellesley, Henry 33 56
Wicar, Jean-Baptiste (-Joseph) 33 154
Worlidge, Thomas 33 380
personal collection 9 229; 13 904; 15 50; 19 757; 28 60
prints 8 838; 12 386; 14 869; 20 601; 25 596, 604; 32 199
drypoints 9 308
engravings 8 838; 9 437; 10 384–5*, 901; 11 56; 22 521; 23 310; 25 605
allegorical 1 656
mythological 1 657
nude figures 23 293
portraits 10 445
religious 6 452; 8 838; 10 385; 12 888; 29 556, 557
etchings 10 549, 550; 23 310
monotypes 21 895; 24 848
woodcuts 6 569; 23 310; 25 243; 26 257; 29 557; 33 353
allegorical 15 85
animal subjects 2 102, 103
inscriptions 23 617
propaganda 26 79
religious 2 223, 223; 4 357; 7 226; 9 431; 12 385; 27 159; 33 352
pupils 3 102, 506; 9 445; 28 215
reproductions in enamel 19 398
reproductions in stained glass 4 870
reproductions on banknotes 3 182
reproductive prints by others
B. G., Master (fl 15th cent.) 20 792
Cartaro, Mario 5 888
Giovanni Antonio da Brescia 12 698
Krüger, Dietrich 18 476
Ladenspelder, Johann 18 619
Lorck, Melchior 19 661
Matham, Jacob 20 812
Musi, Agostino dei 22 369
Dürer, Albrecht (1471-1528) reproductive prints by others—cont.
Negker, Jost de 22 723
Nicoletto da Modena 23 110
Pencz, Georg 24 355
Raimondi, Marcantonio 10 385; 25 858; 26 228
Rota, Martino 27 212
Sadeler, Aegidius, II (1570-1629) 9 446; 27 504
Senefelder, J(ohann) N(epomuk) F(ranz) Alois 19 482; 28 404
Strixner, Johann Nepomuk 29 776
Zoan Andrea 33 689
restorations by others 9 446; 12 168
sculpture 2 800; 6 171; 25 22
stained glass 13 188; 14 572; 15 145; 23 315; 27 256; 29 504
studio 29 853
teachers 9 427; 33 299
writings 12 366; 14 869; 15 93; 21 264; 29 637; 31 299
on architecture 21 578
on fortifications 3 360; 31 298
on human proportions 28 201
on light 19 354
on military architecture 21 565, 571
on proportion 2 356; 14 616; 23 487
translated 8 11
Dürer, Endres 9 427, 436
Dürer, Hans 9 445*; 18 428
collaboration 3 69; 18 574
patrons and collectors 16 866
teachers 9 427
works 18 431, 574; 24 356
Dürer Renaissance 9 443, 445–7*; 12 389; 14 626
engravings 9 446
Duret 8 589
Duret, François-Joseph (c. 1732-1816) 9 447
Duret, François-Joseph (1804-65) 8 472; 9 447*; 11 564
personal collection 24 883
pupils 5 824; 6 468; 8 653; 18 751
works 11 565; 29 574; 30 743
Duret, (Jules-Emmanuel) Théodore 9 447–8*; 15 153, 154, 157; 33 141
Durfort, Louise-Jeanne de, Duchesse de Mazarin see MAZARIN, LOUISE-JEANNE DE DURFORT, Duchesse de
Durga 15 627
Durham 9 448–51*; 10 225
Castle 6 50; 9 451*; 21 839; 26 611, 614, 615
Cathedral of Christ and the Blessed Virgin 3 709; 9 448–50*; 26 578, 590
altars 1 697; 10 322
arches 2 298; 13 36
beakheads 26 589
bronze 26 688
capitals 26 614, 616
Chapter House 2 71; 6 466
chevrons 6 564, 565; 10 228; 26 588
choir 9 449
choir-stalls 7 192
coins 33 136
collections 14 851; 27 617
combs (liturgical) 7 646
door fittings 10 338
doors 9 155
dormitory 21 839, 839, 843, 844
embroidery 2 72, 74, 83, 84; 10 181, 353
font 11 255
galilee porch 12 5, 5
manuscripts 3 710; 26 669, 671
metalwork 32 529

Durham
Cathedral of Christ and the Blessed Virgin—cont.
mouldings 22 216, 218, 220
nave 9 450
Neasham Cross 26 615
Neville Screen 13 82; 24 465
Nine Altars chapel 31 273
piers 26 588
priory 19 289; 21 839
pulpit 25 723
restorations 33 446
screen 28 295
sculpture 9 450–51*; 26 612, 615
textiles 28 715; 30 552
throne 30 779
towers 13 55
transept 31 281
Treasury 9 664
vaults 26 589; 32 90, 92
donjon 21 562
Gulbenkian Museum of Oriental Art and Archaeology see University → Oriental Museum
Kings College see under University
manuscripts 26 661
Oriental Museum see under University
pews 24 576
quilting 25 821
Raby Castle (Co. Durham) 6 61
St Mary the Less 26 615
sculpture 28 241
University 10 375
collections 10 90
King's College 10 375
Oriental Museum 6 925; 7 155; 10 92; 15 744; 24 390; 29 240
Durham, Joseph 9 451*
Durham Cassiodorus 15 874
Durham Earth and Ocean Silk 9 664, 665, 666, 667
Durham Gospels see under GOSPEL BOOKS → individual manuscripts
Duri 27 831
Durieux, Caroline 7 434
Durieux, Tilla see GODEFROY, OTTILIE
Düring, Hans 19 29
Düringer (family) 30 143
Durini (family) 3 355
Durini, Francesco 13 764
Durio, Paco 12 194
Durjanpura 15 467
Dur-Katlimmu see SHEIKH HAMMAD, TELL
Durkheim, Emile 2 137; 28 926
Dur Kurigalzu see AQAR QUF
Durlach 12 430
Durlacher, Alfred 9 451–2*
Durlacher, George L. 9 451–2*
Durlacher, Henry 9 451
Durlet, Franciscus Andreas 3 585, 617, 763
Durm, Josef 9 452*
pupils 4 64; 28 95
works 14 306; 17 817, 818
Durm, Joseph 19 749
Durman Tepe 29 824
Durmensky 6 272
Durmen Tepe 23 608
Dürnbeck, František 8 405
Dürner, Hans 9 452*
Durno, James 5 541; 22 153
Dürnstein Monastery 2 783; 28 123; 29 839; 31 510
Dürr see DIRR
Dürr, Ernst Caspar 33 81
Dürr, Wilhelm 4 616
Durra, Muhanna 9 452*; 17 655
Durrani, Saleem 23 801
Durrani, Timur Shah see TIMUR SHAH, King
Durrazzo see DURRËS
Durrell, Edward 21 397
Durrell, Jonathan 31 634
Durrës 1 537, 538
amphitheatre 1 538
Archaeological Museum 1 546
architecture 1 538
art schools 1 547
Dyrrhachion 9 495*, 511; 26 906; 32 158
mosaics 13 560, 564
painting 1 546
pottery 9 631; 13 534
Dürrheim, Staatssalinen 10 748
Durrie, George Henry 8 276; 9 452–3*
Durrie, John 9 452
Durrieu, Paul 9 453*; 12 524
Durrington Walls 14 387; 23 808; 25 504; 30 434
Dürrnberg 2 774, 776; 9 453*; 12 361; 25 470
cemeteries 6 154, 156
jewellery 25 546, 547
metalwork 6 158; 27 663
Durro 26 642
Durrow 15 877
Dur-Sharrukin see KHORSBAD
Dursley 13 211
Duru, M. 2 846
Duru, Pierre-Louis 14 543; 30 114
Dur-Untash see CHOGHA ZANBIL
Durup, Jean-Baptiste 22 456
Duruthy 25 491
Du Ry (family) 17 834
Du Ry, Charles 4 865, 866; 9 454*
Du Ry, Charles Louis 9 454–5*; 17 834
Du Ry, Louis 31 718
Du Ry, Mathurin 9 454
Du Ry, Paul 9 454–5*
house 17 834
patrons and collectors 14 491; 17 834
pupils 9 454
works 9 454, 455; 12 368, 373; 31 716, 718; 32 339
Du Ry, Simon Louis 9 455–6*; 12 374; 14 492
patrons and collectors 14 492; 17 834, 836
pupils 17 698
works 9 454, 455; 12 413, 475; 13 295; 17 698, 834; 22 361; 23 340
Du Ryer, Pierre 23 680
Duryev 17 866
Dusart, Cornelis 9 456–7*; 13 895; 22 846
personal collection 23 614
teachers 22 840; 23 609
works 5 756; 9 221, 456; 21 415
Dusart, François see DIEUSSART, FRANÇOIS
Duschek, Karl 22 381
Duse, Eleonora 8 109
Du Seigneur, Jean Bernard 11 564
Dušek, Jan Vítězslav 30 221
Dushanbe 6 182; 9 457–8*; 30 251, 252, 253
Aini Opera and Ballet Theatre 29 823
architecture 6 198; 30 252
Bekhzod State Fine Arts Museum see Republican Historical, Regional, and Fine Arts Museum
Donish Institute of History, Archaeology and Ethnography 6 283; 9 458
earrings 9 457
embroidery 6 250
metalwork 6 243
museums 6 282
Republican Historical, Regional and Fine Arts Museum 6 283; 9 458
sculpture 6 214
Dushanbe—cont.
Tajik Republic Museum see Republican, Historical Regional and Fine Arts Museum
Dushan Tepe, Bagh-i Dilgusha 12 83
Dushkyn, Oleksi (Mykhaylovych) 9 458*; 21 349, 350
Dusi, Inge 6 600
Du Sommerard, (Simon-Nicolas-) Alexandre 9 25, 458–9*; 11 663; 13 208; 22 359; 29 515
paintings 9 378
Dussart 3 603
Dusseigneur, Jean 3 288
Düsseldorf 9 459–60*; 12 360, 361, 379
art market 12 474
collections 12 481
Drei-Scheiben-Haus 12 379
Eat Art Gallery 29 420
education (art) 12 479
Ehrenhof 9 460
exhibitions 10 678
Hochschule für Angewandte Kunst 15 823
Kunstakademie 1 107; 9 459, 460; 33 280
collections 18 421; 24 238; 33 284
museums
Kunsthalle 9 460
Kunsthaus 19 719
Kunstmuseum im Ehrenhof
collections 7 903; 9 377, 460; 21 816; 27 491
Kunstsammlung Nordrhein-Westfalen 9 460; 18 114; 28 119; 30 749
Kurfürstliche Galerie 9 11, 18; 22 357
Landesgalerie see Kunstsammlung Nordrhein-Westfalen
Staatliches Kunstmuseum 16 828
painting 12 393; 26 740, 742
Planetarium 4 788
Rheinstadion 22 917
St Margarete 23 647
St Rochuskirche 20 808
Schloss Benrath 12 133; 18 420; 24 784–5; 26 497
Shrine of St Suitbert 12 442
synagogue 17 548
Zoo 33 698
Düsseldorf school 1 119; 9 460–61*; 12 393; 14 535; 25 571
Düsseldorf Secession see SECESSION (DÜSSELDORF)
Dussen, Cornelia van der 27 271
Dussurgey, Adrien see CHABAL-DUSSURGEY, PIERRE-ADRIEN
Dust 'Ali Khan Nizam al-Dawla 30 415
dust-covers see BOOK JACKETS
Dustmann, Hanns 12 379
Dust Muhammad 9 461*; 15 578; 16 318, 320, 325; 17 687
patrons and collectors 7 717; 16 552, 876; 27 514
pupils 28 567
works 1 474; 16 100, 314, 318, 319, 320, 333
writings 16 127, 333
Dusun 20 175
Duszenko, Franciszek 25 116
Dutary, Alberto 9 461–2*; 23 906
pupils 1 739
works 23 905, 905
Dutch Association of Arts and Crafts see NEDERLANDSCHE VEREENIGING VOOR AMBACHTS-EN NIJVERHEIDSKUNST (VANK)
Dutch Classicism 5 542; 22 824–6, 825
Dutch Drawing Society see HOLLANDSCHE TEEKEN-MAATSCHAPPIJ
Dutch East India Company 1 801, 807; 6 622; 15 201; 16 553; 20 163; 29 102, 104; 30 243; 32 417
atlases 2 696
ceramics 7 165; 22 878; 29 116
coins 29 469
collections 7 155; 15 741; 17 429
directors 13 266
fortifications 21 596
furniture 7 166; 15 813
glass 29 118
lacquer 18 612
paper 24 49
porcelain 4 175, 176; 6 331, 332, 919, 920; 16 424; 17 264; 25 649; 30 878
pottery 4 173, 176
sculpture 22 859
silver 29 119
textiles 8 35; 16 449; 22 899
tourism 29 238
Dutch gilt papers see PAPERS → techniques → embossing; gilding
Dutch Guiana see SURINAM
Dutch Italianates 9 462–3*
members
Asselijn, Jan 2 614
Berchem, Nicolaes (Pietersz.) (c. 1620-83) 3 757
Both, Jan 4 486
Breenbergh, Bartholomeus 4 733
Glauber, Johannes 12 801
Heusch, Willem, de 14 499
Huysum, Jan van 15 46
Lingelbach, Johannes 19 420
Poelenburch, Cornelis van 25 65
Pynacker, Adam 25 754
Romeijn, Willem 27 116
Swanevelt, Herman van 30 61
Weenix, Jan Baptist 33 24, 26
works 2 615; 3 758, 759; 4 487, 488; 9 463; 19 420; 25 755, 756; 33 25
Dutch metal see under ALLOYS → types
Dutch mordant see POTASSIUM CHOLORIDE
Dutch pink see under PIGMENTS → types
Dutch Reformed Church 2 148
Dutch Trading Company see NEDERLANDSCHE HANDELSMAATSCHAPPIJ
Dutch West India Company 1 807; 12 136; 13 874, 875
Dutel, Jacques 12 832; 24 147
Duterrau, Benjamin 2 745, 772; 9 464*
Dutert, Charles-Louis-Ferdinand 9 464*
collaboration 10 683
works 11 524; 16 55
Duterte (fl 1850) 24 149
Dutertre, André (1753-1842) 8 542
Duthé, Mlle 8 507
Duthoit, Edmond-Clément-Marie-Louis 9 464–5*; 11 580
Duthoît, L. 23 510
Dutilleul, Roger 9 465*; 11 664; 17 725
Dutilleux, Constant 7 433, 554
Dutillieu, Charles-Gilles 19 142
Du Tillot, Guillaume 3 101; 17 682
Du Toit, Paul 29 109
Dutthagamani Abhaya 29 474
Düttmann, Werner 3 797; 9 465*; 12 380
Dutuit, (Philippe-)Auguste (-Jean-Baptiste) 9 466*
Dutuit, (Etienne-Philippe-) Eugène 9 465*
Dutuit Mount of Olives, Master of the 20 628
Duval, Bertin 9 466
Duval, Elisabeth 9 466
Duval, Jacques 27 429
Duval, Jean 31 227
Duval, Jean-François André 27 429
Duval, John, & Sons 27 336
Duval, Louis David 27 429
Duval, Marc 9 466*; 29 428
Duval, Peter 10 345
Duval, Robert 30 517
Duval, Valentin Jameray 13 922
Duval Le Camus, Jules 9 467*
Duval Le Camus, Pierre 9 466–7*
Duvanli see DOUVANLI
Duvaux, Lazare 9 467*; 20 388; 24 137
ceramics 11 608
frames 11 408
furniture 3 414; 11 591, 593; 32 338
metalwork 9 399; 11 620
Duveen, Henry 9 467
Duveen, Joel Joseph 9 467
Duveen, Joseph, 1st Baron Duveen of Millbank 1 454; 2 560; 3 18, 765; 9 467–8*; 10 367; 11 307, 774; 18 448; 21 90; 31 664
architecture 10 362; 25 235
assistants 9 204
collections 9 298
paintings 3 420; 5 589; 15 29; 18 882
Duveen Brothers 9 200, 467; 12 474; 16 769; 17 777
Duvelleroy 10 781
Duveneck, Frank 1 611; 7 327; 9 468*; 22 304
pupils 11 300; 31 486
works 21 896
Düver see TLOS
Duverger, Erik 30 332
Du Verger de Verville, Jean François 21 573
Duvergier de Hauranne, Jean 17 1
Duvet, Drouhot (fl late 15th cent.) 9 468
Duvet, Drouhot (c. 1485-after 1561) see DUVET, JEAN
Duvet, Jean (c. 1485-after 1561) 9 468–9*; 10 387
works 2 224; 11 533
Duvet, Jean (fl 1540-56) 9 469
Duvet Brothers 32 421
Duvey, Loys 9 469
Du Vivier, Arnould see ARNOULD DU VIVIER
Duvivier, (Pierre-Simon-) Benjamin 9 469*; 20 922
Duvivier, Claude 21 70
Duvivier, Gangulphe 9 469
Duvivier, Henri-Joseph 29 432; 31 220
Duvivier, Jean (fl 1378-1401) see JEAN DU VIVIER
Duvivier, Jean (1687-1761) 9 469*; 20 922
Duwaer, Frans 32 696
Du Wan 7 89; 12 88; 16 858
Duwayr, Tall al- see LACHISH
Duwe, Harald 9 469–70*
Duweir, Tell ed- see LACHISH
Dux 32 756
Dux, Aimone 14 422; 17 445
Dux, Hugo 8 437
Duxford, St John 26 613
Duyck, Eduard 25 347
Duyckinck, Gerardus (1695-1746) 20 679
Duyckinck, Gerret (fl before 1695) 23 46
Duyl-Schwartze, Thérèse van see SCHWARTZE, THÉRÈSE
Duyn, Fanny van
works 22 646
Duys, Herry 29 117

Duyster, Willem (Cornelisz.) **7** 510; **9** 470–71*; **12** 290
works **9** *471*
Duyts, Gustave Den *see* DEN DUYTS, GUSTAVE
Duyts, Jan van **18** 879
Duytscher, Hans de **2** 198
D⨯V, Master *see* VELLERT, DIRK (JACOBSZ.)
Dvārasamudra *see* HALEBID
Dvaravati **30** 785
Dvin **2** *423*, 426; **9** 471–2*, *512*; **16** *105*
Cathedral **7** 261
ceramics **2** 439
jewellery **2** 440
metalwork **2** 441
mosaics **2** 429
pottery **2** 439
sculpture **2** 433
Dvinsk *see* DAUGAVPILS
Dvizheniye **15** 831; **18** 63
Dvor **28** *858*, 862
church **28** 859
Dvořák, Karel **8** 387; **25** 432
Dvořák, Max **2** 833; **9** 472*; **30** 731
assistants **11** 769
pupils **2** 131; **3** 715; **18** 187; **23** 362; **25** 12; **28** 23, 350; **33** 180
teachers **33** 159
works **8** 426
Dvořaková, V. **8** 426
Dvořiště church **8** 377
Dvornikovich, Bishop **31** 786
Dvorský, Bohumír **8** 394
Dwarahat **15** 265
dwarf galleries *see* GALLERIES (ii) (CORRIDORS)
Dwarf Gibson *see* GIBSON, RICHARD
Dwarf Painter **32** 28
Dwight, John **9** 473*; **10** 139
patrons and collectors **28** 168
works **10** *304*, 305, 308; **19** 595
Dwight, Mabel **27** 872
Dwight, Timothy **31** 647
Dworkin, Andrea **10** 486
Dwurnik, Edward **9** 473*; **25** 108
Dwyer Lilac Jadeite **16** IV
D'yachenko, Dmitry M. **31** 552
dyads *see under* SCULPTURE → types
Dyagilev, Sergey (Pavlovich) *see* DIAGHILEV, SERGE (DE)
Dyak **30** 554
D'yakova, Mariya **19** *279*
D'yakovo, St John the Baptist **7** 256; **22** 168; **27** 371
Dyat'kovo Glassworks **27** 415, 416, 417
Dybwad, Peter **14** 631; **19** 111
Dyce, William **2** 524; **9** 473–5*; **10** 373; **28** 274, 275
collaboration **14** 436
groups and movements **26** 740
patrons and collectors **1** 30; **14** 148; **28** 273
works **9** *474*; **10** 252; **14** 580, 587; **19** 614; **22** 328; **28** 238
Dyck, Abraham van *see* DIJCK, ABRAHAM VAN
Dyck, Anthony van **2** 196; **3** 613; **9** 475–88*, *486*; **10** 249; **16** 668, 674; **19** 15, 125, 381; **20** 476; **25** 283
assistants **14** 139; **18** 811; **19** 63; **21** 152; **24** 752
attributions **13** 229; **14** 139, 842; **19** 25; **31** 362; **33** 279
collaboration **23** 381; **27** 298, 299
Algardi, Alessandro **26** 823
Cortona, Pietro da **26** 823
Neeffs, Jacob **22** 717
Pontius, Paulus **10** 391
Rubens, Peter Paul **3** 613
Snyders, Frans **28** 904

Dyck, Anthony van
collaboration—cont.
Steenwijk, Hendrick van (ii) (1580-1649) **29** 592
Vorsterman, Lucas, (i) (*c.* 1595-1675) **10** 391
Vos, Cornelis de **32** 702
Vos, Paul de **32** 706
Wael, Cornelis de **32** 754
copies **21** 128; **24** 553; **25** 664; **29** 487; **32** 824
drawings **2** *314*; **9** *481*, *487*
frames **11** 422, *422*, 424, *430*, 456
groups and movements **3** 264
methods **9** 211; **24** 792; **25** 279, 281, 285; **31** 578
paintings **12** 283; **18** 891
altarpieces **3** 559; **28** 657
literary themes **9** *479*
oil sketches **13** 676, *676*
portraits **3** 560; **9** 245, 278; **10** 248
Amalia von Solms, Princess of Orange (1602-75) **23** 466
Balbi, Marchesa **25** *285*, 286
Cattaneo, Elena Grimaldi, Marchesa **9** *477*; **25** 286
Charles I, King of England and Scotland (*reg* 1625-49) **9** *483*; **29** 424, *802*
children of Charles I **9** *482*
Feilding, William, 1st Earl of Denbigh **10** 861
Henrietta Maria, Queen of England and Scotland (1609-69) **29** 803
Howard, Thomas, 2nd Earl of Arundel and Aletheia Talbot, Countess of Arundel **14** *806*
Jabach, Everard **16** 814
Lomellini (family) **9** *480*
Stuart, Lords John and Bernard **9** *278*
religious **9** *478*, *488*; **11** 403; **31** 90
watercolours **10** 250; **32** 900, VII1
patrons and collectors
Agar-Ellis, George James, 1st Baron Dover **10** 146
Albarelli, Giovanni **5** 432
Alcalá, 3rd Duque de (1583-1637) **26** 307
Altamira (family) **1** 690
Angerstein, John Julius **2** 51
Arenberg, Prosper-Louis, 7th Duke of, Duke of Arschot **2** 382
Arensberg, Engelbert-Marie, 9th Duke of **2** 382
Augustinian hermits **2** 725
Aumale, Henri-Eugène-Philippe-Louis de Bourbon, Duc d' **23** 523
Aved, Jacques (-André-Joseph) **2** 852
Balbi, Costantino, the elder (1676-1740) **3** 90
Baudouin, Silvain-Raphaël **3** 395
Bentivoglio, Guido, Cardinal **3** 745
Bishop's Palace (Kroměříž) **18** 467
Bonaparte, Mathilde, Princess **4** 307
Boyle, Richard, 3rd Earl of Burlington and 4th Earl of Cork **4** 610
Brignole-Sale (family) **4** 811
Bryan, Michael **5** 63
Buchanan, William **5** 71
Buckner, Richard **5** 78
Butler, Charles (1822-1910) **5** 311
Cairo, Francesco **5** 407

Dyck, Anthony van
patrons and collectors—cont.
Carpio, Luis Méndez de Haro y Guzmán, 6th Marqués del **5** 844
Catherine II, Empress of Russia (*reg* 1762- 96) **26** 733
Cavendish, William, 2nd Duke of Devonshire (1671-1729) **6** 116
Cavendish, William, 3rd Duke of Devonshire (1698-1755) **6** 117
Champernowne, Arthur **6** 438
Charles I, King of England and Scotland (*reg* 1625-49) **10** 360; **25** 263; **29** 797, 799, 801
Churchill, John, 1st Duke of Marlborough **7** 286; **10** 364
Clerk, John, 2nd Baronet of Penicuik (1679-1755) **7** 418
Coke, Thomas, 1st Earl of Leicester of the 1st creation (1697-1759) **7** 540
Crozat, Pierre **8** 209
Day, Alexander **8** 582
Duarte, Diego **9** 311
Eertvelt, Andries van **9** 745
Egerton, Francis, 1st Earl of Ellesmere **9** 755
Einden, Jan van den **10** 114
Einden, van den (family) **10** 115
Elizabeth Farnese, Queen of Spain (1692-1766) **4** 559
Emanuel-Philibert, Viceroy of Sicily **28** 8
Flinck, Nicolaes Anthonis **11** 170
Fountaine, Andrew (*d* 1874) **11** 348
Frederick II, King of Prussia (*reg* 1740-86) **14** 652
Frederick Henry, Stadholder of the Netherlands, Prince of Orange (*reg* 1625-47) **22** 904; **23** 463, 465
Frick, Henry Clay **11** 774
Fries, Moritz, Graf von **11** 789
Geest, Cornelis van der **12** 233
Godoy (y Alvárez de Faria), Manuel, Príncipe de la Paz **12** 839
Goering, Hermann (Wilhelm) **12** 843
Grey (family) **13** 645
Groppoli, Anton Giulio Brignole-Sale, Marchese di **4** 811
Guinness, Edward (Cecil), 1st Earl of Iveagh **13** 836
Guzmán, Ambrosio Ignacio Spínola y, Archbishop of Seville **13** 880
Habsburg I., Leopold William, Archduke of Austria, Governor of the Netherlands **13** 919
Hall, Peter Adolf **14** 80
Harrach, Friedrich August, Graf von **14** 190
Heinecken, Karl Heinrich von **14** 314
Henrietta Maria, Queen of England and Scotland (1609-69) **29** 803
Herbert, Philip, 4th Earl of Pembroke and 1st Earl of Montgomery **14** 435
His de La Salle, (Aimé-Charles-) Horace **14** 577
Hohenzollern, Henry, Prince of Prussia **14** 653
Holford, Robert Stayner **14** 675
Hope, John, 5th Earl of Hopetoun **33** 216
Howard (i), Thomas, 2nd Earl of Arundel **14** 806

Dyck, Anthony van
patrons and collectors—cont.
Hudson, Thomas (1701-99) **14** 842
Hume, Abraham, 2nd Baronet **14** 877
Hyde, Edward, 1st Earl of Clarendon **15** 48
Imperiale, Gian Vincenzo **15** 148
Imstenraedt, Franz Gerhard von **15** 158
John V, King of Portugal (*reg* 1706-50) **4** 636
Josephine, Empress of the French (1763-1814) **4** 304
Kelly, Florencio **17** 892
Kneller, Godfrey **18** 146
Knight, Richard Payne **18** 150
Koninklijk Museum voor Schone Kunsten (Antwerp) **3** 616
Lanier, Nicholas **18** 747
Lankrink, Prosper Henry **18** 748
Lee, Eleanor, Countess of Suffolk **25** 282
Leemput, Remi van **19** 63
Leganés, 1st Marqués de **13** 879; **29** 353
Lely, Peter **19** 124
Lempereur, Jean-Denis, II **19** 144
Leopold I, King of Belgium (*reg* 1831-65) **7** 490
Leopold II, King of Belgium (*reg* 1865-1909) **7** 490
Leveson-Gower, George Granville, 1st Duke of Sutherland **19** 270
Liechtenstein-Castelkorn, Karel von, Bishop of Olmutz **8** 423
Louis XIV, King of France (*reg* 1643-1715) **4** 552; **19** 731
Mariette, Pierre-Jean **20** 417
Marquand, Henry G(urdon) **20** 461
Mead, Richard **10** 364
Methuen, Paul (1672-1757) **21** 348
Meynier, Charles **21** 412
Montagu, Ralph, 1st Duke of Montagu **21** 907
Montagu-Douglas-Scott, Walter Francis, 5th Duke of Buccleuch, 7th Duke of Queensberry **21** 908
Murray, Charles Fairfax **22** 351
National Gallery of Scotland **28** 272
Omazur, Nicolas **23** 437
Orléans, Philippe II de Bourbon, 2nd Duc d' (1674-1723) **23** 515, 516
Pallavicini, Agostino **23** 873
Peel, Robert (1788-1850) **24** 322; **33** 190, 216
Percy, Algernon, 10th Earl of Northumberland **12** 243; **24** 389
Poniatowski, Stanisław, Prince **25** 213
Quellinus, Erasmus (ii) (1607-78) **25** 811
Reynolds, Joshua **26** 279, 280
Richardson, Jonathan (1665-1745) **26** 346
Richelieu, Louis-François Armand-Jean Vignerod du Plessis, Duc de (1629-1715) **26** 349
Rockox, Nicolaas **26** 490
Roomer, Gaspar **27** 133
Royal Institution (Edinburgh) **28** 271; **33** 216
Ruffo, Tommaso, Cardinal, Archbishop of Ferrara **27** 316
Salamanca (y Mayol), José, Marqués de **27** 607

Dyck, Anthony van
patrons and collectors—cont.
Savoy, Eugene of, Prince (1663-1736) **28** 15
Schönborn, Lothar Franz von, Bishop of Bamberg, Elector-Archbishop of Mainz **28** 146
Serra, Giovan Francesco, Marqués di Cassano **28** 479
Seymour-Conway, Francis Charles, 3rd Marquess of Hertford **28** 527
Seymour-Conway, Richard, 4th Marquess of Hertford **28** 527
Sheremet'yev, Pyotr (Borisovich), Count **28** 593
Slingelandt, Govert van, Lord of Lindt and West-IJsselmonde **28** 842
Snyders, Frans **28** 904
Spencer (family) **29** 380
Spencer, Robert, 2nd Earl of Sunderland (1641-1702) **29** 381
Spinola, Ambrogio **29** 411
Streeter, Robert (1621-79) **29** 767
Tallard, Marie-Joseph d'Hostun, Duc de **30** 274
Tarnowski, Jan Feliks, Count and Waleria **30** 345
Temple, Richard, 1st Viscount Cobham **30** 451
Vaudreuil, François, Comte de **32** 85
Verrue, Jeanne-Baptiste d'Albert de Luynes, Comtesse de **32** 368
Verstolk van Soelen, Jan Gijsbert, Baron **32** 377
Villiers, George, 1st Duke of Buckingham (1592-1628) **32** 575
Walpole, Robert, 1st Earl of Orford (1676-1745) **32** 824
Watson-Wentworth, Charles, 2nd Marquess of Rockingham **32** 912
Wawra, C. J. **25** 729
Wellesley, Henry **33** 56
William II, King of the Netherlands (*reg* 1840-49) **23** 469
William V, Stadholder of the Netherlands, Prince of Orange (*reg* 1751-95) **23** 469
William VIII, Landgrave of Hesse-Kassel (*reg* 1751-60) **12** 473
Yusupov, Nikolay (Borisovich), Prince (1751- 1831) **2** 417
personal collection **10** 363; **19** 124; **24** 390
prints **25** 596
engravings **25** 606
etchings **3** *560*, 561; **29** 557
portraits **15** 89
pupils **6** 32; **27** 360
reproductions in sculpture **14** 29
reproductive prints by others **25** 221; **27** 645
Baron, Bernard **3** 259
Bolswert, Schelte (Adamsz.) (à) **4** 283
Browne, Alexander **4** 884
Clouwet, Pieter **7** 466
Denon, (Dominique-) Vivant **8** 763
Follin, Bartolomeo **11** 241
Franchoys, Lucas, II (1616-81) **11** 699
Galle, Cornelis (i) (1576-1650) **12** 16
Galle, Cornelis (ii) (1615-78) **12** 17
Heath, Charles (i) (1785-1848) **14** 280
Jode, Arnold de **17** 599

Dyck, Anthony van
  reproductive prints by others—cont.
    Jode, Pieter de (i) (1570-1634) **17** 599
    Jode, Pieter de (ii) (1606-74) **17** 599
    Körnlein, Johannes **18** 387
    Lauwers, Conrad **18** 879
    Lauwers, Nicolaes **18** 879
    Lempereur, Jean-Denis, II **19** 144
    Lombart, Pierre **19** 562
    Louys, Jacob **19** 731
    McArdell, James **19** 867
    Morin, Jean **22** 116
    Neeffs, Jacob **22** 717
    Pontius, Paulus **25** 221
    Robinson, John Henry **26** 473
    Schiavonetti, Luigi **28** 86
    Snyers, Hendrick **28** 904
    Sompel, Pieter van **29** 62
    Strange, Robert **29** 747
    Suyderhoef, Jonas **30** 47
    Vorsterman, Lucas, (i) (*c*. 1595-1675) **19** 348; **32** 699
    Vorsterman, Lucas, (ii) (1624-66) **32** 700
  restorations by others **4** 845
  studio **29** 855
  teachers **3** 107, 559; **27** 287, 298
  writings **25** 221
Dyck, Daniel van den **9** 489*; **12** 914
Dyck, Floris (Claesz.) van **9** 490*; **13** 895; **22** 840
  works **9** *489*; **29** 666
Dyck, Frans van (*fl* 1599) **9** 476
Dyck, Frans Van (*fl* 1877) *see* VAN DYCK, FRANS
Dyck, Frederik van **2** 194; **28** 41
Dyck, Hermann **8** 618
Dyck, J. **4** 21
Dyck, Schloss *see* SCHLOSS DYCK
Dyck, Van, brown *see under* PIGMENTS → types
Dyckerhoff, Friedrich **33** 40
Dyckmans, Joseph-Laurent **5** 290; **25** 269
Dycor Ceramic Studio **29** 117
dyeing
  historical and regional traditions
    Africa **1** 303
    Ancient Near East **1** 880
    Aztec **9** 492
    Cameroon **11** 828
    China **7** 45
    Egypt, ancient **10** 74–5
    Fulani **11** 828
    Indian subcontinent **15** 667–8*
    Japan **17** 308*, *309*, 314
    Mesoamerica, Pre-Columbian **21** 261
    Mexico **9** 492
    New Zealand **23** 74
    Nigeria **11** 828
    Phoenician **1** 880
    Scotland **28** 266
  materials
    alum **30** 557, 560
    arsenic **30** 559
    bamboo **17** 314
    brushes **17** 315
    charcoal **17** 310
    citric acid **30** 559
    clay **30** 557, 558
    copper sulphate **30** 558
    dung **30** 558
    dyes *see* DYES
    flour **30** 558, 560
    gums **30** 557, 558
    inks **17** 310
    iron **30** 560
    iron sulphates **10** 356
    lead **30** 559
    lead nitrate **30** 558
    lead sulphate **30** 558
    lime **10** 356; **30** 558, 560
    limestone **27** 471

dyeing
  materials—cont.
    milk **30** 560
    oxalic acid **30** 559
    plums **30** 560
    rice flour **30** 558, 561
    rice paste **15** 790; **17** 309, 310, *310*, 314; **27** 470
    salt **27** 471
    sodium sulphides **30** 559
    sorghum **30** 557
    soy-beans **17** 310
    sulphuric acid **30** 559
    tartaric acid **30** 559
    waxes **15** 790; **30** 558*
    wheat starch **30** 558
    zinc **30** 558
    zinc oxide **30** 558
  types
    batik *see* BATIK
    bingata see paste resist
    block-resist **17** 308–9*
    bound-resist *see* tie-dying
    discharge **1** 294; **30** *557*, 559*
    ikat *see* IKAT
    overdyeing **9** 491
    paste resist **17** 309, 310, *310*, 315; **27** 470; **30** 557–8*
    resist **15** 668; **30** *557*, 557–8*
      Africa **1** 294
      Bamana **3** 379
      China **7** 45, 52, *144*; **30** 560
      England **10** 356
      Fulani **11** 828
      Gambia, The **3** 379
      Indian subcontinent **15** *669*, 670*, 672*, 673, *673*
      Indonesia **15** 790–92, *791*, 807
      Japan **3** 378; **17** 308–10*, 313, 314, 355; **30** 560–61
      Java **15** 790, *791*
      Malaysia **20** 176
      Mali **20** 198, *199*
      Mesoamerica, Pre-Columbian **21** 261
      Nigeria **3** 379
      Senegal **3** 379
      Sierra Leone **3** 379
      see also BATIK; tie-dyeing
    shibori **17** 309, *311*, *316*
    stencil-dyeing **17** 314, 355
    stitching **30** *555*, 556*
    stitch-resist **17** 309, 314; **21** 261, *261*
    tie-dyeing **30** *555*, 556*
      Africa **9** III2
      China **7** 144; **30** 556
      Indian subcontinent **15** *670*, 670–72*; **30** 556
      Islamic **16** 439
      Japan **17** 309, *309*, 314, 316, *317*; **30** 556
      Mesoamerica, Pre-Columbian **21** 261, *261*
      Nigeria **9** III2
      Yemen **16** 439
    wax resist **7** 144, 145; **17** 309; **30** 558*
  uses
    carpets **5** 832
    cotton **9** 490, 491; **15** 667, 668, 790, *791*, 792
    feathers **9** 490; **21** 249
    felt **10** 872
    fibre art **11** 54
    fibres **9** 490
    gourds **1** 303; **11** 828
    horn **7** 123, 126; **9** 490
    leather **9** 490; **19** 2, 3
    linen **9** 490
    parchment **20** 367
    photography **9** 490
    quills **22** 648, 649
    silk **9** 490, 492; **15** 667, 668, *670*, 790, 792
    skins **9** 490

dyeing
  uses—cont.
    textiles **9** 490, 491; **10** 74–5*; **20** 367; **30** 554–6*, *555*, *557*, 557–8*, 559*
      Indian subcontinent **15** 667–8*, 670*, 672*
      Japan **17** 308, 314
      Mali **20** 198
      Scotland **28** 266
    wool **9** 490, 491, 492
Dyer, Henry **17** 86
Dyer, John **18** 712; **24** 741; **32** 784
Dyer, Roger the *see* ROGER THE DYER
dyer's broom **24** 799
Dyers Cross glassworks **10** 315
dyes **9** 490–93*; **24** 789
  historical and regional traditions
    Africa **1** 294, 295, 299, 343
    Anglo-Saxon **2** 83
    Armenia (Europe) **2** 438; **9** 492
    Aztec **21** 249
    Bali (Indonesia) **15** 806
    Brazil **4** 724
    Britain **9** 492
    Buddhism **29** 477
    Byzantine **9** 612, 664–5
    Canaanite **5** 556
    Central Asia, Western **6** 249, 253; **16** 485
    China **7** 45, 53, 115, 116, 123, 126; **30** 561
    Coptic **7** 826
    Early Christian (*c*. AD 250-843) **9** 612, 664–5
    Egypt **16** 431, 441
    Egypt, ancient **10** 74
    England **9** 493
    France **9** 493; **11** 649
    Germany **23** 786
    Gothic **13** 194
    Guatemala **13** 766
    Hausa **1** 251
    Inca **15** 163
    Indian subcontinent **9** 492; **30** 560
    Indonesia **15** 795
    Iran **16** 449
    Islamic **16** 353, 431, 438, 441, 449, 457, 468, 473, 485
    Japan **9** 492; **17** 219, 277, 308*, *309*, 313, 315, 316, 354, 355*; **30** 561
    Korea **18** 379–80
    Mesoamerica, Pre-Columbian **9** 492; **21** 249, 261
    Mexico **21** 394
    Native North Americans **22** 619–20, 648, 649, 661
    Nigeria **1** *250*
    Portugal **25** 315
    Rome, ancient **27** 112
    Scotland **28** 266
    Spain **5** 834; **19** 3
    Sri Lanka **29** 476
    Tibet **30** 845
    Vietnam **32** 489, 490
    Yemen **16** 438
  materials
    acacia **17** 354
    acorns **7** 45
    akane **9** 492
    alizarin **7** 45; **9** 493; **15** 667–8; **30** 558, 559, 560
    alum **30** 561
    aluminium **9** 490, 491
    aluminium salts **7** 45
    ammonia **9** 492
    bark **6** 253; **15** 163; **22** 648
    brazil-wood **9** 491; **25** 315
    camwood **9** 491
    chromium **9** 490, 493
    coal tar **7** 53
    cochineal **2** 438; **6** 253; **9** 491, 492, 665; **10** 872; **15** 163; **16** 449, 468
    copperas **25** 315
    fuchsine **9** 493

dyes
  materials—cont.
    fucus **9** 492, 665
    gall-nuts **9** 490, 491
    gallotannins **9** 490, 491
    gobaishi **17** 354
    gromwell **7** 45; **17** 308
    henna **1** 343
    indigo **3** 378; **9** 490, 491*, 492, 493; **10** 872; **30** 554, 556, 557, 558, 559, 560, 561
      Africa **1** 294
      Central Asia, Western **6** 253
      China **7** 45
      Early Christian and Byzantine **9** 665
      England **8** 36
      Inca **15** 163
      Indian subcontinent **15** 668, 672
      Islamic **16** 431, 438, 449
      Japan **17** 219, 308, *309*, 316, 354
      Portugal **25** 315
      Sri Lanka **29** 477
    indigot **7** 45; **9** 492
    iron **9** 490, 491
    iron salts **7** 45
    jasmine **7** 45
    kaolin **1** 343
    kermes **2** 83; **9** 492, 665; **16** 431; **19** 3; **25** 315
    lac **9** 492; **15** 667; **16** 431, 449; **18** 607, 655
    lacquer-tree **7** 45
    lake **9** 490
    lichens **9** 492*
    litmus **9** 492
    log-wood **9** 491; **25** 315
    madder **9** 491*, 492, 493; **10** 872; **30** 559, 561
      Anglo-Saxon **2** 83
      Central Asia, Western **6** 253
      Early Christian and Byzantine **9** 665
      Indian subcontinent **15** 667
      Islamic **16** 431, 438, 449, 473, 485
      Japan **17** 308
      Scotland **28** 266
    mauvine **9** 493
    mordants (iii) (dyeing) **15** 667, 672; **17** 308; **30** 559
    mud **1** 295
    natron **16** 431
    oak **7** 45, 115; **17** 354
    pagoda tree **7** 45
    picric acid **9** 493; **24** 789
    Polish cochineal **9** 492
    pomegranates **10** 872
    rice paste **17** 355
    safflower **7** 45; **9** 492; **16** 449; **17** 308
    saffron **9** 492
    sappan-wood **7** 45
    seaweeds **9** 492
    shellfish **9** 492
    soga **30** 558
    sumac **7** 45
    tannins **9** 490
    tin **9** 490
    turmeric **15** 668
    urine **9** 492
    vine leaves **6** 253
    wars **16** 438
    weld **9** 491
    whelks **9** 664
    woad **2** 83; **9** 491, 665; **25** 315
  types
    acid **30** 559
    anilines **4** 724; **9** 493; **22** 661; **23** 786; **30** 562; **32** 816
      Central Asia, Western **6** 254
      Islamic **16** 460, 477
      Japan **17** 277
      Native North Americans **22** 649
      Ottoman **16** 477
      Turkey **16** 477

dyes
  types—cont.
    azo-dyes **9** 493; **18** 656; **24** 789; **30** 558, 559
    cyanine **9** 493
    direct **7** 45; **9** 490, 492, 493; **30** 559
    insect **9** 491–2*
    mordant **7** 45; **9** 490, 491, 493
    natural **9** 490–92*, 493
    orchil **9** 492
    organic **24** 789
    reactive **9** 490, 492; **30** 558, 559
    synthetic **9** 492–3*; **10** 872; **15** 852; **24** 789
    vat **9** 490, 491, 493; **17** *309*
  uses
    carpets **5** 834
    codices **25** 742–3, *743*
    crayons **8** 128
    emulsions **24** 669
    inks **15** 850, 852
    leather **1** 299
    paper **7** 115, 116; **16** 353; **17** 219; **24** 56; **30** 845
    photography **9** 493; **24** 647, 648, 649, 650, 669
    printing **15** 852
    textiles **6** 249; **7** 826; **13** 194
      Islamic **16** 457
    wallpaper **32** 816
dye transfer *see under* PHOTOGRAPHY → processes
Dyffryn Ogwen (Caerns) **32** 787
Dying Gaul **2** 169; **16** 85; **23** 79, 291; **24** 414; **27** 30, 46; **29** 562
Dying Gladiator **23** 353
Dyk, Philip van *see* DIJK, PHILIP VAN
Dyke, Ernest Van *see* VAN DYKE, ERNEST
Dyke, J. C. Van *see* VAN DYKE, J. C.
Dykes Bower, S. E. **5** 287
Dymaean Wall **14** 339
Dymaxion **11** 834–5; **12** 311; **15** 824
  architecture **11** *835*
Dymchurch **21** 569
Dymenge de Legeris **1** 612
Dymond, George **11** 361
Dymshits-Tolstaya, Sof'ya (Isaakovna) **9** 494–5*
DYN **23** 697; **30** 22
Dynamic figurative style **1** 58; **31** 511, *511*
Dynna **26** 409; **32** 522
Dynter, Edmond de *see* EDMOND DE DYNTER
Dyonnet, Edmond **11** 322
Dyrham Park (Avon) **4** 131; **5** 907; **10** 275; **14** 739; **23** 789
Dyrrhachion *see under* DURRËS
Dysart (family) **7** 750
Dysart, Elizabeth Murray, Countess of *see* MURRAY, ELIZABETH, Countess of Dysart
Dysart, François *see* DIEUSSART, FRANÇOIS
Dysart, William Murray, 1st Earl of *see* MURRAY, WILLIAM, 1st Earl of Dysart
Dysart, William Murray, 6th Earl of *see* MURRAY, WILLIAM, 6th Earl of Dysart
Dysert O'Dea (Co. Clare) **16** 19; **26** 618
  church **26** 592
Dyson, James
  works **8** *804*
Dyson, Robert **33** 688
Dyson, Robert H., jr **14** 209
Dyson, Will(iam Henry) **2** 748; **9** 495–6*; **29** 633
Dyson Perrins, Charles William *see* PERRINS, CHARLES WILLIAM DYSON
Dyste, Sven Ingvar **23** 234
Dyste *Virgin* **26** 647
Dyubek, Lev **27** 381

Dyukker, Yevgeny (Eduardovich) *see* DÜKER, EUGEN
Dyukov, Andrey Vladimirovich **18** 569
Dyula **1** 249, 316; **8** 22
Dyushambe *see* DUSHANBE
Dzal-aryk **6** 267
Dzalpak Tepe
glass **6** 267, *267*
Džamonja, Dušan **8** 179; **9** 496*
works **4** 462
Dzantiyev, Aleksandr **27** 433
Dzantiyev, David **27** 433
Dzata **1** 414; **32** 154
Dzenis, Burkards
Dzhabguket **6** 379
Dzhambul *see* ZHAMBYL
Dzhanbas Kala **32** 320
Dzhaparidze, Ucha **31** 398
Dzharkutan **6** 196; **30** 440
Dzhelebova, Nikolina **5** 159
Dzheytun **6** *182*, 195, 275; **9** 496–7*; **31** *458*
Dzhidrov, Krasimir **5** 159
Dzhumadurdyev, Dzhuma **31** 459
Dzhyumabayev, Dzhambul **18** 568
Działdowo, Michał of *see* MICHAŁ OF DZIAŁDOWO
Działyńska, Gryzelda Celestyna, Countess **9** 497
Działyńska, Iza, Countess **9** 497; **25** 138, 139
Działyński, Adam Tytus, Count **9** 497*; **25** 136, 138, 139
Działyński, Jan Kanty, Count **9** 497*
Działyński Library *see under* KÓRNIK
Dzibilchaltún **9** 497–8*; **20** 882, *882*; **21** *372*
Structure 1-sub *see* Temple of the Seven Dolls
stucco **29** 829
talud-tablero **30** 280
Temple of the Seven Dolls **9** 165, 498; **21** 213
Dzibilnocac **21** 231
Dziedzinski & Hanusch **28** 188
Dzięedziora, Jan **2** 502
Dziekónski, Józef Pius **3** 527; **9** 498*; **25** 99, 142; **32** 872
groups and movements **28** 838
Dziko La Malawi *see* MALAWI
Dzików **25** 138
Dziomba, Elza **29** 111
Džmerković, B. **28** 451
Dzulkifli Buyung **20** 172
Dzumalak Tepe **6** 220
Dzveli Gavazi Church **12** 319
Dzveli Shuamta Church **12** 319

E

Eadfrith **19** 409
Eadmer **5** 643
Eads, James Buchanan **9** 499*; **16** 54; **27** 565
Eadui **2** 76; **5** 641; **9** 499*; **20** 330
Eadui Gospels *see under* GOSPEL BOOKS → individual manuscripts
Eadui Psalter *see under* PSALTERS→ individual manuscripts
Eadwine Psalter *see under* PSALTER → individuals manuscripts
Eagar, William **5** 564
Eagle Painter **13** 516
Eagle Pottery **28** 258
Eakins, Benjamin **9** 499
Eakins, Thomas (Cowperthwaite) **9** 499–502*; **24** 600, 671; **26** 108
assistants **2** 130
collaboration **21** 761
groups and movements **26** 57
methods **2** 107; **24** 667
paintings **13** 676
genre **9** *500*; **14** 785; **23** 296; **31** 603, *604*
portraits **11** 498
sporting scenes **9** *501*; **20** 426; **29** 426
patrons and collectors **14** 575; **33** 151
pupils **1** 579; **2** 130; **5** 422; **11** 804; **19** 801; **24** 322; **29** 643; **30** 297
teachers **4** 329
Ealdred, Archbishop **2** 73
Eales, Joseph Herbert **7** 530
Eales Hours *see under* BOOKS OF HOURS→ individual manuscripts
Ealhswith **33** 230
Ealing (Middx)
Gunnersbury House **8** 45; **32** 551, *552*
Pitshanger Manor **10** 234; **20** 485; **28** 906–7; **30** 503
Eames, Charles (Orman) **3** 858; **8** 802; **9** 502–4; **10** 150; **15** 825; **22** 876; **27** 474
collaboration **7** 259; **22** 728; **27** 475; **31** 633
works **6** 391; **15** *825*; **19** 6, 897; **20** 595; **29** 114; **31** *632*, 633; **33** 331
Eames, Ray **6** 391; **8** 802; **9** 502, 503–4; **15** 825; **20** 595; **22** 876; **31** 633
works **15** *825*
Eames chairs *see under* CHAIRS → types
Eames & Young **28** 327
Eanes, João **2** 871
Eannatum (*reg c.* 2470 BC) **29** 614
ear daggers *see under* DAGGERS→ types
Eardley, Joan (Kathleen Harding) **1** 30; **9** 504*; **28** 240
Earl, Augustus *see* EARLE, AUGUSTUS
Earl, Harley T. **15** 824; **20** 594
Earl, James **9** 504
Earl, Ralph **9** 504–5*
reproductive prints by others **9** 148
teachers **33** 92
Earl, Ralph E(leazer) W(hiteside) **9** 504, 505*
Earle, Augustus **2** 744; **9** 504, 505*; **23** 57
Earley, Thomas **9** 321
Earley & Powell **9** 321
Earlier Le **32** 486
Earlom, George **19** 157
Earlom, Richard **9** 505–6*; **21** 416; **29** 675
works **10** 677; **21** 417; **25** 619; **26** 231
Earls, Paul **5** 122; **18** 809; **24** 745; **28** 829
Earls Barton (Northants), All Saints **20** 572; **29** 775, 776
stripwork **29** *776*
Earlshall **9** 727; **28** 230
early Abbasid scripts *see under* SCRIPTS → types
Early Christian **9** 506–669*, *507*, *510*, *511*, *512*, *513*; **18** 823; **26** 140
aesthetics **9** 622
albs **9** 642
allegories **9** 519–20*
altars **1** 693–4*, *693*; **7** 278; **9** 656
alum **9** 665
ambos **7** 278; **9** 590
amices **9** 642
amphorae **9** 632
aprons **9** 643
aquamarines **9** *653*
aqueducts **9** 560
arcades **9** 524
arches **2** 292, 297
architecture **9** 523–8*, 529–32, 533–5, 538*, 542*, 553*, 556–8*, 560, 561*, 731–2; **25** 171
Algeria **30** 727
Armenia (Europe) **2** 428
brick **9** 524, 553, *554*
Cappadocia **5** 673*
Cyprus **8** 357–8*
Greece **9** 538*, 542*
Ireland **16** 6
Italy **16** 623–5*
Mesopotamia **9** 538–41*, 542–3*
military **9** 553–5*, *554*
North Africa **9** 535
Palestine **9** 538–41*, 542–3*
Rhodes (island) **26** 293*
stone **9** 538
Syria **9** 538–41*, 542–3*
Turkey **9** 536–7*, 542*
art legislation **9** 654
audience halls **9** 557
baptisteries **3** 189–91*; **7** 254, 255; **9** 524, 529, 533
Cyprus **3** *191*
Italy **3** *190*; **26** *822*
Mesopotamia **9** 541
North Africa **9** 535
Palestine **9** 541
Syria **9** 541
barbicans **9** 554
basalt **9** 538
baths **9** 553, 560
belts **9** 653
Bibles **4** 3–5*; **9** 602, 606–8*
birri **9** 640
book covers **9** 656
boxes **9** 648
bracae **9** 640
bracelets **9** 653
brick **9** 524
bridges **9** 560
busts **5** 299–300*; **9** 587
calendars **9** 603, 610, 616
campagi **9** 641, 642
camps (military) **9** 553
canon tables **9** 608
capitals **5** *670*; **9** 589
carpets **9** 666
caskets **5** 917, *917*
Early Christian—cont.
catacombs **6** *70*; **9** 562, 570; **26** 798–9; **28** 629
cathedrals **9** 529, *531*, 534, 539
ceilings **9** 654
cenotaphs **6** 170
censers **9** 632, 656
chalices **9** 656
chasubles **9** 642, 643
churches **7** 259–60*, *260*; **9** 522, 523–4, 528–35*, *529*, 536–7, 538*, 542*, 588
ambulatory basilicas **9** 530, *530*
Armenia (Europe) **9** *731*, *732*
basilicas **7** 252*, *252*, 325; **9** 525, 527, 528, 529–32*, *533*, 533–4*, 536–7, *537*, 538*, 542, *542*; **26** 569, 798
Bulgaria **5** *145*; **25** 559
Cappadocia **9** 536
centrally planned **7** 254–5*, *255*
compact-domed basilicas **9** 542
cross-domed **9** 542, *542*
decoration **7** 270–72*; **9** 518
domed basilicas **9** 537
Greece **9** 538*, *542*, 542*
Italy **9** 528–34*, *530*, *532*, *533*; **13** *266*; **16** *624*; **21** *537*; **26** *829*, *835*; **29** *421*
Mesopotamia **9** 538–41*, 542–3*; **31** *435*
Palestine **3** *881*; **9** 538–41*, *541*, 542–3*
rock **26** 483
Roman **26** 859
Syria **7** 259, 260; **9** 538–41*, *539*, *540*, 542–3*
tetraconch **7** 255
tituli **9** 529–30
transept basilicas **9** 538
triconch **7** 255
Turkey **9** *525*, 536; **31** *435*
ciboria (i) (vessels) **9** 656
ciboria (ii) (structure) **7** *278*, 301–2*, *302*; **28** 630
cingula **9** 642, 643
circuses **9** 556, 560
cisterns **9** 560
citadels **9** 554
cloaks **9** 639
coats **9** 643
cochineal **9** 665
coins **9** 635–7*, 638
colophons **9** 605
combs (liturgical) **9** 648
consular diptychs **9** 647, *648*, 648–9
copper **9** 652
cosmologies **9** 616
cotton **9** *640*, 664, *665*
craftsmen and artists **9** 509
crenellations **9** 553
crosses **8** 195, 202; **9** 656, *659*
crowns **9** 653
cups **9** 645
dalmatics **9** 640, 642
damask **9** 665
dictionaries **10** 212
dies (ii) (stamps) **9** 635
diplomatic gifts **9** 509
diptychs **5** 809; **9** 3
domes **9** 85, 525
doors **9** 151–2, 599–600
dosserets **2** 292
drawings **9** 615
dress **9** 251*, 639–44*, *644*
dyes **9** 612, 664–5
earrings **9** 653
embroidery **9** 668–9
enamel **9** 653, 659–63*, *659*
enceintes **9** 553–5, *554*
Early Christian—cont.
enchiria **9** 643
epigonatia **9** 643, *643*
epimanikia **9** 642, *643*
epitrachelia **9** 642, *643*
Evangeliaries **9** 608, 610–11
fans **9** 656; **10** 775
fibres **9** 664*
fibulae **9** 653
filigree **9** 652, 653
fonts (baptismal) **6** 31; **11** 250–51*, *251*
fora **9** 560
fortifications **9** 524, 553–5*, *554*
fortresses **9** 553, 554
forts **9** 554
friezes **29** *817*
frontispieces **9** 608, 610, 611, 613, 615, 616, 617
fucus **9** 665
gilding **9** 654
glass **9** 562, 644–6*
glasses **9** 645
gold **8** 360*; **9** 618, 652–3, *653*, 654*, *659*, 668
gold leaf **9** 617, 623, 645; **19** 356
Gospel books **9** 608–10
guidebooks **26** 799
hats **9** 644
headpieces (manuscripts) **9** 609, 610, 618
headscarves **9** 643
historiography **9** 527–8
hoods **9** 643, *644*
houses **9** 560
human figures **9** 622
iconoclasm **9** 514; **15** 80; **26** 854
iconography **7** 219*; **9** 516*, 517–18*, 519–21*, 562, 572, 573, 575, 595, 596, 609–10, 616, 617, 622, 623, 635; **12** 71–2; **18** 826; **22** 161; **26** 862; **33** 215
icons **9** 517, 518, 621–4*, *624*; **13** 131; **18** *825*; **26** 862; **30** V2
indigo **9** 665
initials (manuscript) **9** 609, 618; **15** 846
insignia **9** 603
interlace **15** 882
ivory **9** 3, *514*; **16** 686, *686*
ivory-carvings **9** *647*, 647–52*, *648*; **16** 798
jewellery **9** 652–4*
kaftans **9** *641*
kermes **9** 665
lamps **9** 656
Lectionaries **9** 611
limestone **9** 538, 590–91
linen **9** 664, 668; **30** 776
lintels **1** *523*
liturgical furnishings **7** 278*
liturgical objects **9** 656
machicolation **9** 554
madder **9** 665
maniples **9** 642
mantles **9** 639, 643
manuscript illumination **9** 602–3*, 604–18*, 619–21*, 622; **19** 356; **22** 519
Egypt **9** 619
England **9** *603*
Italy **16** 654
Lebanon **9** 619
Mesopotamia **9** 619
Syria **9** 619
manuscripts **9** 602–3*, 604–18*, 619–21*
mappae **9** 641, 642
marble **9** 587, 588; **27** 827, *828*
marks **9** 654
Early Christian—cont.
martyria **7** 254–5; **9** 528, 534, 535; **20** 518, *518*, *519*; **28** 629
masonry **9** 553
mausolea **7** 325; **9** 530, 556–7; **20** 865*
metal **9** 668
metalwork **9** 539, 654*
miniatures (manuscript illumination) **4** *4*
mitres **9** 643
monasteries **9** 522, 524, 561; **25** *771*
monuments **22** 43*
mosaics **7** 271, *271*, 272; **9** 561–4*, 568–9*, 570–75*, 645; **19** 356; **22** 161–2; **26** 782; **33** 215
Cyprus **8** 358–9*; **9** 566–7*
England **9** *568*
Greece **7** *278*; **9** 565–6*, *572*
Italy **2** *243*; **3** *190*; **7** *223*; **9** *573*; **16** 654, *761*; **21** *523*; **27** *68*, *782*, 782–3
North Africa **9** 569–70*
Palestine **9** 567–8*, *574*
Spain **6** 177
Syria **9** *567*, 567–8*
Tunisia **9** *569*
Turkey **2** *158*; **9** *564*, 564–5*
narratives **9** 609–10; **22** 519–20*
naturalism **9** 520–21*
necklaces **9** 653, *653*
New Testaments **9** 608–11*
niches **31** *434*
Old Testaments **9** 611–14*
omophoria **9** 642, 643, *643*
ornament **9** 618
painting **9** 561*, 621–4; **16** 653–4*; **19** 356
encaustic **9** 623
fresco **9** 562; **18** 417
Italy **6** 31, *32*
panel **19** 356
secco **9** 562
still-lifes **29** 665
wall **1** 707; **9** 561–3*, 570–75*; **26** *799*; **32** 804*
Cappadocia **5** 675–7*, *676*
Cyprus **8** 358–9*
Italy **6** *70*; **9** *563*; **26** *831*
Syria **9** 416
palaces **9** 524, 529, 553, 556–8*, *558*
pallia (ecclesiastical) **9** 641, 642
patens **9** 656
patronage **7** 217; **9** 519, 521–3*, 539, 623; **16** 761–2
pearls **9** 653, *653*, 668
pendants (jewellery) **9** 645, *659*
periods **8** 356–7*
peristyle courtyards **9** 557
personifications **9** 519–20*
phelonia **9** 643, *643*
phialai **7** 278
piers (ii) (masonry) **24** 750
pigments **9** 612, 623, 664–5
plaques **9** *514*, 590, 647; **16** 686, *686*
plaster **9** 562; **29** 816–17*, *817*
plates **9** 655, *655*
polychromy **25** 171
polykandela **9** 656, *656*
polystauria **9** 643
porphyry **27** 827
portraits **2** 836; **9** 587, 609, 611, 616, 617, 622
author portraits **9** 609, 610
pottery **9** 631–2*
Psalters **9** 604, 611, 613–14
Aristocratic Psalters **9** 613

Early Christian
- Psalters—cont.
  - Marginal Psalters **9** 613
- pyxides (boxes) **9** 648
- reliquaries **9** *647*, 659–60; **26** 143–4*; **28** 629
- representation **9** 622
- revetments **9** 656
- rhipidia **10** 775
- rings **9** 653
- roofs **9** 539
- rotundas **27** 235
- saints' lives **9** 616
- sakkoi **9** 643
- sanctuaries **27** 714
- sarcophagi **9** 594, 596–7; **16** 686; **27** 827*, *828*
- scapulars **9** 644, *644*
- scarves **9** 643
- screens (i) (architectural) **28** 291*
- scriptoria **9** 604
- scripts **9** 604, 606, 610, 612; **28** 305
- sculpture **9** 587–8*
  - architectural **9** 588, 589–92*, 599*
  - Italy **16** 686*
  - marble **9** 587
  - relief **9** 594–7*; **26** 135–6*
  - Spain **29** 287
  - stone **9** 589*, 594–7*
  - wood **9** 599–602*
- seals **9** 635–7*
- sewing **9** 640
- shrines (i) (cult) **9** 656; **28** 629–30*
- silk **9** *640*, *641*, 663–4, *664*, *665*, 665–9
- silver **5** *917*; **8** 360*; **9** 612, 652, 654–6*, *655*, *656*
- *skaramangia* **9** 641
- spolia **9** 531
- spoons **9** 654, 656
- stamps **9** 655
- sticharia **9** 642, *643*
- stoles (ecclesiastical) **9** 642–3
- stone **1** *693*, 693; **9** 538, 562, 589–92*, 594–7*; **27** 827; **30** 776
- stools **30** 776
- stucco **29** 816–17*, *817*
- symbolism (critical term) **9** 519–20*
- tapestries **9** 666
- textiles **9** 663–9*
- theatres **9** 553, 560
- threads **9** 668
- thrones **30** 776*
- tie-bars **9** 599
- togas **9** 639–40
- towers **9** 553, 554, 555
- transepts **9** 530
- treatises **9** 603
- tunics **9** 639, 640, *640*, 641, 643, *644*
- typological cycles **31** 498
- vaults (ceiling) **9** 524; **32** 86
- veils **9** 644
- vestments (ecclesiastical) **9** 641–3*, *643*
- villas **9** 553
- walls **9** 553–4, *554*, 557–8
- weaving **9** 665–6
- weights **9** 645
- woad **9** 665
- women **9** 515
- wood **1** 693; **9** 151–2, 539, 599–602*; **30** 776
- wool **9** 664
- *zonaria* **9** 643, *644*
- *see also* COPTIC; DARK AGE (ii)

Early Cycladic period *see under* CYCLADIC → periods
Early Cypriot period *see under* CYPRUS, ANCIENT → periods
Early Dynastic period *see under* EGYPT, ANCIENT; MESOPOTAMIA → periods
Early English style **13** 34; **26** 361
Early Gothic *see under* GOTHIC → styles
Early Helladic period *see under* HELLADIC → periods
Early Man Shelter **25** 822
Early Minoan period *see under* MINOAN → periods
Early Netherlandish style
- altarpieces **20** *667*, *668*
  - Belgium **3** *641*, *739*; **4** *591*; **8** *551*; **10** *704*; **17** *675*; **21** *101*, *103*, *104*; **30** *165*; **31** *343*, *344*; **33** *119*, *122*
  - Netherlands, the **4** *446*, *447*, *448*; **20** *636*, *656*
- borders (manuscript) **4** *396*
- dossals **3** *609*
- drawings **10** *711*
- embroidery **3** *609*; **10** II2
- justice scenes **4** *592*; **17** *700*
- manuscript illumination **5** *429*; **9** *271*; **12** *524*; **20** *682*, *725*; **31** *449*
- miniatures (manuscript illumination) **3** *727*
  - Belgium **4** *370*; **5** *211*; **13** *660*; **14** *389*; **19** *252*, *340*; **20** *659*, *682*, *687*, *700*, *725*
  - Netherlands, the **5** *443*; **20** *343*, *643*, *644*, *662*
- nude figures **12** *847*
- painting
  - allegorical **4** *450*, *451*
  - flower **29** *665*
  - genre **9** *272*; **31** *703*
  - grisaille **13** *675*
  - *pietàs* **21** *102*
  - religious **4** *594*
    - Belgium **3** *553*; **4** *593*, *595*; **8** *25*, *524*, *552*; **10** *706*, *709*, *710*; **11** *440*; **12** *848*, *849*; **15** *95*; **16** *70*; **20** *660*, *715*, *716*, *780*; **22** *863*; **25** *281*; **29** *692*; **33** *121*, *123*, *125*, *129*
    - Italy **17** *704*
    - Netherlands, the **4** *449*, *841*; **12** *231*, *232*; **20** *773*; **23** *672*; **28** *804*
  - still-lifes **29** *665*
- portraits
  - group **17** *704*
  - miniatures (manuscript illumination) **3** *726*; **20** *724*
  - painting **4** *593*; **20** *670*
    - Belgium **3** *576*; **4** *921*, *922*; **10** *707*, *708*; **20** *676*; **21** *104*; **33** *124*
    - Italy **17** *704*
    - Netherlands, the **7** *239*
  - self-portraits **3** *726*
- woodcuts **3** *556*
- *see also* GHENT-BRUGES SCHOOL; GOTHIC → styles → Late Gothic

Early Predynastic period *see under* EGYPT, ANCIENT → periods
Early Renaissance *see under* RENAISSANCE → styles
Earp, G. B. **2** 757
Earp, Thomas **10** 266; **29** 766; **30** 533; **31** 241
earpicks **7** 102
earplugs **1** 296, 351, 367; **5** 250
earrings **17** 519, 521, 524, 527, 529
- historical and regional traditions
  - Africa **1** 351
  - Ancient Near East **1** 874, 876
  - Bactria **9** *457*
  - Byzantine **9** 653
  - Central Asia, Eastern **6** 310, 312
  - Central Asia, Western **9** *457*
  - China **7** 111
  - Cyprus, ancient **8** 352
  - Early Christian (*c.* AD 250-843) **9** 653
  - Egypt, ancient **10** 31
  - Etruscan **10** *631*
  - Greece, ancient **13** 598, *598*, 599, 601
  - Huastec **14** 831
  - Indian subcontinent **15** *700*
  - Indonesia **15** 814–15
  - Italy **10** *631*; **17** *527*
  - Kenya **1** 351
  - Korea **18** 366, 367, *367*
  - Malaysia **20** 180
  - Mongolia **21** 877
  - Native North Americans **22** 614
  - Phoenician **24** 644
  - Portugal **25** *314*
  - Prehistoric **25** 545
  - Prehistoric art **25** 546
  - Punic **25** 734
  - Rhodes (island) **13** 598, *598*
  - Rome, ancient **27** 102
  - Sasanian **1** 876
  - Tanzania **1** 351
  - Troad **31** *376*
  - Troadic **31** 355
  - Turkey **31** *376*
- materials
  - amber **1** 761
  - cameos **17** *527*
  - electrum **13** *598*
  - gold **7** 111; **9** *457*; **10** *631*; **13** 598; **15** *700*; **17** *527*; **18** *367*; **31** *376*
  - pearls **7** 111; **17** 523–4
  - quartz **25** *314*
  - sapphires **17** *525*
  - shells **14** 831
  - silver **22** 614; **25** *314*
  - turquoise **7** 111
- types
  - girandole **17** 523, 524, *525*, 526

ear-spools **21** 260
earth
- historical and regional traditions
  - Africa **1** 284*; **9** 164
  - China **6** 643–4*
  - Hausa **9** 164
  - Korea **18** 264
  - Nigeria **9** 164
  - Prehistoric art **25** 506
  - Russia **19** 837
- uses
  - architecture **6** 643–4*; **18** 264
  - barrows **25** 506
  - doors **9** 164

earth, rammed *see* PISÉ DE TERRE
earthenwares **6** 325*, 329, 330
- historical and regional traditions
  - Algeria **16** 427
  - Ancient Near East **1** 877
  - Australia **2** 759, *761*
  - Buddhism **18** 337
  - Burma **5** 255
  - Cambodia **5** 506
  - Canada **5** 580–81, *581*
  - Catalonia **29** 328
  - Central Asia, Western **6** *257*, 258; **16** 413
  - China **6** 868, 869, 872, 874, 885; **7** 101
    - Han period (206 BC-AD 220) **6** *686*, 874, 882, *883*
    - Liao period (AD 907-1125) **6** *890*, *891*
    - Northern and Southern Dynasties (AD 310-589) **6** 886
    - Prehistoric **6** 868
    - Qing period (1644-1911) **7** 101, *101*
    - Qin period (221-206 BC) **6** 881–2
    - Shang period (*c.* 1600-*c.* 1050 BC) **6** 870, 875, 879, 880, *880*
    - Tang period (AD 618-907) **4** 172; **6** *887*, 888, *888*, *889*
  - Cuba (Caribbean) **8** 236
  - Czech Republic **8** 404–5
  - Denmark **8** 747
  - Egypt **16** 394, *403*, *405*
  - England **6** 325; **10** 301, *304*, *314*; **29** 495; **30** *877*
  - France **6** 558; **11** *603*
  - Germany **12** 430–33*, *431*, *432*
  - Guinea-Bissau **13** 835
  - Indian subcontinent **15** 685
  - Iran **16** *402*, 413, 425, *426*
  - Iran, ancient **4** 172
  - Iraq **16** *398*, 398, *399*
  - Ireland **16** 28
  - Islamic **16** 393, 394, 395
    - Algeria **16** 427
    - Central Asia, Western **16** 413
    - Egypt **16** 394, *403*, *405*
    - Iran **16** *402*, 413, 425, *426*
    - Iraq **16** *398*, 398, *399*
    - Morocco **16** 427
    - North Africa **16** 427
    - Spain **16** *411*, *419*
    - Syria **16** 406
    - Tunisia **16** 427
    - Turkey **16** 411, 414, 418
  - Italy **10** 527
  - Jamaica **16** 887, *887*
  - Japan **17** *104*, *105*, 244, *245*, 246, 258, 259*, 262*
  - Korea **18** 297, 298, 332–3, 335, 337, 378
    - Buddhism **18** 337
    - Prehistoric **18** *333*, *334*
    - 1st cent. AD **18** *334*
  - Mesoamerica, Pre-Columbian **21** 236
  - Mexico **21** *392*
  - Morocco **16** 427
  - Netherlands, the **22** 877–8, 882, 883
  - New Zealand **23** *69*
  - North Africa **16** 427
  - Prehistoric art **10** 527; **18** *333*, *334*; **29** *228*
  - Ryūkyū Islands **27** 470
  - Scotland **28** *257*
  - South-east Asia **29** *228*
  - Spain **16** *411*, *419*; **29** *324*, *325*, *326*, *327*, 327–8, *328*
  - Sweden **30** *98*
  - Syria **4** 172; **16** 406
  - Thailand **29** *228*
  - Togo **31** 73
  - Tunisia **16** 427
  - Turkey **16** 411, 414, 418
  - Ukraine **31** 563
  - United States of America **4** *482*; **31** 634–7, *636*, *638*
  - Vietnam **32** 484
- materials
  - clay **6** 325
  - enamel **6** 325; **12** *431*; **16** *426*
  - glazes **6** 325, 328, 872; **16** 395
  - slip **6** *257*, 874, 886; **16** 427
- techniques
  - enamel **10** 306; **31** *636*
  - gilding **6** 325
  - impressing **6** 888
  - incising **6** *890*
  - moulding **6** 888
  - overglaze decoration **6** 325, 334
  - painting **6** 874, 888
  - underglaze decoration **6** 325
- uses
  - architectural decorations **18** 337
  - bottles **4** *176*; **28** *257*
  - bowls **2** *761*; **6** *257*; **10** *314*; **16** *398*, *426*
  - busts **29** *328*
  - candlesticks **10** *304*
  - ceramics **2** *761*
  - chess sets **6** 558
  - coffee-services **12** *432*
  - cups **2** *761*
  - dolls **17** 262
  - ewers **6** *888*
  - figurines **6** *887*, 889, *889*; **17** *104*, 262; **18** 298
  - jars **6** *888*; **16** *887*; **18** *334*
  - jugs **10** *314*
  - mirrors **21** 714
  - models **6** *686*, 889
  - plates **16** *399*, *405*
  - pots **18** *333*
  - sculpture **6** *891*; **17** *105*
  - tankards **12** *431*
  - teapots **2** *761*; **7** 101, *101*; **10** *314*
  - tea-services **10** *314*
  - tiles **30** 874, *877*
  - vases **16** *419*; **30** *98*; **31** *638*
- *see also* FAIENCE (ii) (CERAMICS); POTTERY → wares → delftware; lustrewares; tin-glazed wares

Earth Group **9** 672*; **14** 298, 596; **17** 858; **22** 441
- members **8** 179; **15** 66; **25** 12

earth-lodges *see* LODGES
earthquake-proof construction *see* ARCHITECTURE → techniques → anti-seismic
earthworks **21** 562
- England **14** *544*
- Mesoamerica, Pre-Columbian **21** 204
- Native North Americans **21** 597; **22** 570–72, *571*
- Olmec **21** 209
- United States of America **22** 570–72, *571*; **28** 891
- *see also* LAND ART

Earthworks Poster Collective **2** 751
Earthworks Pottery **2** 152
Easby Abbey (N Yorks) **2** 70; **25** *10*
easel paintings *see under* PAINTING → forms
easels **9** 673–4*, 791
easing-chairs *see under* CHAIRS → types
East, Hubert Springford **26** 107
East, W. F. **32** 858
East, William **23** 686
East Africa, German *see* RWANDA
East-Asiatic Company **10** 111
East Boston Crockery Manufactory **4** 482
Eastbourne (E. Sussex) **21** 569
- Pier **24** 748

Eastbury Park (Dorset) **10** 232
East Dereham (Norfolk), St Nicholas **11** 253; **26** 613
East End Dwellings Co. **19** 574
Easter Island **6** 589; **9** 674–6*; **23** *711*
- architecture **23** 715
- barkcloth **23** 713
- body arts **9** 676
- body ornaments **23** 720
- erotic art **10** 487
- feathers **23** 720
- forgeries **23** 738
- headdresses **23** 720
- heritage **23** 737
- platforms **9** 674; **23** 715
- rock art **9** 675; **23** 729
- sculpture **9** 674–5, *675*; **23** 731
- staffs **9** 675
- stone **9** 674–5, *675*; **23** 715
- tourist art **9** 676
- wood-carvings **9** 675, *676*
- writing **9** 676

Eastern Art Club **30** 249
eastern beef-wood **29** 115
Eastern Central Asia *see* CENTRAL ASIA, EASTERN
Eastern Ganga *see*:
- ANANTAVARMAN CODAGANGA, Ruler
- NARASIMHA I, Ruler

eastern kufic script *see* SCRIPTS → types → New Abbasid style
Eastern Luba *see* LUBA (EASTERN)
Eastern Sea Stele *see* SAMCH'ŎK TONGHAE PI
Eastern Sigillata A pottery *see under* POTTERY → wares
Eastern Tombs *see under* ZUNHUA
Eastern Wei period *see under* CHINA → periods
Easter sepulchres **9** 680–81*
Easterwood, Henry **31** 660
East Grafton Church (Wilts) **23** 211
East Grinstead (E. Sussex), Hammerwood Lodge **13** 608; **30** 503
Easthampton (NY), Gates of the Grove synagogue **17** 549
East Harling (Norfolk), SS Peter and Paul **13** 184
East Horndon (Essex), Church of All Saints **4** 779
East India Companies *see* BRITISH; DANISH; DUTCH; FRENCH and SWEDISH EAST INDIA COMPANIES
East India House **19** 311
East Kilbride (Strathclyde) **31** 733
Eastlake, Lady **9** 682, 683*; **32** 748
Eastlake, Charles Lock (1793-1865) **2** 532; **6** 100; **9** 682–3*; **10** 252, 362; **16** 768; **19** 588; **22** 102, 296
  paintings **32** 338
  patrons and collectors
    Albert, Prince of Saxe-Coburg-Gotha (1819-61) **14** 148
    Cavendish, William Spencer, 6th Duke of Devonshire (1790-1858) **6** 117
    Morrison, James **22** 148
    Petty-Fitzmaurice, Henry, 3rd Marquess of Lansdowne **24** 571
    Russell, John, 6th Duke of Bedford **27** 358
    Soane, John **28** 908
  personal collection **21** 824, 825
  reproductive prints by others **10** 396
  writings **10** 191, 199, 281, 298
    on display of art **9** 19
Eastlake, Charles Locke (1836-1906) **7** 714; **9** 682, 684*; **32** 816
  groups and movements **9** 684; **13** 198, 205
  works **1** 171; **6** 391; **13** 209; **17** 469
Eastlake style **9** 684–5*; **31** 630
Eastland (MD), Third Haven Meeting-house **23** 193
Eastley, Max **29** 98
East Liverpool (OH) **31** 636, 637
East London (South Africa), Ann Bryant Art Gallery **29** 121
Eastman, George **3** 250; **8** 579; **9** 685*; **15** 822; **24** 656, 670; **33** 58
Eastman, Seth **7** 840; **9** 685*
Eastman Kodak **9** 493; **15** 822, 824, 825; **24** 650, 653
  see also CAMERAS → types → Kodak; KODAK
Eastman Photographic Materials Co. **8** 579; **15** 822
Eastnor Castle (Hereford & Worcs) **28** 874; **29** 58, 835
Easton, (John) Murray **9** 685–6*
Easton Neston (Northants) **2** 336; **8** 47; **10** 232, 275; **11** 427; **14** *253*, 253–4
Easton on the Hill (Northants) **29** 531
Easton & Robertson **9** 685–6*
East Riddleston Hall (W. Yorks) **28** 302
Eastry **5** 638
East Sutton (Kent), SS Peter and Paul **4** 693
Eastwick, Andrew M. **28** 843
Eastwood (Essex)
  All Saints **9** 155
  St Lawrence **9** 155
Eastwood, J. H. **8** 810
easy-chairs *see under* CHAIRS → types
Eaton, George **20** 3
Eaton, Herbert **29** 515
Eaton, Moses **29** 628
Eaton, Norman **9** 686*
  works **9** 427; **25** 566; **29** 106, *107*
Eaton, T., Company **5** 576, 776; **27** 173
Eaton, Theophilus **23** 25
Eaton Bishop (Hereford & Worcs), St Michael **13** 183
Eaton Hall (Ches) **10** 146; **12** 639; **19** 271; **20** 446; **29** 424, 799
eaves **32** 472
Ebassa, Jacob **28** 692
ebauches **9** 686*
Ebbelaar, Jan **22** 895
Ebbencrone **17** 855
Ebbesen, Torben **8** 742
Ebbo, Archbishop of Reims **9** 686*
  architecture **7** 265
  manuscripts **5** 800, 802; **11** 529; **13** 20; **20** 330; **26** 113
Ebbo Gospels *see under* GOSPEL BOOKS → individual manuscripts
Ebdon, Christopher **23** 782
Ebe, Gustav **9** 686–7*
Ebe & Benda **9** 686–7*
Ebel, Gottfried **15** 144
Ebeling, Ernst **14** 142
Ebelman, Jacques Joseph **6** 924
Ebelmann, Hans Jakob **9** 687*; **13** 776; **28** 138; **29** 747
Ebeltoft
  European Film College **11** 93
  Post House **29** 241
Ebenbach, Franz Georg **9** 687*
Ebendorf, Robert W. **31** 651
Eben Emael **21** 577
ébénistes **9** 687*; **26** 494
Eber, Elk **12** 396; **22** 711
Eberbach Abbey **9** 687–9*; **12** *361*
  dormitory **21** 843
  SS Mary and John the Baptist **9** 688, *688*
Eberdingen-Hochdorf **9** 689–90*; **12** *361*; **25** *470*, 538, 546
  bronze **25** 541
  daggers **25** 540
  drinking-horns **9** *690*
  gold **25** 542
  textiles **25** 546
Eberhard (*fl* 1230) **25** 424
Eberhard, Archbishop of Trier (*reg* 1047-66) **31** 326
Eberhard V, Duke of Wrttemberg (*reg* 1459 -95) **33** 429
Eberhard VIII, Duke of Württemberg (*reg* 1628-74) **14** 324; **24** 588; **33** 429
Eberhard, Franz **9** 690
Eberhard, Johann Richard **9** 690
Eberhard, Konrad **9** 690–91*; **12** 406; **22** 704; **28** 142; **33** 160
  works **9** *691*
Eberhard-Ludwig, Duke of Württemberg (*reg* 1677-1733) **12** 471; **33** 429*
  architecture **19** 779, 780
  collections **33** 429
  frescoes **5** 775
  paintings **11** 857; **14** 834
Eberhard of Brandis, Abbot of Reichenau **13** 169
Eberle, František Josef **8** 413
Eberlein, Gustav (Heinrich) **5** 57; **9** 691–2*; **12** 407
  sculpture **9** *692*
Eberlein, Johann Friedrich **9** 692–3*
  works **17** 769; **21** 64, *65*
Eberlein, Paul **11** 852
Eberler, Mathias **10** 751; **30** 149
Ebermayer **12** 452; **23** 313
Ebersbach, Hartwig **9** 693*
Ebersolt, J. **9** 527
Eberson, John **7** 327
Eberson, L. H. **7** 552
Eberstadt, Rudolf **21** 796
Eberstein, Baronesse von **19** 457
Ebihara, Kinosuke **17** 207
Ebisu kaki see under PUPPETS→ types
Ebla **1** 894; **9** 693–5*; **30** *180*, 184
  architecture **30** 191
  faience (i) (glass) **1** 878
  fortifications **21** 553
  glass **1** 865
  houses **30** 185
  inlays **9** 693
  ivory-carvings **1** 890
  Palace G **1** 862, 893; **9** 693; **23** 806; **30** 184
  ramparts **30** 185
  sculpture **9** 693, 694–5; **30** 186, 192–3
  seals **1** 862; **9** 694
  stele **29** 613
  temples **30** 188
    Temple B1 **30** 185
    Temple B2 **30** 185
    Temple D **30** 185
    Temple G **3**
      stelae **9** *694*
    Temple N **30** 185
  tombs **1** 874
  town walls **30** 190
  trade **30** 179
  writing-tablets **1** 854; **19** 311; **30** 188
Eblaite **1** 854
Eble, Theo **13** 726
Ebner, Jakub **8** 413
Ebner, Louis *see* DEÁK-ÉBNER, LAJOS
Ebo, Archbishop of Reims *see* EBBO, Archbishop of Reims
Eboli, Peter of *see* PETER OF EBOLI
Ebombo **29** 71
ebonite **17** 514; **33** 1
ebony **33** 325, 326
  historical and regional traditions
    Belgium **3** 582, 583, *583*, 585; **11** 445
    Britain **7** 445
    Egypt **16** 488
    Egypt, ancient **3** 482; **6** 559; **9** *828*; **10** 50, 52, 53, 54; **31** *265*
    England **6** 558
    France **9** 687; **11** 587, *587*, 589, *589*, 596; **26** *376*
    Germany **11** *456*; **12** *422*, 423
    Greece, ancient **13** 596
    Hungary **14** 907
    Indian subcontinent **6** 556; **15** 692, 720; **21** 717
    Indonesia **15** 813
    Islamic **16** 488
    Italy **14** *170*
    Japan **17** 399
    Netherlands, the **11** *443*, 444; **22** *872*, *891*, *892*
    Portugal **25** 305
    Scotland **28** 246
    South Africa **29** 114, 115
    Sri Lanka **29** 470
  uses
    beds **3** 482
    boxes **10** 53
    cabinets (ii) (furniture) **3** 582, 583; **5** 350; **9** 687; **11** 587, *587*, 589; **12** 421, *422*
    caskets **14** *170*
    chairs **10** 52
    chess sets **6** 556, 558
ebony
  uses—cont.
    chests **6** 559; **10** 54
    clocks **7** 445
    commodes **11** *589*
    cupboards **22** *872*
    frames **9** 17; **11** 374, *443*, 444, 445, *456*
    furniture **3** 585; **12** 423; **14** 907; **15** 692, 813; **25** 305; **29** 114, 115, 470
    game-boards **31** *265*
    game-pieces **31** 266
    gun stocks **2** 465
    inlays **28** 246
    marquetry **20** 466
    mirror frames **21** 717
    netsuke **17** 399
    palanquins **10** 50
    secretaires **26** *376*
    tablets **9** *828*
    teapots **22** *891*
    tea-services **22** *892*
    veneers **3** *583*; **9** 687; **11** 596
Eboracum *see under* YORK
Eboral, George **28** 878
Eboral, Thomas **28** 878
Ebrach Monastery **12** 365
  church **12** 364; **26** 656
Ebreuil, St Léger Abbey **9** 156; **11** 623
Ebrie **1** 392, 503
Ebstorf Abbey **13** 187
Ebstorf *mappa mundi* **20** 362
Eburnant **23** 652
ebusshi see JAPAN → painters
Ebutametta Hospital **1** 319
Eça de Queirós, José Maria de **25** 871
Ecatepec **21** 230
Ecbatana *see under* HAMADAN
Eccardt, John Giles
  works **32** *825*
eccentric weaving *see* WEAVING → types → curved weft
Ecclesiological Society **2** 320; **10** 237, 335; **13** 207; **28** 561
Ecclesiologist, The **13** 204, 207; **29** 506
Ecclesius, Bishop of Ravenna **26** 35
ECCO (European Confederation of Conservator-Restorers' Organizations) **7** 744
Eced, Vicente **29** 273, 309, 321
Echagüe, José Ortiz *see* ORTIZ ECHAGÜE, JOSÉ
Echagüe Vera, Ofelia **4** 141; **24** 98, 102
Echaurren, Francisco **31** 852
Echavarría, Domingo **9** 117
Echave Ibía, Baltasar de **9** 696*
Echave Ibía, Manuel de **9** 696
Echave Orio, Baltasar de **9** 695–6*; **21** 383
Echave Rioja, Baltasar de **9** 696*
Ech Cheliff **9** 569, 570
  el-Asnam Cathedral **8** 222; **9** 533; **18** 584
    tomb of Bishop Reparatus **7** 267
  Basilica **9** 529
Echeiano, Sanzio *see* TREVISANI, FRANCESCO
Echevarría, Atanasio **21** 384
Echevarria (y Zuricalday), Juan de **9** 696*
Echeverría, Enrique **9** 696*
Echeverría, Pedro Vallenila *see* VALLENILLA ECHEVERRÍA, PEDRO
Echigo **17** 316, 354
echini **9** 697*; **13** *378*, 392, 398; **23** 478, 480
Echizen **17** *11*, *241*
  pottery **9** 697*; **17** 255, 256, 260, 351
    see also under POTTERY → wares
Echochard **23** 799
echoppes **9** 697*; **25** 612
Echser, Heinrich **23** 204
Echter (von Mespelbrunn), Julius, Prince-Bishop of Würzburg and Duke of Franconia **9** 697–8*; **12** 368; **17** 684
  architecture **13** 210; **26** 470; **33** 430–31
  sculpture **23** 616
Echter, Michael **14** 768
Echternach **9** 698–9*; **12** *361*; **19** 826
  Abbey **7** 246; **12** 382; **19** 826
  Denzelt **19** 826
  ivory **23** 660
  manuscripts **5** 805, 806; **9** 698–9; **15** 875; **19** 827; **20** 330, V2; **23** 652, 655, *655*; **25** 743
  SS Peter and Paul **19** 826
  St Willibrordus **7** 264; **13** 18; **19** 826, 827; **23** 651
Echternach Book of Pericopes *see* PERICOPE BOOKS → individual manuscripts
Echternach Gospels *see under* GOSPEL BOOKS → individual mansucripts
Echter von Mespelbrunn (family) **30** 319
Ecija **9** 596, 699*; **29** *258*
  metalwork **29** 334
  Santa Cruz **9** 596
Eck (family) **8** 396
Eck, Adam (*d* 1664) **6** 526; **8** 396
Eck, Barthélemy de *see* EYCK, BARTHÉLEMY D'
Eck, Benedict **13** 275; **23** 708
Eck, Leonhardt von **21** 485
Eck, Veit **13** 776
Ecka, Zrenjanin Picture Gallery **28** 459
Eckartsau, Kinsky hunting lodge **13** 279
Eckbert, Bishop **31** 395
Eckbo, Garrett **1** 490; **7** 286; **12** 143
Eckel, Edmond Jacques **9** 699–700*
Eckel, Hilarius **14** 12
Eckell, Ana **2** 401; **9** 699*
Eckel & Mann **9** 699–700*; **10** 146
Eckerman, Oscar **32** 861
  works **32** *861*
Eckermann, Johann Pieter **22** 101
Eckernførde
  Goschhof **4** 925
  Nikolaikirche **13** 777
    sculpture **13** *777*
Eckernförde factory **8** 748
Eckersberg, C(hristoffer) W(ilhelm) **7** 805; **8** 734, 760; **9** 700–701*
  patrons and collectors **14** 572
  pupils
    Bendz, Wilhelm (Ferdinand) **3** 705
    Dreyer, Dankvart (Christian Magnus) **9** 297
    Frølich, Lorenz **11** 798
    Gurlitt, (Heinrich) Louis (Theodor) **13** 859
    Hansen, (Carl Christian) Constantin **14** 154
    Købke, Christen (Schjellerup) **18** 177, 178
    Larsen, (Carl Frederik) Emanuel **18** 798
    Marstrand, Wilhelm (Nicolai) **20** 480
    Melbye, (Daniel Herman) Anton **21** 76
    Roed, Jørgen **26** 524
    Rørbye, Martinus (Christian Wedelstoft) **27** 144
    Tidemand, Adolph **30** 852
    Vermehren, (Johan) Frederik (Nicolai) **32** 270
  works **8** 734; **9** *701*; **11** *472*
Eckersberg, Erling Carl Vilhelm **9** 701

Eckersberg, J(ohan) F(redrik) **9** 702*; **23** 244
pupils **18** 463; **22** 318; **24** 549; **28** 770, 825
Eckersley, Tom **7** 654; **25** 351, 353
Eckert, Fritz **12** 441
Eckert, Mariano **9** 117
Eckerts, Otto **8** 406
Eckhardt, Anette von **20** 380
Eckhardt, Edris **8** 82; **31** 639, 645
Eckhardt, Ezechiel **9** 702
Eckhardt, Francis **10** 278
Eckhardt, Frederick **10** 278
Eckhardt, Gabriel **9** 702
Eckhardt, Georg (1590-1637) **9** 702
Eckhardt, George (*fl* 1780s) **10** 278
Eckhardt, Hieronymous, the elder (*d* 1572) **9** 702*
Eckhardt, Hieronymous, the younger (*d* 1624) **9** 702
Eckhardt, Rob **22** 869, 877; **31** 576
Eckhardt, Uriel **9** 702
Eckhart, Meister **19** 356
Eckholm, Gordon **7** 645
Eckhout, Albert **4** 715; **9** 702–3*; **25** 325
patrons and collectors **22** 536
works **2** 105; **4** 706, 724; **22** 536; **26** 65
Eckl, Wilhelm *see* EGCKL, WILHELM
Eckman, Carl **4** 712; **27** 808
Eckmann, Otto **9** 703*
groups and movements **2** 565; **3** 511; **10** 215; **12** 416; **17** 441; **28** 341
works **12** 468; **30** 326, *327*
Eckmann type *see under* TYPE-FACES
Eckmuth, Prince d' **14** 482
Eckstein, Franz Gregor Ignaz **8** 391; **13** 258
Eckstein, Frederick **25** 400
Eckstein, Johan Conrad (1722-85) **14** 230
Eckstein, John (*fl* 1792) **4** 86
Eclarté **2** 756, 767
eclecticism **9** 703–5*; **14** 580–81
Bolivia **5** 551
England **9** *704*; **10** 237
France **11** 522–3
Ukraine **23** *354*
Eclipse, L' **5** 758
Ecluse, Charles de L' *see* L'ECLUSE, CHARLES DE
Eco, Umberto **2** 528
Ecochard, Michel **2** 660; **17** 806; **18** 541; **22** 366; **26** 266
Ecole Anglo-Venetienne **4** 321
Ecole d'Alger **1** 634
Ecole d'Art Décoratif Martine **2** 520
Ecole d'Art Public, Paris *see* INSTITUT DES HAUTES ETUDES URBAINES
Ecole d'Aubusson **13** 681
Ecole de Nancy **2** 13, 564; **8** 544; **12** 18; **20** 145; **22** 456; **31** 829
Ecole de Nice **11** 570
Ecole de Paris **4** 718; **6** 383; **9** 705–6*; **12** 892; **24** 800; **32** 136
collections
Dutilleul, Roger **9** 465
Guillaume, Paul **13** 826
Janis, Sidney **16** 906
Loeb, Pierre **19** 537
Marx, Sam and Florene **20** 524
Menil, John and Dominique de **21** 135
MOMA (Museum of Modern Art, New York) **31** 667
René, Denise **26** 193
Sternberg, Josef von **29** 642
Tzanck, Daniel **31** 503
Zborowski, Léopold **33** 627
Ecole de Paris—cont.
members **11** 550; **27** 307
Atlan, Jean-Michel **2** 693
Goncharova, Natal'ya (Sergeyevna) **12** 894
Jilani, Abdulwahab **31** 425
Larionov, Mikhail (Fyodorovich) **18** 791, 793
Lobo, Baltasar **19** 523
Orloff, Chana **23** 529
Richier, Germaine **26** 352
Riopelle, Jean-Paul **26** 414
Tsingos, Thanos **31** 398
Ecole Française d'Extrême-Orient **32** 473
Ecole Nationale de la Mosaïque, Paris **22** 163
Economou, J. **24** 20
écorchés **1** 840; **9** 706*
see also MODELS → types → anatomical; artists'
Ecouen
Château **5** 166; **6** 506; **9** 706–7*, *707*; **11** 514, 656; **13** 226; **23** 492
collections **22** 31
doors **9** 158
grotto **11** 604; **14** 855; **23** 850
leather **19** 5
Musée National de la Renaissance **9** 158, 707
stained glass **29** 512
tiles **11** 604; **30** 885
stained glass **29** 504
Ecouis, Notre Dame **9** 707–8*; **11** *504*; **13** 76
Ecritoire à Globes **9** 398
Ectadja *see* ECIJA
Ecuador **9** 708–15*, *709*; **15** *161*; **29** 125
architecture **9** 710–12*
beads **29** 155
body ornaments **29** 155
cathedrals **9** *711*
ceramics **9** 709
chairs **20** *317*
collages **9** 712
collections **9** 714
education (art) **9** 715*
exhibitions **13** 796
figurines **29** 133
gold **9** 714
guilds **9** 712, 714
hardstones **29** 155
houses **29** *139*
iconography **29** 134
libraries **9** 714*
lithography **9** 714
metalwork **9** 710
monuments **9** *711*
mortars (vessels) **29** 133
museums **9** 714*
painting **9** 712–14*, *713*
paintings **9** 713
patronage **9** 714*
pediments **9** 710
periodicals **9** 749
portraits **9** 713
pottery **29** 150–51
pyramids **25** *689*
retables **26** 252, *252*
rock crystal **29** 155
sculpture **9** 712*, 713*, 714*; **29** 145
shells **29** 217
shrines (i) (cult) **28** 632
silver **9** 714
stone **20** *317*; **29** 145
stone-carvings **29** 155
textiles **9** 709–10
thrones **30** 786
towers **9** *711*
town halls **25** *828*
wood **9** 710
wood-carvers **9** 712
Ecublens **23** 537
ecuelles **9** 715*; **10** 330; **11** *621*; **20** 217
Eczacibasi Ceramic Factory **31** 455
Edades, Victorio **20** 274; **24** 622, 632
Edam
church **22** 821
Nieuwenkamp Museum **23** 125
Edbrooke, Frank E. **9** 715*; **14** 787; **15** 408
Edbrooke, W(illoughby) J. **2** 693; **9** 715*
Edderton Church (Highlands) **28** 227
Eddy, Arthur Jerome **9** 715–16*; **22** 380; **31** 663
Eddy, Don **9** 716*; **24** 686
Eddystone Rock Lighthouse **7** 693; **19** 360, 361
Ede, Charles **4** 366
Ede, Jim (Howard Stanley) **9** 716*; **32** 800
Edelberg, Rudolf Eitelberger von *see* EITELBERGER VON EDELBERG, RUDOLF
Edelfelt, Albert (Gustaf Aristides) **3** 86; **9** 716–18*
works **9** *717*; **11** 95
Edelglas- Mosaik- und Emailwerkstätte **11** 320
Edelglaswerke AG **11** 320
Edelheer Triptych **33** 118
Edelinck, Gaspard-François **9** 718
Edelinck, Gérard **9** 718*; **10** 393; **24** 890; **25** 77
works **14** 83, 84; **19** 65; **22** 684; **24** 805, 890; **26** 388; **28** 506
Edelinck, Jean **8** 525; **9** 718
Edelinck, Nicolas-Etienne **9** 718
Edelkeit, Martha **10** 484
Edelman Goody, Joan *see* GOODY, JOAN EDELMAN
Edelmann, John **29** 913
Edelson, Mary Beth **10** 879
Edelsvärd, Adolf Wilhelm **13** 30; **30** 73, 110
Edelzinn **24** 578, *579*
Edema, Gerard van **9** 718–19*
Eden, F. C. **21** 2
Eden, Garden of *see* GARDEN OF EDEN
Edenshaw, Charles **8** 568; **9** 719*; **26** 107
Edenshaw, Isabella **9** 719
Eder **2** 711
Eder, Lorenz **29** 332
Eder, Otto **2** 804
Eder, Paulus **23** 313
Edessa *see* URFA
Edessa, County of **17** 499–500
Edessa, Mandylion of *see* MANDYLION OF EDESSA
Edfu **9** 719–21*, *774*; **26** *921*
inscriptions **10** 82
mammisi **9** 807; **20** 231, 232
reliefs **9** 891
sacred lake **27** 496
sphinxes **9** 879
stele of Hornakht **9** 879
Temple of Horus **9** 719*, *720*, 832, 834, *834*; **10** 81; **15** 146; **30** 433
chapel **9** 835
inscriptions **9** 827; **10** 62, 68
kiosk **18** 70
sculpture **10** 742; **20** 572
staircases **29** 520
wall paintings **9** 805
Edgar (family) **4** 824
Edgar, King of England (*reg* 959-75) **10** 165
Edgar, Robert **11** 908
Edgar, William **20** 16
Edgar and Nichols **30** 503
Edge, Charles **4** 85
Edge, J. W. **11** 60
edge roll mouldings *see under* MOULDINGS → types
Edgerton, Harold E(ugene) **9** 721*; **24** 653, 669
Edgeware Ceramics **29** 117
Edgewater Tapestry Looms **30** 327, 328; **31** 659
Edgeworth, Maria **16** 27
Edgmore Bridge Company **31** 464
edible gardens *see under* GARDEN → types
Ediciones Estridentistas **10** 543
Edinburgh **9** *722*, 722–9*, *723*, *726*; **24** *657*; **28** *222*
academies and art schools
Academy of St Luke **28** 235, 269, 274
College of Art **9** 725; **28** 275
Drawing School *see* Trustees' Academy of Design
Edinburgh Academy *see under* schools
Institution for the Encouragement of the Fine Arts *see* Royal Institution
Royal Institution **28** 271, 272; **33** 216
see also Royal Scottish Academy
Royal Scottish Academy **1** 106, 108; **9** 725; **13** 610; **25** *36*; **28** 228, 238, 269, 274
see also Royal Institution
School of Applied Art **2** 5; **28** 249, 275
Trustees' Academy of Design **1** 107; **9** 724; **28** 252, 269, 274–5
Winter Academy **28** 274
art forms and materials
architecture **2** 324; **23** 860; **28** 288
cabinetmaking **28** 253
ceramics **28** 257
chairs **28** *253*
dioramas **8** 911
furniture **9** 727*; **28** 256
glass **9** 726*; **28** 259
interior decoration **28** 249
marks **9** 726; **20** 444
metalwork **9** 726*
painting **28** 240
panoramas **24** 17, 18
pewter **28** 262
prints **28** 239
sculpture **28** 242
silverplate **28** 577
textiles **28** 564
Assembly Rooms **2** 617
banks
British Linen Company Bank **3** 175
Commercial Bank *see* Royal Bank of Scotland
Royal Bank of Scotland **26** 288; **28** 228
Bridewell Prison **25** 636
Castle **14** 452; **21** 549, *550*
King's Lodgings **28** 225
St Margaret's Chapel **26** 617
Scottish National War Memorial **28** 250
cemeteries **31** 130
Greyfriars Churchyard **6** 165; **20** 866
Old Calton Burying Ground **6** 165
Charlotte Square **28** 227
City Observatory **23** 340
ecclesiastical buildings
Barclay-Bruntisfield Church **28** 230
Canongate Kirk **28** 227
Greyfriars *see* cemeteries → Greyfriars Churchyard
Holyrood Abbey **26** 617
Nicholson Square Church **21** 347
Reid Memorial Church **28** 231
St Giles Cathedral **28** 224, 243; **29** 414
St John's Episcopal Church **28** 230
Edinburgh
ecclesiastical buildings—cont.
St Mary's Episcopal Cathedral **28** 238, 243
St Stephen's Church, St Vincent St. **28** 230
Tolbooth Church **12** 635–6; **28** 230
education (art) **28** 274
Empire Palace of Varieties **15** 408; **22** 60; **30** 679
foundries **28** 242
Free Church College **25** *36*
guilds **9** 726, 727; **24** 579
Heriot Row **28** 229
Heriot's Hospital *see* schools → George Heriot's School
Heriot-Watt University **28** 275
Holyrood House **4** 889; **9** *725*, *728*, 728–9*; **28** 226, 246; **29** 835
furniture **9** 727
paintings **12** 913; **14** 146; **28** 234; **33** 189
houses and mansions
5 Charlotte Square **28** 252
Drylaw House **28** 242
Duddingston House **6** 412; **23** 860; **25** 266; **28** 227, 247; **32** 553
Gladstone Monument **28** 243
Inverleith House **28** 273
Lauriston Castle **2** 453; **9** 727
Moubray House **28** 245
Prestonfield House **19** 5
8 Queen Street **28** 247
John Watson's Hospital *see* museums → National Gallery of Modern Art
libraries **28** 275
Advocates' Library **28** 254
central library **28** 275
Masonic Temple **10** 97
Moncrieff Terrace **28** 231
monuments and memorials
Albert Memorial **28** 242
Burns Monument **13** 610
National Monument **13** 201, 610
Sir Walter Scott Memorial **6** 171; **28** 242
Wellington Monument **28** 242
museums **28** 272–3
Museum of Antiquities **2** 5
Museum of Science and Art *see* Royal Museum of Scotland
National Gallery of Modern Art **5** 263; **9** 725; **28** 273
National Gallery of Scotland **9** 19, 724, 725; **25** *36*, 267; **28** 228
collections **9** 755; **28** 271, 272
Lothian Bequest **28** 270
Vaughan Bequest **28** 272
National Museum of Antiquities *see* Royal Museum of Scotland
National Portrait Gallery **2** 5; **9** 725; **28** 272
Scottish Photography Archive **28** 272
Outlook Tower **12** 228
Royal Museum of Scotland **9** 724; **11** 360; **28** 273, 274
collections **6** 925; **7** 155; **10** 92; **15** 744; **24** 738; **27** 569
Royal Scottish Museum *see* Royal Museum of Scotland
New Town **12** 635; **28** 227, 269
Orphan Hospital **28** 252
Parliament House **28** 245
Portobello Bathing Pool **19** 332
Ramsay Garden **22** 331
Register House **28** 227
Royal Incorporation of Architects in Scotland **2** 5
Royal Infirmary **14** 782; **28** 227, 228
Royal Observatory **23** 340

Edinburgh—cont.
St Andrew's House **28** 231, 250
St Cecilia's Hall **1** 125; **7** 687
schools
Daniel Stewart's School **28** 156
Donaldson's School **28** 156
Edinburgh Academy **28** 156
Fettes College **9** 724; **28** 288
George Heriot's School **13** 210; **28** 225, 268
Council Chamber **28** 246
John Watson's School **28** 156, 273
Royal High School **9** 723; **13** 610; **25** 268; **28** 156
Scottish National War Memorial *see under* Castle
Scottish Widows Fund Offices **28** 232
shops **28** 227
Trinity College **28** 233
University **9** 723, 725, 727; **28** 271, 273, 275; **31** 674
urban planning **31** 709, 716
Usher Hall **7** 687
Edinburgh Crystal Glass Co. **9** 726; **28** 260
Edinburgh Group **28** 239
Edinburgh & Leith Flint Glass Co. (*fl* 1865-1955) **28** 260; **31** 465
Edinburgh & Leith Glass Co. (*fl* 18th cent) **28** 259
Edinburgh Painter **13** 511
Edinburgh Tapestry Company **7** 573; **28** 250, 266–7; **30** 327, 329
works **28** *267*
Edinburgh Weavers **5** 841; **7** 573; **19** 18
Edingen Aelst, Pieter van **1** 165; **26** 816
Edington, Bishop **33** 238
Edington Priory (Wilts) **13** 183
Edirne **9** 729–30*; **16** *104*
aqueducts **16** 225
baths **16** 224
bazaar **16** 206
Ekmekçioğlu Ahmed Pasha Caravanserai **16** 224
gardens **12** 84
külliye **18** 509
lacquer **16** 535
manuscripts **16** 350
mosques
congregational mosque **16** 222
Eski Cami **16** 205
Lari Çelebi Mosque **16** 222
mosque of Beyazid II **16** 378; **20** 369
mosque of Murad I **4** 172
mosque of Murad II **16** 249, 417; **23** 557
Selimiye Mosque **9** 86, 730, *730*; **16** 223, *224*, 257; **20** 570; **21** 628; **28** 768
Üç Şerefeli Mosque **9** 729; **16** 205, 222, 260; **21** 628; **22** 195, *195*
palaces **23** 816
Rüstem Pasha Han **5** 723, *723*; **16** 224
silk **16** 445
tiles **16** 413
urban planning **16** 266
Edis **8** 403
Edis, R(obert) W(illiam) **3** 501; **4** 37; **7** 470; **9** 730–31*; **31** 763
Edison, Thomas **7** 327, 375, 875; **19** 366; **26** 18; **28** 831
Edith **2** 73
Edition Alecto Limited **20** 607
Editions de la Galerie Simon **13** 671
editions de luxe *see* BOOKS → forms → de luxe
Editions Domberger **20** 607
Edition Staeck **29** 492
Editions Verve **30** 488
Edition Tangente **29** 492
Ēdjmiadzin **2** *423*; **9** *512*, 731–2*; **16** *105*
Alex and Marie Manoogian Treasury Museum **2** 444; **9** 732
Cathedral **2** 425, 428, *435*, 444; **9** *731*, 731–2
Holy Cross of Khotakerats' **2** 442
metalwork **2** 442
sacristy **2** 442, 443
embroidery **2** *443*
khatchk'ars **2** 436; **8** 199; **9** 732
manuscripts **2** 445
Monastery **2** 443; **9** 732
Museum (1872) **2** 444
St Gayane **2** 425; **7** 256
St Hrip'sime **7** 256; **9** 732, *732*
Shoghakat'(Byzantine) *see* Cathedral
Shoghakat' Church (after 1694) **9** 732
Treasury **2** 444
urban planning **2** 428
Ēdjmiadzin Gospels *see under* GOSPEL BOOKS → individual manuscripts
Edkins, Michael **4** 824; **10** 318
Edla, Elizabeth Hensler, Countess d' **4** 385
Edlinger (*fl* 1757) **13** 802
Edlinger, Josef Georg von (1741-1819) **22** 303
works **11** *460*
Edlmannsperger, Johann Jakob **2** 825
Edmerton and Gabriel **14** 251
Edmeston, James **28** 277
Edmond, Maggie **7** 895
Edmond & Corrigan **7** 895
Edmond de Dynter **17** 819
Edmonds, Francis W(illiam) **9** 733*
Edmonton **5** *559*, 561
Art Gallery **5** 591
Citadel Theatre **5** 563
Legislative Building **3** 269
Provincial Museum of Alberta **5** 591
University of Alberta **5** 572
Edmund, King of England (*reg* 939-46) **9** 665
Edmund, Saint, Bishop of Salisbury **27** 624
Edmund Rich, Saint **13** 129
Edney, William **28** 295
Ednie, John **28** 256
Edo (Africa) **3** 718; **9** 733–7*; **23** 131
aesthetics **1** 239
bronze **9** 736
headdresses **9** 734, *734*
masks **1** 290, *335*, 337; **9** 734–5, 736
metalwork **23** 131–2
portraits **1** 268
sculpture **1** 280; **9** 736, *736*
shrines (i) (cult) **9** *736*, 736–7
staffs **9** 735
terracotta **9** 736
textiles **9** 736
tourist art **1** 239
wood-carvings **9** 734, *734*, *735*, *736*
see also BENIN, KINGDOM OF; NIGERIA
Edo (Japan) *see under* TOKYO
Edokoro *see* KYOTO → academies and art schools → Imperial Painting Bureau
Ēdole Church **18** 848
Edom **1** *849*, 857; **9** 737*; **30** 179, 189
Edo period *see under* JAPAN → periods
Edorh, Sokey **31** 73
Edouard **30** 290
Edouard-Joseph, René **10** 212
Edouart, Augustin **28** 714
Edridge, Henry **9** 738*; **14** 597
Edsall, Thomas **4** 478
Edsin Gol **6** 767
Edson, Allan **22** 38
Eduardo 'o Português **25** 295
education (art) **1** 101, 102, 105; **2** 523–4*; **7** 830–31; **13** 823; **26** 236; **33** *311*
historical and regional traditions
Africa **1** 431–4
Albania **1** 546–7*
Algeria **1** 635
Antilles, Lesser **2** 154*
Argentina **2** 405–6*; **7** 848
Australia **2** 769, 771–2*; **9** 464
Austria **2** 831–2*
Bahamas, the **3** 61, 64–5*
Bangladesh **3** 169*
Barbados **2** 154
Belarus' **3** 528, 529; **32** 412
Belgium **3** 617–18*
Bolivia **4** 269–70*
Brazil **4** 725, 727–8*
Britain **2** 475
Buddhism **17** 419; **32** 492
Bulgaria **5** 163–4*
Burma **5** 262–3*
Canada **5** 591–2*; **31** 177
Chile **6** 601–2*
China **6** 775, 811; **7** 147–50*; **28** 553
Christianity **17** 419
Colombia **7** 612*
Costa Rica **8** 18*
Côte d'Ivoire **8** 23
Croatia **8** 181
Cuba (Caribbean) **8** 238*
Czech Republic **8** 425–6*
Denmark **8** 760–61*
Dominican Republic **9** 119*
Ecuador **9** 715*
Egypt **9** 767–8
Egypt, ancient **9** 790
England **2** 524; **10** 252, 371–5*; **19** 165, 621
Ethiopia **1** 433; **10** 578
France **2** 523–4; **11** 668–73*; **21** 412; **24** 138
17th cent. **19** 22; **24** 167–8
18th cent. **1** *105*; **19** 161
19th cent. **19** 38, 39
Gabon **11** 880*
Germany **3** 399, *400*, 400–401, 798; **12** 478–80*
Ghana **12** 510*
Greece **13** 360–61*
Guatemala **13** 770*
Guyana **13** 878
Haiti **14** 59–60*
Hong Kong **7** 150
Hungary **15** 17–18*
India, Republic of **15** 173, 179–80*
Indian subcontinent **15** 208
Indonesia **15** 818–19*
Ireland **16** 37*
Islamic **16** 241, 536
Israel **16** 571–2*
Italy **1** *103*; **16** 777–80*; **23** 294
Jamaica **2** 154; **16** 890*
Japan **17** 27–8, 418–21*; **21** 59
Java **15** 818
Jesuit Order **17** 419
Jordan **17** 654
Kenya **17** 908*
Korea **18** 258, 380–81*
Laos **18** 777*
Lesotho **19** 242
Malaysia **20** 184*
Maori **23** 75
Mexico **21** 397–8*, 404
Native North Americans **22** 594
Neo-Confucianism **17** 419
Netherlands, the **19** 116; **22** 907–8*
New Zealand **23** 75*
Nicaragua **23** 85–6*
Nigeria **1** 432; **23** 138–9*
Northern Ireland **16** 42*
Norway **23** 244*
education (art)
historical and regional traditions—cont.
Ottoman **16** 536
Pacific Islands **23** 736
Pakistan **23** 803–4*
Panama **23** 904, 906
Papua New Guinea **23** 736
Paraguay **24** 102*
Peru **24** 517*
Philippines **24** 632*
Poland **18** 428; **25** 140–42*
Portugal **25** 319*
Puerto Rico **25** 704
Romania **5** 73; **26** 725–6*
Russia **24** 464; **26** 730–31; **27** 441–3*
Saudi Arabia **27** 876
Scotland **28** 271, 274–5*
Senegal **28** 406*
Serbia **28** 451
Sierra Leone **28** 693
Slovenia **28** 863
South Africa **1** 433; **29** 122–3*
Spain **29** 356–7*
Sudan **1** 433
Surinam **30** 16–17
Switzerland **30** 155–6*
Taiwan **7** 150
Tanzania **30** 302*
Thailand **30** 640*
Tibet **30** 812–13*
Trinidad and Tobago **31** 340*
Turkey **31** 455–6
Uganda **31** 528
United States of America **3** 271; **18** 831; **22** 678; **31** 638, 669–70*
Uruguay **31** 758*
Venezuela **32** 172, 180*
Vietnam **32** 492*
Wales **32** 792*
Zaïre **33** 597–8*
Zambia **33** 603*
Zimbabwe **33** 680
types
applied art
Germany **12** 478–80*
Hungary **15** 5
Scotland **28** 274, 275
South Africa **29** 123
Switzerland **30** 155, 156
archaeology **7** 160; **18** 381–2
architecture **1** 105, 106, 108; **20** 561; **28** 498
Argentina **2** 405
Armenia (Europe) **2** 428
Australia **2** 741, 772
Bolivia **32** 568
Brazil **4** 705
England **10** 372, 374; **19** 532; **23** 782
France **9** 420; **11** 670*; **13** 732–3; **24** 170
Germany **3** 399; **9** 421; **19** 532; **26** 102
Greece, ancient **13** 408
Guatemala **13** 770
Hungary **15** 17*
India, Republic of **15** 180
Italy **16** 777–80*
Japan **7** 701; **17** 86
Jesuit Order **25** 142
Korea **18** 261
New Zealand **23** 75
Norway **23** 222, 244*
Pakistan **23** 798
Poland **25** 140, 142
Portugal **25** 319
Romania **26** 725, 726
Rome, ancient **26** 864, 884–5*
Russia **27** 441–3*; **31** 543
South Africa **29** 123; **30** 728
Spain **31** 93
United States of America **31** 669
Uruguay **31** 758
archives **2** 368*
calligraphy **6** 745
education (art)
types—cont.
ceramics **23** 121
conservation **7** 740–43*
crafts **3** 399; **27** 442, 443
Switzerland **30** 155
design **3** 401; **15** 823
Britain **9** 475; **15** 821
Germany **12** 480; **15** 826
Hungary **14** 910
Poland **25** 140
South Africa **29** 123
United States of America **31** 670
drawing **2** 831–2; **15** 17*
embroidery **10** 354
glass **12** 805
industrial drawing **31** 669
photography **3** 403; **24** 678
printmaking **23** 227
scribal **10** 5–6*
sculpture **1** 105; **2** 772
urban planning **3** 410
Educational Alliance **17** 578
Edward, King of Portugal (*reg* 1433-38) **2** 869, 870–71*; **13** 71; **20** 682
architecture **3** *362*, 363
Edward I, King of England (*reg* 1272-1307) **25** 14*
architecture **33** 201
castles **5** 374; **6** 50; **12** 174; **16** 894; **21** 564; **22** 211
chapels **13** 46, 53
churches **32** 828
military **6** 51; **10** 227; **19** 895; **21** 549; **32** 781
palaces **19** 610
towns **6** 560; **31** 711
banners **11** 148
coins **7** 535
furniture **30** 779, *780*
manuscripts **10** 245; **13** 141, *141*; **20** 332
sculpture **8** 197; **22** 44
Edward II, King of England (*reg* 1307-27) **5** 511; **10** 163; **13** 128, 170; **14** 418
Edward III, King of England (*reg* 1327-77) **25** 15*; **33** 202
architecture **6** 51, 57; **7** 420; **10** 163; **14** 75, 454; **19** 566; **25** 885; **33** 523
coats of arms **14** 421
coins **7** 536; **14** 419, *419*
decorative works **30** 780
embroidery **13** 196
interior decoration **19** 612
manuscripts **14** 423; **20** 332
orders (chivalry) **7** 178
paintings **10** 245; **13** 152
textiles **14** 425
Edward IV, King of England (*reg* 1461-83) **9** 738–9*
architecture **3** 882; **5** 514; **10** 163; **13** 55; **14** 75; **24** 466; **33** 248
gold **10** 325
manuscripts **5** 669; **19** 727
stained glass **5** 648
tapestries **10** 348; **13** 634
Edward IV, Master of **3** 555; **9** 739
Edward VI, King of England (*reg* 1547-53) **2** 455; **7** 537; **15** *81*; **19** 567; **28** 313
Edward VII, King of Great Britain (*reg* 1901-10) **26** *78*; **33** *257*
architecture **32** 257
collections **10** 487
furniture **14** 523
manuscripts **30** 749
medals **11** 812
paintings **5** 78; **22** 38
Edward VIII, King of England (*reg* 1936) **10** 487
Edward, Alexander **4** 890
Edward, Charles **30** 266
Edward, John **10** 334

Edwardian Baroque *see* BAROQUE REVIVAL
Edwardian style **9** 739–40*
Edwards (family) **31** 646
Edwards, Alfred **9** 424; **11** 663
Edwards, Amelia B. **10** 80, 90; **24** 561
Edwards, Benjamin **16** 29
Edwards, Edward **9** 212, 740*
Edwards, Edwin **10** 796
Edwards, Ernest **7** 575; **25** 618
Edwards, George **8** 529; **10** 199; **16** 33
Edwards, John (1671-1746) **31** 648
Edwards, John (*fl* 1723-53) **10** 332
Edwards, John (*fl* 1974) **29** 117
Edwards, John Paul **13** 710
Edwards, Jonathan (1703-58) **7** 216
Edwards, Joseph (1814-82) **23** 172; **32** 787
Edwards, Melvin **1** 445
Edwards, Passmore **28** 888
Edwards, Pietro **9** 740*
Edwards, R. (*fl* 1972) **1** 40
Edwards, Richard **7** 161
Edwards, Ruth (1833-1907) **10** 796
Edwards, Samuel (1705-62) **4** 479
Edwards, S. J., & Co. **29** 454
Edwards, Thomas **4** 479
Edwards, (Arthur) Trystan **9** 740–41*
Edwards, Veryan **4** 490
Edwards, William (1719-89) **4** 801
Edwards, William (*fl* early 19th cent.) **10** 334
Edwards, William (*fl* 1857-92) **2** 765
Edwards, W. Joseph (*fl* 1843-67) **24** 637
Edwards & Daniels Associates **27** 642
Edwards Madigan Torzillo & Briggs **2** 743, 771; **5** 602; **18** 890
  works **2** *742*
Edwards of Halifax **4** 354, 355
Edwards & Roberts **22** 744
Edward the Confessor, King of England (*reg* 1042-66) **19** 600
  architecture **2** 64; **19** 564, 600, 608; **23** 211; **26** 587
  metalwork **29** 851
  sculpture **26** 611, 615
Edward the Elder **33** 90
Edwin, King of Northumbria (*reg* 616-32) **33** 541, 546
Edwin, David **30** 853
Edy-Legrand, Edouard Léon Louis **4** 9, 368
Edzani church **12** 321
Edzell Castle **12** 126; **28** 268
Edzná **9** 741*; **20** *882*; **21** *372*; **23** 826
  canals **9** 741
  Cinco Pisos pyramid **9** 741; **21** 204, *204*, 214
  Large Acropolis **9** 741
  Palace of Five Floors *see* Cinco Pisos pyramid
Eeckele, Jan van **20** 665
Eeckhout, Gerbrand van den **9** 741–4*; **22** 871
  collaboration **22** 443
  groups and movements **2** 732
  patrons and collectors **5** 679; **26** 112; **32** 377
  reproductions in tapestry **12** 829
  teachers **22** 843
  works **9** *742*, *743*; **24** 271
Eeckhout, Jan Pietersz. van den **9** 741
Eeden, Frederik (Willem) van **9** 745*
Eeklo **3** 584
Eekman, Nikolas **21** 854
Eenhorn, Lambertus van **22** 879, 880
Eenhorn, Samuel van **7** 166; **22** 879
  works **7** *166*
Eenhorn, Wouter van **22** 879
Eenigen **22** 136
Eertvelt, Andries van **3** 560; **9** 745*; **24** 323; **25** 33
Eesbeeck, van (family) **3** 599
Eesteren, Cornelis van **9** 745–6*; **21** 156; **29** 661
  assistants **31** 867
  collaboration **9** 63
  groups and movements **2** 318; **7** 293; **10** 137; **23** 450
  patrons and collectors **9** 63
  pupils **17** 472
  works **1** 804; **31** 730
Eestrum Church **22** 819
Efate **31** 890, 892
Efendi, Baha **23** 391
Efendi, Ethem, Shaykh **23** 391
Efendi, Necmeddin *see* OKYAY, NECMEDDIN
Efes *see* EPHESOS
EFFanBEE **31** 261
Effettisti **19** 871
Effiat, Antoine Coëffier, Marquis d' **21** 346; **27** 821; **32** 718
effigies **6** 71; **31** 120, 122–7, 128–9
  historical and regional traditions
    England **1** 518; **9** 268; **10** 259–60, 338; **13** 164; **19** 604–5; **25** V2
    France **11** *290*, *898*; **31** 122
    Germany **31** 122
    Gothic **13** 164; **16** *19*
    Ireland **16** *19*
    Italy **3** *138*; **29** *24*
    Kenya **1** 258, *258*
    Native North Americans **1** *153*
    Romanesque **11** *290*; **26** *606*
    Spain **26** *606*
  materials
    alabaster (gypsum) **1** 518
    bronze **10** 338; **13** 164; **31** 122
    granite **26** *606*
    limestone **11** *290*; **25** V2
    marble **11** *898*; **29** *24*; **31** 122
    pipestone **1** *153*
  types
    gisant **12** 744*
  see also BRASSES (MONUMENTAL); SCULPTURE → forms → tomb; TOMBS
Effingham, Catherine Proctor Howard, Countess of *see* HOWARD, CATHERINE PROCTOR, Countess of Effingham
Effingham, Charles Howard, 2nd Baron Howard of *see* HOWARD, CHARLES, 2nd Baron Howard of Effingham
Effner, Carl von **33** 283
Effner, Joseph **9** 746–7*
  architecture
    grottoes **13** 704
    monasteries **23** 636
    palaces **3** 229; **11** 457; **12** 372; **22** 299, 309; **28** 110; **33** 277
    pavilions (buildings) **12** 373
    town houses **9** *747*
  assistants **8** 288
  collaboration **33** 681
  furniture **12** 424
  groups and movements **13** 199
  interior decoration **29** 760; **33** 277
  patrons and collectors
    Maximilian II Emanuel, Elector of Bavaria (*reg* 1679-1706; 1715-26) **22** 308
Effort, L' **5** 37; **19** 539; **30** 726
Efik **1** 348; **5** 753; **8** 231; **15** 61, 65
  masks **15** 62
  trade **15** 61
Efimenko, Petr **18** 400; **21** 413
Efrat, Benni **9** 747*; **29** 769
Efros, Abram (Markovich) **9** 747–8*
Efut **8** 231; **15** 62
Egami, Namio **17** 427
Egan, Barry M. **7** 858
Egan, Felim **16** 18
Egan, John J.
  works **22** *672*
Egan, Pierce **8** 217
Egan, William **7** 858
Egas (*fl* 1189) **25** 295
Egas (family) **31** 88
Egas, Antón **9** 748–9*; **14** 578; **29** 265
  assistants **8** 78
  collaboration **8** 78; **9** 749
  groups and movements **25** 31
  patrons and collectors **27** 605
  pupils **8** 78
  works **1** 586; **8** 78; **27** 605; **31** 87, 91
Egas, Camilo **2** 10; **9** 713, 749*; **25** 829; **27** 155
Egas, Cueman *see* EGAS CUEMAN
Egas, Diego **9** 749
Egas, Enrique (1455-1534) **9** 748–9*; **14** 578; **29** 265
  architecture
    chapels **2** 278; **13** 70; **28** 518; **29** 265
    churches **7** 345; **13** 283; **16** 863; **25** 22; **29** 265, 521; **31** 91
    hospitals **6** 451; **13** 283; **14** 781, *781*; **29** 265, 355; **31** 87
  assistants **8** 78; **32** 493
  collaboration **1** 526, 586; **9** 748; **13** 844
  groups and movements **25** 30, 31
  patrons and collectors **2** 658; **7** 345
Egas, Enrique (*c.* 1500-*c.* 1565) **9** 749; **32** 620
Egas, Hanequin de *see* HANEQUIN DE BRUSELAS
Egas, Pedro **9** 749
Egas Cueman **9** 748*; **14** 134
  collaboration **1** 599; **13** 757
  patrons and collectors **21** 125
  pupils **28** 330
  works **8** 253; **9** *748*; **13** 107, 123, 731, 757; **31** 88, 92
Egas de Bruselas *see* EGAS CUEMAN
Egba **1** 345
Egbado **1** 345
Egbert, Archbishop of Trier **9** 749–50*; **23** 652, 660; **26** 695
  architecture **31** 326
  manuscripts **20** 753; **31** 325
Egbert I, King of Kent (*reg* 664-73) **26** 66
Egbert Codex *see under* CODICES → individual manuscripts → Codex Egberti
Egbor & Associates **23** 135
Egckl, Wilhelm **9** 750*
  collaboration **22** 307; **29** 375; **33** 274
  patrons and collectors **8** 432; **29** 738
  works **12** 366; **22** 299, *307*; **33** 271
Egedius, Halfdan **9** 750–51*; **22** 540
  works **9** *751*; **23** 225
Egell, Augustin **9** 753; **32** 758
Egell, (Johann) Paul **9** 751–3*
  assistants **13** 850; **32** 758
  groups and movements **26** 498
  works **4** 814; **9** *752*; **12** 405; **20** 282
Egen, Geert van **27** 168
Egenau, Juan **6** 598; **9** 753*
Egenberger, Johannes (H.) **2** 575; **21** 175; **22** 848
Egender, Karl **33** 736
Egenhoff **26** 204
Egenolff, Christian von **3** 506
Eger (Czech Republic) *see* CHEB
Eger (Hungary) **9** 754*; **14** *881*; **16** *103*
  Castle **9** 754; **14** 81
  Cathedral of St Michael and St John of Nepomuk **9** 754; **14** 889, 895, 904
  collections **15** 17
  congregational mosque **14** 886
  County Hall **15** 9
    gates **15** *9*; **16** 59
  István Dobo Castle Museum **15** 17
  Jesuit church **14** 887, 894
  Lyceum **9** 754; **10** 531; **14** *887*, 888, 900; **18** 417
  Minorite church **9** 754
Eger cabinets *see under* CABINETS (ii) (FURNITURE) → types
Egeri, Carl von **9** 754–5*
Egermann, Friedrich **8** 410; **12** 787; **23** 264, 271, 272
  works **12** VI2
Egersund Faience Factory **23** 235
Egerton, Daniel Thomas **9** 756*; **21** 385
Egerton, Francis, 1st Earl of Ellesmere **3** 283; **9** 755*; **13** 219; **32** 774; **33** 345
  paintings **19** 271
Egerton, Francis, 3rd Duke of Bridgewater **9** 755*; **33** 221
  collections **19** 587
  paintings **5** 63; **10** 365; **14** 808; **20** 238; **31** 467
Egerton, Francis Henry, 8th Earl of Bridgewater **7** 413; **9** 755; **20** 389
Egerton, John Hume, Viscount Alford **14** 877
Egerton, John Sutherland, 6th Duke of Sutherland **9** 755
Egerton, John William, 7th Earl of Bridgewater **4** 79; **26** 239
Egerton, Thomas, 1st Earl of Wilton **12** 639; **28** 357
Egerton, Thomas, 2nd Earl of Wilton **19** 508
Egerton 1070, Master of **7** 235, 525; **20** 635, 687
Egerton Genesis *see under* BIBLES → individual manuscripts
Egervár Church **14** 894
Egeskov **12** 135
  Castle **4** 781
Egesta *see* SEGESTA
Egg, Augustus (Leopold) **9** 756–7*; **32** 800
  groups and movements **7** 436; **10** 254
  patrons and collectors **10** 755
  works **9** 1, *756*; **24** 667
egg and dart mouldings *see under* MOULDINGS → types
egg and tongue mouldings *see* MOULDINGS → types → egg and dart
Egg chairs *see under* CHAIRS → types
Eggebrecht, Anna Elisabeth **9** 241
Eggebrecht, Peter **9** 241
Eggedal **26** 647
Eggeling, Viking **9** 758–9*; **22** 380; **26** 356
  groups and movements **8** 436, 437
  works **9** *758*; **10** 687
Eggenberg, Hans Ulrich von **2** 782; **13** 330, 918
Eggenberg, Johann Seyfried von, Prince **5** 613; **11** 130; **33** 48
Eggenburg **10** 738
Eggenschwiler, Franz **9** 759*; **30** 140
Eggenschwiler, Urs (1849-1923) **33** 699
Eggenschwiler, Urs Pankraz (1756-1821) **30** 137
Egger, Georg **9** 760
Egger, Hermann **2** 833
Egger, René **25** 375
Eggericx, Jean-Jules **9** 759–60*
  collaboration **3** 551; **11** 724; **31** 875; **32** 380
Egger-Lienz, Albin **2** 797; **9** 760*
Eggers, Bartholomeus **9** 760–61*
  collaboration **22** 858; **25** 812
  patrons and collectors **14** 650
  works **3** 805; **14** 44; **22** 859
Eggers, (Hartwig Karl) Friedrich **9** 761*
Eggers, Johann Karl **22** 704
Eggers, Otto R. **25** 235
Eggert, (Georg Peter) Hermann **9** 761*; **29** 751
  assistants **28** 119
  collaboration **14** 89
  works **14** 142; **23** 341; **25** 856
Eggink, Johann **18** 851
Eggl, Wilhelm *see* EGCKL, WILHELM
Eggleston, William **9** 494, 762*
  works **24** XI1
Eggleston & Oakley **29** 634
eggs **6** 227
  types
    emu **2** 765
    ostrich **1** 297; **25** 735*
  uses
    conservation **28** 340
    grounds **13** 706
    paints **32** 898
    pigments **28** 338
    sealants **25** 174
    secco paintings **28** 338
    tempera **23** 783; **30** 425
    wall paintings **6** 227
egg-shaped kilns *see* KILNS→ types → *zhenyao*
eggshell porcelain *see under* PORCELAIN → types
eggshells **1** 297; **18** 604; **29** 818; **32** 482
egg whites *see* ALBUMEN
Egham (Surrey), Royal Holloway College **7** 639; **14** 688
Egharevba, Jacob U. **3** 723
Eghegnadzor **2** 439
Egidiano, Juan Bautista **17** 513; **24** 502
Egidio da Campione **5** 550
Egidio da Gandria **18** 586
Egidio da Viterbo **26** 817
Egidius de Walcourt **14** 854
El Egido **32** 177
Eginhard *see* EINHARD
Egino, Bishop of Verona **26** 102
Eginton, Francis **24** 637
Eginton, Harvey **5** 314
Egkl, Wilhelm *see* EGCKL, WILHELM
Egle, Ārvids **25** 745
Egler, Harry **11** 299
Egley, William **9** 762
Egley, William Maw **9** 762*
Egli, Ernst **31** 452
Eglinton, Hugh Montgomerie, 12th Earl of *see* MONTGOMERIE, HUGH, 12th Earl of Eglinton
Egloff, Anton **30** 140
Egmond Abbey Church **4** 777; **22** 818, 854
Egmond Breviary *see under* BREVIARIES→ individual manuscripts
Egmont, Arnold van, Count **22** 835
Egmont, Floris von, Count of Buren *see* BUREN, FLORIS VON EGMONT, Count of
Egmont, Justus van **9** 762–3*
  collaboration **9** 476
  patrons and collectors **7** 699
  printmakers **10** 761
  teachers **5** 49; **27** 298
  works **11** 641; **30** 320
Egmont Albums, Master of the *see* HENDRICKSZ. (CENTEN), DIRCK

Egna, Alberto de *see* ALBERTO DE EGNA
Egnatia **13** 581
Egner, Marie **2** 797
Egolzwil **25** 502
Egonu, Uzo **23** 137
Egremont, Charles Wyndham, 2nd Earl of *see* WYNDHAM, CHARLES, 2nd Earl of Egremont
Egremont, George O'Brien Wyndham, 3rd Earl of *see* WYNDHAM, GEORGE O'BRIEN, 3rd Earl of Egremont
Eğret Han **16** 186
Eğrikapılı Hoka Mehmed *see* MEHMED RASIM
Egry, József **9** 763*; **10** 650; **13** 638; **14** 901
Egt, Daniel **29** 119
Eguchi, Katsumi **17** 267
Egville, James D' *see* D'EGVILLE, JAMES
Egyed **27** 87
Egypt **1** *214*, 376; **9** 763–8*; **16** *104*
 alum **16** 431
 aquamarines **9** *653*
 arches **16** 176
 architectural decorations **1** 317; **16** *176*, 176–7, *259*
 architecture **9** 764–5*
  Ayyubid **16** 172, 173, 175
  brick **16** 270
  Coptic **7** 819*
  Fatimid **16** 172
  Islamic **16** 141, 155–6*, 172–7*, 207–13*, 229
  Mamluk **16** 207–13, 257
  military **21** 587–8
  Ottoman **16** 229
  stone **16** 176
  Tulunid **16** 149
  vernacular **32** 312–14*, *313*
  wood **16** 176
 archives **2** 370*
 basins **16** *384*; **20** *228*
 baths **3** 376, 377
 batik **3** 378
 belts **16** 530
 body arts **7** 829*
 bone **16** 523
 book covers **4** 349; **16** 357, *357*
 books **16** 361
 bowls **16** *385*, 415, *518*
 boxes **16** 497
 brass **16** *384*, *385*, *389*
 brick **4** 771–2; **16** 270
 bronze **9** *160*; **16** *506*
 calligraphy **16** *275*; **18** *241*
 carpets **9** 666; **28** 716
  Islamic **16** 466, 468, *472*
  Mamluk **5** 401; **16** *472*, 472–3
 cemeteries **16** 175
 cenobitic cells **7** 819–20*
 cenotaphs **6** 171
 censorship **6** 174
 ceramics **7** 826*; **9** 767
 chests **18** *139*
 churches **7** *820*, 820–21*
 clay **16** 405
 coins **16** 510, 512, *512*, 513, *513*, 514
 copper **16** 404
 cornices **16** 176
 cotton **8** 34; **9** *640*, *665*; **16** 428, 442; **31** 21
 courtyards **16** *210*
 dolls **31** 260
 domes **16** 496
  bulbous **16** 211
  fluted **9** 84
  Islamic **16** 176, 210
  Mamluk **16** 244
  semi-dome **16** 176
 doors **9** 160, *160*; **16** 384, *490*
 doublures **16** 356
 dress **1** 348; **9** 643–4; **16** 431, 452, 453, 454, 456–7, 458
Egypt—cont.
 dyes **16** 431, 441
 earthenwares **16** 394, *403*, *405*
 ebony **16** 488
 education (art) **9** 767–8
 embroidery **16** 431, 432; **28** 716
 enamel **16** 515, 520, *520*
  cloisonné **17** III1
 ewers **16** *519*, 541
 excavations **5** 890
 exhibitions **9** 768
 façades **16** 175
 factories **16** 431, 441
 flasks **16** 540
 flax **16** 428, 431
 forgeries **16** 545
 fortifications **21** 587–8
 frontispieces **16** *129*
 gardens **12** 78
 gateways **5** *396*
 gilding **16** *357*, *520*
 glass **16** 515, 517, *518*, 519, 520, *520*
  Ayyubid **16** 520
  Byzantine **9** 644
  cameo **16** *519*
  Early Christian (*c.* AD 250-843) **9** 644, 645
  lustre **16** *518*
  Mamluk **16** 521
  Roman **27** 78
 glazes **16** 402–3, 404, 415
 gold **9** *653*; **16** *384*, *385*, *389*, *512*, *513*, 529; **17** III1; **21** *718*
 granite **9** *766*
 grilles **16** 496
 guidebooks **13** 810, 811, 812
 harnesses **14** *184*
 headdresses **16** 454, 459
 helmets **16** *504*
 historiography **16** 547
 icons **7** 823*; **9** *624*, *625*, *626*; **28** *762*, *763*
 incising **16** 403, 415
 indigo **16** 431
 inlays **16** *384*, *385*, *389*, 497
 inscriptions **16** 441–2
  Fatimid **16** 176, 258, 512
  Islamic **16** 176, *176*, *259*, 383, 386, 415, 431, 432, 441, 510, 513, 514; **28** 716; **29** *618*; **31** *21*
 iron **16** *504*
 ivory **16** 497
 ivory-carvings **7** *825*; **16** *523*, 523–4*
 jade **16** 861
 jewellery **9** 652; **16** 515, 529–30*
 kermes **16** 431
 khānaqāhs **18** 17, *18*
 knitting **18** 157
 lac **16** 431
 lead **16** 415
 leather **4** 349
 limestone **7** *822*
 linen **9** 247; **16** 431, 432, *433*, 442; **30** IV2; **31** 21, *21*
 liturgical furnishings **7** 280
 madder **16** 431
 madrasas **5** 396; **16** 175–6; **20** 55, 56
 manuscript illumination **4** *14*; **7** 823–4*; **9** 619; **16** *129*, 305–6*, 310–12*
 marble **29** *618*
 markets **10** *831*
 marquetry **16** 490
 mausolea **9** *765*; **16** 175, 207, *209*
 metalwork **9** 766–7
  Islamic **16** 369*, 382–6*, 389–90*
  Mamluk **16** 382
  Ottoman **16** 386
 micrography **21** 475
 mihrabs **16** *176*, 176; **21** 505–6
 minarets **16** 175, *212*; **21** 627
 minbars **16** 496–7; **21** 629
Egypt—cont.
 miniatures (manuscript illumination) **7** *824*; **16** *306*, *312*
 mirrors **21** 718, *718*
 monasteries **21** 833; **27** 813; **28** 761, *761*
 monuments **7** 820*
 mosaics **28** *763*
 mosque lamps **16** *520*
 mosques **5** 401, *404*; **16** *155*, *173*, 173–5, *174*, 209, *210*, *212*
 moulding **16** *403*, 403, 415
 mud-bricks **4** 772
 muqarnas (architecture) **16** 176; **22** 321–2, 323, *324*
 museums **9** 768*; **10** 80; **16** 557
 natron **16** 431
 necklaces **9** *653*
 ornament **16** *129*
 painting **7** 822–4*; **9** 765–6*
  wall **1** 313; **3** *420*; **7** 822–3*, *823*
 paintings
  wall **16** 306
 palaces **16** 257
 palm **16** 487
 paper **24** 48
 patronage **16** 207, 382–3
 pearls **9** *653*
 pendants (jewellery) **17** III1
 photography **24** *663*
 plates **16** *405*
 portals **9** 161
 pottery **1** 285
  Ayyubid **16** 405
  blue-and-white ware **16** 416
  faiyumi ware **16** 403, 405
  Fatimid **16** 404–5
  Fustat Fatimid Sgraffito ware (FFS) **16** 405
  Islamic **16** 402–3*, 404–5*, *405*, 415–17*
  lustreware **16** 393, 404–5, *405*, 415–16*; **22** 515
  Mamluk **16** 415–17
  Pseudo-Samian ware **16** 405
 printing **16** 359, 361
 quartz **16** 405
 railways **5** 399
 ramparts **4** 772
 regalia **16** 539
 rings **16** *504*
 robes **16** 452
 rock crystal **16** 540–41, *541*; **26** 487
 schools **5** *399*; **16** 229
 screens (i) (architectural) **16** *496*
 screens (ii) (furniture) **16** 496
 scripts
  cursive **16** 432
  kufic **16** *176*, 258, *259*
  muḥaqqaq **16** *275*; **18** *241*
  thuluth **16** *275*, 368, 386
 sculpture **7** 821–2*; **9** 591, 765–6*, *766*; **16** 244, 245
 seals **10** 69–70*
 sgraffito **16** 415*
 shadow-puppets **16** 545
 shops **16** 175
 signatures **16** 415, 496
 silica **16** 404
 silk
  Byzantine **9** *640*, *665*, 668
  Early Christian (*c.* AD 250-843) **9** *640*
  Islamic **16** 431, *433*, 441–2, *442*; **28** 715; **31** 21
  Mamluk **16** 430; **28** 716
 silver **16** *384*, *385*, *389*, 404, *504*; **21** *718*
 skins **16** *357*
 slip **16** 405, 415*
 spinning (textile) **16** 432, 468
 squinches **16** 176
 stamping **16** 403
 stamps **16** 517
 stands **16** *389*, 497
 steel **21** *718*
 stelae **7** *822*; **29** *618*
Egypt—cont.
 stone **16** 176
 strapwork **16** 487
 stucco **29** 819
 sugar **31** 260
 swords **16** *506*
 synagogues **17** *550*, 551
 tapestries **7** *827*; **9** *767*; **16** 431, 432, *433*; **30** IV2; **31** 21
 tattoos **7** 829*
 teak **16** *490*
 tents **30** 477
 textiles **7** 826–7*; **16** 431–2*, 441–2*
 thrones **30** 776
 tiles **16** 248
 tin **16** 404
 tiraz **16** 432, *433*, 457; **31** 21, *21*, 22
 tombs **5** *403*; **16** 175, 207, 208–9; **31** *113*
 trade **1** 249
  amulets **25** 734
  carpets **16** 469
  dyes **16** 431
  metalwork **16** 383, 389, 390
  porcelain **16** 403
  pottery **6** 333; **16** 395, 398, 403, 404, 405, 412, 415, 416, 417
  silk **16** 430
  textiles **3** 378; **16** 431, 438, 441
 tughras **31** 417
 tunics **9** *640*
 turbans **16** 456–7
 urban planning **16** *262*
 vaults (ceiling) **16** 270
 weapons **16** 508
 weaving **9** 767; **16** 441
 windows **16** 257
 wood **9** 160; **16** 176; **21** 505
 wood-carvings **7** *829*; **16** 488
 woodwork **7** 828*; **16** 488–91*, *490*, *496*, 496–7*
 wool **9** *767*; **16** 431, *472*; **30** IV2
 writing **10** 1
 yarn **16** 468
Egypt, ancient **9** 769–906*, *774*; **10** 1–95*; **26** *921*
 acacia **6** 559
 adzes **9** 821
 alabaster (gypsum) **10** 54; **22** *690*; **25** 762; **27** 824
 alabaster (limestone) **1** 516; **9** 812–13*, 814; **21** *109*; **29** X1
 alabastra **10** 48
 alloys **21** 329; **30** *396*
 alphabets **10** 1, 4
 altars **1** 691*
 alum **10** 61
 amethyst **10** 29
 amulets **3** 441; **10** 3, 20*, 38–9*, *39*, 47
  Early Dynastic (*c.* 2925-*c.* 2575 BC) **1** 817
  Late Period (664-332 BC) **10** 3; **22** 285
  Old Kingdom (*c.* 2575-*c.* 2130 BC) **10** 69–70
  Predynastic (*c.* 6000-*c.* 2925 BC) **9** 864; **10** 29, 60
  Second Intermediate Period (*c.* 1630-*c.* 1540 BC) **1** *817*
 anhydrite **10** 66, 74
 animal subjects **9** 865, 867; **29** 34
 apartments **9** 852
 apprentices **9** 790
 archaeology **2** 299, 300; **8** 763; **10** 79*, 82
  British School of Archaeology **24** 561
  Centre d'Etudes et de Documentation sur l'Ancienne Egypte (CEDAE) **10** 83
  Deutsche Orient-Gesellschaft **10** 82
  Egypt Exploration Fund **10** 80, 81, 82, 90, 92, 94; **24** 561
Egypt, ancient
 archaeology—cont.
  Egypt Exploration Society **1** 755; **10** 31, 81, 83; **11** 732; **27** 813; **33** 373
  Egyptian Antiquities Service **10** 79–80, 81, 90, 93; **24** 840
  German Archaeological Institute **10** 80, 81
  Institut Français d'Archéologie Orientale (IFAO) **10** 81, 83
  Sudanese Antiquities Service **10** 81
  Swiss Archaeological Institute **10** 81
  UNESCO (United Nations Educational, Scientific and Cultural Organization) **10** 83; **24** 602
 arches **2** 292, 294, 295, 296*
 architects **2** 312; **9** 790, 826*
 architecture **9** 773, 775, 824–6*, 827–35*, 836–8*, 839–41, 842–3*, 849*, 850*, 851–3*; **10** 84; **13** 405; **25** 171
  Amarna (1353-1333 BC) **9** *852*, *853*
  Early Dynastic (*c.* 2925-*c.* 2575 BC) **9** 850*
  Graeco-Roman (332 BC-AD 395) **9** 842*
  Late Period (664-332 BC) **9** 841–2*
  Middle Kingdom (*c.* 1966-*c.* 1630 BC) **9** 838*, 839
  military **9** 843–9*, *845*, *846*, *847*; **21** 554–5*
  New Kingdom (*c.* 1539-*c.* 1075 BC) **9** 839*
  Old Kingdom (*c.* 2575-*c.* 2130 BC) **9** 850*
  Predynastic (*c.* 6000-*c.* 2925 BC) **9** 837*, 849–50*
  Roman **26** 920
  stone **9** 825; **25** 761; **27** 811
  trabeated construction **31** 269
  wood **9** 775, 824
 archives **2** 364
 armour **10** *40*, 41
 arrows **10** 40
 art (imitation of works of) **11** 306
 art history **10** 83–4*, 93
 ashes **10** 55
 astronomy **9** 805*
 axes **9** 820–21; **10** 40–41
 bangles **10** 29
 barges **13** 407
 basalt **9** 813*, 814; **10** 72; **25** 762; **27** 824, 825; **28** 34
 baskets **3** 330, 332; **10** *41*, 41–2*
 beads **1** 864; **7** 80; **9** 815; **10** 28, 47, 56
 beadwork **3** 441
 beakers **10** 72
 bedding **3** 482
 beds **3** 482*; **10** 51, *51*, 53
 bekhen stone **9** 813, *881*; **22** *399*
 bellows (furnaces) **9** 817
 belts **10** 29
 bitumen **24** 792
 body arts **10** 65–8*
 bone **4** 313; **9** 864; **10** 59–60*, *65*
 book illustrations **4** 345; **10** 7
 bookplates **10** 7
 books **4** *341*, 343, *343*, *344*; **10** 3, 5, 6–7*
 Books of the Dead **10** 3, 7
 boomerangs **10** 40
 bottles **12** IV2
 bowls **9** *824*; **10** *25*, 48, 57, *67*
 bows **10** 39–40
 boxes **10** 51, *53*, 53–4
 bracelets **10** 29, *29*
 brick **2** 296; **23** 807
 bronze **5** *71*; **9** 817, 860; **10** 35–7, *36*; **21** 711
  Late Period (664-332 BC) **9** 855, *856*

Egypt, ancient
bronze—cont.
New Kingdom (*c.* 1539-*c.* 1075 BC) **6** 559; **10** 54; **21** *713*
Roman **27** *89*
Third Intermediate Period (*c.* 1075-*c.* 656 BC) **9** *861*, 886
13th Dynasty (*c.* 1756-*c.* 1630 BC) **10** *36*
brushes **5** 32; **9** 898, *898*
builders **9** 826
busts **5** 298*; **22** *723*; **29** 814
cabinets (ii) (furniture) **33** III1
calligraphy **10** 6*
canal-ponds **27** 496
canopic chests **10** 15–16*, 20
canopic jars **5** 298; **10** 14–15*, *15*, 28; **22** 283; **30** 408
canopies (ii) (textile coverings) **10** 51, *51*
capitals **1** *615*; **5** *670*; **9** 834
caricatures **9** 904
carpenters **9** 820, *820*, *821*
cartonnage **10** 10, 12, 13–14*; **22** *284*
cartouches **5** 899
caskets **10** 52
casting **12** 782
casts **6** 9; **10** 68–9
causeways **25** 760, 762
cavetto cornices **10** 51, 52
cedar **6** 559; **10** 54; **33** III1
cenotaphs **6** 170
chairs **6** 388; **10** 50–51, *51*, 52, *52*, 53
chalices **10** 48
chapels **9** *831*; **18** 70
peripteral *see* kiosks
tomb **9** 833, 836, 839, 882
chariots **6** *477*, 478–9; **9** 822; **10** 61
chasing **9** 818
chests **6** 558–9; **10** 54
chisels **9** 814, 815, 821
chronologies **1** 853; **2** 300; **9** 775, *776*; **10** 80; **14** 335; **25** 472
circuses **7** 342
clappers **22** 372
clay **10** 21–2*, 25, 26, 28
clocks **7** 437
clubs (weapons) **10** 40
cobalt **10** 55
cobalt oxides **4** 172
codices **4** *343*; **24** 88
coffins **3** 848; **10** 1, 8–12*, *9*; **33** *580*
coins **13** 588
collars **3** 441; **17** IV2
collections **2** 558; **5** 401; **7** 563; **10** 6–7, 83, 87, 89–91*, 92–4*; **11** 302
colour **10** 1
columns **9** 830, 831; **23** 477; **30** 432
contracts **10** 4
copies **10** 7; **13** *465*
copper **7** 813; **9** 817; **10** 29, *35*, 35, 50, 51
copper oxides **10** 55
cords **10** 61
cornelian **10** 29, 38, 52; **12** 246
corn-mummies **10** 20*
cosmetics **10** 65–8, *66*
cosmetics containers **16** 797
cotton **9** 823
couches **29** 8
craftsmen and artists **9** 789–91*, *814*, *816*, *817*, *818*, *823*, 897, *898*; **10** 35, 61–2, *62*
cryptography **10** 1
crypts **9** 834
daggers **10** 41
dating methods **2** 300; **8** 912; **10** 80
dealing **10** 89*, 91–2*
death-masks **6** 9
decorum **9** 796–8*
determinatives **10** 2
diadems **10** 29

Egypt, ancient—cont.
diorite **9** *869*; **29** 700
dolerite **9** 814
dolls **31** 259, 261
doors **9** 150*
drawings **9** 897–8*, *903*, 903–4*, 906
dress **1** 887; **3** 441; **10** 42–6*, *43*, 61
drills **9** 821
dyeing **10** 74–5*
dyes **10** 74
dynasties *see under* periods
earrings **10** 31
easels **9** 791
ebony **3** 482; **6** 559; **9** *828*; **10** 50, 52, 53, 54; **31** *265*
education (art) **9** 790
scribal **10** 5–6*
electrum **9** 817
emblems **14** *415*
embroidery **10** 75–6*
emeralds **10** 33
enamel **10** 32
entasis **10** 414
epigraphy **10** 81–3*
erasers **10** 5
erotic art **9** 807*; **10** *472*, 473, 487
exhibitions **10** 94–5*
ex-votos **9** 795*; **10** 69
façade decoration **10** 741–2*
façades **9** 825
faience (i) (glass) **6** 559; **7** 80; **9** 788; **10** 3, *17*, 29, 46–9*, *47*, *49*, 50, 51, 52, 53, *65*, *67*; **28** 34
fans **10** 775, *775*
feathers **10** *775*
feldspar **10** 38; **12** 246
festivals **9** 807*; **23** 766
figureheads **28** 611
figurines **9** 865; **10** 47–8, 49, 60, 66
Early Dynastic (*c.* 2925-*c.* 2575 BC) **10** *59*
Faiyum style **27** 111
Late Period (664-332 BC) **10** *49*
Predynastic (*c.* 6000-*c.* 2925 BC) **9** *865*; **18** *238*
flasks **10** 57
flint **9** 775, 816, 865
flutes (columns) **11** 231
flutes (musical instruments) **10** 64
footboards **3** 482
forgeries **10** 85–7*, *88*
fortifications **9** 844; **21** 554–5*
fortresses **9** 844–9, *845*, *846*, *847*, *848*; **21** 554, *555*
friezes **20** *117*
fringes **10** 75*
funerary boats **9** *827*; **10** 17*; **25** 760
funerary equipment **10** 7–20*; **33** *580*
funerary texts **9** 905–6; **10** 7; **25** 761
furniture **1** 869; **10** 2, 49–54*, 58, 61; **14** 494, *495*; **33** 155, 329
galleries (ii) (corridors) **12** *227*
game-boards **10** 48; **31** *265*
game-pieces **10** 60; **16** 797
garden design **12** 66–7
gardens **10** 54*; **12** 65, 66–7*
garnets **10** 29; **12** 246
garrisons **21** 554
gems **12** 246*
Gesamtkunstwerk **12** 497
gesso **3** 482; **9** 898; **12** 501
gilding **3** 482; **6** 559; **10** 50, *51*, *52*, 53; **12** 620, 625
glass **1** 865; **10** 46, 52, 54–9*, *57*, *58*; **12** 782, 785, 788, 789, IV2; **17** IV2
cameo **10** 56, 58
conglomerate **10** 56, 58
glassblowing **10** 56
gold-glass **10** 59

Egypt, ancient
glass—cont.
millefiori **10** 56, 58
mosaic **10** 56, 58
glass paste **10** 46
glazes **4** 172; **6** 333; **9** 788; **10** 46–9*
glues **9** 822
gold **3** 441; **6** 388; **9** 817; **10** 28, 38, 624; **12** 867; **17** IV2
Graeco-Roman (332 BC-AD 395) **10** 33, *39*
Late Period (664-332 BC) **1** 876; **10** 33
Middle Kingdom (*c.* 1966-*c.* 1630 BC) **10** 30, *30*
New Kingdom (*c.* 1539-*c.* 1075 BC) **1** 469; **10** *31*
Old Kingdom (*c.* 2575-*c.* 2130 BC) **10** 29, *37*, 50, 51, 52; **14** 494, *495*
Predynastic (*c.* 6000-*c.* 2925 BC) **10** 29
Third Intermediate Period (*c.* 1075-*c.* 656 BC) **14** *403*
gold leaf **3** 482; **10** 52, 57; **12** 620, 870
granite **9** 773, 813*, 814, 815, 825; **23** 329; **27** 824; **29** 700
black-and-white **29** 700
granodiorite **9** 813
green-grey **29** 700
Late Period (664-332 BC) **9** *889*; **27** 824
Middle Kingdom (*c.* 1966-*c.* 1630 BC) **9** *876*
New Kingdom (*c.* 1539-*c.* 1075 BC) **9** *885*; **14** *758*; **23** *330*, *331*; **30** *297*
Ptolemaic (304-30 BC) **9** *893*; **27** 825
5th Dynasty (*c.* 2465-*c.* 2325 BC) **25** 762
12th Dynasty (*c.* 1938-*c.* 1756 BC) **10** *77*; **28** *492*
13th Dynasty (*c.* 1756-*c.* 1630 BC) **9** *879*
18th Dynasty (*c.* 1539-*c.* 1292 BC) **9** *857*, *862*
19th Dynasty (*c.* 1292-*c.* 1190 BC) **10** 13
guidebooks **13** 807
guilds **10** 6
gums **9** 898
gypsum **29** 814
halls **9** 832, *840*; **13** 405
hammering **9** 818
hammers **9** 814, 815
hardstones **9** 814*; **10** 3; **14** 169
harnesses **14** 179*, *179*
harps **10** *65*, 65; **22** 372
headrests **3** 482; **10** 51, 53, 57
hieroglyphs **9** 881; **10** 1–4*, *5*, 93; **15** 149
horn **10** 29
houses **1** 755; **9** *849*, 849–50, 851, *851*
human figures **9** 801–4*, 853–4, 855, 856–8, 859, 865, 890, 891, 892
hunting scenes **9** 808*, 865
huts **9** 849
hypogea **9** 779
iconography **9** 792–4, *793*, 801–11*, 894; **12** 67
ideograms **10** 1
ideology **9** 796–9*
incising **10** 27–8
industrial scenes **15** 827
inks **15** 851, 852
inlays **9** 822; **10** 1, 28, 47, 48, 52, 58
inscriptions **1** 855; **2** 299; **9** 867; **10** 1, 2, 3, 6, 10
insulae **9** 852
iron **9** 817
isheru waters **27** 496

Egypt, ancient—cont.
ivory **3** 482; **6** 559; **10** 51, 52, 53, *59*, 59–60*, *775*; **22** *488*; **30** 775; **31** 254, *254*, *265*
ivory-carvings **9** 864, 865, *866*; **16** 797
jade **16** 861
jars **6** *329*; **10** *24*, *26*, 74
jasper **1** *817*; **10** 38; **12** 246
jewellery **1** 469; **10** 1, 20*, 28–34*, 38–9, 48, 54, 58, 60; **16** 797
jugs **10** *57*
khekher frieze **9** 825
kilns **10** 22–3
kiosks **9** 830, 831, *831*; **18** 70*
knife-handles **9** *866*, 867–8; **10** 60
knitting **18** 157
knives **10** 60
kohl **10** 67
labels **9** 868; **10** 60; **14** 407
lamps **13** *603*; **27** 104, *104*
languages **10** 1
lanterns (lights) **27** *111*
lapis lazuli **10** 28, 29, 38; **12** 246
lathes **9** 821
lead **10** 46; **18** 902
leather **6** 388; **10** 5, 52, 60–62*; **19** 2; **20** 327; **30** 775
libraries **10** 6–7*
limestone **9** 773, 812*, 814; **10** 72; **27** 14; **29** 614
Amarna (1353-1333 BC) **9** *884*; **22** *723*
Early Dynastic (*c.* 2925-*c.* 2575 BC) **1** *99*; **9** *867*, *868*; **27** 824
First Intermediate Period (*c.* 2130-*c.* 1938 BC) **9** *859*, *873*
Graeco-Roman (332 BC-AD 395) **13** 434
Late Period (664-332 BC) **9** *815*, *891*
Middle Kingdom (*c.* 1966-*c.* 1630 BC) **1** *793*; **10** *17*
New Kingdom (*c.* 1539-*c.* 1075 BC) **9** *882*; **10** *15*, 70, *88*; **28** *34*; **29** *615*; **30** *297*, *696*
Old Kingdom (*c.* 2575-*c.* 2130 BC) **9** 812, 815, *858*, *863*, *872*; **10** 14; **25** 762; **27** 824
Predynastic (*c.* 6000-*c.* 2925 BC) **1** *100*; **10** 72; **18** *238*
Third Intermediate Period (*c.* 1075-*c.* 656 BC) **27** 825
linen **3** 482; **9** 823–4; **12** *226*; **20** 327; **22** 283; **31** 259
literacy **10** 4–5*
looms **9** 824, *824*; **10** 75; **30** 544, 545
lost-wax casting **9** 817, 818; **10** 36, 56
lotus **19** 716, *717*
lutes **10** 65
lyres **10** 65
maces **9** 868, *868*; **10** 40; **21** 554
malachite **10** 29; **24** 793
mallets **9** 814, 815, 821
manganese **10** 55
manuscripts **20** 327
maps **10** 62–3*; **20** 361; **31** 152
marble **9** *895*; **13** *465*; **27** 14
marquetry **20** 466
masks **5** 298; **10** 68
masonry **9** 779, 850; **20** 570, 571
mats **3** 482; **30** 433
mattresses **3** 482
mausolea **20** 863*
measurements **13** 411
metal **30** 775
metalwork **9** 816–18*, *817*, *818*; **10** 30, 34*, 35–8*
mirrors **10** 38, 67; **21** 711*, *713*
models **9** *823*, *849*, 850, *851*
monuments **22** 42*
mosaics **1** *617*; **22** 159
mouldings **9** 825
moulds **9** 818; **10** 56, 57

Egypt, ancient—cont.
mud-bricks **2** 296; **4** 792; **9** 775, 824–5, 844, 850; **23** 807; **30** 433
mummies **1** 342; **9** 842–3; **10** 14*; **20** 327; **22** 283–6*, *284*, *285*; **24** 792
mummy-boards **10** 11, 12, 13
mummy cases **10** *9*, 12, 13–14*, *197*, 197; **22** 285; **25** 276
mummy masks **10** 11, 13*, 14; **22** 284
museums **10** 85, 92–4*
musical instruments **10** 60, 64–5*; **22** 372
narratives **9** 799, 865, 882; **22** *512*, 512–13*; **28** 494
natron **22** 283
necklaces **10** *31*, 47
necropoleis **5** 70; **9** 779, 842–3*, *843*; **12** *766*; **22** 285–6, 716
niello **9** 818; **10** 381
nude figures **27** *89*
obelisks **2** 362; **7** 813; **9** 813, 825; **23** 329–30*, *330*, *331*
offering tables **1** 507; **29** 664
ointment pots **10** 74
onomastica **10** 63
ornament **9** 810–11*; **23** 532–3*
Osiris-beds **10** 20*
ostraca **9** *810*, *903*, 904; **10** 5; **30** 701
paint containers **9** 791
painting **9** 897–903*, *898*; **10** 5, 26; **12** *226*
encaustic **10** 197, *197*
floor **9** 898
landscape **9** 809*
marine **20** 424
still-lifes **29** 664
tomb **9** 790, 791, 897, 898–903; **27** 57; **32** 802
wall **1** 885; **3** 717; **8** 462; **9** 775, *821*, 897–903*; **32** 802*
Amarna style **9** *902*
Early Dynastic (*c.* 2925-*c.* 2575 BC) **9** 899*
First Intermediate Period (*c.* 2130-*c.* 1938 BC) **9** 899–900*; **21** *745*
Middle Kingdom (*c.* 1966-*c.* 1630 BC) **2** *656*; **9** 900*
New Kingdom (*c.* 1539-*c.* 1075 BC) **9** *807*, *809*, *821*, 900–903*, *901*; **14** *179*; **25** 779; **28** *495*; **30** *698*; **32** I1
Old Kingdom (*c.* 2575-*c.* 2130 BC) **9** 899*; **20** *117*
Predynastic (*c.* 6000-*c.* 2925 BC) **14** *514*
Roman **1** *618*; **8** *462*; **27** 57
paints **9** 898; **10** 47
palaces **13** 405; **23** 807*
palanquins **10** 50
palettes **10** 5
ceremonial **9** 844, 868; **14** 407, *415*; **21** 554; **22** *509*; **23** 847–8*
cosmetic **9** 864; **10** 66
painters' **9** *898*; **10** 5
scribes' **10** *4*, 5
palmettes **23** 888
panel paintings **9** 790
papyri **4** *341*; **9** 775, *806*, *904*, 904–6*, *905*; **10** 3, *3*, 4, 5, 6–7, 14, 20; **12** *67*; **20** 329, 336; **23** 692; **26** 557; **30** 701
papyrus **4** *344*; **10** 7; **20** 329; **24** 87–9*; **26** *557*; **31** 259
parchment **4** *343*
pavilions (buildings) **12** 66
pearls **10** 33
pectoral ornaments **10** 29, *30*
pendants (jewellery) **10** 29
pens **10** *4*, 5; **24** 348
periods
26th dynasty **9** 784
Amarathian *see* Naqada I

Egypt, ancient
periods—cont.
Amarna (1353-1333 BC) **1** 505; **9** 781, 782*
Archaic *see* Early Dynastic
Badarian (*c.* 6000-*c.* 4000 BC) **3** 35; **9** 775, *776*
Early Dynastic (*c.* 2925-*c.* 2575 BC) **9** 775, *776*, 778–9; **10** 80
Early Predynastic (*c.* 6000-*c.* 3000 BC) **9** *776*
First Intermediate Period (*c.* 2130-*c.* 1938 BC) **9** 775, *776*, 779*
Gerzean *see* Naqada II
Graeco-Roman (332 BC-AD 395) **9** 775, *778*, 785*
Kushite *see* 25th Dynasty
Late Period (664-332 BC) **9** 775, *777*, 784–5*
Late Predynastic (*c.* 3000-*c.* 2925 BC) **9** *776*
Macedonian Dynasty (332-304 BC) **9** *778*
Mesolithic **9** *776*
Middle Kingdom (*c.* 1966-*c.* 1630 BC) **9** 775, *776*, 779–80*
Naqada I (*c.* 4000-*c.* 3500 BC) **9** 775, *776*; **22** 488
Naqada II (*c.* 3500-*c.* 3000 BC) **9** 775, *776*; **22** 488
Naqada III **9** *777*
Neolithic *see* Predynastic
New Kingdom (*c.* 1539-*c.* 1075 BC) **9** 775, *777*, 780–83*
Old Kingdom (*c.* 2575-*c.* 2130 BC) **9** 775, *776*, 779*
Palaeolithic **9** *776*
Persian *see* 27th Dynasty
Predynastic (*c.* 6000-*c.* 2925 BC) **9** 775*, *776*; **10** 80
Ptolemaic (304-30 BC) **9** 775, *778*, 785
Roman *see* Graeco-Roman
Saite dynasty *see* 26th dynasty
Second Intermediate Period (*c.* 1630-*c.* 1540 BC) **9** 775, *777*, 780*
Thinite **9** 775
Third Intermediate Period (*c.* 1075-*c.* 656 BC) **9** 775, *777*, 783–4*
1st Dynasty (*c.* 2925-*c.* 2775 BC) **9** *776*
2nd Dynasty (*c.* 2775-*c.* 2650 BC) **9** *776*
3rd Dynasty (*c.* 2650-*c.* 2575 BC) **9** *776*
4th Dynasty (*c.* 2575-*c.* 2465 BC) **9** *776*
5th Dynasty (*c.* 2465-*c.* 2325 BC) **9** *776*
6th Dynasty (*c.* 2325-*c.* 2150 BC) **9** *776*
7th and 8th Dynasties (*c.* 2150-*c.* 2130 BC) **9** *776*
9th and 10th Dynasties (*c.* 2130-*c.* 1970 BC) **9** *776*
11th Dynasty (*c.* 2081-*c.* 1938 BC) **9** *776*
12th Dynasty (*c.* 1938-*c.* 1756 BC) **9** *776*
13th Dynasty (*c.* 1756-*c.* 1630 BC) **9** *776*
14th Dynasty (*c.* 1630-*c.* 1523 BC) **9** *777*
15th Dynasty (*c.* 1630-*c.* 1523 BC) **9** *777*
16th Dynasty (*c.* 1630-*c.* 1523 BC) **9** *777*
17th Dynasty (*c.* 1630-*c.* 1540 BC) **9** *777*
18th Dynasty (*c.* 1539-*c.* 1292 BC) **9** *777*
19th Dynasty (*c.* 1292-*c.* 1190 BC) **9** *777*
20th Dynasty (*c.* 1990-*c.* 1075 BC) **9** *777*

Egypt, ancient
periods—cont.
21st Dynasty (*c.* 1075-*c.* 950 BC) **9** *778*
22nd Dynasty (*c.* 950-*c.* 730 BC) **9** *777*
23rd Dynasty (*c.* 823-*c.* 732 BC) **9** *777*
24th Dynasty (*c.* 722-*c.* 715 BC) **9** *777*
25th Dynasty (*c.* 750-*c.* 657 BC) **9** *777*
26th Dynasty (664-525 BC) **9** *777*
27th Dynasty (525-404 BC) **9** 775, *777*
28th Dynasty (404-399 BC) **9** *778*
29th Dynasty (399-380 BC) **9** *778*
30th Dynasty (380-343 BC) **9** *778*
31st Dynasty (343-332 BC) **9** *778*
peristyle courtyards **9** 832
per-neser see SHRINES (i) (CULT)
per-nu see SHRINES (i) (CULT)
per-wer see SHRINES (i) (CULT)
phonograms **10** 2
piers (ii) (masonry) **24** 750
pigments **9** 898; **10** 5
cobalt blue **4** 172
Egyptian blue **24** 790; **32** 802
frit **10** 46, 47, 55; **24** 790
Naples yellow **24** 799
pilgrim flasks **10** 48
pit-graves **9** 836, 837–8, 842
plans **9** 825; **10** 63–4*, *63*
plaques **9** 890; **10** 7, 48, 58; **22** *488*
plaster **2** 541; **6** 9; **10** *16*, 68–9*; **20** *117*; **23** 807; **29** 814*
polishing **9** 815, 818
polychromy **9** *870*; **13** 405; **25** 171
pools **12** 66
porphyry **9** 813; **27** 13
portraits
mummy portraits **29** 814; **30** V1
painting **10** *197*; **30** V1
plaster **29** 814
reliefs **9** 882
sculpture **1** 770, *793*; **2** *659*; **9** 875, 889; **28** *492*
potters **10** 23
potter's wheels **10** 22
pottery **4** 172; **6** 333; **9** *824*, 864; **10** 21–8*, *23*, *24*, *25*, *28*, 46; **20** 593; **31** 261
Black-topped ware **10** 25
Blue painted ware **10** 27, 28
Brown and red painted ware **10** 27
Decorated ware **10** 26
Lotus flower and crosslined ware **10** 27
Naqada II (*c.* 3500-*c.* 3000 BC) **6** *329*; **9** 827, *827*
Scenic ware **10** 27
White background ware **10** 26–7
White crosslined ware **10** 26, *26*
propaganda **14** 226
proportions (human) **9** 799–801*, *800*
pylons **9** 831, 832
pyramid chapels **9** 839
pyramidions **8** *456*, 456
pyramids **2** 362; **8** 456; **9** 779, 812, 813, 836, 838, 842; **10** 96; **20** 117, 863; **23** 338; **25** 760–63*; **31** 107
Early Dynastic (*c.* 2925-*c.* 2575 BC) **27** *810*
Middle Kingdom (*c.* 1966-*c.* 1630 BC) **25** 760, 763
Old Kingdom (*c.* 2575-*c.* 2130 BC) **25** 760, *761*, 762–3, *763*
Ptolemaic (304-30 BC) **9** 779
step **25** 761, *761*; **27** *810*

Egypt, ancient—cont.
quarries **9** 812, 814, 815
quartz **10** 46
quartzite **7** XII; **9** *790*, 813*, 815; **10** 13; **27** 824; **30** *694*; **31** *482*
ramps **25** 761
razors **10** 38, 67
realism (critical term) **10** 1
rediscovery **10** 78–84*
reeds **5** 32; **10** *4*; **24** 348
religion **9** 791–6*, *793*
religious books **10** 4
repoussé **9** 818
representation **1** 505; **9** 788, 796–801*, 854; **10** 1, 3; **28** 47
ring-ponds **27** 496
rings **10** 33, 70
rock art **9** 865
rock crystal **26** 484
rock reliefs **9** 779
rolls **4** *341*, 342; **10** 4, 5, 6, 7; **20** 329; **24** 88; **26** 557, *557*
roofs **13** 404; **27** 127
rushes **6** 388; **10** 5
sacred lakes **9** 832; **27** 496–7*; **30** 432
sanctuaries **9** *828*, *833*; **12** *227*; **29** 386
sandstone **9** 773, 813*, 814, 815, *883*, *887*, *894*, *896*; **10** 5; **22** *512*; **29** 703
sarcophagi **1** 516, *516*; **9** 813, *843*; **10** 12–13*; **27** 823–5*, *824*
satires **9** 805*, *806*; **27** 868
saws **9** 815, 821
scarabs **1** 857; **9** 879; **10** 20, 30, 70–71*, *71*; **22** 285; **28** 34*, *34*
schist **22** *509*; **27** 824, *824*
scribes **9** 897; **10** 3, 4, 5–6*, 7
scripts **9** 896
Coptic **10** 1
cursive **10** 3
demotic **10** 1, 4*, 79
hieratic **10** 1, 2, 3–4*, *3*, 5–6
hieratic, abnormal **10** 4
hieroglyphic **1** 854, 855; **2** 299; **10** 1–4*, 79, 83
sculptors **9** 853, 855
sculpture **9** 779, 813, *815*, *816*, 853–5*, 864*; **10** 55, 57, 68, 84, *472*; **12** 625; **13** 466
Amarna (1353-1333 BC) **9** 883*, *883*
animal subjects **7** XII
architectural **10** 741–2*
block statues **9** 856–7*, *857*, 874
bronze **5** *71*; **9** 855, *856*, 860, *861*, 886
cat statues **5** 70, *71*
chrysaliform figures **9** 866
colossal statues **1** 770; **9** 815, *816*, *862*, 862–3*; **30** *297*, *694*, 694, 695; **31** *482*
composite statues **9** 884
cult statues **8** 261; **9** 795*; **30** 433
dyads **9** 858–9*, *858*, 869–70; **22** 398, *399*
Early Dynastic (*c.* 2925-*c.* 2575 BC) **9** 866–7*, *867*
First Intermediate Period (*c.* 2130-*c.* 1938 BC) **9** 872–3*
Graeco-Roman (332 BC-AD 395) **9** 895–6*, *895*; **13** 465
healing statues **9** 888
kneeling figures **9** 859–60*, 866, 871
Late Period (664-332 BC) **9** 888–90*, *889*
marble **9** *895*; **13** *465*
Middle Kingdom (*c.* 1966-*c.* 1630 BC) **2** *659*; **9** 874–6*, *876*; **10** *77*
naophorous statues **9** 855, 860–61*
New Kingdom (*c.* 1539-*c.* 1075 BC) **9** 880–81*, *881*, 884–5*, *885*; **10** *58*; **28** 407

Egypt, ancient
sculpture—cont.
Old Kingdom (*c.* 2575-*c.* 2130 BC) **9** 869–71*, *869*, *870*; **10** *35*, *37*; **29** X1
Osirid statues **9** 862
praying figures **9** 866
Predynastic (*c.* 6000-*c.* 2925 BC) **9** 864–5*
prostrate figures **9** 861–2*
Ptolemaic (304-30 BC) **9** 892*, *893*, 893–5*
relief **9** 790, *848*, 863–4*; **10** 2; **25** 761; **26** 132, 133–4; **29** 814
Amarna (1353-1333 BC) **9** 884*, *884*
Early Dynastic (*c.* 2925-*c.* 2575 BC) **1** *99*; **9** 867–8*; **14** *494*
First Intermediate Period (*c.* 2130-*c.* 1938 BC) **9** *873*, 873–4*
Graeco-Roman (332 BC-AD 395) **9** 896–7*, *896*; **10** *69*, *507*
Late Period (664-332 BC) **9** 890–92*, *891*
Middle Kingdom (*c.* 1966-*c.* 1630 BC) **2** *656*; **9** 876–8*, *878*; **21** *60*; **24** *88*
New Kingdom (*c.* 1539-*c.* 1075 BC) **1** *100*; **9** 881–2*, *882*, 885–6*; **10** *88*; **17** *714*; **22** *512*; **28** *495*; **30** *696*
Old Kingdom (*c.* 2575-*c.* 2130 BC) **9** *820*, 871–2*, *872*; **10** 82
Predynastic (*c.* 6000-*c.* 2925 BC) **9** 865
Ptolemaic (304-30 BC) **9** *894*, 894–5*
Second Intermediate Period (*c.* 1630-*c.* 1540 BC) **9** 879*
Third Intermediate Period (*c.* 1075-*c.* 656 BC) **9** 887–8*, *887*
18th Dynasty (*c.* 1539-*c.* 1292 BC) **30** *699*
reserve heads **9** 863*, *863*, 870
scribe statues **9** 857–8*, 870, *870*; **14** *758*, 759
seated figures **9** 855–6*, *856*, 866, *867*, 869, *869*, 870, *876*, *879*; **20** 117
Second Intermediate Period (*c.* 1630-*c.* 1540 BC) **9** 878*, 879*
servant statues **9** 854, 871; **10** *16*, 16–17*
squatting statues **9** 859*, *859*
standard-bearers **9** 881
standing figures **9** 855*, 866, 873, *881*, *883*, 888
stelophorous statues **9** 860–61*
stone **9** 815*, 855, 886
theophorous statues **9** 860–61*, *861*
Third Intermediate Period (*c.* 1075-*c.* 656 BC) **9** 886–7*
tomb statues **10** 3
triads **9** 858–9*
wood **2** *659*; **9** 886
5th Dynasty (*c.* 2465-*c.* 2325 BC) **1** 96
18th Dynasty (*c.* 1539-*c.* 1292 BC) **28** *433*
seals **10** 69–71*; **28** 34
serpentine **10** 29; **28** 34
shabti containers **10** *19*, 19–20*
shabtis **10** *17*, 17–19*, 48, 57
shells **10** 29
shields **10** 41
ship-decoration **28** 611
shoes **10** 61
shrines (i) (cult) **9** *827*, 827–35; **30** 432
shrouds **3** 442; **10** 14
signatures **10** 6, 7
signs (emblems) **10** 1–2
silica **10** 55
silk **30** 552

Egypt, ancient—cont.
silver **9** 817; **10** 29, *29*, *36*, 51; **21** 711
silver leaf **3** 482
sistra **10** 48, 64; **22** 372
size **9** 898
slate **9** 864; **14** *415*
slings **10** 40
slip **10** 25
smelting **9** 817–18
soapstone **10** 29, 46, 47, 70, *71*; **12** 246; **28** 34, *433*
soldering **9** 818
soul-houses **9** 850; **10** 17
spears **10** 40
sphinxes **2** 362; **9** 862, 870, 875; **21** *109*; **29** 393–4*, *394*
spindles **30** 540
spinning (textile) **9** 824; **30** 540
spoons **10** *66*
sporting scenes **9** 811*
sprang **10** 76
standards (flags) **14** 407
standards (vexilloid) **11** 150, *150*
statuettes **9** 860; **10** 35–7, 47
Late Period (664-332 BC) **22** *690*
Middle Kingdom (*c.* 1966-*c.* 1630 BC) **10** *47*
New Kingdom (*c.* 1539-*c.* 1075 BC) **10** *36*
Roman **27** *89*
Third Intermediate Period (*c.* 1075-*c.* 656 BC) **10** *36*; **14** *403*
stelae **9** 890; **10** 1, 2, 48; **29** 614–16*
commemorative **9** 868; **29** *615*, 615–16*
Early Dynastic (*c.* 2925-*c.* 2575 BC) **1** *99*
false door **9** 825; **29** 615
funerary **9** 868, 877; **29** 614–15*
New Kingdom (*c.* 1539-*c.* 1075 BC) **9** *790*
rock-cut **29** 614, 616*
Roman **18** 209, *209*
round-topped **29** 615, 616
slab **29** 615
stone **2** 296; **9** 779, 812–16*, 825, 855; **10** 71–4*, *73*; **27** 825; **30** 433
Early Dynastic (*c.* 2925-*c.* 2575 BC) **25** 761; **27** 811
First Intermediate Period (*c.* 2130-*c.* 1938 BC) **22** 159
Old Kingdom (*c.* 2575-*c.* 2130 BC) **27** 824
Predynastic (*c.* 6000-*c.* 2925 BC) **9** 864, 865
Third Intermediate Period (*c.* 1075-*c.* 656 BC) **9** 886
stone-carvings **9** 815; **29** 704
stools **6** 388; **10** 51, 52–3; **23** *533*; **30** 775
stucco **10** 68*, *69*; **29** 813–14*
sundials **23** 338
surveyors **30** 25
sycamore **6** 559
syenite **29** 700
symbols **10** 1
tables **10** 51, 53; **30** 217
table services **30** 218
tablets **9** *828*
talatat-blocks **1** 505; **9** 832, 883
tapestries **10** 44, 75, *75*
tattoos **10** 66, 67, 68; **30** 366
tempera **9** 898
temple-ponds **27** 496
temples **1** 770; **9** 719, *720*, 795, 824, 827*, *831*, *834*, 844; **10** 1, 2, 6; **21** 554; **30** 432–3*
cult **9** 827–35*, *827*, *829*; **18** *19*
Early Dynastic (*c.* 2925-*c.* 2575 BC) **9** 828–9*
funerary **12** 497; **30** 433
Graeco-Roman (332 BC-AD 395) **8** *711*; **9** 834–5*; **24** *603*
Late Period (664-332 BC) **9** 834*; **14** *461*

Egypt, ancient
temples—cont.
mammisi **9** 835; **20** 231–2*
mortuary **9** 827, 835*; **25** 760, 762; **27** 811; **30** 695
New Kingdom (*c.* 1539–*c.* 1075 BC) **9** 831–4*; **30** *433*
Old Kingdom (*c.* 2575–*c.* 2130 BC) **9** 829–30*
peripteral **9** 833
Predynastic (*c.* 6000–*c.* 2925 BC) **9** 827–8*
Ptolemaic (304-30 BC) **2** *422*
rock-cut **1** *95*, 95–6; **9** 830, 831, 833; **12** *227*; **29** 386*
solar **30** 433
sun temples **1** *91*
valley **25** 760, 762
tents **10** 61
terracotta **9** 864, 865, *865*; **27** 111, *111*, 825
textiles **9** 823–4*; **10** 74–6*; **30** *563*
theories (art) **28** 47
threads **30** 540
thrones **29** 393; **30** 774–5*
block-thrones **30** 775
throwsticks **10** 40
tiles **10** 47, 48; **22** 159
tin **4** 688
tombs **9** 836–8*; **10** 1, 2, 3; **20** 863; **31** 107*
chapel **9** 836, 837, 838, 839, 841–2
cist **9** 842
Graeco-Roman (332 BC–AD 395) **9** 842*
Late Period (664-332 BC) **9** 841–2*
mastabas **9** 779, 836, *837*, 839, 899; **20** 596*, 863; **25** 760; **31** 107
Middle Kingdom (*c.* 1966–*c.* 1630 BC) **9** 838*
New Kingdom (*c.* 1539–*c.* 1075 BC) **9** 839–41*, *840*, *841*
Predynastic (*c.* 6000–*c.* 2925 BC) **9** 837*
private **9** 836, 840; **30** *700*
rock-cut **9** *837*; **31** 107
royal **9** 791, 836, *836*, 840–41; **10** 7, 63; **25** 760
saff-tombs **9** 839; **30** 697
see also pyramids
tortoiseshell **10** 29
towers **30** 695
towns **21** 554
toys **31** 254, *254*
trade **9** 785–8*; **21** 652; **30** 185
glass **6** 268; **10** 55
lapis lazuli **9** 814; **10** 28; **12** 246
metalwork **13** 373
pottery **8** 345; **13** 486
silk **6** 621
textiles **16** 438
tin **4** 688
turquoise **10** 28
wood **9** 819
trappings **14** 179*
travel books **10** 82
tunics **30** *563*
turquoise **10** 28, 38; **12** 246
urban planning **9** 850–53, *852*, *853*
urns **13** 539
varnishes **32** 2
vases **10** 28, *28*, 47, 48, *57*
vaults (ceiling) **32** 86, 87, 89
veneers **9** 822; **10** 60; **30** 775
vessels
basalt **10** 72
limestone **10** 72
metal **10** 37–8*
stone **9** *814*, 814–15*, 864; **10** 71–4*, *73*
walls **9** 844, *850*
weapons **10** 39*, *40*
weaving **9** 824; **10** 75*; **30** 551, 552
Egypt, ancient—cont.
wicker **30** 775; **33** 155
windows **33** 245
women **9** 811*, 855, 856, 889–90, 893–4; **22** 722
wood **9** 775, 819–23*, 824; **10** 70; **29** 614; **30** 775; **31** 259
Early Dynastic (*c.* 2925–*c.* 2575 BC) **14** *494*
Middle Kingdom (*c.* 1966–*c.* 1630 BC) **2** *659*; **10** 10; **20** 327
New Kingdom (*c.* 1539–*c.* 1075 BC) **10** 52, *65*
Old Kingdom (*c.* 2575–*c.* 2130 BC) **10** 8; **14** 494
Predynastic (*c.* 6000–*c.* 2925 BC) **10** 29; **30** 433
Third Intermediate Period (*c.* 1075–*c.* 656 BC) **9** 886; **31** 254
18th Dynasty (*c.* 1539–*c.* 1292 BC) **10** *4*, *5*, 5, *66*
wool **9** 823
workshops **9** 790, 815, *823*
wrappings **20** 327
writing **1** 853, 854–5; **10** 1–6*, *3*, *4*, *5*; **20** 329; **24** 88–9
writing boards **10** 5, *5*; **20** 327
see also ANCIENT NEAR EAST; COPTIC; SYRIA-PALESTINE
Egypt, Helen of *see* HELEN OF EGYPT
Egypt Exploration Fund **10** 80, 81, 82, 90, 92, 94; **24** 561
Egypt Exploration Society **1** 755; **10** 31, 81, 83; **11** 732; **23** 36; **27** 813; **33** 373
Egyptian alabaster *see* ALABASTER (LIMESTONE)
Egyptian Antiquities Service **10** 79–80, 81, 90, 93; **24** 840
Egyptian blue *see under* PIGMENTS → types
Egyptian Revival **10** 95–8*; **23** 503
art forms
architecture **10** 83, *97*; **25** 765
gateways **5** *616*
interior decoration **24** 844
regional traditions
Britain **10** 96
France **8** 763
Egyptian Society **2** 164
Egység **1** 132; **24** 440; **31** 541
Ehbisch, Friedrich **8** 740
Ehemant, F. L. **8** 426
Ehingen, Georg von **33** 629
Ehingen Church **12** 372
Ehmcke, Fritz Helmuth **3** 512; **20** 11
Ehmsen, Heinrich **33** 672
Ehn, Karl **10** 98*
works **32** 439, *439*
Ehnder, Johann Gottlieb **21** 64
works **21** *65*
Ehningen Altar, Master of the **20** 660*
Ehninger, John W(hetten) **2** 858; **7** 433; **10** 99*
Ehrenberg, Felipe **10** 99*
Ehrenberg, Ralph E. **2** 368
Ehrenberg, Willem van **7** 833; **8** 663
Ehrenberg Brinkman, Paul **8** 16
Ehrenbill, Lars **27** 169
Ehrenburg, Il'ya **19** 476; **24** 450
Ehrenfeld, William K. **15** 743
Ehrenkrantz, Ezra **26** 19; **28** 159
Ehrenreich, Adám Sándor **10** 99*
Ehrenreich, Johan Ludwig Eberhard **30** 97
Ehrenreich, József **10** 99
Ehrenstrahl, David Klöcker **3** 509; **10** 99–100*
patrons and collectors **14** 288; **30** 117
pupils **8** 453
works **11** 468, *468*; **29** 690; **30** 78, *78*
Ehrenström, Johan Albrecht **10** 218; **13** 611; **14** 371
Ehrenström, Marianne **30** 119
Ehrensvärd, Augustin **20** 484; **30** 3
Ehrensvärd, Carl August **10** 100*; **11** 90, 91
Ehrenzweig, Anton **10** 101*; **25** 684
Ehresman, Donald **4** 24
Ehret, Georg Dionysius (1708-1770) **10** 101*
patrons and collectors **6** 118
reproductive prints by others **6** 87
works **5** 750; **11** 229
writings **11** 229
Ehrlich, Bettina **10** 102
Ehrlich, Christa **22** 892
Ehrlich, Georg (1897-1966) **2** 803; **10** 101–2*; **32** 447
Ehrlich, Hugo **10** 102*
collaboration **18** 412; **19** 651
pupils **1** 578; **8** 766; **12** 887
staff **17** 858
works **33** 593
Ehrmann, Eugene **33** 711
Ehrmann, François Emile **12** 830
Ehrström, E. O. W. **11** 108
Ei, Kyū **10** 102*
Eibar **29** 343
Eibisch, Eugeniusz **10** 102–3*
groups and movements **25** 108
pupils **9** 473; **18** 182; **23** 273; **28** 402
Eichel, Emanuel (1690-1751) **10** 103
Eichel, Emanuel, II (1717-82) **10** 103*
Eichelberger, Ethyl **24** 409
Eichen, Berent van der **8** 733, 754; **30** 322
Eichens, Friedrich-Edward **10** 396
Eicher, Joanne B.
works **1** *348*
Eichermann, Gustavo **21** 381
Eichhardt **14** 79
Eichholtz, Jacob **10** 103*
Eichhorn, Kristoffer **30** 120
Eichhorst, Franz **22** 711
Eichin, Bettina **30** 140
Eichler (family) **2** 719
Eichler, Fritz **15** 826
Eichler, Gottfried, I **10** 103*; **20** 915
Eichler, Heinrich **10** 103
Eichler, Reinhold Max **28** 143
Eichrodt, Ludwig **4** 39
Eichstätt **9** 680
Capuchin church **9** 680
Cathedral **17** 699
monument to St Willibald **14** *450*, 450
Jesuit church **12** 370; **32** 821
Sommerresidenz **14** 696
tapestries **12** 466
Eichthal, Gustave d' **25** 467
Eidlitz, Cyrus L(azelle) W(arner) **10** 103, 104–5*
Eidlitz, Leopold **10** 103–4*; **31** 691
collaboration **26** 340; **31** 690
patrons and collectors **15** 407
pupils **29** 871
staff **10** 104
works **4** 788; **10** 103*; **17** 891; **22** 60
eidographs **24** 22
Eidophusoka **10** 105*; **19** 728; **30** 675, 680
Eidsberg church **13** 102
Eidsvold College **23** 222
Eiebakke, August **10** 105*
Eielson, Jorge Eduardo **24** 510
Eiermann, Egon **10** 105–6*; **12** 379
collaboration **14** 118; **27** 315
groups and movements **8** 826
pupils **31** 579
works **4** 324; **12** 380; **29** 874
Eiermann & Lindner **33** 628
Eiff, Wilhelm von **12** 441; **31** 466
Eiffel, Gustave **10** 106–7*; **25** 856
architecture
aqueducts **2** 242
bridges **4** 389, 803; **23** 453; **25** 293; **30** 27
churches **2** 148
department stores **8** 769, *769*
exhibition architecture **10** *107*, 682, 683; **24** 504
observatories **23** *342*
collaboration **4** 239; **11** 524; **12** 157; **23** 342
sculpture **3** 290
Eiffel Tower *see under* PARIS
Eiga Takuma *see* TAKUMA EIGA
Eigenbilzen **6** 155
Eigen Haard **1** 815; **10** 698; **18** 126; **30** 458
Eigen Haard housing association
architecture **18** *126*
Ei Genshō **33** 492
Eight, Group of *see* EIGHT, THE (iii)
Eight, Society of *see* SOCIETY OF EIGHT
Eight, the (i) (Czech) **8** 249; **10** 107–8*; **18** 492; **25** 433
members **3** 715; **8** 393; **11** 79; **18** 491; **25** 647
Eight, the (ii) (America) **10** 108*, 680; **12** 296; **23** 47; **24** 600; **31** 605
exhibitions **8** 571
members **2** 596; **12** 769; **18** 895; **19** 789; **25** 553; **28** 605, 843
Eight, the (iii) (Nyolcak; Hungary) **1** 131; **10** 108–9*; **14** 882, 896, 901
members **3** 474, 765; **8** 429, 431; **17** 913; **20** 407; **25** 245; **30** 871
Eight, the (iv) (De åtta; Sweden) **33** 566
Eight Eccentrics of Yangzhou **6** 792, 801, 807, 811; **14** 824; **17** 591, 592; **25** 73; **33** 496, 497
works **17** *592*
Eighteen Society **19** 375
Eight Great Artists of the Xiling Region **7** 130
Eighth Street Club *see* 8TH STREET CLUB
Eighties movement *see* TACHTIGERS
Eight Masters of Jinling **12** 899; **22** 459
Eight Masters of Nanjing *see* EIGHT MASTERS OF JINGLING
eight-on-four churches *see under* CHURCHES → types
Eight Talents of Wuxing **25** 780; **33** 646
Eigil **10** 109*
Eigtved, Niels **8** 726, 760, 819; **10** 109–12*; **18** 136
architecture **21** 821
churches **17** 446
palaces **8** 726; **10** *111*; **21** 825; **23** 813; **29** 841
urban planning **7** 802–3; **8** 726; **10** *110*; **31** 715
interior decoration **8** 742–3
Eigtwedt, Niels *see* EIGTVED, NIELS
Eiheiji **10** 112–13*; **17** *11*
Eihōji **12** 98
Eijmer, L. J. **1** 803
Eijnde, Hendrik van den **22** 861
Eikaas, Ludvig **13** 848; **23** 232
Eikai **17** 124
Eike von Repgau **7** 242
Eikoh Hosoe *see* HOSOE, EIKOH
Eikonion *see* KONYA
Eikyūji **17** 157
Eilbertus of Cologne **10** 113–14*
works **7** 583; **10** *113*; **26** 683, 686
Eileithyiaspolis *see* EL-KAB
Eilenberg, Samuel **15** 743, 746; **22** 795
Eilshemius, Louis M(ichel) **10** 114*
Einarsdóttir, Sigrun Olöf **15** 72
Einarsson, Gudhmundur **15** 72
Einaudi **16** 782
Einbeck, Conrad von *see* CONRAD VON EINBECK
Einden, Ferdinand van den **10** 114–15*; **12** 664; **25** 563; **27** 133
Einden, Jan van den **10** 114–15*
Einden, van den (family) **9** 52
Eindhoven
Karregat Centre **29** 428
Stedelijk Van Abbe Museum **22** 906
Ein Gedi
cult centre **30** 183, 188
glass **27** 73
mosaic **17** 542
pottery **30** 197
sanctuary **30** *190*, 191
synagogue **17** 542
Einhard **2** 319; **10** 115*
architecture **4** 776; **5** 794, 797; **12** 363, 471; **32** 637
metalwork **5** 806; **8** 205
reliquaries **10** *115*; **26** 144
Ein Harod Museum of Art **16** 571; **17** 582
Ein Hod **13** 694; **16** 903
Janco Dada Museum **16** 571
Einhorn Presse **19** 31
Einō Kanō *see* KANŌ EINŌ
Einsiedeln, Itinerary of *see* ITINERARY OF EINSIEDELN
Einsiedeln Abbey **10** 116–17*; **13** 18; **22** *61*, 61–2; **30** *124*, 126; **32** 822
Black Madonna **26** 141
church **10** 116; **30** *126*
library **19** 316
manuscripts **24** 269
pilgrim badges **24** 808
sculpture **3** 7; **30** 137
Einsingen Church **8** 215
Einsle, Anton **10** 117*
Einstein, Albert **17** 838; **18** 809; **19** 355; **26** 224; **28** 202
Einstein, Carl **30** 20
Einstein, Mary Small **33** 410
Eiraku Dōzen *see* EIRAKU SOSABURŌ
Eiraku Hozen **10** 117*; **17** 258, 262, 399; **18** 555
Eiraku kiln **18** 538
Eiraku Sosaburō **10** 117
Eiraku Wazen **10** 117; **17** 399; **18** 555
Eirakuya Tōshirō **22** 432
Eirene (*reg* 1340-1) **31** 304
Eirene, Empress of Byzantium (753-805) **13** 547; **33** 307
Eirene, Empress of Byzantium (786-802) **9** 637, 657; **10** 117–18*; **15** 75; **16** 596
Eiri Hosoda *see* HOSODA EIRI
Eiriz, Antonia **8** 234; **25** 209
Eisai **5** 119; **17** 72, 215, 334; **18** 550
Eisaku Wada *see* WADA, EISAKU
Eisch, Erwin **12** 441, 796
Eisdorf, Dorfkirche **9** 156
Eisen, Charles (-Dominique-Joseph) **10** 118–19*
collaboration **20** 421
patrons and collectors **10** 478
reproductive prints by others **9** 365; **12** 515; **19** 136, 268; **20** 914; **32** 502, 720
works **3** 318; **10** *118*
Eisen, Christophe-Charles **10** 118
Eisen, François **10** 118*
collaboration **22** 88
pupils **12** 637
reproductive prints by others **4** 330; **9** 407; **11** 57; **19** 641, 642

Eisen, Jacques-Philippe 10 118
Eisenach Castle *see* WARTBURG CASTLE
Eisenberg, Benedikt 19 110
Eisenberger, Nikolaus 19 111
Eisenburg Castle *see* HUNDEDOARA CASTLE
Eisenerz, St Oswald 2 778
Eisenhoit, Anton 10 119*
Eisen Ikeda *see* IKEDA EISEN
Eisen'in Kanō *see* KANŌ EISEN'IN
Eisen Keisai *see* KEISAI EISEN
Eisenlöffel, Jan 4 73; 10 119*; 22 883; 24 351
 groups and movements 33 323
 works 1 811; 22 892, *892*
Eisenlohr, (Jakob) Friedrich 10 119–20*
 pupils 3 410; 22 185; 29 491; 33 30
 teachers 33 40
Eisenman, Peter D. 10 120–21*; 31 598
 collaboration 13 325; 30 227
 groups and movements 23 50; 25 359; 26 16
 works 8 610; 10 *120*; 18 114; 25 172
Eisenmann, John 7 428
Eisenmenger, August 16 795; 17 517, 897; 18 525; 29 763
Eisen Okuda *see* OKUDA EISEN
Eisenstadt
 Burgenland Landesmuseum 2 831
 Esterházy Palace 2 782; 10 529; 14 886, 888, 899; 29 839
 Jüdisches Museum 17 582
Eisenstaedt, Alfred 10 121*; 24 677
Eisenstein, Johann Eisner von *see* EISNER VON EISENSTEIN, JOHANN
Eisenstein, Sergey 1 744; 5 276; 8 588; 19 80; 25 351; 26 356
Eisenwerth, Fritz Schmoll von 22 306
Eisert, Joseph 9 320
Eisert, Peter 8 410
Eisgrub *see* LEDNICE
Eishi Hosoda *see* HOSODA EISHI
Eishō 22 500
Eisho Chōkōsai *see* CHŌKŌSAI EISHO
Eishōsai Chōki 10 121*
 works 17 276, 285, 287
Eishun Baioken *see* BAIOKEN EISHUN
Eisner, Kurt 23 267
Eisner von Eisenstein, Johann 19 718
Eison 17 125
Eisselburg, Peter *see* ISSELBURG, PETER
Eisui Ichirakutei *see* ICHIRAKUTEI EISUI
Eitelberger von Edelberg, Rudolf 2 831, 833; 10 772; 28 800; 32 446; 33 159
Eitoku Kanō *see* KANŌ EITOKU
Eixeminis, Pedro (*fl* 1383) 29 323
Eiximenis (*fl* 1461) 29 323
Eizaburō Nomura *see* NOMURA, EIZABURŌ
Eizan Kikugawa *see* KIKUGAWA EIZAN
Eizat, Alexander 9 729
Eizenšteins, Mihails
Ejagham 1 425; 8 231; 10 122–4*
 body arts 1 342; 10 124*
 bronze 10 124*
 cement 10 124
 columns 1 261
 masks 1 273; 10 *122*, 122–3*
 regalia 10 124*
 religion 8 231
 sculpture 10 123*, *123*, 124*
 skins 10 *122*, 122
 stone 10 123*, *123*
Ejagham—cont.
 wood 10 *122*, 122–3
 wood-carvings 10 124*
 writing 1 425
Ejin Qi 7 114
Ek 24 440
Ék, Sándor 14 902
Ekaku Hakuin *see* HAKUIN EKAKU
Ekamra *see* BHUBANESHWAR
Ekamraksetra *see* BHUBANESHWAR
Ekbert, Bishop of Bamberg 3 143
Ekeby 26 647
Ekeland, Arne 10 125–6*; 23 226
Ekels, Jan, I (1724-81) 10 126
Ekels, Jan, II (1759-93) 10 126*; 22 846
Ekelund, (Georg) Hilding 10 126–7*
Ekelund, Ragnar 31 886
Eke Sadolin 10 541
Eket 15 61
Ekhmim *see* AKHMIM
Ekholm, Gordon 2 904
Ekholm, Kurt 11 105
Eki 29 70
Ekielski, Władysław 24 441
Ekiti 33 557
Ekkehard IV, Archbishop of Aribo 31 499
Ekkei *see* TENSHŌ SHŪBUN
ekklesiasteria 13 381; 23 349
Ekk Relief 18 848
Eklingji 10 127*; 15 *279*
 Lakulisha Temple 15 273, 489
Eklund, Jarl 11 108; 27 475
Eklund, Sten 30 82
Eklundh, Claes 30 82
Ekman, Carl Anders 10 128
Ekman, Pehr Johan 13 30
Ekman, Robert Wilhelm 10 127–8*; 11 95; 27 337; 31 461, 462
 works 10 *128*
Ekman, Stina 30 87
Ekmekçioğlu Ahmed Pasha 9 730
Ekoi *see* EJAGHAM
Ekolombi 18 484
Ekong, Afi 23 139
Ekperi 9 734, 735
Ekphantos 13 549
Ekphrasis 2 388, 517, 531; 10 128–30*, *130*; 13 807, 810; 16 593
Ekron 24 634, 635
Eksperimentalni atelje *see* EXAT-51
Eksperimenterende Kunstskole 8 736, 741, 759, 761
Ekspresionisti 13 695
Ekspresjoniści Polscy *see* POLISH EXPRESSIONISTS
Eksskole *see* EKSPERIMENTERENDE KUNSTSKOLE
Ekster, Aleksandra (Aleksandrovna) *see* EXTER, ALEXANDRA (ALEXANDROVNA)
Ekström, Gustav 22 730
Ekström, Per 10 131*
Ektachrome *see under* PHOTOGRAPHY → processes
Ekuan, Kenji 21 317
Ekun Fūgai *see* FŪGAI EKUN
Ekweme, Alex (Ifeanyi Chukwu) 1 319; 10 131–2*; 23 135
Ekweme Associates 10 131; 18 200
Elaeussa *see* SEBASTE (TURKEY)
El Alto *see* EL ALTO
Elam, John 23 75
Elamite 1 508, 851, *852*, 854; 10 132–3*; 15 900, 902, 904, 905, 907
 architecture 15 909–10
 bowls 10 132
 bronze 15 *919*
 dress 1 885, 886
 faience (i) (glass) 1 878, 879
 glass 1 868
 iconography 15 *908*
Elamite—cont.
 metalwork 15 919
 reliefs 10 *133*
 rock reliefs 15 *908*, 916, *917*
 scripts 1 854
 sculpture 15 914, *919*; 30 *28*
 stelae 10 *133*
 ziggurats 15 *910*; 33 675
Elamite period *see under* IRAN, ANCIENT → periods
Elan, L' 23 694
Elant Abbey 20 666
Elāpura *see* ELLORA
El Arbolillo *see* EL ARBOLILLO
Elasson, Olympiotissa 9 584, 600
elastomerics *see under* FIBRES → types
Elateia 13 464
Elba 10 *583*
 copper 16 743
 granite 29 700
 iron 27 93
 metalwork 10 624
 Napoleon Museum 20 809
Elbacha, Amine 19 8
Elbasan 1 *537*
 art schools 1 547
 ceramics 1 543
 guns 1 544
 metalwork 1 543
 silver 1 543
Elbasan Woodwork Combine 1 543
El Baúl *see* EL BAÚL
Elberfeld 12 469
 Museum 14 506
Elbfas, Jacob Heinrich 10 133*; 30 77
Elbląg 25 *92*, 116, 120, 126
Elbo, José 10 134*
Elboeuf, Maurice, Prince d' 14 440, 445
El Bosque *see* EL BOSQUE
Elbows Out 13 509
Elburcht, Hans van der 20 249
Elburg, Jan G. 7 489
El Burgo de Osma *see* EL BURGO DE OSMA
Elche 15 59, 60; 30 664
 Dama de Elche 15 58, 59
Elchingen, Jakob von *see* ZWITZEL, JAKOB
Elchinger, Julius 22 306
Elcho, Francis Wemyss-Charteris-Douglas, Lord *see* WEMYSS-CHARTERIS-DOUGLAS, FRANCIS, 10th Earl of Wemyss and March
Elcho Island 1 60
Eldarov, O. G. 2 895
Eldem, Halil Edhem 10 134*; 16 557, 591; 23 604; 31 456
Eldem, Sedad Hakkı 10 134*; 16 587, 591
 collaboration 16 587; 23 441; 31 452
 pupils 5 633
 works 16 241; 31 452
Elder, Louisine (Waldron) *see* HAVEMEYER, LOUISINE (WALDRON)
Elder Balbus 27 46
Elderoğlu, Adidin 31 454
Eldh, Carl 23 615; 30 86
Eldin, John Clerk, Lord *see* CLERK, JOHN, Lord Eldin
Eldoluft 30 103
Elea 9003 15 826
Eleanor, Queen of Castile (*fl c.* 1187-1214) 5 201, 205
Eleanor, Queen of France (1498-1558) 7 865; 11 616; 13 910; 22 64; 26 82
Eleanora of Aragon, Duchess of Ferrara (*fl c.* 1486) 3 92; 26 459; 31 34, 431, 432
Eleanor crosses *see under* CROSSES → types
Eleanor of Aquitaine, Queen of England (1122-1204) 11 290; 29 511
 tomb 27 *829*
Eleanor of Castile, Queen of England (1244-90) 10 270; 16 553; 20 332; 25 14; 29 298
 manuscripts 10 245
Eleanor of Portugal, Holy Roman Empress (1434-67) 25 315
Eleanor of Portugal, Queen of Aragon (*d* 1374) 19 684
Eleanor of Viseu, Queen of Portugal (1458-1525) 2 869, 871*; 14 658; 25 317
 gold 32 406
 paintings 1 213; 11 65; 20 758
Eleanor of Wittelsbach, Holy Roman Empress (1655-1720) 2 824; 20 375
Electa 16 777
Electra Editrice 13 811
electric clocks *see under* CLOCKS → types
electricity 29 97
electric kilns *see under* KILNS → types
electric lamps *see under* LAMPS → types
electric lighting *see under* LIGHTING → types
electric motors *see* MOTORS (ELECTRIC)
electric photographic guns *see under* CAMERAS → types
electric watches *see under* WATCHES → types
electroforming 12 866
electrolysis 21 320*
electronic images *see under* PHOTOGRAPHY → processes
electron microscopy *see under* TECHNICAL EXAMINATION → types
electron-probe microanalysis (EPM) *see under* TECHNICAL EXAMINATION → types
Electron Spin Resonance 2 304
electrophotography *see* PRINTING → processes → electrography
Electroplated Nickel-Silver *see* EPNS
electroplating 10 *135*, 135–7*, *136*, 143; 21 332
 chromium 7 241
 gold 12 870
 nickel 7 241
electroradiographic art *see* PRINTING → processes → xeroradiography
electrostatic copies *see under* COPIES → processes
electrotype casting *see under* CASTING → types
electrotyping 12 866; 25 610; 26 227
 see also PHOTOELECTROTYPING
electrum 12 864
 historical and regional tradition
  Anatolia, ancient 1 834
  Egypt, ancient 9 817
  Greece, ancient 12 864; 13 585, *598*
  Indonesia 15 811
  Rhodes (island) 13 *598*
  Troadic 31 355, *355*
 uses
  coins 13 585; 15 811
  cups 31 *355*
  earrings 13 *598*
Eledzhiyev, Naran 27 433
Eleftheriades, Efstratios *see* TÉRIADE
El Egido *see* EL EGIDO
Eleja Palace 18 851
Elekfy, Jenő 13 638
elektron *see* ELECTRUM
Elema 23 717; 24 76, 77, 78, 79
 masks 24 *77*
Elementarism 10 137–8*; 26 379; 29 661; 32 695
Elem Kalabari 15 124
Elena, Queen of Serbia (*fl c.* 1243-76) 9 583
Eleni 5 150
Eleni, Empress of Byzantium (*fl c.* early 15th cent.) 5 152; 9 629
 works 5 *152*
Elenska Basilica 5 146
Eleonora de' Medici, Duchess of Mantua (1567-1611) 32 403
Eleonora Gonzaga, Duchess of Urbino (*fl* 1520) 24 536; 27 273
Eleonora Gonzaga, Holy Roman Empress (1628-86) 15 166; 30 454
Eleonora of Toledo, Grand Duchess of Tuscany (1522-62) 4 *858*; 16 *746*; 21 *9*, 21–2*
 architecture 11 213; 21 20
 hardstones 21 725
 paintings 4 858
 sculpture 3 160; 24 756
Eleonore, Duchess of Calenberg and Celle (*fl c. 1670)* 6 138
Elephanta 10 138*; 15 195, *276*
 Cave 1 10 138
 pillars 15 277
 reliefs 15 *465*
 sculpture 15 416, 465*
 Shiva Temple 15 275, 277
elephant armour *see under* ARMOUR → types
elephant harnesses *see under* HARNESSES → types
Elephantine *see under* ASWAN
Elephant Silk 9 666; 30 552
elephant trappings *see under* TRAPPINGS → types
Elers, Aarne (Adrian) *see* ERVI, AARNE (ADRIAN)
Elers, David 9 473; 10 138–9*, 305, 306; 29 495
 works 10 *304*
Elers, John Philip 9 473; 10 138–9, 305, 306; 29 495
 works 10 *304*
El Escorial *see* ESCORIAL
Eléspuru, Juan Manuel Ugarte *see* UGARTE ELÉSPURU, JUAN MANUEL
Eleta, Sandra 10 139*
Eleusinian Painter (*c.*355–330 BC) 17 911
Eleusis 10 *139*, 139–40*; 13 *363*; 14 351; 26 *908*
 architecture 13 394
 figurines 13 579
 Greater Propylaia 26 909
 Hall of Mysteries *see* Telesterion
 Lesser Propylaia 5 904; 25 658; 26 909, *909*
 limestone 13 387, 393
 measurements 13 411
 Museum 13 470
 pottery 32 61
 Sanctuary of Demeter and Kore 10 139–40; 13 417; 27 1
 stone 13 387
 Telesterion 13 380, 394; 30 434, 435
 Temple of Demeter *see* Telesterion
 town walls 21 556
Eleusis Painter 32 60
Eleusis Relief 13 431
Eleuthera (Bahamas) 3 *59*, 63
Eleutherai (Greece) 21 557
Eleutherius von Firmian, Leopold Anton, Archbishop of Salzburg *see* FIRMIAN, LEOPOLD ANTON ELEUTHERIUS VON, Archbishop of Salzburg
Eleutherna 8 154; 13 444
Eley, William 7 30
Elfgyfu, Queen of England (*fl c.* 1016-35) 2 76

Elfleda, Queen of England (*d* 916) 2 72, 83
Elf Scharfrichter 24 591
Elgar, Frank 23 8
Elgazzar *see* AL-JAZZAR, ʿABD AL-HADI
Elgg 30 145
Elghammar 30 73
Elgin (Grampian)
Museum 20 14
pulpit 28 251
St Giles 28 230
shops 28 227
Elgin (company) 7 448
Elgin, Thomas Bruce, 7th Earl of *see* BRUCE, THOMAS, 7th Earl of Elgin and 11th of Kincardine
Elgin Marbles 2 555; 10 741; 25 799; 26 134
acquisition 4 889; 10 365, 368; 14 199; 18 893; 33 192
authenticity 5 631
display 2 600; 9 25; 13 468, 469, 606
iconography 26 221; 31 703
polychromy 7 502
Elglund, Bengt 30 111
works 30 *111*
Elgötz, Herman 16 587
El Guereo *see* EL GUEREO
Elhafen, Ignaz 10 140*; 12 405, 460
Elharas 6 *182*; 10 141*; 31 *458*
Elia, Antonio 10 523
Eliá, Santiago Sánchez *see* SÁNCHEZ ELIÁ, SANTIAGO
Elia, Simone 3 772
Elia de Bissone *see* GAGINI, ELIA
Elia di Bartolomeo da Ponte Lombardo 11 896
Elias (*fl* 12th cent.) 26 659
Elias (*fl* 20th cent.) 28 917
Elias, Archbishop of Bari (*reg* 1089-1105) 30 777
Elías, Eduardo Pomareda *see* POMAREDA ELÍAS, EDUARDO
Elias, Etienne 3 565; 19 756
Elias of Cortona 7 905; 11 712
Elias of Dereham 10 141*; 27 625, 627
Eliass, Ģederts 26 384; 31 854
Eliasz., Nicolaes *see* PICKENOY, NICOLAES ELIASZ.
Elibekyan, Genrikh 2 433
Elibekyan, Robert 2 433
Eliche, Marqués de *see* CARPIO, GASPAR DE HARO Y GUZMÁN, 7th Marqués de
Elichpur 15 382
congregational mosque 15 382, 383
Eliézer Toledano 17 565
Eligius, Saint 20 762; 24 132
Elimburga 22 248
Eliot, Charles 4 475; 10 141–2*; 23 422
Eliot, T(homas) S(tearns) 17 850; 21 36; 28 418; 32 700
Elis 13 374
Aphrodite Ourania 24 594
coins 23 432
Heroön 6 170
pottery 13 534
Elisa, Grand Duchess of Tuscany (*reg* 1809-14) 4 *299*, 302, 305*; 7 662
architecture 5 363; 11 181; 23 259
collections 4 298
furniture 16 729, 730
paintings 3 750; 31 72
sculpture 4 301; 7 162
sponsorship 23 259
Elisabeth, Duchess of Austria (*d* 1330) 32 433
Elisabeth Alexeievna, Empress of Russia (1779-1826) 27 429
Elisabeth Dorothea, Landgravine of Hesse-Darmstadt (1635-1709) 8 529
Elisabeth of Hungary, Saint 20 379
Elisabethville *see* LUBUMBASHI
Elisabeth von Reichenstein 19 530
Elisabetta da Rimini 12 556
Elisabetta Gonzaga, Duchess of Urbino (1471-1526) 3 698; 25 897, 898; 27 790
Eliseev, Boris 23 16
Elisenhof 32 532
Eliška Rejčka, Queen of Bohemia (1292-1330) 8 388, 412
Elisofon, Eliot 10 580; 27 164
works 1 *353*, *388*; 10 *579*; 33 *484*
Elissa, Princess 25 732
Elissague, Alberto de Palacio *see* PALACIO ELISSAGUE, ALBERTO DE
Elizabeth, Electress Palatine and Queen of Bohemia (1596-1662) 8 788; 12 133; 21 640; 22 902; 29 799–800*; 32 *231*; 33 *272*
paintings 18 202; 29 797
Elizabeth, Empress of Austria (1837-98) 7 850; 14 483
Elizabeth, Empress of Russia (*reg* 1741-62) 25 745; 26 729, 731*; 28 465
architecture 18 543; 24 546; 26 7, 498; 27 438; 28 837
gardens 12 134
interior decoration 19 219
paintings 27 213, 438
porcelain 27 411, 582
silver 12 357; 27 420
Elizabeth, Holy Roman Empress *see* ELIZABETH, Queen of Germany
Elizabeth, Queen of Belgium (1876-1965) 24 36
Elizabeth, Queen of Bohemia (1286-1335) 4 831
Elizabeth, Queen of Germany (*d* 1330) 33 164
Elizabeth, Queen of Poland (1438-1505) 20 395
Elizabeth, Queen of Romania *see* SYLVA, CARMEN
Elizabeth I, Queen of England (*reg* 1558-1603) 9 322; 10 *247*; 12 *515*; 26 *80*; 28 *313*; 31 412, 415*; 33 *720*
architecture 21 568
astrolabes 28 *210*
collections 10 363
fans 10 780
furniture 10 287
gardens 12 126
imprese 15 150
jewellery 10 *345*; 17 522
miniatures (paintings) 14 546; 21 639
paintings 10 360; 13 240; 19 515; 21 368; 30 411
porcelain 4 177
portraits 25 277, 279
seals 14 546; 33 6
Elizabeth II, Queen of England, Scotland and Northern Ireland(*reg* 1952-) 8 834; 16 889; 23 67, 72; 26 82
Elizabeth Alekseyevna, Empress of Russia (1779-1826) 18 75
Elizabethan Revival 10 142*, 281
Elizabethan style 10 142–3*, 230, *231*; 28 *895*, *896*
Elizabeth Bowes-Lyon, Queen of Great Britain (1900-) 3 447; 29 120
Elizabeth Castle (Jersey) 21 568
Elizabeth de Bourbon, Duchess of Parma (1727-59) 5 379
Elizabeth de Bourbon, Queen of Spain (1602-44) 4 *543*
Elizabeth de Valois, Queen of Spain (1545-68) 14 *2*
Elizabeth Farnese, Queen of Spain (1692-1766) 4 556, *557*, 558–61*, *559*; 16 49; 29 271; 32 130, 332
paintings 29 41, 352
sculpture 27 46
silver 29 336
Elizabeth Kontromanich, Queen of Hungary (1340-87) 2 111
Elizabeth of York, Queen of England (1465-1503) 24 478
Elizabeth Piast, Queen of Hungary (1305-82) 15 10; 25 134
Elizalde, D. 7 484
Elizavetinskaya kurgan 28 323
Elizavetpol *see* GYANJA
Elizondo, Fidias 20 436; 21 389
Elk, Ger(ard Pieter) van 10 143*; 19 756; 22 853; 28 103
Elkab *see* EL-KAB
El Kalas hotel complex 1 320
Elkharas 6 223
elk hide *see under* HIDES → types
Elkington, Frederick 10 143
Elkington, G(eorge) R(ichards) 10 135, 143*; 28 739
works 4 88; 10 335, 343, 347; 17 768; 26 227
Elkington, Henry 10 135, 143
Elkington, Mason & Co. 10 135, 143; 29 575
industrial design 10 *135*
Elkington & Co. 9 295; 32 415
Elkington & Hardman 4 87
Elkingtons 22 28
Elkins (family) 24 600
Elkins Park (PA), Beth Shalom Synagogue 17 549
El'konin, Viktor 27 397
Elkonnen, B. 25 422
El Laberinto de Horta 12 125
El Labrador *see* LABRADOR, EL
Elle, Ferdinand (*c.* 1580-1649) 10 143–4*; 25 385
Elle, Ferdinand, I *see* ELLE, LOUIS (1612–89)
Elle, Ferdinand, II *see* ELLE, LOUIS (1648–1717)
Elle, Louis (1612-89) 3 813; 10 144*; 24 134
Elle, Louis (1648-1717) 10 144
Elle, Pierre 10 144
Ellegaard, Inge 8 736
Ellenius, Allan 30 120
Eller, Poul 8 762
Ellerker, John 10 144
Ellerker, W(illiam) H(enry) 10 144*
Ellerker & Kilburn 10 144*; 24 894
Ellery 29 843
Ellesmere, Francis Egerton, 1st Earl of *see* EGERTON, FRANCIS, 1st Earl of Ellesmere
Ellesmere Chaucer Manuscript (San Marino (CA), Huntington Lib., MS.26.C9) 24 809
Ellet, Elizabeth 33 309
Ellezelles church 13 113
Ellichpur 15 195
Ellicott, Andrew
works 32 *885*
Ellicott, Joseph 5 124
Elliger, Antonie (1701-81) 2 25; 10 145
Elliger, Ottmar, (i) (1633-79) 10 144*; 12 390
Elliger, Ottmar, (ii) (1666-1735) 10 144–5*; 20 147; 22 383
Elling, Christian 8 762
Elling, Pieter 21 156
Ellingen 19 826
church 30 536
Ellinger, Abbot 23 655
Elliot, Archibald 10 145*; 20 868; 28 230, 248
Elliot, Gilbert 28 269
Elliot, James 10 145; 28 230, 248
Elliot, Julian 33 602
Elliot, Walter 1 753
Elliot, William Parker 21 618
Elliot and Sons 33 58
Elliot & Fry 24 661
Elliott, Charles Loring 10 145*
Elliott, Edward 10 756
Elliott, John 7 875
Elliott, John Edmund 7 164
Elliott, Judi 2 764
Elliott, Julian (Arnold) 1 319; 5 668; 10 145–6*; 29 107
Elliott, Thomas 4 353
Elliott, William 28 879
Elliott Collection 17 898
Ellis, Anthony 29 381
Ellis, Charles 10 146
Ellis, Eduardo 2 397
Ellis, Harvey 5 126; 9 699; 10 146–7*; 21 650; 29 653
Ellis, Havelock 3 446
Ellis, John (1701-57) 18 147
Ellis, John (?1710-76) 4 862
Ellis, John L. (*fl* 1841) 30 867
Ellis, Peter 16 54; 19 506
Ellis, Welbore Agar 10 146*; 13 696
Ellis, William 31 635
Ellis and Clarke 10 240; 33 205
Ellison, Gabriel 33 602
Ellmore, W. T., & Son 5 612
Ello, Costanzo da *see* COSTANZO DA ELLO
Ellora 10 147–50*; 15 195, *276*, *285*, *294*, 300
Cave 1 15 275
Cave 2 15 275
Cave 3 15 275
Cave 5 15 277
Cave 6 15 277, 492
Cave 8 15 492
Cave 9 15 277
Cave 10 10 147; 15 277, *277*
Cave 11 15 277, 492
Cave 12 15 277, 492
Cave 14 10 147; 15 277
Cave 15 10 147–8; 15 279
Cave 16 *see* Kailasa Temple
Cave 17 15 277
Cave 21 15 277, 466
Cave 26 15 277
Cave 29 15 277, 466
Cave 32 15 278
cave temples 5 95; 15 275, 277, 492, 493, 558; 26 4; 30 437
Kailasa Temple 10 147, 148–50*, *149*; 15 275, 278, *278*, 543, 558; 30 437
reliefs 15 *492*, 492–3
Kailashanatha Temple 14 77
Lankeshvara Cave 15 278
Little Kailasa 15 278
pillars 15 277
Rang Mahal *see* Kailasa Temple
reliefs 15 214, 215, 227
sculpture 15 416, 465–6*, 492, 527
wall paintings 15 543, 553, 557–8
Ellsworth (ME), Congregational Church 25 268
Ellwangen Jesuit college 12 371
Ellwood, Craig 10 150*
Ellys, John 32 824
elm 33 324
historical and regional traditions
Belgium 3 577
England 10 288, 293
Japan 17 312
uses
furniture 10 288, 293
Elmalı 1 *821*; 10 150–51*; 24 691
ivory-carvings 1 872
wall paintings 13 550
Elmanov, Serami 17 866
elm-bark fibres *see under* FIBRES → types
Elmbreck, Theodoor *see* HELMBREKER, DIRCK
El Mekta *see* EL MEKTA
Elmes, Harvey Lonsdale 7 667; 10 151–2*
works 7 504, 687; 10 236; 18 888; 19 505; 25 268; 31 240
Elmes, Henry John 10 151
Elmes, James 10 151, 374; 14 246; 18 629
Elmhirst, Dorothy 19 235
Elmhirst, Leonard 19 235
Elmina fort 1 318
El Minguillo *see* EL MINGUILLO
El Minya art school *see* EL MINYA ART SCHOOL
Elmley Castle (Hereford & Worcs), St Mary 10 262
Elmore, Alfred 7 436; 10 152*
Elmslie, Essil 11 774
Elmslie, E. W. 2 323
works 2 *324*
Elmslie, George Grant 2 572; 21 649; 25 446, 737; 28 728
Elmzel, William 27 415
El Naranjo *see* EL NARANJO (MEXICO)
Elne, Cathedral of Ste Eulalie 1 696; 26 609, 610
Elno, Karel 2 510; 29 369
El Opeño *see* EL OPEÑO
El Oued *see* EL OUED
Eloul, Kosso 5 571
Eloy, Mário (Jesus de Pereira) 10 152*; 25 299
El Paraíso 19 385; 29 159, 829; 30 447
temple 29 165
El Pardo *see* PARDO, EL
El Paso *see* PASO, EL
El Pedregal *see* EL PEDREGAL
Elphin (Highland) 26 688
Elphinstone Fleeming, Clementina *see* HAWARDEN, CLEMENTINA, Viscountess
El Portón *see* EL PORTÓN
El Pueblo de Nuestra Señora La Reina de Los Angeles *see* LOS ANGELES
El Purgatorio *see* EL PURGATORIO
El Quiché *see* EL QUICHÉ
El Retiro 12 125
El Rosario *see* ROSARIO, EL
Elsa, Juan Francisco 8 234
El Salvador 10 *153*, 153–5*; 21 177; 29 123
architecture 10 153–4
churches 10 *154*
painting 10 154
pottery 10 154
roofs 10 153
sculpture 10 154–5
Els Antigors 3 105
Elsässer, Martin 29 874
Elsässer, Sigmund 13 912
Els Cavalls 29 365
Elscheid, Nikolaus 7 593; 10 155*
Elsden, William 7 532; 8 75; 10 155–6*; 20 32
Else, Joseph 23 259
Elsevier 33 743
Elseviers geïllustreerd maandschrift 24 449
Els Evolucionistes 10 909
Elsheimer, Adam 10 156–61*; 11 735; 16 668, 671; 26 772; 32 194
attributions 3 386; 13 223; 29 528; 32 74; 33 263
collaboration 17 886
commentaries 27 726
groups and movements 30 456
methods 24 493
patrons and collectors 4 567; 8 209; 9 311; 14 682; 18 150, 796; 26 279
pupils 13 222
reproductive prints by others 10 391; 13 222; 24 236; 25 606
teachers 27 228; 31 526

Elsheimer, Adam—cont.
works **7** 814; **10** *157*, *158*, *159*, *160*; **12** 389; **18** 708; **24** VII1; **27** 816
Elsing (Norfolk), St Mary the Virgin **4** 692
Elsinore *see* HELSINGØR
Elsken, Ed(ward) van der **10** 161*; **22** 853
Elsley, Thomas, & Co. **11** 120
Elsloo **25** 500
parish church **13** 115
Elsloo, Master of **13** 115; **22** 857
Elsmaer, Wouter van der **32** 725
Elsmdale Pottery **5** 581
Elsner, Jakob **10** 161–2*
works **10** *162*
Elso, Juan Francisco **8** 229
Elsom, C. H. **30** 516
Elstermann, Kristoffer **30** 102
Elstrack, Renold **10** 162–3*, 248
Elsworth, L. A. **32** 792
Elsworth, William **31** 652
Elte, Harry **4** 221; **10** 163*; **17** 548
El Tejar, Recoleta de la Merced **9** 711
Elten, Hendrik Kruseman van *see* KRUSEMAN VAN ELTEN, HENDRIK
Eltham (Kent)
Eltham Lodge **4** 786; **10** 275
Eltham Palace **6** 407; **10** 163–4*; **14** 75
Great Hall **10** *163*, 163–4
El Tigre *see* EL TIGRE
El Tocuyo *see* EL TOCUYO
Elton, Edmund **10** 312
Elton Hall (Cambs) **25** 639
Eltzner, Adolf
works **14** *141*
Eluard, Gala **8** 465; **30** 17, 21
Eluard, Paul **10** 164*; **16** 808
collaboration **10** 467; **19** 82
collections **24** 369
groups and movements **8** 438, 439, 605; **24** 405; **30** 17, 18, 19, 20, 21, 22
interior decoration **10** 467
personal collection **1** 439
works **3** 673; **10** 467, 838; **20** 414; **21** 709; **24** 726, 801; **27** 799; **30** 20
illustrated **3** 450
Elura *see* ELLORA
Eluru **15** 684
Elvas **10** 164–5*; **25** *288*
Aqueduto das Amoreiras **10** *165*
architecture **25** 289
S Domingos **10** 164; **25** 289, *289*
Elvaston Castle (Derbys) **31** 151
Yew Garden **31** *150*
El Vegón *see* EL VEGÓN
Elven, Martinus Gerardus Tetar van **19** 116
Elven, Pierre Henri Tétar van **4** 306
Elvery, Beatrice **31** 229
Elvetham Hall (Hants) **8** 48; **32** 245
El Viejón *see* EL VIEJÓN
Elvino, Bernardino **7** 777
El Viso, Marqués di Santa Cruz a *see* SANTA CRUZ A EL VISO, MARQUÉS DI
Elwell, Chip **20** 609; **29** 628
Elwell, Francis Edwin **31** 612
Elwin, Verrier **2** 305
Elwood Studio **29** 117
Ely (Cambs) **10** *225*
bronzes **27** 87
Cathedral of the Holy Trinity **1** 723; **3** 708; **4** 63; **10** 165–8*, *166*, 228; **13** 54–5; **15** 32; **18** 827; **19** 59–60; **20** 576; **21** 839; **26** 588; **30** 729
bosses **29** 659
capitals **10** *169*; **29** *659*
Chantry Chapel of Bishop Alcock **13** 84; **32** 89
Ely (Cambs)
Cathedral of the Holy Trinity—cont.
chantry chapels **10** 168*
choir **10** *167*, 168*
choir-stalls **7** 191
clerestory **30** *729*
corbels **7** 837
embroidery **2** 83
galilee porch **10** 167*; **12** 5
gate-house **12** 175
Labyrinth **18** 585
Lady Chapel **2** 295; **6** 458; **7** 277; **8** 611; **10** 168*, 228, 260, 261; **12** 497; **13** 54, *54*, 82, 183; **18** 621, 622; **24** 465
mouldings **22** 221
Octagon **8** 611; **10** 167–8*, 260; **32** 94
piers (ii) (masonry) **24** 751
pinnacles **24** 826
plate **2** 66
presbytery **9** 670; **10** 167*, *167*; **13** 45
Prior Crauden's chapel **7** 275; **30** 501
Prior's Door **10** *169*; **26** 612
restorations **13** 200
sculpture **10** 168–70*, 260; **26** 611, 613, 630
spire **29** 413
throne **30** 778
tomb of a Bishop of Ely **31** *122*
tomb of Bishop Nigellus **31** 122
tracery **31** 271
vaults **32** 91, 92, 93
wall paintings **13** 134
Sextry Barn **30** 853
Ely, Reginald of *see* REGINALD OF ELY
Ely, W. T. **33** 565
Elymais **1** *849*; **10** 133, 170–72*; **15** *901*, 908
coins **1** 889
rock reliefs **15** 917
see also IRAN, ANCIENT
Elys (family) **23** 251
Elyssa **5** 890
Elzner & Anderson **28** 833
Em, David **7** 681
Ema (people) **15** 775
ema see under JAPAN → *ex-votos*
Emae **25** 181
émail see under PIGMENTS → types
émail de plique see ENAMEL → techniques → cloisonné
emakimono see under SCROLLS → types
Emalı **19** 838
Emami, Karim **27** 810; **33** 634
Emanuel, Max, & Co. **19** 719
Emanuel-Philibert, 10th Duke of Savoy (*reg* 1553-80) **28** *2*, 4–5*
architecture **23** 745, 746; **25** 226; **31** 439
ceramics **11** 268
paintings **2** 379; **20** 377
sculpture **25** 576
Emanuel-Philibert, Viceroy of Sicily **9** 478; **28** *2*, 8*
Emanuels, Roy **30** 15
Emar *see under* MASKANA
Ema Saikō **33** 322
Embaros, Hagios Georgios **8** 156; **25** 334
Embekke Temple **29** 450, 477
wood-carvings **29** *478*
Embera **7** 602
Emberton, Joseph **10** 173*; **15** 885; **21** 783; **25** 741
Embil, Jorge de *see* OTEIZA (EMBIL), JORGE (DE)
emblemata *see under* MOSAICS → types
emblem books **4** 358, 359; **10** 173–6*, 725; **15** 83, 150
Belgium **32** 115
Britain **10** 175
emblem books—cont.
Christianity **10** 175
England **20** 478
France **10** 174, 175
Italy **1** 656; **10** 173
Netherlands, the **6** 88
see also PATTERN BOOKS
emblems **10** 173; **14** 416; **15** 149
Belgium **14** *619*
Brazil **8** 231
Cuba (Caribbean) **8** 231
Egypt, ancient **14** *407*
France **10** *174*
Haiti **8** 231
Islamic **14** 427–8; **23** 562–3
Italy **10** 174; **27** 61, *61*, 62
Kongo **8** 231
Luba **19** 741–2*
Netherlands, the **10** *175*
Rome, ancient **26** 750; **27** 61, *61*, 62
Trinidad and Tobago **8** 231
Emborio **10** 177*; **13** *363*, 382; **21** 555; **30** 713
embossing **10** 177–8*; **17** 275, 276
historical and regional traditions
China **7** 116
Etruscan **10** 587
Germany **24** 55
Ireland **16** 33
Italy **10** 587
Japan **17** 275
Mongolia **21** 878
Netherlands, the **22** 888, *889*
Tibet **30** *840*
uses
book covers **4** 354
gold **22** *889*
lead **10** 177
leather **10** 177; **19** 2, *2*
metalwork **21** 878
paper **7** 116; **10** 177; **16** 33; **24** 55–6
prints **10** 178, *178*; **17** 275
silver **22** 888; **30** *840*
wallpaper **10** 177
embrasures **21** 546
Embriachi (family)
workshop **10** 178–80, *179*; **13** 176; **16** 723
see also UBRIACHI
Embriachi, Baldassare **10** 178
Embriachi, Baldassare di Simone d'Aliotto degli **10** 178; **24** 286
Embriachi, Benedetto **10** 180
Embriachi, Lorenzo d'Antonio di Messer Manfredi degli **10** 178, 180
Embroidered Foliage, Master of the **20** 660*
works **5** 46; **20** *660*
embroiderers' guilds *see under* GUILDS → types
embroidery **10** 180–83*; **14** 425; **18** 588; **30** 563
historical and regional traditions
Afghanistan **1** 209–10
Africa **1** *229*, 295, 296, 299, 349
Algeria **16** 448
Anglo-Saxon **2** 83, *84*
Armenia (Europe) **2** 442–3, *443*
Austria **2** *823*, 823–5*, *824*
Azerbaijan **2** 901*
Bangladesh **3** 168*
Belgium **3** 608–10*, *609*; **10** II2
Buddhism **7** 45, *47*, *49*; **17** *306*; **21** 877
Bulgaria **5** 161
Burma **5** 248*
Byzantine **9** *668*, 668–9
Central Asia, Western **6** 248, 250–51*, 252; **16** 451
China **7** 44–5, *47*, 49, *49*, *50*, 50–51, *51*, *53*, 78, *78*, 144, 145
Qing period (1644-1911) **10** I1
Christianity **16** 760
Croatia **8** 180
Cyprus **8** 366
embroidery
historical and regional traditions—cont.
Czech Republic **8** 420–21*
Denmark **8** 753, 755–6*
Early Christian (*c*. AD 250-843) **9** 668–9
Egypt **16** 432; **28** 716
Egypt, ancient **10** 75–6*
England **4** 351; **10** 353–4*, *354*; **13** *194*; **14** 425, *426*
Anglo-Saxon **2** *84*
Arts and Crafts Movement **10** *182*
chinoiserie **7** 167
Gothic **30** *541*
Romanesque **26** 703
11th cent. **3** *427*; **8** *258*; **9** *255*
18th cent. **9** 493
France **11** 647–8*, *648*; **13** 195
Franciscan Order **11** 712
Georgia **12** 331*
Germany **10** *181*; **12** 462–3*, *463*, 464; **23** *337*
Gothic **10** *181*; **13** *194*, 194–7*; **26** *721*; **30** *541*
Greece **9** *668*; **13** 355–7
Hausa **14** *231*, 231–2; **23** 127
Hinduism **15** 548
Hungary **10** II1; **15** 11–12*, *11*
Iceland **15** 73*, *74*
India, Republic of **15** 175–6, *176*
Indian subcontinent **10** I2; **15** 548, 674–6*, *675*, 681, 717, 722, 736, *736*; **21** 717; **25** 316
Indonesia **15** 795
Iran **16** 450–51
Iraq **16** 433–4
Ireland **16** 34
Iroquois **22** 647
Islamic **1** *229*; **16** 124, *430*, 431, 432, 433–4, 448, *448*, 450–51, 459–60, *460*; **28** 716; **31** 20
Italy **13** 195; **16** 758–60*, *759*; **27** *693*
Jainism **15** 674
Japan **14** 429; **17** *306*, 308*, 313, 314, *314*, 315, *316*, 355, *374*; **30** VII2
Jordan **16** *460*
Korea **18** 379*
Kyrgyzstan **18** *569*
Macedonia (ii) (former Yugoslavia) **19** 885*
Malaysia **20** 176
Mali **20** 198
Mande **1** 300
Mesoamerica, Pre-Columbian **21** 261
Mexico **21** *394*
Mongolia **21** 877*
Morocco **16** 448, *448*
Native North Americans **22** *623*, 644*, 645–7*, *645*, 648
see also QUILLWORK
Netherlands, the **13** 196; **22** 897–9*
Nigeria **1** *229*; **14** *231*
Ottoman **16** *460*
Pakistan **23** 802
Paracas culture **24** *89*
Peru **24** 513
Philippines **24** 624
Poland **25** 132
Portugal **25** 316*
Prehistoric art **8** 753
Rhodes (island) **13** *356*
Romanesque **15** 11; **26** 703
Romania **26** 720–21*, *721*
Russia **27** 430–31
Scotland **28** 264–5*, *265*
Serbia **28** 457–8*
Sicily **16** *430*
Slovakia **28** 856*
South America, Pre-Columbian **24** *89*
Spain **13** 195; **29** 349–50*
embroidery
historical and regional traditions—cont.
Sumatra **15** 795
Sweden **30** 115*
Switzerland **30** *150*, 150–51*
Thailand **30** 625, *625*, *626*
Tibet **30** 846
Trinidad and Tobago **2** 146
Turkmenistan **31** 460
Ukraine **31** 564
United States of America **31** 658
materials
appliqué **3** 610; **6** 250; **10** *182*; **16** 759
beads **1** 296; **3** 442; **12** 462, 463; **13** 194; **22** 648
cambric **12** 463
canvas **10** 353
coral **12** 462; **15** *11*
cotton **6** 250; **10** *182*; **12** 463; **17** 355
enamel **13** 194
fustian **10** 353
gems **2** 824; **3** 609; **6** 250; **13** 194; **29** 349
glass **12** 462
gold **2** *823*, *824*; **3** 609, *609*; **7** 50; **12** 463; **13** 194
hemp **10** *182*
inks **7** 50
leather **7** 50
linen **3** *609*; **9** 668; **10** 181, 353; **12** 462, 463; **13** 194, *356*; **15** 12, *74*; **16** *448*, 760; **27** *693*; **28** 264, *265*; **30** *150*, *541*
metal **3** 610; **30** 540
mirrors **21** 717
pearls **3** 609, *609*; **9** 668; **10** II2; **12** 462; **13** 194; **15** 12; **25** 132; **29** 349
sapphires **3** *609*
satin **10** 353
silk **10** 181
Armenia (Europe) **2** *443*
Austria **2** 824
Belgium **3** 609, *609*, 610; **10** II2
Canada **22** *645*
China **7** 44, 45, *49*, 50, *50*, *51*
Early Christian and Byzantine **9** 668
England **10** 353; **30** *541*
France **11** *648*
Germany **10** *181*; **12** 462, 463, *463*; **23** *337*
Gothic **13** 194
Greece **13** *356*
Hungary **15** 12
Italy **16** 760; **27** *693*
Morocco **16** *448*
Scotland **28** 264, *265*
Spain **29** 349, *349*
Switzerland **30** 151
Uzbekistan **6** 250
silver **2** *824*; **12** 463; **13** 194; **15** *11*; **30** *541*
silver-gilt **15** *11*; **30** *541*
threads **10** 181, *181*; **17** 308; **30** 540
topaz **3** *609*
velvet **6** 250; **10** 181, 353; **13** 194; **15** *11*, 12; **29** *349*
wool **10** 353; **11** *648*; **12** 462–3; **15** *74*; **28** 265; **31** 658
types
Assisi **16** 760
Berlin woolwork **2** 767; **31** 658
blackwork **22** 898; **32** 814
broderie anglaise **10** 182; **28** 265
canvaswork **27** 316
cikan **15** 675–6
couching **3** *609*; **6** 250; **30** *567*, 567
count-stitch **7** 45
crewelwork **22** 898; **28** 265; **31** 658
Dresden work *see point de Saxe*

embroidery
types—cont.
false **22** *646*, *647*, 657, 658, 663, *663*
Hedebo **8** 755
Kells **16** 34
machine **30** 151
Marlfield **16** 34
Mountmellick **16** 34
needle-painting **2** 824; **10** 181; **22** 898, *898*
opus anglicanum **10** 181; **13** 195, 196; **14** 425; **23** 460–61*, *461*; **30** 542; **32** 389
opus teutonicum **10** 181; **12** 462
see also whitework
or nué **3** 609, *609*; **10** 181; **16** 759, *759*; **29** 349, *349*
petit point **7** 45
point de Dresde see point de Saxe
point de Saxe **12** 463
whitework **10** 181
Belgium **3** 609
China **7** 53
England **10** 354
Italy **16** 760
Netherlands, the **22** 898
Scotland **28** 265
Switzerland **30** 151
see also opus teutonicum
uses
antependia **29** *349*
aprons **7** 145
bags **18** *569*
beds **10** *354*
blankets **22** *623*
book covers **4** 351
carpets **5** 830–31*
chasubles **15** 11
cloaks **15** 736, *736*
dress
Africa **1** 295, 349
Belgium **3** 609
Central Asia, Western **6** 250–51, 252
China **7** 50, 78, *78*
Islamic **16** 459–60
Italy **16** 760
Japan **17** 314
dresses **10** III; **15** *11*; **16** *460*
epitaphioi **9** *668*
felt **10** 873
hangings **15** *675*; **16** 760
headcloths **20** 176
leather **1** 299
manuscript covers **15** 548
mats **15** 681
patchwork **10** 354
pillows **15** 795
pouches **22** *647*
quilting **10** 353
robes **7** *50*; **10** I1; **30** VII2
rugs **27** 316
shawls **15** 676
silk **28** 716
skirts **30** *626*
tents **15** 717
tunics **1** *229*; **21** *394*; **30** *626*
turbans **30** *626*
vestments (ecclesiastical) **3** 609, 610; **13** 196; **16** *759*; **25** 316
see also NEEDLEWORK; SAMPLERS
Embrun, Cathedral of Notre-Dame **11** 627
embu (effect) **10** 183*
Embu (Kenya)
shields **1** *412*
Embury, Aymar, II **10** 183*; **23** 43
Emch, Peter **30** 135
Emden
railway station **25** 856
Rathaus **12** 367
Emden, Hans van *see* STEENWINCKEL, HANS VAN (i)
Emden, Leendert Claesz. van
works **1** *811*
Emden, Walter **6** 415; **30** 679
Emele, Jakob **12** 369, 372; **33** 671
emerald green *see under* PIGMENTS → types
Emerald Mound **30** 449
emeralds **12** 268, 270, I
historical and regional traditions
Colombia **7** 600, 610; **12** 269; **29** 155
Egypt, ancient **10** 33
Indian subcontinent **6** 556; **12** 252, 253, *253*
Islamic **12** 253; **16** *542*
Ottoman **16** *542*
Peru **29** 155
Sicán culture **29** 155
South America, Pre-Columbian **29** 155
Spain **17** *523*
Turkey **16** *542*
uses
bodice ornaments **17** *523*
canteens **16** *542*
chess sets **6** 556
jewellery **10** 33; **17** 519, 521
monstrances **7** 610
Emeric, King of Hungary (*reg* 1196-1204) **14** 903
Emeric-David, Toussaint-Bernard **10** 183–4*
collaboration **2** 165; **28** 474
works **8** 542; **11** 674; **12** 728
Emericzy, János **3** 224
Emerillon **11** 758
Emerson, E. **10** 669
Emerson, James **4** 685
Emerson, P(eter) H(enry) **8** 579; **10** 184–5*; **24** 669, 738
Emerson, Ralph Waldo **18** 714; **19** 791
Emerson, William (1843-1924) **10** 185*
works **1** 648; **4** 289; **10** 495
Emerson, William (*fl* 1940) **24** 325
Emerson, William Ralph **5** 418; **10** 185–6*
assistants **1** 146
groups and movements **3** 269; **25** 806; **28** 604
staff **17** 897
works **5** *419*; **15** 542
emery **12** 786; **16** 859; **21** 241, 259; **22** 698; **29** 706
Emery, Harold **29** 116
Emery, Irene **29** 178
Emery, Marc **23** 119
Emery, Mary **7** 326
Emery, Michel Particelli, Sieur d' **6** 417; **11** 357; **13** 878; **19** 145; **32** 738
Emery, Walter Bryan **10** 81; **27** 811
Emery Roth & Sons **23** 43
Emes, Alison *see* GERNSHEIM, ALISON
Emes, Rebecca **10** 334
Emes, William **8** 281
Emesa *see* HOMS
Emili, I. **8** 177
Emilie Bell **3** 626; **18** 347
Emirates Fine Art Association **31** 585
Emirgan **16** 271
Sabancı Museum **31** 456
Emishi (Japan) *see* AINU
Emishi (719-90) *see* SAEKI NO EMISHI
Emiya **17** 282
Emlâk Kredi Bank **16** 588
Emlar, Selma **16** 611
Emly Shrine **15** 872; **28** 630, *630*
Emma, Queen of England *see* ELFGYFU, Queen of England
Emma Lake **5** 568, 569, 592
Emmaus Cycle, Master of the **19** 829
Emmens, Jan Ameling **10** 176
Emmerich
St Aldegundis **13** 114
St Martin **8** 223
St Paul **26** 574
Emmerich, D. G. **11** 778
Emmerich, Julius **3** 794
Emmerich, Paul **3** 796; **20** 912–13
Emmerick, R. E. **6** 320
Emmerisch, Richard **32** 759
Emmes, Thomas **10** 393
Emmet, Robert **16** 33
Emmett, John T. **12** 775
Emmett, Maurice **29** 58
Emmett, William **11** 424
Emmichhoven, F. W. Zeylmans van *see* ZEYLMANS VAN EMMICHHOVEN, F. W.
Emmons, Alexander Hamilton **7** 284
Emmons, Donn **33** 428
Emmons, Nathaniel **4** 477
Emmons, Thomas **4** 479
Emokpae, Erhabor **18** 639; **23** 138
Emona *see* LJUBLJANA
Emond, Pierre **5** 572
Emonts (family) **3** 588
Emonts, Gillis **25** 845
Emonts, Johann **25** 845
Emonts, Peter **25** 845
Emo Park **16** 9
emotion **7** 571; **8** 788; **10** 692; **33** 462
Empain, Edouard **2** 124; **5** 400; **9** 764
Empain, Louis **8** 63
Empel, Cornelis van **2** 540
Emperaire, Achille **6** *367*
Emperor's Carpets **16** 475
Emperor tazze *see* ALDOBRANDINI TAZZE
Empire Art Loan Collections Society **29** 122
Empire Marketing Board **7** 377, 652
Empire State Building *see under* NEW YORK → skyscrapers
Empire style **10** 187*; **22** 740; **29** 806
art forms
architecture
France **4** 302; **11** 256, 258, 519, *519*
Russia **27** 375; **29** 554
Turkey **16** 227
frames **11** *396*, 396–7*, 411–13, *412*, *460*, 461
furniture
Cuba (Caribbean) **8** 235
Denmark **8** 745
France **11** *598*; **24** *389*
Germany **12** 426
Netherlands, the **1** 813
interior decoration **10** *186*; **23** 209; **24** 388; **31** 619
metalwork **11** *108*
painting **8** 554
sculpture **4** *301*
regional traditions
France **24** 387; **25** 651
Empire style, Second *see* SECOND EMPIRE STYLE
Empoli
Baptistery **20** *554*
Collegiata **4** 505
glass **16** 740
S Stefano **20** 553–4
Empoli, Jacopo da **10** 187–90*; **16** 673
assistants **30** 798
patrons and collectors **5** 179
pupils **11** 56
works **10** *188*, *189*; **11** 188; **29** 666
Emporiae **10** 190*; **26** *908*; **29** *259*
architecture **26** 904
houses **26** 904
pottery **32** 53
trade **10** 592
Emporio *see* EMBORIO
Emporion *see* EMPORIAE
Emporium **24** 448
empreinte en pâte see PASTEPRINTS
empreinte veloutée prints *see* PRINTS → types → flock
Empresa de Producciones Varias *see* EMPROVA
Empresas Eléctricas **24** 515
EMPROVA **8** 236
Empthusen, Pieter von **14** 469
Empúries *see* EMPORIAE
Empùries, Enric, Comte de **3** 218
Empúries, Master of *see* AMPURIAS, MASTER OF
Empythion **9** *555*, 556
Emrick, Doris **19** 60
Ems, Rudolf von *see* RUDOLF VON EMS
Emshi Tepe **1** 190
Emst, Hamm and Remscheid **17** 853
emu eggs *see under* EGGS → types
Emulation, L' **3** 44; **5** 25; **24** 427, 439
emulsion paint *see under* PAINTS → types
emulsions **9** 493; **10** 191*; **24** 651, 656, 669
cliché-verre **7** 432
film **24** 651
grounds **10** 191; **13** 706*, 707
painting **10** 191
photography **9** 490; **24** 648, 651, 653, 656, 659, 669
En **29** 275; **33** 308
enamel **10** 192–6*; **14** 418, 419, 425
conservation **10** 195–6*
historical and regional traditions
Austria **2** *818*, 818, *820*, 823
Belgium **3** 596; **5** *213*; **26** 692–3*, *693*; **30** 408
Buddhism **7** 68
Byzantine **9** 623, *633*, *645*, 659–63*; **12** V2; **15** I; **16** 750; **32** *212*
Carolingian **5** 806
Celtic **6** 155, *155*
Central Asia, Western **6** 258
China **6** 557, 872, 905, 907, 909, 910, 911; **7** 68, *79*, 79–80*, 86, 109, 111, 112, 132, *133*, 146; **17** 513
Song period (AD 960-1279) **6** 872
Czech Republic **8** 407, *407*, 409, 410, *412*, *414*; **12** VI1
Denmark **8** 752; **26** 694*
Early Christian (*c.* AD 250-843) **9** 659–63*
Egypt **16** 520, *520*
Egypt, ancient **10** 32
England **10** 192, 346–7*; **14** 418, 855
Gothic **10** 322, 344; **13** 170
Romanesque **10** 322; **26** 694*
14th cent. **10** *323*
16th cent. **27** *159*
18th cent. **10** 318, *318*, *347*
France **11** 606, 629–31*
Art Nouveau **17** III1
Celtic **6** *155*
Gothic **11** 614–15, 634; **13** 158, *158*, 167–8, *168*, 169, *169*, 170, *170*
Louis XVI, King of France (*reg* 1774-92) **11** 633
Renaissance Revival **17** III2
Romanesque **7** 720; **26** 691–2*, *692*
13th cent. **14** *418*
14th cent. **11** 615
15th cent. **24** *146*
16th cent. **6** *143*
17th cent. **11** *634*
18th cent. **4** *601*; **11** 632, *633*
Georgia **12** *329*, 329–30*
enamel
historical and regional traditions—cont.
Germany **8** *201*; **10** *113*; **12** *431*, 438, 439, *439*, *445*, 445, 447, 451, 456–7*; **26** *146*; **33** *114*
Gothic **13** 169
Ottonian **4** III
Romanesque **26** 693–4*
Gothic **10** 322, *323*; **11** 614–15; **13** 134, 158, *158*, 167–70*, *168*, *169*, *170*, 194; **32** *213*
Greece, ancient **10** 192; **13** *599*
Hungary **13** 170; **15** *6*, 10, *10*
India, Republic of **15** 174
Indian subcontinent **6** 556; **15** 707, 710–12*, *711*, 723; **16** 515, III2
Insular art **15** *872*
Iran **16** 410*, *410*, *426*, 515–16, *516*
Ireland **15** *872*
Islamic **2** 575; **12** IV1; **16** 410*, *410*, *426*, *504*, 514–16*, *516*, 520, *520*, *521*
Italy **2** *454*; **12** VIII3; **16** *746*, 750*; **26** *144*; **30** *497*; **32** *201*, *212*, *213*
Byzantine **16** 750
Gothic **13** 168, 169
Roman **27** *76*
Japan **17** 242, 256, *263*, 263–4*, 377–9*, 386; **18** *554*, *555*; **23** *196*
Jesuit Order **7** 79
Korea **17** 377; **18** 359*
Laos **18** 776
Mongolia **21** 877
Morocco **16** *504*
Ottoman **16** 516
Ottonian **4** III
Poland **13** 170; **25** *127*, 128; **26** 687
Portugal **25** 312
Prehistoric **25** 541, 547
Romanesque **7** 720; **10** 322; **26** *146*, 687, 691–4*, *692*, *693*
Rome, ancient **27** *76*, 78*
Russia **10** *721*; **27** 212, *415*, *419*, *421*, 426–7*
Scotland **28** *263*
Spain **2** *454*; **13** 169; **14** 419; **16** *504*, 515; **26** 691–2*; **29** 334, *336*, *346*
Switzerland **25** 547; **30** *145*, 148
Syria **16** 520, *520*, *521*
Islamic **12** IV1
Thailand **30** 611, 632*
Turkey **2** 575; **9** *633*; **16** 515
United States of America **4** *480*; **31** *636*
Vietnam **32** 485
materials
antimony oxides **10** 192
brass **7** 79
bronze **7** 68
carnauba wax **33** 1
cobalt oxides **10** 192
copper **6** 905; **7** *70*, 79, *79*, 812; **9** 659, 663; **10** 192; **13** 167, 170; **15** 712*
copper oxides **10** 192
flint **10** 192
glass **13** 134; **17** 386; **25** 547
gold **7** 68, 79; **9** 659, *659*, *660*, *662*, *663*; **10** 192; **12** 866; **13** 168, 170; **15** 707, 710–12*
gold leaf **10** 195
gold oxides **10** 192
iron **6** 905; **7** 80
nitric acid **10** 192
oils **10** 192
platinum **10** 192
potash **10** 192
red lead **10** 192
sand **10** 192

enamel
materials—cont.
silver 7 79; 10 192; 13 168; 15 707, 711, 712*
soda 10 192
sulphuric acid 10 192
uranium oxides 10 192
varnishes 32 2
technical examination 30 407–8*
techniques
basse taille 10 194*; 21 328
England 10 322, 323, 346; 13 170
France 2 112; 10 III1; 11 614, 615, 629, 631; 13 169, 169
Germany 12 456, III2; 13 169
Gothic 10 323, III1; 11 614, 615; 13 134, 163, 163, 168–70*, 169
Italy 13 163, 163, 169, 775
Japan 17 378
Spain 13 169
Sweden 30 112, 112
champlevé 10 193–4*; 21 328; 23 98, 98
Belgium 10 IV2; 26 682, 693
Byzantine 9 659, 661, 663
China 7 27, 68; 10 193
Early Christian (c. AD 250-843) 9 661
England 10 322, 346
France 11 629; 13 167–8, 168; 26 692
Gothic 10 193; 13 167–8*, 168
Indian subcontinent 15 710, 712
Insular art 28 630
Ireland 28 630
Italy 13 168
Japan 17 377
Romanesque 10 194, IV2; 26 692, 693
cloisonné 10 193*; 21 328
Anglo-Saxon 2 79; 17 IV1; 30 44, 44
Byzantine 4 IV2; 8 203; 9 653, 657, 658, 659–63, 660, 662, 663; 10 193
China 7 68–71*, 69, 70, 112; 10 193, III2
Cyprus, ancient 8 352, 352
Early Christian (c. AD 250-843) 9 653, 659
Egypt 16 515; 17 III1
England 10 346; 17 IV1
France 11 614; 13 168; 21 163
Germany 21 502
Gothic 11 614; 13 161, 168*
Hungary 9 662; 13 161; 15 10
Indian subcontinent 10 193
Iran 16 515
Islamic 10 193; 16 514–15; 17 III1
Italy 8 203
Japan 17 377, 378, 379
Merovingian 21 163
Migration period 21 502, 503
Russia 10 193; 27 426
Spain 16 515
Syria 16 515
Ukraine 31 562, 562
émail de plique see cloisonné
engraving 13 168
en résille sur verre 10 194, 195*
en ronde bosse 10 194*, 404*; 17 519
England 10 193, 323, 346
France 10 193, 194; 11 615; 13 170
Gothic 11 615; 13 170*, 170
filigree
Byzantine 9 659, 659
Early Christian (c. AD 250-843) 9 659, 659
Gothic 13 170*
Hungary 15 10
Russia 27 421
gilding 10 193
guilloche 10 IV3; 11 630

enamel
techniques—cont.
moriage 17 378
painted 7 814; 10 195*
China 10 195
England 7 814; 10 195; 29 809
France 11 630, 630; 13 170; 19 397; 24 710
Gothic 13 170*
Mexico 28 784
Netherlands, the 10 195; 28 739
Sweden 28 68
plique à jour 10 194–5*, 194; 13 828; 21 328
England 10 347
France 2 112
Gothic 13 170*
Japan 17 378
Senkschmelz 9 660–63
see also cloisonné
Stuart see Surrey
Surrey 10 195*
transfer (printing) 10 195, 346, 347
Vollschmelz 9 660, 663
see also cloisonné
types
Canton enamel 7 80
opalescent 10 192
opaque 10 192, 193
Schwarzlot 12 439, 439, 788; 14 235
translucent 10 192, 193, 194, 195
transparent 10 192
uses
altarpieces 13 170; 32 213
altars 10 113; 13 168
badges 29 346
basins 10 III2; 15 6
betel sets 18 776
book covers , ; 4 III, IV2
bowls 8 412; 14 171; 27 419
boxes 4 601; 10 347, IV3; 11 630, 633; 30 112
bracelets 17 III2
brooches 15 872
cabinets (ii) (furniture) 12 456
candelabra 7 80
caskets 16 745
ceramics 6 328; 10 199; 16 515; 17 242, 256, 378; 30 611
chalices 2 378; 13 163, 169, 170
chess sets 6 556, 557
chests 7 70
clasps 30 44
clocks 12 III2
combs (hair) 7 109
crosses 8 201, 203, 414
cups 4 480; 10 323, III1; 13 170
daggers 16 516
diadems 13 599
diptychs 9 3
earthenwares 6 325; 10 306; 12 431; 16 426; 31 636
embroidery 13 194
ewers 11 615; 15 6; 29 336
flagons 6 155
flasks 7 69
frames 10 721
glass 8 407, 409; 12 788*; 16 520; 27 76
Austria 2 818, 818
Byzantine 9 645
China 7 86
Czech Republic 8 407, 410; 12 VI1
England 10 318, 318
Germany 12 438, 439, 439; 14 425
Islamic 16 515, 520, 521
Italy 12 VIII3; 32 201
Poland 25 124
Rome, ancient 27 78*
Russia 27 415
Switzerland 30 145
goblets 2 820; 10 194
hairpins 7 111

enamel
uses—cont.
hanap covers 13 168
helmets 16 504
hookas 15 711
icon covers 15 77
icons 9 623; 12 329; 15 I; 32 212
incense burners 7 68
inlays 12 445; 21 328
jars 7 69, 69; 23 196
jewellery 17 519, 522–3, 524, 525, 527, 529
China 7 112
Egypt, ancient 10 32
France 11 634; 17 II1
Germany 21 502
Hungary 15 10
Islamic 16 515
Mongolia 21 877
Prehistoric art 25 547
Scotland 28 263
Ukraine 31 562, 562
kovshy 27 421
lamps 12 IV1
medallions 33 114
metalwork 3 596; 25 547
miniatures (paintings) 14 855; 17 522
mirror-cases 2 112
mirror frames 21 720
mosaics 22 154
murals 22 333
necklaces 11 634
patens 21 163
pendants (jewellery) 10 194; 11 307; 13 170; 15 10, 10; 17 III1
plaques 13 168
porcelain 6 326, 872, 905, 907, 909, 910, 911; 7 79; 14 235; 17 263, 263–4*
pottery 6 258; 10 306; 11 606; 16 410*, 410; 32 485
pyxides (boxes) 13 167
reliquaries 31 535
Belgium 5 213; 10 IV2; 26 693
Byzantine 9 658
France 13 168, 169, 169, 170; 24 146; 26 692
Germany 13 169; 26 146
Ireland 28 630
Italy 13 169; 26 144
retables 13 169
rings 8 352
rosaries 27 159
salts 6 143
scabbards 16 516
sculpture 7 68; 13 169; 30 497
secco paintings 28 339
shrines (i) (cult) 28 630
snuff bottles 7 132, 133
snuff-boxes 2 823; 4 601; 10 346; 11 631, 632, 633; 30 112
spoons 28 739
stained glass 2 485; 29 498
statuettes 13 158
stonewares 6 872; 18 554, 555; 23 196
sword hilts 2 454
swords 2 452
tabernacles (ii) (receptacle) 13 167, 168
tazze 19 397
teapots 25 311
tiles 9 633; 30 874
trappings 25 547
vases 7 27, 79; 17 379
watches 7 444, 446, 447; 11 630; 17 522, 526
Enånger 30 76
Old Church 13 120
Enannatum I, ensi of Lagash 18 638
Enberg, Nils 11 107
Encalada, Lázaro de 29 334
en camaïeu see under PORCELAIN → techniques

Encarnación 24 91
encaustic 10 196
encaustic paintings 1 898; 10 196–9*, 196; 23 784
conservation 10 199*
historical and regional traditions
Byzantine 9 623; 10 197
Early Christian (c. AD 250-843) 9 623
Egypt, ancient 10 197, 197
England 10 198
France 6 121*
Greece, ancient 10 197; 13 393, 544; 24 3
North Africa 10 197
Rome, ancient 24 3
materials
beeswax 1 156; 33 1
casein 10 196
dammar 10 196
ivory 10 197
oils 10 196
pigments 10 196
resins 10 196
spatulas 10 197
styluses 10 197
tempera 10 196
turpentine 10 197
waxes 10 196; 33 5
uses
icons 9 623, 624; 10 197; 28 762
encaustic pottery see under POTTERY → wares
encaustic tiles see under TILES → types
enceintes 8 277; 9 553–5, 554; 21 546; 22 431
Enchin 17 43
enchiria 9 643
enciclopedia, L' 7 779
Enciclopedia dell'arte antica 4 24
Enciclopedia universale d'arte 4 24
Encina, Juan del 30 664
Encke, Erdmann 3 807; 10 200*; 33 296
Enckell, (Knut) Magnus 10 200*
groups and movements 11 96; 28 427
works 11 96; 28 427; 30 284
Enckenvoirt, Cardinal 28 334
enclosed gardens see under GARDENS → types
enclosures 25 504
encolpia 8 203
enconchado 12 915
encre de Chine see under PORCELAIN → wares
Encyclopedia of World Art 4 24; 10 212
encyclopedias 10 200–213*; 14 772; 21 5, 6
China 7 65
England 12 138
France 8 864; 22 24
Italy 20 84; 25 412
Mesoamerica, Pre-Columbian 21 233
encyclopedias of art 2 534, 559; 4 24; 10 203–13*
Britain 10 206
Byzantine 10 213
France 10 206, 209–10; 21 614
Germany 14 234
Japan 17 419
Rome, ancient 25 42
Spain 10 206
Encyclopédie d'Architecture 18 688
Endacott & Goff 12 854
Endara Andrade, Carlos 23 904
Endara Crow, Gonzalo 9 714; 10 214*
Ende see EN
Ende, Hans am 20 14; 26 394; 33 382, 383
Ende, Hermann 10 214*; 32 555
Ende, Jaap van den 8 668

Ende & Böckmann 10 214*
pupils 19 327
staff 22 386; 28 95
works 17 87; 33 698, 699
Endell, August 10 214–15*
groups and movements 2 565–6; 8 825; 12 416
pupils 19 773
staff 25 838
teachers 23 337
works 2 566; 12 376, 468
Endell, Carl Friedrich 33 417
Enden, Martin van den 4 283; 8 534
Ender, Johann Nepomuk 5 85; 14 901; 27 165
Ender, Thomas 2 796; 4 717; 10 215*; 26 414; 32 444
Endere 6 296
fortifications 21 592
Monastery 6 296
stupa 29 867
Enderle, Anton 10 215
Enderle, Johann Baptist 10 215*; 18 497
Enderlein, Caspar 10 216*; 12 453; 23 313; 24 578; 25 22
Endoios 2 679, 681; 10 425
end-papers see under PAPER → types
Endre 26 647
Church 13 120, 185, 190
Endre, Béla 13 333
Endsleigh Cottage (Devon) 33 447
Enebakk 23 224
Church 13 109; 23 228
Enebakk Master 23 228
Enenga 11 878
Enfant, Pierre Charles L' see L'ENFANT, PIERRE CHARLES
Enfants à la Bouche Ouverte, Maître des see OPEN-MOUTHED BOYS, MASTER OF THE
Enfield (Herts), Brooklyn 21 779
Enfield Fire-arms Factory 15 822
enfilades 10 216*; 21 546
En Foco 18 833
engaged columns see under COLUMNS → types
Engalière, Marius 20 473
Engebrechtsz., Cornelis 2 206; 10 216–17*; 18 520
attributions 18 520
pupils 1 166; 18 520; 19 757
works 10 217; 11 441; 19 101; 22 836; 27 256
Engedã, Agaññahu 10 573
Engel, Adolphe Charles Maximilien 8 765
Engel, Andreas 27 146
Engel, (Johann) Carl Ludwig 10 217–20*
architecture 10 218, 219; 11 92; 14 371; 19 318; 23 326, 340; 30 284
urban planning 14 371; 31 461
groups and movements 13 611
restorations by others 27 454; 28 788
works 23 340
Engel, Franz 19 338
Engel, Franz Josef 14 888
Engel, Frederic 29 158
Engel, Józef 14 896
Engelberg 11 805–6; 30 130
Engelberg, Burkhard 4 188; 10 220–21*; 20 561; 33 745, 746
assistants 14 513; 19 825; 33 745
collaboration 33 746
works 4 286; 10 221, 407; 23 204; 31 567, 568
Engelbrecht 3 413
Engelbrecht, Martin 13 897; 24 272; 29 628; 33 617
Engelgrave, Henricus 28 904
Engelhard, Bishop of Naumburg 22 691
Engelhard, H. 9 703

Engelhardt, Christian Mortiz **14** 772
Engelhardt, David **25** 435
Engelhardt, Ludwig **13** 729
Engelhart, Josef **28** 344; **32** 446
Engelhartszell porcelain factory **2** 817
Engelheart, Francis (1713-73) **10** 378*
Engelholm, Olaf **19** 281; **29** 764
Engelmann, Godefroy **10** 221*; **16** 65; **19** 483; **20** 602; **25** 615
 illustrated writings **31** 796
 methods **25** 590
 printmakers **3** 634; **4** 614; **27** 319
 works **19** 484; **25** 623
Engelmann, Paul **33** 284
Engelmüller, Ferdinand **29** 359
Engelram, Master **26** 698
Engels, Friedrich **20** 524–6, 527; **21** 777; **28** 926; **31** 723
Engels, Michel **19** 827
Engelsholm **8** 725
Enger, St Dionysius **26** 632, 683
 memorial to Count Widukind **23** 646, *647*
Enger reliquary **5** 806; **26** 144
Engerth, Eduard **33** 635
Enggano **15** 774
Enghien **3** *539*; **10** 221–2*
 Capuchin church **21** 858
 Château **25** 53
 lace **3** 610
 tapestries **10** 221–2; **30** 317
Engilberts, Jón **10** 222*; **15** 70
engineering (civil) **13** 404, 413; **28** 868; **30** 26
engineering (military) **13** 413; **21** 567
engineers **16** 143, 241; **20** 559, 573
Engineers Union **7** 182
engines (steam) **7** 765; **11** 134
engine sheds **33** 444
England **10** 223–378*, *225*; **26** *905*; **31** 585, *585*
 academies **10** 249; **19** 620
 acanthus **1** 110, 111
 acrylic **17** *529*
 advertisements **10** *420*
 aesthetics **7** 795; **24** 257; **25** 572–3
 agate **10** 347, *347*
 airports **10** *241*
 alabaster (gypsum) **1** 516, 517, *517*, *519*, 520, 707; **10** 227, 260, 261; **13** 84; **25** 183
 alabaster-carvings **1** 517–18*; **23** 258
 allegories **30** XII
 alloys **10** 341, 343; **11** *119*
 almshouses **10** 230; **19** 509
 altarpieces **1** 707; **11** 420–21; **25** 183
  diptychs **9** 4, *4*
  polyptychs **1** *519*
 aluminium **12** *610*, 613; **24** *34*
 amber **1** 761, 762
 amboyna **10** 279, 291, 297
 amethyst **17** *528*
 amulets **17** 516
 animal subjects **29** 424–6
 antiques **10** 284
 apartments **6** *409*; **7** *483*; **11** *808*
 Apocalypses **13** 136; **14** 423
 appliqué **10** *182*
 apprentices **19** 532; **20** 562
 aquatints **2** *238*; **9** *287*; **10** 252; **11** 906
 arbours **12** 126
 arches **2** *65*, 294, 295, 296; **13** 46; **14** 198; **16** *54*
 architects **2** 314–15
 architectural decorations **6** 564; **10** 227, 228; **14** *420*; **30** *504*
 architectural history **2** 64; **10** 897; **23** 860; **33** 211
 architectural models **2** 336, *337*; **23** 687
England—cont.
 architectural publications **14** 66; **22** 211
 architecture **4** 770–71; **10** 226–42*, *232*; **23** *688*; **30** 501–4, 506–7; **33** 204
  Anglo-Saxon **2** 64–7*
  brick **10** 229; **30** 365–6*
  Cistercian Order **10** 227; **13** 43–4; **26** 590
  exhibition **10** *679*
  Gothic **10** 228; **13** 35, 43–7*, 53–6*, 136; **19** 402; **31** 284
  Gothic: Decorated style **13** 54
  Gothic: Early English style **9** 669–70
  Gothic: Early Gothic **13** 43
  Gothic: Perpendicular style **10** 228–9; **13** 55; **24** 465, *466*
  Gothic: Rayonnant style **13** 47
  Gothic Revival **6** *561*
  landscape **12** 126–31
  megalithic **2** 851; **21** *41*
  military **10** 359; **19** 60; **21** 549, 564
  Modernism **19** *747*
  Norman *see* Romanesque
  prefabrication **5** 14; **26** 17, *17*, *19*, 461
  Romanesque **2** 67; **19** 600; **23** 211; **26** 587–90*
  Transitional style **31** 284
  vernacular **8** *830*, 830; **30** *896*, *897*
  Viking **32** 534
  wood **23** 809
  19th cent. **16** 53–4
  20th cent. **2** *309*; **4** *158*
 archives **2** 365, 372
 archivolts **19** *405*
 armoires **10** 288
 armorial bearings **14** *422*, 425, *426*
 armour **2** *471*, 472
 art (reproduction of works of) **26** *231*, *232*, *234*, *235*
 art criticism **26** 271
 art history **10** 376–8*; **32** 826
 artificial stone **2** *541*; **6** 9
 artists' biographies **5** 78; **10** 377
 artists' houses **2** *550*; **6** *551*
 art legislation **10** 370, 373
 art market **2** 559, 560
 art schools **10** 266; **18** 146
 ash **10** 288, 293
 assembly rooms **2** 617, 618, *618*; **4** *613*
 auctioneers **10** 677
 auction houses **2** 559, 560–61; **10** 366; **19** *585*
 auctions **2** 559, 560–61, 706; **21** 614
 avenues **12** 128
 badges **14** *419*
 baleen **23** *539*
 ballflower **3** *121*
 balustrades **10** 275, *275*
 banknotes **1** 121; **3** 180, *181*, 182
 banks **28** *906*
 banners **11** *145*; **12** 272
 baptisteries **3** 191
 barbicans **3** *209*
 barges **3** *232*, 232–3, *234*
 barns **13** *331*; **27** *126*
 barrows **20** 116
 baskets **3** 442
 bays **19** 403
 beads **25** *545*
 beadwork **3** 442
 beakers **10** *337*; **14** *763*
 beakheads **10** 259; **26** 589, 616
 beds **3** 484, 485; **10** 287, 291
  chinoiserie **7** *167*
  Renaissance **10** *289*
  18th cent. **10** *354*
 beech **10** *290*, 293, *296*
 Beer stone **29** 699
 bells **3** *627*
 belvederes **3** *689*
England—cont.
 bench-ends **24** *576*, *577*
 Bibles **4** 6
 bird's-eye views **4** 80
 blinds **10** 279
 bog oak **10** 346
 bonding **4** 779, 787
 bone china **4** 600; **10** 310
 bookbindings **4** 347, 348, 349; **12** 628; **24** 51
 bookcases **23** *547*
 book covers **4** *346*, 349, 350, *350*, 351, *351*, 352, 353–4, *353*; **12** 628; **23** *539*
 book illustrations **4** 366, 367; **10** 254, 255
  17th cent. **9** 375
  18th cent. **4** *362*; **31** *869*
  19th cent. **4** *363*, *885*; **22** *146*
  20th cent. **4** *367*
 Books of Hours **4** 369, 370; **13** *130*
 borders (manuscript) **4** *393*, 394, 395; **14** *424*
 bosses **4** 465, *465*; **13** 83, *83*
 bottles **10** *301*, *304*, *319*
 bowers **6** 407
 bowls **10** 301, *314*, *321*
 boxes **3** 442; **10** 340, *341*, 342, 347–8*, *347*; **14** *763*
 box-wood **33** I2
 bracelets **17** *528*
 brass **4** 685, 688; **10** *268*, 339, 340*, 343
  17th cent. **10** *342*
  18th cent. **10** *341*
  19th cent. **10** 343, 344
 brasses (monumental) **9** 268; **10** 260; **19** *580*
 brick **4** 770–71, *770*, *779*, 785, *785*, 786; **10** 229; **30** 365–6
 bricklaying **4** *770*, 770–71*, 779
 bridge design **26** 206; **28** 868
 bridges **4** *802*; **14** 198; **16** *52*; **19** *574*
  Neo-classicism **27** *715*
  suspension **5** *14*
 brocades **28** *717*; **30** X3
 bronze **10** 339–40; **25** *540*
  Arts and Crafts Movement **11** *256*
  Celtic **6** *161*, 161
  Gothic **13** 164
  Neo-classicism **3** *26*
  New Sculpture **23** *34*; **30** *762*
  New Sculpture (UK) **3** *367*; **11** *303*; **29** *575*
  Romanesque **10** 322
  1st cent. AD **27** *95*
  17th cent. **10** *263*
  18th cent. **27** *467*
  19th cent. **10** *267*; **11** *238*; **19** *600*; **23** *172*
  20th cent. **10** *438*; **11** *157*
 brooches **2** *80*, *595*; **10** 322; **14** 418, *427*
 buckets **10** 341
 buckles **10** 340; **21** II3
 building contractors **7** 420; **8** 248; **20** 561
 building regulations **5** 135
 bureaux **5** 191, 192–3
 burial mounds **5** 292
 busts
  Baroque **24** *753*
  Rococo **27** *243*
  17th cent. **10** *263*
  19th cent. **6** *457*; **16** *799*; **23** *190*
 buttresses **33** 209
 cabinets (i) (rooms) **10** 368; **22** 356
 cabinets (ii) (furniture) **5** 191; **9** 27; **10** *298*; **20** *468*
 cabriole legs **10** 292
 calamander **10** 279
 cameos **10** *345*; **21** II3
 candlesticks **10** *304*, *332*, 341, 343, 344; **26** *688*
England—cont.
 cane **5** 612; **10** 291; **33** 157
 canopies (ii) (textile coverings) **30** *778*
 canvas **10** 353
 capitals **10** 168, *169*; **26** 587, 615–16; **29** *659*
 capriccios **5** 687
 caps **9** 271; **18** 157
 cardboard **31** 258
 cards **7** 548; **10** *420*
 caricatures **5** 756–7*, *757*, 758–9*; **7** 648; **9** 225; **10** 252; **27** 869
  18th cent. **12** *640*
  19th cent. **10** *251*
 carnivals **5** 784, 785
 carpets **5** *836*, 837–9*, *838*, *840*, 840–41*, *841*; **10** 273, 276, 279, 357–8*, *358*; **16** 472
  warp-printed **5** *839*
 caryatids **5** *905*
 caskets **2** *81*; **5** 918; **10** *342*
 casting **22** 28
 cast iron **10** 236, 297, 748; **11** *119*; **16** 52, *53*
 castles **6** *51*, *52*, *55*, 60–61; **10** 226, 359; **21** 561, 563, 564, *569*; **33** *247*, *250*
  concentric **19** 616
  Gothic Revival **5** *194*
  mock **6** 59
  Romanesque **9** *203*; **10** 227
  15th cent. **30** *365*
  17th cent. **6** *60*
  18th cent. **12** *7*
  19th cent. **27** *656*
  20th cent. **6** *62*
 casts **6** 9
 catalogues **10** 377; **31** 276
  auctions **2** 559
  ceramics **7** 161
  collections **2** 600; **6** 77; **32** 825
  exhibitions **10** 299, 677; **21** 265
  sculpture **21** 423
 cathedrals **2** *322*; **10** 359
  Anglo-Saxon **33** *234*
  Baroque **19** *599*
  Byzantine Revival **3** *746*
  eclecticism **9** *704*
  Gothic **4** *825*; **5** *644*, *645*; **10** *167*, *673*; **13** *44*, *45*, *54*; **19** 402, *403*, *597*; **24** *545*; **27** *627*, *628*; **33** *59*, *60*, *61*, *236*, *237*, *548*
  Gothic: Decorated style **8** *611*
  Gothic: Early English style **9** *669*
  Gothic: Early Gothic **33** *62*
  Romanesque **9** *449*, *450*; **10** *166*; **12** *5*; **23** *250*, 250; **26** *588*, *589*; **27** *526*; **33** *235*
  17th cent. **19** *597*
  18th cent. **33** 445–6
  20th cent. **12** *591*
 causeways **23** 685
 cedar **10** 277, 288
 ceilings **10** 271
 cement **2** 692
 cemeteries **25** 539
 censers **13** *164*
 ceramics **6** 329, 558; **10** 281, 300*, 305–15*
  display **9** 29; **29** *221*
 chairs **5** 612; **6** 390; **10** 291, 292, *296*; **19** 592; **30** 783; **31** 682, 684–5
  armchairs **12** *626*
  Arts and Crafts Movement **2** *572*
  back stools **6** 390
  boarded seats **6** 390
  easy-chairs **6** 390
  fauteuils **6** 390
  Polyprop **8** 583
  Roman **6** 388
  sgabello **6** 390
  sleeping-chairs **6** 390; **10** 291, *291*
England
 chairs—cont.
  Sussex **6** 391; **22** *143*
  Trafalgar **27** *139*
  Windsor **14** 522–3
  Windsor (Berks; UK) **10** 293
  X-frame **10** 288, *290*
  18th cent. **10** *295*; **31** *685*
  19th cent. **22** *143*
  20th cent. **10** *300*
 chalices **10** 322, 325
 chalk **14** 544; **29** 699; **31** *527*
 chamber pots **10** 316
 chambers **6** *407*, 407
 chandeliers **6** 443; **10** 319
 chapels
  chantry **7** 282; **10** 260; **13** 84
  Gothic **5** *514*; **12** *799*
  Lady **13** *54*; **18** *621*, 621–2
  Lady chapels **7** 265
  Nonconformist **23** 193–4*, *194*
  Protestantism **7** *283*
  Romanesque **33** *542*
  20th cent. **6** *459*
 chapter houses **6** 465, *465*; **21** 839
 chasubles **14** *426*; **23** *461*; **32** 392
 châtelaines **16** *61*
 chess sets **6** 557, 558
 chests **6** 559, 560; **10** *286*, 286–7, 288
  13th cent. **10** *286*
 chests-of-drawers **8** *804*; **10** 288
 chevrons **6** *565*; **10** 259
 chimney-pieces **6** 604, *604*, 605; **10** 276; **29** *647*
 chintz **10** 276
 choir-stalls **7** *190*
 chronicles **7** 243
 chrysolite **17** *528*
 churches **2** 372; **5** 890; **10** 224, 226, 229, 232, 359; **18** 621; **23** 194; **30** 654
  Anglicanism **25** 266
  Anglo-Saxon **2** *65*, 65–6, *66*, *67*, 67; **10** 227; **21** *887*
  Arts and Crafts Movement **19** *253*
  Baroque **10** *232*; **12** *593*; **14** *256*; **33** *394*, *395*
  basilicas **33** 230
  Gothic **5** *287*; **12** *800*; **13** *46*, *55*, 55–6; **23** *685*
   Late Gothic **12** *818*, *819*
   Perpendicular style **10** *229*
  Gothic Revival **4** *215*; **5** *314*; **24** *307*; **25** *714*; **29** *765*; **30** *533*
  Methodism **21** *347*
  Neo-classicism **8** *493*
  Romanesque **10** 227–9, *228*; **12** 818; **19** *601*, *617*; **23** *685*; **26** *589*
  17th cent. **17** *636*
  19th cent. **30** *502*
 cinemas **7** 327, *328*
 cisterns **12** 126
 clasps **4** 350; **10** 322
 Classicism **7** 380
 clay **6** 325
 clerks of works **7** 420
 cloaks **9** 274
 clocks **7** 438, 439; **10** 291
 cloisters **7** 452, 453, 455, 456, *456*; **12** 799
 closets **9** 11, 14
 clubs (meeting places) **3** *282*; **7** *469*
 clunch **29** 699
 coal **10** 297
 coats **9** 284
 coats of arms **10** 328; **12** 272, 273; **14** *404*, 407, 411, 412, 413, 416, *418*, 418–19, *420*, *422*, *424*, 425, *426*, *427*
 coins **7** 533, 534, 535, 536, 537, *537*, 538; **14** 419, *419*; **19** *581*
 collages **14** *112*
 collars **7** 178

England—cont.
collections 2 559, 560; 9 17; 10 226, 362–71*; 11 140; 18 383; 19 582; 22 356
books 22 356
ceramics 16 395
drawings 9 230
ephemeral art 10 422
erotic art 10 487
imprese 15 150
painting 3 178; 28 273
photographs 10 376*
porcelain 10 276, 371
public 13 605; 20 911; 22 362
reproductions 26 226
royal 7 579; 19 582; 31 220; 33 306
sculpture 9 23–5; 13 299
19th cent. 32 748
colleges 7 566
Gothic 5 511; 7 566; 12 175
Gothick 14 255
Gothic Revival 5 316
Greek Revival 33 192
Mannerism 5 512
15th cent. 33 545
17th cent. 4 785; 23 686, 687
20th cent. 5 513
colonnades 19 573
combs (liturgical) 7 646
commodes 7 657, 659
competitions 7 665, 668, 670, 673*; 10 265
compounds 7 679
concert halls 19 577
concrete 2 600; 7 712, 712; 10 241; 28 874; 33 204–5, 205
conservation 17 209; 23 248
conservatories 5 283; 7 744, 745; 12 137, 791; 24 294
Constitutions of Masonry 20 562
copes 13 194; 30 541
copies 14 638
copings 4 769
copper 2 595; 10 322, 338*, 338, 339, 341, 343
copyright 14 638
coral 6 161
corbels 8 836
corduroy 8 35, 35
corn 31 260
cornelian 20 389
corslets 2 472
costumes 9 245; 30 654, 662*, 663*, 674–5*, 680
cotton 8 35–6, 35, 36; 9 IV2; 10 182, 356*; 21 600
county halls 31 236
court-houses 31 239
courtyards 8 65
craftsmen and artists 10 249, 289, 312; 14 636, 855–7
crests 12 272
crosiers 8 194; 10 322
crosses
altar 8 202
Anglo-Saxon 2 69; 10 322
Eleanor 2 295; 8 197–8*, 198, 611; 13 53, 81; 23 368; 25 14
High 8 195–6*; 10 259; 32 529
Romanesque 26 697
19th cent. 10 343
crowns 12 866
crucifixes 10 338
crypts 10 227; 14 501
cupboards 8 271; 10 288
cups 10 325
communion-cups 10 325
Gothic 10 323
hunt cups 27 108
Renaissance 10 326
trophies 10 334
two-handled 28 740
curtains 10 275, 279
cutlery 8 284
cypress 10 288
damask 10 274; 19 415
Davenports 5 192; 10 297
deal (wood) 10 277; 18 610

England—cont.
dealers 10 677, 679
dealing 2 559, 560; 10 362–8*
decanters 2 570; 10 318
department stores 19 576
designers 10 239
devotional images 8 836, 836
diamonds 10 345
diaper 8 857
dictionaries of architecture 24 87
dictionaries of religious art 25 714
dioramas 8 911, 911
diplomatic gifts 10 324
Diploma works 9 1–2*
disegno e colore 9 8*
display of art 9 11, 14, 16–17, 17, 18–19, 22–5, 26; 10 371
D.I.Y. 10 285
docks 9 58, 59
dolls 31 259, 260, 262
dolls' furniture 31 264
dolls' houses 31 262, 263
domes 10 232; 15 V
donjons 9 143, 144; 10 227, 359; 33 198
door fittings 10 338, 339
doors 9 154; 10 169; 14 681
doorways 7 456; 10 169; 18 50
drainage systems 10 236
drawings 9 225
architectural 12 131; 22 211
Romanticism 23 886
16th cent. 30 763
17th cent. 25 10
18th cent. 2 331
19th cent. 7 665, 668; 27 353
chalk 11 858
Gothic 13 136
ink
Art Nouveau 3 445
Neo-classicism 7 340
Neo-Romanticism 22 752
Romanticism 22 152
17th cent. 3 244, 245
19th cent. 4 87
landscape
17th cent. 9 487
18th cent. 8 95, 95, 96
19th cent. 29 877
life-drawings 19 620
literary themes 31 869
Modernism 22 56
pastel 14 549; 19 818
topographical 9 149; 22 211
17th cent. 19 540
19th cent. 10 479
20th cent. 9 II2
dress 9 244, 253, 269, 271, 278–9*, 282*, 282, 283–4*, 284, 286, 288–9
dresses 10 357; 25 821
drinking-horns 14 763
drypoints 9 308, 309
dyeing 10 356; 30 558
dyes 9 493
earthenwares 6 325; 10 301, 304, 314; 29 495; 30 877
earthworks 14 544
ebony 6 558
ecuelles 10 330
education (art) 2 524; 10 252, 371–5*; 19 165, 621
architecture 10 372, 374; 19 532; 23 782
embroidery 10 354
effigies 1 518; 9 268; 10 259–60, 338; 13 164; 19 604–5; 25 V2
electroplating 10 143
elm 10 288, 293
emblem books 20 478
embroidery 4 351; 10 353–4*, 354; 14 425, 426
Anglo-Saxon 2 84
Arts and Crafts Movement 10 182
chinoiserie 7 167
Gothic see opus anglicanum

England
embroidery—cont.
opus anglicanum 10 181; 13 194, 195, 196; 23 460–61*, 461; 30 541, 542
Romanesque 26 703
whitework 10 354
11th cent. 3 427; 8 258; 9 255
18th cent. 9 493
enamel 10 192, 346–7*; 14 418
basse taille 10 322, 323, 346; 13 170
champlevé 10 322, 346
cloisonné 10 346; 17 IV1
en ronde bosse 10 193, 323, 346
Gothic 10 322, 344; 13 170
painted 7 814; 10 195; 14 855; 29 809
plique à jour 10 347
Romanesque 10 322; 26 694*
Surrey 10 195
16th cent. 27 159
18th cent. 10 318, 318, 347
encyclopedias 12 138
engineering (civil) 28 868
engine sheds 33 444
engravings 10 247–8, 252, 317, 389, 393, 479; 14 418, 638, 675
bird's-eye views 4 81
crayon manner 8 131
Picturesque 24 742
stipple 10 252; 12 640
townscapes 19 568
17th cent. 10 230; 19 569
18th cent. 3 308, 373; 4 362; 6 65; 14 109, 856; 19 570; 27 869; 33 133
19th cent. 3 181; 10 395; 33 542
20th cent. 10 398
erotic art 10 473, 475, 476, 479, 479, 483
etchings 2 471; 10 252
Aesthetic Movement 33 140
colour 27 269
lift-ground 10 559
Picturesque 24 742
relief 7 227; 10 561
soft-ground 10 562; 11 906
17th cent. 14 684
18th cent. 4 117
19th cent. 4 885; 10 556
20th cent. 14 608
exchanges 4 822
exhibitions 9 23–5; 10 255, 677–9*; 25 715; 26 272
Etruscan 10 637
international 10 678
loan 10 678
paintings 19 589
photographs 19 424
South America, Pre-Columbian 29 221
18th cent. 10 678; 20 911
19th cent. 10 679; 20 238, 239; 32 748
20th cent. 33 744
façade decoration 10 744
factories 10 235, 748, 749; 33 205
faience (ii) (ceramics) 22 880
fans 10 781
feathers 28 581
fenders 11 119
fermes ornées 12 128
figurines 10 306, 308, 308
filigree 10 322
films 10 688
fir 10 275
fire-backs 10 340
fire-irons 11 119
fireproofing 16 52
fire-screens 10 343
firing 10 306
flagons 10 327
flint 10 227
floors 10 270, 273, 275–6, 279
fonts (baptismal) 10 338; 11 252, 253, 254, 256; 26 613

England—cont.
forks 8 285; 10 324
fortifications 21 549, 551, 561, 564, 569
forts 10 226; 14 23, 23; 21 576
hill-forts 10 226; 25 537
shore forts 21 561
foundations 28 874
fountains 12 126, 128
frames 9 16; 11 375, 375, 420–38*, 421, 422, 423, 424, 425, 427, 428, 429, 430, 431, 433, 436, 437, 455–7*
friezes 32 V1, 2
frontispieces 14 433
furnaces 12 784
furniture 2 559, 561; 10 278, 284, 285, 286–92*, 293–300*, 328; 19 5; 20 467, 468; 24 62; 28 348; 33 157, 157, 158
Gothic Revival 13 207
Neo-classicism 17 902
water-filled 10 285
18th cent. 7 171
19th cent. 19 593
furniture-makers 10 297
fustian 8 35; 10 353, 356
gables 4 786; 11 876; 30 896
galilees 9 450
galleries (iii) (narrow room) 33 306
galleries (iv) (art) 10 234, 679; 20 911
picture 9 16–17, 17, 18–19, 26; 10 677, 678; 14 539; 20 911; 22 362
sculpture 9 22, 23–5
game-boards 31 265
garden design 3 30; 12 126–31; 25 233; 30 123
gardens 12 104, 126–31*, 136–42; 14 512; 32 552
Chinese 12 131
jardins anglo-chinois 6 411; 12 131
knot gardens 12 126
landscape 26 742; 29 735
pleasure 19 619
sculpture 9 23
16th cent. 12 126
18th cent. 4 806, 876; 7 375; 12 63, 127; 27 259; 29 734; 33 132–3
19th cent. 12 137, 139; 19 820
20th cent. 12 141
garden seating 12 126, 130
garnets 10 322
garnitures 9 29; 10 309
gate-houses 12 175, 176
Gothic 4 770
14th cent. 14 420; 27 526
15th cent. 12 175
16th cent. 6 59; 10 229
gate lodges 12 176
gem-engraving 12 260, 261, 263, 263; 20 389
genealogies 12 271; 14 416
gesso 6 560; 10 292; 18 610
gilding 2 471; 6 560; 11 422, 437; 12 626, 628; 19 4, 5; 28 665
gitterns 33 I2
glass 3 442; 6 443; 10 281, 315–21*; 12 781, 787
air-twists 10 317
à la façon de Venise 10 316
Anglo-Saxon 10 322
Arts and Crafts Movement 2 570
cameo 10 320; 26 227
cased 10 319
cotton twists 10 317, 318
cristallo 10 316
crystal 10 316, 317, 318–19, 319; 19 595; 26 36–7
Crystallo Engraving 10 319
Iron Age 25 545
Pyrex 10 321
Waldglas 10 315, 316

England
glass—cont.
19th cent. 10 335; 16 54
20th cent. 8 279; 10 321
glasses 10 315, 316, 317, 317, 318
baluster-glasses 10 316–17
glazes 6 329; 10 302, 306, 312, 315; 30 681
gloves 3 442
goblets 10 315, 318
gold 10 322–30*, 331–6*, 347*, 355; 12 868; 14 419; 30 542
Anglo-Saxon 2 84; 10 322; 17 IV1
Romanesque 10 322
12th cent. 14 417
14th cent. 14 419
15th cent. 27 159
16th cent. 10 345
17th cent. 2 466; 10 350; 17 522; 28 749
18th cent. 10 347
19th cent. 17 528; 20 389
20th cent. 12 866; 17 529
gold leaf 4 353
goldsmiths 10 328, 331; 14 856
Gospel books 15 874
Gothic 17 612; 29 659
government buildings 10 237; 13 237; 17 903; 19 587; 28 909
gowns 9 274, 275, 276
granite 10 224, 227
graphite 19 540
grates 11 119
greenhouses 10 236; 12 137; 18 4
grottoes 12 127; 13 704
groves 12 126
guidebooks 10 377; 13 811; 33 132–3
guildhalls 19 567
guilds 10 287, 336; 13 822; 14 409; 19 592
gum arabic 10 356
guns 2 461–2, 464, 466, 467, 468; 14 856
gun stocks 2 461, 465, 466
ha has 4 805; 12 128
hair 10 278; 27 641
hairstyles 9 255
halls 14 75–7*
Anglo-Saxon 10 226
Gothic 14 76
Romanesque 10 227; 19 401
11th cent. 19 608
14th cent. 10 270; 14 454
15th cent. 10 163, 164
handkerchiefs 8 35
hangings 10 274, 275; 19 4, 5
hardstones 10 346
Hausmalers 14 235
headdresses 9 271, 274
helmets 2 473; 10 338; 14 412; 27 95
hemp 10 182
henges 2 850; 25 498
heraldry 10 247; 12 272, 273; 14 404, 412, 413, 417, 418, 419, 419, 420, 422, 424, 425, 426
heritage 9 374
hermitages 14 460
hill-figures 10 473; 14 544–5, 544; 31 526–7, 527
hinges 9 155
historicism 14 580
historiography 10 376–8*; 12 128
horn 10 297; 14 763
hornbooks 14 763
Hornton stone 22 57
hospitals 5 14; 10 236; 13 624; 33 385, 398
houses 2 600; 4 780; 10 229–30; 32 276
Africa 1 318
Arts and Crafts Movement 25 634
Baroque 31 860
bungalows 5 173, 174; 28 349

England
houses—cont.
cottage orné **32** 554
country **3** *283*; **8** 42–9*, *43*, *44*, *46*, *48*, *49*; **10** 230, 232, 233; **28** 896; **31** *858*, *859*, *861*; **33** *444*, *445*
Baroque **2** *307*; **6** *515*; **14** *253*; **30** *278*
Elizabethan style **28** *895*, *896*
Gothick **10** *234*; **32** *826*
Gothic Revival **5** *195*
Greek Revival **13** *610*
Neo-classicism **1** *136*; **28** *907*; **30** *386*
Palladianism **4** *612*; **7** *174*; **23** *856*
16th cent. **6** 127
19th cent. **22** *526*; **33** *12*
Egyptian Revival **10** *97*
Elizabethan style **10** *231*
Georgian style **12** 332; **19** *571*
Gothic Revival **13** *203*
Jacobean style **10** *230*
manor **6** 407; **10** 226
Modern Movement **7** *712*
Neo-classicism **2** *550*; **17** *904*
Old English style **10** *238*
Palladianism **4** *610*; **5** *538*, *539*; **10** 364; **33** *224*
prefabricated **26** 17
Queen Anne Revival **22** *810*; **28** *562*
Roman **10** 226
Romanesque **10** 227
town **10** 233; **14** 76
16th cent. **3** 30; **10** 360; **23** *246*; **32** *276*, *277*
17th cent. **32** *277*
18th cent. **23** *247*
19th cent. **12** *315*, *840*; **15** *407*; **22** *528*; **23** *259*
20th cent. **19** *821*; **32** *721*
housing **14** 613
Huguenots **14** 855–7
humanism **14** 868
hunting-lodges **10** 230
hunting scenes **29** 424, 425
iconoclasm **10** 261
iconography **10** 246–7
icons **13** *131*
illusionism **15** 139
imprese **15** 150, *150*
indigo **8** 36; **10** 356
industrial scenes **15** *830*
initials (manuscript) **15** 847
Anglo-Saxon **5** *641*
Gothic **17** *611*; **25** *677*, *807*
Insular art **19** *409*
Romanesque **15** *847*; **20** *341*, V1; **26** 663, 664; **27** *591*; **33** *239*
inlays **10** 288, 290, 291; **20** 468
inns **5** *639*
installations **19** *625*
intarsia **10** 288
interior decoration **10** 269–83*, 284–5*; **14** 856; **23** *790*
Etruscan style **10** *643*
Gothic Revival **19** *614*
Louis Revival **10** *282*
Moorish style **17** *640*; **22** *60*
Neo-classicism **1** *138*; **17** *901*; **22** *737*
Palladianism **33** *225*
Pompeian Revival **25** *193*
Regency style **30** XIV2
Romanticism **28** *908*
16th cent. **10** *271*; **14** *126*
17th cent. **9** *26*; **10** *272*, *274*, *275*
18th cent. **10** *277*, *278*; **28** *581*
19th cent. **10** 142, *280*, *283*; **14** 744, *745*; **26** 84–5; **27** *224*; **29** *646*; **30** XVI
20th cent. **10** *285*

England—cont.
iron **2** *466*; **6** 560; **9** 155–6; **10** *338*, 339, 340, 341–2; **25** *540*
16th cent. **10** *340*
ivory **2** *82*; **10** 288, *326*
ivory-carvings **16** 799; **19** 638
Anglo-Saxon **2** *81*, 82*
Gothic **13** 176*
Romanesque **7** *646*; **8** *194*; **16** *798*; **23** *539*; **26** *697*, 697–8
19th cent. **16** *799*
jack of plates **2** 472
japanning **5** 191; **7** 166; **18** 610–11*, 614; **29** 530
jet **10** 346; **17** *516*, 516–17*
jewellery **10** 344–7*; **17** 516
Anglo-Saxon **2** 79*
Iron Age **25** *545*
mourning **17** *516*, 517
16th cent. **17** 522
18th cent. **17** 525
journeymen **19** 532; **20** 560–61, 562
jugs **10** 302, *302*, 305, *314*, *335*; **14** 425; **15** *820*; **33** 341
kettles **10** 341
kilns **10** 301
king-wood **10** 291
knitting **18** 157
labyrinths **18** 584
lace **10** 355*, *355*; **18** 589, 591, 593
lacquer **6** 560; **7** *167*; **18** 615
imitation **18** 610–11*
lampblack **18** 611
lamps **30** 674
land art **10** 258; **18** 719; **19** 625
law courts **18** 886–7, *888*; **29** *766*
lay figures **18** *898*
lead **10** 264, 338; **11** 253; **18** *903*; **31** *255*
leather **4** *346*, 349, *350*, 351, *351*, 352, 353–4, *353*; **10** 275; **19** 4–5*, *4*
libraries **10** 376*; **19** 315; **22** 356; **23** 686
Baroque **12** *594*; **19** *315*
Greek Revival **28** *874*
19th cent. **19** *318*
20th cent. **33** *218*
lidos **19** 332
lighthouses **28** 868
lighting **9** 13; **10** 677; **14** 539; **30** 679
lime **10** 356
limestone **10** 224, *262*, *674*; **25** V2; **26** *614*, *615*; **29** 700
Purbeck marble **10** 224, 260; **13** 136; **29** XII
Romanesque **10** 227
linen **10** 278, 353; **19** 415, 418; **27** 693; **30** *541*
lithography **1** 121; **19** *484*, 492; **25** *590*; **31** 910
livery halls **19** 508*, *509*
lockets **17** *522*
locks **10** 342
lodgebooks **19** 532
looms **10** 357; **30** *309*, 547
lost-wax casting **12** 612; **19** 60
mahogany **5** 191, 192; **10** 292, 293, 297
mansions **30** 653, 662
manuals
architecture **22** 211; **23** 860
colour **26** 69
drawing **10** 374
gardens **12** 126, 130, 647
iconography **2** 709
interior decoration **23** 789
manuscript **20** 325
painting **3** 228; **19** 818; **31** 480
photography **26** 472
printing **25** 622; **31** 495
scenery **30** 681
urban planning **24** 186

England—cont.
manuscript illumination **15** 874–6; **28** 233
Anglo-Saxon **2** 74–8*, *76*; **10** 242–3*; **20** II; **25** 676
Arts and Crafts Movement **20** *335*
Byzantine **9** *603*
Early Christian (*c.* AD 250-843) **9** *603*
Gothic **3** *879*; **4** *237*; **7** *231*; **13** *130*, *131*, 136, 138, 140, 141–2, 147–8, 152; **17** 611, *611*, 612; **18** *703*; **20** *348*; **24** *175*, *270*; **25** *677*; **33** *200*
Insular art **15** *874*
Romanesque **5** *428*; **10** 243–4*; **26** 670–73*, 677*; **27** *528*; **33** *233*
15th cent. **19** 727
manuscripts **12** 272
maple **2** 465; **10** 297
maps **30** *318*
marble **10** 224, 262, 288, 293; **13** 44
Arts and Crafts Movement **11** *256*
Baroque **10** *264*; **24** *753*
Baroque Revival **22** *28*
Neo-classicism **5** *629*; **8** *587*; **10** *265*; **11** *164*
Rococo **27** *244*
Roman **19** *579*
12th cent. **31** *122*
13th cent. **29** XII
15th cent. **10** *260*
16th cent. **10** *262*
18th cent. **3** *184*; **4** *79*; **10** *293*; **19** *606*; **27** *468*; **28** *64*; **29** *564*; **33** *227*
19th cent. **3** *78*; **6** *456*, *457*; **12** *598*; **19** *600*; **23** *190*; **33** *100*
20th cent. **29** *566*
marbling **23** *790*; **24** 55
markets **11** 330
marks
masons' **20** 440
metalwork **10** 325, 328, 330, 331; **20** 443, 444, *444*
pewter **20** 445
marquetry **10** 297; **20** 467, 468, *468*, 469, VIII1
masonry **10** 226, 227; **20** 571, 572
masons **19** 532; **20** 560–61*, 562*
masons (master) **19** 532; **20** 561; **22** 211
masons' lodges **19** 532; **20** 561
mausolea **20** 866*, 867–8*
Baroque **14** *258*
Greek Revival **20** *868*
Neo-classicism **20** *867*; **33** *444*
mazers **25** 885
mazes **18** 585*
medals **14** 487; **20** 921*, *924*; **28** *749*; **33** 455
metal **10** 342
metalwork **10** 322–30*, 331–7*, 338–44*; **28** 576
Anglo-Saxon **2** 79–80*
Gothic **13** 163–5*
Romanesque **10** 338; **26** 687–8*, *688*
metro stations **19** 575
mezzotints **10** 252; **19** 818; **21** 415, 416–17, *417*; **28** 25; **31** 465
mills (industrial) **10** 748; **16** 52; **21** 600–601
miniatures (manuscript illumination) **33** 90
Anglo-Saxon **2** *75*, *77*; **3** *710*
Benedictine Order **3** *710*
Gothic **2** *222*; **3** *879*; **4** *372*; **13** *130*, *141*, *147*; **14** *415*; **21** *729*; **25** *807*; **28** *66*
Romanesque **4** *6*; **5** *288*; **10** *244*; **26** *670*, *671*, *672*
mirror frames **21** 721

England—cont.
mirrors **6** *153*, 161; **9** 30; **10** 276; **21** 720
back-painted **7** 87
misericords **21** 724, *724*
monasteries **9** 374–5; **10** 229, 259; **21** 834–5, 839, 841
Benedictine Order **3** 708; **21** 836, *839*, *840*
Carthusian Order **21** *841*
Cistercian Order **11** *349*, *350*; **21** *833*; **26** *380*
Dominican Order **21** *842*
Gothic **5** *638*; **11** *349*, *350*; **26** *380*
Romanesque **33** *551*
monuments
Anglo-Saxon **10** 259
equestrian **27** *467*
funerary
Baroque **10** *264*
Neo-classicism **10** *265*; **11** *163*
16th cent. **10** 261–2
17th cent. **29** *714*
18th cent. **19** *606*; **22** 45, *46*; **27** *467*; **28** *64*; **31** *128*; **33** *227*
19th cent. **6** *456*; **19** *600*; **33** *100*
hogback **32** 529
public
Neo-classicism **3** *26*
18th cent. **4** 79, *79*; **7** *340*
19th cent. **7** *673*; **10** *266*; **18** *903*; **23** *172*
20th cent. **22** *48*; **29** *566*
triumphal arches **31** *351*
mosaics **9** *568*; **29** XII
mother-of-pearl **10** 288; **24** *62*
mottes **3** 427
mouldings **10** 278; **22** 211, 213–22
moulds **10** 303, 306
mounts (porcelain) **9** 29
mugs **10** 303, *304*
museums **9** 13, 25, 30; **10** 368–71*; **22** 356, 362; **30** *504*
Greek Revival **7** *504*; **10** *234*; **28** *874*
19th cent. **4** *86*; **9** 30; **22** 362; **23** 259; **32** *905*
musical scores **14** 675
narratives **22** *523*
naturalism **22** 686
necklaces **17** *528*, *529*; **20** *389*; **25** *545*
neck rings **6** 161
needlework **21** 721
nets **10** 355; **18** 589
niches **10** 263; **13** 82
niello **2** *80*; **10** 322
nude figures **10** 265
Neo-classicism **5** *629*
New Sculpture **11** *303*; **23** *34*; **29** *575*
18th cent. **3** *184*
19th cent. **3** *78*; **8** *122*; **10** *646*; **12** *598*; **22** *52*
20th cent. **4** *670*
oak **10** 274, 277, 286, *286*, 288, *289*, 293, 297, 298; **13** *121*; **18** 610
objects of vertu **10** 344*
office buildings **10** 233, 235; **19** 506
Greek Revival **7** *503*
Neo-classicism **1** *139*
New Brutalism **28** *890*
Post-modernism **19** *578*
19th cent. **3** *533*; **28** *563*
20th cent. **14** *674*; **19** *506*; **26** *540*
ogee **23** 368
onyx **10** *345*; **29** XII
opus sectile **29** XII
orangeries **23** *471*
orders (architecture) **23** 491, 492
orders (chivalry) **7** *178*

England—cont.
ornament **23** 541, 542–4, 545, 546
overdoors **23** 678, *679*
painters **5** 656
painting **5** 656; **6** *94*; **10** 242–58*; **23** *790*; **33** *331*
Abstract art **24** *229*
allegorical **15** *81*; **26** *322*; **32** *922*
Pre-Raphaelitism **5** *267*; **15** *25*, *27*
20th cent. **29** *384*
Anglo-Saxon **2** 72*
animal subjects
18th cent. **29** *425*, *810*
19th cent. **1** *449*; **18** *722*, *723*; **32** *326*
architectural **2** *339*; **28** *648*
battle **3** 389–90, *390*
ceiling **17** *851*
colour field **10** 258
Constructivism **10** *257*
conversation pieces **7** 784, *785*, 785–7*, *786*; **10** 249; **21** 148, 149; **33** *694*, 695
18th cent. **10** *277*
Cubism **23** *104*
display **9** 16–17, *17*, 18–19, *26*; **10** *678*
drapery **9** 211
encaustic **10** *198*
fancy pictures **10** *786*; **21** 149
fresco **9** 475; **10** 277–8; **18** *644*; **30** *759*
genre **10** 250; **12** 291, 292–4*
Impressionism **29** *595*
Pre-Raphaelitism **4** *877*, *878*; **10** *253*; **21** *601*
Rococo **13** *324*
social realism **11** *74*
18th cent. **12** *293*; **22** *123*; **24** *366*; **33** *413*
19th cent. **1** *677*; **9** *756*; **10** *255*; **11** *796*; **22** *277*; **27** *841*; **31** *30*; **32** *795*
20th cent. **5** *517*; **12** *644*; **18** *97*; **28** *659*, *660*
Gothic **13** 138, 139, 147–8*, 152–3*
gouache **5** *277*
grisaille **13** 136, 183, *676*; **15** V; **19** 406
hanging **9** 16–17, *17*, 18–19, *26*
hard-edge **10** 258
history **4** *322*; **10** 249–50; **14** 585; **17** *576*; **23** *214*, *451*
Neo-classicism **10** *402*
19th cent. **15** *884*
hunting scenes **29** *425*
industrial scenes **18** III2
Japonisme **33** *138*
Jewish art **17** *576*, 577–8*
landscape **10** 250–52*; **12** 294–5*; **18** 711–15
Gothic **18** *703*
Impressionism **7** *700*
Orientalism **23** *505*
Romanticism **18** *714*; **26** 740, *741*
17th cent. **27** *264*
18th cent. **3** *276*; **8** *97*, *98*; **10** *250*; **11** *910*; **18** *712*; **19** *729*; **27** *716*; **29** *890*; **31** *233*; **33** *221*, *415*, *715*
19th cent. **7** *749*, *752*, *755*, *756*; **8** *185*, *842*; **11** *300*; **18** *905*; **19** *427*; **23** *249*; **26** *238*; **29** *878*; **31** *469*, *474*; **32** *857*
literary themes **17** *641*
Neo-classicism **3** *286*
Pre-Raphaelitism **5** *268*; **14** *850*; **25** *555*; **27** *187*
Rococo **14** *636*
18th cent. **11** *860*, *861*; **12** *646*; **14** *520*; **31** *871*
19th cent. **19** *103*, *240*, *507*; **29** *732*

England
painting—cont.
marine **4** *757*; **20** 424–5*; **31** *468*, *472*
18th cent. **14** *610*
19th cent. **29** *535*
miniatures **9** *26*; **10** 246; **14** 761, 855; **21** 639, 640, 643, 644
16th cent. **14** 545, 546; **30** *412*
murals **22** 333
mythological **8** *122*; **11** *911*; **29** *48*
Aesthetic Movement **11** *436*
Baroque **19** *120*
19th cent. **22** *52*
Op art **23** *449*
Post-Impressionism **10** *256*; **19** *590*
religious
Gothic **13** *138*
Pre-Raphaelitism **11** *785*; **21** *602*
Romanticism **20** *490*
19th cent. **8** *491*; **9** *474*; **10** *646*; **25** *407*
20th cent. **29** *383*
topographical **28** *285*; **31** *155*
vedute **5** *599*
Vorticism **32** *701*
wall **10** 278; **19** 611
Anglo-Saxon **2** 72–4*, *73*
Gothic **13** *128*, 137, 142, 153; **19** *611*, 641
Romanesque **26** 650, 652, *652*
13th cent. **10** 269
watercolours **8** 27; **10** 251; **12** 131; **32** 900, 901
Pre-Raphaelitism **27** *186*
Romanticism **12** *742*, *743*; **23** *885*
17th cent. **32** VII1
18th cent. **26** 76; **27** *278*, *716*; **31** *155*; **32** *825*
19th cent. **4** *121*, *615*; **8** *27*, *29*, *84*; **10** *280*, *282*; **11** *331*; **31** *470*, *473*, *909*; **32** *901*, VIII1
20th cent. **10** *285*; **30** *38*
18th cent. **11** *859*
19th cent. **8** *440*; **26** *69*
20th cent. **3** *28*; **4** *293*; **10** *258*; **14** *612*; **19** *288*; **22** *523*, *525*; **27** *562*
palaces **6** 407; **10** 229, 359; **33** *247*
Baroque **23** 812; **33** *397*
Gothic **19** *609*; **33** *64*
16th cent. **14** *127*; **19** 617, *618*; **23** *197*
17th cent. **17** *635*
see also HOUSES → types → country
palaeography **20** 43
palls **19** 510
panelling **10** 272, *274*, 274–5, 277
panoramas **24** 17–18, *18*, *19*
pantographs **10** 311
pantomimes **8** 911; **30** 675
paper **10** 285; **24** 40, 48, 51, 55; **31** 258, 259
paperweights **24** 57
papier mâché **10** 281, 297; **24** 62, *62*
parks **12** 128; **22** 527; **24** 179, 293
parquetry **10** 275
parterres (i) (gardens) **12** 128
passementerie **24** 237
pastiglia **13** 152
patchwork **10** 354; **24** 252, 253
patens **10** 322, 325
patronage **10** 249, 262–3, 359–62*; **14** 263
royal **19** 582
sculpture **10** 265
stained glass **13** 183
pattern books **14** 855; **24** 269, *270*, 273, 753
architecture **18** 742–3; **24** *275*; **32** 554

England
pattern books—cont.
furniture **10** 280, 296, 299
garden **12** 130
interior decoration **10** 273
ironwork **14** 856
metalwork **30** 871
Rococo **24** 273
sculpture **10** 261
pearls **10** *345*; **17** *522*
pear-wood **18** 610
pedestals **24** 316; **28** *665*
pencils **24** 353
pendants (jewellery) **10** 322, *345*; **13** 170; **17** 522, *528*
pennons **12** 272
performance art **24** *408*
periaktoi **30** 662
periodicals **10** 255; **24** 422, 423–4, 445–6*
Perspex **10** 267
pews **24** 575, *576*, *577*
pewter **10** 340, 341*; **12** 453; **21** II2; **24** 579, *579*, 580, *809*
photocollages **4** *115*
photographic prints
albumen **5** *522*; **24** *668*; **33** *309*
calotypes **30** *269*
daguerreotypes **7** 403
gum bichromate **24** *652*
platinum prints **24** *655*
photography **4** *670*; **10** 252, *483*; **15** 830; **24** 650, 668, 674
calotype process **10** 252
dye transfer **9** *494*
Mass Observation **20** *589*
19th cent. **5** *522*; **22** *389*
pianos **20** VIII1
piers (i) (seaside) **24** *748*
piers (ii) (masonry) **24** 751
clustered **24** 749, *749*
compound **24** *749*
cylindrical **24** 749, *749*
Gothic **24** *751*
pilier cantonné **24** *749*
quatrefoil **24** *749*, 750
Romanesque **33** *547*
pigments **18** 656; **23** 785, 786
pilasters **24** *804*
pilgrim badges **24** *809*
pinchbeck **10** 341
pine **10** 277
pins **10** 340
pipkins **10** 301
pistols **2** *466*
plaster **9** 16; **10** 271, 274, *275*; **29** 834–5*, *836*, 843–5
plastics **10** 285
plate **10** 325
plates **10** *307*, 313
playbills **10** *419*
plywood **10** *300*
pointing (i) (sculpture) **10** 265
polychromy **8** 48; **10** 238; **13** *121*; **25** I2, IV, V2; **30** *533*
porcelain **10** 308–10*
blue-and-white ware **4** 177*
display **10** 276
hard-paste **10** 309, *309*
Parian porcelain **10** *311*, 311
Rococo **10** *308*
soft-paste **4** 600; **10** *308*, 308–9
porringers **10** 341
portals **10** 259; **23** 251
porticos **19** 598; **25** 265, 266, *266*, 267; **33** 10
portraits
artists' **30** *499*
author portraits **20** *341*
cameos **10** *345*; **17** 522
drawings **10** *757*; **33** *720*
Baroque **2** *314*
Renaissance **9** *273*; **10** *246*; **14** *672*
18th cent. **26** *345*
20th cent. **17** *607*
enamel **17** IV1; **24** 553
engravings **10** 248, 393
etchings **25** *210*

England
portraits—cont.
glass **10** *319*
group **21** *148*
Baroque **19** *121*
17th cent. **17** *645*
18th cent. **11** *427*; **19** *584*; **26** *274*; **28** *870*
19th cent. **30** *270*
Kit-cat **18** 96–7
medals **17** 522; **28** *749*
miniatures (manuscript illumination) **5** *641*
miniatures (paintings)
Renaissance **14** *545*, *546*; **21** *639*
16th cent. **14** *761*; **23** *408*
17th cent. **7** *794*
19th cent. **21** *645*
painting **9** 245; **10** 246–7, 248–50*, 360; **14** 545, 546
Aesthetic Movement **33** *139*, *141*
Baroque **9** *278*, *281*, *483*; **19** 120–23*, *121*, *122*, *123*; **29** *802*
Jacobean style **8** *165*; **9** *277*; **19** *583*; **21** *509*
miniatures (paintings) **17** 522
Pre-Raphaelitism **27** *351*
Renaissance **10** *246*, *247*, *666*; **14** *669*, *670*, *671*; **22** *64*; **25** *277*; **31** *414*
Rococo **8** *833*; **33** *693*
watercolours **8** *20*
14th cent. **19** *607*
16th cent. **12** *515*; **13** *239*; **26** *80*; **28** *313*; **31** *889*
17th cent. **9** *56*, *482*; **10** *248*; **11** *424*; **14** *806*; **15** *150*; **17** *645*; **25** *280*; **26** *393*
18th cent. **3** *489*; **4** *611*; **7** *796*, *814*; **8** *26*, *454*; **9** *673*; **11** *427*, *907*, *909*; **14** *114*, *638*, *842*; **18** *143*, *146*, *891*, *892*; **21** *148*; **25** *278*, *283*; **26** *272*, *273*, *274*, *275*, *276*, *277*; **27** *118*, *119*; **29** *31*; **32** *825*
19th cent. **7** *165*; **9** *290*; **14** *147*, *754*; **18** *893*, *894*; **27** *840*; **33** *257*
20th cent. **2** *712*; **3** *29*; **4** *169*; **17** *608*; **26** *78*
photography **24** *655*; **30** *270*; **33** *309*
porcelain **33** *377*
sculpture **4** 79; **30** *499*
18th cent. **29** *564*; **33** *4*
19th cent. **11** *238*
self-portraits **17** 611
Gothic **33** *200*
16th cent. **23** *407*
18th cent. **9** *673*; **14** *638*; **25** *210*; **26** *345*
20th cent. **17** *607*
posters **10** *877*
pots **10** 301, *314*, *343*
potters **10** 301, 312
potter's wheels **10** 301
pottery **10** 300–308*
Barbotine ware **27** *108*
basaltes **10** 642; **33** 21, *21*
blue-and-white ware **4** 177*; **7** 166
Celtic **6** 161
Cistercian ware **10** 302, 303
creamware **6** 333; **10** 306–7, *307*; **22** 882
Delftware **6** 333; **10** 303, 305–6
Developed Stamford ware **10** 302, *302*
encaustic **10** 199
galleyware **10** 303
greenware **10** 301
Jasper ware **10** 306, 345, 642; **21** II3; **33** 21–2
Metropolitan ware **10** 303
Midlands black ware **10** 303

England
pottery—cont.
Midlands yellow ware **10** 303
Nottingham ware **10** 306
Queen ware **15** *822*
Roman **27** *108*
slipwares **10** 303
tin-glazed ware **10** 303, *304*; **30** *875*
Tudor green wares **10** 302, 303
19th cent. **10** 142
power stations **25** *403*; **28** *282*
presses **25** *594*
printing **8** *35*, 36, *36*; **10** 307, 356*; **24** 55; **30** 561–2
colour **25** VII1
colour **3** 421; **4** 367
woodblock **22** *144*
15th cent. **6** 120
printmakers **25** 625
print rooms **9** 26; **11** 430
prints **10** 252; **27** 869
monotypes **4** *118*, *119*
popular prints **25** 243
woodblock **25** VII1
19th cent. **10** *251*
prisons **4** 108; **8** *494*
process art **10** 258, 269
propaganda **25** 651
property development **25** 654–5
prunts **10** *317*
Psalters **25** 676; **26** 660
public buildings **10** 151
Pug mills **4** 785
pulpits **25** 724–5, 726–7
purses **3** 442
pyrometers **33** 22
quilting **10** 353; **25** 821, *821*
quilts **25** 821
racecourses **29** 424
railway stations **3** 246; **10** 236; **16** *54*; **19** *574*; **25** *856*
rapiers **2** *456*
regalia **26** *78*, *80*
reredoses **10** 260
riding houses **25** 249
roads **23** 685
rolls **12** 273; **14** 423
romance manuscripts **26** 564*
roods **27** 124, 125
roofs **16** *54*; **30** 894, 905, 906, 909, 910
cruck **30** *901*, 908
Gothic **19** 609; **30** *904*
hammer-beam **30** *900*
14th cent. **27** *126*
19th cent. **10** 236
ropework **27** 139, *139*
rosaries **13** 164; **27** *159*
rose-wood **5** 192; **10** 279, 297
rotundas **27** 237; **29** *735*
rubies **10** *345*
ruin buildings **12** *130*, 130
saints' lives **13** 136
salts **10** 325; **27** *640*
salvers **28** *738*
samplers **9** 493; **27** 693, 694
sandstone **10** 224
Millstone Grits **29** 703
Old Red **10** 227
Romanesque **10** 227
Yorkstone **29** 703
sapphires **17** *522*
sard **12** *263*
satin **10** 353
satin-wood **5** 192; **10** 293, *293*
satires **7** 648; **25** 651; **27** 869–70*
Rococo **14** *639*
18th cent. **27** *869*
19th cent. **5** *272*
sauceboats **10** 330, *333*
scabbards **6** 160; **30** *394*
scaffolds **30** 653
sceptres **26** 81
schools **10** 241; **23** 194; **26** 461, 476; **28** 156–9
Board schools **25** 804; **28** 157
Gothic Revival **25** I2

England
schools—cont.
Queen Anne Revival **25** 804; **28** *157*
20th cent. **26** *19*
scissors **8** 286, *286*, 287
screenprints **10** 258; **28** *300*
screens (i) (architectural) **10** *270*; **28** 293–5, *294*, *295*, 296
pulpita **28** 292
Renaissance **28** *293*
rood **28** 292
screens (ii) (furniture) **19** 5
screens passages **28** *301*, 301–2*
scripts **28** 305
sculptors **10** 265
sculpture **9** 23–5; **10** 259–69*; **12** 129; **19** 604–5; **30** 499*; **33** 3
Abstract art **5** *790*
allegorical
Baroque Revival **22** *28*
Anglo-Saxon **2** 68–72*; **10** 259
animal subjects
Romanesque **26** *617*
architectural **10** 266, 476, 744
Gothic **33** *62*
Romanesque **5** 645–6, *646*; **10** *169*; **18** 50, *50*
12th cent. **10** *475*
bronze
Neo-classicism **3** *26*
New Sculpture **23** *34*; **30** *762*
19th cent. **11** *238*
20th cent. **10** *438*; **11** *157*
display **9** 22, 23–5
Gothic **7** 456; **10** 266; **13** 80–82*, *81*, *84*, 84–5*, *121*, 121–2*; **33** 550
Decorated style **10** 673
Early Gothic **33** 61
14th cent. **13** 82–3*
marble
Baroque **10** *264*
Baroque Revival **22** *28*
Neo-classicism **10** *265*
Rococo **27** *244*
Roman **19** *579*
16th cent. **10** *262*
18th cent. **3** *184*; **4** *79*; **27** *468*; **28** *64*; **29** *564*
19th cent. **6** *456*; **12** *598*
Modernism **22** *57*
monumental **10** 265–6
mythological **5** *629*; **12** 613
New Sculpture **12** *610*
18th cent. **2** *541*; **3** *184*
19th cent. **12** *598*
New Sculpture **23** *34*; **30** *762*
relief **10** *674*; **19** *404*, *405*
Gothic **9** *681*; **27** *629*
Neo-classicism **8** *587*
New Sculpture (UK) **3** *367*
Romanesque **26** *614*
religious
Gothic **10** *259*; **19** *603*
Neo-classicism **11** *164*
Romanesque **26** *615*
19th cent. **3** *78*
Renaissance **16** 695
Roman **19** *579*
Romanesque **7** 455; **19** 405; **26** 613–17*, 643–4*
stone **13** 80–83*, *81*, *84*, 84–5*; **26** 613–17*, *617*; **32** 529; **33** *62*
tomb
New Sculpture **12** *611*
Renaissance **31** *190*
Rococo **27** *244*
15th cent. **10** *260*
16th cent. **10** *262*
Viking **2** 71*; **32** 529
wood **13** 121–2*; **26** 643–4*
15th cent. **33** 238
17th cent. **7** 236
20th cent. **10** *268*; **14** *401*; **24** *34*

England—cont.
seals **12** 273; **14** 413, 416; **19** *580*; **33** *5*, 6
secretaire-bookcases **5** 192
Seder sets **17** 573
serjeant painters **28** 466*
service stations **28** 488
sets **30** 681, *681*
settees **29** *8*
shafts (wall) **26** 589
shawls **8** 36; **28** 564
shells **28** *581*
shields **6** *161*; **14** 405, 407, 412, 413, 419, 420, 425; **15** 150
shirts **9** 274, 275
showcases **9** 30
shrines (i) (cult) **28** 630
sideboards **28** *665*
signs (markers) **32** *324*, *325*, 326, *327*
silk **2** *84*; **4** 103; **10** *182*, 278, *290*, *350*, *352*, 353, 356–7*, *357*; **21** 600; **23** *461*; **28** 716, 717, *717*; **30** *541*, III2, X3
silver **2** *456*, *466*; **6** 443; **7** 535; **10** 291, 322–30*, *327*, *331*, 331–7*, *332*, *333*, *350*, 355; **14** 418, 856; **23** *461*; **30** *541*, 542
Anglo-Saxon **2** *80;* **10** 322
chinoiserie **7** 167
Modern Movement **10** *337*
New Sculpture **3** 367
Roman **21** I2; **27** *84*
15th cent. **7** *537*
16th cent. **14** *419*
17th cent. **28** *740*
18th cent. **3** *627*; **19** *594*; **25** *737*
19th cent. **10** 142, *335*
silver-gilt **10** *326*, *330*; **13** *164*; **23** *461*; **27** *640*; **28** *738*; **30** *541*
Gothic **10** *323*
19th cent. **10** *334*
silversmiths **10** 331
silver-stain **13** 183; **33** 549
sketch clubs **32** 902–3
sketches **19** *585*
oil **13** *676*
skins **31** 260
skirts **9** 276, 278
skyscrapers **24** *343*
slate **10** 236, 297
slip **6** 325
snuff-boxes **10** 342, 346, 347, *347*
solars **29** 21–2*, *22*
space-frames **29** *250*
spearheads **25** *540*
spires **13** 55–6; **19** 597; **27** 628; **29** *412*, *413*, 413–14*
spoons **8** *284*; **10** 324; **14** *763*
sporting scenes **3** 245; **10** 250; **29** 422, 425; **33** *376*
stables **29** *486*
stage design **17** *638*; **30** 653, *662*, 662–3*, 674–5*, *681*
stage machinery **30** 653, 663, 674
stage scenery **30** 653, 662, 673, 674, *681*, 682
stained glass **29** 505, 506, 507, 508; **30** 654; **33** 549
Anglo-Saxon **2** 83*
Gothic **5** *647*, 647–8, *648*; **13** *135*, 136, 140, 142, 152, 178, 183–5*, *184*; **14** *422*; **19** *406*; **29** 501, 503, II; **33** *64*, *549*
Pre-Raphaelitism **29** *513*, VI2
Renaissance **5** *515*
Romanesque **26** 702
16th cent. **5** 514
19th cent. **22** 143, *143*; **29** *507*
stainless steel **10** *268*
staircases **10** 279; **19** 567; **29** 524
Neo-classicism **6** *412*; **19** *613*
17th cent. **10** *275*

England—cont.
standards (flags) **11** *145*, 148; **12** 272
stands **9** 29, 30
statuettes **11** *303*; **25** IV; **29** 575*, *575*
New Sculpture **10** *267*
steel **10** 284, 341–2, *342*, 345; **16** *61*; **21** II3
16th cent. **2** *471*
stiff-leaf **29** 659, *659*
stockings **18** 157
stoles (ecclesiastical) **2** *84*
stone **1** 707; **10** 224, 236; **11** *254*; **13** 80–83*, *81*, *83*, *84*, 84–5*; **26** 613–17*, *617*; **32** 529
stone-carvings
Anglo-Saxon **2** 68–72*, *69*, *70*, *71*
Romanesque **4** *465*
Viking **2** 71*; **26** *409*; **32** 516, 523, *529*
stone circles **2** *850*; **25** *505*; **29** *717*
stonewares **10** *304*, 304–5, 306, 308, *312*, *314*
stools **10** *290*
stucco **10** 278; **29** 813, 835–7*, *837*
studios **10** 248; **29** 856, 858
studs **30** 896, *896*
sulphides (ceramic) **10** 319
surveyors **7** 420
sword hilts **2** *456*
swords **2** *457*
synagogues **17** 544, 548
tables **10** 288, *292*, 293
Arts and Crafts Movement **2** *572*
gate-leg **10** 290
Greek Revival **30** *218*
Neo-classicism **10** *293*
pedestal **10** *294*
pier **33** *331*
Renaissance **10** *288*
side **9** 30
tankards **19** 4; **24** *579*
tapestries **10** 270, 275, 277, 348–52*; **30** 318, 322, *326*
chinoiserie **7** 167
Pre-Raphaelitism **30** III2
16th cent. **30** *318*
17th cent. **10** *350*
18th cent. **10** *352*
20th cent. **30** IV1
tea-caddies **7** 167; **28** *737*
teapots **10** *314*; **15** *820*
tea-services **10** *314*
tea-urns **10** 341
temples **3** 369; **10** 226; **12** 129
tenements **30** *457*
tents **2** *339*
terraces **9** 367; **12** 127
terracotta **10** 266; **27** *243*; **30** 499*, *499*, 501–4*, *502*, 506*; **32** *905*
textiles **8** 35, 36; **10** 271, 348*; **21** 600–601; **28** *565*; **30** 561–2
Anglo-Saxon **2** 83–4*
Romanesque **26** 703
18th cent. **9** 284
19th cent. **22** *144*; **32** *722*
theatres **30** 660–62*, *662*, 673–4*, *685*
Greek Revival **28** *873*
Renaissance **30** 654
17th cent. **30** *661*, *673*
19th cent. **24** 641
20th cent. **25** *399*
theories
architectural **22** 139; **33** 341, 386, 387
art **5** 777; **7** 570–71, 796; **14** 642; **30** 171–2
garden **12** 130
painting **9** 8; **19** 412; **26** 345; **27** 353
thick-wall structures **10** 228; **30** *729*

England—cont.
thimbles **10** 340
threads **10** *350*; **23** *461*; **30** *541*, 542
thrones **30** 778, *778*, *780*
tiles **4** 787; **10** 311–12; **30** *875*, 876–7*, *877*, XII
encaustic **30** *876*, *877*
timber structures **19** 609; **30** 894, 895, 896, *896*, *897*
tin **4** 688; **18** 615; **22** 893
toilet services **10** 328
tombs **1** 520; **10** 259, 261, 262, 359
ciborium **7** 303
dolmens **21** *40*
Gothic **1** *517*; **13** 84; **19** *605*
Gothic Revival **31** *345*
Neo-classicism **22** *46*
New Sculpture **12** *611*
passage **25** *508*
Renaissance **31** *190*
Rococo **27** *244*
slab **31** *127*
wall **31** *124*, 127
15th cent. **10** *260*
16th cent. **10** *262*
19th cent. **31** *131*
topiary **31** *150*
topographical books **12** 131
topographical illustrations **18** 73
topographical views **10** 250–51; **12** 128, 131; **31** 155–6*; **32** 111; **33** *231*
Totternhoe stone **29** 699
towers **4** *779*; **10** 227; **21** 560; **27** 527
town halls **10** 235, 266; **31** 236, 238–9, *240*
Baroque Revival **10** *239*
Gothic Revival **20** *237*
17th cent. **24** *804*
20th cent. **10** *240*
towns **31** 708, 710
fortified **10** 226
garden cities **1** 146; **8** 810; **10** 239, 284; **11** 785; **14** 277, 809; **16** 891; **24** 185–6, *186*, 187; **25** 805, *805*; **27** 279
industrial model **5** 365; **27** 641; **31** *726*
new **12** 590, 635; **14** 676; **17** 473; **18** 456; **19** 747
townscapes **31** 155–6
toys **31** *255*, 258
tracery **19** 602, 610; **31** 270, 271, 273
bar **13** 46
Gothic **10** 228; **13** 54, 55
trade **6** 624; **10** 278; **15** 201; **25** 304; **28** 456
alabaster-carvings **1** 519
brass **3** 602
brick **3** 588; **4** 778
carpets **5** 835*; **16** 482
ceramics **6** 332, 333; **16** 425; **31** 338
cotton **8** 36; **10** 356; **16** 449
furniture **2** 150; **3** 585; **19** 592
glass **10** 317; **16** 522
hair **16** 449
lace **3** 610
linen **19** 418
manuscripts **4** 372; **16** 553
metalwork **3** 602; **16** 389
mirrors **7** 87
porcelain **4** 177; **6** 624
pottery **2** 152; **6** 332, 333; **10** 303; **16** 28
sculpture **13** 121
silk **6** 624; **28** 717
stonewares **6** 333
tapestries **3** 607
tea-services **7** 29
textiles **6** 624; **7** 53; **15** 722; **25** 315
tin **3** 602; **4** 688; **7** 586
transepts **31** 281
trappers **14** *426*

England—cont.
trappings **6** 161
trays **24** *62*
treatises **23** 690
architecture **10** 231; **28** 645; **31** 297–8*; **33** 387
16th cent. **9** 367; **13** 298
18th cent. **6** 411; **18** 742
19th cent. **21** 620; **25** 713
engravings **10** 393, 757
gardens **6** 411; **12** 61, 64, 127; **30** 123
gem-engraving **12** 263
inks **27** 882
japanning **7** 166; **10** 290; **18** 610, 614; **24** 273; **29** 530
lithography **19** 479
miniatures **14** 547; **21** 639, 640; **23** 208
painting **5** 271; **26** 278–9; **31** 300
paintings **26** 75
perspective **9** 740; **24** 490
pigments **11** 58
theatres **30** 674
varnishing **24** 273; **29** 530
trompe l'oeil **32** *359*
trousers **9** 286
trunks **6** 560
tureens **15** *822*
turntables **10** 301
tympana **10** *169*; **18** *50*
type-faces **31** 494
undercrofts **23** 247
underdrawings **20** *348*
universities **24** *466*; **29** *379*
upholstery **10** 289, *290*; **30** XIV2, XVI; **31** 682, 684–5, *685*, 686
urban planning **10** 226; **33** 230
Indian subcontinent **20** 52
19th cent. **22** *528*
20th cent. **1** 163; **12** 597
urinals **10** 316
urns **12** 130; **28** *665*
vases **10** *311*, *312*
vaults (ceiling) **32** 94
barrel **32** 88
fan **13** 55; **32** 88–9
Gothic **10** 228; **13** 54; **19** 402, *402*, 403, *602*
Gothic: Perpendicular style **19** 602
rib **9** 449; **26** 589
rib: curving **32** 90
rib: lierne **13** 54; **19** 610; **32** 90, 91
rib: net **32** 92
rib: octopartite **5** 638
rib: pendant **32** 92
rib: reticulated **32** 92
rib: star **32** 93
rib: tierceron **13** 45; **32** 93
Romanesque **9** *449*; **19** 402; **26** 589
sail **32** 94
vellum **24** 107
velvet **10** *290*, 353; **29** *8*
veneers **10** 281
Venice turpentine **18** 611
verandahs **32** 240
vernacular art **32** *324*, *325*, *326*, *327*, *329*, *330*
verre églomisé **27** *640*
vestments (ecclesiastical) **32** 392
viaducts **32** *399*
vignettes (Western decoration) **32** *501*
villas **10** 226; **23** 781; **32** 551–2*, 554
Orientalism **4** *809*
Palladianism **23** *858*; **32** *552*, *553*
19th cent. **32** *555*
vulcanite **10** 346
wagons **30** 662
waistcoats **8** 35, *35*, 36; **30** X3
waiters **10** *330*
wall coverings **10** 278

England—cont.
wallpaper **10** 272–3, 278, 281; **19** 5; **32** 810, 814, *814*, *816*, V1-3
chinoiserie **7** 168
flock **10** 275; **32** 813, *815*
Gothic Revival **23** *546*
18th cent. **10** *278*
walls **4** 787; **10** 240; **14** 22–3; **19** *576*; **33** 541
curtain (ii) (non-load-bearing) **8** *279*
walnut **5** 191; **10** 288, *288*, 290, 292, 293, 297
wardens **20** 562
wardrobes **8** 271
warehouses **14** *522*
war memorials **22** *48*
watches **7** 441; **14** 856
watercolour societies **32** 902–3
waxes **19** *580*; **31** *262*; **33** 3, *4*, *5*, 6
waxworks **33** 3, *4*
weathervanes **33** 8
weaving **30** 552
wells **12** 126
whatnots **10** 297
wicker **33** 157, *157*
windows **10** 275; **13** 183; **19** 403; **25** *711*
wine-coolers **10** *331*; **28** *665*; **33** 195
wire **10** 340; **30** *394*
women artists **5** 766; **10** 329, 374, 877–8; **30** 157
wood **2** *572*; **10** 288; **13** 121–2*; **14** 198; **23** 809; **26** 643–4*; **30** *778*; **31** 259
wood-carvings **19** 510
woodcuts **6** 557
15th cent. **33** 350
18th cent. **33** 359*, *359*
19th cent. **7** 413; **25** *244*; **33** 360, 361
wood-engravings **3** *897*; **4** *9*, 366, *367*; **33** *368*
woodwork **31** 422–3
wool **8** 36; **10** 275, 278, *350*, *352*, 353; **13** 196; **30** III2, IV1
workshops **25** *627*
wrought iron **4** *802*; **10** 236; **16** 53–4, *54*
zebra-wood **10** 297
see also ANGLO-SAXON; BRITAIN
England, Richard **20** 212
Englebert, Lambert **3** 600
Englefield, Henry **8** 27
Englefields **10** 344
Engleheart, Francis (1775-1849) **10** 378*
Engleheart, Francis (1713-73) *see* ENGELHEART, FRANCIS
Engleheart, George **10** 378; **21** 644
Engleheart, John Cox Dillman **10** 378
Engleheart, John Dillman **10** 378
Engleheart, Paul **10** 378
Engleheart, Thomas **10** 378
Englische Porcelain-Fabrick (Cologne) **7** 586
English, Josiah **7** 431
English, Michael **25** 353
English, Rose **24** 409
English, Thomas **25** 34
English bond *see under* BONDING
English Domestic Revival **21** 779; **22** 752
English Free Style **23** 498
English garden-wall bond *see under* BONDING
English Harbour Town
Fort Berkeley **2** 148
Naval Dockyard Museum **2** 153
Englishman, the *see* REYSCHOOT, PETRUS JOHANNES
English Muscovy Co. **18** 27
English red *see under* PIGMENTS → types

English Renaissance *see* BAROQUE REVIVAL
English Royal Family Order **7** 178
English Society for the Encouragement of the Arts, Manufactures and Commerce **25** 821
Englund, Ivan **2** 761
Englund, Lars **10** 378*
Engo Kokugon *see* YUANWU KEQIN
Engonopoulos, Nikos **10** 379*; **13** 353
engraving **25** 597
historical and regional traditions
Belgium **3** *594*
Czech Republic **8** *408*
Germany **12** *786*
Gothic **13** 168
Indian subcontinent **15** *708*
Iran **16** 377, 378
Islamic **16** 364, 377, 378
Korea **18** 338, 342
Mesopotamia **10** 381
Netherlands, the **22** 884–5, *885*
Prehistoric art **25** *475*, 476–7, 478, 480, 484, 487, 491–3*, 494
Palaeolithic **10** 381
Rome, ancient **27** 17, 76*
Scotland **28** *259*
types
pressure-engraving **1** *302*, 302–3; **11** 828
pyro-engraving **1** 302, *302*, *303*; **11** 828
stippling **12** *786*, 787; **22** 885
wheel-engraving **10** 317
white-line **3** 182
uses
antlers **25** 491
banknotes **3** *180*, *181*
blades **8** 283
bone **25** 491, 492–3*
chess sets **6** 557
enamel **13** 168
floors **25** 476
gems *see* GEM-ENGRAVING
glass **3** *594*; **8** *408*; **10** *315*, 317, 321, *321*; **12** 439–40, *786*, 786–7*; **13** 914; **14** 425; **22** 884–5, *885*; **27** 76*; **28** *259*; **31** *641*; **32** 202
gold **12** 869
gourds **1** *302*, 302–3, *303*; **11** 828
guns **2** 459
ivory **25** 491
lignite **25** 491
limestone **25** 491
marquetry **20** 466, 468
metalwork **16** 364, 377, 378; **21** 326
pewter **24** 578
plaques **25** 491, 492
pottery **18** 338, 342
quartzite **25** 491
rock *see under* ROCK ART → techniques
rock art **25** *475*, 476–7, 478, 484, 487
rock crystal **26** 485
sandstone **25** 491
sculpture **27** 17
siltstone **25** 491
silver **15** *708*; **28** 740
stone **25** 492–3*
teeth **28** 302, *302*
typography **31** 495
engravings **2** 534; **10** 379–99*, *392*, 554; **14** 418; **15** *90*, *96*; **25** 597, 612, 614, 618; **26** 228, 230, 232, 742
copies *see under* COPIES → types
historical and regional traditions
Argentina **2** 398, 399
Australia **2** 747
Austria **2** *779*, 793; **31** 680
engravings
historical and regional traditions—cont.
Belgium **3** 558*, 561*; **10** 393
Baroque **4** *360*; **27** *503*
Renaissance **7** *556*
16th cent. **12** *16*, *17*, *885*; **27** *502*; **29** *854*
17th cent. **2** 196, *196*
Britain **10** 393–4, 396, 397
Bulgaria **5** 154
China **10** 379
Costa Rica **8** 18
Czech Republic **14** *683*; **25** *432*
Denmark **19** *662*
England **10** 247–8, 252, 389, 393, 479; **14** 418, 638, 675
Picturesque **24** *742*
17th cent. **10** *230*; **19** *569*
18th cent. **3** *308*, *373*; **4** *362*; **6** *65*; **14** *109*, *856*; **19** *570*; **27** *869*; **33** *133*
19th cent. **3** *181*; **10** *395*; **33** *542*
20th cent. **10** *398*
France **10** 392, 393, 396
Baroque **19** *33*, *34*
Mannerism **11** *264*
Rococo **4** *331*, *361*; **26** *493*
16th cent. **13** *231*; **23** *768*; **31** *844*
17th cent. **10** *130*, *690*; **19** *697*, *847*; **20** *457*; **22** *465*; **24** *160*; **27** *589*; **32** *97*
18th cent. **4** *390*; **7** *496*; **10** *118*; **23** *770*; **24** *169*; **25** *798*; **26** *583*
19th cent. **23** *509*; **26** *121*
20th cent. **27** *241*
Germany **10** 381, 396; **25** 651
Dürer Renaissance **9** *446*
Gothic **12** 385
Renaissance **8** *114*; **9** *437*; **10** *385*; **29** *44*, *557*
15th cent. **10** *382*; **20** *746*, *794*; **28** *153*
16th cent. **3** *200*; **8** *838*; **22** *555*, *637*
17th cent. **11** *853*; **18** *44*, *45*; **33** *50*
18th cent. **20** *282*; **33** *37*
19th cent. **12** *274*; **18** *135*
Gothic **12** 385
Guatemala **13** 764
Holy Roman Empire (before 1648) **25** *432*
Hungary **10** *545*; **14** 899
Ireland **16** 24
Italy **2** *170*; **9** 23; **10** 383–4, 394
Baroque **12** *23*; **23** *842*; **26** *310*
Renaissance **5** *534*; **10** *383*; **12** *698*; **15** *92*; **16** *779*; **23** *292*; **25** *160*, *858*, *859*, *904*
16th cent. **5** *184*; **7** *899*; **10** *386*; **11** *180*, *272*; **25** *619*; **26** *229*, *823*; **32** *412*
17th cent. **20** *320*; **28** *6*; **30** *429*
18th cent. **16** *773*; **21** *539*; **23** *753*; **24** 841, 843; **25** *853*
19th cent. **3** *771*
Japan **10** 379; **17** 203
Mexico **10** 393; **21** 385; **24** 418; **25** *321*; **27** 872
Netherlands, the **10** 391, 392; **20** 631
Mannerism **14** 293; **15** *90*; **22** *272*
Renaissance **19** *757*, *758*
16th cent. **10** *388*; **12** *531*, *882*; **15** *96*; **25** *612*
17th cent. **10** *175*, *478*; **13** *223*, *893*; **18** *623*; **24** *235*; **29** *247*; **32** *699*
19th cent. **1** *809*
Peru **24** 506
engravings
historical and regional traditions—cont.
Poland **25** 140
Russia **27** 389
Scotland **12** *776*; **28** 236
South Africa **29** 110
Spain **20** *66*; **29** *302*
Surinam **21** 154, *154*
Sweden **11** 174; **29** *685*; **30** 78
Switzerland **30** *131*
Tunisia **31** *426*
United States of America **3** *180*; **10** 393, 394, 397; **31** 599, 662; **33** *207*
materials
burins (engraving) **10** *379*
burnishers **10** *379*
calcium carbonate **10** 380
copper **14** 293
inks **10** 380, 381; **15** 855
mattoirs **20** 849*
paper **10** 380, 381
presses **10** 380, 381
printing plates **10** 379, 394–6
rockers **10** *379*; **26** 489*
roulettes **10** *379*; **25** 612; **27** 255*
satin **10** 380
silk **10** 380
tools **8** 129; **10** *379*; **25** 494
types
Aberli style **1** 31
alto relievo **19** 515
chiaroscuro **16** 820
crayon manner **2** 239; **4** 330; **8** 129–31*; **10** 391; **25** 597, 614; **26** 231
England **8** 131
France **2** 239; **8** *130*, 130–31*; **11** 723
Sweden **12** 634
dotted prints **9** *189*, 189–90*; **24** 246; **25** 610, 731
see also PRINTS → types → punched
gouache manner **8** 131; **13** 219–21*, *221*; **32** 894
manière criblée see dotted prints
mezzotints *see* MEZZOTINTS
outline **26** 231
pastel manner **4** 330, *331*; **8** 129; **25** 597, 623
Schrotblatt see dotted prints
steel **26** 742
stipple **25** 614, 618; **26** 231; **29** 675–7*; **30** 853
Britain **29** 675–7
England **10** 252; **12** *640*
Germany **13** 258
Russia **29** *676*
white-line **20** 795; **25** 622
uses
art (reproduction of works of) **2** 534; **26** 742
attributions **2** 560
banknotes **3** 180; **10** 396
Bibles **4** 9
book illustrations **4** 345, 356, 357, 359; **10** 380, 389; **20** 631; **21** 579; **26** 742; **32** 199
bookplates **4** 373; **10** 396
catalogues **6** 77
globes **12** 811
maps **10** 389
medical books **21** 6, 7
music (printed) **22** 370
musical scores **14** 675
portraits *see under* PORTRAITS → media
postage stamps **10** 396; **25** 328
puzzles **31** 266
title-pages **10** 389
Engström, Albert **30** 275
Engström, Leander (1886-1927) **10** 399*; **29** 687; **30** 81; **33** 566
Engstrom, Leander (*b* 1914) **10** 399
Engström, Tord **10** 399
Enguerrand (*fl* 12th cent.) **26** 659
Enguerrand III, Lord of Coucy (*fl* 1225-42) **8** 39
Enguerrand VII, Lord of Coucy (*fl* before 1386) **8** 39
Enguidanos, José López *see* LÓPEZ ENGUIDANOS, JOSÉ
Enguidanos (y Perles), Tomás López *see* LÓPEZ ENGUIDANOS (Y PERLES), TOMÁS
Enguidanos, Vicente López *see* LÓPEZ ENGUIDANOS, VICENTE
Enheduanna **1** 509
Enichibō Jōnin **17** 149
Eni-Eri **9** 655
Enikel, Jans **32** 432
Eni-Rabat **30** 307
Enji Tōrei *see* TŌREI ENJI
Enkai **17** 131
Enkaku **17** 125
Enkevoirt, Cardinal **8** 86
Enkhuizen **22** 894
warehouses **32** 861
Westerkerk **22** 821, 857
Enkin Kitamura *see* KITAMURA ENKIN
Enkinshi **17** 391
Enkomi **8** *325*, 330; **10** 399–400*; **13** *362*
architecture **8** 334–5
Ashlar Building **8** 335
bronze **8** 353
copper **8** 353
faience (i) (glass) **8** 350
figurines **8** 326, 339
houses **8** 334
insulae **8** *335*, 336
ivory-carvings **8** 350, *350*, 351
metalwork **14** 355; **21** 329, *334*
sculpture **8** 330
statuettes **8** 353; **10** *400*
Enköping **30** 77
Church of Our Lady **30** 111
Enkū **10** 400–401*; **17** 127, 348
works **5** 120; **17** 43, 98, 348
enlarging **24** 651*, 668
Enlart, Camille **10** 401*; **26** 44
Enlène **25** 492, 493; **31** 360
Enlightened Sarmatism **32** 875
Enlightenment, the **2** 518; **10** 401–2*; **14** 446; **22** 734; **23** 108
Enman, Hans Ersson **30** 116
Enmann group pottery *see under* POTTERY → wares
Enmore Castle (Somerset) **23** 210
Ennabeuren **23** 537
En'nan tea-room **17** 340
Ennedi **1** 370, *376*
Enneking, John Joseph **10** 402–3*; **11** 141
Ennen Hasegawa *see* HASEGAWA ENNEN
Ennezat **26** 601
Enni (Shōitsu Kokushi) **17** 408
Enni Ben'en **18** 550
Ennion **27** 77
works **27** *78*
Ennis, Charles **33** 403
Ennis, Jacob **3** 285
Enniscorthy (Co. Wexford), memorial to the rebellion of 1798 **16** 21
Enniskillen Castle, Fermanagh County Museum **16** 42
Enno, Felice Alberti d', Prince-Bishop of Trent **11** 287
En no Gyōja **17** 42; **18** 67; **22** 348
En no Ozunu *see* EN NO GYŌJA
Eno, Brian **10** 403*; **29** 98
Enoch **2** 733
en résille sur verre enamel *see under* ENAMEL → techniques
Enrico, Antonio d' *see* TANZIO DA VARALLO
Enrico, Giovanni d' **30** 302, 303; **31** 898
collaboration **22** 81; **31** 899, 901
sculpture **27** 499; **31** 899, *900*
Enrico, Melchiorre d' **30** 302; **31** 899
Enrico da Campione **5** 549; **21** 774
Enrico di Ottavio Campione **5** 549
Enrico di Tedice **8** 212; **10** 403*; **24** 854
Enrigus **13** 713
Enrique, Master (*fl c.* 1240-77) **10** 403*; **19** 173; **23** 402
works **13** 104; **19** 171, *172*; **29** 263
Enrique, Master (*fl* early 15th cent.) **23** 402
Enríquez, Alfonso **5** 834; **31** 181
Enríquez, Carlos **8** 233; **10** 403–4*; **22** 718
Enríquez, Fadrique **17** 692
Enríquez, Martín **24** 501
Enríquez, Rafael **20** 274; **24** 622
Enriquez, Ventura **29** 303
Enríquez Borgia, Maria **4** 409
Enríquez de Cabrera *see* CASTILLA, Almirantes de
en ronde bosse enamel *see under* ENAMEL→ techniques
Enryakuji *see under* ŌTSU
Ens, Giuseppe *see* HEINTZ, JOSEPH (ii)
Enschedé, Johannes **22** 370
Enschede, Rijksmuseum Twenthe **22** 906
En school **10** 192*; **17** 98, 120–21
Ensei **10** 192; **17** 120
Enseling, Joseph **3** 891
Ensell, Edward **3** 84
Ensenada, Marqués de **10** 406*; **21** 35
Ensérune **11** 553; **21** 551
Enshū Kobori *see* KOBORI ENSHŪ
Ensingen, Matthäus von **12** 365
Ensingen, Ulrich von **10** 406, 407*; **14** 884; **20** 567
assistants **14** 866
pupils **10** 407
works **4** 187; **12** 365; **14** 117; **18** 515; **29** 754; **30** 136; **31** 567
Ensinger (family) **20** 441
Ensinger, Kaspar **10** 406
Ensinger, Matthias (*d* 1438; elder brother) **10** 406
Ensinger, Matthäus (b c. *1390/1400-63; younger brother)* **9** 191; **10** 406, 407–8*
assistants **10** 408
fonts (baptismal) **9** 192
works **3** 822; **10** *408*; **31** 568
Ensinger, Moritz **10** 406, 408–9*; **18** 518; **22** 306
works **23** 204, 205; **31** 568, 569
Ensinger, Vincenz **3** 822; **10** 406, 408*
Ensor, James (Sidney Edouard), Baron **3** 614; **10** 409–12*, 693; **29** 670
groups and movements **2** 516; **5** 44; **7** 245; **10** 517; **19** 792; **25** 358; **32** 591
paintings **3** 563, *563*; **10** *410*, *411*; **31** 704
patrons and collectors **11** 729
prints **9** 309; **10** 558; **25** 607, 621
Ensor, John **6** 64; **9** 317
Enstone (Oxon) **12** 127
entablature friezes *see under* FRIEZES→ types
entablatures **10** 413*; **22** 211; **23** 477, 478, 480, 484; **26** 878
Greece, ancient **13** 377, *378*, 389, 390, 391, 392, *393*, 414, 415; **21** 341; **25** 11; **27** 692
Rome, ancient **26** 875, 876, 878; **32** *502*

Entartete Kunst **1** 76; **2** 560; **3** 802; **6** 176; **10** 413–14*, 863, 870; **12** 474, 477; **16** 789; **18** 82; **20** 395; **21** 56; **22** 710; **23** 186; **28** 198; **32** 447
books **10** 849
mosaics **30** 760
paintings **1** 160; **3** 480; **12** 396; **17** 767; **18** 112; **21** 855; **28** 112, 169
sculpture **11** 769; **12** 407
woodcuts **24** 14
entasis **2** 362; **7** 502; **10** 414–15*; **24** 368
Buddhism **17** 66
China **6** 640
Egypt, ancient **10** 414
Greece, ancient **2** 676; **10** 414–15; **13** 398, 415
Japan **17** 66
Mesopotamia **21** *283*; **31** 695
Romanesque **10** 415
Rome, ancient **10** 414, 415
Entemena, King of Lagash **21** 303
vases **21** *303*
Enterprise of the Green Shield with the White Lady **7** 178
Entotto, Debra Raguel **1** 315
Entragues, Henriette d' **4** 864
Entrecasteaux, D', Islands *see* D'ENTRECASTEAUX ISLANDS
Entrecolles, François Xavier d' **6** 924; **17** 513
Entremont **6** 159; **11** 528, 553; **21** 551; **25** 538
Entsūji **12** 99
Entzenhoffer, Johann **5** 82
Enugu **1** 429; **23** *129*, 136
Enville Hall (Staffs) **12** 130
conservatory **7** *745*
environment *see* INSTALLATIONS
environmental art **10** 415–17*; **22** 279
collections **24** 24
France **2** 421, *421*; **10** *416*
United States of America **7** 237
environmental design **10** 417*
see also BUILDING REGULATIONS
Environments **17** 805
Enwonwu, Ben **1** 432; **18** 639; **23** 136, 137; **32** 86
enxaquetado rico tiles *see under* TILES → types
enxaquetado tiles *see under* TILES → types
Enyan Abassa
staffs **1** *278*
Enyedi, Ildikó **10** 447
Enyong **15** 61
En'yū, Emperor (*reg* 969-84) **17** 222; **18** 561
Enzelmillner, Joachim **2** 829
Enzer, Joseph **28** 246
Enzo, Giuseppe *see* HEINTZ, JOSEPH (ii)
Enzola, Gianfrancesco (di Luca) **10** 418*; **25** 19
Eoforwic *see* YORK
Eosander, Johann Friedrich **10** 418*
patrons and collectors **14** 651
teachers **30** 522
works **3** 791, 805, 806; **5** 347, 349; **9** 29
Eosander, Nils **10** 418; **29** 744
Eötvos, József, Baron **2** 546; **17** 885
Epan Englianos *see* PYLOS
Epano Zakro **21** 674
Epaux-Bézu Church **3** 443
Epen, J(ohannes) C(hristiaan) van **4** 484; **10** 418–19*
epergnes **6** 32; **10** 419*
Eperjes, Minorite church **14** 894
Epernon, St Thomas **23** 491
Epernon, Duc d' **4** 389; **5** 367; **26** 350
Ephebe of Tralles **5** 743
epheboi lychnophoroi see under CANDELABRA → types
ephemeral art **10** 419–22*; **24** 679
Burma **5** 255–6*
collections *see under* COLLECTIONS → types
Thailand **30** 632–3*
see also ARCHITECTURE → types → temporary; CATAFALQUES
Ephémère, L' **20** 75
Ephesos **1** *849*; **9** *512*; **10** 422–32*, *424*; **13** *362*, *363*; **15** 893; **16** *104*; **26** *908*
Altar of Artemis *see* Temple of Artemis → altar
Altar of Lucius Verus *see* Parthian Monument
aqueduct of C. Sextilius Pollio **26** 911
arcades **9** 524
architecture **9** 524; **10** 423*, 425–7*; **15** 894; **26** 911, 913
Arkadiane **9** 560, 589
Artemision *see* Temple of Artemis
basilica **3** 328
bouleuterion **4** 530
brick **26** 913, *914*
Cathedral of St Mary *see* Church of the Councils
Church of the Councils **3** 191
Baptistery **9** 533
Church of the Virgin *see* Church of the Councils
coins **13** 585
columns **26** 882
Croesus Temple *see* Temple of Artemis
East Baths **26** 872, 912
Flavian temple **10** 426, *426*; **29** 521
fortifications **9** 554
Gate of Mazaeus and Mithridates **26** 913
gymnasium **3** 375; **10** 427; **15** 894; **26** 913
Harbour Baths **26** 913
houses **9** 560
insulae **10** 426–7
ivory-carvings **1** 872; **27** 100
jewellery **13** 597
lamps **13** *603*; **27** *104*
Library of Celsus **10** 426; **13** 414; **19** 312; **23** 483, 484, 534; **26** 883, 913, *914*
marble **29** 702
mosaics **9** 564
Nymphaeum of Trajan **11** 339; **26** 913
orders (architecture) **23** 484
paintings **13** 545, 551; **27** 57
Parthian Monument **27** 39
pottery **13** 484, 536
St John **1** 722; **3** 191; **10** *429*, 429–30; **15** 894; **20** 520; **31** 280
Sanctuary of Artemis **13** 416, 596, 600
Sanctuary of Artemis
Temple of Artemis **10** 430–32*, *431*; **13** *377*, 379, 392, 399, 405, 408, 417, 418, 427, 460, 470; **15** 893; **23** 481, 484; **24** 456; **25** 768
altar **1** 692; **13** 406, 426, 460
Archaic **10** 430–31
Classical, Late **10** 431–2
glass **1** 868
jewellery **13** 598
mouldings **3** 439; **8** 324; **9** 757
paintings **2** 217
sculpture **10** 425, *431*, 675
sculpture **9** *587*; **10** 425*, 427–8*, *428*; **13** 454; **15** 894; **25** 180; **27** 30
stucco **27** 72
Temple of Augustus **27** 45
Temple of Hadrian **2** 297; **10** 426; **15** *894*; **26** 882
urban planning **27** 4
Ephesos—cont.
water pipes **27** 7
Ephoros of Ephesos **2** 217; **13** 551
Ephraim **3** 882; **22** 157; **25** 743
Ephraim, Benjamin V. **12** 474
Ephrussi, Charles **10** 432*
Ephrussi-Rothschild, Charlotte Beatrice **27** 225
Ephyra **10** 432*; **13** *363*
Nekyomanteion **15** 53
Ephyraean goblets *see under* GOBLETS → types
Epi **31** 890
Epiag Porcelain Factory **8** 406
Epicureanism **1** 176
Epidamnos *see* DURRËS
Epidauros **9** *511*; **10** 432–5*; **13** *363*; **26** *908*
Archaeological Museum **13** 470
architecture **13** 389
exedra **10** 671
gutters **13** 390
gymnasium **23** 828
hestiatoria **13** 417
katagogeion **13** 386
limestone **13** 387
masons **13** 389
mosaics **9** 565
poros **13** 387
Sanctuary of Apollo Maleatas **1** 691
Sanctuary of Asklepios **10** 432–4*, *433*; **13** 416, 417, 440; **27** 1, 2
abaton **29** 680
dormitory **27** 712
Temple of Asklepios **10** 432; **13** 374, 379, *379*, 405, 438, 440, *458*, 460; **30** 435
acroteria **1** 128
pediment **24** 319
pronaoi **13** 440
sculpture **10** *434*, 434–5*; **13** 457–8
statue of Asklepios **30** 774
sculpture **13** 454; **25** 179
stadium **13** 403; **29** 488
Stoa of Apollo Maleatas **13** 418
stone **26** 875
Temple of Athena **1** 128
Theatre **13** 385, *402*, 403, 406, 418; **30** 650
Thymele **10** 433; **13** 380, 387, 388, 390, 395, 438; **23** 482; **30** 737
coffering **7** 526, *526*
Epidavros *see* EPIDAUROS
Epignote Painter **32** 37
epigonatia **9** 643, *643*
Epigonos **13** 463; **16** 85*; **24** 414
copies **13** *463*
Epigrafika Vostoka **6** 279
Epigraphers' school **2** 96
Epigraphia Indica **5** 196; **24** 436
Epigraphia Indo-Moslemica **24** 436
epigraphy **8** 369
Afghanistan **16** 166, 169
Central Asia, Western **16** 166, 169
China **6** 762, 764–8; **23** 673; **33** 422
Egypt, ancient **10** 81–3*
Indian subcontinent **15** 197, 198–9*; **20** 862
Islamic **12** 513; **16** 146, 166, 169, 216, 217, 257–60*, 395, 549; **23** 559
Nubia **10** 83
Pakistan **16** 166
Rome, ancient **26** 883–4*
Spain **16** 216, 217
see also under HISTORIOGRAPHY → types
Epikman, Refik **10** 435*; **31** 454
Epiktetos **32** 40*, 49
works **12** 286; **13** *476*, 478, 519
epimanikia **9** 642, *643*
Epimenes **12** 247
Epinal
Museum **18** 867
stencilling **29** 627
woodcuts **15** 142; **25** 244; **33** 360
Epinay, Prosper d', Comte **10** 435*
Epine, L' *see* L'EPINE
Epipalaeolithic period *see under* IRAN, ANCIENT → periods
Epiphania *see* HAMA
Epiphanius, Abbot of San Vincenzo **27** 806
Epiros **13** 561; **25** 331
episcopal palaces *see under* PALACES → types
Episcopius, Joannes *see* BISSCHOP, JAN DE
episkeniai **13** *385*, 386, 406
Episkopi (Cyprus) **18** 408
Museum **8** 366
Episkopi Church (Eurytania) **9** 578
Episkopi Church (Thera) **9** 579
Episkopi-Phaneromeni **8** 330
Episkopi Rotonda (Crete) **8** 155
Epistle books *see* EPISTOLARIES
Epistolaries **28** 487
epistolary cases *see* CASES → epistolary
epistyles **10** 435*
epitaphioi **10** 437*
Byzantine **9** *668*; **10** 437
Gothic **26** *721*
Greece **9** *668*
Romania **26** *721*
Serbia **28** *457*
epitaphs **10** 435–7*; **14** 423; **31** 127
China **6** 741
Czech Republic **8** *390*
Finland **11** 94
France **10** *436*
Germany **10** *436*
Russia **27** *389*
Epitimos **32** 53
epitrachelia **9** 642, *643*
Epitre d'Othéa, Master of the *see* EPITRE MASTER
Epitre Master **5** 208; **7** 235
EPM *see* TECHINCAL EXAMINATION→ types → electron-probe microanalysis (EPM)
EPNS (Electroplated Nickel-Silver) **10** 135
Epoque, L' **5** 44; **31** 866
epoxy resins *see under* RESINS → types
Eppelbaum, Naum **21** 812
Eppelbaum-Marchenko, Brungil'da **21** 812
Eppens, Francisco **21** 380; **22** 164
Epper, Ignaz **30** 135
Epps, Laura (Theresa) *see* ALMA-TADEMA, LAURA (THERESA)
Epstein (family) **25** 136
Epstein (*fl* 19th cent.) **14** 151
Epstein, A., and Sons Inc. **21** 492
Epstein, Elisabeth **4** 132
Epstein, Henri **17** 577
Epstein, Jacob **10** 267, 437–9*; **11** 568; **17** 578, 580; **23** 296; **25** 582
collaboration **12** 631; **14** 107, 674
groups and movements **2** 642; **5** 517; **19** 591, 622, 623; **25** 380; **32** 700, 701
methods **29** 576
patrons and collectors **14** 132; **25** 380, 823; **27** 524
personal collection **1** 438, 439; **22** 55; **23** 742
sculpture **1** 520; **10** 267, *438*; **18** 903; **31** 132, *132*; **33** 181
busts **19** 600
religious **1** 738; **5** 731; **10** 745; **23** 690
Epstein, Jehuda **17** 576
Epstein, Melchior **1** 36
Equatorial Guinea **1** *214*, 393; **10** 439–40*; **11** 880
Equerre, L' **3** 551
equestrian monuments *see under* MONUMENTS → types
Equicola, Mario **10** 442–3*
Equiere Château **6** 509
equilateral arches *see under* ARCHES → types
Equipo 57 (*fl* 1957) **1** 79; **29** 286
Equipo Crónica (*fl* 1964-1981) **10** 443*; **29** 286
Era *see* LAIKMETS
Era, Giovanni Battista dell' **10** 199; **17** 852; **31** 679
(H)Eraclius **8** 609
Eragny Press **4** 366; **24** 885; **33** 361
Eramam, Chalappuratta Shrine **15** 522
Eran **10** 443–4*; **13** 855; **15** *261*, *285*
Narasimha Temple **15** 254
pillar **15** 473
sculpture **15** 457, 468, 469, 473, 750
Erard, Charles *see* ERRARD, CHARLES
Erard, Sébastien **4** 329; **22** 373; **24** 418
Erard & Co.
works **20** VIII1
Erardi, Alessio **5** 131; **10** 444*; **20** 213
Erardi, Stefano **10** 444*; **20** 213
erasers **6** 470; **10** 5
Erasmo da Narni *see* GATTAMELATA
Erasmus (of Rotterdam), Desiderius **3** 612; **4** 752; **10** 445*; **14** 868; **20** 350; **21** *355*, 766; **24** 348
personal collection **14** 666, 668, 869; **21** 355; **25** 18
works **9** 442; **10** 273, 534
illustrated **1** 656; **10** 173; **14** 439; **29** 673
Erasmus, Georg Caspar **10** 444, 445
Erasmus, Johann Georg **10** 445
Erasmus, Nel **29** 109
Erasmus Chest **12** 420
Erasmus of Starhemberg **3** 70
Eraso (family) **32** 179
Eratosthenes **13** 411
Erb, Anselm, Abbot of Ottobeuren **23** 636
Erba, Carlo **27** 788, 789
Erbaba **1** 838
Erbach
Deutsches Elfenbeinmuseum **12** 461
Grossherzogliche Fachschule für Elfenbeinschnitzerei und Verwandte Gewerbe **12** 461
ivory-carvings **12** 461
Erbach-Erbach, Franz I, Graf von **12** 461
Erbach im Odenwald **17** 526
Erbach Painter **13** 524
Erban, Otto **7** 182
Erbar *see under* TYPE-FACES
Erbar, Jacob **31** 497
Erbe, Daniel **11** 713
Erbeler (family) **30** 311
Erben, Anton **23** 271
Erberg, Josef Kalasanc **28** 863
Erberg, Konstantin (Aleksandrovich) **10** 446*
Erbil **1** 851; **21** 275
Erbin, Jorge **2** 397
Erbkam, Georg **14** 594
Erbosi, Giovanni degli **17** 455
Erbslöh, Adolph **22** 921
Ercilla **6** 599
Ercilla, Alonso de **10** 543
Erciyas Dağı **5** 673
Ercker, Lazarus **4** 683

Ercolani (family) **7** 890
Ercolani, Agostino, Conte **10** 446
Ercolani, Filippo, Marchese (*fl* 18th cent.) **10** 446*
Ercolani, Filippo, Prince (*fl* 1699) **8** 146; **10** 446
Ercolani, Lucian R. **14** 523
Ercolani, Vincenzo, Conte **10** 446*
Ercolano
  Accademia Ercolanese di Archaeologia **2** 164; **14** 445; **25** 192, 206
  see also HERCULANEUM
Ercolano, Pietro di Galeotto di *see* PIETRO DI GALEOTTO (DI ERCOLANO)
Ercole I, 2nd Duke of Ferrara, Modena and Reggio (*reg* 1471-1505) **6** 357; **10** *518*, 520*; **26** 459
  architecture **11** 2–3, 6; **31** 714
  books **27** 894
  interior decoration **11** 4
  medals **29** 386
  paintings **4** 194; **20** 904; **24** 342; **26** 459; **31** 431
  tapestries **11** 5
  urban planning **27** 188, 189
Ercole II, 4th Duke of Ferrara, Modena and Reggio (*reg* 1534-59) **9** 183; **10** *518*, 523–4*
  paintings **5** 843; **10** 130
  sponsorship **1** 589
  tapestries **11** 5, 192; **17** 812; **25** 251; **27** 210
Ercole III, Duke of Modena (*reg* 1780-97) **23** 333
Ercole, Master of **11** 8
Ercole del Fiore **16** 826
Ercol Furniture Ltd **14** 523
Ercsi Church **14** 894
Erddig (Clwyd) **9** 202; **10** 292; **32** 818
Erdei, Ferenc **14** 891
Erdeli, Al'dabert I. **31** 560
Erdély, Miklós **4** 84; **10** 446–7*; **14** 896, 897, 902
Erdélyi Szépmíves Céh **18** 395
Erdemli Church **9** 590
Erdenet **21** *870*
Erdene Zuu Monastery **5** 106; **21** *870*, 872, *874*, 875, 886
Erdeven **5** 780
Erdis, Elwood **20** 3
Erdmann, Kurt **10** 447*; **16** 468, 549, 556
Erdmannsdorff, Friedrich Wilhelm (von) **8** 816; **10** 447–8*
  architecture **12** 374; **20** 867; **25** 788; **27** 324; **33** 380
  interior decoration **3** 805; **12** 374; **25** 368; **28** 44
  patrons and collectors **2** 94; **12** 413; **14** 653
  pupils **12** 641
  teachers **7** 415
Erdődy, István, Count **33** 15
Erdody, Simone, Bishop of Zagreb **7** 467
Erdt, Hans Rudi **25** 348
Erebuni *see under* EREVAN
Erech *see* URUK
Erechtheion *see under* ATHENS → Acropolis
Eregli *see* HERAKLEIA (TURKEY)
Eren Eyüboğlu *see* EYÜBOĞLU, EREN
Ererouk *see* YERERUYK'
Eressos **19** 234, *234*
Eretna **17** 864
Eretnid **16** 204
Eretria **10** 448–9*; **13** *363*
  amphorae **13** 517
  baths **13** 562
  chamber **13** 383
  coins **13** 586
  couches **13** 592
  graves **13** 383
Eretria—cont.
  gymnasium **13** 562, 886
  heroön **14** 466
  mosaics **13** 560, 562, 563, 565
  pottery **13** 486, 496, 502, 516, 534
  Sanctuary of Isis **13** 562
  sculpture **10** *449*
  Temple of Apollo **13** 376, 389, 396, 425; **24** 318
  Temple of Apollo Daphnephoros **13** 449
  temples **10** 448
  tholoi **30** 737
  tombs **31** 109
  town walls **21** 556
Eretria Painter **13** 523; **32** 40–41*
Erevan **2** *423*, 428, 429; **9** *507*, *512*; **10** 449–50*; **16** *104*, *105*
  Alexander Myasnikyan Public Library *see* National Library of Armenia
  architecture **2** 428
  Armenian Academy of Sciences **2** 424, 445
  Armenian SSR Government House **2** 436; **30** 281
  Art and Industry Technical College *see* Art College
  Art College **2** 424
  chapel of the Holy Mother of God **10** 449
  Erebuni **31** 699
  Karl Marx Polytechnic Institute **2** 428
  Matenadaran Institute of Ancient Armenian Manuscripts **2** 445; **10** 450
  metalwork **2** 439, 441
  monument to Ghukasyan **2** 436
  monument to the Heroes of the May Uprising in Leninakan **2** 436
  museums **2** 444–5
    Abovyan House Museum **2** 444
    Armenian Museum *see* National Art Gallery of Armenia
    Children's Art Gallery **2** 445
    Erebuni Urartian Citadel **2** 445
    palace **31** 699
    Temple of Haldi **1** 830; **31** 700
    Kotchar Museum **18** 404
    Martiros Saryan Gallery **2** 445
    Museum of Armenian Folk Arts **2** 441
    Museum of Literature and Art **2** 445
    National Art Gallery of Armenia **2** 424; **10** 450
    National Gallery of Armenia **2** 445
    Saryan Museum **13** 653
    State Gallery of Armenia *see* National Gallery of Armenia
    State Historical Museum **2** 441, 444–5
  National Library of Armenia **2** 445
  palace of the Sardars **2** 896
  sculpture **2** 436, 437
  silver **2** 441
  A. Spendiarov Theatre of Opera and Ballet **10** *450*; **30** 281
  Statue of Step'an Shahumyan **2** 437
  Statue of V. I. Lenin **2** 437
  urban planning **2** 428
  Zvart'nots airport **2** 428
Erez (Armenia) *see* ERZINJAN
Erez (Israel) **9** 568
Erfurt **10** 450–53*; **12** *361*
  Angermuseum **10** 451; **14** 285; **29** 516
  churches
    Barfüsserkirche **13** 185
    Cathedral of St Mary **7** 192; **10** *451*, 451–3*; **12** 365
      candelabrum **26** 685
      ciborium **7** 303
Erfurt
  churches
    Cathedral of St Mary—cont.
      stained glass **10** *452*, 453*; **13** 187
    Church of the Canons Regular **2** 724, 725; **29** 502
    Dominican church **29** 502
    Franciscan church **13** 57
    St Severus **10** *451*; **13** 49; **14** 81
  coins **7** *535*
  faience (ii) (ceramics) **10** 451
  Rathaus **31** 241
  tiles **30** 884
Erfurth, Hugo **10** 453*
Erfurt Regler Altar, Master of the **20** 661*
Ergali Mausoleum **17** 866
Ergani Maden **1** 822
Ergo, Engel **18** 3
ergonomic chairs *see under* CHAIRS → types
ergonomics **6** 392; **15** 825; **23** 234
Ergoteles **32** 58
Ergotimos **13** 507; **32** 48
  works **13** *508*
Erhard, Johann Christoph **10** 454*
Erhart (family) **30** 143
Erhart, Bernhard **10** 454
Erhart, Gregor **2** 715; **10** 454, 456–7*; **12** 401; **14** 663
  attributions **10** 455
  collaboration **8** 540, 541; **14** 663
  patrons and collectors **2** 716; **13** 904
  pupils **8** 540; **18** 452
  works **2** 800, *800*; **10** *457*
Erhart, Michel **10** 454–6*; **12** 401; **14** 663; **31** 566
  attributions **10** 456; **13** *118*; **28** 133, 167; **30** 200
  collaboration **8** 540; **28** 171
  pupils **18** 451; **26** 370
  works **1** 710; **10** *455*; **12** 401; **13** 117; **25** 464; **28** *133*; **31** 570
  workshop **13** 117
Erhart, Paulus **14** 663
Erhlen, J. J. **11** 621
Erh-li-t'ou *see* ERLITOU
Eri Ajari **17** 28
Eriba-Adad I (*reg* 1390-1364 BC) **2** 639
Ericero, Antonio **17** 588
Erichsen, Thorvald **10** 457–8*; **23** 226; **29** 78
Erichsen, Vigilius *see* ERIKSEN, VIGILIUS
Erichsson, Nielss **10** 458*
Erici, Andreas **30** 865
Erickson, Arthur (Charles) **10** 458–60*; **16** 101; **28** 557
  collaboration **31** 176
  works **1** 126; **5** 513, 562, 563; **10** *459*; **18** 890; **22** 367; **31** 864
Erickson, Grace **5** 842
Ericson, Estrid **30** 110
Ericson, Sigfrid **10** 460*; **13** 31; **30** 74
Ericsson, Henry **11** 106
Ericsson, John **6** 581
Eridu **1** 892, 894; **10** 460–61*; **21** *267*
  architecture **21** 281, 284, 291
  glass **1** 864
  palace **29** 923
  pottery **21** 270
  religion **21** 277
  Temple VII **10** *460*; **21** 270, 281
  terrace **21** 282
  ziggurat **30** 431; **33** 675
Erie **22** 552, 612
Erie Railroad **32** 866
Erigonos **13** 552
Erik VII, King of Denmark (*reg* 1412-39) **14** 368, 369; **17** 691
Erik XIV, King of Sweden (*reg* 1560-68) **30** 117
  architecture **29** 689; **31** 692
  furniture **30** 92
Erik XIV, King of Sweden (*reg* 1560-68)—cont.
  interior decoration **30** 87
  metalwork **30** 104
  paintings **21** 368
  patronage **31** 707
  regalia **3** 605; **30** 112
  tapestry **30** 114
Erikhson, A. E. **22** 173
Erik of Pomerania *see* ERIK VII, King of Denmark
Eriksberg **26** 691
Eriksen, Christian *see* SKREDSVIG, CHRISTIAN
Eriksen, Gutte **8** 749
Eriksen, Sigurd Alf **23** 238
Eriksen, Vigilius **10** 461*
Eriksson, Anders **30** 116
Eriksson, Christian **14** 221; **30** 86
Eriksson, Liss **30** 86
Eriksson, Nils Einar **10** 461–2*; **13** 31
Eriksson Brothers **30** 110
Erill la Vall **26** 642
Erin Bay style pottery *see under* POTTERY → wares
erinite **11** 763
Erinoid **25** 27
Erishum I (*reg* 1939-1900 BC) **2** 636, 639
Eristave Rati Surameli **31** 906
Erith, Raymond (Charles) **10** 462*; **22** 743; **30** 516
Erith Marshes power station **25** 403
Erith & Terry **30** 516
Eritrea **1** *214*, 378; **10** 564–78*
  architecture **10** 564–7*, 577*
  churches **10** 565–6
  collections **10** 577–8*
  museums **10** 577–8*
  painting **10** 567–74*
  patronage **10** 577–8*
  rock art **1** 373; **10** 568
  sculpture **10** 576–7*
  stelae **10** 565, 577
  tombs **10** 577
Erixson, Sven **10** 462–3*; **32** 274; **33** 30
  groups and movements **10** 805; **29** 687; **30** 81
  pupils **31** 571
Erizzo, Sebastiano **15** 83
Erkens, Adam **3** 762
Erkurgan temple **6** 193
Erlach **2** 799
Erlach, Albert Friedrich von **22** 436
Erlach, Johann Bernhard Fischer von *see* FISCHER VON ERLACH, JOHANN BERNHARD
Erlach, Joseph Emanuel Fischer von *see* FISCHER VON ERLACH, JOSEPH EMANUEL
Erlach, Viktor von **9** 397
Erlangen **12** 468; **30** 324
  Church of the Trinity **1** 700
Erlanger, Baron **4** 597
Erlau *see* EGER
Erler, Andrzej **32** 878
Erler, Erich **10** 463
Erler, Fritz **10** 463*; **14** 89; **25** 748; **28** 143
Erler, Gabriel **32** 878
Erler, Mikołaj **25** 126; **32** 878
Erligang **7** 159
Erling, Konrad von *see* KONRAD VON ERLING
Erlitou **7** 159; **10** 463–4*; **33** 462
  architecture **6** 646
  bronzes **4** 852; **6** 830, *831*, 835, 836, 837, *838*; **10** *464*
  earthenwares **6** *880*
  graves **6** 694
  halberds **6** 841
  jade **7** 3, 90
  palace **6** 679
  turquoise **7** 88
  urban planning **6** 663
Erlouhugou **23** 496
Erlwein, Hans **9** 237
Erman, Adolf **10** 84, 93
Ermanox *see under* CAMERAS → types
Ermans, Giovanni **26** 780
Ermatingen, Schloss Wolfsberg furniture **30** *142*
Ermels, Johann Franz **5** 168; **10** 464*; **12** 390
Ermenak **16** 202
  congregational mosque **16** 202
Ermengau, Matfre **10** 202
Ermenonville **10** 464–5*; **11** *504*; **22** 740
  gardens **12** 124, 724
  tomb of Jean-Jacques Rousseau **6** 171
Ermes, Ali Omer **19** 324
Ermi **8** 337
ermine **9** 255
Ermini, Pietro **8** 19
Erminold Master **12** 399; **13** 87; **20** 661*; **26** 88
Ermisch, Hubert **9** 237
Ermitazh **24** 428
Ermland **25** 130
Ermoldus Nigellus **5** 797
Ermont *see* ARMANT
Ermoupolis **13** 349
Erna, Andrea **4** 832; **19** 55
Ernabella **1** 56; **2** *736*, 768
Ernest, Duke of Saxe-Gotha-Altenburg (*reg* 1605-75) **33** *110*
Ernest, Duke of Styria (*reg* 1386-1424) **2** 792; **13** *900*
Ernest, Elector of Saxony (*reg* 1464-86) **33** *110*, 110–12*
  architecture **2** 480; **21** 62
Ernest I, Duke of Saxe-Coburg and Gotha (*reg* 1826-44) **8** 502; **14** 307; **33** *110*
Ernest II, Duke of Saxe-Coburg and Gotha (*reg* 1844-93) **20** 649
Ernest Augustus, Duke of Saxe-Weimar (*reg* 1748-58) **18** 465; **33** *110*
Ernest Augustus, King of Hannover (*reg* 1837-51) **18** 883
Ernest Augustus III, Duke of Brunswick (*reg* 1913-18) **33** 51
Ernest-Frederick, Margrave of Baden-Durlach (*reg* 1577-1604) **28** 137
Ernest-John, Duke of Kurland (*reg* 1737-40; 1763-69) **17** 472; **26** 7
Ernest-Ludwig, Grand Duke of Hesse (*reg* 1892-1918) **10** 465*
  architecture **8** 529, 531; **23** 393
  decorative works **2** 566; **8** 531
  groups and movements **3** 511; **12** 416, 428
  interior decoration **9** 703
Ernestus **26** 666
Erni, Hans **10** 465*; **30** 135
Ernst, Bernhard **1** 36; **33** 275
Ernst, Georg **12** 445
Ernst, Johan Conrad **8** 726; **16** 863; **23** 221; **25** 29, 30
Ernst, Karl Matthias **20** 915
Ernst, Leopold **2** 808
Ernst, Max(imilian) **5** 882; **6** 558; **10** 466–9*; **11** 550, 569; **12** 396; **13** 801; **23** 48, 296; **24** 144, 428; **25** 6, 583; **30** 21, 22, 298; **31** 607
  architecture **32** 204
  artists' books **20** 336
  book illustrations **2** 409; **4** 366
  collaboration **8** 438; **10** 164; **20** 605
  collages **7** 557; **8** 438; **10** *468*; **11** 549
  dealers **7** 421; **16** 570; **19** 537; **26** 193
  exhibitions **7** 842; **30** 19
  frames **11** 420

Ernst, Max(imilian)—cont.
groups and movements **30** 19
Dada **3** 4; **8** 437, 438; **12** 396; **24** 405
Surrealism **8** 439; **30** 17, 19
jewellery **17** 529
methods **2** 839; **11** 805
objets trouvés **12** 407
paintings **10** *466*, *467*, *469*, 482; **18** 717; **25** 582; **31** 52
patrons and collectors
Arensberg, Walter and Louise **2** 384
Copley, William Nelson **7** 812
Doucet, Jacques (-Antoine) **9** 196
Eluard, Paul **10** 164
James, Edward (Frank Willis) **16** 892
Łódź Museum of Art **2** 409
Menil, de (family) **21** 135
Penrose, Roland **24** 369
Soby, James Thrall **28** 914
photomontages **8** 438
prints **18** 93
cliché-verre **7** 434
collotypes **7** 576
lithographs **19** 491
productions **8** 850; **26** 357
sculpture **8** 438
stage design **3** 120
Ernst, Rodolphe **23** 504
Ernst von Lobming **20** 685
Ernulf, Prior **5** 643; **24** 545
Eroli, Erulo **16** 758; **26** 779; **30** 327
Erős, Gábor **10** 471–2*
Erős, János **10** 472
erotic art **10** 472–87*, *472*, *473*; **23** 294
Austria **10** *481*, 483
Belgium **10** 483
Britain **10** 482
Byzantine **10** 475
China **6** 633; **10** 485*
Christianity **10** 475
Denmark **10** 482
Egypt, ancient **9** 807*
England **10** *475*, 476, 479, *479*, *483*
France **10** 477, 479–80, 483; **11** *267*
Germany **10** 483
Greece, ancient **23** 290
historiography *see under* HISTORIOGRAPHY → types
Indian subcontinent **10** 484–5*; **15** 229*, 566
Ireland **10** 476
Islamic **10** 486*
Italy **10** 476–7, *477*; **12** *764*
Japan **10** *485*, 485–6*
Netherlands, the **10** *478*, 483
Rome, ancient **27** 48, 50
Sweden **10** 483; **21** *644*
United States of America **6** 176; **10** 482
Erp, Dirk van **2** 572; **31** 653
Erp, Theodoor van **10** 487–8*
Erpenius, Thomas (1584-1624) **16** 360
Erpingham, Thomas **23** 250
Errante, Giuseppe **10** 488*
Errard, Charles (*c.* 1570-1630) **10** 488
Errard, Charles (*c.* 1606/9-89) **1** 105; **8** 88; **10** 488–9*; **11** 559; **13** 814; **19** 265; **26** 842
assistants **2** 707; **20** 480
pupils **7** 864
works **11** 744; **20** 481; **26** 204
Errard, J. **31** 720
Errard de Bar-le-Duc, Jean **21** 567, 580
Errazu, Ramón de **20** 60
Errázuriz (family) **2** 405
Errenhausen, Mausoleum of Ruprecht von Eggensburg **2** 781
Errera, I. **3** 620
Erri, Agnolo (degli) **10** 489*; **16** 663
Erri, Bartolommeo (degli) **6** 393; **10** 489; **16** 663
Errico, Teodoro d' *see* HENDRICKSZ. (CENTEN), DIRCK
Erró **10** 490*; **15** 71
Erromango **31** 890, 892
Ersari **6** 254; **16** 485
Ersch, Johann Samuel **4** 21
Érsekújvár Castle **14** 885
Ershov, Igor Alexandrovich **30** 253
Erskine, John, 1st Earl of Mar (*fl* 1572) **28** 268
Erskine, John, 6th Earl of Mar (1675-173) **10** 490*; **12** 593
Erskine, Mary, Countess Marischal **28** *234*
Erskine, Ralph **10** 490–91*; **31** 737
groups and movements **11** 842; **30** 391
works **4** 790; **13** 31; **23** 20; **29** *525*, 526, 686; **30** 75
Erskine, Robert **20** 607
Erskine Bridge **4** 804
Erskine Dinos **32** 67
Erskines of Mar (family) **1** 649
Ersovsky, Eduard (Vladimirovich) **30** 252
Ersson, Anders **30** 116
Erstad-Jørgensen, Erik **29** 76
Erstfeld **6** 155
Ertborn, Florent (Joseph) van **3** 615; **10** 491*
Erté **25** 78
Erthal, Charles Joseph von, Archbishop-Elector of Mainz **18** 174
Erthal, Franz Ludwig von, Prince-Bishop **3** 140
Erthal, Friedrich Carl Joseph von **14** 449
Erthal, Philipp Christoph von **28** 146
Ertinger, Franz Ferdinand **10** 491*; **12** 727
works **5** *345*; **14** 84
Ertle, Sebastian **8** 629; **20** 88
Ertvelt, Andries van *see* ERTVELT, ANDRIES
Erval *see* ERWART
Ervi, Aarne (Adrian) **10** 492*; **11** 92; **30** 368
pupils **24** 370
works **14** 371, 372; **30** 284
Erwart **9** 371
Erwarton, St Mary **25** 175
Erwin (TN) **2** 698
Erwin (*d* 1380) **10** 492*; **12** 356; **29** 754
Erwitt, Elliott **10** 493*; **24** 679
Erwitte, St Laurentius **26** 632
Erythrai **13** 559, 579; **15** 893
Eryx **25** 733
Erzeni, Z.
works **1** *545*
Erzincan (Turkey) **16** 373
Erzinjan (Armenia) **2** 441
Erzurum **10** 493*; **16** *104*
Ahmediye Madrasa **16** 204
architecture **16** 183, 202
Çifte Minareli Madrasa **10** 493; **16** 184, *185*, 204, 246
fortifications **21** 587
tomb of Emir Saltuq **16** 185
Yakutiye Madrasa **16** 204
Er'zya, Stepan (Dmitriyevich) **10** 493–4*; **27** 434; **33** 601
Es, Jacob van **3** 561; **10** 494*; **28** 904
E.S., Master **1** 654; **10** 382; **20** 794–5*; **25** 624; **32** 727
methods **10** 382
pupils **20** 916
works **4** 145; **12** 385, 420; **20** *794*; **24** 271; **25** 622, 632
Esad Yesari **10** 494*; **16** 287
esame artistico e letterario, L' **29** 57
Esarcu, Constantin **5** 73; **26** 722
Esarhaddon (*reg* 680-669) **21** 274
architecture **2** 641; **21** 290; **23** 149, 151
reliefs **21** 290, 297, 299; **33** 685
sculpture **21** 301*; **23** 154
seals **1** 859
Esarhamat **2** 638
Esbeck-Schöningen **25** 500
Esbern Snare **8** 723
Esbjerg, Kunstpavillonen **8** 760
Esbly sur Marne bridge **7** *691*
escalade **21** 546
Escalante, Constantino **21** 386
Escalante, Juan (*fl* 1561) **27** 331; **31** 822
Escalante, Juan Antonio de Frías (*b* 1633) **10** 495*; **26** 438; **29** 282
Escalante, Tadeo **8** 303; **24** 508
escalators **18** 797
Escalente, Constantino **10** 494*
Escallier, Eléonore **8** 607; **11** 606
Escalona Castle **13** 106
Escamaing, d' (family) **4** 692
Escamilla, Luis Tristán de *see* TRISTÁN DE ESCAMILLA, LUIS
Escarpinelli **4** 573
Escayola, Vicente Barroso de la *see* BARROSO DE LA ESCAYOLA, VICENTE
Esch, Jacob van *see* ES, JACOB VAN
Esch, Vincent (Jerome) **10** 495*; **18** 889
Eschach church **33** 629
Eschau **26** 633
Eschauzier, F(rits) A(dolf) **10** 495–6*
Eschay, Jakob **11** 819; **14** 678
Eschel *see under* PIGMENTS → types
Eschenbach, Conrad **27** 217
Eschenbach, Wolfram von *see* WOLFRAM VON ESCHENBACH
Escher, Hans Caspar **10** 496*; **33** 734, 735
Escher, M(aurits) C(ornelis) **10** 496*
methods **28** 202
works **22** 854; **24** 383, 384; **28** *201*
Eschke, Hermann **19** 112
Escholier, Raymond **27** 241
Eschwege, Wilhelm Ludwig, Baron von **4** 639; **10** 496–7*; **25** 293; **28** 781
Eschweiler, Alexander C. **28** 488
Eschweiler, St Antonius Hospital **29** 508
Escobar, Alonso **6** 591
Escobar, José Luis **24** 96
Escobar, Luis **10** 497*
Escobar, Manuel de **20** 460; **24** 502; **32** 25
Escobar, Marisol *see* MARISOL (ESCOBAR)
Escobar, Ticio **24** 101
Escobedo, Diego Vásquez *see* VÁSQUEZ ESCOBEDO, DIEGO
Escobedo, Helen **10** 497*; **12** 844; **28** 330
Escofet, Tejera & Cia **29** 308
Escoffery, Gloria **10** 497*; **16** 884
Escomb Church (Durham) **2** 83; **10** *225*, 497–8*; **20** 572
Escorial **7** 665; **10** 498–504*, *499*, *500*, 534; **14** 516; **22** 694–5; **23** 492, 745–6, 811; **27** 802; **28** 709–10; **29** *258*, 267, 700
architecture **14** 473; **32** 564
Biblioteca **2** 411; **10** 503; **15** 85; **19** 313, 315; **29** 301
collections **2** 411; **3** 188; **13** 922
frescoes **13** 922
interior decoration **29** *300*
Casa de Campo **29** 342
Escorial—cont.
Casa del Infante **29** 272
Casita del Príncipe **4** 566; **12** 925; **29** 272, 305
collections **14** 1
commentaries **27** 754
frescoes **12** 662
furniture **29** 315, 342
gardens **12** 124
Habitaciones de Maderas Finas **29** 306, 318
chairs **29** *318*
imperial stairway **10** *504*; **29** 522
interior decoration **29** *299*, 300–301
ivory-carvings **29** 345
Library *see* Biblioteca
metalwork **13** 922; **29** 339–41, 343
Monastery **10** 500–501
paintings **5** 545; **10** 502–4*; **13** 341, 343, 922; **14** 517; **24** 23, 261; **29** 278, 280, 352; **33** 122, 123, 127
altarpieces **5** 902; **13** 922
frescoes **13** 922
Panteón de los Reyes **10** 501; **20** 866; **25** 226; **29** 269, 336, 341
Patio de los Evangelistas **8** 65; **10** 500–501, 503
pottery **29** 326
reliquaries **26** 148
retables **26** 250
sacristy **7** 523–4; **10** 503; **29** 341, 343
Sala de Batallas **6** 25; **13** 307
sculpture **6** 146, 149; **10** 502–3; **16** 695; **21** 859
S Lorenzo **10** 500, *502*, 502–3; **14** *473*; **31** *93*
Capilla Mayor **11** 486; **12** 260; **29** 291; **30** 802
frescoes **5** *456*, 457
retables **26** 250
tapestries **9** 30; **13** 241; **22** 201
tiles **29** 326; **30** 883, *883*
Escorsat, Dominique **17** 463
Escoto, Miguel D' *see* D'ESCOTO, MIGUEL
Escrin de Charlemagne **5** 807
escritoires *see under* DESKS → types
escritorios see DESKS → types → writing-desks
Escritôrio Técnico F. P. Ramos de Azevedo **2** 903
Escuder, Andrés **3** 220, 221
Escuela de Vallecas **20** 205
Escuela de Gremios *see* FUNDACIÓN DE GREMIOS
Escuela Mexicana de Arquitectura **33** 493
Escuelas Libres de Pintura *see* ESCUELAS DE PINTURA AL AIRE LIBRE
Escuelas de Pintura al Aire Libre **10** 505*; **21** 397, 406; **25** 881; **26** 266
Escuintla **21** 187
Museo de la Democratia **13** 769
escultopintura **28** 784
Escurialene style **10** 534
Esdaile, William **9** 230; **10** 505*; **33** 345
Esdell, William **16** 15
Esdin, Jacquemart de *see* JACQUEMART DE HESDIN
Ese **10** *19*
Eseler, Michael **10** 506
Eseler, Niclas (*c.* 1400/10-after 1482) **10** 506*
works **8** 905, 906; **12** 365; **23** 204, 205; **27** 217, 218
Eseler, Niclas (fl *c. 1492-1509)* **8** 905, 906; **10** 506; **27** 217
E-Series Tarocchi, master of the **20** 661–2*
Esfahan *see* ISFAHAN
Esguerra García, Rafael **21** 4
Eshel-Gershuni, Bianka **16** 568
Esher (Surrey) **10** 195, 346
Esher Place **12** 176; **13** 199
Bishop Waynflete's Tower **4** 770, *770*
Esherick, Joseph **27** 730
Esherick, Wharton **24** 602; **31** 634; **33** 328
Eshira **11** 878
Eshmunazar **28** 667, 668
sarcophagus **28** *667*
Eshnunna *see* ASMAR, TELL
Esie **1** 292; **23** *129*
sculpture **23** 132, *133*
Esir *see* ALI ACEMI
Eskaf **22** 884
Eskelhem **26** 639
Eski Andaval church **5** 675
Eski Gümüs church **5** 678
Eskikahta **16** 411
Eski Krym *see* STARYY KRYM
Eskil, Archbishop **8** 723
Eskilsson, Nils **30** 114
Eskilstuna **30** *65*, 109, 110; **32** 525
Eski Malatya
congregational mosque **23** 561
fortifications **16** 155
Eskimo **10** 506*; **15** 888; **22** 545, 563, 573, 648, 668, 673, 674, 675; **27** 436
beadwork **3** 441
carving **22** 573, 575
maps **20** 362
masks **22** *545*, *573*, 575
tourist art **22** 575
wood-carvings **22** *573*
see also INUIT; YUIT
Eski Mosul region **1** *849*, 895; **10** *506*, 506–7*; **21** *267*, 268, 280
Eskişehir
Anadolu University **31** 456
tomb of Seyit Gazi **16** 186
Eski Stambul *see* PRESLAV
Eskiyapar **1** 834
Esmahan Gevher Sultan **29** 18
Esmelet, Guillaume **4** 546
Esmond-White, Eleanor **29** 110
Esna **9** *774*, 896; **10** 507*; **26** *921*
Deir Manayus wa Shuhada *see* Monastery of the Holy Martyrs
hypostyle hall **26** 920
inscriptions **10** 82
Monastery of the Holy Martyrs **7** 821
sacred lake **27** 496
Temple of Khnum **9** 809, 834, 897; **10** 507*
reliefs **10** *507*
tombs **9** 840
wall paintings **9** 805
Esnauts, Jean **10** 823; **16** 905
Esoteric Buddhism *see under* BUDDHISM → branches
Espacio **24** 510; **30** 214
Espagnat, Georges d' **10** 507–8*; **19** 10; **30** 375
Espalter, Joaquín **3** 219; **29** 283
España, José Casildo *see* CASILDO ESPAÑA, JOSÉ
España Moderna **18** 899
esparto *see* GRASSES → types → sparto
Espeaubourg **11** 623
Espec, Walter **26** 380
especieros de corazón **20** 501
Espejo **29** 336, 337
Espejo, María Antonieta **31** 65
Espellosa, Gerónimo de **8** 237
Espérandieu, Jacques Henry **10** 508*; **20** 473; **32** 83
Espercieux, Jean-Joseph **10** 508–9*
Espinal, Juan de **6** 123; **20** 499; **29** 282
Espinar, Cristobal del **32** 176
Espíndola, Luis de **4** 264
Espine, Jean de l' *see* JEAN DE L'ESPINE

Espinet, Rico 18 834
Espino, C. J. F. 19 174
Espínola Gómez, Manuel 10 509*; 31 756
Espinós, Benito 10 509*
Espinós, José 10 509
Espinosa, Augustin 30 22
Espinosa, Celestino 29 337
Espinosa, Gaspar de 29 213
Espinosa, Gladys Ramírez de *see* RAMÍREZ DE ESPINOSA, GLADYS
Espinosa, Jerónimo Jacinto 10 509–10*; 29 281
attributions 23 571
pupils 27 645
works 10 *510*
Espinosa, Jéronimo Rodriguez de *see* RODRIGUEZ DE ESPINOSA, JÉRONIMO
Espinosa, José María 7 608
Espinosa, Juan Bautista de 10 511*; 29 667
Espinosa, Juan de 10 511
Espinosa, Juan Salazar y *see* SALAZAR Y ESPINOSA JUAN
Espinosa, Manuel (*fl* 1945) 2 604
Espinosa, Onofre de 29 336
Espinosa, Susana 25 702, 703
Espinosa de Castro, Jacinto 10 510
Espinosa Páez, Juan 9 711; 25 829
works 25 *828*
Espinoza, Eugenio 10 511*
Espinoza, Francisco 2 387
Espinoza, Manuel (*b* 1937) 10 511*; 32 180
Espinoza, Nicodemus 24 99
Espinoza Cáceda, Romano 24 509
Espinoza Dueñas, Francisco 10 511*
Espinques, Evrard d' *see* EVRARD D'ESPINQUES
Espirit nouveau, L' 19 40
Espirito Santo, Domingos António de *see* SEQUEIRA, DOMINGOS ANTÓNIO DE
Espírito Santo University *see under* ÉVORA
Espiritu Santo 31 890, 892, 893
Espleghem, Frans Crabbe van *see* CRABBE (VAN ESPLEGHEM), FRANS
Esplugas, A. 10 511–12*
Esplugas, José Oriol Mestres *see* MESTRES ESPLUGAS, JOSÉ ORIOL
Espondaburu, Horacio 31 754
Espoo 14 372
church 11 94
University 29 427
Esposito, Gaetano 10 512*
Esposito, Giovanni 13 764
Esposizione Internazionale d'Arte Decorativa, 1902 *see under* TURIN
Esposizione Universale di Roma *see* ROME → EUR
Espouses (NY), Shrine of the Holy Shroud 28 632
espresso machines 25 218
Esprit, L' 19 897
Esprit nouveau, L' 1 75; 7 293; 11 525; 15 66; 21 782; 23 694; 24 144, 442; 25 740; 26 44
Espuñes, Matilde 29 344
Espuñes, Ramón 29 338
Esquibel, Diego 2 466
Esquiline Treasure 9 520, 655; 18 823, 825; 27 84
Esquillan, Nicolas 33 627
Esquipulas 13 *758*
sanctuary 13 761, *761*
Esquirol, Jean Etienne Dominique 13 625; 21 7
Esquivel, Antonio María 10 512–13*; 28 516; 29 357
patrons and collectors 23 523
works 10 *513*; 29 283
Esquivel, Diego 10 513
Esquivel, Juan de 16 882
Esquivel, Miguel de 10 513*
Esquivias 29 321
Esrom Abbey 8 722
Es Samu Synagogue 17 542
Essaouira 1 527; 21 49; 22 129
Essche, Maurice van 29 109
Esselbeck, Michiel 1 811; 22 888
Esselens, Jacob 10 513–14*
works 5 682; 10 *514*
Esselingen, von *see* BÖBLINGER
Essen 10 514–15*; 12 *360*; 30 729
Collegiate Church 31 273
exchange 10 669
Liberal synagogue 17 548
Minster (Abbey) 10 514–15*, *515*; 26 574
candelabrum 23 659; 26 685
crypt 7 265; 8 223
Essen Virgin (980) 12 399; 22 43; 23 648; 26 145, *145*, 632
reliquaries 26 148
Münsterschatzmuseum 10 515
Museum Folkwang 28 112; 29 608
collections 14 31; 15 745; 21 648; 24 682, 683
see also HAGEN → Folkwang Museum
Opernhaus 30 684
St Liudger 26 684
Steelerstrasse synagogue 17 547
Villa Hügel 15 747
Essen, Gerd-Wolfgang 22 795
Essen, Jacob van *see* ES, JACOB VAN
Essen, Johann von *see* LADENSPELDER, JOHANN
Essendon Church (Herts) 11 255
Essen Madonna (late 11th cent.) 6 389
Essensism 18 106
Essenwein, August Ottmar von 7 589; 10 155, 515–16*; 13 203; 23 317
Esseö, Erzsébeth 20 926
Esser, Johannes Fredericus Samuel 12 502; 28 864
Esser, Max 12 197; 21 66
Esserent, Jean d' *see* JEAN D'ESSERENT
Essex, Arthur Capel, 1st Earl of *see* CAPEL, ARTHUR, 1st Earl of Essex
Essex, Frances Howard, Countess of *see* HOWARD, FRANCES, Countess of Essex
Essex, George Coningsby, 5th Earl of *see* CONINGSBY, GEORGE, 5th Earl of Essex
Essex, Henry VII de Bohun, 6th Earl of *see* BOHUN, HENRY VII DE, 7th Earl of Hereford and 6th Earl of Essex
Essex, Humphrey V de Bohun, 3rd Earl of *see* BOHUN, HUMPHREY V DE, 4th Earl of Hereford and 3rd Earl of Essex
Essex, Humphrey VI de Bohun, 5th Earl of *see* BOHUN, HUMPHREY VI DE, 6th Earl of Hereford and 5th Earl of Essex
Essex, James 10 516*
works 3 741; 5 512; 10 165, 167, 170; 13 200; 32 825, *826*
Essex, Joan de Bohun, Countess of Hereford and *see* BOHUN, JOAN DE, Countess of Hereford and Essex
Essex, Joanna de Bohun, Countess of Hereford and *see* BOHUN, JOANNA DE, Countess of Hereford and Essex
Essex, John 4 692
Essex, Robert Devereux, 2nd Earl of *see* DEVEREUX, ROBERT, 2nd Earl of Essex
Essex, Thomas Cromwell, Earl of *see* CROMWELL, THOMAS, Earl of Essex
Essex, William Capell, 3rd Earl of *see* CAPELL, WILLIAM, 3rd Earl of Essex
Essex and Suffolk Equitable Insurance Company 32 721
Essex Art Pottery Co. 6 65
Essex & Co. 14 53
Esslingen
Frauenkirche 4 187; 10 *408*; 12 365; 13 88
houses 32 282
Rathaus
roof 30 *910*
St Paul 13 49
Spitalkirche St Katharina 4 189, *191*
stained glass 13 186
Esso 13 768; 23 906
Esson, Tomás 8 234
Essor, L' 8 628; 10 517*
members 3 43; 5 44; 8 651, 700, 896; 11 746; 18 23; 26 96
Estache, Pierre L' *see* L'ESTACHE, PIERRE
Estaço, Aquiles *see* STATIUS, ACHILLES
Estampa Popular Catalana 10 443; 25 629; 29 286
Estampe et l'affiche, L' 24 442
Estampe moderne, L' 24 442
Estampes, Robinet d' 6 76
Estanys, José 1 573
Estape, Jules d' 18 659
Estaquería, La *see* LA ESTAQUERÍA
Estarico, Leonardo 2 404
Estate Romana, l' 30 685
Estavayer-le-Lac, St Laurentius 7 192; 21 725
Estavillo, Antonio 24 613
Este (Italy) 16 *618*; 25 *470*
Museo Nazionale Atestino 10 528
Este (i) (family) 10 517–18*, *518*; 24 16
architecture 2 849; 3 744; 11 1; 21 771
coats of arms 14 410
collections 2 161; 16 765
decorative works 31 430
gardens 12 115
manuscripts 20 334; 26 564
paintings 1 595; 4 332, 334; 5 842, 843; 7 893; 12 162; 16 711; 24 760; 31 428
sponsorship 31 428
tapestries 11 4–5, 192
Este (i), Alberto d', Marchese of Ferrara *see* ALBERTO, 11th Marchese of Ferrara
Este, Alberto Maria d' 31 429
Este (ii), Alessandro d' (1783-1826) 10 527
Este (ii), Alessandro d' (*fl* 1864) 10 527
Este (i), Alessandro d', Cardinal (1568-1624) 10 *518*, 525*
Este (i), Alfonso I d', Duke of Ferrara *see* ALFONSO I, 3rd Duke of Ferrara, Modena and Reggio
Este (i), Alfonso II d', Duke of Ferrara *see* ALFONSO II, 5th Duke of Ferrara, Modena and Reggio
Este (i), Alfonso III, Duke of Modena *see* ALFONSO III, 7th Duke of Modena and Reggio
Este (i), Alfonso IV d', Duke of Modena *see* ALFONSO IV, 9th Duke of Modena and Reggio
Este (i), Anna Maria, Duchess of Ferrara, Modena and Reggio *see* ANNA MARIA SFORZA, Duchess of Ferrara, Modena and Reggio
Este (ii), Antonio d' 4 181; 5 679; 10 527
Este (i), Azzo I, Lord of Ferrara *see* AZZO I, Lord of Ferrara
Este (i), Azzo II d', Marchese of Ferrara *see* AZZO II, Marchese of Ferrara
Este (i), Azzo III, 2nd Marchese of Ferrara *see* AZZO III, 2nd Marchese of Ferrara
Este, Baldassare d' *see* BALDASSARE D'ESTE
Este (i), Barbara, Duchess of Ferrara *see* BARBARA OF AUSTRIA, Duchess of Ferrara
Este (i), Beatrice, Duchess of Milan *see* BEATRICE D'ESTE, Duchess of Milan
Este (i), Borso d', Duke of Ferrara *see* BORSO, 1st Duke of Ferrara, Modena and Reggio
Este (i), Cesare d', Duke of Modena *see* CESARE, 6th Duke of Modena and Reggio
Este (i), Eleonora d', Duchess of Mantua *see* ELEONORA DE' MEDICI, Duchess of Mantua
Este (i), Ercole I d', Duke of Ferrara *see* ERCOLE I, 2nd Duke of Ferrara, Modena and Reggio
Este (i), Ercole II, Duke of Ferrara *see* ERCOLE II, 4th Duke of Ferrara, Modena and Reggio
Este (i), Ercole III d', Duke of Modena *see* ERCOLE III, Duke of Modena
Este (i), Francesco I d', Duke of Modena *see* FRANCESCO I, 8th Duke of Modena and Reggio
Este (i), Francesco II, Duke of Modena *see* FRANCESCO II, Duke of Modena
Este (i), Francesco III d', Duke of Modena *see* FRANCESCO III, Duke of Modena
Este, Francesco IV d' *see* FRANCESCO IV, Duke of Modena
Este, Ginevra d' 24 *863*
Este (i), Giovanni Battista *see* ALFONSO III, 7th Duke of Modena and Reggio
Este (ii), Giuseppe d' 10 527
Este (i), Ippolito I d', Cardinal (1479-1520) 10 *518*, 523*; 14 904
architecture 10 544; 11 656; 27 191
collections 6 141
gardens 11 343; 12 115; 26 770
metalwork 6 142
paintings 24 342; 26 459
sculpture 31 62
silver 6 141
Este (i), Ippolito II d', Cardinal (1509-72) 10 *518*, 524*
archaeology 5 843; 19 371
architecture 19 372–3; 28 468; 31 57, 63; 32 692
gardens 32 547
paintings 22 391; 33 718
sculpture 7 331, 332
Este (i), Isabella d', Marchesa of Mantua *see* ISABELLA D'ESTE, Marchesa of Mantua
Este (i), Lionello d', Marchese of Ferrara *see* LIONELLO, 13th Marchese of Ferrara
Este, Lucrezia d', Duchess of Urbino *see* LUCREZIA D'ESTE, Duchess of Urbino
Este, Luigi d', Cardinal 25 227; 32 203
Este (i), Margherita, Duchess of Ferrara *see* MARGHERITA GONZAGA, Duchess of Ferrara
Este, Maria Beatrice d' *see* HABSBURG I., MARIA BEATRICE D'ESTE OF MODENA, Archduchess of Austria
Este, Mary d', Queen of England *see* MARY OF MODENA, Queen of England
Este (i), Niccolò II d', Marchese of Ferrara *see* NICCOLÒ II, 10th Marchese of Ferrara
Este (i), Niccolò III d', Marchese of Ferrara *see* NICCOLÒ III, 12th Marchese of Ferrara
Este (i), Obizzo d' 10 525
Este (i), Obizzo I d', Marchese of Ferrara *see* OBIZZO I, Marchese of Ferrara
Este (i), Obizzo II d', Marchese of Ferrara *see* OBIZZO II, Marchese of Ferrara
Este (i), Rinaldo d', Cardinal 10 526, 527
Este (i), Rinaldo I d', Duke of Modena *see* RINALDO I, Duke of Modena
Este (i), Sigismondo d' 27 190
Este art 6 154; 10 527–8*; 28 807
Este-Austria (family) 2 830
Este-Austria, Francis Ferdinand, Archduke of 4 20; 10 722; 14 11; 23 333; 25 12
Esteban, Bishop of Zamora 33 604
Estéban, Claude 20 75
Esteban, Juan 4 209
Esteban, Martín *see* ESTEVAN, MARTÍN
Esteban, Martin Dominguez 31 193
Esteban, Master 23 900; 27 793
Esteban, Miguel 29 303
Este Collection *see under* VIENNA → museums → Kunsthistorisches Museum
Estefania, Countess of Castile 26 689
Estelé 23 *79*
Estelí 23 85
Estella
metalwork 29 333
sculpture 26 605, 609
S Juan Bautista 26 642
S Pedro de la Rúa 7 455
Estella, Juan Periz de *see* PERIZ DE ESTELLA, JUAN
Estella, Martin Periz de *see* PERIZ DE ESTELLA, MARTIN
Esterbauer, Balthasar 9 752
Esterbrook, Richard 12 26
Esterháza *see* FERTŐD
Esterházy (family) 5 85; 15 13; 18 127
architecture 14 888; 20 494; 28 849
collections 2 829; 15 15
paintings 10 757
portraits 14 899
silver 15 6
Esterházy, Ferenc, Count 24 808
Esterházy, Franz 5 614
Esterházy, Imre, Count 10 531*; 14 894; 15 13; 23 854; 28 857
Esterházy, Imre, Prince-Archbishop, Primate of Hungary 9 145
Esterházy, József, Count 10 531*; 15 2
Esterházy, Károly, Bishop of Vác 14 887, 888; 18 417
Esterházy, Károly, Count 10 531*, 871
architecture 9 754
frescoes 20 856
paintings 14 900
Esterházy, Miklós I, Count (1582-1645) 10 528*; 14 886
Esterházy, Miklós, Count (1711-64) 10 531*

Esterházy, Miklós (József) I, Prince (1714-90) **10** 529*
architecture **6** 554; **11** 31; **14** 298, 887
Esterházy, Miklós II, Prince (1765-1833) **10** 529–31*; **13** 304
architecture **10** *530*; **32** 375
collections **15** 17
sculpture **30** 459
Esterházy, Pál, Prince (1635-1713) **10** 528–31*
architecture **2** 782; **14** 886
paintings **10** 528
Esterházy, Pál, Prince (1786-1866) **3** 203; **10** 530
Esterházy, Princess **18** 843
Esterházy collection *see under* BUDAPEST → museums → Museum of Fine Art
Esterházy-Galantha, Emmerich, Prince-Archbishop of Esztergom **4** 695; **12** 25
Esterházy Madonna **10** 530
Estes, Richard **10** 532*
collaboration **20** 607
groups and movements **24** 686, 687
methods **1** 130
patrons and collectors **23** 7
works **24** *687*; **28** 301
Estete, Miguel de **29** 218
Esteva, Joan **29** 321
Estevan, Martín **10** 532*
Esteve (family) **22** 35
Esteve, Agustín **10** 533; **23** 626
Esteve, Francisco **10** 532
Estève, Maurice **10** 533*; **11** 551
works **10** *533*; **11** *545*; **19** 491
Esteve, Pierre **11** 604
Esteve Bonet, José **10** 532*; **31** 816
Esteve Vilella, Rafael **10** 533*; **31** 816
Esteve y Marques, Agustín **1** 689, 690; **10** 533–4*; **13** 252; **29** 283
Estévez, Fernando **29** 294
Estévez, Jorge **21** 382
esthetics *see* AESTHETICS
Estíbaliz, S María **13** 105
Estienne, Charles (1504-64) **1** 842; **10** 204; **12** 64, 120; **21** 6
Estienne, Charles (*fl* 1950s) **2** 545; **24** 144; **30** 231
Estienne, Henri **10** 534
Estienne, Nicolas **11** 605
Estienne, Robert **4** 8; **10** 534*; **31** 495
Estienne de Bonneuil *see* ETIENNE DE BONNEUIL
Estiennes, Henri **31** 495
estilo chão *see* PLAIN STYLE (PORTUGAL)
estilo desornamentado **10** 534–5*; **12** 920
Estilo Reyes Católicos *see* HISPANO-FLEMISH STYLE
estípites **3** 89; **10** 535*
Estivel (family) **33** 358
Estlander, Carl Gustav **11** 113
Estonia **10** 535–41*, *536*
architecture **10** 536–8*
art schools **10** 539
churches **30** *276*
collections **10** 540*
exhibitions **10** 539; **33** 566
galleries (iv) (art) **10** *537*
insignia **7** 178
limestone **10** 536
lithography **10** 539
museums **10** 540*
painting **10** 538–40*, *540*
portraits **10** *539*
sculpture **10** *538*, 538–40*
stone **10** *538*
wood-engravings **10** 539
Estonian Art Fund **10** 541
Estonian Artists' Group **10** 539, 542*
Estouteville, Guillaume d', Cardinal **10** 542*
architecture **24** 778; **26** 831; **27** 254
sculpture **21** 693, 695
Estouteville, Jacques d' **20** 757
Estrada, Domingo **29** 337
Estrada, Emilio **3** 65; **7** 206; **31** 811
Estrada, Jerónimo Hernández *see* HERNÁNDEZ ESTRADA, JERÓNIMO
Estrada, José de **29** 347
Estrada, José María **10** 542–3*
Estrada, Valentín **10** 154
estrade **12** 109
Estrées, Gabrielle d' **11** *267*
Estrées, Maréchal d' **4** 164
Estrées-sur-Noye villa **32** 542
Estreicher, Dominik **25** 121
Estremoz **25** 308; **29** 702
Estridentismo **1** 739; **8** 254; **10** 543*; **21** 123, 388; **26** 266
Estruch, Juan **10** 543
Estruch y Jordán, Domingo **10** 543
Estudio Cinco **31** 754
Estuna Church **30** 75
Esturmio, Hernando de **10** 543*
Esztergom **10** 544–6*; **14** *881*
Archbishop's Palace **32** 629
Archiepiscopal Library **15** 19
Castle Museum **10** 544, *544*; **14** 883, 884, 890; **15** 17
Chapel **14** 883, 898; **26** 638
Cathedral of St Adalbert **10** *545*, 545–6*; **14** 883, 885, 888, 895
Bakócz Chapel **14** 885
metalwork **11** 615; **26** 687
portal **14** 892
reliquaries **26** 147
sculpture **26** 638
Suky Chalice **13** 162, *162*; **15** 10
Treasury **5** 811; **10** 545; **13** 158, 162; **15** 10, 17
Mint **15** 5
Museum of Christianity **10** 545; **15** 17; **28** 857
Royal Castle *see* Castle Museum
St Anne **14** 888
sculpture **14** 895
silver **9** 655
Etablissement für alle Gegenstände des Ameublements **2** 813; **8** 502
étagère *see under* TABLES → types
Etah **15** 480
Etampes **11** *504*
Château **6** 55; **9** 144
Notre-Dame **10** *546*, 546–7*; **22** 216
St Martin **4** 465; **5** 319
Etampes, Comte d' (*fl* 1367) **30** 312
Etampes, Duchesse d' (*fl* 1552) **25** 208
Etampes, Anne de Pisselieu, Duchesse de **21** 366
Etampes, Margaret of Orléans, Comtesse d' **20** 722
miniatures **20** *723*
Etampes, Robinet d' *see* ROBINET D'ETAMPES
Etaples, Jacques Lefèvre d' *see* LEFÈVRE D'ETAPLES, JACQUES
Etchells, Frederick **10** 547*
groups and movements **13** 712; **23** 437; **26** 59; **32** 700, 701
writings **10** 240
Etchells, Jessie **23** 437
Etchells and Macdonald **4** 366
Etchers Club of Cincinnati **25** 629
Etcheverry, Pierre Dalgare **2** 396
etching **11** 337; **25** 597
historical and regional traditions
England **2** *471*
Sweden **30** *110*
uses
armour **2** 449, 471
etching
uses—cont.
glass **10** 319–20; **12** 787*
steel **30** *110*
swords **2** 449, 452, 453
etching on glass *see* PHOTOGRAPHY → processes cliché-verre
Etching Revival **10** 396, 555–7*; **16** 850; **26** 233; **33** 137
England **14** 106
France **19** 239
etchings **2** 238, 506–7; **10** 547–63*; **18** 706; **25** 597, 612, *613*, 614, 618; **26** 229, 230
historical and regional traditions
Africa **1** *429*
Belgium **3** 561*; **7** *499*; **12** *513*; **13** *701*; **32** *152*
Renaissance **4** *907*
Denmark **8** 731
England **10** 252
Aesthetic Movement **33** *140*
Picturesque **24** *742*
17th cent. **14** *684*
18th cent. **4** *117*
19th cent. **4** *885*; **10** *556*
20th cent. **14** *608*
France **10** 551–3*
Baroque **24** *272*
Cubism **4** *676*
Impressionism **25** *607*
Mannerism **5** *437*, *438*
Realism (style) **22** *688*
17th cent. **3** *633*, *635*; **4** *468*
18th cent. **26** 742
19th cent. **4** 625, *626*; **19** 215; **20** *603*; **21** *171*; **27** *141*
Germany **10** 548, 549–50*, 695
Renaissance **1** *716*; **10** *550*; **14** *574*; **33** *18*
16th cent. **3** *506*; **14** 747, *747*; **18** *876*
18th cent. **5** *29*; **7** *183*; **25** *599*
19th cent. **18** *202*
20th cent. **18** *109*
Iran **15** *899*
Islamic **15** *899*
Italy **10** 550–53*
Baroque **6** *34*; **16** *668*
16th cent. **25** *641*
17th cent. **3** *208*; **4** *89*; **10** *552*; **15** *93*; **27** *153*; **30** *528*
18th cent. **5** 598; **10** *555*; **24** *844*, *845*; **32** *113*
19th cent. **11** *284*
Japan **28** 598
Netherlands, the **10** 549–50*, 553*
Baroque **26** *165*
17th cent. **5** *325*; **10** *553*; **11** 794; **25** *606*; **28** *361*
18th cent. **25** *50*
Nigeria **1** *429*; **23** *136*
Norway **10** *557*
Panama **23** 905
Romania **26** 716
Scotland **28** 236, 238
South Africa **29** 110
Spain **2** *241*; **28** *515*
Switzerland **13** 267; **21** *152*; **25** VII2
United States of America **24** *601*; **33** *140*
19th cent. **17** 441
materials
acids **10** 548–9; **25** 614
albumen **10** 560
alcohol **10** 560
asphalt **10** 560
benzine **10** 560
bitumen **10** 558
carbon papers **10** 548
chalk **10** 548
charcoal **10** 549
copper **10** 562
cotton **10** 561
graphite **10** 548
grease **10** 549
etchings
materials—cont.
grounds **10** 548, 549; **13** 706
gum arabic **10** 559, 560
honey **10** 559
inks **15** 855
leaves **10** 561
linseed oil **10** 560
mordants (i) (acid) **10** 548–9
nitric acid **10** 560
nylon **10** 561
olive oil **10** 560
paper **10** 561
papier mâché **10** 561
petrol **10** 561
petroleum jelly **10** 561
plaster **10** 561
printing plates **10** 548, 549, 562
resins **10** 560
ropes **10** 561
saliva **10** 549
sand **10** 562
sandpaper **10** 562
screens (photographic) **14** 271
silk **10** 561
soap **10** 559, 560
string **10** 561
sugar **10** 559
sulphur **25** 619
tallow **10** 561
textiles **10** 562
tools **9** 697
turpentine **10** 561
varnishes **10** 549, 560, 562; **27** 140; **32** 3
vinegar **10** 560
white lead **10** 560
wood **10** 561
zinc oxide **10** 559
techniques
photogravure **10** 558
stopping-out **29** 719*
wash manner **10** 549
types
Aberli style **1** 31
aquatints *see* AQUATINTS
colour **14** 271; **27** 269
lift-ground **2** 239, 240; **10** *559*, 559–60*; **25** 614; **28** 358
open-bite **2** 241
relief **4** 117; **7** *227*; **10** 555, 560–61*, *561*; **25** 597
soft-ground **10** 548, 555, 557, 561–3*; **25** 597, 614; **27** 141
Britain **10** 555, 562
England **10** *562*; **11** 906
United States of America **10** 562
sugarbite aquatints *see* lift-ground
sugar-lift *see* lift-ground
uses
book illustrations **4** 359, 362; **10** 550
see also ART (REPRODUCTIONS OF WORKS OF); PRINTING → processes → photogravure
Etelhem church **13** 190; **26** 639
Etex, Antoine **3** 289; **8** 192; **10** 563–4*; **11** 565; **27** 311
Etex, Louis-Jules **8** 787
Etgens, Johann Georg **8** 391; **17** 585
ethanol **18** 610; **29** 53
Ethelbald, King of Mercia (*reg* 716-57) **7** 246
Etheldreda, Queen of East Anglia (*reg* 530-79) **10** 165
Etheldreda, Saint (*c.* 630-79) **3** 708
Ethelgar of Abingdon, Archbishop of Canterbury **2** 75
Ethelwald (*fl* 698) **19** 409
Ethelwold, Saint (*c.* 908-84) *see* AETHELWOLD, Saint
ether **24** 649
Ethiopia **1** *214*, 378; **10** 564–78*
altars **1** 694
Ethiopia—cont.
architecture **10** 564–7*, 577*; **21** 43
baskets **1** 295; **3** 442
beadwork **3** 442
canon tables **5** 624
churches **1** *314*, 314–15; **10** 565–6, *566*; **26** 484
coins **1** 362
collections **10** 577–8*
columns **10** 473
cotton **8** 34
education (art) **1** 433; **10** 578
erotic art **10** 473
exhibitions **10** 578
glazes **4** 172
gold **27** 15
houses **1** 311
huts **1** 308
manuscript illumination **1** *380*; **10** 567, 568–9*, *569*, 570
miniatures (manuscript illumination) **10** *570*
models **1** *513*
monasteries **1** 314–15
museums **10** 577–8*
obsidian **29** 702
painting **10** 567–74*, *571*, *573*, *575*
patronage **10** 577–8*
pigments **4** 172
pottery **4** 172
rock art **1** 373; **10** 568
sculpture **10** 576–7*
shields **1** 362
stelae **10** 565, 577
stone **1** 305
tables **1** 366
tombs **10** 577
wraps **1** 348
ethiops **24** 795
ethnographic photography *see under* PHOTOGRAPHY → uses
Ethnographie **24** 430
ethnography **10** *578*, 578–80*, *579*
Africa **21** 480
Brazil **4** 708
Colombia **7** 609
Islamic **16** 107–9*
Mali **21** 480
Middle Niger cultures **21** 480*
Sri Lanka **29** 473
Tibet **30** 848
Ethnos **24** 430
ethos **13** 467; **24** 207
ethylene-vinyl acetate *see* EVA
Etienne *see* STEPHANUS
Etienne d'Auxerre **5** 666; **13** 147
Etienne de Bonneuil **10** 581*
works **13** 50, 102; **31** *693*, 694
Etienne de Lale **14** 759
Etienne de Montbéliard **14** 726
Etienne le Hongrie **15** 11
Etienne le Tur **8** 902
Etienne-Martin **10** 581–2*; **11** 551, 569
collaboration **11** 569; **29** 497
patrons and collectors **19** 848
pupils **7** 645
works **11** *569*
Etiennez, Hippolyte **4** 81
Etikhove, Centrum voor Kunst en Kunstambachten Valerius De Saedeleer **8** 786
Etiolles, Jeanne-Antoinette Poisson d' *see* POMPADOUR, JEANNE-ANTOINNETTE POISSON, Marquise de
Etla **21** 221
Etna group **13** 530, 531; **28** 655
Etoilles **25** 494
Eton (people) **10** 787
Eton College (Berks) **4** 779; **7** 566; **14** 423; **18** 687; **28** 156
architecture **4** 770
Chapel **10** 245
chimneys **4** 779
collections **1** 23; **10** 90, 92
tapestries **30** 328

Etowah (GA) **10** 582*; **22** *544*, 560; **30** 449
Etrog, Sorel **5** 571; **10** 582*
Etropole **5** 160
Etruria *see* ETRUSCAN
Etruria factory *see* WEDGWOOD CERAMICS FACTORY
Etruria Padana **10** 632
Etruscan **10** 582–644*, *583*; **25** 533; **26** *852*
agate **12** 249
alabaster (gypsum) **10** *593*
alphabets **10** 591
altars **1** 692*
amber **1** 761; **10** 635
amphorae **10** *594*, 612
animal subjects **10** 593
antefixes **10** 603
arches **2** 297
architectural decorations **1** 127; **10** 587; **32** *119*
architecture **10** 587, 596–602*; **16** 622; **26** 749, 851
bone **10** 635*
books **10** 589, 590, 636
braziers **10** 613
bronze **6** 388; **10** 587, 588, *590*, *595*, 602, 604–6, *605*, 608, *608*, 624–30*, *625*, *626*, *627*, *628*, *629*, 633, *635*; **16** *684*; **21** 712, *712*; **27** 85
bronzes **10** 638
buckles **10** *625*
bullae **10** 636
busts **10** 604
candelabra **10** 627
cartoons (drawings) **10** 617
caskets **10** 635
casting **10** 587
cemeteries **10** 586
chairs **6** 388
chariots **6** 480*, *481*
cists **10** *629*, 630*
clay **10** 609, 612
coins **10** 586, 632–3*, *632*; **25** 245
collections **10** 637–40*
copies **10** 588
copper **10** 624
cornelian **12** 249, *249*
couches **10** *633*
craftsmen and artists **10** 587, 596
dinoi **10** *614*
dress **10** 635–6*
earrings **10** *631*
embossing **10** 587
erotic art **10** 474
exhibitions **10** 637, 640–41
faience (i) (glass) **10** 591
fibulae **10** *630*; **12** *868*
figurines **10** 602, 604, 625
filigree **10** 631
flax **10** 636
forgeries **10** 637, 638–40*; **13** 516
fortifications **10** 601
frames **11** 379
friezes **10** *607*, 620, *633*
furniture **10** *633*, 633–4*
gem-engraving **12** 248–50*, *249*
gilding **10** 625
gold **10** 624, *630*, 630–32*, *631*, 639; **12** 865, 867, 868, *868*
gold leaf **10** 631
gypsum **10** 606, *606*
harnesses **14** 181*
holmoi **10** *611*
houses **1** 127; **10** *598*, 599–600*; **26** 888
human figures **10** 593–4, 624
huts **10** 587
hydriai **10** *615*; **13** *516*, 516
iconography **10** 587, 588–90, 592–6*, 619
ingots **10** 632
inscriptions **10** 588, 589, *590*, 596, 605, 610, 620, 628, 638; **13** 10
interior decoration **10** *597*
iron **10** 624
Etruscan—cont.
ivory-carvings **1** 872; **10** 593, *634*, 634–5*
jewellery **10** 593, 631–2, 635, 636
jugs **10** 626
kraters **10** *616*
kylikes **10** 612
languages **10** 584, 636, 637; **18** 755
lead **10** 624
limestone **10** 602, *607*
linen **10** 589, 636
looms **10** 635, 636
marble **10** 589, *589*, 602
masks **10** 593
masonry **20** 571
metalwork **10** 587, 593, 624–32*, *630*, *631*
military scenes **10** 595
mints **25** 245
mirror-cases **10** 636
mirror handles **10** 627, 635
mirrors **10** 589, 595, *595*, 627–30, *628*, 639; **21** *712*, 712–13*
modelling **10** 617, 623
models **10** *590*
museums **10** 637, 640*
musical instruments **10** 619
narratives **10** 593, 611, *611*, 624
necropoleis **6** *353*; **22** 716; **23** *584*
nude figures **10** 589, *589*, 595
oinochoai **10** *612*
orders (architecture) **23** 480
painting **12** 287; **16** *652*, 652–3
fresco **10** 617
landscape **18** 701
tomb **10** 591, 594, 617–24*, *618*, *619*, *620*, *621*, *622*, *623*; **30** 346; **32** 118, 744
vase **7** 366; **10** 591, 593, *594*, 611–16, *614*, *615*, *616*
wall **10** 587, 616–24*, *618*, *619*, *620*, *621*, *622*, *623*; **32** 118, 744, 803
palmettes **23** 889
pattern books **10** 617
pediments **24** 317
pendants (jewellery) **10** *635*
periods **10** 587–8*
Archaic **10** 587*
Classical **10** 587–8*
copies **10** 588
Early Iron Age **10** 587*
Hellenistic **10** 588*
Orientalizing **10** 587*
Villanovan *see* Early Iron Age
pigments **10** 617
pithoi **10** 613
plaques **10** 593, 620–21, 634–5; **30** *494*
plaster **10** 617
portraits **10** *608*, 608–9, 620
pottery **10** 587, 593, 609–16*, 641; **13** 540–42, 571
Black-figure **10** *594*, 596, *614*, 614–15*, *615*; **13** 512, 516*, *516*
Black-glazed **10** 616*
Bucchero **6** 353; **10** 593, 611–13*, *612*
Etrusco-Corinthian **10** 613–14*, *614*
Etrusco-Geometric **10** 610–11*, *611*
Greece, ancient **13** 514
impasto ware **10** *599*, 609–10*, *610*
Malacena ware **10** 616
Orientalizing style **10** 611*
Polychrome ware **10** 613
Red-figure **6** 333; **7** 366; **10** 615–16*, *616*; **13** 517
Red ware **10** 613*
pyxides (boxes) **10** *634*
rediscovery **10** 636–8*, 642–4; **13** 10; **18** 755
religion **10** 588–90*, 591
restoration **10** 639–40
Etruscan—cont.
revetments **10** 593, 603
roofs **1** 127
sanctuaries **10** 608
sandstone **10** 602
sarcophagi **10** 588, 592, 594, *607*, 607–8; **27** 823, 826*
sardonyx **12** 249
scarabs **12** 248–50, *249*
sculpture **10** 602–9*, *603*, *604*, *606*, 639; **16** 683; **27** 9
architectural **10** 588, 593, 595, 596, 603–4, *604*
bronze **10** 587, 602, 604–6, *605*, *608*; **16** *684*
korai **10** 593
kouroi **10** 593
marble **10** 589, *589*
monumental **10** 588, 593
mythological **10** *589*
relief **10** 593, *593*, 604
stone **10** 602, 606–8; **32** 744
Wiry Geometric style **10** 604
signatures **10** 629
silver **10** 624, 625, 630–32*, *632*
slip **13** 571
sporting scenes **10** 594, *594*
statuettes **10** 587, 627
stelae **10** 587, 594
stone **6** 388; **10** 588, 602, 606–8; **27** 826; **32** 744
stools **6** 388; **10** *633*, 634
streets **10** 602
stucco **29** 814*
tables **10** *633*
temples **2** *355*, *356*; **10** 588, 593, 596, *600*, 600–601*, *601*, 603–4; **26** 865, 886; **27** 712; **30** 435
terracotta **1** 127; **10** 587, 588, 593, 602–4, *603*, *604*, 608, *633*; **27** 9, 826; **30** 494, *494*; **32** *119*
textiles **10** *635*, 635–6*
thrones **10** 633, *633*
tiles **1** *126*; **30** 494
tin **10** 624
togas **10** 636
tombs **10** 587, 588, 597–9*, 603, 617–24*; **13** 486, 506; **20** 863; **30** 346; **31** 109
arch door **10** 597*
caditoia **10** 598*
chamber **10** 593, *597*, 597–9
corbel **10** 597*
lunette **10** 597*
rock-cut **10** *597*
three-cell **10** 598*
two-cell **10** 598*
trade **10** 584–5, 590–92*, 609
armour **10** 592
bronze **2** 557; **10** 590, 592
chariots **10** 591
coins **10** 591
copper **10** 591; **14** 333
faience (i) (glass) **10** 590
fans **10** 591
glass **2** 557; **10** 591
iron **10** 591
ivory-carvings **10** 591; **24** 643
jewellery **10** 590, 591, 592
metalwork **10** 591; **13** 372
ostrich eggs **10** 590
parasols **10** 591
pottery **10** 591, 592; **13** 486
shells **10** 590
shoes **10** 591
silver **10** 590
vases **10** 612, 614, 616
weapons **10** 592
trappings **14** 181*
tripods **10** *626*, *627*
tufa **10** 602
tumuli **10** 598
urban planning **10** 587, 602; **20** *529*
urns **10** 588, 593, 594
biconical **10** *610*
canopic *see* funerary
Etruscan
urns—cont.
funerary **7** *176*; **10** 588, 593, *593*, 594, 602–3, *603*, 607, 608, 609; **27** 9
hut **10** 587, *599*
vases **10** 587, 609, 610–16, 631
walls **10** 601–2
weaving **10** 635
weights **10** 636
wool **10** 636
Etruscan School **8** 6; **10** 641*; **14** 809; **22** 51; **26** 776
Etruscan Study *see* Gabinetto Etrusco
Etruscan style **1** 137; **10** 276, 637, 641–4*, *643*; **11** 84; **13** 702; **25** 192
see also ARABESQUE STYLE
Etrusco-Corinthian pottery *see under* ETRUSCAN → pottery
Etrusco-Geometric pottery *see under* ETRUSCAN → pottery
Etselo *see* HEZELO
Etsingol **6** 290
Ettal Abbey **33** 270
church **7** 257; **26** 498; **29** 838
Ettamanur **15** 543
Ettedgui, Joseph **17** 593
Ettenhofer, Johann Georg **22** 299; **32** 602
Ettinger, Pavel (Davydovich) **10** 644*
Ettinghausen, Richard **10** 645*; **16** 549, 557, 558
Ettlingen Schloss
fountains **28** *138*
Ettore d'Antonio de' Bonacossi *see* BONACOSSI, ETTORE D'ANTONIO DE'
Ettumanur Shiva Temple **15** 336, 524, 649, 721
Etty (family) **12** 591
Etty, John **14** 197
Etty, William **10** 645–7*; **14** 587; **32** 197; **33** 545
exhibitions **19** 507
groups and movements **26** 740
methods **4** 184
patrons and collectors **5** 78; **12** 638; **22** 314, 719; **32** 338; **33** 251
pupils **14** 197
reproductive prints by others **9** 148; **10** 396; **28** 693
works **10** 252, *646*; **21** 760
Etulo **15** 101
Etung
masks **10** *122*
Etzatlán **10** 647*; **21** *372*
tombs **21** 216; **31** 118
Etzina *see* KARAKHOTO
Etzlaub, Erhard **12** 815
Eu, Nôtre Dame et St Laurent **13** 79
Eu, Geoffroy d' *see* GEOFFROY D'EU
Euagoras I (*reg* 411-374/3 BC) **8** 332, 341; **27** 608
Euainetos **13** 587; **30** 175
works **13** *587*
Euaion **13** 489
Euaion Painter **13** 523
Euboia **8** *304*; **14** *332*, 360
Galataki Monastery **25** 336
Euboulides (*fl c.* 371 BC) **10** 647*
Euboulides (*fl c.* 191/90 BC) **10** 647–8*
Euboulides (*fl* late 2nd cent. BC) **10** 648*
Eucalyptus School **19** 701
Euceda, Maximiliano **14** 715, 716
Eucharides Painter **13** 511
Eucheiros **13** 510
Euclid **1** 113; **2** 345, 347, 354; **11** 743; **24** 486, 657; **28** 202
Eudaimonoiannis, Nikolaos **21** 860
Eude, Peter **5** 827
Eudes de la Perrière *see* ODO, Abbot of Cluny
Eudes de Montreuil **24** 774
Eudokia, Empress of Byzantium **17** 489; **19** 787
Eudovic, Joseph **2** 149
Eudoxos of Knidos **2** 649
Euelthon **8** 332, 349
Euenor **13** 451, 551; **24** 206
Euergides Painter **13** 519; **32** 40
Euffigneix **6** 159
Eufrasius, Bishop **1** 694
Eugen, Adam **22** 310
Eugene, Field-Marshal of Savoy *see* SAVOY, EUGENE OF, Prince
Eugene, Frank **5** 7; **10** 648–9*; **24** 739, *739*
Eugene (OR), Hult Center for the Performing Arts **1** 126
Eugénie, Empress of the French (1826-1920) **4** 306; **11** 635; **13** 680; **24** 36, 141; **26** 500; **32** 374
architecture **9** 420; **28** 346
collections **4** 307
dress **9** 287
furniture **3** 889; **6** 376; **12** 741; **22** 744
jewellery **17** 527
metalwork **11** 622
paintings **3** 396; **4** 306; **5** 342; **14** 121; **16** 876; **19** 115
portraits **5** 826
sculpture **7** 841
Eugenikos, Manuel *see* MANUEL EUGENIKOS
Eugenios, Metropolitan **22** 405
Eugenius III, Pope (*reg* 1145-53) **26** 811, 831
Eugenius IV, Pope (*reg* 1431-47) **2** 37
architecture **23** 97; **26** 755, 820
metalwork **26** 766
paintings **19** 444
sculpture **11** 71; **12** 543; **26** 766
swords **2** 453
Eugowra **2** *736*
Andrews Farmhouse **2** 743
Eugrammos **10** 616
Eugrippius **2** 776
Euhemeros **22** 411
Euhodus, C. Junius
sarcophagus **22** *411*
Euing, William **12** 777
Eukleidas **13** 587; **30** 175
Eukratidea *see* AI KHANUM
Eulalios **18** 211
Eulo **26** 293
Eumaros **10** 649*; **18** 58; **25** 44
Eumathios Philokales **9** 580; **18** 411
Eumelos of Corinth **15** 85
Eumenes (engraver) **30** 175
Eumenes I, King of Pergamon, (*reg* 263-241 BC) **24** 412
Eumenes II Soter, King of Pergamon (*reg* 197-60 BC) **24** 410
architecture **24** 411
manuscripts **19** 312
mosaics **13** 567
museums **9** 20
parchment **24** 106
sculpture **13** 469
stoa **2** 667; **13** 369, 406; **29** 681
Eumorfopoulos, George **6** 868; **7** 111; **10** 649*; **14** 604
Eupalinos of Megara **13** 411; **27** 687; **30** 26
Euphiletos Painter **13** 511; **23** 146
Euphranor **10** 649–50*; **13** 458; **25** 44
attributions **13** 460, *460*
pupils **13** 546
teachers **2** 412
works **2** 686, *686*; **13** 459, 545, 548, 551, 554
writings **31** 301

Euphrasius, Bishop **9** 573; **25** 252; **29** 816
Euphronios **13** 484, 520, 535; **32** 41–2*, 63
  collaboration **32** 60
  patrons and collectors **5** 536, 537; **10** 592; **13** 542, 606
  pupils **32** 49
  teachers **32** 65
  works **13** 489, 518, *518*, 520
Euphrosyne Komnena Dukaena Palaiologina **23** 831
Euphrosyne Palaiologina **23** 830
Euphrosynos **22** 228; **25** 333
Eupolemos **2** 407
Eupompos **13** 551, 554; **23** 900
Eupraxia **28** 457
Eurasburg, Schloss *see* SCHLOSS EURASBURG
Eureka (CA), Carson House **9** 685
Eureka clocks *see under* CLOCKS → types
eurhythmia **13** 467
Eurich, Richard **20** 425
Euriowie **22** 62
Euripides **23** 480
Euro-Disney **6** 63
Euromos **5** 742
  Temple of Zeus **5** 742, *742*
Europa (1803-5) **28** 107
Europa (after 1910) **31** 368
Europa ewer **12** 445
Európai Iskola *see* EUROPEAN SCHOOL
Európai Iskola Könyvtáta **10** 651
European Confederation of Conservator-Restorers' Organizations *see* ECCO
Europeans, the *see* EUROPEAN SCHOOL (EURÓPAI ISKOLA)
European School (Európai Iskola) **10** 650–51*; **14** 901; **17** 833; **21** 77
  members **3** 111; **11** 887; **25** 246
Europus *see* CARCHEMISH
Eusebi, Luis **10** 651*
Eusebio (di Jacopo di Cristoforo) da San Giorgio **3** 858; **10** 651–2*; **15** 60
  collaboration **3** 858; **24** 524, 525, 831
  teachers **3** 55
  works **24** 832
Eusebios of Caesarea **5** 624; **9** 608, 622; **10** 652*; **20** 339; **22** 411; **28** 487
  works **8** 259; **15** 75; **17** 498; **31** 494, *494*
Eustace, Bishop of Ely **10** 167; **12** 5
Eustace, John Chetwode **13** 298, 304
Eustace workshop **2** 846
Eustachio, Bartolomeo **1** 841
Eustathios (*fl* 10th cent.) **28** 764
Eustathios Boilas (*fl* 11th cent.) **9** 625, 657
Eustathios Makrembolites (*fl* 12th cent.) **10** 129
Eustolios **18** 408
Euston Hall (Suffolk) **32** 575
Euston Road School **10** 652–3*; **19** 591, 623
  members **3** 631; **7** 547; **10** 257, 375; **22** 243; **23** 333; **24** 228
  sponsorship **4** 169
  works **23** 297; **31** 706
eutectic soldering *see* METALWORK → techniques → granulation
Euteknios **9** 617
Euthydomos **13** 409
Euthykartides **13** 439; **22** 700
Euthykrates **33** 461
Euthymides **32** 42*, 63
  pupils **13** 520; **32** 34, 49
  works **13** 489, 518
Euthymius, Archbishop **23** 270
Euting, Julius **2** 254; **27** 877
Eutresis **10** 653*; **13** *363*; **14** 351
  houses **14** 338, 339
Eutychianos, Bishop **9** 656
Eutychides **10** 653*; **13** 429; **27** 28
  copies **2** *156*
  works **2** 157; **9** 249; **13** 370, 462; **28** 383; **29** 567
Eutychios
  attributions **9** 585; **13** 265
  works **2** 646; **9** 584; **19** 884; **23** 373, 374; **28** 446, 448; **29** 551; **30** 718
Euxenidas **2** 412; **13** 551
Euxitheos **13** 606; **32** 41, 60
EVA **26** 244
Evangeliaries **5** 800; **9** 608, 610–11, 616; **23** 652; **28** 487
  individual manuscripts
    Aribert Evangeliary (Milan, Cathedral, MS. Inv. 1431) **21** 533
    Codex Millenarius Maior (Kresmünster, Stiftsbib. Cim. 1) **2** 790; **18** 447
    Codex Millenarius Minor (Kresmünster, Stiftsbib. Cim. 2) **18** 447
    Evangeliary of Abbess Uta of Niedermünster (Munich, Bayer. Staatsbib., Clm. 13601) **23** *654*, 654
    Evangeliary of Egmond (The Hague, Kon. Bib., MS. 76F) **22** 833
    Godescalc Evangeliary (Paris, Bib. N., MS. nouv. acq. lat. 1203) **5** 800, 801, *801*; **6** 483; **7** 246; **20** *337*; **25** 743
    Grimani Evangeliary (Venice, Bib. N. Marciana, MS. lat. I. 103) **7** 467
    Miroslav Evangeliary (Belgrade, N. Mus.) **22** 16
    Sainte Chapelle Evangeliary (Paris, Bib. N., MS. lat. 8892) **2** 846; **11** 530
  see also LECTIONARIES
Evangelista da Reggio **10** 653*; **16** 848
Evangelista di Pian di Meleto **10** 653–4*; **25** 908; **27** 790
Evangelista Romano **2** 184
Evangelisti, Filippo **3** 713
Evangelistiaries *see* EVANGELIARIES
Evangelist Master **4** 20
Evangelist portraits *see under* PORTRAITS → types
Evans, Allen **11** 848
Evans, Arthur (John) **2** 300; **10** 654*; **14** 360; **21** 651, 653, 655, 663
  assistants **33** 373
  excavations **2** 304; **18** 165; **21** 678, 692
  personal collection **12** 266; **13** 542
Evans, Bernard Walter **4** 86
Evans, Clifford **7** 206; **20** 371
Evans, Edmund (William) **4** 363; **8** 121; **10** 654*; **13** 615; **33** 361
Evans, Edward **24** 601
Evans, Ernest A. **22** 276
Evans, Frederick H(enry) **10** 654–5*; **24** 674, 688
Evans, Garth **10** 268
Evans, George de Lacy **24** 894
Evans, John **2** 299; **10** 91
Evans, Merlyn (Oliver) **10** 655*
Evans, Myfanwy **24** 839
Evans, Richard **14** 58, 60
Evans, Walker **10** 656–7*; **24** 673; **31** 606
  pupils **19** 280
  works **10** *656*; **25** 653; **28** 919
Evans Collection *see under* OXFORD → Ashmolean Museum
Evans & Shalev **27** 563
Evanston (IL), Patten House **6** 578
Evansville (IN), Museum of Arts and Sciences **13** 716
Evarts, William Maxwell **27** 556
Evaux **13** 211
Evdir Han **16** 186
Eve, Claix **26** 745
Eve, George W. **4** 373
Eve, Joseph **3** 61
Eveillard, Pierre-Louis, Marquis de Livois *see* LIVOIS, Marquis de
Eveleigh, John **3** 371; **23** 782
Evelyn, John **10** 657–8*; **15** 47; **33** 3
  personal collection **4** 249; **10** 787
  works **12** 120; **13** 299, 619; **25** 629
    on architecture **10** 204, 376; **20** 879; **23** 857
    on cemeteries **6** 165
    on gardens **5** 344; **12** 61, 127; **32** 552
    on greenhouses **7** 744
    on landscape **12** 128
    on museums **28** 496
    on urban planning **19** 569
    on villas **32** 551
Evelyn, Mary **10** 657
Evelyn, W. A. **33** 545
Evelyn. John **32** 797
Even, E. Van *see* VAN EVEN, E.
Evenepoel, Henri (-Jacques-Edouard) **3** 563; **10** 658*; **19** 490; **20** 603
Evenky **27** 436
Events **24** 403
Everaerts (family) **3** 600
Everard, Bishop of Norwich **7** 351; **11** 288; **21** 838
Everard, Bertha **29** 108
Everard, Ruth *see* HADEN, RUTH EVERARD
Everard Group **29** 108
Everardus von Greiffenclau **20** 786
Everberg, Philippe Evrard Vander Noot, Count of, Bishop of Ghent **27** 133
Everdingen, Allart van **10** 658, 659, 660–61*; **13** 895; **22** 843
  collaboration **3** 757
  patrons and collectors **2** 382; **10** 864; **31** 342
  personal collection **28** 359
  pupils **3** 84; **9** 718
  works **10** *661*; **18** 710; **30** 78
Everdingen, Caesar (Bovetius) van **10** 658, 659–60*; **13** 895; **22** 839
  collaboration **4** 377; **14** 46
  works **10** 659, *659*; **14** 46, 584
Everdingen, Pieter van **10** 658
Everett, Bruce **19** 702
Evergetis, Paul of *see* PAUL OF EVERGETIS
Evergood, Philip **10** 661–2*; **23** 48; **25** 653
Evergreen, The **12** 780
Everitt, Allen Edward **4** 86
Everlöv **30** 76
Evers, Antonius *see* EVERS, TÖNNIES
Evers, Henri (Hendrik Jorden) **4** 57; **10** 662*
Evers, Inge Dorothea **10** 875
Evers, J. Brink **10** 662
Evers, Tönnies, I (*d* 1584) **10** 662
Evers, Tönnies, II (1550/2-1613) **10** 662*; **12** 409
Evers, Tönnies, III (*fl* 1613) **10** 662
Eversley, Fred **1** 444
Evertsberg **13** 120
Evertsen, Cornelis **20** 81
Evert van Soudenbalch **20** 662
Evert van Soudenbalch, Master of **20** 662–3*; **22** 836
  works **20** *662*
Evesham, Epiphanius **10** 262, 662–3*
Evesham Abbey (Hereford & Worcs) **26** 613; **30** 778
Eveux-sur-l'Arbresle, Ste Marie de La Tourette **6** 467; **7** 453; **11** 527; **19** 46
  Sainte-Sacrement **6** *460*, 461
Evgenikos, Kir Manuil **12** 324
  works **12** *324*
Evian, Villa Sapinière **4** 626
Evicera, Conde d' **25** 820
E. V. of Braşov **26** 720
  works **26** *720*
Evol, Guillem de So, Vescomte d' **20** 757
Evola, Julius **8** 436
Évora **10** 663–5*; **25** *288*, 318; **26** *908*
  Archbishop's Palace *see* Museu de Évora
  architecture **25** 291
  Biblioteca Pública **32** 538
  Casa Pia **30** 880
  churches
    Cathedral **10** 663–4; **13** 101; **19** 777; **25** 289, 300
    Church of the Lóios
      azulejos **3** *815*
    Espírito Santo **10** 664; **17** 511
    Nossa Senhora da Graça **10** *664*
    Nossa Senhora das Mercês **26** 254
      retables **26** *253*
    Nossa Senhora d'Espinheiro **25** 295
    Nossa Senhora do Carmo **26** 254
    Nossa Senhora dos Remédios **1** 72; **26** 254
    S Francisco **13** 125; **14** 395; **17** 595; **25** 295
  Espírito Santo University **10** 664
  gold **25** 312
  metalwork **25** 313
  Museu de Évora **10** 664; **25** 318; **32** 539
  Paço de Évora **25** 291
  painting **25** 295
  Palacio de los Condes de Cadaval **5** 364
  Passeio Público **25** 293
  sculpture **25** 301
  stained glass **13** 192
  tiles **30** 880
Évora, Alvaro d' *see* PIREZ, ALVARO
Évora Altarpiece **12** 846
Évora Altarpiece, Master of the **20** 663*
Évora-Monte **25** 291
Evrard, Saint **7** 646
Evrard, Perpète **21** 641
Evrard de Fouilloy, Bishop of Amiens **1** 777
Evrard d'Espinques **16** 854
Evrard des Pitons, Louis *see* PITONS, LOUIS EVRARD
Evrard d'Orléans **9** 708; **10** 665*; **12** 723; **13** 77; **24** 132
  attributions **5** 666
  collaboration **5** 666
  patrons and collectors **5** 666
Evrecy **26** 597
Evreux **11** *504*
  Cathedral of Notre-Dame **10** 665*; **13** 42, 61; **22** 216
    choir-stalls **13** 125
    stained glass **13** 181; **29** 503, 512
  St Taurin **11** 614; **13** 158; **28** 631
Evreux, Louis-Henri de La Tour d'Auvergne, Comte d' **11** 657; **21** 823
Evron **9** *513*, 567
  Notre-Dame de l'Epine **13** 59, 179; **29** 414
Evry **2** 11, 700; **6** 534; **7** 343; **24** 131; **31** 735
Ewald, Johannes **1** 34
Ewan, J. **16** 889
Ewart, David **23** 631
Ewart, John **31** 176
Ewart, William **10** 370
Ewe **1** 282, 392, 503; **14** 55; **31** 73
  carvings **31** 73
  cotton **30** VIII1
  textiles **31** 73
Ewe-fon **8** 230
Eweka II
  altar **3** *721*
Ewelme (Oxon) **4** 779
  Almshouses **4** 770; **14** 781
  St Mary **13** 84
Ewen, Paterson **5** 569
  works **5** *569*
Ewenni **32** 789
Ewenny Priory (Mid Glam.) **26** 590, 618
ewers **10** 666*
  historical and regional traditions
    Afghanistan **16** *375*, *378*
    Belgium **3** *597*
    Central Asia, Western **6** *239*, 245, *246*; **16** *378*
    Chile **6** 599
    China **6** *875*, *878*, 888, *888*, *892*, *918*; **7** 23
    Crete **21** *688*
    Cycladic **8** *314*
    Czech Republic **32** *401*
    Egypt **16** *519*, 541
    France **11** *605*, *615*, *636*
    Germany **12** 445, 452; **28** I1
    Gothic **11** *615*
    Hungary **15** *6*
    Indian subcontinent **12** V1; **15** *714*
    Iran **16** 369, *371*, 375, *408*, *519*
    Iraq **16** 369, *370*
    Islamic **10** *832*; **16** 365, 369, *370*, *371*, 375, *375*, *378*, *381*, *408*, *519*, 541
    Italy **23** *540*
    Japan **17** *254*
    Korea **18** *338*
    Minoan **21** *688*
    Netherlands, the **22** *881*, 890
    Nupe **23** *303*
    Prehistoric **6** *878*
    Sogdiana **6** *239*
    Spain **29** *336*
    Sweden **30** *111*
  materials
    agate **11** *636*
    brass **12** 452; **16** *378*, *381*; **23** *303*
    bronze **2** *237*; **6** *246*; **16** *370*, *375*; **21** *688*; **26** 685–6*
    copper **30** *111*
    earthenwares **6** *888*
    enamel **11** *615*; **15** *6*; **29** *336*
    faience (ii) (ceramics) **11** *605*
    glass **12** V1; **16** *519*
    gold **11** *636*
    inlays **16** *375*, *378*, *381*
    lapis lazuli **11** *636*
    porcelain **6** *918*
    pottery **22** *881*
    rock crystal **10** *832*; **16** 541
    sardonyx **11** *636*
    shells **28** I1
    silver **6** *239*, 599; **7** 23; **16** *371*; **22** 890; **32** *401*
    silver-gilt **3** *597*; **11** *615*; **15** *6*; **28** I1; **29** *336*; **32** *400*
    stonewares **6** *892*; **17** *254*
  types
    aquamanilia **2** 237–8*, *237*; **12** 452; **26** 685–6*
Ewes, Simonds d' **14** 177
Ewondo **5** 523
Eworth, Hans **10** 666–7*
  attributions **10** 246; **14** 297; **21** 369
  patrons and collectors **19** 793
  works **9** 275; **10** 246, *666*
Ewoutsz., Jan **1** 806
Ewout Verhagen, E. **16** 873

Ewuare **3** 718
Ewu Palace **9** 735
exaleiptra *see* KOTHONES
Exat-51 **8** 179; **10** 667*; **24** 733
excavations **2** 299–300, 301–3*, *303*; **5** 890; **30** 346
exchange **22** 562, 565; **23** 741
Exchange Club **10** 669–70*
exchanges **10** 667–9*
England **4** *822*
Finland **29** *64*
France **29** *92*
Gothic **31** *815*
Italy **32** *507*
Netherlands, the **10** *668*; **22** *830*
Russia **27** *375*
Spain **14** *474*; **31** *815*
see also MARKETS
exedrae **5** *21*; **10** *670*, 670–71*
Exekias **13** 485, 489, 508, 509; **32** 42–6*
attributions **32** 46
inscriptions **13** 490
methods **13** 550; **22** 410
narratives **13** 508–9; **22** 513
patrons and collectors **13** 542
pupils **13** 511; **32** 54
works **9** 247; **13** 472; **32** *44*
exempla **5** 800
Exeter (Devon; UK) **10** *225*, 671–5*
Assembly Rooms **2** 617
baths **3** 375
carpets **5** 838, *838*; **10** 358, *358*
Cathedral of St Peter **10** 228, 260, 671–3*, *672*; **12** 5; **13** 45, 54; **23** 491; **26** 590; **32** 92, 93
bosses **4** 465
choir-stalls **29** 413
Lady Chapel **18** 622
manuscripts **26** 669
misericords **21** 724
mouldings **11** 420; **22** 222
nave **10** *673*
sculpture **10** 673–4*, *674*, 743; **13** 82, 83; **29** 96
stained glass **10** 674–5*; **13** 183
throne **30** 778, *778*
tracery **31** *272*
vaults **32** 92
wall paintings **7** 275
Guildhall **31** 239
houses **10** 227
Isca Dumnoniorum **10** 671
metalwork **10** 323
pews **24** 576
pottery **10** 301
Rougemont Castle **6** 56; **12** 173; **33** 199
Royal Albert Memorial Museum **10** 370; **12** 270
Exeter (NH; USA), Philips Exeter Academy Library **19** 365
Exeter, John Cecil, 5th Earl of *see* CECIL, JOHN, 5th Earl of Exeter
Exeter, Thomas Cecil, 1st Earl of *see* CECIL, THOMAS, 1st Earl of Exeter
Exeter Gospels *see under* GOSPEL BOOKS → individual manuscripts
exhibition architecture *see under* ARCHITECTURE → types
exhibitions **1** 104, 106, 108; **2** 366, 369, 372; **10** 675–85*; **14** 690; **28** 340
catalogues *see under* CATALOGUES → types
historical and regional traditions
Aboriginal Australia **1** 67*
Africa **1** 437–8*; **31** 490
African American art **1** 446
Albania **1** 546
Anatolia, ancient **1** 839–40*
Arabia **2** 275*
Argentina **2** 404
Assyrian **21** 310
Australia **1** 67; **2** 369, 754
Barbados **5** 746
exhibitions
historical and regional traditions—cont.
Belgium **33** 8
Belize **3** 624
Bhutan **3** 916*
Bolivia **4** 263
Brazil **4** 725, 727
Britain **4** 27; **15** 821; **29** 426
Burma **5** 246
Canada **22** 598, 670
Caribbean Islands **5** 745–6*
Central Asia, Eastern **6** 321–2*
Central Asia, Western **6** 285–7*
China **7** 131, 157–8*; **30** 850
Colombia **7** 609
Costa Rica **8** 17
Côte d'Ivoire **8** 23
Cuba (Caribbean) **5** 746
Czech Republic **17** *581*
Denmark **2** 370; **8** 729, 760
Dominican Republic **5** 745, 746
Ecuador **13** 796
Egypt **9** 768
Egypt, ancient **10** 94–5*
England **9** 23–5; **10** 255, 677–9*; **25** *715*; **26** 272
Etruscan **10** 637
South America, Pre-Columbian **29** *221*
18th cent. **10** *678*; **20** 911
19th cent. **10** *679*; **20** 238, *239*; **32** 748
20th cent. **33** 744
Estonia **10** 539; **33** 566
Ethiopia **10** 578
Etruscan **10** 637, 640–41
France **10** 676, 677, 678, 679–80*; **24** 138, 139, 140, 168, 171–2
17th cent. **10** *676*
18th cent. **20** 135
20th cent. **31** 607
Gabon **11** 880
Germany **9** 239; **10** 95, 678; **24** 677
Greece, ancient **10** 675; **13** 469–71*, 606*
Guatemala **13** 768
Guyana **13** 876
Haiti **14** 60
Honduras **14** 716
Iceland **15** 70
India, Republic of **15** 169
Indian subcontinent **15** 747–8*
Iran, ancient **15** 923*
Iraq **16** 2
Islamic **16** 559–60*
Italy **6** 80; **10** 675–6; **14** 867; **15** 826
Etruscan **10** 637
17th cent. **27** 171
Jamaica **5** 746
Japan **17** 345, 424, 435–7*, *436*
Jewish art **17** *581*
Jordan **17** 654
Korea **18** 325–6, 384–5*
Latvia **18** 851
Lithuania **19** 498; **26** 403; **27** 446
Mesoamerica, Pre-Columbian **21** 264–5*, *265*
Mesopotamia **21** 310*
Mongolia **21** 886*
Native North Americans **22** 595, 598, 674, 677, 678–9*
Nepal **22** 795
Netherlands, the **1** 808; **14** 42
Nicaragua **23** 84
Nigeria **23** 135, 139*
Norway **23** 602
Nubia **10** 94
Pacific Islands **23** 740–41*
Paraguay **24** 101
Poland **25** 139, 141
Puerto Rico **5** 746
Romania **5** 74, 634
Rome, ancient **10** 675; **27** 31, 47, 115–16
exhibitions
historical and regional traditions—cont.
Russia **10** 680; **16** 808
Scotland **11** 338
South Africa **29** 121, 122*
South America, Pre-Columbian **7** 609; **29** 220*, 221*, *221*
Spain **29** 294
Sri Lanka **29** 478
Surinam **30** 16
Sweden **29** *688*
Syria-Palestine **30** 199
Taiwan **30** 248–9
Tanzania **30** 302
Tibet **30** 850*
Trinidad and Tobago **5** 746
Ukraine **2** 634
Union of Soviet Socialist Republics **18** 793
United States of America **2** 559; **4** 23, 27
Armory Show, 1913 **2** 447; **10** 680; **23** *47*; **31** 605, 664
18th cent. **24** 820
19th cent. **10** 683; **25** 5
20th cent. **1** 438; **10** 95; **22** 674, 677; **24** 673; **28** 925; **31** 607, 669
Uruguay **31** 756
Vietnam **32** 483
Wales **32** 791
Zimbabwe **33** 680
types
architecture **17** 620
calligraphy **17** 239
ceramics **31** 639
conceptual art **4** 202
dealers **6** 79–80*; **10** 680
fine art **6** 79–80; **15** 883
industrial **10** 678; **15** 883
international **6** 79*; **10** 678, 680, 681–5; **15** 883–5*; **22** 363
loan **6** 80*; **10** 676, 678, 679, 680
one-man **10** 675
Australia **3** 124
France **10** 680
Iceland **30** 757
Palestine **28** 548
Russia **32** 724
ōtsue **33** 491
paintings **7** 157, 158; **19** *589*
photographs **3** 421; **8** 652; **24** 675, 683*
England **19** 424
Italy **1** 643
posters **19** 488
private **18** 57
sculpture **17** 135–6, 137–8
stained glass **29** 516*
tapestries **30** 332
textiles **2** 767
Exhibitions of Famous Works of the Occident *see* TAISEI MEIGATEN
existentialism **1** 78; **10** 685–6*; **24** 144; **27** 853
ex libris *see* BOOKPLATES
Exloo **25** 531
Exmouth (Devon), The Barn **25** *634*
Exner, Johan Julius **8** 735; **26** 406
Exodus Master **33** 71
Expedición Botánica **7** 601, 608, 611
Expédition du Morée **23** 427
Experimental Atelier *see* EXAT-*51*
Experimental Creative Production Combine (Moscow) **27** 411
experimental films *see under* FILMS → types
Experimental Workshop **33** 488
Experimentele Groep **1** 810; **22** 852
members **2** 230; **4** 669; **7** 489, 758, 864; **19** 768; **27** 137
Expert, Roger-Henri **4** 597; **10** 689*; **17** 451; **24** 267
Expertise **20** 566–7*
Expo '92 *see under* SEVILLE
Export, Valie **10** 879
export licences *see* ART LEGISLATION
exports and imports *see* INDIVIDUAL COUNTRIES; CULTURES; PEOPLES → trade
Exposición Iberoamericana, 1929 *see under* SEVILLE
expositions *see* EXHIBITIONS
exposition universelle *see* EXHIBITIONS → types → international
Exposure **24** 434
exposures, multiple *see under* PHOTOGRAPHY → processes
expression **10** 689–93*, *690*; **26** 221; **30** 18
China **10** 692–3*
facial **33** 462
Expressionism **10** 693–8*; **23** 7; **26** 743; **30** 169; **31** 503
art forms
altars **9** *239*
architecture **10** 696–8*; **11** 869; **21** 781
Germany **10** *697*, *698*; **21** *119*, *120*, 782; **25** *69*
Netherlands, the **18** *126*
Poland **21** 780
brick **4** 789
collections **9** 189; **20** 880; **28** 273
drawing **18** *206*
drawings **18** *80*
etchings **10** 695
lithographs **10** 695; **19** *489*
nude figures **22** *257*
painting **10** 693–5*; **28** 394; **29** 669, 670
Austria **28** *90*
Belgium **3** *565*; **24** *459*
Croatia **8** 178
France **29** *246*
Germany **3** *477*, *478*; **10** *694*; **12** *395*, 395–6; **14** *284*; **18** *79*, *81*, IV2; **20** *381*; **22** *257*; **23** *186*, *187*; **24** *311*
Guatemala **13** *765*
Hungary **8** *806*
Jordan **9** 452
Macedonia (ii) (former Yugoslavia) **19** 325
Norway **23** *226*; **29** *78*
portraits **3** *479*, *480*; **17** *452*; **21** *55*; **28** *89*
Russia **27** *396*
sculpture **9** *239*; **10** 695–6*; **12** *408*; **18** *78*
woodcuts **10** 695*, *695*; **22** *293*; **25** *582*; **29** 871
commentaries **4** 27
exhibitions **8** 431; **28** 920; **31** 605; **32** 775
periodicals **24** 427
regional traditions
Austria **2** 797; **10** 696; **23** 2; **28** 88
Belgium **10** 696; **18** 626; **31** 502
Bolivia **4** 262
Brazil **28** 354
Cuba (Caribbean) **25** 209
Denmark **17** 481
Finland **17** 771; **23** 266; **27** 633
France **10** 696
Germany **4** 893; **7** 562; **9** 239; **10** 683, 693–6*, 849; **14** 284, 644; **15** 828; **18** 77; **22** 114; **28** 77, 343; **29** 642
Hungary **1** 131
Japan **33** 488
Netherlands, the **1** 814, 815
Norway **10** 696; **29** 78
Poland **11** 317; **25** 100, 649
Russia **27** 394
Scandinavia **10** 693
South Africa **29** 108
Sweden **33** 566
Expressionism
regional traditions—cont.
Switzerland **30** 135
Expressionist Group *see* EKSPRESIONISTI
Expressionova **13** 877
Exter, Alexandra (Alexandrovna) **10** 699–700*; **19** 80; **23** 694; **27** 378
assistants **22** 268; **31** 502
exhibitions **4** 236; **15** 857
groups and movements **8** 251; **16** 817
patrons and collectors **8** 10
productions **30** 686
pupils **24** 334; **26** 70; **30** 389
works **9** 292; **10** *699*; **26** 504; **29** 872
Exter, Julius **24** 566
Exton (Leics)
dovecot **9** 202
SS Peter and Paul **10** 262
extrados **2** 292, *292*; **10** 700*
extrusion *see* wirecutting
exultet rolls *see under* ROLLS → types
Exuma **3** 64
ex-votos **10** 701–2*
historical and regional traditions
Christianity **8** 835, 836; **10** 701
Crete **2** 415
Egypt, ancient **9** 795*; **10** 69
France **27** 110–11
Germany **10** *702*
Greece, ancient **13** 376; **18** 409; **27** 111, 712
India, Republic of **15** 174
Indonesia **15** 812*
Italy **16** 749; **27** 109–10*
Japan **17** *25*, 33, 153, *346*, 346–7
Minoan **2** 415
Prehistoric **27** 835
Rome, ancient **26** 858, 859; **27** 52, 109–12*, 712
Sardinia **27** 835
Scandinavia **32** 523
Spain **27** 111
Viking **32** 523
materials
banana leaves **15** 812
flowers **15** 812
fruit **15** 812
nuts **15** 812
palm leaves **15** 812
rice **15** 812
terracotta **13** 376; **27** 109–12
waxes **16** 749
see also DEVOTIONAL OBJECTS; SCULPTURE → types → votive statues
Ey, Johanna **24** 13
Ey, Mutter *see* EY, JOHANNA
Eyak **22** 612
Eyambo, King **26** 18
Eyb, Albrecht von **20** 744
Eyben, Bruno Ninaber van *see* NINABER VAN EYBEN, BRUNO
Eybl, Franz **10** 702–3*; **18** 419; **24** 568; **26** 501
works **10** *703*
Eyck, Aldo van **10** 715–16*
groups and movements **7** 294, 295; **11** 527, 842; **20** 475; **30** 391
patrons and collectors **32** 623
pupils **14** 485
staff **4** 454
works **10** *715*; **22** 832
writings **31** 867
Eyck, Barthélemy d' **2** 115; **10** 703, 713, 716*; **11** 531; **20** 614
works **20** 708; **31** 308
Eyck, Gaspard van **9** 745
Eyck, Hannie van **10** 716
Eyck, Hubert van **10** 703–5*; **13** 806
catalogues **6** 78
collaboration **3** 612; **12** 521; **22** 837; **26** 184; **31** 795

Eyck, Hubert van—cont.
methods **19** 354
patrons and collectors **1** 154; **10** 363; **11** 666; **31** 449
pupils **10** 705
works **1** 710; **3** 553; **10** 703, *704*; **12** 519; **13** 674, *675*; **18** 704; **30** 654
Eyck, Jan van **3** 612; **4** 920; **9** 269; **10** 703, 705–14*; **13** 156; **14** 41; **19** 381; **31** 815; **33** 8
attributions **2** 178, 179; **3** 323; **7** 239; **9** 221; **19** 529; **26** 779; **28** 1; **31** *449*
catalogues **6** 78
collaboration **3** 612; **12** 521; **22** 837; **26** 184; **31** 795
copies **8** 87
drawings **10** *711*
frames **11** *442*
methods **7** 627; **12** 501, 803; **13** 706, 708; **19** 352, 354; **23** 376; **24** 4, 5, 492
paintings **3** 553; **10** 703; **24** 90
altarpieces **12** 628; **13** 674, *675*; **18** 827; **23** 293; **30** 654
diptychs **9** 4
polyptychs **1** 710; **10** 704, *704*, 705; **12** 519; **18** 704
triptychs **13** 674; **31** *343*, *344*
architectural **2** 339
miniatures (manuscript illumination) **16** 722
portraits **6** 442; **10** *707*; **25** 281, 284; **26** 184, *185*
Arnolfini, Giovanni di Arrigo and Cenami, Giovanna **1** 761; **3** *576*; **7** 784; **10** *708*; **12** 287; **19** 356; **21** 719
Eyck, Jan van
paintings
portraits—cont.
Binchois, Giles **11** 439
Leeuw, Jan de **4** *921*; **13** 159
religious **4** 920; **10** *706*, *709*, *710*; **11** 439; **15** 135; **19** 356; **25** *281*; **31** 154, 246
still-lifes **29** 665
patrons and collectors
Aders, Carl **1** 154
Albert I, Duke of Bavaria-Straubing (*reg* 1347-1404) **22** 901
Alfonso I, King of Naples (*reg* 1435-58) **2** 178, 276; **7** 543; **16** 658
Beurnonville, Etienne-Edmond Martin, Baron de **3** 890
Boisserée, Melchior and Sulpiz **4** 242
Boisserée, Sulpiz (Melchior Damiticus) **4** 242
Brukenthal, Samuel, Baron von **5** 9; **26** 722
Burgundy (House of) **4** 918
Elizabeth I, Queen of England (*reg* 1558- 1603) **10** 363
Ertborn, Florent (Joseph) van **10** 491
Fesch, Joseph, Cardinal **11** 32
Geest, Cornelis van der **12** 233
Georg van der Paele, Canon **3** 612
Howard (i), Thomas, 2nd Earl of Arundel **14** 807
Isabella d'Este, Marchesa di Mantua (1474-1539) **16** 658
Eyck, Jan van
patrons and collectors—cont.
John III, Duke of Bavaria-Straubing (*reg* 1417-25) **22** 901
Johnson, John G(raver) (1841-1917) **17** 618
Lorenzo the Magnificent, Lord of Florence (*reg* 1469-92) **16** 770
Margaret of Austria, Duchess of Savoy and Regent of the Netherlands (1480-1530) **13** 905
Margaret of Cleves, Duchess of Bavaria (*fl* 1358- 1404) **22** 901
Marquand, Henry G(urdon) **20** 461
Mary of Hungary, Regent of the Netherlands (1505-58) **13** 909
Medici (family) **16** 658
Mellon, Andrew W(illiam) **21** 90
Philip II, King of Spain (*reg* 1556-98) **13** 922
Philip the Good, 3rd Duke of Burgundy (*reg* 1419- 67) **5** 210
Rockox, Nicolaas **26** 490
Saint-Morys, Charles Paul Jean-Baptiste de Bourgevin Vialart de **27** 568
Solly, Edward **29** 46
Thyssen-Bornemisza, Heinrich, Baron von **30** 795
Vincenzo I, 4th Duke of Mantua (*reg* 1587- 1612) **12** 912
Vischer, Jacob **26** 554
Eyck, Jan van
patrons and collectors—cont.
William II, King of the Netherlands (*reg* 1840–9) **23** 470
Winders, Maxime **33** 245
Wittelsbach (House of) **22** 835; **31** 449
pupils **2** 178; **7** 240; **20** 707
reproductive prints by others **26** 233
Eyck, Lambert van **3** 553; **10** 703, 714*
Eyck, Margaret van **10** 703
Eyckelsbeeck, N. van **1** 812
Eycken, J. B. van **22** 697
eye cups *see under* CUPS → types
eye idols *see under* FIGURINES → types
Eyfells, Jóhann **15** 71
Eyice, S. **4** 67
Eykens, Frans *see* YKENS, FRANS
Eylatan **6** 196; **10** 896
Eyles, George **24** 294
Eymoutiers, St Etienne **11** 614
Eynard, Edouard **19** 848
Eynatten **3** 588
Eynde, Cornelis van den **10** 717
Eynde, Hubert van den **3** 570; **10** 716, 717*
pupils **10** 717; **23** 11
Eynde, Jan van den **3** 546; **10** 717–18*
Eynde, Norbert van den **3** 570; **10** 717*
Eynde, Sebastian van den **10** 717*
Eynden, Roeland van **22** 910
Eyo, Ekpo **10** 123; **15** 105
Eyquem, Miguel **6** 594
Eyre, Ivan **5** 569
Eyre, Samuel **27** 626
Eyre, Vi **2** 760
Eyre, Wilson **10** 718*
groups and movements **7** 619, 876; **25** 807; **28** 604
works **11** 748; **24** 598
Eyrecourt Castle (Co. Galway) **16** 22
Eysen, Louis **10** 718–19*; **12** 394
Eyserbeck, Johann August **25** 368
Eysmont, Nikolay (Gehodorovich) **27** 417
Eysselinck, Gaston **3** 579, 587, 616
Eystein, Archbishop **13** 50
Eytan, Dan **10** 719*; **16** 566
Eyüboğlu, Bedri Rahmi **10** 719*; **31** 454, 455
Eyüboğlu, Eren **10** 719
Eyüp *see* ISTANBUL
eyvan *see* IWAN
Eyzies, Les *see* LES EYZIES
Ezaki, Issei **17** 267
Ezbet Rushdi **9** 830
Ezcurra, Héctor de **2** 397
Ezechia da Vezzano *see* VEZZANO, EZECHIA DA
Ezekial Master **24** 158
Ezekiel **20** 564
Ezero **31** 354
Ezine **29** 700, *700*
Ezinge **14** 73
Ezo *see* AINU
Ezquerra, Jerónimo **5** 435, 875
Ezr, Catholicos **9** 732
Ezra, St George **7** 255
Ezra Master **33** 71
Ezzelino III da Romano **23** 752

F

F 15 Kontakt 24 452
Faaberg 13 143
Fabbri, Agenore 16 709
Fabbri, Pietro 20 497
fabbriche de' nostri tempi per ciò che è disegno, ordine e misura in riguardo all'ornamento pubblico, Le 24 447
Fabbricotti, C. 19 793
Fabbroni, Carlo Agostino, Cardinal 7 860; 19 816
Faber, A. W. 13 677
Faber, Frédéric 3 591; 5 51
Faber, Henri 3 591; 5 51
Faber, Jacob 31 414
Faber, Johann, II 6 360; 10 720*
Faber, Johann Joachim 10 720*
  works 12 394
Faber, Johann Ludwig 23 313
Faber, John, the elder (*c.* 1660-1721) 10 720*
Faber, John, the younger (1695-1756) 10 720
  works 10 785; 14 841; 18 145; 21 148, 416; 31 869
Faber, Martin Hermansz. 10 720–21*
Faber, Oscar 28 282
Faber, Traugott 26 46
Faber & Faber 33 304
Fabergé 27 421, 422, 584
  works 27 *421*
Fabergé, Agathon 10 721
Fabergé, (Peter) Carl (Gustavovitch) 10 721–2*; 11 109; 14 172; 19 596; 27 416, 421, 426, 584
  enamel 10 194, IV3
  glass 27 *416*
  gold 12 865
  jade 16 860
  jewellery 27 429
  methods 12 869
  patrons and collectors 11 301; 14 117; 26 353, 729, 734
  pupils 12 450
  rock crystal 26 486
  sculpture 33 601
  workshop 10 *721*; 11 631; 27 428; 28 741
Fabergé, Gustav (Petrovich) 10 721
Faberger 10 721
Faber pencil factory 24 353
Fabi (family) 2 319
Fabiaan, Jan 4 923
Fabiani, Martin 4 366
Fabiani, Max 10 722–3*
  groups and movements 28 670
  pupils 28 403
  works 19 516; 28 860; 30 885
Fabiani, Wilhelm 26 719
Fabianus 31 349
Fabiger *see* FABERGER
Fabius Pictor 25 44; 26 764; 27 52
Fabkris Aktiebolaget Herkules 29 689
Fable of the Ancients, The *see* MASHEL HA-KADMONI
fables 4 *357*; 10 723–6*
Fåborg 8 *720*
  Museum for Fynsk Malerkunst 7 233; 8 728, 758, 760; 18 136; 24 549; 30 158
Fabre, François-Xavier, Baron 10 726–7*; 22 35
  collections 22 35
  patrons and collectors 4 106
  personal collection 9 229
  teachers 8 556
  works 8 561; 10 *726*; 13 303
Fabre, Jaume 3 220; 10 727*
Fabre, João María 10 728
Fabre, Valentin 2 699
Fabregat, José Joaquín 21 384
Fabre Perrotet and Cattani 30 684
Fabrés, Antonio 10 727*; 14 468; 21 387
Fabrés, Cayetano 10 727
Fabri, Charles 8 677
Fabri, Francesco Saverio 10 727–8*
  collaboration 4 637; 5 376; 8 9
  patrons and collectors 12 889
  works 25 293
Fabriano 10 381
  paper 10 728*; 24 48; 25 598
  watermarks 32 908
Fabriano, Antonio da *see* ANTONIO DA FABRIANO
Fabriano, Francesuccio da *see* GHISSI, FRANCESUCCIO (DI CECCO)
Fabriano, Gentile da *see* GENTILE (DI NICCOLÒ DI MASSIO) DA FABRIANO
Fabriano, Giovanni Andrea Gilio da *see* GILIO DA FABRIANO, GIOVANNI ANDREA
Fabriano, Jacopo da *see* JACOPO DA FABRIANO
Fabriano Altarpiece, Master of the *see* PUCCIO DI SIMONE
Fábrica Cerâmica Viúva Lamego Ld.a 19 467, 468; 25 310
Fábrica da Rua de Campo de Ourique 25 310
Fábrica da Torrinha 23 455; 25 310
Fábrica da Vista Alegre 10 728–9*; 25 *288*, 304, 311
  production 25 *311*
Fábrica da Viuva Antunes 25 310
Fábrica de Castelo Picão 26 52
Fábrica de Cerâmica Constância 19 467, 468; 25 310; 30 881
Fábrica de Darque *see* FÁBRICA DE VIANA
Fábrica de Faianças das Caldas da Rainha 5 421
Fabrica de Grecia 9 678
Fábrica de Janelas Verdes *see* FÁBRICA DE CERÂMICA CONSTÂNCIA
Fábrica del Buen Retiro 1 462; 2 285; 4 564, 566; 5 348; 9 29; 20 69, 71; 29 293
Fábrica de los Cinco Cremios de Madrid 10 509
Fábrica de Massarelos 23 454, 455; 25 310; 26 479
Fábrica de Miragaia 23 454; 25 310; 26 479
Fábrica de Porcelana del Buen Retiro 29 341
Fábrica de Santo Antonio do Vale de Piedade 23 454, 455; 26 479
Fábrica de S António do Vale de Piedade 25 310
Fábrica de Viana 10 729*; 25 *288*, 310
Fábrica do Capitão-Mor *see* REAL FÁBRICA DA BICA DO SAPATO
Fábrica do Custodio Ferreira Braga 25 310
Fábrica do Juncal 10 729*; 25 *288*, 310
Fábrica do Rocio de S Clara 23 454; 25 310; 31 865
Fábrica dos Marianos *see* FÁBRICA DE CERÂMICA CONSTÂNCIA
Fabricius, Adam 11 798
Fabricius, Georg 26 848
Fabriczy, Cornelius von 4 64; 10 729–30*; 11 770
Fabriek voor Metaalbewerking 22 876
Fabrini, Giuseppe Antonio 8 83
Fabrique Royale de Berlin, La 12 459
fabriques 12 105
Fabris (family) 16 738
Fabris, Emilio De *see* DE FABRIS, EMILIO
Fabris, Fiorina 16 739
Fabris, Pietro 10 730*; 13 304; 14 113
Fabritius, Barent 10 730, 732–4*; 22 843
  works 10 *733*
Fabritius, Carel 10 730–34*; 22 844
  attributions 10 734
  groups and movements 8 669
  methods 24 491
  patrons and collectors 4 614
  pupils 32 260
  teachers 10 730; 22 843
  works 8 667; 10 *732*; 22 844
Fabritius, Frederik, I (1688-1755) 8 753
Fabritius, Frederik, II (1740-1829) 8 752
Fabritius, Johannes 10 730
Fabritius, Kilian 5 9; 8 895
Fabritius, Paul 13 914
Fabritius, Pieter Carelsz. 10 730, 732
Fabro, Luciano 2 526; 10 734–5*; 16 682
Fabry, Emile 3 564; 8 701; 10 735*; 14 770
Fabry Ottó 17 855
Fabulator 13 103
  works 13 *103*
Fabullus *see* FAMULUS
Fabunwe 1 429
Fabyan, Robert 18 585
façade decoration 10 735–45*
  historical and regional traditions
    Assyrian 10 742
    Austria 10 737, 741; 30 *885*
    Babylonian 10 742
    Belgium 10 745, *745*
    Czech Republic 10 737, 741
    Egypt, ancient 10 741–2*
    England 10 744
    France 10 744–5
    Germany 10 737, *737*, 740, 741, 745
    Gothic 10 741, 743–4
    Greece, ancient 10 742*
    Iran, ancient 10 742
    Italy 4 774; 10 736, 737, *740*, 740–41, 742, 743, 744; 25 865
    Mesopotamia 10 742*
    Netherlands, the 10 745
    Poland 10 741
    Romanesque 10 742–3
    Rome, ancient 10 742*
    Spain 10 743–4
    Switzerland 10 737, *739*, 741
  materials
    alabaster (gypsum) 10 742
    arriccio 10 740
    limestone 10 742
    marble 4 774; 25 865
    mud-bricks 10 742
    plaster 10 740
    sculpture 10 741–5*, *744*, *745*
    terracotta 10 742
    tiles 30 876, *885*
façade decoration—*cont.*
  techniques
    cartoons (drawings) 10 740
    painting 10 735–9*, *736*, *737*, *739*
    sgraffito 10 *740*, 740–41*
  see also ARCHITECTURAL DECORATIONS; PAINTING → types → architectural
façades 14 420
  historical and regional traditions
    Africa 1 317
    Champa 6 *423*
    Egypt 16 175
    Egypt, ancient 9 825
    France 5 371, *371*; 20 *296*; 21 366; 24 *123*
    Germany 13 49, 56, *57*; 22 *437*
    Gothic 2 *2*; 13 49, 56, *57*, *64*; 16 627
    Greece, ancient 8 *686*; 13 385, 391*, 407; 21 341
    Hausa 1 317
    Iran 28 *615*
    Iraq 16 179; 18 *483*
    Islamic 16 142, *148*, 175, 179, 221
    Italy 4 776; 26 318
      Baroque 29 *80*
      Gothic 2 *2*; 13 *64*; 16 627
      Gothic Revival 28 *393*
      Neo-classicism 17 *443*
      Renaissance 26 *398*, *399*; 27 *772*; 31 *743*
      14th cent. 10 *744*
      17th cent. 4 *426*; 10 *736*
    Ottoman 16 221
    Portugal 25 *186*
    Romanesque 5 371, *371*
    Rome, ancient 2 541; 26 863, 873, 923
    Russia 22 184
    Sasanian 18 *483*
    Spain 14 *579*; 21 *126*
    Syria 16 *148*, 179
    Turkey 16 221
    United States of America 23 *39*
    Vietnam 6 *423*
  materials
    artificial stone 2 541
    cast iron 23 *39*
    iron 4 228
    marble 27 *772*
    stucco 2 541; 4 776
    tiles 28 *615*; 30 875
  techniques 31 592, *592*
  types
    neck *see under* GABLES → types
Faccenna, Domenico 24 20; 27 523
Faccini, Bartolommeo 19 373
Faccini, Girolamo 19 373
Faccini, Pietro 10 531, 745–6*; 31 307
  works 10 *746*
Faccioli, Girolamo 20 796
face 21 546
face masks *see under* MASKS → types
face roll mouldings *see under* MOULDINGS → types
faceting *see* CUTTING
face-to-face weaving *see under* WEAVING → types
face-towers *see under* TOWERS → types
Facetti, Germano 4 369
Fa-chao *see* FAZHAO
Fachblatt für Innen-Dekoration 24 427
Facht, Jacob 10 746–7*
  works 19 29; 28 498, *498*
facings 21 213; 26 900
Facio, Bartolomeo 10 747*; 13 755
  works 2 276, 277; 16 780; 24 90
Facio, Sara 10 747*; 23 506
Facio Hébequer, Guillermo 2 399
Facius, Friedrich Wilhelm 12 264
Facius, Georg Sigmund 29 676
Facius, Johann Gottlieb 29 676
Fackel, Die 18 442
facsimiles 2 364; 11 306; 26 227
Facteur Cheval 23 334
factories 10 748–9*; 14 580; 20 593; 21 600
  historical and regional traditions
    Austria 23 358
    Denmark 16 *828*
    Egypt 16 431, 441
    England 10 235, 748, *749*; 33 *205*
    France 10 748
    Germany 3 *512*; 10 697; 21 *780*; 25 *69*
    Islamic 16 431, 436, 441
    Italy 11 *63*
    Netherlands, the 4 *815*
    Poland 19 *536*
    Russia 27 *377*
    Spain 16 436
    United States of America 10 749; 17 *722*; 25 893; 31 *596*
  lighting 17 721
  materials
    cast iron 10 748
    concrete 33 *205*
    glass 10 697
    steel 10 697
Factory Additions 25 626
factory design 5 271
Facundus manuscript 2 222
FAD (Sociedad de Foment de les Arts Decoratives) 29 308, 309, 319, 322
  see also ADI-FAD
Fadel, Sérgio Sahione *see* SAHIONE FADEL, SÉRGIO
Fader, Fernando 2 399; 7 847
Fadil, Faizal 28 775
Fadlun 2 898
Fadrique, Villa de Don *see* VILLA DE DON FADRIQUE
Fadrique de Portugál, Bishop of Sigüenza 28 709
Fadrusz, János 7 471; 10 750*; 14 896; 30 890
Faé, Geoffroy 10 665
Faed, James 10 750*
Faed, John 10 750*
Faed, Thomas 10 750*; 11 301; 28 237, 238, 748
Fællesforeningen for Danmarks Brugsforeninger 21 791
Faenza 10 751*; 16 *618*
  Cathedral 20 112, *112*
    S Savino Monument 20 113–14
  ceramics 14 425
  Galleria dei Cento Pacifici 12 583
  maiolica 10 755; 16 732, 733, 734, 735; 20 234
  Museo Internazionale delle Ceramiche 16 776
  Palazzo Conti Sinibaldi 12 583
  Palazzo Laderchi 12 584; 16 677
  Palazzo Milzetti 12 584; 16 677
  tiles 30 886
Faenza, Antonio Gentili da 3 817; 10 751*

Faenza, Carlo II Manfredi, Lord of see MANFREDI, CARLO II
Faenza, Francesco da see FRANCESCO DA FAENZA
Faenza, Jacopo da see JACOPO DA FAENZA
Faenza, Marchetti Marco da 26 818
  works 21 11
Faenza, Petrus Andrea da 5 85
Faenza, Pier Maria da 11 191
Faenze, Marco da 13 628
Faerno, Gabriele 19 371
Faesch, Claus 10 751
Faesch, Johann Jakob 10 751, 752–3*
Faesch, Johann Rudolf 10 751; 30 146
Faesch, Paul 10 751, 752
Faesch, Remigius (i) (d 1533/34) 10 751–2*; 30 643
Faesch, Remigius (ii) (1596-1667) 10 751, 752*; 30 154
Faesch, Romey see FAESCH, REMIGIUS (i) (d 1533/34)
Faesch, Ruman see FAESCH, REMIGIUS (i) (d 1533/34)
Faesulae 1 692
Fafertin Church 9 541
Fafi 31 434
Fagan, Robert 10 366, 753*; 13 650; 16 15
Făgăraş 26 705, 707, 713
Fage, Raymond La see LAFAGE, RAYMOND
Fagel, Cornelis 10 754
Fagel, François 20 458
Fagel, Greffiers 8 87
Fagel, Hendrick (1765-1838) 10 754
Fagel, Hendrik (1706-90) 10 753*
Fagerlin, Ferdinand 6 130
Fagervik Manor House 11 91
Fagg, Bernard 15 105; 23 179
Fagg, William 1 232; 15 105
Faggis, Angelo de, Abbot of Montecassino 22 10
Fagioli, Nicola 4 407
Fagiuoli, Ettore 32 342
Fagiuoli Emilianus, Hieronymus see FACCIOLI, GIROLAMO
Fagnano Olona School 16 651
Fagolino, Marcello 10 562
Fagon, Louis 19 646
Faguays, Le 29 576
Fagus, Félicien 22 538
Faharet Çeşme 24 690
Fahd, King (reg 1982-) (Saudi) 27 876
Fahlcrantz, Carl Johan 3 111; 10 754*; 23 875; 30 79; 33 697
Fahlström, Anders 30 97
Fahlström, Öyvind 10 754–5*; 22 523
  dealers 7 842
  groups and movements 25 232
  works 7 649; 30 81, 82
Fahmi, Mustafa 9 764
  works 9 765
Fahr, Klosterkirche 30 132
Fahrafeld 17 897
Fahraj Mosque 16 154
Fahr al-Din ʿAli ibn al-Husayn see SAHIB ATA
Fahrenkamp, Emil 10 755*; 22 711; 25 403
Fåhreu, Klas 30 118
Fahri, Otto 23 342
Fahringer, Karl 14 33
Fahrner, Theodor 12 456
Fa-hsien see FAXIAN
fahua see under PORCELAIN → wares
Faichtmayer see FEUCHTMAYER
Faida 2 640; 20 220; 21 300; 23 153
Faidherbe, Lucas see FAYDHERBE, LUCAS
Faiella, Silvestro 7 704
faience (i) (glass) 10 48, 755*
  historical and regional traditions
    Ancient Near East 1 877–9*, 878; 31 531
    Babylonian 21 308
    Crete 8 153; 21 658, 682*, 683–4*, 683
    Cyprus, ancient 8 349–50*; 18 98
    Egypt, ancient 6 559; 7 80; 9 788; 10 3, 17, 29, 46–9*, 47, 49, 50, 51, 52, 53, 65, 67; 28 34
    Elamite 1 878, 879
    Greece, ancient 13 589–90*, 590; 14 358, 358–9*
    Helladic 14 358, 358–9*
    Kerma culture 10 48
    Mesopotamia 21 308
    Minoan 8 153; 14 358; 21 658, 682*, 683–4*, 683
    Mycenaean 14 358, 358–9*
    Nubia 10 48
    Prehistoric art 25 531
    Punic 25 734*
    Rhodes (island) 1 878; 13 589
    Syria-Palestine 1 878
  uses
    alabastra 10 48
    amulets 10 3, 47; 25 734
    architectural decorations 1 879*
    aryballoi 13 590
    beads 1 877; 3 440; 10 47
    bowls 1 878; 10 48, 67
    boxes 10 51, 53
    brick 1 879
    caskets 10 52
    chairs 10 50, 52
    chalices 10 48
    chests 6 559
    containers 1 878
    figurines 10 47, 48, 49, 49; 21 683
    game-boards 10 48
    goblets 1 878
    harps 10 65
    inlays 10 48; 21 684
    jewellery 1 877; 10 29, 48; 21 683–4; 25 531
    pendants (jewellery) 1 877
    pilgrim flasks 10 48
    plaques 1 879; 10 48
    rhyta 18 98
    scarabs 28 34
    seals 1 877–8; 21 684
    shabtis 10 17, 48
    sistra 10 48
    statuettes 10 47, 47
    stelae 10 48
    tiles 10 47, 47, 48
    vases 10 48; 13 590, 590
faience (ii) (ceramics) 10 751, 755*
  historical and regional traditions
    Austria 2 815, 815
    Belgium 3 588, 589–90, 590
    Brazil 25 310
    Czech Republic 8 404, 404
    Denmark 8 747, 747–8; 30 883
    England 22 880
    Finland 11 105
    France 5 918; 6 333; 11 604–6, 604, 605, 606; 22 880; 30 885
    Germany 6 333; 12 430–31, 431; 22 880
    Hungary 15 1, 2, 2
    Indian subcontinent 15 374–5
    Islamic 16 248, 395
    Netherlands, the 22 879–80, 881–2
    Norway 23 234, 234–5
    Poland 25 122, 123
    Portugal 19 468; 25 309, 309–10*
    Russia 27 410
    Sweden 30 97
    Switzerland 30 143, 144
  techniques
    painting 14 235
faience (ii) (ceramics)—cont.
  uses
    architectural decorations 15 374–5
    caskets 5 918
    crucifixes 15 1
    ewers 11 605
    jugs 2 815
    mosaics 16 248
    murals 3 588
    plates 11 604; 25 309
    stoves 30 144
    tiles 30 875
    trays 30 97
    tureens 23 234
    vases 15 2
  see also POTTERY → wares → Delftware; lustreware; tin-glazed ware
Fai Fo 6 425, 432
Faigenbaum, Patrick 11 553
Faile, E. H. 2 522
Fain, Pierre 8 684; 11 905
Fainsilber, Adrian 11 528; 14 522; 24 132; 26 333
Fairbairn, Thomas 9 757; 10 755*; 15 28; 20 238, 493
Fairbairn, William 10 748
Fairbanks, Avard 22 126
Fairbanks, Douglas, jr 14 511
Fairbanks, Semantha 28 541
Fairfax, Charles B. 1 146
Fairfax, James 2 756
Fairfax, Robert 10 757
Fairfax, Thomas 33 10
Fairfax Murray Sketchbook see under SKETCHBOOKS → individual manuscripts
Fairfield DuBois see DUBOIS PLUMB PARTNERSHIP
Fairfield Pottery 2 152
Fairford, St Mary 13 55, 185
Fairford designer 5 515
Fairholt, Frederick William 10 209
  works 5 639
Fairn, Leslie (Raymond) 10 756*
fairs, trade see TRADE FAIRS
fairs, world see EXHIBITIONS → types → international
Fairservis, Walter A., jr 25 817
Fairweather, George Earnest 10 173; 20 13; 25 741
Fairweather, Ian 10 756*
fairy-tales 4 360
Faisalabad 15 411
  Serena Hotel 23 799
Faisant, Pierre 31 384
Faistauer, Anton 10 756*
  groups and movements 23 1, 2; 28 88
  works 2 797; 27 664, 665
Faistenberger, Andreas, I (1588-1625) 10 756
Faistenberger, Andreas, II (1647-1736) 10 756; 12 748; 29 760
  patrons and collectors 33 276
  pupils 27 873; 31 358
  works 22 302
Faistenberger, Anton 2 581, 795; 8 880; 10 757*
Faistenberger, Balthasar 10 756*
Faistenberger, Benedikt 10 756
Faistenberger, Joseph 10 757
Faistenberger, Wilhelm 10 756, 757
Faita, Pietro, Abbot of Brescia 20 585
Faithorne, William (1616-91) 10 393, 757–8*; 19 818
  pupils 14 538
  reproductive prints by others 31 871
  teachers 24 296
  works 4 373; 8 454; 10 757; 14 268; 17 915; 32 797
Faithorne, William, the younger (1655-1710) 10 758
Faivre, Jules Abel 25 349
Faix, Josef 9 303
Faiyum 7 819; 9 507, 773, 774, 823; 10 62, 758, 758–60*; 16 104; 26 921
  architecture 9 825; 16 208
  Deir al-Malak Mikha'il see Monastery of St Michael
  Monastery of St Michael 7 823
  mosque of Princess Asal-bay 16 259
  mummies 22 286
  mummy masks 10 13
  red lead 24 796
  sculpture 9 875; 10 35; 27 12
  stele 7 822
  textiles 7 826
faiyumi ware see under POTTERY → wares
Faiyum portraits 9 623; 10 197, 197, 199, 759; 22 285; 27 52, 58; 30 425, V1
Faizabad 15 409, 592, 654
Faizullayev, R. 31 782
Faja, Enver 1 539
Fajardo, Carlos 4 728
Fajardo y Chacón, Pedro, 1st Marqués de los Vélez see VÉLEZ, PEDRO, 1st Marqués de los
Fa Jo-chen see FA RUOZHEN
Fakaofo 31 75
fakes see FORGERIES
Fakeye, Lamidi 1 228, 428
  works 1 427
al-Fakhar, Tell 1 864
Fakhariyah 1 862
Fakhr al-dawla, Amir (reg 983-97) (Buyid) 16 372, 435
Fakhr al-Din Razi 18 524
Fakhri 16 355
Fakhr-i Muddabir 15 678
Fakhry, Ahmed 10 81; 28 810
Faktour, Benedikt 11 819
Falaise 6 54
  La Trinité 13 60
Falaise, Charles-Philippe Chennevières (-Pointel), Marquis de see CHENNEVIÈRES(-POINTEL), CHARLES-PHILIPPE, Marquis
Falamin 24 73, 74
Falamir, Abelardo José 32 538
Falardeau, Pierre 5 569
Fałat, Antoni 25 108
Fałat, Julian 10 760*; 18 398, 428; 25 141
Falbe, Joachim Martin 12 391
Falʻbov, Porphiriy (Ivanovich) 30 253
Falca, Alessandro 19 634
Falca, Pietro see LONGHI (ii), PIETRO
Falcate, Antonio Rodrigues see RODRIGUES FALCATE, ANTONIO
Falcetti, Giovanni Battista 3 229
Falch, Johann 26 362
Falciatore, Filippo 22 479
Falcieri, Biagio 13 746; 20 391
Falcini, Angiolo 16 730
Falcini, Luigi (fl 19th cent.) 16 730
Falcini, Luis (1889-1973) 2 399; 5 355
Falcini, Mariano 10 760–61*; 17 547; 20 809; 25 61
Falck, Hans 20 803
Falck, Jeremias 10 761*; 19 16; 25 106
  patrons and collectors 25 675
  works 4 43; 7 795
Falcke, Isaac 3 522
Falcó, Jacobo Fitz-James Stuart y, 17th Duque de Alba see ALBA, 17th Duque de
Falcon, Jean Philippe 16 850
Falconbridge 9 118
Falcone, Andrea 10 761–2*; 27 133
Falcone, Aniello 10 761, 762–3*; 16 673; 22 478, 479
  assistants 25 252
  attributions 20 741
  collaboration 11 321; 20 741
  patrons and collectors 10 115; 22 21
  pupils 6 108; 19 434; 27 149; 29 253
  works 3 388; 10 762
Falcone, Bernardo 10 763*; 16 701; 19 630
Falcone pyxis 13 531
Falconer, William 25 61
Falconet, Etienne-Maurice 10 763–5*; 11 561, 663; 22 859; 27 389; 28 521; 30 219
  dealing 27 438
  patrons and collectors 2 417; 5 380, 530; 7 528; 10 442; 11 658; 18 660; 27 223
  pupils 7 574; 25 209
  sculpture 25 118
    equestrian monuments 10 442, 876; 22 45; 27 575; 29 565
    mythological 10 764
    statuettes 11 577; 23 295; 29 573
  teachers 19 142
Falconet, Louis 10 764
Falconet, Pierre 10 763
Falconet-Collet, Marie Anne 22 859
Falconete, Pedro Sanchez see SANCHEZ FALCONETE, PEDRO
Falconetto, Giovanni Maria 10 765–7*
  architecture 10 767; 23 752, 862; 27 304; 30 655
  assistants 21 647; 31 824
  collaboration 22 130
  paintings 10 766; 32 341
  patrons and collectors 7 862, 863
  stucco 23 756
Falconetto, Jacopo 10 765
Falconetto, Tommaso 10 766
Falcon glassworks 10 318, 319; 19 595; 24 57
  production 10 319
Falconi, Bernardo see FALCONE, BERNARDO
Falconi, Giovanni Battista 10 768*; 25 97
  patrons and collectors 19 751
  works 18 693; 25 63, 114; 29 839; 33 259
Falconieri (family) 4 434; 12 533
Falconieri, Alessandro 10 769; 12 533, 534
Falconieri, Giuliana see GIULIANA FALCONIERI, Saint
Falconieri, Guido Orazio Gabrielli di Carpegna, Conte di 10 769
Falconieri, Orazio 10 768, 769*; 11 741
Falconieri, Ottavio 10 769; 21 27
Falconieri, Paolo 10 769; 21 28, 29, 53; 25 690; 30 267
Falconieri, Paolo di Pietro 10 768
Falconieri, Paolo Francesco (1626-96) 10 768–9
Falcon Press 20 609
Falcon Works 13 22
Falda, Giovanni Battista 10 769*; 12 115, 117
  works 11 740, 741; 12 116; 26 758, 846; 29 251; 32 111, 112, 236
Faldoni, Bernardo see FALCONE, BERNARDO
Faldoni, Gianantonio 6 91; 10 769–70*; 24 894; 33 613
faldstools see CHAIRS → types → X-frame
Falens, Karel von 23 516
Falerii Novi 2 297; 7 366; 10 583, 602; 26 887
Falerii Veteres see CIVITÀ CASTELLANA

Faletans, Hippolyte Thierry, Comte de **4** 749
Falguière, Alexandre **5** 879; **10** 770–71*; **11** 563; **12** 488
assistants **31** 488
groups and movements **11** 565
pupils
Bourdelle, Emile-Antoine **4** 568
Costa, Tomás **25** 302
Lamourdedieu, Raoul **18** 682
Larche, Raoul(-François) **18** 786
Laszczka, Konstanty **18** 822
MacMonnies, Frederick William **20** 30
Mercié, (Marius-Jean-)Antonin **21** 147
Morlon, Pierre-Alexandre **22** 125
Niederhäusern, Auguste de **23** 114
Puech, Denys **25** 697
Prud'homme, Georges (-Henri) **25** 669
Ringel d'Illzach, (Jean-)Désiré **26** 408
Valbudea, Ştefan **31** 802
teachers **17** 667
Fali **1** 312
Falier, Antonio **10** 771*
Falier, Giovanni **5** 626; **10** 818
Falier, Ordelafo, Doge of Venice (*reg* 1102-18) **32** 213
Falier, Vitale, Doge of Venice (*reg* 1084-96) **32** 206
Falize, Alexis **10** 771
Falize, Lucien **10** 771*; **11** 622; **17** 527; **24** 147
Falk, János **9** 754
Falk, Jeremij *see* FALCK, JEREMIAS
Fal'k, Robert (Rafailovich) **3** 529; **9** 747; **10** 771–2*; **32** 661
groups and movements **12** 871; **16** 817, 818; **22** 178, 508; **27** 392, 394
pupils **7** 291
Falke, Jakob von **10** 772*; **26** 190
Falke, Otto von **24** 445
Falkenau *see* FALKNOV
Falkenberg **8** 824; **30** 370
Falkenlust
Chinese House **12** 412
grotto **12** 412
Falkenstein, Claire **10** 772*
Falkenstein, Kuno von, Archbishop **31** 326
Falkentorp, Ole **3** 410; **8** 728
Falkirk (Central)
Carron Co. Museum **11** 119
Museum **11** 119
St Francis Xavier **28** 244
Falkirk Iron Co. **3** 741; **28** 255
Falkland Palace (Fife) **28** *222*, 225, *225*, 234, 251, 268
Falknov **8** *374*, 407, 408; **10** 772–3*
Falla, Julián **10** 773*; **13** 764
Falla Bonet **8** 232
Fallaga Salām, Ala **10** 573
Fallenter, Hans **20** 803
Falling Creek (VA) **31** 652
Fallingwater *see under* BEAR RUN (PA)
Fallon, Conor **16** 22
Falloppi, Giovanni di Pietro *see* GIOVANNI DA MODENA
Falmer (E. Sussex) **4** 808
Sussex University **3** 243; **29** 379
Falmouth (Jamaica) **16** *878*
architecture **16** 882
barracks *see* school
Barrett House **16** 882
church **16** 883
Court House **16** 883, *883*
school **16** 883
Falmouth (VA; USA), Gari Melchers Memorial Gallery **21** 77
Falqua **7** 87
Falque, Jeremij *see* FALCK, JEREMIAS
Falqués, F. **3** 216
Falqui, Enrico **28** 212
false arches *see under* ARCHES → types
false domes *see under* DOMES → types
false doors *see under* STELAE → types
false embroidery *see under* EMBROIDERY → types
false sandarach *see under* PIGMENTS → types
Falster **23** 536
Fălticeni, Ion Irimescu Museum **16** 49
Faltz, Raimund **10** 773*; **14** 651
Falu **30** 104
Faludi, Eugenio Giacomo **23** 753
Fal'ul, St Michael **7** 255
Falun **30** *65*; **31** 718
Christina church **30** 70
Falus, Elek **17** 876
Faluschi, Antonio **7** 915
Falz, Raymund *see* FALTZ, RAIMUND
Famabalasto culture **29** 190
Famagusta **8** *325*, 361; **10** 773–4*; **32** *158*
archaeological museum **8** 366
fortifications **32** 159
Lala Mustafa Mosque *see* Latin Cathedral of St Nicholas
Latin Cathedral of St Nicholas **8** 362; **10** 774*, *774*
metalwork **8** 363
Nestorian church **8** 362
Orthodox Cathedral of St George of the Greeks **8** 362, *362*
palace **8** 361
pottery **8** 343
St George of the Latins **8** 362
SS Peter and Paul **8** 362
textiles **8** 366
Famiglia Artistica, La (19th cent.) **5** 848; **7** 690; **21** 527
Família Artística Paulista (1930s) **4** 718; **28** 213; **32** 690
famille jaune porcelain *see under* PORCELAIN → wares
famille noire porcelain *see under* PORCELAIN → wares
famille rose porcelain *see under* PORCELAIN → wares
famille verte porcelain *see under* PORCELAIN → wares
Famin, Auguste-Pierre (1776-1859) **13** 295; **24** 387
Famin, Auguste Pierre Sainte-Marie (1791-1854) **19** 250
Famin, Charles **10** 775*; **17** 628
Famine Stele **2** 657
Fāmiya *see* APAMEIA
Famulus **25** 44; **26** 789; **27** 52
works **26** *788*
Fanari Karditsas **13** 358
Fancelli, Carlo **10** 782
Fancelli, Chiarissimo **24** 752
Fancelli, Cosimo **10** 782*; **16** 696; **26** 810; **27** 486; **29** 251
Fancelli, Domenico (Alessandro) **10** 783–4*; **29** 289
patrons and collectors **2** 279; **9** 112
pupils **23** 494
tombs **23** 494; **29** 289
works **2** *278*, 864; **7** 345; **10** *783*; **13** 283
Fancelli, Giacomo Antonio **10** 782; **26** 810; **27** 486
Fancelli, Giovanni **11** 214
Fancelli, Luca **10** 784*; **21** 532; **24** 523
attributions **11** 213
collaboration **1** 556; **12** 906
patrons and collectors **12** 907; **20** 319
Fancelli, Luca—cont.
works **1** 564; **11** 40; **12** 906, 914; **18** 862
Fancelli, Pandolfo di Bernardo **29** 496
Fancelli, Petronio **20** 497
Fancelli, Pietro **20** 497
Fan Ch'i *see* FAN QIH
fancy pictures *see under* PAINTING → types
Fan Daosheng **20** 286
Fane, John, 7th Earl of Westmorland **22** 138
Faneca, Juan de Soler y *see* SOLER Y FANECA, JUAN DE
Fanegas, Jaime **29** 267
Fanelli, Francesco **10** 263, 786–7*
patrons and collectors **10** 360; **29** 801
works **19** 606
Fanelli, Gaetano **20** 415
Fanelli, Virgilio **29** 341
Faneuil, Peter **4** 472
Fanfare Press **33** 304
Fanfrolico Press **19** 413
Fang **10** 440, 787–92*; **11** 878
aesthetics **1** 237
art criticism **2** 519
craftsmen and artists **1** 244
hairstyles **10** 792*
headdresses **1** 351
masks **10** *791*, 791–2*
metalwork **10** 792
musical instruments **1** 358
patronage **1** 241
sculpture **1** 231, 232, *232*, 282, 322, 323, 324, 359; **10** *788*, 788–92*, *789*, *790*
wood **1** *232*; **10** *788*, *789*, *790*, *791*
wood-carvings **10** 792
Fang Chao-ling *see* FANG ZHAOLING
Fang Chieh *see* FANG JIE
Fang Chün-i *see* FANG JUNYI
Fang Congyi **10** 793*
fang ding see under VESSELS → types
Fang Hanyuan **17** 184
Fang Hsi-yüan *see* FANG XIYUAN
Fang Jie **7** 62
Fang Junyi **6** 867
Fangor, Wojciech **10** 793–4*; **15** 122; **29** 52
Fang Shishu **2** 96; **33** 496
Fang Ts'ung-i *see* FANG CONGYI
Fang Xiyuan **17** 184
fang yi see under VESSELS → types
Fang Yulu **7** 93, 94
Fang Zhaoling **10** 794*; **14** 722
fan-holders **15** *119*
Fan Kuan **6** 773, 797, 817, 819; **10** 794–5*; **29** 67
groups and movements **29** 244
works **6** 789, 791; **10** *795*; **32** 842
Fanlo **26** 643
Fanlong **6** 783
Fan-lung *see* FANLONG
Fan Min **6** 729; **25** 800
Fannière, Auguste **11** 622
Fannière, François-Auguste **5** 392; **11** 622; **13** 680
Fannière, François-Joseph-Louis **5** 392; **13** 680
Fannière, Joseph **11** 622
Fano
basilica **26** 890, 924
bastion **3** 359
gates **7** 358
printing **16** 360
Fano, Giovanni da *see* GIOVANNI DA FANO
Fano, Girolamo da **26** 769
Fano, Isola di *see* ISOLA DI FANO
Fano, Ulisse da **10** 737
fanons **32** 387*
Fanourakis, Thomas **8** 157
Fan Qi **12** 899; **22** 459, 460
works **22** *460*
fans **10** 775–82*, *780*; **20** 595
historical and regional traditions
Africa **10** 778–9*
Asante **10** 779
Aztec **10** 779, *779*
Benin Republic **10** 778, 779
Buddhism **10** 778
Byzantine **9** 656
Chancay **10** 780
China **6** 791; **7** 103; **10** 776–7, *776*; **11** 152; **22** 234; **28** *554*
Cook Islands **7** 791; **10** 779
Early Christian (*c.* AD 250-843) **9** 656; **10** 775
Egypt, ancient **10** 775, *775*
England **10** 781
Fiji **10** 779
France **10** 780, 781, *781*
Greece, ancient **10** 775
Hawaii **10** 779
Indian subcontinent **10** 778*; **15** 727
Indonesia **10** 778
Italy **10** 781
Japan **3** *144*; **10** 776–7, *777*; **17** 160, 167–8
Java **10** 778
Korea **10** 777; **18** 380
Malaysia **10** 778
Marquesas Islands **10** 779
Marshall Islands **10** 779
Maya **10** 779
Mesoamerica, Pre-Columbian **10** *779*, 779–80*; **21** 250
Moche (culture) **10** 780
Native North Americans **10** 780*; **22** 654
Netherlands, the **10** 781
Niger **10** 779
Pacific Islands **10** 779*
Papua New Guinea **10** 779
Peru **10** 780
Rome, ancient **10** 775
South America, Pre-Columbian **10** 779–80*
South-east Asia **10** 778*
Spain **10** 782
Switzerland **10** *781*
Taiwan **10** 777
Tonga (Pacific Islands) **10** 779
Yoruba **10** 779
materials
bamboo **10** *779*; **18** 380
brocades **18** 380
cypress **10** 776
feathers **10** *775*, 778, *779*, 782; **21** 250; **22** 654
gold **10** *777*
gold leaf **10** *781*
horn **10** *781*
iron **10** *777*
ivory **7** 103; **10** *775*, 777; **16** 799
lace **10** 782
leather **10** 778
paper **10** 776; **18** 380
silk **10** 776
silver **9** 656; **10** *777*
techniques
painting **6** 791; **10** 776, 777; **17** 160
Fans, Maximiliaen **25** 668
Fansago, Cosimo *see* FANZAGO, COSIMO
Fanserif *see under* TYPE-FACES
Fanshan **19** 302
Fanshawe, Henry **3** 186
Fanta, A. **8** 416
Fanta, Josef **8** 379, 401; **10** 795–6*; **18** 462; **25** 429
Fantacchiotti, Odoardo **16** 705
Fan Tao-sheng *see* FAN DAOSHENG
Fantastici, Agostino **3** 485; **10** 97; **16** 730
Fantastic Realism *see* PHANTASTISCHER REALISMUS
Fantastic style pottery *see under* POTTERY → wares
Fante **1** 289, 311, 314, 331, 503; **5** 753, 761
shrine **1** *332*
Fanti **1** 265, 392
Fanti, Ercole Gaetano **19** 55
Fanti, Gaetano **5** 774; **21** 84; **32** 459
Fanti, Vincent Anton Jozeph **19** 337
Fantin-Latour, (Ignace-)Henri (-Théodore) **10** 796–7*
dealers **30** 425
groups and movements **17** 440; **19** 90; **26** 55; **33** 137
lithographs **19** 490; **20** 602; **25** 607
paintings **19** 487
flower **11** 229, *229*
literary themes **22** 379
portraits **6** 439; **9** 673; **10** *797*; **11** 417
still-lifes **29** 669
patrons and collectors **1** 614; **5** 278; **14** 246; **15** 894, 895; **19** 230; **22** 93; **24** 638; **30** 375
prints **25** 626
teachers **13** 806; **19** 39
Fantin-Latour, Jean-Théodore **10** 796
Fantin-Latour, (Marie-Louise-) Victoria **10** 796, 797–8*
Fantoni (family) **3** 772; **16** 728
Fantoni, Andrea **3** 772, 773; **10** 798*; **16** 728
Fantoni, Giacomo **6** 89; **10** 798–9*; **27** 304
Fantoni, Grazioso **10** 798
Fantoni, Venturino **10** 798
fan tracery *see under* TRACERY → types → bar
Fantuzzi, Antonio **2** 185; **10** 799*; **11** 532
groups and movements **11** 262, 264
works **10** 551; **11** 572; **13** 700; **27** 210
Fanum, Basilica **3** 328
fan vaults *see under* VAULTS (CEILING) → types
Fanzago, Cosimo **10** 799–801*; **22** 477
architecture **16** 639
chapels **29** 251
churches **9** 182; **10** *801*; **13** 801
cloisters **22** *485*
gates **16** 744
monasteries **16** 703; **22** 10, 477
attributions **7** 704
collaboration **11** 17
grilles **9** 158
inlays **16** 747
interior decoration **22** 485
pupils **10** 761; **31** 788
sculpture **3** 827; **5** 360; **10** *800*; **16** 703; **19** 139; **22** 484; **28** 367; **31** 788
Fanzolo di Vedelago, Villa Emo **23** 867; **32** 548
FAP *see under* WORKS PROGRESS ADMINISTRATION
Faq'ous, Tell **20** 549
Fara, Tell **1** *849*; **10** 802*; **21** *267*
seals **1** 860; **10** *802*
writing-tablets **1** 853
Farab *see* OTRAR
Faraghan carpets *see under* CARPETS → types
Faragó, Ferenc **31** 797
Faragó, Géza **17** 876
Faragó, Ödön **14** 908
Farah, Empress (1939-) (Pahlavi) **15** 900; **16** 539; **30** 415
Far'ah, Tell el- (North) **1** 857, 858; **30** 196
Far'ah, Tell el- (South) **1** 857
Farahabad **12** 82
Farahani, Abdallah **30** 301
Farahani, Iddi Abdallah **30** 301
Farain, Tell el- **9** 773, *774*; **10** 802*

Faraj (fl 1005) 16 524
  works 16 525
Faraj, Sultan (reg 1399-1405; 1405-12) (Mamluk) 5 397; 16 211; 20 230*
Farakhshah see VARAKHSHA
Farama, Tell el- see PELUSIUM
Faraoui and de Mazieres 1 320
Faras 9 774; 10 803*; 23 276, 278, 286, 287
  Cathedral 1 379; 10 803; 23 287, 288
    wall paintings 23 288, 289
  ceramics 23 289
  church 23 288
  Northern Monastery 23 287
  Rivergate Church 23 287
  Temple of Tutankhamun 23 280
Farasan 32 315
Faraz, Antonio 11 713; 29 333, 334
Faraz, Juan 11 713
Farbenindustrie, I. G. 25 69; 29 777
Farcetti, Abbé 7 416
Farcinade, F. 23 510
Fard, Kambakhsh-e 17 773
Fardon, Richard
  works 6 406
Farelli, Giacomo 10 803*; 20 411; 22 479
Farès, Bishr 10 804*; 16 549
Farey, Cyril 2 333
  works 4 158
Farfa 7 262; 10 804–5*; 16 620
  Abbey Church 10 804; 26 576, 698
  manuscripts 26 665
Farfa Customary 10 805
Farfan 30 447
Farfán, Fernando de la Torre y see TORRE Y FARFÁN, FERNANDO DE LA
Farfa Register 10 804
Fargas, Francesc Isaura i see ISAURA I FARGAS, FRANCESC
Farge, C(hristopher) Grant La see LA FARGE, C(HRISTOPHER) GRANT
Farge, Oliver La see LA FARGE, OLIVER
Farghana see FERGHANA
Färg och Form 10 463, 805*; 14 595; 19 428; 30 81
Fargue, La see LA FARGUE
Fargue, Léon-Paul 4 588; 24 334
Farhad (fl 1477) 16 328; 28 617
Farhad (fl c. 1650-70) 6 236
Farhad-Beg Yailaki 18 29
  Monastery 6 296
Farhat, Ammar 31 425
Farhat, Safia 31 426
Faría, José Custodio de Saa y see SAA Y FARÍA, JOSÉ CUSTODIO DE
Faria Lobo, Silvestre de see LOBO, SILVESTRE DE FARIA
Faridabad 15 409
Farid Bukhari, Shaykh 15 369, 371, 409
Faridpur 3 166
Fariello, Francesco 25 792
Farigoule, Louis (-Henri-Jean) see ROMAINS, JULES
Farill 17 721
Farinacci, Roberto 16 680, 681
Farinati, Giambattista 10 805
Farinati, Paolo 10 805–6*; 32 343
  collaboration 5 617
  patrons and collectors 12 910; 32 348
  teachers 12 658
  works 5 31; 20 446; 33 356
Farinelli, Carlo Broschi 3 385; 4 561; 10 806*
Faringdon (Berks), All Saints 9 155
  tracery 31 272
Faringdon, Alexander Henderson, 1st Lord see HENDERSON, ALEXANDER, 1st Lord Faringdon
Faringdon Abbey (Oxon) 7 350
Farington, George 10 807; 15 652
Farington, Joseph 10 806*; 21 901; 23 690
  pupils 7 749
  reproductive prints by others 9 506
  teachers 10 372; 19 157; 33 220
  works 4 607; 10 369; 29 491
  writings 19 586
Faris, James C.
  works 1 344; 23 275
Faris al-Shidyaq (1804-87) 16 361
Farius, Jan 13 221
Farjat, Benoît 6 502
Farkas, Zoltán 13 638
Farkasházi-Fischer, Jenö 14 449
Farkasházi-Fischer, Móric 14 449; 15 2
Farkë 1 543
Farleigh, John 4 367; 28 808; 33 369
  works 4 367
Farley, Lilias 5 571
Farmakovsky, Boris (Vladimirovich) 10 807*; 23 427
Farmer, John 3 475
Farmer & Brindley 3 367, 746; 10 266; 25 187; 28 278; 31 241
Farmer & Co. 2 755
Farmer & Dark 25 403
Farmer & Rogers 17 440; 19 311
Farmer Scythian 28 320
farmhouses see under HOUSES → types
Farmington (CT), Hill-Stead Museum 25 234
farmsteads see HOUSES → types → farmhouses
Farnborough, Amelia Long, Lady see LONG, AMELIA, Lady Farnborough
Farnborough, Charles Long, 1st Baron see LONG, CHARLES, 1st Baron Farnborough
Farnese (family)
  architecture 4 47; 25 260; 27 742; 32 502, 627
  collections 4 558; 16 764; 26 768; 27 114, 115
  gardens 12 115
  imprese 5 864
  interior decoration 31 372
  maps 20 365
  medals 33 586
  metalwork 12 309
  paintings 5 858; 30 41; 33 717
  sculpture 2 168, 169; 22 166; 25 256; 27 46
Farnese, Alessandro, 3rd Duke of Parma see ALESSANDRO, 3rd Duke of Parma
Farnese, Alessandro, Cardinal (1468-1549) see PAUL III, Pope
Farnese, Alessandro, Cardinal (1520-89) 5 789; 10 807, 809–11*; 24 24
  architecture 11 318; 23 745; 32 505
    churches 1 595; 16 635; 17 510; 32 506, 507
    palaces 26 838; 27 740
    villas 5 683; 6 59; 32 506
  bronzes 10 624
  collections 12 151; 19 372
  decorative works 24 419; 26 838
  gardens 26 785
  gold 10 751
  hardstones 14 171
  manuscripts 7 468–9
  medals 3 817; 4 340; 33 586
  metalwork 12 309; 16 742
  paintings 13 910; 23 577; 26 89; 32 22; 33 718
    allegorical 32 12
Farnese, Alessandro, Cardinal (1520-89)
  paintings—cont.
    frescoes 2 493; 3 858; 7 777; 27 652; 29 428; 32 12
    history 3 471
    mythological 15 87
    portraits 27 705
    religious 25 729; 32 237
  rock crystal 16 745
  sculpture 3 827; 10 811
Farnese, Elizabeth, Queen of Spain see ELIZABETH FARNESE, Queen of Spain
Farnese, Francesco 21 539
Farnese, Girolamo 18 870
Farnese, Isabella 11 872
Farnese, Margaret of Austria, Duchess of Parma see MARGARET OF AUSTRIA, Duchess of Parma, Regent of the Netherlands
Farnese, Mario, Duca 4 656; 21 754; 27 723
Farnese, Odoardo, 5th Duke of Parma and Piacenza see ODOARDO, 5th Duke of Parma and Piacenza
Farnese, Odoardo, Cardinal 5 850; 10 807, 811*; 12 266; 23 577; 26 770
  altarpieces 5 864
  architecture 26 839
  decorative works 26 838
  frescoes 5 857; 9 88
  gardens 5 684
  interior decoration 5 864, 867
  paintings 5 861, 865, 868; 26 839
Farnese, Orazio 21 79
Farnese, Ottavio, 2nd Duke of Parma see OTTAVIO, 2nd Duke of Parma
Farnese, Pier Luigi, 1st Duke of Parma see PIER LUIGI, 1st Duke of Parma
Farnese, Ranuccio, Cardinal 10 807, 811*
  architecture 23 745; 26 838; 32 505
  decorative works 26 838
Farnese, Ranuccio I, 4th Duke of Parma see RANUCCIO I, 4th Duke of Parma
Farnese, Ranuccio II, 6th Duke of Parma, see RANUCCIO II, 6th Duke of Parma
Farnese Atlas 10 810; 12 812
Farnese Bull 2 168, 229; 3 921; 10 812*; 13 430, 605; 26 292, 838; 27 46
Farnese Casket 3 817–18; 10 810; 14 171; 25 21
Farnese Cup 5 866; 12 250, 265; 14 169, 170; 21 14
Farnese Eros 25 456
Farnese Flora 2 168; 10 810
Farnese Hercules 2 168; 10 810, 812*; 13 303; 25 256; 26 795, 838; 27 46
Farnese Hours see under BOOKS OF HOURS → individual manuscripts
Farnese Table 25 256; 32 506
Farnesina see ROME → villas → Villa Farnesina
Farnham (Surrey) 6 55
  Castle 4 779, 779; 6 60; 9 144
Farnham, Paulding 31 650
  works 31 650
Farnikat 6 379
Farny, Henry F. 7 327; 33 184–5
  works 33 184
Faro 10 728; 25 313
Faro, António da Costa 10 812–13*; 32 616
Faroe Islands 3 332; 10 813*; 32 513
Farouq I, King (reg 1936-52) (Muhammad Ali's Line) 10 92
Farquar, John 3 477
Farquet, Jean 29 336
Farquhar, Robert D. 8 568
Farquharson, Joseph 10 813*
Farra, Muhammad 16 241
Farrand, Beatrix Jones 10 814*
  works 4 142; 12 142, 143
Farrar (family) 5 581
Farrar, Ebenezer Lawrence 10 814
Farrar, George Henry 10 814
Farrar, George Whitfield 10 814*
Farrar, Moses 10 814
Farrell, Edward 10 335
Farrell, Micheal 3 117; 10 814*; 16 18
Farrell, Terence 9 322; 10 815; 13 667
Farrell, Terry 10 814–15*
  works 10 242; 19 578, 578
Farrell, Thomas 9 322; 10 815*; 16 21
Farrell, William 19 869
Farren, Elizabeth 18 892
Farrer, James 20 81
Farrer, T. C. 25 556
Farreras, Francisco 10 815*
Farrés, Arturo 29 330
Farriol, Josep Pey i see PEY I FARRIOL, JOSEP
Farrobó, Conde de 11 249; 19 533
Farroukh, Mustafa 19 8
Farrukhabad 15 409, 592
Farrukh Beg 10 815–17*; 15 586
  works 8 848; 10 816; 15 587; 22 259
Farrukh Chela 10 817–18*
  works 10 818
Farrukh Husayn 10 817; 15 639
Farrukhsiyar, Emperor (reg 1713-19) (Mughal) 15 612
Fars 15 901, 902, 904, 905; 16 105, 377
  metalwork 16 373
  rock reliefs 15 916, 917
  standards (vexilloid) 11 151
Farsetti, Antonfrancesco 10 819
Farsetti, Daniele 10 819
Farsetti, Filippo 5 625; 10 818–19*; 25 323; 32 196
Farsi, Mohammed Said 27 875, 876
farthingales see SKIRTS → types → hooped
Faruffini, Federico 10 819*
  groups and movements 21 527; 28 34
  teachers 3 857
  works 16 678
Farum, Midtpunkt 8 729
Fa Ruozhen 10 819–20*
Faryumad, congregational mosque 16 193
Fās see FEZ
Fasanotti, Gaetano 3 437
Fäsch, Remigius see FAESCH, REMIGIUS (ii)
fasciae 10 820*; 13 393; 23 478
fasciculated piers see under PIERS (ii) (MASONRY) → types
Fascism 10 820–22*; 28 792–3
  architecture 10 821; 19 304, 305; 21 521
  murals 25 652
  propaganda 25 652
fashion 24 678
fashion plates 10 823, 823–4*, 824
fasil 21 546
Fasiledes, Emperor of Ethiopia (reg 1632-67) 1 315; 10 566
fāsī script see under SCRIPTS → types
Fasmer, Hendrich J. 23 231
Fasoldt, Charles 7 448
Fasoli, Alfredo 9 182
Fasolis, Florentius de' 28 532
Fasolo, Bernardino 3 393
Fasolo, Giovanni Antonio 3 200; 10 824–5*; 20 86; 32 349, 550
  works 9 265
Fasolo, Lorenzo 3 199; 4 729
Fassbender, Joseph 10 825*; 14 48; 31 328
Fassett, Francis H. 29 648
Fassett & Stevens 29 648
Fassin, Adolphe 3 572
Fassin, Nicolas Henri Joseph 5 10; 9 366; 10 825*; 14 834; 18 794
Fassler, John 10 825–6*; 17 603; 20 484; 29 106
Fassola see FAZOLA
Fastarabad 6 266
Fastnet Rock Lighthouse 19 361
Fastolf, John 10 270, 287, 289, 325; 20 664
Fastolf Master 7 236; 20 664*, 772
Fatahillah 16 873
Fatehabad 6 444
  caravanserai 15 374
Fatehpur (Rajasthan) 15 611
Fatehpur (Uttar Pradesh) 15 261
Fatehpur Baori see RAWALPINDI
Fatehpuri Begum (Mughal) 8 675
Fatehpur Sikri 10 826, 826–30*; 15 196, 261, 360, 363; 16 105
  Ambiya Wali Mosque 15 340
  architecture 15 409, 410
  Birbal's House 10 829
  brocades 15 662
  Buland Darvaza 10 828
  carpets 15 682
  ceramics 6 918
  congregational mosque 10 826, 828; 21 630
  Divan-i ʿAm 10 829
  gardens 12 73; 15 361
  Hiran Minar 10 826, 829–30
  Jodh Bai Mahal 10 828–9; 23 818
  Khwabgah 10 826
  Maryam's Palace 10 829
  Panch Mahal 10 829
  Pathan Mosque 15 340
  Rangin Mahal see Maryam's Palace
  sandstone 15 414
  Sonahra Makan see Maryam's Palace
  Stonecutters' Mosque 10 826, 827
  tomb of Shaykh Salim Chisti 10 828; 15 345; 16 257; 31 114, 115
  Turkish Sultana's Palace 10 829
  urban planning 16 239
  wall paintings 15 544
Fateh Singh, Rana of Mewar (reg 1884-1930) (Rajput) 15 601
Fateh Singh Rao III, Maharaja (reg 1949-) (Gaekwad) 15 182
Fath, Jacques 9 294
  works 9 293
Fath ʿAli Shah, Shah (reg 1797-1834) (Qajar) 16 536; 25 770*
  architecture 17 830; 20 548; 28 748; 30 414, 415
  book covers 22 260; 28 27
  dress 16 465
  enamel 1 637; 16 515
  interior decoration 16 80
  manuscripts 16 341, 341; 21 723
  metalwork 16 393
  paintings 3 193; 16 535; 21 506
  palaces 16 234
  porcelain 16 425
  regalia 16 539
  talars 16 234
Fathallah 16 534
al-Fath ibn Khaqan 12 79
Fathy, Hassan 10 830–31*; 16 242
  pupils 32 770
  works 1 319; 9 764; 10 831; 16 241
Fátima, Shrine of the Virgin 24 36; 28 632
Fatimid 10 832, 832–3*; 16 113, 121
  architecture 21 504, 582; 22 323; 23 815
  ewers 10 832

Fatimid—cont.
rock crystal 10 *832*
silk 28 716
see also:
AL-'AZIZ, Caliph
AL-HAFIZ, Caliph
AL-HAKIM, Caliph
AL-MANSUR, Caliph
AL-MU'IZZ, Caliph
AL-MUSTA'LI, Caliph
AL-MUSTANSIR, Caliph
AL-ZAHIR, Caliph
Fatma Sultan 16 350, 447
Fatmev Mosque 6 277
Fatqua 7 87
fats 8 127; 15 849; 24 106; 33 2
Fatsan *see* FOSHAN
Fa-tsang *see* FAZANG
Fattah, Ismail 10 833*
works 3 52; 16 2, *3*
Fattore, Il *see* PENNI, GIOVAN FRANCESCO
Fattoretto, Giovanni Battista 17 512
Fattori, Giovanni 10 833–6*; 11 190; 14 588; 16 678; 19 512
groups and movements 18 715; 19 870, 871; 20 482
patrons and collectors 31 757
pupils 23 192; 28 319
works 2 107; 10 *834*, *835*; 11 397; 16 678
Fattori, Giovanni, Museo Civico *see under* LIVORNO
Fattori, Liborio 31 315
Fattorini *see* SCHIAVON
Fattu 15 632; 22 439
fatty acid spue 19 6
Fatuhiva *see* MARQUESAS ISLANDS
Fatullayev, N. 2 897
Fat'yanovo culture 27 367
Fau, Julien 1 845
Fauchery, Antoine Julien 2 745; 8 460
Fauchery, Auguste 26 333
Fauchet, Claude 2 162
Fauchier (family) 20 474
Fauchier, Balthazar 10 836
Fauchier, Joseph 11 605; 20 474
Fauchier, Laurent 10 836*
Faucit, Helen 16 33
Faucon, Bernard 24 679
Fauconberg, Thomas Belasyse, 4th Viscount *see* BELASYSE, THOMAS, 4th Viscount Fauconberg
Fauconnet, François 24 147
Fauconnier, Jacques-Henri 11 621, 622
Faugeron, Jean 24 130
Faujas de Saint-Fond, Barthélemy 12 209
Fauju 15 629
Faulchot 10 836
Faulchot, Colleçon 10 836*
Faulchot, Gérard, I (*d* 1540) 10 836*
Faulchot, Gérard, II (*d* 1606) 10 836
Faulchot, Jean 10 836
Fauler 33 357
Faulhaber, Johann 5 763
Faulkbourne Hall (Essex) 4 779
Faulkner, Barry 5 530
Faulkner, Charles 14 809; 22 143
Faulkner, John 10 837*
Faulkner, William 1 84; 8 63
Faulte, Jean 3 547; 5 40; 10 837*; 13 831
Fauno, Lucio 26 848
Fauquez, Pierre Joseph 3 590; 31 220
Fauré, Camille 11 631; 19 396
Faure, Félix, Mme 20 821
Fauré, Gabriel 32 591
Faure, Jean-Baptiste 10 837*
paintings 4 655; 15 154; 21 864; 24 883
sponsorship 28 795
Faure-Favier, Louise 18 863
fausse-braye 21 546
Faust, Isaac 12 453
Faust, Séverin *see* MAUCLAIR, CAMILLE
Faustini, Modesto 14 479
Faustin Soulouque, Emperor of Haiti (*reg* 1849-59) 14 58, 60
fauteuils see under CHAIRS → types
fauteuils de commodité see under CHAIRS → types
Fauteux, Roger 2 839
Fautrier, Jean 10 837–9*; 11 569
groups and movements 1 78; 2 515, 543, 544; 11 551; 20 846
patrons and collectors 21 135; 23 371; 24 24
works 10 *838*; 11 550; 28 920
Fauveau, Félicie de 10 839*; 31 374
Fauveau, Hippolyte 10 839
Fauvism 5 529; 7 630; 8 773; 10 839–42*; 18 717; 20 821; 22 747; 27 239; 32 668
art forms
lithography 19 *491*
painting 29 670
painting (allegorical) 20 *823*
painting (genre) 9 *134*; 22 *851*
painting (landscape) 10 *840*; 32 *668*
painting (townscapes) 20 *465*
portraits 5 *529*
collections 3 251; 19 282; 27 343; 29 642; 33 36
commentaries 30 231
exhibitions 10 680; 12 870, 871; 16 817; 25 356; 31 605
regional traditions
Belgium 5 44; 23 399; 30 726
see also BRABANT FAUVISM
France 20 464; 21 776; 24 143; 25 752; 32 96
faux bois see under PAINTING → techniques
faux marbre see under PAINTING → techniques
Fauzan Omar 20 172
Fava, Alessandro, Conte 8 158; 20 902; 21 539
Fava, Filippo 5 852
Fava, Marc Antonio 2 455
Favanne, Henri (-Antoine) de 6 121; 10 842*
Favard, Baronessa 25 74
Favard, Fiorella 11 190
Favarger, Pierrette 30 144
Favart, Charles-Simon 4 515; 30 369
Faventinus, Marcus Cetius 26 884, 924
Favenza, Vincenzo 3 179
Faveran, Dominique de *see* DOMINIQUE DE FAVERAN
Faveran, Jacques de *see* JACQUES DE FAVERAN
Favereau, Gabriel 3 210
Faverey, Alphonse 30 16
Faversham Abbey (Kent) 26 615
Favier (family) 11 604; 22 35
Favier, Philippe 11 553; 19 848
Favorino, Varino 31 905
Favorite Palace 26 547; 33 594
Spiegelkabinett 5 349
Favorsky, Vladimir (Andreyevich) 10 843*; 22 178; 27 395, 433, 443; 32 661; 33 370
collaboration 5 276
groups and movements 11 358; 27 395
pupils 8 844; 24 818
works 27 411
Favray, Antoine de 10 843*; 20 213
Favre, Pierre 11 354
Favretto, Giacomo 10 844*; 16 678; 32 197
works 32 197, *197*
Favrile glass *see under* GLASS → types
Favro, Murray 5 572; 10 844*
Fa'w al-qibli 7 820
Fawcett, Benjamin 4 363, 369
Fawcett, James 2 766
Fawkener, Everard 6 533; 29 432
Fawkes, Lionel Grimstone 5 751
Fawkes, Walter Ramsden 31 470
Fawley Court (Bucks) 10 642; 24 415; 25 192
Faworski, Józef 25 105
fax art *see* PRINTING → processes → telecopy
Faxian 1 210; 6 320; 17 831, 857; 24 264; 28 624, 637, 720
Faxiang Buddhism *see under* BUDDHISM → sects
Faxian's Cave 29 445
Fay, András 2 546
Fay, Josef 33 228
Fayan Buddhism *see under* BUDDHISM → sects
Fayan Wenyi 5 110
Faydherbe, Hendrik 10 844
Faydherbe, Jan Lucas 10 844
Faydherbe, Lucas 3 570; 10 844–5*
assistants 3 894; 8 21
pupils 4 220; 8 663; 18 742; 32 121, 255
teachers 27 298
works 3 545, 604; 5 39; 11 502; 14 488; 30 495
Faydysh-Krandiyevsky, A.
works 22 *179*
Faye, Mbor 28 405
Faye, Mor 28 405
Faye, Ousmane 28 405
Fa-yen Wen-i *see* FAYAN WENYI
Fayet, Gustave 12 193; 26 72
Fayet, Jean 11 514
Fayet, Simon 12 832
Faylaka Island 2 *246*, 251; 15 912
coins 2 261
figurines 2 260
fortress 2 251
glass 2 263
pottery 2 268
sculpture 2 257
seals 2 270, 271
stone vessels 2 272
temples 2 251–2
Faynum
textiles 30 *563*
Faysal I, King of Iraq (*reg* 1921-33) (Hashimid) 16 2
Fayyad, Najib 19 7
Fayyaz, Mohammad 23 804
Fayzl Khodzha 18 195
Fazang 5 109
Fazhao 5 109
Fazil Haravi 12 81
Fazio, Bartolomeo *see* FACIO, BARTOLOMEO
Fazio, Gano di *see* GANO DI FAZIO
Fazio, Giuliano De *see* DE FAZIO, GIULIANO
Fazl 15 594
al-Fazl, Abu *see* ABU AL-FAZL
Fazl'ali 22 266
Fazola, Henrik 9 754; 10 845*; 15 9; 16 59
works 15 *9*
Fazola, Lénéard 10 845
Fazzi, Ignazio 17 544
Fazzini, E. 17 622
Fazzini, Pericle 6 345; 10 845–6*; 11 802; 16 709; 24 279; 26 777
Fazzolari, Fernando 2 401; 10 846*
F.C., Master *see* CRABBE (VAN ESPLEGHEM), FRANS
Fea, Carlo 7 726; 10 846*
Fearn, William 7 30
Fearnley, Thomas 8 451; 10 846–7*; 23 225
feathers 10 847–8*, *847*
display 7 732
historical and regional traditions
Aboriginal Australia 1 53
Africa 1 296, 349, *405*
Aztec 2 908; 7 636; 10 *779*, 848; 21 249, *250*
Brazil 4 707, *707*
Britain 10 848
Chimú 29 207
China 7 65, 113
Cook Islands 23 720
Easter Island 23 720
England 28 *581*
Guyana 13 875
Hawaii 10 847, 848, *848*; 14 248–9; 23 720
Hopi 22 *583*
Inca 10 848; 15 163, 164
Indian subcontinent 10 778; 15 733
Indonesia 31 264
Inuit 10 848
Japan 10 848
Maasai 10 848
Maori 10 848; 23 720
Marquesas Islands 23 720
Maya 21 249
Mende (Sierra Leone) 10 848
Mesoamerica, Pre-Columbian 10 *779*; 21 245, 249–50*, *250*, 261
Moche (culture) 29 207
Native North Americans 3 331; 10 847, 848; 22 *549*, *583*, 652–4*, *653*; 31 260
Nazca 29 207
New Guinea 10 848
Pacific Islands 23 720, 721
Papua New Guinea 10 847; 23 721; 24 *75*, *84*
Paraguay 24 93
Peru 29 *207*
Society Islands 28 *922*
South Africa 10 848
South America, Pre-Columbian 29 155, *207*, 207–8*
Tarascan 21 249; 30 342
Tonga (Pacific Islands) 31 143
Torres Strait Islands 31 186
United States of America 22 *549*, *653*
Zaïre 1 *405*
techniques 9 490; 21 249
types
birds of paradise 24 75
duck 21 249
humming-bird feathers 21 249
kingfisher 7 108, 110, 111, *111*, 112; 10 848
ostrich 1 349; 10 *775*
peacock 30 654
powisi 30 16
quetzal 10 848; 21 249
uses
amulets 22 652
aprons 21 249
arrows 10 848
baskets 3 331; 10 848; 22 652
belts 22 652, 653
blankets 22 652
body ornaments 23 720
brushes 5 32; 7 65
canoes 10 848
charms 22 652
cloaks 10 848; 14 248–9, *249*; 22 652; 30 342
costumes 30 654
crowns 7 110, 111, *111*, 112; 13 875
dolls 22 *583*; 31 260
dolls' furniture 31 264
dress 7 636; 15 163; 22 653; 28 *922*
fans 10 *775*, 778, *779*, 782; 21 250; 22 654
footwear 1 349
hair ornaments 7 108
hammocks 10 848
feathers
uses—cont.
hats 1 296; 17 524
headbands 22 652
headdresses 1 53; 4 *707*; 10 848; 15 733; 21 249, 250; 22 652, 653, *653*; 23 721; 24 75, *75*, *84*; 30 342; 31 143, 186
headpieces (body ornament) 22 652
helmets 10 848; 14 249; 21 245
interior decoration 28 *581*
jewellery 7 112; 17 530; 30 16
kites 7 113
masks 1 *405*
pens 24 349
pipes (smoking) 22 653
quivers 22 652
regalia 22 *549*, 653, 654
sashes 14 249
sculpture 10 *848*
shields 10 848; 21 245, 249, *250*; 22 653; 30 342
skirts 22 652
spears 10 848
standards (vexilloid) 30 342
tepees 22 653
textiles 21 261; 29 207–8
topknots 22 652
tunics 29 *207*
upholstery 31 684
wall coverings 10 848
Featherston, Grant 2 756, 759
featherworkers' guilds *see under* GUILDS → types
Febre, Valentin le 32 356
Febure, Thomas Le *see* LE FEBURE, THOMAS
Febvre, Le (family) *see* LE FEBVRE (FAMILY)
Febvre-Caters, Le *see* LE FEBVRE, JACQUES, II
Febvrier 30 885
Febvrier, Jacques 19 382
Febvrier, Pierre-Louis 18 745
Fécamp
Abbey 13 36; 31 284
La Trinité 3 710; 11 656, 727; 26 597; 30 782; 32 603
Benedictine liqueur factory 10 748
chalets 6 395
Fechheimer, Edwin S. 14 518
Fechner, Gustav Theodor 25 684
Fechter, Charles 30 682
Fechter, Johann Jacob 3 334
Fechter, Paul 10 848–9*
Fedders, Jūlijs (Voldemars) *see* FEDERS, JŪLIJS (VOLDEMARS)
Feddersen-Wierde 14 73; 32 532
Feddes van Harlingen, Petrus 10 849*; 23 908
Fede, (Giuseppe), Conte 10 849*
Fede, Matteo Pagano della *see* PAGANO DELLA FEDE, MATTEO
Fedele da S Biagio 10 488
Fedeli *see* MAGGIOTTO
Fedeli, Ercole dei 2 453
Fedeli, F. 4 310
Fedeli, Luigi 5 762
Fedeli, Matteo 4 643
Fedeli, Stefano de' 3 695; 21 525
Feder, Gottfried 31 730
Federación de Fundaciones Privadas 32 179
Federal Arts Project (FAP) *see under* WORKS PROGRESS ADMINISTRATION (WPA)
Federal Capital Commission 5 602
Federal Relief Project 22 672
Federal Society for Arts and Humanities 23 139
Federal style 10 849–52*; 20 7
architecture 10 *850*; 31 591, *591*
furniture 8 235; 31 628, *628*
interior decoration 31 618
tea-urns 10 *851*
see also NEO-CLASSICISM

Fédération, La 24 439
Fédération Internationale de la Médaille (FIDEM) 20 926
Federation style 2 740; 10 852*
Federici, Domenico Maria 10 852–3*
Federico I, 3rd Marchese of Mantua (*reg* 1478-84) 12 *904*, 907*
  architecture 10 784; 20 319
  paintings 20 311; 21 18
  sculpture 2 140
Federico II, 5th Marchese and 1st Duke of Mantua (*reg* 1519-40) 12 903, *904*, 909*; 20 319
  architecture 12 749, 753–7
  maiolica 31 747
  paintings 6 39; 7 891; 16 667; 19 200; 22 413; 29 84; 31 34, 35
  sculpture 10 521; 19 551
  silver 16 742
  swords 2 455
  tapestries 17 812; 20 323
Federighi, Antonio 10 853–4*
  collaboration 16 845
  patrons and collectors 24 732
  works 10 *854*; 16 843; 23 585; 28 675, 681, 684
  workshop 11 254
Federigo II, 1st Duke of Urbino (*reg* 1444-82) 22 12–13*; 31 *741*
  architecture 11 688; 12 717; 16 630; 18 861; 25 216
    palazzi 1 556; 16 630; 18 861; 29 859, 860; 31 739, 740, 742
  collections 14 870
  furniture 16 722
  imprese 15 150
  interior decoration 16 711, 723; 31 740
  manuscripts 2 697; 3 917; 11 687, 722; 12 721; 20 689; 31 740; 32 384
  marquetry 20 467
  paintings 3 844; 5 782; 16 659, 661; 17 702, 704; 20 623; 24 764
  sculpture 25 157
  Studiolo 29 *860*
  tapestries 13 196, 634
  teachers 12 905
  weapons 20 552
Federigo Memmi *see* TEDERIGHO MEMMI
Federigo Parmense *see* BONZAGNA, GIAN FEDERICO
Federigui, Juan 22 343
Federle, Helmut 30 135
Federoff, George 22 575
Feders, Jūlijs (Voldemars) 10 854–5*; 18 850
Fédi, Antonio 33 154
Fedi, Pio 3 357; 16 706
Fedier, Franz 30 135
Fedkowicz, Jerzy 18 429; 33 416
Fedorkov, Anatoly (Fedorovich) 27 418
Fedorová, Silvia 28 856
Fedorovitch, Sophie 30 687
Fedoskino 24 62
Fedotov, Pavel (Andreyevich) 10 855–7*; 27 389, 390
  works 4 40; 10 *856*
Feduchi, Luis M. 29 273, 309, 321, 322
Fedusko of Sambor 31 557
feeders 13 536
feeding bottles *see under* BOTTLES → types
Feeley, Paul 11 729; 24 213
Feer, Petermann 30 149, 311
Feer tapestry 30 311
Fegolmin 24 73, 74
Fehér, László 14 902
Fehling, Heinrich Christoph 10 857*
  collaboration 29 547
  pupils 33 685
Fehling, Heinrich Christoph—cont.
  teachers 4 507; 12 478
  works 9 242
Fehling, Hermann 10 857*
Fehmer, Carl 10 185
Fehn, Sverre 10 857–8*; 23 222
Fehner, Christian 14 543
Fehr, Friedrich 23 185
Fehr, Gertrude 10 858*
Fehr, Henry 10 267
Fehr, Jules 10 858
Fehr, William, Collection *see under* CAPE TOWN
Fehre, Johann Gottfried 3 67
  works 3 *67*
Fei, Alessandro (di Vincenzio) 10 858*; 21 22; 32 17
Fei, Paolo di Giovanni *see* PAOLO DI GIOVANNI FEI
Feibush Ashkenazi *see* JOEL BEN SIMEON
Feicheng, Guo (Family) Shrines 6 697
Feichtmayer, Anton 10 858, 860
Feichtmayer, Franz Xaver (i) (1698-1763) 10 858, 860*
  assistants 26 24
  collaboration 10 859; 24 370; 26 24; 31 511
  patrons and collectors 33 278
  pupils 10 860
  works 11 124; 31 512
Feichtmayer, Franz Xaver (ii) (1735-1803) 10 858, 860–61*; 11 127; 26 498
Feichtmayer, Johann Michael 10 858, 859–60*
  collaboration 10 860; 31 511, 512; 32 466
  works 7 211; 10 *859*; 11 124, 125, 127; 23 636; 25 728
Feichtmayer, Michael 10 858, 860
Feichtmayer, Simpert 10 858
Feichtmayr, Jacob 33 240
Feick, George 25 737
Feiffe, Jules 27 872
Feige, Johann Christian 9 241
Feigen, Richards L., and Co. Inc. 14 685
Feigl, Friedrich 10 107, 108; 13 711
Feigler, Ignác 28 850
Fei-hsien *see* FEIXIAN
Feilchenfeldt, Walter 5 924
Feilden, Bernard (Melchior) 10 861*
Feilding, Basil 10 861*; 22 696
Feilding, William, 1st Earl of Denbigh 10 861
Feilner, Simon 11 730; 14 606
Feilner, Tobias 28 100
Feinauer, Albert 12 450
Feininger, Andreas (Bernhard Lyonel) 10 861, 863*; 12 396; 28 78
Feininger, Lyonel 10 861–3*
  collaboration 14 571
  exhibitions 32 775
  groups and movements 10 861
    Aktion, Die 24 585
    Arbeitsrat für Kunst 2 288
    Bauhaus 3 400, 402; 10 698; 12 396
    Black Mountain College (NC) 4 109
    Blaue Reiter 4 133
    Blue Four 4 177; 17 766; 18 111
  house 2 552
  patrons and collectors 14 295; 23 121; 25 629
  pupils 2 381; 12 634
  works 10 *862*; 11 465; 12 497; 33 363
Feininger, T(heodore) Lux 10 861, 863*
Feinstein, Daniel Isaac *see* SPOERRI, DANIEL
Feint, Adrian 2 756, 759
Fei Qinghu 17 189
Feira 10 729
Feistel-Rohmeder, Bettina 10 413
Feistenberger *see* FAISTENBERGER
Feitama, Isaac 10 864
Feitama, Sybrand (1620-1701) 10 864
Feitama, Sybrand, the younger (1694-1758) 1 808; 10 863–4*
Feitelson, Lorser 19 702; 31 607
Feito, Luis 10 864*; 29 286
Feixian 4 173
Fejérváry, Gabriel 28 857
Feješ, Emerik 22 440
  works 22 *441*
Feke, Robert 4 477, 599; 10 864*; 31 600
Fekheriya, Tell 2 283
Fel, Marie 18 *842*
Felaata *see* FULANI
Felber, Hans 10 865*; 14 322; 18 515; 23 204
Felbinger, Bartol 8 176; 10 865–6*; 33 592
Felbrigge Psalter *see under* PSALTERS → individual manuscripts
Felbrigg Hall (Norfolk) 3 920; 5 295; 9 17; 32 111
Feldbauer, Max 28 143
Feldbergs, Ojārs
Feldebrő 14 898; 26 638, 687
  parish church 14 883
Feldenkirchen, Toni 31 328
Felderhoff, Reinhold Karl 10 866*; 28 52
Feldiora Fortress 26 706
Feldman, Eugene 19 493
Feldman, Morton 5 381
Feldmann, Julius 12 821
feldspar 6 324
  historical and regional traditions
    Egypt, ancient 10 38; 12 246
    Japan 17 242
    Prehistoric art 25 477
  uses
    amulets 10 38
    glazes 6 324, 326, 329; 17 242
    paints 25 477
    rock art 25 477
Feleart, Dieric *see* VELLERT, DIRK (JACOBSZ.)
Feleo, Roberto 24 620
Felgenhauer, Fritz 33 197
Felguérez, Manuel 5 881; 10 866–7*; 21 389, 406; 28 330
  collaboration 12 844
  works 22 21
Félibien, André 10 690, 867*; 13 468; 22 378; 24 167
  drawings 6 416; 9 94
  engravings 7 545; 19 *352*; 27 549
  groups and movements 24 169; 25 398
  patrons and collectors 6 489
  writings 6 570; 10 205
    on art 10 204; 23 489; 24 494; 31 296, 300
    on artists 10 204; 11 674
    on caricatures 5 760
    on *disegno e colore* 9 8
    on painting 12 289; 18 700
Félibien, J. F. 19 16
Félibien, Michel 10 867
Félibien des Avaux, Jean-François 10 867
Felice, Matteo 10 868*
Felice di Michele 20 413
Felice Peña 23 80
Felici, A. 1 122
Felicia, Queen of Castile-León (*d* 1085) 26 642, 689
Feliciangeli, Silvio 24 96
Feliciano, Felice 2 161, 166; 10 868*; 15 50; 25 557
Feliński, Roman 19 836
Felipe V, King of Spain *see* PHILIP V, King of Spain
Felipe, Alejandro Sánchez *see* SÁNCHEZ FELIPE, ALEJANDRO
Felipe, Diego 2 386
Felipe Pablo de San Leocadio 24 28
Felípez de Guzmán, Diego, Marqués de Leganés *see* LEGANÉS, 1st Marqués de
Felix (*fl* 1160-4) 26 669
Felix (*b* 1720) *see* BERNABÉ, FELIX
Felix IV, Pope (*reg* 526-30) 9 534; 26 835
Felix V, (Anti-) Pope *see* AMADEUS VIII, Count of Savoy
Félix, Benjamin 22 21
Felix, LaFortune 14 58
Felix Gem 12 907; 14 807; 23 326
Felix Meritis Society 1 808; 13 295; 19 116; 22 827
Felixmüller, Conrad 10 868–70*
  groups and movements 4 208
  works 10 *869*; 12 396; 29 871; 33 363
Fell, Thomas 17 526
Fellbach-Schmiden 6 159; 25 538, 545
Fellenstein, Nicholas 20 186
Fellerer, Max 2 789, 815; 10 870*
Felletin 30 326, 329
  carpets 11 652
  tapestries 2 703, 704; 11 639, 640, 642, 643; 30 322
Fellheimer & Wagner 7 326; 32 851
Felli, Domenico 23 513
Fellig, Arthur *see* WEEGEE
Fellig, Usher *see* WEEGEE
Fellini, Federico 25 194; 28 337
Fellner, Ferdinand (*fl* 1840s) 10 871
Fellner, Ferdinand (1847-1916) 10 871*; 17 630; 18 692; 31 551
  collaboration 5 149; 14 367; 23 353; 33 593
  staff 2 415; 29 777
  works 2 786, 808; 8 176; 13 330; 23 340, *354*; 30 678, 679; 33 735
Fellner, Jakob 10 871*
  patrons and collectors 10 531
  works 9 754; 14 *887*, 888
Fellner, Simon 11 851
Fellowes-Prynne, G. H. 29 765
Fellows, Charles 19 838; 33 459
Fellowship of Experimental Art (TEII) 27 581
Fellowship of St Luke 10 871–2*; 25 108; 32 877
Fellowship of South Russian Artists 18 399
Fellowship of Travelling Exhibitions *see* WANDERERS
Fell's Cave 29 204
Feloix, Louis-Gabriel 11 627; 24 893
Felsburg 29 700
Felsina *see under* BOLOGNA
Felsing, Otto 25 600
Felsőelefánt *see* Horná Lefantovce
felt 10 872–5*, *875*; 30 549
  historical and regional traditions
    Afghanistan 10 872, 874
    Albania 1 544
    Anatolia, ancient 10 873
    Britain 10 875
    Central Asia 10 872, 873–5
    Central Asia, Western 6 248, 251; 10 *874*; 16 485
    China 10 873–4; 30 *475*
    Czech Republic 10 875
    Georgia 10 874
    Germany 3 *891*; 10 875
    Greece, ancient 10 875
    Iceland 10 875
    Indian subcontinent 10 875
    Iran 10 872, 873, 874
    Iraq 10 874
    Ireland 16 33
felt
  historical and regional traditions—cont.
    Islamic 16 124, 466, 485
    Japan 10 873
    Mongolia 10 873, 875; 21 877
    Morocco 10 875
    Rome, ancient 10 875
    Scandinavia 10 875
    Siberia 10 873, *873*
    Slovakia 10 875
    Sweden 10 875
    Tibet 10 875; 30 846
    Turkey 10 872, 874; 30 *474*
  materials
    hair 10 872
    jute 10 872
    vegetable fibres 10 872
    wool 10 872
  techniques
    dyeing 10 872
    embroidery 10 873
    quilting 21 877
  uses
    appliqué 10 872
    bags 10 873
    carpets 10 874; 16 466
    dolls 31 260
    doors 10 874
    dress 6 251
    fibre art 11 54
    hangings 10 873, *875*
    harnesses 10 873
    hats 10 872, 875
    mantles 10 873
    mats 10 873
    pens 24 350
    rugs 10 873, *874*; 27 316
    saddlery 10 873
    sculpture 3 *891*
    tents 10 873, 874; 16 485; 30 470, 473, *474*, *475*
    wagons 10 874
Fel'ten, Yury (Matveyevich) 10 876*
  collaboration 27 585; 31 828
  patrons and collectors 26 731
  works 24 290, 546; 25 746; 27 376, 575
Felten & Guilleaumme 18 140
Felton, Alfred 2 769, 770; 10 876–7*
Féltorony, Harrach Palace 14 886
felt paper *see under* PAPER → types
Feltre, Morto da *see* MORTO DA FELTRE
Feltre, Vittorino da *see* VITTORINO DA FELTRE
Feltrini, Andrea (di Giovanni di Lorenzo) 10 877*
  collaboration 11 704; 12 556; 27 848
  works 3 16
Feltrini, Andrea di Cosimo 27 849
felt-tip pens *see* PENS → types → fibre-tip
Felwer, Hanns *see* FELBER, HANS
Female Half-Lengths, Master of the 14 190; 20 664–6*
  works 20 *665*
Fémes Beck, Vilmos *see* BECK (ii), VILMOS FÉMES
Femine, Giulio Cesare de 12 890
feminism 2 538; 10 258, 483, 486, 877–83*; 15 100; 28 927; 29 390
  installations 10 *877*, *879*, *880*, *881*, *882*
  United States of America 6 577; 31 673
  see also WOMEN ARTISTS
Feminist Art Journal 10 878; 24 429
Feminist Art News 10 879; 24 429
Fenaille, Maurice 11 675
fences 1 311; 12 94
fenders 11 119, *119*
Fendi, Peter 2 796; 10 883–4*; 12 294; 19 339; 32 444
Fendour, John 28 250

Fenékpuszta Villa 26 906, 907
Fénelon, François de Salignac de la Mothe- 3 259; 10 884*
Fénéon, Félix 3 826; 10 884–5*; 19 36; 22 538; 30 231
  collections 1 438
  groups and movements 22 745, 746
  works 7 630
Fenest, Johann 14 18
fenestellae 1 694; 8 222; 10 885*
Feng 33 660
Fenga Hill 1 371
  rock art 1 376
Fengate 25 503
Fengchu (Qishan)
  architecture 6 646, 647
  palace 33 660
Fenger, Ludwig
  illustrated works 25 11
Feng Hetu 7 23
Feng Ho-t'u see FENG HETU
Feng Hsi-lu see FENG XILU
Feng Huang 25 800
Feng Sufou 7 83
Feng Tse-kai see FENG ZIKAI
Feng Tzu-chen see FENG ZIZHEN
Feng Tzu-K'ai see FENG ZIKAI
Fengxiang 6 696, 854; 7 140
Feng Xilu 7 62
Fengyang
  Huang ling 6 701, 732
  jade 7 10
  sculpture 6 732
  urban planning 6 665
Feng Yingke 7 66
Feng Ying-k'o see FENG YINGKE
Feng Zikai 10 885–6*
Feng Zizhen 6 752
Feni, Dumile see DUMILE (FENI)
Feni, Zwelidumiloe Geelboi Mgxaji Mslaba see DUMILE (FENI)
Fenioux Church 26 600
Fenis Castel 17 445
Fenn, Howard 10 337
Fenner, William 31 422
Fenoglio, Pietro 10 886*; 16 721
Fenollosa, Ernest Francisco 10 887*; 11 748; 17 133, 200, 420, 798; 21 59
  collections 17 431, 434
  sculpture 17 108
  works 17 194
  writings 17 439
Fenton 29 495
Fenton, Christopher Webber 4 482; 31 636, 637
Fenton, Jonathan 4 482
Fenton, Richard Lucas 4 482
Fenton, Roger 10 887–8*; 24 666, 668
  dealers 1 454
  works 24 664, 665, 667
Fenton's Cabinet Establishment 16 886
Fenwick, Kathleen 25 238
Fényes, Adolf 10 888*; 14 901
  groups and movements 30 211
Fenzone, Ferraú 19 383
Feodor I, Tsar of Moscow (reg 1584-98) 27 430
Feodor III, Tsar of Moscow (reg 1676-82) 18 207
Feodosiya see KAFFA
Feodosy 8 908; 10 890; 22 184; 25 342
Feofan Grek see THEOPHANES THE GREEK
Feognost, Metropolitan 22 181
Feoli, Vincenzo
  works 9 12; 16 773
Feoli Painter 10 614
Fer, Nicholas de 21 580
Ferabosco, Martino 26 840
Ferabosco, Pietro 10 888–9*; 32 442
  attributions 32 456
Ferabosco, Pietro—cont.
  patrons and collectors 13 910, 915
  works 2 212, 780; 4 695; 14 885; 32 455, 456
Ferahan see FARAGHAN
Feraklos 26 294
Férand, Gaspard 22 242
Ferapont 10 889
Ferapontov Monastery 10 889, 889–90*; 27 363
  Cathedral of the Nativity of the Virgin 8 909; 25 342
  iconostasis 25 337
Ferari, Procopio de 28 476
Ferber (Silvers), Herbert 10 890–91*; 17 580; 18 162; 24 213
Ferdinand (c. 1580-1649) see ELLE, FERDINAND
Ferdinand, Archduke of Austria see FERDINAND II, Holy Roman Emperor
Ferdinand, Archduke of Austria, Count of Tyrol (reg 1564-95) 2 827; 13 899, 900, 911–12*
  architecture 2 780; 8 422; 15 864, 866
  armour 9 31
  collections 2 830; 6 76; 15 866; 22 675
  coral 7 835
  fountains 24 331
  furniture 26 103; 32 777
  glass 2 818
  gold 6 142
  guns 2 458
  hardstones 11 635; 27 815
  lacquer 18 612
  manuscript illumination 14 619
  maps 11 270
  metalwork 13 646; 19 152
  paintings 11 270; 12 720
  porcelain 9 28
  sculpture 9 340; 24 331
  silver 29 738
Ferdinand, Count of Flanders (reg 1212-33) 12 521
Ferdinand, Duke of Parma ((reg 1765-99) 4 560; 13 805
Ferdinand, Emperor of Austria (reg 1835-48) 1 687; 14 267; 19 522
Ferdinand, Infante of Castile 16 439
Ferdinand, King of Bohemia and Hungary see FERDINAND I, Holy Roman Emperor
Ferdinand, King of Naples and Sicily see FERDINAND II, King of Aragon and Sicily
Ferdinand I, Holy Roman Emperor (reg 1558-64) 13 899, 900, 908*
  altarpieces 3 877
  architecture 1 667; 2 212, 778; 8 377; 25 425; 29 371, 624, 738; 31 23; 32 434, 442
  coins 18 876
  collections 18 520
  drawings 29 738
  gardens 12 114
  glass 2 818; 15 3
  hardstones 21 725
  manuscripts 14 620
  maps 14 573; 29 85
  medals 8 790; 22 924
  metalwork 16 899
  paintings 4 207; 18 877; 20 191; 28 377, 378; 32 680
  sculpture 1 763; 8 384
  silver 18 139
  statuettes 29 571
Ferdinand I, King of Castile-León (reg 1035-65) 2 222; 8 213; 19 178; 20 689; 26 689; 29 288
Ferdinand I, King of Naples (reg 1458-94) 2 275, 276–7*
  architecture 22 470; 27 735, 736; 32 545
  books 12 655
  drawings 21 14
  manuscripts 20 144
  paintings 8 14
  sculpture 11 28; 30 498
Ferdinand I, King of Portugal (reg 1367-83) 19 463; 32 539
Ferdinand I, King of Spain (reg 1035-65) 26 605
Ferdinand I, King of the Two Sicilies (reg 1759-1825) 4 557; 5 555; 14 17, 445; 29 676
  architecture 3 920; 16 646; 22 472, 474, 487
  collections 14 445
  drawings 5 908
  excavations 27 58
  paintings 5 908; 10 488; 14 17; 27 201
  porcelain 16 737; 22 482; 25 193
  sculpture 4 562
  tapestries 25 411
Ferdinand II, Holy Roman Emperor (reg 1619-37) 2 827; 13 900, 901, 917–18*; 15 865
  architecture 5 771; 19 769; 33 303
  armour 2 821
  collections 18 521
  engravings 18 43; 27 504
  furniture 32 448
  glass 10 773
  hardstones 25 436
  medals 1 35
  metalwork 2 819, 821; 12 446; 16 900
  paintings 2 794; 25 187; 32 706; 33 388
  sculpture 1 36
  weapons 2 455
Ferdinand II, King of Aragon and Sicily (reg 1479-1516) 2 275, 277–8*
  architecture 2 658; 4 647; 9 112; 13 283; 18 587; 20 61; 27 605; 28 519
  coats of arms 29 298
  collections 13 922; 26 306
  hardstones 17 515
  interior decoration 29 298
  metalwork 29 333
  paintings 3 844; 12 650
  palaces 13 286
  sculpture 2 278
  silk 28 716
Ferdinand II, King of León (reg 1157-88) 7 362; 19 171
Ferdinand II, King of Portugal (1816-89) 4 631, 632, 638–9*, 639; 33 110
  architecture 10 496; 25 293, 317; 28 781
  furniture 4 629; 25 308
  paintings 2 206; 8 163; 11 249; 21 348, 349; 26 517; 28 736
Ferdinand II, King of the Two Sicilies (reg 1830-59) 1 745; 4 333, 557; 22 98, 474
Ferdinand III, Holy Roman Emperor (reg 1637-58) 13 901, 918–19*
  architecture 19 770
  fortifications 25 426
  furniture 32 448
  hardstones 21 726; 25 436
  ivory 33 669
  paintings 13 919; 19 831; 27 725; 29 612
  sculpture 32 442
Ferdinand III, King of Castile-León (reg 1217-52) 9 699; 13 103; 16 440; 28 511
Ferdinand IV, King of Bohemia and Hungary (reg 1646-54) 13 901
Ferdinand IV, King of Naples see FERDINAND I, King of the Two Sicilies
Ferdinand V, King of Castile see FERDINAND II, King of Aragon and Sicily
Ferdinand VI, King of Spain (reg 1746-59) 4 556, 557, 561*
  architecture 2 285; 20 67; 29 271
  collections 4 560
  gardens 2 285
  military works 13 694
  paintings 1 784; 5 435, 436; 11 172; 12 587, 923; 19 648
  sculpture 6 67, 68
  sponsorship 4 441
Ferdinand VII, King of Spain (reg 1808; 1814-33) 4 557, 557, 566*; 20 70; 29 354
  architecture 32 565
  bronze 29 342
  collections 17 628
  interior decoration 29 306
  metalwork 29 342
  paintings 10 651; 19 659; 20 59; 21 35; 26 308, 517, 738; 29 352
  sculpture 1 742; 3 199; 5 544
Ferdinand, Anders Nicolaus 30 97
Ferdinand, Louis 18 745
Ferdinand-Charles, Count of Tyrol (reg 1632-62) 6 126; 13 845
Ferdinande, Joseph see FERNANDE, JOSEPH
Ferdinand Maria, Elector of Bavaria (reg 1651-79) 1 787; 25 672; 33 273, 276*
Ferdinand Maximilian, Archduke of Austria see MAXIMILIAN OF HABSBURG, Emperor of Mexico
Ferdinando, 6th Duke of Mantua (reg 1612-26) 12 904, 912–13*
  architecture 20 320; 28 337; 32 404
  collections 18 747
  jewellery 27 815
  medals 21 804
  paintings 1 535; 4 813; 11 39–41; 13 785; 22 83; 26 197
  sculpture 1 625
Ferdinando I, Grand Duke of Tuscany (reg 1587-1609) 21 7, 8, 9, 23–4*; 23 157, 158; 32 546; 33 722
  architecture 7 311; 19 511; 23 140; 32 547
  art policies 16 766
  collections 11 188
  decorative works 9 182
  gold 20 903
  hardstones 8 418; 11 29; 16 724; 24 779
  interior decoration 11 213
  metalwork 32 161
  paintings 4 567; 5 708; 7 311; 11 180, 803; 20 266; 27 723; 30 355; 32 732
  porcelain 16 736
  sculpture 3 231; 5 360; 12 576; 31 787, 825
  stage scenery 3 226
Ferdinando II, Grand Duke of Tuscany (reg 1621-70) 11 192; 21 9, 26*
  architecture 11 181
  carpets 16 473
  furniture 12 461; 14 51
  paintings 4 65; 14 312
    battle 27 296
    ceiling 11 188
    frescoes 11 22
    landscape 9 376
    modelli 11 839
    portraits 8 186; 19 122
    religious 6 348; 27 851
    still-lifes 1 165; 28 169
  sculpture 15 101; 21 29; 30 228, 229
  tapestries 11 194
Ferdinando III, Grand Duke of Tuscany (reg 1814-24) 3 750; 5 363; 11 31; 12 355; 16 730; 17 852; 22 113; 27 623; 29 378
Ferdinando-Carlo, 10th Duke of Mantua (reg 1665-1708) 6 37; 12 903, 904, 914*
Ferdinando de la Cerda 10 322
Ferdinand of Cifer 31 353
Ferdinand the Catholic, King of Aragon and Sicily see FERDINAND II, King of Aragon and Sicily
Ferdon, Edwin 31 140
Feré, Jean (d 1447) 10 891
Feré, Jean (d 1454) 10 891
Feré, Pierrot (fl 1395-1429) 2 496; 10 891*; 30 313
Feré, Pierrot (d 1448) 10 891
Fère-en-Tardenois, La see LA FÈRE-EN-TARDENOIS
Fereman, Jacob 16 570
Ferenc II Rákóczy, Prince of Transylvania (1676-1735) 14 900, 900, 904; 15 4; 20 350; 28 856
Ferenc Golberger 15 11
Ferenc Kluge 15 11
Ferenc Lotharingiai 15 11
Ferenczy, Béni 10 892, 893–4*; 14 896
  groups and movements 13 638
  pupils 29 61; 32 498
  works 10 894
Ferenczy, István 5 85; 10 895–6*; 15 18
  collaboration 16 811
  personal collection 20 400; 28 857
  pupils 16 811
  works 10 546; 14 895
Ferenczy, Károly 10 891, 892–3*; 14 901
  groups and movements 13 638; 22 434
  pupils 30 212
  teachers 14 687
  works 10 892
Ferenczy, Noémi 10 892, 895*; 13 638; 15 12; 30 327
Ferenczy, Valér 10 892
Ferentino 26 871
  Cathedral 30 777
  Mercato Romano 32 87
  S Ippolito 13 98
  S Lucia 13 98
  S Maria Maggiore 13 98
  S Pancrazio 13 98
feretories 10 896*
Ferg, Adam Pankraz 10 896; 13 277
Ferg, Franz de Paula 2 795; 4 662; 10 896*
Ferghana 6 182; 10 896*; 16 105; 31 781
  architecture 31 782
  cotton 6 249, 250
  fortifications 6 199
  ikat 16 451
  museums 6 282, 283
  temples 6 200
Fergioni, Bernardino 2 26; 19 524; 20 270
Fergola, Alessandro 31 100
Fergola, Salvatore 14 17
Ferguson, Amos 3 62, 64
Ferguson, Frank 8 110; 12 926
Ferguson, Henry 7 171
Ferguson, James 12 815
Ferguson, John Calvin 7 161
Ferguson, Kenneth 31 640
Ferguson, William Gouw 10 897*; 20 141; 28 234
Fergusson, James 1 483; 10 897–8*; 15 211, 747
  groups and movements 2 642, 643
  works 1 500; 15 403

Fergusson, J(ohn) D(uncan) 10 898–9*
collections 28 274
groups and movements 12 777; 28 289, 290
pupils 9 9
works 28 238, *239*, 240, 243
Fergusson, Louis 5 516
Fergusson Gallery *see under* PERTH (SCOTLAND)
Feridun Jah, Nawab of Bengal (*reg* 1824-58) 15 380
Ferit Bey 23 695
Ferka 23 286
Ferlandin 3 728
Ferloni, Pietro 25 411; 26 778
Ferlov Mancoba, Sonja 7 488; 8 741; 10 899*; 20 243
fermes ornées 8 461; 12 122, 128, 129
Fermín Arias, Pedro 32 177
Fermo
Cathedral 10 181; 16 541; 26 703; 29 349
S Lucia 16 825–6
Fermo da Caravaggio *see* GHISONI, FERMO (DI STEFANO)
Fermont, A. A. 15 770
Fermor, Henrietta Louisa, 1st Countess Pomfret 23 690
Fermor, Thomas, 1st Earl of Pomfret 13 782
Fermor, William, 1st Baron Leominster 8 47; 14 253
Fernach, Hans 21 524, 533
Fernande, Joseph 10 899*
Fernandes, Antonio 25 295
Fernandes, Diogo 32 147
Fernandes, Eduardo (Manuel) Batarda *see* BATARDA (FERNANDES), EDUARDO (MANUEL)
Fernandes, Fatima 22 245
Fernandes, Fernando 25 302
Fernandes, Garcia 10 899–900*; 25 295
collaboration 1 213; 2 874; 11 65; 14 395; 19 655
teachers 19 655
works 25 296
Fernandes, J. B., Trust Company 31 339
Fernandes, Joseph *see* FERNANDE, JOSEPH
Fernandes, Manuel (*fl* after 1515) 10 900
Fernandes, Manuel, I (*d* 1515) 10 900*
Fernandes, Mateus, I
collaboration 4 245
patrons and collectors 2 872
works 3 363; 13 71; 20 325; 25 290
Fernandes, Pero 30 416
Fernandes, Vasco 10 900–902*; 25 320; 26 253
collaboration 32 98
paintings 28 730
patrons and collectors 2 873
pupils 32 98
works 10 *901*; 25 295; 32 616
Fernandes Barros, Manuel 10 729
Fernandes da Cunha, Lygia da Fonseca *see* FONSECA FERNANDES DA CUNHA, LYGIA DA
Fernandes da Fonseca, José Luís 10 729
Fernandes d'Almada, Rodrigo 9 439
Fernandes da Silva, Manuel 28 911
Fernandes de Arruda, Miguel 2 500
Fernandes Novais, Manuel 31 813
Fernandes Pinto Alpoim, José *see* ALPOIM, JOSÉ FERNANDES PINTO
Fernández, Agustín 10 902*; 18 834
Fernández, Alejo 9 699; 10 902*; 29 277
Fernández, Antonio Arias *see* ARIAS FERNÁNDEZ, ANTONIO
Fernández, Antonio Susillo *see* SUSILLO (FERNÁNDEZ), ANTONIO
Fernandez, Armand *see* ARMAN
Fernández, Carmelo 7 609; 31 229
Fernández, Francisco 17 586; 32 557
Fernández, Gregorio 10 902–5*; 27 703
collaboration 25 419
patrons and collectors 14 6
pupils 10 905; 26 517
teachers 26 404
works 5 427, 883; 10 *903*; 25 23; 29 291; 31 823; 32 630
Fernandez, Honrado 24 620
Fernández, Jorge 10 902; 26 249
Fernández, José María 21 385
Fernández, Juan (*d* 1572) 10 904*; 28 519
Fernández, Juan (*fl* 1570-1603) 29 326; 30 883
works 30 *883*
Fernández, Juan (*fl* 1615) 2 285
Fernández, Juan (*d* 1657) *see* LABRADOR, EL
Fernández, Juan (*fl* mid 18th cent.) 31 195
Fernández, Juan Antonio Ribera y *see* RIBERA Y FERNÁNDEZ, JUAN ANTONIO
Fernandez, Louis 10 904–5*
Fernández, Lucas 30 664
Fernández, Luis (*fl* 1542-81) 23 704
Fernández, Luis (?1594-1654) 10 905*
Fernández, Pedro (*fl* 1519-21) 11 484
works 11 *484*
Fernández, Pedro (*fl* 1806) 8 232
Fernández, Rafael 8 18
works 8 *17*
Fernández Blandon, Antonio *see* BLANDON, ANTONIO FERNÁNDEZ
Fernández Cantero, Antonio 11 713; 29 336
Fernández Corredor, Juan 9 117, 119
Fernández de Araujo, Diego 32 178
Fernández de Cabrera y Bobadilla, Pedro, Conde de Chinchón *see* CHINCHÓN, PEDRO FERNÁNDEZ DE CABRERA Y BOBADILLA, Conde de
Fernández de Castro, José María 29 321
Fernández de Castro Andrade y Portugal, Pedro, Conde de Lemos *see* LEMOS, Conde de
Fernández de Córdoba, Alfonso 4 18
Fernández de Córdoba, Francisco 8 15; 23 80
Fernández de Laredo, Juan 26 438
Fernández de la Vega, Luis 10 905*; 29 292
Fernández del Campo, Pedro *see* MEJORADA, Marqués de
Fernández del Moral, Lesmes 2 391; 29 339
Fernández de Medrano, Sebastián 10 905*
Fernández de Navarrete, Juan *see* NAVARRETE, JUAN FERNÁNDEZ DE
Fernández de Valdez, Pedro 20 460
Fernández de Velasco, Juan 10 905–6*
Fernández Granell, Eugenio *see* GRANELL, EUGENIO FERNÁNDEZ
Fernandez Islands, Juan *see* JUAN FERNANDEZ ISLANDS
Fernández-Jardón, César Portela *see* PORTELA FERNÁNDEZ-JARDÓN, CÉSAR
Fernández Ledesma, Gabriel 10 906*; 21 388
Fernández Muro, José Antonio 2 401, 546; 10 906*; 13 655
Fernández Noseret, Luis 10 906*; 12 28
Fernández Trevejos, Antonio 8 231
Fernández Urbina, José María 20 500; 23 392
Fernández Varela, Manuel 29 21
Fernandi, Francesco *see* IMPERIALI
Fernandi, Joseph *see* FERNANDE, JOSEPH
Fernando, Prince 22 68
Fernando I, King of Naples *see* FERDINAND I, King of Naples
Fernando II, King of Aragon and Sicily *see* FERDINAND II, King of Aragon and Sicily
Fernando, Ranjit 29 468
Fernando de Sepúlveda 29 333
Fernando Spagnuolo 19 516
Fernan Nuñez, Conde de 15 889
Fernbach 2 13
Fernbach, Franz Xavier 10 199
Fernbach, Henry 10 104
Ferneley, Claude Lorraine 10 907
Ferneley, John (1782-1860) 2 106; 10 907*; 13 314; 20 477; 29 425
Ferneley, John, jr (1815-62) 10 907
Ferneley, Sarah 10 907
Fernelmont, H. de 28 41
Ferner, F. J. 14 235
Fernhout, Edgar (Richard Johannes) 8 506; 10 907*; 22 853
Fernhout-Pellecaan, Rachel 10 907
Ferniani (family) 16 736
Fernie, Eric 2 64
Fernkorn, Anton Dominik 2 802; 10 907–8*; 32 445
collaboration 19 113
pupils 16 811
works 8 178; 10 *908*
Fernow 26 128
ferns 3 331
Feroci, Corrado 30 608, 616, 617, 640
Feron, Marin 26 478
Feroni, Giuseppe 12 9
Ferrabosco, Giovanni Battista 29 830
Ferrabosco, Martino 10 908–9*
collaboration 5 767; 32 9
patrons and collectors 13 908
works 26 807
Ferrabosco, Pietro 28 852; 33 303
Ferrai, Kosmosoteira Theotokos monastery 9 579
Ferrajuoli, Nunzio 8 159; 22 27
Ferramola, Floriano 22 106, 107
Ferramolino, Antonio 12 761; 28 656
Ferramosca (family) 28 30
Ferrán, Guillén 5 362
Ferrand, Jacques-Philippe 10 909*
Ferrand de Monthelon, Antoine 11 665; 26 113
Ferrant, Alejandro 4 378; 25 419
Ferrant, Angel 3 843; 8 538; 10 909–10*; 29 296
works 10 *910*
Ferrant, Luis 1 464
Ferrante I, King of Naples *see* FERDINAND I, King of Naples
Ferrante, Callisto 22 5; 30 746
Ferrara 11 1–8*; 16 *618*
Addizione Erculea 27 189–90
art forms and materials
book jackets 24 50
engravings 10 383
furniture 31 682
gardens 12 115
Ferrara
art forms and materials—cont.
ketubbot 18 3
maiolica 16 732
manuscripts 4 *16*; 17 564
painting 16 661, 667; 18 707, 708
sculpture 16 688
stage design 30 656
tapestries 11 4–5*; 16 755, 756, 757; 30 314, 319
bastion 3 359
Castello Estense 11 *2*
Camerini d'Alabastro 3 306, 660; 10 443, 522; 14 870; 22 413; 31 34
paintings 5 843; 10 524
Salone dei Giochi 10 524
Castello Vecchio *see* Castello Estense
Cathedral of S Giorgio 11 5–6*; 16 625, *626*; 20 820
altarpiece 1 711
apse 27 190
organ shutters 31 *430*
Porta dei Mesi 26 621
relief sculpture 11 *6*
sculpture 7 642; 16 691; 23 101; 26 621
Certosa 12 722
monument to Niccolò III d'Este 1 555
Museo Boldini 11 4
Museo Nazionale Archeologico 11 3; 12 161; 27 191
Museo di Spina 16 775
palazzi 16 629
Palazzo Belfiore 10 519; 16 711; 29 859; 31 429
Palazzo Bentivoglio 3 744
Palazzo Bevilacqua 3 896
Palazzo Comunale 11 2–3, 843; 16 681
paintings 16 *681*
Palazzo del Corte *see* Palazzo Comunale
Palazzo Costabili 13 294
Palazzo dei Diamanti 27 *189*, 190; 28 38
paintings 5 850, 857; 10 525
see also Pinacoteca Nazionale
Palazzo Fabiani Freguglia 11 76
Palazzo di Ludovico il Moro *see* Museo Nazionale Archeologico
Palazzo Massari *see* Museo Boldini
Palazzo del Paradiso 1 553
Palazzo Roverella 27 190
Palazzo Schifanoia 10 520; 11 6–8*; 14 868; 32 549
alabaster-carvings 1 518
frescoes 16 659
interior decoration 9 97
Salone dei Mesi 1 655; 2 650; 7 925; 11 4, *7*, 7–8; 22 412; 26 456
Palazzo Scrofa-Calcagnini *see* Palazzo Costabili
patronage 16 763
Pinacoteca Nazionale 11 4
see also Palazzo dei Diamanti
S Benedetto 27 190
S Cristoforo 11 76; 27 190
S Domenico
paintings 12 *42*
S Francesco 27 *191*
Teatro di S Lorenzo 30 666, 667
urban planning 27 189–90; 31 714
Ferrara, Antonio (di Guido) Alberti da *see* ALBERTI (DA FERRARA), ANTONIO (DI GUIDO)
Ferrara, Carel de 18 3
Ferrara, Costanzo da *see* COSTANZO DA FERRARA
Ferrara, Girolamo da *see* CARPI, GIROLAMO DA
Ferrara, Jakie 11 8*
Ferrara, Luigi 13 795
Ferrara, Taddeo da *see* CRIVELLI, TADDEO
Ferrara, Vicino da *see* VICINO DA FERRARA
Ferrara T 585 group 10 616
Ferrarese 29 763
Ferrari, Bartolommeo 3 249
Ferrari, Defendente 11 11–12*
collaboration 29 366
patrons and collectors 23 873
works 11 *11*; 31 443
Ferrari, Ettore 11 12*, 15; 16 707; 29 566
Ferrari, Eusebio 11 12*
Ferrari, Filippo 11 12
Ferrari, Francesco (*fl* 18th cent.) 8 267
Ferrari, Francesco de' (*fl* 1476-93) 7 899
Ferrari, Francesco de' Bianchi *see* BIANCHI FERRARI, FRANCESCO DE'
Ferrari, Gaudenzio 11 13–14*; 21 525; 27 499
assistants 19 545
attributions 31 899
patrons and collectors 22 26
pupils 18 747
works 11 *13*; 15 137; 18 747; 27 497, *497*
Ferrari, Giacomo Bernardino 27 744
Ferrari, Giolito de' 9 74
Ferrari, Giovanni 5 625; 31 187
Ferrari, Giovanni Andrea de' 11 14*
pupils 5 724; 6 26, 32; 21 145; 25 62
teachers 29 784
Ferrari, Giovanni Battista 12 115; 18 735
Ferrari, Giuseppe (1755-1819) 24 865
Ferrari, Giuseppe (1811-70) 12 633
Ferrari, Giuseppe de' (*d* 1768) 11 8
Ferrari, Gregorio de' 11 8–10*; 16 675; 24 836
assistants 11 10
collaboration 12 283; 14 27; 24 835, 836
patrons and collectors 3 90; 4 811
restorations 2 127
teachers 11 53
works 11 *9*, *10*; 15 138; 20 371
Ferrari, Juan 11 14
Ferrari, Juan Manuel 11 14–15*; 31 754
Ferrari, L. 27 192
Ferrari, Lorenzo de' 11 8, 10–11*
collaboration 11 9
patrons and collectors 29 411
teachers 11 10
Ferrari, Luca 11 15–16*
works 11 *15*
Ferrari, Luigi 17 442
Ferrari, Marco *see* AGRATE, MARCO D'
Ferrari, Maria de, Duchessa di Galliera *see* GALLIERA, MARIA DE FERRARI, Duchessa di
Ferrari, Orazio de' 2 127, 619; 11 16*; 21 830
Ferrari, Pompeo 11 17*; 25 98
collaboration 32 895
restorations by others 11 739
works 12 824; 25 408
Ferrari, Tommaso Maria, Cardinal 7 682; 26 827
Ferrario, Carlo 20 275
Ferrario, Giulio 10 208
Ferraris, Federico 5 872
Ferraro, Nunzio 2 731
Ferrarons, Pedro 25 879
Ferrassie, La *see* LA FERRASSIE

Ferrata, Ercole 11 17–18*; 21 29; 26 771, 773
 assistants 20 909; 27 346
 collaboration 8 202; 13 814; 20 909; 26 810
 patrons and collectors 23 900; 32 8
 pupils 16 699
  Caffa, Melchiorre 1 631; 5 376
  Cateni, Giovanni Camillo 6 86
  Foggini, Giovanni Battista 11 234; 16 700
  Gabbiani, Anton Domenico 11 873
  Maglia, Michele 29 831
  Marcellini, Carlo Andrea 20 385
  Ottoni, Lorenzo 23 644
  Piamontini, Giuseppe 24 696
  Retti, Leonardo 29 831
  Rossi, Francesco de' 1 630
  Soldani (Benzi), Massimiliano 29 29
 restorations 32 236
 teachers 1 630, 631
 works 1 629; 5 376; 11 *18*; 16 699; 26 810; 28 681; 29 251
 workshop 5 376, 377
Ferrat brothers 22 242
Ferrato, Bartoli di Sasso *see* BARTOLI DI SASSO FERRATO
Ferraz de Almeida Júnior, José *see* ALMEIDA JÚNIOR, JOSÉ FERRAZ DE
Ferrazzi, Ferruccio 11 18*; 16 680
Ferrazzi, Stanislao 11 18
Ferré (family) 25 704
Ferré, Luis A. 25 703
Ferreira, Alexandre Rodrigues 4 706
Ferreira, Chucho Reyes *see* REYES FERREIRA, JESÚS
Ferreira, Custodio 32 535
Ferreira, Gaspar 11 18–19*; 17 595
Ferreira, Hestnes 25 294
Ferreira, Jesús Reyes *see* REYES FERREIRA, JESÚS
Ferreira, José Mamede Alves *see* ALVES FERREIRA, JOSÉ MAMEDE
Ferreira, Luís 30 881
Ferreira, Manuel 2 853
Ferreira, Simoão 11 19*; 25 313
Ferreira Amarante, Carlos Luis *see* AMARANTE, CARLOS LUIS FERREIRA
Ferreira Chaves, J. 27 615
Ferreira da Costa, J. C. 22 245
Ferreira das Tabuletas *see* FERREIRA, LUÍS
Ferreira de Castro Neto, Vicente 4 715
Ferreira Jácome, Manuel 4 710
Ferreira Pinto, Inácio 26 412
Ferreira Pinto Basto, Augusto 10 728
Ferreira Pinto Basto, João Teodoro 10 729
Ferreira Pinto Basto, José 10 728; 25 311
Ferreira Vilaça, José de Santo António 2 286
Ferreirim, Igreja Matriz 11 65
Ferreiroa 26 642
Ferrer, Jaume 20 515
Ferrer, Joan 29 350
Ferrer, Miguel 25 701
Ferrer, Mosén Pedro García *see* GARCÍA FERRER, MOSÉN PEDRO
Ferrer (Garcia), Rafael (Pablo Ramón) 11 19–20*; 18 833
Ferrera, Raúl 3 273
Ferreri, Andrea 20 903; 24 834
Ferrerio, Domenico *see* FERRIERO, DOMENICO
Ferrers, de (family) 10 302
Ferretti, Francesco 21 579
Ferretti, Giovanni Domenico 11 20–21*; 16 674
 patrons and collectors 12 355; 21 31
Ferretti, Giovanni Domenico—cont.
 pupils 3 308
 reproductive prints by others 3 308
 works 11 *21*
Ferretti, Prospero 17 203
Ferrey, Benjamin 11 21–2*; 23 211; 25 710; 33 64, 192
Ferrey, Edmund Benjamin 11 22
Ferreyra, Francisco 6 591
Ferreyra, Gonzalo 6 591
Ferrez, Gilberto 4 728
Ferrez, Marc 4 716; 10 580; 11 22*; 13 295
 works 24 664, *664*
Ferrez, Zéphrin 4 716; 13 295
Ferri 25 419
Ferri, Antonio Maria 7 897; 12 6; 21 30; 28 735
Ferri, Ciro 7 913; 11 22–4*; 20 214; 21 29; 26 771
 altars 7 912
 architecture 7 913; 10 769; 11 214; 20 385; 26 840
 assistants 7 910
 attributions 10 769
 ciborium 20 385
 collaboration 6 585; 16 673; 24 696; 26 810
 drawings 2 139; 30 42
 frescoes 3 773; 10 769; 11 *24*, 741; 21 28; 25 861
 interior decoration 7 910; 11 188
 mosaics 26 810
 patrons and collectors 10 768, 769; 21 26, 29; 24 225
 pupils 11 18; 16 699
  Cateni, Giovanni Camillo 6 86
  Foggini, Giovanni Battista 11 234; 16 700
  Gabbiani, Anton Domenico 11 873
  Marcellini, Carlo Andrea 20 385
  Odazzi, Giovanni 23 347
  Piamontini, Giuseppe 24 696
  Puglieschi, Antonio 25 718
  Redi, Tommaso 26 69
  Rivalz, Antoine 26 424
  Rocca, Michele 26 477
  Soldani (Benzi), Massimiliano 29 29
 reliefs 6 86
 reproductive prints by others 4 *272*; 6 502; 29 399
 teachers 7 913
Ferri, Giovanni Stefano 11 22
Ferri, Pompeo *see* FERRARI, POMPEO
ferric chloride 10 548; 24 655
ferric oxide 16 394
Ferrier, C. M. 23 447
Ferrier, Fernando Garreaud *see* GARREAUD FERRIER, FERNANDO
Ferrier, Gabriel 1 782; 4 98; 19 77; 24 560; 25 237, 752
Ferrier, Leonard Joseph 3 600
Ferrière 14 57
 works 14 *57*
Ferrières, Raoul de *see* RAOUL DE FERRIÈRES
Ferrières Château 7 841
Ferrières-en-Brie Church 13 39
Ferriero, Domenico 27 764
Ferrini, Benedetto 11 25*; 28 530
Ferris, George Washington 15 883
Ferriss, Hugh 7 838; 11 25–6*; 31 729
 works 2 *551*
Ferris Wheel 15 883
Ferro, Giacomo 31 899, 901
Ferro, Giovanni 16 747
Ferro, Giovanni Battista 32 874
Ferro, Gregorio 4 565; 11 26*, 218; 20 57
Ferro Caveiro, Miguel 29 272
ferro-concrete *see* CONCRETE → types → reinforced
Ferron, Marcel 2 840
Ferron, Monique Bourbonnais *see* BOURBONNAIS FERRON, MONIQUE
Ferrone, Francesco 7 542
Ferroni, Egisto 16 678
Ferroni, Giovanni Battista 4 565; 20 70; 29 304, 315, 337, 341, 342
ferronières 17 526, 527
ferrotypes *see under* PHOTOGRAPHIC PLATES → types
Ferroud 5 296
Ferrouillat & Cie 9 370
Ferrucci, Andrea di Michelangelo di 24 752
Ferrucci, Andrea di Piero (di Marco) 2 15, 17; 11 26, 27–9*
 collaboration 7 918
 pupils 7 918; 20 271; 22 32
 works 10 546; 11 *28*, 198
Ferrucci, Bernardo 11 26
Ferrucci, Domenico 11 697
Ferrucci, Francesco (di Giovanni) (i) 11 26, 27, 29*
Ferrucci, Francesco di Simone 4 276; 11 26–7*
 patrons and collectors 25 690
 teachers 32 366
 works 11 *27*; 18 673; 31 744, 745
Ferrucci, Giovanni 11 29
Ferrucci, Giovanni Domenico 8 497
Ferrucci, Pompeo 26 840
Ferrucci, Romolo 11 29; 21 755
Ferrucci, Simone di Nanni 11 26, 382
Ferrucci del Tadda, Francesco 6 147; 16 746
ferrules 5 *32*, 33
Ferry, Jules 21 371
Ferry, William 2 760
Ferry & Barber 1 798
Ferry de Clugny, Cardinal 20 638, 777; 29 398; 32 729
Fersfield, St Andrew 13 121
Ferstel, Heinrich von 2 808; 11 29–30*
 assistants 19 327; 20 386
 groups and movements 13 202
 patrons and collectors 3 746
 pupils 14 724; 20 894; 23 326; 25 648; 28 800; 29 777
 teachers 31 873
 works 2 786, 787, 802, 808, 830; 4 833; 11 *30*; 22 363; 32 437
Ferstel, Max von 23 372
Ferster, Hans 11 31*; 30 69, 70
Ferté, Denis-Pierre-Jean Papillon de La *see* PAPILLON DE LA FERTÉ, DENIS-PIERRE-JEAN
Fertőd 11 31*; 14 *881*
 Esterházy Castle 10 529; 11 31; 14 887, 900, 906, *906*
Fesch, Joseph, Cardinal 11 31–2*
 collections 4 298, 304; 8 549
 jewellery 22 103
 paintings 5 536; 13 308; 19 399; 24 396
 sponsorship 8 21
Fesch, Musée *see under* AJACCIO
Fesel, Christoph 18 498; 29 658
Feselen, Melchior 11 32–3*; 22 302, 918; 33 271
Feshin, Nikolay (Ivanovich) 11 33*; 27 434
Fesinger, Klemens Ksawery 19 836
Fesinger, Sebastian 19 836; 25 115
Fesira 1 269; 20 36, 37–8
 works 20 *38*
Fessard, Etienne 3 318; 4 514; 6 402; 14 85; 19 144; 22 682; 27 531
Festa, Tano 26 778; 28 657
Festbücher 10 175, 176
Festenburg 14 18
Fester, Henri 2 516
Fester, Théodore 17 527
Festetits, Samuel, Graf von 11 33*
festival barges *see under* BARGES
festival mosques *see* MOSQUES → types → *musalla*
Festival of Britain, 1951 *see under* LONDON → exhibitions
festivals 23 765–71*
 Bahamas, the 3 *60*
 China 7 143
 Egypt, ancient 9 807*; 23 766
 France 5 *814*; 23 766, *768*, *770*
 Indian subcontinent 15 730*
 Japan 18 *549*
 Spain 23 766
 Venezuela 32 167
 see also CARNIVALS
festoon curtains *see under* CURTAINS → types
festoons 11 33–4*
Festos *see* PHAISTOS
Festsaal 11 34*
Festschriften 4 25, 26*; 16 550
Fesulis, Andrea de *see* ANDREA (DI GUIDO) DA FIESOLE
Feszl, Frigyes 5 82; 11 34*; 14 889
fêtes champêtres see under PAINTING → types
fêtes galantes see under PAINTING → types
Fetherstonhaugh, Harry 26 239
Fetherstonhaugh, Matthew 3 382; 4 845; 11 39*
Fethiye *see* TELMESSOS
Feti, Domenico *see* FETTI, DOMENICO
Fétis, E. 3 619
fetishes 3 171; 14 378; 22 669
Fetish-Finish school 31 609
fetish-houses *see* CULT HOUSES; SHRINES (i) (CULT)
Fetter 18 618
Fetternear Banner 28 264–5, *265*
Fetti, Domenico 11 39–42*; 16 675; 32 194
 patrons and collectors 11 662; 12 912; 13 920; 19 731; 26 283; 29 800; 32 576
 teachers 7 313
 works 11 *40*, *41*
Fetti, Giovanni 13 94
Fetti, Giustina 11 40, 41
Fetti, Mariano 3 305
Fetti, Pietro 11 39, 41
Fetti, Vincenzo 11 40, 41
Fetting, Rainer 10 483; 12 397
fettling *see under* POTTERY → techniques
Feuchère, Jacques-François 11 42
Feuchère, Jean-Jacques 11 42*, 564, 622; 14 282; 20 119
Feuchère, Lucien-François 33 48
Feuchères, Léon 10 508
Feucht, Jacob *see* FACHT, JACOB
Feuchtmayer (family) 30 137
Feuchtmayer, Franz Joseph 11 42–3*; 12 404; 29 838
Feuchtmayer, Gervasius 11 42
Feuchtmayer, Johann Michael 11 42, 43*; 29 838
Feuchtmayer, Joseph Anton 3 823; 11 42, 43–5*
 assistants 9 6
 collaboration 3 57, 58
 groups and movements 26 498
 pupils 33 163
 works 10 117; 11 43, *44*, *45*; 12 404; 27 555; 29 838
 workshop 12 405
Feuchtwanger Altar, Master of the 33 300, 301
Feuerbach, Anselm 11 45–7*
 patrons and collectors 17 818; 19 151; 26 406; 28 40
 pupils 15 49
 teachers 8 76; 28 104; 29 16
 works 2 797; 11 *46*, 462, *463*; 12 394; 22 329
Feuerstein, Bedřich 8 380; 11 47*
Feuillade, François de la, Duc d'Aubusson *see* AUBUSSON, FRANÇOIS DE LA FEUILLADE, Duc de Roannez, Duc d'
Feuillâtre, Eugène 11 623, 631, 635
Feuille, La 20 602
Feuillet 29 833
Feuquières, Comtesse de 4 455; 19 141
Feure, Georges de 11 47*
 collaboration 11 904
 groups and movements 2 564
 works 2 *564*; 4 71; 11 582, 600; 19 398, 490
Feuter, Daniel Christian 31 649
Fevère, Andrea 11 47
Fevère, Filippo 11 47, 194; 32 205
Fevère, Francesco 11 47
Fevère, Giovanni 11 47, 48
Fevère, Jacopo 11 47
Fevère, Pietro 11 47–8*, 194; 16 758; 30 322
Feversham, Charles William Reginald Duncombe, 2nd Earl of *see* DUNCOMBE, CHARLES WILLIAM REGINALD, 2nd Earl of Feversham
Fewkes, Jesse Walter 22 594
Fewkes, V. 29 546
Fey, Hans 12 472
Feyen-Perrin, (François-Nicolas) Auguste 11 48*
Feyen-Perrin, Eugène 11 48
Feyerabend, Ägidius 11 48
Feyerabend, Charles-Sigismond 11 49
Feyerabend, Sigmund 1 788; 11 48–9*; 29 44
Feyo, Barata 25 302
Feyo, Salvador Barata *see* BARATA FEYO, SALVADOR
Fez 1 *376*; 11 49–51*; 15 103; 16 *103*
 art forms and materials
  architecture 1 315; 16 217; 22 128
  ceramics 22 129
  embroidery 1 378; 16 448; 22 129
  jewellery 16 532
  minbars 21 629
  paper 24 48
  pottery 16 427
  scripts 16 282
  silk 16 440
  stained glass 16 257
  textiles 16 447
  woodwork 16 492
 Bab Agdal 21 584
 Batha Palace 11 50
 baths 16 218
 Dar Batha Museum 22 129
 factories 16 436
 fortifications 21 583, 584, 585
 Funduq al-Tattawiniyyin 5 724
 houses 16 218, 263
 Ibn-Denan synagogue 17 551
 Islamic religious buildings
  Abdallah Mosque 16 240
  Abu'l-Hasan Mosque 16 217
  'Attarin Madrasa 16 *218*, 244, 250, 387, 495; 29 820
  brass 4 *687*
  Bu 'Inaniyya Madrasa 16 218, 250; 20 *56*, 57
  congregational mosque 16 217
  Hamra Mosque 16 217
  Karouine Mosque *see* Qarawiyyin Mosque
  Lala al-Zhar Madrasa 16 218
  madrasas 20 57
  minarets 21 626
  Mosque of the Andalusians 16 157, 188, 387, 493, 495
  Qarawiyyin Mosque 11 50, *50*; 15 103; 16 90, 157, 188, 190, 218, 495; 22 324; 27 506
  chandelier 16 387

Fez
Islamic religious buildings
Qarawiyyin Mosque—cont.
minbar 11 50; 16 494
pavilions (buildings) 16 240
woodwork 16 493
Sba'iyyin Madrasa 16 218
Sharratin Madrasa 16 240
Shrabliyin Madrasa 16 218
market 16 260
storehouses 16 218
urban planning 16 262
FFKR, Inc. 27 642
ffoulkes, Charles 2 450
Ffoulkes, Jocelyn 22 102
Ffynone Villa 32 783
Fialetti, Odoardo 11 51*
collaboration 23 879
patrons and collectors 33 387
pupils 4 455
works 1 842; 21 759
Fialka, Olga von 10 892
Fialko, I. I. 28 747
Fialova, Eva 8 421
Fiamberti, Tommaso 11 51*; 20 721
Fiaminghi, Hermelindo 4 719
Fiamma, Galvanno 12 684
Fiammenghini, I see Rovere (ii), della
Fiammingho, Egidio see Vliete, Gillis van den
Fiammingo, Adriano 7 311; 11 51*
Fiammingo, Arrigo see Broeck, Hendrik van den
Fiammingo, Carlo 21 53
Fiammingo, Giovanni see Vasanzio, Giovanni
Fiammingo, Paolo 11 52*
works 11 52, 819
Fiandra, Jacomo d'Angelo di see Jacomo d'Angelo di Fiandra
Fiandra, Pietro di Andrea di see Pietro di Andrea di Fiandra
Fiasella, Domenico 11 52–3*; 16 675
assistants 11 8
collaboration 11 14; 23 265
patrons and collectors 3 90; 15 148
pupils 6 26; 11 8; 25 62
teachers 23 772
works 5 769; 11 53
Fiasella, Giovanni 11 52
Fiat (Fabbrica Italiana Automobili Torino) 2 727; 15 826; 16 765; 31 443
Fiatalok see Young, the (Fiatalok)
Fiat Ritmo see under Cars → models
Fibich, Johann Caspar 2 795
Fibichová, Zdena 8 388
Fibonacci, Leonardo 21 172
fibre art 1 15; 11 54–5*, 54; 25 134; 30 329
fibreboard 31 283; 33 328
fibreglass 11 55–6*; 25 23, 27
historical and regional traditions
Chicano 18 831
Mexico 18 831
Scotland 11 55
United States of America 15 825; 18 831
uses
architecture 25 24
casts 6 7
chairs 6 392; 15 825
conservation 24 7
moulds 11 55
panel paintings 24 7
relining 26 142
sculpture 11 55, 55; 18 831; 25 26
tables 30 218
fibres 9 490
historical and regional traditions
Africa 1 293*, 295–6*, 355, 405
fibres
historical and regional traditions—cont.
Angola 7 198
Brazil 4 724
Byzantine 9 664*
China 7 43
Early Christian (c. AD 250–843) 9 664*
Japan 17 306
Luba 1 355
Lwena 7 198
Senufo 28 422
Zaïre 1 405
types
acrylic 30 543*
animal 30 538–9*
banana 7 43; 17 355; 21 477
bast 7 43; 17 305, 306, 312, 313, 353; 30 537*
bromelia 24 92
cellulose 9 490, 491; 30 542
elastomerics 30 543*
elm 17 312
elm-bark 30 VII2
kudzu 17 312
lime-wood 17 312
man-made 30 542–3*, 543
orchid 7 43
palm 17 209
paper mulberry 17 312
polyalkenes 30 543*
polyamides 30 542–3*
polyester 1 156; 5 33, 34; 26 244; 30 543*
protein 9 490, 491
reeds 5 32
seed hairs 30 538*
synthetic 5 33, 655, 832; 9 493; 30 542–3*
vegetable 10 872; 20 329; 25 477
wisteria 17 312
uses
brushes 5 32, 33; 17 209
canvas 5 655
carpets 5 832
felt 10 872
fibre art 11 54–5
masks 1 405; 7 198; 28 422
paper 20 329; 24 40
papier mâché 24 61
robes 30 VII2
sashes 21 477
staffs 1 355
see also Hemp; Jute; Paper; Rami; Silk
fibrous concrete see under Concrete → types
Fibrous Plaster see under Stucco → types
fibrous slab 24 62
fibulae
historical and regional traditions
Berber 16 532
Buddhism 30 841, 841
Byzantine 9 653
Crete 8 154; 13 601
Cyprus, ancient 8 352
Dacian 30 773
Early Christian (c. AD 250–843) 9 653
Etruscan 10 630; 12 868
Germany 21 162, 502
Greece, ancient 13 600, 600–601, 601
Islamic 16 532
Italy 10 630; 12 868
Merovingian 21 162
Migration period 21 502
Morocco 16 532
Rhodes (island) 13 601
Tibet 30 841, 841
Visigothic 32 618
materials
bronze 8 154; 13 600, 600–601, 601; 30 841
garnets 21 162
gold 10 630; 12 868; 21 162
fibulae
materials—cont.
iron 8 154
silver 30 773
see also Brooches
Ficherelli, Felice 11 56*, 697; 20 385
fiches see Microfiches
Fichet, Alexandre 31 425
Fichev, Nikola 5 148, 156; 32 149
works 5 148
Fichi, Ercole 29 251
Fichte, Johann Gottfried 22 540
Ficino, Marsilio 1 656; 11 56*; 14 868, 869; 16 658; 21 10; 22 749
groups and movements 22 412
works 15 85
Fick, Angelika see Hoerle, Angelika
Fick, Wilhelm 25 837; 29 869
Ficke, Nicolaes 33 391
Fico group 2 450
Ficoroni, Francesco de 11 57*; 13 605; 26 849
Ficoroni Cist 10 629, 629; 11 57; 13 605; 25 420; 26 860; 27 85
Ficquet, Etienne 11 57*
Fidanovski, Nicola 19 885
Fidasi Khan Koka 15 367
fiddles 5 508; 15 816, 816; 21 880
Fidelle, Isidor Coridon see Folkema, Jacob
FIDEM see Fédération Internationale de la Médaille
Fidenza, Cathedral of S Donnino 26 690
Fidler, A. G. Sheppard 4 86
Fidler, Hans Christoph 12 440
Fidler, Peter 22 584
Fiechter, Ernst Robert
works 13 385
Fiedler, Johann Christophe 8 408
Fiedler, Konrad 11 57–8*, 315; 20 405; 22 329
Fieffé, Charles-Jean 4 391
Field, Erastus Salisbury 7 787; 11 58*; 12 54
Field, George 11 58–9*
Field, Hamilton Easter 18 868
Field, Henry 19 756
Field, John 15 116
Field, Marshall, III 6 575; 25 235
Field, R(obert) N(ettleton) 11 59*; 23 60, 62, 68, 69
Field, Robert 11 59*
Field and Tuer 4 364
Fielding (family) 4 66
Fielding, Amelia 11 59
Fielding, Anna Maria see Hall, Anna Maria
Fielding, (Anthony Van Dyck) Copley 11 60*
patrons and collectors 25 41
pupils 11 60; 20 483; 27 350
reproductive prints by others 11 60
teachers 31 909
Fielding, Frederick Felix Ferdinand Raffael 11 60*
Fielding, Henry 8 218; 27 868
Fielding, Nathan Theodore 11 59–60*
Fielding, Newton (Limbird Smith) 11 60*
Fielding, Temple 13 807
Fielding, Thales 11 60*
Fielding, Theodore Henry Adolphus 3 373; 11 59–60*
pupils 3 745; 5 439
writings 10 559; 25 627
Fieldler 8 83
Field Museum of Natural History see under Chicago (il) → museums
Field of the Cloth of Gold see under Balinghem
Fiennes, Celia 11 61*
Fiennes, Gaspard-Moyse-Augustin de Fontanieu, Marquis de 20 138
Fiennes, Mary, Lady Dacre 10 666
Fiennes de Clinton, Edward see Clinton, Edward Fiennes de
Fieravante, Aristotele di see Fioravanti, Aristotele
Fieravante di Ridolfo 11 115
Fieravino, Francesco see Maltese, Francesco
Fierens, Paul 3 619; 4 618
Fierens-Gevaert, H. 3 619
Fierlants, Nicolaas Maerten 12 285
Fierro, Francisco see Fierro, Pancho
Fierro, Pancho 11 61*; 24 508
Fieschi (family) 12 280
Fieschi, Lorenzo 3 742
Fieschi-Morgan Reliquary 9 659, 660
Fiesole 10 583
Badia Fiesolana see under San Domenico di Fiesole
Centro Documentario Avanguardie Storiche Fondazione Primo Conti 7 779
Museo Dupré 9 405
sandstone 10 602
sculpture 10 608, 609
S Domenico 2 31
vases 10 613
Villa Medici 12 110, 111; 28 283; 32 545
Fiesole, Andrea (di Guido) da see Andrea (di Guido) da Fiesole
Fiesole, Domenico di Antonio da see Domenico di Antonio da Fiesole
Fiesole, Filippo da 33 615
Fiesole, Giovanni da (c. 1395/1400–1455) see Angelico, Fra
Fiesole, Giovanni da (1507–47) see Giovanni da Fiesole
Fiesole, Giovanni di Martino da (fl 1423) see Giovanni di Martino da Fiesole
Fiesole, Jérôme de see Jérôme de Fiesole
Fiesole, Michele di Giovanni da see Michele di Giovanni da Fiesole
Fiesole, Mino da see Mino da Fiesole
Fiesole, Silvio da see Cosini, Silvio
Fiesole Bible see under Bibles → individual manuscripts
Fiette 2 152
Fietz, Gerhard 33 635
Fieubet, Gaspard de 11 61*; 18 626; 19 248
Fieuzal, Léonce de 2 843
Fieve, Carlos Luis Ribera y see Ribera y Fieve, Carlos Luis
Fife, Phyllis 22 599
Fife, William Duff, 1st Earl of see Duff, William, 1st Earl of Fife
Fife Pottery 28 258
Fifteen 2 575; 8 583
Fifth Moon Group see Wuyue Huahui
Fifty New Churches Commission 12 593; 14 255–6; 16 893
Figari, Filippo 27 836
Figari, Pedro 11 62*; 22 24; 31 758
patrons and collectors 31 757, 758
works 31 755, 755
Figdor, Albert 2 829; 11 62*; 20 666; 32 447
Figdor Deposition, Master of the 20 666*; 22 835
Figeac 13 211
Figeac Sacramentary see under Sacramentaries → individual manuscripts
Figge, Eddie 30 81
Figgis, T. Phillips 21 349
Figini, Luigi 1 578; 10 822; 11 62–4*; 13 728; 15 885; 21 422; 26 15
Figini and Pollini 3 93, 94; 11 62–4*
collaboration 3 438; 16 649
groups and movements 13 728; 26 15
works 10 749; 11 63; 31 731
Figino, (Giovan) Ambrogio 7 646; 11 64–5*; 26 770
collaboration 21 525
patrons and collectors 4 425, 471; 26 245
teachers 19 546
works 11 64
fig-juice 8 127
Figline, Master of see Fogg Pietà, Master of the
Figline, Ospedale Serrostori 32 16
Figueira, Baltazar Gomes see Gomes Figueira, Baltazar
Figueira, Basilia Gomes see Gomes Figueira, Basilia
Figueiredo, Cristóvão de 11 65*
attributions 2 871
collaboration 1 213; 10 899; 14 395; 19 655
patrons and collectors 2 874
works 25 295
Figueiredo, João de 25 310
Figueiredo, Manuel Marques de see Marques de Figueiredo, Manuel
Figueiredo, N. 20 371
Figueiredo Seixas, José de 22 534
Figuera, Juan 11 482; 27 836
Figueres
Fundació Gala-Salvador Dalí 29 357
Teatre-Museu Dalí 8 468
Figueroa (family) 7 607
Figueroa, Ambrosio de 7 289
Figueroa, Antonio Matías de 9 699
Figueroa, Baltasar de 7 607
Figueroa, Carlos Zúñiga see Zúñiga Figueroa, Carlos
Figueroa, Celestino 11 66
Figueroa, Garcia Silva see Silva Figueroa, Garcia
Figueroa, Gaspar de 4 233; 7 607, 612
Figueroa, José Santos 11 66
Figueroa, Juan de 27 606; 29 336, 337
Figueroa, Leonardo de 11 65–6*
groups and movements 7 289
works 7 289; 28 513, 520; 29 270, 271, 841
Figueroa, Lorenzo Suárez de see Suárez de Figueroa, Lorenzo
Figueroa, Miguel 11 66
Figueroa, Pedro de 6 596
Figueroa, Pedro José 7 608; 11 66*
Figueroa Aznar, Juan Manuel 24 518
Figuration Narrative 11 552; 24 145
figureheads 15 810; 16 45; 28 611, 612–14, 612, 613, 614; 29 49, 49
figure sculptures see under Sculpture → types
figurines 9 29; 11 66*
historical and regional traditions
Africa 1 269, 270, 271–3*, 272, 275, 277, 281, 330
Anatolia, ancient 1 823, 825, 825, 832, 834
Ancient Near East 10 461; 31 530
Angola 2 86
Antilles, Greater 2 145

figurines
historical and regional traditions—cont.
Antilles, Lesser **2** 144
Asante **1** 273
Austria **25** 489, *541*; **33** 197, *198*
Aztec **21** 243
Bamileke **1** *277*
Bangladesh **15** *726*
Beguines **3** 503
Benin Republic **1** 271–2, *272*
Buddhism **7** 104–5, *105*
Burkina Faso **1** 273
Cameroon **1** 273, *277*
Central Asia, Eastern **6** 298, 315–16
Central Asia, Western **6** 276
Chad Republic **1** *330*
China **6** *856*, *860*, *861*, 862, 883, *887*, 887–8, 889, *889*, *901*, 907, 910; **7** *55*, 104–6, *105*, *106*, 125, *126*, 140, 141, 143, 247; **28** *618*
Chorrera culture **30** *512*
Colombia **22** 266
Congo, Republic of **1** *275*; **3** *694*
Costa Rica **9** 677; **29** *143*
Côte d'Ivoire **1** 273, *281*
Crete **8** 154; **13** 578; **21** 656, 657–8, 678–80, *679*, *680*, 681*, 683*, *683*
Cucuteni culture **25** 512
Cycladic **1** 795; **8** 308, 314–15*, *315*, *316*, 316*
Cyprus, ancient **8** 337–8*, 339–40; **19** 131
Hellenistic **8** 342
Prehistoric **8** *329*, 337*, 338–9
Czech Republic **9** 80; **25** 488
Daoism **7** 105–6, *106*
Dogon **1** 273
Ecuador **29** 133
Egypt, ancient **9** 865; **10** 47–8, 49, 60, 66
Early Dynastic (*c.* 2925–*c.* 2575 BC) **10** *59*
Faiyum style **27** 111
Late Period (664–332 BC) **10** *49*
Predynastic (*c.* 6000–*c.* 2925 BC) **9** *865*; **18** *238*
England **10** 306, 308, *308*
Etruscan **10** 602, 604, 625
Fon **1** 271–2, *272*
France
Prehistoric **18** 875–6; **19** 243, *243*; **25** 489
Roman **27** 110–11
18th cent. **28** *521*
Funnel Beaker culture **25** 512
Germany **1** *762*; **12** *433*, 450
Palaeolithic **25** 489, *489*, *490*
Prehistoric **32** 679
Rococo **6** I2
20th cent. **12** *437*
Ghana **1** 272, *272*
Greece, ancient **1** *761*; **12** 286; **13** 433, 571–4*, *572*, *574*, 578–82*; **23** 427; **27** 111
Archaic **13** 578–9*, *579*
Attica **13** *580*
Boeotia **13** *579*, *580*
Classical **13** 579–81*, *580*
Hellenistic **13** *581*, 581–2*
Gulf Coast, Mesoamerica **21** *218*
Gumelniţa culture **25** 512
Helladic **14** 352, *352*
Hemba **14** 378
Hinduism **15** *783*
Huastec **14** 830–31
Inca **29** 218
Indian subcontinent **15** 414, *421*, 450, 695, 718, 719, 728, 730; **30** *510*
Baluchistan **15** 213

figurines
historical and regional traditions
Indian subcontinent—cont.
Indus civilization **15** 213, *412*, 415, 417–20*, *418*, *419*, 421–2*, 718
Rajasthan **15** 724
Tamil Nadu **15** *729*
Indonesia **15** *783*
Indus civilization **15** 213, *412*, 415, 417–20*, *418*, *419*, 421–2*, 717–18
Iran, ancient **15** *903*, 903
Italy **16** *737*
Etruscan **10** 625
Palaeolithic **25** 489
Renaissance **8** *101*
Roman **27** 109–10*
18th cent. **22** *681*
Japan **17** *97*, *102*, 102–4, 262, *263*, *264*, *265*, 348–9*
Jōmon period (*c.* 10,000–*c.* 300 BC) **17** 30, *97*, *104*, 371, 629
Java **15** *783*
Jōmon culture **17** *97*
Kongo **1** *275*
Kuba (iii) (Zaïre) **1** *269*
Lega **1** 273; **19** *72*, 73–4
Lobi **1** 272, *272*
Mali **1** 273, *281*
Maya **21** *239*, 247, 251, 256
Mende (Sierra Leone) **21** 117
Mesoamerica, Pre-Columbian **18** *881*; **21** 195, 235*, 236–40, 242, 250, 256; **30** 511–12
Aztec **21** 243
Huastec **14** 830–31
Maya **21** *239*, 247, 251
Mexico **8** 255; **18** *881*; **21** *218*, *238*, *239*; **33** *619*
Olmec **21** 241; **23** 418
Palaeolithic **21** *193*
Pre-Classic (*c.* 2000 BC–*c.* AD 250) **21** *218*
Remojadas **26** 181
West Mexico **21** 196, *236*; **33** *102*
Zapotec **33** *619*
Mesopotamia **7** *186*; **9** *45*; **21** 276, 277, 293*, 295; **28** *22*
Mexico **8** 255; **18** *881*; **21** *194*, *218*, *238*, *239*; **33** *619*
Minoan **21** 678–80, 681*, 683*
Early Minoan (*c.* 3500/3000–*c.* 2050 BC) **21** 656
Late Minoan (*c.* 1600–*c.* 1050 BC) **21** *679*, *680*
Middle Minoan (*c.* 2050–*c.* 1600 BC) **21** 657–8, 679, *683*
Moche (culture) **29** 134
Moldova **25** 489
Mossi **1** 273
Muisca **22** 266
Mycenaean **14** 352, *352*
Nabataea **22** 420
Native North Americans **22** 573, 582, *669*
Nepal **22** 790
Nigeria **1** *270*, 273
Olmec **18** *881*; **21** *218*; **23** 417, 418
Parthian **24** 218
Pende **1** 273
Philistine **24** 635
Phoenician **24** 642–3*
Prehistoric art **8** *329*, 338–9; **25** 472, 473, 488–91*, 494
Anatolia, ancient **1** *823*, 825, *825*
Austria **33** 197–8, *198*
Bronze Age **25** 527, 528
Cucuteni culture **25** 512
Cyprus, ancient **8** 337–8*, *338*
France **16** 615; **18** 875–6; **19** 243, *243*
Funnel Beaker culture **25** 512
Germany **25** *489*, *490*; **32** 679

figurines
historical and regional traditions
Prehistoric art—cont.
Gumelniţa culture **25** 512
Iron Age **25** *541*, 542
Japan **17** 30, *102*, 102, *104*, 629
Neolithic **25** 512
Palaeolithic **9** 80; **16** 797
Sardinia **25** 512; **27** 834, 835, *835*
Serbia **25** *528*; **32** *581*
South-east Asia **29** 228
Thailand **29** 228
Tisza culture **25** 512
Tripol'ye culture **25** 512
Vinča culture **25** 512; **32** *581*
Punic **25** 733–4
Remojadas **26** 181
Rhodes (island) **13** 578
Rome, ancient **27** 109–12*
Russia **25** 489
Samarran culture **21** 269
Sardinia **25** 512; **27** 834, 835, *835*
Senufo **1** 273, *281*
Serbia **25** *528*; **32** *581*
Siberia **25** 489
Sicily **13** 580, 581
South Africa **1** 273
South America, Pre-Columbian **9** 677; **18** 835; **22** 266; **29** 134, *185*, 218; **30** 511
Chorrera culture **30** *512*
Costa Rica **29** *143*
Inca **29** 218
South-east Asia **29** 228
Spain **27** 111
Sri Lanka **29** 471, 475, *476*
Sumerian **9** *45*
Switzerland **30** *147*
Syria-Palestine **5** *186*; **21** *331*; **30** 182, 185, 195, *195*
Tanagra **15** 895
Tanzania **1** 273
Teke **1** 273
Thailand **29** 228; **30** *511*
Tisza culture **25** 512
Toltec **31** 100
Tripol'ye culture **25** 512
Turkey **1** *729*; **31** *700*
United States of America **22** *669*
Urartian **1** *729*; **31** *700*
Valdivia culture **31** 811–12
Vietnam **32** 480
Vinča culture **25** 512; **32** 581*, *581*
West Mexico **21** 196, *236*; **33** 102, *102*
Yoruba **1** *270*
Zaïre **1** *269*, 273, *275*; **19** *72*
Zapotec **33** *619*
Zulu **1** 273
materials
alabaster (gypsum) **5** *186*; **9** *45*; **28** *22*
amber **1** 761, *761*, *762*
antlers **25** 488
basalt **21** *218*
bone **21** 247; **24** 218; **25** 488, *490*
bronze **21** *331*; **25** *541*
Anatolia, ancient **1** *825*
Ancient Near East **31** 530
China **6** *856*, *860*, *861*, 862; **17** *587*
Crete **8** 154
Etruscan **10** 604
Greece, ancient **13** 571–2*, 573*
Indian subcontinent **15** *412*, 417–20*
Sardinia **27** 835, *835*
Urartian **31** *700*
ceramics **1** *330*

figurines
materials—cont.
clay
China **7** 141
Cyprus **8** 338
Mexico **21** *193*
Prehistoric art **25** 488, 512
United States of America **22** *669*
Vinča culture **32** *581*
West Mexico **33** *102*
Zapotec **33** *619*
earthenwares **6** *887*, 889, *889*; **17** *104*, 262; **18** 298
faience (i) (glass) **10** 47, 48, *49*, 49; **21** *683*
gold **15** *783*
gypsum **9** *45*
horn **7** 125, *126*
ivory **16** 797
China **7** 104–6, *105*, *106*
Czech Republic **9** 81
Egypt, ancient **10** *59*, 60
Indian subcontinent **15** 450, 695, 724
Japan **17** *102*
Lega **19** *72*
Prehistoric art **19** *243*; **25** 488, *489*, 490; **32** 679
Urartian **1** *729*
jasper **15** *418*
lead **21** *331*
lignite **25** 488
limestone **8** 338; **9** *45*; **18** *238*; **33** *198*
marble **8** *315*, *316*
marls **25** 488
picrolite **8** 337, *338*; **19** 131
porcelain
China **6** *898*, 907, 910
England **10** *308*
France **28** *521*
Germany **6** I2; **12** *433*, *437*
Italy **16** *737*
Japan **17** *263*, *264*, *265*
pottery
China **6** 883, 887–8; **7** *55*
Costa Rica **9** 677
Cyprus, ancient **8** *329*, 338, *339*
Mesoamerica, Pre-Columbian **21** *236*, *238*, *239*
Prehistoric art **25** *528*
sandstone **25** 488
shells **29** 218
silk **7** 140
siltstone **25** 488
silver-gilt **30** *147*
silver leaf **21** *331*
soapstone **15** *419*, *903*
stone **2** *145*; **9** 677, 865; **15** 417–20*; **25** 488; **29** *143*, *185*
stonewares **28** *618*
terracotta **15** *421*
Central Asia, Eastern **6** 315–16
Central Asia, Western **6** 276
Crete **8** 154
Cyprus, ancient **8** 339
Egypt, ancient **9** 865, *865*
Greece, ancient **13** 578–82*, *579*, *580*, *581*; **23** 427
Huastec **14** 830–31
Indian subcontinent **15** 213, 414, 421–2*, 718, 719, 728, *729*; **30** *510*
Italy **8** *101*; **22** *681*
Mesopotamia **7** *186*; **21** 295
Minoan **21** *680*
Mycenaean **14** *352*
Nepal **22** 790
Phoenician **24** 642–3*
Rome, ancient **27** 109–12
South America, Pre-Columbian **30** 511–12, *512*
South-east Asia **29** 228
Thailand **30** *511*

figurines
materials—cont.
wood **1** *269*, *270*, *272*, *275*, *277*, *281*; **2** *86*; **3** *694*; **7** 140, 141; **15** *783*; **22** 582
techniques
moulding **6** 887; **13** 578
types
Akua'ba **1** 503; **2** 588*, *588*
cuchimilcos **6** 440
eye idols **4** 641, *641*; **21** 272
pendants (jewellery) **25** 489
plank figurines **8** 338, *339*
see also STATUETTES
Fiigenschoug, Elias **14** 244, 245; **23** 224
Fijałkowski, Stanisław **11** 66–7*
Fiji **11** 67–70*; **23** *711*
barkcloth **11** 69; **23** 713, 735
baskets **3** *330*
body ornaments **11** 69
bone **4** 314
bowls **11** 68, *68*
breastplates **11** *69*
canoes **11** 68; **23** 725; **27** 234
carpenters **11** 67
clubs (weapons) **11** 69; **27** 234
coral **7** 834
drums (musical instruments) **11** 68
fans **10** 779
forgeries **23** 737
headrests **11** 69
houses **11** 69
ivory **11** *69*
mats **11** 69; **23** 713; **27** 235
pandanus **3** *330*
pottery **11** 70; **23** 727, 728
rock art **23** 728
scrapers **27** 234
sculpture **11** 68
shells **11** *69*
stencilling **11** 69; **29** 627
tattoos **11** 70; **27** 234
textiles **11** 69
weapons **23** 734
wood **11** 68, *68*
Fijt, Jan *see* FYT, JAN
Fikellura style pottery *see under* POTTERY → wares
Fila **25** 181
Fila, Rudolf **28** 853
Filacciano, Elena Orsini, Baroness of **23** 575
Filadelfia **31** 717
Filago, Agostino **5** 414
Filālī *see* 'ALAWI
Filandia **29** 212
metalwork **29** *212*
Filangieri, Gaetano **11** 70*
Filaret, Patriarch **7** 172
Filarete **9** 157; **11** 71–3*; **12** 110; **16** 67; **18** 898; **22** 44; **26** 766
architecture **14** 781; **29** 22, 23; **31** 712
attributions **8** 135
collaboration **24** 232
doors **11** *71*; **16** 691; **26** *766*, 808
drawings **16** 630
patrons and collectors **16** 630; **26** 766; **28** 530
sculpture **11** *72*; **16** 691; **25** 19; **29** 568; **30** 501
writings **2** 356, 518
Trattato di architettura **7** 257; **13** 708; **16** 630; **21** 537; **23** 486, 487; **25** 635; **31** 295, *295*, 302; **32** 639
Filareto, Apollonio **4** 352
Filatov, Vladimir **27** 417
Filat'yev, Ivan **27** 387
Filat'yev, Tikhon **22** 177, 184
filbert brushes *see under* BRUSHES → types
Fildes, Alan **28** 326
Fildes, (Samuel) Luke **11** 74–5*
collaboration **8** 863
competitions **10** 373
groups and movements **14** 680

Fildes, (Samuel) Luke—cont.
  patrons and collectors 14 688; 19 270
  reproductive prints by others 1 454; 2 234; 4 807; 21 606
  works 10 254; 11 *74*; 12 296; 18 100; 26 *78*; 28 919
File 12 275; 24 430
filé *see* THREADS → materials → gold
Filefjell 26 691
Filevich 31 561
Filfila 27 13; 29 702
Filgueiras Lima, João 4 714; 11 75*
  works 4 *714*; 27 644
Filho, João Camara *see* CAMARA FILHO, JOÃO
Filho, José Mariano *see* MARIANO FILHO, JOSÉ
Filho, Rodolpho Ortenblad *see* ORTENBLAD FILHO, RODOLPHO
Filhol, Antoine-Michel 6 77
Filhol, François 33 470
Fili, Church of the Protective Veil of the Virgin 27 372
Filiberti, Giuseppe 9 158
fili di sinopia 28 778
Filiger, Charles 11 75*; 13 232; 25 215; 27 639
filigrana *see under* GLASS → techniques
filigree 11 76*; 21 328
  historical and regional traditions
    Anglo-Saxon 2 79; 10 322
    Cambodia 5 500
    Central Asia, Western 6 274, *274*
    China 7 68, 108, 109, *109*, 110, 111, 112, *112*
    Crete 21 687
    England 10 322
    Etruscan 10 631
    France 21 *163*
    Germany 21 *162*
    Gothic 13 *162*, 163
    Hungary 13 *162*
    Ireland 32 *530*
    Islamic 12 868; 16 531
    Italy 10 631; 13 163
    Kurdistan 16 531
    Malta (Republic of) 20 216*
    Merovingian 21 *162*, *163*
    Mexico 21 254
    Migration period 21 503
    Minoan 21 687
    Portugal 25 314
    Russia 27 418, *423*, *425*, 426
    Scandinavia 32 524, 531
    Viking 32 524, *530*, 531
  materials
    gold 7 108, *109*, 111, 112, *112*; 12 867–8; 13 *162*; 20 216; 21 687; 27 101, *102*; 32 *530*
    lacquer 5 500
    silver 7 111, 112; 12 868; 20 216; 32 531
  types
    opus interrasile 9 652, 653; 21 327; 27 101, 102, *102*
    opus veneticum 13 163
  uses
    chalices 13 *162*
    crowns 7 110, 111–12
    fibulae 21 *162*
    hair ornaments 7 108
    jewellery 6 274, *274*; 7 111, 112; 16 531
    patens 21 *163*
    pendants (jewellery) 27 *423*
    shrines (i) (cult) 32 *530*
filigree enamel *see under* ENAMEL → techniques
Filipelli, Cafiero 28 319
Filipepi, Alessandro (di Mariano di Vanni) *see* BOTTICELLI, SANDRO
Filipeştii de Pădure 26 708
Filipini, Francesco 29 341
Filipović, Franjo 14 596
Filipovič, M. 3 529
Filippi, Camillo 11 4, 76*; 25 736
  collaboration 12 162
  patrons and collectors 10 523
  pupils 11 76
  teachers 9 187
  works 11 5
Filippi, Cesare 11 76
Filippi, Giovanni Maria 11 77*
  attributions 25 426, 438
  collaboration 14 320; 29 372
  patrons and collectors 13 915
  works 8 378; 25 54, 426, 438; 33 637
Filippi, Minuccio 28 684
Filippi, Sebastiano, I (*d* 1523) 11 76
Filippi, Sebastiano, II (*c.* 1532–1602) 11 4, 76–7*
  assistants 10 524
  works 11 5; 16 757; 19 373
Filippi, Tommaso 22 702
Filippini *see* ORATORIANS
Filippini, Francesco 29 341
Filippini, Giovanni Antonio 9 376; 30 527
Filippis, Giuseppe de 22 481
Filippo, Master 2 1
Filippo Benizi, Saint 28 489
Filippo da Fiesole 19 496
Filippo Maria, 3rd Duke of Milan (*reg* 1412–47) 32 609, 611–12*
  frescoes 24 861; 33 624
  manuscripts 3 531; 20 783
  paintings 21 463; 24 782
  tarot cards 3 695
Filippo Neri, Saint 7 276; 11 78*; 23 472
Filippo Rapicano *see* RAPICANO, FILIPPO
Filippo Veris da Milano 32 256*
Filippuccio (*fl* 1273–93) 21 107
Filippuccio, Memmo di (1288–1324) *see* MEMMO DI FILIPPUCCIO
Filitosa 11 78*, *505*; 25 *470*, 523, 529
Filla, Emil 11 79–80*
  groups and movements
    Cubo-Expressionism 8 249
    Czech Cubism 8 373; 16 902
    Eight, the (i) (Czech) 8 393; 10 107, 108; 18 492; 25 433
    Group of Plastic Artists 10 108; 13 711
    Mánes Union of Artists 20 254
    Sphinx, De 29 397
  works 8 393; 11 *79*
Fillans, James 28 243
Fillastre, Guillaume, Bishop of Tournai 7 243; 20 451; 31 147
filled-in *urushi* *see under* LACQUER → types
filleted roll mouldings *see under* MOULDINGS → types
Fillet group 13 532
fillet mouldings *see under* MOULDINGS → types
Filley (family) 31 652
Filley, Oliver 31 652
Fillia 11 80*; 16 681
  collaboration 27 853
  groups and movements 1 166; 8 771; 11 867; 25 447; 31 446
  writings 27 853
Fillian, John 10 758
Filliger, Charles *see* FILIGER, CHARLES
filling 32 817
Filliou, Robert 11 80–81*
  collaboration 27 215; 30 748
  groups and movements 4 731; 11 232
  works 24 407
Fillmore, Millard 32 828
Filloeul, Gilbert 11 81
Filloeul, Pierre 11 81*
film 24 669, 743
  materials
    celluloid 24 669
    emulsions 24 651
  types
    35mm 24 677, 678
    colour *see* panchromatic
    holographic 14 690
    infra-red 24 653
    iridescent 11 54
    panchromatic 9 493; 24 647, 655, 663
    Polaroid 24 655
    roll 20 406; 24 647, 651, 656, 669
    sheets 24 651, 669
  uses
    cliché-verre 7 432
    fibre art 11 54
  see also CAMERAS; PHOTOGRAPHIC NEGATIVES
Film and Photo League 24 685; 28 794
films 7 375; 8 911; 24 662, 678; 26 236; 31 607
  animation 9 10
  avant-garde *see* experimental
  experimental 10 686–9*, *687*; 22 380
  fine art *see* experimental
  see also TRANSPARENCIES
film sets 31 *82*
film studios 18 193
Filocalus 5 801
Filomarino, Ascanio, Cardinal 9 411; 11 81*; 18 736; 22 478
Filomarino, Isabella 11 114
Filonov, Pavel (Nikolayevich) 11 82–3*; 27 392, 394, 442
  groups and movements 17 732; 18 30; 22 750; 31 583
  pupils 12 804; 18 412
  works 11 *82*
Filotesio, Nicola *see* COLA DELL'AMATRICE
Filotheos 21 344
Filottrano 6 157
Filsak, Karel 25 430; 29 438
Filser, Martin 10 529
Filteau, Jacques-Richard 1 786
Fina Buzzacarina, Lady of Padua 5 871; 21 112
Finaguerra, Maso 9 30
Fiñana 16 436
Finance Corporation of Bahamas Ltd (FinCo) 3 64
Finch, Alfred William 11 83*, 104, 105
  groups and movements 3 563; 7 245; 11 96; 22 746; 28 427; 32 591
  pupils 13 699
  works 3 592; 11 449
Finch, Francis Oliver 1 897; 23 884; 31 909
Finch, Heneage, 4th Earl of Aylesford 11 83–4
  architecture 4 333; 22 738
  decorative works 26 388
  etchings 27 271
  groups and movements 10 644
  interior decoration 25 192, *193*
  prints 25 631
Finch, Isabella 17 904
Finch, John 9 79
Finch, Raymond 4 444; 5 731
Finch, William 28 710
Fincham, St Martin 26 613
Finchingfield, St John's 9 152
Finch & Westerholm 22 468
FinCo *see* FINANCE CORPORATION OF BAHAMAS LTD
Find, Ludvig (Frederik) 11 84*
Finden, Edward Francis 8 66; 11 84; 14 680; 29 691
Finden, William 4 885; 8 66; 11 84; 14 680; 28 748; 29 634, 691
Findon, John *see* FENDOUR, JOHN
Fine, Jud 19 703
Fine, Oronce
  works 28 *211*
Fine, Perle 24 213
fine art 30 382
fine art exhibitions *see under* EXHIBITIONS → types
fine art films *see* FILMS → types → experimental
Fine Arts Association 33 58
Fine Art Society 10 679; 33 140
Fine Arts Quarterly Review 24 446
Fine Arts Squad 19 703
Fine Arts Union (sindicatul Artelor Frumoase) 5 74
Fine Grey ware *see under* POTTERY → wares
Fine-line style pottery *see under* POTTERY → wares
Finelli, Carlo 28 756; 29 639
Finelli, Giuliano 11 84–5*; 22 477
  assistants 13 814
  collaboration 3 838
  patrons and collectors 22 21
  pupils 1 631
  works 3 840; 11 81; 16 699, 703; 20 73
Fineman, Eleanor *see* ANTIN, ELEANOR
Fine Orange ware *see under* POTTERY → wares
Finetti, Giuseppe De *see* DE FINETTI, GIUSEPPE
finger cups *see under* CUPS → types
finger marks 25 476, 478, *478*
fingernail script *see under* SCRIPTS → types
finger paintings *see under* PAINTING → forms
finger rings *see under* RINGS → types
Fingo 1 417, 418, 419
Fini, Léonor 10 483; 11 85*; 30 22
Fini, Tommaso di Cristofano *see* MASOLINO
finials (architectural) 11 86*
  Africa 1 328
  China 6 668, 686, 691; 7 143
  Maya 21 207
  Mesoamerica, Pre-Columbian 21 207*
  New Caledonia 23 18, *18*
  see also ACROTERIA
finials (scrolls) 17 569–70*, *570*
Finiguerra, Antonio 11 86
Finiguerra, Maso 11 86*
  attributions 3 96
  collaboration 3 99; 12 549
  methods 10 381
  patrons and collectors 12 897
  pupils 3 96
  reproductive prints by others 27 176
  works 11 *86*; 16 750; 20 111; 23 115, *115*
Finike *see* PHOINIKOS
Finja Church 30 75
Fink, Jacob 11 161
Fink, Johann Lorenz 3 140
Fink, Larry 11 87*
Fink, Lotte 19 522
Finkelstein, Nathan I. 14 157*
Finland 11 *87*, 87–113*; 32 513
  architects 11 90; 31 461
  architecture 11 88–9*, 92–3*; 30 284
    International Style 11 *93*
    vernacular 32 286–9*
    wood 32 286–7
  archives 2 369
  art history 11 113*
  art schools 31 461
  auction houses 2 369
  birch 8 *803*; 11 98
  bowls 11 *106*
  boxes 11 *108*
  bronze 11 *100*
Finland—cont.
  bureaux 11 *103*
  busts 11 *100*
  carpets 5 829, 841; 11 109, *109*, 110–11; 27 316
  cast iron 30 284
  cathedrals 14 *371*; 31 *462*
  ceramics 11 105–6*
  chairs 1 8
  churches 11 *88*, 89–90*, 91*
  coins 7 539
  collections 11 111–12*
  concrete 19 411
  dealing 11 111–12*
  epitaphs 11 94
  exchanges 29 *64*
  faience (ii) (ceramics) 11 105
  frames 11 *474*, *477*, *478*
  furniture 11 102–4*
  glass 11 106–7*, *107*
  gold 11 107, 108
  government buildings 10 *218*
  granite 11 *88*, 100
  historicism 14 580
  historiography 11 113*
  houses 32 286, 287–8, *288*
  interior decoration 11 101–2*, *102*
  jewellery 11 108–9*
  libraries 10 *219*; 11 112*
  maiolica 11 105
  marble 11 *99*
  marks 11 108
  marquetry 11 *103*
  metalwork 11 107–8*
  monuments 11 99, *99*
  moss 32 286
  museums 11 112*; 14 *373*
  oak 11 98
  painting 11 93–7*, *97*
    genre 9 *717*; 10 *128*
    landscape 11 *96*, 96; 17 *448*
    wall 11 94, *94*, *102*
    19th cent. 12 *20*
  patronage 11 111–12*
  pattern books 6 581
  periodicals 24 452*
  photoarchives 11 112
  porcelain 11 105, *106*
  portraits 11 94
  pottery 11 105
  railway stations 27 *473*
  rock art 11 93
  sanatoria 15 *886*
  schools 11 *90*
  screenprints 11 97; 23 207
  sculpture 11 97–9*, *98*, 100–101*, 106
    Baroque 11 *99*
    Gothic 11 98
    19th cent. 28 814
  silver 11 107, *108*
  sports centres 29 427
  stained glass 13 190
  stools 8 *803*
  stoves 11 105
  täkänäs 11 109
  textiles 11 109–10*
  theatres 14 *372*
  tiles 30 884*
  timber structures 32 287
  town halls 1 *10*
  towns 1 9; 10 492
  trade 11 108
  urban planning 31 461
  vernacular art 11 110–11*
  women artists 2 317
  wood 32 286–7
  wood-carvers 11 98
  wood-carvings 11 *98*, 98–9
  wool 5 829; 11 *109*
  see also SCANDINAVIA
Finland, Tom of *see* TOM OF FINLAND
Finlay, Alan 2 760
Finlay, David 21 90
Finlay, Ernest 2 760
Finlay, Hugh 3 129; 10 852

Finlay, Ian Hamilton **7** 699; **11** 113*; **28** 240, 273, 316
Finlay, John **3** 129; **10** 852
Finlay, Karen **10** 882; **24** 409
Finlay, Kirkman **14** 108
Finlayson, Adrian C. **25** 700
Finlayson, James **30** 284
Finley, James **4** 803
Finmar **28** 548
Finn, Alfred C. **14** 802
Finnberg, Gustaf Wilhelm **11** 95, 113–14*
Finne, Gunnar **19** 408
Finne, Henrik **23** 227
Finnish Academy of Art (Suomen Taideakatemian Säätiö) **11** 112
Finnish Art Association (Suomen Taideyhdistys) **11** 95, 111, 112; **14** 372
Finnish Society of Artists **14** 373
Finoglia, Paolo Domenico **11** 114*; **22** 484
Finot, Louis **11** 114–15*
Finsler, Hans **4** 90; **5** 279; **11** 115*; **24** 676
Finson, Louis **5** 702; **10** 721; **11** 115*; **23** 908
Finspång **30** *65*, 109, 113
Castle **30** 118
Finster, Barbara **16** 549
Finsterlin, Hermann **10** 697, 698
Finsterwalder, Ignaz **18** 120; **26** 24
Finström Church **11** 92
Finta, Jószef **14** 891
Fintinele **14** 899
Fiocchi, A. **1** 736
Fiocchi, Mino **16** 649; **23** 263; **25** 218
Fiocco, Giuseppe **11** 115*; **22** 337
Fioravanti, Alfredo **10** 639
Fioravanti, Aristotele **4** 271; **11** 115–16*
attributions **4** 643
patrons and collectors **16** 790; **27** 437
works **11** *116*; **22** 169, 181; **27** 371
Fioravanti, Benedetto **20** 220
Fioravanti, Cosimo **31** 524
Fioravanti, José **2** 400
Fiore, del (family) **32** 190
Fiore, Ercole del *see* ERCOLE DEL FIORE
Fiore, Jacobello del *see* JACOBELLO DEL FIORE
Fiore, Joseph **4** 109
Fiore, Quentin **20** 29
Fiorelli, Giuseppe **16** 774; **25** 194, 207
Fiorentino, Adriano *see* ADRIANO FIORENTINO
Fiorentino, Domenico *see* DOMENICO FIORENTINO
Fiorentino, Francesco *see* FRANCISCUS ITALUS
Fiorentino, Giuliano *see* GIULIANO FIORENTINO
Fiorentino, Mario **16** 650
Fiorentino, Niccolò *see* SPINELLI, NICCOLÒ DI FORZORE
Fiorentino, Niccolò di Giovanni *see* NICCOLÒ DI GIOVANNI FIORENTINO
Fiorentino, Nicolás *see* DELLI, DELLO (DI NICCOLÒ)
Fiorentino, Pier Francesco *see* PIER FRANCESCO FIORENTINO
Fiorentino, Pier Maria *see* SERBALDI DA PESCIA, PIER MARIA
Fiorentino, Rosso *see* ROSSO FIORENTINO
Fiorentino, Stefano *see* STEFANO FIORENTINO
Fiorentinus, Francesco *see* FRANCISCUS ITALUS
Fiorentinus, Johannes *see* JOHANNES FIORENTINUS
Fiorentinus, Niza *see* NIZA FIORENTINUS
Fiorenza, Nicholo da *see* BARONCELLI, NICCOLÒ
Fiorenzi (family) **6** 35
Fiorenzo di Lorenzo (di Cecco di Pascolo) **11** 116–18*; **24** 520
attributions **5** 672; **20** 679
pupils **24** 829
works **11** *117*
Fiorenzuola **6** 139
Fiori, Ambrogio de' **4** 620
Fiori, Ernesto de **4** 718
Fiori, Mario dei *see* MARIO DEI FIORI
Fiorillo, Johann Dominicus **11** 118*; **29** 358
Fiorini, Bernardino **24** 342
Fiorini, Giovanni Battista **2** 388
Fiorini, Lorenzo **20** 541
Fiorini, Marcel **4** 98
Fioroni, Giosetta **26** 778
Fiorucci, Elio **9** 294
Fiozzi, Aldo **8** 436
fir **10** 275; **18** 361; **33** 324
Firdawsi **16** 545; **21** 704; **22** 515
works **15** *572*; **16** *302*
Fire, De **19** 799; **27** 643
firearms *see* GUNS
fire-backs **10** *340*; **11** 118
fire-boards *see* CHIMNEY-BOARDS
fire-clays *see under* CLAY → types
fire curtains *see under* CURTAINS → types
fire-dogs *see* ANDIRONS
fire gilding *see under* GILDING → types
fire-grates *see* GRATES
fire-holders **33** *708*
fire-irons **11** 119, *119*
Firens, Pierre **15** 34
Firenze, Andrea da *see* ANDREA DA FIRENZE
Firenze, Antonio di Cristoforo da *see* ANTONIO DI CRISTOFORO DA FIRENZE
Firenze, Desiderio da *see* DESIDERIO DA FIRENZE
Firenze, Giovanni da *see* GIOVANNI DA FIRENZE
Firenze, Guido da *see* GUIDO DA FIRENZE
Firenze, Luca di *see* LUCA DI FIRENZE
Firenze, Marco da *see* MARCO DA FIRENZE
Firenze, Maturino da *see* MATURINO DA FIRENZE
Firenze, Michele da *see* MICHELE DA FIRENZE
Firenze, Nicolò Coccari da *see* NICOLÒ COCCARI DA FIRENZE
Firenze, Pacio da *see* PACIO DA FIRENZE
Firenze, Sisto di *see* SISTO DI FIRENZE
Firenze, Tommaso da **27** 498
Firenze, Zanobi da *see* ZANOBI DA FIRENZE
Firenze, Zebo da *see* ZEBO DA FIRENZE
Firenzuola, Agnolo **1** 178
fireplace furnishings **11** 118–20*; **28** 263
fireplaces
historical and regional traditions
Belgium **3** 575, 576, 578, 588
Britain **4** 778
France **11** 574
Germany **12** 410
Netherlands, the **22** 862
Russia **27** *407*
materials
brick **3** 588; **4** 778
steel **27** *407*
tiles **3** 576; **30** 876
fireproofing **7** 693; **28** 830
Britain **31** 240
England **16** 52
fireproofing—cont.
Russia **19** 837
United States of America **6** 486; **33** 174
fire puppets *see under* PUPPETS → types
fire-screens **3** 442; **10** 343
fireside companions **11** 119
fireworks **23** 769
firing **6** 328, 329–30*
historical and regional traditions
Byzantine **9** 633
Greece, ancient **13** 480, 482–3*
Japan **17** 242–3
Korea **18** *333*
Mesopotamia **4** 771
types
biscuit **6** 325, 326; **10** 306
glost **6** 325, 326, 329
uses
brick **4** 767–8*, *768*
stained glass **29** 499*, *499*
firing glasses *see under* GLASSES → types
Firka *see* FERKA
Firkovich, A. S. **7** 248
Firlej (family) **13** 774; **25** 135
Firlej, Andrzej **13** 774
Firle Place (E. Sussex) **8** 83
Firm, The **13** 9
Firmazeau **2** 704; **11** 643
Firmian, Franz Alphons von **11** 120
Firmian, Franz Lactanz von, Graf **11** 120*
Firmian, Karl Joseph von, Graf **4** 310; **7** 916; **11** 120*; **18** 162, 163
Firmian, Leopold Anton Eleutherius von, Archbishop of Salzburg **11** 120*
Firmin-Didot **24** 846
Firmin-Didot, Ambroise **2** 499; **8** 867*
Firminy-Vert, Unité d'Habitation **19** *45*
firmitas **2** 362
Firnhaber, Charles **2** 765
First Garden City Ltd **24** 187
First Gothic *see* GOTHIC → styles → Early Gothic
First Group **1** 636
First Intermediate Period *see under* EGYPT, ANCIENT → periods
First Kennicott Bible *see under* BIBLES → individual manuscripts
First National Architectural Style **32** 108
First New Service **27** 584
First of May Factory **27** 414
First Prayerbook of Maximilian, Master of the *see* OLDER PRAYERBOOK OF MAXIMILIAN, MASTER OF THE
First Romanesque *see under* ROMANESQUE → styles
First State Textile Factory **25** 239
First Style *see under* ROME, ANCIENT → mosaics; painting → wall
First Working Group of Constructivists **29** 632
Firtaler, Barthlmä *see* FIRTHALER, BARTHLMÄ
Firth, Cecil **10** 81
Firth, Ian **23** 69
Firth, Mark **1** 738
Firth, Thomas, & Sons **8** 285
Firthaler, Andre **11** 120
Firthaler, Barthlmä **11** 120*
Firth of Forth Bridge **16** 55
Firth Vickers **29** 484
Firuz, Khan (*reg c.* 1469–95) (Dandani) **15** 351
Firuzabad Mosque (Deccan; India) **15** 356
Firuzabad (Delhi; India) *see under* DELHI
Firuzabad (Iran) **11** 121–2*; **15** *901*, 906, 912
garden palace **11** 121; **23** 807
iwans **16** 801
relief of Ardashir I **1** 887
rock reliefs **11** *121*, 121–2
Firuzabadi **22** 321
Firuz Bey **16** 202
Firuz Khalji **8** 675
Firuz Shah, Sultan (*reg* 1351–88) (Tughluq) **15** 341, 342, 343, 716; **17** 451; **31** 416
architecture **8** 673; **15** 341
canals **8** 675
carpets **15** 682
gardens **12** 73
Fisac Serna, Miguel **9** 113; **11** 122*; **29** 274, 309
Fiscali, Filippo **20** 535
Fischart, Johann **29** 673
Fischbach, Johann Heinrich **17** 885
Fischbeck **26** 685
Fischel, Oskar **11** 122*
Fischer, Adam **8** 741
Fischer, Adolf **7** 155, 584
Fischer, August **1** 548; **5** 413; **14** 482
Fischer, Daniel **28** 853
Fischer, Eberhard
works **1** *291*; **8** *488*
Fischer, Edward Francis Gunter **2** 765
Fischer, Egon **8** 741
Fischer, Emil **14** 687
Fischer, Ernst **28** 927
Fischer, Franz **2** 804
Fischer, Georg **2** 305; **11** 123*
Fischer, J. (*fl* 1808–11) **25** 428
Fischer, Jiří *see* FISCHER, GEORG
Fischer, J. J. (*fl* 17th or 18th cent.) **6** 526
Fischer, Johann **32** 437
Fischer, Johann Baptist **11** 129
Fischer, Johann Bernhard **27** 665
Fischer, Johann Georg **3** 58; **11** 123*; **18** 120; **33** 41
Fischer, Johann Martin **2** 802; **10** 883; **11** 123–4*; **18** 127; **24** 586
Fischer, Johann Michael **11** 124–7*
architecture
churches **10** 859; **11** *125*; **12** 372
Osterhofen Abbey Church **2** 581; **32** 822
Ottobeuren Abbey Church **11** *126*; **23** 636, 637; **28** 130
Our Lady of the Snows (Aufhausen) **23** *473*
St Anna am Lehel (Munich) **12** 372; **22** 299
SS Marinus and Anianus (Rott am Inn) **12** *372*; **13** 851
Zwiefalten Abbey Church **12** 497
libraries **19** *316*
collaboration **29** 760, 761; **32** 822; **33** 682
gardens **33** 434
groups and movements **26** 498
patrons and collectors **23** 473
Fischer, Johann Sigismund **5** 671; **16** 738; **23** 262
Fischer, Joseph (1764–1822) **10** 860; **14** 901
Fischer, József (1769–1822) **10** 530
Fischer, József (*b* 1901) **2** 416; **11** 128*
collaboration **20** 460
groups and movements **14** 890; **15** 886
Fischer, Jürgen Lit **7** 681
Fischer, Karl von **11** 128–9*
assistants **3** 155
pupils **12** 167; **23** 371; **33** 673
restorations **18** 123
works **12** 374; **22** 300, 308
Fischer, Lili **11** 129*
Fischer, Lothar **29** 435
Fischer, Oskar **29** 872
Fischer, Otto **22** 921; **25** 348
Fischer, Susanne **20** 894
Fischer, Theo (*fl* 1907) **30** 153
Fischer, Theodor (1862–1938) **11** 129*
assistants **4** 309
collaboration **12** 378; **28** 177
dealing **12** 474
groups and movements **8** 824; **28** 341
pupils
Böhm (ii), Dominikus **4** 235
Borbiró, Virgil **4** 378
Forbát, Fred **11** 299
Häring, Hugo **14** 175
Hikisch, Rezső **14** 523
Kauffmann, Richard (1887–1958; architect) **17** 853
May, Ernst (1886–1970) **20** 878
Mendelsohn, Erich **21** 118
Oud, J(acobus) J(ohannes) P(ieter) **23** 662
Welzenbacher, Lois **33** 66
staff **19** 283; **26** 402; **30** 370
teachers **28** 374; **30** 733
works **14** 362; **29** 874
Fischer, (Josef) Vincenz **11** 122–3*; **21** 512; **25** 154; **33** 256
Fischer, Walter **33** 736
Fischer-Galaţi, H. **26** 723
Fischer-Lueg, Konrad **25** 153
Fischer von Erlach, Johann Bernhard **11** 129, 130–34*; **32** 435, 443
architecture **5** 773; **12** 356; **14** 402
architectural decorations **19** 316
castles **11** 120
catafalques **6** 72
chapels **4** 843; **33** 417
churches **2** *782*, 827; **11** *133*; **25** 266; **27** 661; **32** 435, 453–4, 760
gates **2** 782
halls **23** 812
libraries **13** 279; **32** 456, *457*
mausolea **2** 781
palaces **2** 828; **4** 698; **11** *132*; **14** 528; **23** 811, 812; **25** 427; **32** 460
stables **19** 55
staircases **29** 525
assistants **20** 250
attributions **20** 250
collaboration **1** 667; **2** 783, 819; **12** 748; **20** 494; **25** 449; **32** 442
gardens **32** 460
groups and movements **3** 261
patrons and collectors **3** 689; **8** 378; **13** 918, 921; **28** 15; **30** 793
pupils **11** 134
restorations by others **23** 698
sculpture **4** 844
altars **27** *661*
funerary monuments **4** 844; **25** 766
monstrances **25** 443
public monuments **5** *264*
stucco **13** 330
teachers **11** 274
writings **2** 833; **4** 362; **10** 96; **12** 368; **14** 402; **16** 143, 547; **20** 131; **23** 489; **31** 298
Fischer von Erlach, Joseph Emanuel **11** 130, 134–6*; **32** 435
architecture **3** 791; **7** 881; **32** 456
ecclesiastical buildings **1** 668; **14** 887; **30** 914; **32** 453
government buildings **32** 456
libraries **2** 784; **11** 131; **32** 456, *457*
public monuments **13** 888; **14** 894
riding houses **26** 363
assistants **1** 668

Fischer von Erlach, Joseph Emanuel—cont.
collaboration **1** 668; **7** 881; **20** 494
engravings **2** *779*; **11** *135*
patrons and collectors **13** 921, 922; **28** 836
writings **14** 402
Fisches, Isaak **12** 390; **18** 46; **27** 319; **29** 400
Fischetti, Fedele **5** 914; **11** 136*; **22** 481
Fischetti, Fedele Alessandro **11** 136
Fischinger, Oskar W. **10** 687, 688; **11** 137*; **19** 702; **31** 607
Fischl, Eric **11** 137*; **21** 897; **31** 609
Fischli, Max **33** 737
Fisco, Claude (Antoine) **3** 547; **5** 40; **11** 137*
Fise-le-Marsal Church **13** 114
Fisen, Englebert **11** 166
fish **15** 850
Fish, Janet **29** 671
Fishbourne (W. Sussex) **10** *225*, 226; **11** 137–8*; **26** *905*
gardens **12** 70; **32** 544
mosaics **27** 62
paintings **10** 242
palace **11** 137–8
Fisher (family) **10** 265; **33** 545
Fisher, Adrian **4** 790
Fisher, Alexander **2** 570; **10** 336, 347; **12** 450; **17** 528; **28** 215
Fisher, Alvan **11** 138*; **31** 601; **32** 753
Fisher, Andrea **6** 600
Fisher, Angela
works **3** *756*
Fisher, Brian **5** 569
Fisher, Charles **11** 138
Fisher, C. S. **3** 883; **21** 47; **27** 669
Fisher, Eberhard **15** 748
Fisher, Edward **11** 139*; **19** 645; **21** 416; **26** 278
Fisher, Elmer H. **28** 327
Fisher, Emil **5** 85
Fisher, Henry **8** 66; **25** 635
Fisher, Ignác **5** 85
Fisher, John (i) (1736-1804) **11** 138*
Fisher, John (ii) (1760-1839) **11** 138
Fisher, John (iii) (*b* 1786) **11** 138
Fisher, John (*fl* 1802) **7** 752, 753
Fisher, Jonathan **16** 16
Fisher, Karl **31** 566
Fisher, Kitty **26** *277*
Fisher, Richard (*b* 1690) **11** 138
Fisher, Richard (1786-1819) **11** 138
Fisher, Samuel, the elder (*fl* 1771-80) **11** 138
Fisher, Samuel, the younger (*d* 1812) **11** 138
Fisher, Samuel (*fl* 1830-55) **25** 836
Fisher, Sandra **18** 93
Fisher, Thomas **19** 483
Fisher, William **11** 138
Fisher of York *see* FISHER, JOHN (i)
Fisher-Price Toys **31** 259
Fishkill (NY), Fowler House **11** 361
Fishlake (S. Yorks), St Cuthbert **26** 614
Fishpool (Notts) **12** 627
Fiske, J. W. **31** 653
Fisker, Kay (Otto) **11** 139*; **29** 77
collaboration **14** 392; **21** 820; **29** 601
competitions **25** 850
groups and movements **8** 728
staff **21** 820
teachers **17** 755
works **8** 728, *728*
Fiskerton (Lincs) **6** 160
Fisk University *see under* NASHVILLE (TN)
fission-track dating *see under* DATING METHODS → types
Fisson, J. B. **3** 578
Fistaine, Jean-François **8** 753
Fister, Hans *see* PFISTER, HANS
Fitalis, Georgios **11** 140; **13** 354
Fitalis, Ioannis **11** 140
Fitalis, Lazaros **11** 140; **13** 354
Fitalis, Markos **11** 140
Fitch, John **6** 115, 116; **13** 614
Fitch, Simon **9** 504
fitched brushes *see under* BRUSHES → types
Fiter **18** 47
Fiter, Antoni Serra i *see* SERRA I FITER, ANTONI
Fitero Abbey **29** 263
S María la Real **13** 50; **16** 524
Fittinghof, I. F. **25** 791
Fitton, James **2** 553
Fitton, Peter **18** 814
Fitzalan, Henry, 12th Earl of Arundel **11** 140*; **19** 792; **23** 198
Fitz-Alwyne **5** 135
Fitz-Foy, Walter **6** 411
Fitzgerald (family) **16** 36
FitzGerald, Desmond **11** 140–41*
works **9** 317; **16** *11*, 12, 38, 40
FitzGerald, Edward **11** 798; **32** 109
Fitzgerald, Elizabeth **7** 436
Fitzgerald, G. M. **3** 883
Fitzgerald, James, 1st Duke of Leinster **6** 63; **19** 867; **33** 158
Fitzgerald, Kit **32** 421
FitzGerald, Lionel LeMoine **5** 567; **11** 141*; **13** 711
Fitzgerald, Richard **24** 698
Fitzgerald, William Robert, 2nd Duke of Leinster **2** 598; **26** 462
Fitzharding, Robert **4** 824
Fitzherbert, Henry Valentine, 9th Baron Stafford **7** 839
Fitz-James Stuart y Falcó, James, *see* ALBA, 17th Duque de
Fitz-James Stuart y Silva, Carlos Miguel, 14th Duque de Alba *see* ALBA, 14th Duque de
Fitzmaurice, Francis Thomas, 3rd Earl of Lansdowne **29** 805
Fitzmaurice, Henry Charles Keith, 5th Marquess of Lansdowne **12** 75
Fitzpatrick, Francis W. **5** 126
Fitzroy, Augustus Henry, 3rd Duke of Grafton **14** 833
Fitzroy, Blanche **19** 413
Fitzroy, Charles, 2nd Duke of Grafton **4** 758; **17** 904
Fitzroy Picture Society **30** 1
Fitzroy Street Group **5** 516, 517; **12** 644; **13** 9; **23** 23; **24** 884; **26** 10
works **5** *517*
FitzStephen, Ralph **12** 799
Fitzwarin Psalter *see under* PSALTERS → individual manuscripts
Fitzwilliam, Richard, 6th Viscount Fitzwilliam **9** 317
Fitzwilliam, Richard, 7th Viscount Fitzwilliam **11** 141*
collections **10** 369; **32** 835; **33** 345
paintings **2** 598; **5** 65
Fitzwilliam, William Wentworth, 2nd Earl Fitzwilliam **2** 598; **26** 490
Fitzwilliam Album *see under* ALBUMS → individual manuscripts
Fitzwilliam Museum *see under* CAMBRIDGE (UK) → museums
Fiumicelli, Lorenzo **3** 470
Five, The **2** 197
Five Dynasties *see under* CHINA → periods
five-element pagodas *see under* PAGODAS → types
Five Senses **2** 148
fixatives **1** 155; **7** 747; **11** 141–2*; **17** 210
materials
agar-agar **11** 142
barium hydroxide **32** 809
casein **11** 142
dammar **11** 142
funori **11** 142
gum arabic **11** 142
mastic **11** 142
parylene **11** 142
polymers **11** 142
shellac **11** 142
varnishes **32** 3
waxes **11** 142
uses
drawings **6** 470
pigments **11** 141
wall paintings **11** 142; **32** 809
see also ADHESIVES; CONSERVATION; CONSOLIDANTS
Fizelle, Rah **2** 771; **3** 124
Fizuli **2** *890*
Fjaestad, Gustaf (Edolf) **11** 142*; **30** 114
groups and movements **22** 540
works **22** *541*
Fjaestad, Maja **11** 142
Fjelie Church **30** 75
Fjell, Kai (Breder) **11** 142–3*; **23** 226
Fjellström, Pehr **28** 95
Fjenneslev Church **8** 758
Flacco, Orlando **32** 343
Flachat, Eugène **11** 143*; **27** 591
Flachat, Stéphane **11** 143; **27** 591
Flack, Audrey **1** 130; **11** 143*; **24** 686; **29** 671
Fladmoe, Torsten Christensen **32** 497
Flageoulot, Charles-Antoine **8** 51
Flagg, Ernest **11** 143–4*; **26** 75; **28** 833; **30** 458; **31** 595
Flagg, James Montgomery **25** 349, 652
works **25** *651*
Flagler, Henry Morrison **5** 875; **14** 277; **21** 421; **27** 532
flagons
historical and regional traditions
Belgium **6** 155
Celtic **6** *155*, 155–6
England **10** *327*
France **6** 155, *155*
Germany **6** 155; **12** 444
Hungary **15** 8
La Tène culture (*c*. 450-.*c* 50 BC) **6** *155*
Netherlands, the **22** 893, *893*
materials
bronze **6** *155*
coral **6** *155*
enamel **6** *155*
pewter **15** 8; **22** *893*; **24** 580
silver **10** *327*
types
Bauchkannen **30** 146
Stitzen **30** 146
flags **11** 144–53*; **14** 404, 416, 425, 429
historical and regional traditions
China **11** 145*
Crusaders **11** 147
France **11** 148
Germany **11** 149
Holy Roman Empire (before 1648) **11** 147
Islamic **11** 146*
Japan **11** 145–6*, *146*; **14** 429; **17** 363
Poland **11** 150
Rome, ancient **11** 146*
Sri Lanka **29** 477, *477*
flags
historical and regional traditions—cont.
United States of America **7** 408
materials
cotton **11** 145
linen **11** 145
silk **11** 145
types
colours **11** 150
prayer *see* PRAYER FLAGS
see also BANNERS; GONFANONS; GUIDONS; PENNONS; STANDARDS
Flagstaff (AZ), Museum of Northern Arizona **22** 677
flagstones **13** 387
Flahaut, Charles-Claude *see* ANGIVILLER, CHARLES-CLAUDE DE FLAHAUT DE LA BILLARDERIE, Comte de
flails **6** 305
Flak, Stanislaus **18** 425
Flake, Otto **8** 436
flake white *see under* PIGMENTS → types
flak jackets **2** 474
Flamand, Pierre **11** 618
Flamand Christensen, Sigrid *see* CHRISTENSEN, SIGRID FLAMAND
Flamboyant style *see under* GOTHIC → styles
Flamen, Albert **7** 194; **11** 155*; **29** 572
Flamen, Anselme **11** 156*; **20** 481; **24** 165
Flameng, Auguste **25** 751
Flameng, François **11** 156*
Flameng, Léopold **11** 156; **14** 390; **19** 282; **25** 868; **26** 234
Flamengrie, La *see* LA FLAMENGRIE
Flament, A. (*fl* 1692) **11** 155
Flament, Andre le (*fl* 1520-1) **1** 766
Flamma, Galvanno *see* FIAMMA, GALVANNO
Flammarion **2** 733; **4** 368
Flammarion, Ernest **2** 733
Flammingo, Paolo **31** 15
flamsk tapestries *see under* TAPESTRIES → types
Flanagan, Barry **11** 156–7*
groups and movements **10** 269; **25** 646
works **10** 269; **11** *157*; **29** 13
Flanchet **6** 533; **29** 432
Flander, Brita **11** 107
Flanders *see* BELGIUM
Flanders, Countess of **12** 521
Flanders, Ferdinand, Count of *see* FERDINAND, Count of Flanders
Flanders, Louis II de Mâle, Count of *see* LOUIS II, Count of Flanders and Duke of Brabant
Flanders, Mathilde of Portugal, Countess of *see* MATHILDE OF PORTUGAL, Countess of Flanders
Flandes, Arnao de **13** 191; **32** 247
Flandes, Juan de *see* JUAN DE FLANDES
Flandin, Eugène (Napoléon) **8** 19; **16** 547; **21** 299; **27** 854
Flandria, Cornelio de *see* CORNELIO DE FLANDRIA
Flandrin, (René-) Auguste **11** 157–9*
patrons and collectors **17** 667
pupils **11** 158, 159
teachers **15** 839; **19** 847
Flandrin, Fernand Maillaud **11** 644
Flandrin, Hippolyte (-Jean) **11** 157, 158–9*, 544, 659
assistants **11** 159
collaboration **3** 126; **12** 809; **24** 736
methods **10** 199
Flandrin, Hippolyte(-Jean)—cont.
pupils **8** 659, 794; **31** 29
teachers **15** 839; **19** 847
works **7** 876; **11** *158*, 159, 520; **14** 593; **22** 329
Flandrin, Jean-Baptiste-Jacques **11** 157
Flandrin, Jules **11** 160*; **20** 126
Flandrin, (Jean-) Paul **11** 157, 159–60*, 659
collaboration **12** 809
teachers **11** 158; **19** 847
works **11** 159; **12** 830
flanking towers *see under* TOWERS → types
flanks **21** 546
Flannagan, John B(ernard) **11** 160–61*
Flann Sinna, King of Meath and High King of Tara (*reg c*. 908) **7** 459
Flaño, Hernan **6** 595
Flascoen, Laurent **10** 222
Flascoen, Quentin **10** 222
Flash Art **24** 429, 449
flash bulbs **24** 651
flashing **29** 498
flash photography *see under* PHOTOGRAPHY → processes
flasks
historical and regional traditions
China **6** *890*, *910*; **7** *69*; **23** *553*
Colombia **29** *212*
Crete **21** *670*
Cyprus, ancient **8** *343*
Egypt **16** 540
Egypt, ancient **10** 57
Greece, ancient **6** III1
Hungary **15** *3*, 3
Iran **16** *424*
Islamic **16** *424*, 540
Japan **17** *252*, *257*
Minoan **21** *670*
Mongolia **21** 878
Prehistoric **8** *343*; **25** 543
South America, Pre-Columbian **29** *212*, 212–13
Vietnam **32** 487
materials
amber **1** 761
earthenware **6** *890*
enamel **7** *69*
glass **10** 57; **15** *3*
porcelain **6** *910*; **16** *424*; **23** *553*
pottery **6** III1; **8** *343*; **21** *670*
rock crystal **16** 540
silver-gilt **15** *3*
stonewares **17** *252*, *257*
tumbaga **29** *212*
flasks, pilgrim *see* PILGRIM FLASKS
flasks, powder *see* POWDER FLASKS
Flat, Paul **24** 838
flat arches *see under* ARCHES → types
Flatatunga **15** *68*, 69; **32** 517, 524
Flathead **22** 616
Flatman, Thomas **3** 444; **11** 161*; **21** 640
Flato, Paul **31** 655
Flatow, Louis Victor **11** 161*, 796; **14** 511; **19** 588
flat roofs *see under* ROOFS → types
flats (housing) *see* APARTMENTS
flats (theatre) *see* WINGS
flat-topped vaults *see under* VAULTS (CEILING) → types
Flatz, (Johann) Gebhard **11** 161*
Flaubert, Gustave **4** 242; **8** 596; **18** 783
Flaugier, Josep **29** 305
Flaum, Franciszek **25** 115
Flavacourt, Guillaume de, Archbishop of Rouen *see* GUILLAUME DE FLAVACOURT, Archbishop of Rouen
Flavier Pablo, Severino **24** 622

Flavigny-sur-Ozerain, St Pierre 5 795; 7 265; 8 222; 26 601
Flavin, Dan 11 162*
  dealers 6 23
  groups and movements 1 79; 10 416; 21 645
  methods 28 203
  patrons and collectors 24 24; 32 623
  works 15 869; 19 355; 22 748; 31 615
Flavitsky, Konstantin (Dmitriyevich) 11 162*
Flavius Diogenes 23 893
Flavius Felix 7 772; 9 648
Flavius Furius Aptus, C. 10 427
Flavius Mithridates see GUGLIELMO RAIMONDO
Flavius Pantainos 2 668, 685
Flavius Philostratus 2 670
flavone 9 491
flavonol 9 491
Flawford, St Peter's 1 518
flax 30 537
  historical and regional traditions
    Ancient Near East 1 879
    Egypt 16 428, 431
    Etruscan 10 636
    Islamic 16 352, 428, 431
    Italy 10 636
    Maori 3 331
    New Zealand 23 73*, 712
    Pacific Islands 23 712
    Syria 16 428
  uses
    baskets 3 331
    canvas 5 654
    cloaks 20 358
    paper 16 352
    textiles 16 431
    wicks 5 610
Flaxman, John 7 480; 10 372; 11 162–5*; 13 302; 15 820; 26 231; 33 22
  attributions 3 78–9
  book illustrations 13 246; 22 415; 23 295
  collaboration 10 334; 33 100
  drawings 9 225
  groups and movements 22 734, 737, 741; 26 85, 742
  interior decoration 26 541
  patrons and collectors 3 179; 14 485, 744; 24 893; 28 908; 33 453
  personal collection 20 335
  pottery 10 307, 307
  pupils 3 78; 13 213
  reproductive prints by others 1 845
  sculpture 5 751; 9 24; 10 264, 265; 11 164; 16 884; 27 197, 357; 30 503; 31 130; 33 3
    architectural 28 894
    monuments 10 265; 11 163; 19 599, 606; 20 389; 31 115, 130
    relief 8 83
  silver 10 334; 27 336; 29 723
  surveys 23 22
  teachers 10 372
Flé, G. 31 889
fleaseed 24 55
Fleason, Plunkett 24 602
Flecha, Giuseppe see FRECHA, JOSÉ
Flecha, José see FRECHA, JOSÉ
Flechtheim, Alfred 11 165*; 12 474; 13 698
Fleck, Marian 33 386
Fledborough (Notts), St Gregory 9 680, 681
Fleece Press 25 628
Fleecy Clouds, Master of the 20 662
Fleeming, Clementina Elphinstone see HAWARDEN, CLEMENTINA, Viscountess
Fleetwood Pier 24 748
Fleetwood-Walker, Bernard 4 87
Flegel, Friedrich 11 165
Flegel, Georg 11 165*
  collaboration 31 804
  pupils 12 389; 20 406
  works 11 227; 12 389; 29 666
Flegel, Jacob 11 165
Flegenheimer, Julien 12 276; 19 43; 22 732
Fleischaker & Baum see EFFANBEE
Fleischer, Karl Christoph 5 30
Fleischmann 22 304
Fleischmann, Anneliese see ALBERS, ANNI
Fleischmann, Richard 8 414
Fleischmann & Bloedel 31 261
Flémal, Bertholet 9 198; 11 166*; 19 344
  pupils 5 766
  works 3 559; 11 166
Flémal, Renier 11 166
Flémalle, Henri de 3 600; 14 392
Flémalle, Master of 5 549; 8 524; 20 666–72*, 730
  attributions 3 581; 20 614; 26 568
  commentaries 31 94
  methods 19 354; 20 671–2; 24 5
  patrons and collectors 28 377
  pupils 33 117, 119
  reproductive prints by others 20 622
  works 2 3; 3 553; 11 438; 13 674; 20 667, 668, 670; 29 665; 30 165, 166; 31 154
Fleming, Erik, Baron 4 480; 30 108, 113
Fleming, Francis 3 82
Fleming, Hans 11 166–7*; 30 84
Fleming, Herman 11 90
Fleming, Ian 28 239
Fleming, Isabella see CZARTORYSKA, ISABELLA, Princess
Fleming, Richard, Bishop of Lincoln 23 686
Fleming, William 10 330
Flemingia grahamiana see WARS
Flemish bond see under BONDING
Flemish Caravaggisti 26 746
  works 26 746
Flemish Primitives see EARLY NETHERLANDISH STYLE
Flemish stretcher bond see under BONDING
Flemister, Frederick 1 443; 33 370
Flemming, Robert 11 167*; 32 384
Flenoy, Mary E. 33 308
Flensborg Kobbermølle 8 751
Flensburg Court of Appeal 11 798
Flers, Camille 5 343; 7 434; 9 423; 11 167*
Fles, Moritz S. 29 721
Fleschi, Giacomo 11 897
Fleschi, Matteo 11 897
flesh puppets see under PUPPETS → types
Fleskum 23 225; 28 826
Fletcher, Banister (1833–99) 11 167, 168
Fletcher, Banister (Flight) (1866–1953) 11 167–8*
Fletcher, Benjamin 15 823; 33 157
Fletcher, Edward Taylor 5 560
Fletcher, Herbert Phillips 11 167
Fletcher, Isaac D. 12 615
Fletcher, Jean 30 226, 227
Fletcher, Norman Collings 30 226, 227
Fletcher, Thomas 31 650
Flettner, Peter see FLÖTNER, PETER
Fletton (Cambs), St Margaret 2 70
Fleurance 4 780
Fleuri, Geoffroi de 31 478
fleurons 11 168*; 17 519
Fleury (France) 20 330
  Saint-Benoît-de-Fleury see SAINT-BENOÎT-SUR-LOIRE ABBEY
Fleury (1821–89) see CHAMPFLEURY
Fleury, Charles Rohault de see ROHAULT DE FLEURY, CHARLES
Fleury, Georges Rohault de see ROHAULT DE FLEURY, GEORGES
Fleury, Hubert Rohault de see ROHAULT DE FLEURY, HUBERT
Flexible, Den 7 805
flexographic printing see under PRINTING → processes
Flexor, Samson 4 719
Flicke, Gerlach 11 168*; 19 793
Fliegende Blätter 4 39
Flight, Barr & Barr 6 408; 10 310; 14 147; 33 378
Flight, Claude 4 107; 19 430; 25 624
Flight, Thomas 6 408; 33 377
Flight & Barr 10 309; 33 378
flijs see under CARPETS → types
Flinck, Govaert 11 168, 169–70*
  attributions 31 341
  patrons and collectors 13 266; 14 650; 22 901
  teachers 16 833; 22 843; 26 163, 167
  works 1 813; 4 250; 11 169, 170; 22 843; 23 675
Flinck, Nicolaes Anthonis 6 116; 11 169, 170–71*
  collections 33 79
  drawings 9 230; 26 167
Flinders, Matthew 2 743; 33 95
Flindt, Paul, I (fl 1567–82) 11 171
Flindt, Paul, II (c. 1567–1631) 11 171*; 23 310; 25 731
Flines, Jacob de 12 801; 18 652
Flin-Flon Provincial Center 14 521
Flint (Clwyd) 31 711; 32 780
  Castle 16 894
flint 6 324; 29 699*
  historical and regional traditions
    Denmark 25 515, 516
    Egypt, ancient 9 775, 816, 865
    England 10 227
    Indian subcontinent 15 192
    Iran, ancient 15 902–3
    Islamic 16 420
    Mesoamerica, Pre-Columbian 21 259
    Ottoman 16 420
    Prehistoric art 8 283; 15 902–3; 25 472, 493, 515, 516
    Romanesque 10 227
    Rome, ancient 26 874
  uses
    abrasives 16 859
    architecture 26 874
    blades 8 283
    ceramics 6 330
    daggers 25 516
    enamel 10 192
    masonry 20 570, 571
    porcelain 6 325; 29 699
    pottery 16 420
    Ransome's Stone 29 699
    tools 15 192; 25 472, 493, 515
  see also CHERT
Flint, William Russell 7 576; 11 171*
flintlocks see under GUNS → types
Flintoe, Johannes 9 702; 13 776; 14 483; 23 231
Flintridge China Co. 31 639
Flipart, Charles-François 11 171
Flipart, Charles-Joseph 11 171, 172*
  collaboration 1 785
  patrons and collectors 4 561
  teachers 1 784
  works 20 70
Flipart, François 5 884
Flipart, Jean-Charles 11 171
Flipart, Jean-Jacques 5 884; 11 171–2*; 13 642; 32 428
Flitcroft, Henry 11 172–3*
  architecture 11 427; 19 570; 29 733
    assembly rooms 2 618
    country houses 8 47; 13 645
    garden buildings 2 541; 14 598; 27 237; 29 734, 734
  assistants 11 428
  attributions 25 726
  collaboration 4 805
  groups and movements 23 858
  patrons and collectors 4 893
float glass see under GLASS → types
floating bridges see under BRIDGES → types
floats 23 768–9
float stitch see under STITCHES
Floccon 24 491
Floch, Guillaume 11 616
Floch, Joseph 32 447
Flockhart, William 1 163; 14 538; 20 34
Flockinger, Gerda 10 346; 17 530
flock prints see under PRINTS → types
flock wallpaper see under WALLPAPER → types
Flocon, Albert 3 18
Floda Church 20 866; 29 840; 30 85
Flodin, Hilda 11 100
Floding, Per Gustaf 2 239–40; 11 173–4*; 24 137
  pupils 28 461
  teachers 26 98
  works 30 78
Flodingska Gravyrskola 11 174
Floetner, Peter see FLÖTNER, PETER
floor decorations 15 174, 178, 726
floor frames see under TIMBER STRUCTURES → types
floor paintings see under PAINTING → forms
floors
  historical and regional traditions
    Belgium 3 575, 577, 578
    England 10 270, 273, 275–6, 279
    Germany 12 409, 413
    Greece, ancient 13 556–7, 560–61, 566–7*
    Indian subcontinent 15 393
    Islamic 16 250
    Italy 27 61–2
    Japan 17 47*, 53
    Prehistoric art 25 487, 502
    Romanesque 26 680
    Rome, ancient 26 877; 27 59–65*
  materials
    brick 3 575
    clay 25 502
    oak 3 577; 10 273
    pebbles 13 556
    plaster 13 556
    stone 3 575, 577, 578
    tiles 3 575, 577; 16 250; 26 877; 29 75; 30 874, 876
    varnishes 32 2
    wood 3 578
  techniques
    engraving 25 476
    parquetry 3 578; 20 467
  types
    caves 25 487
    chip 13 565
    terrazzi 30 515*
    tessellated 29 75
Floors Castle (Borders) 18 585; 29 7
Floquet, Lucas 2 198
Flora, Master of 1 19; 11 266; 20 672–4*
  works 1 17
Flora, Paul 2 797
Flora Ann Pottery 29 117
Floral Bone China 29 117
floral marquetry see under MARQUETRY → types
Floral style mosaics see under GREECE, ANCIENT; ROME, ANCIENT → mosaics
Floral style pottery see under POTTERY → wares
Flore, Maître de see FLORA, MASTER OF
Floréal see under BRUSSELS
Floreffe Abbey 20 331; 26 146, 666, 667; 30 907
Floreffe Bible see under BIBLES → individual manuscripts
Floreins, Jan 21 102
Florence 11 174–217*, 178; 16 616, 618, 620; 26 183–4
  academies 11 215*
    Accademia di Bandinelli 16 778, 779
    Accademia di Belle Arti 16 774, 779; 24 25
      collections 31 764
      Galleria dell'Accademia 25 74
      gallery 16 774
    Accademia Columbaria 13 10
    Accademia e Compagnia del Disegno see Accademia del Disegno
    Accademia del Disegno 1 102; 2 523; 11 215–17*; 16 664, 778–9; 24 91; 27 747
      collections 11 845
      exhibitions 10 676
      members 4 408; 6 87; 12 308; 21 19; 22 448; 24 733; 30 851; 31 55
    Medici Academy 1 102; 11 217*; 16 778
    Platonic Academy 14 868; 21 10
  art forms and materials
    altarpieces 11 183–4*; 25 183
    architecture 16 628, 634*
    busts 5 300
    cassoni 6 1–4*, 1, 2, 3, 6, 7
    chandeliers 6 443
    coats of arms 14 410
    coins 7 535, 536, 536, 537; 14 419
    coral 16 750
    crucifixes 16 655
    drawings 3 765
    embroidery 10 181; 13 195; 16 759
    engravings 10 383
    façade decoration 10 737, 739, 740, 741
    flags 11 150
    frames 11 382, 386, 387, 390, 390, 397, 397
    furniture 16 723, 724, 727, 729, 730
    glass 16 740
    gold 16 741, 742
    hardstones 11 192*; 12 462; 14 171; 16 746, 747; 24 779; 29 315
    jewellery 16 751, 752; 17 526
    ketubbot 18 3
    lacquer 18 614
    maiolica 16 732, 733, 733
    manuscripts 4 372; 11 186; 13 823; 16 655; 20 331, 333; 31 49
    marks 20 441
    medals 20 919
    models 2 336
    mosaics 11 192
    musical instruments 22 372
    objects of vertu 11 191–2*
    painting 9 14; 11 183–4; 18 704–5; 29 301; 31 142
      Baroque 16 669, 673–4
      frescoes 11 185
      Mannerism 16 664*
      Renaissance 16 657, 660, 661–2*, 663*
      still-lifes 29 668
      16th cent. 9 7

Florence
art forms and materials—cont.
porcelain **4** 176; **6** 923; **7** 165; **11** 191*; **16** 736, *736*
prints **25** 614, 625
rock crystal **26** 486
scagliola **28** 28
sculpture **11** 192; **12** 111; **13** 93; **16** 689–91*, 694–6*, 699–700*; **26** 624; **30** 497*
relief **11** *184*
silk **11** *193*; **13** 197; **16** 752, 753; **28** 716
statuettes **29** 568–9, 572
tapestries **11** 192–4*, *193*; **16** 756, *757*; **30** 319, *319*
terracotta **30** 497*
threads **11** *193*
velvet **16** 714
woodcuts **33** 350, 351
wool **11** *193*
wrought iron **16** 743
Bargello *see* museums → Museo Nazionale del Bargello
Berta Municipal Stadium **29** 489
Bigallo **11** 891
Boboli Gardens **7** 332; **11** *214*, 214–15*; **12** 115, 117
fountains **16** 696
Grotticina di Madama **13** 703
Grotto Grande **13** 703
Ocean Fountain **7** 672; **12** 569
sculpture **5** 360; **6** 144, 149; **25** 76; **27** 203, *203*
botanic garden **4** 483
building regulations **5** 135
Carcere delle Stinche *see under* museums → Palazzo Vecchio
Casa Buonarroti *see under* museums
Casa Vasari **1** 662; **2** 550
frescoes **32** *16*
Casa Vecchia **11** 384
Casino di S Marco **8** 275; **21** 25; **27** 178
Casino Mediceo **12** 569
Castello di Sammezzano **16** 720
catalogues **6** 77
chronicles **7** 243
collections **4** 408
Collezione della Ragione **11** 191
display of art **9** 18
ecclesiastical buildings **11** 195*
Badia Fiorentina **2** 484
Chiostro degli Aranci **12** 710–11, *711*
painting **19** *448*
sculpture **26** 624
tomb of Count Ugo of Tuscany **16** 691
Baptistery **3** 192; **5** 26; **7** 256; **11** 198–9*, *199*; **16** 625; **23** 485; **26** 182, 576
altar **13** 168; **16** 741, *741*
Coscia monument **21** 467
crosses **8** 201
crucifix **13** 124
doors **11** 199–200*
Gates of Paradise **9** 156; **12** *540*, 540–41*, *541*; **14** 870; **26** 136, 183
monument to anti-Pope John XXIII **16** 690
mosaics **11** 199*; **20** 720; **22** 163, 165
North doors **7** 664, 671; **9** 156; **12** 537–8*, *538*; **16** 689, 690; **24** 90; **26** 183
polychromy **25** 171
sculpture **13** 93; **16** 689; **32** 362–3
South doors **9** 154, 158; **11** *200*; **13** 93; **16** 688, 743; **24** *874*, 874–5; **26** 136
vestments (ecclesiastical) **16** 759, *759*
Brancacci Chapel *see under* S Maria del Carmine

Florence
ecclesiastical buildings—cont.
Campanile **11** 200*; **13** 65, 133
reliefs **1** 654
sculpture **11** 200–201*, *201*; **16** 689, 691; **22** 411; **24** 875
Cathedral of S Maria del Fiore **2** 480, 482, 484; **11** 195–6*, *196*, 198*, 201–2*; **13** 53, 63, 65; **16** 627, 646; **20** 263; **30** 272; **31** 513, 710
Cantoria **16** 690; **26** 442–3, *443*
dome **2** 336; **5** *15*, 15–16; **7** 664, 692; **9** 82, 84, 85, 86; **16** 628, 629; **20** 579; **26** 183; **32** 88
doors **9** 157, 159
exedrae **5** 21, *21*
frescoes **16** 659; **26** 184; **28** 490; **31** *513*
furniture **16** 724
lantern **5** 20–21, *21*
manuscripts **26** 666
metalwork **13** 163
monument to Filippo Brunelleschi **5** *128*
monument to Niccolò da Tolentino **6** *13*; **13** 676; **29** 565
monument to Sir John Hawkwood **13** 676; **22** 44; **29** 565
nave **13** *66*
north sacristy **20** 111
painting **11** 197–8*
polychromy **25** 171
Porta della Mandorla **12** 701; **13** 94
sculpture **2** *482*; **3** *159*; **10** 743; **11** 197*; **13** 93; **16** 689, 774; **18** 673; **19** 753; **22** 44; **26** 187; **27** *769*; **30** 497
shrine of St Zenobius **7** 671; **12** 542; **27** 830
stained glass **11** 198*; **29** 504
textiles **10** 182
tomb of Antonio d'Orso **31** 4
Cestello *see* S Maria Maddalena dei Pazzi
Church of the Scalzi **7** 457; **13** 676
Convento delle Oblate **8** 212
Misericordia **26** 187
Monastery of S Marco **2** 34–7*; **9** 112; **21** 10, 467–8, *468*
altarpiece **1** 711; **2** 35; **27** 495, 496
chapter house **6** 466
cloister of S Antonino **7** 457
cloister of S Domenico **7** 458
crucifix **8** 216
education (art) **16** 777
frescoes **2** 35–7*, *36*, *37*; **7** 218; **16** 659; **26** 184; **28** 490; **32** *809*
library **14** 867; **19** 313; **32** 384
paintings **16** 664
screen **28** 293
see also museums → Museo di S Marco
Ognissanti **23** 140
altarpiece **1** 708; **12** *689*
frescoes **28** 490
paintings **12** 690
refectory **21** 846
Orsanmichele **11** *202*, 202–4*; **26** 186; **30** 273
capitals **1** 110
crucifix **13** 124
paintings **15** 85
railings **16** 743
reliefs **11** *184*
sculpture **3** 173; **9** 123–4; **12** 538–9, *539*, 541–2; **13** 94, 824; **16** 689, 694; **22** 44, *461*; **26** 183; **32** *360*, 360–61
stained glass **13** 192

Florence
ecclesiastical buildings
Orsanmichele—cont.
tabernacle **7** 334, *334*; **13** 65
Pazzi Chapel *see under* Santa Croce
Peruzzi Chapel *see under* Santa Croce
S Agata **25** 690
S Ambrogio
altarpiece **20** 530–31
Cappella del Miracolo **27** 175, *175*
frescoes **9** *263*, 263
SS Annunziata **1** 696; **7** 257; **11** 204–5*; **21** 469, *470*; **28** 489, 490
cartoons (drawings) **10** 675
Chapel of S Barbara **28** 490
Corboli Chapel **6** *13*
crucifix **8** 216
exhibitions **10** 676
ex-votos **16** 749
frescoes **9** 264; **16** 674; **25** 222; **27** *846*, 847–8; **28** 489, *489*, 490; **32** *805*
rock crystal **16** 745
tomb of Mario Nari **1** 790
S Apollonia **26** 184
Cenacolo **16** 659, 660
frescoes **5** 443; **6** 12; **15** 135; **26** *184*
refectory **21** 846
SS Apostoli
paintings **27** *732*; **32** *12*
Scalzo *see* Church of the Scalzi
Santa Croce **2** 484; **11** *205*, 205–6*, 711; **13** 63, 65; **16** 627, 646; **20** 641; **21** 468; **25** 172; **30** 501
altarpieces **1** 712; **16** 664; **25** 463; **31** 532–4, *533*
Bardi Chapel **3** 173, 919; **11** 708, 709, *709*, 712; **12** *691*; **16** 837; **20** *551*, 551–2
Baroncelli Chapel **11** 888, *889*; **13** 673; **19** 354; **29** 665
cemetery of the cloisters **16** 706
choir **11** *891*, 892
crucifix **8** 211, 215
frescoes **5** 443; **11** 709; **12** 690; **13** 135; **21** *845*; **25** 379
monument to Galileo Galilei **31** 129
mouldings **22** 221
paintings **7** 316–17
Pazzi Chapel **5** *18*, 18–19, *19*, *20*; **6** 465; **7** 257; **11** 388; **16** 628; **21** 842; **23** 486; **24** 299; **30** 501
Pazzi Chapel: coffers **7** 527
Pazzi Chapel: dome **9** 86
Pazzi Chapel: polychromy **25** 171
Pazzi Chapel: sculpture **26** *444*; **30** 497
Peruzzi Chapel **3** 173; **11** 712; **12** *692*; **32** 805
pulpit **20** *114*; **25** 724
refectory **11** *890*; **21** 845
reliefs **26** 137
Rinuccini altarpiece *see* RINUCCINI ALTARPIECE
rock crystal **16** 745
screen **28** 293
sculpture **30** 497
stained glass **13** 132, 192
tomb of Carlo Marsuppini **8** *797*, 797–8; **16** 690; **27** 830
tomb of Countess Sophia Zamoyska **16** 706, *706*
tomb of Gastone della Torre **31** *3*, 3–4
tomb of Leonardo Bruni **8** 797–8; **16** 690; **27** *180*, 180–81, 830
tomb of Pietro Mellini **20** 114

Florence
ecclesiastical buildings
Santa Croce—cont.
tomb of Vittorio Alfieri **16** 705
S Egidio **24** 492; **30** 497
S Felicita
Annunziata Chapel **23** 486
Barbadori Chapel **5** 16
Capponi Chapel **7** 628; **16** 663; **25** 223, *223*
frescoes **28** 490
S Filippo Neri **16** 646
S Gaetano **7** 704
S Giovanni della Calza **21** 846
S Lorenzo **1** 110; **5** 17–18; **7** 254; **9** 86; **11** 174, 206–8*, *207*; **20** 278; **23** 486; **26** 183, 187; **32** 94
Biblioteca Laurenziana **1** 164; **2** 336, 596; **16** 634, 724; **19** 313, *314*; **20** 278; **21** 12, 451*, *452*; **29** 523; **30** *357*
Chapel of the Princes **11** 191–2; **16** 641; **23** 140
façade **21** 451*
manuscripts **11** 295
model **2** 336
New Sacristy **5** *17*; **7** 527; **16** 634, 695; **20** 865; **21** 438–9*, 451*; **23** 488; **26** 187
Old Sacristy **1** 164; **5** *17*; **9** 126–7, 156; **11** 206; **16** 628, 691, 694; **26** 183
paintings **15** 135
pilasters **24** 805
pulpits **18** 677; **25** 724, *725*; **26** 136
reliquaries **26** 148
sculpture **22** *32*; **32** 361
tabernacle **8** 799
tomb of Giovanni di Bicci de' Medici and his wife Piccarda **27** 830
tomb of Giuliano de' Medici, Duc de Nemours **27** 830
tomb of Lorenzo de' Medici, Duke of Urbino **21** *438*; **27** 830
tomb of Piero I de' Medici and Giovanni de' Medici **1** 110; **6** 458; **27** 830; **32** *361*
tombs **14** 870; **25** 283
S Lucia dei Magnoli
paintings **16** *846*
S Marco **28** *735*
S Maria degli Angeli **5** 449, 450; **16** 628
altarpieces **5** 450; **19** 681
frescoes **5** 450, 451; **12** *528*
Scolari Oratory **5** *18*, 19–20; **7** 257
S Maria del Carmine **14** 870
altarpiece **5** 778
Brancacci Chapel **2** 339; **4** 658; **5** *778*, 778; **7** 627; **11** *185*; **16** 837; **19** 446; **20** *534*, 534–5, 553, 554–6, *555*; **22** 521; **26** 183
Corsini Chapel **11** *235*; **16** 674, 700
education (art) **16** 777
frescoes **5** 778; **16** 659; **20** 530
S Maria Maddalena dei Pazzi **27** 734–5, *735*
altarpiece **31** *54*, *55*
S Maria Maggiore
altarpieces **13** 124; **25** 462
Carnesecci Chapel **20** 531
paintings **7** 817
woodwork **16** 725
S Maria Novella **1** 562–3; **7** 254; **9** 111; **11** 208–9*, *209*; **13** 52; **16** 627, 629; **21** 842; **26** 186; **29** 782; **30** 272–3
altarpieces **1** 712; **16** 664
Cappella Maggiore **16** 763; **25** 379
Chiostro Grande **7** 457

Florence
ecclesiastical buildings
S Maria Novella—cont.
Chiostro Verde **7** 453, 457; **26** 184; **31** *514*, 514
crucifix **8** 215, *215*; **12** *694*
frescoes **8** 212; **9** 264; **15** 85; **16** 659; **24** 487; **26** 187; **28** 490; **29** 360, *360*; **32** 805
Gaddi chapel **9** 182; **11** 893
Gondi Chapel **27** 737
paintings **9** 111
pulpit **7** 267
screen **28** 293
Spanish Chapel **1** 654; **2** 15–16, *16*; **6** 466; **9** 108; **15** 85
spire **29** 414
stained glass **13** 192, 193
Strozzi altarpiece *see* STROZZI ALTARPIECE
Strozzi Chapel **7** *333*; **16** 659; **19** 450, *450*, 451; **20** 279
Tornabuoni chapel **12** 551; **31** 173
Trinity fresco **7** 527; **11** 381; **15** 135; **20** *533*, 533–4; **21** 763; **26** 183
S Maria Nuova *see* hospitals → Arcispedale di S Maria Nuova
S Miniato al Monte Abbey Church **1** 723; **2** 348; **4** 774; **8** 836; **11** 209–11*, *210*; **16** 625; **23** 485; **26** 182, 576, 579
arches **2** 294
chapel of the Cardinal of Portugal **11** *186*; **16** 659, 691; **27** 183, *184*; **30** 497
crypt **8** 224
mosaics **22** 165
paintings **16** *839*
polychromy **25** 171
pulpit **26** 624
roof **30** 905
sculpture **26** 624
S Pancrazio **28** 490
Rucellai Chapel **1** *563*, 563–4
S Paolo dei Convalescenti
relief sculpture **26** *446*
S Pietro Martire **2** 31–2
S Salvatore al Monte **8** 187–8, *188*; **16** 635
S Salvi **27** *850*
paintings **32** 364, *364*
Santo Spirito **5** 20, 22, 360; **7** 254; **16** 628; **26** 183, *183*; **27** 655–6, 734; **32** 94
chapels **5** *17*
Corbinelli Altar **16** 694
paintings **19** 448–9, *449*
sculpture **5** *361*
stained glass **13** 193
tomb of Neri Capponi **27** 830
Santa Trìnita **24** 867
altarpiece **1** 708
Bartolini Salimbeni Chapel **19** *681*, 681–2
frescoes **11** 712; **16** 659, 763, *763*; **31** 124
paintings **7** 316; **13** 146
Sassetti Chapel **11** 384; **12** *552*; **16** *660*
tomb of Francesco Sassetti **27** 830
tomb of Nera Corsi **27** 830
tomb of Onofrio Strozzi **27** 830
education (art) **16** 778
English Cemetery **16** 706
festivals **23** 766
Forte di Belvedere **3** 689
Fortezza da Basso **3** 359; **21** 566
Fortezza di S Maria Belvedere *see* Forte di Belvedere
Galleria Corsini *see under* palazzi → Palazzo Corsini
Grand Ducal workshops, tapestry factory *see* ARAZZERIA MEDICEA

Florence—cont.
grottoes **13** 703
guidebooks **1** 572; **21** 496
Harvard University Centre of Humanistic Studies **3** 765
hospitals
Arcispedale di S Maria Nuova **5** 450; **14** 781; **16** 779; **30** 497
Ospedale di S Martino alla Scala **4** 494
Spedale degli Innocenti **2** 290; **5** 16; **14** 781, 784; **16** 143; **26** 183; **30** 501; **32** 94
Loggia **16** 628; **23** 485
reliefs **30** *501*
Women's Cloister **23** 486
humanism **14** 867
Institute for Etruscan Studies **10** 638
Istituto Nazionale di Studi sul Rinascimento **7** 782; **27** 635
kilns **4** 774
libraries
Biblioteca Laurenziana *see under* ecclesiastical buildings → S Lorenzo
Biblioteca Marucelliana **16** 776
prints **16** 777
Biblioteca Nazionale Centrale **16** 648
collections **16** 777
Biblioteca Riccardiana *see under* palazzi → Palazzo Medici-Riccardi
Kunsthistorisches Institut **2** 366, 370; **16** 777
Loggia dei Lanzi **13** 65; **22** 44
sculpture **6** 139, 144, *145*; **12** 570–71, *571*, 573; **16** 695
Loggia della Signoria **19** 673, 752
Mercato Vecchio **11** *180*
monument to Ferdinand I **10** 441
museums
Casa Buonarroti **2** 552; **8** 275
directors **31** 94
drawings **21** 453, 455
frescoes **6** 126; **32** 499
paintings **1** 672; **4** 53; **5** 179; **7** 492, 702; **10** 189; **12** 706; **27** 178; **32** 499
sculpture **8** 215; **21** 432, 433
Galleria dell'Accademia *see under* academies → Accademia di Belle Arte
Galleria Antica e Moderna *see* academies → Accademia di Belle Arte → Galleria dell'Accademia
Jewish museum **17** 582
Museo Archeologico di Firenze
collections **2** 22; **10** 91, 94, 639, 640; **16** 774; **27** 46
Museo Topografico dell'Etruria **10** 638
Museo degli Argenti *see under* Palazzo Pitti
Museo Bardini **3** 228
Museo del Bigallo **11** 176
Museo di Firenze com'era *see* ecclesiastical buildings → Convento delle Oblate
Museo della Fotografie Fratelli Alinari
Alinari photograph collection **2** 367, 370; **16** 777
Giacomo Brogi photograph collection **16** 777
James Anderson photograph collection **16** 777
Museo Horne **7** 297; **8** 188; **14** 764; **29** 380
Museo Nazionale del Bargello **23** 835; **31** 236
collections **5** 871; **6** 11; **13** 128; **16** 774; **28** 393
directors **30** 4
Museo dell'Opera del Duomo **16** 774

Florence
museums—cont.
Museo di S Marco **5** 791
see also ecclesiastical buildings → Monastery of S Marco
Museo della Specola *see* Museo Zoologico 'La Specola'
Museo Stibbert **16** 774
Museo di Storia della Scienza **16** 775
Museo Topografico dell'Etruria *see under* Museo Archeologico di Firenze
Museo Zoologico 'La Specola' **8** 19; **16** 749; **33** 3
Palazzo Pitti **1** 792; **7** 912; **9** 17; **11** 192, 212*, 213*, *213*; **16** 634; **20** 280; **21** 26; **23** 836; **24** 404, 895; **25** 60
amber **1** 762
bathroom **29** 833
Boboli Gardens *see* Boboli Gardens
cameos **27** 197
collections **4** 404, 813; **9** 142; **11** 51; **12** 591; **20** 97; **22** 357, 529; **24** 299; **25** 59; **26** 397
coral **7** 835
display **9** 14, 15, 19, 27
frames **11** 397
furniture **11** 192; **16** 729
hardstones **31** 851
interior decoration **7** 908–10; **11** 213–14*; **16** 713, 714, 719
Museo degli Argenti **11** 846; **12** 257, 258, 265; **14** 169, 171; **16** 742; **21** 725
paintings (allegorical) **1** 659; **8** 464; **12** 355; **32** 14
paintings (battle) **27** 150, 292, 296
paintings (cabinet pictures) **3** 42
paintings (ceiling) **26** 323
paintings (frescoes) **1** 659; **6** 126; **12** 707; **15** 138; **16** 673, 674; **21** 26, 30; **26** 321; **27** 150, 479
paintings (history) **14** 267; **30** 40
paintings (landscape) **23** 850; **25** 66; **27** 150; **28** 705, 706
paintings (portraits) **5** 920; **6** 111; **7** 863; **8** 186; **9** 478; **25** 271; **30** 40, 41, 42
paintings (religious) **4** 53; **5** 713; **8** 142; **10** 159, 446, 811; **11** 389, 873; **12** 713; **20** 586; **25** 905; **28** 433; **30** 41; **32** 11
paintings (still-lifes) **3** 690
paintings (*vedute*) **33** 269
Palazzina della Meridiana **3** 904; **16** 646
Sala della Stufa **5** 179; **7** 908, 911; **16** 673; **27** 178
Sala delle Allegorie **11** 679
Sala di Apollo **7** 910; **11** 22–3
Sala di Bona **19** *511*
Sala di Giove **7** *908*, 910; **21** 732
Sala di Marte **7** 910; **16** *713*
Sala di Saturno **7** 910; **11** 23
Sala di Venere **7** 910
Sala Terrena *see* Museo degli Argenti
sculpture **5** 454; **6** 146; **9** 403, 404; **11** 234; **16** 705; **22** 414; **24** 316, 697; **29** 683
silver **4** 62
Stanza del Pranzo **16** 719
stucco **29** 830
tapestries **9** 30; **29** 424
Palazzo Vecchio **11** 211–12*, *212*; **13** 63; **16** 627; **20** 572; **21** 21, 22; **22** 799; **23** 809; **30** 357; **31** 236, 237, 851; **32** 14
altarpiece **19** 446

Florence
museums
Palazzo Vecchio—cont.
Camera Verde **12** 557
Cappella di Eleonora **4** 856
Carcere delle Stinche **7** 333
collections **16** 763; **19** 538
frescoes **4** 494; **5** 697; **21** *11*; **28** 928
Guardaroba **8** 513; **20** 365; **22** 357
Guardaroba Secreta **9** 28
Hall of the Mercanzia **4** 493
interior decoration **1** 657; **3** 15; **16** 712; **28** 928
machicolation **19** 895
paintings **3** 14; **15** 87; **32** *14*
Quartiere degli Elementi **12** 527; **32** 14
Quartiere di Eleonora di Toledo **29** 741
Quartiere di Leone X **32** 14
Ricetto **27** 480
Sala dei Cinquecento **3** 15, 159, 743; **4** 408; **7** 676; **8** 187; **14** 583; **16** 663; **19** 184, 374; **21** *20*, 21; **31** 237; **32** 14
Sala dei Cinquecento: sculpture **5** 360
Sala dei Gigli **4** 494; **12** 551; **16** 659
Sala dei Settanta **24** 522
Sala del Dugento **3** 15; **7** 560; **27** 650
Sala del Gran Consiglio *see* Sala dei Cinquecento
Sala dell'Orologio *see* Sala dei Gigli
Sala dell'Udienza **9** 148; **16** 724; **27** 203, 650, *651*
Sala del Maggior Consiglio *see* Sala dei Cinquecento
Sala del Mappamondo **16** 771
Sala di Clemente VII **3** 387
Sala di Cosimo il Vecchio **21** 12
Sala di Gualdrada **11** 193
Scrittoio di Calliope **21** 21
sculpture **3** 156; **12** 571; **16** *694*, 774; **32** 367
staircases **29** 523
Studiolo **21** 22; **25** 76; **29** 860–61, *861*; **32** *17*
Studiolo: collections **5** 317; **16** 770
Studiolo: frescoes **15** 828; **25** 241; **29** *741*
Studiolo: interior decoration **1** 670, *670*; **4** 409; **6** 112; **7** 815; **8** 512; **9** 14; **10** 858; **16** 664, 712; **19** 872; **22** 447, *448*; **25** 262; **27** 732; **29** 741; **32** 16
Studiolo: paintings **31** 54
Studiolo: sculpture **3** 161, *162*; **9** 21; **19** 673
tapestries **11** 192, *193*
tiles **30** 886
woodwork **16** 724
Uffizi **1** 671; **2** 365; **5** 629; **8** 19; **9** 403; **11** 215*; **13** 236; **16** 634, 771; **20** 278; **21** 21, 23; **22** 739; **23** 359; **31** 236, 268; **32** 14, *15*
Alberti archive **1** 550
artists' portraits **18** 470
catalogues **3** 701; **18** 755
collections **3** 701; **7** 782; **10** 637, 638; **16** 771, 772, 774; **22** 355, 356, 357; **25** 74; **26** 364
courtyard **11** *180*
directors **25** 690–91; **26** 364
drawings **3** 904; **4** 54; **5** 846, 866; **7** 903; **8** 497; **9** 230; **10** 190, 726; **12** 506; **20** 96; **21** 28; **24** 529; **29** 410; **31** 269, 764; **32** 22
engravings **16** 777

Florence
museums
Uffizi—cont.
frames **11** 392
Gabinetto Disegni e Stampe **22** 113
Galleria della Statue **9** 11
hanging **9** 17, 18
interior decoration **5** 317
paintings **1** 730; **5** 920; **9** 15; **21** 28; **26** 386, 420
prints **25** 631
Sala delle Niobi **1** 574
sculpture **2** 169; **5** 626; **9** 23; **27** 46
Teatro Mediceo **30** 656, 657
Tribuna **9** 12, 14–15, *15*, 21, 28; **13** 303; **20** 90; **23** 352; **24** 25
weapons **9** 31
Ospedale di S Maria Nuova *see* hospitals → Arcispedale di S Maria Nuova
palazzi **16** 629
Palazzo Almeni **10** 737, 738
Palazzo Altoviti **5** 361
Palazzo dell'Antella **10** *736*, 737; **12** 706
Palazzo Baldovinetti **23** 835
Palazzo Barberini **16** *764*
Palazzo Bardi **23** 835
Palazzo Bargello *see* museums → Museo Nazionale del Bargello
Palazzo Bartolini Salimbeni **3** 16, *16*
Palazzo Borgherini *see* Palazzo Rosselli del Turco
Palazzo dal Borgo **10** 738
Palazzo Capponi **16** 713; **25** 59, 890
Palazzo Corsi *see* museums → Museo Horne
Palazzo Corsini **16** 713
chapel **20** 377
frescoes **16** 674
Galleria Corsini **8** 498; **9** 19; **11** 81, 697; **19** 35; **20** 374; **30** 42
library **24** 212
Palazzo Davanzati **13** 281
Palazzo Ducale *see* museums → Palazzo Vecchio
Palazzo Fenzi **28** 733
Palazzo Gerini **11** 873
Palazzo Giraldi-Taddei **25** 890
Palazzo Gondi **16** 629; **27** 735
Palazzo Guadagni **2** 295
Palazzo Incontri **11** 874
Palazzo Marucelli **16** 674; **26** 321
Palazzo Medici *see* Palazzo Medici-Riccardi
Palazzo Medici-Riccardi **3** 173, 174; **9** 21; **20** 552, 572; **21** 468, *469*; **23** 809, 835, *836*; **26** 242
Biblioteca Riccardiana **11** 391
Chapel **13** 260; **16** 629; **21** 12–13; **26** 186
courtyard **8** 65
façade **16** 629
frescoes **15** 138; **16** 659, 674
Galleria Riccardiana **12** 662; **22** 414
interior decoration **16** 629
paintings **16** 660; **31** 514–15
reliefs **3** 860
Sala Grande **24** 538; **25** 158, 160
scrittoio **29** 859
sculpture **9** 21; **11** 29; **16** 770; **21** 10, 17
stables **29** 485
staircases **29** 521
statuettes **3** 860
Studiolo **16** 770; **18** 521; **26** 444
study **16** 711; **21** 12
tapestries **32** 500

Florence
palazzi—cont.
Palazzo Niccolini **3** 161; **31** 268
Palazzo Nonfinito **1** 670; **19** 672; **27** 648
Palazzo dell'Opera di S Giovanni **27** 184
Palazzo Pandolfini **23** 836
Palazzo di Parte Guelfa **5** 19; **16** 711; **29** 550
Palazzo Pazzi-Quaratesi **16** 629
Palazzo Pitti *see under* museums
Palazzo del Podestà *see* museums → Museo Nazionale del Bargello
Palazzo dei Priori *see* museums → Palazzo Vecchio
Palazzo del Proconsolo **6** 11
Palazzo Rosselli del Turco **4** 404; **16** 711
Palazzo Rucellai **1** 562, *562*; **16** 629; **23** 486, 539, 836; **24** 804; **27** 182; **31** 150; **33** 246
Palazzo Sabatier **23** 633
Palazzo Salviati *see* Palazzo Nonfinito
Palazzo della Signoria *see* museums → Palazzo Vecchio
Palazzo Strozzi **4** 776; **8** 187; **16** 629, *629*; **23** 809; **28** *733*, 733–4
collections **30** 656
Palazzo Strozzino **20** 111–12
Palazzo Taddei **30** 231
Palazzo degli Uffizi *see* museums → Uffizi
Palazzo Valori *see* Palazzo Altoviti
Palazzo Vecchio *see under* museums
Palazzo Venturi-Ginori **21** 26
Palazzo Vespucci **29** 362
patronage **11** 185–6
piazzas
Piazza della Signoria **11** 176, *212*; **22** 44
Fountain of Neptune **1** *791*; **3** 160; **7** 672; **11** 342; **16** 695, 696; **21** 21; **22** 44
monument to Cosimo I de' Medici **10** 441; **12** *573*; **16** 695; **26** 137; **29** 565
sculpture **3** 158, *158*; **6** 144–5; **12** 573; **21** 17; **28** 928
Piazza S Marco
Medici garden **16** 770
Piazza SS Annunziata **11** *177*; **16** 699; **31** 712, 717
fountain **16** *700*
Piazza Vittorio Emanuele **16** 646
Ponte Santa Trinita **4** 801
Ponte Vecchio **4** 801
Spedale degli Innocenti *see under* hospitals
Stazione S Maria Novella **16** 650; **21** 471; **25** 855
tapestries **26** 779
synagogue **17** 547
Teatro della Pergola **11** 873; **30** 229, 667
Teatro Mediceo *see under* museums → Uffizi
towers **4** 776
University **31** 674
urban planning **5** 22; **16** 646; **31** 711, 714
Vasari's House *see* Casa Vasari
villas
Il Riposo **32** 106
Villa Carducci **14** 869; **16** 660
frescoes **6** *12*, 13; **24** 1
Villa di Poggio alla Scaglia
frescoes **27** *522*
Villa Gallina **25** 157
Villa I Tatti **3** 765; **7** 336; **24** 838; **28** 283
Villa Lappeggi **21** 27

Florence
villas—cont.
Villa La Quiete 12 707
Villa Lemmi 4 496, 503; 10 432; 31 173
Villa Medicea della Petraia see LA PETRAIA, VILLA MEDICEA
Villa Poggio Imperiale 1 574; 8 275; 22 357; 29 833; 31 268
Villa Quaracchi 12 110
walls 31 710
water supply 31 711
workshops 11 185
Zuccaro's house 33 718
Florence, Hercules 24 659
Florence mosiac see PIETRE DURE
Florence of Worcester's Chronicle (Oxford, Corpus Christi Coll., MS. 157) 14 423
Florence Painter 13 523
Florence Phillips 29 121
Florence Pontificale see under PONTIFICALS → individual manuscripts
Florensa, Adolf 3 216; 23 260
Florensky, Pavel (Aleksandrovich) 11 217–18*; 27 444
Florentia, Raffaelle de see RAFFAELLINO DEL GARBO
Florentim, António see António Florentim
Florentin (fl 1928) 7 294
Florentín, Andrés 29 290
Florentin, Dominique see BARBIERE, DOMENICO DEL
Florentín, Francisco 32 147
Florentín Demestri, Pedro 24 99
Florentine finishes 21 326
Florentine mosaic see COMMESSO DI PIETRE DURE
Florentino, Francesco 29 265, 267
Florentino, Jacopo 20 2; 29 265
Florentino, Nicolao see DELLI, NICCOLÒ
Florentins, Les 8 653; 11 565
Florentius 22 248
Flores 15 751
architecture 15 756
baskets 15 810
beads 15 814
bracelets 15 814
dress 15 813
ikat 15 795
jewellery 15 814, 815
Flores, Antonio 8 253
Flores, Bartolomé 6 591
Flores, Joseph 29 303
Flores, Juan 2 201; 3 588; 11 219; 29 326; 30 883
works 30 883
Flores, Las see LAS FLORES
Flores, Leonardo 4 261
Flores, Salvador Ortega see ORTEGA FLORES, SALVADOR
Flores, Simón 24 622
Flórez, Antonio 29 273
Florian, Alexie Lazăr 26 719
Floriana
Eucharistic Congress Memorial 20 214
statue of Grand Master Vilhena 20 214
Floriani, Pietro Paolo 20 212; 21 580
Florianus see BLUEMNER, OSCAR
Floridablanca, Conde de 11 218*
Florida Islands 29 50
Florigerio, Sebastiano 11 218–19*; 24 342
Florindo, Alonso Ruiz de see RUIZ DE FLORINDO, ALONSO
florins see under COINS → types
Floris IV, Count of Holland (reg 1222-34) 14 45
Floris V, Count of Holland (reg 1256-96) 14 38, 45; 22 265, 822
Floris, Carmelo 27 836
Floris, Claudius 11 219
Floris, Cornelis, I (c. 1435-1538) 11 219, 220
Floris, Cornelis, II (1513-75) 3 544, 569, 598; 11 219–21*, 634; 25 382
architecture 2 192, 203, 203; 31 238
ornament 2 194; 11 875; 22 870; 29 747
attributions 3 545; 22 823
collaboration 24 237
patrons and collectors 17 740; 23 395
prints 3 576; 10 326; 12 422; 23 540; 25 607
pupils 4 146; 17 918
reproductive prints by others 3 558; 7 499; 9 64; 29 44
sculpture 2 195; 3 568, 569; 7 303; 8 739; 11 219; 26 470; 27 168
teachers 11 219
writings 3 569, 581; 10 745; 12 421; 13 701; 20 281
Floris, Cornelis, III (1551-1615) 11 716
Floris, Frans 11 219, 220–22*; 22 839; 25 129
assistants 7 428; 25 382
attributions 3 24
collaboration 7 427; 14 296
groups and movements 26 728
house 11 220
patrons and collectors 3 90, 615; 5 325; 7 711; 17 643; 26 307
pupils 4 148, 839, 840; 8 103; 11 716; 14 296; 25 382; 30 59; 32 708
reproductions in tapestry 2 199
reproductive prints by others 3 558; 4 442; 7 499, 799, 899; 9 64; 12 15; 14 505; 33 169
teachers 19 547
works 2 195; 3 557; 4 839, 923; 7 712; 11 221, 222; 17 700; 20 281; 26 470
Floris, Hans 14 542
Floris, Jacob (1524-81) 29 747
Floris, Jacques 11 219
Floris, Jan (fl 1450) see VRIENDT, JAN FLORISZ. DE
Floris, Jan (d 1567) see FLORES, JUAN
Floris van Egmond, Count see EGMOND, FLORIS VAN, Count
Floris van Langren, Jacob 12 814
Florit, José María 29 300
Flors linen manufactory 19 418; 30 115
Flosche, Daniel (von) see FRÖSCHL, DANIEL (VON)
Flötner, Peter (1485/96-1546) 11 223–4*; 12 401; 23 312, 540
attributions 12 225
collaboration 3 69, 70; 18 574; 28 144; 29 563
fountains 11 223
furniture 8 271, 271; 12 420, 421
jewellery 12 455
metalwork 3 70, 98; 25 126
patrons and collectors 16 866; 25 454
prints 12 386, 815; 19 813; 33 353
sculpture 12 409
fountains 12 401; 23 309
plaquettes 25 21, 22
reliefs 12 402; 18 574
Flötner, Peter, the younger (fl 1581-1618) 25 21
Flouquet, Pierre-Louis 3 399, 564; 5 44
flour 7 116
dyeing 30 558, 560
frescoes 11 764
grounds 13 706, 708
paints 32 898
paper 7 116; 24 56
resins 7 116
Flower, Barnard 5 514; 13 185
Flower, Cyril, Baron Battersea 22 60
Flower, Joseph 4 823
Flower, Marmaduke 23 346
flower arrangements 17 342, 379–82*, 380; 30 632–3
Flower Borders, Master with the 20 628
Flower Breughel see BREUGHEL, JAN, I
flowered jasper see under JASPER → types
flower gardens see under GARDENS → types
flower pagodas see under PAGODAS → types
flower painting see under PAINTING → types
Flower Renaissance 7 471
flowers 15 812; 17 341
flowing tracery see TRACERY → types → bar → curvilinear
Fludd, Robert 18 522; 21 152
Flügelaltar see under ALTARPIECES → types
Flühli 30 124
glass 30 145, 145
Flühliglas see under GLASS → types
Fluocaril 29 546
fluorescent lamps see under LAMPS → types
fluorine 12 781
fluorite 14 167
Flurer, Franz Ignaz 11 230*; 28 860
flurosilicate 29 813
Flury, Samuel 16 549
flushwork masonry see under MASONRY → types
Flute-blowing Hare, Master of the see GUDEWERT, HANS (i)
fluted domes see under DOMES → types
flutes (columns) 11 231*, 231; 13 377, 389, 398, 415; 23 478; 26 878
flutes (glasses) 3 594
flutes (musical instruments) 22 374
historical and regional traditions
China 7 58
Egypt, ancient 10 64
Indonesia 15 817
Japan 17 397
Maya 22 375
Mesoamerica, Pre-Columbian 21 257*
Thailand 30 637
materials
bamboo 7 58
bone 21 257
greenstone 21 257
jade 21 257
pottery 21 257
Fluxus 2 447; 7 895; 11 231–2*; 24 407; 29 97
collections 8 759; 29 16; 32 714
commentaries 8 609
members 13 779
Armleder, John (M.) 2 447
Ben 3 698–9
Brecht, George 4 731
Filliou, Robert 11 80
Flynt, Henry 7 685
Friedman, Ken 7 895
Kirkeby, Per 18 84
Köpcke, Arthur 8 736
Paik, Nam June 10 688; 23 777
Schippers, Wim T(heodor) 28 103
Spoerri, Daniel 29 420
Vostell, Wolf 32 714
multimedia 22 279, 381
performance art 1 34; 22 381; 24 403, 407
Flying Angel Painter 13 520
Flying Art School 2 772
flying buttresses see under BUTTRESSES → types
flying squirrel-hair see under HAIR → types
flying white script see SCRIPTS → types → hihaku
Flynn, Dan 2 766
Flynt, Henry 7 685; 24 407
Flynt, Paul, II see FLINDT, PAUL, II
fly-whisks see WHISKS
FMR 24 449
Foa, Tobias ben Eliezer 27 482
fob seals see under SEALS → types
Fobsen, Jacob van see ES, JACOB VAN
Focal Press 28 878
Foce del Sele 13 447
Sanctuary of Hera 13 425
Temple of Hera 13 470
Foch, Niels 29 202
Focillon, Henri (-Joseph) 11 233*; 31 672
pupils 1 154; 6 502; 24 321; 29 638
works 11 676; 26 44
Focillon, Victor-Louis 11 233
Fock, Hermanus 10 559; 20 400
Fockedey, Hippolyte 4 130
Focsaneanu, Paul 29 721
Fodor, Carel Joseph 6 89; 11 233*
Fodor, Eugene 13 807, 811
Foeng, Jules Chin A. 30 16
Foerk, Ernő 26 241; 28 172
Foerster, Karl 14 118
Foerster, Wilhelm 23 342
F. of Bruges 20 795
Fogdö 30 76
Fogdö, Master of 20 159, 674*
Fogel, Anders 14 230
Fogelberg, Andrew 10 333; 29 723
Fogelberg, Bengt Erland 11 234*; 29 1; 30 86, 107; 31 362
Fogelino, Marcello
works 32 409
Fogg Art Museum see under CAMBRIDGE (MA) → Harvard University
Foggia, Bartolomeo da see BARTOLOMEO DA FOGGIA
Foggia, Nicola di Bartolomeo da see NICOLA DI BARTOLOMEO DA FOGGIA
Foggia, Riccardo da see RICCARDO DA FOGGIA
Foggini, Giovanni Battista 11 188, 192, 234–5*; 20 214
assistants 11 322; 20 385; 24 697; 29 30
caskets 14 170
collaboration 6 86; 24 697; 26 148; 28 735; 31 129
engravings 21 30
patrons and collectors 10 140; 21 29, 31
pupils
Baratta, Giovanni di Isidoro 3 198
Cateni, Giovanni Camillo 6 86
Cornacchini, Agostino 7 860; 16 700
Fuga, Ferdinando 11 813
Galilei, Alessandro (Maria Gaetano) 12 6
Ghinghi, Francesco 12 547
Piamontini, Giuseppe 24 696
Rastrelli, Bartolomeo Carlo 26 6
Ticciati, Girolamo 30 851
Valle, Filippo della 31 826
Weber, Lorenzo Maria 33 15
sculpture 16 700
fountains 16 700; 21 30
monumental 11 189
reliefs 11 205, 235; 20 385; 28 735; 31 187
statuettes 29 572
tomb 12 826
teachers 11 18, 23
Foggini, Giulio 31 129
Foggini, N. 4 492
Foggini, Vincenzo 24 24; 31 129; 32 912
Foggo, George 11 235*
Foggo, James 11 235*
Fogg Pietà, Master of the 20 674–5*
works 20 675
Fogolino, Francisco 11 235
Fogolino, Marcello 11 235–6*
collaboration 26 727
works 2 594; 5 180; 9 308; 10 737
Fogolino, Matteo 5 180
Fogong Temple see under YING XIAN
Foguang Temple see under MT WUTAI
Fohr, Carl Philipp 11 236–7*
works 11 236; 12 393; 27 322
foils (i) (tracery) 11 237*
foils (ii) (metal) 11 237*
foils (iii) (swords) 29 469
Foix, Gaston (fl early 15th cent.) 20 625
Foix, Gaston (d before 1517) 3 138
Foix, Gaston II, Comte de (fl 1330) 23 409
Foix, Louis de 19 360; 29 917
Foix, Margarita de 4 817
Foix, Roger Bernat III, Comte de 2 10
Fojnica 4 459
Franciscan Monastery 4 462
Fokine, Mikhail 2 108; 3 119; 30 686
Fokke, Arend 11 237
Fokke, Jan 11 237
Fokke, Simon 3 900; 11 237*; 18 176; 25 649; 31 367
Fol, Walter 12 266; 14 121
Foladi 1 202
Folan, William 5 411
Folarin, Agbo 15 57
Folch, Jaime 1 741
Folchart Psalter see under PSALTERS → individual manuscripts
Folchetti, Stefano 11 237*
Folch i Torres, Joaquín 5 509
Folcker, Gustaf 30 107
folding-books see BOOKS → types → accordion books
folding chairs see under CHAIRS → types
folding knives see under KNIVES → types
folding stools see under STOOLS → types
Foler, Antonio 32 77
Foley, Daniel 7 857
Foley, Fiona 1 65
Foley, James W. 33 146
Foley, John Henry 11 237–9*; 16 21
pupils 4 835; 18 527
teachers 3 79, 509
works 10 266; 11 238; 22 47; 28 278
Foley, Paul 10 292
Foley, Thomas, Baron 18 677; 22 726
Foley, Thomas Henry, 4th Baron Foley 8 441
Folgore, Luciano 25 447
Folgueras 29 273
Folia historiae artium 24 441
Folies Bergère 25 375
Foligno
Cathedral 26 625
Palazzo Trinci 28 778
patronage 16 763
Sassovivo 7 921, 922
Foligno, Niccolò da see NICCOLÒ DA FOLIGNO
Folingsby, George 19 873
Folingsby, G. F. 5 175
Folio Society 4 366

folk architecture see ARCHITECTURE → types → vernacular
folk art 11 239–41*
India, Republic of 15 175–7*
Japan 17 44–5*, 344–59*, 347
Edo period (1600-1868) 17 45
see also VERNACULAR ART
Folke Egerstrom (family) 3 273
Folkema, Anna 11 241
Folkema, Jacob 11 241*; 30 297
Folkema, Johannes 11 241
Folkestone, Jacob Bouverie, 1st Viscount see BOUVERIE, JACOB, 1st Viscount Folkestone
Folkestone Pier (Kent) 24 748
folk houses see HOUSES → types → minka
Folkingham Castle (Lincs) 14 418
Folkton 25 511
Folkung, Magnus III, King of Sweden see MAGNUS III, King of Sweden
Folkung, Magnus IV, King of Sweden see MAGNUS IV, King of Sweden
Folkwang-Auriga 26 195
Folleville Church, Tomb of Raoul de Lannoy and Jeanne de Poix 11 556, 898
Folli, Giuseppe 26 778
follies 11 242–3*, 243
see also GROTTOES
Follin, Bartolomeo 5 908; 11 241*; 23 530
Follot, Paul 11 241–2*, 583, 601
collaboration 6 551; 10 284
groups and movements 2 520, 521
pupils 24 475
works 5 841; 11 601
Folo, Giovanni 23 173
Folpard van Amerongen 31 449
Folperti, Mauro dei, Abbot of Padua 20 307
Folquera, Francesc 23 260
Folstadt 31 659
Fol-Straub, Marianne 20 592
Foltýn, František 8 393
Foltz, Ludwig von (i) (fl 1810-20) 11 243
Foltz, Ludwig von (ii) (1809-67) 11 243
Foltz, Philipp von 8 883; 11 243–4*; 19 97
Folwell, Jody 22 606
Foment de les Arts Decoratives see FAD
Fomin, Igor' (Ivanovich) 11 244, 245*
collaboration 19 273; 27 313; 29 388
pupils 27 313
works 27 380
Fomin, Ivan (Aleksandrovich) 4 312; 11 244–5*; 27 378, 580
assistants 12 234
groups and movements 29 529
pupils 19 273; 25 170; 27 284; 31 371
staff 9 458
teachers 3 734
works 3 527; 21 98; 22 174; 27 378, 379; 32 412
Fomison, Tony 11 245–6*
Fon 1 425; 3 727; 11 246–7*
architecture 3 728
ceramics 1 329
currency 1 363
figurines 1 271–2, 272
gesture 1 265
gourds 1 303
houses 1 311
iconography 1 282, 284
iron 11 246
palaces 1 309
patronage 1 241
portraits 1 267, 268, 270
sculpture 1 278; 11 246, 246–7*
Fon—cont.
textiles 1 295, 424
tunics 1 348
wood 1 272
wood-carvings 11 247
Foncez (family) 3 599
Foncières, Philippe de see PHILIPPE DE FONCIÈRES
Foncin, Jean 3 128; 21 575
works 21 575
fondachi 32 184
fondaci see CLUBS (MEETING PLACES)
Fondation Arp see under CLAMART
Fondation François-et-Souza-Desnoyer see under SAINT-CYPRIEN
Fondation Léon Alègre see BAGNOLS-SUR-CÉZE → Musée Léon Alègre
Fondation Maeght see under SAINT-PAUL-DE-VENCE
Fondation Nourhan Fringhian 2 445
Fondazione Giuliano Gori 1 15
Fondazione Querini-Stampalia see under VENICE → foundations
Fondi
Cathedral of S Pietro 7 922
Via Appia 27 7
Fonditore, Rosso 24 870
Fondo Nacional para las Artes 25 703
fonds 2 363
Fonds Mexicains 20 see CODICES → individual manuscripts → Aubin Manuscript 20
Fonds Portugais see under PARIS → Bibliothèque Nationale
Fondukistan 1 186, 849; 5 102; 11 247–8*
Niche E 1 203
sculpture 1 189, 192, 193, 198, 199; 11 247
stucco 1 197
wall paintings 1 201, 202
Fonduli, Agostino 11 248–9*; 21 525
collaboration 3 384; 4 644
Fonduli, Bartolomeo 11 248
Fonduli, Giovanni Paulo 11 248*; 20 800; 29 569
collaboration 3 636, 860
competitions 7 672
pupils 11 248
Fonduliis, Fondulino de see FONDULINO DE FONDULIIS
Fondulio, Giovanni Paulo see FONDULI, GIOVANNI PAULO
Fondulli, Giovanni Paulo see FONDULI, GIOVANNI PAULO
Fondulo see FONDULI
Fondulo, Agostino 5 697
Fongario, Bernardino see FUNGAI, BERNARDINO (CRISTOFANO DI NICHOLO D'ANTONIO DI PIETRO)
Fongbé 8 230
Fonghaia, Bernardino da see FUNGAI, BERNARDINO (CRISTOFANO DI NICHOLO D'ANTONIO DI PIETRO)
Fonhave, Hinrik see FUNHOF, HINRIK
Fonmon Castle (Glams) 32 788
Fonnesbech-Sandberg, Elna 8 759
Fonoll, Reinard des see REINARD DES FONOLL
fons see CHALICES
Fonseca, Alonso de, Archbishop of Santiago de Compostela (fl 1521) 1 526
Fonseca, Alonso de, Archbishop of Seville (1418-73) 4 784; 7 491
Fonseca, Alonso de, Bishop of Avila (fl 1469-85) 15 835
Fonseca, António Manuel da 11 249*
pupils 3 360; 4 639; 8 163; 19 805; 21 128, 348; 26 516
sponsors 4 638
works 19 468
Fonseca, Antonio Tejeda see TEJEDA FONSECA, ANTONIO
Fonseca, António Tomáas da 25 293
Fonseca, Bernardino José 10 729
Fonseca, Gonzalo 11 249*; 30 275; 31 755
Fonseca, João Tomás da 11 249
Fonseca, José Calado da see CALADO DA FONSECA, JOSÉ
Fonseca, José Luís Fernandes da see FERNANDES DA FONSECA, JOSÉ LUÍS
Fonseca, Juan de (fl 1627) 4 210
Fonseca, Juan Rodríguez de, Bishop of Palencia (fl 15th cent.) 17 601, 674
Fonseca, Maria de (fl 15th-early 16th cent.) 21 124
Fonseca, Maria Inês Carmona Ribeiro da (b 1926) see MENEZ
Fonseca, Oscar 13 311
Fonseca Azevedo, Bento da 17 595
Fonseca e Evora, José Maria de 21 831
Fonseca e Silva, Valentim da 4 708, 711, 716; 11 249*
works 26 413
Fonseca Fernandes da Cunha, Lygia da 4 728
Fonseca Lima, José da 28 731, 732; 31 2
Fonseca y Acevedo, Alonso de, Archbishop of Toledo 11 250*
architecture 1 526; 28 726; 32 116
gold 29 333
sculpture 3 846
Fonseca Zamora, Carlos 13 771
Fonseca Zamora, Oscar 9 677
Fonsié, Adamou 3 152
Fonson, Alexandre 3 598
Fonson, Charles-Auguste 11 250*
Fonson, Pieter Jozef 3 599, 613
Font, Anna 29 346
Fontaine, Cecile 10 689
Fontaine, Marie-Jo La see LA FONTAINE, MARIE-JO
Fontaine, Nicholas 4 9
Fontaine, Pierre-François-Léonard 11 256–8*, 523; 12 731
architecture 11 519; 24 163; 26 743; 33 217
chapels 11 519; 23 522
façades 24 123
libraries 11 257; 25 408
mausolea 20 867, 869
collaboration 8 593; 9 12; 19 251; 21 411; 22 47; 23 544; 24 123, 387–8; 31 351
drawings 2 332
furniture 3 485; 4 42; 6 390; 11 597; 29 315
groups and movements 10 186; 13 201; 22 734, 740; 24 387; 26 189
interior decoration 1 110; 6 390; 11 579; 13 702; 24 317; 29 305, 305
metalwork 11 305
patrons and collectors 4 301, 302, 306, 565; 11 597; 27 536
pupils 12 167; 13 295; 19 812; 24 352; 26 191, 525; 29 490
silver 11 621
staff 22 25
stucco 29 834
teachers 24 582; 32 80
writings 3 584; 11 520; 25 193
illustrated 23 209
Fontainebleau 11 259–63*, 504
Château 4 248, 780; 6 505, 506; 7 916; 11 259, 259–61*, 262, 512, 513, 515, 556, 656, 659, 661; 13 700; 19 18, 692; 23 540, 810; 26 449; 31 848
Appartement des Bains 11 263
Ballcourt 3 118
Boudoir Turc 13 234
Cabinet de la Reine 9 87
Cabinet du Roi 31 848
Cabinets de Medailles et Antiquités 3 48
carpets 5 837; 27 896
Chambre de la Duchesse d'Etampes 1 19; 6 506; 11 532, 572, 572; 25 578, 579; 31 848
Chambre de la Reine 4 337; 6 506; 19 723; 25 578; 26 376; 31 848
Chambre du Roi 3 646; 9 13; 11 263; 25 578; 31 848
Chapelle de la Ste-Trinité 11 267, 755; 17 627; 18 643; 29 833; 31 341
Cour du Cheval Blanc 11 257
Cour Ovale staircase 11 513
Escalier du Roi 25 579
fountains 11 342, 343
frames 11 400
frescoes 10 130
furniture 7 658; 11 592, 596; 29 683
Galerie Basse 31 848
Galerie de Diane 4 36; 6 519; 18 867; 19 37; 21 425; 26 264, 334
Galerie des Cerfs 4 337
Galerie d'Ulysse 1 18; 6 491, 506; 10 799; 13 700; 15 137; 25 579–80, 580; 30 787; 31 848
Galerie François I 1 657; 6 506; 9 11, 14, 21; 11 571–2; 13 700; 20 278, 281; 23 810; 25 578, 579; 27 209; 29 747, 833; 31 848
tapestries 30 318
Galerie Henrie see Salle de Bal
gardens 12 113, 121; 13 703; 31 849; 32 503
Grand Cabinet 20 860
Grande Salle 6 604; 16 855
Grotte du Jardin des Pins 23 541; 25 579; 31 848
interior decoration 2 245; 3 621; 4 301, 303; 9 398; 10 187; 11 260, 532, 533, 571; 13 701
Jardin de Diane 3 925
Jardin de la Reine 3 210; 24 812
locks 16 59
Musée Chinois 4 307
paintings 1 898; 4 303, 305, 537, 744; 9 328; 10 477; 11 266; 12 271; 13 665; 17 465; 18 642, 708; 19 66, 646, 649; 22 734; 23 293; 27 209–10; 29 255, 623, 887; 31 379; 32 584, 718
park 24 179
Pavillon de Pomone 31 848
Pavillon des Poêles 9 328
Porte Dorée 6 141–2, 504; 10 744; 11 513; 16 695; 25 579; 31 848
Salle de Bal 11 266, 532; 19 692
sculpture 4 305, 337; 8 650; 10 509; 13 790; 16 695; 25 79, 577; 31 849
staircase 29 524, 524
stucco 29 833, 834
Study of Théagène and Chariclée 11 574
tapestries 3 461; 29 424
Grand Ferrare 11 656; 14 789
painting 22 414
St Louis 31 341
tapestries 11 262*, 639; 30 318
Fontainebleau school 10 477; 11 262–7*, 656; 20 281; 25 191, 578; 26 229
members 9 328; 10 799; 11 260
works 11 264, 267
Fontaine-Henri, Château of 11 513
Fontaines, Robin de see ROBIN DE FONTAINES
Fontana see under TYPE-FACES
Fontana (v) (family) 11 191, 348; 16 735; 31 741
Fontana, Alberto 1 17
Fontana, Annibale 11 278–80*
collaboration 19 673; 27 815
patrons and collectors 1 625
works 8 407; 11 279, 280; 14 171; 21 529; 26 486; 29 570
Fontana, Baldassare 11 280–81*; 18 428; 23 425
works 8 386; 18 467; 25 98, 114
Fontana, Bill 29 98
Fontana (v), Camillo 11 268; 31 741
Fontana (iv), Carlo (1638-1714) 3 266, 838; 11 274–7*
architecture 19 736; 27 195
catafalques 11 276
churches 1 532; 9 82, 86; 11 275, 277; 15 121; 25 852; 26 758, 826, 833; 27 195; 31 713
government buildings 25 636, 636
hospices 23 352
palaces 20 494
palazzi 3 835; 11 181; 23 492; 26 759; 29 831
restorations 27 758
theatres 30 667
villas 32 549
assistants 11 277; 18 699; 21 473; 27 319
collaboration 6 585; 10 232; 16 562; 25 861, 862; 26 810; 29 830
drawings 23 644; 26 829
ivory-carvings 12 460; 29 520
metalwork 30 704
patrons and collectors 1 532; 6 584, 585; 8 378; 15 861–2; 16 638; 23 898; 28 908
pupils
Bizzacheri, Carlo Francesco 4 104
Buratti, Carlo 5 186
Fontana, Baldassare 11 280
Fontana (iv), Francesco (Antonio) 11 277
Fontana (v), Girolamo, II 11 277
Gibbs, James 12 593
Hildebrandt, Johann Lukas von 14 527
Juvarra, Filippo 17 706
Ludovice, João Frederico 19 775
Specchi, Alessandro 29 373
Tessin, Nicodemus (1654-1728) 30 522
Vaccarini, Giovanni Battista 31 788
sculpture 19 768
stucco 4 434; 25 852
Fontana (iv), Carlo Stefano (1675-1740) 11 277*
Fontana (iv), Domenico 11 116, 270, 271–3*; 16 641; 26 769
architecture
catafalques 6 72
chapels 29 82
churches 8 224; 10 809; 11 272; 26 821, 832
libraries 19 313; 26 814
palazzi 4 648; 19 167; 22 477; 26 819, 819–20, 839, 840
portals 26 836
tombs 26 833; 29 82
urban planning 11 271; 26 757
assistants 9 340; 20 43

Fontana (iv), Domenico—cont.
  collaboration 8 513; 20 46; 22 472; 25 260; 29 82; 31 787
  engineering 25 259; 26 757
  fountains 29 82; 30 344; 32 9
  patrons and collectors 23 96; 24 398–9; 26 814; 28 529; 31 831
  pupils 6 22; 25 860
Fontana, Felice 1 844
Fontana (v), Flaminio 11 191, 268; 31 741
Fontana (iv), Francesco (Antonio) 1 532; 11 277*
Fontana, Franco 11 281*
Fontana, Gerolamo 27 787, 788
Fontana (iii), Giovanni 11 270–73*
  assistants 20 43
  collaboration 6 22; 25 227
  patrons and collectors 24 398
  works 2 212; 4 405; 11 272, 273, *740*, 741; 20 46; 26 757, 840
  writings 6 23
Fontana (ii), Giovanni Battista 11 270*
  attributions 2 88
  collaboration 11 270
  works 2 374; 3 648; 15 866, 867
Fontana, Giovanni Maria 19 563; 27 573; 28 41
  works 27 *574*
Fontana (v), Girolamo, II 11 277*
  patrons and collectors 7 621
  works 9 *11*; 16 771
Fontana (ii), Giulio 11 270*
  collaboration 11 270
  patrons and collectors 11 270
  works 11 270; 15 *92*; 19 139; 31 43
Fontana (iii), Giulio Cesare 11 273; 22 472
Fontana (v), Guido 11 268; 22 31; 31 741, 747
  works 31 *742*
Fontana, Jakub 17 756
  architecture 3 527; 25 99, 212; 32 870, 879
  furniture 25 121; 32 879
  patrons and collectors 25 118
  pupils 21 158
Fontana (i), Lavinia 11 268, 269*; 16 668, 780; 26 771; 30 798; 33 308
  patrons and collectors 10 525
  works 4 276; 9 266, 267; 11 *269*; 16 668
Fontana, Lucio 11 281–3*; 16 681, 775; 21 528
  collaboration 3 438
  dealers 7 421; 16 820
  groups and movements 1 79, 90; 7 782, 894; 9 201; 10 416; 13 729; 17 694; 29 370
  pupils 5 451; 19 209
  teachers 33 183
  works 2 401; 10 822; 11 *282*, 398; 12 437; 16 681, 708, 709; 21 892; 22 748
Fontana, Luigi 24 866
Fontana (iii), Marsilio 11 270
Fontana (v), Mauro 11 274, 277–8*
Fontana (v), Nicolo 11 268
Fontana (v), Orazio 11 268; 19 689; 28 4; 30 880; 31 741
  works 6 11
Fontana, Paolo Antonio 19 750; 25 98
Fontana, Pietro 23 173
Fontana (i), Prospero 4 276; 11 268–9*; 24 419
  collaboration 6 361; 32 14; 33 716
  patrons and collectors 10 446
  pupils 5 441, 851, 856; 11 269; 25 640; 27 480; 30 798
  reproductive prints by others 4 309
  restorations by others 29 892
Fontana (i), Prospero—cont.
  teachers 15 863
  works 4 276; 30 801; 32 22
Fontana, Virgilio 5 616
Fontana Martina 32 678
Fontane, Peter 11 283
Fontane, (Henri) Theodor 11 283*; 19 335
Fontaner, Karl 2 780
Fontanesi, Antonio 2 10; 11 283–5*; 16 678; 17 133, 198, 203, 420; 21 59
  pupils 2 578; 5 425; 30 256
  works 7 434; 11 *284*, *285*
Fontanesi, Francesco 23 87
Fontanet, Jaume 12 740
Fontanges caps 17 523
Fontanieu, Gaspard-Moyse-Augustin de, Marquis de Fiennes *see* FIENNES, GASPARD-MOYSE-AUGUSTIN DEFONTANIEU, Marquis de
Fontanieu, M. de 11 595
Fontanieu, Moyse-Augustin de 20 138
Fontanieu, Pierre-Elizabeth de 20 138; 26 376
Font'Arcada, Abbey Church 25 289
Font de Gaume 11 285–6*, *505*; 25 *470*, 475, 482, 484, 487
  rock art 25 *483*
Fonte, Bartolomeo della *see* BARTOLOMEO DELLA FONTE
Fonte, Jacopo della *see* JACOPO DELLA QUERCIA
Fontebasso, Andrea 16 739
Fontebasso, Francesco 9 48; 11 286–7*
  pupils 33 721
  works 11 *287*; 16 719
Fontebasso, Giuseppe 16 739
Fontebuoni, Anastagio 12 763; 18 733; 21 25; 31 886
fonteghi *see* FONDACHI
Fontem 1 *394*; 3 170
Fontenai, Abbé de 10 206; 11 288*; 12 179
Fontenals, Pablo Milà i *see* MILÀ I FONTENALS, PABLO
Fontenay, Abbé de *see* FONTENAI, Abbé de
Fontenay, Eugène 17 527
Fontenay, Julien de 11 635; 12 259
Fontenay Abbey 7 267, 351; 11 288–9*, *289*, *504*; 13 38; 21 837, 838, *838*
  arches 2 298
  chapter house 6 464, *464*; 22 218
  church 11 510; 26 584
  cloister 7 453, 455
  dormitory 21 843
  mouldings 22 216, 218
Fontenay-Mareuil, François du Val, Marquis de 19 300
Fontenella *see* SAINT-WANDRILLE
Fonteny, H. de 30 569
Fonteo, Giovanni Battista 13 914
Fontes e Abrantes, Marquês de 11 289*
Fontevrault Abbey 11 290–91*, *504*, 510; 21 837; 26 586, *599*
  capitals 26 599
  chapter house 6 467
  effigy of Henry II 11 *290*
  piers (ii) (masonry) 24 751
  tomb of Eleanor of Aquitaine 27 829, *829*; 31 122, 125
  tombs 13 72
Fontfroide Abbey 7 350, 454
Fontgombault Abbey 4 63
Fonthill Abbey (Wilts) 3 476; 10 235, 280, 361; 13 200, 206; 29 890; 33 *445*
  armour 9 31
  gallery 9 12
  gardens 26 743
  model 2 337
  paintings 20 731
Fonthill Abbey (Wilts)—cont.
  stained glass 29 515
Font i Carreras, Augusto 3 220, 764; 11 291*; 21 315; 26 533
Fontigny Abbey 13 38
Fontpertuis 20 137
Fontpertuis, Louise-August Angran, Vicomte de *see* ANGRAN, LOUISE-AUGUST, Vicomte de Fontpertuis
fonts (baptismal) 7 282; 11 250–56*, 340
  historical and regional traditions
    Belgium 3 *566*
    Byzantine 9 *591*
    Czech Republic 8 415, *415*
    Early Christian (*c*. AD 250–843) 6 31; 11 250–51*, *251*
    England 10 338; 11 252, 253, *254*, *256*; 26 613
    France 9 *191*; 11 253, 623
    Germany 11 253; 12 452; 13 160; 32 *604*
    Gothic 9 *191*; 13 160
    Greece, ancient 11 339
    Holy Roman Empire (before 1648) 26 684*
    Italy 11 254*
    Mexico 21 *374*
    Ottonian 23 659
    Palestine 11 *251*
    Romanesque 10 338; 26 613, *640*, 684*; 30 83
    Sweden 26 *640*; 30 83
    Syria 9 *591*
  materials
    brass 3 *566*; 32 *604*
    bronze 11 253*, *256*; 26 684*
    copper 12 452
    lead 11 253*, 623; 18 902
    limestone 9 *591*
    marble 11 *256*
    pewter 8 415, *415*; 11 253; 24 580
    stone 9 *191*; 11 252*, *254*
    wood 11 252*
fonts (typographic) *see* FOUNTS
Fontseré i Mestres, Josep 12 179
Fonvizin, Artur (Vladimirovich) 9 145; 11 291–2*; 20 151; 27 394, 396
Fonvizin, D. I. 27 438
Fónyi, Géza 4 84
food 17 341, 382–3*, *383*
food containers *see* BOXES → types → *bentō*; CONTAINERS → uses → food
Foon, Pat Chu *see* CHU FOON, PAT
Foord, George 11 433
Foord & Dickinson 11 433
Foot, Samuel 24 691
Football World Cup 29 489
footboards 3 482, 483
Foote, Robert 30 750
Foote, Samuel 33 693
Footner, William 11 292*; 22 36
foot rings *see under* RINGS → types
footstools *see under* STOOLS → types
footwear 1 349*; 32 487, *487*
Foppa, Cristoforo *see* CARADOSSO
Foppa, Gian Maffeo 5 696
Foppa, Vincenzo 4 747; 11 292–4*; 14 868; 16 663; 20 741; 21 525
  collaboration 3 695; 5 127
  patrons and collectors 6 357; 11 32; 21 11; 25 144; 27 272; 28 530, 531; 29 411
  works 3 771; 4 729; 11 *293*, *294*
Foppes van Essen, Jacob van *see* ES, JACOB VAN
Foppesz., Pieter Jan 22 837
fora 11 327–8*; 12 497; 26 781–5, 863, 867, 890, 905; 27 3
  Britain 26 905
  Byzantine 9 560
fora—cont.
  Early Christian (*c*. AD 250–843) 9 560
  Greece 7 *852*; 15 894
  Italy 11 *327*; 26 *748*, 889
  Rome, ancient 26 889
  see also AGORAI; MARKETS
Fora, Bartolomeo di Giovanni (di Miniato) del 3 300; 11 295
Fora, Gherardo di Giovanni (di Miniato) del 11 295–7*; 20 847
  collaboration 2 697; 11 296, 297; 12 553; 20 413
  patrons and collectors 13 644
Fora, Monte di Giovanni (di Miniato) del 11 295, 296–7*; 20 847
  collaboration 2 697; 4 197; 11 295, 296; 12 553
  pupils 2 697
Forabosco, Girolamo 8 427; 11 297*; 16 675
  patrons and collectors 8 427; 13 920
  pupils 18 901
Forain, Jean-Louis 5 701; 11 297–8*; 20 603; 27 240
  works 5 758; 11 *298*
Forbát, Fred 3 795; 11 299*; 14 890
Forbes, Alexander 28 261
Forbes, Anne 9 725; 28 235
Forbes, Elizabeth (Adela) Stanhope 9 309; 11 300–301*; 23 26
Forbes, James Staats 11 301*; 14 47
Forbes, John 10 851
Forbes, Malcolm (Stevenson) 11 301*
Forbes, Mansfield 19 890
Forbes, Stanhope (Alexander) 11 299–300*
  education (art) 23 26
  groups and movements 3 628; 10 254; 23 22, 26
  patrons and collectors 30 359
  works 11 *300*, 435; 20 425
Forbes, William 28 268
Forbes, William Nairn 5 418; 15 403
Forbes, W. J. Waldie 14 603
Forbes & Paterson 28 272
Forbici, Giuseppe Archinto alle, Conte *see* ARCHINTO ALLE FORBICI, GIUSEPPE, Conte
Forbidden City *see under* BEIJING
Forbin, (Louis Nicolas Philippe) Auguste, Comte de 11 301–2*
  groups and movements 9 363; 31 373
  patrons and collectors 4 303
  personal collection 26 452
  sponsorship 13 790; 15 42
  teachers 1 497; 7 762
  works 14 482; 26 264
Forbin, Jacques 32 571
Force, Anne-Marie de Bosmelet, Duchesse de la 31 *378*
Force, Jean-Aimar Piganiol de la *see* PIGANIOL DE LA FORCE, JEAN-AIMAR
Force, Juliana 23 48
Forces Murales 30 328
Forces Nouvelles 11 302*, 550; 20 387; 30 271
Forcett, Edward 10 316
Forchoudt 2 196; 4 448; 19 430; 32 713
Forchoudt, Alexander 19 336
Forchoudt, Marcus 4 224
Forchoudt, Wilhelm 19 336
Forchtenau, Esterházy Palace 14 886
Ford (family) 28 259
Ford, Brian 33 602
Ford, Brinsley, Collection *see under* LONDON
Ford, C. R. 2 705; 13 844; 33 58
Ford, Edward Onslow 4 599; 11 302–3*
  works 11 *303*
Ford, Ford Madox 30 680
Ford, George Burdett 31 728, 729
Ford, Henry, I (1863–1947) 4 789; 8 802; 15 822–3; 17 722; 20 593; 30 390
Ford, Henry, II (*b* 1917) 24 183
Ford, Jazaniah 31 266
Ford, John (*fl* 1819–35) 9 726; 28 259
Ford, John F. (*fl* 20th cent.) 22 795
Ford, Michael 9 397
Ford, Model T *see under* CARS → models
Ford, Richard 11 304*; 12 270; 13 810; 22 352
Ford, William (*fl* 1810; glassmaker) 28 259
Ford, William (*fl* 1810–28; architect) 14 810
Forde Abbey (Dorset) 21 843
Fordell Castle (Fife) 13 211
Förderer, Otto and Zwimpfer 11 304
Förderer, Walter Maria 11 304–5*; 30 129
Ford Foundation 33 7
Fordham, Daniel Porter 9 200
Ford House 28 226
Fordinois 4 532
Ford Motor Co. 15 822, 824; 32 501
  architecture 30 390; 31 596; 32 558
  production 8 802; 20 *594*
  sponsorship 15 829; 24 683; 31 662
Fordrin, Louis 30 872
Ford Works 28 259
forecourts 5 474
Foreestier, Pauwels *see* ALBERDINGK THIJM, JOSEPHUS ALBERTUS
Forel, Auguste 17 *197*
Foreman, Richard 24 409
Foremark (Derbys), St Saviour 28 295
Förening för konst 29 688
Förening för nutida konst 29 688
Fores, S. W. 8 217
Forest, Jean-Baptiste 11 305*; 24 805
Forest, Lockwood de 7 577; 15 408; 30 868
Forest, Pierre 11 305
Forest de Bélidor, Bernard 4 804; 10 206; 15 402
Forestel, Jean de Wavrin, Lord of 3 555; 20 785
Forester, Cecil George Wilfred Weld-Forester, 7th Baron *see* WELD-FORESTER, CECIL GEORGE WILFRED, 7th Baron Forester
Forest Hills Gardens (NY) 2 698
Foresti, Alba 5 877
Foresti, Jacobus Philippus 3 699
Forestier (family) 26 376
Forestier, A. 13 876
Forestier, Auguste 4 106
Forestier, Etienne 9 399; 11 305*
Forestier, Etienne-Jean 11 305*
Forestier, Jean-Claude-Nicolas 24 128
  collaboration 3 450
  works 14 241; 24 181; 28 514; 29 273; 31 728
Forestier, Julie 15 836
Forestier, Pierre-Auguste 11 305*; 28 809
Forestier-Walker, Robert 19 519
Forestier-Walker & Born 14 784
  works 14 *783*
Forfar (Tayside), Ethie House 28 250

Forgách, Count, Bishop of Nagyvárad **26** 317
Forgeais **25** 691
Forgeois, Michèle **3** 366
forgeries **1** 174; **2** 835; **6** 76; **7** 561, 830; **11** 305–11*; **21** 38; **26** 226
  dating methods **30** 404, *404*
  historical and regional traditions
    Africa **1** 434–6*
    Anatolia, ancient **1** 839
    Ancient Near East **1** 875, 896*
    Aztec **21** 266
    China **2** 558; **11** 307
    Crete **21** 690–91*
    Cycladic **8** 314, 316*
    Easter Island **23** 738
    Egypt **16** 545
    Egypt, ancient **10** 85–7*
    Etruscan **10** 637, 638–40*; **13** 516
    Fiji **23** 737
    Greece, ancient **13** 516
    Hawaii **23** 738
    Helladic **14** 360*
    Indian subcontinent **15** 750*; **16** 545
    Iran **16** 545, 546
    Islamic **16** 545–6*
    Italy **2** 558; **10** 637, 638–40*
    Maori **23** 737, 738
    Marquesas Islands **23** 737, 738
    Maya **21** 266
    Mesoamerica, Pre-Columbian **21** 266*
    Minoan **21** 690–91*
    Mycenaean **14** 360
    Native North Americans **22** 668
    New Caledonia **23** 737
    Olmec **21** 266
    Pacific Islands **23** 737–8*
    Prehistoric art **25** 475
    Rome, ancient **2** 558; **27** 105
    Society Islands **23** 737
    Solomon Islands **23** 738
    South America, Pre-Columbian **29** 222*, 223–4*
    Syria **16** 545
    Syria-Palestine **1** 896
    Turkey **1** 896
    Zapotec **21** 266
  patinas **24** 258
  technical examination **11** 309–10*
  types
    armour **2** 450
    carpets **16** 546
    ceramics **16** 396
    coins **11** 310; **12** 627
    figurines **21** 690–91
    furniture **3** 585; **11** 307, 308
    ivory-carvings **21** 690–91
    jewellery **11** *307*, 310
    metalwork **1** 896; **11** 309
    painting **11** *306*, 308, *308*; **15** 750
    photography **11** 310, *311*
    postage stamps **25** 329
    pottery **29** 223
    reliefs **10** *88*
    rings **21** 691
    rock art **25** 475
    scientific instruments **11** 310
    scrimshaw **11** 307; **28** 302
    sculpture **11** 308; **24** 258
      Greece, ancient **7** 561
      Italy **7** 562
      Maori **23** *738*
      Pakistan **15** 750
      Rome, ancient **7** 561
    seals **21** 691
    vessels **11** 310
  see also ART (ORIGINAL WORKS OF); COPIES
Forges-Chimay **3** 592
Forget, Louis **6** 513
forging *see* HAMMERING
Forjas, José **22** 245
forks **8** *283*, 285
  England **8** 285; **10** 324
  Ireland **8** *284*
forks—cont.
  Sierra Leone **1** 327
Forlani, Bonaventura **10** 818
Forlano, Giuseppe **19** 806
Forlati, Bruna **11** 312*
Forlati, Ferdinando **11** 311–12*; **32** 206
Forlì
  bastion **3** 359
  Cathedral **7** *308*; **33** 350
  Forum Livi **27** 3
  Palazzo Albicini **7** 308
  S Francesco **30** 887
Forlì, Ansuino da *see* ANSUINO DA FORLÌ
Forlì, Francesco Menzocchi da *see* MENZOCCHI DA FORLÌ, FRANCESCO
Forlì, Giustino del fu Gherardino da *see* GIUSTINO DEL FU GHERARDINO DA FORLÌ
Forlì, Lodovico da *see* LODOVICO DA FORLÌ
Forlì, Melozzo da *see* MELOZZO DA FORLÌ
Forlimpopoli **3** 359
form **11** 312–14*; **17** 801; **24** 383
Form **24** 451
Forma **1** 112; **11** 314–15*; **26** 777
  members **7** 725, 782; **9** 168; **16** 681, 709; **31** 436
Forma **24** 441
formaldehyde plastics **25** 27*
formalin **28** 813
Formalism **11** 312, 313, 315*; **15** 879–80
Forman, Alfred **24** 894
Forman, Charles **4** 801
Forman, John **33** 543
Formanoli, Antonio **25** 218
Forma nueva **29** 309
Formello **10** 591
Formello, Donato da **26** 809; **32** 17
Forment, Damián **11** 316*; **31** 815
  patrons and collectors **4** 409
  works **11** 483; **25** 58; **26** 249; **27** 818; **29** 290, 335
Formentera **3** 106
Formenton, Tommaso **4** 643; **11** 316*
Formes **2** 510; **3** 565; **29** 369
Formes **24** 442
Formes Utiles *see* UNION DES ARTISTES MODERNES
Form Function Finland **24** 452
Formia, Villa of Cicero **27** 65
Formica **25** 23, 26, 27
Formica Corp. **31** 634
Formigé, Jean-Camille **3** 123; **4** 48; **10** 683; **11** 317*
Formigé, Jules **27** 539, 543
Formigine, Andrea da **4** 272; **11** 384
Formilli, C. T. G. **23** 473
Formiści *see* FORMISTS
Formism **11** 317; **25** 116
Formists **11** 317*; **18** 429; **25** 108, 649; **26** 266; **32** 877; **33** 607
  members **7** 292; **8** 431; **29** 582; **30** 199
Formosa *see* TAIWAN
Formosul **30** 559
Formscheyder **14** 616
Formsens **11** 759, 760
Form System **31** 134
form watches *see under* WATCHES → types
formwork (i) (support) *see* CENTERING
formwork (ii) (concrete) *see* SHUTTERING
Fornace, Michele da *see* MICHELE DI MATTEO DA BOLOGNA
Fornaguera, Bonaventura **29** 336
Fornaretto Mantovano **27** 483
Fornari, Anselmo **16** 725
Fornari, Duke **9** 383
Fornari, Manfredi de **11** 294
Fornaroli, Antonio **16** 650
  works **16** *93*
Fornåsa Church **30** 75
Fornels, Eugenio **3** 826
Fornenburgh, Johannes Baptista van **11** 226
Forner, Raquel **2** 400; **11** 317*; **18** 415
Forney **4** 24
Forni, Ludovico **1** 455
Forni, Ulisse **11** 318*
fornices **26** 888, *888*
Fornovo, Giovanni Battista **11** 318*
Foroughi, Mohsen **15** 922
forowa **2** 590
Forres, Sueno's Stone **24** 738
Forrest, Bodrug & Associates **5** 573
Forrest, Theodosius **18** 672
Forrest, William **20** 421
Forrestall, Tom **5** 569
Forrester, James **16** 14
Forrester and Lemon **23** 54
Fors, Pulp factory **4** 790
Forsberg, Nils (1842-1934) **11** 318*
Forsberg, Nils (*b* 1870) **11** 318
Forschauer, Christoffel **4** 178, 179
Forsell, Ulla **30** 103
Forshaw, J. H. **1** 29
Forshem Church **26** 639
Forsmann, Franz **12** 376; **27** 335; **33** 228
  works **27** *335*
Forsmark **30** 72
Forssell, Christian (Didrik) **3** 870; **30** 80
Forssman, Erik **30** 120
Forstenried, Pilgrimage Church of the Holy Cross **26** 646
Forster, Charles **11** 320
Forster, Conrad **12** 366
Förster, Emil von **2** 787; **23** 813; **28** 859
Forster, François **11** 318–19*
Förster, G. **10** 761
Forster, Georg **11** 319*
Förster, Hans *see* FERSTER, HANS
Forster, Hendrik **2** 766
Förster, Ludwig **11** 319*; **24** 438
  assistants **32** 760
  collaboration **2** 786; **14** 150
  teachers
  works **2** 786; **4** 833; **8** 379; **17** 547; **32** 437
Forster, Thomas **11** 319*
Förster, Wieland **8** 134; **11** 320*
Forster & Try **22** 39
Forstner, Leopold **11** 320*; **13** 330; **18** 130
Forsyth, Alexander **1** 734
Forsyth, Douglas **7** 159
Forsyth, Gordon **7** 798
Forsyth, James **22** 809; **30** 533
Forsyth, Joseph **13** 304
Fort, Enrique **2** 215
Fort, Louis **24** 726
Fort, Paul **4** 325; **22** 421; **25** 747; **32** 739
Fort Adams **21** 575
Fortaleza **4** *705*
  Museu Artur Ramos **4** 708
Fortaleza S Teresa **31** 752
Fort-Brescia, Bernardo **2** 494
Fort Canning **28** 773
Fort Caroline **21** 573
Fort Center (FL) **11** 320–21*, *321*; **22** *544*
Fort Clinch **21** 575
Fort Cumberland (Highland) **21** 569
Fort Cunningham (Bermuda) **21** 576
Fort-de-France Cathedral **2** 148
Fort du Plessy, Claude Le *see* LE FORT DU PLESSY, CLAUDE
Forte, Luca **11** 321*; **22** 478
Fortebraccio, Bernardino **5** 672
Fortebraccio, Braccio **1** 553
Forte Netto, Luiz **4** 715; **12** 43
Fortescue-Brickdale, (Mary) Eleanor **11** 322*
Fortetsa **1** 867
Fortezza, Horatio **8** 180
  works **16** *744*
Fort George (Highlands; UK) **21** 549, 569, *569*; **28** 227
Fort George (Vido Island) **21** 574, *574*
Fort Hare **1** 433
Forth Bridge **4** 799, 802
Forti, Simone **24** 407
Fortier, Benoît de **19** 268
Fortier, Bruno **13** 716
Fortier, Gustave **10** 729; **25** 311
Fortier, Jean **5** 836
fortifications **3** 359–60, *360*; **21** 545–99*, *571*
  historical and regional traditions
    Africa **1** 311; **21** 596–7*
    Algeria **1** 311
    Anatolia, ancient **1** *831*; **21** 552–3*
    Ancient Near East **21** 552–4*, *553*
    Antilles, Lesser **2** 148
    Arabia **2** 250–51*; **21** 588
    Assyrian **21** 552
    Austral Islands **25** 896
    Austria **2** 780
    Azerbaijan **2** 892
    Aztec **21** 598, 599
    Babylonian **21** 552
    Belarus' **3** 526
    Belgium **25** 503
    Britain **21** 568–9*, 573–5*, *574*; **26** 905
      Indian subcontinent **5** 417
    Bulgaria **21** 551
    Byzantine **9** 524, 553–6*, *554*, 558*; **21** 562, *563*
    Canaanite **30** 185
    Canada **21** 575
    Central Asia **21** 591*
    Central Asia, Eastern **6** 296; **21** 592*
    Central Asia, Western **6** 197, 199; **21** 591–2*
    Chach **6** 199
    Champa **21** 595
    Chimú **21** 599
    China **21** 593–4*
    Corsica **21** 551
    Crete **32** 159
    Croatia **32** *159*
    Crusaders **18** 422
    Cuba (Caribbean) **8** 231
    Cycladic **8** 310, 311
    Cyprus **32** 159
    Cyprus, ancient **21** 555
    Czech Republic **21** 551
    Denmark **8** 721, 724; **21** 570
    Early Christian (*c.* AD 250-843) **9** 524, 553–5*, *554*
    Egypt **21** 587–8
    Egypt, ancient **9** 844; **21** 554–5*
    England **21** 549, 551, *561*, 564, *569*
    Etruscan **10** 601
    Ferghana **6** 199
    France **21** 549, 550, *567*, 567–8*, 573*
      Mauritius **21** 573
      North America **21** 573
      Prehistoric **21** 551
      13th cent. **8** 40
      17th cent. **32** 79–80
    Germany **12** 369–70; **21** 571*; **31** 195
      Prehistoric **21** 551; **25** 503
      Roman **26** 905
    Greece, ancient **13** 396, 403; **21** 551, 555–8*, *556*, *557*; **26** 909
    Gumelniţa culture **25** 503
    Haiti **14** 57
    Hausa **21** 597
fortifications
  historical and regional traditions—cont.
    Helladic **14** 338, 339, 340
    Hittite **1** *831*; **30** 186
    Indian subcontinent **5** 417; **15** 248, 340; **21** 574, 590, *590*
    Indonesia **21** 596, *596*
    Iran **21** 588–9
    Iran, ancient **21** 553–4*
    Iraq **16** 151; **21** 588
    Ireland **21** 551
    Islamic **16** 141; **21** 581–9*
      Arabia **21** 588
      Egypt **21** 587–8
      Indian subcontinent **15** 340
      Iran **21** 588–9
      Iraq **16** 151; **21** 588
      Morocco **21** 585
      Ottoman **21** 585–7, *586*
      Sicily **16** 172
      Spain **21** 584–5
      Syria **21** 582–3, *583*, 587–8
      Tunisia **16** 156
      Turkey **16** 155; **21** 585–6, *586*
    Italy **10** 601; **21** 565–7*, *566*
    Japan **17** 46; **21** 595*
    Korea **21** 594*
    Lebanon **21** *563*
    Libya **21** *560*
    Linear Pottery culture **25** 503
    Malta (Republic of) **21** 574, 580
    Mauritius **21** 573, 574
    Maya **21** 598, 599
    Mesoamerica, Pre-Columbian **21** 208*, *598*, 598–9*; **24** 367
    Mesopotamia **21** 552*
    Mexico **24** 367
    Morocco **1** 311; **21** 585
    Mozambique **21** 572
    Mycenaean **14** 340
    Native North Americans **21** 597–8*
    Netherlands, the **7** 521; **21** 569–70*, *570*, 572–3; **22** 822
    North America **21** 573–4, 575–6
    Nubia **21** 554–5
    Nupe **21** 597
    Ottoman **21** 585–7, *586*
    Parthian **2** 251
    Philippines **21** 596
    Poland **21** 551
    Portugal **21** 551, 572; **25** 291
    Prehistoric art **21** 551–2*; **25** 498, 503–4*, 522, 535–6
      Bulgaria **21** 551
      Czech Republic **21** 551
      England **21** 551
      France **21** 551
      Germany **21** 551
      Ireland **21** 551
      Poland **21** 551
      Scotland **21** 551
      Spain **21** 551
    Puerto Rico **25** *700*
    Punic **25** 733
    Romania **21** 551; **26** 707
    Rome, ancient **21** 548, 558–61*, *560*, *561*; **26** 905, 907, 909
    Russia **21** 561; **27** 370
    Sarawak **21** 596
    Sardinia **21** 551
    Sasanian **21** 554
    Scandinavia **21** 570*
    Scotland **21** 549, 551, *569*; **28** 223
    Sicily **16** 172; **21** 556, *557*
    Singapore **21** 575
    Slovakia **21** 551
    Sogdiana **6** 199
    South America, Pre-Columbian **21** 599*
    South-east Asia **21** 595–6*
    Spain **21** 551, 573*, 584–5; **25** 733
    Sri Lanka **21** 572, 575
    Sweden **21** 570

fortifications
historical and regional traditions—cont.
Syria **18** 422; **21** 582–3, *583*, 587–8
Syria-Palestine **21** 553, *553*; **30** 185, 186, 190–91, *190*
Thailand **21** 595
Tibet **21** 592–3*
Tokharistan **6** 199
Tripol'ye culture **25** 503
Tunisia **16** 156
Turkey **16** 155; **21** 585–6, *586*; **31** *700*
United States of America **21** 575–6
Urartian **21** 553; **31** *700*
Venetian Empire **21** 550; **32** 159, *159*
Venezuela **32** 168–9
Vietnam **21** 595, 596
Wales **32** 781
Yoruba **21** 597
materials
brick **31** 195
stone **21** 559, 561–2
tamarisk **6** 296
wood **21** 561–2
types
concentric **8** 277; **21** 562, 564, *564*
fortification rasante **21** 546
see also ARCHITECTURE → types → military; BARBICANS; BASTIONS; CASTLES
Fortification Tablets **1** 117, 118
fortified houses *see under* HOUSES → types
fortified monasteries *see under* MONASTERIES → types
fortified palaces *see under* PALACES → types
fortified towns *see under* TOWNS → types
Fortin, Auguste **24** 387
Fortin, Felix **20** 214
Fortin, Jean **12** 814
Fortin, Jean-Baptiste-Auguste **20** 214
Fortin, Marc-Aurèle **11** 322*
Fortin, Teresita **14** 716
Fortini, Giovacchino **3** 812; **11** 322*; **29** 572
Fort Jaffna *see under* JAFFNA
Fort Lamy *see* N'DJAMENA
Fort Leavenworth (KS) **21** 576
Fort Lupin **21** 568
Fort Macon **21** 575
Fort MacPherson **22** 640
Fort Michilimaquinac **22** 616
Fort Moro **21** 573
Fort Nassau **13** 875
Fort Nelson **21** 575
Fort Neuf **21** 574
Fort Niagara **21** 573
Fortnum, C(harles) D(rury) E(dward) **11** 323*
Fortnum & Mason **11** 323
Forton Service Station (Lancs) **28** 488
Fort Ontario **21** 573
Fortoul, Hippolyte **11** 323–4*; **32** 82
Fort Pitt **21** 573
Fort Rae **22** 639
Fort Raleigh **21** 573
fortresses **3** 359; **6** 49; **12** 173; **21** 546
historical and regional traditions
Armenia (Europe) **2** 427
Bhutan **3** 913, *913*
Byzantine **9** 553, 554, 555–6*
Crete **8** 156
Early Christian (*c*. AD 250-843) **9** 553, 554
Egypt, ancient **9** 844–9, *845*, *846*, *847*, *848*; **21** 554, *555*
France **21** *567*
Georgia **12** 318; **30** *388*
fortresses
historical and regional traditions—cont.
Honduras **14** 713
Hungary **16** 228
Inca **15** *162*
Islamic **16** 141, 156, 217, 228; **20** *157*
Italy **11** *688*
Knights Hospitaller **21** 574
Korea **18** 260, 265, 279; **21** 594
Netherlands, the **29** 452
Nubia **9** 844, 847; **21** 554–5, *555*; **23** 278
Ottoman **16** 228
Portugal **29** 452
Romania **26** 706
Rome, ancient **23** 300; **25** 423
Russia **17** *872*; **22** *181*; **25** *679*; **27** *211*, 370, 371
Serbia **28** 440, *444*
South America, Pre-Columbian **15** *162*
Spain **16** 217; **20** *157*; **31** 588
Sri Lanka **29** 452
Tunisia **16** 156
Ukraine **31** *549*
United States of America **27** *532*; **31** 588
Urartian **3** 356; **31** 699
Venetian Empire **8** 156
see also ARCHITECTURE → types → military; FORTS
Fortress Liechtenau **12** 370
Fortrey, Samuel **18** 5
Fort Rhijnauwen **21** 570
Fort Royal, Fort Saint Louis **2** 148
forts **3** 359; **6** 49; **21** 545, 546, 572, 573, 576–7
historical and regional traditions **1** *461*
Africa **1** 318
Belgium **21** *577*
Britain **1** 318; **21** 568, *574*; **26** 907
Byzantine **9** 554
Canada **21** 575
Crete **8** 154
Cyprus, ancient **8** 334
Early Christian (*c*. AD 250-843) **9** 554
England **10** 226; **14** 23, *23*; **21** *576*
France **26** 907
Germany **21** 571
Greece, ancient **21** *557*
Indian subcontinent **1** *461*; **15** 311; **21** *574*
Ireland **9** 390–91; **21** 552
Islamic **16** 151
Mozambique **21** *572*
Netherlands, the **21** *572*
Portugal **1** 318; **21** *572*
Prehistoric art **9** 391; **21** 552
Romania **26** 707
Rome, ancient **6** 68–9*; **21** 558–61; **25** 423
Britain **26** 907
England **14** 23, *23*
France **26** 907
Serbia **28** 439
Scotland **21** *569*
Serbia **28** 439
Sicily **21** *557*
Sri Lanka **21** *572*
United States of America **21** *575*, 575–6
types
coastal **21** 568, 576
hill-forts
Bronze Age **25** 519
Byzantine **9** 554
Early Christian (*c*. AD 250-843) **9** 554
England **10** 226; **25** *537*
Ireland **21** 551
Prehistoric art **21** 551; **23** 808; **25** 522, 535–6, *537*
Scotland **21** 551
forts
types
hill-forts—cont.
Spain **21** 551
pentagonal **21** 547
ring **21** 547
shore forts **21** 560, *561*
star **21** 547
tetrapyrgia **9** 554, 555; **21** 547, 563, *563*
see also ARCHITECTURE → types → military; FORTRESSES
Fort St George *see* GEORGETOWN (GUYANA)
Fort St Sebastian **21** 572, *572*
Fort S Felipe **21** 574
Fort S Leonardo **21** 574
Fort Tilbury (Essex) **21** 569
Fort Totten Reservation (ND), Four Winds School **22** 671
Fortuna, Alessandro **9** 92
Fortuna Faience Factory **11** 105
Fortunatus **13** 266
Fortunatus, Venatius *see* VENATIUS FORTUNATUS
Fortune **4** 586; **15** 829, 831
Fortuny, Museo *see under* VENICE → museums
Fortuny cupola *see under* STAGE SCENERY → types
Fortuny i Baró, Maria **11** 324
Fortuny Tablet **16** 418; **20** 158; **22** 535
Fortuny y Carbo, Mariano **31** 757
Fortuny y Madrazo, Mariano **11** 324, 326–7*
house **2** 552; **16** 721
works **9** 245; **16** 418; **30** 685
Fortuny y Marsal, Mariano (José Bernardo) **11** 324–6*; **16** 678; **26** 776
groups and movements **23** 504; **24** 829
works **11** *324*, *325*; **29** 284
Fort Vaudreuil **21** 573
Fort Worth (TX) **31** 735
Amon Carter Museum **2** 852; **12** 647
gardens **11** 347
Kimbell Art Museum **17** *724*, 725; **22** 367; **28** 584; **31** 597, 667
lighting **19** 365
Forty, F. J. **19** 577
Forty, Jean-François **11** 627
Fort Yukon (AK) **22** 640, 645
Fort Zeelandia (Formosa) **6** 331
Fort Zeelandia (Guyana) **13** 875
Forum *see under* TYPE-FACES
Forum **10** 716; **22** 832; **24** 449; **31** 867
Forum: Maandschrift voor architectur en gebonden kunsten **24** 450
Forum Cornelii *see under* IMOLA
Forum Group **26** 425
Forum Livi *see under* FORLÌ
Forward (Vperyod) group **4** 231
Forzore di Spinelli **29** 407
Foscari (family) **3** 317
Foscari, Francesco, Doge of Venice (*reg* 1423-57) **11** 328*; **13** 95
Foscari, Nicolò **11** 328
Foscarini, Marco **2** 163; **3** 380; **24** 842
Foschi, Pier Francesco **10** 858; **27** 732, 851
Foschini, Arnaldo **24** 694; **26** 762
Foshan **6** *614*, 621; **11** 328–9*
Foshchevataya **32** 528
Foss, Harald Frederik **30** 757
Fossa, S Maria **13** 124
Fossacésia, S Giovanni in Vénere **26** 625
Fossanova Abbey **7** *347*; **13** 51, 98; **16** 627, 762
Fossati, Carlo Giuseppe **11** 329
Fossati, Davide Antonio **11** 329*; **13** 277; **14** 900
Fossati, Domenico **11** 329; **13** 740
Fossati, E. Radice **3** 438
Fossati, Gaspare Trajano **11** 329*
collaboration **16** 595
works **9** 527; **16** 221, 593
Fossati, Giorgio **11** 329; **22** 388; **25** 144
Fossati, Giovanni Battista **29** 841
Fossati, Giuseppe **9** 527; **11** 329; **16** 221, 593, 595
Fossati, Joan Battista **8** 742
Fossati, Pietro **2** 395
Fossatum Africae **21** 559
Fossberg, Petrus **30** 110
Fossé, Jacques **1** 497
Fosse, Jean-François **19** 801
Fosse-la-Ville, Collégiale St Feuillen **3** 541
Fossen, Jacob van *see* ES, JACOB VAN
Fossi, Giulo **5** 868
Fossin **17** 526
Fossum **11** 330*; **25** *470*, 532; **30** *65*
rock art **25** *532*
Fossum Master **23** 229
Foster, Ben **31** 141
Foster, Birket **4** 868
Foster, John (1648-81) **4** 476; **11** 330–31*
works **4** *476*
Foster, John, I (1759-1827) **11** 330*; **19** 505
Foster, John, II (1787-1846) **7** 502; **11** 330*; **19** 505
Foster, Myles Birket **4** 363, 868; **10** 254; **11** 331*; **32** 502
works **11** *331*
Foster, Nathaniel G. **3** 6
Foster, Norman **11** 332–4*; **26** 540
architecture **1** 737; **3** 217; **10** 285; **12** 794; **19** 578
airports **1** 495
banks **3** 177; **11** *333*; **14** 721; **16** 55
curtain walls **8** *279*
factories **10** 749; **14** *522*; **30** 468
space-frames **29** *250*
university buildings **10** 371; **22** 366; **23** 248; **27** 524; **29** 250
collaboration **14** 521
furniture **14** 522
groups and movements **2** 309
Foster, Richard **4** 789; **17** 620
Foster, Wendy Ann **11** 332; **26** 540
Foster, William **5** 668
Foster Associates **1** 495; **10** 242; **14** 521; **19** 578
works **10** *241*
Fot (*fl* 11th cent.) **32** 525
Fót (Hungary) **14** 889
Roman Catholic church **14** 889
Fota **16** 24
Fothergill, John (1712-80) **3** 310
Fothergill, John (*d* 1782) **2** 456; **4** 540; **10** 333, 342
works **10** *333*
Fothergill, John (*fl* 1820-30) **29** 634
Fothergill, Watson **23** 258
Fotiades, Theodoros **8** 364; **11** 334*
Fotoform group **17** 878; **23** 9; **29** 608, 780
Fotograf **31** 566
Fotografia **9** 50
fotografia, La **24** 452
Fotografia artistica, La **24** 447, 739
Fotografický obzor **24** 440
Fotografie **24** 440
Fotografisk tidskrift **24** 451
Fotograf Lyubitel **25** 648
fotoleos **4** 262
Fotologia **24** 449
Foto Ringle + Pit **29** 641
fototesta **24** 255
Fototipia Laurent **18** 868
Fotuna **31** 893
fou see under VESSELS → types
Fouard, Moïse-Jean-Baptiste **24** 397
Foucart, Georges **10** 81
Foucault, Léon **24** 655
Foucault, Michel **11** 334–5*; **25** 361; **26** 62
Foucault, Nicolas-Joseph **11** 335*; **18** 626
Foucher, Alfred Charles Auguste **11** 335*
collections **15** 744
pupils **9** 401
surveys **1** 211
writings **1** 211; **15** 211; **19** 690; **28** 535; **30** 848
Foucher, Blaise **11** 630
works **11** *630*
Fouchier, Bertram de **4** 53
Foucou, Jean-Joseph **11** 335–6*; **22** 85
collaboration **13** 234
patrons and collectors **20** 897
pupils **10** 509
Foucquet, Bernard **11** 336*; **29** 689; **30** 85
Foucquet, Jacques **11** 336*; **29** 689; **30** 88
Foucquet, Nicolas *see* FOUQUET, NICOLAS
Fouere, Olwen **7** 552
Fougères **3** 359; **21** 565
Fougeron, André **11** 302, 336–7*, 550, 551
Fougoumba congregational mosque **1** 317
Fougstedt, Arvid **30** 81
Fouilhoux, Jacques André **14** 199, 735, 813; **15** 885, 886
works **5** *136*
Fouilloy, Evrard de *see* EVRARD DE FOUILLOY
Fouilloy, Hugh of *see* HUGH OF FOUILLOY
Foujita, Tsugouharu **3** 120; **11** 337*, 550; **23** 384; **26** 113
foul-biting **11** 337*
Foulc *Madonna* **8** 798; **20** 303
Fould, Achille **16** 876
Fould, Louis **11** 337–8*
Foulis, Andrew **1** 648; **28** 269, 271, 274; **31** 495
Foulis, Robert **11** 338*; **12** 776; **28** 274
patrons and collectors **28** 269
pupils **1** 648
works **28** 271; **31** 495
Foulis Academy *see under* GLASGOW
Foulis Easter Church (Tayside) **28** 233
Foulis Press **11** 338
Foullet **17** 666
Foullon, Guillaume Elie Le *see* LE FOULLON, GUILLAUME ELIE
Foulon, Benjamin **7** 466; **31** 851
Foulston, John **10** 97; **14** 786
Foum al-Hassan **1** *376*; **22** 129
Foumban **1** *394*; **3** 151, 152; **5** 525
royal palace **3** 152
foundations **6** 640, 690; **25** 216; **27** 137; **28** 830, 874
founders **20** 218
Founders' Company **10** 339
Founder's Cup (1541) **3** 597
Foundress's Cup (1507) **14** 418
foundries **6** 830*, 865; **12** 401; **28** 242
Foundry Painter **13** 521, 571; **32** 36
Fountain, Marian **23** 73
works **23** *72*
Fountain Brush Co. **1** 494
fountain courts **16** 202, *203*
Fountaine, Andrew (1676-1753) **10** 364; **11** 347–8*; **14** 435

Fountaine, Andrew (*d* 1874) **11** 348
fountain houses **11** 339; **13** 381–2; **21** *899*
Fountain of Hercules and Antaeus **12** 812
fountain pens *see under* PENS → types
fountains **11** 338–47*; **12** 105, 109
historical and regional traditions
China **3** *517*; **11** 338
Czech Republic **33** *435*
England **12** 126, 128
France **7** 531; **11** 341, 343; **12** 113, 120
Baroque **11** *344*, *560*
Renaissance **11** *342*; **13** *226*
19th cent. **1** *497*
Germany
Gothic **11** *341*
Mannerism **12** *347*
Renaissance **11** *223*; **28** *138*
16th cent. **23** *252*
20th cent. **12** *196*
Gothic **11** *340*, *341*
Greece, ancient **11** 339; **13** 381–2; **26** 910
Indian subcontinent **11** 340
Indonesia **12** *102*
Islamic **11** 339–40*; **16** 141, 142
Indian subcontinent **11** 340
Ottoman **16** 225, *226*, 265
Sicily **12** *78*
Spain **11** 340; **16** *368*
Syria **11** 340
Turkey **16** 225, *226*, 265
Italy **9** 21; **12** 110, 114, 116, 117
Baroque **11** *343*; **16** 698, *700*; **22** *45*; **27** *647*
Gothic **11** *340*
Mannerism **1** *791*; **11** *341*
Renaissance **16** 696; **19** *372*; **22** 33
Roman **12** *68*; **27** *66*
Romanesque **26** *623*
stile liberty **16** *648*
16th cent. **25** *259*; **31** *321*
Nepal **22** 759–60
Netherlands, the **12** 131
Ottoman **16** 225, *226*, 265
Palestine **20** *231*
Romanesque **26** *623*
Rome, ancient **11** 339; **12** 69; **22** 161; **26** 863
Greece **26** 910
Italy **12** *68*; **27** *66*
Russia **24** *547*
Sicily **12** *78*
Spain **11** 340; **16** *368*
Switzerland **11** *346*; **30** 136
Syria **11** 340
Turkey **16** 225, *226*, 265
United States of America **11** *345*
lighting **7** 531
materials
bronze **16** *368*; **33** *435*
mosaics **27** *66*
sculpture **12** *347*; **16** 696; **29** 563–4
types
drinking fountains **2** 510; **11** 340, 346
wine-fountains **23** 767–8
Fountains Abbey (N. Yorks) **7** 351, 353; **10** *225*; **11** 348–50*, *349*, *350*; **12** 6, 128, 312; **21** *833*, 836, 837; **22** 716; **26** 381, 590; **29** 861
chapter house **6** 464
dormitory **21** 843, 844
Infirmary **14** 780
restoration **2** 321
Fountains Hall (N.Yorks) **11** 348
fountain-spouts **20** 51
founts **31** 495, *497*
Fouquay, Nicolas **27** 249
Fouque, Joseph **22** 242
Fouque Arnoux **11** 606
Fouquet, Alphonse **26** 191
works **17** III2
Fouquet, Bernard **8** 190
Fouquet, François **11** 355, 356, 726
Fouquet, Georges **2** 521, 565; **11** 635; **12** 869; **17** 529; **22** 253
works **2** *521*
Fouquet, Jean (*c.* 1415/20–*c.* 1481) **11** 350–55*; **18** 827; **24** 471; **31** 226
attributions **20** 703, 788
collaboration **7** 595
copies **31** 842
manuscript illumination **4** 395; **6** *463*; **7** 243; **9** 221; **11** *353*, *354*, 399; **31** 228
paintings **11** 532
diptychs **11** *454*
history **9** 270; **24** *116*
portraits **11** *353*, 399; **26** 765; **31** 843
religious **11** *351*
patrons and collectors
Aumale, Henri-Eugène-Philippe-Louis de Bourbon, Duc d' **23** 523
Berry, Charles de Valois, Duc de **31** 844
Charles, Duke of Orléans (*reg* 1407-65) **31** 842
Charles VII, King of France (*reg* 1422-61) **31** 832, 843
Chevalier, Etienne **6** 562
Durrieu, Paul **9** 453
Ertborn, Florent (Joseph) van **10** 491
Louis XI, King of France (*reg* 1461-83) **31** 843
Nemours, Jacques d'Armagnac, Duc de (1433-77) **16** 854
Niccolò III, 12th Marchese of Ferrara (*reg* 1393-1441) **10** 519
Peter II, Duke of Bourbon (*reg* 1488-1503) **4** 545
Robertet, Jean **7** 596; **26** 454
Thompson, Henry Yates **30** 749
pupils **20** 639, 707
Fouquet, Jean (1899-1984) **2** 521; **17** 529
Fouquet, Louis **11** 355, 356
Fouquet, Nicolas **11** 356–7*; **20** 137; **31** 321
architecture **6** 508; **11** 516, 657; **12** 747; **19** 264, 265, 721; **32** 96
books **31** 322
collections **11** 662
gardens **12** 121; **19** 162
interior decoration **11** 573, 574
manuscripts **17** 449
medals **3** 856
paintings **4** 552; **19** 21
productions **31** 165
sculpture **2** 92; **14** 804; **25** 79, 705
stucco **12** 725; **19** 76; **29** 833
tapestries **11** 641; **30** 321; **32** 96
Fouquet, Pieter **18** 628; **28** 166
Fouquier, Jacques **11** 357–8*
patrons and collectors **26** 349
pupils **6** 433; **25** 33
reproductive prints by others **22** 116; **24** 397
works **11** *357*; **18** 710
Fouquières, Louise-Marie Becq de *see* BECQ DE FOUQUIÈRES, LOUISE-MARIE
Four, The **2** 562; **11** 358*; **12** 780; **20** 22; **25** 347; **28** 275
members **12** 780; **19** 875–6
Four Arts Society of Artists **11** 358*; **22** 178; **27** 394
members **5** 26; **10** 843; **18** 444, 527; **21** 735; **24** 566; **31** 572
four-centred arches *see under* ARCHES → types
Fourchambault Iron Works **15** 828
Fourché, Léonard **31** 382
four-colour painting *see under* PAINTING → types
Fourcy, Henry de **11** 574
Fourcy, Jean de, Sieur de Corbinière *see* CORBINIÈRE, JEAN DE FOURCY, Sieur de
Fourdinois, Alexandre George **28** 155
Fourdinois, Henri **5** 350; **11** 599; **28** 155
works **5** *350*
Four Dog Palette **23** 847
Fourdrinier, Henry **32** 816
Fourdrinier, John **24** 43
Fourdrinier, Paul **14** 856
Fourdrinier, Sealy **24** 43; **32** 816
Four from the Xiling Region, The **7** 130
Four from the Xi Region, The **7** 130
Four Gentlemen of Jiading **19** 378
Four Great Calligraphers of the Northern Song **14** 825; **21** 419
Four Great Masters (Japan) **17** 198
Four Great Masters from Abroad (Japan) **17** 189
Four Great Pupils of Kanō Tan'yū **18** 537
Four Hours of the Day Clock **11** 626
Fourier **3** 313
Fourier, Charles **11** 358, 521; **12** 144; **24** 591; **30** 458
Fourierism **11** 358–9*
Fourmaintraux factory **30** 885
Four Masters of the Yuan **6** 790, 820; **14** 822; **23** 165, 168; **25** 73; **29** 244; **32** 845
Fourment, Daniel **3** 615; **27** 296
Fourment, Hélène **25** 274, *274*; **27** *298*
Fourment, Susanna **25** *284*
Fourment-Piqueri (family) **10** 717
Fourment-Stappaert (family) **10** 717
Fourmile style **22** 604
Fourmois, Théodore **3** 562; **11** 359*; **18** 877
Fournel, Victor **7** 304
Fournérat, Nicolas **11** 609; **19** 397
Fournier, Fortuné **11** 581
Fournier, Jacques, Cardinal *see* BENEDICT XII, Pope
Fournier, Jean **14** 42
Fournier, Lionel **22** 795; **30** 834
Fournier, Louis-Antoine **7** 806
Fournier, Pierre-Simon **4** 360; **11** 359*
works **22** 370; **31** 495, *495*
writings **31** 495
Fournival, Richard de *see* RICHARD DE FOURNIVAL
Four Per Cent Industrial Dwellings Co. **19** 574
Four Purists **11** 365; **14** 732; **19** 423
Fourquevaulx, Marquis de **13** 325
Four Rens **26** 215
Fourrier, Marcel **30** 19
Four Small Wangs **23** 581
Fourth dimension **1** 75; **4** 201; **8** 244; **11** 359–60*; **20** 851, *851*; **26** 40; **30** 7; **31** 763
Fourth Group **10** 872
Fourth Style painting *see under* ROME, ANCIENT → painting → wall
Four Wangs **32** 842, 843
Fous, J. **25** 430
Foussadier (family) **30** 327; **31** 659
Fouta Djallon **1** 313
Fouzé **7** 778
Fowke, Francis **11** 360–61*
assistants **30** 162
works **1** 798; **7** 687; **9** 319, 724; **10** 682; **14** 149; **16** 54; **22** 363; **28** 273; **30** 503, *504*
Fowler, Charles **2** 324; **11** 361*; **27** 358
Fowler, Cylford **28** 692
Fowler, Daniel **5** 564
Fowler, John (1817-98) **4** 802; **16** 55; **21** 349
Fowler, John (1906-77) **10** 284
works **10** *285*
Fowler, Michael **32** 797
Fowler, Orson Squire **11** 361*; **16** 62
Fowler, Thaddeus Mortimer **4** 81
Fowler Architectural Collection *see under* BALTIMORE (MD) → John S. Hopkins University
Fowler & Colefax **10** 284
Fowles, Francis **2** 744
Fowles, Joseph **2** 772
Fox **22** 552, 627
Fox, A. R. **12** 316
Fox, C. **32** 274
Fox, (Georgiana) Caroline, Baroness Holland *see* LENNOX, (GEORGIANA) CAROLINE, Baroness Holland
Fox, Cecil Croker **20** 30
Fox, Charles **10** 681; **11** 362*
Fox, Charles James **5** 303; **23** *190*; **27** 853
Fox, Charles Richard **11** 362
Fox, E(manuel) Phillips **11** 362–3*; **14** 307
Fox, Ethel Carrick **11** 363*
Fox, George **11** 785; **31** 265
Fox, Henderson & Co. **5** 13; **12** 791; **24** 293
works **26** *17*
Fox, Henry, 1st Baron Holland **11** 362
Fox, Henry Edward, 4th Baron Holland **11** 362; **29** 380
Fox, Henry Richard Vassall, 3rd Baron Holland **4** 322; **10** 726; **11** 362
Fox, Mary *see* MARY, Princess of Liechtenstein
Fox, Revel (Albert Ellis) **5** 668; **9** 427; **11** 363*; **29** 106
Fox, Richard *see* FOXE, RICHARD
Fox, Sheldon **18** 193*
Fox, Stephen **11** 362
Fox, Terry **29** 99; **32** 420
Fox, The **6** 486
Fox, Vincent *see* VOLPE, VINCENT
Fox, William **7** 327
Fox-Davies, A. C.
works **14** *415*
Foxe, John **10** 246
Foxe, Richard **5** 515; **10** 260, 325; **23** 686; **33** 236, 238
Fox Hill **3** 61
foxing **11** 363*
Foxley (Hereford & Worcs) **12** 131
Fox-Strangways, W(illiam) T(homas) H(orner) **11** 363–4*
Fox Talbot, William Henry *see* TALBOT, WILLIAM HENRY FOX
fox teeth *see under* TEETH → types
Foyatier, Denys **11** 364*; **12** 10
Foy & Gibson Ltd. **24** 894
Foynitsky, Aleksandr **21** 811
Foys **30** 366
Foy Suzor-Coté, Marc-Aurèle de *see* SUZOR-COTÉ, MARC-AURÈLE DE FOY
Foz, Marquêses de **4** 630; **10** 728; **25** 318
Fraass, Erich **33** 30
Fracanzan, Giovanni Battista **22** 388
Fracanzano, Alessandro **11** 364
Fracanzano, Cesare **11** 364*
Fracanzano, Francesco **11** 364–5*; **16** 673; **27** 149
Fracanzano, Michelangelo **11** 364
Fracassini, Cesare **5** 527
Fraccaroli, Innocenzo **16** 705
Fracchia, Giuseppe di Luciano *see* FRECHA, JOSÉ
Frączkiewicz, Antoni **25** 114
Frade, Ramón **25** 701
Fradeletto, Antonio **32** 197
Fraenkel, Paul **8** 438; **24** 405
Fraenkel, T. O. **28** 121
Frafra **1** 289, 312
Fragelli, Marcelo (Aciolly) **4** 714; **11** 365*
Fraget, Józef **32** 878
Fragiacomo, Pietro **24** 708; **32** 197
Fragner, Jaroslav **11** 365–6*
groups and movements **14** 732
works **8** 380, 381; **25** 438; **28** 850
Fragnicourt **25** 518
Fragonard, Alexandre-Evariste **11** 370–71*
dealers **2** 614
groups and movements **31** 374
teachers **11** 366, 369
works **11** *370*; **20** 924; **21** 761, *761*; **28** 523
Fragonard, Jean-Honoré **11** 366–70*; **24** 136
attributions **3** 852; **21** 643
book illustrations **2** 412; **4** 361
collaboration **12** 336; **14** 791, 846
drawings **2** 84; **18** 713
etchings **10** 554
exhibitions **10** 679
frames **11** *407*, *408*
groups and movements **31** 373
interior decoration **11** 579; **23** 678
paintings **11** 540
fêtes galantes **11** 37, *368*; **18** 712
genre **12** 292; **28** 384; **32** 429
mythological **5** 884; **11** *367*; **22** 415
oil sketches **23** 381
portraits **27** *571*
patrons and collectors **11** 658
André, Edouard (-François) (1833-94) **16** 851
Azincourt, Barthélémy-Augustin Blondel d' **2** 904
Bache, Jules Semon **3** 18
Bergeret de Grancourt, (Pierre-) Jacques-Onésyme **3** 776
Beurdeley, (Emmanuel-) Alfred (1847-1919) **3** 889
Beurnonville, Etienne-Edmond Martin, Baron de **3** 890
Caffiéri, Philippe (ii) (1714-74) **5** 380
Clark, Robert Sterling **7** 377
Cognacq, (Théodore-) Ernest **7** 528
Doucet, Jacques (-Antoine) **9** 196
Du Barry, (Marie-Jeanne Bécu,) Comtesse **9** 313; **10** 478
Filomarino, Ascanio, Cardinal **11** 81
Frick, Henry Clay **11** 774
Groult, Camille **13** 705
Hall, Peter Adolf **14** 80
Hawkins, John Heywood (1803-77) **14** 252
La Caze, Louis **18** 588
Livois, Marquis de **19** 510
Morgan, J(ohn) Pierpont (1837-1913) **22** 111
Morny, Charles-Auguste, Duc de **22** 127
Papillon de La Ferté, Denis-Pierre-Jean **24** 63
Pâris, Pierre-Adrien **24** 177
Péreire (family) **24** 396
Rothschild (family) **27** 223
Saint-Morys, Charles Paul Jean-Baptiste de Bourgevin Vialart de **27** 568
Saint-Non, Richard de, Abbé **27** 570, 571
Seymour-Conway, Richard, 4th Marquess of Hertford **28** 527

Fragonard, Jean-Honoré
patrons and collectors—cont.
Sireul, Jean-Claude Gaspard de **28** 790
Véri (-Raionard), Louis-Gabriel, Marquis de **32** 255
Voyer, Marquis de **32** 719
Wallace, Richard **28** 528
Yusupov, Nikolay (Borisovich), Prince (1751- 1831) **33** 579
pupils **11** 370; **12** 336; **19** 25
reproductions in ceramics **6** 462
reproductive prints by others **20** 914
Beauvarlet, Jacques-Firmin **3** 463
Gautier-Dagoty, Louis-Charles **12** 209
Launay, Nicolas de (1739-92) **18** 858
Launay, Robert de **18** 858
Saint-Non, Richard de, Abbé **27** 570
studio **29** 856
teachers **4** 513; **19** 646; **22** 683
Fragonard, Théophile **11** 366
Fragrant Hill Resort Hotel **14** 788
Frähn, C. M. **16** 547
Fraigevise, Frédéric *see* FRÉGEVIZE, FRÉDÉRIC
Fraikin, Charles-Auguste **3** 572; **11** 371*; **21** 369; **25** 64
Fraile, Alfonso **11** 371–2*
Frain an der Thaya, Schloss *see* VRANOV NAD DYJÍ
Fraisinger, Caspar *see* FREISINGER, CASPAR
Fraisse, Abraham **18** 873
Fraisse, Jean-Antoine **6** 455; **11** 577
Fraknó *see* FORCHTENAU
Frakno, Bishop **30** 210
frame-and-mat *see under* ARCHITECTURE → techniques
framemakers **11** 377–8*, 382–3, 384
frames **9** 12, 17–18; **11** *372*, 372–499*; **25** 664
historical and regional traditions
Africa **1** 306
Belgium **11** 438–50*, *442*, *450*
Byzantine **9** 658; **11** 374
Carolingian **11** 374
Denmark **11** *469*, 472, *472*, 473, *475*, *476*, *478*
England **9** 16; **11** 375, *375*, 420–38*, *421*, *422*, *423*, *425*, *427*, *428*, *430*, *431*, *433*, *436*, *437*, 455–7*
Etruscan **11** 379
Finland **11** *474*, *477*, *478*
France **9** 18; **11** *373*, 375, 377, 398–420*, *399*, *400*, *401*, *402*, *403*, *407*, *408*, *409*, *412*, *413*, *414*, *415*, *416*
Germany **11** 375, 450–65*, *451*, *453*, *454*, *456*, *457*, *458*, *459*, *460*, *461*, *462*, *463*, *464*
Gothic **11** 376, 379–81, *380*, *381*, 398–9, *399*, 420–21, *421*, 438–40, 450–54*, *451*, *452*, *453*, 465–6, *466*, *479*, 479–83*, *481*
Ireland **16** 26
Italy **9** 14; **11** 374, 375, 376, 379–98*, *380*, *381*, *382*, *383*, *384*, *385*, *386*, *388*, *389*, *390*, *391*, *392*, *393*, *394*, *395*, *396*, *397*; **24** 5
Netherlands, the **11** 373, 438–50*, *440*, *441*, *443*, *447*; **23** *542*
Norway **11** 465–6, *466*, *472*, *474*
Rome, ancient **11** 379
Russia **9** 18; **10** *721*
Scandinavia **11** 465–78*
frames
historical and regional traditions—cont.
Spain **11** 373, 375, 376, 479–96*, *481*, *484*, *486*, *488*, *489*, *492*, *493*, *495*, *496*
Sweden **11** *468*, *469*, *470*, *471*, 471–2, *472*, *474*, *475*, *476*
Switzerland **11** *452*
United States of America **11** *496*, 496–9*, *497*, *498*
historiography *see under* HISTORIOGRAPHY → types
materials
acrylic **8** 129
candle holders **11** 383
clay **4** 254
coral **7** 835
ebony **9** 17; **11** 374, *443*, 444, 445, *456*
enamel **10** *721*
glass **8** 129; **11** 407
gold **9** 17; **10** *721*
lace **11** 461, *461*
mouldings **24** 4
pastiglia **11** *383*, *384*, *393*
plaster **9** 16; **11** 377
silver **9** 658
walnut **11** *383*
wood **11** 373
techniques
carving **11** 374
gilding **9** 17; **11** 373–4, *383*, *385*, *386*, *389*, *390*, *394*, *422*, *437*, *440*, *441*, *443*, *488*, *489*
types
aedicular **11** *383*, 383–4, *390*, *400*, 435, *436*, *484*; **31** 627
Auricular **11** 391–2, *392*, 423–4*, *424*, 446
Canaletto **11** 395, *395*
Carlo Maratta **11** 394–5, *429*, 429–30
cassetta **11** *384*, 384–7, *385*, *386*, 421, *454*, *463*, 483, *488*, 490
cusped **5** 164
Kneller **11** 424
leaf **11** 392
Lely **11** 424, *425*
Lutma **11** 446
Salvator Rosa **11** 393–4, *394*
Sansovino **11** *390*, 391, *391*
Sunderland *see* Auricular
tabernacle *see* aedicular
tambour *see* TAMBOUR (i) (EMBROIDERY)
tondo **11** 387–9, *388*
uses
altarpieces **11** 374, 379–81, 420–21; **24** 4, 5
drawings **8** 129; **9** 26; **11** 407
frescoes **11** 763
icons **24** 4
miniatures (paintings) **9** 27
mosaics **11** 374
painting **9** 14; **11** 372
panel paintings **9** 14; **11** 379; **24** 4–5
pastels **11** 407
photography **24** 674
polyptychs **24** 5
prints **9** 26; **11** 407
rock art **11** 374
watercolours **9** 26; **11** 407
see also DOORFRAMES; MIRROR FRAMES; WINDOW-FRAMES
frames, drawing *see* DRAWING-FRAMES
Frameworks **24** 429
Framlingham (Suffolk) **6** 56
Castle **12** 173
St Michael **10** 261
tomb of Thomas Howard, 3rd Duke of Norfolk **10** *262*
Frampton, Christabel **11** 500
Frampton, George (James) **11** 499–500*
groups and movements **23** 34, 35
Frampton, George (James)—cont.
patrons and collectors **14** 132
works **5** 270; **20** 925
Frampton, Hollis **10** 688
Frampton, Kenneth **31** 672
Frampton, Meredith **11** 500
Frampton-on-Severn (Glos), St Mary **10** 338; **11** 253; **18** 902; **26** 688
Franc, Martin Le *see* MARTIN LE FRANC
França, José-Augusto **25** 320
Français, Atelier *see* ATELIER FRANÇAIS
Français, François-Louis **11** 500–501*
collaboration **3** 259
teachers **1** 642; **12** 608
works **11** *501*
Français, Louis, Musée *see under* PLOMBIÈRES-LES-BAINS
Française Legère *see under* TYPE-FACES
Francalancia, Riccardo **26** 776
Francart, Jacob **7** 487; **14** 621
Francart, Jacques **11** 501–2*
assistants **9** 412
patrons and collectors **13** 917
pupils **21** 149
works **3** 545, *546*
Francart, Jacques (before 1550-1601) **11** 501
Francastel, Pierre **2** 536; **11** 502*, 676; **24** 145
works **28** 926
Francavilla **13** 580
Francavilla, Pietro **11** 502–3*; **24** 855
collaboration **4** 401–2; **5** 360; **12** 570, 575
patrons and collectors **4** 548; **7** 699; **21** 24; **23** 87
pupils **3** 925; **4** 401
works **5** 360; **9** 706; **10** 441; **11** *503*, 558, *558*
France **11** 503–676*, *504*, *505*; **23** *99*; **26** *904*, *905*
academies **8** 788; **19** *34*; **20** 135
academy figures **1** 108
acanthus **1** 110
aesthetics
18th cent. **1** 898; **3** 386; **9** 327; **25** 799
19th cent. **4** 124; **8** 661; **10** 183–4; **14** 396
20th cent. **18** 587; **27** 853–4
agate **11** *636*
alabaster (gypsum) **1** 516; **17** *459*; **33** *28*
alcoves **19** 262
allegories **30** II2
altarpieces **1** 707; **9** 3, 4
Gothic **13** *109*, *174*; **20** *742*, *762*
14th cent. **9** 4
15th cent. **20** *451*, *731*
altars **1** 693, *693*, 697
amaranth **11** 595
amber **1** 761
ambulatories **1** 767, *767*
amethyst **26** *147*
amphitheatres **2** *418*; **23** 147
anatomical studies **1** 841–2
animal subjects **2** 105; **29** 426
apartments **11** *519*; **24** *128*, *129*; **27** *880*
apprentices **11** 585
apses **5** 371
aquatints **2** 239; **4** 330; **24** *724*
aqueducts **2** 242
archaeology **6** 95; **8** 868
arches **2** 294, 295; **7** *694*; **30** 658
architects **2** 313–14, 315
architectural history **9** 351, 420
architectural publications **19** 144–5
France—cont.
architecture **4** 790; **7** 531, 693; **9** 464; **11** 508–28*; **26** 743; **27** 879
brick **4** 780*
Carolingian **11** 509*; **12** 485; **27** 539
cavity-walling **4** 789
Cistercian Order **13** 37–8
exhibition **10** *416*, *682*; **15** *884*; **16** *55*
Gothic **11** 510–11*; **13** 35, 36–43*, 50, 59–61*; **27** 539; **31** 284
Flamboyant style **9** 48; **13** 59
High Gothic **13** 39; **14** 518
Late Gothic **8** 789
opus francigenum **13** 42
Rayonnant style **13** 41–3*, 59
Indian subcontinent **15** 401
Iron Age **25** 538
Jesuit Order **17** 511
Mannerism **11** 514
megalithic **5** 780, *780*; **21** 43
Merovingian **11** 509*; **25** 85, 88
military **21** 549, 550, 567–8*, 573*
Neo-classicism **19** 725
Prehistoric **25** 502–3*
Renaissance **11** 511–14*
restoration **2** *321*
Roman **11** 509*; **26** 904
Romanesque **4** 780; **11** 509–10*; **23** 211; **24** 104; **26** 571, 582–6*; **27** 566, *566*; **31** 224
stone **32** 278
United States of America **31** 589
vernacular **32** 278–80*, 290
16th cent. **13** 224
18th cent. **20** 416
19th cent. **16** 53; **32** *595*
archives **2** 365, 366, 369, 370*; **4** 332
armoires **8** 271; **11** 589, 593; **20** VII
armour **2** 473
art (classification of) **8** 845
art (illustrations of works of) **10** 212
art (reproduction of works of) **26** *233*, *234*
art criticism **18** 630; **26** 411; **30** 756
art history **6** 502; **8** 900; **9** 453; **10** 867; **11** 674–6*; **22** 357; **28** 528–9
artists' biographies **10** 208, 210, 212; **11** 57; **19** 144, 216
17th cent. **8** 525; **13** 830
18th cent. **8** 846
19th cent. **28** 744
artists' houses **2** 391
art legislation **2** 554, 560; **11** 667–8*
art market **2** 558–9
art policies **11** 667–8*; **24** 139
art schools **2** 366; **9** *312*; **11** 229; **24** *173*
ateliers **32** 81
auction houses **2** 369; **24** 141
auctions **2** 559, 707
avenues **12** 120
balconies (theatres) **30** 670
ballets **30** 659
banknotes **3** 182
baptisteries **3** 191; **25** *86*
barns **24** 104, *105*
bas-de-page **3** *323*
basins **11** *617*
bastions **3** 359; **21** 567–8, 581
beadwork **3** *440*, 442; **4** II
beakheads **3** *443*
beds **3** 484*, *484*; **11** *576*, 585, 588, 593, *594*, 598; **31** *684*
beech **3** *484*; **11** 589, *594*, 595
Bibles
Bibles moralisées **13** *140*, 140, 141, 179
Carolingian **5** *804*
France
Bibles—cont.
Gothic **13** 140
billboards **25** 345
binders **18** 118
bird's-eye views **4** 80
biscuit **29** 573
bodice ornaments **17** *525*
bone **11** 637; **25** *491*
bone-carvings **25** *491*, *492*
bookbindings **4** 347, 348, 349; **24** 51
book covers **4** 349, 350, 351, *351*, 352, *353*, 354, *354*, IV3; **5** *811*
book illustrations **4** 356, 359, 360, 364*, 365–6
Rococo **4** *361*
17th cent. **6** 518
20th cent. **7** *508*
bookplates **4** 373
books **19** 870
Books of Hours **13** *148*; **20** *637*
borders (manuscript) **4** 394, *394*, 395
bosquets **12** 119, 121
bosses **4** 465
bowls **11** *608*
boxes **3** *440*, 442; **4** *601*; **11** 630, 631–3*; **24** 147; **28** I2
box-wood **29** 571
bracelets **17** III2
brass **11** 624
brick **4** 780*, 790
bridges **4** 801; **7** *691*; **12** 206; **24** 479
brocades **11** *645*, *646*
bronze **11** 623, 625–7*; **29** 571, *572*, 573, 574–5
Baroque **7** *423*; **24** *786*
Carolingian **5** *806*
Celtic **6** *155*
Cubism **9** *362*
Empire style **11** 629
Mannerism **11** *558*; **24** *814*
Migration period **21** *503*
Neo-classicism **14** *798*; **27** *311*
Roman **27** 89, 90
Romanesque **26** *682*
Romanticism **3** *313*, *315*; **8** *565*
15th cent. **11** 624
16th cent. **11** 624; **27** *548*
17th cent. **8** *94*; **27** *822*
18th cent. **5** *381*; **11** *589*, *626*, *627*; **26** *112*
19th cent. **2** *100*; **26** *510*, *511*
20th cent. **4** *661*; **12** *566*; **20** *825*, *828*; **26** *351*
buckles **2** *565*; **21** *503*
buffets **8** 271; **9** 30; **11** 586, *586*, 587, 589
bureaux **5** 191, 192, *192*, 193; **7** 657; **11** 589, *591*, 593, 597; **18** I2; **26** 84
18th cent. **32** *337*
busts **5** 304
Baroque **3** *833*
Gothic **17** *459*
Neo-classicism **14** *797*
Romanticism **8** *565*
18th cent. **19** *141*
19th cent. **5** *303*, *304*, *826*; **7** *163*
buttresses **6** 493
cabinetmaking **11** 595–7
cabinets (i) (rooms) **5** 344, *345*, 349; **9** 11
cabinets (ii) (furniture) **5** 350, *350*; **9** *28*; **11** 587, *587*, *588*, 589, *599*, *627*; **12** *831*; **24** *150*
calendars **20** *612*
cameos **12** 259, *262*, *264*
cameras (ii) (photography) **20** 406
canals **2** 242
candlesticks **14** 419; **26** 493, *493*, *682*
cane **33** 157
capitals
historiated **27** *534*

France
capitals—cont.
Merovingian 17 665
Romanesque 5 372; 7 232, 477; 17 686; 19 224; 22 115; 25 88; 26 596, 597–9, 598, 601, 601–2, 610; 27 534, 534, 552; 31 211, 225
capriccios 5 686, 687; 18 654; 26 450
caps 9 271; 18 157
cards 24 660; 31 266
caricatures 5 756, 757–8*; 8 510; 27 871
19th cent. 5 303; 27 870
carnivals 5 785, 787
carpets 5 835–7*, 837, 839–40*, 841*; 11 651*; 27 894–6
Brussels 5 839, 840
Islamic 16 466
Wilton (Wilts) 5 840
17th cent. 5 I; 27 895
19th cent. 11 651
cartoons (drawings) 6 536
cartoons (comic strips) 26 742
cartoons (satirical) 27 871
carving 11 587, 587, 589, 595
caryatids 11 558; 13 227
caskets 5 917, 918
cast iron 3 524; 9 86; 11 522; 18 582; 30 671
castles 6 49, 50, 54, 504; 21 549, 561, 563, 564
mock 6 59
12th cent. 6 512
13th cent. 2 49; 8 40
15th cent. 31 844
see also châteaux
catafalques 6 72
catalogues 2 559; 6 545
auctions 6 80; 11 662; 19 25; 20 416
collections 6 77; 8 209; 17 667; 19 216, 782
museums 3 712; 6 77
oeuvre 10 212
18th cent. 28 221
cathedrals
Gothic 1 577, 778; 2 46, 497; 4 578, 579, 579; 6 494, 495; 8 74; 13 36, 37, 40, 41; 18 757, 758, 759; 19 127; 22 505; 24 152, 153, 154; 26 115, 116; 27 250, 254; 28 414, 415; 29 753, 754, 881; 31 383
Flamboyant style 6 414
High Gothic 2 844; 3 457, 458; 29 17
Rayonnant style 11 510; 26 45
Romanesque 2 321; 5 388; 11 509; 26 584
18th cent. 4 165
19th cent. 32 83
cave art 25 476, 476–7, 483
cedar 11 599
ceilings 11 574
cemeteries 6 154, 166; 20 868; 25 539
cenotaphs 4 533
censorship 6 175, 176
ceramics 9 28; 11 603*; 14 425
chairs 6 390; 11 585, 586, 587, 589, 594–5, 597, 598, 599; 30 783; 31 684, 685
armchairs 11 598, 600
Art Nouveau 11 600
bergères 6 390; 11 589
boarded seats 6 390
caquetoire 6 390
chaise au vertagadin 6 390
duchesse brisée 19 723; 26 84
fauteuils 6 390; 11 587, 589, 594–5
fauteuils de commodité 6 390; 31 684
Roman 6 388
sièges courants 6 390
sièges meublants 6 390

France
chairs—cont.
19th cent. 30 XV
chaises longues 11 594
chalices 11 616; 21 163
chalk 29 699
chandeliers 6 443; 9 13; 29 573
chapels 6 460
funerary 20 865
Gothic 2 862
Modernism 19 46, 368
Renaissance 19 691
Saintes-Chapelles 27 550
two-storey 5 371
17th cent. 20 297
chapter houses 6 464
chariot fittings 6 155
châteaux 4 865; 6 51, 59, 503–10*; 23 806, 809; 32 369
Baroque 32 369
Neo-classicism 4 224; 11 257, 883; 19 800; 32 767
Renaissance 2 27; 6 505, 545; 9 351, 352; 11 512, 905
Rococo 11 884; 32 373
16th cent. 6 416; 9 706, 707; 11 261; 27 559; 28 467
17th cent. 6 507; 11 356; 19 266; 20 288, 290, 291, 449, 457; 29 917
18th cent. 6 509
cherry-wood 2 459, 460; 11 596
chess sets 6 557, 558
chests 6 559, 560; 11 585
chests-of-drawers 20 469
chevets (beds) 3 484
children's books 4 364
chimney-pieces 6 604, 605
choir-stalls 7 191; 13 126
chromolithography 25 620
chronicles 7 242, 243, 243
chronologies 25 486
churches 3 125; 7 693
Baroque 20 294; 24 164
basilicas 7 253
Benedictine Order 4 869; 17 685
Carolingian 12 484
Gothic 5 728; 7 578; 13 38, 42, 60, 178; 24 156; 25 220; 26 121; 27 253, 541, 542; 31 206
Early Gothic 27 533
Flamboyant style 13 59
Rayonnant style 31 385
Gothic Revival 13 202
Gothic survival 13 211
hall 14 80, 82; 26 585
Knights Templar 18 154
Neo-classicism 6 397; 26 13; 29 93
Protestantism 30 431
Romanesque 5 370, 371; 7 232; 11 529; 17 685; 19 527; 23 14; 24 103; 25 87; 26 122; 31 207, 209, 224; 32 396, 464
17th cent. 11 516; 19 135; 20 289
18th cent. 7 840; 28 486
19th cent. 11 520, 525; 14 593; 32 84
cinemas 19 368
clasps 4 350; 14 418
Classicism 7 380, 383
clay 25 476–7
clerestories 6 493; 13 40
clocks 3 753; 7 438, 439, 442, 446, 447; 11 626; 26 304; 29 573
cloisters 5 369; 7 454, 455, 455–6; 26 604
coats of arms 12 272; 14 408, 409, 413, 414, 418, 419, 425, IV
coffeepots 24 147
coffrets 11 622
coins 7 533, 534, 535, 536, 537, 538, 539; 14 419

France—cont.
collages 4 675; 8 242; 10 468; 23 260; 24 726
collections 2 558–9; 7 561; 11 660–68*; 17 430; 22 359; 24 138, 163; 26 230
curiosities 11 661
drawings 19 143
furniture 7 565
Gothic 13 153
manuscripts 5 210
medals 3 288; 9 298
paintings 7 563; 28 273
plaquettes 9 298
public 13 605; 22 357–8
royal 3 304; 7 561; 9 418; 19 216; 20 133; 24 138
sculpture 7 562
colleges 2 724; 19 265
commercial art 7 652
commodes 6 I3; 7 657–8, 658; 11 589, 589, 591–3, 592; 26 84, 84
competitions 24 138; 25 637
architecture 7 665–6, 670; 24 170
painting 19 161
sculpture 7 672–3*
concrete 7 693, 694, 697; 11 771
prestressed 7 691; 11 771
reinforced 7 531, 693; 14 388; 24 128, 128, 472, 473
conservatories 7 744
contracts 25 794
copies 26 514
copper 11 628, 629; 13 167; 20 922, VII
coral 6 155; 7 835
cornices 11 412
costumes 30 659*, 660*, 660, 671, 671–2*
cotton 8 36–7; 11 649*; 23 331; 30 X1
couches 11 589, 593–4
court-houses 27 246
courtyards 8 65; 19 237
cradles (i) (cots) 24 389
craftsmen and artists 4 240; 14 855; 19 3; 24 139
crockets 8 183
crosses 8 197*
crypts 13 636
cupboards 8 271; 11 587, 590, 593; 27 682
cups 10 III1; 13 170; 28 522
curtains 3 484
cutwork 11 649
damask 11 589, 645
dealing 2 558–9; 11 660–64*; 23 778
death-masks 31 840
decadence and decline 8 596
decalcomania (ii) (printing) 9 105
department stores 4 239; 8 769
desks 5 192; 11 591, 598
diamonds 11 634, 634; 17 II3, III2
dictionaries of architecture 6 378; 32 598
dictionaries of art 2 869; 10 206, 208, 209–10, 212; 11 288
disegno e colore 9 8–9*; 19 22; 25 398
display of art 7 561; 9 11, 14, 18, 22, 23, 25, 28; 22 357–8, 358, 359; 24 138, 139
docks 9 58
dolls 31 259, 262
dolls' houses 31 262
domes 3 524; 9 85, 86; 26 584–5
donjons 8 902, 902
doors 9 152, 156, 158; 26 511, 641; 27 544, 681
doorways 27 142
dormitories 21 843
drawbridges 8 902
drawings 9 222, 225; 12 273
allegorical 8 883

France
drawings—cont.
architectural 7 666; 21 568; 22 211
Gothic 2 326; 13 142; 31 275; 32 569
Rococo 4 164
13th cent. 32 569
16th cent. 19 694
18th cent. 4 532; 24 582
19th cent. 2 332
aux trois crayons 9 I2
chalk
Baroque 32 716
Mannerism 5 814
Rococo 32 918
17th cent. 21 85
18th cent. 4 509; 6 400
19th cent. 25 671
crayon 28 503
graphite 26 513
ink
Art informel 2 544
Baroque 3 632
Gothic 13 137; 20 742
17th cent. 8 883
18th cent. 2 709; 12 596; 22 87; 27 531
19th cent. 13 879
20th cent. 2 839
leadpoints 32 570
mythological 18 626; 21 764
pastel 5 922; 8 624; 15 VI1; 23 296; 24 III; 31 705
topographical 2 27; 11 259; 21 568
townscapes 2 859
wash 4 244; 32 334
dress 9 244, 269, 277, 278*, 279–85*, 281, 283, 285; 30 672
dresses 4 II
drypoints 9 309–10
dyes 9 493; 11 649
earrings 17 525
earthenwares 6 558; 11 603
ebony 9 687; 11 587, 587, 589, 589, 596; 26 376
ecuelles 11 621
education (art) 2 523–4; 11 668–73*; 21 412; 24 138
architecture 9 420; 11 670*; 24 170
17th cent. 19 22; 24 167–8
18th cent. 1 105; 19 161
19th cent. 13 732–3; 19 38, 39
effigies 11 290, 898; 31 122
emblem books 10 174, 175
emblems 10 174
embroidery 11 647–8*, 648; 13 195
enamel 11 606, 629–31*
Art Nouveau 17 II1
basse taille 2 112; 10 III1; 11 614, 615, 629, 631; 13 169, 169
Celtic 6 155
champlevé 11 629; 13 167–8, 168; 26 692
cloisonné 11 614; 13 168; 21 163
en résille sur verre 10 195
en ronde bosse 10 193, 194; 11 615; 13 170
Gothic 11 614–15, 634; 13 158, 158, 167–8, 168, 169, 169, 170, 170
guilloche 11 630
Louis XVI style 11 633
painted 11 630, 630; 13 170; 19 397; 24 710
plique à jour 2 112; 10 194
Renaissance Revival 17 III2
Romanesque 7 720; 26 691–2*, 692
13th cent. 14 418
14th cent. 11 615
15th cent. 24 146
16th cent. 6 143

France
enamel—cont.
17th cent. 11 634
18th cent. 4 601; 11 632, 633
encyclopedias 8 864; 22 24
encyclopedias of art 10 206, 209–10
engineering (military) 21 567
engravings 10 392, 393, 396
Baroque 19 33, 34
crayon manner 2 239; 8 130, 130–31*; 11 723
gouache manner 13 220–21*, 221
Mannerism 11 264
Rococo 4 331, 361; 26 493
16th cent. 13 231; 23 768; 31 844
17th cent. 10 130, 690; 19 697, 847; 20 457; 22 465; 24 160; 27 589; 32 97
18th cent. 4 390; 7 496; 10 118; 23 770; 24 169; 25 798; 26 583
19th cent. 23 509; 26 121
20th cent. 27 241
epitaphs 10 436
erotic art 10 477, 479–80, 483; 11 267
etchings 10 551–3*
Baroque 24 272
Cubism 4 676
Impressionism 25 607
Mannerism 5 437, 438
Realism (style) 22 688
relief 10 561
17th cent. 3 633, 635; 4 468
18th cent. 26 742
19th cent. 4 625, 626; 19 215; 20 603; 21 171; 27 141
ewers 2 237; 11 605, 615, 636
exchanges 29 92
exhibitions 10 676, 677, 678, 679–80*; 24 138, 139, 140, 168, 171–2
dealers 10 680
industrial 10 678
loan 10 679
one-man 10 680
photographs 3 421
17th cent. 10 676
18th cent. 20 135
20th cent. 31 607
ex-votos 27 110–11
façade decoration 10 744–5
façades 5 371, 371; 20 296; 21 366; 24 123
factories 10 748
faience (ii) (ceramics) 5 918; 6 333; 11 604–6, 604, 605, 606; 22 880; 30 885
fans 10 780, 781, 781
fashion plates 10 823, 824
fermes ornées 12 122
festivals 5 814; 23 766, 768, 770
figureheads 28 612
figurines 18 875–6; 19 243, 243; 25 489; 27 110–11; 28 521
filigree 21 163
film 20 406
films 10 688
fireplaces 11 574
flagons 6 155, 155
flags 11 148
follies 11 243
fonts (baptismal) 9 192; 11 253, 623
fortifications 21 549, 550, 567, 567–8*, 573*
Mauritius 21 573
North America 21 573
Prehistoric 21 551
13th cent. 8 40
17th cent. 32 79–80
fortresses 21 567
forts 21 568; 26 907
fountains 7 531; 11 341, 343; 12 113, 120
Baroque 11 344, 560

France
fountains—cont.
drinking fountains 2 510
Renaissance 11 342; 13 226
19th cent. 1 497
frames 9 18; 11 373, 375, 377, 398–420*, 399, 400, 401, 402, 403, 407, 408, 409, 412, 413, 414, 415, 416
friezes 32 IV3
frontispieces 24 468
furniture 2 561; 11 576, 585–6*, 587–602*, 617–18; 19 723; 20 467, 468, 469; 26 227; 33 157
Louis XVI style 19 723
Régence style 26 83–4*, 84
18th cent. 4 531
gables 13 42
galleries (iv) (art) 9 14, 18, 21, 22, 23; 23 778
garden buildings 19 212
garden design 4 605; 12 112–13, 119–24, 121, 122, 123
gardens 12 104, 119–24*, 121, 122, 123; 20 133, 868
Chinese 12 123
jardins à la française 12 122, 123
jardins anglais 12 123
jardins anglo-chinois 12 123, 123
jardins paysagers 12 123
Renaissance 12 112–13*, 113
Roman 12 70, 70
sculpture 32 372
17th cent. 6 454; 12 61; 19 162, 164; 20 449
gargoyles 12 150
gate-houses 12 174, 175–6
gates 23 147
gem-engraving 12 255, 257, 257, 259–60, 262, 264
genealogies 12 271
gilding 7 441, 658; 11 589, 591, 592, 594, 595, 598, 625–7*, 626, 627; 13 109; 18 I2; 26 376
glass 11 602, 610–11*, 612–13*
Art Nouveau 2 563
cameo 12 18
crystal 9 13
marqueterie de verre 12 18
plate 11 407
19th cent. 12 18
20th cent. 12 793; 18 659
goblets 11 611
gold 11 613–23*, 631–3*; 27 15; 28 I2
Gothic 7 720; 10 III1; 13 168
Merovingian 21 163
Renaissance Revival 17 III2
12th cent. 23 99
14th cent. 2 112; 26 147
15th cent. 24 146
16th cent. 6 143
17th cent. 5 836; 11 636
18th cent. 4 601; 11 631, 632, 633; 24 147
gold dust 25 620
gold leaf 4 351
government buildings 2 172; 6 534; 22 454
gowns 9 275, 276
granges 25 668
granite 12 211
graves 6 155; 25 508, 511
grilles 22 455
grottoes 12 120; 13 703–4, 704; 23 850
guidebooks 13 809, 810
guilds 11 585, 588, 655, 669*
guns 2 459, 460–61, 460, 463, 463–4, 465, 465, 467; 14 856
gun stocks 2 459, 460, 460, 461, 463, 465
gypsography 26 480
hair ornaments 17 525
halls 14 74, 74–5*
hanap covers 13 168
hangars 11 771, 771

France—cont.
hangings 3 484, 484; 19 3
hardstones 9 30; 11 632, 635–6*; 12 830–31
Hausmalers 14 235
helmets 6 157
hemp 11 637
henges 25 498
heraldry 12 273; 14 404, 408, 409*, 413, 418, 419, IV
heritage 6 95; 9 25; 19 159; 24 662
hinges 9 156
historiography 11 674–6*
hoardings 8 277
hoods 9 275
hospitals 11 511; 14 780, 782; 24 126, 164; 29 91
hôtels particuliers
Régence style 29 751
17th cent. 14 790; 19 263, 264; 20 288
18th cent. 4 225; 7 416; 11 515
houses 4 780; 11 656; 32 278, 279, 279–80, 280
Gothic 4 584
Modern Movement 19 653
Neo-classicism 19 56, 57
Renaissance 29 750
town 29 751; 32 72
18th cent. 24 121
20th cent. 12 793; 19 41–2
housing 5 56, 362–3; 12 160; 19 43, 45; 24 131
Huguenots 14 854–5
humanism 14 868
hunting scenes 29 424
iconography 13 179
ideograms 2 226
illusionism 15 137
imprese 15 150
industrial scenes 15 829
initials (manuscript) 5 804; 7 514; 15 848; 20 339; 21 729; 31 226
inlays 2 461
insignia 7 178
interior decoration 11 571–2*, 573, 573–84*, 576; 26 494; 31 687
Baroque 32 371
Empire style 10 186; 23 209
Gothic 26 555
Louis XV style 19 722
Louis XVI style 19 723
Modernism 19 45
Neo-classicism 11 579
Régence style 23 458; 26 83–4*
Renaissance 11 572; 19 692
Rococo 11 578
Second Empire style 11 581
18th cent. 14 791
19th cent. 32 597
20th cent. 11 582, 583
inventories 13 153
iron 3 125; 9 156, 464; 11 623; 14 592; 16 53; 24 722; 30 21
ivory 5 917; 6 558; 9 3; 11 588, 636–7*; 19 243; 21 720; 29 571, 574; 31 255
ivory-carvings
Carolingian 5 811; 11 636
Gothic 13 172–6*, 173, 174
Ottonian 23 660
Prehistoric 16 798
Romanesque 26 696–7
13th cent. 16 799
japanning 7 166; 18 614
jars 20 471
jewellery 11 633–5*; 17 519, 527, II1, 3
joinery 11 595
kaolin 11 607
keys 11 625
king-wood 11 596; 26 84
knitting 18 157
knives 8 283, 284, 285
labyrinths 18 584, 585

France—cont.
lace 6 455; 11 649–51*, 650; 18 589, 590, 591, 593
lacquer 11 632; 18 I2; 26 376
lamps 2 563; 11 574
lapis lazuli 11 636
law courts 4 867; 9 337; 18 887–8
lawns 12 121, 122
lead 1 133; 11 253, 623
leather 4 349, 351, 351, 352, 353, 354, 354, IV3; 11 587; 19 3*
libraries 11 673–4*; 13 153; 18 582, 583
lighting 2 510; 7 531; 23 778; 30 679
lime 33 326
limestone 4 546, 583; 7 477, 478; 11 290, 554; 25 477; 29 701; 31 211
linen 11 650; 18 589; 19 418
lithography 19 483*, 486–90, 491; 22 252; 25 345, 346, 347, 348, 350; 31 214
Art Nouveau 20 602
Fauvism 19 491
Impressionism 20 260
Japonisme 17 441
Romanticism 8 640
19th cent. 3 775; 4 750; 6 549–50; 8 545, 545, 828; 17 604; 19 486, 487; 26 71; 27 870
20th cent. 19 490, 513
looms 2 838; 16 850; 30 309
machine aesthetic 19 896
magazines 32 82
mahogany 7 658; 11 595, 597, 598, 598
maiolica 30 885
mansions 30 653, 653
manuals
architecture 2 869; 5 167; 9 350; 19 26
carpentry 19 26
etching 10 551, 563; 18 658
gardens 8 846; 12 118, 122
libraries 19 313
painting 24 806; 28 485
perspective 9 352
print collecting 9 466
printing 4 468
scenery 30 681
typography 11 359; 31 495
manuscript illumination 5 804–5; 13 673; 20 756; 28 233
Carolingian 5 804; 9 686; 31 226
Gothic 4 10; 7 242, 243; 13 133, 136, 138, 140, 140, 141–2, 142, 148, 148–9*, 153–5, 674; 17 462; 20 332, 647; 26 562; 31 836
Late Gothic 19 389, 392, 394
Transitional style 31 285
Jewish art 17 562–3*
Late Antiquity 26 863
Romanesque 10 201; 26 668–70*, 677*; 27 247
Style au fonds d'or 13 136
14th cent. 13 827; 25 692, 693
15th cent. 4 371; 7 598, 599; 11 353, 354; 17 454; 19 350; 31 388
manuscripts 5 800, 804–5; 12 272
Byzantine 9 603
Early Christian (c. AD 250–843) 9 603
maple 2 465
maps 20 367
marble 7 657; 8 94; 11 589, 592; 31 122
Baroque 2 91; 3 833; 12 725, 726; 24 785, 786; 25 706; 28 846; 29 563
Baroque Revival 5 879
Cubism 33 590
Mannerism 24 813
Merovingian 17 665

France
marble—cont.
Neo-classicism 4 301; 6 517; 8 566; 10 764; 11 561
Renaissance 7 596; 11 557
Rococo 8 70, 71; 28 845
Romanesque 31 209
16th cent. 4 338; 11 503, 898; 24 133; 27 547
18th cent. 4 510; 7 450; 19 141; 23 795
19th cent. 5 304, 826; 6 468; 7 163; 11 564
20th cent. 2 491; 4 660; 20 120
markets 3 125
marks
ceramics 20 441
furniture 20 442
metalwork 11 613; 13 158; 20 443, 444
ormolu 20 445
marquetry 5 192; 11 588, 589, 589, 590, 596; 20 467, 468, 469, 469, VII
boullework 11 596; 20 467
floral 11 596
masonry 29 636
masons 19 532
masons' lodges 19 532
master printers 20 602–4
mausolea 20 864, 867*, 868–9*
mazes 12 123
medals 14 419; 20 922–3*, 924, 925
16th cent. 20 920*
17th cent. 20 922; 32 864
medical books 1 844
menhirs 25 505
metal 11 602; 27 879; 30 542
metalwork 11 613*, 623–5*, 628–9*, 629
Gothic 13 157, 158–9*
Romanesque 7 720; 26 681–2*
metro stations 21 349
meuble à deux corps see BUFFETS
mezzotints 21 416
miniatures (manuscript illumination)
Gothic
Late Gothic 24 116; 31 309
miniatures (manuscript illumination)
Carolingian 5 804
Gothic 2 313; 3 643; 5 207; 7 765; 11 530; 13 140, 153, 154; 14 414; 16 852; 20 340, 342, 637, 706, 707, IV; 28 487
Renaissance 20 334; 25 405
Romanesque 26 668, 677
13th cent. 14 725
14th cent. 4 525
15th cent. 2 114; 4 763; 6 463; 7 235; 11 725; 20 452, 562, 625, 626, 629, 633, 634, 646, 701, 723, 735; 31 838
16th cent. 24 472; 30 529
mirror-cases 2 112
mirror frames 21 720; 24 821
mirrors 9 12; 11 589; 21 720, 720; 26 492
mixed-media 18 119
modelli 21 764, 771
models 2 337
monasteries 13 210
Benedictine Order 3 708; 21 836
Carthusian Order 5 894
Cistercian Order 21 837, 838
Cluniac Order 7 476
Gothic 11 510; 21 844; 22 40
Romanesque 7 476; 26 583; 27 560
12th cent. 7 372
18th cent. 7 774
monograms 2 733
monstrances 26 493
monuments
equestrian 10 442

France
monuments—cont.
funerary 7 596; 27 822; 28 846; 31 132
public 1 497; 8 473; 11 561; 22 45–7; 24 124; 26 112
triumphal arches 2 286–7, 287; 24 469; 26 112; 31 351
16th cent. 4 338
morceaux de réception 22 85–6*
mosaics 12 485; 26 681; 27 62; 32 542
mother-of-pearl 4 601; 11 632; 28 I2
mottes 21 562
mouldings 22 211, 215, 216–22
roll-and-fillet 22 215
mounts (furniture) 11 589, 590
mounts (guns) 2 460
museums 2 366; 3 873; 6 77; 9 25; 11 664–8*; 19 848; 22 357–8, 358, 359, 362; 24 138
Baroque 24 163
Modernism 24 131; 28 483
18th cent. 20 139
19th cent. 5 536; 11 301–2; 23 126; 32 82
20th cent. 20 208; 24 127
music-halls 30 679
naturalism 22 687–8*, 688
necklaces 11 634
nefs 11 616
neon 22 748
newspapers 6 491; 8 545; 13 306
nickel-brass 7 539
nude figures 23 294, 294–5, 296
Baroque 12 725; 25 706; 29 572
Cubism 9 355
Mannerism 20 673
Neo-classicism 4 301; 6 517; 12 730; 14 798; 24 172, 736
Neo-Impressionism 28 503
Orientalism 6 501; 15 844
Realism (style) 26 56
Rococo 4 515, 516; 17 627; 25 275; 28 845; 29 573
Rococo Revival 11 545
16th cent. 11 503
18th cent. 4 510; 10 726; 23 795; 26 93
19th cent. 4 528; 5 342, 825; 26 509, 510
20th cent. 20 120, 825, 828
oak 5 192; 8 271; 11 585, 589
objects of vertu 11 629*
objets trouvés 23 334
observatories 23 339, 342
office buildings 11 527; 14 388
olive-wood 11 596
onyx 12 262
opals 17 II1
opera houses 11 882; 12 156, 157
orangeries 23 470
orders (architecture) 24 170
Doric 2 173
giant 5 166; 19 693; 23 492, 493
17th cent. 31 297
organ shutters 23 500
ormolu 11 590; 23 531
ornament 23 542, 543, 544
orthostats 12 211
overdoors 14 791; 23 678
overmantels 14 791
pageants 23 768, 770
painting 11 528–53*; 24 720
Abstract art 1 74; 8 657; 9 334; 12 806; 14 206; 20 816, 828; 25 148; 32 577; 33 305
Abstraction-Création 1 89
allegorical 1 660; 4 125; 19 142; 20 891
Baroque 19 23
Fauvism 20 823
Neo-classicism 7 384; 32 429
Realism (style) 8 53
Rococo 11 539

France
painting
allegorical—cont.
Romanticism **15** *88*
Symbolism (movement) **5** *880*
17th cent. **4** *128*
20th cent. **19** *82*
animal subjects
Romanticism **2** *107*
Romanticism **8** *449*
18th cent. **14** *846*; **23** *668*
19th cent. **24** *141*
architectural
Impressionism **21** *865*
Romanticism **8** *449*
Troubadour style **13** *309*
18th cent. **26** *448, 449*
Art brut **2** *515*
battle
Baroque **19** *20, 22*
19th cent. **11** *370*; **21** *412*
20th cent. **8** *605*
bird's-eye views **25** *84*
cabinet pictures **24** *138*
ceiling **9** *417*; **19** *248*
conversation pieces **30** XIV1
Cubism **4** *676, 677*; **8** *244*; **9** *355*; **12** *806*; **13** *670*; **18** *636*; **19** *77*; **21** *364*; **24** *719*
Dada **8** *435*; **11** *549*; **24** *709*
display **9** 14, 18, 22; **10** *676*; **24** 139
drapery **9** 211
encaustic **6** 121*
fêtes champêtres **18** *693*; **20** *255*
fêtes galantes **11** *37*, *368*; **32** *914, 915*, 915–17, *916*
flower **11** 228, *229, 230*; **20** *257*; **26** *73*; **29** *256*
fresco
Gothic **2** *863*; **12** *697*; **13** 135, 150; **32** *573*
Mannerism **16** 877
16th cent. **25** *579*
19th cent. **1** *759*
genre **12** 289*, 291, 292*, 294*
Barbizon school **21** *611, 612*
Baroque **11** *535*; **19** *146, 147, 148, 149*
Fauvism **9** *134*
Impressionism **8** *622*; **9** *289*; **11** *298*; **15** *153*, VIII; **20** *259*; **24** *879*; **26** *208, 209*
Mannerism **11** *533*
Neo-classicism **32** *428*
Néo-Grec **24** *58*
Neo-Impressionism **22** *746*; **28** *502, 698*
Orientalism **7** *760*, II2; **15** *844*
Post-Impressionism **6** *370*; **31** *213, 215, 216*
Realism (style) **4** *339, 754*; **8** *51, 52, 54, 56*; **12** *295*; **26** *54, 56*
Rococo **4** *514*; **17** *627*; **31** *380*
17th cent. **18** *839*; **19** *247*
18th cent. **6** *473, 474*; **8** *500*; **12** *638*; **13** *639, 640, 641*; **17** *465*; **19** *217, 220*; **23** *788*; **32** *921*
19th cent. **2** *142*; **3** *434*; **5** *441*; **8** *448, 599*; **9** *286*; **19** *295*; **21** *69*; **25** *750, 751*; **26** *451*; **32** *739, 740, 742*
20th cent. **4** *326, 327*; **9** *373*; **20** *827*; **29** *493*
Gothic **11** 530–31*; **13** 147*, 153–5*
grisaille **13** 136, *137*, 148, *148*, 181, 673, *674*; **29** VI1
hanging **9** 14, 18
history **2** 53; **3** 451; **11** 538*, 540*; **14** 583, 584–5; **24** 138; **25** 638; **31** 373
Baroque **14** *583*; **24** *212*
Neo-classicism **8** *555, 559*; **11** *541, 900*; **12** *732*; **13** *792*; **15** *846*; **19** *255*; **22** *735*; **24** *172, 381, 583*

France
painting
history—cont.
Orientalism **26** *92*
Realism (style) **14** *587*
Rococo **14** *585*
Romanticism **8** *643*; **12** *352*; **13** *690*; **26** 737, 738–40
Troubadour style **26** *265*
15th cent. **11** *353*
16th cent. **9** *276*
17th cent. **4** *574*; **8** *784*; **18** *648*; **19** 246; **24** *476*; **29** *623*
18th cent. **4** *744*; **9** 209; **13** *643*; **18** *642*; **21** *902*; **26** *424*; **30** *46*; **32** *670*
19th cent. **3** *396*; **8** *76, 654*; **11** *546*; **14** *311*; **15** *840*; **16** *66*; **18** *865*; **21** *761*; **24** *816*; **28** *67*; **32** *336*
20th cent. **8** *714*; **24** *143*
hunting scenes **23** *667*; **32** *335*
Impressionism **9** *288*; **11** *38*
industrial scenes **19** *767*
Jewish art **17** 577*
juste-milieu style **12** *809*
landscape **18** 704, 708, 711–14
Art informel **10** *838*
Baroque **24** *211*
Fauvism **10** *840*; **32** *668*
Gothic **5** 428; **13** 154
Impressionism **12** *188*; **15** *151*; **21** *866*; **22** *119*; **24** *880, 881*; **28** *795*
naive art **27** *261*
Pointillism **18** *716*
Post-Impressionism **6** *368*
15th cent. **20** 452
17th cent. **21** *609*; **24** *254*; **25** *393*
18th cent. **9** 416; **18** *661*; **31** *817*
19th cent. **3** *212*; **7** *878, 879*; **8** *539, 859*; **11** *501*, 543–4*; **14** *189, 847*; **18** *713*; **21** *429*; **26** 741; **27** *266, 267*; **31** *387, 479*
20th cent. **20** *272*
literary themes **8** *639*; **26** *739*; **27** *143*; **32** *510*
marine **20** 426*; **32** *333, 684*
18th cent. **24** *811*
19th cent. **4** *523*
military scenes **12** *349*; **24** *256*
miniatures **7** 463; **21** 638, 641, 642, 643–4
Modern Movement **18** *118*
murals **22** 329, 330, *330*, 333
mythological
Baroque **4** *535, 537*; **17** *672*; **32** *717*
Mannerism **1** *17*; **9** *328*
Neo-classicism **12** *730*; **13** *794*; **24** *736*
Rococo **3** *855*; **4** *515, 516*; **11** *367*; **22** *683*; **23** *294*
Rococo Revival **11** *545*
Romanticism **8** *642*
17th cent. **18** *632*; **19** 246; **21** *498*; **25** *387, 390, 392*
18th cent. **14** *84, 85*; **24** *136*; **26** *93*
19th cent. **1** *641*; **4** *528*; **5** *342*; **18** *713*
naive art **27** *262*
Orientalism **20** *420*
pietàs **20** *207*; **25** *796*
Pittura Metafisica **8** *603*
Post-Impressionism **7** *675*; **25** *357*
Purism **23** *694*; **24** *144*; **25** *739*
Realism (style) **19** *381*
religious
Baroque **6** *434*; **8** *90*; **11** *534*; **17** *671*; **19** *24*; **25** *708*; **32** *715, 718*
Gothic **3** *640*; **11** *399*; **25** *794*
Mannerism **3** *399*; **18** *663*

France
painting
religious—cont.
Orientalism **6** *501*
Rococo **19** *647*
Symbolism (movement) **12** *190*; **22** *90*
14th cent. **17** *456*
15th cent. **11** *351, 800*; **20** *613, 651*
16th cent. **19** *341, 342*
17th cent. **7** *864*; **9** *175*; **11** *166*; **18** *838, 840*; **24** VII2; **25** *391*; **30** *354*
18th cent. **8** *795*; **9** *208*; **10** *726*; **24** *773*; **26** *247*; **28** *743*
19th cent. **3** *358*; **4** *527*; **12** *158*
20th cent. **13** *714*
Romanesque **11** 529–30*
screen **28** *298*
sporting scenes **8** *620*; **12** *351*; **19** *297*
still-lifes **29** 664, 668
Cubism **29** *670*
Post-Impressionism **6** *369*; **29** *669*
17th cent. **11** *535*; **21** *891*
18th cent. **6** *472, 475*; **8** *812, 813*; **11** *539*; **24** *135*; **29** *669*
19th cent. **22** *29*
Surrealism **4** *700*; **10** *467, 469*; **30** *20, 292*
Symbolism (movement) **30** *170*
Synthetism **28** *484*
Tachism **20** *816*
topographical **27** *559*; **31** *156*
townscapes **31** *156*
Fauvism **20** *465*
Impressionism **5** *391*; **15** VII; **24** *882*; **28** *796*
19th cent. **8** *718*
urban life
Impressionism **15** VI2; **21** *863, 864*; **23** III, IV
Neo-Impressionism **28** *501*
vanitas **31** 883
wall **32** 806
Gothic **13** 140
Prehistoric **25** 650
Roman **27** 56, *56*
Romanesque **11** *529*; **26** *650, 651*; **27** 590
Romanticism **15** *88*
17th cent. **11** *755*
19th cent. **11** *158*
watercolours **8** *641*; **18** *678*
Orientalism **32** VII2
Post-Impressionism **6** *373*
Symbolism (movement) **22** *91*
19th cent. **8** *547*
19th cent. **24** *138, 139, 713*
20th cent. **3** *127*; **8** *604, 774*; **9** *335*; **10** *533*; **11** *545, 552*; **19** *79, 81*; **20** *591*; **21** *706, 707*; **24** *224, 715, 718, 721, 723*; **27** *239*; **31** *775*
paints **18** 118
palaces
Baroque **8** *33*
Gothic **13** 59
Neo-classicism **23** 812
Renaissance **23** 810–11
16th cent. **19** *237*
17th cent. **4** *866*; **19** *134*; **20** *896*
see also CHATEAUX
panoramas **9** 370; **24** 18
paper **24** 40, 48, 51, 55; **31** 258, 259
paperweights **24** 57
papier collé **13** *669*
papier mâché **24** 62; **31** 262
parasols **3** 442
parquetry **11** 596; **20** 467; **26** 84
parterres (i) (gardens) **12** 119, 121
parterres de broderie **21** 822

France—cont.
parures **17** *525*
passementerie **24** 237
patens **21** *163*
patronage **2** 366; **11** 652–60*; **13** 76–7, 178, 181; **20** 131
Gothic **13** 153
17th cent. **11** 356
pattern books **24** 269, 271, *272*
architecture **9** 350, 351; **10** 110; **22** 925; **32** 554
guns **2** 461, 463, 466
interior decoration **6** 535
ironwork **14** 856
Renaissance **9** 351
typography **11** 359
pavilions (buildings) **32** *374*
pearls **11** *634*
pedestals **24** 316
perfume containers **3** 442
periaktoi **30** 659
periodicals **8** 476; **11** 359; **12** 208; **13** 663; **24** 421–2, 423, 442–3*
perspective **18** 704
pewter **11** 624, 628*, 629; **24** 578, *579*
photoarchives **11** 674
photographic prints **4** 130; **19** *87*; **22** *724*; **24** *660, 662*
photography **4** *690*; **5** *897*; **24** 646, 658, 662, 663, 676
architecture **3** 422
chronophotography **20** 406
cliché-verre **7** *433*
20th cent. **3** 289; **5** 896; **24** *672*
piers (ii) (masonry) **13** 40, 43; **24** 749, 750–51
pigments **23** 78; **25** *478, 479*
pillars **27** *142*
pine **11** 595
pinnacles **24** *825*
plans **21** 568
plaques **7** *718*; **13** 168; **24** *149*
plaquettes **25** 22
plaster **4** *568*; **5** *303*; **9** 14; **12** *564*; **24** *821*; **29** 833–4*, 843; **30** *21*
plates **11** *604*
platters **12** *357*
polishing **11** 595
polychromy **11** 589; **13** *109, 126*; **29** 574
pommels (guns) **2** *465*
pools **12** 120
poplar **33** 326
porcelain **5** 918; **11** 591, 607–10*; **24** *149*
display **9** 30
hard-paste **6** 333; **11** 607, 609–10*, *610*; **28** *522, 523, 524*; **29** 753
soft-paste **6** 923; **11** 607–9*, *607, 608*; **28** *521*; **32** *583*
18th cent. **6** I3; **28** *521*
porches **13** *60*
portals
Gothic **4** 581; **8** *892*; **9** 708; **18** *759*; **27** *544*
Early Gothic **2** *47*; **10** *546*
Romanesque **2** *728*; **4** *581*; **29** *94*
porticos **25** 267
portraits
aquatints **16** *905*
artists' **23** *379*
drawings **7** 462
Impressionism **25** *278*
Renaissance **7** *463*
17th cent. **9** *387*
18th cent. **20** *417*
19th cent. **15** *838*
20th cent. **14** *363*; **20** *829*
drawings (pastel)
18th cent. **18** *842*; **19** *436*; **24** *243*, V
20th cent. **24** *244*
enamel **10** IV1
engravings **10** 392
16th cent. **4** *547*

France
portraits
engravings—cont.
17th cent. **9** *9*; **20** *473*
group
Baroque **9** *280*; **18** *788*
18th cent. **25** *670*
19th cent. **15** *838*
lithography **8** *764*; **12** *896*
manuscript illumination **7** 463
miniatures (manuscript illumination) **4** *571, 572*
miniatures (paintings) **21** *641*
painting **11** 539; **31** 834
Baroque **9** *280*; **11** *537*; **18** *788, 789*; **21** *497, 498*; **31** *378*
Expressionism **29** *246*
Fauvism **5** *529*
Gothic **13** *131*
Impressionism **8** *619*; **9** *288*
Mannerism **7** *465*; **11** *267*; **25** *282*
Neo-classicism **8** *556, 558*; **18** *660*; **19** *67*; **23** *520*; **26** *81*; **32** *585*
Post-Impressionism **6** *367, 370*; **12** *858*
Realism (style) **8** *55*; **11** *544*
Renaissance **7** *426, 462, 866*
Rococo **4** *512*; **9** *283*; **25** *275*; **27** *571*
Romanticism **8** *646*; **12** *335, 353*; **13** *691*
Second Empire style **4** *307*
watercolours **16** *64*
15th cent. **20** *733*
16th cent. **11** *400, 532*; **31** *849*
17th cent. **4** *550*; **6** *435, 436, 443*; **20** *473*; **24** *134*; **25** *394*; **26** *349, 385*
18th cent. **2** *851*; **8** *507, 866, 890*; **9** *285, 302, 365, 400*; **18** *576*; **22** *685*; **24** *542*; **25** *670, 884*; **26** *248, 387*; **31** *69*; **32** *495, 496*
19th cent. **4** *303, 329*; **5** *813*; **10** *797*; **12** *18*; **18** *866*; **23** *521*; **25** *279*
20th cent. **9** *2, 292*; **14** *330*; **21** *788*; **29** *604*
photography **22** *424*; **24** *660, 661*
sculpture **11** 561–2*
Neo-classicism **11** *561*
18th cent. **7** *450*; **24** *137*
19th cent. **4** *458*; **6** *468*
20th cent. **4** *661*
self-portraits
Neo-classicism **32** *585*
17th cent. **9** *9*; **25** *394*
18th cent. **9** *365*; **18** *576, 842*; **24** *243*; **32** *496*
19th cent. **8** *764*
20th cent. **14** *330*
posters **2** 510; **7** 652; **22** *252*; **25** 345–7, *346, 347, 348*, 349–50, *350*; **31** *214*
19th cent. **6** 550, *550*
pottery **11** 603–7*
blue-and-white ware **4** 177*; **7** 166
creamware **11** 606
La Tène culture (*c.* 450–*c.* 50 BC) **25** *543*
lead-glazed ware **11** *603*, 603–4
Rhenish ware **27** 108
St Porchaire ware **6** 333
terra sigillata **27** 107–8
terres jaspées **23** 849
tin-glazed ware **30** 875
printing **4** 130; **8** 36–7; **11** 649*; **19** 870; **20** 861; **23** 331; **24** 55; **30** 562, X1
colour **12** 208
printmakers **10** 210
print publishers **18** 745; **25** 626
prints **11** 540–41*; **21** 896, *896*; **24** 883; **25** 731; **31** *705*

France—cont.
prisons **19** 11
prizes (artists') **24** 138, 140; **25** 637
promenades **4** *390*
propaganda **25** 650, 651
proportions (architecture) **2** *360*
proportions (human) **14** *872*
pulpits **23** *98*
purses **3** 442
pyramids **25** *766*
pyxides (boxes) **13** 167
quartz **11** *622*
rafraîchissoirs **22** 14
railway stations **11** 524; **18** *664*; **24** *126*; **25** *855*
realism (critical term) **22** 687–8, *688*
regalia **26** *81*
reliquaries **11** 616
Gothic **13** 42, 158, 168, 169, *169*, *170*; **24** *146*; **26** *147*
Gothic Revival **32** *598*
Ottonian **7** 720
Romanesque **26** *692*
rock art **19** 229; **25** 475, *486*
carvings **18** 806; **25** 509, 511
engraving **12** 149; **25** *475*, 480, 487
painting **12** 149; **25** *478*, *479*, 487; **29** 422; **31** *360*
Prehistoric **2** 63; **18** 806, *807*; **23** 77–8; **24** *310*; **31** 360–61, 410
reliefs **25** *477*
rock crystal **11** 633; **12** *257*; **26** *147*
rocks **12** 120
romance manuscripts **14** 408; **26** 561–3*
roods **27** 124
roofs **14** 592; **30** 671, 907, 909, 910
rose-wood **11** 596
rubbings **2** 461
salons **19** 264
salts **6** *143*
sapphires **11** *634*; **17** *525*, II3
sarcophagi **27** *829*
sardonyx **11** *636*; **12** *264*
satin-wood **11** *592*, 595
satires **25** 651; **27** *870*, 870–71*
scaffolds **30** 653
scena per angolo **30** 672
sceptres **26** 81
schools **28** 156, 157
scissors **8** *286*, 287
screens (i) (architectural) **28** 292, *292*
screens (ii) (furniture) **28** 298, *298*
scripts **28** 305
sculpture **11** 553–71*; **30** 498–500*; **33** 3
allegorical
Baroque **24** *785*; **25** *706*
Empire style **4** *301*
Neo-classicism **4** *301*; **27** *311*
Rococo **8** *71*
19th cent. **26** *510*
animal subjects **2** *100*; **3** *313*, *315*
Rococo **8** *71*
architectural **10** 744–5
Baroque **11** *558*
Gothic **2** *47*; **6** *497*; **26** *118*, *119*; **27** *544*; **28** *416*
Neo-classicism **8** *566*
Romanesque **2** *841*, 842, *842*; **4** *581*; **26** 596, *596*; **27** 534
20th cent. **4** *568*
biomorphism **2** *491*
bronze **4** *661*; **7** *423*; **8** *94*; **9** *362*; **12** *566*; **14** *798*; **26** *509*; **27** *822*
Baroque **24** *786*
Mannerism **11** *558*
Neo-classicism **27** *311*
Romanticism **3** *313*, *315*

France
sculpture
bronze—cont.
20th cent. **20** *825*, *828*; **26** *351*
column statues **1** *781*; **6** *403*, *495*; **7** 642, *642*; **9** *257*; **13** 73, *74*; **26** 602; **29** 902
Constructivism **24** *574*
Cubism **2** *311*; **9** *362*; **18** *863*; **24** *716*; **33** *590*
display **9** 22, 23, 25
Gothic **7** 455–6; **13** 72–7*, *76*, 125–6*, 169; **24** 159
15th cent. **13** 77–9*
Jewish art **17** 577*
marble **8** *94*; **25** *418*; **28** *846*; **29** *563*
Baroque **2** *91*; **12** *725*, *726*; **24** *785*, *786*; **25** *706*
Baroque Revival **5** *879*
Cubism **33** *590*
Mannerism **24** *813*
Neo-classicism **6** *517*; **10** *764*; **11** *561*
Rococo **8** *71*; **28** *845*
16th cent. **11** *503*; **24** *133*
18th cent. **4** *510*; **7** *450*; **23** *795*
19th cent. **6** *468*
20th cent. **2** *491*; **4** *660*; **20** *120*
monumental **13** 140, 141
mythological
Baroque **1** *133*; **7** *423*; **12** *725*; **29** *563*
Baroque Revival **5** *879*
Neo-classicism **6** *517*; **10** *764*; **14** *798*
Rococo **28** *845*
16th cent. **11** *503*
18th cent. **4** *510*; **23** *795*
19th cent. **30** *500*
Neo-classicism **25** *418*
Nouveau Réalisme **6** *354*
Prehistoric art **25** *544*
primitivism **12** *194*
relief **11** 588; **25** 477, *477*
Gothic **8** *892*; **24** *155*
Mannerism **24** *814*
Neo-classicism **27** *310*
Prehistoric art **25** *476*
Renaissance **11** *557*; **13** *226*
Romanesque **7** *224*; **21** *798*, *799*; **29** *94*; **31** *209*; **32** *397*
19th cent. **5** *825*
religious **4** *583*
Gothic **13** *126*; **24** *157*; **28** *866*; **31** *382*
Gothic: Late Gothic **19** *138*
Mannerism **24** *813*
Renaissance **26** *185*
Romanesque **7** *478*; **11** *554*
14th cent. **11** *555*
16th cent. **4** *546*; **24** *133*
Renaissance **16** 695
restorations **32** 596–7
Roman **12** *70*; **27** 31
Romanesque **2** 728; **7** 454; **26** 596–7*, 600–601*, 641*; **31** 225
Auvergne **26** 601*
Burgundy (region) **26** 601–2*
First Romanesque **26** 609
Languedoc **26** 602–3*
Loire Valley **26** 598–9*
Normandy **26** 597–8*
Provence **26** 603–4*
Roussillon **26** 604*, 609–10*
Romanticism **26** 742
stone **13** 72–9*, *74*, *75*, *76*; **26** 596–9*, *596*, 600–604*, 609–10*
Baroque **11** *558*
Gothic **13** *78*
Iron Age **25** *544*
Surrealism **12** *564*; **30** *21*
tomb
Baroque **2** *91*; **12** *726*; **24** *786*; **28** *846*

France
sculpture
tomb—cont.
Gothic **13** *78*
Mannerism **16** *856*
Renaissance **1** *766*; **7** *596*
16th cent. **3** *210*; **27** *547*, *548*
17th cent. **8** *94*; **27** *822*
wood **4** *661*; **13** 125–6*, *126*; **24** *716*; **26** 641*
16th cent. **26** *350*
18th cent. **2** 53
19th cent. **11** *564*
20th cent. **4** *662*; **7** *697*; **8** *773*; **9** *356*; **11** *569*, *570*; **12** *184*, *566*; **21** *787*; **22** *748*; **24** *722*; **26** *351*; **30** *924*
seals **14** *408*, 413
secretaires **11** 591; **26** *376*
sets **30** 672
settlements **25** 473, 502
shawls **28** 564
shells **11** *616*
shell structures **28** *583*
shields **14** 409, 413
ship-decoration **28** 612
shops **24** *121*
showcases **9** 31
shrines (i) (cult) **23** *99*; **28** 632
shutters (window) **9** 12
signs (markers) **2** 510
silk **9** 279; **11** 589, *638*, *640*, 644–7*, *645*, *646*, *648*; **16** 850; **24** 810; **28** 716, 717; **30** I1, II2
bizarre **4** 103; **11** 646
chinoiserie **7** 167
point rentré **19** 850
8th cent. AD **9** *252*
silver **11** 613–23*
Rococo **21** *70*
Roman **27** *82*, 82–3
16th cent. **6** 443; **11** *616*
17th cent. **2** *463*; **9** 30; **11** 576, *618*; **14** *418*
18th cent. **8** 68; **11** *620*, *621*; **12** *357*; **24** *147*
19th cent. **4** *458*; **5** 836; **11** *622*
20th cent. **11** *622*
silver dust **25** *620*
silver-gilt **11** *615*, *617*; **13** *158*, *168*, *169*, *170*; **24** *146*
skirts **9** 276, 278
snuff-boxes **4** *601*; **7** 167, *194*; **11** *608*, *631*, 632, *632*, 633, *633*; **24** 62
sofas **2** *564*; **11** 594
spear-throwers **25** *491*
spires **29** 412–13, 414*
sporting scenes **29** 426
squares (town) **31** 717
Louis XIV style **11** *517*
17th cent. **11** 518; **24** *117*, *119*
18th cent. **8** *889*; **22** *454*, *455*; **24** *123*; **26** *205*
stables **29** *485*
stage design **30** 653, 659–60*, 671–2*, 686
stage machinery **30** 654, 658
stages **30** *653*
stage scenery **30** 681
stained glass **29** 504, 505–6, 508
Gothic **3** *459*; **4** *582*; **6** 494, *498*; **13** 135, 136, *136*, 140–41*, 142, *143*, 149, 178–81*, *179*, *180*; **16** *837*; **24** *158*; **26** *120*, 123; **27** *549*; **29** 501, 503, *510*, *511*, *759*, I, VI1
Channel style **13** *143*
Early Gothic **28** *417*
Romanesque **19** 129; **26** *700*, 702, *703*
20th cent. **29** *509*
staircases **19** 264; **24** *474*; **29** 521, *523*, 524, *524*
Renaissance **4** *156*
16th cent. **13** 224
17th cent. **29** 523–4

France—cont.
statuettes **29** 571–2*, 573–5*
Baroque **29** *572*
Carolingian **5** *806*
Gothic **13** *158*, 172–4, *173*
Rococo **29** *573*
Roman **27** 89, 90
13th cent. **16** 799
18th cent. **5** *381*
19th cent. **2** *100*
steel **11** *625*; **16** *55*
stereotomy **19** *691*; **29** *636*
stone **1** *693*, 707; **9** *191*; **11** *558*; **13** 72–9*, *74*, *75*, *76*; **25** *544*; **26** 596–9*, *596*, 600–604*, 609–10*; **32** 278
Gothic **13** *78*
Prehistoric **25** 502–3*
stone-carvings **12** *211*; **26** 595
stonewares **11** 604
stools **11** 587
strapwork **13** 700
streets **2** 510; **20** *474*
stucco **11** *572*; **25** *579*; **26** 123; **29** 833–4*, *834*, 843, *844*
studios **11** 544*, 671*; **23** *788*; **29** 855, *857*, *858*
Surrealism **2** *514*
sycamore **11** *591*
synagogues **17** 545, 547, 548
tabernacles (ii) (receptacle) **13** 167, *168*; **25** 183
tables **11** 587, 589, 590–91*, 599, *602*
console tables **7** *746*; **11** 575, 589, 595
en cabaret **11** 591
pedestal **11** 590
tric-trac **11** 590
tabourets see STOOLS
tapestries **11** 589, 637–44*; **12** 829; **30** 312–14*, 318, 321–4
à alentours **11** 643
Baroque **30** *321*
chinoiserie **7** 167, *168*
Gothic **2** 49–51, *50*, 111; **11** *638*; **13** *195*, 196
Mannerism **8** *67*
Renaissance **11** 571
14th cent. **30** *313*
15th cent. **20** *777*; **29** *423*; **30** I1
17th cent. **11** *640*; **12** *829*; **21** *366*, *367*; **30** II2
18th cent. **2** *703*; **3** *462*; **11** *642*; **30** *323*
20th cent. **11** *644*; **13** 681; **19** *808*
taste **1** 898
tazze **11** 617; **19** *397*
teapots **11** *607*
temples **23** *148*; **26** 858; **30** 434, 436
terraces **12** 120
terracotta **14** *797*; **27** 110–11; **29** *573*; **30** 498–500*, *500*, *501*
textiles **9** 284; **11** 574, 576, 637*; **26** 703; **30** 562
theatre boxes **30** 670
theatres **26** 432; **30** *653*, 658–9*, 669–71*
anatomy **22** *739*
Neo-classicism **19** *726*; **32** *768*
Post-modernism **4** *228*
Renaissance **30** 654
Roman **30** *652*
17th cent. **30** *658*
18th cent. **29** 91; **30** *670*
theories
architectural **4** 533; **18** 857; **24** 469; **32** 79
art **31** 820–21
17th cent. **1** 897–8; **25** 392
19th cent. **8** 661; **10** 183–4; **18** 631; **25** 659–60; **30** 174, 239
20th cent. **1** 524; **3** 784; **10** 164; **13** 232; **20** 436–7; **27** 854

France
theories—cont.
colour **6** 564; **14** 396; **22** 745; **28** 504
garden **8** 845; **12** 124
landscape **8** 771
painting **1** 73; **8** 782; **9** 8–9; **18** 630; **30** 170
proportions (architecture) **24** 469
representation **11** 334
thick-wall structures **5** 370, 371
threads **30** 542
thrones **30** 781–2
tiles **11** 603; **30** 885–6*, *886*
timber structures **30** 895; **32** 278–9
tin **10** 624
toilet services **5** 611; **11** *618*
tokens **4** *509*
tombs
Baroque **2** *91*; **12** *726*; **24** *786*
ciborium **7** 303
dolmens **9** 80
Gothic **13** *78*
Mannerism **16** *856*
megalithic **21** 42
passage **5** 780–81; **25** 511
Prehistoric **25** 506
Renaissance **1** *766*
Romanesque **11** *290*
tower **12** *770*
wall **31** *124*, 125
14th cent. **17** 459
16th cent. **11** 556; **26** *350*; **27** *547*
17th cent. **8** *94*
topographical views **31** 156–7*
tortoiseshell **11** 590
towers
flanking **8** *277*
réduits modèles **21** 568
tours modèles **21** 568
19th cent. **10** *107*
20th cent. **23** 262
town halls **3** *465*; **11** *566*; **14** *448*; **22** 330; **31** 235, 241–2
towns
fortified **1** *482*, 482–3
garden cities **2** 391; **3** 226; **11** 526; **12** 145; **24** 128, 129, *129*; **29** 900
industrial model **11** 724
new **2** 11, 700; **4** 227; **5** 609, *610*; **6** 534; **7** 343; **12** 185; **13** 716; **18** 809; **21** 346; **24** 131, *131*; **25** 375; **26** 346–7; **29** 420, 918; **31** 735; **32** 26, 769
toys **31** *255*, 258
tracery **31** 270, 271, 273
bar **31** 270
blind **7** 860
Gothic **11** 153, *154*; **13** 59
plate **31** *270*, 271
trade **6** 624; **10** 592
ceramics **6** 332; **11** 605
cotton **11** 649
damask **19** 418
dress **1** 347
fans **10** 781
feathers **1** 250
furniture **3** 584
glass **16** 522
iron **14** 57
lace **3** 610; **11** 649
lacquer **32** 482
manuscripts **16** 553
paper **24** 48
papier mâché **3** 578
plaster **3** 578
porcelain **11** 607, 610
pottery **6** 333
ribbons **16** 448
silk **11** 645; **28** 717
tapestries **3** 607
textiles **7** 53; **15** 722; **16** 448; **25** 315
wallpaper **3** 578

France
trade—cont.
wood **11** 587
transfer (printing) **11** 606
trappings **6** 155
treatises **19** 9
aesthetics **9** 372
16th cent. **31** 197
18th cent. **2** 15
architecture **23** 487–8, 489; **28** 371; **31** 296–7*
Gothic **31** 835
16th cent. **5** 166; **19** 693–4
17th cent. **2** 168; **6** 417; **10** 489; **12** 310
18th cent. **7** 774, 840; **8** 793; **19** 34
19th cent. **22** 362; **26** 270; **27** 123; **32** 427, 598
art **25** 660
bridges **12** 206; **24** 479
collections **2** 904
drawing **25** 396
engravings **10** 390
fortifications **21** 567; **29** 376
gardens **12** 64, 120, 122, 132, 724; **21** 822
gem-engraving **20** 416
grottoes **13** 704
jewellery **17** 524
locks **16** 59
painting **31** 300
encaustic **3** 19
landscape **31** 817
17th cent. **11** 743; **23** 748; **24** 805
18th cent. **8** 500
19th cent. **10** 199
20th cent. **8** 774; **12** 806
palaeography **19** 865
perspective **8** 786; **24** 335, 490, 494
photography **19** 86
portraits **15** 31
prisons **25** 637
silk **11** 645
stage design **30** 659
stained glass **29** 506
stencilling **29** 628
stereotomy **8** 775; **11** 771
stone-cutting **8** 787
terracotta **6** 378
wood **19** 26
wood-engravings **4** 360
trompe l'oeil **8** 525; **11** *604*; **15** 140; **27** 56; **29** 668
tulip-wood **11** 596; **26** 84
tureens **11** *620*, *622*; **12** *357*; **21** *70*; **32** *583*
turning **11** 587
tusks **11** 636
tympana **7** *224*, *719*; **11** *554*; **26** *600*; **27** *544*; **31** *493*
Gothic **13** *75*; **19** *128*; **27** *543*; **31** *493*
Romanesque **26** *600*
typography **31** *495*
typological cycles **29** *510*
upholstery **11** 587; **30** XV; **31** 684, *684*, 685, *687*
urban planning **8** 217; **31** 724, 737
Modernism **19** *50*
Neo-classicism **22** *34*
16th cent. **29** 376
valances **3** 484
vases **11** 635, 636; **30** *495*
La Tène culture (*c.* 450-.*c* 50 BC) **25** *543*
19th cent. **11** *610*; **28** *523*
20th cent. **11** *612*; **28** *524*
vaults (ceiling)
flat-topped **7** 774
Gothic **3** 458; **13** 59
nave **26** 586
rib **13** 36; **26** 586; **32** 90
rib: jumping **32** 90
rib: lierne **32** 90
rib: net **32** 92

France
vaults (ceiling)—cont.
rib: octopartite **25** 667
rib: quadripartite **32** 92
rib: sexpartite **5** 371
rib: tierceron **32** 93
Romanesque **26** 586
19th cent. **32** *599*
vautoir **22** 726
velvet **7** 442
veneers **11** 588, *588*, 589, 596, *602*; **20** 468
verandahs **32** 240
villas **32** 541, 551, 553–4, 555
Cubism **11** *525*
Modernism **19** *42*
Roman **26** 906; **32** 543
20th cent. **32** *556*
see also châteaux
violet-wood **11** 596
viols **22** *374*
wallpaper **9** 370; **24** 63; **32** 810, 813, 814, 815, III, IV1; **33** 711
flock , ; **32** IV2, 3
wall passages **5** 371
walls **8** *277*
walnut **5** *350*; **8** 271; **11** 585, *586*, 587, 589, 595, *600*; **27** *682*; **28** *298*; **33** 326
war cemeteries **6** 166
war memorials **19** *823*
watches **7** 441, *441*, 447; **11** *630*
water towers **22** *34*
wax **31** 840
waxes **21** *771*; **31** 262; **33** 3
waxworks **33** 3
weaving **30** 552
weepers **33** *28*, 28
wicker **33** 157
willow **33** 157
windows **9** 12
band **13** *136*, 178, 181; **29** VI1
clerestory **13** 179, 181
lancet **13** 181
medallion **13** 178, *179*, 181
rose **26** *45*; **31** *270*
women **7** 235
women artists **11** 672*; **12** 336; **21** 412; **24** 138, 139, 141, 142
3rd cent. AD **10** 197
19th cent. **4** 318; **14** 282
wood **4** *661*; **9** 152; **11** 595–6, 598, 601; **13** 125–6*, *126*; **24** *716*, *821*; **26** 641*
wood-carvings **26** 641; **27** *681*
woodcuts
images d'Epinal **15** 142*; **25** 244
Post-Impressionism **25** *583*
15th cent. **33** 350*
16th cent. **10** *174*; **33** 357*
18th cent. **25** *243*; **33** 359–60*
19th cent. **6** 491; **17** 441; **19** 214, *215*; **31** 830, *830*; **33** 360, 361, *361*
20th cent. **33** 362
wood-engravings **9** *170*; **13** *307*; **29** *857*; **33** 369, *369*
wool , ; **2** *703*; **5** 836, I; **11** *638*, *640*, *648*; **27** *895*; **30** *313*, I1, II2
workshops **29** 852
wrought iron **3** 524; **11** 585, 624, 628
France, Adelaïde de *see* BOURBON, ADELAÏDE DE
France, Anatole **2** 733; **4** 368, 589; **14** 553
Francé, Johannes Franciscus **23** 299
France, Joseph Angelo de **13** 922
France, Marie de *see* MARIE DE FRANCE
France, Sophie de **5** 767
France, Victoire de *see* BOURBON, VICTOIRE DE
France, William **11** 431
Francés, Esteban **30** 22
Francés, Matías *see* MATÍAS FRANCÉS

Francés, Nicolás **11** 482, 676–8*
works **11** *677*
Francesca, Pierro della *see* PIERO DELLA FRANCESCA
Francesca da Firenze **16** 780
Franceschi, Caterina dei *see* CATERINA DEI FRANCESCHI
Franceschi, Domenico de' **32** 199
Franceschi, Edgar **18** 834
Franceschi, Francesco de' *see* FRANCESCO DE' FRANCESCHI
Franceschi, Piero de' *see* PIERO DELLA FRANCESCA
Franceschini (family) **3** 863
Franceschini, Baldassarre **4** 277; **11** 678–9*; **32** 691
collaboration **12** 707
patrons and collectors **3** 97; **21** 26, 27, 28; **23** 87; **24** 834; **28** 489
pupils **11** 697; **29** 29
teachers **27** 179
works **11** 205, 214, 389, *678*; **16** 674
Franceschini, Bartolomeo **17** 443
Franceschini, Giacomo **11** 682
Franceschini, Guasparri **11** 678
Franceschini, Marcantonio **4** 277; **11** 679–82*; **16** 670
collaboration **4** 320; **7** 308; **14** 27; **20** 902; **29** 775
patrons and collectors **3** 90; **5** 178; **7** 779; **27** 316; **28** 13
pupils **1** 733; **4** 320; **5** 358; **12** 23, 25; **20** 390
reproductive prints by others **3** 308; **12** 582
teachers **7** 309
works **11** *680*, *681*; **12** 284; **25** 893; **26** 810
Franceschini, Vincenzo **22** 480
Francesco I, 4th Capitano of Mantua (*reg* 1382-1407) **12** 903–4*, *904*; **16** 710; **20** 318
architecture **3** 298
Francesco I, 4th Duke of Milan (*reg* 1450-66) **11** 116; **16** 630; **24** 284; **28** 529–31*
architecture **11** 25, 72; **21** 516, 532; **29** 22
decorative works **22** 104
manuscripts **20** 697
paintings **3** 695; **28** 531
sculpture **8** 799
Francesco I, 8th Duke of Modena and Reggio (*reg* 1629-58) **5** *302*; **10** 517, *518*, 526–7*
architecture **2** 849; **18** 685; **32** 492
collections **16** 767
paintings **3** 745; **12** 308; **18** 685; **27** 150; **28** 39
Francesco I, Grand Duke of Tuscany (*reg* 1574-87) **21** 7, *8*, *9*, 22–3*; **26** 779
architecture **5** 183; **11** 212, 215; **16** 771; **29** 860
military **19** 511
art policies **9** 21
collections **11** 187; **32** 106
decorative works **8** 274; **24** 250
drawings **32** 22
fountains **11** 343
gardens **25** 452
gold **4** 53; **20** 903
hardstones **11** 191; **14** 171; **16** 746
interior decoration **16** 664, 712; **29** 741
manuscripts **6** 148
metalwork **13** 922
paintings **5** 317; **6** 112; **7** 815; **25** 241; **27** 732, 851; **31** 54
allegorical **4** 409
display **9** 14
frescoes **25** 77
history **19** 374
industrial scenes **10** 858; **15** 828
marine **1** 670

Francesco I, Grand Duke of Tuscany (*reg* 1574-87)
paintings—cont.
mythological **19** 872; **32** 16
religious **4** 859; **20** 311
parks **12** 116
porcelain **4** 176; **6** 923; **16** 736
sculpture **3** 161; **6** 146; **8** 512; **9** 21; **10** 441; **12** 21, 569, 570, 571, 576; **19** 673; **21** 440; **25** 76; **27** 204; **29** 569
Studiolo **29** *861*
tapestries **11** 194
teachers **5** 182
Francesco I, Lord of Padua (*reg* 1355-88) **5** 871; **24** 559; **30** 232
Francesco II, 10th Duke of Milan (*reg* 1521-35) **28** 529, 533*
architecture **19** 200
manuscripts **4** 76; **20** 791
paintings **21** 525; **27** 891
Francesco II, 4th Marchese of Mantua (*reg* 1484-1519) **10** *518*; **12** *904*, 908*; **25** 151
architecture **19** 551; **20** 319
collections **2** 140
medals **20** 322
paintings **3** 656, 818; **4** 335; **20** 312; **26** 454; **31** 432
sculpture **1** 162
Francesco II, Duke of Modena (*reg* 1662-94) **16** 747
Francesco II, Lord of Padua (*reg* 1390-1405) **5** 872; **6** 168; **14** 433
Francesco III, Duke of Modena (*reg* 1737-80) **12** 473; **13** 746; **16** 752
Francesco IV, 5th Duke of Mantua (*reg* 1612) **25** 383
Francesco IV, Duke of Modena (*reg* 1814-46) **23** 333
Francesco V, Duke of Modena (*reg* 1846-59) **4** 20
Francesco, Bartolommeo di *see* BARTOLOMMEO DI FRANCESCO
Francesco, Bernardo di *see* BERNARDO DI FRANCESCO
Francesco, Domenico di *see* DOMENICO DI MICHELINO
Francesco, Francesco di Antonio di *see* FRANCESCO DI ANTONIO DI FRANCESCO
Francesco, Giovanni di (1412-59) *see* GIOVANNI DI FRANCESCO (DEL CERVELLIERA) (i)
Francesco, Giovanni di (*fl* 1444-*d* *c.* 1460) *see* GIOVANNI DA PISA (i)
Francesco, Guido *see* FRANÇOIS, GUY
Francesco, Juan **8** 202
Francesco, Lupo di *see* LUPO DI FRANCESCO
Francesco, Mariotto di *see* MARIOTTO DI FRANCESCO
Francesco, Stefano di *see* STEFANO DI FRANCESCO
Francesco Bologna **20** 350
Francesco da Barberino **12** 683; **31** 4
Francesco da Camerino **12** 285
Francesco da Faenza **6** 11
Francesco dal Prato **21** 19
Francesco da Milano **2** 111
Francesco da Niguarda **3** 783
Francesco d'Antonio (di Bartolommeo) **6** 2; **11** 683*; **12** 302; **16** 741; **20** 536
Francesco d'Antonio (Zacchi) da Viterbo **11** 683–4*; **32** 628
Francesco da Parma **16** 723
Francesco da Pavia **3** 393; **4** 729
Francesco da Pisa **8** 767
Francesco da Pozzo **1** 531
Francesco da Rimini **4** 275
Francesco da San Simone **24** 854
Francesco (di Giacomo) da Sant'Agata *see* SANT'AGATA, FRANCESCO (DI GIACOMO) DA

Francesco da Tieri **12** 702
Francesco de Cotignola *see* ZAGANELLI, FRANCESCO (DI BOSIO)
Francesco de Filippo da Firenze **3** 307
Francesco de' Franceschi **11** 684*; **32** 199
Francesco del Borgo **11** 684–5*; **24** 731; **26** 811
Francesco del Cossa *see* COSSA, FRANCESCO DEL
Francesco della Chiesa **3** 810
Francesco del Valente **12** 705; **31** 707
Francesco di Andrea **28** 687
Francesco di Antonio **8** 180; **10** 713
Francesco di Antonio del Chierico **11** 685–7*; **26** 326
attributions **2** 186
collaboration **2** 697; **20** 689
patrons and collectors **2** 276; **31** 845
pupils **2** 697; **4** 197; **27** 176
works **11** *686*; **32** 384
Francesco di Antonio di Francesco **12** 717
Francesco di Bartolommeo **8** 797, 799
Francesco di Bettini **20** 657
Francesco di Cristofano Giudicis *see* FRANCIABIGIO
Francesco di Giorgio (1439-1501) **30** 230
Francesco (Maurizio) di Giorgio Martini (1439-?1501) **2** 161; **11** 687–94*; **15** 136; **16** 661, 662; **21** 532, 565, 567, 571, 578; **22** 44; **28** 676; **31** 742
architecture
churches **7** 905; **11** *689*, *690*; **28** 683
domes **23** 349
fortifications **3** 359; **11** *688*
monasteries **18** 862
palazzi **2** 1; **18** 862; **31** 742, 745
stables **31** 740
studioli **29** 859
urban planning **31** 712
assistants **3** 253; **8** 100
attributions **2** 277; **8** 101; **13** 772; **18** 861; **24** 533; **26** 836; **28** 675; **31** 744, 746; **32** 104
collaboration **3** 253; **9** 75; **14** 784; **18** 697; **25** 216; **28** 702
copies **22** 805
drawings **19** 194; **29** 522
methods **21** 768; **28** 201
paintings **2** 339; **11** 692–3*
cassoni **6** 4
frescoes **28** 683
panel **20** 684; **32** 104
spalliere **29** 362
still-lifes **29** 665
patrons and collectors **2** 277; **22** 13; **23** 349
sculpture **11** *693*, 693–4*; **16** 692; **26** 137; **28** 681; **29** 568
plaquettes **25** 20
writings **5** 905; **8** 100; **12** 110; **19** 687; **23** 486, 487; **31** 235, 295; **32** 639
Francesco di Giovanni (1428-95) *see* FRANCIONE
Francesco di Giovanni (*fl c.* 1470-80) **32** 366
Francesco di Giovanni di Domenico *see* BOTTICINI, FRANCESCO
Francesco di Neri di Ubaldo *see* SELLAIO
Francesco di Niccolò **19** 199, 200
Francesco di Pietro della Biada *see* BENAGLIO, FRANCESCO
Francesco di Rinaldo **28** 684
Francesco di Segna **28** 365
Francesco di Stefano *see* PESELLINO

Francesco di Valdambrino 11 696*
attributions 13 626; 16 841
collaboration 16 840
competitions 7 671
works 7 330; 28 681
Francesco di Vannuccio 11 696–7*; 24 28
Francesco di Vito 22 484
Francesco Felle Pecore see MOSCA, FRANCESCO DI SIMONE
Francesco Griffo da Bologna 31 494
Francesco-Maria I, Duke of Urbino 27 273–4*; 31 35
architecture 3 683; 12 278; 24 534, 536; 27 274, 323
drawings 21 450
interior decoration 27 760
paintings 7 560; 9 185; 11 701
sculpture 15 101
Francesco-Maria II, Duke of Urbino 27 274–5*
architecture 23 348; 27 482
furniture 23 348
paintings 3 257; 9 175; 32 626; 33 719
sculpture 3 161; 5 533; 29 561
Francesco Napoletano 25 466
Francescuccio di Fabriano see GHISSI, FRANCESCUCCIO (DI CECCO)
Frances Sibyl Augusta, Margravine of Baden-Baden (reg 1675-1737) 4 890; 26 547; 33 593, 594*
Francés y Pascual, Plácido 29 306, 307
Francés y Sanchez-Heredero, José 11 697*
Francey, S. & T. 12 597
Francheville, Pierre de see FRANCAVILLA, PIETRO
Franchi, Alessandro 11 697*; 22 384; 28 381, 689
Franchi, Antonio 7 780; 11 697–8*; 16 674; 24 26; 25 549
Franchi, Giuseppe 7 662; 20 390; 24 758
Franchi, Rossello di Jacopo 4 31; 6 2; 7 457; 11 197, 698*
Franchina, Carlo 29 271
Franchina, Nino 11 802
Franchini see LAFRANCHINI
Franchini, Girolamo 16 739
Franchoys, Lucas, I (1574-1643) 7 699; 11 698–9*
Franchoys, Lucas, II (1616-81) 11 698, 699*
Franchoys, Pieter 11 698–9*
Francia, Alexandre 11 703
Francia, Ali de see FRANCIA, JUAN DE
Francia, Domenico 13 802; 29 689
Francia, Francesco 11 699–702*; 16 662
attributions 13 294
collaboration 2 607; 4 276; 8 3
patrons and collectors 1 731; 3 743; 5 700; 27 350; 31 448
pupils 3 55; 11 702; 15 862; 24 393; 25 736, 858; 32 629
reproductive prints by others 22 466
restorations by others 6 115
works 4 *271*; 11 384, *700*, *701*; 16 750; 23 115
Francia, Giacomo 11 699, 701, 702*
works 11 *702*
Francia, Giulio 11 699, 701, 702
Francia, Il (15th cent.) see FRANCIA, FRANCESCO
Francia, Il (16th cent.) see PARIGI (DI SANTI) ALFONSO
Francia, Juan de 32 124
Francia, (François-)Louis (-Thomas) 11 702–3*
dealers 4 66
Francia, (François-)Louis (-Thomas)—cont.
groups and movements 12 742; 25 264; 32 903
patrons and collectors 21 901
Francia, Nicolò di see NICOLÒ DI FRANCIA
Francia, Rubinetto di see RUBINETTO DI FRANCIA
Francia, Zanino di (*fl c.* 1491-1507) see ZOHANNE DE FRANZA
Francia, Zanino di (*fl* 1422-42) see ZANINO DI FRANCIA
Franciabigio 11 703–4*; 16 766; 27 846
attributions 27 847
collaboration 12 719; 25 222; 27 740, 848, 849
patrons and collectors 3 15; 20 142; 21 18; 25 76
reproductive prints by others 18 476
teachers 1 572
works 11 204, 388, *704*; 21 16, 846; 31 581
Francin, Claude (-Clair) 8 70, 72; 11 704–5*
Francin, François-Alexis 11 704
Francin, Guillaume 11 705; 21 424
Francine, François de 11 344
works 11 *344*
Francini (family) 12 120
Francini see LAFRANCHINI
Francini, Alexandre 4 548; 11 343; 12 120
Francini, François 12 120, 121
Francini, Thomas 4 548; 21 346
aqueducts 4 548
fountains 11 343
gardens 27 314; 29 917
grottoes 4 548; 12 120; 13 704; 27 559
stage design 30 659
Francione 11 705*
collaboration 25 216; 27 733
pupils 25 216
works 11 211
Francioni, Bernabeo 20 373
Franciosino, Il see CORDIER, NICOLAS
Francis, Duke of Saxe-Coburg-Saalfeld (reg 1800-06) 33 *110*
Francis, Saint 25 229
Francis I, Duke of Brittany (reg 1442-50) 4 827*
Francis I, Duke of Lorraine, Grand Duke of Tuscany see FRANCIS I, Holy Roman Emperor
Francis I, Emperor of Austria (reg 1792-1835) 5 631; 13 899; 14 11; 26 59; 31 680
books 11 789
collections 22 675
paintings 13 783; 18 418
prints 33 116
sculpture 33 624
Francis I, Holy Roman Emperor (reg 1745-65) 13 *901*; 14 11; 18 683
architecture 2 612, 784; 16 862; 19 800
collections 1 637; 2 830; 18 670
faience (ii) (ceramics) 14 677; 15 2; 28 856
gems 24 734
hardstones 11 192
mosaics 33 691
tapestries 11 194; 30 324
Francis I, King of France (reg 1515-47) 7 *426*; 14 869; 20 132, 137, *334*; 25 276, *282*; 31 *833*, 847–9*, *849*
architecture 19 90; 20 133; 23 810; 24 133, 754; 31 834
châteaux 11 727
Amboise 23 809
Blois 4 155; 11 512
Francis I, King of France (reg 1515-47)
architecture
châteaux—cont.
Chambord 6 59, 415, 416–17; 21 550
Château de Madrid (Paris) 4 780; 11 513
Fontainebleau 4 780; 6 505; 11 259–60, 262, 513, 556; 19 18
Saint-Germain-en-Laye 27 558
Vincennes 32 582
military 19 690; 28 468
palaces 6 506; 9 94; 11 513; 24 116, 161
art policies 11 656
carpets 11 651
ceramics 26 447
collections 6 139; 9 387; 10 487; 20 280; 23 855; 27 114
coral 4 337
enamel 19 398
furniture 11 586; 16 766
gardens 12 113
gems 11 634; 12 258, 259, 266
gold 18 662
heraldry 5 913
interior decoration 11 571; 13 700; 25 578
jewellery 17 520
maiolica 16 734
manuscripts 4 571; 7 463; 11 532; 12 837; 20 334; 21 638
metalwork 2 455; 9 468; 11 616; 24 146
miniatures (manuscript illumination) 30 530
musical instruments 22 374, *374*
paintings 4 569; 7 426, 462, 464; 10 477; 11 508, 532, 661; 19 185; 24 471; 27 848
allegorical 4 857; 8 4; 21 499; 27 209
anamorphic 19 186
battle 27 740
erotic 23 293
landscape 26 30
portraits 12 750
religious 3 305; 7 425
parks 24 179
patronage 11 656
pottery 11 604
rock crystal 16 745
salts 6 139, 142, *143*, 149; 12 865; 27 640; 30 219
sculpture 3 160; 4 337; 6 141–3; 7 562; 11 513, 556; 16 695; 22 32; 25 578; 26 768; 27 46, 546; 29 562, 571; 32 503
silver 6 141
stained glass 3 460
staircases 4 *156*
stucco 29 833
tapestries 11 262, 572, 639; 24 15; 26 779; 27 132; 30 318
Francis I, King of the Two Sicilies (reg 1825-30) 4 *557*; 27 58
Francis I style see FRANÇOIS IER STYLE
Francis II, Duke of Brittany 4 827–8*; 21 565; 31 845
Francis II, Holy Roman Emperor see FRANCIS I, Emperor of Austria
Francis II, King of France (reg 1559-60) 20 133; 25 580; 31 *833*
Francis II Gospels see under GOSPEL BOOKS → individual manuscripts
Francis III, Duke of Lorraine (reg 1726-39) see FRANCIS I, Holy Roman Emperor
Francis, Caroline 2 766
Francis, Dennis 28 300
Francis, Field & Francis 31 256, 264
Francis, Ivor 2 749
Francis, John F. 9 451; 11 705–6*; 23 171
Francis, Martin 26 333
Francis, Sam(uel Lewis) 11 706*
collaboration 31 869
dealers 16 820
groups and movements 2 545; 25 361; 31 607
patrons and collectors 9 189; 27 277; 33 45
teachers 19 83
works 1 130; 19 492; 21 897
Franciscan Breviary, Master of the 20 675–6*
Franciscan Order 4 724; 5 689; 7 214, 231; 11 707–12*; 15 860
architecture 11 711–12; 19 566; 21 841–2*; 33 571
Bolivia 4 260
Brazil 4 709–10
Denmark 8 723
Gothic 13 51, 52
Ireland 16 7
Italy 13 52; 26 755
Mexico 21 373, 375; 33 571
Paraguay 24 *94*, 94–5
Sardinia 27 836
United States of America 22 567; 31 588
embroidery 11 712
iconography 11 708–11*; 13 127
painting 11 *710*
fresco 11 *709*, *710*; 12 *691*, *692*, *693*; 20 *506*
patronage 11 711–12*; 13 132; 16 762
sacrimonti 27 498
sculpture 24 98
shelters 33 571
stained glass 11 712
Francisco, Carlos V. 24 622
Francisco, Juan 11 713*; 29 333, 334
works 29 *334*
Francisco de Baeza 28 709
Francisco de Córdova 32 167
Francisco de Osona 23 605; 29 277
Francisco de San Gil 14 609
Francisco de São José 30 799
Francisco el Grande 30 3
Francisco Henriques see S LORENZO DELLA COSTA, MASTER OF
Franciscus de Castello Italico de Mediolano 20 847
Franciscus de Retza 4 146
Franciscus Italus 11 713*; 18 427, 431; 25 96
patrons and collectors 16 866
works 25 111
Franciscus Niger 22 369
Francis Ferdinand, Archduke of Este-Austria see ESTE-AUSTRIA, FRANCIS FERDINAND, Archduke of
Francis-Joseph, Prince of Liechtenstein (reg 1772-81) 19 338*
Francis Joseph I, Emperor of Austria-Hungary (reg 1848-1916) 14 12*
architecture 2 787; 32 456
furniture 12 172; 19 113; 24 817
glass 19 522
interior decoration 32 460
metalwork 8 428
paintings 1 141; 4 838; 10 117; 14 315, 509
sculpture 3 732; 14 365
sponsorship 14 11
Francis of Assisi, Saint 7 231; 11 205, 707
Francisque 11 637
Francistown 4 490
Franciszek of Sieradz 25 102
Franck, Charles 2 517; 3 587
Franck, François 2 516, 517; 3 585, 587, 614
Franck, Franz Friedrich 12 390
Franck, Hans see LÜTZELBURGER, HANS
Franck, Hans Ulrich 2 719; 11 713–14*; 12 390; 20 796
Franck, Heynken 16 833
Franck, Jean-Michel 18 864
Franck, Kaj 11 105, 106
Franck, Laureys 21 609
Franck, Louis 2 516; 3 614
Franck, Maximilian 29 740
Franck, Pauwels see FIAMMINGO, PAOLO
Franck, P. H. see FRUYTIERS, PHILLIP
Franck, Simon 8 118
Franck, Valentin 14 138
Franckaert, Jacob see FRANCART, JACQUES
Francke, A. H. 30 848
Francke, Master 11 714–15*; 13 155, 156; 14 101
works 11 98, *715*; 12 223, 383
Francke, Paul 11 715–16*
works 33 52, 292, 293
Francke, Pauline 29 609
Francke, Pauwels see FLAMMINGO, PAOLO
Francke & Heidecke 18 417
Francken, Ambrosius, I (*c.* 1544-1618) 11 716, 717*
collaboration 23 201; 32 712
pupils 11 717
reproductive prints by others 3 126
teachers 11 222
works 3 558
Francken, Ambrosius, II (*c.* 1590-1632) 11 716, 717
Francken, Ambrosius, III (1614-62) 11 716
Francken, Frans, I (1542-1616) 11 716, 717–18*; 12 242; 29 592
collaboration 2 341
pupils 11 717, 718
works 3 558
Francken, Frans, II (1581-1642) 11 716, 718–20*; 32 251
assistants 3 41
attributions 11 717
collaboration 2 341; 4 913
Bassen, Bartholomeus Cornelisz. van 3 352
Breughel, Jan, I (1568-1625) 4 915; 5 352; 11 443
Coques, Gonzales 7 833
Jordaens, Hans, III (*c.* 1595-*d* 1643) 17 647
Momper, Josse de, II (1564-1635) 21 830
Neefs (family) 22 718
Vrancx, Sebastiaen 32 724
patrons and collectors 3 613; 5 353; 6 77; 23 468; 26 490; 32 7
works 1 663; 3 559; 5 352, *353*; 9 22; 11 442, *442*, 443, *718*, *719*; 22 *372*, 373
Francken, Frans, III (1607-67) 11 716, 720*; 22 201, 718
Francken, Hieronymus, I (1540-1610) 11 716–18*
attributions 11 718
pupils 4 150; 11 717, 718; 17 918
Francken, Hieronymus, II (1578-1623) 5 352; 11 716, 717–18*
Francken, Hieronymus, III (*b c.* 1611) 11 716
Francken, Nicholas 11 716
Francken, Thomas 11 716
Franckenberg, Conrait von see KUENE VON DER HALLEN, KONRAD
Franckenberg, Johann von 18 497
Franckenberger, Tobias 4 747
Franckenstein, Johann Goll van 10 864
Franckenstein, Philipp Anton von, Bishop of Bamberg 30 866

Franco, Armando 12 920
Franco, (Giovanni) Battista 11 720–22*; 13 541; 26 770
patrons and collectors 3 203; 10 753; 13 658, 659
pupils 3 253
works 4 664; 11 *721*; 22 391; 27 274; 32 223, 647
Franco, Carlos 13 6
Franco, Cesare 5 532
Franco, Chagas 27 141
Franco, Francisco 8 74; 25 302
Franco, Giacomo (1550-1620) 6 25; 23 879
Franco, Giacomo (1818-95) 8 532; 11 722*
Franco, Rodrigo 1 680
Franco, Salvatore di 12 748
Franco Bolognese 4 274
Franco da Pesaro 12 285
Franco dei Russi 11 722*
collaboration 8 172; 12 733; 27 807
patrons and collectors 4 18; 11 4; 12 666
pupils 2 186
works 32 198
François, Alessandro 10 637
François, Alphonse 10 396
François, Ange 11 724
François, Auguste 6 597, 601
François, Chief Associate of Maître *see* JACQUES DE BESANÇON, MASTER OF
François, Claude 5 564; 11 722–3*; 22 37; 24 805; 32 737
François, Guy 11 534, 723*; 27 817
François, Jean-Charles 11 723*; 22 456
methods 10 562
patrons and collectors 29 537
pupils 4 330
works 2 239; 8 130, 131; 13 220
François, (Pierre-)Joseph (-Célestin) 11 723–4*
pupils 20 52; 22 696
teachers 14 480; 19 166
François, Lucien 11 724*
François, Maître 11 724–5*; 20 626, 699
collaboration 20 699
patrons and collectors 16 854
works 11 *725*
François d'Orléans 12 723; 31 840
François-et-Souza-Desnoyer Foundation *see under* SAINT-CYPRIEN
François Ier style 11 726–7*
François Vase 6 480; 10 591; 13 485, 489, 508, *508*, 549; 30 775; 32 48
Francolin, Hans 18 877
Francolise, San Rocco Villa 26 869; 32 541, *541*
Franconville-la-Garenne 6 171
Francotay 8 448
Francq, Léon 24 128
Francuart, Jacques 12 16
Francucci, Innocenzo *see* INNOCENZO DA IMOLA
Francz, Master 3 853
Francz de Welize 25 434
Franczke, Peter 25 111
Franenholz 18 584
Frangeš-Mihanović, Robert 3 86
Frangipane, Mario 1 626
Frangk, Jacoff *see* HAYLMANN, JACOB
Frangopoulos, Ioannis *see* IOANNIS FRANGOPOULOS
Frank, Alfred 19 112
Frank, Bálint 15 7
Frank, Christian 2 804
Frank, Einar Utzon 23 392
Frank, Hans 33 353
Frank, Hans Ulrich *see* FRANCK, HANS ULRICH
Frank, Jean-Michel 11 584, 727*; 12 564, 567
Frank, Josef 2 815, 826; 7 *294*; 11 727–8*; 32 448
collaboration 19 809; 29 777; 32 439
groups and movements 8 826
pupils 14 25; 25 48
staff 25 48
works 2 788, 789, 810, *810*, 815; 30 755
Frank, Mary 21 897
Frank, Richard 4 823
Frank, Robert 11 728–9*; 24 678
assistants 12 599; 19 851
collaboration 10 688
works 11 *728*; 24 679
Frank, Sebastian 9 443
Frank, Waldo 1 772
Franke, Günther 11 729*; 23 7
Fränkel, Adolf 3 429
Fränkel, L. 19 719
Frankel, Wolfgang 26 364
Franken, H. G. 17 466
Frankenberg Church 14 81
Frankenstein, Clare 16 820
Frankenthal 11 609; 12 389, 467; 29 753
Frankenthaler, Helen 11 729–30*; 31 609
collaboration 20 606
dealers 18 162
groups and movements 1 88; 25 361; 31 607
methods 25 24
teachers 14 633
works 1 129, 130; 7 636; 11 *730*; 25 25; 31 *608*; 33 364
Frankenthal Porcelain Factory 11 730–31*; 12 434, 435; 26 498
designers 12 434; 19 772; 33 280
directors 12 433
production 12 *434*
Frankenthal school 7 710; 11 731–2*; 12 389; 18 707; 21 710; 28 165
Frankfort, Henri 1 893; 9 44; 10 81; 11 732*; 21 276
Frankfurt, Johhanes of *see* JOHHANES OF FRANKFURT
Frankfurt, Master of 2 206; 3 554; 20 676*, *676*
teachers 17 601
works 9 *272*; 11 735; 20 *676*
Frankfurt am Main 11 732–6*; 12 *361*
Altes Rathaus 26 255; 29 611; 32 120
Bahā'ī temple 30 451
books 21 636
Börse 10 669
Cathedral of St Bartholomäus 12 *492*, 492; 13 58, 188; 32 90
cemetery 31 131
ceramics 22 879
coins 7 *534*
collections 12 481
Convention Centre 28 835
cupboards 8 271; 12 423
Deutsche Bibliothek 12 482
exchange 10 669
façade decoration 10 737
faience (ii) (ceramics) 12 430
Frankfurter Hof 14 786
Frobenius-Institut 1 439
guilds 24 579
Hauptbahnhof 25 856, 857
Jewish cemetery 17 555
Karmeliterklosterkirche *see* museums → Museum für Vor- und Frühgeschichte
lamps 17 *571*, 573
Leonhardskirche 11 *733*
marks 11 736
metalwork 11 736*
museums
Archäologisches Museum 11 735
Frankfurt am Main museums—cont.
Deutsches Architekturmuseum 11 735; 12 380, 498, *498*; 31 580
Deutsches Filmmuseum 11 735
Deutsches Postmuseum 11 735
Jüdisches Museum 11 735; 17 581, 582
Liebighaus 11 735
Museum Alter Plastik *see* Leibighaus
Museum für Kunsthandwerk 7 155; 11 735; 21 56; 22 367; 30 332
Museum für Moderne Kunst 11 735, *736*; 14 685
Museum für Völkerkunde 11 735; 29 240
Museum für Vor- und Frühgeschichte 11 735
Schirn Kunsthalle 11 735
Städelsches Kunstinstitut und Städtische Galerie 9 230; 11 735; 14 569; 24 234, 326; 29 487; 32 120
painting 12 389, 390, 391, 394
Pauluskirche 13 729
pewter 12 453
pottery 4 176, *176*; 27 108
Praunheim estate 12 379
Römerstadt estate 12 379; 20 *879*
Rothschildpalais *see* museums → Jüdisches Museum
Salzhaus 32 282
Schauspielhaus 30 684
Schillerschule 28 158
silver 12 449
Stadt-und Universitätbibliothek 27 225
synagogues 17 544, 547, 548
terracottas 27 110
tiles 30 884
trade fair 12 446
urban planning 20 878–9; 31 728
Villa Metzler *see* museums → Museum für Kunsthandwerk
Westhausen estate 12 379
yokes (animal) 25 547
Frankfurt an der Oder 24 181
Frankfurt black *see under* PIGMENTS → types
Frankfurt Crucifixion, Master of the *see* RIMINI, MASTER OF
Frankfurter Aufbau AG 2 216
Frankfurt Garden of Paradise, Master of the 20 677*
frankincense *see under* RESINS → types
Frankinet, Edouard 6 91
Frankish art 8 527; 9 253
see also CRUSADERS; MEROVINGIAN
Frankl, Paul 2 522; 11 736–7*; 29 514, 880; 31 632
Franklin, Benjamin 10 401; 24 47, 596; 25 655; 28 885; 31 652
Franklin, Harry 1 439
Franklin, Maud 33 141
Franklin Institute *see* PHILADELPHIA (PA) → Atwater Kent Museum
Frankonovurd *see* FRANFURT AM MAIN
Frankovich, Andrey 31 563
Franks 21 500
see also FRANKISH ART; MEROVINGIAN
Franks, Augustus Wollaston 7 161; 11 737–8*
Franks Casket 2 81, *81*; 32 523
Franks Collection *see under* LONDON → museums → British Museum
Franque, François 11 738*
Franque, Jean-Baptiste 11 738
Franque, Jean-Pierre 8 561; 11 738–9*; 25 581
Franque, Joseph (-Boniface) 4 305, 333; 11 738, 739*; 25 581
Franquelin, Jean-Augustin 22 243
Frans, Franchois 2 25
Franschhoek
Huguenot Memorial Museum 30 728
La Provence 5 662
Frans Hendrickx *see* S LORENZO DELLA COSTA, MASTER OF
Fransquin (family) 3 600
František of Dietrichštejn 8 422
Frantz, Johann Philipp 5 30
Frantz, Karol Marcin 11 739*; 25 98
Frantz, Marcin 11 739*; 19 815
Frantzén, Johan Otto 30 97
Franz, Duke of Pomerania-Stettin (*reg* 1618-20) 30 203
Franz I, Emperor of Austria *see* FRANCIS II, Holy Roman Emperor
Franz, Heinrich Gerhard 2 833; 6 320
Franz, Julius 9 764; 16 557
Franza, Zohanne de *see* ZOHANNE DE FRANZA
Franz-Dreber, (Karl) Heinrich *see* DREBER, (KARL) HEINRICH
Franzén, John-e 30 82
Franzen, Ulrich 14 803
Franzheim, Kenneth 14 802
Franzi, Juan 27 511
Franz Josef, Emperor of Austria *see* FRANCIS JOSEPH, Emperor of Austria
Franz Josef, Prince of Liechtenstein *see* FRANCIS JOSEPH, Prince of Liechtenstein
Franz Ludwig, Elector of Trier 30 370
Franzone (family) 1 628, 629
Franzone, Agostino (i) (*fl* 1678) 11 739*; 21 483
Franzone, Agostino (ii) (*d* 1705) 11 739*
Franzone, Giacomo, Cardinal 11 739*
Franzone, Stefano 11 739
Franzoni, Francesco Antonio 23 701; 24 846; 25 8
Franz von Bocholt 20 795
Frapier, Edmond 19 491; 25 600
Frari Triptych 11 382, *382*
Frascati 11 740–41*; 16 *620*
fountains 13 703
Palazzo Vescovile 18 524
S Pietro 11 277
S Romualdo di Camaldoli 5 450, 451
urban planning 21 79
Vescovile Palace 25 105
Villa Aldobrandini 1 595–6; 11 *740*, 740–41; 12 115, 117; 15 837; 32 548, 550
fountains 11 343
frescoes 9 89
gardens 9 22; 32 547
sculpture 27 357
Villa Arrigoni-Muti 18 734
Villa Falconieri 5 414; 11 23, *24*; 12 534; 13 656
Villa Mondragone 11 *741*
Villa Montalto Grazioli 24 10
Villa Muti 7 906
Frasconi, Antonio 10 725; 11 742*; 31 756; 33 364
Fraser, Alexander 11 742*; 28 236, 237
Fraser, Charles 11 742*
Fraser, Donald 28 260
Fraser, Furness & Hewitt 11 848
Fraser, Haden 28 260
Fraser, James Baillie 5 419; 15 655
Fraser, James Earle 3 30; 27 360; 33 150
Fraser, John 11 848
Fraser, John Arthur 5 565; 11 742–3*; 22 38
Fraser, Patrick Allan 28 255
Fraser, Thomas E. 23 341
Fraser, William 15 208, 655; 28 268
Frasinelli, Roberto 2 215
Frass, Wilhelm 2 803
Frassinelli, Gian Piero 30 3
Frassinoro, S Maria Assunta e S Claudio 26 690
Frate, Cecchino del *see* CECCHINO DEL FRATE
Frate, Domenico del 23 173; 31 172
Frate, El *see* MANCINI, GIACOMO
Fratelli Alinari, Presso Bardi 1 643
Fratelli Alinari IDEA 1 643
Fratellini, Giovanna 11 743*
Fratelli Toso factory 32 204
Frater, Jock 2 772
Frater, William 5 63
Fraternal Society of Knighthood of St George 7 177
Fratin, Christophe 2 99; 11 564
Fratina, Giovanni *see* DEMIO, GIOVANNI
Fratrel, Joseph 10 199
Fratsta 3 587
Fratta, Domenico 8 160
Frattale 27 835
Fratta Polesine, Villa Badoer 23 866; 32 548, *549*
Fratte di Salerno *see* SALERNO, FRATTE DI
Frauberger, Heinrich 17 581, 582
Frauen, Asmus 8 150
Frauenburg *see* FROMBORK
Frauenchiemsee, St Maria Abbey 23 651; 26 648
wall paintings 26 *649*
Frauenhofer, Joseph 23 340
Frauenholz, Johann Friedrich 25 454
Fraueninsel 14 235
Frauenkirchen, Church of the Blessed Virgin 14 886
Frauenpreiss, Matthias 2 473
Frauenstein, Wallfahrtskirche 2 800; 10 456
Fraula, de (family) 3 418
Fray 19 324
Fray Bentos 31 *751*
Museo Solari 31 758
Frazee, John 8 124; 25 267; 31 610
Frazzanò, Monastery of S Filippo di Fragalà 28 655
Freake, Elizabeth 20 *677*
Freake Painter 20 677–8*
works 20 *677*; 31 599
Fréart (de Chantelou), Paul 11 743, 744*; 25 390, 391; 29 886
paintings 11 356, 662; 19 354; 23 173; 25 389, 392, 395
Fréart (de Chambray), Roland 10 489; 11 743–4*; 19 197; 23 856; 29 886
works 11 674; 23 487
translated 1 179; 10 204, 376, 658; 20 879
Fréart, Sieur de *see* FRÉART, PAUL
Freccia, Pietro 8 19
Frecha, José 10 502; 29 301
Frechen 7 586; 22 877
Frecherus, Daniel 25 104
Frechrieu, Pierre 7 720
Freckenhorst, St Bonifatius 11 252; 26 632
Frecskai, Endre 12 839
Freddie, Wilhelm 8 736; 10 483; 11 744–5*; 30 22
Frédeau, Ambroise 11 745*; 24 330; 26 423; 31 207
Fredeau, Matthieu 18 745
Fredeman, W. E. 4 27
Fredensborg 8 *720*, 726; 11 745–6*; 18 453
chapel 8 740

Fredensborg—cont.
gardens 12 135
interior decoration 8 733
Ladies' Apartment 8 743
stucco 29 540, 840
Frédéric, Léon (Henri Marie) 3 563; 5 44; 10 517; 11 746*; 12 296
Frederica, Queen of Prussia, Countess Lichtenau (1751-1805) 28 44
Frederica Sophia Wilhelmina, Margräfin of Bayreuth *see* WILHELMINA, Margräfin of Bayreuth
Frederici, Paolo di Giovanni *see* PAOLO DI GIOVANNI FEI
Frederick, Archbishop of Cologne 26 660
Frederick, Duke of Mecklenburg-Schwerin (*reg* 1756-85) 20 848; 23 669
Frederick, Emperor of Germany (*reg* 1888) 14 *648*, 655*
Frederick, King of Bohemia *see* FREDERICK V, Elector Palatine and King of Bohemia
Frederick, King of Sweden *see* FREDERICK IV, King of Denmark and Norway
Frederick, Margrave of Ansbach (*reg* 1486-1536) 4 376; 14 *648*; 31 286
Frederick, Margrave of Bayreuth (*reg* 1735-63) 3 428; 11 241; 14 *648*; 18 418; 27 587, 777
Frederick, Prince of Wales *see* HANOVER, FREDERICK, Prince of Wales
Frederick I, Duke of Württemberg (*reg* 1593-1608) 4 817; 11 766; 28 87, 137; 31 719; 33 434
Frederick I, Elector of Brandenburg (*reg* (1415-40) 14 647
Frederick I, Elector of Saxony (*reg* 1423-8) 19 830
Frederick I, Grand Duke of Baden (*reg* 1858-1907) 11 46; 17 818; 28 104
Frederick I, Holy Roman Emperor (*reg* 1152-90) 14 646*
architecture 1 1; 6 525; 12 245; 23 305
castles 22 822
chandeliers 6 442; 26 686
liturgical objects 1 4
metalwork 26 683
paintings 33 153
Frederick I, King of Denmark and Norway (*reg* 1523-34) 8 738
Frederick I, King of Prussia (*reg* 1701-13) 3 798; 8 447; 14 *648*, 650-51*
architecture 4 217; 5 347; 10 418; 12 479; 22 803; 31 715
art policies 12 478
collections 9 28; 12 475; 13 605; 21 264
drawings 3 500
enamel 12 457
engravings 14 53
furniture 12 424; 20 852
glass 12 440
medals 10 773; 19 290
metalwork 12 446
paintings 14 387; 19 749; 24 541; 26 564; 30 517
pottery 13 541
sculpture 3 198; 14 647; 22 436; 28 115
sponsorship 19 642
Frederick I, King of Württemberg (*reg* 1806-16) 19 780; 28 351; 30 767
Frederick I, Landgrave of Hesse-Kassel *see* FREDERICK IV, King of Denmark and Norway
Frederick I Barbarossa, Holy Roman Emperor *see* FREDERICK I, Holy Roman Emperor
Frederick II, Duke of Württemberg *see* FREDERICK I, King of Württemberg
Frederick II, Elector of Brandenburg (*reg* 1440-71) 19 111
Frederick II, Elector of Saxony (*reg* 1428-64) 33 *110*
Frederick II, Elector Palatine (*reg* 1544-45) 3 877; 12 815; 14 653; 23 618; 28 58
Frederick II, Holy Roman Emperor (*reg* 1212-50) 1 5; 14 646-7*; 16 762; 26 628
architecture 3 140, 234; 5 689; 6 57, 83; 7 383; 16 172, 627; 18 784; 22 44, 469, 475; 24 774; 25 450; 30 176; 32 451
military 6 16; 8 138; 33 417
banners 11 148
cathedrals 31 278
coins 7 536
gardens 12 110
gems 12 256
groups and movements 26 182
manuscripts 3 879; 17 505; 26 564; 29 423
sculpture 13 98; 22 44; 24 866-7
Frederick II, King of Denmark and Norway (*reg* 1559-88) 8 *732*; 23 395-6*
architecture 8 725; 14 368, 369, *370*, 542; 23 328; 29 593
glass 8 749
paintings 8 732, 758; 19 662
sculpture 13 682; 18 575; 33 434
tapestries 8 732, 754; 14 369; 18 149; 30 320
Frederick II, King of Prussia (*reg* 1740-86) 14 *648*, 649, 652*; 33 *377*
architecture 3 791-2, 806; 12 374, 902; 18 159, 160; 19 76; 23 812, 861; 25 367, 368; 26 496, 497; 30 676
palaces 14 750
collections 12 473, 476; 25 150; 30 274
frames 11 458
furniture 12 424; 14 750; 18 853; 29 403; 32 337
gardens 12 134
gems 8 12; 12 266; 29 724
hardstones 12 462
interior decoration 12 410, 413; 14 750; 22 436
medals 20 921
miniatures (paintings) 21 643
musical instruments 22 374
paintings 3 381; 11 663; 18 693; 19 644, 649; 24 256, 396, 541-2; 26 247, 732; 30 714
porcelain 3 804
sculpture 1 133, 633; 8 72; 19 141; 24 785; 30 353; 32 76
silk 12 464
sketches 14 751; 25 366
snuff-boxes 12 459
stage design 12 25, 26
writings 21 59
Frederick II, Landgrave of Hesse-Kassel (*reg* 1760-85) 14 491, 492*
architecture 12 374, 475; 19 57; 22 361
sponsorship 17 698
urban planning 9 455
Frederick III, Duke of Holstein-Gottorp (*reg* 1616-59) 13 777; 23 674
Frederick III, Elector of Brandenburg (*reg* 1688-1701 *see* FREDERICK I, King of Prussia (*reg* 1701-13)
Frederick III, Elector of Saxony (*reg* 1486-1525) 33 *110*, 112*
architecture 21 99; 33 110
collections 8 541
manuscripts 10 162
paintings 3 200; 5 199; 8 113, 115, 116; 9 433, 435; 12 387; 33 84
sculpture 21 71
sponsorship 8 114
woodcuts 33 365
Frederick III, Elector Palatine (*reg* 1559-76) 11 731
Frederick III, Holy Roman Emperor (*reg* 1440-93) 2 775; 13 899, *900*, 901-2*; 14 649
architecture 2 777; 13 329; 24 550; 31 329
armour 2 471; 15 867
coats of arms 14 420
manuscripts 19 830; 20 512
sculpture 12 341, 344
stained glass 33 301
swords 2 452
textiles 2 824
Frederick III, King of Denmark and Norway (*reg* 1648-70)
architecture 8 725
collections 8 759; 9 702; 18 523; 22 536
paintings 20 249
sponsorship 14 244, 245; 21 406
thrones 8 752; 30 782, *782*
Frederick III of Simmern *see* FREDERICK III, Elector Palatine
Frederick IV, Count of Tyrol (*reg* 1406-39) 15 863
Frederick IV, Elector Palatine (*reg* 1583-1610) 13 218; 14 305; 20 281; 28 137
Frederick IV, King of Denmark and Norway (*reg* 1699-1730)
architecture 8 726; 11 469, 745; 22 388; 31 317
diplomatic gifts 23 238
gardens 8 726; 12 135; 18 453
glass 12 897; 32 203
interior decoration 8 742; 19 36
paintings 1 449; 32 765
sculpture 3 198; 33 460
sponsorship 8 819
Frederick IV, King of Naples (*reg* 1496-1501) 4 570; 22 481
Frederick V, Duke of Styria *see* FREDERICK III, Holy Roman Emperor
Frederick V, Elector Palatine (*reg* 1610-23) and King of Bohemia (*reg* 1619-20) 14 41; 22 7, 902; 28 137; 32 231, *231*; 33 *272*
architecture 3 353; 5 763; 14 305
gardens 6 95
paintings 11 357; 14 730; 25 65
sculpture 13 218
Frederick V, King of Denmark and Norway (*reg* 1746-66) 7 802; 8 733; 29 386, 540
academy 8 758, 760
architecture 10 110, 111; 31 715
collections 8 758, 759; 27 558; 33 196
sponsorship 14 815
Frederick V, Margrave of Baden-Durlach (*reg* 1677-1709) 3 334, 336; 14 834; 21 640; 27 196; 33 593
Frederick VI, Burgrave of Nuremberg *see* FREDERICK I, Elector of Brandenburg
Frederick VI, King of Denmark and Norway (*reg* 1808-39) 8 759; 16 863; 30 763
Frederick VII, King of Denmark (*reg* 1848-63) 8 753, 758; 16 863
Frederick, John 12 262
Frederick-Augustus I, Elector of Saxony *see* AUGUSTUS II, King of Poland
Frederick-Augustus II, Elector of Saxony *see* AUGUSTUS III, King of Poland
Frederick-Augustus III, Elector of Saxony *see* FREDERICK-AUGUSTUS I, King of Saxony
Frederick-Augustus the Strong, Elector of Saxony *see* AUGUSTUS II, King of Poland
Frederick-Christian, Elector of Saxony (*reg* 1763) 5 878; 13 268
Frederick-Eugene, Duke of Württemberg (*reg* 1795-7) 14 497
Frederick-Franz I, Grand Duke of Mecklenburg-Schwerin (*reg* 1815-37) 29 905
Frederick-Franz II, Grand Duke of Mecklenburg-Schwerin (*reg* 1883-97) 8 706
Frederick Henry, Stadholder of the Netherlands, Prince of Orange (*reg* 1625-47) 14 41; 15 40; 22 824, 902; 23 462, *463*, 464-5*
architecture 3 353; 9 299; 14 38; 22 825, 902; 25 324, 327; 26 392
drawings 15 41; 29 799
furniture 2 385
gardens 12 131; 21 822
paintings 4 656; 13 337; 22 844, 904; 25 65; 26 157; 27 518; 31 780, 807; 32 705
allegorical 3 23
ceiling 4 377
flower 28 364
literary themes 4 151, 152; 19 473
portraits 7 832; 14 730; 22 94
religious 19 348; 22 842; 26 157, 163
sculpture 22 858
Frederick of Toggenburg 7 241
Fredericksberg Public Library 19 319
Fredericksen, Burton B. 25 665
Frederick the Great, King of Prussia *see* FREDERICK II, King of Prussia
Frederick the Great, Museum *see under* POZNAŃ
Frederick the Wise, Elector Palatine *see* FREDERICK II, Elector Palatine
Frederick William, Elector of Brandenburg (*reg* 1640-88) 3 798; 14 647, *648*; 21 153
architecture 3 790; 25 366
atlases 2 696
coins 12 410
collections 22 536
drawings 9 702
enamel 12 457
furniture 8 447; 12 410
glass 4 666; 12 440
paintings 3 42; 7 832; 10 144; 11 169; 12 473; 19 349; 30 517; 31 779; 32 262
patronage 9 53
sculpture 9 53, 760, 761; 17 913
silk 3 804
tapestries 3 804; 9 703; 12 468
Frederick William I, King of Prussia (*reg* 1713-40) 12 479; 14 *648*, 651*
architecture 3 791; 26 560
art policies 3 798
frames 11 458
metalwork 4 62
paintings 15 47
Frederick William II, King of Prussia (*reg* 1786-97) 14 *648*, 649, 653*; 28 42
architecture 3 806; 8 461; 11 242; 12 641
art policies 22 358
collections 10 448; 12 476
drawings 11 283
Frederick William II, King of Prussia (*reg* 1786-97)—cont.
furniture 26 530
gardens 25 368
interior decoration 12 413, 414
sculpture 6 97; 28 43
Frederick William III, King of Prussia (*reg* 1797-1840) 14 *648*, 649, 653-4*
architecture 28 98
art policies 22 358
collections 4 330; 10 92
drawings 18 476
furniture 26 303
gardens 3 807
medals 28 98
paintings 2 560; 3 497; 4 135; 11 780, 894; 12 763; 29 46
porcelain 3 805
sculpture 28 44
Frederick William IV, King of Prussia (*reg* 1840-61) 10 93; 14 490, *648*, 649, 650*, 654*; 22 426
architecture 2 478; 3 792, 793, 794; 4 243; 7 588; 12 376, 476; 13 202; 24 290, 484, 485; 25 367, 368; 28 99, 101, 102; 29 736, 863
art policies 3 807
ceramics 2 869
gardens 19 156; 28 102
interior decoration 12 414, 416; 25 193
paintings 3 497; 11 780; 14 527; 17 856
sculpture 14 304; 15 144; 26 377; 29 609
Fredericton 5 *559*
Beaverbrook Art Gallery 1 496; 5 590
Christ Church Cathedral 5 561; 33 212-13
St Anne's Chapel 33 213
University of New Brunswick 5 590
Frederiksberg 19 799
Frederiksborg Slot *see under* HILLERØD
Frederiksdal
château 8 742
Sparrow Hideaway *see* Spurveskjul
Spurveskjul 1 34; 8 728
Frederiksen, Anton 13 216
Frederikssund, J. F. Willumsens Museum 8 760; 33 214
Frederikstad 23 *218*, 220
Frederiksværk 8 751
Fredi, Bartolo di *see* CINI, BARTOLO DI FREDI
Frediani, Gian Battista 17 856; 19 496
Frediani, Vincenzo (di Antonio) 11 747*; 20 653; 22 567
Frédou, Jean-Martial 11 723
Fredriksen, Stinius 14 229; 23 230
Fredrikson, Franz 18 449
Fredrikstad, Østfold County Central Hospital 23 232
Free Architects' Association 3 409
Free Art Schools (Copenhagen) *see* KUNSTNERNES STUDIESKOLER (COPENHAGEN)
Free Art Studios *see* SVOMAS
Free Classic style *see* QUEEN ANNE REVIVAL
Freed, James Ingo *see* PEI, I(EOH) M(ING)
Freed, Leonard 11 747*; 24 677
Freedberg, David 26 64
Freedberg, Sydney 31 672
Freedman, Ann 18 162
Freedman, Barnett 4 366, 369; 11 747-8*
Freedom group 18 55
Free Field style pottery *see under* POTTERY → wares
Freeman, Ralph 4 803; 30 159

Freeman Fox & Partners 4 804
Freemasons 20 559, 562
Freemasons' Lodge 32 877
Freenthal, Franz Adolf von 18 467
Free Ones, the *see* VAPAAT
Freepainters' Lodge 10 872
Freer, Charles Lang 11 748*
  bronzes 6 868
  ceramics 6 925; 16 395; 22 59
  collections 10 887; 15 742; 17 431; 31 662
  etchings 33 141
  paintings 8 841; 31 393
Freer Canteen 16 365, 381
Freer Gallery of Art *see under* WASHINGTON (DC) → museums
Freese, Johann Georg von 31 26
Free Society of Artists 19 586
free-standing fillet mouldings *see under* MOULDINGS → types
Free State Art Studios *see* SVOMAS
Free Studio association 33 740
Freeth, Hubert Andrew 4 87
Freetown 1 *386*; 28 691
  architecture 28 691
  carnivals 5 788
  fortifications 21 574
  Fulah Town Mosque 28 691
  Hill Station Reservation 28 691
  House of Parliament 28 691
  Law Courts 28 691
  Maroon Church 28 691
  National Art Centre 28 693
  Odeon Cinema 28 691
  Paramount Hotel 28 691
  Railway Terminal Station 28 691
  St Charles's Regent 28 691
  St George's Cathedral 28 691
  Secretariat 28 691
  Sierra Leone Museum 28 692
  State House 28 691
Free University *see under* URBINO
free-word painting *see* DIPINTO PAROLIBERO
freeze-drying 7 730
Fregenae 10 586
Fregenal de la Sierra, S Maria 21 393
Frégevize, Edouard 11 748
Frégevize, Frédéric 11 748*
Fregoso, Federico, Cardinal 25 465
Frei, Hans 11 748–9*
Freiberg 11 749*; 12 *361*
  Cathedral 11 749*
    brasses 4 693
    Golden Portal 11 749; 13 87
    sculpture 13 86
    Tulpenkanzel 20 798
  Schloss Freudenstein 33 113
  sculpture 12 399
  stonewares 12 428
  tapestries 12 466
Freiberger, Anton, Abbot of Im Lavanttal 19 748
Frei Bühne 30 685
Freiburg, Egon, Herzog von 11 750
Freiburg, Johann von, Graf von Neuenburg *see* NEUENBURG, JOHANN VON FREIBURG, GRAF VON
Freiburg, Michael von *see* MICHAEL VON FREIBURG
Freiburg im Breisgau 11 749–52*; 12 *361*
  Augustinermuseum 30 332
  Franciscan church 22 222
  houses 32 281
  Institute of Applied Arts 19 499
  rock crystal 26 485
  St Martin 26 74
  sculpture 8 384; 12 399; 13 85, 88
  stained glass 13 186
  tapestries 14 422
Freiburg im Breisgau—cont.
  Unsere Liebe Frau Cathedral 11 750*; 12 362, 365; 13 49, 56, 89; 24 189
    Altar of the Three Kings 33 *31*
    choir 13 57
    metalwork 5 212
    sculpture 11 750–51*, *751*; 13 87, 88
    spire 11 452; 20 581; 29 414
    stained glass 11 751–2*; 13 187, 188; 29 501, *502*
    Tomb of Christ 13 88
    tracery 31 271
    vaults 32 90
Freie Künstlervereinigung 32 244
Freie Sezession *see* SEZESSION, FREIE
Freie Strasse 14 845
Freie Vereinigung Berliner Künstler 22 291
Freie Vereinigung Münchener Künstler 3 511; 22 304; 28 341
Freilicher, Jane 29 670
Freinburg, Heinrich von *see* HEINRICH VON GMÜND
Freire, María 31 755
Freire de Andrade, Gomes 26 412
Freisaal 2 793
Freising
  Cathedral of SS Maria and Corbinian 2 582; 22 305; 26 634
    altarpiece 5 *607*
  manuscripts 5 805
  Martinskirche 4 777
  Residenz 12 366
Freising, Johann Theodor von, Prince-Bishop 8 288; 11 124
Freising, Otto of *see* OTTO OF FREISING
Freisinger, Caspar 11 752*
  works 11 *752*
Freising Visitation, Master of the 18 450; 20 678*
Freitag, Wolfgang 4 26
Freitas, Nicolau de 2 188; 3 815; 30 881
Freitas, Pinto 24 395
Freitas Valle, José de 4 726
Fréjus 9 *510*
  Baptistery 7 256; 9 533; 21 163
Fréjus *Aphrodite* 13 423, 454, *454*; 17 742
Frelander, Max 11 108
Frélaut, Jacques 25 628
Frélaut, Robert 25 628
Fremantle 2 740
Fremel, Constantin François 22 449; 25 124
Fremiet, Emmanuel 11 659, 753*
  assistants 31 802
  collaboration 5 825; 10 771
  patrons and collectors 23 794
  pupils 12 610
  works 2 100; 11 599, *599*; 15 56; 22 48; 26 723
Frémiet, Louis 27 309
Frémiet, Sophie 27 309
Frémin, Jean
  works 4 *601*
Frémin, Michel de 26 12
Frémin, René 11 559, 754*
  collaboration 3 867; 30 733
  patrons and collectors 4 558, 560, 588
  works 4 587; 11 345; 12 125; 23 458; 27 753, *753*, 754
Fréminet, Louis 11 755
Fréminet, Martin 11 533, 656, 754–5*; 24 134
  groups and movements 9 328; 11 260, 262, 267
  patrons and collectors 4 548
  reproductive prints by others 30 746
  works 11 260, *755*
Fréminet, Médéric 9 328; 11 754
Fremlin Carpet 15 682
Fremont culture 22 582
Frémy, Claudy 25 443
French, Daniel Chester 11 755–6*; 25 5
  assistants 33 42
  collaboration 3 30, 31; 32 793
  groups and movements 7 875
  teachers 26 401
  works 3 30; 4 477; 12 614; 22 48; 27 565; 31 611
French, Daniel Chester, Studio and Museum *see* STOCKBRIDGE (MA, USA) → Chesterwood
French, David 5 615
French, Jared 12 216
French, J. C. 2 306; 15 742
French, John 3 71
French, Leonard 2 763; 11 756*
  works 2 763, *763*; 29 509
French, William Merchant 7 430
French Archaeological Mission 2 227
French Congo *see* GABON
French East India Company 8 35; 11 605; 21 573
French Equatorial Africa *see* CHAD REPUBLIC; GABON
French Gallery 14 47
French Gramophone Company 7 375
French Group 11 775
French Guiana 11 *756*, 756–60*; 29 128
  architecture 11 757–8*
  headdresses 11 *758*
  houses 11 *757*, 758
  jewellery 11 759
  sculpture 11 759
  textiles 1 424
French horse 20 466
French pewter *see* ALLOYS → types → hard metal
French polishing 11 595; 18 610, 611
French Somaliland *see* DJIBOUTI
French Sudan *see* MALI
French Territory of the Afars and the Issas *see* DJIBOUTI
French windows *see under* WINDOWS → types
Frener, Johann Baptist 13 764
Frenkel, Vera 5 569
Frenkel, Yitzhak 16 567, 571
Frente group 7 376; 14 464; 23 382; 28 476
Frentzen, Georg 7 582; 25 856
Frenzel, Johann Gottfried Abraham 11 760*; 12 634
Freppa, Giovanni 3 357
Frere, Bartle 4 288
Frère, (Pierre) Edouard 11 760–61*
Frere, Eustace 32 773
Frère, Théodore 11 761; 23 504
Freres, Dirk 14 538
Fréron, Elie-Catherine 11 761*
Fresca, Matteo Acqua *see* ACQUA FRESCA, MATTEO
Freschel, Daniel (von) *see* FRÖSCHL, DANIEL (VON)
Fresco, Antonio 15 832
Fresco Brotherhood *see* FRESKOBRØDERNE
frescoes 7 735; 11 761–4*; 22 333; 23 381, 784; 28 337; 30 4; 32 802, 808
  conservation 19 395; 29 892
  historical and regional traditions
    Afghanistan 16 169
    Augustinian hermits 2 *725*
    Austria 2 *794*, *795*; 13 *278*; 27 *664*; 31 *357*
    Benedictine Order 28 *702*
    Buddhism 15 570
    Byzantine 8 155; 9 562, 576; 18 417
    Carmelite Order 5 *778*
    Central Asia, Western 16 169
    China 6 776
frescoes
  historical and regional traditions—cont.
    Crete 2 *879*; 8 155, 156
    Czech Republic 17 *820*
    Denmark 8 730, 732; 14 154
    Early Christian (*c.* AD 250-843) 6 31, *32*; 9 562; 18 417
    Ecuador 9 *713*
    Egypt, ancient 8 462; 9 898
    England 9 475; 10 277–8; 18 *644*; 30 *759*
    Etruscan 10 617
    France
      Gothic 2 *863*; 12 *697*; 13 135, 150; 32 *573*
      Mannerism 16 877
      16th cent. 25 *579*
      19th cent. 1 *759*
    Franciscan Order 11 *709*, *710*; 12 *691*, *692*, *693*; 20 *506*
    Germany 12 390–91
      Baroque 2 *579*, *580*, *583*; 28 109
      Nazarenes 12 *392*
      Renaissance 28 *59*
      Rococo 1 *785*; 3 *780*; 12 *391*; 14 *695*
      18th cent. 33 *672*
    Gothic 13 133–4*
      Czech Republic 17 *820*
      France 2 *863*; 12 *697*; 13 135, 150; 32 *573*
      Italy 11 888, *889*, *890*, *891*, 892; 13 132, 135, 136, 144, 145, *145*; 20 *506*, *775*; 29 *405*, *406*; 32 II2
      Spain 13 135, 150; 29 *276*
    Greece, ancient 13 393
    Indian subcontinent 15 570; 30 *643*
    Islamic 16 169
    Italy 7 457–8; 11 761; 13 *803*; 16 710–11; 20 509, 553; 28 *337*
      Baroque 5 *863*; 6 *28*; 7 *908*; 9 *92*; 11 *9*, *24*, *53*, *681*; 13 *786*; 16 *669*, *674*; 18 *733*, *735*; 27 *488*; 29 *40*; 30 *372*, *858*
      Benedictine Order 28 *702*
      Carmelite Order 5 *778*
      Early Christian (*c.* AD 250-843) 6 31, *32*
      Etruscan 10 617
      Franciscan Order 11 *709*, *710*; 12 *691*, *692*, *693*; 20 *506*
      Gothic 11 888, *889*, *890*, *891*, 892; 13 132, 135, 144, 145, *145*; 20 *506*, *775*; 29 *405*, *406*; 32 II2
      Grotesque 31 *523*
      Mannerism 2 *494*; 7 *886*; 8 *182*; 12 *283*, *755*, *756*; 15 IV; 21 *444*, *447*; 24 *420*; 25 *222*, *223*; 26 *816*; 27 *649*, *651*, *653*; 29 *741*; 30 *800*; 32 *350*
      Neo-classicism 21 *528*
      Renaissance 2 *36*, *37*, *38*, *607*, *725*; 4 *194*, *317*; 5 *816*; 6 *12*, *13*; 7 *457*; 8 *504*; 9 *263*, *265*; 11 *13*, *117*, *185*, *293*, *710*; 12 *550*; 13 *261*; 16 *613*, *664*, *763*; 19 *444*, *450*; 20 *305*, *533*, *534*; 21 *11*, *97*; 22 *413*; 24 *522*, *531*, *755*, *762*, *764*, *831*, *862*; 25 *250*, *901*; 26 *457*; 27 *846*, *850*; 28 *80*, *658*, *702*, *703*; 29 *360*; 31 *513*, *514*; 32 *16*
      Renaissance: Early Renaissance 11 *7*; 16 *660*; 26 *184*
      Romanesque 1 *819*; 27 *784*
      13th cent. 2 *622*, *623*, *624*; 6 *103*, *104*; 7 *315*; 20 *697*, 698, *713*; 21 *107*
frescoes
  historical and regional traditions
    Italy—cont.
      14th cent. 1 *726*, *727*; 2 *16*, *187*, *338*, *626*, *627*; 9 *260*; 11 *709*; 12 *682*, *684*, *685*, *687*, *688*, *691*, *692*, *693*, 695; 19 *665*; 20 *551*; 21 *113*, *845*; 24 VIII1; 28 *489*, *685*, *686*; 31 *104*
      15th cent. 1 *554*; 6 14; 9 *262*; 12 *704*; 16 *710*; 20 *554*, *555*, *558*; 26 *827*; 27 *175*; 28 *682*, *687*; 33 *625*
      16th cent. 1 *17*; 3 *859*; 4 *271*, *840*; 5 *455*; 11 *762*; 18 *707*; 26 *727*; 27 *497*; 28 *688*; 33 *716*, *717*, *719*
      17th cent. 1 *552*; 4 *813*; 11 *216*, *874*; 27 *121*
      18th cent. 4 *277*; 8 *192*; 12 *528*
      19th cent. 28 *136*
    Korea 18 302
    Maya 21 251
    Mesoamerica, Pre-Columbian 21 226*, *228*, 229, *230*, 251
    Mesopotamia 32 803
    Minoan 2 *879*
    Romanesque 1 *819*; 26 *649*; 27 *784*; 30 *368*
    Romania 26 710
    Rome, ancient 8 462; 18 *702*; 27 51
    Servites 28 *489*
    Slovenia 28 860
    Spain 10 *504*; 29 275
      Gothic 13 135, 150; 29 *276*
      Romanesque 30 *368*
      16th cent. 5 *456*
      17th cent. 21 732
      18th cent. 3 *425*; 12 *924*
    Switzerland 22 385
    Syria-Palestine 30 197
    United States of America 5 9; 22 336
    Venetian Empire 8 156
    Zapotec 21 *230*
  materials
    adhesives 11 764
    arriccio 11 762
    beeswax 11 764
    charcoal 11 762
    consolidants 7 747
    flour 11 764
    frames 11 763
    gold leaf 11 764
    intonachino 11 762
    intonaco 11 761, 762, 763
    lime 19 394; 32 802
    mortars (building) 11 762, 764
    mud 21 226
    paints 11 763–4
    pigments 11 761, 763–4*; 24 788
    plaster 11 761, 762; 21 226, 229
    resins 11 764
    tin leaf 11 764
    varnishes 11 764
    waxes 10 197; 33 5
  techniques
    cartoons (drawings) 11 763
    giornate 11 763, *763*; 13 145
    highlighting 11 763
    modelling 6 569
    pontate 11 763
    pouncing 11 *761*, 763; 32 *806*
    sgraffito 28 534
    sinopie 28 778, *778*, 779
    spirit fresco 12 33
    squaring up 11 *762*, 763
    stamping 20 509
    transfer (conservation) 29 892
  uses
    cloisters 7 *457*
  see also MURALS; SECCO PAINTINGS; WALL PAINTINGS
Fresdeval Monastery 13 106, 108

Fresez, Jean-Baptiste **19** 827
Freshfield Album *see under* ALBUMS → individual manuscripts
Freskobrøderne **18** 465; **26** 554
Fresnaye, Roger de La *see* LA FRESNAYE, ROGER DE
Fresne, Jean **10** 144
Fresne, Raphaël Trichet du *see* TRICHET DU FRESNE, RAPHAËL
Fresnel, Augustin **19** 361
Fresnel, Fulgence **3** 9
Fresnoy, Charles-Alphonse Du *see* DU FRESNOY CHARLES-ALPHONSE
Fressingfield (Suffolk), SS Peter and Paul **24** 577
Frestrom, Oscar **4** 819
Fresvik **13** 119; **25** 175
fret *see* MEANDER
Fréteval **6** 54
Frettabréf sím **24** 452
Frette, Guido **11** 62; **13** 728
fretwork **11** 764*
Freud, Anna **25** 683
Freud, Ernst **11** 764, 765
Freud, Lucian **11** 764–5*
groups and movements **10** 258; **32** 912
patrons and collectors **1** 496; **28** 273; **30** 795
works **10** *258*, 482; **21** 761; **23** 297
Freud, Sigmund **1** 78; **11** 765*; **18** 587; **23** 297; **30** 18; **31** *757*
groups and movements **28** 343
works **22** 416; **25** 681–3; **28** 206
Freudenberg, Phillip **14** 632
Freudenberger, Sigmund **3** 823; **11** 766*; **18** 224, 858; **30** 133
Freudenstadt **11** 766–7*; **12** *361*; **28** 87; **31** 719
fortifications **12** 369
Stadtkirche **12** 369, 399; **19** 815; **26** 646
urban planning **12** 368
Freudweiler, Daniel Albert **8** 790
Freudweiler, Heinrich **11** 767*; **33** 424, 736
Freund, Georg Christian **11** 768
Freund, Gisèle **11** 767*
Freund, Hermann Ernst **11** 767–8*; **17** *478*
pupils **17** 481
teachers **8** 740
works **8** 744, *744*, 746
Freund, Vilmos **20** 447; **28** 87; **29** 398
Freunde, Die **31** 539
Freundlich, Otto **3** 802; **11** 569, 768–9*
groups and movements **1** 90; **8** 438; **13** 727
pupils **6** 392
works **3** 801
Frew, Alexander **20** 32
Frewin, John **4** 874
Frey, Albert **1** 736; **18** 186; **19** 51
Frey, Dagobert **2** 833; **11** 769*
Frey, Hans **18** 475; **23** 311
Frey, Hans Heinrich **11** 770
Frey, Hermann-Walther **11** 770
Frey, Hyacinth **12** 263
Frey, Jakob **29** 76; **30** 144
Frey, Jan Zachariasz **32** 678
Frey, Johannes Jakob (1813-1865) **11** 769–70*
Frey, Johann Jakob, I (1681-1752) **3** 109; **7** 682; **11** 770*; **13** 625; **26** 229
Frey, Karl **11** 770*
Frey, Lajos **14** 889
Frey, Martin **12** 346
Frey, Pierre **11** 584
Frey, Samuel **11** 769
Frey, Vilma **12** 839
Frey and Kocher **1** 736
Freydanck, Carl Daniel
works **28** *101*
Freye, Georg-Herman **7** 346
Freyer, Grattan **16** 29
Freymuth, Alfons **22** 853
Freyre, Gilberto **4** 708, 718
Freyre, Manuel Villarán *see* VILLARÁN FREYRE, MANUEL
Freyssinet, Eugène **7** 696; **11** 770–71*; **28** 583
groups and movements **24** 174
works **4** 803; **7** *691*, 694; **11** 525, *771*
Freystadt, Maria-Hilf-Kirche **12** 372
Freytag, Gustav **24** 591
Freytag & Berndt **2** 512
Freytag-Loringhoven, Elsa **8** 435; **28** 51
Freywald, G. **26** 725
Freze, Gert *see* PHRAEZE, JORIS
Freze, Varvara **27** 413
Frézier, Amédée-François **11** 771–2*; **23** 488; **26** 12; **29** 637; **31** 721
Frezza, Orazio **3** 521
Friano, Maso da San *see* SAN FRIANO, MASO DA
Friant, Emile **22** 456
Fri Arkitektsforening *see* FREE ARCHITECTS' ASSOCIATION
Friars Minor, Order of *see* FRANCISCAN ORDER
Friars Preachers *see* DOMINICAN ORDER
friary chairs *see under* CHAIRS → types
Frias, Juan de **2** 865; **32** 576
Frias, Nicolau de **11** 772*; **14** 662; **32** 539
Frias, Sebastião de **11** 772
Frias, Teodósio de (*d* 1634) **11** 772
Frias, Teodósio de, the younger **11** 772
Frias da Mesquita, Francisco de **4** 709; **11** 772*
Frías Escalante, Juan Antonio de *see* ESCALANTE, JUAN ANTONIO DE FRÍAS
Friazin, Bon **22** 169
Friberg, Berndt **30** 99
Friberg, Roy **30** 82
Friborg, Jørgen **14** 542
Fribourg **11** 773*, *773*; **30** *124*, 126
Cathedral of St Nicholas **13** 126; **30** 126, 136
ceramics **30** 143
Cordeliers-Kirche **30** 130
Couvent de la Visitation **30** 126
fountains **30** 136
glass **30** 145
gold **30** 145
houses **30** 126, 127
Rathaus **30** 126
St Augustin *see* St Maurice
St Maurice **30** 136
sculpture **30** 136
town walls **30** 126
Fribourg, Claux de *see* CLAUX DE FRIBOURG
Frič, Martin **33** 599
Frich, Joachim **14** 483; **23** 232
Frichye, V. M. **27** 444
Frick, F. **12** 641
Frick, Henry Clay **2** 560; **11** 774*; **18** 161; **21** 90
architecture **25** 5
collections **10** 367; **12** 474; **31** 668
paintings **9** 200, 467
sculpture **3** 228
Frick, Johann Friedrich **18** 202
Frick Collection *see under* NEW YORK → museums
Frickx, Robert **28** 751
Fričovce, Berthóthy Castle **28** 849
Fricxs, Bernard **18** 69
Frid, Tage **31** 634
Friday Club **3** 631; **4** 168; **11** 774*; **19** 359; **23** 15
Fridegaudus **31** 227
Fridell, Axel **30** 81
Fridericianum, Museum *see under* KASSEL
Fridericus **7** 583; **26** 683, 686
Friðfinnsson, Hreinn **11** 774–5*; **15** 71
Fridlyand, Semyon (Osipovich) **11** 775*
Fridman, D. A. **19** 732
Fridolin, Samuel **29** 871
Fridolin, Stephan **12** 385; **23** 310; **33** 301
Fridrich (family) **8** 407
Fridrihsons, Kurts **11** 775*
Fridugisus, Abbot of Tours **5** 802
Fried, Elaine *see* DE KOONING, ELAINE
Fried, Michael **21** 645; **26** 63; **31** 673
Fried, Nancy **10** 483
Friedau, Schloss *see* SCHLOSS FRIEDAU
Friedberg Pilgrimage Church **32** *253*
Friedeberg, Pedro **11** 775*
Friedeberger, Klaus **11** 775–6*
Friedel, Johann Friedrich **14** 750
Friedell, Clemens **31** 650
Friedhoff, Gijsbert **11** 776*
Friedl, J. **8** 402
Friedlaender, (Gotthard) Johnny **4** 728; **11** 776*
pupils **3** 827; **12** 29; **13** 339; **25** 880
Friedlaender, Walter **11** 776–7*; **31** 672
Friedland (Czech Republic) *see* FRÝDLANT
Friedland, Maud **16** 568
Friedland Church (Germany) **14** 81
Friedlander, Lee **3** 673; **11** 777*
Friedländer, Marguerite **12** 437
Friedländer, Max Jacob **2** 204, 532, 535; **7** 715; **11** 777–8*; **30** 731
collections **22** 909
works **18** 701
Friedländer, Salomon **29** 872
Friedman, Alschuler and Sincere **21** 492
Friedman, André *see* CAPA, ROBERT
Friedman, Harry G. **17** 581
Friedman, Ken **7** 895; **11** 232
Friedman, Yona **11** 527, 778*; **24** 130
Friedmann, Robert **17** 548
Friedrich II, Archbishop of Salzburg **27** 660
Friedrich, Caspar David **11** 778–83*
groups and movements **9** 239; **22** 540; **26** 736, 737, 741; **29** 891
patrons and collectors **26** 111, 406
pupils **18** 77; **32** 119
works **1** 712; **2** 342; **9** 225; **11** 462, *462*, *779*, *780*, *781*, *782*; **12** 393, 853; **18** 714; **19** 355; **30** 166, *167*; **33** 361
Friedrich, Karl **31** 568
Friedrich, Martin **7** 209
Friedrich, Nikolaus **11** 784*
Friedrich, Walter **4** 146
Friedrich of Villach **2** 574; **11** 784*; **17** 604
Friedrichs **27** 439
Friedrichshafen Church **29** 838
Friedrich Ulrich, Duke of Brunswick-Wolfenbüttel (*reg* 1613-34) **11** 715
Friedrich von Hochstaden, Provost **33** 458
Friedrich von Pfalzen **27** 755
Friedsam *Annunciation* **15** 95, *95*
Friend, Albert M. **31** 672
Friend, Donald (Stuart Leslie) **2** 749, 767; **11** 784–5*
Friends, Religious Society of *see under* CHRISTIANITY → sects
Friends of Finnish Handicrafts **22** 540; **28** 105
Friends of Puerto Rico (New York) **18** 833
Friends of the Arts Society (Iraq) **16** 2
Friends of the Museum of Fine Arts (Hungary) **15** 16
Fries (family) **2** 829; **32** 879
Fries, Adriaen de *see* VRIES, ADRIAEN DE
Fries, (Jacob Daniel Georg Gottlieb) Bernhard **11** 786, 787*
Fries, Christian Johann von, Graf **14** 645; **33** 623
Fries, Ernest (*b* 1934) **2** 766
Fries, Ernst (1801–33) **11** 786–7*
works **11** *463*, 787; **12** 393
Fries, Hans **11** 787–8*; **20** 796; **30** 131
works **11** *788*
Fries, Joachim **12** 445
Fries, Josef, Graf von **11** 789; **33** 623
Fries, Moritz, Graf von **2** 829; **11** 789*; **32** 377; **33** 623
Fries, Theresia, Countess **31** *27*
Fries, Wilhelm **11** 786
Friesach **2** 777; **26** 655
Dominican church **2** 799
Rathaus **26** 635
Friese, Hans **12** 114, 135
Frieseke, Carl **33** 142
Friesen family **4** 507
Friessach, Henna von Gurk, Gräfin von *see* HENNA VON GURK, Saint
Friestas, S Fins **26** 611
Friesz, (Emile) Othon **11** 789–90*; **19** 80
groups and movements **10** 839, 841
pupils
Bălăcescu, Lucia Dem. **3** 88
Basaldúa, Héctor **3** 318
Berni, Antonio **3** 826
Braque, Georges **4** 673
Butler, Horacio **5** 311
Douglas, Aaron **9** 199
Drysdale, Russell **9** 310
Forner, Raquel **11** 317
Grau, Ricardo **13** 322
Gruber, Francis **13** 714
Preller, Alexis **25** 550
Resende, Júlio (Martins da Silva Dias) **26** 243
works **19** *91*, 92; **27** 343
Frie Udstilling **7** 805, *806*; **11** 790*; **28** 847
friezes **11** 790–92*; **23** 477, 478, 480, 481
historical and regional traditions
Achaemenid **2** 213
Byzantine **29** *817*
Central Asia, Western **6** *230*, *231*
Chimú **6** *441*, *607*
Crete **21** 675*
Cyprus **29** *817*
Early Christian (*c*. AD 250-843) **29** *817*
Egypt, ancient **20** *117*
England **32** V1, 2
Etruscan **10** *607*, 620, *633*
France **32** IV3
Greece, ancient **2** 648; **3** 341; **10** 742; **11** 790–91*, *791*; **13** 377, *378*, 379, 390, 391, 393, 401, 426, 432*, 447; **27** 692
Archaic, Late **13** *447*
Classical, Early **2** *680*
Classical, High **13** *426*
Italy **21** *342*
Turkey **14** *69*
friezes
historical and regional traditions—cont.
Hurrian **15** 33
Indian subcontinent **15** *230*
Iran, ancient **2** 213
Islamic **31** *573*
Italy **10** *607*, *633*; **21** *342*; **26** *792*, *890*; **27** *26*
Maya **31** 778
Mesoamerica, Pre-Columbian **31** 99, *99*, 778
Mesopotamia **11** *792*
Mexico **31** *99*
Minoan **21** 675*
Mitannian **15** 33
Peru **6** *607*
Rome, ancient **11** 791; **26** 792, *792*, *890*; **27** 24–5, *26*, 33, 35, 38, 39, 40, 41, 44, *44*
Sogdiana **6** *230*, *231*
South America, Pre-Columbian **6** *607*
Sweden **30** 116*
Syria **31** *573*
Toltec **31** 99, *99*
Turkey **14** *69*
materials
limestone **10** *607*
marble **13** *426*; **27** *26*
mud **6** *441*, *607*
plaster **20** *117*; **29** *817*
sandstone **15** *230*
stucco **31** *573*
terracotta **10** *633*; **21** *342*
uses
furniture **11** 792
metalwork **11** *792*; **28** 806
pottery **10** 612
situlae **28** 806
wallpaper **11** 792; **32** 812, 817, IV3, V1, 2
frigidaria **13** 386
Frigimelica, Bonifacio **28** 84
Frigimelica, Girolamo, Conte **12** 119; **25** 561; **28** 859; **29** 736; **32** 410
Frigmelica, Giovanni **19** 516
Friis, Ewert **11** 792–3*; **30** 85
Friis, Johan **4** 68
Friis, Jørgen, Bishop of Viborg **8** 724
Friis, Knud **11** 793*
Frijoles Canyon (NM) **22** 594
Frijsenborg **8** 745
Frikh-Khar, Isidor (Grigorevich) **27** 411
Fri Konst **10** 462
Frimkiss, Michael **31** 640
Frimmel, Theodor von **8** 513
fringes **3** 483; **24** 237
Africa **1** 300
Egypt, ancient **10** 75*
Native North Americans **22** 644, 655
Trinidad and Tobago **31** *332*, 332–3
Frink, Elisabeth **10** 880; **11** 793*; **30** 782
Fripp, Alfred Downing **4** 619
Fripp, Charles Edward **3** 389, 390; **31** 864
Fripp, R. Mackie **32** 414
Fripp, Thomas **31** 864
Friquet, Jacques **4** 756
Friquet de Vauroze, Jacques **4** 575
Frisbee, William **29** 723
Frisch, Ferdinand Helfreich **11** 793
Frisch, Heinrich **12** 770
Frisch, Johann Christoph **10** 199; **11** 793*; **30** 353
Frisching Factory **30** 144
Fris factory **22** 884
Frisians **21** 500, 501
Frisingen Missal *see under* MISSALS → individual manuscripts
Frisio, Johan *see* VREDEMAN DE VRIES, HANS

Frisius, Rainer Gemma **12** 814
Frisius, Simon (Wynhoutsz.) **4** 812; **10** 391; **11** 794*; **13** 222; **14** 709; **27** 885; **32** 588
Friso, Alviso dal **32** 354
Frisone, Giovanni Battista **29** 830
Frisoni, Donato Giuseppe **12** 372, 405
  pupils **25** 828; **26** 257
  works **19** 779–80, *780*; **28** 129; **33** 41, 429
Fristobaldo, Leonardo **31** 189
frit **6** 324; **11** 794*
  historical and regional traditions
    Central Asia, Western **6** 258
    China **6** 888
    Egypt, ancient **10** 46, 47, 55; **24** 790
    Iran **6** IV3; **16** *394*, *408*, 408–9*, *413*
    Islamic , ; **6** IV1, 3; **16** 393, *394*, *406*, *408*, 408–9*, 412, *413*, *416*, *418*, 419, 420, 421, *421*, *422*
    Japan **17** 242
    Ottoman **16** 419, 420, 421, *421*, *422*
    Syria **16** *406*, *416*, *417*
    Turkey **6** IV1; **16** *418*
  uses
    amulets **10** 47
    beads **10** 47
    ceramics **17** 242
    glazes **6** 888; **10** 47; **11** 794
    inlays **10** 47
    paints **10** 47
    pigments **24** 790
    porcelain **6** 326
    pottery , ; **6** 258, IV1, 3; **16** 393, *394*, *406*, 408–9, 412, *413*, *416*, *417*, *418*, 419, 420, 421, *422*
    vases **10** 47
Fritchly, E. W. **22** 404
Frith, David **32** 790
Frith, Francis **11** 794–5*; **24** 657, 664
  groups and movements **23** 504
  methods **28** 206
  staff **30** 36
  works **5** 401
Frith, William Powell **11** 795–7*; **19** 588
  assistants **9** 762
  collaboration **2** 128
  dealers **1** 453; **11** 161; **12** 30; **26** 233
  groups and movements **7** 436; **9** 756; **10** 254
  methods **9** 673
  patrons and collectors **14** 148, 688; **19** 269
  photography **14** 813
  pupils **30** 384
  reproductive prints by others **2** 692; **13** 327; **14** 680
  works **9** 1, 286, 287; **10** 253, 678; **11** *796*; **12** 295; **14** 147; **21** 761; **29** 425; **31** 704
Frith, William Silver **3** 367; **5** 66; **10** 267; **11** 499; **23** 34; **25** 187
Frithestan, Bishop of Winchester **2** 72, 83
Fritsch, Bohumir **8** 386
Fritsch, Elizabeth **10** 315; **11** 797*
  works **10** *314*
Fritsch, Gustav **10** 580
Fritsch, Theodor **11** 797*
Fritsche, William **33** 13
Fritts-Richard organ *see* SEATTLE (WA) → St Alphonsus
Fritz, Erwin **2** 661–2
Fritzki **32** 879
Fritzlar, St Peter's **6** 398; **26** 686
  Treasury **6** *398*
Frizé, Bernard **11** 553
Frizeau, Gabriel **4** 391; **19** 297; **26** 72
Frizell, William **29** 800, 804
Frizon, Jehan le *see* JEHAN LE FRIZON
Frizzi, Giuseppe **31** 442
  works **31** *442*
Frizzoni, Federico **11** 797
Frizzoni, Giovanni **11** 797
Frizzoni, Gustavo **11** 797–8*; **22** 102
Frizzoni, J. **1** 648
Frobel, Balthasar **8** 386
Froben, Johann **3** 335; **10** 445; **20** 796
Frobenius, Leo **1** 435; **9** 64; **15** 105; **18** 484
Frobenius Master **19** 744
Frobisher, Martin **33** 146
Frochot, Nicolas-Thérèse-Benoît **25** 671
frock-coats *see under* COATS → types
Frodl-Kraft, Eva **29** 514
Froebel, Friedrich **31** 254
Froelicher, C.-M.-A. **20** 868
Froelicher, J. A. **4** 556
Froen, Olaf **3** 62
Frög **25** 542
frog drums *see* DRUMS → types → Heger III
Froger, W. A. **27** 634
Froggatt, F. G. **19** 414
Frog service **10** 307, *307*
Fröhlich, Lorenz *see* FRØLICH, LORENZ
Frohner, Adolf **2** 797; **32** 447
Froidevaux, Y. **8** 74
Froidevaux, Y. M. **22** 40
Froimont, Jean Clemens de **20** 281
Froissart, Jean **2** 449; **7** 243; **19** 340
Fröjel Church **27** 125
Froli, Adriatico **13** 764
Frølich **9** 237
Frølich, Lorenz **8** 755; **11** 798*; **17** 720
Frölich, Max **12** 451; **30** 147
Frölicher, Johann Peter **30** 136
Frölicher, Otto **11** 798*; **29** 600; **30** 134
Frolick, Gloria **18** 529
From, Henrik Christian **4** 68
Fromantiou, Hendrik de **12** 473; **14** 650; **31** 779; **33** 389
Frombork **30** 535
  Cathedral **4** 783; **25** 114
Frome (Somerset) **2** 325
Fromel, Gerda **16** 22
Froment (-Delormel), (Jacques-Victor-) Eugène (1820-1900) **8** 281; **11** 798–9*; **19** 282, 767
Froment, Eugène (1844-1900) **12** 205
Froment, Nicolas **11** 799–800*
  patrons and collectors **1** 497; **2** 115; **9** 453
  works **2** 860; **9** 4; **11** 531, *800*; **13** 675
Fromentin, Eugène (Samuel Auguste) **9** 766; **11** 800–801*
  dealers **4** 655
  groups and movements **23** 504
  pupils **7** 859; **12** 496
  works **2** 106
    illustrated **20** 126
    translated **17** 593
Froment-Meurice (family) **11** 621, 622
Froment-Meurice, Emile **11** 636
Froment-Meurice, François-Désiré
  designers **11** 42, 622
  exhibitions **24** 147
  groups and movements **13** 208; **26** 190
  patrons and collectors **24** 147
  works **11** 621, 622, *622*, 636; **17** 527
Fromery, Pierre **12** 457
Fromiller, Josef Ferdinand **11** 801*
Frómista **29** *258*
  S María de Husillos **26** 606
  S Martín **11** 801*; **26** 581, 606, 607; **29** 262
Frommel, Carl Ludwig **11** 802*
Frommel, Otto **11** 802
Frommer, Arthur **13** 807, 811
Frondsberg, Schloss *see* SCHLOSS FRONDSBERG
Fronsperger **1** 788
Frontaura, Carlos **23** 606
Frontebosc, Guillaume Toustain de *see* TOUSTAIN DE FRONTEBOSC, GUILLLAUME
Frontenac, Louis **25** 801, 802
Fronte Nuovo delle Arti **11** 802*; **32** 197, 403
  members **1** 446; **5** 923; **7** 881; **16** 681; **22** 125; **27** 799; **31** 436; **32** 109, 403
Frontier, Jean-Charles **8** 542
frontier art *see* WILD WEST AND FRONTIER ART
Frontier Films **29** 745
Frontinus, Sextus Julius **11** 802–3*; **26** 884
  writings **4** 804; **11** 339, 341; **12** 656; **19** 256; **25** 144; **26** 751; **27** 2, 6
frontispieces
  Belgium **12** *885*
  Buddhism **17** *148*
  Byzantine **9** 608, 610, 611, 613, 615, 616, 617
  Carolingian **30** *487*
  Central Asia, Eastern **6** 307
  Early Christian (*c.* AD 250-843) **9** 608, 610, 611, 613, 615, 616, 617
  Egypt **16** *129*
  England **14** *433*
  France **24** *468*
  Germany **33** *712*
  Indian subcontinent **15** *679*
  Iran **16** *293*
  Islamic **16** *129*, 291, *293*
  Italy **4** *397*; **6** *98*; **20** III; **23** *92*; **25** *411*; **26** *841*
  Japan **17** *148*, 219
  Netherlands, the **22** *355*
frontlets *see* HEADBANDS
Frood, Millie **12** 777; **28** 240
Froschauer, Christof **30** 151; **32** 680
Fröschl, Daniel (von) **11** 803*
  patrons and collectors **2** 104; **13** 914; **21** 640
  works **11** *803*; **21** *640*
Fröskog **13** 119
Frosne, Jean **28** 506
Frossley, Daniel (von) *see* FRÖSCHL, DANIEL (VON)
Frost, A(rthur) B(urdett) (1851-1928) **4** 364; **11** 804*
Frost, Arthur Burdett (1887-1917) **11** 804; **23** 570
Frost, Charles **14** 813
Frost, Charles Sumner **7** 485
Frost, Edward Sands **27** 317
Frost, John **8** 528
Frost, Robert **10** 355
Frost, Terry **1** 78; **3** 373; **11** 804*; **27** 563
Frost, William Edward **11** 804*
Frosterley (Durham) **10** 227
Frosterus, Sigurd **4** 789; **11** 805*; **29** 769
Frosterus-Sâltin, Alexandra **7** 251; **10** 127
Frote & Westermann **20** 118
Frothingham, Benjamin (*fl* 1730s) **11** 805
Frothingham, Benjamin (1734-1809) **4** 479; **11** 805*; **31** 626
Frothingham, Benjamin, III (1774-1832) **11** 805
Frothingham, James **27** 613
frottage **10** 467–71; **11** 805*; **30** 19
  see also RUBBINGS
frottis **11** 805*
Froude, James **16** 886
Frowinus, Abbot of Engleberg **11** 805–6*
Frowinus Bible *see under* BIBLES → individual manuscripts
Fruchter, Lajos **13** 638; **15** 16
Frueauf, Rueland (i) (*c.* 1440/50-1507) **2** 792; **11** 806*; **20** 684; **27** 664
Frueauf, Rueland (ii) (?1470s-after 1545) **11** 806*
  works **11** *806*
Fruela I, King of Asturias (*reg* 757-68) **23** 681
Fruela II, King of Asturias (*reg* 910-25) **23** 682
Frühlicht **30** 370
Fruhtrunk, Günter **11** 807*; **12** 397
Frühwirth, Johann **26** 25
fruit **15** 812
Frujinescu, Grigore **26** 713
Frullini, Luigi **11** 190, 397; **16** 730
  works **16** *730*
Frulovisi, Titi Livio **18** 686
Frunza, Giotta **20** 105
Frunze *see* BISHKEK
Fruosino, Bartolomeo di *see* BARTOLOMEO DI FRUOSINO
Fruosino, Battista di *see* BATTISTA DI FRUOSINO
Frutiger, Adrian **31** 497
Frutos, Hugo González *see* GONZÁLEZ FRUTOS, HUGO
Frutti, Gobbo dei *see* BONZI, PIETRO PAOLO
Fruwirth **25** 617
Fruytier, Wilhelmina **30** 330
Fruytiers, Philip **11** 807*; **22** 717
Fry, Drew & Partners **9** 297; **11** 808; **25** 571
Fry, E(dwin) Maxwell **9** 297; **10** 321; **11** 807–9*; **13** 688; **21** 783; **23** 134; **32** 86
  collaboration **2** 578; **17** 463; **18** 386; **19** 46; **23** 134; **33** 382
  groups and movements **20** 475
  staff **8** 508; **26** 479
  teachers **26** 111
  works **1** 319; **6** 445, *445*; **11** *808*; **15** 168
Fry, Roger (Eliot) **1** 181; **2** 532, 536; **5** 517; **10** 377, 547, 680, 693; **11** 774, 809–10*; **13** 313; **18** 793; **22** 379; **24** 424
  collaboration **10** 284; **14** 764
  exhibitions **10** 255; **19** 589; **21** 776
  furniture **28** 298
  groups and movements **4** 168, 169; **5** 841; **19** 591, 623; **23** 22, 437–8; **25** 355–6
  paintings **19** *590*; **22** 373
  personal collection **10** 367; **19** 590
  writings **7** 631; **8** 613; **11** 315; **31** 300
Fryazin, Bon **27** 371
Frycz, Karol **12** 602; **17** 802; **18** 429
Frýdlant
  Castle **8** 378, 384
  Dekanatskirche **14** 316
Frydrych, Piotr **7** 837
Frye, Thomas **4** 600; **11** 810*; **19** 595
  pupils **24** 551
  reproductive prints by others **24** 551
  works **10** 308; **16** 15; **21** 416
Frytom, Frederik van **4** 176; **22** 879
FSA *see* WORKS PROGRESS ADMINISTRATION (WPA) → Farm Security Administration
fu *see under* VESSELS → types
Fu Baoshi **11** 810–11*
Fucecchio, Master of **11** 388; **28** 70
Fucecchio *Crucifix* **3** 808
Fu Cha **30** 48
Fuchigami, Hakuyō **11** 811*
Fu-chou *see* FUZHOU
Fuchs, A. **33** 76
Fuchs, Bohuslav **11** 812*
  assistants **18** 439
  groups and movements **21** 783
  teachers **18** 405
  works **4** 833; **8** 380; **28** 850
Fuchs, Eduard **10** 486
Fuchs, Emil **11** 812*; **20** 925
Fuchs, Ernst **11** 812–13*
  groups and movements **2** 797; **24** 592; **25** 863; **32** 447
  pupils **33** 695
  works **10** 483
Fuchs, Heinrich Maximilian **15** 145
Fuchs, Johann Gregor **19** 110
Fuchs, Josef **8** 380; **25** 430; **31** 492
Fuchs, Leonhard **4** 358; **14** 433; **28** 206
Fuchs, Paul **29** 97
Fuchs, Peter **11** 813*; **32** 683
fuchsine **9** 493
fuchsite **21** 241, 243, 251
Füchsl, Fréd *see* FORBÁT, FRED
Fucina degli Angeli factory **12** 795
fucus **9** 492, 665
Fudeng **33** 318
Fude no Ayamaru *see* KITAGAWA UTAMARO
Fudeya Myōki **14** 703
Fudōji, Taitokuin **18** 239
Fuederer, Ruprecht **11** 806
Füeg, Franz **30** 128
Fuenciscla **29** 336
Fuenleal, Sebastián Ramírez de, Bishop **8** 253
Fuensalida, Casa Galiana **29** 263
Fuente, Enrique Yañez de la *see* YAÑEZ DE LA FUENTE, ENRIQUE
Fuente de Guarrazar, La *see* LA FUENTE DE GUARRAZAR
Fuentelaencina Church **11** 485
Fuenteovejuna **29** 334
Fuentes, Manuel Anastasio **19** 386; **24** 504
Fuentes de Nava, S Pedro **29** 278
Fuentidueña, S Martín **26** 607
Fueter, Daniel Christian **20** 924
Fueter, Max **30** 138
Fufeng
  bronzes **6** 842, 868
  Famen Temple **6** 714; **7** 89; **16** 518
    Asoka stupa **29** 868
    metalwork **7** 23, 24
    reliquaries **26** 150
    silver **7** *24*
Fufluna *see* POPULONIA
Fug, Hans **23** 311
Fuga, Ferdinando **11** 813–16*; **26** 842
  attributions **18** 785
  collaboration **11** 136; **24** 11; **25** 808
  competitions **12** 657
  patrons and collectors **3** 707, 708; **4** 562; **7** 897, 898; **10** 769; **22** 473
  works **5** 186; **7** 898; **11** *814*, *815*; **23** 843; **24** 240; **26** 819, 832, 833, 840; **29** 82; **32** 651
Fūgai Ekun **11** 816–17*; **17** 193
Fugarolas, Mateo **8** 236
Füger, Heinrich Friedrich **2** 796; **11** 817*; **18** 670; **22** 480; **32** 444
  patrons and collectors **10** 531; **11** 789
  pupils **1** 728; **8** 445; **18** 418, 526, 683; **28** 135; **29** 658; **32** 759
  works **1** 28; **21** 643; **33** 623
Fugére, Henry **11** 637
Fugetsu Magosuke **22** 432

Fugger (family) **2** 716; **12** 386, 452, 471
architecture **2** 713; **14** 513, 678; **33** 746
brass **32** 605, 608
imprese **29** 740
manuscripts **4** 760
musical instruments **22** 376
paintings **1** 763; **4** 401, 759; **12** 648; **17** 719; **20** 191; **28** 189; **30** 34; **33** 274
portraits **1** 5
sculpture **5** 768; **12** 345, 346
Fugger, Albrecht, Graf von **13** 919
Fugger, Anton, I **4** 760; **11** 818*
Fugger, Georg **10** 220
Fugger, Hans **11** 818–19*; **29** 738; **32** 649; **33** 271
architecture **14** 678; **30** 34
decorative works **8** 881
drawings **29** 738
interior decoration **5** 768
paintings **11** 52; **13** 701; **17** 711
sculpture **5** 531, 768; **12** 345, 348, 403
Fugger, Hans Jakob **2** 161
Fugger, Jakob, II (1459-1525) **10** 220; **11** 817–18*
architecture **2** 713
paintings **12** 753
sculpture **20** 104
Fugger, Jakob (*fl* 1573) **14** 678
Fugger, Markus **14** 678; **30** 34
Fugger, Marx **8** 881
Fugger, Octavian Secundus **2** 713; **11** 819*
Fugger, Ottheinrich **22** 725
Fugger, Philipp Eduard **11** 819
Fugger, Raymund **11** 818
Fugger, Ulrich **10** 220
Fugger-Museum *see under* BABENHAUSEN
fugitive **11** 820*
Fuglesang, Signe Horn **32** 534
Fuglevaag, Brit **23** 239
Fuhaku Kawakami *see* KAWAKAMI FUHAKU
Fu Hao **6** 695, 726, 828, 836, 840, 841; **7** 3, 32, 74, 152, 631; **28** 550
tomb **7** *4*
Fuhr, Xaver **11** 729
Führer, A. **1** 469
Führich, Joseph von **11** 820*
collaboration **4** 106
pupils **29** 885; **30** 210, 641
works **11** 462; **15** 146; **22** 273; **23** 677; **32** 444
Fuhrlohg, Christopher **10** 295; **14** 230
Fuhrmann, Ernst **26** 195
Fuina, Gesualdo **6** 22
Fujayra **2** *246*, 248
architecture **31** 584
museums **2** 275; **31** 585
see also UNITED ARAB EMIRATES
Fuji, Masazo **17** 203
Fujii, Hiromi **11** 820*; **17** 92
Fujii, Kōyū **17** 135
Fujii, Seidō **17** 414
Fujiidera
Mitsuzuka tombs **17** 59
Tsudoshiroyama **17** 57
Fujii Shigeyoshi **12** 100
Fujikawa, Yūzō **14** 762; **17** 135
Fujiki Atsunao **17** 236
Fujimori, Shizuo **23** 441
Fujimoto Tesseki **17** 192
Fujina **17** 353
Fujinobu Yamamoto *see* YAMAMOTO FUJINOBU
Fujinoki Tomb **11** 820–21*; **17** *11*, 320; **27** 832
Fujinomiya, Fuji Art Museum **17** 433
Sengen Shrine **22** 231
Fujino Shūhō **17** 230
Fujio Kitade *see* KITADE FUJIO
Fujisan *see* MT FUJI
Fuji Sankei Communications Group **17** 433
Fujishima, Takeji **11** 821*; **21** 59
pupils **14** 213; **17** 874; **33** 668
teachers **17** 204
works **17** 204
Fujishiro **17** 388
Fujita, Denzaburō **17** 429; **23** 595
Fujita, R. **18** 259
Fujita, Tsuguji **17** 207, 436
Fujiwara (family) **11** 822*; **14** 302, 565; **17** 21, 52, 154
architecture **18** 552
paintings **17** 152
scrolls **17** 160
works **17** 156
Fujiwara (Japan) **11** 821–2*; **17** *11*, 93–4, *93*, *94*; **23** 822
architecture **17** 68
Chōdōin **23** 822
Daigokuden **23** 822
Fujiwara, Ginjirō **17** 429
Fujiwara, Kei **17** 267, 433
Fujiwara, Ken **17** 267
Fujiwara, Yū **17** 267
Fujiwara Mitsunobu *see* TOSA MITSUNOBU
Fujiwara no Akihira (986-1066) **17** 346
Fujiwara no Akihiro (1114-1204) *see* FUJIWARA NO SHUNZEI
Fujiwara no Fusasaki **17** 218
Fujiwara no Gōshin **17** 161
Fujiwara no Hidehira **14** 565, 566, 567
Fujiwara no Kanesuke **28** 625
Fujiwara no Kanshi **5** 334
Fujiwara no Kintō **11** 823; **17** 223, 828
Fujiwara no Kiyohira **14** 565, 566, 567
Fujiwara no Korefusa **11** 823; **17** 223
Fujiwara no Koretsune **17** 224, 226
Fujiwara no Koreyuki **17** 224, 226; **29** 902
Fujiwara no Kōzei **11** 822–3*
groups and movements **11** 822; **17** 221, 227; **23** 445
works **17** 215, 222, *222*, 227
Fujiwara no Michinaga **11** 823; **17** 423; **18** 68
architecture **18** 549; **30** 445
gardens **12** 97
metalwork **17** 321; **18** 68
painting **17** 156
sculpture **17** 119, 597
Fujiwara no Mitsushige **31** 199
Fujiwara no Moromichi **17** 224; **18** 68
Fujiwara no Motohira **14** 565, 566, 567
Fujiwara no Motomitsu
works **18** *223*
Fujiwara no Mototoshi **17** 224
Fujiwara no Nobuzane **11** 825–6*
works **11** 824; **13** 213; **17** 154, 161, 166, 829, *829*
Fujiwara no Norinaga **17** 224
Fujiwara no Reishi *see* INMEIMON'IN
Fujiwara no Sadaie *see* FUJIWARA NO TEIKA
Fujiwara no Sadanobu **11** 823*
works **17** 212, *212*, 219, 223
Fujiwara no Sadayori **17** 809
Fujiwara no Sari **11** 822*; **17** 215
groups and movements **11** 822; **17** 221, 227; **23** 445
works **17** 215, 222, 227
Fujiwara no Seika **17** 409
Fujiwara no Shōshi **17** 155, 598
Fujiwara no Shunzei **11** 824–5*; **17** 215, 224
Fujiwara no Sukemasa *see* FUJIWARA NO SARI
Fujiwara no Tadamichi **11** 823–4*; **17** 224
Fujiwara no Takanobu **11** 824–5*
pupils **11** 825
works **17** 154, 161, *161*
Fujiwara no Tamehisa **17** 746
Fujiwara no Tameie **11** 825; **17** 829
Fujiwara no Tameuji **11** 825
Fujiwara no Tanetsugu **22** 427
Fujiwara no Teika **11** 824, 825*
patrons and collectors **17** 342, 343
works **17** 215, 224–5
writings **17** 343
Fujiwara no Toshinari *see* FUJIWARA NO SHUNZEI
Fujiwara no Yasuhira **14** 565
Fujiwara no Yorimichi **5** 335; **14** 302; **17** 423; **18** 68
architecture **5** 118, 334; **17** 156
sculpture **17** 598
Fujiwara no Yoritsune **17** 747
Fujiwara no Yoshitsune *see* GOKYŌGOKU YOSHITSUNE
Fujiwara no Yukihiro **31** 199
Fujiwara no Yukimitsu **31** 199
Fujiwara no Yukinari *see* FUJIWARA NO KŌZEI
Fujiwara no Yukitsune **11** 823
Fujiwara Tamemitsu **17** 69
Fukae Roshū **17** 179; **23** 365
Fukami, Sueharu **17** 268
Fukami Gentai *see* KŌ TEN'I
Fukase, Masahisa **11** 826*
Fukashijō *see* MATSUMOTO CASTLE
Fukawa *see under* NAGATO
Fukaya, Koki **12** 101
fukibokashi see KIRIFUKI
Fukiji, Amida Hall **5** 119
Fukomoto, Shuko **11** 54
Fukō Temple **18** 348
Fukuda, Heihachirō **11** 826*
Fukuda, Kodōjin **17** 199
Fukuda, Shigeo **25** 354
Fukuhara, Rosō **11** 826
Fukuhara, Shinzō **11** 826*
Fukuhara Gogaku **23** 594
Fukuhara Shōshū **17** 412
Fukui, Ichijodani **9** 697
Fukui Cave **17** 244, 629
Fukui Tan'in **17** 413
Fukuoka **17** 18, 95
Art Museum **3** 170; **17** 433
Fukuoka Bank **3** 177
Higashiyama Saruyama **30** 259
Il Palazzo Hotel **27** *192*
Monjudō **17** 126
Nishi Saruyama **30** 259
Zendoji **18** 306
Fukurai Masatomo **17** 393
Fukushima **17** 433
Fukuyama, Myōō'in **17** 74, 829
Fukuzawa, Ichirō **11** 826–7*; **17** 206, 207
Fula *see* FULANI
Fulani **1** 299, 304, 393; **5** 216; **10** 580; **11** 827–30*; **12** 32; **13** 834, 835; **14** 231; **20** 861; **23** 127, 128, 302; **28** 404, 690
basketwork **23** 127
blankets **11** 829–30, *829*
body arts **1** 288; **11** 830*
cloaks **1** 348
cotton **11** 830
craftsmen and artists **1** 246
dyeing **11** 828
engraving **11** 828
goatskin **1** *307*
gourds **1** *302*, 303, 382; **11** 827–9*, *828*
gowns **23** 302
grasses **1** 307
hairstyles **1** 343; **11** 830
houses **1** 308
iconography **1** 373
jewellery **23** 127
mosques **1** 317
patronage **1** 240, 241
religion **1** 230
Fulani—cont.
scarification **11** 830
shelters **1** 307
tattoos **1** 346
tents **1** *307*, 307
textiles **11** 829–30*; **20** 198; **23** 128
weaving **11** 829–30
wool **11** *829*, 829–30
Fulbe *see* FULANI
Fulbert, Bishop of Chartres **6** 492; **7** 266; **13** 37
Fulcaro, Francesco **4** 457
Fuld **23** 670
Fuld, Gertrude *see* FEHR, GERTRUDE
Fulda **11** 831–2*; **12** *361*; **13** 18
Abbey Church *see* Cathedral of St Salvator and St Bonifatius
Cathedral of St Salvator and St Bonifatius **3** 709; **5** *793*, 794; **7** 263, 265; **10** 109; **11** *831*, 831–2*; **12** 372, 471; **26** 10
ciborium **7** 303
cloister **7** 453
transept **31** 280
faience (ii) (ceramics) **11** 832*; **12** 430, 431
manuscripts **5** 803, 806; **23** 652, 653, 654, 655
Orangery **12** 373
paintings **12** 382
porcelain **12** 433
Residenzschloss **5** 349
St Andreas **23** 651
St Michael **11** 832*; **12** 363; **28** *427*, 428
Schloss Biebrich **12** 373
Schloss Fasanerie **9** 71
sculpture **12** 399
tapestries **30** 324
Fulda Codex *see under* CODICES → individuals manuscripts
Fülep, Lajos **10** 108; **24** 440
Fulford, M. G. **5** 436
Fulgentius **22** 412
fulgurik **12** 781
Fulham Pottery **6** 122; **9** 473; **10** 305; **20** 485
production **10** *304*
Fulì, Ansuyn da *see* ANSUINO DA FORLÌ
Fulk **26** 657
Fulk III Nerra, Count of Anjou (*reg* 987-1040) **2** 45; **6** 50; **19** 526, 527
Fulk IV Rechin, Count of Anjou (*reg* 1067-1109) **24** 36
Fulk de Saundford, Archbishop of Dublin **9** 322
Fulla, Ludovit **28** 853
works **28** *853*
Fullah **28** 690
Fullaondo, Juan Daniel **27** 511
Fullarton, William **15** 593
Fulleda **29** 330
Fuller, George **11** 832–3*
Fuller, George E., & Company **27** 138
Fuller, Isaac **5** 900; **11** 833*; **26** 393
Fuller, Jack **11** 243
Fuller, James Augustus **4** 288; **18** 889
Fuller, James Franklin **16** 25
Fuller, John Augustus **4** 289; **29** 647
Fuller, Loïe **25** *620*; **30** 686
Fuller, Margaret **33** 309
Fuller, Meta Vaux **1** 441, 442; **11** 834*; **33** 314
Fuller, Nicholas **20** 478
Fuller, R(ichard) Buckminster **2** 362; **5** 562; **7** 882; **11** 834–6*; **15** 824; **24** 407; **26** 20; **28** 488; **30** 467
collaboration **11** 332
groups and movements **4** 109, 110
Fuller, R(ichard) Buckminster—cont.
works **2** 361; **10** 685; **11** *835*; **12** 311, *311*; **25** 24; **29** 250
Fuller, S. J. **14** 861
Fuller, Sue **10** 397
Fuller, Thomas (*fl* 1650) **7** 431
Fuller, Thomas (1823-98) **5** 561; **11** 836–7*
groups and movements **13** 203
pupils **24** 641
works **5** 561; **11** *837*; **13** 237; **23** 631, 632; **26** 340; **31** 176, 242
Fuller, Thomas William (1865-1951) **11** 837
Fuller Brooch **2** 80, *80*; **10** 322; **33** 89
Fuller Collection *see under* CHICAGO (IL) → museums → Field Museum of Natural History
Fuller & Gingell **11** 836
Fuller & Jones **11** 836
Fullerö Manor House **30** 70
Fuller's **10** 677
Fullman, Ellen **29** 99
Füllmaurer, Heinrich **11** 838*
Füll von Windach, Sebastian, Pfalzgraf **3** 354
Fullwood, Albert Henry **2** 602
Fulper Pottery Co. **31** 261, 639
Fulton, Hamish **10** 258, 269; **11** 838*; **18** 695
Fulton, James **29** 489
Fulton, Robert **18** 845; **24** 18; **33** 92
Fulvio, Andrea **1** 572; **11** 838–9*; **26** 767, 848
Fulvius Nobilior **19** 888; **33** 640
Fumagalli, Angelo **5** 384
fumage **23** 697; **30** 21
Fumai Matsudaira *see* MATSUDAIRA FUMAI
Fumal, Jean **11** 773
Fu-ma Tseng *see* FUMA ZENG
Fuma Zeng **7** 25
Fumée, Nicolas **24** 813
Fumiani, Giovanni Antonio **7** 779; **11** 839*
Fumiere & Gavignot **10** 771
Fumihiko Maki *see* MAKI, FUMIHIKO
Fumio Asakura *see* ASAKURA, FUMIO
Fumo, Franciszek **32** 876
Fumon Mukan *see* MUKAN FUMON
Fumu **30** 418
Funafuti **31** 484
Funaki, Kenji **21** 634
Funaki, Michitada **21** 634
Funakoshi, Katsura
works **17** *137*
Funakoshi, Yasutake **17** 137; **27** 872
Funan *see under* CAMBODIA
Funayama Tomb **17** 320
Funchal
Cathedral **25** 295
Instituto Superior de Arts Plásticas **25** 319
Funck, David **14** 747
Funcke, Cornelius **9** 241
Functionalism **7** 293; **8** 613; **11** 835, 839–42*; **15** 886; **19** 897; **21** 780–81; **23** 498
art forms
architecture **26** 14
Czech Republic **11** 365
Denmark **8** *728*
Finland **10** 126; **31** 461
France **11** 526
Germany **21** 782
Indonesia **15** 770
Netherlands, the **11** *840*; **23** 663, *664*
Scandinavia **23** 222
Slovenia **28** 860

Functionalism
art forms
architecture—cont.
Sweden **1** 475; **30** *74*, 74–5
Switzerland **11** *841*
furniture **8** 746; **12** 428
regional traditions
Belgium **31** 874
Croatia **1** 578
Czechoslovakia **14** 247, 732; **29** 553; **31** 492
Denmark **8** 728
Finland **1** 8; **5** 67; **11** 104; **15** 39; **19** 407
Germany **3** 399, 401, 402, 403; **12** 416
Italy **19** 533; **27** 853
Mexico **21** 381
Netherlands, the **22** 868–9; **29** 531; **33** 215
Poland **5** 8
Sweden **20** 437; **30** 92
Fundación Alberto *see under* MADRID
Fundacion Carvajal **25** 703
Fundación de Gremios **29** 309, 347
Fundación de Puerto Rico **25** 703
Fundación Generalísimo *see* FUNDACIÓN DE GREMIOS
Fundación Polar **32** 179
fundame see under LACQUER → types
Fundenii **26** 713
Fundi, John **20** 150
Fundulli, Giovanni Paulo *see* FONDULI, GIOVANNI PAULO
Funen *see* FYN
funeral books **6** 71
funeral pyres **6** 72
Funeral Rites, Master of the *see* ST FRANCIS'S OBSEQUIES, MASTER OF
funerary boats *see under* BOATS → types
funerary chapels *see under* CHAPELS → types
funerary equipment
Central Asia, Eastern **6** 289
Egypt, ancient **10** 7–20*; **33** *580*
Greece, ancient **13** 478, 482, 483, 485
see also COFFINS; SARCOPHAGI
funerary monuments *see under* MONUMENTS → types
funerary objects **18** 777
Africa **1** 257–8*, 339
Benin, Kingdom of **1** 258
Ife (kingdom of) **1** 258
Laos **18** 776, 777
Nigeria **1** 258
West Mexico **33** 103
funerary reliefs *see* STELAE → types
funerary statuettes *see* SCULPTURE → types → servant statues; SHABTI
funerary stelae *see under* STELAE → types
funerary temples *see under* TEMPLES → types
funerary texts **9** 905–6; **10** 7; **25** 761
funerary urns *see under* URNS → types
Fünfkirchen *see* PÉCS
Fung, Rosa **6** 523
Fungai, Bernardino (Cristofano di Nicholo d' Antonio di Pietro) **11** 842*; **23** 698; **29** 362, 763
Funghoff, Hinrik *see* FUNHOF, HINRIK
Funhof, Hinrik **4** 418; **11** 843*; **12** 384
Funi, Achille **5** 849; **11** 843–4*; **20** 522; **27** 788
exhibitions **10** 821
groups and movements **10** 821; **16** 680; **20** 522; **21** 528; **23** 263
Funi, Achille—cont.
pupils **1** 143; **8** 161; **9** 201
works **16** 681, *681*; **27** 789
funicular arches *see under* ARCHES → types
Funk, Hans **11** 844*; **20** 796
Funk, Johann Georg **11** 125
Funk art **17** 694; **31** 609, 640
Funk ceramics **2** 762
Funke, Jaromír **11** 844–5*
Funnel Beaker culture **25** 504, 507, 512, 514
Funnel group **10** 616
funnels **28** 614
funori **7** 747; **11** 142
Funsai *see* ZŌROKU II
Fu Pao-shih *see* FU BOASHI
fur
display **7** 732
historical and regional traditions
Africa **1** 295, 296
Islamic **16** 456
Mesoamerica, Pre-Columbian **21** 261
Native North Americans **22** 551, 656
United States of America **22** 551
uses **1** 296; **16** 456; **21** 261; **22** 656
baskets **1** 295
see also HAIR
Furck, Sebastian **21** 152
Furcy-Raynaud **11** 675
Fürdung **19** 532
Fures y Muñoz, Gerónimo **11** 845*
Furet, François **3** 392
Furetière, Antoine **10** 205
Fürich, Wenzel **11** 820
Furiet, Paul **24** 824
Furietti, Giuseppe Alessandro **26** 286
Furietti Centaurs **9** 20
Furini, Filippo **11** 845
Furini, Francesco **11** 845–6*; **16** 673
attributions **6** 126
collaboration **21** 26
patrons and collectors **21** 26; **27** 648
pupils **12** 4; **24** 801
teachers **1** 673; **27** 179
works **10** 476; **11** *846*; **23** 294
Furlanetto, Ludovico **5** 55; **27** 719
Furna, Dionysios of *see* DIONYSIOS OF FURNA
furnaces **12** 784–5*; **21** 320
historical and regional traditions
Africa **1** 287, *287*
Belgium **4** *685*
England **12** 784
Indian subcontinent **4** 681, *681*, *682*; **21** *320*
Japan **17** 319
Togo **1** *287*
types
blast **7** 97, 98
Catalan hearth **16** 50
induced-draught **1** 287
Furner, A(rthur) Stanley **11** 847*; **29** 106
Furnerius, Abraham **3** 386; **11** 847*; **22** 843
Furnerius, Johannes Claesz. **3** 386; **11** 847
Furnerius, Maria **11** 847
Furnese, Henry **29** 381
Furness, Frank **11** 847–50*; **24** 600
works **3** 175; **11** *848*, *849*; **24** 598; **25** 4; **31** 593
Furness, William Henry **11** 847
Furness Abbey (Cumbria) **13** 43–4; **22** 217
Furness & Evans **11** 848; **14** 811
works **11** *849*
Furness & Hewitt **11** 848
works **11** *848*
furniture **2** 561
conservation **7** 727–8, 729
furniture—cont.
display **22** 355
historical and regional traditions
Africa **1** 365–6*
Albania **1** 541–3*
Ancient Near East **1** 866, 867, 890*
Antilles, Lesser **2** 150–51
Australia **2** 757–9*
Austria **2** 811–15*, *812*, *814*; **33** 156
Azerbaijan **2** 898
Bahamas, the **3** 63*
Bamum **3** 152–3*
Barbados **2** 150
Belgium **3** 580–88*, *583*, *587*; **8** 633; **25** 303; **33** 157
Brazil **4** 720–22*
Britain **29** 471
Bulgaria **5** 157–8*
Canada **5** 576–80*
Caribbean Islands **5** 752
Catalonia **29** 319–21
Central Asia, Eastern **6** 311–12*, 313
China **7** 30–42*, *32*, *34*, *35*, *36*, 145–6; **25** 303
Cuba (Caribbean) **8** 234–6*, *235*
Cyprus **8** 365*
Czech Republic **8** 394–403*
Denmark **8** 745–7*
Egypt, ancient **1** 869; **10** 2, 49–54*, 58, 61; **14** 494, *495*; **33** 155, 329
England **2** 559, 561; **10** 278, 284, 285, 286–92*, 293–300*, 328; **19** 5; **20** 467, 468; **24** 62; **28** 348; **33** 157, *157*
Gothic Revival **13** *207*
Neo-classicism **17** *902*
18th cent. **7** *171*
19th cent. **19** *593*
Etruscan **10** *633*, 633–4*
Finland **11** 102–4*
France **2** 561; **11** 576, 585–6*, 587–602*, 617–18; **19** 723; **20** 467, 468, 469; **33** 157
Louis XVI style **19** *723*
Régence style **26** 83–4*, *84*
18th cent. **4** *531*
Germany **9** 234; **12** 419–22*, *420*, *421*, *422*, 425–8*, *427*, 445, 448, 462; **33** 156–7
Baroque **12** 422–3*
Functionalism **12** 428
Rococo **12** 423–5*
18th cent. **26** *530*
Gothic **14** 903
Greece **13** 357–8*
Greece, ancient **13** 390, 591*, 592*, 596–7; **33** 155
Guatemala **13** 768*
Helladic **14** 354
Hungary **14** 902–10*
Iceland **15** 72*
India, Republic of **15** 174
Indian subcontinent **15** 692–4*, 696, 697; **25** 303
Indonesia **15** 813*
Ireland **16** 25–8*
Islamic **16** 498, 516–17*
Italy **16** 721–32*, 746, 748; **25** 303, 306; **28** 28
Etruscan **10** *633*, 633–4*
Neo-classicism **24** *845*
Surrealism **16** *721*
18th cent. **16** *727*
19th cent. **23** *830*
Jamaica **16** 885–7*
Japan **14** 429; **17** 297, 302, 341, 357–8*, 384–5*; **25** 303
Jesuit Order **8** 398
Kassite **1** 869
Kenya **30** 57
Korea **18** 359–63*, *360*
Laos **18** 776
Madagascar **20** 40*
Malta (Republic of) **20** 215*
Mesopotamia **21** 304
furniture
historical and regional traditions—cont.
Mexico **21** 391*
Mongolia **21** 883
Netherlands, the **15** 813*; **22** 869–77*, *872*, *873*, *874*, *876*; **29** 470; **33** 157
New Zealand **23** 65–8*
Norway **23** *233*, 233–4*
Ottoman **16** 498
Peru **24** 514–15*
Philippines **24** 629*
Phoenician **16** 573
Poland **25** 119–22*
Portugal **25** 303, 304–8*; **29** 470
Romania **26** 717–18*
Rome, ancient **26** 875; **27** 94, 99–100*; **33** 155
Russia **9** 30; **27** 406–10*
Scotland **28** 244–5, 248, 250–55*, *254*, 256*
Serbia **28** 454*
Shakers **28** 542
South Africa **29** 114–16*
Spain **29** 309–17*, 318–22*
Sri Lanka **29** 470–71*
Surinam **30** 16*
Swahili **30** 57*
Sweden **20** 468; **30** 92–6*
Switzerland **30** 142–3*; **33** 157
Syrians **16** 573
Syria-Palestine **30** 187
Trinidad and Tobago **31** *337*, 337–8*
United States of America **2** 561; **10** 851–2; **20** 468, 469; **24** 601; **31** 249, 616, 617, 618, 619, 623–34*, *633*; **33** 155, 158
Federal style **31** *628*
Neo-classicism **31** *628*
Rococo **31** *627*
17th cent. **31** *616*
18th cent. **31** *618*
19th cent. **3** 685; **31** *620*
Vietnam **32** 482, 488
Wales **32** 788–9*
marks *see under* MARKS
materials
alder **14** 905
amboyna **3** 584; **10** 297; **15** 813
ash **10** 288, 293; **14** 905
Australian black-wood **29** 116
bamboo **7** 31, 145, 146
bentwood **30** 753
black-wood **15** 813
box-wood **12** 426
brass **25** 306
bronze **10** 633; **12** 424
camphor-wood **7** 31
cane **5** 612, 752; **15** 693; **29** 471; **33** 155, 156, 157
cast iron **3** 585; **10** 297; **12** 426; **28** 255
cedar **2** 757; **4** 721
cherry-wood **12** 425; **14** 907
chromium **7** 241; **31** 654
coal **10** 297; **28** 255
coromandel **29** 115
eastern beef-wood **29** 115
ebony **3** 585; **12** 423; **14** 907; **15** 692, 813; **25** 305; **29** 114, 115, 470
elm **10** 288, 293
fir **18** 361
glass **10** 58; **11** 602
glues **1** 156
gold **9** 30; **10** 52; **12** 423; **14** 494, *495*
gold leaf **1** 867
granadilla **29** 315
hardstones **12** 462, 831; **16** 724, 746
horn **10** 297
imbuia **29** 116
inlays **16** 799; **29** 311; **32** 488; **33** 332–3
furniture
materials—cont.
iron **3** 580; **27** 94; **31** 629
ivory **1** 890; **12** 423; **13** 596–7; **15** 693, 696, 697; **16** 798, 799; **25** 303, 305; **29** 470
jacaranda **4** 720, 721; **29** 315, 319
labels **20** 442
laburnum **28** 252
lacquer **3** 585; **6** 313; **7** 31; **12** 423; **15** 813; **17** 297, 302, 384; **18** 361; **22** 874; **29** 114; **32** 482
laminates **3** 685; **28** 256; **33** 331
leather **10** 61; **19** 5–6*
lignum vitae **29** 315
lime **14** 905
lime-wood **14** 903
mahogany **11** 851
Brazil **4** 721
Canada **5** 578
Caribbean Islands **5** 752
Czech Republic **8** 399
England **10** 292, 293, 297
France **11** 598
Germany **12** 425, 426
Hungary **14** 907
Ireland **16** 26
Jamaica **16** 886
Scotland **28** 252
United States of America **31** 625
maple **10** 297; **14** 905
marble **3** 583; **13** 592
metal **3** *587*; **7** 31; **11** 602; **17** 384; **25** 305; **31** 633
Monel metal **31** 654
mulberry **4** 721
oak
Belgium **3** 580, 582, 583, 585
Czech Republic **8** 399
England **10** 286, 288, 293, 297, 298
France **11** 585
Germany **12** 425
paper **10** 285; **32** 814
papier mâché **10** 297; **24** 62; **31** 629
paulownia **18** 361
pear-wood **18** 361
pine **3** 585; **11** 595; **14** 903, 905; **18** 361
plastics **10** 285; **22** *876*; **31** 634
rose-wood **3** 585; **8** 399; **10** 297
satin-wood **10** 293; **29** 115
silver **9** 30, 234; **10** 291, 328; **11** 576, 617–18; **12** 423, 445, 448
silver-gilt **12** 424
slate **10** 297
steel **10** 284; **16** 61
stink-wood **29** 114, 115, 116
stone **26** 875
straw **29** 763
sycamore **14** 903, 907
teak **15** 813; **29** 114
tortoiseshell **3** 585; **11** 590; **16** 748
tubular steel **7** 241; **8** 402; **29** 321; **30** 755
varnishes **7** *603*; **17** 384; **24** 258; **32** 2; **33** 335
veneers **11** 588, 596, 851; **12** 421; **32** 156*; **33** 332
walnut **8** 399; **10** 288, 290, 292, 293, 297; **11** 585, 595; **12** 425, 426; **14** 903, 905, 907; **24** 601; **28** 246; **29** 311
wicker **6** 311; **31** 629; **33** 155–8, *157*
willow **18** 361; **33** 156
wire **31** 629
wood **1** 365; **7** 30–31, 145; **10** 52; **11** 595–6, 598, 601; **13** 592; **14** 494; **16** 498; **17** 384; **18** 776; **20** 40; **22** *876*
wrought iron **3** 580; **11** 585
zebra-wood **10** 297

furniture
materials—cont.
zelkova **18** 361
see also UPHOLSTERY → materials
patinas **24** 258
restoration **7** 729
techniques
carving **11** 589, 595
French polishing **11** 595; **18** 610, 611
gilding **11** 595; **12** 626*
intarsia **8** 395; **33** 332
japanning **24** 61
joinery **7** 31–2, *32*; **11** 595; **17** 384; **33** 329–31*
lattice work **29** 311
marquetry **11** 590, 596; **12** *420*; **20** 467; **33** 332
mass production **28** 255
painting **13** 592; **23** 790; **24** 258; **33** 331–2
parquetry **11** 596; **20** 467
types
dolls' *see* DOLLS' FURNITURE
ergonomic **23** 234
fireplace *see* FIREPLACE FURNISHINGS
Mission furniture **31** 631–2
office **31** 633–4
reproduction *see under* REPRODUCTIONS
suites **31** 630–31
vernacular **11** 850–51*
water-filled **10** 285
see also:
ARMOIRES; BEDS; BUREAUX; CABINETS; CHAIRS; CHESTS; CUPBOARDS; DESKS; STOOLS; TABLES
furniture-makers **10** 297; **16** 726
furniture-makers' guilds *see under* GUILDS → types
Furnius, Abraham **18** 228
Furnius, Pierre **19** 547
Furnos Minus
Basilica I **9** 570
mausoleum **9** 570
Furse, Charles Wellington **11** 851*
Fursov, P. **18** 400
Furst, Emilio **2** 404
Fürst, Moritz **20** 925
Fürst, Paulus **31** 680
Furstemberg, François-Egon de **8** 93
Fürstenau, Baurat **25** 409
Fürstenberg (family) **3** 57; **13** 684; **29** 674
Fürstenberg, Caspar von **10** 119
Fürstenberg, Dietrich von, Prince-Bishop of Paderborn **10** 119
Fürstenberg, Pontus **11** 851*; **30** 117, 118
paintings **18** 801; **33** 187
Fürstenberg, Pontus—cont.
sculpture **14** 221
sponsorship **18** 801
Fürstenberg, Theodor Caspar von **21** 414; **28** 671
Fürstenberg Porcelain Factory **11** 851–2*; **26** 498; **33** 54
designers **7** 806; **24** 460; **32** 757; **33** 49
directors **12** 433
Fürstenfeld
Mariä Himmelfahrt **32** 822
Monastery **12** 372
Fürstenzell Monastery **11** 125
Furtenagel, Lucas **2** 716; **25** 278
Furtenbach, Hans *see* H.F., MASTER
Furtenbach, Josef *see* FURTTENBACH, JOSEF, the elder
Furter, Michael **20** 793, 794
Furth, Jan **8** 386
Fürth Synagogue **17** 544
Furtmeyr, Berthold **11** 852*; **20** 512
Furtres, Ruprecht **18** 451
Furttenbach, Josef, the elder (1591-1667) **10** 739; **11** 852–3*
reproductive prints by others **11** *853*
works **14** 782
writings **6** 165; **12** 368; **13** 809; **25** 635; **31** 298
Furttenbach, Josef, the younger (1632-55) **11** 853
Furtun, Candeğer **31** 455
Fürtwängler, (Johann) Adolf (Michael) **11** 854*; **13** 468, 613; **23** 476
Furukawa, Takahisa **17** 267
Furukawa, Toshiko **17** 267
Furuta Oribe **11** 854–5*; **12** 98
personal collection **17** 343
pottery **17** 261
pupils **14** 704; **17** 343; **18** 180
works **15** 108; **17** 336
Furuyama Moroshige **14** 577
Fusagasugá **7** *601*
Fernando Mazuera **7** 606
Fusainkai *see* FYŪZANKAI (SKETCHING SOCIETY)
Fusain Society *see* FYŪZANKAI (SKETCHING SOCIETY)
Fusajirō Abe *see* ABE, FUSAJIRŌ
Fusaro, Jean **19** 848
Fusasaki, Fujiwara no *see* FUJIWARA NO FUSASAKI
Fuschini, A **8** 74
Fusconi (family) **26** 768
Fuse **24** 430
Fuseli, Henry **11** 857–62*; **30** 125, 132; **33** 736
dealing **19** 588
exhibitions **19** 507
groups and movements **26** 736, 737; **29** 891
Fuseli, Henry—cont.
paintings **4** 607
patrons and collectors **2** 51; **13** 637; **19** 98; **20** 25; **28** 908; **33** 251, 453
pupils **19** 284; **32** 677
reproductive prints by others **5** 216; **13** 871; **17** 630
teachers **11** 857
works **2** 164; **7** 226; **9** 1, 224; **10** 479, *479*; **11** *858*, *859*, *860*, *861*; **19** 483; **21** 417; **23** 295; **25** 630
Fusetsu Nakamura *see* NAKAMURA, FUSETSU
Fu Shan **6** 761; **11** 855–6*
works **6** *762*; **11** *855*
Fushekati, Myrteza **1** 540
Fushimi **17** 373
Castle **17** 84, 323
Fushimi, Emperor (*reg* 1287-98) **11** 856*; **17** 225, 227, 228; **29** 66
Fushimi Jisaburō **17** 400
Fushimi Sadafusa **17** 167
Fusina, Andrea da **11** 856–7*
Fussell, Solomon **27** 887
Fussel's Lodge **25** 507
Füssen, St Mang **23** 651
Füssenich **26** 646
Füssli (family) **30** 146
works **30** *146*
Füssli, Anna **11** 857
Füssli, Elisabeth **11** 857
Füssli, Hans Caspar (1706-82) *see* FÜSSLI, JOHANN CASPER
Füssli, Hans Caspar (1743-86) **11** 857
Füssli, Hans Rudolf **11** 857
Füssli, Johann Caspar **11** 857*; **24** 453
pupils **11** 857; **21** 408
works **30** 156
Füssli, Johann Heinrich (1741-1825) *see* FUSELI, HENRY
Füssli, Johann Heinrich (1745-1832) **10** 206
Füssli, Melchior **5** 168
Füssli, (Johann) Rudolf (1709-93) **10** 206; **30** 156
Füssli, (Johann) Rudolf (1737-1806) **11** 857*; **24** 438
Füssli, Wilhelm Heinrich **11** 857
Fust, Johannes **4** 344, 357; **7** 189, 625; **13** 866; **22** 369; **25** 622; **33** 349
al-Fustat *see under* CAIRO
Fustat Fatimid Sgraffito ware *see under* POTTERY → wares
Fuster, Alberto **21** 386
fustian **8** 35; **10** 353, 356; **30** 561
fustic **24** 799
fusuma see under PARTITIONS → types
Futa-Djallon **11** 830
al-Futaih, Fuad **33** 520
Futamura Baizan **17** 409
Futcher, Raphael **25** 308
Fu-teng *see* FUDENG
Fu Tianchou **6** 733
Fu T'ien-ch'ou *see* FU TIANCHOU
Futuna **25** 181
Futura *see under* TYPE-FACES
Futurism **2** 225; **3** 115, 784; **4** 200; **10** 415; **11** 862–9*; **19** 355; **24** 404, 427; **26** 51, 224, 235; **28** 202; **31** 503, 605
art forms
architecture **11** *868*, 868–9*; **16** 648*; **21** 781
drawing **27** *788*
film **10** 686
industrial scenes **15** 828
multimedia **5** 849
music and art **27** 446; **29** 96
painting
Czech Republic **18** *493*
England **23** 15
France **23** 570
Italy **3** 115, *116*; **4** *200*; **5** *848*; **11** *864*; **16** 679; **27** *446*; **28** *507*, *792*
Russia **12** *893*
sculpture **4** *201*; **11** *866*
collections **33** 254
exhibitions **10** 699, 885; **16** 906; **31** 519; **32** 753, 775
regional traditions
Belgium **28** 119
England **10** 255
France **28** 507
Hungary **20** 104
Italy **1** 74, 166; **3** 114; **4** 198, 199; **7** 895; **8** 770; **10** 822; **11** 80, 360, 868; **16** 707; **19** 896; **21** 776; **22** 288; **24** 404; **25** 446; **27** 156, 445, 853; **28** 506, 792; **29** 373, 872; **31** 74
Japan **17** 205
Portugal **27** 786
Russia **8** 250; **10** 699; **11** 360; **12** 893; **18** 22; **20** 851, 886–7; **24** 404–5; **27** 394; **30** 7, 361
United States of America **28** 508
writings **4** 340; **5** 219, 848; **9** 191; **20** 426–8, *427*; **24** 63; **31** 583
see also CUBO-FUTURISM
Futurismo **24** 448
Futurist Art Society *see* MIRAIHA BIJUTSU KYŌKAI
Fuurstrøm Fajancefabrik **8** 749
Fuwah **27** 593
Fu Wen **6** 779
Fux, Hanns Georg *see* FUX, JOHANN GEORG
Fux, Hieronymus **31** 371
Fux, Johann Georg **11** 869*
Fuyō Kō *see* KŌ FUYŌ
Fuyuki (family) **17** 179; **23** 364
Fuzellier, Jean-Baptiste **11** 626
Fuzellier, Nicolas Barthélemy **11** 626
Füzesabony **25** 528
Fuzhenko, Anatoly S. **31** 561
Fuzhou **6** *614*, *623*; **11** 869–70*; **28** *719*, 721
tomb of Huang Sheng **6** 700; **7** 26, 77
trade **6** 624
Fužine Castle **28** 862
FVB, Master **3** 555; **10** 383; **20** 795*
works **3** *556*
Fyfe, Arthur **29** 768
Fyfe, Theodore **1** 29
Fyfield Manor (Oxon) **30** 909
Fyn **9** 156; **13** 167
Fynboerne painters *see* FYN PAINTERS
Fyn painters **8** 735, 760; **14** 155, 572; **30** 157; **33** 595
Fyns Glasværker **4** 743; **8** 749, 750
Fynson, Jacques **11** 115
Fyodorko **31** 550
Fyodor of L'viv **31** 558
Fyodorov, German **32** 661
Fyodorov, Perfily **27** 401, 407, 427
Fyodorov, Pyotr **27** 406
Fyodorov, Revel' **27** 434
Fyodorov-Davydov, Aleksey (Aleksandrovich) **11** 870*; **27** 444
Fyodorov Gospel *see under* GOSPEL BOOKS → individual manuscripts
Fyodorovna, Mariya **4** 745
Fyodorovsky, Fyodor **18** 573; **27** 396, 425
Fyol, Conrad **20** 676
Fyot de La Marche, Claude-Philibert **8** 834; **19** 161
Fyot de La Marche, Jean-Philippe **32** 766
Fyring, Dirich **8** 752
Fyrkat **8** 721
fortresses **32** 532–3, *533*
Fyrwald, Friedrich **30** 112
Fyt, Jan **11** 871–2*
assistants **6** 29
patrons and collectors **4** 559; **5** 9; **26** 722; **30** 118
pupils **4** 221
teachers **28** 903, 904
works **3** 561; **11** *871*; **29** 666, 668
Fytton, Peter **21** 27
Fyūzankai (Sketching Society) **17** 205, 436; **33** 552
Fyvie **31** 230
Fyvie Castle **3** 383

G

G **7** 771; **8** 437; **26** 356
G58-Hessenhuis group **3** 565, 573; **31** 879
G: Material zur Elementaren Gestaltung **24** 428
Gaag, Lotti van der **22** 861
Gaál, Endre **15** 5
Gaal, Konrad **28** 856
Ga'anda **1** 254, 303, 346, 381; **30** 509
  pottery **1** *286*
  scarification **1** *255*
Gaasbeek Kasteel **3** 616
Gabae *see* ISFAHAN
Gabal al-Silsila *see* GEBEL EL-SILSILA
Gabashvili, Georgy (Ivanovich) **11** 873*; **12** 326, 329
Gabashvili, Gigo *see* GABASHVILI, GEORGY (IVANOVICH)
Gabashvili, I. **12** 327
Gabb, George **3** 624
  works **3** *624*
Gabbiani, Anton Domenico **11** 873–4*
  collaboration **12** 528; **26** 242
  patrons and collectors **5** 451; **7** 897; **21** 29
  pupils **11** 743; **14** 848; **19** 816; **25** 890; **26** 69
  reproductive prints by others **3** 308
  teachers **8** 498
  works **11** 188, *874*; **16** 674; **21** 30; **25** 77
Gabburri, Francesco Maria Niccolò **3** 306; **11** 188, 874–5*; **24** 707
  decorative works **7** 860
  drawings **2** 26; **9** 230; **26** 245
  personal collection **17** 900
Gabe, Dora **3** 874
Gabe, Ron *see* PARTZ, FELIX
Gaberbocchus Press **30** 704
Gabès **16** 436
  Museum of Popular Arts and Traditions **31** 427
Gabet, Charles Henri Joseph **10** 208
Gabetti, Roberto **16** 650, 651; **22** 747
Gabicce, Giacomo delle **24** 535
Gabicce, Girolamo di Lanfranco delle **24** 535
Gabii **26** 865, *886*, 889
  temple **12** 70
Gabillou **25** 485
Gabion, Jeanne-Elisabeth *see* CHAUDET, JEANNE-ELISABETH
Gabla *see* BYBLOS
Gabler, Ambrosius **10** 454; **18** 115
Gabler, George Christian **1** 769
Gabler, Stefan **18** 511
gables **11** *875*, 875–6*; **30** 897
  historical and regional traditions
    Belgium **3** 544; **5** *40*; **11** 875–6
    Cambodia **5** 476
    China **6** 692
    Czech Republic **11** 876
    Denmark **11** 876
    England **4** 786; **11** 876; **30** *896*
    France **13** 42
    Germany **11** 876; **30** 897
    Gothic **13** 42
    Hungary **11** 876
    Japan **17** 48; **20** 835
    Netherlands, the **11** 875–6
    Palau **23** 833, *833*
    Poland **11** 876
    South Africa **11** 876
    Sweden **11** 876
gables—cont.
  materials
    brick **4** 785–6
  types
    neck **4** 785; **32** 588
    pignon chantourné see scrolled
    pignon en cloche see scrolled
    scrolled **4** 785; **11** 875
    spout **4** 785
    step **1** 801, *802*; **4** 785
    welsche Giebel **11** 876
gablets **20** 564, *565*; **28** 128–9, 497
Gabo, Naum **7** 772; **11** 569, 877–8*; **19** 477; **23** 603; **24** 440, 573; **27** 394
  collaboration **23** 103; **24** 574; **25** 25
  exhibitions **3** 802
  groups and movements **1** 76, 77, 90; **3** 120; **7** 547, 770; **18** 62; **27** 563
    Abstract art **1** 76
  methods **28** 202
  productions **8** 850; **24** 574; **30** 686
  works **2** 838; **10** 267; **11** *877*; **12** 408; **14** 785; **16** 57; **21** 897; **25** 25, *25*
  writings **1** 132; **7** 772; **24** 574
Gabon **1** *214*, 393; **11** 878–80*
  architecture **11** 879*
  basketwork **11** 878
  collections **11** 880*
  cult houses **1** 395
  dress **11** 879
  education (art) **11** 880*
  exhibitions **11** 880
  masks **1** 399, *399*; **11** 878
  musical instruments **1** 358
  painting **11** 879*
  patronage **11** 880*
  popular art **11** 879*
  religion **11** 878
  sculpture **1** 282, 359; **11** 879*, *879*
  serpentine **11** 879
  soapstone **11** *879*
  tourist art **1** 252; **11** 879, *879*
  trade **1** 250
  wood **1** *399*
Gabor, Dennis **14** 689
Gaboria **19** 382
Gaborone **1** *413*
  National Art Gallery **4** 490
  National Museum, Monuments and Art Gallery **4** 490
Gaboury, Etienne-Joseph **5** 563; **11** 880*
Gabra **17** 906
Gabrea, Florin **26** 722
Gabrėnas, Kazimieras **19** 498
Gabri, Antonio **4** 832
Gabri, Pietro **4** 832; **5** 79
Gabriel, Albert (-Louis) **11** 886*; **16** 548
Gabriel, Ange-Jacques **11** 880, 882–4*; **20** 136
  architecture **11** 518, 881
    châteaux **6** 509; **7** 195; **9** 313, 314; **11** 261; **19** 232
    chimney-pieces **5** 380
    façades **31** 373
    government buildings **20** 139
    hermitages **18** 815
    hôtels particuliers **11** 405
    maisons de plaisance **20** 131
    pavilions **11** 658; **23** 812; **24** 290; **32** *374*, 553
    schools **11** 518; **19** 161; **24** 122; **25** 80
Gabriel, Ange-Jacques
  architecture—cont.
    squares (town) **4** 226, 389; **24** 122, *122*
    theatres **9** 84; **30** 670
  assistants **32** 240, 768
  collaboration **2** 172; **7** 773; **11** 881; **25** 363; **28** 847
  competitions **7** 666
  frames **11** 408
  gardens **4** 389; **7** 677
  groups and movements **22** 738; **23** 861; **24** 170
  interior decoration **11** *882*, *884*
  patrons and collectors **4** 554; **6** 396; **7** 677; **11** 658; **25** 80, 81; **32** 370, 372, 373, 374
  personal collection **19** 141; **25** 363
  plans **11** *883*
  pupils **5** 662; **13** 831; **30** 728
  sculpture **8** 72
Gabriel, Ferdinand **2** 814
Gabriel, Frigyes **14** 910
Gabriel, Jacques, I (*fl c.*1610) **11** 880
Gabriel, Jacques, II (*b* 1605) **11** 880
Gabriel, Jacques, III (1637-97) **11** 880
Gabriel, Jacques, IV (*c.* 1637-86) **11** 261, 880–81*; **20** 293
Gabriel, Jacques, V (1667-1742) **11** 880, 881–3*
  assistants **11** 882; **19** 27
  attributions **2** 701
  collaboration **2** 701
  patrons and collectors **2** 701; **11** 882
  works **4** 389; **7** 195; **8** 33, 889; **10** 668; **11** 883; **23** 509, 510; **24** 163, 221; **26** 204, *205*; **31** 372, 717
Gabriel, Maurice, I (1602-49) **11** 880
Gabriel, Maurice, II (1639-93) **11** 880
Gabriël, Paul Joseph Constantin (1823-1903) **11** 885*; **14** 46; **22** 849; **26** 528
Gabriël, Paulus Joseph (1784-1834) **11** 884–5*; **29** 723; **30** 736
Gabriel, Richard **29** 468
Gabriel Bethlen, Prince of Transylvania (*reg* 1613-29) **14** 880, 885; **15** 3, 11, 13; **26** 722
Gabriele **11** 684
Gabriele di Battista **11** 896
Gabriele di Bertoni **18** 586
Gabrieli, Gabriel de' **11** 886*; **12** 373; **19** 337; **26** 257
Gabrieli, Gaspar de **9** 209; **16** 14
Gabrieli, Marchiò **31** 821
Gabrielino **22** 550
Gabriel of Salamanca *see* ORTENBERG, GABRIEL OF SALAMANCA, Graf von
Gabriel von Eyb **14** 450
Gabrini, Pietro **8** 786
Gabron, Guilliam **25** 812
Gabrova, St John the Baptist **31** 393
Gabrovo **5** 158
Gaceta de árte **30** 22
Gaceta del arte **11** 886*; **24** 452
Gachet, Paul (-Ferdinand) (1828-1909) **6** 375; **11** 887*; **12** 842; **15** 153, 154
Gachet, Paul (1873-1962) **11** 887
Gachupin, Laura **22** 608
Gács **15** 2
Gács, György Z. **15** 5
Gad, Dora **22** 366
Gadag
  temples **15** 324, 325
Gadaladeniya **29** 450, 460
Gadamer, Hans-Georg **1** 183; **14** 458, 459; **26** 62
Gadányi, Jenő **10** 650; **11** 887*; **14** 902
Gadara **17** 655
Gaddang **24** 624, 625, 626
Gaddesby (Leics), St Luke's **24** 576
Gaddi (ii) (family) **3** 161; **16** 749; **20** 93
Gaddi (i), Agnolo **11** 887, 891–3*; **13** 149
  collaboration **12** 681; **19** 673; **23** 95
  methods **7** 627
  patrons and collectors **8** 535
  pupils **1** 553; **3** 299; **6** 168; **19** 678; **29** 550, 597
  restorations by others **7** 332; **19** 443
  works **5** 443; **11** 709, *891*, *892*; **16** 655; **24** 539; **31** 513
Gaddi, Camillo (*fl* 1607) **7** 312
Gaddi (i), Gaddo (di Zanobi) **11** 887–8*; **20** 697
Gaddi (i), Giovanni **11** 887, 890–91*; **12** 681
Gaddi (ii), Giovanni de' **5** 789; **11** 893*; **21** 768; **27** 770
Gaddi (ii), Niccolò **9** 181; **11** 887, 893*
  collections **11** 188
  drawings **32** 22
  personal collection **14** 806
Gaddi (i), Taddeo **11** 887, 888–93*; **13** 149
  attributions **11** 203, 891; **19** 683
  methods **13** 133, 138
  patrons and collectors **5** 509; **8** 763; **29** 46
  pupils **6** 168; **11** 890; **12** 702; **23** 95
  reproductive prints by others **27** 346
  teachers **12** 686
  works **7** 333; **11** 206, 210, 709, *889*, *890*; **13** 136, 673; **16** 655; **19** 354, 356; **20** 552; **21** 845, *845*; **24** 855, 860; **29** 665
Gaddiano, Anonimo *see* MAGLIABECHIANO, ANONIMO
Gade, H. A. **4** 290
Gadebridge Park (Herts) **32** 542
Gadegaard, Poul **8** 736, 758
Gādhinagara *see* KANNAUJ
Gadio, Bartolomeo da *see* BARTOLOMEO DA GADIO
Gadir *see* CÁDIZ
Gadner **8** 882
Gadner, Georg **31** 311
Gadō, Bertil **15** 142
Gadō Ono *see* ONO GADŌ
Gádor, István **15** 2
Gadzhibababekov, Kasym-bek **25** 800
Gadzhinsky, M. I. **2** 893
Gaekwad, Fateh Singh Rao III, Maharaja *see* FATEH SINGH RAO III, Maharaja
Gaekwad, Sayaji Rao III *see* SAYAJI RAO III, Maharaja
Gaekwad, Sayaji Rao III, Maharaja *see* SAYAJI RAO III, Maharaja
Gael, Barend **4** 131; **33** 391
Gaertner, Eduard **11** 894*; **24** 490
  works **3** 799, *806*; **11** *894*; **28** *100*; **31** 156
Gaertner, Peter *see* GERTNER, PETER
Gaesbeeck, Adriaen van **19** 102
Gaeta
  Cathedral of SS Erasmo e Marziano **26** 624, 665
  S Lucia **26** 624
  tomb of L. Munatius Plancus **20** 864
  tomb of L. Semproniu Atratinus **20** 864
Gaeta, Zucca da **22** 12
Gaetani (family) **26** 765
Gaetani, Niccolò, Duca di Laurenzano *see* LAURENZANO, GAETANI NICCOLÒ, Duca di
Gaetani, Onorato II *see* ONORATO II, Lord of Fondi
Gaetani, Onorato II, Lord of Fondi **2** 183
Gaetano, il *see* PULZONE, SCIPIONE
Gafa, Lorenzo **20** 212
Gafar, Melchiorre *see* CAFFA, MELCHIORRE
Gaffé, René **33** 744
Gaffron **29** 221
Gaffurio, Franchino
  works **22** *377*
Gaffurri, Giorgio **14** 171
Gafsa **16** 486; **18** 49; **31** 426
Gafurri, Bernardino **21** 529
Gafurri, Cristofano **21** 529
Gafurri, Giorgio **21** 22, 529
Gaga *see* METZGER, LOUISE
Gagarin (family) **27** 439, 441
Gagarin, Feofil, Prince **29** 779
Gagarin, Grigory (Grigor'yevich) **11** 894–5*; **12** 331; **30** 915
Gagarin, I. A. **27** 438
Gagarin, N. S., Prince **4** 599
Gagarin, Princess **14** 768
Gagarino **25** 490; **27** 364
Gage, Diana, Viscountess Gage **8** 83
Gage, Frances **5** 571
Gage, George **11** 895*
Gage, John **4** 692
Gagen, Robert F. **32** 795
Gages **17** 514
Gages-Boussies, Marquis de **3** 599
Gaget, Gauthier & Cie **3** 290
Gaggin & Gaggin **28** 327
Gaggini *see* GAGINI
Gaggini, Giuseppe **3** 195; **16** 705
Gaggini, Pace **24** 286
Gagik, King of Vaspurakan (*reg* 785-*c.* 800) **1** 451; **2** 426, 444
Gagik I, King of Armenia (*reg* 989-1020) **2** 97, 426, 430
Gagini (family) **23** 843; **28** 657
Gagini, Antonello **9** 338; **11** 895, 898–9*; **28** 657
  works **20** 214
  workshop **20** 214
Gagini, Antonio (1478/9-1536) *see* GAGINI, ANTONELLO
Gagini, Antonio (*b* before 1514) **11** 899
Gagini, Domenico **11** 895–8*
  pupils **11** 898
  works **11** *896*; **18** 859, 860; **22** 487; **23** 845
  workshop **20** 214
Gagini, Elia **11** 895, 896–7*
Gagini, Fazio **11** 895, 899
Gagini, Giacomo **11** 899
Gagini, Giandomenico **11** 899

Gagini, Giovanni 11 895, 897*; 26 503
Gagini, Nabilo 16 742
Gagini, Pace 11 897–8*
 collaboration 3 868; 11 895, 905; 23 709; 25 254–5
 patrons and collectors 11 556
 works 11 898
Gagini, Pasio see GAGINI, PACE
Gagini, (Giovan) Vincenzo 11 899; 23 843
Gagliardi, Filippo 6 35; 18 871; 26 820; 27 489; 32 101
Gagliardi, Giuseppe 16 743
Gagliardi, Pietro 30 364
Gagliardi, Rosario 11 899*; 28 769
 collaboration 28 769
 works 16 640; 23 258; 28 657
Gagliardo Primario 2 109, 110
Gagnaire, Herménégilde Joseph Alexandre, Baron de Joursanvault see JOURSANVAULT, HERMÉNÉGILDE JOSEPH ALEXANDRE GAGNAIRE, Baron de
Gagneraux, Bénigne 11 669, 899–901*
 works 11 900
Gagnières, Roger de 4 827
Gagnon, Charles 5 568; 11 901*; 22 39
Gagnon, Clarence (Alphonse) 5 67, 566, 593; 11 901–2*
Gagnot 7 783
Gagny, Augustin Blondel de see BLONDEL DE GAGNY, AUGUSTIN
Gagny, Gaillard de 7 194
Gagra 12 320
Gahagan, Sebastian 23 190
Gahlin, Sven 15 741
Gahō Hashimoto see HASHIMOTO GAHŌ
Gahona, Gabriel Vicente see PICHETA
Gahuku 24 75
Gahungu, Mopela 5 285
Gahungu, Pierre 5 285
Gahura, František L. 8 380
Gai (family) 32 195
Gai, Antonio 9 158; 11 902*; 32 195
Gai, Francesco 11 902
Gai, Giovanni Maria 11 902
Gaiani, Egisto 16 730
Gaibach Church 28 145
Gaibano, Giovanni da see GIOVANNI DA GAIBANO
Gaignat 8 867
Gaignat, Jean 7 194
Gaignat, Louis-Jean 11 902*
Gaigneur, Louis Constantin Le see LE GAIGNEUR, LOUIS CONSTANTIN
Gaignières, Robert de 7 407
Gaignières, (François-) Roger de 11 902–3*; 12 273; 16 853; 31 842
 drawings 4 386, 552; 6 562; 7 595; 13 168; 254; 16 856; 17 670; 26 39
 engravings 11 352; 24 159
Gaii, Atelier see ATELIER GAII
Gail, Jean-Baptiste 4 238
Gailbach Schloss 5 349
Gailde, Jean 11 903*; 13 79; 31 382
Gailde-Halins (family) 13 79
Gailhabaud, Jules 11 722
Gailhoustet, Renée 11 903–4*
Gaillac 7 693
Gaillard, Eugène 4 71; 11 635, 904*; 13 318
 groups and movements 2 564
 works 11 582, 600
Gaillard, Ferdinand 26 233
Gaillard, René 13 642
Gailley, Antoine 8 890
Gaillon Château 1 766; 6 504; 7 595; 8 684; 11 504, 512, 556, 661, 726, 904–5*, 905; 14 460
 chapel 11 556
 façade 20 906
 fountains 3 868; 11 341, 897; 23 709; 25 254
 gardens 11 905*; 12 110, 112
 misericords 21 725
Gaing, Pierre V de, Abbot of Cadouin 5 369
Gainsborough, Charles Noel, 1st Earl of see NOEL, CHARLES, 1st Earl of Gainsborough
Gainsborough, Thomas 3 368, 372; 9 400–401; 10 249; 11 906–13*
 assistants 31 139
 attributions 18 570
 collaboration 13 29
 dealers 7 234
 drawings 25 572
  facsimiles 19 484
 exhibitions 19 586
 frames 11 428, 429
 groups and movements 22 740; 26 740
 methods 5 657; 10 559; 18 899; 23 378; 25 279, 281
 paintings 14 785; 20 911
  animal subjects 2 105
  conversation pieces 7 785
  fancy pictures 10 785–6, 786; 12 294
  glass 20 92
  landscape 10 251; 11 910; 18 712, 712
  mythological 11 911
  portraits 9 283, 284, 284; 11 907, 909
 patrons and collectors 10 361
  Alba, 17th Duque de (1878-1953) 1 529
  Baring, John 3 239
  Bate-Dudley, Henry 3 366
  Beit, Otto (John) 3 522
  Benson, R(obert) H(enry) 3 740
  Cambó y Batlle, Francisco de Asís 5 509
  Charlotte, Queen of Great Britain (1744-1818) 14 144
  George III, King of Great Britain (reg 1760-1820) 14 144
  George IV, King of Great Britain (reg 1820-30) 14 146
  Getty, J(ean) Paul 12 504
  Gillott, Joseph 12 638
  Grosvenor, Richard, 1st Earl Grosvenor (1731-1802) 13 696
  Grosvenor, Robert, 2nd Earl of Grosvenor and 1st Marquess of Westminster 13 696
  Groult, Camille 13 705
  Guinness, Edward (Cecil), 1st Earl of Iveagh 13 836
  Harvey, Thomas 8 184
  Hawkins, John Heywood (1803-77) 14 252
  Holloway, Thomas 14 688
  Horne, Herbert (Percy) 14 764
  Huntington, Henry E(dwards) 15 29
  Huntington Art Gallery 19 703
  Jennens, Charles 17 476
  Knight, Richard Payne 18 150
  Lázaro Galdiano, José 18 900
  Lever, William Hesketh, 1st Viscount Leverhulme 19 270
  Long, Charles, 1st Baron Farnborough 19 624
  Macklin, Thomas 20 25
  Marquand, Henry G(urdon) 20 461
  Monro, Thomas 21 901
  Montagu-Douglas-Scott, Walter Francis, 5th Duke of Buccleuch, 7th Duke of Queensberry 21 908
Gainsborough, Thomas
 patrons and collectors—cont.
  Morgan, J(ohn) Pierpont (1837-1913) 22 111
  Neeld, Joseph 22 719
  Petty, William (Fitzmaurice), 2nd Earl of Shelburne and 1st Marquess of Lansdowne 24 570
  Petty-Fitzmaurice, Henry, 3rd Marquess of Lansdowne 24 571
  Pleydell-Bouverie, Jacob, 2nd Earl of Radnor 25 39
  Rothschild (family) 27 223
  Rushout, John, 2nd Baron Northwick 27 350
  Sackville, John Frederick, 3rd Duke of Dorset 27 494
  Spencer, John, 1st Earl Spencer 29 381
  Temple-Nugent-Grenville, George, 1st Marquess of Buckingham 13 637
 prints 2 240; 10 555, 562, 562
 reproductive prints by others 3 309, 366; 13 327; 18 237, 728; 27 277; 28 283; 32 652
 teachers 13 324; 14 269
Gainza, Martín de 28 512, 518; 29 266
Gaiole, Giovanni da see GIOVANNI DA GAIOLE
Gairalt, Antoni Puig see PUIG GAIRALT, ANTONI
Gairard, Raymond 12 1*; 31 207
Gaitero, Damian 29 303
Gaitonde, Vasudev S. 4 290, 291; 8 677; 12 1–2*
Gaitov, Rais 27 435
Gaius 27 111
Gaius Matius 31 150
Gaius Verres 28 654
Gajapati, Kapilendradeva see KAPILENDRADEVA, Ruler
Gajassi, Vincenzo 24 509
Gajnipur see Rawalpindi
Gaj Singh, Maharaja of Bikaner (reg 1745-87) (Rajput) 15 390, 609
Gaj Singh, Maharaja of Marwar (reg 1620-38) (Rajput) 15 614
Gakhar (family) 26 40
GaKhn 3 196; 15 857; 27 444
Gakojō see MATSUMOTO CASTLE
Gaku Onogi see ONOGI, GAKU
Gakuō Zōkyū 30 466
Gakutei Yashima see YASHIMA GAKUTEI
gala see KANDHARA
Galaktionov, Stepan (Filippovich) 12 2*
Galalith 25 27
Galán, Rufino 14 716
Galand, Mikuláš 28 853
Galanis, Demetrios 12 2*, 546
Galántai, György 14 897
Galante, Nicola 31 446
Galantini, Ippolito 11 743
Galard, Gustave de 4 391
Galardi, Alberto 21 824
Galasek, Ludwig 12 821
Galassi, Andrea 27 836
Galassi, Galasso 3 876
Galassio da Correggio 32 612
Galatali, Atilla 31 455
Galati 2 427; 26 709
Galats see GALATI
Galaunė, Paulius 19 498
Galaz, José de 7 610
Galbán, José 27 644
galbanum 32 1
Gal'berg, Samuil (Ivanovich) 12 2–3*; 23 531
Galbraith, John Kenneth 15 743
Galbraith, Thomas 28 234, 268
Galcerán, Vicente 21 815
Galdi, Vincenzo 12 817
Galdiano, José Lázaro see LÁZARO GALDIANO, JOSÉ
Galdieri, Eugenio 16 550
Galdikas, Adomas 19 498, 499
Galdós, Benito Pérez see PÉREZ GALDÓS, BENITO
Galdzak 12 235
Gale, Joseph 19 424
Gale, Martin 16 18
Gale, Richard C. 33 232
Gale, Richard P. 17 431
Gale, Mrs Richard P. 17 431
Gale, Thomas 33 401
Galeazo, José Vallejo y see VALLEJO Y GALEAZO, JOSÉ
Galeazzo II, Lord of Milan (reg 1322-8) 2 18; 21 524; 32 609, 610–11*
Galeazzo, Giovanni 30 731
Galeazzo da Sanseverino 4 76
Galeazzo Maria, 5th Duke of Milan (reg 1466-76) 5 128; 28 531*
 architecture 11 25, 691
 frescoes 3 695
 manuscripts 25 465, 465
 paintings 5 127; 11 292, 293; 13 213
 sculpture 1 747
Galebada 29 450
Galecio, Galo 9 714
Galeka 1 419
Galen 21 5
Galen, Bernhard von, Prince-Bishop of Münster 13 684; 24 740
Galen, Gijsbert Diederik 28 166
Galen, Heinrich von 13 683
galena 1 713; 17 353
Galenzovsky, Stefan 18 658
Galeotti, Andrea 13 764
Galeotti, Antonio 12 4
Galeotti, Giovanni Battista 12 3
Galeotti, Giuseppe 12 3*; 25 226
Galeotti, Leopoldo 8 616
Galeotti (di Ercolano), Pietro di see PIETRO DI GALEOTTI (DI ERCOLANO)
Galeotti, Pietro Paolo 12 3–4*; 20 919
Galeotti, Sebastiano 11 20; 12 3*, 529; 29 411
Galeotti Torres, Rodolfo 12 4*
Galepin 9 383
Galera 24 645; 25 733
Galeria Kryzwe Koło 32 878
Galerie contemporaine 24 661
Galerie Grossgörschen 35 12 397
Galerie Koller 8 428
Galerie Miethke see under VIENNA → galleries
Galerie Rosen see under BERLIN
Galerie Simon, Editions de la see EDITIONS DE LA GALERIE SIMON
Galerie Würthle see under VIENNA → galleries
Galerius, Emperor of Rome (reg 305-11) 27 43
 architecture 9 556; 19 881; 28 439; 30 716
  palaces 9 556
  temples 30 719
  triumphal arches 27 43, 45; 30 719; 31 350
 mosaics 9 565
Galestruzzi, Giovan Battista 12 4*; 32 236
Galettoi, Pietro Paolo 7 672
Galfetti, Aurelio 4 491; 12 4–5*; 26 16
Galgada, La see LA GALGADA
Galgagno 9 655
Galgani, Niccoló, Fra 12 714
Galgario, Fra Vittore see GHISLANDI, GIUSEPPE
Galí, Francesc 21 705; 23 260
Galia, José Miguel 32 171
Galiani 32 641, 642
Galiari, Gaspare 21 495
Galibi 11 758, 759
Galić, Drago 15 66
Galić, Risto 19 883
Galich see HALICH
Galiche 30 773
Galicia, Fede 33 308
Galicnik, Museum of Djordji Pulevski 19 886
Galilee 24 252
galilees 9 450; 12 5, 5–6*
Galilei, Alessandro (Maria Gaetano) 12 6–9*
 collaboration 16 23; 24 305; 25 808
 patrons and collectors 7 897; 21 29, 908; 31 860
 works 12 7, 8; 13 301; 16 639; 20 866; 26 820, 821
Galilei, Galileo 2 105; 12 9*; 20 567
 collaboration 24 772
 groups and movements 6 360
 patrons and collectors 21 25
 pupils 7 312
 works 5 649; 20 576; 24 91; 28 210
Galimard, (Nicolas-) Auguste 12 10*
Galimbayeva, Aisha 17 867
Galimberti, Sándor 12 10–11*
Galimberti, Valéria 12 10*
Galindo, Beatriz 18 681
Galindo, Juan 21 262
Galitsko-Volynsky 27 381
Galitzin, Dimitri (Alekseyevitch), Prince 14 797; 30 714
Galizia, Fede 12 11*; 16 668; 28 496
Galizia, Nunzio 12 11
Gałkowski, Helena 12 11–12
Gałkowski, Stefan 12 11–12*
Gall, Saint 27 554
Gall, Leonhard 22 710
Gallaccini, Teofilo 12 12*; 20 242; 23 861; 31 296; 32 615
Gallagher, Glen 30 387
Gallait, Louis (-Joseph) 12 12–13*; 14 587
 pupils 6 344; 14 457
 teachers 28 68
 works 3 562; 11 448; 31 218
Galland, Auguste 27 882
Galland, Jacques 12 13
Galland, P(ierre) V(ictor) 12 13*
 collaboration 28 349
 pupils 10 658; 14 482
 works 29 306, 308
Gallant, George 9 320
Galla Placidia 9 533, 571; 12 13–14*
Gallarati, Giovanni Pietro 3 783
Gallardo, Mateo 12 14*
Gallarus Oratory 12 14*; 16 5; 32 88
Gallas, Franz Ferdinand, Count of the Holy Roman Empire 5 613
Gallatin, A(lbert) E(ugene) 12 15*; 24 600; 26 127
 collections 10 90; 31 665, 667
 groups and movements 1 772
 paintings 8 708; 14 329
Gallatly, John 8 841
Gallatown Pottery see FIFE POTTERY
Gallay, Jacques 29 750
Galle (Sri Lanka) 6 623; 29 440, 452
 fortress 29 452
Galle (family) 27 299
Galle, André 12 17*; 23 666
Galle, Claude 11 305
Galle, Cornelis (i) (1576-1650) 12 15, 16–17*
 collaboration 10 391
 pupils 12 17
 works 9 78; 10 158; 12 17; 17 599

Galle, Cornelis (ii) (1615-78) **9** 718; **12** 15, 17*; **22** 717; **24** 890
works **11** 807
Galle, Dirck *see* GALLE, THEODOR
Gallé, Emile (Charles Martin) **2** 13; **11** 600, 613; **12** *18*, 18–19*, 787; **19** 801; **30** 506
assistants **25** 662
exhibitions **15** 883
groups and movements **2** 562, 564; **8** 544; **22** 252, 456
works **2** *563*; **5** 24; **6** 391; **11** 582; **20** 469; **23** 547
workshop **20** 442
Galle, Joannes **12** 15, 17*
Galle, Philip **2** 195, 411; **7** 427, 557; **10** 387, 389; **11** 222; **12** 15–16*; **14** 294
collaboration **12** 514; **32** 725
engravings **3** 558
printmakers **12** 879; **32** 708; **33** 169
pupils **7** 556; **12** 16
reproductive prints by others **7** 556
teachers **7** 799
works **2** 104, 411; **4** 149, 251; **7** 555; **11** 717; **12** *16*; **13** 664; **15** *90*; **17** 182; **29** 741, *854*; **32** 711
Galle, Theodor **12** 15, 16*
works **1** 658; **7** 556; **17** 599; **20** 769
Gallego, Fernando **12** 19*
works **7** 363; **11** 482; **27** 603; **29** 276; **33** 605
Gallego, Francisco **7** 363; **12** 19
Gallego, José **16** 863
Gallego, Juan **13** 756
Gallegos, Roberto **21** 737
Gallego y Burín **13** 284
Gallehus **32** 519
Gallén, Axel *see* GALLEN-KALLELA, AKSELI (VALDEMAR)
Gallenius, Lars **11** 94
Gallen-Kallela, Akseli (Valdemar) **11** *100*, 110; **12** 19–21*
groups and movements **4** 891; **22** 540, 541; **24** 591; **33** 379
pupils **28** 746
sponsors **11** 111
works **11** 95, 100, 105, *477*, 477–8, *478*; **12** *20*, 498; **22** 331
Gallen-Kallela, Jorma **12** 21
Galleotti, Giuseppe **10** 501
Galleotti, Sebastiano **29** 411
Gallé-Reinemer, Charles **12** 18; **25** 662
Galleria dei Lavori *see* OPIFICIO DELLE PIETRE DURE (FLORENCE)
Gallerie des modes et costumes français, La **10** 823
Galerie Georges Giroux **5** 44
gallerie nazionali italiane, Le **24** 448
galleries (i) (upper storey internal area) **12** 21*; **26** 572; **31** 321
galleries (ii) (corridors) **2** 290; **12** 21*; **19** 315
Byzantine **9** 555
Cambodia **5** 468, 474, 475, *475*
Egypt, ancient **12** *227*
Germany **12** 364
Romanesque **12** 364
see also ARCADES; LOGGIAS
galleries (iii) (narrow room) **12** 21*; **19** 314; **33** 306
galleries (iv) (art) **2** 365, 369, 557; **9** 11–13, 14; **12** 21*; **22** 355, 358–9; **31** 235
historical and regional traditions
Antilles, Lesser **2** 153
Australia **2** 771
Austria **32** 446
Barbados **2** 153
Bosnia **4** 463
Bulgaria **5** 150
galleries (iv) (art)
historical and regional traditions—cont.
Canada **5** 590
Cuba (Caribbean) **8** 238
England **10** 234, 679; **20** 911
Estonia **10** *537*
France **9** 14; **23** 778
Germany **12** 475; **14** *176*; **33** 53
Greece, ancient **13** 402
Herzegovina **4** 463
Italy **9** *11*; **16** 771*; **31** 446
Jordan **17** 655
Martinique **2** 153
Nicaragua **23** 84
Nigeria **23** 139
South Africa **29** 121
United States of America **3** 129; **23** 46, *49*; **24** *697*, 820; **31** 665
Venezuela **32** 179
types
picture **7** 562, 563; **9** 11, 13–20*, 27; **14** 869; **22** 356, 361; **25** 279
Austria **9** 19
Belgium **7** *563*; **9** 15–16, 22
England **9** 16–17, *17*, 18–19, *26*; **10** 677, 678; **14** 539; **20** 911; **22** 362
France **9** 14, 18, 22
Germany **9** 18
Greece, ancient **7** 561; **10** 675; **13** 554–5
Italy **9** *15*; **26** *775*
Netherlands, the **9** 15
Rome, ancient **9** 13
Russia **9** 18
Spain **9** 15, 18
sculpture **7** 562; **9** 11, 14, 20–26*; **22** 356
Belgium **9** 22
England **9** 22, 23–5
France **9** 21, 22, 23
Germany **22** 362
Greece, ancient **9** 20
Italy **9** *15*, 20–22, 23; **16** *773*
Netherlands, the **9** 15, 22
Rome, ancient **9** 20
Sweden **9** 23, *24*
see also CABINETS (i) (ROOMS); CLOSETS; MUSEUMS; STUDIOLIS
gallery graves *see under* GRAVES → types
Gallery House (Tayside) **28** 226
Galles **2** 196
galleting *see under* MASONRY → types
galleyware *see under* POTTERY → wares
Galli, Aldo **26** 289
Galli, Domenico **22** 374
Galli, Francesco **25** 466
Galli, Giacomo **29** 252
Galli, Giovanbattista **9** 76
Galli, Giovanni Antonio *see* SPADARINO, LO
Galli, Giovanni Maria **3** 530; **19** 497; **29** 839
works **19** *496*
Galli, Jacopo **12** 21*
architecture **32** 229
sculpture **9** 21; **12** 607; **21** 433; **26** 299
Galliani, Carlantonio **6** 568
Galliano
Baptistery **16** 625
S Vincenzo **16** 625, 654; **22** 520; **23** 649
Galliano, John **30** 688
Galliard, Claude Ferdinand **10** 396
Galliardi, Gottlieb Anton **14** 900
Galliari, Bernardino **12** 22*; **30** 669
pupils **12** 914
works **12** *22*; **16** 719
Galliari, Fabrizio (1709-90; uncle) **12** 22–3*; **30** 669
collaboration **12** 22
pupils **12** 914
works **16** 719
Galliari, Fabrizio (*fl* late 18th cent.; nephew) **12** 22
Galliari, Gasparo **12** 22
Galliari, Giovanni (i) (*c.* 1680-1720) **12** 22
Galliari, Giovanni (ii) (1746-1818) **12** 22; **16** 719
Galliari, Giovanni Antonio **12** 22, 914
Galliari, Giuseppe **12** 22
Galli-Bibiena (family) **30** 676
competitions **12** 22
pupils **17** 626
works **1** 124; **4** 277; **5** 686; **15** 139; **24** 490
Galli-Bibiena, Alessandro **12** 23; **13** 725; **20** 281, 282; **27** 587; **33** 280
Galli-Bibiena, Antonio **12** 23, 25–6*; **15** 13; **25** 448
collaboration **7** 882
patrons and collectors **11** 120; **28** 857; **31** 510
pupils **12** 583; **31** 268
works **4** 695; **5** 82; **10** 531; **14** 900; **20** 320; **23** 855; **28** 852; **30** 667
Galli-Bibiena, Carlo **12** 23, 26*
collaboration **12** 24; **30** 676
patrons and collectors **14** 652
works **3** 428
Galli-Bibiena, Ferdinando **12** 23–5*
assistants **12** 25
collaboration **26** 320
patrons and collectors **1** 633; **10** 811, 812
pupils **5** 358; **12** 24; **18** 696; **19** 117
works **12** *23*; **14** 402; **21** 30; **23** 606; **25** 893; **30** 668, *668*
writings **31** 296
Galli-Bibiena, Francesco **12** 23, 24*
attributions **9** 190
collaboration **21** 146
patrons and collectors **10** 811, 812
pupils **23** 359; **24** 9
works **4** 273; **21** 30; **30** 667
Galli-Bibiena, Giovanni Carlo **4** 636; **12** 23; **23** 406
Galli-Bibiena, Giovanni Maria **4** 562; **11** 679; **12** 23
Galli-Bibiena, Giuseppe **12** 23, 24–6*
assistants **12** 25, 26; **27** 136
collaboration **28** 163; **30** 676
patrons and collectors **14** 652
works **3** 428; **12** *25*; **21** 84; **30** 668
Galli-Bibiena, Maria Oriana **12** 23
gallic acid **24** 649
Gallien, Edme-Jean **11** 626
Gallien & Cie, L. Galy **19** 417
Gallienus, Emperor of Rome (*reg* 253-68) **27** 41, 42, 97
Gallier, James (i) (1798-1866) **8** 462, 574; **12** 26*; **23** 31
collaboration **14** 786; **31** 232
works **18** 629; **23** *31*, 31
Gallier, James (ii) (1827-68) **12** 26*; **23** 31
Gallier, Thaddeus **12** 26
Galliera, Duc de **9** 313
Galliera, Maria de Ferrari, Duchesa di **4** 811; **12** 284, 650
Gallier & Dakin **12** 26
Gallier & Esterbrook **12** 26
Gallieriasamling **30** 118
Gallimard **20** 208
Gallimard, Paul **27** 880
Gallimore, Ambrose **6** 93
Gallina, Eduardo Rosales *see* ROSALES MARTÍNEZ, EDUARDO
Gallina, Marco **21** 463
Gallinazo **12** 27*; **29** *156*
adobe **29** 162
pottery **12** 27
pyramids **21** 750
textiles **29** 180
Gallini, Giovanni Andrea Battista **1** 125; **7** 687
Gallino, Cayetano **31** 754
Gallio, Conte **5** 775
Galliori, Giulio **24** 824
Gallipoli **9** 554
Gallissà, Antoni Maria **29** 308
Gallista *see* ORMOPHOKLISIA
Gallizioli, Costantino **3** 772; **5** 872
gall-nuts **9** 490, 491; **15** 849
Gallo (*fl* 17th cent.) **2** 376
Gallo, Agostino **6** 359
Gallo, Antonio Maria, Cardinal **5** 415
Gallo, Francesco **32** 632
Gallo, Miguel Mujica *see* MUJICA GALLO, MIGUEL
Gallo, Pietro **31** 285
Gallo, Santino **25** 446
Gallo, Vincenzo d'Angelo del **32** 202
Galloche, Louis **12** 27*
collaboration **6** 121; **10** 842
patrons and collectors **2** 724
pupils **19** 142; **22** 682
Gallois Duquette, Danielle
works **4** *55*
Gallon Château **9** 21
galloon **24** 237
Gallori, Emilio **16** 707; **27** 492
gallotannins **9** 490, 491; **15** 849, 851
Galloway, Charles **5** 310
Galloway Mazer **28** 261
Gallucci, Andrea **12** 27
Gallucci, Nicola **8** 201; **12** 27–8*
Gallup (NM), Inter-tribal Indian Ceremonial **22** 677
Gallurus Oratory **16** 7
Gallus, Joannes **33** 367
Galluzzi, Andrea **4** 310; **24** 9
Galluzzi, Giovanni Battista **4** 310; **26** 519
Galluzzo, Certosa **5** 894, 895
Galman, Jan **2** 416
Galofré, José **29** 357
Galon, Col. **4** 683
Galopin, Mathurin **4** 390
Galo Polychrome ware *see under* POTTERY → wares
Galović, R. **25** 464
Galque, Adrian Sánchez *see* SÁNCHEZ GALQUE, ADRIAN
Galsted **23** 536
Galstyan, Vruyr **2** 433
Galsworthy, John **4** 367
Galt **4** 81
Galt, James **31** 255
Galtes, Charles **3** 220
Galtrim **16** 24
Galván, Jesús Guerrero *see* GUERRERO GALVÁN, JESÚS
Galván brothers **4** 264
Galván Candela, José Maria **12** 28*
Galvani **25** 721
Galvano di Rinaldo da Vigo **4** 274
galvanograph **21** 896
Galvão, Duarte **14** 658
Galveston (TX), Moody Gardens **12** 143
Gálvez (family) **2** 143; **13** 764
Gálvez, Antonio Joseph de **12** 28*; **21** 159
Gálvez, Cristina **24** 511
Gálvez, Francisco Javier de **12** 28*; **26** 251
Gálvez, José Jacobo **13** 730
works **13** *730*
Gálvez, Juan **4** 378; **10** 504
Gálvez, Vicente de **12** 28*; **26** 251
Gálvez Suárez, Alfredo **12** 28*; **13** 765
Galvin's Gorge
rock art **1** *57*
Galwa **11** 878
Galway **16** *5*, 20, 37
Queen's College **16** 11
Galzetta Bianca, Matteo *see* WITHOOS, MATTHIAS
Gama, Vasco da *see* VASCO DA GAMA
Gamann, Franz **28** 184
Gamard, Christophe **19** 233
Gamarra, Francisco González *see* GONZÁLEZ GAMMARA, FRANCISCO
Gamarra, Gregorio **4** 261; **18** 777; **24** 507
Gamarra, José **12** 29*; **23** 85; **31** 756
Gamatai *see* GUINAN
Gamazo, Germán Valentín **31** 815
Gamba, Bartolommeo **19** 510
Gamba, Crescenzo la **22** 486
Gamba, Enrico **12** 29*; **29** 611
Gamba, Francesco **12** 29*
Gambacorti (family) **11** 888
Gambar **2** 896
Gambara, Antonio **23** 843
Gambara, Gianfrancesco, Cardinal **3** 56; **11** 343
Gambara, Giovanni **23** 843
Gambara, Lattanzio **3** 767; **12** 29*; **26** 727–8
Gambarelli, Crescenzio **22** 805
Gambarin, Martin **25** 438
Gambarini, Carlo, Count **14** 436
Gambarini, Giuseppe **5** 178; **12** 29–30*
Gambart, (Jean Joseph) Ernest (Théodore) **11** 761, 796; **12** 30–31*; **19** 588; **26** 232
paintings **1** 677; **11** 796; **15** 26; **25** 41
printmakers **26** 233
Gambart & Co. **8** 190; **21** 604
Gambartes, Leónidas **2** 400
Gambart & Junin **12** 30
Gambarto, Girolamo **27** 655
Gambassi, Cieco da *see* GONNELLI, GIOVANNI FRANCESCO
Gambatelli, Girolamo **26** 817, 818
Gambello, Antonio (di Marco) **2** 502; **7** 516; **12** 31*; **19** 553
works **16** *631*
Gambello, Vittore **12** 31*; **19** 208; **28** 436
attributions **27** 780
patrons and collectors **13** 657
works **3** 690; **20** 918; **21** 16; **29** 569
Gamber, Ortwin **2** 450
Gamberelli, Antonio *see* ROSSELLINO, ANTONIO
Gamberelli, Bernardo *see* ROSSELLINO, BERNARDO
Gamberelli, Domenico **27** 179–80
Gamberelli, Giovanni **27** 179–80
Gamberelli, Matteo **27** 179–80
Gamberelli, Tomaso **27** 179–80
Gamberini, Domenico **6** 22
Gamberini, I. **21** 471
Gamberucci, Cosimo **7** 457; **22** 448; **24** 860
Gamberucci, Marco **12** 590
Gambia, The **1** *214*, 380; **12** 31–2*
architecture **12** 32*
dyeing **3** 379
gold **1** 288
masks **12** 32
trade **1** 250
Gambier Islands **23** *711*; **31** 403–4*
human figures **31** 403, *404*
Gambier-Parry, Thomas **12** 32–3*
architecture **33** 372
frescoes **33** 5
methods **22** 331; **32** 806

Gambier-Parry Wallet 16 381
Gambin, Giulio 11 604; 19 849; 23 13
Gamble, Ellis 14 637
Gamble, James 1 648; 11 360; 30 162
Gambo, Francisco de *see* ZUMAYA, FRANCISCO DE
Gamboa, Diane 19 703
Gamboa, Fernando 21 396
gamboge 12 623, 803; 17 277; 24 800
Gambogi, Raffaello 28 319
Gamborg, Frederik 8 758
Gamborino, Miguel 12 33*
gambrel roofs *see under* ROOFS → types
Gambrill, Charles Dexter 11 848; 25 327; 26 338; 28 591
Gambrill & Richardson 26 338
Gambroon *see* BANDAR ABBAS
Gambs, Heinrich 26 530; 27 408, 583
  works 27 *583*
Gambs, Peter Heinrichovich 27 584
Gamburd, Moisey 21 811
game-boards 1 762; 10 48; 15 730; 31 265, *265*, 266*
Game-Cock Salt 10 326
Gamelin, Jacques 1 845; 12 33–4*; 26 841
Gamelin, Jacques-François 12 34
game-pieces 31 265
  historical and regional traditions
    Egypt, ancient 10 60; 16 797
    Japan 17 386
  materials
    amber 1 761
    clay 31 266
    ebony 31 266
    glass 17 386
    gold 31 266
    ivory 10 60; 16 797, 798; 31 254, 266
    stone 31 266
    wood 31 266
Gameren, Tylman van 12 34–5*, 133; 25 135
  attributions 12 224
  patrons and collectors 19 752
  works 12 *35*; 18 426, 428, 440, 693; 21 158; 23 113; 25 98, *98*; 28 115; 32 869, 870, 880
games 21 187; 26 872; 31 254*, 265–7*
  see also TOYS
Games, Abram 25 352, 652
  works 25 *353*
Games, Master of the 20 678*
Gamio, Manuel 1 713; 8 255; 18 784; 21 263; 30 483
Gamla Synagogue 17 541
Gamla Uppsala, St Peter's 26 593
Gamle Estrup 19 5
Gamma 27 616
gammalu 29 477, *478*
Gammelgarn 13 120
Gamoike Tomb 17 59
Gampert, Jean-Louis 2 700
Gampert, Otto 10 563
Gampola 17 769; 29 *440*
Gampopa 5 105
Gamrekeli, I. 12 327
Gamucci, Bernardo 9 181; 26 848
Gamundi, B. 25 703
Gamundi, Mari 25 703
Gamzigrad 9 556; 28 439
  palace 9 565; 28 439
  Romuliana 28 *437*
GAN *see* ADRIAN-NILSSON, GÖSTA
Gan (company) *see* HAHN
Gan, Aleksey (Mikhaylovich) 12 35–6*
  groups and movements 7 768; 15 857; 29 632; 32 382
  works 7 768, 769
Gan, E. 4 469
Gana, Ali 19 324
Ganada, Francisco Alves 12 762
Ganado (AZ) 22 626
Ganagobie Monastery 11 *505*; 12 36*; 26 604
Ganapuram 15 539
Ganasobba 1 485; 15 526
  works 15 *527*
Ganay, Hubert de, Marquis 11 664
Ganbarē Hāylu, Qaññgēta 10 573
Gance, Abel 6 167
Gand *see* GHENT
Gand, Gilbert de, Earl of Lincoln 14 408
Gand, Juste de *see* JUSTUS OF GHENT
Gand, Olivier de *see* OLIVIER OF GHENT
Ganda 1 369
Gandara, Antonio de La 4 670; 12 36*
Gándara, Jerónimo de la 1 464
Gandaraditya, Ruler (*reg c.* 954-8) (Chola) 15 234
Gandarias, Justo de 12 28; 13 764
Gand-dehra, Shakti-Devi Temple 15 626, 627
Gandellini, Francesco Gori *see* GORI GANDELLINI, FRANCESCO
Gandellini, Giovanni Gori *see* GORI GANDELLINI, GIOVANNI
Gandellini, Pietro Gori *see* GORI GANDELLINI, PIETRO
Gandelsonas, Mario 1 463
Ganden 12 36–7*; 30 *806*
  Monastery 30 819, 820, 821
Gandersheim 29 818
Gandersheim, Hrosvita von 18 512
Gandersheim Casket 2 82
Gandhara 1 *186*; 6 *182*; 12 37*
  columns 15 448
  dress 1 887
  forgeries 15 750
  furniture 6 311
  iconography 1 206
  jewellery 15 700
  metalwork 1 206
  narratives 22 516
  schist 15 *446*, *447*
  sculpture 1 195; 5 91, 95; 9 34, *34*, *35*; 15 220, *222*, 416, 439, 445–9*, *446*, *447*, 452, 458; 24 218; 30 784
  stucco 1 196; 29 824
  wall paintings 15 543
Gandharadi temples 15 283
Gandhi, Indira, National Centre for the Arts *see under* DELHI
Gandhi Memorial Museum *see under* AHMADABAD → museums
Gandhu 22 439
Gandía, Enrique de 2 405
Gandía, Luisas Géigel de *see* GÉIGEL DE GANDÍA, LUISAS
Gandia Church 29 335
Gândirea 26 716
Gandja 2 *890*, 894; 12 37*; 16 *105*, 160
  administrative building 2 894
  carpets 2 438, 901
  gates 9 160
  jewellery 2 900
  Nizami Picture Gallery 12 37
  textiles 2 900
Gandja/Karabagh carpets *see under* CARPETS → types
Gandolfi, Clementina 12 38
Gandolfi, Democrito 12 38
Gandolfi, Gaetano 12 37, 39–42*; 16 670
  patrons and collectors 31 307
  pupils 12 42; 24 320, 321
  teachers 31 164
  works 11 *394*, 395; 12 *40*, *41*, 42
Gandolfi, Giovanni Battista 12 38
Gandolfi, José Maria 12 43*
Gandolfi, Mauro 12 37, 42–3*
  works 11 396; 12 *42*
Gandolfi, Roberto Luiz 12 43
Gandolfi, Ubaldo 12 37, 38–9*; 16 670
  assistants 24 320
  patrons and collectors 31 307
  pupils 24 320, 321
  teachers 31 164
  works 12 *39*; 13 740
Gandolfi, Ubaldo Lorenzo 12 38
Gandolfi, Venancio 9 711
Gandolfo, Antonio 28 213
Gandon, James 5 197; 12 43–5*
  assistants 3 81; 28 894
  collaboration 14 500
  competitions 7 666
  patrons and collectors 2 597
  teachers 16 24
  works 2 617; 6 94; 9 317; 12 *44*; 16 9, 21; 18 886, 887; 23 258; 25 268
Gandra, Hernâni 1 752
Gandria, Egidio de *see* EGIDIO DE GANDRIA
Gandria, Pietro de *see* PIETRO DE GANDRIA
Gandussis (family) 5 51
Gandy, James 16 13
Gandy, Joseph Michael 2 333; 12 45–6*
  collaboration 5 169
  patrons and collectors 28 908
  works 2 332, 333; 3 373; 5 688; 25 207
Gandy, William 19 583
Gandy-Deering, John Peter 12 26; 25 268; 33 192
Gandzasar Monastery Complex 2 892
  church 2 434, 435, 893, 895
Gane, Crofton 10 299
Gane, P. E. 7 483
Ganegoda 29 460
Ganeshra 15 451
Ganfei, S Salvador 25 289; 26 611
Ganga *see* EASTERN GANGAS; WESTERN GANGAS
Gangaikondacholapuram 12 46*; 15 *294*, 333
  Brihadīśvara Temple 30 *439*
  Gangaikondacholishvara *see* Rajendra Cholishvara
  Rajendra Cholishvara 15 333, 518
Ganganelli, Lorenzo (Giovanni Vincenzo Antonio), Cardinal *see* CLEMENT XIV, Pope
Gangapura, Chennakeshava Temple 15 538
Gangar Sagar
  sculpture 15 *216*
Ganga Singh, Maharaja of Bikaner (*reg* 1887-1944) (Rajput) 4 58
Gangasiripura *see* GAMPOLA
Gangaw 5 *221*, 247
Ganghegui, Luis Peña *see* PEÑA GANGHEGUI, LUIS
Ganghofer, Jörg *see* JÖRG VON HALSBACH
Gangl, Joseph 20 926
Gangnat, Maurice 26 209
Gangotena, Alfredo 9 714
Ganguly, Manmohan 15 212
Gani 23 641
Ganja *see* GANDJA
Ganj 'Ali Khan 3 377; 16 230; 18 85
Ganj Dareh 12 46–7*; 15 *901*, 903, 909, 913, 920
Ganjin 17 98, 117, *130*; 22 502, 504
ganjira see under PINNACLES → types
Gankevich, V. V. 11 245
Ganku Kishi *see* KISHI GANKU
Gann, Thomas 7 484; 27 786
Gannat 9 156
Gano da Siena *see* GANO DI FAZIO
Gano di Fazio 2 42; 12 47*; 13 93
Ganovski, Mito 5 159
Ganquan 7 83
Gansauge, Johannes *see* GANSSOG, JOHANNES
Gansenji 17 119
Ganses, Paul 9 119
Gansevoort Limner 20 678–9*; 31 872
Ganssog, Johannes 12 47*
Ganstaug, Johannes *see* GANSSOG, JOHANNES
Gant, Copin de *see* COPIN DE GANT
Gantai Kishi *see* KISHI GANTAI
Gante, Giovanni di *see* GIOVANNI DI GANTE
Gante, Pedro de 21 382, 397
Gante, Pippo di *see* PIPPO DI GANTE
Ganter Bridge 4 804
Gantner, Joseph 12 47–8*; 21 407; 30 157
Gantrel, Etienne 4 536; 14 84; 19 154
Gantzow, Johannes *see* GANSSOG, JOHANNES
Ganushev, Nikola 5 154
Ganweriwala 15 246
Gan Yang 18 60
Ganymed (1919-25) 24 445
Ganymed (1949-63) 7 576
Ganymede Painter 13 530; 32 45*
Ganymede Silk 16 435
Ganymed Graphische-Anstalt 26 236
Ganz, Paul 30 157
Ganzhou *see* CHANGYE
Ganzo, Robert 10 838
Gao 1 *381*
  architecture 1 316
  mosque-tomb of Askia-al-Hajj Muhammed 1 316
  Museum 20 199
Gao Cen 12 899; 22 459
Gaochang *see* KHOCHO
Gaocheng 6 840
  see also TAIXI
Gaodi, Emperor (*reg* 206-195 BC) 14 133; 33 464
Gaodi, Emperor (Southern Qi; *reg* 479-83) 7 152
Gao Fenghan 12 48–9*; 33 497
  works 12 *49*
Gaofeng Yuanmiao 6 756
Gao Jianfu 12 49–50*; 19 421, 422, 423, 866
Gao Jun 17 184
Gao Kan 17 184
Gao Kegong 7 151; 12 50*; 14 136
Gao Lian 7 37
gaols *see* PRISONS
Gaona, Ignacio 31 589
Gao Pian 32 478
Gaoping County, Kaihua Temple 6 778
Gao Qifeng 12 49; 19 421, 422, 423
  works 19 *422*
Gao Qipei 6 781, 811; 12 50–51*; 19 469
  works 12 *51*
Gaoquan 17 409
Gao Shiqi 7 153; 12 51–2*
Gaotlhalehwe, Speedo 4 489
Gaoua 1 *386*
  Musée des Civilisations du Sud-Ouest 5 217
  shrine 19 *522*
Gao Xiang 33 497
Gao Yi 6 697; 25 800; 33 500
Gao Yongzhi 26 *216*
Gao Yuangui 7 35
Gaozong, Emperor (Tang; *reg* 649-83) 29 904
  paintings 6 808; 33 492, 498, 648
  tomb 6 *698*, 698; 25 780
  writings 6 745, 746
Gaozong, Emperor (Song; *reg* 1127-62) 6 618, 750–51, 754; 7 152; 12 52*
  calligraphy 14 825
  ceramics 6 892
  jade 7 7
  paintings 6 809; 17 590; 33 468
  sculpture 19 639
Gaozong, Emperor (Qing; *reg* 1736-96) *see* QIANLONG EMPEROR
Gaputytė, Elena 19 499
Gara, Giovanni di 21 636
Garabetta, Angelo 29 830
Garabit Viaduct 4 799, 803; 30 27
Garáfulic, Lily 6 598; 31 812
Garagay *see under* LIMA
garages *see* SERVICE STATIONS
Garaku 17 400
Garamond, Claude 10 534; 31 495
Garamszentbenedek *see* ZIÁR NAD HRONOM
Garanin, Anatoly (Sergeyevich) 12 52–3*
Garanjeau 8 902
Garatti, Vittorio 8 233; 13 213
Garau, Amalia 22 242
Garavelli Antonelli, Cristóbal *see* ANTONELLI, CRISTÓBAL GARAVELLI
Garavelli Torres, Juan Bautista *see* ANTONELLI, JUAN BAUTISTA (iii)
Garavito, Humberto 12 53*; 13 765
Garay, Antonio 28 884
Garay (Caicedo), Epifanio 7 609, 611; 12 53*; 23 904, 906
Garay, Juan de 2 392, 394
Garay, Pedro de 2 285
Garázda (family) 14 904
Garb, Anton 14 678
Garbers, Karl 3 242
Garbett, William 33 237
garbhagrha 15 243*
Garbieri, Lorenzo 12 53–4*, 763; 20 586
Garbisch, Bernice Chrysler 12 54*
Garbisch, Edgar William 12 54*
Garbo, António Baptista 12 54; 19 776
Garbo, Carlos Baptista 12 54*; 19 776; 20 85
Garbo, Giovanni Battista 12 54
Garbo, Raffaellino del *see* RAFFAELLINO DEL GARBO
Garbrant, Adrien 12 874
Garcés, Juan, Fray 32 167
Garcia III, Count of Castile (*reg* 1035-54) 26 689
García, Adrián 18 833
García, Alfonso Sánchez *see* SÁNCHEZ GARCÍA, ALFONSO
Garcia, Antonio 7 605; 25 233
García, Antonio López *see* LÓPEZ GARCÍA, ANTONIO
García, Antonio Muñoz *see* MUÑOZ GARCÍA, ANTONIO
García, Aurelio 24 98
Garcia, Aurora 3 624
Garcia, Carmelita 3 624
García, Domingo 12 55*; 18 833
García, Felipita Aguilar 22 607
García, Felo 8 17
García, Gabriel 9 714
García, Gay (Enrique) 12 55*; 18 834
García, Jerónimo Francisco 12 54*
García, Joaquín Torres *see* TORRES GARCÍA, JOAQUÍN
García, Josep Torres *see* TORRES GARCÍA, JOSEP
García, José Villagrán *see* VILLAGRAN (GARCÍA), JOSÉ
García, Leo 14 714
García, Manuel 25 701
Garcia, Maria 3 624
García, Martín 25 702
García, Miguel Jerónimo 12 54*

García, N. 21 396
García, Pablo Antonio 7 608
García, Pedro 32 560
Garcia, Piedad 3 624
García, Rafael Esguerra *see* ESGUERRA GARCÍA, RAFAEL
Garcia, (Frederico) Ressano 12 55*; 19 466; 22 14; 25 293
García, Reynaldo González *see* GONZÁLEZ GARCÍA, REYNALDO
García, Roberto 32 169
works 32 *169*
García, Romualdo 12 56*
Garcia, Rupert 18 832
García, Silvestre Antonio 10 154
García, Simón 12 619; 31 297
Garcia, Sylvia 3 624
García, Víctor Manuel *see* VÍCTOR MANUEL (GARCÍA)
Garcia Benito, Edouard 10 824
García Bravo, Alonso 21 401; 31 721
García Buch, Mirta 8 236
Garcia Cabrera, Pedro 11 886
García Crespo, Luis 12 56
García Crespo, Manuel 12 56*; 27 606; 29 337
Garcia d'Ávila, Casa da Torre 4 709
García de Asucha, Ignacio 4 233
Garcia de Barco 20 620
García de Benabarre, Pedro 9 264
works 9 *264*
García de Coca, Luís 29 337
García del Molino, Fernando 22 96
García de los Reyes, Bernabé 6 67; 29 336
García de Miranda, Juan 12 56*; 29 282
García de Pradas, Juan 13 283
García de Quiñones, Andrés 7 288; 12 56–7*; 27 603
García de Quiñones, Jerónimo 7 288; 12 57
García Ferrer, Mosén Pedro 21 375
García Guerrero, Luis 12 57*
Garci-Aguirre, Pedro 10 773; 12 57*; 13 761, 770
García Hevia, Luis 7 608, 611, 612; 11 66
García Hidalgo, José 12 57–8*; 20 66
assistants 7 689
pupils 2 497
works 12 *58*; 20 *66*; 29 *302*, 357
García Huidobro, Carlos 6 594
García Joya, Mario *see* MAYITO
García Mercadal, Fernando 7 *294*; 12 58*, 177; 21 783; 29 273
García Mesa, José 4 262, 269; 12 59*
García-Moreno, Sergio Larraín *see* LARRAÍN GARCÍA-MORENO, SERGIO
García Moya, Antonio 4 712; 28 394
García Nava, Francisco 2 289
Garciandía, Flavio 8 234
García of Castile 16 437
García Payón, José 5 433; 30 254
García Ponce, Fernando 12 59*
García Ponce, Juan 12 59
García Reinoso, Antonio 12 59*
Garcia-Trujillo, Tina 22 606
García Uriburu, Nicolás 2 401
García Vega, Agustín 18 784
García y Delgado, Mauricio 8 303; 24 507
Garcilasso 12 71
Garcimuñoz 8 16
Garcí Núñez, Julián Jaime 2 396
Garcí Sevilla, Ferran 3 220
Garda 30 75
Gardberg, Bertel 11 108
Garde, Fanny 7 807
Garde, Jacques de La *see* LA GARDE, JACQUES DE
Gardecki, Józef 29 791
garde-corps 9 258
Gardel, Pierre-Gabriel 11 257
Gardella, Ignazio 12 59–60*
collaboration 1 578; 3 439; 25 792; 27 192
groups and movements 15 886
pupils 4 490
works 4 790; 16 650; 30 684
Gardelle, Daniel 19 435
Gardelle, Robert 12 60*
Garde-meuble ancien et moderne, Le 13 831
Garde Meuble de la Couronne *see under* MAISON DU ROI
Garden, Hugh M(ackie) G(ordon) 6 578; 25 446; 28 121, 122
garden buildings 19 *212*
Garden carpets *see under* CARPETS → types
garden cities *see under* TOWNS → types
Garden City (NY) 17 891; 29 651
Garden City Association 8 824; 12 145
garden design 5 344; 12 61–70*, 104–9*, 136–44*; 18 902; 24 741
Ancient Near East 12 66*
Britain 24 740
Cambodia 12 102
China 12 85–93, *91*, *92*
Egypt, ancient 12 66–7
England 3 30; 12 126–31; 25 233; 30 123
France 4 605; 12 112–13, 119–24, *121*, *122*, *123*
Greece, ancient 12 67–8
Indonesia 12 102
Italy 12 110–12, 114–19, *117*, *118*
Japan 12 95–101*, *97*, *99*, *100*, *101*, *102*; 18 567
Korea 12 93–5
Netherlands, the 12 *106*, 131–2, *132*
Rome, ancient 12 68–70
Thailand 12 102
United States of America 9 204
see also PATTERN BOOKS → types → garden
Gardener, Jon 12 107
garden-farms *see* FERMES ORNÉES
Garden Grove (CA), Crystal Cathedral 12 794; 16 *56*; 19 365
garden mazes *see under* MAZES → types
Garden of Eden 12 66, 106, 107; 24 90
Garden Party relief 1 886, 890, 891; 2 641, *641*; 22 511; 30 774
garden pattern-books *see under* PATTERN-BOOKS → types
gardens 11 225; 12 60–144*, *108*, *109*
historical and regional traditions
Afghanistan 16 197–8
Ancient Near East 12 66*
Australia 12 142
Austria 12 133–4*; 32 *461*
Aztec 12 71, 136
Brazil 5 *218*; 7 884
Britain 12 70, 105
Buddhism 12 85, *97*, 97–9, *101*; 18 *560*, *562*, *563*
Byzantine 12 71–2*
Cambodia 12 102–4*
Canada 12 136
Central Asia, Western 12 81–3*; 16 197–8, 238
China 6 631, 632, 692, 795; 11 338; 12 85–93*, *89*, *91*; 30 49
Ming period (1368-1644) 12 63, *88*, *91*
Qing period (1644-1911) 6 682–4; 12 89, *90*, *92*
Confucianism 12 93
Czech Republic 12 133–4*
gardens
historical and regional traditions—cont.
Denmark 12 135; 16 863
Egypt 12 78
Egypt, ancient 10 54*; 12 66–7*
England 12 104, 126–31*, 136–42; 14 512; 32 552
16th cent. 12 *126*
18th cent. 4 *806*, *876*; 7 *375*; 12 *63*, *127*; 27 *259*; 29 *734*; 33 132–3
19th cent. 12 *137*, *139*; 19 *820*
20th cent. 12 *141*
France 12 104, 119–24*, *121*, *122*, *123*; 20 133, 868
Renaissance 12 112–13*, *113*
Roman 12 70, *70*
17th cent. 6 *454*; 12 *61*; 19 *162*, *164*; 20 *449*
Germany 12 133–4*; 14 469; 17 698; 33 380
Baroque 28 110
Mannerism 6 95
Rococo 12 *133*; 26 497; 32 120
19th cent. 22 381
Greece, ancient 12 65, 67–8*
Inca 12 71
Indian subcontinent 12 72–3*
Bengal 12 73
British-Indian 12 75–6*, *76*
Gujarat 12 73
Islamic 12 73–5*, *75*; 16 239
Mughal 11 340; 12 62, 73–5, *75*; 15 361
Indonesia 12 102–4*
Iran 12 81–3*, *83*
Iraq 12 77
Ireland 12 127, 128, 129, 131
Islamic 11 340; 12 76–8*, 83–5*; 16 129, 141
Afghanistan 16 197–8
Central Asia, Western 12 81–3*; 16 197–8, 238
Egypt 12 78
Indian subcontinent 12 73–5*, *75*; 16 239
Iran 12 81–3*, *83*
Iraq 12 77
Morocco 12 78
North Africa 12 78
Sicily 12 *78*
Spain 12 78–81*, *80*, *81*
Syria 12 77
Turkey 12 83–5*, *84*
Italy 11 340; 12 114–19*, *117*, *118*; 32 547
Baroque 11 *740*, *741*
Renaissance 12 110–12*, *111*, *112*; 16 633
Roman 12 *68*, 70; 26 *899*
16th cent. 4 *287*; 12 *60*, *62*
17th cent. 12 *116*
Japan 11 338; 12 85*, 95–101*, *99*, *100*, *102*; 17 337, 340; 18 *560*, *562*, *563*
Korea 12 85*, 93–5*, *94*
Maya 12 71
Mesoamerica, Pre-Columbian 12 71*
Morocco 12 78
Netherlands, the 12 104, 131–2*, *132*; 33 691
North Africa 12 78
Norway 12 135, *135*
Poland 12 133–4*
Portugal 12 124–5*, *125*
Rome, ancient 12 65, *68*, 68–70*, *70*; 26 862, *862*, *899*; 27 29, 48; 32 543–4
Russia 12 134*, *134*
Scandinavia 12 135*, *135*
Scotland 12 126, 128, 129, *129*
Sicily 11 340; 12 *78*
South Africa 12 142
South America, Pre-Columbian 12 71*
gardens
historical and regional traditions—cont.
Spain 2 284; 12 124–5*
Baroque 27 *753*
Islamic 12 78–81*, *80*, *81*
Sri Lanka 29 448
Sweden 12 135
Syria 12 77
Thailand 12 102–4*, *103*
Tunisia 12 70
Turkey 12 83–5*, *84*
United States of America 12 62, 136*, *136*, *142*, 143, *143*
Vietnam 12 104*
Wales 12 131
historiography *see under* HISTORIOGRAPHY → types
types
allotment 12 61
botanic 4 *483*, 483–4*; 12 61, 93, 103–4, 115, 125; 22 131
chār bāgh 8 679; 12 73; 15 361
Chinese 12 123, 131
cloister 12 61, 108
community 12 61
courtyard 12 65, 66
dry-landscape 12 61
Buddhism 18 *563*, 564
Japan 12 85, *97*, 98; 18 556, *560*, *562*, *563*, 564; 31 *400*
edible 12 61
enclosed 12 107, *107*
flower 12 61
four-fold 12 78
hanging 12 65
ḥayr 12 77
herbularius see physic
hortus see vegetable
hortus conclusus 3 503; 12 106, 108; 18 704
Italy 12 110, 112
jardins à la française 12 122, 123; 26 471
jardins anglais 12 123
jardins anglo-chinois 6 411; 12 123, *123*, 131
jardins paysagers 12 123
see also PARKS
kepoi 12 68
knot gardens 12 61, *64*, 126
landscape 2 414; 12 61; 26 742; 29 *735*; 32 564
locus amoenus 12 109
nursery 12 61
paradeisoi 11 340; 12 62, 65; 24 90*
peace 12 61
physic 12 107
pleasure 12 61; 19 *619*; 24 90
public 12 61, 93, 106
remembrance 12 61
riyāḍ 12 77
rock 12 61, 105
roof 18 854
sculpture 9 25; 12 61; 28 314–16*, *315*; 29 563–4
England 9 23
France 32 372
Italy 9 21; 26 *845*
Japan 12 101
Rome, ancient 12 287
United States of America 23 *176*
secret *see hortus conclusus*
tea 12 93, 98–9
terraced 18 *646*
vegetable 12 61, 107
victory 12 61
water 12 61, *102*
winter 7 744; 12 61
see also CONSERVATORIES
zoological *see* ZOOS
see also TOPIARY
garden seating 12 109, 126, 130
Gardens of Love, Master of the 20 620, 679*, 785
Gardez 1 *186*, 198, 199
Gardie, Magnus Gabriel De la *see* DE LA GARDIE, MAGNUS GABRIEL
Gardien, Fernand 19 51
Gardijn, Karel du *see* DU JARDIN, KAREL
Gardin, Gianni Berengo *see* BERENGO GARDIN, GIANNI
Gardiner, A. H. 10 1–2
Gardiner, Bishop 33 236
Gardiner, J. & J. 28 255
Gardiner, John 30 741
Gardiner, Luke 9 316
works 9 *315*
Gardiner, Margaret 32 800
Gardiner, Peter 28 258
Gardiner, Robert Hallowell 31 689, 691
Gardiner, Sidney 31 650
Gardiner, W. F. K. 32 414
Gardner, Alexander 4 627; 12 145–6*; 24 667
collaboration 4 627
staff 23 625
works 15 830; 24 *666*, 667
Gardner, (Ernest) Arthur 12 146*
Gardner, Briar 23 68
Gardner, Daniel 12 146–7*
Gardner, Francis 22 180; 27 412
Gardner, Helen 2 535
Gardner, Isabella Stewart 2 560; 12 147*
architecture 8 266; 29 870
collections 4 477; 16 769; 31 664, 667
paintings 7 579; 20 679; 33 705
Gardner, Isabella Stewart, Museum *see under* BOSTON (MA; USA) → museums
Gardner, Robert W. 32 95
Gardner, Samuel (1817-93) 5 570
Gardner, Samuel (*fl* 1870s) 12 146
Gardner Annunciation, Master of the 20 679*
Gardner Museum *see under* TORONTO
Gardner Porcelain Factory 27 412, 413
production 27 *412*
see also DMITROV FACTORY
Gardone Riviera, Vittoriale degli Italiani 16 721
Garduño, Mario Schjetnan *see* SCHJETNAN GARDUÑO, MARIO
Gare, Church of the Annunciation 5 156
Gareau de la Seynie, Jean-Baptiste-Joseph du 19 397
Garega I 3 147
Garelli, Tommaso 12 717
Garemijn, Jan Antoon 12 147*
works 3 *561*, 562; 31 341
Garemyn, Jan 29 668
Gareth, Benedetto 30 1
Gargallo, Pablo 11 569; 12 148*
groups and movements 11 568; 23 260
works 12 *148*; 16 57, *57*; 29 295
Gargallo, Pablo, Museo *see under* SARAGOSSA
Gargallo i Catalán, Pau 29 329
Gargar 17 499
Gargas 11 *505*; 12 149*; 25 *470*, 476, 477, 478, 484, 485
Gargilesse 26 599
Gargiolli, Giovanni 12 149*
patrons and collectors 13 915
works 2 212; 8 378; 25 426, 438
Gargiulo, Domenico *see* SPADARO, MICCO
gargoyles 12 149–50*, *150*; 13 390
Garh Dhanaura 12 150–51*; 15 *285*, 467
Garhi *see* TELIAGARHI
Garh Mauryan 29 824
Garibaldi (family) 16 725
Garibaldi, Giuseppe 1 152

Garífuna 2 145; 3 621, 622; 5 754; 14 712
garilla 21 546, 562
Garimberto, Gerolamo 12 151*; 13 541
Garin (family) 20 664
Garin, Abbot of Saint-Michel-de-Cuxa 27 567
Garka, Peter 5 156
Garlake, Peter 15 105, 107
Garland 2 364
Garland, Colin 12 151*; 16 884
Garland, Henry 29 426
Garland, John of 23 679
Garland, Nicholas (Withycombe) 12 151–2*
garlands 17 519
garlic 12 621
Garlick, Beverly 12 152*
Garlick & Cranwell 23 66
Garm 30 *252*
Garmendia, Francisco 31 753
Garmerwolde Church 22 819
Garnaas, Jørgen 23 238
Garnache, Jehançon 6 414; 10 836; 31 384
Garncarsko 25 109
Garner, Harry (Mason) 7 155; 12 152*
Garner, Matthew 10 305
Garner, Robert 33 136
Garner, Thomas 2 594; 4 214; 5 731; 16 824; 25 836; 28 279; 30 743
Garneray, Auguste (-Simon) 4 303; 12 153–4*
Garneray, Hippolyte (-Jean-Baptiste) 12 153
Garneray, Jean-François 4 556; 8 556; 12 153*
Garneray, (Ambroise-) Louis 12 153*
garnets 12 268, I
historical and regional traditions
Afghanistan 1 *206*
Ancient Near East 1 876
Anglo-Saxon 10 322; 30 *44*
Aztec 22 164
Buddhism 1 *206*
Czech Republic 8 *414*, 416–17*
Egypt, ancient 10 29; 12 246
England 10 322
Germany 21 *162*
Greece, ancient 12 248
Merovingian 21 162, *162*
Mesoamerica, Pre-Columbian 22 164
Rome, ancient 27 *103*
uses
abrasives 7 11; 16 859
bowls 14 *171*
clasps 30 *44*
crosses 8 *414*
fibulae 21 *162*
jewellery 10 29; 17 525
mosaics 22 158, 164
necklaces 27 *103*
reliquaries 1 *206*
seals 12 248
Garni 2 *423*; 12 154–5*
jewellery 2 440
khatchk'ars 2 435
mosaics 2 429
temple 2 425, 433; 12 *154*
Garnier, Antoine 18 745
Garnier, (Jean-Louis-) Charles 5 824; 10 683; 12 155–7*
architecture 25 172
casinos 21 830
observatories 23 *342*
opera houses 3 465; 8 281; 9 326; 11 522, *525*, 546, 565, 659; 12 *156*, *157*; 22 330; 23 546; 24 125; 29 525, 843, *844*; 30 677
assistants 14 87
collaboration 14 238; 19 153; 22 732; 23 342; 24 221
Garnier, (Jean-Louis-) Charles—cont.
competitions 7 666
drawings 2 334
groups and movements 2 643; 26 500; 28 345, 346
interior decoration 3 396
pupils 18 116
staff 12 746
Garnier, Daniel 6 443; 10 329
Garnier, Etienne-Barthélemy 9 417; 12 158*; 31 373
works 12 *158*
Garnier, François 12 159; 15 97; 21 797; 27 494
Garnier, Louis 12 159*; 31 56
Garnier, Paul 7 447
Garnier, Pierre (1720-1800) 11 591; 12 159*
Garnier, Pierre (*b* 1928) 7 699
Garnier, Tony 7 695; 11 525; 12 159–61*
assistants 8 589, 894
collaboration 25 663; 31 243
groups and movements 21 780; 26 15
pupils 22 120
staff 8 63
works 3 176; 11 526; 12 *160*; 19 847; 24 129; 31 728
workshop 24 130
writings 11 526; 31 235
Garnier de Rochefort, Abbot of Clairvaux 7 352
Garnish (family) 23 251
garnitures 9 28, 29; 10 *309*
Garo 3 165
Garofalini, Giacinto 4 320; 11 679
Garofalo 11 4; 12 161–2*; 25 736
collaboration 5 843; 9 185; 11 76
methods 18 898
patrons and collectors 4 411; 5 848; 10 523; 11 5; 19 238; 24 833; 27 729; 32 774
pupils 5 842
teachers 4 195
works 11 5; 12 *162*
Garolli, Pierfrancesco 5 614
Garon, Annie de 12 824
Garona, Tommaso, da 30 793
Garouste, Elizabeth 11 584
Garouste, Gérard 11 553; 12 162*
Garovaglio *see* ALLIO
Garovaglio Painter 10 614
Garove, Michelangelo 12 163*; 13 750; 17 707, 708; 28 14, 15
Garovo, Leonardo 33 637
Garranes (Co. Cork) 15 872
Garrard 10 335; 11 621; 12 163–4*
Garrard, George 12 164*
patrons and collectors 14 146; 27 358
reproductive prints by others 1 647
teachers 12 646
works 2 99; 27 357
Garrard, James 12 163
Garrard, James Mortimer 12 163
Garrard, Mary D. 31 673; 33 312
Garrard, R., J. & S. 12 163
Garrard, Robert (1758-1818) 12 163
Garrard, Robert (1793-1881) 12 163
Garrard, R. & S. 12 163
Garrard, Sebastian 12 163
Garrard, Sebastian Henry 12 163
Garrard & Co. Ltd 10 346; 12 164; 19 594, 596
Garreau, Louis E. F. 10 126
Garreaud, Eduardo 6 598
Garreaud Ferrier, Fernando 24 518
Garreta, Raimundo Madrazo *see* MADRAZO GARRETA, RAIMUNDO
Garrett, Daniel 6 66; 11 242; 14 808; 23 780, 860; 24 275; 26 474
Garrett, Thomas 29 419, 496
Garrez, Pierre-Joseph 6 377; 12 164*
Garrick, David 12 164–5*; 19 728; 30 675; 33 217
architecture 1 138
costumes 30 675
furniture 7 171, 172, 486; 8 528
paintings 7 786; 14 640; 24 810; 33 692
productions 7 340
sculpture 6 528; 27 243
silver 10 333
staff 30 680
Garrick St Ring 19 579
Garriga y Roca, Miguel 12 165*; 21 315
Garrison, Edward B. 12 165*
Garrison Collections *see under* LONDON → Coutauld Institute
garrisons 21 554
Garro, Bernardo de 29 337
Garro, Fermín 29 336
Garro, Lamberto de 29 337
Garrod, Dorothy 2 63
Garrowby Hall (N. Yorks) 31 37
Garrucci, Raffaele 12 165–6*
Garrus 16 407
Garshin, Vsevolod (Mikhaylovich) 12 166*
Garstang, John
excavations
Hazor 14 273
Hierakonpolis 14 513
Jerico 1 893; 17 483, 484
Meroë 21 160
Mersin 1 893; 19 519; 21 166
Sakça Gözü 1 893; 27 598
Garsten Abbey 2 781, 783; 29 838
Garstin, Alethea 12 166
Garstin, John 5 418; 15 402; 31 241
Garstin, Norman 4 657; 12 166*; 16 17; 23 26
Gartenberg, Wolko 24 309
Garter, Order of the *see* ORDER OF THE GARTER
garters 22 *651*
Garthorne, George 10 329, 330
Garthwaite, Anna Maria 10 357; 26 500
works 10 *357*; 30 X3
Gartman, Viktor (Aleksandrovich) 1 72; 12 166*; 27 580; 28 837
Gärtner, Andreas (Johann) 12 167*; 22 308; 28 186
Gärtner, Christoph *see* GERTNER, CHRISTOPH
Gärtner, Eduard *see* GAERTNER, EDUARD
Gärtner, Friedrich von 12 167–8*
architecture 12 *167*; 18 123; 22 300; 33 282
churches 7 871; 33 282
libraries 12 376; 19 317
monuments 33 282
palaces 2 673, *674*; 11 128; 13 348, 359; 18 124
synagogues 17 547
villas 2 591; 32 554
groups and movements 13 612; 25 193, 789; 27 334, 336
patrons and collectors 33 282
pupils 5 217; 11 34; 14 212; 17 518; 18 493; 32 683; 33 30
teachers 11 129; 33 40
Gärtner, Georg, I (*d* 1612) 12 168; 15 145
Gärtner, Georg, II (*c.* 1575/80-1654) 9 446; 12 168–9*; 17 711; 33 130
Garton Slack 6 481
Gärtringen Church 32 821
Garvagh *Madonna* 25 906
Garvey, Marcus 1 442
Garwood, G. F. 25 817
Gary, Elbert 11 774
Garza, Silvia 33 472
Garza Treviño, Fernando 21 397; 22 21
Garzi, Luigi 12 169*; 19 816; 20 805
Garzoni (family) 12 118
garzoni 12 169*
Garzoni, Giovanna (?1600-70) 11 229; 12 169–70*; 28 8
Garzoni, Giovanni (*fl c.* 1500) 1 554
Gascar, Henri 10 249; 12 170*
Gascar, Pierre 12 170
Gascard, Henri *see* GASCAR, HENRI
Gascars, Henri *see* GASCAR, HENRI
Gasch, Sebastià 8 465
Gaschin, Anna Barbara von, Countess 25 122
Gascoigne, Edward 12 7
Gascon, Ponciano Ponzano y *see* PONZANO Y GASCON, PONCIANO
Gascoyne, David 30 22
Gąsiorowski, Feliks 10 760
Gaskell, Elizabeth 9 384
Gaskin, Arthur Joseph 4 87; 10 336; 17 528
books 4 *87*
Gaskin, Georgina 17 528
gaslight papers *see under* PHOTOGRAPHY → materials
gas-liquid chromatography *see under* TECHNICAL EXAMINATION → types
gasoliers *see under* LAMPS → types
gasometers 23 325
Gaspar, Bartolomeu 20 464
Gaspar, Jean-Marie 3 572
Gaspari, Antonio 3 202; 19 629, 630; 24 537; 30 669; 32 188
Gaspari, Giovanni Paolo 30 669
Gaspari, Maksim 28 860
Gaspari, Pietro 1 598; 30 669
Gasparini, Gaspare 19 689
Gasparini, Matteo 29 304, 341
works 29 *304*
Gasparini, Paolo 12 170–71*
Gasparino di Antonio 24 520
Gasparoni, Francesco 24 447
Gasparo Padovano 12 171*, 907; 27 807
attributions 20 III
Gaspars, John Baptist 9 211; 19 123, 124; 26 393
Gasperini, Gian Carlo 8 181*
Gasq, Paul 10 771; 22 92
Gasquet, Joachim 25 747
Gasse, Luigi 22 474; 23 340
Gasse, Stefano 22 474; 23 340
Gassel, Lucas 3 554; 12 171–2*
works 12 *171*; 18 706
Gassen, Pierre 3 610
Gasser, Franz 12 172
Gasser, Hans 2 802; 12 172*
collaboration 16 811
pupils 14 364; 16 811
works 10 907; 26 378
Gasser, Josef 2 802; 30 888
Gasset, José Ortega y *see* ORTEGA Y GASSET, JOSÉ
Gassion, Master 27 799
Gassner, Hyazinth, Abbot of Steingaden 33 172
Gasson, Barry 22 367
Gasson, Barry, Architects 28 232, 273
works 28 *231*
gas stations *see* SERVICE STATIONS
Gastaldi, Andrea 13 695
Gastaldi, Giacomo 2 696
Gastaldi, Panfilo 10 853
Gasteiz *see* VITORIA
Gastellu, Mario 2 397
Gastón, Miguel 25 823
Gaston de Phebus 3 879
Gasulla 29 365
see also REMIGIA
Gasur *see* NUZI
Gat, Dora 16 566; 17 493
Gat, Moshe 16 567
Gatch, Lee 13 214
Gatchell, George 32 903
Gatchell, Jonathan 32 903
Gatchina 12 173*; 27 *363*, 376; 33 579
palace 4 745; 12 173; 27 402
GATCPAC (Grup d'Artistas i Tècnicos Catalans per el Progrés de l'Arquitectura Contemporània) 12 177; 29 309, 321
members 28 483; 29 87; 31 184
see also GATEPAC
Gate, Simon 8 803; 14 65; 30 102
Gåtebo 32 523
Gatecliff Shelter 2 *302*
gate-houses 3 209; 12 173–6*; 14 420; 21 550; 24 *275*
England 4 *770*; 6 59; 10 229; 12 175, *175*, 176; 14 *420*; 27 *526*
France 12 *174*, 175–6
Gothic 4 *770*
gate-leg tables *see under* TABLES → types
Gatell, Josep Mirabent *see* MIRABENT GATELL, JOSEP
gate lodges 12 *176*, 176–7*
GATEPAC (Grupo de Artistas y Técnicos Españoles para el Progreso de la Arquitectura Contemporánea) 3 219; 12 177*
collaboration 3 217
members 12 58; 29 273
periodicals 24 452
works 22 365
see also GATCPAC
gates 7 357–61*
historical and regional traditions
Assyrian 7 *813*
Austria 2 *822*
Buddhism 18 280
Byzantine 27 *344*
China 7 361*
Confucianism 18 280
France 23 *147*
Germany 7 *358*
Greece, ancient 7 358
Hungary 15 *9*
Indian subcontinent 7 360–61*; 13 886; 15 283
Iran 16 264
Islamic 16 216, 264
Italy 7 *360*; 16 *634*; 32 *342*
Japan 7 361*; 16 *786*; 17 215
Korea 18 *262*, 279–80*
Malta (Republic of) 20 *217*
Poland 7 *359*
Rome, ancient 7 358, *358*; 23 *147*; 32 *342*
Spain 5 *202*; 16 216
Syria 27 *344*
Syria-Palestine 30 185
Thailand 30 639
materials
copper 7 *813*
iron 12 174
silver 20 *217*
wood 30 639
wrought iron 2 *822*; 15 *9*
see also DOORWAYS; PORTALS
Gates, Bill 13 301
Gates, William 27 720
Gateshead, Team Valley Trading Estate 10 749
Gateway of the Sun *see under* TIAHUANACO
gateways 6 56*
historical and regional traditions
Austria 2 *778*, *786*
Buddhism 31 *160*, 160–61*
Cambodia 2 *60*
China 6 675
see also PAILOU
Czech Republic 25 *433*
Egypt 5 *396*
Germany 4 *777*

gateways
historical and regional traditions—cont.
Greece, ancient 13 391; 24 417; 26 909, 909
Helladic 22 396
Indian subcontinent 4 290; 15 377; 31 160, 160–61*
Indonesia 15 768
Ireland 26 475
Islamic 5 396; 21 582, 583–4, 584
Italy 5 616; 24 886; 26 891; 27 761, 762
Java 15 768
Micronesia, Federated States of 23 716
Morocco 21 584
Mycenaean 22 396
Nepal 5 103
Pacific Islands 23 716
Rome, ancient 26 864, 891, 909, 909
Russia 32 663, 663
Spain 27 481
Syria-Palestine 30 190, 190
Taiwan 30 246
Turkey 24 417
materials 26 891
brick 4 777
types
candi bentārs 15 767, 768
gopuras
Cambodia 5 474
Indian subcontinent 6 580; 13 3–5*, 4; 15 239, 329, 333–4, 335, 398, 398; 20 74
toraṇas 5 103; 15 431; 31 160, 160–61*
see also PROPYLAIA
Gathering of Manna, Master of the 20 680*; 22 835
gatherings 4 342; 16 353
Gatineau 23 632
Gatley, Alfred 26 288
Gatling, John 26 411
Gatta, Bartolomeo della *see* BARTOLOMEO DELLA GATTA
Gatta, Saverio della 22 480
Gattamelata 3 636
Gattamelata, Jacopo 3 658
Gattapone 2 42, 628; 13 65
Gattapone, Matteo di *see* MATTEO DI GATTAPONE
Gatteaux, Jacques-Edouard 12 177–8*
Gatteaux, Nicolas-Marie 2 25; 12 177*; 20 922
Gatti, Annibale 4 507; 20 482; 25 74
Gatti, Bernardino 12 178*
assistants 29 428
collaboration 12 29
pupils 2 92, 93
works 2 128; 24 196; 25 250
Gatti, Gasparo de' 32 215
Gatti, Giovan Battista 16 730
Gatti da Urbino, Battista de 16 736
Gatti da Urbino, Camillo de 16 736; 31 741
works 31 742
Gattinara, Francesco di 12 719
Gattucci, Giambattista 5 845
Gatwick Airport (W. Sussex) 1 494
Gau, Franz Christian 12 178*
pupils 28 398
works 3 123; 11 521; 25 172
writings 20 901
Gaübe, Güdrün 21 67
Gaubert 2 660
Gaucelm, Jaubert 20 757
Gaucher, Charles-Etienne 12 178–9*; 19 11; 27 484
Gaucher, François-Tranquille 9 421
Gaucher, Yves 12 179*; 13 2; 22 39; 25 28
Gaucher de Reims 26 114
Gaucherel, Léon 5 23; 25 868
Gauchez, Léon 6 519
Gaucourt, Charles de 11 724; 20 699
Gauda, Shashanka *see* SHASHANKA, Ruler
Gaudefroy-Demombynes, Maurice 10 804
Gaudêncio, Amadeu 8 164
Gaudernack, Gustav 23 236
Gaudhu 15 632
Gaudí (i Cornet), Antoni 12 179–83*; 25 172, 173; 29 307, 308, 320
architecture 29 273
apartments 2 216; 19 171
architectural decorations 23 333, 547; 29 329; 30 506
buttresses 20 581
cathedrals 3 106
chapels 4 789
churches 3 216; 7 277; 12 182; 29 886
housing 12 181
presbyteries 23 881
skyscrapers 28 833
stereotomy 29 637
villas 25 II2
assistants 29 321
collaboration 3 764; 17 679; 27 304; 29 321; 31 183
furniture 29 319, 320, 320, 321
groups and movements 2 568; 3 216, 219; 10 697; 13 204; 21 779; 26 14
interior decoration 29 308, 308
models 2 337
mosaics 21 IV2; 22 158, 163, 164
parks 24 181
patrons and collectors 13 782–3
stained glass 29 508
tiles 22 158; 29 308
Gaudibert, Louis-Joachim 12 207
Gaudibert, Mme 9 288
Gaudier, Henri *see* GAUDIER-BRZESKA, HENRI
Gaudier-Brzeska, Henri 11 568; 12 183–4*; 26 59
groups and movements 19 622; 23 437; 25 380; 32 700, 701
patrons and collectors 9 716; 14 132; 25 823
works 10 267; 12 184
Gaudin, Henri 12 185*
Gaudin, Paul 2 218; 33 553
Gaudissart, Emile 3 462; 5 841; 11 644; 27 322
Gaudotos 13 552
Gaudreaus, Antoine-Robert 12 185*
attributions 7 194
collaboration 7 657
patrons and collectors 4 554; 11 626; 28 527
works 1 110; 5 379; 7 657, 658; 11 590, 591, 593, 596
Gaudreaus, François-Antoine 12 185
Gaudron, Aubertin 11 589
Gauermann, Carl 12 185
Gauermann, Friedrich (August Matthias) 2 796; 12 185–6*; 19 339; 32 444
Gauermann, Jakob 2 796; 12 185
Gauffier, Faustine 12 186
Gauffier, Louis 12 186*
Gauffier, Pauline *see* CHATILLON, PAULINE
gaufrage 10 178; 17 275
Gaugain, (Armand-Pierre-) Henri 12 186–7*
Gaugain, Thomas 12 187*; 30 374
Gauger, V. 12 856
gauges 13 411
gauging 4 786, 787
Gauguin, Jean 8 749; 24 549
Gauguin, Paul 2 149; 7 674; 11 667; 12 187–96*, 497; 15 156; 25 582, 584; 30 290
attributions 5 529
ceramics 6 462
collaboration 11 606
dealers 9 425; 19 10; 26 107; 32 686
exhibitions 2 447; 10 680; 24 142; 26 546; 28 171
frames 11 418
groups and movements
Cloisonnism 7 451, 452
Frie Udstilling 11 790
Golden Fleece (Zolotoye Runo) 12 870
Impressionism 15 155, 156
Nabis 10 693; 22 421
Pont-Aven 18 717; 25 214, 215
Post-Impressionism 25 355, 356, 358
Symbolism (movement) 30 168–9, 170
Synthetism 30 173–4
methods 5 654, 655; 7 630
paintings 7 675; 10 414; 11 547; 12 193; 30 170, 174
genre 12 296
landscape 12 196
religious 12 190
still-lifes 29 670
patrons and collectors 30 361
Barnes, Albert C. 3 251; 12 769
Cochin, Denys (-Pierre-Augustin-Marie), Baron 7 496
Cone (family) 7 702
Courtauld, Samuel (1876-1947) 8 62
Degas, (Hilaire-Germain-) Edgar 8 622
Fürstenberg, Pontus 11 851
Lurcy, Georges 24 183
Maitland, Alexander 28 272
Matisse, Henri (Emile Benoît) 20 822
Morozov, Ivan (Abramovich) (1871-1921) 22 135, 136
Ōhara, Magosaburō 23 371
Reber, Gottlieb Friedrich 26 59
Rouart, Henri(-Stanislas) 27 238
Sadler, Michael 22 55
Schuffenecker, (Claude-) Emile 28 172
Shchukin, Sergey (Ivanovich) 28 569
Śleẃinski, Władysław 28 841
Stein, Leo 29 604
Tetzen-Lund, Christian 30 532
Whitney, John Hay 33 150
Wildenstein, Georges 33 182, 183
personal collection 6 375; 15 154; 24 883
prints 25 624
lithographs 19 488, 490
monotypes 21 896; 25 616
woodcuts 12 195; 25 583, 624; 29 557; 33 361, 361–2
pupils 14 89; 21 410; 22 421; 28 484
reproductive prints by others 21 869
sculpture 11 567, 568; 12 191, 194
tapestries 30 326
writings 2 732; 22 379
Gauguin, Paul René 23 227
Gauhati
Kamakhya Hill 15 396
State Museum of Assam 15 181
Gaul *see* FRANCE
Gaul, August 12 196–7*
dealers 5 924
groups and movements 2 642
pupils 21 66; 29 491
reproductions in porcelain 21 67
teachers 12 407
works 2 100; 12 196; 14 644
Gaul, Winfried 13 727
Gauld, David 12 197*; 29 508
Gaulle, Edme 27 309, 547
Gaulli, Giovanni Battista 12 197–203*; 26 842
collaboration 5 770; 31 370
drawings 12 202
frames 11 393, 394
mosaics 26 810; 31 314
paintings
frescoes 12 199; 15 138; 16 671; 17 510; 25 852; 26 823; 29 830; 32 101
oil sketches 12 201; 23 381
portraits 27 172
patrons and collectors 1 728; 6 584, 585; 11 32; 17 509; 24 225; 26 824
pupils 1 732; 3 920; 5 770; 20 903; 23 348
reproductive prints by others 29 399
Gaulon, C.-C.-M.-N. 13 249; 19 486
Gault, Jacques-Joseph de 11 633, 636
Gault de Saint-Germain, Pierre-Marie 12 203*
Gaultier, Germain 4 866; 20 288; 26 204
Gaultier, Jacques 4 390
Gaultier, Jean 24 775
Gaultier, Jean-Paul 9 294
Gaultier, Léonard 10 392; 12 203–4*
collaboration 33 669
works 4 746; 5 814; 9 388
Gaultier, Pierre 12 203
Gaumont film studios 30 216
Gaunt, Adrian 2 336
Gaunt, T., & Co. 2 766
gauntlets 2 469
Gaur 12 204*; 15 279, 370; 16 105
architecture 15 195, 351, 352–3*
Chiragh Minar 15 352
citadel 15 352
Dakhil Darwaza 15 352
Firuza Minar *see* Chiragh Minar
fortifications 21 591
Hajatgah tomb 15 352
Kutwali Darwaza 15 352
mosques
Bara Sona Mosque 15 352, 353
Chamkatti Mosque 15 352
Chhota Sona Mosque 15 353
Darasbari Mosque 15 352, 686
Gumnant Mosque 15 353
Jahanian Jahangasht Mosque 15 352
Jan Janiyan Mosque *see* Jahanian Jahangasht Mosque
Lattan Mosque 15 352, 353
Qadam Rasul Mosque 15 352
Tantipara Mosque 15 352
'Umar Ghadi Mosque *see* Tantipara Mosque
Putol tomb 15 352
Gauricus, Pomponius 12 204–5*; 22 377
works 2 356; 23 487; 28 509; 30 496; 31 302
Gauron, Nicolas-François 8 776; 21 137
Gausachs, Josep 9 117
Gausdal 25 175
Gausel 15 873
Gaussel, Jean 24 159
Gaussian curvature 20 579
Gausson, Léo 12 205*; 22 745
Gaustad 23 221
Gauszke, Briccius *see* GAUTSZKE, BRICCIUS
Gautama, Siddharta *see* SIDDHARTA GAUTAMA
Gautamiputra 15 430
Gautamiputra Yajna Satakarni, King (*reg c.* late-2nd cent.) (Satavahana) 27 866
Gautelmi of Trets, Melchior 6 469
Gautherot, Claude (1729-1802) 12 205
Gautherot, Claude (1769-1825) *see* GAUTHEROT, PIERRE
Gautherot, Pierre 12 205–6*
Gauthey, Emiland-Marie 12 206*; 24 174
Gauthier, Charles 30 417
Gauthier, Jean 9 325
Gauthiot d'Ancier, Fernand 11 586; 27 682
Gautier, Amand (-Désiré) 8 820; 12 206–7*; 19 381
Gautier, Henri 4 804
Gautier, Lucien Marcelin 20 473
works 20 474
Gautier, (Pierre-Jules-) Théophile 12 207–8*
groups and movements 20 498; 26 500
personal collection 15 843; 17 440
works 2 530; 10 555; 21 778; 24 837
illustrated 26 481; 33 669
Gautier-Dagoty (family) 21 416
Gautier-Dagoty, Arnault-Eloi 12 209
Gautier-Dagoty, Edouard 12 209; 18 810; 21 416; 25 623
Gautier-Dagoty, Fabien 12 209
Gautier-Dagoty, Jacques-Fabien 11 541; 12 208–9*; 13 220; 21 6; 25 590, 623
Gautier-Dagoty, Jean-Baptiste-André 12 208, 209
Gautier-Dagoty, Louis-Charles 12 209
Gautier-Dagoty, Pierre-Edouard 4 391
Gautier de Marvis, Bishop of Tournai 3 542; 31 221
Gautier de Mortagne 18 757
Gautier de Varinfroy 13 42
Gautr 32 530
Gautreau, Mme 27 840
Gautron, Christophe-Paul, Marquis de Robien *see* ROBIEN, CHRISTOPHE-PAUL GAUTRON, Marquis de
Gautron de Robien, Paul-Christophe *see* ROBIEN, PAUL-CHRISTOPHE GAUTRON DE
Gautszke, Briccius 2 480; 12 209*
Gauvain, Mansuy 22 455
Gauvain of Bordeaux 2 467
Gauvreau, Claude 2 839; 26 77
Gauvreau, Pierre 2 839; 5 568; 26 76
Gauw, Gerard 10 391
gauze 28 715; 30 551*
China 7 46; 30 551
Japan 17 306, 313; 30 551
Mesoamerica, Pre-Columbian 21 261
Vietnam 32 489
Gauzelin, Saint 11 614
Gauzfredus 9 152; 12 209*; 26 641
Gauzlin, Abbot of Saint-Benoît-sur-Loire 27 533
Gauzlin Gospels *see under* GOSPEL BOOKS → individual manuscripts
gavākṣa see CANDRAŚĀLĀ
Gavard, Jacques-Dominique-Charles 12 723
Gavarni, Paul 10 781; 12 209–11*; 24 605
patrons and collectors 30 32
works 4 364; 5 758; 12 210, 896; 19 484; 20 602; 25 345; 27 871; 31 704
Gavarron, Isoarde 25 793
Gavassa, Quintilio 7 612
Gavet, Emile 9 424; 21 613; 24 551

Gavilán, Baltazar 24 508
works 24 *507*
gavit‘ see under HALLS → types
Gavrilenko, Grigory I. 31 560
Gavrilov, Fyodor 27 434
Gavrinis 11 *504*; 12 211*; 25 *470*, 508
rock art 25 511
stone-carvings 12 *211*
tombs 5 780–81
Gawharshad (Timurid) 30 917, 919*
architecture 14 430; 16 196, 197, 200; 20 548; 22 194
Gawhar Sultan 16 334
Gawilgarh 15 382
Chhoti Mosque 15 382
Great Mosque 15 382
Gawra, Tepe 2 639; 12 211–12*; 21 *267*, 271
acropolis 12 *212*, 212
architecture 21 281
jewellery 1 873
pottery 1 894; 21 *305*, 306; 31 152
seals 1 856, 877; 21 270
temples 21 270, 281
tokens 21 270
Gay, Derrick 31 339
Gay, G. Yu. 21 696
Gay, Jan Jakub 12 212*; 25 99; 32 871
Gay, John 4 361; 9 379; 13 324; 17 904; 28 221
Gay, Nikolay (Nikolayevich) *see* GE, NIKOLAY (NIKOLAYEVICH)
Gay, Victor 10 209
Gay, Walter 3 156; 12 212–13*
Gaya 4 213*; 15 *279*
Gayakarna, Ruler (*reg* 1123-53) (Haihaya) 14 51
gay and lesbian art 10 476, 482, 483; 12 213–19*, *214*, *215*, *216*, *217*, *219*; 23 297
Gayane, Saint 9 732
Gayangos, Juan 32 169
Gaya Nuño, Juan Antonio 12 220*
Gaydarov, Stoyan 5 159
Gaye, Giovanni (Johann Wilhelm) 12 220–21*
Gaye, Howard 2 333
Gayer-Anderson, R(obert) G(renville) 2 306; 10 90, 92; 15 742
Gayet, Albert 10 82
Gayfere, Thomas 32 825; 33 446
Gayfetjyan, Vahram 2 432
Gaykhatu, Khan (*reg* 1291-5) (Ilkhanid) 16 360
Gaymanovaya Mogila 4 111
Gay Men's Press 12 218
Gaynor, John P(lant) 12 221*
works 14 787; 23 39; 27 730; 28 830; 31 592, *592*
Gayo 15 795
Gayrard, Paul 12 221
Gayrard, Raymond 12 221*
gayrawānī script *see under* SCRIPTS → types
Gaytán, Joaquín 13 768
Gayū Sekichin 24 436; 30 256
Gaywood, Richard 3 244; 12 221–2*
Gaza 23 847
mosaic 17 542
pottery 9 632
St Stephen 12 71
synagogue 9 562; 17 542, 558; 27 61
Gaza, Teodoro 8 370
illustrated works 20 III
Gazan 15 483
gazebos 3 185; 12 222*
see also BELVEDERES; PAVILIONS (BUILDINGS)
Gazette des Beaux-Arts 1 154; 4 124; 10 432; 20 524; 24 423, 442; 26 58; 33 183
Gazette du bon ton, La 2 520; 10 824
Gazi 21 654, *680*
Gaži, Dragan 14 596
Gaziantep 9 564; 17 499
Gazini *see* GAGINI
Gazoldo, Maria Diana da 8 427
Gaztelu de Tudela, Martín 29 267
Gazur Gah 16 200
tomb of ‘Abdallah Ansari 16 197, 802; 28 634
Zarnigarkhana 16 200
Gažvič, Vladimir 28 854
Gazzard, Don(ald) 30 161
Gazzard, Donald, & Associates 2 743
Gazzard, Marea 2 762
Gazzarini, Tommaso 19 70; 31 763
Gazzettino delle arti del disegno 20 482; 24 448
Gazzini *see* GAGINI
Gazzola, Conte 12 657
Gazzola, Piero 22 77; 24 2
Gazzotto, Vincenzo 17 443
Gbaguidi Nicolas 3 728
Gbande 1 263; 19 310
Gbaya 1 369
Gboho 21 597
GCI *see* GETTY CONSERVATION INSTITUTE
Gdańsk 12 222–4*, *223*; 23 328; 25 *92*, 135, 137
altars 25 111
amber 1 760, 762, *762*; 7 90
architecture 25 96
Arsenal 4 786
Artus Hall 25 134
churches 13 58
Confraternity of St George 4 783
damask 12 469
embroidery 12 463
fortifications 21 571
furniture 25 118, 119, 120–21
gold 25 126, 127, 137
houses 4 785
interior decoration 25 118
Jewish museum 17 581
metalwork 12 447; 13 162; 25 129, 130
painting 12 390; 25 135
pewter 25 129
railings 25 130
St Mary 1 519; 4 783; 12 223; 25 96, 102, 111
Chapel of Eleven Thousand Virgins 25 110
reliquaries 26 146
Schadius epitaph 10 436
sculpture 13 117; 25 176
textiles 28 715
sashes 25 133
sculpture 13 85; 25 111, 113
State Higher School of Fine Arts 25 142
tiles 25 122
Town Hall 4 783; 17 700; 25 104; 31 237
Great Chamber 4 147, *148*
Small Chamber 4 147
warehouses 32 861
water supply 31 711
GDL *see* GESELLSCHAFT DEUTSCHER LICHTBILDNER
Gdynia 25 *92*, 100, 136
ge see CHINA → halberds
Ge, Nikolay (Nikolayevich) 12 224–5*; 27 391, 579; 31 565; 32 835
GEAM *see* GROUPE D'ETUDE D'ARCHITECTURE MOBILE
Gear, A. M. 22 719
Gear, William 4 87; 7 489; 28 240
gearings 7 765
Gebauer, Christian David 29 72
Gebauer, Kurt 8 388
Gebedzhe 5 159
Gebeil *see* GIBELET
Gebel, Mathes 2 716; 12 225*; 20 920; 23 309, 311
groups and movements 9 447
works 3 70; 9 440; 12 402
Gebel Ahmar 9 813; 30 694
Gebel Barkal 22 467
ceramics 23 284
colossal statue 23 283; 30 237
palace (B1200) 23 281
palace of Amanitore 23 283
sanctuary of Amun 23 281
sculpture 23 282; 29 34
shrines (i) (cult) 23 281
statue of Akhratan 23 282
statue of Aramatelqo 23 282
stelae 23 282
temples 29 386; 30 237
Temple 700 23 283
Temple of Amun 23 281
Gebel Dosha 9 833
Gebelein 9 *774*; 12 225–6*
dress 10 45
paintings 5 655; 12 *226*
reliefs 9 876
stele 9 868
tombs (private)
Ini 12 225
Iti 9 900; 12 225
Gebelein, George Christian 4 480; 31 651
Gebel el-Arak 9 *774*, 827; 12 226*
ivory 10 60
reliefs 9 867, 868
Gebel el-Mawta 28 810
Gebel el-Silsila 9 773, *774*; 12 227*
cenotaph of Senenmut 28 407
sandstone 9 773, 813, 814
Speos of Horemheb 9 811, 833; 12 227, *227*; 29 386
Gebel Hardan Temple 23 283
Gébelin, Antoine Court de *see* COURT DE GÉBELIN, ANTOINE
Gébelin, François 12 227*
Gebel Kibli 10 59
Gebel Qatrani 9 813; 25 775
Gebel Tarif *see* THEBES (i) (EGYPT) → el-Tarif
Gebel Uweinat 9 865
Gebetbuch Kaiser Maximilians 12 385
Gebhard, Archbishop of Salzburg 27 660
Gebhard, Bishop 1 160
Gebhard, Otto 26 88
Gebhardt, Eduard von 10 539; 21 76
Gebrauchsgraphik 4 369
Gebrüder Leistler 19 113
Gebsattel, Johann Philip von 33 294
Gebtu *see* KOPTOS
Gebu 9 876
Gebze
Çoban Mustafa Caravanserai 16 224
Çoban Mustafa Pasha Hamamı 3 376
congregational mosque 16 222
Gechter, (Jean-François-) Théodore 11 564; 12 228*
Gechū 17 400
Gedatsubō *see* JŌKEI (1155-1213)
Geddes, Andrew 9 309; 12 228*; 22 531
Geddes, Margaret Sarah *see* CARPENTER, MARGARET SARAH
Geddes, Norman Bel *see* BEL GEDDES, NORMAN
Geddes, Patrick 12 228–9*; 31 728
collaboration 6 387
groups and movements 12 780
works 17 492; 22 331; 28 238, 240; 30 421
Geddes, Robert 12 229*
Geddes, Wilhelmina 16 41; 29 507; 31 229
works 16 *41*
Geddes Brecher Qualls Cunningham 12 229
Geddington, Eleanor cross 8 197; 22 220
Gedeler, Elias von 12 478
Gedi 1 *407*, 410; 30 56
palace 1 315
Gedikli 1 824
Gediz Church 9 590
Gedko, Bishop of Kraków 32 748
Gedo, Ilka 14 902
Gedon, Lorenz 26 190; 28 374
Gedong Songo 15 *753*, 758, 759
temple 15 756
Gedovius, Germán 12 229–30*; 14 468; 21 386, 387, 397
Geefs (family) 3 572
Geefs, E. 28 41
Geefs, Guillaume 3 613; 5 43; 12 230*
assistants 6 487
collaboration 25 64
pupils 23 1; 32 590
teachers 12 230
works 3 572
Geefs, Jean 12 230
Geefs, Joseph 6 487; 8 831; 12 230; 17 664; 18 670
Geel, Jan Frans van 3 570; 12 230*; 22 839
pupils 8 764; 12 230; 27 282
teachers 14 479
works 25 727, 728
Geel, Jan Lodewijk van *see* VAN GEEL, JAN LODEWIJK
Geel, Jean-François van *see* GEEL, JAN FRANS VAN
Geel, Jean-Louis van 12 230
Geelong, Corio Villa 2 738
Geelong Gold Cup 2 765
Geer, Gerard de, Baron 2 302
Geeraedts, Martin 19 643
Geer-Bergenstrahle, Marie-Louise De *see* DE GEER-BERGENSTRAHLE, MARIE-LOUISE
Geers, de (family) 30 118
Geertgen tot Sint Jans 4 752; 12 230–33*
altarpieces 22 835
attributions 20 636, 637; 22 199
groups and movements 30 456
patrons and collectors 13 919
works 4 752; 12 *231*, *232*; 19 356; 20 723
Geerts, Charles Henri 3 423, 585, 884
Geertsen, Ib 8 736
Geervliet 22 855
Geese Bearer, Master of the *see* PEISSER, HANS
Geest, Cornelis van der 12 233*; 14 23; 27 291
dealing 3 615
paintings 2 196; 3 558; 5 353; 8 464; 10 710; 27 290
Geest, Julius Felix de 12 233
Geest, Symon Juckes de 12 233
Geest, Wybrand (Symonsz.) de, I (1592–*c.* 1662) 12 233*; 28 92
Geest, Wybrand de, II (*d* before 1716) 12 233
Geestigheit *see* CABEL, ADRIAEN VAN DER
Geet, Jacob Sigfridsson 11 94
Geffels, Franz 6 37; 12 913, 914
Geffroy, Gustave 4 626; 12 234*
Géfin, Gyula 30 212
Geflecht 29 435
Gefle Porslinsfabrik 30 101
Gegechkori *see* MARTIVILI
Gegello, Aleksandr 11 244; 12 234*
collaboration 23 144, 391
works 27 578, *578*
Gegello, Alexander I. 17 867
Gegenbach, Joseph *see* CANABAS
Gegerfelt, Victor von 13 30
Gegerfelt, Vilhelm von 7 251
Geghard Monastery 2 *423*; 12 234–5*, *235*
Church of the Mother of God 12 235
Kat'oghike Church 2 435
khatchk‘ars 2 436; 8 198
Gegner, Der 24 427
Gego 12 235*; 33 317
Geguti Palace 9 558
Gehenna Press 3 333
Gehlert, George 12 452
Ge Hong 6 626
Gehr, Ernie 10 688
Gehrmann, Johann Michael 17 677
Gehron & Seltzer 30 468
Gehry, Frank O(wen) 12 236*
house 1 737; 2 552, *552*
works 1 737; 12 *236*; 19 701, 703; 21 650; 33 45
Geiami Shingei *see* SHINGEI GEIAMI
Geigel, Johann Philipp 3 140; 32 120; 33 434
Géigel de Gandía, Luisas 25 702
Geiger, Benno 30 144
Geiger, Johann 10 99
Geiger, Nepomuk 30 205
Geiger, Nicolaus 28 164
Geiger, Peter 13 702
Geiger, Rupprecht 12 237*; 33 635
Geiger, Willi 12 237*
Geiges, Fritz 11 752
Geikie, Walter 12 237–8*; 28 237, 238
Geiler, Hans 30 136
geisa 13 377, *378*
Geisberg, Max (Heinrich) 12 238*
Geiser, Karl 33 737
Geislingen 12 449, 460
Geismar, Hans von *see* HANS VON GEISMAR
Geiss, Johann Conrad 3 804
Geisselbrunn, Jeremias 12 238–9*; 21 127
Geissenklöster 25 490, 493
Geissler, Karl Gottfried 33 417
Geissler, Niklaus 30 136
Geist, C. L. 30 276
Geitlinger, Ernst 13 267
Geizkofler, Zacharias 14 320
Gekel', Yegor 18 851
Gekkei *see* MATSUMURA GOSHUN
Gekkō Ogata *see* OGATA, GEKKŌ
Gekko Otomo *see* OTOMO GEKKO
Gekkōtei Shōjin 17 846
Gela 13 *362*; 21 342
figurines 13 579, 580
pottery 13 499
reliefs 13 *582*
terracotta 13 *582*
town walls 13 389
Gelaesenhuys, Het 3 593
Gelati, Lorenzo 28 318
Gelati Gospels *see under* GOSPEL BOOKS → individual manuscripts
Gelati Monastery 12 *239*, 239–40*, *317*
church 7 262; 12 320
mosaics 12 323
wall paintings 12 323, 324
enamel 12 330
gates 9 160
icons 12 328
metalwork 12 328
St George 25 344
gelatin
forgeries 11 310
glues 1 155
grounds 13 706
moulds 6 7; 21 321
paints 23 792
paper 24 38
photography 9 490, 494; 24 646, 647, 649, 650, 651, 653, 655, 658

gelatin—cont.
printing 6 328; 7 575; 24 650
stucco 29 813
see also SILVER GELATIN
gelatin dry plates see under PHOTOGRAPHIC PLATES → types
gelatin silver papers see under PAPER → types; PHOTOGRAPHY → materials
Gelbke, C. H. von 25 623
Geld, Hendrik van der 28 595
Gelder, Arent de 12 240–41*; 22 846
patrons and collectors 32 377
teachers 14 739; 22 843, 845; 26 166
works 5 657; 9 169; 12 241
Gelder, Dirk van 22 854
Gelder, Godefroy van 14 709
Gelder, J(an) G(errit) van 12 242*
Gelder, Pieter Smidt vom see SMIDT VOM GELDER, PIETER
Gelderen, Willem van 23 450
Gelder-Jost, Ingrid van 12 242
Geldersman, Vincent see SELLAER, VINCENT
Geldorp, George 12 242, 243*, 341
Geldorp, Gortzius 12 242*, 389
Gelduinus, Bernardus see BERNARDUS GELDUINUS
Geldulf, Provost 19 862
Gelede 3 728
Gelemiș see PATARA
Gelfrein, V. G. 19 319
Gel'freykh, Vladimir (Georgiyevich) 12 243*
assistants 3 685
collaboration 15 890; 27 285, 379; 28 570, 571
groups and movements 29 529
pupils 27 284
works 22 174; 27 379, 379
Gelgel 15 785
Gelhi 15 875
Gelhor, Jan 13 162; 25 126
Gelhor, Peter 13 162
Gelibolu see GALLIPOLI
Gelino di Geri 31 141
Gell, William 12 45, 243–4*; 25 193, 207
Gellée, Claude see CLAUDE LORRAIN
Gellerstedt, Albert Theodor 30 80
Gellert, Leon 2 756, 759
Gelli, Edoardo 11 397
works 11 397
Gelli, Giovanni Battista 12 244*; 16 781
Gellius, Aulus 25 45
Gellone Sacramentary see under SACRAMENTARIES → individual manuscripts
Gelmírez, Diego 27 793
Gelnhausen Palace 6 57; 12 245, 245–6*, 361, 364
Gelon 12 802; 30 174*
Gelosi (family) 29 422
Gelosi (company) 30 659
Gelovani, A. 12 327
Gelpke, André 12 246*
Gelsdorp, Gortzius see GELDORP, GORTZIUS
Gelsenkirchen Theatre 18 118
Geltrú 29 330
Gelu, Duke of Wallachia (reg 10th cent.) 26 706
Gelugpa Buddhism see under BUDDHISM → sects
Gely, Fran Cervoni see CERVONI GELY, FRAN
Gem-Aten see KAWA
Gemayel, César 19 8
Gembecki, Piotr, Bishop of Kraków 25 120
gemeenschapskunst see SYMBOLISM (MOVEMENT) → art forms → painting → Netherlands, the
gemellions 14 419
gem-engraving 12 246–67*; 17 520; 26 132
collections see under COLLECTIONS → types
historical and regional traditions
Byzantine 12 254, 254–5*, 255
Carolingian 5 811–12; 12 256
England 12 260, 261, 263, 263; 20 389
Etruscan 12 248–50*, 249
France 12 255, 256, 257, 259–60, 262, 264
Germany 12 260
Greece, ancient 12 246–8*, 247, 248; 13 598
Indian subcontinent 12 252–3*, 253
Islamic 12 253*
Italy 3 817; 12 256, 256, 257–9, 257, 258, 259, 260, 261–3, 263, 264
Levant 16 573
Rome, ancient 12 250, 250–52*, 252
uses
portraits see under PORTRAITS → media
Gemini, Thomas
works 28 210
Geminiano, Bongiovanni di see BONGIOVANNI DI GEMINIANO
Geminiano, Domenico di see DOMENICO DI GEMINIANO
Gemini GEL 10 178; 19 492, 702; 20 607–8; 25 626
Geminus, Thomas 1 841; 10 326; 21 6
Gemito, Vincenzo 12 267–8*; 22 480
collaboration 8 275
groups and movements 32 256, 257
works 12 268; 16 707
Gemlich, Ambrosius 2 455
Gemma, Cornelis 19 64
Gemma Augustea 12 250; 13 914; 24 330
Gemma Claudia 12 251; 14 II2
Gemmai 23 276, 286
Gemma Tiberiana 24 330
Gemmeh, Tell 30 190
Gemmingen, Konrad von, Prince-Bishop of Eichstätt 32 771
Gemmingen, Ulrich von, Archbishop of Mainz 13 720
Gemological Institute of America (GIA) 12 268
Gemoser, Max 7 575
gems 12 268–70*,
historical and regional traditions
Austria 2 824
Belgium 3 609; 26 145
Brazil 12 268; 17 525
Burma 12 268
Byzantine 9 657, 660, 662; 32 212
Carolingian 5 808; 7 513
Central Asia, Western 6 250, 273
China 7 90, 95
Egypt, ancient 12 246*
Georgia 12 329
Germany 4 III; 12 447, 451; 26 145
Gothic 13 194; 32 213
Greece, ancient 13 375
Hungary 9 662
Indus civilization 12 252
Italy 5 808; 16 751; 32 212, 213
Japan 17 387
Ottonian 4 III; 26 145
Romanesque 26 145
Rome, ancient 25 45
Russia 27 419
Spain 29 349
Sri Lanka 29 471
Thailand 12 268
Visigothic 32 617
gems—cont.
technical examination 30 401
techniques
cutting 8 417; 12 269, 269–70*; 17 522
engraving see GEM-ENGRAVING
heating 12 270
irradiation 12 270
polishing 17 522
types see DIAMONDS; EMERALDS; RUBIES; SAPPHIRES
uses
altarpieces 32 213
beads 3 440
book covers 4 III; 7 513; 13 159
bowls 12 V2; 27 419
crosses 8 201
crowns 32 617
embroidery 2 824; 3 609; 6 250; 13 194; 29 349
icons 12 329; 32 212
inkstones 7 95; 17 387
jewellery 6 273
reliquaries 5 808; 26 145
see also HARDSTONES
Genava see GENEVA
Genazzano, Nymphaeum 4 651; 13 703
Genbō 22 496
Gendai Nihon Bijutsu Ten (Contemporary Japanese Art Exhibition) 17 136
Gendall, John 1 121; 12 270*
Gendje see KIROVABAD
Gendre Factory 30 144
Gendron, (Etienne-) Auguste 12 270–71*; 24 396; 30 32
Gendt, A. D. N. van 1 803; 12 271; 21 58
Gendt, Adolf Leonard van (1835-1901) 1 803; 8 299; 10 418; 12 271*
Gendt, A. L. van (d 1986) 14 688
Gendt, J. G. van (fl 20th cent.) 1 803; 12 271; 21 58
Gendt, Johan Godart van (fl 19th cent.) 12 271
genealogies 12 271–3*; 14 416; 21 235; 25 275; 26 557
Genealogy, Masters of the 17 820
Genebelli, Federico 21 568
Geneleos Group 13 430, 445, 592; 15 893; 27 689
Geneleos of Samos 13 444; 27 688
Genelli, (Giovanni) Bonaventura 12 273–4*; 25 550; 28 40
works 12 274
Genelli, Friedrich 12 273
Genelli, Hans Christian 12 273*; 20 867
Genelli, Janus 12 273; 21 370
Genelli, Johann Franz Joseph 12 273
Gen'emon Kinkōzan see KINKŌZAN GEN'EMON
Genepin 22 73
Generación del '52 2 475; 4 262, 265, 268, 270; 7 493; 15 144; 29 51
Generación del Trece 6 597; 13 9
General Dutch Union of Foreign Travel 7 655
Generalić, Ivan 12 274*; 14 595, 596; 22 441
Generalić, Josip 14 596
General Idea 5 569; 12 275*; 24 409
General Motors 8 802; 15 824; 17 722; 20 926
Generation of 1970 2 397
Genesis Initial, Master of the 26 659; 33 240
Genesis Master (fl c. 1235) 2 846
Genesis Master (fl c. 1390) 33 71
Genest, François 24 148
Genet, Jean 3 754; 10 688; 24 144
Geneta Iyasus see AZEZO
Geneva 9 510; 12 275–7*, 276; 26 905; 30 124
Academy 1 107; 12 276
apartments 30 127
art forms and materials
enamel 12 445
lace 30 151
metalwork 30 147
mosaics 9 569
objects of vertu 30 148
pewter 24 579
sculpture 27 12; 30 136
watches 30 148
see also under WATCHES → types
art market 2 561
auction houses 2 561
Bibliothèque d'Art et d'Histoire 30 156
Bibliothèque de la Classe des Beaux-Arts 30 156
Bibliothèque de l'Ecole d'Architecture et des Ecoles d'Art see BIBLIOTHÈQUE D'ART ET D'HISTOIRE
Bibliothèque publique 2 418
Cathedral of St Peter 1 623; 7 257; 12 276, 277*; 13 41; 26 908; 30 125
altarpiece 33 287
choir-stalls 30 136
sculpture 26 635
Collections Baur 7 156; 17 434
Ecole des Beaux-Arts 12 277
Ecole des Arts Décoratifs-Ecole Supérieure d'Arts Appliqués 30 156
Ecole Supérieure d'Art Visuel 30 156
exhibitions 12 277; 16 560
Fondation Diday 8 864
Galerie Ecart 2 447
Hôtel Champbel-Beau-Séjour 8 150
houses 30 126
Maison Clarté 19 44
Musée d'Art et d'Histoire 8 864; 12 277; 25 418; 30 155
Collection Coutan 25 410
Musée de l'Athénée 12 277
Musée Barbier-Mueller 1 437; 23 742
Musée d'Ethnographie 22 795
Musée d'Histoire Naturelle 30 155
Musée Mondiale 22 365
Musée Olympique 25 878
Musée Rath 12 277; 30 127, 154
Palace of the League of Nations 7 293, 669; 11 841; 13 238
Protestant cemetery 6 165
Reformation Monument 5 445, 446
Temple de la Fusterie 30 126
Geneva, Counts of 12 276
Geneva, Peter, Count of 30 313
Geneva Boccaccio, Master of the 20 612, 703, 706
Geneva Latini, Master of the see ROUEN ECHEVINAGE, MASTER OF THE
Geneva School 18 794; 31 363
Genevilliers 24 129
Genevoix, Domingo see DOMINGO GENEVOIX
Genevrière, Marcel 11 601
Genga, Bartolommeo 3 683; 12 278–9*; 27 274; 31 742
Genga, Bernardino 1 845; 9 706
Genga, Girolamo 12 277–8*; 27 273
architecture 12 278
assistants 3 682; 4 856; 7 560
collaboration 3 698; 32 629
patrons and collectors 27 274, 760
pupils 12 278; 18 690; 23 745
Genga, Girolamo—cont.
works 24 536, 567; 27 323; 28 677; 32 546
Genga, Simone 18 690, 691
Genghis Khan (reg 1206-27) (Great Khans) 11 151; 21 882
Geng Wei 6 762
Geng Zhaozhong 7 153
Genichirō Inokuma see INOKUMA, GENICHIRŌ
Génicot, L.-F. 3 620
Gen Iryō 17 412
Génisson, Jules-Victor 3 884
Genius 20 404; 24 445
Geniza documents 16 430, 457, 516; 24 48; 32 312
Genji 31 200
Genk, Openluchtmuseum Bokrijk 3 616
Genkei 17 122
Genkei Araki see ARAKI GENKEI
Genke-Meller, Nina 2 634
Genkichi Takahashi see TAKAHASHI, GENKICHI
Genki Kita see KITA GENKI
Genki Komai see KOMAI GENKI
Genklene 29 53
Genkov, Nikola 31 393
Genlis, Félicité Ducrest de Saint-Aubin, Comtesse de 12 154
Gennadius, Joannes 13 361
Gennadius, Saint 22 247
Gennadiyev, Andrey (Borisovich) 27 581
Gennady, Ivanov 17 868
Gennai Hiraga see HIRAGA GENNAI
Gennari (family) 9 230
Gennari, Bartolommeo 12 279
Gennari, Benedetto (d 1610) 13 785
Gennari, Benedetto, I (1563-1658) 12 279*
Gennari, Benedetto, II (1633-1715) 6 116; 8 141; 12 279–80*
assistants 12 30
teachers 13 785
Gennari, Cesare 12 279; 13 785; 21 539
Gennari, Ercole 12 279
Gennari, Lorenzo 12 279
Gennaro, Antonio Maria 1 732
Genneco, Germán Samper see SAMPER GENNECO, GERMÁN
Genoa 12 280–85*; 16 616, 618
aqueduct 2 242
art forms and materials
ceramics 12 285*
coats of arms 14 410
coins 7 535
coral 7 835; 16 750
cotton 8 37, 37
damask 12 284
embroidery 16 760
façade decoration 10 737
frames 11 393
furniture 5 192; 16 728; 29 304
jewellery 16 750; 17 526
lace 16 754
lacquer 18 614
lampas 12 284
maiolica 16 735
maps 20 363
painting 15 138; 16 674–5
sculpture 16 688, 701–2*; 26 619
shawls 8 37, 37
silk 12 284–5*; 13 197; 16 752, 753; 28 716
staircases 29 523
stucco 29 831
tapestries 16 756
textiles 16 753
velvet 12 284; 16 714; 30 553
Banca d'America e d'Italia 29 411
Camera di Commercio see palazzi → Palazzo Carrega Cataldi
Camposanto di Staglieno 6 166; 31 131

Genoa—cont.
Cemetery of Stalieno 16 706
Collegio dei Gesuiti see palazzi → Palazzo dell'Università
ecclesiastical buildings
Cathedral of S Lorenzo 12 280; 16 627, 725
Chapel of S Giovanni Battista 11 896; 27 775, 776
metalwork 16 742
monument to Giuliano Cybo 25 256
Chiesa delle Vigne 29 831
Grimaldi Chapel 26 137
reliefs 12 574
Oratory of S Giacomo della Marina 6 27
S Ambrogio 1 695, 696; 16 725
SS Annunziata del Vastato 2 127
paintings 24 836
S Bartolomeo degli Armeni 9 658
S Carlo 16 701
S Filippo Neri 11 682; 16 701, 702
S Luca 16 701; 29 831
S Maria Assunta 1 605–6, 607; 16 701
S Maria del Castello 9 264
S Stefano 12 750–51
Forte di Quezzi complex 16 650
gardens 12 115
MacKenzie Castle 16 721
museums
Galleria Nazionale di Palazzo Spinola 29 411
frames 11 392
see also palazzi → Palazzo Spinola (Piazza Pellicceria 1)
Museo Villa Croce 16 777
Palazzo Bianco 1 578; 6 24; 8 552; 24 836
Palazzo Rosso 4 811
collections 16 775; 18 740
drawings 11 9
frames 11 392
frescoes 11 9, 9; 13 816; 15 138
paintings 9 174; 11 9, 393; 24 836, 862
stucco 29 831
palazzi
Palazzo Airoli-Negrone 2 619; 23 539; 24 203
Palazzo Balbi-Senarega 16 647
paintings 6 28, 28
Palazzo Belimbau
frescoes 30 372, 373
Palazzo Bianco see under museums
Palazzo Bombrini 30 373
Palazzo Brignole 24 837
Palazzo Cambiaso 28 396
Palazzo Carrega Cataldi 6 24; 16 712
Palazzo Cataldi see Palazzo Carrega Cataldi
Palazzo Cattaneo
frescoes 5 455, 455
Palazzo Centurione 13 816; 24 836
Palazzo Doria Pamphili 1 657; 3 54; 9 173; 12 281; 25 250
frescoes 5 455; 9 172; 12 283
garden 22 33
gardens 9 173; 12 116
interior decoration 16 712; 24 419
paintings 23 680
Palazzo Doria-Quartara 11 897
Palazzo Doria-Tursi see Palazzo Municipale
Palazzo Ducale 16 647; 30 864
Sala del Maggior Consiglio 8 554
Palazzo Durazzo 29 831, 832
Palazzo Durazzo Bombrini 29 40

Genoa
palazzi—cont.
Palazzo Durazzo-Pallavicini 5 857, 858; 9 480, 485, 487; 13 787; 26 196
Palazzo Ferretti 24 837
Palazzo de Franchi 6 26
Palazzo Granello 2 619; 11 9
Palazzo Grimaldi (via Garibaldi 9) see Palazzo Municipale
Palazzo Grimani see Palazzo Spinola (Piazza Pellicceria 1)
Palazzo Lercari-Parodi 28 396
Palazzo Lomellini Doria 3 34; 7 682
Palazzo della Meridiana 5 455; 6 24
Palazzo Municipale 29 523
Palazzo Negrone see Palazzo Airoli-Negrone
Palazzo Pallavicini-Pessagno 28 395; 29 411
Palazzo Patrone
frescoes 11 53, 53
Palazzo Podestà see Palazzo Stefano Pallavicini
Palazzo Ravashieri-Negroni 12 3
Palazzo Reale 5 555; 6 28; 11 9, 396; 16 701, 702
Palazzo Rosso see under museums
Palazzo Sanfelice 29 525
Palazzo Sauli 11 10; 24 837
Palazzo S Giorgio 11 897; 25 254
Palazzo Spinola (Piazza Pellicceria 1) 11 10, 11; 12 3
see also museums → Galleria Nazionale di Palazzo Spinola
Palazzo Spinola Pessagno (Piazza Corvetto 3) see Palazzi Pallavicini-Pessagno
Palazzo Stefano Pallavicini 6 24; 11 682
Palazzo Tomaso Spinola see Palazzo Pallavicini- Pessagno
Palazzo dell'Università 3 922–3; 29 524
Porta del Molo 1 607
Porta Siberia see Porta del Molo
Stadio Luigi Ferraris 29 489
Strada Nuovissima (Via Balbi) 3 922
Teatro Carlo Felice 3 195; 16 647; 30 684
trade 24 48
urban planning 31 711, 717
Villa Cambiaso 16 712; 32 547
Villa Centurione-Carpaneto 29 783
Villa delle Peschiere see Villa Pallavicino
Villa Doria 9 174; 13 703
Villa Durazzo 24 202
Villa Giustiniani Cambiaso 1 606, 606–7; 5 455
Villa Grimaldi Fortezza 29 372
Villa Gropallo 11 9
Villa Imperiale-Scassi 12 116
Villa Pallavicino 1 607; 13 703; 32 547, 548
interior decoration 16 712
wall paintings 6 24
Villa Spinola di San Pietro 2 126; 29 411
Genod, Michel 26 264
Genoels, Abraham, I (fl 1628-37) 12 285
Genoels, Abraham, II (1640-1723) 4 521; 12 285*, 832; 27 133
Genoels, Peeter 12 285
Genois, Alardin 4 692
Genouillac, Henri de 18 86; 30 422
Genoux & Cie 3 110
Genovés, Juan 12 286*; 13 725; 29 287
Genovese, Gaetano 16 645; 22 474
Genovese, Giuseppe 22 474
Genovesino, il see MIRADORI, LUIGI
Genpaku Sōtan 18 560
Genpaku Sugita see SUGITA GENPAKU
Genpei Akasegawa see AKASEGAWA, GENPEI
genre painting see under PAINTING → types
genre pittoresque 19 723; 26 493–4
Genroku Okumura see OKUMURA GENROKU
Genro Suiō see SUIŌ GENRO
Genryō 27 470
Gensei 17 129
Gensfleisch zur Laden, Johann see GUTENBERG, JOHANN
Genshin 5 118
Genshirō Yamanoto see YAMANOTO GENSHIRŌ
Genshō, Empress 22 501
Gent, Joos van see JUSTUS OF GHENT
Gent, Justus van see JUSTUS OF GHENT
Gente, Jehan de la 32 582
Genthe, Arnold 12 298*
Genthon, István 13 638
Gentil, François 31 382
Gentil, Jean Baptiste 15 654, 702, 714, 741; 16 553
Gentile (family) 6 21; 16 735
Gentile see PRIMO, LUIGI
Gentile (di Niccolò di Massio) da Fabriano 12 298–302*; 13 139, 155; 22 413; 24 16; 28 676; 32 189
assistants 3 648; 12 302
attributions 27 619
collaboration 16 824; 24 861
drawings 25 557
methods 19 354
paintings 16 135, 660
altarpieces 11 184; 12 299, 300; 16 661; 24 861; 29 423
frescoes 16 659; 24 861; 26 765; 32 220
predellas 9 262; 12 301; 25 464
religious 19 356
patrons and collectors 4 747; 7 218, 620; 27 729; 28 271; 29 781
pupils 3 647, 648
religious 12 298
workshop 24 270
Gentile (Partino) da Montefiore del Aso, Cardinal 2 627; 12 303–4*; 20 505
Gentileschi, Artemesia 3 862; 12 304, 306–9*, 308; 16 780
attributions 5 695
collaboration 29 803
groups and movements 30 456
patrons and collectors 12 308; 14 7; 26 307
pupils 12 304; 23 897
reproductive prints by others 17 599
teachers 30 356
works 1 663; 10 476; 12 306, 307
Gentileschi, Francesco 12 304, 306, 308
Gentileschi, Giulio 12 306
Gentileschi, Orazio 12 304–8*; 16 670; 23 294
attributions 6 112; 21 701
collaboration 12 307, 308; 30 355
groups and movements 30 456
patrons and collectors
Aldobrandini, Pietro (ii), Cardinal (1571-1621) 1 595
Borghese, Scipione, Cardinal 30 356
Carol I, King of Romania (reg 1866-1914) 5 792

Gentileschi, Orazio
patrons and collectors—cont.
Charles I, King of England and Scotland (reg 1625-49) 29 801
Charles-Emanuel I, 11th Duke of Savoy (reg 1580-1630) 28 7
Churchill, John, 1st Duke of Marlborough 7 286
Doria, Marcantonio 9 174
Grenville, Richard, 2nd Earl Temple (1711-79) 13 637
Henrietta Maria, Queen of England and Scotland (1609-69) 29 803
Marie de Medici, Queen of France (1573-1642) 4 549
Philip IV, King of France (reg 1285-1314) 14 755
Serra, Giovan Francesco, Marqués di Cassano 28 479
Villiers, George, 1st Duke of Buckingham (1592-1628) 32 576
pupils 12 307
works 2 493; 4 405; 10 805; 11 393, 423; 12 305, 306, 307; 30 355
Gentili, Antonio 12 309*
collaboration 8 202
patrons and collectors 10 524; 25 7
works 16 742
Gentili, Eraclito 26 779
Gentili, Pietro 10 751
Gentilini, Franco 12 309*
Gentilis, Cosmato 1 519
Gentillastre, Henri 16 853
Gentillâtre, Jacques 12 309–10*
Gentils, Vic 3 573; 12 310*
Gentleman, David 4 367
Gentleman's Magazine 2 319
Gentofte
library 8 729
school 28 159
Gentot, Blaise 14 161; 30 872
Gentsche Bijdragen tot de Kunstgeschiedenis 24 439
Gentse Meubel 3 587
Gentz, (Johann) Heinrich 12 310–11*
collaboration 3 792; 12 375; 28 98
patrons and collectors 14 654
teachers 12 902
works 3 792, 807; 12 374; 20 867, 868; 23 490; 28 44; 33 37
Genu, Marie Joseph Gabriel 4 42
Genua see GENEVA
Gen Yamaguchi see YAMAGUCHI, GEN
Genzui Gessen 17 196
geodesic domes see under DOMES → types
Geodesics Inc. 11 835
Geoffrey I, Count of Anjou (reg 958-87) 19 525, 526
Geoffrey II de Villehardouin 7 180
Geoffrey II Martel, Count of Anjou (reg 1040-60) 19 527; 27 552
Geoffrey V Plantagenet, Count of Anjou (reg 1129-51) 14 412, 420; 25 13
Geoffrey de Loudun, Bishop 19 129
Geoffrey de Mountbray, Bishop 8 73; 11 654
Geoffrey de Noiers 33 62
Geoffrey of Monmouth 14 416; 26 564
Geoffrey of Villehardouin 25 51
Geoffrin, Marie-Thérèse 12 312*; 24 136; 25 212
furniture 11 626
paintings 4 517; 19 646; 32 428
sculpture 13 805
Geoffroi d'Ainai 7 351, 371; 11 348; 12 312*
Geoffroy-Dechaume, Adolphe-Victor 12 312–13*; 24 158; 29 610
Geoffroy d'Eu, Bishop of Amiens 1 777
Geoghegan, Trevor 16 18
geography see REGIONALISM (i)
Geoksyur 6 255, 275
geological books 4 360
geomancy
China 6 667, 675, 690, 696, 698, 699; 12 89, 313*, 313; 23 773
Japan 12 95; 17 33
Korea 12 93; 18 268, 269
Vietnam 32 471, 477
geometric abstraction see ABSTRACTION, GEOMETRIC
geometrical centre 2 292
Geometrical Compartment Binder 4 353
Geometric Cut 21 568
geometric tracery see under TRACERY → types → bar
geometry 1 101; 14 407
Greece, ancient 13 400, 400, 413–15*, 414
Islamic 16 133–4*, 143
Rome, ancient 26 924
see also PROPORTIONS (ARCHITECTURE)
geometry (constructive) 20 564–6*, 565; 28 497–8; 29 636–7
Georg, Edouard 11 550
Georg-August-Universität see under GÖTTINGEN
George, Duke of Landshut (reg 1479-1503) 26 365
George, Duke of Saxony (reg 1500-39) 3 69; 8 540; 13 58; 32 830, 831
George, Prince, Duke of Cumberland (1653-1708) 8 454
George, Prince of Wales see GEORGE IV, King of Great Britain
George I, Elector of Hannover see GEORGE I, King of Great Britain
George I, King of Great Britain (reg 1714-27)
architecture 18 634
gardens 33 257
interior decoration 10 277; 14 127; 17 901
metalwork 25 759; 30 299
paintings 13 229; 17 507; 19 165
George I, King of Greece (reg 1863-1913) 24 632; 33 677
George I, Landgrave of Hesse-Darmstadt (reg 1567-96) 8 529
George I Rákóczy, Prince of Transylvania (reg 1630-48) 14 885; 15 7
George II, Duke of Saxe-Meiningen (reg 1866-1914) 30 682
George II, King of Great Britain (reg 1727-60)
gardens 4 805
metalwork 4 62, 63; 24 22
paintings 4 601; 14 640; 17 507; 19 165; 33 675
seals 20 144
George II, Landgrave of Hesse-Darmstadt (reg 1626-61) 8 529
George III, Elector and King of Hannover see GEORGE III, King of Great Britain
George III, King of Great Britain (reg 1760-1820) 10 365; 14 142–5*; 21 409
architecture 6 410; 33 446
books 6 411
cartoons (drawings) 10 368
ceramics 33 377
coaches 10 295
coins 24 887

George III, King of Great Britain (reg 1760-1820)—cont.
collections 2 559; 8 474; 25 412; 28 884; 29 796
decorative works 14 833; 33 226
drawings 1 533; 6 36; 8 95, 474; 9 229, 230; 27 521
pastel 27 359
engravings 3 308; 13 614; 14 79, 280; 27 463; 28 597; 33 373
furniture 32 540
gardens 4 875; 18 5
gems 9 28
gold 12 163; 14 382
jewellery 27 336
medals 20 921
paintings 5 593, 878; 8 105, 474; 10 366; 14 599; 18 892; 25 881; 26 274, 319
history 8 493; 14 586; 33 91
marine 28 481, 482
miniatures 8 83
portraits 25 883; 33 694
religious 33 91, 715
vedute 32 111
porcelain 22 482; 25 193
prints 25 631
sculpture 7 480; 31 477
silver 2 722
sponsorship 25 871
George III, Prince of Montenegro (reg 1490-96) 22 17
George IV, King of Great Britain (reg 1820-30) 9 13; 10 365; 14 142*, 145–7*, 147; 19 586; 25 283
architecture 4 809; 10 297, 361; 14 681; 15 406; 22 527; 25 249; 26 85, 743; 33 249, 447
armour 9 31
ceramics 29 419; 33 377
chandeliers 6 443
coins 24 887
collections 2 559; 7 561; 8 20; 10 487; 26 500
decorative works 27 336; 30 747; 33 448
drawings 10 479
pastel 27 359
engravings 12 640; 27 278
furniture 4 883; 5 192; 8 448; 10 296, 297; 25 712; 30 783; 33 48
gardens 17 905
gems 12 263
gold 12 163
interior decoration 3 79; 8 105; 10 277, 279; 26 84, 85
manuscripts 12 272; 16 341; 21 723; 25 770
paintings 3 239; 8 474; 9 17; 27 853; 28 370, 527; 33 190
allegorical 22 277
animal subjects 1 450; 6 402; 20 477
battle 8 886; 14 754
genre 4 78; 7 572
landscape 11 912
marine 7 431; 28 78
miniatures 14 717
portraits 18 893; 25 283; 29 810; 32 496
porcelain 9 29
porphyry 30 113
prints 7 579
sculpture 2 559; 5 630; 7 480, 502; 14 635; 27 197
silver 9 30; 10 334; 26 85; 28 140; 29 723
George IV, King of Hanover see GEORGE IV, King of Great Britain
George V, Elector of Hanover (reg 1851-66) 17 856
George V, King of Great Britain (reg 1910-36) 3 232; 5 521; 8 675; 14 523; 30 367
George, Ernest 12 315–16*; 25 688
George, Ernest, & Yates 12 315; 17 897
George, Jean 11 630, 632
George, Milton 12 314*; 16 885
George, Stefan 19 31
George, Waldemar 3 753; 17 577; 31 268
George, Walter Sykes 12 314*; 19 822
George, W. S.
works 7 278
George-Frederick, Margrave of Baden-Durlach (reg 1577-1622) 33 434
George-Frederick, Margrave of Brandenburg-Ansbach (d 1603) 4 146
Georgeham (Devon), St George 28 295
George of Antioch 23 845; 26 680; 28 655
George of Kolozsvár 13 160; 14 892; 20 492–3*; 26 710, 719
George of Poděbrady, King of Bohemia (reg 1457-71) 12 314*; 25 425
George & Peto 12 315–16*
pupils 19 819
staff 3 81; 8 580
works 12 315; 25 805; 30 504
Georges, Master 2 115
Georges, Paul 11 410
Georgescu, Ion 12 316*; 29 721
works 26 714, 715
Georges de Saluces 29 397
Georget, Etienne-Jean 12 353
Georget, Jean-Joseph 29 348
Georgetown (Guyana) 13 873, 874, 875
Burnham mausoleum 13 877
Cathedral of the Immaculate Conception 13 875, 876
Church of the Sacred Heart 13 875
City Engineer's Office 13 875
City Hall 13 875
Magistrates Court 13 875
National Art Collection 13 877
National Cultural Centre 13 876
National Insurance Scheme Building 13 876
Parliament Building 13 875
railway station 13 875
St Andrew 13 875
St George's Cathedral 13 875
Seaman's Hospital 13 875
Smith Congregational Church 13 875
Stabroek Market 13 875
State House 13 875
University of Guyana 13 875
Victoria Law Courts 13 875
Georgetown (Malaysia) 20 162
Kapitan Keling Mosque 20 166
George William, Duke of Calenberg and Celle (reg 1665-1705) 6 138; 33 53*
George William, Margrave of Bayreuth (reg 1712-26) 3 428, 429
Georgi, Hadji 5 157
Georgi, Walter 28 143
Georgia 12 316–32*, 317; 16 104, 105
architecture 9 548–9; 12 318–20*
barrows 12 318
book design 12 327
bronze 12 322
carnivals 5 785
carpets 16 481
cathedrals 12 319
churches 12 318–20
basilicas 12 318, 318
Byzantine 7 262; 9 548–9; 30 305, 306
centrally planned 7 256
decoration 7 273, 274; 12 321–2, 323–4
6th cent. AD 12 318; 22 251
Georgia
churches—cont.
10th cent. AD 4 34
12th cent. 31 907
13th cent. 18 69; 30 388
collections 12 331*, 332*
decorative arts 12 328–30*
domes 9 84
embroidery 12 331*
enamel 12 329, 329–30*
felt 10 874
fortresses 12 318; 30 388
gems 12 329
gilding 12 328
gold 12 328–9*, 329
icons 9 623; 12 322–3*, 325–6*, 326, 328, 329; 15 77; 25 341*
languages 12 317
liturgical furnishings 7 279
manuscript illumination 12 317, 322–3*, 324–5*, 325
masonry 12 318
metalwork 12 328–30*
monasteries 8 567; 12 239; 30 305
monuments 12 322
mosaics 12 322–3*
museums 12 332*
ornament 12 318
painting 12 323–4*, 325*, 326–8*, 327
wall 12 322–4*; 30 305
Post-Byzantine 25 344*
Romanesque 8 567
9th cent. AD 12 323
14th cent. 12 324
palls 12 331
patronage 12 331*
plaques 9 658
pottery 12 330*
sculpture 7 274; 12 321–2*, 321, 322
silver 9 658; 12 328, 328–9*, 329
stone 12 318
textiles 12 330–31*
writing 12 317
Georgiades, Pefkios 8 365
Georgiadis, Nicholas 30 688
Georgian Group 5 338
Georgian Society 16 38
Georgian style 12 332–3*; 19 571; 22 743
Georgia Straits see STRAITS OF GEORGIA
Georgic 18 700
see also PASTORAL
Georgiev, Georgi 17 808
Georgiev, Pencho 12 333*
Georgios 21 345
Georgius Codinus 13 808
Georgius Zotori Zapari Fenduli see HERMANNUS DALMATA
Georg van der Paele, Canon 3 612; 10 710; 13 909
paintings 10 709
Georg von Liechtenstein, Prince-Bishop of Trent 2 824; 5 180; 14 433; 18 704
Georgy, I. 27 412
Gepids 21 500, 501
Geppert, Eugeniusz 8 303
Gera 30 793
Gera, Bartolomeo, Bishop 32 689
Geraardsbergen see GRAMMONT
Gerace, Cathedral of the Assumption 16 626; 26 580
Gerada, Mariano 12 333*; 20 214
Gera da Pisa 28 656
Geraerdts, Stephanus 24 357
Gerakan Seni Rupa Baru 15 808
Geraki 9 511; 12 333–4*
churches 9 579; 12 333–4
houses 14 339
Gerald of Wales 31 289
Geraldton, St Francis Xavier Cathedral 2 741
Gerallt Cymro 32 781
Gerard II, Abbot of Echternach 9 698
Gérard, François (-Pascal-Simon) 11 541; 12 334–6*
assistants 13 790
collaboration 4 36; 13 793
groups and movements 26 738
patrons and collectors 11 542
Berry, Caroline de Bourbon, Duchesse de 4 556
Caroline Murat, Queen of Naples (1782-1839) 22 338
Denon, (Dominique-) Vivant 8 764
Isabey, Jean-Baptiste 16 64
Josephine, Empress of the French (1763-1814) 4 303
Louis XVIII, King of France (reg 1814-24) 4 555
Napoleon I, Emperor of the French (reg 1804-14) 4 300
Pourtalès-Gorgier, James-Alexandre, Comte de 25 383
Zamoyski, Stanisław 33 607
pupils 4 836; 6 490; 18 418; 28 132; 29 658
reproductions on porcelain 17 445
reproductive prints by others 2 702; 8 864; 11 319
works 4 303; 8 867; 9 286; 11 541; 12 335; 23 295; 24 140
Gérard, Henri 12 336
Gérard, Jean 3 48
Gérard, Jean-Baptiste 13 306
Gerard, J. G. 1 210
Gerard, John 14 434; 24 296; 26 542; 33 146
works 14 433
Gérard, Marguerite 11 542; 12 336*
collaboration 11 369
patrons and collectors 14 396
teachers 11 366, 369
Gérard, Marie-Anne 21 643
Gérard, Noël 11 596
Gérard de Conchy, Bishop of Amiens 1 777
Gérard de Lenoncourt see JACQUEMIN, GÉRARD
Gerardi, Nicolaus see GERHAERT, NICOLAUS
Gerardo di Pietro 4 274
Gerard of Alsace 22 453
Gerard of Cremona 2 348, 650
Gerardus see GERHARD
Gerard van der Meire 8 501
Gerasa see under JERASH
Gerasime 12 324
Gerasimov, Aleksandr (Mikhaylovich) 12 339–40*; 28 918
groups and movements 2 633; 27 395
works 28 918
Gerasimov, Mikhail M. 20 209
Gerasimov, Sergey (Vasil'yevich) 3 529; 12 340*; 27 396
groups and movements 20 151
pupils 18 392; 28 394; 31 64
Geras Painter 13 520
Gérault d'Areaubert, Claude-Charles 23 510
Gerber, Samuel 2 661–2
Gerbert of Aurillac see SYLVESTER II, Pope
Gerbier, Balthazar 10 363; 12 340–41*; 19 582; 21 615
assistants 23 208
collaboration 12 243
dealing 32 575
pupils 33 244
works 9 480
Gercken, Andreas 8 739
Gercken, Didrik 8 739; 33 161
Gerdts, W. 4 27
Gere, Charles 4 87; 25 556
Gere, John 6 78
Geremia, Cristoforo di see CRISTOFORO DI GEREMIA
Gérente, Henri 3 288; 29 506
Gerevich, Tibor 14 890
Gerf Hussein 9 833, 863; 23 280; 25 874; 29 386
Gerfrid, Bishop of Laon 18 757
Gergely, S. 25 246
Gerger see GARGAR
Gerhaert, Nicolaus 12 341–4*; 16 69; 20 736; 28 149; 29 757; 31 327
assistants 19 771
attributions 13 100; 14 454; 23 205; 33 164
collaboration 29 726
patrons and collectors 13 902
pupils 18 451
works 2 800; 12 343, 344, 401; 13 91, 117; 14 49; 27 125; 31 127; 32 441, 453
Gerhaert, Peter 12 341
Gerhard 12 345*
works 7 588; 13 48, 48
Gerhard II, Archbishop of Bremen 4 742
Gerhard, Eduard 10 627, 637, 639
Gerhard, Hubert 12 345–8*; 22 302; 26 103
assistants 2 44; 26 103
attributions 10 524
collaboration 5 768; 8 881
patrons and collectors 11 819; 13 916; 33 275
pupils 12 238; 13 315; 18 478
works 2 714, 800; 7 554; 12 346, 347, 403; 29 571; 33 274, 746
Gerhard of Luxeuil 23 652
Gerhardt, Greta see DOMNICK, GRETA
Gerhardus, Master 26 684
Geri, Betto di see BETTO DI GERI
Geri, Gelino di see GELINO DI GERI
Gericault, (Jean-Louis-André-) Théodore 7 385; 10 479; 11 542, 543, 567, 659; 12 348–54*; 24 140; 27 248
book illustrations 8 867; 30 385
collaboration 20 602
commentaries 18 836
drawings 18 744
frames 11 413
groups and movements 26 736, 737, 739, 740, 742; 29 891
lithographs 18 678; 19 486, 487; 25 607, 628
methods 6 570
paintings 21 760; 25 651
history 11 542, 543; 12 352; 14 586; 20 426
military scenes 11 542; 12 349
portraits 12 353; 25 275
sporting scenes 2 106; 12 351; 29 425
still-lifes 29 669
watercolours 32 900
patrons and collectors 5 278; 6 548; 8 72, 73, 638, 705; 11 233, 302; 12 609; 14 577; 31 397
reproductive prints by others 28 170
studio 29 856
teachers 13 794
Gericke, Samuel Theodor 14 651
Geri di Bartolommeo 8 797, 799
Gérin, Claude-Humbert 6 454; 11 608; 32 582
Gérin, Jacques-Albert 32 913
Gérines, Jacques de 3 602; 5 210; 8 662; 12 354–5*; 13 159
Gering, Giles 23 198
Gering, Ulrich 26 556
Gerini, Andrea, Marchese 8 12; 12 355*; 26 242; 33 691
Gerini, Carlo (1733-96) 12 355
Gerini, Carlo, Marchese (1616-73) 12 355*
Gerini, Giovanni 12 355
Gerini, Lorenzo di Niccolò 23 95

Gerini, Pierantonio **14** 367
Gerino da Pistoia **24** 525, 526
Gérin-Richard, Henri de **27** 142
Gerkan, A. von **19** 660
Gerl, Joseph
works **9** 754; **10** 531, 871; **14** *887*, 888
Gerl, Joseph Ignaz **12** 356
Gerl, Matthäus (Franz) **9** 754; **12** 356
Gerlach (family) **25** 127
Gerlach, Johann Carl **2** 127
Gerlach, Johannes **12** 356*; **29** 754, 755
Gerlach, Martin **18** 131; **22** 187
Gerlach, Philipp **3** 790, 791; **14** 651; **18** 475; **25** 366
Gerlach and Schenk **28** 344
Gerlachs Jugendbücherei **8** 428
Gerlachus **26** 702; **29** 758
works **26** *701*
Gerlach & Wiedling **8** 428
Gerlamoos, Master of *see* ARTULA VON VILLACH, THOMAS
Gerlannus **26** 595
Gerling, Sonja **29** 117
Germ: Thoughts towards Nature in Poetry, Literature and Art, The **24** 426; **25** 554; **27** 188
Germa, Rossend Gelabert **29** 344
Germain, François-Thomas **11** 619; **12** 357–8*
collaboration **3** 122; **13** 234
patrons and collectors **3** 841; **4** 635; **11** 619; **24** 147
works **11** 619, 626; **12** *357*; **23** 518; **24** *147*; **25** 313
Germain, Henri **4** 597
Germain, Pierre **1** 110; **11** 588, 620; **12** 356
Germain, Thomas **10** 764; **11** 619, 626; **12** 356–7*
assistants **26** 470
groups and movements **26** 493
patrons and collectors **24** 147
pupils **4** 520
works **4** 635; **11** 619; **12** 357; **25** 313
Germaine, John **30** 278
German **1** 543
German, A. D. **32** 861
German Archaeological Institute **10** 80, 81
German East Africa *see* RWANDA
Germaniceia *see* MARAŞ
Germanicus **27** 115
Germanicus Caesar **2** 649; **14** II2
Germano **32** 217
Germanos I, Patriarch of Constantinople **9** 641
German silver *see under* ALLOYS → types
Germanus of Auxerre, Saint **2** 844
Germanus of Paris, Saint **24** 115
Germany **12** 358–483*, *360*, *361*
academies **3** 400; **9** *459*; **28** 343
aesthetics
18th cent. **3** 411; **14** 99, 446; **17** 800–802; **21** 121; **28** 94, 109; **29** 921–2
19th cent. **8** 899; **14** 298–300, 434; **28** 56, 73, 161
20th cent. **19** 457
agate **12** *459*; **14** 167
alabaster (gypsum) **1** 516; **21** *72*; **22** *280*
alabaster-carvings **1** 517
alphabets **10** 592
altarpieces **1** 710; **3** *865*; **12** 401; **18** 714
Baroque **8** *627*
diptychs **13** *177*
Flügelaltar **1** 709
Gothic **1** *709*; **11** 450–53, *451*; **12** 383, 400; **13** 131; **23** *254*; **26** *371*, *372*; **29** *730*
polyptychs **12** *383*; **20** *758*; **29** *772*
Renaissance **4** *759*; **13** *721*, *722*
Germany
altarpieces—cont.
Rococo **1** *712*
Schnitzaltar **1** 710; **28** 133, *133*
triptychs **25** 183; **31** 344;
Renaissance **5** *200*; **8** *116*
14th cent. **3** *865*, *866*
15th cent. **7** *722*, *723*, *724*; **19** 528; **20** *192*; **22** *188*; **33** *301*, *630*
16th cent. **12** *401*; **18**611; **19** *106*; **20** *611*; **31** *286*; **33** *31*; *287*
17th cent. **5** *607*; **27** *725*
18th cent. **28** *145*
altars **1** 698, 699; **12** 461
Expressionism **9** *239*
Gothic **17** *741*
Mannerism **33** *738*
portable **29** IX1
Rococo **19** *364*
Romanesque **10** *113*; **26** *535*
12th cent. **26** 534
17th cent. **17** *689*, *690*
amber **1** *762*; **6** 558; **28** 168
ambulatories **1** 768
anatomical studies **1** 841
Andachtsbilder **2** 3; **24** 776
antefixes **26** 878
antependia **12** 462, 466, 469; **23** *657*
apartments **21** *783*; **25** *839*
Apocalypses **2** *223*
apprentices **19** 532; **20** 563
arches **2** 294, 480; **3** *791*, 793, 795
architectural models **12** *366*; **14** 513
architecture **12** 362–76*, *370*, 471, 472; **26** 743
Baroque **12** 370, 389
brick **4** 776–7*; **12** 362
Cameroon **5** 523
Carolingian **12** 362–3*; **26** 100
cavity-walling **4** 789
Cistercian Order **4** 776; **12** 471; **13** 47–8, 57
Dominican Order **13** 57
exhibition **10** *685*; **21** *491*; **23** *394*; **30** *370*
Gothic **12** 362, 364–6*; **13** 35, 47–9, 56–8*; **20** 87; **31** 284
Jesuit Order **17** 511
military **21** 571*
Namibia **22** 450
Nazism **22** 711*
Neo-classicism **12** 374
Ottonian **12** 363–4*
prefabrication **26** *18*
Premonstratensian Canons **12** 471
Renaissance **12** 366–8*
Renaissance Revival **12** 376
Romanesque **12** 363–4*; **17** 482; **26** 571–5*
Rundbogenstil **12** *167*
stone **32** 281
Transitional style **31** 284
vernacular **32** 281–3*
20th cent. **12** 378–81*; **19** *168*
archives **2** 370*, 372
armour **2** 469, 470–71, *470*, 472
arm rings **6** 155, *157*
arsenals **12** *370*
art (reproduction of works of) **12** 442
art history **12** 482–3*; **20** 246
artists' biographies **14** 314; **20** 483; **22** 920
artists' houses **2** *550*
art market **2** 560; **12** 473–4
art schools **1** 107–8; **12** *378*; **28** *100*
ash **8** *271*
ashtrays **3** *402*
assemblages **28** *197*
asylums **2** 657
atlases **2** *695*
auctions **2** 559, 707
Germany—cont.
automata **2** *838*; **12** 445
badges **14** III1
bags **3** 442
banknotes **3** 182
baptisteries **3** 192
barrows **6** 154; **25** 507
basilicas (non-ecclesiastical) **31** *324*
basins **12** 445; **17** *888*
bastions **21** 551
baths **31** 323
beads **12** 440, 462, 463
beadwork **3** 442
beakers **12** *439*, 444; **14** 425
beams **18** 883
beds **3** 484, *485*; **12** 420, 424, 426, *427*
birch **12** 426
block-books **4** 143, 144, 146*, *357*; **12** 385
bone **25** *490*
bookbindings **4** 347, 348, 349; **17** 566–7*; **24** 51
book covers **4** 349, 351, 352, 354, III, IV2; **5** *809*; **12** 442; **22** *520*; **26** 695
book illustrations **4** 365, 366; **14** 869; **25** 872
Gothic **12** 385
Ottonian **12** 382
Renaissance **9** *436*
15th cent. **4** *357*
19th cent. **5** *291*
bookplates **4** *373*
books **10** 724; **12** 385; **13** 866
Books of Arms **12** 272
bosses **22** *693*
bottles **4** *176*; **12** *429*
bowls **27** *75*
boxes **9** 240; **12** 452; **16** *900*; **24** 62
box-wood **12** 423, 426; **19** *108*; **29** *728*; **33** 326
bracelets **12** *454*
brass **3** *402*; **4** 682, *689*; **12** 451–2*, *452*; **13** 160–61; **32** *604*, *605*, *606*
brasses (monumental) **4** *693*; **32** 604
brick **4** 776–7*, *777*; **12** 362; **31** 195
calcium silicate **4** 788
hollow **4** 788
bronze **11** 253; **12** 451–2*
Baroque **3** *798*; **23** *309*
Celtic **18** 120
Gothic **28** IV2
Holy Roman Empire (before 1648) **13** *160*, 160–61
Mannerism **12** *346*, *347*; **26** *104*
Ottonian **7** *381*; **9** *153*; **12** *399*; **23** *658*
Prehistoric **9** 689, *690*
Renaissance **11** *223*; **12** *402*
Rococo **12** 424, *425*
Roman **27** *86*, *88*
Romanesque **26** *146*, *535*
16th cent. **28** 492
20th cent. **20** *396*
brooches **14** 418
bureaux **5** 191, *191*
burial mounds **9** 689; **25** *539*; **32** 773
busts **12** *406*
cabinets (i) (rooms) **5** 347; **21** 64
Chinese **12** 412
mirror **5** 347, *348*, 349; **12** 412
porcelain **5** 347–8, *348*; **12** 412
cabinets (ii) (furniture) **12** 421–2, 461
Cantourgen **12** 424
17th cent. **2** *45*, *716*; **12** *422*, *456*, *460*
cambric **12** 463
cameos **21** *162*
camps (military) **26** 905, 907
candlesticks **12** 452, *453*, 454
cane **33** 156
Germany—cont.
capitals **26** *573*, 573
caps **3** 442; **18** 157
cards **20** *746*; **31** 266
caricatures **5** 758*
carnivals **5** 785, 786, 787
carpenters **12** 420
carpets **12** 468–9*; **14** 65
cars **15** *824*
cartoons (drawings) **23** *315*
cartouches **18** 43
casting **12** 454
cast iron **3** 793; **12** 426
castles **6** 57*; **33** 88
Baroque **19** *780*
Renaissance **12** *367*
Romanesque **32** *883*
16th cent. **22** *918*
17th cent. **2** 591
19th cent. **6** *62*
catalogues **12** 475, 482
collections **5** 338; **9** 18
portraits **10** 213
prints **14** 688
18th cent. **23** 108
cathedrals **3** *141*
Baroque **12** *371*, *404*
double **9** 534
Gothic **4** *189*; **7** *587*, *588*; **10** *451*; **12** *492*; **13** *47*, *48*; **20** *87*; **28** *182*; **31** *569*
Transitional style **31** *284*
Romanesque **12** *364*; **20** *128*; **26** *575*; **29** *392*; **31** *326*
cenotaphs **13** *610*
censers **6** 173, *174*
censorship **6** 176
centrepieces **12** *450*; **16** *899*
ceramics **12** 428*
chains **12** 450
chairs **6** 388; **12** 419, 426, 427, *428*, 428, 461
chalices **12** 442
chancels **12** 363
chandeliers **6** 443; **12** 452, 454
chapels **1** *3*; **26** 574; **29** 392
chapter houses **20** *859*
chasubles **12** *463*, *464*, 469; **32** 392
cherry-wood **2** *458*; **12** 425, 426
chess sets **6** 557, 558, *558*
chests **6** *559*, 560; **12** 419, 420–21, 454; **16** *59*
chevets (chapels) **26** 572
chrysography **7** *246*
churches **4** 776–7; **8** *531*; **11** *45*; **12** 370, 371–2; **14** *101*, *569*
Baroque **2** *584*; **8** *873*, *875*; **23** *473*; **24** *562*; **32** *822*
Carolingian **5** *795*; **26** *100*, *101*
Gothic **4** *191*; **8** *906*; **10** *408*, *451*, *515*; **11** *733*; **13** *49*, *57*; **18** *724*; **19** *745*; **20** *379*; **23** *314*, *316*; **31** *327*, *567*; **33** *457*
Late Gothic **18** *828*; **23** *205*
Gothic Revival **13** *200*
Greek Revival **25** *366*
hall **2** *118*; **4** *665*; **5** *76*; **13** 49, *49*, 58; **14** 80, 81, *81*, 157; **19** 29; **23** *205*; **28** 497; **29** *5*
Modernism **3** *292*
Neo-classicism **16** *804*; **33** *39*
Oratorians **23** *473*
Protestantism **12** 373; **31** 166; **33** 278
Rococo **12** *372*; **26** *497*, 497–8; **32** *467*; **33** *683*
Roman **12** 362
Romanesque **1** *723*; **7** *591*, *594*; **9** *688*; **14** *533*, *534*; **17** *483*; **26** *572*, *573*
sepulchre **28** *427*
wall-pillar **32** 821–2, *822*
17th cent. **3** *67*, *229*; **28** *88*
18th cent. **4** *235*; **11** *125*, *126*; **30** *791*
ciboria (i) (vessels) **12** 442
ciboria (ii) (structure) **7** 303
Germany—cont.
cinemas **7** 328
clasps **4** 350, 355; **23** *658*
clocks **7** 439, *440*, 442, 447; **12** III2
clothes-presses **12** 426
coats of arms **12** 272; **14** 409–10, *412*, 421, 425, 426, III1
coffeepots **12** 446, *447*, 447, *451*
coffee-services **12** *432*; **21** *65*
coffering **8** *881*
coifs (dress) **12** 469
coins **7** *535*, 537, 538, *538*, 539; **12** 444, 447; **14** 419
collages **7** *558*; **10** *466*; **14** *605*
collections **2** 367, 560; **12** 446, 473–4*, 475–7; **17** 434
engravings **19** 111
porcelain **5** *348*; **12** 412
portraits **10** 213
prints **33** 280
public **12** 476
royal **22** 358
18th cent. **21** 64
19th cent. **33** 282
colophons **7** *625*, 625
columns **26** 905
commercial art **7** 651, 656
commodes **7** 658; **12** 424, *425*
competitions **12** 853
concert halls **28** *56*
concrete **19** 502
confessionals **7** 703
connoisseurship **17** 818; **26** 358
conservatories **12** 415
Constitutions of Masonry **20** 562–3
containers **15** *825*
copper **12** 451–2*; **13** 161
coral **12** 462; **18** *522*
costumes **28** *111*
cotton **8** 37; **12** 463
couches **9** 689
courtyards **18** *455*
craftsmen and artists **3** 400
crests **14** *412*
crosses **8** *200*, *201*; **12** 442
crucifixes **8** 216; **24** *544*
Gothic **7** 593; **8** *214*; **12** *343*
Ottonian **7** 590; **8** *213*; **12** 399
crypts **8** *224*, 224; **26** 572; **29** 391
cupboards **8** 271; **12** 420, *420*, 421, 422, 423, 425
Baroque **12** *422*
cabinet-cupboards **12** 422–3
sacristy **12** 423
two-tiered **8** 271, *271*; **12** 421
vitrine **12** 423
16th cent. **12** *421*
18th cent. **12** *426*
cups **12** 443, 444, 445, 447, *449*; **14** 418
Baroque **16** *901*
communion-cups **12** 444
grape **24** 573
16th cent. **12** *444*
currency **12** 440
curtains **12** 413; **17** 570
cushion covers **12** 467
daggers **1** *593*
damask **12** 464, 469; **19** 418
dealers **12** 472
dealing **2** 560; **12** 473–4*
decadence and decline **8** 595
department stores **12** *377*; **21** *120*
design **8** 802*
desks **5** 192; **12** 423, 425, 426
diamonds **12** *459*
dictionaries of art **30** 731
diplomatic gifts **14** 323
diptychs **9** 4
display of art **9** 14, 18, *27*; **22** 358
dolls **31** 259, 261, *261*, 262
dolls' furniture **31** 264
dolls' houses **31** 262, 263, *263*
domes **9** 84, 86; **30** 685, 734
doors **9** *153*; **12** 452, 454; **23** *658*

Germany—cont.
drawings **9** 225, 440
architectural **19** 532; **22** 211
Gothic **2** *327*; **4** *189*, *191*
15th cent. **28** 497
18th cent. **33** *40*
chalk **13** *723*
charcoal **7** *872*
genre **9** *226*
ink
Gothic **12** *385*, *387*
Renaissance **3** *102*; **4** *760*
16th cent. **24** *355*; **33** *130*
19th cent. **7** *871*
landscape **8** *514*
life-drawings **9** 430
metalpoints **21** 340
mythological **24** *355*
oil transfer **18** *111*
pastel **18** *80*; **24** *245*, VI
Renaissance **12** 386
silverpoints **21** *340*; **27** *147*
townscapes **3** *793*; **23** *305*
wash **9** *214*; **11** *752*
dress **9** 269, 273, 279, 288
drinking-horns **9** *690*
drypoints **9** 310; **20** 693; **25** *605*
dyes **23** 786
earthenwares **12** 430–33*, *431*, *432*
ebony **11** *456*; **12** *422*, 423
education (art) **3** 399, *400*, 400–401, 798; **12** 478–80*
applied art **12** 478–80*
architecture **3** 399; **9** 421; **19** 532; **26** 102
crafts **3** 399
design **12** 480; **15** 826
urban planning **3** 410
effigies **31** 122
embossing **24** 55
embroidery **10** *181*; **12** 462–3*, *463*, 464; **23** *337*
enamel **8** *201*; **10** *113*; **12** *431*, 438, 439, *439*, *445*, 445, 447, 451, 456–7*; **26** *146*; **33** *114*
basse taille **12** *456*, III2; **13** 169
cloisonné **21** *502*
Gothic **13** 169
Ottonian **4** III
Romanesque **26** 693–4*
Schwarzlot **12** 439, *439*; **14** 235
encyclopedias of art **14** 234
engines (steam) **11** 134
engravings **10** 381, 396; **12** *786*; **25** 651
bird's-eye views **17** *817*; **33** *431*
dotted prints **9** 190
Dürer Renaissance **9** *446*
Gothic **12** 385
Renaissance **8** *114*; **9** *437*; **10** *385*; **29** *44*, *557*
stipple **13** 258
townscapes **2** *714*; **23** *307*
white-line **20** 795
15th cent. **10** *382*; **20** *746*, *794*; **28** *153*
16th cent. **3** *200*; **8** *838*; **22** *555*, *637*
17th cent. **11** *853*; **18** *44*, *45*; **33** *50*
18th cent. **20** *282*
19th cent. **12** *274*; **18** *135*
epitaphs **10** *436*
erotic art **10** 483
etchings **10** 548, 549–50*, 695
Renaissance **1** *716*; **10** *550*; **14** *574*; **33** *18*
16th cent. **3** *506*; **14** 747, *747*; **18** *876*
18th cent. **5** *29*; **7** *183*; **25** *599*
19th cent. **18** *202*
20th cent. **18** *109*
ewers **2** 237; **12** 445, 452; **28** I1
exhibitions **9** 239; **10** 95, 678; **24** 677
ex-votos **10** *702*
façade decoration **10** 737, *737*, 740, 741, 745

Germany—cont.
façades **13** 49, 56, *57*; **22** *437*
factories **3** *512*; **10** 697; **21** *780*; **25** *69*
faience (ii) (ceramics) **6** 333; **12** 430–31, *431*; **22** 880
felt **3** *891*; **10** 875
fibulae **21** *162*, *502*
figurines **1** *762*; **12** *433*, 450
Palaeolithic **25** 489, *489*, *490*
Prehistoric **32** 679
Rococo **6** I2
20th cent. **12** *437*
filigree **21** *162*
films **10** 687
film studios **18** 193
finials (scrolls) **17** *570*
fireplaces **12** 410
flagons **6** 155; **12** 444
flags **11** 149
floors **12** 409, 413
fonts (baptismal) **11** 253; **12** 452; **13** 160; **32** *604*
fortifications **12** 369–70; **21** 571*; **31** 195
Prehistoric **21** 551; **25** 503
Roman **26** 905
forts **21** 571
foundries **12** 401
fountains
Gothic **11** *341*
Mannerist **12** *347*
Renaissance **11** *223*; **28** *138*
16th cent. **23** *252*
20th cent. **12** *196*
frames **11** 375, 450–65*
Art Nouveau **11** *464*
Baroque **11** *456*, *457*
Biedermeier **11** *461*
cassetta **11** *454*, *463*
Empire style **11** *460*
Gothic **11** 450–54*, *451*, *453*
Gothic Revival **11** *463*
Neo-classicism **11** *460*, 460–61*
Renaissance **11** *454*, 454–5*
Rococo **11** 457–60*, *458*, *459*
19th cent. **11** *462*, *463*
20th cent. **11** *464*
frontispieces **33** *712*
furniture **9** 234; **12** 419–22*, *420*, *421*, *422*, 424, 425–8*, *427*, *428*, 445, 448, 462; **33** 156–7
Baroque **12** 422–3*
Functionalism **12** 428
Rococo **12** 423–5*
18th cent. **26** *530*
gables **11** 876; **30** 897
gablets **28** 128
galleries (ii) (corridors) **12** 364
galleries (iv) (art) **12** 475; **14** *176*
picture **9** 18
sculpture **22** 362
18th cent. **33** 53
games **31** 266
gardens **12** 133–4*; **14** 469; **17** 698; **33** 380
Baroque **28** 110
Mannerism **6** 95
Rococo **12** *133*; **26** 497; **32** 120
19th cent. **22** 381
garnets **21** *162*
gates **7** *358*
gateways **4** *777*
gay and lesbian art **12** *215*
gem-engraving **12** 260
gems **4** III; **12** 447, 451; **26** *145*
Gesamtkunstwerk **32** 763
gilding **2** *458*; **7** *440*, *443*; **12** *443*, 445, III2; **24** 55; **26** *146*, *535*; **28** IV2; **29** 818, IX1
glass **10** 697; **12** 374, 438–41*, 456, 462; **14** 425
Bauhaus **15** *825*
à la façon de Venise **12** 439
Byzantine **9** 646
crystal **12** 440
porcelleinglas **12** 440
Roman **7** 586; **27** *75*

Germany
glass—cont.
Waldglas **12** 438, *438*
Zierglas **12** *441*, 441
17th cent. **12** *439*
glasses
Berkemeyer **12** 438
claw-beakers **12** 438
humpen **12** 438
Krautstrunk **12** 438
Kurfürstenhumpen **12** 438
Maigelein **12** 438
Nuppenbecher **12** 438
Passglas **12** 438
Reichsadlerhumpen **12** 438
roemers **12** 438
Stangenglas **12** *438*, 438
glazes **12** 429
Gnadenpfennige **17** 522
goblets **12** 442
gold **9** 689–90; **12** 442–50*, 463, 868
Baroque **12** 423
Celtic **6** 155, *157*; **18** 120
Gothic **12** 442
Merovingian **21** *162*
Ottonian **4** III; **23** *657*, *658*
Prehistoric **9** *690*
Romanesque **28** *631*
6th cent. AD **21** *502*
11th cent. **2** *452*
12th cent. **26** *145*
13th cent. **10** *181*
14th cent. **12** 464
15th cent. **28** 129
16th cent. **12** 446, *455*
18th cent. **12** *447*, *459*
19th cent. **21** 66
20th cent. **12** 450–51*, *451*
Goldschmelz **2** 453
government buildings **3** *793*; **22** *300*
gowns **9** 275
graves **18** 119–20; **25** 508
gravestones **21** *164*, *502*
grottoes **12** 412; **13** 704–5
guidebooks **12** 482; **13** 810
guildhalls **4** *742*
guilds **12** 403, 420, 442, 469; **13** 823
guns **2** *458*, 459, 460, 464
gun stocks **2** *458*, 459; **20** *853*
Gutenberg Bible **4** *9*; **25** *589*
hair **3** *672*
hair-nets **12** 469
half-shafts **26** 573
halls **3** *513*, 795; **14** 74*; **23** 317; **27** 610
hangings **12** 412
hardstones **7** 91; **8** *201*; **12** 445, 457–9, *458*, 461–2*
Hausmalers **14** 235
hemp **12** 464
heraldry **14** 404, 407, 409–10*, 419, III1
heritage **14** 492
historicism **14** 580
historiography **2** 531–2; **12** 482–3*
hospitals **3** 140; **14** *678*
houses **32** *281*, *282*, 283
Baroque **28** *106*
Expressionism **10** *698*
organic architecture **23** *499*
prefabricated **26** 18, *18*
Roman **26** 906
town **28** *106*
17th cent. **11** *853*; **33** *294*
20th cent. **8** *826*
housing **3** *796*; **20** *879*; **30** 371
humanism **14** 868
ice buckets **12** *436*
iconography **2** 3; **22** 711; **26** 654
illusionism **15** 139
industrial design **15** 824*, 825–6*
industrial scenes **3** *800*
inks **10** 381
inlays **12** 423, 445
intarsia **12** 421, 423

Germany—cont.
interior decoration **12** 408–19*, *409*, *410*, *412*, *414*, *415*, *417*, *418*, 462; **31** *686*
Renaissance **10** 662; **22** *307*
Rococo **3** *429*; **26** *496*
18th cent. **12** *411*
19th cent. **2** *550*
iron **3** 804*; **9** *690*; **12** 374, 454*, *454*; **13** 161; **16** *59*
ivory **2** *45*; **12** 423, *460*, 460–61*; **22** *520*; **23** *661*; **24** *543*, *544*; **26** *146*; **29** 574; **32** 679; **33** *670*
ivory-carvings **16** 799; **29** 520
Carolingian **5** *809*
Gothic **13** 176–7*, *177*
Ottonian **23** 660, *661*; **28** *805*
Palaeolithic **25** *489*
Romanesque **26** 695, *696*; **29** IX1
17th cent. **2** *44*; **20** *853*
jade **16** 861
jars **21** *64*
jewellery **3** 804*; **12** 454, *455*, 455–6*; **17** 530
journeymen **19** 532; **20** 561, 563
jugs **6** 333; **12** 452; **27** *86*
justice scenes **3** *40*; **17** 699
kaolin **29** 574
kettles **15** *823*
knitting **12** 469; **18** 157, 158
Kunstkammern **9** 14; **12** 461, 475; **18** *522*
lace **11** *461*; **12** 463, 469–70; **18** 158, 590, 593
lacquer **12** 423
lamps **17** 571, *571*, 573
lead **25** *22*
leather **4** 349, 351, 352; **23** 254
lecterns **12** 452
libraries **9** 455; **12** 481–2*; **19** *316*, 318
Libri amicorum **12** 273
lidos **19** 332
lighting **30** 734
limestone **8** *541*; **14** *450*; **29** 700
lime-wood **8** *627*; **10** *455*, *457*; **12** *401*; **13** *316*; **19** *106*; **22** *281*; **23** *887*; **26** *371*; **29** *729*, *730*, *761*; **33** *31*
linen **7** 167; **12** 462, 463, 464, *464*, 465, 469; **13** 194; **19** 418; **27** 693
linocuts **19** 429, *429*
lithography **10** 695; **12** 392; **19** 481–2*, 490–91; **25** *349*; **28** 404; **29** 776; **31** *256*
Nazarenes **23** *411*
20th cent. **3** *892*; **14** *571*
lithophanes **12** 435
locks **12** 454; **16** *59*
lodgebooks **19** 532
mahogany **3** *485*; **12** 425, *426*, 426
manuals
architecture **3** 410; **4** 203; **22** 61; **33** 297
building **19** 532
glass **4** 666
manuscript **20** 325
painting **22** 923
writing **22** 920
manufacturing **15** 824*, 825–6*
manuscript illumination
Carolingian **12** *381*, 382
Gorze, Order of **13** *19*
Gothic **4** *11*; **10** *723*; **13** 137, 140, 142, 151
Jewish art **4** *15*
Ottonian **20** *754*
Romanesque **26** 673–4*, 675*; **33** *293*
15th cent. **20** *324*
manuscripts **12** 272
maple **5** *191*; **12** 426
maps **2** *695*; **20** *365*
marble
Baroque **12** 423
Gothic **12** *400*

Germany
marble—cont.
Neo-classicism **9** *691*
Rococo **1** *712*
18th cent. **28** *42*, *43*
19th cent. **9** *692*; **14** *526*
marbling **12** 413; **24** 55
marks **12** 440, 442; **20** 440, 445
marquetry **5** *191*; **12** 423, 424, *425*; **20** 467
boullework **12** 422; **29** 60
martyria **9** 534
masks **28** *111*
masonry **26** 574; **28** 129
masons **19** 532; **20** 561, 562–3*
masons (master) **19** 532; **20** 563
masons' lodges **3** 399; **19** 532; **20** 562–3
master printers **20** 607
mausolea **20** 867*, 868*
measures **12** 453
medals **20** 920*, *920*, 923*, 926, *926*; **26** 127; **28** 190
medical books **1** 844; **21** *6*
metal **12** 463; **30** 542
metalcuts **21** 337, *339*
metalwork **12** 442*, 451–4*, *452*, *453*, *454*
Celtic **6** 155
Gothic **13** 160–61*
Renaissance **33** *18*
mezzotints **21** 414, 415, *415*
miniatures (manuscript illumination)
Gothic **3** *472*; **33** *589*
Ottonian **20** V2; **23** *653*, *654*, *655*; **26** *78*
Romanesque **26** *673*, *674*, *675*
15th cent. **2** *713*
mirror frames **21** 721
mirrors **12** 412, *424*
monasteries **12** 369, 372, 471
Baroque **23** *5*
Benedictine Order **3** 709
Carolingian **19** *698*
Gothic **7** *206*
monstrances **12** 442, 447
monuments **12** 407, 471, 472
equestrian **3** *142*, *798*; **26** *23*; **32** 832
funerary **12** *399*
public **7** *381*
triumphal arches **3** *791*
mortars (vessels) **12** 452
mosaics **21** III1; **26** 681; **27** 62; **30** 506
mother-of-pearl **12** 424, *425*, 450
mouldings **22** 211, 219, 220, 221, 222
museums **3** 807; **12** 374, 475–7*; **14** 492; **22** 358, 362; **31** *736*
Baroque **25** *240*
Greek Revival **18** *122*
Nazism **22** *710*
Neo-classicism **12** *375*
Renaissance Revival **18** *124*
16th cent. **33** 274
18th cent. **9** 455, *455*; **14** 491
19th cent. **22** *362*
20th cent. **7** *386*, *585*; **11** *736*; **12** *498*; **22** *368*
neck rings **6** 155, *157*
nickel **3** *402*
nude figures **23** 294; **24** *543*
Baroque **23** *309*
Expressionism **22** *257*
Gothic **10** *455*; **26** *370*
Mannerism **3** *103*; **14** *320*
Neo-classicism **8** *509*
Neue Sachlichkeit **22** *922*
Renaissance **3** *102*; **11** *223*; **12** *402*; **29** *557*
Surrealism **3** *672*
16th cent. **3** *200*; **21** *72*
17th cent. **11** *803*
19th cent. **7** *856*; **9** *692*; **14** *526*; **20** *405*
20th cent. **19** *95*; **20** *396*, *808*
numismatics **24** 848

Germany—cont.
oak 6 559; 12 423, 425; 13 118; 33 326
objects of vertu 12 455*
observatories 14 491; 21 119
office buildings 18 417
opera houses 33 429
orangeries 23 470
orders (architecture) 23 490
organic architecture 11 841; 14 175
organs 32 832
painting 12 381–97*; 14 423; 23 375; 24 3
Abstract art 17 763, 765, 767; 22 379, 701
acrylic 25 153
allegorical
Expressionism 3 480
Neue Sachlichkeit 12 396
Renaissance 8 117
Rococo 1 785
Romanticism 11 781; 22 379
16th cent. 19 132
17th cent. 32 230
19th cent. 23 676; 29 847
animal subjects 4 132; 20 381
architectural 4 136; 14 664
Art informel 12 397
Baroque 12 389–91*
battle 12 388
Carolingian 12 381–2
Dada 8 434; 12 395
display 9 18; 22 362
Expressionism 3 478; 10 694; 12 395, 395; 22 257; 23 187; 24 311
flower 14 626
fresco 12 390–91
Baroque 2 579, 580, 583; 28 109
Nazarenes 12 392
Renaissance 28 59
Rococo 1 785; 3 780; 12 391; 14 695
18th cent. 33 672
genre 12 294; 30 740
Baroque 12 390
Biedermeier 12 414; 28 196
Expressionism 14 284
Gothic 12 108
Neue Sachlichkeit 9 42; 22 922
Romanticism 30 167
19th cent. 12 415; 19 334; 22 304; 29 416; 33 383
20th cent. 21 785; 28 840
glass 12 798
Gothic 12 382–3*, 385*; 13 135, 142–3, 151
hanging 9 18
hard-edge 12 397
history 12 472
Mannerism 30 35
Realism (style) 21 140, 141
16th cent. 33 85
17th cent. 2 716
19th cent. 11 46; 24 587; 26 740
hunting scenes 18 175
Jesuit Order 12 389
Jewish art 17 578–9*
landscape 1 714; 18 77, 714
Baroque 28 148
Expressionism 3 477; 18 81, IV2
Renaissance 1 715–16
Romanticism 4 135; 11 779, 780, 782; 12 393; 26 359, 742
18th cent. 18 174
19th cent. 4 206; 8 898; 18 183; 26 741; 27 232
20th cent. 17 762; 18 31; 28 125, 342
Mannerism 3 103
marine 10 862
miniatures 11 803; 21 640, 640

Germany
painting—cont.
murals 22 328, 329, 330, 332, 333
mythological
Baroque 27 228; 28 147
Mannerism 14 320
Neo-classicism 26 128
17th cent. 27 886
19th cent. 4 204; 7 856
Nazism 22 711*
Neo-classicism 12 391
Neue Sachlichkeit 3 802; 12 396
Ottonian 12 382
panel 12 383; 13 151
Realism (style) 12 393–4; 19 97
religious
Baroque 19 706; 27 227
Expressionism 23 186
Gothic 11 715; 12 384; 14 455; 20 765; 26 507
Mannerism 8 882
Renaissance 1 717, 718; 5 59; 8 113; 9 432; 13 723; 17 601; 26 188; 28 48, 189
Romanticism 11 462
15th cent. 12 409; 16 71; 19 529; 20 654; 25 40; 28 150, 151, 171
16th cent. 3 473; 26 11
17th cent. 17 720; 22 249
18th cent. 12 411
19th cent. 23 676; 28 135; 31 538
Renaissance 12 385–7*
Rococo 12 390–91*
Romanesque 12 382
Romanticism 12 393
Socialist Realism 12 397
still-lifes 29 664
townscapes
18th cent. 3 677
19th cent. 3 806; 12 604
20th cent. 11 735
urban life 18 79
vanitas 29 725
vedute 4 663
wall
Carolingian 5 799
Gothic 13 134, 138, 139, 143
Gothic: Zackenstil 32 805
Jewish art 17 558
Ottonian 23 649, 650, 650–51; 26 101
Roman 27 56
Romanesque 26 649, 651, 653
16th cent. 33 278
watercolours
Jewish art 17 578
Renaissance 9 430, 433, 440
16th cent. 18 510; 33 32
20th cent. 12 215; 18 110
19th cent. 20 405
20th cent. 3 324, 803; 12 397, 398; 14 327, 623; 20 12; 23 357; 25 841; 26 355; 28 177; 32 695
palaces 12 371; 18 159; 32 682; 33 37
Baroque 3 266; 9 236, 237, 747; 22 309; 23 3, 4, 811–12, 812; 25 367; 28 110, 117
Gothic 13 58
Neo-classicism 23 813; 28 101
Renaissance 24 230; 29 739
Rococo 26 495–6, 496
Romanesque 12 245
16th cent. 29 875
17th cent. 27 196; 33 54
18th cent. 8 530; 17 835
19th cent. 23 814
panelling 12 409, 410
paper 10 381; 24 40, 48, 51, 55, 56; 31 258
papercuts 24 56
papier mâché 24 62; 28 111; 31 262
parks 12 472
parliament buildings 12 377

Germany—cont.
paste 24 56
pasteprints 24 245, 246
patens 12 444
patronage 12 446, 470–72*
pattern books 24 271; 32 680
architecture 9 687; 12 368; 17 837; 20 804; 28 143, 497
16th cent. 9 687
furniture 31 680
interior decoration 12 409
jewellery 17 521
metalwork 12 446; 33 17
sculpture 4 187
textiles 12 469
pavilions (buildings) 8 289; 24 290
pearls 12 447, 462
pear-wood 12 426; 33 II1
pencils 24 353
pendants (jewellery) 12 455; 17 521
performance art 24 406
periodicals 12 416, 641; 23 108; 24 421, 423, 443–5*
pewter 12 423, 452–4*, 453; 13 161
photoarchives 2 366, 370; 12 481–2*
photographic prints 24 667, IX
photography 24 663, 673, 674, 676, 677
photo-engraving 7 686
20th cent. 24 675; 27 718
photomontages 3 801; 13 698; 14 604; 24 686; 27 872
piers (ii) (masonry) 24 749, 751
pietàs 24 776
pietra paesina 12 461
pigments 23 786
pillars 6 156
pine 33 326
pinnacles 28 128
pitchers 12 442
plants 12 415
plaques 7 686; 16 799; 26 696
plaquettes 12 447; 25 21–2, 22
plaster 3 243; 12 406; 29 838*, 843
polychromy 10 457; 32 253
pommels (guns) 2 459
poplar 12 408; 33 326
porcelain 4 493; 6 558, 558; 9 239; 12 406, 433–7*, 434, 435, 436, 437, 472; 22 880; 31 261, 261
blue-and-white ware 4 176–7*
display 5 348; 12 412
hard-paste 6 333; 21 63–7, 66
Rococo 6 I2; 26 498
18th cent. 9 234, 238; 12 433; 21 64
porphyry 20 798; 29 IX1
portals 11 749; 12 410; 29 6
Gothic 31 569
porticos 25 267
portraits
author portraits 5 802
double 21 484
drawings 9 428, 429; 18 206
drawings (pastel) 24 242
drypoints 9 309
engravings 1 592; 18 47; 20 916
group 13 904; 27 339, 340
medallions 33 114
medals 17 522; 28 191
painting 12 383
Expressionism 3 479; 17 452; 21 55
Gothic 33 300
Impressionism 19 335
Late Gothic 25 91
Neo-classicism 31 27
Renaissance 1 763; 3 507; 5 60; 9 431, 439; 10 162; 14 665; 20 191; 23 306; 25 274
Romanticism 27 339, 340
watercolours 22 101

Germany
portraits
painting—cont.
16th cent. 21 484; 22 924; 26 408; 33 85
17th cent. 32 231
18th cent. 11 459; 12 852; 19 111
19th cent. 11 236; 22 101; 32 120
20th cent. 10 869; 13 698; 19 151, 335
relief sculpture 24 807
sculpture 13 679; 18 420; 28 42
Gothic 9 257; 22 264, 692
self-portraits 9 429; 19 151
Expressionism 3 479; 18 206
Gothic 18 420
Impressionism 19 335
Renaissance 9 429, 431; 24 807
19th cent. 11 236; 32 120
20th cent. 9 309
woodcuts 13 903; 33 290
posters 7 651; 25 348, 349, 350, 652, 652
pots 12 443, 452
pottery 6 558
blue-and-white ware 4 176, 176–7*
Böttgerporzellan 21 63
Jaspisporzellan 6 332; 21 63, 64
tin-glazed ware 12 430; 30 875
power stations 25 402
predellas 25 464
presses 10 381
printing 7 625; 8 37; 13 866
printmakers 9 440
prints 12 391; 18 82
devotional prints 8 837, 837, 838
flock 11 173
punched 25 731
propaganda 25 651, 652, 652
prunts 12 438, 438
pulpits 25 727–8; 29 760
pump rooms 14 840
purses 3 442
quartz 12 450
racecourses 10 215
railway stations 25 856
refectories 20 859
regalia 26 78, 79
reliquaries 12 442, 447
Carolingian 10 115
Gothic 13 169; 26 371
Ottonian 26 145
Romanesque 26 146
representation 12 384
ribs 29 392
rock art 25 511
romance manuscripts 26 563–4*
roods 27 124, 125; 33 17
roofs 27 127; 30 909
rosaries 12 455
roundels 27 255
rugs 12 409, 413
ruin buildings 27 323
runes 10 592
samplers 27 693, 694
sanctuaries 26 905
sandstone 3 142; 11 751; 12 343, 344; 13 86, 91, 92, 683, 684; 26 370, 372; 29 6; 32 830
satires 27 869, 871, 871–2*
sawmills 12 419
sceptres 12 442
schools 4 61; 27 335; 28 156, 158
scientific instruments 28 209
scissors 8 286, 287
screens (i) (architectural) 12 399; 28 292; 33 17
scripts 3 512; 28 307
sculpture 12 398–405*, 406–8*, 472; 23 254
allegorical 18 478
architectural 10 745
Baroque 28 116
Gothic 20 89; 22 315; 29 6

Germany
sculpture—cont.
Baroque Revival 12 406
bronze 28 492
Baroque 3 798
Gothic 13 160
Mannerism 12 346, 347; 26 104
Renaissance 11 223; 12 402
20th cent. 20 396
Carolingian 12 398
chryselephantine statues 29 576
colossal statues 3 155; 28 186
display 22 362
Expressionism 10 695–6*; 18 78
Gothic 12 344; 13 86–7, 160; 20 129
Early Gothic 12 399–400; 22 692
Late Gothic 13 316; 32 605
group 16 799
Holy Roman Empire (before 1648) 26 634*
Jugendstil 12 407
Lutheranism 12 403
marble
Gothic 12 400
Neo-classicism 9 691
18th cent. 28 42
19th cent. 14 526
monumental 3 498, 498; 26 377
mythological 4 376; 8 509; 9 691; 12 402
Renaissance 11 223; 33 II1
Rococo 22 303
Nazism 12 408; 22 711–12
Neo-classicism 12 406
Ottonian 7 590; 12 399
palmesels 23 887
pietàs 9 239; 28 76
Protestantism 12 402, 403
relief
Expressionism 12 408
Gothic 13 86; 22 280; 29 818
Mannerism 33 739
Ottonian 7 381
Protestantism 12 402, 405
Renaissance 8 541; 32 606, 830
16th cent. 19 108
18th cent. 28 43
religious 10 455, 457; 24 461; 26 370; 29 761
Baroque 9 752; 13 684, 777
Gothic 7 589; 11 751; 12 400; 13 91, 92; 22 281; 29 728, 729
Mannerism 12 346; 26 104
Renaissance 14 450
Rococo 1 712
Romanesque 26 632
16th cent. 21 72
18th cent. 13 851; 32 253
Rococo 26 498
Roman Catholicism 12 402–3
Romanesque 12 399; 26 632–3*, 634*
sandstone 13 92
stone 13 86–7, 88, 91; 22 264, 692; 26 632, 632–3*, 634*
Surrealism 3 672
tomb 18 479; 32 833
votive statues 10 702
wood 9 752; 22 303; 24 461; 32 253
16th cent. 26 103
19th cent. 9 692; 14 526
20th cent. 3 243, 891; 19 95; 20 808
seals 14 413
secretaires 12 421, 423, 425, 426
settlements 25 502
shells 28 I1
shields 14 409–10, 421
shops 31 876
Art Nouveau 2 566
shrines (i) (cult) 12 442; 23 99, 311; 28 630, 631, 632, IV2
shrines (ii) (altarpieces) 28 641

Germany—cont.
 silk 10 181; 12 462, 463–4*, 463, 464, 467, 469; 23 337
 silver 6 173, 557; 12 442–50*, 449, 463
  Baroque 12 423
  Gothic 23 311
  Roman 27 81
  Romanesque 6 173, 174
  9th cent. AD 10 115
  12th cent. 7 535
  15th cent. 12 443
  16th cent. 2 718; 7 440; 12 444; 16 900
  17th cent. 7 538; 9 234; 18 522
  18th cent. 12 435, 445; 13 679
  19th cent. 12 450
  20th cent. 12 450–51*, 451
 silver-gilt 2 453; 8 200, 201; 12 424, 444, 445, 449; 16 899, 901; 17 888; 28 II
 situlae 28 805
 skyscrapers 28 834, 835
 snuff-boxes 12 457–9*, 458, 459
 sofas 12 426
 spice-boxes 17 572, 572
 spires 13 56, 58; 29 414
 squares (town) 14 492; 28 802
 stage design 30 685, 686, 687
 stages, revolving 30 685
 stained glass 23 315; 29 503–4, 506, 508
  Gothic 2 720; 7 590; 10 452; 12 382; 13 135, 142, 185, 185–8*, 186; 22 693; 29 502, III
  Renaissance 14 572
  Romanesque 26 701, 702
  16th cent. 27 255; 29 512
 staircases 25 188; 29 522; 33 433
 stairs, holy 23 5
 statuettes 12 406, 445; 24 543; 27 88; 29 574*
  Baroque 23 309
 steel 10 697; 12 454*; 16 59; 30 734
 stencilling 24 56
 stone 1 709; 4 776; 6 156; 13 86–7, 88; 22 264, 692, 693; 26 632, 632–3*, 634*; 32 281, 679
 stone-carvings 6 156; 21 164, 502; 26 595
 stonewares 12 428–30*, 429
 stoups 31 567
 stoves 12 410, 411
 stucco 11 44; 12 372; 26 632; 29 838*, 843
  Baroque 12 404; 28 130
  Gothic 29 818, 818
  Rococo 10 859; 29 838; 33 682
  Romanesque 12 399
  18th cent. 28 131
 swords 2 452, 453, 453
 synagogues 17 543, 544, 546, 547, 548, 548, 549; 33 40
 tables 12 419–20, 423, 424, 426; 14 426
  console tables 12 423, 424, 424
  sewing-tables 12 426
 tankards 12 431, 435, 444, 447
 tapestries 12 464–8*; 14 422; 30 310–12*, 319, 324, 327
  chinoiserie 7 167
  Gothic 13 194, 196
  Romanesque 14 65; 26 703
  12th cent. 12 465
  15th cent. 12 466; 30 312
  17th cent. 5 606, 606
  20th cent. 30 328
 tas 17 569, 570
 tazze 12 444
 teak 20 808
 teapots 12 447
 tea-services 12 434
 teddy bears 31 260
 tempera 12 383
 tension structures 30 469
 terracotta 4 376; 26 104

Germany—cont.
 textiles 12 462*, 463, 469–70*; 26 703
 theatres 14 491; 30 676*, 678, 683, 684; 32 339
  Baroque 14 469
  Expressionism 10 697
  Neo-classicism 28 99
  Renaissance Revival 28 398, 399
  Rococo 8 290
  19th cent. 7 582
  20th cent. 31 877
 theories
  architectural 4 179, 504; 11 853; 12 368–9; 27 334; 28 119, 400
  art
   17th cent. 27 726
   18th cent. 12 852; 14 99, 446; 17 801–2; 18 880
   19th cent. 14 298–300, 526; 26 369–70; 28 107–8, 109, 160–61
   20th cent. 1 73; 3 400, 731, 891; 18 110; 20 527; 24 16–17; 33 383–4
  colour 1 74; 12 853; 18 449; 27 341
  painting 19 245; 22 385
  representation 19 327
  sculpture 12 407; 14 446
 threads 10 181; 12 463, 464; 30 542
 tiles 12 409, 430; 30 506, 884–5*
 timber structures 30 895, 896; 32 283
 tin 31 256, 263
 tombs 14 421
  Baroque 26 25; 32 833
  dolmens 9 80
  Gothic 13 160; 30 535; 32 607
  megalithic 21 41
 tools 32 679
 tortoiseshell 12 423, 424, 425
 towers 13 56; 31 568, 569
 town halls 19 746; 31 237
  Baroque 4 324; 23 317
  Mannerism 14 679
  Renaissance 2 714; 19 110; 23 317
  20th cent. 12 380
 towns 3 139; 12 471
  garden cities 8 824; 9 237; 11 797; 12 145; 14 362; 26 374; 28 177; 30 370, 521; 31 728
  new 28 87
 toys 31 255, 256, 258
 tracery 13 48, 56, 57; 31 270, 271, 273
  bar 13 48
 trade 28 456
  copper 3 602
  faience (ii) (ceramics) 25 310
  furniture 19 592
  hardstones 7 91
  iron 14 57
  metalwork 16 389
  paintings 23 224
  paper 24 48
  porcelain 22 882
  pottery 6 333
  stonewares 6 333
  tapestries 3 607
 trade fairs 12 446
 trade schools 12 479
 tragacanth-sugar 21 65
 trappings 14 182
 treatises 30 709–10
  architecture 12 369; 31 298*
   16th cent. 4 178; 8 882; 12 366
   17th cent. 10 444; 11 853; 29 872
   20th cent. 22 386
  calligraphy 22 920
  Celtic art 16 830
  engraving 22 320; 31 26
  fortifications 9 441; 12 369; 21 578

Germany
 treatises—cont.
  gardens 14 570
  painting 31 300
   landscape 18 174
  papermaking 24 40
  proportion 9 441
 tree trunks 3 891
 trompe l'oeil 23 8
 tubular steel 3 402; 12 428
 tureens 12 436
 tympana 20 798
  Gothic 13 88
 typography 31 494, 497
 upholstery 31 686
 urban planning 12 471; 31 724, 737; 33 51
  6th cent. BC 14 498
  17th cent. 12 368
  20th cent. 11 797; 14 524
 vases 21 66
 vaults (ceiling) 3 793
  barrel 22 307
  cellular 13 58
  Gothic 10 221
  groin 29 392
  rib: curving 32 90
  rib: Gothic 14 268
  rib: jumping 32 90
  rib: net 12 366; 32 92
  rib: reticulated 32 92
  rib: star 32 93
  rib: tierceron 32 93
  rib: triradial 12 493
  Romanesque 12 366; 26 575
 velvet 12 464
 veneers 12 421, 421, 424, 425, 426; 20 467
 Vesperbilder 24 776
 vestments (ecclesiastical) 32 391
 villas 26 906; 28 102; 32 554–5
 wallpaper 19 429; 32 810, 817
 wall passages 26 574
 walnut 5 191, 191; 8 271; 12 423, 425, 426; 33 326
 watches 7 439, 443
 waxes 10 702
 weaving 12 463, 464, 465, 468
 westworks 12 363; 19 697; 26 574; 33 107
  Ottonian 33 108
 wicker 33 156–7
 willow 33 156, 326
 windows 12 408, 409
 wings (theatre) 25 788
 women artists 3 401; 18 206
 wood 2 45; 3 672; 9 752; 12 362; 17 741; 22 303; 24 461; 28 111; 31 255; 32 253
 wood-carvings 23 254
 woodcuts 4 373; 10 695; 12 383; 14 182
  animal subjects 2 103
  chiaroscuro 5 199, 294; 33 365–6
  Expressionism 10 695; 25 582
  Gothic 12 385
  Lutheranism 19 814
  Mannerism 4 864
  Renaissance 1 721; 2 103, 223; 5 199; 9 431; 12 386; 23 617; 26 79; 28 58; 29 434; 33 19, 352
  townscapes 7 584
  15th cent. 3 334; 4 8, 357; 7 648; 8 837; 10 725; 25 589
  16th cent. 2 719; 12 495; 21 579; 28 144; 32 680
  17th cent. 33 358*
  19th cent. 26 256
  20th cent. 4 893; 33 362–3
 wool 12 462–3, 464, 465, 467, 469; 18 158
 workshops 3 399; 28 492
 writing sets 18 522
 Wunderkammern 12 475
 yad 17 570
 zoos 33 699

Germersheim 12 361, 483–4*
Germi 15 921
Germigny-des-Prés 7 256, 257; 11 504; 12 484, 484–5*
 architecture 12 484–5*
 mosaics 7 275; 11 529; 12 485*; 22 162; 30 707
 Oratory chapel 3 541; 5 794, 799; 11 509
 piers (ii) (masonry) 24 750
 sculpture 12 485*
 stucco 11 553
Germisoni, Filippo 3 712
Germiyanid 16 204
Germolles Castle 5 207
Germundsson, Lars 30 77
Gernes, Poul 8 736, 741, 761
Gernrode
 St Cyriakus 1 722; 12 363; 23 646, 647; 24 750; 26 572; 33 107
  arches 2 294
  roof 27 129
  stucco 26 632
 sculpture 26 632
Gernsheim, Alison 12 486*
Gernsheim, Helmut 12 485–6*
Gero, Archbishop of Cologne 23 647, 652; 26 145
Gerő, Lászlo 14 891
Gero Codex see under CODICES → individual manuscripts
Gero Crucifix see under COLOGNE → churches → Cathedral of St Peter and St Maria
Gerofabriek 22 894
Gerolamini 6 99
Gerolamo see CAMPAGNA, GIROLAMO
Gerolamo, Paolo 24 836
Gerolamo di Bartolomeo Strazzarolo da Aviano see GIROLAMO DI BARTOLOMEO STRAZZAROLO DA AVIANO
Gerolamo di Giovanni Pennacchi see GIROLAMO DI GIOVANNI PENNACCHI
Gerolamo Padovano 12 733
Gerolamo Roberto Bresciano 21 905
Gérôme, Jean-Léon 9 766; 11 547, 567, 664, 671; 12 486–8*; 14 588
 collaboration 14 363
 dealers 2 858; 13 228
 groups and movements 2 530; 22 744, 745; 23 503; 24 171; 28 345
  Orientalism 23 504
 patrons and collectors 4 308; 7 377; 19 755, 875; 22 127; 29 651; 31 870; 32 829
 pupils
  Ahmet, Ali 1 475
  Backer, Harriet 3 22
  Bakst, Léon 3 86
  Berndtson, Gunnar (Fredrik) 3 821
  Brush, George de Forest 5 35
  Bunker, Dennis Miller 5 174
  Burnand, Eugène 5 265
  Cassatt, Mary (Stevenson) 5 921
  Cox, Kenyon 8 85
  Dagnan-Bouveret, P(ascal)-A(dolphe)-J(ean) 8 447
  Eakins, Thomas (Cowperthwaite) 9 500
  Edelfelt, Albert (Gustaf Aristides) 9 716
  Fox, E(manuel) Phillips 11 362
  Gandara, Antonio de La 12 36
  Glaize, (Pierre-Paul-) Léon 12 770
  Helleu, Paul César (François) 14 363
  Henry, Lucien (Felix) 14 397
  Hynais, Vojtěch 15 49
  Josephson, Ernst 17 662
  Laszczka, Konstanty 18 822

Gérôme, Jean-Léon
 pupils—cont.
  La Thangue, Henry Herbert 18 830
  Lecomte du Nouÿ, (Jules) Jean (Antoine) 19 38
  Léger, Fernand 19 77
  Osman Hamdi 23 604
  Peel, Paul 24 322
  Raffaëlli, Jean-François 25 846
  Rappard, Anthon (Gerhard Alexander) van 26 2
  Redon, Odilon (Bertrand-Jean) 26 71
  Robinson, Theodore 26 474
  Roll, Alfred(-Philippe) 26 558
  Schjerfbeck, Helene (Sofia) 28 104
  Thayer, Abbott Handerson 30 648
  Vuillard, Edouard 32 738
  Wauters, Emile (-Charles) 32 924
  Weir, Julian Alden 33 43
 reproductive prints by others 12 724
 studio 29 856
 teachers 8 654; 12 810
 works 2 106; 5 401; 9 245; 11 414, 414, 416, 544, 545; 12 487; 14 588; 29 574
Geron, Matthias see GERUNG, MATTHIAS
Gerona see GIRONA
Geroni, Pietro Antoni 4 441
Geronthrai see GERAKI
Gerrard, Charles 1 637
Gerraud, Gastón 24 510
Gerrish Nunn, Pamela see NUNN, PAMELA GERRISH
Gerritsz., Abraham 8 291
Gerritsz., Gerrit (1565-1644) 8 291
Gerritsz., Hessel 32 588
Gerritsz., Jacob see CUYP, JACOB (GERRITZ.)
Gerritsz., Pieter 20 615
Gerritsz., Reijer 32 724
Gerritsz., Willem 13 255
Gersaint, Edmé-François 2 559; 8 883; 11 663; 12 489*; 24 137; 25 815
 dealing 4 167; 11 663
 drawings 14 162; 18 626
 paintings 2 852; 24 255
 writings 4 331; 6 78; 11 662; 18 796; 25 815
Gersbach, Egon 14 498
Gersdorff, Hans von 21 6; 33 18
Gershov, Solomon (Moiseyevich) 27 581
Gershovich, Boris 24 350
Gershuni, Moshe 12 489–90*; 16 568; 31 566
Gerson, Horst (Karl) 12 490*; 14 635
Gerson, Jacob, Consul General for Saxony 20 649
Gerson, Jean 9 429; 33 18
Gerson, Susi 20 97
Gerson, Wojciech 12 490*; 25 107, 136, 141
 groups and movements 25 106
 pupils 6 532; 18 413; 24 11; 25 63; 29 538; 30 207; 33 450
 works 32 876, 877
Gerspach, E. 22 163
Gersprach, Edouard 28 350
Gerstein, Noemí 2 401; 12 490–91*
Gerstelinck, Bernard 2 199
Gerstenberg, Kurt 29 65
Gerstens, Jakob 22 302
Gerstens, Wolfgang Jacob 12 411
Gerster, Kálmán 28 850
Gerster, Károly 11 34; 14 889
Gersting 32 879
Gerstl, Emil 8 402
Gerstl, Richard 2 797; 10 696; 12 491*; 28 138; 32 446

Gerstl, Wilhelm 8 134; 28 380
Gerstner, Franz 19 718
Gerstner, Karl 1 79; 7 546–7; 23 262; 30 135
Gerthener, Johann 12 491
Gerthener, Madern 12 491–3*
works 11 733, 734; 12 *492*
Gertler, Mark 10 374; 12 493*; 17 578
groups and movements 19 623
patrons and collectors 16 42; 20 476
pupils 11 784; 14 111; 24 241
teachers 19 591; 31 146
Gertner, Christoph 12 494*; 28 60
Gertner, Peter 12 494*
Gertrude 12 419
Gertsch, Franz 24 686
Gerulata 4 694
Gerunda *see* GIRONA
Gerung, Hans 12 494
Gerung, Matthias 12 494–5*
works 11 838; 12 *495*; 33 354
Gervais, Paul 12 652
Gervais de Château-du-Loir, Archbishop of Reims 26 121
Gervaisot de Dueil 31 841
Gervase (*fl c.* 1200) 5 643; 27 124
Gerverot, Louis 22 882
Gervex, Henri (Alexandre) 12 495–6*
pupils 4 127; 9 382; 10 648; 18 177
teachers 5 342; 29 645
works 22 93
Gervin I, Abbot of Saint-Riquier (*fl* 1045-75) 27 589
Gervin II, Abbot of Saint-Riquier (*fl* 1075-96) 27 589
Gervis, Sir George 11 22
Gerzean *see* NAQADA
Gerzean period *see* EGYPT, ANCIENT → periods → Naqada II
el-Gerzeh 10 59
Gerzso, Gunther 12 496*; 21 406
Gesamtkunstwerk 2 807; 12 496–8*; 13 687; 15 868; 18 125; 22 379; 28 344; 32 763
Gesäter Church 26 647
Geschichte und Darstellung des Geschmacks 12 413
Geschwent, Jan 8 398
Gesell, Georg *see* GSELL, GEORG
Gesellen see JOURNEYMEN
Gesellius, Herman 12 498; 19 407; 27 473
Gesellius, Lindgren & Saarinen 12 498–9*; 27 473, 475
groups and movements 2 571; 22 541
staff 23 391
works 11 92; 14 371; 19 407; 30 284
Gesellius, Loja 27 473
Gesellschaft der Künste 23 121
Gesellschaft Deutscher Lichtbildner (GDL) 10 453
Gesellschafter, Der 13 773
Gesellschaft für Goldschmiedekunst 12 450
Gesellschaft für Radierkunst 25 629
Gesellschaft für Sammlung & Conservierung von Kunst- & historischen Denkmälern des Judentums 17 581
Gesellschaft zur Erforschung Jüdischer Kunstdenkmäler 17 581, 583
Gesner, Konrad 4 21; 24 353
Gessan 17 196
Gessen Genzui *see* GENZUI GESSEN
Gesseri Tomb 10 631
Gessert, M. A. 29 514
Gesshin Wada *see* WADA GESSHIN
Gesshō Chō *see* CHŌ GESSHŌ
Gessi, Francesco 12 499*
attributions 25 717; 26 283
collaboration 26 197, 200; 28 395
patrons and collectors 31 307
pupils 5 651; 31 359
Gessinger, Christian 12 369
Gessingh, Balten 22 872
Gessner, Abraham 30 147
Gessner, Andreas 1 789
Gessner, Franz 8 379
Gessner, Hubert 8 379; 18 467; 32 439
Gessner, Jacob 4 179
Gessner, (Johann) Konrad 12 500–501*
collections 30 154
pupils 14 303; 32 677
works 2 102–3; 19 *482*, 483; 28 206
Gessner, Robert S. 1 666
Gessner, Salomon 11 857; 12 499–500*; 29 73; 30 132, 133; 33 736, 737
pupils 12 500
reproductive prints by others 18 201
works 12 *500*; 20 914; 26 258; 33 737
Gessner, Thobias 4 179
gesso 12 501*
historical and regional traditions
Buddhism 6 717, 779
China 6 717, 725, 779
Egypt, ancient 3 482; 9 898; 12 501
England 6 560; 10 *292*; 18 610
Gothic 13 135, 139
Indian subcontinent 31 259
Italy 12 501
Japan 17 393, *394*
Scotland 19 *876*
materials
calcium sulphate 12 501
chalk 12 501
glues 1 156
size 12 501
techniques
gilding 12 626
types
gesso grosso 12 501
gesso sottile 12 501; 24 248
gesso spresato see under PLASTER → types
uses
beds 3 482
chests 6 560
dolls 31 259
fibre art 11 54
grounds 12 501; 13 135, 706*, 707, 708; 30 426
japanning 18 610
lacquer 18 609
masks 17 393, *394*
paintings 6 779; 9 898; 12 501; 13 135, 139; 28 339
sculpture 6 717, 725; 12 501, 626
tables 10 *292*
Gestalt psychology 24 383–4
Geste, Le 4 577
Geste, Vasily (Ivanovich) *see* HASTIE, WILLIAM
Gestel, Dimmen 12 501
Gestel, Leo 12 501–2*; 22 851
groups and movements 19 792; 21 775; 28 864
works 22 851
Gestetner, David 15 824, 825; 19 538; 28 299
Gesti, Vasily (Ivanovich) *see* HASTIE, WILLIAM
Gestingthorpe 27 17
Gestosa Parish Church 13 125
Gestoso y Pérez, José 12 502*
gestural painting *see* ACTION PAINTING
gesture 1 264–6*; 12 502–4*
Gesù, Il *see under* ROME → ecclesiastical buildings
Gesualdo, Alfonso, Cardinal 30 649
Gesuati Polyptych 27 765, *766*
Al Gesù glassworks 32 203
production 32 *203*
Getae 1 452
Getashen 2 440
Gether, Suzanne 2 767
Gethsemane *see under* JERUSALEM
Getov, Vilyam 5 159
Getrouw, Rudi 30 16
Getsova, Ekaterina 5 159
Getty, J(ean) Paul 12 504*; 25 194
collections 13 606; 31 667
sculpture 2 600; 13 470
Getty, J. Paul, Museum *see under* MALIBU (CA)
Getty, J. Paul, Trust 2 369
Getty Bronze 13 462
Getty Conservation Institute (GCI) *see under* MARINA DEL REY (CA)
Getty Epistles, Master of the 20 789, 790
Getty Grant Programme 7 742
Getz, Leon 23 262
Getzschmann, Robert 31 797
Geubels (family) 30 317, 320
Geubels, Frans 5 49
Geubels, Jacob 5 49; 32 6
Geuder, Martin 24 331
Geurin, Maurice de 26 536
Geurmaz, Abdulkader 1 635
Geurts, Marie-Ann 20 382
Geutebrück, Albert 19 457
Geva, Avital 31 566
Gevaş, Tomb of Halime Hatun 16 204
Gevelsberg 26 646
Gevorg IV 2 444
Ge ware *see under* POTTERY → wares
Gewecke, Hans 18 79
Gewerbehalle 24 444
Gewerbeschulen *see* TRADE SCHOOLS
Geyer, Ludwig 19 536; 32 763
Geyer, (Karl Ludwig) Otto 12 505*
Geyers, Nepomuk 2 813
Geyger, Ernst Moritz 12 505*
Geyler von Kayserberg 20 796
Geymueller, Heinrich von 12 506*; 29 600
Geymüller, Johann Heinrich 2 808
Geymüller, Johann Jakob 2 808
Geyre *see* APHRODISIAS
Geza I, King of Hungary (*reg* 1074-7) 9 *662*
Géza II, King of Hungary (*reg* 1141-62) 5 80; 10 544
Gezāw, Tāddasa 10 577
Gezer 16 *565*
fortifications 16 573; 17 553; 21 553, *553*; 30 190
glass 1 865
metalwork 30 196
pottery 24 634
urban planning 30 190
Gezer, Hüseyin 12 506*; 31 454
GGG Photo Studio 31 875
G.G.N., Monogrammist 33 357
Ghadames 1 315, *376*; 19 3, 324
Ghafadaryan, Karo 9 471
Ghaffari, Abu'l-Hasan 12 506, 507*; 25 769, 770
works 16 341, 342, 535
Ghaffari, Abu'l-Hasan Mustawfi 12 506–7*
Ghaffari, Muhammad 12 506, 507*; 15 898; 16 536; 25 769; 30 415
Ghaga-shahr 18 499; 24 216
iconography 24 218
paintings 18 *499*
palace 15 922
stucco 29 814, 815
wall paintings 24 218; 33 708
see also KUH-I KHWAJA
Ghaibi *see* GHAYBI
Ghalekuti 1 786
Ghana 1 *214*, 380, 386; 12 507–10*
architectural decorations 1 312
architecture 1 312; 12 508*
beads 1 297
body arts 1 288
cement 1 331, *332*
ceramics 1 330
coffins 12 *509*
cotton 30 VIII1
doors 9 164
education (art) 12 510*
figurines 1 272, *272*
houses 1 311, 320
iconography 1 262, 282
masks 1 342
metalwork 16 383
monuments 1 331
mud 1 284; 9 164
painting 1 240, *246*, 289, *290*; 12 *508*, 508–9*
palaces 23 824
patronage 1 240; 12 510*
posubans 1 314
pots 1 369
regalia 3 132
scarification 1 345
sculpture 1 331; 12 *509*, 509–10*
shrines (i) (cult) 1 289, 309, *332*
silk 1 293
spoons 1 369
staffs 1 *278*
terracotta 1 285
tourist art 2 588
trade 1 249; 16 383
weaving 1 293
weights 1 277–8, 363, 428
women artists 1 *246*
wood 1 *272*; 12 *509*
wood-carvers 1 435
Ghanada 2 271
Ghanapur 15 539
Chennakeshava Temple 15 328
sculpture 15 *539*
Ghanauli 15 483, 484
Ghandini, Alessandro 33 367
Ghanerao 15 615, 643
Mahavira Temple 15 273, 489
Palace 15 643
Ghani 16 526; 21 718
works 16 *527*
Ghani, Muhammad 3 53; 16 2
al-Ghanim, Jabr Jassim 18 541
ghanta 15 243*
Ghantasala 15 250, 438; 23 817
Ghanzi 1 *413*
Gharapuri *see* ELEPHANTA
el-Gharbaniyat 9 848
Ghardaia 1 *376*, 634; 3 755
architecture 1 315, 320
carpets 1 636
congregational mosque 1 316
Gharighat 15 452
Ghar-i Mar *see* AQ KUPRUK II
il-Ghariyeh 9 543
Ghasi (*fl c.* 1790s) 15 610
Ghasi (*fl c.* 1820-36) 15 601
Ghassoub, Youssef 19 8
Ghassul, Teleilat el- 12 510–11*; 30 *180*
architecture 30 191
cult centre 30 183
wall paintings 12 *511*; 30 183, 198
ghatapallava 15 243*
Ghathu 15 629
Ghatotkaca 15 257
ghats 31 *903*
ghatti gum *see under* GUMS → types
Ghayb Beg 1 583, 584; 16 552
Ghaybi 12 511*; 16 417
Ghayrat Khan 15 366
Ghazali 23 289
al-Ghazali 16 100; 23 561
Ghazan, Khan (*reg* 1295-1304) (Ilkhanid) 15 133; 16 193, 314; 20 371; 30 477
Ghazanfar 8 674
Ghazi al-Din Haydar, Nawab of Avadh (*reg* 1814-27) 15 654
Ghazi ibn ʿAbd al-Rahman al-Dimashqi 16 311
Ghazi Malik *see* GHIYATH AL-DIN TUGHLUQ, Sultan
Ghazna 1 *186*, 207; 6 *182*; 12 511–12*; 16 *105*
coins 6 266
excavations 16 550
inscriptions 16 259
mausoleum of Salar Khalil 29 825
metalwork 16 373
minaret of Bahramshah 16 166, 169
minaret of Masʿud III 16 166, 168
palace of Masʿud III 16 167, 169, 258; 29 825
sculpture 16 246
Ghaznavid 12 512–13*; 16 115
see also:
ʿABD AL-RASHID, Sultan
BAHRAMSHAH, Sultan
MAHMUD, Ruler
MASʿUD I, Ruler
MASʿUD III, Sultan
Ghazni *see* GHAZNA
Ghedini (family) 8 3
ghee 4 684
Gheeraerts, Marcus (i) (*c.* 1520-*c.* 1590) 12 513–14*
pupils 12 514
works 4 80, 920; 10 247, 725; 12 *513*, 514; 20 109
Gheeraerts, Marcus (ii) (1561-1635) 12 514–15*; 23 689
attributions 15 150
groups and movements 10 142
teachers 14 297
works 8 828; 9 278; 12 *515*
Ghein, van den (family) 3 603
Ghelniţa Church 26 710
Ghemen, Gotfred of *see* GOTFRED OF GHEMEN
Ghendt, Emmanuel Jean de 12 515–16*; 19 641
Ghent 3 *539*, 565; 12 516–23*, *517*, *518*
Achtersickel *see* Music Conservatory
Archaeological Museum *see* Byloke Abbey
art forms and materials
architecture 22 822
armour 2 471
brass 3 602
brasses 4 692
brick 4 778
embroidery 3 610
faience (ii) (ceramics) 3 590
gables 11 875
lace 3 610
manuscripts 3 552, 555; 4 372; 20 333; 26 563
marks 3 601; 20 *443*
metalwork 3 597
painting 3 559
pewter 3 603
sculpture 3 567, 570, 572; 13 113; 26 630
silver 3 598, 600
stained glass 27 255
tapestries 3 606; 12 519–20*
weathervane 33 8
Bischops Huis 3 548, 578; 9 411
craftsmen and artists 13 133
De Zwarte Moor 13 110
ecclesiastical buildings
12 520–21*
Begijnhof St Elisabeth 3 503; 13 110

Ghent
ecclesiastical buildings—cont.
Byloke Abbey 3 552; 12 521–2*
Hospital 12 521–2*, *522*; 14 780; 30 853, 901, 909
wall paintings 3 *551*
Church of the Saviour 10 704
Dominican Monastery 13 110, 182
Leugemeete Chapel 3 552; 13 110
Pand 27 256
St Bavo's Abbey (10th cent.) 3 567
church 3 541; 12 *520*, 520–21
manuscript illumination 3 552
manuscripts 3 553
textiles 3 609
wall paintings 3 552
St Bavo's Cathedral (13th cent.) 10 703, 704; 12 521; 13 211
altar 1 699
altarpiece
ciborium 7 303
metalwork 3 598
monument to Antoine Triest 9 412–13, *413*
monument to Eugène-Albert d'Allamont, 9th Bishop of Ghent 3 570, *571*
sculpture 13 113
St Jacobskerk 3 541; 4 *219*
St Jan *see* St Bavo's Cathedral
St Michielskerk 3 545
St Niklaaskerk 3 567
SS Peter and Paul 13 128
St Pieter's Abbey 13 211
St Pieterskerk 3 546; 15 45
education (art) 3 617, 618
Exposition Universelle et Industrielle, 1913 15 883
Fish Market 14 326
Gravensteen Castle 3 *541*, 541; 8 138
Guard House *see* Handelsbeurs commercial exchange
guilds 3 596
Handelsbeurs commercial exchange 33 179
Hoger Sint-Lukasinstituut 3 548, 618, 619; 12 519
Hôtel Brunin 26 285
Hôtel Falligan 3 546, *547*
Hôtel d'Hane-Steenhuyse 26 285
Hôtel Oombergen *see* Koninklijke Vlaamse Academie
Hôtel Vanden Boogaerde 26 285
Hôtel Verhaegen
Koninklijke Academie voor Schone Kunsten 8 594
Koninklijke Vlaamse Academie 3 546
Law Courts 3 547
Lousbergs hôtel 3 578
Museum Arnold Vander Haeghen 9 196
museums 3 616
Museum voor Hedendaagse Kunst 3 617, 618; 12 519
Museum voor Sierkunst 3 617; 12 519; 30 332
Music Conservatory 13 113
Opera 3 578
Oudheidkundig Museum van de Bijloke *see* Byloke Abbey
Pakhuis 3 546
Rijksuniversiteit 3 551, 588, 619; 10 187; 19 320
shops 4 790
Spanjaardskasteel 3 544
Stadhuis 2 294, 296; 3 543, 545; 12 523*, *523*; 31 238
Tanners' House 13 113
Town Hall *see* Stadhuis
University 12 836
warehouses 32 861
Ghent, Justus of *see* JUSTUS OF GHENT
Ghent, Olivier of *see* OLIVIER OF GHENT
Ghent Altarpiece 10 *704*, 707; 12 519, 521; 19 529
commentaries 31 795
dress 10 706
frame 11 439
grisaille 13 674, *675*
patrons and collectors 3 612; 10 363, 704–5; 29 46
realism (critical term) 1 710; 3 553; 18 704; 19 354, 529; 23 293; 26 184
restoration 4 161; 22 837
style 18 827
Ghent and Flanders, Master of the Privileges of *see* PRIVILEGES OF GHENT AND FLANDERS, MASTER OF
Ghent Associates 20 725, 727
Ghent-Bruges school 3 555; 12 519, 523–5*; 13 659; 20 736, 737; 21 638
works 4 *370*, *396*; 12 *524*; 13 *660*; 21 *637*
see also EARLY NETHERLANDISH STYLE
Ghent Calvary Triptych, Master of the 8 501
Ghéon, Henri 27 281
Gheorgiu, Ion (Alin) 12 525*
Gheraert van Brugghe, Meester *see* DAVID, GERARD
Gherardesca Tomb, Master of La 24 854
Gherardi, Antonio 12 525–6*
pupils 25 690
teachers 7 913
works 12 *526*; 21 893; 29 831
Gherardi, Cristofano 1 551; 12 527*; 32 11, 12, 14
Gherardi, Filippo 12 527*; 15 138
collaboration 7 553; 13 292; 32 215
patrons and collectors 7 622
works 16 671, 714; 26 320
Gherardi, Pietro 13 746
Gherardi, Sebastiano 7 553; 12 527
Gherardini, Alessandro 12 3, 527–9*
works 7 458, 897; 12 *528*
Gherardini, Maurizio, Marchese 5 432
Gherardini, Melchiorre 6 338, 340; 31 901
Gherardino da Forlì *see* GIUSTINO DEL FU GHERARDINO DA FORLÌ
Gherardo delle Notti *see* HONTHORST, GERRIT (HERMANSZ.) VAN
Gherardo di Giovanni da Minato 12 734
Gherardo Fiammingo *see* HONHORST, GERRIT (HERMANSZ.) VAN
Gherarducci, Silvestro dei 5 451; 12 529*
Gherarduccio Master 4 274
Ghercke, J. 30 276
Gheria el-Garbia 21 560, *560*
Gheri di Mannaia 13 775
Gherla Castle 14 885
Gherwen, Reynier van der 22 843
Ghetti, Bartolomeo 32 580
Ghetti, Pietro 32 580
Gheyn, Jacques de, I (1537/8-?81) 12 529
Gheyn, Jacques de, II (1565-1629) 10 387; 12 529–32*; 13 895; 14 41; 25 626
collaboration 9 79; 27 507
patrons and collectors 2 105; 11 225
pupils 32 621
teachers 12 879
Gheyn, Jacques de, II (1565-1629)—cont.
works 4 152; 11 225, 229; 12 *531*, 532, 881; 13 896; 20 247; 22 839; 23 464; 30 531, 878; 31 881, 882, *882*
Gheyn, Jacques de, III (?1596-1641) 12 529, 532*
Gheyn, Willem de 19 16
Ghezzi, Biagio di Goro *see* BIAGIO DI GORO GHEZZI
Ghezzi, Franceso 3 918
Ghezzi, Giuseppe 8 563; 10 676; 12 532–3*; 26 771; 27 486
collaboration 26 246
personal collection 8 563
pupils 1 795; 3 920; 12 533
works 16 720; 18 733
Ghezzi, Pier Leone 12 532, 533–6*, *534*
collaboration 1 795; 24 240
patrons and collectors 3 707; 10 769; 25 213; 29 724
personal collection 18 421
reproductive prints by others 13 300; 25 210
teachers 12 533
works 5 756, *756*; 9 225; 12 *535*; 13 300, *300*; 26 827
Ghezzi, Sante 28 472
Ghezzi, Sebastiano 12 532
Ghiață, Dumitru 12 536*; 26 716
Ghiberti, Buonaccorso (di Vittorio) 1 162; 12 536, 545*; 32 639
Ghiberti, Lorenzo (di Cione) 5 26; 12 536–45*, *542*; 14 869; 16 689, 690, 741; 20 432; 21 *11*; 28 676
assistants 13 259; 21 461, 465; 26 442; 29 407
collaboration 5 15; 11 185, 196, 201; 21 466, 467; 24 539; 31 201
competitions 7 664, 671
copies 3 854
domes 11 202
frames 11 382; 19 441
methods 11 184; 28 202
patrons and collectors 2 32; 3 173; 7 620; 13 824; 21 11; 26 766; 29 782; 32 22
personal collection 11 893; 27 45; 32 22, 639
pupils 9 122; 11 71, 86; 12 545; 20 553; 25 156; 27 180; 31 512
reproductive prints by others 13 303, 625; 24 252
restorations by others 14 690
sculpture 3 99; 16 690
doors 9 156; 11 200; 12 *538*, *540*, *541*; 14 870; 15 85; 16 614, 689; 24 90; 26 136, 183; 30 496
fonts (baptismal) 11 254; 16 692, 842; 28 681
reliefs 7 *671*; 12 *540*
sarcophagi 27 830
shrines (i) (cult) 11 198
statues 11 184, 204; 12 *539*; 16 689; 22 44
stained glass 6 11; 11 198; 29 504; 31 513
studio 29 853
writings 2 518; 13 863; 16 780; 31 302
on art 2 531; 12 685–8; 24 487; 25 46
on artists 5 124; 7 319; 12 683, 684, 691; 13 133; 29 598
on sculpture 22 44
Ghiberti, Tommaso 12 536, 544
Ghiberti, Vittorio, I (1418/19-1496) 12 536, 545*; 22 799
assistants 13 259
collaboration 12 544
pupils 32 22
works 9 158; 11 192
Ghiberti, Vittorio, II (1501-42) 12 536; 32 10
Ghica, Alexandru Dimitrie, Prince of Wallachia (*reg* 1834-42) 30 202
Ghica, Grigore II 26 708
Ghiesen, Peter 2 486
Ghieteel, Frans 16 867
Ghiglia, Oscar 12 545–6*; 16 679
Ghiglia, Paolo 12 546
Ghiglia, Valentino 12 546
Ghijsels, Jean-Pierre 5 45
Ghika, Matilda *see* GHYKA, MATHYLA
Ghika, Niko 12 546–7*; 13 353
works 12 *546*; 13 353
Ghika-Budeşti, Nicolae 12 547*; 13 204
Ghil, René 1 21
Ghilardy, Olinto 30 236
Ghilini, Marchese 1 622
ghilleems *see* KILIMS
Ghimnazia Vasiliană 26 725
Ghinelli, Pietro 2 2
Ghinghi, Francesco 12 547*; 16 747; 22 481
patrons and collectors 12 262
pupils 3 812
works 22 481
Ghinghi, Vincenzo 12 547
Ghini, Giovanni di Cristofano 28 687
Ghini, Giovanni di Lapo 30 272
Ghini, Simone (di Giovanni) 9 157; 24 731
Ghinucci, Tommaso 3 56, 57; 11 343
Ghiordes *see* GÖRDES
Ghiringhelli, Gino 6 582; 10 822; 25 838
Ghiringhelli brothers 10 822
Ghirlandaio, Benedetto 3 916; 12 547, 556*
collaboration 20 123
patrons and collectors 4 544
works 11 209, 211
Ghirlandaio, Davide 12 547, 555–6*
collaboration 11 687; 12 549, 550, 552, 553, 554–5; 20 123; 32 386
patrons and collectors 25 690
Ghirlandaio, Domenico 2 161; 11 184; 12 547, 548–56*; 26 765, 766; 29 853
assistants 3 300; 12 555
attributions 13 644; 19 445
collaboration 7 676; 26 186, 815
Antoniazzo Romano 2 184
Attavanti, Attavante (Vante di Gabriello di Vante Attavanti) 2 697
Botticelli, Sandro 4 494
Francesco di Antonio del Chierico 11 686, 687
Hamilton Xenophon, Master of the 20 689
Lippi, Filippo (di Tommaso) 19 445
Maiano, Benedetto da 20 113
Mainardi, Bastiano 20 123
Perugino 24 523
Rosselli, Cosimo 27 175
Vespucci, Guidantonio 32 386
drawings 9 *217*; 12 *554*; 20 124; 25 557
frames 11 384, 388
groups and movements 26 187
methods 24 *7*
paintings
frescoes
chapel of St Fina (Collegiate Pieve, San Gimignano) 12 *550*; 20 114; 27 751
Ognissanti (Florence) 4 494; 10 713
Palazzo Vecchio (Florence) 16 659
Ghirlandaio, Domenico
paintings
frescoes—cont.
Sassetti Chapel (Santa Trinita, Florence) 11 186, 712; 16 660, *660*, *763*
Sistine Chapel (Rome, Vatican) 4 840; 24 521; 26 815
S Maria Novella (Florence) 9 263; 11 56; 15 85; 18 704; 29 360, *360*
S Maria Novella (Florence): Cappella Maggiore 7 333; 16 711
S Maria Novella (Florence): Tornabuoni Chapel 18 725
panel
altarpieces 3 300; 27 734
portraits 16 751; 25 152
religious 9 77; 12 *552*; 16 659; 21 846; 25 690
patrons and collectors 4 494
Alexander, Francis 1 611
Benson, R(obert) H(enry) 3 740
Coke, Thomas, 1st Earl of Leicester of the 1st creation (1697-1759) 27 161
Drury Lowe (Holden), William (1802-1877) 9 306
Hieronymites 14 517
Kann, Rodolphe 17 777
Lorenzo the Magnificent, Lord of Florence (*reg* 1469-92) 21 14
Ryerson, Martin A(ntoine) 27 463
Sassetti, Francesco (di Tommaso) 16 763; 27 863; 31 124
Sixtus IV, Pope (*reg* 1471-84) 16 661; 27 271
Strozzi, Filippo, the elder (1428-91) 29 782
Thyssen-Bornemisza, Heinrich, Baron von 30 795
Tornabuoni, Giovanni 31 173
Tornabuoni, Lorenzo 31 173
pupils 1 102, 572; 5 129; 12 556; 13 280; 20 123; 21 432
stained glass 13 193
workshop 16 661; 26 815
Ghirlandaio, Michele di Ridolfo del *see* TOSINI, MICHELE
Ghirlandaio, Ridolfo 12 548, 556–7*
collaboration 10 877; 11 721; 27 740
patrons and collectors 23 855; 29 58
personal collection 20 536
pupils 10 858; 24 419; 25 262, 721; 31 205
teachers 12 556
works 12 *556*
Ghirri, Luigi 12 557*
Ghirshman, Roman 1 894; 7 187; 12 765; 15 922, 923
Ghirza 12 557*; 31 109
Ghiselin, Cesar 31 648
Ghisi, Giorgio 2 195, 455; 7 499; 10 386, 389; 12 557–8*; 28 316
methods 10 386
pupils 7 899
teachers 28 316
works 3 850; 4 860; 12 558; 20 322; 24 365; 25 605; 26 229
Ghisi, Teodoro 12 557, 558*
collaboration 2 20
reproductive prints by others 12 558
works 2 793, *793*; 32 404
Ghisilardi (family) 24 531
Ghislieri (family) 1 104
Ghisilieri, Antonio, Marchese 12 559*
Ghisilieri, Ettore 4 277; 12 559
Ghisilieri, Francesco 12 559*

Ghislain de Busbecq, Ogier see BUSBECQ, OGIER GHISLAIN DE
Ghislandi, Defendente 12 559
Ghislandi, Domenico 12 559
Ghislandi, Giuseppe 3 772; 12 559–60*
  patrons and collectors 5 872
  works 12 560
Ghislandi, Vittore 4 292; 31 883
Ghisleni, Giovanna Battista see GISLENI, GIOVANNI BATTISTA
Ghislieri (family) 21 539
Ghislieri, Michele see PIUS V, Pope
Ghisolfi, Ambrogio 26 503
Ghisolfi, Bernardino 4 335
Ghisolfi, Giovanni 5 289, 845; 12 560*; 13 347
Ghisoni, Fermo (di Stefano) 12 561*
Ghissi, Francescuccio (di Cecco) 12 561*
Ghiyath (fl c. 1600) 16 449
Ghiyath al-Din (fl 14th cent) 14 260; 16 316; 26 4; 30 223
Ghiyath al-Din (fl 15th cent) 30 921
Ghiyath al-Din, Ruler (reg 1397) (Bahmani) 15 356
Ghiyath al-Din, Sultan (reg 1469-1500) (Khalji) 15 573, 739
Ghiyath al-Din al-Kashi 22 322
Ghiyath al-Din Balban, Sultan (reg 1266-87) (Mamluk of Delhi) 15 410
Ghiyāth al-Dín Baysunghur see BAYSUNGHUR
Ghiyath al-Din Jami 16 474
Ghiyath al-Din Kay Khusraw I, Sultan (reg 1192-6 1204-10) (Saljuq of Anatolia) 17 864
Ghiyath al-Din Kay Khusraw II, Sultan (reg 1237-46) (Saljuq of Anatolia) 16 186
Ghiyath al-Din Muhammad ibn Sam, Sultan (reg 1174-1203) (Ghurid) 14 429, 431; 15 689; 16 167, 169; 21 627
Ghiyath al-Din Tughluq, Sultan (reg 1320-5) (Tughluq) 8 672, 678; 15 337, 340; 16 201, 373; 31 416
  coins 15 688
Ghorid see GHURID
Ghose, Ajit 15 618
Ghosh, Amalananda 1 469; 17 738; 30 378
Ghosh, Gopal 5 420
Ghositarama 17 857
Ghosundi 15 213
Ghujdivan Madrasa 6 203
Ghulam 12 561*
Ghulam ‘Ali Khan 15 208, 593, 594, 655
Ghulam Husayn 30 352
Ghulam Muhammad Warith 15 681
Ghulam Murtaza Khan 15 208, 593
Ghumli Temple 15 267
Ghuri see:
  DILAVAR KHAN HUSAYN GHURI, Sultan
  HUSHANG SHAH, Sultan
Ghurid 12 561–2*
  see also:
    ‘ALA’ AL-DIN MUHAMMAD IBN SAM, Sultan
    GHIYATH AL-DIN MUHAMMAD IBN SAM, Sultan
Ghurisa
  Gopala Lakshmi Temple 15 396
  Raghunatha Temple 15 395
Ghuys, Joris 28 899
Ghyka, Mathyla 9 70; 14 874
Ghysmans, Hendrik 11 731
GIA see GEMOLOGICAL INSTITUTE OF AMERICA
Giacchetti, Gian Ambrogio 11 636; 12 831
Giacchino miniatore see GIOACCHINO DI GIGANTIBUS DE ROTTENBURG
Giachetto di Benedetto 28 687
Giachetto di Benedetto da Razzo 16 756; 26 778
Giachi, Giovanni 27 788
Giac Hours see under BOOKS OF HOURS → individual manuscripts
Giacoboni, Giorgio 3 199
Giacomelli, Giovan Battista 10 524
Giacomelli, Mario 12 562*
Giacomelli, Sophie 16 906
Giacometti, Alberto 10 638; 11 550, 568, 569; 12 563–7*; 23 296; 24 144, 453; 30 125
  collaboration 11 727; 20 603
  dealers 16 906; 20 75
  groups and movements 9 758; 24 144; 25 6; 27 854; 30 20, 21
  patrons and collectors
    Cooper, Douglas 7 797
    Fondation Maeght (Saint-Paul-de-Vence) 20 76
    Guggenheim, Peggy (Marguerite) 13 801
    Hirshhorn, Joseph H(erman) 14 575
    Knox, Seymour H(orace) 18 170
    Matisse, Pierre 20 832
    National Gallery of Modern Art (Edinburgh) 28 273
    Noailles, Charles de, Vicomte and Marie-Laure de, Vicomtesse 23 169
    Rockefeller, Blanchette Hooker 26 489
    Schreiber, Taft and Rita Bloch 28 167
    Thompson, G(eorge) David 30 749
    Watson, Peter (Victor William) 32 912
  pupils 21 621
  works 12 564, 566; 19 491; 21 745, 769; 25 582; 29 575; 30 21, 139, 488
Giacometti, Augusto 8 434; 12 563*; 22 921; 30 134
Giacometti, Diego 11 727; 12 563, 565, 567*; 27 524
Giacometti, Giovanni 12 562–3*; 24 570; 30 134
Giacomini, Filippo 9 182
Giacomini, Giacomo Andrea 17 444
Giacomo II, Lord of Padua (reg 1345-50) 5 871
Giacomo, Nicolò 21 650
Giacomo, Salvatore di 21 495
Giacomo, Scilla see LONGHI, SILLA
Giacomo, Zuane see ZUANE GIACOMO
Giacomo Bellanti di Terra d’Otranto 20 323
Giacomo da Campione 5 551; 13 318; 21 533; 32 611
Giacomo da Damiano 19 181
Giacomo da Iseo 1 820
Giacomo da Porlezza 32 409
Giacomo da Sagramoro see GIACOMO DA SANCINO
Giacomo da Sancino 10 519
Giacomo di Corso 27 765
Giacomo di Cosmate Romano 7 918
Giacomo di Giovanni d’Antonio Loiani 20 624
Giacomo di Mannaia 13 775
Giacomo di Mino del Pellicciaio 12 567*
Giacomo di Paolo Sulmona 28 744
Giacomo di Vita 28 687
Giacomo Jaquerio see JAQUERIO, GIACOMO
Giacomotti, Félix (-Henri) 3 873; 11 546; 12 567–8*
Gia Dinh, School of Fine Arts 32 483, 492
Giai pham 32 483
Gialdi, Giorgio 4 832
Giallinas, Angelos 13 352
giallo antico see under MARBLE → types
giallolino see PIGMENTS → types → lead-tin yellow
giallorino see PIGMENTS → types → lead-tin yellow
Giamalakis 21 692
Giambellino see BELLINI, GIOVANNI
Giamberti, Antonio di Francesco di Bartolo see SANGALLO, ANTONIO DA (i)
Giamberti, Antonio di Sandro di Paolo see MARCONE
Giamberti, Francesco 27 732–3*
Giambologna 11 502; 12 117, 568–74*, 577; 16 689
  assistants 5 768; 9 158; 26 103; 30 31
  attributions 7 332; 21 770
  collaboration 3 631; 11 503; 12 346; 18 869; 21 903; 32 730
  competitions 7 672
  copies 26 389
  garden buildings 11 242
  groups and movements 20 281
  methods 21 769, 770
  patrons and collectors
    Alcalá, 3rd Duque de (1583-1637) 26 307
    Cosimo I, Grand Duke of Tuscany (reg 1569- 74) 13 910
    Cosimo II, Grand Duke of Tuscany (reg 1609- 21) 21 25
    Ferdinando I, Grand Duke of Tuscany (reg 1587-1609) 21 24
    Ferdinando II, Grand Duke of Tuscany (reg 1621-70) 21 26
    Ford, Richard 11 304
    Francesco I, Grand Duke of Tuscany (reg 1574-87) 10 441; 21 22, 23; 29 861
    Gondi, Bartolomeo 12 897
    Marczibányi, Imre 20 400
    Marie de Medici, Queen of France (1573-1642) 4 548
    Nollekens, Joseph 30 496
    Praun, Paulus 25 454
    Salviati (family) 27 648
    Tessin, Carl Gustav, Count 30 524
    Vecchietti, Bernardo 11 188; 32 105, 106
    Villiers, George, 1st Duke of Buckingham (1592-1628) 9 23; 32 575
    Vladislav IV Vasa, King of Poland (reg 1632-48) 32 7
    Watson-Wentworth, Charles, 2nd Marquess of Rockingham 32 912
  pupils 5 605; 16 699; 22 422; 23 252; 26 103; 30 227
  reproductive prints by others 2 20; 13 625; 30 803
  restorations by others 5 363; 19 117
  sculpture 7 783; 9 21; 11 503; 16 696, 703; 20 278; 22 44; 24 90; 32 106
    allegorical 20 279, 280; 21 23; 25 452
    animal subjects 12 572
    crucifixes 8 216; 12 403; 33 274
    doors 9 157
    equestrian monuments 4 402; 10 441; 11 187, 558; 12 573; 29 565
    fountains 4 272; 11 341, 342, 343; 16 696
Giambologna
  sculpture—cont.
    history 12 571
    marble 21 22
    modelli 12 570, 574; 21 769
    monumental 26 103
    monuments 7 311
    mythological 9 21; 11 214, 215; 12 572; 23 782
    nude figures 23 293
    portraits 11 503
    reliefs 10 743; 11 205; 20 278; 26 137
    religious 16 689, 695, 696
    statuettes 16 696; 21 22; 29 569, 569
  workshop 4 551; 11 188; 12 727
Giambone, P. O. M. P. 19 161
Giambono, Michele 12 579–81*
  assistants 6 11
  attributions 11 684
  collaboration 3 649
  pupils 8 166
  works 12 579, 580; 22 163; 32 189, 212
Giambono da Bissone 5 550; 24 194
Giambullari, Pier Francesco 4 408
Giammpiccoli, Sebastiano 4 736
Giampiccoli, Giuliano 12 582*
Giampiccoli, Marco Sebastiano 12 582*
Giampietrino, il see RIZZOLI, GIOVANNI PIETRO
Giana, Giovanni
  works 12 118
Gian Battista of Venice 25 96
Gian Cristoforo Romano 12 582–3*; 19 688
  attributions 6 103
  collaboration 4 817
  patrons and collectors 10 521, 522; 12 908; 15 861
  works 5 300; 12 583; 19 688; 20 918; 24 286
Gianda, Giovanni 12 119
Giandemaria, Marchese 29 32
Gianetti, Matteo see GIOVANETTI (DA VITERBO), MATTEO
Gianfattori, Carlo Ferrante see FERRANTE, CARLO
Gianfrancesco, 1st Marchese of Mantua (reg 1407-44) 12 904, 905*
  architecture 20 319
  coins 20 322
  paintings 16 661
  tapestries 20 323
Gianfrancesco da Tolmezzo 25 249
Gian Galeazzo, 1st Duke of Milan (reg 1378-1402) 21 534; 29 22; 32 609, 610–12*
  architecture 3 298; 5 894; 16 627; 21 516, 530, 841; 24 284
  books 4 76; 5 871
  heraldry 7 179
  interior decoration 16 711
  ivory-carvings 13 176
  manuscripts 2 123; 13 318; 24 779; 32 612
  paintings 20 321
Gian Gastone, Grand Duke of Tuscany (reg 1723-37) 21 7, 9, 31*
  cameos 2 22
  drawings 14 848
  tapestries 11 20
Giani, Alberto 27 420
Giani, Carl 2 826
Giani, Felice 12 583–5*
  assistants 24 822
  collaboration 7 493; 23 829; 31 679
  groups and movements 14 875
  interior decoration 29 640
  methods 10 199
  patrons and collectors 26 722
Giani, Felice—cont.
  works 5 555; 12 585; 16 677; 26 840
Giani, Giambattista 27 420
Giannattasio, Ugo 16 680
Giannino 13 817
Giannotti, Silvestro 19 117
Giannotti, Tommaso see RANGONE, TOMMASO
Gianotis, Bernardino Zanobi de see ZANOBI DE GIANOTIS, BERNARDINO
Gianotti, Francesco 2 396
Giansimoni, Niccolà 25 790
giant order see under ORDERS (ARCHITECTURAL) → types
Giant Salt see HUNTSMAN SALT
Gianyar 15 806, 807
  Gedung Arca Museum 29 239
Giaquinto, Corrado 12 586–9*; 16 673; 22 479; 26 774
  assistants 12 923
  collaboration 7 682
  patrons and collectors 4 561, 562; 10 806; 11 32; 27 316; 31 341
  pupils 5 902; 6 47
  reproductions in tapestry 6 47
  teachers 7 682; 27 201; 29 43
  works 12 588, 589, 923; 15 139; 20 72, 73; 29 283, 350
Giarde, Arrigo 29 830
Giardini, Alessandro 12 590
Giardini, Giovanni (1646-1721; silversmith) 12 590*
  collaboration 15 862
  works 7 746; 16 742; 24 273; 26 780
Giardini, Giovanni (d 1721; architect) 2 701
Giardini da Forlì, Giovanni 20 214
Giardino Barnabo 20 423
Giardoni, Francesco 32 375
Giardoni, Giuseppe 29 337, 341, 342
Giauque, Elsi 30 330
Gibaja, Arminda 23 414
Gibb, John 7 210; 23 58
Gibb, Robert (1801-37) 28 248
Gibb, Robert (1845-1932) 3 390
Gibberd, Frederick 12 590–91*
  pupils 6 409
  staff 10 145; 25 399
  works 7 258; 9 2; 10 242; 12 591; 19 506, 578; 27 527; 31 243, 733
Gibbings, Robert 4 366; 33 369
Gibbon, Edward 8 595; 13 303
Gibbons, Grinling 10 263, 273; 11 424; 12 591–2*; 32 358
  assistants 4 79
  collaboration 11 426; 20 880; 25 813
  groups and movements 33 199
  interior decoration 10 275; 23 467
    Christ Church Cathedral (Canterbury) 30 781
    Kensington Palace (London) 23 470
    Petworth House (W. Sussex) 12 592; 23 542; 33 453
    St Lawrence (Little Stanmore) 5 65
    St Paul’s Cathedral (London) 7 192; 19 599
    Windsor Castle (Berks) 33 249
  mirror frames 21 721
  monuments 19 606
  patrons and collectors 4 137; 6 128; 7 286, 298; 14 127; 29 58
  picture frames 11 423
Gibbons, John 9 757
Gibbons, Orlando 14 675
Gibbons, Rechucher Charlie 23 833
Gibbs, Henry Hucks, 1st Baron Aldenham 12 592*

Gibbs, James **8** 47; **10** 232–3; **12** 593–5*; **28** 878; **29** 736
- architecture **4** 422; **5** 65, 512; **12** 6
  - churches **7** 254; **12** *593*, *594*; **14** 257; **19** 314, 570; **25** 266
  - garden buildings **27** 466; **30** 451, 452
  - houses **17** 633
  - libraries **3** 83; **9** 86; **23** 688; **27** 237
  - mausolea **20** 866
  - orders (architecture) **23** 488
  - villas **32** 553
- assistants **10** 278; **27** 466
- collaboration **4** 805; **13** 782; **19** 606; **29** 835
- drawings **29** 715
- groups and movements **3** 266; **13** 199; **23** 860; **26** 499
- models **2** 337
- patrons and collectors **7** 175; **10** 490; **14** 178; **25** 635; **30** 451
- sculpture **4** 79; **5** 827; **10** 264, 278; **19** 606; **29** 30
- stucco **18** 634
- teachers **11** 274
- writings **2** 314; **5** 749; **24** 275; **31** 298

Gibbs and Canning **30** 504
Gibelet **17** 501; **19** 8; **24** 641
- architecture **5** 331–2; **24** 642; **30** 191
- Byblos **1** *849*, 850; **5** 331–2*; **16** 572; **30** 179, *180*
- Castle **19** 9
- coins **5** *332*; **30** 187
- dyes **1** 880
- fort **21** 563, *563*
- fortifications **21** 553, 587
- glass **1** 865
- halls **30** 191
- harbour **24** 642
- inscriptions **1** 855
- Maison des Morts **30** 182
- metalwork **5** 332; **30** 186, 188, 195
- mosaics **13** 546, 554
- pebbles **30** 182
- pottery **30** 196
- St John **17** 502
- sanctuary **30** 191
- sarcophagus of King Ahiram **30** 187, 193
- sculpture **5** 332; **24** 642; **30** 185
- seals **1** 856, 857, 862
- tombs **30** 195
- trade **9** 786

Gibelin, Esprit-Antoine **12** 595–6*
- works **12** *596*

Gibellina **28** 657
- Centro Civico e Culturale **28** 657

Gibert, Jean-Baptiste **19** 254
Gibert, Joseph **6** 366
Gibert, Pablo **29** 295
Giberti, Giovanni Matteo **12** 750; **31** 161
Gibil Gabib group **13** 530
- works **13** *530*

Gibney, Arthur **16** 12
Gibon *see* SENGAI GIBON
Gibraleón **29** 334
Gibraltar **12** 596–7*
- architecture **21** 574
- Calahorra **21** 585
- fortifications **12** 596–7; **21** 574, 584
- *ketubbot* **18** 3
- weapons **16** 505

Gibran, Gibran Khalil **19** 7, 9
Gibside, Durham **20** 868
Gibson, Allyson **3** 64
Gibson, Benjamin **12** 597, 598, 599
Gibson, Charles Dana **4** 365
Gibson, Donald (Evelyn Edward) **12** 597*; **28** 158
Gibson, Helena **30** 103
Gibson, James **28** 207
Gibson, J. B. **3** 250; **4** 627
Gibson, J. G. S. **31** 242
Gibson, John (i) (1790-1866) **5** 751; **12** 597–9*; **19** 507; **32** 786, 787
- groups and movements **32** 415
- patrons and collectors **3** 454; **6** 117; **14** 148; **22** 719
- pupils **14** 778; **30** 703
- reproductions in hardstones **12** 265
- teachers **24** 293
- works **10** 311; **12** *598*; **19** 614; **23** 295; **25** 175; **27** 878

Gibson, John (ii) (1817-92) **12** 599*
- teachers **3** 283
- works **3** 176; **12** 774; **19** 573; **31** 241; **32** 783

Gibson, J. S. **33** 193
Gibson, Kenneth **10** 421
Gibson, Patrick **12** 237
Gibson, Ralph **12** 599–600*
Gibson, Richard **12** 600*; **21** 29, 640; **23** 467
Gibson, Robin **2** 770; **4** 819
Gibson, R. W. **5** 124
Gibson, Solomon **12** 597, 599
Gibson, Susan Penelope *see* ROSSE, SUSAN PENELOPE
Gibson, Thomas **12** 600*; **33** 377
- works **11** *425*

Gidal, Peter **10** 688
Gidayū Takemoto *see* TAKEMOTO GIDAYŪ
Gidding, Jaap **22** 867, 900; **23** 450
Gide, André **12** 600–601*; **15** 888
- architecture **4** 332
- paintings **24** 838
- writings **4** 364, 765; **8** 715; **20** 126, 387

Gide and Baudry **9** 340
Gideon, Sampson **12** 601*
Gideon Associates **15** 56
Gidō Shūshin **17** 169; **30** 522
Gié, Maréchal de **3** 924; **11** 661
Giecz Piast residence **25** 94
Giedion, Sigfried **7** *294*; **11** 839; **12** 601*; **31** 672
- architecture **27** 214
- groups and movements **7** 293, 294, 296, 344; **21** 782; **29** 661
- pupils **14** 596
- writings **1** 666; **19** 896; **26** 735

Giedroge, Prince **30** 31
Giegerich, Jill **27** 277
Gieng, Hans **3** 822; **11** 773; **30** 136
Gien Jūgō **18** 557
Gierdegom, Joseph Franciscus Van *see* VAN GIERDEGOM, JOSEPH FRANCISCUS
Giergl, Henrik **15** 4
Giergl, Kálmán **14** 889
Gierke, Jakob **25** 129
Gierlach **19** 425
Gierløf, Christian **8** 747
Gierowski, Stefan **12** 602*; **32** 878
- groups and movements **25** 108
- pupils **17** 739; **18** 387

Giers, N. K. de **10** 90
Giers, Walter **29** 98
Giersing, Harald **8** 735; **12** 602–3*
- works **12** *602*

Gierymski, Aleksander (Ignacy) **12** 603–4*; **25** 107; **32** 876
- works **12** *604*

Gierymski, Maks(ymilian) **12** 603*; **25** 107; **32** 876
- works **25** *107*

Gies, Ludwig **12** 604–5*; **27** 308
- works **12** 407; **20** 926, *926*

Giese, Ernst **28** 95
Giese, Joachim Ulrich **30** 97
Giese, Johann Heinrich **12** 452
Giesecke, A. **23** 703
Gieseke, Wilhelm **13** 677
Gieselmann, Reinhard **31** 579
Giesen, J. H. L. **1** 804; **33** 616
Giesler, Daniel **25** 129
Giesler, Hermann **12** 605*
Giesser, Lenart **28** 862
Giessübel-Talhau **25** 542
Gife, Eugène **3** 763
Giffard, Pierre **14** 84
Giffard Bible *see under* BIBLES → individual manuscripts
Gifford (Lothian), Yester House **28** 246, 251
Gifford, Edward **16** 805
Gifford, Henry **30** 673
Gifford, Richard **8** 501
Gifford, Robert Swain **20** 604
Gifford, Sanford Robinson **12** 605–6*
- groups and movements **14** 843; **18** 715; **19** 791; **31** 602
- works **12** *606*

Gifu, Ōzōji **17** 125
Gigante, Achille **12** 606
Gigante, Ercole **12** 606
Gigante, Gaetano **12** 606
Gigante, Giacinto **12** 606–7*; **22** 480; **32** 400
- groups and movements **16** 678; **28** 317
- teachers **24** 893
- works **12** *607*

Gigantibus *see* GIOACCHINO DI GIGANTIBUS DE ROTTENBURG
Gigen **5** 145; **30** 769
Gigl, Hans Georg **24** 370; **27** 554; **33** 76
Gigl, Mathias, II (*fl c.* 1761-9) **24** 370; **27** 554; **33** 76
Gigli, Ottavio **12** 607–8*; **26** 473
Gigliardi, Domenico *see* GILLARDI, DOMENICO
gigliati see under COINS → types
Giglio **13** 372; **29** 700
Giglio, Carlo Vicentini dal, Conte **16** 739
Giglio, Livino di *see* LIVINO DI GIGLIO
Gigliotti, Vittorio **25** 273
Gignilliat, Antoine **18** 873
Gignous, Eugenio **12** 608*; **28** 34, 318
Gignoux (family) **2** 714, 717
Gignoux, Régis-François **12** 608*; **15** 858; **18** 627
Gigoux, Jean (-François) **3** 873; **12** 608–9*
- pupils **3** 259, 877; **11** 500; **18** 658
- works **19** 487

Gigthis **19** 889; **26** 919
Gihaut **6** 487
Giheta, School of Art **5** 285
Gijón
- Instituto Asturiano Jovellanos **17** 673
- Palacio de La Trinidad **3** 240
- Universidad Laboral **29** 273

Gijón, Francisco Ruiz *see* RUIZ GIJÓN, FRANCISCO
Gijsbrecht van Brederode, Bishop of Utrecht **20** 663
Gijsbrecht van Brederode, Master of **20** 663; **22** 836
Gikai **10** 112
Gil, Alvar Carrillo *see* CARRILLO GIL, ALVAR
Gil, Celeste Woss y *see* WOSS Y GIL, CELESTE
Gil, Isidro **25** 786
Gil, Jerónimo Antonio **12** 609*
Gil, Vicente **1** 587; **20** 621
Gilabert, Antonio **31** 814
Gilabertus **12** 609*; **26** 602, 610
- works **26** 595; **31** 211, 212

Giladi, Aharon **23** 25
Gilan **1** 786; **15** 919
Gila Polycrome ware *see under* POTTERY → wares
Gilardi, Domenico *see* GILLARDI, DOMENICO
Gilarte, Mateo **12** 57
Gilbert, Adrian **31** 863
Gilbert, Alfred **12** 610–13*
- collaboration **4** 221; **19** 60
- groups and movements **23** 33, 34
- patrons and collectors **14** 132
- teachers **10** 373
- works **6** 9; **10** 266; **12** *610*, *611*; **19** 600, 606; **20** 925; **22** 48; **25** 175, IV; **27** 831; **29** 575, *575*; **31** 132

Gilbert, André-Louis **11** 596
Gilbert, Araceli **9** 713; **12** 613*
Gilbert, Bradford **23** 42; **28** 830
Gilbert, Cass
- assistants **14** 317
- collaboration **23** 43
- groups and movements **7** 357; **32** 793
- restorations by others **14** 174
- staff **7** 838; **11** 25; **26** 42
- teachers **20** 19
- works **7** 326; **10** 683; **21** 649; **22** 363; **23** 42; **27** 565; **28** 831; **30** 507; **31** 595; **32** 861

Gilbert, C(harles) P(ierrepont) H(enry) **12** 615*
- works **23** 40, *40*

Gilbert, Dominique **19** 397
Gilbert, Edward **28** 295
Gilbert, Emile (-Narcisse-Jacques) **11** 520; **12** 615–17*
- collaboration **4** 171; **8** 879–80; **9** 312
- pupils **8** 544; **27** 768; **32** 84
- works **9** 338; **11** 521, 523; **12** *616*; **25** 637

Gilbert, John **4** 868; **12** 617*; **33** 369
Gilbert, John Graham *see* GRAHAM-GILBERT, JOHN
Gilbert, Michèle **19** 397
Gilbert, P. **3** 620
Gilbert, Stephen **7** 489
Gilbert, Walter Raleigh **15** 653
Gilbert, (Charles) Web(ster) **2** 753; **12** 617*
Gilbert, W. S. **12** 315; **30** 504
Gilbert and George **12** 617–18*; **19** 591
- groups and movements **10** 269
- works **10** 483, *483*; **24** 408; **31** 706

Gilbertine Order **21** 840
Gilbert Islands *see under* KIRIBATI
Gilbert-Lecomte, Roger **24** 405; **28** 745; **30** 20
Gilbert of Whitleigh **7** 420
Gil Blas **20** 602
Gilbody, Samuel **19** 508
Gilchrist, Alexander **27** 188
Gilcrease, (William) Thomas **12** 618*
Gildas **14** 408
Gil de Castro (y Morales), José *see* CASTRO (Y MORALES), JOSÉ GIL DE
Gil de Hontañón, Juan (i) (1480-1526) **12** 618–19*; **14** 578; **29** 265
- collaboration **12** 619
- pupils **12** 619
- works **13** 70; **24** 280; **27** 605; **28** 369, 518; **29** 265

Gil de Hontañón, Juan (ii) (*fl* 1521-31) **12** 618, 619*
- collaboration **26** 299
- works **27** 605

Gil de Hontañón, Rodrigo **1** 586; **7** 362; **10** 498, 534; **12** 618, 619–20*; **19** 171; **29** 265, 267; **31** 674, 822
- assistants **2** 375
- collaboration **12** 619, 920; **26** 299
- patrons and collectors **9** 112
- works **5** 362; **7** 345; **12** 618, *619*; **14** 475; **25** 23; **27** 605; **28** 369, 726; **29** 265, 267; **30** 501
- writings **20** 567; **31** 297

Gil de Liendó, Rodrigo *see* LIENDÓ, RODRIGO GIL DE
Gildemeester, Jan (1705-79) **28** 780
Gildemeester, Jan (Jansz.) (1744-99) **9** 298; **12** 620*; **22** 904; **24** 810
Gildemeister **8** 428
Gildemijn, L. **3** 885
Gilder, Helena de Kay **27** 557
Gilder, Richard Watson **27** 557
gilder's compo **12** 629
gilding **10** 135–6; **12** 620–29*
- conservation **12** 628–9*, *629*
- historical and regional traditions
  - Afghanistan **12** III1; **29** 825
  - Anglo-Saxon **10** 338
  - Belgium **3** 575, 576, 577, 582; **26** *145*
  - Britain **7** *444*, 445
  - Buddhism **6** *300*; **15** *501*; **17** *34*, 110–12, *111*, *112*, *113*; **18** *287*, *294*, *295*, *296*, *607*; **22** *497*; **28** *582*; **29** *460*; **30** *844*
    - China **6** 706, 707, *708*, *710*, *719*, *720*, *722*
    - Japan **17** *107*
    - Korea **18** *285*
  - Burma **5** 256, 261, *261*; **12** 626; **18** *607*
  - Byzantine **9** *645*, 654
  - Central Asia, Eastern **6** *300*
  - Central Asia, Western **6** 269, 274
  - China **6** 706, 707, *708*, *710*, *719*, *720*, *722*, 832, 859, 863, 866, 874, 905; **7** 22, *24*, *25*, *26*; **12** 623, 625; **18** 607
  - Czech Republic **8** *397*
  - Denmark **8** *746*
  - Early Christian (*c.* AD 250-843) **9** 654
  - Egypt **16** *357*, *520*
  - Egypt, ancient **3** 482; **6** 559; **10** 50, *51*, *52*, 53; **12** 620, 625
  - England **2** *471*; **6** 560; **11** *422*, *437*; **12** *626*, 628; **19** *4*, 5; **28** *665*
  - Etruscan **10** 625
  - France **7** *441*, *658*; **11** *589*, *591*, *592*, *594*, 595, *598*, 625–7*, *626*, *627*; **13** *109*; **18** I2; **26** *376*
  - Georgia **12** *328*
  - Germany **2** *458*; **7** *440*, *443*; **12** *443*, 445, III2; **24** 55; **26** *146*, *535*; **28** IV2; **29** 818, IX1
  - Gothic **13** *109*, 136, 139; **28** IV2
  - Greece, ancient **8** 262; **12** 625; **13** 393, 435, 537, 539
  - Hinduism **22** *772*
  - Holy Roman Empire (before 1648) **28** IV2
  - Indian subcontinent **6** 555; **12** V1; **15** 414, *501*; **29** 825
  - Iran, ancient **15** *920*
  - Ireland **32** *530*
  - Islamic **12** 625, 627, II1; **16** 357, *357*, *520*, *521*
  - Italy **6** 7, *7*; **11** *383*, *385*, *386*, *389*, *390*, *394*; **12** *538*, *540*, *541*, 628; **16** *728*; **27** *10*; **32** *193*, *201*
  - Japan **12** 621, 626; **17** *34*, 100, 101, *112*, 319, *321*; **18** 607; **22** *497*
    - Asuka period (AD *c.* 552-645) **17** *107*
    - Hakuhō period (AD 645-710) **17** 110–12, *111*
    - Heian **17** 321
    - Nara period (AD 710-94) **17** *113*
  - Korea **18** *285*, *287*, *294*, *295*, *296*, *364*
  - Madagascar **20** *39*

gilding
historical and regional traditions—cont.
Malaysia **20** 176
Moche (culture) **29** 212
Morocco **12** 628
Nepal **22** *755*, *772*, *774*, 774, *775*, *776*
Netherlands, the **11** *440*, *441*, *443*
Poland **25** *120*
Romanesque **1** *708*; **26** *145*, *146*, *535*; **29** IX1
Rome, ancient **12** 625, 626, 627; **27** *10*, 15, 29
Sasanian **15** *920*
Slovenia **28** *862*
South America, Pre-Columbian **29** 212
Spain **11** *488*, *489*; **12** 628; **19** 3; **29** *343*
Sri Lanka **29** *460*
Sweden **30** *94*
Syria **16** *357*, *520*, *521*
Thailand **12** 625, II2
Thracian **30** 769
Tibet **28** *582*; **30** *844*
Vicús culture **29** 212
Viking **32** *530*
materials
albumen **1** 156; **12** 621
alloys **12** 621, 627
aluminium **12** 621, 623
bronze **12** 623, 627, 629
clay **4** 254
copper **24** 55
garlic **12** 621
glazes **12** 623, 626
gold **12** 623*, 624*, 625–6*, 627–8*, 629, 869–70*
gold dust **24** 55
gold leaf **12** 620, 621, 622, 623*, 625, 626, 627, 629, 870
grounds **13** 707
gum arabic **12** 621
honey **6** 328; **12** 623
laminates **12** 621
mahogany **7** *658*
mercury **6** 328; **9** 663; **12** 623, 624*, 869–70; **17** 101; **21** 331; **22** 774
mordants (ii) (gilding) **7** 245–6; **12** 622, 625
mosaic gold **12** 623
ochre **24** 56
palladium **12** 621
platinum **12** 621, 627
red lead **24** 56
salt **12** 623
shellac **12** 621
silver **12** *328*, 627; **17** 321
silver leaf **12** 621; **19** 2
size **6** 328; **12** 628, 629; **24** 55; **28** 813
tin **24** 55
tin leaf **12** 621, 625; **19** 2
tools **12** *622*
transfer (printing) **12** 621
waxes **12** 629
zinc **24** 55
types
cold-gilt **6** 329
fire gilding **7** 813; **12** 624*, 626, 627; **21** 331
oil **12** 621, 622, 626, 627
water **12** 622, 626, 627
uses
altarpieces **1** *708*; **12** 625, 626; **13** *109*
altars **26** *535*; **29** IX1
armour **2** *471*
banners **17** *321*
beds **3** 482, 582; **10** *51*; **11** *594*
body arts **30** 654
bookbindings **12** 623, 627–8*
book covers **12** 627–8*, III1; **13** *159*; **16** 357, *357*; **30** 836
boxes **10** 53; **20** *39*
gilding
uses—cont.
bronze **6** 832
China **6** 707, *708*, *710*, *719*, *720*, 859, 866
France **11** *589*, 625–7*, *626*, *627*; **23** 531; **29** *343*
Japan **17** 100, 101, 319
Rome, ancient **27** *10*
Viking **32** *530*
bronzes
Etruscan **10** 625
bureaux **18** I2
cabinets (ii) (furniture) **16** *728*
cassoni **6** 7, *7*
ceramics **6** 328–9, 336
chairs **8** *746*; **10** 50, *51*, *52*; **12** *626*
chalices **2** *378*; **6** 398
chess sets **6** 555
chests **6** 559, 560
clocks **7** *440*, 445; **8** *397*; **12** III2
coffins **33** *580*
coins **12** 627
commodes **7** *658*; **11** *592*; **30** *94*
copper **12** 624; **17** 319
crowns **7** *25*
cult statues **8** 262
desks **11** *591*, *598*
doors **12** *538*, *540*
earthenwares **6** 325
enamel **7** 813; **10** 193
frames **9** 17; **11** 373–4, *383*, *385*, *386*, *389*, *390*, *394*, *422*, *437*, *440*, *441*, *443*, *488*, *489*
furniture **11** 595; **12** 626*
gesso **12** 626
glass **5** 256; **6** 269; **9** *645*; **12** 788*, V1; **16** *520*, *521*; **32** *201*
guns **2** *458*
icons **12** 625
ivory **16** 797
jewellery **6** 274; **17** 524
lacquer **12** 623, 626; **18** 607*
leather **3** 575, 576, 577; **12** 621, 623; **19** *1*, 2, 3, *4*, 5
manuscript illumination **12** 621, 623, 625; **13** 136
masks **30** 654
metalwork **12** 627*
miniatures (manuscript illumination) **12** 625
mirrors **6** 863; **21** *721*
ormolu **12** 627
painting **12** 624–5*; **13** 139
paper **24** 55, 56
pedestals **28** *665*
pediments **12** II2
photographic plates **24** 660
plates **15** *920*
polychromy **13** 393
porcelain **6** 326, 874, 905
pots **12** *443*
pottery **13** 537, 539
reliquaries **18** *364*; **26** *145*, *146*
sculpture **4** 851; **12** 625–6*, 627; **25** 175
Buddhism **18** *607*
Central Asia, Eastern **6** *300*
China **6** 706, 707, *708*, *710*, *719*, *720*, *722*
Greece, ancient **13** 435
Indian subcontinent **15** 414, *501*
Japan **17** *34*, *110*, 110–12, *111*, *112*, *113*; **22** *497*
Korea **18** *285*, *287*, *294*, *295*
Nepal **22** *755*, *772*, *775*, *776*
relief **12** *540*, *541*; **18** *296*
Rome, ancient **27** *10*, 15, 29
Slovenia **28** *862*
Sri Lanka **29** *460*
secretaires **26** *376*
shrines (i) (cult) **28** IV2
sideboards **28** *665*
silver **7** *24*, *26*; **12** 445, 624
gilding
uses—cont.
stucco **29** 818, 825; **32** *193*
tempera **30** 427
textiles **12** 621
threads **30** 541
thrones **25** *120*
trumpets **28** *582*; **30** *844*
urns **28** *665*
wall paintings **12** 625
wallpaper **32** 812
watches **7** *441*, *443*, 444, *444*
wine-coolers **28** *665*
wood-carvings **5** *261*; **12** 626
woodwork **12** 626*
gilding metal *see under* ALLOYS → types
Gildon, Charles **14** 637
Gilduin, Bernard *see* BERNARDUS GELDUINUS
Gilebertus **9** 155; **33** 247
Giles, Godfrey Douglas **3** 389
Giles, Herbert Allen **6** 612; **7** 161
Giles, James **10** 309, 318; **14** 857; **33** 377
Giles, John **1** 897; **23** 884
Giles of Bridport, Bishop of Salisbury **27** 627
Giletto de Alemania **13** 98
Gilfillan, J. A. **23** 58
Gilf Kebir **9** 865
Gilgal **30** 181, 182
Gilgamesh **21** 552
Gilgardi, I. D. **13** 611
Gilgit **5** 101, 102; **15** 544; **23** 798
Gilhofer **2** 829
Gilhooly, David **17** 694; **31** 640
Gili, Jerónimo **2** 284
Gili, Paoli **16** 742
Gili Moros, Joaquim **13** 725
Gilio da Fabriano, Giovanni Andrea **12** 629–30*; **16** 614; **25** 71
Gilioli, Emile **12** 630*
Gill, André **5** 758; **11** 297; **12** 630–31*
Gill, Charles Lovett **26** 336; **32** 257
Gill, David **3** 65
Gill, De Lancey
works **22** *642*
Gill, (Arthur) Eric (Rowton) **12** 631*; **17** 631, 632; **32** 786
collaboration **14** 674; **30** 744
groups and movements **2** 553, 571
patrons and collectors **10** 487
scripts **28** 307
teachers **17** 625
works **4** 9, *9*, 366, 373, 789; **10** 267, 482; **14** 107; **19** 606; **20** 121; **22** 117; **26** 133; **31** 497; **33** 362
writings **31** 498
Gill, Harry P. **6** 123
Gill, Irving (John) **12** 631–2*
collaboration **33** 407
groups and movements **21** 781
staff **33** 407
works **12** *632*; **19** 701; **27** 720, *720*
Gill, Louis J. **27** 721
Gill, Maud Ethel **2** 516
Gill, S(amuel) T(homas) **2** 745, 771; **12** 633*
Gill, William **31** 634
Gill, Winifred **23** 437
Gillar, Jan **8** 402
Gillard, Eugène **16** 788
Gillardi, Domenico **12** 633*; **18** 116; **27** 404
assistants **13** 654
collaboration **27** 376
pupils **5** 332
works **17** 869; **22** 172
Gillardi, Giovanni Battista **12** 633; **13** 653
Gillberg, Jakob **12** 634*; **26** 98
Gille **24** 149
Gille, Christian Friedrich **8** 451; **12** 634*
Gillen, F. J. **1** 67
Gilleron, Emile **8** 602
Gilles, A. (*fl* 1895-1910) **22** 20
Gilles, Antoine (*fl* early 19th cent.) **27** 659
Gilles, Jean-Baptiste *see* COLSON, JEAN-BAPTISTE
Gilles, Jean-François *see* COLSON, JEAN-FRANÇOIS
Gilles, Werner **12** 634–5*
Gilles de Blackere **10** 709
Gilles de Liège **13** 99
Gilles de Walcourt *see* EGIDIUS DE WALCOURT
Gilles le Muisis, Abbot **3** 553
Gillespie, James **12** 927
Gillespie, J. J. **4** 183
Gillespie, John **31** 335
Gillespie, John Gaff **7** 530; **27** 636*
Gillespie, Kidd & Coia **5** 513; **7** 530; **14** 863; **28** 232
Gillespie Graham, James **12** 635–6*
assistants **25** 712
groups and movements **28** 288
works **9** 723; **12** 773; **28** 230, 248, 254
Gillespie & Steel Associates **2** 148; **13** 876; **31** 335
Gilles van den Bossche **5** 53
Gillet, Arsène **8** 859
Gillet, Nicolas-François **12** 636*
pupils **13** 5; **18** 415; **20** 517; **25** 647; **28** 568, 643
works **32** 580
Gillet, Pierre-Joseph **21** 544
Gillgren, Sven Arne **30** 108
Gilliam, Sam **12** 636*; **32** 890
works **1** 443, 445, *445*
Gilliardi, Domenico *see* GILLARDI, DOMENICO
Gillick, Ernest George **12** 636–7*
Gillick, Mary **12** 636–7*
Gillier, Melchior **25** 390
Gillies, Max **8** 495
Gillies, W(illiam) G(eorge) **9** 725; **12** 637*; **28** 239, 240
Gilliland, Hector **30** 160
Gilliland, James **25** 842
Gillinder & Sons **24** 57; **31** 644
Gilling Castle (N. Yorks) **29** 835
Gillis, Antoni-Frans **12** 637*
Gillis, François **12** 637
Gillis, Jacob **10** 494
Gillis, Jan Baptist **14** 326
Gillis, Jean Michel **12** 637
Gillis, Nicolas **22** 840; **29** 666
Gillis, Pieter **3** 612
Gillis van Everen **3** 492
Gillot, Charles **10** 561; **13** 317
Gillot, Claude **11** 537; **12** 637–8*
assistants **32** 913
patrons and collectors **25** 815; **30** 523
pupils **17** 667; **18** 692
reproductive prints by others **2** 709; **15** 31
works **2** 467; **4** 360; **11** 36, 538; **12** *638*; **13** 701; **29** 748; **30** 672
Gillot, Firmin **10** 561
Gillott, Joseph **12** 30, 638–9*
paintings **4** 86; **19** 427; **31** 472
pens **24** 350
Gillow (family) **12** 639*; **31** 683
designers **30** 266
Gillow, Richard (1734-1811) **12** 639
Gillow, Richard (1806-66) **12** 639
Gillow, Robert **12** 639
Gillow & Co. **2** 755; **3** 893; **10** 282, 297; **28** 255
Gillray, James **5** 756; **12** 639–41*
assistants **8** 217
groups and movements **26** 742
Gillray, James—cont.
works **4** 607; **5** 756, *757*; **7** 648; **10** 252, 479, 555; **12** *640*; **25** 283, 651; **27** 869
Gill Sans *see under* TYPE-FACES
Gillsland, James *see* GILLILAND, JAMES
Gilly, David **3** 799; **12** 641–2*; **24** 443; **26** 13; **33** 228
pupils **12** 641; **14** 87; **18** 122; **28** 97
works **12** 374; **25** 408
Gilly, Friedrich **12** 641–3*
collaboration **12** 375
groups and movements **13** 201, 609; **22** 738; **26** 743
pupils **18** 122
teachers **10** 448
works **3** 792; **6** 171; **12** 310, 374, *642*; **20** 867; **23** 490; **25** 366, *366*; **28** 44, 97
Gilman, Arthur Delavan **12** 643*; **25** 327
collaboration **5** 64; **11** 836; **23** 41; **28** 831; **29** 870
groups and movements **26** 190
works **4** 473
Gilman, Harold **10** 374; **12** 643–4*
groups and movements **1** 666; **3** 894; **5** 516; **8** 264, 265; **10** 255; **13** 9; **19** 622
works **10** 256; **12** *644*
Gilman, Kendall & Post **31** 593
Gilman Paper Company **24** 683
Gil Master **1** 587; **20** 621
Gilmor, Robert **8** 575; **9** 199; **12** 644–5*; **13** 621; **31** 232
Gilmor, Mrs Robert **29** *918*
Gilmore, Joseph **3** 370
works **3** *370*
Gilot, Françoise **19** 492; **24** 724
Gilpin, John Bernard **12** 645
Gilpin, Laura **12** 647*; **24** 676; **33** 146
Gilpin, Sawrey **3** 277; **12** 645–7*
patrons and collectors **14** 144, 146
pupils **12** 164, 647; **28** 883
teachers **28** 285
works **2** 105; **12** *646*; **29** 425
Gilpin, William (1724-1804) **12** 645–6*
groups and movements **24** 741–2
works **18** 700, 713; **25** 572; **26** 740
illustrated **12** 646
Gilpin, William Sawrey (1762-1843) **12** 645, 647*; **32** 903
Gilsemans, Isaac **23** 57
Gilson, Jean-Henri **25** 872
gilt bronze *see* ORMOLU
gilt-engraved ***urushi*** *see under* LACQUER → types
Giltlingen, Johann von, Abbot of Augsburg *see* JOHANN VON GILTLINGEN, Abbot of Augsburg
Giltlinger, Andreas **12** 648
Giltlinger, Christoph, I **12** 647
Giltlinger, Christoph, II **12** 648
Giltlinger, Florian **12** 648
Giltlinger, Gumpolt, I **12** 647, 648*
Giltlinger, Gumpolt, II **12** 647
Gimac, Carlos **11** 19, 289
Gimenez, Rafael **32** 538
Gimeno, Eduardo **13** 252
Gimignani, Alessio **12** 648*
Gimignani, Giacinto **12** 648*
patrons and collectors **21** 27; **23** 87; **27** 172
pupils **12** 648
teachers **7** 913
works **11** 194; **26** 837
Gimignani, Ludovico **12** 648–9*
collaboration **12** 648
patrons and collectors **16** 82; **27** 172
Gimlinge Church **8** 730

Gimmeland 32 515
brooches 32 *514*
Gimmi, Wilhelm 12 649*; 30 134
Gimo 30 72
Gimond, Marcel 5 683; 9 60; 11 568; 12 506; 22 342; 31 94; 33 698
Gimont Church 4 780
gimp 24 237
Gimpel 10 680
Gimpel, René 3 18; 11 664; 28 384
Gimson, Ernest (William) 12 649–50*; 19 253
collaboration 19 253; 25 634; 29 843
groups and movements 2 569, 570, 575
staff 4 171
studio 29 858
teachers 28 347
works 6 391; 10 298, 299; 28 174; 30 782
gin 23 792
Ginain, Paul-René-Léon 2 391; 9 464; 12 650*, 746
Gindel, Hynek Prokop 8 414
Gindel, Prokop 8 414
Gindelach, Matthias *see* GUNDELACH, MATTHÄUS
Gindinarti Church 23 288
Ginebra, Danilo Caro *see* CARO GINEBRA, DANILO
Ginebra, José A. Caro *see* CARO GINEBRA, JOSÉ A.
Giner, Tomás 12 650–51*
Ginés, José 4 565; 12 651*; 29 293
Ginés de Aguirre, Andrés 12 651*
Ginestarre de Cardós 11 479
Gingee 12 651–2*; 15 *294*
fortifications 21 590
temples 15 398
wall paintings 15 646
Gingell, William Bruce 11 836
gingko 18 363
Ginjirō Fujiwara *see* FUJIWARA, GINJIRŌ
Ginkakuji *see under* KYOTO
Ginkel, D. van 30 391
Ginkel, H. P. D. Van *see* VAN GINKEL, H. P. D.
Ginkhuk *see* INKHUK
Ginn, Henry 19 287
Ginna, Arnaldo 10 687
Ginnasio, Cardinal 19 430
Ginner, Charles (Isaac) 12 652*
groups and movements 1 666; 3 894; 5 516, 517; 8 264, 265; 10 255; 13 712; 19 591, 622
patrons and collectors 16 42
teachers 2 62
works 10 256; 11 *437*; 14 107
Ginori (family) 11 206
Ginori, Carlo, Marchese 9 57, 58; 11 188; 16 737; 29 30, 572
Ginori, Richard 16 721
Ginotti, Giacomo 16 706
Gins, Madeline H. 2 282
Ginsberg, Jean 12 652–3*; 14 295; 19 747
Ginsberg, Jorge 13 725
Gintsburg, Il'ya (Yakovlevich) 12 653*
Ginzburg, B. 2 894
Ginzburg, Moysey (Yakovlevich) 7 770; 12 653–5*; 17 867; 18 445; 27 379; 32 661
assistants 19 207
collaboration 3 287; 21 622
groups and movements 7 769; 22 178; 23 590
works 7 770; 12 *654*; 27 379, 405, 409; 32 382
Ginzke, Ignaz 8 419
Gioacchino, Toma 31 100–101*
Gioacchino di Gigantibus de Rottenburg 1 127; 12 655*
Gioanetti, Vittorio Amedeo 16 739
Giöbel, Selma 14 594
Giocchi, Arnoldo 5 156
Giocondo (da Verona), Giovanni 3 359; 11 585; 12 655–7*; 20 133, 350; 25 906; 31 316
collaboration 26 804, 805
patrons and collectors 2 277; 21 16; 31 845, 847
works 5 285; 11 512; 12 *656*; 24 116; 26 454; 31 712
writings 2 161; 5 905; 6 357, 358; 31 295; 32 640
Giocondo, Lisa del 9 *263*
Gioffredo, Mario Gaetano 11 136; 12 657*
works 22 473
Giolfino (family) 32 343
Giolfino, Nicola 10 805; 12 658*
Giolfino, Nicolò 12 658
Gioli, Paolo 12 658*
Giolito 10 725
Gionima, Antonio 8 145; 12 658*
Gionima, Simone 12 658
Gion Nankai 12 658–9*; 17 188
works 17 189, *190*, 236
Giordani, Angelo 3 179
Giordani, Pietro 12 659*
Giordano, Antonio 12 660
Giordano, Luca 2 171; 10 114; 12 659–64*; 16 673; 20 66; 22 479; 32 194
attributions 9 52
groups and movements 3 261
metalwork 32 580
methods 23 377
paintings 16 673; 20 66
allegorical 15 138
altarpieces 16 676
ceiling 16 674; 20 71; 31 90
frescoes 10 504, *504*; 12 *663*; 13 801; 20 72; 31 89
literary themes 30 358
mythological 12 *661*; 22 414
oil sketches 23 381
portraits 12 *660*
religious 5 874; 12 *662*; 13 732; 22 10, 485; 26 436; 31 *90*
patrons and collectors
Andreini, Pietro Andrea 2 22
Balbi, Costantino, the elder (1676-1740) 3 90
Bardini, Stefano 3 228
Borromeo (family) 16 562
Carol I, King of Romania (*reg* 1866-1914) 5 792
Cecil, John, 5th Earl of Exeter 10 364; 13 299
Charles II, King of Spain (*reg* 1665-1700) 14 11; 27 802; 29 352
Colebrooke, George 7 552
Corsini, Filippo 7 896, 897
Curzon, Nathaniel, 1st Baron Scarsdale 8 281
Einden, van den (family) 10 114
Ensenada, Marqués de 10 406
Fetherstonhaugh, Matthew 11 39
Filangieri, Gaetano 11 70
Fries, Moritz, Graf von 11 789
Godoy (y Alvárez de Faria), Manuel, Príncipe de la Paz 12 839
Harrach, Aloys Thomas, Graf von 14 191
Harrach, Ferdinand Bonaventura, Graf von 14 190
Medinaceli, Luís de la Cerda Fernández de Córdoba Folch de Cardona y Aragón, 9th Duque de (1660-1711) 21 35
Orléans, Philippe II de Bourbon, 2nd Duc d' (1674-1723) 23 516
Pallavicini, Maria Camilla, Princess of Gallicano 23 874
Peñaranda, Gaspar de Bracamonte y Guzmán, 3rd Conde de 4 619
Giordano, Luca
patrons and collectors—cont.
Rosso, Andrea del (1640-1715) 27 205
Ruffo, Tommaso, Cardinal, Archbishop of Ferrara 27 316
Sackville, John Frederick, 3rd Duke of Dorset 27 494
Spinola (family) 29 411
Talbot, Charles, 1st Duke of Shrewsbury (1660-1718) 30 267
pupils 7 681; 20 841
reproductions in tapestry 6 47
reproductive prints by others 3 463; 8 763; 11 218; 26 517
restorations by others 6 47; 12 587
Giordano, Stefano 25 149
Giordano, Tommaso 8 807
Giordano di Giovanni 2 178; 27 658
Giorgetti, Antonio 23 644; 29 251
Giorgi VIII, King of Georgia (*reg* 1446-65) 12 331
Giorgi, Antonio de' 2 232
Giorgi, Bruno 4 718; 12 665*
works 4 713, 714, 719, *720*
Giorgini, Simone 4 104
Giorgio, Francesco 2 355; 22 378
Giorgio Alegretto da Ragusa 31 431
Giorgio da Firenze 31 443
Giorgio da Gubbio *see* ANDREOLI, GIORGIO
Giorgio d'Alemagna 4 20; 12 665–6*; 24 247; 31 428
works 12 *666*
Giorgio da Sebenico 12 666–8*; 28 85; 32 159
attributions 18 861
collaboration 1 604
pupils 23 89
works 2 1, *2*; 8 175, 178; 9 330; 12 *667*; 23 93
Giorgio della Chiesa 33 625
Giorgioli, Carlo Giuseppe 19 752
Giorgioli, Francesco Antonio 12 668*; 19 752; 30 132
Giorgione 6 85; 12 668–78*; 16 665; 32 193
attributions 3 179; 11 662; 18 708; 19 300; 24 390; 25 569; 26 358, 364; 28 332; 31 32–3, 362
collaboration 5 535; 28 332; 31 32
methods 7 628; 23 376
paintings 16 665
allegorical 1 656; 12 *668*
altarpieces 12 *673*; 26 364; 27 496
façade decoration 10 737, 738
fêtes champêtres 11 34, 35, *35*
frescoes 3 670; 19 663; 32 191
genre 12 288
landscape 12 *670*; 18 707; 32 191
mythological 10 476; 12 *672*; 22 414; 23 292; 32 191
portraits 12 *669*, *671*; 25 276
religious 10 476; 24 90
patrons and collectors
Art Gallery and Museum (Glasgow) 28 273
Augustus II, King of Poland (*reg* 1697-1706; 1709-33) 33 115
Barbarigo, Agostino, Doge of Venice (*reg* 1486- 1501) 3 201
Benson, R(obert) H(enry) 3 740
Bourbon I., Louis de, le Grand Dauphin (1661-1711) 4 553
Contarini, Taddeo 7 775
Crozat, Pierre 8 209
Everdingen, Allart van 10 660
Grimani, Domenico, Cardinal, Patriarch of Aquilea 13 657
Giorgione
patrons and collectors—cont.
Grimani, Giovanni, Patriarch of Aquileia 13 659
Habsburg I., Leopold William, Archduke of Austria, Governor of the Netherlands 13 919
Hamilton, James, 3rd Marquess and 1st Duke of Hamilton 10 861
Herbert, Philip, 4th Earl of Pembroke and 1st Earl of Montgomery 14 435
Hesselin, Louis (-Cauchon) 14 492
Imperiale, Gian Vincenzo 15 148
Jabach, Everard 16 814
Leemput, Remi van 19 63
Leyland, F(rederick) R(ichard) 19 290
Michiel, Marcantonio 21 474
Nave, Bartolomeo della 22 696
Piles, Roger de 24 805
Ruffo, Tommaso, Cardinal, Archbishop of Ferrara 27 316
Strange, John 29 746
Tallard, Marie-Joseph d'Hostun, Duc de 30 274
Vendramin, Gabriele 16 767; 32 156
Villiers, George, 1st Duke of Buckingham (1592-1628) 32 575
pupils 28 331; 31 32, 161, 523
reproductive prints by others 5 534; 8 267; 9 407; 25 858; 26 229
restorations by others 24 343; 27 321
Giorgis, G. 4 101
Giori, Angelo, Cardinal 4 538, 540; 7 394; 12 679–80*
giornale artistico, Il 20 483; 24 448
Giornale degli architetti 24 447
Giornale de' letterati 2 163
giornale dell'arte, Il 24 449
Giornale delle belle arti e della incisione antiquaria, musica e poesia 24 447
Giornale di belle arti ossia pubblicazione mensuale delle migliori opere degli artisti... 24 447
Giornale di fotografia 24 447
giornate 11 763, *763*; 12 680*; 13 145
Giornico, S Niccolò 26 635
Giosafatti (family) 2 594
Giosafatti, Antonio 12 680
Giosafatti, Giuseppe 2 594; 12 680*
teachers 22 103
works 2 594
Giosafatti, Lazzaro 12 680*
Giosafatti, Lorenzo 12 680
Giosafatti, Pietro 12 680
Giosafatti, Silvio 12 680
Giosuè, Abbot of San Vincenzo 27 806
Giosuè di Santi 22 800
Giottino (*fl* 1368) 12 681*; 20 551
attributions 2 625, 626
collaboration 11 890
works 26 815
Giottino (1770-1849) *see* HUMBERT DE SUPERVILLE, DAVID PIERRE
Giotto (di Bondone) 2 558, 625; 6 107; 12 681–95*; 13 135, 144, 145; 14 868; 23 292, 753
architecture 11 176, 200; 13 65, 133; 16 627, 777; 24 875; 30 272
assistants 8 471; 20 552
Giotto (di Bondone)—cont.
attributions 1 640; 2 *338*, 625, 627; 6 100; 19 683; 20 697, 712; 25 *463*; 26 246, 541; 29 405
competitions 7 676
copies 2 576
methods 6 569; 7 627; 12 621; 13 133, 135, 138; 19 353; 24 5, 486, 492; 32 805
mosaics 16 613; 22 163; 26 803
paintings
frescoes
Arena Chapel (Padua) 5 443; 6 1, 460; 9 245, 260; 12 *682*, *684*, *685*, *687*, *688*; 13 145–6, 673; 15 135; 16 655, 837; 18 676; 22 521; 23 756–7; 24 VIII1; 26 182
Castelnuovo (Naples) 13 150; 22 486
Old St Peter's (Rome, Vatican) 29 596
Palazzo Visconti (Milan) 21 524
Santa Croce (Florence) 11 183, 206, *709*; 12 *691*, *692*
S Francesco (Assisi) 2 624; 12 *693*; 25 230
S Francesco (Rimini) 26 398
panel
altarpieces 1 708; 4 275; 11 380; 16 847; 24 854; 25 462
crucifixes 8 212; 11 209; 12 *694*
religious 12 *689*
patrons and collectors
Artaud de Montor, Jean-Alexis-François 2 514
Azzo(ne), Lord of Milan (*reg* 1328-39) 32 609, 610
Bardi (i) (family) 3 173, 226; 11 712
Bodemuseum (Berlin) 9 200
Butler, Charles (1822-1910) 5 311
Coningham, William 7 709
Davenport Bromley, Walter 8 549
Fesch, Joseph, Cardinal 11 32
Gardner, Isabella Stewart 12 147
Gondi, Bartolomeo 12 897
Graham, William 13 272
Hervey, Frederick Augustus, 4th Earl of Bristol 14 485
Horne, Herbert (Percy) 14 764
Lorenzo the Magnificent, Lord of Florence (*reg* 1469-92) 16 770
Metropolitan Museum of Art (New York) 9 200
Peruzzi (family) 3 173; 11 712
Petrarch, Francesco 5 871; 24 559
Poniatowski, Stanisław, Prince 25 213
Robert, King of Naples and Jerusalem (*reg* 1309-43) 2 109, 110; 13 150–51
Scala, della (family) 32 343
Scrovegni, Enrico 3 173
Solly, Edward 29 46
Stefaneschi, Giacomo Gaetani, Cardinal 26 765; 29 596
photographed works 22 702
pupils 5 661; 6 168; 8 441; 11 888; 20 504, 551
reproductive prints by others 13 303; 24 252
restorations by others 3 919; 19 442; 27 321
sculpture 11 200
teachers 7 319
workshop 11 888; 13 132, 135; 22 476
Giotto de Maestro Stefano *see* GIOTTINO (*fl* 1368)

Giovan Battista da Siena *see* SIENA, GIOVAN BATTISTA DA
Giovane, Palma 25 227; 27 274
giovane artista moderno, Il 24 448
Giovanelli, Benedetto 28 676
Giovanello di Maffeo, Matteo di *see* GATTAPONE
Giovanetti (da Viterbo), Matteo 12 696–7*
patrons and collectors 7 411
works 2 862; 12 *697*; 13 150; 32 *573*, 574
Giovanna Battista, Regent 6 19
Giovanna da Piacenza 7 322, 886–7
Giovannetti, Matteo 32 628
Giovanni, Fra 18 697
Giovanni, Master 28 683
Giovanni IV, Abbot of Benevento 3 716
Giovanni, Agostino di *see* AGOSTINO DI GIOVANNI
Giovanni, Antonio di Agostino di ser *see* ANTONIO DA FABRIANO
Giovanni (di Tomaso), Apollonio di *see* APOLLONIO DI GIOVANNI (DI TOMASO)
Giovanni, Bartolomeo di *see* BARTOLOMEO DI GIOVANNI
Giovanni (di Marco), Berto di *see* BERTO DI GIOVANNI (DI MARCO)
Giovanni, Bertoldi di *see* BERTOLDI DI GIOVANNI
Giovanni, Brenni 33 276
Giovanni, Buonaiuto di *see* BUONAIUTO DI GIOVANNI
Giovanni, Francesco di *see* FRANCIONE
Giovanni, Giordano di *see* GIORDANO DI GIOVANNI
Giovanni (da Pisa), Gualtieri di *see* GUALTIERI DI GIOVANNI (DA PISA)
Giovanni, Guido di *see* GUIDO DI GIOVANNI
Giovanni, Lattanzio di *see* LATTANZIO DI GIOVANNI
Giovanni (da Firenze), Leonardo di Ser *see* LEONARDO DI SER GIOVANNI (DA FIRENZE)
Giovanni, Luigi de 7 316
Giovanni, Matteo di *see* MATTEO DI GIOVANNI
Giovanni, Mino di *see* MINO DA FIESOLE
Giovanni, Piero di *see* LORENZO MONACO
Giovanni, Sandrino di *see* SANDRINO DI GIOVANNI
Giovanni, Ser *see* RICCIARDO DI NANNI, SER
Giovanni, Tommaso di *see* MASACCIO
Giovanni Agostino da Lodi 12 698*; 21 485
Giovanni Andrea *see* ZOAN ANDREA
Giovanni Angelo di Antonio da Camerino 20 623
Giovanni Antonio da Brescia 12 698–9*
collaboration 20 314
works 9 308; 10 384; 12 *698*; 13 700
Giovanni Antonio da Parma 5 913
Giovanni Antonio d'Arezzo 10 784; 12 906
Giovanni Balducci *see* GIOVANNI DI BALDUCCIO
Giovanni Battista da Sesto *see* SESTO, GIOVANNI BATTISTA DA
Giovanni Battista di Jacopo Rosso *see* ROSSO FIORENTINO
Giovanni Battista Egnazio 21 474
Giovanni Boniforte da Concorezzo 20 319
Giovanni Carlo di Bretagna 31 428
Giovanni Cristoforo Romano *see* GIAN CRISTOFORO ROMANO
Giovanni da Campi 30 272, 273
Giovanni da Campione 2 212; 3 771, 772, 773; 5 550, 551; 13 94
Giovanni da Castel Bolognese *see* BERNARDI, GIOVANNI (DESIDERIO)
Giovanni da Como *see* GIOVANNI DA MILANO
Giovanni da Cremona *see* FONDULI, GIOVANNI PAULO
Giovanni da Fano 12 699*
Giovanni da Fiesole (*c.* 1395/1400-1455) *see* ANGELICO, Fra
Giovanni da Fiesole (*fl* 1472) 16 724
Giovanni da Fiesole (1501-47) 24 419
Giovanni da Firenze 22 476
Giovanni da Gaibano 32 197
Giovanni da Gaiole 20 264
Giovanni d'Agostino 1 457*; 28 679, 680, 681
Giovanni d'Alemagna 12 699*; 32 229, 652
collaboration 3 876; 20 304; 23 754; 27 495; 32 653–4
teachers 12 581
works 12 581; 25 9; 32 *228*, *654*
Giovanni d'Alesso d'Antonio *see* UNGHERO, NANNI
Giovanni dall'Acqua 7 898
Giovanni Dalmata 12 699–700*; 14 893; 31 359
attributions 4 737
collaboration 4 737; 21 694; 24 278; 26 767
patrons and collectors 27 271
works 8 178; 14 884; 26 809; 31 359
Giovanni dal Monte 19 496
Giovanni da Lodi *see* BATTAGGIO, GIOVANNI DI DOMENICO
Giovanni dal Ponte 12 700*
patrons and collectors 5 509
pupils 6 11
works 4 31; 6 2; 13 169
Giovanni da Maiano *see* MAIANO, GIOVANNI DA
Giovanni d'Ambrogio 11 197, 892; 12 701*; 13 94
Giovanni d'Ambrogio, Pietro di *see* PIETRO DI GIOVANNI D'AMBROGIO
Giovanni da Milano 12 702–3*; 25 731
assistants 11 891
collaboration 11 890; 12 681
patrons and collectors 29 693
works 12 *702*, *703*; 26 815
Giovanni da Minato, Gherardo di *see* GHERARDO DI GIOVANNI DA MINATO
Giovanni da Modena 12 703–4*
collaboration 21 462
works 12 *704*
Giovanni da Monte Cassino 12 704*
Giovanni da Murrovalle 12 693; 20 712
Giovanni da Napoli *see* MARIGLIANO, GIOVANNI
Giovanni da Nola *see* MARIGLIANO, GIOVANNI
Giovanni da None 12 683
Giovanni d'Antonio *see* PIFFERO
Giovanni da Oleggio 2 18
Giovanni (di Giuliano) da Oriolo 12 705*
Giovanni da Piacenza 4 276
Giovanni da Piamonte 24 762
Giovanni (di Pietro) da Pisa (i) (*fl* 1401-23) 12 705*
Giovanni da Pisa (ii) (*fl* 1444-*d c.* 1460) 9 130; 12 705*; 25 9; 31 707
Giovanni d'Aragona, Cardinal 12 171; 20 144; 26 2; 27 806
Giovanni d'Arbosio *see* JEAN D'ARBOIS
Giovanni d'Aria 32 603
Giovanni da Rimini 12 705–6*
Giovanni (di Andrea) da Riolo 12 705
Giovanni da San Giovanni 12 706–7*; 27 179
collaboration 11 845; 21 26
patrons and collectors 3 744, 745; 5 179; 21 25, 26; 33 579
works 10 *736*, 737; 11 214, 846; 12 *707*; 21 26
Giovanni da Trau 2 2
Giovanni da Verona 12 707–8*; 16 726; 25 849; 32 343
Giovanni de Bonsignori 23 680
Giovanni degli Studiuoli *see* VASANZIO, GIOVANNI
Giovanni de Grassi 21 530, 531; 24 270
Giovanni del Biondo 12 708–9*
works 11 380; 12 *708*; 13 149
Giovanni delle Corniole *see* GIOVANNI DELLE OPERE
Giovanni delle Opere 12 257; 16 746, 751; 20 800
works 12 *257*
Giovanni dell'Opera *see* BANDINI, GIOVANNI (DI BENEDETTO)
Giovanni del Virgillio 23 679
Giovanni di Alberto 19 686
Giovanni di Andrea di Domenico 32 366
Giovanni di Balduccio 12 709–10*; 13 93; 24 854
patrons and collectors 32 609
works 4 275; 13 *94*, 94, 96, 124; 16 688; 21 524
Giovanni di Bartolo (*fl* 1365-85) 13 169; 28 676
Giovanni di Bartolo (*fl* 1419-35) *see* NANNI DI BARTOLO
Giovanni di Bartolomeo (*fl* 1384) 22 680
Giovanni di Bartolommeo da Firenze (*fl* 1429) 18 674; 20 552
Giovanni di Benedetto (*fl* 1361) 28 686
Giovanni di Benedetto da Como (*fl c.* 1378) 12 710*; 20 710
Giovanni di Bernardo 5 130
Giovanni di Bertino 12 710*
Giovanni di Bindino 3 707
Giovanni di Bonino 2 632; 20 674
Giovanni di Bonsignori 15 82
Giovanni di Cecco 28 678, 679
Giovanni di Consalvo 12 710–12*
works 12 *711*
Giovanni di Contaldino di Meuccio 32 360
Giovanni di Cosma *see* COSMATI, JOHANNES
Giovanni di Cristofano 4 32
Giovanni di Cristoforo 5 913
Giovanni di Domenico di Piero 4 505
Giovanni di Francesco (del Cervelliera) (i) 1412-59) 12 712–13*; 20 748
attributions 20 704
collaboration 19 445; 24 754
works 16 847; 19 442; 26 399
Giovanni di Francesco (ii) (*fl* 1444-*d c.* 1460) *see* GIOVANNI DA PISA (i)
Giovanni di Francesco Ciambella 24 525
Giovanni di Francesco da Imola 16 841, 842; 31 450
Giovanni di Francesco Ribaldi *see* RIBALDI, GIOVANNI DI FRANCESCO
Giovanni di Francia (*fl* 1389) *see* ZANINO DI PIETRO
Giovanni di Francia (*fl c.* 1491) *see* ZOHANNE DE FRANZA
Giovanni di Gante 16 66
Giovanni di Gherardo da Prato 12 713–14*
Giovanni di Giovanni 11 192
Giovanni di Giuliano da Piacenza 26 457
Giovanni di Gualtieri 13 733
Giovanni di Guido *see* RAINERIUS, JOHANNES GUITTONIS
Giovanni di Lorenzo 26 844
Giovanni di Magré 21 904
Giovanni di Marco *see* GIOVANNI DAL PONTE
Giovanni di Martino da Fiesole 13 95; 18 674; 21 747
Giovanni di Niccolò 12 539
Giovanni di Nicolò (da) Barbagelata *see* BARGAGELATA, GIOVANNI DI NICOLÒ (DA)
Giovanni di Paolo (di Grazia) 12 714–16*; 13 149; 30 233
attributions 4 30
patrons and collectors 19 92; 29 763
pupils 11 842
works 5 884; 6 4; 11 383; 12 *714*, *715*; 16 662
Giovanni di Pietro (i) (*fl* 1401-23) *see* GIOVANNI (DI PIETRO) DA PISA (i)
Giovanni di Pietro (di Giovanni) (ii) (*b c.* 1403-*d* before 1479) 12 716–17*; 20 844; 24 760
Giovanni di ser Francesco 12 580
Giovanni di Ser Giovanni Guidi *see* SCHEGGIA
Giovanni di Simone 24 857
Giovanni di Stefano (*c.* 1446-1506) 3 298; 12 717*; 20 745; 28 681
Giovanni di Stefano da Siena (*fl* 1366-91) 7 303; 13 97
Giovanni di Tomé 32 366
Giovanni di Traù *see* GIOVANNI DALMATA
Giovanni di Turino 16 750; 28 687; 31 450
Giovanni di Vita 28 687
Giovanni Dominici 7 218
Giovanni Donato da Montorfano 9 112; 19 183
Giovanni Francesco da Rimini 12 717–18*
Giovanni Giorgio da Pavia 3 227
Giovanni Luigi di Bernardo di Maestro Jacopo da Verona *see* JACOPO DA VERONA
Giovanni Marcanova Antenoreo 10 868
Giovanni Maria di Bartolommeo *see* ZOPPO, ROCCO
Giovanni Maria Platina 16 725
Giovanni Martini da Udine 12 737
Giovanni Miniato 11 295
Giovannini, Giacomo Maria 9 30
Giovanni of Bruges 32 205
Giovanni Pietro da Oriolo 12 705
Giovanni Siro Cattaneo da Bermano 11 294
Giovanni Todeschino 4 570
Giovanni Zenone da Vaprio 12 718*
Giovannoni, Gustavo 12 718–19*; 16 648; 26 762; 31 729
collaboration 24 693
exhibitions 21 422
pupils 24 2
works 16 648, 731
writings 31 731
Giovannozzi, Luigi 11 190
Giovannozzi, Ottaviano 11 190
Giovanonni, Gustavo 3 124
Giove, Asdrubale Mattei, Duca di *see* ROCCA SINIBALDI, ASDRUBALE MATTEI, Duca di
Giovenone, Gerolamo 12 719; 18 748
Giovenone, Giovanni Battista 12 719*
Giovenone, Pietro 12 719
Giovio, Benedetto 6 359; 12 719
Giovio, Giovanni Battista, Conte 12 720
Giovio, Paolo 10 173, 810; 12 719–20*; 15 86; 16 348; 18 705; 22 355; 27 849
dealing 10 809
patrons and collectors 21 17; 25 76
personal collection 1 730; 3 656; 4 411, 426, 856, 858, *923*, 923; 7 777; 16 770; 27 210
works 9 185; 16 781; 29 673
Gipfel, Gabriel 2 454
Gipkens, Julius 25 348
Gips, A. F. 22 892
Giral, Antoine 12 720*
Giral, David 12 721*
Giral, Etienne (i) (1689-1763) 12 720, 721
Giral, Etienne (ii) (1723-99) 12 721*
Giral, Jacques 12 720, 721*; 32 427
Giral, Jean 12 720–21*
Giral, Jean-Antoine 11 738; 12 721*; 22 34
works 22 *34*
Giraldi, Guglielmo 11 4; 12 721–2*
works 12 *722*
Giraldi, Lilio Gregorio 1 656; 15 83; 22 414
Giraldo, Lucas 2 865
Giraldus 4 584
Giralte, Francisco 3 847; 12 722–3*; 20 67; 26 249; 31 89
Giralte de Bruselas *see* BRUSELAS, GIRALTE DE
Girandole, Bernardo delle *see* BUONTALENTI, BERNARDO
girandole earrings *see under* EARRINGS → types
girandoles 28 215
Girard, Alexis-François 30 353
Girard, Dominique 12 723*
collaboration 33 698
patrons and collectors 28 15
works 5 7; 12 133; 22 309; 28 110; 32 458; 33 277
Girard, François 19 9
Girard, Jean 23 512; 27 536
Girard, Laurent 11 354
Girard, Stephen 24 597
Girard d'Arcy, Abbot 32 396
Girard de la Chapelle 17 456
Girard d'Orléans 12 723*; 17 461
attributions 31 834; 33 428
patrons and collectors 31 832, 834
works 13 *131*
Girarde, Eugène-Alexandre 23 504
Girardet, Charles-Samuel 12 723
Girardet, Edouard (-Henri) 7 529; 12 723–4*
Girardet, Jean 2 722; 16 64; 19 800; 29 537
Girardet, Karl 12 723, 724
Girardet, Paul 5 265; 12 723; 19 260
Girardin, Claude 25 705
Girardin, François 31 341
Girardin, Laurent 25 570
Girardin, Lepelletier de *see* LEPELLETIER DE GIRARDIN
Girardin, Louis-René, Marquis de 10 464; 12 124, 724*; 22 740
Girardin, Maurice 12 724*; 13 681
Girardin, Nicolas-Claude 3 453; 12 724–5*
Girardo il Franco 28 655
Girardon, François 4 551; 11 559; 12 725–7*; 19 118, 243; 26 91
assistants 12 159; 19 88
catalogues 23 457
collaboration 19 76; 20 480; 31 408

Girardon, François—cont.
patrons and collectors 4 303, 551; 7 546; 11 356; 19 731; 32 824
personal collection 6 490; 9 22, 409
pupils 4 224; 6 490, 518; 8 150; 11 754; 19 118; 28 845; 29 840
reproductive prints by others 26 229; 28 756
sculpture 19 88, 118; 22 44; 32 96, 372
equestrian monuments 3 833; 9 481; 10 442; 11 558; 29 565
funerary monuments 3 853
medallions 27 548
modelli 3 258; 8 70; 19 213
mythological 11 559; 12 725; 26 449
restorations 25 456
statuettes 29 571, 572
stucco 29 833, 834
tombs 12 726; 31 128
Girardon, Nicolas 12 725
Girardot, Louis Auguste 33 455
Girardot de Marigny, Jean 14 798; 32 333
Girardoux, Jean 30 390
Girard-Perregaux 7 448
Girardus 2 129
Girart de Roussillon 32 395
Girart de Roussillon, Master of the 3 555; 17 454–5; 19 350; 20 680*
Girart of Nivelles 17 456
Giraud, Charles
works 5 536
Giraud, Eugène 4 308; 11 581; 23 126
Giraud, Jean-Baptiste 12 727–8*
Giraud, Louise Emilie 19 115
Giraudoux, Jean 3 796
Girault, Charles-Louis 12 728*
collaboration 11 524
patrons and collectors 3 616
teachers 8 545
works 10 683; 11 668; 22 363; 24 127, 127
Girault de Prangey, Joseph-Philibert 12 728*; 13 285; 16 547; 22 59
Giray Khans see:
HAJJI GIRAY, Khan
MENGLI GIRAY I, Sultan
MENGLI GIRAY II, Khan
girder bridges see under BRIDGES → types
girders (beams) 13 391; 28 874
girders (kiln furniture) 6 330
Girdhapur 15 441
Girdlers Carpet 15 682; 16 476
girdles (ecclesiastical) see CINCTURES
girdles (secular) 17 520
Gire, Joseph 3 66
Girga 9 778
Giriama 1 410
Girieud, Pierre (Paul) 12 728–9*; 22 921
Giriktepe 24 266
Girke, Raimund 12 397
Girl-in-a-Swing factory 10 308
Girnar see under JUNAGADH
Girodet (de Roussy-Trioson), Anne-Louis 11 541, 543; 12 729–33*
collaboration 13 793
competitions 25 638
groups and movements 22 741; 23 503; 26 735, 738
patrons and collectors 3 687; 4 300, 565; 7 677; 8 868; 11 666; 14 396, 577; 24 418
pupils 2 702; 3 854; 4 836; 8 829; 13 778; 17 920; 18 744; 21 797, 889; 26 455; 31 857
reproductions in hardstones 3 687
Girodet (de Roussy-Trioson), Anne-Louis—cont.
reproductions on porcelain 17 445
reproductive prints by others 2 702; 11 319; 17 453; 19 487
teachers 8 560
works 8 561, 867; 11 411, 541; 12 334, 730, 732; 24 138, 140
Girola, Claudio 2 400, 546, 604
Girolamo (di Meo del Guasta) 3 751
Girolamo Bologni da Treviso 3 649
Girolamo da Carpi see CARPI, GIROLAMO DA
Girolamo da Cremona 12 733–5*
attributions 11 692
collaboration 20 413; 27 766
patrons and collectors 4 397
teachers 23 754
works 3 531, 751; 6 5; 12 734, 906; 19 306, 307; 31 570; 32 198
Girolamo da Fiesole see JÉRÔME DE FIESOLE
Girolamo da Gualdo 20 844
Girolamo Dai Libri see LIBRI, GIROLAMO DAI
Girolamo da Salerno 6 355
Girolamo da Sermoneta see SICIOLANTE, GIROLAMO
Girolamo da Treviso (i) (1475-97) 12 735*; 31 316
pupils 8 817
works 7 862; 31 316
Girolamo (di Tommaso) da Treviso (ii) (1498-1544) 12 735–6*
attributions 27 892
collaboration 4 280; 7 331
patrons and collectors 6 41; 31 413
reproductive prints by others 5 856; 22 466
works 12 736; 23 355; 28 716
Girolamo da Udine 7 323; 12 737*
Girolamo del Buda 3 156
Girolamo del Crocifissaio see MACCHIETTI, GIROLAMO (DI FRANCESCO DI MARIOTTO)
Girolamo di Bartolomeo Strazzarolo di Aviano 12 735
Girolamo di Benvenuto 29 362
Girolamo di Giovanni da Camerino 2 131; 12 737*
Girolamo di Giovanni Pennacchi 12 735
Girolamo di Romano see ROMANINO, GEROLAMO
Giroldo (di Jacopo) da Como 11 254; 12 737–8*
Giroldo da Lugano see GIROLDO (DI JACOPO) DA COMO
Girometti, Giuseppe 12 264, 738*; 16 752
Girometti, Pietro 6 341; 12 265, 738
Giron, Charles 3 824
Girón, Juan Tellez, Count of Ureña see UREÑA, JUAN TELLEZ GIRÓN, COUNT OF
Girón, Patricio 13 767
Girona (family) 21 315
Girona 12 738–40*; 29 259
Cathedral 12 738–9*; 13 50, 67, 68, 211; 20 566; 29 263
Baldacchino 29 332
cloister 7 454
cross 13 165
doors 9 156
embroidery 10 181
enamel 13 169
manuscripts 22 248
metalwork 22 248; 29 332, 333
retable 11 484, 484
sculpture 12 739*; 26 610, 642
stained glass 12 739–40*, 740; 13 191
Girona
Cathedral—cont.
textiles 29 349
throne 30 778
tomb of Bishop Bernat de Pau 13 107
Chapter House 29 350
gold 13 165; 29 332
metalwork 29 332
Museu Diocesà de Girona 12 738
Palacio Episcopal see Museu Diocesà de Girona
sculpture 13 106
S Domingo in Puigcerda 13 150; 29 263
S Feliú 9 596; 13 68; 29 288
S Pere de Galligants 7 455; 12 738; 26 610; 29 263
Girona, Mario 8 233
Girona Bible see under BIBLES → individual manuscripts
Girona Master 4 274; 20 680–81*
Gironcoli, Bruno 2 804
Gironella, Alberto 12 740*; 21 389, 406; 30 23
Giron & Löngren 30 113
Girón y Guzmán, Pedro Téllez, 3rd Duque de Osuna see OSUNA, 3rd Duque de
Girón y Pacheco, Pedro de Alcántara Téllez see OSUNA, 9th Duque de
Girost, Jean 13 171
Giroust, Marie-Suzanne see ROSLIN, MARIE-SUZANNE
Giroux, Alphonse-Gustave 11 663; 12 740; 26 500
Giroux, André 12 740, 741
Giroux, Archille 8 616; 21 426
Giroux, François-Simon-Alphonse 12 740*; 14 861
Giroux, Olympe 12 740
girovago farfalla, Il 24 447
Girri, Alberto 1 684
Girshman, R. 4 91
Girsu see TELLOH
Girtin, Thomas 12 741–4*; 33 545
collaboration 28 883; 31 467
groups and movements 26 740; 32 903
patrons and collectors 8 98; 21 901; 26 282; 33 251
pupils 19 625
reproductive prints by others 14 813; 19 284
teachers 8 584
works 10 251, 374, 555, 562; 12 742, 743; 18 714; 24 18; 25 596; 31 155, 155; 32 901
Girvon, Jasmine 16 889
Giry, Arthur 18 856
Gisalrich 32 432
gisant see under EFFIGIES → types
Gisbert, Teresa 4 269, 270; 21 3
Gisbert Pérez, Antonio 12 744*; 29 284
Giscard d'Estaing, Valéry 11 660
Gisel, Ernst 12 744*
Gisela 23 657
jewellery 23 658
Gisela Cross 26 87
Gisela Treasure 23 537
Gishitsu 17 226
Gishubi 5 285
Giske Church 23 228; 26 647
Gislebertus 7 478, 922; 12 745*; 26 602; 32 397
patrons and collectors 2 840
works 2 841, 842, 842; 11 554, 554; 23 291; 26 133, 595
Gisleni, Giovanni Battista 12 745*
attributions 18 431
patrons and collectors 28 908; 32 5, 7
works 25 97; 32 578, 874, 875
Gismondi, Italo 27 115
works 26 796
Gismondi, Luigi 31 679
Gismondi, Paolo 12 746*
Giso, Bishop of Wells 33 59
Gisors (France) 6 53, 54, 55; 9 144
Gisors, Alphonse (-Henry) de 6 397; 12 746*; 24 165
Gisors, (Alexandre-Jean-Baptiste-) Guy de 12 746*; 24 388
Gisors, Jacques-Pierre 11 519; 12 746*
Gisors, Jean de see JEAN DE GISORS
Gisors, Louis (-Henry-Georges Scellier) de 2 391; 12 159, 746
Gispen, Willem Hendrik 22 868, 876; 23 450
Gissey, Germain 31 305
Gissey, Henri 20 137; 30 660
Gistan Kara ibn Jani Beg 16 237
Gisulfo, Abbot of Montecassino 22 10
Gitai-Weinraub 30 421
Gitega 1 407
Professional Centre 5 285
Gitiadas 13 391
Gitksan 22 657
Gits, Bernard Toon 29 397
Gitschmann von Ropstein, Hans 11 752
Gitskan 22 547
Gittard, Daniel 2 840; 6 453; 12 747*; 24 169
gitterns 33 12
Giudecca 16 651; 32 186
Giudice, Carlo Giovanni Francesco see GIUDICI, JOHANNES FRANCISCUS
Giudice, Filippo del 12 747–8*
Giudice, Francesco Maria Del see DEL GIUDICE, FRANCESCO MARIA
Giudice, Gennaro del 12 748*; 27 757
Giudice, Giuseppe del 12 748*; 27 757
Giudice, Michele del
works 23 842
Giudice, Niccolo del, Cardinal 11 813; 20 805
Giudicelli, Paul 9 115, 117
works 9 118
Giudici, Carlo Maria 2 232; 21 533
Giudici, Johannes Franciscus 12 748*
Giudici, Reinaldo 32 415
Giudicis, Francesco di Cristofano see FRANCIABIGIO
Giudienov, Dimiter 5 154
Giudobano (family) 27 893
Giuffrè, Antonino 28 656
Giugni (family) 1 792
Giuliana Falconieri, Saint 28 489
Giuliani, Giovanni 12 748*
assistants 27 873
patrons and collectors 28 836
pupils 9 145
works 2 801; 8 386; 14 309; 32 443
Giuliano (family) 17 527
Giuliano, Carlo 4 99; 6 20; 12 265; 17 527; 26 191
Giuliano, Giovanni di see GIOVANNI DA ORIOLO
Giuliano da Rimini 9 260; 12 693, 749*; 24 779
Giuliano d'Arrigo, see PESELLO
Giuliano da Sangallo see SANGALLO, GIULIANO DA
Giuliano di ser Andrea 12 540, 544
Giuliano di Taddeo 29 496
Giuliano Fiorentino 13 107
Giuliari, Bartolomeo 32 342
Giulia Varano, Duchess of Urbino (fl 1547) 25 280
Giulini, Marchese 3 856
Giulio Cesare see under SHIPS → named vessels
Giulio di Scipione 12 257
Giulio Romano 12 749–58*; 25 191; 26 769; 31 714
architecture 3 850; 8 81; 23 539
courtyards 12 24
grottoes 13 703
loggias 23 865
orders (architecture) 23 488, 488
palazzi 12 752, 754; 16 633, 712; 20 280; 23 492, 680, 836, 863; 32 546
restorations 3 849; 10 805
villas 9 84; 32 546
assistants 3 419, 646; 7 560; 20 322; 28 316
attributions 4 401, 807; 13 703
collaboration 21 17; 23 492; 26 818
Chigi, Agostino (i) (1466-1520) 6 583
Colle, Raffaello (di Michelangelo di Luca) dal 7 560
Girolamo (di Tommaso) da Treviso (ii) (1498-1544) 12 736
Lampi, Vincenzo 8 537
Lombardo, Cristoforo 4 280
Parmigianino 24 200
Penni, Giovan Francesco 24 365
Polidoro da Caravaggio 25 148
Primaticcio, Francesco 25 578
Raphael 25 902, 908
Rinaldo Mantovano 26 404
Udine, Giovanni da 31 523
copies 5 286; 21 609
drawings 9 221; 12 755; 16 712
floats 19 561
groups and movements 10 95; 20 281
house 2 547; 20 572
interior decoration 11 263
jewellery 9 244
metalwork 16 742; 23 540, 540
methods 21 766; 25 379; 29 84
paintings 2 340
frescoes 16 633
Cathedral of S Maria Maggiore (Verona) 5 31; 31 161
Palazzina (Mantua) 3 849
Palazzo Ducale (Mantua) 12 756
Palazzo del Te (Mantua) 1 657; 10 477; 12 755; 13 700; 15 137; 20 279; 22 413; 25 72; 27 323
S Maria della Steccata (Parma) 2 128; 24 200
Vatican Palace (Rome) 3 387
Villa Madama (Rome) 25 905, 907
oil
altarpieces 3 858
mythological 10 130
religious 12 753; 16 665
patrons and collectors
Alfonso III, 7th Duke of Modena and Reggio (reg 1628-9) 10 525
Bankes, William John 3 179
Charles I, King of England and Scotland (reg 1625-49) 29 800
Clement VII, Pope (reg 1523-34) 21 17
Egerton, Francis, 1st Earl of Ellesmere 9 755
Ercole II, 4th Duke of Ferrara, Modena and Reggio (reg 1534-59) 10 523; 11 5
Federico II, 5th Marchese and 1st Duke of Mantua (reg 1519-40) 12 903, 909; 16 667; 20 319; 31 35
Flinck, Nicolaes Anthonis 11 170
Francesco I, 8th Duke of Modena and Reggio (reg 1629-58) 10 526

Giulio Romano
patrons and collectors—cont.
Francis I, King of France (*reg* 1515-47) 31 849
Fugger, Jakob, II (1459-1525) 11 818
Gondi, Benedetto 12 897
Gonzaga (family) 20 318
Gonzaga, Cesare 12 911
Gonzaga, Ercole, Cardinal 12 909
Guastalla, Ferrante Gonzaga, Duca da 12 910
Jabach, Everard 16 814
Lely, Peter 19 124
National Gallery (London) 27 350
Orléans, Philippe II de Bourbon, 2nd Duc d' (1674-1723) 23 515
Périer, Casimir 24 418
Rangone, Tommaso 25 889
Reynolds, Joshua 26 280
Sabbioneta, Vespasiano Gonzaga, Duca da 12 910
Simonelli, Niccolò 28 754
Tallard, Marie-Joseph d'Hostun, Duc de 30 274
Thiene, Giovanni Galeazzo 30 731
Thiene, Marcantonio 30 731
Turini, Baldassare 31 448
Urban VIII, Pope (*reg* 1623-44) 3 205
pupils 7 467; 12 561; 26 404; 29 84, 737
reproductive prints by others 26 229
Bergeret, Pierre-Nolasque 19 483
Biard, Pierre (ii) (1592-1661) 3 925
Bisschop, Jan de (1628-71) 4 96
Bos, Balthazar van den 4 442
Caraglio, Giovanni Jacopo 5 699
Cock, Hieronymus (Wellens) 7 499
Cort (van Hoorn), Cornelis 7 899; 17 183
Davent, Léon 8 549
Fantuzzi, Antonio 10 799
Flipart, Jean-Jacques 11 171
Ghisi, Giorgio 12 557, 558
Jode, Pieter de (i) (1570-1634) 17 599
Lanier, Nicholas 18 747
Milan, Pierre 21 538
Musi, Agostino dei 22 369
Pencz, Georg 24 356
Raimondi, Marcantonio 2 387; 10 385, 487; 25 860
Scultori, Adamo 28 316
Scultori, Diana 10 386; 28 317
Scultori, Giovanni Battista 28 316
Tardieu, Nicolas-Henry 30 344
Vicentino, (Giuseppe) Niccolò 32 407
Villamena, Francesco 32 560
restorations by others 19 645; 32 *810*
stage design 30 656
stucco 29 830
tapestries 17 812; 20 323; 22 191
teachers 25 909
Giunta, Domenico (di Giovanni) *see* GIUNTI, DOMENICO (DI GIOVANNI)
Giunta, Jacopo 27 606
Giunta, Lucantonio (di) 4 9; 7 189
Giunta di Capitino *see* GIUNTA PISANO
Giuntalochi, Domenico (di Giovanni) *see* GIUNTI, DOMENICO (DI GIOVANNI)
Giuntalodi, Domenico (di Giovanni) *see* GIUNTI, DOMENICO (DI GIOVANNI)
Giunta Pisano 12 759–60*; 24 854
attributions 2 622
works 4 275; 8 212; 12 *760*; 16 655
Giunti, Domenico (di Giovanni) 12 760–61*
attributions 27 482
works 12 *761*; 21 517, *518*
writings 32 20
Giunti, Giovanni 12 760
Giuochi Borromeo, Master of the 12 718
Giuone, Giulio 29 841
Giurdignano, S Salvatore 26 484
Giurgin Island 26 707
Giurgola, Romaldo 7 670; 21 732*
Giusaffa di Filippo di Meo 28 687
Giuseppe 20 323
Giuseppe Padovano 18 872
Giusti (family) 13 224
Giusti, Agostino 32 343
Giusti, Alessandro 12 762–3*
assistants 19 893; 32 424
collaboration 23 757
patrons and collectors 4 636
works 1 680; 12 *762*; 20 86; 25 301
Giusti, Antonio (1479-1519) 11 556; 17 596; 27 547
Giusti, Antonio (1624-1705) 8 497; 21 30; 27 521
Giusti, Ercole, Conte 29 32
Giusti, Giovanni (1485-1549) 11 556; 17 596; 27 547
Giusti, Gomberto, Conte 29 32
Giusti, Pietro 3 179
Giusti, Tommaso 14 141, 469
Giustiani (family) 32 216
Giustinian, Marco Antonio 14 106
Giustiniani (i) (family) 25 388
architecture 21 466
collections 8 653
paintings 5 815; 29 40
sculpture 4 886; 14 435; 20 812; 27 46
Giustiniani (ii) (family) 16 736
Giustiniani (i), Andrea di 12 763; 14 563
Giustiniani (ii), Antonio 12 764
Giustiniani (i), Benedetto, Cardinal 12 763*; 18 669
Giustiniani (i), Giuseppe 12 763
Giustiniani (ii), Ignazio 12 764*
Giustiniani (i), Luca 5 455; 19 806; 27 878
Giustiniani, Michele 10 709
Giustiniani (ii), Nicola 12 764
Giustiniani (i), Orazio, Cardinal 20 495
Giustiniani (i), Vincenzo, Marchese 12 763–4*
architecture 18 669
catalogues 2 163
collections 4 330; 22 384; 26 773; 27 114
drawings 30 526
paintings 5 708, 711; 6 26; 11 52; 14 653; 16 771; 20 266; 26 94; 27 725; 32 715
frescoes 1 534
genre 5 706
portraits 5 706
religious 3 8; 5 702, 711; 14 728; 20 704, 840; 28 179
sculpture 9 410
writings 3 265
Giustiniani stele 24 204
Giustino del fu Gherardino da Forlì 12 765*
Giusto (Manzini), Andrea di *see* ANDREA DI GIUSTO (MANZINI)
Giusto da Guanto *see* JUSTUS OF GHENT
Giusto da Incisa 16 724
Giusto di Andrea (di Giusto) 12 765*
attributions 9 96
collaboration 22 800
pupils 9 148
Giusto di Andrea (di Giusto)—cont.
teachers 22 802
Giverny 15 156; 21 868
Musée Américain 24 481
Musée Claude Monet 2 552; 21 867
Givry, Cardinal de 8 67; 11 639
Giyan, Tepe 12 765–6*, 838; 15 *901*, 903, 921; 19 812
ceramics 15 *921*
pottery 15 920
seals 1 856
Giza 9 773, *774*; 10 80, 93; 12 *766*, 766–8*
figurines 9 809
funerary boat of Cheops 9 819, 822; 10 81
Great Sphinx 9 *829*, 862, 870; 25 762; 29 394, *394*
inscriptions 10 82
Muhammad Mahmud Khalil collection 9 768
Muhammad Naghi Museum 9 768
mummies 22 284
Museum 10 92
pyramids 9 825; 10 78, 79; 24 750; 25 171
Chephren (*reg c.* 2520–*c.* 2494 BC) 20 863; 25 762
Great Pyramid 2 294; 9 779, 838; 10 80; 12 767; 20 863; 22 42; 23 338; 25 761, *761*, 762; 31 107; 32 88, 89
Grand Gallery 25 762
King's Chamber 25 762
Queen's Chamber 25 762
sarcophagus 27 824
Khentkawes 9 850
Mycerinus 9 813; 10 79; 20 863; 25 762
Neuserre 10 66
Pyramid of Cheops *see* Great Pyramid
valley temple of Cheops 25 762
reliefs 9 872
sculpture 9 863, *863*
statuettes 10 16
temples
mortuary temple of Cheops 9 813; 25 762
mortuary temple of Mycerinus 25 762
Temple of the Sphinx 9 *829*, 830
valley temple of Chephren 9 150, 813, 825; 12 767; 27 127
valley temple of Mycerinus 9 826, 850, *850*; 10 72; 25 762
sculpture 9 871
tomb chapels 9 833, 838
tombs 9 *837*; 20 596
tombs (private) 10 96
Iason 10 50
Kawab 9 859
Khafreankh 9 872
Qar 10 50, 51
Rawer 9 859, 870
Seneb 9 858, 872
tombs (royal)
Hetepheres I 9 822, 823; 10 51; 14 494–5*, *495*
furniture 6 388; 10 50, *51*; 30 775
jewellery 10 29, *29*
Khamerernebty I 9 862
Meresankh III 9 789; 10 43, 50, 51
sculpture 9 870
Mycerinus 22 398
Nebemakhet 10 51
workers' camp 25 761
Gizella, Queen of Hungary (1856-1932) 15 11
Gizella Cross 15 5
Giziński, Antoni 12 821
GJ, Master 32 152
Gjakevë 1 543
Gjeçovi, Shtjefën 1 545
Gjellerup Church 8 722
Gjergj I 1 544
Gjernes, Liv Mildred 23 234
Gjesing 26 640
Gjirokastër 1 *537*, 538
art schools 1 547
ceramics 1 543
furniture 1 542
houses 1 539; 16 228
metalwork 1 543
Museum of the National Liberation War 1 546
Museum of Weapons 1 546
National Renaissance Museum 1 546
Gjøl 26 640
Gjon 1 539
Gjörvell, Christoffer 29 686
Gjörwell, Carl Christopher 11 91; 30 73; 31 461
Gjøvik Glassverk 23 235
Gla 12 768*; 13 *363*; 14 *332*, 340, 348
megaron 21 46
Glabbais, Aegidius de 33 261
Glabbeeck, Jan van 22 843
glacis 8 277; 21 546
glacite 3 576
Glackens, William J(ames) 12 768–9*; 14 393; 24 600; 31 605
dealing 3 251
groups and movements 2 596, 597; 10 108; 23 47; 28 925
works 21 897
Gladbic, J. 25 90
Gladding-McBean Co. 31 639
Gladkov, Boris 10 700
Gladstone, Charles 26 107
Gladstone, William Ewart 28 509
glair *see* ALBUMEN
glaives 2 448
Glaize, Auguste-Barthélemy 5 57; 12 769–70*; 26 315
Glaize, (Pierre-Paul-) Léon 11 156; 12 770
Glaize, Maurice 2 56, 59
Glamis Castle (Tayside) 27 129
Glamoč 4 *459*
basilica 4 459
Glantschnigg, Ulrich 12 770*
Glanum 11 *505*; 12 770–71*; 25 538; 26 *908*
Arc Municipal 31 369
baths 3 375; 26 872
bouleuterion 4 530
forum 11 327
houses 26 904
Mausoleum of the Julii 12 *770*, 771; 20 *864*, 865; 21 892; 26 883; 31 109
urban planning 27 3
Glanz, Joseph 10 907
Glänz, Joseph Dominikus 33 32
Glaoua 16 486
Glaoui (family) 3 755
Glarean, Heinrich 12 810
Glarner, Fritz 12 771*; 21 855
groups and movements 1 666; 30 135; 31 607
works 12 15
Glaser, Eduard 2 830; 33 520
Glaser, Hans 3 604
Glaser, Milton 4 369; 7 292; 12 771–2*; 25 354
Glasere, Marc de 13 910
Gläserne Kette 2 288; 10 697; 12 378, 792; 19 773; 21 781, 782; 28 55; 30 370, 371
Glasewald, Ephraim Wolfgang 27 323
works 27 *323*
Glasgow 12 772–9*, *774*; 28 *222*
Archbishop's Palace 31 230
art forms and materials
architecture 28 228
Glasgow
art forms and materials—cont.
cabinetmaking 28 252, 254
carpets 28 266
ceramics 28 257
furniture 28 *254*, 256
glass 28 259–60
interior decoration 28 248, 249
prints 28 239
art schools 28 275
Glasgow School of Art 2 569; 7 668; 9 739; 12 776; 15 888; 20 22, *22*; 21 779; 27 129; 28 229, 238, 258, 265, 270, 275
collections 2 561; 20 20
library 28 275
Mackintosh School of Architecture 28 275
School of Design 2 524; 8 802
churches
Caledonia Road United Presbyterian Church 25 267
Cathedral of St Mungo 12 777–9*, *778*; 28 224, 251, 267; 29 506
choir 13 45
Elgin Place Congregational Church 25 267
Queen's Cross Church 20 21
St Andrew's Parish Church 25 266; 28 227
St Benedict 28 232
St George's Tron 12 *773*
St Vincent Street Free Church 28 254
Wellington Church 28 231
City Chambers 12 *775*; 14 397
Clyde Regional Centre 4 790
Court-house *see* Justiciary Courts
education (art) 28 274, 275
exhibitions 12 776
factories
Fairfields Engine Works 28 228
North British Diesel Engine Works 28 228
Randolph Elder Engine Works 28 228
Templeton's Carpet Factory 4 788; 10 748
Forum Hotel 28 231
Foulis Academy 11 338; 12 776; 28 252, 271, 274
foundries 28 242
Glasgow Herald Building 20 20–21
Goldsmiths' Company 28 261
Great Western Terrace 28 229
houses, flats and tenements 2 325
Craigen Court 28 231
Kelvincourt 2 216
Mackintosh House 28 249
Pollok House *see under* museums
Red Road flats 28 231
International Exhibition, 1901 24 739; 28 273
Italian Centre 28 232
Justiciary Courts 13 610; 18 887; 25 268
Kirklee Bridge 4 801
Lion Chambers 7 694
Lunatic Asylum 2 658
Martyrs' School 20 21
Metro stations 21 349
Mitchell Library 11 338; 28 275
Moray Place 28 254
museums 28 273
Art Gallery and Museum 12 777; 28 273
collections 13 273; 20 20; 29 746
directors 24 372
exhibitions 2 119
library 28 275
sculpture 11 499
Burrell Collection 5 278; 7 155; 22 367; 28 *231*, 232, 272
ceramics 6 925

Glasgow
  museums
    Burrell Collection—cont.
      collections **29** 516; **30** 332
    Gallery of Modern Art **28** 273
    Hunterian Museum and Art Gallery *see under* University
    Pollok House **13** 344; **28** 273
    St Mungo Museum of Religious Life and Art **28** 273
  Nithsdale Road **28** 254
  Queen Margaret Medical College **20** 21
  Royal Bank of Scotland **28** 228
  Royal Exchange **25** 268
  St Andrew's Halls **7** 687
  St Vincent Crescent **28** 229
  Scotland Street School **28** 229
  shops and warehouses **28** 227
    Ca' d'Oro warehouse **28** 228
    Cleland, Jack, Paterson & Co. **28** *254*
    Gardner's warehouse **28** 228
    Jamaica Street warehouses **26** 18
    Wylie & Lochead warehouse **28** 228
  Stock Exchange **12** *773*; **28** 228
  tea rooms **28** 270
    Argyle Street Tea-rooms *see* Crown Lunch and Tea Rooms
    Buchanan Street Tea Rooms *see* Cranston's Tea Rooms
    Cranston's Tea Rooms **20** 23
    Crown Lunch and Tea Rooms **6** 391; **20** 23; **28** 255, 256
    Willow Tea Rooms **16** 60; **20** 23; **28** 256; **29** 508
    furniture **6** *391*
  Tobacco Exchange **28** 228
  town walls **31** 710
  Trades House **28** 227
  Union Bank **28** 231
  University **28** 229
    Chapel **28** 243
    collections **33** 142
    Hunterian Museum and Art Gallery **12** 777; **15** 29; **20** 20, 921; **27** 115; **28** 249, 254, 273; **29** 548
      Mackintosh House *see under* houses, flats and tenements
    library **28** 275
  urban planning **31** 723, 724
Glasgow Art Club **12** 776
Glasgow Art Union **12** 776
Glasgow Boys **7** 406; **12** 776, 779–80*; **21** 99; **22** 439; **23** 22; **28** 238
  collections **20** 23; **26** 12
  members **5** 521; **8** 125; **13** 868; **18** 882; **19** 891; **32** 834
  patrons and collectors **26** 107; **28** 270
  works **19** 109
Glasgow Corporation **28** 271
Glasgow Dilettanti Society **12** 776
Glasgow Group **12** 777
Glasgow Improvement Trust **2** 119
Glasgow Institution for Promoting and Encouraging the Fine Arts in the West of Scotland **12** 776
Glasgow League of Artists **12** 777
Glasgow Pottery (Canada) **5** 581
Glasgow Pottery (Strathclyde Region) **28** 257
Glasgow Society of Lady Artists **12** 776
Glasgow Society of Painters and Sculptors **12** 777
Glasgow style **2** 562, 569; **6** 164; **12** 780*; **19** 876; **28** 275
  chairs **6** *391*
  members **18** 65; **32** 835
Glasier, John **23** 689
glass **6** 324; **12** 780–97*; **14** 425
  cleaning **12** 797*
glass—cont.
  conservation **12** *796*, 796–7*
  historical and regional traditions
    Achaemenid **1** 868
    Africa **1** *233*, 296, 297, *297*
    Albania **1** 543*
    Anatolia, ancient **1** 865–6*
    Ancient Near East **1** 864–8*, *867*, 877; **12** 785; **28** 384
    Anglo-Saxon **10** 322
    Arabia **2** 263*
    Armenia (Europe) **9** 646
    Asante **2** *585*, *588*
    Australia **2** 762–4*; **21** 801
    Austria **2** 817–19*, *818*; **19** *523*
    Azerbaijan **2** 898*
    Bahrain **2** 263
    Bali (Indonesia) **15** 806
    Belgium **3** 575, 576, 583, 592–4*, 595–6*
    Brazil **4** 722*; **12** *794*
    Britain **12** 791
    Buddhism **6** 717; **7** 82
    Bulgaria **5** 159*
    Burma **5** 256*; **18** 604
    Byzantine **9** 562, 644–6*, *645*, 657; **12** 788
    Cambodia **5** 500
    Canada **5** 582–4*, *583*
    Catalonia **29** 330–31, *331*
    Celtic **6** 159
    Central Asia, Western **6** 267–9*, *267*, *268*
    China **7** 80–87*, *81*, 109, 111; **12** 789
      Buddhism **7** 82
      export **7** 86–7*, *87*
      Ming period (1368-1644) **7** 18, 110, 111
      Qing period (1644-1911) **7** 19, *84*, *85*, *86*, 132, *133*; **12** IV3
      Song period (AD 960-1279) **6** 717
      Sui period (AD 581-618) **7** *82*, *107*
      Zhou period (*c.* 1050-256 BC) **7** *81*, 107; **21** 714
    Croatia **8** 180
    Czech Republic **8** 406–11*, *407*, *408*, *410*; **12** *786*, 788, VI1, VI2, VI3; **21** 721
    Denmark **4** 743; **8** 749–50*, *750*
    Early Christian (*c.* AD 250-843) **9** 562, 644–6*
    Egypt **16** 515, 517, *518*, 519, 520, *520*; **27** 78
      Ayyubid **16** 520
      Byzantine **9** 644
      Early Christian (*c.* AD 250-843) **9** 644, 645
      Mamluk **16** 521
    Egypt, ancient **1** 865; **10** 46, 52, 54–9*, *57*, *58*; **12** 782, 785, 788, 789, IV2; **17** IV2
    Elamite **1** 868
    England **3** 442; **6** 443; **10** 281, 315–21*; **12** 781, 787
      Anglo-Saxon **10** 322
      Arts and Crafts Movement **2** *570*
      Iron Age **25** *545*
      19th cent. **10** *335*; **16** *54*
      20th cent. **8** *279*; **10** *321*
    Finland **11** 106–7*, *107*
    France **11** 602, 610–11*, 612–13*; **12** *793*
      Art Noveau **2** *563*
      19th cent. **12** 18
      20th cent. **12** *793*; **18** *659*
    Germany **10** 697; **12** 374, 438–41*, 456, 462; **14** 425
      Bauhaus **15** *825*
      Byzantine **9** 646
      Roman **7** 586; **27** *75*
      17th cent. **12** *439*
    Gothic **13** 134, 135, 139
    Greece, ancient **13** 393, 435, *593*, 593–5*, *594*; **22** 160
    Helladic **1** 865
glass
  historical and regional traditions—cont.
    Hittite **1** 865
    Hungary **15** *3*, 3–5*
    Hurrian **1** 864, 865; **15** 33
    Iceland **15** 72*
    Indian subcontinent **12** V1; **15** *694*, 694–5*; **21** 717
      Gujarat **15** 723
      Islamic **16** 522
      Maurya period **15** 700
      Mughal **16** 522
    Iran **12** V2; **16** 522
    Iran, ancient **1** 866*, 868; **4** 172
    Iraq **12** V2
    Ireland **6** 443, *443*; **12** 787; **16** 29–30*, *30*; **32** *530*
    Islamic **7** 90; **9** 645; **12** 788, 789; **14** 427; **16** 255, 256, 517–21*, 522*; **21** 718
      Egypt **16** 515, 517, *518*, *519*, 519, 520, *520*
      Indian subcontinent **16** 522
      Iran **16** *519*, 522
      Ottoman **16** 221, 522
      Palestine **16** 517, 519
      Syria **12** IV1; **16** 515, 517, 519, 520, *520*, *521*
      Turkey **16** 221, 522
      Yemen **16** *533*
    Italy **16** 740*
      Byzantine **9** 646
      Roman **12** VIII2; **27** 66, *76*
      15th cent. **12** VIII3; **32** *201*
      16th cent. **32** *202*
      20th cent. **32** *205*
    Japan **17** 371, *373*, 381, 385–7*, *387*, 398; **25** 176
    Kenya **1** *297*
    Kongo **1** *233*
    Korea **18** 266, *364*, 364–5*
    Kyrgyzstan **6** *267*
    Malta (Republic of) **20** 215–16*
    Merovingian **21** 163
    Mesopotamia **1** 864–5*, 866, *867*, 868*; **12** 782, 785, 787
    Mexico **21** 392
    Mitannian **1** 865; **15** 33
    Mycenaean **1** 865
    Netherlands, the **12** *786*; **22** 884–5*
    New Zealand **23** 56, 70*
    Northern Ireland **3** 536
    Norway **23** 221, 235–6*
    Ottoman **16** 221, 522
    Palestine **9** 644; **16** 517, 519
    Phoenician **1** 867, 868; **24** 645*; **25** 734
    Poland **25** 124–5*, *125*
    Portugal **25** 311*
    Prehistoric **12** 789; **25** 531, *545*, 546–7*
    Punic **25** 734*
    Rhodes (island) **1** 868; **13** 593
    Romania **26** 718–19*
    Rome, ancient **12** 783, 785, 786, 787, 788, 789, 790; **21** 713; **26** 855, 871; **27** 66, 72*, 74–7*, *78*, *79*
      Central Asia, Western **6** *267*
      Egypt **27** 78
      Germany **7** 586; **27** *75*
      Italy **12** VIII2; **27** *76*
      Kyrgyzstan **6** *267*
      Netherlands, the **22** 884
      Spain **29** 330
      Switzerland **30** 144
    Russia **27** 414–18*, *415*, *416*, *418*
    Sasanian **7** 83; **9** 645
    Scotland **28** 231, *259*, 259–60*
    Seleucid **28** 384
    Slovakia **28** 856*
    Slovenia **28** 862
    South Africa **29** *118*, 118–19*
    Spain **29** 330–32*, *331*
    Sweden **30** *101*, 101–3*, *103*
glass
  historical and regional traditions—cont.
    Switzerland **9** 646; **30** 144–5*, *145*
    Syria **16** 515, 517, 519, 520
      Ayyubid **16** 520
      Byzantine **9** 644
      Early Christian (*c.* AD 250-843) **9** 644
      Islamic **12** IV1; **16** *520*, *521*
      Mamluk **16** 521
    Syria-Palestine **1** 865*, 867, 868
    Thailand **18** 604; **30** 633*
    Thracian **30** 769
    Turkey **16** 221, 522
    Ukraine **31** 563
    United States of America **3** 84; **10** 852; **12** *794*, *795*, VII2; **20** 593; **28** 488; **31** 641–5*, *641*, *643*, *645*
    Venetian Empire **16** 521
    Venezuela **32** 171, *171*
    Viking **32** *530*
    Wales **32** 790
    Yemen **16** *533*
  materials
    antimony **10** 55; **13** 594; **30** 408
    antimony sulphides **12** 782
    ashes **10** 55
    barium **7** 81; **12** 781
    cadmium sulphides **12** 782
    chalk **12** 439
    chromium **12** 782
    cobalt **10** 55; **30** 407
    cobalt oxides **12** 781; **24** 791
    copper **7** 80, 84; **10** 55; **30** 407
    copper oxides **10** 55; **12** 781; **16** 518
    enamel **12** 788*; **16** *520*
      Austria **2** 818, *818*
      Byzantine **9** *645*
      China **7** 86
      Czech Republic **8** 407, 410; **12** VI1
      England **10** 318, *318*
      Germany **12** 438, 439, *439*; **14** 425
      Islamic **16** 515, 520, *521*
      Italy **12** VIII3; **32** *201*
      Poland **25** 124
      Rome, ancient **27** 78*
      Russia **27** *415*
      Switzerland **30** *145*
    fluorine **12** 781
    frit **11** 794
    gold **12** 782; **16** 520
    gold leaf **13** 594
    inscriptions **16** 521
    iron **12** 782
    lead **7** 81; **12** 781; **17** 385, 386
      see also types → crystal
    lead oxides **10** 55, 316; **12** 439
    lime **12** 781
    magnesium **7** 80, 82
    manganese **10** 55; **30** 407
    manganese dioxide **32** 200, 201
    potash **10** 315; **12** 438, 439, 781; **29** 497; **30** 407
    potassium **7** 82; **10** 55; **24** 791
    potassium carbonate **12** 781
    sand **29** 497
    selenium **12** 782
    silica **7** 80; **10** 55; **12** 781; **32** 200
    silver **12** 782
    silver chloride **12** 788
    silver oxides **16** 518
    soda **10** 317; **12** 438, 781; **29** 497; **30** 407; **32** 200
    soda-lime **7** 82; **10** 315; **12** 438; **17** 385
    sodium **10** 55
    sulphides (ceramic) **12** 789*
    tin **30** 408
    uranium oxides **12** 782
  reproductions *see under* REPRODUCTIONS
  restoration **12** 797*
glass—cont.
  technical examination **12** 796–7*; **30** 393, 400, 401, *407*, 407–8*
  techniques
    air-twists **10** 317; **12** 786
    cane **1** 866
    carving **7** 84–6, *85*
    casting **12** 782–3*; **13** *594*, 594–5; **27** 74*
    combing **12** 785*
    cotton twists **10** 317, *318*; **12** 786
    crizzling **7** 84, *84*; **8** 173*; **26** 36
    Crystallo Engraving **10** 319, *319*
    cutting **6** 269, 443; **8** 407–8, *408*, 409, *410*; **10** 318–19, *319*, 321; **12** 787*; **16** 30, *30*, 518; **17** *387*; **27** 75–6*, *416*
    enamel **8** *407*, 409; **27** *76*
    engraving **3** *594*; **8** *408*; **10** *315*, 317, 321, *321*; **12** 439–40, *786*, 786–7*; **13** 914; **14** 425; **22** 884–5, *885*; **27** 75–6*; **28** *259*; **31** *641*; **32** 202
    etching **10** 319–20; **12** 787*
    filigrana **32** 201, *202*, 203
    flashing **29** 498
    gilding **5** 256; **6** 269; **9** *645*; **12** 788*, V1; **16** *520*, *521*; **32** *201*
    glassblowing **12** 783–4*, *784*; **28** 384
      Central Asia, Western **6** 268
      China **7** 82–3
      Egypt, ancient **10** 56
      Islamic **16** 517
      Japan **17** 386
      Rome, ancient **12** 784; **27** 72–3*, 74–5*, 77–8*
      United States of America **19** 501
    grinding **21** 720
    inlay **5** 256
    iridization **2** 818
    Lorraine method **22** 156; **25** 124
    lost-wax casting **10** 56; **12** 782
    marbling **1** 865
    mass production **31** 643
    moulding **12** 782, 783*, *783*
      Ancient Near East **1** 865
      Egypt, ancient **10** 56, 57
      England **10** 320, 321
      Greece, ancient **13** 594
      Islamic **16** 517
      Rome, ancient **27** 73, 74
    overlaying **7** 84–6, *85*, *86*
    painting **12** 788*; **14** 235; **27** 78*; **32** 202
    pâte-de-verre **11** 794; **12** 782
    polishing **10** 320
    pressing **7** 81; **10** 320, 321; **12** 783; **31** 643, *643*
    sand-blasting **12** 787*
    staining **12** 788*
    stamping **16** 517
    trailing **12** 785*; **27** 73*, 75*, 77–8*
  types
    à la façon de Venise **3** 593; **10** 316; **12** 439; **22** 884
    antique **29** 497
    aventurine **7** 84; **12** 782; **24** 57; **32** 203
    cameo **12** 787*
      China **12** 787
      Egypt **16** *519*
      Egypt, ancient **10** 56, 58
      England **10** 320; **26** 227
      France **12** 18
      Iran **16** *519*
      Islamic **16** 518, *519*
      Rome, ancient **12** 787, *787*; **27** 73–4*, 76–7*, *77*, 78*; **30** *407*
      Switzerland **27** *77*
    cased **10** 319
    chalcedony **3** 270; **12** VIII1; **32** 201, 203, 204
    conglomerate **10** 56, 58

glass
types—cont.
cristallo **3** 270; **10** 316; **21** 719; **32** 201, *201*
crown **12** 790
crystal **12** 781
Belgium **3** 593, 594
England **10** 316, *317*, 318–19, *319*; **19** 595; **26** 36–7
France **9** 13
Germany **12** 440
Japan **17** 100
Russia **27** 415–16
Cypriote **30** 868
dalles de verre **29** 498
Favrile **2** 568; **30** 868*
float **12** 793
Flühliglas **30** 145, *145*
gold-glass **12** 788
Ancient Near East **1** 867
Austria **2** 818
Egypt, ancient **10** 59
Greece, ancient **13** 594
Islamic **16** 518
ice **12** 788*
ice glass **32** 202
iridescent **15** 4, *4*
lattimo **3** 270; **32** 201, *202*, 203, *203*
Lava **30** 868
lead *see* crystal
lustre **16** 518, *518*
marqueterie de verre **12** 18
milk *see lattimo*
millefiori **10** 56, 58; **12** 788; **15** 871–2; **24** 57; **32** 204
mosaic **12** 788*
Ancient Near East **1** 865, *866*
Egypt, ancient **10** 56, 58
Greece, ancient **13** 594
Iran, ancient **1** *866*
Islamic **16** 518
Mesopotamia **1** 865
Norman slab **29** 497
Paris jet **17** 514
plate **11** 407; **12** 791
porcelain *see* lattimo
porcellana contrafacta **32** 203, *203*
porcelleinglas **12** 440
porporino **24** 568
pot-metal **13** 178; **29** 498
Pyrex **7** 875; **10** 321
reamy **29** 498
Sandwich **4** 483
Schaffhausen **30** 145
stained *see* STAINED GLASS
streaky **29** 498
sulphide **27** *418*
Vaseline **12** 782
Vauxhall **17** 514
vetro porcellano see lattimo
Waldglas **8** 407; **10** 315, 316; **12** 438, *438*; **22** *885*
window **3** 594
Zierglas **12** *441*, 441
uses
alabastra **12** VII1
altar sets **7** 86, *86*
amphorae **12** *787*
amulets **25** 734
architectural decorations **16** 221
architecture **12** 790–94*; **19** 320; **20** 560; **22** 365; **28** 65
Brazil **12** *793*
England **8** *279*
France **12** *793*
Germany **12** 374
Ireland **3** 536
Korea **18** 266
New Zealand **23** 56
Scotland **28** 231
United States of America **12** *794*
Venezuela **32** 171, *171*
beads **3** 440, 442; **25** 546–7
Africa **1** 296, 297
Cambodia **5** 500
Cameroon **3** 145, *147*, *149*

glass
uses
beads—cont.
China **7** 80, *81*
Egypt, ancient **1** 864; **10** 56; **12** 789
Iran **4** 172
Italy **32** 202
Japan **17** 385–6
Kenya **1** *297*
Korea **18** 364
Micronesia, Federated States of **21** *477*
Punic **25** 734
Thailand **30** 633
beakers **1** *866*; **16** *521*; **27** *79*
bells **3** 628
belthooks **7** 81, 107
belts **7** 109, 111
bottles **6** *268*; **9** 646; **10** *319*; **12** IV2; **15** *4*
bowls
China **7** *84*; **12** IV3
Czech Republic **8** *410*; **12** VI3
Egypt, ancient **10** 57
England **10** *321*
Greece, ancient **13** 594, *594*
Indian subcontinent **15** *694*
Iran **12** V2
Iraq **12** V2
Islamic **16** *518*
Rome, ancient **6** *267*; **12** VIII2; **27** *75*, *77*
boxes **17** 386
bracelets **7** 109
cabinets (ii) (furniture) **3** 583
candlesticks **7** 86, *86*
chairs **10** 52
chandeliers **6** 443, *443*; **9** 13; **12** 789
chess sets **6** 555
cladding **14** 200
cliché-verre **7** 432
clocks **7** 439
collars **17** IV2
combs (hair) **17** 386
containers **3** 592; **15** *825*
crowns **7** 110
cups **7** 81, 82, *85*; **18** *364*; **27** *76*
decanters **2** *570*; **17** *387*; **27** *416*
discs **7** 81
dolls **17** 371, *373*
dolls' furniture **31** 264
dolls' houses **31** 262
doors **3** 575
dress **25** 546
embroidery **12** 462
enamel **13** 134; **17** 386; **25** 547
ewers **12** V1; **16** *519*
factories **10** 697
flasks **10** 57; **15** *3*
flower arrangements **17** 381
frames **8** 129; **11** 407
furniture **10** 58; **11** 602
game-pieces **17** 386
goblets **6** 268; **10** *315*, *318*; **11** *611*; **12** VIII3; **27** *415*; **28** *259*; **30** *101*; **31** *641*
hair ornaments **17** 386
headrests **10** 57
incense burners **7** 86, *86*
inkwells **6** 269
inlays **1** 865, 867; **7** 81; **10** 58; **12** 789; **13** 594, 595; **17** 386
jars **7** *82*; **29** *118*
jewellery **7** 111; **10** 54, 58; **25** 531, 546
jugs **10** *57*, *335*; **12** VIII1; **27** *78*
knife-handles **17** 386
kogoks **18** 364
lacquer **7** 18, 19; **18** 604
lamps **2** *563*; **12** 789, IV1; **16** *520*, 521; **30** *868*, 868–9
light bulbs **7** 875
medals **20** 926
mirror frames **21** 717, 721
mirrors **3** 576; **7** *87*; **12** 789; **17** 386, 387; **21** 713, 714, 718, 719, 720; **32** 202

glass
uses—cont.
mosaics **9** 562, 645; **12** 622, 789, 790; **16** 255, 256; **22** 155, 156; **27** 66
necklaces **7** *109*; **16** *533*
netsuke **17** 386, 398
paintings **13** 139; **15** 806
see also under PAINTING → forms
paperweights **12** 789; **17** 386; **24** 57; **32** 204
pendants (jewellery) **9** 645
photography **24** 646, 648, 649, 650, 651
plaques **1** 865; **9** 646; **10** 58; **12** *786*
plates **5** *583*
pottery **25** 546
printing **7** 575
reliquaries **3** 593; **7** 82; **18** 364
roofs **13** 619; **16** *54*
rosaries **17** 386
sceptres **17** 386
scroll rollers **17** 386
sculpture **1** *233*; **2** *588*; **6** 717; **10** 55, 57, *58*; **12** *795*, 795–6*, VII2; **17** 100; **25** 176
service stations **28** 488
shabtis **10** 57
shrines (i) (cult) **32** *530*
snuff bottles **7** 86, 132, *133*
stools **2** *585*
sword fittings **7** 81
swords **17** 386
textiles **25** 546
toys **17** 386; **31** 254
trappings **17** 386
tripods **7** 86
unguent vessels **25** 734
vases **1** *867*; **7** *85*; **8** *750*; **10** *57*; **11** *612*; **12** VI2; **27** *418*; **30** *103*; **31** *645*
weights **9** 645
wind chimes **17** 386
windows **6** 269; **12** 790; **23** 221; **26** 871
Glass, D. **4** 27
Glass, Gertrude *see* GREENE, GERTRUDE
Glass, Peter **20** 469
Glass, Philip **24** 407, 409; **33** 223
Glass, William **20** 890
glassblowing *see under* GLASS→ techniques
Glass Bottleworks **28** 259
Glassby, Robert **4** 221
glasses
historical and regional traditions
England **10** 317
Ireland **16** 29
Netherlands, the **12** *786*; **22** 884, 885
materials
gold leaf **9** 645
types
Amen **10** 318
baluster-glasses **10** 316–17
balustroids **10** 317
Berkemeyer **12** 438
claw-beakers **10** 315; **12** 438, 785
firing **10** 317
flutes **10** 316
gold **9** 645
humpen **12** 438; **25** 124
Jacobite (Stuart) **10** 318
Krautstrunk **12** 438
Kurfürstenhumpen **12** 438
Maigelein **12** 438
Nuppenbecher **12** 438
Passglas **12** 438
Ranftbechern **2** *818*
Reichsadlerhumpen **12** 438, VI1
roemers **10** 316, *317*; **12** 438, 785; **22** *885*
Rüsselbecher see claw-beakers
Silesian **10** 317
Stangenglas **12** *438*, 438

glasses
types—cont.
toastmasters' **10** 317
Welcome **25** 124
see also CUPS; GOBLETS
glassfibre reinforced polyester *see* FIBREGLASS
glass holders **1** *811*; **22** 887, 889
glasshouses *see* GREENHOUSES
Glassie, Henry **16** 550; **32** 304, 328
glassmakers' guilds *see under* GUILDS → types
Glassow, M. **10** 647
glass paste **11** 794
historical and regional traditions
Egypt, ancient **10** 46
Greece, ancient **12** 247, 248
Ireland **16** 33
Scotland **28** *242*
uses
cameos **17** *525*
jewellery **16** 33; **17** 524, 525
medallions **28** *242*
mosaics **22** 154, 163
seals **12** 247, 248
glass reinforced plastic (GRP) *see* FIBREGLASS
Glass Ware House (Dublin) **9** 320
glassworks **28** 862
glassy faience *see* FAIENCE (i) (GLASS)
Glastonbury (Somerset) **10** *225*
Abbey **2** 66; **9** 397; **10** 227; **12** 5, 798–800*; **13** 44; **21** 836; **23** 491; **26** 590
choir **22** 217
cloister **7** 455
Great Church **12** *800*, 800
Lady Chapel **12** *799*, 799–800; **18** 622; **26** 617
sculpture **13** 84; **26** 616
stained glass **2** 83
crosses **2** 68
pottery **6** 161
wood-carvings **25** 545
Glastonbury Master **12** 800
Glas Towie **25** 511, *512*
Glasværket i Aalborg **8** 749
Glatz **8** 389
Glatz, Oszkár **9** 81; **22** 434
Glauber, Diana **12** 801
Glauber, Jan Gottlieb **12** 801
Glauber, Johannes **12** 801–2*
collaboration **18** 652; **21** 411
groups and movements **9** 462
teachers **3** 759; **18** 155
works **12** *801*
Glaubitz, Jan Krzysztof **12** 802*
works **3** 526; **19** 497; **32** 579
Glaukias of Aigina **1** 481; **12** 802*
Glaukion of Corinth **2** 664
Glaukos (*fl c.* 590 BC) **7** 169
Glaukos (*fl* mid-5th cent. BC) **13** 374
Glaukytes **13** 510
Glavas Tarchaneiotes, Michael *see* MICHAEL GLAVAS TARCHANEIOTES
Glavinica Epitaph **1** 544
Glavka, Iozef **28** 838
Glavkustprom (Chief Directorate for Cottage Industry) **27** 422
Glavna, Iosif **31** 553
Glaz **21** 571
glazes **6** 330; **12** 802–3*
conservation **6** 334
historical and regional traditions
Ancient Near East **1** 877; **4** 769; **6** 333
Belgium **3** *589*
Byzantine **9** 633
Cambodia **5** 506
Canada **5** 581, *581*, *582*
Central Asia, Western **6** 207, 257, 258; **16** 239, 248
China **6** 869, 872–3*, 879, 881, 882, 885, 886, 887, 888, 893, 894, 895
Egypt **16** 402–3, 404, 415

glazes
historical and regional traditions—cont.
Egypt, ancient **4** 172; **6** 333; **9** 788; **10** 46–9*
England **10** 302, 306, *312*, 315; **30** 681
Ethiopia **4** 172
Germany **12** 429
Greece, ancient **13** 480–81, 482, 504, 536
Hungary **15** 2
Indian subcontinent **15** 686
Iran **4** 172; **16** 165, 248, 401, 402, 408, 412, 413, 426
Iraq **16** 399, 433
Ireland **16** 28
Islamic **6** 333; **16** 248, 393–4, 395; **31** 21
Central Asia, Western **16** 239, 248
Egypt **16** 402–3, 404, 415
Iran **16** 165, 248, 401, 402, 408, 412, 426
Iraq **16** 399, 433
North Africa **16** 427
Ottoman **16** 420
Syria **16** 415
Timurid **16** 413
Turkey **16** 411
Italy **2** 178; **12** 803; **26** 443
Japan **17** 242*, 247–9, 252*, 258, 350, 352, 353, *405*; **28** 495
Edo period (1600-1868) **17** 255, 262
Heian period (AD 794-1185) **17** 242, 250–51; **27** 699
Muromachi period (1333-1568) **17** 253
Nara period (AD 710-94) **17** 247, *248*, 250
Shōwa period (1926-89) **17** 266
Khmer **30** 610
Korea **18** *335*, 336, 337, 338, 340
Mesopotamia **6** 333; **21** 308
Native North Americans **22** 604
Netherlands, the **12** 803
North Africa **16** 427
Ottoman **16** 420
Phoenician **4** 172
Portugal **25** 309
Scotland **28** 258
Syria **4** 172; **16** 415
Syria-Palestine **30** 197
Thailand **30** 610
Turkey **16** 411
Vietnam **32** 484
materials
alizarin **12** 623
aloe **12** 623
alum **12** 803
alumina **6** 324, 329
amber **23** 792
annatto **12** 623
antimony **16** 394
arsenic **16** 394
ashes **6** 329, 873; **10** 315; **17** 242, 250–51; **18** *335*, 340; **27** 699
borax **6** 326
camphor **25** 309
chalk **12** 803
china stone **6** 329
clay **17** 242
cobalt **6** 869, 872, 888, 902, 906, 909; **16** 248, 394, 407, 414
cobalt oxides **4** 172
copal **12** 803
copper **6** 869, 873, 905, 910; **10** 302
copper oxides **6** 872, 885, 895, 899; **16** 394, 426
dammar **12** 803
dragon's-blood **12** 803
feldspar **6** 324, 326, 329; **17** 242
ferric oxide **16** 394
frit **6** 888; **10** 47; **11** 794

glazes
materials—cont.
galena 17 353
gamboge 12 623, 803
iron 6 869, 905; 17 242, 253
iron oxide 6 329, 872, 873, 881, 885, 894, 899, 909
kaolin 6 329
lac 12 623
lead 6 326, 328, 329, 333; 30 874
Central Asia, Western 6 257
China 6 872, 882, 886, 887, 888
Egypt, ancient 10 46
England 10 306
Ireland 16 28
Islamic 16 395, 399, 415, 420, 427
Japan 17 242, 247–9
Portugal 25 309
lead oxides 6 872
lime 6 326, 329, 873, 881, 895
limestone 17 242
manganese 6 869; 16 394, 402, 407
manganese oxide 6 872
mastic 12 803
oils 2 178; 12 803
pigments 12 803; 18 656
potash 6 329; 16 394
potassium oxide 6 872, 873
quartz 6 872; 16 394
red lead 16 393
resins 12 803; 23 792
saffron 12 623
salt 3 *589*; 4 769; 5 581; 6 329; 10 *312*, 315; 12 429; 16 394, 427; 28 258; 30 875
saltpetre 6 872
sandarac 12 803; 23 792
silica 6 329, 873; 16 404
silver oxides 16 394
slip 6 329
smalt 6 869; 12 803
soda 6 329; 16 394
solvents 23 792
starch 16 433
tin 6 257, 329; 16 393, 399, 402, 404, 413
see also FAIENCE (ii) (CERAMICS); POTTERY → wares → delftware; lustrewares; tin-glazed wares
titanium oxide 6 873
turquoise 16 407
verdigris 12 623, 803
zinc 6 329
technical examination 30 401
techniques
overglaze decoration 6 910
underglaze decoration 6 910
wax resist 6 874, 888
types
Bristol 6 329
hare's fur *see temmoku*
leadless 30 874, 875
liuli 6 890
oil spot 6 896
temmoku 6 873, 896
tobacco spit 31 636
uses
architectural decorations 16 194
beads 10 47
brick 4 769
ceramics 4 172; 6 324, 328, 329*, 869, 872–3*; 11 794; 16 393–4; 17 242, 266; 28 495
drawings 11 407
earthenwares 6 325, 328, 872; 16 395
gilding 12 623, 626
paintings 12 802; 24 789
oil 2 178; 23 375
watercolours 11 407
paper 17 *405*
porcelain 6 326, 329, 894, 899
pottery 6 333; 13 480–81; 22 604
Central Asia 6 257
glazes
uses
pottery—cont.
China 6 879, 881, 882, 886, 888, 893, 895
Early Christian and Byzantine 9 633
Egypt, ancient 10 46
England 10 315
Greece, ancient 13 504, 537
Ireland 16 28
Islamic 16 399, 401, 402, 408, 411, 412, 413, 415, 420, 426, 427
Japan 17 247, 250–51, 252, 253, 255, 258
Korea 18 336
Mesopotamia 21 308
Syria-Palestine 30 197
prints 11 407
revetments 16 248
sculpture 25 175
stage scenery 30 681
stonewares 5 506; 6 328, 329, 872, 873, 893; 17 350, 352; 18 *335*, 337, 338; 27 699; 32 484
terracotta 26 443; 30 505
textiles 16 433; 31 21
tiles 16 165, 239, 248; 30 874–5*, 876*
wallpaper 32 811, 818
Glazier, John *see* JOHN GLAZIER
Glazier Codex *see under* CODICES → individual manuscripts
glaziers 20 560; 22 157
Glazinis, Hugh de, Abbot of Marseille *see* HUGH DE GLAZINIS, Abbot of Marseille
Glazunov, Il'ya (Sergeyovich) 12 804*; 27 397
Gleadowe, R. M. Y. 10 337
works 10 *337*
Gleanings in Science see JOURNAL OF THE ASIATIC SOCIETY OF BENGAL
Gleason, Roswell 4 481; 31 652
Gleave, John Lee 9 117
Glebova, Tat'yana (Nikolayevna) 11 82; 12 804*; 18 412; 27 581
Gleeson, Evelyn 9 318
Gleeson, James 2 749; 12 804–5*
Gleeson, William 2 763; 12 805*; 33 680
Gleichen Russwurm, Heinrich Ludwig von 10 560
Gleichmann, Otto 12 805*
Glei'eh Fort 14 21
Gleismüller, Sigmund 33 84
Gleissner, Franz 19 482; 28 404
Gleize, La *see* LA GLEIZE
Gleizes, Albert 11 548; 12 805–7*; 16 17
exhibitions 32 775
groups and movements
Abbaye de Créteil 1 21
Abstract art 1 76
Abstraction-Création 1 89, 90
Cubism 8 240, 241, 244, 246, 247
Dada 8 435, 436
Jack of Diamonds (Bubnovy Valet) 16 817
Moderne Kunstkring 21 775
Orphism 23 569, 570
Puteaux group 9 361; 19 78; 25 747
Salon des Réalités Nouvelles 24 574
Section d'Or 2 225; 28 347
Society of Independent Artists (USA) 28 925
patrons and collectors 2 383, 409; 13 800
pupils 4 107; 14 718; 17 473; 30 348
reproductive prints by others 32 577
works 12 *806*
Gleizes, Albert—cont.
writings 20 851; 21 363, 364; 25 747; 31 300
Gleizes, Jean-Antoine 'Auguste' 25 581
Glele 1 389; 11 246
Glenbeigh Towers (Co. Kerry) 12 840
Glencoe (IL), Congregation Israel 17 549
Glendale (CA), Forest Lawn Memorial Park 18 *101*; 29 515
Glendalough (Co. Wicklow) 12 807–8*; 16 *5*
Round Tower 12 *807*
St Kevin's Church 19 869–70
St Kevin's Kitchen 12 *807*, 808; 26 592
St Saviour's 26 592
Glen Dimplex 16 35
Glendurgan House (Cornwall) 18 585
Glenfesk (Co. Kerry), St Agatha 16 11
Glenfinnan Viaduct 4 803
Gleninsheen Gorget 12 869
Glenkiln (Dumfries & Galloway) 28 315
Glenlyon estate (Tayside) 28 230
Glenn, Mildred 24 890
Glennie, Fred 5 668
Glenorchy, Colin Campbell, 8th Laird of *see* CAMPBELL, COLIN, 8th Laird of Glenorchy
Glenrose 29 743
Glenrothes (Fife) 31 733
Glenstal Castle (Co. Limerick) 23 211
Glenstone Hall (Yorks) 25 268
Glesker, Jost 12 808
Glesker, Justus 3 705; 12 404, 808*
Glesscker, Justus *see* GLESKER, JUSTUS
Glessner, J. J. 26 342
Glevum *see* GLOUCESTER (GLOS; UK)
Gleyre, (Marc-)Charles (-Gabriel) 1 106; 9 766; 11 671; 12 808–10*; 30 125
dealers 13 228
groups and movements 23 504
patrons and collectors 2 614
pupils
Anker, (Samuel) Albert 2 116
Bachelin, (Rodolphe-)Auguste 3 20
Bazille, (Jean-)Frédéric 3 434
Bocion, François (-Louis-David) 4 202
Du Maurier, George (Louis Palmella Busson) 9 384
Gérôme, Jean-Léon 12 486
Grigorescu, Nicolae 13 651
Hamon, Jean-Louis 14 120
Henry, E(dward) L(amson) 14 396
Hermans, Charles 14 457
Jobbé-Duval, Félix (Armand Marie) 17 597
Laso (de la Vega de los Ríos), Francisco 18 812
Lecomte du Nouÿ, (Jules) Jean (Antoine) 19 38
Lepic, Ludovic (-Napoléon) 19 215
Monet, (Oscar-)Claude 21 862
Oller (y Cestero), Francisco 23 415
Pina, José Salomé 24 818
Poynter, Edward John 25 406
Prinsep, Val(entine Cameron) 25 587
Simon, Friedrich Rudolf 28 750
Sisley, Alfred 28 795
Wallis, Henry 32 800
Whistler, James (Abbott) McNeill 33 137
teachers 14 482
Gleyre, (Marc-)Charles (-Gabriel)—cont.
works 12 *809*; 30 133
Glick, John 31 640
Gliddon, George Robins 10 90
gliders 30 364
Gligorova, Ilinka 19 884
Glimm, Albrecht 9 433
Glimmingehus (Sweden) 30 67, 87
Glimminghus Castle (Denmark) 8 738
Glinica 25 122
Glinitz *see* GLINICA
Glinsky, Y. 18 39
Glinton, Sabrina 3 63
Glinucci, Girolamo, Cardinal 1 605
Glit Ltd 15 72
Gloag, John 20 475
Glob, Peter 3 69
Globe Cup 1 771
Globe Goblet 30 147
Globe Potteries 29 116
globes 2 649; 12 810–15*, *811*, *814*; 23 339
Globular Amphora culture 25 516
globus tables *see under* TABLES → types
Glockendon, Albrecht, I (father) 12 815
Glockendon, Albrecht, II (son) 12 815–16*
Glockendon, Gabriel 12 815
Glockendon, Georg, I (grandfather) 12 815*
Glockendon, Georg, II (grandson) 12 815
Glockendon, Jakob 12 815
Glockendon, Nikolaus (father) 12 815, 816*; 14 649
Glockendon, Nikolaus (son) 12 815
Glockendon, Sebastian 12 815
Glockendon, Wolf 12 815
Glöckle, Michael 11 731
Glöckner, Hermann 12 816–17*
Gloddaeth 32 781
Gloeden, Wilhelm von 12 215, 817*
Glogów 21 571; 31 718
Glomy, Jean-Baptiste 11 663
Glons Parish Church 3 566
glories 12 817*
see also LIGHT
Glorification of St Thomas Aquinas, Master of the 3 247
Glorification of the Virgin, Master of the 12 384; 20 681*
Głos plastyków 24 441
glossaries 10 204, 205, 209, 211–12
Glossop, William 11 119
glost firing *see under* FIRING → types
Glot, Richard 11 606
Glothau, Hans 12 223
Głotowo Church 25 130
Glotsch, L. C. 10 445
Gloucester (Glos; UK) 10 *225*; 12 817–20*
Abbey *see* Cathedral of St Peter and the Holy Trinity
Cathedral of St Peter and the Holy Trinity 12 817–20*; 13 55; 23 491
ballflower 3 121
choir 8 611; 31 273
choir-stalls 7 191
cloister 7 453; 12 *819*; 13 55; 19 312; 28 308
monument to Edward II 12 818
mouldings 22 216
piers (ii) (masonry) 24 751
presbytery 12 *818*
screen 13 200
sculpture 10 260, 262
stained glass 13 152, 183, *184*; 29 422, 503, 507
stiff-leaf 29 659
Gloucester (Glos; UK)
Cathedral of St Peter and the Holy Trinity—cont.
tomb of Robert Curthose, Duke of Normandy 13 121
tracery 31 271
transept 24 465
vaults 32 88, 89
pottery 10 301
St Oswald 2 66, 72
sculptors 10 265
shire hall 18 887
The PackAge Revisited 10 422
urban planning 27 4
Whitefield Presbyterian Chapel 23 194
Gloucester (Ont; Canada) 23 632
Gloucester, Eleanor de Bohun, Duchess of *see* PLANTAGENET, ELEANOR, Duchess of Gloucester
Gloucester, Gilbert de Clare, Earl of *see* CLARE, GILBERT DE, Earl of Gloucester
Gloucester, Henry Stuart, Duke of *see* STUART, HENRY, Duke of Gloucester
Gloucester, Humfrey, Duke of *see* PLANTAGENET, HUMFREY, Duke of Gloucester
Gloucester, John of *see* JOHN OF GLOUCESTER
Gloucester, Mary, Duchess of *see* HANOVER, MARY, Duchess of Gloucester
Gloucester, Thomas of Woodstock, Duke of *see* PLANTAGENET, THOMAS, OF WOODSTOCK, Duke of Gloucester
Gloucester, William Frederick, Duke of *see* HANOVER, WILLIAM FREDERICK, Duke of Gloucester
Gloucester, William Henry, Duke of *see* HANOVER, WILLIAM HENRY, Duke of Gloucester
Gloucester Candlestick 5 611; 10 322, 338; 26 688, *688*
glove puppets *see under* PUPPETS → types
Glover, Ablade 12 509
works 12 *508*
Glover, George 12 820*
Glover, John 2 745, 769; 4 882; 12 821*; 32 903
Glover, Thomas 22 429
gloves 3 442; 32 389
glove stretchers 4 *314*
Głowacki, Jan Nepomucen 12 821*; 25 106
Gluck, Christoph Willibald 30 672
Glück, Heinrich 16 549
Gluckstadt, Emil 8 759
Glucq, Jean 17 684
glues 1 155; 20 367
historical and regional traditions
Afghanistan 1 202
Aztec 21 249
Bhutan 3 914
Buddhism 1 202
China 7 92
Egypt, ancient 9 822
Indian subcontinent 15 548
Islamic 16 356; 29 818
Japan 17 138, 140, 213, 281, 387, 388
Korea 18 302
Mesoamerica, Pre-Columbian 21 249
materials
antlers 15 850
fish 15 850
gelatin 1 155
hides 7 92
horn 7 92; 15 850
seaweeds 17 138
skins 15 850; 31 282
starch 1 155, 156; 28 312

glues—cont.
technical examination 30 410*
uses
bookbindings 16 356; 24 107
conservation 17 138; 28 312
consolidants 7 747
crayons 8 127
dolls 31 261
feathers 21 249; 22 652
furniture 1 156
gesso 1 156
grounds 13 706, 708
inks 7 92; 15 849, 850; 17 213
insksticks 7 92; 17 387, 388
marquetry 20 466
paintings 1 202; 15 548; 17 140; 18 302; 24 4, 5; 28 338, 339; 32 808
paints 3 914; 9 39
paper 1 156
prints 11 173; 17 281
relining 26 142
scagliola 28 28
stucco 29 813, 818
textiles 1 156
toys 31 258
transfer (conservation) 31 282
wicker 33 155
see also ADHESIVES; SIZE
Glukhov 31 562, 563
Glukhov, A. 27 423
Glume (family) 29 376
Glume, Friedrich Christian 9 687; 26 497
Glume, Johann Georg (1679-1765) 14 651; 28 118
Glume, Johann Gottlieb 12 391; 25 367
Glusberg, Jorge 2 401; 13 725
Glushchenko, Nikolay P. 31 560
Glyadenovo 27 367
glycerin 28 813; 29 813; 32 898
Glyfada, Pierides Gallery 13 359
Glykon 10 812
Glymes (family) 22 64
Glyndebourne Festival Opera 30 684, *685*, 687, *688*
Glynne Cup 10 326
glyphography 25 610
Glyptal *see under* PAINTS → types
glyptics *see* SEALS
Gmelin, W. G. 14 17
Gmünd, Heinrich von *see* HEINRICH VON GMÜND
Gmünd, Johann von *see* JOHANN VON GMÜND
Gmünd, Michael von *see* MICHELI VON FREIBURG
Gmund am Tegernsee, St Ägidius 32 822
Gmunden 2 *776*, 815; 12 821–2*
Gmundner Keramik 12 822; 25 404; 33 166
Gmundner Tonwarenfabrik 12 821
Gmundner Werkstätten 12 821
GMW Partnership 12 875
Gnadenpfennige 17 522
Gnaios 12 250
Gnathia ware *see under* POTTERY → wares
Gnauth, (Gustav) Adolf 3 511; 12 822*; 13 852; 14 164
Gndevank' Church 2 429, 434
gneiss *see under* LIMESTONE → types
Gnezdo 29 89
Gnezdovsky, Yury 27 381
Gniew 30 536
Gniezno 12 822–4*; 25 *92*
architecture 25 94
Cathedral of the Assumption of the Virgin and St Adalbert 12 *823*, 823–4*; 13 57; 25 95, 126, 127, 129, 134; 26 668
chapel of Teodor Potocki 25 130
doors 9 153; 25 110, 134, 137; 26 684
Gniezno
Cathedral of the Assumption of the Virgin and St Adalbert—cont.
mausoleum of Jan Łaski 20 865
metalwork 13 162; 25 129; 26 682, 687
St Adalbert's shrine 12 823
sculpture 25 110
tomb of Primate Baranowski 25 114
tomb of St Adalbert 25 111; 26 148
chalices 25 126
metalwork 26 686
Gnoli, Domenico (i) (1838-1915) 12 824*; 24 448
Gnoli, Domenico (ii) (1933-70) 12 824–5*; 16 682
Gnoli, Umberto 12 824
Gnome, The (Rūķis) 12 825*; 18 852
members 25 745; 27 284; 31 854; 33 601
gnomons 22 572
Gnosis 12 826*; 13 557
works 13 557, 558, 560, *563*, 564; 24 338
Gnosticism 1 818; 12 251–2*, *252*
Gnyozdovo 32 527
Gō, Junzō 17 414
Goa 12 826–7*; 15 200, *276*, 401
cabinets (ii) (furniture) 20 VIII2
Cathedral 25 291
churches 17 512
fort 25 291
furniture 15 693; 25 305
Panaji 15 411
printing 15 679
sculpture 15 724
wood-carvings 15 542
Goa, Old *see* GOA VELHA
Goa Gajah 15 *754*, 763, 784
goat-hair *see under* HAIR → types
goatskin *see under* SKINS → types
Goa Velha 12 826–7
Archaeological Museum 12 826
Basilica of Bom Jesus 12 826
Cathedral of S Caterina 12 826; 26 254
Church of Our Lady of the Rosary 12 826
Church of St Cajetan 12 827
St Francis of Assisi 12 826
Goa You Porcelain Factory 30 389
gobaishi 17 354
Gobbo dei Carracci *see* BONZI, PIETRO PAOLO
Gobbo dei Frutti *see* BONZI, PIETRO PAOLO
Gobedra 10 576
Gobel, Bartholomeus 20 792
Gobel, Berthold 20 792
Göbel, Johann Philip 1 700
Gobelin (family) 12 827
Gobelinmanufaktur (Munich) 12 468
Gobelins factory 2 558; 4 552; 7 545; 11 576, 652, 659; 12 827–32*; 19 21–2; 20 133, 139; 22 725; 24 146
bronze 31 409
cabinets (ii) (furniture) 8 251; 12 *831*, 832
collections 14 145; 17 777; 27 430; 28 527; 33 19
designers 2 105; 3 621; 5 837; 6 376; 11 644; 12 874; 20 135; 23 381; 24 15, 137; 25 81
Alix, Yves 1 645
Anquetin, Louis 2 124
Audran, Claude, III (1658-1734) 2 708
Begeyn, Abraham (Jansz.) 3 500
Belle, Clément (-Louis-Marie-Anne) 3 639
Berain, Jean, I (1640-1711) 3 752
Berthélemy, Jean-Simon 3 852
Gobelins factory
designers—cont.
Blanc, (Paul) Joseph 4 124
Boel, Pieter 4 222
Boizot, Louis-Simon 4 248
Boucher, François 4 514, 517
Boudewijns, Adriaen Frans 4 522
Boullogne, Bon 4 535
Boullogne, Louis de (1654-1733) 4 536
Bracquemond, Félix (-Auguste-Joseph) 4 626
Bracquemond, Pierre 4 627
Cassas, Louis-François 5 921
Coypel, Antoine 8 91
Coypel, Charles-Antoine 8 93
Denon, (Dominique-) Vivant 8 763
Desportes, (Alexandre-) François 8 811, 814
Dufy, Raoul 9 374
Duplessis, Joseph-Siffred 9 399
Durn, Pierre-Louis 30 114
Eckhout, Albert 9 703
Erixson, Sven 10 463
Flamen, Albert 11 155
Friesz, (Emile) Othon 11 790
Galland, P(ierre) V(ictor) 12 13
Genoels, Abraham, II (1640-1723) 12 285
Gole, Pierre 20 467
Guyot, Laurent 13 878
Hallé, Claude-Guy 14 84
Hallé, Noël 14 84
Jobbé-Duval, Félix (Armand Marie) 17 597
Laurens, Jean-Paul 18 865
Le Brun, Charles 10 275; 21 367; 24 470; 30 530
Lépicié, Nicolas-Bernard 19 217
Leroux, (Louis) Hector 19 231
Loir, Nicolas-Pierre 19 542
Loo, (Charles-)Amédée (-Philippe) van 19 649
Lurçat, Jean 19 808
Maignan, Albert (-Pierre-René) 20 118
Malaine, Joseph-Louis 33 711
Mathieu, Georges 20 815
Meissonnier, Juste-Aurèle 21 69
Merson, Luc Olivier 21 166
Monnoyer, Jean-Baptiste 21 891
Moreau, Gustave 22 91
Mosnier, Pierre 22 191
Oeben, Jean-François 23 356
Oudry, Jean-Baptiste 23 667; 29 424
Passavant, Claude 5 838
Pillement, Jean (-Baptiste) 24 810
Prassinos, Mario 25 450
Singier, Gustave 28 777
Soufflot, Jacques-Germain 29 92
Steinheil, Louis-Charles-Auguste 29 610
Survage, Léopold 30 25
Suvée, Joseph-Benoît 30 46
Troy, Jean-François de 31 379
Vanloo, Carle 19 646
Verdier, François 32 242
Vien, Joseph-Marie, Comte (1716-1809) 32 428
Winck, Johann Christian Thomas 33 240
directors 12 234; 18 614; 30 323
drawing schools 1 107; 26 510
dye-works 6 564
exhibitions 10 678
furniture 11 588, 617; 19 722; 24 147; 30 783
hardstones 11 636; 12 830–31*
japanning 18 614
pupils 4 338
school 11 669
silver 12 832
tapestries 12 828–30*
16th cent. 11 640
Gobelins factory
tapestries—cont.
17th cent. 4 550; 11 48, 576, 641, 642; 12 *829*; 22 536; 23 512; 30 321, II2
18th cent. 2 *703*; 7 167; 8 755; 9 313; 10 277; 11 643; 12 412; 19 382; 29 92, 350; 30 *309*, *323*
19th cent. 4 302; 5 839; 11 643; 25 193; 27 896; 30 325, 326
20th cent. 3 450; 10 895; 11 644; 30 327, 328, 329
Gobelins weaving *see under* WEAVING → types
Gobelsburg, Mariae Geburt 26 634
Gober, Robert 12 218, 832*
Gobert, André 12 832
Gobert, Claude-Thomas 12 833
Gobert, Jean 12 832
Gobert, Jean-Baptistse 12 832
Gobert, Louis-François 11 625
Gobert, Pierre 12 832–3*; 26 376
Gobert, Thomas (*d c.* 1644) 12 833
Gobert, Thomas (*c.* 1630-1708) 12 833*
Gobertus, Master 6 173
works 6 *174*
Gobertus of Trier *see* GOBERTUS, MASTER
Gobiendes, Church of Santiago 29 261
Gobillard, Jeannie 31 820
Gobillard, Paule 31 820
Gobin, Michel 29 668
Gobin, Robert 33 350
Goblé, Steven 20 400
Goblet, Alexander 23 190
goblets
historical and regional traditions
Ancient Near East 1 *878*
Austria 2 *820*
Byzantine 9 *634*
Central Asia, Western 6 268
China 7 12
Crete 21 *669*, 671
Cycladic 8 *313*
Cyprus 9 *634*
Czech Republic 8 404, *408*; 21 *726*
England 10 *315*, *318*
France 11 *611*
Germany 12 442
Greece, ancient 14 *170*, 338
Helladic 14 338, *344*
Holy Roman Empire (before 1648) 21 *726*
Italy 12 VIII3
Minoan 21 *669*, 671
Mycenaean 14 338
Norway 10 *194*
Poland 25 *125*
Russia 27 *415*
Scotland 28 *259*
Sweden 30 *101*, 102
Syria-Palestine 1 *878*; 30 *197*
United States of America 31 *641*
materials
amber 1 762
bloodstone (chalcedony) 21 *726*
enamel 2 *820*; 10 *194*
faience (i) (glass) 1 *878*
glass 6 268; 10 *315*, *318*; 11 *611*; 12 VIII3; 27 *415*; 28 *259*; 30 *101*; 31 *641*
lacquer 7 12
pottery 9 *634*; 14 *343*; 21 *669*; 30 *197*
sard 14 *170*
silver-gilt 2 *820*
types
Ephyraean 14 338, *344*
see also CUPS; GLASSES
Gobustan 1 823; 2 *890*; 12 833*; 25 *471*
Gocadiguse group 28 330
Gočár, Josef 8 401; 12 833–4*; 25 437
collaboration 18 570
groups and movements 7 182; 8 373; 13 711; 16 902; 21 781; 32 449
pupils 3 736; 6 345; 14 247
teachers 18 405
works 8 249, 380, 401, 402, 423; 25 429, 430
Goczemski, Józef 25 106
God, Antoine 33 289
Goda, Kiyoshi 17 204
Godagiri 15 701
Godalming (Surrey)
Charterhouse School Chapel 6 459, *459*
power station 25 402
Godapura 15 522
Godard, André 12 834*; 15 922; 16 548; 19 812; 30 415; 33 688
collections 15 922
works 15 899; 17 717
Godard, Yedda 12 834
Goday, Josep 3 216
Goddard (family) 31 626
Goddard, H. 6 408
Goddard, John (1723-85) 12 834–5*; 23 32; 31 249, 626
Goddard, John, jr (*d* 1843) 12 835
Goddard, John Frederick 24 660
Goddard, Stephen 12 835
Goddard, Thomas 12 835
Goddard, Townsend 12 835
Goddard & Gibbs 29 513
Godde, Etienne-Hippolyte 8 816; 12 835*; 19 250; 26 190, 545
Godderis, Jack 17 518
Gode, Ludwig 4 695; 14 894; 28 855
Godeau, Simon 12 133
Godebski, Cyprian 18 430; 25 130
Godecharle, Gilles-Lambert 3 571; 12 835–6*
patrons and collectors 3 613; 4 302
teachers 8 699
works 5 43; 22 33
Godeffroy, J. C. 23 742
Godefried 12 471
Godefroid de Claire *see* GODEFROID OF HUY
Godefroid of Huy 12 836*; 26 683; 33 153
patrons and collectors 26 146
Godefroy 16 852
Godefroy, Adrien 14 192
Godefroy, A. N. 29 433
Godefroy, Denys *see* DENIS GODEFROY
Godefroy, (Jean Maur) Maximilian 12 836–7*
pupils 21 371
works 3 128; 10 850; 18 845; 33 195
Godefroy, Ottilie 5 924; 8 181
Godefroy, Stefano *see* STEFANO GODEFROY
Godefroy-Durondeau 5 51
Godefroy le Batave 7 463; 11 532; 12 837*
Godehard, Bishop of Hildesheim 9 153; 14 535; 23 658
Godelin, Gervaise 19 238
Godeman, Abbot of Thorney 1 184; 2 75; 33 232
Goderamus, Abbot of Hildesheim 7 594
Goderan 3 552; 26 666
Godert von Sante Druden 29 5
Godescalc 12 837–8*
works 5 800, 801, *801*; 6 483; 12 382; 25 743
Godescalc Evangeliary *see under* EVANGELIARIES → individual manuscripts

Godescalc Gospel Lectionary see EVANGELIARIES → individual manuscripts → Godescalc Evangeliary
Godet 29 305
Godewijk, Margareta van 20 81; 22 898
Godfrey 30 366
Godfrey (family) 23 66
Godfrey, Elizabeth
works 28 737
Godfrey, L. J. 23 66
Godfrey of Huy see GODEFROID OF HUY
Godi, Girolamo de' 23 862
villa 23 863
Godier, Jean 11 426
Godin, Denis-Germain 4 536
Godin, Jean-Baptiste 11 358; 30 458
Godin, Louis 23 340
Godinho Leal, Manuel 5 421
Godin Tepe 1 894; 10 132; 12 838*; 15 901, 904, 909, 910, 921
architecture 15 905
hypostyle hall 15 911
seals 1 863
town walls 21 554
Godl, Stefan 12 838*
patrons and collectors 13 904; 28 492; 29 571
works 2 800, 800; 6 171; 15 865; 20 104
Godlavidu 15 539
Godley, Frederick 14 735
works 5 136
Godley, John Robert 7 210; 33 374
Godman, C. E. 12 838
Godman, Frederick Ducane 12 838–9*; 16 395, 554; 22 59
Godmanchester (Cambs) 13 211
Godmersham Court Lodge (Kent) 28 301
Godo, José 29 337
Gödöllő 14 881, 894
Grassalkovich Palace 14 887; 15 13
Sun School 14 890
Gödöllő colony 12 839*; 14 901, 908; 15 12; 18 388; 21 4; 22 433; 30 762
members 3 474
works 18 394; 22 433
Godolphin, Sidney, 1st Earl Godolphin 30 267
Godon, François-Louis 9 379
Godowsky, Leopold 24 653
Godoy, Francisco de 5 362
Godoy, García 9 119
Godoy, Juan Silvano 24 100, 101
Godoy (y Alvárez de Faria), Manuel, Príncipe de la Paz 12 839–40*
collections 29 353
furniture 28 593
paintings 5 784; 11 218; 13 244; 22 338; 26 734
Godoy, Terryl 3 624
Godson, William 33 231
Godunov (family) 27 385
Godunov, Boris, Tsar of Russia see BORIS GODUNOV, Tsar of Russia
Godunov school 22 176
Godwin 30 877
Godwin, Beatrice 33 141
Godwin, E(dward) W(illiam) 8 109; 10 282; 12 840–41*; 19 311
collaboration 28 349
groups and movements 1 170; 10 238; 17 440; 25 805
houses 33 180
patrons and collectors 14 132
works 9 29; 10 282; 11 436; 12 840; 16 25; 17 469; 19 574; 23 547; 31 241; 33 140, 143
Godwin, E(dward) W(illiam)—cont.
writings 10 298
Godwin, George (1789-1863) 12 841
Godwin, George (1813-88) 12 841*; 24 446
Godwin, Henry 12 841
Godwin, John 14 755; 23 134
Godwin, Ted 4 169; 5 569
Godwin, William 22 277
Godwin Hopwood 14 755
Godwin Hopwood Kuye Architects 14 755
Goebbels, Joseph 1 166; 10 413, 414; 22 710; 25 652
Goebel, Carl 12 842*
Goebel, Carl Peter 12 842
Goebel, Jenő Paizs see PAIZS GOEBEL, JENŐ
Goeblange 19 826
Goecke, Irma 12 468; 30 328
Goecke, Theodor 28 801; 30 370
Goedewaagen 22 884; 23 120, 121
Goedhard, Johan 29 99
Goedicke, Hans 10 83
Goed Wonen, Stichting see STICHTING GOED WONEN
Goeimare, Joss 27 885
Goeldi, Emílio, Museu Paraense see under BELÉM (ii) (BRAZIL)
Goeldi, Oswaldo 4 717; 12 842*
Goelet, John 15 745
Goelet, Ogden 15 22
Goeller, Adolf 14 434
Goemai 1 382
Goemans, Camille 30 20
Goeneutte, Norbert 12 842*
Goenka, Jagdish 15 742
Goenka Academy of Art and Music 15 742
Goeree, Jan 12 843
Goeree, Willem 12 842–3*; 22 907
Goerg, Edouard 11 336; 29 26; 33 36
Goering, Hermann (Wilhelm) 2 560; 12 843*
architecture 23 814; 26 402
collections 12 474
paintings 10 414; 21 39
Goeritz, Erich 16 570, 571
Goeritz, Marianne 12 844
Goeritz, Mathías 3 273; 12 843–4*; 21 390; 28 330
groups and movements 28 330
pupils 11 775; 28 330
works 7 696; 21 396; 28 731
writings 21 381
Goerlich Lleo, Javier 31 815
Goertz, Jürgen 1 738
Goerz 24 669
Goes, Church of Mary Magadalen 22 820
Goés, Domingos de 4 725
Goes, Felip de 20 832
Goes, Hugo (fl 1509) 10 272
Goes, Hugo van der (1440-82) 5 43; 12 519, 844–50*; 22 836
attributions 20 705, 717
collaboration 20 789
copies 8 553
groups and movements 26 186
methods 19 354; 24 4; 25 281
patrons and collectors 3 553, 612, 890; 4 379; 5 212; 9 724; 13 919; 16 659; 25 270; 28 233, 268
works 1 710; 3 596; 4 595, 920; 5 214; 9 4; 12 845, 846, 847, 848, 849; 13 806; 18 676, 704; 23 501; 26 186
workshop 11 149
Goes, Marinus Robyn van der 12 851*; 21 765; 22 717; 32 700
Goes, Pieter 5 62
Goés Calmon, Francisco 4 725
Goeschl, Roland 12 851*
Goetghebuer, Pierre Jacques 3 619; 31 864
Goethals, Charles 32 591
Goethals, Hugo 4 692
Goethe, August von 28 44
Goethe, Johann Caspar 13 807; 26 529
Goethe, Johann Wolfgang von 1 106, 180, 660; 5 286; 12 851–3*, 852; 13 303; 18 739; 21 409; 22 379; 28 657; 33 37
architecture 33 117
collaboration 30 767
dealing 17 916
house 33 37
methods 5 519
patrons and collectors 2 383
personal collection 6 98; 11 732; 27 338; 30 854
productions 21 59
sculpture 18 107
silhouettes 28 714
teachers 17 713; 23 359; 31 27
writings 6 148; 13 807; 14 18; 24 421, 425, 443; 29 753; 33 117
illustrated 4 364; 7 183, 870; 8 640; 26 258
on collecting 13 541
on colour 1 74; 7 629
on decorum 8 613
on Dürer 9 443
on Pompeii 25 207
translated 9 682; 20 370; 28 286
Goethem, Nicolas van see YENEN
goethite 24 792, 798
Goetkind, Antoon 3 607
Goetkindt, Pieter 4 913
Goetz, Gottfried Bernhard 25 38
Goetz, Henri 5 725, 726
Goetz, Hermann 12 853–4*; 15 182, 211
Goetz, Johann Lorenz 29 750, 755
Goetz, Karl Xaver 12 854*; 20 926
Goevaerts, Abraham see GOVAERTS, ABRAHAM
Goez, Gottfried Bernhard see GÖZ, GOTTFRIED BERNHARD
Goff, Bruce (Alonzo) 12 854–5*
works 12 855
Goff, Clare 19 812
goffering 17 275
GoFukakusa, Emperor (reg 1246-60) 17 225
GoFushimi, Emperor (reg 1298-1301) 11 856; 17 225
Gogaku Fukuhara see FUKUHARA GOGAKU
Gogel, Daniel 10 857
Gogen, Aleksandr (Ivanovich) 12 855–6*; 32 72
Göggingen 12 430, 431
Gogh, Theo van
dealing 4 589; 13 829; 15 155; 18 696; 21 868
frames 11 449
paintings 12 190
publications 22 29
sponsorship 12 857; 13 228
Gogh, Vincent van (1820-88) 4 588; 12 856; 13 228; 20 351
Gogh, Vincent (Willem) van (1853-90) 7 674; 10 693; 11 547, 672; 12 189, 856–61*; 14 43; 20 871; 22 29, 379, 815, 851
attributions 11 308
commentaries 9 745
dealers 3 826; 7 234; 26 107; 30 290; 32 686
exhibitions 2 447; 3 813; 10 680; 11 790; 14 43; 19 10; 26 546
forgeries by others 11 308, 309
frames 11 448–9
groups and movements 12 870; 15 156; 24 585; 25 355, 356, 358; 26 57
house 2 552
methods 7 630; 13 709; 24 349
paintings 22 905
Gogh, Vincent (Willem) van (1853-90)—cont.
patrons and collectors 2 561, 707; 10 414; 12 474; 28 344
Barnes, Albert C. 3 251; 12 769
Bond, Alan 2 561
Bremmer, H(endricus) P(etrus) 22 905
Bührle, Emil Georg 5 132
Camondo, Isaac de, Comte 5 530
Clark, Robert Sterling 7 377
Courtauld, Samuel (1876-1947) 8 62
Dale, Chester 8 463
Gachet, Paul (-Ferdinand) (1828-1909) 11 887
Hammer, Armand 14 117
Kröller-Müller, Hélène 4 743; 18 466; 22 906
Maitland, Alexander 28 272
Matisse, Henri (Emile Benoît) 20 822
Metropolitan Museum of Art (New York) 2 560
Morozov, Ivan (Abramovich) (1871-1921) 22 135, 136
Museu de Arte de São Paulo 4 726
Phillips, Duncan 24 638
Schuffenecker, (Claude-) Emile 28 172
Shchukin, Sergey (Ivanovich) 28 569
Tetzen-Lund, Christian 30 532
Tōgō Seiji Museum 17 433
Whitney, John Hay 33 150
Wildenstein, Georges 33 183
Yasuda Fire and Marine Insurance Company 2 561
personal collection 14 453; 22 29; 24 832
works 7 674, 675, III1; 9 216; 10 693; 12 296, 857, 858, 859, 861; 17 287; 18 717; 19 488; 22 849; 24 243
Gogh, Vincent van (1866-1911) 22 905
Gogh, Vincent van, Rijksmuseum see under AMSTERDAM → museums
Gogh-Bonner, Johanna van 12 861
Gogol, Nikolay (Vasil'yevich) 12 862*
productions 17 812; 32 579
works 27 868
illustrated 6 384; 30 488; 33 607
Gogollari, Dhimo 1 543; 12 862*
Gogoşu 26 719
Goguen, Jean 25 28
GoHanazono, Emperor (reg 1428-64) 17 173
Gohar 2 438; 16 480
rugs 2 438
Goh Beng Kwan 28 774
Goh Ee Choo 28 774
Gohl, Theodor 3 823
Gohlke, Frank 23 37
Gō Hokushō 17 413; 20 75
GoHorikawa, Emperor (reg 1221-32) 11 825
Goicoles y Zañartu, Juan José de 6 592
Going, Richard 4 824
Goings, Ralph 29 671
Goi Ranshū 17 236
Góis, Damião de 2 874; 4 453; 14 659
Gois, Edmé-Etienne-François 12 863; 31 374
Gois, Etienne-Pierre-Adrien 6 516; 12 862–3*; 25 876; 28 847
Goitia, Francisco 12 863*
Gojan 1 543
Gojō 17 83
Gokle 20 54
GoKōgon, Emperor (reg 1351-71) 17 226; 29 66
GoKomatsu, Emperor (reg 1382-1412) 2 599; 17 167
Gokstad 23 227; 32 517
Gokul Das II, Rawat of Deogarh (reg 1786-1821) (Rajput) 15 600
Gokyōgoku see under JAPAN → calligraphy
Gokyōgoku Yoshitsune 17 224
Gola 1 236, 242–3, 245, 247, 256, 342; 19 309; 21 115
Gola, Emilio 12 863*
Golani, Rivka 33 696
Golconda 12 863–4*; 15 294, 637; 16 105
Bala Hisar 15 381, 382, 541
Bala Hisar Darvaza 15 381, 382
calligraphy 15 681
ceramics 6 918
Chahar Gunbad 31 113
Fateh Darvaza 15 541
fortifications 15 381
manuscripts 16 343, 345
mausoleum of A'zam Khan 29 825
mausoleum of Khayr Khan 29 825
Naya Qil'a 15 381
paintings 15 640–42*, 641
Qutb Shahi palace 15 381
Qutb Shahi tombs 15 384, 384
textiles 15 673
water supply 15 382
gold 12 864–70*; 14 418; 17 525; 21 319
alloys 12 864–5
copper 5 747; 12 865; 17 318; 29 211; 30 240, 240; 32 238
palladium 12 865
silver 9 657; 12 864, 865; 17 318; 29 211
zinc 12 865
historical and regional traditions
Achaemenid 1 118; 21 III
Afghanistan 1 204, 205, 206; 16 375
Africa 1 286, 288, 296, 350
Akan 1 392; 8 22
Akye 1 515
Anatolia, ancient 1 521, 834, 836, 874
Ancient Near East 1 873–5, 873, 876; 21 III; 31 531
Anglo-Saxon 2 79, 83, 84; 10 322; 17 IV1
Antilles, Lesser 2 152
Argentina 2 401–2*
Armenia (Europe) 2 441–2; 27 15
Asante 1 288, 352, 353; 2 585, 586, 587
Assyrian 1 875
Australia 2 764
Austria 2 819–21*, 820, 823*, 823, 824
Aztec 21 252
Bactria 9 457; 30 891
Bali (Indonesia) 15 793
Bangladesh 3 169
Baule 3 408, 409; 8 22
Belgium 3 596–602*, 606, 607, 609, 609; 5 213; 14 413; 18 591
Bhutan 3 914
Black Sea Colonies 1 118
Bolivia 4 265–6*
Brazil 4 723–4*
Britain 27 15
Buddhism 1 206; 7 21, 23, 24, 25, 27; 18 351–2; 30 823, 836
Bulgaria 5 160; 25 517
Burma 20 329
Byzantine 6 173; 7 763; 8 203; 9 606, 611, 618, 623, 636, 652–3, 653, 654*, 656*, 658, 659, 659, 660, 662, 663, 668; 15 I; 19 351; 22 162; 32 212
Cambodia 5 507

gold
historical and regional traditions—cont.
Canaanite **1** 874
Canada **5** 584–6*, *585*
Caribbean Islands **5** 747
Carolingian **5** *808*; **7** *513*
Celtic **6** 155, *157*, 158; **12** *867*; **18** 120; **25** 542
Central Asia, Western **6** 236–42*, 250, *259*, *260*, 261, 273, *273*, 274, *274*; **9** *457*; **27** *599*; **30** *891*
Champa **6** 432
Chavín culture **29** *214*
Chile **6** 599*
China **6** *632*; **7** *20*, 21–7*, 45, 68, 79, 106, 108, 109, 111, 112, 116, 128, 632; **21** 715
Buddhism **7** 21, 23, 24, 25, 27
Han period (206 BC–AD 220) **7** 108
Liao period (AD 907-1125) **7** 110
Ming period (1368-1644) **7** 17, *27*, 50, *50*, *53*, 110, 111, *111*
Northern and Southern Dynasties (AD 310-589) **21** 715
Qing period (1644-1911) **7** 19, *19*, 20, 51, *51*, 111, 112
Shang period (*c.* 1600–*c.* 1050 BC) **7** 106, 107
Song period (AD 960-1279) **6** 895; **7** 15, 110
Sui period (AD 581-618) **7** *109*
Tang period (AD 618-907) **7** 14, *14*, 109
Yuan period (1279-1368) **7** 50
Zhou period (*c.* 1050-256 BC) **6** 853, 855; **7** *22*, 88, *98*, 107, *107*, 108; **21** 714
20th cent. **7** *112*
Coclé culture **7** 507; **29** *151*
Colombia **7** 600, 610–11*; **28** *781*; **29** 135, 152, *211*; **30** 240, *240*
Côte d'Ivoire **8** 22
Crete **8** 153; **21** 686–7*, *686*, *687*, 688*, *688*
Croatia **8** 180
Cuba (Caribbean) **8** 237
Cupisnique **8** 272
Cycladic **8** 322*
Cyprus **8** 360*
Cyprus, ancient **8** 349, 351, *352*, 352, 353; **24** *644*
Czech Republic **8** 411–14*
Dacian **30** 773
Denmark **8** 750–51*, 752; **32** *516*
Early Christian (*c.* AD 250-843) **8** 360*; **9** 618, 652–3, *653*, 654*, *659*, 668
Ecuador **9** 714
Egypt **9** *653*; **16** *384*, *385*, *389*, *512*, *513*, 529; **17** III1; **21** *718*
Egypt, ancient **1** 469, 876; **3** 441; **6** 388; **9** 817; **10** 28, 29, 30, *30*, *31*, 33, *37*, 38, *39*, 50, 51, 52, 624; **12** 867; **14** *403*, 494, *495*; **17** IV2
England **10** 322–30*, 331–6*, 347*, 355; **12** 868; **14** 419; **30** 542
Anglo-Saxon **2** *84*; **10** 322; **17** IV1
Romanesque **10** 322
12th cent. **14** *417*
14th cent. **14** *419*; **19** *581*
15th cent. **27** 159
16th cent. **10** *345*
17th cent. **2** *466*; **10** *350*; **17** *522*; **28** *749*
18th cent. **10** *347*
19th cent. **17** *528*; **20** *389*
20th cent. **12** *866*; **17** *529*
Ethiopia **27** 15

gold
historical and regional traditions—cont.
Etruscan **10** 624, *630*, 630–32*, *631*, 639; **12** 865, 867, 868, *868*
Finland **11** 107, 108
France **11** 613–23*, 631–3*; **27** 15; **28** I2
Gothic **7** 720; **10** III1; **13** 168
Merovingian **21** *163*
Renaissance Revival **17** III2
12th cent. **23** *99*
14th cent. **2** *112*; **26** *147*
15th cent. **24** *146*
16th cent. **6** *143*
17th cent. **5** 836; **11** *636*
18th cent. **4** *601*; **11** *631*, *632*, *633*; **24** 147
Gambia, The **1** 288
Georgia **12** 328–9*, *329*
Germany **9** 689–90; **12** 442–50*, 463, 868
Baroque **12** 423
Celtic **6** 155, *157*; **18** 120
Gothic **12** 442
Merovingian **21** *162*
Ottonian **4** III; **23** *657*, *658*
Prehistoric **9** *690*
Romanesque **28** *631*
6th cent. AD **21** *502*
11th cent. **2** *452*
12th cent. **26** *145*
13th cent. **10** *181*
14th cent. **12** 464
15th cent. **28** 129
18th cent. **12** *447*, *459*
19th cent. **21** 66
20th cent. **12** 450–51*, *451*
Gothic **13** 136, 139, 168, 170, 194
France **7** 720; **10** III1; **13** 168; **26** *147*
Germany **10** *181*
Hungary **13** *162*
Italy **32** *213*
Netherlands, the **13** *159*
Spain **29** *333*
Gran Chiriquí culture **13** 291, *291*
Greece, ancient **6** 388; **12** 865, 867, 868, *869*; **13** 390, 391, 435, 568–71*, *570*, 596, 597–9*, *599*; **17** I; **27** 15; **32** 250
Guatemala **13** 767–8*
Haiti **14** *55*
Helladic **14** 354–5*, *355*, 357, *357*
Hinduism **15** *783*
Hittite **8** 261
Holy Roman Empire (before 1648) **26** 683*
Hungary **9** *662*; **13** *162*; **15** 5–8*, *10*
Inca **15** 164
Indian subcontinent **6** 556; **7** 634; **15** 200, 564, 616, 663, 668, 675, *688*, *700*, 706–7*, *707*, 710–12*, 736; **17** II2; **21** 717
17th cent. **15** *678*
Indonesia **15** *783*, 793, 794, 802, 811, 812, 814, *816*, *817*
Insular art **15** *872*, 872
Iran **16** 292–3, *376*, 450, *506*, *512*, *516*, *530*; **20** *448*
Iran, ancient **14** *211*; **15** 905; **21** II1
Ireland **12** *867*; **15** 872, *872*; **16** 30–32*, 34; **25** 526; **32** *530*
Islamic **4** 688; **6** 556; **12** 868; **16** 292, 363, 364, 371–3*, *508*, 520, 531; **21** 718, *718*
Afghanistan **16** *375*
Almohad **1** 682
Ayyubid **16** 520

gold
historical and regional traditions
Islamic—cont.
Egypt **16** *384*, *385*, *389*, *512*, *513*, 529; **17** IV1
Iran **16** 292–3, *376*, 450, *506*, *508*, *512*, *516*, *530*; **21** I1
Mamluk **16** *383*
Ottoman **16** *513*, 532
Pakistan **16** *513*
Sicily **16** *430*
Spain **7** 534; **16** *513*
Syria **16** 311, *384*, *511*
Turkey **16** *507*, *513*, *542*
Italy **7** 536; **16** 690, 741–3*; **19** 351; **32** 212
Byzantine **8** *203*; **32** *212*
Carolingian **5** *808*
Early Christian (*c.* AD 250-843) **26** *144*
Etruscan **10** 624, *630*, 630–32*, *631*; **12** *868*
Gothic **32** *213*
Roman **27** 15
13th cent. **7** *536*
15th cent. **12** *583*
16th cent. **2** *454*, *472*; **7** *834*, *835*
17th cent. **16** *753*
19th cent. **16** *752*; **17** *527*
Jainism **15** 564, 616
Jamaica **16** 888
Japan **17** 220, 297, 298, *305*, 313, 318, 319, *334*, 370, 372
Edo period (1600-1868) **10** *777*; **17** *370*
Momoyama period (1568-1600) **17** 370
Muromachi period (1333-1568) **17** *228*, *301*, *362*
Nara period (AD 710-94) **17** 219
Java **15** *783*
Jewish art **17** 574
Knights Hospitaller **20** 216
Korea **18** 249, 339, 349–52*, *350*, 366, *367*, 370
Kurdistan **16** 531
Laos **18** 770, 776
Malaysia **20** 173, 174, 175, 176, 179
Malta (Republic of) **20** 216–17*
Maya **16** 803; **21** *253*
Merovingian **21** *162*, *163*
Mesoamerica, Pre-Columbian **12** 866; **16** 803; **21** 250, 252, *253*, 253; **22** 158
Mesopotamia **1** 874, 875; **12** 864, 867; **21** 303, 304
Mexico **21** 392–3*
Minoan **8** 153; **21** 686–7*, *686*, *687*, 688*, *688*
Mixtec **21** *253*, 737
Mongolia **7** 21; **21** 882, 884
Morocco **1** 682
Muisca **29** *211*
Mycenaean **14** 355*, *355*, 357, *357*
Nepal **12** 867; **22** 788
Netherlands, the **13** *159*; **22** 885–92*, *889*, 897*
New Zealand **23** 70–72*
Nicaragua **23** 83*
Norway **23** 236
Nubia **9** 817
Ottoman **16** *506*, *507*, *508*, *513*, 532, *542*, *860*
Ottonian **4** III; **22** *43*; **23** 647, 656–7*, *657*, *658*; **26** *145*
Pakistan **16** *513*; **23** 803
Panama **29** 132, *151*
Peru **8** 272; **28** *651*; **29** *214*
Philippines **24** 626, 627*
Phoenician **24** 644, *644*
Phrygian **1** 836
Poland **25** 125–8*, *127*, *133*, 137

gold
historical and regional traditions—cont.
Portugal **25** 312–14*; **32** *406*
Prehistoric art **25** 517, *517*
Bronze Age **25** *525*, 525–6, *526*, 531
Germany **9** *690*
Iron Age **25** 540, 542*, 546
Punic **25** 735
Rhodes (island) **12** *869*
Romanesque **10** 322; **19** 351; **26** 683*, 703; **28** *631*
Rome, ancient **8** 263; **21** 1; **25** 43; **27** *15*, 15–16, 79*, 80*, *103*
Russia **10** *721*; **27** 418–23*, *419*, *421*, *429*; **28** *320*, *322*, *325*
Sardinia **6** 158
Sarmatian **28** *325*
Scandinavia **32** *516*, 523, 524
Scotland **28** 260–62*, *263*
Scythian **2** *101*; **28** *320*, 321, 322, *322*
Senegal **1** 288
Sicán culture **28** 651, *651*, *652*
Sicily **16** *430*, 742
Sinú **28** *781*
South Africa **12** 864; **29** 103, 105
South America, Pre-Columbian **12** 866; **13** *291*; **28** 651, *651*, *652*, *781*, 800; **29** 132, *151*, 152, 211
Chavín culture **29** *214*
Coclé culture **7** 507
Colombia **29** 135, *211*; **30** 240, *240*
Cupisnique **8** 272
Gran Chiriquí culture **13** *291*
Muisca **29** *211*
Panama **29** 132
Peru **8** 272; **29** *214*
Tairona **30** 240, *240*
Veraguas culture **32** 238
Spain **2** *454*; **7** 534; **17** *523*; **29** 301, 332–8*, *333*, *346*, 349
Sri Lanka **20** 329; **29** 472, *473*, 474–5
Sudan **9** 817
Sumatra **15** 794, 811
Sumerian **1** 874
Sweden **30** 104–9*, 112*, *112*, *113*
Switzerland **6** 155; **17** *520*; **27** 15, *15*; **30** 145–6, 147, 151
Syria **16** 311, *384*, *511*; **21** *718*
Syria-Palestine **30** 195
Tairona **30** 240, *240*
Tajikistan **27** *599*
Thailand **30** *619*, 631, 635–6*
Thracian **30** 769, 770
Tibet **30** 823, *836*, 836, 839, 840, 841, *841*
Troad **31** *376*
Troadic **31** 355*
Turkey **16** *508*, *513*, *542*, *860*; **31** *376*
Ukraine **31** 562, *562*
United Arab Emirates **2** *264*
United States of America **31** 646, *650*, *655*
Urartian **1** 836
Uruguay **31** 756*
Varna **25** 517
Venezuela **32** 176–7*
Veraguas culture **32** 238
Vietnam **6** 432; **32** 487
Viking **32** *516*, 523, 524, *530*
Visigothic **32** *617*
Wales **25** *525*
marks *see under* MARKS
patinas **21** 329*
reuse **7** 565
technical examination **30** 408
techniques
beating **12** 621, *621*
blocking **12** 865

gold
techniques—cont.
brazing **12** 866
burnishing **12** 622
carving **12** 869
casting **12** 865; **29** *211*
chasing **12** 868–9
cutting **12** 866*
electroforming **12** 866
electroplating **12** 870
electrotyping **12** 866
embossing **22** *889*
engraving **12** 869
filigree **7** *112*
granulation **1** 874; **6** 273; **7** *107*, 108; **10** 30; **12** 867; **15** *700*; **21** 328
guilloche **12** 869
lost-wax casting **12** 865; **28** *781*
patrix-working **30** 770
pattern-punching **30** 770
piercing **12** 866
raising **12** 865
repoussé **12** 865, 868–9; **16** 364; **21** *253*; **29** *214*
riveting **12** 866
sgraffito **12** 626
sinking **12** 865
snarling **12** 868
soldering **12** 866–7; **24** 793
spinning **12** 865
types
mosaic *see* MOSAIC GOLD
shell **12** 623, 625, 626
uses
altarpieces **32** *213*
amulets **3** 441; **10** 38, *39*
antependia **23** *657*
arm-bands **17** I
armlets **1** *876*
armour **17** *362*
arm rings **6** 155, 158
badges **29** *346*
beads **1** 296; **3** 440, 441; **14** *357*; **31** 355
beakers **14** *211*
beds **10** 51
belthooks **7** *98*, 107
belts **7** 109, 110, 111
betel sets **20** 175; **30** 631
bodice ornaments **17** *523*
bookbindings **1** 682; **24** 107
book covers , ; **4** III, IV2; **7** *513*; **13** *159*
bowcases **6** *259*
bowls **7** 22; **12** V2; **14** *171*; **18** 351; **22** *435*; **24** *644*; **27** *419*; **30** 769; **31** 531
boxes **2** 823*; **4** *601*, 601–2*; **7** *19*, *20*; **8** 752; **10** 51, 347*, *347*, *721*; **11** 631–3*; **22** 897*; **24** 147; **28** I2; **30** 112*
bracelets **6** *20*; **7** 109, 111; **16** *530*, *752*; **17** *528*, III2; **31** 355
braids **30** 542
brooches **14** *417*; **15** *872*; **17** *520*; **27** *429*; **31** *655*
buckles **7** 108
busts **27** *15*
calligraphy **17** 219, 220, *228*
canopies (ii) (textile coverings) **10** 51
canteens **16** *542*
caps **18** 351
carpets **5** 836
caskets **10** 52; **18** 351, 352
ceilings **9** 654
censers **6** 173
ceramics **6** 328, 329
chains **7** *107*, 108; **16** 532
chairs **6** 388; **10** 50, 52
chalices **2** *378*; **5** *585*; **13** *162*; **21** *163*
chandeliers **9** 13
chess sets **6** 556
ciboria (i) (vessels) **5** *585*

gold
uses—cont.
clasps **6** *273*; **23** *658*; **30** *44*, *891*
coins **7** 533, 534, 536, 537; **12** 866; **14** 419
Afghanistan **1** 204
Belgium **14** *413*
Byzantine **9** *636*
Cyprus, ancient **8** 349
England **14** *419*; **19** *581*
Etruscan **10** 632
Indian subcontinent **15** *688*
Indonesia **15** 811, 812
Islamic **16** *511*, *512*, *513*
Italy **7** *536*
Japan **17** 318, 370, *370*
Malaysia **20** 179
collars **17** IV2
combs (hair) **7** 109
crosses **8** 201, 203, *203*, 204; **9** *659*
crowns **7** 110, *111*; **12** *866*; **18** *350*, 350–51; **23** 656; **29** *214*; **32** *617*
cult statues **8** 261, 263
cups **10** III1; **21** *688*; **22** *889*; **30** 769; **32** *516*
daggers **6** 261; **16** *516*
diadems **13** *599*, 599; **28** *325*
diplomatic gifts **9** 657
diptychs **9** 3
dolls **17** 372
doors **13** 390, 391
drinking-horns **9** *690*
earrings **7** 111; **9** *457*; **10** *631*; **13** 598; **15** *700*; **17** *527*; **18** *367*; **31** *376*
electroplating **10** 135
embroidery **2** *823*, *824*; **3** 609, *609*; **7** 50; **12** 463; **13** 194
enamel **7** 68, 79; **9** 659, *659*, *660*, *662*, *663*; **10** 192; **12** 866; **13** 168, 170; **15** 707, 710–12*
ewers **11** *636*
fans **10** *777*
fibulae **10** *630*; **12** *868*; **21** *162*
figurines **15** *783*
filigree **7** 108, *109*, 111, 112; **12** 867–8; **13** *162*; **20** 216; **21** 687; **27** 101, *102*; **32** *530*
frames **9** 17; **10** *721*
fringes **3** 483
furniture **9** 30; **10** 52; **12** 423; **14** 494, *495*
game-pieces **31** 266
gilding **12** 623*, 624*, 625–6*, 627–8*, 629, 869–70*
glass **12** 782; **16** 520
guns **2** *466*
hair ornaments **7** 108, *112*
hairpins **7** 109
headdresses **1** *873*; **7** 109; **28** *651*; **31** *376*
headrests **10** 51
helmets **2** *472*; **16** *507*
horns **25** *526*
icons **9** 623, 625, 626; **12** *329*; **15** 1; **32** *212*
inks **15** 564, 851, 852
inlays **3** 914; **4** 688; **6** 853, 855; **7** 14, 22, 107; **14** *55*; **15** 712; **16** 364, *375*, *376*, *383*, *384*, *385*, *389*; **21** 328; **30** *841*
jewellery **10** 29, 30; **17** 519, 522, 527
Afghanistan **1** 205
Africa **1** 350
Ancient Near East **1** *873*
Arabia **2** *264*
Central Asia, Western **6** 273, 274
China **7** 106, 107, 112
Early Christian and Byzantine **9** 652–3
Egypt, ancient **10** 28, 29, 33
Finland **11** 108
Germany **21** *502*
gold
uses
jewellery—cont.
Greece, ancient **13** 597–9*
Helladic **14** 357
Indian subcontinent **15** 736
Indonesia **15** 814, *815*
Islamic **16** 529
Korea **18** 366
Mesoamerica, Pre-Columbian **21** 253
Minoan **21** 686, 687
Nepal **22** 788
Ottonian **23** 657
Philippines **24** 626
Phoenician **24** 644
Prehistoric **25** 531
Sri Lanka **29** *473*
Troadic **31** 355
Ukraine **31** 562, *562*
Vietnam **32** 487
jugs **16** 372
keris **15** *817*; **20** 174
knives **28** *651*
kovshy **27** *421*
lace **10** 355; **16** 34; **18** 590, *591*; **30** 151, 542
lacquer **7** *14*, 15, 17, 19, 20, 25, 107; **17** 297, 298, *301*, *305*; **18** 370, 604; **30** *619*
laminates **12** 621
lockets **17** *522*
manuscript illumination **9** 606; **13** 136; **15** 564, 616; **16** 292–3, 311; **19** 351; **20** 336; **30** *836*
manuscripts **9** 611, 618
masks **14** *355*; **17** *334*; **28** 651
medallions **7** *763*; **13** 599; **21** 1; **27** *96*
medals **12** *583*; **16** 690; **20** 917; **28** *749*
mirror-cases **2** *112*
mirror frames **21** 717, 718, 719
mirrors **21** 714, 715, *718*
monstrances **5** *585*; **29** *333*; **32** *406*
mosaics **19** 351; **22** 155, 156, 158, 161, 162
mounts (porcelain) **9** 28, 29
necklaces **17** *527*, *529*
Byzantine **9** *653*
China **7** *109*, 111
Egypt, ancient **10** *31*
England **20** *389*
Greece, ancient **13** 599
Islamic **16** 531
Rome, ancient **27** *103*
Sweden **30** *113*
Troad **31** *376*
neck rings **6** 155, *157*, 158; **12** *867*
paintings **7** 627; **13** 139; **18** 770; **19** 351, 352
palanquins **10** 50
papal roses **24** 36, *36*
paper **7** 116
patens **9** 657; **21** *163*
pectoral ornaments **7** *107*; **10** *30*; **12** *869*
penboxes **21** I1
pendants (jewellery) **11** *307*; **17** III1
Baule **3** *409*
Byzantine **9** *663*
Central Asia, Western **6** *274*
China **7** 111
Early Christian (*c*. AD 250–843) **9** *659*
England **10** *345*
Helladic **14** *357*
Hungary **15** *10*
Indian subcontinent **15** 736
Islamic **17** III1
Minoan **21** *687*
Scotland **28** *263*
Sinú **28** *781*
South America, Pre-Columbian **13** *291*; **29** *151*
gold
uses—cont.
pens **24** 349
photographic plates **24** 660
photography **24** 647
pigments **7** 632, 634; **15** 802
pilgrim badges **24** 809
pitchers **22** *435*
plaques **2** *101*; **6** *632*; **7** *27*, 108; **25** *517*; **27** *599*; **32** 523
plaquettes **25** 19
plates **9** 656
porcelain **6** 895; **21** 66
printing **15** 668
printing plates **23** 114, 115
prints **15** 855
regalia **1** 352
reliquaries **31** *535*
Afghanistan **1** *206*
Belgium **5** *213*
Byzantine **9** *658*, *663*
France **24** *146*; **26** *147*
Germany **26** *145*
Italy **5** *808*; **26** *144*
Ottonian **22** *43*
rings **6** 158; **7** 109, 111; **8** *352*; **10** 33; **17** 574, II2; **21** *686*
rosaries **27** *159*
salts **6** *143*
scabbards **15** *678*, *817*; **16** *506*, *508*, *516*
sculpture **3** 407; **10** *37*; **13** 435, 596; **23** 647; **27** 15–16; **30** 823
seals **7** 128; **21** *686*, 882
shields **21** 250
shrines (i) (cult) **23** *99*; **28** *631*; **32** *530*
snuff-boxes **2** 823; **4** 601, *601*; **10** 347, *347*; **11** *631*, *632*, *633*; **12** *459*; **30** *112*
standishes **29** 535
statuettes **14** *403*
stoles (ecclesiastical) **2** *84*
stonewares **18** 339
stools **1** 353; **2** *585*
sword grips **6** *260*
sword guards **16** *506*
sword hilts **2** *454*; **7** *835*
sword ornaments **2** *587*
swords **2** *452*; **6** 261; **7** *22*; **15** *678*; **16** *508*
tables **9** 656
tankards **16** *860*
tapestries **3** 606, *607*; **5** *48*
tea-services **2** *820*
textiles **15** 793, 794; **16** *753*; **17** 313; **20** 175; **28** 716; **29** 152
threads **10** 181; **30** 308, 540, 541–2
Anglo-Saxon **2** 83, *84*
Belgium **10** II2; **14** III2; **30** III1, 2
Central Asia, Western **6** 250
China **7** 45, 50, *50*, 51, *51*, *53*
Early Christian and Byzantine **9** 668
England **10** *350*
France ,
Germany **12** 463, 464
Gothic **10** *181*; **13** 194
Indian subcontinent **15** 663, 675
Islamic **16** *430*, 450
Malaysia **20** 176
Poland **25** *133*
Romanesque **26** 703
Spain **29** 301, 349
thrones **9** 656; **15** 707, *707*
vases **31** *650*
vessels **7** 88; **20** *448*
wallpaper **32** 812
watches **7** 444
weaving **12** 464
weights **1** 392
wire **7** *107*, 110, 111; **21** 324
writing *see* CHRYSOGRAPHY
see also PLATE
Gold, Francis **4** 78
Goldbach, Sylvesterkapelle **23** 650–51
Goldbeater, Thomas **23** 248
goldbeating *see under* GOLD → techniques
Goldberg, Bertrand **28** 488
Goldberg, Glenn **18** 161
Goldberg, Michael **16** 820; **29** 113
Goldberg, Peg L. **2** 556
Goldblatt, Sidney **29** 108
Gold Club **8** 6; **26** 776
Gold Coast *see* GHANA
gold dust
historical and regional traditions
China **7** 20
France **25** *620*
Japan **17** 276
uses
boullework **20** 466
chromolithography **25** *620*
gilding **24** 55
lacquer **7** 20; **18** 602, 604, 605, 606, 607
marquetry **20** 466
prints **17** 276
threads **30** 540
Goldefroid, Marie-Eléonore **12** 336
Goldegg, Schloss *see* SCHLOSS GOLDEGG
Goldemberg, Jorge **2** 397
Golden, Daan **12** 870*; **22** 853
Golden, Eunice **10** 484
Golden Altar *see under* MILAN → ecclesiastical building → S Ambrogio
Golden Altar of Lüneburg, Master of the **20** 681*
Goldenberg, Edward *see* ROBINSON, EDWARD G(OLDENBURG)
Golden Bull of Charles IV **13** 153
Golden Cockerel Press **4** 9, 366; **12** 631; **17** 632; **26** 39
Golden Compass **10** 389
golden cut *see* GOLDEN SECTION
Goldenes Rössl **10** 194; **11** 615; **13** 158, 170, *170*; **31** 840, 841
Goldene Tafel of Lüneberg, Master of the *see* GOLDEN ALTAR OF LÜNEBERG, MASTER OF THE
Golden Fleece (*Zolotoye Runo*) **1** 21; **4** 178; **12** 870–71*; **27** 458
contributors **3** 692; **4** 156; **10** 446; **18** 482
exhibitions **10** 680; **16** 817
Fal'k, Robert (Rafailovich) **10** 771
Girieud, Pierre (Paul) **12** 729
Goncharova, Natal'ya (Sergeyevna) **12** 892
Konchalovsky, Pyotr (Petrovich) **18** 215
Larionov, Mikhail (Fyodorovich) **18** 792
Mashkov, Il'ya (Ivanovich) **20** 548
Tatlin, Vladimir (Yevgrafovich) **30** 361
Golden Gate, Master of the **29** 763
Golden Globe **12** 814
Golden Gospels *see under* GOSPEL BOOKS → individual manuscripts
Golden Haggadah *see under* HAGGADOT → individual manuscripts
Golden Horn ware *see under* POTTERY → wares
Golden Legend **16** 837–8; **28** 402
Golden Man *see under* ISSYK
golden mean *see* GOLDEN SECITON
Golden section **2** *348*, 349, 353; **12** 871*; **13** 413; **14** 874; **25** 349; **28** 200, *200*
Golden Service **3** 599
Golden Stool **1** 353; **2** 585, *585*
Golden Targe **30** 329
Golden Tower **6** 423
Goldewski, Michał **13** 215
Goldfinch, John **10** 421
Goldfinger, Ernö **12** 871*
collaboration **2** 578; **14** 399; **28** 809
groups and movements **10** 241
staff **25** 571
works **28** 158
gold foil *see* GOLD LEAF
gold-glass *see under* GLASS → types
Gol'dgor, D. S. **29** 388
Goldie, C(harles) F(rederick) **2** 706; **12** 872*; **23** 59
Golding, John **8** 240, 522
Goldingen *see* KULDĪGA
Goldingham, John **15** 402; **20** 53; **29** 526
gold leaf **21** 330, 331
historical and regional traditions
Ancient Near East **1** 867
Bali (Indonesia) **15** 806
Baule **3** 407
Buddhism **17** *116*
Byzantine **9** 617, 623, 645; **19** 356
Cambodia **5** 501
Caribbean Islands **5** 747
China **7** 15, 92
Early Christian (*c*. AD 250–843) **9** 617, 623, 645; **19** 356
Egypt, ancient **3** 482; **10** 52, 57; **12** 620, 870
England **4** *353*
Etruscan **10** 631
France **4** *351*
Gothic **13** 134
Greece, ancient **12** 870; **13** 482, 594
Indonesia **3** 331; **15** *798*
Italy **4** *352*; **10** 631; **12** 621
Japan **17** 100, *116*, 140, 277, 298, *309*, 314, *314*
Java **15** *798*, 798
Korea **18** 371
Malaysia **20** 176
Mesoamerica, Pre-Columbian **21** 246
Rome, ancient **27** 15, 51
Russia **32** *527*
Ryūkyū Islands **27** 471
Sumatra **15** 810
Thailand **30** 618
Vietnam **32** 482
Viking **32** *527*
techniques
painting **12** 623
punching **12** 623; **25** *730*
sgraffito **12** 623, 625
uses
altarpieces **12** 623
atlatls **21** 246
axes **32** *527*
baskets **3** 331; **15** 810
beds **3** 482
book covers **4** *351*, 352, *352*, *353*
ceramics **6** 328
chairs **10** 52
costumes **17** *314*
drawings **15** 806
dress **17** *309*, 314
enamel **10** 195
fans **10** *781*
furniture **1** 867
gilding **12** 620, 621, 622, 623*, 625, 626, 627, 629, 870
glass **9** 645; **13** 594
icons **9** 623
inksticks **7** 92
ivory-carvings **12** 621
lacquer **7** 15; **17** 298; **18** 602, 607; **27** 471; **30** 618; **32** 482
manuscript illumination **19** 356; **20** 347
manuscripts **9** 617

gold leaf
uses—cont.
mosaics **9** 645; **12** 622; **22** 155
painting **5** 501; **11** 764; **12** 621; **13** 134; **17** 140; **19** 356; **27** 51
papier mâché **24** 61
pastiglia **24** 248
postage stamps **25** 329
pottery **13** 482
prints **17** 277
puppets **15** *798*, 798
sculpture **5** 747; **17** 100, *116*; **27** 15
shabtis **10** 57
textiles **20** 176
threads **30** 540
Goldman, Edouard **14** 58
Goldman, György **14** 896
Goldman, Hetty **10** 653; **21** 166
Goldman, Philip **22** 795
Goldman Manufacturing Co. **2** 759
Goldmann, Lucien **28** 926
Goldmann, Nikolaus **10** 668; **12** 872*; **29** 872; **31** 298
Goldoni, Carlo **4** 362
gold oxides **10** 192
Goldsaddle, Richard **19** 530
Goldsborough (N. Yorks) **17** 516
St Mary **10** 327
Goldscheider, Alois **12** 872
Goldscheider, Friedrich **12** 872*; **32** 450
works **2** 816
Goldscheider, Ludwig **12** 873*; **14** 767
works **26** *235*
Goldscheider, Regina **12** 872
Goldscheider'sche Porzellan-Manufaktur und Majolika-Fabrik **2** 816; **12** 872; **32** 450
Goldschmelz **2** 453
Goldschmid (family) **8** 414
Goldschmidt, Adolph **12** 483, 873*
assistants **23** 395
pupils **5** 187; **21** 478; **33** 285
Goldschmidt, Ernst **8** 762
Goldschmidt, Erwin **2** 706
Goldschmidt, Gertrudis *see* GEGO
Goldschmidt Collection **29** 88
Goldschmied, Bernhard *see* BERNHARD GOLDSCHMIED
Goldschneck, Stanislav **8** 384
Gold Scrolls, Master of the **20** 681
Gold Scrolls Group **2** 871; **3** 555; **20** 624, 681–2*
works **20** *682*
Goldsmidt, Jakob **21** 91
Goldsmith, Mrs **33** 3
Goldsmith, Myron **12** 873–4*; **16** 868; **28** 818, 834
Goldsmith, Oliver **4** 363; **8** 218; **30** 384
goldsmiths **14** 417
England **10** 328, 331; **14** 856
Gothic **13** 167
Inca **15** 163
Islamic **16** 262
Malta (Republic of) **20** 216*
United States of America **31** 646
Goldsmiths Corporation (Paris) **11** 657; **14** 83
goldsmiths' guilds *see under* GUILDS → types
Goldsmiths & Silversmiths Co. **19** 596
Goldstein, Emanuel **22** 291
Goldstein, Franz **10** 210
Goldstein, Zvi **12** 874*
Goldsworthy, Andy **28** 206
Goldwater, Robert **4** 576; **24** 433
Gole, Cornelius **10** 290
Gole, Jacob **21** 415
Gole, Pierre **12** 874*; **20** 139; **24** 150
patrons and collectors **19** 722; **23** 513
pupils **29** 60
Gole, Pierre—cont.
works **7** 166; **11** 575, 576, 588, *588*, 589; **12** 832; **20** 467; **33** 333
Golenischchov, Roman **12** 856
Golenishchev, Vladimir Semyenovich **10** 90; **27** 440; **31** 401
Golenkina, Alisa **27** 413
Golescu (family) **26** 718
Goleşti
House of Stroe Leurdeanu **26** 708
House of the Golescu family **26** 718
Golf Book *see under* BOOKS OF HOURS → individual manuscripts
Golferich, Macario **27** 304
Golgi **8** 335, 341, 342
Golgotha *see* CALVARY
Gol Gumbaz *see under* BIJAPUR
Goli **15** 438, 476
Golia **26** 708, 712
Golikov, Ivan Ivanovich **23** 837
Golikova, Nina (Anatol'yevna) **27** 423
Goli masks *see under* MASKS → types
Golini, Giulio **28** 85
Golitsyn (family) **5** 332; **12** 134; **22** 170
Golitsyn, Aleksandr **10** 461
Golitsyn, A. N. **17** 870
Golitsyn, D. M. **27** 438
Golitsyn, Dmitry (Alekseyevich), Prince **26** 732; **27** 438
Golitsyn, M. A., Count **26** 734
Golitsyn, M. P. **27** 439
Golitsyn, V. V. **27** 438
Golius, Jacob **16** 553
Goll, Ivan **19** 79; **30** 18
Goll, J. H. **26** 476
Gollán, Agustín Zapata *see* ZAPATA GOLLÁN, AGUSTÍN
Gollattagud **29** 824
Golle, Pierre, *see* GOLE, PIERRE
Göller **1** 834
Goller, Bruno **12** 874–5*; **14** 26; **18** 106
Gollerbakh, Erikh (Fyodorovich) **12** 875*
Göllersdorf
Nepomukkapelle **21** 893
Schloss Schönborn **7** 303
Gollins, Frank **12** 875
Gollins, Melvin, Ward **10** 242; **12** 875*
Göllner, Miklós **30** 207
Göllü Dağ **24** 690
Goll van Franckenstein, Johann, I (1722-85) **1** 808; **6** 89; **12** 876*; **27** 271
Goll van Franckenstein, Johann, II (1756-1821) **12** 876*
Goll van Franckenstein, Pieter Hendrik **12** 876*
Golombek, Lisa **16** 548
Goloni **28** 320
Gołoński, Andrzej **32** 871
Golosov, Il'ya (Aleksandrovich) **12** 876–7*; **32** 661
collaboration **21** 92
groups and movements **23** 590
works **12** *877*; **22** 174; **27** 378, 380
Golosov, Pantaleymon (Aleksandrovich) **12** 876*; **22** 174; **27** 379
Golosy, Oleg **31** 560
Goloubew, Victor **2** 57; **15** 742, 744, 745
Golovin, Aleksandr (Yakovlevich) **12** 877–8*; **27** 392
collaboration **4** 312; **25** 146; **33** 487
groups and movements **33** 379
patrons and collectors **22** 135
productions **8** 849; **20** 232
Golpayegan Mosque **22** 321
Gols, Hendrik *see* GOLTZIUS, HENDRICK
Goltho **2** 66, 67; **10** 226
Goltots, Antonín Petr **6** 363
Gol'ts, Georgy (Pavlovich) **6** 526; **12** 878–9*
Goltyr Painter **13** 508
Goltz, Hans (*fl* 1920) **18** 111
Goltz, Jan, I (*fl* 1532-50) **12** 879
Goltz, Jan, II (1534-after 1609) **12** 879
Goltzius, Hendrick **1** 104; **10** 384, 386–7; **12** 15, 879–85*; **13** 894, 895; **20** 244, 812; **22** 839; **25** 625
assistants **9** 79
collaboration **20** 246; **27** 507; **33** 167
drawings **12** *880*; **18** 710; **22** *840*
groups and movements **9** 446; **26** 728
methods **5** 294; **8** 128
paintings **12** *884*
patrons and collectors **3** 890; **4** 614; **5** 325; **14** 92, 563; **23** 113; **27** 270; **32** 8, 377, 707
prints **25** 605
engravings **2** 162; **7** 867; **13** 896; **23** 294; **26** 229; **29** 431; **32** 711
allegorical **1** 658, 662, 663; **15** *96*
genre **3** 230
mythological **10** *388*; **12** *882*
religious **7** 520
woodcuts **12** *883*; **13** 896; **33** 355
landscape **25** 606; **33** 358
marine **33** *168*
mythological **33** 367
pupils **4** 701; **8** 664; **12** 340, 529; **13** 222, 337; **17** 598; **22** 272
reproductive prints by others **7** 556, 557; **9** 79; **11** 794; **12** 16; **17** 598; **18** 387; **22** 272; **25** *612*; **27** 503, 507
teachers **7** 799
Goltzius, Hubertus **12** 884–5*; **25** 17, 280, *280*
patrons and collectors **26** 490
reproductive prints by others **19** 343
teachers **19** 547, 548
works **4** *360*; **12** *885*; **25** 622; **33** 365
Goltzius, Julius **12** 885
Goltzsche, Dieter **12** 886*
Goltz von Hinsbeck, Hubrecht **12** 879
Golu **15** 623
Golub, Leon (Albert) **6** 576; **12** 886*; **14** 589
groups and movements **6** 576
works **25** 654; **31** 609
Golubac **28** *437*, 439, 440
Golubaya Roza *see* BLUE ROSE
Golubić, Grgur **23** 373
Golubkina, Anna (Semyonovna) **12** 887*; **27** 392
Gołuchów **25** 99, 138
Castle Museum **9** 497; **25** 139
Golus, J. **4** 148; **25** 422
Golvin **25** 771
Golyamo Delčevo **25** 501
Golytsin, Illarion **27** 397
Golzius, Geldorp **19** 260
Gomar, Francí **12** 650
Gombad-e Qabus *see* GUNBAD-I QABUS
Gombart, Johann Carl **2** 719
Gombauld, Jean Ogier de *see* OGIER DE GOMBAULD, JEAN
Gombe
gourds **1** *248*
Gomberville, M. de **8** 525
Gomboš, Stjepan **12** 887*; **17** 858
Gombrich, Ernst (Hans Josef) **2** 834; **12** 887*; **18** 458, 701; **26** 224; **28** 207, 917
teachers **28** 115
works **1** 182; **2** 138; **7** 783; **8** 613; **15** 91, 880; **20** 528; **24** 385; **25** 361, 683; **26** 63; **29** 880, 881
on aesthetics **1** 174
on caricatures **5** 760
on expression **10** 691
Gombroon *see* BANDAR ABBAS
Gomel' *see* HOMIEL
Gómera, Ali de *see* ALI DE GÓMERA
Gomes, António **12** 888*; **26** 253
Gomes (de Oliveira), Augusto **12** 888*
Gomes, Dórdio (Simão César) *see* DÓRDIO (SIMÃO CÉSAR) GOMES
Gomes, Ferñao **12** 888*; **25** 296; **26** 253
Gomes, Manuel Cipriano **5** 421
Gomes, Pero **2** 874
Gomes Batista, João **19** 460
Gomes Chaves, Pedro **4** 710
Gomes d'Alvelar, Francisco **5** 421
Gomes da Silva, Aires **6** 452
Gomes da Silva, João **2** 189
Gomes de Andrade, Manuel **8** 858
Gomes do Avelar, Francisco **10** 728; **12** 888–9*
Gomes Figueira, Baltazar **2** 877, 878; **25** 297
Gomes Figueira, Basilia **2** 878
Gómez, Bernardo Lira *see* LIRA GÓMEZ, BERNARDO
Gomez, Henry da Costa *see* COSTA GOMEZ, HENRY DA
Gómez, Javier Sánchez *see* SÁNCHEZ GÓMEZ, JAVIER
Gómez, José Miguel **14** 714
Gómez, Juan de Alfaro y *see* ALFARO Y GÓMEZ, JUAN DE
Gómez, Juna Nepomuceno *see* NEPUMOCENO GÓMEZ, JUAN
Gómez, Luis Duque *see* DUQUE GÓMEZ, LUIS
Gómez, Marte R. **21** 395
Gomez, Modesto Brocos y *see* BROCOS Y GOMEZ, MODESTO
Gómez, Pedro Nel *see* NEL GÓMEZ, PEDRO
Gomez, Vicente **24** 108
Goméz, Vicente Salvador *see* SALVADOR GÓMEZ, VICENTE
Gomez Chavez, Pedro **23** 669
Gómez Cornet, Ramón **2** 400; **6** 10
Gómez de Ceballos, Pedro Vicente **29** 336
Gómez de Llarenas, Carlos **32** 171
works **32** *171*
Gómez del Rio, Bernabé **6** 45
Gómez de Mora, Juan *see* MORA (i), JUAN GÓMEZ DE
Gómez de Trasmonte, Juan **21** 401
Gómez de Valencia, Felipe **12** 889*
Gómez Gavazzo, Carlos **31** 758
Gómez Grau, Enrique **4** 234; **7** 607
Gómez Jaramillo, Ignacio **7** 609, 611
Gómez Moreno, Manuel **12** 889*; **13** 285; **24** 452; **31** 172
Gómez Palacio, Gonzalo **21** 381
Gómez Pinzón, José **7** 606
Gómez Villaseñor, Juan **10** 502
Gomide Graz, Regina *see* GRAZ, REGINA GOMIDE
Gomis, Joaquim **3** 219; **12** 889–90*
GoMizunoo, Emperor (*reg* 1611-29) **17** 179, 233, 380, 383; **18** 553, 567
Gomm, William **26** 529
Gommatagiri **29** 438
Gomme, Bernard de **21** 569
Gomme, Ebeneezer **10** 300; **14** 523
Gomme, James **14** 522
Gomoa Mankesim
shrines (i) (cult) **1** *332*
Gomolava **25** 499
Gomon Miura *see* MIURA GOMON
Gompertz, G. St G. M. **18** 259
Gomperz, Lucie *see* RIE, LUCIE
Gomringer, Eugen **7** 698
Gomzin, Ivan **3** 733; **33** 599
Gon, Andrey **28** 628
Gonanwa **1** 415
GoNara, Emperor (*reg* 1526-57) **17** 781; **31** 198
Gonçalves, André **12** 890*; **25** 297, 814
collaboration **19** 655
education (art) **25** 319
pupils **5** 903
teachers **3** 815
works **26** 254
Gonçalves, Eurico **25** 300
Gonçalves, Fernão **31** 101
Gonçalves, João **25** 295
Gonçalves, Nuno **12** 890–92*; **29** 101
attributions **2** 860, 871; **25** 320
works **12** *890*, *891*; **25** 295, *296*; **26** 252; **27** 802; **32** 26
Gonçalves de Rosa, Antonio **4** 710
Gonçalves do Riba Fria, Gaspar **28** 780
Gonçalves Neto, Estevão **12** 892*; **25** 297
Gonçalves Ribas, João **2** 286
Gonçalves Soares, José **8** 268
Gonchar, Ivan **31** 563
Goncharov (family) **33** 517
Goncharov, Andrey **27** 396; **28** 924; **33** 370
Goncharov, Sergey (Mikhaylovich) **12** 892
Goncharova, Natal'ya (Sergeyevna) **12** 892–5*; **18** 793; **22** 350; **27** 392
collaboration **18** 474
exhibitions **3** 802
groups and movements
Acmeism **1** 121
Cubism **1** 73
Cubo-Futurism **8** 251
Donkey's Tail **9** 144–5; **22** 178
Golden Fleece (*Zolotoye Runo*) **12** 870, 871
Jack of Diamonds (Bubnovy Valet) **16** 817
Neo-primitivism **22** 750
Post-Impressionism **25** 356
Rayism **26** 40
Union of Youth **31** 583
patrons and collectors **8** 10; **22** 135
productions **3** 119; **8** 850; **30** 686
works **3** *119*; **12** *893*, *895*; **18** 792; **19** 491; **27** 431; **29** 872
Gonchary, Church of the Dormition **27** 372
Goncourt, Edmond de **9** 231; **10** 480; **12** *896*, 896–7*; **20** 446
personal collection **4** 816; **9** 418; **17** 440; **18** 842
works **11** 675; **18** 642; **25** 847; **26** 501
Goncourt, Jules de **9** 231; **12** *896*, 896–7*; **20** 446
personal collection **4** 816; **9** 418; **17** 440; **18** 842
works **11** 675; **25** 847; **26** 501
Gond **15** 734, 735
Gonda, Alexander **23** 636
Gonda, Jan **19** 542
Gondar **1** *379*
architecture **1** 379; **10** 566
Bath of Fasilides **10** 566
Church of Attatami Qeddus Mika'el **10** 566
Church of Elfen Giyorgis **10** 566

Gondar—cont.
Church of Gemjabet Maryam **10** 566
library of Emperor Yohannes I **10** 566
painting **10** 570
palace of Empress Mentewab **10** 566
palace of Fasiledes **10** 566
Reception Hall of Emperor Baqaffa **10** 566
Saddle Castle **10** 566
Gondelach, Franz **12** 440, 897*; **14** 491; **26** 486
Gondelach, Georg **4** 666
Gondelach, Matthias *see* GUNDELACH, MATTHÄUS
Gondi (family) **12** 576
Gondi, Bartolomeo **12** 897
Gondi, Benedetto **12** 897
Gondi, Giovanni Battista **12** 897
Gondi, Giuliano **27** 735
Gondi, Jean-François de, Archbishop of Paris **27** 535, 536
Gondi, Mariotto **22** 801
Gondoin, Jacques **12** 898*
collaboration **22** 47
groups and movements **22** 734, 738; **24** 173
works **11** 518; **12** 650; **22** *739*
Gondola, Andrea di Pietro della *see* PALLADIO, ANDREA
Gondola, La **22** 27; **26** 548
Gondolach, Matthias *see* GUNDELACH, MATTHÄUS
gondole chairs *see under* CHAIRS → types
Gondophares, Ruler (*reg c.* 20-50) (Pahlava) **15** 819
Gondorf **21** 164
Gondouin, Jacques *see* GONDOIN, JACQUES
Gondrin, Antoine-Louis de Pardaillon de *see* ANTIN(, Duc) d'
Goneim, Zakaria **10** 81; **27** 812
Gonesse Church **30** 907
roof **30** *906*
gonfanons **11** 146, *147*
gong see under VESSELS → types
Gong, King (Lu; *reg* 154-128 BC) **6** 815
Gong Banqian *see* GONG XIAN
Gong Bell Manufacturing Co. **31** 257
gong-chimes **5** 258, 508
Gongchu *see* CHEN RONG
Gong Chun **33** 535
Gong Fu **12** 88
gong hammers **3** 407
Gong Kai **12** 898–9*; **30** 49
Góngora, Antonio Caballero y *see* CABALLERO Y GÓNGORA, ANTONIO, Bishop of Córdoba
Góngora, Caballero **20** 501
Góngora, José Cayetano Sigüenza y *see* SIGÜENZA Y GÓNGORA, JOSÉ CAYETANO
gongs **22** 376
historical and regional traditions
Bali (Indonesia) **15** 816
Buddhism **18** 348
Indonesia **15** 816
Java **15** 816
Korea **18** 348
Mixtec **21** 737
South-east Asia **4** 855
Thailand **30** 637
Zande **33** 610
materials
bronze **4** 855; **18** 348
wood **1** *359*
types
double **31** 331
slit-gongs **1** *359*, 360*
Gong Xian (1619-89) **6** 791; **12** 899–901*; **22** 458, 460; **25** 783
groups and movements **22** 459; **33** 496
patrons and collectors **8** 457
pupils **22** 460
works **6** 792; **7** 148; **12** *900*
writings **22** 461
Gong xian (Henan) **6** *615*; **12** 901*; **30** 443
caves **6** 691, *691*
ceramics **6** 330; **7** 151
kilns **6** 885
pottery **6** 885
sculpture **6** 710, 711, 726; **12** 901
tombs **6** 655, 699
Yongtai ling **6** 699, *699*
Yongxi ling **6** *700*
Yong Zhao ling **6** *731*
see also TIESHENGGOU
Goñi, Hermenegildo Otero *see* OTERO GOÑI, HERMENEGILDO
Gonin, Francesco **12** 901–2*; **16** 720; **24** 448; **31** 445
Gonjō Butsuzen **17** 409
Gonneau, Michel **4** 544
Gonnelli, Giovanni Francesco **12** 902*
Gönnersdorf **25** *470*, 491, 492, 494
figurines **25** *489*
Gonon, Honoré **8** 566
Gonord **24** 149
Gonord, Pierre **8** 130; **19** 144
Gonschior, Kuno **12** 397
Gonseki *see* FUJIWARA NO KŌZEI
Gonsenheimer **26** 379
Gonsirovsky, Feliks **23** 354
Gontard, Karl Philipp Christian von **3** 428; **12** 902*
assistants **18** 476
collaboration **19** 76
patrons and collectors **12** 413; **14** 652, 653; **25** 368
pupils **12** 310
works **3** 428, 791; **12** 374; **25** 366, 367; **27** 323
Gontella, Carlos **18** 867
Gonthier, Linard *see* GONTIER, LINARD
Gontier, Château *see* CHÂTEAU GONTIER
Gontier, Jean **12** 903
Gontier, Linard (1562–*c.* 1642) **12** 903*; **31** 382, 384
Gontier, Linard, the younger (*fl* 1640s) **12** 903
Gontier, Nicolas **12** 903
Gontshwanetse, Mokwaledi **4** 489
Gonur 1 **6** 196
Gonzaga (family) **10** 442; **12** 903–4*, *904*; **14** 869; **20** 318; **23** 92
architecture **3** 298; **19** 558; **20** 318
coats of arms **14** 410
collections **5** 764; **11** 40, 661, 662; **16** 767, 814; **19** 833; **20** 322; **27** 504; **28** 173
drawings **16** 815
dress **12** 558
gems **14** 806; **24** 572
imprese **15** 150
manuscripts **12** 722; **20** 334; **26** 564
medals **6** 102
metalwork **6** 140
paintings **2** 20; **4** 335; **16** 667; **24** 227; **31** 5, 14
frescoes **28** 434
history **11** 40; **19** 834
mythological **7** 891
portraits **11** 662
religious **8** 4
sculpture **7** 562
tapestries **19** 834; **20** 323; **30** 331
Gonzaga, Alfonso, Lord of Novellara *see* NOVELLARA, ALFONSO GONZAGA, Lord of
Gonzaga, Anne Catherine *see* ANNE CATHERINE GONZAGA, Archduchess
Gonzaga, Arrivabene Valenti, Count *see* VALENTI GONZAGA, ARRIVABENE, Count
Gonzaga, Barbara, Marchesa of Mantua *see* BARBARA OF BRANDENBURG, Marchesa of Mantua
Gonzaga, Camillo **24** 250
Gonzaga, Carlo I, Duke of Mantua *see* CARLO I, 8th Duke of Mantua
Gonzaga, Carlo II, 9th Duke of Mantua *see* CARLO II, 9th Duke of Mantua
Gonzaga, Cecilia **24** *863*
Gonzaga, Cesare **12** 151, 761, *904*, 911*; **32** 692
Gonzaga, Eleonora, Duchess of Mantua *see* ELEONORA DE' MEDICI, Duchess of Mantua
Gonzaga, Eleonora, Empress *see* ELEONORA GONGAZA, Empress
Gonzaga, Elisabetta, Duchess of Urbino *see* ELISABETTA GONZAGA, Duchess of Urbino
Gonzaga, Ercole, Cardinal **12** *904*, 909–10*
architecture **3** 849; **12** 757
paintings **10** 805; **12** 561; **32** 348
seals **6** 140, 141
tapestries **20** 323
Gonzaga, Federico I, 3rd Marchese of Mantua *see* FEDERICO, 3rd Marchese of Mantua
Gonzaga, Federico II, 5th Marchese and 1st Duke of Mantua *see* FEDERICO II, 5th Marchese and 1st Duke of Mantua
Gonzaga, Ferdinand II, Duca da Guastalla *see* GUASTALLA, FERDINAND II GONZAGA, Duca da
Gonzaga, Ferdinando, 6th Duke of Mantua *see* FERDINANDO, 6th Duke of Mantua
Gonzaga, Ferdinando-Carlo, 10th Duke of Mantua *see* FERDINANDO-CARLO, 10th Duke of Mantua
Gonzaga, Ferrante, Duca da Guastalla *see* GUASTALLA, FERRANTE GONZAGA, Duca da
Gonzaga, Ferrante, II **12** 911
Gonzaga, Francesco, Cardinal **12** *904*, 907*
manuscripts **13** 833; **27** 806
paintings **12** 558
tapestries **2** 20
Gonzaga, Francesco I, 4th Capitano of Mantua *see* FRANCESCO I, 4th Capitano of Mantua
Gonzaga, Francesco II, 4th Marchese of Mantua *see* FRANCESCO II, 4th Marchese of Mantua
paintings **24** 471
Gonzaga, Francesco IV, 5th Duke of Mantua *see* FRANCESCO IV, 5th Duke of Mantua
Gonzaga, Gianfrancesco, 1st Marchese of Mantua *see* GIANFRANCESCO, 1st Marchese of Mantua
Gonzaga, Gianfrancesco, Lord of Ródigo *see* RÓDIGO, GIANFRANCESCO GONZAGA, Lord of
Gonzaga, Gianlucido **3** 531
Gonzaga, Guglielmo, 3rd Duke of Mantua *see* GUGLIELMO, 3rd Duke of Mantua
Gonzaga, Laura, Duchess of Mantua *see* LAURA GONZAGA, Duchess of Mantua
Gonzaga, Leonora, Duchess of Urbino *see* LEONORA GONZAGA, Duchess of Urbino
Gonzaga, Louisa Maria, Queen of Poland *see* LOUISA MARIA GONZAGA, Queen of Poland
Gonzaga, Ludovico (1539-95) **11** 611; **12** *904*
Gonzaga, Ludovico, Bishop of Mantua (1458-1511) **5** 697; **12** 903, *904*, 908*
sculpture **2** 139, 140–41; **6** 102
Gonzaga, Ludovico II, 2nd Marchese of Mantua *see* LUDOVICO II, 2nd Marchese of Mantua
Gonzaga, Luigi Valenti *see* VALENTI GONZAGA, LUIGI
Gonzaga, Margherita, Duchess of Ferrara *see* MARGHERITA GONZAGA, Duchess of Ferrara
Gonzaga, Ottavio, Marchese **6** 37
Gonzaga, Paola **12** 905
Gonzaga, Pietro di Gottardo **24** 292
Gonzaga, Sigismondo **13** 833
Gonzaga, Silvio Valenti, Cardinal *see* VALENTI GONZAGA, SILVIO, Cardinal
Gonzaga, Vespasiano, Duca da Sabbioneta *see* SABBIONETA, VESPASIANO GONZAGA, Duca da
Gonzaga, Vincenzo I, 4th Duke of Mantua *see* VINCENZO I, 4th Duke of Mantua
Gonzaga, Vincenzo II, 7th Duke of Mantua *see* VINCENZO II, 7th Duke of Mantua
Gonzaga Vase **12** 908
Gonzago, Francesco **31** 845
Gonzago, Pietro di Gottardo **2** 417; **12** 134, 914*; **27** 376
Gonzague, Catherine de, Duchesse de Longueville *see* LONGUEVILLE, CATHERINE DE GONZAGUE, Duchesse de
Gonzalès, Eva **12** 915*; **20** 256
Gonzales Associates **22** 568
González (y Alvarez Osorio), Aníbal **12** 916*; **28** 514; **29** 273
Gonzalez, Antonio, Bishop of Caracas **3** 95
González, Bartolomé **9** 5; **12** 916*; **14** 6
González, Beatriz **7** 610; **33** 316
González, Carlos **12** 916–17*; **31** 755, 758
Gonzalez, Christopher **12** 917*; **16** 889
González, Concordio **12** 918
González, D. Augustin **30** 883
Gonzalez, Diego Méndez *see* MÉNDEZ GONZALEZ, DIEGO
González, Domingo **29** 342
González, Fernan **13** 105
González, Fernando Cardénas *see* CARDÉNAS GONZÁLEZ, FERNANDO
Gonzalez, Gabriel **8** 253
González, Guillermo **9** 116
González, Hernán **10** 498
González, Joan **12** 918
González, José Ramón **8** 237
González, Juan (*fl* 1425-59) **29** 333
González, Juan (*fl* 1662-1717) **12** 915–16*
González, Juan (*b* 1945) **12** 917*; **18** 835
González, Juan Francisco **6** 597; **12** 917–18*
pupils **13** 9; **14** 367; **22** 114
González, Juan Francisco—cont.
works **6** 597
González, Juan Mora *see* MORA GONZÁLEZ, JUAN
González, Julia **8** 236
González (-Pellicer), Julio (1876-1942) **11** 568; **12** 918–19*; **24** 721, 726; **29** 285
collaboration **14** 206; **16** 57
groups and movements **1** 90
works **12** *919*; **29** 295
González, Julio (*fl* 1970s) **24** 99
González, Manuel **12** 922
González, Manuel de la Cruz **1** 783; **8** 18; **12** 919*; **25** 826
González, Marino **6** 523
González, Matías **29** 347
González, Miguel **12** 915–16*
González, Norberto **33** 472
González, Pascasio **10** 154
González, Pedro Angel **12** 919–20*
González, Pedro Ruíz *see* RUÍZ GONZÁLEZ, PEDRO
González, Rafael **29** 336
González, Rose **12** 915*; **22** 606
González, Sancha **26** 689
González, Santiago **13** 763, 764, 770; **26** 522; **33** 518
González, Simón (1856-1919) **6** 597
González, Simón (*d* 1627) **5** 886
Gonzalez, Tsé-Pe **12** 915
González Bogen, Carlos **12** 920*; **20** 234; **32** 568
González Bravo **3** 482
González Camarena, Jorge *see* CAMARENA, JORGE GONZÁLEZ
González Darna, Castor **8** 236
González de Benavides, Julián **2** 174
Gonzalez de Clavijo, Ruy *see* CLAVIJO, RUY GONZALEZ DE
González de Lara, Hernán **12** 920*; **31** 87
González de la Vega, Diego **26** 438
González de León, Teodoro **12** 920–21*
collaboration **21** 381, 397, 404; **33** 584
works **21** 381, *381*
González de Medina Barba, Diego **12** 921*
González de Mendoza, Pedro (*d* 1385) **13** 731; **21** 124*
González de Mendoza, Pedro, Cardinal (1428-95) **14** 578; **21** 125–6*; **29** 264; **31** 87, 88, 822; **32** 100
González de San Pedro, Pedro **1** 847; **32** 98
González de Sepúlveda, Pedro **17** 673
González Frutos, Hugo **24** 99
González Gamarra, Francisco **24** 509
González García, Reynaldo **25** 483
González Gortázar, Fernando **12** 921–2*; **21** 382
González Goyri, Roberto **12** 922*; **13** 765
González Merguete, José **2** 394; **4** 256; **7** 847; **29** 893
González-Montes, Francisco Cubas y *see* CUBAS Y GONZÁLEZ-MONTES, FRANCISCO
González Perez, José Victoriano Carmelo Carlos *see* GRIS, JUAN
González Reyna, Jorge **7** 696
González Romero, Raúl **27** 621
González Ruiz, Antonio **12** 922*
González Rul, Manuel **12** 922–3*; **14** 462; **21** 381; **31** 186
González Trujillo, Alejandro **24** 509

González Valcárcel, José Manuel see VALCÁRCEL, JOSÉ MANUEL GONZÁLEZ
González Velázquez, Alejandro 12 923–4*; 29 304; 31 90
González Velázquez, Antonio 12 923–4*
collaboration 12 587
patrons and collectors 4 561; 31 341
pupils 3 424; 20 77
teachers 12 587
works 12 587, 924; 29 283, 304
González Velázquez, Castor 12 923, 925*
González Velázquez, Isidro 1 743; 12 923
works 2 285; 4 565; 9 23; 11 494; 29 272, 305; 32 565
González Velázquez, Luis 12 923–4*
collaboration 12 924
patrons and collectors 4 561
works 12 587; 29 304; 31 90
González Velázquez, Pablo 12 923
González Velázquez, Zacarías 12 923, 924–5*
collaboration 5 453
patrons and collectors 31 808
works 5 452, 453; 9 23; 12 924
González Zuleta, Guillermo 7 606
Go Oc Eo see OC EO
Good, John Willis 4 221
Goodall, Edward 12 925*; 13 697
Goodall, Edward Alfred 12 925; 13 876
Goodall, Eliza 12 925
Goodall, Frederick 12 925–6*
dealers 12 30
groups and movements 23 504; 32 903
reproductive prints by others 12 925
Goodall, Thomas F. 10 184
Goodall, Walter 12 925
Goodchild, Doreen 2 760
Goode, Joe 19 492, 702; 25 232; 31 608; 33 45
Gooden, Stephen 10 397
Gooderick, Matthew 24 752; 29 321
Good Furniture Group 10 299
Goodhart Master 9 349
Goodhart-Rendel, H(arry) S(tuart) 12 926*
staff 28 622
works 4 810; 10 240; 17 600
Good Hope, Great House 16 886
Goodhue, Bertram (Grosvenor) 12 926–7*; 31 596
collaboration 8 110; 14 68
groups and movements 31 595
patrons and collectors 31 680
staff 14 199, 734
works 6 459; 10 684; 12 927; 27 720
Goodison, Benjamin 10 294; 11 426, 428; 17 902
Goodman, Nelson 1 174, 182; 10 691; 24 380; 26 222; 29 880
Goodman, Percival 10 120; 17 549
Goodnough, Robert 13 1*
Goodnow & Jenks 4 480
Goodrich, Daniel 28 539
works 28 540
Goodrich, Lloyd 13 1*
Goodrich Castle (Hereford & Worcs) 3 209
Goodrich Court (Herts) 9 31; 10 280
Goodridge, Henry Edmund 3 372, 477; 10 151
Good Samaritan Master (fl early 13th cent.) 4 582
Good Samaritan Master (fl 1537-45/6) 28 218
works 4 582
Goodwin, Albert 4 879; 13 1–2*; 14 850
Goodwin, Betty 5 569; 13 2*; 22 39
Goodwin, Francis 4 80
Goodwin, Henry 9 705
Goodwin, John (fl early 20th cent.) 22 744; 33 22
Goodwin, John (fl 1953) 15 105
Goodwin, Philip L. 17 723; 22 365; 29 716
Goodwin, Robin 28 591
Goodwin, Sydney 9 705
Goodwood Cup 10 334, 334; 12 163; 29 723
Goodwood House (W. Sussex)
architecture 19 157
collections 19 157, 158
grotto 11 243; 28 581
paintings 5 598, 686; 19 157
sculpture 8 481
Goody, Clancy and Associates 13 2
Goody, Joan Edelman 13 2*
Goody, Marvin E. 13 2
Goodyear, Charles 31 260
Goodyear, Joseph 25 836
Gookin, Frederick W. 17 431
Gool, Jan van 13 2–3*; 14 42, 795; 30 297
works 22 902, 910
Goold, Bruce
works 2 768
Goos 13 682
Goose Creek (SC), St James 4 786
goose-foot lamps see under LAMPS → types
Goose Lake Castle see MATSUMOTO CASTLE
Goovaertz, Agustin 7 606; 21 4
Gooyer, Salomon (Jacobsz.) de see RUYSDAEL, SALOMON (JACOBSZ.) VAN
Gop, Old Temple 15 266, 463
Gopagni see GWALIOR
Gopal 15 610
Gopalas 22 766
Gopas, Rudolf 7 211; 13 3*; 18 529
Gopeshwar Temple 15 264
Gopinath 20 54
Gopinatha Rao, T. A. see RAO, T. A. GOPINATHA
Göppert, Michael 17 887
Göppingen Church 12 370
Gopsall Hall (Leics) 17 476
gopuras see under GATEWAYS → types
Göransson, Åke 10 805; 13 31; 30 81
Gorantla, Madhavarayasvami Temple 15 539
Goravsky, Apollinary see HARASÛSKI, APALINARY
Gorbunovo peat-bog 13 5*; 25 471; 27 362, 365, 366
Gorchakov (family) 27 439, 441
Gordaneer, James 32 414
Gördes 16 472, 476, 478
carpets 16 478
Gördes carpets see under CARPETS → types
Gordes Château 32 10
Gordeyev, Boris 27 379
Gordeyev, Fyodor (Gordeyevich) 13 5*; 25 647; 27 389, 579
Gordian III, Emperor of Rome (reg 238-44) 15 918
Gordillo, Luis 13 5–6*
works 13 6; 29 287
Gordion 1 821, 827, 849; 13 6–8*; 23 806; 24 689
architecture 1 831
bronze 1 836
burial mounds 1 830
citadel 13 6–7*
coins 2 261
fortifications 21 553
furniture 1 890; 33 335
glass 1 867
iron 1 836
Gordion—cont.
ivory-carvings 1 870, 872
Megaron 2 1 890; 13 7
Midas tomb 13 8; 31 108
mosaics 1 890; 13 561; 22 159
pottery 1 837
sculpture 1 833; 24 690
textiles 1 881
tumuli 13 7–8; 24 691
wall paintings 13 550
Gordon, Alex (b 1917) 5 732
Gordon, Alexander (1692-1754) 10 79
Gordon, Alexander (fl 1799) 5 71
Gordon, Alexander (fl 1927) 28 772
Gordon, Alexander, 4th Duke of Gordon (1743-1827) 9 727
Gordon, Arturo 6 597; 13 9*
Gordon, Charles 25 35
Gordon, Charles George 29 884
Gordon, D. 4 27
Gordon, D. H. 15 551
Gordon, George, 4th Earl of Aberdeen 33 192
Gordon, George, 4th Earl of Huntly 28 245; 31 230
Gordon, Harry 21 573, 574; 25 4
Gordon, Hortense 23 790
Gordon, Ishbel Maria, Countess of Aberdeen 16 32
Gordon, John 5 540
Gordon, J. R. 18 888
Gordon, Lucy Duff see LUCILE
Gordon, Max 27 478
Gordon, Robert (Jacob) 29 108
Gordon, William 3 383
Gordon Lennox, Augusta, Duchess of Richmond 17 851
Gordon's Pottery 28 258
Gore, Charles 8 96; 13 304; 18 149
Gore, Spencer (Frederick) 13 9*; 19 589
groups and movements 1 666; 5 516, 517; 10 255; 19 591, 622
patrons and collectors 16 42
works 14 107
Górecki, Józef 7 837
Gorecki, Tadeusz 25 673
Gorée 28 405
Musée Historique d'Afrique Occidentale 28 406
Goree, Willem 8 128
Gorei Maekawa see MAEKAWA GOREI
Göreme 5 673; 9 512
Çarıklı Kilise 5 678; 9 581
churches 5 674; 9 576; 26 483, 484
Elmalı Kilise 5 678; 9 581
Karanlık Kilise 5 674, 678; 9 581, 581
Merymana 5 678
St Eustace 5 677
Tokalı Kilise 5 675
New Church 5 674, 674, 676, 677; 7 279; 9 580, 640
Old Church 5 677
Gores, Landes 17 620
Goret de Saint-Martin, François 25 79
Gorey, Edward 4 368
Gorezyn, Jan Aleksandr 25 106
Gorgan 15 905; 16 105
Gorgasus 10 617; 26 764
gorge 21 546
Gorge, H. 8 402
Gorge Meillet, La see LA GORGE MEILLET
Gorgi, Abdelaziz 31 426
Gorgi, Abdelkadir 31 426
Gorgolewski, Zygmunt 25 408
Gorgona group 8 179
Gorgon Painter 13 507; 32 45*
Gorgora 10 566
Gorgora, Church of Debre Sina 10 572
Gorgy, Habib 9 766
Gorham see GORHAM MANUFACTURING CO.
Gorham, J., & Son 13 9
Gorham, Jabez 13 9*
Gorham, John 13 9
Gorham, Webster & Price 13 9
Gorhambury House 3 31; 24 845
Gorham Manufacturing Co. 4 480; 10 135; 13 9*; 31 649, 650, 654, 655
Gorham & Thurber 13 9
Gori (Georgia) 12 320
Gori (family) 16 775
Gori, Agnolo 4 65
Gori, Antonio Francesco 10 637, 642; 13 10*; 33 613
groups and movements 2 164
illustrated works 5 55
pupils 32 237
Gori, Lamberto Cristiano 28 28
Gorica 28 862
Gori collection see under CELLE DI PISTOIA
Gori Gandellini, Francesco 13 10
Gori Gandellini, Giovanni 13 10*
Gori Gandellini, Pietro 13 10
Gorin, (Albert) Jean 13 10*
groups and movements 1 90; 27 639
patrons and collectors 2 409
works 11 419; 22 749
Gorin, Stanislas 26 71
Gorinchem 22 855
Göring, Hermann (Wilhelm) see GOERING, HERMANN (WILHELM)
Goris 2 428
Goris, Gerard 13 10*
Goritz, Johann 27 776
Gorívar, Javier 9 712
Gorka, Géza 5 86; 15 2
Gorkha Palace 22 764
Gor Khatri see PESHAWAR
Gorki Leninskiye, V. I. Lenin Museum 27 381, 381
Gorky see GORODETS
Gor'ky see NIZHNY NOVGOROD
Gorky, Arshile 5 531; 13 11–13*; 31 607
groups and movements 1 78, 83, 85, 90; 30 22; 31 607
methods 8 128
patrons and collectors 14 575; 18 170; 28 167; 31 663; 33 45
pupils 20 568
works 2 839; 4 75; 13 11, 12
Gor'ky, Maksim 9 51; 13 11, 13–14*
groups and movements 4 231
illustrated works 1 731
productions 28 757
Gorlaeus, Abraham 12 266
Gorlero, Baudés 2 525
Gorleston Psalter see under PSALTERS → individual manuscripts
Gorlov, Dmitry (Vladimirovich) 27 411
Gorm, Estrid 27 167
Gorm, Harald Bluetooth, King of Denmark see HARALD I, King of Denmark
Gorm, Knut IV, King of Denmark see KNUT IV, King of Denmark
Gorm, Valdemar II, King of Denmark see VALDEMAR II, King of Denmark
Gorman, Chester 3 154
Gorman, Rudolph Carl 13 14*; 22 666
works 22 598, 599
Gorman company 16 889
Gormaz, García de San Esteban y see SAN ESTEBAN Y GORMAZ, GARCÍA DE
Gorm the Old, King of Denmark (reg c. 900-c. 950) 17 473
Gorn 24 428
Gornea see GARNI
Gornjak 22 79
Gornji Grad Monastery 28 857, 858, 858, 861
church 28 859
Gornoshit 27 428
Gornostajev, Aleksander 14 371
Gornostayev, Aleksey (Maksimovich) 27 579
Gornostayev, F. F. 27 443
Gornostayev, Nikolay 21 98
Gornostayev, Vasily M. 29 555
Gornyy Badakhshan 32 321
Goro see BIAGIO DI GORO GHEZZI
Goro, Niccolò di see NICCOLÒ DI GORO
Gorobei 31 765
Gorodets 13 14*; 27 363, 430
wood-carvings 13 14
Gorodetsky, Sergey 1 121; 2 895; 33 740
Gorodetsky, Vladislav V. 31 551
Gorodets style 13 14
Goro di Gregorio 13 15*, 93; 28 676
Goro di Guccio Ciuti 13 15
Gorodishche, Church of the Annunciation 27 383
Gorokhovsky, Eduard 27 397
Gorosaburō Kanaya see KANAYA GOROSABURŌ
Gorōyama Tomb 17 143
Gorp, Henri Nicolas van 18 858
Görres, Johann Joseph von 1 660; 7 870; 13 15–16*
Gorron, Geoffrey, Abbot of St Albans 26 671
Gorsium 9 557
Gorska, Tamara see DE LEMPICKA, TAMARA
Gorski Kotar 8 180
Gorson, Aaron 25 5
Gorston, Nicholas see GOSTON, NICHOLAS
Gort, John Standish Surtees Prendergast Vereker, 6th Viscount see JOHN STANDISH SURTEES PRENDERGAST VEREKER, 6th Viscount Gort
Gortázar, Fernando González see GONZÁLEZ GORTÁZAR, FERNANDO
Gortiz, Johann 25 904
Gorton, Bishop of Coventry 30 782
Görtschacher, Urban 2 792
Gortyn 8 154, 155; 9 511; 13 16–18*, 17, 362; 21 651; 26 908
architecture 8 154
bouleuterion 4 530
busts 13 443, 443
church 8 155
Hagios Titos 8 155; 9 538
measurements 13 410, 411
odeion 26 910
Odeum 8 155
Pythion see Temple of Apollo Pythios
reliefs 13 443
sculpture 8 154
Temple of Apollo Pythios 8 154, 155
Temple of Isis and Serapis 8 155
Gortyn Apollo 8 154
Gortyn Athena 8 154
Gortys 3 374; 21 45; 26 908
Asklepieion 13 407
Görtz, Sebastian see GÖTZ, SEBASTIAN
Goryany 31 550
St Nicholas 31 556
Goryayev, Vitaly 27 396
Gorys, Gerard see GORIS, GERARD
Goryunova, Nonna 15 831
Goryushkin-Sorokopudov, Ivan 30 299, 361

Gorze, Order of **13** 18–19*
manuscript illumination **13** *19*
Gos, Jan **32** 156
Go Sanh **6** 432
Gosanke (family) **17** 788
Gosbecks **25** 538; **26** 905
Gosberg **25** 529
Goscelin of St Bertin **2** 64, 73
Göschl, Roland **2** 804
Gościsiszowice, Master from **25** 111
Gościsiszowice, Parish Church **25** 111
Goscombe John, William *see* JOHN, WILLIAM GOSCOMBE
Gosebruch, Ernst **18** 81
Goseda, Yoshimatsu **17** 203
Goseda Hōryū **17** 198
Göser, Simon **33** 76
GOSET **9** 747
Gosford House (Lothian) **28** 227; **29** 7
Gosforth (Cumbria) **32** 523
Gosforth Cross **32** 529, *529*
Goshavank'
Horonios monastery **7** 262
khatchk'ars **2** 436
Gosh Church **2** 429
Goshen, Eri **10** 719
Gōshin, Fujiwara no *see* FUJIWARA NO GŌSHIN
Go Shion **17** 411
GoShirakawa, Emperor (*reg* 1155–8) **10** 192; **11** 824; **12** 96; **15** 159; **17** 120, 121; **22** 496
replicas **12** *96*
gosho see under DOLLS → types
Goshoshiki kiln **27** 873
Goshun Matsumura *see* MATSUMURA GOSHUN
Gosizdat **12** 875
Goslar **12** *360*; **13** 161
Brusttuch house **27** *127*
Cathedral of SS Simon, Judas and Matthias **12** 419
copper **12** 452
Liebfrauenkirche **14** 81
metalwork **23** 659; **26** 683
Palace **13** 19–20*; **14** 74; **26** 575
Rathaus **12** 442, *443*; **13** 161; **20** 683
silver **28** 737
Goslar *Bergkanne* **12** 442, *443*; **23** 311
Goslar Gospels *see under* GOSPEL BOOKS → individual manuscripts
Goslar Sibyls, Master of the **20** 683*
Goslavsky, I. V. **2** 893; **3** 88
Gosling, David **31** 733, 738
works **31** *737*
Gospa od Škrpjela Church **22** 16, 17
Gospel Book of Bernward of Hildesheim *see under* GOSPEL BOOKS → individual manuscripts
Gospel books **4** 3; **5** 624; **13** 20–22*; **20** 339–40
historical and regional traditions
Armenia (Europe) **2** 430
Bulgaria **5** 160, *160*
Byzantine **7** 222; **9** 608–10, 620, 651; **13** 21
Carolingian **5** 800, 801, 802; **13** *20*, 20
Early Christian (*c.* AD 250–843) **9** 608–10
England **15** *874*
Insular art **13** 20; **15** 871, 873–5, *874*; **17** 889–90; **20** 330, 339
Ireland **13** 20; **17** 889–90
Ottonian **13** 20; **23** 652
Scotland **28** 233
individual manuscripts
Aachen Gospels (Aachen, Domschatzkam.) **1** 4; **5** 802
Gospel books
individual manuscripts—cont.
Ada Gospels (Trier, Stadtbib., MS. 22) **23** 537
Adishi Gospels (Mestia, Mus. Hist. & Ethnog) **12** 324
Alaverdi Gospels (St Petersburg, Saltykov-Shchedrin Pub. Lib., MS. A484) **12** 325
Arenberg Gospels (New York, Pierpont Morgan Lib., MS. M. 869) **2** 74
Aschaffenburg Golden Gospels (Aschaffenburg, Schloss Johannisburg, Hof- & Stiftsbib., MS. 13) **13** 142
Assamani Gospels (Rome, Vatican, Bib. Apostolica, MS. Vat. Slav. 3) **5** 152
Averbode Gospels (U. Liège, Bib. Gén., MS. 363C) **3** 552; **13** 21; **26** 667; **31** 499
Awag Vank' Gospels (London, BL, Or. MS. 13654) **2** 430
Bamberg Cathedral Gospel Book (Bamberg, Staatsbib. MS. Bibl. 94) **23** 655
Barberini Gospels (Rome, Vatican, Bib. Apostolica, MS. Barb. lat. 570) **15** 875
Berti Gospels (Tbilisi, Acad. Sci., Inst. MSS) **12** 328; **23** 452
Book of Dimma (Dublin, Trinity Coll. Lib., MS. 59) **15** 875; **16** 12
Book of Durrow (Dublin, Trinity Coll. Lib., MS. 57) **15** 847, 873–4, 882, *882*; **16** 12; **17** 889; **23** 537; **28** 233
Book of Kells (Dublin, Trinity Coll. Lib., MS. 58) **15** 871, 874, 875, 877; **16** 12, 36; **17** 888, 889–90*; **24** 738; **28** 233
borders (manuscript) **9** 219; **15** 882
canon table **5** 624
initials (manuscript) **15** 847, *847*
miniatures **16** *13*; **17** *890*
scripts **28** 305
Book of Mulling (Dublin, Trinity Coll. Lib., MS. 60) **16** 12
Canterbury Codex Aureus *see* Stockholm Codex Aureus
Chad Gospels *see* Lichfield Gospels
Codex Aureus (London, BL, MS. Harley 2788) **32** 852
Codex Aureus of Echternach (Nuremberg, Ger. Nmus., Cod.2 **9** 698, 749; **23** 655, 656, 660; **25** 743; **28** 24
Codex Aureus of St Emmeram (Munich, Bayer. Staatsbib., Clm. 14000) **5** 804, 808, 810; **6** 485; **7** 512–13*; **9** *253*, 253; **11** 614; **23** 653, 654; **25** 743, *743*; **30** 779
book cover (gold) **7** *513*
book cover (ivory) **4** IV2
Codex Caesarius Upsaliensis (Uppsala, U. Lib.) **9** 698; **27** 617
Codex Escorial (Madrid, Escorial, Bib. Monasterio S Lorenzo, MS. Vit. 17) **9** 698; **18** 587; **20** V2; **27** 616
Copenhagen Gospels (Copenhagen, Kon. Bib. MS. G.1) **33** 232
Coronation Gospels (London, BL, Cotton MS. Tib. A. II) **33** 90
Gospel books
individual manuscripts—cont.
Coronation Gospels of Charlemagne (Vienna, Schatzkam. SCHK XIII) **1** 4; **5** 802, *802*; **6** 389, 483; **12** *381*, 382; **13** 20; **20** 330; **32** 458
Cutbercht Gospels (Vienna, Österreich. Nbib., Cod. 1224) **15** 875; **27** 663
Dobreisho Gospels (Sofia, Nat. Lib., MS. 18) **5** 153
Dobromilov Gospels (Moscow, Lenin Lib.) **31** 556
Durham Gospels (Durham, Cathedral Lib., MS. A.II.17) **15** 874
Eadui Gospels (Hannover, Kestner-Mus., MS. WM. XXIa 36) **5** 641
Ebbo Gospels (Epernay, Bib. Mun., MS. 1) **2** *836*; **5** 802; **6** 388; **9** 686; **11** 529; **20** 330; **26** 113; **31** 774
canon table **5** 624
Echternach Gospels (Paris, Bib. N., MS. lat. 9389) **9** 698; **15** 874; **20** 330
Ēdjmiadzin Gospels (Erevan, Matenadaran Inst. Anc. Armen. MSS, MS. 2374) **2** 430; **5** 624; **9** 732, 733*; **10** 450
Exeter Gospels (Paris, Bib. N. MS., lat. 14782) **26** 671
Francis II Gospels (Paris, Bib. N., MS. lat. 257) **5** 804
Fyodorov Gospel (Yaroslavl', A. Mus.) **27** 383
Gauzlin Gospels (Nancy, Trésor Cathédrale) **31** 227
Gelati Gospels (St Petersburg, Saltykov-Shchedrin Pub. Lib., MS. 908) **12** 325
Golden Gospels (Nuremberg, Ger. Nmus., MS. 20.156. 142) **7** 246
Goslar Gospels (Goslar, Rathaus) **14** 535
Gospel Book of Bernward of Hildesheim (Hildesheim Diözmus. & Domschatzkam., MS. 18) **6** 564
Gospel of Kars (Jerusalem, Gulbenkian Lib., MS. 2556) **2** 430
Gospel of Nikephoros Phokas *see under* LECTIONARIES → individual manuscripts
Gospel of Vukan (St Petersburg, Saltykov-Shchedrin Pub. Lib., F.n.I. 82) **22** 16; **28** 449
Gospels of 1038 (Erevan, Mantenadaran Inst. Anc. Armen. MSS, MS. 6201) **10** 450
Gospels of 1053 (Erevan, Matenadaran Inst. Anc. Armen. MSS., MS. 3593) **2** 430
Gospels of 1260 (Jerusalem, Armen. Patriarch., MS. 251) **31** 177
Gospels of 1268 (Erevan, Matenadaran Inst. Anc. Armen. MSS, MS. 10675) **31** 177
Gospels of Abbess Theophanu (Essen, Münsterschatzmus.) **26** 695
Gospels of Abbot Ellinger (Munich, Bayer. Staatsbib., Clm. 18005) **23** 655
Gospels of Haghpat (Erevan, Matenadaran Inst. Anc. Armen. MSS, MS. 6288) **2** 430
Gospel books
individual manuscripts—cont.
Gospels of Henry III (Madrid, Escorial, Bib. Monasterio S Lorenzo, Cod. Vit. 17) **23** *655*
Gospels of Henry IV (Kraków, Wawel Cathedral, MS. 208) **26** 660, 674
Gospels of Henry the Lion (Wolfenbüttel, Herzog August Bib., Cod. Guelf, 105 noviss. 2; Munich, Bayer. Staatsbib., Clm. 3055) **5** 29; **7** *246*; **13** 21; **26** 659, 660, 662, 675; **33** 51, *293*
Gospels of Hitda of Meschede (Darmstadt, Hess. Landes- & Hochschbib., Cod. 1640) **23** 654
Gospels of Mathilda (New York, Pierpont Morgan Lib., MS. M. 492) **20** 820
Gospels of Otto III (Munich, Bayer. Staatsbib., Clm. 4453) **1** 4; **7** 246, 302; **12** 254; **13** 20, 21*; **23** 652, *653*, 654, 660; **26** 101; **28** 24
Gospels of Prince Vasak (Jerusalem, Gulbenkian Lib., MS. 2568) **2** 444
Gospels of Queen Felicia (New York, Met.) **26** 642
Gospels of Queen Keran (Jerusalem, Gulbenkian Lib., MS. 2563) **2** 444
Gospels of Queen Mariun (Jerusalem, Gulbenkian Lib., MS. 1973) **2** 444
Gospels of Queen Mlk'e (Venice, Lazzaro degli Armeni Bib., MS. 1144/86) **2** 430, 444; **13** 21–2*
Gospels of St Margaret of Scotland (Oxford, Bodleian Lib., MS. lat. liturg. F.5) **2** 78*
Gospels of S Maria ad Martyres (Trier, Stadtbib., MS. 23) **31** 325
Gospels of Trebizond (Venice, Lib. Mekhitharists, MS. 1400) **2** 430
Gospels of Zeyt'oun (Istanbul, Arm. Patriarch Treasury) **31** 177
Grimbald Gospels (London, BL, Add. MS. 34890) **2** 76; **9** 499
Grimensky Gospels (St Petersburg, Saltykov-Shchedrin Pub. Lib.) **31** 558
Guntbald Gospels (Hildesheim, Diözmus., Cod. 18) **14** 532
Haghpat Gospels (Erevan, Matenadaran Inst. Anc. Armen. MSS, MS. 6288) **10** 450
Hannover Gospels (London, BL, MS. Arundel 155) **9** 499
Harley Golden Gospels (London, BL, Harley MS. 2788) **13** *20*, 20; **15** 848; **31** 48
Helmarshausen Gospels (Trier, Domschatz, Cod. 139) **26** 683
Hereford Gospels (Hereford, Cathedral Lib., MS. P. I. 2) **15** 875
Hillinus Gospels (Cologne, Erzbischöf. Diöz. -& Dombib., MS. 12) **7** 583
Jruchi Gospels (Tbilisi, Acad. Sci., Inst. MSS, MS. H1660) **12** 324
Kalist Gospels (London, BL) **28** 822
Kederminster Gospels (London, BL, Loan MS. 11) **2** 77; **33** 232
Gospel books
individual manuscripts—cont.
Kievan Gospels (St Petersburg, Saltykov-Shchedrin Pub. Lib.) **31** 558
Krupnik Gospels (Rila Monastery, National Museum) **5** 160, *160*
Leofric Gospels (Oxford, Bodleian Lib., MS. Auct. D.2.16) **26** 666
Lichfield Gospels (Lichfield, Cathedral Lib., s.n.) **15** 874; **32** 784
Limburg Gospels (Cologne Cathedral, Treasury, MS. 218) **7** 591
Lindau Gospels (New York, Pierpont Morgan Lib., MS. M. 1) **5** 806, 808; **11** 614; **22** 111
Lindisfarne Gospels (London, BL, Cotton MS. Nero D. IV) **4** *343*; **8** 38, 196; **10** 243; **15** 871, 874, *874*, *882*; **19** 409*; **20** 329; **23** 537; **29** 851
borders (manuscript) **9** 219; **15** 882
initials (manuscript) **15** 847; **19** *409*
scripts **28** 305
London Gospels (London, BL. Add. MS. 39627, fol.3r) **5** *153*
Lorsch Gospels (Alba Iulia, Batthyaneum Lib.; Rome, Vatican, Bib. Apostolica, MS. Pal. lat. 50) **5** 809
Lothair Gospels (Paris, Bib. N., MS. lat. 266) **5** 803; **14** 408; **31** 226
Lutsk Gospels (Moscow, Rus. Lib.) **31** 558
Macregol Gospels (Oxford, Bodleian Lib., MS. Auct. D. 2. 19) **15** 875
Mainz Golden Gospels (Aschaffenburg, Schloss Johannisburg, Hof- & Stiftsbib., MS. 13) **33** 588, *589*
Manchester Gospels (Manchester, John Rylands U. Lib., MS. 98) **23** 654
Mariinsko Gospels (Moscow, Rus. Lib., Grig, 6M1689) **5** 152
Médard Gospels *see* Soissons Gospels
Mokvi Gospels (St Petersburg, Saltykov-Shchedrin Pub. Lib., MS. Q902) **12** 325
Mstiž Gospels (Vilnius, Pub. Lib.) **3** 527
Mughni Gospels (Erevan, Matenadaran Inst. Anc. Armen. MSS, MS. 7736) **2** 430; **10** 450
Nonnberg Gospels (Munich, Bayer. Staatsbib., Clm. 15904) **2** 790
Orsha Gospels (untraced) **3** 527
Orshanka Gospels (St Petersburg, Acad. Sci., Lib.) **31** 556
Ostromir Gospels (St Petersburg, Saltykov-Shchedrin Pub. Lib.) **31** 556
Pantaleon Gospels (Cologne, Hist. Arch., MS. 312A) **26** 673
Parma Gospels (Parma, Bib. Palatina, MS. gr. 5) **9** 608, 610
Patriarchate Gospels (Istanbul, Gr. Orthdx Patriarch., Cod. gr. 3) **9** 610
Peresopnitsky Gospels (Kiev, Cent. Lib. Acad. Sci.) **31** 558

Gospel books
individual manuscripts—cont.
Peshitta Gospels (untraced) **25** 833
Prague Gospels (Prague Cathedral, Cim. 2) **5** 804
Quedlinburg Gospels (New York, Pierpont-Morgan Lib., MS. M. 755) **23** 653; **28** 24
Rabbula Gospels (Florence, Bib. Medicea-Laurenziana, MS. Plut. I.56) **5** 442, 624; **7** 219; **9** 518, 608, 620, *620*; **13** 20; **22** 520; **25** 833*; **31** 436
Rossano Gospels (Rossano, Mus. Dioc.) **2** 836; **7** 221, 246; **9** 606, 608; **13** 20; **18** 824; **22** 520; **25** 743; **27** 173–4*, *174*; **31** 48
St Augustine Gospels (Cambridge, Corpus Christi Coll., MS. 286) **9** 602, *603*; **13** 20; **15** 875; **16** 654; **20** 330; **22** 520; **27** 532–3*
St Cuthbert Gospel of St John (London, BL, Loan MS. 74) **4** 346, *346*, 348, 351
Sainte-Chapelle Gospels (Paris, Bib. N., MS. lat. 8851) **20** 754; **31** 325
St Gall Gospels (St Gall, Stift.-Bib., Cod. 51) **15** 875
St Médard Gospels *see* Soissons Gospels
St Willibrord Gospels *see* Echternach Gospels
Sava Gospel Book (Moscow, Cent. Archv. Anc. Doc.) **5** 152
Sinope Gospels (Paris, Bib. N., MS. suppl. gr. 1286) **7** 246; **9** 608; **25** 743; **27** 174
Sion Gospels (London, Victoria and Albert Museum) **4** 111
Siysk Gospel (untraced) **27** 383
Small Bernward Gospels (Hildesheim, Diözmus., Cod. 13) **14** 532
Soissons Gospels (Paris, Bib. N., MS. lat. 8850) **5** *624*, 801, 810; **6** 483; **7** 246, 512; **11** 340; **30** *166*
canon table **5** 624
Stockholm Codex Aureus (Stockholm, Kun. Bib., MS. A. 135) **5** 640; **7** 246; **25** 743; **33** 90
Stonyhurst Gospel *see* St Cuthbert Gospel of St John
Stuttgart Gospels (Stuttgart, Württemberg. Landesbib., MS. II. 40) **5** 802
Targmantchats Gospels (Erevan, Matenadaran Inst. Anc. Armen. MSS, MS. 2743) **2** 430; **10** 450
Tbeti Gospels (St Petersburg, Saltykov-Shchedrin Pub. Lib.) **12** 325
Trier Gospels (Trier, Domschatz, Cod. 61) **5** 810; **9** 698; **15** 875
Trinity Gospels (Cambridge, Trinity Coll., MS. B.10.4) **2** 77; **33** 232
Tskarostavi Gospels (Tbilisi, Acad. Sci., Inst. MSS) **12** 328; **23** 452
Valerianus Gospels (Munich, Bayer. Staatsbib., Clm. 6224) **15** 847; **19** 549
Vani Gospels (St Petersburg, Saltykov-Shchedrin Pub. Lib., MS. A1335) **12** 325
Vehap'at's Gospels (Erevan, Matenadaran Inst. Anc. Armen. MSS, MS. 10780) **2** 430, *431*; **5** 624; **32** 118*

Gospel books
individual manuscripts—cont.
York Gospels (York Minster, Chapter Lib., Add. MS. 1) **2** 77; **9** 499
see also NEW TESTAMENTS
Gospel Lectionaries *see* EVANGELIARIES
Gospil, Thomas **28** 900
Gospodov Dol Church **5** 150
Göss
Pfarrkirche **2** 778
vestments (ecclesiastical) **2** 823; **32** *388*
Goss, W. H., Ltd **6** 164
Goss, William Henry **13** 22*
Gossart, Jan **2** 204, 206; **13** 22–8*; **21** 124; **23** 112, 294; **33** 355
collaboration **14** 296
groups and movements **9** 462; **26** 728
methods **31** 577
patrons and collectors
Beurnonville, Etienne-Edmond Martin, Baron de **3** 890
Boisserée, Melchior and Sulpiz **4** 243
Charles I, King of England and Scotland (*reg* 1625–49) **29** 800
Christian II, King of Denmark and Norway *reg* 1513–23) **8** 758; **23** 395
Clark, Robert Sterling **7** 377
Howard (ii), Frederick, 5th Earl of Carlisle **14** 808
Howard (ii), George James, 9th Earl of Carlisle **14** 809
Margaret of Austria, Duchess of Savoy and Regent of the Netherland (1480–1530) **13** 905
Nassau, Hendrik III, Count of **22** 535
Philip of Burgundy, Bishop of Utrecht **5** 214; **22** 901
Richards, John Inigo **26** 335
Siciliano, Antonio **10** 713
Tallard, Marie-Joseph d'Hostun, Duc de **30** 274
pupils **21** 167; **28** 215
reproductive prints by others **11** 794
sponsors **5** 206
works **2** 340; **3** 554; **5** *625*; **10** 476; **11** 440; **13** *24*, *25*, *26*, *27*, 659, 661; **22** 836–7; **27** 256; **31** 881
Gossart, Nicasius **13** 27
Gossart, Pierre **13** 27
Gosschalk, I. **1** 803
Gosse, Edmund (William) **13** 29*; **23** 33, 34
Gosse, Ellen **1** 678
Gosse, Philip **16** 886
Gosse, Sylvia **13** 29; **28** 661
Gosseal, Pedro **9** 710, 715; **25** 829
Gösser, Wilhelm **3** 393
Gosset, Adolphe-François **7** 434
Gosset, Alphonse **26** 113
Gosset, Isaac **13** 29*; **14** 856
Gosset, Matthew **13** 29
Gosset de Guines, Louis-Alexandre *see* GILL, ANDRÉ
Gossuin of Metz **10** 202
Gostinopol' Monastery, St Nicholas **25** 337, 342
Gostomski, Zbigniew **13** 29–30*
Goston, Nicholas **10** 325
Gostyń **25** 98, 103, 115
Gosudarstvennyy Institut Khudozhestvennoy Kultury *see* GINKHUK
Gosukōin *see* FUSHIMI SADAFUSA
Goswamy, Brijen **15** 212, 748
Got, Bertrand du *see* CLEMENT V, Pope
Gotard, Jan **10** 871
Gotarzes II **4** 94
Gotay, Consuelo **25** 702

Gotch, Thomas Cooper **4** 657; **13** 30*; **23** 26
Gote, Pieter van der **31** 147
Göteborg **13** 30–31*; **21** 570; **30** 64, *65*; **31** 718
Classical High School *see* Hvitfeldska Gymnasiet
Haga Church **30** 73
High School for Girls **18** 801
Hvitfeldska Gymnasiet **18** 802
jewellery **30** 112
Lennart Torstensson's Palace **30** 84
metalwork **30** 106
museums
City Museum **13** 30
Etnografiska Museum **29** 241; **30** 119
Historical Museum **13** 30
Konstmuseum **1** 466; **10** 460; **11** 234, 851; **13** 31; **22** 730
Military Museum **13** 30
Röhss Museum of Arts & Crafts **13** 31
Oskar Fredrikskyrka **30** 73
painting **30** 80
railway station **30** 73, 110
stadium **29** 489
University **30** 119
Göteborgskolorister **13** 31; **30** 81
Göteborgs Konstnärsklubb **24** 451
Goten, Cornelis van der **29** 350
Goten, Jacob van der *see* GOTEN, JACQUES VAN DER
Goten, Jacques van der **2** 199; **29** 350; **30** 324
Goten, Jan van der **2** 199, 200
Gotfred of Ghemen **8** 731
Gotfredus, Archbishop of Milan **21** 522, 533; **23** 659; **28** 805–71*
Gotgelf, G. M. **21** 810
Gotha
porcelain **30** 793
Schloss Friedenstein **5** 345–6; **8** 115, 120; **20** 695; **32** 907
Gotha Altarpiece **12** 495
Gothart Nithart, Mathis *see* GRÜNEWALD, MATTHIAS
Göthe, Erik Gustav **13** 31*; **21** 471; **30** 109
Göthe, Johann Friedrich Eosander *see* EOSANDER, JOHANN FRIEDRICH
Gothein, Marie-Louise **12** 65
Gothein, Werner **18** 79
Gothic **13** 31–197*
alabaster (gypsum) **1** *517*, *519*; **3** *456*; **13** 84; **17** *459*; **22** *280*; **33** *28*
altarpieces **12** 626; **13** 127, 130–31, 170; **24** 3
Austria **11** *806*
Belgium **4** *416*; **13** 110
Catalonia **13** 106; **14** *858*
diptychs **9** 3, *4*; **11** *451*; **13** *177*
England **11** 420–21
France **13** *109*; **20** *742*, *762*
Germany **1** *709*; **11** 450–53; **12** 383, 400; **13** 131; **23** *254*; **26** *371*, *372*; **29** *730*
Holy Roman Empire (before 1648) **13** 116
Italy **7** *329*, *334*; **9** *342*, *347*; **13** 130, 146, *146*; **20** *728*; **32** *213*
International Gothic **12** *299*, *300*, *301*
Late Gothic **7** 111; **19** *680*, *681*
Netherlands, the **13** 110–11, *114*
Norway **11** 465; **13** 143, *144*
Poland **29** *727*
polyptychs **13** 130
England **1** *519*
Germany **12** *383*
Italy **4** *31*; **7** *333*; **9** *345*; **11** *380*, *382*; **13** *129*, 139; **20** *675*
Slovakia **19** *281*
Slovakia **19** 281; **28** *854*

Gothic
altarpieces—cont.
Spain **3** *218*; **11** 479–83, *481*, *677*; **13** 69, 123, 169; **28** *517*, 518
Sweden **13** 120; **23** *255*; **30** 83
Switzerland **11** *452*
triptychs **16** *825*
France **13** *174*
Italy **3** *696*; **4** *37*; **7** *335*; **10** 179; **32** *228*
altars **2** *481*; **11** *479*; **13** 168; **17** *741*
ambulatories **2** *864*
amethyst **26** *147*
Andachtsbilder **13** 115, 116, 129
antependia **11** *466*; **13** 130, 135, 143, *144*; **24** 3
Antiphonaries **13** 130
Apocalypses **13** 130, 136
apses **2** 347
arcades **4** 141, *141*
arches
basket **2** 292
catenary **2** 292
containing **2** 292
cusped **2** 294
Decorated style **2** 295
equilateral **2** 294
four-centred **2** 294
horseshoe **2** 294
interlace **2** 294
keel **2** 295
lancet **2** 295
ogee **2** 295; **13** 46, 54
Perpendicular style **2** 294
pointed **2** 295, 298*; **13** 35, 51
shouldered **2** 295
stilted **2** 295
trefoil **2** 296
architecture **12** 497; **13** 35–71*, 210; **25** 172
Austria **2** 777–8; **13** 56
Belarus' **3** 526
Belgium **3** 542–4; **13** 61–3*
brick **12** 362; **13** 61; **24** 347
churches **13** 210
Cistercian Order **13** 35, 37–8, 47–8, 50, 51, 57
commentaries **3** 741; **27** 352
Czech Republic **8** 376–7; **13** 56, 57
Denmark **13** 50, 56; **26** 304
Dominican Order **13** 52, 57
Early Gothic **31** 284
England **10** 228; **13** 35, 43–7*, 53–6*, 136; **19** 402; **31** 284
Decorated style **13** 54
Early English style **9** 669–70
Early Gothic **13** 43
Perpendicular style **13** 55–6; **24** 465
Rayonnant style **13** 47
France **11** 510–11*; **13** 35, 36–43*, 50, 59–61*; **27** 539; **31** 284
Flamboyant style **9** 48; **13** 59
High Gothic **13** 39; **14** 518
Late Gothic **8** 789
opus francigenum **13** 42
Rayonnant style **13** 41–3*, 59
Franciscan Order **13** 52
Germany **12** 362; **13** 35, 47–9, 56–8*; **20** 87, *87*; **31** 284
Early Gothic **12** 364–5
High Gothic **13** 49
Late Gothic **12** 365–6*; **13** 58
Rayonnant style **13** 56–7*
Holy Roman Empire (before 1648) **13** 47–9*
Hungary **13** 56
Ireland **9** 321; **13** 56; **16** 7
Italy **13** 35, 51–3*, 63–6*; **16** 627*
Lithuania **13** 58; **19** 495
maniera tedesca **13** 35
marble **13** 35–53*
Netherlands, the **13** 61–3*; **22** 819–21*

Gothic
architecture—cont.
Norway **31** 363
opus francigenum **13** 35; **23** 462*
Poland **12** 823; **13** 56, 57; **24** 347; **31** 394
Portugal **3** 362; **13** 70–71*; **25** 289–90
Sardinia **27** 836
Scandinavia **13** 50*, 56–8*
Scotland **13** 56
Slovakia **28** 849
Slovenia **28** 858–9
Spain **13** 35, 50–51*, 66–70*; **19** 171; **29** 263, 265
Sweden **13** 50, 56
Switzerland **30** 125–6
Transitional style **31** 283–4
art history **9** 453
ballflower **3** *121*
bas-de-page **3** *323*
bays **19** 403
beads **13** 194
Bestiaries **13** 130
Bibles **4** 3, 7; **13** 129, 130, 136
Bible historiale **4** 12–13*
Bibles moralisées **4** 10–11*; **13** 140, *140*, 141, 179; **31** 500
Biblia pauperum **4** 11–12*; **31** 500
France **13** 140
block-books **12** 385
book covers **13** *159*
book illustrations **12** 385
books **12** 385
Books of Hours **13** 127, 129, 130, *130*, *148*; **20** *637*
borders (manuscript) **4** *393*, *394*; **14** *424*; **20** 338–9
bosses **13** *83*, 83; **22** *693*
box-wood **29** *728*; **33** 12
brass **13** 159–61; **32** *605*
brasses (monumental) **4** *693*; **19** *580*
Breviaries **13** 130
brick **4** 782; **12** 362; **13** 61, 64; **24** 347
bricklaying **4** *770*
bronze **11** *200*; **13** 159–61, *160*, 164; **24** *874*; **28** IV2
busts **17** *459*
buttresses **5** 319; **9** 672; **14** 519
cabinets (ii) (furniture) **3** *581*
calendars **13** 137
capitals **5** *670*; **29** *659*
castles **13** 53
Balearic Islands **3** *106*
Czech Republic **8** *376*
Italy **6** *17*; **13** 64
Poland **20** *185*
Romania **14** *880*
Slovakia **4** *695*
Sweden **14** *368*
Wales **16** *896*
cathedrals **12** 497; **20** 573, 574, 575, 582*
Austria **32** *451*
Belgium **5** *52*; **31** *221*; **33** *568*
Catalonia **7** *282*
Cyprus **10** *774*; **23** *112*
Czech Republic **25** *440*
Denmark **27** *167*
England **4** *825*; **5** *644*, *645*; **8** *611*; **9** *669*; **10** *167*, *673*; **13** *44*, *45*, *54*; **19** *402*, *403*, *597*; **24** *545*; **27** *627*, *628*; **33** *59*, *60*, *61*, *236*, *237*, *548*
England: Early Gothic **33** *62*
France **1** *577*, *778*; **2** *46*, *497*; **4** *578*, 579, *579*; **6** *493*, *494*; **8** *74*; **13** *36*, *37*, *40*, *41*; **18** *757*, *758*, *759*; **19** *127*; **20** *582*; **22** *505*; **24** *152*, *153*, *154*; **26** *115*, *116*; **27** *250*, *254*; **28** *414*, *415*; **29** *753*, *754*, *881*; **31** *383*
France: Flamboyant style **6** *414*
France: High Gothic **2** *844*; **3** *457*, *458*; **29** *17*

Gothic
cathedrals—cont.
France: Rayonnant style **11** *510*; **26** *45*
Germany **4** *189*; **7** *587*, *588*; **10** *451*; **12** *492*; **13** *47*, *48*; **28** *182*; **31** *569*
Germany: Transitional style **31** *284*
Greece **2** 11
Ireland **5** *915*, 916; **9** *321*
Italy **8** *134*; **13** 63, *66*; **16** 627; **18** *785*; **21** *530*, *531*; **25** *451*; **28** *678*, *679*; **31** *329*
Netherlands, the **13** *62*; **28** *595*
Poland **12** *823*; **18** 431
Scotland **12** *778*
Spain **2** *864*; **5** *203*; **13** *67*, 68, *69*; **19** *172*; **23** *881*; **27** *605*, *606*; **28** *708*; **31** *91*, *814*; **33** *604*
Sweden **31** *693*
Switzerland **12** *276*; **14** *518*
censers **13** *164*
chalices
England **10** 322
Hungary **13** 161–2, *162*, 170
Italy **13** *163*, 169
Poland **13** 170
Spain **13** 169
chalk **13** 135
chapels **13** 127
chantry **7** 267; **13** 84
Czech Republic **33** *742*
England **5** *514*
France **2** *862*
Lady **12** *799*; **13** *54*, *55*
Saintes-Chapelles **27** *550*
chapter houses **6** *465*; **20** *859*
chasubles **13** *197*; **32** *388*
chests **6** 559, *559*
chevets (chapels) **25** *439*
choir-stalls **7** *190*, *191*; **13** *118*, 123, 126
chronicles **13** 130
churches **1** 123; **7** 267–8*; **13** 53, 132; **29** 902
Austria **2** *777*; **14** *309*
Belgium **2** 191, *202*; **3** 542, *543*
Czech Republic **17** *585*; **18** *539*
decoration **7** *274*
England **5** *287*; **10** *229*; **12** *800*, *818*, *819*; **13** *46*, *55*, 55–6
France **5** *728*; **7** *578*; **13** *38*, *42*, *60*, 178; **24** *156*; **25** *220*; **26** *121*; **27** *253*, *541*, *542*; **31** *206*
France: Early Gothic **27** *533*
France: Flamboyant style **13** *59*
France: Rayonnant style **31** *385*
Germany **4** *191*; **8** *906*; **10** *408*, *451*, *515*; **11** *733*; **13** *49*, *57*; **18** *724*; **19** *745*; **20** *379*; **23** *314*, *316*; **31** *327*, *567*; **33** *457*
Germany: Late Gothic **18** *828*; **23** *205*
hall **13** 49, *49*, 50, *52*, 58; **23** *205*; **29** *5*
Hungary **14** *886*; **29** *75*
Italy **4** *279*; **7** *347*; **11** *205*; **13** *52*; **19** *686*; **22** *483*; **32** *215*
Lithuania **19** *495*
Netherlands, the **1** *812*; **13** *61*; **19** *100*; **22** *820*
Poland **5** *28*; **6** *531*; **8** *590*
Portugal **25** *290*; **31** *102*
Slovakia **3** *224*
Slovenia **28** *859*
Spain **3** *215*; **12** 619–20; **13** *70*
ciboria (i) (vessels) **7** *300*
clerestories **13** 40, 132
cloisters **5** *369*; **7** 455–6*, *456*
coffers **3** *580*
collections **13** 153, 155
colleges **5** *511*; **7** *566*; **12** *175*
colour **13** 135–7
commentaries **21** 620
Gothic—cont.
contracts **13** 133
copes **13** *194*; **30** *541*
copper **13** 161, 166, 167, 170
corbels **8** *836*
craftsmen and artists **13** 132–3*; **20** 332–3
crockets **8** 183, *183*
crosiers **10** 322; **13** 176
crosses **13** 165, *165*; **21** 893
crucifixes
Denmark **13** *171*
Germany **7** 593; **8** *214*; **12** *343*
Italy **8** *212*; **13** 123–4, *124*, *176*; **28** *753*
Spain **13** 122, *122*
cups **10** *323*, III1; **13** 170
custodia **29** *333*
devotional images **8** *836*; **13** 129
devotional objects **13** 129
diaper **8** 856, *857*
dictionaries **10** 209
domes **13** 65; **33** *604*
doors **27** *544*
doorways **7** *456*
drawings **2** 792; **13** 133, 136, 138
architectural **2** 347; **28** 497
Austria **2** *328*
France **2** *326*; **13** 142; **31** *275*; **32** *569*
Germany **2** *327*; **4** *189*, *191*
ink
France **13** *137*; **20** *742*
Germany **12** *385*, *387*
leadpoints **32** *570*
dyes **13** 194
effigies **13** 164; **16** *19*
embroidery **10** *181*; **13** *194*, 194–7*; **26** *721*; **30** *541*
enamel **13** 134, *158*, 167–70*, 194; **32** *213*
basse taille **10** *323*, III1; **11** 614, *615*; **13** 134, 163, *163*, 168–70*, *169*
champlevé **10** 193; **13** 167–8*, *168*
cloisonné **11** 614; **13** 161, 168*
England **10** 322; **13** 170
en ronde bosse **11** 615; **13** 170*, *170*
filigree **13** 170*
France **11** 614–15; **13** 158, 167–8, *168*, 169, *169*, 170, *170*
Germany **13** 169
Hungary **13** 170
Italy **13** 168, 169
painted **13** 170*
plique à jour **13** 170*
Poland **13** 170
Spain **13** 169
engraving **13** 168
engravings **12** 385
epitaphioi **26** *721*
ewers **11** *615*
exchanges **31** *815*
façade decoration **10** 741, 743–4
façades **2** *2*; **13** 49, 56, *57*, *64*; **16** 627
filigree **13** *162*, 163
fonts (baptismal) **9** *191*; **13** 160
fountains **11** *340*, *341*
frames **11** 376, 379–81, *380*, *381*, 398–9, *399*, 420–21, *421*, 438–40, 450–54*, *451*, *452*, *453*, 465–6, *466*, 479–83*, *481*, *496*
furniture **14** 903
gables **13** 42
gargoyles **12** 149
gate-houses **4** *770*
gems **13** 194; **32** *213*
Gesamtkunstwerk **12** 497
gesso **13** 135, 139
gilding **12** 626; **13** *109*, 136, 139; **28** IV2
gitterns **33** I2
glass **13** 134, 135, 139, 178
Gothic—cont.
gold **13** 136, 139, 168, 170, 194
France **7** 720; **10** III1; **13** 168; **26** *147*
Germany **10** *181*
Hungary **13** *162*
Italy **32** *213*
Netherlands, the **13** 159
Spain **29** *333*
gold leaf **13** 134
goldsmiths **13** 167
Graduals **13** 130
grounds **13** 135
guildhalls **19** *567*
guilds **13** 133, 137, 155
gypsum **13** 135
halls **3** *774*; **14** *45*, *74*, *76*; **23** 317
hanap covers **13** 168
heraldry **13** 128
hospitals **11** *511*
houses **4** *584*, *920*; **11** 773
iconography **7** 224; **13** 73, 127, 128–9, *131*; **28** 402
Christianity **13** 179
France **13** 179
International Gothic **13** 155
Italy **13** *129*
icons **13** *131*
incising **13** 139
initials (manuscript) **13** 137
Belgium **7** *189*
Czech Republic **4** *7*
England **17** *611*; **25** *677*, *807*
France **20** *339*
Iceland **15** *69*
Italy **19** *456*; **23** *506*
interior decoration **13** 128; **26** *555*
inventories **13** 153
iron **13** 160, 161, 166
ivory **13** 171; **21** *720*
ivory-carvings **13** *171*, 171–7*, *173*, *174*, *176*, *177*; **16** 799
jewellery **17** 519
labyrinths **18** 584, *585*
lecterns **13** 159
libraries **13** 153, 155
limestone **2** *799*; **10** *674*; **13** *90*, *101*, 103, 136
lime-wood **13** *316*; **22** *281*; **23** *887*; **29** *727*, *729*, *730*
linen **13** 194; **30** *541*; **32** *389*
liturgical books **13** 130, 136
luminance **13** 135
manuals **13** 133, 137
manuscript illumination **4** *13*; **9** *268*, *269*, *270*; **13** 128, 129–30*, 136–8*; **24** *179*
Austria **2** 792*
Catalonia **4** 764
Czech Republic **13** 137, 151
England **4** *237*; **7** *231*; **13** *130*, *131*, 136, 138, 140, 141, 147–9, 152; **17** 611, *611*, 612; **18** *703*; **20** *348*; **24** *175*; **25** *677*; **33** *200*
France **4** *10*; **7** *242*, *243*; **13** 133, 136, 138, *140*, 140, 141–2, *142*, *148*, 148–9*, 153–5, *674*; **17** *462*; **20** *332*, *647*; **26** *562*; **31** *836*
Late Gothic **19** *389*, *392*, *394*
Transitional style **31** *285*
Germany **4** *11*; **10** *723*; **13** 137, 140, 142, 151
Italy **13** 133, 137, 149; **18** *684*; **20** *331*, *650*
Late Gothic **12** *666*
Netherlands, the **22** *833*
Spain **13** 144; **29** 275, *852*
Style au fonds d'or **13** 136
Switzerland **13** 151; **30** 130*
manuscripts **3** *879*; **20** 331–3*; **28** *306*
marble **2** *482*, *483*; **13** 44, *94*, *96*, *97*, *108*; **20** *728*; **23** *587*; **24** *869*, *870*, *872*, *873*, *875*; **32** *227*
Germany **12** *400*
Gothic
marble—cont.
Italy **7** *334*
marks **13** 157, 158, 165
masonry **4** 782
mausolea **13** 71
metalwork **13** 135, 157*, 158–61*, 162*, 163–7*, *164*, *165*
Germany **13** 160–61*
Hungary **13** 161–2*
mimesis **13** 128, 138–9
miniatures (manuscript illumination) **12** *107*, *109*; **13** 130; **21** 637; **33** *308*
Czech Republic **33** *71*
England **2** *222*; **3** *879*; **4** *372*; **13** *130*, *141*, *147*; **14** *415*; **21** *729*; **25** *807*; **28** *66*
France **2** *313*; **3** *643*; **5** *207*; **7** *765*; **11** *530*; **13** *140*, *153*, *154*; **14** *414*; **16** *852*; **20** *340*, *342*, *637*, *706*, *707*, IV; **24** *116*; **28** *487*; **31** *309*
Germany **3** *472*; **33** *589*
Italy **19** *679*
Switzerland **3** *188*
mirror frames **21** *720*
mirrors **21** *720*
misericords **21** *724*
Missals **13** 130
modelling **13** 139
monasteries
Cistercian Order **11** *349*, *350*; **26** *380*; **32** *746*
Czech Republic **32** *746*
England **5** *638*; **11** *349*, *350*; **26** *380*
France **11** 510; **21** *844*; **22** *40*
Germany **7** *206*
Portugal **1** *590*
monstrances **13** 162; **29** *333*
monuments **13** 94–5; **22** 44*
mosaics **13** 134–5, 145
mouldings **22** 211, 215, 216–22*
angle-fillet **22** 213–15
Decorated style **22** 215, 219, 220, 221
Flamboyant style **22** 215, 219, 220, 221
Perpendicular style **22** 219, 220, 221, 222
Rayonnant style **22** 217, 219, 220, 221, 222
Sondergotik **22** 219
narratives **13** 128, 129, *129*
naturalism **13** 128–9*
niches **13** 82
nude figures **10** *455*; **26** *370*
oak **3** *580*, *581*; **6** *559*; **13** *114*, *118*, *119*, *121*, 135; **25** *726*
oils **13** 134
painting **13** 126–56*, *134*
Austria **2** 791–2*
Channel style **13** 140–42*
Croatia **8** 178
Czech Republic **13** 151–2*; **30** 706
England **13** 147*, 152–3*
France **11** 530–31*; **13** *142*, 147*, 153–5*
fresco **13** 133–4*; **20** *506*
Czech Republic **17** *820*
France **2** *863*; **12** *697*; **13** 135, 150; **32** *573*
Italy **11** 888, *889*, *890*, *891*, 892; **13** 132, 135, 136, 144, 145, *145*; **20** *775*; **29** *405*, *406*; **32** II2
Spain **13** 135, 150; **29** *276*
genre **12** *108*
Germany **12** 382–3*; **13** 142–3*, 151
Late Gothic **12** 385*
grisaille **13** 137, 178; **29** VI1
England **13** 136, 183
France **13** 136, *137*, 148, *148*, 181, *674*
history **13** *134*
Gothic
painting—cont.
Holy Roman Empire (before 1648) **13** 142–3*, 151–2*
Iceland **13** 143
International Gothic **13** 155–6*
Italy **13** 133, 138, 146, 149*, 155; **16** 661
landscape **5** 428; **13** 154; **18** *703*
Late Gothic **23** 256
Norway **13** 143; **23** 223
panel **13** 127, 129, 130–32*, 134–5, 136, 137; **24** 3
Austria **2** 792*; **13** 151
England **13** 138–9
Germany **13** 135, 142, 151
Italy **13** 146
Norway **13** 135, 143
Spain **13** 143, 150
pietàs **20** *207*; **25** *796*
Poland **25** 101, *102*
religious **3** *640*
Austria **13** *151*
Czech Republic **13** *152*; **17** *819*; **25** *431*; **30** *706*
England **13** *138*
France **11** *399*; **25** *794*
Germany **11** *715*; **12** *384*; **14** *455*; **20** *765*; **26** *507*
Hungary **14** *898*
Italy **3** *808*; **9** *344*; **11** *381*, *892*; **13** *129*, *146*; **16** *826*; **19** *674*, *684*; **20** *507*, *508*, *509*, *675*; **24** XII4
Italy: Gothic (Late) **12** *579*, *580*; **19** *680*
Italy: International Gothic **3** *248*; **12** *298*; **29** *598*
Netherlands, the: Late Gothic **20** *782*
Norway **13** *144*
Spain **29** *277*
Switzerland **30** *130*
Scandinavia **13** 143*
secco **13** 132, 133–4*, 135
Spain **13** 143–4*, 149–50*; **29** 275–6
Style of 1200 *see* TRANSITIONAL STYLE
Transitional style **13** 139–40*
wall **13** 127, 132*, 133–5*, 136, 137, 139, 142; **32** 805*
Austria **2** 791–2*, *791*; **7** *274*
Catalonia **3** *339*
Czech Republic **13** *134*, 151
Denmark **8** *731*
England **13** *128*, 137, 142, 153; **19** *611*, 641
France **13** 140
Germany **13** 134, 138, 139, 143
Italy **13** 144–7*
Spain **13** 144, *150*
Sweden **30** 75–7, *76*, *77*
Switzerland **30** 129–30*
palaces **13** 53
Croatia **9** *330*
England **19** *609*; **33** *64*
France **13** 59
Germany **13** *58*
Spain **13** *283*
Wales **27** *539*
palazzi **4** *775*; **13** *64*; **24** *519*; **28** *675*, *683*; **32** *628*
pastiglia **13** 139, 152
patens **10** 322
patronage **13** 127–8*, 130, 132, 133, 137, 155
France **13** 153
Italy **13** 130
sculpture **13** 76–7
stained glass **13** 178, 181, 183
pattern books **4** *187*; **13** 155
pearls **13** 194
pendants (jewellery) **13** 170
pewter **13** 161
piers (ii) (masonry) **13** 40, 43; **20** 574; **24** 749, *749*, 751, *751*; **33** *259*
pigments **13** 137

Gothic—cont.
pine **13** 135
pinnacles **24** *825*, 826
plaques **13** 168
polychromy **10** *457*; **13** *109*, *115*, *119*, *121*, *122*, *124*, *126*, 132; **25** 172
Pontificals **13** 130
poplar **13** 135
porches **13** *60*
porphyry **20** *798*
portals
France **2** *47*; **4** 581; **8** *892*; **9** 708; **10** *546*; **18** *759*; **27** *544*
Germany **29** *6*; **31** *569*
Spain **13** *282*
Switzerland **18** *875*
portraits
painting **12** 383; **13** *131*, 131–2; **25** *91*; **31** 834; **33** *300*
sculpture **2** *483*; **5** *204*; **9** *257*; **18** *420*; **22** *264*, *692*
self-portraits **18** *420*; **33** *200*
proportions (architecture) **2** 344–9*; **12** 619
proportions (human) **14** *872*
Psalters **13** 129, 136
pulpits **24** *872*; **25** *724*, 725, *726*
punching **13** 139
pyxides (boxes) **13** 167
red lead **24** 796
refectories **20** *859*
reliquaries **9** *3*; **26** 146–7*
Belgium **5** *213*
France **13** 42, 158, 168, 169, *169*, *170*; **24** *146*; **26** *147*
Germany **13** 169; **26** *371*
Italy **13** 169; **31** *535*
representation **12** 384; **13** 128–9, *129*
rock crystal **26** *147*
romance manuscripts **12** *107*; **13** 130
roods **27** *125*; **33** *17*
roofs **27** 128, 130; **30** 907
England **19** 609; **30** *904*
hammer-beam **30** *900*
Italy **13** 64
rosaries **13** 164
saints' lives **13** 128, 130, 136
sandstone **11** *751*; **12** *343*, *344*; **13** *86*, *91*, *92*, 102; **29** *6*
Germany **26** *370*, *372*
screens (i) (architectural) **13** 127
choir-screens **12** 399
rood **13** 127; **28** *292*; **33** *17*
scripts **28** 305–6*, *306*
sculpture **7** 455*; **13** 71–126*; **28** 402
allegorical **5** *176*
architectural **10** 741, 743
Austria **32** *441*
England **33** *62*
France **2** *47*; **6** *497*; **26** *118*, *119*; **27** *544*; **28** *416*
Germany **20** *89*; **22** *315*; **29** *6*
Italy **5** *430*; **13** *93*; **26** *400*; **32** *227*
Spain **10** 743–4
Switzerland **14** *318*
Austria **2** 798–9*
Belgium **8** 662; **13** 98–101*, 109–15*, *112*
bronze **13** *160*
Cistercian Order **13** 97–8
column statues **1** *781*; **6** *495*; **7** 642; **9** *257*; **13** 73, *74*
Denmark **13** 118; **26** 304
England **7** 456; **10** 266; **13** 80–82*, *81*, *84*, 84–5*, *121*, 121–2*; **33** 550
Decorated style **10** 673
Early Gothic **33** 61
14th cent. **13** 82–3*
France **7** 455–6; **13** 72–7*, *76*, 125–6*, 169; **24** 159
15th cent. **13** 77–9*

Gothic
sculpture—cont.
Germany **12** *344*; **13** 86–7, *160*; **20** *129*
Early Gothic **12** 399–400; **22** 692
Late Gothic **13** *316*; **32** *605*
Holy Roman Empire (before 1648) **13** 85*, 86–7*, 115–18*, *160*
Hungary **14** 893
Italy **13** 87–92*, 93*, 123–4*; **16** 688*
Campania **13** 98*
Emilia-Romagna **13** 95–6*
Late Gothic **16** 692*
Lazio **13** 97–8*
Lombardy **13** 94–5*
Tuscany **13** 93–4*
Umbria **13** 96–7*
Veneto **13** 95*
limestone **13** *90*
marble **13** *94*, *96*, *97*, *108*; **20** *728*; **26** *400*
Italy **2** *482*, *483*; **24** *873*, *875*
monumental **13** 140, 141
Netherlands, the **13** 98–101*, 109–15*
Norway **13** 102, 119
palmesels **23** *887*
pietàs **2** *799*; **8** *383*
Poland **25** 110
Portugal **13** 101–2*, 124–5*; **25** *301*
relief
England **9** *681*; **10** *674*; **27** *629*
France **8** *892*; **24** *155*
Germany **13** *86*; **22** *280*; **29** *818*
Italy **7** *334*; **11** *200*; **16** *687*; **23** *586*, *587*; **24** *869*, *870*, *874*
Poland **31** *394*
Spain **19** *173*
Sweden **13** *103*
religious **4** *583*; **10** *455*, *457*; **19** *603*; **26** *370*
Belgium **13** *99*, *100*, *111*
Czech Republic **13** *90*
England **10** *259*
France **13** *126*; **24** *157*; **28** *866*; **31** *382*
France: Late Gothic **19** *138*
Germany **7** *589*; **11** *751*; **12** *400*; **13** *91*, *92*; **22** *281*; **29** *728*, *729*
Hungary **14** *892*
Italy **2** *482*; **20** *728*; **24** *873*, *875*; **28** *680*
Italy: Lombardy **13** *94*
Netherlands, the **3** *456*; **13** *114*, *115*
Norway **13** *119*
Poland **25** *111*
Spain **13** *109*
sandstone **13** *92*
Scandinavia **13** 102–3*, 118–20*
Spain **13** 103–8*, 122–3*; **29** 288–9
stone **13** 72–9*, *74*, *75*, *76*, 80–83*, *81*, *84*, 84–5*, 86–92*, *88*, *91*, 93–108*, *93*, *99*, *100*, *104*, *109*; **22** *264*; **33** *62*
France **13** *78*
Sweden **13** 102, 119, 120; **30** 83
Switzerland **30** 136
tomb
France **13** *78*
Italy **13** *96*, *97*
Portugal **13** *101*
Spain **13** *107*, *108*; **28** *724*
Switzerland **22** *919*
wood **13** 109–20*, *111*, *112*, *115*, 121–6*, *126*; **14** *892*
sgraffito **13** 139
shields **14** 405

Gothic—cont.
shrines (i) (cult) **13** *94*; **23** *311*; **28** IV2
silk **11** *638*; **13** 194, 197*; **30** *541*, 552; **32** *389*
Germany **10** *181*
Italy **13** *197*, 197
Sicily **13** 197
Spain **13** 197
silver **9** *3*; **13** 135, 159, 168, 194; **23** *311*; **30** *541*
silver-gilt **7** *300*; **13** *158*, 166; **30** *541*
England **10** *323*
France **11** *615*; **13** *168*, *169*, *170*
Italy **13** *163*
Spain **29** *333*
silver-stain **13** 178, 183
soapstone **13** 102
spires **13** 55, 56, 58, 62–3; **27** 628; **29** *412*, 412–13, *413*
stained glass **13** 127, 132*, 134, 135–6, 178*, 189*; **19** 356; **29** 501–3
Austria **13** 151, 186, *188*; **29** IV
Belgium **13** 181–3*, *182*
Cistercian Order **13** 136
Czech Republic **13** 187, 189
Denmark **13** 190
England **5** *647*, 647–8, *648*; **13** *135*, 136, 140, 142, 152, 178, 183–5*, *184*; **14** *422*; **19** *406*; **29** 501, 503, II; **33** *64*, *549*
Finland **13** 190
France **3** *459*; **4** *582*; **6** *498*; **13** 135, *136*, 136, 140–41*, 142, *143*, 149, 178–81*, *179*, *180*; **16** *837*; **26** *120*, 123; **27** *549*; **29** 501, 503, *510*, *511*, *759*, I, VI1
Channel style **13** *143*
Early Gothic **28** *417*
Germany **2** *720*; **7** *590*; **10** *452*; **12** 382; **13** 135, 142, *185*, 185–8*, *186*; **29** *502*, III
Early Gothic **22** 693
Holy Roman Empire (before 1648) **13** 185–8*; **29** 502, *503*
Italy **13** 192–3*, *193*
Norway **13** 190
Poland **13** 189, *189*
Portugal **13** 192*
Romania **13** 189
Scandinavia **13** 190–91*
Spain **12** *740*; **13** *191*, 191–2*; **19** *174*
Sweden **13** 190–91, *190*
Switzerland **13** 186; **30** 130*
Wales **13** 183, 184
statuettes **13** *158*, 172–4, *173*
stiff-leaf **29** *659*
stone **1** *709*; **5** *430*; **8** *382*; **9** *191*; **13** 72–9*, *74*, *75*, *76*, *78*, 80–83*, *81*, *84*, 84–5*, 86–92*, *88*, 93–108*, *93*, *99*, *100*, *103*, *104*, *105*, *107*; **22** *264*, *692*, *693*
stucco **29** 818, *818*
styles
Backsteingotik **4** 776; **7** 206; **13** 56*
Beautiful Style *see schöner Stil*
Channel **30** 745
Court **12** 383
Curvilinear **8** 610
Decorated **3** 121; **5** 374–5; **8** 610–11*, *611*; **9** 670; **13** 34; **23** 251; **26** 361
Early English **3** 895; **9** 669–70*; **13** 34
Early Gothic **9** 671–2*; **13** 34; **31** 283
First Gothic *see* Early Gothic
Flamboyant **2** 295; **8** 611; **10** 401; **11** 153–5*, *154*; **13** 34; **24** 115
France **11** 511

Gothic
styles
Flamboyant—cont.
Poland **25** 126
Spain **14** 134
tracery *see under* TRACERY → types → bar
Geometric **8** 610
High Gothic **11** 510; **13** 34; **14** 518–19*
Hochgotik see High Gothic
International Gothic **18** 827
Late Gothic **2** 204; **8** 611; **11** 153; **13** 34; **18** 826–8*, *828*
England **12** 818
France **11** 153–5
Germany **13** 211; **18** 419; **29** 65*
Poland **25** 96
see also ANTWERP MANNERISM; EARLY NETHERLANDISH STYLE; GOTHIC SURVIVAL
opus francigenum **23** 462*
Perpendicular **11** 153; **13** 34; **24** 465–6*, *466*; **26** 361; **33** 202
Premier art gothique *see* Early Gothic
Rayonnant **6** 530; **13** 34, 53, 142; **14** 519; **24** 115, 132, 774; **26** 44–6*, 453
France **11** 510–11
reduced Gothic *see* Reduktionsgotik
Reduktionsgotik **12** 823; **13** 34; **26** 74*
schöner Stil (Beautiful Style) **13** 155
Czech Republic **13** *90*
Holy Roman Empire (before 1648) **13** 89–90
Poland **25** 110, *110*
Soft style *see weicher Stil*
Sondergotik **11** 153; **13** 34; **29** 65*
Spätgotik see Late Gothic
Style of 1200 *see* TRANSITIONAL STYLE
weicher Stil (Soft Style) **13** 155
Germany **12** 383
Holy Roman Empire (before 1648) **13** 89–90, 187
Netherlands, the **20** 688
Slovenia **28** 861
Zackenstil **28** 860; **32** 805; **33** 588*
synagogues **25** *444*
tabernacles (ii) (receptacle) **3** *568*; **13** 167, *168*
tapestries **2** 49–51, *50*, 111; **11** *638*; **13** 194–7*, *195*
tempera **13** 134, 135
textiles **13** 194–7*
theories **13** 34
thick-wall structures **30** 729
threads **10** *181*; **13** 194
tiles **30** *876*
tin **13** 139
tombs
England **1** *517*; **13** 84; **19** *605*
France **13** *78*
Germany **13** 160; **30** *535*; **32** *607*
Italy **13** 95–6, *96*, *97*; **31** *3*, *4*
Portugal **13** *101*
Spain **13** *107*, *108*; **28** *724*
Switzerland **30** 136
wall **31** *124*
towers
Belgium **13** 62–3
bell-towers **13** 64; **28** *675*
England **4** *779*
Germany **13** 56; **31** *568*
Ireland **5** *915*
Italy **27** *751*
Netherlands, the **13** *62*, 62–3
Spain **13** 68

Gothic—cont.
town halls
Belgium **3** *544*; **4** *925*; **5** *53*; **12** *523*
Czech Republic **4** *833*
Italy **13** *773*
Poland **30** *203*; **31** *196*; **33** *417*
Slovakia **3** *224*
tracery **31** 270
bar **13** 46, 48, 53, 178; **14** 519
blind **7** 860
England **10** 228; **13** 54, 55
France **11** 153, *154*; **13** 59
Germany **13** 56, *57*
Perpendicular **31** 273
plate **13** 40; **31** *270*
Rayonnant style **31** 273
treatises
architecture **12** 619–20; **31** 835
colour **13** 138
manuscript illumination **13** 136
tympana
France **13** *75*; **19** *128*; **27** *543*, *544*; **31** *493*
Germany **13** *88*; **20** *798*
Spain **13** *104*, *109*
typological cycles **29** *510*
underdrawings **20** *348*
universities **13** 130
varnishes **13** 134
vaults (ceiling) **20** *583*
cellular **13** 58
Czech Republic **25** *441*
England **10** 228; **13** 54; **19** 402, *402*, 403, *602*, 602
fan **13** 55; **19** *602*
France **3** 458; **13** 59
Germany **10** *221*; **12** 366
Perpendicular style **19** *602*
Poland **13** 57
rib **6** 178; **13** 35, 36, 51
rib: curving **32** 90
rib: Germany **14** 268
rib: jumping **13** 57
rib: lierne **13** 54, 69
rib: net **12** 366
rib: quadripartite **32** 92
rib: sexpartite **32** 93
rib: star **13** 57; **24** *347*, 348; **33** *259*
rib: tierceron **13** 45
rib: triradial **12** 493; **32** 747
velvet **13** 194
verre églomisé **13** 139
vestments (ecclesiastical) **13** 196
weaving **30** 552
weepers **33** *28*
windows **13** 35, 132, 136
band **13** 136, 178, 181, 183; **29** 502, VI1
clerestory **13** 179, 181
England **19** 403
lancet **13** 181
medallion **13** 178, *179*, 181, 183; **29** 501
medallions **13** 135, *135*
oriel **25** *711*
rose **13** 191; **26** *45*; **31** *270*
women artists **33** *308*
wood **8** *383*; **13** 109–20*, *111*, *112*, *115*, 121–6*, *122*, *124*, *126*; **14** *892*; **17** *741*
wood-carvings **13** 143; **30** 136
woodcuts **2** 792; **12** 385
wool **11** *638*; **13** 194
workshops **29** *852*
Gothic, Modern *see* MODERN GOTHIC STYLE
Gothic bond *see under* BONDING
Gothic clocks *see under* CLOCKS → types
Gothick **10** 276; **12** 176; **13** 198–9*; **29** 890
architecture **14** 255; **17** 877; **28** 227
colleges **14** *255*
gardens **12** 129
houses **10** *234*; **32** *826*
tracery **31** 271

Gothic Majesty, Master of the **10** 244; **26** 677; **31** 284; **33** 240
Gothic order *see under* ORDERS (ARCHITECTURAL) → types
Gothic Revival **9** 739; **13** 33, 198–209*; **14** 580; **23** 209, 498; **25** 711; **26** 737; **27** 352; **32** 414
art forms
architecture **13** *202*
Australia **32** *858*
Austria **13** *204*
Belgium **3** *548*; **5** 320; **13** *208*; **33** 307
Britain **23** 498
Canada **3** *73*; **11** *837*
Ecuador **9** *711*
England **4** *215*; **5** *194*, *195*, *314*, *317*; **6** *561*; **10** *237*; **12** 926; **13** *203*; **18** *888*; **20** *237*; **24** *307*; **25** *714*, I2; **29** *765*, *766*; **30** *533*
France **7** 774; **11** 521–2*; **12** 178; **13** *202*
Germany **13** *200*; **26** 102
Hungary **14** *888*
Indian subcontinent **4** *289*
Ireland **16** *10*
Italy **28** *393*
Netherlands, the **8** *299*; **22** 828–9
Norway **23** 233
Russia **27** *376*, 377
Scotland **25** *36*
United States of America **8** *575*; **11** *849*; **12** *927*; **17** 877; **24** *281*; **26** *214*; **31** 232, 592, 595, 688, *690*
brick **4** 787
crockets **8** 184
dictionaries **10** 208
frames **11** *463*
furniture **2** *758*; **8** 235; **13** *207*; **29** *318*; **30** 782; **31** 629
gargoyles **12** 149
interior decoration **11** 580; **16** 24; **19** *614*; **31** 620
metalwork **8** 202; **10** 335, 342; **30** 107
mouldings **22** 211, 212
ornament **23** 546
polychromy **30** *533*
reliquaries **32** *598*
stained glass **29** 497
tiles **30** 876, *877*
title-pages **31** 49
tombs **31** 131, *345*
tracery **31** 271
wallpaper **23** *546*
commentaries **14** 748
regional traditions
Austria **2** 787
Belgium **3** 578, 585, 618, 762, 885; **18** 66; **33** 7
Britain **2** 569; **13** 198; **26** 738
Canada **5** 560–61; **33** 213
Caribbean Islands **5** 749
Czech Republic **21** 757
England **7** 663; **10** 235, 236–7, 280, 281–2, 295, 298; **13** 206, 207, 209; **26** 743; **29** 764; **32** 824; **33** 445–6
France **3** 288; **13** 206, 208; **28** 346
Germany **12** 415, 452; **13** 206, 208; **14** 227; **17** 699; **23** 372; **29** 576; **31** 580; **33** 380, 745
Honduras **14** 713
Hungary **29** 607
Indian subcontinent **4** 288, 289
Ireland **16** 10–11
New Zealand **22** 230
Romania **26** 709
Scotland **28** 229, 230, 248
Spain **29** 343
United States of America **8** *110*; **13** 208; **33** 134, 213, 263
Venezuela **32** 170
Gothic Revival—cont.
see also HIGH VICTORIAN GOTHIC; PERPENDICULAR GOTHIC REVIVAL
Gothic survival **3** 545; **13** 199, 209–11*, *211*
see also GOTHIC → styles → Late Gothic
Goths **14** 182; **21** 500, 501, 502, 503; **30** 64
Gøti **26** 640
Götke, Conradt **19** 496
Gotland **8** 738; **13** 103, 120; **30** *65*, 66–7, 75
Gotlib, Henryk **13** 212*
Gotō (family) **17** 29, 424; **31** 81
Gotō, Shuichi **17** 249
GoToba, Emperor (*reg* 1183-98) **10** 192; **13** 212–13*; **17** 225
Gotoh, Keita **17** 429
Gotō Saijirō **18** 537
Götsch, Joseph **12** 405
GoTsuchimikado, Emperor (*reg* 1464-1500) **31** 197, 198
Gott, Joseph **13** 213*
Gottardi (Folin), Roberto **8** 233; **13** 213*
Gottardo de Scottis **13** 213–14*
Göttel, Jakobus **8** 824
Gottereau, Paul **5** 72; **26** 709, 718
works **26** *709*
Gottfried, Johann Ludwig **21** 152
Gottfried Keller-Stiftung *see under* WINTERTHUR (SWITZERLAND)
Gottfriedt, Johann **18** 851
Gottfried von Strassburg **26** 563
Gotthelf, Jeremias **2** 116
Gottifredi, Francesco **21** 27
Götting, Gottfried **13** 214*
Gotting, Johann Peter **13** 214
Götting Church **32** 822
Göttingen
Barfüsserkirche **20** 683
Georg-August-Universität **11** 118
houses **32** 282
Jakobikirche **14** 81, *81*
Johanniskirche **14** 81
observatory **23** 340
Göttingen Model Book **20** *324*, 325; **24** 270
Göttinger Barfüsseraltar, Master of the **20** 683–4*
Gottlieb, Adolph **13** 214–15*
dealers **16** 820; **18** 162; **24** 213
groups and movements **1** 78, 84, 85, 87; **27** 219; **31** 138, 607
patrons and collectors **9** 189
works **13** *215*; **17** 568; **18** 718; **21** 897
Gottlieb, Conrad **2** 805; **15** 866; **32** 777
Gottlieb, Filip **13** 215
Gottlieb, Leopold **13** 215
Gottlieb, Marceli **13** 215
Gottlieb, Marcin **13** 215
Gottlieb, Maurycy (Moses) **13** 215–16*; **17** 576, 580
Gottlob, Ernst **2** 240
Gottlob, Kaj **13** 216*
Gottorp Castle **8** 738
Gottorp Giant Globe **12** 811
Gottschalk, Albert **13** 216*
Gottsched, Joachim Christoph (*fl* 1760) **10** 207; **24** 443
Gottsched, Johann Christoph (1700-66) **13** 216–17*
Gottwald, Hynek **8** 402
Gottwaldov *see* ZLÍN
Göttweig Monastery **2** 780, 783, 825, 828; **3** 876; **28** 123
Götz, Gottfried Bernhard *see* GÖZ, GOTTFRIED BERNHARD
Götz, Hermann **4** 64; **33** 343
Götz, Johann Georg **13** 217
Götz, Joseph Matthias **11** 127; **12** 403, 404; **13** 217*
Götz, Karl-Otto **13** 217–18*
dealers **7** 842
Götz, Karl-Otto—cont.
groups and movements **2** 545; **7** 489; **12** 397; **21** 341; **25** 786
patrons and collectors **14** 238
pupils **25** 153; **26** 355; **32** 834
Götz, Sebastian **13** 218*; **28** 138
Götzenberger, Jakob **13** 218–19*
Gotzens **15** 139
Götzinger, Hans **6** 363
Gotzkowsky, Johann Ernst **3** 804; **12** 473; **26** 732
gouache *see under* PAINTS → types
gouache manner *see under* ENGRAVINGS → types
gouache paintings *see under* PAINTING → forms
Goubau, Alexander **27** 291
Goubau, Antoni, I **13** 221–2*; **18** 787
works **2** 164; **26** *772*
Goubau Lithographic studios **18** 877
Goubault (family) **3** 598
Goubauw, Alexander (*fl* 1633) **12** 851
Goubeau, Antoni, I, *see* GOUBAU, ANTONI, I
Gouda **13** 222*; **22** *813*
ceramics **22** 878
St Janskerk **13** 222*; **22** 836; **29** 504, 505
stained glass **8** 102–3, *103*; **22** 901
Stadhuis **22** 822
Stedelijk Museum Het Catharina Gasthuis **22** 906
tapestries **22** 897; **30** 318
tiles **30** 878
Gouda, Cornelis van **14** 293
Goudargues **26** 603
Goudeau **33** 198
Goudge, Edward **6** 515; **10** 274; **29** 835; **33** 244
Goudin-Thebia, Serge **11** 760
Goudon **23** 536
Goudréaux, Pierre **12** 391
Goudt, Hendrik **10** 157; **13** 222–3*
patrons and collectors **5** 325; **32** 7
works **10** 159, 160, 161, 391; **13** *223*
Goudvink *see* FYT, JAN
Goudy, Frederic William **13** 223–4*; **31** 496
works **31** *496*
Gouers, Daniel **11** 632
works **11** *632*
Gouffier, Adrien de, Bishop of Albi **1** 577
Gouffier, Artus **13** 224
Gouffier, Claude, Duc de Roannez *see* ROANNEZ, CLAUDE GOUFFIER, 1st Duc de
Gouffier, Guillaume (i) (*c.* 1420-95) **13** 224
Gouffier, Guillaume (ii) (*c.* 1488-1525) **13** 224
Gouffier, Louis **13** 224
Gouge, Edward **26** 394
Gough, A. **4** 823
Gough, Frederick, 5th Baron Calthorpe **30** 533
Gough, Hugh Roumieu **28** 349
Gough, Piers **13** 224–5*
Gough, Richard **13** 225*
Goujon, Jean **1** 766; **11** 637; **13** 225–7*
architecture **10** 744; **11** 258, 265
caryatids **5** 905; **13** *227*
châteaux **9** 706
ecclesiastical buildings **24** 159
façades **10** 744; **24** 161
fountains **11** 342, *342*, 513; **13** *226*; **23** 795; **24** 133
hôtels particuliers **20** 292
museums **11** 656
assistants **22** 448
attributions **11** 265, 532; **24** 812; **27** 247
Goujon, Jean—cont.
book illustrations **20** 489
collaboration **9** 176; **11** 557; **19** 237; **20** 488; **22** 448
groups and movements **20** 281
patrons and collectors **7** 778; **22** 31
Goujon, Paul **12** 832
Goulandris (family) **13** 359
Goulandris, N. P. **8** 323
Goulandris Foundation *see under* ANDROS (GREECE)
Goulandris Master **8** 315
Goulburn
Cathedral **2** 738
law courts **18** 888
Gould, Carl F. **28** 327
Gould, James **8** 492
Gould, Jay **14** 223, 482; **18** 161
Gould, John **4** 362
Gould, William **12** 134
Goulding, Frederick **19** 488; **25** 628; **33** 140
Goulet, Michel **5** 572
Goulet, Yann **16** 21
Goullon, Louis **21** 641
Goullons **11** 630
Goulon, Jules Du *see* DU GOULON, JULES
Goulton-Constable, J. **18** 585
Goult Priory **26** 597, *598*
Goulty, H. N. **1** 146
Goumenitsa **14** 358
Gounaropoulos, Giorgos **13** 227–8*, 353
Gounaropoulos Museum *see under* ATHENS → museums
Gounod, Charles **20** 387
Gounouilhiou, Simon **30** 148
Goupil, (Jean-Michel-) Adolphe **2** 499; **4** 588; **8** 463; **10** 680; **11** 325; **12** 488; **13** 228*; **16** 876; **20** 351; **24** 141; **25** 617
engravings **12** 724
paintings **3** 437; **4** 252; **6** 532; **8** 717; **18** 696; **22** 99; **30** 32
Goupil, (Jules) Adolphe **11** 663, 664; **28** 68
Goupil, Adolphe, & Co. **14** 43
paintings **10** 727; **14** 47; **15** 155; **19** 869; **24** 883
photographs **22** 723; **24** 661; **30** 569
prints **12** 30; **18** 161; **26** 233; **29** 723
staff **12** 856, 857
Goupil, Albert **4** 588; **16** 554, 556, 559; **19** 755
Goupil, Vibert & Co. **19** 260; **29** 382
Goupil gallery **4** 589; **6** 519; **25** 868
Goupilgravure *see under* PRINTING → processes
Goupy, C.-M. **19** 161
Goupy, Joseph **13** 228–9*
collaboration **30** 890
groups and movements **14** 638
patrons and collectors **5** 65; **14** 143
pupils **6** 87; **14** 144
Goupy, Louis **4** 609; **13** 228
Gouraud, François **29** 245
Gourdaine, Jan Piotr Norblin de la *see* NORBLIN DE LA GOURDAINE, JAN PIOTR
Gourdelle, Pierre **7** 464; **12** 203
Gourdon **21** 162, *163*
gourds **13** 229*
historical and regional traditions
Africa **1** *302*, 302–4*, *303*, 367, 382
Argentina **13** 229
Asante **1** 303
Cameroon **1** 303; **11** 828
China **7** 113, 141, 147; **13** 229*
Fon **1** 303
gourds
historical and regional traditions—cont.
Fulani **1** *302*, 303, 382; **11** 827–9*, *828*
Hausa **1** 303, 382; **14** 233
Ibibio **1** 303
Igbo **1** 303
Japan **17** 400
Kenya **3** 442
Mesoamerica, Pre-Columbian **21** 256
Niger **11** 828, *828*
Nigeria **1** *248*, 302, *302*, 303, *303*; **11** 828
Nuba **23** 275
Peru **13** 229; **24** 500
South America, Pre-Columbian **13** 229*; **29** 159, *159*, 188
Tarascan **30** 341
Yoruba **1** 303
techniques
beadwork **3** 442
carving **1** 303; **7** 141; **29** 159
dyeing **1** 303; **11** 828
engraving **1** *302*, 302–3, *303*; **11** 828
painting **1** 303
uses
boxes **1** 367
kites **7** 113
musical instruments **1** 302
pipes (smoking) **1** 367
rattles **21** 256
Gourgue, Jacques Enguerrand **14** 58
Gourley, R. **28** 483
Gourlier, Charles-Pierre **13** 231*
Gourma **31** 73
Gourmont (family) **13** 231
Gourmont, François de **13** 232; **33** 357
Gourmont, Gilles **13** 231
Gourmont, Jean de (i) (*c.* 1483-*c.* 1551) **10** 387; **13** 231*
works **13** *231*; **20** 793
Gourmont, Jean de (ii) (*c.* 1537-*c.* 1598) **13** 231–2*
Gourmont, Remy de **13** 232*; **17** 449; **33** 361
collaboration **11** 75
works **8** 629; **10** 508
Gourmont, Robert **13** 231
Gourna, New *see under* THEBES (i) (EGYPT)
Gournay, Michel Amelot de **24** 805
Gournay-sur-Aronde **6** 157; **25** 538
Gournia **4** 607; **13** 232–3*, *362*; **21** *651*
bronzes **21** 688
faience (i) (glass) **21** 683
ivory-carvings **21** 680, 682
pottery **21** 667, *669*
shrines (i) (cult) **21** 654
silver **21** 658, *658*, 688
tombs **21** 656
towns **21** 664
wall paintings **8** 153
Goury, Jules **16** 547; **22** 59; **25** 172, 623; **28** 398
Goussé, Thomas **19** 249
Gousset, Pierre **26** 556
Goussi-Desylla, Eleni **2** 175
Goust, L. **6** 397; **28** 414
Gout, Paul Emile Antoine **22** 40
goût grec **11** 518; **13** 233*
see also NEO-CLASSICISM → regional traditions → France
Goutheinze **29** 834
Gouthière, Pierre **11** 625, 627; **13** 233–4*
attributions **26** 182; **33** 48
collaboration **9** 379; **11** 627; **26** 376
groups and movements **10** 96
patrons and collectors **20** 897; **27** 223; **28** 527

Gouthière, Pierre—cont.
pupils **30** 747
works **3** 523; **11** *626*, 627, 636
Goutsteen, Peeter **32** 709
Goutzwiller, Charles **14** 390
Gouvaert, Abraham *see* GOVAERTS, ABRAHAM
Gouverneur Factory **5** 343
Gouy **25** 475
Gouyn, Charles **6** 533; **10** 308; **29** 432
Govaers, Daniel *see* GOUERS, DANIEL
Govaerts, Abraham **5** 352; **11** 718, 720; **13** 234*; **17** 647
Govaerts, Willem **13** 234
Govancroft Pottery **28** 258
Govardhan (*fl c.* 1596-1640) **13** 235–6*; **15** 587, 589, 594, *594*
works **13** *235*; **15** 584; **16** 346
Govardhan (*fl* 1720-40) **15** 591
Goven, Jan van **13** 895
government buildings **13** 236–9*; **31** 235, 236
Argentina **2** *396*
Australia **2** *737*; **5** *602*
Belarus' **21** *696*
Belgium **5** *42*
Brazil **4** *713*; **23** *119*
Canada **11** *837*
Chile **6** *593*
Denmark **14** *152*
England **10** *237*; **13** *237*; **17** *903*; **19** *587*; **28** *909*
Finland **10** *218*
France **2** *172*; **6** *534*; **22** *454*
Germany **3** *793*; **22** *300*
Hungary **14** *888*
Indian subcontinent **19** *47*
Japan **17** 46, *88*, *92*
Netherlands, the **9** *368*
Pakistan **16** *93*
Peru **19** *387*
Russia **22** *174*; **26** *730*; **33** *600*
Sri Lanka **29** *455*
Switzerland **11** *841*
Union of Soviet Socialist Republics **19** *207*
United States of America **8** *470*; **13** *238*, *611*; **26** *352*; **31** *591*
Federal style **31** *591*
18th cent. **4** *473*
19th cent. **29** *771*
20th cent. **31** *598*
Uruguay **31** *753*
Venezuela **32** *169*
see also CURIAE; LAW COURTS; SENATE- HOUSES; TOWN HALLS
see also PARLIAMENT BUILDINGS
Govinda III, Ruler (*reg c.* 794-814) (Rashtrakuta) **10** 150
Govindaswami, S. K. **15** 560
Govindnagar **15** 455, 458; **20** 816, 819
Govind Sharma **15** 648
Govone Castello **16** 720
Govora Monastery **25** 340
Gow, Leonard **14** 604
Gowan, James **7** 788; **12** 793; **13** 239*; **29** 677
Gowane **22** 244
Gowenius, Peder **20** 910
Gower, George **13** 239–40*; **28** 466
collaboration **19** 515
groups and movements **10** 142
patrons and collectors **31** 415
works **10** 246, *247*; **13** *239*
Gower, Henry de *see* HENRY DE GOWER
Gower, John **28** 66
Gower, Lady **12** 742
Gower, Ronald (Charles) **19** 271*
Gowin, Emmet **13** 240*
Gowing, Lawrence **10** 652
gowns **9** 269–70, 274, 275, 276; **23** 302
Goya (y Lucientes), Francisco (José) de **3** 425; **6** 124; **11** 218; **13** 240–53*, *248*; **19** *660*; **27** 819; **29** 283
assistants **10** 534; **17** 681
attributions **6** 48; **12** 923; **19** 762, *763*
catalogues **9** 60
collaboration **3** 426; **5** 453
copies **18** 678
drawings **9** 224; **29** 283
exhibitions **1** 154
frames **11** 488, 489, *493*
groups and movements **26** 736, 738, 740, 742
paintings **14** 586; **20** 67; **25** 285
frescoes **5** 368
grisaille **5** 453
history **3** 389; **13** *246*; **20** 64; **22** 522
mythological **13** *248*
nude figures **9** 244
oil sketches **23** 381
portraits **1** *528*; **13** *244*, *245*; **25** *286*
religious **31** 90
satirical **27** 868, 870*
still-lifes **29** 669
patrons and collectors
Alba, Maria Teresa Cayetana Silva y Alvárez y Toledo, 13th Duquesa de **1** 528
Altamira, Vicente Joaquín Osorio Moscoso y Guzmán, 11th Conde de **1** 690
Beisteguy y Benítez, Carlos de **3** 522
Bellio, Georges de **3** 671
Beruete (y Moret), Aureliano (de) **3** 869
Borbón y Braganza, Sebastián Gabriel **4** 378
Bourbon II., Luis Antonio, Infante of Spain **4** 564
Brame, Hector (-Henri-Clément) **9** 424
Ceán Bermúdez, Juan Agustín **6** 124
Charles III, King of Spain (*reg* 1759-88) **4** 564
Charles IV, King of Spain (*reg* 1788-1808) **4** 566; **29** 352
Contini Bonacossi, Alessandro, Conte **7** 782
Esterházy, Miklós II, Prince (1765-1833) **10** 530
Ferdinand VII, King of Spain (*reg* 1808; 1814-33) **4** 566
Godoy (y Alvárez de Faria), Manuel, Príncipe de la Paz **12** 839
Groult, Camille **13** 705
Harris, Tomás **14** 195
Iriarte, Bernardo de **16** 48
Jovellanos, Gaspar Melchor de **17** 673
López Cepero, Manuel **19** 658
Louis-Philippe, King of the French (*reg* 1830-48) **23** 521; **30** 385
Martínez Pérez, Sebastián **20** 502
Museo Nacional de Bellas Artes (Buenos Aires) **2** 404
Museu de Arte de São Paulo **4** 726
Osuna, Duques de **29** 353
Osuna, Duquesa de (1752-1834) **23** 626
Péreire (family) **24** 396
Pollok House **28** 273
Salamanca (y Mayol), José, Marqués de **27** 607
Stirling-Maxwell, William **29** 680
Valde-Iñigo, Marqués de **31** 808
prints **5** 757; **7** 648; **20** 602; **25** 596, 599
aquatints **13** *243*
Goya (y Lucientes), Francisco (José) de
prints—cont.
etchings **2** 240, *241*; **5** 685; **25** 72, 607, 619; **27** 870
lithographs **19** 486; **20** 602; **25** 345
reproductions in tapestry **10** 504
reproductive prints by others **1** 776; **12** 28
tapestries **4** 566; **9** 30; **29** 350; **30** 325, *325*
Goya, Javier **13** 246, 252; **27** 607
Goya, Mariano **13** 249
Goya: Revista de arte **5** 529; **24** 429, 452
Go Yayanagi *see* YAYANAGI, GO
Goybault, Paoul **13** 254*
Goyen, Jan (Josephsz.) van **7** 673; **13** 255–7*; **14** 41
attributions **18** 155; **28** 360
methods **24** 493; **31** 578
patrons and collectors **5** 679; **12** 504; **21** 485; **27** 266, 463
pupils **3** 757; **5** 343; **19** 101; **29** 585
teachers **19** 101; **30** 60; **32** 137
works **5** 682; **13** *256*, *257*; **18** 710; **20** 424; **22** 840, 844; **29** 375
Goyeneche, Juan de **7** 287; **29** 331
Goyen-Matignon, Jacques III de, Comte de Thorigny *see* THORIGNY, JACQUES III, Comte de
Goyer, Jacob Jansz. de **27** 455
Goyer, Salomon (Jacobsz.) de *see* RUYSDAEL, SALOMON (JACOBSZ.) VAN
Goyers (family) **3** 585
Goyō Hashiguchi *see* HASHIGUCHI, GOYŌ
Gōyō Hirata *see* HIRATA, GOYO
Goyot, Laurent **2** 703
GoYōzei, Emperor (*reg* 1586-1611) **17** 233, 728, 784; **18** 181, 558
Goyrand, Claude **14** 394; **15** 31
Goyri, Roberto González *see* GONZÁLEZ GOYRI, ROBERTO
Goys, Antoine de **4** 442
Goyvaert, Abraham *see* GOVAERTS, ABRAHAM
Göz, Gottfried Bernhard **2** 719; **13** 258*; **18** 106
groups and movements **26** 498
teachers **3** 779
Göz, Johann **19** 781
Gozaemon Tamura *see* TAMURA GOZAEMON
Gozalvo, Pablo **31** 90
Gozbert, Abbot of St Gall **5** 795; **12** 363; **21** 835; **27** 554, 555–6
Gozbertus, Master **26** 684
Goźlice Church **26** 637
Gözlükule **21** 166
Gozo **20** 218
Qala Sanctuary **20** 213
Temple of Nadur **24** 866
Gozón Castle **2** 654
Gozo of Abomey **1** 313
Gozzadini (family) **8** 3
Gozzadini, Annibale **7** 925
Gozzadini, Bonifazio **24** 199
Gozzadini, G., Count **32** 562
Gozzi, Alvisio **20** 278
Gozzi, Gasparo **12** 292; **13** 258*
Gozzo **18** 446
Gozzoli, Benozzo **13** 259–62*
assistants **12** 765; **24** 754
collaboration **2** 38; **9** 96; **12** 544; **27** 174
frescoes **2** *725*; **11** 56
patrons and collectors **2** 725; **11** 712; **14** 148
pupils **19** 894; **23** 89
restorations by others **4** 493
Gozzoli, Benozzo—cont.
works **13** *259*, *261*; **14** 517; **16** 629, 659, 660; **18** 704; **21** 12, 468; **22** 680; **23** 586; **24** 855, 860; **26** 186, 765; **27** 750, 751; **29** 423
G Plan Ltd **14** 523
Graadt van Roggen, Johannes Mattheus **23** 125
Graaff-Reinet **1** 318; **5** 662; **18** 887
Graat, Barent **1** 808; **13** 262*; **27** 134
Grabacki, Jan **18** 429
grabado, El **2** 399
Grabar, André **5** 163; **9** 528; **13** 262–3*; **19** 231
Grabar', Igor' (Emmanuilovich) **2** 890; **13** 263*; **27** 391, 440
collaboration **18** 899; **25** 89
groups and movements **12** 870; **27** 444; **31** 582
pupils **31** 64
works **22** 178; **27** 444
Grabar', Mirona (Vladimirovna) **27** 417
Grabar, Oleg **16** 549
Graben, Rumprecht von *see* RUMPRECHT VON GRABEN
Graber, Johann Peter **19** 815
Gráber, Margit **24** 457
Grabinski, Count **25** 893
Gräbner, Julius Wilhelm **28** 95
Grabow Altarpiece **1** 710; **3** 865; **12** 382, *383*; **13** 116, 151
Grabowski, Stanisław, Bishop of Warmia **28** 105
Grabska, Elżbieta **2** 502
Grabuloski-Grabul, Jordan **13** 263–4*; **19** 885
Graburn, Nelson **2** 137; **22** 674
Grabuset, Jean **13** 264
Grabuset, Thomas **11** 800; **13** 264*
Gračanica **9** *511*; **28** *437*
Church of the Dormition **9** 552, 585; **13** *264*, 264–5*; **25** 343; **28** 442, 446
icons **25** 339
Grace, Bill **2** 152
Grace, Della **12** 219
Grace Dieu, Diocesan Teachers' Training College **29** 123
Grachev, T. P. **27** 422
Grachev & Co. **27** 584
Gracht, Adriaan van der **12** 520
Gracht, Jakob van der **28** 519
Gracia, Manuel de **24** 621
Gracian, Ballasor **18** 817
Gracías **14** *711*, 712
church **14** 713
Gracien, Gilles **16** 854
Gracq, Julien **30** 22
Grada, Raffaele De *see* DE GRADA, RAFFAELE
Gradać **28** *437*
Church of the Annunciation **9** 552, 582, 583; **28** 441
Monastery **9** 561
Gradefes, Monastery of S Maria **13** 123; **29** 263
Gradenigo (family) **32** 216
Gradenigo, Antonio **17** 443; **28** 392
Gradista Muncelului *see* SARMIZEGETHUSA
Gradizzi, Francesco Aloisii **1** 598
Gradl, Hermann **11** 852; **12** 437
Grado **9** *510*; **13** 265–6*; **16** *618*
Cathedral of S Eufemia **9** 534; **13** 265; **16** 625
Baptistery **3** 189
Treasury **26** 690
mosaics **22** 161
S Giovanni Evangelista **3** 189; **13** 265–6
S Maria delle Grazie **13** 265, *266*
Graduals **7** 188; **13** 130; **28** 486, 487
individual manuscripts
Aarau Gradual (Aarau, Aargau. Kantbib., MS. Bibl. Wett fol. Max.3) **13** 151
Piteglio Gradual (Pistoia, Mus. Civ.) **23** 744
St Michel Gaillac Gradual (Paris, Bib. N., MS. lat. 776) **26** 670
see also ANTIPHONALS; CHOIR-BOOKS
Graebe, Carl **18** 655; **24** 796
Graebner, Julius Wilhelm *see* GRÄBNER, JULIUS WILHELM
Graeff (family) **4** 383
Graeff, Cornelis de **13** 266*
Graeff, Jacob de **25** 327
Graeser, Camille **1** 666; **13** 266–7*; **30** 135; **33** 737
Graeve, Siger van der **21** 803
Graevenitz, Gerhard von **13** 267*; **18** 63; **23** 262
Graevius, (Johann) Georgius **2** 163; **8** 220; **18** 595
Graf (family) **30** 143
Graf, Gottfried
works **11** *464*
Graf, Hans **10** 757, 896
Graf, Hug (*d* 1527/30) **13** 267
Graf, Hugo (*fl* 20th cent.) **9** 502
Graf, Johann *see* GRAF, HANS
Graf, Johann Michael **18** 849
Graf, Salomon **25** 549
Graf, Theodor **10** 92
Graf, Urs **3** 335, 387; **13** 267–8*; **30** 131, 146
patrons and collectors **1** 771; **10** 752
works **10** 549; **13** *268*; **25** 610, *610*; **30** 131, *131*; **33** 354
Grafenberg, Wirnt von *see* WIRNT VON GRAFENBERG
Graff, Anton **9** 238; **10** 539; **13** 268–9*; **17** 713; **33** 736
patrons and collectors **14** 653; **19** 111
pupils **11** 767; **12** 500; **28** 408; **30** 353
reproductive prints by others **13** 773
works **3** 799; **12** 392; **19** *111*; **30** 132
Graff, Dorothea **21** 154
Graff, Frederick **18** 845
Graff, G. **30** 276
Graff, Ignatz **29** 912
Graff, Jan Michał **25** 212
Graff, Johann Andreas **21** 151, 153; **31** 371
Graff, Laurence **10** 346
Graffart, Charles **3** 595
Graffi, Carlo **21** 824
graffiti **13** 269–71*, *270*; **22** 336; **29** 464; **31** 609
Grafica society **26** 723
Grafico, Camillo **24** 239
Grafiknytt **24** 451
Gräfle, Albert **19** 150
Grafley, Charles **31** 612
grafoscopio **25** 217
Grafton, Augustus Henry Fitzroy, 3rd Duke of *see* FITZROY, AUGUSTUS HENRY, 3rd Duke of Grafton
Grafton, Charles Fitzroy, 2nd Duke of *see* FITZROY, CHARLES, 2nd Duke of Grafton
Grafton Group **4** 168
Graglia **27** 498
Graham, Anderson, Probst & White **5** 274; **7** 429; **13** 271*; **30** 505
Graham, Bruce **6** 574; **28** 818
Graham, Burnham & Co. **5** 274; **13** 271
Graham, Dan(iel Harry) **13** 271–2*; **24** 403, 408; **32** 421

Graham, Ernest **5** 274; **13** 271; **23** 42
Graham, Frances **5** 268
Graham, Fred **13** 272*; **20** 359
Graham, Geoffrey **30** 160
Graham, George **7** 442
Graham, Ian **26** 411
Graham, James, 1st Duke of Montrose **10** 292
Graham, James Gillespie *see* GILLESPIE GRAHAM, JAMES
Graham, Johan (1706-76) **14** 794
Graham, John (1754-1817) **1** 649; **5** 271; **12** 237; **19** 515; **28** 274; **32** 912; **33** 188
Graham, John (*fl* 1778-85) **7** 486
Graham, John (1794-1866) *see* GRAHAM-GILBERT, JOHN
Graham, John (1881-1961) **13** 272*; **28** 875
groups and movements **1** 83; **21** 645
personal collection **1** 438
Graham, John A. (*fl* 1976) **1** 14
Graham, Maria *see* CALCOTT, MARIA
Graham, Maria Dundas, Lady Calcott **5** 434; **33** 309
Graham, Martha **23** 175; **30** 688
Graham, Paddy **16** 18
Graham, Richard **19** 119
Graham, Robert **10** 482
Graham, Mrs Thomas **11** *909*
Graham, William **13** 272–3*
frames **11** 434
musical instruments **22** 373
paintings **5** 266, 267; **21** 604; **25** 555; **27** 187; **32** 795
Grahame, Kenneth **24** 210
Graham-Gilbert, John **12** 776; **13** 273*
Grahamstown **29** 103, *103*, 105
School of Art **29** 123
Grahamstown Potteries **29** 117
Grahor, Janko (Nikola) **13** 273*
Grahor, Janko Josip **8** 176; **13** 273
Grahor and Klein **13** 273
Graillon, César **13** 274
Graillon, Félix **13** 274
Graillon, Pierre-Adrien **13** 273–4*
Graimberg, Count **26** 372
Grain, Jean le *see* ZIARNKO, JAN
Graincourt-lès-Havrincourt *see* GRAINCOURT TREASURE
Graincourt Treasure **27** 82
Graindorge (ceramics) **19** 382
Graindorge (textiles) **19** 418
Graindorge, F. C. **3** 614
grain elevators **13** 274*; **26** 709
Grainger, Richard **9** 55; **23** 20
Grainger Candlestick **10** 341
Grainger & Co. **10** 309, 310; **33** 378
Grainger & D'Ebro **2** 705; **23** 54
graining *see under* PAINTING → techniques
grain lake *see under* PIGMENTS → types
Grain Power Station **25** 403
Graispach, Gabriel **22** 305
Grajeda Mena, Guillermo **13** 274*, 765
Grajera y Hebroso, José **13** 274–5*; **29** 294
Grajos, Los *see* LOS GRAJOS
Gramatica, Antiveduto **4** 567; **12** 912; **13** 275–6*; **18** 747; **26** 842
assistants **5** 704
patrons and collectors **5** 451; **20** 841; **24** 399; **28** 271
works **5** 450; **13** *276*
Gramática, Rosina **2** 397
Gramcko, Elsa **13** 276*
Grame, Samuel **4** 481
Gramiccia, Lorenzo **13** 276–7*; **18** 674
Grammichele **28** 657
Grammont **3** *539*, 610; **13** 277*
Grammont, Duc de **23** 515
Gramont, Marshal of France **19** 263
Gramont, Antoine-Charles, Duc de **25** 377
Gramophone Company (London) **7** 375
Gramsci, Antonio **28** 927
Gran *see* ESZTERGOM
Gran, Daniel **13** 277–9*; **15** 18
collaboration **11** 329; **19** 378
pupils **23** 358
works **1** *659*, 660; **2** 795, 828; **8** 392; **13** *278*; **15** 139; **32** 444, 457
Grana, Dossa **14** 141, 469
Granacci, Francesco **13** 280–81*
collaboration **27** 740, 848
patrons and collectors **3** 15; **4** 404; **8** 147; **16** 711; **23** 855
works **13** *280*; **26** 816; **29** 362
Granada (Nicaragua) **23** *79*
architecture **23** 80
education (art) **23** 85
La Merced **23** 80
Mercados Municipales **23** 80
Museo de Antropología **23** 85
Puerta de Los Leones **23** 80
S Francisco **23** 80
Granada (Spain) **13** 281–9*; **16** *103*, 215; **29** *258*
Alcázar Genil **12** 81; **16** 216, 494
Alhambra **13** 285*, *286*, 287–8*; **14** *618*; **16** 142, 143, 189, 215; **23** 815; **25** 172; **29** 264
Alcazaba **13** 285–7*
architecture **13** 285*
Bab al-Ghudur **16** 216, 217
Bab al-Shari'a **13** 287; **16** 216, 217; **21** 584
Casita del Partal **13** 287; **16** 216, 217
ceilings **2** 529
ceramics **20** 158
coats of arms **14** 428
Cuarto Dorado **16** *217*
fortifications **21** 584
Fountain of the Lions **11** 340; **16** 137
fountains **11** 340
furniture **29** 311
gardens **12** 76, 79, 80; **13** 289*
gates **16** 215
Generalife **13** 287
inscriptions **16** 259
Justicia Gate *see* Bab al-Shari'a
Mirador de Daraxa **16** 257; **18** 71
muqarnas (architecture) **22** 324
Museo Nacional de Arte Hispanomusulmán *see under* Palace of Charles V
Museo Provincial de Bellas Artes *see* Palace of Charles V
Palace of Charles V **7** 901; **13** *283*, 288*; **14** 474; **20** *2*, 2–3*; **23** 492, 811; **29** 266; **30** 882
courtyard **8** 65
interior decoration **29** 299
Museo Nacional de Arte Hispanomusulmán **16** 556
sculpture **23** 343
Palacio de Comares **12** 80; **13** 287*; **16** 216, 217, *217*; **23** 815
ceiling **2** 529; **16** 494, *495*
doors **16** 495
façade **16** 495
Palacio de los Leones **13** 287–8; **16** 216; **23** 815
Palacio del Partal **16** 246, 494
Patio de la Acequia **13** 289
Patio de los Arrayanes **8** 64, *65*
Granada (Spain)
Alhambra—cont.
Patio de los Leones **8** 65; **11** 340; **12** 79, 80; **13** *288*, 289; **16** 216; **22** 255
ceilings **16** 495
doors **16** 495
fountains **16** 246
portals **16** 216
Puerta de la Justicia **16** 495
Puerta del Vino **16** 250
Qalahurra **13** 288*
Qubba Major *see* Sala de Dos Hermanas
Riyāḍ Palace *see* Patio de los Leones
Sala de Dos Hermanas **16** 216; **29** 310
Sala de la Barca **2** 529
Sala de la Justicia *see* Sala de los Reyes
Sala de los Abencerrajes **16** 216
Sala de los Reyes **16** 216; **19** 3
Sultan's Palace *see* Palacio de Comares
tiles **14** 428; **30** 882
Torre de Comares **4** 784
Torre de la Cautiva **13** 287; **16** 216, 217
Torre de las Damas **16** 253
Torre de las Infantas *see* Qalahurra
Torre del Peinador **16** 216
towers **16** 215
vaults (ceiling) **16** 142
Vela Tower **21** 585
Alixares **12** 80
architecture **2** 529
armour **16** *504*
Audiencia *see* Chancellery
Bab al-Rambla **16** 216
Bab al-Tawwabin **16** 216
Bab Ilbira **16** 216
baths **3** 377
Cartuja de Jerez **29** 841
Casa de Chapiz **22** 256
Casa del Cabilo Antigno *see* Yusufiyya Madrasa
Casa del Gallo **33** 8
Casa de Zafra **16** 216
catafalques **6** 71
ceramics **13** 285
chairs **29** 311
Chancellery **29** 268
Corral del Carbón **5** 724; **16** 216
Cuarto Real de Santo Domingo **16** 215, 216, 494
Dar al-Hurra Palace **16** 216
Dar al-Manjara al-Kubra *see* Cuarto Real de Santo Domingo
dress **16** 458
ecclesiastical buildings
Cathedral of S María de la Encarnación **5** 620–21; **28** 725–6, *726*; **29** 266, 269
Capilla Real **13** 70, *282*; **23** 494; **26** 249; **29** 265
Sagrario **29** 271
sculpture **13** 112; **29** 292
stained glass **29** 504, 505, V
hermitage of S Sebastian **16** 215
monastery of the Cartuja **29** 292
sacromonte **27** 498
Salvador church **16** 215
S Cruz la Real **9** 112
S Jerónimo **29** 266
S Juan de los Reyes **16** 216
fortifications **21** 584
furniture **29** 311, 314
gardens **12** 80–81
Generalife **16** 215, 494; **29** 264
gardens **12** 79, 80, *81*; **16** 129
glass **29** 331
guilds **29** 312
Hospital de S Juan de Dios **14** 782
Hospital Real de Dementes **2** 658; **29** 265
Granada (Spain)—cont.
House of the Bride **12** 80
ivory-carvings **16** 525
leather **19** 3
madrasa **20** 55
manuscripts **16** 291
Maristán **16** 216
Mauror Hill **16** 493
metalwork **16** 386, *387*
painting **29** 280
Palacio Real
Capilla Real **2** 278
Patronato de la Alhambra **29** 358
pottery **16** 404, 412, 419; **29** 322
sculpture **15** 59; **29** 292
silk **29** 348; **30** VII1
synagogue **22** 254
textiles **16** 429
tiles **30** 882
University **31** 674
Yusufiyya Madrasa **16** 216
granadilla **29** 315
granaries **1** 263, 310–11, *310*; **9** 68; **13** 407; **14** 339; **17** 54; **23** 275; **24** *265*; **30** 639; **33** 511
Granát **8** 417
Granbury (TX), Hood County Court House **18** 888
Granby, John Manners, Marquess of *see* MANNERS, JOHN, Marquess of Granby
Gran Chiriquí culture **13** 290–91*; **23** *902*
alloys **13** 291
gold **13** 291, *291*
metalwork **13** 291
pendants (jewellery) **13** *291*
pottery **13** 290
sculpture **13** 290–91
Gran Colombia *see* COLOMBIA; ECUADOR; PANAMA; VENEZUELA
Grancourt, (Pierre-) Jacques-Onésyme Bergeret de *see* BERGERET DE GRANCOURT, (PIERRE-)JACQUES-ONÉSYME
Grancsay, Stephen **2** 450
Grand, Toni **11** 552, 570
Granda **29** 344
Granda, Ramón **29** 338
grand appareil **26** 569
Grand Bahama **3** *59*
Grand Bassam **1** *386*; **8** 22
grands cabinets see under CABINETS (i) (ROOMS) → types
Grand Canal **6** 620; **29** 905
Grand Dauphin, Le *see* BOURBON I., LOUIS DE, Le Grand Dauphin
Grand Duché du Luxembourg *see* LUXEMBOURG
Grand Duchy of Luxembourg *see* LUXEMBOURG
Grande, Antonio del **13** 292*
collaboration **3** 198; **6** 23
patrons and collectors **7** 621; **9** 175; **23** 899
works **4** 434; **5** 344; **7** 621; **9** *11*; **11** 277; **16** 771
Grande Anse, Spice Islands Hotel **2** 148
Grande Erculanèse **14** 442, 445
Grandes Chroniques de France, Master of Charles V's *see* CHARLES V'S GRANDES CHRONIQUES DE FRANCE, MASTER OF
Grandes Heures *see under* BOOKS OF HOURS → individual manuscripts
Grandes Heures de Rohan *see under* BOOKS OF HOURS → individual manuscripts → Rohan Hours
Grandes Heures of Anne of Brittany *see under* BOOKS OF HOURS → individual manuscripts
Grandes Heures of Philip the Bold, Duke of Burgundy *see under* BOOKS OF HOURS → individual manuscripts
Grande Tuilerie d'Ivry **22** 270
grandfather clocks *see under* CLOCKS → types
Grandhomme, Paul **26** 191
works **17** III2
Grandi, Ercole (1463-before 1525) **13** 293–4*
works **13** *293*
Grandi, Ercole (di Giulio Cesare) de' (1455/6-96) *see* ROBERTI, ERCOLE (D'ANTONIO) DE'
Grandi, Gian Matteo **13** 292; **26** 331
Grandi, Giovanni Girolamo **13** 292–3*; **23** 754; **32** 646
Grandi, Giuseppe **13** 294–5*
groups and movements **21** 527; **28** 34
pupils **27** 206; **33** 183
teachers **30** 215
works **13** *294*; **16** 706, 707; **21** 533
Grandi, Lorenzo **13** 292
Grandi, Vincenzo **5** 180; **13** 292–3*; **23** 754; **26** 331; **32** 646
Grandidier, Ernest **6** 925; **7** 155
Grandis, Alvise **27** 719
Grandisson, John, Bishop of Exeter **10** 672, 674; **13** 147, 176
Grandjean, Esprit **3** 521
Grandjean, Jean **1** 808; **2** 25; **13** 295*
Grandjean de Montigny, Auguste-Henri-Victor **4** 711; **13** 295–6*; **18** 122; **26** 413
collaboration **8** 593
groups and movements **26** 189
patrons and collectors **4** 302, 637
pupils **4** 711
works **12** 414; **13** *296*
Grand Jeu, Le **26** 306; **28** 745; **30** 20; **33** 304
Grandmaison, Aubin-Louis Millin de *see* MILLIN DE GRANDMAISON, AUBIN-LOUIS
Grandma Moses *see* MOSES, GRANDMA
Grand Manner **12** 292; **13** 296–7*; **22** 686
Grandmont **26** 692
Grandmont, Vedeau de **19** 248
Grandon, Charles **13** 638
Grandpierre-Deverzy, Adrienne **1** 28
Grand Pressigny **25** 515
Grand Prix de Rome Architecture **25** 637
Grand Rapids (MI) **13** 297*; **31** *587*, 629, 631
Grand Rapids Chair Co. **13** 297
Grand style pottery *see under* POTTERY → wares
Grand Tour **2** 161, 559; **5** 686; **7** 561, 562, 563; **9** 23; **10** 79, 249, 364; **13** 297–304*, 809; **15** 202; **18** 814; **27** 115; **33** 409
paintings **3** 380, 382–3; **5** 685; **18** 711
porcelain **6** 333
Grand Trianon *see under* VERSAILLES → Château
Grand Union **24** 407
Grand-Vabre Church **13** 79
Grandville, J(ean-) J(acques) **13** 306–7*; **24** 605; **25** 345; **33** 369
works **4** 364; **5** 758; **10** 726; **13** *307*; **27** 871
Granell, Eugenio Fernández **11** 19; **25** 701; **30** 22
Granello, Niccolosio (*fl* before 1550) **13** 307

Granello, Nicolás (c. 1550-93) 6 24; 13 307*
collaboration 5 457; 6 25
patrons and collectors 13 922
pupils 6 24
works 10 503; 30 372
Grañen, Blasco de 13 307–8*
Graner, Lluis 21 699; 23 194
Granet, André 10 689
Granet, François-Marius 13 308–9*
assistants 8 538
groups and movements 9 363; 31 373
patrons and collectors 2 514; 4 303, 305; 8 73, 649
teachers 7 762
works 1 497; 13 309
Granfors 11 105
Grange, Jacques 11 584
Grange, Jean de la, Cardinal see JEAN DE LA GRANGE, Cardinal
Granger, James 13 309; 33 94
Granger, Jean-Pierre 8 538; 19 239
Granger, N. 10 79
grangerize 13 309*
granges 25 668
Granges, David des 13 309–10*
works 18 591
Granges-sur-Lot 4 780
Granie, Joseph 19 297; 25 747
Granier (fl 20th cent.) 25 375
Granier, Pierre (1635-1715) 12 159
Granikos monument 14 443
Granit 5 85
granite 6 324; 29 699–700*
historical and regional traditions
Chavín culture 29 167
Czech Republic 8 376
Egypt 9 766
Egypt, ancient 9 773, 813*, 814, 815, 825; 23 329; 27 824; 29 700
Late Period (664-332 BC) 9 889; 27 824
Middle Kingdom (c. 1966-c. 1630 BC) 9 876
New Kingdom (c. 1539-c. 1075 BC) 9 885; 14 758; 23 330, 331; 30 297
Ptolemaic (304-30 BC) 9 893; 27 825
5th Dynasty (c. 2465-c. 2325 BC) 25 762
12th Dynasty (c. 1938-c. 1756 BC) 10 77; 28 492
13th Dynasty (c. 1756-c. 1630 BC) 9 879
18th Dynasty (c. 1539-c. 1292 BC) 9 857, 862
19th Dynasty (c. 1292-c. 1190 BC) 10 13
England 10 224, 227
Finland 11 88, 100
France 12 211
Hinduism 15 508, 514, 515, 518, 519
Indian subcontinent 15 233, 329, 508, 514, 515, 518, 519, 534, 538; 17 761
Italy 29 700
Japan 17 102
Korea 18 264, 280, 283, 288, 298, 302; 23 775; 29 869
Malawi 20 161
Peru 29 167
Prehistoric 12 211; 25 515
Romanesque 10 227; 26 606
Rome, ancient 26 874, 876–7; 27 14; 29 700
Scandinavia 11 100
South America, Pre-Columbian 29 131, 167
Spain 26 606; 29 700
types
black-and-white 29 700
Granite of the Column 29 700
granodiorite 9 813
granite
types—cont.
green-grey 29 700
marmor claudianus 29 700
marmor troadense 29 700, 700
Mysian 29 700
violet see marmor troadense
uses
architecture 8 376; 9 773; 18 264; 26 874
bridges 18 280
churches 11 88
effigies 26 606
obelisks 9 813, 825; 23 329, 330, 331; 29 131
pagodas 23 775
pyramids 25 762
relief sculpture 15 233, 538
rock reliefs 15 508, 514
sarcophagi 10 13; 27 824, 825
sculpture
Egypt 9 766
Egypt, ancient 9 815, 857, 862, 876, 879, 885, 889, 893; 10 77; 14 758; 28 492; 30 297
Finland 11 100
Indian subcontinent 15 515, 518, 519, 534; 17 761
Japan 17 102
Korea 18 283, 288, 298, 302
Malawi 20 161
Nubia 23 279
Rome, ancient 27 14
South America, Pre-Columbian 29 167
stupas 29 869
temples 15 329
tools 25 515
granitelle 30 113
Granja de San Ildefonso, La see SAN ILDEFONSO
Granjon, Robert 16 360; 27 637
Granmichele 31 717
Gran Nicoya culture 13 310–12*
hardstones 29 153, 154
jade 13 311–12, 312
jars 13 311
metates 13 310–11; 29 141, 142
pendants (jewellery) 13 311, 312
pottery 13 310, 311; 29 147, 148, 149
Pataky 13 310
sculpture 13 310–11; 29 142
Grano, Antonino 28 477
Grano, Giorgio Gandini del 3 487
granodiorite see under GRANITE → types
Granollers 29 329, 330
Granovsky, Timofey 33 583
Gran Pajatén 6 380; 13 312*; 29 156, 171
Granpré Molière, Marinus Jan 13 312–13*; 22 186; 27 230
groups and movements 8 669, 670; 22 831; 23 450
pupils 29 531
Granpré Molière, Verhagen & Kok 13 313
Gransdorf 6 481
Grant, Albert 18 169; 21 604
Grant, Duncan (James Corrowr) 3 631; 10 374; 13 313–14*; 19 591
collaboration 10 284, 547
exhibitions 10 255
groups and movements 4 168, 169; 5 517; 10 256; 19 623; 23 437, 438; 25 356
house 2 552
patrons and collectors 20 476
studio 29 858
works 4 169, 369; 7 434; 9 20; 18 688; 22 332, 380; 28 299
Grant, Francis 13 314*
patrons and collectors 6 117, 118
reproductive prints by others 2 692; 6 451; 10 750
works 29 425
Grant, Francis, Lord Cullen of Monymusk (1658-1726) 28 869
Grant, James 14 109
Grant, Mary 11 239; 28 243
Grant, Peter 16 22
Grant, W. H. 5 668
Grantham, Thomas Philip Robinson, 3rd Baron see GREY, THOMAS PHILIP DE, 2nd Earl de Grey
Grantham, Thomas Robinson, 2nd Baron see ROBINSON, THOMAS, 2nd Baron Grantham
Granthomme, Jean 33 357
Granucci, Bartolomeo 31 789
granulation see under METALWORK → techniques
Granvelle, Cardinal 29 649
Granvelle, Antoine Perrenot de, Cardinal 22 63
architecture 3 545
collections 1 5; 3 873; 11 665
drawings 9 443
medals 13 862; 17 643
paintings 4 453, 908; 18 5; 22 64
Granvelle, Jean Perrenot de 4 161
Granvelle, Nicolas Perrenot de 3 873; 4 856
Granville, Edward Montagu Stuart, 3rd Baron and 1st Earl of Wharncliffe 25 406
Granville, Walter L. B. 5 418; 17 798; 18 889
works 18 889
Grão Vasco see FERNANDES, VASCO
Grapaldi, Francesco Maria see GRAPALDO, FRANCESCO MARIA
Grapaldo, Francesco Maria 13 314–15*
grape cups see under CUPS → types
Graphic, The 12 296; 15 830; 28 919; 32 415
Graphic Design 24 437
GraphicStudio see under TAMPA (FL) → University of South Florida-Tampa
Graphicus 24 449
Graphies 8 63
Graphis 4 369; 25 352
Graphische Künste: Gesellschaft für vervielfältigende Kunst 24 423, 438, 444
graphite 8 128; 13 315*; 24 789
historical and regional traditions
China 7 92, 632
England 19 540
Prehistoric 25 514
uses
drawings 2 330; 9 217; 19 540
etchings 10 548
inks 7 92
pencils 13 315; 24 353
pigments 7 632
pottery 25 514
underdrawings 13 315
graphotypes 25 611
Grapiglia, Giovanni Girolamo 6 89; 32 216
Grapp, Wendling see DIETTERLIN, WENDEL
Grard, Georges 3 573
Gras, Caspar 13 315*
patrons and collectors 13 916
teachers 12 347
works 2 800; 10 441; 12 347, 404; 15 864, 865
Gras, Domenech Sugrañes i see SUGRAÑES I GRAS, DOMENECH
grāsamālā see GRĀSAPAṬṬI
grāsamukha see KĪRTIMUKHA
grāsapaṭṭi 15 243*
Grasmeir, Johann Georg 15 865
Grasmere group 10 614
Grass, Philippe 29 758
Grassalkovich, Antal, Graf 14 887; 15 13; 20 892; 23 462
Grass and Earth Society 13 315–16*; 18 87; 33 149
Grässel, Hans 28 374
Grasser, Erasmus 12 401; 13 316–17*; 18 450, 451; 22 301
works 13 316; 26 186
grasses
historical and regional traditions
Africa 1 295, 306, 307, 308, 426; 3 331
China 7 115
Fulani 1 307
India, Republic of 15 173
Indian subcontinent 15 551, 727
Indonesia 15 809
Japan 17 365
Kenya 1 307
Native North Americans 3 331, 332; 22 570, 647, 655, 656, 663; 31 260
Sudan 1 306, 307
United States of America 1 426; 22 570
types
beargrass 3 331
galleta 22 661
sparto 3 331; 24 6, 40; 30 538
uses
architecture 1 307
baskets 1 426; 3 331, 332; 15 809; 22 655, 656, 661, 662, 663
bonsai 17 365
brushes 15 551
cladding 1 307
dolls 31 260
houses 22 570
mats 15 809
paper 7 115; 24 40
roofs 1 306, 307
sculpture 15 727
thatch 1 307, 308
trays 15 727
see also STRAW
Grasset, Eugène (-Samuel) 11 600; 13 317–18*
groups and movements 22 252
pupils 3 854; 4 717, 722; 11 241; 12 563; 27 280; 32 614
reproductions in ceramics 22 270
works 11 600; 19 490; 25 346, 347
Grassi, Anton 13 320; 32 449
Grassi, Giorgio 12 380; 16 650, 651; 18 114, 456; 26 16; 30 455
Grassi, Giovannino de 13 155, 318–19*; 21 524, 533
assistants 13 319
patrons and collectors 32 611, 612
works 3 531; 4 395; 9 219; 13 149; 14 433
Grassi, Józef 8 372; 13 320*; 25 212; 26 258
Grassi, Luigi 2 517, 518
Grassi, Niccolò 18 47
Grassi, Orazio 1 626; 3 923; 9 91; 13 320–21*; 15 121; 17 510
Grassi, Porrino de 13 319*
Grassi, Salomone de 13 319*
works 3 531; 13 319, 319; 32 612
Grassman, Marcello 4 719
Grass-roots art 2 515
grass script see SCRIPTS → types → cursive
Grasten, Viola 32 817
Graswangtal, Schloss Linderhof 12 376, 416; 23 546, 813; 33 283
paintings 3 702
stucco 29 843
Venus grotto 13 705
Gratama, Jan 1 814; 13 321*, 632; 17 910
Grate, Eric 13 321–2*; 30 86, 110
grates 11 119, 119
Gratian 8 614
works 8 614; 20 696
Gratianopolis see GRENOBLE
Gratien, Koumba 11 879
Gratien, Zossou 3 728
grattage 10 470; 13 322*
Grattarolo 10 763
Grattoni, Matteo 16 726
Grattoni, Severino 6 323
Graty, M. I. 21 813
Gratz, Hanss von see NIESENBERGER, HANS
Gratzen see NOVÉ HRADY
Gratzl, Philipp 2 812
Grau, Enrique 7 610; 13 322*
Grau, Enrique Gómez see GÓMEZ GRAU, ENRIQUE
Grau, Francisco 28 367
Grau, J. Torres see TORRES GRAU, J.
Grau, Juan 28 367
Grau, Ricardo 13 322*; 14 875; 24 510; 28 604
Graubner, Gotthard 12 397; 13 322–3*; 14 238
Grauer, Sherry 5 572
Graufesenque, La see LA GRAUFESENQUE
Graulière, La see LA GRAULIÈRE
Graux de la Bruyère, Jean Baptiste François 21 720
GRAV see GROUPE DE RECHERCHE D'ART VISUEL
Graval, Jehan de 26 148
Gravant, François 11 608
Gravant, Louis-François 6 454
Grave, Jan Evert 6 89
Grave, Jean 8 204; 13 323*
Grave, Josua de 13 323–4*
Grave Creek (WV) 22 571
Graveley, Edmund 10 163
Gravelot 10 249; 13 324–5*; 19 136; 26 499
assistants 11 906
collaboration 14 269; 22 88
pupils 11 906; 20 144
reproductive prints by others 9 365; 12 515; 14 132; 19 144, 642; 28 221; 31 871
works 3 318; 4 360, 361; 10 348; 11 631; 13 324; 32 501
Gravely, F. H. 15 211
grave markers 24 630*; 29 616–17*
see also GRAVESTONES; STELAE → types → funerary
Graverol, Jane 30 23
gravers see BURINS (ENGRAVING)
graves
historical and regional traditions
Arabia 2 248–50
Austria 14 87
Bahrain 2 249
Bolivia 29 133
Celtic 14 87
Germany 18 119–20; 25 508
Greece, ancient 13 383
Helladic 14 339
Moche (culture) 21 749
Netherlands, the 25 508
Prehistoric 18 119–20; 25 506–9*, 538–9*, 540, 542
Scythian 6 212
Tiahuanaco 29 133
types
catacomb 25 507
chariot 6 155; 25 539; 28 549
gallery 25 507–8*, 511*
passage 25 508*
pit-graves 9 836, 837–8, 842; 13 383, 396
timber 25 507
see also TOMBS
Graves, Algernon 4 27
Graves, H. E. 5 667
Graves, Henry, & Co. 2 234; 11 362, 796; 13 327; 21 604; 28 283; 29 634; 31 137
Graves, Michael 13 325–6*; 23 490; 31 633
collaboration 10 120
groups and movements 9 705; 23 50; 25 359
works 7 386; 13 326; 25 172, 174; 27 721; 28 835; 31 598, 598, 633, 633

Graves, Morris (Cole) **13** 326–7*; **28** 167, 328; **31** 607
Graves, Nancy **13** 327*
assistants **27** 217
dealers **18** 161
works **6** 9; **19** 492; **31** 615
Graves, Richard **4** 481; **31** 651
Graves, Robert **13** 327*; **16** 820
Gravesande, Arent Arentsz. van 's *see* ARENTSZ. VAN 'S GRAVESANDE, ARENT
Gravesande, Carel Nicolaas Storm van 's *see* STORM VAN 'S GRAVESANDE, CAREL NICOLAAS
gravestones **14** 277*
Bosnia **4** 461, *461*
Costa Rica **9** *679*
Cuba (Caribbean) **8** 233
Cyprus, ancient **8** 341
Denmark **8** 738
Este art **10** 528
Germany **21** *164*, *502*
Jewish art **17** 555
Malaysia **20** 170
Merovingian **21** *164*
Migration period **21** *502*
Poland **25** 115
South America, Pre-Columbian **9** *679*
United States of America **31** 610
see also STELAE → types → funerary
graveyards *see* CEMETERIES
Gravier, Charles, Marquis de Vergennes *see* VERGENNES, CHARLES GRAVIER, Marquis de
Graville, Louis Malet de *see* MALET DE GRAVILLE, LOUIS
Graville-Sainte-Honorine **26** 598
Gravina, Stefano Regio, Principe di Aci **11** 816
Gravisca **10** *583*, 585, 613, 617, 638; **30** 346
Gravura **2** 903; **25** 185; **27** 799
gravure (rotary) **26** 235
gravure sur bois debout *see* WOOD ENGRAVINGS
Gray, Musée Baron Martin **8** 649
Gray, A. E., & Co. Ltd **7** 798
Gray, Basil **13** 327–8*; **16** 549
Gray, Charles (*d* 1847) **4** 868
Gray, Charles M. (*fl* 1930s) **9** 502
Gray, David **28** 261
Gray, E., & Sons **19** 596
Gray, Edward **5** 71
Gray, Eileen **11** 584; **13** 328*; **16** 28; **18** 615
patrons and collectors **9** 196; **11** 582
works **7** 241; **11** 583, 601; **28** 298
Gray, George **29** 381
Gray, Gustave Le *see* LE GRAY, GUSTAVE
Gray, Mrs Hamilton **10** 637
Gray, Henry **1** 845
Gray, Henry Peters **15** 30
Gray, James **28** 261
Gray, Thomas **3** 741; **4** 361, *362*; **32** 825
Gray, William **13** 328–9*
Graydon-Stannus, Mrs **10** 320
Grays Library **4** 789
Grayswood (Surrey), New Farm **7** *712*
Graz **2** *776*; **13** 329–30*
Alte Galerie **29** 516
Barmherzigenkirche **2** 783
Burg **2** 778, 779
Cathedral of St Ägidius **8** 836
mausoleum of Ferdinand II **2** 781; **13** *329*, 918
fortifications **2** 780
glass **2** 818
Kunstverein **1** 438
Landeszeughaus **2** 449
Landhaus **2** 779, 806, 822
Leechkirche **2** 798; **28** 861; **30** 535
manuscript illumination **2** 792
Graz—cont.
metalwork **2** 821
monument to Francis I of Austria **20** *390*
painting **2** 793
Schloss Eggenberg **2** 782; **12** 369; **13** 330; **33** 48
Steiermärkisches Landesmuseum Joanneum **2** 830, 831; **13** 330, 918; **14** 11; **22** 203
Universitätskirche **2** 781
Graz, Charles des **29** 88
Graz, John **4** 717
Graz, Regina Gomide **4** 724
Grazia (*fl* 1232-4) **24** 193
Grazia da Pistoia, Leonardo **28** 657
Graziadio **6** 139
Graziani (family) **24** 760
Graziani, Ercole, I (1651-1726) **8** 159; **29** 32
Graziani, Ercole, II (1688-1765) **8** 160; **12** 38; **13** 330*
Graziani, Mateo **19** 386; **24** 504
Graziani, Paolo **18** 635
Grazioli, Donato **27** 637
Grazioli, Francesco **7** 862
Graz School **30** 214
Grazzini, Giovan Francesco **12** 707
Grbić **29** 546
Grdan, Vinko **9** 672
Grdzelishvili, K. **12** 327
grease **10** 549; **33** 2
Great, Albert the *see* ALBERT THE GREAT
Great Abaco Island **3** *59*, 63
Great Anstey (Herts), St George **26** 613
Great Antonine Altar **27** 38
Greatbach, Daniel **1** 772; **31** 636
earthenware **31** *636*
great basinets *see under* HELMETS → types
Greatbatch, William **10** 306; **15** 820; **29** 495; **33** 20, 136, 137
Great Bed of Ware **3** 484; **10** 288, *289*
Great Bible of Mortier *see under* BIBLES → types
Great Bradley (Suffolk), St Mary **26** 613
Great Brington (Northants), St Mary **1** 520
Great Britain *see* BRITAIN
Great Cameo of France **1** 652, *652*; **12** 251
Great Chalfield Manor (Wilts) **8** 43
Great Chesters (Northumb.) **6** 162
Great Coucher Book of the Duchy of Lanchester (London, PRO, MS. D of L/42) **14** 423
Great Council Altarpiece **3** 304
Great Coxwell Barn (Oxon) **10** *225*; **13** 331*, *331*; **32** 860
Great Dixter (E. Sussex) **31** 151
Great Ejaculator **8** 338
Great Elector *see* FREDERICK WILLIAM, Elector of Brandenburg
Greater Antilles *see* ANTILLES, GREATER
Greater London Council (GLC) *see* LONDON COUNTY COUNCIL (LCC)
Great Exhibition, 1851 *see under* LONDON → exhibitions
Great Gallery (Barrier Canyon, UT) **13** 332*, *332*; **22** *544*
Great Harris Papyrus **4** *341*; **26** 556
great helms *see under* HELMETS → types
Great Khans *see*:
GENGHIS KHAN, Khan
GÜYÜK, Khan
MENGU, Khan
OGEDEI, Khan
Great Khans—cont.
QUBILAY, Khan
Great Kimble (Bucks), St Nicholas **26** 613
Great Malvern Priory (Hereford & Worcs) **13** 184; **30** *904*
Great Mongol *Shāhnāma* **8** 707; **15** 134; **16** 292, 294, 295, 296, 303, 316, *316*, 317
Great Packington Church (Warwicks) **13** 608
Great Paxton (Cambs), Holy Trinity Church **1** 723; **2** 67; **26** 589; **31** 281
Great Plains Artists Association **31** 174
Great Plains painting *see under* HUNGARY → painting
Great Ponton (Lincs), Church of the Holy Cross **5** 319
Great Pyramid *see under* GIZA → pyramids
Great Queen Street Academy *see under* LONDON → academies
Great Serpent Mound (OH) **22** *571*, 572
Great Style *see* GRAND MANNER
great towers *see under* TOWERS → types
Great Trajanic Frieze *see under* ROME → Arch of Constantine
Great Vehicle Buddhishm *see* BUDDHISM → branches → Mahayana
Great Wall (Thrace) **9** 554
Great Wall of China **4** 795; **6** *614*, 643, 648; **13** 333–4*; **20** 571; **21** 593, *870*
Great Wardrobe tapestry workshop (London) **10** 275; **19** 596
Great Warley (Essex), St Mary the Virgin
font **11** *256*
Great Western Railway **15** 830
greatwheels **7** 764
Great Zimbabwe **1** 305, 308; **13** 334–6*; **20** 570, 571; **23** 824; **28** 621; **33** 678
architecture **13** 335–6
Elliptical Building **13** *336*
sculpture **1** 415, 418
walls **1** 414
Gréau Collection **22** 111
greaves **2** 469; **13** 584; **30** 771
Greaves, Derrick **18** 97, 98; **28** 880
Greaves, Henry **13** 337; **33** 144
Greaves, John **2** 163; **10** 78, 96
Greaves, Stanley **2** 152; **13** 876
Greaves, Walter **13** 336–7*; **33** 144
Grébaut, Eugène **10** 80
Grebber, de (family) **21** 350
Grebber, Frans (Pietersz.) de **13** 337, 895; **19** 119; **22** 839; **27** 508, 885
Grebber, Pieter (Fransz.) de **13** 337*; **22** 839
collaboration **14** 46; **21** 827
groups and movements **10** 660
patrons and collectors **28** 18
pupils **3** 757; **5** 542; **14** 291, 366; **19** 292
teachers **12** 883
works **9** 308; **14** 584
Grebe, Johannes George **22** 891
Grebenshchikov, Afanasy **27** 410
Greber, Henri-Léon **11** 753
Gréber, Jacques **3** 225; **11** 526; **12** 58; **13** 337–8*; **23** 631
Gréber, Maison **8** 132
Grebnev, P. **27** 425
Grebo **1** 391–2
Greca, Felice della **6** 585; **13** 338*; **26** 759
Greca, Giulio della **23** 576
Greca, Vincenzo della **4** 433; **13** 338*; **22** 5; **24** 371; **29** 250
Greceanu, Olga **26** 716, 721
Greche, Domenico dalle **13** 338*
Grechetto, il (*fl* 1538-64) *see* CESATI, ALESSANDRO
Grechetto, il (1616-70) *see* CASTIGLIONE, GIOVANNI BENEDETTO
Grechin, Olisey *see* OLISEY GRECHIN
Greco (family) **6** 571
Greco, Alberto **2** 401; **13** 338–9*
Greco, El **6** 45; **8** 157; **13** 339–45*; **25** 333; **32** 160, 190
attributions **21** 73
collaboration **21** 858, 859
dealers **9** 424
frames **11** *486*, 488, 490
methods **13** 708; **23** 377
paintings **7** 226; **11** 710; **20** 280; **29** 280; **31** 89, 90
genre **12** 287
history **13** *342*
portraits **13** *343*
religious **7** *225*; **9** 110, 267; **10** 502; **13** *340*, *343*; **14** 784; **21** 159; **28** 709; **29** 278
topographical **13** *344*; **31** 154
patrons and collectors
Altamira (family) **1** 690
Arcos, Pedro Laso de la Vega, 1st Conde de **23** 156
Benavente, 10th Conde de (1584-1653) **3** 700
Beruete (y Moret), Aureliano (de) **3** 869
Borbón y Braganza, Sebastián Gabriel **4** 378
Bowes, John **4** 600
Brudenell, George, 4th Earl of Cardigan and 1st Duke of Montagu **4** 893
Burrell, William (1861-1958) **28** 273
Cambó y Batlle, Francisco de Asís **5** 509
Carol I, King of Romania (*reg* 1866-1914) **5** 792; **26** 722
Castilla, Diego de **6** 44
Castro, Rodrigo de, Bishop of Cuenca **6** 44
Coningham, William **7** 709
Contini Bonacossi, Alessandro, Conte **7** 782
Degas, (Hilaire-Germain-) Edgar **8** 622
Farnese, Alessandro, Cardinal (1520-89) **10** 810
Havemeyer, Louisine (Waldron) **14** 244
Hieronymites **14** 516, 517
Jovellanos, Gaspar Melchor de **17** 673
Koehler, Bernhard (1849-1927) **18** 187
Lane, Hugh (Percy) **18** 727
Lerma, Francisco Gómez de Sandoval y Rojas, Duque de **27** 723
Louis-Philippe, King of the French (*reg* 1830-48) **23** 521
Montpensier, Antoine-Marie-Philippe-Louis de Bourbon, Duc de **23** 523
Museu de Arte de São Paulo **4** 726
Orsini, Fulvio **23** 577
Péreire (family) **24** 396
Robinson, John Charles **26** 473
Ryerson, Martin A(ntoine) **27** 463
Salazar de Mendoza, Pedro **27** 612
Sandoval y Rojas, Bernardo de, Cardinal Archbishop of Toledo **27** 724
Santiago, Francisco Esteban Rodríguez de los Ríos, 1st Marqués de **27** 792, 793
Wrightsman, Charles B(ierer) **33** 416
personal collection **31** 347
Greco, El—cont.
pupils **30** 711; **31** 41, 347
reproductive prints by others **2** 645
Greco, Emilio **13** 346–7*
collaboration **17** 622
patrons and collectors **24** 279
works **16** 709; **23** 588, 754; **26** 810
Greco, Gennaro **13** 347*
Greco, Il *see* CESATI, ALESSANDRO
Greco, Vincenzo **13** 347
Grecolini, Giovanni Antonio *see* CRECCOLINI, GIOVANNI ANTONIO
Grècque, François *see* ERNI, HANS
Greda group **22** 335
Grée, Peter de **16** 14
Greece **13** 347–62*, *362*
architectural decorations **4** 774; **9** 547
architecture **13** 348–51*
brick **9** 547
Byzantine **7** 170; **9** 545–7*, 550–51*
Early Christian (*c*. AD 250-843) **9** 538*, 542*
vernacular **32** 289, 290, 293–4
archives **2** 370*
art legislation **2** 561
brick **4** 774; **9** 547
bricklaying **7** 273
cathedrals **2** 11
ceramics **13** 358*
churches **2** 509
basilicas **3** 329; **9** 538*, *542*, 547
Byzantine **7** *260*; **9** 542*, 545–7*, *546*, *547*, 550–51, *551*, *552*; **14** *776*; **17** *839*; **18** 571; **21** *860*; **30** *725*
cross-domed **9** *542*
cross-in-square **9** 545–7, *546*
cross-vaulted **7** 253
decoration **7** 273
domed octagon **7** 170; **9** 547
Early Christian (*c*. AD 250-843) **9** 538*, 542*, *542*
Greek-cross octagon **9** *547*; **14** 776
rock **26** 483
transept basilicas **9** 538
ciboria (ii) (structure) **7** *278*
coins **7** 532, 539; **9** 639
collections **13** 359–60*
copper **13** 359
dealing **13** 360*
domes **2** 510
doors **9** 151, *600*
education (art) **13** 360–61*
embroidery **9** *668*; **13** 355–7
epitaphioi **9** *668*
fora **7** *852*; **15** 894
furniture **13** 357–8*
guidebooks **33** 136
heraldry **14** 411
hotels **13** *351*; **18** 232
houses **13** *350*; **25** *499*, 500; **32** *294*
icons **9** *601*, *630*; **15** III; **24** 3; **25** 333, 334; **31** 554
ikat **30** 554
interior decoration **13** *357*, 357–8*
ivory **9** *600*
knitting **18** 157
libraries **13** 361*
mansions **32** *294*
manuals **8** 910
manuscript illumination **9** *607*, *609*, *611*, *614*, *615*; **28** *764*
marble **29** *702*
masonry **4** 773; **9** 547, *551*
metalwork **13** 358–9*
miniatures (manuscript illumination) **9** *607*, *609*, *611*, *614*, *615*
monasteries **21** 343, *343*; **22** *226*, 226, *227*
mosaicists **29** 87

Greece—cont.
mosaics
Byzantine **7** 170; **9** 565–6*, *572*, 577–9, *585*, *630*; **22** *162*; **30** *721*, *723*
Early Christian (*c.* AD 250–843) **7** *278*; **9** 565–6*, *572*
mosques **2** *672*; **30** 716
museums **7** *852*
office buildings **9** *207*
orders (architecture) **13** 387
painting **9** 206; **13** 351–3*
genre **13** *352*
panel **24** 3
religious **20** 51
wall
Byzantine **9** 577–9, *578*, *584*, 585; **17** *839*; **22** *406*, *407*, *409*
Post-Byzantine **25** *330*, 334–6*, *335*
palaces **2** *674*
parekklesia **9** 547; **24** 110*
patronage **13** 359*
photoarchives **13** 361*
plaster **13** *354*
portraits **13** *353*
pottery **8** 901
sculpture **9** *598*; **13** 353–5*, *354*
seals **7** 532
settlements **25** 499
silk **9** *668*; **13** 355
silver **13** 358–9
synagogues **17** 540, 543
textiles **13** 355–7*
trade **6** 624
treatises **5** 215; **25** 7
trousers **9** 640
walls **21** 735
wood **9** *600*
see also Byzantine; Cycladic; Greece, ancient; Helladic; Mycenaean
Greece, ancient **13** 361–606*, *362*, *363*; **14** *332*; **26** *908*
abaci (capitals) **13** *378*, *393*
abata **13** 417
acanthus **1** 109, *111*; **13** 415; **23** 534
acoustics **1** 123
acroteria **8** *689*; **10** *434*; **13** 390, 391, 426, 432; **23** *429*
adhesives **13** 483
adyta **13** *376*, 377, 398
aesthetics **1** 175–6*; **13** 375, 412, 413, 467; **25** 31–2; **33** 461–2
agate **12** 247, *247*
agorai **1** 455*; **2** *684*; **13** 380, 381, *381*, 419
alabastra **13** *475*, 477, 569, *569*
allegories **1** 651–2; **22** 411
alphabets **10** 1, 591; **13** 490; **24** 641
altars **1** 691–2*, *692*; **13** 376, 380, 393, 406, 417; **24** *412*; **27** 712–13
amber **1** 761, *761*
ambulatories **13** 379
amphitheatres **26** 910
amphorae **10** 612; **13** 474, 475, 478, 491, 504, *514*, 514, *591*
Attica **13** *517*, *519*, *522*
belly **13** 475, *475*
belly-handled **13** 492, *494*
Euboia **13** 516
neck **13** 475, *475*, 491, *492*, *495*, 495, *507*, *510*, 518
Nolan **13** 475, 536
one-piece **13** 475, *475*, 501
Orientalizing style **13** *501*, *503*
Panathenaic **13** 478, 479, 484, 485, 486, 491, 539
Proto-Attic **13** *501*
shoulder-handled **13** 491, *494*
transport **13** 474
Type A **32** 43, *44*
amphoriskoi **13** *475*, 477, 536, *593*
amulets **1** 816, 817; **14** 360
Greece, ancient —cont.
anathyrosis **13** 387
andrones **13** 383, 386, 556; **23** 434
animal subjects **13** 493, 501, 505, 506
antefixes **2** 131*, *131*; **13** 390
anthemia **2** *134*
apodyteria **10** 670
appliqué **13** 540
aqueducts **13** 381; **26** 910
arches **2** 295, 297*; **13** 403, 404; **26** 909
architects **2** 312; **13** 394–5*, 408
architectural decorations **23** 533–4
architecture **13** 368, 373–4*, 375–416*, *384*, *385*, *402*, *414*, *416*, *418*, *420*; **25** 171; **29** 805–6
Archaic **13** *367*
Classical **2** 666; **13** *367*
criticism **13** 409
Dark Age (*c.* 1050–*c.* 750 BC) **13** *367*
Hellenistic **13** *367*
Ionia **15** 893, 894
Italy **16** 622
military **21** 551, 555*, *557*, 558
Roman **13** *367*
Rome, ancient **26** 908–11*
stone **13** 386–9*
trabeated construction **13** 390; **31** 269, *269*
5th cent. BC **15** 132
architraves **13** 377, *378*, 379, 393
arm-bands **17** I
armour **13** 583–4*, *584*
arrises **13** 377, 389
arrow-shooters **21** 557
arsenals **13** 381
art (imitation of works of) **11** 306
art criticism **13** 467–9*, 553–4*
art history **2** 531; **22** 686
artists' biographies **8** 535
art market **9** 20
art movements **13** 518
aryballoi **13** *475*, 478, *499*, *500*, *590*
askoi **13** 519, 537
atlantids **2** *695*; **13** 415; **23** 477
attributions **32** 26–7
auditoria *see theatra*
barges **13** 407
basilicas (non-ecclesiastical) **26** 910
bastions **21** 551
bath-gymnasia **15** 894
baths **3** 374–5*; **13** 386, 407, 556
Roman **26** 909–10
beads **13** 393, *600*, 602
beds **3** 482–3*
blazons **13** 583
bolsals **13** 536
bone **12** 247; **13** 595*; **21** 712
Bronze Age **14** 353–4*
bosses **13** 388, *388*
bouleuteria **13** 380–81, *381*, 405, *405*, 407; **14** 73; **23** 349
bowls **10** 474; **13** 476, 490, 536, 594, *594*
Homeric **13** 539
Long-petal **13** 540
Megarian **13** 477, 491, 539, *540*
Shield **13** 540
bracelets **13** *600*, 601
brass **4** 682, *686*
brick **13** 404
bronze **1** 123; **2** 451; **3** 483; **4** 849, 850–52*; **8** *690*; **13** 390, 391, 422, 434–5*, 437–8*, *442*, *453*, 568, 571–7*, *572*, *574*, 583–4, 588, 597, *600*, 600–602*; **21** *712*; **24** 258; **25** *179*
Archaic **8** 262, 458; **13** 572–3*; **24** *328*; **30** *339*; **32** *660*
Archaic, Late **13** 448
Boeotia **13** *601*
Greece, ancient
bronze—cont.
Classical **8** 262, *696*; **13** 573*
Classical, Early **1** 481; **13** 433, *573*; **25** 177, *178*; **29** 567, *567*
Classical, High **13** *429*; **26** *297*
Classical, Late **13** *460*
Geometric (*c.* 900–*c.* 700 BC) **13** 441, 572*
Hellenistic **13** 573–4*, 589
Italy **30** 339
Proto-Daidalic **13** *443*
4th cent. BC **13** *577*
5th cent. BC **6** 9; **13** 438, 586; **23** 290
6th cent. BC **13** *575*, *576*
7th cent. BC **13** *584*; **21** 712
8th cent. BC **8** *262*
buckets **13** 475
bucrania **13** 392
builders **13** 395
building contractors **13** 395
building regulations **13** 395
burial mounds **13** 383, 384
busts **5** 298–9*; **13** *443*, 583*
cables **13** 411
caldaria **13** 386
calendars **2** 648
callipers **13** 438
cameos **12** 248
candelabra **5** *604*
capitals **5** *670*; **10** 742; **13** 376, 377, 387, 391, *392*, 393, 399, 401, 405, *413*, 415
Aiolic **15** 893
Corinthian **1** 109; **3** 341; **17** 742
carpenters **13** 394
cartoons (drawings) **13** 556
caryatids **5** 904*, *904*; **13** 415; **23** 477
casting **13** *437*, 437–8*, *594*, 594–5
casts **6** 9; **7** 562; **27** 30
catapults **21** 557
cauldrons **13** 371, 492, 575–6, *575*
caves **15** 98
ceilings **13** 390, 392
cellae **13** 376, *376*, 377, 405, 415
cement **13** 404
cemeteries **13** 396
cenotaphs **6** 170
censers **6** 173
chains **13** 411
chairs **6** 388; **13** 591*
diphros **6** 388; **13** 591
diphros okladias **13** 591
klismos **6** 388, *388*; **13** 591; **33** 330
thronos **6** 388; **13** 591
chalcedony **12** 247, 248
chariots **6** 480*
chattering **13** 537
chests **13** 592*
chiaroscuro **2** 227; **13** 472
chimneys **13** 390
chisels **13** 436
chitones **9** 246, 249
choes **13** *475*, 476, 479
chronologies **13** *367*
cinnabar **13** 535, 536
circuits **21** 555, 556
cisterns **7** 354; **13** 381, 383, 391
clamps **13** *389*, 391
Classicism **7** 382
clay **13** *436*, 436–7*, 479, 515, 535, *550*; **22** 160; **29** 814
white **13** 479
clocks **13** 382
codices **20** 327
coffering **7** *526*, 526–7*; **13** 390, 392
coins **1** 203; **4** *686*; **5** 298; **13** 585*; **14** 407; **21** 1
Archaic **13** 585–6*, *585*
Classical **13** 586–8*, *587*
colts **13** 585
Hellenistic **13** 588–9*, *588*
Greece, ancient
coins—cont.
Italy **13** 586
owls **13** 585
Sicily **13** *587*
tetradrachms **13** *585*, 588, 589
turtles **13** 585
collections **7** 561; **13** 424, 604–6*; **14** 867
erotic art **10** 487
paintings **7** 562; **13** 554–5*
pottery **13** 540–42*
sculpture **7** 561–2, 564; **9** 23; **13** 469–71*; **27** 10, 45
colonnades **13** 379, 381, 391, 397, *397*, 415, 417
colour **2** 227
columns **13** 376–7, *376*, 379, 388, 389, 391, 392, 393, 398, 399, 410, 412, 415–16
Corinthian **2** 666; **11** 231, *231*; **13** 379, 380, 401, 405, 415
Doric **11** 231, *231*; **13** 398
engaged **13** 401
Ionic **11** 231, *231*; **13** 377, 379, 398, 399, 401
Roman **26** *909*
Turkey **10** *431*
combs (hair) **13** 595
compasses **13** 411
competitions **10** 675; **13** 375, 394
construction machinery **7** 764; **13** 387, *388*, 400
contrapposto **7** 783; **13** 422, 453
copies **2** 557; **13** 423
coins **13** 587
sculpture **2** 558; **7** 561; **10** 311; **13** *422*, *423*, 438–9*, *450*, *454*, *462*, *463*, *465*, 469; **16** 685; **18** *148*; **19** *853*; **23** *291*; **24** 416, *593*; **26** 854; **27** 10, 30, 39, 40
copper **13** 573; **21** 712
copper hydroxide chloride **13** 536
corbels **7** 837; **13** 396
cornelian **12** 247; **13** *599*
cornices **13** 377, 392, 393, *393*
costumes **9** 248; **30** 650
couches **13** 383, 386, 591*, *591*, 596–7
courts **13** 383
courtyards **8** 64; **13** 382
craftsmen and artists **10** 587; **13** 371, 375, 394–5*, 433, 439*, 440*, 444, 467, 468, *481*, *483*, 484–6*, *485*
cranes **13** 400
cups **10** 474; **13** 476–7, 478, 510, *535*, 539–40, *570*
Attica **13** 518–19, 520, *520*, 523, *537*
band **13** *475*, 476
bilingual **13** 518
Castulo **13** 538
eye **13** 476
eye (Type A) **13** *475*, 475; **32** 43
eye (Type B) **13** *475*, 476
eye (Type C) **13** *475*, 476
Ionian Little Masters **13** 515
Italy **13** *437*
komast **13** *475*, 476, 507
Lakonian **13** 512, *512*; **32** 57
Lakonian droop **32** 47
lip **13** *475*, 476; **32** 37
Little Master **13** 490, 510
mastos **13** 477
Merrythought **32** 37
one-handler **13** 536
Protogeometric **13** 492
Rheneia **13** 536
Siana **13** *475*, 476, 508; **32** 37
cup-skyphoi **13** *475*, *476*, 477
cypress **13** 390
decorators **13** 395
dentils **11** 791; **13** 377
derricks **7** 764; **13** 387
diadems **13** 599, *599*, 601
dies (ii) (stamps) **13** 585
dinoi **13** *507*, *509*
Greece, ancient —cont.
dioptra **13** 412
display of art **9** 13, 20; **13** 604*
ditches **21** 558
dolls **31** 259
domes **9** 85
doors **9** 150–51*, *151*; **13** 390, 391, 415
doorways **13** 387
dowels **13** 391
drapery **9** 246; **13** 422
drapery, sculpture **13** *423*
drawings **18** 108
architectural **13** 395, 409–10*, 412
figure **13** 472, 535
dress **1** 887; **9** 245–9*
drills **13** 436
dromoi **29** 487
earrings **13** 598, *598*, 599, 601
ebony **13** 596
echini **13** *378*, 392, 398
education (architectural) **13** 408
ekklesiasteria **13** 381; **23** 349
electrum **12** 864; **13** 585, *598*
emery **22** 698; **29** 706
enamel **10** 192; **13** *599*
engineering (civil) **13** 404, 413
engineering (military) **13** 413
entablatures **13** 377, *378*, 389, 390, 391, 392, *393*, 414, 415; **21** 341; **25** I1; **27** 692
entasis **2** 676; **10** 414–15; **13** 398, 415
episkeniai **13** *385*, 386, 406
erotic art **10** 474; **23** 290
exedrae **10** *670*, 671*
exhibitions **10** 675; **13** 469–71*, 606*
ex-votos **13** 376; **18** 409; **27** 111, 712
façade decoration **10** 742*
façades **8** *686*; **13** 385, 391*, 407; **21** 341
faience (i) (glass) **13** 589–90*, *590*; **14** *358*, 358–9*
fans **10** 775
fasciae **13** 393
feeders **13** 536
felt **10** 875
fibulae **13** *600*, 600–601, *601*
figureheads **28** 611
figurines **1** *761*; **12** 286; **13** 433, 571–4*, *572*, *574*, 578–82*, *579*, *580*, *581*; **23** 427; **27** 111
firing **13** 480, 482–3*
flagstones **13** 387
flasks **6** II1
floors **13** 556–7, 560–61, 565–7*
flutes (columns) **11** 231, *231*; **13** 377, 389, 398, 415
fonts (baptismal) **11** 339
forgeries **7** 561; **13** 516
fortifications **13** 396, 403; **21** 551, 555–8*, *556*, *557*; **26** 909
forts **21** *557*
fountain houses **13** 381–2
fountains **11** 339; **13** 381–2; **26** 910
friezes **2** 648; **3** 341; **10** 742; **11** 790–91*, *791*; **13** 377, *378*, 379, 390, 391, 393, 401, 426, 432*, 447; **27** 692
Archaic, Late **13** *448*
Classical, Early **2** *680*
Classical, High **13** *426*
Italy **21** *342*
Turkey **14** *69*
frigidaria **13** 386
funerary equipment **13** 478, 482, 483, 485
furniture **13** 390, 591*, 592*, 596–7; **33** 155
galleries (iv) (art) **13** 402
picture **7** 561; **10** 675; **13** 554–5
sculpture **9** 20
garden design **12** 67–8
gardens **12** 65, 67–8*
gargoyles **13** 390

Greece, ancient —cont.
  garnets 12 248
  gates 7 358
  gateways 13 391; 24 417; 26 909, 909
  gauges 13 411
  gay and lesbian art 12 213
  geisa 13 377, 378
  gem-engraving 12 246–8*, 247, 248; 13 598
  gems 13 375
  geometry 13 400, 400, 413–15*, 414
  gilding 8 262; 12 625, 626; 13 393, 435, 537, 539
  girders (beams) 13 391
  glass 13 393, 435, 593, 593–5*, 594; 22 160
    gold-glass 13 594
    millefiori 12 788
    mosaic 13 594
  glass paste 12 247, 248
  glazes 13 480–81, 482, 504, 536
  goblets 14 170, 338
  gold 6 388; 12 865, 867, 868, 869; 13 390, 391, 435, 568–71*, 570, 596, 597–9*, 599; 17 I; 27 15; 32 250
  gold leaf 12 870; 13 482, 594
  granaries 13 407
  grave markers 29 616–17*
  graves 13 383, 396
  greaves 13 584
  grilles 13 390
  guidebooks 13 807*
  guilloche 13 392, 830
  guttae (i) (architectural ornament) 11 790; 13 377, 378
  gutters 13 390, 392, 393
  gymnasia 3 374; 8 694; 10 670; 13 386, 403, 406–7, 416
  gypsum 29 814
  haematite 13 536
  hairstyles 9 248
  half-timbering 13 389
  halls 13 380, 405, 407; 14 73*
    assembly 13 386
    audience 13 407
    dining 13 381, 386, 396, 417
  hardstones 13 599; 14 169
  harmony 13 412
  harnesses 14 180–81*
  helmets 13 583, 584
  herbals 14 432
  heroa 13 380; 14 466–7*; 20 863
  hestiatoria 13 417
  himatia 9 246, 249
  hoards 13 568
  hotels 13 386
  houses 13 382, 382–3*, 389, 396, 396, 407, 419, 420, 556
    Classical 23 434–5
    farmhouses 21 341
    pastas 13 382, 382, 383, 556; 23 434, 434
    prostas 13 382–3, 382; 25 575
    Rhodian 13 383, 407
    town 8 687; 25 575
    4th cent. BC 24 337
    9th cent. BC 13 396
  human figures 10 649; 13 415, 422, 428, 453, 492, 493, 505; 18 409; 25 177
  huts 13 389
  hydriai 13 474, 475, 479, 514, 576
    Attica 13 510, 511, 523
    Etruscan 13 516, 516
    Hadra vases 13 539
    kalpis 13 576
  hypocausts 3 374; 13 407
  iconography 10 211; 13 370, 472–4*, 544–7*, 553; 22 410; 33 241
    Etruscan 10 587, 595–6
  illusionism 15 135
  impluvia 13 383
  incising 13 504
  industrial scenes 15 827

Greece, ancient —cont.
  inlays 13 393, 573, 594, 595
  inscriptions 2 299; 13 385, 387, 485, 487–91*, 488, 489, 490, 507
    Classical, High 13 456–7
  insulae 13 407, 420; 15 894
  interior decoration 13 389
  interlace 15 881
  inventories 6 76
  iron 13 568
  ivory 6 388; 12 247; 13 390, 435; 16 798
    Bronze Age 14 353–4*
  ivory-carvings 13 441, 595–7*, 596
    Bronze Age 14 353, 354
    Geometric (*c.* 900–*c.* 700 BC) 13 442
  jasper 12 247, 248
  jet 1 816
  jewellery 13 597–9*, 600–602*; 14 360
  jugs 13 476
  kadoi 13 475
  kantharoi 13 475, 477, 477, 492, 493, 513
  kaolinite 13 535
  katagogeia 13 386
  kilns 13 482–3
  kithara 22 372
  kothones 13 475, 477, 513
  kotylai 13 475, 476, 477
  kotyle pyxides 13 477
  kraters 13 474, 476, 477, 478, 492, 504, 576, 577
    Attica 13 518, 522
    bell 13 370, 475, 476, 531, 536, 539
    Black-figure 13 515
    calyx 2 134; 13 473, 475, 476, 518, 522, 533, 534; 32 43
    column 13 475, 476, 505, 506, 509
    France 32 660
    Geometric (*c.* 900–*c.* 700 BC) 13 497
    Italy 13 527, 528
    kotyle 13 477, 496, 501
    Neo-Attic 22 733
    volute 13 475, 476, 508
  kyathoi 13 513, 513
  kylikes 13 475, 476, 477; 22 410
  labels 13 485, 488
  lagynoi 13 476
  lamps 13 602*, 603; 19 364; 27 104, 104
  landscape 13 418, 418–19
  languages 13 369
  law courts 13 381
  lead 13 568; 22 160
  lebetes 13 475, 476
  lebetes gamikoi 13 475, 478, 479
  lekanides 13 475, 478, 513, 536
  lekythoi 13 456, 475, 478, 491, 507, 535–6
  levels 13 411
  lewises 13 388
  libraries 19 311–12*; 26 909
  limestone 12 246; 13 387, 393, 395, 434*, 443; 27 14, 825
    andesite (volcanic) 13 387
    gneiss 13 387
    St Elias 13 387
  linen 9 246, 247
  lions' heads 13 392, 393
  looms 30 546
  lost-wax casting 13 435, 437–8, 571, 572, 575; 21 321
  lotus 19 716
  louteria 13 538
  loutrophoroi 13 456, 475, 478, 529
  lydion 13 478
  macella 19 888; 26 910
  malachite 13 536
  manuals 25 177
  manuscripts 13 369
  maps 20 362

Greece, ancient —cont.
  marble 13 387, 388, 389, 393, 422, 423, 427, 433, 434*, 436, 438, 457, 592; 27 825; 29 701–2
    Archaic 8 688, 695, 870; 18 244, 409, 410; 22 699, 699; 27 688, 689
    Archaic, Early 13 445
    Archaic, Late 10 449; 13 447, 448, 449; 18 244
    Archaic, Middle 13 446
    Classical 2 679
    Classical, Early 1 480; 8 697; 13 425, 426, 452; 25 179
    Classical, High 8 262, 689; 10 139, 434; 13 428, 454, 455, 456, 458; 23 433; 25 576; 29 616
    Classical, Late 13 459; 19 853; 23 291
    Geometric (*c.* 900–*c.* 700 BC) 12 246
    Hellenistic 13 371; 24 414; 27 692
    Hellenistic, High 22 514
    Hellenistic, Late 13 466
    Neo-Attic 22 733
    Parian 8 457
    Roman 5 604; 26 875; 27 14
    Turkey 14 69, 70
    5th cent. BC 23 432; 24 205
    6th cent. BC 29 368
  markets 19 888; 20 438
  marks 13 487, 488
  masks 13 438, 582*
  masonry 13 387, 395, 396, 397, 400, 403; 20 570
    broken ashlar 13 388
    Cyclopean 20 571
    dry-stone 20 571
    headers 13 388
    isodomic 13 388
    Lesbian 13 388
    parpend stones 13 388
    pseudo-isodomic 13 388
    rustication 20 572
  masons 13 394–5*
  mausolea 13 407; 14 71
  meander 13 391; 20 912
  measurements 13 386, 410, 410–15*, 411, 413, 414
  measuring instruments 13 411–12
  medallions 13 599
  medical books 21 5
  megara (buildings) 13 382, 382–3, 397; 25 500
  merchants 13 486
  metalwork 13 391, 393, 568*, 574–7*, 575, 576, 577; 26 544
  metopes 10 742; 11 790; 13 377, 378, 390, 391, 392, 393, 398, 425–6, 432*, 445, 446–7
    Classical, High 13 425
    5th cent. BC 23 432
  military scenes 13 493
  mimesis 1 175; 2 413; 25 32
  mirror handles 21 712
  mirrors 13 577*; 21 711–12*, 712, 713
  modelli 21 768
  modelling 2 227
  models 13 376, 395, 409–10*, 438–9*; 24 374
  modules 13 412*
  monopteroi 21 892–3*, 893
  monuments
    funerary 13 371, 383–4*, 384; 20 863
    public 22 42–3*
  mortars (building) 13 403, 404
  mosaics 8 691; 13 383, 556–61*, 557, 558, 559, 560, 562–7*, 562, 563, 564, 566; 22 159–60; 24 411
    Floral style 13 558, 561, 562, 563, 563–4
    opus tessellatum 13 556
    Roman 27 63

Greece, ancient
  mosaics—cont.
    4th cent. BC 23 435
  mouldings 13 389, 391–2*, 392, 393, 393, 394, 399; 20 912; 22 211
    astragal 13 392
    bead and reel 3 439; 13 392, 393
    cyma recta 13 392, 393
    cyma reversa 10 431; 13 392, 393
    egg and dart 8 869; 9 757, 757; 13 392, 392, 393, 393
    fillet 13 377, 392, 393
    hawksbeak 13 392, 393
    leaf and dart 13 392, 392, 393, 393
    ovolo 13 392
  moulds 13 480, 539, 578, 594
  mud-bricks 4 772; 13 376, 389, 394
  mugs 13 476, 537
  museums 13 469–71*, 604*; 22 354
  mutules 11 790; 13 377, 378, 393
  mythology 22 410–11
  nails 9 151
  narratives 13 451, 464, 472, 493; 22 513–14*, 514
  necklaces 13 599
  neck rings 13 601
  nestoroi 13 526
  niello 10 381
  nude figures 13 422, 449, 459, 459, 463; 18 148, 409, 410; 19 853; 22 699; 23 290–91*, 291; 24 328, 414; 25 456, 456; 26 297; 30 339
    Classical 25 178, 179
    Classical, High 13 429
    Hellenistic 25 179
    Hellenistic, Late 13 466
  nymphaea 26 910
  ochre 13 536
  odeia 13 386; 23 349, 350; 26 910; 27 712
  oeci 13 382
  oinochoai 13 436, 476, 488, 491, 503, 507, 569, 569
  olpai 13 476
  opisthodomoi 13 376, 376, 398
  orchestras 13 385, 385–6; 30 650
  orders (architecture) 13 377, 396, 398–400*, 404, 407, 408, 412, 424; 23 429, 477; 27 690
    Aiolic 13 398
    Corinthian 13 387, 391, 401, 405, 415, 416; 23 477, 482, 534
    Doric 2 676, 677; 7 851; 13 377, 378, 387, 388, 389, 390, 391–2, 393, 398, 401, 405, 406, 408, 415, 416; 23 429, 477, 478, 479, 481, 481, 533
    Ionic 8 692; 13 377, 387, 388, 389, 391, 393, 393, 398–400, 399, 401, 402, 405, 408, 415, 416; 15 893; 19 232; 23 477, 481, 482, 533; 27 687, 688
    Turkey 18 580
  ornament 23 533–5*
  orthostats 13 376, 388
  outworks 21 557, 558
  painters 13 547–9
  painting 2 217; 8 262; 13 374–5*, 543–55*, 592; 24 3; 25 44; 29 665; 30 715
    Archaic 13 545*, 549–53*
    Classical 13 545–6*, 548–9, 550–51*
    display 7 561; 9 13
    encaustic 10 197; 13 393, 544; 24 3
    four-colour 2 217; 13 535, 535
    fresco 13 393
    genre 12 286–7*
    Geometric (*c.* 900–*c.* 700 BC) 13 545*, 549–53*

Greece, ancient
  painting—cont.
    Hellenistic 13 544, 546–7*, 549, 551–3*
    Italy 16 652
    landscape 8 704; 18 701
    marine 20 424
    mythological 13 545
    Orientalizing style 13 545*, 549–53*, 550
    still-lifes 29 664–5
      see also xenia
    vase 3 466; 9 247, 248; 10 591; 12 286; 13 485, 489, 583; 14 407; 16 830; 22 410, 410, 411, 513; 31 254; 32 26–7*
      Attica 13 517–19*, 517, 518, 519, 520, 522, 523, 524, 591; 29 396
      5th cent. BC 2 134; 32 44, 50
      see also pottery
    wall 1 450; 13 389, 393, 394, 543–55*; 23 291; 25 176–7; 32 250, 803*
      Bronze Age 14 338
      Classical 13 543, 546, 548–9
      Hellenistic 13 547, 549, 552
      Roman 13 546, 547
      Turkey 10 151
      4th cent. BC 32 250
  paints 13 544
  palaces 13 404, 405, 407; 23 808*
  palaestrae 13 386, 406; 23 828
  palmettes 23 888
  papyri 13 369; 20 329
  papyrus 26 556, 557
  paraskenia 13 385, 385, 406
  parks 24 178
  patronage 7 561; 13 371, 373–5*, 485–6, 487
  pattern books 13 546
  pavements 13 395, 395
  pebbles 22 159–60; 23 435
  pectoral ornaments 12 869
  pedestals 13 393
  pediments 13 377, 378, 390, 391, 398, 414, 424–5, 431–2*, 432, 445–6; 24 317–19*, 319
    Archaic 7 849
  pelikai 13 475, 475, 478, 518, 524
  pendants (jewellery) 13 600, 601–2
  peploi 9 246, 248
  periods 13 368
    Archaic 13 367, 368, 471
    Classical 13 367, 368, 471
    Dark Age (*c.* 1050–*c.* 750 BC) 8 527; 13 366–8, 367
    Dimini (*c.* 5000 BC) 25 500
    Geometric (*c.* 900–*c.* 700 BC) 13 367
    Hellenistic 13 367, 369, 471
    Roman 13 367
    Sesklo (*c.* 6000 BC) 25 500
  perirrhanteria 16 612, 612
  peristyle courtyards 13 382, 382; 24 456
  peristyles 13 376–7, 376, 380, 383, 397
  perspective 13 472; 24 486
  phialai 13 477, 569, 575
  piers (ii) (masonry) 13 406; 24 750
  pigments 13 481, 544
    coral red 13 536
    Egyptian blue 13 535, 536
    sinopia 28 778
  pilasters 13 376, 376, 391; 24 805
  pilgrim flasks 13 492
  pillars 13 415
  pins 13 600, 600
  pithoi 13 383, 474, 538
  plaques 13 370, 443, 550, 582*, 595; 32 67
  plaster 13 389, 438; 29 814*
  plates 13 478, 536
  platforms 13 385, 386
  plumblines 13 411
  pointing (i) (sculpture) 13 438–9

Greece, ancient —cont.
polychromy **4** 851; **13** 377, 392–4*, 398, 405, 498; **21** 341; **25** 171, 799, I1; **26** 134–5; **29** VIII1
porches **13** 382, 415
poros **13** 387, 388, 389, 393
porphyry **27** 14
porticos **13** 396; **25** 264; **29** *681*
portraits
coins **13** 587, 588*, 589
sculpture **5** 298; **13** 429, 451, 454, 465–6; **14** *70*; **25** *576*
self-portraits **13** 546
three-quarter **2** 217
potters **13** *480*
potter's wheels **13** 479–80
pottery **7** 851; **13** 370, 471–542*, *475*, *480*, *485*, *490*; **16** 830; **20** 912
Arcadia **13** 496
Archaic **13** 472
Argolid **13** 493, 495–6, 498
Attica **13** *436*, 493–5*, *494*, *495*, 571
Black and White style **13** 501
Black-figure **3** 466; **13** *367*, 368, 471, 472, 474, 475, *480*, 481–2, *482*, *483*, 486, 487, 488, 504*, 539, 549; **14** 498; **23** 145, 290; **24** 331; **32** *44*
Attica **13** 500, 501, 504, 506–11*, *507*, *508*, *509*, *510*, *511*, *512*, *591*
Boeotia **13** 513–14*, *513*
Caeretan **13** 516*, *516*
Chalcidian **13** *515*, 515–16*
Corinth **13** 499, 504*, 505–6*, *505*, *506*
Euboia **13** 516–17*
Ionia **13** 503, *514*, 514–15*
Lakonia **13** *512*, 512–13*
Black-glazed **13** 471, 479, 480–83, *481*, *482*, *483*, 536–8*
Attica **13** *537*
Boeotia **13** 536
Lakonia **13** 536
black ware **13** 472
Boeotia **13** 493, 496, 498, 513
Bronze Age **14** 337–8, 359
Bucchero **13** 571
Calenian Ware **13** 540
Campana C ware **13** 538
Campana group **13** 514
Classical **13** 472–3, *473*
coiling **13** 479
Corinth **13** 495, 496
Corinthian **13** *367*
Eastern Sigillata A **13** 538
Enmann group **13** 514
Etruscan **13** 514
Euboia **13** 493, 496–7, *497*
Fikellura style **13** 487, 503, *503*
First Black-figure style **13** *499*, 499
Geometric (*c.* 900–*c.* 700 BC) **13** 368, 471, 493–8*, *494*, *495*, *497*; **21** 95
Geometric **13** *367*
Geometric (*c.* 900–*c.* 700 BC) **13** 472; **22** 410, 513
Gnathia ware **13** 539
Grand style **13** 504
Grey bucchero ware **13** 491
Hellenistic **13** 538–40*, *539*, *540*
Ionia **15** 893
Italy **13** 473, 525–33*, 538
Apulian **13** 526–30*, *527*, *528*, *529*
Campania **13** *531*, 531–2*
Lucanian **13** 525–6*, *526*
Paestan **13** 532–3*, *533*
Kabeirion style **13** 513–14
Kerch' style **13** 524, *524*
Klazomenian ware **13** 487, 514, *514*, 515
Knipovitch group **13** 514

Greece, ancient
pottery—cont.
Lakonia **13** 474, 496; **32** 36
Late Helladic IIIC (*c.* 1180–*c.* 1050 BC) **13** *367*
lead-glazed ware **13** 540
Northampton group **13** 514
Orientalizing style **13** 471, 472, 496, 498–501*, *499*, 502–4*; **32** 30
Lakonia **13** 498
Ornate style **13** 524, 526
Pergamene appliqué ware **13** 540
Plain style **13** 524, 526
Proto-Attic **13** *367*, 498, 500–501*, *501*
Proto-Corinthian **13** *367*, 498, 499–500*
Protogeometric **13** *367*, 368, 471, 472, 491*, 492–3*
Achaia **13** 492
Argolid **13** 492
Attica **13** 491–2*, *492*
Boeotia **13** 492
Corinth **13** 492
Dodecanese **13** 492
Euboia **13** 492–3
Ionia **13** 492
Ithaka (Greece) **13** 492
Lakonia **13** 492
Thessaly **13** 492
Protogeometric B **13** 493
Red-figure **2** *134*; **3** 466; **6** 333; **12** 286; **13** *367*, 368, *437*, 471, 472, 475, *476*, *477*, *481*, 481–2, *482*, 488, *489*, 517*, 525–34*, *526*, *527*, *528*, *529*, *530*, *531*, *533*; **23** 290; **30** 339; **32** 31, *35*, 55, 65
Attica **13** *370*, *436*, *437*, 510, 517–25*, *517*, *518*, *519*, *520*, *522*, *523*, *524*; **29** *396*
Boeotia **13** 513–14, 533–4, *534*
Corinth **13** 534
Lakonia **13** 534
Red-glazed ware **13** 538
restoration **13** 483
Rhodes (island) **26** 290
Second Black-figure style **13** 499, *500*
Sicily **13** *530*, 530–31*
Six's technique **13** 482
Sub-Mycenaean (*c.* 1050–*c.* 1000 BC) **13** *367*, 471
Sub-Protogeometric **13** 492
Thessaly **13** 496
West Slope ware **13** 481, 539
White-ground **6** II1; **13** 471, 482, 535–6*, *535*
Attica **13** 511
Wild Goat style **13** 503, *503*; **15** 893
8th cent. BC **24** 892
promenades **13** 381
pronaoi **13** 376, *376*
proportions (architecture) **2** 344, 350–51; **13** 408, 409, 410, 412–13*, *413*
proportions (human) **13** 422
propylaia **13** 417; **25** *657*, 657–8*; **26** 909, *909*; **27** 712
proskenia **13** 385–6, *385*, 406; **30** 651
protomes **13** 435, 575, *575*, 582–3*
prytaneia **13** 380; **25** 674–5*
psykters **13** 476, 518
ptera **13** 376
pumice **29** 706
pyramids **20** 863; **25** 766
pyxides (boxes) **13** *475*, 478
pyxides (vases) **13** 479, 492, 493, *505*, *530*
quadrigas **20** 863
quarries **13** 387
quartz **12** 248
ramparts **4** 772
rams **21** 556, 557

Greece, ancient —cont.
realism (critical term) **2** 227
rediscovery **26** 263; **27** 45
red lead **13** 387
refinements (architecture) **10** 414; **13** 413–15*, *414*
regulae (i) (architectural ornament) **11** 790; **13** 377, *378*, 393
religion **10** 591; **13** 369–71*
replicas **7** 562
representation **13** 422; **19** 853; **25** 177, 768
reservoirs **13** 381
revetments **13** 424
rhyta **13** 477, 569
rings **13** 601
rock crystal **12** 247
rolls **4** 342; **20** 329; **26** 556, 557
roofs **2** 668; **13** 390, 397; **27** 127; **30** *493*, *902*, 902–3*
Hellenistic **2** *667*
Roman **2** 408
trussed **13** 381, 390, 407
rosettes **13** 392, 393
rouletting **13** 537
rules **13** 411
running tracks **13** 381, 386, 403, 406
sacred groves **12** 68; **13** *418*, 418–19
sanctuaries **8** 692, *692*, 868; **13** 369, 371, 376, 380, 381, 386, 396, *404*, 416–17*, *416*, *418*, 418–19*, 420, 568; **18** *393*; **27** 711–14*, *712*; **29** 680
sand **29** 706
sarcophagi **13** 383, 515; **26** 855; **27** 825–6*
sard **14** *170*
sardonyx **12** 248
satires **27** 868
scaenae **13** 385–6, *385*, 406; **26** 910; **30** 650, 651
scarabs **12** 247, *247*, *248*
schools **13** 381
science and art **28** 200
scotiae **13** 393
scripts **13** 490–91*
sculptors **13** 395; **25** 455
sculpture **2** 678–82; **7** 783; **8** 457; **9** 34; **12** 286–7, 625; **13** 374*, 392, 421–71*, *423*, 433–9*, 440*, 441*, 450*, 467–71*; **22** 733; **24** 258, 318–19*, *319*; **25** 177, 179, *456*; **29** 559
acro-elephantine **13** 597
acrolithic **1** 127*; **8** 262; **13** 434
Archaic **13** *367*, 444*; **22** 699; **27** *689*
Archaic, Early **13** 442–5*
Archaic, Late **13** 447–9*, *447*
Archaic, Middle **13** 445*, *446*
architectural **10** 742*; **13** 391, 392, 393, 424–7*, 431–2*, 445–7, 469–70
Archaic **2** 679, *679*; **7** *849*
Classical **2** 679–81; **10** *434*
Classical, Early **2** *680*; **13** *432*, 451–2
Classical, High **13** *425*, *426*
Classical, Late **13** 460*
Hellenistic **2** *667*
Sicily **28** *387*
Attica **8** 155; **13** 447
Boeotia **13** 455; **18** 409
bronze **1** 481; **6** 9; **8** 262, *262*, 458, *696*; **13** 422, *429*, 433, 434–5*, 438, 441–2, *442*, *443*, 448, *453*, *460*; **23** 290; **24** 258, *328*; **25** 177, *178*, *179*; **26** *297*; **30** 339
chryselephantine statues **8** 262, 458; **13** 387, 435*, 596; **16** 798; **24** 593
Classical **13** *367*; **25** *178*
Classical, Early **2** 681–2; **13** 450–52*

Greece, ancient
sculpture—cont.
Classical, High **2** 682; **13** 452–8*; **24** *593*
Classical, Late **2** 682; **13** *459*
collections **13** 469*
colossal statues **8** 262; **24** 593; **27** 689
cult statues **2** *686*; **8** 262, *262*; **10** 423; **13** 370, 424; **27** 711; **29** 567
Daidalic **13** 442–4*
Dark Age (*c.* 1050–*c.* 750 BC) **13** 441*
display **7** 561; **9** 20
fountain houses **11** 339
Geometric (*c.* 900–*c.* 700 BC) **2** 681; **13** *367*, *441*, 441–2*
group **13** 424, 458; **27** 689
Hellenistic **2** 682; **9** *248*; **13** *367*, 461–2*; **25** *179*
Hellenistic, Early **13** *462*, 462–4*, *463*
Hellenistic, High **13** 464–5*, *465*
Hellenistic, Late **13** 465–7*
herms **5** 298–9; **13** 429; **14** 455–6
Ionia **15** 893
Italy **30** 339
korai **8** 688; **13** 371, 422, 429, 444–5, 451; **18** 243–5*, *244*; **29** 559, VIII1
kouroi **13** 371, 422, 429, 444–5, *446*, *449*, 451; **18** *409*, 409–10*, *410*; **22** 699, *699*; **23** 290; **24** *328*; **27** 689, *689*; **29** 559
Lakonia **13** 441, 442, *442*, 455
marble **13** *422*, 433, 436; **23** *433*
Archaic **2** 679; **8** 262, *688*, *870*; **13** 434*; **18** *244*, *409*, *410*; **22** 699, *699*; **27** 688, *689*
Archaic, Early **13** 445
Archaic, Late **13** *448*, *449*; **18** *244*
Archaic, Middle **8** *695*; **13** *446*
Classical, Early **1** *480*; **8** *697*; **13** *452*; **24** *205*; **25** *179*
Classical, High **8** *689*; **13** 438, *454*; **25** *576*
Classical, Late **13** *459*; **14** *69*, *70*; **19** *853*; **23** *291*
Hellenistic **27** *692*
Hellenistic, Late **13** *466*
Roman **13** 438
monumental **13** 368, 421–71*; **23** 290–91
Archaic **27** 689
Archaic, Late **13** *431*
Classical, Early **13** *432*
Classical, Late **13** 458–61*
Hellenistic, High **13** 465
Ripe Archaic *see* Archaic, Late
mythological **8** *688*, *689*; **10** *449*
Classical, Early **1** *480*
Classical, High **13** *429*
Classical, Late **7** *854*; **13** *460*
Geometric (*c.* 900–*c.* 700 BC) **13** *442*
Proto-Daidalic **13** *443*
5th cent. BC **24** *205*
nude figures **25** 456
Orientalizing style **13** 442
portraits **13** 604
Proto-Daidalic **13** 442*
relief **8** *690*; **10** *139*; **11** 791; **13** 370, *371*, 424, 427–8*, 430–32*, 582*; **22** *514*; **24** *415*; **26** 134–5*, *292*
Archaic **13** *582*; **30** *645*
Archaic, Late **13** *431*, *447*
Classical, Early **13** *432*, 451
Classical, High **13** *455*, 455–8
Classical, Late **13** 461*
record **13** 428*, *428*, 456–7
Rich style **13** *456*, *458*
Turkey **10** *431*; **14** *69*

Greece, ancient
sculpture
relief—cont.
votive **13** 427–8*
6th cent. BC **29** *368*
restoration **9** 21
Rich style **13** 452, 455, 456–8
Roman **13** *367*
Severe style (i) (Greece, ancient) **13** *450*, 450–52, 468
stone **8** 262; **13** 435–6*; **29** *710*
tomb **13** 424
Turkey **8** *870*; **14** *70*
votive statues **13** 424
wood **8** 262; **13** 433–4*, 442
5th cent. BC **23** *433*
seals **12** 246–8*; **13** 595; **14** 338, 359*, *359*, 360
seating **13** 380, 385, *385*, 386
serpentine **12** 246, 247
set squares **13** 411
shaft graves **13** 383
shields **13** 583, 584; **14** 407; **15** 149
ship-decoration **28** 611
shops **13** 381
shrines (i) (cult) **13** 418–19
siege engines **13** 413; **21** 556–7
siege-sheds **21** 556, 557
signatures **7** 830; **13** 439, 440, 484, 488, 489*, *489*, 490, 587; **20** 441; **24** 892; **32** 27
silhouettes **13** 481, 492, 493, 498, 504, 535
silver **3** 483; **13** 390, 391, 568–71*, *569*, *570*, 573, 585, *585*, *587*, *588*, 588, 589
sinopie **13** 556
skyphoi **13** *475*, 476, 478, 492, 533
souvenirs **13** 478
specifications (*syngraphe*) **13** 409
specimens (*paradeigma*) **13** 409
sphinxes **8** *695*; **13** 429; **29** 395–7*
sporting scenes **29** 422, 423
stadia **13** 386, 403, 418; **16** 612; **27** 712; **29** 487–8*, *488*
stage buildings **13** 385–6, *385*, 391
stage design **1** 450; **30** 650–51*
stages **13** *385*, 386, 406; **30** 651
stage scenery **1** 450; **30** 650
staircases **13** 385, *385*
stairs **13** 387
stamnoi **13** *475*, 476, *485*
stamps **13** 537, *537*
standardization **14** 564
statuettes **13** 433, 436, 571–4*, *572*, *573*, *574*, 578–82*, 595–6, *596*; **29** 567*, *567*
Italy **30** *339*
stelae **6** *388*; **13** *544*; **29** 616–17*
Attica **29** 616
funerary **13** 427*, 430–31, *431*, 456, *457*; **26** *292*; **29** *616*
Rich style **13** *457*
steps **13** 380
stoas **8** *686*; **13** 381, *381*, 386, 389, 402–3, 406, 416, 417, 418; **27** 712, 714; **29** 680–81, *681*; **31** 294
6th cent. BC **13** *402*
7th cent. BC **27** 687
stone **1** *692*; **8** 262; **13** 376, 386–9*, *388*, *389*, 393, 435–6*, 439, 445, 543; **22** 160; **29** *710*
stone-throwers **21** 557
stools **6** 388
straight-edges **13** 411
stucco **13** 383, 389, 602–4*; **29** 813, 814*
stylobatai **13** *376*, 414
supports **13** 543
surveyors **30** 25
surveys **13** 411–12
swords **2** 451
symbolism (critical term) **13** 415–16*

Greece, ancient —cont.
symmetry **13** 412
tables **13** 592*; **30** 217
taeniae **11** 790; **13** 377, *378*, 393
tattoos **30** 367
tempera **13** 393, 544
templates **13** 409, 556
temples **2** 362, *664*, *672*, *688*; **8** *370*, *685*; **13** 375, *375*, *376*, 376–80, *377*, 387, 390, 391–2, 393, 394, *395*, 396, 397–401*, *400*, *404*, 405–6, *406*, 408, 409, 412, 414, *414*, 415, *416*, 424, 431–2*, 443, 445, 556; **21** 46; **22** 354; **23** 429, 477; **27** 712; **30** 434–5*, 902–3
amphiprostyle **13** 376
Archaic **7** 849
colossal **13** 399
Corinthian **13** 405
Crete **18** *210*, 210–11
cult **13** 396, 417
dipteral **13** 376
distyle **13** *376*
Doric **1** *479*, 511, *511*; **2** *677*, 684; **13** 377–9, *378*, 387, 401, 405, *414*, 415; **17** *745*; **23** *759*; **30** *435*; **31** *269*
funerary **20** 863
hekatompeda **13** 397, 415
Hellenistic **13** 410
hexastyle **13** 398
Ionia **15** *894*
Ionic **13** *379*, 379, 398–400, 415
Italy **16** *622*; **30** 339
Libya **8** *367*
Lydia **19** 841
Naxos (Greece) **22** *698*
peripteral **10** 423; **13** 376, *397*, 397, 398, 415
peristyle **13** 397; **24** 456*
prostyle **13** 376
pseudo-dipteral **13** 378, 405
Roman **26** 910–11
sanctuary-temples **30** 434–5
Sicily **13** 378
treasury-temples **30** 434, 435
tripteral **13** 376
Turkey **5** *742*; **8** *869*
5th cent. BC **13** *401*
6th cent. BC **7** *852*
7th cent. BC **28** 893
tepidaria **13** 386
terracotta **7** *854*; **10** 742; **13** 376, 390–91, 393, 424, 433*, 436–7*, 441, *441*, *443*, 450, 577–83*, *603*; **21** *342*; **22** 160; **23** 427, *433*; **24** *374*; **27** 825; **29** 567; **30** *493*, 493–4; **31** 259
Archaic **13** 578–9*, *579*, *582*
Attica **13** *580*
Boeotia **13** *579*, *580*
Classical **13** 579–81*, *580*
Daidalic **13** 443
Hellenistic **13** *581*, 581–2*
Roman **27** 111
textiles **13** 604*
theatra **13** 380, 385–6, *385*; **30** 650
theatres **1** 123; **13** 380, 385–6*, *385*, 391, 403, 406, 418; **19** 234; **21** 341; **29** 488; **30** 650–51*, *651*
Hellenistic **24** *413*
Roman **26** 910
4th cent. BC **13** *402*
theories **13** 467–9*
architectural **13** 403, 408–9*; **25** 768
art **13** 545, 548; **25** 31–2, 177
form **13** 468; **25** 31
painting **13** 553–4*
perspective **13** 553
sculpture **13** 467–9*
thericleians **13** 537
tholoi **8** 692, *694*; **13** 380, 390, 401; **14** 73; **27** 691; **29** 367
thrones **13** *452*; **30** 775*
tile graves **13** 383
Greece, ancient —cont.
tiles **13** 387, 390, 411, *411*; **30** *493*, 493–4
title-pages **31** 48
toichobatai **13** 388, 389
tombs **13** 383, *384*, 391, 396, 407, *407*, 568; **31** 107–9*, *108*
chamber **13** 383, 384, 396
cist **13** 383, 396
Macedonian **13** 391, 404, 407
peribolos **13** 384
rock-cut **31** 108
tholos **13** 383; **31** 108
tools **13** 371
towers **2** *667*; **21** 557
towns **13** 419
toys **31** 254
trade **9** 786; **10** 591–2; **13** 372–3*; **21** 652
art **2** 557
coins **1** 203; **10** 591
marble **26** 855
metalwork **10** 591
obsidian **8** 306
pottery **6** 333; **10** 591, 592, 610; **13** 486–7*, 525; **28** 654
sculpture **1** 480; **26** 292, 854
Scythian **28** 323
shoes **10** 591
terracotta **13** 578
textiles **6** 290
vases **10** 614
trappings **14** 180–81*
treasuries **13** 376, 379, 380, 390; **27** 712; **31** 293–4*, *294*
6th cent. BC **13** *399*
treatises **13** 394, 554; **24** 414
architecture **13** 408–9; **14** 461; **23** 482
painting **10** 650; **13** 549; **31** 298
perspective **13** 553
sculpture **31** 301–2*
urns **13** 539
trees **13** *418*, 418–19
triglyphs **11** 790; **13** 377, *378*, 379, 393, 398
tripods **13** *575*, 575–6
trompe l'oeil **13** 389; **22** 160
trophies **31** 368–9
tufa **13** 387
tumuli **13** 383, 384; **31** 107
underdrawings **13** 543–4
urban planning **13** 382, 401–2, 416, 417, 419–21*, *420*
4th cent. BC **25** 573–5
6th cent. BC **21** 341
varnishes **2** 217; **13** 544
vases **10** 474; **13** *475*, 477–8, 480, 483, *488*, 489, 590, *590*; **16** 830
bilingual **13** 517; **32** 65
Chalcidian **13** 515
Lakonia **13** 512
vaults (ceiling) **13** 391, 403, 404, 407; **29** 488
barrel **8** 694; **32** 87
verandahs **13** 383
vessels
bronze **13** 574
metal **13** 574–7*
volutes **13** 377, 391, 392, 393, 399
wall decorations **13** 383, *392*, 393, *393*
walls **13** 388–9, 393, 396
curtain (i) (castle) **21** 557–8
defensive **21** 555–6, 557
Roman **26** 909
town **13** 389, 403, 404; **21** *312*, 549
water pipes **13** 419
waterspouts **13** 390, 392
water supply **2** 241
waxes **20** 327
weapons **13** 391, 583–5*
weathervanes **33** 8
well-heads **33** 56–7, *57*
wells **13** 381
white lead **23** 141
wicker **33** 155
Greece, ancient —cont.
wine-coolers **13** 476
wings (theatre) **13** 385
women **13** 415, 423; **25** 456
wood **1** 450; **8** 262; **9** 151; **13** 376, 389–90, 433–4*, 442, 543, 592, 604*; **20** 327; **21** 712; **27** 825
wool **9** 246; **13** 604
workshops **13** 371
wreaths **13** 598, 599
writing **10** 4; **13** 369, 490–91; **20** 329
writing-tablets **4** 342; **20** 327
xenia **29** 665
see also CYCLADIC; HELLADIC; MACEDONIA (i) (GREECE); MYCENEAN
Greef, Bastiaan de **29** 433; **33** 48
Greef, Ben de **13** 607
Greef, Jan de **13** 607*; **22** 828
collaboration **22** 828
works **1** 803; **26** 268; **29** 8, 433
Greek crosses *see under* CROSSES → types
Greek-cross octagon churches *see under* CHURCHES → types
Greek key design *see* MEANDER
Greek pitch **28** 339
Greek Revival **10** 850; **13** 607–13*; **18** 887; **22** 735; **25** 267; **28** 248; **33** 195
art forms
architecture **13** 608, *610*, *611*; **20** *868*; **25** 172; **29** 805–6
England **7** *503*, *504*; **10** *234*; **13** 608; **20** *868*; **28** *873*, *874*; **33** *192*
Germany **3** *791*; **13** 608–9, 610, *610*; **18** *122*; **25** *366*
Greece **2** *674*
Ireland **16** *9*, 9–10
Scotland **13** 610
United States of America **8** *574*; **13** 610–11; **18** 629; **21** *617*; **29** 771; **31** *232*; **32** *827*
brick **4** 787
furniture **28** 253
interior decoration **31** 619, 620
regional traditions
Britain **33** 191
England **10** 235; **13** 609–10; **30** *218*
Germany **18** 122, 741; **28** 98
Scotland **9** 723
United States of America **21** 617, 618; **28** 641; **31** 591–2
green *see under* PIGMENTS → types
Green (family) **31** 652
Green, Anthony **11** 437; **13** 614*
Green, Benjamin (*c.* 1736-1800) **8** 131; **10** 562
Green, Benjamin (1811-58) **23** 20
Green, Curtis **25** 402
Green, Edward B. **5** 124
Green, F. D. Lycett **33** 545
Green, Frederick **14** 673
Green, Frederick W. **10** 80; **14** 513
works **14** *514*
Green, Guy **19** 508; **29** 495; **30** 877
Green, Henry **10** 176
Green, J. G. **10** 319
Green, John **14** 198; **23** 20
Green, Joseph (*fl* 1801) **11** 432, 433
Green, Joseph H. (*fl* 1839) **1** 154
Green, Julien **32** 669
Green, Leslie W. **21** 349
Green, Robert A. **5** 175
Green, Rupert **13** 615
Green, Thomas **13** 614*
Green, Valentine **13** 614–15*; **21** 416
teachers **14** 132
works **3** 280; **8** 21; **21** 417; **24** 367; **26** 231; **33** 413
Green, William Curtis **10** 240; **13** 615*; **33** 205
Green-and-white ware *see under* POTTERY → wares
Greenaway, Henry **10** 333
Greenaway, John **13** 615
Greenaway, Kate **4** 363; **10** 420; **13** 615*; **22** 744; **33** 361
Greenaway, Peter **7** 681
Greenaway, Thomas **3** 370
green belt **7** 326; **12** 144; **22** 283; **27** 380
Greenberg, Clement **2** 536; **11** 706; **13** 615–16*; **21** 776; **25** 360; **31** 608
groups and movements **1** 78, 86; **8** 240; **21** 645; **23** 791; **27** 563
works **2** 518; **5** 569; **7** 636, 783; **8** 613; **11** 315; **25** 360; **31** 300, 672
Greenberg, Johannes **10** 540
green bice *see* PIGMENTS → types → green verditer
Green City Mountain *see* MT QINCHENG
Green Count *see* AMADEUS VI, Count of Savoy
Greene, Balcomb **1** 771; **31** 138
Greene, Belle da Costa **13** 616–17*; **22** 111
Greene, Charles (Sumner) **2** 572–3; **13** 617–18*; **31** 595, 632
works **2** *572*
Greene, Connie **10** 484
Greene, David **2** 308; **7** 788
Greene, Gertrude **31** 614
Greene, Godfrey **16** 55
Greene, Henry (Mather) **2** 572–3; **13** 617–18*; **31** 595, 632
Greene, John **10** 316
Greene, John Holden **5** 78; **13** 202, 617*; **25** 666; **27** 884
Greene, Stan **22** 589
Greene Collection **8** 537
Greene & Greene **13** 617–18*
works **5** 173; **6** 391; **13** *618*
green-glazed ware *see under* POTTERY → wares
green-grey granite *see under* GRANITE → types
Greenhall, Mickey **10** 483
greenheart **33** 325
Greenhill, John **5** 900; **13** 618–19*; **19** 123
Greenhills (OH) **7** 326
greenhouses **7** 744; **12** 791; **13** 619*
Britain **13** 619
England **10** 236; **12** 137; **18** *4*
Rome, ancient **13** 619
United States of America **13** 619
see also CONSERVATORIES; ORANGERIES
Greenland **5** *559*; **13** 620–21*; **32** 513
amulets **13** 620
architecture **32** 533
cloaks **3** 441
tapestries **13** *620*
tattoos **30** 366
Greenlaw, Jean **1** 433
Greenless, Robert **20** 276
Greenock (Strathclyde) **28** 254
Custom House **28** 228
law courts **28** 288
St Patrick's **28** 243
Green Oribe ware *see under* POTTERY → wares
Greenough, Horatio **11** 189; **13** 621–2*; **31** 610, 662
pupils **13** 622
works **12** 645; **22** 47; **31** 611, *611*
writings **11** 840
Greenough, Richard Saltonstall **13** 622*; **31** 611
Greenpoint Glass Works **9** 171
Greens, Herb **12** 855
Greenslade, Sidney K. **19** 319
Greensmith, Peter **24** 181
Green Spring Plantation (VA) **31** 634
Greensted (Essex), St Andrew **2** 67; **30** 894
greenstone
historical and regional traditions
Ancient Near East **1** *859*
Maori **23** *734*
Maya **21** 251, *251*
Mesoamerica, Pre-Columbian **21** *185*, 240–41, 242, 251, *251*, 257; **23** 418
Olmec **21** *185*; **23** 418
Pacific Islands **23** *734*
Punic **25** 734
South America, Pre-Columbian **29** 155
uses
clubs (weapons) **23** *734*
flutes (musical instruments) **21** 257
masks **21** 251
scarabs **25** 734
sculpture **21** *185*
seals **1** *858*
see also JADE
green verditer *see under* PIGMENTS → types
Greenwald, Herbert S. **21** 492, 493
greenware *see under* POTTERY → wares
Greenway, Francis (Howard) **2** 737; **13** 622–3*; **23** 36
works **2** *737*, 738; **4** 167; **13** *622*; **18** 887; **30** 158; **32** 249
Greenwich (Kent) **13** 623–4*
armour **2** *471*, 472, 473
arsenal **2** 502
Charlton House **4** 785; **8** 45
Hospital *see* Royal Naval College
National Maritime Museum **3** 232; **7** 789; **10** 367; **13** 624; **14** 849; **32** 143
Observatory **23** 339, 340
Palace **8** 794; **12** 126; **13** 623*; **19** 582; **23** 208; **30** 660; **33** 10
collections **10** 363
King Charles block **13** 623
Queen's House **8** 45; **10** 270, 290, 292, 360; **13** 623; **29** 801, 803; **32** 551
Queen's House **2** 358; **17** 634; **25** 265
Ranger's House **7** 900
Royal Naval Hospital **10** 232, 249, 360; **13** 623–4*, *624*; **14** 254, 782; **33** 398, *398*
Chapel **25** 727
model **2** 336
Painted Hall **3** 267; **10** 277; **14** 784; **30** *759*
paintings **30** 758–9
St Alfege **14** 256
Town Hall **4** 788
Vanbrugh Castle **6** 60; **10** 232; **13** 200; **23** 210; **31** *860*
Greenwich glasshouse **10** 316
Greenwich Mural Workshop **22** 333
works **22** *333*
Greenwood, Frans **9** 169; **10** 317; **22** 885; **28** 166
Greenwood, John **4** 477; **10** 366; **13** 624*
Greenwood, Thomas (*d* 1797) **30** 675
Greenwood, Thomas (*fl* 1810) **27** 139
Greenwood Hare, Cecil **4** 215
Greer, Howard **9** 292
greeting cards *see under* CARDS → types
Grefrath **1** 519
Greg, R. H. **10** 90
Gregan, John Edgar **20** 237
Gregg, Noel **23** 72
Grégoire, Henri-Charles-Martin **13** 625*; **27** 247, 254

Gregolini 18 791
Gregoor, Jan 8 862
Gregori, Antonio 6 146
Gregori, Carlo 13 625*; 32 424
Gregori, Ferdinando 13 625*
Gregori, Gaspar 29 267
Gregori, Guido 6 146
Gregorian, Marcos 15 898
Gregoriano Etrusco, Museo see under ROME, VATICAN → museums
Gregoriis, Giovanni de' 4 196; 13 625
works 4 196
Gregoriis, Gregorio de' 13 625*
works 4 196, 196; 16 360
Gregorini, Domenico 13 625–6*; 23 637
works 16 639
Gregorini, Ludovico 13 625
Gregorio, Antonio di see ANTONIO DI GREGORIO
Gregorio, Bartolommeo di see BARTOLOMMEO DI GREGORIO
Gregorio, Goro di see GORO DI GREGORIO
Gregorio, José 2 397
Gregorio, Marco De see DE GREGORIO, MARCO
Gregorio di Catino 10 804
Gregorio di Cecco (di Luca) 13 626*; 30 232
Gregorio di Lorenzo 11 26
Gregoriopolis 23 620
Gregorius, Albert 4 877
Gregorius, Petrus 8 127; 24 241
Gregory, Abbot of Saint-Michel-de-Cuxa 27 568
Gregory, Bishop of Tours 8 203, 222; 11 653; 13 626–7*; 31 226
Gregory, Saint see GREGORY I, Pope
Gregory I, Pope (reg 590-604) 8 259; 13 627*
architecture 8 222; 20 520; 26 801
manuscripts 19 549
metalwork 8 203
reliquaries 26 143
translated writings 33 89
Gregory IV, Pope (reg 827-44) 5 779; 23 620; 26 833
Gregory VII, Pope (reg 1073-85) 7 474
Gregory IX, Pope (reg 1227-41) 14 726; 19 787; 26 803
Gregory X, Pope (reg 1271-76) 23 461
Gregory XI, Pope (reg 1370-77) 11 654; 29 5
Gregory XIII, Pope (reg 1572-85) 4 311; 13 627–8*
architecture 9 339; 18 699; 19 631; 24 399; 25 260; 26 757, 814, 831, 840; 31 820
military 23 746
art policies 1 102; 16 768
collections 28 30
manuscripts 4 318
maps 8 513; 20 366
medals 4 322, 339
metalwork 32 213
mosaics 26 809
paintings 2 492; 4 812; 5 442, 735; 18 870; 22 392; 26 89, 835; 30 428
frescoes 27 480
sculpture 1 791; 2 139; 31 787
urban planning 11 272
Gregory XIV, Pope (reg 1590) 4 323; 28 529*
Gregory XV, Pope (reg 1621-3) 13 785; 19 205, 778*; 26 758
Gregory XVI, Pope (reg 1831-46) 8 867; 12 738; 13 628–9*; 24 846; 26 820
Gregory, Bruce 19 83
Gregory, Eric (Craven) 13 629*
Gregory, Gregory 27 656
Gregory, Padraig 16 39
Gregory, Peter see GREGORY, ERIC
Gregory, Richard 28 207
Gregory, Waylande 8 82; 31 639
Gregory Master see REGISTRUM GREGORII, MASTER OF THE
Gregory of London 23 460
Gregory of Nazianzus, Bishop 9 570, 614, 620; 10 129; 24 177
Gregory of Nyssa, Saint 7 212; 9 570
Gregory the Great, Pope see GREGORY I, Pope
Gregotti, Vittorio 11 63; 13 629–30*; 16 650
groups and movements 22 747
works 13 630; 18 114; 28 657; 29 274, 489, 490
Gregotti Associati 13 629
Gregović, Marko 22 17
Gregson, T. S. 5 418
Gregynog Press 4 366; 32 791
Greif, Johann Georg 22 302
Greifen, Philip, Duke of Pomerania-Stettin see PHILIP, Duke of Pomerania-Stettin
Greifen, Vratislav VIII, Duke of Pomerania-Wolgast see POMERANIA-WOLGAST, VRATISLAV VIII, Grand Duke of
Greiffenklau, Everardus von see EVERARDUS VON GREIFFENKLAU
Greiffenklau, Johann Philipp von, Prince-Bishop of Würzburg 2 843; 23 2; 32 120
Greiffenklau, Karl Philipp von, Prince-Bishop of Würzburg 2 843; 13 631–2*; 30 858
Greiffenklau Missal see under MISSALS → individual manuscripts
Greif Studio 27 717
Grein, E. 28 133
Grein, Jack 30 685
Greinburg Palace 2 779
Greine, Ludwig 31 262
Greiner, Dick 13 632*
Greiner, Otto 13 632*; 14 687
Greipel, Johann 21 512
Greis, Otto 12 397; 13 632*; 25 786
Greisch 19 826
Greither, Elias, I 8 627; 13 633*
Greither, Johann 13 633
Greive, P. F. 1 650; 13 633
Grekov, Aleksey 20 147
Grekov, Mitrofan (Borisovich) 2 633; 13 633*; 27 395
Grekov Studio of Military Artists 13 633; 32 737
Greku, E. L. 21 812
Greku, Mikhail 21 811
Grela, Juan 2 399, 400; 26 216
Grellet, Gabriel 11 609; 19 397
Grellet, Pierre 11 609; 19 397
Gremi, Church of the Archangels 12 331; 25 344
gremiales 32 390*
Grémio Artístico 28 736
Gremislavsky, Ivan Yakovlevich 28 757
Gremm, Willem 9 470; 33 427
Grenada 2 144, 149; 5 745
architecture 2 148
barracks 2 148
houses 2 147
libraries 2 153
museums 2 153
painting 2 150
patronage 2 153
see also ANTILLES, LESSER; WINDWARD ISLANDS
Grendey, Giles 7 485; 10 294; 13 634*; 19 592
works 10 294; 29 316
Grenfell, Bernard 23 692
Grenfell, Francis Wallis 10 91
Grenfell, William 27 317
Grenier (family) 13 195
Grenier, Antoine 13 634
Grenier, Colinet 13 634
Grenier, Imbert 13 634
Grenier, Jean 10 348; 13 634; 31 219
Grenier, Pasquier 13 196, 634*
attributions 2 871
dealing 13 195; 30 314; 31 218
patrons and collectors 5 211; 9 738
works 31 218, 219
Grenier-Wambersie (family) 24 885
Gréningaire 29 628
Grenoble 11 505; 13 635, 635–6*
Bibliothèque Municipale d'Etude et d'Information 11 673
festivals 23 770, 770
Maison de la Culture 30 684
museums 11 668
Musée des Beaux-Arts 11 665, 666
Musée Dauphinois 13 635
Musée de Grenoble 10 798; 19 66
Musée Stendhal 13 635
St Laurent 11 509
Oratory of St Oyand 13 636*, 636; 21 163
silver 11 620
Villeneuve de Grenoble 2 700
Visitation convent of Ste-Marie-d'en-Haut see museums → Musée Dauphinois
Grenoble, Alexandre see JACQUET, ALEXANDRE
Grenoble, Matthieu Jacquet de see JACQUET DE GRENOBLE, MATTHIEU
Grent, William 29 377
Grenville, Richard, 2nd Earl Temple (1711-79) 4 422; 13 636–7*; 29 736; 30 452
Grenville, Richard, 3rd Duke of Buckingham and Chandos (1776-1839) 8 597; 32 540
Grenzhausen 12 429
Greppel, Rudolf 28 856
Greppi, Cristoforo 20 841
Grès, Mme 9 293
Gresford (Clwyd), All Saints 32 782, 790
Gresham, Richard 11 348
Gresham, Thomas 6 127; 19 568
Gresham group 13 637–8*; 14 901; 22 434
members 3 766, 820; 9 763; 30 212
Gresik 15 753, 792
mosque-tomb complex of Sunan Giri 15 757
Gresley, Nigel 27 717
Gresnicht, Carl 3 890
Gresse, John Alexander 14 548
Gretor, Willy 29 775
Gretsch, Hermann 12 437; 32 757
Gretzer 29 221
Gretzinger, Salomon 14 319
Greus, Gregor 8 742; 11 467; 23 635
Greuter, Elias, I see GREITHER, ELIAS, I
Greuter, Johann Friedrich 6 502; 18 735; 20 499; 32 716
works 3 207
Greuter, Matthäus 2 105, 707; 3 293, 353; 8 882
Greuze, Jean-Baptiste 8 481; 11 508, 658, 672; 13 638–44*; 22 85; 24 135, 136, 167
attributions 9 398
collaboration 18 661
exhibitions 10 679
groups and movements 26 740
patrons and collectors
Augustin, Jean-Baptiste (-Jacques) 2 722
Greuze, Jean-Baptiste
patrons and collectors—cont.
Canino, Lucien Bonaparte, Prince of (1775-1840) 4 304
Caraman, Duc de 5 700
Catherine II, Empress of Russia (reg 1762- 96) 26 732
Cognacq, (Théodore-) Ernest 7 528
Delessert, (Jules-Paul-) Benjamin (1773-1847) 8 664
Demidoff, Nicolas 8 704
Du Barry, (Marie-Jeanne Bécu,) Comtesse 9 313
Houssaye, (François-) Arsène 14 802
La Live de Jully, Ange-Laurent de 11 658; 18 660
Livois, Marquis de 19 510
Marigny, Marquis de 25 82
McLellan, Archibald 28 271
Morny, Charles-Auguste, Duc de 22 127
Paul I, Emperor of Russia (reg 1796-1801) 26 733
Péreire, Jacob-Emile & Isaac 24 396
Périer, Casimir 24 418
Ramsay, Allan (1713-84) 28 271
Rushout, John, 2nd Baron Northwick 27 350
Seymour-Conway, Richard, 4th Marquess of Hertford 28 527
Sparre, Gustaf Adolf 29 366
Véri (-Raionard), Louis-Gabriel, Marquis de 32 255
Wille, Jean-Georges 33 196
Yusupov, Nikolay (Borisovich), Prince (1751- 1831) 33 579
pupils 9 365; 14 657; 20 890; 33 195, 196
reproductive prints by others 3 463; 5 884; 6 563; 11 171–2; 13 871; 19 261, 262; 20 584; 21 800; 22 88; 28 754; 32 720
sponsors 8 372
works 2 53, 105; 7 384; 8 764; 10 785; 11 408, 540; 12 291, 292; 13 639, 640, 641, 643; 18 660; 19 118
Greuze, Jean-Louis 13 638
Greve (family) 23 236
Grevenbroeck, Henric van 2 201; 3 588
Grevenmacher 19 826
Grevenmacherberg 19 826
Greverade, Adolf 21 103; 23 255
Greverade, Heinrich 21 103; 26 507
Grevesmühlen Church 14 81
Greville, Charles 13 644; 26 541
Greville, Charles Francis 2 240; 13 644*; 14 114
Greville, Charles John 13 644
Greville, Francis, 1st Earl Brooke and 1st Earl of Warwick (1719-73) 13 644*
Greville, Francis, 5th Earl Brooke and 5th Earl of Warwick (1853-1924) 13 644
Greville, Fulke 13 644
Greville, George, 2nd Earl Brooke and 2nd Earl of Warwick 13 644*; 14 114; 28 883
Greville, John, Earl of Bath 29 717
Grévin, Alfred 13 644–5*
Grey, Amabel de, Countess de Grey 8 95; 13 645
Grey, Anthony de, 11th Earl de Grey 13 645; 25 759
Grey, Edward 22 148
Grey, Elmer 19 319
Grey, Forde, 1st Earl of Tankerville 9 386; 30 278
Grey, George 1 58, 67
Grey, George Harry, 5th Earl of Stamford 13 301
Grey, Henry de, 12th Earl de Grey 13 645
Grey, Henry de, 1st Duke and 11th Earl of Kent 5 827
Grey, James 26 263
Grey, Jemima de, Marchioness de Grey 13 645
Grey, Ormson and Brown
works 7 745
Grey, Sophia de, 1st Duchess of Kent 5 827
Grey, Spalding 24 409
Grey, Thomas Philip de, 2nd Earl de Grey 13 645; 26 475
Grey, Walter de, Archbishop of York 33 547
Grey Canyon Collective 22 598
Greyfriars 25 805
Grey Minyan ware see POTTERY → wares → Minyan ware
Grey school see HAGUE SCHOOL
Greyss, Benedetto de 9 21
greywacke see BEKHEN STONE
Grèze, La see LA GRÈZE
Grez-sur-Loing 3 776; 30 79
members 12 779
Bussière, Gaston 5 296
Krohg, Christian 18 463
Larsson, Carl (Olof) (1853-1919) 18 801
Liljefors, Bruno (Andreas) 19 379
Netti, Francesco 22 916
Nordström, Karl (Fredrik) 23 205
Skredsvig, Christian 28 825
Strindberg, (Johan) August 29 774
Griaciani-Marchand 25 703
Griaule, Marcel 9 64–5, 66, 68
Gribanov, B. N. 27 439
Gribble, Herbert Augustine 23 30, 473
Gribbon, Edward 3 274
Gribeauval, Jean-Baptiste Vaquelte de 21 567
Gribelin, Simon, II 13 645–6*; 14 161
works 7 796; 10 328, 330; 14 419, 856; 25 759
Gribloch 28 231
Gricci, Giuseppe 13 646*; 16 737
works 2 285; 5 348, 671; 9 29; 16 718, 737; 20 69; 29 329
Gricci, Stefano 5 348
Grice, H. P. 7 661
Grice, Malcolm Le see LE GRICE, MALCOLM
Grice, Michael 2 318
Grič-Zagreb see under ZAGREB
Gridhrakuta see RAJGIR
Griebel, Otto 22 923
Grieder, Terence 18 637
Grieg, Edvard 22 540
Grieg, Per 23 222
Griego, el see ALVAREZ DE LA PEÑA, MANUEL FRANCISCO
Griegst, Arje 8 753
Griekse A 22 879, 880, 881; 30 878
Griemert, Hubert 12 432
Grien, Hans Baldung see BALDUNG, HANS
Grieneisen 10 105
Griepenkerl, Christian
pupils
Czeschka, Carl Otto 8 428
Faistauer, Anton 10 756
Gerstl, Richard 12 491
Iveković, Oton 16 795
Jungnickel, Ludwig Heinrich 17 691
Kurzweil, Max(imilian) 18 533
Lefler, Heinrich 19 69
Schiele, Egon 28 88
Strauch, Ludwig Karl 29 763
Šubic, Jurij 29 885
Grierson, Amier & Draffin 2 705

Grierson, John **7** 547; **33** 74
Grierson, Ronald **5** 841
works **5** *841*
Griesbeck von Griesbach, Florian **8** 377, 422; **13** 646*; **29** 625
Gries Church **2** 799; **23** 707; **28** 134
Griese, Johann August **12** 426
Grieshaber, H. A. P. **2** 134; **29** 693; **33** 364
Griespeck, Florián **8** 395; **29** 582
Grieve (family) **30** 680
Grieve, David **2** 766
Grieve, Johan Conrad **13** 633*
Grieve, John Henderson **30** 679, 681
Grieve, Thomas **30** 679, 681
Grieve, William **30** 679
Griffa, La **9** 191
Griffenfeld **14** 245
Griffi, Ambrogio **11** 294
Griffier, Jan, I (?1645-1718) **9** 327; **13** 647*; **27** 518
Griffier, Jan, II (*fl* 1738-73) **13** 647; **27** 518
Griffier, Robert **13** 647; **27** 518
Griffin, James S. **22** 539
works **22** *539*
Griffin, Marion Mahony **13** 647–8*; **31** 595
groups and movements **6** 578; **25** 446
works **13** *647*
Griffin, Walter Burley **2** 759; **5** 337, 602; **7** 670; **13** 647–8*; **31** 595
groups and movements **2** 572; **6** 578; **25** 446
staff **4** 65; **19** 453
works **2** 740, *741*, 741, 756; **5** 601; **13** *647*; **19** 775; **30** 159; **31** 729
Griffin Bird Painter **13** 508
Griffith, F(rancis) L(lewellyn) **10** 81, 82; **18** 209; **22** 467; **33** 481
Griffith, James **23** 690
Griffith, John **15** 656
Griffith, Milo ap **32** 787
Griffith, Moses **15** 892
Griffith, Thomas **31** 472
Griffith Park Observatory **23** 342
Griffiths, D. W. **1** 21
Griffiths, Henry **28** 894
Griffo, Ambrogio **4** 817
Griffo, il *see under* TYPE-FACES
Griffo, Sebastiano **19** 849
Griffo da Bologna, Francesco *see* FRANCESCO GRIFFO DA BOLOGNA
Griffoni, Floriano **7** 926
Grifi, Ambrogio *see* AMBROGIO GRIFI
Grifoni (family) **3** 161; **11** 180
Grifoni, Giuseppe *see* GRISONI, GIUSEPPE
Grifoni, Ugolino **1** 792
Grigg **2** 151
Griggs, F(rederick) L(andseer Maur) **13** 648–9*
Griggs Crucifixion, Master of the *see* TOSCANI, GIOVANNI
Grigi, Giovanni Giacomo de' **13** 650*, 659
Grigi, Guglielmo de' **5** 177; **13** 649–50*
patrons and collectors **19** 663
works **5** 177; **13** *649*
Grignion, Charles (1717-1810) **1** 844; **4** 361; **13** 324, 650; **15** 29; **22** 153
works **4** *362*
Grignion, Charles (1754-1804) **13** 650*
Grignon, J.-B. **5** 838
Grigny
Chanteloupe des Vignes **24** 131, *131*
La Grande Borne **1** 489
Grigoletti, Michelangelo **8** 135; **33** 611
Grigolia, L. **12** 327
Grigor **2** 601
Grigor I Mamikonian, Prince **25** 686
Grigorashchenko, Leonid **21** 812
Grigorescu, Georghe **13** 651
Grigorescu, Lucian **13** 650–51*; **26** 716
Grigorescu, Nicolae **13** 651–2*; **26** *714*
assistants **2** 22
patrons and collectors **26** 723
pupils **24** 559
works **5** 73; **13** *652*; **26** 714, 723
Grigorescu, Octav **13** 653*
Grigorie, Master **25** 341
Grigorievna Shcherbatova, Princess Maria *see* SHCHERBATOVA, MARIA GRIGORIEVNA, Princess
Grigorios, Archbishop **23** 373
Grigorios, Bishop of Devol **23** 373
Grigorovich, Victor (Ivanovich) **27** 440
Grigorovich, Yury **32** 601
Grigorovich-Barsky, Ivan (Grigor'yevich) **13** 653*; **18** 35; **31** 551, 552
Grigor the Illuminator, Saint **2** 425; **9** 732
Grigory **31** 556
Grigoryan, Gevorg **2** 433
Grigoryan, Mark (Vladimir) **13** 653*
works **2** 445; **10** 450
Grigor'yev, Afanasy (Grigor'yevich) **13** 653–4*; **27** 376, 404
collaboration **12** 633
groups and movements **13** 611
works **22** 172
Grigor'yev, Aleksandr **2** 633; **27** 434
Grigor'yev, Boris (Dmitriyevich) **13** 654*; **27** 392
collaboration **33** 486
groups and movements **18** 507
Grigor'yev, Boris A. **19** 273
Grigor'yev, Dmitry **33** 507
Grigoryev, Viktor **31** 560
Grigson, Geoffrey **32** 800
Grijalva, Juan de **21** 256
Grijó, Monastery of S Salvador **13** 102; **25** 291
Grill, Andries **1** 811; **14** 42; **22** 887
Grill, Anthony **1** 811
Grill, Johannes **1** 811
Grillande, Nicholo delle **12** 548
Grillandi *see* GHIRLANDAIO
Grillaud **24** 394
Grillenzoni, Francesco **7** 889
Grillenzoni, Orazio **10** 524
grilles
historical and regional traditions
Egypt **16** 496
France **22** *455*
Greece, ancient **13** 390
Indian subcontinent **16** 257
Iran **16** 502
Islamic **6** 171; **16** 256, 257, 487, 496, 500, 502
Morocco **16** 257
Ottoman **16** 257
Spain **29** *339*
Turkey **16** 257
Yemen **16** 500
materials
iron **29** *339*
marble **16** 256
stucco **16** 257
wood **16** 487, 496, 502
wrought iron **22** *455*
Grillet **6** 116, 515
Grillo (family) **12** 284
Grillo, Duca di **1** 574
Grillo, Yusuf **1** 432; **18** 639
Grillon, Fernando **24** 99
grills, window *see* WINDOW-GRILLS
Grilo, Sarah **2** 401, 546; **13** 654–5*
Grima, Andrew **17** 530
Grimaldi (family; Genoa) **1** 605; **12** 280, 281, 283, 284
Grimaldi (family; Monaco) **11** 16
Grimaldi, Alessandro Maria **33** 380
Grimaldi, Alexander **33** 380
Grimaldi, Fabrizio **13** 655*; **20** 44; **30** 649
Grimaldi, Francesco *see* GRIMALDI, FABRIZIO
Grimaldi, Francesco Maria **19** 354
Grimaldi, Gerolamo, Cardinal **6** 24
Grimaldi, Giacomo **13** 655*
patrons and collectors **26** 802
works **2** 482; **26** 800, 802, *803*
Grimaldi, Giovanni Battista **4** 352; **6** 24
books **4** *352*
Grimaldi, Giovanni Franceso **13** 655–6*
collaboration **1** 628; **6** 585
patrons and collectors **6** 585; **7** 622; **9** 22; **23** 899
reproductive prints by others **12** 4
works **9** 222; **11** 741; **13** *656*; **18** 709; **26** 840; **27** 486
Grimaldi, Honoré II, Prince of Monaco *see* HONORÉ II, Prince of Monaco
Grimaldi, Mary Catherine, Princess of Monaco *see* MARY CATHERINE, Princess of Monaco
Grimaldi, Nicolò **12** 281
Grimaldi, William **33** 380
Grimani (family) **23** 332
Grimani, Antonio **13** 657*
Grimani, Domenico, Cardinal, Patriarch of Aquilea **13** 637, 657–9*; **21** 104
collections **2** 162; **13** 658; **16** 767; **32** 193
gems **12** 265
manuscripts **7** 467; **13** 659
paintings **4** 447, 452; **12** 670
plaquettes **21** 784; **25** 20
sculpture **13** 678; **16** 770; **27** 769
Grimani, Gerolamo, I (father) **13** 657
Grimani, Gerolamo, II (*d* 1570; son) **13** 650, 657, 659*
Grimani, Giovanni, Patriarch of Aquileia **13** 657, 659*
architecture **27** 772
collections **2** 162; **13** 657, 658; **32** 193, 222
hardstones **16** 747
interior decoration **13** 658
manuscripts **13** 657
paintings **11** 722; **27** 649; **33** 718
sculpture **2** 162, 608; **16** 770
stucco **31** 524
Grimani, Marco, Patriarch of Aquileia **13** 657, 658*; **28** 469
Grimani, Marino, Cardinal, Patriarch of Aquileia **13** 657, 658–9*
collections **13** 659
manuscripts **7** 467; **13** 657
paintings **4** 452; **13** 657
sculpture **5** 626; **13** 657
Grimani, Ottaviano **32** *648*
Grimani, Vettor **13** 657, 658*
architecture **13** 658
interior decoration **13** 658
paintings **27** 649
stucco **31** 524
tapestries **27** 210
Grimani Breviary *see under* BREVIARIES → individual manuscripts
Grimani Breviary, Master of the David Scenes in the *see* DAVID SCENES IN THE GRIMANI BREVIARY, MASTER OF THE
Grimani Evangeliary *see under* EVANGELIARIES -individual manuscripts
Grimaud, B. P., & Cie **31** 266
Grimb, Mořice *see* GRIMM, MAURIZ
Grimbald Gospels *see under* GOSPEL BOOKS → individual manuscripts
Grimbergen, Abbey Church of St Servaas **3** 546, 570; **7** 703; **33** 685–6
Grimbolt **7** 195
Grimbosc Castle **6** 53
Grimenski Gospels *see under* GOSPEL BOOKS → individual manuscripts
Grimer *see* GRIMMER
Grimes Graves **10** 473; **25** 515
Grim & Leeds **31** 263
Grimm, David **3** 527
Grimm, Franz Anton **13** 661–2*
Grimm, (Johann) Georg **4** 717; **6** 10; **13** 662*; **24** 206
Grimm, German **12** 856
Grimm, Hermann **2** 365; **12** 873; **26** 236
Grimm, Jacob Ludwig Carl **8** 218; **22** 540
Grimm, Jakob **12** 365; **23** 316
Grimm, Johann **1** 31
Grimm, Ludwig Emil **13** 662*
Grimm, Marx **18** 493
Grimm, Mauriz **4** 833; **13** 661–2*
Grimm, (Friedrich) Melchior, Baron von **8** 865; **11** 663; **13** 663*
dealing **26** 731
paintings **27** 438
sculpture **24** 787
Grimm, Samuel Hieronymous **13** 663–4*
Grimm, Sigismund **14** 747; **20** 743, 744
Grimm, Vince **2** 546
Grimm, V. V. **6** 280
Grimm, Wilhelm Carl **8** 218; **22** 540
Grimm, Willem **29** 64
Grimma, Mořice *see* GRIMM, MAURIZ
Grimmaer *see* GRIMMER
Grimmel, Elias **20** 147
Grimmel, Johann **17** 689
Grimmer, Abel **3** 107, 560; **5** 352; **13** 664–5*
Grimmer, Abraham **13** 664
Grimmer, Adam **31** 526
Grimmer, Jacob **3** 560; **7** 428, 498; **13** 664*
Grimmer, Johann **31** 526
Grimmon, A. A. M. **31** 576
Grimnitz **4** 666; **7** 209
Grimoard de Pestels de Lévis, Anne-Claude-Philippe de Tubières, Comte de Caylus *see* CAYLUS, Comte de
Grimod (family) **6** 563
Grimod, Pierre-Marie-Gaspard, Comte d'Orsay *see* ORSAY, PIERRE-MARIE-GASPARD GRIMOD, Comte d'
Grimod de la Reynière, Laurent **2** 245; **7** 416; **10** 643; **11** 663; **25** 192
Grimod du Fort, Pierre **13** 665
Grimou, Alexis **8** 793; **13** 665–6*
Grimsby Docks (Humberside) **9** 58
Grimschitz, Bruno **2** 833
Grimshaw, Arthur **13** 666
Grimshaw, (John) Atkinson **13** 666–7*
Grimshaw, Louis H. **13** 666
Grimshaw, Nicholas **1** 737; **10** 242, 814; **13** 667*
Grimsthorpe Castle (Lincs) **10** 345; **14** 639; **30** 123, 783
Grimston (N. Yorks) **10** 302
Grimston (family) **8** 95
Grimstone, Edward **6** 129
Grimston-Lyles Hill pottery *see under* POTTERY → wares
grinaldas tiles *see under* TILES → types
Grinberg, Aleksandr **27** 379
Grinberg, P. M. **4** 469
Grīnbergs, Andris **13** 667*
Grīnbergs, Teodors *see* ZAĻKANS, TEODORS
Grindaker **26** 646
Grindel, Eugène (-Emile-Paul) *see* ELUARD, PAUL
grinders, tea *see* TEA-GRINDERS
grinding **21** 720
Griñon, Ignacio **29** 338
Grip Church **13** 114
Gripenberg **30** *65*
Gripiotes, Ioannes **13** 339
Grip Ltd **13** 711; **19** 471, 877
Gripper Axminster carpets *see under* CARPETS → types
Grippo, Víctor **2** 401; **13** 667*, 725
Gripsholm Castle **4** 781; **13** 667–8*; **18** 801; **30** *65*, 68, *68*, 72
collections **30** 118
frames **11** 470
furniture **5** 350; **30** 92, 93, 96
interior decoration **30** 77, 87, *88*, 91
paintings **5** 436; **11** 468; **27** 357
sculpture **25** 114
Statens Porträttsamling **13** 668
theatre **30** 72, 677
White Drawing Room **11** 471
Gripsholm Coffer **18** 613, *613*
Gris, Juan **3** 366; **7** 385; **13** 668–72*; **24** 143; **29** 285
dealers **11** 165; **17** 725; **27** 162
exhibitions **13** 711
groups and movements **3** 120; **8** 240, 242, 243, 245, 246; **9** 705; **28** 347; **30** 3
methods **28** 202
patrons and collectors
Arensberg, Walter and Louise **2** 383
Cooper, Douglas **7** 797
Gallatin, A(lbert) E(ugene) **12** 15
Lefèvre, André **19** 66
Magnelli, Alberto (Giovanni Cesare) **20** 97
Reber, Gottlieb Friedrich **26** 59
Rupf, Hermann and Margrit **27** 343
Stein, Getrude **29** 605
Thompson, G(eorge) David **30** 749
Vallenilla Echeverría, Pedro **32** 178
productions **8** 850
studio **29** 858
works **7** 557; **11** 495; **13** *669*, *670*; **29** 670
Gris, Ludwig **29** 97
grisaille paintings **6** 569; **13** 672–7*
historical and regional traditions
Belgium **13** 674–5, *675*
Cistercian Order **26** 702
England **13** 136, 183, *676*; **15** V; **19** 406
France **13** 136, *137*, 148, *148*, 181, 673, *674*; **29** VI1
Gothic **13** 136, 137, *137*, 148, *148*, 178, 181, 183, *674*; **29** VI1
Italy **13** 673, 676
Romanesque **26** 702
uses
manuscript illumination **13** *148*, 148, 673*, *674*
stained glass **13** 136, *136*, 178, 181, 183, 672–3*; **19** 406; **26** 702; **29** 502–3, VI1

grisaille paintings—cont.
 see also PAINTING → types → monochrome
Grisanty, Aurelio 9 118
Grisebach, August 3 794
Grisebach, Hans 13 677*; 28 95
Griselda Master 20 684*
 collaboration 16 660; 28 700, 701, 702
 works 16 659; 29 362
Griselini 21 48
Grisolles Bridge 7 693
Grison, Pierre Joseph see GRISONI, GIUSEPPE
Grisone, Romualdo, Archbishop 2 129
Grisoni, Giuseppe 11 20, 194; 13 677–8*; 14 178, 598
Grisotti, Marcello 3 94
Grissell and Peto 28 277
Griswold, Ashbil 31 652
Gritchenko, Alexis see HRYSHCHENKO, OLEKSA
Gritsyuk, Mikhail Ya. 31 561
Gritti, Andrea, Doge of Venice (reg 1523-39) 13 678*; 27 637; 32 193
Gritti, Camillo Bernardino 3 864
Grivolas, Pierre 6 378
Grixopolus 20 321
Grizedale Forest Park (Cumbria) 28 316
Grob, Rita 6 600
Grob, Ulrik 8 758
Grob-art 28 669
Grobinya 32 527
Grobon, François 2 232
Grobon, Jean-Michel 4 244
Grodecki, Louis 29 514
Grodekov, N. I. 6 281
Grodno see HORADNIA
Grodtschilling, Bendix, I 8 752
Grodzisk Wielkopolski Church 4 295; 25 97
Groebli, Isaac 30 563
Groeger, Friedrich Carl 29 376
Groenendijk Collection see under AMSTERDAM → museums → Stedelijk Museum
Groenendoelen, Jan Hendrik Troost van see TROOST VAN GROENENDOELEN, JAN HENDRIK
Groenesteyn, Anselm F(ranz) Ritter zu see RITTER ZU GROENESTEYN, ANSELM F(RANZ)
Groenewegen, Gerrit 13 678–9*
Groenewegen, J. H. 2 318; 13 679*
Groenewegen-Frankfort, H. A. 10 84
Groenkan, Gerard A. van de 26 378
Groenrijs, Hans 13 234
Groep 32 4 221; 10 163; 14 693; 18 212; 22 831; 29 484; 33 616
Gröer, Etienne de 19 467; 25 294
Groesbeek, St Anthony 8 669
Grof, Charles de 13 680
Grof, Guillielmus de 12 405; 13 679–80*; 22 302
 patrons and collectors 33 277
 pupils 32 253
 works 13 679; 22 309
 workshop 12 405
grog 6 325, 330
Grogan, Nathaniel 16 14
Gröger, Friedrich Carl 12 394
Groger-Wurm, Helen 1 66
Grognard, Alexis 11 157; 26 264, 333
Grohar, Ivan 13 680*; 16 874; 28 860
Grohé, Guillaume 11 598, 599; 13 680*
Grohé, Jean-Michel 11 598; 13 680
Grohmann, Adolf 16 549
Grohmann, Jeroným 8 414
Grohmann, Will 3 803; 13 680–81*
groin vaults see under VAULTS (CEILING) → types
Groitzsch, Dedo von, Count 33 16
Grojec Synagogue 17 546, 559
Grolais, Jean Villiers de La see VILLIERS DE LA GROLAIS, JEAN
Groland, Sebald 25 40
Grolier, Jean, Vicomte d'Agnisy 13 681*; 20 800
 book covers 4 352
 books 4 351; 14 616
 plaquettes 25 18
Grolier Club 14 616; 17 898
Grolier Codex see under CODICES → individual manuscripts
Groll, J. 33 177
Gromaire, Marcel 11 550; 12 830; 13 681*; 30 328
 assistants 6 84
 collaboration 19 808
 groups and movements 10 696
 patrons and collectors 12 724
 pupils 1 468; 6 10; 28 828; 31 94
 works 11 644
Gromann, Nikolaus 12 366; 31 166; 33 36
Gromort, Georges 5 634; 17 832
gromwell 7 45; 17 308
Gron, Edith 23 81, 84
Grønbæk 26 648
Grøndal, F. V. 7 807
Grone, Johann Baptist 9 242
Grøngård 8 725
Gröningen Abbey (Germany) 12 399; 26 632
Groningen (Netherlands, the) 22 813, 819, 887, 894, 895
 Groninger Museum 14 635; 22 906
 Martinikerk 13 62; 22 819
Groningen (family) 18 590
Grøningen, Gert van 13 682*
Groningen, Hendrik van 13 682
Groningen, Henry Horst von 25 113
Groningen, Johan van 13 682*
Gröninger (family) 12 402; 22 315, 316
Gröninger, Dietrich (Theodor) 13 683–4*
Gröninger, Gerdt 13 682*
Gröninger, Gerhard 13 682–3*
 works 13 683
Gröninger, Gertrud 13 683
Gröninger, Heinrich 13 682*; 23 749
Gröninger, Johann Mauritz 13 683–4*
 works 13 684
Gröninger, Johann Wilhelm 13 684–5*
Gronk 18 831; 19 703
Grønningen 7 805; 14 228
Gronovius, Jakob 2 163
Gronowski, Tadeusz 26 296
Gronsveld Diepenbroick-Impel, Bertram, Count 22 882
Grönvall, Johan Petter 30 107
Grönvold, Bernt 26 546
Grönvold, Holger 17 646
Groombridge, Leyswood 23 398
Groombridge, William 12 645
Grooms, Red 24 407; 25 231
Groosman, E(rnestinus) F(lorimond) 13 685*
Groosman Partners 13 685
Groot, Cornelis Hofstede de see HOFSTEDE DE GROOT, CORNELIS
Groot, Guillaume De see DE GROOT, GUILLAUME
Groot, Hugo de 12 529; 22 909
Groot, Jan de 23 609
Groot, José Manuel 11 66
Groot Constantia see under CAPE TOWN
Groote, Cristián de 6 595
Groote, Gerard 4 751–2
Groote Adoration, Master of the von 2 204; 20 783–4*
Grooth, Georg Christoph 2 409; 26 731; 27 388, 420
Grooth, Johann Friedrich 27 438
grooved roll mouldings see under MOULDINGS → types
Gropelli, Marino 9 331
Gropina, S Pietro 16 688; 26 624
Gropius, Carl Wilhelm 11 894
Gropius, Martin (Philipp) 13 685*
 pupils 20 386
 sculpture 9 691
 teachers 4 505
 works 13 717; 22 363; 28 672
Gropius, Walter (Adolf Georg) 2 397, 524; 3 795; 4 475; 7 385, 482, 771, 772; 8 803; 10 241, 375; 11 526; 12 497; 13 686–9*; 19 591, 897; 21 793; 30 458; 31 596; 32 750; 33 38
 architecture 12 380
  apartments 13 688; 26 19
  art schools 8 816; 12 378; 21 782; 27 129
  department stores 8 379
  factories 4 788; 13 686; 21 780, 781
  houses 2 552; 3 401; 26 18, 19; 29 858
  mosques 16 242
  museums 30 227
  theatres 30 683, 684
  urban planning 3 797; 17 817
 collaboration 3 795; 10 749; 12 379, 792
  Bartning, Otto 3 293
  Behrens, Peter 3 512
  Belluschi, Pietro 3 682
  Breuer, Marcel (Lajko) 4 761, 762
  Forbát, Fred 11 299
  Fry, E(dwin) Maxwell 11 808
  Meyer, Adolf (1881-1929) 21 407
  Williams, Amancio 33 203
 competitions 7 669, 670
 education (art) 12 480
 exhibitions 12 417
 furniture 12 428
 groups and movements 3 401; 7 296; 8 8, 247; 10 697, 698; 26 15
  Bauhaus 2 288; 3 399, 400, 400, 401, 402, 403, 801; 12 378, 396, 450; 15 824
  Black Mountain College (NC) 4 109
  CIAM 7 293, 294
  Deutscher Werkbund 7 582; 8 825, 826; 10 683; 21 490
  Modern Movement 15 885; 21 779, 781, 782
  Ring, Der 26 405
  St Ives group 1 77
  TAC (The Architects Collaborative) 30 226
 house 2 552
 pupils 3 252; 14 90; 17 421, 620, 803; 27 313; 28 374
 staff 4 761; 20 837; 23 273
 writings 1 107–8; 18 111; 26 18; 28 548
Gropper, William 1 772; 5 759; 15 830; 17 578; 23 48; 27 872; 31 606
Groppo, Cesare 26 478
Groppoli, Anton Giulio Brignole-Sale, Marchese di 4 811*
Gros, Antoine-Jean 1 106; 11 543, 544, 659, 671; 13 689–92*; 15 666
 collaboration 20 873
 competitions 25 638
 groups and movements 23 503; 24 171; 26 737, 738; 31 373
 methods 21 760
Gros, Antoine-Jean—cont.
 paintings
  military scenes 24 140
  portraits 4 303
 patrons and collectors
  Beisteguy y Benítez, Carlos de 3 522
  Chéramy, Paul-Arthur 6 548
  Coutan, Louis-Joseph-Auguste 8 72, 73
  Denon, (Dominique-) Vivant 8 763
  Forbin, (Louis Nicolas Philippe) Auguste, Comte de 11 302
  His de La Salle, (Aimé-Charles-) Horace 14 577
  Louis XVIII, King of France (reg 1814-24) 4 556
  Napoleon I, Emperor of the French (reg 1804-14) 4 300
  Yusupov, Nikolay (Borisovich), Prince (1751- 1831) 33 579
 pupils
  Barye, Antoine-Louis 3 313
  Begas, Carl (Joseph) (i) (1794-1854) 3 497
  Bellangé, (Joseph-Louis-) Hippolyte 3 634
  Bonington, Richard Parkes (1802-28) 4 321
  Charlet, Nicolas-Toussaint 6 487
  Courbet, (Jean-Désiré-) Gustave 8 51
  Court, Joseph-Désiré 8 61
  Couture, Thomas 8 75
  Delaroche, Paul (Hippolyte) 8 653
  Diday, François 8 864
  Gechter, (Jean-François-) Théodore 12 228
  Gudin, (Jean-Antoine-) Théodore 13 778
  Healy, George Peter Alexander 14 277
  Hesse, Nicolas-Auguste 14 489
  Huet, Paul 14 847
  Jollivet, Pierre-Jules 17 628
  Lami, Eugène(-Louis) 18 678
  Langlois, (Jean-)Charles 18 744
  Martinet, Louis 20 497
  Mazer, Carl Peter 20 898
  Moine, Antoine-Marie 21 797
  Monnier, Henry (Bonaventure) 21 889
  Passavant, Johann David 24 234
  Philipon, Charles 24 605
  Raffet, (Denis-)Auguste (-Marie) 25 849
  Robert, (Louis) Léopold 26 450
  Robert-Fleury, Joseph Nicolas 26 455
  Roqueplan, Camille (-Joseph-Etienne) 27 142
  Rousseau, Philippe 27 265
  Schnetz, (Jean) Victor 28 132
  Signol, Emile 28 699
  Simonau, François 28 751
 reproductions in tapestry 12 830
 reproductive prints by others 17 453; 19 636
 teachers 8 560
 works 3 389; 11 412, 541, 542, 643; 13 690, 691; 14 586; 19 483; 20 602; 24 163, 166; 26 53
Gros, de 12 177
Gros, Jean-Antoine 13 689; 16 706
Gros, Jean de see JEAN DE GROS
Grosbois Château 11 515; 19 14
Grosch, Christian Henrich 5 165; 13 611, 693*
 works 23 221, 231, 602
Grosch, Heinrich August 3 111; 13 693
groschen see under COINS → types
Groschwitz, Gustave von 19 492
Grosclaude, Louis 4 202
Grose, Francis 13 693*
 works 2 450; 5 760; 10 377; 16 38; 32 799
Groselin, Giuliano 1 730
Grosell, Martin 8 759
Grosholtz, Marie see TUSSAUD, Mme
Grosjean, Roger 11 78
Groslier, Bernard-Philippe 2 56; 13 693
Groslier, George 2 56; 5 482, 500; 13 693*
Grosman, Maurice 19 492
Grosmont (Gwent) 30 907
 Castle 29 22
 roof 30 908
gros point see under LACE → types
gros point de Venise see under LACE → types
Gross, Anna 33 300
Gross, Anthony 4 367; 13 694*; 25 627
Gross, Chaim 13 694*; 17 578
Gross, Cornelis
 works 12 III2
Gross, František 2 546; 8 394
Gross, Henning 10 720; 14 502
Gross, Michael 13 694*
Gross, Oskar 3 177
Gross, Philip 23 317
Gross, Professor 9 501
Gross, Richard Oliver 23 72
Grossberg, Carl 22 923
Grossberg, Yitzroch Loiza see RIVERS, LARRY
Grossbirkach Church 23 646; 26 634
Grossbreitenbach 30 793
Grossbungen 9 655
Grosschedel, Franz 2 473
Grosschedel, Wolfgang 2 473
Grosse, E. 1 235
Grosse, Franz 27 408
Grossé, Louis 3 610; 18 66
Grosse, Michael 14 469
Grossen, Françoise 11 54
Grossen Bären 33 77
Grosse Pointe (MI), Edsel Ford House 31 595
Grosseteste, Robert 1 176; 19 356
Grosseto 13 93; 16 732; 18 690
 Museo Archeologico e d'Arte della Maremma 10 640
Grossgmain, Master of 2 792; 11 806; 20 684–5*
Grossgörschen 35 3 803; 14 613; 31 532
Grossheim, Karl von 17 864–5*
grossi see under COINS → types
Grossi, João 3 920; 13 694–5*; 18 578
Grossi, Silvio 26 779
Grossi, Tommaso 12 902; 14 267
Grosslobming, Master of 2 799; 14 158; 20 685*
Grossman, József 9 754; 10 871
 works 14 887
Grossman, Nancy 10 483; 13 695*
Grossman, Peter 27 813
Grossman, Sid 24 685
Grossman, Tatyana 19 492; 20 606; 25 626
Grossmann, Christian Gotthelf 19 781
Grossmann, Hedwig 16 568
Grossmann, Peter 1 93
Grossmann, Rudolf 8 658
Grosso (family) 1 578
Grosso, Alfonso 28 516
Grosso, Giacomo 5 740; 13 695*; 31 446
Grosso, Nicola 2 396
Gross-Schönau 12 469; 19 418
grossular 16 857
gros tournois see under COINS → types
Grosvalds, Jāzeps 13 695–6*; 26 384
Grosvenor (family) 19 570

Grosvenor, Hugh Lupus, 1st Duke of Westminster **13** 697*
architecture **9** 200
furniture **12** 639
interior decoration **8** 106
paintings **20** 446; **32** 922
Grosvenor, Hugh Richard Arthur, 2nd Duke of Westminster **1** 496
Grosvenor, Richard, 1st Earl Grosvenor (1731-1802) **13** 696*; **14** 641; **25** 249; **29** 808
paintings **8** 474
Grosvenor, Richard, 2nd Marquis of Westminster (1795-1869) **4** 172; **13** 696
Grosvenor, Robert, 2nd Earl of Grosvenor and 1st Marquess of Westminster **10** 146; **13** 696*
Grosvenor, Thomas, 2nd Earl of Wilton **12** 639
Grosvenor, Thomas, 3rd Baronet **13** 696
Grosvenor Museum *see under* CHESTER (CHES)
Gros Ventre **22** 551, 650
Grosz, George **12** 395; **13** 697–8*; **25** 651
collaboration **14** 845
dealers **11** 165
groups and movements **3** 801, 802; **8** 433, 436, 437; **10** 695; **12** 396; **22** 922, 923; **23** 267; **24** 405; **25** 6
methods **24** 349
personal collection **2** 370
pupils **3** 672; **25** 887; **28** 887
works **3** 801; **4** 366; **5** 758; **8** 597; **10** 481; **12** 396, *396*; **13** *698*; **19** 491; **24** 685; **25** 653; **27** *871*, 871–2; **28** 920; **31** 705; **32** 902
Grötefend, Georg Friedrich **1** 891
Grotell, Maija **4** 73; **13** 699*; **31** 640
Grotesque **10** 642; **13** 699–702*; **25** 191
art forms
etchings **13** *701*
frescoes **31** *523*
interior decoration **13** *669*
historical and regional traditions
Belgium **13** *701*
France **13** 700, 701
Italy **13** *669*, 700
Rome, ancient **13** 699; **26** 789; **29** 665
Sweden **13** 864
see also MASCARONS
Groth, Anthonius **30** 112
Groth, Jan **23** 227
Groth, Klaus **29** 376
Grotius, Hugo *see* GROOT, HUGO DE
Grotjahn (*fl* 1769) **26** 529
Grotjan (*fl* 1897) **14** 87
Grotko, Wacław **25** 128; **32** 878
Grötlingbo Church **13** 190; **26** 639
Grotowski, Jerzy **3** 486
Grotta **8** *304*, 309; **22** 698
Grotta del Bue Marina **27** 834
Grottaferrata **26** 680
Abbey Church **26** 624
Grottes, Sebastian *see* GÖTZ, SEBASTIAN
Grottger, Artur **13** 702*; **25** 106
Grottger, Jan Józef **13** 702
Grotti **10** 615
grottoes **11** 242–3; **12** 61, 62; **13** 702–5*; **26** 477; **27** 323; **28** 581
England **12** 127; **13** 704
France **12** 120; **13** 703–4, *704*; **23** 850
Germany **12** 412; **13** 704–5
Italy **5** *183*; **9** 21; **12** 110, 115, 116; **13** 703, *703*; **16** 696
Netherlands, the **12** 530
Rome, ancient **22** 161; **27** 29
grottoes—cont.
see also FOLLIES; HERMITAGES; NYMPHAEA
Groult, André **2** 521; **11** 601, 602; **18** 863
Groult, Camille **13** 705*
ground drawings *see under* DRAWINGS → forms
grounds **13** 705–9*; **25** 581
historical and regional traditions
Buddhism **29** 462
Central Asia, Eastern **6** 301
Central Asia, Western **6** 224
Gothic **13** 135
Sri Lanka **29** 462
Turkmenistan **6** 224
materials
acrylic **13** 707*
ashes **13** 708
asphalt **10** 548; **13** 706
calcium sulphate **25** 174
ceramics **6** 224
chalk **6** 224; **13** 135, 706*; **24** 798; **25** 174; **30** 426
charcoal **25** 174
clay **6** 301; **13** 708; **25** 174
dolomite **25** 174
eggs **13** 706
emulsions **10** 191; **13** 706*, 707
flour **13** 706, 708
gelatin **13** 706
gesso **12** 501; **13** 135, 706*, 707, 708; **30** 426
glues **13** 706, 708
gypsum **6** 301; **13** 135; **24** 798
hair **6** 301
iron oxide **25** 174
kaolin **29** 462
lime **25** 174
mastic **10** 548
mica **25** 174
mud **21** 226
oils **10** 548; **13** 706–7*, 708
papier mâché **25** 175
petroleum jelly **10** 548
plaster **3** 914; **9** 623; **27** 51
red lead **25** 174
resins **13** 706, 707
sand **6** 224, 301; **25** 174
sawdust **25** 174
shells **25** 174
silk **18** *315*
silver **13** 135
size **13** 706; **28** 812
stone **6** 224
straw **6** 301
tallow **10** 548; **13** 706
textiles **3** 914
waxes **10** 548; **13** 706
white lead **13** 708; **25** 174
technical examination **30** 401
types
Armenian bole **13** 707
blended colourgrounds *see irisé*
bole (red) **13** 707*
composite **13** 707*
irisé **32** 812; **33** 711
uses
aquatints **13** 706
canvas **5** 654; **13** 706
etchings **10** 548, 549; **13** 706
gilding **13** 707
mezzotints **13** 706
paintings **13** 135, 706–9; **23** 377, 378; **24** 6, 798
sculpture **25** 174–5*
supports **13** 705, 708
tempera **30** 426
textiles **13** 708
wallpaper **32** 812
Grounds, Romberg & Boyd **2** 742, 743; **13** 709
Grounds, Roy (Burman) **13** 709*
collaboration **4** 605; **26** 744
staff **4** 605
works **2** 742, 770; **21** 76, *76*
group, 10+ *see* 10+ GROUP
Group, 1922 *see* 1922 GROUP
group, 30-30 *see* 30-30 GROUP
Group, 43 *see* 43 GROUP
Group, 54 *see* 54 GROUP
Group, Abstract *see* ABSTRACT GROUP
group, Ada *see* COURT SCHOOL OF CHARLEMAGNE
Group, Åfors *see* ÅFORS GROUP
Group, Ahrend *see* AHREND GROUP
group, Aka *see* AKA GROUP
Group, American Artist *see* AMERICAN ARTIST GROUP
group, Anteo *see* ANTEO GROUP
Group, Antiope *see* ANTIOPE GROUP
group, Antipodean *see* ANTIPODEAN GROUP
Group, Aphrodite *see* APHRODITE GROUP
Group, Apollonia *see* APOLLONIA GROUP
group, a.r. *see* A.R. GROUP
group, Ar Livre *see* AR LIVRE GROUP
Group, Arron *see* ARRON GROUP
Group, Artist Placement *see* ARTIST PLACEMENT GROUP
Group, Artists *see* ARTISTS GROUP
group, Artiture *see* ARTITURE GROUP
Group, Ashington *see* ASHINGTON GROUP
Group, Atelier *see* ATELIER GROUP
group, AV *see* AV GROUP
group, Baratzite *see* BARATZITE GROUP
group, Basara *see* BASARA GROUP
Group, Beaver Hall Hill *see* BEAVER HALL HILL GROUP
Group, Behshahr Industrial *see* BEHSHAHR INDUSTRIAL GROUP
group, Bernardelli *see* BERNARDELLI GROUP
Group, Birmingham *see* BIRMINGHAM GROUP
group, Black fury *see* BLACK FURY GROUP
group, Block *see* BLOCK GROUP
Group, Bloemfontein *see* BLOEMFONTEIN GROUP
Group, Bloomsbury *see* BLOOMSBURY GROUP
group, BMPT *see* BMPT GROUP
group, Boiotian Dancers *see* BOIOTIAN DANCERS GROUP
group, Boreas-Florence *see* BOREAS-FLORENCE GROUP
group, Borelli *see* BORELLI GROUP
Group, Borgia *see* BORGIA GROUP
Group, British Surrealist *see* BRITISH SURREALIST GROUP
Group, Calcutta *see* CALCUTTA GROUP
Group, Calgary *see* CALGARY GROUP
group, Çallı *see* ÇALLI GROUP
Group, Camden Town *see* CAMDEN TOWN GROUP
group, Campanizing *see* CAMPANIZING GROUP
group, Canaanites *see* CANAANITES GROUP
Group, Canosa *see* CANOSA GROUP
Group, Casablanca *see* CASABLANCA GROUP
group, Chicago Imagist *see* CHICAGO IMAGIST GROUP
Group, Chicago Mural *see* CHICAGO MURAL GROUP
Group, Circle Art *see* CIRCLE ART GROUP
group, Clusium *see* CLUSIUM GROUP
Group, Cock *see* COCK GROUP
Group, Conran Design *see* CONRAN DESIGN GROUP
Group, Contemporary *see* CONTEMPORARY GROUP
Group, Contemporary Art *see* CONTEMPORARY ART GROUP
Group, Cumberland Market *see* CUMBERLAND MARKET GROUP
group, Cvijeta Zuzorić *see* CVIJETA ZUZORIĆ GROUP
Group, D *see* D GROUP
group, Danaid *see* DANAID GROUP
group, Denes *see* DENES GROUP
Group, Design *see* DESIGN GROUP
Group, Dolphin *see* DOLPHIN GROUP
group, Dot-rosette *see* DOT-ROSETTE GROUP
Group, Duane Street *see* DUANE STREET GROUP
Group, Earth *see* EARTH GROUP
Group, Estonian Artists' *see* ESTONIAN ARTISTS' GROUP
group, Etna *see* ETNA GROUP
Group, Everard *see* EVERARD GROUP
Group, Expressionist *see* EKSPRESIONISTI
group, Ferrara T 585 *see* FERRARA T 585 GROUP
group, Fico *see* FICO GROUP
group, Fillet *see* FILLET GROUP
Group, First *see* FIRST GROUP
Group, Fitzroy Street *see* FITZROY STREET GROUP
group, Forward (Vperyod) *see* FORWARD (VPERYOD) GROUP
group, Fotoform *see* FOTOFORM GROUP
group, Freedom *see* FREEDOM GROUP
Group, French *see* FRENCH GROUP
group, Frente *see* FRENTE GROUP
Group, Fuji Sankei Communications *see* FUJI SANKEI COMMUNICATIONS GROUP
group, Funnel *see* FUNNEL GROUP
group, G58-Hessenhuis *see* G58 HESSENHUIS GROUP
Group, Geneleos *see* GENELEOS GROUP
Group, Georgian *see* GEORGIAN GROUP
group, Gibil Gabib *see* GIBIL GABIB GROUP
Group, Glasgow *see* GLASGOW GROUP
group, Gocadiguse *see* GOCADIGUSE GROUP
Group, Gold Scrolls *see* GOLD SCROLLS GROUP
Group, Good Furniture *see* GOOD FURNITURE GROUP
group, Gorgona *see* GORGONA GROUP
Group, Grafton *see* GRAFTON GROUP
group, Grasmere *see* GRASMERE GROUP
group, Greda *see* GREDA GROUP
group, Gresham *see* GRESHAM GROUP
Group, Guyanese Art *see* GUYANESE ART GROUP
Group, Haimon *see* HAIMON GROUP
group, Halmstad *see* HALMSTAD GROUP
group, Hanover *see* HANOVER GROUP
group, Harvey *see* HARVEY GROUP
group, Henri Rousseau *see* ROUSSEAU, HENRI, GROUP
group, Hesse *see* HESSE GROUP
group, Horse Bird *see* HORSE BIRD GROUP
group, Human Mask *see* HUMAN MASK GROUP
group, *Husohoe* *see* HUSOHOE GROUP
group, Inatos *Niobe* *see* INATOS NIOBE GROUP
Group, Independent *see* INDEPENDENT GROUP
group, Indigenista *see* INDIGENISTA GROUP
group, Indigo *see* INDIGO GROUP
Group, Informele *see* ART INFORMEL
group, Ivy Leaf *see* IVY LEAF GROUP
group, Jung Jiddisch *see* JUNG JIDDISCH GROUP
Group, Kinodoni Art *see* KINODONI ART GROUP
Group, Komast *see* KOMAST GROUP
group, Kraków *see* KRAKÓW GROUP
group, Kras *see* KRAS GROUP
Group, Late Metz *see* LATE METZ GROUP
group, La Tolfa *see* LA TOLFA GROUP
Group, Leafless *see* LEAFLESS GROUP
group, Leagros *see* LEAGROS GROUP
group, Le Falot *see* LE FALOT GROUP
group, Lentini-Manfria *see* LENTINI-MANFRIA GROUP
Group, Lewes *see* LEWES GROUP
Group, Lion *see* GRUPO DO LEÃO
group, Lipari *see* LIPARI GROUP
Group, Lisbon Surrealist *see* LISBON SURREALIST GROUP
Group, Liuthard *see* LIUTHARD GROUP
Group, London *see* LONDON GROUP
group, Ludovisi *Gaul* *see* LUDOVISI GAUL GROUP
group, MA *see* MA GROUP
Group, MARS *see* MARS GROUP
group, Massad *see* MASSAD GROUP
group, Mediala *see* MEDIALA GROUP
group, Memphis *see* MEMPHIS GROUP
Group, Merioola *see* MERIOOLA GROUP
group, Metope *see* METOPE GROUP
Group, Modern Architects *see* MODERN ARCHITECTS GROUP
group, Movement *see* MOVEMENT GROUP
group, Müksala *see* MÜKSALA GROUP
Group, Mutual Improvement *see* MUTUAL IMPROVEMENT GROUP
group, Neo-Concrete *see* NEO-CONCRETE GROUP
Group, New *see* NEW GROUP
Group, New Scottish *see* NEW SCOTTISH GROUP
Group, New Sculpture *see* NEW SCULPTURE GROUP
Group, New Vision *see* NEW VISION GROUP
Group, New Wing *see* NEW WING GROUP
group, Nichegoki *see* NICHEGOKI GROUP
Group, Niobe *see* NIOBE GROUP
Group, Norwid's *see* GROUP OF FIVE
Group, November *see* NOVEMBER GROUP
group, Nueva Figuración *see* NUEVA FIGURACIÓN GROUP
Group, Number Ten Architectural *see* NUMBER TEN ARCHITECTURAL GROUP
Group, Nuttall *see* NUTTALL GROUP

group, October see OCTOBER GROUP
group, Oktyabr see OKTYABR GROUP
Group, One Art see ONE ART GROUP
group, One-dimension see ONE-DIMENSION GROUP
group, Önningeby see ÖNNINGEBY GROUP
group, Orvieto see ORVIETO GROUP
group, Palangana see PALANGANA GROUP
group, Panique see PANIQUE GROUP
Group, PAS see PAS GROUP
Group, Pasquino see PASQUINO GROUP
group, Phantom see PHANTOM GROUP
Group, Pioneer see PIONEER GROUP
group, PKP see PKP GROUP
group, Plan see PLAN GROUP
group, Polychrome see POLYCHROME GROUP
group, Portico see PORTICO GROUP
Group, Portonaccio see PORTONACCIO GROUP
Group, Praesens see PRAESENS GROUP
group, Praxias see PRAXIAS GROUP
group, Prism see PRISM GROUP
Group, Progressive Artists' see PROGRESSIVE ARTISTS' GROUP
group, Puteaux see PUTEAUX GROUP
group, R '33 see R '33 GROUP
Group, RA see RA GROUP
group, Racken see RACKEN GROUP
Group, Realists see REALISTS GROUP
Group, Research Libraries see RESEARCH LIBRARIES GROUP
group, Revolt see REVOLT GROUP
Group, Rhondda see RHONDDA GROUP
group, Rhythm see RHYTHM GROUP
group, Riga Artists' see RIGA ARTISTS' GROUP
group, Roman Urbanist see ROMAN URBANIST GROUP
Group, Royal Doulton Tableware see ROYAL DOULTON TABLEWARE GROUP
Group, Rutgers see RUTGERS GROUP
group, St Ives see ST IVES GROUP
group, Sakitama tomb see SAKITAMA TOMB GROUP
group, Septem see SEPTEM GROUP
group, Sezon see SEZON GROUP
group, Škreta see ŠKRETA GROUP
group, Sokra see SOKRA GROUP
group, Spiral see SPIRAL GROUP
group, Spurinas see SPURINAS GROUP
group, Stiffneck see STIFFNECK GROUP
Group, Stupid see STUPID GROUP
group, Suma see SUMA GROUP
Group, Surrealist see SURREALIST GROUP
Group, Sydney see SYDNEY GROUP
Group, Tattoo see TATTOO GROUP
group, Témoignage see TÉMOIGNAGE GROUP
Group, The 2 705; 7 210
Group, Transvaal see TRANSVAAL GROUP
group, Turin Futurist see TURIN FUTURIST GROUP
Group, Tyrrhenian see TYRRHENIAN GROUP
group, U-Bahn see U-BAHN GROUP
Group, Urban Innovations see URBAN INNOVATION GROUP
group, Valori Primordiali see VALORI PRIMORDIALI GROUP
Group, Varberg see VARBERG GROUP
Group, Vernacular Architecture see VERNACULAR ARCHITECTURE GROUP
group, Vitelleschi see VITELLESCHI GROUP
group, Vittskövle see VITTSKÖVLE GROUP
Group, Wedgwood see WEDGWOOD GROUP
Group, Wednesday Art see WEDNESDAY ART GROUP
group, White Stag see WHITE STAG GROUP
Group, Wrocław see WROCŁAW GROUP
Group, Young Painting see YOUNG PAINTING GROUP
Group 5 see GRUPPE 5
Group 9 4 107
Group 42 7 182; 8 394; 18 201; 25 433
Group 55 4 234; 29 582
Group 1890 15 170; 28 577; 30 58
Group Architects 23 56
Group of the Dresden Lekanis 13 507
Group E 13 508; 32 45–6*
Groupe d'Art Constructif et Mouvement 3 485
Groupe des Artistes Radicaux 8 436
Groupe d'Art Monumental 8 701; 10 735; 22 1
Groupe Bogolan Kasobane 20 198
Groupe Ecart 2 447
Groupe Espace 1 7, 79; 8 857
Groupe d'Etude d'Architecture Mobile 11 778
Groupe d'Etude d'Architecture Moderne 14 155
Groupe Fromagé 1 445
Group of Eight see EIGHT, THE (iii)
Groupe des IX 31 502, 878
Groupe Luc Bois 2 447
Groupe des Maisons Ouvrières 24 128
Groupe de Recherche d'Art Visuel (GRAV) 1 79; 2 401; 10 416; 13 709–10*; 18 63; 19 355; 21 746; 28 914
exhibitions 23 262
members 11 551; 19 209; 22 97; 23 449; 26 193
Groupe du Rouge-Cloître 23 398
Groupe des Six 25 52
Groupe Surréalisme Révolutionnaire 5 45
Groupe Yenga 29 764
Group f.64 1 143; 8 270; 13 710*; 33 105
Group of Fine Artists 16 902
Group of Five (Indonesia) 15 808
Group of Five (Poland) 33 291
Group of Four 28 788
Group of the Huge Lekythoi 32 46*
Group Material 12 218
Group of Munich 883 10 615
Group N 23 145
Group of New Art see GRUPAL DE ARTĂ NOUĂ
Group of Painters, Canadian see CANADIAN GROUP OF PAINTERS
Group of Painters, Transcendental see TRANSCENDENTAL GROUP OF PAINTERS
Group of Plastic Artists 8 249, 373, 401; 13 711*
exhibitions 13 711*
Group of Plastic Artists—cont.
members 3 715; 5 662; 8 393; 10 108; 11 79; 12 834; 14 632; 20 254; 25 647; 29 359
group portraits see under PORTRAITS → types
Group R 13 536; 32 46*, 66
Group of Riga Artists see RĪGA MĀKSLINIEKU GRUPA
group sculpture see under SCULPTURE → types
Group of Seven (Canada) 5 566, 593; 13 711–12*; 18 718; 31 177
collections 5 589, 590
members 5 846; 11 141; 14 194, 676; 16 818; 19 471, 877; 30 753; 31 910
works 13 *712*
Group of Seven (Israel) 2 487
Group of Ten 10 719; 13 212; 31 454
Group of Ukrainian Artists 26 70
Group of Vatican 265 10 615
Group of Vatican G 57 23 145
Group X 8 265; 9 55; 13 712–13*; 14 107; 17 850; 19 287
Group of Young Artists 17 802; 18 429
Group Zero see ZERO GROUP
Grousset, René 29 642
Groux, Charles (-Auguste-Corneille) De see DE GROUX, CHARLES(-AUGUSTE-CORNEILLE)
Groux, Henry De see DE GROUX, HENRY
Grove, Arthur 25 634
Grove, David C. 6 393
Grove, Helga 32 414
Grove, James 2 764
Grove, Jan 32 414
Grove, John (*d* 1676) 29 835
Grove, John (*d* 1708) 29 835, 843
Grove Hardy Ltd. 14 173
groves 12 61, 126
Groves-Raines, Nicholas 28 231
Grow, Henry 27 642
Growse, F. S. 20 820
Grozdanić, M. 28 452
Grozer, Joseph 22 123
Grozie 26 710
Grozny Fortress 27 433
GRP see FIBREGLASS
Gruamons see GRUAMONTE
Gruamonte 13 713*; 26 623
Gruato (family) 32 190
Gruaz 11 284
Grubačević, R. 9 331
Grubenhäuser see under HOUSES → types
Grubenmann, Hans Ulrich 4 801; 13 713*
Grubenmann, Jakob 13 713*
Grubenmann, Johannes 4 802; 13 713*
Grubenmann, Ulrich 13 713
Gruber, Esaias 2 800
Gruber, Francis 11 302; 13 713–14*
works 11 551; 13 *714*; 28 920
Gruber, Gabriel 19 516
Gruber, Georg 3 527
Gruber, Jacques 13 713; 22 456; 29 508, 516
Gruber, Johann Erhardt 10 528
Gruber, Karl 14 306
Gruber, L. Fritz 27 718
Gruber, Veit 28 696
Grubicy, Alberto 13 715; 25 568; 28 355
Grubicy (De Dragon), Vittore 8 136; 9 40; 13 714–15*; 16 678; 28 355
Gruché, Pierre 14 856
Grude, Klaus 13 161
Grue (family) 6 21; 16 735
Grue, Carlo Antonio 16 735
Grue, Francesco Antonio Xaverio 6 21; 13 715*; 16 735
Grue, Rinaldo 11 5
Grueby, William Henry 13 715–16*; 30 887; 31 638
Grueby Faience Co. (1895-1908) 2 572; 4 482; 13 715; 30 887
Grueby Faience & Tile Co. (1908-19) 13 715
Gruen, Victor (David) 13 716*
staff 24 342
works 19 701; 28 623; 31 735, 864
Gruenwald, Alfred Emanuel Ferdinand see BAARGELD, JOHANNES THEODOR
Grumbach, Antoine 13 716*
Grummaert see GRIMMER
Grummellier, Johan 11 107
Grünau Hunting-lodge 14 451; 33 278
Grünbaum, Viktor see GRUEN, VICTOR
Grünberg, B. 18 433
Grünberg, Martin 2 502; 3 790; 22 803; 23 339
Grund, František Karel 13 717
Grund, Kristián 13 717
Grund, Norbert 8 391; 13 717*
Grund, Petr Pavel Christian 13 717
Grund Church 15 *68*, 72
chairs 15 *72*
Gründerzeit 13 717*
Grundig, Hans 9 239; 13 717–18*; 18 1
Grundig, Lea 13 717, 718*; 17 579; 22 923
Grundmann, Johann Basilius 11 31
Grundmann, Otto 3 740; 30 343
Grundy, Anne Hull 13 718*
Grundy, John Hull 13 718
Grunembergh, Carlos 23 257; 30 176
Grunenberg, Johannes 8 115
Grünenplan, mirror-glass factory 33 54
Gruner, Elioth (Lauritz Leganyer) 2 749; 13 718–19*
Grüner, (Wilhelm Heinrich) Ludwig 6 563; 9 25; 14 148; 30 503; 31 132
Grüne Regenbogen 25 842
Grünestein, Anselm F(ranz) Ritter zu see RITTER ZU GROENESTEYN, ANSELM F(RANZ)
Grünewald, Isaac (Hirsche) 13 719*; 14 594; 29 687; 30 81; 33 566
Grünewald, Matthias (1475-1528) 13 719–23*; 20 693
attributions 2 835; 12 495
commentaries 27 726
copies 28 41
forgeries by others 11 308
patrons and collectors 9 195; 14 647, 649; 21 90; 31 526
works 1 710; 2 591; 7 226; 9 435; 11 455; 12 386; 13 676, *721*, *722*, *723*; 14 32, 784; 19 356; 26 188; 28 134
Grung, Geir 10 857; 30 391
Grunhof, Hélène 8 436
Grünhut, Josef 28 670
Grüninger, Johann 2 223; 30 487
Grünpeck, Joseph 20 690
Grunt, Jaroslav 8 402
Grünwald, Béla Iványi see IVÁNYI GRÜNWALD, BÉLA
Grunwald, Henryk 13 724*; 25 130; 32 878
Grünwald, Matěj (*fl* 1641) 3 224
Grünwedel, Albert 6 320; 13 724*; 15 211; 18 26, 105, 494; 28 624; 31 438
collections 6 321
excavations 33 505
Grupa 55 32 878
Grupa Czwarta see FOURTH GROUP
Grupa Krakowska see KRAKÓW GROUP
Grup d'Artistas i Tècnicos Catalans per el Progrés de l'Arquitectura Contemporània see GATCPAC
Grupa Samokształceniowa see MUTUAL IMPROVEMENT GROUP
Grupello, Gabriel 3 571; 13 725*; 33 279
collaboration 25 812
copies 29 540
patrons and collectors 9 460; 33 280
teachers 12 405; 25 812
works 1 813; 8 216; 29 571
Grupo Sí 25 697
Grupo, 103 see 103 GRUPO
Grupo de Arte Constructivo 31 183
Grupo Arte Fotográfico 21 409
Grupo Arte Nuevo Juan 24 510
Grupo Austral 2 397; 4 315; 33 202
Grupo de Boedo 2 399
Grupo Carlos Federico Sáez 10 509
Grupo CAYC 2 401; 3 485, 712; 13 667, 725*
Grupo dos Cinco 30 348
Grupo de Diseño Urbano 21 382
Grupo de Florida 2 400
Grupo H_2O/Talleres de Comunicación 10 99
Grupo Hondo 12 286; 13 725*
Grupo do Leão 4 386; 19 466; 25 298, 299, 870, 871; 27 615; 28 736; 32 98
Grupo Manos 25 703
Grupo de Montparnasse 6 597; 22 114; 32 416
Grupo Neoconcreto 6 66
Grupo Ocho 8 18; 12 919
Grupo de los Once 8 233; 21 544
Grupo Orión 2 400
Grupo Parpalló 1 620; 12 286
Grupo R 13 725–6*; 20 516; 29 87, 273
members 3 217
Grupo Rectángulo 6 598
Grupo Signo 6 598
Grupo Surrealisto de Lisboa 25 300
Grupo Taller 8 18
Grupo Totem 8 18
Grupo de los Trece see GRUPO CAYC
Grupo UQUXKAH 10 154
Gruppa 12 602; 25 108
Gruppe 5 13 726*
Gruppe XI 14 481; 18 136
Gruppe 33 2 513; 4 216; 13 726–7*; 30 135
Gruppe 37,2 9 693
Gruppe 53 2 545; 5 26; 12 397; 13 727*; 14 620
Gruppe, Rote see ROTE GRUPPE
Gruppe D 3 4
Gruppe der Elf see VEREINIGUNG DER ELF
Gruppe G see SCHOLLE, DIE
Gruppe *H* 3 393
Gruppe der Neuen Prächtigkeit 13 729
Gruppe der Progressiven see GRUPPE PROGRESSIVER KÜNSTLER
Gruppe Progressiver Künstler 1 160; 13 727*; 25 838
Gruppe Rih 28 113
Gruppe Spur see SPUR
Gruppo 7 10 820; 13 728*; 16 649; 21 783; 26 15
collaboration 11 62
members 11 62; 19 304; 26 15; 30 512
works 16 649
Gruppo 40 25 447

Gruppo di Como 25 838; 26 289
Gruppo MISA 6 103
Gruppo N 1 79; 2 528; 13 728*; 16 681; 18 63; 23 262
Gruppo Nuove Tendenze 11 843
Gruppo Origine 5 279, 671; 7 555; 16 681; 26 777
Gruppo degli Otto 6 103
Gruppo degli Otto Pittori Italiani 13 727–8*; 16 681; 31 436; 32 197
  members 11 802; 22 125; 27 799; 32 109
Gruppo di Portonaccio 26 777
Gruppo Primordiale Futurista 19 330
Gruppo Sei 16 649; 24 484
Gruppo T 1 79; 2 528; 13 728–9*; 16 681; 18 63; 23 262, 298
Grupul de Artă Nouă 20 877
Grupul Nostru (Our Group) 13 651; 25 237
Grupul Plastic (Plastic Group) 25 237
Grus, Jaroslav 8 394
Grüssau Monastery 12 390
Grust, Otto Friedrich Theodor 21 66
Grut, Torben 29 489
Grützke, Johannes 11 734; 13 729*
Grützner, Eduard 22 304
Gruuthuse, Louis de see LOUIS DE GRUUTHUSE
Gruyter, Jacob de 27 230
Gruzenberg, Sergey 3 809
Gruzhino 27 414
Gruzinets, Vasily 32 617
Gryaznov, M. P. 24 297
Grygiel, Ruszard 25 516
Grylls, Thomas John 7 410
Grymbault, Paoul see GOYBAULT, PAOUL
Grymer see GRIMMER
Gryparis, Georgios 25 334
Gryspek, Florian see GRIESBECK VON GRIESBACH, FLORIAN
Grzegorz 32 878
Grzimek, Sabine 13 729*
Grzimek, Waldemar 13 729
Grzymała, Tadeusz see STRYJEŃSKA, ZOFIA
Grzywacz, Zbylut 25 108; 29 742, 743
Gschwandtner, Ernst 3 393
Gschwandtner, Káspar 8 413
Gsell (family) 2 829; 11 33
Gsell, Georg 13 729*; 21 151; 26 729
Gsell, Stéphane 1 636
Gsellhofer, Carl 12 842
Gsteu, Johann Georg 2 287
gu see under VESSELS → types
Gua 3 848
Guacialoti, Andrea 2 277; 3 859; 13 729–30*
Guadagni (family) 19 672
Guadalajara (Mexico) 13 730–31*; 21 265, 372
  Archivos del Estado de Jalisco 21 381
  Cathedral 21 375
  College of S Tomás 21 376
  education (art) 21 397
  glass 21 392
  Government Palace 23 567, 568
  Hospicio Cabañas 14 785; 21 378; 25 653
  IBM Building 21 381
  Instituto Nacional de Antropología e Historia (INAH) 21 395
  Museo de Arqueología del Occidente de Mexico 13 731
  Museo Regional de Antropología e Historia 21 396
  pottery 21 392
  Teatro Degollado 13 730
Guadalajara (Spain) 29 258
  astrolabes 16 369
  jet 17 515
  mausoleum 29 272
  Palacio de Cogolludo 29 299
  Palacio del Infantado 7 837; 13 731, 731–2*, 756, 756; 14 578; 29 264, 267, 299
  Puerta de Toledo 29 263
Guadalcanal 29 50, 51
Guadalcazar, Marqués de 29 306
Guadalimar 24 452
Guadalquivir, Marqués de Las Marismas del see LAS MARISMAS DEL GUADALQUIVIR, Marqués de
Guadalupe (Mexico)
  Basilica 21 377
  Capilla del Pocito 13 797
  Carmelite church 25 57
  Instituto Nacional de Antropología e Historia (INAH) 18 784
  Museo Regional de Guadalupe 21 396
  Nuestra Señora 24 502; 30 502
  Pocito Chapel 21 377
  Shrine of the Virgin 24 36
Guadalupe (Spain) 29 258
  embroidery 29 349
  Monastery of Nuestra Señora de Guadalupe 4 784; 7 458; 11 490–91; 13 68, 107, 732*; 14 516, 517; 22 255; 29 264
    Museo de Bordados 13 732
    Museo de Cantorales 13 732
    paintings 14 516; 33 732
Guadalupe (fl 1970s) 9 118
Guadalupe, Alonso de 29 334
Guadalupe, Antón Sánchez de see SÁNCHEZ DE GUADALUPE, ANTÓN
Guadalupe Victoria, José 21 396
Guadalupe Zuno, José 13 796
guadameci see under LEATHER → types
Guadelipe Hidalgo 10 505
Guadeloupe (country) 2 144, 149; 5 745
  body ornaments 5 747
  libraries 2 153
  museums 2 154
  pottery 5 747; 29 199
  see also ANTILLES, LESSER; WINDWARD ISLANDS
Guadet, Julien Azais 13 732–3*; 20 582
  collaboration 3 465
  groups and movements 26 14
  pupils 6 527; 14 115; 21 631; 24 472; 31 575
  teachers 2 14; 18 581
  writings 3 465; 11 523
Guadet, Paul 13 733
Guadix 16 386
Guaiacum wood 16 879
Guaita, Karl von 29 611
Guajibo 7 602
Guajiro 7 602
Gual, Bartoloméu 3 220
Gual, Jaime Sabartés y see SABARTÉS Y GUAL, JAIME
Gualandi, Michelangelo 1 551; 13 733*; 16 782
Gualandi Urn 10 603
Gualdi, Pedro 6 67
Gualdo, Bernardo da see BERNARDO DA GUALDO
Gualdo, Girolamo da see GIROLAMO DA GUALDO
Gualdo, Matteo da see MATTEO DA GUALDO
Gualdorp, Gortzius see GELDORP, GORTZIUS
Gualino, Riccardo 23 764
Gualöv 13 118
Gualterio 1 713
Gualterio, F. A. 13 541
Gualtieri
  Palazzo Bentivoglio see Palazzo Comunale
  Palazzo Comunale 3 744; 12 707
Gualtieri, Cardinal 12 547
Gualtieri, Cornelio I Bentivoglio, Marchese di 3 743, 744*; 19 373
Gualtieri, Cornelio II Bentivoglio, Marchese di 3 744
Gualtieri, Enzo Bentivoglio, Marchese di 3 743, 744*; 12 706
Gualtieri, Lorenzo 21 28
Gualtieri, Rinaldo di see WOUTERSZ., REINAUT
Gualtieri di Giovanni (da Pisa) 13 733*; 23 93
  collaboration 3 707
Gualtiero 3 700
Gualupita las Dalias 21 598
Guam 20 411; 23 711, 735
Guamán, Diego Cusi see CUSI GUAMÁN, DIEGO
Guambiano 7 602, 603
Gu An 30 49
Guaná 29 202
Guanabacoa Church 8 231
Guanajuato 21 250
  Alhóndiga de Granaditas 21 378
  Church of Carmen de Celaya 21 378; 31 307
  Church of La Valenciana 21 377, 395
  Hidalgo market 21 378
  Museo-Casa Olga Costa-José Chávez Morado 8 8
  Museum 21 396
  pottery 21 392
  Teatro Juárez 21 378
Guanare 32 165
  S Francisco 32 168
Guanauato 21 250
Guan Daosheng 33 319, 646
Guané 29 152
guang see VESSELS → types → gong
Guangala 13 735*; 27 610; 29 151, 217
Guanghan 6 615; 7 138, 159; 13 735–6*
  bronzes 6 726, 843; 7 3, 160
  gold 7 21
  lacquer 7 16
  Pit 1 13 736*
  Pit 2 13 736*, 736
Guangjiqiao 7 46
Guangshan 6 851
Guangwudi, Emperor (Han; reg AD 25-57) 14 134
Guangxu, Emperor (Qing; reg 1875-1908) 7 71
Guangyuan 30 443
  Qianfo Cliff 6 715
Guangzhou 6 614, 623; 13 736–7*; 28 719, 721
  art forms and materials
    ceramics 14 425
    coins 7 72
    enamel 6 911; 7 71, 79, 80
    furniture 7 34
    glass 7 81, 83
    hardstones 7 91
    horn 7 126
    ivory-carvings 7 103, 104
    jade 7 6, 7
    lacquer 7 18
    marks 7 30
    metalwork 6 624
    porcelain 6 920
    silver 7 29, 30
  Cherish the Sage Mosque see Huaisheng si
  Dacheng dian 6 674
  glass 7 87
  Guanxiao Temple 7 99; 23 773
  Huaisheng si
    Guang ta 6 676, 677
    Light Tower see Guang ta
  Liurong Temple 6 668, 718
  minaret 21 628
Guangzhou—cont.
  mirrors 7 87
  Municipal Academy of Art 7 149
  Tomb 5054 7 89
  tomb of Zhao Mo, King of Nanyue 22 466*
  trade 6 332, 557, 624
Guangzong, Emperor (Song; reg 1190-94) 19 856
Guanji Monastery 15 51
Guan Lianchang see TINGQUA
Guanmiaoshan 8 582
Guano 9 709
Guan Qiaochang see LAMQUA (i)
Guan Shanyue 19 423
Guan Shicun see LAMQUA (ii)
Guanto, Giusto da see JUSTUS OF GHENT
Guan Tong 6 773; 13 737–9*
  groups and movements 29 244
  works 13 738
Guan ware see under POTTERY → wares
Guan xian
  Erwang miao 6 724
  Fulong miao 6 724, 728, 729
  sculpture 6 733
  Taming the Dragon Temple see Fulong miao
Guanxiu 6 783; 13 739*
Guanzi 21 593
Guan Zuolin see SPOILUM
Guaqui 4 255
  church 4 258
Guaram I, King of Iberia (reg 588-90) 22 250
Guarana, Jacopo 13 740*
  pupils 13 740
  works 14 785; 24 865; 29 736
Guarana, Vincenzo 13 740*
Guaraní 2 392; 24 92–3; 29 128, 132, 191; 31 752
  architecture 24 93
  sculpture 24 93, 97, 97
  textiles 24 100
Guarantee Photos 31 875
Guarda Cathedral 7 703; 13 71
Guarda, Ferdinand Aviz, Duque de 2 869, 874*; 3 725; 14 658
Guarda, Gabriel 6 594
Guardi, Agostinho de 13 695
Guardi, Andrea 2 17; 24 858
Guardi, Antonio see GUARDI, GIOVANNI ANTONIO
Guardi, Domenico 13 740; 32 194
Guardi, Francesco 13 740, 742–5*; 16 676, 677; 31 155; 32 194
  attributions 13 741, 742
  collaboration 13 742
  methods 5 519
  patrons and collectors 28 271
    Agar-Ellis, George James, 1st Baron Dover 10 146
    Akademie der Bildenden Künste (Vienna) 2 831
    Bonaparte, Mathilde, Princess 4 308
    Buckner, Richard 5 78
    Camondo, Moïse de, Comte 5 530
    Loeser, Charles Alexander 19 538
    Mocenigo, Alvise IV, Doge of Venice (reg 1763–79) 21 147
    Mond, Ludwig 21 849
    Museu Nacional de Belas Artes (Rio de Janeiro) 4 726
    Napoleon III, Emperor of France (reg 1852–70) 4 306
    Poniatowski, Stanistaw, Prince 25 213
    Sasso, Giovanni Maria 27 864
    Strange, John 29 746
    Walker, (Byron) Edmund 32 794
  reproductive prints by others 27 720; 31 821
  teachers 30 862
Guardi, Francesco—cont.
  works 2 342; 3 231; 5 686; 9 223; 13 743, 744; 23 231; 29 669, 736; 31 155, 248; 32 112, 195
Guardi, Giacomo 13 740, 745; 32 194
Guardi, Giovanni Antonio 13 740–42*; 32 194
  patrons and collectors 28 173
  pupils 5 907
  works 5 883; 9 223; 13 741, 742; 30 358
Guardi, Nicolò 13 740, 741, 745; 23 231
Guardi, Pietro Antonio 13 741
Guardia, Alejandro 4 265
Guardia, Nicolò della 26 809
Guardiagrele, Nicola da see GALLUCCI, NICOLA
Guardini, Michele 20 556
Guardiola, Josep 29 329
Guarducci, Michele di Giovanni 31 165; 32 384
guar gum see under GUMS → types
Guarienti, Pietro Maria 13 746*; 25 319
Guariento (di Arpo) 13 746–7*; 23 753; 28 397
  patrons and collectors 2 725
  pupils 25 442
  works 5 871; 7 862; 8 212; 12 299; 13 747; 32 190, 220
Guarini, Francesco see GUARINO, FRANCESCO
Guarini, Giovanni Battista 1 601
Guarini, Guarino 13 748–53*; 16 637; 31 443
  architecture 12 163; 16 641–3
    churches 12 790; 32 410
      Annunziata dei Teatini (Messina) 28 657
      Chapel of the Holy Shroud (Cathedral of S Giovanni Battista, Turin) 13 750; 16 642; 21 144, 893; 28 632; 31 447
      Ste Anne-la-Royale (Paris) 24 118
      S Lorenzo (Turin) 13 749; 31 441
      S Maria della Divina Providenza (Lisbon) 13 751; 23 489
      S Vincenzo (Modena) 2 849
    palaces 4 422; 21 75
    palazzi 13 752; 23 836
  groups and movements 3 262, 267
  patrons and collectors 23 473; 28 13; 30 649
  writings 2 358; 16 643; 23 489, 489; 29 637; 31 296; 32 643
Guarino, Francesco 13 753–4*; 22 479
  patrons and collectors 22 486
  pupils 29 36
  teachers 29 544
  works 13 754
Guarino, Giovanni Tommaso 13 753
Guarino da Verona 13 754–5*; 14 866; 15 85; 29 859
  pupils 8 601; 10 747; 13 328
  works 2 42; 10 130; 25 46; 31 429
Guarinoni, Hyppolytus 2 781; 13 755*
Guarita 29 192, 193, 194
Guarnacci, Mario 10 642
Guarneri, Giuseppe 8 135
Guarnieri, Carlo 16 743
Guarnieri, S. 21 471
Guarrazar, La Fuente de see LA FUENTE DE GUARRAZAR
Guarrazar Treasure 29 345
Guas, Bonifacio 13 756
Guas, Enrique 13 756

Guas, Juan 12 618; 13 756–7*
architecture
arches 2 865
cathedrals 2 863; 31 91
chapels 2 865
cloisters 24 280; 28 369
colleges 31 822
façades 3 45; 13 108, 731, *756*; 31 *823*
monasteries 13 69, 70, *70*; 14 578; 28 368; 29 263; 31 87, 88
portals 28 369
presbyteries 11 483
collaboration 9 748; 27 703
groups and movements 14 578
patrons and collectors 2 278; 9 112; 21 124, 125
pupils 2 865
restorations by others 21 81
Guas, Pedro 13 756; 14 134; 21 125
Guasave 2 904; 21 203
Guasp (family) 33 358
Guaspre, le *see* DUGHET, GASPARD
Guastalla, Ferdinand II Gonzaga, Duca da 8 537
Guastalla, Ferrante Gonzaga, Duca da 12 *904*, 910*
architecture 12 760–61; 21 517
medals 31 319
paintings 5 547; 7 488; 12 561; 28 335
urban planning 28 460
Guastalla, Pauline Bonaparte, Duchessa di *see* BONAPARTE, PAULINE, Princess Borghese
Guastalla, Piazza Roma 16 697
Guastavillani, Filippo, Cardinal 20 541
Guastavino (y Moreno), Rafael 13 757*; 20 18
Guastavino Fireproof Construction Company 13 757
Guastavino vaults *see under* VAULTS (CEILING) → types
Guastavino y Esposito, Rafael 13 757
Guatamiputra (*reg c.* late 1st-early 2nd cent. AD) (Satavahana) 15 451
Guatemala 13 757–70*, *758*; 21 177, *178*, *193*
acrylic 13 766
architecture 13 760–63*; 24 *744*
banks 13 *762*
cathedrals 2 *143*
churches 13 *761*
collections 13 768–70*
cotton 13 766
dealing 13 768–9*
dolls 31 261
dress 13 760
dyes 13 766
education (art) 13 770*
engravings 13 764
exhibitions 13 768
furniture 13 768*
gold 13 767–8*
guilds 13 766, 770
ikat 30 554
jade 16 859; 23 418
jadeite 16 861; 21 241; 29 152–3
libraries 13 769*
looms 13 766; 30 544
mahogany 13 *767*
maiolica 13 768
marks 13 767
museums 13 769–70*
painting 10 154; 13 760, 763–6*, *765*
patronage 13 768–9*
pedestals 13 *767*
pilasters 13 761
pottery 13 768*; 31 261
prints 13 764
pyramids 24 *744*
rayon 13 766
retables 26 251
Guatemala—cont.
sculpture 10 154; 13 763–6*, *767*
silk 13 766
silver 13 *767*, 767–8*
spinning-wheels 13 766
stelae 29 *620*
temples 24 *744*
textiles 13 766–7*, *766*
tombs 17 *754*
vaults (ceiling) 13 760
weaving 13 766
wool 13 766
Guatemala City 13 *758*, 770–71*
Academia de Bellas Artes *see* Escuela Nacional de Artes Plásticas
Academia de Geografía e Historia
library 13 769
architecture 13 761–2
Avenida de la Reforma 13 762
Banco de Guatemala 13 763
Banco Occidente 13 *762*, 763
Biblioteca Nacional 13 763
Cathedral 13 761, 762, 767
Central de Correos 13 763
Corte Suprema de Justicia 13 763
Crédito Hipotecario Nacional 13 763
Edificio Sanidad Pública 13 763
Escuela de Dibujo 12 57; 13 770
Escuela Nacional de Artes Plásticas 13 765, 770
Facultad de Medicina 13 763
furniture 13 768
Galería DS 8 859
Gran Teatro 13 763; 26 66
Instituto de Antropología e Historia 13 769
Monastery of S Francisco 14 714
museums
Museo de Arte Contemporáneo 13 769
Museo Cafarnaum 13 769
Museo Fray Francisco Vázquez 13 769
Museo Ixchel de Traje Indígena 13 769
Museo Nacional de Arqueología y Etnología 13 769; 21 265
Museo Nacional de Arte Moderno 13 769
Museo Nacional de Artes e Industrias Populares 13 769
Museo Nacional de Historia 13 769
Museo Nacional de Historia y Bellas Artes 13 769
Museo Popol Vuh 13 769
Nuestra Señora de las Mercedes 13 767
Olympic City 13 763
Palacio Municipal 13 763
Palacio Nacional 12 28; 13 763
Policía Nacional 13 763
pottery 13 768
Registro de la Propiedad Inmueble 13 762
San Carlos Gran Hotel 12 28
S Augustín Acasaguastlán 13 767
sculpture 13 *767*
Seguro Social building 13 763
S Francisco 13 762
Teatro Nacional 13 762, 764
Templo de Minerva 13 763, 764
Terminal Aérea 13 763
textiles 13 766
Universidad de San Carlos 13 770
Universidad Mariano Gálvez de Guatemala 13 770
Universidad Rafael Landívar 13 770
Guattani, Giovanni Antonio 26 849; 32 613
Guay, Jacques 12 262; 13 771*
patrons and collectors 25 80
pupils 11 635; 25 80
reproductive prints by others 25 80
Guay, Jacques—cont.
works 4 517; 12 *262*
Guayabo de Turrialba 13 771–2*; 29 *136*, 143
Guayaquil 9 *709*
architecture 9 712
Banco Central de Ecuador 29 221
Cathedral 9 711, *711*
Centro Cultural 9 714
Museo Antropológico y Pinacoteca del Banco Central del Ecuador 9 714
Museo Municipal 9 714
Universidad Laica 'Vicente Rocafuerte' de Guayaquil 9 715
Guayasamín, Oswaldo 9 713; 13 772*; 23 85; 28 920
works 9 *713*
Guayde, Jehan *see* GAILDE, JEAN
Guazzalotti, Andrea 20 918
Guazzo, Stefano 7 646
Gubba, Tell 14 128
Gubbay Toilet Service 10 329
Gubbio 13 772–3*; 16 *620*
imprese 15 150
Palazzo dei Consoli 2 42; 13 *773*; 16 627; 31 236, 237
staircase 29 521
Palazzo Ducale 11 690; 16 659, 724
Studiolo 22 13; 29 860
Palazzo Pretorio 2 42
Piazza della Signoria 2 42; 31 236
pottery 14 425
lustreware 16 734
maiolica 13 773*; 16 734
S Agostino 2 725
S Domenico 16 724
S Francesco 13 52
urban planning 23 898
Gubbio, Giorgio da *see* ANDREOLI, GIORGIO
Gubbio, Mello di *see* MELLO DI GUBBIO
Gubbio, Niccoló da *see* NICCOLÓ DA GUBBIO
Gubbio, Oderisio da *see* ODERISIO DA GUBBIO
Guben, Wolf House 4 788
Gubitz, Anton 13 773
Gubitz, Friedrich Wilhelm 13 773*
Gubitz, Johann Christoph 13 773
Gubler, Friedrich 7 *294*
Gubler, Max 30 135
Gucci, Giovanni 13 773
Gucci, Santi 13 773–4*; 18 425; 25 96
patrons and collectors 33 606
works 12 114; 13 *774*; 18 433, *433*; 22 168; 25 113; 31 238
Guccio Ciuti, Goro di *see* GORO DI GUCCIO CIUTI
Guccio di Mannaia 13 774–5*; 16 741
patrons and collectors 23 96
pupils 31 141
works 2 632; 10 194; 13 163, *163*, 169
Gucevicius, Laurynas Stuoka *see* GUCEWICZ, WAWRZYNIEC
Gucewicz, Wawrzyniec 13 775–6*; 19 497; 32 579; 33 615
Gucht, Maximilian van der 9 703; 23 465
Guckeisen, Jakob 6 560; 9 687; 13 776*
Gudaitis, Antanas 19 499
gūdamaṇḍapa 15 243*
Guda of Westphalia 26 659; 33 308
Gudbrandsdal 30 326
tapestries 23 238; 30 320, 324
textiles 23 240
wood-carvings 11 240, *240*
Gude, Hans Fredrik 13 776*; 23 232
collaboration 30 852
Gude, Hans Fredrik—cont.
pupils
Bergh, (Johan) Edvard 3 776
Cappelen, (Herman) August 5 679
Hertervig, Lars 14 483
Holmberg, (Gustaf) Werner 14 689
Kielland, Kitty (Lange) 18 32
Krohg, Christian 18 463
Leistikow, Walter 19 112
Lindholm, Berndt (Adolf) 19 408
Munsterhjelm, (Magnus) Hjalmar 22 316
Rydberg, Gustaf (Fredrik) 27 460
Sinding, Otto Ludvig 28 770
Thaulow, Frits (Johan Fredrik) 30 647
Wahlberg, (Herman) Alfred (Leonard) 32 765
Wright, Magnus von 33 411
teachers 28 104
works 23 225
Gude, Nils 13 776
Gudea, *ensi* of Lagash 1 884; 21 295, *295*; 29 X2
Gudenberg, W. W. von 7 552
Gudeon, Regnault 1 765
Gudewerdt, Hans (i) (*d* before 1642) 13 777*
Gudewerdt, Hans (ii) (*c.* 1600–71) 13 777–8*
works 13 *777*
Gudhem Abbey Church 13 102
Gudhjonsson, Jens 15 73
Gudhnadóttir, Jonina 15 72
Gudiashvili, Lado (Davidovich) 12 326, 332; 13 778*
Gudimallam 13 778*; 15 *294*, 416, 438–9
sculpture 15 *438*
Gudin, (Jean-Antoine-) Théodore 12 732; 13 778–9*; 29 248
Gudiol i Cunill, Josep 13 779*
Gudiol i Ricart, Josep 13 779*
Gudjonsdóttir, Sigrun 15 72
Guðmundsson, Guðmundur *see* ERRÓ
Guðmundsson, Kristján 13 779–80*; 15 71
Guðmundsson, Sigurður (1833–74) 15 70; 22 540
Guðmundsson, Sigurður (*b* 1942) 13 780*; 15 71; 22 853, 862
Guðnason, Svavar 7 488; 13 780*; 15 70
Gué, Julien-Michel 8 548
Guebwiller 13 57; 26 633
Guedes, Amancio (d'Alpoim Miranda) 13 780–81*; 30 391
works 1 319; 13 *781*; 22 245; 29 107
Guedes, João Bernardo 23 454
Guedes, Joaquim 4 715; 13 781–2*
works 13 *782*
Guedes, Manuel 25 313
Gueffier, Etienne 26 760
Guégan, Pierre 30 231
Guelders, Arnold, Duke of 32 823
Guelf (family) *see* WELF (FAMILY)
Guelfi (family) 28 677
Guelfi, Giovanni Battista 4 611; 10 264; 12 595; 13 782*; 19 606
Guëll (family) 12 180
Guëll (i Bacigalupi), Eusebi, Baron 13 782–3*
Guelph (House of) *see* WELF (HOUSE OF)
Guelphi, Giovanni Battista *see* GUELFI, GIOVANNI BATTISTA
Güemes, Pedro de 7 363
Güemes, Septien 27 605
Güemes Bracamante, Gonzáles de 23 681
Güemes Pacheco, Juan Vicente de, Conde de Revillagigedo, Viceroy of New Spain 21 402
Guénebault, Louis Jean 10 209, 211
Guénégaud, Claude de 13 783
Guénégaud, Henri de 13 783*
architecture 20 293
Guenepin, François-Jean-Christophe 28 349
Guennol Collection 20 642
Guenther, Egon 18 514; 29 110
Guenzel, Louis 9 305
Guépière, Phillippe de La *see* LA GUÉPIÈRE, PHILLIPPE DE
Guérard, Bernhard von 13 783
Guérard, Eugene von 2 771; 13 783–4*
patrons and collectors 4 882
works 2 745, *745*; 13 *784*; 23 58
Guérard, Henri 12 915; 21 895, 896
Guérard, Nicolas (*d* 1719) 3 762
Guérard, Nicolas (*fl c.* 1720) 2 467
Guerard, Thomas de *see* THOMAS DE GUERARD
Guercia, Jacopo della *see* JACOPO DELLA QUERCIA
Guercino 9 90; 11 3; 12 279; 13 784–9*; 16 669
assistants 12 279
attributions 3 211; 4 291
caricatures 5 756
collaboration 3 211; 4 334; 18 689; 30 356; 32 593
drawings 8 *42*; 9 26, 222; 13 *788*; 15 *856*; 25 558; 32 *884*
frames 11 387
groups and movements 3 265
methods 8 128
paintings 2 2; 16 670
altarpieces 17 509; 26 810
frescoes 13 *786*; 15 137; 24 695; 27 693; 32 550
history 23 294
literary themes 30 358
religious 5 450; 10 476; 13 *785*, *787*
patrons and collectors
Albarelli, Giovanni 5 432
Alcalá, 3rd Duque de (1583–1637) 26 307
Aldrovandi, Filippo 1 597
Alfonso III, 7th Duke of Modena and Reggio (*reg* 1628–9) 10 525
Aved, Jacques (-André-Joseph) 2 852
Bourbon del Monte, Francesco Maria, Cardinal 4 567
Bourbon I., Louis de, le Grand Dauphin (1661–1711) 4 553
Bouverie, John 4 596; 25 665
Brydges, James, 1st Duke of Chandos 5 65
Camuccini, Pietro 5 554
Caraman, Duc de 5 700
Carr, William Holwell 5 848
Cavendish, William, 1st Duke of Devonshire (1640–1707) 6 116
Champernowne, Arthur 6 438
Charles IV, King of Spain (*reg* 1788–1808) 4 565
Charles-Emanuel I, 11th Duke of Savoy (*reg* 1580–1630) 28 7
Coke, Thomas, 1st Earl of Leicester of the 1st creation (1697–1759) 7 540
Colonna, Girolamo, Cardinal (1604–66) 7 620, 621
Créquy, Charles de Blanchefort de 19 238
Dalton, Richard 8 475
Denon, (Dominique-) Vivant 8 763
Ercolani (family) 10 446
Este (i), Alessandro d', Cardinal (1568–1624) 10 525

Guercino
patrons and collectors—cont.
Ferdinando, 6th Duke of Mantua (*reg* 1612-26) **12** 913
Francesco I, 8th Duke of Modena and Reggio (*reg* 1629-58) **10** 526
Gennari (family) **9** 230
George III, King of Great Britain (*reg* 1760-1820) **8** 474
Gerini, Carlo, Marchese (1616-73) **12** 355
Ghisilieri, Ettore **12** 559
Giori, Angelo, Cardinal **12** 680
Gregory XV, Pope (*reg* 1621-3) **19** 778
Hawkins, John Heywood (1803-77) **14** 252
Hervey, Frederick Augustus, 4th Earl of Bristol **14** 485
Howard (ii), Frederick, 5th Earl of Carlisle **14** 808
Hudson, Thomas (1701-99) **14** 842
Isham, Thomas **13** 300
John VI, King of Portugal (*reg* 1816-26) **4** 725
Laborde-Méréville, François (-Louis- Joseph) de **18** 579
Lancellotti, Tiberio **18** 689
Lanier, Nicholas **18** 747
La Vrillière, Louis Phélypeaux de **18** 885
Ludovisi (family) **3** 744
Ludovisi, Ludovico, Cardinal **19** 779
Lumague, Barthélémy **19** 790
Lumague, Charles **19** 790
Medici, Leopoldo de', Cardinal **21** 28
National Gallery of Scotland **28** 272
Patrizi, Costanzo **24** 267
Polignac, Melchior de, Cardinal **25** 150
Poniatowski, Stanisław, Prince **25** 213
Reynolds, Joshua **26** 280
Reynst (family) **26** 283
Royal Institution (Edinburgh) **28** 271
Ruffo, Tommaso, Cardinal, Archbishop of Ferrara **27** 316
Sauli (family) **27** 878
Savoy, Eugene of, Prince (1663-1736) **28** 15
Serra, Giacomo **4** 334; **28** 478
Spencer, John, 1st Earl Spencer **29** 381
Tarnowski, Jan Feliks, Count and Waleria **30** 345
Thibaudeau, Narcisse-Adolphe, Comte de **30** 727
Udney, John **31** 524, 525
Udney, Robert **31** 524
Uffelen, Lucas van **31** 526
Waldegrave, William, 1st Baron Radstock **32** 774
pupils **4** 291; **5** 383, 651; **10** 526; **12** 279; **24** 833; **25** 562; **27** 893
reproductions in tapestry **22** 481
reproductive prints by others
Bartolozzi, Francesco **3** 308; **8** 474; **26** 230
Coriolano, Giovanni Battista **7** 857; **33** 358
Couvay, Jean **8** 77
Cunego, Domenico **8** 267
Dorigny, Nicolas **9** 176
Lélu, Pierre **19** 119
Mattioli, Lodovico **20** 849
Traballesi, Giuliano **31** 268
restorations by others **29** 892
teachers **4** 277
Guere *see* WE
El Guereo **4** 260
Guéret, Louis-Jean **14** 365; **32** 920; **33** 153
Guergour **16** 486
Guerin (family) **20** 664
Guérin, Charles (-François-Prosper) **13** 789–90*
pupils **3** 318; **9** 495; **13** 695; **14** 499; **22** 92
Guérin, Félix **13** 791
Guérin, Gabriel-Christophe **4** 816; **14** 390
Guérin, Gilles **13** 790*
collaboration **12** 725; **26** 91; **27** 821
patrons and collectors **7** 699; **14** 492
works **19** 212, 642
Guérin, Gustave **13** 790*; **26** 704
Guérin, Isabelle **13** 791
Guérin, Jean-Pierre Philibert **13** 791
Guérin, Jules **5** 275
works **31** *727*
Guérin, (Jean-Baptiste) Paulin **8** 73; **12** 336; **13** 790–91*; **24** 171; **25** 11
Guérin, Pierre (-Narcisse) **11** 542, 544, 659, 671; **13** 791–4*
assistants **8** 638
competitions **25** 638
groups and movements **31** 373
paintings **24** 212
patrons and collectors **4** 304, 556; **11** 666
pupils
Cibot, (François-Barthélemy-Michel-)Edouard **7** 304
Cogniet, Léon **7** 528
Fogelberg, Bengt Erland **11** 234
Gericault, (Jean-Louis-André-) Théodore **12** 349
Henriquel-Dupont **14** 394
Huet, Paul **14** 847
Lauréus, Alexander **18** 870
Orsel, (André-Jacques-) Victor **23** 572
Scheffer, Ary **28** 67
Sigalon, (Alexandre-François-) Xavier **28** 694
reproductive prints by others **11** 319
teachers **26** 93
works **11** 543; **13** *792, 794*
Guérin Earthenware Factory **3** 592
Guérineau **25** 578
Guerini, Giovan Francesco *see* GUERRIERI, GIOVAN FRANCESCO
Guerini, Giulio Cesare **5** 852
Guerini, Liborio **12** 889
Guerini, Rochus *see* LYNAR, ROCHUS QUIRINUS
guérisseur see SCULPTURE → types → healing statues
Guerlain **18** 659
Guermonprez, Trude **11** 54; **31** 660
Guernesi
painting **1** *290*
Guerney, Charles de **2** 417
Guernier, Alexandre Du *see* DU GUERNIER, ALEXANDRE
Guernier, Louis Du *see* DU GUERNIER, LOUIS
Guerniero, Giovanni Francesco **11** 345; **14** 491; **17** 834, 835
works **17** *835*
Guerra, Alfonso **8** 275; **13** 795*
Guerra, Camillo **6** 136; **13** 795; **22** 78, 97
Guerra, Cristoforo **32** 107
Guerra, Eugenio **21** 73
Guerra, Gabriel **13** 795*; **21** 403; **23** 207
Guerra, Gaspare **3** 644; **5** 123; **13** 795
Guerra, Giovanni **13** 795*; **19** 383; **22** 715; **24** 399
works **1** 791
Guerra, Giovanni Battista **13** 795
Guerra, Marco **9** 710; **17** 514
Guerra, Miguel **13** 767
Guerra, Valentín Gutiérrez *see* GUTIÉRREZ GUERRA, VALENTÍN
Guerre, Louis **25** 211
Guerreiro da Costa, Jorge **26** 254
works **26** *253*
Guerreri, Giovan Francesco *see* GUERRIERI, GIOVAN FRANCESCO
Guerrero, Amalia **18** 833
Guerrero, Enrique **2** 280; **33** 493
Guerrero, José **13** 796*
Guerrero, Juan (*fl* 18th cent.) **28** 516
Guerrero, Juan Agustín (*fl* 19th cent.) **9** 712; **13** 796*
Guerrero, Juan Carlos (*fl* 20th cent.) **2** 397
Guerrero, Lorenzo **24** 622
Guerrero, Manuel **24** 819
Guerrero, Pedro **10** 153
Guerrero, Vicente **29** 151
Guerrero, Xavier **13** 796*
Guerrero Galván, Jesús **13** 796–7*
Guerrero y Torres, Francisco Antonio de **13** 797*; **21** 377, 401
Guerri, Dionisio **11** 42
Guerrico, José Prudencio de **2** 404
Guerrico, Manuel J. de **2** 404
Guerrieri, Camilla **13** 797
Guerrieri, Giovan Francesco **13** 797*
Guerrieri Gonzaga, Giovanni Battista **32** 403
Guerrilla Girls **6** 175
Guerrini, Mino **9** 168; **11** 314; **16** 681
Guerrino, Tondino di *see* TONDINO DI GUERRINO
Guersi, Guido **13** 721
Guesdon, Alfred **4** 80
Guest, (Thomas) Douglas **13** 797–8*
Guesten Hall (Worcs) **30** 909
roof **30** *908*
Guétin, Canal Latéral à la Loire **2** 242
Guevara, Alejandro **29** 34
Guevara, Antonio de **17** 692; **27** 606
Guevara, Diego de **4** 446
Guevara, Felipe de **29** 335, 352
Guevara, Fernando Niño de, Cardinal *see* NIÑO DE GUEVARA, FERNANDO, Cardinal
Guevara, Gloria **29** 34
Guevara, Juan Niño de *see* NIÑO DE GUEVARA, JUAN
Guevara Moreno, Luis **13** 798*; **32** 175
Guevara y Tassis, Iñigo Vélez de *see* OÑATE Y DE VILLAMEDIANA, Conde de
Guévrékian, Gabriel **7** *294*; **13** 798*; **23** 169
Gueydan, de **25** 280
Guezo **11** 246
Guffens, Gottfried Egide **22** 329
Gu Fuzhen **33** 496
Gugark' **2** 426
Guge
painting **30** *810*
Gugel, Eugen **13** 798–9*; **23** 121
Gugelot, Hans **15** 826
Gugenmus, Antoni **32** 878
Gugenmus, Franciszek **32** 878
Gugenmus, Michał **32** 878
Gugga **4** 640; **6** 566; **15** 483
Guggenbichler, Georg **13** 799
Guggenbichler, (Johann) Meinrad **13** 799–800*
works **2** 801, *813*; **13** *799*
Guggenheim, John Simon, Memorial Foundation **31** 663
Guggenheim, Olga **13** 800
Guggenheim, Peggy (Marguerite) **2** 560; **10** 469; **13** 800–801*; **19** 590; **23** 48; **31** 607, 665
groups and movements **30** 22
sculpture **10** 772
Guggenheim, Simon **13** 800
Guggenheim, Solomon R(obert) **2** 560; **7** 782; **13** 800*; **24** 574
collections **23** 48; **26** 58; **31** 668
Guggenheim, Solomon R., Museum *see under* NEW YORK → museums
Guggenheim, Willy *see* VARLIN
Guggiari, Hermann **13** 801*; **24** 98, 100
Guggisberg, Monica **30** 145
Gught, Maximiliaan van der **22** 897; **30** 320
Gught, Michael van der **32** 378
Guglak Fortress **2** 427
Guglielmada, Giovanni Battista **20** 921
Guglielmelli, Arcangelo **10** 800; **13** 801–2*
Guglielmelli, Marcello **13** 802*
Guglielmi, Gregorio **2** 795; **13** 802–4*
patrons and collectors **7** 898; **28** 18; **31** 341
works **2** 714; **13** *803*; **31** 444; **32** 460
Guglielmi, O.Louis **25** 462
Guglielmo (*fl c.* 1138; painter) **8** 211
Guglielmo (*fl c.* 1138; sculptor) *see* GUGLIELMUS
Guglielmo (*fl* 1158-65; sculptor) **13** 804*
attributions **24** 858
collaboration **4** 297
works **24** 854, 856, 858; **25** 723; **26** 623
Guglielmo, 3rd Duke of Mantua (*reg* 1550-87) **3** 850; **12** *904*, 911*
collections **12** 151
paintings **2** 20; **8** 4; **12** 558; **31** 14
tapestries **17** 812
Guglielmo, Master **21** 515
Guglielmo da Pisa **13** 804*
collaboration **24** 868
teachers **24** 854
works **4** 279; **18** 677; **24** 872; **25** 724
Guglielmo del Magro *see* GIRALDI, GUGLIELMO
Guglielmo di Verdelay **2** 109
Guglielmo (lo) Monaco **2** 276; **9** 157
Guglielmo Raimondo **2** 650
Guglielmo Tedesco *see* TETRODE, WILLEM DANIELSZ. VAN
Guglielmus **8** 211; **13** 804*; **26** 619; **32** 342, 344
Gugliemi Collection **10** 640
Gugong bowuyuan yuangan **24** 435
Gugong xueshu jikan **24** 435
Gugon wenwu Yuekan **24** 435
Gu Hongzhong **6** 809, 812; **7** 36, 76
works **7** *35*
Guhrs, Pam **33** 602
gui see under VESSELS → types
Guiana, British *see* GUYANA
Guiana, Dutch *see* SURINAM
Guiana, French *see* FRENCH GUIANA
Guiard, Laurent **11** 627; **13** 805*
Guiart, Jean **23** 738, 739
Guiart des Moulins **4** 12
Guiaud, Jacques **13** 306
Guibal, Barthélemy **13** 805*; **22** 454, 456; **29** 537
Guibal, Nicolas **11** 817; **13** 805–6*; **22** 273; **33** 429
Guibert, Honoré **11** 408, 410
Guibert, J. B.
works **31** *709*
Guibert, Philip **19** 592
Guibert de Nogent **5** 894; **8** 260
Guicardo, Innocento **28** 10
Guicciardini, Francesco **14** 7; **32** 502
Guicciardini, Lodovico **13** 806*; **19** 343
Guichard **19** 850
Guichard, Alexandre **14** 58
Guichard, E. **11** 600
Guichard, Joseph (-Benoît) **4** 625; **13** 806*; **19** 847; **22** 119
Guidalotti, Buonamico di Lapo **2** 15
Guidé, Jean-Baptiste **24** 255
guidebooks **2** 531; **4** 21; **13** 807–12*; **22** 352
Arabia **13** 811
Armenia (Europe) **13** 811
Azerbaijan **13** 811
Belgium **13** 808, 810
Britain **13** 809
Byzantine **13** 808
China **13** 812
Early Christian (*c.* AD 250-843) **26** 799
Egypt **13** 810, 811, 812
Egypt, ancient **13** 807
England **10** 377; **13** 811; **33** 132–3
France **13** 809, 810
Germany **12** 482; **13** 810
Greece **33** 136
Greece, ancient **13** 807*
Indian subcontinent **13** 812
Iran **13** 812
Iraq **13** 812
Italy **13** 299, 304, 808, 809, 810, 811; **20** 243; **26** 755
7th cent. AD **26** 799
16th cent. **1** 554; **13** 808
17th cent. **18** 814
18th cent. **26** 345
Japan **13** 812; **17** 274
Java **13** 812
Latin America **13** 811
Mexico **13** 811
Morocco **13** 812
Netherlands, the **13** 810
Palestine **13** 808
Peru **13** 811
Rome, ancient **13** 807–8*
Spain **11** 304; **13** 809, 810
Sudan **13** 811
Switzerland **13** 810
Syria **13** 811
Tibet **13** 812
Turkey **13** 811
United States of America **13** 811
see also TRAVEL BOOKS
Gui de Pileo **1** 697
Guidetti, Guidetto **13** 813*
attributions **26** 832
patrons and collectors **6** 360
pupils **25** 258
works **16** 634
Guidetto **13** 813*, 817; **19** 765, 766; **24** 858; **26** 624
Guidetto da Como **25** 450
Guidi, Antonio **7** 332
Guidi, Domenico **13** 814–15*; **26** 773
collaboration **11** 17; **25** 863
teachers **1** 630, 631
works **1** 629, 630, 631; **10** 501; **11** 740; **13** *815*; **15** 861; **16** 699; **27** 172
Guidi, Giovanni di Ser Giovanni *see* SCHEGGIA
Guidi, Guido **21** 6
Guidi, Jacopo di Piero **11** 892; **13** 94; **19** 674, 752
Guidi, Virgilio **4** 278; **13** 816*; **16** 680
Guido **24** 858; **25** 863; **28** 684
Guido, Angel **21** 314
Guido, Ercolino di *see* MARIA, ERCOLINO DE

Guido, Lombardo di see LOMBARDO DI GUIDO
Guidobaldo I, 2nd Duke of Urbino (reg 1482-1508) 22 12, 13*; 27 790; 31 741
books 27 790; 32 385
paintings 17 704; 25 898; 31 413
Guidobaldo II, 4th Duke of Urbino (reg 1538-74) 27 274*
architecture 12 278; 24 534; 31 745, 746
ceramics 6 I1; 11 268; 31 741; 33 720
decorative works 4 856
paintings 11 721; 31 35
sculpture 1 789; 4 664
sponsorship 23 878
Guido Bonatti 2 650
Guidobono, Bartolomeo 4 811; 13 816–17*; 14 27; 24 563
Guidobono, Domenico 13 816, 817; 28 14
Guidobono, Giovanni Antonio 13 816
Guidobono, Master 13 817; 19 765
Guido da Colonna 7 242; 20 512
Guido da Como 5 550; 13 817*; 24 867
works 19 765; 24 854, 859; 25 723; 26 624
Guido da Corno 13 813
Guido da Firenze 2 15
Guido da Pavia, Bishop of Pisa 24 856
Guido da Siena 9 341; 13 817–20*
works 2 389; 11 379; 13 818, 819; 16 655
Guido di Giovanni 28 681
Guido di Meo d'Antonia see ANTONIA, GUIDO DI MEO D'
Guido di Merlino 9 425; 31 741
Guido di Piero da Mugello see ANGELICO, Fra
guidons 11 148, 150
Guidoriccio da Foligno 31 534
Guidotti, Dario 9 131
Guidotti, Paolo 24 860
Guidus de Como 13 817
Guiette, René 2 545; 3 79, 551; 20 846
Guiffrey, Jules (-Marie-Joseph) 11 675; 13 820–21*
Gui Fu 6 764, 765
Guignard, Alberto da Veiga 4 718; 6 66; 13 821*
Guignard, J. G. 6 563
Guignebert, Vincent 11 644
Guignet 24 794
Guigo I, Prior 5 893, 894
Guigou, Paul 11 887; 13 821–2*; 20 473; 22 29
Guigues, Louis-Jacques 26 351
Guiguet, Jacques
works 6 166
Guijano, Gerónimo see QUIJANO, JERÓNIMO
Guilá Naquitz 21 260
Guilbert, Yvette 25 278, 279
Guilde de la Gravure 19 491
Guildford (Australia), Hall Collection Museum 24 496
Guildford (Surrey; UK)
Abbot's Hospital 10 230
Castle 6 55
Cathedral 4 790
Grammar School 10 230
school 28 156
Guildford, Henry 14 668
guildhalls 14 76; 18 886; 31 235, 236–8*
Belgium 3 544
England 19 567
Germany 4 742
Gothic 19 567
see also LIVERY HALLS
Guild of Glass Engravers 10 321
Guild of Handicraft 2 594, 595, 766; 10 298, 336, 344, 346; 19 596; 20 437
frames 11 434
jewellery 17 528
silver 10 336
Guild of St Barnulphus 21 129
Guild of St George 6 408; 27 352
Guild of St George, Master of the 20 686*
Guild of St Joseph and St Dominic 12 631
Guild of St Thomas and St Luke 33 7
Guild of Sculpture (Ont.) 5 592
Guild of the Cloth Refiners, Florence 32 362
guilds 7 830; 13 822–4*; 14 409; 20 599
historical and regional traditions
Belgium 3 588, 598, 605, 617; 5 46
Benin, Kingdom of 1 242; 3 722
Bolivia 4 269
China 6 787; 7 147
Ecuador 9 712, 714
Egypt, ancient 10 6
England 13 822; 14 409; 19 592
France 11 655, 669*
Germany 13 823
Indian subcontinent 15 207
Ireland 16 25
Italy 1 102; 24 521; 28 676; 32 189–90, 223
Mexico 21 397
Native North Americans 22 650, 666
Netherlands, the 1 806; 22 886, 894
Nupe 23 302
South-east Asia 29 236
Spain 17 515
Switzerland 30 154
Tibet 30 843
types
architects' 15 245*
builders' 6 690
carpenters' 12 420; 17 52; 29 312
embroiderers' 22 898
featherworkers' 21 249
furniture-makers' 10 287; 11 585, 588; 22 870; 25 119; 29 315; 32 448
glassmakers' 25 124; 32 200
goldsmiths' 3 596; 8 180; 12 442; 23 236; 25 312; 27 419; 29 332, 336
knitters' 12 469
masons' 20 561–2; 32 189
metalsmiths' 10 336; 22 789; 25 128; 28 262
painters'
Belgium 2 194
Gothic 13 133, 137, 155
Guatemala 13 770
Italy 16 780; 28 676; 32 189
Mexico 21 382
Netherlands, the 1 104; 22 907
Poland 25 101
Spain 14 8
pewterers' 3 603; 22 893; 24 579
printmakers' 25 624–5*
publishers' 7 624
sculptors' 12 403; 26 855
silversmiths' 8 237
tapestry-weavers' 12 519
textiles 16 445
weavers' 3 606; 13 766; 17 311
wood-carvers' 32 189
Guilermo de la Monta 11 482
Guilford (CT) 31 623
Guilford, Francis North, 1st Earl of see NORTH, FRANCIS, 1st Earl of Guilford
Guilford, Frederick North, 5th Earl of see NORTH, FREDERICK, 5th Earl of Guilford
Guilfoyle, William 12 142
Guilhelme, Master 13 192
Guilhermy, (Roch François) Ferdinand (Marie Nolasque), Baron de 13 824–5*; 27 545
Guilin 6 716, 732; 30 443
Mt Fubo 6 716
Mt Xi 6 716
sculpture 6 732
tomb 6 703
Guillain, Henry 20 138
Guillain, Nicolas 13 825*
assistants 27 821
collaboration 13 825; 16 856; 31 305
pupils 13 825
Guillain, Simon, I (1589-1658) 11 557; 13 825*
collaboration 3 853; 13 825; 31 305
pupils 2 91
teachers 1 631; 13 825
Guillain, Simon, II (1618-54) 1 465
Guillard 11 257
Guillard, Charles 20 777
Guillaume, Abbot of Saint-Benoît-sur-Loire 27 533
Guillaume IV, Abbot of Saint-Trond 3 641
Guillaume, Eugène 4 308; 7 170; 18 751; 24 509
Guillaume, Jean-Baptiste-Claude-Eugène 11 563, 566; 13 826*; 28 346
Guillaume, Paul 1 230, 438; 8 603, 775; 13 826*; 18 445; 21 787
Guillaume, Victor 22 456
Guillaume au Vaissel 11 639
Guillaume d'Arondel 31 835
Guillaume de Bez 11 653
Guillaume de Cantiers, Bishop of Evreux 29 512
Guillaume de Croy 3 545
Guillaume de Dammartin 22 464
Guillaume de Deguilleville 1 653
Guillaume de Estourtville, Cardinal 11 904
Guillaume de Flavacourt, Archbishop of Rouen 27 252
Guillaume de Hellande, Bishop of Beauvais 5 549; 11 799; 14 422; 30 314; 31 219
Guillaume de Joinville 26 114
Guillaume de Lorris 12 107
Guillaume de Machaut 13 154, 826–7*; 20 652
works 13 153, 154, 827
Guillaume de Marcillat 13 827*
patrons and collectors 9 112; 27 273
pupils 24 250; 32 10
works 2 390; 29 504, 504
Guillaume de Nourriche 26 453
Guillaume de Pierre see GUILLAUME DE MARCILLAT
Guillaume d'Harcourt 10 665
Guillaume di Brabante 10 519
Guillaume Julien 13 828*
patrons and collectors 5 666
works 13 158, 168; 24 132
Guillaume le Clerc 3 878; 26 563
Guillaume of Champeaux 7 371
Guillaumet, Gustave (-Achille) 13 828*; 23 504
Guillaumin, (Jean-Baptiste) Armand 7 674; 13 828–9*
exhibitions 15 154, 155
groups and movements 15 151, 152
patrons and collectors 30 375
works 15 828
Guillaumot, Charles-Axel 12 746
Guillebert de Lannoy 14 389
works 14 389
Guillebert de Lannoy, Master of 17 455
Guillebert de Metz 20 686
Guillebert de Metz, Master of 3 555; 20 686–7*, 721
pupils 20 749
works 7 235; 20 451, 687
Guillebon, Jeanne-Claude de see CHRISTO AND JEANNE-CLAUDE
Guillelmus 5 371
Guillem, Oscar Tusquets see TUSQUETS GUILLEM, OSCAR
Guillemard, Gilberto 23 31
Guillem de So, Vescomte d'Evol see EVOL, GUILLEM DE SO, Vescomte d'
Guillem de Torrelles 3 339
Guillemer, Jean 17 458
Guillemet, (Jean-Baptiste-) Antoine 13 829–30*
Guillemín, G. F. 16 803
Guillén, Abraham 24 518
Guillén, Arnoldo 25 455
Guillen, Arturo 14 716
Guillén, Asilia 13 830*
works 23 81, 82
Guillén de Holanda 2 23; 14 609
Guillén de Levi 17 676
Guilleré, René 11 601
Guillermin, Jean-Baptiste 11 637
Guillermo 29 330
Guillermo de Pereirs, Cardinal 4 737
Guillermo Gonzalez Zueleta 1 744
Guillery, Marcantonio
works 4 352
Guillet, Georges see GUILLET DE SAINT-GEORGES
Guillet, Marie see CAZIN, MARIE
Guillet, Père Marie Joseph 31 335
Guillet de Saint-Georges 13 830*
Guillibaud, Jean-Baptiste 11 605; 27 249
Guillielmus see GUGLIELMO
Guillim, John 14 406
Guilliod, Jayme 14 58
guilloche 12 869; 13 830–31*, 831
Greece, ancient 13 392, 830
Italy 11 384, 386
Rome, ancient 13 830
Guillon, Guillaume see LETHIÈRE, GUILLAUME
Guillon, Jacques 5 573, 580
Guillot, Anatole 22 271
Guillot, Claude 10 839
Guillou, Constant 10 669
Guillou, Jeannine 29 493
Guilmant, Félix 10 83
Guilmard, Desiré 13 831*
Guimarães 13 831*; 25 288
Castle 8 138
gold 25 312
metalwork 25 313
Misericórdia 31 813
Museo Arqueológico de Martins Sarmento 25 318
Museu de Alberto Sampiao 25 318
sculpture 26 648
S Francisco 26 253
silk 25 315
silver-gilt 13 166
Guimarães, João Francisco 1 753
Guimard, (Gilles) Barnabé 3 547; 13 831–2*; 22 33
collaboration 5 40; 22 33
works 3 274, 547
Guimard, Hector (-Germain) 11 525; 13 318, 832–3*
groups and movements 2 510, 562, 564, 568; 21 779; 26 14
reproductions in ceramics 22 270
works 4 48, 74; 11 525, 600, 628, 629; 17 548; 21 349, 349; 23 547; 24 128; 29 508
Guimard, Marie-Madeleine 11 368; 19 56, 115
Guimerá, Gasper Galcerán de Gurrea Aragón y Pino, Conde de 13 862, 863*; 18 817; 33 469
Guimet, Emile 13 833*
Guimet, Jean-Baptiste 13 833; 24 791
Guimet, Musée see under PARIS → museums
Guinan 6 835; 21 714
Guindaleri, Pietro 13 833–4*
works 13 834
Guinea 1 214, 386; 13 834–5*
compounds 1 312
currency 1 363
gongs 1 359, 360
headdresses 3 46
huts 1 308
iconography 1 261, 262
masks 1 336, 336
mythology 1 281
photography 10 580
sculpture 1 359; 3 46
stone 1 292
tools 1 364
wood 1 359; 3 46, 47
Guinea, Equatorial see EQUATORIAL GUINEA
Guinea-Bissau 1 214, 386; 13 835*
earthenwares 13 835
museums 1 440
textiles 13 835
Guines, Pedro 13 106
Guinigi (family) 20 709
Guinigi, Niccolò Lazzaso 23 92
Guinigi, Paolo 16 839
Guinness (company) 11 748
Guinness, Arthur Edward, 1st Lord Ardilaun 16 25
Guinness, Edward (Cecil), 1st Earl of Iveagh 1 454; 10 367; 13 836*; 33 565
Guinness, Mary Catherine see GUINNESS, MAY
Guinness, May 13 836*
Guinness, Rupert Edward, 2nd Earl of Iveagh 4 672
Guinness Peat Aviation 16 35
Guinness Trust 19 574
Guino, Richard 26 210
Guinovart, Josep 3 219; 8 538; 13 836*; 29 287
Guinti (da Lodi), Domenico 12 910
Guionnet, Alexandre 2 99; 5 392
Guionnet, Remonnet 4 547
Guiot de Beaugrant see BEAUGRANT, GUYOT DE
Guipal, Nicolas 8 508
Guiragossian, Paul 19 8
Guirand de Scevola, Lucien-Victor 5 530
Guiritti, Bernardino 21 98
Guiron le courtois, Master of the 20 687–8*
Guisachan 28 249
Guisard 15 842
Guiscard, Robert, Duke of Apulia see ROBERT GUISCARD, Duke of Apulia
Guise (family) 11 656; 25 580
Guise (France), Familistère 11 358; 30 458
Guise, Antoinette de Bourbon, Duchesse de 3 210
Guise, Charles de, Cardinal 3 210; 21 366; 27 653
Guise, Claude I, Duc de 4 400
Guise, Elisabeth-Marguerite d'Orléans, Duchesse de 18 633
Guise, François de Lorraine, 2nd Duc de 11 266
Guise, Gen. 9 230
Guise, Henri, 5th Duc de 9 76, 379
Guise, Jacques de see JACQUES DE GUISE
Guise, Jean, Cardinal of Lorraine 4 400
Guise, John 10 365; 13 837*; 23 690; 28 560
Guise diamond, Le 11 634
Guise Master 31 843
Guitarro Cave 29 179

guitars **22** 374
Guitet **12** 830
Guitry, Lucien **21** 371
Guitti, Francesco **3** 744; **30** 666
Guittonis, Johannes *see* RAINERIUS, JOHANNES GUITTONIS
Guiyang Buddhism *see under* BUDDHISM → sects
Guizebert, Pierre **4** 544
Guizot, François (-Pierre-Guillaume) **13** 837*
Guizzardi, Giuseppe **21** 824
Gujarati, C. D. **15** 742
Gujer, Lise **18** 80; **30** 151
Gujral, Satish **8** 677; **13** 837–8*
 works **15** 169, 172, *172*
Gujranwala **23** 803
Gujrat **15** 713; **23** 803
Gu Kaizhi **6** 635, 773, 785, 808, 812, 816; **11** 307; **13** 838–9*; **17** 588; **30** 49
 attributions **33** 318, 465
 copies **7** *34*
 works **5** 36; **6** 773, 776, 779, 796, 816; **7** 13, 108, 706
 writings **6** 630, 821; **25** 72
Gukei Sumiyoshi *see* SUMIYOSHI GUKEI
Gukei Ue *see* UE GUKEI
Gulácsy, Lajos **13** 839–40*; **14** 901; **20** 103
Gulbarga **13** 840*; **15** *294*; **16** *105*
 architecture **15** 356; **16** 201
 Chor Gunbad **15** 356
 congregational mosque **15** 356
 fortifications **21** 591
 Haft Gunbad **13** 840; **15** 356
 Langar ki Masjid **15** 358
 mosque of Qalandar Khan **15** 358
 mosques **15** 358
 Shah Bazar Mosque **15** 356
 shrine of Gisu Daraz **15** 356
 tomb of Da'ud Shah **15** 356
 tomb of Firuz Shah **15** 356; **29** 825
 tombs **15** 356
Gulbenkian, Calouste, Museu *see under* LISBON → museums
Gulbenkian, Calouste Sarkis **2** 444; **10** 90; **13** 840–41*; **16** 555
Gulbenkian Apocalypse *see under* APOCALYPSES → individual manuscripts
Gulbenkian Carpet **15** 683
Gulbrandsen, Inger **23** 241
Gulbrandsen, Nora **23** 235
Gulbransson, Olaf **5** 758; **13** 841*
Guldager, (Amandus) Christian *see* GULLAGER, (AMANDUS) CHRISTIAN
Guldara **1** *186*; **13** 841*; **15** *264*
 plaster **29** 824
 sculpture **1** 196
 stucco **29** 824
 stupa **1** 191, *192*; **15** 249
Guldberg, Ove Høegh **16** 863
Guldenmund, Hans **28** 143; **29** 44, 719
Güldenpfennig, Arnold **28** 46
Guldsmedsaktiebolaget **30** 108
Guler **15** *619*, 630
Gulf Coast, Mesoamerica **21** *178*, 197–8, 200
 basalt **21** *218*
 figurines **21** *218*
 pottery **21** 237–8
 sculpture **21** 218–19*, 220*
Gulf Formational culture **25** 398
Gulf Oil **28** 488
Gulgee, Ismail **13** 842*; **23** 799
 works **23** 800, *801*
Gulgong **2** 745
Gu Liaoding **7** 60
Gulielmo da Modena *see* WILIGELMO
Gulin Qingmou **17** 804
Gu Linshi **32** 844
Gulistan, Ibrahim **15** 900
Gulistan Dam **16** 198
Gull, Gustav **13** 842*; **18** 91; **27** 214; **30** 127; **33** 735, 736
Gullager, (Amandus) Christian **13** 842*
Gullah culture **1** 424
Gulland, William Giuseppi **7** 155
Gullar, Ferreira **4** 719
Gullers, Karl **17** 623
Gulleson, Haaken **13** 120; **30** 83
Gullichsen, Harry **1** 9
Gullichsen, Kairamo & Vormala **11** 92
Gullichsen, Kristian **13** 842–3*
Gullichsen, Maire **1** 9; **11** 100
Güllü Dere
 Hermitage of Niketas the Stylite **5** 675, 676
 St John **5** 676, 677, *677*
Gully, John **13** 843*; **23** 58
Gulpayagan **16** 164, 165
 congregational mosque **16** 162
Güls, St Servatius **27** 335
Gülşehir, Karşi Kilise **5** 676, 678
Gulshanābād *see* NASIK
Gulshan Album *see under* ALBUMS → individual manuscripts
Gulyamova, Erkinoy **9** 457; **14** 860; **28** 26
Gulyás, Gyula **14** 897
Gum **15** 483
Gumaiyima **10** 58
Gumani **15** 606
gum arabic **1** 155; **13** 843; **23** 783; **24** 789
 historical and regional traditions
  Bhutan **3** 914
  England **10** 356
  Indian subcontinent **15** 668
  Islamic **16** 356
  Malaysia **20** 176
 uses
  bookbindings **16** 356
  crayons **8** 127
  etchings **10** 559, 560
  fixatives **11** 142
  gilding **12** 621
  inks **15** 851
  paints **23** 783, 792; **32** 898
  photography **24** 651
  plaster **29** 813
  printing **10** 356; **15** 668
  scroll paintings **3** 914
  secco paintings **28** 338
  textiles **20** 176
  varnishes **32** 2, 3
Gumbel, David **16** 568
gum bichromate process *see under* PHOTOGRAPHY → processes
Gu Mei **33** 320
gum elemi **18** 610
Gumelniţa culture **25** 503, 512, 514, 516
 houses **25** 501
Gumery, Charles **5** 825
Gumiel, Manuel **4** 262
Gumiel, Pedro **13** 844*; **29** 265
 assistants **32** 493
 patrons and collectors **19** 793; **21** 126
 works **1** 586; **7** 345
Gumilyov, Nikolay **1** 121
Gumley, John **10** 292; **11** 431
Gumlösa Church **4** 781
Gummer, William Henry **2** 705; **13** 844*; **23** 56; **33** 58
Gummer & Ford **23** 56
Gumpp, Christoph **2** 783; **13** 844–5*
 collaboration **28** 162
 works **2** 781; **15** 864; **29** 388
Gumpp, Elias **13** 845
Gumpp, Georg Anton **2** 783; **13** 844, 846*; **15** 865
 collaboration **13** 845
 works **13** *846*
Gumpp, Johann Anton **13** 844, 845–6*; **22** 302
 collaboration **29** 602
 patrons and collectors **33** 277
 pupils **29** 602
 works **22** 308; **27** 553; **28** 109
Gumpp, Johann Baptist **13** 844
Gumpp, Johann Martin (1643-1729) **2** 783; **13** 844, 845–6*; **29** 388
Gumpp, Johann Martin (1686-1765) **13** 845
Gumpp, Michael **22** 302
gums **13** 843*
 historical and regional traditions
  Central Asia, Western **6** 227
  China **6** 736
  Egypt, ancient **9** 898
  Khwarazm **6** 227
 types
  arabic *see* GUM ARABIC
  cherry **13** 843
  ghatti **13** 843
  guar **13** 843
  locust **13** 843
  tamarind seed mucilage **13** 843
  tragacanth **13** 843; **23** 792; **32** 898
 uses
  calligraphy **6** 736
  crayons **8** 127
  dyeing **30** 557, 558
  inks **6** 736; **15** 850, 851, 852
  manuscript illumination **13** 136, 843
  miniatures (paintings) **13** 843
  paints **13** 843; **23** 783; **32** 898
  papier mâché **24** 61
  wall paintings **6** 227; **9** 898
Gümüşkesen **20** 863
Gum Vihara **5** 103
Gun **1** 329
Gun, A. L. **27** 428
Gun, Karl (Fyodorovich) *see* HŪNS, KĀRLIS (TEODORS)
Gunbad-i Qabus **13** 846*; **16** *105*, 159
 muqarnas (architecture) **22** 321
 niches **16** 161
 tiles **16** 165
 tomb tower **16** *160*; **31** 113
gun-cotton *see* COLLODION
Gund, Graham **4** 476
Gunda Anivaritachari **24** 267
Gunda Gundé, Monastery of Debre Gerzen **10** 570
Gundaya of Vengi **15** 535
 works **15** *534*
Gundel, Baron **19** 338
Gundelach, Franz (*fl* 1660) **12** 897
Gundelach, Franz (1663-1714) *see* GONDELACH, FRANZ
Gundelach, Hans **13** 847
Gundelach, Hans Wilhelm **13** 847
Gundelach, Johann Heinrich **12** 440
Gundelach, Matthäus **13** 847*; **18** 47
 collaboration **18** 225
 patrons and collectors **13** 912, 916
 pupils **14** 321
 reproductive prints by others **18** 46
 works **13** *847*
Gundersen, Gunnar S(igmund) **13** 847–8*
Gundersen, Robert M. **22** 240
Gundersheimer, Herman S. **17** 583
Gundestrup **8** *720*
Gundestrup Cauldron **6** 159; **13** 848–9*, *849*; **22** *371*; **25** *470*, 542; **26** 133; **30** 772, 773
Gundi Kabul **14** 19
Gundlach, F. C. **13** 849*
Gundrada, Countess of Surrey
Gundry, Thomas **18** 743
Gundulf, Bishop of Rochester **13** 849–50*; **19** 615; **26** 588
Gundulič, Ivan **8** 178
Güner, Güngör **31** 455
Gunetzhainer, Johann Baptist **8** 290; **11** 124; **22** 299, 300, 307; **32** 822; **33** 682
Gunetzhainer, Martin **32** 602; **33** 276
Güngören Church **9** 543; **31** 435, 436
Gunhild Cross **8** 201, 758
gunmetal *see under* ALLOYS → types
Gunn, James **28** 239
Gunning, Maria, Countess of Coventry **19** *436*
Gunnis, Rupert **10** 212, 377
Gunnlögsson, Halldor **13** 850*
Gunolt, August **13** 330
guns **2** 448, 457–68*
 historical and regional traditions
  Africa **1** 362
  Albania **1** 543–4; **8** 862
  Austria **2** 821
  Azerbaijan **2** 900
  Catalonia **2** 467
  England **2** 461–2, 464, 466, 467, 468; **14** 856
  France **2** *460*, 460–61, *463*, 463–4, 465, *465*, 467; **14** 856
  Germany **2** 464
  Iran **16** 509
  Islamic **16** 508–9
  Italy **2** 462, 464–5, 466, 467
  Netherlands, the **2** 464
  Ottoman **16** 508–9
  Scotland **2** 462, 464, 467
  Spain **2** 462, 464, 466, 467
  United States of America **15** 822; **20** 593
 materials
  gold **2** *466*
  iron **2** *466*
  mounts **2** *460*, 466
  steel **16** 508
 pattern books *see under* PATTERN BOOKS → types
 techniques
  engraving **2** 459
  gilding **2** *458*
 types
  flintlocks **2** 460
  matchlocks **2** 457; **17** 363; **29** 469
  wheellocks **2** 457, *458*, 459, 460
Guns, A. I. **3** 733
Gunst, Ignaz **29** 760
gun stocks **2** 458, *458*, 459, 460, *460*, 461, 462, *463*, 465, *466*; **16** 499; **20** *853*
Guntbald **23** 654
Guntbald Gospels *see under* GOSPEL BOOKS → individual manuscripts
Gunter, Edmund **19** 617
Gunter, John **30** 687
Gunter, Marcus **17** 523, 524
Günter of Kevernburg **14** 413
Günther, Anton, Count of Oldenburg *see* ANTON GÜNTHER, Count of Oldenburg
Günther, (Franz) Ignaz **4** 375; **13** 850–52*; **22** 302
 attributions **5** 305; **12** 447
 groups and movements **26** 498
 reproductions in metalwork **22** 305
 teachers **9** 753; **29** 761
 works **11** 125, 127; **12** 405, 406; **13** *851*; **33** 278
 workshop **12** 405
Günther, Jeremias **13** 916
Günther, (Johann) Joachim **9** 753; **13** 852*
Günther, Johann Georg **13** 850
Günther, Karl **8** 410
Günther, Matthäus **13** 852–3*
 collaboration **10** 860; **13** 631; **24** 370
 groups and movements **26** 498
Günther, Matthäus—cont.
 patrons and collectors **33** 429
 personal collection **14** 695
 teachers **2** 580; **3** 779
 works **11** 127; **12** 391; **15** 139, 865
Günther, Otto **7** 855
Günther, Rafael Yela *see* YELA GÜNTHER, RAFAEL
Gunther Tapestry **9** 519, 665, 666
Gunther & Wagner **8** 885
Gunung Cibodas **15** 781
Gunungtua **15** 787
Gunz, Anton **25** 438
Günzberg, David **17** 576
Gunzburg, Simeon Levi **21** 636
Günzburg Frauenkirche **12** 372; **32** 823
Gunzenhäuser, Elias **33** 36
Gunzo **7** 474; **13** 853–4*
Guo, Prince **7** 50
Guo Baichuan *see* KUO PAI-CH'UAN
Guomindang *see* KMT
Guo Moruo **6** 768; **7** 160
Guo Ruoxu **2** 519; **6** 816, 822; **17** 229; **18** 316
Guo Shonjing **23** 339
Guo Shun **19** 857
Guo Si **6** 797; **13** 854
Guo Xi **6** 773, 789, 817, 819; **13** 854–5*; **29** 67
 groups and movements **33** 528
 works **6** 789, 819; **7** 148; **13** *855*; **17** 881; **28** 311; **33** 476
 writings **6** 788, 789, 797
Gupta **13** 855*
 see also:
  CHANDRAGUPTA II, Ruler
  KUMARAGUPTA, Ruler
  RAMAGUPTA, Ruler
  SAMUDRAGUPTA, Ruler
  SKANDAGUPTA, Ruler
Gupta, Sunil **10** 882
Gur **8** 21
Gurah **15** 780
Guramishvili, David **12** 326
Guran **5** 160
Güran, Nazmi Ziya **2** 634; **13** 856*; **16** 805; **31** 454
Guran, Tepe **15** 903, 909, 920
Gurb, Arnaldo de *see* ARNALDO DE GURB
Gur Baksh **15** 623
Gurchinovo **30** 770
Gure *see* BAGIS
Gure, Desmond **13** 856*
Gurensi **1** 240, 284
Gurevich, Yelena (Moiseyevna) **27** 411
Gurgan **16** 372, 396, 409; **23** 562
Gurganj *see* KUNYA-URGENCH
Gurganj Minaret **16** 160
Gurgen, King of Lorē (*reg c.* 981) **14** 36
Gurgen II, King (*reg* 975-1008) **30** 306
Gurgi **15** 290, 497
guri see under LACQUER → types
Gur-i Mir *see under* SAMARKAND
Gurjaani Church **12** 319
Gurjara-Pratihara **13** 856*, 881
 see also MIHIRA BHOJA, Ruler
Gurk **2** *776*
 Cathedral of Mariae Himmelfahrt **13** 857–8*, *857*; **26** 575
  Bishop's Chapel **13** 858
  crypt **2** 777; **13** 857–8
  doors **9** 152, *152*; **26** 646
  sculpture **2** 802; **9** 147; **26** 634
  wall paintings **2** 791, *791*, 793; **13** 139, 143, 858*; **26** 654
Gurk, Henna von, Saint *see* HENNA VON GURK, Saint
Gurlitt, Cornelius **3** 262; **13** 858*
Gurlitt, Fritz **3** 800; **4** 205
Gurlitt, Hildebrand **10** 413
Gurlitt, (Heinrich) Louis (Theodor) **13** 859*

Gurlitt, Wilhelm 8 885
Gurmantche 22 196
Gurney, Eustace 21 32
Gurney, Mrs Russell 14 764; 28 601
Guro 1 392; 8 21; 13 859–61*
aesthetics 1 236
chairs 13 861
craftsmen and artists 13 861*
currency 1 363
divination instruments 1 357
heddle pulleys 13 861
masks 1 236, 392; 13 859–60*, 860
sculpture 8 22
spoons 13 861
wood 13 860
wood-carvings 13 861*
Guro, Yelena (Genrikhovna) 13 862*; 20 850
groups and movements 18 507; 20 851; 30 7; 31 583
teachers 33 740
Gurob Shrine Plan 10 63
Gurowski, Władysław 32 878
Gurrea Aragón y Pino, Gasper Galcerán de, Conde de Guimerá see GUIMERÁ, GASPER GALCERÁN DE GURREA ARAGÓN Y PINO, Conde de
Gurrea y Aragón, Martín, Duque de Villahermosa see VILLAHERMOSA, MARTÍN GURREA Y ARAGÓN, Duque de
Gurre Castle 8 724
Gurri, Salvador 3 218; 5 544
Gurría, Angela 13 863*; 28 330
Gurruwiwi, Mandjuwi 13 863*
Gurruwiwi, Murupula 13 863
Gurteens 16 29
Gurugal-hinna 29 474
Guruli, V. 12 329
Gurumpawo 6 406
Guru Nanak see NANAK, GURU
Gurung 22 757, 766
Gurunovo 27 412
Gurunsi 5 216, 217, 328–30*
masks 5 328–30*, 329
Gurvich, José 30 275
Guryev 17 865
Gus Glassworks 27 415, 416, 417
Gush Halav Synagogue 17 541, 542
Gusho Masuda see MASUDA (YAMAGUCHI) GUSHO
Gusii 17 907
Gusman, Pierre 33 369
Gusmão, Adriano de 25 320
Gusmin of Cologne 2 112; 13 863*
Gusnasco di Pavia, Lorenzo 10 522
Guspini, S Nicola di Mira 27 836
Gusrud, Svein 23 234
works 23 233
Gussage All Saints 25 541
Gussmann, Otto 17 921; 24 311
Gussow, Karl 18 134, 463
Gustav I, King of Sweden (reg 1523-60) 32 5*
architecture 7 568; 13 668; 14 371; 19 424; 26 357; 29 689; 30 68, 92; 31 692
collections 30 118
gardens 12 114, 135
interior decoration 30 87
paintings 18 801; 31 707
sculpture 4 602
tapestries 30 114, 322
Gustav II Adolf, King of Sweden (reg 1611-32) 9 167; 12 421; 13 30; 14 52; 18 613; 24 21; 31 692
Gustav III, King of Sweden (reg 1771-92) 11 470; 14 692*; 30 64, 71, 119
architecture 11 242; 13 668, 865; 29 685; 30 72, 117, 467
art policies 13 864; 29 687
Gustav III, King of Sweden (reg 1771-92)—cont.
collections 27 115; 30 119, 524
decorative works 24 846
drawings 14 692
engravings 11 173
furniture 13 864; 14 230; 30 95
gardens 29 691
interior decoration 26 99; 29 689; 30 89, 89
museums 29 690
paintings 8 815; 11 663, 900; 14 543, 815; 18 635; 24 812; 30 79, 118; 33 86
sculpture 6 97; 9 23; 28 462
silver 8 161; 30 107
stage design 8 815; 9 379
Gustav IV Adolf, King of Sweden (reg 1792-1809) 14 230
Gustav VI Adolf, King of Sweden (reg 1950-73) 13 863–4*; 30 119
ceramics 6 925
collections 7 156; 17 815
silver 4 480
Gustavian style 11 103, 103; 13 864–5*; 14 692; 30 89, 94
Gustavsberg Ceramics Factory 8 803; 30 98, 99, 100, 101; 32 792
Gustavsberg Studio 30 99
Gustavsberg-Vänge 30 98
Gustavus IIIs Antikmuseum see under STOCKHOLM → museums
Gusti Madé Rundu 15 808
Guston, Philip 13 865–6*
groups and movements 1 84; 31 138, 607
patrons and collectors 9 189
pupils 8 577; 29 613
works 13 865; 19 492; 29 670
Gustorf choir-screens 26 633
Güstrow
Cathedral of St Maria 4 667–8; 11 452
parish church 13 112
Gusyatyn 31 560
Gutai 1 78; 7 895; 13 866*; 17 207; 23 595
exhibitions 23 298
members 33 562
works 24 407
Gutai Bijutsu Kyōkai (concrete art society) see GUTAI
Gutbrod, Rolf 8 631; 23 635; 29 428, 874; 30 469
Gutekunst, H. G. 30 153
Gutekunst, Otto 7 579
Gutekunst, Richard 30 153
Gutenberg, Johann 13 866–7*; 15 853; 25 588–9
works 4 344; 21 338; 24 809; 25 589
Gutenberg Bible see under BIBLES → types
Gütersloh, Albert Paris von 2 797, 826; 13 867*; 32 446, 447
groups and movements 2 804; 23 1, 2; 24 592; 28 88; 32 447
pupils 4 697; 14 818; 18 93
Gutfreund, Otto 13 867–8*; 25 433
collaboration 12 834
groups and movements 8 249, 373; 13 711; 16 902
works 8 249, 387, 387, 406
Guth, Josef 2 399, 405; 22 96
Guthe, Carl 5 591; 30 383
Guthe, Grace 5 591
Guthfrithsson, Anlaf 7 534
gūṭhīs 22 769
Guthlac Roll see under ROLLS → individual manuscripts
Guthmann, Johannes 3 478
Guthrie, George 2 760
Guthrie, James 13 868*
collaboration 8 125
groups and movements 12 779, 780; 19 891; 28 238
works 28 238
Guthrie, J. & W. 29 508
Guthrie Bell Shrine 28 260
Guthrie & Larnach 23 66
Guthrie & Wells 12 197
Guthwerdt see GUDEWERDT
Gutians 21 273
Gutiéra, Antonio Mohedano de la see MOHEDANO (DE LA GUTIÉRA), ANTONIO
Gutiérrez, Baltazar 19 173
Gutiérrez, Carlos 2 405
Gutiérrez, Cipriano Toledo y see TOLEDO Y GUTIÉRREZ, CIPRIANO
Gutiérrez, Domingo 32 172
Gutiérrez, Fadrique 8 17
Gutiérrez, Felipe S(antiago) 13 868*
Gutiérrez, Francisco 4 562; 20 67; 29 293
Gutiérrez, Joaquín 7 608, 611
Gutiérrez, José 13 730
Gutiérrez, Juan Martínez see MARTÍNEZ GUTIÉRREZ, JUAN
Gutiérrez, Juan Simón 13 869*
Gutiérrez, Pedro 13 870; 29 350
Gutiérrez, Raúl 32 558
Gutiérrez, Rodrigo 13 869*; 21 385
Gutiérrez, Santiago 21 405
Gutiérrez Alarcón, Sérvulo 13 869*; 24 510, 514
Gutiérrez Cabello, Francisco 3 470; 13 869*
Gutiérrez Camarena, Marcial 22 71
Gutierrez Cossio, Pancho see COSSIO, PANCHO GUTIERREZ
Gutiérrez de la Vega, José 13 870*; 29 283
Gutiérrez de los Ríos, Gaspar 13 870*
Gutiérrez Guerra, Valentín 29 337
Gutiérrez Navarrete, Alonso 9 116
Gutiérrez Navarrete, Antón 9 116
Gutiérrez Sencio, Miguel 24 501
Gutiérrez Solana, José see SOLANA, JOSÉ (GUTIÉRREZ)
Gutiérrez Soto, Luis 29 273, 321
Gutkind, Erwin 3 796
Gutman, Nahum 16 567; 17 566, 579
Gutmann, John 13 870*
Gutmann, Joseph 17 583
Gutmann, Rolf 30 391
Gutrecht, Matthäus 4 208
Gutsa, Tapfuma 33 679
Gutschow, Konstanty 12 379
Gutt, Michael 13 871
Gutt, Romuald 13 870–71*; 14 155; 17 874; 23 113; 28 838
guttae (i) (architectural ornament) 11 790; 13 377, 378, 871*
guttae (ii) (vessel) 13 871*
gutta-percha 25 23
Guttenberg, Carl 13 871; 20 915
Guttenberg, Heinrich 13 871
Guttenbrunn Glassworks 2 818
Guttenburg, Johann Gottfried von, Prince-Bishop of Würzburg 29 60
gutters 13 390, 392, 393
Gutti, Rosina Mantovani 28 381
Guttierez, Martin 18 834
Guttiérrez Alea, Tomás see ALEA, TOMÁS GUTTIÉRREZ
Guttmann, Alfred see HAJÓS, ALFRÉD
Guttmann, Hermann 17 548
Gutton, Henri 2 13; 18 664
Guttuso, Renato 13 871–3*; 24 448; 26 777; 28 920; 31 436
groups and movements 7 894; 11 802; 16 681; 26 777
patrons and collectors 7 797
works 10 822; 13 872; 16 681
Gutwillig, József 20 447
Guwei cun (Hui xian) 6 695
Guxing zhen (Zhengzhou) 7 98
Guy 5 370
Guy, Francis 12 645; 13 873*
Guy, P. L. O. 21 47
Guy, Seymour Joseph 31 870
Guy, Walter 11 547
Guyana 13 873, 873–8*; 29 128
aprons 3 441; 13 875
architecture 13 875*, 876, 877
baskets 3 331
basketwork 13 874
beads 13 875
beadwork 3 441
body arts 13 874
canoes 13 874
cathedrals 13 876
crowns 13 875
drawings 13 876
education (art) 13 878
exhibitions 13 876
feathers 13 875
hammocks 13 874, 875
houses 13 875
insignia 13 875
knitting 18 158
liana 3 331
lithography 13 876
painting 13 876–7*
patronage 13 877–8*
photography 10 580; 13 876
pottery 13 874
sculpture 13 877, 877
timber structures 13 875
trade 13 874
wood 13 877
Guyane, La see FRENCH GUIANA
Guyanese Art Group 13 876
Guyang Caves see under LONGMEN
Guyau, Jean-Marie 28 916, 926
Guy de Chauliac 21 5
Guy de Dammartin see DAMMARTIN, GUY DE
Guy de Mello, Bishop of Auxerre 2 846
Guy de Monceau, Abbot of Saint-Denis 27 550
Guy de Turno 20 451
Guyenne, Louis de Valois, Duc de, le Dauphin 12 723; 20 625, 633
Guy of Warwick Mazer 10 323
Guyon, Jean-Louis 11 642; 22 456
works 11 642
Guyot, Guillaume-Germain, Abbé 2 15
Guyot, Laurent 8 594; 13 219, 220, 878*
Guyot de Beaugrant see BEAUGRANT, GUYOT DE
Guys, (Ernst-Adolphe-Hyacinthe-) Constantin 3 392; 13 878–9*
commentaries 3 392
works 8 596; 13 879; 31 704
Guyski, Marceli 25 115
Guy the Venerable, Bishop of Auxerre 29 501
Guyuan, Tomb of Li Xian 7 23, 83
guyue xuan see under PORCELAIN → wares
Güyük, Khan (reg 1246-9) (Great Khans) 21 882; 30 470
Guzana see HALAF, TELL
Güzel sanatlar birligi see ASSOCIATION OF OTTOMAN PAINTERS
Guzmán, Alberto 13 880*; 24 511
Guzmán, Alvaro de Bazán y, 1st Marqués de Santa Cruz see SANTA CRUZ, ALVARO DE BAZÁN Y GUZMÁN, 1st Marqués de
Guzmán, Ambrosio Ignacio Spínola y, Archbishop of Seville 13 880*; 28 515
Guzmán, David J., Museo Nacional see under SAN SALVADOR
Guzmán, Domingo de see DOMINIC, Saint
Guzmán, Gaspar de (fl 1560-84) 29 334
Guzmán, Gaspar de Bracamonte y (1596-1676) see PENARANDA, GASPAR DE BRACAMONTE Y GUZMÁN, 3rd Conde de
Guzman, Jaime de 24 622
Guzmán, Jerónimo de 19 657
Guzmán, Luis Méndez de Haro y, Marqués de Carpio see CARPIO, LUIS MÉNDEZ DE HARO Y GUZMÁN, 6th Marqués de
Guzmán, Pedro Téllez Girón y, 3rd Duque de Osuna see OSUNA, 3rd Duque de
Guzmán, Ramiro Nuñez de, Duque de Medina de las Torres see MEDINA DE LAS TORRES, RAMIRO NUÑEZ DE, Duque de
Guzmán Blanco, Antonio 5 692; 32 169, 170, 179
Guzmán de Rojas, Cecilio 4 267, 268; 13 880*
patrons and collectors 4 267
pupils 23 706
teachers 23 174
works 4 262; 25 366
Guzmán y Pimentel, Gaspar de, Conde-Duque de Olivares see OLIVARES, Conde-Duque de
Guzzi, Giuseppe 16 746
Gvāliyar see GWALIOR
Gvaliyari, Nand 13 882
Gvelesiani, D. 12 327
Gvelesiani, Romanoz 12 326
Gvozdenović, Nedeljko 4 461; 28 451
Gvozdetz Synagogue 17 559
Gwal 15 629
Gwalior 13 880–83*; 15 261, 285, 292, 360
Archaeological Museum 13 882; 15 181, 498, 498, 686
architecture 15 355
Assi Khambha 15 372; 29 635
calligraphy 15 497
Chaturbhuja Temple 13 881; 15 288, 495
congregational mosque 15 373
fort 15 372, 498
fortifications 21 590
Gujari Mahal see Archaeological Museum
Laderi 15 372
Man Mandir 13 881, 882; 15 391, 498, 686; 23 818; 32 323
kiosks 18 72
tiles 15 687
manuscript illumination 15 564, 566, 567, 568–9
Palace of Raja Kirtti Singh 15 386
Palace of Shah Jahan 15 373
Sas-Bahu temples 13 881, 881; 15 292–3, 497
sculpture 15 495
shrine of Muhammad Ghaus 15 372
Teli ka Mandir 15 287, 495
temples 15 263
Vaishnava temples see Sas-Bahu
wall paintings 15 544
Gwani, Baban 23 133
Gwari 14 231; 30 509
Gwathmey, Charles 5 609; 13 883–4*; 23 50
Gwathmey, Robert 26 410
Gwijde van Dampierre, Count of Flanders 3 614
Gwilt, George 28 559
Gwilt, Joseph 2 359; 3 281; 14 173
Gwóźdź, Andrzej 17 757
Gwoździec see GVOZDETZ
Gwydyr, Peter Burrell, 2nd Lord see BURRELL, PETER, 2nd Lord Gwydyr and 19th Lord Willoughby de Eresby
Gwyn, Nell 32 244
Gwynedd County Architects' Department 32 784

Gwynn, John **13** 884*; **19** 585; **23** 688; **32** 778
Gwynne, Patrick **22** 719
Gwynne, S. **10** 377
Gwyther, W. W. **29** 768
Gyaltsendrak **30** 829
Gyalus, László **16** 872
Gyandjyan, Kamo **2** 437
Gyantse **13** 884–5*; **30** *806*
bronzes **30** 849
carpets **30** 846
Kumbum **30** 812, 818, 832
palace **21** 593
Palkhor Choide Lamasery **13** 884–5, *885*
Pango Chorten *see* Kumbum
Pelkor Chode *see* Palkhor Choide Lamasery
sculpture **22** 775
temple **30** 812, 818
Gyaraspur **13** 885–6*; **15** *261*, *285*, 292
Char Khambha **15** 288, 495
Hindola Torana **13** 886
Maladevi Temple **15** 288, 495
sculpture **15** 494
temples **15** 262, 287; **24** 102
toraṇas **31** 160
Gyárfás, Jenő **13** 886*
Gyarmathy, Tihaner **14** 902
gyeltsen **30** 842
Gyldén, Emma **7** 251
Gyldenløve, Ulrik Frederik, Count **12** 801
Gyles, Henry **29** 506; **33** 545, 550
Gyllenhielm, Carl Carlsson **8** 481
Gyllenhielm, Sofia **11** 108
Gyllenstierna, Carl **30** 93
gymnasia **13** 886–7*; **23** 828
Greece, ancient **3** 374; **8** 694; **10** 670; **13** 386, 403, 406–7, 416
Japan **30** *289*
Libya **8** *368*
Rome, ancient **8** *368*; **26** 872
see also BATHS; BATH-GYMNASIA
Gymnicus, Johann **33** 289
Gynaikokastron **9** 556
Gyōda, Inariyama tomb **15** 160*
Gyōgi **17** 422; **20** 361
Gyōja, En no *see* EN NO GYŌJA
Gyōkai **17** 124, 730
Gyōki **17** 746; **18** 68
Gyokoshū Kuwayama *see* KUWAYAMA GYOKOSHŪ
Gyokudō *see* URAGAMI GYOKUDŌ
Gyokudō Kawai *see* KAWAI, GYOKUDŌ
Gyokuei Keifukuin *see* KEIFUKUIN GYOKUEI
Gyokuen Bonpō **13** 887–8*
works **13** *888*; **17** 170–71
Gyokujundō *see* IKENAGA DŌUN
Gyokuran, Ikeno Machi *see* IKE GYOKURAN
Gyokurin **33** 322
Gyokurin'in, Saan **17** 340
Gyokusen Mochizuki *see* MOCHIZUKI GYOKUSEN
Gyokushō, Kawabata *see* KAWABATA GYOKUSHŌ
Gyokuso *see* OUCHI, JIEMON
Gyōmyō Shamon *see* SHAMON GYŌMYŌ
Győr **13** 887–8*; **14** *881*
Ark of the Covenant monument **14** 894
Carmelite church **14** 900
Cathedral **13** 161, 162, 888; **14** 900; **15** 10
collections **15** 17
education (art) **15** 18
János Xantus Museum **13** 888
Margit Kovács Museum **13** 888
Marian column **14** 894
St Ignatius **14** 886; **29** 839
altarpiece **14** 893, 894, *894*, 900
paintings **14** 900
pulpit **14** 894
Széchény Pharmacy **13** 888
Györgyi, Alajos **13** 889
Györgyi, Dénes **13** 889*; **14** 890; **18** 394
Györgyi, Géza **13** 889
Gyōsai **17** 125
Gyōsai Kawanabe *see* KAWANABE KYŌSAI
Gyoshū Hayami *see* HAYAMI, GYOSHŪ
Gyōtoku Gyokuyō **17** 413
gypsography **25** 611; **26** 480
gypsum **14** 167; **29** 698
historical and regional traditions
Afghanistan **1** 202
Africa **1** 305
Ancient Near East **29** 814
Buddhism **1** 202
Central Asia, Eastern **6** 301
Egypt, ancient **29** 814
Etruscan **10** 606, *606*
Gothic **13** 135
Greece, ancient **29** 814
Iran, ancient **15** 912
Islamic **16** 268, 269; **29** 818
Italy **10** *606*
Mesopotamia **9** *45*; **21** 296
Parthian **29** 814
Rome, ancient **27** 13
Sumerian **9** *45*; **29** *923*
Syria-Palestine **30** 196
United States of America **26** *401*
types
alabaster *see* ALABASTER (GYPSUM)
uses
architecture **16** 269
conservation **7** 737
figurines **9** *45*
gypsum
uses—cont.
grounds **6** 301; **13** 135; **24** 798
mortars (building) **15** 912; **16** 268
paintings **1** 202; **13** 135; **28** 338
plaster **29** 812; **30** 196
reliefs **29** 814
sculpture **10** 606, *606*; **26** *401*; **27** 13; **29** *923*
stucco **29** 813, 818, 845
see also GESSO
Gyraldus, Lylius *see* GIRALDI, LILIO GREGORIO
Gyrr **7** 805
Gyrzhavka **21** *810*
Monastery **21** 810
Gys, Charles **6** 415
Gysbrechts, Cornelis **15** 140
Gysels, Pieter **13** 889*
Gysin, Brion **13** 889–90*
Gysis, Nikolaos **1** 141; **13** 359, 890*; **18** 490
pupils **19** 69, 283; **20** 455
works **13** 352, *352*
Gytheion **13** 512
Gyulafehérvár *see* ALBA IULIA
Gyulakuta *see* FINTÎNELE
Gyurdjyan, Gabriel **2** 431, 432
Gyzes, Nikolaos *see* GYSIS, NIKOLAOS
Gzhel **27** 410, 411, 412, 414

H

H, Master **2** 471
H, Monogrammist **10** 246
H2SO4 **8** 437
HA, Monogrammist *see* AESSLINGER, HANS
Haacke, Hans **13** 891*; **23** 49
  groups and movements **7** 686
  pupils **9** 72
  works **7** *686*
  writings **6** 176
Haag, Carl **13** 891–2*
Haag, Richard **28** 328
Haag, Tetar Philip Christiaan **22** 905
Haagen, Abraham van der **13** 892
Haagen, Cornelis van der **13** 892
Haagen, Jacobus van der **13** 892
Haagen, Joris Cornelisz. van der **13** 892
Haagen, Joris van der **13** 892*; **14** 41; **32** 144
Haagsche Kunstkring **4** 203; **14** 43; **31** 147
Haagse Aquarellisten **32** 903
Haagse Ets Club **33** 46
Haakon IV Haakonsson, King of Norway (*reg* 1217-63) **3** 774; **23** 219
Haám, Ignacio de **2** 658; **31** 88, 92
Haan, Benno **2** 824
Haan, David de **12** 764
Haan, Hermann *see* HAHN, HERMAN (1574-1627/8)
Haan, Johannes de **14** 794
Haan, Jurjen de **14** 43
Haan, Remy van *see* HAANEN, REMIGIUS (ADRIANUS) VAN
Haanen, Casparis **13** 892
Haanen, Remigius (Adrianus) van **13** 892*
Haanstra, Johann **1** 510
Haaren, Groot-Seminarie **22** 831
Haarlem **1** *585*; **13** 892–6*; **22** *813*
  ABC (Architectuur-Bouwhistorisch Centrum) **13** 894
  academy **1** 104; **13** 895; **22** 907
  art forms and materials
    ceramics **22** 878
    choir-stalls **22** 856
    damask **19** 416, *416*, 418; **22** 899
    engravings **10** 391
    glass **22** 884
    painting **12** 290; **18** 710; **22** 835, 839–40*
    pewter **22** 893
    portraits **13** *895*
    silk **22** 899
    silver **22** 887
    stained glass **27** 255
    textiles **22** 900
    tiles **30** 878
  Butchers' Hall **18** 7
  Commandery church **12** 231
  Frans Halsmuseum **13** 893, 894; **22** 906
  guilds **13** 893–4*
  Historisch Museum Zuid-Kennemerland **13** 894
  Keramisch Centrum **22** 908
  Kunstnijverheidsschool **22** 908
  New Church *see* St Anna
  Nieuwe Gracht 74 **22** *865*
  Nieuwe Kerk *see* St Anna
  Pavilioen Welgelegen **22** 827, *827*
  St Anna **5** 543
  St Bavo **13** 62, 896*; **22** 820, 837
    altarpiece **13** 111
    organ shutters **22** 835
    sculpture **22** 859
Haarlem—cont.
  Stadhuis **4** *702*; **13** *893*; **22** 822; **31** 239
  Stedelijk Museum **13** 894
  Stichting Foto- en Grafisch Centrum **13** 894
  Teylers Foundation **13** 894; **14** 386; **22** 902; **32** 8
  Teylers Museum **22** 827; **30** 568; **32** 466
    collections **22** 905, 906; **23** 353; **24** 712; **26** 177, 246; **28** 132; **33** 47
    drawings **9** 230
    paintings **21** 488
  theatres **30** 665
Haarlem, Cornelis Cornelisz. van *see* CORNELISZ. VAN HAARLEM, CORNELIS **7** 773
Haarlem, Coster of *see* COSTER OF HAARLEM
Haarlem, Hendrik van *see* HENDRIK VAN HAARLEM
Haarlem, Jacob Jansz. van *see* JACOB JANSZ. VAN HAARLEM
Haarlem, Jan Joest van *see* JOEST (VON KALCAR), JAN
Haarlem Academics *see* HAARLEM CLASSICISTS
Haarlem Ateliers **22** 908
Haarlem Bible, Master of the **22** 835
Haarlem Classicists **10** 660; **13** 337
Haarlemmerhout **12** 132
Haas, F. **24** 566
Haas, Georg **13** 897*
  works **2** 805, *805*, 806; **32** 448
  writings **12** 409
Haas, Hans-Peter **20** 607
Haas, Leo **17** 579
Haas, P. **24** 309
Haas, Philipp, & Söhne **2** 826
Haas, Richard **15** 140
Haas, V. **8** 405
Haas brothers **20** 253
Haase, Jacob de **6** 346
Haase, Volkmar **9** 121
Haas & Söhne **29** 722
Haász, Gyula **20** 206
Haaxman, P. **17** 841
Habachi, Labib **2** 657
Habana, La *see* HAVANA
Habash Kahn **15** 368
Habbeke, Aegidius **14** 617
Haber, Abraham **24** 386
Haberland, Christoph **18** 849; **26** 383
Haberle, John **13** 897*; **15** 140; **31** 603
Haberli **31** 436
Habermann, Eugen **10** 537; **30** 276
Habermann, Franz Xaver **2** 719; **13** 897–8*
  patrons and collectors **32** 535
  works **12** 446; **24** 272
Habermann, Hugo von
  groups and movements **12** 394; **28** 341
  pupils **18** 434; **29** 791; **31** 145, 399; **33** 161
Habermel, Erasmus **13** 914
Haberschrack, Mikołaj **25** 102
Habershon, William **10** 185
Habershon & Pite **22** 230
Haberstumpf (family) **6** 526
Habert, Nicolas **13** 898*
Habeşeşti **21** 551
Habib **16** 277
Habiballah **16** 339; **27** 514
Habib Allah, King (*reg* 1901-19) (Barakzay) **17** 717
Habiballah ibn ʿAli Bahajani
  works **16** *378*
Habib Bourguiba **17** 731
Habib Fida ʿAli **17** 806; **23** 799
  works **23** *799*
Habib Gorgy, Sophie **9** 767
Habib Khan Sur **15** 369
Habib Lotfallah, Emir **2** 689
Habich **14** 247
Habich, Ludwig **8** 531; **23** 393
Habiganj, Shankarpasha mosque **30** 162
Habikino **17** 82
  houses **17** *82*
Habinnas **27** 28
Habiru **30** 186
Habitat **7** 725; **8** 804; **10** 285, 300; **20** 595
Hablingbo
  church **13** 119; **26** 639
  memorial stone **32** 522
Habraken, Nicolaas (John) **13** 898–9*
Habrecht, Isaak **31** 570
Habrodiaitos *see* PARRHASIOS
Habsburg (House of) **13** 899*
Habsburg I. (Austrian House of) **2** 827; **13** 899–901*, *900*, *901*
  armour **9** 31
  catafalques **6** 71
  collections **2** 828, 830; **21** 264; **22** 356, 357; **26** 229; **27** 115; **32** 446
  drawings **30** 519
  ivory-carvings **12** 460
  manuscripts **4** 760
  metalwork **16** 900
  paintings **4** 908; **9** 18; **30** 519
  patronage **3** 612–13
  sculpture **24** 806
  stained glass **30** 130
  tapestries **30** 331
Habsburg I., Agnes, Queen of Hungary *see* AGNES, Queen of Hungary
Habsburg I., Albert, Archduke of Austria, Regent of the Netherlands *see* ALBERT, Archduke of Austria, Regent of the Netherlands
Habsburg I., Albert II, Duke of Austria *see* ALBERT II, Duke of Austria
Habsburg I., Albert III, Duke of Austria *see* ALBERT III, Duke of Austria
Habsburg I., Albert V, Duke of Austria *see* ALBERT II, Holy Roman Emperor
Habsburg I., Amalia Wilhelmina, Holy Roman Empress *see* AMALIA WILHELMINA, Holy Roman Empress
Habsburg I., Andreas, Cardinal-Archduke of Austria, Prince-Bishop of Brixen **26** 103, 104
Habsburg I., Anne of Austria *see* ANNE OF AUSTRIA, Queen of France
Habsburg I., Bianca Maria, Holy Roman Empress BIANCA MARIA SFORZA, Holy Roman Empress
Habsburg I., Caroline Augusta, Empress of Austria *see* CAROLINE AUGUSTA, Empress of Austria
Habsburg I., Charles, Archduke of Austria, Duke of Styria *see* CHARLES, Archduke of Austria, Duke of Styria
Habsburg I., Charles, Archduke of Austria, Prince-Bishop of Breslau *see* CHARLES, Archduke of Austria, Prince-Bishop of Breslau
Habsburg I., Charles Francis Joseph, Emperor of Austria *see* CHARLES, Emperor of Austria
Habsburg I., Charles I, King of Spain *see* CHARLES V, Holy Roman Emperor
Habsburg I., Charles Joseph, Archduke of Austria **13** 920, 921
Habsburg I., Charles Ludwig, Archduke of Austria **1** 141
Habsburg I., Charles VI, Holy Roman Emperor *see* CHARLES VI, Holy Roman Emperor
Habsburg I., Claudia, Countess of Tyrol *see* CLAUDIA DE' MEDICI, Countess of Tyrol
Habsburg I., Eleonora Gonzaga, Empress *see* ELEONORA GONZAGA, Holy Roman Empress
Habsburg I., Eleonore, Archduchess of Austria (1582-1615) **17** 918
Habsburg I., Elizabeth *see* ELIZABETH, Queen of Poland
Habsburg I., Elizabeth, Empress of Austria *see* ELIZABETH, Empress of Austria
Habsburg I., Ernest, Archduke of Austria **4** 897; **7** 413; **13** *900*, *901*, 915–16*; **15** 16
  paintings **3** 613; **4** 453, 902
Habsburg I., Ernest, Duke of Styria *see* ERNEST, Duke of Styria
Habsburg I., Ferdinand, Archduke of Austria, Count of Tyrol *see* FERDINAND, Archduke of Austria, Count of Tyrol
Habsburg I., Ferdinand, Archduke of Austria, Duke of Breisgau **2** 232; **16** 646; **20** 90; **24** 757
Habsburg I., Ferdinand, King of Bohemia and Hungary *see* FERDINAND I, Holy Roman Emperor
Habsburg I., Ferdinand-Charles, Count of Tyrol *see* FERDINAND-CHARLES, Count of Tyrol
Habsburg I., Ferdinand I, Holy Roman Emperor *see* FERDINAND I, Holy Roman Emperor
Habsburg I., Ferdinand II, Holy Roman Emperor *see* FERDINAND II, Holy Roman Emperor
Habsburg I., Ferdinand III, Holy Roman Emperor *see* FERDINAND III, Holy Roman Emperor
Habsburg I., Ferdinand IV, King of Bohemia and Hungary *see* FERDINAND IV, King of Bohemia andHungary
Habsburg I., Frederick, Duke of Styria *see* FREDERICK III, Holy Roman Emperor
Habsburg I., Frederick III, Holy Roman Emperor *see* FREDERICK III, Holy Roman Emperor
Habsburg I., Frederick V, Duke of Styria *see* Frederick III, Holy Roman Emperor
Habsburg I., Isabella, Archduchess of Austria *see* ISABELLA, Archduchess of Austria
Habsburg I., Joanna, Grand Duchess of Tuscany *see* JOANNA OF AUSTRIA, Grand Duchess of Tuscany
Habsburg I., Joanna, Queen of Castile *see* JOANNA, Queen of Castile
Habsburg I., Leopold I, Duke of Austria *see* LEOPOLD I, Duke of Austria
Habsburg I., Leopold II, Duke of Styria *see* LEOPOLD II, Duke of Styria
Habsburg I., Leopold V, Archduke of Austria, Count of Tyrol *see* LEOPOLD V, Archduke of Austria and Count of Tyrol
Habsburg I., Leopold William, Archduke of Austria, Governor of the Netherlands **11** 872; **13** *901*, 919–21*, *920*; **26** 390
  cabinet pictures **30** *463*
  catalogues **32** 700
  collections **2** 829, 830; **3** 615; **13** 921; **16** 767; **17** 647; **22** 696; **27** 504; **32** 444
  furniture **8** 396; **9** 412
  metalwork **8** 790
  paintings **3** 230; **8** 125; **9** 16, 194; **14** 381, 616; **22** 841; **27** 725; **28** 898; **30** 461; **33** 389
    allegorical **30** 734
    cabinet pictures **3** 613; **5** 354; **6** 77; **9** 12, 15; **30** 463
    genre **7** 428; **8** 464; **21** 487
    portraits **7** 832
    religious **2** 876; **32** 705, 754
    still-lifes **20** 220; **32** 706
  portraits **30** 744; **32** 728
Habsburg I., Leopold William, Bishop of Breslau *see* LEOPOLD WILLIAM, Archduke of Austria, Governor of the Netherlands
Habsburg I., Margaret of Austria, Duchess of Savoy *see* MARGARET OF AUSTRIA, Duchess of Savoy and Regent of the Netherlands
Habsburg I., Margaret of Austria, Duchess of Parma, Regent of the Netherlands *see* MARGARET OF AUSTRIA, Duchess of Parma, Regent of the Netherlands
Habsburg I., Margaret of Austria, Queen of Spain *see* MARGARET OF AUSTRIA, Queen of Spain
Habsburg I., Margaret of Spain, Holy Roman Empress *see* MARGARET OF SPAIN, Holy Roman Empress
Habsburg I., Maria Anna Josepha, Queen of Portugal *see* MARIA ANNA JOSEPHA, Queen of Portugal
Habsburg I., Maria Beatrice d'Este of Modena, Archduchess of Austria **20** 90
Habsburg I., Maria Christierna, Archduchess of Austria (1574-1621) **17** 918

Habsburg I., Maria Christina, Archduchess of Austria, Duchess of Saxe-Teschen (1742-98) **6** 98; **10** 899
Habsburg I., Maria Christina of Austria, Queen of Spain *see* MARIA CHRISTINA OF AUSTRIA, Queen of Spain
Habsburg I., Maria Ludovica of Modena, Empress of Austria *see* MARIA LUDOVICA, Empress of Austria
Habsburg I., Maria Maddalena, Grand Duchess of Tuscany *see* MARIA MADDALENA OF HABSBURG, Grand Duchess of Tuscany
Habsburg I., Maria of Bavaria, Archduchess of Austria *see* MARIA OF BAVARIA, Archduchess of Austria
Habsburg I., Maria-Theresa, Queen of Hungary and Bohemia, Holy Roman Empress *see* MARIA-THERESA, Queen of Hungary and Bohemia
Habsburg I., Marie-Antoinette, Queen of France *see* MARIE-ANTOINETTE, Queen of France
Habsburg I., Mary Anne of Austria, Queen of Spain *see* MARY ANNE OF AUSTRIA, Queen of Spain
Habsburg I., Mary of Burgundy, Holy Roman Empress *see* MARY OF BURGUNDY, Holy Roman Empress
Habsburg I., Mary of Hungary, Regent of the Netherlands *see* MARY OF HUNGARY, Regent of the Netherlands
Habsburg I., Matthias, Holy Roman Emperor *see* MATTHIAS, Holy Roman Emperor
Habsburg I., Maximilian, Archduke of Austria, Count of Tyrol *see* MAXIMILIAN, Archduke of Austria, Count of Tyrol
Habsburg I., Maximilian Joseph, Archduke of Austria (1782-1863) **19** 434
Habsburg I., Philip I, King of Castile *see* PHILIP I, King of Castile
Habsburg I., Rudolf, Archduke of Austria, Cardinal-Archbishop of Olomouc **18** 467
Habsburg I., Rudolf I, Holy Roman Emperor *see* RUDOLF I, Holy Roman Emperor
Habsburg I., Rudolf II, Holy Roman Emperor *see* RUDOLF II, Holy Roman Emperor
Habsburg I., Rudolf IV, Duke of Austria *see* RUDOLF IV, Duke of Austria
Habsburg I., Sigismund-Francis, Count of Tyrol *see* SIGISMUND-FRANCIS, Count of Tyrol
Habsburg I., Wilhelmina Amalia, Holy Roman Empress *see* AMALIA WILHELMINA, Holy Roman Empress
Habsburg II. (Spanish House of) **14** 1–2*, *2*; **20** 866
Habsburg II., Anne of Austria, Queen of Spain *see* ANNE OF AUSTRIA, Queen of Spain
Habsburg II., Balthasar Carlos, Infante of Spain **19** 770; **20** 899
Habsburg II., Charles II, King of Spain *see* CHARLES II, King of Spain
Habsburg II., Elizabeth de Bourbon, Queen of Spain *see* ELIZABETH DE BOURBON, Queen of Spain
Habsburg II., Elizabeth de Valois, Queen of Spain *see* ELIZABETH DE VALOIS, Queen of Spain
Habsburg II., Ferdinand, Cardinal-Infante of Spain **8** 125; **14** *2*, 10*; **25** 274; **27** 296; **28** 898
Habsburg II., Ferdinand I, King of the Two Sicilies *see* FERDINAND I, King of Naples and the Two Sicilies
Habsburg II., Ferdinand IV, King of Naples *see* FERDINAND I, King of the Two Sicilies
Habsburg II., Francesco V, Duke of Modena *see* FRANCESCO V, Duke of Modena
Habsburg II., Isabella Clara Eugenia, Archduchess of Austria, Regent of the Netherlands *see* ISABELLA CLARA EUGENIA, Archduchess of Austria
Habsburg II., Isabella of Portugal, Queen of Spain *see* ISABELLA OF PORTUGAL, Holy Roman Empress
Habsburg II., Joanna, Queen of Castile *see* JOANNA, Queen of Castile
Habsburg II., Joanna of Austria, Princess of Portugal **9** *267*; **14** *2*, 5*; **23** 746
Habsburg II., Margaret of Austria, Duchess of Parma, Regent of the Netherlands *see* MARGARET OF AUSTRIA, D. of Parma, R. of the Netherlands
Habsburg II., Margaret of Austria, Queen of Spain *see* MARGARET OF AUSTRIA, Queen of Spain
Habsburg II., Margaret of Spain, Holy Roman Empress *see* MARGARET OF SPAIN, Holy Roman Empress
Habsburg II., Maria Anna of Austria, Queen of Spain *see* MARIA ANNA OF AUSTRIA, Queen of Spain
Habsburg II., Maria-Louisa of Parma, Queen of Spain *see* MARIA-LOUISA OF PARMA, Queen of Spain
Habsburg II., Maria of Portugal, Princess **14** *2*
Habsburg II., Maria-Theresa, Queen of France *see* MARIA-THERESA, Queen of France
Habsburg II., Marie Louise, Queen of Spain *see* MARIE LOUISE D'ORLÉANS, Queen of Spain
Habsburg II., Philip I, King of Castile *see* PHILIP I, King of Castile
Habsburg II., Philip II, King of Spain *see* PHILIP II, King of Spain
Habsburg II., Philip III, King of Spain *see* PHILIP III, King of Spain
Habsburg II., Philip IV, King of Spain *see* PHILIP IV, King of Spain
Habsburg II., Philip the Fair, Duke of Burgundy *see* PHILIP I, King of Castile
Habsburg II., Philip V, King of Spain *see* PHILIP V, King of Spain
Habsburg-Lorraine (House of) **14** 11*
Habsburg-Lorraine, Ferdinand, Archduke of Austria *see* FERDINANDO III, Grand Duke of Tuscany
Habsburg-Lorraine, Ferdinand III, Grand Duke of Tuscany *see* FERDINANDO III, Grand Duke of Tuscany
Habsburg-Lorraine, Ferdinand Maximilian, Archduke of Austria *see* MAXIMILIAN OF HABSBURG, Emperor of Mexico
Habsburg-Lorraine, Francis, Duke of Lorraine *see* FRANCIS I, Holy Roman Emperor
Habsburg-Lorraine, Francis Ferdinand, Archduke of Austria *see* ESTE-AUSTRIA, FRANCIS FERDINAND, Archduke of
Habsburg-Lorraine, Francis I, Emperor of Austria *see* FRANCIS I, Emperor of Austria
Habsburg-Lorraine, Francis I, Holy Roman Emperor *see* FRANCIS I, Holy Roman Emperor
Habsburg-Lorraine, Francis II *see* FRANCIS II, Holy Roman Emperor
Habsburg-Lorraine, Francis II, Holy Roman Emperor *see* FRANCIS I, Emperor of Austria
Habsburg-Lorraine, Frederick, Archduke of Austria (1856-1936) **31** 807
Habsburg-Lorraine, John, Archduke of Austria **2** 796, 830; **14** 11
Habsburg-Lorraine, Joseph (Antony), Archduke of Austria, Palatine of Hungary **10** 117; **14** 11
Habsburg-Lorraine, Joseph II, Holy Roman Emperor *see* JOSEPH II, Holy Roman Emperor
Habsburg-Lorraine, Leopold, Archduke of Austria (1823-98) **14** 11, 151
Habsburg-Lorraine, Leopold I, Grand Duke of Tuscany *see* LEOPOLD II, Holy Roman Emperor
Habsburg-Lorraine, Ludwig Viktor, Archduke of Austria **11** 30
Habsburg-Lorraine, Maria Carolina, Queen of Naples *see* MARIA CAROLINA, Queen of Naples
Habsburg-Lorraine, Maria Dorothea of Württemberg, Archduchess of Austria **10** 117
Habsburg-Lorraine, Marie-Louise, Empress of the French *see* MARIE-LOUISE, Empress of the French, Duchess of Parma
Habsburg-Lorraine, Maximilian, Archduke of Austria, Electoral Archbishop of Cologne **7** 900
Habsburg-Lorraine, Maximilian, Archduke of Austria, Emperor of Mexico *see* MAXIMILIAN, Emperor of Mexico
Habsburg-Lorraine, Rainer, Archduke of Austria **14** 11
Habsburg-Lorraine, William, Archduke of Austria (1827-94) **14** 151
Habsburgs, Master of the **20** 688*
Habsenas *see* MERCIMEKLI
Habspurg *see* HABSBURG
Habuba Kabira **1** *849*; **14** 12–14*, *13*; **21** *267*, 271; **30** 178, *180*
  architecture **21** 281
  pottery **21** 306; **30** 183
  seals **1** 862
  temple **30** 183
  town walls **21** 552
  trade **30** 179
Hachette **13** 811
Hachijōnomiya (family) **17** 80
Hachijō Toshihito, Prince **18** 565, 566
Hachijō Toshitada, Prince **17** 791; **18** 565, 566
  works **18** *566*
Hachimonjiya Jishō **23** 161
Hachiōji Miyata **17** 103; **30** 258
  figurines **17** *97*
Hachirō Nakagawa *see* NAKAGAWA, HACHIRŌ
Hachirō Takatori *see* TAKATORI HACHIRŌ
Hachisuka (family) **17** 304
Hachizan Takatori *see* TAKATORI HACHIZAN
Hächler, Peter **30** 140
Hachmann, R. **17** 753
Hach'ŏn *see* KO UN
Hacı bin Musa **16** 205, 810
Hacılar **1** *821*, 823, 824, *849*; **14** 14–15*; **31** 456
  architecture **1** 830; **27** 127
  figurines **1** 823, *823*, 832; **10** 473
  fortifications **21** 552
  pottery **1** 823, *823*, 824, 837, 894; **14** *14*
  wall paintings **1** 838
Hacı Mengimberti **16** 497
Hack, Jan, III **18** 6
Hack, Rien **22** 860
Hackaert, Jan **14** 15–16*; **22** 843
  collaboration **3** 757
  patrons and collectors **14** 375
  teachers **4** 488
  works **14** *15*
Hacken, Joseph van **30** 499
Hackeney (family) **7** 425
Hackeney, Nikasius **7** 424; **20** 691
Hackensack (NJ), Ackerman House **31** *590*
Hacker, Dieter **14** 16*
Hacker, Frederick **5** 560
Hacker, Johann David **26** 530
Hackert, Carl Ludwig **14** 16; **19** 399
Hackert, Georg (Abraham) **14** 16, 17, 18*; **33** 116
Hackert, Johann Gottlieb **14** 16
Hackert, Philipp (*d* 1768) **14** 16; **32** 114
Hackert, (Jacob) Philipp (1737-1807) **13** 304; **14** 16–18*
  patrons and collectors **8** 83; **14** 486, 539; **18** 149; **30** 451; **33** 116
  pupils **9** 395; **12** 853
  reproductive prints by others **14** 18
  works **2** 164; **8** 96; **12** 392; **14** *17*, 285; **28** 317
Hackert, Wilhelm **14** 16
Hackett, G. **12** 173
Hackhofer, Johann Cyriak **14** 18*
Hackin, Joseph **1** 212; **3** 502; **15** 695; **29** 642; **30** 848
Hackin, Ria **3** 502; **15** 695
Hackl, Gabriel von **20** 380; **21** 37; **25** 743; **29** 638, 791
Hackman & Co. **11** 107
Hackmey, Joseph **16** 570
Hackner, Christoph **33** 417
Hackney, Rod(erick Peter) **14** 18–19*; **31** 737
Hacquin, Jean-Louis **24** 730
al-Hada **2** 268
Hadatu *see* ARSLAN TASH
Hadda **1** *186*, 211; **11** 335; **14** 19*
  sculpture **1** 193, 195–6; **15** 458
  stucco **1** 196
  stupas **1** 192
  wall paintings **1** 200, 201; **6** 302
Haddad, Salim **19** 7
Haddad, Tell Temple **14** 128–9
Haddej **31** 424
Hadden, G. J. **15** 832
Hadden, Thomas **28** 263
Haddenham **25** 507
Haddington (Lothian)
  St Mary **28** 224
  Town Hall **31** 239
Haddington, Thomas Baillie, 7th Earl of *see* BAILLIE, THOMAS, 7th Earl of Haddington
Haddiscoe (Norfolk), St Mary **26** 613
Haddon, Robert (Joseph) **2** 740, 756; **14** 19*
Haddon Hall (Derbys) **8** 43
  banqueting hall **10** *270*
  dining-room **10** 271, *271*
  Long Gallery **10** 272
  screen **10** 270
Haddon stone **2** 541
Hadejia **23** *129*
Hadeland Glasverk **23** 235–6
Haden, Ruth Everard **29** 108
Haden, (Francis) Seymour **10** 255; **14** 20*; **25** 629
  methods **10** 556
  prints **25** 630
  pupils **10** 796; **32** 795
  works **9** 204, 309; **10** 556, *556*; **14** 251; **21** 418
Hadëri, Shaban **1** 541; **14** 20*; **25** 869
Haderslev Church **8** 723
Hadfield, George **8** 20; **14** 20*; **30** 761
  works **20** 869; **32** 886, 892
Hadfield, Joseph **13** 875
Hadfield, Maria (Louisa Caterina Cecilia) *see* COSWAY, MARIA (LOUISA CATERINA CECILIA)
Hadfield, Octavius **33** 57
Hadid, Zaha **14** 20–21*; **18** 236
Hadigaon
  Ganesha Temple **22** 759
  Kotal-Tol **22** 759
  Satya Narayana temple **22** 759
  sculpture **22** 758, *758*, 766, 771, 796
Haditha **1** 895
Haditha region **1** *849*; **14** 21–2*; **21** *267*
Hadjiadamos, Andy *see* ADAMOS, ANDY
Hadjibekov, N. **2** 894
Hadji Boškov, Petar **14** 22*; **19** 885
Hadjida, Vera **8** 364
Hadjimichail, Theophilos *see* THEOPHILOS (*c.* 1868-1934)
Hadjinicolaou, Nicos **28** 917, 927
Hadjiyev, E. **2** 896, 902
Hadjiyeva, B. **2** 897
Hadlaub, Johannes **33** 736
Hadleigh (Suffolk), Deanery Tower **4** 771; **12** 176; **30** 501
Hadley (MA) **31** 623
Hadley, James **33** 378
al-Ḥaḍr *see* HATRA
Hadramawt **16** 271
Hadrancourt-le-Haut-Clocher **13** 211
Hadra vases *see under* HYDRIAI → types
Hadrian, Emperor of Rome (*reg* 117-38) **8** 477; **9** 896; **13** 369; **14** 22*; **16** 684; **27** *37*
  architecture
    temples **1** 498
      Pantheon **1** 463; **9** 85; **16** 623; **24** 21; **26** 751, 792, 890, *898*; **30** 436
      Temple of Olympian Zeus **2** 688; **24** 331
      Temple of Venus and Rome **26** 782, 892, 925; **30** 436
  amphitheatres **26** 874
  aqueducts **16** 578; **26** 910
  architecture **2** 155, 669–70; **8** 368; **11** 174; **16** 809; **23** 619; **26** 884, 896–9*
    arches **31** 350
    barracks **23** 621
    baths **1** 463
    bridges **23** 19
    fora **26** 784, 785, 866
    fortifications **21** 559
    granaries **28** 893
    harbours **31** 303

Hadrian, Emperor of Rome (*reg* 117-38)
architecture—cont.
libraries **19** 312; **26** 785, 908, *909*
mausolea **20** 864, *864*; **26** *794*, 795; **27** 235
military **21** 559
palaces **23** 808, 809; **26** 895
reservoirs **2** 156
urban planning **27** 3
villas **16** 623; **26** 870, *899*; **27** 59, 61, 62, 67; **31** 57, 58, *59*, 61
coins **2** 416; **27** 97
collections **2** 558
Edirne **9** 729
Hadrian's Villa **11** 339; **26** 853; **27** 72; **31** 58–9
mosaics **31** *62*
sculpture **3** 708; **8** 155; **9** 20; **10** 95; **24** 570; **26** 861; **27** 37–9; **31** *60*
Hadrian I, Pope **31** 57
Hadrian's Villa *see under* TIVOLI
Hadrian's Wall **10** *225*, 359; **14** 22–3*, *23*; **21** 547, 559; **26** 875, 906, *908*
forts **10** 226
Hadrumetum *see under* SOUSSE
Hadstock (Essex), St Botolph **9** 155; **26** 589
Hadza **1** 304, 306
Hadzhi-Abbas **2** 893
Hadziewicz, Rafał **12** 603; **18** 413; **25** 106; **33** 450
Hadžifejzović, Jusuf **4** 462
Haecht, Godevaard van **33** 169
Haecht, Tobias van *see* VERHAECHT, TOBIAS
Haecht, Willem van, II **14** 23*
patrons and collectors **5** 353; **6** 77; **12** 233
printmakers **32** 708; **33** 169
teachers **32** 250
works **1** 663; **7** *563*; **9** 15, *16*, 22; **10** 710; **32** 586; **33** 169
writings **10** 174; **15** 84
Haecken, Joseph van *see* AKEN, JOSEPH VAN
Haefeli, Max **7** *294*; **14** 24
Haefeli, Max Ernst **14** 24*
collaboration **22** 187; **29** 603
works **29** *603*; **30** 128, *128*
Haeflinger, Paul **30** 160
Haeften, Benedictus van **10** 175
Haegang *see* KIM KYU-JIN
Haegen, V. Van der *see* VAN DER HAEGEN, V.
Haeghen, Arnold Vander, Museum *see under* GHENT → Museum Arnold Vander Haeghen
Haeghen, Jan-Baptiste van der **14** 24*
Haeght, Jan van **4** 592
Haeinsa **21** 846
Haein Temple **18** 254, 261, *261*
books **18** 355
library **18** 265
paintings **18** 308, 309, 310, 311
sculpture **18** 293
Haelen, François Van *see* VAN HAELEN, FRANČ4IS
Haelwech, Wynant **22** 898
works **22** *898*
Haelwegh, Albert **8** 733; **14** 25*
haematite
historical and regional traditions
Greece, ancient **13** 536
Islamic **12** 253; **16** *543*
Maya **21** 718
Mesoamerica, Pre-Columbian **1** 713; **21** 241, 719
Native North Americans **21** 718
Panama **21** 718
Rome, ancient **12** 251, 252, *252*
South America, Pre-Columbian **21** 718
haematite—cont.
uses
abrasives **16** 859
amulets **12** 251, 252, *252*
burnishing **12** 622
mirrors **21** 718, 719
pigments **13** 536; **25** 175
polishing **21** 241
seals **16** *543*
Haemmaat *see* SOLEB
Haen, Abraham de, II (1707-48) **3** 900; **29** 402
Haen, Antony de **33** 391
Haen, David de **3** 7
Haen, Jan de **20** 81
Haenam, Taehŭng-sa Temple **12** 94
Haenel, Erich **28** 120
Haenel, Karl Moritz **14** 25*
Haenen, Babs **22** 884
Haenggi, Mme **9** 385
Haensbergen, Johan van **19** 474; **25** 68
Haentz, Zacharie *see* HEINCE, ZACHARIE
Haerdtl, Oswald **2** 789, 815; **14** 25*, 629
collaboration **2** 810
pupils **28** 187
works **2** 789
Haeredes Pauli **32** 354
Haes, Carlos de **14** 25–6*
pupils **2** 285; **3** 869; **20** 860; **26** 96, 298
works **29** 284, *285*
Haesaerts, Luc **5** 44
Haesaerts, Paul **3** 619; **5** 44; **26** 236
Haese, Günter **14** 26*
Haese, Roel d' **3** 573; **8** 846*
Haesler, Otto **6** 138; **21** 494; **26** 405
Hafen, John **22** 126
Hafenbrädl, Friedrich **19** 718
Haffenecker, Anton **25** 438
Haffner, Antonio Maria **14** 26, 27*
Haffner, Enrico Giovanni **14** 26–7*; **16** 670
collaboration **5** 653; **11** 679, 680; **14** 27
works **15** 138
Haffner, Wilhelm **11** 472
Hafid, Assam Abdul **16** 2
Hafit *see* JABAL HAFIT
Hafiz (*fl c* 1390) **22** 322; **27** 513; **28** 616
al-Hafiz, Caliph (*reg* 1131-49) (Fatimid) **20** 368
tapestries **16** *433*
al-Hafiz, Farghali Abd **9** 766
Hafiz-i Abru **16** 196, 303, 322, 551
Hafiz Osman **1** 584; **14** 27*; **16** 285, 287, 590
Hafod (Dyfed) **12** 131
Hafod Uchtryd **32** 783
Hafshuya Mosque **16** 193
Hafsid **14** 27–8*; **16** 114
see also:
AL-MUNTASIR, Ruler
ABU ZAKARIYA, Ruler
'ATF
Hafsten, Halvdan **23** 243
Hafstrom, Jan **30** 82
Haftavan Tepe **14** 28*; **15** *901*
fortress **15** 905
Haft Tepe **14** 28–9*; **15** *901*, 905
palace **23** 807
stucco **29** 814
temple **15** 909
Haga **12** 135
interior decoration **11** 471
Pavilion **30** 72, 89, *89*, 117
furniture **30** 95
interior decoration **13** 864
Turkish Tent **11** 242; **18** 73
Hagan, Charlotte **12** 509
Hagar Qim **25** 512
Hagarsa, Tomb of Meryaa **9** 874
Hagberg, Rune **30** 81
Hagbolt, Jacob **14** 29*
Hagbolt, Ludwig **14** 29
Hagborg, (Vilhelm Nikolaus) August **14** 29*
Hagby Church **30** 66
Hage, Bartholomeus vander **10** 222
Hage, Johannes **8** 758, 759
Hagedorn, Christian Ludwig von **1** 105; **9** 238; **12** 478; **14** 29–30*, 835
Hageladas *see* Ageladas
Hagemann, Friedrich **28** 45
Hagemann Portfolio **27** 472
Hagemeister, Karl **14** 30*
Hagen **12** *360*; **14** 30–31*
Folkwang Museum **14** 30; **21** 648; **26** 546; **31** 876
see also ESSEN → Museum Folkwang
Hohenhagen **14** 31
Karl Ernst Osthaus Museum **14** 31
Stadhuis **30** 760
Hagen, August Matthias **10** 539
Hagen, Chad Alice **10** 875
Hagen, Christiaen van der **29** 644
Hagen, Gaspar van der **27** 466
Hagen, G. B. **30** 750
Hagen, Hugo **1** 548; **18** 527; **25** 402; **28** 91, 672
Hagen, Oscar **31** 672
Hagen, William van der **13** 892; **14** 31*; **16** 14
Hagenau **19** 734
Hagenau, Haincelin de *see* HAINCELIN DE HAGENAU
Hagenau, Niclaus **12** 401
Hagenauer, Friedrich **2** 718; **14** 31–2*; **20** 920; **26** 204
Hagenauer, Johann Baptist **14** 32*; **25** 34, 322; **27** 665; **33** 623
Hagenauer, Nikolaus **14** 31, 32*; **29** 757
works **11** 455; **13** 721; **28** 134
Hagenauer, Wolfgang **2** 783; **14** 32; **27** 665
Hagenbeck, Karl **33** 699
Hagenbund **2** 797; **3** 21; **14** 33*; **20** 254; **32** 447
members **10** 756; **18** 489; **19** 69; **32** 446
Hagener **23** 712
Hagen-Haspe Friedhofskapelle **23** 502
Hagenmeyer **22** 807
Hager, Carl Otto **14** 33*; **29** 105
Hagesandros **14** 33–4*; **29** 389
attributions **13** 468
collaboration **18** 756; **25** 45
works **13** 464; **26** 292; **27** *8*
Hagesawa Sakon **14** 215
Hagesawa Sōtaku **14** 215
Hagesawa Soya **14** 215
Hagesias *see* HEGIAS
Hägg, Axel Herman *see* HAIG, AXEL HERMAN
Haggadot **14** 34–5*, *35*; **17** *537*, 563, 565–6*
individual manuscripts
Ashkenazi Haggadah (London, BL, MS. Add. 14762) **17** 600
First New York Haggadah (New York, Jew. Theol. Semin. America Lib., MS. Mic. 4481) **17** 600
First Nuremberg Haggadah (Jerusalem, Schocken Lib., MS. 24086) **17** 600
Golden Haggadah (London, BL, Add. MS. 27210) **14** 34, *35*; **17** 536, *536*, 562
Kaufmann Haggadah (Budapest, Lib. Hung. Acad. Sci., MSA 422) **14** 34
Rylands Haggadah (Manchester U Lib.,Heb. MS.6; copy London, BL, MS.1404) **14** 34
Haggadot
individual manuscripts—cont.
Second New York Haggadah (New York, Jew. Theol. Semin. America Lib., MS. Mic. 8279) **17** 600
Second Nuremberg Haggadah (Jerusalem, Schocken Lib., MS. 24087) **14** 34; **17** 563
Washington Haggadah (Washington, DC, Lib. Congr., Hebr. MS. I) **17** 600
Yahuda Haggadah (Jerusalem, Israel Mus., MS. 180/50) **14** 34; **17** 563
Haggerty, John **30** 741
Haghe, Die **22** 875
Haghe, Louis **25** 587, 623, 626; **26** 463
works **13** *635*; **25** *715*
Haghpat Monastery **2** *423*; **14** 36*, *36*
bell-tower **14** *36*
Church of the Holy Sign **2** 429, 434; **14** 36
hall of Hamazasp **2** 427
khatchk'ars **2** 436; **8** 199
library **2** 427
Treasury **2** 444
Hagi **14** 36–7*; **17** *11*, *241*
pottery **17** *256*
Hagia Triada *see* AYIA TRIADA
hagiographies *see* SAINTS' LIVES
Hagios Georgios Diassoritis **22** 700
Hagios Ioannis 'stou Adissarou' **22** 700
Hagios Meletios Monastery **25** 336
Hagios Neophytos monastery **8** 367
Hagios Nikolaos tis Stegis **8** 358, 359; **9** 580, 628
Hagios Varnavas *see under* SALAMIS
Hagiwara, Hideo **17** 296
Hagiwara, Kyōjirō **17** 293; **20** 874
Hagley Hall (Hereford & Worcs) **10** 277; **12** 130; **13** 608
furniture **17** 623
garden bridge **4** 801
interior decoration **11** 428
portico **25** 267
ruin buildings **12** *130*; **27** 323
sculpture **27** 468
temple of Theseus **22** 735; **29** 806
Haglund, Birger **30** 109, 113
works **30** *113*
Hagmann, John S. **29** 642
Hagn, Ludwig von **17** 885
Hagnow, Nikolaus von *see* HAGENAUER, NIKOLAUS
Hagnower, Nikolaus *see* HAGENAUER, NIKOLAUS
Hagop Bilo **29** 227
Hagos, Dastā **10** 574
Hagström, Eric **30** 113
Hague, Anderson **20** 239
Hague, The **9** 28; **14** 37–46*; **22** *813*
academy **1** 104, 105
Accijnhuisje **22** 828
Akademie voor Beeldende Kunst **14** 43
art forms and materials
architecture **22** 826
brass **22** 895
bronze **22** 894
ceramics **22** *883*
furniture **14** 44*; **22** 873
glass **22** 884, 885
metalwork **22** 891
painting **22** 844–5*
pewter **22** 893
porcelain **22** 882
silver **22** 887, 888, *888*
Bijenkorf, De **18** *437*
Hague, The—cont.
Binnenhof **12** 131; **14** 38, 44–5*, *45*; **18** 653; **22** 846
Grote Zaal *see* Ridderzaal
Loterijzaal *see* Ridderzaal
Brugmanshuis **22** *868*
Buitenhof **12** 530
Schilderijenzaal Prins Willem V **22** 905, 906
churches
Grote Kerk **14** 44*; **22** 820, 821
Nieuwe Kerk **2** 385
St Jacobskerk *see* Grote Kerk
St Willebrorduskerk **22** 828
Willemskerk **22** 828
De Volharding building **22** 831
Dr Anton Philips Concert Hall **1** 126
equestrian statue of William the Silent **14** 42
Gothische Zaal **22** 828
Haagsche Teeken-Academie **14** 42
Huis Patras **22** 827
Huis Schuylenburch **29** 837
Huis ten Bosch **1** 658; **14** 45–6*; **22** 825, 826, 902; **25** 324, *325*; **32** 551
gardens **12** 131
Great Hall *see* Oranjezaal
Lacquer Cabinet **5** 349
Oranjezaal **10** 660; **13** 337; **14** 46*, 584, 730; **17** 649; **19** 349; **22** 844; **23** 465–6; **25** 324
paintings **11** 170; **22** 844; **29** 247
sculpture **8** 884
White Dining Room **11** 447
see also Nationale Konstgalerij
Iconographisch Bureau **22** 909
Koninklijke Bibliotheek **22** 909; **23** 469
Koninklijk Kabinet van Schilderijen *see* museums → Mauritshuis
Koninklijk Teater **22** 827
Kröller House **2** 337
Mauritshuis *see under* museums
monument to Liberty **14** 42
Müller head office **19** 32
museums
Bredius Museum **4** 732; **22** 905
Gemeentearchief **18** 628
Gemeentelijke Museum voor Schoone Kunsten **29** 478
Gemeentemuseum **3** 788; **14** 40, *40*, 43
collections **7** 155; **22** 906; **26** 527; **33** 47
library **22** 909
paintings **21** 855
Historisch Museum **18** 628; **22** 906
Mauritshuis **4** 786; **5** 542, *542*; **14** 39; **15** 40; **22** 536, 824, 906; **23** 469, 492; **32** 551
collections **4** 732; **5** 345; **14** 42; **22** 906; **23** 463, 469
directors **3** 769; **4** 732; **14** 635; **29** 591
interior decoration **24** 341
paintings **23** 469; **28** 842; **32** 268
paintings (ceiling) **18** 823
Nationale Konstgalerij **14** 42
Nederlands Kostuummuseum **22** 906
Panorama Mesdag **22** 906
Rijksmuseum Hendrik Willem Mesdag **21** 176; **22** 906
Rijksmuseum Meermanno-Westreenianum **21** 39; **33** 106
Nieuwe Kunstschool **22** 908
Nirwana apartment block **22** 831
Noordeinde **4** 302; **14** 729; **22** 828
Oude Hof **22** 844
Oude Stadhuis **22** 823
Paleis Noordeinde **14** *38*; **22** 904

Hague, The—cont.
Peace Palace 30 506
Raadhuis *see* Royal Palace
Ridderzaal 22 822
Rijksbureau voor Kunsthistorische Documentatie (R.K.D) 2 371; 12 490; 19 782; 22 909, 911
Rijksdienst Beeldende Kunste 2 371
Royal Palace 22 822, *866*; 33 261
Shell Building 22 831
Stadhuis *see* Oude Stadhuis
studios 22 908
urban planning 14 39
Villa Carel Henny 32 555
Vredespaleis 4 874
Hague, William 14 46*
Hague Convention 2 555
Haguenau 11 606; 26 633; 29 753
Hague school (painting; 19th cent.) 4 59, 203; 11 885; 14 46–7*; 18 715; 20 435, 871; 22 849–50*, 851; 26 57, 527; 33 45
collections 5 278; 9 305; 13 715; 22 906; 26 107; 28 271; 32 794
members 2 224, 575; 3 398; 14 43; 16 573; 20 432, 434; 21 175; 29 723; 30 736; 33 47
works 2 106; 20 *433*, *872*; 26 *528*
Hague school (architecture; 20th cent.) *see* NIEUWE ZAKELIJKHEID
Hagura Katei 17 413
Hagurozan 17 322
Hah *see* ANITLI
ha has 4 805; 12 128; 14 47*
Hahn 27 422, 429, 584
Hahn, Daniel Meinerts 31 335
Hahn, Emanuel 5 570; 33 343
Hahn, Erzsébet Forgách 10 650; 14 896
Hahn, Frederick, Graf von 26 506
Hahn, Herman (*fl* 1570s) 14 47
Hahn, Herman (1574-1627/8) 14 47*; 32 6
Hahn, Hermann 14 47–8*; 17 832; 29 491
Hahn, Johann Michael 33 670
Hahn, Otto 2 528
Hahn, Reynaldo 25 661
Hahn, Ulrich 3 423
Hahn, Wolfgang 14 48*
Hähnel, Ernst Julius 9 239; 14 48–9*
assistants 28 94
pupils 3 510, 732; 26 408
works 2 802; 26 378
Hahnloser, Hans Robert 28 115; 30 157
Hahnloser-Bühler, Arthur 30 152, 153
Hahnloser-Bühler, Hedy 30 152, 153
Hahn Missal *see under* MISSALS → individual manuscripts
Hahoe 18 300, 378
masks 18 *378*
Hahr, August 30 120
Haichang 7 126
Haid, Anna Barbara 27 319
Haid (i), Johann Elias 10 103
Haid (i), Johann Gottfried 14 49; 21 416, 417, 512
Haid (i), Johann Jakob 10 103; 13 268
Haid (i), Johann Lorenz 7 183; 14 49; 23 146; 24 707
Haid (i), Johann Valentin 14 49
Haida 8 568; 14 49*; 22 547, 564, 565, 614, 657, 668, 674, 676
architecture 22 *564*
dress 22 632
mats 22 *657*
sculpture 22 580–81*
Haida *see* NOVÝ BOR (CZECH REPUBLIC)
Haidenreich, Erhard *see* HEIDENREICH, ERHARD
Haidenreich, Ulrich *see* HEIDENREICH, ULRICH
Haider, Andreas (i)(*fl c.* 1500) 14 49
Haider, Andreas (ii)(*d* 1544-5) 14 49
Haider, Hans 14 49; 16 68, 69
Haider, Michael 14 49
Haider, Simon 12 343; 14 49*; 16 68, 69; 18 233
Haider, Thomas 14 50
Haider, Zulqarnain 23 800
Haidra 31 427
Haidt, John Valentine 14 50*
Haifa 16 *565*
houses 16 565
Israel Institute of Technology *see* Technion
Mané-Katz Museum 16 571; 20 252
Mt Carmel 17 854
Museum of Art Library 16 572
Museum of Modern Art 17 434
Music and Ethnology Museum 17 582
Technion 3 43; 16 572
Danciger Teaching Laboratory 16 566, *566*
Faculty of Architecture Library 16 572
Tikotin Museum of Japanese Art 16 571
University 16 570, 572
Media Department library 16 572
Haig, Axel Herman 2 333; 5 196; 7 664; 14 50*
works 7 *665*
Haig, Thomas (*d* 1803) 7 171, 172
Haig, Thomas, & Co. (*fl c.* 1825) 10 852
Haight, Charles C(oolidge) 14 50–51*, 244
Haihai 22 547, 579
Haihaya 14 51*
see also:
GAYAKARNA, Ruler
SHANKARAGANA, Ruler
Haiko, Edelfelt Museum 9 717
Ha'il 21 588
Hailes Abbey (Glos) 4 465; 7 275, 350, 352, 353; 13 46
Haile Selassie, Emperor of Ethiopia (*reg* 1930-6; 1941-74) 10 567
Hailu, Kegngetta Jenbere *see* JENBERE HAILU, KEGNGETTA
Haimhausen, Sigismund, Graf von 23 324
Haimon Group 13 511
Haimon Painter 23 146
Hain, M. 33 599
Haina Abbey 13 49
Hainauer, Oscar 9 467; 12 474; 25 19
Hainault, Jacoba, Countess of *see* JACOBA, Countess of Hainault
Haincelin, Jean 7 525; 20 625; 31 842
Haincelin de Hagenau 5 208; 7 525; 20 625, 633; 31 841
Haine, Claus de *see* CLAUS DE HAINE
Hainhofer, Melchior 14 678
Hainhofer, Philipp 5 607; 9 28; 12 461; 14 51–2*; 19 790
architecture 13 631
collaboration 2 44; 27 229
furniture 5 350; 12 422; 18 522; 19 152; 21 127; 32 772
paintings 17 719
Hainleinn, Michael 22 375
Hains, Raymond 11 551; 14 52*
dealers 7 421
groups and movements 8 608; 23 260; 30 924
patrons and collectors 14 48
Hains, Raymond—cont.
works 7 557; 23 260, *260*
Hainsch, Johann Georg *see* HEINTSCH, JOHANN GEORG
Hainsse, Zacharie *see* HEINCE, ZACHARIE
Hainz, Johann Georg 12 390
Hainzelin, Toussaint 26 351
Hainzelmann (family) 2 719; 14 53
Hainzelmann, Elias 14 53*
Hainzelmann, Johann 14 53*; 18 788
Haiphong 29 *225*; 32 *468*
Hang Kenh Temple 32 *479*, 480
hair
historical and regional traditions
Africa 1 307, *404*
Angola 7 *197*
Bhutan 3 914
China 6 877; 7 65
Chokwe 1 *404*; 7 *197*
England 10 278
Germany 3 *672*
Indian subcontinent 15 551, 734
Japan 17 368
Korea 18 303
types
alpaca hair 4 *266*; 27 641; 29 *182*; 30 538, 539*
badger-hair 5 32, 33, 34, *34*; 25 477
bear-hair 5 32
camel hair 6 299, 301; 10 872; 16 466; 18 48; 30 538, 539*; 32 899
Islamic 16 430
cat-hair 17 368
deer-hair 5 32; 17 209, 227
dog-hair 17 368
ermine 5 32
fox-hair 5 32
goat-hair 5 32, 830; 10 872; 18 48; 30 470, 471, 538, 539*
Africa 1 307
Berber 1 307
Iran 16 449; 30 *473*
Islamic 16 430, 449, 466
Japan 17 209
Kashmir 16 430
Tibet 30 845
hog-hair 17 209
horsehair 11 54; 17 *334*, 368; 18 589; 22 649; 30 151; 31 260, 684
human hair 5 32–3; 10 872; 31 261
Japan 17 371, *373*, 407
Marquesas Islands 23 720
Native North Americans 31 260
Pacific Islands 23 720
Samoa 23 720
llama-hair 30 538, 539*; 32 177
miniver 5 32, 33; 9 255; 30 426
mink 5 32
mohair 16 430, 445; 30 539*; 31 261
moose-hair 22 647, 650, 663
mountain goat-hair 22 619, 620
Mustela 5 32
ox-hair 5 32, *32*, 33, 34
polecat-hair 5 32
rabbit-hair 17 227, 368
raccoon-hair 17 368
rats' whiskers 7 66
sable 5 32, *32*, 33, 34; 30 426; 32 899
sheep *see* WOOL
squirrel-hair 5 32, 33, 34
stoat-hair 5 32
vicuña-hair 15 163; 30 539*
weasel-hair 5 32
wolf-hair 5 32; 17 368
yak-hair 3 915; 17 407; 22 791; 30 845
hair—cont.
uses
brushes 3 914; 5 32–3, 35; 6 736, 877; 7 65; 15 551; 17 209, 227, 368; 18 303; 32 899
carpets 5 830; 16 466
dolls 17 371, *373*; 31 260, 261
felt 10 872
grounds 6 301
headdresses 23 720
kilims 18 48
lace 18 589
masks 15 734; 17 *334*
plaster 29 813
puppets 17 407
sculpture 1 *404*; 3 *672*; 6 299; 7 *197*
stucco 10 278; 29 813
tents 1 307; 30 470, 471, *473*
textiles 3 915; 16 449; 22 791
threads 30 538, 539*
upholstery 31 684
hairbrushes 4 *314*
hairdryers 20 594
Haireddo Sentā *see* HI-RED CENTER
hair-nets 12 469
hair ornaments 17 521, 523, 524, 526, 527
historical and regional traditions
China 7 108, 112, *112*, 836
Cyprus, ancient 8 352
France 17 *525*
Japan 17 386
Malaysia 20 180
Mongolia 21 877
Native North Americans 22 649
Rome, ancient 27 *102*
Tunisia 27 *102*
materials
coral 7 836
feathers 7 108
glass 17 386
gold 7 108, *112*
pearls 7 *112*; 27 *102*
quills 22 649
sapphires 17 *525*; 27 *102*
silver-gilt 7 108
turquoise 7 108
hairpins
historical and regional traditions
China 7 102, 109, 110, 111, 145
Korea 18 367, 368
Prehistoric art 25 546
materials
amber 1 761
bronze 7 109
enamel 7 111
gold 7 109
ivory 7 102
silver 7 109
turquoise 7 109
hairstyles 9 255, 256, 258
Africa 1 342–3, *343*
Central Asia, Eastern 6 310
China 7 74
England 9 255
Fang 10 792*
Fulani 1 343; 11 830
Greece, ancient 9 248
Hamar 1 285
Indian subcontinent 15 736
Iran 16 464, 465
Islamic 16 464, 465
Native North Americans 22 628*, 631
Norman 9 255
Rome, ancient 9 249–50
Vietnam 32 486
Hairy-Who 31 609
Haisla 22 547, 564, 579
Haité, George 14 53; 33 372
Haité, George Charles 14 53*
Haiti 2 144; 5 744, *745*; 14 53–60*, *54*
architecture 14 56–8*
carnivals 5 788
coins 7 539
Haiti—cont.
collections 14 60
dujos 14 54, *55*
education (art) 14 59–60*
emblems 8 231
exhibitions 14 60
fortifications 14 57
gold 14 *55*
ground drawings 14 56, *56*
houses 1 *421*; 14 56–7
metal 14 58
museums 14 60
oil-drums 14 58
painting 1 425*; 14 58–9*, *59*
palaces 14 *57*
patronage 14 59–60*
pottery 14 54
sculpture 14 58
tourist art 14 59
trade 14 57
trigonolites 14 54
vèvè *see* ground drawings
wood 14 *55*
wood-carvings 14 54
see also HISPANIOLA (ISLAND)
Haitze, Pierre-Joseph 8 525
Haiweng *see* LIU HAISU
Haix, Duco dela 26 243
Hajar am-Dhaybiyya 2 266
Hajar Bin Humayd 2 *246*, 260, 263, 268
Hajas, Tibor 14 897
Hajdina Church 28 858
Hajdu, Etienne 10 178, 650; 11 569; 12 437
works 10 *178*
Hajdúsámson 14 60*, *881*; 25 *471*, 526
Hajek, Otto Herbert 14 60–61*; 29 875
Hajek-Halke, Heinz 23 9; 29 608
Haji Begum 8 679
Hajib Mas'ud ibn Ahmad al-Naqqash 16 374
works 16 *366*
Hajii 16 236
Hajii Shuja' 16 232
Haji Mahmud 15 573
Hajime Katō *see* KATŌ, HAJIME
Hajime Yatsuka *see* YATSUKA, HAJIME
Hajipur 15 595; 16 345
congregational mosque 15 368
Haji Shah Morr 29 824
Haji ware *see under* POTTERY → wares
al-Hajjaj (*c.* 661-714) 16 363
al-Hajjar 2 270, 272
Hajjara 16 271
Hajji, Sultan (*reg* 1346-7) (Mamluk) 16 384
Hajjiabad 15 912, 922; 29 815, 816
Hajji 'Abbas 16 391, 393, 509
al-Hajj Ibrahim ibn Mehmed 12 84
Hajji Firuz 15 913
Hajji Giray, Khan (*reg* 1426-56; 1456-66) (Giray Khans) 7 248; 29 553
Hajji Isma'il 16 381
Hajji Mahmud 16 331
Hajji Muhammad 1 894; 21 270
Hajji Muhammad Bakhshi Uyghur 1 644; 16 326; 28 811
al-Hajj Yusuf ibn al-Ghawabi 16 383
Hajong 3 165
Hajós, Alfréd 14 61*
Ha Jublie 19 241
Haka Chin 5 250
al-Hakam II, Caliph (*reg* 961-76) (Umayyad)
architectural decorations 2 528; 7 527; 9 645; 16 188, 256, 493; 21 629
architecture 7 845; 20 49; 22 193
ivory-carvings 16 524
manuscripts 7 845; 16 272, 306
Håkansson, Clemet 30 116
Håkansson, Nils 30 76

Hakata 12 97; 17 355, 373, 411
Hakataya 22 600
Hakendover, St Salvator 3 568; 13 111, *111*
Hakendover, Master of 20 688*
attributions 3 568; 14 63
works 13 100, 111, *111*
Hakenlandberg Triptych 11 452
Hakewill, Henry 28 156
Hakewill, James 4 614; 5 750; 16 884, 886; 18 721
al-Hakim, Caliph (*reg* 996-1021) (Fatimid) 5 402; 16 174, 432, 489; 22 194
Hakim 'Ilm al-Din *see* WAZIR KHAN
Hakka 6 661, 692; 7 45
architecture 6 *693*
Hakkâri 1 823
Hakkyō Asakawa *see* ASAKAWA, HAKKYŌ
Hakluyt, Richard 14 708
Hakman, Kosta 4 461
Hakob, Bishop of Dvin 2 429; 30 360
Hakobyan, Hakob 2 433
ha-Kohen, Solomon 17 565
Hakola, Antti 11 90
Hakola, Matti 11 90
Hakone
Art Museum 7 154
Open-air Museum 17 138, 433, *433*
Hakoris (*reg* 393-380 BC) 9 *778*, 888, 892
Hakp'o *see* YANG P'AENG-SON
Haksan *see* YUN CHE-HONG
Hakubakai (White Horse Society) 2 211; 11 821; 17 204, 435; 18 531; 22 444
hakudō *see under* ALLOYS → types
Hakuho Hirano *see* HIRANO, HAKUHO
Hakuhō period *see under* JAPAN → periods
Hakuhō style *see under* JAPAN → sculpture
Hakuin Ekaku 5 120; 14 61–3*; 17 165
works 14 *62*; 17 *192*, 193–4, 231
Haku Maki *see* MAKI, HAKU
Hakurei Yoshida *see* YOSHIDA, HAKUREI
Hakuryū Miyasaka *see* MIYASAKA HAKURYŪ
Hakusai Ōkuni *see* ŌKUNI, HAKUSAI
Hakuseki Arai *see* ARAI HAKUSEKI
Hakutei Ishii *see* ISHII, HAKUTEI
Hakuyō Fuchigami *see* FUCHIGAMI, HAKUYŌ
Hal 3 *539*
Hôtel de Ville 9 409
Notre-Dame-de-Hal 3 598; 9 156; 13 62; 14 63*; 22 220
altar 21 *858*
monstrances 31 843
sculpture 3 567, 568; 13 99, 100
stained glass 13 182
Onze Lieve Vrouwebasiliek *see* Notre-Dame-de-Hal
porcelain 3 591
St Martin *see* Notre-Dame-de-Hal
Hal, Jacob van 33 261
Hala 15 687; 23 *797*, 802
Halab *see* ALEPPO
Halabala, Jindřich 8 402
Halabiyeh 9 641, 663, 664
fortifications 9 554
praetorium 32 89
tunics 9 *252*
Zenobia 9 *513*
Halabyan, Karo 2 428
Halaf, Tell 2 283; 14 63–4*; 21 *267*; 30 *180*, 187
ivory-carvings 1 870
palace 30 194
pottery 1 894; 21 269; 30 196
reliefs 30 194
Halaf, Tell—cont.
sculpture 30 187
Temple-Palace 1 839; 14 *64*; 21 290
Halaf culture 21 269–70*; 30 737
Halaf period *see under* MESOPOTAMIA; ANCIENT NEAR EAST → periods
Halaf pottery *see under* POTTERY → wares
Halai 13 579
Hala Sultan Teke 8 *325*; 13 *362*; 14 64*
bronze 8 353
copper 8 353
Halász, István 10 472
Halász, Péter 14 896
Halász Gyula *see* BRASSAÏ
Halász-Hradik, Elemér 18 141
Halásztelek, St Elizabeth 14 891
Halauska, Ludwig 28 170
Halawa 30 197
Halaward *see* KHELAVERD
Halbax, Michael Wenzel 8 390; 25 548; 27 553
Halbehrr, Frederico 14 275
halberds 2 448
historical and regional traditions
China 6 841, 848; 7 3
Japan 17 361, 362
Korea 18 345
materials
bronze 6 841, 848; 18 345
inlays 6 841
steel 17 361
Halberstadt 12 *360*; 14 65*
Cathedral of St Stephanus 13 49; 26 571, 572
gems 12 255
rock crystal 26 485
rood 27 123, 124, *125*
sculpture 13 86
stucco 29 818
textiles 9 668; 12 462, 465, *465*, 467, 468; 26 703; 30 310–11, 331
Treasury 9 657
westwork 7 265
Liebfrauenkirche 12 399; 26 632; 28 293
sculpture 26 632
stained glass 13 187
Halbherr, Federico 2 879; 13 16; 14 65*; 15 98; 24 589
Halbig, Johann von 18 527; 33 726
Halbwachs, Maurice 31 728
Halcrow & Partners 4 803
Halcyon Days Ltd 10 347; 19 596
Hald, (Nils Tov) Edward 8 803; 14 65*; 30 99, 100, 884; 33 566
works 30 99, 100, 102, *103*
Haldane, J. B. S. 30 411
Haldane, William 'Deacon' 13 297
Haldeman and Goronsson, Architects 29 52
Haldenstone, James, Prior 27 529
Haldenwang, Christian 11 802
Haldenwang, Johann Christian 23 410
Halder, Jacob 2 472
Halderen, Jan van 2 486; 22 856
Haldner, Matthäus 18 451
Haldner, Max 18 451
Haldon Belvedere (Devon) 11 242
Hale, F. A. 27 642
Hale, George 23 342
Hale, Herbert D. 26 538
Hale, William 28 830
Halebid 14 65–6*; 15 *294*
Hoysaleshvara Temple 14 65–6; 15 327, *532*, 533
Kedareshvara Temple 15 533
Parshvanatha Temple 15 533
reliefs 15 227
Santinatha Temple 15 533
sculpture 15 744
temples 15 532
Halen, Arnoud van 25 823
Halen Siedlung 30 128
Halentei, Ishi 23 141
Halepagen 8 615
Halepagen Altar, Master of the *see* DEDEKE, WILM
Halepas, Yannoulis 14 66*
works 13 354, *354*
Hales (Norfolk), St Margaret 26 613
Hales, John *see* HAYLS, JOHN
Halevi, Samuel 4 784
Halévy, Daniel 25 660
Halévy, Joseph 33 520
Halewijn, Joanna van 16 69
half columns *see under* COLUMNS → types
Halfer, Josef 24 55
half-Gobelins weaving *see under* WEAVING → types
half-hipped roofs *see under* ROOFS → types
Halfpenny, John 7 167; 14 66
Halfpenny, Joseph 33 545
works 33 *542*
Halfpenny, William 14 66*
groups and movements 23 860
works 7 167; 18 72; 24 275
half roll-and-fillet mouldings *see under* MOULDINGS → types
half-shafts 26 571, 573
half-silk *see under* SILK → types
half-timbering 13 389
half-tone block *see under* PRINTING → processes
half-tones *see under* PRINTS → types
half-uncial script *see under* SCRIPTS → types
HALI: The International Journal of Carpets and Textiles 24 446
Halič Fortress 28 852
Halich 14 67*; 31 *546*, 548, 552, 563
Cathedral of the Dormition 31 548, 561
Church of the Nativity of Christ 31 550
Church of the Prophet Elijah 27 369
Church of the Saviour 27 369
Monastery of SS Boris and Gleb 31 548
St Panteleymon 27 369; 31 549, 561
Halıcılar Köşkü Madrasa 16 224
Halicka, Alicia 20 399
Halieis 13 401; 26 910; 29 487
Halier, Carl 27 643
Halifax (i) (W. Yorks; UK) 10 *225*; 14 67*
All Souls 28 *278*
carpets 10 358; 14 67
cotton 8 36
Piece Hall 2 324
Square Congregational Chapel 23 194
Town Hall 31 241
Halifax (ii) (NS; Canada) 5 *559*; 14 67–8*; 21 574, 575
Army Museum 14 67
Dalhousie University 5 592
education (art) 5 592
Keith Hall 5 *561*
Mechanics Institute *see* Nova Scotia Museum
Nova Scotia College of Art and Design 5 592; 14 68; 20 609
Nova Scotia Museum 5 590, 591
Victoria School of Art and Design *see* Nova Scotia College of Art and Design
Halifax, Charles Montagu, 1st Earl of *see* MONTAGU, CHARLES, 1st Earl of Halifax
Halikarnassos 5 741, 742; 13 *363*; 14 *68*, 68–72*; 20 871; 26 *908*
Bodrum Museum 14 71
Castle of St Peter 14 69, 420; 18 152
figurines 13 579, 580
Halikarnassos—cont.
fortifications 21 557
Mausoleum 13 384, 407, 430, 432; 14 69–72*, *71*; 20 863, 865; 22 42; 23 482; 24 205; 25 766, 768; 30 405, *406*; 31 109
frieze 13 426
reliefs 14 *69*
roof 27 131
sculpture 5 64; 13 459, 460, 470; 14 69, *70*, 70, 71–2
Palace of Mausolos 13 389, 407
reliefs 14 *69*
Tomb of Mausolos and Artemesia *see* Mausoleum
town walls 21 556
Halim Abdelhalim 22 325
Halin 5 *221*, 223, 225
architecture 5 237
coins 5 255
sculpture 5 238, *239*
Halins, Nicolas 20 645
Haliotis shells *see under* SHELLS → types
Halkomelem 22 589
Hall (Austria) 2 819
Abbey Church 2 780
Hall (Sweden) 26 647
Hall, Ann 18 66
Hall, Anna Maria 14 79*
Hall, Augusta 32 790
Hall, Benjamin 7 448
Hall, Bernard 2 771; 25 884
Hall, David 32 420
Hall, Denis Clarke 28 158
Hall, D. J. 19 702
Hall, Edwin Stanley 9 686
Hall, Elizabeth Johstone 14 *539*
Hall, Eric 26 99
Hall, Francis 9 61
Hall, Fred 4 657; 23 26
Hall, George Henry 14 79*
Hall, George O. 19 700
Hall, Harry 32 789
Hall, Herbert James 3 50
Hall, H.R. 31 508
Hall, John (*fl* 1732) 3 232
Hall, John (1739-97) 14 79*; 25 857
Hall, John (*fl* 1862) 2 738; 4 818
Hall, John (*b* 1943) 5 569
Hall, L. Bernard 21 77
Hall, Linsey 10 81
Hall, Margaret Bernardine
works 33 *313*
Hall, Morgen 32 790
Hall, Nigel 1 738
Hall, Peter 30 687
Hall, Peter Adolf 14 79–80*; 19 797; 21 643; 24 137; 33 196
Hall, Richard 13 335
Hall, Samuel (*fl* 1822) 31 334
Hall, Samuel Carter (1800-89) 14 78*
illustrated writings 16 16; 20 28; 29 634; 32 855
periodicals 24 422, 446
Hall, Mrs S. C. 15 35
Hall, William 5 560
works 5 *560*
Hallaç Monastery 5 674, 675, *675*; 9 544
Hallaert, Dionys 15 866
Hallard, Johan Abraham 30 107
Hallart, L.
works 5 *82*
Hallbergs, C. G. 30 108
hall churches *see under* CHURCHES → types
hall crypts *see under* CRYPTS → types
Hall & Dods 9 61
Halle (Belgium) *see* HAL
Hallé, Charles 19 413
Hallé, Claude-Guy 14 83–4*
Hallé, Daniel 14 83*; 25 70
Halle, Joseph Jean 20 914
Halle, Josset de *see* JOSSET DE HALLE
Hallé, Michel-Robert 11 630
works 4 *601*; 11 *631*
Hallé, Noël 14 83, 84–5*; 23 299; 24 137
patrons and collectors 4 554; 11 540; 14 585; 25 212
pupils 3 851; 8 763; 9 395; 20 421
reproductive prints by others 19 216
works 11 406; 14 *84*, *85*
Halle an der Saale
Burg Giebichenstein 12 456
Cathedral 12 471
Landesmuseum für Vorgeschichte 18 444
Marktkirche 12 365; 13 211; 19 815
Neue Stift 12 402
St Moritz 7 721; 13 90
Unsere Liebe Frau *see* Marktkirche
Hallek, Enno 30 82, 86
Hallen, Hans (Heyerdahl) 9 427; 14 85–6*; 29 106
Hallen, Konrad, Kuene von der *see* KUENE VON DER HALLEN, KONRAD
Hallen and Theron 29 107
Haller 6 171
Haller, Albrecht von 1 844; 21 6
Haller, Franz 24 370
Haller, Fritz 14 86*; 30 128
Haller, Hermann 14 31, 86*; 30 138; 33 737
Haller, Jan Kryštof 8 413
Haller, Johann Nepomuk 3 155
Haller, Jost 14 86–7*; 28 150
Haller, Martin 14 87*, 102
Haller, Oswald 15 865
Haller, Philipp 28 161
Haller, Ulrich 14 421
Haller von Hallerstein, Karl 7 502; 14 87*
excavations 3 340; 13 612; 23 490
works 25 267; 32 606
Hallet, Stephen 32 892
Hallett, Henry 30 330
Hallett, William 10 294, 295; 19 592; 32 540
Halley, Peter 1 81
Halliday, James T. 28 281
works 25 *403*
Halliday, Thomas (*fl* 1920s) 33 370
Halliday, Thomas Symington (*b* 1902) 28 244
Hallin, Frans August 7 807
Halling, Else 23 232
Hall-in-Tirol 2 818
Hallman, Per Olof 29 686
Hallmann, Anton 28 175
hallmarks *see* MARKS → metalwork
Hall of Lu *see* LINGGUANG DIAN
Hall of Numinous Brilliance *see* LINGGUANG DIAN
Hall & Prentice 2 741; 4 818
halls 6 407; 8 43; 14 73–8*; 23 809
historical and regional traditions
Anglo-Saxon 10 226; 14 73–4
Assyrian 30 187
Austria 15 866
Buddhism 14 77; 17 *815*; 30 575
Cambodia 5 *482*
China 3 *518*; 6 *639*, *649*, *651*, *653*, 656–8, *657*, *659*, *660*, *682*; 14 78*
Daoism 6 *672*
Czech Republic 23 809; 26 *367*
Egypt, ancient 13 405
England 14 75–7*
Anglo-Saxon 10 226
Gothic 14 *76*
Romanesque 10 227; 19 *401*
11th cent. 19 608
14th cent. 10 *270*; 14 454

halls
historical and regional traditions
England—cont.
15th cent. 10 163, 164
France 14 74, 74–5*
Germany 3 513, 795; 14 74*; 23 317
Gothic 3 774; 14 45, 74, 76; 23 317
Greece, ancient 13 380, 405, 407; 14 73*
Hungary 14 904
Indian subcontinent 14 77*; 15 313, 320, 325
Buddhism 14 77; 17 815
Islamic 14 77
Indonesia 14 78
Iran 30 222
Islamic 14 77; 16 800; 30 222
Italy 31 745
Japan 14 78; 18 551; 20 76; 28 606
Mangbetu 20 268
Netherlands, the 14 45
Norway 3 774
Parthian 6 198; 24 216
Poland 3 768; 19 748
Romanesque 10 227; 19 401
Rome, ancient 14 73
Scandinavia 32 532
South-east Asia 14 77–8*
Syria-Palestine 30 187, 191
Taiwan 30 245
Thailand 30 575
Viking 32 532
types
apadanas 2 213*
Achaemenid 15 912
Ancient Near East 24 483
Indian subcontinent 23 817
Iran, ancient 14 210; 15 911; 24 483
see also hypostyle halls
audience halls 9 557; 13 407; 15 356, 365; 23 817
see also BIT HILANI
caityas see CAITYAS
city halls see CITY HALLS
colonnaded see STOAS
columned 15 335, 335
concert halls see CONCERT HALLS
county halls see COUNTY HALLS
dining 13 381, 386, 396, 417
gavit' 2 426–7; 14 36; 27 701
guildhalls see GUILDHALLS
halls of columns 33 101
honden 16 812, 812; 23 597, 597
shoden see JAPAN → sanctuaries
hondō 17 66, 73, 73–4, 74
hypostyle 9 832, 840; 15 53*
see also apadanas
Japan 16 812, 812; 23 597
livery see LIVERY HALLS
meeting halls 17 842; 18 886
music-halls see music-halls
sale terrene 14 906; 27 610–11*, 611
town halls see TOWN HALLS
zhamatun see GAVIT'
see also SCUOLE
Hallstatt 2 774, 776; 6 154; 14 87–8*; 25 470, 533
cemetery 25 538
daggers 25 540
Grave 507 14 88
Grave 994 14 88
iron 16 59
jewellery 25 545
swords 25 540
Hallstatt/Baudische-Werkstätte 2 816
Hallstatt culture (c. 750–c. 450 BC) 6 152; 14 87; 25 533
situlae 28 806
swords 2 451
trade 10 592
Hallström, Althins 14 595
Hallström, Eric 14 88*; 30 81
Hallström, Gunnar August 14 595
Hallström, Staffan 19 798; 30 81
hall temples see under TEMPLES → types
hallucinogenic drugs 25 681
Hallur 15 301
Hallwachs, Michael Wenzel see HALBAX, MICHAEL WENZEL
Hallwyl, Franz-Joseph 19 55
Hallwyl, Walther, Count von 14 88*; 30 118
Hallwyl, Wilhelmina, Countess von 14 88–9*; 30 118
Hallwylska Museet see under STOCKHOLM → museums
Hallynckbroot, Lodewijk van 10 713
Halm, Peter 29 578
Hălmagiu 26 713
Halmahera 15 810
Hălmeag Church 26 710
Halmhuber, Gustav 9 761; 14 89*; 20 282; 32 801
Halmstad group 14 89*; 30 81
halogen lamps see under LAMPS → types
Haloi, Ganesh 5 421
Halonen, Eemil 11 100; 14 89
Halonen, Pekka 11 96; 14 89–90*; 22 540
works 11 96
Halpax, Michael Wenzel see HALBAX, MICHAEL WENZEL
Halpern, Deborah 2 762
Halpern, Stanislaw 2 761
Halprin, Anna 24 407
Halprin, Lawrence 7 286; 11 346; 14 90*; 21 650; 28 328
Halprin & Associates 28 328
Hal Qesari see CAESAREA (ISRAEL)
Hals, Anthonie 14 91
Hals, Claes see HALS, NICOLAES
Hals, Dirck 14 90, 91, 96–7*
groups and movements 13 895
reproductive prints by others 28 79
teachers 14 95; 22 840
works 12 290
Hals, Franchoys 14 90
Hals, Frans (1581/5-1666) 13 894, 895; 14 90, 91–5*; 25 138
attributions 19 293; 32 74
collaboration 21 827
forgeries by others 21 39
groups and movements 13 895
methods 24 793
patrons and collectors 10 365
Art Institute of Chicago 27 463
Bellio, Georges de 3 671
Boymans, F(rans) J(acob) O(tto) 4 614
Cappelle, Jan van de 5 679
Coats, W. A. 28 272
Duveen, Joseph, 1st Baron Duveen of Millbank 9 467
Everdingen, Allart van 10 660
Frans Halsmuseum (Haarlem) 22 906
Guinness, Edward (Cecil), 1st Earl of Iveagh 13 836
Huntington, Arabella D(uval) 15 29
Jennens, Charles 17 476
Johnson, John G(raver) (1841-1917) 17 619
Kann, Rodolphe 17 777
La Caze, Louis 18 588
Marquand, Henry G(urdon) 20 461
Mauritshuis (The Hague) 3 769
Mead, Richard 10 364
Mellon, Andrew W(illiam) 21 90
Museu de Arte de São Paulo 4 726
Pourtalès-Gorgier, James-Alexandre, Comte de 25 383
Hals, Frans (1581/5-1666)
patrons and collectors—cont.
Proby, William, 5th Earl of Carysfort 25 639
Reimer, Georg Andreas 26 112
Seymour-Conway, Richard, 4th Marquess of Hertford 28 527
Städelsches Kunstinstitut und Städt- ische Galerie (Frankfurt) 29 487
Trolle-Bonde, Gustaf, Count 31 362
William VIII, Landgrave of Hesse-Kassel (reg 1751-60) 14 491
pupils 4 870; 7 510; 19 292, 293; 21 813; 23 609; 26 532; 32 376, 592; 33 389
reproductive prints by others 4 242; 18 237; 26 234; 30 47; 32 140
works 7 511; 11 774; 12 290; 13 824, 895; 14 91, 92, 93; 22 840; 24 357, 580; 25 327, 362
Hals, Frans (1618-69) 14 90
Hals, Harald 14 97*; 17 854; 23 222
Hals, Harmen 14 90
Hals, Johannes 14 91, 95
Hals, Nicolaes 14 91; 27 329; 32 728
Hals, Reynier 14 91
Halsbach, Jörg von see JÖRG VON HALSBACH
Halsband, Frances 26 441
Hälsingborg see HELSINGBORG
Halsmuseum, Frans see under HAARLEM
Haltern Fort 6 68
Halwachs, Michael Wenzel see HALBAX, MICHAEL WENZEL
Halyday, James 23 66
Ham (France) 21 564
Ham (Surrey; UK)
Keir Collection 16 555
Hama 14 97–8*, 592; 16 104; 30 180, 185, 187
architecture 16 208; 30 177
congregational mosque 16 496; 22 192
glass 1 865; 16 517, 519
houses 16 269
inscriptions 1 893
ivory-carvings 1 870, 871
Museum 14 98
pottery 16 406, 416; 30 184
sculpture 30 187
seals 1 862
trade 30 179
Hamada, Chimei 14 98*; 17 293, 296
Hamada, Kōsaku 6 867; 17 426; 18 259
Hamada, Shōji 14 98–9*; 17 353; 21 635; 28 627
collaboration 18 901
groups and movements 4 110; 21 634
patrons and collectors 23 371
pupils 17 266
works 17 265; 18 555
Hamadan 15 897, 898, 902, 910; 16 105, 372; 28 721
apadana 2 213
carpets 16 483
Ecbatana 15 901; 24 215; 28 719
Royal Palace 25 171
Gunbad-i 'Alaviyyan 16 128; 21 506
mausoleum of Esther and Mordechai 16 501
metalwork 16 369, 371
Hamaguchi, Yozō 14 99*; 17 293, 296
Hamah, Tell el- 1 881
Hamakita 17 21
Hamam, El 9 568
Hamama 16 486
Hamamatsu 17 389, 389
Hamamlıköy Church see DOLISHHAN CHURCH
Hamangia culture 6 344–5
Hamann, Johann Georg 14 99*
Hamann, Richard 2 366; 14 99–100*
Hamar 23 218, 219
Cathedral 26 593
hairstyles 1 285
Hedmarksmuseum 23 222, 231
mud 1 285
Hamath see HAMA
Hamaya, Hiroshi 14 100*
Hamazasp 14 36
Hambidge, Guy 23 566
Hambleden (Bucks) 6 161; 32 542
Hambledon Hill (Dorset) 21 42, 551; 25 504
Hambleton, Toni 25 703
Hambling, Maggi 14 100*
Hambridge, Jay 3 681
Hambruch, Paul 22 693
Hamburg 12 360, 379, 469; 14 100–103*
art forms and materials
altarpieces 12 400
architecture 12 376
books 21 636
collections 12 476
cupboards 12 423
drinking vessels 14 102
earthenwares 12 430
faience (ii) (ceramics) 25 310
flagons 12 444
furniture 7 166
gold 14 102–3*; 30 112
ketubbot 18 3
lacquer 18 614
painting 12 384, 390, 391, 394; 13 131; 29 666
pewter 12 452
pottery 4 176
silver 12 443, 449; 14 102–3*
tapestries 12 467; 30 319
auction houses 2 559
Bibliothek Warburg see LONDON → Warburg Institute
Chilehaus 10 698, 698; 14 644; 30 506
guilds 24 579
Hamburger Theatersammlung und Zentrum für Theaterforschung 7 407
Hauptbahnhof 25 857
Johanneum 12 376; 27 335, 335
Johanniskirche 11 714; 12 383
Kunstgewerbeschule 1 107; 28 178
Kunsthalle 2 560; 12 476, 481; 14 102; 23 394; 28 342; 29 376
Landesstelle für Bild Dokumentation 2 370
libraries 19 314
monument to Bismarck 29 566
Museum für Hamburgische Geschichte 28 178
Museum für Kunst und Gewerbe 9 703; 14 102
collections 4 71; 15 745; 30 332; 33 296
library 12 481
Museum für Völkerkunde 2 275; 21 265
collections 1 67; 9 64; 15 745; 23 302, 740; 29 240
exhibitions 23 740
Nikolaikirche 7 668; 13 204
Oberstrasse synagogue 17 548
Opera House 30 676, 677
Panoptikum 33 4
Petrikirche 12 383; 13 116, 161
PPS-Galerie 13 849
Rathaus 7 668; 12 416; 17 700; 18 889
St Katharina 14 101
St Michaelis 19 815
Stadttheater 29 843
State Opera House 30 684
Hamburg—cont.
urban planning 31 728
Zoo 33 699
Hamburg-Amerika 21 371
Hamburger, Bernard 27 838
Hamburger, Jurgen 29 117
Hamburger's Pottery 29 117
Hamburg-Wandsbeck, Reemtsma cigarette factory 14 644
Hamby, William 22 728
Hambye Abbey 22 220
Ham Che-gŏn 14 103*
Hamdanid, Sayf al-Dawla see SAYF AL-DAWLA, Ruler
Hamdi, Osman see OSMAN HAMDI
Hamdi Bey see OSMAN HAMDI
Hamdullah, Şeyh 1 473; 14 103*; 16 285; 23 641
Hameel, Alart du see ALART DU HAMEEL
Hämeenlinna 11 103
Castle 4 781; 11 89
church 11 91
Hamel, Théophile 4 542; 5 564; 14 103*; 22 38; 25 11
Hameln, Haus Rike 33 87
Hamels (Herts) 8 461
Hämelschenburg Schloss 33 88
Hamengkubuwono I, Sultan of Yogyakarta (reg 1755-92) 15 775, 802
Hamengkubuwono IX, Sultan of Yogyakarta (reg 1939-49) 33 538
Hamen y (Gómez de) León, Juan van der 14 16, 104–5*; 25 208
works 4 209; 14 104; 29 668
Hamer, Stefan 29 44
Hamerani (family) 20 921
Hamerani, Alberto 14 105
Hamerani, Anna Cecilia 12 260
Hamerani, Beatrice 14 105
Hamerani, Ermenegildo 14 105*; 20 921
Hamerani, Gioacchino 14 106
Hamerani, Giovanni 14 105*; 20 921
Hamerani, Johan Andreas 14 105
Hamerani, Ottone 14 106*; 20 922
works 20 922
Hamerlitz, F. 17 808
Hamersleben Church 7 303
Hamerton, Philip Gilbert 14 106*; 22 379; 23 886; 24 423
Hamesse, Adolphe 14 106
Hamesse, Georges 14 107*
Hamesse, Léon 14 107*
Hamesse, Paul 14 106–7*
Ham House see under RICHMOND (SURREY; UK)
Hamhŭng 18 328, 368
Hami 6 288, 308; 28 719, 720
tower 28 720
Hamid 15 366
Hamid Aytaç 23 695
Hamidouch 21 585
Hamill, Samuel W. 27 721
Hamilton (Ont.; Canada) 5 559
Art Gallery of Hamilton 5 591
Queen Victoria memorial 5 570
Hamilton (New Zealand), Waikito Museum of Art and History 23 75
Hamilton (Strathclyde; UK) 28 266
Hamilton (family; panorama exhibitors) 24 19
Hamilton (watchmakers) 7 448
Hamilton, Duchess of 28 246
Hamilton, Alexander, 10th Duke of Hamilton and 7th Duke of Brandon 14 107*
architecture 19 873; 33 217
collections 3 477; 33 345
paintings 4 330; 8 560
sculpture 2 558
Hamilton, Andrew 24 596
Hamilton, Catherine, Lady 14 16
Hamilton, Charles 12 130; 23 782

Hamilton, Cuthbert **13** 712; **14** 107*; **22** 352; **23** 437; **26** 59
Hamilton, David **12** 773; **14** 107–8*
assistants **26** 481; **33** 217
works **12** *773*; **25** 268, 619; **28** 229
Hamilton, E. **10** 377
Hamilton, E. A. **1** 151; **33** 408
Hamilton, Edward **33** 7
Hamilton, Emma **14** 445; **27** *119*
Hamilton, Franz de **14** 111
Hamilton, Gavin **10** 366; **13** 303; **14** 108–9*, 585; **22** 480; **26** 774; **27** 115
collaboration **2** 612
dealing **2** 164; **24** 845; **30** 268; **31** 244; **33** 453
excavations **31** 245
groups and movements **13** 297; **22** 736
patrons and collectors **8** 281; **24** 570; **25** 8; **29** 381; **30** 451; **33** 20
personal collection **4** 886; **6** 97
pupils **1** 649
reproductive prints by others **4** 331; **8** 267; **14** *109*; **21** 416; **32** 689
teachers **20** 806
works **4** 407; **14** 586; **22** 415; **28** 235
illustrated **8** 267
Hamilton, Gawen **14** 110*
personal collection **19** 643
reproductive prints by others **3** 259
works **19** *584*; **32** 378; **33** 377
Hamilton, George, 1st Earl of Orkney **8** 794
Hamilton, Gustavus **16** 15
Hamilton, Hector **29** 529
Hamilton, Hildegarde **3** 63
Hamilton, Hugh Douglas **14** 110*; **16** 15
copies **25** 843
patrons and collectors **33** 20
works **16** 14, 15
Hamilton (of Finnart), James (i) (*c*. 1496-1540) **14** 110–11*
Hamilton, James (ii) (1819-78) **14** 111*
Hamilton, James (*d* 1862) **14** 108; **26** 481
works **12** *773*
Hamilton, James, 1st Duke of Abercorn (*fl* 1835) **16** 25
Hamilton, James, 2nd Earl of Arran **28** 244
Hamilton, James, 3rd Marquess and 1st Duke of Hamilton **10** 861; **21** *509*; **22** 696
Hamilton, James, 8th Earl of Abercorn (*d* 1789) **6** 411; **28** 227
Hamilton, James Douglas-Hamilton, 5th Duke of *see* DOUGLAS-HAMILTON, JAMES, 5th Duke of Hamilton
Hamilton, James Douglas-Hamilton, 6th Duke of *see* DOUGLAS-HAMILTON, JAMES, 6th Duke of Hamilton
Hamilton, Johann Georg de **14** 111
Hamilton, John, Archbishop of St Andrews **27** 530
Hamilton, Karl Wilhelm de **2** 717; **14** 111
Hamilton, Peter **14** 113
Hamilton, Philipp Ferdinand de **14** 111*
Hamilton, Richard **10** 375; **14** 111–13*; **23** 21; **24** 229; **25** 628; **30** 749
collaboration **10** 258; **20** 607; **27** 215
collages **7** 558; **14** *112*
exhibitions **24** 229
Hamilton, Richard—cont.
groups and movements **10** 258; **15** 166; **19** 590; **25** 231
methods **7** 681; **25** 25, 624
models **19** 396; **25** 26
photographs **9** 494, *494*
prints **7** 576; **19** 493; **25** 596; **28** 300
pupils **5** 77; **18** 687
ready-mades **26** 51
Hamilton, R. J. Ozege **28** 692
Hamilton, R. W. **16** 550; **18** 20; **23** 153
works **16** *149*
Hamilton, Susan Euphemia, Duchess of Hamilton **1** 583
Hamilton, Thistle- *see* HAMILTON, KARL WILHELM DE
Hamilton, Thomas, sr (*fl* 1794) **14** 113
Hamilton, Thomas, jr (1784-1858) **14** 113*
groups and movements **13** 610; **22** 741
works **9** 723; **25** 268; **28** 156
Hamilton, William (*fl* 1750; woodworker) **14** 107
Hamilton, William (i) (1730-1803; collector) **2** 559; **7** 384; **10** 366, 642, 644; **13** 303, 304; **14** 113–14*, *114*; **25** 192; **33** 208
catalogues **14** 131
collections **2** 164; **10** 487; **13** 605
decorative works **14** 109; **24** 845
drawings **2** 40
gems **12** 266; **33** 385
glass **5** 337; **10** 320
paintings **17** 641
pottery **10** 365, 368; **11** 162; **13** 541; **14** 744; **26** 230
writings **10** 730; **13** *302*; **31** 28
Hamilton, William (ii) (1751-1801; painter) **10** 90; **14** 115*
patrons and collectors **8** 281
reproductive prints by others **3** 309; **5** 216; **20** 400; **29** 675; **31** 137
teachers **10** 372
Hamilton, William (*fl* 1787-8; architect) **10** 850
Hamilton, William (*fl* 1835; archaeologist) **31** 456
Hamilton, William (*fl* 1850; mason) **2** 758
Hamilton, William Alexander Douglas-Hamilton, Duke of *see* DOUGLAS-HAMILTON, WILLIAM ALEXANDER, Duke of Hamilton
Hamilton, William Richard (1777-1859) **5** 631
Hamilton Bible *see under* BIBLES → individual manuscripts
Hamilton-Chichester, Lady **20** 219
Hamilton Glass Co. **5** 583
Hamilton-Gordon, George William **30** 385
Hamilton & Inches **28** 262
Hamilton Palace (Lanarks) **2** 560; **12** 129; **28** 226
furniture **10** 291
interior decoration **28** 246, 248
Hamilton Xenophon, Master of the **2** 697; **11** 687; **20** 688–9*
Hamina **11** 90, 104
Hamipré **6** 481
Hamlin, A(lfred) D(wight) F(oster) **14** 115*
Hamlin, Samuel **31** 652
Hamlin, Talbot F(aulkner) **14** 115–16*
Hamm, Bartholomäus von *see* BARTHOLOMÄUS VON HAMM
Hammad, Mahmud **30** 177
Hammad ibn Buluggin, Ruler (*reg* 1015-28) (Hammadid) **25** 770
Hammadid, Hammad Ibn Buluggin, Ruler *see* HAMAD IBN BULUGGIN, Ruler
Hammam al-Sarakh **3** 376; **16** 148; **17** 656
Hammamet **31** 424
Villa Sebastian **31** 424
Hammam et-Turkman, Tell **21** 306
el-Hammamiya **9** 849; **10** 59
Hammam Lif Synagogue **17** 543
hammams *see* ISLAMIC → baths
Hamman (*fl* 1491) **2** 186
Hamman, Edouard (-Jean-Conrad) **14** 116*
Hammann, Jean Martin Herman **10** 559
Hammarsköld, Lorenzo **30** 119
Hammath-Tiberias
mosaics **17** 542, 558
synagogue **9** 562; **17** 542, 570
wall paintings **17** 556
Hamme, Guillaume van **14** 116*
Hamme, Jan Ariens van **10** 304; **30** 877
Hammel, Friedrich von **13** 218
Hammels Park **28** 905
Hammer, Armand **14** 116–17*; **18** 161
Hammer, Barbara **10** 689
Hammer, Friedrich **14** 117
Hammer, Hans **14** 117*; **25** 725; **29** 755, 757
Hammer, Marius **23** 236
Hammer, Victor **14** 116
Hammerbacher, Herta **14** 117–18*
hammer-beam roofs *see under* ROOFS → types
hammering
historical and regional traditions
Buddhism **17** 320
China **6** 830
Egypt, ancient **9** 818
Japan **17** 320
South America, Pre-Columbian **29** 211
uses
bronze **4** 851
coins *see* STRIKING
iron **21** 323
medals *see* STRIKING
metalwork **6** 830; **9** 818; **21** 322–3*, *324*; **29** 211
prints *see* PRINTS → techniques → repoussage
Hammermen's Incorporation of Edinburgh **28** 262
Hammer-Purgstall, J. von **16** 547
hammers **2** 448
Egypt, ancient **9** 814, 815
Prehistoric art **25** 493
South America, Pre-Columbian **29** 211
hammers, bush *see* BOUCHARDES
hammers, war *see* WAR HAMMERS
Hammersbøen, Vebjørn **23** 242
Hammershøi, Svend **14** *119*, 119–20*; **17** 720
Hammershøi, Vilhelm **14** 118–19*
groups and movements **7** 805; **11** 790
patrons and collectors **14** 572
pupils **14** 119
works **8** 735; **14** *119*
Hammersley, Frederick **19** 702
Hammerstein, Oscar, II **30** 687
Hammid, Alexander **10** 688
hammocks **13** 874, 875; **29** 194*; **32** 166
Hammond, Harmony **12** 217
Hammond Lucy, George **13** 541
Hammonds, David (*b* 1943) **1** 445
Hammons, David **3** 338
Hammuda Pasha **17** 730
Hammudid, Yahya I *see* YAHYA I, Ruler
Hammurabi, King of Babylon (*reg* 1792-1750 BC) **3** 11; **29** 614
Hammurabi's Code of Laws stele *see* CODE OF HAMMURABI
Hamnett, Katharine **7** 482; **9** 294; **23** 549
Hamnett, Nina **14** 120*; **23** 437; **28** 808
works **11** *437*
Hamon, Jean-Louis **12** 487, 810; **14** 120–21*; **22** 745
Hamon, Kristóf **5** 81
Hamont Church **13** 110
Hamoudi, Jamil **16** 2
Hampaté Ba, Amadou **1** 373
Hampe, Karl Friedrich **12** 393
Hampel, Sigmund Walter **28** 670
Hampi **14** 121–5*, *122*, *124*; **15** *294*
ceramics **6** 918
Hazararama Temple **15** 533
Ramachandra Temple complex **14** 124–5; **15** 329
stucco **29** 824
temples **15** 329
Tiruvengalanatha Temple **15** 331
urban planning **15** 409
Vijayanagara **14** 121–5, *122*, *124*
fortifications **21** 590
palace **23** 817
Ramachandra Temple complex **22** 516
sculpture
bronze **15** 533
colossal statues **15** 533
Virupaksha Temple **14** 122–3; **15** 330, 533, 648
Vitthala Temple complex **14** 123; **15** 330, *330*, 533
Garuda shrine **15** 331, *331*
Hampp, John **29** 506
Hampton Court Palace (Middx) **4** 786; **6** 60; **10** *225*, 229, 232, 275, 276, 360; **14** 76, 126–8*, *127*; **19** 568; **22** 717; **23** 466; **30** 871; **33** 199, 397, *397*
architectural decorations **30** 502
Ballcourt **3** 118
cartoons **11** 679
catalogues **3** 81
ceramics **9** 28
chimney-pieces **6** 604
chimneys **4** 769
collections **8** 186; **10** 363, 368; **11** 361
Fountain Court **8** 65
Fountain Garden *see* Privy Garden
fountains **8** 273
frames **11** 426
frescoes **32** 359
furniture **10** 291, 292
Gallery **23** 253
gardens **4** 875; **12** 114, 126, 127, 128; **19** 622; **33** 199, 257
Great Hall **10** 229; **14** 75, *126*; **22** 717; **23** 809
hangings **16** 760
hunting scenes **29** 424
interior decoration **10** 274
ironwork **14** 856
maze **18** 585
orangeries **23** 470
paintings **9** 14; **26** 283
animal **4** 232
architectural **29** 767
copies **10** 156
genre **14** 291; **27** 643
history **2** 340, 558; **14** 144, 849; **16** 659; **17** *704*; **20** 311; **22** 13; **29** 801; **31** 35; **33** 387
landscape **8** 495; **31** 71
mythological **3** 844; **12** 279; **29** 803; **32** 718
portraits **2** 162, 558; **7** 426; **8** 4; **12** 515, 750; **13** 26, 240; **19** 712; **23** 467; **24** 23, 356; **28** 313; **29** 804; **31** 37; **32** 244; **33** 387
religious **5** 384; **14** 147; **23** 883; **24** 419; **26** 322; **27** 496; **29** 800, 803; **31** 205; **32** 107, 358
satire **29** 799
still-lifes **14** 755
Hampton Court Palace (Middx)—cont.
porcelain cabinet **7** 166
portraits **21** 355
Privy Garden **10** 342; **16** 59
restoration **7** 729
Royal Collection **29** 717
sculpture **7** 298; **10** 261, 264; **19** 250; **20** 116
staircases **29** 522
tapestries **30** 322, 331; **33** 306
Textile Conservation Centre **7** 742
tiles **10** 273; **30** 878
weapons **9** 31
William III apartments **14** 420
Wolsey's Closet **10** 271
Hampton in Arden **23** 398
Hampton & Sons **22** 744
Hampton University (VA) **1** 442
Hamrath **20** 863
Hamrin region **1** *849*; **14** 128–9*; **21** *267*, 268
faience (i) (glass) **1** 878
houses **14** *128*
pottery **21** 270, 306
Hamsah, T. R., & Yeang Sdn Bhd **20** 169
Haṃsavatī *see* PEGU
Hamsíková, Květa **8** 420
Ham Spray **5** 881
Hamsun, Knut **20** 591
Hamwih **2** 65, 83
Ham Yun-dŏk **14** 129*
Hamza al-Isfahani **16** 304
Hamza ibn Muhammad al-ʿAlawi **33** 482
Hamza Mirza (Safavid) **33** 626
Hamzič, Mihajlo **8** 178; **25** 340
Han (Chinese) **6** 616
Han (Native American Indian) **22** 546
Han, Baltasar **17** 657
Han, Dou Wan *see* DOU WAN
Han, Herman **25** 104
Han, Hermann (1574-1627/8) *see* HAHN, HERMAN
Han, Liu Sheng *see* LIU SHENG
Han, Oscar **28** 788
Han, Ulrich **22** 369
Hana **17** 836
Hana, H. **27** 634
Hanabusa Itchō **14** 129*; **17** 797
Hanabusa Ittei *see* UTAGAWA KUNISADA I
Hanabusa school **14** 129
Hanada, Kiyoteru **14** 129–30*; **23** 385
Hanak, Anton **2** 831; **14** 130*; **31** 755
groups and movements **14** 33
pupils **33** 386
restorations **23** 425
teachers **14** 365
works **2** 803; **14** 628
Hanamaki **17** 373
Hanamkonda **14** 130–31*; **15** *294*, 534
reliefs **15** *538*
sculpture **15** 538
'Thousand-pillared' Temple **15** 328, 538
sculpture **15** *538*
Han Aneybe **21** 560
hanap covers **13** 168
Hanap de la Vigne et des Métiers **10** 771
Hanau
Deutsches Goldschmiedehaus **12** 450, 451
gold **12** 450, 451
jewellery **12** 455; **17** 526
silver **12** 448, 449
Staatliche Zeichenakademie **12** 448, 455, 479
Hanau, Princess of **17** 834
Hanau Faience Factory **12** 430, 431; **14** 131*
Hanawa **17** 355

Hanaya, Kanbei 22 445
Hanazono, Emperor (reg 1308-18) 11 856; 17 225, 228; 29 66
Hanbei see KUSUMI MORIKAGE
Hanbei Shōkōsai 17 288
Hanbei Yoshida see YOSHIDA HANBEI
Hanbijutsu (Anti-art Society) 17 207
Hanbury (Staffs), St Werburgh 1 517
tomb of John de Hanbury 1 517
Hancarville, Pierre François Hugues, Baron d' 10 642; 14 131*
patrons and collectors 14 114; 33 208
sponsors 31 245
works 2 164; 22 739; 24 273; 26 230
Hanchi 6 740
Han Cho see HAN ZHUO
Hanch'ŏn see YI CHAE
Han Chong-ju 18 375
Han Chong-yu 18 52
Hancı, Abdurrahman 5 633
Hancock (MA) 28 541
Round Barn 28 539, 540
Hancock, C. F. 22 28
Hancock, James 29 116
Hancock, John 25 655
Hancock, John, Insurance Company 4 476
Hancock, Joseph 10 331; 28 577
Hancock, Robert 6 93; 10 346; 14 131–2*
pupils 13 614
works 10 309; 33 377, 377
Hancock, Samuel 24 580
Hand, John Oliver 6 78
Hand A see PAREMENT DE NARBONNE, MASTER OF THE
Handan 6 663
palace 6 679
Handarbetets Vänner 30 114, 115
handbooks see MANUALS
Hand C see HOURS OF THE HOLY GHOST, Master of the
hand-drums see under DRUMS → types
Hand E see LIMBOURG, DE
Handel, George Frideric 5 907; 7 446; 13 229; 17 476; 23 637; 29 564; 30 675
HANDICO see TANZANIAN HANDICRAFTS MARKETING CORPORATION
Handke, Johann Christoph 8 391; 23 425
handkerchiefs 8 35, 36
Handler (family) 29 76
Handler, Ferdinánd see HANDLER, NÁNDOR
Handler, Jakab 14 132*
Handler, József 14 132
Handler, Nándor 14 132*, 889
handles, brush see BRUSH HANDLES
Handley-Read, Charles 14 132–3*
Handley-Read, Lavinia 14 132–3*
Handmann, (Jakob) Emanuel 11 766; 14 133*
hand mirrors see under MIRRORS → types
Handōgame kiln 17 811
Han Dōsei see FAN DAOSHENG
handpins see under PINS → types
hand-puppets see under PUPPETS → types
Handschick, Brigitte 14 133*
Handschuh, Andreas 11 731
Handscomb, Terrence 23 62
handscrolls see under SCROLLS → types
hand stencilling see under STENCILLING → types
hand-tinted prints see under PRINTS → types
hand weaving see under WEAVING → types
handwriting see SCRIPTS
Handy, Levin 4 628
Han dynasty see:
GAODI, Emperor
WENDI, Emperor
XUANDI, Emperor
see also CHINA → periods → Han period
Handyside 13 619
Hanedoes, L. 26 482
Hänel, Karl Moritz see HAENEL, KARL MORITZ
Hanequin de Bruselas (1448-70) 9 748; 14 134–5*; 27 703
assistants 1 599
pupils 13 756
works 8 253; 13 69; 14 578; 31 90, 92
Hanequin de Bruselas (fl 1448-70) 14 135
Hanequín de Cuéllar 29 265
Hanequin de Egass see HANEQUIN DE BRUSELAS (1448-70)
Hanette (family) 4 692
Hanfstaengl, Franz (Seraph) 14 135*; 24 312, 659, 661; 26 232
Hanga geijutsu 24 437
Hangal temples 15 325, 326
Han Gan 6 799, 816; 14 135–6*
works 14 136
Hangard-Maugé, E. I. 26 234
hangars 11 771, 771
hanging gardens see under GARDENS → types
hangings 3 483, 485; 11 54; 30 774; 31 681
historical and regional traditions
Africa 1 307
Anatolia, ancient 9 490
Angola 2 87
Austria 2 825
Bulgaria 5 161, 162
Burma 5 249
England 10 274, 275; 19 4, 5
France 3 484, 484; 19 3
Germany 12 412
India, Republic of 15 176
Indian subcontinent 10 I2; 15 636, 643, 646, 647, 675, 723
Indonesia 15 794, 812*
Italy 16 760
Netherlands, the 20 365
Norway 23 239, 240
Rome, ancient 27 114
Scotland 28 265
South Africa 29 104
Spain 19 3; 29 298
Sumatra 15 794
Ukraine 31 564
materials
appliqué 5 249
cotton 2 87; 15 675, 794
damask 10 274
embroidery 15 675; 16 760
felt 10 873, 875
leather 19 2, 3, 5, 5
silk 15 675
textiles 15 636
wool 5 249
types
bed 15 176; 31 658
kalaga 5 248
see also BANNERS
hanging scrolls see under SCROLLS → types
Hang Trong see HANOI
Hanguk Kogohagoe (Korean Archaeological Society) 18 382
Hanguk Kogohakpo 18 382
Hanguk Kogohak Yŏn'guhoe (Society of Korean Archaeological Studies) 18 382
Hanguranketa 29 450
Hangzhou 6 615; 7 151, 153, 159; 14 136–7*
calligraphy 6 753
caves 30 443
Feilai feng 5 112; 6 720
Fenghuang Temple 6 677
jade 7 10
kilns 6 892, 894
lacquer 7 18
Lingyin Temple 23 773
Liuhe ta 6 655
National Academy of Art 7 149
paper 7 116
porcelain 4 173; 6 898
prints 7 118, 119
seals 7 131
shrine of Yue Fei 28 638
Six Harmonies Pagoda see Liuhe ta
tomb of Yue Fei 6 726; 7 99
tombs 6 699
urban planning 6 664
Wu family house 6 688, 689
Zhejiang Provincial Museum 6 772; 14 823
Hanhausen, J. 17 832
Han Ho 14 137*
works 18 330, 330
Hanina 17 557
haniwa see under SCULPTURE → types
Hanjirō Sakamoto see SAKAMOTO, HANJIRŌ
Han Kan see HAN GAN
Hankar, Paul 14 137–8*; 28 482
collaboration 10 735; 14 604
groups and movements 2 563; 3 579
house 3 550
pupils 28 899
staff 14 106
teachers 3 44, 898
works 3 550, 586; 10 735
Hanko Kajita see KAJITA, HANKO
Hankō Okada see OKADA HANKŌ
Hankou 6 621
Hanks, Nancy 31 663
Hanley (Staffs) 29 495
Hanlin Painting Academy 6 635, 816, 817
Hanly, Patrick 2 706; 14 138*; 23 61
Hanmer, Thomas 13 324
Hann, Sebastian 14 138*; 15 7; 26 720; 28 649
Hanna, Denis O'D. 16 42
Hanna, Dennis 23 69
Hanna, Henry Bathurst 15 742
Hanna, Leonard C(olton) 7 429; 14 138–9*; 31 667
Hannaert, Johannes 14 42
Hannaford, Samuel 7 326
Hannas, Marx Anton 33 359
Hannay, Arthur 7 245
Hannema, D. 4 614; 27 231
Hanneman, Adriaen 14 41, 139–40*; 22 844; 26 38
groups and movements 14 41
patrons and collectors 15 40
reproductive prints by others 8 495
works 14 139; 17 645
Hannequin, Gilles 31 846
Hannes, Pierre 11 355
Hannibal, Martin 8 453
Hanning, Gerald 19 535
Hanning, Tony 2 764
Hanno, (Andreas Friedrich) Wilhelm von 14 140*; 18 101; 22 319
Hannon, Edouard 5 24
Hannon, Théo 7 245; 28 921
Hannong (family) 19 734
Hannong, Balthasar 29 753
Hannong, Charles François 11 605, 730; 29 753
Hannong, Joseph-Adam 11 606, 730; 29 753
works 11 606
Hannong, Paul Antoine 11 606, 609, 730; 29 753
Hannong, Pierre-Antoine 16 739; 29 753
Hannosset (family) 3 600
Hannover 12 360, 379; 14 140–42*, 141
architecture 4 787
Christuskirche 4 787
faience (ii) (ceramics) 12 430
Hannoverscher Anzeiger building 14 644
Hauptbahnhof 25 854
museums
Historisches Museum am Hohn Ufer 12 380
Kestner Gesellschaft 28 119
Kestner-Museum 10 93; 14 142; 17 922
Kunstgewerbemuseum 14 230
Museum für Kunst und Wissenschaft 14 212
Niedersächsisches Landesmuseum 14 142; 17 922
Provinzialmuseum see Niedersächsisches Landesmuseum
Sprengel Museum 14 142; 18 114
Opera House (1845-52) 25 871
Opernhaus (1748) 30 676
painting 12 394
Rathaus 14 615
silver 12 446
tapestries 30 324
Technische Hochschule 14 230
Theater Leineschloss 25 871
urban planning 18 883
Hannover, Abstrakten see ABSTRAKTEN HANNOVER
Hannover, Emil 8 761; 14 572
Hannover Gospels see under GOSPEL BOOKS → individual manuscripts
Hannoversche Kunstblätter 24 421
Hannoversch Münden, Eberlein Museum 9 692
Hannss von Esslingenn see BÖBLINGER, HANS VON (II)
Hannukah lamps see under LAMPS → types
Hano (AZ) 22 609
Hanoi 29 225; 32 468, 469
Art School 32 492
Central History Museum of Vietnam 29 240
Cultural Palace 32 476
Dien Huu see One-pillar Temple
Ecole des Beaux-Arts de l'Indochine de Hanoi 32 480, 482, 492
Great Church 32 476, 476
kilns 32 484
Lotus Temple see One-pillar Temple
mausoleum of Ho Chi Minh 32 476, 476
One-pillar Temple 32 472, 472
prints 32 481
Thanh Loi Hotel 32 476
urban planning 32 477
Van Mieu 32 474, 474–5
Hanoot, Jan 4 925
Hanoteau, Hector 8 57
Hanover (Germany) see HANNOVER
Hanover (House of) 12 476; 14 142–3*
Hanover, Adelaide, Queen of Great Britain see ADELAIDE, Queen of Great Britain
Hanover, Albert, Prince of Saxe-Coburg-Gotha see ALBERT, Prince of Saxe-Coburg-Gotha
Hanover, Alfred, Duke of Edinburgh and Duke of Saxe-Coburg-Gotha see ALFRED, Duke of Saxe-Coburg-Gotha
Hanover, Anna, Princess of Orange see ANNA OF HANOVER, Princess of Orange
Hanover, Arthur, Duke of Connaught (1850-1942) 15 407
Hanover, Augusta, Princess of Wales (1719-72) 6 410; 10 378; 12 600; 18 4
Hanover, Augustus Frederick, Duke of Sussex 10 753; 12 263; 14 166, 275, 285; 22 86
Hanover, Caroline Elizabeth, Princess 21 148
Hanover, Caroline Mathilda, Queen of Denmark and Norway see CAROLINE MATHILDA, Queen of Denmark and Norway
Hanover, Charlotte, Princess see CHARLOTTE, Queen of Belgium
Hanover, Charlotte, Queen of Great Britain see CHARLOTTE, Queen of Great Britain
Hanover, Edward, Duke of Kent 3 72; 14 67
Hanover, Edward Augustus, Duke of York 7 469; 8 493; 25 630; 33 217
paintings 4 845
Hanover, Elizabeth, Princess 9 26; 24 57
Hanover, Ernest Augustus, Duke of Cumberland see ERNEST AUGUSTUS, King of Hannover
Hanover, Ernest Augustus, King of Hannover see ERNEST AUGUSTUS, King of Hannover
Hanover, Frederica, Duchess of York 6 402; 28 42
Hanover, Frederick (Louis), Prince of Wales (1707-51) 13 837; 14 142–3*; 21 148
architecture 6 410; 19 585, 619
barges 3 232, 232
catalogues 18 143; 32 379
decorative works 8 149; 17 902; 26 182; 28 486
engravings 20 144
frames 11 426, 427
furniture 10 294
gardens 18 4
gold 33 158
interior decoration 10 378
paintings 8 501; 9 397; 13 229; 19 645; 21 148; 24 633; 33 685
salts 27 641
silver 10 332; 29 432
silver-gilt 33 158
Hanover, Frederick Augustus, Duke of York 4 882; 5 286; 14 681; 24 22; 33 447
Hanover, George I, Elector of Hannover see GEORGE I, King of Great Britain
Hanover, George I, King of Great Britain see GEORGE I, King of Great Britain
Hanover, George II, Elector of Hannover see GEORGE III, King of Great Britain
Hanover, George II, King of Great Britain see GEORGE II, King of Great Britain
Hanover, George III, Elector and King of Hannover see GEORGE III, King of Great Britain
Hanover, George III, King of Great Britain see GEORGE III, King of Great Britain
Hanover, George IV, King of Great Britain see GEORGE IV, King of Great Britain
Hanover, George IV, King of Hannover see GEORGE IV, King of Great Britain
Hanover, Henry Frederick, Duke of Cumberland 25 630
Hanover, Louise, Princess 4 220; 5 590

Hanover, Mary, Duchess of Gloucester 3 489
Hanover, Victoria, Queen of Great Britain see VICTORIA, Queen of Great Britain
Hanover, William, Duke of Clarence see WILLIAM IV, King of Great Britain
Hanover, William Augustus, Duke of Cumberland 14 142–4*; 27 715; 33 221
  carpets 10 675
  etchings 27 716
  metalwork 4 62
  paintings 12 646
  teachers 11 172
Hanover, William Frederick, Duke of Gloucester 3 490; 14 275; 19 730
Hanover, William Henry, Duke of Gloucester 12 263
Hanover, William IV, King of Great Britain see WILLIAM IV, King of Great Britain
Hanover County Courthouse (VA) 18 887
Hanrath, J. W. 10 418
Hanrath, T. 8 206
Hanroku Saeki see SAEKI HANROKU
Hans, Alfred 3 110
Hans, Jean 8 661
Hans, Master 13 262; 19 111
Hansa (Baltic) see HANSEATIC LEAGUE
HANSA (Bolivia) 4 260
Han Sai Por 28 774
Hansan Temple 18 267
Hanschuher, Christian 8 880
Hanseatic League 11 108; 13 56; 19 568
Hanselaere, Pieter van 4 877
Hansen, Al 2 698; 24 407
Hansen, Anna see SYBERG, ANNA
Hansen, Carl Martin 7 807
Hansen, C(hristian) F(rederick) 8 719; 14 151–4*
  architecture 8 726, 727
    chapels 27 168
    churches 8 727; 11 768; 14 149, 153; 24 549; 30 764
    country houses 8 727
    government buildings 18 887
  assistants 14 497
  furniture 8 744
  groups and movements 13 611
  paintings 14 152
  pupils 13 693; 14 149
  restorations by others 4 184
Hansen, (Hans) Christian 13 358; 14 149–50*
  groups and movements 13 612
  pupils 14 150
  teachers 14 497
  works 13 348, 359
Hansen, (Carl Christian) Constantin 8 735, 746; 11 473; 14 154–5*; 30 766
Hansen, Emil see NOLDE, EMIL
Hansen, Ernst 10 482
Hansen, Frida 22 540; 23 239; 30 326
  works 23 240
Hansen, Fritz 8 746
  works 8 747
Hansen, Hans 8 751
Hansen, Hans Munk 4 184; 31 776
Hansen, Heinrich 8 754; 11 467; 14 542
Hansen, Jens 23 72
Hansen, Johannes 8 759
Hansen, Karl-Heinz see HANSEN-BAHIA
Hansen, Kristian Møhl 8 756
Hansen, Oskar 14 155*, 219; 17 448
Hansen, Peter Marius 8 735; 14 155*; 33 595
Hansen, Ragnar 2 766
Hansen, Svend Wiig see WIIG HANSEN, SVEND
Hansen, Theophilus (Edvard) 2 808, 814; 14 150–51*; 19 522; 24 817
  architecture 2 786, 787; 4 833; 28 850, 859; 32 437
    concert halls 1 125
    exchanges 10 669
    government buildings 2 787; 13 237, 238; 14 150; 25 268
    monuments 18 517
    museums 4 106
    observatories 23 340
    palaces 2 787, 808
    public buildings 13 348; 17 719
    universities 14 149
  assistants 32 760
  collaboration 2 786, 802; 11 319; 14 364; 18 517; 32 437
  groups and movements 13 612; 26 190; 28 838
  patrons and collectors 14 11
  pupils 2 711
  staff 17 858; 33 677
  teachers 14 497
Hansen, Vilhelm 8 759
Hansen-Bahia 10 574
Hansen Reistrup, Karl 17 720
Hansen von Ulm 13 188
Hansenzhai (Xi'an) 7 89
Hansford, Sidney Howard 14 155*
Hansfstaengl, Edgar 14 135
Hanshan 6 785; 7 3
Hanshan Deqing 5 112
Han-shan Te-ch'ing see HANSHAN DEQING
Hansi Fort 15 340
Han Si-gak 14 156*
Hansins, Andries 4 161
Hans Maler see KNIEPER, HANS
Hans Maler von Bruneck 27 756
Hansman, J. 28 537
Hans of Cologne see BESSER, HANS
Hansom, Charles Francis 1 151; 14 156
Hansom, Edward Joseph 14 156
Hansom, Joseph Aloysius 4 85; 10 235; 12 599; 14 156*; 25 268; 31 240
Hansom, Joseph Stanislaus 14 156
Hanson, Alan 23 739
Hanson, Duane 6 9; 14 156–7*; 24 686, 687; 27 872
Hanson, Francis 16 888
Hansøn, Johan 23 224
Hanson, Louise 23 739
Hanson, Norman Leonard 1 319; 8 82; 14 157*; 17 603; 20 8, 484
Hanson, Tomkin, Finkelstein 14 157*; 29 106
Hansŏng New Palace 18 275
Han Sŏn-guk 14 156
Hanssen 14 87
Hans Sigersdorfer 23 311
Hansson, Holger 20 630; 31 767
Hansson, Rolf 30 82
Hanss von Cöln see CÖLN, HANS VON
Hanss von Gratz see NIESENBERGER, HANS
Hans van Antwerpen 10 326; 22 896
Hans von Ache 29 758
Hans von Böblingen see BÖBLINGEN, HANS VON, I
Hans von Burghausen 14 157–8*
  works 4 777; 12 365; 13 58; 18 723, 724; 27 660; 32 821
Hans von Cöln see CÖLN, HANS VON
Hans von Elchingen 33 745
Hans von Ess(e)lingen (i) see BÖBLINGEN, HANS VON, I
Hans von Esslingen (ii) see BÖBLINGER, HANS, II
Hans von Freiburg 20 566; 21 530
Hans von Geismar 14 158*
Hans von Gmünd 13 107
Hans von Judenburg 2 799; 4 286; 14 158–9*; 20 764
Hans von Liechtenstein 32 454
Hans von Nussdorf 30 136
Hans von Reutlingen 1 5; 26 147; 29 333
Hans von Stetheimer see HANS VON BURGHAUSEN
Hans von Tübingen 20 764
Hans von Worms 14 159*
Hantai, Simon 2 545; 11 551; 14 159–60*; 30 23
Hantanpo 7 114, 116
Hanthawadi see PEGU
Hanto, Bishop of Augsburg 25 743
Hantumhuizen Church 22 819
Hanula, Josef 28 853
Hanušová, Blanka 8 421
Hanusz 25 111
Hanuš z Olomouce 14 160*
Hanway, Jonas 4 353
Hanwell, William 29 835
  works 29 836
Hanwell Asylum 2 658
Hanwŏndang see KIM KWAN-P'IL
Han Yŏng-un 18 332
Hanytkiewicz, A. 19 155
Han Yu-dong 18 60
Han Zhixun see HON CHI-FUN
Han Zhuo 6 797, 817
Hao 33 660
Hao Hui 33 500
Hao Tianguan 6 723
Haozous, Allan see HOUSER, ALLAN
Haozous, Robert 14 801; 22 665
Hapiru see HABIRU
Happart, Johannes Philips 11 872
Happel, Eberhard Werner 19 662
Happenings 10 416; 15 869; 17 805; 22 279, 381; 24 403, 407; 25 231
  Argentina 2 401
  Bolivia 4 264
  collections 29 16
  commentaries 8 609
  France 10 490; 21 698
  Mexico 21 390
  Sweden 30 81
  United States of America 8 902; 23 397; 27 668
haptics 26 369
Hapuseneb 9 826
Hapwood, Joseph 14 863
Haq, Commodore 17 806
Haqla Mosque 16 215
Hara, Brian 20 162
Hara, Hiromu 14 160–61*
Hara, Hiroshi 14 161*; 17 92
  pupils 33 488
  works 1 737; 17 91, 92
Hara, Kiyoshi 17 266
Hara, Sankei 14 161*
Hara, Tomitarō 17 424
Harache, Pierre, I (c. 1630-1700) 10 330; 14 161*; 19 593
  patrons and collectors 6 116
  pupils 24 22
  works 10 329; 14 856; 28 740
Harache, Pierre, II (fl 1698-1717) 14 161
Harada, Naojirō 17 204; 30 256
Haradum see KHIRBET ED-DINIYEH
Haraha Shiva Temple 15 260
Harai, Shin 17 402
Hara Jihei see UNKOKU TŌGAN
Harakta 16 486
Harald 26 639
Harald Bluetooth, King of Denmark see HARALD I, King of Denmark
Harald I, King of Denmark (reg c. 950-85) 8 758; 17 473; 27 166, 167; 32 513, 517
Harald III, King of Norway (reg 1047-66) 23 601
Haranee see QASR KHARANA
Haranger, Pierre-Maurice, Abbé 14 162*
Harappa 8 269; 14 162*; 15 192, 193, 246, 264, 408; 23 797, 798
  Archaeological Museum 23 804
  architecture 4 793
  bronze 4 853
  figurines 15 213, 418, 421
  gems 12 252
  Granary 15 246
  ivory 15 695
  ivory-carvings 16 798
  pottery 15 685
  sculpture 15 417–18, 747
  seals 15 420, 747
Harappa civilization see INDUS CIVILISATION
Harar 1 379, 379; 10 567, 568
Harare 1 413
  architecture 1 319
  Batanai Gardens 33 678
  BAT Workshop School 33 680
  National Gallery 33 678, 679, 680
  Regional School of Art and Design 33 680
  University Land Management Building 33 678
  Zanu-PF Headquarters 33 678
  ZIMCOR Building 33 678
Harari, Ralph (Andrew) 14 162–3*; 16 372; 17 432
Harasûski, Apalinary 3 529; 14 163*
Haraszty, István 14 897
Haraucourt, Edmond 28 423, 750
al-Harawi 13 812
Hara Yōyūsai 17 399
Harb 2 262
Härbel, Nikolaus Friedrich 6 572; 20 839; 27 574
Harbeson, Benjamin, & Son 31 653
Harbison, C. 15 91
Harbiyya 16 150
Harbledown (Kent), St Nicholas 10 323
Harbord, William 4 758
Harbottle, E. H. 10 674
Harbour Island 3 59
harbours 8 154
Harbrecht, Isaac 7 439
Harcourt, Comtesse d' 24 786
Harcourt, Duchesse d' 11 595
Harcourt, Geoffrey D. 32 756
Harcourt, George Simon, 2nd Earl Harcourt 8 95; 14 163; 20 569
Harcourt, Guillaume d' see GUILLAUME D'HARCOURT
Harcourt, Simon, 1st Earl Harcourt of Stanton Harcourt and 2nd Earl Nuneham 14 163–4*
hardboard see under BOARDS → types
Harde and Short 30 507
Hardegg (family) 3 488
Hardegger, August 14 164*
Hardenberg, Friedrich Leopold von 22 540
Hardenberg, Lambertus 22 847
Hardenberg, Torben 8 753
Hardenbergh, Henry Janeway 14 164–5*
  restorations by others 14 174
  teachers 19 346
  works 2 216; 4 474; 14 788; 23 41
Harder, Charles M. 31 640
Harder, Hans 2 799
Härder, Johann Christian 26 530
Harders, Claus 22 204
Harderwijk 22 813
  Grote Kerk 22 820
Hardham (W. Sussex), St Botolph 2 74; 26 650, 654, 657
Hardie, Martin 10 367, 377; 14 165*; 25 627
Hardin, Helen 14 165*; 22 596
Harding, Chester 14 165–6*; 29 683; 33 345
Harding, G. R. 28 426
Harding, J. 14 166
Harding, J(ames) D(uffield) 14 166*
  patrons and collectors 23 322
  pupils 4 756; 8 830; 27 350
  works 5 827; 19 484; 25 587, 592, 626
Harding, Morris 3 537
Harding, Stephen, Abbot of Cîteaux 4 6; 7 348, 352; 26 669
Harding, Thomas 7 236
Harding, Valentine 30 411
Harding, Wilbert 2 152
Hardinge, Henry, 1st Viscount 8 830
Hardingstone (Northants), Eleanor cross 8 197, 198; 13 81
Hardiot, Michelin 31 384
Hardivilliers, Noël 11 630, 633
Hardman, John 3 884; 8 202; 10 335, 343; 14 167*; 25 712, 714, 715, 716, 717; 29 506
  groups and movements 13 207
  works 4 85; 10 343; 19 614; 27 538; 29 766
Hardman, John, & Co. 4 88, 826; 9 321; 10 343; 25 717
Hardorf, Rudolf 3 288
Hardorff, Gerdt 17 853; 21 540; 23 394; 27 337; 29 376
Hardouin, Michel 20 288
Hardouin, Raphaël 20 293
Hardouin Mansart, Jules see MANSART, JULES HARDOUIN
Hardouin Mansart de Jouy, Jean see MANSART DE JOUY, JEAN HARDOUIN
Hardouin Mansart de Sagonne, Jacques see MANSART DE SAGONNE, JACQUES HARDOUIN
Hardoy, Jorge 2 397; 4 315; 15 886; 29 321
hard-paste porcelain see under PORCELAIN → types
hardstones 14 167–72*
  historical and regional traditions
    Antilles, Lesser 29 198–9
    Aztec 2 908; 21 243
    Buddhism 7 91; 22 787; 28 582
    Byzantine 8 199; 9 623, 657; 14 170; 15 I
    Carolingian 14 170
    Cedrosan Saladoid culture 29 198–9
    Central Asia, Western 6 273
    Chavín culture 29 185
    Chimú 29 186
    China 6 632; 7 27, 88–91*, 107, 112
    Coclé culture 29 154
    Costa Rica 9 679–80; 29 153–4
    Cupisnique 29 185
    Czech Republic 8 417, 417–18*
    Ecuador 29 155
    Egypt, ancient 9 814*; 10 3; 14 169
    England 10 346
    France 9 30; 11 632, 635–6*; 12 830–31
    Germany 7 91; 8 201; 12 445, 457–9, 458, 461–2*
    Gran Nicoya culture 29 153, 154
    Greece, ancient 13 599; 14 169
    Inca 29 186
    Indian subcontinent 7 91; 15 697–9*
    Ireland 32 530
    Italy 14 170, 170–71; 16 690, 724, 744*, 746–8*
    Java 29 227
    Longshan culture 7 107
    Manteño culture 29 155
    Maya 29 153
    Mesoamerica, Pre-Columbian 1 713; 21 218, 240–44*

hardstones
historical and regional traditions—cont.
Mesopotamia **14** 169
Mixtec **21** 243
Moche (culture) **29** 186
Mongolia **21** 875, 877
Nepal **22** *787*
Nubia **23** *286*
Olmec **21** 241; **29** 154
Portugal **25** 314
Prehistoric art **7** 107
Recuay culture **29** 185
Rome, ancient **14** 169–70
Russia **27** 427–8*
Siberia **14** 172
South America, Pre-Columbian **9** 679–80; **29** 152–4*, 155*, 184–6*, 198–9
South-east Asia **29** 227
Tarascan **30** 341
Tiahuanaco **29** 185
Tibet **7** 91; **28** *582*
Viking **32** *530*
techniques
abrasion **21** 241
carving **14** 168–9*
cutting **14** *168*, 168–9*
drilling **21** 241; **29** 153
polishing **21** 241
Reliefmosaik **12** 459
sawing **21** 241
Zellenmosaik **12** 458
uses
adzes **29** 227
altars **12** 461
amulets **10** 3
cabinets (ii) (furniture) **12** 421, 461
caskets **14** *170*
chalices **2** *378*
crosses **8** *199*, *201*
crowns **23** *286*
furniture **12** 462, 831; **16** 724, 746
icons **9** 623; **15** I
inlays **7** 91; **12** 445
interior decoration **12** 462
jewellery **6** 273; **7** 107, 112; **10** 346; **21** 877; **22** *787*
medals **16** 690
mosaics **22** 154
pendants (jewellery) **29** 154
pietre dure **14** 168–9
plaques **6** *632*; **7** *27*
pommels (swords) **2** 452
shrines (i) (cult) **32** *530*
snuff bottles **7** 91
snuff-boxes **11** 632; **12** 457–9, *458*
sword grips **2** 452
thumb rings **21** 875
trumpets **28** *582*
vases **11** 635, 636; **14** 170, 171
see also GEMS
Hardtmuth, Joseph **2** 785; **19** 55, 338
Hardwick, Bess of *see* TALBOT, ELIZABETH, Countess of Shrewsbury
Hardwick, Elizabeth *see* TALBOT, ELIZABETH, Countess of Shrewsbury
Hardwick, Philip **14** 173*
collaboration **9** 58; **19** 573; **25** 854
groups and movements **26** 190
pupils **9** 684; **33** 449
staff **24** 307
works **2** 324; **3** 885; **19** 506, 510
Hardwick, Philip Charles **14** 173, 786
Hardwick, Thomas **14** 172–3*
collaboration **25** 637
pupils **14** 173; **31** 466
works **18** 886; **28** 875
Hardwicke, Philip Yorke, 1st Baron *see* YORKE, PHILIP, 1st Baron Hardwicke
Hardwicke, Philip Yorke, 2nd Earl of *see* YORKE, PHILIP, 2nd Earl of Hardwicke
Hardwicke, Philip Yorke, 3rd Earl of *see* YORKE, PHILIP, 3rd Earl of Hardwicke
Hardwick Hall (Derbys) **8** *44*, 45; **10** 143, 230, 360; **14** 422; **24** 290; **28** 894, 895; **30** 266*; **32** 551
carpets **9** 30
Chapel **10** 271
dress **10** 353
floors **10** 273
frames **11** 421
furniture **10** 288, *288*; **20** 467
gazebo **12** 222
High Great Chamber **10** 271, 272
interior decoration **10** 271
leather **19** 5
Long Gallery **9** 30
overdoors **23** 678
paintings **3** 886; **19** 531
plaster **29** 834
quilts **15** 675
tapestries **1** 165; **30** 331
windows **12** 790
Hardy, B. C. **14** 29
Hardy, Bert **14** 173*
Hardy, Dudley **14** 174*; **25** 347
Hardy, Frederick Daniel **8** 121
Hardy, George **8** 121
Hardy, Hugh Gelston **14** 174*
Hardy, James, Pty Ltd **2** 772
Hardy, Jean **14** 174*
Hardy, Leopold **10** 682
Hardy, T. B. **14** 174
Hardy, Thomas **24** 743; **33** 401
Hardy Brothers **2** 765
Hardy Holzman Pfeiffer Associates **1** 126; **14** 174*; **19** 286; **21** 650
Hare **22** 546
Hare, Cecil Greenwood *see* GREENWOOD HARE, CECIL
Hare, David **14** 175*; **23** 48; **31** 614
exhibitions **18** 301
groups and movements **30** 22
patrons and collectors **13** 801
works **31** *613*
Hare, H. T. **3** 269
Hare, James H. **24** 677
Hare & Hare **14** 802
Hare-Naylor, Georgiana **11** 163
Harenc, Jean **11** 352
Harengau **24** 82
Harer, Fredrick **11** 499
hare-wood **20** 466
Harewood (W. Yorks), All Saints **1** 519
Harewood, Edwin Lascelles, 1st Baron *see* LASCELLES, EDWIN, 1st Baron Harewood
Harewood, Gloria **31** 339
works **31** *338*
Harewood, Henry George Charles Lascelles, 6th Earl *see* LASCELLES, HENRY GEORGE CHARLES, 6th Earl of Harewood
Harewood, Henry Lascelles, 1st Earl of *see* LASCELLES, HENRY, 1st Earl of Harewood
Harewood House (W. Yorks) **10** 233, 643
furniture **7** 171, 172, 659; **11** 119; **24** 317; **28** 665, *665*
interior decoration **11** 430, 431
Music Room **5** 687
paintings **3** 316; **11** 384; **12** 742; **31** 467
Hargeïsa **1** *379*; **29** 57
Hargesheimer, Carl-Heinz *see* CHARGESHEIMER
Hargreaves, Harold **15** 419, 420
Hargreaves, James **30** 540
Hargreaves, Thomas **19** 507
Haribans **14** 175*
hari-bor see under LACQUER → types
Haricharan **15** 631
Harichavank' Church **2** 434
Harigoyen, Emanuel von **2** 591
Hariharālaya *see under* ROLUOS
Harihar̃laya *see under* ROLUOS
Häring, Hugo **7** *294*; **12** 378; **14** 175–6*
collaboration **3** 293, 795; **11** 299; **27** 657; **32** 439
groups and movements **7** 293; **8** 826; **11** 841–2; **21** 781, 782; **23** 498–500; **26** 405
teachers **11** 129
works **14** *176*; **23** *499*
Haring, Keith **12** 218; **14** 177*
works **9** 213, 227; **12** 218; **13** 270; **25** 620; **31** 609
Haringey (Herts), Salisbury public house **25** 688
Harington, John, 2nd Lord Harington of Exton **27** 356
Harington, Lucy *see* RUSSELL, LUCY, Countess of Bedford
Haripur **15** 628
al-Hariri **11** 146; **16** 456
works **16** *455*
Hariri, Tell *see* MARI
Harishena, Ruler (*reg c.* 460-78) (Vakataka) **15** 555
Hari Singh Nalva **24** 540
Haritch **2** 435
Haritsu Ogawa *see* OGAWA HARITSU
Hariulf, Abbot of Saint-Riquier **27** 588
Harivarman I, King of Champa (*reg c.* 803) **6** 419
Hariya **22** 429
Hariyupia *see under* HARAPPA
Har Jaimal **15** 623
Härkeberga Church **30** *65*, 76
wall paintings **30** *77*
Harker, Joseph **30** 681
Harkhu **15** 626
Harkhuf **2** 656
Harkness, John Cheesman **30** 226
Harkness, Sarah Pillsbury **30** 226
Harkova, Ali **1** 544
Harlaxton Manor (Lincs) **10** 142; **29** 835
Harlay, François II de **17** 685
Harlay, Henry de **20** 455
Harlebeke Church **3** 547
Harlech (Gwynedd) **32** *780*, 788
Castle **6** 53, 56; **9** 144; **16** *895*, *896*; **21** 564
gate-house **12** 173, 174
Harlem, Simon van *see* SIMON VAN HARLEM
Hårleman, Carl **14** 177*; **30** 88, 93, 106
assistants **1** 152; **8** 189
collaboration **30** 522
patrons and collectors **14** 692
personal collection **5** 167
pupils **8** 189; **9** 455
sponsorship **26** 98
works **11** 91; **20** 866; **29** 689, 691; **30** 71, 93; **31** 693, 694
Hårleman, Johan **14** 177
Harlem Renaissance **1** 441–2; **31** 606; **33** 370
Harleston, Elise **33** 308
Harley, Edward, 2nd Earl of Oxford **14** 178*; **19** 165; **27** 466
architecture **12** 593
gardens **4** 805
manuscripts **10** 368; **14** 259; **28** 844; **32** 852
paintings **8** 454; **33** 376
Harley, Milton **16** 884
Harley, Robert, 1st Earl of Oxford **4** 353; **14** 177–8*; **32** 852
Harleyford Manor (Bucks) **8** 47; **32** 553
Harley Golden Gospels *see under* GOSPEL BOOKS → individual manuscripts
Harley Psalter *see under* PSALTERS → individual manscripts
Harlingen **22** 881; **30** 878, 879
A. C. W. Schefferschool **4** 790
Harlingen, Petrus Feddes van *see* FEDDES VAN HARLINGEN, PETRUS
Harlow (Essex) **10** 303; **12** 590; **19** 577; **31** 733
Town Hall **31** 243
Harlow, George Henry **7** 435; **14** 178*
Harls, Anton **2** 394
Harmal, Tell **1** *849*; **9** 46*; **21** *267*, 286
temple **21** 287
see also DIYALA REGION
Harman, Jeremiah **18** 579
Harman Chapel **26** 711
Harmon, Arthur Loomis **28** 628–9
Harmon, William E. **1** 442
Harmon Foundation *see under* NEW YORK → foundations
harmony **1** 559–60; **13** 412; **14** 869; **22** 377, 378; **28** 200–201
Harmose **10** 65
Harms, Antoine Frédéric **10** 205
Harms, Johann Oswald **14** 141
harnesses **14** 179–87*
historical and regional traditions
Assyrian **14** *180*
Central Asia **10** 873
Egypt, ancient **14** *179*
Korea **14** 184
Native North Americans **22** *650*
Poland **25** 128
Scythian **14** *180*
types
camel **14** 186–7*, *187*
elephant **14** 185–6*
horse **14** 179–81*, 182, 183–4*, *184*, 185*, 418, 419; **25** 541
harness leather *see under* LEATHER → types
harness-mounts **32** *512*, *513*, *515*
Harnett, William Michael **14** 187–8*; **31** 603
groups and movements **24** 686
methods **31** 578
works **15** 140, *141*; **24** 379, 555; **29** 669
Härnevi Church **30** 76
Harnier, Wilhelm von
works **11** *461*
Harnoncourt, René d' **22** 674, 677, 679
Haro, S Tomás **29** 265
Haro, Etienne-François **9** 424; **14** 188*; **15** 843
Haro, García Avellaneda y *see* CASTRILLO, GARCÍA AVELLANEDA Y HARO, Conde de
Haro, Henri **14** 188
Haro, Jules **14** 188
Haro, Pedro Fernández de Velasco, 2nd Conde de **5** 203; **21** 124; **29** 333; **32** 124–5*
Harootian, Koren der **14** 858
Harosteguy, Emilio Duhart *see* DUHART HAROSTEGUY, EMILIO
Haroué **26** 449
Haro y Guzmán *see* CARPIO, Marquéses de
Haro y Guzmán, Gaspar de *see* CARPIO, GASPAR DE HARO Y GUZMÁN, 7th Marqués de
Haro y Guzmán, Luis Méndez de *see* CARPIO, LUIS MÉNDEZ DE HARO Y GUZMÁN, 6th Marqués de
Haro y Guzmán, Luis Méndez de, Marqués de Carpio *see* CARPIO, LUIS MÉNDEZ DE HARO Y GUZMÁN, 6th Marqués de
Harpalos **14** 461; **20** 863
Harper **1** *386*
William V. S. Tubman Museum **19** 310
Harper & Brothers **1** 22; **4** 364; **11** 804; **17** 881
Harper & Row **13** 811
Harper's Bazaar **18** 476
Harper's Weekly **5** 758; **15** 830; **27** 872
Harpignies, Henri-Joseph **14** 188–90*
pupils **22** 93, 137; **26** 558
works **11** 415; **14** *189*; **32** 902
Harpley (Norfolk), St Lawrence **9** 152; **24** 577
harps **22** 374, 375, 376
Africa **1** 359
Ancient Near East **1** 891
Burma **5** *259*, 259
Cambodia **5** 508
Egypt, ancient **10** *65*, 65; **22** 372
Mangbetu **1** 359
Sumerian **22** 372
Zaïre **1** 359
Zande **33** 610
harpsichords **22** 372, *372*
Harput **9** 620
tomb of Mansur Baba **16** 204
tomb of Seyh Seraffedin **16** 204
Harrach (family) **3** 488; **8** 422; **14** 528
Harrach, Aloys Thomas, Graf von **14** 190, 191–2*; **27** 201; **32** 332
Harrach, Ernst Adalbert, Archbishop of Prague **5** 771
Harrach, Ernst Guido, Graf von **8** 12; **14** 190; **23** 271
Harrach, Ferdinand Bonaventura, Graf von **2** 829; **14** 190*; **20** 494
Harrach, Franz Anton, Prince-Archbishop of Salzburg **9** 145
Harrach, Franz Ernst, Graf von **14** 190
Harrach, Friedrich August, Graf von **14** 190*
Harrach, Leonhard III, Graf von (1468-1527) **14** 190
Harrach, Stephanie, Gräfin von **14** 190
Harrach codices **2** 808
Harrache (family) **10** 347
Harrachhütte glassworks **19** 522
Harrachov glass works **14** 191
Harrack, Norma Rodney **16** 888
Harran **1** *821*; **14** 192*; **16** *104*; **21** *267*; **30** *180*
architecture **9** 543
Great Mosque **16** 180; **22** 323
metalwork **16** 369
trade **30** 179
Harran Census **2** 503
Harrania
architecture **5** 401
ceramics **9** 767
Habib Gorgy Sculpture Museum **9** 768
Wissa Wassef Art Centre **9** 765, 767, *767*, 768
Wissa Wassef Tapestry Museum **5** 401; **9** 768
Harrer, Anton **19** 107
Harrewijn, Jacobus **9** 408
Harrich, Jobst **9** 435, 446; **11** 734; **12** 168; **17** 711; **33** 130
Harries, Katrine **29** 110
Harriet, Fulchran-Jean **14** 192*; **25** 638
Harriman, E. H. **31** 659
Harrington, John **10** 289
Harrington, Oliver **5** 759
Harrington's Photographic Journal **24** 438
Harringworth, Robert Curzon, 14th Baron of *see* CURZON, ROBERT, 14th Baron of Harringworth
Harriot, Thomas **33** 146
Harris, Ann Sutherland **33** 310
Harris, Anthony Charles **10** 90

Harris, Daniel 23 690
Harris, E(mmanuel) Vincent 14 193–4*
groups and movements 22 743
staff 7 435
teachers 29 695
works 5 731; 20 238
Harris, George Francis Robert, Baron, Governor of Trinidad 31 339
Harris, Harwell Hamilton 14 194*; 19 701
Harris, Hywel 32 783
Harris, Ina-Maria 19 242
Harris, James 31 768
Harris, James Russell 28 879
Harris, Jeffrey 23 61
Harris, Joel Chandler 11 804
Harris, John (*fl* 1640s) 2 545
Harris, John (?1667-1719) 4 80; 10 205
Harris, John the elder (*fl* 1693-1719) 4 80
Harris, John the younger (*fl* 1715-55) 4 80
Harris, John (1756-1846) 31 265
Harris, John (*b* 1931) 10 211
Harris, John Castle 2 760
Harris, Lawren P. 14 195
Harris, Lawren S(tewart) 14 194–5*
groups and movements 5 566; 13 711; 16 818; 30 711
works 14 *195*
Harris, Lionel 14 195
Harris, May 23 69
Harris, Michael 14 200
Harris, Noel Chandler 4 364
Harris, Peter 20 172
Harris, Robert 5 566; 14 193*; 26 108
Harris, Rolfe 3 62
Harris, Thomas (*d* 1820) 9 401
Harris, Thomas (1830-1900) 7 619
Harris, Tomás 14 195–6*
Harris, Vincent 19 319
Harris, W. 28 385
Harris, William 14 146
Harris, William Critchlow 14 193*
Harris, William Laurel 24 281
Harris, William Wade 1 514
Harris Lebus Ltd 10 299
Harris Master *see* SÁNCHEZ, PEDRO, II
Harrison 14 280
Harrison, Austen St Barbe 14 196*; 17 492; 23 689
Harrison, Benjamin 9 715; 14 252
Harrison, Charles (*fl* 1850s) 8 586
Harrison, Charles (*b* 1942) 2 512
Harrison, C. W. 16 21
Harrison, George Henry 14 196
Harrison, Harriet 14 196
Harrison, Henry 3 239
Harrison, Hinemea 14 196
Harrison, J. E. K. 23 134
Harrison, John 8 34
Harrison, John Augustus Charles 4 373
Harrison, John Edwin 4 155; 29 848
Harrison, Joseph 6 88
Harrison, J. Stockdale 9 724
Harrison, Margaret 10 879
Harrison, Maria 14 196
Harrison, Mary P. 14 196*
Harrison, Pakiriki 14 196*
Harrison, Peter 14 197–8*; 23 32; 31 590
groups and movements 23 860
works 4 472; 14 *197*; 17 545
Harrison, Sarah Cecilia 17 472
Harrison, Stephen 18 73
Harrison, T. Alexander 11 362
Harrison, Thomas (1744-1829) 14 198–9*
collaboration 14 260
groups and movements 13 609
Harrison, Thomas (1744-1829)—cont.
works 4 802, 889; 6 561; 10 235; 18 887; 19 505; 20 237; 29 549
Harrison, Tom (1911-76) 20 589, 590
Harrison, Wallace (*fl* 1949; painter) 11 729
Harrison, Wallace K(irkman) (1895-1981; architect) 7 838; 14 199–200; 18 186
architecture 13 238, *238*; 23 43, 118; 30 684
Harrison, William Frederick 10 230; 14 196
Harrison and Abramovitz 14 199–200*
staff 12 185; 30 260
works 1 736; 8 278; 14 203; 25 5
Harris Papyrus I 24 634
Harris Queensway 10 300
Harrisson, Tom 3 629
Harrow School (Middx) 10 92; 30 749
Butler Museum 6 439; 25 804
Harsdorff, C(aspar) F(rederik) 14 201*; 25 874
assistants 14 151
pupils 14 151
works 8 726, 727, 743, 745; 11 746; 21 77; 23 221; 27 168
Harsha 15 738
Harshavarman I, King of Cambodia (*reg* 900-*c.* 922) 5 468, 469
Harsiese (*reg* 131 BC) 9 *778*
Harsnet, Samuel 17 693
Harsthorne, Robert 6 528
Hart, Abraham van der 14 201–2*; 22 827
works 1 802; 22 827, *865*
Hart, Frederick 19 398
Hart, George Overbury 9 310; 26 488
Hart, Heinrich 8 824
Hart, James McDougal 14 202*; 20 488; 31 870
Hart, Julius 8 824
Hart, Laurent Joseph 20 925
Hart, Percival 10 316
Hart, Samuel 14 202
Hart, Solomon Alexander 14 202*; 17 576
works 17 *576*
Hart, William 14 202
Hart, William Howard 7 875
Harta *see* NAKRASON
Hart Beers Kempson, Julie *see* KEMPSON, JULIE HART BEERS
Harte, Abraham van der 33 674
Harte, Neville A. 32 153
Hartel, Auguste 29 751
Härtel, H. (Rudolf) 10 577
Härtel, Herbert 6 320; 20 816
Härtel, Hermann 12 274
Hartel, Wilhelm von 33 159
Hartel & Neckelmann 19 318
Harter, Hieronymus 14 678
Hartford (CT) 14 202–3*; 31 *587*
Hartford Arch 30 505
Phoenix Mutual Life Insurance building 14 200
silver 31 649
Wadsworth Atheneum 2 858; 22 359; 32 753
collections 1 895; 14 202; 22 112; 31 666
Greek collection 13 470
sculpture 27 47
Harth-Terré, Emilio 19 387
Hartigan, Grace 14 203*; 16 820; 20 606, 607
Hartington, Adam of *see* ADAM OF HARTINGTON
Hartlaub, Gustav F. 22 922
Hartlauer, Fritz 2 804
Hartlepool Monastery (Cleveland) 2 68
Hartley, James
swords 2 *457*
Hartley, Jesse 2 324; 9 59; 19 506; 32 861
works 9 *59*
Hartley, Marsden 14 203–4*; 22 381; 23 48; 31 605
collaboration 20 604
exhibitions 31 490
groups and movements 8 435
patrons and collectors 3 251; 14 575; 29 655, 657
teachers 6 500
works 12 216; 14 *204*
Hartley, Mary 18 891
Hartley Courthouse 18 887
Hartman, Carl V. 9 677; 13 310; 29 219, 222
Hartman, Mauno 11 101
Hartman, Viktor (Aleksandrovich) *see* GARTMAN, VIKTOR (ALEKSANDROVICH)
Hartmann, Bishop 16 434, 443
Hartmann, Anton 10 545
Hartmann, D. 31 298
Hartmann, Ferdinand 26 375
Hartmann, Frédéric 21 613
Hartmann, Heinz 25 683
Hartmann, Johann Heinrich 18 449
Hartmann, Johann Jakob 2 795
Hartmann, Joseph (*c.* 1674-1734) 13 217
Hartmann, József (*fl* 1744-64) 14 894
Hartmann, Meister 14 204–5*; 31 569, 570
Hartmann, Oluf 8 736
Hartmann, Risler & Cie 33 711
Hartmann, (Carl) Sadakichi 14 205*; 29 655
Hartmann von Dillingen, I 22 796
Hartman van Coesvelt, Jan 26 284
Hartmeyer, T. A. 31 488
Hartnell, Norman 9 294
Hart Nibbrig, F(erdinand) *see* NIBBRIG, F(ERDINAND) HART
Hartrick, Archibald Standish 19 492
Hartsherne, Ebenezer 4 478
Hartsinck, Andries 15 772
Hartt, Frederick 2 535; 31 672, 673
Hartung II, Bishop of Regensburg 26 656
Hartung, Hans 3 778; 11 551, 644; 14 205–6*; 26 352
dealers 26 193
groups and movements 1 78; 2 543, 544; 30 231; 33 635
patrons and collectors 7 842; 9 121
works 3 462; 14 *206*; 19 491
Hartung, Hugo 28 47
Hartung, Karl 3 803; 7 325; 12 408; 14 206–7*, 606
Hartwell (Bucks)
Hartwell House 22 716
St Mary 13 200
Hartwell, Alonzo 4 880
Hartwell, Henry Walker 14 207*
Hartwell & Richardson 14 207*
Hartwig relief 24 319, 320
Hartwig von Stade 17 482
Hartzer, Ferdinand (Carl Emmanuel) 14 207*
Harue Koga *see* KOGA, HARUE
Harumura Kurokawa *see* KUROKAWA HARUMURA
Harun al-Rashid, Caliph (*reg* 786-809) (Abbasid)
dress 16 456
mosques 25 778
paper 16 351; 24 48
porcelain 16 398
reliquaries 5 806
tents 30 476
urban planning 16 151
Harunobu Suzuki *see* SUZUKI HARUNOBU
Harusato Matsudaira *see* MATSUDAIRA FUMAI
Harushige Suzuki *see* SHIBA KŌKAN
Haruta 17 364
Harvard Hannibal, Master of the 7 525; 20 615, 689*
Harvard University *see under* CAMBRIDGE (MA)
Harvard University Press 31 680
Harvelay, Mme de 5 440
Harvest *see* HØST
Harvester Vase 21 654, 659, 663, 689
Harvest jugs *see under* JUGS → types
Harvey, Bryan 2 309
Harvey, Don 32 414
Harvey, Elisabeth 8 864
Harvey, Fred, Company 22 568, 615, 668, 676
Harvey, George (1800-78) 19 791
Harvey, George (1806-76) 14 208*, 540; 28 238
Harvey, Isaac 18 169
Harvey, James 14 193
Harvey, John 3 370
Harvey, Lewis J. 2 759, 760, 771
Harvey, Thomas 8 184; 31 465
Harvey, W. Alexander 5 365; 11 785
Harvey, William 14 208*
Harvey group 5 597
Harvey Wiley Corbett Associates 7 839
Harwa 9 859, 892
Harwan 15 458
plaques 15 *459*
Harwein, Joseph 17 493
Harwennefer (*reg* 205-199 BC) 9 *778*; 25 687
Harwich (Essex) 21 569
Harwood, Francis 8 83
Harzuilens, De Haar Castle 22 829
Hasam, Chile 20 604
Hasan (*fl* 16th cent) 29 18
Hasan, Sultan (*reg* 1347-51; 1354-61) (Mamluk) 18 507; 20 229*
architecture 5 404; 16 *210*
metalwork 16 382, 384
Hasan II, King (*reg* 1962-) ('Alawi) 1 527; 22 128
mosques 22 *128*
Hasan, Nakkaş 14 208–9*; 16 348
Hasan, Pirzada Najam ul- 23 800
Hasan, Qamrul 3 168
Hasan, Zaki Muhammad 14 209*; 16 549
Hasan al-Quhadi 31 902
Hasan Beg 16 231
works 16 *232*
Hasan Çelebi 1 473
Hasanefendić, Seid 4 461
Hasan ibn Husayn 6 172; 16 502
al-Hasan ibn Juban ibn 'Abdallah al-Qunawi 16 290
Hasan ibn Piruz 9 41
Hasankeyf 4 801; 16 204
Hasanlu 14 209–11*; 15 899, *901*, 902, 907, 910, *911*, 921
architecture 14 209
Burned Buildings complex 14 *209*, 210
glass 1 865, 866
gold 15 919
ivory-carvings 1 866, 870, 872
jewellery 1 874–5
metalwork 14 *211*, 211; 15 919
palace 1 894; 23 807; 31 700
town walls 21 554
Hasan of Kashan 16 372
Hasanoğlan 1 834
Hasan Pasha 27 698, 699
Hasan Shah (*d c.* 1526) (Sur) 15 368; 27 858
Hasa Tal'at Bey 23 391
Hasat Bin Salt 2 270
Hasaya Chone 5 246
Haschenperg, Stefan von 14 211–12*; 21 568
Hase, Conrad Wilhelm 14 212*
assistants 23 459; 28 46
groups and movements 13 202
pupils 9 382; 13 677; 23 661
works 4 787; 14 142
Hasegawa (family) 18 557
Hasegawa, Itsuko 14 212–13*; 17 92
Hasegawa, Kiyoshi 14 213*; 17 296
Hasegawa, Saburō 14 213*; 17 207
Hasegawa Ennen 17 413; 20 75
Hasegawa Kyūzō 14 215
Hasegawa Sadanobu 17 289
Hasegawa school
works 17 *164*
Hasegawa Tōhaku 14 213–15*; 17 164, 419, 784; 31 253
attributions 18 558
patrons and collectors 31 253
works 14 *214*; 17 *335*; 18 559, 560
Haseji 17 126
Haseki Hürrem Sultan 16 92
Haseki Sultan 16 224
Haselberger, L. 10 415
Haseldine, John 3 521
Haseler, Thomas 29 764
Haseler, W. H. 4 88; 10 336, 344
Haseltine, Charles F. 14 215
Haseltine, Herbert 18 161
Haseltine, James H. 14 215
Haseltine, William Stanley 14 215*
Hasenauer, Karl 14 216*
collaboration 28 400; 32 437, 457; 33 131
pupils 3 398; 14 627; 31 702
works 2 *786*, 787, 808, 830; 9 12; 22 364; 23 813; 28 *399*; 29 525
Hasenbanck, Matthäus 12 444
works 12 *444*
Hasenburk Missal *see under* MISSALS → individual manuscripts
Hasenclever, Johann Peter 9 460; 14 216–17*, 535
Hasenclever, Walter 23 267
Hashem al-Khattat *see* HASHEM MUHAMMAD AL-BAGHDADI
Hashem Muhammad al-Baghdadi 14 217*; 16 1
Hashiguchi, Goyō 17 294
Hashim 14 217–18*; 15 586, 587, 590
works 14 *217*
Hashimid, Faysal I *see* FAYSAL I, King of Irak
al-Hashimiyya 3 51; 16 150
Hashimoto, Chikanobu 17 177
Hashimoto, Heihachi 14 218*
Hashimoto, Kansetsu 17 201
Hashimoto Gahō 14 218–19*
groups and movements 17 200, 797–8
pupils 17 200, 860; 28 603
works 31 253
hashirae see under PRINTS → types → *ukiyoe*
Hashmi, Salima 23 800
Hasht Bihisht Palace *see under* ISFAHAN
Hashtnagar 15 446
Hasior, Władysław 14 219*; 25 108, 116
Haskell, Ernest 21 896
Haskell, Llewellyn S. 8 575; 31 592
Haskell, Stevens 20 388
Hasket Derby, Elias *see* DERBY, ELIAS HASKET
Haskins, Sam 24 656
Haslemere (Surrey) 2 569
Haslinger, Johann 2 783
Haslund, Ole 8 759
Haslund-Christensen, H. 21 886
Hasōhai *see* CHŌDENSU MINCHŌ
Haspel, Jerg 33 349

Hassall, Joan **4** 366, 367
Hassall, John **25** 347
Hassam, (Frederick) Childe **14** 219–21*; **31** 603
exhibitions **2** 447
groups and movements **15** 156; **23** 47; **30** 452; **31** 487, 603
patrons and collectors **11** 141; **24** 638
works **4** 478; **14** *220*
Hassan, Faik **14** 221*; **16** 2
groups and movements **10** 833; **16** 2
works **16** 2
Hassan, Fatima **22** 129
Hassan, Ijaz ul- **23** 800
Hassan, Selim **10** 82
Hassan al-Mulla **25** 777
al-Hassani, Mahdi **16** 1
Hassani Mahaleh **1** 786
Hassan iqbal al-Hakimi **22** 382
Hassaniyya **33** 97
Hassan Sharif **31** 585
Hassaût **6** 248; **9** 663
silk **6** *248*
Hasse, Johann **29** 119
Hasse, Johann Adolf **12** 24
Hasselberg, (Karl) Per Åkesson **14** 221*; **30** 86
Hasselberg-Olsson, Elisabeth **30** 115
Hassell, John **10** 374
Hassell & Partners **1** 152
Hasselqvist, Arne **2** 151
Hassels, Warner **18** 672
Hasselt **3** *539*, 601, 603
church **22** 820
Hasselt, Jean de *see* JEAN DE HASSELT
Hassuna **1** 894; **2** 639; **21** 269, 305
Hassuna culture **21** 269*, 305
Hassuna period *see under* MESOPOTAMIA → periods
Hastie, William **5** 521; **14** 221–2*; **18** 36; **31** 551
collaboration **27** 345
works **25** 746; **27** 576; **29** 554
Hastinapura **8** 670; **14** 222*; **15** *261*; **22** 758
Hastings (New Zealand) **23** 56
Hastings (E. Sussex; UK)
Castle **3** 427
St Clement **11** 253
Hastings, Elizabeth **21** 102
Hastings, Francis Rawdon-Hastings, Marquess of *see* RAWDON-HASTINGS, FRANCIS, 1st Marquess of Hastings
Hastings, Hubert de Cronin **14** 222*; **20** 475
Hastings, Jack **22** 332
Hastings, Rafael (Eduardo Indacochea) **14** 222–3*
Hastings, Thomas **5** 875–6*; **11** 774; **20** 19; **32** 793
Hastings, Warren **14** 611; **15** 697, 741, 744; **25** 39; **33** 695
Hastings, William, Baron Hastings **20** 737
Hastings Hours *see under* BOOKS OF HOURS → individual manuscripts
Hastrup **9** 156
Hasui Kawase *see* KAWASE, HASUI
Hasuike Hideaki **17** 781
Haszard, Rhona **23** 60
Hata (family) **17** 311, 312; **18** 548
Hata Chikashi **17** 811
Hata Chitei **17** 157
Hatakeyama, Issei **17** 429
Hatampura *see* ALAMPUR
Hata no Kawakatsu **18** 548, 555
Hatathli, Ned, Center **22** 568
Hata Zoroku **17** 323
Hat Bathu *see* BATH
hat bo *see* VIETNAM → operas
Hatch, Chester **5** 579
Hatch, Stephen D(ecatur) **14** 223*
hat cheo *see* VIETNAM → operas
hatchets **21** 245
hatching **6** 569; **13** 138; **14** 223*
Hatfield (Herts) **31** 733
Comet **25** 689
St Leonard **31** 122
Hatfield, Charles **25** 4
Hatfield, Thomas of *see* THOMAS OF HATFIELD
Hatfield House (Herts) **4** 785; **6** 127; **8** 45; **10** 270; **16** 823
collections **6** 128; **8** 165
furniture **10** 291
mosaics **33** 387
paintings **12** 243; **32** 245
sculpture **7** 236, 641
Hatfield Regis Priory (Essex) **7** 190
Hathaway, Rufus **14** 223*
Hathial Mound *see under* TAXILA
Hathigumpha **16** 869
Hatillo, El **14** 223–4*; **29** *136*, 140
el Hatillo ware *see under* POTTERY → wares
Ha Tlebere **19** 241
Hatnub **3** 848; **9** 813, 816, 832; **29** 616
Hatogamine Shrine **17** 129
Hatoula **30** 182
Hatra **1** *849*; **14** 224–6*; **15** *901*; **16** 2; **21** *267*, 275
architecture **21** 275, 292; **24** 216
dress **16** 455
Great Temple complex **14** *225*, 225–6
iwans **16** 801; **21** 292
jewellery **24** 218
sculpture **1** 887; **2** 257; **24** 217
Temple of Allat **14** *226*
hats **14** 416; **17** 523
historical and regional traditions
Africa **1** 296, 349
Algeria **16** 459
Byzantine **9** 644
Central Asia, Western **6** 252
China **7** 145
Early Christian (*c*. AD 250-843) **9** 644
Indian subcontinent **15** 733
Indonesia **15** 810
Iran **10** 872
Islamic **16** 456, 459, 462
Malaysia **20** 182
Morocco **16** 459
Native North Americans **22** 613, *659*
Nigeria **1** 348
Ottoman **16** 462
Peru **24** *512*
South America, Pre-Columbian **29** 151
Trinidad and Tobago **31** *332*, 332–3
Turkey **16** 462
Vietnam **32** 487, *487*, 491
Viking **9** 254
Zaïre **1** 296
materials
basketwork **1** 296; **22** *659*
beads **1** 296
feathers **1** 296; **17** 524
felt **10** 872, 875
fringes **31** *332*, 332–3
fur **1** 296
jewellery **17** 523
metal **22** 613
raffia **1** 296
silver **24** *512*
velvet **24** *512*
Hatshepsut (*reg c*. 1479–*c*. 1485 BC) **9** *777*, 807, 882; **10** 80, 81, 86, 94; **14** 226–7*; **25** 776; **28** 407; **30** 689
architecture **24** 750
gardens **10** 54
obelisks **23** 329, *330*
sculpture **1** 691; **9** 880
wall paintings **9** 903
Hatshepsut (*reg c*.1470–*c*. 1485 BC)
architecture **30** 692
Hatshepsut (*reg c*. 1470–*c*. 1485 BC)—cont.
fortresses **9** 824
temples **3** 717; **9** 781
Buhen **9** 847; **10** 803
Luxor **30** 692
mortuary temple (Deir el-Bahri) **9** 825, 826, 835; **10** 80; **11** 231; **12** 497; **20** 231; **30** 693
Hatshepsut, mortuary temple of *see under* THEBES (i) (EGYPT) → mortuary temples
Hattem Church **22** 820
Hattenheim, St Vincenz **9** 156
Hatterman, Nola **30** 16
Hattersley, Ralph **31** 525
Hatti *see* HITTITE
Hatton, Christopher, 1st Baron Hatton **3** 186; **9** 374; **10** 287, 349; **29** 714
Hattori Nankaku **17** 236
Hattula Church **4** 781; **11** 88, 94, 98
Hattusa *see* BĞAZKŸ
Hatun Cañar *see* INGAPIRCA
Hatuncolla **31** 46
Hatvan Hospital **14** 887
Hatz, Elizabeth **14** 227*
Hatzfeld, Karl, Graf **18** 741
Hau, Johannes **10** 539
Hauberat, Guillaume de **14** 227*; **19** 268; **20** 281
Hauberat, Jean **14** 227
Hauberg, Niels **30** 750
Hauberg Stele **29** 620
Hauberisser, Georg (Joseph) von **12** 376; **13** 330; **14** 227–8*; **22** 301
hauberks **2** 468, 469; **6** 261
Haubert, Francisco de Leygonier y *see* LEYGONIER Y HAUBERT, FRANCISCO DE
Haubrichs, Josef **7** 585
Hauchin, Martin de **17** 700
Hauck, Guido **24** 491
Hauck, John Maurice **33** 545
Haudebourt, Louis-Pierre **14** 228
Haudebourt-Lescot, (Antoinette-Cécile-) Hortense **14** 228*; **28** 170; **31** 373
Hauduroy, Louis **13** 645
Hauduroy, Samuel **4** 131; **14** 856
Hauer, Bonaventura Gottlieb **14** 767
Hauer, Daniel Adam **13** 871
Hauer, Johann **29** 762
Hauers, Wilhelm **14** 87
Haufler, Max **13** 726
Haugen Sørensen, Arne **8** 736; **14** 228
Haugen Sørensen, Jørgen **8** 741; **14** 228*
Haugesund **23** *218*
City Hall **23** 222
Haughton, Moses **4** 86; **11** 860; **28** 693
Haughton Castle (Northmb.) **19** 895
Haughwout, E. V., & Co. **12** 221
Hauguet, Ferdinand **8** 73
Haugwitz, Johann von, Bishop of Meissen **18** 461
Hauke, César M. de **10** 885
Haukeland, Arnold (Martin) **1** 12; **14** 228–9*; **23** 231
Haukipudas Church **11** 95
wall paintings **11** *94*
Haumonté, Paul **28** 500
haunches **2** 292, *292*
Hau-Nebut **9** 778
Haungooah *see* SILVERHORN
Haunoo **24** 630
Haupt, Adam **25** 116
Haupt, Albrecht (Karl) **14** 229–30*; **19** 428
Haupt, Elias **14** 230
Haupt, Georg **14** 230*
groups and movements **13** 864
Haupt, Georg—cont.
works **7** 194; **10** 293, *293*, 295; **20** 468; **30** *94*, 95
Hauptmann, Carl **33** 383
Hauptmann, Johann Gottlob **9** 236
Hauranne, Jean Duvergier de *see* DUVERGIER DE HAURANNE, JEAN
Hauré, Jean **3** 715; **11** 305
Hauror **2** 510
Haury, Emil **32** 233
Hausa **1** 383; **11** 827; **14** 230–33*; **17** 680; **23** 127, 128, 133
aluminium **1** 247
architectural decorations **1** 317, *318*
architecture **1** 249; **4** 793; **14** 233*; **23** 127, 134
basketwork **14** 233; **23** 127
calligraphy **14** 233
ceramics **14** 232*
cities **1** 251
compounds **1** 312
cotton **1** *218*
craftsmen and artists **1** 246, 251
cushion covers **1** *218*
doors **9** 164
dress **1** 249; **14** *231*
dyes **1** 251
earth **9** 164
embroidery **14** *231*, 231–2; **23** 127
façades **1** 317
footwear **1** 349
fortifications **21** 597
gourds **1** 303, 382; **14** 233
houses **1** 251, 305, 308, *318*
leather **1** *218*, 299; **14** 233*
looms **14** 231
masks **1** 342
metalwork **1** 247; **14** 233
mosques **1** 316
mud-bricks **4** 793
ostrich feathers **1** 349
palaces **1** 284, 315; **23** 824
palm leaves **1** 305
patronage **1** 241, 242
pottery **1** 246; **14** 232
regalia **1** 242, *242*
robes **1** 349
scarification **1** 345
spoons **1** 247
tattoos **1** 346, 347
textiles **1** 251; **14** 231–2*
trade **1** 249, 251
trappings **14** 233
trousers **1** 348
veils **1** 349
wall decorations **14** *232*, 233*
weaving **14** 231
wood-carvings **14** 233
Hauschild, Wilhelm **22** 308
Hausdorf, Georg **9** 117
Hausen, Max Clemens von **8** 631
Hausenius, George Friedrich **29** 119
Hausenstein, Wilhelm **14** 234*
Hauser, Anton Xaver **33** 76
Hauser, Arnold **2** 537; **14** 234*, 901; **28** 926
pupils **14** 156
works **20** 528; **28** 917
Hauser, Carry **32** 447
Hauser, Erich **14** 234–5*
Hauser, Hans **12** 379
Hauser, Walter **10** 81
Haushofer, Max **5** 70; **14** 235*, 247; **18** 395; **20** 372
Hausinger, Adam **22** 306
Hausknecht, M. **25** 428
*Hausmaler*s **14** 235*
Hausmann, Karl **10** 718
Hausmann, Raoul **3** 802; **14** 235–7*, 604; **24** 427
groups and movements **3** 801; **8** 433, 436, 437; **12** 396; **23** 267
productions **3** 801; **26** 357
Hausmann, Raoul—cont.
works **3** 801; **12** 407; **14** *236*; **24** 685
Hausmann, Victor **14** 235
Hausner, Jan **8** 406
Hausner, Rudolf **2** 797, 831; **14** 237*; **24** 592; **32** 447
Haus-Rucker-Co. **14** 237–8*
Häusser, Elias David **8** 726, 742, 819; **10** 110
Häusser, Robert **14** 238*
Haussmann, Carl **11** 731
Haussmann, Georges Eugène, Baron **4** 306; **14** 238*
assistants **24** 174
patrons and collectors **1** 685
urban planning **24** 123, 125–6
works **1** 685; **9** 338; **11** 508, 523, *524*, 659; **24** *124*, 179; **28** 346; **31** 724, *724*
Haussmann, Raoul **13** 727
haus tambaran *see under* HOUSES → types
Haus und Garten **2** 810, 815, 826; **11** 728
Hauswald, Karl **18** 851
Hauswirth, Johann Jakob **14** 238–9*
Hauszmann, Alajos **14** 239*, 908; **30** 212
assistants **14** 865; **20** 447
collaboration **2** 415; **3** 412
pupils **18** 212, 655
works **5** 86; **14** 889; **16** 903
Haute-Claire, Atelier de *see* ATELIER DE HAUTE-CLAIRE
Hautecoeur, Louis (-Eugène-Georges) **11** 676; **14** 239*
Hautecombe Church **13** 202
Hautefeuille **23** 515
Hauteville, Roger Borsa de, Duke of Apulia *see* ROGER BORSA, Duke of Apulia
Hauteville, Roger de, Count *see* ROGER OF HAUTEVILLE, Count of Naples and Sicily
Hauteville, Roger II de, King of Naples and Sicily *see* ROGER II, King of Naples and Sicily
Hauteville, Tancred de, Prince of Antioch *see* TANCRED, Prince of Antioch
Hauteville, William II de, King of Naples and Sicily *see* WILLIAM II, King of Naples and Sicily
Haute-Volta *see* BURKINA FASO
Haut-Ittre **30** 905
Haut-Koenigsbourg **6** 51
Hautrage **13** 110
Hautrage-Nord **25** 190
Hautrive, Marquis d' **4** 552
Hautsch, Georg **20** 923
Hauttmann, Johann **33** 283
Hautvillers **5** 802; **11** 529; **31** 773
Hauxton (Cambs), St Edmund **26** 613
Hauzinger, Josef **33** 256
Havana **8** 227, 228, *228*, 231; **14** 240–42*, *241*; **31** 721
Academia de San Alejandro *see* Escuela Nacional de Bellas Artes San Alejandro
Aldama mansion **8** 232
Bacardi offices **8** 232
Balaguer mansion **8** 232
ballet school **8** 233
Casa Cultura de Velasco **8** 233
Casa de Correos **5** 749
Casa de Gobierno **5** 749
Casa-Moré **8** 232
Cathedral **8** 237
Centro de Arte Internacional **8** 238
Centro Gallego **8** 232
ceramics **8** 236
Cetro de Oro flats **8** 232
convent of S Clara de Asís **8** 231
Coppelia ice-cream parlour **8** 233

Havana—cont.
Cuban Telephone Company **8** 232
Customs House **8** 231
drama school **8** 233
Escuela de Artes Dramáticas **13** 213
Escuela Nacional de Bellas Artes San Alejandro **8** *232*, 238
Escuelas Nacionales de Arte de Cubanacán **8** 232
Espíritu Santo **8** 231
exhibitions **5** 746
Faculty of Farming and Animal Husbandry Sciences **8** 233
Fortaleza Vieja **8** 231
fortifications **8** 231; **21** 573
Fototeca de Cuba **8** 239
Franciscan Hospital **8** 231
Franciscan Monastery **8** 231
Free Studio for Painters and Sculptors **8** 238
Galería Habana **8** 238
Hospital of S Francisco de Paula **8** 231
Hotel Nacional **8** 232
Instituto Superior de Arte **8** 238
José Antonio Echevarria University **8** 233
La Compañía **8** 231
López Serrano flats **8** 232
Los Tres Reyes del Morro **8** 231
metalwork **8** 237
Museo de la Ciudad **27** 865
Museo Nacional de Arte Decorativo **8** 239
Museo Nacional de Bellas Artes **8** 238, 239
music school **8** 233
National Capitol **8** 232
Noval house **8** 232
Oficinas de Mecánica Agrícola **8** 233
Palacio de Bellas Artes *see* Museo Nacional de Bellas Artes
Palacio de los Capitanes Generales **8** 231
Palacio de las Convenciones **8** 233
Palacio Presidencial **8** 232
Palacio del Segundo Cabo **8** 231
Prison **8** 231
Real Fuerza **8** 231
Retiro Odontológico **8** 232
San Salvador de la Punta **8** 231
Santiago de las Vegas Workshop **8** 236
S Domingo **8** 231
Seguro del Médico **8** 232
S Francisco de Asís **8** 231
Teatro Tacon **8** 232
Town Hall **8** 231
Tribunal de Cuentas **8** 232
Vidaña house **8** 232
Havana chests **8** 235
Havana jamb **8** 235
Havard, Henry **14** 242*; **18** 658
Havard, James **22** 599
Havasupai **22** 634, 661, 669
Havatsky, Anton **3** 528
Havcuba, Jiří **8** 411
Have, Theodor de *see* HAVEUS, THEODORE
Havelberg **13** 187
hāvelī see under INDIAN SUBCONTINENT → temples
Havell, Daniel **14** 242
Havell, Ernest Binfield **5** 420; **14** 242, 243*; **15** 211, 653, 656, 657; **20** 54
collections **15** 742, 747
Havell, Frederick James **7** 433; **14** 242
Havell, Robert, I (1769-1832) **14** 242, 243; **20** 604
Havell, Robert, jr (1793-1878) **14** 242, 243*
collaboration **20** 604
copies **17** 616
Havell, Robert, jr (1793-1878)—cont.
works **2** 710; **4** 80, 364
Havell, Robert, & Sons **2** 745
Havell, William **7** 433; **14** 242*; **32** 903
Havelock North, Taurua **23** 56
Havemeyer, Henry Osborne **14** 244*
ceramics **16** 554
collections **5** 922; **18** 161; **31** 667
paintings **18** 672; **23** 156; **31** 664
Havemeyer, Louisine (Waldron) **5** 922; **8** 621; **14** 244*; **31** 664, 667
paintings **27** 238
Haven, Lambert van **8** 725, 758; **14** 244, 245*; **23** 224
collaboration **14** 245
teachers **14** 244
works **8** 725, *726*, 733, 742; **14** 543
Haven, Michael von **14** 244–5*; **23** 224
Haven, Nikolaj van **14** 244
Haven, Parkman B. **33** 135
Haven, Solomon von **14** 244–5*; **23** 224
Haverfordwest (Dyfed) **31** 710
Haveri, Siddheshvara Temple **15** 325, 531
Havering Palace (Essex) **14** 422
Haverkamp, Wilhelm **28** 779
Haverkamp-Begemann, E. **28** 362
Haverman, Hendrik Johannes **14** 245*; **32** 258
Haverman, Margareta **11** 228; **15** 47; **29** 668
Haverö **30** 83
church **26** 647
Havers, Mandy **10** 483
Haverty, Joseph **16** 16
Haverty Bequest **7** 377
Haveus, Theodore **14** 245*
Haviland, Charles **5** 284; **6** 462; **14** 246
Haviland, D. **14** 246
Haviland, Daniel **14** 246
Haviland, David **14** 245
Haviland, D. G. **14** 246
Haviland, Edward **14** 246
Haviland, Georges **14** 246
Haviland, John **14** 246–7*
collaboration **25** 4
pupils **32** 827
works **25** 637; **31** 592
Haviland, Robert **14** 246
Haviland, Théodore **14** 246
Haviland Brothers & Co. **14** 246; **19** 397
Haviland China Co. **14** 246
Haviland & Co. **14** 246; **19** 397
Haviland pottery and porcelain factories **6** 462; **27** 724; **29** 58; **31** 638
designers **2** 700; **4** 625, 626
Haviland studio (Auteuil) **6** 462; **11** 606; **14** 246; **19** 397; **24** 148
Haviland studio (Vaugirard) **6** 462; **11** 606
Havilland, Thomas Fiott de **15** 403; **20** 53
Havinden, Ashley **7** 653; **25** 351
Havlica, J. **28** 850
Havlice, P. **4** 27
Havlíček, Josef **14** 247*
collaboration **14** 732; **25** 430
works **8** 380, 402, 406
Havn *see* COPENHAGEN
Havránek, Bedřich **14** 235, 247*
Havre, Le *see* LE HAVRE
Havri, Siddheshvara Temple **15** 325, *326*
Havuts T'ar Monastery **2** 436
Hawaii **14** 248–51*; **23** *711*
barkcloth **14** 249
bedding **14** 249
body ornaments **14** 249; **23** 720
bone **4** 314
Hawaii—cont.
canoes **23** 724, 737
cloaks **14** 248–9, *249*
dress **14** 249
fans **10** 779
feathers **10** 847, 848, *848*; **14** 248–9; **23** 720
forgeries **23** 738
headdresses **10** 848; **23** 720
helmets **10** 848; **14** 249
ivory-carvings **14** 249
platforms **23** 715
rock art **23** 728
sashes **14** 249
sculpture **10** *848*; **14** 250; **23** 731
shells **28** 581
tattoos **14** 249–50; **23** 719
teeth **23** 720
weapons **23** 734
wood-carvings **14** *250*, 250
Hawara **9** *774*; **10** 758; **14** 251*
mortuary temple of Ammenemes III **1** 793; **9** 875; **10** 759
sculpture **1** *793*
mummy masks **10** 13
pyramid of Ammenemes III **1** 793; **10** 759; **14** 251; **25** 763
red lead **24** 796
tombs
Artemidorus **10** 13
Djedbastetefankh **10** *15*
Haward, Francis **25** 619
Haward, Sidney **19** 359
Hawarden, Clementina, Viscountess **14** 251*; **33** 308, 310
works **33** *309*
el-Hawawish **1** 506
Hawelti **10** 576
Hawes, John Cyril **2** 741; **14** 251–2*
Hawes, Josiah Johnson **29** 245
Hawes, Nancy **29** 245
Hawick **28** 266
Hawikuh (NM) **22** 608
Hawkchurch (Devon)
bungalows **5** *174*
Hawke, W. **32** 792
Hawke & McKinley **3** 269
Hawkes, Samuel **29** 644
Hawkes, T. G., & Co. **5** 730; **14** 252*; **29** 644
Hawkes, Thomas Gibbons **5** 730; **14** 252; **29** 644; **31** 644
Hawkes, Townsend **29** 644
Hawke's Bay Museum *see under* NAPIER
Hawkesworth, Frank **14** 480
Hawkesworth, J.
works **23** *725*
Hawkins **25** 617
Hawkins, E. J. W. **18** 411; **33** 151
Hawkins, Ernest **2** 602
Hawkins, G.
works **28** *873*
Hawkins, John (1783-1831) **4** 288
Hawkins, John (*fl* 1828) **16** 799
Hawkins, John Heywood (1803-77) **14** 252*
Hawkins, Richard **23** 690
Hawkins, Waterhouse **4** 37
Hawk-priestess Statuette **13** 596
hawksbeak *see under* MOULDINGS → types
Hawkshaw, John **3** 246; **25** 856
works **19** *574*
Hawkshead, Beatrix Potter Gallery **25** 372
Hawksmoor, Nicholas **2** 314; **10** 232; **12** 594; **14** 252–8*; **19** 595; **33** 398
architecture **10** 232; **23** 688, *688*; **31** 234
canopies (i) (architecture) **30** 781
churches **13** 199; **14** *256*; **19** 570, 602
colleges **7** 567; **13** 199; **14** *255*
Hawksmoor, Nicholas architecture—cont.
country houses **8** 47; **14** *253*; **31** 859
garden buildings **31** 862
hospitals **13** 623
libraries **19** 314
mausolea **6** 66; **14** *258*; **20** 866
models **2** 336
orangeries **12** 791; **23** *471*
pulpits **25** 727
pyramids **25** 766
screens (i) (architectural) **28** 295
attributions **6** 65
collaboration **7** 378; **8** 47; **16** 893; **23** 470; **31** 234, 858, 859, 862
groups and movements **3** 266, 267; **10** 96
patrons and collectors **4** 137, 138; **13** 645; **14** 807, 808
restorations by others **26** 337
Hawkstone Park (Salop) **33** 448
Hawksworth, John
works **30** *367*
Hawley, Christine **7** 788
Haworth, Henry **3** 356; **28** 242
Haworth, Jann **25** 231; **29** 12
Haworth, Samuel **8** 840
Haworth, William **28** 242
Hawran **29** 816
Hawthorne, Charles W. **8** 863; **20** 568; **27** 212
Hawthorne, Nathaniel **8** 528; **14** 258*
Hawton (Notts), All Saints **9** 681; **13** 54, 82
Haxhiu, Fatmir **1** 540; **14** 258–9*
Hay, Andrew **10** 366; **14** 259*; **32** 824
Hay, Cornelis **14** 668
Hay, David Ramsay **25** 36; **26** 288; **28** 248, 272
Hay, Douglas **5** 65
Hay, Elisabeth-Sophie Le *see* CHÉRON, ELISABETH-SOPHIE
Hay, George **9** 726; **14** 259; **28** 259
Hay, G. S. **20** 238
Hay, James (*fl* 1737) **13** *300*
Hay, James M. (*fl* 1888) **7** 664; **9** 705
works **9** *704*
Hay, Jean *see* HEY, JEAN
Hay, John, jr (*fl* 1850) **33** 219
Hay, John (*fl* 1885) **26** 342
Hay, Louis **22** 468
Hay, Richard Augustine, Father **27** 171
Hay, Robert (1799-1863) **4** 586; **10** 78, 82, 85
Hay, Robert (1808-90) **16** 855*
Hay, Thomas, 7th Earl of Kinnoul **12** 593
Hay, William **5** 561; **14** 259*; **18** 743
Haya, Diego de la **3** 847
Haya, Martín de **2** 868
Hayakawa, Kunihiko **14** 259*; **17** 92
Hayami, Gyoshū **14** 260*; **17** 201, 202
Hayanari *see* TACHIBANA NO HAYANARI
Hayart, Ben **19** 827
Hayasdan *see* ARMENIA (EUROPE)
Hayashi, Tadamasa **17** 204, 430, 435, 441
Hayashi Kodenji **17** 378
Hayashi Moriatsu **17** 416
Hayashi Razan **17** 234, 409, 788
Hayashi Rōen **23** 594
Hayashiya Shichiemon **17** 844
Hayatsor *see* ÇAVUŞTEPE
Hayball, Gunn **17** 898
Haybat Khan **15** 368
Hayberger, (Johann) Gotthard **1** 160; **14** 260*; **27** 553
Haycock, Edward (1790-1870) **14** 260*
Haycock, Edward (*d* 1882) **14** 260
Haydar (*d* 1325) **14** 260–61*; **16** 283
pupils **1** 25
teachers **33** 503
works **16** 283; **22** 538
Haydar (*fl* 1487) **16** 538
Ḥaydarābād *see* HYDERABAD
Haydar Ali (*fl* 17th cent.) **15** 640
Haydar 'Ali, Khan of Mysore (*reg* ?1761-82) **3** 163; **16** 81, 82; **22** 517
Haydar Ra'is **14** 261*; **16** 348
Hayden, Ferdinand V. **16** 821
Hayden, Henri **14** 261*
Hayden, Palmer **1** 442
Haydenreich, Erhard *see* HEIDENREICH, ERHARD
Haydenreich, Ulrich *see* HEIDENREICH, ULRICH
Haydocke, Richard **9** 8; **14** 547; **19** 547; **23** 690; **31** 300
Haydon, Benjamin Robert **1** 844; **10** 372, 373; **14** 261–3*, 587; **19** 621, 720
assistants **14** 208
groups and movements **13** 297
patrons and collectors **3** 454; **14** 147, 744
pupils **9** 682; **15** 32; **18** 688, 721, 722
reproductive prints by others **4** 845
teachers **11** 860
works **10** 250, 252; **14** *262*; **19** 587
Haydt, John Valentine **22** 80
Haye, Corneille de la *see* LYON, CORNEILLE DE
Haye, Reinier de la **14** 140
Hay-Eadie, Gerd **16** 42
Hayek, Hans von **17** 853; **24** 591
Hayer, Georg **18** 177
Hayes, Atwell **7** 857
Hayes, Edward **14** 263*
Hayes, Edwin **16** 16
Hayes, Michael Angelo **14** 263–4*
Hayet, Louis **14** 264*; **22** 745
Hayez, Francesco **14** 264–7*; **21** 527
collaboration **23** 829
groups and movements **26** 740
patrons and collectors **3** 687
pupils **3** 856; **5** 726; **8** 135; **15** 819
reproductions in hardstones **3** 687
reproductions in ivory **3** 49
teachers **7** 306; **20** 91
works **14** *265*, *266*, 587; **16** 677; **21** 527
Hay & Henderson **9** 61
Hayley, Edward **18** 712
Hayley, William **4** 120; **11** 163; **32** 910
Hayling Island **25** 538
Hayllar, Edith **14** 268
Hayllar, James **14** 267
Hayllar, Jessica **14** 267
Hayllar, Kate **14** 268
Hayllar (Wells), Mary **14** 268
Haylmann, Jacob **14** 268*
works **2** 117, 118; **8** 377; **12** 366; **30** 682
Hayls, John **14** 268–9*
patrons and collectors **24** 373; **25** 280, 281
works **11** *423*; **25** *280*
Hayman, Francis **14** 269*
assistants **11** 906, 907
attributions **33** 226
collaboration **13** 324; **32** 778
commentaries **10** 377
groups and movements **14** 638; **19** 585; **28** 924
methods **18** 898
patrons and collectors **17** 476; **20** 33, 911; **21** 91; **33** 693
pupils **6** 409; **8** 493; **10** 249; **11** 906

Hayman, Francis—cont.
reproductive prints by others 26 30; 32 652
works 7 785; 10 785; 11 426; 12 165, 293; 14 638; 19 619
Haymhaussen, Carlos 6 592, 599, 601
Haynes, Doug 5 569
Hayonim Cave 30 181
Hayq see Armenia (Europe)
Hayreddin (d 1512) 1 757; 9 729–30; 14 270*; 23 641
Hayreddin Pasha (fl 1380) 16 205, 810
ḥayr gardens see under Gardens → types
Hayrik, Khrimian 2 444
Hays 16 213, 214; 33 520
Hays, Barton S. 6 499
Hayter, Charles 14 270
Hayter, George 14 270–71*
patrons and collectors 27 358
pupils 25 630
reproductive prints by others 4 845; 28 283
Hayter, John 6 118; 14 270
Hayter, S(tanley) W(illiam) 5 531; 10 397; 14 271*; 20 604; 25 628; 31 508
assistants 26 68
collaboration 20 605
methods 10 380, 557, 560, 561
pupils
Antúnez, Nemesio 2 190; 6 598
Corneille 7 865
Downey, Juan 9 204
Masson, André 20 591
Olsen, John 23 425
Pollock, (Paul) Jackson 25 166
Reddy, Krishna 26 67
Sonderborg, K(urt) R(udolf) H(offmann) 29 65
Thieler, Fred 30 730
Toledo, Francisco (b 1940) 31 92
Vieira da Silva(, Marie-Helène) 32 423
staff 18 805; 23 12
works 9 310; 10 178, 398, 563; 25 620, 624; 28 52
Haytley, Edward 11 907; 14 271–2*
works 11 428
Hayton, John 31 289
Haytoum, John see Hayton, John
Hayward, Edward 2 771
Hayward, Gordon 3 124
Hayward, John (1808-91) 2 450; 33 212
Hayward, John (fl 1962) 2 450
Hayward, Richard 3 183; 6 528; 11 255; 17 476; 23 21
Hayward & Sons 28 549
Haywire Press 11 777
Hayyim ben Israel 17 561
Ház, A 20 206
Hazan Itaya see Itaya, Hazan
Hazara (people) 1 188, 209
Hazara Congregational Mosque 16 159
Hazarian, Harut'iwn 2 444
Hazart, Cornelius 8 877
Haze, Jacob de 19 650
Haze, Jan de 5 46, 211; 19 382; 30 314
works 14 III2
hazel 3 331
Hazel, Helsby see Helsby (Hazel), Alfredo
Hazelwood see Churchill
ḥaẓīra 16 197
Hazlitt, John 14 272
Hazlitt, William 13 812; 14 272*; 23 214; 25 283
al-Haẓm 2 255
Hazor 1 892; 14 273–4*; 16 565, 573; 17 553; 30 180, 185
architecture 16 566; 30 192
Hazor—cont.
fortifications 16 573; 17 553; 21 553, 553; 30 190
glass 1 865
Hazor Museum for Antiquities 16 570
orthostats 30 186
palaces 17 553
reliefs 30 193
sculpture 14 273
seals 1 857
stelae 29 613
Stelae Temple 8 261
stele 30 193
temples 30 185, 188
town walls 30 190
urban planning 30 190
Ha-Zore'a, Wilfrid Israel House of Oriental Art 16 571
Hazoume Romuald 3 728
Hazzidakis, Joseph 2 415; 14 275*; 20 203; 31 492
H. B. see Doyle, John
he see under Vessels → types
H.E., Master see H.F.E., Master
Head, Edmund (Walker) 14 275*
Head, Guy 14 275*
Head, Tim 10 269; 14 275–6*
headbands 1 351; 17 519; 21 878; 22 613, 652
headboards 3 483; 25 305
headcloths 15 792; 20 175, 176, 180
see also Headdresses; Headscarves
Headcorn (Kent) 32 277
headdresses 9 258
historical and regional traditions
Aboriginal Australia 1 53
Africa 1 254, 349*, 351, 386, 391
Algeria 16 448, 459
Ancient Near East 1 873, 883, 884, 885
Antilles, Lesser 2 147
Baga 1 391; 3 46, 47*
Belgium 9 271
Brazil 4 707
Cambodia 5 504
Central Asia, Eastern 6 310, 311
China 7 2, 109, 110; 10 848
Cook Islands 23 720
Easter Island 23 720
Edo (Africa) 9 734, 734
Egypt 16 454, 459
England 9 271, 274
Fang 1 351
French Guiana 11 758
Guinea 3 47
Hawaii 10 848; 23 720
Igbo 15 112, 113
Ijo 15 124, 125–6
Inca 15 164
Indian subcontinent 15 733, 734
Indonesia 15 814
Iran 16 454, 465, 466
Islamic 16 448, 454, 459, 461, 462, 465, 466
Laos 18 774
Lebanon 16 459
Marquesas Islands 23 720
Maya 21 249
Mende (Sierra Leone) 1 236
Mesoamerica, Pre-Columbian 21 246, 249, 250
Mongolia 3 441; 7 836; 21 877, 878
Native North Americans 22 652, 653, 653; 28 II1
Ndebele 1 349
Nigeria 9 734
Ottoman 16 454, 461
Pacific Islands 23 720, 721*
Papua New Guinea 23 721; 24 75, 75, 84, 84
Peru 28 651
Samoa 23 720
Santa Cruz Islands 27 779
Sicán culture 28 651
headdresses
historical and regional traditions—cont.
Society Islands 28 922, 922
Solomon Islands 27 779
South America, Pre-Columbian 28 651
Spain 9 260, 264
Syria 16 454, 459
Syria-Palestine 1 885
Tarascan 30 342
Thailand 3 441
Tibet 30 840
Tonga (Pacific Islands) 31 143
Torres Strait Islands 31 186
Trinidad and Tobago 31 332
Troad 31 376
Tunisia 16 459
Turkey 16 461, 462; 31 376
Vanuatu 31 891
Yoruba 1 349; 33 557
Zapotec 21 249
Zulu 1 351; 33 724
16th cent. 9 273–4
materials
beadwork 3 441
copper 28 651
coral 7 836
cornelian 1 873
feathers 1 53; 4 707; 10 848; 15 733; 21 249, 250; 22 652, 653, 653; 23 721; 24 75, 75, 84; 30 342; 31 143, 186
gold 1 873; 7 109; 28 651; 31 376
hair 23 720
jade 7 2
lapis lazuli 1 873
nuts 31 186
pearls 7 110
quills 22 652
raffia 1 382
shells 28 II1; 31 186
silver 7 109, 836; 28 651
skulls 31 891
tortoiseshell 31 186
turquoise 7 836
wood 1 391; 3 47; 15 124
types
tombstone 31 332
see also Headcloths; Headscarves
Heade, Martin Johnson 14 276–7*; 16 884; 31 602
groups and movements 14 843; 18 715; 19 791
works 14 276; 18 715; 20 425
header bond see under Bonding
headers see under Masonry → types
Headingly, Adolphe Smith 30 753
Headington (Oxon) 23 684
head-ornaments 17 519, 520
headpieces (body ornament) 22 652
headpieces (manuscripts) 9 609, 610, 618; 14 277*
see also Manuscript illumination
headrests
historical and regional traditions
Africa 1 366, 403, 411, 411, 416, 416–17*
Egypt, ancient 3 482; 10 51, 53, 57
Fiji 11 69
Kenya 1 411
Luba 19 743*, 744
Shona 1 416, 416–17*; 28 621, 621
Zulu 1 366, 416, 417; 33 724, 724
materials
aluminium 1 411
beads 1 411
copper 1 411
glass 10 57
gold 10 51
hides 1 411
headrests
materials—cont.
ivory 10 53
wood 1 403, 411, 416; 19 744; 28 621
see also Pillows
heads, colossal see under Sculpture → types
headscarves
Algeria 16 459
Byzantine 9 643
Early Christian (c. AD 250-843) 9 643
Islamic 16 459
Morocco 16 459
Tunisia 16 459
see also Headcloths; Headdresses; Scarves
headstones see Gravestones
Heal, Ambrose 10 299; 14 277*; 28 888; 29 484
Heal, John Harris 14 277
Healey, Giles 4 295
Healey, Robert 16 14
Healing, Annie 22 452, 609
healing statues see under Sculpture → types
Heal & Son 3 485; 10 284, 299; 15 824; 33 50
Healthy and Artistic Dress Union (London) 9 290
Healy, George Peter Alexander 14 277–8*
Healy, Giles 21 231
Healy, Michael 29 507
Healy, Robert 14 278*
Heaphy, Charles 14 279*; 23 57
Heaphy, Thomas (1775-1835) 1 121; 14 278*
Heaphy, Thomas Frank (1813-73) 14 278–9*
Heard, Augustine 13 734
Hearn, Lafcadio 20 834
Hearne, Thomas 14 279*
patrons and collectors 18 149; 21 901; 24 18
reproductive prints by others 24 742, 742
works 2 162; 18 713
Hearst, Phoebe Apperson 10 80; 14 279; 29 221
Hearst, William Randolph 14 279*; 24 423
architecture 6 63; 22 112; 28 193
collections 10 91
Comic-strip art 7 648
sculpture 21 850; 27 47
stained glass 29 515
Hearst Foundation see San Simeon (CA) → Hearst Castle
heart brooches see under Brooches → types
Heartfield, John 3 802; 14 279–80*
groups and movements 3 801; 8 433, 436, 437; 24 405
works 3 801; 4 369; 5 758; 24 685, 686, 686; 25 350, 652; 27 872
hearth brooms 11 119
Heat-Colour (Zhar-tsvet) 22 178
Heath, Charles (i) (1785-1848) 14 280*
assistants 25 753
collaboration 27 459; 29 715; 31 471
pupils 9 148; 18 727
works 14 550
Heath, Charles (ii) (fl 1825) 14 280*
Heath, James 4 607; 7 839; 10 378, 394; 14 280*, 813; 28 86; 30 853
Heath, John (fl c. 1760-70) 31 649
Heath, John (fl c. 1765) 8 776; 9 368
Heath, Thomas 10 306
Heath, William 14 280*
Heathcoat, John 10 355; 16 34; 18 589
Heathcote, David
works 14 231, 232
Heatherley, Thomas 10 373; 12 610; 13 30; 24 832; 32 331; 33 452
Heath Hall (N. Yorks) 26 499
Heath Robinson, William 4 367
Heathrow (Middx) 25 538; 30 434
Airport 1 494, 495
heating 12 270
heating systems 2 692; 7 734; 15 51, 51, 52, 52; 26 879; 28 831
see also Hypocausts
Heaton, Butler & Bayne 14 281*; 23 690; 29 507; 31 241
designers 14 677
staff 8 583; 14 281
works 29 766
Heaton, Clement (1824-82) 14 281
Heaton, Clement J(ohn) (1861-1940) 14 281*; 22 920
Heaton, Ellen 14 849
Heaton, Maurice 14 281; 31 645
Heaton, Ralph, & Son 5 255, 507
Heaton & Butler 7 410
Heaton Hall (Lancs) 10 235, 642; 12 639; 25 192
Heaton's Cloisonné Mosaics Ltd 14 281
Hebanowski, Stanislas 25 408
Hebbel, Markus see Hebel, Markus
Hebborn, Eric 11 308; 25 664
Hebdomon, St John the Baptist 9 537
Hebebrand, Werner 12 379
Hebel, Markus 11 468; 14 281–2*; 30 85
Hebenstreit, Andreas 2 825
Hebenstreit, Józef 5 84; 14 894; 31 787
Hebenstreit, Sigmund 33 271
Hebenu see Zawyat tel-Mayitin
Hébequer, Guillermo Facio see Facio Hébequer, Guillermo
Heberdey, Rudolf 23 508
Hébert (fl c. 1750s) 3 414; 8 161
Hébert (ii), Adrien 11 322; 14 282–3*
Hébert (i), (Pierre-Eugène-) Emile 14 282
Hébert, (Antoine-Auguste-) Ernest 9 424; 14 283*; 20 433
Hébert, François 24 148
Hébert (i), Héléna 14 282*
Hébert, Henri 5 570; 14 283
Hébert, Jules 32 95
Hébert, Julien 5 580
Hébert (ii), Louis-Philippe 5 570; 8 256; 14 282*
Hébert, Nicolas 18 812
Hebert, Pedro 14 283–4*
Hébert (i), Pierre 14 282
Hébert, Thomas-Joachim 4 532; 11 596; 32 368
hebigama kilns see Kilns → types → climbing
Hebra, Ferdinand von 21 7
Hébrard, Adrien 5 127
Hébrard, André 20 431
Hébrard, Ernest 10 689; 21 735; 30 718
works 29 417
Hebrew 1 855
Hebrews 1 830
Hebron 16 208, 459, 565; 17 500
Avraham Avinu synagogue 17 552
Haram al-Khalil Mosque 21 629
Shrine of Abraham 16 90; 28 634; 31 111
Shrine of Husayn 16 490
Hebron Moravian Mission 5 561
Hebroso, José Grajera y see Grajera y Hebroso, José
Hebsgaard, Per Steen 10 813
Hebster, Hans see Herbst, Hans
Hecataeus of Miletus 13 807

Hecatompylos see SHAHR-I QUMIS
Hecht, Joseph 10 397; 14 271
Hecht, Reuben 16 570
Hecht Behecht see ISFAHAN → Hasht Bihisht Palace
He Chuo 17 591
Hecke, Jan-Frans van den 5 50; 24 15
Hecke, Jan van (1699-1777) 10 899
Hecke, Jan van den (*fl c.* 1575-1600) 2 199
Hecke, Jan van der (1620-84) 19 349
Hecke, Leo van den 5 49
Hecke, van den (family) 30 320
Hecke de Jonge, Peter van 3 615
Heckel, Augustin 25 460
Heckel, C. 4 507
Heckel, Erich 4 892, 893; 10 638; 14 284–5*; 17 818; 25 600
  groups and movements
    Arbeitsrat für Kunst 2 288
    Brücke, Die 4 132, 891; 10 694, 695, 841; 12 395; 16 817; 18 77; 28 124
  patrons and collectors 11 729
  works 4 *893*; 9 310; 12 396, 407, 408, 450; 14 *284*; 18 717; 19 429, *429*, 491; 29 871; 33 363
Heckel, Hans (*fl* 16th cent.) 14 49
Heckel, Jan (*d* before 1786) 32 878
Hecken, Abraham van der 22 843
Hecker, Christian Friedrich 12 263; 14 285*
Hecker, Christopher 28 105
Hecker, Isaac Thomas 24 281
Hecker, Waldemar 24 591
Hecker, Zvi 16 566
  works 16 *566*
Heckfield Place (Hants) 12 *137*
Heckington (Lincs), St Andrew 9 681, *681*; 12 150; 13 54
  sculpture 13 82
Heckscher, William S. 10 176
Hecquet (*fl c.* 1715-26) 11 592, 596
Hecquet, Robert 3 463; 8 544
Hector Painter 13 522
Heda, Gerrit (Willemsz.) 14 287; 22 840; 29 666
Heda, Willem (Claesz.) 13 894, 895; 14 286–7*
  patrons and collectors 28 904
  works 14 *286*; 22 840; 23 113; 29 666; 31 882
Hedared Church 30 67
Heddal 9 156
  church 6 389, *389*; 11 465; 23 219; 26 691
  Mellem-Ryen 23 *232*
Heddal *Madonna* 25 175
Heddeley & Riland 31 653
heddle pulleys 3 407; 13 861
Hedebo embroidery see under EMBROIDERY → types
Hedeby 32 524, 533
Heden 8 755
Hedensted 26 648
Hederich, Benjamin 10 206
Hédervàry, János, Bishop of Győr 13 888
Hedgeland, George 25 398
hedges 21 597
Hedges, Warren T. 19 878
Hedges, William 13 876
Hedin, Sven (Anders) 6 320, 767; 7 159; 14 287*; 19 727; 21 885, 886
  personal collection 6 321
Hedlinger, Johann Anton 14 287
Hedlinger, Johann Baptist 14 287
Hedlinger, Johann Karl 14 287*; 20 915, 924; 30 85
Hedlund, Hans 13 31
Hedman, Karl 11 111, 112
Hedon, Hugh 33 548
Hédon, Jules 27 248
Hédouin, (Pierre-)Edmond (-Alexandre) 4 242; 11 156; 14 288*
Hedvig Eleanora, Queen of Sweden (1639-1715) 12 135; 14 288*; 29 690
  architecture 13 668; 30 117, 522
  furniture 30 93, *93*
  interior decoration 10 100
  paintings 3 509; 5 544; 33 421
Hedwig, Electress of Brandenburg (1513-73) 3 70
Hedwig, Electress of Saxony (*fl c.* 1600) 19 93
Hedwig, Saint 16 520
Heed, Martin Johnson see HEADE, MARTIN JOHNSON
Heek, van (family) 22 906
Heel, Johann Wilhelm 12 440, 446
Heel, Peter 3 6
Heely 12 130
Heem, Cornelis (Jansz.) de 11 227; 14 288, 289, 290*
Heem, David (Cornelisz.) de 14 288, 290*
Heem, Jan Davidsz. de (1606-83/4) 14 288, 289–90*; 22 844
  collaboration 32 116, 705
  patrons and collectors 11 229; 26 112; 28 271
  pupils 14 290; 23 447
  works 11 225, 227, *227*; 14 *289*, *290*; 22 841; 29 *666*, 667; 31 882, *883*
Heem, Jan Jansz. de (*b* 1650) 14 288, 289, 290*
  works 14 *290*
Heemskerck, Egbert (Jaspersz.) van, I (1634/5 1704) 4 873; 14 291*
Heemskerck, Egbert van, II (1645-1744) 14 291
Heemskerck, Jacobus van 32 232, 588
Heemskerck, Maarten van 14 291–4*, 869; 22 837–8, 871; 26 768; 28 217
  collaboration 7 799
  drawings 2 162, *320*; 9 21; 12 21; 14 *292*; 16 770, *770*; 26 *801*, 845, *845*; 27 182
  groups and movements 9 462; 26 728
  paintings 1 806; 2 164; 8 666; 13 895; 14 *293*; 22 *837*
  patrons and collectors 3 889; 7 867; 14 93
  prints 1 658; 7 799; 25 604; 33 355
  reproductive prints by others 3 558; 4 442; 7 499, 899; 12 15; 15 *90*; 17 598; 25 605; 26 *768*; 31 825
  stained glass 27 256
  teachers 22 837
Heemskerck van Beest, Jacoba (Berendina) van 14 294–5*; 22 852, 854; 29 871, 872; 32 775
  groups and movements 21 775
Heemskerck van Beest, Jacob Eduard van 14 294; 33 72
Heemskerk, Willem Jacob van 22 885
Heemstede 12 132; 14 295*; 22 *813*
Heenvliet 22 822
Heep, (Adolf) Franz 4 713; 12 652; 14 295–6*
Heer, Gerrit de 25 369
Heer, Guillaume de 20 235
Heer, Margaretha de 20 235
Heeramaneck, Alice 22 795; 30 849
Heeramaneck, Munchersa 14 296
Heeramaneck, Nasli M. 8 707; 14 296*; 30 849
  collections 7 156; 15 742, 745, 746; 22 795
  sculpture 15 746
Heeramaneck Galleries 14 296
Heerberg am Kocher Church 33 630, *630*
Heerden, Johan van 29 112
Heere, Jan de, the elder (1502/5-76/8) 14 296*; 26 470
Heere, Jan de, the younger (*fl* 1577) 14 296
Heere, Lucas de 13 806; 14 296–7*; 20 664
  attributions 10 666
  patrons and collectors 7 436; 26 307
  pupils 8 165; 12 514; 20 244; 24 301
  teachers 7 466; 11 222
  works 12 520; 22 910
Heermann (family) 8 385
Heermann, Johann Georg 8 385, 396
Heermann, Paul 8 385; 21 64
Heermann, Zacharias 8 385
Heerschoop, Hendrick 14 287
Heerup, Henry 7 488; 8 741; 14 297*
Hees, Gerrit van 23 614
Hees, Willem van see HESIUS, WILLEM
Heeswijk-Dinther, Berne monastery 22 870
Hefat 21 744
Hefele, Melchior 14 297–8*; 30 212
  patrons and collectors 10 529
  works 4 695, *696*; 11 31; 13 888; 14 888; 20 494; 28 850
Hefetz, Magdalena 16 568
Heffernan, James 6 457
Heftige Malerei 12 397
Hegedüs, Ármin 5 83
Hegedušić, Krsto 14 298*
  assistants 32 148
  groups and movements 8 179; 9 672; 14 595–6; 22 441
  pupils 30 37
Hegedušić, Željko 9 672
Hegel, Georg Wilhelm Friedrich 1 179; 10 685; 14 298–300*; 15 210; 28 925; 33 630
  on aesthetics 1 180–81; 3 799; 12 482
  on art 2 518
  on art history 2 532, 533; 29 879
  on colour 7 629
Hegel, Konstanty 32 877
Hegel, Vladimir 16 877
Hegel, Wladislaw 26 715, 723
Hegemann, Marta 8 437; 25 837; 29 869
Hegemann, Werner (Manfred Maria Ellis) 14 300*; 31 728
Hegenauer 12 405
Hegendorf, Hans 19 111
Heger, Hilde 27 665
Heger, Rolf 15 816
Heger drums see under DRUMS → types
Hegermann-Lindencrone, Effie 7 807
Hegesias see HEGIAS
Hegeso Stele 6 *388*; 13 431
Hegewald, Michael 14 301
Hegewald, Zacharias 14 301*; 32 833
  works 32 *833*
Hegi, Franz 33 424, 736
Hegias 14 301*; 24 592
Hegu de Lowenfeld, Henry-Michel, Baron 11 635
Hegvald 26 639
Hegylos 8 458
Hehl, Christoph (Carl Adolf) 14 301*
Heholl (family) 33 300
He Hong 7 115
Heian see under KYOTO
Heiankyō see under KYOTO
Heian period see under JAPAN → periods
Heiberg, Edvard 3 749; 8 728
Heiberg, Jean (Hjalmar Dahl) 14 302*; 23 226, 603; 28 828
Heiberg, Kasper 8 741
Heide, Henning von der 8 615; 12 401; 13 120; 14 302–3*; 23 256
Heideck, Carl Wilhelm 14 303*
Heidegger, John James 17 626
Heidegger, Martin 1 179, 182; 10 685, 686; 14 303–4*, 458, 459; 26 62
Heideken, P. G. 10 754
Heidel, Hermann Rudolf 14 304*
Heidelberg 12 *361*; 14 304–6*, *305*; 25 *470*
  Bibliotheca Palatina 19 314; 33 278
  Friedrichsbau 10 745; 12 369; 13 218
  Heiliggeist Foundation 33 278
  Kurpfälzisches Museum 14 306
  Orangery 23 470
  Ottheinrichsbau 10 745
  Ruprecht-Karls-Universität 10 93, 640; 12 442; 25 686
  Schloss 12 *367*, 369; 14 305–6
    furniture 29 60
    Gläsener Saalbau 12 366
    Hortus Palatinus 6 95–6; 11 343; 12 133; 13 704
    Ottheinrichsbau 12 367
  sculpture 6 156
  University 12 481
Heidelberger, Ernst Johann 8 384, 396; 14 306*; 18 191; 25 446
Heidelberger, Thomas 14 306*
Heidelberg Painter 13 508; 32 47*
Heidelberg school 2 746, 747, 769; 14 306–7*; 19 413; 21 76
  members 2 747; 7 700; 8 571; 19 873; 26 464; 29 767; 30 39; 33 263
  works 2 *746*; 29 *767*
Heideloff, Carl Alexander von 14 307–8*; 27 217
Heideloff, Franz Joseph (Ignatz Anton) 14 307
Heideloff, N. 29 592
Heideloff, Victor (Wilhelm Peter) 14 307
Heidenreich, Erhard 14 308*
Heidenreich, Ulrich 14 308*
Heidenreichstein 6 57
Heidetränk 6 159
Heidnischwerk see under TAPESTRIES → types
Heidt, John Valentine 33 91
Heiemon Okano see OKANO HEIEMON
heightening 14 308*
Heihachi Hashimoto see HASHIMOTO, HEIHACHI
Heihachirō Fukuda see FUKUDA, HEIHACHIRŌ
Heijde Church 13 190
Heijō see under NARA
Heikel, Axel Olai 21 885
Heikel, Elia 19 411
Heikkinen, Mikko 11 93
Heil, Leon van 7 915
Heilbronn, Kilianskirche 12 366; 24 806; 30 161
Heilbuth, Hermann 8 759
Heiligenberg Schloss 6 604
Heiligenkreuz Abbey 2 *776*, 777, 781; 13 49, 56; 14 308–9*, *309*; 22 219
  church 2 777
  manuscript illumination 2 791
  sculpture 2 801; 12 748
  stained glass 13 142, 186
Heiligenkreuz-Gutenbrunn Church 2 795
  frescoes 2 *795*
Heiligenleiten 9 156
Heiliger, Bernhard 3 803; 12 408; 14 310*
Heiligkreuztal Altarpiece 20 770
Heilmann, Jacob see HAYLMANN, JACOB
Heilmann, Johann Caspar 6 563
Heilmann, Josué 30 151, 563
Heilmann & Littmann 19 502
Heilsberg see LIDZBARD WARMIŃSKI
Heilsbronn Minster 21 845; 31 286, *286*
Heiltsuk 22 547, 579
Heim, François-Joseph 11 659; 14 310–11*; 33 673
  works 14 *311*
Heim, Jacques 8 658; 13 798
Heim, Joseph 14 310
Heimatschutz 4 143; 14 312; 28 175
Heimatstil 11 129; 14 311–12*; 30 143
Heimatwerk 14 312
Heimbach, Wolfgang 14 312–13*
Heimberg 30 144
Heimberger, Richard 11 104
Heimo workshop 19 863; 26 631
Heimsch, Johann Georg see HEINTSCH, JOHANN GEORG
Heince, Zacharie 14 313*
Heinczlin Glaser 25 434
Heindl, Franz Anton 14 313
Heindl, Franz Xaver 14 313
Heindl, Ignaz 14 313
Heindl, Wolfgang Andreas 14 313*
Heindrickx, Loys 12 523
Heine, Gustav 2 478
Heine, Heinrich 24 223
Heine, Maurice 30 20
Heine, Thomas Theodor 14 313–14*; 27 871
Heinecken, Karl Heinrich von 14 314*; 33 115
  works 6 78; 10 206, 207; 33 115
Heinecken, Robert 14 314*; 19 702
Heine-Geldern, Robert 14 315*; 29 242
Heineman Hours see under BOOKS OF HOURS → individual manuscripts
Heinemann 4 367; 22 304
Heinemann, William 23 102
Heinersdorff 14 295
Heinesen, Zakarias 10 813
Heiningen 12 462
Heinitz, Friedrich Anton, Freiherr von 1 105; 12 479
Heinitz, Karl Friedrich von 5 885
Heinouchi (family) 17 52
Heinouchi Masanobu 2 317; 14 315*; 17 418
Heinrich (*fl c.* late 14th cent.) 27 217
Heinrich, Duke of Saxony see HENRY, Duke of Saxony
Heinrich IV, King of Germany see HENRY IV Holy Roman Emperor
Heinrich VIII, Prince-Bishop of Bibra 11 832
Heinrich, Annemarie 10 747
Heinrich, E. 31 759
Heinrich, Ede 14 315–16*
Heinrich, Georg 3 797
Heinrich, Gerhard see HEINRIK, GERARD
Heinrich, Johann Georg see HEINTSCH, JOHANN GEORG
Heinrich of Werl, Bishop of Paderborn 1 697; 20 671; 26 534
Heinrichs, Georg 19 168
Heinrichskelch 6 398
Heinrich von Cleve, Abbot of Liesborn 20 718
Heinrich von Freiburg see HEINRICH VON GMÜND

Heinrich von Gmünd **13** 89; **20** 567; **21** 530; **24** 191*
attributions **4** 832; **7** 589; **20** 493; **25** 441, *442*
works **7** 583; **8** 382; **13** 89
Heinrich von Konstanz **30** 136
Heinrich von München **7** 242
Heinrich von Veldeke **14** 423; **19** 863; **26** 561
Heinrich von Virneburg, Archbishop of Cologne **7** 590
Heinrici, Johann Martin **11** 632, 731
Heinrik, Gerard **14** 316*
Heins, Dietrich, I *see* HEINS, JOHN THEODORE
Heins, George Lewis **14** 317*
Heins, John Theodore (*c.* 1697-1756) **14** 316*
Heins, John Theodore (1732/3-71) **14** 316
Heins, Sacharie *see* HEINCE, ZACHARIE
Heinsch, Johann Georg *see* HEINTSCH, JOHANN GEORG
Heinse, (Johann Jakob) Wilhelm **14** 316–17*; **24** 443
Heinsen, Hein **8** 741
Heinsius, Daniel **10** 175
Heinsius, Johann Ernst **11** 410; **14** 317*
Heinsius, Johann Julius **14** 317
Heins & La Farge **7** 277; **8** 111; **14** 317*; **18** 628
Heintsch, Johann Georg **14** 317–18*
Heintz, Daniel (i) (1530/35-96) **3** 336; **14** 318–19*
works **14** *318*
Heintz, Daniel (ii) (1575-1633) **14** 318, 321*
works **14** 319
Heintz, Daniel (iii) (1640-1709) **14** 318
Heintz, Ferdinand **13** 847
Heintz, Giuseppe *see* HEINTZ, JOSEPH (ii)
Heintz, Jiří Antonín **8** 386
Heintz, Johann **18** 848
Heintz, Joseph (i) (1564-1609) **8** 390; **13** 847; **14** 318, 319–21*; **22** 839, 918; **24** 231
collaboration **11** 77; **14** 679
methods **21** 764
patrons and collectors **12** 387; **13** 912; **29** 429
reproductive prints by others **18** 42
works **1** 550; **12** 368, 370, *370*; **14** *320*; **22** 918; **26** 104; **32** 821; **33** 279
Heintz, Joseph (ii) (*c.* 1600-78) **14** 318, 321–2*
pupils **31** 313
reproductive prints by others **18** 46
teachers **13** 847
works **32** 111
Heintz, Regina **14** 318
Heintz, Tobias **18** 848
Heintz di Augusta *see* HEINTZ, JOSEPH (ii)
Heintze, Andreas Heinrich **22** 449; **25** 124
Heintze, Johann Christian **14** 317
Heintze, Johann Heinrich **22** 449; **25** 124
Heinz, Günther **2** 834
Heinze, Johann Ernst *see* HEINSIUS, JOHANN ERNST
Heinzelmann, Konrad **12** 365; **14** 322*; **23** 204, 316
Heinz Graffunder Collective **3** 805
Heinzmann, Carl Friedrich **14** 322–3*
Heir, Tell el- **9** 848; **28** 760, *760*
Heise, Carl Georg **3** 242
Heise, Jacob **14** 323*
Heise, Wilhelm **22** 304
Heisecke, María Victoria **24** 102
Heisei period *see under* JAPAN → periods
Heisel, Heinz **17** 548, 549
Heiser, Karel Vilém Kristián **8** 419
Heisig, Bernhard **14** 323–4*; **19** 112
Heisig, Walter **12** 480; **14** 323
Heisler, Jindrich **30** 22, 23; **31** 250
Heiss, Elias Christoph **2** 719; **18** 47
Heiss, Johann **10** 103; **12** 390; **14** 324*; **18** 46; **29** 400
Heister, Lorenz **21** 6
Heisterbach Abbey **32** 88
Heisterbach Altar, Master of the **20** 690*
Heisterkamp, Peter *see* PALERMO, BLINKY
Heito I, Abbot of Reichenau (*reg* 806-23) **21** 835; **26** 100; **27** 556
Heito III, Abbot of Reichenau (*reg* 888-913), Archbishop of Mainz **23** 650; **26** 101
Heiton, Andrew **19** 109; **28** 289
Heitzinger, Jakob **22** 302
Heizei, Emperor (*reg* 806-9) **18** 503
Heizer, Michael **14** 324–5*; **23** 49
methods **9** 310
works **7** 697; **18** 694, 695, 822
Heizer, Robert **8** 255; **18** 881
Hejduk, John **14** 325*; **23** 50
Hejia cun **6** *615*; **14** 325–6*
glass **7** 82
hardstones **7** *89*, 90
metalwork **7** 23
Hejing *see* CHAWUHUGOU
Hejna, Václav **8** 394
Hejnum **13** 119
Hekanefer **23** 279
Hekareshu **10** 57
Hekatomnids **1** 888
hekatompeda see under TEMPLES → types
Hektoridas **10** 434; **13** 460
Hel, Abraham del **2** 716
Helander, Vilhelm **19** 114
Helbig, Jules **3** 619; **31** 856
Helbig, Walter **8** 434; **10** 639; **12** 649
Helchis, Jakob **2** 816; **16** 737
Held, Al **8** 110; **14** 326*; **24** 585
Held, Robert **5** 583
Helden **30** 772, 773
Heldenberg **2** 802
Helderberg, Jan Baptiste **14** 326*
Helderberg, Lieven Jan **14** 326
Helderenberg, Jan Baptiste *see* HELDERBERG, JAN BAPTISTE
Heldmann, Ignaz **11** 741; **24** 240
Heldt, Werner **14** 326–8*
groups and movements **3** 803
works **3** 802; **14** *327*
Heldua **9** 543
Hele, Ivor **2** 749
Helen, Duchesse d'Orléans and Grand Duchess of Mecklenburg-Schwerin (1814-58) **8** 705
Helena, Saint, Empress (*c.* 255-330) **3** 880; **5** 443; **7** 217; **33** 458
Helen of Egypt **33** 307
Helen Painter **17** 911
Helensburgh (Strathclyde) **28** 229
Hill House **20** 24, *24*; **28** 249, 270
Long Croft **28** 230
Helft, Jacques **27** 163
Helgadóttir, Gerður **14** 328*; **15** 71
Helgeland Bridge **4** 804, *804*
Helhesten **7** 488; **17** 658
He Liangjun **25** 73
Helice **9** 749
Helin, Pekka **14** 328*
Helin and Siitonen **14** 328–9*
Helinge'er *see* HELINGOL
Helingol **6** 648, 808; **30** 912
ceramics **6** *891*
Heliodorus (*fl c.* 150/100 BC; ambassador) **3** 874; **15** 213, 430
Heliodorus (*fl c.* 1st cent. BC; sculptor) **12** 911
Heliogabalus, Emperor of Rome (*reg* 218-22) **26** 787, 900
heliography *see under* PRINTING → processes
heliogravure *see* photogravure; PHOTOGRAPHY → processes
Hélion, Jean **14** 329–30*
groups and movements **1** 76, 89, 90, 772; **5** 776; **7** 698, 772; **11** 550
patrons and collectors **2** 409; **12** 15
works **1** *89*; **11** 550; **14** *330*; **22** 749
writings **13** 727
Heliopolis (Egypt) **9** *774*; **14** 331*
benben **14** 331; **23** 329
necropoleis **9** 843
obelisk of Sesostris I **14** 331; **23** 329
obelisk of Tuthmosis III **23** 331
reliefs **9** 868
sanctuary **9** 827, 828
Heliopolis (Lebanon) *see* BAALBEK
Helios *see* MUYBRIDGE, EADWEARD
Héliot, Berthelot **11** 637
heliotrope *see* BLOODSTONE (CHALCEDONY)
heliotype process *see under* PHOTOGRAPHY → processes
Hell, Xavier Hommaire de *see* HOMMAIRE DE HELL, XAVIER
Helladic **14** 331–61*, *332*
alabastra **14** *344*
amulets **14** 360
architecture **14** 336, 338–41*
armour **14** 356
arrowheads **14** 356
askoi **14** *342*
beads **14** 357, *357*
bone **14** 353–4*
bowls **14** *342*, *345*, *347*
bronze **14** 356*, *356*; **22** *397*
cemeteries **23** 476
chronologies **14** *334*, 334–5*, 337*
cists **14** 339
citadels **14** 340
collections **14** 360–61*
columns **14** 340
craftsmen and artists **14** 335, 341
cups **14** *344*, 344, 355
daggers **14** 355; **22** *397*
doorways **14** 340
dromoi **14** *340*
faience (i) (glass) **14** *358*, 358–9*
figurines **14** 335, 352, *352*
forgeries **14** 360*
fortifications **14** 338, 339, 340
furniture **14** 354
gateways **22** *396*
glass **1** 865
goblets **14** 338, *343*, *344*
gold **14** 354–5*, *355*, 357, *357*
granaries **14** 339
graves **14** 339
houses **14** *336*, 336, 338–9
human figures **14** 335
iconography **14** 333–4*
inlays **22** *397*
ivory **14** 353–4*, *354*
ivory-carvings **14** *353*, *354*
jars **14** *343*, *345*, *347*
jewellery **14** 356–8*, 360
jugs **14** *343*, *344*, *356*
kantharoi **14** *343*
kraters **14** *345*, *347*
kylikes **14** *345*, *358*
masks **14** 338, *355*
masonry **22** *396*
megara (buildings) **14** 338, 340; **21** *46*, 46
metalwork **14** 354*
Helladic—cont.
museums **14** 360–61*
palaces **14** 338, *339*, 340; **23** 476–7; **25** *754*; **31** *25*, 25–6
pendants (jewellery) **14** *357*
periods **14** 334
Early Helladic (*c.* 3600/3000-*c.* 2050 BC) **14** *334*, 335–6*, *336*
Early Helladic I (*c.* 3600/3000-*c.* 2900/2600 BC) **14** *334*
Early Helladic II (*c.* 2900/2600-*c.* 2400 BC) **14** *334*
Early Helladic III (*c.* 2400-*c.* 2050 BC) **14** *334*
Final Neolithic (*c.* 4500-*c.* 3600/3000 BC) **14** *334*
Late Helladic (*c.* 1600-*c.* 1050 BC) **14** *334*, 337–8*
Late Helladic I (*c.* 1600-*c.* 1500 BC) **14** *334*
Late Helladic IIA (*c.* 1500-*c.* 1440 BC) **14** *334*
Late Helladic IIB (*c.* 1440-*c.* 1390 BC) **14** *334*
Late Helladic IIIA:1 (*c.* 1390-*c.* 1360 BC) **14** *334*
Late Helladic IIIA:2 (*c.* 1360-*c.* 1335 BC) **14** *334*
Late Helladic IIIB:1 (*c.* 1335-*c.* 1240 BC) **14** *334*
Late Helladic IIIB:2 (*c.* 1240-*c.* 1180 BC) **14** *334*
Late Helladic IIIC (*c.* 1180-*c.* 1050 BC) **14** *334*
Middle Helladic (*c.* 2050-*c.* 1600 BC) **14** *334*, 337*
Mycenaean *see* Late Helladic IIIC (*c.* 1180-*c.* 1050 BC)
Sub-Mycenaean (*c.* 1050-*c.* 1000 BC) **14** *334*
pithoi **14** 341, 342, *344*
plaques **14** 354
plaster **14** *352*
plates **14** *342*
pottery **14** 341–7*, 359
Argive Close style **14** 346, *347*
Argolid **14** 341, 343, 346
Attica **14** 341
Ayia Marina ware **14** 342
Boeotia **14** 341
Corinthian **14** 341
Cyprus, ancient **8** 346
Early Helladic (*c.* 3600/3000-*c.* 2050 BC) **14** 335–6, 342*, *342*
Euboia **14** 342
filled style *see* Metope style
Late Helladic (*c.* 1600-*c.* 1050 BC) **14** 337–8, 341, *344*, 344–7*, *345*, *347*
Lefkandi I **14** 342, *342*
Lerna IV Patterned ware **14** 342, *342*
Mainland Polychrome style **14** *343*, 344
Matt-painted ware **14** 337, 343, *343*, 344, 345
Metope style **14** *347*
Middle Helladic (*c.* 2050-*c.* 1600 BC) **14** *343*, 343–4*, *344*
Minyan ware **14** 333, 337, 343, *343*; **23** 475
Octopus style **14** *347*
Palatial style **14** *344*
Pictorial style **14** *345*, *347*
Talioti ware **14** 342
Thessaly **14** 341
pyxides (vases) **14** *345*
religion **14** 333–4*
rhyta **14** 355
sauceboats **14** 342, *342*
saucers **14** *342*
sculpture **14** 351–3*
Early Helladic (*c.* 3600/3000-*c.* 2050 BC) **14** 351*
Late Helladic (*c.* 1600-*c.* 1050 BC) **14** 351–2*
mythological **14** *352*
relief **14** 352–3*
Helladic—cont.
seals **14** 359*, *359*
cylinder **14** 358
Early Helladic (*c.* 3600/3000-*c.* 2050 BC) **14** 336
Late Helladic (*c.* 1600-*c.* 1050 BC) **14** 338
Popular group **14** 360
settlements **14** 336, 338, 340
silver **14** 354–5*
spearheads **14** 356
stelae **14** 338
stools **14** 354
swords **14** 356
tankards **14** *342*
terracotta **14** *352*
theatres **19** 234
tombs
Late Helladic (*c.* 1600-*c.* 1050 BC) **14** 340–41
tholos **14** 338, 339, *340*, 340; **23** 476
trade **14** 331–3*, 335, 337; **21** 652
wall paintings **14** 338, 340, 348–51*, *349*, *350*; **23** 477
walls **14** 340
Hellande, Guillaume de *see* Guillaume de Hellande
Helland-Hansen, Peter **23** 232
Hellat, Georg **10** 537
Hell Brueghel *see* BRUEGHEL, PIETER, II
Hellbrunn Schloss **2** *776*, 782; **14** 361*; **27** 610; **29** 27
automata **2** 837
gardens **12** 105, 133; **14** 361*
grottoes **13** 704
Mirror Grotto **13** 703
Orpheus grotto **13** 703
ruin-grotto **13** 703; **27** 323
Helldén, David **3** 43; **18** 664; **19** 284; **30** 75, 684
Hellebæk, Utzon's house **8** 729
Hellebæk Værk **8** 751
Hellenikon **13** 384
Hellenraedt, Edmond **14** 362*
Hellens, Franz **18** 577
Helleputte, Georges *see* HELLEPUTTE, JORIS
Helleputte, Joris **3** 548; **14** 362*
education (art) **3** 618
pupils **7** 460
teachers **3** 885
works **19** 260
Heller, Ben **33** 45
Heller, Carl **13** 360
Heller, Isidore **6** 573
Heller, Jakob **9** 435; **13** 720; **17** 711
Heller, Joseph **9** 444
Heller, Juan **29** 337
Heller, R. **29** 435
Heller Altarpiece **9** 435, 443, 445; **13** 720, *721*
Hellerau **8** 824; **9** 237; **12** 145, *360*, *361*, 378; **14** 362–3*; **26** 374; **28** 177; **30** 520; **31** 728
Festspielhaus **30** 682
furniture **12** 428
Heller Designs **32** 500
Helleu, Alice **14** *363*
Helleu, Paul César (François) **14** 363–4*
methods **9** 216
patrons and collectors **22** 22; **25** 150
works **9** 309; **14** *363*
Hellewich, Laurens Heinrich **30** 460
Hellicar, Evelyn **26** 336
Hellich, Josef Vojtěch **14** 364*
Hellinck, Nicolaas **10** 222
Hellington (Norfolk), St John the Baptist **26** 613
Hellinus, Abbot **3** 566
Hellion, Martha **10** 99
Hellmer, Edmund (von) **2** 803; **14** 364–5*
assistants **3** 511

Hellmer, Edmund (von)—cont.
pupils **10** 750; **14** 130
works **2** 803; **32** 456
Hellmer, Hermann **2** 808; **18** 692
Hellmuth, George F. **22** 366
Hellmuth, Obata & Kassabaum **1** 495; **5** 124; **8** 470; **26** 433
Hellot, Jean **11** 609; **32** 582
Hellsted, Frederik Ferdinand **30** 2
Hellweg (family) **22** 891
Hellyar, Christine **14** 365*; **23** 63
Helm, Willem (Leendertsz.) van der **14** 365*; **18** 886; **19** 99, 100
Helman, Isidore-Stanislas-Henri **14** 365–6*
works **24** *176*
Helmantike *see* SALAMANCA
Helmarshausen, Roger of *see* ROGER OF HELMARSHAUSEN
Helmarshausen Abbey **12** *360*; **14** 366*; **26** 683
manuscripts **7** 246, *246*; **12** 382; **26** 660, 675
Helmbach Glassworks **8** 408
Helmbreker, Dirck **7** 509; **14** 366–7*; **22** 208
Helme, Corbett and Harrison **14** 199
Helmer, Herman **14** 367*; **30** 678; **31** 551
collaboration **5** 149; **8** 176; **10** 871; **13** 330; **23** 340, 353; **30** 679; **33** 593, 735
staff **2** 415; **17** 630; **29** 777
works **23** *354*
helmet masks *see under* MASKS → types
Helmet of Boabdil **16** 505
helmets **2** 469; **14** 412–13, *413*, 421
historical and regional traditions
Ancient Near East **1** 883
Anglo-Saxon **10** *338*; **14** 412
Aztec **22** 164
Celtic **6** 157
Central Asia, Eastern **6** 306
Central Asia, Western **6** 261, 262
China **7** 55, *55*
Crete **8** 154
Dacian **30** 773
Egypt **16** *504*
England **10** *338*; **14** 412; **27** *95*
France **6** 157
Greece, ancient **13** 583, 584
Hawaii **10** 848; **14** 249
Indian subcontinent **30** *564*
Iran **16** *504*
Iraq **16** *504*
Islamic **16** *504*, 505, 507, *507*
Italy **6** 157
Japan **17** 300, 302, 362, *362*, 363
Mesoamerica, Pre-Columbian **21** 245; **22** 164
Morocco **16** *504*
Native North Americans **14** *746*
Ottoman **16** *504*, 507, *507*
Romania **30** *770*
Rome, ancient **27** *95*
Scandinavia **14** 412
Slovenia **28** 807
Spain **16** *504*
Syria **16** *504*
Thracian **30** *770*, 770–71
Turkey **16** *504*
United States of America **14** *746*
materials
amethyst **16** *507*
antlers **14** *746*
bronze **6** 261; **7** 55, *55*; **8** 154; **13** 583; **27** *95*
copper **10** *338*; **14** *746*
enamel **16** *504*
feathers **10** 848; **14** 249; **21** 245
gold **2** *472*; **16** *507*
iron **10** *338*; **16** *504*, 505, *507*; **30** 773
lacquer **17** 300, 302
helmets
materials—cont.
paper **21** 245
rubies **16** *507*
satin **30** *564*
silver **30** *770*
skins **21** 245
steel **2** *470*, *472*; **6** 261; **16** 507
turquoise **16** *507*
techniques
damascening **2** *472*
types
armets **2** 470, *470*
basinets **2** 469
burgonet **2** 472, *472*
Corinthian **13** 583
great basinets **2** 469
great helms **2** 469
kettle-hats **2** 469
morions **2** 472
potts **2** 473
sallets **2** 470
Spangenhelm **2** 468
helmet shells *see under* SHELLS → types
Helmhack, Abraham **23** 313
Helmholtz, Hermann von **24** 376; **28** 203
Helmholtz resonator **1** 124
Helmholz, F. **12** 173
Helmholz, Hermann von **24** 738
Helmle, Corbett & Harrison **7** 838
Helmle, Frank J. **7** 838
Helmle & Corbett **7** 838
Helmle-Merzweiler **11** 752
Helmond **22** 900
Castle **22** 822
Helmore & Cotterill **23** 55
helm roofs *see under* ROOFS → types
Helms, Jacob **8** 761
Helmschmied, Desiderius **2** 472
Helmschmied, Koloman **2** 472
Helmschmied, Lorenz **2** 470, 472, 716
Helmsdorf **25** 523, 524, 529
Helmsley **6** 56
Helmstedt University **31** 674
Helorus **28** 655
Helpidius, Rusticus *see* RUSTICUS HELPIDIUS
Helpman, Robert **4** 606
Helsby (Hazel), Alfredo **6** 597; **12** 917; **14** 367*
Helset, Edvin **23** 234
Helsingborg **14** 367–8*; **30** *65*
Castle **4** 781; **8** 723, 724; **14** 367–8*, *368*
St Michael **8** 723
Helsinge Church **8** 723
Helsingfors *see* HELSINKI
Helsingør **8** *720*; **14** 368–70*
76, Stengade **4** 781
Carmelite church **8** 723, 738
Krogen *see* Kronborg Castle
Kronborg Castle **4** 781; **8** 719, 725, 732, 739; **14** 369–70*, *370*, 730; **23** 328
interior decoration **29** 748
paintings **16** 63; **30** 734
tapestries **8** 732, 754, 758; **14** 542; **18** 149
Lundehave *see* Marienlyst
Marienlyst **8** 744
Ørekrog *see* Kronborg Castle
St Marie **14** 369
St Olai **8** 723
Helsinki **10** 218–19; **11** *87*, 92; **14** 370–73*; **31** 718
Academy of the Visual Arts **11** 112; **14** 372
Bank of Finland **11** 97
Cathedral **11** 92; **14** *371*
furniture **11** 104
gold **11** 108
guilds **11** 103
Itäkeskus Tower and Commercial Centre **11** 92
Kaisaniemenkatu *see* Keskuskatu
Helsinki—cont.
Keskuskatu **27** 473
metalwork **11** 108
Municipal Theatre **14** *372*
Murtokatu **27** 473
museums
Anderson, Amos, Museum of Art **11** 112; **14** 372
Artegrafica **14** 373
Art Exhibition Hall **11** 112; **14** 372
Athenaeum Art Museum **11** 111, 112; **14** *373*, 656; **28** 814
collections **11** 112; **14** 372
see also National Gallery
City Art Museum **14** 372, 373
Didrichsen Art Museum **14** 372; **29** 241
Galeri Hagelstam **14** 373
Galeri Hörhammer **14** 373
Juhani Kirpilä's House **14** 372
Kansallismuseo *see* National Museum of Finland
Kluuvi Gallery **14** 372
Lauri and Lasse Rietz Collection **14** 372
Museum of Contemporary Art **11** 112
Museum of Finnish Architecture **11** 112; **27** 454
Museum of Foreign Art **11** 112
National Gallery **11** 112; **14** 372
see also Athenaeum Art Museum
National Museum of Finland **11** 92, 100, 112; **12** 21, 498; **14** 371; **19** 408
collections **11** 112; **21** 886
Suomen Kansallismuseo *see* National Museum of Finland
Villa Gyllenberg **14** 372
National Theatre **11** 92
observatory **23** 340
Olympic Stadium **11** 100; **29** 489
Parliament Building **11** 92
Pohjola Insurance Company Building **11** 100
Postal Savings Bank **31** 886
Puu-Käpylä **31** 821
railway station **11** 92; **27** 473, *473*
Senate House **10** *218*; **11** 92
Senate Square **13** 611
Sibelius monument **11** 101
Stock Exchange **29** *64*
Stockmann department store **4** 789; **11** 92
Teollisuuskeskus Building **26** 260
University **10** *219*, 422; **11** 92, 104; **19** 318
University of Industrial Arts **11** 112
Uschakoff Building **3** 177
Villa and Art Gallery Didrichsen **26** 261
Ylätuvanpolku **14** 328–9
Helst, Bartholomeus van der **1** 806; **14** 373–4*; **24** 735
collaboration **3** 84; **33** 26
patrons and collectors **31** 342
reproductive prints by others **33** 25
works **11** *443*; **14** *374*
Helst, Lodewijk van der **14** 374
Helsted, Axel (Theophilus) **14** 374–5*
Helt, Nicolaes de **31** 341
Heltái, Gaspar **19** 772
Helt Stockade, Nicolaes de **1** 806; **22** 843
He Lu **30** 47
Helvetii **6** 152; **18** 828
Helvetisches Journal für Literatur und Kunst **24** 453
Helvétius, Claude-Adrien **24** 787
Helwan **9** 765, 812, 813; **29** 615
Helwig, J. **19** 496
Helyer, J. S. **5** 562; **31** 863
Helzingen **19** 826
Hem, Den **20** 656
Hem, Herman van der **14** 375
Hem, Laurens van der **14** 375*
drawings **9** 150; **14** 15; **27** 518; **28** 73
Hemachandra **15** 720
Hemadri **15** 317
hematite *see* HAEMATITE
Hemavati **14** 375*; **15** *294*, 534; **23** 182
Doddeshvara Temple **15** 530
reliefs **15** 530
sculpture **15** 529, 537
Siddeshvara Temple **15** 529, *530*
Virupaksha Temple **15** 530
Hemba **14** 375–9*; **29** 68
divination instruments **1** 357
fetishes **14** 378
figurines **14** 378
masks **1** 405; **14** 378
portraits **1** 269
regalia **1** 365
sculpture **1** 403; **14** 376–8*, *377*
stakes **14** 378
stools **1** 365; **14** 378, *378*
wood **14** *377*, *378*
wood-carvings **14** 378–9*
Hembicki, R. **3** 529
Hemel Hempstead (Herts) **17** 473; **31** 733
Hemerken, Thomas *see* KEMPIS, THOMAS À
Hémery, Antoine François **20** 5
Hemery, Michel Particelli, Sieur d' *see* EMERY, MICHEL PARTICELLI, Sieur d'
Hemessen, Catharina van **14** 381, 382*
Hemessen, Gillis van **14** 379
Hemessen, Hans van **14** 379
Hemessen, Jan Sanders van **3** 554; **14** 379–82*
attributions **20** 792
patrons and collectors **5** 792
pupils **14** 382
teachers **7** 427
works **14** *379*, *380*; **31** 882
Heming, Thomas **14** 382*; **19** 593
collaboration **10** 333
patrons and collectors **33** 208
teachers **2** 304
works **4** 540; **10** 333; **14** 857
Hemingway, Ernest **21** 706
Hemis **14** 383*; **15** *264*; **30** *806*
temple **30** 819
hemispeoi **29** 386
hemispherical domes *see under* DOMES → types
hemlock **22** 563
Hemmaberg **2** 776
Cathedral **9** 529
Hemmel von Andlau, Peter **2** 115; **14** 383*
assistants **20** 648
patrons and collectors **33** 429
works **2** 721; **11** 752; **13** 188, *188*; **23** 316; **27** 664; **29** 503, IV
workshop **12** 385
Hemmerlin, Laux **3** 20
Hemming, Samuel **26** 18
Hemmings **26** 18
Hemmor **27** 87
Hémon, Louis **11** 902; **30** 50
Hemony, François **1** 810, 812; **3** 627; **22** 894
Hemony, Pieter **1** 810; **3** 627; **22** 894
hemp **5** 653
historical and regional traditions
Central Asia, Eastern **6** 304, 314
Central Asia, Western **6** 251
China **7** 43, 45, 63, 64, 114; **17** 101; **18** 601
England **10** *182*
France **11** 637
Germany **12** 464
Islamic **16** 352
hemp
historical and regional traditions—cont.
Japan **17** 101, 139, 209, 219, 297, 312, 389, 403
Korea **18** 373
types
Indian **22** *663*
uses
banners **6** 304
baskets **22** *663*
bookbindings **7** 63
brushes **17** 209
canvas **5** 653, 654
dress **6** 251
embroidery **10** *182*
kites **17** 389
lacquer **17** 297; **18** 601
paper **6** 314; **7** 64, 114; **16** 352; **17** 139, 219, 403; **24** 40
sculpture **17** 101
tapestries **11** 637
textiles **7** 43, 45
threads **30** 537–8*
weaving **17** 312
Hempel, Eberhard **14** 383*
Hempel, Sven **10** 462
Hempel, Willi **33** 635
hempseed oil *see under* OILS → types
Hemricourt, Jacques de *see* JACQUES DE HEMRICOURT
Hems, Harry **10** 266
Hemse rood **12** 626; **26** 647, *647*; **27** 123, 124
Hemudu **6** *615*, 685; **7** 12, 138; **14** 384*
Hemudu culture **6** 877, 878; **7** 159
Hemy, Bernard Benedict **14** 384
Hemy, Charles Napier **14** 384*
Hemy, Thomas Madawaska **14** 384
Hénard, Antoine-Julien **14** 384
Hénard, Eugène Alfred **11** 525; **14** 384–5*; **24** 128; **25** 658; **29** 843; **31** 728
Henares, Diego de **5** 691
Hénault, Charles-Jean-François **6** 527; **7** 495; **11** 81
Hénault, G. **23** 510
Hénault, Lucien Ambrose **6** 593, 602; **27** 791
Henchir Kasbat *see* THUBURBO MAIUS
Henchir Souar *see* SOUAR, HENCHIR
Henckels
works **8** *286*
Hencze, Tamás **14** 902
Hendecourt, Bernard d', Vicomte **9** 451
Henderick, G. **3** 579
Henderikse, Jan **2** 422; **8** 668; **23** 298; **28** 159
Henderson, Alexander **11** 743; **14** 385*
Henderson, Alexander, 1st Lord Faringdon **12** 315; **32** 907
Henderson, Anketell Matheson **26** 74
Henderson, David **1** 772
Henderson, D. & J. **1** 772; **31** 636
Henderson, George **10** 681
Henderson, Gregory **18** 259
Henderson, John (*d* 1786) **2** 617
Henderson, John (1764-1834) **21** 901; **32** 903
Henderson, John (1804-62) **14** 259
Henderson, Kingsley **4** 605
Henderson, Nigel **14** 385*; **15** 166; **19** 590; **24** 34
Henderson, P. L. B. **10** 97
Henderson Box **16** 379
Hendery, Robert **5** 585, 586
Hendery & Leslie **5** 586
Hendler, David **31** 747
Hendley, Thomas **15** 742
Hen Domen **6** 53, 56
Hendon Synagogue **17** 548

Hendra **15** 808
Hendrick de Borchgrave **1** 526
Hendricks, Geoff **11** 232
Hendricks, J. **8** 681
Hendricksz. (Centen), Dirck **14** 385–6*; **15** 147
Hendrickx, Ernest **3** 549; **14** 386*
Hendrickx, Henri **14** 386
Hendricx, Gillis **4** 283
Hendricxz., Lieven **19** 348
Hendrik, Gerard **8** 384
Hendriks, Wybrand **14** 386*; **20** 400; **22** 846; **30** 568
Hendrik van den Bogarde **4** 144
Hendrik van Diependale **19** 260
Hendrik van Haarlem **20** 636
Hendrik van Pede *see* PEDE, HENDRIK VAN
Hendrik van Tienen **13** 62
Hendrik van Wueluwe **20** 676
Hendrix, Jimi **4** 608
Hendrix, L. **3** 885
Hendrychová, Dagmar **8** 406
Hendtzschel, Gottfried **23** 224
Henegouwe, Jan van *see* GOSSART, JAN
Henein, Georges **30** 22
Henekin, Simon **18** 899
Henen-nesut *see* HERAKLEOPOLIS MAGNA
Henequin, Jean **2** 461
Heng, Amanda **28** 775
Hengelose Trijpweverij **23** 125
henges **2** *850*; **14** 387*; **21** 40; **23** 808; **25** 498, 505–6*; **30** 434
Hengnan **7** 26
Hengrave Hall (Suffolk) **8** 44; **10** 273; **12** 176; **14** 76
Hengstenberg, Rudolf **22** 332
Henjeru *see* HEMAVATI
Henkel (family) **17** 2
Henkels, George J. **3** 685
Henle, Fritz **14** 387*
Henlein, Peter **7** 441
Henley, Robert **25** 399
Henley, William Ernest **4** 364
Henley-on-Thames Glasshouse (Oxon) **10** 316
Henman & Cooper **3** 537
henna **1** 343; **23** 803
Henna von Gurk, Saint **1** 160
Henne, Joachim **8** 752; **14** 387*
Henne, Jost **14** 388*; **33** 72
Henneberg, Hugo **14** 388*; **18** 501; **24** 738; **32** 924
Henneberger, Georg Rudolf **14** 159
Hennebert **19** 807
Hennebique, François **11** 525; **14** 388*
  collaboration **16** 55; **21** 4
  methods **7** 693
  works **4** 803; **7** 693; **8** 30; **10** 748; **24** *128*, 473; **26** 18, 762
Hennecart, Jean **14** 389*
  collaboration **5** 213; **8** 69; **19** 736
  patrons and collectors **5** 213
  works **14** *389*
  workshop **11** 149
Hennekin (family) **3** 600
Hennell, R. G., & Sons **10** 346
Henneman, Nicolaas **30** 269
Hennepin, Louis **5** 564
Hennequart, Jean *see* HENNECART, JEAN
Hennequin, Philippe-Auguste **8** 556; **14** 389–90*
  pupils **12** 12
Hennequin de Haacht **5** 207
Hennequin de Liège *see* JEAN DE LIÈGE (i)
Hennequin de Marville *see* JEAN DE MARVILLE
Hennequin du Vivier *see* JEAN DU VIVIER
Henner, Georg
  works **2** *812*
Henner, Jean-Jacques **14** 390*
  pupils **4** 319; **28** 188
Henner, Jean-Jacques—cont.
  teachers **9** 300; **24** 737
  works **7** 832
Hennessy, Basil **12** 510
Hennessy, J. B. **24** 336
Hennessy Hours *see under* BOOKS OF HOURS → individual manuscripts
Hennesy, Hennesy & Company **29** 106
Hennevogel, Jan Vilém **8** 399
Hennevogel, Johann **18** 443
Hennezell, de (family) **10** 316
Hennicke, Georg **25** 188; **27** 611
Henniges, Peter, I **12** 444
Hennin, A. D. **33** 147
Hennin, Jean de **18** 691
Henning, Gerhard **7** 807; **8** 741; **14** 391–2*
Henning, John (i) (1771-1851) **14** 391*
  assistants **14** 391
  collaboration **14** 391
  works **28** 243
Henning, John (ii) (1802-57) **14** 391*
Henning, Paul Rudolf **3** 795; **11** 299
Henning, Petter **30** 105
Henning, Samuel (*fl* 1760-80) **14** 391
Henning, Samuel (*d* 1832) **14** 391
Hennings, Emmy **3** 113; **8** 433, 434; **24** 405
Henningsen, Poul **3** 749; **14** 392*; **19** 799; **27** 643
Henningsen, Thorkild **3** 749
Hennin-Liétard, Jean de, Count **3** 545; **9** 329
Henny, A. B. **14** 625
Henrard, Robert Arnold **8** 661; **14** 392–3*
Henri, Florence **14** 393*
Henri, Robert **14** 393*; **24** 600; **31** 604
  exhibitions **10** 680
  groups and movements **2** 596–7; **10** 108; **23** 47
  pupils
   Amador, Manuel E(ncarnación) **1** 749
   Bellows, George (Wesley) (1882-1925) **3** 680
   Bruce, Patrick Henry **4** 888
   Davis, Stuart **8** 577
   Glackens, William J(ames) **12** 769
   Gottlieb, Adolph **13** 214
   Hopper, Edward **14** 751
   Kent, Rockwell **17** 899
   Kuniyoshi, Yasuo **18** 518
   Man Ray **20** 287
   Pach, Walter **23** 701
   Russell, Morgan **27** 360
   Spencer, Niles (Maurice) **29** 382
  teachers **2** 130
  works **21** 897
Henrichemont **4** 865; **29** 918; **31** 720
Henri Christophe, King of Northern Haiti (*reg* 1811-20) **14** 57, 58, 60
Henrici, Carlo (1737-83) **4** 286
Henrici, Karl (1842-1927) **7** 581
Henricksz., Gerrit **14** 316
Henricus *see* JANSEN, HENDRICUS
Henricus, Basil **29** 467
Henricus, George **29** 467
Henricus, Master **31** 384
Henri d'Aubersque **31** 842
Henri de Beaumetiel **5** 548
Henri de Braine, Archbishop of Reims **26** 114, 120
Henri de Cheraux **20** 644
Henri de le Pasture **33** 117
Henri de Lorraine, Bishop of Metz **3** 21
Henri de Vulcop *see* VULCOP, HENRI DE
Henri di Brabante *see* ARRIGO DI BRABANTE
Henriet, Claude, II (*c* 1540-1603/4) **14** 394
Henriet, (Charles-) Frédéric **14** 394*; **19** 295
Henriet, Israël **14** 394*; **25** 626; **28** 742
  patrons and collectors **28** 742
  printmakers **3** 632; **5** 438
  pupils **28** 742
Henrietta Maria, Queen of England and Scotland (1609-69) **4** *543*; **29** 802–3*
  architecture **6** 96; **13** 623; **17** 634, 635; **29** 797
  furniture **10** 291
  gardens **12** 127; **21** 822
  gold **24** 36
  interior decoration **10** 275
  metalwork **8** 884
  paintings **9** 482; **12** 306; **23** 208; **24** 553; **26** 198
  portraits **25** 283
  sculpture **19** 250
  stage design **17** 637
Henriettental **2** 818
Henriksson, Peter **11** 94; **30** 865
Henrion, Adrien-Joseph *see* ANRION, ADRIEN-JOSEPH
Henriquel, Louis-Pierre *see* HENRIQUEL-DUPONT
Henriquel-Dupont **3** 870; **13** 228; **14** 394–5*; **26** 232, 233
Henriques, Francisco **10** 899; **14** 395*
  assistants **19** 655
  attributions **13** 192
  patrons and collectors **2** 871
  works **3** 363; **25** 295
Henriques, L. A. **16** 889
Henriques, Paul **16** 889
Henriques Toledo, Aldary **4** 713
Henríquez, Alfonso **14** 716
Henríquez, Angel Vega *see* VEGA HENRÍQUEZ, ANGEL
Henriquez, Richard **31** 864
Henriquez and Todd **31** 864
Henríquez de Ribera, Fadrique **11** 898
Henri Rousseau group *see* ROUSSEAU, HENRI, GROUP
Henry (*fl c.* 1760-70) **24** 893
Henry, Duke of Saxony (*reg* 1539-41) **8** 682; **33** *110*, 110, 113*
Henry, King of Navarre *see* HENRY IV, King of France
Henry, King of Portugal (*reg* 1578-80) **19** 654; **30** 518
Henry, Prince of Great Poland *see* HENRY III, Prince of Silesia
Henry, Prince of Wales *see* STUART, HENRY, Prince of Wales
Henry I, Count of Champagne (*reg* 1152-81) **25** 667; **31** 381
Henry I, Duke of Brabant (*reg* 1183-1235) **5** 52; **28** 594
Henry I, Holy Roman Emperor *see* HENRY THE FOWLER, Holy Roman Emperor
Henry I, King of Cyprus (*reg* 1218-53) **8** 361
Henry I, King of England (*reg* 1100-35)
  architecture **7** 473; **14** 508; **23** 491; **26** 50, 615
  menagerie **24** 178; **33** 698
Henry I, Landgrave of Hesse (*reg* 1265-1308) **17** 834
Henry I, Prince of Silesia (*reg* 1201-38) **31** 394
Henry II, Bishop **2** 719
Henry II, Duke of Brunswick-Wolfenbüttel (*reg* 1514-68) **33** 50, 292
Henry II, Duke of Lorraine (*reg* 1608-24) **5** 438; **8** 783; **11** 657; **19** 35; **21** 89
Henry II, Holy Roman Emperor (*reg* 1002-24) **9** 661; **10** 181
Henry II, King of Cyprus (*reg* 1285-1324) **8** 363
Henry II, King of England (*reg* 1154-89) **25** 13*
  architecture
   castles **6** 51, 55; **8** 138; **9** 203; **12** 173; **21** 563; **23** 19; **33** 247
   chapels **19** 127
   hospitals **2** 45
   manor houses **14** 75
   monasteries **5** 894; **11** 290; **32** 416
  interior decoration **10** 269
  manuscripts **26** 660
  mazes **18** 585
  paintings **26** 655
  stained glass **29** 511
Henry II, King of France (*reg* 1547-59) **31** *833*, 850*
  architecture **9** 351; **11** 513; **19** 690; **20** 133; **24** 116
   châteaux **31** 834
    Anet **2** 27; **4** 780
    Palais du Louvre **6** 506; **24** 116
    Saint-Germain-en-Laye **19** 693; **27** 559
    Saint-Léger-en-Yvelines **19** 691
    Vincennes **19** 692; **32** 582
   monasteries **19** 693
   town halls **24** 116
  art policies **11** 656
  collections **9** 387
  decorative works **3** 645
  enamel **19** 396, 398
  glass **11** 611
  interior decoration **25** 580
  jewellery **17** 521
  medals **29** 534
  paintings **7** 466, 865
  productions **30** 659
  regalia **26** 82
  sculpture **13** 226; **27** 547
  swords **2** 455
  tapestries **24** 366
Henry II, Landgrave of Hesse (*reg* 1328-76) **17** 834
Henry II Jasomirgott, Duke of Austria (*reg* 1141-71) **32** 432
Henry II of Bavaria, Holy Roman Emperor (*reg* 1002-24) **26** *78*; **28** 24, 25*
  architecture **3** 139, 333; **22** 917
  coats of arms **14** 408
  furniture **25** 723
  gold **23** *657*
  liturgical objects **1** 4
  manuscripts **2** 222; **7** 246; **22** 11, 520; **23** 652, 654; **28** 487
  metalwork **3** 337; **23** 657
  rock crystal **16** 541
  textiles **12** 462
Henry II of Lusignan, King of Jerusalem (*reg* 1192-97) **17** 506
Henry II of Trastamara, King of Castile-León (*reg* 1366-67; 1369-79) **7** 362, 846
Henry III, Holy Roman Emperor (*reg* 1039-56) **13** 19; **23** *655*; **27** 616–17*
  architecture **14** 81
  churches **22** 817
  manuscripts **7** 246; **9** 698; **23** 655
Henry III, King of Castile-León (*reg* 1390-1406) **24** 280
Henry III, King of England (*reg* 1216-72) **25** 13–14*
  architecture **7** 420; **10** 141, 359
   castles **6** 54; **9** 204; **19** 615; **21** 549; **33** 247
   monasteries **10** 224; **13** 46; **19** 601
   palaces **6** 407; **19** 610
  coats of arms **14** 422
  embroidery **23** 460
  interior decoration **10** 269; **13** 128
  sculpture **17** 612; **27** 124
Henry III, King of England (*reg* 1216-72)—cont.
  stained glass **14** 422
Henry III, King of France (*reg* 1574-89) **31** *833*, 851*
  architecture **7** 665; **9** 353; **21** 345; **24** 117; **31** 834
  books **14** 616
  orders (chivalry) **7** 178
  paintings **9** 387
  productions **30** 659
  tapestries **14** 297
Henry III, Prince of Silesia (*reg* 1306-09) **33** 416
Henry IV, Count of Luxembourg *see* HENRY VII, Holy Roman Emperor
Henry IV, Duke of Bavaria (*reg* 1393-1459) **18** 723–4
Henry IV, Holy Roman Emperor (*reg* 1065-1104) **27** 616, 617*
  architecture **12** 471; **20** 128; **26** 575
  cathedrals **29** 390, 391
  gold **9** 657
  manuscripts **26** 660, 666, 674
  tapestries **9** 519
Henry IV, King of Castile-León (*reg* 1454-74) **5** 882; **13** 732; **19** 896; **20** 61; **29** 298
Henry IV, King of England (*reg* 1399-1413) **10** 163, 323; **30** 534
  swords **2** 452
  tapestries **10** 270
Henry IV, King of France (*reg* 1589-1610) **4** 542, *543*, *547*, 547–8*; **11** 661; **21** *9*
  architecture **7** 916; **9** 350, 353; **20** 133–4; **24** 117–18
   cathedrals **23** 510
   châteaux **11** 260; **21** 345; **27** 559
   military **6** 503
   palaces **9** 353; **24** 161
   squares (town) **11** 656; **20** 289
   town halls **24** 116
   urban planning **11** 515
  art policies **11** 651
  collections **9** 387; **10** 487
  decorative works **30** 659
  fountains **11** 343
  furniture **11** 587
  gardens **12** 120
  gems **3** 48; **12** 266
  interior decoration **6** 604; **11** 573, 574; **16** 855
  paintings **3** 449; **9** 328, 385, 387; **11** 266, 533; **24** 134
   mythological **9** 398
   portraits **9** 466
   religious **11** 754
  pottery **11** 604
  sculpture **19** 249; **25** 577
  silk **29** 348
  tapestries **11** 640; **13** 878; **30** 321
  textiles **2** 703
Henry V, Duke of Bavaria (*reg* 1004-26) **14** 408
Henry V, Holy Roman Emperor (*reg* 1106-25) **26** 662
Henry V, King of England (*reg* 1413-22)
  architecture **4** 779; **5** 895
  coins **7** 536
  furniture **8** 107
  gold **25** 16
  sculpture **18** 687
Henry VI, King of England (*reg* 1422-61; 1471) **18** 687*
  architecture **5** 511, 513; **10** 163; **23** 686; **24** 466; **28** 156
  carpets **10** 270
  coins **7** 536
  furniture **19** 5
  manuscripts **5** 288; **20** 624
  tapestries **10** 348
Henry VII, Holy Roman Emperor (*reg* 1308-13) **19** 827–8*

Henry VII, King of England (*reg* 1485-1509) 31 412–13*
alabaster-carvings 1 518
architecture 5 514; 13 623; 14 781; 17 10; 19 567; 24 466; 31 412; 32 378
coats of arms 14 424
coins 7 *537*
gardens 12 126
manuscripts 4 569
paintings 10 360
sculpture 31 189
silk 16 753
silver 24 146
stage machinery 30 653
tapestries 10 348; 13 634; 20 651
tomb 31 *190*
Henry VIII, King of England (*reg* 1509-47) 10 *246*; 14 *670*, *761*; 28 313; 31 412, 413–15*, *414*; 32 690
architecture 7 420; 22 717; 26 71
colleges 5 511
military 12 736; 14 211, 862; 19 60; 21 550, 568, *569*; 26 538; 31 217
palaces 8 273; 10 229; 14 75; 19 568
Bridewell Palace (London) 19 567
Eltham Palace (Kent) 10 163
Greenwich Palace (Kent) 13 623
Hampton Court Palace (Middx) 14 126, *127*; 23 809
Nonsuch Palace (Surrey) 6 59; 11 140; 23 197
Windsor Castle (Berks) 33 248
theatres 30 660
armour 2 *471*, 472
books 2 161; 19 114
carpets 5 835; 10 357
collections 10 363
decorative works 32 378; 33 408
furniture 10 289, 290
gardens 12 126; 23 198
glass 17 737
gold 1 746; 10 324, 326; 24 36
interior decoration 10 226; 14 *126*
jewellery 10 344
manuscripts 4 760; 31 751
metalwork 2 455
miniatures (paintings) 21 638
mirrors 21 720
orders (chivalry) 7 179
paintings 12 387; 14 666, 670–71, 673; 19 515; 30 131, 411; 31 205
parks 24 179
sculpture 3 157, 451, 706; 10 270, 360; 20 116; 31 189
tomb 27 831
ship-decoration 4 880
silver 10 324
stained glass 32 150
stucco 23 198; 29 835
swords 2 455
tapestries 1 165; 10 271, 349; 27 132; 30 331
tents 2 *339*
terracotta 30 502
Henry XII, Duke of Bavaria *see* HENRY THE LION, Duke of Saxony
Henry, Bon-Thomas 14 395–6*
Henry, Charles 14 396*; 19 355
collaboration 8 192; 10 199
groups and movements 30 168
works 28 201
illustrated 28 698
Henry, E(dward) L(amson) 14 396–7*
Henry, Françoise 16 38
Henry, Frederick 26 154
Henry, George (1858-1943) 12 779; 14 397*; 19 891; 26 107; 28 238
Henry, George (*b* 1930) 13 876
Henry, Grace 14 397
Henry, Joseph 5 *756*
Henry, J. S., & Co. 3 741
Henry, Lucien (Felix) 2 740, 756, 758; 14 397*
Henry, Maurice 30 20, 21
Henry, Olive 16 41
Henry, Patrick 25 655
Henry, Paul 3 537; 14 397–8*; 16 17, 36
Henry, Robert 11 644
Henry de Bruisselles 31 384
Henry de Gower 14 398*
works 27 538, *539*; 32 781
Henry de Mamesfeld 23 689
Henry Julius, Duke of Brunswick-Wolfenbüttel (*reg* 1589-1613) 3 77; 11 715; 13 915; 33 51, 52*
architecture 23 252
paintings 12 494
Henryków Church 4 782; 7 *280*; 25 95
Henry of Blois, Bishop of Winchester 14 398*; 26 755; 33 235
architecture 10 259; 12 799
enamel 26 694
manuscripts 33 233
metalwork 26 688
oliphants 23 400
sculpture 7 473; 26 611, 616; 33 238
Henry of Ellerton 5 373
Henry of Huntingdon's Chronicle (Baltimore, Walters A. G., MS. 793) 14 423
Henry of Passau 29 511
Henry of Reyns 13 46; 19 601; 33 247
Henry the Bald 28 260
Henry the Fowler, Holy Roman Emperor (*reg* AD 919-36) 4 665; 21 62, 562
Henry the Lion, Duke of Saxony (*reg* 1142-80); Duke of Bavaria (*reg* 1156-80) 13 21; 19 746; 22 297; 33 50, 51–2*, *293*
architecture 5 29; 19 745; 33 50
manuscripts 7 246; 14 366; 26 659, 660, 662, 675
metalwork 26 683
sculpture 26 646, 685
Henry the Rich *see* HENRY IV, Duke of Bavaria
Henschel, Charles 18 161
Hensel, Wilhelm 14 398–9*
Henselmann, Hermann 12 380; 14 399*
Hensel of Siegersdorf *see* HANS SIGERSDORFER
Henshaw, Frederick Henry 4 86
Hensius, Daniel 32 588
Henslowe, Philip 30 662
Henszlmann, Imre 5 85; 14 889; 15 18
Hentel 30 206
Hentia, Sava 26 714
Hentrich, Helmut 12 379; 14 399–400*; 24 568
Hentrich & Heuser 24 568
Hentrich-Petschnigg & Partner (HPP) 14 399; 24 568
Hentschel, Johannes Rudolf 12 436; 21 66
Hentschel, Julius Conrad 21 66
Hentschel, Konrad 12 436
Hentur 9 858
Hentz, Adler and Shutze 28 645
Hentzer, Paul 5 835
Henzada 5 *221*, 247, 261
Hepdjefa 2 659; 17 911
Hephaistion (*fl* 324 BC) 10 873
Hephaistion (*fl* 2nd cent. BC) 13 557; 14 400*; 29 87
works 13 558, *558*, *559*, 567; 24 411
Hephaistos Painter 13 521
Hephthalites *see* HUNS
Hephthalite scripts *see under* SCRIPTS → types
Hepp, Sebastian 13 631
Heppener, Johannes 33 47
Hepplewhite, Alice 24 273
Hepplewhite, George 14 400*
works 6 390; 10 297; 12 333
writings 24 317; 25 307; 26 85; 28 253
Heptachord Painter 10 611
heptastyle 14 400*
heptaychs *see under* ALTARPIECES → types
Hepworth, Barbara 10 375; 14 400–402*, 452; 19 590; 23 103
dealers 16 820
groups and movements 1 77, 90; 7 772; 10 258; 19 591, 623; 27 563; 28 506; 31 673
patrons and collectors 9 716; 13 629; 28 274
teachers 27 219
works 1 738; 10 267; 14 *401*; 19 492; 28 314
Hepworth, Barbara, Museum *see under* ST IVES (CORNWALL)
Hepworth, Philip D. 8 810; 33 382
Heqaib 2 656; 10 77, *77*
Hequet, Diógenes 31 754
Hera Borghese 13 454
Heracanas 10 621
Heraclea Lyncestis, Large Basilica 7 271; 9 566
Heraclius 2 518; 20 324; 26 657; 31 299
Heraea, Metta 30 115
Heraeus, Karl Gustav 13 921; 14 402*; 32 453
Heraia 14 354
Heraios 6 215; 18 16
heraki see under MARKS
Herakleia (Italy) 13 525
Herakleia (Sicily) 13 485, 486, 581, 587
Herakleia (Turkey) 4 110, 112; 9 630; 13 *363*
Herakleia Lynkestis *see* BITOLJ
Herakleia under Latmos 5 742; 14 402–3*
ekklesiasterion 13 407
town walls 21 557
Herakleides 30 286
Herakleion 8 155, 156; 21 565
Archaeological Museum 8 157; 14 275; 17 808; 18 165; 24 35, 589
collections 21 673, 690, 691
directors 20 423
architecture 32 159
Armoury *see* Town Hall
Ayios Markos 32 159
bastion 3 359
Candia 32 *158*
Hagias Minas 25 334
Hagios Markos 8 156
Historical and Ethnographic Museum of Crete 8 157
icons 8 157; 25 331; 32 159, 454
Loggia 8 156
Rocca al Mare 8 156; 21 550
St Catherine 8 157, *157*
St Matthew 8 157
Town Hall 8 156
Herakleitos 13 370
Herakleopolis Magna 7 *819*; 9 *774*; 10 758; 14 403*; 26 *921*
bone-carvings 7 825
gables 7 821
monuments 7 820
reliefs 9 873, *873*
sculpture 7 821; 9 873; 14 *403*
temples 9 831
Heraklides 13 552
Heraklios, Emperor of Byzantium (*reg* 610-41) 8 356, 360; 9 543, 636, 667; 22 519
Heraklios I (*reg* 610-41) 14 403–4*
Heraldic Cocks cycle 10 614
heraldic manuscripts 12 271–3*; 26 557
heraldic sculpture *see under* SCULPTURE → types
heraldic tables *see under* TABLES → types
heraldry 2 469; 4 373; 6 332; 10 247; 11 147–8, 376; 12 271–3; 13 128, 137; 14 404–29*, *415*, *416*, *417*, *418*, *419*, *420*, *421*, *422*, *424*, *426*, *427*, *429*, ; 15 149, 150; 16 247; 17 302; 22 *341*, 562; 25 328; 28 611, 614; 29 513
carpets 14 425
charges 4 63; 14 427–8
sculpture 14 *421*
seal bags 14 425
see also COATS OF ARMS; GENEALOGIES; PEDIGREES *and under* MANUALS → types
Heran, Henri 20 603
Hera of Ephesos 10 425
Heras, Arturo 31 816
Herăstrău 30 773
Herat 1 *186*, 207, 209; 6 *182*, 186; 14 429–31*; 16 *105*, 366; 30 919
art forms and materials
architecture 1 207; 16 196
book covers 12 III; 16 *358*, 358
carpets 14 431*; 15 682; 16 475, 482, 483
coins 6 266
inscriptions 16 169
manuscripts 1 208; 6 234; 14 431*; 16 *122*, *276*, 292, 294, 296, 301, 303, 321, 323, *324*, 325, 326, *326*, 328, 331, 332, 335, 358, *552*; 20 VI
metalwork 1 208; 14 430–31*; 16 364, *366*, 373, *375*, 377, *378*, 390
paintings 16 122
papercuts 16 *354*
plaster 16 200
silk 1 209
Bagh-i Jahanaray 12 82; 16 198
citadel 16 198
congregational mosque 16 197, 373; 22 194
fortifications 21 589
Friday Mosque 16 166; 24 877
Ghurid mausoleum 16 168, 169
tiles 16 169
gardens 12 82; 16 198
Gawharshad's complex 16 197, 199, 200; 23 562; 30 919; 31 112
Ikhlasiyya complex 16 196, 198
madrasa of Husayn 16 198
madrasas 20 55
mosques 22 354
Musalla *see* Gawharshad's complex
urban planning 16 264
Heraud, Gabriel 32 566
Hérault, Anne-Auguste 15 38
Hérault, Antoinette 6 502
Hérault, Charles-Antoine 15 38
Héraut, Henri 11 302, 550
Herbage, Juan 6 592
Herbal of Macer Floridus 14 433
herbals 4 358; 12 108; 14 406, 432–4*; 21 6; 26 661
individual manuscripts
Carrara Herbal (London, BL, Egerton MS. 2020) 5 872; 32 198
Herbart, Johann Friedrich 14 434–5*
Herbatte 3 595
Herbe, Paul 20 450
Herbel, Charles 11 642; 22 456
Herberger, Dominikus Hermenegild 7 212
Herberstein, Sigmund von 14 574
Herbert (family)
architecture 10 231
collections 10 364
Herbert (family)—cont.
paintings 10 248; 24 396
reliefs 25 665
sponsorship 6 96
Herbert, Arthur John 14 437
Herbert, Cyril Wiseman 14 437
Herbert, Edward, 1st Baron of Churbury 18 795
Herbert, George 7 698; 25 726
Herbert, George Edward Stanhope Molyneux, 5th Earl of Caernarvon 5 889; 10 81, 86
Herbert, Henry, 10th Earl of Pembroke 33 226
Herbert, Henry, 9th Earl of Pembroke 13 300; 14 435, 436*
architecture 7 287; 8 47
bridges 4 801
collaboration 22 138
drawings 9 230
gardens 33 226
paintings 3 372; 14 810; 33 220
sculpture 11 348
works 32 553, *553*
Herbert, Henry John George, 3rd Earl of Carnarvon 3 283; 10 237
Herbert, Jocelyn 30 687
Herbert, J(ohn) R(ogers) 14 436–7*; 19 614; 24 604
Herbert, Philip, 4th Earl of Pembroke and 1st Earl of Montgomery 14 435*
architecture 6 96; 17 635; 33 10, 225
heraldry 14 413
paintings 12 600; 15 158; 19 120; 24 753
tapestries 10 350
Herbert, Philip, 5th Earl of Pembroke 8 495; 14 435
Herbert, Robert 31 673
Herbert, Thomas 24 481
Herbert, Thomas, 8th Earl of Pembroke 12 763; 14 435–6*; 32 824
Herbert, Wilfred Vincent 14 437
Herbert, William 22 528
Herbert, William, 3rd Earl of Pembroke 14 435, 806; 27 356; 32 699
Herbert, Winston 31 660
Herberts, Kurt 3 411
Herbig, Wilhelm 31 288
Herbin, Auguste 3 366; 14 437*; 19 381
dealers 26 193; 27 162
groups and movements 1 76, 89, 90; 6 342; 8 240, 246; 21 775; 24 574; 27 639; 28 347
patrons and collectors 32 178
pupils 8 482
Herbo, Léon 10 517
Herbrot, Jacob 4 760
herbs 17 365
Herbst, Hans 14 437–9*, 666
works 14 *438*
Herbst, Marion 22 896
Herbst, Michael 14 678
Herbst, Peter 4 606
Herbst, René 11 584, 602; 31 581, 582
herbularius see GARDENS → types → physic
Herburg, Heinrich I von, Archbishop of Mainz 7 *535*
Herceg-novi 22 *17*
Herck, Jan, I 3 598
Herckenrode Abbey 3 575, 588
Hercolani (family) *see* ERCOLANI
Herculaneum 2 164; 10 641; 14 439–46*, *440*; 16 *621*; 25 191, 194; 26 230, *886*; 27 115
architecture 16 623
Basilica 14 443, *444*; 27 58
baths 14 441, 445
bronzes 27 86
candelabra 5 604
collections 13 470

Herculaneum—cont.
College of Augustales **14** 444
excavations **2** 299; **13** 605
Forum Baths **27** 61
gardens **12** 68
houses and villas **14** 441–2
House of Neptune and Amphitrite **14** 445; **27** 52, 66
House of Stags **14** 445; **27** 67
House of the Bicentenary **14** 444
House of the Black Hall **14** 444
House of the Deer **27** 99
House of the Great Portal **27** 58
House of the Mosaic Atrium **14** 444
House of the Papyri **14** 444
House of the Stags **14** 444; **26** 869; **27** 58
Samnite House **14** *441*, 444; **27** 53
Villa of the Papyri **14** 442; **26** 869; **27** 29, 30, 31, 32; **28** 383
busts **28** *383*
gardens **12** 69
sculpture **14** 443; **27** 20, 46
statuettes **27** 87
inscriptions **26** 856
jewellery **27** 102, 103
lamps **27** 87
mosaics **14** 444–5*; **22** 161; **23** 534
paintings **13** 545, 546
palaestra **14** 441, 443
rediscovery **14** 445–6*
sculpture **13** 423; **14** 442–3*, *443*; **27** 12, *12*, 30, 46; **29** 572–3
statuettes **27** 88, 89
Suburban Baths **27** 70, 71
Temple of Magna Mater **14** 441
textiles **27** 112
theatre **14** 440–41
wall paintings **1** 898; **5** 685; **12** 287; **14** 443–4*; **16** 653; **23** 291; **26** 857; **27** 49, *49*, 50, 53, 58, 74
workshops **27** 55
see also ERCOLANO
Herculaneum pottery **19** 508
Herculaneum Service **25** 193
Herculano, Alexandre **5** 902
Hercules **2** 453
Hercules and Telephus **27** 46
Herculia *see* SZÉKESFEHÉRVÁR
Herczeg, Zsigmond **3** 412
Herdegen, Seitz **23** 311
Herder, Johann Gottfried **1** 660; **10** 83; **14** 446*; **33** 37
groups and movements **22** 540
works **1** 180
Herdgen, J. **19** 497
Herdman, Robert **14** 447*
Herdman, William Gawin **19** 507; **24** 491
Herdonia **19** 889; **27** 3
Héré, Emmanuel **14** 447–8*
collaboration **13** 805
patrons and collectors **29** 537
works **11** 723; **14** *82*, *448*; **19** 800, *800*; **22** 454, *454*, 455; **31** 718
Héré, Paul **14** 447
Heredia **8** *15*
Basílica S Domingo **8** 16
parish church **8** 16
Heredia, Juan Talavera y *see* TALAVERA (Y HEREDIA), JUAN
Hereford
Bishop's Chapel **7** 257; **23** 491; **26** 574, 590
Bishop's Palace **14** 75
Cathedral of St Mary the Virgin and St Ethelbert the King **10** 227; **13** 55
ballflower **3** 121
Bishop's Chair **6** 389
capitals **26** 616
furniture **10** 286
Hereford
Cathedral of St Mary the Virgin and St Ethelbert the King—cont.
Mappa mundi **20** 362, *363*
restorations **33** 446
screen **13** 209; **28** 296
sculpture **10** 476
shrine **28** 630
stiff-leaf **29** 659
guilds **24** 579
Old Town Hall **31** 235
shire hall **18** 887
Hereford, Earls of *see* BOHUN, DE
Hereford, Walter of *see* WALTER OF HEREFORD
Hereford Beacon **18** 585
Hereford Gospels *see under* GOSPEL BOOKS → individual manuscripts
Herefordshire school **18** 50; **26** 616
works **18** *50*
Hereke **2** 439; **16** 445, 479
Hérémence, Centre Paroissial **30** 129
Herend Ceramics Factory **14** 449*, *881*; **15** 2, 3
Hérent, Augustinian convent **13** 112
Herentals
Fraikin-Museum **11** 371
St Waldetrudis **13** 112
Herero **1** 254, 348, 349, 351, 414, 419
Heresies **10** 878
Hereşti, Cazan Năsture **26** 708
Herford, Marienkirche **14** 81
Herford, Laura **10** 374
Hergiswil **30** *124*, 145
Hergla
bridge **16** 156
ribāṭ **16** 156
Hergt, Toni **24** 406
Herholdt, Johan Daniel **8** 727; **14** 497
Heribert (scribe) **23** 652, 653
Heribert, Archbishop of Cologne **7** 580
Herickx, Gordon **4** 87
Herigoyen, Emanuel Joseph von **14** 449*
Herimann **14** 366; **26** 659, 675; **33** 52
Herimar, Abbot of Reims **26** 122
Hering, Charles **4** 354
Hering, Doman *see* HERING, THOMAS
Hering, Frederick **22** 743
Hering, Henry **3** 30
Hering, Loy **12** 401; **14** 449–51*
works **2** 800; **12** 402; **14** *450*
workshop **12** 402
Hering, Martin **14** 451; **22** 918
Hering, Michael **14** 449, 451
Hering, Thomas **1** 170; **14** 451
Heriot, George (1563-1624) **28** 268; **31** 889
Heriot, George (1759-1839) **5** 564; **8** 81; **14** 451*; **22** 37
Heriot-Watt University *see under* EDINBURGH
Herisset, Antoine **19** 10
heritage **1** 546; **2** 366; **9** 374; **14** 451–3*; **24** 662; **28** 172
Belgium **16** 907
Britain **14** 452–3
Canada **32** 414
Chile **6** 601
China **14** 452
Easter Island **23** 737
France **6** 95; **9** 25; **19** 159; **24** 662
Germany **14** 492
India, Republic of **15** 183–4
Italy **3** 770; **10** 846; **14** 451
Japan **14** 452; **18** 556
Norway **23** 243
Pacific Islands **23** 737
Poland **32** 678
heritage—cont.
United States of America **14** 452; **21** 422
see also ARCHITECTURE → conservation
Heritage, Robert **10** 299
Heritage Club **4** 366
Heritage Foundation **14** 452
Héritier de Brutelle, Charles-Louis L' *see* L'HÉRITIER DE BRUTELLE, CHARLES-LOUIS
Heriz carpets *see under* CARPETS → types
Herkenrath, Peter **14** 48
Herkner, Friedrich **16** 22, 37
Herkomer, Hubert von **10** 373; **14** 453–4*; **21** 418, 615
assistants **11** 123
competitions **10** 373
groups and movements **14** 680
patrons and collectors **11** 301
pupils **23** 102
reproductive prints by others **4** 807
works **9** 2; **10** 254; **12** 296; **21** 896; **28** 919; **31** 704
Herkomer, Johann Jakob **3** 58; **15** 864; **23** 636; **33** 41
Herkomer, Lorenz **14** 453
Herkotypes *see* SPONGOTYPES
Herland, Hugh **14** 454*; **19** 609; **25** 17
Herland, William **14** 454; **33** 248
Herle, Leonhard **31** 563
Herle, Wilhelm von *see* WILHELM OF COLOGNE, MASTER
Herlein **30** 15
Herlin, Friedrich **14** 454–5*
collaboration **20** 736
pupils **28** 57
staff **18** 650
works **12** 342, 385; **14** *455*; **20** 736; **23** 205; **27** 218; **29** 726
Herlin, Hans **14** 454
Herlufsholm *Christ* **8** 737, 738; **13** 171, *171*, 172
Herlufsholm School *see under* NÆSTVED
Herluin, Abbot of Glastonbury **12** 799
Hermalle-sous-Huy **26** 644
Heřman (*fl c.* 1144) **25** 442
Herman, Bishop **26** 590
Herman, Giacomo **16** 727; **26** 780
Herman, Johannes *see* HERRMANN, HANS (EMIL RUDOLF)
Herman, Josef **12** 777; **14** 456*; **32** 786
Herman, Oskar **8** 178
Herman, Sam **2** 763; **28** 260
Herman de Voghele **5** 53
Herman de Waghemakere **2** 192; **3** 544; **13** 62; **17** 883
Herman d'Italie *see* SWANEVELT, HERMAN VAN
Hermann **12** 471
Hermann I, Duke of Swabia (*reg* 926-49) **29** 873
Hermann I, Landgrave of Thuringia **32** 882
Hermann, Franz Anton **20** 129
Hermann, Franz Benedikt **14** 456
Hermann, Franz Georg (1640-89) **14** 456*
Hermann, Franz Georg (1692-1768) **14** 456–7
Hermann, Johann Eucharius **7** 211
Hermann, Joseph Karl Gottlieb **28** 91
Hermann, Martin **7** 211
Hermann, Master **13** 161
Hermann, Paul *see* HERAN, HENRI
Hermann of Munster **21** 362
Hermann-Paul **14** 457*; **19** 490
Hermannsburg **1** 56, 63
Hermannstadt *see* SIBIU
Hermannus Dalmata **2** 650
Herman of Cologne **5** 207; **20** 207; **28** 66, 866
Hermans, Anne **7** 466
Hermans, Charles **5** 44; **14** 457*
Hermans, Jacob **7** 708
Hermans, Willem **23** 501
Hermant, André **31** 582
Hermant, Jacques **7** 531; **14** 458*
Hermant, Pierre **22** 421
Hermant, Pierre-Antoine-Achille **14** 457–8*
Hermanville-sur-Mer Parish church **30** 907
hermas **25** 126
Hermeling, Gabriel **12** 449; **13** 209
hermeneutics **1** 183; **8** 899; **14** 458–9*; **26** 62; **28** 109
Hermes, Gertrude **1** 147; **10** 344
Hermes Ludovisi **13** 453
Hermessen, Caterina van **33** 308
Hermetic Cubism *see under* CUBISM → types
Hermias **13** 411
Hermione **26** 910
Hermitage Museum *see under* ST PETERSBURG → museums
hermitages **11** 243; **14** 460*; **27** 323
Cappadocia **5** 675
Coptic **7** 820
England **14** *460*
see also GROTTOES
Hermit atoll **24** *64*, 82
Hermite, Jean L' *see* L'HERMITE, JEAN
Hermit Islands *see* HERMIT ATOLL
Hermodoros of Salamis **26** 856, 865, 885, 887
Hermogenes (*fl c.* 560-*c.* 520 BC; potter) **13** 510
Hermogenes (*fl* ?late 3rd-early 2nd cent. BC; architect) **14** 461*
architecture **13** 380, 412; **15** 894; **20** 98; **23** 482; **30** 482
patrons and collectors **24** 411
works **13** 409
writings **13** 403, 408, 409; **26** 924; **32** 634
Hermolaus Barbarus **25** 46
Hermolykos **18** 448
Hermonax **13** 521; **32** 34
Hermonthis *see* ARMANT
Hermopolis Magna **1** 756; **7** *819*; **9** 773, *774*, 852; **14** 461–2*
brackets **7** 828
Cathedral **7** 820, *820*
ivory-carvings **27** 100
necropolis **9** 843; **22** 716
pylon **9** 831
reliefs **9** 877; **10** 86
sacred lake **27** 496
Temple of Thoth **14** *461*
tombs
Ankhor **9** 843
Petosiris **9** 842; **24** 555*
altar **1** 691
coffin **10** 58
reliefs **9** 811, 818, 821, 892; **14** 462
Hermopolis West *see* TUNA EL-GEBEL
Hermosilla, José de **16** 547; **29** 271; **32** 564
Hermoso, Pedro **3** 199
herms *see under* SCULPTURE → types
Hermsdorf, Stephan **19** 111; **31** 166
Hernandarias de Saavedra *see* SAAVEDRA, HERNANDARIAS DE
Hernández, Abdel **8** 234
Hernández (Navarro), Agustín **14** 462–3*
collaboration **12** 922; **21** 381; **31** 186
studio **21** 381
works **21** 381
Hernández, Daniel **6** 48; **14** 463*
pupils **5** 527; **25** 827; **29** 434; **32** 581
works **24** 509
Hernández, Diego **29** 340
Hernández, Domingo Ximénez *see* XIMÉNEZ HERNÁNDEZ, DOMINGO
Hernandez, Gómez de **2** 387
Hernández, José **6** 10
Hernández, Julio Antonio Rodríguez *see* JULIO ANTONIO (RODRÍGUEZ HERNÁNDEZ)
Hernández, Julio L(ópez) **14** 463*
works **29** 297
Hernández, Manuel **7** 610, 611; **23** 903
Hernández, Marco **29** 334
Hernández, Mateo **5** 651; **11** 568, 569; **14** 463*; **29** 295
Hernandez, Miriam **18** 833, 834
Hernández, Santiago **14** 464*; **16** 48; **21** 386
Hernández Acevedo, Manuel **25** 702
Hernández Callejo, Andrés **2** 866
Hernández Cruz, Luis **14** 464*; **25** 702
Hernández Estrada, Jerónimo **14** 464*
pupils **23** 300, 342, 683
works **9** 699; **23** 626
Hernandez-Lakota, Ron **22** 671
Hernández Ortega, Gilberto **9** 117
Hernández-Pijuan, Joan **3** 219; **29** 287
Hernández Prieto, Enrique Antonio **32** 172
Hernan Nuñez Arnalte **20** 493
Herne Bay Pier **24** 747
Herne-Saint-Hubert **10** 197
Herning
Angligården **20** 352
Carl-Henning Pedersen og Else Alfelts Museum **8** 758; **24** 316
Kunstmuseum **8** 760
Hernmarck, Helena Barynina **30** 330
heroa **13** 380; **14** 466–7*; **20** 863
see also SANCTUARIES
Herod Agrippa I **17** 488
Herodes Atticus **14** 464–5*
architecture **2** 670; **23** 350, 431; **26** 909, 910; **29** 488
sculpture **26** 857
Herodian **6** 72
Herodium **17** 556
synagogue **17** 541
Herodoros **29** 652
Herodotos of Olynthos **29** 652
Herodotus **1** 886; **13** 373; **14** 465*; **26** 295, 296; **27** 687
works **2** 298; **30** 848
on Achaemenids **1** 115
on Arabs **16** 454
on architecture **2** 361, 666
on cauldrons **13** 575
on cities **18** 407
on devices **14** 407
on fortifications **21** 556
on gold **15** 706
on hypogea **15** 52
on monuments **22** 42
on pyramids **25** 761
on Scythians **1** 188; **28** 320, 321, 323, 324
on tattooing **30** 769
on tents **21** 885
on Thracians **30** 768
on trade **13** 372
on weapons **15** 677
on ziggurats **21** 286
Herod Tapestry **23** 241
Herod the Great **14** 465*; **27** 670
architecture **2** 156; **17** 488, 493, *494*, 494–5, 539; **20** 539; **26** 914, 916, 917; **27** 1
gardens **12** 70
Herold, Christian Friedrich **14** 767

Herold, J. (*fl* 1554) 15 83
Hérold, Jacques 30 22, 23
Herold, Johann Gregorius *see* HÖROLDT, JOHANN GREGORIUS
Heron, Hilary 16 22
Heron, Patrick 14 465–6*; 25 628
groups and movements 1 77; 2 545; 10 258; 27 563
works 10 257; 11 *437*
Heron, Robert Methren 28 258
Heron of Alexandria 2 344, 349, 350, 837; 9 618; 11 343; 13 410, 704; 21 577; 30 26
Heroöpolis *see* MASKHUTA, TELL EL-
hero stones *see under* MONUMENTS → types
Herp, Willem van, I (1614-77) 5 353; 14 467*
works 3 42; 5 351, *351*
Herper, Adolf Friedrich 18 182
Herpin, Master of the 20 804
Herport, Albrecht 29 644
Herr, Michael 14 467*; 17 656
Herrad von Landsberg, Abbess 1 653; 10 202; 14 467–8*, 772; 26 661; 33 308
works 1 *653*
Herraiz workshop 29 321
Herráiz y Silo, Pascual 1 464
Herrán, Saturnino 6 21; 10 727; 14 468*; 21 387, 405
Herrard von Landsberg 12 382
Herrebø 23 *218*
Herrebø Faience Factory 23 234–5
works 23 *234*
Herrenberg 19 826
Herrenberg Altarpiece 26 *11*
Herrenchiemsee, Schloss *see under* HERRENINSEL
Herrenchiemsee Monastery Church 12 370; 32 822
Herrenhausen 12 133, *360*; 14 469*; 20 869
Herreninsel, Schloss Herrenchiemsee 12 416, 463; 23 546, 813, *814*; 33 283
paintings 3 702
sculpture 33 726
stucco 29 843
Herrera, Alejandro Rivandeneyra *see* RIVADENEYRA HERRERA, ALEJANDRO
Herrera, Alonso de 29 45
Herrera, Antonio 24 612
works 24 *612*
Herrera, Carlos María 8 267; 31 754
Herrera, Carlos Salazar *see* SALAZAR HERRERA, CARLOS
Herrera, Carmen 18 834
Herrera, Francisco de (i) (*c.* 1590-1656) 14 469–70*; 28 515
patrons and collectors 18 899; 27 792
pupils 16 48; 19 517; 32 125
works 4 211; 14 *470*; 28 515; 33 730
Herrera (y Aguilar), Francisco de (ii) (1622-85) 14 469, 470–72*; 20 66; 28 515
assistants 31 183
collaboration 6 343
groups and movements 7 290
patrons and collectors 4 566; 14 10; 23 437; 27 792
works 13 880; 14 *471*; 22 313; 29 269, 281, *281*
Herrera, Jerónimo de Bustamante de *see* BUSTAMANTE DE HERRERA, JERÓNIMO DE
Herrera, Joe Hilario 22 595, 596; 24 351
Herrera, Juan Alfonso de Pimental y, 8th Conde de Benavente *see* BENAVENTE, 8th Conde de
Herrera, Juan de 14 472–7*; 29 267, 356
architecture 10 499; 14 *474*; 19 227; 29 267, 300; 31 88, 822
cathedrals 7 288; 14 *475*; 25 455; 26 299; 31 823
chapels 2 284
churches 10 502; 13 284; 14 *473*; 29 268
conservatories 2 284
exchanges 28 512
libraries 19 313
monasteries 10 499
palaces 2 284; 10 *499*, *500*, 501, 534; 13 288; 23 811; 31 93, 94
staircases 10 499, *504*; 29 523
town halls 25 455
urban planning 20 63
attributions 1 740; 10 503; 20 62; 25 291
collaboration 8 65; 23 492; 29 522; 32 156
engravings 10 503
furniture 29 301
gardens 2 284
metalwork 10 502
patrons and collectors 6 44; 13 922; 14 517
pupils 22 66; 32 560
reproductive prints by others 24 475
retables 11 486; 20 66; 26 250; 31 319; 33 578
sculpture 10 502
teachers 31 93
writings 31 297
Herrera, Juan Francisco Alfonso de Pimental y, Conde de Benavente *see* BENAVENTE, 10th Conde de
Herrera, Velino 14 477–8*; 22 594
works 14 *477*
Herrera Aguilar, Juan de 14 469
Herrera Barnuevo, Antonio de 14 478*
Herrera Barnuevo, Sebastián de 14 478*; 22 69; 29 269
groups and movements 7 290
works 2 285
Herrerabarría, Adriano 14 479*; 23 905
Herreras, Rodrigo de 19 174
Herrera style 10 534; 11 485–7*, *486*; 24 511
Herrera Toro, Antonio 14 479*; 32 180
assistants 26 548
pupils 4 670; 5 354; 21 832, 902; 26 262
works 32 175, 178
Herrera Velarde, Francisco de 4 261; 25 365
Herrera y Sotomayor, Juan de 5 886
Herrería, Julián de la 14 479*; 24 98, 101, 102
Herrería, Julián de la, workshop 1 70
Herrero, Alejandro 1 149
Herrestad 6 389
Herreyns, Guillaume 14 479
Herreyns, Guillaume-Jacques 14 479–80*
pupils 8 764; 11 723; 12 230; 29 255, 256
teachers 3 873
Herreyns, Jacques 14 479
Herreyns, W. J. 33 170
Herri *see* ERRI
Herriman, George 5 759; 7 649
works 7 *649*
Herri met de Bles *see* BLES, HERRI MET DE
Herring, Benjamin (1806-30) 14 480*
Herring, Benjamin (1830-71) 14 480*
Herring, Charles 14 480*
Herring, J(ohn) F(rederick) (1795-1863; father) 4 808; 10 250; 14 480*; 29 425
Herring, Mrs J. F. 14 480*
Herring, J(ohn) F(rederick) (1820-1907; son) 14 480*
Herring, William 28 817
herringbone masonry *see under* MASONRY → types
Herrliberger, David 33 736
Herrmann, Franz Ludwig 30 132
Herrmann, Hans (Emil Rudolf) 14 480–81*
Herrmann, Karl-Ernst 30 688
Herrmann-Neisse, Max 13 *698*; 21 *55*
Herrnhuters *see* CHRISTIANITY → sects → Moravian Brethren
Herron, Jorge
works 22 *23*
Herron, Ron 2 308, 309; 31 734
works 2 *309*
Herrón, Willie 18 831
Herrterich, L. 22 433
Herry, Maître 4 150
Hers 27 756
Hersak, Dunja
works 29 *70*
Hersbruck High Altar, Master of the 20 690*
Herschel, John (Frederick William) 5 518; 14 481*; 24 646, 650, 654
Herscher, Josef 8 386
Hersele, Joost van, I (*fl* late 16th cent.) 12 467
Hersele, Joost van, II (*fl* 1589-1621) 12 467
Hersent, Louis 14 481–2*
patrons and collectors 11 542; 23 523
pupils 4 678; 6 535; 10 839; 12 809; 19 218; 28 196; 31 345
reproductive prints by others 2 702
teachers 26 93
works 19 466
Hersent, Louise-Marie-Jeanne 21 412
Hersfeld Abbey Church 5 794; 12 363, 471; 13 18; 31 280
Hershmann, Saloh 16 566
Herst, Auguste 25 78
Herstmonceux Castle (E. Sussex) 4 779
Hersúa 12 844; 28 330
Hertel, Andrea 14 893
Hertel, Hilger 22 316
Hertel, Johann Georg 10 103; 13 897; 24 272
Herten, Georg 18 574
Hertenstein, Jacob von 14 664, 666
Herter, Albert 3 176; 30 327; 31 659
Herter, Christian 14 482*; 31 621, 630
groups and movements 1 171
staff 2 699
works 31 870
Herter, Ernst 7 850; 14 482–3*; 33 296
Herter, Gustave 14 482
Herter Brothers 2 699; 14 482
Hertereich, Ludwig 11 320
Herterich, Heinrich Joachim 27 337; 29 376
Herterich, Johann Caspar 16 72; 26 419
Herterich, Ludwig 18 205; 28 54
Herter Looms 30 327, 328; 31 659
Hertervig, Lars 14 483*
Hertford Castle 4 770
Hertford, Edward Seymour, 1st Earl of *see* SEYMOUR, EDWARD, 1st Duke of Somerset
Hertford, Francis Charles Seymour-Conway, Marquess of *see* SEYMOUR-CONWAY, FRANCIS CHARLES, 3rd Marquess of Hertford
Hertford, Gilbert de Clare, Earl of *see* CLARE, GILBERT DE, Earl of Hertford
Hertford, Richard Seymour-Conway, Marquess of *see* SEYMOUR-CONWAY, RICHARD, 4th Marquess of Hertford
Herting, Carl 32 816
Hertlein, Hans 3 795
Hertoft, Nanna 8 756
Hertogs, J. 28 41
Hertonäs Oäkta Porcelain Factory 11 105
Hertz, Bram 12 266
Hertz, Mary 32 854
Hertzberg, Ewald Frederick, Graf von 26 506
Hertzberger, Herman 14 483–5*
works 7 688; 14 *484*; 18 114; 22 832
writings 31 867
Hertzberger, Menno 14 688
Hertzfelde, Wieland 8 436
Hertzhauser 6 91
Herut'yunyan, Ara 2 437
Hervart, Barthélemy 19 264; 21 498
Hervartó Church 14 899; 28 852
Hervé, Daniel 11 426
Hervé, François 10 296; 26 85
Hervé de Buzançais 31 227
Hervey 5 289
Hervey, Frederick Augustus, 4th Earl of Bristol 14 485–6*; 16 35; 22 86
collections 5 553
models 2 337
paintings 3 750; 4 234; 5 554; 9 18; 10 753; 13 303, 304; 16 36; 17 640; 22 271; 31 308
sculpture 3 184; 11 163
Hervey, John, 1st Earl of Bristol 3 245; 7 500; 26 558
Hervey, John I, Baron Hervey of Ickworth (1665-1751) 14 485
Hervey, John II, Baron Hervey of Ickworth (1696-1743) 14 485
Hervey de Stanton 5 511
Hervey Islands *see* COOK ISLANDS
Hervier, (Louis-Henri-Victor-Jules-François) Adolphe 9 309; 14 486*
Hervier, Marie-Antoine 14 486
Hervieu, Jean 2 14
Hervieu, Louis (*fl* 18th cent.) 26 376
Hervieu, Louise (1878-1954) 14 486*
Hervilly, Ernest d' 13 645
Herwijck, Steven van 14 486–7*; 20 921
works 16 868
Hery, Claude de 23 412; 31 851
Herz, Johann Daniel (1693-1754) 10 103; 24 443
Herz, Johann Daniel (*fl* 1755) 24 421
Herz, Max 9 764; 16 241, 557
Herzeele, Joos van 2 198, 199
Herzegovina 4 458–63*, *459*; 33 571
architecture 4 459*
collections 4 462–3*
decorative arts 4 462*
galleries (iv) (art) 4 463
metalwork 4 462
museums 4 462–3*
painting 4 460–62*
rock art 25 475
sculpture 4 460–62*
silver 4 462
textiles 4 462
Herzfeld, Ernst (Emil) 14 487*; 15 899; 16 252, 548, 549, 550; 19 812; 27 680
excavations 12 77; 16 252; 24 481; 27 678, 680
works 18 *499*; 27 846
Herzfelde, Helmuth *see* HEARTFIELD, JOHN
Herzfelde, Wieland 13 697; 14 845
Herzliya 17 854
Herzog, Anton 18 417
Herzog, Fülöp 14 889; 28 87; 30 762
Herzog, George 33 246
Herzog, Jacques 30 129
Herzog, Oswald 2 288; 3 801
Herzogenburg 2 783, 828
Abbey Church 2 783
Hesbay 12 272
Hesbene, Pierre de 3 609
Heschler, David 14 487–8*
Heschler, Sigmund 12 405; 14 487
Hesdin
château 4 841; 13 76
park 24 178
shields 14 419
Hesdin, Jacquemart de *see* JACQUEMART DE HESDIN
Hesekiel, Georg Christoph 12 415; 13 199; 33 380
Heseltine, J. P. 9 231; 19 782
He Shaoji 6 767
Heshbon 9 737
Heshen 7 132, 153
Heshterek *see* ORTACA
Heshuo *see* XINTALA
Hesilriges (family) 21 148
Hesiod 1 175; 9 618; 21 885; 22 410
Hesione Painter 10 616
Hesius, Willem 14 488*
attributions 3 546
collaboration 25 813
works 19 260
Hesketh 9 56
Hesketh, Robert 29 768
Heski, Ksawery Dominik 25 841
hesmen kem see under ALLOYS → types
Hespel, César d', Bishop of Lille 33 153
Hespéris-Tamuda 22 129
Hess (family) 11 33
Hess, Andreas 5 84
Hess, Carl Ernst Christoph 13 662; 25 789
Hess, David 30 133
Hess, Felix 29 98
Hess, Heinrich Maria von 14 488*; 33 282
pupils 8 790
works 18 123; 33 37
Hess, Hieronymus 14 488*; 28 115; 29 848; 30 133
Hess, Johannes 12 439
Hess, Johann Friedrich Christian 11 735
Hess, Ludwig 14 489*; 33 424
Hess, Martin 20 693
Hess, Mathias 31 256
Hess, Peter von 25 789
works 11 *461*
Hess, Thomas B. 14 489*; 24 433
Hesse, Alexandre-Jean-Baptiste 8 664; 11 544; 14 489–90*
Hesse, Carl 14 490
Hesse, Ernest-Ludwig, Grand Duke of *see* ERNEST-LUDWIG, Grand Duke of Hesse
Hesse, Eva 14 490*; 23 49
groups and movements 25 645, 646
teachers 1 549
works 15 869; 29 *12*, 13; 31 615, *615*
Hesse, Friedrich von, Cardinal 25 550
Hesse, Gertrude 17 878
Hesse, Hans 29 630

Hesse, Henri-Joseph **14** 489
Hesse, Ludwig I, Grand Duke of *see* LUDWIG I, Grand Duke of Hesse
Hesse, Ludwig III, Grand Duke of *see* LUDWIG III, Grand Duke of Hesse
Hesse, Ludwig Ferdinand **12** 416; **14** 490*; **25** 368
Hesse, Maria, Princess of *see* MARIA ALEXANDROVNA, Empress of Russia
Hesse, Nicolas-Auguste **12** 10; **14** 489*
Hesse, Philip III von **31** 526
Hesse, Rudolf **14** 490
Hesse, Wilhelmina, Grand Duchess of *see* WILHELMINA, Grand Duchess of Hesse
Hesse, William I, Elector of *see* WILLIAM I, Elector of Hesse
Hesse, William II, Elector of Hesse *see* WILLIAM II, Elector of Hesse
Hesse-Darmstadt, Alexandra, Princess of *see* ALEXANDRA FYODOROVNA, Empress of Russia (1872-1918)
Hesse-Darmstadt, Elisabeth Dorothea, Landgravine of *see* ELISABETH DOROTHEA, Landgravine of Hesse-Darmstadt
Hesse-Darmstadt, Ernest-Ludwig, Grand Duke of Hesse *see* ERNEST-LUDWIG, Grand Duke of Hesse
Hesse-Darmstadt, Frederica, Queen of Prussia *see* FREDERICA, Queen of Prussia
Hesse-Darmstadt, George I, Landgrave of *see* GEORGE I, Landgrave of Hesse-Darmstadt
Hesse-Darmstadt, George II, Landgrave of *see* GEORGE II, Landgrave of Hesse-Darmstadt
Hesse-Darmstadt, Ludwig VIII, Landgrave of *see* LUDWIG VIII, Landgrave of Hesse-Darmstadt
Hesse group **10** 616
Hesse-Homburg, Friedrich VI Joseph, Landgrave of **21** 821
Hesse-Kassel (House of) **14** 490–91*
Hesse-Kassel, Amelia Elizabeth, Landgravine of *see* AMELIA ELIZABETH, Landgravine of Hesse-Kassel
Hesse-Kassel, Augusta Hohenzollern, Electress *see* AUGUSTA HOHENZOLLERN, Electress of Hesse
Hesse-Kassel, Charles, Landgrave of *see* CHARLES, Landgrave of Hesse-Kassel
Hesse-Kassel, Frederick I, Landgrave of *see* FREDERICK, King of Sweden
Hesse-Kassel, Frederick II, Landgrave of *see* FREDERICK II, Landgrave of Hesse-Kassel
Hesse-Kassel, Marie von, Grand Duchess of Mecklenburg-Strelitz *see* MARIE, Grand Duchess of Mecklenburg-Strelitz
Hesse-Kassel, Maurice, Landgrave of *see* MAURICE, Landgrave of Hesse-Kassel
Hesse-Kassel, Maximilian **17** 834
Hesse-Kassel, William IV, Landgrave of *see* WILLIAM IV, Landgrave of Hesse-Kassel
Hesse-Kassel, William IX, Landgrave of *see* WILLIAM I, Elector of Hesse
Hesse-Kassel, William VIII, Landgrave of *see* WILLIAM VIII, Landgrave of Hesse-Kassel
Hessel, Ehrenfried **17** 549
Hesselagergård **4** 781; **8** 742
Hesselberg **23** 231
Hessèle, Charles **20** 603
Hesselin, Louis (-Cauchon) **4** 126, 573, 574; **14** 492*; **19** 262
Hesselius, Gustavus **14** 492–3*; **31** 600
Hesselius, John **14** 493*
Hessels, Willem **22** 93
Hessenberg's Lithography Shop **28** 535
Hessenfeld Bros **31** 261
Hessen-Homburg, Elisabeth, Landgräfin von **28** 142
Hesse Painter **13** 546
hessian **5** 655; **9** 19
Hessing, Leonard **30** 160
Hessing, Mona **2** 767
Hessing, Valjean **22** 597
Hesski, Daminik Xavier **3** 528
Hessler, Melchior **11** 734
Hessus, Helius Eobanus **9** 440
Hestaux, Louis **12** 18
Hester, Joy **2** 750; **14** 493*; **31** 410
Hesterberg, Rolf **2** 661–2
Hestercombe (Somerset) **12** 141
garden **12** *141*
Hesterek Church **9** 543
Hestiaios **13** 374
hestiatoria **13** 417
Hesyre **9** 822, 868, 899; **10** 50; **14** 493–4*, *494*; **20** 596; **27** 812; **29** 615
tomb **27** *811*
Hesz, János Mihály **10** 546; **15** 18
hét, A **24** 440
Hetaozhuang (Minhe) **20** 143
Hetek see SEVEN
Hetep **9** 857, 874
Hetepdief **9** 860
Hetepheres I **10** 29, 51; **14** 494–5*
furniture **6** 388; **9** 823; **10** 50, *51*; **14** *495*; **30** 775
jewellery **10** *29*
Hetepsekhemwy **9** *776*; **27** 811
Heteren, Adriaan Leonard van **22** 904
Heteren, Hendrick van **22** 904
Hetet, Rangimarie **14** 495*; **20** 360; **30** 418
Heteti
shabtis **10** *17*
Het Huis oud en nieuw **8** 299
Het Jonge Moriaenshoofd **8** 668; **22** 879
Het Loo **10** 274; **14** 495–6*; **22** *813*, 826, 864, 906; **26** 560; **33** 199
bedroom of Queen Mary II **20** *459*
fountains **9** 22; **11** 345
gardens **12** 61, 105, 132, *132*
interior decoration **14** 855
library **5** 349
paintings **1** 659; **12** 801; **22** 846, 904
porcelain cabinet **7** 166
stucco **29** 837
Hetnefert **10** 10
Het Overzicht **3** 564; **24** 439
Hetsch, G(ustav) F(riedrich) **8** 727; **14** 497*
porcelain **7** 807
pupils **14** 149
works **8** 727, 744, 751; **17** 547
Hetsch, Philipp Friedrich von **14** 496–7*, 586
pupils **18** 182; **28** 86, 351
works **12** 392
Het'um I, King of Lambron (*reg* 1226-69) **31** 177
Hetzel, J **3** 849; **6** 582
Hetzelt, Friedrich **12** 379
Hetzendorf, Franjo Conrad von **8** 178
Hetzendorf von Hohenberg, Johann Ferdinand *see* HOHENBERG, JOHANN FERDINAND (HETZENDORF) VON
Heuback, Gebrüder **12** 437
Heuglin, Johann Erhard, II **12** 446; **24** 271
Heumann, Georg Daniel **20** 914
Heumann, J. W. **14** 103
Heun, Arthur **25** 446
Heuneburg **12** *361*; **14** 497–8*, *498*; **21** 551; **23** 808; **25** *470*, 538
bronze **25** 541
hill-fort **25** 535
metalwork **25** 535
potter's wheels **25** 543
pottery **25** 543
Heur, Cornelis d' **32** 241
Heurich, Jan (1873-1925) **14** 498–9*; **25** 136; **32** 872
Heurich, Jan Kacper (1834-87) **14** 498; **20** 397; **32** 872
Heusch, Jacob de **9** 462; **14** 499; **32** 112
Heusch, Willem, de **9** 463; **14** 499*
Heuser, Hans **14** 399
Heusner, Rachel **3** 623, 624
Heussen, Claes van **14** 94
Heusser, Hans **8** 434
Heuvel, Antoon van den **3** 559; **12** 519; **14** 499*
Heuvick, Gaspard **17** 699; **23** 665
Hevelius, Johannes **12** 812, 813
Heveningham Hall (Suffolk) **10** 643–4; **30** *386*
gardens **4** 876, *876*
Orangery **23** 470
Hever (Kent)
Castle **2** 646; **31** 151
St Peter **7** 178
Heverlee **30** 326, 327
Celestine church **3** 569; **21** 858
Heversham Cross **2** 69
Hevesi, Ludwig **28** 343
Hevia, Luis García *see* GARCÍA HEVIA, LUIS
Hevía, Victor **29** 295
Heward, (Efa) Prudence **5** 67, 567; **14** 499*; **22** 39
Hewelke, Maria **16** 737
Hewelke, Nathaniel Friedrich **8** 101; **16** 737; **32** 200
Hewell Grange **16** 824
hewers **20** 559
Hewetson, Christopher **14** 500*
patrons and collectors **5** 541; **14** 486; **24** 893; **30** 268; **33** 208
works **14** *500*; **16** 21
Hewison, Robert **14** 453
Hewitt, Edgar **22** 594
Hewitt, George and William **31** 390
Hewitt, George Watson **11** 848; **24** 600
Hewitt, Graily **28** 307
Hewitt, John **2** 450
Hewitt, Samuel **12** 315
Hewitt's Willow Pottery **31** 261
Hewlett, Alfred **33** 565
Hewlett, James (*fl c.* 1807) **19** 271
Hewlett, James Monroe (1869-1941) **11** 834
Hews, Abraham **4** 482
Hewson, John **10** 852
Hewson, Stephen **33** 545
Hewton, Randolph **5** 567; **14** 499
Hexagons **20** 169
hexastyle **14** 500*
Hexham Abbey (Northumb.) **2** 65; **10** *225*; **13** 44; **14** 501*
crosses **2** 69
crypt **8** 222; **14** *501*
furniture **30** 776
plaques **10** 322
sculpture **2** 68
Hey, Jean **14** 502*; **20** 731, 733–4; **26** 556
Heybeli, Panagia Kamariotissa **7** 256; **9** 547
Heyblocq, Jacobus **5** 682; **33** 263
Heyboer, Anton **14** 502*; **22** 854
Heyde, Henning von der *see* HEIDE, HENNING VON DER
Heydeck, Carl Wilhelm *see* HEIDECK, CARL WILHELM
Heyden, Adolf von **18** 544
Heyden, Cornelis van der **33** 268
Heyden, Goris van der **14** 503
Heyden, Isaac van der **14** 503
Heyden, Jacob van der **14** 502–3*
works **14** *503*
Heyden, Jan van der (*fl* 1590) **14** 502
Heyden, Jan van der (1637-1712; father) **14** 503–4*; **31** 155
collaboration **22** 843; **32** 145
patrons and collectors **4** 618; **15** 40
printmakers **14** 683
works **2** 338; **8** 427; **11** *431*; **14** *504*; **22** 686; **25** *325*; **31** 246, *247*, 704
Heyden, Jan van der (*fl* 1660s; son) **14** 504
Heyden, J(acques) C(ornelis) J(ohan) van der **14** 504*; **22** 853
Heyden, Johannes van der **14** 502
Heyden, Pieter van der **10** 389; **14** 504–5*
copies **13** 664
works **2** 411; **4** 911; **11** 222
Heyden, Sylvia **30** 331; **31** 660
Heydenreich, Erhard *see* HEIDENREICH, ERHARD
Heydenreich, Ludwig Heinrich **14** 505*; **19** 718
Heydenreich, Ulrich *see* HEIDENREICH, ULRICH
Heydenryk, Henry **11** 499
Heydour (Lincs), St Michael's **13** 183
Heydt, August von der **14** 506*
Heydt, Eduard von der **1** 438; **15** 742, 745; **17** 432; **19** 542
Heye, George **22** 673
Heyenbroek, Herman **26** 75
Heyer, Georg **3** 797
Heyerdahl, Hans (Olaf Halvor) **10** 105; **14** 506–7*; **23** 225
works **14** *506*
Heyerdahl, Thor **9** 674
Heylan, Ana **14** 507
Heylan, Bernardo **14** 507
Heylan, Francisco **14** 507*; **19** 628
Heylan, José **14** 507
Heylbrouck, F. **26** 285
Heylmann, Jacob *see* HAYLMANN, JACOB
Heylyn, Edward **4** 600; **11** 810
Heymann, J. D.
works **12** *417*
Heymann, Moritz **14** 632
Heymann, Violette **24** *244*
Heymanns, Joseph **31** 875
Heymans, Adrien Joseph **3** 562; **14** 507*; **19** 792
Heymans, Pieter **30** 203, 319
Heymel, Alfred Walter **33** 383
Heymüller, Matthias Gottlieb **12** 405
Heyn, Miguel **24** 99
Heyne, Christian Gottlob **14** 876
Heyne, Johann Christoph **31** 651
Heynicke, Kurt **29** 872
Heyns, Jan **1** 526; **28** 595
Heyns, Zacharias **31** 881
Heyrman, Hugo **23** 906
Heys, George **25** 565
Heysen, (Ernst) Hans (Franz) **2** 769; **14** 507–8*
works **1** 152; **2** 748, *748*
Heysham (Lancs), St Patrick's Chapel **2** 72
Heystee **29** 482
Heythrop House (Oxon) **2** 307, *307*
Heythum, Antonín **8** 402
Heyward, F. J. **23** 212
Heyward, Julia **24** 409
Heyward, William **4** 692
Heywood, Thomas **7** 236
Heywood Bros. **33** 156
Heywood-Wakefield Co. **33** 158, 410
Hezelo **7** 474; **13** 854; **14** 508*
Hezenmans, L. C. **28** 595
He Zhen **7** 130
Hezilo, Bishop of Hildesheim **14** 531, 532; **26** 686
He *zun* **3** 187
H.F., Master **20** 796*
H.F.E., Master **20** 796*
H. G., Master **20** 797
el-Hiba **10** 93
Hiba, Tell al- *see* LAGASH
Hibberd, Shirley **12** 140
Hibbert, George **5** 63
Hibernian Silk Warehouse **16** 34
Hiberno-Saxon art *see* INSULAR ART
Hibino, Gōhō **17** 240
hibi-nuri see under LACQUER → types
Hibis, Temple of Amun **9** 803, 834, 892; **18** *19*, 20
Hick, Benjamin **19** 508
Hickel, Anton **14** 508–9*
Hickel, Johann **14** 508
Hickel, Joseph **14** 508*
Hickey, Dale **2** 751; **14** 509*
Hickey, John **14** 509*
Hickey, Thomas **3** 373; **14** 509
hickory **3** 331
Hickox, Elizabeth **14** 509–10*; **22** 660
works **22** *660*
Hickox, Louise **14** 510; **22** 660
Hicks, David (Nightingale) **10** 285; **14** 511*
Hicks, Edgar **12** 54
Hicks, Edward **11** 785; **14** 510*
Hicks, George Elgar **11** 161; **14** 511–12*
Hicks, James **16** 28
Hicks, Sheila **14** 512*; **30** 331
works **11** 54, *54*
Hicks, Thomas **14** 510–11*
Hicks & Parr **14** 511
Hidai, Nakoku **17** 240
works **17** *239*
Hidai, Shoha **17** 240
Hidai, Shokin **17** 240
Hidai, Tenrai **17** 239, 240
Hidaka Tetsuō **17** 189, 199; **23** 298
Hidalga (y Musitu), Lorenzo de la **14** 512*; **21** 378, 402
Hidalgo, Felix Resurrección **20** 274; **24** 622
Hidalgo, José García *see* GARCÍA HIDALGO, JOSÉ
Hidalgo, Miguel **21** 392
Hida Takayama **17** 357
Hidatsa **22** 551
dress **22** 650
feathers **22** 653
headdresses **22** *653*
quillwork **22** 648, 649, 650
sculpture **22** 584
Hidcote Manor Garden (Glos) **10** *225*; **12** 142; **14** 512*; **31** 151
Hidehira, Fujiwara no *see* FUJIWARA NO HIDEHIRA
Hideichirō Kinoshita *see* KINOSHITA, HIDEICHIRŌ
Hidemaro II **17** 286
Hideo Hagiwara *see* HAGIWARA, HIDEO
Hideo Sakurai *see* SAKURAI, HIDEO
Hideo Sugita *see* EI, KYŪ
Hideo Takeda *see* TAKEDA, HIDEO
hides **19** 1
historical and regional traditions
Africa **1** 295, 307, *411*
Cambodia **5** 505
Java **15** 798

hides
historical and regional traditions—cont.
Kenya **1** *411*
Mesoamerica, Pre-Columbian **21** 234
Native North Americans **22** 592, 654–5*
Prehistoric art **25** 477
types
buffalo **1** 299; **15** *798*; **22** *592*, 654, *654*, 655
elk **22** 655
water-buffalo **7** 92
uses
baskets **1** 295
glues **7** 92
headrests **1** *411*
manuscripts **21** 234
painting **22** 592, *592*
pouches **22** *557*
puppets **5** 505; **15** *798*, 798
rock art **25** 477
shields **22** *562*
see also LEATHER; SKINS
Hidetada Tokugawa *see* TOKUGAWA HIDETADA, Shogun
Hidetake Andō *see* ANDŌ, HIDETAKE
Hidetoshi Nagasawa *see* NAGASAWA, HIDETOSHI
Hideyori Kanō *see* KANŌ HIDEYORI
Hideyori Toyotomi *see* TOYOTOMI HIDEYORI
Hideyoshi Toyotomi *see* TOYOTOMI HIDEYOSHI, Taikō
Hideyuki *see* SAKURAI, HIDEO
Hidta Codex *see under* CODICES → individual manuscripts
Hiebel, Johann **25** 416
Hieber, Hans **2** 336; **14** 513*
works **12** *366*, 367; **23** 617; **33** 354
Hieber, Placidus, Abbot of Lambach **18** 668
Hieber, Ulrich **28** 48
Hiecke, Robert **25** 804
Hieda no Are **17** 214
Hieizanji *see* ŌTSU → Enryakuji
Hien, Daniel **22** 271
Hienheim **25** 500
Hiepes, Tomás **14** 513*
Hierakonpolis **9** *774*, 778; **10** 64; **14** 513–14*
cult statues **9** 797
Decorated Tomb *see* Tomb 100
figurines **10** 60
houses **9** 850
ivory **10** 59
Painted Tomb *see* Tomb 100
sculpture **9** 867; **10** 35, *35*, *37*
statuettes **10** 37
Temple of Horus **23** 848
Temple of Khasekhemwy **9** 827, 828, 868; **30** 433
Tomb 100 **10** 80; **14** 513–14, *514*
wall paintings **9** 827, 828, 899, 901
tomb of Horemkawef **14** 514
town walls **9** 844; **21** 554
Hierakonpolis Palette **9** 868
Hierapetra **8** 154; **21** *651*
Archaeological Collection **8** 157; **21** 691
Hierapolis **5** 742; **9** *512*, *513*; **13** *362*; **14** 514–15*; **26** *908*
bath-gymnasium **3** 375; **26** 912
north necropolis **14** 515
St Philip **7** 254; **9** 537; **20** 520
sculpture **14** 515*
hieratic script *see under* SCRIPTS → types
Hiernle, Karl Josef **8** 386, 398; **14** 515–16*
hieroglyphic script *see under* SCRIPTS → types
hieroglyphs **22** 414
Egypt, ancient **9** 881; **10** 1–4*, *5*, 93; **15** 149
Maya **17** 753; **20** 883; **22** 443; **27** 607
Mesoamerica, Pre-Columbian **21** 219; **22** 443; **27** 607
Spain **6** 72
Hieron (*fl* early 5th cent. BC; Greek potter) **32** 55
Hieron (*fl* early 4th cent. BC; Etruscan potter) **10** 622
Hieron II (*reg* 270-16 BC) **13** 561
Hieronymites **10** 498; **14** 516–17*
painting **14** *516*
Hierosolymitan order *see under* ORDERS (ARCHITECTURE) → types
Hierschel (family) **17** 444
Hiesmayr, Ernst **32** 440
Higashiyama, Kaii **14** 517*; **17** 428; **28** 627
Higgens, Dick **11** 232; **24** 407; **27** 215
Higgins, David Paul **25** 235
Higgins, Eugene **21** 897
Higgins, Frances **31** 645
Higgins, John Woodman **29** 515
Higgins, Michael **31** 645
Higginson, Augustus Barker **14** 517–18*
Higgs, Cecil **29** 108
Higham (Suffolk), Barhams Manor House **10** 271
Higham Ferrers (Northants), St Mary **4** 693; **27** 125
Highclere Castle (Hants) **3** *283*; **10** 238
High Crosses *see under* CROSSES → types
Higher (State) Artistic and Technical Workshops *see* VKHUTEMAS
Higher Institute of Architecture and Building, Moscow *see* MOSCOW ARCHITECTURE INSTITUTE
Higher State Art-Technical Institute *see* VKHUTEIN
High Gothic *see under* GOTHIC → styles
Highland Park (IL)
Ford factory **4** 789
Ward Willits House **21** 780; **31** 595, *595*; **33** *401*
Highland Stoneware **28** 258
highlighting **11** 763; **13** 138–9
high looms *see under* LOOMS → types
Highmore, Anthony **14** 520
Highmore, Joseph **10** 372; **14** 519–20*; **18** 146
assistants **1** 504
patrons and collectors **20** 911; **21** 91
reproductive prints by others **24** 335; **31** 871
works **5** 76; **7** 785; **11** 426; **14** *520*
Highmore, Thomas **14** 519; **30** 758
Highnam Court (Glos) **12** 33
high-performance liquid chromatography *see under* TECHNICAL EXAMINATION → types
High Renaissance *see under* RENAISSANCE → styles
high-speed photography *see under* PHOTOGRAPHY → processes
High Tech **10** 749; **14** 520–22*; **19** 897
architecture **1** *737*; **2** 308; **11** 334; **14** *522*; **15** 887
high-tin bronze *see under* ALLOYS → types
High Victorian Gothic **5** 315
England **14** 746
New Zealand **22** 230
High Victorian Gothic—cont.
United States of America **25** 371, 372; **31** 593
high-warp looms *see under* LOOMS → types
High Wycombe (Bucks) **10** *225*; **14** 522–3*
furniture **10** 293, 297, 299
Wycombe Chair Museum **14** 523
Higis **1** 346
Higonnet, Léon **19** 769
Higuchi, Hiroyasu **30** 392
Higuchi Shūgetsu **17** 400, 401
Higuera, La *see* LA HIGUERA
Higueras, Fernando **21** 861
Higueras, Jacinto **29** 295
hibaku see under SCRIPTS → types
hibakutai see under SCRIPTS → types
Híjar **17** 565
Hijara, Ismail **2** 491
Hijares, Rafael **21** 380
Hijazis **1** 317
ḥijāzī script *see under* SCRIPTS → types
Hijikata, Teiichi **14** 523*
Hijrat al-Felle **16** 215
Hi Kangen *see* FEI QINGHU
Hikaru, Yamada **33** 480
Hikisch, Rezső **14** 523*
Hikohichirō Matsumoto *see* MATSUMOTO, HIKOHICHIRŌ
Hikone **17** 95, *95*
Genkyūen **12** 99
keep **17** 83
Hikone Screen **17** 175
Hilair, Jean-Baptiste **14** 366
Hilarion **25** 120
Hilarius, Bishop of Arles (*reg* 429-49) **2** 418
Hilarius, Pope (*reg* 461-68) **26** 752, 821
Hilberseimer, Ludwig (Karl) **14** 523–4*
collaboration **21** 493
groups and movements **8** 826; **12** 378; **26** 405
works **12** 378; **31** 730
Hilbert, Georges **11** 568
Hilbert, Kamil **25** 428, 439, 441
Hilbig, Gustav **18** 850
Hild, János **14** 524, 888
Hild, József **5** 81; **14** 524–5*; **23** 747
assistants **33** 172
pupils **11** 34
works **5** 82; **9** 754; **10** *545*, 546; **14** 889; **15** 14; **25** 155; **33** 515
Hilda, Saint **21** 835
Hildburgh, Walter Leo **14** 525*
Hildburghausen, Friedrich Wilhelm Eugen von, Prince **30** 793
Hildebert II, Abbot of Mont-Saint-Michel **22** 39
Hildebrand, Adolf von **11** 190, 315; **14** 525–6*, 896; **22** 304
collaboration **20** 405; **22** 329
competitions **3** 498
teachers **20** 405; **33** 726
works **5** 304; **12** 407; **14** *526*
writings **12** 407
Hildebrand, Hans **18** 828
Hildebrand, Henri Théophile **19** 767
Hildebrand, Maciej **32** 878
Hildebrand Brandenburg **4** 372
inscription **4** *373*
Hildebrandt, Carl Ludwig **25** 366
Hildebrandt, Eduard **14** 527*
Hildebrandt, Fritz **14** 527
Hildebrandt, Johann Lukas von **2** 782; **12** 373; **14** 402, 527–30*; **16** 904; **29** 789; **32** 435, 443; **33** 431
architecture
cabinets (i) (rooms) **5** 349
catafalques **6** 72
chapels **21** 893
Hildebrandt, Johann Lukas von architecture—cont.
churches **8** 378; **12** 356; **16** 904; **19** 433; **23** 4
ciboria (ii) (structure) **7** 303
government buildings **32** 456
halls **2** 695; **27** 610, *611*
monasteries **2** 828; **3** 877; **24** 808
palaces **2** 782–3, 828; **14** *528*, *529*, 886; **23** 811, 812; **27** 661; **32** 458, *459*
pavilions (buildings) **33** 432
stables **29** 485
staircases **23** 812, *812*; **25** 188; **29** 525
collaboration **1** 667; **8** 875; **20** 494; **23** 2, 3, 4; **28** 123; **29** 789; **33** 65, 698
gardens **12** 723
groups and movements **3** 266; **26** 495
patrons and collectors **3** 689; **14** 191; **28** 15, 146; **32** 458
pupils **8** 874
teachers **11** 274
Hildebrandt, (Ferdinand) Theodor **9** 460; **14** 216, 838; **16** 63; **23** 204; **26** 255; **33** 697
Hildegard, Holy Roman Empress (*d* 783) **12** 837
Hildegard of Bingen **19** 356; **33** 308
Hilder, J(essie) J(ewhurst) **14** 531*
Hildesheim **12** *360*, 382, 471; **14** 531–5*
altars **29** IX1
Cathedral of St Mariae **14** 531*, 532*
altarpieces **9** 752
Bernward Cross **8** 200, *200*, 201; **14** 532; **23** 657
brasses **4** 693
chandeliers **26** 686
Column of Christ **7** 381, *381*; **14** 532; **22** 43; **23** 658
crosiers **8** 194
doors **4** 688; **9** 152, 153, *153*; **23** 538, 657, 658, *658*; **26** 684
font **11** 253; **26** 684
manuscripts **23** 654
paintings **30** 310
shrine of St Godehard **28** 630
Treasury **14** 532*
Virgin **12** 399
wall paintings **26** 654
westwork **7** 265
Kaiserhaus **12** 367
Knochenhaueramthaus **32** 282
Magdalenenkirche **23** 657
metalwork **8** 205; **23** 657; **26** 683
painting **12** 391
Roemer-Pelizaeus-Museum **10** 48, 90, 93
St Godehardikirche **7** 192; **26** 660, 671, *672*
St Michael **1** 723, *723*; **7** 265; **12** 363; **13** 18; **14** 532–5*, *533*, *534*; **22** 216; **23** 645; **26** *572*, 572–3, *573*
ambulatory **1** 768
candelabrum **26** 686
choir-screen **12** 399; **26** 632
doors **9** 153; **22** 520
manuscripts **26** 675
paintings **12** 382; **13** 142; **14** 535*
piers (ii) (masonry) **24** 750
screen **28** 293
sculpture **14** 535*; **23** 646
stucco **29** 818, *818*
transept **31** 280
vaults **32** 87
wall paintings **26** 653
sculpture **12** 399; **26** 632
Hildesheim Cope **12** 462
Hildesheim Missal *see under* MISSALS → individual manuscripts
Hildesheim Service **12** 448
Hildesheim Treasure **27** 80, *81*, 81, 100
Hildevert de Lavardin, Bishop of Le Mans **19** 127
Hilditch factory **10** 310
Hildoard Sacramentary *see under* SACRAMENTARIES → individual manuscripts
Hildyard **5** 295
Hilebrand, Friedrich **8** 413
Hileq **14** 34
Hilger, Wolf, I **13** 630
Hilgers, Carl **14** 535*
Hili **2** *246*, 254, 266, 272
Hilinos **32** 65
Hilker, Georg C. **8** 746; **11** 473; **14** 154
Hill (*fl* 15th cent.) **1** 518
Hill, Aaron **30** 675
Hill, Anthony (*fl* 1840-52) **32** 783
Hill, Anthony (*b* 1930) **7** 772; **14** 536–7*
Hill, Carl Fredrik **14** 537*; **30** 79
Hill, Charles **1** 152
Hill, David Octavius **2** 119; **14** 539–40*; **28** 237, 243, 274
works **14** *539*
Hill, Francis **27** 626
Hill, Gary **32** 421
Hill, George **5** 570
Hill, George Francis **2** 262; **14** 537*
Hill, Harold D.
works **9** *46*
Hill, Joan **14** 538*; **22** 595
works **22** *596*
Hill, John (1770-1850) **14** 536*
pupils **14** 536
works **23** 46; **28** 560; **31** 602; **32** 799
Hill, John (*fl* 1780s) **32** 903
Hill, John Henry **14** 536
Hill, John William **14** 536*; **25** 556; **31** 603; **32** 799
Hill, Noel, Ist Lord Berwick **13** 650
Hill, Oliver **14** 538*
pupils **28** 283
works **10** 241, 284; **25** 689
Hill, Rowland **25** 328; **33** 448
Hill, Stuart **10** 344
Hill, Thomas (*fl* 1568) **12** 126
Hill, Thomas (1661-1734) **10** 758; **14** 538–9*; **29** 536
Hill, Thomas (1829-1908) **31** 603
Hill, Thomas Noel, 2nd Baron Berwick **14** 539*
Hill, W. Burrough **4** 798
Hill, William (1827-89) **31** 241
Hill, William McKinley (*fl* 1930) **14** 538
Hillah **4** 772
Hillan, Christian **10** 332
Hill and Adamson **9** 725; **14** 539–40*; **24** 661
groups and movements **24** 738
patrons and collectors **9** 725; **12** 486
works **14** *539*
Hill Court (Hereford & Worcs), Painted Bedroom **23** 789, *790*
Hille, Klaas **1** 815; **10** 698; **18** 126
Hille, Maria **30** 925
Hille, S., & Co. **19** 592
Hillebrand, A. **26** 708
Hillebrand, Lucy **21** 431
Hillebrandt, Franz Anton **14** 540–41*
collaboration **5** 81
works **4** 695; **5** 86; **10** 546; **14** 887, 888; **26** 317; **30** 206; **31** 353; **32** 457
Hillebrandt, Joseph **14** 541
Hillebrecht, Rudolf **12** 379; **14** 142; **18** 883

Hillegaert, Paulus van (1595/6-1640) **17** 881
Hillegaert, Paulus van, II (1631-55) **32** 673
Hillegers, Frans **29** 119
Hille International **6** 391; **8** 583; **10** 299; **20** 595
 furniture **10** *300*; **20** *595*
Hill End **2** 745
Hiller, Karol **14** 541*
Hiller, Susan **10** 879; **14** 541*; **24** 409
Hillerød **8** *720*; **14** 541–3*
 Frederiksborg Slot **5** 920; **8** 719, 724, 725, 727, 732, 739, 742; **14** 541–3*, *542*; **19** 815; **22** 897; **32** 772
  audience room **8** 733
  collections **1** 686; **8** 759; **14** 154; **17** 478
  fountain **32** 731
  gardens **12** 135
  interior decoration **8** 742; **11** 467
  paintings **14** 244; **18** 818; **19** 36; **20** 249; **32** 765; **33** 421, 422
  Pancake Kitchen **30** 883
  portraits **4** 292; **30** 59
  tapestries **8** 754
 Nationalhistoriske Museum på Frederiksborg *see* FREDERIKSBORG SLOT
Hillers, John K. **10** 580
Hillersberg, Lars **30** 82
Hilleström, Carl Peter **14** 543
Hilleström, Pehr **14** 543*
 works **9** *24*; **11** *471*; **30** 79, 114
hill-figures **10** *473*; **14** *544*, 544–5*; **31** 526–7, *527*
Hillfon, Curt **30** 82
Hillfon, Hertha **30** 99
hill-forts *see under* FORTS → types
Hill Hall (Essex) **28** 886
Hillhouse, James Abram **31** 232
Hillhouse, May **29** 110
Hilliard, John **14** 548*
Hilliard, Laurence **14** 545, 547, 548*; **21** 639
Hilliard, Nicholas **4** 847; **14** 545–8*
 attributions **10** 246; **28** 357
 groups and movements **10** 142
 patrons and collectors **9** 367; **14** 548; **21** 908; **31** 415
 pupils **14** 548; **19** 531; **23** 407
 reproductive prints by others **18** 570
 teachers **30** 412
 works **4** 847; **8** 828; **9** 244, 275; **10** 246; **14** *545*, *546*; **17** 522; **20** 921; **21** 639, *639*; **25** 279
 writings **28** 666; **31** 300
Hilliard, Richard **14** 545
Hilliard, Winifred **1** 64
Hillier, Jack **17** 271
Hillier, Tristram **31** 673
Hilliger (family) **4** 692
Hillingdon Civic Centre (Middx) **4** 790; **31** 243
Hillinger, Franz **30** 371
Hillinus **23** 652
Hillinus Gospels *see under* GOSPEL BOOKS → individual manuscripts
Hillmann, Hans **25** 353
Hills, Alexander **4** 609
Hills, Joan **4** 608
Hills, Robert **14** 548–9*; **26** 476; **32** 903
Hillsboro Court-house (NC) **18** 887
Hill-Stead Museum *see* FARMINGTON (CT), HILL-STEAD MUSEUM
Hilltop Factory **33** 341
Hilly, John **15** 24
Hilmer, Heinz **12** 381
Hilmor **7** 483
Hilo *see* HADDA
Hilpert, Andreas **31** 255
Hilprecht, Herman V. **1** 892
Hils, Karl **7** 325; **30** 644
Hilský, Václav **19** 423
Hiltensperger, (Johann) Georg **12** 603; **18** 125
Hiltipure **26** 685
Hilton **1** 518
Hilton, John **22** 39
Hilton, Roger **6** 588; **14** 549–50*
 groups and movements **2** 545; **10** 258; **27** 563
 works **14** *549*
Hilton, Walter **1** 518
Hilton, William (1752-1822) **14** 550
Hilton, William (1786-1839) **11** 84; **14** 550*; **19** 98; **32** 338
 reproductive prints by others **10** 378
Hilton & Baird **22** 39
Hilton of Cadboll **24** 738; **28** 233, 241
 crosses **24** *737*
Hilts, Alvin **5** 571
Hiltunen, Eila **11** 101
Hiltz, Johann *see* HÜLTZ, JOHANN
Hilversum
 carpets **22** 900
 Raadhuis *see* Stadhuis
 Stadhuis **4** 788; **9** 368, *368*; **22** 831; **31** 243
 Zonnestraal Sanatorium **4** 57, *57*; **21** 783; **22** 830
Hilz, Sepp **12** 396
Him, George **25** 353
Hima **1** 411
himatia **9** 246, 249, 251
Himeji **14** 550–52*; **17** *11*
 Castle **14** 551–2*, *552*; **17** 46, 49, 83, 84–6*, *85*; **21** 595; **33** 245
 Shirasagijō *see* Castle
Himera **13** *362*; **14** 552–3*; **16** *621*; **21** 556
Himid, Lubaina **10** 882; **14** 553*
Himiko, Princess **17** 312
Himi Munetada **17** 393
Himyar **2** 268
hina see under DOLLS → types
hinagata-bon see JAPAN → pattern-books
Hinako, Jitsuzō **17** 135
Hinard, Jean-Baptiste **3** 752
Hinart, Louis **3** 460; **11** 641
Hinayana Buddhism *see* BUDDHISM → branches → Theravada
Hinaya Ryūho **17** 829
Hinchcliffe, Mark **28** 261
Hinckeldeyn, Karl **25** 409
Hincmar, Archbishop of Reims **5** 803; **26** 122
Hincz, Gyula **14** 553*
Hind, Arthur Mayger **14** 553–4*
Hind, William (*fl* 1680-90) **13** 614
Hind, William G(eorge) R(ichardson) (1833-89) **14** 554*
Hindagala **29** 464
Hindaun **15** 346
 Jachchaw ki Ba'oli **15** 345
Hindemith, Paul **30** 390
Hindenlang, Charles **13** 726
Hinder, Frank **3** 124
Hinder, Margel **2** 753
Hinderbach, Giovanni **5** 180
 works **5** *181*
Hindoo style *see* MOORISH STYLE
Hindriksson, Lorens **30** 109
Hinds, Patrick Swazo *see* SWAZO HINDS, PATRICK
Hinds, René **25** 786; **28** 174
Hindsgavl **25** *470*
 daggers **25** *516*
Hinduism **14** 554–62*; **26** 140
 art forms and materials
  altars **1** 701, 706
  amulets **1** 818
  architecture **6** 420; **15** 758; **20** 165*; **29** 448
Hinduism
 art forms and materials—cont.
  book illustrations **22** *786*
  brick **5** *487*
  bronze **15** *219*, *516*, *517*, 523, *728*
  busts **6** *429*
  chlorite **15** *504*
  copper **22** *772*
  cosmologies **5** 463, 467–8, 474
  cotton **15** *673*
  embroidery **15** 548
  figurines **15** *783*
  gilding **22** *772*
  gold **15** *783*
  granite **15** *508*, *514*, *515*, *518*, *519*
  jewellery **15** 702
  lacquer **15** 548
  limestone **15** *510*
  manuscript covers **15** 548
  manuscript illumination **15** 545, 566, *567*, 616
  manuscripts **15** 544, 548, 549
  metal **22** 772–3
  narratives **5** 487; **15** 226–8*, 780; **22** 516–17*
  nude figures **15** *218*
  ornament **23** 555–6
  painting **14** *556*, *558*, *559*; **15** *79*, *217*, 599, *602*, *622*, *628*, *633*, *673*, 674; **15** 544
  paubhās **22** 781
  prints **15** 177–8, *178*
  rock crystal **26** 487
  rock reliefs **15** *465*, *477*, *508*, *510*
  sanctuaries **15** 762
  sandstone **5** *485*, *488*, *489*, *492*, *493*, *494*; **15** *214*, *218*, *495*, *496*, *497*
  schist **28** *544*
  scrolls **22** 784
  sculpture **15** *496*; **17** *761*
   Afghanistan **1** 199
   Bangladesh **15** *502*
   bronze **15** *219*, *516*, *517*, 523, *728*
   Burma **5** 240*
   Cambodia **5** 484–5, *485*, 486–90, *487*, *488*, *489*, *492*, *493*
   Champa **6** 427, 428–9*, *429*, 430
   India, Republic of **15** *79*
   Indian subcontinent **1** *485*; **5** 95; **15** *214*, *216*, *218*, *219*, *416*, *417*, *438*, 443–4*, *463*, *468*, *469*, *471*, *472*, *480*, *481*, *482*, *484*, *488*, *489*, *490*, *492*, *495*, *496*, *497*, 502, *502*, *503*, 503–5, *504*, 507–20, *514*, *515*, *516*, *517*, *518*, *519*, 523, *524*, *530*, 535, *536*, *728*; **20** *224*; **23** 832; **28** *544*
   Indonesia **15** 778–9, 780
   Java **15** 778, 780
   Laos **18** *769*
   liṅga **15** *438*
   Malaysia **20** 170*
   Nepal **5** *121*; **6** *449*; **22** *767*, 767–8, *768*, 770, *770*, 771, *772*, 772–3
   South-east Asia **14** *561*; **29** 231
   stone **6** *449*; **15** *463*, *482*, *484*, *488*, *502*, *503*, *504*; **22** *767*, 767–8, *768*, 770, *770*, 771
   Thailand **30** 574, 598
   Vietnam **6** 427, 428–9*, *429*, 430
  wood **15** *524*
 shrines (i) (cult) **14** 559; **15** *331*; **19** *695*; **25** 169; **28** 635
 silver **15** *502*
 slate **15** *216*
Hinduism
 art forms and materials—cont.
  stone **6** *429*, *449*; **15** *463*, *482*, *484*, *488*, *502*, *503*, *504*; **22** *767*, 767–8, *768*, 770, *770*, 771
  temple-mountains **5** 464, *466*, 466, *469*, *471*
  temples **30** 431
   Bali (Indonesia) **3** *872*
   Cambodia **5** 463–7*, *465*, *469*, *470*, *471*, 473
   Champa **6** 420
   Indian subcontinent **1** *484*; **3** *911*; **13** *882*; **14** 77, 559; **15** 257, *263*, *282*, *286*, *287*, *289*, *291*, *310*, *312*, 312, *315*, *316*, *318*, *320*, *321*, *323*, 329, *330*, *332*, *334*; **17** *760*; **18** *13*, *14*; **20** *224*; **29** *481*; **30** 437*, *439*; **31** *542*
   Malaysia **20** 156
   rock-cut **15** 465–6, 477, 521–2; **30** 431
   Shaivism **1** *485*; **3** *911*
   Singapore **28** 773
   South Africa **29** 105
   South-east Asia **14** 560
   Trinidad and Tobago **5** *755*
   Vaishnavism **15** 394
   Vietnam **6** 420
  textiles **15** 176, 548, 599, 669, 673
  tower-sanctuaries **5** *466*
  wood **15** *524*, *783*; **18** *769*
 astrology **14** 560
 censorship **6** 174
 iconoclasm **15** 79
 iconography **5** 92
  Cambodia **5** 461–2
  Indian subcontinent **7** 633; **14** *556*, 556–8, *557*, *558*; **15** 213–14*, 219*; **20** 818
   Ganapatya **15** 216–17*
   Saura **15** 216
   Shaivism **15** 214–15*
   Shakta **15** 217–19*
   Vaishnavism **15** 215–16
  Indonesia **15** 756–7*, 777
  Java **15** 777
  Nepal **22** 756*
  Sri Lanka **29** 443–4
 patronage **15** 206
 pilgrimages **14** 559; **31** 902
 regional traditions
  Afghanistan **1** 188, 189
  Bali (Indonesia) **29** 226
  Bangladesh **14** 554
  Cambodia **5** 461–2, 463, 473
  Caribbean Islands **14** 554
  Champa **6** 419–20*
  India, Republic of **14** 554
  Indian subcontinent **5** 93; **14** 554–60*; **15** 190, 195, 202, 203, 204
  Indonesia **15** 756
  Malaysia **20** 164
  Nepal **22** 755–6
  Pacific Islands **14** 554
  South-east Asia **14** 560–62*; **29** 234
  Sri Lanka **14** 554; **29** 442, 443–4
  Vietnam **6** 419–20*
 rituals **14** *559*, 559–60
 sects
  Ganapatya **15** 216–17*
  Saura **15** 216
  Shaivism **5** 473; **14** 555; **30** 642
   Cambodia **5** 461
   Champa **6** 419*
   Indian subcontinent **15** 214–15*
   Vietnam **6** 419*
  Shakta **15** 217–19*
  Tantric **5** 96
  Vaishnavism **5** 473; **6** 419; **15** 215–16
Hine, Lewis W(ickes) **14** 562–3*
 patrons and collectors **27** 164
 pupils **27** 164; **29** 744
 works **15** 830; **24** 673, 675
Hine, T. C. **23** 258, 259
 works **23** *259*
Hine Taizan **17** 188, 192, 199
Hingbon **17** 804
hinges **9** 155, 156; **22** 238
Hingham (MA), Old Ship Meeting-House **31** 589
Hinglajgarh **14** 563*; **15** *285*
Hinis **12** 66
Hinkson, Jackie **31** 336
Hinloopen, Michiel (Thijmensz.) **1** 807; **14** 563*; **23** 112, 113; **28** 362
Hino (family) **5** 119
hinoki (Japanese cypress) *see under* CYPRESS-→ types
Hino Tomiko **31** 198
Hinrik van dem Kroghe **26** 507
Hinsbeck, Hubrecht Goltz von *see* GOLTZ VON HINSBECK, HUBRECHT
Hinse, Zacharie *see* HEINCE, ZACHARIE
Hinterfultigen, Schwandbach Bridge **4** 803; **7** 694; **20** *119*
Hinton, Alfred Horsley **19** 424; **24** 739
Hinton, Denys, & Partners **23** 194
Hinton, Howard **2** 769
Hinton House (Somerset) **19** 531
Hinton Martell (Dorset), Gaunt's House **8** 30
Hinton St Mary (Dorset) **9** *510*
 mosaics **9** *568*, 569; **18** 825
Hintz, Zacharie *see* HEINCE, ZACHARIE
Hintze, Hans, IV **12** 443
Hintze, Johann Ferdinand Julius **3** 799
Hinxman, John **8** 576
Hinz, Georg **29** 666
Hiolle, Ernest-Eugène **14** 564*; **23** 794
Hiolle, Maximilien-Louis **14** 564
Hiorne, David **17** 476
Hiorne, William **17** 476
Hiorns, Arthur H. **24** 258
Hiorthoy, Edvard **7** 546
Hipkins, Roland **33** 58
hipped roofs *see under* ROOFS → types
Hippert, H. **3** 619
Hippias **19** 771
Hippiatrika Codex *see under* CODICES → individual manuscripts
Hippius, Gustav Adolf **10** 539
Hippius, Otto-Pius **10** 537; **30** 277
Hippocrates **21** 5; **28** 324
Hippodamos **2** 312; **13** 421; **14** 564*
 pupils **26** 291
 works **13** 401, 419; **15** 894; **21** 542; **24** 327
hippodromes *see* CIRCUSES (ROMAN)
Hippolita Master *see* IPPOLITA MASTER
Hippolite, Hector *see* HYPPOLITE, HECTOR
Hippolyte **32** 582
Hippo Regius *see under* EL-'ANNĀBA
al-Hira **15** 610; **16** 397, 399
 church **2** 275
 stucco **2** 273
 writing **16** 277
Hirabayashi Atsunobu **17** 235
Hirado
 kilns **17** 811
 porcelain **4** 175, 176; **17** 264, *265*, 399
Hirafuku, Hyakusui **17** 201
Hirafuku Tomb **17** 106, *106*
Hiraga, Meigin **17** 402

Hiraga Gennai **14** 564–5*; **17** 185; **23** 347; **27** 865
hiragana *see under* SCRIPTS → types
Hiragushi, Denchū **17** 135
Hiraide **17** 54, 56, 103
Hiraizumi **14** 565–7*; **17** *11*
  Art Museum **14** 565
  Chūsonji **14** 566–7*; **30** 446
    collections **17** 428
    Konjikidō **5** 119; **14** 566*; **17** 68, 120, 300, *300*, 321
    Treasure House **14** 565
  Kōdaijuin *see* Chūsonji
  Mōtsuji **12** 95; **14** 567*
  Museum **14** 565
Hiraki, Shinji **17** 430
hiramakie *see under* LACQUER → types
Hirano, Hakuho **17** 294
Hirano Ihei Morikiyo **17** 792
Hirapur **15** 505
Hiraqla **16** 153
Hirasa kiln **27** 873
Hirasawa **17** 357
Hirashimizu **17** 258, 353
Hirata, Gōyō **17** 371
Hirata Hikoshirō **17** 377
Hirata Suiseki **23** 390
Hirata Tentsū **27** 470
Hiratsuka, Un'ichi **17** 295; **22** 287; **33** 363
Hirayama, Ikuo **14** 568*; **17** 202
Hirazawa Kyokuzan **17** 416
Hirder, Sebald **18** 575; **22** 918
Hire, Laurent de La *see* LA HYRE, LAURENT DE
Hi-Red Center **14** 568*; **30** 256
Hirn, Jean-Georges **11** 229
Hirn, Konrad **2** 717
Hirnl, Karl Josef *see* HIERNLE, KARL JOSEF
Hiroaki Morino *se* MORINO, HIROAKI
Hiroatsu Takada *see* TAKADA, HIROATSU
Hirochika **31** 199
Hiroi, Tsutomu **28** 829
Hirokage **2** 9
Hiromi Fujii *see* FUJII, HIROMI
Hiromi Tsuchida *see* TSUCHIDA, HIROMI
Hiromitsu Nakazawa *see* NAKAZAWA, HIROMITSU
Hiromori Sumiyoshi *see* SUMIYOSHI HIROMORI
Hiromu Hara *see* HARA, HIROMU
Hironao Sumiyoshi *see* SUMIYOSHI HIRONAO
Hirosada II **17** 289
Hirosada Konishi *see* KONISHI HIROSADA
Hirosada Utagawa *see* UTAGAWA HIROSADA
Hiroshige II (1826-69) **17** 290
Hiroshige III (1842-94) **17** 290
Hiroshige Andō *see* ANDŌ HIROSHIGE
Hiroshige Suzuki *see* SUZUKI HIROSHIGE
Hiroshige Utagawa *see* ANDŌ HIROSHIGE
Hiroshi Hamaya *see* HAMAYA, HIROSHI
Hiroshi Hara *see* HARA, HIROSHI
Hiroshi Izue *see* IZUE, YUTAKA
Hiroshi Kawanishi *see* KAWANISHI, HIROSHI
Hiroshima **14** 568*; **17** *11*, 18, 84
  City Museum of Contemporary Art **17** 92; **18** 532, *533*
  Museum of Art **17** 433
  Peace Memorial Museum **17** 53, 89
Hiroshi Nakajima *see* NAKAJIMA, HIROSHI
Hiroshi Nakamura *see* NAKAMURA, HIROSHI
Hiroshi Oe *see* OE, HIROSHI
Hiroshi Seto *see* SETO, HIROSHI
Hiroshi Tateishi *see* TATEISHI, HIROSHI
Hiroshi Teshigahara *see* TESHIGAHARA, HIROSHI
Hiroshi Yoshida *see* YOSHIDA, HIROSHI
Hirotaka Terasawa *see* TERASAWA HIROTAKA
Hirotsura Sumiyoshi *see* SUMIYOSHI HIROTSURA
Hiroyasu Sumiyoshi *see* SUMIYOSHI HIROYASU
Hiroyoshi Sumiyoshi *see* SUMIYOSHI HIROYOSHI
Hiroyuki Iwamoto *see* IWAMOTO, HIROYUKI
Hiroyuki Sumiyoshi *see* SUMIYOSHI HIROYUKI
Hirozo Murata *see* MURATA, HIROZO
Hirsau Abbey **3** 709; **7** 266; **14** 569
  Abbey **7** 231
  choir-stalls **7** 191
  manuscripts **26** 666, 674; **12** 382
  St Aurelius-Kirche **14** 569
  SS Peter and Paul **12** 364; **14** 569
Hirsau Congregation **14** 569*
  architecture **14** *569*
Hirsau Passional *see under* PASSIONALS → individual manuscripts
Hirsch **27** 238
Hirsch, Abraham **19** 847
Hirsch, Alfredo **2** 404
Hirsch, Alphonse **17** 441
Hirsch, E. D. **14** 459
Hirsch, Elizabeth **2** 404
Hirsch, Richard **4** 483
Hirsch, Robert von **14** 569–70*; **30** 154
Hirsch, Silvia **2** 397
Hirsch, Stefan **25** 461
Hirsch, Walter **14** 570*
Hirschberg
  Gnadenkirche **12** 373
  Holy Cross Church **19** 815
Hirschely, Kašpar Jan **8** 391
Hirschfeld, Christian Cay Laurenz **14** 570*; **28** 178
Hirschfeld-Mack, Ludwig **14** 570–72*; **18** 62; **22** 380; **24** 406
  works **14** *571*
Hirschfeld Painter **13** 494; **32** 47*
Hirschhorn, Edith **12** 821
Hirschlanden **25** 538, *539*, 544–5
Hirschler, Moritz **8** 568
Hirschmann, Johann Leonhard **18** 146
Hirscholm Palace **8** 754
Hirschsprung, Heinrich **7** 806; **14** 572*
  collections **8** 758, 759
  groups and movements **28** 814
  sponsorship **8** 758
Hirschsprung, Pauline **8** 759
Hirschsprungske Samling *see under* COPENHAGEN → museums
Hirschvogel (family) **23** 315; **29** 504
Hirschvogel, Augustin **14** 572, 573–4*; **33** 303
  attributions **19** 256
  groups and movements **8** 514
  patrons and collectors **10** 531
  teachers **14** 837
  works **2** 794; **10** 550; **14** *574*; **18** 706; **25** 606; **27** 256; **32** 434
Hirschvogel, Hans **14** 572, 573
Hirschvogel, Heinz **14** 572
Hirschvogel, Lienhard **24** 355
Hirschvogel, Sebald **14** 572
Hirschvogel, Veit (1543-74) **14** 572
Hirschvogel, Veit, the elder (*d* 1485) **12** 386; **14** 572–3*, *572*; **15** 145; **23** 308
Hirschvogel, Veit, the younger (1485-1553) **14** 572, 573
Hirsfogel *see* HIRSCHVOGEL
Hirshfield, Morris **14** 574–5*; **16** 906
Hirshhorn, Joseph H(erman) **14** 575*; **31** 665, 668
Hirshhorn Museum and Sculpture Garden *see under* WASHINGTON (DC) → museums
Hiršl, M. E. **8** 400
Hirst, Brian **2** 764
Hirst, Damien **19** 591
Hirszenberg, Samuel **16** 567
Hirt, Aloys **12** 476; **14** 575–6*; **22** 358
  pupils **18** 122; **26** 22
  works **12** 374; **20** 867
Hirt, J. **17** 584
Hirth, Georg **14** 576*; **22** 304; **28** 341, 374
Hirth, Kenneth **33** 472
Hirtshals **8** 727
Hirtz, Hans **14** 576*; **20** 693, 705
Hirtz, Johann von *see* JOHANN VON HIRTZ
Hirvimäki, Veikko **11** 101
Hirzhorn, Eucharius *see* CERVICORNUS, EUCHARIUS
Hisakazu Minami **6** 586
Hisako Kajiwara *see* KAJIWARA, HISAKO
Hisamasa Matsuya *see* MATSUYA HISAMASA
Hisar (Bulgaria) *see* AUGUSTAE
Hisar (India) **15** 342
  Gujari Mahal **15** 342
  Jahaz Kothi **15** 342
  Lat ki Mosque **15** 342
  palace **15** 342
Hisar-i Firuza *see* HISAR (INDIA)
Hisarlık *see* TROY
Hisashi Matsuoka *see* MATSUOKA, HISASHI
Hisatsugu Zōami *see* ZŌAMI HISATSUGU
Hischylos **32** 40
His de La Salle, (Aimé-Charles-) Horace **10** 432; **14** 576–7*
Hisham, Caliph (*reg* 724-43) (Umayyad) **16** 245, 251, 538; **25** 775; **27** 344
Hisham II, Caliph (*reg* 976-1009; 1010-13) (Umayyad) **16** 436
Hisham al-Mazloum **31** 585
Hishida, Shunsō **14** 219, 577*; **17** 180, 200
Hishikawa Kichizaemon **14** 577
Hishikawa Morofusa **14** 577
Hishikawa Moronobu **14** 577*
  works **10** 485; **17** 176, 273, 280; **24** 276
Hisht-tepe **6** *182*; **14** 577–8*; **30** *252*
Hislop, A. D. **7** 530
HISM *see* HOLLANDSCHE IJZEREN SPOORWEG-MAATSCHAPPIJ (HISM)
Hisn, Tell *see* HELIOPOLIS
Ḥiṣn al-Akrād *see* KRAK DES CHEVALIERS
Ḥiṣn Salʿ *see* PETRA
Hispalis *see* SEVILLE
Hispaniola (Island) **2** 144; **5** 744; **9** *114*; **14** 53, *54*; **29** 128
  ceramics **5** 752
  see also DOMINICAN REPUBLIC; HAITI
Hispaniola (Dominican Republic) *see* SANTO DOMINGO (DOMINICAN REPUBLIC)
Hispano-Flemish style **2** 278; **13** 756; **14** 578–9*; **29** 263, 298; **31** 87
  architecture **13** *731*, 757; **14** *579*
  interior decoration **29** *298*
  painting (religious) **8** *872*
  retables **3** *845*
  sculpture **13** 107
Hispano-Guaraní Baroque **24** 92, 97
  works **24** *97*
Hispano-Maghribi *see* HISPANO-MORESQUE STYLE
Hispano-Moresque style **16** 215, 216
  architecture **16** 217
  pottery **6** IV2
  swords **2** 452
  textiles **16** 439; **28** 716; **29** 349
Hispano-Muslim style *see* HISPANO-MORESQUE STYLE
Hispano-Suiza **23** 694
Hissar (Bulgaria) **9** 458
  Basilica **2** **5** 155
  tombs **5** 150
Hissar, Tepe (Iran) **6** *182*; **14** 579*; **15** *901*, 902, 904, 909, 920, 921
  metalwork **15** 918, 919
  palace **23** 807
Hissar Fortress (Tajikistan) **6** *182*, 198; **14** 579*; **16** *105*; **30** *252*, 252
Hist, Friedrich **10** 542
Histia, Mary **22** 608
Historia Friderici et Maximiliani, Master of the **1** 714; **20** 690–91*
Historia scholastica *see* BIBLES → types → *Bible historiale*
historiated initials *see* INITIALS (MANUSCRIPT)
Historia y cultura **24** 435
Historical Glass Museum (Biidoro Shiryōkō) **17** 385
historicism **2** 532; **9** 704; **14** 580–81*
historic monuments *see* HERITAGE
historie *see* ISTORIE
histories **7** 241–4*
  see also CHRONICLES
historiography **2** 530–33, 535–9; **4** 20; **13** 807; **22** 360
  historical and regional traditions
    Aboriginal Australia **1** 67–8*
    Afghanistan **1** 210–11*
    Africa **1** 235, 436*
    Austria **2** 833–4*
    Belgium **3** 619–20*
    Benin, Kingdom of **3** 723–4*
    Bulgaria **5** 163–4*
    Byzantine **2** 880; **8** 872; **9** 527–8
    Central Asia, Eastern **6** 320*
    Central Asia, Western **6** 278–81*
    China **7** 160–61*
    Czech Republic **8** 426*
    Denmark **8** 761–2*
    Early Christian (*c*. AD 250-843) **9** 527–8
    Egypt **16** 547
    England **10** 376–8*
    Finland **11** 113*
    France **11** 674–6*
    Germany **2** 531–2; **12** 482–3*
    Indian subcontinent **7** 793; **15** 210–12*
    Iran **16** 548
    Ireland **16** 38*
    Islamic **16** 546–50*
    Italy **2** 531; **3** 851; **16** 780–82*; **18** 756
    Japan **7** 160; **17** 439*
    Jewish art **17** 583*
    Kazakhstan **6** 280*
    Korea **18** 259*
    Kyrgyzstan **6** 280*
    Maya **21** 234
    Mesoamerica, Pre-Columbian **21** 234
    Mongolia **21** 884–5*
    Native North Americans **22** 673–4*
    Netherlands, the **22** 909–11*
    Norway **23** 244–5*
    Pacific Islands **23** 738–9*
    Poland **25** 142–3*
    Portugal **25** 319–20*
    Russia **27** 443–4*
historiography
  historical and regional traditions—cont.
    Scandinavia **32** 534*
    Sicily **16** 547
    South-east Asia **29** 241–3*
    Spain **11** 304; **16** 547; **29** 358–9*
    Sweden **30** 119–20*
    Switzerland **30** 156–7*
    Tajikistan **6** 279–80*
    Tibet **30** 848*
    Turkestan (region) **6** 278–9*
    United States of America **19** 246; **31** 411, 671–3*
    Viking **32** 534*
  types
    architecture **3** 619–20; **32** 274*, 304*
    armour **2** 450–51*
    bronzes **6** 867–8*; **7** 160
    caricatures **5** 760*
    ceramics **7** 160, 161
    epigraphy **16** 547
    erotic art **10** 486*
    frames **11** 378*
    gardens **12** 65, 100, 104, 128
    manuscript illumination **16** 295–6
    painting **7** 161
    photography **12** 486
    sculpture **7** 160, 161
    stained glass **29** 513–14*
    weapons **2** 450–51*
  see also ART HISTORY
history of architecture *see* ARCHITECTURAL HISTORY
history of art *see* ART HISTORY
history of gardens *see* GARDEN HISTORY
history painting *see under* PAINTING → types
Histria **26** *852*, *906*, 907
Hitchcock, Alford & Co. **14** 590
Hitchcock, Alfred **8** 468
Hitchcock, De Witt Clinton **25** 611
Hitchcock, George **14** 589*
Hitchcock, Henry-Russell **3** 271; **14** 589–90*; **17** 620; **31** 672
Hitchcock, Lambert **14** 590*; **31** 628
Hitchcock Chair Co. **14** 590
Hitchcock chairs *see under* CHAIRS → types
Hitchcock Museum *see under* RIVERTON, (CT)
Hitchcocksville (CT) *see* RIVERTON (CT)
Hitchens, Ivon **14** 590–91*
  groups and movements **10** 257; **22** 751; **23** 333; **28** 506
  works **18** 718
Hitchins, John **26** 239
Hitda, Abbess **23** 652, 654
Hite, Isaac **25** 152
Hitler, Adolf **12** 605; **22** 709; **25** 652; **31** 368
  architecture **23** 814; **27** 316; **29** 378; **33** 38
  urban planning **29** 752
Hitomi Chikudo **17** 234
Hitoshi Komatsu *see* KOMATSU, HITOSHI
Hitoshi Watanabe *see* WATANABE, HITOSHI
Hitoyoshi **17** 106
Hitt, S. R. **25** 235
Hittite **1** 822, 825–7, 851, *852*, 854; **14** 591–2*
  arches **2** 296*
  architecture **1** 826, 831; **20** 540*
  dress **1** *884*, 885
  fortifications **1** *831*; **30** 186
  glass **1** 865
  gold **8** 261
  iconography **1** 828–30*; **33** 513
  inscriptions **1** 827
  ivory-carvings **1** 870
  limestone **1** *833*

Hittite—cont.
- masonry 1 826, *831*
- metalwork 1 827
- palaces 1 826; 20 540, *540*; 23 806
- pottery 1 826, 838; 15 159–60
- religion 1 828–30*
- rock reliefs 1 832–3
- scripts 1 827, 829, *854*, 855, 893; 14 591
- sculpture 1 522, 827, 832–3, *833*; 4 *231*; 8 261; 14 *592*; 33 *513*
- seals 1 827, 857*, *857*
- silver 8 261
- temples 1 826; 15 159
- writing 4 230
- writing-tablets 1 853, 865

Hittorff, Jacques-Ignace 7 502; 14 592–3*
- assistants 33 616
- collaboration 14 238; 24 123; 25 855; 26 545
- excavations 13 612
- groups and movements 13 607, 612; 24 173
- patrons and collectors 4 555
- staff 26 338
- works 1 798; 11 520, 523, 524; 14 *593*; 16 53; 24 125, *126*; 25 172, 267

Hitzig, (Georg Heinrich) Friedrich 14 593–4*; 25 136
- assistants 32 682, 801
- groups and movements 26 190
- sculpture 9 692
- works 3 793, 794; 12 376; 13 717; 14 142; 26 3

Hitzig, Samuel 32 449
Hitzl, Franz 28 186
Hivaoa 20 462; 23 720
- painting 12 *193*
- *see also* MARQUESAS ISLANDS

Hiw *see* DIOSPOLIS PARVA
Hiyakuren Ono *see* ONO, HIYAKUREN
Hiyamizu-Tateno kiln 27 873
Hizen 17 264
Hjaltalín, Thorsteinn Illugason 15 70
Hjelholt, Berit 8 756; 30 331
Hjertén, Sigrid (Maria) 13 719; 14 594–5*; 30 81; 33 566
Hjorth, Bror 10 805; 14 595*; 29 688; 30 81, 86
Hjorth, Hans 14 595
Hjorth, Lauritz Adolph 8 748; 14 595*
Hjorth, Olsen 23 602
Hjorth, Peter 14 595
HKPA *see* HOWELL KILLICK PARTRIDGE & AMIS
H.L., Master 12 401; 20 796–7*
- works 12 401, *401*

Hla, M. T. 5 246
Hladik, Jan 30 331
Hlava, Pavel 8 411; 17 816
Hlávka, Josef 8 423; 25 429
Hlebaŭ, A. 3 531
Hlebine 8 *174*
Hlebine school 8 179; 12 274; 14 298, 595–6*; 22 441
Hleza, Austin 30 63
Hlito, Alfredo 2 546, 604; 14 596*
Hložník, Ferdinand 28 853
Hložník, Vincent 28 853, 854
Hluboká 6 364; 8 404
Hlukhiv *see* GLUKHOV
Hlungwani, Jackson (Mbhazima) 14 596*; 29 113
Hmawza *see* SRIKSHETRA
Hmong 18 762; 29 239; 30 571
- dress 18 774; 30 623, 624–5*
- jewellery 18 775; 30 634
- metalwork 29 239
- musical instruments 30 637, *637*
- textiles 11 759

HMS 29 603
HMS Colossus see under SHIPS → named vessels

Ho, Tao 14 596–7*
Hoaching 7 30
Hoadley, David 14 597*; 23 25
Hoa Lai 6 *418*, 421, *421*, 427, 432
Hoa Lu 32 486
- tomb of Dinh Tien Hoang 32 475

Hoang Dang Nhuan 32 483
Hoar, Frank 1 494
hoardings 8 *277*, 277–8
hoards 13 568; 25 518
Hoare (i) (family) 3 173; 10 361
Hoare (i), (Richard) Colt 5 434; 13 303, 304; 14 597, 598*
- architecture 29 735
- drawings 8 96
- frames 11 427
- furniture 13 634
- paintings 9 366; 31 467

Hoare, Frances 17 851
Hoare (i), Henry Ainslie 14 597
Hoare (i), Henry Hugh Arthur 14 597
Hoare (i), Henry the elder (1677-1724) 14 597; 29 733
Hoare (i), Henry the younger (1705-85) 14 597–9*
- collections 2 27
- furniture 13 634
- gardens 12 130; 22 740; 29 733, *734*
- paintings 3 372; 14 597
- sculpture 14 599; 27 468; 29 734

Hoare, John 7 875
Hoare (ii), Mary 14 598
Hoare, Michael *see* HALFPENNY, WILLIAM
Hoare (ii), Prince, I (*c.* 1711-69) 3 372; 14 598, 599*
Hoare (ii), Prince, II (1755-1834) 3 372; 14 598, 599*; 33 20
Hoare (i), Richard 14 597
Hoare (ii), William 3 372; 14 598–9*
- patrons and collectors 3 239; 13 637; 14 486
- pupils 18 891
- reproductive prints by others 14 803
- teachers 15 149
- works 14 597

Hoashi Kyōu 17 198; 30 299
Hoban, James 14 600*
- competitions 7 666
- pupils 21 615
- works 10 850; 25 267; 31 591, 662; 32 892, 893, *894*

Hobart 2 *736*
- Customs House *see* Parliament House
- furniture 2 757
- Lady Franklin Museum 2 738, 770; 4 107
- Parliament House 2 738
- St George 2 738
- synagogue 17 547
- Van Dieman's Land Mechanics School of Art 2 772

Hobart, Henry 8 45
Hobart, John, 2nd Earl of Buckinghamshire 32 540
Hobashira kiln 17 811
Hobbema, Meindert 14 600–603*; 29 375
- collaboration 3 757, 775; 22 843; 32 145
- copies 26 124
- patrons and collectors
  - Altman, Benjamin 1 731
  - Arenberg, Auguste-Marie-Raymond, 6th Duke of 2 382
  - Beurnonville, Etienne-Edmond Martin, Baron de 3 890
  - Egerton, Francis, 1st Earl of Ellesmere 9 755
  - Faesch, Johann Jakob 10 753
  - Fesch, Joseph, Cardinal 11 32
  - Frick, Henry Clay 11 774
  - Harvey, Thomas 8 184

Hobbema, Meindert
- patrons and collectors—cont.
  - Kann, Rodolphe 17 777
  - Leopold I, King of Belgium (*reg* 1831-65) 7 490
  - McLellan, Archibald 28 271
  - Moltke, Adam Gottlob, Count 21 825
  - Morny, Charles-Auguste, Duc de 22 127
  - Peel, Robert (1788-1850) 10 365; 24 322
  - Seymour-Conway, Richard, 4th Marquess of Hertford 28 527
  - Wallace, Richard 28 528
- reproductive prints by others 4 886
- restorations by others 21 429
- teachers 22 843; 27 326
- works 14 *601*, *602*; 18 710

Hobbes, James R. 10 208
Hobbes, Thomas 13 300
Hobbs, Alfred C. 15 822
Hobbs, Brockunier & Co. 14 603*; 31 644
Hobbs, John H. 14 603
Hobbs, John L. 14 603
Hobbs, Joseph John Talbot 2 740; 14 603*; 24 496
Hobby Horse, The 12 780; 15 142; 24 426; 33 361
Hobé, Georges 14 603–4*; 18 436; 25 190; 28 482
- works 3 550, 579; 14 138

Hobrecht, James 3 794; 31 724
Hobro Church 4 69
Hobson, Geoffrey 29 88
Hobson, Robert Lockhart 7 161; 14 604*
Hobson, William 2 705
Hobun Kikuchi *see* KIKUCHI, HOBUN
Hoburgh, Christian 10 175
Hoby, Thomas 13 298
Hocentonji (family) 3 728
Hoch 5 876
Hoch, Franz 24 591
Höch, Hannah (Johanne) 14 604–5*
- groups and movements 3 801; 8 433, 436, 437; 24 405
- works 3 801; 14 *605*; 24 685

Hochanova, Lamberto 24 620
Hochberg-Fürstenstein, Hans Heinrich IV, Reichsgraf von 31 28
Hochdorf (Eberdingen) *see* EBERDINGEN-HOCHDORF
Hochdos 7 51
Hocheder, Karl 7 694; 14 605–6*; 28 374; 30 520
Hochelten 26 146
Ho Chen *see* HE ZHEN
Hochgotik see under GOTHIC → styles
Hochheimer, C. F. A. 8 128
Ho-chia-ts'un *see* HEJIA CUN
Hōchiku Yoshida *see* YOSHIDA, HŌCHIKU
Ho Chi Minh 32 482
Ho Chi Minh City 29 *225*; 32 *468*, *469*
- Cathedral of Notre-Dame 32 476
- Musée Blanchard de la Brosse *see* National Museum
- National Museum 9 401; 29 240
- Phien An 21 596; 32 477
- Presidential Palace 32 476

Ho Ch'o *see* HE CHUO
Hochob 21 231; 26 412
- Temple II 9 *166*

Hochon 27 682
Hochosterwitz, Schloss *see* SCHLOSS HOCHOSTERWITZ
Hochreith, Wittgenstein hunting lodge 2 809
Hochstaden, Friedrich von, Provost *see* FRIEDRICH VON HOCHSTADEN, Provost
Hochstaden, Konrad von, Archbishop of Cologne *see* KONRAD VON HOCHSTADEN, Archbishop of Cologne
Höchst Ceramic Factory 3 804; 12 430, 431, 433; 14 606*; 19 734; 26 498
- designers 12 434; 19 772

Hochstetter, Daniel 10 339
Hōchū Nakamura *see* NAKAMURA HŌCHŪ
Höckelmann, Antonius 14 606*
Hocken, Thomas 23 75
Höcker, Paul 24 279; 28 143
Höckert, Johan Fredrik 14 607*; 17 9; 18 468; 30 79
Hockly, Daniel 29 120
Hockney, David 12 217; 14 607–9*; 19 591; 30 329
- collaboration 20 607, 608
- computer art 7 681
- electrography 10 135
- erotic art 10 483
- groups and movements 10 258; 19 702; 25 231
- methods 5 655; 10 191; 24 354
- paintings 12 217, 296; 18 719; 21 761
  - acrylic 12 *217*; 19 *702*; 25 25
  - conversation pieces 7 787
  - nude figures 23 297
  - watercolours 32 902
- patrons and collectors 7 797
- prints 2 241; 10 258; 25 619
  - etchings 10 557, 563; 14 *608*
  - lithographs 19 493
  - telecopy 25 620
- productions 30 687
- screens (ii) (furniture) 28 298
- stage design 30 *688*
- teachers 10 375

Hocquart, Gilles 19 56
Hod 30 604
Hodart, Filipe 14 609*; 19 139
Hoddle, Robert 21 75
Hodegetria Icon 19 787
Hodgdon, Charles A. 28 591
Hodge, Albert 27 636
Hodge, David 17 593
Hodge, Edward Grose 29 88
Hodge, Frederick Webb 8 282
Hodge, Robert 28 252
- works 28 *253*

Hodge, Tom 29 88
Hodges, Charles Howard 14 609–10*; 18 480; 22 846, 848; 26 282
Hodges, William 2 743; 8 494; 10 807; 14 610–11*; 15 210, 406
- sponsors 30 451
- teachers 33 220
- works 14 *610*; 15 679; 23 57; 28 *923*
- writings 22 59; 32 240

Hodgeson, Alan 32 414
Hodgetts, Richardson & Son 10 320
Hodgins, Robert 29 109, 111
Hodginson, Vi *see* EYRE, VI
Hodgkin, Howard 14 611–12*; 30 688
- works 7 681; 11 437; 14 *612*; 15 748; 19 492; 25 621

Hodgkins, Frances (Mary) 14 612–13*; 22 804; 23 60; 28 506; 31 673
Hodgkins, William Mathew 14 612; 23 58
Hodgkinson, Eaton 16 53
Hodgkinson, Patrick 14 613*; 19 578
Hodgson, Brian Houghton 22 795
Hodgson, Charles 11 362
Hodgson, J. E. 27 564
Hodgson, Kirkman 20 493
Hodgson, Solomon 3 898
Hodgson, Tom 23 790
Hodgson & Graves 29 918
Hod Hill (Dorset) 27 94
Hödicke, K(arl) H(orste) 3 803; 12 397; 14 613–14*; 31 532
Hodin, Jacquemart de *see* JACQUEMART DE HESDIN
Hodiše 28 861
Hodler, Alfred 3 823
Hodler, Ferdinand 3 824; 12 277; 14 614–15*; 21 135; 30 125
- collaboration 6 66; 14 89
- exhibitions 23 114
- groups and movements 10 693; 25 357; 27 639; 28 344; 30 169
- works 12 497; 14 *615*; 18 717; 22 330; 30 134; 33 736

Hódmezővásárhely 13 332, 333; 15 1, 3
- János Tornyai Museum 31 174
- *see also* HUNGARY → painting → Great Plains painting

Hodne, Thomas 22 671
Hodne-Stageberg Partnership 22 670, 671
Hodorovich, F. 12 322
Hodowica Altar 25 115
Hodson, George Frederick 25 402
Hoe, Robert 14 616*
Hoechst, I. G.-Farben dye-works 4 789
Hoechstetter (family) 4 760
Hoeck, van den (family) 14 5
Hoecke, Adriaen van 22 888
Hoecke, Caspar van den 9 762; 14 616
Hoecke, Jan van den 3 559; 5 49; 14 616–17*; 30 320
- reproductive prints by others 12 851
- works 5 *50*; 14 *617*

Hoecke, J. Van *see* VAN HOECKE, J.
Hoecke, Robert van den 14 616
Hoecker, Willem 4 73
Hoeckgeest, Gerrit *see* HOUCKGEEST, GERRIT
Hoef, Christiaan J. van der 22 883, 894
Hoefel, Johann Nepomuk 10 99
Hoefnagel, Georg *see* HOEFNAGEL, JORIS
Hoefnagel, Jacob 8 390; 13 914; 14 620, 682; 21 640
Hoefnagel, Joris 3 613; 14 618–20*
- collaboration 20 90; 23 579
- patrons and collectors 2 104; 13 914; 14 682; 33 274
- portraits 13 *913*
- reproductive prints by others 27 504
- teachers 4 251
- works 2 696; 4 896; 7 900; 8 390; 11 229; 14 *618*, *619*, 643; 18 706; 21 640; 23 198; 31 246

Hoegaarden Church 3 547
Høegh, Aka 13 620
Høegh-Guldberg, Ove 8 758
Hoehme, Gerhard 13 727; 14 620–21*; 25 153
Hoeimaker, Hendrik 3 545; 11 502; 14 621*
Hoeker, Willem 22 883, 892
Hoeker & Zoon 23 120; 28 867
Hoek van Holland 23 *664*
Hoel, Bishop of Le Mans 19 126–7
Hoelzel, Adolf *see* HÖLZEL, ADOLF
Hoemacker, Jean van 2 194
Hoen Nishiyama *see* NISHIYAMA HOEN
Hoentschel, Georges 5 881; 11 600; 22 111
Hoerle, Angelika 8 438; 25 838; 29 869
Hoerle, Heinrich 8 437, 438; 13 727; 22 923; 25 837, 838; 29 869
Hoermann, Hans
- works 26 *909*

Hoernle, A. H. A. 6 320
Hoesch 21 32

Hoeschotype *see* PRINTING → processes → collotype
Hoesen, Beth van 10 398
Hoesslin, Bartholomäus 2 718
Hoesslin, Philipp 2 718
Hoeswinkel, Eduard van 32 708
Hoet, Gerard (i) (1648-1733) 14 621–2*
pupils 14 622
Hoet, Gerard (ii) (1698-1760) 14 621, 622*; 27 134
dealing 27 271
reproductive prints by others 30 297
works 12 473; 13 3; 22 910
writings 13 2
Hoet, Hendrick Jacob 14 621; 19 397
Hoet, Moses 14 621
Hoeterickx, Emile 10 517
Hoetger, Bernhard 4 743; 12 407; 14 622*
groups and movements 8 531; 10 695, 697
house 4 789
patrons and collectors 14 506
works 4 789; 8 531
Hoets, Digby 29 117
Hoevenaar, Jos 21 789
Hoey, Claude d' 19 65
Hoey, Jean d' 31 382
Hoey, Nicolas de 8 890
Hoeydonck, Paul van *see* VAN HOEYDONCK, PAUL
Hofen-Friedrichshafen 32 822
Hofer, Karl (Johannes Christian) 3 802; 14 622–4*
groups and movements 22 921
works 3 802, 803; 14 *623*
Hofer, Otto 8 176; 33 131
Hofer, Philip 4 359; 14 624*
Hoff, Arne 2 451
Hoff, Paul Oscar 14 97; 17 853; 23 222
Hoff, Povl Ernst 14 624–5*
Hoff, (George) Rayner 2 741, 753, 772; 8 684; 14 625*
Hoff, Robert van t' 3 490; 14 625*; 21 781; 29 660
Hoff, Torsten 23 237
Hoffart, Johannes 22 917
Hoffer, O. 33 593
Höffert 10 453
Hoffman, Benjamin Gottlob 12 458
Hoffman, Georg 30 115
Hoffman, Gottfried 25 364
Hoffman, J. G. Samuel 2 760
Hoffman, José 32 567
Hoffman, Nathan
works 21 *743*
Hoffman, Peter 23 635
Hoffman, Wilhelm 25 435
Hoffman Brick Co. 2 760
Hoffman-La Roche 27 658
Hoffmann, Adam 29 743
Hoffmann, Armin 25 354
Hoffmann, Elias 31 526
Hoffmann, Emanuel 8 410; 17 816
Hoffmann, Ernst Theodor Amadeus 22 379; 33 673
Hoffmann, Eugen 29 733
Hoffmann, F. B. 21 421
Hoffmann, Ferdinand, Baron 2 374
Hoffmann, Friedrich Gottlob 14 625–6*
Hoffmann, Hans 14 626*; 23 308
groups and movements 9 446
patrons and collectors 10 531; 25 454
works 14 *626*
Hoffmann, Hans Ruprecht 14 627*
works 12 402; 25 726; 31 325, 327
Hoffmann, Heinrich (1576-1623) 14 627
Hoffmann, Heinrich (1809-94) 4 362
Hoffmann, Hubert 19 773
Hoffmann, J. H. 10 90
Hoffmann, Johann Friedrich 8 410; 17 816
Hoffmann, Josef (Franz Maria) 2 567, 788, 789, 826; 7 669; 10 346; 11 526; 12 822; 14 627–31*; 15 823; 19 719; 24 438; 32 446
architecture 8 379; 12 497; 18 135; 28 344
houses 2 789; 3 550, 579; 18 130; 21 819
palaces 12 497; 14 *629*
pavilions (buildings) 3 513
restorations 23 425
sanatoria 14 *628*; 32 438
assistants 3 393; 13 798
ceramics 2 816, 817; 32 450, *450*
collaboration 2 809, 810; 14 130; 19 539; 22 187; 27 665; 32 439
exhibitions 15 883
furniture 2 814; 3 485, 587; 6 391; 8 802; 18 192; 32 448
glass 2 818; 8 411; 19 522, *523*; 23 548
groups and movements
Art Nouveau 2 562
Deutscher Werkbund 21 780
Klimtgruppe 28 344
Modern Movement 21 779
Secession (Vienna) 2 776; 28 343; 32 762
Siebenerklub 3 398; 28 670
Wiener Werkstätte 2 571; 8 802; 22 187; 32 449; 33 165–6
interior decoration 2 809; 3 *579*; 18 533
jewellery 17 528
patrons and collectors 29 693; 32 764
pupils 10 870; 19 522; 22 892; 25 673
silver 2 821
staff 14 25
Hoffmann, Karl (1815-86) 14 631*
Hoffmann, Karl (1838-after 1900) 14 631
Hoffmann, Lorenz 6 76
Hoffmann, Ludwig (Ernst Emil) (1852-1932) 3 795; 14 631–2*; 26 405
assistants 28 119
collaboration 30 350
pupils 31 367
works 3 795, 807; 18 890; 19 111; 21 311
Hoffmann, Samuel *see* HOFMANN, SAMUEL
Hoffmann, Thomas 27 505
Hoffmann, Wolfgang 14 630
Hoffmann kilns *see under* KILNS → types
Hoffmann-Lederer, H. 1 722
Hoffmeister, K. 8 401
Hoffnagel, Peter 23 235
Hoffstadt, Friedrich 13 204; 28 371
Hoffstädter, Bedrich 28 853
Hoflehner, Rudolf 2 804; 14 632*
Höfler, Georg 12 260
Höflich, Johann Jakob 19 781
Hofman, Vlastislav 7 182; 8 401, 406, 416; 14 632*
groups and movements 8 373; 12 834; 13 711; 16 902; 33 710
works 8 249, 380
Hofmann, Hans (Georg Albert) (1880-1966) 14 632–3*; 31 607
assistants 6 135
dealers 24 213
groups and movements 1 78, 83, 84, 85; 31 607
patrons and collectors 13 801
pupils 1 771
Adams, Mark 1 145
Hofmann, Hans (Georg Albert) (1880-1966)
pupils—cont.
Albizu, Olga 18 832
Cavallon, Giorgio 6 111
Clausen, Franciska 7 405
Diller, Burgoyne 8 896
Eames, Ray 9 503
Frankenthaler, Helen 11 729
Goodnough, Robert 13 1
Jensen, Alfred (Julio) 17 477
Johnson, Lester 17 619
Kaprow, Allan 17 805
Kocamemi, (Ahmet) Zeki 18 182
Krasner, Lee 18 441
Nevelson, Louise 23 12
Rivers, Larry 26 430
Stankiewicz, Richard 29 539
Tollu, Cemal 31 94
Tryggvadóttir, Nína 31 393
works 14 *633*
Hofmann, Hans (*d* 1957) 3 335
Hofmann, Johann-Benedikt, II 21 757
Hofmann, Julius 12 416; 13 209; 29 843; 33 283
Hofmann, Ludwig von (1861-1945) 24 591; 28 342
Hofmann, Peter 33 736
Hofmann, Samuel 14 634*; 21 407; 30 131; 33 736
Hofmann, Werner 5 760; 28 917
Hofmannsthal, Hugo von 5 760; 8 596; 18 491
Hofmeister, Oskar 24 674, 738
Hofmeister, Theodor 24 674, 738
Hofstätter, Béla 14 634
Hofstätter & Domány 14 634–5*
Hofstede de Groot, Cornelis 12 490; 14 635*; 22 909, 910; 30 731
Hōfu, Tsuki Katsura 12 100; 31 400*
works 31 *400*
Hofuf 2 *246*, 261
Museum 2 275
Hofwijck 14 635*; 22 *813*; 25 324
gardens 12 132
Hog, Robert 28 252
works 28 *253*
Hōgai Kanō *see* KANŌ HŌGAI
Hogan, Bernardo 25 703
Hogan, Cecil 23 736
works 23 *736*
Hogan, James 10 321; 29 513
Hogan, João (Manuel Navarro) 14 635*
Hogan, John 14 635–6*; 16 21
Höganäs-Keramik 30 99
hogan houses *see under* HOUSES → types
Hogarth, D. G. 10 423, 425, 430; 17 843
Hogarth, Paul 2 553
Hogarth, William 9 *673*; 11 907; 12 291; 14 269, 636–42*, *638*, 856; 19 586, 619; 27 *243*; 28 206, 466, 740
attributions 31 869
caricatures 9 225
collaboration 13 29; 18 672; 32 778; 33 377
commentaries 19 327; 27 258
decorative works 14 419; 28 *738*
education (art) 10 361, 372; 19 584; 26 499
exhibitions 32 327
frames 11 *425*, *428*
paintings 10 249, 677; 14 784; 20 911
conversation pieces 7 785, *785*
fancy pictures 10 785
history 14 585
narrative 10 479; 12 293; 14 *636*, *639*
oil sketches 19 584, *585*
portraits 9 673; 10 249; 14 *638*
Hogarth, William—cont.
patrons and collectors 3 63
Algarotti, Francesco 1 633
Angerstein, John Julius 2 51
Beckford, William (1760-1844) 3 476
Caulfeild, James, 1st Earl of Charlemont 6 94
Fox, Henry, 1st Baron Holland 11 362
Garrick, David 12 165
Gigoux, Jean(-François) 12 609
Grosvenor, Richard, 1st Earl Grosvenor (1731-1802) 13 696
Howard, Hugh 14 810
Marquand, Henry G(urdon) 20 461
Mellon, Paul 21 91
Miles, Philip John 21 541
Rushout, John, 2nd Baron Northwick 27 350
Soane, John 28 907, 908
Wyndham, George O'Brien, 3rd Earl of Egremont 33 453
personal collection 18 147
prints 7 648
engravings 7 500; 10 392; 14 280, *856*; 25 688; 26 230; 31 704
narrative 10 252; 26 221
satirical 27 869, *869*
trade cards 4 361; 10 420, *420*
etchings 5 756; 10 555; 11 908
woodcuts 33 359
reproductive prints by others
Baron, Bernard 3 259
Earlom, Richard 9 506
McArdell, James 19 867
Ravenet, Simon Francis, the elder (1706-74) 26 30
Scotin, Gérard (-Jean-Baptiste), II (1698-after 1755) 28 221
Vandergucht, John 31 871
teachers 30 759
writings 5 760; 19 354; 31 300
Hogarth Club 4 604; 5 284; 19 103; 28 348; 32 800; 33 251
Hogarth Press 3 631
hogback monuments *see under* MONUMENTS → types
hog bristle 5 33, *33*, *34*
Högby 9 156
Hogenberg, Abraham 14 643, 683
Hogenberg, Franz 14 643–4*; 21 580
assistants 14 643
collaboration 26 408; 31 154
works 2 696; 3 558; 4 80, 898; 7 581; 14 618; 26 533; 31 71
Hogenberg, Johann (1500-*c*.1539) *see* HOGENBERG NICOLAS
Hogenberg, Johann (1550-*c*.1614) 14 643
Hogenberg, Nicolas 3 556; 8 102; 10 550; 14 643*
works 32 271; 33 355
Hogenberg, Remigius 14 643
Hōgen En'i 17 150, 154
Högenwald, Matthias 28 380
Höger, (Johann Friedrich) Fritz 14 644*
groups and movements 10 698
works 10 *698*; 14 *101*, 102, 142; 30 506
Höger, Josef 19 339
Hogevank' 2 426
Högg, Hans 16 587
Hogg, Ima 14 803
Hogg, William 2 764
Hoggar 1 370, *371*
Hogguer 8 589
Hoghton, Henry 8 832
Höglander, J. E. 30 95
Högler, Anton Joseph 5 339
Höglund, Erik 30 103
Högsrum 26 647
Hohauser, Henry 21 421
Hohen, Alexander von *see* GOGEN, ALEKSANDR (IVANOVICH)
Hohenaspergle *see* KLEINASPERGLE
Hohenberg (family; ceramicists) 12 822
Hohenberg (family; painters & engravers) *see* HOGENBERG
Hohenberg, F.
works 31 *713*
Hohenberg, Johann Ferdinand (Hetzendorf) von 2 785; 14 645*
pupils 25 155
works 2 785, 808; 28 837; 32 460, 461; 33 623
Hohenberg, Johann Martin *see* ALTOMONTE, MARTINO
Hohenberg/Gmundener Keramik 2 816
Hohenbourg, Herrad of *see* HERRAD OF HOHENBOURG
Hohenbourg, Herrad von, Abbess *see* HERRAD VON LANDSBERG, Abbess
Hohenburg, Herwart von 10 83
Hohenems (Austria), Karl-Borromäuskirche 2 800
Hohenems (family) *see* ALTEMPS
Hohenems, Marcus Sitticus von, Prince-Archbishop of Salzburg 14 645–6*
architecture 2 780, 782, 828; 14 361; 27 661; 29 27
gardens 12 133
paintings 2 793
Hohenfurth Abbey *see* VYŠŠÍ BROD ABBEY
Hohenhagen colony 23 120
Hohenheim 8 508; 13 200; 27 324
Hohenkirchen Church 11 252
Hohenlohe, Wolfgang II, Graf von 26 470; 33 36
Hohenlohe-Langenburg, Joachim Albrecht, Graf von 29 60
Hohenstaufen (House of) 12 256; 14 410, 646*
Hohenstaufen, Frederick Barbarossa, Holy Roman Emperor *see* FREDERICK I, Holy Roman Emperor
Hohenstaufen, Frederick I, Holy Roman Emperor *see* FREDERICK I, Holy Roman Emperor
Hohenstaufen, Frederick II *see* FREDERICK II, Holy Roman Emperor
Hohenstein, Adolfo 25 348
Hohenstein, Thun- *see* THUN-HOHENSTEIN
Hohensünderin, Maria Susanna 2 825
Hohenzollern (House of) 12 473; 14 647–9*, *648*; 17 740; 33 296
Hohenzollern, Albert, Prince of Prussia (1809-72) 28 102; 29 737
Hohenzollern, Albert of Brandenburg, Cardinal, Elector-Archbishop of Mainz (*reg* 1514-45) 12 442; 14 647, *648*, 649*
Hohenzollern, Augusta, Electress of Hesse-Kassel *see* AUGUSTA OF HOHENZOLLERN, Electress of Hesse-Kassel
Hohenzollern, Augusta, Queen of Prussia and Empress of Germany *see* AUGUSTA, Empress of Germany
Hohenzollern, Augustus, Prince of Prussia 12 335; 28 102
Hohenzollern, Augustus William, Prince of Prussia 13 663; 14 *648*
Hohenzollern, Barbara, Marchioness of Mantua *see* BARBARA OF BRANDENBURG, Marchioness of Mantua

Hohenzollern, Charles, Prince of Prussia 2 478; 14 654; 28 102; 29 737, 863
Hohenzollern, Charlotte Alexandra, Princess of Prussia *see* ALEXANDRA FYODOROVNA, Empress of Russia (1798-1860)
Hohenzollern, Christian Ernest, Margrave of Bayreuth *see* CHRISTIAN ERNEST, Margrave of Bayreuth
Hohenzollern, Ferdinand, Prince of Prussia 13 663
Hohenzollern, Frederica, Princess of Prussia *see* HANOVER, FREDERICA, Duchess of York
Hohenzollern, Frederick, Margrave of Bayreuth *see* FREDERICK, Margrave of Bayreuth
Hohenzollern, Frederick I, Elector of Brandenburg *see* FREDERICK I, Elector of Brandenburg
Hohenzollern, Frederick I, King of Prussia *see* FREDERICK I, King of Prussia
Hohenzollern, Frederick II, Elector of Brandenburg *see* FREDERICK II, Elector of Brandenburg
Hohenzollern, Frederick II, King of Prussia *see* FREDERICK II, King of Prussia
Hohenzollern, Frederick III, Elector of Brandenburg *see* FREDERICK I, King of Prussia
Hohenzollern, Frederick III, King of Prussia *see* FREDERICK, Emperor of Germany
Hohenzollern, Frederick the Great, King of Prussia *see* FREDERICK II, King of Prussia
Hohenzollern, Frederick VI, Burgrave of Nuremberg *see* FREDERICK I, Elector of Brandenburg
Hohenzollern, Frederick William, Elector of Brandenburg *see* FREDERICK WILLIAM, Elector of Brandenburg
Hohenzollern, Frederick William I, King of Prussia *see* FREDERICK WILLIAM I, King of Prussia
Hohenzollern, Frederick William II, King of Prussia *see* FREDERICK WILLIAM II, King of Prussia
Hohenzollern, Frederick William III, King of Prussia *see* FREDERICK WILLIAM III, King of Prussia
Hohenzollern, Frederick William IV, King of Prussia *see* FREDERICK WILLIAM IV, King of Prussia
Hohenzollern, George William, Margrave of Bayreuth *see* GEORGE WILLIAM, Margrave of Bayreuth
Hohenzollern, Henry, Prince of Prussia 13 663; 14 *648*, 649, 653*; 18 741; 29 403
Hohenzollern, Joachim Frederick, Elector of Brandenburg *see* JOACHIM FREDERICK, Elector of Brandenburg
Hohenzollern, Joachim I, Elector of Brandenburg *see* JOACHIM I, Elector of Brandenburg
Hohenzollern, Joachim II, Elector of Brandenburg *see* JOACHIM II, Elector of Brandenburg
Hohenzollern, John Cicero, Elector of Brandenburg *see* JOHN CICERO, Elector of Brandenburg
Hohenzollern, John George, Elector of Brandenburg *see* JOHN GEORGE, Elector of Brandenburg
Hohenzollern, Louise, Queen of Prussia *see* LOUISE OF MECKLENBURG-STRELITZ, Queen of Prussia
Hohenzollern, Louise-Henrietta, Electress of Brandenburg *see* LOUISE-HENRIETTA, Electress of Brandenburg
Hohenzollern, Louis Ferdinand, Prince of Prussia 12 642
Hohenzollern, Marianne of Orange Nassau, Princess of Prussia 18 188; 20 433; 28 102
Hohenzollern, Sophia Charlotte, Electress of Brandenburg *see* SOPHIA CHARLOTTE, Queen of Prussia
Hohenzollern, Victoria, Empress of Germany *see* VICTORIA, Empress of Germany
Hohenzollern, Wilhelmina, Margravine of Bayreuth *see* WILHELMINA, Margravine of Bayreuth
Hohenzollern, Wilhelmina, Princess of Prussia *see* WILHELMINA OF HOHENZOLLERN, Queen of the Netherlands
Hohenzollern, William, Crown Prince of Germany 1 763; 30 350
Hohenzollern, William I, King of Prussia *see* WILLIAM I, Emperor of Germany
Hohenzollern, William II, Emperor of Germany *see* WILLIAM II, Emperor of Germany
Hohenzollern-Ansbach, Albert of, Duke of Prussia *see* ALBERT OF HOHENZOLLERN-ANSBACH, Duke of Prussia
Hohenzollern-Ansbach, Frederick, Margrave of Ansbach *see* FREDERICK, Margrave of Ansbach
Hohenzollern-Ansbach, Sophie, Margravine of Ansbach *see* SOPHIE, Margravine of Ansbach
Hohenzollern-Hechingen, Joseph Wilhelm, Prince of 16 804
Hohenzollern-Sigmaringen (House of) 14 570
Hohenzollern-Sigmaringen, Karl, Prince of *see* CAROL I, King of Romania
Hohenzollern-Sigmaringen, Karl Anton, Prince of (1811-85) 5 791
Hohe Ufer 24 427
Hohe Warte 24 438
Hohhot 7 56; 21 *870*
  Ih Zuu Monastery 21 872
  Inner Mongolian Museum 21 875, 886
Hohlenstein-Stadel 25 488, 490
Hohlt, Albrecht 12 437
Hohlt, Görge 12 437
Hohlwein, Ludwig 7 652; 25 348
  works 7 *651*; 25 *652*
Hohmichele 25 538, 546
Höhn, Johann 20 923
Höhne, Anthony 25 408
Hohne & Rosling 12 452
Hohokam 22 550, 554; 32 233
  architecture 22 566
  burial mounds 31 116
  jewellery 22 642
  pottery 22 600, *601*, 601–2, 603
  shells 22 642
  textiles 22 622
Höhr 12 429
Hohr, Joseph 17 824
Ho Hung *see* HE HONG
Hŏ Hyŏng 14 744
Hoi An 6 425; 32 *468*
Hoida Tadatomo 17 414
Höijer, (Carl) Theodor 14 371, 656–7*
  works 14 *373*
Hoin, Claude (-Jean-Baptiste) 8 891; 14 657*
Hoischhügel Cathedral 9 529
hoists 7 764, 765, 766, 767
Hoit, Price & Barnes 2 522; 17 799
Hōitsu Sakai *see* SAKAI HŌITSU
Højen Church 8 730
Høje Tåstrup, Station and City Centre 8 729
Hōjō (Japan) 17 348
  Iwaya Kōrai kiln 1 448
Hōjō (family) 17 161, 430, 746; 33 539
Hōjō (1663-1706) 17 409
Hōjō Masako 17 746; 18 224
Hōjō Munemasa 17 747
Hōjō Nagatoki, Shogunal Regent (*reg* 1256-64) 17 747
Hōjō Sadatoki, Shogunal Regent (*reg* 1284-1301) 17 747
Hōjō Shigetoki 17 747
Hōjō Tokimasa, Shogunal Regent (*reg* 1203-05) 17 122; 31 675
Hōjō Tokimune, Shogunal Regent (*reg* 1268-84) 17 747, 749; 25 892
Hōjō Tokiyori, Shogunal Regent (*reg* 1246-56) 17 747, 748
Hōjō Tsunetoki, Shogunal Regent (*reg* 1242-46) 17 747
Hōjō Yasutoki, Shogunal Regent (*reg* 1224-42) 17 746
Hōjō Yoshitoki, Shogunal Regent (*reg* 1205-24) 17 747
Hŏju *see* YI (ii) CHING
Hoju Itani *see* ITANI HOJU
HOK 22 366
Hokeah, Jack 22 595
Hokkaido 17 10, *11*, 18
Hokkei Toyota *see* TOYOTA HOKKEI
Hokoham 28 897
Hōkōji *see* ASUKADERA
Hoko River 22 587
Hokuba Tessai *see* TESSAI HOKUBA
Hokuei Shunkōsai *see* SHUNKŌSAI HOKUEI
Hokuju Shōtei *see* SHŌTEI HOKUJU
Hokusai Katsushika *see* KATSUSHIKA HOKUSAI
Hokusho Gō *see* GŌ HOKUSHO
Hokushū Shunkōsai *see* SHUNKŌSAI HOKUSHŪ
Hokusō *see* HANABUSA ITCHŌ
Ho Kwong Yew & Sons 20 169
Holabird, John 10 684
Holabird, William 6 577; 14 657–8*; 17 476
Holabird & Roche 14 657–8*; 31 594
  collaboration 6 573; 30 505
  staff 13 271; 23 9
  works 28 833; 31 242, 595
Holabird & Root 14 658; 21 492
Holaday, Sarah 10 329
Holalagundi, Siddheshvara Temple 15 647
Holan, Karel 8 393
Holand, Juan de *see* JOEST (VON KALCAR), JAN
Holanda, Alberto de 13 192
Holanda, António de 14 658–61*
  collaboration 14 661; 25 295
  patrons and collectors 2 874
  pupils 14 661
  works 3 725
Holanda, Cornielis (de) 2 865; 14 662*; 29 289
Holanda, Cristiano de 7 345
Holanda, Francisco de 14 658, 659–62*; 25 278, 320
  collaboration 11 772; 14 659
  patrons and collectors 2 873
  sponsors 2 873
  works 2 162; 9 20; 14 *659*, *661*; 21 *566*; 25 291, 296; 26 299, 830; 31 825
  writings 14 658; 24 90; 26 767, 769; 31 297, 299
  translated 25 320
Holanda, Guillén de *see* GUILLÉN DE HOLANDA
Holanda, Teodoro de
  works 29 V
Holas, Bohumil 8 23
Holbach, Paul Henri, Baron d' 23 668
Holbeach (Lincs), All Saints 29 413
Holbein (family) 1 771
Holbein, Ambrosius 14 665–6*
  collaboration 14 671; 30 131
  patrons and collectors 1 771
  works 14 *665*; 33 354
Holbein, Hans (i) (*c*. 1460/5-1524) 2 715, 716; 11 734; 12 386; 14 663–6*; 20 693; 28 313
  assistants 28 57, 58
  collaboration 3 473; 8 540; 10 456; 14 666, 671; 20 916; 32 759
  frames 11 453
  paintings 2 715; 5 198; 14 *664*
  patrons and collectors 1 771; 2 716; 4 638; 11 818; 33 275
  portraits 10 221; 27 *147*, 147; 32 759
  pupils 18 451
  stained glass 12 648; 17 699
  woodcuts 4 358
Holbein, Hans (ii) (1497/8-1543) 2 715; 3 333; 8 595, 910; 10 226, 667; 14 663, 666–73*; 22 374; 25 653; 30 125, 131
  assistants 17 610
  attributions 5 60; 9 682; 14 437, 439, 848; 33 287
  book illustrations 10 445
  collaboration 14 664, 665; 19 515, 825
  copies 14 488; 19 63; 27 823
  decorative works 30 660
  drawings 9 221; 17 457
    portraits 14 *672*
      Brandon, Henry, 2nd Duke of Suffolk 14 *671*
      Henry VIII, King of England (*reg* 1509-47) 10 *246*
      More, Thomas, and family 7 784; 9 *273*, 274
  façade decoration 10 736, 737, 738, 739
  frames 11 454, 455, 456
  glass 17 737
  jewellery 9 244; 10 344; 17 520
  metalwork 10 326
  methods 21 766; 25 284
  paintings 16 470; 19 617
    altarpieces 14 *667*
    frescoes 3 336; 15 137
    history 30 782
    miniatures 10 246; 21 639, *639*
    organ shutters 23 501
    portraits 14 869
      Cheseman, Robert 29 423
      Christina of Denmark, Duchess of Milan (*fl* 1538) 25 280
      Erasmus (of Rotterdam), Desiderius 10 445
      Guildford, Lady 9 274
      Henry VIII, King of England (*reg* 1509-47) 5 835; 9 274; 14 *670*; 19 510, 583; 26 221, 222
      More, Thomas 25 *277*
Holbein, Hans (ii) (1497/8-1543)
  paintings
    portraits—cont.
      Polisy, Jean de Dinteville, Seigneur de, and Selve, Georges de, Bishop 14 *669*; 29 437
      Tuke, Brian 31 417
    religious 8 530
  patrons and collectors
    Amerbach, Basilius 1 771
    Art Institute of Chicago 27 463
    Augustus III, King of Poland (*reg* 1733-63) 1 633
    Becker, Herman (*c*. 1617-78) 3 475
    Caroline of Brandenburg-Ansbach, Queen of England (1683-1737) 9 26
    Christina, Queen of Sweden (*reg* 1632-54) 30 118; 32 7
    Cromwell, Thomas, Earl of Essex 8 187
    De la Gardie, Magnus Gabriel 30 118
    Duarte, Diego 9 311
    Duveen, Joseph, 1st Baron Duveen of Millbank 9 467
    Evans, Frederick H(enry) 10 655
    Everdingen, Allart van 10 660
    Faesch, Remigius (ii) (1596-1667) 10 752
    Fitzalan, Henry, 12th Earl of Arundel 11 140
    Francesco I, 8th Duke of Modena and Reggio (*reg* 1629-58) 10 526
    Harley, Robert, 1st Earl of Oxford 14 178
    Henry VIII, King of England (*reg* 1509-47) 10 246, 360; 12 387; 31 414
    Herbert, Philip, 4th Earl of Pembroke and 1st Earl of Montgomery 14 435
    Howard (i), Aletheia, Countess of Arundel 14 807
    Howard (i), Thomas, 2nd Earl of Arundel 10 363; 14 806
    Imhoff, Willibald 15 145
    Imstenraedt, Franz Gerhard von 15 158
    Jabach, Everard 11 662; 16 814, 815
    Le Brun, Jean-Baptiste-Pierre 19 25
    Lely, Peter 19 124
    Lindsay, Alexander (William Crawford), 25th Earl of Crawford and 8th Earl of Balcarres 19 412
    Loo, Andreas de 19 644
    Lumley, John, 1st Baron Lumley 19 793
    Maximilian I, Duke of Bavaria (*reg* 1598–1651) and Elector of Bavaria (*reg* 1623–51) 33 275
    Mead, Richard 10 364; 20 910
    Montagu-Douglas-Scott, Walter Francis, 5th Duke of Buccleuch, 7th Duke of Queensberry 21 908
    More, Thomas 22 87; 25 277
    Pleydell-Bouverie, Jacob, 2nd Earl of Radnor 25 39
    Potocki, Stanisław Kostka 25 364
    Pourtalès-Gorgier, James-Alexandre, Comte de 25 383
    Solly, Edward 29 46
    Spencer, Robert, 2nd Earl of Sunderland (1641-1702) 29 381
    Stuart, Henry (Frederick), Prince of Wales 29 799

Holbein, Hans (ii) (1497/8-1543)
patrons and collectors—cont.
Tarnowski, Jan Feliks, Count and Waleria **30** 345
Thyssen-Bornemisza, Heinrich, Baron von **30** 795
Torlonia (family) **31** 172
reproductive prints by others **3** 259; **22** 723; **28** 693; **29** 676; **32** 699
stained glass **29** 504
weapons **2** 455
woodcuts **1** 656, 840; **4** 9; **25** 651; **30** 131; **33** 354
Holbein, Johann Caspar **31** 510
Holbein, Michael **14** 663
Holbein, Sigmund **3** 473; **14** 663
Holbein carpets *see under* CARPETS → types → Large-pattern Holbein; Small-pattern Holbein
Holbein daggers *see under* DAGGERS → types
Hölbling, Johann **5** 84
Holburne, William **3** 373
Holburne of Menstrie Museum *see under* BATH (AVON)
Holck, Vilhelm **14** 543
Holck Colding, T. *see* COLDING, T. HOLCK
Holcomb, Adele **33** 309
Holcombe (Devon) **6** 161
mirrors **6** *153*
Holcot (Beds), St Nicholas **10** 229
Holden, Charles (Henry) **14** 673–4*
collaboration **10** 437, 439
works **4** 823; **10** 240; **14** *674*; **19** 319, 575, 577; **21** 349
Holden, Gregory **11** 105
Holden, Isaac **28** 843
Holden, Richard **2** 473
Holdenby House (Northants) **3** 186; **10** 349
Holden Jara, Roberto **24** 102
Holder, Boscoe **31** 335
Holder, Edwin **4** 798
Holder, Preston **13** 710
Holdermann, Georg **14** 675*
Holderness, Countess of **10** 754
Holderness, Robert d'Arcy, 4th Earl of *see* ARCY, ROBERT D', 4th Earl of Holderness
Holdgate **25** 627
Holdship, Richard **8** 776; **9** 368
Holdsøe, Poul **8** 728
Hole, William **10** 248; **14** 675*
Holéczyová, Elena **28** 856
Holewell, Thomas **13** 84
Holewinski, Jan de **1** 666
Holfelder, Jan **25** 132
Holford, Evelyn *see* BENSON, EVELYN
Holford, Robert Stayner **10** 281; **14** 675*
catalogues **3** 740
decorative works **29** 646
paintings **19** 413
Holford, William (Graham) **14** 676*
collaboration **6** 409; **14** 674; **19** 519
teachers **26** 111
works **10** 749; **19** 577
Holgate, Edwin H(eadley) **5** 567; **13** 711; **14** 676*; **22** 39
Holger, Dirk **30** 329
Holguín, Melchor Pérez de **4** 261, 269; **13** 880; **14** 676–7*
Holgvín, Rafael Urdaneta *see* URDANETA HOLGVÍN, RAFAEL
Holics Ceramics Factory **14** 677*, *881*; **15** 2; **28** 856
works **15** *1*
Holiday, Henry (George Alexander) **14** 677*; **18** 882; **23** 690
collaboration **6** 439
house **6** 439
Holiday, Henry (George Alexander)—cont.
pupils **8** 864
works **5** 194; **14** 281; **24** 641; **25** 398
holiday camps *see* CAMPS (HOLIDAY)
Holjac, Janko **8** 176
Holke, Jan Jerzy **32** 878
Holker, John **10** 356
Holker Hall (Cumbria) **19** 735; **33** 177
Holkham Bible Picture Book *see under* BIBLES → individual manuscripts
Holkham Hall (Norfolk) **4** 757–8, 787; **7** 540; **9** 17, 84; **10** 233, 361; **23** 856, *856*, 859, *859*; **24** 290; **33** 442
Blue Satin Dressing Room **9** 26
collections **10** 364, 365
frames **11** 426
furniture **10** 294
manuscripts **8** 563
Marble Hall **7** 541
miniatures (paintings) **14** 547
paintings **3** 382; **5** 907; **7** 396, 397, 540, 541; **9** 18, 377; **14** 707; **15** 148; **20** 588; **21** 442; **25** 644; **27** 161, 740, 893
portico **25** 266
sculpture **4** 758; **7** 541; **9** 23; **14** 391; **19** 672
tapestries **10** 351
textiles **13** 302
Holkonda **15** 358
Holl, Benedikt **2** 813
Holl (ii), Charles **14** 680
Holl (i), Christian **14** 678
Holl (i), Christoph **14** 678
Holl (i), Elias, I (1573-1646) **14** 677, 678–9*; **22** 918; **33** 746
assistants **33** 294
attributions **12** 369
collaboration **14** 320
works **2** 714, *714*; **11** 876; **12** 368, 370, *370*; **14** *678*, *679*; **18** 225; **31** 239; **33** 746
writings **14** 678
Holl (i), Elias, II (*b* 1611) **14** 678
Holl (i), Esaias **14** 677
Holl (ii), Francis (1815-84) **14** 680
Holl (ii), Frank (Montague) **14** 680*
house **18** 903
patrons and collectors **14** 148
works **10** 254; **12** 296; **28** 919
Holl (ii), Henry Benjamin **14** 680
Holl (i), Jakob **14** 677
Holl, Jan Gotfryd **25** 127
Holl (i), Jeronimus **14** 678
Holl (i), Johannes, I (1512-1594) **14** 677, 678*
Holl (i), Johannes, II (1542-*d* before 1594) **14** 677
Holl (i), Johannes, III (1597- *c.* 1615) **14** 678
Holl (i), Johannes, IV (*b* 1616) **14** 678
Holl (i), Jonas **14** 677, 678
Höll, Maria Katharina *see* PRESTEL, MARIA KATHARINA
Holl (i), Mattäus **14** 678
Holl (i), Sebastian **14** 677
Holl, Steven **11** 93
Holl (ii), William (1771-1838) **14** 680
Holl (ii), William (1807-71) **14** 680
Hollamby, Henry **31** 423
Holland (country) *see* NETHERLANDS, THE
Holland (company) **21** 818; **22** 883
Holland, Arnolphus, Count of **12** 884
Holland, Caroline **18** 746
Holland, Henry (1712-85) **14** 680
Holland, Henry (1745-1806) **5** 731; **14** 680–81*
architecture **19** 571, 572; **22** 527
castles **5** 194
clubs (meeting places) **7** 469
conservatories **7** 744; **27** 357
country houses **8** 47, *48*, 105
dairies **8** 461
theatres **30** 674
villas **4** 809; **7** 437
assistants **28** 905; **30** 361
collaboration **10** 162
furniture **10** 295, 296; **26** 85; **27** 357
groups and movements **26** 84
interior decoration **10** 277, 279; **11** 431
patrons and collectors **8** 461; **14** 145; **27** 357; **30** 451
personal collection **28** 908; **33** 99
teachers **4** 875
Holland, Henry Edward Fox, 4th Baron *see* FOX, HENRY EDWARD, 4th Baron Holland
Holland, Henry Fox, 1st Baron *see* FOX, HENRY, 1st Baron Holland
Holland, Henry Rich, 1st Earl of *see* RICH, HENRY, 1st Earl of Holland
Holland, Henry Richard Vassall Fox, 3rd Baron *see* FOX, HENRY RICHARD VASSALL, 3rd Baron Holland
Holland, James **2** 553; **14** 682*
Holland, Jan van *see* JAN VAN HOLLAND
Holland, Philemon **8** 38; **20** 863; **25** 46
Holland, Richard **8** 105
Holland, Thomas, Duke of Surrey **5** 895; **21** 840
Holland, William **14** 682
Hollande, d' **29** 834
Hollander, Irwin **19** 492; **20** 609
Hollander, Jan de *see* AMSTEL, JAN VAN
Hollander's Workshop **20** 609
Hollandismus **18** 173
Holland Land Company **5** 124
Hollands and Bantings **33** 145
Hollandsche Ijzeren Spoorweg-Maatschappij (HISM) **23** 670
Hollandsche Kunstenaarskring **1** 810
Hollandsche Teeken-Maatschappij **20** 435, 871
Holland & Sons **10** 297; **14** 682*; **15** 821; **19** 592
designers **30** 266
staff **10** 282
Hollar **25** 433
Hollar, Vaclav *see* HOLLAR, WENCESLAUS
Hollar, Wenceslaus **10** 657; **12** 389; **13** 299; **14** 682–5*; **19** 597
book illustrations **2** 601; **4** 359, 360; **7** 431; **10** 725
catalogues **6** 78
collaboration **22** 717
drawings **10** 250; **30** *661*, 662; **32** 900
patrons and collectors **14** 178, 563, 806; **20** 416; **24** 373
prints **2** 876; **9** 244; **25** 626
engravings
architectural **9** 375; **11** 140; **14** 454; **19** 598, 609
landscape **2** 540
portraits **12** 515, 670
topographical **10** 250; **33** *249*
townscapes **7** 583; **14** *683*; **19** *568*, 583
etchings **10** 252; **25** 664
allegorical **14** *684*
mythological **10** 160
natural history **10** 757
genre **25** 605
satirical **5** 756
Hollar, Wenceslaus—cont.
pupils **12** 221; **25** 10
reproductive prints by others **19** *597*; **31** 871
teachers **21** 152
Hollar Association **8** 393
Holle, William *see* HOLE, WILLIAM
Hollegha, Wolfgang **2** 797
Hollein, Hans **2** 815; **14** 685*; **15** 408; **16** 101
groups and movements **25** 359; **30** 391
works **2** 789, 810; **11** 735, *736*; **12** 380, 498; **15** 900; **18** 114, 456; **22** 368, *368*; **32** 440
Holleman, Gerard **10** 270
Holleman, Marius **10** 562
Hollemans, Garret (i) (*fl c.* 1584-96) **14** 685–6*
Hollemans, Garret (ii) (*b* 1607) **14** 686
Hollemans, Jasper **1** 520; **14** 685–6*
Hollemans, Richard **14** 686
Höller, Franz Xaver **12** 441
Holles, John, 1st Duke of Newcastle **9** 44
Holliday, A(lbert) Clifford **14** 686*; **17** 492
hollie point lace *see under* LACE → types
Hollins, Michael Daintry **21** 697
Hollins, Peter **4** 86; **10** 265; **14** 686*
Hollins, William **14** 686
Hollis, Douglas **28** 315; **29** 99
Hollis, Thomas (1720-74) **4** 353; **5** 598; **14** 687*; **17** 475; **20** 911
Hollis, Thomas Brand (*fl* after 1774) **14** 687
Hollman, Margot *see* WITTKOWER, MARGOT
Hollman, Ottmar **27** 876
Holló, Barnabás **14** 896
Hollo, Eva *see* VECSEI, EVA
Holló, László **13** 333
Hollóháza Ceramics Factory **14** 687*, *881*; **15** 3
Hollola
church **4** 781; **11** 98
swimming baths **14** 329
Hollósy, Simon **14** 687–8*, 901; **16** 794
groups and movements **22** 434
pupils
Buri, Max (Alfred) **5** 215
Csontváry (Kosztka), Tivadar **8** 226
Czigány, Dezső **8** 429
Dobuzhinsky, Mstislav (Valerianovich) **9** 57
Favorsky, Vladimir (Andreyevich) **10** 843
Ferenczy, Valér **10** 892
Galimberti, Sándor **12** 10
Grosvalds, Jāzeps **13** 695
Kernstok, Károly **17** 913
Kravchenko, Aleksey (Il'ich) **18** 444
Krzyżanowski, Konrad **18** 482
Narbut, Georgy (Ivanovych) **22** 506
Rerrich, Béla **26** 241
Réti, István **26** 256
Ternovets, Boris (Nikolayevich) **30** 491
Tscharner, Johann (Wilhelm Jan) von **31** 396
works **15** 18
hollow and bead *see under* MOULDINGS → types
hollow and roll *see under* MOULDINGS → types
Holloway, G. H. **7** 559
Holloway, Thomas **14** 688*
hollow bricks *see under* BRICKS → types
hollow-building *see under* POTTERY → technique
hollow-casting *see under* CASTING → types
hollow chamfer mouldings *see under* MOULDINGS → types
hollow mouldings *see under* MOULDINGS → types
hollow roll mouldings *see under* MOULDINGS → types
hollow wall tubes *see* TUBULI
Hollstein, F(riedrich) W(ilhelm) H(einrich) **14** 688*
Hollstein und Puppel **14** 688
Hollweg, Bethmann **1** 119
holly **20** 466
Hollyer, Frederick **14** 688*
works **24** *655*
Hollywood (CA)
Dodge House **21** 781
Kings Road complex **28** 96
Holm, Andreas **8** 751
Holm, Bill **8** 562; **14** 688–9*; **28** 330
Holm, Christian **19** 797
Holm, Hans Jørgen **17** 755
Holm, Per Daniel **14** 537
Holm, T. Cedar **33** 310
Holman, Francis **19** 802; **20** 424
Holman, W. A. **13** 844
Holman Hunt, William *see* HUNT, WILLIAM HOLMAN
Holmberg, August **31** 397
Holmberg, (Gustaf) Werner **14** 689*
pupils **27** 337
works **11** 95, *474*
Holme **13** 50
Holme, Charles **9** 295; **24** 739
Holme, Randle **14** 177
Holme, Thomas **24** 596
Holmegaards Glasværker **7** 807; **8** 749, 750
designers **8** 750
works **8** *750*
Holmenkollen **23** *218*
Hotel **23** 232, 233
Holmens Church **11** 468
Holmes, Arthur W. **7** 718
Holmes, Charles John **3** 81
Holmes, George **4** 78
Holmes, Oliver Wendell *see* WENDELL HOLMES, OLIVER
Holmes, Randle **29** 90
Holmes, Sandra **1** 66; **33** 534
Holmes, William Henry **22** 673
Holmes à Court, Robert **1** 66; **2** 770
Holmes & Aubert **17** 469
Holmgren, Christer **8** 750
Holmgren, Herman Teodor **30** 73; **31** 693
holmoi **10** *611*
Holmsbu, Billedgalleri **29** 79
Holmstrup **13** 190
Holmul **21** 214, 237
Holo **1** 357, 403, 405, 406; **2** 86
holograms **14** 689–90*; **24** 657; **25** 329; **26** 236; **28** 204; **30** 395–6
holographic contouring *see* TECHNICAL EXAMINATION → types → contouring (holographic)
holographic film *see under* FILM → types
holographic interferometry *see* TECHNICAL EXAMINATION → types → interferometry (holographic)
Holographics International **24** 446
holography *see under* TECHNICAL EXAMINATION → types
Holoholo **1** 403
Holon, Centre for Technological Education **16** 572
Hološka, Karol **28** 856
Holosphere **14** 690
Holownia, Thaddeus **29** 99
Holper, Hieronymus **23** 311
Holroyd, Charles **3** 81

Holsbeek Church 13 114
Holscher, Knud 8 729; 14 690*
Holschuh, Jan 12 461
Holsman, Holsman, Klekamp and Taylor 21 492
Holsøe, Carl (Vilhelm) 14 119, 119, 691*
Holst, Hermann von 13 648
Holst, Richard (Nicolaüs) Roland 14 691*; 22 851, 854, 908
collaboration 21 122
groups and movements 1 815
studio 29 483
works 22 851
Holstebro, Kunstmuseum 8 760; 22 367
Holstein Beck, Helena Maria, 4th Duquesa de Palmela see PALMELA, HELENA MARIA DE HOLSTEIN BECK, 4th Duquesa de
Holstein-Gottorp (House of) 14 692*
Holstein-Gottorp, Christian Albert, Duke of see CHRISTIAN ALBERT, Duke of Holstein-Gottorp
Holstein-Gottorp, Frederick III, Duke of see FREDERICK III, Duke of Holstein-Gottorp
Holstein-Gottorp, Gustav III, King of Sweden, see GUSTAV III, King of Sweden
Holstein-Gottorp, Karl Peter Ulrich, Duke of see PETER III, Emperor of Russia
Holstein-Gottorp, Karl XIII, King of Sweden see KARL XIII, King of Sweden
Holstein-Gottorp, Louisa Ulrica, Queen of Sweden see LOUISA ULRICA, Queen of Sweden
Holstein-Gottorp, Sofia Albertina, Princess 11 471; 26 99
Holstein-Gottorp, Sophia Magdalena, Queen of Sweden see SOPHIA MAGDALENA, Queen of Sweden
Holstein-Plön, Joachim II, Herzog von 17 7
Holstensius, Luca 6 584
Holsteyn, Pieter, II 32 590
Holt (Norfolk)
Home Place 9 739
Kelling Place see Home Place
Holt, George 19 507
Holt, G(erard) H(endrik) M(aria) 4 57; 14 693*; 22 832
Holt, Henrik van 33 458
Holt, James 2 765
Holt, Nancy 18 695; 28 890; 31 615
Holter, Turid 23 241
Holtermann, Bernard Otto 2 745; 3 427
Holtom and Fox 31 241
Holtruger Madonna, Master of the 20 711
Holty, Carl 1 772; 26 126
Holtzhey, Johann George 14 693*; 20 923
Holtzhey, Martin 14 693; 20 923
Holtzman, Harry 1 772; 21 855
Ho Lu see HU LU
Holubice 8 376
Holveque, Juan 2 284
Holweck, Oskar 33 636
Holý, Miroslav 8 393
Holy Blood, Master of the 4 921; 20 691*
Holycross Monastery 16 7, 7
Holy Crown of Hungary 9 653, 662, 662
Holy Family, Master of the 7 583
Holy Ghost, Master of the Hours of the see HOURS OF THE HOLY GHOST, MASTER OF THE
Holy Kinship, Master of the 7 590; 12 384; 20 612, 691–2*; 29 46
Holy Mandylion see MANDYLION OF EDESSA
holy mountains see SACRIMONTI
Holy Office of the Inquisition 6 175
insignia 29 346
Holy Roman Empire (before 1648)
altarpieces 13 116
Andachtsbilder 13 115, 116
architecture 13 47–9*; 26 570, 571–5*
banners 11 148–9
bells 26 686*
bloodstone (chalcedony) 21 726
box-wood 29 570
brass 26 684–6*
bronze 5 301; 13 160; 26 684–6*, 685; 28 IV2
busts 5 301; 21 II4
candelabra 26 686*
chalices 6 398
chapels 1 3
choir-stalls 13 118
chronicles 7 243
copper 26 686*
craftsmen and artists 29 570
crucifixes 26 684–5
doors 26 684*
engravings 25 432
ewers 26 685–6*
flags 11 147
fonts (baptismal) 26 684*
gilding 28 IV2
goblets 21 726
gold 26 683*
heraldry 14 404
insignia 7 178
justice scenes 17 700
metalwork 13 160–61*; 26 683–6*
oak 13 118
orders (chivalry) 7 178
painting 1 6; 13 142–3*, 151–2*
paintings 13 847
patens 6 398
portraits 25 432; 28 377
sculpture 26 634*
bronze 13 160; 26 684–5*, 685
Gothic 13 85*, 86–7*, 115–18*, 160
palmesels 26 646
Romanesque 26 631–5*, 632, 634, 645–6*, 684–5*, 685
stone 13 85*, 86–7*; 26 631–5*, 632, 634
wood 13 115–18*; 26 645–6*
shrines (i) (cult) 28 IV2
silver 26 683*
silver-gilt 6 398
spires 29 414*
stained glass 13 185–8*; 29 502, 503
statuettes 29 570–71*
stone 13 85*, 86–7*; 26 631–5*, 632, 634
stucco 26 632
theatres 30 665*
tombs 26 684*
wood 13 115–18*; 26 645–6*; 29 570
woodcuts 33 348, 348–9*, 351–4*, 355
see also AUSTRIA; CZECH REPUBLIC; GERMANY
Holyrood Flint Glassworks 9 726; 28 259
Holy Sepulchre school 26 629
Holy Shroud of Turin see SHROUD OF TURIN
holy stairs see STAIRS, HOLY
Holywood (Co. Down), Ulster Folk and Transport Museum 16 8, 40, 42
Holywood, John 33 349
Holz, Ferdinand Wilhelm 3 794; 25 856
Holzapfel, Johan Lorenz 22 896
Holzbauer, Franz Xaver 29 777
Holzbauer, Wilhelm 14 693–4*
collaboration 2 789
groups and movements 2 287–8
works 2 789; 27 663; 32 439
Hölzel, Adolf 14 694*; 29 875
assistants 1 120
groups and movements 28 344
pupils 3 400, 411; 13 266; 14 570, 762; 16 788; 21 409; 23 185; 28 111
Hölzer, Gottlob August 30 758
Holzer, Jenny 14 694*
exhibitions 10 882
groups and movements 3 338; 7 686
works 9 227; 18 822; 31 609, 609
Holzer, Johann Evangelist 2 719; 14 694–6*
personal collection 13 852
reproductive prints by others 23 146
teachers 3 779
works 12 391; 14 695
Holzer, Rainer Michael 7 798
Holzer-Kjellberg, Friedl 11 105
works 11 106
Holzgerlingen 6 156
Holzhausen, J. H. von 11 734
Holzheu, Max 8 859
Holzinger, Franz Josef Ignaz 1 668; 12 405; 14 696*; 27 553, 554
Holzinger, Johann Georg 14 696
Holzman, Malcolm 14 174*
Holzmeister, Clemens 2 789, 831; 10 870; 14 696–7*; 16 591; 31 452
collaboration 3 393
pupils 14 693; 24 326
works 2 789; 19 434; 27 662
Holzschuher, Franz 5 46
Holzschuher, Fritz 31 287
Holzschuher, Lazarus 18 512
Holzschuher von Asbach (family) 3 70
Holzstich see WOOD-ENGRAVINGS
Homa, Giovanni Battista 28 7
Homann 20 364
maps 20 365
Homar, Lorenzo 3 44; 14 697*; 18 832, 833; 20 513; 25 702
Homar i Mezquida, Gaspar 29 307, 308, 320, 321
Homberg, auf 14 407
Homberg, Daniel Brendel von, Archbishop of Mainz 26 470
Homberg, Oscar 16 554
Homberg, Wilhelm 29 724
Homberg collection 13 175
Homberg-Hannema, Nita 22 899
Hombo 14 376, 377, 378
Homborg, Signe 2 317
Hombrechtikon Plaque 2 255–6, 256
Homburg, Schloss Karlsberg 30 783; 33 281
Home, George 9 727
Home, Henry, Lord Kames 2 358; 14 697–8*
Home, Jehan le see LOME, JEHAN
Home, Robert 15 654, 693; 17 852
Home Arts and Industries Association 2 569
Homebase Ltd 10 285
Homem, Diogo 14 698*
Homem, Lopo 14 698*
Homer 2 300; 10 248; 22 410, 415
Homer, Augusta 27 556
Homer, Winslow 14 698–701*; 31 603
dealers 18 161
groups and movements 26 57; 30 887
methods 31 578
Homer, Winslow—cont.
patrons and collectors 7 377, 379; 27 463; 33 151
reproductive prints by others 25 450
works 2 107; 3 61; 9 225; 14 588, 700, 701; 20 425; 22 371; 29 426; 31 603
Homeric bowls see under BOWLS → types
Homiel 3 525
Cathedral of SS Peter and Paul 3 526
maternity home 3 527
Rumyantsev Palace 3 526
synagogue 3 527
Hommaire de Hell, Xavier 16 548
Homme-Témoin 14 701–2*; 21 628
Homoet Hours see under BOOKS OF HOURS → individual manuscripts
Hŏ Mok 14 702*; 18 314, 330
Homolka 21 551
Homolka, J. 8 426
homosexual art see GAY AND LESBIAN ART
Homs 16 208; 30 177, 179, 180
coins 16 511
minarets 21 627
Ho-mu-tu see HEMUDU
Honamhwap'a 14 817
Hon'ami (family) 14 702*
Hon'ami Kōetsu 9 738; 14 702–5*; 17 165, 177, 178–9, 409; 18 552; 30 376
assistants 25 869
books 17 397
collaboration 17 303; 30 375, 376
groups and movements 17 215, 232
pupils 17 233; 23 362
works 14 703, 704; 17 228, 232, 271, 343; 18 553; 22 231; 23 364
Hon'ami Kōho 14 702, 704, 705*
works 14 705
Hon'ami Kūchūsai see HON'AMI KŌHO
Honanisto see HOWLING WOLF
Hon Chi-fun 14 722
Honda 15 827
Hondainville Château 27 568
Honda Tadamasa 14 551
Honda Tadayoshi 17 342
Hondecoeter, Melchior d' 14 706–7*
patrons and collectors 29 7
teachers 33 26
works 14 707; 23 466; 29 666, 667
Hondecouter, Nicolaes de, II (1605–c. 1671) 14 706
Hondecoutre, Gijsbert Gillisz. de 14 706
Hondecoutre, Gillis (Claesz.) de 14 706*; 19 564; 22 843
Hondecoutre, Hans de 14 706
Hondecoutre, Nicolaes (Jansz.) de, I (d 1609) 14 706
Hondius, Abraham (Danielsz.) 14 709–10*
collaboration 4 439
patrons and collectors 20 33
reproductive prints by others 6 547
works 14 710
Hondius (ii), Hendrik, I (1573–1650) 14 41, 707, 708–9*; 32 251
collaboration 32 725
pupils 15 40
works 11 226, 794; 22 910; 25 606; 27 885; 29 431, 649; 31 881; 32 140; 33 181
Hondius (i), Hendrik, 'II' (1597–1651) 10 391; 14 707, 708*
Hondius (ii), Hendrik, II (1615–77) 14 708, 709*; 27 504
Hondius (i), Jacomina 14 707, 708
Hondius (i), Jodocus, I (1563–1612) 10 391; 14 707–8*; 29 377
works 2 696; 9 314; 12 812, 814; 20 364; 23 197; 32 588
Hondius (i), Jodocus, II (1593–1629) 14 707, 708
Hondius (i), Jodocus, III (1622–55) 14 708
Hondius (ii), Willem 14 708; 19 539; 20 14; 32 7
hondō see under HALLS → types
Hondt, Abraham (Danielsz.) de see HONDIUS, ABRAHAM (DANIELSZ.)
Hondt, Antoon Johan de 3 599
Hondt, Christiaan de, Abbot of Ter Duinen 10 713; 20 789
Hondt, Daniel Abramsz. de 14 709
Hondt, Lambert de (father) 3 388; 10 351
Hondt, Lambert de (son) 3 388
Honduras 14 710–17*, 711; 21 177, 178, 193; 29 123
architecture 14 712–14*
ballcourts 20 883
cathedrals 14 713
collections 14 716–17*
exhibitions 14 716
fortresses 14 713
jade 23 418
lithography 14 716
marble 29 153
museums 14 716–17
painting 14 714–16*, 715
patronage 14 716–17*
sculpture 7 801; 14 714–16*
stelae 7 801
trade 21 252
vases 29 153
Honduras, British see BELIZE
Hone, Evie (Sydney) 9 321; 14 717, 718*; 16 17; 29 507
works 14 718
Hone, Galyon 5 514; 13 185
Hone, Horace 14 717*; 16 15
Hone, John Camillus 14 717
Hone, Nathaniel (i) (1718–84) 14 717*; 21 643
personal collection 25 664
pupils 3 74
works 10 785; 16 13
Hone, Nathaniel (ii) (1831–1917) 14 717–18*; 16 16, 17
Hone, Philip 14 718–19*, 843
Hone, Samuel 14 717
Hone, William 8 217
Hønefoss 23 218
Honegger, Denis 11 773
Honegger, Gottfried 14 719*; 21 892; 30 135, 140
Hōnen 5 119; 17 22
Honents, Tigran see TIGRAN HONENTS
honey
etching 10 559
gilding 6 328; 12 623
inks 15 851
size 28 813
Honey, W(illiam) B(owyer) 14 719*
Honeyman, John 12 774; 20 20, 21; 28 228
Honeyman, Robert Wemyss 24 372
Honeyman, T. J. 24 372; 28 289
Honeyman & Keppie 20 20, 21, 22
honeysuckle (ornament) see ANTHEMIA; PALMETTES
Honga 14 376, 377
Hongdong see YONGNINGBAO (HONGDONG)
Hong Fok company 27 314
Honghuatao (Yidu) 8 582
Hongje see CHŎNGJO, KING
Hong Kong 6 614; 14 719–22*
art forms and materials
calligraphy 6 772

Hong Kong
art forms and materials—cont.
collections 6 772; 7 154
jewellery 7 112
painting 14 721–2*
sculpture 6 562
silver 7 29, 30
topographical views 14 *721*
toys 31 259
Arts Centre 14 597, 722
Bank of China Tower 14 *720*, 721
banks 11 *333*
Chinese University, Art Gallery of the Institute of Chinese Studies 7 154
City Hall Art Gallery *see* Museum of Art
education (art) 7 150
Flagstaff House Museum of Teaware 7 154; 14 720
Government House 14 720
Hongkong & Shanghai Bank 1 737; 3 177; 10 242; 11 332, *333*; 14 721; 16 55; 28 835
Kowloon-Canton Railway Terminal 14 720
law courts 18 890
Legislative Council Building 14 720
mass production 22 667
Museum of Art 7 62, 154; 14 722
St John's Cathedral 14 720
skyscrapers 14 *720*
Tsui Museum of Art 7 154
University of Hong Kong
Fung Ping Shan Museum 7 154
Main Building 14 720
Hong Kong Art Club 14 722
Hong Kong Sculptors Association 14 722
Hong Kong Visual Arts Society 14 722
Hong Kye-hui 18 355
works 18 *355*
Honglou (Dongshan) 7 43
Hongnŭng, tomb of Emperor Kojong 18 300
Hongō, Shin 17 135, 137, 433
Hongre, Etienne Le (1628-90) *see* LE HONGRE, ETIENNE
Hongren 2 95; 14 722–3*
works 2 95; 14 *723*
Hongrie, Etienne le (*fl* late 14th cent.) *see* ETIENNE LE HONGRIE
Hong Se-sŏp 14 723–4*; 18 317
works 14 *724*
Hongshan 7 2
Hongshan culture 7 *2*, 159
Hong Shin-yu 18 52
Hong Sik 33 532
Hong Sŏk-ch'ang 18 326
Hong Sŏk-gyun 18 372
Hong Tae-yong 18 259
Hongwolhon *see* KIM (iii) TŬK-SIN
hong wood 7 31
Hongwu emperor (Ming; *reg* 1368-98) 6 622
architecture 6 661; 13 333; 22 458, 459
paintings 6 779, 817
sculpture 6 732
Hongyi 5 113
Hongzhi, Emperor (Ming; *reg* 1488-1505) 6 817; 10 216; 32 840; 33 437
Hönig, Eugen 22 710
Honigberger, Martin 1 211; 13 841
Hönigsberg, Lav 14 724*
Hönigsberg & Deutsch 14 724*; 33 593
Honington Hall (Warwicks) 10 276; 19 5
Honiton 18 593
lace 10 355, *355*
Honka, Matti 11 90
Honma, Takusai 17 324
Honnecourt, Villard de *see* VILLARD DE HONNECOURT
Honnervogt, Jacques 12 203; 19 257
Honnet, Gabriel 9 385
hōnoki 17 356
Honolulu (HI)
Academy of Arts 6 735, 826; 7 156; 12 927; 18 384
Bishop Museum 23 739, 740, 741; 28 921
Honoratus, Saint 19 226
Honoré 24 148, 149
Honoré, Master 13 138; 14 724–6*
assistants 26 334
attributions 11 531
methods 6 569
patrons and collectors 4 764; 5 666
works 4 394; 8 857; 13 142; 14 *725*
Honoré II, Prince of Monaco (*reg* 1612-62) 21 830; 23 748
honorific arches *see* MONUMENTS → types → triumphal arches
Honorius Augustodunensis 7 454; 10 202; 26 674; 29 500
Honorius I, Pope (*reg* 625-38) 26 799
Honorius II, Pope (*reg* 1124-30) 24 193
Honorius III, Pope (*reg* 1216-27) 14 726–7*; 26 680, 765
Honorius of Autun 6 174
Honour, Hugh 13 811
Honselaarsdijk 8 878
collections 9 28
gardens 12 131
Indiaense Cabinet 5 349
paintings 4 151, 152, 377, 656; 13 337; 14 730; 19 473; 22 844; 25 68
Honshu 17 10, 18, *241*
Hontañón, Gil de *see* GIL DE HONTAÑÓN
Honthoir, Jean Arnold de 3 570; 14 393, 727*
Honthorst, Gerrit (Huygensz.) van (*fl c.* 1575) 14 727
Honthorst, Gerrit (Hermansz.) van (1592-1656) 1 104; 11 188; 14 41, 727–31*; 23 466; 26 772; 31 771
attributions 20 640; 29 253, 388
collaboration 4 377; 14 46
copies 4 657
groups and movements 5 1; 9 462; 22 843; 30 456; 31 772
methods 19 353
patrons and collectors
Canino, Lucien Bonaparte, Prince of (1775-1840) 4 304
Carleton, Dudley, 1st Viscount Dorchester 5 764
Charles I, King of England and Scotland (*reg* 1625-49) 29 801
Christian IV, King of Denmark and Norway (*reg* 1588-1648) 14 369, 370; 23 396
Cosimo II, Grand Duke of Tuscany (*reg* 1609- 21) 21 25
Elizabeth, Electress Palatine and Queen of Bohemia (1596-1662) 29 799
Frederick Henry, Stadholder of the Netherlands, Prince of Orange (*reg* 1625-47) 22 844, 904; 23 465
Frederick William, Elector of Brandenburg (*reg* 1640-88) 12 473
Henrietta Maria, Queen of England and Scotland (1609-69) 29 803
Huygens, Constantijn (i) (1596-1687) 15 40
Nisbet, William Hamilton 28 271
Statens Museum for Kunst (Copenhagen) 8 758
Honthorst, Gerrit (Hermansz.) van (1592-1656)
patrons and collectors—cont.
Villiers, George, 1st Duke of Buckingham (1592-1628) 32 576
Wotton, Henry 33 387
pupils 4 150, 486, 846; 27 725; 29 696
reproductive prints by others 28 671; 30 47
teachers 4 151, 153; 5 1
works 1 658; 12 290; 14 *727*, *728*, *729*, *731*; 23 465
Honthorst, Herman (Gerritsz.) van (*fl c.* 1611-6) 14 727
Honthorst, Herman (Hermansz.) van (*fl* 1629-32) 14 727
Honthorst, Willem (Hermansz.) van 3 798; 14 650, 727, 730
Hontondji (family) 11 247
Honzík, Karel 14 732*
collaboration 14 247; 25 430
groups and movements 8 829; 11 365
works 8 380, 402
Hoobrouck de Mooreghem, E. van 24 885
Hooch, Pieter de 5 187; 14 732–4*; 22 843; 27 230
attributions 8 427; 32 268
forgeries by others 3 889; 21 39
groups and movements 8 669
methods 24 370
patrons and collectors
Altman, Benjamin 1 731
Arenberg, Prosper-Louis, 7th Duke of, Duke of Arschot 2 382
Boymans, F(rans) J(acob) O(tto) 4 614
Delessert, (Jules-Paul-) Benjamin (1773-1847) 8 664
Drummond, George A(lexander) (1827-1910) 9 305
Faesch, Johann Jakob 10 753
George IV, King of Great Britain (*reg* 1820-30) 14 146
Johnson, John G(raver) (1841-1917) 17 619
Martínez Pérez, Sebastián 20 502
National Gallery (London) 4 602
Peel, Robert (1788-1850) 24 322
Périer, Casimir 24 418
Ryerson, Martin A(ntoine) 27 463
Salamanca (y Mayol), José, Marqués de 27 607
Stuart, John, 3rd Earl of Bute (1713-92) 29 796
teachers 3 759
works 8 667; 11 444, 446; 12 290–91, *291*; 14 *733*, *734*; 22 844, 894; 30 878; 31 246
Hood, Anthony *see* HILDER, J(ESSIE) J(EWHURST)
Hood, Dorothy 14 803
Hood, Godley & Fouilhoux 7 838; 17 838
works 26 *488*
Hood, Henry 4 237, 238
Hood, John 21 138
Hood, Raymond (Mathewson) 14 734–5*
collaboration 14 813; 28 833; 31 595
competitions 7 669
groups and movements 13 204; 15 885, 886
works 5 *136*; 7 *669*; 14 *735*; 23 43; 28 833; 30 507, *507*
Hood, Robert 8 81
Hood, Thomas 14 735–6*
hood mouldings *see under* MOULDINGS → types
Hōōdo *see* UJI→ Byōdōin → Phoenix Hall
hoods 9 275, 643, *644*
Hooee, Daisy 22 608
Hooft, Gerrit Hendriksz. 20 81
Hooft, Pieter Cornelisz. 10 175
Hooftman, Gilles 32 709
Hoogenberg *see* HOGENBERG
Hoogerwou, W. J. van 23 125
Hoogewerff, G(odefridus) J(ohannes) 14 736*; 15 90; 22 911
Hooghe, Ignace de 12 273
Hooghe, Pieter de *see* HOOCH, PIETER DE
Hooghe, Romeyn de 14 736–7*
works 5 756; 14 *737*; 29 557
Hooghly 15 722
Hoogsteder-Naumann Mercury 24 450
Hoogstoel, Louis 3 585
Hoogstraeten, Antoine de Lalaing, Count of 13 905; 17 884
Hoogstraten, St Katharinakerk 13 63; 21 725
Hoogstraten, Master of 20 692*
Hoogstraten, Dirck van 14 737–8
Hoogstraten, François van 14 741
Hoogstraten, Hans van 14 737
Hoogstraten, Samuel van 9 169; 14 737–41*
attributions 10 734
groups and movements 28 92
methods 6 470
patrons and collectors 32 377
personal collection 28 362
pupils 12 240; 14 794; 28 49
reproductive prints by others 28 49
teachers 22 843, 845; 33 169
works 14 *739*, *740*; 15 140; 22 907; 24 323, *489*, 490
writings 8 128; 14 584; 18 700; 31 300
Hook, James Clark 14 742*
Hook, Judith 10 378
hookas 15 *711*
Hooke, Robert 14 742–3*; 28 210
collaboration 21 615; 33 394
teachers 19 123
works 2 658; 7 503; 8 46; 10 273; 19 569; 20 567; 33 393
illustrated 4 360
hooked rugs *see under* RUGS → types
Hooker, Blanche *see* ROCKEFELLER, BLANCHE HOOKER
Hooker, Philip 14 743*
Hooker, Samuel 14 743
Hooker, William 18 5
Hooker Creek 1 56
Hooker's green *see under* PIGMENTS → types
Hool, Jan Baptist van 12 230
Hoole, Charles 4 360
Hoole, Henry E., & Co. 10 343; 16 60; 29 646; 30 162
Hoop, Adriaan van der 22 904; 32 708
hooped skirts *see under* SKIRTS → types
Hooper, Basil Bramston 14 743–4*; 23 55
Hooper, James 1 439
Hooper, Thomas 19 869; 31 863
Höör Church 26 639
Hoorebeke, van (family) 3 599
Hoorn 22 884; 32 861
Grote Kerk 14 *737*
Hoorn, Cornelis Cort van *see* CORT (VAN HOORN), CORNELIS
Hoorn, W. van 22 875
Hoose, Marie 20 788
Hoosemans, François 3 602
Hootz, Reinhardt 13 811
hooves 24 4
Hooykaas, Bernard 4 814
Hoozee, R. 3 619
Hop (Hopkins, Livingston) 2 747
Hŏ Paek-nyŏn 14 744*
Hŏ Paeng-hyŏn 18 326
hopanes 24 792
Hope Plas Teg 32 782
Hope, Adrian 4 95; 28 262
Hope, A(lexander) J(ames) B(eresford) 14 745–6*
architecture 4 862; 5 314
collaboration 5 640
groups and movements 9 705; 13 201
Hope, Anthony 4 365
Hope, Charles, 1st Earl of Hopetoun 28 269
Hope, Charles, 2nd Earl of Hopetoun 27 469
Hope, Emily 2 766
Hope, Henry 14 744; 22 827; 26 389
Hope, Henry Philip 11 164
Hope, John (1737-84) 4 95; 14 744
Hope, John, 4th Earl of Hopetoun (1765-1823) 33 216
Hope, John, 5th Earl of Hopetoun 33 216
Hope, Terje 23 234
Hope, Thomas 14 744–5*; 19 599
architecture 2 692; 25 267
book illustrations 23 545
collaboration 32 554
collections 10 753; 13 605; 14 114
drawings 9 26; 11 163
frames 11 431
furniture 27 139, *139*; 30 *218*
groups and movements 9 704; 10 96–7; 22 741; 25 193
interior decoration 1 110; 10 *97*; 14 *745*
paintings 9 12; 14 262; 15 406
pottery 9 29; 13 541
sculpture 9 24; 21 850; 24 317; 30 764
writings 2 332; 5 340; 10 279, 296; 23 *888*, 889; 26 85
Hopea, Saara 11 106
Hope and Reeler 33 602
Hope Diamond 11 634
Hope Goblet 11 308
Hope *Hygieia* 21 850
Hopetoun, Charles Hope, Earl of *see* HOPE, CHARLES, Earl of Hopetoun
Hopetoun House (Fife) 9 727; 27 469; 28 227, 246, 269
collections 33 216
paintings 24 233
Yellow Drawing Room 28 247
Hope Town 3 *59*
Wyannie Malone Historical Museum 3 64
Hopewell 14 746; 22 554, 571–2, 610, 611, 617; 31 116
burial mounds 22 *571*
metalwork 14 *746*; 22 *617*
Hopewell Furnace 31 652
Hopewell Mounds 14 746–7*; 22 *544*
metalwork 14 *746*; 22 *617*
Hopfer (family) 9 446; 12 386
Hopfer (*fl* 1611) 27 229
Hopfer, Daniel 2 455; 14 747–8*
patrons and collectors 2 716
works 10 549; 12 386, 420; 14 *747*; 25 607
Hopfer, Hieronymus 10 549; 14 747
Hopfer, Lambert 10 549; 14 747
Hopfgarten 29 21
Hopi 14 748*; 22 452, 562, 563, 676
architecture 22 567
baskets 3 *332*; 22 661
costumes 22 *583*
cotton-wood 22 583, *583*
dolls 22 *583*, 583–4, 669; 31 259
feathers 22 *583*

Hopi—cont.
fetishes 22 669
historiography 22 673
jewellery 22 615, 629, 669
masks 22 583
metalwork 22 614
painting 17 716
pottery 22 451, 562, 604, 609
religion 22 557
wall paintings 2 876
weaving 22 626; 27 599
Hŏ P'il 14 748*
Hôpital de la Salpêtrière see under PARIS → hospitals
Hopkin, Robert 8 821
Hopkins, C. 9 416
Hopkins, John Henry, Bishop 14 748*
Hopkins, John William 14 748*
Hopkins, Lawford & Nelson 14 748*
Hopkins, Mary 20 17
Hopkins, Michael 1 737; 21 91
Hopkins, Michael, & Partners 14 521; 29 490; 30 684
works 30 685
Hopkins, Stephen 12 835
Hopkins & Hopkins 16 32
Hopkinson, Tom 4 670; 14 173
hoplon see under SHIELDS → types
Hoppe, Anton 14 748
Hoppe, Emil (1876-1957) 14 748–9*; 28 155
Hoppé, E(mil) O(tto) (1878-1972) 14 749–50*
Hoppe, Erik 8 736
Hoppe, Paul 14 749
Hoppenbrouwers, Johannes Franciscus 2 224; 26 482; 28 72
Hoppenhaupt, Johann Christian 14 750–51*
collaboration 11 459; 14 750; 22 436
patrons and collectors 14 652; 25 368
reproductive prints by others 21 59
works 12 412, 413; 14 750
Hoppenhaupt, Johann Michael, I (fl c. 1705-35) 7 746; 14 750
collaboration 11 459
patrons and collectors 14 652; 25 368
works 12 412, 413
Hoppenhaupt, Johann Michael, II (1709-78/86) 14 750–51*
collaboration 14 750, 751; 22 436
reproductive prints by others 21 59
works 22 436
Hoppenstede, Servaes 12 410
works 12 410
Hopper, Edward 14 751–2*; 31 606
groups and movements 1 773
patrons and collectors 14 575; 26 488; 33 151
teachers 21 606
works 12 296; 14 752; 15 828; 31 705
Hopper, Robin 32 414
Hopper, Thomas 14 753*
groups and movements 23 210
patrons and collectors 14 145; 21 541
works 6 61; 23 210; 30 268; 32 784
Hoppesteyn (family) 8 668
Hoppesteyn, Jacob Wemmersz. 22 879
Hoppin, Augustus 2 858
Hoppin, Francis L(aurens) V(inton) 14 753*; 33 132
Hoppin, Howard 14 753
Hoppin, Thomas 31 689
Hoppin Painter 13 526
Hoppner, John 14 753–5*
patrons and collectors 13 705; 14 146; 19 98; 25 39; 28 527
Hoppner, John—cont.
pupils 5 434
reproductive prints by others 7 579; 17 630; 28 882; 32 856; 33 191
works 9 1; 10 249; 14 754
Hoppō Bunka (Northern Culture) Museum see under YOKOGOSHI
Hopps, Walter 18 33; 19 702
H. O. Project 23 382
Hops, Franz Magnus 7 212; 12 405
Hopton, Arthur 14 755*; 18 580
Hopwood, Gillian 14 755*; 23 134
Hor 9 859
Horace
villas 31 58
writings 27 868
illustrated 4 361
on art dealers 2 558
on decorum 8 612
on Etruscan bronzes 10 625
on poetry and painting 14 869; 31 767
on Tivoli 18 701
Horadnia 3 525, 525; 14 755–6*
architecture 31 548
Cistercian church 3 526
fortress 3 526
Historical and Archaeological Museum 3 526; 14 756
Jesuit church 3 526
Lower Castle 3 527
Murovanka Church 3 526
Palace of Stephen Bathory see Historical and Archaeological Museum
SS Boris and Gleb 3 526; 4 781
Sapieha Palace 3 527
sashes 25 133
Upper Castle 3 526
Hōrai (fl 16th cent.)
works 17 394
Hōrai (1677-1751) see GION NANKAI
Hōraku 17 401
Horapollo 1 655; 15 83, 149; 22 414
Horat, Carla 10 398
Horatius Flaccus, Quintus see HORACE
Horb, Max 10 107
Horben, Schloss see SCHLOSS HORBEN
Horbling (Lincs), St Andrew 9 680
Horbowy, Zbigniew 25 125
Horb Synagogue 17 546, 559
wall paintings 17 558
Hörby 26 691
Horcheimer, Nicholas 23 313
Horčička, František 8 423; 14 756*; 25 433
Hord, Donal 27 721; 30 255
Horder 26 640
Horder, Percy Morley 10 462
Hordliczka, Ignacy 25 124
Hore, Somnath 5 420; 14 756*
Horeau, Hector 7 745; 14 756–7*
Hōreda 10 536
manor house 10 537
Horejc, Jaroslav 8 406, 411, 414, 416; 19 522; 23 271; 25 435
Horemans, Jan Josef, I (1682-1752) 3 562; 9 28; 14 757*
Horemans, Jan Josef, II (1714-after 1790) 14 757–8*
Horemans, Peter Jacob 14 757*; 22 302, 309
Horemheb (reg c. 1319-c. 1292 BC) 9 777, 791, 839; 10 80; 14 758, 758–9*
architecture 2 850; 12 227; 14 461; 23 280; 27 812; 30 691
reliefs 9 885
sculpture 9 885
stele 29 616
tomb 27 811
wall paintings 9 903
Horemkawef 14 514
Horenbout, Gerard 12 519; 14 759–61*; 20 635, 700
attributions 20 692
collaboration 3 555
groups and movements 12 524
patrons and collectors 13 905
works 4 76; 13 661; 14 760
Horenbout, Lucas 14 759, 761*; 20 635
attributions 14 761
patrons and collectors 31 414
teachers 14 759
works 10 246; 21 639
Horenbout, Susanna 14 759, 761*; 30 412
Horer, Balthasar 33 623
Hörger, Ferenc Antal 5 84; 15 13
Hörhammer, Ivar 11 112
Hori (family) 17 323
Hori, Keikin 17 240
Hori, Kosai 17 207
works 17 208
Hori, Ryūjo 17 371
Hořice 8 425
Museum of Applied Art 8 424
Horie, Masaaki 17 203
Horiguchi, Sutemi 14 761–2*; 17 88; 33 488
Hori Kyōan 17 788
Hori Naonori 17 439
Hořín Castle 8 379; 11 458; 26 496
Horinger see HELINGOL
Horinouchi shell-mound 17 245
Hōrin Shōshō 18 553
Horio Yoshiharu 20 834
Horisada 17 415
Hörisch, Carl Gottlieb 9 241
Hörisch, Christiane Sophie von 9 241
Horiuchi (family) 2 6
Horiuchi, Masakazu 14 762*
Horiuno III 17 415
Horiyoshi 17 415
Horizon 32 912
horizontal draught kilns see under KILNS → types
horizontal ground looms see under LOOMS → types
horizontal Phakpa script see under SCRIPTS → types
horizontal scrolls see SCROLLS→ types → handscrolls
Horizonte 10 543
Horkheimer, Max 20 527
Hörling 14 133
Hörmann, Franz Benedikt see HERMANN, FRANZ BENEDIKT
Hörmann, Franz Georg see HERMANN, FRANZ GEORG
Hörmann, Johannes 18 142
Hörmann, Theodor von 14 762*
Hormayr, Josef von 10 883
Hormiguero 26 412
Hormizd, Kushanshah 33 510
Hormuz 6 623; 15 201; 16 449
Horn (Austria)
Externsteine 9 680; 26 632
Georgskirche 2 780
Horn (Netherlands)
Castle 4 778
horn 14 762–4*; 25 23; 31 195
historical and regional traditions
Bamana 3 135
China 1 760
Egypt, ancient 10 29
England 10 297; 14 763
Indian subcontinent 6 556
Japan 14 764; 17 398
materials
inscriptions 7 124
techniques
carving see HORN-CARVINGS
dyeing 7 123, 126; 9 490
types
buffalo 7 126
deer 7 92
narwhal 8 835
ox 1 367
horn
types—cont.
rhinoceros 7 102, 103, 109, 123–8*, 125, 126, 127, 130; 14 763
unicorn 8 835
uses
beakers 14 763, 763
belts 7 109, 124
book covers 14 763
boxes 14 763, 763
brush backs 14 763
buttons 14 763
chess sets 6 556
combs (hair) 14 763
cups 7 123–5, 126, 126, 127, 128; 14 763
cutlery 14 763
drinking-horns 14 763, 763
fans 10 781
figurines 7 125, 126
furniture 10 297
glues 7 92; 15 850
hornbooks 14 763
jewellery 10 29
knife-handles 8 285
knife scales 14 763
lanterns (lights) 14 763
marquetry 20 466
masks 3 135
netsuke 14 764; 17 398
plaques 7 124
powder horns 14 763
seals 7 130
shoe horns 14 763
snuff-boxes 1 367
spoons 8 284; 14 763
stands 7 125
stoppers 14 763
toggles 14 763
trumpets 14 763
watches 7 447
Horn, Andrew 25 808
Horn, E. W. 5 30
Horn, Rebecca 10 882; 14 764*; 24 403, 409
Horna, Juan de see JUAN DE HORNA
Hornakhte 9 879
Horná Lefantovce 14 885
church 14 900
Hornay, Erasmus see HORNICK, ERASMUS
Hornbach Sacramentary see under SACRAMENTARIES → individual manuscripts
Hornbæk 17 605; 18 470
hornbeam 33 324
hornbill, helmeted see HELMETED HORNBILL
Hornblower & Marshall 24 638
hornbooks 14 763
Hornbostel, Christian Georg 2 825
Hornbostel, Henry 5 776; 14 734
Hornby, Frank 31 257
Hornby Hall (Lancs) 6 451; 10 294
horn-carvings 7 125, 125, 126, 127; 27 365; 28 302
Horndon on the Hill Market (Essex) 20 438
Horne, Cleeve 5 571
Horne, Herbert (Percy) 11 190; 14 764*
groups and movements 6 322
patrons and collectors 31 680
teachers 20 26
works 4 503; 20 476; 21 32; 28 601
Horne, Jean 5 571
Horne, T. H. 26 463
Horne, William (Cornelius) van see VAN HORNE, WILLIAM (CORNELIUS)
Horne & Allen 17 469
Horneck, Erasmus see HORNICK, ERASMUS
Horned God 8 353
Hornel, E(dward) A(tkinson) 12 779; 14 397, 765*; 26 107; 28 238
collections 28 274
Horne Presentation Casket 2 765
Horner, Johan (fl 1752)
frames 11 469
Horner, Johann Jacob (1772-1831) 24 453
Horner, W. 12 469
Hornes, Marguerite of see MARGUERITE DE HORNES
Horne Triptych, Master of the 23 743
Hornhausen
gravestones 21 502
Hornick, Erasmus 2 455; 3 598; 14 765–6*; 23 312
works 10 326; 12 455; 17 521
Hornick, Jean 17 521
Hörnickh, Erasmus see HORNICK, ERASMUS
Hornicsek, László 14 910
Horniman Museum see under LONDON→ museums
Horninck, Erasmus see HORNICK, ERASMUS
Hørning Plank 8 721, 729
Horno-Popławski, Stanisław 25 116
horns 1 326, 327, 328; 16 797; 21 117; 22 372; 23 400–402; 25 526, 526
see also OLIPHANTS
Hornsey Town Hall 4 788; 31 243
Hornslet Church 8 730
Hornton stone 22 57
Hornung, Zbigniew 25 143
hornworks 21 546, 570
Horny, Conrad 14 766
Horny, Franz Theobald 12 393; 14 766*
Horodenka Altar 25 115
Höroldt, Johann Gregorius 14 766–7*; 21 64
works 12 434; 21 65
Höroldt, Rachel Eleonore 14 767
Horologgi, Francesco 28 4; 31 439
Horomos Monastery 2 435
Hororata, Glen Alton Farm 23 64
Horová, Julie 8 406; 28 856
Hořovice 8 416
Horovitz, Bela 12 873; 14 767*
Horovitz, Josef 16 549
Horovitz, Leopold 14 767*; 17 576; 18 128
Horozco, Sebastián de Covarrubias see COVARRUBIAS HOROZCO, SEBASTIÁN DE
Horoztepe 1 821, 834
figurines 1 825, 825
metalwork 1 522, 824, 834, 835
ritual objects 1 825
Horpit 9 895
Hörr, Josef 33 76
horrea see WAREHOUSES
Horrix, Matthien 14 767
Horrix, Willem 14 767
Horrix factory 14 44, 767*; 22 873
horror vacui 14 767*
Horrues Church 13 113
Horschelt, Theodor 4 671; 14 768*
Horse, Master of the 5 213
horse armour see under ARMOUR → types
Horse Bird group 13 513
horsehair see under HAIR→ types
horse harnesses see under HARNESSES→ types
Horsens 8 720
Vor Frelser 8 739, 740
horses, white see HILL-FIGURES
Horse Sand Fort (Hants) 21 569
horseshoe arches see under ARCHES→ types
horse trappers see TRAPPERS
horse trappings see under TRAPPINGS → types

Horsewell, William 31 651
Horsey, Edward 5 560; 14 768*
Horsfall, T. C. 20 239
Horsfield, George 24 556
Horsham (W. Sussex), St Faith Priory 10 244; 26 653
Horsley, Gerald Callcott 2 575; 14 768
Horsley, John Callcott 14 768*
groups and movements 8 121
patrons and collectors 7 548; 28 576
reproductive prints by others 3 646
works 19 614
Horsnaile, Christopher 10 263; 29 542, 543
Hörsne Church 13 190
Horšovský Týn Castle 8 376
Horst 14 768–9*
Horst, Gerrit van der 2 855; 22 843
Horst, Hendrick ter 22 894
Horst, J. H. 15 769; 16 874
Horstok, Johannes Petrus van 3 211
Horta, Victor 3 550; 7 669; 14 769–71*; 21 369
architecture 5 *41*, 42; 14 *771*; 25 172, 173; 31 218
assistants 9 759
collaboration 5 24; 6 487; 10 735; 18 670
groups and movements 2 510, 562–3, 564; 4 74; 21 779; 22 252; 26 14
house 2 552; 3 586; 10 735; 25 173; 31 888
see also BRUSSELS → museums → Musée Horta
interior decoration 3 579, 586; 11 449
metalwork 16 55; 23 547
patrons and collectors 2 369
pupils 5 24; 8 63
stained glass 29 508
staircases 14 *770*; 29 525
teachers 3 44, 89, 898
Hortemels, Louise-Magdeleine 7 495
Hortense de Beauharnais, Queen of Holland (1783-1837) 4 298, *299*, 305*; 9 364; 12 154; 16 64; 31 478; 33 48
Hortensius 13 555
Horthemels, Marie-Nicole 3 639
Horti, Pál 14 908, 909; 15 8, 12
horticulture *see* GARDENS
Hortinus, Julius Roscius 10 175
Hortleder, Friedrich 31 371
Hortobágyi, Endre 14 902
Horton, William 7 480
Hortulus Animae, Master of the 20 692–3*
hortus see GARDENS → types → vegetable; ROME, ANCIENT → gardens
hortus conclusus see under GARDENS → types
Hortus deliciarum 1 653, *653*; 12 382; 14 467, 772*, *772*; 24 269
Horvat, Lavoslav 9 672
Horvat 'Anim Synagogue 17 542
Horvat Dikke Synagogue 17 541
Horváth, Antal 14 132
Horváth, Márton 15 5
Horvat ha-'Amudim Synagogue 17 541
Horvat Ma'on Synagogue 17 542
Horvat Rimmon Synagogue 17 542
Horvat Shema' Synagogue 17 542
Horvat Summak Synagogue 17 542
Horvat Suseya Synagogue 17 542
Hørve Church 8 723
Horverk, Niklas 28 113
Hörwarth (family) 14 450
Horwood, John 5 562
Hory, Elmyr de 11 307, 309, 310
Hŏ Ryŏn 18 315, 325
Hory u Dobré 8 407
Hōryū Goseda *see* GOSEDA, HŌRYŪ
Hōryūji *see under* IKARUGA
Hosaenggwan *see* CH'OE PUK
Hosaholalu, Lakshmi-Narayana Temple 15 327, *327*
Hōsai Kameda *see* KAMEDA BŌSAI
Hosan *see* CHO HŬI-RYONG
Hosch, Edward 18 875
Hoschedé, Ernest 3 671; 15 154; 21 864
hose 9 255, 265, 267
Hösel, Erich 21 66
Hosenfeller, Christian Friedrich 14 775
Hosenfeller, Heinrich Christian Friedrich 14 775*; 23 225, 235
Höser, Vitus 12 370
Ho Shao-chi *see* HE SHAOJI
Ho-shen *see* HESHEN
Hoshiarpur 15 721
Punjab Government Museum Sadhu Ashram 15 484
Hoshino, Satoru 17 268
Hoshiyama Chūji 27 873
Hoshō Totoki *see* TOTOKI HOSHŌ
Hoshour Associates 22 671
Hōshubana 17 390
Hosiasson, Philippe 14 776*
Hosios Loukas 9 *511*; 14 776–7*
architectural decorations 16 135
Church of the Theotokos 4 774; 7 221, 260, *260*; 9 526, 527, 545, 546, 547; 20 571
capitals 9 592
crypt 7 261; 24 110
sculpture 7 273; 9 592
coins 13 586
glass 9 645
Katholikon 9 576, 578, *578*, 592; 14 *776*; 22 519; 28 291; 29 817
Monastery 9 593
mosaics 8 212; 14 776–7; 19 356; 22 162
St Barbara *see* Church of the Theotokos
wall paintings 14 776–7
Hosios Meletios Monastery 9 593; 21 834, 844
Hoskins, George Alexander 19 484
Hoskins, G. O. 31 240
Hoskins, John (i) (*c.* 1590-1665) 7 793; 14 777–8*
copies 20 476
patrons and collectors 29 803
pupils 7 793
works 21 640
Hoskins, John (ii) (*c.* 1620/30- *d* after 1692) 14 777, 778*
Hosmer, Charles 5 589
Hosmer, Harriet 12 598; 14 778*; 31 611; 33 309
groups and movements 19 286
works 23 295
hosoban see under PRINTS → types → *ukiyoe*
Hosoda Eiri 17 285
Hosoda Eishi 14 778*; 17 285; 31 53
Hosoda Shūji 18 530
Hosoe, Eikoh 14 779*; 17 860; 22 120; 31 106
Hosoi Kōtaku 14 779*; 17 235, 409, 413; 33 491
works 17 *236*
Hosoi Kyūkō 17 410
Hosokawa (family) 12 100
Hosokawa Katsumoto 18 561
Hosokawa Masamoto 18 561
Hosokawa Rinkoku 17 413
Hosokawa Tadaoki 1 448
Hosokawa Takakuni 17 780
Hosokawa Yūsai 17 215; 18 558
Hospet 14 125
hospices 16 202–4, 237
see also HOSPITALS
Hospitalfield House (Tayside) 25 11
hospitaliae 30 652, 656
Hospitaller, Knights *see* KNIGHTS HOSPITALLER
Hospital Nacional 13 763
hospitals 14 779–85*
Belgium 14 *783*
Byzantine 9 561
Cambodia 5 479
England 10 236; 13 *624*; 33 385, *398*
France 11 *511*; 14 *780*, *782*; 24 126, *164*; 29 *91*
Germany 3 140; 14 *678*
Gothic 11 *511*
Islamic 8 *478*; 16 141, 181, 184–5, 202–4
Italy 11 72, *72*; 25 *853*; 31 *894*
Malta (Republic of) 20 216
Netherlands, the 4 *57*; 19 116
Norway 23 221
Rome, ancient 21 559
Russia 17 *870*; 31 *544*
Spain 8 *79*; 14 *781*; 31 *509*
Sri Lanka 25 169
Syria 8 *478*; 16 181
Turkey 16 184–5, 202–4
see also HOSPICES
Hospodka, Josef 7 210; 23 271
Hossauer, George 13 207
Hossenfeller, Heinrich Christian Friedrich *see* HOSENFELLER, HEINRICH CHRISTIAN FRIEDRICH
Hosshin, Abbot of Myōhōin 15 129
Hosshōji *see under* JAPAN → calligraphy
Hossō Buddhism *see under* BUDDHISM → sects
Høst 7 488; 20 243
Høst, Oluf 8 736
Höste, Einar 30 86
Hoste, Huib 3 551, 579, 587; 7 *294*
Hostess Tableware Ltd. 10 314
Hostettler, Hans 2 661–2
Hosté Villa 32 542
Hostun, Marie-Joseph d', Duc de Tallard *see* TALLARD, MARIE-JOSEPH D'HOSTUN, Duc de
Hōsui Yamamoto *see* YAMAMOTO, HŌSUI
Hōsun 24 436
Hotaka, Rokuzan Art Museum 23 369
Hotan *see* KHOTAN
Hotchin, Claude 24 496
Hotchkiss 15 824
Hôtel des Invalides *see under* PARIS → hospitals
Hotel Koyokan 12 101
hotels 14 786–8*
Greece 13 *351*; 18 232
Greece, ancient 13 386
Japan 27 *192*
Netherlands, the 23 *671*
Norway 23 221
Portugal 25 *294*
United States of America 12 *794*; 14 786, *787*, 787–8, *788*; 17 891; 21 *421*; 25 270–71
hôtels particuliers 10 110; 14 789–92*; *264*; 20 288
Régence style 29 *751*
17th cent. 14 *790*; 19 *263*, *264*
18th cent. 4 *225*; 7 *416*; 11 *515*
see also HOUSES → types → town
Hotere, Ralph 14 792*; 20 359; 23 61
Hötetter, Ambrosius 10 220
Hotevilla 22 567
Hoteville 22 567
hothouses *see* GREENHOUSES
Hothuys, Andreas 22 856
Hoti-Mardan *see under* MARDAN
hotoke mawashi see under PUPPETS → types
Hoton, William 33 548
Hottentot *see* KHOIKHOI
Hottinger, Franz 22 703
Hottinger, Johann Konrad 23 675; 24 587
Hotz, Theo 30 129; 33 736
Hötzel, Elsa 28 111
Hötzendorf, Hugo Conrad 18 472
Houaïlou 23 19
Houasse, Michel-Ange 14 792, 793*; 29 282
patrons and collectors 4 558
pupils 12 922; 24 351, 461
works 4 184; 14 *793*; 29 350
Houasse, René-Antoine 8 70; 12 832; 14 792, 793*
collaboration 12 828; 19 22; 21 891
groups and movements 25 398
pupils 6 121; 10 842
Houbigant 18 659
Houbraken, Antonyna 14 794
Houbraken, Arnold 14 737, 794–5*
pupils 14 795
works 22 907, 910
writings
illustrated 14 795
Houbraken, Jacobus 14 794, 795*
collaboration 32 378
dealing 28 362
personal collection 25 631
pupils 30 297
reproductive prints by others 11 906
teachers 14 794
works 14 794; 18 143; 25 363, 823; 30 297; 31 367; 33 25
Houbraken, Nicola van 29 669
Houcheong 7 30
Hou-chu, Emperor (Later Shu; *reg* AD 583-9) *see* HOUZHU, Emperor
Houckgeest, Gerrit 3 352; 14 795–6*; 22 844
groups and movements 8 669
works 2 341, 342; 8 667; 14 *796*
Houdan 6 55
Houdard de la Motte, Antoine 4 360; 12 638
Houdé, François 5 583
Houdon, Jean-Antoine 14 796–9*
attributions 19 756
collaboration 12 835
groups and movements 24 171
patrons and collectors
Angiviller, Charles-Claude de Flahaut de la Billarderie, Comte d' 11 561
Catherine II, Empress of Russia (*reg* 1762- 96) 13 663
Charles Augustus, Grand Duke of Saxe-Weimar (*reg* 1775-1828) 33 117
Cognacq, (Théodore-) Ernest 7 528
Gulbenkian, Calouste Sarkis 13 841
Hohenzollern, Henry, Prince of Prussia 14 653
Josephine, Empress of the French (1763-1814) 4 303
Morny, Charles-Auguste, Duc de 22 127
Musée Fabre (Montpellier) 22 35
Napoleon I, Emperor of the French (*reg* 1804-14) 4 301
Orléans, Louis-Philippe-Joseph de Bourbon, 5th Duc d' (1747-93) 23 519
Seligmann, Jacques 28 384
Seymour-Conway, Richard, 4th Marquess of Hertford 28 527
Wrightsman, Charles B(ierer) 33 416
Houdon, Jean-Antoine—cont.
pupils 30 747
teachers 28 847
works 3 26; 5 302; 9 706; 11 562; 14 *797*, *798*; 22 45; 24 136, *137*; 30 499; 31 610
Houdon, Jean-François 11 627
Hoüel, Jean-Pierre-Louis-Laurent 2 904; 8 703; 14 799*; 28 657
Houel, Nicolas 5 813
Houfe, E. A. S. 26 337
Houffalize, Ste Catherine
tomb of Thierry d'Houffalize 13 99
Houghton, Amory (1813-82) 7 874
Houghton, Amory (1837-1909) 7 875
Houghton, Arthur Amory 16 552; 29 644
Houghton, Arthur Boyd 10 254; 14 799–800*
works 4 363, 868; 25 598
Houghton, Georgiana 11 310
Houghton, John (*d c.* 1775) 16 21, 26
Houghton, John Michael (1797-1874) 14 799
Houghton, J. R. 28 742
Houghton, Mifflin & Co. 31 680
Houghton, Richard Moncton Milnes, 1st Baron *see* MILNES, RICHARD MONCTON, 1st Baron Houghton
Houghton Hall (Norfolk) 10 233, 276, 361; 23 859; 32 824
catalogues 6 77; 32 824, 825
collections 10 364
furniture 10 294
interior decoration 11 426
Marble Hall 17 *901*
paintings 9 506; 13 301; 23 874
sculpture 27 466
stables 29 486, *486*
staircase 10 293
tapestries 10 351
textiles 13 302
Houlbert, John 9 729; 28 246
Houlden, John 4 353
Houle, Robert 22 598
Houma (China) 6 *615*; 14 800–801*
bronze 6 636, 832–3, 852, 854
bronzes 6 832
gold 7 21
jade 7 4
moulds 6 *833*; 14 *800*
tombs 6 655; 33 660
Houma (North America) 22 663
Houmt Souk, Museum of Popular Arts and Traditions 31 427
Hōun Ohara *see* OHARA, HŌUN
Houphouet-Boigny, Félix 8 23
houppelandes see GOWNS
Hourin Country Club 12 101
Hourmouziades 8 901
Hours of Alfonso, Duca di Calabria *see under* BOOKS OF HOURS → individual manuscripts
Hours of Alfonso I d'Este *see under* BOOKS OF HOURS → individual manuscripts
Hours of Anne, Duchess of Bourbon *see under* BOOKS OF HOURS → individual manuscripts
Hours of Anne of Brittany *see under* BOOKS OF HOURS → individual manuscripts → Grandes Heures of Anne of Brittany
Hours of Ascanio Sforza *see under* BOOKS OF HOURS → individual manuscripts
Hours of Blanche of Savoy *see under* BOOKS OF HOURS → individual manuscripts

Hours of Bonaparte Ghislieri *see under* BOOKS OF HOURS → individual manuscripts
Hours of Bona Sforza *see under* BOOKS OF HOURS → individual manuscripts
Hours of Catherine of Cleves *see under* BOOKS OF HOURS → individual manuscripts
Hours of Charles de France *see under* BOOKS OF HOURS → individual manuscripts
Hours of Charles the Noble *see under* BOOKS OF HOURS → individual manuscripts
Hours of Duke Louis, Master of the **28** 1
Hours of Edward I of Portugal *see under* BOOKS OF HOURS → individual manuscripts
Hours of Elizabeth the Queen *see under* BOOKS OF HOURS → individual manuscripts
Hours of Engelbert of Nassau *see under* BOOKS OF HOURS → individual manuscripts
Hours of Etienne Chevalier *see under* BOOKS OF HOURS → individual manuscripts
Hours of Folpard van Amerogen *see under* BOOKS OF HOURS → individual manuscripts
Hours of Francesco Maria Sforza *see under* BOOKS OF HOURS → individual manuscripts
Hours of Frederick III of Aragon *see under* BOOKS OF HOURS → individual manuscripts
Hours of Gijsbrecht van Brederode *see under* BOOKS OF HOURS → individual manuscripts
Hours of Henry VII *see under* BOOKS OF HOURS → individual manuscripts
Hours of Isabella di Chiaromonte *see under* BOOKS OF HOURS → individual manuscripts
Hours of Isabella of Castile, Master of the *see* TOMASINO DA VIMERCATE
Hours of Isabella Stuart, Duchess of Brittany *see under* BOOKS OF HOURS → individual manuscripts
Hours of Isabella the Catholic *see under* BOOKS OF HOURS → individual manuscripts
Hours of Jacques de Langeac *see under* BOOKS OF HOURS → individual manuscripts
Hours of Jacques d'Estouteville *see under* BOOKS OF HOURS → individual manuscripts
Hours of James IV and Margaret Tudor *see under* BOOKS OF HOURS → individual manuscripts
Hours of Jeanne de Savoie *see under* BOOKS OF HOURS → individual manuscripts
Hours of Jeanne d'Evreux *see under* BOOKS OF HOURS → individual manuscripts
Hours of Jean Robertet *see under* BOOKS OF HOURS → individual manuscripts
Hours of Joanna of Navarre *see under* BOOKS OF HOURS → individual manuscripts
Hours of John the Fearless *see under* BOOKS OF HOURS → individual manuscripts
Hours of Kaetzaert van Zaer *see under* BOOKS OF HOURS → individual manuscripts
Hours of Katharina von Lokhorst *see under* BOOKS OF HOURS → individual manuscripts
Hours of King Manuel *see under* BOOKS OF HOURS → individual manuscripts
Hours of Laudomia Medici *see under* BOOKS OF HOURS → individual manuscripts
Hours of Lorenzo the Magnificent & Clarice Orsini *see under* BOOKS OF HOURS → individual manuscripts
Hours of Louis de Laval *see under* BOOKS OF HOURS → individual manuscripts
Hours of Maréchal de Boucicaut *see* BOOKS OF HOURS → individual manuscripts → Boucicaut Hours
Hours of Margaret, Duchess of Clarence *see under* BOOKS OF HOURS → individual manuscripts
Hours of Margaret of Cleves *see under* BOOKS OF HOURS → individual manuscripts
Hours of Marguerite of Foix *see under* BOOKS OF HOURS → individual manuscripts
Hours of Marguerite of Rohan *see under* BOOKS OF HOURS → individual manuscripts
Hours of Maria of Navarre *see under* BOOKS OF HOURS - individual manuscripts
Hours of Mary of Burgundy *see under* BOOKS OF HOURS → individual manuscripts
Hours of Mary Stuart *see under* BOOKS OF HOURS → individual manuscripts
Hours of Mary van Vronenstein *see under* BOOKS OF HOURS → individual manuscripts
Hours of Philippe de Commyne *see under* BOOKS OF HOURS → individual manuscripts
Hours of Philippe of Cleves *see under* BOOKS OF HOURS → individual manuscripts
Hours of René II of Lorraine *see under* BOOKS OF HOURS → individual manuscripts
Hours of René of Anjou *see under* BOOKS OF HOURS → individual manuscripts
Hours of René of Lorraine *see under* BOOKS OF HOURS → individual manuscripts
Hours of Saluces *see under* BOOKS OF HOURS → individual manuscripts
Hours of Sophia von Bylant *see* BOOKS OF HOURS → individual manuscripts → Homoet Hours
Hours of the Holy Ghost, Master of the **31** 448
Hours of Thiebaut de Luxembourg *see under* BOOKS OF HOURS → individual manuscripts
Hours of Yolande de Soissons *see under* BOOKS OF HOURS → individual manuscripts
Hours of Yolande of Flanders *see under* BOOKS OF HOURS → individual manuscripts
House, Harlan **14** 801*
  works **5** 582, *582*
House and Garden **10** 284
houseboards **24** *73*, 73–4*
Housebook **20** 694
Housebook Master **1** 654; **14** 87; **20** 693–5*, 804; **29** 504
  attributions **28** 149
  reproductive prints by others **20** 792
  works **9** 308; **12** 385; **20** *693*, *694*; **25** 605, *605*
house churches *see* CHURCHES → types → *domus ecclesiae*
Houseman, Jacob *see* HUYSMANS, JACOB
Housemark ♖, Master of the **24** 246
House of Dun **28** 246
House of Photography **1** 23
House of Saudi Arts **27** 876
House of Strathbogie *see* PALACE OF HUNTLY
House of the Anchor **23** 366
House of the Niobid **12** 150
houseplants *see* PLANTS
Houser, Allan **14** 801*; **22** 595
houses **32** 297–8
  historical and regional traditions
    Afghanistan **1** 208
    Africa **1** 295, 305–7, 308, 311–14, *313*, 318, *318*, 319, 320, *421*; **4** *792*
      Islamic **1** 308, 315–16
    Ainu **1** 493
    Albania **1** 539; **16** 228
    Algeria **16** 218–19
    Angola **1** 320
    Antilles, Lesser **2** 146
    Arabia **2** 247–8; **16** 270–71
    Argentina **33** *203*
    Asante **1** 311, 313
    Australia **32** *307*
    Austria **25** *37*
    Aztec **21** 208; **32** 305
    Bahamas, the **3** *61*
    Bali (Indonesia) **15** 772–3
    Bamileke **1** 307
    Belarus' **32** 298
    Belgium **3** 575
      Art Nouveau **5** *41*
      Baroque **2** *549*
      Gothic **4** *920*
      Modern Movement **3** *551*
      17th cent. **5** *40*
      20th cent. **14** *629*
    Benin Republic **1** 311, 312
    Bhutan **3** 913
    Bolivia **4** *260*; **5** *887*
    Botswana **1** 320
    Brazil **13** *782*
    Britain **32** 276–7
      Prehistoric **25** 503*
      South Africa **29** 105
      United States of America **31** *590*
      19th cent. **28** 874
    Bulgaria **5** 147–8, 156
    Burkina Faso **1** 311, 312; **21** 597
    Burma **5** 236–7*
    Byzantine **9** 560, 561
    Cambodia **5** 483*, *483*
    Cameroon **1** 307
    Canaanite **5** 557; **30** 185
    Canada **5** *573*
    Carib **30** 13
    Caribbean Islands **5** 749
    Central Asia, Western **6** 200, *200*, 229–30; **16** 154
    China **6** *647*, 661, 684–92*, *685*, *686*, *689*, *693*; **7** 143
    Creole **11** *757*, 758
    Crete **13** 396; **21** 655–6
    Cucuteni culture **25** 501–2*
    Cyprus, ancient **8** *333*, 333–4
    Czech Republic **8** *377*, *380*; **25** *430*
    Dan (Africa) **8** 489–90*
    Denmark **32** 285, 286
    Dominican Republic **5** 749; **9** 116
    Early Christian (*c.* AD 250-843) **9** 560
    Ecuador **29** *139*
    Egypt, ancient **1** 755; **9** *849*, 849–50, 851, *851*
    England **2** 600; **4** 780; **10** 229–30; **32** *276*
      Africa **1** 318
      Arts and Crafts Movement **25** *634*
      Baroque **31** *860*
      Egyptian Revival **10** *97*
houses
  historical and regional traditions
    England—cont.
      Elizabethan style **10** *231*
      Georgian style **12** 332; **19** *571*
      Gothic Revival **13** *203*
      Jacobean style **10** *230*
      Modern Movement **7** *712*
      Neo-classicism **2** *550*; **17** *904*
      Old English style **10** *238*
      Palladianism **4** *610*; **5** *538*, *539*; **10** 364; **33** *224*
      Queen Anne Revival **22** *810*; **28** *562*
      Roman **10** 226
      Romanesque **10** 227
      16th cent. **3** 30; **10** 360; **23** *246*; **32** *276*, *277*
      17th cent. **32** *277*
      18th cent. **23** *247*
      19th cent. **12** *315*, *840*; **15** *407*; **22** *528*; **23** *259*
      20th cent. **19** *821*; **32** *721*
    Ethiopia **1** 311
    Etruscan **1** 127; **10** *598*, 599–600*; **26** 888
    Fiji **11** 69
    Fon **1** 311
    France **4** 780; **11** 656; **32** *278*, *279*, 279–80, *280*
      Gothic **4** *584*
      Modern Movement **19** *653*
      Neo-classicism **19** *56*, *57*
      Renaissance **29** *750*
      18th cent. **24** *121*
      20th cent. **12** *793*; **19** 41–2
    French Guiana **11** *757*, 758
    Fulani **1** 308
    Germany **32** *281*, *282*, 283
      Baroque **28** *106*
      Expressionism **10** *698*
      organic architecture **23** *499*
      Roman **26** 906
      17th cent. **11** *853*; **33** *294*
      20th cent. **8** *826*
    Ghana **1** 311, 320
    Gothic **4** *584*, *920*; **11** 773
    Greece **13** *350*; **25** *499*, 500; **32** *294*
    Greece, ancient **13** *382*, 382–3*, 389, *396*, 396, 407, 419, 420, 556
      Classical **23** 434–5
      4th cent. BC **24** *337*
      9th cent. BC **13** 396
    Grenada **2** 147
    Gumelniţa culture **25** 501
    Guyana **13** 875
    Haiti **1** *421*; **14** 56–7
    Hausa **1** 251, 305, 308, *318*
    Hungary **32** 298
    Igbo **1** 284, 331
    India, Republic of **15** 168
    Indian subcontinent **5** 418; **15** *390*; **32** *323*, 323–5
      Bengal **15** 402
      Colonial period **15** 402
      Islamic **15** 345
    Indonesia **3** 144; **15** 770, 771–5*, *774*, 789, *807*
    Iran **16** 154, 163, 264
    Iraq **16** 152–3, *270*; **32** *314*, 315
    Ireland **16** 8
    Islamic **16** 263, 267–71*; **32** *316*
      Africa **1** 308, 315–16
      Albania **16** 228
      Algeria **16** 218–19
      Arabia **16** 270–71
      Central Asia, Western **16** 154
      Indian subcontinent **15** 345
      Iran **16** 154, 163, 264
      Iraq **16** 152–3, *270*; **32** *314*, 315
      Morocco **16** 218–19
      Ottoman **16** 266, *266*, 271
      Philippines **24** *611*
      Saudi Arabia **32** *316*
      Syria **16** 152, 269; **32** 315
houses
  historical and regional traditions
    Islamic—cont.
      Turkey **16** *266*, 266, 269; **32** 318–19, *319*
      Yemen **32** *317*
    Italy **26** *843*
      Etruscan **1** 127; **10** *598*, 599–600*
      Prehistoric **25** 500–501
      Renaissance **3** *850*
      Roman **14** *441*; **25** *199*; **26** 888
      16th cent. **19** *203*
      19th cent. **4** *246*
    Jamaica **16** 882
    Japan **17** 46, 54–5, *55*, 56
      Jōmon period (*c.* 10,000–*c.* 300 BC) **17** 629
      Shōwa period (1926-89) **16** *784*
      Yayoi period (*c.* 300 BC–*c.* AD 300) **33** 511
    Java **15** 772
    Jewish art **17** 552
    Jordan **3** 514
    Kenya **1** 307, 320
    Korea **18** 262, 264, 274*, 276–9*, *278*
      Prehistoric **18** 260
      19th cent. **18** *277*
    Kuwait **18** 540–41
    Laos **18** 764, 766, 767*
    Latvia **26** *383*
    Lesotho **1** 311
    Liberia **1** 319
    Malawi **1** 320
    Malaysia **20** 167
    Maldives, Republic of **20** 188–9
    Mali **1** 317; **20** 198
    Maya **21** 208; **32** 307
    Mesoamerica, Pre-Columbian **21** 204, 207–8*; **32** 305
    Mesopotamia **21** 280–81, 284, 287
    Mexico **32** 305
    Minoan **21** 655–6
    Mongolia **6** 692
    Morocco **16** 218–19
    Mozambique **1** 320
    Native North Americans **21** *174*; **22** 570, 572–3
    Ndebele **1** *313*
    Nepal **22** 766
    Netherlands, the **2** *193*; **4** 786
      Modern Movement **21** *781*
      Régence style **22** *826*
      Renaissance **1** *802*
      South Africa **29** 104
      17th cent. **32** *589*
    Nigeria **1** 284, 305, *318*
    North Africa **26** 870, 920
    Norway **23** 219
    Ottoman **16** 228, 266, *266*, 271
    Pacific Islands **23** *717*
    Papua New Guinea **23** *736*
    Paraguay **24** 94
    Philippines **24** *611*, *615*, 615–16*, *616*
    Poland **25** *97*; **32** 297, *297*, 298, *299*
    Portugal **25** 292
    Prehistoric art **25** 473, 519–22
      Britain **25** 503*
      China **6** *685*
      Cucuteni culture **25** 501–2*
      Cyprus, ancient **8** *333*
      France **25** 503
      Greece **25** *499*, 500
      Gumelniţa culture **25** 501
      Iron Age **25** 536
      Italy **25** 500–501
      Japan **17** *55*, *629*
      Jordan **3** 514
      Korea **18** 260
      Lengyel culture **25** 500
      Neolithic **25** 498–503*, *499*, *501*
      Rössen culture **25** 500

houses
historical and regional traditions
Prehistoric art—cont.
Scotland 28 815, 815
Stroke-ornamented Pottery culture 25 500
Switzerland 25 502*
Tripol'ye culture 25 501–2*
Turkey 25 499
Ukraine 25 501
Punic 25 732
Renaissance 1 802
Romanesque 10 227
Rome, ancient 26 856, 868–70, 877, 891
England 10 226
Germany 26 906
Italy 14 441; 25 199; 26 888
Russia 3 433; 32 298
St Lucia 2 147
Samoa 27 683
Scandinavia 32 532, 533
Scotland 20 23, 24; 28 815, 815
Senegal 1 313
Shona 1 313
Singapore 28 773–4
Sogdiana 6 200, 200, 229–30
South Africa 1 313; 5 662; 29 104, 105, 107
South America, Pre-Columbian 29 139
South-east Asia 29 226
Spain 29 274; 32 291
Sudan 1 306, 307, 311, 319
Sumatra 15 771–2*
Surinam 30 15
Sweden 32 532
Switzerland 3 75; 11 773; 25 502*
Syria 9 560; 16 152, 269; 32 315
Syria-Palestine 10 173; 30 182, 185, 186
Tanzania 1 311; 30 300, 302
Thailand 30 591–2, 639
Togo 1 305, 311, 312
Tokharistan 6 200
Trinidad and Tobago 31 335
Tripol'ye culture 25 501–2*
Tuareg 1 306
Turkey 16 266, 266, 269; 25 499; 32 318–19, 319
Uganda 1 311
Ukraine 25 501
United States of America 15 22; 31 589–90, 591–2, 593; 32 893
Chicago school 31 595
Colonial period 31 590
Colonial Revival 7 619
Modernism 10 120; 23 10; 28 96
Modern Movement 2 551; 5 649; 21 493
Native North Americans 22 567, 570, 572–3
Queen Anne Revival 25 805
Romanesque Revival 3 128; 23 40
Shingle style 20 17
18th cent. 6 486; 32 300, 301, 302
19th cent. 15 22; 27 613; 32 894
20th cent. 11 835; 12 632, 855; 29 35; 30 870; 33 401, 405
Venezuela 32 166, 169
Vietnam 32 471, 477*, 477
Viking 32 532, 533
Wales 32 781–2, 782
Yemen 32 317; 33 519
Yoruba 1 311
Zaïre 1 295
Zambia 4 792
Zande 1 308
Zimbabwe 1 320
materials
adobe 6 691
bamboo 3 144; 5 236; 15 770
houses
materials—cont.
basketwork 1 295
beach-rock 2 248
brick 3 575; 4 780
cement 1 331
concrete 2 600; 7 712, 712; 26 18
domes 16 270
grasses 22 570
mica 1 284
mud 33 519
mud-bricks 4 792; 13 396; 16 266; 20 198; 21 280; 26 877
palm leaves 2 247; 15 770
plaster 18 277
shells 1 284
stone 3 575
stucco 18 277
vaults (ceiling) 16 270
wood 3 575; 5 236; 7 143; 18 277; 23 717
types
almshouses see ALMSHOUSES
apsidal 14 336
artists' see ARTISTS' HOUSES
atria 26 869, 904
baby see DOLLS' HOUSES
banqueting see BANQUETING HOUSES
Basle Mission 1 319
bungalows 5 173–4*; 6 395; 7 678
Africa 1 318
Britain 5 173–4
Canada 5 173
England 5 173, 174; 28 349
Indian subcontinent 5 173; 32 324
Singapore 28 773
Sri Lanka 29 453
United States of America 5 173; 13 618
canoe-houses 23 726; 29 50–51
chattel 2 147, 147; 16 883; 31 334
circular 25 473
Corinthian 26 869
corridor 14 336, 338–9
cottage orné 8 30*; 32 554; 33 447
council see BOULEUTERIA; TOWN HALLS
country 20 814
Crete 8 153; 21 664*
Denmark 8 727
England 3 283; 8 42–9*, 43, 44, 46, 48, 49; 10 230, 232, 233; 28 896; 31 858, 859, 861; 33 444, 445
England: Baroque 2 307; 6 515; 14 253; 30 278
England: Elizabethan style 28 895, 896
England: Gothick 10 234; 32 826
England: Gothic Revival 5 195
England: Greek Revival 13 610
England: Neo-classicism 1 136; 28 907; 30 386
England: Palladianism 4 612; 7 174; 23 856
England: 16th cent. 6 127
England: 19th cent. 22 526; 33 12
France see CHÂTEAUX
Indian subcontinent 19 774
Ireland 6 411; 16 9, 9, 22–3, 24–5; 23 861; 24 305
Minoan 8 153; 21 664*
Netherlands, the 22 827
Poland 25 98, 99
Russia 1 71; 27 377
Scotland 28 226, 230, 289
United States of America 9 204; 15 22; 31 592
houses
types
country—cont.
see also ARCHITECTURE → types → landscape; CHÂTEAUX; GARDEN DESIGN; VILLAS
courtyard
China 6 648, 661, 686, 688, 689, 690, 692
Iraq 16 267, 268
Islamic 16 260, 267, 267–8, 268, 270
dachas 27 377
displuviate 26 869
dolls' see DOLLS' HOUSES
farmhouses
Africa 1 318
Denmark 32 285, 285
Finland 32 286, 287–8, 288
Greece, ancient 21 341
Iceland 32 533
Japan 17 81–2, 82; 18 173
Netherlands, the 32 283–5, 284
Norway 32 286, 287, 287–8
Prehistoric art 25 536
Rome, ancient 26 869
South Africa 1 318; 5 662, 662
Sweden 32 286, 287–8
Switzerland 30 126–7, 127
Viking 32 533
fortified 1 539; 6 49
greenhouses see GREENHOUSES
Grubenhäuser 2 64; 32 532
haus tambaran 23 716, 717
hogan 22 568
ice-houses see ICE-HOUSES
laird's 28 225–6
lodges see LODGES
longhouses
Indonesia 15 773–4
Lengyel culture 25 500
Linear Pottery culture 25 500
Malaysia 20 167–8
Prehistoric 25 500
Prehistoric art 25 503
Rössen culture 25 500
Stroke-ornamented Pottery culture 25 500
machiya 17 46
maisons de plaisance 10 110
manor 1 440; 6 407; 8 175, 725; 10 226; 16 22
mbari 1 289, 314, 331; 15 110, 114, 115
minka 17 46, 81–3*, 82; 21 648*
model 3 489
nōka 17 46
pastas 13 382, 382, 383, 556; 23 434, 434
peristyle 26 869, 870, 888, 904, 920
Pètési 1 319
pigeon 5 673
pile dwellings 17 54, 56; 25 502*
pit dwellings 17 54, 55, 55, 56, 384–5
pithouses 22 566
plank 22 563–5, 564
prefabricated 10 681; 22 719; 26 18–19*
Africa 1 318
Britain 26 18, 19
England 26 17
Germany 26 18, 18
United States of America 26 19; 31 596
prostas 13 382–3, 382; 25 575
public see PUBLIC HOUSES
pueblo 22 566, 567
rest see REST-HOUSES
Rhodian 13 383, 407
shinden 17 46, 68–70, 70, 71, 384–5
shoin 2 599; 17 46, 75–81, 76, 77, 78, 79, 80, 81, 335, 385; 18 563, 564, 565
shop-houses 20 168; 28 773, 773
houses
types—cont.
sōan 17 337
summer-houses 23 220
taighean tugha 28 229
teahouses
Japan 16 811–12; 17 46, 52, 79–81*, 88, 335–6, 337, 340; 18 565, 566; 33 562
Netherlands, the 12 132
terrace 4 786
testudinate 26 869
tetrastyle 26 869
torogan 24 610–11, 611
tower 6 54; 31 229–31*
Ireland 6 59; 16 8, 22; 31 229
Italy 16 627
Scotland 6 59; 28 224, 288; 31 229–31, 231
Yemen 33 519–20
town
Austria 13 846
Crete 21 662, 664*
England 10 233; 14 76
France 29 751; 32 72
Germany 28 106
Greece, ancient 8 687; 25 575
Ireland 6 64
Minoan 21 662, 664*
Netherlands, the 5 542
Romania 26 707–8
Rome, ancient 32 72
Russia 27 377
South Africa 5 662
Switzerland 30 127
United States of America 27 730
see also APARTMENTS; HÔTELS PARTICULIERS; INSULAE; TENEMENTS
tripartite 14 128, 128
Tsangli 25 500
Tuscan 26 869
Usonian House 31 596; 33 404, 405
wada 15 393–4, 394
wikiup 22 567
see also CHALETS; TENEMENTS
Housesteads fort 14 23
housing
historical and regional traditions
Austria 32 439
Brazil 26 110
Catalonia 12 181
France 5 56, 362–3; 12 160; 19 43, 45
Germany 20 879
Japan 18 41
Netherlands, the 1 804; 8 670; 10 715
Russia 12 654, 877; 18 620
types
mass
Bulgaria 5 150
England 14 613
France 24 131
Germany 3 796; 30 371
Modern Movement 30 128
Netherlands, the 18 126
Russia 21 622; 27 578
Switzerland 3 841
United States of America 11 144
row-housing 30 521
Housman, Laurence 8 109
Houssaye, (François-) Arsène 14 802*; 24 837
Housser, Bess 14 194
Housset, (François-) Arsène see HOUSSAYE, (FRANÇOIS-)ARSÈNE
Houston (TX) 14 802–3*; 31 587
Astrodome 29 489
Best Products Co. Inc. 28 799
Contemporary Arts Museum 14 802, 803
Cullen Sculpture Garden 14 803
Glassell School of Art 14 803
Indeterminate Façade 4 790
Houston (TX)—cont.
Jesse Jones Hall for the Performing Arts 7 688
Majestic Cinema 7 327
Menil Collection 14 521, 803; 21 135; 24 697, 698; 26 333
Museum of Fine Arts 14 802, 803; 23 177; 29 763; 30 120
North Carolina National Bank 3 177; 17 621; 28 835
Pennzoil Place 31 598
RepublicBank Center see North Carolina National Bank
Rice University 5 340
Rothko Chapel 14 803
skyscrapers 14 803
Houston, James 22 575
Houston, John 9 725; 28 240
Houston, Richard 14 803*; 21 416
works 5 76; 14 132; 21 148; 24 366; 26 278
Hout see DUBOIS, LOUIS (JEAN-BAPTIST)
Houtaing Church 13 113
Houte, Adriaen van den see ADRIAEN VAN DEN HOUTE
Houten, Ignaz van 20 666
Houten, Jan van 25 649
Houten, Sientje van 14 43; 21 175
works 14 43
Houten, Van see VAN HOUTEN
Houtman, Aart 8 668
Houtman, Frederik 12 812
Houwaert, J. B. 19 64
Houzeau, Jacques 14 804*; 19 225
Houzhu, Emperor (Later Shu; reg AD 583-9) 6 537, 816
Hova see MERINA
Hovaida, 'Abbas 15 900
Hovd, Tugeemel Amarjuulagch Monastery 21 872
Hove (E. Sussex) 4 808
Town Hall 31 241
Hove, Anne-Birth 13 620
Hove, Bartholomeus Johannes van 14 804*; 22 860
patrons and collectors 33 46
pupils 4 443; 19 99; 23 321; 32 379; 33 46
Hove, Denys van 32 705
Hove, Huib van 20 433
Hove, Nicolas ten 9 366
Hove, Victor Van see VAN HOVE, VICTOR
Hovenden, Thomas 14 393, 804*; 31 603
Hovens Greve 30 391
Hovenweep National Monument 22 566
Hovhannavank' Monastery, Church of the Forerunner 2 435
Hovhannēs (fl 895-906) 9 733; 30 360
Hovhannēs III Imastaser, Katholikos, Bishop of Odzun (reg 717-20) 23 355
Høvikodden, Henie-Onstad Kunstsenter 14 229; 23 243, 244
Sonja Henies og Niels Onstads Stiftelser see Henie-Onstad Kunstsenter
Hoving, Viktor 11 111
Hoving, Walter 30 867
Hovingham Hall (N. Yorks) 5 907; 29 485
Hovnat'an, Naghash 14 804, 805
Hovnat'anian (family) 9 732
Hovnat'anian, Agafon 14 805
Hovnat'anian, Hakop (fl 18th cent.) 14 804
Hovnat'anian, Hakop (1806-81) 2 431; 12 326; 14 805
Hovnat'anian, Harut'un 14 804
Hovnat'anian, Hovnat'an 14 804
Hovnat'anian, Mkrtum 14 805
Hovsep'yan, Artashes 2 437
Hovvi, Church of the Shepherd 2 426

Howald, Ferdinand 8 708; 20 287, 422
Howard (i), Aletheia, Countess of Arundel 11 895; 14 807*
Howard, Catherine, Queen of England see CATHERINE HOWARD, Queen of England
Howard, Catherine Proctor, Countess of Effingham 8 26
Howard, Charles 31 607
Howard, Charles, 10th Duke of Norfolk (1720-86) 7 171
Howard, Charles, 11th Duke of Norfolk (1746-1815) 23 210
Howard, Charles, 2nd Baron Howard of Effingham 3 389; 10 349; 20 366; 30 318; 32 732
Howard (ii), Charles, 3rd Earl of Carlisle 14 807–8*
architecture 6 65; 14 257, 807; 31 858
decorative works 21 891
sculpture 5 827; 18 902; 23 253
silver 14 161
Howard, Constance 10 354
Howard, Ebenezer 12 144; 14 809*; 31 728
collaboration 24 185
works 11 797; 12 144, 145
Howard, Edward, 9th Duke of Norfolk 4 422, 758
Howard, Frances, Countess of Essex 23 408
Howard (ii), Frederick, 5th Earl of Carlisle 14 808*
architecture 6 66
collections 14 807; 19 587
paintings 5 63; 9 755; 10 365; 19 270; 32 774
pottery 31 308
silver 10 334; 30 361
Howard (ii), George James, 9th Earl of Carlisle 14 808–9*
collections 14 807
groups and movements 10 641
paintings 8 6, 121
pupils 23 102
Howard, Gerrard 11 426
Howard, Henry 14 810*
works 23 31; 28 908
Howard, Henry, 12th Earl of Suffolk 4 758
Howard, Henry, 1st Earl of Northampton 10 350; 22 897
Howard (ii), Henry, 4th Earl of Carlisle 14 808*
architecture 6 66
gems 12 266
paintings 5 598; 13 301
sculpture 14 807
Howard, Henry, 6th Duke of Norfolk 10 658
Howard, Henry Fitzalan, 1st Duke of Norfolk 23 247; 28 280
Howard (i), Henry Frederick, 3rd Earl of Arundel 23 208
Howard, Hugh 9 230; 14 435, 810*; 16 13
Howard (i), James, Lord Maltravers 14 807
Howard, John 7 666; 25 636
works 25 636
Howard, John G(eorge) 5 560; 14 810*
Howard, John Galen 18 664; 20 19; 25 737; 27 730
Howard, Ralph, Viscount Wicklow 27 356
Howard, Robert 31 607
Howard (i), Thomas, 14th Earl of Arundel see HOWARD (i), THOMAS, 2nd Earl of Arundel
Howard (i), Thomas, 1st Earl of Suffolk 8 45; 10 229
Howard (i), Thomas, 2nd Earl of Arundel 2 163; 10 204; 13 299; 14 805–7*, 806; 17 693; 19 583; 23 208; 24 300, 571–2
architecture 32 552
Howard (i), Thomas, 2nd Earl of Arundel—cont.
collections 5 847; 10 363, 368; 11 140; 13 605; 14 435, 810; 15 145; 19 582
drawings 9 229, 230; 17 633; 25 664; 27 270; 28 33; 33 612
engravings 32 699
etchings 14 684
gems 23 326
manuscripts 31 773
paintings 4 912; 5 764; 9 477, 483, 486; 14 755; 15 158; 16 767; 19 124, 644; 21 509; 23 208, 326; 29 800; 32 575
prints 18 745
sculpture 1 895; 8 884; 9 22; 10 658; 14 253; 23 22, 690; 26 348
sponsorship 14 683
Howard, Thomas, 3rd Viscount Howard of Bindon 6 128
Howard, Thomas, 8th Duke of Norfolk (d 1732) 25 759
Howard, William 14 810
Howard (i), William, Viscount Stafford 14 807
Howard Grace Cup 10 325, 326
Howard & Sons 6 484
Howard University see under WASHINGTON (DC)
Howatson 4 303
Howbridge (Essex), White Hall 10 284
How Caple (Hereford & Worcs), SS Andrew and Mary 28 295
Howden (N. Humberside)
Abbey 13 82
St Peter's 31 271
Howe, Frank Maynard 10 683; 31 863
Howe, George 11 849; 14 811*
collaboration 3 177; 17 723; 19 235; 24 598; 28 833; 29 718; 31 597
groups and movements 15 885, 886
patrons and collectors 20 142
teachers 18 664
works 22 365
Howe, James 25 402
Howe, Lois Lilley 20 282
Howe, Oscar 14 811–12*; 22 595, 596
patrons and collectors 22 677
pupils 28 142
works 14 811
Howe, Richard Curzon, 1st Earl see CURZON, RICHARD, 1st Earl Howe
Howe, Ruperta 29 800
Howe, Timothy 22 240
Howe & Lescaze 18 186; 19 235
Howell, Alfred 5 570
Howell, C. A. 27 187
Howell, Charles Henry 33 565
Howell, William Gough 14 812; 20 475; 30 391
Howell Killick Partridge & Amis 4 790; 14 812*; 23 689
Howells, John Mead 14 812–13*
collaboration 14 735; 28 833; 31 595
competitions 7 669
groups and movements 13 204
works 7 669; 14 735; 30 507
Howells and Stokes 7 619
works 7 619
Howie, Lawrence H. 2 760
Howitt, Alfred 1 67
Howitt, Arthur 17 581
Howitt, T. Cecil 23 258; 25 403
Howland, William Ford 5 573
Howlett, Bartholomew 14 813*
Howlett, Robert 11 796; 14 813*
Howlett, Victoria 2 762
Howley, William, Archbishop of Canterbury 4 170
Howling Wolf 14 814*
works 14 814
Howson, Peter 12 777
Howzer, Hans Jacob, II 14 814
Howzer, Wolfgang 10 328, 329; 14 814–15*
Hoy 4 81
Hoya Missal see under MISSALS→ individual manuscripts
Hoyau, Germain 33 357
Hoyberger, Gotthard see HAYBERGER, GOTTHARD
Hoyeck, Youssef 14 815*; 19 8
Høyen, N(iels) L(auritz Andreas) 8 735, 760; 14 815*; 18 178
works 8 761
Høyer, Bizzie 4 62; 10 899
Høyer, Cornelius 8 734; 14 815*; 21 643
Hoyer, David 32 765
Hoyland, John 1 81; 14 816*; 21 897; 28 804
Høylandet Church 23 240
Hoyle, Alexander 8 111
Hoyle, Doran & Berry 8 111
Hoyle, Rafael Larco see LARCO HOYLE, RAFAEL
Hoym, Comte D' see D'HOYM, Comte
Hoym, Karl, Graf(1739-1807) 18 741
Hoym, Karl-Heinrich, Graf von 32 706
Hoyningen-Huene, George 14 816*
Hoyo, Pedro de 10 498
Hoyos, Ana Mercedes 7 610
Hoysala 3 688; 14 65, 816*
see also:
BITTIGA, Ruler
NARASIMHA I, Ruler
Hoyt, Charles B. 6 925; 7 156
Hoyt, Edward H. 33 135
Hoyte, J(ohn) (Barr) C(lark) 2 706; 14 817*; 23 58
Hoytema, Theo(door) van 14 817*
Hŏ Yu 14 744, 817*; 18 331
höyük 1 851
Hōzan see TAKAHASHI KUMAKICHI
Hōzan Tankai 17 127
Hozen Eiraku see EIRAKU HOZEN
Hozen Konan see EIRAKU HOZEN
Hozier (family), d' 32 386
Hozo, Dževad 4 462
H(igh-) P(erformance) L(iquid) C(hromatography) see under TECHNICAL EXAMINATION → types
HPP see HENTRICH-PETSCHNIGG & PARTNER
Hrabanus Maurus, Abbot see RABANUS MAURUS, Abbot
Hrabnicki, Florian 3 526
Hradec (family) 8 422; 20 89
Hradec, Adam 8 395
Hradec, Adam, II 14 818*
Hradec, Jáchym 14 817–18*
Hradec, Zachariáš of see ZACHARIÁŠ OF HRADEC
Hradec Králové 12 834
architecture 8 376
Bishop's Residence 8 412
Cathedral 4 783; 8 376
church 8 378
iron 8 416
Museum of Applied Art 8 424
pewter 8 415
Town Museum 8 401; 18 405
Hradisko Monastery 8 386
Hradiště see TÁBOR
Hranush, Queen (fl 1063) 2 444
Hrastnik, Glass Museum 28 863
Hrastovec Castle 28 859
Hrastovlje, Holy Trinity church 28 858, 858
Hrbek, Marek 8 413
H. & R. Daniel 10 310
Hrdlička, Aleš 24 367
Hrdlicka, Alfred 2 804; 12 469; 14 818*
Hrdlička Museum of Anthropology see under PRAGUE → Charles University
Hrebeljanovich, Lazar I, Prince of Serbia see LAZAR I, Prince of Serbia
Hrelyu see KHRELYU
Hriňová glassworks 28 856
Hrodbert, Bishop of Worms 27 659
Hrodek, Karel 23 271
Hŕomkla Monastery 2 430; 31 177
Hronsky Svaty Benadik 26 711
Hrozný, Bedřich 1 893
Hrube, Alexander 3 531
Hrubý, Josef 8 251; 25 430
Hrusice, St Wenceslas 26 637
Hrymfaxe 24 451
Hryncewicz, Ludwik 19 497; 32 579
Hryniewiecki, Jerzy 14 818–19*; 25 142; 32 873
Hryshchenko, Oleksa 14 819*
Hrzán z Harasova, Jan Adam 25 257
H.S., Master 12 420; 20 797*
Hsalè 5 242
Hsaya Sa 5 246
Hsia Kuei see XIA GUI
Hsi-an see XI'AN
Hsia Nai see XIA NAI
Hsiang Chün see XIANG JUN
Hsiang K'ai see XIANG KAI
Hsiang Mo-lin see XIANG MOLIN
Hsiang Sheng-mo see XIANG SHENGMO
Hsiang Yü see XIANG YU
Hsiang Yüan-pien see XIANG YUANBIAN
Hsiao Chao see XAO ZHAO
Hsiao Ch'en see XAO CHEN
Hsiao Ch'in 30 249
Hsiao Chün-hsien see XIAO JUNXIAN
Hsiao Feng see XIAO FENG
Hsiao Hsien see XIAO XIAN
Hsiao I see YUANDI, Emperor (Liang; reg AD 552-5)
Hsiao Shu-fang see XIAO SHUFANG
Hsiao-tsung, Emperor (Sung; reg 1163-90) see XIAOZONG, Emperor
Hsiao-wen-ti, Emperor (Wei; AD 471-99) see XIAOWENDI, Emperor
Hsiao Yün-ts'ung see XIAO YUNCONG
Hsia period see under CHINA → periods
Hsia Shen see XIA SHEN
Hsia Wen-yen see XIA WENYAN
Hsia Yang 30 249
Hsieh, Empress see XIE, Empress
Hsieh Chih-liu see XIE ZHILIU
Hsieh Ho see XIE HE
Hsieh Huan see XIE HUAN
Hsieh Kung-ch'iao see XIE GONGQIAO
Hsieh Ling-yün see XIE LINGYUN
Hsieh Pin see XIE BIN
Hsieh Sun see XIE SUN
Hsien-yang see XIANYANG
Hsien-yü Shu see XIANYU SHU
Hsi-hsüan, Marquis see XIXUAN, Marquis
Hsi Kang see XI GANG
Hsi K'ang see XI KANG
Hsinbyushin, King of Burma (reg 1763-76) 25 889
Hsin-cheng see XINZHENG
Hsing T'ung see XING TONG
Hsin-yang see XINYANG
Hsin Yüeh see TŌKŌ SHIN'ETSU
Hsüan-te emperor (Ming; reg 1426-35) see XUANDE emperor
Hsüan-ti, Emperor (Han; reg 74-49 BC) see XUANDI emperor
Hsüan-tsang see XUANZANG
Hsüan-tsung, Emperor (T'ang, reg 712-56) see XUANZONG, Emperor (Tang, reg 712-56)
Hsüan-t'ung emperor (Ch'ing; reg 1909-11) see PU YI
Hsüan-wu-ti, Emperor (Wei; reg AD 500-505) see XUANWUDI, Emperor
Hsü Chen-ch'ing see XU ZHENQING
Hsü Chien-kuo see XU JIANGUO
Hsüeh Chi see XUE JI
Hsüeh Ching-shih see XUE JINGSHI
Hsüeh Shang-kung see XUE SHANGGONG
Hsüeh Su-su see XUE SUSU
Hsüeh Yao see XUE YAO
Hsü Hsi see XU XI
Hsü Ku see XU GU
Hsün-tzu see Xunzi
Hsü Pang-ta see XU BANGDA
Hsü Pei-hung see XU BEIHONG
Hsü Ping-fang see XU BINGFANG
Hsü Shen see XU SHEN
Hsü Shih-tai see XU SHITAI
Hsü Su-pai see XU SUBAI
Hsü Ta see XU DA
Hsü Tao-ning see XU DAONING
Hsü Wei see XU WEI
Hsü-yün see XUYUN
hu see under VESSELS→ types
Hu, Mary Lee 31 651
Hua (family) 33 439
Huaca de la Centinela 29 174
Huaca del Dragón 29 168
reliefs 29 168
Huaca del Loro 14 820*; 22 706; 29 156
headdresses 28 651
Huaca de los Reyes 6 522, 523; 8 272; 29 168, 213, 829
Huaca El Corte 3 365; 29 174
Huaca La Florida 30 447
Huaca La Mayanga 3 365
Huaca Las Ventanas 3 363, 365; 28 651
Huacaloma 6 523
Huaca Lucia, Temple of Columns 3 364
Huaca Oro 3 365
pyramid 3 364
Huaca Pintada 29 173
Huaca Prieta 29 156, 158, 219
architecture 29 158
gourds 13 229; 29 159, 159
snuff trays 29 133
textiles 23 564; 29 159, 180
Huaca Rejada 29 215
Huaca Rodillona 28 652
Hua Feng 7 83
Hua Hin, Railway Hotel 30 590
Huahine 28 921
Huai, Leonard Charles see LYE, LEN
Huai-jen see HAIREN
Huaikui-Varbanova, Sun 31 905
Huairen 6 745
Huaisu 5 36; 6 747; 14 820*
patrons and collectors 6 772
works 6 747, 747
Huaiyin 6 788
Huaiyuan 7 10
huali 7 31
Huamán, Venancio Shinki see SHINKI HUAMÁN VENANCIO
Huamanga see AYACUCHO
Huambo Church 2 86
Huancané 24 498, 512
Huand Hatun see under KAYSERI
Huang (family) 7 119
Huangbao zhen see TONGCHUAN
Huang Binhong 6 768; 14 820–21*; 28 553
groups and movements 2 96; 6 774

Huang Binhong—cont.
 works 14 *821*
Huangcai *see under* NINGXIANG
Huang Ch'üan *see* HUANG QUAN
Huang Chucai 6 803
Huang Chün-pi 14 822*; 30 249
Huang Chü-pao *see* HUANG JUBAO
Huang Ch'u-ts'ai *see* HUANG CHUCAI
Huang Daozhou 6 544
Huang Deshi 7 119
Huang Ding 23 581
Huangfu Fang 33 69
Huang Gongwang 6 773, 785, 790, 819; 14 822–3*; 23 582
 collaboration 23 167
 groups and movements 25 73; 29 244; 32 845
 patrons and collectors 32 838; 33 427
 works 6 760, 790, *819*; 14 *822*, *823*; 17 189; 33 570
 writings 6 798
Huang Hsiu-fu *see* HUANG XIUFU
huang huali 7 31, *38*, *39*, *40*, 141, *141*
Huang I *see* HUANG YI
Huang I-feng *see* HUANG YIFENG
Huang Jubao 7 148
Huang Junbi *see* HUANG CHÜN-PI
Huang Kung-wang *see* HUANG GONGWANG
Huangliangmeng, Lu Sheng Shrine 28 638
Huang of the South *see* HUANG BINHONG
Huang Pin-hung *see* HUANG BINHONG
Huang Quan 6 799; 7 148; 14 823–4*
Huang Renkui *see* YANK WONG
Huang Shen 6 811; 14 824–5*; 33 497
 works 14 *825*
Huang Sheng 6 700; 7 26, 77
Huang Tao-chou *see* HUANG DAOZHOU
Huang Te-shih *see* HUANG DESHI
Huang Thanh 6 424, *424*
Huang Ting *see* HUANG DING
Huang T'ing-chien *see* HUANG TINGJIAN
Huang Tingjian 6 748, 749, 750, 752, 771, 818; 14 825*
 patrons and collectors 6 772
 works 6 *749*, 823; 17 231
Huang Xiufu 6 822
Huang Yi 7 130
Huang Yifeng 7 119
Huang Ying-tsu *see* HUANG YINGZU
Huang Yingzu 7 119
Huang Yongyu 14 825–6*
 works 14 *826*
Huangyueling (Jiangpu), tomb of Zhang Tongzhi 7 26
Huang Zhu 26 215
Huantaiji 6 684, 704
Huánuco Pampa 14 826–7*; 15 *161*; 29 *156*, 162, 166, 167
 temple 29 166
Huari 14 827–9*
 Chejo Wasi 14 *827*
Huaricoto 30 447
Huari culture 14 820, 827, 828–9; 21 749; 23 565; 29 *156*, 161
 architecture 14 828*; 29 161
 palaces 23 826
 pottery 14 828–9*
 sculpture 14 829*; 29 171
 shells 29 218
 tapestries 29 *181*
 textiles 14 829*; 29 180
 tunics 29 *181*
Huari Forger 29 223
Huarmey 29 214
Huaro 24 *498*
Huarochiri Narrative 29 131, 132
Huarpa 29 177
Huart, Adrien 13 644
Huart, Clément 16 559
Huart, Louis 24 605
Huart, Marguerite
huaru 7 130
Huastec 14 829–31*; 21 177, 200, 217
 architecture 14 829
 bone-carvings 21 248
 earrings 14 831
 ear-spools 21 260
 figurines 14 830
 pectoral ornaments 14 831
 pendants (jewellery) 21 260
 pottery 14 831; 21 238
 pyramids 25 764
 sandstone 14 *830*, 830
 sculpture 14 *830*, 830–31; 21 188, 222*
 seals 21 *258*
 shells 14 831; 21 260
 stelae 29 620
 terracotta 14 830–31
 wall paintings 14 831; 21 227
Huating school 33 652
Huaud (family) 7 444; 30 148
Huaud, Ami(cus) 12 457
Huaud, Jean-Pierre 12 457
Huaxtepac 12 71
Hua Yan 6 763; 14 *831*, 831–2*; 33 497
Huayan Buddhism *see under* BUDDHISM → sects
Hua Yen *see* HUA YAN
Huaytara 29 167; 30 447
Hubáček, Karel 8 381; 14 832*
Hubacher, Carl 29 602, 603; 30 *128*; 33 735
Hubacher, Hermann 30 138; 33 737
Huban, István Dési *see* DÉSI HUBAR, ISTVÁN
Hubard Profile Gallery 12 633
Hubbard, Elbert 2 572; 14 832*; 31 631, 653
Hubbard, Eric Hesketh 10 212
Hubbard Amphora 8 347
Hubbell, Benjamin S. 7 429; 22 365
 works 7 *429*
Hubbell, J. Lorenzo 22 626, 676
Hubbo Church 13 120
Hubbock, A. B. 20 168
 works 20 *168*
Hubbuch, Karl 14 832–3*; 17 818; 22 923
Hübel, Mert 4 832
Huber (family) 12 277
Huber, Anton 14 834*
Huber, Charles 2 254; 27 877
Huber, Conrad 18 497
Huber, Hans 14 835
Huber, Hermann 12 649
Huber, Hunt & Nichols 7 327
Huber, Jakob Wilhelm 12 606
Huber, Jean 14 833–4*; 30 125
 patrons and collectors 13 663; 31 363
 pupils 14 834
 works 28 714, *714*; 30 132
Huber, Jean-Daniel 14 833, 834*; 31 363
Huber, Jenő 13 888
Huber, Johann Kaspar 14 303; 21 735
Huber, Johann-Rudolf 14 834–5*; 28 72
Huber, Jörg 14 835*; 28 58; 29 727
Huber, Joseph Daniel 32 436
Huber, József 14 895
Huber, Max 1 666
Huber, Michael 2 792; 14 835*
Huber, Patriz 2 566; 8 531; 12 416, 450
Huber, Rudolf Carl 29 763
Huber, Stephan 12 369
Huber, Wolfgang 14 835–7*; 22 302
 groups and movements 2 792; 8 513; 18 705; 26 189
 pupils 32 400
 works 9 221; 11 455; 12 387, *387*; 14 *836*, *837*; 27 256; 33 354
Hubert, Edgar 23 333
Hubert, Jean 4 827
Hubert, Josef 28 850
Hubert, Pierre Alain 28 829
Hubert, Pirrson & Company 23 41
Huberti, Edouard (-Jules-Joseph) 3 562; 4 529; 14 838*; 32 380
Huberti, Jacques 3 600
Hubert Walter, Archbishop of Canterbury 10 141; 26 688
Hubert Walter chalice 16 30
Hubley Manufacturing Co. 31 257
Hübner, Bartholomäus 20 915
Hübner, Emil 14 864
Hübner, Heinrich 5 924
Hübner, (Rudolph) Julius (Benno) 9 239, 460; 12 394; 14 838–9*
Hübner, Karl Wilhelm 9 460
Hübner, Paul 8 413; 25 22
Hübner, Philipp Rudolf 12 494
Hübner, Ulrich 5 924
Hübsch, (Gottleib) Heinrich (Christian) 14 839–40*
 groups and movements 9 704; 27 334
 patrons and collectors 17 817
 pupils 29 491; 33 30
 teachers 33 40
 works 12 376; 14 *840*; 17 817; 22 363; 27 334–5; 30 503
Huby, Marmaduke, Abbot of Fountains 7 351; 11 349
Huc, Evariste Régis 13 812
Hu Cao 12 899; 22 460
Huchenggang (Anxiang) 6 878
Hu Cheng-yen *see* HU ZHENGYAN
Huchon de Boulone 5 207
Huchtenburgh, Jan van 3 762; 11 396; 21 415; 28 18; 32 592
huckaback-diaper 19 415
Huckel, John H. 22 676
al-Hudaydah 33 519
Huddersfield Railway Station (W. Yorks) 25 268
Hudeček, Antonín 8 393; 14 840–41*
Hudeček, František 2 546; 8 394
Hudnut, Joseph (Fairman) 14 841*
Hudson, Edward 19 819
Hudson, H. 24 380
Hudson, James 22 102
Hudson, John 3 737
Hudson, Julian 1 440
Hudson, Robert 31 609, 615, 640
Hudson, S. G. 31 241
Hudson, Thomas (1701-99) 14 841–2*
 assistants 1 504, 505
 collaboration 33 377
 methods 9 211
 patrons and collectors 33 693
 personal collection 25 631; 26 346
 pupils 17 475; 22 151; 24 366, 548; 26 271; 31 139; 33 217, 412
 teachers 26 345
 works 10 249; 11 *425*; 14 *842*
Hudson, Tom (*b* 1922) 14 816
Hudson, Tony 19 242
Hudson River school 9 391; 14 843–4*; 17 899; 18 715; 19 791; 26 742; 29 891; 31 602
 collections 7 379, 840
 members
  Casilear, John William 5 917
  Church, Frederick Edwin 7 284
  Colman, Samuel (ii) (1832-1920) 7 577
Hudson River school members—cont.
  Durand, Asher B(rown) 9 418
  Fisher, Alvan 11 138
  Gifford, Sanford Robinson 12 606
  Gignoux, Régis-François 12 608
  Johnson, David 17 616
  Shattuck, Aaron Draper 28 559
  Wall, William Guy 32 799
 works 4 *44*; 9 *419*; 15 828; 18 IV1; 31 *602*
Hudson's Bay Company 22 546, 668; 32 413
Hudud al-'Alam 21 885
Hue 6 *418*; 14 844–5*; 29 *225*; 32 *468*, *469*
 Archaeological Museum 29 240
 Citadel 6 426; 14 844, *844*
 Imperial City 32 476
 kilns 32 484
 Royal Palace 23 823
 School of Fine Arts 32 483, 492
 tomb of Gia Long 32 475
 tomb of Khai Dinh 32 476
 tomb of Minh Mang 32 475
 tomb of Thieu Tri 32 476
 tomb of Tu Duc 32 *475*, 476
 tombs 32 475–6
 urban planning 32 477
Huë, Jean-François 11 666; 14 845*; 32 333, 334
Hué, Michael 11 426
Hueber, Andrä (*fl c.* 1750-63) 2 783; 28 776
Hueber, Andree (*fl* 1554-89) 33 274
Hueber, Josef 1 160; 13 330; 14 260
Huebler, Douglas 7 685, 686
Huebner, Georg 31 634
Huebner, Johann Cristoph 12 461
Hue de Boulogne 4 841, 842; 5 210
Huejotzingo
 Franciscan Monastery 21 373, 375, 383, *383*
 S Miguel 21 375
Huejutla 14 829
Huelgas, Las *see* LAS HUELGAS
Huelsen, Christian 2 833
Huelsenbeck, Richard 3 113; 14 845*; 24 428
 groups and movements 3 801; 8 433, 434, 436, 437, 438; 24 405; 31 503
 productions 26 357
 works 2 488; 24 405
Huelva 24 100
 Monastery of La Rábida 22 255
Huene, Stephan von 29 98
Huerfanas, Niñas 8 858
Huerta, Juan de la *see* JUAN DE LA HUERTA
Huerta, Moises de 29 295
Huerta Rendón, F. 7 206
Huertas, Luis de 25 700
Hues, Johann 14 103
Huesca 26 642
 Cathedral of Roda d'Isábena 26 249; 29 310, 335
 Church of Loreto 29 268
 metalwork 29 335
 sculpture 13 106; 26 642
 S Pedro el Viejo 26 607
 textiles 16 436
 University 31 674
Huet, Alexandre 7 190
Huet, Christophe 14 845–6*
 collaboration 28 776
 reproductive prints by others 11 81
 works 7 167, 168; 14 791; 18 614; 28 *776*
Huet, François 14 845
Huet, Jean-Baptiste (-Marie), I 14 845, 846*
 collaboration 14 791; 23 331
 patrons and collectors 5 530
Huet, Jean-Baptiste (-Marie), I—cont.
 reproductive prints by others 4 331; 8 703
 works 2 105; 3 461; 11 649; 14 *846*
Huet, Jean-Baptiste, II (*b* 1772) 14 845
Huet, Michael
 works 1 *336*, *337*
Huet, Nicolas, I (*b* 1718) 14 845, 846
Huet, Nicolas, II (*b* 1788) 14 845
Huet, Paul 14 847–8*
 groups and movements 26 500, 741
 patrons and collectors 4 306
 teachers 13 692
 works 7 433, 434; 14 *847*; 19 487
Huet, René-Paul (*b* 1844) 14 848; 25 752
Huetter, Sigmund 20 678
Huet-Villiers, François 4 555
Huexotla 21 208
Huf, Fritz 2 488
Huffel, Albert Van *see* VAN HUFFEL, ALBERT
al-Hufuf 27 875; 32 316
 fortifications 21 588
 Qasr 'Abid 21 588
 Qasr Ibrahim 21 588
Hugé, Emile 2 396
Hugenois, Lieven 3 609
Hugford, Enrico 14 848; 28 28
Hugford, Ignazio Enrico 7 897; 14 848*
 illustrated writings 13 625
 paintings 13 303
 pupils 3 308; 7 339
Huggins, William John 14 849*
Huggler, Arnold 30 138
Hugh, Bishop of Grenoble 5 893
Hugh, Dean 7 352
Hugh, Saint 7 474; 21 840
Hugh I, Earl of Chester 6 561
Hugh II, Duke of Burgundy (*reg* 1102-43) 2 840
Hugh II, King of Cyprus (*reg* 1253-67) 8 361
Hugh III, Duke of Burgundy (*reg* 1162-92) 8 888
Hugh IV, King of Cyprus (*reg* 1324-59) 3 638; 8 362, 363; 16 383
Hughan, Harold 2 761
Hugh Capet, King of France (*reg* 987-96) 11 653
Hugh de Balsham 5 510
Hugh de Glazinis, Abbot of Marseille 20 475
Hugh de Sainte-Marie 27 535
Hughes, Arthur 14 849–50*
 groups and movements 10 253; 25 554, 555
 patrons and collectors 25 41
 pupils 13 1
 works 11 434; 12 295; 14 *850*
Hughes, George R. 10 83
Hughes, Griffith 5 750
Hughes, H. R. 22 809
Hughes, Hugh 32 785, 791
 works 32 *785*
Hughes, John (1865-1941) 14 850*; 16 21; 30 61
Hughes, John (1903-77) 19 506
Hughes, Richard (Henry) 14 850–51*; 22 387
Hughes, Robert (1811-92) 32 785
Hughes, Robert Ball 32 753
Hughes, Roger 31 864
Hughes, Shirley 4 368
Hughes, Thomas 14 850
Hughes, Trajan 14 851*
Hughes de Comminelles 32 384
Hughes-Stanton, Blair 4 366
Hugh of Cluny, Saint 3 871; 7 473; 24 103; 26 583
Hugh of Fouiloy
 works 7 *348*

Hugh of Le Puiset, Bishop of Durham 14 851*; 26 590
architecture 6 50, 407; 9 448, 450; 14 75; 26 615
metalwork 26 688
Hugh of St Albans 13 147; 25 15
Hugh of St Victor 24 269; 29 500; 32 416
Hughtenburgh, Jan van 3 759; 4 521
Hügin, Karl 33 737
Hugli 7 678
Hugnet, Georges 14 271, 852*; 30 21
Hugo, Charles (-Victor) 14 853*; 31 792
Hugo, François 14 853
Hugo, Herman 10 175
Hugo, Ian 10 397
Hugo, Jean 3 120; 7 508
Hugo, Master 14 853–4*; 20 331
works 5 289; 9 153; 10 244, 244; 26 652, 659, 672, 672, 688
Hugo, Valentine 30 20, 21
Hugo, Victor (-Marie) 5 303; 14 852–3*
collaboration 25 847
groups and movements 26 739
productions 4 529; 30 385
sponsorship 4 749
works 2 319
illustrated 4 529, 816; 11 156, 799; 17 605; 18 865; 21 462; 26 481; 29 609; 30 353; 31 213
Hugo de Walcourt see HUGO D'OIGNIES
Hugo d'Oignies 14 854*
works 3 593; 13 159, 159; 26 683
Hu Gongshou 17 199
Hugo Pictor 26 659, 669
Hugo van der Goes see Goes, HUGO VAN DER
Hu Guangyu 6 866
Hugué, Manuel Martínez see MANOLO
Huguenots 14 854–7*
Hugues, Pierre-François, Baron d'Hancarville see HANCARVILLE, PIERRE-FRANÇOIS HUGUES, Baron d'
Hugues de Thil, Lord of Saint-Beury see SAINT-BEURY, HUGUES DE THIL, Lord of
Hugues d'Orgues, Archbishop of Rouen 11 654; 27 253
Huguet 14 857*
patrons and collectors 2 870, 871
works 3 362, 362, 363; 13 71, 101; 25 290
Huguet, François
works 26 205
Huguet, Jaume 3 218; 14 857–8*; 29 276
collaboration 11 483
pupils 20 812; 27 818
works 11 480, 482; 14 858
Huguet, Philippe-Jean-Baptist 11 621
Huguet, Pierre (fl late 18th cent.) 5 584, 585
Huguet, Pierre (fl 1887-97) 11 759
Huguetan, Adriana Margareta 14 39; 20 459
Hugur og hönd 24 452
Huhn, Carl (Theodor) see HŪNS, KĀRLIS (TEODORS)
Hui 6 616
Huichong 6 783
Hui-ch'ung see HUICHONG
Huidobro, Borja 2 699, 700; 6 534; 7 343
collaboration 24 132
works 6 534
Huidobro, Carlos García see GARCÍA HUIDOBRO, CARLOS
Huidobro, Vicente 8 438; 13 671
Huie, Albert 14 858*; 16 884
Huijazoo 21 230, 231
Huiji see MUNJONG
Huillard, Paul 29 899
Huilliot, Pierre-Nicolas 26 386
Huineng 5 109
Hŭi-on see CHO SOK
Hui school see ANHUI SCHOOL OF SEAL CARVERS
Hui Sheng 6 320; 28 637
Huisman, Nele 30 213
Huismans, Sipke 8 506
Huis Plantin-Moretus see ANTWERP → museums → Plantin-Moretus Museum
Huis ter Heide 21 781
Huitoto 7 602; 29 132
Hui-tsung, Emperor (Sung; reg 1101-25) see HUIZONG, Emperor
Huitzilapa 21 217
Huitzilopochco 21 374
Hui xian 7 56, 97
see also GUWEI CUN; LIULIGE
Huiyuan 6 796
Huizar, Pedro 31 589
Huizhou 6 661, 687; 7 142, 151
Huizinga, Johan 13 155; 14 858–9*; 28 917
Huizinge Church 22 819
Huizong, Emperor (Song; reg 1101-25) 5 389; 6 618, 636; 7 152; 12 52; 14 859–60*; 29 67
albums 1 581
art policies 6 816
attributions 18 559
bronzes 6 865
ceramics 6 892
coins 7 72, 73
collections 6 772
education (art) 7 148; 21 418
gardens 12 87
horn 7 124
jade 7 8
paintings 6 631, 800, 804, 817, 822; 9 140; 14 135; 17 697; 33 649
writings 13 738
Hu Kaiwen 7 93
Huki Atan, Carlos 9 676
Huki Atan, Joel 9 676
Huki Atan, Pedro 9 676
Hukin & Heath 4 88; 9 295
Huki Tekena, Melchor 9 676
Hu Kuang-yü see HU GUANGYU
Hulagu, Khan (reg 1256-65) (Ilkhanid) 15 134; 16 193; 20 370; 30 470, 477
Hulaylan 15 920
Hulbeck, Charles R. see HUELSENBECK, RICHARD
Hulbuk 6 182, 233, 269; 14 860–61*; 30 252
governors' palace 14 860*
ivory-carvings 6 271
plaster 29 822
stucco 29 822
wall paintings 16 253
Huldschinsky, Oscar 4 209; 12 474
Hülegü see HULAGU, Khan
Hulewicz, Jerzy 25 108; 26 266
Hulin, Mme 14 861*
Hulin de Loo, Georges 3 619; 14 861*
Hulk, Abraham 32 592
Hull (Qué.; Canada) 23 630, 632
Canadian Museum of Civilization 5 575, 591, 592, 732; 23 632
National Museum of Canada see Canadian Museum of Civilization
Hull (Humberside; UK) 10 225; 14 861–3*
ceramics 14 863*
Congregational Chapel, Albion Street 23 194
docks 9 58
fountain 4 779
School of Art 30 506
town walls 4 778, 779
Hull (Humberside; UK)—cont.
University Collection of South-east Asian Art and Traditional Craftsmanship 29 240
Hull, Charles Wager 10 669
Hull, John 4 479; 31 647
Hull Dock Company 9 58
Hulle, Anselmus van 3 559; 25 221
Hull Grundy see GRUNDY, HULL
Hull Grundy Collection see under LONDON → museums → British Museum
Hullmandel, Charles Joseph 14 863*; 19 483; 25 615
methods 25 590
printmakers 4 614
works 4 362; 19 484, 484, 486; 25 623
writings 20 602
Hulme, Captain 19 802
Hulme, T(homas) E(rnest) 14 863–4*; 26 49; 32 700
Hulne Monastery 5 778
Hulot, Guillame 3 798; 14 651
Hulot, L.-J. 1 14
Huls, Robert 7 708
Huls, Samuel van 5 326
Hülsemann, Johann Heinrich 12 412; 25 368
Hülsen, Christian 14 864*
Hulsen, Clara van 21 102
Hulsen, Esias van 14 865*; 21 151
Hülsenbeck (family) 18 574; 26 727; 27 339; 28 144
Hulsmann, Johann 10 464
Hulst
St Willibrordusbasiliek 13 62; 22 820
Stadhuis 22 822
Hulst, Cornelia Aletta van 2 25
Hulst, Jan Baptist van der 23 470
Hulst, Van 30 879
Hulswit, Jan 3 211
Hulswit, M. J. 15 770
Hultén, C(arl) O(tto) 14 865*
groups and movements 15 142; 21 696; 30 81
Hulten, Pontus 30 81
Hültl, Dezső 14 865*
Hültz, Johann 10 407; 14 117, 865–6*; 17 695; 29 754
Hulusi, Mehmed 2 883; 23 695
Hulwith 33 538
Hum, Peter, Prince of 28 455
Humaco 25 698
Casa Roig 25 704
Humahuaca 2 393
church 2 398
Humahuaca culture 29 190
human figures 10 578; 14 869; 23 290–97; 25 276, 685; 32 635
Africa 1 321–2
Anatolia, ancient 2 504
Ancient Near East 2 504
Bamum 3 151, 152
Brazil 29 194
Britain 14 544, 544
Byzantine 9 622
Cambodia 5 484
Cameroon 3 151
Celtic 6 159
China 7 3, 104–6
Cycladic 8 315
Early Christian (c. AD 250-843) 9 622
Egypt, ancient 1 505; 9 801–4*, 853–4, 855, 856–8, 859, 865, 890, 891, 892
Etruscan 10 593–4, 624
Gambier Islands 31 403, 404
Greece, ancient 10 649; 13 415, 422, 428, 453, 492, 493, 505; 18 409; 19 853; 25 177
Helladic 14 335
Ife (kingdom of) 15 106
Indian subcontinent 15 206
Iran, ancient 15 917
Irian Jaya 16 43, 44, 46
Italy 10 593–4, 624
human figures—cont.
Japan 17 105–6, 158
Mali 21 479, 479
Marquesas Islands 20 463
Mesoamerica, Pre-Columbian 21 218
Mesopotamia 2 504; 21 296
Middle Niger cultures 21 479, 479*
Moche (culture) 29 176
Native North Americans 1 153
Nigeria 15 106, 106, 118; 23 180, 180–81
Olmec 21 218
Palau 23 834
Polynesian outliers 25 182
Prehistoric art 1 149, 150; 25 481, 490*
Rome, ancient 27 29
Scandinavia 32 520–21*
South America, Pre-Columbian 29 176, 194
Syria-Palestine 1 491–2, 492; 30 181
Viking 32 520–21*
Yoruba 15 106
see also FIGURINES; NUDE FIGURES
humanism 10 693; 12 110; 14 866–70*; 16 658; 26 183
Human Mask group 10 614
Humann, Christian 15 743
Humann, Karl 14 655; 22 731; 24 415; 25 573
human proportions see PROPORTIONS (HUMAN)
Humareda, Víctor 14 875*; 24 510, 515
Humartash 16 162
Humayun (Nizam Shahi) 15 637
Humayun, Emperor (reg 1530-40; 1555-6) (Mughal) 15 410, 578, 582
albums 15 547
architecture 8 675, 679; 15 362, 372; 22 258
dress 15 691
fortifications 24 540
manuscripts 16 272
paintings 1 25; 21 722
sculpture 1 502
tents 15 716
Humber Bank Pottery 14 863
Humber bridge 4 803
Humberstone, Samuel 14 875
Humberstone, Simon Thomas 5 581; 14 875
Humberstone, Thomas, sr (1776-1849) 14 875
Humberstone, Thomas, jr (1811-95) 14 875
Humberstone, Thomas Allan 14 875
Humbert, Abbot of Echternach 27 616
Humbert I, King of Italy see UMBERTO I, King of Italy
Humbert, Albert Jenkins 14 148; 20 869; 31 132
Humbert, Charles 4 59
Humbert, Ferdinand 4 127; 9 382
Humbert, Jean 14 42, 875
Humbert, Provost 19 862
Humbert de Superville, David Pierre 4 471; 14 875–6*; 28 474
Humberville, William 23 686
Humblot, Robert 11 302, 550
Humboldt, Alexander von 10 92; 21 262, 264; 29 220; 33 472
Humboldt, August von 18 183
Humboldt, Caroline von 14 876*
Humboldt, (Karl) Wilhelm von 12 476; 14 876*
Humboldt Celt 21 183
Humbracht, Claus 20 676
Humbret 7 578
Humcha 15 530
Bogara Basti 15 530
Panchakuta Basti 15 530
Hume, Abraham, 2nd Baronet 14 876–7*; 26 279
Hume, Bertram 10 462
Hume, David 10 401; 14 877–8*
works 1 172, 180; 4 601; 8 613
illustrated 7 413; 23 213, 452; 25 626
Hume, James 2 738; 4 108; 30 158
Humenné Castle 28 853
humeral veils 32 390*
humidifiers 7 734
humidistats 7 734
Humlebæk 8 720
Louisiana Museum 4 183; 7 806; 8 729, 758, 759; 22 366, 367; 28 315
Hummel, Daniel 13 726
Hummel, Erdmann 4 39; 12 393
Hummel, Johann Erdmann 12 274; 14 878*; 24 490
Humml, Theodor 4 616
Humor
church 25 344; 26 707; 31 101
iconostasis 26 718
Monastery 25 341; 26 717
humpen see under GLASSES → types
Humphrey, George 23 741
Humphrey, Hannah 8 217; 12 640; 28 25
Humphrey, H. Noel 19 485
Humphrey, Jack (Weldon) 14 878–9*
Humphrey, Tom 14 307
Humphrey, William (fl 1565) 10 339
Humphrey, William (c. 1740-c. 1810) 12 639
Humphreys, George 4 158
Humphreys, Hugh 32 791
Humphreys, Noel 26 234
Humphreys, Richard 10 851; 31 649
works 10 851
Humphreys, William, Art Gallery see under KIMBERLEY
Humphrey's Journal 24 432
Humphry, Ozias 3 373; 14 879*; 15 654; 19 157; 21 644; 31 233
Humplik, Josef 2 803
Humpolec 8 419
Hun 21 871
Huna see:
DHANYAVISHNU, Ruler
MATRVISHNU, Ruler
YASHODHARMAN, Ruler
Hunaeus, Hermann 14 142
Hunain, Georges 2 511
Hunde 19 74
Hundertpfundt, Anton 14 837
Hundertwasser, Friedensreich 2 797, 826, 831; 14 879*
works 28 300; 33 364
Hundrieser, (Franz Richard) Emil 12 505; 14 879*
Hundrieser, Hans 14 879
Hundsgruppe 11 812; 25 863
Hunedoara Castle 14 880*, 880, 884, 889; 26 705; 30 793
Hunefer 9 905
mummy 9 904
Hünerwadel, Marcus 30 144
Hunfalvi Chest 14 905, 905
Hung, Francisco 14 880*
Hungana 1 350, 403
Hungarian Academy of Sciences 14 882
Hungarian Activism see Activists
Hungarian green see MALACHITE
Hungarian Impressionists and Naturalists see MIENK
Hungarian National Association for Fine Arts 15 14
Hungary 14 881, 881–910*; 16 103
alder 14 905
altarpieces 14 894; 30 206
apartments 14 907

Hungary—cont.
 architecture 13 56; 14 883–91*; 26 594
 art history 14 888
 ash 14 905
 banks 14 889
 basins 15 6
 beds 14 905
 bookcases 14 903
 bottles 15 4
 bronze 14 897
 cast iron 15 9
 castles 5 82; 10 544
 cathedrals 10 545; 14 890
 ceramics 15 1–3*
 chairs 14 903, 904, 908
 chalices 13 161–2, 162, 170
 chapels 10 544
 chasubles 15 11
 cherry-wood 14 907
 chests 14 903, 905, 905
 choir-stalls 14 903, 904
 churches 14 886; 16 872; 29 75
 coats of arms 14 411, 418, IV
 coins 7 535; 14 411; 15 6
 collections 10 530; 15 15–17*
 colleges 14 887
 copper 15 9
 coral 10 II1; 15 11
 cotton 15 11
 crosiers 26 687
 crucifixes 15 1
 cupboards 14 906
 cups 15 6
 dealing 15 16
 dress 16 463
 dresses 10 II1; 15 11
 ebony 14 907
 education (art) 14 910; 15 5, 17–18*
 embroidery 10 II1; 15 11–12*, 11
 enamel 9 662; 13 161, 170; 15 6, 10, 10
 engravings 10 545; 14 899
 ewers 15 6
 faience (ii) (ceramics) 15 1, 2, 2
 filigree 13 162
 flagons 15 8
 flasks 15 3, 3
 floors 29 75
 fortresses 16 228
 furniture 14 902–10*
 gables 11 876
 gardens 18 854
 gates 15 9
 gems 9 662
 glass 15 3–5*, 3, 4
 glazes 15 2
 gold 9 662; 13 162; 15 5–8*, 10
 government buildings 14 888
 halls 14 904, 906
 heraldry 14 411*, IV
 heritage 28 172
 historicism 14 580
 houses 32 298
 inlay 14 905
 interior decoration 14 902–10*, 906, 909
 iron 15 9
 jewellery 15 10
 lace 15 12*
 larch-wood 14 903
 libraries 15 19*
 lime 14 905
 limestone 5 86
 lime-wood 14 903, 903
 linen 15 12
 mahogany 14 907
 maple 14 905
 maps 10 472
 marble 14 895
 marks 15 5, 8
 marquetry 14 904
 metal 15 11, 12
 metalwork 13 161–2*; 15 5–9*; 26 687, 687
 monuments 31 787
 museums 15 16–17*
 objects of vertu 15 10–11*
Hungary—cont.
 painting 10 892; 14 898–900*, 901
  allegorical 8 780
  Expressionism 8 806
  genre 30 209
  Great Plains painting 13 332–3*; 22 433; 31 174
  history 3 703; 15 13; 30 205
  religious 14 898
  watercolours 31 541
  19th cent. 20 42
  20th cent. 8 226; 14 902
 passementerie 15 12*
 patronage 15 13, 15*
 pattern books 14 888
 pearls 9 662; 15 12
 pendants (jewellery) 15 10, 10
 periodicals 24 440–41*
 pewter 15 8
 photoarchives 15 19*
 pine 14 903, 905
 pitchers 15 3
 porcelain 15 2
 portraits 14 900; 15 13; 25 246; 26 419
 posters 25 348
 regalia 15 11
 sculpture 14 891*, 893–7*
  bronze 14 897
  Gothic 14 892, 893
  marble 14 895
  relief 24 314
  Romanesque 26 636, 638*
  stone 26 638*
  wood 14 892
  15th cent. 5 86
 shields 14 411
 silk 15 11, 12
 silver 15 5–8*, 11
 silver-gilt 15 3, 6, 11
 squares (town) 14 890
 stained glass 12 839
 stone 26 638*
 stonewares 15 2
 stoves 14 904
 sycamore 14 903, 907
 synagogues 17 544, 547
 tables 14 903, 907
 tapestries 15 12*
 textiles 14 904; 15 11–12*
 threads 15 11, 11, 12
 tiles 5 85; 16 422
 vases 15 2
 velvet 10 II1; 15 11, 12
 walnut 14 903, 905, 907
 wood 14 892
 wrought iron 15 9, 9
Hungbŏp Temple 29 869
Hung-chih, Emperor (Ming; reg 1488-1505) see HONGZHI, Emperor
Hŭngdŏk, King (reg 826-36) 18 298
Hŭngdŏk Temple 18 356
Hunger, Christoph Conrad 12 433; 27 411; 30 97; 32 398, 449
Hŭngguk Temple 18 307
Hung-i see HONGYI
Hung-i Kamalvand 10 171
Hung-i Nauruzi 1 849; 10 171; 24 217, 218
Hung-i Yar Alivand 10 172
Hung-jen see HONGREN
Hung Thanh 6 418
Hung-wu, Emperor (Ming; 1368-98) see HONGWU, Emperor
Huni (reg c. 2600-c. 2575 BC) 2 296; 9 776; 20 117, 863; 25 762
Hunjirō, Sakamoto 23 141
Hunkuyi
 wall decorations 14 232
Hunn, Johann C. 12 453
Hunneman, William C. 4 481; 31 653
Hunold, Friedemann 23 412
Hunov, John 8 759
Huns 6 188, 188; 21 500, 501
Hūns, Kārlis (Teodors) 15 19*; 18 852
Hünsdorf 19 826
Hunstanton School (Norfolk) 5 56; 10 242; 28 158, 889
Hunt, Abbot of Bristol 4 825
Hunt, Alfred William 7 647; 15 23–4*
Hunt, Andrew 15 23
Hunt, Arthur 23 692
Hunt, Gary 23 73
Hunt, Gertrude 16 36
Hunt, Henry 2 395
Hunt, Jarvis 17 799
Hunt, John (fl before 1978) 16 36
Hunt, John Horbury (1838-1904) 2 740; 4 108; 15 24*
Hunt, John S. (fl 1822) 27 336; 29 723
Hunt, Kay 10 879
Hunt, Leigh 23 701
Hunt, Myron 6 578; 19 319; 25 446
Hunt, Richard (Howard) 1 444, 445; 6 576; 15 24*
Hunt, Richard Howland 15 23; 23 40
Hunt, Richard Morris 5 274; 6 513; 15 20–23*; 31 593, 622
 groups and movements 7 619; 25 806; 26 190
 patrons and collectors 31 870
 pupils 11 848; 31 862; 32 859
 staff 25 327; 27 216
 works 2 216; 3 290; 6 573; 10 683; 15 22; 20 869; 23 32, 33, 39, 40, 41, 341; 28 831; 29 653; 31 593, 622
Hunt, Steven 33 401
Hunt, Sumner P. 33 452
Hunt, Tony (b 1942; museum official) 22 589; 32 414
Hunt, Tony (fl 1984; engineer) 14 521
Hunt, William 20 589
Hunt, William Henry 15 24*
 patrons and collectors 7 647; 11 331; 12 638; 21 901
 reproductive prints by others 11 362
 teachers 31 909
 works 10 251, 253; 11 229
Hunt, William Holman 8 828; 9 766; 15 24–8*; 19 588; 23 379
 dealers 1 453; 12 30; 26 233
 dress 9 289
 frames 11 375
 groups and movements 10 253; 21 602; 23 503, 504; 25 554, 555, 556; 26 56; 27 185
 patrons and collectors 9 757; 10 755; 19 270; 25 41; 33 251
 pupils 20 493
 reproductive prints by others 12 30; 28 748; 29 486
 works 2 107; 5 658; 7 226, 647; 11 433, 433, 434, 435; 12 295; 15 25, 27; 28 664
Hunt, William Morris 15 19–20*
 personal collection 28 560
 pupils 11 755; 16 892; 18 627
 teachers 8 76
 works 15 20
hunt cups see under CUPS → types
Hunter, Alexander 15 656; 20 54
Hunter, Alexis 10 880
 works 10 880
Hunter, Andrew 12 773
Hunter, Clementine 32 329
Hunter, Edmund 10 357
Hunter, Henry 23 327
Hunter, John 2 744; 28 206; 29 809
Hunter, (George) Leslie 24 372; 28 238, 289, 290
Hunter, Robert 15 28*; 16 13
Hunter, Roy 31 733
Hunter, William (1718-83) 10 372; 15 28–9*; 28 205, 206
 book illustrations 21 7
 collections 12 777; 28 273
 manuscripts 21 6
 methods 9 706
 paintings 29 809
 writings 1 844; 10 293
Hunter, William (fl 1765) 29 804
Hunterian Museum and Art Gallery see under GLASGOW → University of Glasgow
Hunters' Palette 11 150; 23 848
Hunterston Brooch 1 761; 15 872; 28 264
Huntingdon law courts 18 886
Huntingdon (family) 9 467
Huntingdon, Charles Philip 25 373
Huntingdon, Collis P. 32 109
Huntingdon, David, Earl of see DAVID I, King of Scotland
Huntingdon, James 25 373
Huntingdon, William Balle 25 373
Huntingdon Frères 25 373
Huntingdon's, Henry of, Chronicle see HENRY OF HUNTINGDON'S CHRONICLE
Huntingfield Psalter see under PSALTERS → individual manuscripts
hunting-lodges 10 230; 16 238
Hunting Palette 9 827, 868
hunting scenes 29 422, 423–5*
 Assyrian 29 423
 Belgium 28 903; 32 706; 33 182
 Egypt, ancient 9 808*, 809, 865
 England 29 424, 425, 425
 France 23 667; 29 423, 424; 32 335
 Germany 18 175
 Indian subcontinent 15 604, 606
 Iran, ancient 15 917
 Italy 6 38; 19 635; 28 12; 31 515
 Korea 18 319
 Netherlands, the 14 710; 20 343
 United States of America 14 700
 see also SPORTING SCENES
Huntington, Anne Hyatt see HYATT HUNTINGTON, ANNA
Huntington, Arabella D(uval) 15 29*
Huntington, Archer M(ilton) 7 515; 15 29, 30*
Huntington, Collis P(otter) 15 29*
Huntington, Daniel 7 840; 10 367; 15 30*; 27 556
Huntington, Henry E(dwards) 15 29–30*; 19 703
Huntington, John 30 848
Huntington, Robert 10 79
Huntington Art Gallery see AUSTIN (TX) → University of Texas
Huntington Hartford Art Gallery see under NEW YORK → museums
Huntington Library see under SAN MARINO (CA)
Huntingtower Castle (Tayside) 28 244
Huntley & Palmer 17 640
Huntly, George Gordon, 4th Earl of see GORDON, GEORGE, 4th Earl of Huntly
Hunt Museum see under LIMERICK
Hunt Painter 13 512; 32 47*
Hunt & Roskell 3 78; 19 594, 596; 27 336; 29 723
Huntsman, Benjamin 16 60
Huntsman and Acanthus-scroll Silk 9 665
Huntsman Salt 27 640
Hünxe, Otto Pankok Museum 24 14
Hunyadi, John, Regent of Hungary 14 880, 884
Hunza (Pakistan) 23 798
Hunza (Colombia) see TUNJA
Hunzinger, George 22 744; 31 631
Huocheng, Tomb of Tughluq Timur 6 658
Huo Ch'iu-ping see HUO QUBING
Huo Ch'ü-ping see HUO QUBING
Huong Que
 sculpture 6 428, 429
Huong Tich Temple 32 473
Huo Qubing 6 697, 727; 14 134
Huot, Jean-Louis 18 797
Hupa 22 549, 641, 659
 caps 22 659
Hupa-iya 29 128
Hupeau 24 479
Hupeau, Jean 23 509
Huppe, Aemilius 5 440
Huppe, Samuel 5 440
Huquier, Gabriel 11 663; 15 31*; 26 229
 printmakers 2 853; 4 514; 18 661; 33 44
 works 6 490; 8 209; 12 638; 23 458, 514; 24 271; 26 493
Huquier, Jacques-Gabriel 9 395; 15 31
Hurault, Jacques, Bishop 3 304
Hurayda 2 263
Hurbat Rosh Zayit 17 553
Hurd, Jacob 4 479; 31 648
Hurd, Nathaniel 11 805; 31 649
Hurd, Peter 33 451
Hurdal Verk 23 235
Hurel Baatar 21 881
Huret, Grégoire 8 77; 15 31*
Hurezi 26 708, 725
 Monastery 25 340; 26 713, 720, 722
Hurlestone, Richard 33 414
Hurley, (James) Frank 15 31–2*
Hurley, Tyndall Hogan
 works 7 269
Hurley, William 10 168, 170, 260; 13 55; 15 32*
Hürlimann, Johann 5 168
Hürlimann, Martin 23 8
Hurlstone, Frederick Yeates 15 32*
Huron 22 552; 31 175
 architecture 21 597
 embroidery 22 647
 pottery 22 612
 quillwork 22 650
 textiles 22 628
Hurrell, Harold 2 512
Hürrem 17 491
Hürrem Sultan (Ottoman) 23 641; 28 767
Hurrian 1 851, 854; 2 661; 15 32–3*; 21 730; 31 698
 animal subjects 15 33
 bronze 15 33
 friezes 15 33
 glass 1 864, 865; 15 33
 iconography 33 513
 inscriptions 15 32
 pottery 15 33
 scripts 1 827
 sculpture 15 33
 seals 15 33
 see also MITANNIAN
Hurst, John 14 603
Hurst Fenn 25 503
Hurt, Henry 27 336
Hurtado, Angel 15 33*
Hurtado, Emma 26 428
Hurtado del Puenta, Sancho 5 791
Hurtado de Mendoza, Diego, Cardinal Archbishop of Seville 7 614; 21 126; 29 333, 353
Hurtado de Mendoza, Diego de, Conde de Mendoza-Infantado see MENDOZA-INFANTADO, DIEGO DE HURTADO DE MENDOZA, Conde de
Hurtado de Mendoza, Gregorio 23 410
Hurtado de Mendoza, Juan 21 124
Hurtado Izquierdo, Francisco 15 33–4*
 collaboration 27 708; 29 292

Hurtado Izquierdo, Francisco—cont.
groups and movements **7** 289
works **9** 407, 408; **11** 492; **13** 284; **20** 157; **24** 280; **27** 708; **29** 271, 292
Hurtado Manrique, Juan **5** 692; **32** 170, 179
works **5** *692*
Hurtault, Maximilien-Joseph **11** 261
Hurten, Charles **10** 312
Hurtrelle, Nicolas **15** 34
Hurtrelle, Simon **15** 34*; **20** 897; **22** 34; **24** 165
Hurtu, Jacques **15** 34*
Hurtubise, Jacques **5** 568; **25** 28
Hurum **9** 156
church **29** 580
Hurum, Per **23** 230
Hurworth **23** 65
Hus **23** 219
Hus, R. W. **29** 811
Husaby Church **6** 389; **26** 593; **30** 66
Husain, Maqbool Fida **4** 291; **8** 677; **15** 34–5*
groups and movements **4** 290; **15** 169
works **15** 169, 748
Husayn (*fl* late 19th cent.) **16** 426
Husayn I, Shah (*reg* 1694-1722) (Safavid) **2** 648; **6** 172; **16** 231; **27** 512
Husayn'ali *see* 'ALI
Husayn Bayqara, Sultan (*reg*1470-1506) (Timurid) **7** 717; **16** 528; **30** 917, 922–3*
architecture **3** 113; **14** 430
bookbindings **16** 358
book covers **16** *358*
calligraphy **29** 919
gardens **12** 82
manuscripts **1** 208; **4** 49, 50; **16** 272, 286, 296, 304, 325, 326, 344, 552; **27** 675; **30** 918, *922*
metalwork **1** 208; **16** 378
papercuts **16** 354, *354*
Husayn Beg **1** 584; **16** 480, 552
Husayni, Mansur Negargar **15** 898
Husayn ibn Abi Talib Damghani **4** 100
Husayn ibn 'Ali (*fl* before 1000) **16** 372
Husayn ibn 'Ali (*fl* 15th cent.) **16** 502
Husayn ibn Jawhar **16** 541
Ḥusayn ibn Manṣūr ibn Bayqara *see* HUSAYN BAYQARA
Husayn ibn Muhammad al-Mawsili **16** 379, 382, 383
Husayn ibn Salama, Ruler (*reg c.* 1000) (Ziyadid) **33** 584
Husayn ibn Talib al-Damghani **2** 316
Husayn Nizam Shah I, Ruler (*reg* 1554-65) (Nizam Shahi) **15** *637*, 637
Husayn Pasha Fahmy **16** 241
Husayn Quli Khan **15** 371
Husayn Shah, Sultan of Jaunpur (*reg* 1458-79) (Sharqi) **15** 344
Husby-Långhundra **30** 83
Huseinov, G. U. **2** 898
Hüsgen, Heinrich Sebastian **9** 443
Hüsgen, Wilhelm **24** 591
Hushang Shah, Sultan of Malwa (*reg* 1405-35) (Ghuri) **6** 444; **15** 354; **20** 250
Husifa **9** 567
Huskisson, Leonard **15** 35
Huskisson, Robert **11** 432; **15** 35*
Husly, Hans Jacob **23** 633
Husly, Hendrik **23** 633
Husly, (Hans) Jacob Otten *see* OTTEN-HUSLY, (HANS) JACOB
Husn, Tell el- *see* BETH SHAN
Husnik, Jakob **7** 575
Husohoe group **18** 60
Husrau Parwiz **6** 173
Husrefbey **27** 819
Huss, József **28** 838; **32** 872
Hussain, Imtiaz **23** 801
Hussain, Iqbal **23** 799, 800
Hussain, Saddam *see* SADDAM HUSSAIN
Hussain, Taha **9** 766
Hussa Sabah al-Salem al-Sabah, Shaykha (al-Sabah) **16** 553; **18** 541
Hussein, M. M. **23** 150
Hussein, Muhie al-Din **9** 767
Hussein, Oswald **13** 877
Hussem, Willem (Frans Karel) **15** 36*; **22** 852
Husser, Joseph **6** 573
Husserl, Edmund **10** 685; **24** 594; **26** 62
Hussey, Philip **15** 36*
Hussey, R. C. **26** 361
Hussey, Walter **15** 36*
Hussmann, Heinrich **17** 816
Husson, Jules (-François-Felix) *see* CHAMPFLEURY
Husson, Pierre-Arsène-Denis **6** 518
Hussum, Willem **14** 43
Husterknupp, Der **21** 562
Hustin, Ferdinand **4** 392
Hustin, J. A. **3** 547
Hustin, Jacques **4** 391
Hustin, Victoire **4** 392
Huston, Joseph **11** 849
Huston & Kurtz **24** 688
Huszadik század **24** 440
Huszár, Adolf **14** 896; **16** 811
Huszár, Vilmos **15** 36*; **22** 852
collaboration **26** 379; **33** 215
groups and movements **14** 901; **22** 875; **29** 660, 661
patrons and collectors **2** 409
works **22** 868, *868*
Hu Tang **7** 130
hutch chests *see under* CHESTS → types
Hutcheson, David **19** 875
Hutcheson, Francis **1** 180; **15** 37*
Hutchings, R. T. **1** 845
Hutchinson, Allen **23** 62
Hutchinson, Charles L. **6** 575; **27** 463
Hutchinson, Henry **5** 512; **26** 361
Hutchinson, John **15** 37–8*; **19** 357; **29** 801; **32** 797
Hutchinson, Peter **18** 695
Hutchinson, William **19** 361
Hutchison, Alexander C. **24** 470
Hutchison, John **18** 68; **20** 20
Hutchisson, Joseph **14** 132
Huth, Eilfried **30** 214
Hutheesingh (family) **15** 408
Huth Hours *see under* BOOKS OF HOURS → individual manuscripts
Huth-Schmölz, Walde **15** 38*; **28** 127
Hutian **17** 589
Hu T'iao-hsin *see* HU TIAOXIN
Hu Tiaoxin **15** 74
Hutin, Charles-François **15** 38–9*
assistants **15** 39
pupils **18** 121
reproductive prints by others **15** 39
teachers **28** 846
Hutin, François **15** 38*
Hutin, Jean-Baptiste **15** 38
Hutin, Pierre-Jules **15** 38, 39*
Hütl, Dező **14** 634
Hutou *see* GU KAIZHI
huts
historical and regional traditions
Africa **1** *306*, 307–8, *311*
Egypt, ancient **9** 849
Etruscan **10** 587
Greece, ancient **13** 389
huts
historical and regional traditions—cont.
Indian subcontinent **15** 235, *235*
Italy **10** 587
Mesopotamia **16** 801
Nuba **23** 275
South Africa **1** *311*
Sudan **1** *306*
Surinam **30** 13
Zaïre **1** 311
Zulu **1** *311*
types
chalets *see* CHALETS
clochans **16** 7; **28** 817
cylindrical *see* rondavel
dome **1** 308
rondavel **1** 307, 308
Hu Ts'ao *see* HU CAO
Hutson, Bill **1** 444
Hutson, Peter **23** 68
Hutsul'shchyna **31** 562, 563, 564
Hutte, Hieronimus **25** 113
Hutten, Franz Christoph von, Prince-Bishop of Speyer **4** 891; **13** 852; **33** 671
Hutten-Czapski, Emeryk **25** 139
Huttenlocher, Ferdinand **21** 796
Hutter, Albrecht **2** 127
Hutter, Wolfgang **2** 797; **13** 867; **24** 592; **32** 447
Hüttinger, Eduard **30** 157
Hüttl Porcelain Factory **5** 85
Hutton, Addison **25** 573; **28** 843
Hutton, C. **3** 505
Hutton, David Con **23** 75
Hutton, Edward **15** 39*
Hutton, Graham **28** 878
Hutton, James **2** 299
Hutton, William, & Sons **10** 336
Hutton, William S. **25** 737
Hutton Castle (Borders) **29** 515
Huttunen, Erkki **15** 39*
Hutu **5** 285; **27** 458
hut urns *see under* URNS → types
Hutz, Lucas **28** 48
Hutz Portrait, Master of the **21** 157
Huuva, Rose Marie **27** 472
Huvé, Jean-Jacques **17** 628; **32** 427
Huvé, Jean-Jacques-Marie **18** 653; **24** 387; **32** 509, 594
Hu Wenming **6** 866
Huxley, Paul **28** 805
Huy
brass **3** 602, 603; **4** 688
glass **3** 593
marks **3** 601
Notre-Dame **6** 248, 285; **13** 99
St Mort **13** 110, 114
sculpture **13** 114
shrine of St Odile **3** 552
silver **3** 598
Huy, Godefroid of *see* GODEFROID OF HUY
Huy, Jean Pépin de *see* JEAN PÉPIN DE HUY
Huy, Rainer of *see* RAINER OF HUY
Huybrechts, Adriaan **33** 169
Huybrechts, Gaspar **9** 718; **16** 15
Huybs, Nicolaas **8** 26
Huydecoper, Joan, I (1599-1661) **15** 40*; **22** 901–2; **26** 153
Huydecoper, Joan, II (*fl* 1674) **14** 503; **15** 40
Huygelen, Frans **3** 604
Huygens, Christian **19** 354
Huygens, Constantijn (i) (1596-1687) **14** 39, 584; **15** 40*; **18** *10*; **22** 842, 902; **25** 324
architecture **14** 39, 635; **22** 824
collections **22** 904
dealing **23** 465
etchings **14** 736
gardens **12** 132
interior decoration **23** 465
paintings **14** 730; **19** 348; **26** 157, 158; **27** 509
Huygens, Constantijn (i) (1596-1687)—cont.
patrons and collectors **14** 46; **15** 40
Huygens, Constantijn (ii) (1628-97) **13** 324; **15** 41–2*
groups and movements **4** 868
illustrated writings **32** 231
patrons and collectors **15** 40
works **15** *41*; **25** 382
Huyot, Jean-Nicolas **8** 18; **15** 42*
assistants **3** 843
pupils **2** 14; **9** 336; **13** 231; **19** 69; **26** 270
works **6** 397; **9** 337
Huys, Frans **4** 896; **15** 42, 43*; **27** 258
works **5** 61; **11** 222
Huys, Modest **19** 792
Huys, Pieter **3** 554; **15** 42–3*
works **2** 194; **11** 441; **15** 43; **19** 64
Huysmans, Charles-Marie-Georges *see* HUYSMANS, JORIS-KARL
Huysmans, Cornelis **9** 378; **15** 43*
Huysmans, Hendrik **15** 43
Huysmans, Jacob **4** 884; **10** 249; **15** 43–4*; **17** 599
Huysmans, Jan Baptist **15** 43
Huysmans, Joris-Karl **8** 596; **11** 567; **15** 44*; **19** 36
collaboration **25** 847
groups and movements **27** 239; **30** 168
Huysmans, Pieter **15** 43
Huysmans, Pieter Balthasar (1684-1706) **15** 43
Huysmans, Victor-Godfried **15** 44
Huyssens, Peter **15** 45*
patrons and collectors **17** 511
works **1** 467; **2** 192, *192*; **3** 545–6; **4** 920
Huysum, Caspar van **15** 45
Huysum, Jacobus van **15** 45–6*
Huysum, Jan van **15** 45, 46–7*; **22** 847, 848
patrons and collectors **12** 620; **14** 146; **19** 338, 436, 847
pupils **15** 46
reproductive prints by others **9** 506; **25** 619
teachers **3** 759
works **11** 228, *228*; **15** *46*; **22** 847; **29** 668
Huysum, Justus van, I (1659-1716) **15** 45
Huysum, Justus van, II (1685-1707) **15** 45
Huysum, Maria van **15** 46
Huysum, Michiel van **15** 46
Huyter, Jan de **8** 666
hüyük **1** 851; **21** 268
Hu Yukun **22** 460
Huyvetter, Jean-Augustin d' **24** 885
Huzao *see* DALVERZIN TEPE
Hu Zhengyan **7** 120
Huzhou **6** 637, 864; **7** 66
Huzhou school of ink-bamboo **6** 804
Hval **4** 460
Hvar **8** 174, *174*
arsenal **8** 175
city tower **8** 175
Dominican Monastery **8** 180
Franciscan Monastery **8** 180
loggia **8** 175
theatre **8** 175
Hvedekorn **24** 451
Hvitträsk **12** 498–9
H W, Master **20** 797–8*
works **2** 118; **20** *798*
Hwang Chip-jung **15** 47*
Hwang In-Chung **18** 344
Hwang Ki-no **18** 329
Hwang Su-yŏng **18** 259
Hwaŏm Buddhism *see* BUDDHISM → sects → Avataṁsaka
Hwaŏm Temple **18** 308, 310, 311; **23** 775
Hwawang-toin *see* SŎNG SE-CH'ANG
Hwt-hery-ib *see* ATHRIBIS
Hxtal NYLI epoxy resin **33** 6
hyacinth **12** 252; **14** *171*
Hyakinthos **9** 591
Hyakudō *see* SENGAI GIBON
Hyakufuchi Dōji *see* JIUN SONJA
Hyakusen Sakaki *see* SAKAKI HYAKUSEN
Hyakusui Hirafuku *see* HIRAFUKU, HYAKUSUI
Hyalith **23** 264
hyalopsite *see* OBSIDIAN
Hyannisport **7** 679
Hyat, Fazal **23** 804
Hyatt, Anna **15** 30
Hyatt, John W. **16** 797; **25** 25; **26** 244
Hyatt, Thaddeus **7** 693
Hyatt Huntington, Anna **15** 47*
Hybert, Fabrice **11** 553
Hybrid Enterprises **24** 639
Hyckes, Richard **10** 349; **30** 318
Hyde, Anne, Duchess of York **19** *122*; **25** 279
Hyde, Edward, 1st Earl of Clarendon **8** 46; **10** 360, 657; **15** 47–8*; **19** 123
Hyde, Eugene **15** 48*; **16** 884; **32** 910
Hyde, Frank **21** 761
Hyde, George Taylor **23** 170
Hyde, Henry, 2nd Earl of Clarendon **15** 48; **30** 278
Hyde Park (NY), Vanderbilt Mansion **14** 452
Hyderabad (India) **15** 48–9*, *294*, *637*; **16** *105*
architecture **15** 381–2; **21** 44
British Residency **15** 402
calligraphy **15** 681
carpets **15** 684
Char Minar **15** *48*, 381
Chaumahalla **15** 381–2
enamel **15** 711
High Court **18** 889
ikat **15** 672
Jagdish and Kamla Mittal Museum of Indian Art **15** 742
Mecca Mosque **15** 382
metalwork **15** 713, 714; **21** 330
paintings **15** 642
printing **16** 361
Salar Jung Museum **15** 182, 184, 681, 742
State Museum **15** 182
textiles **15** 664, 665, 672
Hyderabad (Pakistan) **15** 712
State Archaeological Museum **23** 804
Hyde's Weekly Art News *see* ARTNEWS
Hydman-Vallien, Ulrica **30** 103
Hydra **32** 294
hydraulic works **11** 338, 343, 344
Cambodia **5** 459
Islamic **11** 339
Nabataea **22** 419; **24** 556
Rome, ancient **26** 864
hydriai **15** 49*
historical and regional traditions
Etruscan **10** *615*; **13** *516*, 516
Greece, ancient **13** 474, *475*, 479, 514, *576*
Attica **13** *510*, *511*, *523*
Etruscan **13** *516*, 516
Italy **10** *615*
materials
bronze **13** *576*
pottery **10** *615*; **13** *510*, *511*, *516*, *523*
types
Hadra vases **13** 539
kalpis **13** 576
hydrochloric acid **10** 548
hydrogen peroxide **6** 335; **33** 1

hydrogen plasma **7** 730
Hyech'o **6** 320; **17** 831
Hyehŏ **18** 306
Hyères, Villa Noailles **11** *525*, 526, 584
Hyesan *see* YU SUK
Hyewŏn *see* SIN YUN-BOK
Hyghalmen Roll *see under* ROLLS→ individual manuscripts
Hyginus (*fl* 1st cent. AD) **6** 68; **21** 558
Hyginus (*fl* 2nd cent. AD) **2** 649; **15** 82
Hyginus Grommaticus **27** 2
hygrometers **7** 734
Hyksos **9** 780, 824, 831, 851
Hylaea **13** 862; **18** 22; **20** 886
Hylestad Church **29** 580
Hylton Castle (Tyne & Wear) **21** 549
Hymans, Henri **3** 619
Hymas, Alison **5** 573
Hynais, Vojtěch **15** 49*; **25** 433
pupils **16** 874, 908; **17** 592
works **8** 392
Hynckes, Raoul **15** 49*; **22** 852
Hyngeller, János **14** 894, 907
Hyngeller, Johan **30** 206
Hyōbu Bokkei **29** 13
Hyobu Saiyo **17** 173
Hyōe Ishiō *see* ISHIŌ HYOĒ
Hyōgo *see* KOBE
Hyojong, King (*reg* 1659-74) **18** 330
Hyŏndae misulga hyŏphoe (Modern Artists Association) **18** 326
Hyŏn'gwang **5** 114
Hyŏnjae *see* SIM SA-JŎNG
Hyŏnong *see* YUN TŎK-HŬI
Hyŏnsunja *see* AN KYŎN
Hyperborean **28** 320
Hyperion **24** 444
hyperpyra see under COINS → types
Hyper Realism *see* PHOTOREALISM
Hypnerotomachia Poliphili **1** 655; **4** 358; **5** 685; **12** *64*, 64, 105, 112; **15** 50*; **22** 377; **32** 198, 550
hypo **24** 649, 656
hypocausts **15** 51–2*; **26** 879
China **15** 51–2*, *52*
Greece, ancient **3** 374; **13** 407
Islamic **3** 377
Italy **26** 888
Korea **15** 52*
hypocausts—cont.
Mongolia **15** 52
Rome, ancient **3** 374; **13** 404; **15** 51*, *51*; **26** 871, 879, 888
hypogea **6** 165; **9** 779; **15** 52–3*; **31** 110
see also CEMETERIES; MAUSOLEA; TOMBS
hypogées see under TOMBS → types
Hypo-Kulturstiftung **12** 472
hypostyle *see under* HALLS → types
hyposulphite *see* HYPO
Hyppis **13** 546, 552
Hyppolite, Hector **5** 753; **14** 58; **15** 53*; **30** 23
Hyppolite, Jean **10** 685
Hypšman, Bohumil **8** 379
Hyrcanus **16** 3
Hyre, Laurent de La *see* LA HYRE, LAURENT DE
Hyre, Philippe de La *see* LA HYRE, PHILIPPE DE
Hyrlau, St George **25** 344
Hyromos *see* EUROMOS
Hyrtakina *Pan* **8** 154
Hysing, Hans **8** 454; **15** 53–4*; **25** 881; **30** 78
Hyuhyudang *see* YI KYE-HO
Hyŭjŏng **18** 330
Hyzer & Lewellyn **30** 887
Hyzler, Giuseppe **15** 54*; **20** 213
Hyzler, Vincenzo **15** 54*; **20** 213

I

I, Monogrammist **21** 338; **23** 618
I 10 **21** 854; **29** 661
Iacobovits, Marta **26** 719
Iacopo, Cosma di *see* COSMA DI IACOPO
Iacovleff, Alexandre *see* YACOVLEV, ALEKSANDR (YEVGENIYEVICH)
Iahnefer **9** 879
Iaia of Cyzicus **13** 549, 552; **25** 44; **33** 307
Iakovidis, Georgios **13** 352, 360; **15** 55*
Ialysos **13** *363*; **26** *289*, 290, 291
jars **26** *290*
pins **13** *600*
pottery **26** 290
sculpture **26** 292
wall paintings **21** 674
Iamblichus **22** 749
IAM of Zwolle, Master **20** 799*
Iancu, Marcel *see* JANCO, MARCEL
Ianelli, Alfonso **5** 337; **12** 854
Iaşi **15** 55–6*; **26** *705*, 710
Academia Mihăileană **26** 725
architecture **2** 427
Dosoftei House-Museum **15** 55
education (art) **26** 725, 726
Ion Cantacuzino's house **26** 708
Museum of Art **15** 56; **26** 724
Palace **26** 708, 719
St Spiridon **26** 708
School of Engineering **26** 725
Trei Ierarhi **26** 708, 712, 721, 722
Iasil, St Theodore **25** 341
Iason **10** 50
Iasos **4** 530; **5** 741, 742; **27** 13
Iatali **12** 330
Iatmul **23** 721, 722, *722*; **24** 66, 68
masks **24** *72*
Iatrus **21** 560
I.B., Master **19** 501; **20** 799–800*; **24** 331
Iba **17** 346
Ibadan **15** 56–7*; **23** *129*
architecture **23** 134
houses **1** 319
painting **23** 136
textiles **33** 559
University **1** 228, 319, 432; **23** 134, 135
workshops **1** 429
Iban **5** 11; **15** 789, 796; **20** 163, 182, 183
architecture **15** 773, 774; **20** 167
boats **20** 179
textiles **20** 175, 176
wood-carvings **20** 181
Ibáñez, Genaro **4** 262, 267
Ibañez, Marcos **13** 761, 770
Ibarra **22** 97
Ibarra, Hilarión **32** 173
Ibarra, Joachin **4** 362
Ibarra, José de **7** 883; **15** 57*; **21** 384, 397
Ibarra, Juan de *see* ALAVA, JUAN DE
Ibarra, Pedro de **7** 362
Ibarrola, Agustín **29** 286
Ibb **16** 213, 214
Asadiyya Madrasa **16** 213
Malhuki Mosque **16** 214
Ibbetson, Julius Caesar, the elder (1759-1817) **1** 612; **15** 57–8*; **18** 713
Ibbetson, Julius Caesar, the younger (1783-1825) **15** 58
Ibels, Henri-Gabriel **15** 58*
groups and movements **8** 714; **22** 421, 422
methods **17** 276
Ibels, Henri-Gabriel—cont.
patrons and collectors **4** 71
works **19** 490
Iberia (Georgia) **9** *512*; **12** 316, 318
Iberia (peninsula) **15** 58–60*
alphabets **12** 889
sandstone **15** 59, *60*
sculpture **15** 59
stelae **15** 59, *60*
Ibero y Odriozola, Francisco de **27** 767
Ibi (*reg* 2140 BC) **27** 812
Ibi (*fl c.* 650 BC) **9** 822, 891; **12** 227–8
Ibi, Sinibaldo **3** 858; **15** 60–61*
Ibía, Baltasar de Echave *see* ECHAVE IBÍA, BALTASAR DE
Ibía, Francisco de *see* ZUMAYA, FRANCISCO DE
Ibía, Manuel de Echave *see* ECHAVE IBÍA, MANUEL DE
Ibibio **15** 61–5*
aesthetics **1** 237
body arts **1** 342, 344; **15** 65*
brass **15** 65
cement **1** 331, 332
colour **7** 635
craftsmen and artists **15** 61*
divination instruments **1** 356
drums (musical instruments) **15** 65*
gourds **1** 303
masks **1** 256, 273–4, *273*; **15** 61–2*, *62*
monuments **1** 331
murals **15** 64
portraits **1** 268
puppets **15** 65*
sculpture **1** 332; **15** *63*, 63–4*, *64*, 65
shrines (i) (cult) **1** 310
textiles **15** 64, *64*
wood **1** *273*
wood-carvers **15** 111, 112
wood-carvings **15** 61
Ibiza **25** 732
amulets **17** 514
Cathedral of S Maria de las Nieves **3** 106; **29** 332
copper **25** 734
eggs **25** 735
figurines **25** 733
moulds **25** 734
Museo Arqueológico **3** 106
Museo de Arte Contemporáneo **3** 106
razors **25** 734
S Eulalia del Rio **3** 106
Ibler, Drago **8** 177; **15** 66*
groups and movements **9** 672; **25** 12
pupils **17** 858; **25** 12
works **19** 883
Iblis, Tall-i **15** 904
IBM **12** 472; **23** 273; **25** 589, 887; **31** 661
IBM Pavilion **25** 24
Ibn 'Abbad **16** 372
Ibn Abi' Amir *see* AL-MANSUR (*d* 1002)
Ibn al-Bawwab **15** 66*; **16** 259
patrons and collectors **16** 551
works **3** 53; **5** 322; **16** 272, *275*, 282–3, *283*, 289, 545
Ibn al-Durayhim **16** 311
works **16** *311*
Ibn al-Fuwati **16** 313
Ibn al-Haytham **5** 519; **19** 356; **24** 487; **28** 202
Ibn al-Jayyāb **13** 287
Ibn al-Khatib **12** 80; **13** 287, 289
Ibn al-Nadim **7** 716
Ibn al-Razzaz al-Jazari **2** 575; **7** 438
clocks **7** *437*
Ibn al-Suyufi **16** 209
Ibn al-Wahid *see* SHARAF AL-DIN MUHAMMAD IBN SHARAF IBN YUSUF
Ibn al-Zayn *see* MUHAMMAD AL-ZAYN
Ibn al-Zubayr **16** 144, 529; **20** 914
Ibn 'Arabshah **16** 196, 321
Ibn 'Aziz **16** 252
Ibn Babawayh (family) **2** 316
Ibn Badis *see* AL-MU'IZZ IBN BADIS
Ibn Bakhtishu **16** 545
Ibn Bassal **12** 80
Ibn Battuta **13** 812
on architecture **16** 193
on arms and armour **15** 678
on carpets **15** 682; **16** 469
on Colombo **7** 613
on gardens **12** 83
on masks **1** 229
on metalwork **16** 373
on Mongolia **21** 885
on palaces **1** 308; **15** 340
on sculpture **1** 381
on tents **15** 716
on textiles **16** 443
Ibn Butlan **14** 432; **21** 5
Ibn Fadlan **31** 546
Ibn Ghaybi al-Tawrizi **12** 511
Ibn Hajji Muhammad 'Ali **16** 287
Ibn Hamdis **16** 246
Ibn Hani *see under* UGARIT
Ibn Hawqal **13** 811; **18** 810
Ibni Neccar Mosque **16** 498
Ibn Jubayr **20** 914; **21** 32; **23** 561
Ibn Khaldun **16** 106, 207, 539
Ibn Khurdadhbih **18** 483
Ibn Kilis **31** 22
Ibn Luyun **12** 64, 81
Ibn Mardanish **12** 80
Ibn Miskawayh **31** 546
Ibn Muqla **15** 66–7*; **16** 259, 273
patrons and collectors **16** 551
works **16** 282
Ibn Sa'id **5** 833; **16** 368, 379
Ibn Sina *see* AVICENNA
Ibn Tulun mosque *see under* CAIRO → Islamic religious buildings
Ibn Tumart **16** 191
Ibn Yazid **3** 338; **16** 369
works **16** *370*
Ibn Zamrak **13** 288
Ibn Zaydun **12** 79
Ibo (Jamaica) **16** 880
Ibo (Nigeria) *see* IGBO
Ibolo **1** 345
Ibragimov, U. **22** 446
Ibrahim (*fl c.* 1675-1700) **15** 608
Ibrahim, Sultan (*reg* 1640-48) (Ottoman) **16** 610; **22** 384
Ibrahim II, Governor (*reg* 875-902) (Aghlabid) **17** 731
Ibrahim, Abdel Halim **9** 765
Ibrahim, Farouk **9** 766
Ibrahim, L. A. **16** 550
Ibrahim, Master **16** 604
Ibrahim 'Adil Shah II, Ruler (*reg* 1579-1626) ('Adil Shahi) **1** 157; **4** 51, 52; **15** 587, 638, *639*, 739
architecture **4** *51*
Ibrahim Ağa Müstahfizan **5** 398; **16** 210
Ibrahim b. Ghana'im **20** 227
Ibrahim Hakkı **16** 350
Ibrahim Hussein **20** 172
Ibrahim ibn al-Aghlab, Governor (*reg* 800-12) (Aghlabid) **1** 451; **17** 731
Ibrahim ibn Jami' **16** 491
Ibrahim ibn Mawaliya **16** 379
Ibrahim ibn Muhammad al-Raqqam **16** 386
Ibrahim Iskandar, Sultan (*reg* 1648-87) **20** 189
Ibrahim Khalil, Khan (*reg* 1759-1806) (Jiwanshir) **28** 644
Ibrahim Khan (*fl* 17th cent.; painter) **15** 640
Ibrahim Khan Kakar (Dilavar Khan) (*fl* 1605-8; ruler) **15** 369
Ibrahim Mirza (Safavid) **2** 235; **7** 717; **16** 301, 334, 335; **27** 514; **28** 567
miniatures **16** *336*
Ibrahim Mustafa **31** 584
Ibrahim Müteferrika **15** 67; **16** 360
Ibrahim Paha **15** 67*; **16** 610; **19** 280
Ibrahim Scharbatchizade **16** 285
Ibrahim Sultan (Timurid) **30** 917, 920–21*
architecture **1** 25
manuscripts **16** 290, *322*, 324–5*; **28** 616
'Ibri **23** 436
Ibrim *see* QASR IBRIM
Ibru, Roye **32** 86
Ibru, Vaughan-Richards Partnership **32** 86
Ibrulj, Mustafa **4** 462
Ibsen, Henrik **8** 109, 596; **11** 142; **30** 682; **33** 608
Ibu **9** 877
I.B. with the Bird, Master *see* PALUMBA, GIOVANNI BATTISTA
ICA (Institute of Contemporary Arts) *see under* LONDON → museums; WASHINGTON (DC)
Ica (people) **7** 602; **29** 181; **30** 240
ICA (International Council on Archives) **2** 365, 369
Ica (Peru) **24** 514
Museo Regional **24** 516
Ica-Chincha **15** 67*
Icarte, Hilda **6** 600
Icaza, Francisco **3** 625
Icaza, Teresa **23** 905
ICCROM (International Centre for the Study of Preservation and Restoration of Cultural Property) **2** 323; **7** 742, 743
ice boxes *see under* BOXES → types
ice buckets **12** *436*
ice-chests *see under* CHESTS → types
ice cream cups *see under* CUPS → types
ice glass *see under* GLASS → types
ice-houses **15** 67–8*; **16** 232
Iceland **15** *68*, 68–74*; **32** 513
architecture **15** 71–2*; **32** 533
baskets **3** 332
ceramics **15** 72*
chairs **15** *72*
churches **32** 517
embroidery **15** 73*, *74*
exhibitions **15** 70; **30** 757
farmhouses **32** 533
felt **10** 875
furniture **15** 72*
glass **15** 72*
initials (manuscript) **15** *69*
interior decoration **15** 71–2*
knitting **15** 73*; **18** 158
Iceland—cont.
linen **15** *74*
manuscripts **15** 69
metalwork **15** 73*
painting **13** 143; **15** 69–71*, *71*; **30** *757*
pattern books **24** 269
periodicals **24** 452*
sculpture **15** 69–71*
silver **15** 73*
textiles **15** 73–4*
wood **15** *72*
wood-carvings **15** 69; **32** 524
wool **15** *74*
Iceland agate *see* OBSIDIAN
Iceland Review **24** 452
Ichcatec **21** 736, 738
Ichibei Izumiya *see* IZUMIYA ICHIBEI
Ichibei Shirakoya *see* SHIRAKOYA ICHIBEI
Ichiguchi **17** 364
Ichihashi, Toshiko **17** 371
Ichijō, Emperor (*reg* 986-1011) **17** 222
Ichijōji Pagoda **23** 776
Ichijusai *see* UTAGAWA KUNIMASA
Ichikawa (Japan)
ceramics **17** *245*
Ichikawa (family) **17** 332
Ichikawa Beian **15** 74–5*; **17** 216, 237, 412; **32** *896*
Ichikawa Danjūrō I **17** 333
Ichikawa Danjūrō II **17** 333
Ichikawa Kansai **15** 74; **17** 237
Ichimatsu dolls *see under* DOLLS → types
Ichimonjiya Sukezaēmon **18** 553
I-ching *see* YIJING
Ichinojō Koretomi *see* OGATA KŌRIN
Ichinomiya Oyama Shrine **17** 363
Ichinyū Raku *see* RAKU ICHINYŪ
Ichirakutei Eisui **17** 285
Ichiraku Tsuchiya *see* TSUCHIYA ICHIRAKU
Ichirō Fukuzawa *see* FUKUZAWA, ICHIRŌ
Ichiroku Iwaya *see* IWAYA ICHIROKU
Ichiryūsai (1735-1814) *see* UTAGAWA TOYOHARU
Ichiryūsai (1773-1829) *see* UTAGAWA TOYOHIRO
Ichiryūsai (1797-1858) *see* ANDŌ HIROSHIGE
Ichiyōsai (1769-1825) *see* UTAGAWA TOYOKUNI
Ichiyōsai (1786-1864) *see* UTAGAWA KUNISADA I
Ichiyo Shunjuike *see* SHUNJUIKE ICHIYO
Ichiyūsai (1797-1858) *see* ANDO HIROSHIGE
Ichiyūsai (1797-1861) *see* UTAGAWA KUNIYOSHI
Ichizō Kobayashi *see* KOBAYASHI, ICHIZŌ
I.C.I. **30** 543
Iciar, Juan de **32** 590
Icí i D'Allà, D' **8** 538
Icklingham (Suffolk), All Saints **10** 339
Ickworth (Suffolk) **25** 193
metalwork **26** 558
model **2** 337
paintings **3** 383; **9** 18; **13** 303; **14** 485; **22** 86; **32** 496
portico **25** 266
sculpture **14** 485
silver **14** 485

Icod de los Vinos **8** 237
Icographic **24** 446
ICOM (International Council of Museums) **2** 369, 370, 556; **7** 743; **12** 477; **30** 155
ICOMOS (International Council on Monuments and Sites) **2** 323; **7** 744
Iconclass **4** 27; **15** 78, 97
icon covers **15** 77–8*, *77*
Iconium *see* KONYA
icon manuals *see under* MANUALS → types
iconoclasm **6** 175; **10** 652; **15** 78–81*; **26** 140
 Africa **1** 228
 Buddhism **15** 79–80
 Byzantine **6** 175; **9** 514; **12** 71; **15** 75, 80
 China **15** 78
 Cistercian Order **15** 80
 Early Christian (*c.* AD 250-843) **9** 514; **15** 80; **26** 854
 England **10** 261
 Hinduism **15** 79
 Indian subcontinent **15** 79
 Islamic **15** 80–81; **16** 99–100, 245
 Jewish art **6** 175
 Mesoamerica, Pre-Columbian **23** 417–18
 Navajo **15** 78
 Olmec **23** 417–18
 Sikhism **15** 79
iconographic handbooks *see under* MANUALS → types
iconographic programmes **15** 84–8*
iconography **2** 532; **4** 27; **6** 76; **10** 175, 206, 208, 213; **14** 868; **15** 89–97*, *90, 91, 92, 93, 94, 95, 96*; **18** 215; **26** 225; **30** 166
 Achaemenid **1** 117
 Afghanistan **1** 188–9*, 198, 206
 Africa **1** 260–64*, 271–9*, 280–84*, 312, 334–6, 352
 Aguada culture **29** 190
 Anatolia, ancient **1** 828–30*, 834–5
 Ancient Near East **1** 859
 Arabia **2** 254, 257
 Aramaean **1** 830
 Asante **1** 262
 Augustinian Canons **2** 724–5*
 Aztec **21** 186, 189
 Baga **1** 262, 263
 Bamana **1** 263, 280
 Bamileke **3** 146–7
 Beguines **3** 503*
 Benedictine Order **3** 709–11*
 Benin Republic **1** 282, 284
 Bhutan **3** 914
 Bon (religion) **30** 810–11
 Brazil **29** 134
 Buddhism **5** 87–8, *88*, 90–92*, 224, 462–3; **15** 779; **29** 458, 459
  Afghanistan **1** 188–9, 198, 206
  Burma **5** 237, 240
  Cambodia **5** 495, 496, 499–500
  Central Asia **5** 102
  Central Asia, Eastern **6** 292–3*, 302, 303
  Central Asia, Western **6** 194–5*
  Champa **6** 427
  China **5** 91; **6** 627–8*, 721, 799; **7** 34, 104–5, *105*
  Esoteric **5** 91, 92, 116; **7** 633; **15** 757
  Indian subcontinent **3** 907; **5** *92*, 93, *96*; **7** 633; **15** 220–24*, 229, 416, 425, 428–9, 431–2, 446–8, 501
  Indonesia **15** 757*, 777
  Japan **5** 116, 118; **17** 33–9*, 107, 108, 109, 146–8, 168
  Java **15** 777
  Korea **5** 91; **18** *254*, 254–5, 305–6, 307–9
  Lamaism **7** 104–5

iconography
 Buddhism—cont.
  Laos **18** 763
  Mahayana **5** 91, 116
  Mongolia **5** 91; **21** 872–3, 880
  Nepal **5** 103; **22** 756–7*
  Pure Land **5** 118
  South-east Asia **5** 91
  Sri Lanka **29** 442–3, *443*
  Thailand **29** 826; **30** 573–4*, 594
  Tibet **5** 91; **30** 809–11*, 813, 822, 825–6, 845
  Vietnam **6** 427; **32** 470
 Burkina Faso **1** 280
 Burma **5** 223–4*, 237, 240
 bushidō **17** 42*
 Byzantine **7** 220–22*; **9** 516*, 517–18*, 519–21*, *520, 521*, 572, 573, 575, 576, 583, 595, 596, 609–10, 616, 617, 622, 623, 625–6, 629, 635; **10** 209, 437; **12** 71–2; **15** 76; **19** 169; **22** 162; **23** 374
 Camaldolese Order **5** 450*
 Cambodia **5** 461–3, 467, 495, 496, 499–500, 501–2
 Cameroon **1** 263, 276
 Cao dai **32** 471
 Carmelite Order **5** 778*
 Carthusian Order **5** 895*
 Central Asia **5** 102
 Central Asia, Eastern **6** 292–3*, 302, 303
 Central Asia, Western **6** 192–3*, *193*, 194–5*
 Champa **6** 419–20*, 427
 Chavín culture **6** 521–2*; **29** 133, 134
 Chicano **18** 831–2
 Chile **6** 596
 Chimú **29** 133
 China **6** 627–8*, 629–33*, 803; **7** 75, 76
  Buddhism **5** 91; **6** 627–8*, 721, 799; **7** 34, 104–5, *105*
  Confucianism **6** 628*
  Daoism **5** 107; **6** 628*; **7** 61, 105–6, *106*; **10** 485
 Chokwe **1** 261
 Christianity **1** 652; **2** 2–4, *3*, 237; **5** 443, 807; **7** 219*, 220*, 223–5*, 273, 627; **8** 210–11, 835; **11** 340; **12** 108; **13** 775; **14** 660; **15** 89, 881; **16** 837, 897; **18** 676–7; **19** 788, *788*; **20** 251; **22** 411, 412; **24** 775; **25** 650; **26** 58, 329; **27** 158–60, 494–6; **28** 915–16; **30** 707; **32** 86
  Byzantine **5** 677; **7** 220–22*; **9** 595, 596, 609–10, 616, 622, 623, 624, 625–6, 629, 635; **23** 374
  Calvinism **5** 447; **28** 915
  Early Christian (*c.* AD 250-843) **5** 676; **7** 219*; **9** 595, 596, 609–10, 616, 622, 623, 624, 635; **24** 336; **33** 215
  France **13** 179
  Germany **2** 3; **26** 654
  Gothic **7** 224; **13** 73, 127, 128–9*, *129, 131*, 179
  Lutheranism **19** 815
  Nestorianism **6** 293
  Philippines **24** 610*
  Post-Byzantine **7** 222–3*
  Protestantism **7** 226–7*
  Renaissance **7** 225
  Roman Catholicism **6** 596; **7** 225–6*
  Romanesque **7** 224; **26** 605, 616, 651, 654–5*, 702
  Spain **26** 605
  Vietnam **32** 470–71
  14th cent. **25** 679
  15th cent. **19** 813
  18th cent. **8** 910
 Colombia **29** 134

iconography—cont.
 Confucianism **6** 628*; **17** 40–42*; **18** 256; **32** 470
 Crete **21** 677
 Cycladic **8** 306–7*
 Cyprus **8** 326–7*
 Cyprus, ancient **8** 327*
 Daoism **8** 516–17
  China **5** 107; **6** 628*; **7** 61, 105–6, *106*; **10** 485
  Japan **17** 39–40*
  Korea **18** 255
  Vietnam **32** 470
 Denmark **8** 757*
 Dogon **1** 261, 263, 275, 280
 Dominican Order **9** 107–11*; **13** 127
 Early Christian (*c.* AD 250-843) **7** 219*; **9** 516*, 517–18*, 519–21*, 562, 572, 573, 575, 595, 596, 609–10, 616, 617, 622, 623, 635; **12** 71–2; **18** 826; **22** 161; **26** 862; **33** 215
 Ecuador **29** 134
 Egypt, ancient **9** 792–4, *793*, 801–11*, 894; **12** 67
 Elamite **15** *908*
 England **10** 246–7
 Etruscan **10** 587, 588–90, 592–6*, 619
 Fon **1** 282, 284
 France **13** 179
 Franciscan Order **11** 708–11*; **13** 127
 Fulani **1** 373
 Germany **2** 3; **22** 711; **26** 654
 Ghana **1** 262, 282
 Gothic **7** 224; **13** 73, 127, 128–9*, *131*; **28** 402
  Christianity **13** 179
  France **13** 179
  International Gothic **13** 155
  Italy **13** *129*
 Greece, ancient **10** 211, 587, 595–6; **13** 370, 472–4*, 544–7*, 553; **22** 410; **33** 241
 Guinea **1** 261, 262
 Hebrew **1** 830
 Helladic **14** 333–4*
 Hieronymites **14** 517*
 Hinduism **5** 92
  Cambodia **5** 461–2
  Indian subcontinent **7** 633; **14** *556*, 556–8, *557, 558*; **15** 213–14*, 219*; **20** 818
   Ganapatya **15** 216–17*
   Saura **15** 216
   Shaivism **15** 214–15*
   Shakta **15** 217–19*
   Vaishnavism **15** 215–16
  Indonesia **15** 756–7*, 777
  Java **15** 777
  Nepal **22** 756*
  Sri Lanka **29** 443–4
 Hittite **1** 828–30*; **33** 513
 Hurrian **33** 513
 Igbo **1** 261, 275
 Indian subcontinent **7** 633; **15** 206, 210, 213*, 229–30*, 232–4*, 706, 729, 749; **23** 290
  Buddhism **3** 907; **5** *92*, 93, *96*; **7** 633; **15** 220–24*, 229, 416, 425, 431–2, 446–8, 501
  Chola **15** 522–3
  Indus civilization **15** 213, 229
  Jainism **15** 224–6*
 Indonesia **15** 756*, 782, 814–15, *815*
  Buddhism **15** 757*, 777
  Hinduism **15** 756–7*, 777
  Islamic **15** 757–8*
 Indus civilization **15** 213, 229
 Iran, ancient **15** 907–8*, *908*, 916
 Islamic **15** 757–8*; **16** 127–38*, 429, 468; **18** 242; **24** 609–10*; **28** 915
 Italy **22** 413; **25** 71–2
  Byzantine **9** *520*

iconography
 Italy—cont.
  Etruscan **10** 587, 588–90, 592–6*, 619
  Gothic **13** *129*
  Renaissance **14** 866
 Jainism **15** 224–6*; **23** 290
 Japan **17** 30*, 44–5*, 322, 345–50
  Buddhism **5** 116, 118; **17** 33–9*, 107, 108, 146–8, 168
  bushidō **17** 42*
  Confucianism **17** 40–42*
  Daoism **17** 39–40*
  Neo-Confucianism **17** 41
  Prehistoric **17** 30–31*
  Shinto **10** 485; **17** 31–3*
  Shugendō **17** 42–4*
 Java **15** 777, 797–8
 Jesuit Order **17** 509–10*; **22** 414
 Jewish art **9** 517; **17** 533–7*; **28** 915
 Kissi **1** 263
 Knights Hospitaller **18** 152*
 Knights Templar **18** 153–4
 Kongo **1** 261
 Korea **18** 253–6*, *255*, 316, 375
  Buddhism **5** 91; **18** *254*, 254–5, 305–6, 307–9
  Confucianism **18** 256
  Daoism **18** 255
  shamanism **18** 253–4
 Kuba (iii) (Zaïre) **1** 263
 Laos **18** 763
 Late Antiquity **18** 823–5; **26** 862–3, *863*
 Luba **19** 738–9*
 Mali **1** 280
 Manichaeism **6** 293
 Maya **21** *184*, 187, 189, 190
 Mende (Sierra Leone) **1** 263
 Mesoamerica, Pre-Columbian **21** 182–3*, *184*, 184–6*, 187–90*, 218, 373–4, *374*, 739; **29** 133
 Mesopotamia **15** 916; **21** 276–9*
 Mexico **18** 831–2; **21** 373–4; **26** 426
 Minoan **21** 653–4*, 677
 Mixteca-Puebla **21** 186, 739, *739*
 Moche (culture) **29** 133, 134
 Mongolia **5** 91; **21** 872–3*, 880
 Mycenaean **14** 333–4*
 Native North Americans **22** 559–61*, 665
 Nazism **22** 711
 Neo-Confucianism **17** *41*, 41
 Nepal **22** 755–6*, 757*
  Buddhism **5** 103; **22** 756–7*
  Hinduism **22** 756*
  Tantra **5** 103
 Nigeria **1** 261
 Oratorians **23** 472–3*
 Parthian **24** 218
 Pende **1** 261
 Peru **29** 134
 Philippines **24** 609–10*
 Phoenician **1** 830
 Phrygian **1** 830
 Pictish art **24** 737
 Post-Byzantine **7** 222–3*
 Prehistoric **17** 30*
 Romanesque **7** 224; **26** 605, 616, 651, 654–5*, 702
 Rome, ancient **5** 801; **9** 517; **10** 211; **22** 411; **26** 857, *858, 859*, 859–63*, *862*; **27** 11–12*, 31, 47–50*; **32** 86; **33** 241
  Late Antiquity **26** 862–3, *863*
 Scandinavia **32** 519–24*
 Senufo **1** 275, 280
 Servites **28** 489–90*
 Shinto **10** 485; **17** 31–3*
 Shugendō **17** 42–4*
 Sicán culture **28** 651
 Sierra Leone **1** 261
 South America, Pre-Columbian **29** 129–34*
  Aguada culture **29** 190
  Chavín culture **6** 521–2*

iconography
 South America, Pre-Columbian—cont.
  Sicán culture **28** 651
 South-east Asia **5** 91
 Spain **26** 605
 Sri Lanka **29** 442–4, *443*, 458, 459
 Switzerland **30** 136
 Syria-Palestine **30** 188–9*
 Tantra **5** 103
 Thailand **29** 826; **30** 573–4*, 594, 635
 Theatine Order **30** 648–9*
 Thracian **30** 771
 Tibet **5** 91; **30** 809–11*, 813, 822, 825–6, 845
 Togo **1** 282
 United States of America **18** 831–2; **31** 672
 Urartian **1** 830
 Valdivia culture **29** 134
 Vietnam **6** 419–20*, 427; **32** 470–71*
 see also ALLEGORIES; ICONOGRAPHY; SYMBOLISM (CRITICAL TERMS) **32** 470
 Viking **32** 519–24*
 West Mexico **33** 103
 Yaka **1** 262
 Yoruba **1** 261, 276, 280–81, 282–4
 Zaïre **1** 261, 262, 263, 282
 Zambia **1** 282
 Zoroastrianism **6** 192–3*, *193*; **33** 706–8*
 see also ALLEGORIES; ICONOLOGY; SYMBOLISM (CRITICAL TERMS)
iconology **2** 532; **10** 207; **15** 89–97*, *90, 91, 92, 93, 94, 95, 96*, 211
 see also ALLEGORIES; ICONOGRAPHY; SYMBOLISM (CRITICAL TERMS)
iconostases *see under* SCREENS (i) (ARCHITECTURAL) → types
icons **9** 3, 13; **15** 75–7*, *77*
 historical and regional traditions
  Belarus' **3** 527, 528, *530*; **25** 341*
  Bulgaria **5** 151–2*, *152*, 154; **9** 633; **25** 338–9*, 559
  Byzantine **2** 3; **7** *221*, 222, 230; **9** 517, 518, 597–8, 601*, 621–30*, 632, 633, 658; **10** 197; **13** 131; **15** 75*, 76, *76*, I, II3, III; **24** 3; **26** 332; **31** 343; **32** *212*
   Bulgaria **5** 151–2, *152*
   Crete **9** 622
   Cyprus **9** 627
   Egypt **9** *624, 625, 626*; **28** *762, 763*
   Greece **9** *630*; **15** II1
   Jerusalem, Latin Kingdom of **9** 627
   Macedonia (ii) (former Yugoslavia) **9** *628*
   Palestine **9** 627
   Russia **9** 629; **15** *76*, II2; **27** *383, 384*; **30** V3
   Syria **9** 627
   Ukraine **26** *141*; **31** *555*
  Christianity **19** *788*, 788–9
  Coptic **7** 823*
  Crete **7** 850
   Byzantine **9** 622
   Post-Byzantine **8** 157; **25** 331–2*, *332, 333*, 333–4*
   Venetian Empire **8** 157, *157*
  Cyprus **8** 359; **9** 623, 624, 626, 627
  Early Christian (*c.* AD 250-843) **9** 517, 518, 621–4*, *624*; **13** 131; **18** *825*; **26** 862; **30** V2
  Egypt **7** 823*; **9** *624, 625, 626*; **28** *762, 763*
  England **13** *131*

icons
historical and regional traditions—cont.
Georgia **9** 623; **12** 322–3*, 325–6*, *328*, *329*; **15** 77
Post-Byzantine **25** 341*
12th cent. **12** *326*
Gothic **13** *131*
Greece **9** *630*; **15** II1; **24** 3; **25** 333, 334; **31** 554
Indian subcontinent **15** 416
Italy **19** *788*; **30** V2; **32** *212*
Japan **10** 400; **17** 341
Jerusalem, Latin Kingdom of **9** 627
Knights Hospitaller **26** 293
Macedonia (i) (Greece) **9** 624
Macedonia (ii) (former Yugoslavia) **9** *628*
Palestine **9** 624, 625, 627
Poland **25** 341*
Post-Byzantine **8** 157, *909*; **25** 331–2*, *332*, 333–4*, *333*, *337*, 337–41*, *339*; **27** *385*, *386*
Rhodes (island) **26** 293, 295
Romania **25** 340–41*
Russia **24** 3; **27** 305, 382–6; **31** 555
Byzantine **9** 629; **15** *76*, II2; **27** *305*, *383*, *384*; **30** V3
Post-Byzantine **8** *909*; **25** *337*, 337–8*; **27** *385*, *386*
Serbia **25** *339*, 339–40*; **28** 447–9*, *448*
Syria **9** 627
Ukraine **25** 341*; **26** *141*; **31** 554–5*, *555*, 557*, 558
Venetian Empire **8** 157, *157*; **32** 159
materials
enamel **9** 623; **12** *329*; **15** I; **32** *212*
encaustic paintings **9** 623, *624*; **10** 197; **28** *762*
frames **24** 4
gems **12** *329*; **32** *212*
gold **9** 623, 625, 626; **12** *329*; **15** I; **32** *212*
gold leaf **9** 623
hardstones **9** 623; **15** I
icon covers *see* ICON COVERS
lapis lazuli **9** 623
marble **7** *221*
mosaics **9** 623, 627, 630, *630*; **15** II3; **28** *763*
mounts **9** 622, 625
pigments **9** 623
plaster **9** 623
pottery **9** 632, 633
silver **5** 152; **9** 623, 658; **12** *328*, *329*
silver-gilt **9** 623
tempera **30** 425
techniques
gilding **12** 625
types
architrave **9** 622, 623, 625, 626–7, 628, 629, 630
calendar **25** 183
despotic **9** 622, 626, 629
double-sided **9** 622, 626, 629
relief **9** 597–8, *601*
see also PAINTING → types → religious
I(nductively) C(oupled) P(lasma) S(pectrometry) *see under* TECHNICAL EXAMINATION → types
Iculisma *see* ANGOULÊME
Ida, Shōichi **17** 296
Ida Bagus Kembeng **15** 808
Ida Bagus Madé (Poleng) **15** 808
Ida Bagus Madé Djata(sura) **15** 809
Ida Bagus Madé Pugug **15** 809
Ida Bagus Madé Togog **15** 809
Ida Bagus Rai **15** 809
Idaean cave **8** 154; **13** *362*; **15** 98*; **21** *651*; **29** 396
Idah **15** 108; **23** *129*
masks **15** *108*
Idah, Ovia **1** 332
Idaho Falls Mormon temple (ID) **22** 126
Idaian cave *see* IDEAN CAVE
Ida Keishi **17** 414
Idalion **8** *325*
alabastra **1** 868
bowls **24** *644*
houses **8** 337
ivory-carvings **8** 351
sculpture **8** 342
Idang *see* KIM ŬN-HO
Idar-Oberstein **12** 455, 456
Idasse **22** 245
Id Dêr **21** 834
Iddibal Tapapius **19** 221
Idea **24** 437
idea art *see* CONCEPTUAL ART
ideale Heim, Das **14** 312
Ideal Home **10** 284
Ideal Home Exhibition, 1908 *see under* LONDON → exhibitions
idealization **22** 686; **25** 284–5
Ideal Toy Co. **31** 260, 261
Idee **29** 547
Idehen, Festus **18** 639
Idelson, Benjamin **16** 565; **28** 557; **33** 507
Idemitsu, Sazō **17** 430
Idensen Church **26** 651, 657
ideograms
Ancient Near East **1** 853
China **17** 211
Egypt, ancient **10** 1
France **2** *226*
Mesoamerica, Pre-Columbian **21** 248
Mixtec **21** 248
ideographs *see under* SCRIPTS → types
ideology **9** 796–9*; **15** 98–101*
Idera Tomb **17** 59, 143
Idfū *see* EDFU
'idgāhs see under MOSQUES → types
Idhra *see* HYDRA
Idikushari **18** 26
Iding **18** 484
Idjevan **2** 428, 439
'Idjl **2** 255
idocrase **16** 857
Idogro, Pedro Caro *see* CARO IDOGRO, PEDRO
Idol see IDOLINO
idolatry **15** 78
Idolino **15** 101*; **25** 179; **27** 22, 46; **29** 561, *562*
idols, eye *see under* FIGURINES → types
Idoma **1** 383; **15** 101–3*
aesthetics **1** 236
costumes **1** 270
masks **1** 383; **15** 101–2, *102*
sculpture **15** 102
Idrieus **18** 580
Idrimi, King of Alalakh (statue *c.*1500 or 1250 BC) **1** 816; **30** 193
Idris I, Ruler (*reg* 789-93) (Idrisid) **11** 49; **15** 103; **16** 493
Idris II, Ruler (*reg* 793-828) (Idrisid) **11** 49; **15** 103; **16** 493
Idris, Effendi **10** 92
al-Idrisi **5** 833; **29** 323
Idrisid **15** 103*
see also:
IDRIS I, Ruler
IDRIS II, Ruler
Idromeno, Andrea **15** 103
Idromeno, Arsen **15** 103
Idromeno, Kol **15** 103–4*
personal collection **1** 545
works **1** 540; **15** *103*
Idstein Unionskirche **19** 815
Idubor, Felix **18** 639; **23** 137, 139; **32** 86
Idut **27** 812
tomb **9** *872*; **27** *811*
Idźkowski, Adam **7** 837; **15** 104*
IED (Integrated Environmental Design) **10** 417
Iehiro Konoe *see* KONOE IEHIRO
Ieli **12** 328
Iemitsu Tokugawa *see* TOKUGAWA IEMITSU, Shogun
Ienaga Sansaburō Masachika **17** 262
Ieper *see* YPRES
Ierapetra *see* HIERAPETRA
Ieremia, Prince **26** 721
Iermilov, Vasyl' **2** 634
Iermonahul, Gavril **26** 711
Iernu Mureș **26** 707
Iernut Palace **14** 885
Ieshige Kawachi Daijō *see* KAWACHI DAIJŌ IESHIGE
Ietsugu Ao *see* AO IETSUGU
Ieuan ap Sullen **32** 784
Ieyasu Tokugawa *see* TOKUGAWA IEYASU, Shogun
Ifaluk **23** 723
IFAN *see* OUAGADOUGOU → Institut Français de l'Afrique Noire
IFAO *see* INSTITUT FRANÇAIS D'ARCHÉOLOGIE ORIENTALE
Ife (Nigeria) **1** 222, *386*; **15** 104–7*; **23** *129*; **33** 553
art forms and materials
architecture **1** 309; **33** 554
beads **1** 297; **33** 559
brass **4** 854
painting **23** 136
pots **1** 329
terracotta **1** 350
fortifications **21** 597
Museum of the Ife Antiquities **23** 139
University **23** 135
Ife (Kingdom of) **1** 436; **33** 553
brass **1** 250; **15** *106*
copper **15** *104*, *105*
funerary objects **1** 258
human figures **15** *106*
masks **15** *104*
metalwork **23** 131
regalia **1** 352
sculpture **15** *105*, *106*, 107*, *107*; **23** 131; **33** 555*, 559
stone-carvings **1** 292
terracotta **1** 329; **15** *107*; **30** 509
Ifejike-Obukwelu, Kate **1** 247
Iffley (Oxon), St Mary **6** 564; **26** 589, *589*, 614
Ifield (Sussex), St Margaret **11** 253
IFLA (International Federation of Library Associations and Institutions) **2** 369
Iford Manor (Wilts) **12** 141
Ifran **17** 551
Ifugao **24** 607, 609
basketwork **24** *628*, 628
body ornaments **24** 625, 626
containers **24** 626–7
dress **24** 628
sculpture **24** 617, *618*
textiles **24** 623, 624
I Fukyū *see* YI FUJIU
Iga **17** *11*, *241*
ceramics **15** 108*
pottery **17** 255, 260–61, 438
Igalu **1** 383; **15** 108–9*
costumes **1** 270
doors **1** 383
masks **15** *108*, 108–9*
scarification **1** 345
wood-carvings **15** 109*
Igami, Bonkotsu **17** 295
Igarashi (family) **17** 303, 304, 424; **31** 81
Igarashi Dōho **17** 303, 304
Igarashi Magobei **14** 704
Igarashi Shinsai **17** 304
Igarashi Sōo **14** 704
Igarra **9** 736
Iga ware *see under* POTTERY → wares
Igbide **9** 736
Igbira **1** 270
Igbo **1** 243; **14** 55; **15** 109–17*; **23** 128; **31** 331
anklets **1** 292, 351
architecture **23** 134
body arts **1** 288, *289*, 343, 344; **15** 115
brass **15** 109
caricatures **5** 761
cement **1** 331
ceramics **1** 329, 330
colour **7** 635
costumes **1** 270; **15** *111*
craftsmen and artists **1** 244
divination instruments **1** 356
doors **9** 164
dress **15** 115
drums (musical instruments) **1** 243; **10** 124
gesture **1** 266
gourds **1** 303
hairstyles **1** 343
headdresses **15** 112, 113
houses **1** 284, 289, 314, 331; **15** 110, *114*, 115
mbari **1** 331
iconography **1** 261, 275
ivory **1** 292, 293
masks **1** 256, 273, 274, 290, 301, 338, 341, 342; **15** 110–13*, *111*
meeting-houses **1** 310; **15** 116
mixed-media **1** 301
mud **1** 331
painting **23** 137
patronage **1** 241, 243
pottery **1** 246
scarification **1** 344, 345
sculpture **1** 274, 330, 331; **5** 761; **15** 109, *112*, *113*, 113, 114, 115*, *115*
shells **1** 284
shrines (i) (cult) **1** 289; **15** 113*
temples **1** 309
terracotta **30** 509
textiles **1** 349
wall paintings **1** 289
wigs **1** 343
wood **9** 164; **15** *113*, *115*
wood-carvings **15** 116
wrought iron **15** 109
Igbo Isaiah **15** 116, 117
body arts **1** 345
bronze **15** 118, *118*, *119*
copper **15** 119
iron **15** 120
pottery **15** 120
Igbo Jonah **15** 116–17
copper **15** 120
iron **15** 120
pottery **15** 120, *120*
Igbomina **1** 345; **33** 557
Igbo Richard **15** 116, 117
armlets **1** 351
copper **15** 119, *119*
iron **15** 120
pottery **15** 120
Igbo-Ukwu **1** 222, 224, *386*, 436; **10** 124; **15** 109, 116–20*; **23** *129*
bowls **4** *854*
bronze **1** 288; **15** *118*, 118–19*, *119*
copper **15** 117–18, *119*, 119–20*
iron **15** 120*
lost-wax casting **15** 117
metalwork **1** 288, 342; **23** 131
pots **1** 329
pottery **15** 120*, *120*
sculpture **4** 854
tin **15** 118
Igede **1** 342
Igel **26** 861
Igelshofer, Franz **14** 573
Iggensbach Church **26** 686
Iglau *see* JIHLAVA
Igler, Hans *see* KNABENSBERG, HANS
Iglesia, Francisco Ignacio Ruiz de la *see* RUIZ DE LA IGLESIA, FRANCISCO IGNACIO
igloos **9** 165
Ignas, Vytautas **19** 499
Ignatios of Constantinople **9** 638
Ignatius Loyola, Saint **7** 215; **10** 175; **15** 121*; **19** 736
Ignatiyev **25** 475; **27** 364
Ignatov, N. **12** 327
Ignatov, Vasily **27** 434
Ignatovich, Boris (Vsevolodovich) **15** 121–2*; **28** 643
Ignatovich, Ol'ga **15** 122
Ignatovich, Yelizaveta **15** 122
Ignat'yev, Fyodor **33** 507
Ignaz, Pavel **6** 363
Igneris *see* SALADOID
Igołomia **18** 429
Igorot **24** 607, 626, 631
Iguácel
sculpture **26** 643
S María **26** 582, 607
Iguel, Charles-François-Marie **3** 824; **33** 55
Igusa Yoshisaburō *see* UTAGAWA KUNIYOSHI
I Gusti Madé Deblog **15** 809
I Gusti Nyoman Lempad **15** 809
Ihara Sikaku **17** 348; **23** 594
Ihei Kimura *see* KIMURA, IHEI
Ihei Toshimaya *see* TOSHIMAYA IHEI
Ih huree *see under* ULAAN BAATAR
Ihlara
churches **5** 677
Eğri Taş Kilisesi **5** 676, 677
Karagedik Kilise **9** 544
Kokar Kilise **5** 677
St Michael **5** 676
Yılanlı Kilise **5** 677
Ihlow Abbey **4** 776
Ihnasya el-Medina *see* HERAKLEOPOLIS MAGNA
Ihnatowicz, Zbigniew **15** 122*; **29** 52; **32** 872
Ihne, Ernst Eberhard **3** 43, 794, 795, 807; **15** 122*
Ihriský, Vojtěch **28** 855
Ihrwach, Sebastian *see* IRRWOCH, SEBASTIAN
Ihuatzio **30** 340; **31** 118
sculpture **30** *341*
Ihy **9** 877
Ii (family) **17** 429
IIC *see* INTERNATIONAL INSTITUTE FOR CONSERVATION OF HISTORIC AND ARTISTIC WORK
Iida City Museum **14** 161
Iida Hyakusen **17** 235
Iittala Glassworks **11** 107
vases **11** *107*
Iittala-Nuutajärvi Co. **11** 107
Iizuka, Shirohatayama **30** 258
Iizuka (family) **17** 304
Iizuka Tōyō **17** 304, 399
Iizumiya Shichiemon **17** 400
Ijebu-Ode **23** *129*
Ijebu-Yoruba **33** 557
sculpture **1** *270*
Ijjasz de Murcia, Ernese **1** 744
Ijkens, Frans *see* YKENS, FRANS
Ijo **15** 123–6*
headdresses **15** *124*, 125–6
masks **15** 124
portraits **1** 267
screens (ii) (furniture) **1** 257; **15** 125, *125*
sculpture **15** 124, *125*
textiles **1** 349
women artists **1** 247
wood-carvings **15** *124*, 125
Ij Shrine **16** 801, 802
IJsselstein
church **13** 114; **22** 823
tombs **22** 855

IJssewijn, Michiel *see* YWYNS, MICHIEL
Ika 15 62
ikakeji see under LACQUER → types
Ikalto Church 12 319
Ikao 9 734
Ikaria, Sanctuary of Dionysos 13 385
Ikaros *see* FAYLAKA ISLAND
Ikaruga
Chūgūji 23 597
Hōryū Gakumonji *see* Hōryūji
Hōryūji 2 655; 5 116; 14 773–5*, *774*; 16 783; 17 *11*, 46, 65, 66, 67, 94, *107*, *109*, 325, 397; 18 260; 30 445, *445*
bronze 17 110
chūmon 12 174
collections 17 428
Daihōzōden 14 773
Daikōdō *see* Great Lecture Hall
Denpōdō 14 774; 17 69, 101, 115; 30 913
doors 9 162
Edono 17 157; 28 625
Great Lecture Hall 17 66
Hokiji 17 66
Hōrinji 4 625; 17 66
Ikaruga no Miya 14 773
Ikaruga no Tera *see* Wakakusadera
Jōguōden *see* Tō'in
kondō 4 625; 5 118; 14 773–4; 17 48, 66, 97, 107, 145
Kudara Kannon 17 108–9*
Lecture Hall 30 913
Main South Gate 14 775
masks 17 391, 392
Middle Gate 7 361; 17 99
pagoda 17 66, 113; 23 776
Picture Hall *see* Edono
roofs 30 913
Sai'in 14 773–5
scrolls 17 270
sculpture 6 835; 14 773; 17 101, 107, 109, 124, 131
Shaka Triad 17 107–8*, 211
Shōryō'in 14 775
Tachibana Shrine 14 773; 17 34–5, 110–11, *111*; 23 553; 28 639
Tamamushi Shrine 14 773; 17 66, 110, 145, *145*, 158, 299; 28 639
textiles 17 312, 313, 374
Tō'in 14 774
Treasure House 17 108
Wakakusadera 14 773; 23 597
wall paintings 17 139
Yumedono 14 774; 17 68, 108, 130; 19 317
Yumedono Kannon 17 99, *99*, 108*
Ikaruga no Daiji *see* Hōryūji
Ikaruga no Soji *see* Hōryūji
ikat 30 554–6*, *555*
Afghanistan 30 554
Africa 1 294
Bali (Indonesia) 15 793
Burma 5 248*; 30 554
Cambodia 5 502, *502*, 503
Central Asia, Western 16 451
Chile 6 *599*
China 7 144
Côte d'Ivoire 8 22
Ferghana 16 451
Greece 30 554
Guatemala 30 554
Indian subcontinent 15 670, 671–2*; 30 554, 556
Orissa 30 555
Indonesia 9 III1; 15 792, 793, 794, *795*, 795–6, *796*; 30 554
Iran 30 554
Islamic 16 *438*, 439, 451; 31 21, 22
Japan 17 307–8, 316–17, *317*, *354*, 354–5; 30 554, 556
ikat—cont.
Java 15 792
Khmer 5 *502*
Laos 18 771
Malaysia 20 176; 30 554
Mesoamerica, Pre-Columbian 21 261
Peru 24 513
Ryūkyū Islands 27 471
Sumatra 15 794
Syria 30 554
Thailand 5 502, 503; 30 554
Turkestan (region) 30 554
Turkey 30 554
Yemen 16 *438*, 439; 31 21, 22
IKB (International Klein Blue) 18 118
Ikdang *see* KONGMIN
IKEA 20 595; 30 92
ikebana see JAPAN → flower arrangements
Ikebana International 17 382
Ikebe, Kiyoshi 15 128*
Ikeda, Kurehaza 17 331
Ikeda, Masuo 15 128*
Ikeda Eisen 15 128–9*; 17 417; 31 53
Ikeda Koson 17 180
Ikeda Taishin 17 399; 28 600
Ikeda Terumasa 14 551; 17 84
Ikeda Tsunamasa 23 386
Ike Gyokuran 15 126, 127–8*; 17 234; 33 321, 577
teachers 17 190; 33 492
works 33 *321*
Ikemura, Leiko 30 135
Ikenaga, Hajime 17 429
Ikenaga Dōun 15 129*; 17 409, 410, 413
works 17 *410*
Ikenobō Sen'ei 17 380
Ikenobō Sengyō 17 380
Ikenobō Senkō II 17 380
Ikenobō Senno 17 380, 417
Ikere, Palace of the Ogoga 9 *164*; 33 *554*
Ike Taiga 15 126–8*; 17 165, 194; 18 552; 33 321, 561
patrons and collectors 17 433
pupils 17 190, 234; 18 60, 542; 23 594
teachers 33 492
works 1 582; 15 *127*; 17 190, 216, 237, 238; 20 287; 22 231
Ikhshid 27 671
Ikin, Humphrey 23 67
works 23 *67*
Ikisada, Latmos Church 4 9 550
İkiztepe 1 *821*, 824, 834
Ikkei Kanō *see* KANŌ IKKEI
Ikkei Ukita *see* UKITA IKKEI
Ikkeri 15 398
Aghoreshvara Temple 15 398, 533
Ikko (family) 17 186
Ikko Narahara *see* NARAHARA, IKKO
Ikko Tanaka *see* TANAKA, IKKO
Ikkyū *see* IKKYŪ SŌJUN
Ikkyū Sōjun 15 129–31*; 18 560
pupils 22 339; 28 624
works 15 *130*, *131*; 17 342
Ikom 1 *381*; 23 *129*
masks 10 *122*
Ikot Abassi 15 61
Ikot Abia Osom 15 61
Ikot Ekpene 1 *386*; 9 735, 736; 15 61, 62
IKOY Partnership 14 521
Ikramov, Iskandr 31 783
Iksan
Kodo 18 292
Mirŭk Temple 12 94; 18 260, 267; 30 444
pagoda 23 775
sculpture 18 283
Wanggung 18 351, 365
Ikshvaku *see*:
CHANDASIRI, Queen
Ikshvaku—cont.
see: VASHISHTHIPUTRA CAMTAMULA I, King
Ikšķile 18 *847*
church 18 847
Iktinos 2 312; 13 394; 15 131–2*
collaboration 2 676; 17 742
works 2 679; 3 340, 341; 7 502; 13 379, 394, 400–401, *401*
writings 2 351
Ikuma Arishima *see* ARISHIMA, IKUMA
Ikuno 17 318
Ikunum 2 636
Ikuo Hirayama *see* HIRAYAMA, IKUO
Ikuta, Susumu 17 267
Ila 1 368
Ilam Gautama 15 559
Ilande 29 70
Ilaro 1 *381*
masks 1 *239*, *241*
Ila Tonga 1 311
Ilavský, Svetozaźr 28 853
Ilceda, Cristobal Sandoval y Rojas, Duque de 27 723
Ilchester, 4th Earl of *see* FOX-STRANGEWAYS, W(ILLIAM) T(HOMAS) H(ORNER)
Ileana 5 73; 26 715
Ile-aux-Noir 21 575
Ile-Bouchard, L' *see* L'ILE-BOUCHARD
Ile de France *see* MAURITIUS
Ile de La Gonâve 14 54, *54*
Ile Longue 25 508
Ile Royale 11 *756*, 759
Iles, Frank 8 707
Iles, Raoul de, Abbot of Mont-Saint-Michel 22 40
Iles du Salut 11 *756*, 758
Ilesha 21 597
Il'f 18 504
Ilford Ltd 24 649, 656
Ilfov, Snagov Monastery 4 783; 25 344; 26 712
Ilg, Albert 28 800
Ilgın
baths 3 377
complex of Lala Mustafa Pasha 16 224
Ilgynly Tepe 6 275
Ilha de Moçambique 22 245
Museu de Arte Sacra 22 245
Palacío de São Paolo 22 245
Ilho *see* NAM KYE-U
Iliazd *see* ZDANEVICH IL'YA
Ilić, Boža 28 451
Il Idrísí 13 812
Iliescu-Călineşti, Gheorghe 15 132*
Ilin, Ephraim 16 570
Il'in, Lev (Aleksandrovich) 3 88; 15 132–3*; 18 114
Il'in, T. 23 76
Il'ina, Lidiya Alexandrovna 18 568
Ilion *see* TROY
Ilioneus 13 914
Ilissos Relief 13 431
Iliupersis Painter 13 528–9
works 13 *528*
Ilkhanid 15 133–4*; 16 116; 23 815
see also:
ABAQA, Khan
ABU SA'ID, Sultan
ARGHUN, Khan
GAYKHATU, Khan
GHAZAN, Khan
HULAGU, Khan
ULJAYTU, Sultan
Ilkić, Jovan 28 444, 838
Ilkley (W. Yorks), Heathcote 19 *821*
Illasi, Villa Pompei-Carlotti 3 109
Illchester Carpet 15 683
Illescas 29 263
Hospital de la Caridad 14 784; 29 267, *268*
Illescas, Sixto 12 177; 29 87
Illinois 22 552
Illinois Glass Co. 19 304
Illiński (family) 25 138
illite 25 477
Illmitz 25 529
Illouschegg, Franc *see* JELOVŠEK, FRANC
Illunga, Enoch 33 603
illusionism 8 910–11; 10 736; 15 134–42*, IV; 27 *497*
see also MIMESIS
Illustrated London News 12 617; 15 830; 17 877; 25 244; 26 742
Illustration, L' 6 491; 15 830
Illustration nouvelle, L' 5 364
illustrations, book *see* BOOK ILLUSTRATIONS
illustrations of works of art *see* ART (ILLUSTRATIONS OF WORKS OF)
Illustratore 2 18; 4 274; 20 695–6*
collaboration 20 787
works 14 898; 20 *696*
Illustrazione Italiana 11 869
Illyrian 1 537
Illzach, (Jean-)
Désiré Ringel d' *see* RINGEL D'ILLZACH, (JEAN-)DÉSIRÉ
Ilmenau 30 793
ilmenite 21 241, 718
Ilminster School (Somerset) 28 156
Ilobasco 10 *153*, 154
Ilongot 24 625
Ilorin 1 297, *386*; 23 *129*
University 23 135
Ilovšek, Franc *see* JELOVŠEK, FRANC
Ilpenstein collection 13 266
Ilp'yŏnun *see* SIN YUN-BOK
Ilsenberg 12 452
Ilsted, Peter 14 119
Ilsung (family) 14 678
Ilsung, Georg 32 777
Ilta 18 332
Iltners, Edgars
Iltutmish, Sultan (*reg* 1211-36) (Mamluk of Delhi) 8 672, 677, 678; 15 339, 340; 20 226
Ilue-Ologbo 9 736
Ilushuma 2 636, 639
Ilvessalo, Kirsti 11 110
Il'ya 18 37
Ilyas Bey 16 601
Ilychovo 28 323
Ilyinič, Jury, Prince 3 526
Imad, Bishop of Paderborn 23 648; 26 646
'Imad al-Din, Ruler (*reg* 1127-46) (Zangid) 22 202
'Imad al-Din Mahmud Shirvani 17 830
Imād al-Ḥasanī *see* MIR 'IMAD
Imado ware *see under* POTTERY → wares
Imad Virgin 12 399
Imaemon Imaizumi XIII *see* IMAIZUMI, IMAEMON, XIII
Imagawa (family) 17 778
Imagawa Ujichika 22 432
Image 12 510; 24 434
Image, Selwyn 6 322; 10 354; 15 142*
image-houses 25 169; 29 443, 448–51*, *449*
images d'Epinal see under WOODCUTS → types
Imagier, L' *see* TABARANT, ADOLPHE
imagines maiorum see under PORTRAITS → types
Imaginistgruppen 14 865; 15 142–3*; 30 53, 81
Imagism 1 121
Imagists 6 577
Imai, Kenji 15 143*; 17 90
Imai, Toshimitsu 15 143*
Imaichō 17 97
Imai Isshikensofu 17 381
Imai Junsai 17 409
Imai Sōkyū 23 347
Imaizumi (family) 17 267
Imaizumi, Imaemon, XIII 17 267; 22 421
Imam, 'Ali 23 799, 804
imambaras 15 380
Imam Dur 31 112
Imami (family) 15 143–4*
Imami, Javad al- *see* JAVAD AL-IMAMI
Imami, Muhammad al-Husayni al- *see* MUHAMMAD AL-HUSAYNI AL-IMAMI
Imami, Mustafa al- *see* MUSTAFA AL-IMAMI
Imami, Nasrallah *see* NASRALLAH IMAMI
Imami, Riza *see* RIZA IMAMI
Imamura, Shikō 14 260; 17 201
works 17 *203*
Imana, Gil 4 263; 15 144*; 22 335; 29 894
Imanishi (family) 17 83
Imao, Abdulmari 24 620
imarets 16 224
Imari 4 174; 17 263
Imari ware *see under* PORCELAIN → wares
Imatra 1 9
Imbach, Mariae Geburt 13 57
Imbe 17 255
Imber de Rangel, Sofía 32 179
Imbert 20 270
Imbert, Gabriel 24 212
Imbert, Joseph-Gabriel 9 399
Imbert, Oscar 9 117
Imbonate, Anovelo da *see* ANOVELO DA IMBONATE
Imbrechts, Antoon 11 698
imbuia 29 116
Imdang, Tomb 6A 18 351
Imenj-jatu 9 876, *876*
Imera *see* HIMERA
Imereti 12 316
Imery, Carlos Alberto 10 154
Imfeld, Nikolaus II, Abbot of Einsiedeln 3 7
Imgur-Enlil *see* BALAWAT
Imhof, Heinrich Max 15 144*; 20 385; 28 115; 30 137
Imhoff (family) 3 726; 9 429; 16 900; 18 419; 20 620; 32 605
Imhoff, Andreas 16 900
Imhoff, Hans, IV 12 816; 15 144; 23 316
Imhoff, Johann Joseph (1739-1802) 15 145
Imhoff, Johann Joseph (1796-1860) 15 146
Imhoff, Konrad (*d* 1449) 15 144; 20 696
Imhoff, Konrad (1463-1519) 15 144
Imhoff, Peter (*fl* 1507) 32 605
Imhoff, Peter Joseph (1768-1844) 15 145–6*
Imhoff, Regina 14 679
Imhoff, Willibald 9 443, 446; 14 626; 15 145*
Imhoff Altar, Master of the 15 144; 20 696*
Imhoff Cup 12 444
Imhotep 2 312; 9 789, *856*; 15 146*; 20 863
works 14 331; 19 471; 25 761; 27 811; 31 107
Im Hui-jae 18 329
Im Hŭi-ji
works 18 *323*
I.M.Imprimit 25 628
Imiris-gora 9 85
Imirzek 2 435, 436
imitation *see* MIMESIS
imitation carved *urushi see under* LACQUER → types
imitation lace *see under* LACE → types

imitation lacquer *see under* LACQUER → types
Imitation Lustreware *see under* POTTERY → wares
imitation plaster *see under* PLASTER → types
Imitation Realism **4** 882
imitations of works of art *see* ART (IMITATIONS OF WORKS OF)
imitation stucco *see under* STUCCO → types
Im Lavanttal, St Paul Abbey **2** *776*; **15** 146*
Imlin **11** 620
Immaculate Conception, Master of the *see* FREDIANI, VINCENZO (DI ANTONIO)
Immaculates, the *see* PRECISIONISM
Immendorff, Jörg **14** 589; **15** 146–7*
collaboration **24** 354
groups and movements **25** 360
works **12** 397, *398*
Immenraet, Philips Augustin **31** 523
Immerseel, Chrysostoom van **30** 461; **32** 713
Immerzeel, Christian van **11** 718
Immerzeel, Johannes **10** 208
IMO **4** 812; **18** 536
Im Ok-sang **18** 327
Imola
bastion **3** 359
Forum Cornelii **27** 3
S Agostino **16** 699
S Domenico **13** 96
Imola, Antonio di Giovanni da **11** 20
Imola, Giovanni di Francesco da *see* GIOVANNI DI FRANCESCO DA IMOLA
Imola, Innocenzo da *see* INNOCENZO DA IMOLA
Imola, Obizzo Alidosio d' **15** 150
Imola Psalter *see under* PSALTERS → individual manuscripts
Imparato, Francesco **5** 693
Imparato, Gerolamo **15** 147*; **31** 790
Imparato, Gioacchino **16** 748
impasto **5** 34; **15** 147*
impasto ware *see under* POTTERY → wares
Impe, van **4** 790
Imperato, Ferrante **16** 770
Imperial Axminster carpets *see under* CARPETS → types
Imperial Baroque *see* BAROQUE REVIVAL
Imperial Bronze Foundry (Vienna) *see* KUNSTERZGIESSEREI (VIENNA)
Imperial China and Glassworks (St Petersburg) **27** 416
see also IMPERIAL GLASS FACTORY (ST PETERSBURG)
Imperial Cross **8** 201
Imperial Crown style **17** 89; **31** 242; **32** 896
Imperiale (family) **15** 147–8*
Imperiale, Davide **5** 694
Imperiale, Gian Giacomo (1550-1622) **15** 147
Imperiale, Gian Giacomo (1627-63) **15** 148
Imperiale, Gian Vincenzo **6** 35; **15** 147–8*; **29** 543
Imperiale, Vincenzo **5** 455; **15** 147; **25** 226
Imperial Glass Factory (St Petersburg) **27** 415, 416, 582
designers **28** 642
see also IMPERIAL CHINA AND GLASSWORKS (ST PETERSBURG)
Imperial Household Agency (Japan) **14** 773; **17** 57, 430; **18** 565, 567
Imperiali (1679-1740) **7** 418; **14** 598; **15** 148–9*; **22** 190; **25** 882; **27** 356; **28** 271
works **4** 611; **15** *148*
Imperiali, Cardinal (*fl* 1703) **22** 288
Imperial Menologia **9** 616
Imperial Painting Bureau *see under* KYOTO → academies and art schools
Imperial Porcelain Factory *see* LOMONOSOV PORCELAIN FACTORY (ST PETERSBURG)
Imperial Roof style *see* IMPERIAL CROWN STYLE
Imperial War Graves Commission **4** 158; **8** 811; **19** 822
Impey, Elijah **15** 653, 741; **16** 553
Impey, Elizabeth **15** 593, 653
Impey, Mary **15** 741
Impicchati, Andreino degli *see* CASTAGNO, ANDREA DEL
impluvia **13** 383
imports and exports *see* INDIVIDUAL COUNTRIES; CULTURES; PEOPLES → trade
imposts **2** 292, *292*; **22** 216
imprese **10** 173, 175; **12** 272; **14** 404, 414, 419, 426; **15** 149–50*, *150*
Impressed ware *see under* POTTERY → wares
impressing
Africa **1** 286
Central Asia, Western **6** 275
China **6** 874, 876, *876*, 882, *884*, 888, *891*, 892
Prehistoric art **6** *876*; **25** 514
Impressionism **5** 389–90; **7** 629, 638; **8** 547, 579, 619, 621, 625; **12** 188, 294; **15** 151–7*; **18** 715–16; **19** 355; **21** 613, 862; **22** 745; **24** 667; **25** 38; **30** 168; **31** 704; **33** 611
art forms
drawings **8** *624*; **23** *296*; **31** *705*
drawings (pastel) **15** VII; **24** III
etchings **25** *607*
frames **11** 375, *416*, 416–18
lithography **20** *260*
modelli **21** *771*
nude figures **18** *531*; **23** 295
painting (general) **32** 902
France **11** 297–8; **28** 794, 796
Turkey **2** 634
painting (architectural) **21** *865*
painting (*fêtes champêtres*) **11** *38*; **20** *255*
painting (flower) **20** *257*
painting (genre)
England **29** *595*
France **8** *622*; **9** *288*, *289*; **11** *298*; **15** *153*, VIII; **20** *259*; **24** *879*; **26** *208*, *209*
Japan **18** *531*
Netherlands, the **22** *850*
painting (landscape)
Australia **2** *746*
England **7** *700*
France **12** *188*; **15** *151*; **21** *866*; **22** *119*; **24** *880*, *881*; **28** *795*
painting (sporting scenes) **8** *620*
painting (still-lifes) **29** 669
painting (townscapes) **5** *391*; **15** VII; **24** *882*; **28** *796*
painting (urban life) **15** VI2; **23** III, IV
France **21** *863*, *864*
Italy **33** *612*
United States of America **14** *220*
portraits **8** *619*; **9** *288*; **19** *335*; **25** *278*
Impressionism—cont.
collections **2** 404, 559, 561; **3** 251, 800; **8** 62; **9** 424, 447; **11** 778; **14** 244; **18** 186, 466; **19** 239; **23** 882; **24** 183, 551; **25** 234; **26** 113; **30** 375
Canada **5** 589; **31** 880
Denmark **8** 759
France **10** 837
Romania **26** 722
United States of America **31** 664
commentaries **1** 613; **18** 631; **19** 232; **20** 483; **24** 708; **26** 432; **30** 231
exhibitions **2** 559; **5** 921; **6** 368; **10** 680; **11** 887; **22** 425, 687, 745; **23** 633; **24** 140, 142, 784, 878, 880; **25** 846; **26** 207–8; **28** 698; **31** 605
France **4** 625, 626; **22** 119–20; **28** 171, 344
periodicals **24** 426
regional traditions
Australia **14** 307
see also HEIDELBERG SCHOOL
Canada **5** 593
Denmark **24** 633
England **5** 516; **23** 22; **29** 595
Finland **11** 83, 95; **33** 96
France **6** 366; **11** 546–7; **12** 295–6; **19** 871; **21** 863–4; **22** 687, 688; **26** 207, 431–2; **28** 340, 501
Germany **28** 342
Hungary **10** 108
Italy **29** 255
Japan **30** 258
Mexico **7** 405
Sweden **30** 118
United States of America **15** 156; **24** 481; **26** 474; **30** 452; **31** 487, 603
Uruguay **31** 754
Impressionisten **23** 603
Impressionists (Iraq) **16** 2
Impressionniste, L' **24** 426, 442; **26** 432
impressions **7** 128; **11** 306; **19** 439
imprimatura **13** 705, 708; **15** 158*
Imprimerie Arte **20** 75
Imprimerie Lithographique **4** 614
Imprimerie Photographique **4** 130
Imprimerie Royale **4** 359; **31** 321
Improved Dwellings and Lodging House Company **24** 894
Improved Industrial Dwellings Company (*c.*1863) **30** 458
Impruneta
S Maria **1** 709
altarpiece **1** *709*
Villa Mezzomonte **6** 126
Imray, John **7** 436
Imshaug, St Mary **29** 580
Imstenraedt, Bernhard Albert von **15** 158*
Imstenraedt, Franz Gerhard von **15** 158*
Im Yong-ryŏl **33** 530
Inaba (family) **17** 342
Inaba Tsūryū **17** 400
Inagaki Tsuru-jo **33** 318
Inage Okuzan **17** 412
Inamgaon **15** 159*, 247, 718
I-nan *see* YI'NAN
İnandıktepe **1** 522, *821*, 829; **15** 159–60*
İnandık Vase **1** 838, 891; **15** 159–60; **22** 511
in antis **2** 131; **9** 39; **13** 376
Inariyama tomb **15** 160*; **17** *11*
In Arte Libertas **8** 6, 601, 701; **16** 678; **19** 869; **26** 776
Inatos *Niobe* group **8** 155
Inbe **4** 103
INBO *see* INVERSIONES BOLIVIANAS
Inburi **30** 632
inbutsu see under PRINTS → types
Inca **10** 580; **15** 160–64*, *161*; **24** 497; **29** 127, 161, 191
adobe **29** 164
altars **1** 701
architects **29** 135
architecture **15** 162–3*; **29** 166
armour **29** 205
aryballoi **15** 163; **29** *175*
bark **15** 163
bone **15** 163
bowls **29** *186*
building regulations **5** 135
citadels **20** *3*
clubs (weapons) **29** 205
cochineal **15** 163
cotton **30** IX
craftsmen and artists **15** 163; **29** 134*
cups **15** 163
doors **9** 166
dress **15** 162, 163–4; **29** *183*, 183–4
dyes **15** 163
feathers **10** 848; **15** 163, 164
figurines **29** 218
fortresses **15** *162*
gardens **12** 71
gold **15** 164
goldsmiths **15** 163
hair **15** 163
hardstones **29** 186
headdresses **15** 164
indigo **15** 163
jewellery **15** 164
looms **15** 163
masks **29** 209
masonry **15** 163; **23** 415; **29** 163–4*, *164*
masons **15** 163
masons (master) **29** 135
mass production **29** 135
metal **21** 718
metalwork **15** 164*; **29** 133, 210, 211
mirrors **21** 718
musical instruments **15** 164; **29** 216
observatories **23** 338
painters **29** 135
painting **15** 162
palaces **15** 162; **23** 826
patios **15** 162
patronage **15** 162
potters **29** 135
pottery **15** 163*
quipus **15** 162
religion **29** 129–30*
roads **15** 162
roofs **27** 128
sculptors **29** 135
sculpture **15** 163*; **29** 171–2
shells **15** 163
shields **14** 411
shrines (i) (cult) **28** *641*
silver **15** 164
squares (town) **15** 162
stone **29** *186*
stone-carvings **15** 163; **29** 145
storehouses **15** 162
sundials **23** 338
tapestries **15** 163
temples **29** *166*; **30** 447–8
terraces **15** 162
textiles **15** 163–4*; **29** 135, 181, 207
tombs **31** 119
tunics **29** 183; **30** IX
urban planning **15** 162–3
walls **15** 162
weaving **15** 163
wood-carvings **15** 163; **29** 135
Inca, Garcilaso de la Vega el *see* VEGA EL INCA, GARCILASO DE LA
Inca, Juan Tomás Tuyru Tupac *see* TUYRU TUPAC INCA, JUAN TOMÁS
Inca, Sebastián Acosta Tupac *see* ACOSTA TUPAC INCA, SEBASTIÁN
Incallacta **29** 166, 167
incandescent lamps *see under* LAMPS → types
Incarnation, Marie de l' **25** 801
Inca Roca (*reg c.* 1250–*c.* 1315) **23** 826
In Castel Durante Painter **6** 18
incastellamento **6** 57
Ince, Joseph Murray **15** 164*
Ince, William **15** 164–5
furniture **7** 659, 746; **10** 295; **20** 468
pattern books **8** 529; **11** 119; **20** 350
Ince *Athena* **4** 181
Ince Blundell Hall (Merseyside) **10** 712; **12** 639
Pantheon **4** 181
Ince Blundell marbles **4** 182
Ince Hall *Virgin and Child* **10** 712
Ince & Mayhew **15** 164–5*; **16** 27
works **10** 295
writings **10** 294
incense **17** 341
incense boats **4** *723*
incense burners
historical and regional traditions
Arabia **2** 269
Bahrain **2** 269
Buddhism **7** 68; **18** *348*, 348–9
China **6** 785, 795, *859*, *875*, *882*, 900; **7** 68, 86, *86*, 110
Daoism **6** 785
Iran **16** *374*
Islamic **16** 365, 372, *374*
Japan **17** *265*
Korea **18** *348*, 348–9
Maya **20** 884
Peru **24** 512
Punic **25** 733
Vietnam **32** 486, 488
materials
bronze **6** *859*; **16** *374*; **18** *348*, 348–9
ceramics **20** 884
enamel **7** 68
porcelain **17** *265*
pottery **6** *882*, 900
silver **7** 110; **24** 512
incense containers **17** *301*
incense smoke **7** 102
Incensu, Complex of Kara Mustafa Pasha **16** 224
Incent, John **28** 156
Incerti, Achille **1** 640
Inch Abbey (Co. Down) **16** 7
Incharraundiaga, Pedro **8** 253
Inchbold, J(ohn) W(illiam) **10** 253; **15** 165*; **25** 554
Inchcolm Abbey (Fife) **28** 233
Inchō **15** 159
Inch'ŏn **18** *248*, 262, 301
Inchtuthil **21** 559
incidendo **6** 569
incidere **13** 138
incinerators **2** *741*
Incir Han **16** 247
Incirköy **16** 522
Incisa, Giusto da *see* GIUSTO DA INCISA
incising
historical and regional traditions
China **6** 874, 882, *890*, 892, 901, 905
Egypt **16** 403, 415
Egypt, ancient **10** 27–8
Gothic **13** 139
Greece, ancient **13** 504
Iran **16** 425
Ireland **25** 511
Islamic **16** 364, *388*, 395, 403, 415, 425
Ottoman **16** *388*
Prehistoric art **25** 511, 514
Syria **16** 415
Turkey **16** *388*

incising—cont.
uses
brass **16** *388*
ceramics **16** 425
earthenwares **6** *890*
lacquer **18** 602*
metalwork **16** 364
paintings **13** 139
porcelain **6** 905
pottery **6** 874, 882, 901; **10** 27–8, *301, 612, 614*; **13** 504; **16** 395, 403, 415; **25** 514
rock art *see under* ROCK ART → techniques
stonewares **6** 892
Incorporated Society of Artists **10** 372; **19** 586
see also SOCIETY OF ARTISTS OF GREAT BRITAIN
incunabula **4** 344, 357; **7** 513; **15** 165*; **32** 198
incuse method **13** 586
Indargarh **15** 603, 606
painting **15** *606*
palace **15** 606
Indar Sal, Raja of Indargarh (*reg c.* 1660) (Rajput) **15** 606
Indau, Johann **11** 457; **15** 166*
Inden *see* KORNELIMÜNSTER
Indenbaum, Léon **17** 577
Indented Bar and Concrete Engineering Company **33** 204
Independence (MO), Harry S. Truman Library **3** 748
Independent, The **12** 152
Independent Art Society (abstract art) *see* JIYŪ BIJUTSU KYŌKAI
Independent Art Society (Fauvist) *see* DOKURITSU BIJUTSU KYŌKAI
Independent Gas Light and Coke Company **14** 391
Independent Group **10** 258; **14** 385; **15** 166*; **19** 590; **22** 279; **25** 231; **31** 463
members **3** 172; **14** 111; **28** 889; **33** 218
Independents *see under* CHRISTIANITY → sects
Independents Group *see* ONAFHANKELIJKEN, DE
Independientes, Los **24** 510; **31** 531
Inderpat **8** 670
Inder Vijai Singh **15** 621
indexes **2** 364, 367, 368; **4** 22, 25–6; **5** 386; **10** 204, 205, 212, 213; **15** 96–7
Index Iconologus **4** 27
Index Islamicus **16** 550
Index of American Design **5** 386; **31** 663, 672
India - before 1947 *see* INDIAN SUBCONTINENT; after 1947 *see* INDIA, REPUBLIC OF
India, Bernardino **5** 617; **15** 167*
India, Republic of **15** 167–84*, *178, 261, 279, 285, 294*
advertisements **15** 177
alloys **15** 174
antiquities **15** 183–4
appliqué **15** 175, 176
archaeology **15** 183
architecture **15** 167–9*, *168*
art history **2** 530
art legislation **15** 183–4*
art schools **15** 171, 179
bags **15** 175
bamboo **15** 173, 174
baskets **15** 173, 174
billboards **15** 177
boxes **15** 174, 175
brass **15** 174
brick **15** 168
bronze **15** 175
calendars **15** 178
cement **15** 169
clay **15** 174
coins **15** 689
India, Republic of—cont.
collections **15** 178–9*, 180–83*
commercial art **15** 180
competitions **15** 169
concrete **15** 168
costumes **15** 175–6
cotton **15** *176*
dowries **15** 175
dung **15** 174
education (art) **15** 173, 179–80*
architecture **15** 180
embroidery **15** 175–6, *176*
enamel **15** 174
exhibitions **15** 169
ex-votos **15** 174
floor decorations **15** 174, 178
folk art **15** 175–7*
furniture **15** 174
grasses **15** 173
hangings **15** 176, *176*
heritage **15** 183–4
houses **15** 168
jewellery **15** 174
leather **15** 174
libraries **15** 184*
marble **15** 174
metal **15** 175
mirrors **15** *176*
monuments **15** 183
mud-bricks **15** 169
museums **7** *882*; **15** 180–83*, 184
painting **15** *79*, 169–71*, *170*, 175, 178
scroll **15** 175
wall **15** 174
watercolours **15** *175*
papier mâché **15** 174
patronage **15** 178–9*
periodicals **4** 290
photoarchives **15** 184*
plaques **15** 174
plaster **15** 174
popular art **15** 177–8*, *178*
posters **15** 177
pottery **15** 174
prints **15** 177–8, *178*
quilts **15** 175, 176
reeds **15** 173
rickshaws **15** 177
ritual objects **15** 174
sculpture **15** *79*, 171–3*, *172, 173*, 174, 175, 177
shawls **15** 175, 176
steel **15** 169
studios **9** *180*
textiles **15** 175–7*
tourist art **15** 173, 175
trade **15** 175, 184
vernacular art **15** 174–5*, *175*
willow **15** 174
workshops **15** 179
see also INDIAN SUBCONTINENT
India, Tullio **15** 167
India ink *see under* INKS → types
Indiana, Robert **12** 217; **15** 184–5*
collaboration **20** 607
groups and movements **25** 232
patrons and collectors **32** 623
works **12** 217; **25** 354; **28** 300
Indiana Illustrating Company **26** 536
Indian Antiquary **5** 196; **24** 436
Indianapolis (IN)
court-house **18** 888
Indiana State Capitol **31** *232*
Museum of Art **6** 826
Public Library **8** 152
Indian Art and Letters **24** 446
Indian Arts and Crafts Association **22** 670
Indian Arts and Crafts Board **22** 575, 670, 677
Indian Church *see* LAMANAI
Indian Hill (MA) **2** 698
Indian Institute of Architects **2** 317
Indian lake *see* LAC
Indian red *see under* PIGMENTS → types
Indian Society of Oriental Art **5** 420; **15** 657
Indian subcontinent **15** 185–750*, *191, 261, 276, 279, 285, 294, 619*; **16** *105*; **30** 438
adhesives **15** 551
aesthetics **7** 634; **15** 206
agate **15** 697–8*
albums **1** 582–3*, *583*; **15** 547, 585–6, *586*; **22** 235–6
alizarin **15** 667–8
alloys **4** 687; **15** 706; **21** 330
aloe **15** 549
altars **1** 705*; **4** 793; **15** 237*, 731
alum **15** 667, 668
amber **1** 762
ammonites **15** 729
aquatints **15** 210
arcades **13** *882*
arches **2** 294, 297*; **8** 269; **15** 317, *326*, 327, 387; **16** 201, 239; **23** 368
architects **2** 317*; **15** 207, 208, 245
architectural decorations **15** 262, 342, 354, 374–5, 680, 719
architecture **3** 194; **15** 209*, 212, 234–408*, 548; **25** 292
Andhra Pradesh **15** 293–302*, 324*, 328*
Avadh **15** 376–8*
Bengal **15** 351–3*, 378–80*; **16** 201
Bhauma **3** 909
brick **3** 908; **4** 793–4*; **15** 263, 337, 351
Buddhism **15** 311, 406
Chalukyas of Badami **15** 293–300; **24** 267
Chalukyas of Kalyana **15** 324
Chalukyas of Vengi **15** 301
Chandella **15** 290
Chola **15** 331–4*
Colonial period **15** 242*, 401–4*
commentaries **10** 897–8
Deccan **15** 355–8*, 380–85*
Gujarat **15** 311–15*, 347–9*, 393–5*; **16** 201
Gupta **15** 252–7*
Gurjara-Pratihara **15** 288, 738
Haihaya **15** 290–91
Himachal Pradesh **15** 309–11*
Indus civilization **15** 246–7*
Islamic **4** *51*; **8** 670; **15** 207, 234, 241–2*, 260, 306–7*, 308–9*, 336–59*, 387; **16** 166, 192, 201*, 239*
Kachchhapaghata **15** 292–3
Karnataka **15** 293–302*, 324–8*
Kashmir **15** 264–6*
Kerala **15** 306*, 336*, 358*
Kosala **15** 283–4*
Ladakh **15** 311*
Madya Pradesh **15** 285–93*, 322–4*
Maharashtra **15** 275–9*, 315–17*
Malwa **15** 353–5; **16** 201
Maratha period **15** 393–5
megalithic **15** 192; **21** 43–4*
military **15** 541; **16** 239; **21** 574, 590–91*
Mughal **8** 679; **15** 207, 359–67*, 368–73*, 384, 388–9; **16** 220
Pallava period **15** 302–4
Paramara **15** 291–2
post-and-plank **15** 286, *286*
Prehistoric **15** 245–6*, 247*
Punjab **15** 374–5*
Rajasthan **15** 311–15*, 349–51*, 385–90; **16** 201
Rajput **15** 385–93*
Rashtrakuta **15** 300
Sikhism **15** 375
Sind **15** 338
Solanki **15** 311
stone **4** 794; **16** 239
Sultanate **15** 339–46*
Tamil Nadu **15** 302–5*, 331–4*, 358–9*
Indian subcontinent
architecture—cont.
Uttar Pradesh **3** 908; **15** 260–64*
vernacular **15** 235–6*; **32** 322–5*
Vijayanagara period **15** 328–31*, 335–6*
wood **15** 721
Yadava **15** 315–17
20th cent. **15** 242
armour **14** *186*; **15** 676–9*
arrowheads **15** 677
art history **4** 883; **7** 792–3; **15** 210–12*; **18** 458
artists' biographies **15** 681
art market **2** 558
art schools **15** 656
ash **15** 720
ashes **15** 667
assembly rooms **2** 618
astrology **14** 560
awnings **15** 288
balconies (houses) **15** 288
bamboo **15** 551
bangles **15** 700
banners **15** 563, 570, 647
bark **15** 544, 548, 549, 551; **20** 327
basalt **15** 328
baskets **3** 331, 332; **15** 727
baths **15** 193, *246*, 382
batik **3** 378; **15** 670
bazaar art *see* Popular art
beads **1** 850
beadwork **15** 676
beakers **15** *708*
beetles **15** 618
betel sets **15** 727
boats **15** 721
body arts **15** 734
bone **4** 314
book covers **4** IV1; **15** 549, 563–4, 570; **16** 359
book illustrations **15** 207
books **15** 549, 679–80*
bowls **15** *694, 727*
bows **15** 676, *677*, 677
boxes **15** *696*
box-wood **15** 721
brackets **10** *827*; **15** *431, 531*
brass **4** *682*, 683–4, 687*, 853, 854; **15** 712, *714*, 733, 735, *735*
18th cent. **15** *708*
brick **4** *793*, 793–4*; **15** 256–7*, 262, 263, 280, 328, 413
Islamic **15** 337, 351
Uttar Pradesh **3** 908
brocades **15** 662–4*, *663, 664*, 716
bronze **4** *853*, 853–4*, 855; **15** 414, 459, *523*, 730; **21** 716; **22** 447
Buddhism **15** *223*, 476; **26** *150*
Colonial period **15** *725*
Hinduism **14** *557*; **15** *219, 728*
Indus civilization **15** *412*, 417–20*
Jainism **15** 453
Karnataka **15** *530*, 530–31
Kerala **15** 521, 522, 523, 524, *525*, 708–9
Tamil Nadu **15** *516*, 516–17, *517*
brushes **15** 551
bureaux **15** *693*
burial practices **15** 192
cabinets (ii) (furniture) **20** VIII2
cairns **21** 44
caityas **1** *500*; **10** 147; **15** 237, 249; **17** *815*
calendars **15** 199*
Brhaspati **15** 199
Gupta **15** 199
Kalachuri-Chedi **15** 199
Kollam **15** 199
Laukika *see* Saptarshi **15** 199
Saptarshi **15** 199
Shaka **15** 199
Valabhi *see* Gupta **15** 199
Indian subcontinent
calendars—cont.
Vikrama **15** 199
Western Ganga **15** 199
calligraphers **15** 207, 546
calligraphy **15** 199, 338, 354, 497, 680–81*, *680*, 727
cameos **15** 723
canals **15** 192
cane **15** 693
capitals **5** *669*; **15** *259*, 430
Buddhism **27** *844*
Maurya **15** *413*, 415, 750
1st cent. BC **15** *428*
caravanserais **15** 202, 364
cards **15** 730
carpets **5** 829, 833; **15** 681–4*, *683*; **16** 466, 476*, 485*
carving **4** *793*, 794
caskets **15** 696
casting **4** *853*; **15** 414
cat's-eye **12** 252
caves **3** 194; **15** 194, 236, *250*, 275–9, *277, 278*, 302–4; **18** 18; **24** 887–8
Buddhism **5** 94; **15** *236*, 236, 252–3, 257–9, *258*
cedar **15** 721; **21** 717
ceilings **15** 313, *313*, 325
cemeteries **6** 165
cenotaphs **15** 389
ceramics **15** 685*
chairs **15** *697*
chariots **6** 479, 481*; **15** 193
charters **20** 328, *328*
chasing **15** *708*
chess sets **6** 555–6*, *556*, 557
chintz **15** 717; **30** 559, VI2
chlorite **15** *504*
chronologies **15** 199*
churches **7** 494; **15** 524
cists **21** 43–4
clay **15** 192; **30** *220*
cloaks **15** 736, *736*
coffins **15** 192
coins **7** 532, 533; **8** 269; **15** 193, 194, 200, 213, 219, 231, 687–9*, *688*; **16** 513, 514; **23** 772; **29** 469
collections **15** 211, 737, 739–46*
erotic art **10** 487
Mandi **15** 634
Mughal **16** 552
paintings **15** 610, 611, 740
prints **15** 617
17th cent. **15** 594
18th cent. **15** 618
19th cent. **15** 618
colleges **15** *404*
colonnades **15** 399, *400*
colour **7** 633–4*; **15** 228
columns **15** 330, *335*, 336, 386, 393
Gandhara **15** 448
half **15** 393
Maurya **15** 737
combs (hair) **15** 726, 734
connoisseurship **7** 717*; **15** 740
copies **15** 749–50*
copper **4** 853; **15** *223*, 336, 687, 712*; **20** 328, *328*
Indus civilization **15** 420
coral **12** 252
coral-wood **15** 721
corbels **10** *828*; **15** 338
cornices **15** 258
cosmetic palettes **15** 446
cosmologies **15** 703
cotton **5** 829; **8** 34; **10** I2; **15** 660–61*, 664–5*, 667, 668–70, 674; **20** 327
Hinduism **15** *673*
Islamic **31** 21
17th cent. **15** *675, 683*
18th cent. **15** *691*
19th cent. **8** 36; **15** *669*
coverlets **30** VI2

Indian subcontinent—cont.
craftsmen and artists 15 207–8*, 209, 245, 401; 30 812
Chamba (i) (India) 15 626
Islamic 15 347
Mughal 15 546
16th cent. 15 608
crowns 15 730
cups 15 699
damascening 15 712, 713*
dance 7 634
dating methods 15 199*
decorative arts 15 722–5*
deodar 15 310, 720
diamonds 12 252
dolls 15 731; 31 259
domes 4 52; 9 83; 15 359; 16 201, 239
doorjambs 9 161
doors 9 161, 161–2*
doorways 15 272; 31 520
dowries 15 730
drawings 3 320; 8 534; 15 210, 626
dress 15 689–92*, 690, 733, 734
drums (musical instruments) 22 376
dung 15 548
dyeing 15 667–8*
paste resist 30 557, 558
resist 15 668, 669, 670*, 672*, 673, 673
tie-dyeing 15 670–72*, 670; 30 556
wax resist 30 558
dyes 9 492; 30 560
earrings 15 700
earthenwares 15 685
ebony 6 556; 15 692, 720; 21 717
education (art) 15 208
embroidery 10 I2; 15 548, 674–6*, 675, 681, 717, 722, 736, 736; 21 717; 25 316
emeralds 6 556; 12 252, 253, 253
enamel 6 556; 10 193; 15 707, 710–12*, 711, 723; 16 515, III2
engraving 15 708
epigraphy 15 197, 198–9*; 20 862
erotic art 10 484–5*; 15 229*, 566
ewers 12 V1; 15 714
exhibitions 15 747–8*
faience (ii) (ceramics) 15 374–5
fans 10 778*; 15 727
feathers 10 778; 15 733
felt 10 875
festivals 15 730*
figurines 15 414, 421, 450, 695, 718, 719, 728, 730; 30 510
Baluchistan 15 213
Indus civilization 15 213, 412, 415, 417–20*, 418, 419, 421–2*, 718
Rajasthan 15 724
Tamil Nadu 15 729
flint 15 192
floor decorations 15 726
floors 15 393
forgeries 15 750*; 16 545
fortifications 5 417; 15 248, 340; 21 574, 590, 590
forts 1 461; 15 311; 21 574
fountains 11 340
friezes 15 230
frontispieces 15 679
furnaces 4 681, 682; 21 320
furniture 15 692–4*, 696, 697; 25 303
game-boards 15 730
gardens 12 72–3*, 75
Bengal 12 73
British-Indian 12 75–6*, 76
chār bāgh 8 679; 12 73; 15 361
Gujarat 12 73
Islamic 12 73–5*, 75; 16 239
Mughal 11 340; 12 62, 73–5, 75; 15 361
gates 7 360–61*; 13 886; 15 283
gateways
Avadh 15 377

Indian subcontinent
gateways—cont.
gopuras 6 580; 13 3–5*, 4; 15 239, 329, 333–4, 335, 398, 398; 20 74
toraṇas 15 431
20th cent. 4 290
gem-engraving 12 252–3*, 253
gesso 31 259
ghats 31 903
gilding 6 555; 12 V1; 15 414, 501; 29 825
glass 12 V1; 15 694, 694–5*, 700, 723; 16 522; 21 717
glazes 15 686
glues 15 548
gold 6 556; 7 634; 15 200, 564, 616, 663, 668, 675, 678, 688, 700, 706–7*, 707, 710–12*, 736; 17 II2; 21 717
government buildings 19 47
granaries 24 265
granite 15 233, 329, 508, 514, 515, 518, 519, 534, 538; 17 761
grasses 15 551, 727
grilles 16 257
guidebooks 13 812
guilds 15 207, 245*
gum arabic 15 668
hair 15 551, 734
hairstyles 15 736
halls 14 77*; 15 313, 320, 325
apadanas 23 817
audience 15 356, 365; 23 817
Buddhism 14 77; 17 815
columned 15 335, 335
Islamic 14 77
hangings 10 I2; 15 636, 643, 646, 647, 675, 723
hardstones 7 91; 15 697–9*
harnesses 14 181*, 183–4*, 185, 186*
hats 15 733
headdresses 15 733, 734
helmets 30 564
hero stones 15 231
historiography 7 793; 15 210–12*
hookas 15 711
horn 6 556
houses 5 418; 15 390; 32 323–5, 324
Bengal 15 402
bungalows 5 173; 32 324
Colonial period 15 402
country 19 774
Islamic 15 345
wada 15 393–4, 394
human figures 15 206
hunting scenes 15 606
huts 15 235, 235
hyacinth 12 252
iconoclasm 15 79
iconography 7 633; 15 206, 210, 213–34*, 428–9, 706, 729, 749; 23 290
Buddhism 3 907; 5 92, 93, 96; 7 633; 15 220–24*, 229, 416, 425, 428–9, 431–2, 446–8, 501
Chola 15 522–3
Hinduism 7 633; 14 556, 556–8, 557, 558; 15 213–14*, 219*; 20 818
Ganapatya 15 216–17*
Saura 15 216
Shaivism 15 214–15*
Shakta 15 217–19*
Vaishnavism 15 215–16*
Indus civilization 15 213, 229
Jainism 15 224–6*
iconology 15 211
icons 15 416
'idgāhs 15 340, 343
ikat 15 670, 671–2*; 30 554, 555, 556
imambaras 15 380
indigo 15 668, 672; 30 560
inks 15 564, 850

Indian subcontinent—cont.
inlays 4 687; 15 354, 414, 693, 707, 712, 714
inscriptions 15 192, 193, 198–9*, 233, 310, 443, 688, 688
Indus civilization 15 198, 420
Islamic 15 680; 16 513
Kannada 15 197
Kushana 15 440, 445–6
Maurya 15 194, 197, 750
Mughal 16 514
Sanskrit 15 197
Tamil 15 197
interior decoration 21 717
iron 15 193, 667, 668, 734
ivory 6 555, 556, 556, 557; 15 450, 549, 693, 693, 695–7*, 696, 697, 724; 21 717
iwans 23 817
jackfruit-wood 15 720, 730
jade 15 698–9*, 699, 701; 16 860, III2; 21 717, 717
jasper 15 418
jewellery 15 423, 699–702*, 703, 723, 726, 733, 735, 736
jute 5 829
khānaqāhs 15 357; 18 17
kiosks 18 71–2*, 72
labyrinths 18 584
lac 15 667; 16 431; 21 717
lacquer 6 555; 15 548
insect 18 608, 609
Islamic 16 535
Kashmir 4 IV1
Mughal 15 546
ladles 15 729
lamps 15 708, 708–9, 729; 17 573
languages 15 193, 197–9*
lapis lazuli 15 564
lathes 6 556
law courts 18 889, 889; 20 53
leather 15 681, 715
libraries 15 208, 546; 16 344
limestone 15 510
lintels 9 161
lithography 15 679, 679
lockets 15 726
looms 30 546, 547
lost-wax casting 15 727, 735
lotus 19 716, 717
madder 15 667
madrasas 15 341, 357
maṇḍalas 5 96; 26 139
manuals
architecture 15 237, 242, 249, 312, 315, 403, 409
iconography 15 749
painting 15 550
sculpture 15 415
manuscript covers 15 546, 548, 549
manuscript illumination 15 228–9, 230, 549–50, 563–9*, 570–71*, 647, 739
Assam 15 548
Bengal 15 570, 571, 634
Bihar 15 570–71*
Buddhism 5 92, 96, 96; 15 544, 545, 549, 563, 568, 569, 570–71, 739
Candāyana 15 576, 576–7*
Caurapañcāśikā 15 574–6*, 575
Deogarh 15 227, 548
Gujarat 15 564, 616–17*, 617
Hinduism 15 545, 566, 567, 616
Islamic 15 571, 571–4*, 572, 573, 739–40; 16 330–31*, 344–6*
Jainism 15 544, 545, 549, 561, 563–9, 565, 616–17, 617, 739; 16 869
Kashmir 15 650–51*, 651
Kota 15 606
Mamluk 15 571–2
Mughal 15 230, 545–7, 549, 579–84*, 740
16th cent. 1 26; 15 546, 577, 579, 582, 583, 586; 21 727; 22 517

Indian subcontinent
manuscript illumination
Mughal—cont.
17th cent. 15 585
Mysore 15 649
Orissa 15 547, 570, 636, 636
Pala 15 545
Rajasthan 15 564
Rajput 15 227, 548
11th cent. 22 517
16th cent. 15 690
17th cent. 15 648
manuscripts 15 208, 544–9*, 563–6*, 749; 20 327
Hinduism 15 544, 548, 549
Islamic 15 545*
Jainism 15 226, 549, 563
Kashmir 15 548
Mughal 16 304, 344
Pahari 15 547
Pala 15 570
poṭhī 15 547
Rajput 15 547
maps 15 703–5*, 704
marble 15 340, 354; 16 239
marks 15 707
marquetry 20 VIII2
masks 15 705–6*, 731, 734, 734–5
masonry 15 307
mass production 4 793; 15 448
mats 15 727
mausolea 6 165; 15 383; 27 858, 858
measurements 15 210
medical books 21 5
memorial posts 15 730
metal 6 556; 15 499, 500, 501, 505, 549, 729–30
metalwork 15 706*, 708–14*, 727, 732
Bengal 15 709
Bidri ware 15 713–14, 714, 724; 21 326
dhokra 15 727, 727
Islamic 15 709
Kashmir 15 709
kuftkārī ware 21 330
Maratha period 15 709
Rajput 15 709
mica 15 653, 724
mihrabs 15 338, 351; 21 506
minarets 8 672
minbars 15 340; 21 630
miniatures (manuscript illumination) 15 576, 716
mirror frames 21 717, 717
mirrors 21 716–17*, 717, 718
models 15 724
modules 15 210
monasteries 1 499; 15 311; 21 847*
Buddhism 3 905; 22 447
monuments 15 735; 27 866–8*, 867
mordants (iii) (dyeing) 15 667, 668, 672, 673
mortars (building) 15 351
mosaics 15 374–5
mosques 1 502; 15 48, 207, 344; 16 239
Bengal 15 353
four-iwan 22 195
Kerala 15 359
Mughal 8 679; 15 361, 366
8th cent. AD 15 307, 338–40
12th cent. 15 339
14th cent. 15 345, 351
15th cent. 1 472; 15 348, 350
18th cent. 15 379
mother-of-pearl 6 556
mouldings 15 241, 312, 317, 326
moulds 15 423, 750; 29 825
mounts (works on paper and scrolls) 22 235–6*
mud 15 548
museums 15 743–6*; 22 364, 364
musical instruments 22 376

Indian subcontinent—cont.
muslin 15 660–61
narratives 15 226–9*, 442, 448, 563, 564; 22 516–17*, 517
naturalism 15 206
nim 15 721
nude figures 15 218; 20 818; 23 290
observatories 23 338, 339
opals 12 252
pagodas 23 772
painters 15 207, 550*
painting 5 419; 7 616; 15 206, 228, 230, 543–658, 673–4*; 28 309; 30 559–60
Andhra Pradesh 15 647–8, 650, 650
battle 15 589
Bengal 15 634–5*, 635
Bengal School 5 420
Bihar 15 570
Bilaspur 15 624*
Buddhism 15 570, 570
Bundi (Rajasthan) 15 603–7*
ceiling 15 562, 645
Chamba (i) (India) 15 625–7*, 626
Company 2 306; 5 419; 8 676; 15 651–5*, 654, 724; 16 522
Deccan 15 637–42*, 643*
Deogarh 15 597–601*, 601, 602, 603, 643
fresco 15 570; 30 643
Garhwal 15 627–8*, 628
glass 16 522
Golconda 15 640–42*
Gujarat 15 565
Guler 15 217, 628–9*, 629
Hinduism 14 556, 559; 15 217, 599, 602, 622, 628, 633, 673, 674
Islamic 12 74
Jainism 15 225, 563–6, 566, 674
Jammu 15 630, 630–31*
Jasrota 15 631, 631–2*
Kachchh 15 617–18*, 618
Kangra 15 217, 632, 632–3*
Kashmir 15 650–51
Kerala 15 650
Kishangarh 15 611–13*, 613
Kota 15 605–6
Kulu 15 620–21*, 621
Kutch see KACHCHH
landscape 15 565, 566
Malwa 15 597, 602, 602–3*, 603
Mandi 15 633, 633–4*
Mankot 15 619, 621–2*, 622
Maratha period 15 647
Marwar 15 613–16*, 614
miniatures 15 578, 724
Mughal 15 575, 577–8*, 584–7*, 588–93*
Sub-imperial 15 593–7*, 594, 595, 596
16th cent. 1 26; 10 816, 818; 15 231, 578; 17 922
17th cent. 12 74; 13 235; 14 217; 15 585; 18 657; 20 301
18th cent. 15 591; 22 438
Mysore 15 649
Nurpur 15 623, 623–4*
Orissa 15 635–6*
Pahari 7 VI1; 14 611; 15 618–19*, 620, 620–22*, 621, 623, 623–4*, 625–9*, 626, 629, 630, 630–34*, 631, 632; 22 438
Punjab 10 485
Rajasthan 7 VI2; 10 485; 15 596, 597–601*, 599, 600, 601, 608–16*, 608, 610, 611, 613, 614, 617–18*, 618, 740
Rajput 15 211, 597–601, 603–7*, 608, 608–16*, 610, 611, 613, 617–18*, 618, 643
Ramkot see Mankot
scroll 15 563, 617, 643, 647; 28 309, 311–12

Indian subcontinent
painting—cont.
secco **15** 548
Shekhavati **15** 609*, 611*
Timurid **15** 638
wall **7** 494; **15** 543–4*, 548*, 551, 553–62*, *559*, 563*, 643–50*, 726; **32** 804
Bengal **15** 563
Bihar **15** 563
Buddhism **1** 500; **15** *562*; **32** 804
Bundi (Rajasthan) **15** *604*
Bundi school **15** *604*, *606*
Chamba (i) (India) **15** 627
Chola **15** 560
Hinduism **15** *544*
hunting scenes **15** *604*
Islamic **15** 354
Karnataka **15** 648
Kerala **15** 649–50
Mysore **15** 649
Nayaka **15** 646–7
Orissa **15** 636
Pahari **15** 627
Vijayanagara period **15** *644*, 644–6, *645*
5th cent. AD **15** *554*, *556*, *557*, *558*; **32** *324*
6th cent. AD **15** *558*
11th cent. **15** *560*
watercolours
Bundi school **15** *606*, *607*
Company painting **15** *652*, *655*
Hinduism **14** *558*
Mughal **20** *284*
17th cent. **1** *583*
13th cent. **15** 206
15th cent. **15** 569
16th cent. **15** 574–6*, *575*
18th cent. **15** 648
19th cent. **5** *420*
20th cent. **15** *656*
palaces **15** 235, 248–9; **23** 816–20*
Avadh **15** *378*
Colonial period **15** *402*
Islamic **15** *354*
Madya Pradesh **23** *818*
Malwa **15** *354*
Mughal **15** 242, *369*, *371*
prāsādas **23** 817
Rajput **15** 242, 385–93, *386*, *387*, *388*, *389*, *391*, *392*; **23** *819*
16th cent. **7** *494*
palm **15** 720
palm leaves **15** 544, 547, 548, 561, 636, 727; **20** 327
Buddhism **5** *96*; **15** 570
Jainism **15** 545, 563–4
paper **15** 545, 549, 706; **20** 327; **28** 310, 635
Islamic **15** 549
Jainism **15** 564
papier mâché **18** 609; **24** 62
parasols **11** 151
parks **24** 178
patronage **15** 206, 207, 208, 324, 334, 651, 737*
architecture **15** 737–8*
Buddhism **5** 95; **15** 737, 739
Gupta **15** 738
Hinduism **15** 206
Islamic **15** 206, 207, 738, 739–40
Jainism **15** 737, 739
painting **15** 739–40*
Rajput **15** 724
sculpture **15** 737–8*
Vijayanagara (ii) (Indian dynasty) **15** 738
pattern books **16** 823
pavilions (buildings) **3** 38; **10** *829*; **15** 258, 346; **29** *480*
pearls **6** 556; **12** 252
pedestals **15** 448
pendants (jewellery) **15** 736
periodicals **24** 436*

Indian subcontinent—cont.
periods
Kushana **15** 445–6
photography **10** 580; **15** 616
pigments **7** 633; **15** 548
black **7** 634
blue **7** 634
blue-black **7** 634
carmine **15** 564
peori **16** 330
red **7** 634
ultramarine **15** 551, 564; **24** 790
white **7** 634
yellow **7** 634
pilasters **15** 330
pilgrimages **5** 93; **14** 559; **15** 202; **31** 902
pillars **15** 236–7*, 277, 302, 303, 317, 325, 424, 442, 733; **27** 844*
Buddhism **15** *415*, 422–3; **27** 867
Maurya **15** 194, 341, 413
2nd cent. BC **15** 430–31
5th cent. AD **15** 258, *259*
7th cent. AD **15** 303
pine **15** 720
plaques **4** 794; **15** 226, *459*, 695, 718
Buddhism **15** *221*
Jainism **15** 226, 443
Shunga period **15** *718*
plaster **4** 793; **15** 319; **29** 824–5*
poetry **25** 72
polychromy **15** 354
pools **20** *74*
poplar **15** 311
popular art **5** 419, *420*
portraits **15** 206, 231–2*
cameos **15** *702*
coins **15** 231
donor **15** 233, *233*, 234
drawings **15** *581*
Gupta **15** 231
Kushana **15** 231
manuscript illumination **8** *543*
Mughal **15** 231–2
Pahari **15** 232
painting **15** 232, *607*, 619, *637*
Bilaspur **15** *624*
Deccan **15** 638, *639*, 639–40, *641*
Golconda **15** *641*, 641–2
Islamic **15** 637
Mughal **1** *92*; **3** *92*; **4** *91*; **15** 580, *580*, *586*, 586–7, *587*
Pahari **15** 621, 622, 623, *624*
Rajput **15** 614, *614*
19th cent. **15** *657*
photography **15** 232
Rajput **15** 232
sculpture **15** 232–4*, *233*, 540, 737–8
self-portraits **8** *543*
pots **15** 708
potters **15** *729*
potter's wheels **15** 685
pottery **15** 193, 194, 685–6*, *686*
pouches **3** 442
printing **15** 668–70*, 679; **16** 361
prints **15** 679–80*
proportions (architecture) **15** 210
puppets **7** 122; **15** 714–15*, *715*
quilting **25** 821
quilts **15** 674–5, 727
railings **15** *425*, 428, *429*, *437*; **27** 844*
railway stations **4** *289*
reeds **15** 730
religion **15** 192, 202–4*, 205*, 226; **28** 711–12; **33** 706
reliquaries **15** *686*, *698*; **26** 149–50, *150*, *151*
repoussé **15** 713
rest-houses **15** 202
retables **26** 254
rice **3** 331
rings **17** II2

Indian subcontinent—cont.
ring stones **15** 423–4
ritual objects **15** 726, 727, 729–30*
rituals **14** *559*, 559–60
roads **15** 202
robes **15** *691*
rock art **10** 138; **15** 192, 551–2*, *552*
rock crystal **15** 697–8*, *698*; **16** 542; **21** 717, *717*; **26** 487
rock reliefs **15** *236*, *437*, *464*, *465*, *466*, 477, *477*, *508*, *510*, *677*
rolls **15** 731
roofs **15** 336
rose-wood **15** 720
rubies **6** 556; **12** 252; **17** II2; **21** *717*
sandalwood **15** 720, 721, 724
sandstone **15** *452*
Islamic **15** 340; **16** 239
2nd cent. BC **15** *253*, *430*
3rd cent. BC **15** *423*; **27** *844*
1st cent. AD **15** *427*, *444*; **20** *818*
2nd cent. AD **15** *440*, *441*, *442*
3rd cent. AD **20** *819*
5th cent. AD **8** *768*; **15** *455*, *456*
6th cent. AD **15** *457*, *460*
7th cent. AD **15** *229*, *495*
8th cent. AD **15** *214*, *495*
9th cent. AD **15** *536*
10th cent. AD **15** *218*, *230*, *496*, *537*
11th cent. **15** 324, *497*
15th cent. **15** *498*
17th cent. **27** *867*
19th cent. **15** *413*, *542*
sapphires **12** 252
sarcophagi **15** 686
sardonyx **15** 698, *702*
sārīs **15** *670*, 692
sashes **3** 442
satin **30** *564*
scabbards **15** *678*
schist **15** *222*, *446*, *447*, 448, *461*, 499; **28** *544*
schools of painting **15** *597*, *619*, *637*
screens (i) (architectural) **23** 803
scripts **15** 192, 193, 198–9*, 338; **16** 514
sculptors **15** 207, *414*, 414–15*, 543
sculpture **15** 206, *229*, 411–543*, 548, 719, 727, 733; **23** 290; **29** 438, 824; **30** 510
Andhra Pradesh **15** 438–9*, 533–41*, *534*
architectural **15** 206, 326, 397–8, *398*, *400*, 412–13*; **30** *642*
Hinduism **15** *496*; **17** *761*
Islamic **15** 413
Madya Pradesh **15** *496*
Maha-Gurjara **15** 274
Maharashtra **15** 275
Nolamba **15** *531*
Orissa **15** 505
Vijayanagara period **15** 335, *335*
Bengal **15** 498–503*, 541
Bhil **15** *735*, 735
Bihar **15** 498–503*
bronze **14** *557*; **15** *223*, 453, 476, 516–17, 521, 522, 523, *523*, 524, *525*, 530–31, 708, *728*, 730
10th cent. AD **15** *530*
11th cent. **15** *219*, *516*, *517*
19th cent. **15** *725*
Buddhism **10** 484; **15** *222*, *223*, 415–16, *431*, 439–42*, *440*, *441*, 451, 453–4*, *457*, *462*, 476, 499–502, 505, *505*, 521, *530*; **17** 857; **20** 818–19
2nd cent. BC **15** *425*
1st cent. AD **15** 446–9
2nd cent. AD **15** 446

Indian subcontinent
sculpture
Buddhism—cont.
5th cent. AD **15** *455*, *456*, *470*
7th cent. AD **15** *500*
10th cent. AD **15** *500*
11th cent. **15** *501*; **30** *220*
12th cent. **15** *501*
Chalukyas of Kalyana **15** 531–2
Chandella **15** 481
Chola **15** 514–18*
colonialism **7** *616*
Colonial period **15** 542–3*
colossal statues **15** 528, *528*; **29** 438
cult statues **15** 727–9*, 730
dvārapāla **15** 507, *534*, *542*
equestrian **15** *735*
figure **15** 415, 424, 539–40, 734
Gandhara **15** *222*, 416, 445–9*, 452, 458
Gujarat **15** 449–50*, 461–3*, *462*, 484–91*, 541
Gupta **8** 768; **15** 194, 454–8*, 475–6*
Gurjara-Pratihara **15** 480–81, 486
Haryana **15** 484*, *484*
Himachal Pradesh **15** 483*
Hinduism **5** 95; **15** 443–4*, 502, *503*, 503–5, *519*, 520, 523, *524*; **23** 832; **28** *544*
Saura **15** *216*, 444, *478*, *504*
Shaivism **1** *485*; **15** *214*, *438*, *463*, *479*, *480*, *481*, *482*, *488*, *496*, *497*, *502*, *530*, 535, *728*
Shakta **15** *218*
Vaishnavism **15** *472*, *484*, *495*, *502*
5th cent. AD **15** *416*, *468*, *469*, *471*
8th cent. AD **15** *417*
10th cent. AD **15** *515*
11th cent. **15** *219*, *504*, *516*, *517*
16th cent. **15** *518*
Hoysala **15** 532–3
Indus civilization **15** 417–22*
Islamic **15** 497
Jainism **5** 95; **15** *442*, 442–3*, 453, 467, 497–8, 508, 522, 523, 531; **20** 817
Jammu **15** *482*, 482–3*
Karnataka **15** 525–33*, 541
Kashmir **15** 458–9, 482–3*
Kerala **15** 521–5*, *523*, *525*, 541
Kushana **6** 215; **15** 439–41*, *444*, 444
Kushana period **15** 416, *440*, *442*, 451, 452–3*
liṅga **15** 332, 412, *438*, 443–4, 729
Madya Pradesh **15** 467–75*, 494–8*, *496*
5th cent. AD **15** *468*, *469*, *470*, *471*, *472*
7th cent. AD **15** *495*
8th cent. AD **15** *495*
Maharashtra **15** 450–51*, 463–6*, 491–3*
Malwa **15** 460, *460*, *461*
Maratha period **15** 493
Mathura **7** 793
Maurya period **15** 422–4, *423*
monumental **15** 194
Naga (people) **15** *733*
nāga **15** 444
Nayaka period **15** 519–20*
Nolamba **15** 529–30
Orissa **15** 503–6*
Pala-Sena period **15** 498–503*
Pallava **15** 509–14
Punjab **15** 483–4*
Rajasthan **15** 449–50*, 459–60*, 484–91*, *487*, *488*, 541
Rashtrakuta **15** 492–3

Indian subcontinent
sculpture—cont.
relief **15** *230*, *233*, *235*, *251*, 413, 499, 719; **23** 803
Andhra Pradesh **15** *536*, *537*, *538*, *539*
Buddhism **5** *88*, *95*; **9** *35*; **15** *248*, *415*, 425–6, *429*, *435*, *437*, 442, 448, 453, *454*; **20** *819*
Chalukyas of Badami **15** *527*
Gandhara **9** *34*; **15** *446*, *447*
Gujarat **15** *490*
Gupta **8** *768*; **15** *476*
Hinduism **15** 443, *489*, *490*, *492*, 507–14, *514*, *536*; **20** *224*
Hoysala **15** *532*
Kerala **15** *521*
Kushana **15** *452*; **20** *818*
Madya Pradesh **15** *497*, *498*
Maharashtra **15** *451*, *492*
Rajasthan **15** *489*, *542*
Tamil Nadu **15** 507–14
Vijayanagara period **15** *540*
1st cent. BC **15** *235*
2nd cent. BC **15** 428, *434*
5th cent. AD **31** 520, *520*
Shunga period **15** 425
stone **15** 412, 414, 452, *463*, *502*, *505*; **23** 832
7th cent. AD **15** *500*, *503*
9th cent. AD **15** *482*, *484*, *488*
10th cent. AD **15** *487*
11th cent. **15** *414*, *501*, *504*
Tamil Nadu **15** 506–20*
Uttar Pradesh **15** *479*, *481*, *482*
Vidarbha **15** 463–4*
Vijayanagara period **15** 329, 518–19*, 533, 539
Western Ganga **15** *528*
wood **7** *616*; **15** 412, 414, 523–4, *524*, 721, *733*
yakṣa **15** 413, 426–7, *427*, 429–30, *430*
yakṣī **15** 413, *425*, 429–30
7th cent. AD **15** 478–9*
8th cent. AD **15** 479–80*
seals **15** 192
cylinder **1** 850; **15** 421
Gupta **15** 476
Indus civilization **15** 213
stamp **15** 420–21
serpent-stones **15** 728, *728*
settlements **15** 192
shawls **15** 665*, 666, *666*, 676, 723; **28** 564
shells **15** 729, 734
shrines (i) (cult) **15** 249–51*, 309, 310–11, 324, 325–8, *326*, *327*, 727–9*; **25** 303; **28** 635*, III2
Buddhism **28** 635
circular **15** 249–50, *250*
elliptical **15** 251
Hinduism **14** 559; **15** *331*; **28** 635
Islamic **15** *308*
Kerala **15** 336
square **15** 249
tree-shrines **15** 249, 728
Vijayanagara period **15** 330, *331*
signatures **15** 208, 415, 532
silk **15** 661–5*, *663*, *664*, 667, 668, 670, *670*, *675*; **28** 717, 718
silver **4** 687; **6** 556; **15** 200, *223*, *500*, *502*, 664, 668, 687, *688*, 707–8*, *708*, *711*, 712*, *714*; **21** 717
silversmiths **15** 723
sissoo **25** 303
slate **15** *216*
smelting **21** *320*
soapstone **15** 192, 324, 327, *419*, 420; **26** *151*
spinning (textile) **15** 660
spires **15** 318, *318*, 319
spolia **15** 207, 338
sporting scenes **29** 422

Indian subcontinent—cont.
spruce **15** 720
squinches **15** 340
staircases **29** 526–7*, *527*
stairwells **29** 526
standards (vexilloid) **11** 151–2
stands **15** 729
statuettes **4** 687
steel **15** *678*; **16** 51, 60
stelae **15** 231, 413, 448, 499; **29** 619
stencilling **30** 561
stepwells **15** 192, 341, 343, 349; **29** 635–6*, *635*
stone **4** 794; **15** 253–6*, 412, 414, 417–20*, 452, *502*, *505*; **27** 844*; **29** 444
Islamic **16** 239
2nd cent. AD **15** *454*
5th cent. AD **15** *463*
7th cent. AD **15** *500*, *503*
9th cent. AD **15** *482*, *484*, *487*
10th cent. AD **15** *488*
11th cent. **15** *414*, *501*, *504*, *540*
13th cent. **15** *539*
stone-carvings **15** 338
straw **15** 548
stucco **15** 338, 413, 414, 448, 475, 499; **29** 824–5*
stupas **1** *500*, *754*; **4** 794; **5** 94, *95*; **15** 194, 220, 237*, 249*, *262*, 431; **23** 772; **27** *709*; **29** 863–4*, *864*
Jainism **15** 226; **29** 864
superstructures **4** 794; **15** 286, *397*
sword hilts **15** 696
swords **15** 677, 678, *678*
symbolism (critical term) **15** 424*
symbols **15** 412
talismans **15** 726, 734
tattoos **15** 733, 735
teak **6** 555; **15** 720, 721; **25** 303
temples **4** *793*, 794; **9** 161–2; **13** 885; **15** 195, 206, 207, 234, 237–41*, 250, 253*, 260, 266–75*, 279–83, 304–5, 309, 317–22, 385, 393, 405–6; **26** 48; **30** 436–7*
Andhra Pradesh **15** 293–302*, 328*, 534
apsidal **15** *251*, 251–2*, 259
Assam **15** 396*
Bengal **15** 279–81*, 395–6*, *396*
Bihar **15** 279–81*, 321–2*
Buddhism **3** *905*; **15** *280*; **30** 437
Chalukyas of Badami **15** *297*, *298*, *299*, 526–7
Chalukyas of Kalyana **15** *326*
Chalukyas of Vengi **15** 301, *301*
Chandella **15** *289*
Chola **7** 200; **15** 305, 331–4, *332*, *334*
Deccan **15** 240
drāviḍa **15** 239–41, *240*, 258, 259–60, 278–9, 293–8, *296*, 300, 302–3, 317, 324–7, 328, 333; **30** 437–9*
elliptical **15** 251
Gujarat **15** 266–7, *267*, *268*, *272*, *274*
Gupta **15** 194, 237, 252–7*, *253*, *254*, *255*, *256*
hall **15** 300
hāvelī **15** 394–5
Himachal Pradesh **15** *310*, 396–7*, *397*
Hinduism **1** *484*; **3** *911*; **13** *881*; **14** 77, 559; **15** 257, *282*, 312, *312*, *315*, *316*, *318*, *320*, *321*, *330*, *332*, *334*; **17** *760*, *761*; **18** *13*, *14*; **20** *224*; **29** *481*; **30** 437–9*, *439*; **31** *542*
Shaivism **1** *485*; **15** *263*, *286*, *287*, *289*, *291*, *310*, *323*, 329

Indian subcontinent
temples—cont.
Hoysala **15** *327*, 327–8
Jainism **15** 301, 312, *313*, 313, *314*, 314, 528
Kalinga **15** 317
Karnataka **15** 293–302*, 324–8*
Kashmir **15** 264–6, *265*
Kerala **15** 336*
Kosala **15** 283–4, *284*
Kulu **15** *310*
kūṭina **15** 239, *240*
Ladakh **15** 397
latina **15** *238*, 239, 284, 298
Madya Pradesh **15** 285–93, *286*, *287*, 322–4, *323*
Maha-Gurjara **15** 268, 270, 271–5, *272*, *273*, *274*
Maha-Maru **15** 267–71, *269*, *270*, *271*, 275
Maharashtra **15** 315–17, 493
Maru-Gurjara **15** 271, 275, 311–15, *312*, *314*
nāgara **15** *238*, 239, 260, 266–75, 277–8, 298–300, 309–11, 316, 318, 326, 327, 328, 405; **30** 437–9*
5th cent. AD **15** 258
Nayaka **15** 397–400, *398*, *400*
Orissa **15** 281–3*, 317–20*, *318*, *320*, 395*; **18** 213, *214*
Pallava **15** *304*, *305*
Paramara **15** *291*
Rajasthan **15** 267–75, *269*, *270*, *271*, *273*
Rashtrakuta **15** 527–8
rock-cut **1** *485*; **15** *250*, 252–3, 275–9, 293, 302–4, 464–6, 477, 492, 507, 521–2; **30** 437*
2nd cent. BC **15** *251*
7th cent. AD **15** *277*, 534, 535
8th cent. AD **10** *149*; **15** *278*, 306
sāndhāra **22** 423
Sikhism **15** *375*
Surashtra style **15** 266, *267*, *268*
Tamil Nadu **15** 240
Tripura **15** 396*
Uttar Pradesh **15** 260–63; **31** *904*
Vaishnavism **15** 394
Vanga **15** 320–21*, *321*
Vijayanagara period **15** 328–31, *330*, *335*, 335–6, 644
vimāna **15** *297*, *298*, 301–2, 325–6, 333
Western Ganga **15** 529
Yadava **15** *315*, *316*
8th cent. AD **15** 262
9th cent. AD **15** 306
11th cent. **30** 642
17th cent. **20** *74*
20th cent. **15** *405*
tents **15** *716*, 716–17*; **30** *472*
terracotta **15** 395, 414, *421*, 453, 717–20*, 727, 728; **30** 510*, *510*
Baluchistan **15** 213
Bangladesh **15** *726*
Gond **15** *734*
Gupta **15** 719
Indus civilization **15** 213, 420, 421–2*
Kushana period **15** 719
Maurya period **15** 718
Pala period **15** 719
Pala-Sena period **15** 499
Prehistoric **15** 686
Rajasthan & Gujarat **15** 449
Satavahana period **15** 719
Shunga period **15** *718*, 718
Tamil Nadu **15** *729*
4th cent. AD **15** *459*, *462*
9th cent. AD **15** *221*
20th cent. **15** 719, 729, 730
textiles **15** 200, 201, 548, 549, 562, 658–76*, 722–3; **30** 559–60, 561
Assam **15** 662

Indian subcontinent
textiles—cont.
Bengal **15** 201, 723
Deccan **15** 664
Gujarat **15** 202, 671*, 672, 723
Hinduism **15** 599, 669, 673
Islamic **15** 664*; **16** 452*
Jainism **15** 565, *566*
kalamkārī **15** 673–4*
maśrū **15** 664*
Mughal **15** 201
Orissa **15** 636
Punjab **15** 669
Rajasthan **15** 669–70, 671*
8th cent. AD **28** 309
18th cent. **15** 548; **29** *233*
theories (art) **15** 205
threads **15** 663, 675
thrones **15** 693, 707, *707*; **30** 784–5*
tiles **15** 336, 337, 338, 342, 354, *374*, 374–5, 686–7*, *687*
tiraz **31** 21
tombs **6** 165; **15** 686, 734; **31** 114–15*
Bahmani **15** 356, 358
Deccan **15** *384*
Ghurid **20** *251*
Islamic **15** *337*, 342, 343, 349; **31** 111, 113, 114, *115*
megalithic **21** *44*
Mughal **1** *459*; **8** *679*; **15** *364*; **28** *711*
Prehistoric **21** *44*
Punjab **15** *374*
15th cent. **8** *674*
16th cent. **8** *674*
17th cent. **15** *373*
tools **15** 192, 193; **29** 444
topaz **12** 252
tortoiseshell **6** 556
tourist art **15** 732, 750
towers **10** *830*; **15** 330
town halls **31** 241
toys **15** 724, 730, 731
trade **15** 192, 196, 200–202*; **26** 855; **29** 230, 231
books **16** 343
carpets **5** 842
ceramics **6** 331, 917–18*
chintz **22** 899
Chola **15** 200
coral **16** 750
cornelian **1** 350
cotton **8** 35; **11** 649
furniture **7** 166; **15** 693; **25** 303
glass **7** 87; **16** 522
gold **15** 706
hair **16** 449
hardstones **7** 91
ikat **15** 671
indigo **16** 449
iron **29** 228
ivory **1** 195, 250; **25** 303
lac **18** 655
lapis lazuli **15** 548
manuscripts **15** 572; **16** 342
mirrors **21** 716, 720
Mughal **15** 722
pigments **15** 551; **24** 795, 799
porcelain **4** 175
pottery **16** 409, 427
puppets **7** 122; **17** 406
shawls **15** 666
shrines (i) (cult) **25** 303
stone **16** 199
textiles **3** 378; **15** 201, 202, 658–9, 669; **17** 314; **29** 231, 232–3; **30** 622
wood **2** 248
trappings **14** 181*, 183–4*, 185, 186*; **15** 736
travel books **15** 202*
trays **15** 727
treatises **15** 190, 208–10*; **30** 642
aesthetics **15** 206
architecture **15** 206, 208–10*, 315, 324; **29** 868
automata **15** 573

Indian subcontinent
treatises—cont.
fortifications **21** 590
gems **15** 701
mosques **15** 208
painting **15** 206, 208–10*
sculpture **15** 206, 208–10*, 541
urban planning **15** 209
tribal art **15** 731–6*
tughras **31** 417
turmeric **15** 668
turrets **15** 322, *323*
urban planning **1** 648; **15** 193, 242, 248, 398, 408–11*
England **20** 52
Gupta **15** 409
Indus civilization **15** 192, 408
Islamic **15** 409–10
Rajput **15** *411*
urns **15** 192
vaults (ceiling) **15** 343
velvet **15** *678*, 716
verandahs **32** 239, 240, *240*
vernacular art **15** 498, 726–31*
vihāras **1** 501; **15** 275–7
viridian **6** 556, *556*
walls **15** 409
walnut **15** 720, 721
weapons **15** 676–9*, 696, 712
weaving **15** 660*, 727, 732
wheels **15** 193
whisks **10** 778
women **15** 637
wood **15** 412, 414, 523–4, *524*, 544, 549, 706, 724; **18** 609; **31** 259
Naga (people) **15** *733*
18th cent. **7** *616*
wood-carvings **15** 309, 336, 491, 541, *722*, 733; **33** 325
woodwork **15** 720–22*
wool **15** 665–7*, *666*, *683*
workshops **15** 414–15, 550, 722; **16** 468
writing **15** 192, 193, 198–9*; **20** 327, *328*
yarn **15** 659
zinc **15** 713
see also BANGLADESH; INDIA, REPUBLIC OF; NEPAL; PAKISTAN
Indian yellow *see under* PIGMENTS → types
Indica **24** 425
Indigenism **4** 265; **25** 829; **27** 485
Bolivia **4** 262, 264, 267
Ecuador **9** 713
Indigenista group **24** 509
indigo **9** 491
historical and regional traditions
Africa **1** 294; **7** 635
Brazil **4** 724
Byzantine **9** 665
Central Asia, Western **6** 253
China **7** 45; **18** 600; **30** 561
Early Christian (*c.* AD 250–843) **9** 665
Egypt **16** 431
England **8** 36; **10** 356
Inca **15** 163
Indian subcontinent **15** 668, 672; **30** 560
Iran **16** 449
Islamic **16** 431, 438, 449
Japan **17** 219, 277, 308, *309*, 316, 354; **18** 600; **30** 561
Netherlands, the **8** 36
Nigeria **1** *250*
Portugal **25** 315
Rome, ancient **23** 785
Yemen **16** 438
Yoruba **7** 635
uses
dyes **3** 378; **7** 45; **9** 490, 491*, 492, 493; **10** 872; **30** 554, 556, 557, 558, 559, 560, 561
Africa **1** 294
Central Asia, Western **6** 253
China **7** 45

indigo
uses
dyes—cont.
Early Christian and Byzantine **9** 665
England **8** 36
Inca **15** 163
Indian subcontinent **15** 668, 672
Islamic **16** 431, 438, 449
Japan **17** 219, 308, *309*, 316, 354
Portugal **25** 315
Sri Lanka **29** 477
inks **15** 852, 853
lacquer **18** 600, 608
pigments **7** 635; **17** 277; **23** 785; **24** 791*
printing **10** 356
Indigo group **10** 447
indigot **7** 45; **9** 492; **24** 791
Indiketes **10** 190
indirubin **9** 491
indiscret chairs *see under* CHAIRS → types
Indivini, Domenico d'Antonio **11** 691
Indo-Aryans **15** 193, 213; **29** 440
Indo-Caribbean culture **5** 754–5*
Indochina *see* SOUTH-EAST ASIA
Indonesia **15** 750–819*, *751*, *752*, *753*, *754*
altars **1** 706
amboyna **15** 813
amulets **1** 817
appliqué **15** 792, 795
architecture **15** 758–68*, 769–70*, 771–5*, 806
Buddhism **15** 758
Hinduism **15** 758
Islamic **15** 768*
megalithic **15** 754, 756; **21** 45
military **21** 596, *596*
axes **15** 754, 756
bamboo **3** 144; **15** 770, 807, 809, 817; **20** 327
banana leaves **15** 812
barkcloth **15** 807
baskets **3** 331; **15** 809–10*
basketwork **15** 809–10*
batik **3** 379, *379*; **9** IV1; **15** 790–92, *791*, 796; **30** XI
beadwork **15** 814–15*
betel sets **15** 810, 813
black-wood **15** 813
blouses **15** 795
boats **15** 789, 810–11*
bracelets **15** 814
brick **4** 796
bronze **15** 776, 777
buckles **15** 814
calligraphy **15** 757
candi *see* sanctuaries
cane **15** 809
canoes **15** 810; **23** 724
ceramics **15** 811*
chairs **15** 813
chalk **15** 807
cloves **15** 810
coconuts **15** 807
coffins **15** 812, *812*
coins **15** 811–12*, 814
colour **15** 806
containers **15** 807
copper **15** 812
cosmetics **15** 802
costumes **15** 802
cotton **9** III1, IV1; **15** 790, *791*, 792, 793, 794, *794*, *795*; **30** XI
craftsmen and artists **15** 791; **29** 236
dance **15** 802*
dolls' furniture **31** 264
domes **9** 86
doors **15** 785
drawings **15** 804–9*, *806*
chalk **15** 807
dress **15** 792, 794, *796*, 807, 812–13*

Indonesia—cont.
drums (musical instruments) **15** 754, 756, 783, 787, 817
Dong Son **15** 816; **29** 229
Heger I **15** 816
Pejeng **15** 816
dyeing **15** 790–92, *791*, 807; **30** 556
dyes **15** 795
earrings **15** 814–15
ebony **15** 813
education (art) **15** 818–19*
electrum **15** 811
embroidery **15** 795
ex-votos **15** 812*
fans **10** 778
feathers **31** 264
fiddles **15** 816, *816*
figureheads **15** 810
figurines **15** *783*
flowers **15** 812
flutes (musical instruments) **15** 817
fortifications **21** 596, *596*
fountains **12** *102*
fruit **15** 812
furniture **15** 813*
garden design **12** 102
gardens **12** *102*, 102–4*
gateways **15** *767*, 768, *768*
gold **15** *783*, 793, 794, 802, 811, 812, 814, *815*, *817*
gold leaf **3** 331; **15** *798*
gongs **15** 816
grasses **15** 809
halls **14** 78
hangings **15** *794*
hats **15** 810
headcloths **15** 792
headdresses **15** 814
hides **15** *798*
houses **3** 144; **15** 770, 771–5*, *774*, 789, *807*
longhouses **15** 773–4
iconography **15** 756*, 782, 814–15, *815*
Buddhism **15** 757*, 777
Hinduism **15** 756–7*, 777
Islamic **15** 757–8*
ikat **9** III1; **15** 792, 793, 794, *795*, 795–6, *796*; **30** 554
iron **15** 817, *817*; **29** 228
ivory **15** 814
jewellery **15** 814–15*, *815*
keris **15** 757, 817–18, *817*
lacquer **3** 331; **15** 813
languages **29** 226
leather **10** 778
limestone **15** *781*
looms **15** 792, 793, 794
lost-wax casting **15** 816
mantles **15** *795*
manuscript illumination **15** 804, *805*
manuscripts **20** 327
marks **15** 813
masks **15** 802–4*, *803*
mats **15** 809, 810
meeting-houses **15** *771*
metal **15** 795
mosques **15** 757, 768–9
mounds **15** 754
musical instruments **15** 816–17*; **22** 376
narratives **15** 779, 780
nuts **15** 812
ornament **23** 554–5
painting **15** 804–9*, *807*, *808*
scroll **15** 801, *801*
palaces **15** *769*, 775
palm leaves **15** 770, 809, 812
pandanus **15** 809
pastels **29** *234*
periodicals **24** 437
photography **10** 580
pigments
black **15** 802, 807
red **15** 802, 807
Turkey red **15** 795
Indonesia
pigments—cont.
white **15** 802, 807
pillows **15** 795
plaster **15** 779
portraits **15** 780
puppets **15** 797, *797*, *798*, 800, *800*
rafters **15** 787
rattles **15** 817
religion **15** 755–8*
rice **15** 812
rice paste **15** 790
rings **15** 814
roofs **15** 773, *774*
sanctuaries **4** 419, *419*; **15** 758–68*, *759*, *761*, *765*, *766*
sarcophagi **15** 788; **27** 831, *831*
sarongs **15** 791, 793, 795, *796*; **30** XI
sashes **15** 792
scabbards **15** *817*
scripts **15** 757
scrolls **15** *801*, 801–2
sculpture **15** 776*, 777–89*, *781*
bronze **15** 776, 777
Buddhism **15** 776, *778*, 778–9, *782*
Hinduism **15** 778–9
relief **15** 779, 780, 781–3, *786*
stone **4** *420*; **15** *778*, *782*
wood **15** 784, 785–7*, *786*, 789
sequins **15** 795
settees **15** 813
ship-decoration **15** 810–11
ships **15** 810
silk **15** 790, 792, 793, 794
silver **15** 813*
skull troughs **15** 754
spears **15** 818
stone **4** *420*; **15** 777, *778*, *782*; **27** *831*
stupas **29** 865, *866*
swords **15** 818
symbolism (critical term) **15** 758
tattoos **15** 809
teak **15** 813
temples **15** 758–68*, 785
rock-cut **15** 763–4
textiles **15** 758, 789*, 790–92*, 793*, 794–6*, 807, 810; **29** 239
theatre **15** 797*, 802–4*
puppets **15** *800*, 800–801*
shadow **15** 797–800*, *797*, *798*, 804
wayang beber **15** *801*, 801–2*
thrones **30** 785
tombs **15** *763*
towers **15** 812*
trade
ceramics **6** 330, 331; **30** 609
ivory **15** 814
textiles **15** 790
wood **3** 584
tufa **15** *786*, 787
urban planning **15** 775–6*
villages **15** 772
waxes **15** 790
weapons **15** 817–18*
windows **15** 785
women **15** 771
wood **15** 757, *783*, 784, 785–7*, *786*, 789
wood-carvings **15** 757, 776
wraps **15** 792
xylophones **15** 817
yarn **15** 795
see also SOUTH-EAST ASIA
Indonesians **5** 459
Indo-Parthian **15** 819*; **24** 215
see also PAHLAVA
Indore
Central Museum **15** 181
Gargaj Mahadev Temple **15** 495
Shiva Temple **15** 287
Indo-Saracenic style *see* MOORISH STYLE
Indragarh **15** 495
Indraprastha **8** 670
Indrapura **6** 418; **9** 133
Indratataka *see* LOLEY BARAY
Indravarman I, King of Cambodia (*reg* 877-89) **5** 464, 466; **26** 558
Indravarman II, King of Champa (*reg c.* 854) **6** 418; **9** 133
Indravarman III, King of Champa (*reg c.* 918) **6** 428
Indrica **18** *847*
St John the Baptist **18** 849
Indslev **9** 156
induced-draught furnaces *see under* FURNACES → types
inductively coupled plasma spectrometry *see under* TECHNICAL EXAMINATION → types
Indulkana **1** 64
Induno, Domenico **15** 819*; **16** 678; **21** 527
Induno, Gerolamo **15** 819*; **16** 678; **21** 527
induśālikā *see* CANDRAŚĀLĀS
Indus civilization **14** 162; **15** 192–3; **20** 478; **23** 798
architecture **4** 772; **15** 246–7*
arrowheads **15** 677
baths **15** 193, *246*
beadwork **3** 442
brick **4** 772
bronze **4** 853; **15** *412*, 417–20*
copper **15** 420
dress **15** 689
figurines **15** 213, *412*, 415, 417–20*, *418*, *419*, 421–2*, 717–18
gems **12** 252
iconography **15** 213, 229
inscriptions **15** 198, 420
ivory **15** 695
jasper **15** *418*
jewellery **15** 700
pottery **15** 685
scripts **15** 192, 193; **25** 468
sculpture **15** 417–22*
seals **15** 213, 420–21
settlements **15** 192
soapstone **15** *419*, 420
stone **15** 417–20*
stucco **29** 824
swords **15** 677
terracotta **15** 213, 420, 421–2*, 717–18
trade **15** 200
urban planning **15** 192, 408
writing **25** 468
industrial design **1** 107; **2** 372; **8** 801; **15** 820–27*; **31** 497
see also MANUFACTURING
industrial drawing education *see under* EDUCATION (ART) → types
industrial exhibitions *see under* EXHIBITIONS → types
industrial lacquer *see under* LACQUER → types
industrial model towns *see under* TOWNS → types
industrial scenes **3** *800*; **15** 827–31*, *829*, *830*; **18** III2; **19** *767*; **30** 79
Industrie Femminile Italiane **16** 755, 760
Indus Valley script *see under* SCRIPTS → types
Indy, Vincent d' **24** 838
Ine, King of Wessex (*reg* 688-726) **12** 799
Inegöl, Mosque of Ishak Pasha **18** 509
Ineichen, Peter **30** 153
Ineni **9** 901; **10** 54
Inerti *see* GEBELEIN
Infantado, Duque de Mendoza- *see* MENDOZA-INFANTADO, RODRIGO DIAZ DE VIVAR, Duque de
Infantado, Duques de *see* MENDOZA
Infantado, María de Luna, Duquesa de **19** 793; **24** 28; **28** 330
Infantado, Rodrigo de Silva, 4th Duque de Pastrana, Duque del **21** 125
Infantado y Pastrana, Gregorio Mariá de Silva Mendoza y Sandoval, Duque del **21** 125, *125*
Infante, Francisco **15** 831*; **27** 397
Infante, Juan José Díaz *see* DÍAZ INFANTE, JUAN JOSÉ
Infante, Sérgio **4** 636
infirmaries **14** 780
Inflanty Polskie *see* LATGALE
Informalism *see* ART INFORMEL
information art *see* CONCEPTUAL ART
information theory **7** 659
Informele Group *see* ART INFORMEL
Infrangipani, Marsilio **11** 116
infra-red light *see* LIGHT → infra-red
infra-red photography *see under* PHOTOGRAPHY → processes
infra-red spectrometry *see under* TECHNICAL EXAMINATION → types
Infregliati, Battista **7** 905
Infroit (family) **11** 411
Infroit, Claude **11** 410
Infroit, Etienne-Louis **11** 404
Ing, Jackson & Park-Ross **9** 427; **29** 106
Inga, Juan Zapaca *see* ZAPACA INGA, JUAN
Ingachungana **15** 832
Ingalik **22** 546, 639
Ingannati, Pietro degli **3** 667; **15** 831–2*
Inganni, Angelo **21** 495, 527
Ingapirca **15** 832*; **29** *136*, 140, 145; **30** 448
Ingarden, Roman **1** 182; **26** 62
Ingatestone Hall (Essex) **31** 682
Ingeborg, Queen of France (1180-1223) **25** 677
Ingeborg Psalter *see under* PSALTERS → individual manuscripts
Ingegno, L' **2** 632; **24** 525
Ingelard **24** 132
Ingelbrechts (family) **20** 730
Ingelheim, Frank von **11** 734
Ingelheim am Rhein, Altes Rathaus **18** 385
Ingelheim Palace **5** 794, 797
Ingelmunster **30** 326
Ingelow, Jean **24** 832
Ingelrams, Cornelis **28** 388
Ingelran **27** 250
Ingemann, Poul **8** 729
Ingenheim synagogue **17** 547
Ingen Ryūki **11** 870; **15** 832–3*; **17** 409
collaboration **20** 286, 287
groups and movements **17** 231, 234
pupils **9** 73; **17** 234; **21** 802
works **15** *833*; **20** 286; **21** *803*
Ingerl, Ignaz **28** 186
Ingermann (family) **9** 240
Ingermann, Christian Heinrich **12** 447
Ingermann, Mathäus **19** 751
Ingersoll, Robert H. **20** 593
Ingersoll & Co. **7** 448
Ingestre (Staffs), St Mary **25** 727; **28** 295
Ingham, Charles Cromwell **12** 645; **14** 718; **15** 834*
Ingharra *see* KISH
Inghirami (family) **19** 443
Inghirami, Francesco **10** 627, 637
Ingholt, Harald **14** 97; **23** 894
Ing Idisz **1** 160
Ingjong, King (*reg* 1544-5) **18** 330
Inglada, Alexandre de Riquer i *see* RIQUER I INGLADA, ALEXANDRE DE
Inglada, José Aparicio *see* APARICIO INGLADA, JOSÉ
inglaze decoration *see under* CERAMICS → techniques
Inglefield, Julia **20** 217
Inglés, Jorge **15** 834–5*
works **9** 264; **15** *834*
Inglis, James **31** 880
Inglott, Anton **15** 835*; **20** 213
Ingobertus **5** 803
Ingolstadt **12** *361*; **15** 835*
Augustinerkirche **11** *125*
Liebfrauenmünster **4** 777; **12** 365, 366; **14** 308
Maria de Victoria church **15** 139
Ingolstadt, Ludwig VII of, Duke of Bavaria *see* LUDWIG VII, Duke of Bavaria
Ingombe Ilede **1** 288
Ingot God **8** 353
ingots **10** 632; **21** 320
Ingrain carpets *see under* CARPETS → types
Ingram, Arthur **33** 543
Ingram, Bruce **10** 367
Ingram, James **28** 228
Ingres, Jean-Auguste-Dominique **7** 385, 629; **9** 9; **11** 189, 543, 659, 663; **14** 188; **15** 835–46*; **16** 677; **26** 776; **29** 877; **31** 142
assistants **11** 157
book illustrations **30** 385
catalogues **6** 80
collaboration **3** 125; **6** 377; **12** 809; **23** 829; **28** 746
competitions **25** 638
dealers **14** 188
decorative works **10** 781
drawings **9** 225; **12** 178; **13** 304; **15** *838*
cartoons **32** 597
education (art) **2** 524; **11** 671, 672
exhibitions **2** 447; **20** 497; **24** 140, 142
frames **11** 414, *414*
groups and movements **22** 742; **23** 504; **24** 171; **26** 738; **28** 345; **31** 373, 374
methods **21** 760, 764; **24** 354, 667; **25** 279, 284; **31** 578
paintings **31** 480
altarpieces **1** 712
history **11** 541; **12** 214; **14** 587; **15** *846*; **24** *172*; **25** 193; **30** 783
murals **22** 329
mythological **7** *384*
nude figures **10** 479; **15** *844*; **23** 295
portraits **3** 294, 295; **7** 502; **11** *412*; **17** 525; **23** 522; **25** *279*, 286; **26** *81*
religious **2** 840; **11** 543; **15** *840*
patrons and collectors **11** 659; **23** 522
Alba, 14th Duque de (1794-1835) **1** 529
Artaud de Montor, Jean-Alexis-François **2** 514
Aumale, Henri-Eugène-Philippe-Louis de Bourbon, Duc d' **23** 523
Beisteguy y Benítez, Carlos de **3** 522
Beurnonville, Etienne-Edmond Martin, Baron de **3** 890
Blacas, Pierre-Louis-Jean-Casimir de Blaces d'Aulps, Duc de **4** 106
Bonaparte, Napoléon (-Jérôme), Prince **4** 308
Camondo, Isaac de, Comte **5** 530

Ingres, Jean-Auguste-Dominique
patrons and collectors—cont.
Caroline Murat, Queen of Naples (1782-1839) 22 338
Coutan, Louis-Joseph-Auguste 8 73
Delafontaine, Pierre-Maximilien 8 649
Demidov, Anatoly, Prince 8 705
Didot, Saint Marc 8 868
Forbin, (Louis Nicolas Philippe) Auguste, Comte de 11 302
Haro, Etienne-François 14 188
Ionides, Constantine Alexander 15 895
Musée Ingres 2 370
Napoleon I, Emperor of the French (*reg* 1804-14) 4 300, 302
Péreire, Jacob-Emile & Isaac 24 396
Petit, Francis 24 551
Polignac, Winnaretta, Princesse Edmond de 25 150
Pourtalès-Gorgier, James-Alexandre, Comte de 25 383
Rothschild, James Mayer de, Baron (1792-1868) 27 223
Turpin de Crissé, Lancelot-Théodore, Comte de 31 478
prizes (artists') 24 171
pupils
Amaury-Duval, Eugène-Emmanuel 1 759
Américo de (Figueiredo e) Melo, Pedro 1 774
Bertin, Edouard (-François) 3 854
Bonnassieux, Jean-Marie-Bienaimé 4 328
Chassériau, Théodore 6 500
Chenavard, Paul (-Marc-Joseph) 6 535
Cornu, Sébastien (Melchior) 7 876
Desgoffe, Alexandre 8 794
Flandrin, Hippolyte (-Jean) 11 158, 159
Flandrin, (Jean-)Paul 11 159
Galimard, (Nicolas-) Auguste 12 10
Guichard, Joseph (-Benoît) 13 806
Haro, Etienne-François 14 188
Janet-Lange 16 904
Janmot, (Anne-François-) Louis 16 907
La Chevreuse, Louis-Marie-François Jacquesson de 31 393
Lehmann, (Charles Ernest Rodolphe) Henri (Salem) 19 93
Menn, Barthélemy 21 135
Mottez, Victor(-Louis) 22 207
Nègre, Charles 22 723
Oudiné, Eugène(-André) 23 666
Spence, William Blundell 29 380
Stevens, Alfred (Emile-Léopold) (1823- 1906) 29 645
Stürler, Franz Adolph von 25 741
Ziegler, Jules-Claude 33 673
reproductions in hardstones 12 265
reproductive prints by others 4 625
stained glass 29 506
studio 29 856
teachers 8 559; 27 143
Ingres, Jean-Marie-Joseph 15 835; 19 755
Ingres, Musée *see under* MONTAUBAN
Ingress, Edward 18 890
Inguapí 29 212
Ingulph, Abbot of Croyland 7 453
Ingush 27 433
Inhapy 9 841
Ini 12 225
Iñiguez, Diego Angulo *see* ANGULO IÑIGUEZ, DIEGO
Inis Cealtra, St Caimin's 26 592
Initial Binder 4 352
initials (manuscript) 4 345; 15 846–8*; 20 338; 28 304
Anglo-Saxon 5 *641*
Belgium 7 *189*; 26 666
Byzantine 9 609, 618
Carolingian 5 801, *804*; 15 848; 21 *729*; 31 *226*
Czech Republic 4 *7*
Early Christian (*c*. AD 250-843) 9 609, 618; 15 846
England 15 847
Anglo-Saxon 5 *641*
Gothic 17 *611*; 25 *677*, *807*
Insular art 19 *409*
Romanesque 15 *847*; 20 *341*, V1; 26 663, 664; 27 *591*; 33 *239*
France 5 *804*; 7 *514*; 15 *848*; 20 *339*; 21 *729*; 31 *226*
Gothic 13 137
Belgium 7 *189*
Czech Republic 4 *7*
England 17 *611*; 25 *677*, *807*
France 20 *339*
Iceland 15 *69*
Italy 19 *456*; 23 *506*
Iceland 15 *69*
Insular art 15 *847*, 848; 19 *409*
Ireland 15 847
Italy
Gothic 19 *456*; 23 *506*
Romanesque 26 666
15th cent. 7 *188*; 25 *465*
Lombard art 19 549
Merovingian 15 847
Romanesque 9 *256*; 15 847; 26 663–4
Belgium 26 666
England 15 *847*; 20 *341*, V1; 26 663, 664; 27 *591*; 33 *239*
France 15 *848*
Italy 26 666
see also MANUSCRIPT ILLUMINATION
Injae *see* KANG HŬI-AN
Injalbert, (Jean-)Antoine 15 849*
pupils 2 52; 4 59; 23 746; 32 512; 33 589
Injō 15 158; 17 120
Injuid 16 316
Ink, Jack 19 523
Inkaku 15 159; 17 120
Inkawasi 29 166
Inkei 15 159
Inken 17 124
Inkhuk 1 75; 15 856–7*; 17 764; 20 301; 22 509; 26 504; 27 443
members 2 578, 603; 4 812; 18 457, 536; 20 194; 25 239, 735; 27 284; 29 626, 632; 30 8, 338; 31 520; 32 382
patrons and collectors 8 10
teachers 3 196; 18 620
Working Group of Architects 9 73
inkle looms *see under* LOOMS → types
Inkombank 27 440
Inkoo Church 11 94
ink painting *see under* PAINTING → forms
Inkpen hill-figure (Berks) 14 544
Ink photos *see* PRINTING → processes → collotype
inks 15 849–56*
conservation 15 855–6*, *856*
historical and regional traditions
Central Asia 15 850
China 6 736; 7 50, 62, 91–4*, *93*; 15 852; 24 790; 29 617
Egypt, ancient 15 851, 852
Germany 10 381
inks
historical and regional traditions—cont.
Indian subcontinent 15 564, 850
Islamic 16 276
Jainism 15 564
Japan 15 850; 17 140, 212–13*, 310, 392
Korea 15 850, 852; 18 303
Mongolia 15 850
Netherlands, the 15 852
Rome, ancient 15 851
South-east Asia 15 850, 851
Taiwan 15 850
Thailand 15 850
Tibet 15 850
materials
bark 15 850
binders 7 92
bistre 9 216; 15 852, 855
bone 15 851
bronze 25 598
camphor 7 91; 15 850
carbon blacks 15 849, 850, 851, 853
charcoal 15 851
copper 15 852
cuttle fish 15 852
dyes 15 850, 852
fats 15 849
gall-nuts 15 849
gallotannins 15 849, 851
glues 7 92; 15 849, 850; 17 213
gold 15 564, 851, 852
graphite 7 92
gum arabic 15 851
gums 6 736; 15 850, 851, 852
honey 15 851
indigo 15 852, 853
iron oxide 15 852
iron salts 15 851
ivory black 15 851
lacquer 7 92; 15 849; 17 213
lampblack 6 736; 7 91, 92; 15 849, 851, 853; 17 213; 24 790; 25 598
musk 7 91; 15 850
oil black 17 213
oils 15 849, 851, 853; 25 598
orpiment 15 852
petroleum products 15 850
pigments 15 849, 851, 852
red lead 15 852
resins 15 851, 853; 17 213; 25 598
sepia 15 852, 855
silver 15 851, 852
soap 15 853; 25 598
soot 6 736; 7 91, 92, *93*; 15 849, 851, 852; 16 276; 17 213
tannins 15 851
tin 15 852
turpentine 25 598
umber 15 855
verdigris 15 852
vitriol 15 851
waxes 33 1
yeast black 15 851
technical examination 15 *850*
types
black 15 849–52*, *850*
brown 15 852*
Chinese 15 849–50, *850*, 854
green 15 852
grey 15 852
India 15 852
iron-gall 9 216; 15 849, 851, 855, 856, *856*
printer's 7 432; 10 380; 33 1
red 15 851, 852
stone 7 92; 15 849
vermilion 15 851
white 15 851
yellow 15 851, 852
uses
aquatints 2 239, 240
calligraphy 6 736; 15 853–4*; 17 212–13; 23 *801*
cliché-verre 7 432
inks
uses—cont.
drawings *see under* DRAWINGS → forms
dyeing 17 310
embroidery 7 50
engravings 10 380, 381; 15 855
etchings 15 855
lithography 15 853, 855
manuscript illumination 13 136; 15 852, 855; 20 347
marquetry 20 466
masks 17 392
paintings 15 *850*, 853–4*; 17 140
see also under PAINTING → forms
paper 15 851; 24 55
photography 24 648, 650, 653, 655
postage stamps 25 329
printing 7 575; 15 849, 852–3*, 854–5*; 24 650, 653; 25 589; 27 882
prints 25 598*, 612
rubbings 29 617
screenprints 15 853, 855
scripts 15 855
seals 15 851
stencilling 15 855
tattoos 30 366
wallpaper 32 811, 812, 814, 818
watercolours 15 853
woodcuts 15 855
writing 7 62, 92; 15 849–52*, 853, 855*; 17 212–13
writing-tablets 4 342
inkstands 29 535
see also STANDISHES
inksticks 6 736; 7 91–4*, *93*; 15 850, 851, 852, 854; 17 213, 227, 387, 388*
inkstones 6 736; 7 92, 94–6*, *94*, *96*, 134–5; 17 213, 387–8*
inkwells 6 269; 9 657; 16 276, 365, 390
Inland Architect and Builder 24 432
Inland Architect and News Record 24 432
inlays
historical and regional traditions
Afghanistan 16 *366*, *375*, *378*
Ancient Near East 1 865, 867, *869*; 24 336, *336*
Azerbaijan 2 902
Bhutan 3 914
Buddhism 18 *348*
Cambodia 5 500
Central Asia, Western 16 *378*
China 6 808, 832; 7 88, 101; 18 603, *612*
Ming period (1368-1644) 7 17–18
Qing period (1644-1911) 7 19–20, 91
Shang period (*c*. 1600-*c*. 1050 BC) 6 841; 7 12, 88, 107
Song period (AD 960-1279) 6 *865*, *866*
Tang period (AD 618-907) 6 863; 7 14
Yuan period (1279-1368) 7 15–16
Zhou period (*c*. 1050-256 BC) 6 853–4, 855; 7 22, 81, 107
Crete 21 682*, 684*
Egypt 16 *384*, *385*, *389*, 497
Egypt, ancient 9 822; 10 1, 28, 47, 48, 52, 58
England 10 288, 290, 291; 20 468
France 2 461
Germany 12 423, 445
Greece, ancient 13 393, 573, 594, 595
Helladic 22 *397*
Hungary 14 905
inlays
historical and regional traditions—cont.
Indian subcontinent 4 687; 15 354, 414, *693*, 707, 712, *714*
Iran 16 375–6, *376*, 377, 378
Iraq 16 379, *380*, 381–2
Islamic 16 364, *381*, *383*, 487
Afghanistan 16 *366*, *375*, *378*
Central Asia, Western 16 *378*
Egypt 16 *384*, *385*, *389*, 497
Indian subcontinent 15 354
Iran 16 375–6, *376*, 377, 378
Iraq 16 379, *380*, 381–2
Ottoman 16 499, 528
Syria 16 *99*, 381–2, *384*, 389, 497
Turkey 16 498
Yemen 16 500
Italy 20 467
Japan 17 298*, 386; 18 603, 604, *613*
Jordan 24 336, *336*
Korea 18 338–9, *339*, 341, 344*, *348*, 603
Mesopotamia 1 865
Minoan 21 682*, 684*
Mycenaean 22 *397*
Ottoman 16 499, 528
Parthian 24 218
Portugal 25 306
Scotland 28 246
South America, Pre-Columbian 29 218
Spain 29 311, 313, *313*
Sumerian 1 *869*; 31 *696*
Syria 16 *99*, 381–2, *384*, 389, 497
Syria-Palestine 1 *869*
Thailand 30 636*, *636*
Tibet 30 *841*
Turkey 16 498
Vietnam 32 482, 488*
Yemen 16 500
materials
amber 1 761
amboyna 10 291
beads 5 500
bone 4 313, 314; 16 487; 29 313
brass 15 712, *714*
casuarina 32 488
chinaberry 32 488
copper 6 832, 853; 7 101; 13 573; 16 364, *366*, 375, *381*; 21 329
coral 3 914; 7 835
ebony 28 246
enamel 12 445; 21 328
faience (i) (glass) 10 48; 21 684
frit 10 47
glass 1 865, 867; 7 81; 10 58; 12 789; 13 594, 595; 17 386
gold 3 914; 4 688; 6 853, 855; 7 14, 22, 107; 14 *55*; 15 712; 16 364, *375*, *376*, *383*, *384*, *385*, *389*; 21 328; 30 *841*
hardstones 7 91; 12 445
iron 21 329
ivory 10 288; 15 *693*; 16 487, 497, 500, 797, 799; 28 246; 29 *313*
jade 16 528
king-wood 10 291
lacquer 5 500; 7 12
lapis lazuli 31 *696*
limestone 31 *696*
limewater 32 488
lime-wood 32 488
malachite 7 88
marble 10 288; 12 423; 15 340, 354
mirrors 5 256
mother-of-pearl 7 15–16, *16*, 17–18, 19–20, 101; 10 288; 16 499, 500; 18 *612*, *613*; 24 218; 30 636*, *636*; 32 488
pewter 20 467; 21 329
poon 32 488

inlays
materials—cont.
sandalwood **32** 488
scagliola **28** 28
shells **7** 14; **29** 218; **31** *696*
silver **3** 914; **4** 687, 688; **6** 853, 855; **7** 14, 22, 107; **13** 573; **15** 707, 712, *714*; **16** *99*, 364, *366*, 375, *375*, *376*, *378*, *380*, *381*, *383*, *384*, *385*, 389, *389*; **18** *348*; **21** 329
teak **32** 488
tortoiseshell **12** 423; **28** 246; **31** 195
turquoise **3** 914; **6** 832, 841; **7** 88
uses
altarpieces **10** *179*
basins **16** *384*
bowls **16** *385*
bronze **6** 832, 855; **7** 107
buckets **16** *366*
canteens **16** *99*
chairs **10** 52
daggers **22** *397*
desks **29** 313, *313*
ewers **16** *375*, *378*, *381*
furniture **16** 799; **29** 311; **32** 488; **33** 332–3
glass **5** 256
gun stocks **2** 461
halberds **6** 841
hieroglyphs **10** 1
incense burners **18** *348*
inscriptions **10** 1
iron **7** 107
jewellery **10** 28
lacquer **7** 14; **17** 298; **18** 603–4*, *612*, *613*; **30** *636*; **32** 482
metalwork **16** 364, 375–6, 377, 378, 379, 381–2; **21** 328–9* *see also* DAMASCENING
mirrors **6** 863; **30** *841*
paintings **13** 139; **32** 488
penboxes **16** *376*
polychromy **13** 393
porcelain **18** 344*
pottery **18** 338–9
sculpture **3** 914; **15** 414
stonewares **18** *339*, 341
tiles **30** 874
trays **16** *380*
vessels **6** 853–4, *865*, *866*
weapons **15** 712
wood **7** 107
woodwork **2** 902; **16** 487, 497, 498, 499, 500
Inle **5** 258, 263
Inmaculada Concepción castle **23** 80
Inman, Henry **15** 857–8*
patrons and collectors **12** 645; **26** 75
pupils **29** 583
teachers **17** 450; **23** 630
Inmeimon'in **18** 224
Innendekorationen **12** 416
Inner Asia *see* CENTRAL ASIA
Inner Mongolia *see* MONGOLIA
Innes, George **28** 244
Innes, James Dickson **5** 516; **10** 374; **11** 774; **15** 858*; **32** 786
Innes House (Grampian Region) **28** 226
Inness, George **15** 858–9*; **31** 141, 603
dealers **18** 161
patrons and collectors **7** 379
pupils **30** 867
works **15** 828, *859*
Innocent II, Pope (*reg* 1130-43) **26** 655, 833, 834, 835
Innocent III, Pope (*reg* 1198-1216) **15** 860*; **16** 762; **26** 802, 811
Innocent IV, Pope (*reg* 1243-54) **14** 415; **23** 460; **24** 36; **26** 811
Innocent VI, Pope (*reg* 1352-62) **2** 860, 862; **5** 895; **12** 697
Innocent VIII, Pope (*reg* 1484-92) **10** 630; **12** 655; **15** 861*; **20** 311; **26** 811
Innocent IX, Pope (*reg* 1591) **4** 323
Innocent X, Pope (*reg* 1644-55) **23** 898–9*
architecture **3** 198; **4** 432, 433; **13** 292; **16** 638, 639; **25** 861; **26** 758, 821; **29** 251
fountains **3** 832
medals **21** 805
paintings **9** 375, 376; **33** 25
sculpture **1** 628, 630; **11** 23, 739; **26** 810
stucco **29** 830
Innocent XI, Pope (*reg* 1676-89) **12** *202*; **23** 352; **26** 810; **27** 593
paintings **23** 352–3
Innocent XII, Pope (*reg* 1691-1700) **11** 275; **15** 861–2*; **27** 593; **30** 704
Innocent XIII, Pope (*reg* 1721-24) **15** 862*; **24** 10; **29** 374
Innocent, C. F. **32** 274
Innocenti, Camillo **21** 424
Innocenzo da Imola **15** 862–3*
patrons and collectors **10** 446; **19** 238
pupils **11** 268; **18** 680; **25** 578
teachers **1** 572
Innovationists **16** 2
inns **5** *148*, *639*; **14** 786; **27** 50
Innsbruck **2** *776*; **15** 863–7*, *865*
armour **2** 471, 473
bronze **29** 571
clocks **7** 442
ecclesiastical buildings
Cathedral of St Jakob **2** 800; **11** 123; **15** *864*
Hofkapelle *see under* Hofkirche
Hofkirche **15** *864*, 866*
Fürstenchor **32** 777
Hofkapelle **2** 780
Hofkapelle: tomb of Maximilian I **2** 800, *800*, 821; **6** 170; **7** 554, *554*; **15** 866; **20** 104; **28** 492; **33** 28
monument to Andreas Hofer **2** 802
woodwork **2** 805
Jesuit church **2** 780
Mariahilfkirche **2** 781
St Jakobskirche *see* Cathedral of St Jakob
Galerie im Andechshof **15** 866
Harnaschhaus **10** 736
Helblinghaus **11** 876
Hofburg **2** 779, 813; **15** *864*
Hofglashütte **2** 818; **13** 912
interior decoration **2** 805
Landhaus **13** 846, *846*
Leopold Fountain **2** 800; **13** 315
metalwork **2** 821
monument to Archduke Leopold I **10** 441
monument to Maximilian I *see* ecclesiastical buildings → Hofkirche → Hofkapelle: tomb of Maximilian I
Neuer Hof **15** 864
Rathaus **15** *864*
Schloss Ambras **2** 793; **13** 912; **15** 866–7*, *867*
armour **9** 31; **11** 270
collections **2** 830; **13** 899, 912, 921; **15** 866–7*; **21** 264
coral **7** 835; **31** 285
dining-room **11** 270
façade decoration **10** 738
frescoes **11** 270
gold **6** 142
Kunstkammer **2** 819, 821, 830; **13** 918; **18** 521, *522*; **24** 331; **27** 815
lacquer **18** 612
metalwork **2** 822
Innsbruck
Schloss Ambras—cont.
paintings **4** 913; **6** 126; **19** 662; **30** 519
porcelain **9** 28
sculpture **13** 916; **24** 806
Spanischer Saal **2** 779, 805, *805*; **15** 866
Tiroler Landesmuseum Ferdinandeum **2** 831; **14** 834; **15** 866
Tiroler Volkskunstmuseum **15** 866
tower **14** 420
Innuit *see* INUIT
Inokuma, Genichirō **17** 206
Inoue, Manji **17** 266
Inoue, Yasuji **17** 290; **18** 172
Inoue, Yūichi **17** 240
Inoue Kinga **17** 751
inpainting **15** 867*
Inquisition *see* HOLY OFFICE OF THE INQUISITION
inrō **17** 303–4, 398, *400*; **18** 11
Ins **25** 546
Insalato di Jacopo **7** 817
In school **15** 158–9*; **17** 98, 120–21
Inscription Painter **13** 515
works **13** *515*
inscriptions **6** 76; **11** 308; **12** 105
historical and regional traditions
Achaemenid **1** *116*
Afghanistan **1** 187; **16** 166, 169
Anatolia, ancient **1** 827, 828, 830; **33** 684
Ancient Near East **1** 854, 855, 859, 860, 891, 895; **2** 299
Buddhism **6** 777; **17** 126; **30** 809
Byzantine **4** 774; **9** 576, 660
Cambodia **5** 463, 464, 491
Central Asia, Western **6** 208, 274; **16** 166, 169, 248, 378, 492
Champa **6** 418, 420
China **6** 735–9, *736*, *738*, *739*, *740*, *743*, *744*, 745, 750, *753*, 755, 762–8, *763*, *765*, 772, 774, 777, 805, 823, 826, 836, 840*, 842, 857, 863, 865, 900, 903; **7** 65, 96, 124, 128, 130, 152; **29** 617
Crete **8** 154
Egypt **16** 441–2
Fatimid **16** 176, 258, 512
Islamic **16** 176, *176*, *259*, 383, 386, 415, 431, 432, 441, 510, 513, 514; **28** 716; **29** *618*; **31** *21*
Egypt, ancient **1** 855; **2** 299; **9** 867; **10** 1, 2, 3, 6, 10
Graeco-Roman (332 BC-AD 395) **10** 1
Etruscan **10** 588, 589, *590*, 596, 605, 610, 620, 628, 638; **13** 10
Greece, ancient **2** 299; **13** 385, 387, 485, 487–91*, *488*, *489*, *490*, 507
Classical, High **13** 456–7
Hittite **1** 827
Hurrian **15** 32
Indian subcontinent **15** 192, 193, 198–9*, 233, 310, 443, 688, *688*
Indus civilization **15** 198, 420
Islamic **15** *680*; **16** 513
Kannada **15** 197
Kushana **15** 440, 445–6
Maurya **15** 194, 197, 750
Mughal **16** 514
Sanskrit **15** 197
Tamil **15** 197
Indus civilization **15** 198, 420
Iran **16** *123*, 165, 193, 232, 250, 377, 378, 390, 391, 414, 425, 430, 450, 492, 510, 513
Ilkhanid **16** 513
Safavid **16** 514
Iran, ancient **1** *116*
inscriptions
historical and regional traditions—cont.
Iraq **16** 381, 399, 433, 434, 510
Islamic **14** 428; **16** 128, 130–31, 134–5, 138, 143, 243, 248, 257–60*, 367–8, 372, 395, 467, 509, 510–14, 521, 542–3, *543*, 547, 549; **29** 617, 619; **31** 20–22
Afghanistan **16** 166, 169
Central Asia, Western **6** 208; **16** 166, 169, 248, 378, 492
Egypt **16** 176, *176*, *259*, 383, 386, 415, 431, 432, 441–2, 510, 513, 514; **28** 716; **29** *618*; **31** *21*
Ghaznavid **12** 513
Indian subcontinent **15** *680*; **16** 513
Iran **16** *123*, 165, 193, 232, 250, 377, 378, 390, 391, 414, 425, 430, 450, 492, 510, 513
Iraq **16** 381, 399, 433, 434, 510
Khurasan **16** 378
Ottoman **16** *137*, 514
Pakistan **16** 166
Spain **16** *387*, 524
Syria **16** 147, 277, 381, 383, 415, 441–2, 510
Turkey **16** *137*, 497, 514
Yemen **16** *438*, 439
Italy **10** 588, 589, *590*, 596, 610, 638
Japan **17** 107, 126, 230, 234, 321, 348, 369, 391
Khurasan **16** 378
Korea **18** 356, *356*
Malaysia **20** 170
Maya **20** 883, 884; **21** 264; **24** 743
Mesoamerica, Pre-Columbian **21** 264; **24** 743; **29** 620
Mesopotamia **2** 299; **4** 771; **21** 276–7, 297
Neo-Assyrian (*c.* 883-*c.* 612 BC) **1** *854*
Mongolia **21** 883
North Africa **16** 512, 513
Ottoman **16** *137*, 260, 514, 810
Pakistan **16** 166
Phoenician **1** 828
Phrygian **1** 830
Punic **25** *733*
Rome, ancient **26** 861, 864; **27** 2, 32, 61
South-east Asia **29** 231
Spain **14** 410; **16** *387*, 513, 524
Syria
Fatimid **16** 512
Islamic **16** 147, 277, 381, 383, 415, 441–2, 510
Umayyad **16** 258
Tibet **13** 885; **30** 809, 813
Turkey **16** *137*, 497, 514, 810
Urartian **1** 830
Vietnam **6** 420
Yemen **16** *438*, 439
materials
brick **4** 774
bronze **6** 736
inlays **10** 1
linen **10** 589
mosaics **27** 61
pottery **17** 234
tiles **16** 165, 248
techniques
casting **17** 321
uses
architectural decorations **12** 513; **16** 147, 176, *176*, 243, 248, 257–60*, *259*
architecture **16** 134, 143, 165, 166, 169, 193, 250, 810
armour **16** 509
bowls **16** *123*
brick **4** 771
calligraphy **17** 230
carpets **16** 467
inscriptions
uses—cont.
ceramics **16** 395, 425
chandeliers **16** *387*
coffins **10** 10
coins **15** 688, *688*; **16** 510–14; **17** 369; **18** *356*
copper **18** 356
glass **16** 521
heraldry **14** 410
horn **7** 124
inkstones **7** 96
ivory-carvings **16** 524
jewellery **6** 274
jugs **16** 372
masks **17** 391
medals **20** 917
metalwork **16** 135, 367–8, 377, 378, 381, 383, 386, 390, 391
mirrors **6** 863
paintings **6** 774, 777, 805
porcelain **6** 903
portraits **25** 285
pottery **6** 900; **10** 610; **13** 485, 487–90*, *488*, *489*, *490*, 491*; **16** 399, 414, 415
prints **20** 601; **25** 599–600*
relief sculpture **9** 867; **13** 457
scrolls **28** 310
sculpture **15** 440, 443; **17** 107, 126
seals **7** 128; **16** 542–3, *543*
shirts **16** *137*
silk **28** 716
stelae **29** 617, *618*, 619
textiles **16** 430, 431, 432, 433, 434, *438*, 439, 441–2, 450; **31** 20, *21*
tiles **6** 208
vessels **6** 826, 836, 840*, 842, 857, 865
woodwork **16** 492, 497
insect lacquer *see under* LACQUER→ types
insect repellants **7** 115
Insel, Die **2** 565; **24** 427, 444
Inselin, C.
works **31** *217*
Insfrán, Edgar L. **24** 101
Inshaw, David **4** 823
Inshō **15** 159; **17** 392
Insho, Domoto **30** 247
Insight *see* ZIMBABWE INSIGHT
insignia **7** 177, 178–9*; **14** 409, 414, 416; **15** 149; **17** 524, 525; **29** *346*
Byzantine **9** 603
Early Christian (*c.* AD 250-843) **9** 603
Estonia **7** 178
France **7** 178
Guyana **13** 875
Holy Roman Empire (before 1648) **7** 178
Italy **32** 394
Japan **14** 428
Latvia **7** 178
Lithuania **7** 178
Native North Americans **22** 652
Poland **14** *410*
Rome, ancient **32** 394
Inskeep **1** 374
Inskip, George Charles **31** 763
Insom, Giovanni **3** 294
Inson **15** 159; **17** 122
installations **9** 26; **15** 868–9*; **22** 279, 748
Canada **12** *219*
England **19** *625*
feminism **10** *879*, *881*
United States of America **10** *879*, *881*; **15** *868*
instant photographs *see under* PHOTOGRAPHY → processes
Institut del Disseny Industrial *see* FAD
Institute for Conservation (UK) **7** 742

Institute of Artistic Culture *see* INKHUK
Institute of British Architects *see* LONDON → Royal Institute of British Architects
Institute of Contemporary Arts (ICA) *see under* LONDON → museums; WASHINGTON (DC) → museums
Institute of Painters in Watercolours **32** 903
Institute of Paper Conservation **7** 744
Institute of Proletarian Fine Art (St Petersburg) *see* INSTITUTE OF PAINTING, SCULPTURE AND ARCHITECTURE (ST PETERSBURG)
Institut Européen de l'Aquarelle **32** 903
Institut Français d'Archéologie Orientale (IFAO) **10** 81, 82, 83
Institut Khudozhestvennoy Kultury *see* INKHUK
Institut National de la Culture et les Arts Haïtiens **14** 60
Instituto Cultural Peruano Norteamericano **24** 515
Instituto de Cultura Puertorriqueña **25** 703
Instituto de Diseño Industrial *see* FAD
Instituto del Diseño Industrial *see* ADI-FAD
Instituto Feminino de Estudios Superiores **13** 770
instruments, astronomical *see* ASTRONOMICAL INSTRUMENTS
instruments, divination *see* DIVINATION INSTRUMENTS
instruments, measuring *see* MEASURING INSTRUMENTS
instruments, medical *see* MEDICAL INSTRUMENTS
instruments, musical *see* MUSICAL INSTRUMENTS
instruments, optical *see* OPTICAL INSTRUMENTS
instruments, scientific *see* SCIENFIFIC INSTRUMENTS
insulae **30** 457
 Egypt, ancient **9** 852
 Greece, ancient **13** 407, 420; **15** 894
 Rome, ancient **10** 426–7; **15** 869–70*, *870*; **23** *621*; **26** 863, 868, 869, 887, 891; **27** 4, 55
 see also APARTMENTS
Insular art **15** 870–78*; **25** 533
 amber **15** *872*
 author portraits **4** *343*
 bookbindings **4** 348
 book covers **4** *346*, 349
 bowls **15** 871
 bronze **15** *872*, *873*; **28** *630*
 brooches **15** 871, *872*, 872, 873
 canon tables **5** 624
 carving **21** 326
 chalices **2** 377–8*, *378*; **8** *782*
 crosiers **15** 873
 crosses **7** *460*; **15** *877*; **17** *889*
 enamel **15** *872*; **28** *630*
 glass **15** 871–2
 gold **15** *872*, 872
 Gospel books **13** 20; **15** 871, 873–5, *874*; **17** 889–90; **20** 330, 339
 handpins **15** 871
 initials (manuscript) **15** *847*, 848; **19** *409*
 interlace **15** 882, *882*
 latchets **15** 871
 leather **4** *346*, 349
 manuscript illumination **15** 873–6*, *874*; **17** 889–90; **20** 339; **28** 233
 manuscripts **28** *304*
 metalwork **15** 871–3*, *873*
Insular art—cont.
 miniatures (manuscript illumination) **4** *343*; **15** 874; **16** *13*; **17** *890*; **21** 637
 ornament **23** 537
 plaques **15** *873*
 reliquaries **15** 872; **28** *630*
 sarcophagi **5** 916
 scripts **28** *304*, 305
 sculpture **15** 876–8*
 shrines (i) (cult) **28** *630*
 silver **2** *378*; **8** *782*; **15** *872*, 873
 stone **7** *460*
 stone-carvings **15** *876*
 workshops **29** 851
 see also PICTISH ART
Insular Museum of Ethnology, Natural History and Commerce (Burma) **29** 238
Insular Saladoid ware *see under* POTTERY → wares
Insulis, Alanus de *see* ALANUS DE INSULIS
intaglio carving *see under* CARVING → types
intaglio prints *see under* PRINTS → types
In Tao Art Association **14** 722
intarsia **15** 878*; **20** 465, 466
 historical and regional traditions
  Czech Republic **8** 395, *396*, *397*
  England **10** 288
  Germany **12** 421, 423
  Islamic **16** 524
  Italy **20** 467; **29** *860*
  Netherlands, the **22** 871
 uses
  chests **8** *396*
  clocks **8** *397*
  furniture **8** 395; **33** 332
  tables **12** 423
  woodwork **16** 524
Intef **9** 874, 875
Integral **20** 877; **21** 79; **26** 716
integralism **26** 716
 see also CONSTRUCTIVISM → regional traditions → Romania
integral tripack processes *see* PHOTOGRAPHY → processes → tripack
Integrated Capital Service Ltd **9** 180
Integrated Consultants **10** 132
Integrated Environmental Design *see* IED
Inten (Institute exhibitions) **17** 134, 436
intensity **15** 878*; **19** 351
intention **7** 661; **15** 878–80*; **26** 222
Interbau, 1957 *see under* BERLIN → exhibitions
inter-connected looping textiles *see under* TEXTILES → techniques
Interdiszciplináris Gondolkodás *see* INDIGO GROUP
interferometry *see under* TECHNICAL EXAMINATION → types
Interguglielmi, Elia **15** 880–81*
Interián de Ayala, Juan **15** 881*
Interieur, Das **24** 427, 438
interior decoration **14** 420
 historical and regional traditions
  Afghanistan **1** 208, *209*
  Albania **1** 541–3*, *542*
  Antilles, Lesser **2** 150–51*
  Australia **2** 754–7*, *755*
  Austria **2** 805–10*, *805*, *810*; **33** 48
   Rococo **2** *806*, *807*
   Rococo Revival **2** *809*
   19th cent. **20** *146*
  Azerbaijan **2** 898–9*
  Bahamas, the **3** 63*
  Barbados **2** 150, 151
  Belgium **3** 575–9*
   Art Nouveau **3** *579*
   15th cent. **3** *576*
interior decoration
 historical and regional traditions
  Belgium—cont.
   17th cent. **3** *577*
  Bolivia **4** 262
  Bulgaria **5** 156–7*, *157*
  Canada **5** 572–6*, *573*, *575*
  Caribbean Islands **5** 755
  Catalonia **29** 305, *308*
  Central Asia, Western **16** 200
  Cuba (Caribbean) **8** *235*
  Cyprus **8** 365*
  Czech Republic **8** 394–403*
  Denmark **8** 742–5*, *743*, *744*, 757*, 759
  England **10** 269–85*; **14** 856; **23** *790*
   Etruscan style **10** *643*
   Gothic Revival **19** *614*
   Louis Revival **10** *282*
   Moorish style **17** *640*; **22** *60*
   Neo-classicism **1** *138*; **17** *901*; **22** *737*
   Palladianism **33** *225*
   Pompeian Revival **25** *193*
   Regency style **30** XIV2
   Romanticism **28** *908*
   16th cent. **10** *271*; **14** *126*
   17th cent. **9** *26*; **10** *272*, *274*, *275*
   18th cent. **10** *277*, *278*; **28** *581*
   19th cent. **10** 142, *280*, *283*; **14** 744, *745*; **26** 84–5; **27** *224*; **29** *646*; **30** XVI
   20th cent. **10** *285*
  Etruscan **10** *597*
  Finland **11** 101–2*, *102*
  France **11** 571–84*, *573**, *576*; **26** *494*; **31** *687*
   Baroque **32** *371*
   Empire style **10** *186*; **23** 209
   Gothic **26** *555*
   Louis XV style **19** *722*
   Louis XVI style **19** *723*
   Modernism **19** *45*
   Neo-classicism **11** *579*
   Régence style **23** *458*; **26** 83–4*
   Renaissance **11** *572*; **19** *692*
   Rococo **11** *578*
   Second Empire style **11** *581*
   18th cent. **14** *791*
   19th cent. **32** *597*
   20th cent. **11** *582*, *583*
  Germany **12** 408–19*, *409*, *410*, *412*, *414*, *415*, *417*, *418*, 462; **31** *686*
   Renaissance **10** 662; **22** *307*
   Rococo **3** *429*; **26** *496*
   18th cent. **12** *411*
   19th cent. **2** *550*
  Gothic **13** 128; **26** *555*
  Greece **13** *357*, 357–8*
  Greece, ancient **13** 389
  Hungary **14** 902–10*, *906*, *909*
  Iceland **15** 71–2*
  Indian subcontinent **21** 717
  Iran **16** 195, 200
  Ireland **16** 22–5*, *24*
  Islamic **16** 195, 200, 428; **29** 297; **32** *312*
  Italy **16** 709–21*
   Baroque **16** *715*
   Etruscan **10** *597*
   Grotesque **13** *669*
   15th cent. **16** *710*
   16th cent. **2** *548*
   17th cent. **16** *713*
   18th cent. **16** *717*, *718*
   19th cent. **16** *720*
   20th cent. **16** *721*
  Jamaica **16** 885–7*
  Mexico **21** 391*
  Mustique **2** 151
  Native North Americans **22** *580*
  Netherlands, the **22** 862*, 863–70*, *868*, *869*, *870*; **31** *683*
   Biedermeier **22** *866*
interior decoration
 historical and regional traditions
  Netherlands, the—cont.
   Neo-classicism **22** *865*
   15th cent. **22** *863*
   17th cent. **20** *459*; **22** *864*
  New Zealand **23** 63–5*, *64*
  Norway **23** 231–2*, *232*
  Poland **25** *117*, 117–19*, *118*, 128, 131; **32** *874*, *880*, *882*
  Portugal **25** *303*, 303–4*
  Romania **26** 717–18*
  Rome, ancient **25** 191–4; **29** 665
  Russia **27** 399–404*, 405*
   Neo-classicism **27** *403*; **29** *839*
   Rococo **27** *402*
   17th cent. **27** *399*
  Scotland **28** 244–5*, *245*, *247*, 247, 248–50*, *249*, 252, *286*
  Serbia **28** 454*
  South Africa **29** 113–14*
  Spain **29** 297–309*, *298*, *299*, *300*, *302*, *304*, *305*, *307*; **31** *90*
  Sweden **13** 864; **29** *690*; **30** 87–92*, *88*, *89*, *90*, *91*
  Switzerland **30** 140–41*, *142*
  Trinidad and Tobago **31** *337*, 337–8*
  Tunisia **32** *312*
  United States of America **1** *171*; **31** 615–23*, *616*, *618*, *620*, *621*, *622*
  Wales **32** 788*, *788*
 materials
  amber **1** 762
  damask **3** 576; **9** 15
  feathers **28** *581*
  glacite **3** 576
  hardstones **12** 462
  hessian **9** 19
  lacquer **12** 412
  leather **3** 577
  mirrors **5** 349*; **12** 412; **21** 717
  paper **5** 755
  papier mâché **30** 90
  plants **12** 415
  plaster **16** 23–4; **32** *788*
  prints **16** 24
  rice **5** 755
  shells **28** *581*
  silk **28** 717; **30** 90
  stucco **29** *839*
  textiles **3** 578; **11** 574, 576; **22** 864
  tiles **28** 246; **30** 875, 876
 techniques
  painting **23** 789–90*, *790*; **30** 90
Interioristas, Los **7** 917
Interiors **22** 728; **24** 431
interlace **15** 881–2*
 Ancient Near East **15** 881, *882*
 Borneo **15** 882
 Early Christian (*c.* AD 250–843) **15** 882
 Greece, ancient **15** 881
 Insular art **15** 882, *882*
 Islamic **15** 882
 Italy **15** *882*
 Kuba (iii) (Zaïre) **15** 882
 Lombard art **19** 550*
 Rome, ancient **15** 881
interlace arches *see under* ARCHES → types
interlaced masonry *see under* MASONRY → types
Interlocking style *see* PLAYA GRANDE STYLE
internal buttresses *see under* BUTTRESSES
Internari, Giovanni Battistta **3** 714
International Auction Records **4** 23
International Centre for the Study of Preservation and Restoration of Cultural Property *see* ICCROM
International Copper Co. **31** 654
International Council of Museums *see* ICOM
International Council on Archives *see* ICA
International Council on Monuments and Sites *see* ICOMOS
Internationale Bau-Ausstellung, 1957 *see* BERLIN → exhibitions → Interbau, 1957
Internationale Bau-Ausstellung, 1979, 1984, 1987 *see under* BERLIN → exhibitions
Internationale des Artistes Expérimentaux **7** 489
Internationale revue i 10 **24** 449
Internationales Archiv für Ethnographie **24** 430
Internationale Situationniste **7** 759
International Exhibition of Modern Art *see* NEW YORK → exhibitions → Armory Show, 1913
International exhibitions *see under* EXHIBITIONS → types
International Foundation of SS Cyril and Methodius **5** 163
International Garden Cities and Town Planning Association **12** 145
International Gothic *see under* GOTHIC → styles
International Graphic Arts Society **25** 629
International Harvester **19** 538
International Institute for Conservation of Historic and Artistic Works (IIC) **7** 743
International Institute for the Unification of Private Law *see* UNIDROIT
International Paper and Fiber Co. **24** 41
International Petroleum Company **24** 515
International Phases **26** 475
International Sculpture Center **32** 890
International Silver Co. **31** 650
International Situationist Movement **17** 658; **29** 435
International Studio: An Illustrated Magazine of Fine and Applied Art **24** 426, 431
International Style **7** 615; **10** 417; **14** 590; **15** 885–7*; **17** 620; **23** 498; **25** 741; **26** 14; **33** 205
 Belgium **3** 551; **4** 577
 Brazil **4** 706
 Britain **6** 527; **30** 242
 Canada **5** 573; **28** 557
 Colombia **7** 606
 El Salvador **10** 154
 Finland **11** *93*; **15** *886*
 Germany **13** 686
 Honduras **14** 714
 Japan **17** 53, 86, 88; **27** 597
 Mexico **21** 380
 Nigeria **23** 134
 South Africa **20** 8; **29** 577
 United States of America **5** *136*; **14** 811; **15** *887*; **17** 838; **31** 597, *597*
 Venezuela **5** 692; **32** 170
 see also MODERN MOVEMENT; MODERNISM
International Tapestry Network **31** 661
interpretation of works of art *see* ART (INTERPRETATION OF WORKS OF)
intersecting tracery *see under* TRACERY → types → bar
Intha **5** 248
Intimate Gallery **29** 657
intimisme **4** 325; **15** 888*
 drawings **21** *87*
Intimnaya Masterskaya **17** 732
intonachino **11** 762
intonaco **11** 761, 762, 763; **15** 888*; **27** 51; **32** 802

intonarumori 27 445
intrados 15 888*
see also SOFFITS
INU (Istituto Nazionale di Urbanistica) 25 792
Inuit 10 506; 13 620; 15 888*; 16 861; 22 545, 556, 557, 655, 656, 668, 674
amber 1 761
amulets 1 816, 818
baskets 22 656
basketwork 22 656
beadwork 22 638*
dolls 31 259, 260
dress 22 629, 630
feathers 10 848
games 31 266
iron 21 319
ivory 31 254, 259
leather 31 260
maps 31 152
parkas 22 629–30*, 630
toys 31 254
Inuit Art 24 430
Inupiaq 22 545, 630, 631
Inurria, Mateo 29 295
Inuvialuit 22 630
Inuyama 17 373
Joan tea-room 17 338, 340
Meiji-Mura Museum 17 433, 434
invalid chairs *see under* CHAIRS → types
Invalides, Les *see* PARIS → hospitals → Hôtel des Invalides
Inventaire Général des Monuments et des Richesses Artistiques de la France 32 278
inventories 2 366, 368, 561; 6 75, 76; 7 560; 11 309
China 17 229
France 13 153
Gothic 13 153
Greece, ancient 6 76
Italy 16 768
Japan 17 229
Inveralmond (Tayside) 28 260
Inveraray (Strathclyde) 28 227
Castle 6 60; 13 200; 28 227
paintings 9 302; 21 34
Inverness (Highlands) 28 222
cabinetmaking 28 254
Episcopal Cathedral 28 230
Fort Augustus 21 549
St Mary's Gaelic Kirk 28 251
inverse segregation 1 834
Inversiones Bolivianas (INBO) 4 268
inverted arches *see under* ARCHES → types
investment 2 557, 561; 7 561; 15 888*
Native North Americans 22 668
Netherlands, the 7 562
Invrea (family) 6 34
inweaving *see under* WEAVING → types
Inwood, Charles Frederick 15 889
Inwood, Edward 15 889
Inwood, Henry William 5 905; 10 235; 15 889*; 25 268
Inwood, William 10 235; 15 889*; 25 268; 30 503
Inyotef I (*reg c.* 2081–*c.* 2065 BC) 9 776, 839
Inyotef II (*reg c.* 2065–*c.* 2016 BC) 9 776, 839, 873
Inyotef III (*reg c.* 2016–*c.* 2008 BC) 9 776, 839, 873
Inza, Joaquín 4 565; 13 252; 15 889*; 16 48
IO, Master 2 469
Ioakim, Abbot of Krušedol 25 339
Ioan (*fl* 1678–88) 7 763
Ioann (*fl* 1161) 25 90
Ioannes (*fl* 1637) 21 345
Ioannina 9 511; 15 889–90*
Archaeological Museum 13 534; 18 232
Castle 18 243
Ioannina—cont.
Cathedral 13 358
Dilios Monastery 25 335
Eleousa Monastery 25 336
gold 15 890
metalwork 13 359
Philanthropinoi Monastery 7 222; 25 335, 336
silver 13 358, 359; 15 890
textiles 13 356
Ioannis Frangopoulos 22 408
Ioannis the illustrator 9 628
Ioasaf, Archbishop of Rostov (*fl* 1490) 10 889
Ioasaph (*fl* 1391) 9 610
iodine 24 650
Iofan, Boris (Mikhaylovich) 15 890*
assistants 3 685
collaboration 12 243; 27 285; 28 571
competitions 7 670
groups and movements 29 529, 530
works 13 238; 22 174; 27 379
Iofan, Dmitry 15 890
IO.FF, Master 20 800*
works 25 20, 20
Ioganson, Boris (Vladimirovich) 2 633; 15 891*; 27 395
Ioganson, Karl 7 768
Iohannes (*fl* 997) 23 649
Iohannes de Mutiglianus 26 621
Iol *see* CHERCHEL
Iolas, Alexandros 13 359; 20 102; 21 134
Iolkos 13 363
Iolkos *see under* VOLOS
Iommi, Ennio 2 400, 546, 604; 15 891*
Ion, Master
works 26 712
Ion, Prince 26 721
Iona 15 870, 892*; 21 834; 28 222
crosses 8 197; 15 892; 24 738
manuscript illumination 28 233
manuscripts 15 847, 874; 17 890; 28 233
marble 29 702
St John's Cross 15 892, 892
sculpture 28 241
Iona Psalter *see under* PSALTERS → individual manuscripts
Ionescu, Eugène 16 808
Ionescu, Grigore 15 893*
Ionescui-Mihăeşti, Constantin 26 723, 725
Ionescu-Pascanu, C. 26 719
Ionescu-Valbudea, Ştefan *see* VALBUDEA, ŞTEFAN
Ionia 1 821; 13 363; 15 893–4*
Ionian Little Masters *see under* CUPS → types
Ionic capitals *see under* CAPITALS → types
Ionic columns *see under* COLUMNS → types
Ionic order *see under* ORDERS (ARCHITECTURAL) → types
Ionic temples *see under* TEMPLES → types
Ionides (family) 19 90; 27 187
Ionides, Aleco 15 895; 17 466
Ionides, Alexander Constantine 15 894–5*; 32 921
Ionides, Basil 10 284
Ionides, Constantine Alexander 5 267; 15 894–5
I'Ons, Frederick (Timpson) 29 108
Ios 8 304; 29 701
Iosadzhenov, I. S. 27 439
Iosifo-Volokolamsky Monastery 15 895*; 27 363
Ioulis *see* KHORA
Iowa 22 551, 616
I.P., Master 2 800; 6 364; 8 383, 515; 20 800*
Ipacaraí 24 100
Ipai 22 550
Ipiales, Museo Arqueológico 7 612
I Ping-shou *see* YI BINGSHOU
Ipiutak 22 546, 574
combs (hair) 22 574
Ipkhi 12 330
Ipoh 20 162, 168, 169, 170
Padang 20 170
Paloh Mosque 20 166
Town Hall 20 170
Ipóly 26 724
Ipolyi, Arnold, Bishop of Banská Bystrica 15 17; 28 857
Ipoustéguy, Jean (Robert) 11 570; 15 895–6*
Ippei Okamoto *see* OKAMOTO, IPPEI
Ippen 5 119
Ippitsusai Bunchō 15 896*; 17 283, 844
Ippō *see* IKENAGA DŌUN
Ippolita Master 20 697*
Ippolito del Donzello *see* DONZELLO, IPPOLITO DEL
Ippo Mishosai 17 381
Ippo Mori *see* MORI IPPO
Ippu *see* SIN YUN-BOK
Iprari 12 323
Ipsley (Hereford & Worcs), St Peter's 1 520
Ipswich (Suffolk; UK)
Cardinal's College 28 156
Christchurch Mansion 26 613
metalwork 6 161
power station 25 402
Prison 25 636
St Nicholas 26 613
St Peter 26 613
Willis, Faber & Dumas Building 8 279, 279; 11 332; 12 794
Ipswich (MA; USA) 31 661
Whipple House 12 136
Ipuia 27 812
Ipuky 9 789, 820, 821, 840; 10 52
Ipuy 9 840; 10 46; 25 875
Ipy 9 790, 903
Iqbal, Khalid 23 799, 800
Iquique 6 590
Iracoubo 11 756
church 11 758, 759
Iradat Khan 15 363
Irakleion *see* HERAKLEION
Irakli II, King of Georgia (*reg* 1744–98) 14 804
Iraku Uozumi *see* UOZUMI, IRAKU
Iram 23 436
Iran 6 181; 15 896–900*, 897; 16 104, 105; 21 267
albums 16 318–19
aqueducts 16 231
arches 2 292, 295
architects 16 232
architectural decorations 16 165, 194–5, 233, 233, 234, 244, 249; 21 718
architecture 15 897–8*; 16 142, 153–4*, 158–65*, 166, 192–200*, 229–35*, 264*
Abbasid 16 150
ā'inakārī 16 257
Aqqoyunlu 16 196, 198
Bawandid 16 158
brick 4 791; 16 154, 158, 160, 164, 164–5, 199–200
brick dust 32 320
Buyid 16 158
Ilkhanid 16 192
Jalayirid 16 192
Kakuyid 16 160
Khwarazmshah 16 158
military 21 588–9
Muzaffarid 16 192, 193
Qajar 16 229, 233, 234–5, 249
Qarakhanid 16 158
Qaraqoyunlu 16 195, 198, 248
Safavid 16 220, 229–33
Great Saljuqs 16 158, 162
Samanid 16 158
stone 16 199
Iran
architecture—cont.
Timurid 16 192, 195–8
vernacular 32 319–20*
wood 16 199
Zand 16 229, 233–4
Ziyarid 16 158
astrolabes 2 648
axes 16 509
baths 16 193
belts 16 463
bookbindings 18 609
book covers 16 358–9
book illustrations 16 196
bowls 6 IV3; 12 V2; 16 123, 402, 410, 410, 413, 426, 554
boxes 16 376
bracelets 16 530
brass 16 373, 376, 391, 392, 392–3, 506; 32 161
brick 4 791; 16 154, 158, 160, 164, 164–5, 199–200, 244; 32 320
bannā'ī 16 195, 199
bricklaying 23 559
bridges 16 231, 232
bronze 2 648; 16 370, 373, 374, 504, 506; 19 810, 811
calligraphers 16 232
calligraphy 16 232, 286
candlesticks 16 375, 376
caps 16 454
caravanserais 16 154, 193, 198, 232
caricatures 5 761
carpets 5 829, 830, 833, IV; 9 492; 12 77, 77; 15 899; 16 466, 467, 469, 474–5*, 475, 476, 482, 482–4*, 483
casting 16 370
cast iron 16 504
cenotaphs 6 172, 172; 16 249
ceramics 9 34; 16 419, 423–5*, 515; 29 618
chess sets 6 556
china stone 16 393
cisterns 16 232
citadels 16 264
clay 16 393, 408
coats 16 464, 465
cobalt 16 414
cochineal 16 449
coins 16 510, 511, 512, 513, 513, 514
collections 1 896; 15 900; 16 230, 424, 551–2
colour 7 634
columns 16 502
copper 16 375, 394
corbels 16 164
cosmetics 16 465, 466
cotton 5 829; 16 449, 450; 18 48; 31 21
courtyards 16 142, 154, 264
craftsmen and artists 16 232*, 331
culs-de-sac 16 264
daggers 16 516
dalmatics 16 444
damask 16 441
diplomatic gifts 16 413
domes 16 161, 162, 164, 164, 193, 199, 270
doors 9 160
doublures 16 356
dovecots 9 203
dress 16 452, 453, 454, 457, 458, 463–6*
dyes 16 449
earthenwares 16 402, 413, 425, 426
embroidery 16 450–51
enamel 16 410*, 410, 426, 515–16, 516
engraving 16 377, 378
etchings 15 899
ewers 16 369, 371, 375, 408, 519
façades 28 615
felt 10 872, 873, 874
Iran—cont.
flasks 16 424
forgeries 1 896; 16 545, 546
fortifications 21 588–9
frit 6 IV3; 16 394, 408, 408–9*, 413
frontispieces 16 293
gardens 11 340; 12 81–3*, 83
gates 16 264
glass 12 V2; 16 519, 522
glazes 4 172; 16 165, 248, 401, 402, 408, 412, 413, 426
gold 16 292–3, 376, 450, 506, 512, 516, 530; 20 448
grilles 16 502
guidebooks 13 812
guns 16 509
hair 16 449; 30 473
hairstyles 16 464, 465
halls 30 222
harnesses 14 183
hats 10 872
headdresses 16 454, 465, 466
helmets 16 504
historiography 16 548
houses 16 154, 163, 264
ice-houses 15 68; 16 232
ikat 30 554
incense burners 16 374
incising 16 425
indigo 16 449
inkwells 16 390
inlays 16 375–6, 376, 377, 378
inscriptions 16 123, 165, 193, 232, 250, 377, 378, 390, 391, 414, 425, 430, 450, 492, 510, 513
Ilkhanid 16 513
Safavid 16 514
interior decoration 16 195, 200
iron 16 504
ivory-carvings 16 526*
iwans 16 161, 162, 193–4, 801
jackets 16 463, 466
jade 16 528, 528
jewellery 16 464, 465, 530–31*
jugs 16 528
khānaqāhs 18 18
kilims 18 48, 48, 49
kilns 16 394, 409
kiosks 18 70, 71
Korans 16 290
lac 16 449
lacquer 16 533, 534; 18 609
insect 18 609
lampstands 16 391, 391
languages 16 108
lithography 16 342
maces 16 504, 506, 509
madder 16 449
madrasas 16 163, 197; 20 54, 55, 57
maidans 16 230, 231
manganese 16 402
manuscript illumination 4 49; 16 124, 290, 292–3, 295, 302–3, 313–17*, 315, 316, 317, 318–29*, 331–40*, 341–2*; 18 609; 22 515
manuscripts 16 290, 296, 302–3, 304, 321; 30 919
maqṣūras 20 369
marbling 24 55
marks 16 424
masonry 16 160
matrices 16 506
mausolea 15 898; 16 159–60, 194, 194, 197, 230
medical books 21 5
metalwork 15 899; 16 368, 369*, 370*, 372, 373–8*, 390–91*, 392*
Timurid 16 377–8
mihrabs 16 161, 244, 249, 492; 21 506; 29 820
minarets 16 160, 163, 164, 165, 194; 21 627
minbars 21 630

Iran—cont.
miniatures (manuscript illumination) **16** *301*, *302*, *319*, *322*, *325*, *328*, *333*, *336*, *338*, *341*; **18** *70*; **30** *477*
mirror-cases **16** *534*
mirrors **16** 257; **21** 717–18
monograms **16** 425
mosaics **16** 195, 199, 248, *249*
mosques **15** 338; **16** 142, 153–4, *154*, 159, 161–3, *164*, 193–4, 196–7, 198, 234, *234*; **30** *224*
congregational **33** 624
courtyard **16** 153–4
four-iwan **16** 163; **22** 194, *194*
hypostyle **16** 159
kiosk-mosque **16** 162
musallas **16** 163; **22** 354
Timurid **30** 919
14th cent. **33** *512*
15th cent. **16** *77*
17th cent. **16** *78*
mud-bricks **16** 199
muqarnas (architecture) **16** 161, 164, 169, 194, *233*; **22** 321, 322
museums **15** 899–900*; **16** 557
narratives **22** *515*
necklaces **16** 531
niches **16** 161
nude figures **23** 290
observatories **16** 193
ochre **16** 248
painting **15** 898–9*; **16** *125*, 160, *254*; **21** 507
glass **16** 522
oil **16** 535–6*
Safavid **16** 331, 337
wall **16** 200, 233, 253–4, 331; **32** 804
15th cent. **7** V
17th cent. **16** *464*
palaces **16** 160, 234–5, 246, *265*
Hasanwayhid **16** 160
Islamic **16** *80*
Safavid **23** *816*
paper **24** 55
papier mâché **16** 533; **24** 62
patronage **16** 126, 374
pigments **4** 172; **16** 248, 249
pishṭāq **16** 160, 164
plaster **16** 165, 200
plates **16** *394*
porcelain **4** 172; **16** 423, 424, *424*, 425, *425*
portals **16** 194
portraits **16** *127*, *341*, *536*; **25** 770
pottery **15** 899; **16** 123, *123*, 124, 395, 400–402*, 407–10*, *408*, *410*, 412–14*, *413*, *414*, 423–7*, *554*
Aghkand ware **16** 407
Amol ware **16** 407
blue-and-white ware **9** *36*; **16** 413, 414, *414*, 424
champlevé ware **16** 407
Ilkhanid **16** 412–13, *413*
Kashan style **16** 409–10
lājvardīna ware **6** IV3; **16** 412, 413
Laqabi ware **16** 408
lustreware **16** 393, *394*, 401, 404, 409–10*, 412, 413, 423, 425, 427
Miniature style **16** 409
Monumental style **16** 409
Qajar **16** 425–7
Great Saljuqs **16** 407
Samanid **16** 401–2
Timurid **16** 413–14
tin-glazed ware **16** *426*, 426
Zand **16** 425
printing **16** 361, 450
quartz **16** 408, 413
quilting **25** 821
regalia **16** 538, 539
revetments **16** 199, *234*, *249*
ribāṭs **16** 154
ribs **16** 164

Iran—cont.
robes **16** 463, 464, 465
rock crystal **16** 540
rock reliefs **30** *337*
sabres **16** *506*
safflower **16** 449
salvers **32** *161*
sashes **16** 465
satin **16** 449, *450*
scabbards **16** *516*
scissors **8** *286*, 287
scripts **16** 273
figural **16** 375–6
nastaʿlīq **16** *286*, 368, 378, 390, 391, 514
Pahlavesque **16** 510
thuluth **16** 514
sculpture **16** 246
sgraffito **16** *402*, 402, 407–8*
shears **8** *286*
shirts **16** 463, 464
shrines (i) (cult) **25** 830; **28** IV1
signatures **16** 232, 331, 410
silk **5** 829; **16** 428, 430, 435, *435*, 443, *444*, 449, *450*, 465, 474, *475*; **18** 48, 49; **25** 131; **28** 715, 716
silver **16** *371*, 375, *376*, 450, *511*, *513*
silver-gilt **16** *372*
skirts **16** 466
slip **16** 408*
smalt **16** 394
souvenirs **16** 414
squares (town) **27** 512
squinches **16** 161, 164
stained glass **16** 257
steel **16** 391, *508*, *516*
stelae **29** 618, 619
stone **16** 199
stucco **16** 158, 160, 165, *200*, *233*, *244*; **21** 506; **29** 818, *820*
sword guards **16** *506*
swords **16** *508*
takyas **16** 234
talars **16** 234
tents **16** 193; **30** *472*, 473, 480*
terracotta **16** 165
textiles **16** 435*, 443, 449, 450, 451*, 546
threads **16** 450; **18** 48, 49
tiles **1** *98*; **6** 172; **16** 165, 193, 195, *199*, 199, *234*, 248, 249, *249*, 412, 425; **28** *615*
tin **16** 402, 413
tiraz **31** 21
tombs **16** 158, 159–60, 163–4, 197, 492; **31** *112*
Firuzanid **16** 160
Kakuyid **16** 159
tower **16** 158, 159–60, *160*, 194; **23** *559*
towers **16** 232
towns **2** 378; **8** 861; **10** 719
trade **16** 331
carpets **5** 835, 841; **16** 482
ceramics **6** 332; **16** 425
cobalt **6** 622
cochineal **16** 449
cotton **16** 449
glass **7** 83
hair **16** 449
indigo **16** 449
lac **16** 449
manuscripts **15** 572; **16** 328
porcelain **4** 175; **16** 412, 424, 425
pottery **6** 333; **16** 398, 401, 402, 413, 425, 427
silk **16** 430, 445, 449
smalt **6** 869; **16** 394
stone **16** 199
textiles **16** 441, 444, 451
wool **16** 449
trappings **14** 183
trays **16** *372*
trousers **16** 465, 466
turbans **16** 452, 454, 464
turquoise **16** *530*

Iran—cont.
underclothes **16** 464, 466
urban planning **16** 230, 264*
vaults (ceiling) **16** 192, 194, *195*, 199, *200*, 232, *233*
velvet **16** 449
vessels **20** *448*
villas **16** 230
war hammers **16** *504*
weaving **16** 443, *444*, 449, *450*, *467*
wind catchers **33** 243
wood **6** *172*; **9** 160; **16** 199
woodwork **16** 491–2*, 501–2*, *502*
wool **5** IV; **16** 449, *467*; **18** *48*
workshops **16** 468
see also ANCIENT NEAR EAST; IRAN, ANCIENT; LURISTAN
Iran, ancient **1** 822; **15** 900–923*, *901*
agate **15** 902
alabaster (gypsum) **15** 913
animal subjects **15** 907–8
architecture **15** 909–13*, *911*
Iron Age **15** 910–11
military **21** 553–4*
arsenic **15** 918
axes **7** *187*
beads **4** 172
beakers **1** *866*; **14** *211*
blackstone **1** *856*
bowls **33** *688*
brick **15** 912
bridges **4** 800
bronze **15** 902, 905, 918, *919*; **21** *712*
bullae **28** 537
ceramics **15** 903, 904, 905, 920–21*, *921*
chariots **6** 480
chlorite **15** 902, 904, 913, 914
chronologies **1** *852*, 853
citadels **24** *482*
coins **27** *855*
collections **15** 922*
copper **15** 902, 918
cornelian **15** 902
dress **1** 883, *884*, 886
earthenwares **4** 172
exhibitions **15** 923*
façade decoration **10** 742
figurines **15** 903, *903*
fire-holders **33** *708*
flint **15** 902–3
fortifications **21** 553–4*
friezes **2** 213
gardens **12** 62
pleasure **24** 90
gilding **15** *920*
glass **1** 866*, *866*, 868; **4** 172
gold **14** *211*; **15** 905; **21** III1
gypsum **15** 912
halls **2** 213; **14** 210; **15** *911*; **24** *483*
harnesses **14** 180*
human figures **15** 917
hunting scenes **15** 917
iconography **15** 907–8*, *908*, 916
inscriptions **1** *116*
iron **15** 919
ivory **15** 902, *915*
jewellery **1** 874–5
lapis lazuli **15** 902; **33** *688*
lead **15** 918
limestone **15** 914, *914*
lost-wax casting **15** 904, 905, 918
magnesite **15** *914*
metal **21** 302
metalwork **1** *118*; **15** 904, 918–20*; **26** 544
mirrors **21** *712*
mortars (building) **15** 912
mud-bricks **28** 537
museums **15** 922*
painting **15** 922*; **18** *499*
palaces **23** 807*
parks **24** 178

Iran, ancient—cont.
periods
Baradostian **15** 902
Chalcolithic (*c*. 5500–*c*. 3500 BC) **1** *852*; **15** 904*
Elamite (*c*. 3500–*c*. 7th cent. BC) **1** *852*
Epipalaeolithic **15** 903
Epipalaeolithic/Mesolithic (before *c*. 8500 BC) **1** *852*
Islamic **1** *852*
Neolithic (*c*. 8500–*c*. 5500 BC) **1** *852*; **15** 903–4*
Palaeolithic **15** 902–3*
Zarzian **15** 902
phialai **1** *118*
pigments **4** 172; **33** *688*
plaster **29** *815*
plates **15** *920*; **27** *856*
pottery **1** *786*, 851; **33** 504
rediscovery **1** 894*
reliefs **15** 915–18*
religion **15** 907–8*, *908*
rhyta **15** 905, *915*
rock art **15** 902
rock reliefs **1** *116*; **4** *92*; **15** *908*, 915, 916, 917, *917*, *918*, 920; **24** 217
Parthian **10** *171*
sanctuaries **15** 913
scripts **24** 481
sculpture **15** 913–15*, *914*
architectural **10** 742
bronze **15** *919*
Elamite **15** *919*
Prehistoric **15** 913*
relief **15** *914*; **24** *220*; **33** *707*
seals **1** 868; **15** 904
cylinder **1** 850, 856, 858, *863*, 863–4
stamp **1** *856*, 858
silk **1** 882, *882*
silver **1** *118*; **7** *187*; **15** 905, *920*; **27** *855*; **30** 770
silver-gilt **27** *856*
soapstone **15** *903*
squinches **15** 912
stelae **29** 614
stucco **29** *815*
temples **15** *911*, 912, 913; **30** 432
tents **30** 476
textiles **1** *882*, 882–3
tin **15** 902
tombs **15** 904
tools **15** 902–3*
towers **33** 707, *707*
trade **1** 882; **6** 258, 267, 621; **24** 298
trade routes **15** 901–2
trappings **14** 180*
vaults (ceiling) **15** 912; **28** 537, *537*
weaving **1** *882*
wood **15** 902
writing **15** 904
writing-tablets **1** 854
ziggurats **15** *910*
see also ACHAEMENID; ELYMAIS
Iranamadu Formation *see under* BUNDALA
Irani, Askari Mian **23** 800
Iranian Calligraphers Association **15** 898
Iranian Carpet Company **15** 899
Iranis **33** 706
Iranistan **15** 407
Iraq **2** 638; **16** 1–3*, *104*, *105*; **21** 266, *267*
albums **16** 318–19
archaeology **3** 629; **21** 310
arches **16** 150
architectural decorations **16** *247*
architecture **16** 1, 149, 158*, 178–82*
Abbasid **16** 150–53*, *150*, 243
brick **16** 182
Jalayirid **16** 192
military **21** 588
stone **16** 150

Iraq
architecture—cont.
vernacular **32** 314–15*
archives **2** 370*
astrolabes **2** *647*
bowls **12** V2; **16** 398, *398*; **23** *558*
brass **16** 379, *380*
brick **16** 182
bronze **2** *647*; **16** *370*, *538*
calligraphy **16** 1, *283*
cantonments **16** 151
carpets **16** 468
ceramics **9** 34
chess sets **6** 556
clay **16** 398
coins **16** 510, *512*
collections **16** 3
cotton **16** 434; **31** 21
courtyards **16** 152
crowns **16** *538*
damascening **16** *516*
dating methods **16** 399*
domes **16** 182
doors **16** *489*
dress **16** 455–6
earthenwares **16** *398*, 398, *399*
embroidery **16** 433–4
ewers **16** 369, *370*
exhibitions **16** 2
façades **16** 179; **18** *483*
felt **10** 874
finials (scrolls) **17** 569
fortifications **16** 151; **21** 588
gardens **12** 77
glass **12** V2
glazes **16** 399, 433
guidebooks **13** 812
helmets **16** *504*
houses **16** 152–3, *267*, *268*, *270*; **32** *314*, 315
inlays **16** 379, *380*, 381–2
inscriptions **16** 381, 399, 433, 434, 510
iron **16** *504*
iwans **14** *225*; **16** 142, 153
jewellery **16** 530–31*
jugs **16** 399
lamps **17** 573
lead **16** 399
madrasas **3** *52*; **16** 180
manganese **16** 400
manuscript illumination **16** *114*, 307–10*, 313–17*, 318–21*, 327–9*
mausolea **16** 159, 181
Megillat **21** 48
metalwork **16** 369*, 379*, 380–81*
minarets **16** 180; **21** *626*
miniatures (manuscript illumination) **16** *308*, *309*, *320*
mosques **16** *151*, 151, 152, 179–80; **27** 680
mouldings **16** 182
mud-bricks **16** 150
muqarnas (architecture) **22** 322
painting **16** 1–2, 434
palaces **16** *152*, 152–3, 160, 182; **18** *483*
patronage **16** 380*
plates **16** 398, *399*
polo grounds **16** 153
pottery **2** *492*; **16** 393, 396, 397–400*
blue-on-white ware **16** 397, *398*, 400
lustreware **16** 393, 397, 399, *399*, 400, 404; **23** *558*
tin-glazed ware **16** 399
printing **16** 434
racecourses **16** 153
reeds **16** 269; **32** *314*
regalia **16** *538*
scientific books **16** 309–10
scripts **16** *283*
sculpture **16** *3*, 243, 245, *247*
relief **14** *226*
seals **1** 858

Iraq—cont.
shrines (i) (cult) **28** *633*
signatures **16** 399
silk **16** 433, 434–5; **28** 715
silver **16** *380*, *512*
slip **16** 399
starch **16** 433
stone **16** 150
stucco **16** 153, 243; **27** *681*; **29** 819
swords **16** *506*
synagogues **17** 550
tapestries **16** 434
teak **16** 488, *489*
terracotta **16** *247*
textiles **16** 433–5*
tikim **17** *568*
tiles **16** 400, 404
tin **16** 399
tiraz **16** 433; **31** 21
tombs **16** 159
trade
ceramics **16** 397, 398
dress **16** 456
fur **16** 456
metalwork **16** 379
pottery **6** 333; **16** 401, 402, 403, 404, 417
textiles **16** 438
tiles **16** 400
trays **16** *380*
urban planning **16** 150–51
vaults (ceiling) **16** 150, 153, 181; **18** 483
weaving **16** 434–5
wood-carvings **16** 488
woodwork **16** 488–91*, *489*
wool **16** 434, 455
ziggurats **2** *236*; **33** 675
see also ANCIENT NEAR EAST; MESOPOTAMIA
'Iraq al-Amir **13** *362*; **16** 3–4*
Iraq Consult **6** 382
Iraqi Oil Company **6** 387
Iraqw **1** 311, 409; **3** 442
skirts **1** *410*
Irarrázabal, Mario **6** 598; **16** 4*
Irascibles **29** 534
Irazábal, Juan Pérez de *see* PÉREZ DE IRAZÁBAL, JUAN
Irazusta, Miguel de **27** 644
Irbach, Sebastian *see* IRRWOCH, SEBASTIAN
Irbid, Yarmouk University **17** 655
Irbil **32** 314
Irby, Florance George Henry, Lord Boston **18** 169
I Regig **15** 808
Ireland **16** 4–38*, *5*; **31** 585; **32** 513
airports **16** *11*
amber **15** *872*
aquatints **6** *64*
archaeology **16** 36
architecture **16** 6–12*
Cistercian Order **16** 7; **21** 87
Dominican Order **16** 7
Early Christian (*c*. AD 250-843) **16** 6
Franciscan Order **16** 7
Gothic **9** 321; **13** 56; **16** 7
Romanesque **5** 915, 916; **7** 459; **12** 807–8; **16** 7; **26** 592*
18th cent. **12** *44*
art history **16** 38*
assembly rooms **2** 617
bookcases **16** *27*
bowls **6** 152; **16** 31
boxes **16** 32, *32*
bronze **15** *872*, *873*; **16** *21*; **28** *630*; **32** *530*
brooches **15** 871, 872, *872*, 873
bureaux **16** *27*
canals **9** 341
candlesticks **16** 31, *31*, 32
canvas **16** 33
capitals **16** 19
carpets **5** 841
cashels *see* forts

Ireland—cont.
castles **6** 61; **16** 7–8; **21** 564
cathedrals **5** *915*, 916; **9** *321*
cemeteries **19** 720
ceramics **16** 28–9*
chalices **2** 377–8*, *378*; **8** *782*, 782–3; **16** 30
chandeliers **6** 443, *443*
chapels **26** *592*
chevaux-de-frise **9** 391
chimney-pieces **16** *23*
churches **2** 72; **7** *269*; **12** *807*; **16** 7, *10*, 10–11
clocks **16** 26
coins **7** 538
collections **10** 487; **16** 24, 36–7*
colleges **9** *323*; **18** *753*
compasses **6** 161
comports **16** *29*
corbels **12** 14
cotton **16** 33, *34*
craftsmen and artists **16** 25; **32** 529
crochet **16** 34
crosiers **15** 873
crosses **1** 468; **15** 876–8*
High **7** *460*; **8** *196*, 196–7*; **15** *877*; **16** 18–19; **17** 888–9*, *889*; **26** 618; **31** 402
Insular art **15** *877*
processional **8** *202*
cups **6** 161; **16** 31
damask **19** 417
dealing **16** 36*
decanters **16** *30*
decorative arts **32** 529–30*
dish rings **16** 32
earthenwares **16** 28
education (art) **16** 37*
effigies **16** *19*
embossing **16** 33
embroidery **16** 34
enamel **15** *872*; **28** *630*
engravings **16** 24
erotic art **10** 476
felt **16** 33
fermes ornées **12** 129
filigree **32** *530*
forks **8** *284*
fortifications **21** 551
forts **9** 390–91; **21** 551, 552
frames **16** 26
furniture **16** 25–8*
gardens **12** 127, 128, 129, 131
gateways **26** 475
gilding **32** *530*
glass **6** 443, *443*; **12** 787; **16** 29–30*, *30*; **32** *530*
millefiori **15** 871–2
glasses **16** 29
glass paste **16** 33
glazes **16** 28
gold **15** 872, *872*; **16** 30–32*, 34; **32** *530*
Celtic **12** *867*
Prehistoric **25** 526
Gospel books **13** 20; **17** 889–90
guilds **16** 25
handpins **15** 871
hardstones **32** *530*
henges **25** 498
heraldry **14** 409
historicism **14** 580
historiography **16** 38*
houses **16** 8
country **16** 9, 22–3, 24–5; **24** *305*
Greek Revival **16** *9*
Neo-classicism **6** *411*
Palladianism **23** *861*
manor **16** 22
tower **6** 59; **16** 8, 22; **31** 229
town **6** *64*
huts **16** 7; **28** 817
incising **25** 511
initials (manuscript) **15** 847
interior decoration **16** 22–5*, *24*
jewellery **16** 33
jugs **16** 31

Ireland—cont.
jumpers **18** 158
kilns **16** 28, 29
knitting **18** 158
lace **16** 34; **18** 593
latchets **15** 871
lead **16** 28
libraries **16** 38*
linen **5** 654; **16** 33, *34*; **19** 418
looms **16** 33, 34
mahogany **16** 23, 26, *26*, *27*
mansions **12** 6
mantles **16** 33
manuscript illumination **15** 873–4, 875; **16** 12–13; **17** 889–90
maps **9** *314*
marks **16** 32; **20** 444, *444*
metalwork **13** 164, 165; **15** *873*; **26** 688–9*
mezzotints **16** 24; **21** 416
miniatures (manuscript illumination) **16** *13*; **17** *890*
Insular art **4** *343*
mirrors **16** 26, 30
misericords **16** 25
monasteries **16** *7*; **21** *88*, 834
monuments **16** *20*, 21
funerary **14** *500*
mouldings **22** 217
museums **16** *10*, 36–7*
neck rings **12** *867*
objects of vertu **16** 33*
oratories (i) (chapels) **12** 14
overmantels **16** *23*
painting **2** 72; **16** 12–18*
history **20** *29*
landscape **16** 14, *15*
religious **14** *718*
urban life **16** *16*
20th cent. **16** *17*
paper **16** 33
parliament buildings **9** *316*
patronage **16** 35*
periodicals **16** 42
periods **6** 162
photoarchives **16** 38*
piggins **16** 30
plaques **15** *873*
plaster **16** *23*, 23–4; **29** 829
poplin **16** 34
porcelain **16** *29*, 29
portals
Romanesque **26** *618*
portraits **9** *2*; **16** 13–14, *14*
drawings **19** *19*
self-portraits **19** *19*
potter's wheels **16** 28
pottery **16** 28; **25** 544
printing **16** *34*; **30** 562
print rooms **16** 24
prints **16** 15–16, 24
reliquaries **15** 872; **28** *630*
rock art **18** *169*, 169–70; **25** *509*, 510, 511, 531
salvers **16** 31
sarcophagi **5** 916
scripts **28** 305
sculpture **16** 18–22*
architectural **10** 476; **31** *402*
bronze **16** *21*
Dark Age (ii) (*c*. 5th-8th cent. AD; Western Europe) **15** 876–8*
marble **14** *500*
Romanesque **7** 458; **26** 618–19*
stone **26** *618*, 618–19
tomb **14** *500*
shrines (i) (cult) **28** *630*; **32** *530*
silk **16** 33–4
silver **2** *378*; **8** *782*; **15** *872*, 873; **16** 30–32*, *31*, *32*, 34; **32** *530*
stained glass **29** 507, VII
stone **1** 468; **7** *460*; **12** 6; **26** *618*, 618–19
stone-carvings **15** *876*; **23** 23, *24*
stucco **29** 835
studios **9** *319*
tables **16** *26*, *27*

Ireland—cont.
teapots **16** 31
textiles **16** 33–5*, *34*; **30** 562
tiles **30** 877
tombs **9** 80; **16** 19–20; **25** 508–9, 510
towers **5** *915*
tracery **31** 273
trade **16** 28, 36
treatises
aesthetics **15** 37
tweeds **16** 34
urban planning **16** 8
villas **32** 553
walls **9** 391
walnut **16** *27*
weaving **16** 33
windows **24** 305
wood-carvings **16** 25
wool **16** 33
workshops **29** 851
Ireland, Northern *see* NORTHERN IRELAND
Ireland, W. H. **10** 420
Ireland, William of *see* WILLIAM OF IRELAND
Ireli
meeting-houses **1** *309*
Irena (GA) **21** 597
Irenaeus, Bishop of Lyon **1** 693; **9** 608
Irevani, Mirza Kadym **2** 901
Iri **9** 736
Wongwang University **18** 381
Iria, Temple of Dionysos **22** 699
Irian Barat *see* IRIAN JAYA
Irian Jaya **15** *751*; **16** 42–7*; **23** *711*
architecture **23** 715
canoes **16** 43, 44
figureheads **16** 45
human figures **16** *43*, 44, 46
korwar **16** *43*, 43–4
languages **16** 43
posts **16** 45, *45*
rock art **23** 729
sculpture **16** *43*; **23** 733
shields **16** 47, *47*
spirit poles **16** 46
wood **16** *43*, *45*, *47*; **23** 715
wood-carvings **16** 43–5, *45*, 46–7, *47*
Iriarte (family) **15** 889
Iriarte, Agustín **12** 28
Iriarte, Bernardo de **6** 46; **16** 48*
Iriarte, Domingo de **16** 48*
Iriarte, Francisco **6** 523
Iriarte, Hesiquio **14** 464; **16** 48*; **21** 385
Iriarte, Ignacio de **16** 48–9*
Iriarte, Rafael **13** 765
Iriarte, Tomás de **16** 48*; **28** 389
Iriarte, Valero **16** 49*; **29** 282
Iribe, Paul **2** 520; **9** 196; **10** 824; **11** 582, 601; **19** 85
iridescent film *see under* FILM → types
iridescent glass *see under* GLASS → types
iridization **2** 818
Irie, Shikai **17** 199
Irigoyen, Juan Manuel Besnes y *see* BESNES Y IRIGOYEN, JUAN MANUEL
Irimescu, Ion **16** 49*; **26** 716
Irind Church **2** 426
Iris, El **19** 399
irisé grounds *see under* GROUNDS → types
Iris Factory **11** 83, 104, 105; **12** 21; **28** 427
Irish Decorative Art Association **16** 41
Irish Exhibition of Living Art **16** 18; **19** 891
Irish Linen Board **16** 33
Iriya **23** 367
Irizarry, Carlos **18** 833

Irizarry, Epifanio **18** 832; **25** 701, 702
Irkutsk **16** 49*; **27** *362*, 374, 436
Art Museum **16** 49
Irlbacher **11** 464
Irmandade de S Lucas **25** 297, 317
Irmingard, Empress **5** 803
Irminger, Johann Jacob **12** 447; **21** 64
works **12** *447*
Irmisch, Hans **29** 485; **33** 113
Irodikromo, Soeki **30** 16
irogane see under ALLOYS → types
iroko-wood **33** III2
iron **7** 735; **16** 49–60*; **21** 319
conservation **7** 748
historical and regional traditions
Africa **1** *233*, 286, 287, 288, 296, *297*, 350, 385
Anatolia, ancient **1** 834, 836
Anglo-Saxon **10** *338*
Arabia **16** *506*
Austria **2** 822
Bamana **3** 133–4
Belgium **3** 575, 580; **13** 160
Benin Republic **3** 728; **11** *246*
Britain **7** 445
Buddhism **6** 706, 721; **18** *290*, *291*
Bulgaria **5** 160–61
Burma **29** 228
Cameroon **1** 287
Celtic **6** 157
Central Asia, Eastern **6** 313
Central Asia, Western **6** *260*, 261
China **6** 706, 725, 869; **7** 94, 96–100*, 146
Five Dynasties (AD 907-60) **7** *99*
Ming period (1368-1644) **6** 721, 905
Song period (AD 960-1279) **6** *724*, 731; **7** *100*
Tang period (AD 618-907) **6** 730
Zhou period (*c*. 1050-256 BC) **7** 56, *98*, 107
20th cent. **7** 80
Côte d'Ivoire **8** 22, *23*
Crete **8** 154
Cyprus, ancient **8** 353, *354*
Czech Republic **8** *388*, 415–16*
Dacian **30** 773
Denmark **8** 752
Dogon **9** *69*
Egypt **16** *504*
Egypt, ancient **9** 817
England **2** *466*; **6** 560; **9** 155–6; **10** *338*, 339, 340, 341–2; **25** *540*
16th cent. **10** *340*
Etruscan **10** 624
Fon **11** *246*
France **3** 125; **9** 156, 464; **11** 623; **14** 592; **16** 53; **24** *722*; **30** *21*
Germany **3** 804*; **9** 690; **12** 374, 454*, *454*; **13** 161; **16** *59*
Gothic **13** 160, 161, 166
Greece, ancient **13** 568
Hungary **15** 9
Indian subcontinent **15** 193, 667, 668, 734
Indonesia **15** 817, *817*; **29** 228
Inuit **21** 319
Iran **16** *504*
Iran, ancient **15** 919
Iraq **16** *504*
Islamic **16** 363, 503, *504*, 505, *507*
Italy **10** 624; **16** *708*, 744; **25** 533
Japan **17** 47, 102*, 242, 253, 308, 318, 358
Edo period (1600-1868) **10** *777*; **17** 370
Kofun period (*c*. AD 300-710) **17** 361

iron
historical and regional traditions
Japan—cont.
Muromachi period (1333-1568) **17** *323*
Kenya **1** *297*
Kongo **1** *233*
Korea **18** 249, 289, *290*, *291*, 352–3*
Malaysia **20** 174; **29** 228
Malta (Republic of) **20** 218
Mesopotamia **21** 269, 304
Minoan **2** 451
Mongolia **21** 882
Morocco **16** *504*
Native North Americans **22** 612, 613
Netherlands, the **13** 160; **22** 894*
Nigeria **23** 130, 180
Northern Ireland **3** 536
Norway **9** 156; **23** 237
Ottoman **16** *504*
Ottonian **23** 658
Philippines **29** 228
Philistine **24** 635
Phrygian **1** 836
Portugal **13** 166; **22** 14
Prehistoric art **9** *690*; **16** 59; **25** *540*, 540–41*, 547; **29** 228–9
Romanesque **9** *155*; **26** 691
Romania **30** 769
Rome, ancient **27** 93–4*
Russia **16** 53; **32** *527*
Scandinavia **26** 691
Scotland **2** 462; **28** 228
Shona **28** 621
South-east Asia **29** 228–9
Spain **12** *148*; **16** *57*, *504*; **29** 338–9*, *339*, 340, 341
Gothic **13** 166
Sri Lanka **16** 59; **29** 468, 474
Sweden **9** *155*, 156; **30** 109–10*
Switzerland **30** 139
Syria **16** *504*
Syria-Palestine **30** 194
Thailand **29** 228
Thracian **30** 769
Tibet **30** 841
Turkey **16** *504*
United States of America **4** 228; **29** 651; **31** *264*, 652–3*
Urartian **1** 836; **31** 700
Viking **32** *527*
patinas **21** 330*
technical examination **30** 397, 409
techniques
casting **6** 725; **7** 98; **12** 454
electroplating **10** 136
hammering **21** 323
inlays **7** 107
lost-wax casting **7** 99
moulding **7** 97, 98
smelting **7** 98; **16** 50; **17** 318; **28** 263
welding **7** 169
types
cast *see* CAST IRON
corrugated *see* CORRUGATED IRON
pig **7** 98
wrought *see* WROUGHT IRON
uses
altars **3** 728
architecture **3** 536; **9** 464; **12** 374; **16** 51–4*; **28** 228; **29** 651
armour **2** 448, 469; **16** 503
arrowheads **6** 261
axes **7** 97; **16** *504*; **32** *527*
beads **1** 296, *297*
beds **3** 485
bells **3** 627
belthooks **7** 97, *98*
bracelets **12** *454*; **22** 613
bridges **4** 801
iron
uses—cont.
candle holders **29** 338
candlesticks **5** 611; **12** 454
cauldrons **7** 97
chairs **6** 388, 389
chandeliers **12** 454
chests **6** 560; **12** 454; **16** 59, *59*
chests-of-drawers **17** 358
churches **3** 125
clocks **7** 445
coffers **3** 580
coins **17** 370
crossbow-bolts **7** 97
cupboards **8** 270
dolls' furniture **31** *264*
domes **3** 524
door fittings **10** 339; **26** 691
doors **3** 575; **9** 154*, *155*; **12** 454
drinking-horns **9** *690*
enamel **6** 905; **7** 80
façades **4** 228
fans **10** *777*
fibulae **8** 154
fire-backs **10** *340*
furniture **3** 580; **27** 94; **31** 629
gates **12** 174
girders (beams) **13** 391
glass **12** 782
glazes **6** 869, 905; **17** 242, 253
grilles **29** *339*
guns **2** *466*
gun stocks **2** 462
helmets **10** *338*; **16** *504*, 505, *507*; **30** 773
hinges **9** 155
inkstones **7** 94
inlays **21** 329
jewellery **1** 350; **3** 804*; **12** 454
keris **15** 817, *817*; **20** 174
kettles **17** *323*
locks **16** 59
mills (industrial) **21** 600
mirrors **21** 714, 719
mordants (iii) (dyeing) **9** 490, 491; **15** 667, 668; **17** 308; **30** 559, 560
necklaces **22** 613
portcullises **12** 174
presses **25** 592
printing plates **10** 548; **25** 612
roofs **14** 592
sabres **16** *506*
scabbards **6** 157; **15** *817*
scissors **8** 286
sculpture **6** 730, 731; **10** 702; **16** 56–8*
Africa **1** *233*, 385
Bamana **3** 133–4
Benin Republic **11** *246*
China **6** 706, 721, *724*
Côte d'Ivoire **8** *23*
Czech Republic **8** *388*
France **24** *722*; **30** *21*
Italy **16** *708*
Japan **17** 102*
Korea **18** 289, *290*, *291*
Spain **12** *148*; **16** *57*
Switzerland **30** 139
seals **21** 882
shields **30** 773
shutters (window) **9** *69*
spearheads **25** *540*
stands **8** *354*
statuettes **17** 323
stools **6** 388
sword grips **6** *260*
sword guards **16** *506*
swords **2** 451; **7** 56, 97; **23** 658; **27** 93
talismans **15** 734
tools **7** 97; **8** 154; **15** 193; **17** 47; **29** 228; **31** 700
toys **31** 256
tracery **31** 270
trappings **25** 547–8
vaults (ceiling) **22** 14
walls **7** 98
iron
uses—cont.
watches **7** 441
weapons **8** 154, 353; **16** 503; **17** 361; **18** 353; **29** 474
wheels **25** 547
Ironbridge and Coalbrookdale (Salop) **4** 802; **15** 828; **18** III2
Iron Bridge **16** 52, *52*
iron chromate **24** 799
Iron Crown of Lombardy **5** 807
Iron Gates Helmet **30** 770, 771
iron-glazed ware *see under* POTTERY → wares
Ironimus *see* PEICHL, GUSTAV
iron oxide **6** 324, 325, 328; **10** 740; **24** 790; **25** 477
historical and regional traditions
China **6** 872, 873, 881, 885, 899, 909
Japan **17** 246
Korea **18** 339, 342, *342*, 343
uses
ceramics **6** 330
glazes **6** 329, 872, 873, 881, 885, 894, 899, 909
grounds **25** 174
inks **15** 852
pigments **13** 480; **24** 795
pottery **6** 885; **17** 246
stained glass **29** 498
iron salts **7** 45; **15** 851; **18** 600; **24** 650, 655
iron sand **17** 358
iron sulphates **10** 356
iron-wood **17** 399
Iroquois **16** 61*; **21** 597; **22** 552, 556, 557, 558, 559, 562, 663, 666, 670, 673
bags **22** 627
beadwork **22** 643
embroidery **22** 647
pottery **22** 612
shells **28** 582
textiles **22** 628
weaving **22** 628
Irradiador **10** 543
irradiation **12** 270; **19** 352
Irrawang **2** *736*, 759
Irrer, Hans **33** 279
irrigation systems **7** 185; **12** 66; **21** 269
Irrsdorf, Master of **20** 800
Irrsdorf Reliefs **2** 800
Irrwoch, Sebastian **16** 61–2*
Irsee Abbey, Mariae Himmelfahrt **25** 727
stucco **28** *130*
Irtyertia
mummy **22** *284*
Irua, palace **9** 735
Irunilakode **15** 521
Irvine (Strathclyde) **31** 733
Irvine, James (*fl* 1799-1802) **5** 71
Irvine, James (1833-99) **5** 847; **6** 438; **16** 62*; **28** 271
Irving, Col. (*fl* 1767) **5** 577
Irving, Charles R., & Robert Casson Co. **4** 479
Irving, Henry **25** 674; **30** 680, 681
productions **30** *681*
Irving, John **3** 61
Irving, Washington **3** 63; **4** 364, 365, 367; **5** 422; **8** 528; **10** 99
Irving, William **19** 158
Irwin, Lady (*fl* 1688) **23** 253
Irwin, 7th Viscount (*fl c.* 1733-54) **10** 294
Irwin, Harriet Morrison **16** 62*
Irwin, Henry **18** 889; **20** 53; **22** 404; **28** 748
works **20** *53*
Irwin, Robert **16** 62*; **19** 702
groups and movements **10** 416; **31** 609
patrons and collectors **24** 24; **33** 45
pupils **4** 168
Irwoch, Sebastian *see* IRRWOCH, SEBASTIAN
Isa **15** 608
Isaac, Bishop of Dijon **8** 893
Isaac, Nelson **23** 71
Isaac ben Israel **17** 561
Isaac ben Solomon ibn Sahula **17** 565; **21** 176
Isaac de Corbeil **17** 563
Isaac Hiyo Caro **17** 562
works **17** *562*
Isaachsen, Olaf **16** 63*; **23** 225
Isaachsen, Ole Wilhelm *see* ISAACHSEN, OLAF
Isaac Master **20** 697–8*
methods **32** 805
works **2** 624; **13** 144; **20** *697*, 712; **24** 159
Isaac Moheb ben Ephraim **7** 846
Isaacs, Av **5** 590
Isaacs, Lazarus
works **31** *641*
Isaacsz., Pieter (Fransz.) **16** 63*
attributions **30** 734
patrons and collectors **23** 396
pupils **2** 854; **20** 249; **23** 124
teachers **1** 6; **17** 924
works **8** 733
Isaak II Angelos, Emperor of Byzantium (*reg* 1185-95; 1203-04) **9** 555
Isabayev, Isataj **17** 867
Isabeau of Bavaria, Queen of France (1371-1435) **20** 207; **31** *833*, 840–41*; **33** *272*
enamel **13** 170
gold **13** 158
manuscripts **7** 235, *235*; **20** 625, 647; **31** 832
metalwork **31** 840
paintings **7** 544
tapestries **7** 544
Isabel la Católica *see* ISABELLA, Queen of Castile-León
Isabel de Valois, Queen of England (1389-1409) **25** 16
Isabella, Duchess of Brittany (*fl c.* 1448) **2** 113; **4** 827*
Isabella, Queen of England (1292-1358) **10** 163, 348; **13** 147; **25** 15, 17
Isabella I, Queen of Castile-León (*reg* 1474-1504) **2** 275, 277–9*; **10** 906; **14** 578; **28** 724
architecture **2** 658; **4** 647; **9** 112; **13** 283, 757; **20** 62; **28** 368, 519; **31** 87
palaces **13** 286
coats of arms **29** 298
collections **13** 922
gold **24** 36; **29** 333
hardstones **17** 515
interior decoration **29** 298
manuscripts **20** 659, 682, 737; **25** 405; **26** 563; **31** 88, 103; **32** 728
metalwork **29** 333
paintings **3** 554, 811, 844; **4** 446; **17** 674; **28** 803, 804; **29** 299; **33** 118
sculpture **2** *278*
silk **28** 716
Isabella II, Queen of Spain (*reg* 1833-68) **4** 557, *557*, 566–7*; **10** *513*; **20** *68*
architecture **10** 501; **25** 226
paintings **5** 906; **10** 512; **13** 248; **19** 762; **21** 126; **26** 308; **30** 418
photographs **7** 435
sculpture **21** 36; **24** 839; **31** 829
Isabella Clara Eugenia, Archduchess of Austria, Regent of the Netherlands (*reg* 1599-1633) **13** *901*, 917*; **14** *2*; **24** *23*; **27** 296, *705*
architecture **15** 45; **32** 115
drawings **9** 388
interior decoration **29** *299*
medals **17** 643
Isabella Clara Eugenia, Archduchess of Austria, Regent of the Netherlands (*reg* 1599-1633)—cont.
metalwork **5** 52
paintings **1** 687; **2** 104; **3** 558, 613; **4** 913, 915; **7** 368, 413; **8** 125; **9** 480; **19** 650; **22** 7; **25** 382; **27** 291, 295; **28** 898
tapestries **1** 686; **28** 899; **31** 501
Isabella da Robecca **29** 23
Isabella d'Este, Marchesa di Mantua (1474-1539) **10** 517, *518*, 520–22*, *521*; **12** 908; **19** 834; **20** 322
architecture **8** 81
ceramics **31** 741
collections **2** 140; **6** 41; **12** 582; **16** 770
decorative works **5** 697
fountains **29** 25
furniture **9** 97
gems **2** 98; **12** 257, 265
imprese **15** 150
interior decoration **16** 711
maiolica **24** 535; **31** 747
manuscripts **13** 834
medals **12** *583*
musical instruments **10** 522; **22** 376
paintings **2** 558; **3** 303, 818; **6** 39; **7** 562; **16** 658, 659, 661; **19** 183, 200; **24** 523; **27** 790; **29** 860; **31** 34
allegorical **1** 656; **3** 660; **7** 891; **8** 4; **10** 130; **14** 582; **15** 86; **20** 312; **22** 412; **24** 527; **26** 349
mythological **14** 870
portraits **26** 459; **28** 335
sculpture **2** 139, 140; **9** 21; **13** 920; **20** 311; **29** 568
Isabella di Chiaromonte, Queen of Naples (*fl c.* 1460) **7** 544; **10** 868
Isabella of Aragon, Duchess of Milan (1470-1524) **4** 284
Isabella of Aragon, Queen of Portugal (1271-1336) **13** 166
Isabella of Bavaria, Queen of France *see* ISABEAU OF BAVARIA, Queen of France
Isabella of Portugal, Duchess of Burgundy (1397-1472) **2** 871; **8** 893
Isabella of Portugal, Holy Roman Empress (1503-39) **6** 71; **13** 906; **14** 658; **20** 70; **29** 334; **31** 191
Isabella Psalter *see under* PSALTERS → individual manuscripts
Isabella the Catholic *see* ISABELLA, Queen of Castile-León
Isabelline style *see* HISPANO-FLEMISH STYLE
Isabey, (Louis-)Eugène (-Gabriel) **16** 64, 65–6*
patrons and collectors **4** 556; **23** 522
pupils **4** 232, 880; **9** 422; **14** 42, 486, 527; **17** 643
reproductive prints by others **4** 364
works **4** 364; **16** *66*; **19** 487; **20** 602; **30** 385
Isabey, Jean-Baptiste **12** *335*; **16** 64–5*; **21** 643; **22** 456
patrons and collectors **4** 303; **33** 607
personal collection **12** 334
pupils **12** 153; **31** 579
reproductive prints by others **8** 595
works **16** *64*; **19** 483; **20** 602; **21** 644
Isacco da Imbonate **21** 533
Isacs, Pieter (Fransz.) *see* ISAACSZ., PIETER (FRANSZ.)
Isaeus, Magnus **30** 73

Isaia da Pisa **16** 66–7*
collaboration **24** 28, 29; **26** 808
patrons and collectors **24** 731
pupils **12** 582
works **11** 895; **16** 691; **22** 487; **26** 808
Isaiah Master **2** 846; **24** 158, 159
'Isa ibn Ahmad al-Razi **16** 534; **20** 49
'Isa ibn 'Ali **31** 543
'Isa ibn Muhammad ibn Aydın **10** 430
'Isa ibn Musa (Abbasid) **31** 543
Isakson, Karl (Oskar) **8** 735; **16** 67–8*; **30** 81; **33** 595
Isami Matsumoto *see* MATSUMOTO, ISAMI
Isamu Komada *see* KOMADA, ISAMU
Isamu Wakabayashi *see* WAKABAYASHI, ISAMU
Isapur **15** 737
Isar **31** 420
Isarn, Abbot of Marseille **20** 475
Isaura **21** 558
Isaura i Fargas, Francesc **29** 338, 343, 344
Isaurikos, Leo III, Emperor of Byzantium *see* LEO III ISAURIKOS, Emperor of Byzantium
Isava, Casimiro **32** 169
Isavoy Mogum **18** 195
Isca *see* CAERLEON
Isca Dumnoniorum *see under* EXETER (DEVON)
İscehisar *see* DOKIMEION
Ischali **1** *849*; **9** 46*; **21** *267*
architecture **21** 274
Temple of Ishtar-Kititum **9** *46*; **21** 286; **30** 432, *432*
see also DIYALA REGION
Isches **27** 689
Ischia *see* PITHEKOUSSAI
Ischia, Marchese d' *see* CANOVA, ANTONIO
Ischia di Castro
pottery **10** *612*
Ischyrios, Nikephoros **9** 580
Iscovescu, Barbu **26** 713
Ise **17** *11*, 412
Ise, Lady **17** 223
Isefjordmaster **8** 731
Iselburg, Peter *see* ISSELBURG, PETER
Iseli, Rolf **9** 310; **16** 68*; **30** 135
Iselin, Heinrich **14** 49; **16** 68–9*
Iselin, Ludwig **1** 771
Ise Nakajima *see* NAKAJIMA ISE
Isenbrandt, Adriaen **2** 206; **3** 554; **4** 921; **16** 69–71*
patrons and collectors **8** 552
works **16** *70*
Isenburg, Salentin von, Archbishop of Cologne **30** 531
Isenhagen Monastery **12** 462
Isenheim (family) **11** 628
Isenheim Altarpiece **1** 710; **7** 226; **11** 455; **12** 386; **13** 721–2, *722*; **14** 32, 784; **19** 356; **26** 188; **28** 134
Isenmann, Anton **19** 769
Isenmann, Caspar **7** 579; **12** 384; **16** 71–2*; **28** 154
works **16** *71*
Isenring, Johann Baptist **19** 525
Iseo, Giacomo da *see* GIACOMO DA ISEO
Iser, Iosif **16** 72*, 903; **20** 877; **26** 715, 716, 723
Iser, Wolfgang **26** 62, 63
Iserecker, Ulrich **16** 874
Iserenhod(t), Anton *see* EISENHODT, ANTON
Iserlohn **12** 452
Isern, Ramon **13** 726; **20** 515
Ise Shrine **16** 72–4*; **17** 19, 46, 60, 61–2, *62*, 98, 345, 346; **28** 638
architecture **2** 655
Ise Shrine—cont.
gardens **12** 95
Gekū **16** 72–4
kōtai jingū see Naikū
Naikū **16** 72–4, *73*
Toyouke daijingū see Gekū
Isesi **27** 812
Iseum *see* BEHBEIT EL-HAGAR
Isfahan **3** 168; **15** *897*; **16** 74–81*, *75*, *105*, 235; **27** 514
All Saviour's Cathedral *see under* New Julfa
art forms and materials
architecture **16** 161, 196, 229–30
carpets **15** 682, 899; **16** 474, 482
enamel **16** 515
felt **10** 874
glass **16** 522
inscriptions **16** 232
lacquer **16** 534
manuscripts **2** 431; **16** 317, 322, 327, 328, 331, 338–40*
metalwork **16** 369, 391, 392, *392*
paintings **16** *127*, 253
portals **16** 194
pottery **4** 172
rock crystal **16** 542
scripts **16** 280
textiles **16** 449, 450; **31** 21
tiles **16** 249
woodwork **15** 899; **16** 491, 502
Bazaar **9** 83; **16** 79*
Qaysariyya (Royal Bazaar) **16** 265
Bethlehem Church *see under* New Julfa
bridges **16** 231
Allahverdi Bridge **16** 253
Khwaju Bridge **4** 801; **16** 231, *232*
Si-o-sih pul **16** 230
caravanserais **5** 723
ceramics **2** 440
Chahar Bagh **12** 82; **16** 230, 265
craftsmen and artists **16** 232
dovecots **9** 203
gardens **12** 82
Hazar Jarib **12** 82
houses **16** 269
Anguristan House **16** 502
Islamic religious buildings
'Ali Mosque **16** 230, 232
Darb-i Kushk **16** 199
Friday Mosque **16** *77*, 77–8*, 153–4, 159, 160, 161–2, *162*, 164, *164*, 199, 230, 254, 550; **22** 194
domes **4** 792; **16** 164
inscriptions **16** 259, 260
iwans **16** *801*, 801
maqṣūra **20** 369
mihrab **16** 245; **21** 506
minbar **16** 501
mosaics **16** 232
muqarnas (architecture) **22** 321, 322
squinches **16** 164
stucco **29** 820, *820*
vaults (ceiling) **4** 792
Hakim Mosque *see* Jurjir Mosque
Jurjir Mosque **16** 160, 161; **24** 877
Madar-i Shah Madrasa **16** 231; **20** 57
caravanserai **16** 232
Madrasa-i Imami **16** 194
Masjid i Jum'a *see* Friday Mosque
Masjid-i Shah *see* Shah Mosque
minarets **16** 160, 163
mosques **22** 354
Muzaffarid madrasa **20** 57
Qutbiyya Mosque **16** 230
Shah Mosque **8** 64; **16** 78*, *78*, 100, 129, 230, 232, 265; **22** 194; **24** 878
Isfahan
Islamic religious buildings—cont.
Shaykh Lutfallah Mosque **16** 79*, 100, 230, *249*, 260; **22** 322
dome **16** 248
stained glass **16** 257
Julfa *see* New Julfa
Maydan-i shah *see* Royal Maidan
museums **15** 900
New Julfa **2** 428; **16** 80–81*, 230, 265, 391
carpets **2** 438
churches **16** 80
All Saviour's Cathedral **2** 428, 444
Bethlehem Church **2** 428
khatchk'ars **8** 198
manuscript illumination **2** 425
metalwork **2** 441
paintings **16** 331
Petros Valijanian House **16** 233
palaces **16** 231, *265*
'Ali Qapu Palace **15** 897; **16** 79*, 517; **23** 816
column **16** *502*
Music Room **16** 233, *233*; **29** 820
porticos **16** 502
Chihil Sutun **15** 897; **16** 79–80*, *80*, 230, 231, 257, 502; **18** 71; **23** 816
doors **16** 502
muqarnas (architecture) **22** 322
murals **22** 262
porticos **16** 502
stained glass **16** 257
wall paintings **16** 233, 254, *254*, 535; **22** 261
Hasht Bihisht Palace **15** 897; **16** 80*, 230, 231; **18** 71; **23** 816, *816*
gardens **12** 76
porticos **16** 502
Talar-i Ashraf **16** 231
Pul-i Khwaju *see* bridges → Khwaju Bridge
Royal Maidan **16** 78*, 230, *231*
tombs and mausolea
Darb-i Imam **16** 198, 200, 248, 257
Harun-i Vilayat **16** 230
Imamzada Baba Qasim **16** 195, 232
Imamzada Ja'far **16** 194
Imamzada Zayd **16** 233, 254
tomb of Shaykh Abu Mas'ud **16** 198
town walls **21** 584
urban planning **16** 230, 264–5; **27** 512
Isfahani, Ahmad *see* AHMAD (*fl* 1880)
Isfahani, Aqa Baba *see* AQA BABA
Isfahani, Haydar 'Ali *see* HAYDAR 'ALI
Isfahani, Ja'far *see* JA'FAR
Isfahani, Muhammad Isma'il *see* MUHAMMAD ISMA'IL
Isfahani, Muhammad Kazim *see* MUHAMMAD KAZIM
Isfahani, Muhammad Riza *see* MUHAMMAD RIZA ISFAHANI
Isfahani, Najaf 'Ali *see* NAJAF 'ALI
Isfandiyaroğlu Ismail Bey **25** 51
Isfara **6** 277; **30** *252*, 252, 253
Isfijab **6** 249
Ishaković-Hranušić, Ishakbey **27** 819
Isham (family) **7** 298
Isham, Justinian **33** 10
Isham, Norman **25** 666
Isham, Samuel **16** 82*
Isham, Thomas **10** 364; **13** 300; **16** 82*; **19** *123*, 540
İşhan *see* ISHKHANI
Ishana of Kanyakubja **15** 286
Ishanapura **5** 464
Ishanavarman I, King of Cambodia (*reg c.* 615–*c.* 635) **5** 464
Ishān Baḥrīyāt *see* ISIN
I-shan I-ning *see* YISHAN YINING
Ishaq, Kamala Ibrahim **29** 896
Ishbaljir **21** 873
Ishbīliya *see* SEVILLE
Isheda Benin, Temple to Ogun Igbo **1** 309
isheru waters **27** 496
Isherwood, Christopher William Bradshaw **21** 36
Ishibashi, Mitsuru **10** 399
Ishibashi Foundation **17** 433
Ishibutai tomb *see under* ASUKA → Shimanosho
Ishida Yūtei **20** 522
Ishigaki, Tōrinji **27** 470
Ishiguro, Munemaro **17** 266
Ishiguro Collection **1** 896
Ishii, Hakutei **2** 579; **17** 204
Ishii, Teiko **17** 204
Ishii, Tsuruzō **17** 134, 135
Ishikawa, Kōmei **17** 133
Ishikawa, Toraji **17** 295
Ishikawa Jōzan **16** 83*; **17** 234, 409
Ishikawa Kazumasa **20** 835
Ishikawa Masamochi **16** 84; **18** 494; **31** 253
Ishikawa Tatsuemon Shigemasa **17** 393
Ishikawa Toyomasa **16** 84
Ishikawa Toyonobu **16** 83–4*; **17** 281, 282
Ishikawa Yasunaga **20** 835
Ishikawa Yukimoto **15** 896
Ishimoto, Yasuhirō **16** 84*
Ishin Sūden **18** 558, 559
Ishiwatari, Koitsu **17** 294
Ishiyama *see under* OSAKA
Ishiyama, Osamu **16** 84*; **17** 92
Ishiyamadera **17** 67, 132; **23** 776
Ishizaki (family) **17** 186
Ishizaki Yūshi **17** 186, 187
Ishkhani **30** 305
Cathedral (late 10th cent.) **12** 328
church (early 9th cent.) **12** 323; **30** *305*, 305–6
Ishmaku, Burhan **1** 543; **16** 84–5*
'Ish Muhammad **16** 342
Ishō Hyōe **17** 393
Ishoven, J. L. van **4** 844
'Ishratabad, palace **16** 235
Ishtikhan **23** 608
Ishvari Singh, Maharaja of Jaipur (*reg* 1743–50) (Rajput) **16** 871
Ishwari Sen **15** 634
Isidore of Charax **17** 773
Isidore of Seville, Saint **7** 452; **19** 313
writings **3** 878; **10** 201, 203; **20** 361; **22** 411; **24** 348; **31** 289
on allegories **1** 652
on proportion **2** 351
Isidoros of Miletus **2** 135; **16** 592
works **16** *592*
Isigonos **16** 85*
Isimila Museum **30** 302
Isin **16** 85*; **21** *267*, 278, 295
Isinai **24** 623
Isinda **19** 838
Isin-Larsa period *see under* MESOPOTAMIA → periods
Is'ird *see* SIIRT
Isiskhemheb **10** 61
Iskandar, Popo **15** 808
Iskandar Munshi **12** 82
Iskandar Sultan (Timurid) **30** 917, 919–20*
manuscripts **16** 299, 301, 322*; **28** 616
Iskandaryan, Khatchatur **2** 437
Iskenderun **17** 500; **28** 384; **30** 478
Iskodar **6** 277; **16** *105*, 161, 492
mihrab **16** *492*
Iskowitz, Gershon **5** 569
Iskra **29** 631
Iskusstvo **10** 446; **24** 450, 451; **27** 444
Iskusstvo i promyshlennost' **24** 450; **27** 438
Iskusstvo kommuny **4** 812; **22** 508; **24** 450
Iskusstvo Leningrada **24** 451
Iskusstvo Molodykh *see* IMO
Iskusstvo odevat'sya **24** 450
Iskusstvo trudyashchimsya **24** 450
Iskusstvo v massy **24** 450
Isla Cano **29** 147
Isla de Cabras, El Cañuelo **25** 704
Isla de Gracia *see* VENEZUELA
Isla de la Juventud *see* CUBA
Isla del Sol **31** 47
Isla de Sacrificios **7** 202; **21** 264
Isla Española *see* HISPANIOLA
Islam **1** *852*; **16** 85–92*, *88*, *89*, *90*, 99–101*, 270, 429; **18** 239
branches
Kharijite **16** 111
Mu'tazilism **16** 86
Shi'ite **16** 86, 111, 119, 454
Sufism **16** 87, 116–17, 129
Sunni **16** 86, 112, 115, 116
iconoclasm **15** 80–81
iconography **28** 915
patronage **16** 90–92*
pilgrimages **16** 87–8*, 453, 454
regional traditions
Afghanistan **1** 189
Africa **1** 228–9*, 230
Brunei **29** 226
China **6** 626
Indian subcontinent **14** 555; **15** 202, 204
Indonesia **15** 756
Malaysia **20** 164, 165
South-east Asia **29** 233–4
Sri Lanka **29** 442
Sudan **1** 229, 230
Islam, Aminul **3** 168
Islamabad **15** *264*; **16** 93–4*; **23** *797*, 798
Folk Heritage Museum **23** 804
Frontier House **23** 799
Government Officers' Hostel **16** 93
Housing and House Building Finance Corporation buildings **23** 799
National Assembly **23** 799
National Council for the Arts **23** 804
National Film Development Corporation cinemas **23** 799
Presidency **16** 94; **23** 799
Sadequain Museum **27** 505
Secretariat **16** *93*, 93; **23** 799
Shah Faisal Mosque **16** 94, 242
Sherazad Hotel **23** 799
University **23** 799
Islamic **16** 94–560*, *103*, *104*, *105*
acacia **16** 500
aesthetics **15** 206
albums **1** 583–4*; **16** 271, 272, 283, 318–19; **22** 235–6
alloys **16** 363
alphabets **16** 273, *274*, 278
alum **16** 431
amethyst **16** *507*
amulets **1** 818; **17** 516
apartments **16** 241
appliqué **16** 466
aqueducts **2** 242; **16** 224, 231
arabesques **2** 244–5*, *245*; **16** 133; **23** 557
archaeology **16** 550
arches **2** 297–8*; **16** 142
Afghanistan **16** 167, *168*
Africa **1** 315
blind **2** 292
Central Asia, Western **16** 167
corbelled **2** 294
cusped **2** 294
diaphragm **2** 294
equilateral **2** 294
flat **2** 294

Islamic
arches—cont.
four-centred **2** 294
horseshoe **2** 294; **16** 158, 168, 188, *188*; **21** 548
Indian subcontinent **16** 201
interlace **2** 294
joggled **2** 294
keel **2** 295; **16** 176
Morocco **16** 190
ogee **2** 295; **16** 239
pointed **2** 295; **16** 150, 153
relieving **2** 295
segmental **2** 295
stilted **2** 295
trefoil **2** 296
Tudor **2** 296
two-tiered **2** 296
architects **2** 316*; **16** 143*, 220–21, 232, 241
architectural decorations **16** 133, 142–3*, 146, 243–7*, 248–54*, 255*, 256*, 257–60*, 395; **22** 154
Afghanistan **16** 169
Africa **1** 317–18
Algeria **16** 190
Central Asia, Western **16** 169, 239, 245
Egypt **16** *176*, 176–7, *259*
Ghaznavid **12** 513
Indian subcontinent **15** 342, 354, 680
Iran **16** 165, 194–5, 233, *233*, *234*, *244*, *249*; **21** 718
Iraq **16** *247*
Morocco **16** 190, 191, 250
Ottoman **16** 221
Spain **16** *189*
Syria **16** 146, 245, *255*
Turkey **16** 186, 221, 245
Umayyad (Syria) **16** 145
architecture **16** 133, 134, 140–271*; **25** 171
Abbasid **16** 149–50*
Afghanistan **1** 207–8*; **16** 166–9*, 195–200*
Africa **1** 315–18*
ā'inakārī **16** 257
Albania **16** 228
Algeria **16** 170–71*, 187*, 190, 217–19*, 229
anti-seismic **16** 239
Arabia **16** 229
Azerbaijan **2** 891
Bosnia **16** 228
brick **4** 791–2*; **15** 337; **16** 140, 160, 199–200, 268, 269
Central Asia, Western **16** *159*, 169, 239
Egypt **16** 270
Indian subcontinent **15** 351
Iran **16** 154, 158, *164*, 164–5
Iraq **16** 182
Turkey **16** 186
brick dust **32** 320
Central Asia, Western **6** 201–3*, 204–5*; **16** 142, 153–4*, 158–61*, 166–9*, 195–200*, 235–9*, *236*, 264
China **6** 676–7*
Egypt **16** 141, 155–6*, 172–7*, 207–13*, 229
Empire style **16** 227
Fatimid **16** 170*
Indian subcontinent **4** *51*; **8** 670; **15** 207, 234, 241–2*, 260, 306–7*, 308–9*, 336–59*, 387; **16** 166, 192, 201*, 239*
Indonesia **15** 768–9*
Iran **4** 791; **16** 142, 150, 153–4*, 158–65*, 166, 192–200*, 229–35*, 264–5*
Iraq **16** 149, 150–53*, *150*, 158, 182*
Java **15** 768–9*
Jordan **16** 155
Macedonia (ii) (former Yugoslavia) **16** 228

Islamic
architecture—cont.
Malaysia **20** 165–6*
military **4** 464; **16** 186, 206, 239, 240; **21** 581–9*, *583*, *586*, *588*
Morocco **16** 157–8*, 187*, 190–91*, 217–19*, 239–41*
North Africa **16** 190*
Orientalism **16** 227
Ottoman **16** 143, 199, 201, 205–7*, 220–29*, *228*, 265–7*
Pakistan **16** 166–9*
Philippines **24** 610–11*
Sicily **16** 171–2*
Spain **16** 157–8*, 187–91*, 215*; **29** 287–8
stone **16** 141, 150, 176, 182, 186, 199, 239, 266, 269
Syria **4** 791; **16** 145–9*, 155–6*, 178–82*, 207–13*, *228*, 228–9
Tajikistan **16** 166
Tunisia **16** 156–7*, 170–71*, 219–20*, 229
Turkey **16** 183*, 186*, 201–2*, 204, 205–7*, 221*, 265–7*
Umayyad **16** 145
Umayyad (Syria) **16** 145–9*
Uzbekistan **16** 166
vernacular **16** 123, 142; **32** 309–12*, *310*, *313*, 314–16*, 317–22*
Egypt **32** 312–14*
wood **16** 141, 176, 199, 216, 222, 269, 491–2, 494–5
Yemen **16** 177–8*, 207, 213–15*, 229
armour **16** 503–10*, *504*, *506*
arsenic **16** 394
art criticism **2** 519
art history **16** 468–9, 546–50*; **26** 332
astrolabes **2** 646–8, *647*, *648*; **16** 369, 386
astrology **16** 138
axes **16** *504*, 508, 509
balconies (houses) **16** 269
banners **11** 146; **14** 427; **16** 429
barracks **16** 225
basins **6** IV1; **16** *384*, 397
baths **3** 375–8*; **16** 142, 252
Central Asia, Western **6** 211
Egypt **3** 376, 377
Indian subcontinent **15** 382
Iran **16** 193
Jordan **3** 376
Ottoman **16** 224
Palestine **16** *149*
Syria **3** 376, 377; **16** 148
Turkey **3** 376, 377, *377*; **16** 204–5, 224
bazaars **6** 211; **16** 205, 206
beakers **16** 520, *521*
belts **16** 462, 463, 530
belvederes **16** 266
bitumen **4** 688; **16** 269
boats **14** 428
bone **16** 487, 503, 523
bonnets **16** 459
bookbindings **12** 627; **16** 271, 353, *355*, 355–9*, 533
Iran **18** *609*
Morocco **1** 682
bookcases **16** 487
book covers **12** 627; **15** 549; **16** 355–9*, *357*, *358*
Afghanistan **12** II1
Spain **16** 357
book illustrations **16** 196
books **15** 549; **16** 360–62*, *361*
bowcases **16** 505
bowls **6** IV3; **16** 365–6, 394
Azerbaijan **2** *899*
Egypt **16** *385*, 415, *518*
Iran **16** *123*, *402*, 410, *410*, *413*, *426*, *554*
Iraq **16** 398, *398*; **23** *558*
Ottoman **16** *421*
Spain **16** 404, 419

Islamic—cont.
bows **16** 508
boxes **16** 365, *376*, *383*, 487, 497
penboxes **21** I1
writing-boxes **20** VIII3
bracelets **16** *530*, 532
brass **4** 688*; **16** 363, *381*, *383*, *543*; **21** I1
Afghanistan **16** *378*
Central Asia, Western **16** *378*
Egypt **16** *384*, *385*, *389*
Iran **16** 373, *376*, *391*, *392*, 392–3, *506*; **32** *161*
Iraq **16** 379, *380*
Khurasan **16** 377
Ottoman **16** *388*
Syria **16** *99*, 379, *384*
Turkey **16** *388*; **32** *161*
brick **4** 791–2*; **16** 140, 143, 268, 269; **20** 166; **29** 618; **32** 320
Afghanistan **16** 169
Africa **1** 315, 317
bannā'ī **16** 195, 199, 250, 259
Central Asia, Western **6** *206*; **16** 154, *159*, 160, 169, 199–200, 239
Egypt **16** 270
Indian subcontinent **15** 337, 351
Iran **16** 154, 158, 160, *164*, 164–5, 199–200, 244
Iraq **16** 182
Ottoman **16** 207
Turkey **16** 186, 207
bricklaying **16** 269; **23** *559*
bridges **16** 141
Iran **16** 231, *232*
Ottoman **4** 801; **16** 207, 225
Spain **16** 217
Turkey **16** 207
bronze **2** *647*, *648*; **4** 855; **9** *160*; **16** *135*, 363, 364, 503, *504*; **21** 717
Afghanistan **16** *366*, *375*
Iran **16** 370, 373, *374*, *506*
Iraq **16** *370*, *538*
Khurasan **16** 370
Spain **16** *368*, 386, *387*; **20** 51
Syria **16** *511*
Transoxiana **16** 370
buckets **16** *366*
builders **16** 143
burnishing **16** 394
calendars **23** 338
calligraphers **16** 232, 273, 276–7*, 283, 285
calligraphy **4** 344; **14** 217; **16** 124, 126, 134, 273–9*, *275*, 280–84*, *284*, 285–8*, 354; **18** *240*
Abbasid **16** *279*, *280*
Afghanistan **16** *276*, *354*
black exercise **16** 287
Egypt **16** *275*; **18** *241*
Indian subcontinent **15** 338, 354, 497, *680*, 680–81*, 727
Indonesia **15** 757
Iran **16** 232, *286*
Iraq **16** *283*
North Africa **16** *281*
Ottoman **14** 27; **22** *235*
Spain **16** 215
Syria **16** *275*
zoomorphic **16** 287, *288*
candlesticks **16** 364, 375, *376*, *388*
canopies (ii) (textile coverings) **16** 429
canteens **16** *99*, *542*
cantonments **16** 151
capitals **5** *669*; **16** 145, 188, 191, 243
caps **16** 454, 457, 459, 462
caravanserais **5** 722–4*; **16** 141, 246, 260, 262
Central Asia **16** 163
Central Asia, Western **6** 201, *202*; **16** 154, 238
Iran **16** 154, 193, 198, 232
Ottoman **16** 206, 224, 266

Islamic
caravanserais—cont.
Syria **16** 148, 228
Turkey **5** *723*; **16** 141, 186, 205, 206, 224, 266
caricatures **5** 761*
carpets **16** 123, 124, 428, 429, 466–87*, *480*
Afghanistan **16** 466
Afshar **16** 484
Algeria **16** 486
animal **16** 470, *470*
Azerbaijan **16** 481, 483
Bakhtiari **16** 484
Baluch **16** 484
Belgium **16** 466
Bellini **16** 471
Berber **16** 486
Britain **16** 466
Central Asia **16** 468
Central Asia, Western **16** 466, 469, 484–5*
Chichaoua **16** 486
China **16** 466
commentaries **16** 468
Compartment **16** 473
Crivelli **16** 471
Dragon **16** 479–80, *480*
Egypt **16** 466, 468, *472*
England **16** 472
Faraghan **16** *483*, 484
flījs **16** 486
France **16** 466
Gandja/Karabagh **16** 481
Garden **12** *77*; **16** 475
Gördes **16** 478
Heriz **16** 483
Indian subcontinent **16** 466, 476*, 485*
Iran **5** IV; **16** 466, *467*, 469, 474–5*, *475*, 476, *482*, 482–4*
Iraq **16** 468
Kazakh/Borchaly **16** 481, *481*
Kırşehir **16** 478
Konya **16** 469
Kuba **16** 481
Kurdistan **16** 483–4
Lâdik **16** *478*, 478
Lilihan **16** 484
Lotto **16** 471, *471*
Mamluk **5** 401; **16** *472*, 472–3, 486
Memling **16** 471
Milâs **16** 478
Morocco **16** 486, *487*
Mucur **16** 478
North Africa **16** 473, 485–7*
Ottoman **5** II; **16** 470–72*, *471*, 476–9*
Ottoman Court **16** 473
Para-Mamluk **16** 473
Polonaise **16** 475
prayer rugs **5** III; **16** 467, *478*
Qashqa'i **16** 484
qtīfs **16** 486
Romania **16** 466
ṣaff **16** 467
Sanguszko **16** 475
Serabi **16** 483
Small-pattern Holbein **16** 471
Spain **16** 430, 466, 468, 471
Sultanabad **16** 483
Syria **16** 466
Tajikistan **16** 466
tanchras **16** 486
Transylvanian **16** 472
Tunisia **16** 486
Turkey **5** II; **16** 430, 466, 469, *470*, 470–72*, *471*, 476–9*
Turkmenistan **16** 466
Turkoman **16** *484*, 484–5
United States of America **16** 466
Ushak **5** II; **16** 471–2
Uzbekistan **16** 466
Vase **16** 475
Ziegler **16** 483
cartouches **16** 215, 216, 260
carving **16** 248, 395

Islamic—cont.
caskets **16** 365, 524, 525, *525*
casting **16** 363, 370
cast iron **16** *504*
castles **32** *321*
ceilings **2** 528–9; **16** 216, 494–5, *495*
cemeteries **16** 175
cenotaphs **6** 171–2*, *172*, *207*; **16** 249, *500*, 500–501
ceramics **14** 427; **16** 393–428*, 515
chains **16** 532
chandeliers **16** 365, 386–7, *387*
chargers **16** *418*
chasing **16** 364, *388*
chess sets **6** 556–7*; **16** 523
chests **16** *499*, 517; **18** *139*
chevrons **6** 564
china stone **16** 393
cisterns **16** 217, 232
citadels **6** 210; **16** 130, 141, 215–16, 264, 266
clay **6** 556; **16** 269, 393, 398, 405, 408
clocks **7** *437*, 438
cloisters **16** 184, 204
coats **16** 457, 462, 464, 465
cobalt **16** 248, 394, 414
cochineal **16** 449, 468
codices **16** 271
coffering **7** 527*
coins **7** 533; **14** 428; **16** 130, 510–14*; **21** 504
Central Asia, Western **6** 264–6*, *265*
Egypt **16** 510, 512, *512*, 513, *513*, 514
Indian subcontinent **15** 689; **16** 513
Iran **16** 510, *511*, *512*, 513, *513*
Iraq **16** 510, *512*
Malaysia **20** 179
Ottoman **16** *513*, 514
Pakistan **16** *513*
Saudi Arabia **16** 514
Spain **7** 534; **16** *513*
Sumatra **15** 811
Syria **16** 510, *511*
Tunisia **16** *512*
Turkey **16** *513*, 514
Umayyad (Syria) **21** *505*
collages **16** 354
collections **8** 759; **16** 551–8*
armour **2** 450
calligraphy **16** 551–2
carpets **16** 554–5
ceramics **16** 395–6*
dress **16** 445
manuscript illumination **16** 551–2
porcelain **16** 122, 230, 393, 424
textiles **16** 448
weapons **2** 450
colophons **7** 625–6*, *626*
colour **7** 634–5*; **16** 457
columns
Afghanistan **16** 168
Central Asia, Western **16** 168, 502
colonnettes **16** 142
Iran **16** *502*
Spain **16** 188
concrete **16** 143, 241
connoisseurship **7** 716–17*
consoles **16** 142, 202
copies **15** 750
copper **14** 428; **16** 363, 364, *381*, 394; **21** 717
Afghanistan **16** *366*
Egypt **16** 404
Iran **16** 375
copper oxides **16** 394, 518
coral **16** 269
corbels **15** 338; **16** 164
cordia **16** 500
cornelian **12** 253; **16** 543, *543*
cornices **16** 142, 176
cosmetics **16** 465, 466

Islamic—cont.
cotton **16** 428, 434, *438*, 438–9, 442, 445, 449, 450, 462, 466, 473; **31** 21
courtyards **8** 64, *65*; **16** 142, 260, 263
Central Asia, Western **16** *238*
Egypt **16** *210*
Iran **16** 142, *154*, 264
Iraq **16** 152
Morocco **16** *218*
Ottoman **16** 221
Spain **13** *288*
Syria **16** *148*, *181*
Tunisia **16** *156*
Turkey **16** 142, 183, 184, 221
craftsmen and artists **16** 126–7*, 262
Indian subcontinent **15** 347
Iran **16** 232*, 331
Ottoman **16** 346, 387
Syria **16** 146
Turkey **16** 346, 387
crowns **16** 537–9*, *538*
culs-de-sac **16** 261, 264
cups **16** 365–6
curtains **16** 448; **30** VII1
cushions **16** 429
dados **16** 216
daggers **16** 504, *506*, 509, *516*
dalmatics **16** *444*
damascening **16** *516*
dating methods **16** 399*
découpages **16** 354
dies (ii) (stamps) **16** 510
diplomatic gifts **16** 429, 445
domes **9** 86*; **16** 130, 137, 142, 182; **28** 634
Algeria **16** 190
bulbous **9** 83; **16** 211, 239
Central Asia, Western **16** 161, 164, *237*, 238
cut-off **9** 83
Egypt **16** 176, 210, 244, 496
fluted **9** 84
Indian subcontinent **15** 359; **16** 201
Iran **16** 161–2, 164, 193–4, 199, 270
Iraq **16** 182
melon **9** 84
Morocco **16** 190
muqarnas (architecture) **22** 322
Ottoman **16** 205, 221, 222–3
Palestine **16** *147*
pumpkin **9** 84
semi-dome **9** 84; **16** 176
Syria **16** 182, 270
Turkey **16** 141, 205, 222–3
Yemen **16** 214–15
door fittings **16** 366
doors **9** 160–61*
Central Asia, Western **16** 492, 501–2
Egypt **9** 160, *160*; **16** 384, *490*
Iran **9** 160
Iraq **16** *489*
Ottoman **9** 160
Spain **16** 495
Turkey **9** 160
Yemen **16** 500
doublures **16** 356
dress **15** 692; **16** 429, 448, 452–62*, *462*, 463–6*
Ottoman **16** 454, 458, 460–63*, *462*
dresses **16** *460*, 461, 462
dyeing **16** 439
dyes **16** 353, 431, 438, 441, 449, 457, 460, 468, 473, 477, 485
earthenwares **16** 393, 394, 395
Algeria **16** 427
Central Asia, Western **16** 413
Egypt **16** 394, *403*, *405*
Iran **16** *402*, 413, 425, *426*
Iraq **16** *398*, 398, *399*
Morocco **16** 427
North Africa **16** 427
Spain **16** *411*, *419*

Islamic
earthenwares—cont.
Syria **16** 406
Tunisia **16** 427
Turkey **16** 411, 414, 418
ebony **16** 488
education (art) **16** 241, 536
eggshells **29** 818
emblems **14** 427–8; **23** 562–3
embroidery **16** 124, 459–60; **31** 20
Africa **1** *229*
Algeria **16** 448
Central Asia, Western **16** 451
Egypt **16** 431, 432; **28** 716
Iran **16** 450–51
Iraq **16** 433–4
Jordan **16** *460*
Morocco **16** 448, *448*
Nigeria **1** *229*
Ottoman **16** *460*
Sicily **16** *430*
emeralds **12** 253; **16** *542*
enamel **16** 514–16*, 520
cloisonné **10** 193; **16** 514–15; **17** III1
Egypt **16** 515, 520, *520*
Indian subcontinent **16** 515
Iran **16** 410*, *410*, *426*, 515–16, *516*
Morocco **16** *504*
Ottoman **16** 516
Spain **16** *504*, 515
Syria **12** IV1; **16** 515, 520, *520*, *521*
Turkey **2** 575; **16** 515
engineers **16** 143, 241
engraving **16** 364, 377, 378
epigraphy **12** 513; **16** 146, 166, 169, 216, 217, 257–60*, 395, 549; **23** 559
erotic art **10** 486*
etchings **15** *899*
ethnography **16** 107–9*
ewers **16** 365, *381*
Afghanistan **16** *375*, *378*
Central Asia, Western **16** *378*
Egypt **16** *519*, 541
Fatimid **10** *832*
Iran **16** 369, *371*, 375, *408*, *519*
Iraq **16** 369, *370*
exhibitions **16** 559–60*
façades **16** 142, *148*, 175, 179, 221
factories **16** 431, 436, 441
faience (ii) (ceramics) **16** 248, 395
felt **16** 124, 466, 485
fibulae **16** 532
filigree **12** 868; **16** 531
flags **11** 146*
flasks **16** *424*, 540
flax **16** 352, 428, 431
flint **16** 420
floors **16** 250
forgeries **16** 396, 545–6*
fortifications **16** 141, 151, 155, 156, 172; **21** 581–9*, *583*, *586*
Indian subcontinent **15** 340
fortresses **16** 141, 156, 217, 228; **20** *157*
forts **16** 151
fountain courts **16** 202, *203*
fountains **11** 339–40*; **16** 141, 142
drinking **11** 340
Indian subcontinent **11** 340
Ottoman **16** 225, *226*, 265
Sicily **12** *78*
Spain **11** 340; **16** *368*
Syria **11** 340
Turkey **16** 225, *226*, 265
fountain-spouts **20** 51
friezes **31** *573*
frit, ; **6** IV1, 3; **16** 393, *394*, *406*, *408*, 408–9*, 412, *413*, *416*, *417*, *418*, 419, 420, 421, *422*
Ottoman **16** *421*
frontispieces **16** *129*, 291, *293*
funerary stelae **29** 617–19*, *618*

Islamic—cont.
fur **16** 456
furniture **16** 498, 516–17*
gardens **11** 340; **12** 76–85*; **16** 129, 141
Afghanistan **16** 197–8
Central Asia, Western **12** 81–3*; **16** 197–8, 238
Egypt **12** 78
four-fold **12** 78
ḥayr **12** 77
Indian subcontinent **12** 73–5*, *75*; **16** 239
Iran **12** 81–3*, *83*
Iraq **12** 77
Morocco **12** 78
North Africa **12** 78
riyāḍ **12** 77
Sicily **12** *78*
Spain **12** 78–81*, *80*, *81*
Syria **12** 77
Turkey **12** 83–5*, *84*
gates **16** 216, 264
gateways **5** *396*; **21** 582, 583–4, *584*
gatherings **16** 353
gem-engraving **12** 253*
geometry **16** 133–4*, 143
gilding **12** 625, 627, II1; **16** 357, *357*, *520*, *521*
glass **7** 90; **9** 645; **12** 788, 789; **14** 427; **16** 255, 256, 517–21*, 522*; **21** 718
cameo **16** 518, *519*
Egypt **16** 515, 517, *518*, *519*, 519, 520, *520*
glassblowing **16** 517
gold-glass **16** 518
Indian subcontinent **16** 522
Iran **16** *519*, 522
lustre **16** 518, *518*
mosaic **16** 518
Ottoman **16** 221, 522
Palestine **16** 517, 519
Syria **12** IV1; **16** 515, 517, 519, 520, *520*, *521*
Turkey **16** 221, 522
Yemen **16** *533*
glazes **6** 333; **16** 248, 393–4, 395; **31** 21
Central Asia, Western **16** 239, 248
Egypt **16** 402–3, 404, 415
Iran **16** 165, 248, 401, 402, 408, 412, 426
Iraq **16** 399, 433
North Africa **16** 427
Ottoman **16** 420
Syria **16** 415
Timurid **16** 413
Turkey **16** 411
glues **16** 356; **29** 818
gold **4** 688; **6** 556; **12** 868; **16** 292, 363, 364, 371–3*, 520, 531; **21** 718, *718*
Afghanistan **16** *375*
Almohad **1** 682
Ayyubid **16** 520
Egypt **16** *384*, *385*, *389*, *512*, *513*, 529; **17** III1
Iran **16** 292–3, *376*, 450, *506*, *508*, *512*, *516*, *530*; **21** I1
Mamluk **16** *383*
Ottoman **16** *513*, 532
Pakistan **16** *513*
Sicily **16** *430*
Spain **7** 534; **16** *513*
Syria **16** 311, *384*, *511*
Turkey **16** *507*, *508*, *513*, *542*
goldsmiths **16** 262
grilles **6** 171; **16** 256, 257, 487, 496, 500, 502
guilds **16** 445
gum arabic **16** 356
guns **16** 508–9
gun stocks **16** 499
gypsum **16** 268, 269; **29** 818
haematite **12** 253; **16** *543*

Islamic—cont.
hair
camel **16** 430, 466
goat **16** 430, 449, 466
mohair **16** 430, 445
hairstyles **16** 464, 465
halls **14** 77; **15** 356; **16** 800; **30** *222*
harnesses **14** 183, *184*
hats **16** 456, 459, 462
haẓīra **16** 197
headdresses **16** 448, 454, 459, 461, 462, 465, 466
headscarves **16** 459
helmets **16** *504*, 505, 507, *507*
hemp **16** 352
heraldry **14** 410, 427–8*, *427*; **16** 247
herbals **14** 432
historiography **16** 546–50*
epigraphy **16** 547
manuscript illumination **16** 295–6
hospices **16** 202–4, 237
hospitals **8** *478*; **16** 141, 181, 184–5, 202–4
houses **16** 263, 267–71*; **32** *316*
Africa **1** 308, 315–16
Albania **16** 228
Algeria **16** 218–19
Arabia **16** 270–71
Central Asia, Western **16** 154
courtyard **16** 260, *267*, 267–8, *268*, 270
Indian subcontinent **15** 345
Iran **16** 154, 163, 264
Iraq **16** 152–3, *270*; **32** *314*, 315
Morocco **16** 218–19
Ottoman **16** 266, *266*, 271
Philippines **24** *611*
Saudi Arabia **32** *316*
Syria **16** 152, 269; **32** 315
Turkey **16** *266*, 266, 269; **32** 318–19, *319*
Yemen **32** *317*
hunting-lodges **16** 238
hydraulic works **11** 339
hypocausts **3** 377
ice-houses **16** 232
iconoclasm **16** 99–100, 245
iconography **16** 127–38*, 429, 468; **18** 242
Indonesia **15** 757–8*
Philippines **24** 609–10*
'idgāhs **15** 340, 343
ikat **16** *438*, 439, 451; **31** 21, 22
imarets **16** 224
incense burners **16** 365, 372, *374*
incising **16** 364, *388*, 395, 403, 415, 425
indigo **16** 431, 438, 449
inks **16** 276
inkwells **16** 276, 390
inlays **16** 364, *381*, *383*, 487
Afghanistan **16** *366*, *375*, *378*
Central Asia, Western **16** *378*
Egypt **16** *384*, *385*, *389*, 497
Indian subcontinent **15** 354
Iran **16** 375–6, *376*, 377, 378
Iraq **16** 379, *380*, 381–2
Ottoman **16** 499, 528
Syria **16** *99*, 381–2, *384*, 389, 497
Turkey **16** 498
Yemen **16** 500
inscriptions **14** 428; **16** 128, 130–31, 134–5, 138, 143, 243, 248, 257–60*, 367–8, 372, 395, 467, 509, 510–14, 521, 542–3, *543*, 547, 549; **29** 617, 619; **31** 20–22
Afghanistan **16** 166, 169
Central Asia, Western **6** 208; **16** 166, 169, 248, 378, 492
Egypt **16** 176, *259*, 383, 415, 431, 432, 441–2, 510, 513, 514; **28** 716; **29** *618*; **31** *21*
10th cent. AD **16** 432
11th cent. **16** *176*

Islamic
inscriptions
Egypt—cont.
15th cent. **16** 386
Ghaznavid **12** 513
Indian subcontinent **15** *680*; **16** 513
Iran **16** 193, 250, 377, 390, 391, 450, 510, 513
9th cent. AD **16** 430
10th cent. AD **16** *123*, 492
12th cent. **16** 165
15th cent. **16** 378, 414
17th cent. **16** 232, 425
Iraq **16** 381, 399, 433, 434, 510
Khurasan **16** 378
Ottoman **16** *137*, 260, 514
Pakistan **16** 166
Spain **16** *387*, 524
Syria **16** 147, 277, 381, 383, 415, 441–2, 510
Turkey **16** *137*, 497, 514
Yemen **16** *438*, 439
intarsia **16** 524
interior decoration **16** 428
Central Asia, Western **16** 200
Iran **16** 195, 200
Spain **29** 297
Tunisia **32** *312*
interlace **15** 882
iron **16** 363, 503, *504*, 505, *507*
ivory **6** 556; **16** 487, 503, *508*; **21** 718
Egypt **16** 497
Morocco **21** *630*
Spain **16** *506*
Syria **16** 497
walrus **16** 526
Yemen **16** 500
ivory-carvings **16** 522–6*, *523*, *525*, *527*, 799
iwans **16** 142, 800–802*; **23** 815
Afghanistan **16** 167
Central Asia, Western **16** 167
Iran **16** 162, 193–4, *801*
Iraq **16** 142, 153
T-shaped **16** 153
Turkey **16** 186
jackets **16** 463, 466
jade **16** 503, 527–8, *528*, 860; **21** 718
jade-carvings **16** 527–8*
jars **16** 394, 397, *416*
jasper **16** *543*
jewellery **16** 124, 464, 465, 515, 529–33*
joinery **16** 487, 497
joining **16** 487
jugs **16** 372, 399, *528*
kaftans **16** *446*, 456, 460, 461
kerchiefs **16** 448
keris **15** 757
kermes **16** 431
khānaqāhs **16** 117, 141; **18** 17–18*
Central Asia, Western **6** 211
Egypt **18** 17, *18*
Indian subcontinent **15** 357; **18** 17
Iran **18** 18
Ottoman **16** 265
Tunisia **16** 220
Turkey **16** 265
Yemen **16** 214–15
kilims **2** *901*; **16** 477, 478; **18** *48*, 48–9*
kilns **16** 394, 409
kiosks **18** 70–71*, *70*
kitchens **16** 141
knitting **18** 158
knots **16** 466
Korans **16** 128, 273, 275, 282, 288–91, *289*, *290*; **18** 239–42*
külliye **1** 538; **16** 221–4; **18** 507–9*, *508*
lac **16** 431, 449, 533
lacquer **16** 533–5*, *534*; **18** 608, *609*; **26** 303

Islamic—cont.
lamps **14** 427; **16** 364
mosque **12** 789, IV1; **16** *520*, 521
oil **16** 394
Ottoman **16** 421, 422
Syria **16** 397, *520*
Turkey **16** 394
lampstands **16** *391*, 391
languages **16** 107, 258*
lanterns (architecture) **16** 216
lapis lazuli **12** 253; **16** *543*
lead **16** 257, 363, 395, 415, 420
Iraq **16** 399
North Africa **16** 427
Syria **16** 415
leather **6** 557; **12** II1; **16** 124, 356, *358*, 503, 544, *544*
cuir-bouilli **16** 503
libraries **16** 272; **19** 316–17*
light **16** 138
lime **29** 818
linen **16** *137*, 352, 356, 428, 431, 432, *433*, 442, *448*; **31** 21, *21*
Linotype composition machines **16** 361
lithography **16** 342, 361
lost-wax casting **16** 363
lotus **19** 717
maces **16** *504*, 505, *506*, 508, 509
madder **16** 431, 438, 449, 473, 485
madrasas **16** 141, 158, 246; **20** 54–7*
Central Asia, Western **6** 201, *205*, 211; **16** 237
Egypt **5** 396; **16** 175–6; **20** 55, 56
Indian subcontinent **15** *341*, *357*
Iran **16** 163, 197; **20** 54, 55, 57
Iraq **3** *52*; **16** 180
Morocco **16** 218; **20** *56*, 57
North Africa **16** 215
Ottoman **16** 222, 223, 265, 810
Syria **16** 180, *181*; **20** 56
Tunisia **16** 219
Turkey **10** 493; **16** *184*, 184–5, *185*, 202–4, 222, 223, 265; **20** 56, 57; **27** 632
Yemen **16** 214
maidans **16** 230, *231*
maiolica **16** 250, 418
manganese **16** 248, 394, 400
Iran **16** 402
mantles **16** 459
manuals **16** 100
manuscript illumination **7** *437*; **16** 128, 131–2, 136, 288–99*, *298*, 300–301*, 302–4*, 305*, 310*, 331*, *455*; **22** 515–16
Afghanistan **1** 208*; **16** *122*, *289*, *290*, *552*
Azerbaijan **2** *896*
Central Asia, Western **16** 252, 321–7*, 342–3*
Egypt **16** *129*, 305–6*, 310–12*
Indian subcontinent **15** *571*, 571–4*, *572*, *573*, 739–40; **16** 330–31*, 344–6*
Iran **4** *49*; **16** 124, 290, 292–3, *295*, 302–3, 313–17*, *315*, *316*, *317*, 318–29*, 331–40*, 341–2*; **18** *609*; **22** *515*
Iraq **16** *114*, 307–10*, 313–17*, 318–21*, 327–9*
Morocco **16** *300*
North Africa **16** 306–7*
Ottoman **16** *118*, 304, 329–30, 346–51*; **23** *642*; **30** *478*
Spain **16** *300*, 306–7*
Syria **16** 307–12*, *311*
Transoxiana **16** 290
Turkey **12** *84*; **16** *118*, 304, 307–10*, 329–30*, 346–51*; **23** *642*
manuscripts **16** 271–351*; **18** 242; **33** *504*
animal subjects **16** *311*

Islamic
manuscripts—cont.
Indian subcontinent **15** 545*
Iran **16** 290, 302–3
Malaysia **20** 171
Morocco **27** 506
Ottoman **16** 304
Transoxiana **16** 290
Turkey **16** 304
maps **31** 152
maqṣūras **16** 121, 130, 487; **20** 368–70*
Iran **20** 369
Morocco **20** 369
Spain **16** 188, *188*; **20** 368
Tunisia **20** *369*
marble
Egypt **29** *618*
Indian subcontinent **15** 340, 354; **16** 239
Ottoman **16** 221
Syria **21** *505*
Turkey **16** 221
marble powder **29** 818
marbling **16** 353, *353*
markets **16** 141, 260–61, 262, 430; **20** 438; **31** 235
Central Asia, Western **16** *237*, 238
Egypt **10** *831*
Turkey **16** 266
marks **16** 424
marquetry **16** 487, 490; **20** VIII3
martyria **17** *489*, *495*
mashrabiyya **16** 132, 494
masks **1** 229
masonry **20** 570
ablaq **16** 182; **33** 614
Central Asia, Western **16** 160
interlaced **16** 180
Iran **16** 160
spolia **16** 131, 141, 221, 243
Turkey **16** 186
matrices **16** *506*
mats **16** 262
mausolea **16** 130, 158, 246; **27** 681
Afghanistan **16** 166
Central Asia, Western **5** 137, 139; **6** 201, *206*; **16** *140*, *159*, 159–60, 166, 197
Egypt **16** 175, 207, *209*
Iran **15** *898*; **16** 159–60, 194, *194*, 197, 230
Iraq **16** 181
Syria **16** 181, 207
Turkey **16** 204
measurements **16** 143
medallions **16** 372–3
medical books **21** 5
mercury **21** 718
metal **9** 160; **16** 443
metalwork **14** 427; **16** 135, 363–93*
Azerbaijan **16** 378
Central Asia, Eastern **6** 314
Central Asia, Western **16** 370*, 377
Egypt **16** 369*, 382–6*, 389–90*
Ghana **16** 383
Indian subcontinent **15** 709
Iran **16** 368, 369*, 370*, 372, 373–8*, 390–91*, 392*
Iraq **16** 369*, 379–82*
Khurasan **16** 377, 392
Morocco **16** 386–7
North Africa **16** 386–7*
Ottoman **16** 386, 387–9*
Spain **16** 368–9*, 386–7*; **20** 51
Syria **14** *427*; **16** 367, 369*, 379*, 380*, 381–6*, 389–90*
Turkey **16** 378, 379, 387–9*
Veneto-Saracenic **32** 160–62*, *161*
mi'dhana **21** 625
mihrabs **16** 100, 130, 141, 146, 492; **21** 504–6*, *505*; **22** 192
Afghanistan **16** *163*

Islamic
mihrabs—cont.
Central Asia, Western **16** 161, 245, *492*
Egypt **16** 176, *176*; **21** 505–6
Indian subcontinent **15** 338, 351; **21** 506
Iran **16** 161, *244*, 249; **21** 506; **29** *820*
Morocco **16** *240*
Saudi Arabia **21** 32
Spain **16** 188, *188*
Sudan **21** 505
Syria **1** *603*; **21** 505, *505*
Tajikistan **16** *492*
Turkey **21** 506
Yemen **16** 178
minarets **16** 100, 130, 138, 141, 142, 158; **21** 625–8*
Afghanistan **16** 166, *167*
Central Asia, Western **6** 201; **16** 160, 166, 237
Egypt **16** 175, *212*; **21** 627
Indian subcontinent **8** *672*
Iran **16** 160, 163, 164, 165, 194; **21** *627*
Iraq **16** 180; **21** *626*
Morocco **16** 190; **21** *626*
North Africa **16** 190
Ottoman **21** 628
Spain **21** 626
Syria **16** 180; **21** 627
Turkey **16** 202; **21** 628
Uzbekistan **5** *140*
Yemen **16** 178, 215
minbars **16** 130, 487; **21** 629–30*; **22** 192; **30** 784
Egypt **16** 496–7; **21** 629
Indian subcontinent **15** 340; **21** 630
Iran **21** 630
Morocco **11** 50; **16** *493*, 495; **21** *630*
North Africa **16** 493–4
Spain **16** *493*
Syria **16** 496–7; **21** 629
Turkey **16** *498*; **21** 630
miniatures (manuscript illumination) **16** 293
Afghanistan **16** *324*, *326*; **20** VI
Central Asia, Western **16** *343*
Egypt **16** *306*, *312*
Iran **16** *301*, *302*, *319*, *322*, *325*, *328*, *333*, *336*, *338*, *341*; **18** *70*; **30** *477*
Iraq **16** *308*, *309*, *320*
Ottoman **16** *348*, *349*, *446*, *454*
Turkey **16** *329*, *348*, *349*, *446*, *454*
mirror-cases **16** *534*
mirror frames **16** *527*; **21** 718
mirrors **16** 257, 365; **21** 717–18*, *718*
mortars (building) **15** 351; **16** 268
mosaics **16** 248, 250, 255*, 259, 466, 487; **22** 154, 162
Central Asia, Western **16** 199, 248
Indian subcontinent **15** 375
Iran **16** 195, 199–200, 248, *249*
Ottoman **16** 199, 260
Spain **16** 216
Syria **16** 146, 147, 148, *255*
Tunisia **16** 256
Turkey **16** 199
mosques **16** 128, 141, 144, 145, 158, 241, 243, 246, 487; **20** 368; **22** 191–6*
Afghanistan **16** 166
Africa **1** 229, *316*, 316–17
Albania **1** 538
Algeria **16** 190, 217
Arabia **16** 229
basilica **16** 183, 202
Bosnia **4** *460*
Bulgaria **5** 148
Caribbean Islands **5** 755

Islamic
mosques—cont.
Central Asia, Western **6** 202, 211; **16** 153–4, 159, 166, 236–7
China **6** 676–7
circular **16** 145
congregational mosques **6** 201; **16** 130, 221, 260, 262
courtyard **16** 153–4
domed **16** 213–14; **22** *195*, 195–6*
Egypt **5** 401, *404*; **16** *155*, *173*, 173–5, *174*, 209, *210*, *212*
four-iwan **16** 162–3; **22** *194*, 194–5*
Greece **2** *672*; **30** 716
hypostyle **16** 145, 146–8, 183, 202; **22** 192–4*, *193*
Indian subcontinent **1** *502*; **15** *48*, 207, 338, *344*, 351; **16** 239
8th cent. AD **15** *307*
12th cent. **15** *339*
14th cent. **15** *345*, *359*
15th cent. **1** *472*; **15** *348*, *350*, *353*
16th cent. **15** *361*
17th cent. **15** *366*
18th cent. **15** *379*
Indonesia **15** 757
Iran **15** 338; **16** *78*, 142, 153–4, *154*, 159, 161–3, *164*, 193–4, 196–7, 198, 234, *234*; **22** *194*; **30** *224*; **33** *512*
Iraq **16** 151, *151*, 152, 179; **27** 680
kiosk-mosque **16** 162
Malaysia **20** *166*, 166
Mali **20** 198
Morocco **11** *50*; **16** 190–91, *191*, 217–18, 240, *240*; **22** *128*
multi-unit **16** 205
musalla **16** 152, 163
North Africa **16** 190, 493
Ottoman **9** *730*; **11** 339; **16** 142, 205, *206*, 221, *223*, *224*, 226, 228, 229, 257, 265, 266; **22** *195*
Palestine **22** *193*
Philippines **24** 611
Qatar **16** *242*
Saudi Arabia **21** 32, *33*; **27** *876*
Singapore **28** 772
single-domed square **16** 183, 202, 205
single-unit **16** 222
South Africa **29** 105
Spain **7** *845*; **16** 157–8, 188
Sudan **1** 284
Syria **8** 479–80, *480*; **16** *148*, 179–80
T-plan **16** 205–6, 240, 810
Tunisia **16** *156*, 156–7, *170*, 219
Turkey **5** *282*; **9** *526*; **16** 183–4, 202, *203*, 221, 226, 265, 266; **28** *766*, *767*, *768*
12th cent. **16** *179*
14th cent. **16** *203*, 205–6, *206*, 497
15th cent. **22** *195*
16th cent. **9** *730*; **16** *223*, *224*
17th cent. **16** 221
Umayyad (Syria) **16** 146
Uzbekistan **5** *139*
Yemen **16** 177, *178*, *214*
mother-of-pearl **9** 160; **16** 256, 499, 500
moulding **16** 394, *403*, 403, 415
mouldings **15** *241*; **16** 182
moulds **16** 352, 517
mounts (works on paper and scrolls) **22** *235*, 235–6*
mud-bricks **4** 791; **16** 140
Afghanistan **16** 168
Central Asia, Western **16** 168, 199–200
Iran **16** 199

Islamic
mud-bricks—cont.
Iraq **16** 150
Ottoman **16** 266
Turkey **16** 266
mulberry **16** 429
muqarnas (architecture) **16** 138, 142, 158, 215; **22** 321–5*; **26** 139
Algeria **16** 170, 190
Central Asia, Western **6** 202; **16** 161, 169
Egypt **16** 176; **22** 321–2, 323, *324*
Iran **16** 161, 164, 169, 194, *233*; **22** 321, 322
Iraq **22** 322
Spain **16** 216, 494; **22** 324
Syria **22** 322–3
Turkey **22** 323, *323*
museums **16** 555–8*
musical instruments **16** 498
mythology **16** 137
nails **16** 500
nakkashane **16** 346
narratives **22** *515*, 515–16*, 517*
natron **16** 431
necklaces **16** 531, 532, 533, *533*
niches **16** 161
niello **16** 364
numismatics **16** 547
observatories **16** 193, 198; **23** 338
ochre **16** 248
ogee **23** 368
oliphants **16** 526
onyx **16** *543*
oratories (i) (chapels) **16** 141
orders (architecture) **16** 241
ornament **16** *129*, 132–3, 134, 146; **23** 556–63*
painting **16** 250*, 487, 535*
Algeria **1** 634
Central Asia, Western **16** 160
floor **16** *251*
fresco **16** 169
glass **16** 522*
Indian subcontinent **12** *74*
Iran **7** V; **16** 160, 331, 337, *464*, 535–6*
Iraq **16** 434
Italy **16** 525–6
landscape **16** 136
Ottoman **16** 221, 536–7*, *537*
Sicily **16** 525–6
Turkey **16** 221, 497, 535, 536–7*, *537*
wall **12** 625; **16** 250–54*
Central Asia, Western **6** 202; **16** 200, 252, 253
Egypt **16** 306
Indian subcontinent **15** 354
Iran **16** 200, 233, 253–4, *254*, 331
Ottoman **16** 254
Syria **16** 148
Turkey **16** 254
Umayyad (Syria) **16** 252
watercolours **1** *635*, *636*; **16** *125*, *132*
palaces **16** 130, 141, 146, 243–4, 246, 800; **23** 814–16*
Afghanistan **16** 167
Africa **1** 315
Central Asia, Western **6** *203*; **16** 160, 167, *238*
Egypt **16** 257
fortified: Spain **20** *157*
Indian subcontinent **15** *354*
Iran **16** *80*, 160, 234–5, 246, *265*; **23** *816*
Iraq **16** *152*, 152–3, 160, 182
Jordan **16** *556*
Morocco **16** 240; **23** 816
Ottoman **16** 225, 227, 266; **23** 816
Spain **13** *288*; **16** 187, 215, 217, *217*
Syria **16** 148, 182, 245

Islamic
palaces—cont.
Turkey **16** 186, 204, 225, 227, 266
palm **16** 269, 487
palmettes **23** 556
paper **16** 271, 275, 351–4*, *353*; **24** 41, 45*, 48*; **25** 598
Central Asia, Western **27** 673
Indian subcontinent **15** 549
papercuts **16** *354*, 354–5*
papier mâché **16** 359, 533
papyrus **16** 275
paratacamite **24** 793
parchment **16** 274, 351, 356
pasteboard **16** 356
patronage **16** 121–6*, 296–7
architecture **16** 143*
Central Asia, Western **16** 235*
Egypt **16** 207, 382–3
Indian subcontinent **15** 206, 207, 738, 739–40
Iran **16** 374
Mamluk **16** 130
metalwork **16** 380*
Ottoman **16** 122, 133
Syria **16** 146, 207, 382–3
pattern books **16** 305
pavements **16** 145, 250
pavilions (buildings) **15** 346; **16** 197, 204, *225*
pearls **16** *430*
pendants (jewellery) **17** III1
pendentives **16** 142
pens **16** 276; **24** 348
periodicals **16** 550
piercing **16** 364
piers (ii) (masonry) **16** 145, 190
pigments
black **7** 635
blue **7** 635
cobalt blue **16** 420, 427
green **7** 635; **16** 129, 248
peori **16** 330
pink **16** 249
purple **16** 448
red **16** 421, 485; **30** 477
tomato red **16** 249
white **7** 635
pīshṭāq **16** 160, 164, 801; **24** 877–8*
plans **16** 143, 196
plaques **16** 528
plaster **16** 140, 142, 269; **29** 818–20*
Central Asia, Western **16** 200
Iran **16** 165, 200
plates **16** *394*, 398, *399*, *405*, *422*
poetry **25** 72
polo grounds **16** 153
polychromy **7** 634; **15** 354; **25** 171
pools **16** 142
poplar **16** 269
porcelain **16** 423, *424*, *425*
blanc de chine **16** 425
blue-and-white ware **16** *424*
Kraak ware **16** 424
Kubachi ware **16** 423, 424
soft-paste **16** *424*, *425*
portals **16** 142
Central Asia, Western **6** *203*
Egypt **9** 161
Iran **16** 194
Syria **8** *478*
Tunisia **16** *170*, *219*
Yemen **16** 178
porticos **16** 145, 222
portraits **15** 637; **16** *127*, *341*, *536*
potter's wheels **16** 394
pottery **6** 333; **16** 396*, 404*, 412*
Abraham of Kütahya ware **16** 418
Afghanistan **16** 407
Aghkand ware **16** 407
Algeria **16** 404, 427
Amol ware **16** 407

Islamic
pottery—cont.
Baba Nakkaş ware **16** 418
Barbotine ware **16** 394
blue-and-white ware , ; **4** *172*, 172–3*; **6** IV1, 2; **9** *36*; **16** 413, 414, *414*, 416, *417*, 418, *418*, 420, 424, 427; **30** XIII1
blue-on-white ware **16** 397, *398*, 400
Brittle ware **16** 397
Central Asia, Western **16** 123, 400–402*, 407–10*, 412–14*
champlevé ware **16** 407, 411
cuerda seca ware **16** 411, 412
Damascus ware **16** 420
Egypt **16** 402–3*, 404–5*, *405*, 415–17*
faiyumi ware **16** 403, 405
Fustat Fatimid Sgraffito ware (FFS) **16** 405
Golden Horn ware **16** 420, 421
Iran **6** IV3; **16** 400–402*, 407–10*, 412–14*, 423–7*
Timurid **16** 413
10th cent. AD **16** 123, *123*
12th cent. **16** *410*
13th cent. **16** 124, *394*, 395, *408*
14th cent. **16** *413*, *554*
15th cent. **16** *414*
Iraq **16** 396, 397–400*
Iznik ware **16** 124
Jordan **16** 396, 397
Kashan style **1** 98; **16** 409–10
lājvardīna ware **6** IV3; **16** 412, 413
Laqabi ware **16** 406, 408
Late Roman C **16** 396
lustreware **6** 333, IV2; **16** 393, 394, *394*, 395, 399, *405*, 409–10*, 412, 415–16*; **22** 515
Egypt **16** 404–5
Iran **16** 401, 404, 412, 423, 425, 427
Iraq **16** 397, *399*, 400; **23** *558*
North Africa **16** 411
Spain **16** 404, 412, 418, 419, *419*
Syria **16** 404, 406, *406*, 407, *416*
Mesopotamia **16** 401
Miletus ware **16** 418, 420
Miniature style **16** 409
Monumental style **16** 409
Morocco **16** 412, 418, 427
North Africa **16** 403–4, 411–12*, 418–19*, 427–8*
Ottoman **16** 419, 420, *421*, *422*
Palestine **16** 397
Pseudo-Samian ware **16** 405
Raqqa ware **16** 405, 406
Red Slip ware **16** 396
Sicily **16** 411
Spain **16** 403–4*, 411–12*, 418–19*; **29** 322
Syria **16** 396–7*, *397*, 405, *406*, 406–7*, 413, 415–17*, *416*, *417*
tin-glazed ware **16** 399, *426*, 426
Tunisia **16** 403, 404, 411, 427
Turkey **16** 406, 411*, 413, 418*, *418*
Umayyad Palace ware **16** 396, *397*
printing **16** 359–62*, *361*, 434, 450, 451
propaganda **16** 145
punching **16** 364
pyxides (boxes) **16** 525
qaysariya **16** 262
qibla **16** 141, 144, 145; **22** 192
quartz **16** 394, 405, 408, 413, 420
quilts **16** 429
quivers **16** 528
racecourses **16** 153
raising **16** 363

Islamic—cont.
red lead **16** 393
reeds **16** 269, 276; **24** 348; **32** *314*
regalia **16** 537–9*, *538*
repoussé **16** 364
reuse **16** 245
revetments **16** 143, 243–5, 248, 250, 381
Central Asia, Western **16** 199
Iran **16** 199, *234*, *249*
ribāṭs **16** 151, 154, 155, 156
ribs **16** 142, 164
rings **16** *504*
roads **16** 151
robes **16** *430*, 452, 459, 460, 462, 463, 464, 465
rock crystal **6** 556; **12** 253; **16** 540–42*, *541*, *542*; **26** 487
rolls **16** 271
roofs **16** 141, 269; **27** 127
ropes **16** 262
rubies **12** 253; **16** *507*, *542*
rubrics **16** 291
sabres **16** 503, *506*, 508
safflower **16** 449
salvers **32** *161*
sandstone **15** 340; **16** 239
sapphires **12** 253
sashes **16** 429, 461, 462, 465
satin **16** 449, *450*
saz **16** 133, 349, 388
scabbards **16** *508*, *516*
schools **5** *399*; **16** 141, 229, 241, 265
science and art **28** 201
scientific books **16** 132, 297–9*, *298*, 309–10
screens (i) (architectural) **16** 257, 269, *496*, 500
screens (ii) (furniture) **16** 487, 496, 500
scripts **15** 198; **16** 166, 216, 217, 273, 285–7*, 367–8
andalusī **16** 282
Arabic **4** 344; **16** 258, 277–8, 359; **29** 619
bihārī **16** 286
cursive **12** 513; **16** 169, 258, 259–60, 368, 432
dīvānī **16** 287
early Abbasid **16** 278–9*, *279*, 280
fāsī **16** 282
figural **16** 375–6
fingernail **16** 276
gayrawānī **16** 282
ḥijāzī **16** 278; **18** *240*
Kufesque **16** 135
kufic **15** 338; **16** 169, *176*, 215, 216, 258–9, *259*, 273, *275*, 278, 367, 510–12, 542–3, *543*; **29** *618*, 619
maghribī **16** 280, *281*, 281–2*
muḥaqqaq **16** *275*, 282; **18** *241*
naskh **15** 338; **16** *275*, 278, 282, *283*, 285, 386, 513
nasta'līq **16** 285–6, *286*, 368, 378, 390, 391, 514
New Abbasid style **16** 280–81*, *280*
Pahlavesque **16** 510
Persian **16** 258, 285, 329
proportioned **15** 67
rayḥān **16** *275*
riqā' **16** 282
shikasta nasta'līq **16** 287
Six Pens **16** 280, 282–4*
sūdānī **16** 282
ta'līq **16** 286
tawqī' **16** 282
thuluth **16** 169, *275*, 282, 285, 368, 386, 513, 514
Turkish **16** 258
sculpture
architectural **15** 413; **16** 243–7*
bronze **16** *135*
Central Asia, Western **16** 239
Indian subcontinent **15** 497
Malaysia **20** 170–71*

Islamic
sculpture—cont.
Philippines **24** 618*
relief **6** 222; **16** *247*
seals **16** 542–3*, *543*, *552*; **33** 5
serge **16** 445
sewing **16** 356
sgraffito **16** 248, 250, *402*, 402, 407–8*, 411, *411*, 415*
shadow-puppets **16** 543–5*, *544*
shamsa **16** 291
shields **14** 428; **16** 503, 505, 507
shirts **16** *137*, 459, 460, 463, 464
shoes **16** 452, 461
shops **16** 141, 175, 266
shrines (i) (cult) **28** 632–5*
Central Asia, Eastern **28** 637
Central Asia, Western **28** 636
Indian subcontinent **15** *308*
Iran **28** IV1
Iraq **28** *633*
Kazakhstan **16** *198*
shutters (window) **16** 500
signatures **16** 126, 127, 232, 325, 331, 399, 410, 415, 496, 508
silica **16** 404
silk **16** 124, 428–9, 430, *430*, 431, *433*, 434–5, *435*, 436–7, *437*, *439*, 440, 441–2, *442*, 443, *444*, 445, 446, *446*, 447–8, *448*, 449, *450*, 462, 465, 466, 473, 474, *475*, 508; **28** 715–16; **31** 21
half-silk **16** 433; **31** 21
Spain **30** VIII1
silver **4** 688; **6** 556; **16** 363, 364, 371–3*, *381*, *383*, *504*, 532; **21** *718*
Afghanistan **16** *366*, *375*, *378*
Algeria **16** 532
Central Asia, Western **16** *378*
Egypt **16** *384*, *385*, *389*, 404; **21** I1
Iran **16** *371*, 375, *376*, 450, *511*, *513*; **21** I1
Iraq **16** *380*, *512*
Syria **16** *99*, *384*, 389, 510, *511*
Tunisia **16** *512*
Umayyad (Syria) **21** *505*
Yemen **16** *533*
silver-gilt **16** *372*
silver oxides **16** 394, 518
sinking **16** 363
size **16** 352
skins **16** *357*
skirts **16** 466
slip **16** 395, 399, 405, 408*, 415*, 420, 422
Small *Shāhnāmas* **16** 296
smalt **16** 394
soot **16** 276
souks **16** 262
souvenirs **16** 414
spinning (metalwork) **16** 363
spinning (textile) **16** 432, 468
spolia **15** 338
squinches **15** 340; **16** 142, 161, 164, 168–9, 176
stained glass **16** 256*, 257
stamping **16** 403
stamps **16** 517
stands **16** *389*, 487, 497, *501*, 517
starch **16** 433
steel **16** 143, 363, *508*, *516*; **21** *718*
Iran **16** 391
Ottoman **16** 507, 508
stepwells **15** 343, 349
stitches **31** 21
stone **6** 557; **16** 141, 142, 243, 255, 256, 269; **20** 166; **21** 630
Central Asia, Western **16** 199
Egypt **16** 176
Indian subcontinent **16** 239
Iran **16** 199
Iraq **16** 150
Ottoman **16** 266
Syria **16** 182
Turkey **16** 186, 266

Islamic—cont.
stone-carvings **2** *245*; **15** 338
stonewares **16** 406
stools **16** 516
strapwork **6** 557; **16** 487; **23** 560; **31** 784
streets **16** 206, 261–2, *266*
stucco **16** 133, 140, 243–5, 250, 257; **21** 506; **29** 818–20*
Afghanistan **16** *163*; **29** 825
Algeria **16** 190
Central Asia, Western **16** 160
Egypt **29** 819
Indian subcontinent **15** 338; **29** 825
Iran **16** 158, 160, 165, *200*, *233*, *244*; **29** 818, *820*
Iraq **16** 153, 243; **27** *680*; **29** 819
Jordan **29** *819*
Morocco **16** 190, 257
Ottoman **16** 257
Spain **16** *189*, 217
Syria **31** *573*
Turkey **16** 248, 257
Yemen **16** 214, 215
studios **16** 122
swastikas **23** 562
sword guards **16** *506*
sword hilts **16** 527, 528
swords **2** 452; **16** 503–4, 505, *506*, 508, *508*, 509
symbolism (critical term) **16** 136, 468
takyas **16** 234
talars **16** 234, 238, *238*
talismans **16** 137, *137*, 245, 453
tamarisk **16** 500
tanks **16** 246
tanneries **16** 262
tapestries **16** 431, 432, *433*, 434; **31** 21
teak **16** 269, 488, *489*, *490*
tents **15** 716–17*; **16** 124, 193, 197, 429; **30** *472*, 476–80*
Central Asia, Western **16** 485
terracotta **16** 140, 143
Afghanistan **16** 166, 169
Central Asia, Western **16** 166, 169, 245
Iran **16** 165
Iraq **16** *247*
Pakistan **16** 166
textiles **6** 557; **14** 428; **16** 124, 428–87*, 503; **31** 20–22
Afghanistan **16** 451
Algeria **16** 448*
Baghdad Group **16** 436
Central Asia, Western **16** 435, 443, 451
Egypt **16** 431–2*, 441–2*
India, Republic of **15** 176
Indian subcontinent **15** 664*; **16** 452*
Indonesia **15** 758
Iran **16** 435*, 443, 448*
Iraq **16** 433–5*
Java **15** 758
maśrū **15** 664*
metal-ground **16** 450
Morocco **16** 447–8
North Africa **16** 436–7*, 439–40*, 447–8*
Ottoman **16** 121, 444–7*
Sicily **16** 437
Spain **16** 436–7*, 439–40*
Syria **16** 441–2*
Transoxiana **16** 435, 443
Tunisia **16** 448
Turkestan (region) **16** 451
Turkey **16** 444
Uzbekistan **16** 451
Yemen **16** 438–9*
zandanījī **16** 435
theatre **16** 544–5
theories (art) **15** 206
threads **16** *430*, 443, 450
thrones **16** 516; **30** 784*

Islamic—cont.
tiles **16** 140, 143, 158, 248–50*, 259, 269, 395; **21** 506; **22** 154
Afghanistan **16** 169
Central Asia, Western **6** 202, 204, *207*; **16** *140*, 169, 199, *236*, 239, 248
cuerda seca **16** 199, 239, 249, 250
Indian subcontinent **15** 337, 338, 342, 354, 686
Iran **1** *98*; **6** 172; **16** 165, 193, *199*, 199–200, *234*, 248, *249*, 425
Iran: 13th cent. **16** 195
Iraq **16** 400, 404
lājvardīna **16** 249, 412
lustre **16** 216, 248, 249; **28** 634
mīnā'i **16** 249
Morocco **16** 250
North Africa **16** 427
Ottoman **16** 206, 221, 260, 419, 420, 421, 422, 423
painted **16** 248–9
Spain **16** 216, 217
Syria **16** 422
Tunisia **16** 250, 427
Turkey **16** 206, 221, 248, 418; **30** XIII1
Yemen **16** 215
timber structures **16** 269
tin **16** 363, 393, 395, 399, 402, 404, 413, 420
tiraz **16** 121, 455, *455*; **31** 20–22*
Egypt **16** 432, *433*, 457; **31** *21*
Iraq **16** 433
Spain **16** 436
Yemen **16** 438
tombak **16** 388
tombs **16** 90, 128, 141, 142; **28** 633–5; **31** 110–13*
Afghanistan **16** *163*
Central Asia, Western **16** 159–60, 163–4, 197, 237, 492
Egypt **5** *403*; **16** 175, 207, 208–9; **31** *113*
Indian subcontinent **15** *337*, 342, 343, 349; **31** 111, 113, 114, *115*
Iran **16** 159–60, 163–4, 197, 492; **31** *112*
iwan **16** 186
Morocco **16** 240, *240*
Ottoman **16** 206
Syria **16** 207
tower **16** 158, 159–60
Central Asia, Western **16** 159
Iran **16** 159–60, *160*, 194; **23** *559*
Turkey **16** 185–6, 204; **31** 113
Tunisia **16** 220
Turkey **16** 185–6, 206; **31** *114*
Uzbekistan **27** *675*
Yemen **16** 177, 214–15
topographical illustrations **16** 347
tortoiseshell **16** 499
towers **16** 142; **21** 546
Azerbaijan **2** *892*
China **6** *677*
pigeon **16** 232
Spain **16** 215, 216
Syria **21** 583
tracery **31** 273
trade **16** 106–7*, 126, 331
armour **16** 505
bitumen **16** 269
books **16** 343, 360, 361
carpets **16** 468, 469, 470, 476, 479, 481, 482
ceramics **16** 393, 397, 398, 419
cobalt **16** 394
cochineal **16** 449
cotton **16** 449
craftsmen and artists **16** 146
dress **16** 456
dyes **16** 431, 438
fur **16** 456
glass **16** 221, 257, 522; **28** 723
guns **16** 508
Islamic
trade—cont.
hair **16** 449
indigo **16** 449
iron **16** 59
lac **16** 449
manuscripts **16** 328, 342, 346
metalwork **16** 368, 379, 383, 389, 390
mirrors **21** 718, 720
paper **16** 351, 352
porcelain **16** 124, 393, 403, 420
pottery **6** 333*; **16** 401, 412, 413, 415, 416, 417, 553
Egypt **16** 403, 404, 405
Iraq **16** 398, 402
Ottoman **16** 420
Syria **16** 396, 397
ribbons **16** 448
silk **16** 428, 429, 445, 449; **28** 721
smalt **16** 394
stone **16** 199
teak **16** 269
textiles **16** 428, 429, 441, 444, 448, 449, 463, 553
textiles: Egypt **16** 431
textiles: Yemen **16** 438
tiles **16** 400
tin **16** 393
weapons **16** 505
wood **16** 487, 488
wool **16** 449
trappings **14** 183; **16** 429
trays **16** 366, 372, *372*, *380*
treatises **16** 136
aesthetics **16** 455
architecture **2** 316; **16** 143, 221
automata **15** 573
calligraphy **16** 126, 277*, 284, 286
ceramics **16** 394
design **16** 143
gems **16** 412, 527
pottery **1** 98
scientific instruments **2** 647
vaults **22** 322
trousers **16** 460, 461, 462, 465, 466
tufa **16** 269
tughras **14** 428; **16** 135, 514; **31** 416–17*
tunics **1** *229*; **16** 454, 458, 461
turbans **16** 429, 452, 455, 456–7, 459, 464, 537, 539
turquoise **12** 253; **16** *507*, *530*, 531
type-faces **16** 361
underclothes **16** 458, 461, 464, 466
uniforms **16** 461
universities **16** 241
urban planning **16** 260–64*, 268
Central Asia, Western **6** 210–11*, *211*; **16** 264
Egypt **16** *262*
Indian subcontinent **15** 409–10
Iran **16** 230, 264–5*
Iraq **16** 150–51
Ottoman **16** 265–7*
Syria **16** *261*
Turkey **16** 265–7*
varnishes **16** 356, 533
vases **16** 419, *419*
vaults (ceiling) **16** 140, 142
barrel **16** 150, 153, 270; **32** 88
cellular **32** 88
Central Asia, Western **6** 202; **16** 199
Indian subcontinent **15** 343
Iran **16** 192, 194, 199, *200*
muqarnas (architecture) **16** 142, *171*, 181, 190, *195*, 199; **22** 322–3
rib **16** 142, 232, *233*
Spain **16** 217
Turkey **16** 186
veils **16** 453
velvet **16** 430, 446, 449; **23** *560*
Islamic—cont.
veneers **16** 499
vessels **16** 527, 528
villas **16** 230, 241
walls **6** 211; **16** 141; **21** 583
walnut **16** *499*
warehouses **16** 141, 262
war hammers **16** *504*
wars **16** 438
watermarks **16** 352
water supply **2** 242
waxes **33** 5
weapons **16** 503–10*, *504*, *506*, 528
weaving **16** 466
Central Asia, Western **16** 443
Egypt **16** 441
inweaving **16** 436
Iran **16** 443
Iraq **16** 434–5
knotted-pile **16** 466–7, *467*, 469
lampas **16** *444*, 449, *450*; **30** VII1
Morocco **16** 429
North Africa **16** 440, 447–8
Ottoman **16** 476–7, 478–9
Spain **16** 439–40
Syria **16** 441
Turkey **16** 444, 476–7, 478–9
wicker **16** 507
wind catchers **16** 270
windows **16** 256, 257
women **15** 637
women artists **16** 476
wood **6** 171, 556; **9** 160; **16** 141, 142, 269, 356, *383*, 503; **21** 505, 629–30
Central Asia, Western **16** 199
Egypt **16** 176
Iran **6** *172*; **16** 199
Malaysia **20** 166
Morocco **16** *493*; **21** *630*
North Africa **29** 618
Ottoman **16** 222
Spain **16** 216, *493*, 494–5, *506*
Turkey **16** 202, 222
Yemen **16** *500*, 500–501
wood-carvings **16** 487
Central Asia, Western **6** 277–8; **16** 492
Indonesia **15** 757
Iraq **16** 488
Philippines **24** 618
Turkey **16** 497
Yemen **16** 500
woodwork **16** 487–502*, 524
Central Asia, Western **16** 491–2, *492*, *501*, 501–2*
Egypt **16** 488–91*, *490*, *496*, 496–7*
Iran **16** 491–2*, 501–2*, *502*
Iraq **16** 488–91*, *489*
Kazakhstan **16** *501*
North Africa **16** 492–5*
Ottoman **16** 498–9*, *499*
Spain **16** 492–5*
Syria **16** 488–91*, 496–7*
Tajikistan **16** 491, *492*
Turkey **16** 497–8*, *498*
turning **16** 487
Yemen **16** *500*, 500–501*
wool **5** II, III, IV; **16** 428, 429, 430, 431, 434, 445, 449, 455, 466, *467*, *470*, *471*, *472*, *478*; **18** *48*
workshops **16** 468
wraps **16** 459
writing **16** 134–5*, 273–6*, *274*, *275*, 277–8*; **29** 617
yarn **16** 468
zinc **16** 363
zulla **16** 144
Islamic Art **16** 550
Islamic Art Foundation **23** 804
Isla Molina **24** 105
Islam Shah, Sultan (*reg* 1545-53) (Sur) **30** 9
Islam Shah Sur, Sultan of Delhi (*reg* 1510-34) **15** 409; **27** 858
Island (Co. Cork) **25** 508
Island Gems **12** 247
Isla Plana **25** 733
Isla Venado **29** 151
Isle-Adam, Philippe-Auguste de Villiers de l', Comte *see* VILLIERS DE L'ISLE-ADAM, PHILIPPE AUGUSTE, Comte de
Isle-Adam, St Martin **10** 476
Isle d'Abeau, L' *see* L'ISLE D'ABEAU
Isle Jourdain, Bertrand de l', Bishop of Toulouse *see* JOURDAIN, BERTRAND DE L'ISLE, Bishop of Toulouse
Íslensk grafík *see* SOCIETY OF ICELANDIC PRINTMAKERS
Isle of Man
crosses **32** 516
decorative arts **32** 530*
memorial stones **32** 522
stone-carvings **32** 523, 530*
Isle of May Lighthouse **19** 361
Isle of Pines **23** 17, 18
Isle of Whithorn (Dumfries & Galloway), St Ninian's Chapel **28** 241
Isle of Wight County (VA), Old Brick Church **4** 786
Islet, L *see* L'ISLET
Isleta (NM) **22** 568, 606
Isleworth **10** 339
Islip Roll *see under* ROLLS → individual manuscripts
Isma'il, Khedive (*reg* 1863-79) (Muhammad Ali's Line) **5** 399, 401; **9** 764; **16** 557; **17** 640
Isma'il, Sultan (*reg* 1672-1727) ('Alawi) **1** 527; **10** 291; **16** 240; **21** 73, 585; **23** 816
Isma'il I, Shah (*reg* 1501-24) (Safavid) **4** 49; **12** 83; **16** 230, 332, 390; **30** 478
Isma'il I, Sultan (*reg* 1313-25) (Nasrid) **13** 282, 286, 287
Isma'il I bin Ahmad, Amir (*reg* 892-907) (Samanid) **5** 139
Isma'il II, Shah (*reg* 1576-7) (Safavid) **16** 337; **22** 260; **27** 506; **28** 811; **33** 626
Isma'il, Adham **30** 177
Ismail, Namık **2** 634; **31** 454; **33** 628
Isma'il 'Adil Shah, Ruler (*reg* 1510-34) ('Adil Shahi) **15** 572
Isma'il Ghalib **16** 553
Ismail Hakkı Sami *see* SAMI
Isma'il ibn Ward al-Mawsili **16** 379
Isma'iliya **9** 765, 767
Isma'il Jalayir **16** 536, 561*; **22** 260
Ismailov, Aubakir **17** 867
Ismailov, E. **2** 894; **12** 37
Ismailov, Gulfairus **17** 867
Ismailov, I. **22** 446
Ismailovo **12** 134
Isma'il Quli Khan **15** 371
Isma'il Zühdü Efendi **22** 385
Ismaning **13** 852
Ismat al-Dunya **16** 325; **18** 29
İsmayil Hakki Baltacıǧlu **16** 287
Isneg **24** 625
Isnos **27** 700
Isny, Jörg of *see* JÖRG OF ISNY
Isoda Koryūsai **16** 561–2*; **17** 281
works **16** *561*; **17** 276, 278, *282*, 283; **31** 53
isodomic masonry *see under* MASONRY→ types
Isohachi Wakasugi *see* WAKASUGI ISOHACHI
Isoko **9** 736–7
sculpture **9** *736*
Isokon Furniture Co. **4** 762; **7** 482, 483; **10** 299; **13** 688
Isokrates **13** 372
Isokyrö Church **11** 94
Isola, Aimaro D' **16** 650, 651; **22** 747
Isola, Maija **11** 110
Isola Bella **16** 562–3*, *618*
gardens **12** 115, 118
Palazzo Borromeo **16** *562*, 562–3
monument to Camillo Borromeo **27** 830
Museo Borromeo **4** 427; **16** 563
sculpture **4** 816, 817
Isola Comacina **27** 500
Isola di Fano **10** 590
Isola di San Vittore *see* ISOLA BELLA
Isola Sacra **27** 72; **31** 109
Isola S Giorgio **32** 182
S Giorgio Maggiore **4** 774; **5** 533; **16** 635; **23** 868; **26** 478; **31** 14; **32** 187, 214–15*, *214*
altar **5** *533*
refectory **23** 867
sculpture **16** 697
isometric perspective *see under* PERSPECTIVE→ types
Isono Bunsai **17** 285–6
Isopata **21** *651*
jewellery **21** *686*
isopropanol **29** 53
isotope analysis *see under* TECHNICAL EXAMINATION → types
Isotta de Terzaga **21** 111
Isotype **7** 482
Isoya Yoshida *see* YOSHIDA, ISOYA
Isozaki, Arata **3** 217; **16** 563–4*; **30** 288
staff **26** 549; **33** 509
works **1** 737; **16** *564*; **17** *91*, 92; **18** 114; **19** 320, 703; **22** 367
Isparta **16** 477; **31** 455
Israel **13** *362*; **16** *104*, 564–72*, *565*; **17** 531; **30** 178, *180*, 187
architecture **16** 564–7*
archives **2** 370*
brass **16** *569*
ceramics **16** 568*
chairs **16** *569*
collections **16** 570*, 571*; **17** 582*
dealing **16** 570*
education (art) **16** 571–2*
garden cities **17** 853
libraries **16** 572*
metalwork **16** 568–9*
moshavim **17** 854
museums **16** 571*; **17** *492*, 582*
painting **16** *567*, 567–8*; **17** 579–80*
patronage **16** 569–70*
photoarchives **16** 572*
rugs **16** 569
sandstone **17** *579*
sculpture **16** 567–8*; **17** *579*, 579–80*
textiles **16** 569*
trade **1** 880
universities **16** *566*
urban planning **17** 854
walnut **16** *569*
see also ANCIENT NEAR EAST; JEWISH ART; PALESTINE; SYRIA-PALESTINE
Israel, Marvin **18** 476
Israelite **1** *852*; **16** 572–3*; **30** 187, 189
craftsmen and artists **16** 573
metalwork **30** 195
seals **16** 573
Israel Phoenix Assurance Company **16** 570
Israels, Isaac (Lazarus) **14** 47; **16** 575–6*; **22** 850, 851
Israëls, Jozef **16** 573–5*; **17** 576; **22** 850
groups and movements **14** 43, 46, 47
patrons and collectors **11** 301; **28** 271
reproductive prints by others **19** 734; **33** 677
teachers **18** 481; **24** 745
works **16** *574*; **22** 849

Israel Stele 9 783
Israyelyan, Rafayel (Sarqis) 10 450; 16 576*
Issac-la-Tourette Church 1 518
Issai 17 400
Issakovitch, Serge (Ivan) *see* CHERMAYEFF, SERGE (IVAN)
Issam Shreida 31 584
Issanchou, Jean-Baptiste 19 396
Issan Ichinei *see* YISHAN YINING
Issarda 15 575
Issedones 2 100
Issei Ezaki *see* EZAKI, ISSEI
Issei Hatakeyama *see* HATAKEYAMA, ISSEI
Issei Suda *see* SUDA, ISSEI
Issel, Alberto 16 731; 28 318
Issel, Werner 14 399
Isselburg, Peter 16 576*
  pupils 27 725; 31 370
  works 12 242; 14 467; 33 131
Isshi 17 170
Isshi Bunshu 17 193, 233; 30 263
Isshikensofu Imai *see* IMAI ISSHIKENSOFU
Isshin, Ogawa 24 739
Isshō *see* MARUYAMA ŌKYO
Isshō Miyagawa *see* MIYAGAWA ISSHŌ
Issiakhem, M'hamed 1 635; 16 577*
Issogne 12 287
Issoire, St Austremoine 26 601, 641
Issott, Thomas 7 758
Issoudun
  La Tour Blanche 6 *54*, 55; 8 278; 9 144
  Notre-Dame 26 599
Issō Yagi *see* YAGI, ISSŌ
Issyk 6 *182*; 16 577*; 17 *865*
  burial chamber 6 212; 16 577
  gold 2 101
  Golden Man 6 237
  jewellery 6 273
  metalwork 6 242
  textiles 6 251
Istakhr 16 397, 407
al-Istakhri 15 308; 18 21
Istalif 1 210
Istana Nurul Imam 5 11
Istana Satu *see* Terengganu Royal Palace
Istanbul 3 168; 16 *103*, *104*, 447, 577–612*
  academies and art schools
    Academy of Fine Arts 16 221, 536, 590–91; 31 452, 454, 455
      directors 12 506
    Artillery School 16 591; 31 453
    Military Academy 16 591; 31 453
    State School of Applied Arts 31 456
  aqueducts 2 242; 9 632; 16 224
    Aqueduct of Valens 2 242; 9 560
  arsenal 2 502
  art forms and materials 16 423, 479
    altarpieces 32 213
    architecture 2 428; 4 773, 774; 9 523, 550; 16 220; 31 452, 453; 32 318
    armour 16 *507*
    bookbindings 16 359
    books 14 35; 16 360
    bronze 9 154
    carpets 2 439; 16 470, 473; 28 716
    coins 9 639
    curtains 2 442
    doors 9 581
    dress 16 460
    embroidery 2 443
    enamel 16 516
    fonts (baptismal) 11 251
    glass 9 645, 646
    gold 2 442; 16 531
Istanbul
  art forms and materials—cont.
    heraldry 14 411
    icon covers 15 77
    icons 9 623, 625, 626, 627, 628, 629, 630, 633
    ivory-carvings 9 648, 649, 652; 16 *527*
    jewellery 9 652
    ketubbot 18 3
    linen 9 664
    manuscript illumination 2 425, 431; 9 605, 612, 617; 14 432; 16 *118*, 346, 350; 17 535; 31 48
    marks 13 358
    metalwork 16 387
    mosaics 9 576–7, 584, 633, 645; 16 589; 22 156
    paintings 9 576–7, 586; 10 197
    photography 16 591
    pottery 9 632, 633, 634
    rock crystal 16 540
    sculpture 9 588; 23 432; 27 45
    seals 9 635
    silk 9 664, 666, 667; 28 715, 716
    silver 8 360; 22 519
    spolia 16 583
    stamps 9 655
    textiles 16 445
    weapons 16 *506*, 507
    weights 9 645
  Ataköy housing complex 16 588
  baths 3 375, 377; 16 224
    Ayasofya Hamamı 16 224
    Barbaros Hayreddin Pasha Hamam 3 376; 16 224
    Haseki Sultan Hamamı 3 376, *377*
    Baths of Zeuxippos 9 557, 633
    see also under Islamic religious buildings → Kiliç Ali Pasha complex; Süleymaniye mosque complex
  Bosporus Bridge 4 803
  bridges 16 588
  Byzantion 16 578*
  Central Post Office Building 16 227
  churches *see* ecclesiastical buildings
  Çinili Hammam *see* baths → Barbaros Hayreddin Pasha Hamam
  Çinili Kiosk *see under* museums
  cisterns
    Binbirdirek 7 354
    Cisterna Basilica 7 354, *354*; 32 89
    Karakgümrük Cistern 32 94
  coins 16 *513*
  collections 13 555
  Constantinople 7 762; 9 *507*, *511*, *512*, 536, 560, 561; 13 369; 16 578–84*, *579*, *581*, *583*, *584*, 761; 26 854, 875; 32 *158*
  Covered Market *see* Grand Bazaar
  craftsmen and artists 16 588–9, 590
  ecclesiastical buildings 16 600
    Blachernai Church 9 521
    Cathedral *see* Hagia Sophia
    Christ Pantepoptes 9 543, 544, *544*, 545, *545*
    Christ Pantokrator Monastery 7 228; 9 522, 526, 544, 545, 588; 16 582, 595–7*
      chapel of St Michael 9 545; 24 110
      enamel 32 214
      Hospital 9 561; 14 780
      mosaics 9 576
      screens (i) (architectural) 7 279
      sculpture 9 590
      South Church (Virgin Eleousa) 16 *596*
      stained glass 9 646
Istanbul
  ecclesiastical buildings—cont.
    Christ the Saviour in Chora 4 773; 9 523, 544, 550, 645; 16 597*; 31 456, 579
      capitals 9 592, 598
      icons 7 222
      inscriptions 4 774
      katholikon 9 584–5
      mosaics 9 562; 16 591, 597–9*, *598*; 22 163
      parekklesion 9 585; 24 *110*, 110
      sculpture 9 592, 593; 16 599*
      stained glass 9 646
      wall paintings 16 597–9*; 22 520; 28 446; 32 III
    Church of the Holy Apostles 9 536, 537, 557; 10 129; 16 603*; 20 520, 865; 22 43, 156
      mosaics 9 576
      see also Islamic religious buildings → Fatih complex → Fatih Mosque
    Church of the Kyriotissa 9 575, 576, 634; 16 599–600*
    Church of the Theotokos (Blachernai Palace) 9 536
    Constantine Lips Monastery 9 592; 20 571
      bricklaying 7 *273*
      chapel of St John the Baptist 9 550; 24 110
      Church of the Theotokos *see* North Church
      mosaics 9 633
      North Church 7 260; 9 544, 545, 588, 592, 593, 597
      parekklesia 24 110
      sculpture 9 592
      South Church 9 550, 593
    Convent of Our Lady of Good Hope 7 228; 9 617
    Crimean War Memorial Church 7 668
    Hagia Eirene 7 252, 279; 9 524, 536, 537, 542; 16 580, 592, 600*; 26 584; 31 456
      arcades 1 722
      armour 2 450
      mosaics 9 575
      plaques 9 592
      tie-bars 9 599
      vaults 32 86, 88
    Hagia Euphemia 7 255; 9 584
    Hagia Sophia 9 514, 524, 525, 529, 536, 537, 654; 10 129; 12 71; 16 581, 591–5*, *592*; 19 362; 20 573; 22 195; 23 485; 27 235; 31 456
      altar 1 694; 7 278
      ambo 1 764; 7 278
      Baptistery 3 190
      capitals 1 *110*; 9 590
      crowns 19 356
      Deesis mosaic 9 583, *583*; 22 157, *157*; 23 831
      domes 4 774; 9 82, 84, 85, 525, 550; 19 *363*; 20 579, 580; 26 584, 923; 32 89
      gallery 30 853
      library 16 498
      mausoleum of Mehmed III 16 499
      mausoleum of Selim II 16 499
      metalwork 9 654, 656, 657
      mosaics 7 *220*, 221; 9 522, 562, 576–7, *577*, 645; 12 813; 16 593–5, *594*; 19 356; 21 III2; 22 161, 162, 163; 33 151
      Patriarchal Palace 9 557, 577
      phiale 7 278
      proportions (architecture) 2 350; 16 593
      screens (i) (architectural) 7 278; 28 291
      silver 9 588
Istanbul
  ecclesiastical buildings
    Hagia Sophia—cont.
      skeuophylakion 7 259
      synthronon 7 279
      templon 28 291
      tie-bars 9 599
    Hagios Demetrios 31 120
    Hodegon Monastery 9 610; 16 589; 23 831
    Kilise Cami 9 544, 550, 584
    monasteries 16 582–3; 21 834
    Myrelaion 9 84, 544, 545, 576
    Nea Ekklesia 9 543; 22 156
    St Akakios 16 580
    St George at Mangana 9 522, 598; 24 110
    Sant Iren Kilisesi *see* Hagia Eirene
    St John Stoudios 7 252, 278; 9 524, *525*, 536; 16 600–601*
      manuscripts 9 604, 610, 613; 16 589
      sculpture 9 589, 590
    St Mary Pammakaristos 9 550, 593, 625; 16 601–2*; 22 156; 24 110
      inscriptions 4 774
      parekklesion 7 221, 273; 9 526, 544, 584; 16 *601*
      south façade 4 *771*
    St Mokios 16 580
    St Nicholas 9 575
    SS Peter and Paul 16 602
    St Polyeuktos 2 98–9; 9 523, 537, 588, 592, 618; 16 596
      screen 28 291
      sculpture 9 589, 590, 597
    St Saviour Pantepoptes *see* Christ Pantepoptes
    SS Sergios and Bakchos 2 323; 7 255; 9 84, 537, *537*; 16 602–3*; 23 485
      sculpture 1 *111*; 9 589, 590, 593; 16 603
    St Theodore *see* Kilise Cami
    St Sophia *see* Hagia Sophia
    Theotokos Chalkoprateia 9 536
    Virgin of the Pharos 9 592, 593
    Virgin Pege 9 657
  education (art) 16 536
  Elementary School 16 227
  Eski Saray *see* Topkapı Palace
  fortifications 9 524, 553, *554*, 555
    Golden Gate 9 519, 520, 555
    Rumeli Hisar 16 206; 21 585, *586*
    town walls 16 266
      Land Wall 4 773; 7 692; 21 558, 562, 586
    Yediküle 21 586
  Forum Tauri 30 706
  Forum of Theodosios *see* Forum Tauri
  Fourth Vakif Han 16 227
  gardens 12 85
  government buildings 16 227
    Public Debts Administration Building 31 452
    Social Security Complex 31 452
  Grand Bazaar 16 611–12*
  guilds 16 588, 590
  Haydarpasa barracks 16 225
  Hilton Hotel 14 788; 31 452, 455
  Hippodrome 7 342; 9 587, 596; 10 440, 743; 18 823
  Hospice of Sampson 9 560
  houses 16 266, 586
  Imperial College of Military Engineering 16 221
  Islamic religious buildings 16 221, 222, 224, 227, 241
    Aya Sofya Cami *see* ecclesiastical buildings → Hagia Sophia
    Azapkapı Mosque 16 223
    Bali Pasha Mosque 16 222
    Bayezid II Mosque 16 222, 498, *499*; 18 509; 20 369
    Bebek Mosque 16 227
Istanbul
  Islamic religious buildings—cont.
    Bezmialem Valide Sultan Mosque 16 227; 21 630
    Blue Mosque *see* Sultan Ahmed I Mosque
    Bodrum Cami *see* ecclesiastical buildings → Myrelaion
    Edirnekapi Mihrimah Sultan Mosque *see* Mirimah Sultan Mosque
    Eski Imaret Cami *see* ecclesiastical buildings → Christ Pantepoptes
    Fatih complex 19 317; 20 369
      Fatih Mosque 16 222, 603*, 604*; 18 509; 20 57
      Fatih Mosque *see also* ecclesiastical buildings → Church of the Holy Apostles
    Fenari Isa Cami *see* ecclesiastical buildings → Constantine Lips Monastery
    Fethiye Cami *see* ecclesiastical buildings → St Mary Pammakaristos
    Firuz Ağa Mosque 16 222
    Hadim Ibrahim Pasha Mosque 16 222
    Hamidiye Mosque 16 241
    Haseki Hürrem Sultan complex 16 224
      Mosque 16 222
    Imrahor Cami *see* ecclesiastical buildings → St John Stoudios
    Iskele Mosque 16 222, 223; 28 *767*
    Ivaz Efendi Mosque 16 222
    Jetty Mosque *see* Mihrimah Sultan Mosque
    Kalenderhane Cami *see* ecclesiastical buildings → Church of the Kyriotissa
    Kara Ahmad Pasha Mosque 16 222
    Kariye Cami *see* ecclesiastical buildings → Christ the Saviour in Chora
    Kiliç Ali Pasha complex 16 224
      Mosque 16 257
    Kilise Cami *see under* ecclesiastical buildings
    Kücük Aya Sofya Cami *see* ecclesiastical buildings → SS Sergios and Bakchos
    Laleli complex 18 509
      Mosque 16 226
    madrasas 16 222
    Mehmed II Fatih complex *see* FATIH COMPLEX
    Mihrimah Sultan Mosque 16 223, 257
    Molla Gürânî Mosque *see* ecclesiastical buildings → Kilise Cami
    Nişancı Mehmed Pasha Mosque 16 223
    Nuruosmaniye complex 18 509
      Mosque 16 226
    Nusretiye Mosque 16 227; 18 509
    Ramazan Efendi Mosque 16 222
    Rüstem Pasha Madrasa 16 224
    Rüstem Pasha Mosque 16 221, 223, 249; 21 506
    Şehzade Mehmed Mosque 9 84; 16 222; 28 *766*, 767
    Sokollu Mehmed Pasha Mosque 9 84; 16 223, 249; 21 506; 28 *768*
    Süleymaniye mosque complex 16 224, 604–5*; 18 *508*, 509; 20 57; 28 767
      baths 16 224
      fountain 16 91

Istanbul
Islamic religious buildings
Süleymaniye mosque complex—cont.
Mosque **16** 221, 222, *223*, 257, 422, 498, *585*; **21** 628; **22** 196, 323; **24** 878
Museum of Turkish and Islamic Art *see under* museums
Sultan Ahmed I Mosque **11** 339; **16** 223, 257, 605*; **21** 628
Takkeci Ibrahim Ağa Mosque **16** 222
Yeni Valide Mosque **16** 223, 257
Zeyrek Cami *see* ecclesiastical buildings → Christ Pantokrator Monastery
Kapalı Çarşı *see* Grand Bazaar
monuments
Arch of Theodosios **9** 589
Column of Arkadios **9** 519, 595, *595*
Column of Marcian **9** 596
Column of Theodosios **9** 589, 595
Obelisk of Theodosios **9** 595; **27** 45
Obelisk of Tuthmosis III *see* Obelisk of Theodosios
Serpentine Column **18** 825; **23** 330
museums **16** 591
Archaeological Museum **16** 591; **31** 456
collections **31** 355
directors **10** 134
Greek collection **13** 470; **31** 356
Armenian Patriarchate Treasury **2** 444
Çinili Kiosk **16** 199, 225, 557, *589*, 591; **18** 71; **23** 815; **31** 456
collections **16** 557
directors **23** 604; **31** 454
Iş Bankası collection **31** 456
Military Museum **2** 450
Mimar Sinan University Museum of Painting and Sculpture **16** 591; **31** 456
Museum of the Ancient Orient **16** 591; **31** 456
Museum of Turkish and Islamic Art **12** 84; **16** 225, 557, 591; **31** 456
Museum of Turkish Ceramics *see* Çinili Kiosk
Topkapı Palace Museum **6** 331; **16** 387
armour **2** 450; **16** 507
ceramics **6** 925; **7** 155
collections **16** 591; **31** 456
dress **16** 461
guns **16** 508
porcelain **4** 172; **6** 898, 916; **16** 393
see also palaces → Topkapı Palace
Vakıflar Carpet Museum **16** 557, 591; **31** 456
Vakıflar Kilim and Flat-Woven Rug Museum **16** 557, 591; **31** 456
palaces **23** 816
Beylerbeyi Palace **16** 227
Blachernai Palace **9** 519, 520, 524, 555, 558
Church of the Theotokos *see under* ecclesiastical buildings
mosaics **9** 576
Dolmabahçe Palace **16** 227, *587*; **23** 816
Great Palace **4** 773; **9** 519, 524, 557, 558; **16** 581, 605–7*, *606*
Audience Hall *see* Chrysotriklinos
baths **9** 561

Istanbul
palaces
Great Palace—cont.
Chalke Gate **9** 623; **30** 705
Chrysotriklinos **9** 537; **16** 581; **19** 502
manuscripts **17** 664
metalwork **9** 656
mosaics **9** *564*, 565, 574; **12** 71; **22** 161
Mouchroutas **9** 558
Nea Ekklesia *see under* ecclesiastical buildings
peristyle courtyard **9** 557
Virgin of the Pharos *see under* ecclesiastical buildings
Mangana Palace **9** 558, 633; **16** 608
New Palace *see* Topkapı Palace
Palace of Antiochos **9** 557
Palace of Ibrahim Pasha **12** 84
Palace of Lausos **9** 557; **18** 825
Palace of Theodore Metochites **9** 559
Sacred Palace *see* Great Palace
Tekfur Saray **9** 524, 559, *559*; **16** 423
Topkapı Palace **16** 142, 225, 266, 584, 608–11*, *609*; **23** 816
Armoury **16** *504*
Baghdad Kiosk **16** 221, 225, *225*, 257, 499; **18** 71; **23** *638*
Chamber of the Holy Mantle *see* Hırka-i Saadet Dairesi
Circumcision Room **16** 225, 249, 421
collections **16** 552, 591
Fountain of Ahmed III **16** 226, *226*
gardens **12** 84
Harem **9** 160; **16** 499
Hırka-i Saadet Dairesi **28** 633
kitchens **16** 221
Library **16** 295
Osman III Pavilion **16** 226
paintings **16** 536
Revan Kiosk **16** 225, 499; **18** 71
Sünnet Odası *see* Circumcision Room
Treasury **16** 542
see also museums → Topkapı Palace Museum
parks
Emirgan Park **24** 182
Yıldız Park **24** 182
patronage **16** 589–90
Research Centre for Islamic History, Art and Culture (IRCICA) **31** 456
School of Civil Engineering *see* Technical University
schools and colleges **31** 455
Darüssafaka School **31** 453
Galatasaray High School **31** 454
shops **16** 612
Sirkeci railway terminal **16** 227; **31** 452
Technical University **16** 221; **31** 452, 455
Tercümen Newspaper Offices **31** 453
Tiled Kiosk *see* museums → Çinili Kiosk
tombs **16** 227
mausoleum of Ahmed I **16** 498
mausoleum of Eyüp Ensari **28** 634
Naksidil Sultan Türbe **9** 84
tomb of Constantine **20** 865
tomb of Mahmud II **16** 227
tomb of Mihrişah Sultan **16** 226
tomb of Şehzade Mehmed **16** 498
town walls *see under* fortifications
trade **9** 597; **28** 716
urban planning **16** 241, 266, 586, 587

Istanbul—cont.
Yambul synagogue **17** 551
Yerebatan Saray *see* cisterns → Cisterna Basilica
Isthmia **13** *363*; **16** 612–13*; **26** *908*
baths **26** 909
Sanctuary of Poseidon **1** 691; **21** 892–3; **26** 909
stadium **29** 487, 488
Temple of Poseidon **13** 376, 394, 549; **16** *612*; **23** 481
Istituto Italiano per il Medio ed Estremo Oriente **15** 897
Istituto Nazionale di Studi sul Rinascimento *see under* FLORENCE
Istituto Nazionale di Urbanistica *see* INU
Istituto Nazionale per la Ricerca Matematica e Operativa per l'Urbanistica (IRMOU) **22** 106
Istler, Josef **8** 394; **20** 254; **30** 23
Istomin, Konstantin **11** 358
Istomin, Nazary **25** 338
Istoriato ware *see under* POTTERY → wares
istorie **1** 558; **16** *613*, 613–14*; **25** 71
see also PAINTING → types → history
Istros **4** 110
architecture **4** 113
coins **4** 112
pottery **4** 112
walls **4** 113
Isturitz **11** *505*; **16** 615*; **25** *470*
bone-carvings **25** *492*
contours découpés **25** 493
figurines **25** 488, 489
István Báthori, Voivode of Transylvania (*fl* 1470s) **23** 324
Istvánffy, Ferenc **14** 687
István Kassai *see* STEFAN (*fl* before 1464; *d* before 1499)
I Sukaria **15** 808
Isuwa **17** 875
Iswari Narain Singh **15** 654
Isyakhim, M'hammad *see* ISSIAKHEM, M'HAMED
Itá **24** *91*, 97
ita bokashi **17** 275
Itaboraí, Casa de Câmara **4** 711
Italia, Angelo **16** 615–16*, 640; **23** 258; **28** 657
Italia artistica, L' **24** 448
Italianates, Dutch *see* DUTCH ITALIANATES
Italiani di Parigi **8** 772; **16** 680; **31** 268
italic *see under* SCRIPTS → types; TYPE-FACES
Italica *see under* SANTIPONCE
Italica, Shalom **21** 48
Italie, Herman d' *see* SWANEVELT, HERMAN VAN
Italien, Pierre l' *see* PIERRE L'ITALIEN
Italiens de Paris *see* ITALIANI DI PARIGI
Italo-Moresque ware *see under* POTTERY → wares
Italus, Franciscus *see* FRANCISCUS ITALUS
Italus, Matteo *see* MATTEO ITALUS
Italy **10** 582, *583*, 584–6; **13** *362*; **16** 616–782*, *616*, *618*, *620*, *621*; **26** 595, *886*; **31** 166
academies **16** *779*; **24** 733
aesthetics **11** 56; **19** 546–7; **30** 745; **32** 20
15th cent. **10** 747
20th cent. **8** 182–3
agate **14** I1
airports **11** *868*
alabaster (gypsum) **1** 516; **10** *593*
allegories **1** 654–7*, 659; **30** *319*
allegories of art **1** *663*
alphabets **10** 591

Italy—cont.
altarpieces **1** 707, 708–9, 710–12; **11** 379–81; **15** 85; **24** 4, 5; **27** 495–6; **32** 213
Baroque **1** *711*; **9** *90*; **11** *681*; **13** *815*; **20** *904*; **22** *478*
Gothic **7** *329*, *334*; **9** *342*, *347*; **13** 130, 146, *146*; **20** *728*; **32** *213*
International Gothic **12** *299*, *300*, *301*
Late Gothic **7** I11; **19** *680*, *681*
heptatychs **31** 534
Mannerism **1** *710*; **3** *486*; **12** *673*; **31** *38*
Order of Poor Clares **25** *229*
polyptychs **9** *100*; **13** 130; **24** 5; **25** 183–4, *184*; **27** *766*
Gothic **4** *31*; **7** *333*; **9** *345*; **11** *382*, *397*; **13** *129*, 139; **20** *675*
Renaissance **8** *168*, *170*; **9** *102*; **21** *145*; **32** *654*, *656*
14th cent. **12** *702*; **20** *760*; **24** *32*
15th cent. **3** *697*
Renaissance **2** *32*, *180*; **3** *663*, *917*; **4** *284*; **7** *738*; **8** *4*; **11** *28*, *701*; **12** *162*; **19** *181*, *441*, *711*, *713*, *785*; **20** *312*, *531*, *787*; **21** *904*, *905*; **22** *477*, *798*, *799*, *800*; **24** *286*, *526*, *761*; **26** *445*, *457*; **27** *495*, *860*, *861*; **31** *533*; **32** *104*; **33** *634*
High Renaissance **3** *304*, *305*
triptychs **1** *530*; **4** *32*; **5** *307*; **18** *698*; **31** 344
Gothic **3** *696*; **7** *335*; **10** *179*; **16** *825*; **32** *228*
Renaissance **9** *99*, *101*; **30** *232*
14th cent. **8** *442*; **21** *112*; **23** *323*
15th cent. **4** *620*
16th cent. **29** *28*
13th cent. **25** *229*
14th cent. **1** *709*; **5** *164*; **7** *337*; **12** *689*; **28** *366*
15th cent. **3** *697*; **4** *730*; **12** *714*; **20** *739*; **29** *550*
16th cent. **2** *128*; **31** *54*, *55*
altars **1** *695*, 698
Baroque **1** *695*; **5** *533*; **19** *374*; **32** 195
Carolingian **5** *807*
Gothic **2** *481*; **13** 168
Roman **26** *890*; **27** *23*
14th cent. **1** *696*
16th cent. **32** *649*
amber **10** 635
ambos **7** *919*
amphitheatres **1** *797*; **25** 198, 748; **26** 789–91, 888, 889, *894*; **32** 340
amphorae **10** *594*
amulets **17** 574
anatomical studies **1** 840–41, *841*, *842*
animal subjects **10** 593
antependia **11** 379
appliqué **16** 759
apprentices **12** 169; **16** 777
aqueducts **2** 242
arcades **26** 888, *888*, *894*
archaeology **14** 867; **31** 61
arches
horseshoe **2** 294
ogee **32** 207
pointed **13** 51
proscenium **30** 666
Roman **26** 887, *887*
round **2** 298*
triple **7** 917
architects **2** 313
architectural decorations **1** 127; **10** 587; **32** *119*
architectural publications **27** 762

Italy—cont.
architecture **4** 790; **16** 622–51*; **30** 501
Baroque **16** 636–9*; **20** *541*; **32** 217
brick **4** 774–6*; **23** *621*; **31** 442
Cistercian Order **13** 51; **16** 627
Dominican Order **13** 52
Early Christian (*c*. AD 250–843) **16** 623–5*
Etruscan **10** 596–602*; **16** 622
exhibition **19** *305*
Franciscan Order **13** 52
Futurism **16** 648*
Gothic **13** 35, 51–3*, 63–6*; **16** 627*
Greece, ancient **16** 622
Mannerism **16** 634–5*; **20** 278–9
marble **26** 889
military **3** *360*; **21** 565–7*
Neo-classicism **16** 643–8*
Neo-Liberty **16** 650*
Post-modernism **16** 651*
Razionalismo **3** *438*; **16** 649–50*
Renaissance **4** 642, 652; **16** 628–35*
Rococo **16** 639
Roman **16** 623; **26** 886–9*
Romanesque **16** 625–7*; **26** 575–80*, *579*
stile liberty **16** 648*
vernacular **32** 289, 290, 291–2*
wattle-and-daub **10** 587
13th cent. **23** 585
20th cent. **16** 648–51*
archives **2** 365, 370*; **32** 204
arks **17** 570
armour **2** 469, 471, 472
arsenals **32** *183*
art (reproduction of works of) **26** 230
art criticism **4** 454; **18** 699; **32** 18, 20
art history **6** 101; **12** 165; **16** 780–82*; **20** 242; **21** 538
Renaissance **32** 18–22
15th cent. **12** 543
16th cent. **12** 244; **16** 766
19th cent. **32** 233
artists' biographies **16** 780–81; **21** 909; **23** 507; **28** 35
Renaissance **32** 18–22
14th cent. **12** 684; **32** 561
15th cent. **20** 263
16th cent. **4** 64; **12** 719; **20** 84, 93; **26** 49
17th cent. **3** 97–8, 673–4; **8** 535; **24** 238
18th cent. **9** 120; **11** 875; **19** 636; **24** 225
artists' houses **2** *547*, *548*
art legislation **2** 561; **10** 821; **16** 765, 766, 768–9
art market **2** 558; **10** 676
askoi **32** *563*
auditoria **30** 667
bacini **16** 100, 395, 404, 411; **30** 886
balustrades **9** 21
banks **10** *821*
banners **11** 149
baptisteries **3** *190*, 192, *192*; **11** *199*; **26** *822*
basilicas (non-ecclesiastical) **3** *328*; **7** 917; **26** *748*, *797*, *868*, 888
bastions **3** 359, *360*; **21** 561, 566, *566*; **24** *532*; **28** 309
baths **3** *374*; **26** 888
beads **16** 744
beadwork **3** 442
beds **3** 483, *483*, 484; **9** 14; **16** 722
bekhen stone **27** *14*
Bibles **4** 6; **26** 660, 666
biccherne **4** *29*; **14** 424
bird's-eye views **19** *764*
bone **10** *179*, 635*

Italy—cont.
- bookbindings 4 347, 348, 349; 12 628; 17 566*; 24 51
- book covers 4 349, 350, 351, 352, 352, 353, 354; 12 628
- book illustrations 3 674; 4 196, 359; 11 685; 14 424
- books 10 589, 590, 636; 15 50; 32 198
- Books of Hours 4 370; 12 710
- borders (manuscript) 4 395
- *boschi* 12 114, 119
- bosquets 12 119
- bowls 12 VIII2; 25 543; 27 107
- bracelets 6 20; 16 752
- brass 16 743, 744
- braziers 10 613
- brick 4 774–6*, 788, 790; 13 64; 23 621; 26 877, 878; 30 667; 31 442
- bridges 14 388; 32 186
- brigandines 2 472
- bronze 9 152, 153–5, 158–9; 10 587; 16 689, 690, 743
  - Baroque 2 609, 610; 5 532, 533; 16 700; 27 830; 29 29
  - Etruscan 10 587, 588, 590, 595, 605, 608, 624–30*, 625, 626, 627, 628, 629, 633, 635, 638; 16 654
  - Futurism 4 201
  - Gothic 11 200; 24 874
  - Greece, ancient 30 339, 339
  - Mannerism 1 791; 3 162, 469; 6 142, 144, 145; 12 572, 573; 29 569
  - Prehistoric 10 527
  - Renaissance 1 162, 556; 2 140, 141; 3 636, 637, 860, 861; 8 796; 9 127, 130, 156–7, 157; 11 71, 693; 12 538, 539, 539, 540, 541; 16 690; 19 202, 208; 20 622; 21 II4; 24 863; 25 20, 725; 26 327, 327, 329, 330, 766; 29 408, 561; 32 105, 360, 362, 363
  - Roman 14 443; 25 202; 27 9, 10
  - Romanesque 26 690; 32 342
  - 16th cent. 5 415; 9 340
  - 17th cent. 7 842; 24 696
  - 19th cent. 32 122
  - 20th cent. 9 159; 16 707; 20 353, 429
- buckles 10 625
- building regulations 26 887
- bullae 10 636
- busts 5 300–302, 304; 9 21, 23
  - Baroque 1 630; 4 406; 5 302; 20 902; 26 773
  - Mannerism 6 144
  - Neo-classicism 6 129
  - Renaissance 5 300; 9 124; 16 691; 21 692, 693, II4; 25 V1
  - Roman 27 12, 110
  - 15th cent. 18 860
  - 16th cent. 3 924; 5 415; 32 648, 649
- cabinets (ii) (furniture) 5 191, 192, 350; 16 728
- cafés 17 443; 24 553
- cameos 12 256, 258, 258–9; 16 690, 746, 746; 17 527
- candelabra 5 604; 10 627
- candle holders 11 383
- candlesticks 7 919; 16 541, 742; 26 328–30, 329
- capriccios 5 685–7; 20 414
- caricatures 5 755–6*, 756; 9 220; 12 535
  - 17th cent. 5 866
  - 18th cent. 13 300
- carnivals 5 785, 786
- cartellini 19 440
- cartography 18 635
- cartoons (drawings) 5 898; 9 102; 10 617; 16 757; 25 902; 26 565

Italy—cont.
- cartouches 5 899
- carving 9 128; 26 136
- casinos (i) (garden) 19 371
- caskets 5 917; 10 635; 14 170; 16 746; 24 249
- cassoni 6 1–7*, 1, 2, 3, 4, 6, 7, 560; 9 14; 14 426; 16 722, 722, 724, 726; 22 413
- casting 10 587; 27 18
- castles 6 17, 57*, 59; 13 64; 21 515, 564, 566
  - 14th cent. 11 2
- casts 27 18, 19
- catacombs 6 70
- catafalques 6 72; 11 276
- catalogues
  - collections 16 767; 27 114
  - exhibitions 6 80; 10 676
  - prints 18 635
  - print-sellers' 18 635
  - 18th cent. 32 237
- cathedrals 9 529
  - Baroque 3 836
  - Byzantine 31 162
  - Early Christian (*c.* AD 250-843) 9 531
  - Gothic 8 134; 13 63, 66; 16 627; 18 785; 21 530, 531; 25 451; 28 678, 679; 31 329
  - Renaissance 11 196; 20 112; 24 747; 31 447
  - Romanesque 12 280; 19 766; 21 772; 23 585; 24 193, 288, 855, 857, 858; 26 576; 32 185, 206
- ceilings 30 357; 32 404
- cemeteries 10 586; 28 36; 32 562–3
- centrepieces 32 203–4
- ceramics 16 732*
- *certosina* 20 467
- chairs 6 390; 16 722; 19 5
  - Etruscan 6 388
  - *sgabello* 6 390
  - 16th cent. 16 725
  - 18th cent. 5 54
- chalcedony 14 I1
- chalices 13 163, 169
- chandeliers 6 443; 32 204
- chapels 31 674
  - Baroque 12 526
  - Renaissance 1 563; 5 18, 19, 20; 11 186
  - 14th cent. 23 756
- chapter houses 6 467
- chariots 6 480*, 481
- chasubles 13 197; 32 392
- chess sets 6 557
- chests-of-drawers 16 732
- Choir-books 7 188
- choir-stalls 16 722
- chronicles 7 242, 243
- churches 2 365; 4 774–5
  - ambulatory basilicas 9 530
  - Barnabites 3 249
  - Baroque 3 249, 355; 4 430, 431, 432, 435; 7 912, 913; 9 339; 11 275; 13 750; 16 638, 638, 641; 17 707, 708; 19 28, 628, 629, 634; 20 44; 23 331; 25 886; 26 318, 758, 759, 760, 807, 823; 28 735; 29 80; 31 674; 32 644
  - basilicas 7 252, 325; 9 529–32*, 533, 533–4*; 19 686
  - Capuchins 5 690
  - centrally planned 7 255, 257–8; 16 629, 632, 637
  - Cistercian Order 7 347
  - decoration 7 275, 276
  - Early Christian (*c.* AD 250-843) 9 529–34*, 530, 532, 533; 13 266; 16 624; 21 537; 26 829, 835; 29 421
  - Gothic 4 279; 7 347; 11 205; 13 52; 22 483; 32 215
  - hall 13 52

Italy
- churches—cont.
  - Lazio 7 918
  - Mannerism 16 634–5, 636; 23 869; 30 802; 32 214
  - Neo-classicism 31 800
  - Palladianism 30 424
  - Post-modernism 25 272
  - Renaissance 1 564, 566, 567, 606; 3 385, 772; 4 644, 652; 7 516; 8 188; 11 202, 207, 209, 689, 690; 21 470, 516; 24 196; 25 216; 27 734, 735, 739, 743; 31 278; 32 630
    - Early Renaissance 5 16, 17; 16 631; 26 183
    - High Renaissance 16 633
  - rock 26 483
  - Romanesque 2 389; 3 235; 4 281, 748; 11 210; 16 626; 21 535; 26 577, 833; 31 316
  - sepulchre 28 428
  - 6th cent. AD 26 34, 35, 36
  - 13th cent. 23 755
  - 15th cent. 19 554; 27 191
  - 16th cent. 25 260; 26 806; 32 503, 631
  - 17th cent. 7 781; 10 801; 25 861, 862
  - 18th cent. 11 815; 12 8
  - 19th cent. 22 473
- ciboria (ii) (structure) 1 695; 7 302, 303
- circuses 7 342
- cists 10 629, 630*
- clasps 4 350
- Classicism 7 383; 12 9
- clay 10 609, 612
- clocks 7 439; 16 726
- cloisters 7 455, 457, 457–8
  - Baroque 22 485
  - Romanesque 3 716
  - 13th cent. 7 920
- clubs (meeting places) 29 370
- coats of arms 14 409, 410–11, 412, 415, 420, 424, 425, 426
- coffering 16 712
- coins 7 533, 534, 535, 536, 537, 538, 539
  - didrachm 10 632
  - Etruscan 10 586, 632–3*; 25 245
  - florins 7 536
  - Greece, ancient 13 586
- collections 2 558; 4 408; 14 867; 16 760–69*, 770–76*; 22 356; 27 114–15; 32 106, 212
  - casts 7 562
  - erotic art 10 487
  - Etruscan 10 637–40*
  - glass 32 204
  - manuscripts 6 151
  - paintings 22 357
  - photographs 16 777
  - portraits 7 726; 9 15
  - prints 16 777
  - public 13 605
  - Renaissance 16 770–71
  - sculpture 2 168–9; 7 562; 13 470; 26 768
  - 15th cent. 13 469
- colleges 7 566, 566; 26 319
- colonnades 26 34
- colophons 32 384
- colour 7 627
- columns 27 40
- commodes 7 659
- competitions 7 664–5, 671, 671–2*; 10 675; 16 639
- concrete 7 692*; 14 388; 22 805, 806; 26 887
- confessionals 7 703
- connoisseurship 21 28; 22 102
- conservation 7 738–9
- contracts 22 157
- contrapposto 7 783
- copies 10 588; 14 867; 16 685
- copper 10 624; 16 743
- coral 3 442; 7 834, 835; 16 750*
- cornelian 12 257

Italy—cont.
- corslets 2 472
- costume books 32 107
- costumes 30 657*, 669*
- cotton 8 37, 37
- couches 10 633
- courtyards 8 65; 23 810
  - Renaissance 16 631, 632; 21 519; 22 132; 27 741
  - 16th cent. 11 180
- craftsmen and artists 10 596; 13 823; 16 660–61*; 32 189–90
- credenze 9 30
- crosiers 13 176
- crucifixes 8 210, 211–12, 216
  - Baroque 5 532
  - Gothic 8 212; 13 123–4, 124, 176; 28 753
  - Renaissance 8 215
  - Romanesque 8 211
  - 13th cent. 7 317, IX; 8 767; 12 III1; 20 761; 24 854
  - 14th cent. 7 317; 12 694; 13 747
- crypts 8 223
- cupboards 8 271; 16 730
- cups 13 437; 27 76
- curtains 17 571
- damascening 2 472
- dealers 16 766
- dealing 16 765–9*
- decadence and decline 8 595
- design 6 42; 8 803*
- dictionaries 10 204
- dictionaries of art 3 98; 16 781
- dinoi 10 614
- diptychs 9 4
- *disegno* 32 19, 21
- *disegno e colore* 9 6–8*
- display of art 9 11, 11, 12, 14–15, 15, 18, 20–22, 22, 23, 26; 14 867; 26 837
- dolls' houses 31 262
- domes 26 903
  - Baroque 13 749; 16 642; 26 809; 32 645
  - Gothic 13 65
  - Neo-classicism 2 177
  - Renaissance 5 15; 27 761
  - Roman 26 793
  - segmental 9 84, 86
  - 5th cent. AD 26 32
- doors 9 152, 153–5, 158–9
  - Early Christian (*c.* AD 250-843) 9 151–2
  - Neo-classicism 1 574
  - Renaissance 9 156–8*, 157; 11 71; 12 538, 540
  - Romanesque 16 687; 32 342
  - 20th cent. 9 159
- doublets 9 265
- drawings 9 26, 222, 223
  - anatomical studies 1 841, 842
  - animal subjects 24 861
  - architectural 2 328–30
    - Futurism 27 788
    - Renaissance 2 329, 330; 5 15
    - 16th cent. 2 330; 14 659; 26 801
  - chalk 5 855, 886
    - Baroque 3 54; 5 866; 7 911; 8 42
    - Mannerism 6 141
    - Renaissance 9 I1; 19 186, 193; 21 758; 25 558, 909; 29 883
    - 17th cent. 21 807
  - charcoal 24 706
  - ink
    - Baroque 2 126; 13 788; 21 766; 24 836
    - Mannerism 19 545; 23 575; 24 199
    - Neo-classicism 12 585
    - Renaissance 3 157; 9 220; 14 871; 19 184, 192; 22 237; 24 861; 32 13
    - 15th cent. 29 407
    - 16th cent. 1 103, 663
    - 17th cent. 6 37

Italy
- drawings
  - ink—cont.
    - 19th cent. 2 320
  - landscape 7 391; 9 218, 223; 13 656
  - life-drawings 21 758
  - metalpoints 3 652; 21 340
  - mythological 5 866; 12 214, 755; 27 209
    - Baroque 11 10
    - Mannerism 6 141
  - pastel 5 878; 24 IV
  - presentation 19 449; 25 557–8*, 558
  - religious 12 554; 26 770; 32 354
    - Baroque 24 835
    - Renaissance 3 651; 19 449; 21 763
  - Renaissance 9 220–21
  - silverpoints 9 217; 19 191, 192
  - wash 26 770; 32 17, 884
  - 16th cent. 25 221; 26 845
  - 17th cent. 7 911
  - 18th cent. 24 846
- dress 9 259, 260–61*, 262–7*; 10 635–6*; 16 760
- drypoints 9 308
- earrings 10 631; 17 527
- earthenwares 10 527
- ebony 14 170
- *écorchés* 9 706
- education (art) 16 777–80*; 23 294
- education (architectural) 16 777–80*
- education (art) 1 103; 16 779
- effigies 3 138; 29 24
- emblem books 1 656; 10 173
- emblems 10 174; 14 416; 27 61, 61, 62
- embossing 10 587
- embroidery 13 195; 16 758–60*, 759; 27 693
- enamel 16 750*; 32 213
  - *basse taille* 13 163, 163, 169, 775
  - Byzantine 16 750
  - champlevé 13 168
  - cloisonné 8 203
  - Early Christian 26 144
  - Gothic 13 168, 169
  - Renaissance 30 497
  - Roman 27 76
  - 11th cent. 32 212
  - 15th cent. 12 VIII3; 32 201
  - 16th cent. 2 454; 16 746
- encyclopedias 20 84; 25 412
- end-papers 4 349
- engravings 9 23; 10 383–4, 394
  - allegorical 28 6
  - architectural 12 23; 24 843
  - Baroque 23 842; 26 310
  - bird's-eye views 24 535; 31 713
  - Renaissance 5 534; 10 383; 12 698; 15 92; 16 779; 23 292; 25 160, 858, 859, 904
  - topographical views 4 272
  - 16th cent. 7 899; 10 386; 11 180, 272; 25 619; 26 229, 823; 32 412
  - 17th cent. 20 320; 28 6; 30 429
  - 18th cent. 16 773; 21 539; 23 753; 24 841
  - 19th cent. 3 771
- erotic art 10 476–7, 477; 12 764
- espresso machines 25 218
- etchings 10 550–53*
  - Baroque 6 34; 16 668
  - 16th cent. 25 641
  - 17th cent. 3 208; 4 89; 10 552; 15 93; 27 153; 30 528
  - 18th cent. 5 598; 10 555; 24 844, 845; 32 113
  - 19th cent. 11 284
- ewers 23 540
- exchanges 32 507
- exedrae 5 21

Italy—cont.
exhibitions **6** 80; **10** 675–6; **14** 867; **15** 826
Etruscan **10** 637, 641
loan **10** 676
photographs **1** 643
17th cent. **27** 171
ex-votos **16** 749; **27** 109–10*
façade decoration **4** 774; **10** 736, 737, *740*, 740–41, 742, 743, 744; **25** 865
façades **4** 776; **26** 318
Baroque **29** *80*
Gothic **2** *2*; **13** *64*; **16** 627
Gothic Revival **28** *393*
Neo-classicism **17** *443*
Renaissance **26** *398*, *399*; **27** *772*; **31** *743*
14th cent. **10** *744*
17th cent. **4** *426*; **10** *736*
factories **11** *63*
fans **10** 781
fibulae **10** *630*; **12** *868*
figurines **16** *737*
Etruscan **10** 625
Palaeolithic **25** 489
Renaissance **8** *101*
Roman **27** 109–10*
18th cent. **22** *681*
filigree **10** 631; **13** 163
finials (scrolls) **17** 569
flax **10** 636
floors **27** 61
fondachi **32** 184
fonts (baptismal) **11** 254*
fora **11** *327*; **26** *748*, 889
forgeries **2** 558; **7** 562; **10** 637, 638–40*
fornices **26** 888, *888*
fortifications **10** 601; **21** 565–7*, *566*
fortresses **11** *688*
foundations **25** 216
fountains **9** 21; **12** 110, 114, 116, 117
Baroque **11** *343*; **16** 698, *700*; **22** *45*; **27** *647*
Gothic **11** *340*
Mannerism **1** *791*; **11** *341*
Renaissance **16** 696; **19** *372*
Roman **12** *68*; **27** *66*
Romanesque **26** *623*
stile liberty **16** *648*
16th cent. **25** *259*; **31** *321*
framemakers **11** 382–3, 384
frames **9** 14; **11** 374, 375, 376, 379–98*, *380*, *381*, *382*, *383*, *384*, *385*, *386*, *388*, *389*, *390*, *391*, *392*, *393*, *394*, *395*, *396*, *397*; **24** 5
friezes **10** *607*, *633*; **21** *342*; **26** *792*, *890*; **27** *26*
frontispieces **4** *397*; **6** *98*; **20** III; **23** *92*; **25** *411*; **26** *841*
furniture **16** 721–32*, 746, 748; **25** 303, 306; **28** 28
Etruscan **10** *633*, 633–4*
Neo-classicism **24** *845*
Surrealism **16** *721*
18th cent. **16** *727*
19th cent. **23** *830*
furniture-makers **16** 726
galleries (iv) (art) **9** *11*; **31** 446
Baroque **16** 771*
picture **9** *15*; **26** *775*
Renaissance **16** 771*
sculpture **9** *15*, 20–22, 23; **16** *773*
garden design **12** 110–12, 114–19, *117*, *118*
gardens **11** 340; **12** 114–19*, *117*, *118*; **32** 547
Baroque **11** *740*, *741*
botanic **4** *483*; **12** 115; **22** 131
hortus conclusus **12** 110, 112
Renaissance **12** 110–12*, *111*, *112*; **16** 633
Roman **12** *68*, 70; **26** *899*
sculpture **9** 21; **26** *845*

Italy
gardens—cont.
16th cent. **4** *287*; **12** *60*, *62*
17th cent. **12** *116*
gates **7** *360*; **16** *634*; **32** *340*
gateways
Egyptian Revival **5** *616*
Neo-classicism **24** *886*
Renaissance **27** 761, *762*
Roman **26** *891*
gay and lesbian art **10** 476; **12** *214*
gem-engraving **12** 256, *256*, 257–9, *257*, *258*, *259*, 260, 261–3, *263*, 264
16th cent. **3** *817*
gems **5** *808*; **16** 751; **32** *212*, *213*
gesso **12** 501
gilding **6** 7, *7*; **11** *383*, *385*, *386*, *389*, *390*, *394*; **12** *538*, *540*, *541*, 628; **16** *728*; **27** *10*; **32** *193*, *201*
glass **16** 740*
aventurine **32** 203
Byzantine **9** 646
chalcedony **3** 270; **12** VIII1; **32** 201, 203, 204
cristallo **3** 270; **21** 719; **32** 201, *201*
ice **32** 202
lattimo **3** 270; **32** 201, *202*, *203*, 203
millefiori **32** 204
porcellana contrafacta **32** 203, *203*
Roman **12** VIII2; **27** 66, *76*
15th cent. **12** VIII3; **32** *201*
16th cent. **32** *202*
20th cent. **32** *205*
glazes **2** 178; **12** 803; **26** 443
glaziers **22** 157
globes **12** *814*
goblets **12** VIII3
gold **7** 536; **16** 741–3*; **19** 351; **32** 212
Byzantine **8** *203*; **32** *212*
Carolingian **5** *808*
Early Christian (*c*. AD 250-843) **26** *144*
Etruscan **10** 624, *630*, 630–32*, *631*, 639; **12** *868*
Gothic **32** *213*
Renaissance **16** 690
Roman **27** 15
13th cent. **7** *536*
15th cent. **12** *583*
16th cent. **2** *454*, *472*; **7** *834*, *835*
17th cent. **16** *753*
19th cent. **16** *752*; **17** *527*
gold leaf **4** *352*; **10** 631; **12** 621
granite **29** 700
grottoes **9** 21; **12** 110, 115, 116; **13** 703
Renaissance **16** 696
16th cent. **5** *183*; **13** *703*
guidebooks **13** 299, 304, 808, 809, 810, 811; **20** 243; **26** 755
7th cent. AD **26** 799
16th cent. **1** 554; **13** 808
17th cent. **18** 814
18th cent. **26** 345
guilds **1** 102; **28** 676; **32** 189–90, 223
artists' **24** 521
glassmakers' **32** 200
masons' **32** 189
painters' **16** 780; **28** 676; **32** 189
wood-carvers **32** 189
guilloche **11** *384*, *386*
guns **2** 459, 462, 464–5, 466, 467
gun stocks **2** 459, 465
gypsum **10** *606*
halls **31** *745*
hangings **16** 760
hardstones **14** *170*, 170–71; **16** 690, 724, 744*, 746–8*
harpsichords **22** 372
helmets **2** 470, *470*, *472*; **6** 157

Italy—cont.
heraldry **14** 404, 406, 410–11*, 412, *415*
herbals **14** 432, 433
heritage **3** 770; **10** 846; **14** 451
historiography **2** 531; **3** 851; **16** 780–82*; **18** 756
holmoi **10** *611*
hose **9** 265
hospitaliae **30** 656
hospitals **11** 72, *72*; **25** *853*; **31** *894*
houses **26** *843*
Etruscan **1** 127; **10** *598*, 599–600*
peristyle **26** 888
Prehistoric **25** 500–501
Renaissance **3** *850*
Roman **14** *441*; **25** *199*; **26** 888
tower **16** 627
16th cent. **19** *203*
19th cent. **4** *246*
human figures **10** 593–4, 624
humanism **14** 866–8*; **16** 658
huts **10** 587
hydriai **10** *615*
hypocausts **26** 888
iconographic programmes **15** 85
iconography **22** 413; **25** 71–2
Byzantine **9** *520*
Etruscan **10** 587, 588–90, 592–6*, 619
Gothic **13** *129*
Renaissance **14** 866
icons **19** *788*; **30** V2; **32** *212*
illusionism **15** 135–40, IV; **27** *497*
imprese **15** 149, 150
incunabula **32** 198
industrial design **15** 826*
ingots **10** 632
initials (manuscript)
Gothic **19** *456*; **23** *506*
Romanesque **26** 666
15th cent. **7** *188*; **25** *465*
inlays **20** 467
inscriptions **10** 588, 589, *590*, 596, 610, 638
insignia **32** 394
insulae **23** *621*; **26** 887
intarsia **20** 467; **29** *860*
interior decoration **16** 709–21*
Baroque **16** *715*
Etruscan **10** *597*
Grotesque **13** *669*; **31** 523
15th cent. **16** *710*
16th cent. **2** *548*
17th cent. **16** *713*
18th cent. **16** *717*, *718*
19th cent. **16** *720*
20th cent. **16** *721*
interlace **15** *882*
inventories **16** 768
iron **10** 624; **16** *708*, 744; **25** 533
istorie **16** *613*, 613–14*
ivory **1** 707; **5** 192; **16** 686, *686*; **23** *660*; **30** *776*
ivory-carvings **16** 799
Etruscan **10** 593, *634*, 634–5*
Gothic **13** 176*, *176*
Islamic **16** 525–6*
Ottonian **23** 659–60, *660*
Romanesque **26** 698
jade **16** 861
japanning **5** 192
jars **16** *733*
jasper **14** I1
jewellery **16** 750–52*; **17** 526
archaeological **17** *527*
Etruscan **10** 593, 631, 635, 636
jugs **10** 626; **12** VIII1
ketubbot **18** *2*, 3
kraters **10** *616*; **13** *527*, *528*, *531*, *533*
kylikes **10** 612
labyrinths **12** 114, *118*, 119
lace **16** *754*, 754–5*; **18** 589, 590, 593
lacquer **18** 614

Italy—cont.
lamps **9** *520*; **17** 573; **27** 103–4, *104*
languages **10** 637
lanterns (architecture) **5** *21*
lapis lazuli **14** I1; **16** *747*
lathes **20** 90
lead **1** *35*; **10** 624; **16** 743
leather **4** 349, 351, 352, *352*, 353; **19** *3*, 3–4*, 5, 6; **30** 657
cuir-bouilli **19** 4
letters **2** 166–7
libraries **2** 365; **8** 601; **14** 867; **16** 776–7*; **21** 468
Mannerism **19** *314*; **21** *452*
17th cent. **4** *426*
lighting **9** *12*; **30** 657, 669
limestone **10** *607*; **29** 701; **31** 523
linen **10** 589, 636; **16** 760; **19** 418; **27** *693*
loggias **12** 110; **19** *634*; **25** *907*
looms **10** 635, 636
loutrophoroi **13** *529*
maiolica **6** 333, I1; **14** 425; **16** 732–6*, *733*, *734*, *735*; **30** 886, *886*; **31** *742*, 747
mantles **17** 569
manuals
architecture **1** 607; **3** 863; **24** 25
drawing **11** 51; **31** 359
gardens **12** 115
iconography **4** 521; **26** *415*, 415–16
manuscript illumination **8** 588
manuscripts **20** 324–5
mythology **22** 412, 414
painting **21** 74
printing **4** 217
stage design **27** 482
manufacturing **15** 826*
manuscript illumination **14** 424; **32** 197–8
Early Christian (*c*. AD 250-843) **16** 654
Gothic **12** *666*; **13** 133, 137, 149; **18** *684*; **20** *331*, *650*
Jewish art **17** 564–5*
Renaissance **4** *19*; **13** *834*; **20** III; **27** *807*
Romanesque **26** 664–6*
12th cent. **16** *655*
14th cent. **1** *640*; **8** *614*; **14** *432*; **15** *93*; **31** *500*
15th cent. **3** *532*; **19** *306*
manuscripts
Byzantine **9** 605
Early Christian (*c*. AD 250-843) **9** 605
maps **16** *584*; **20** 363, *366*
marble **31** 523
Baroque **1** *627*, *629*, *630*, *711*; **3** *262*, *828*, *829*; **4** *406*, *621*; **5** *302*, *377*; **9** *410*; **11** *18*, *189*, *235*, *280*; **13** *815*; **16** *698*; **19** *88*; **20** *47*, *902*, *909*; **26** *773*; **27** *830*; **29** *563*; **31** *790*; **32** *195*
Carolingian **5** *796*
Dominican Order **9** *106*
Etruscan **10** 589, *589*
Gothic **2** *482*, *483*; **7** *334*; **13** *94*, *96*, *97*; **16** *687*; **20** *728*; **23** *587*; **24** *869*, *870*, *872*, *873*, *875*; **26** *400*; **28** *680*; **31** *3*, *4*; **32** *227*
Lombard art **19** *550*
Mannerism **1** *790*, *791*; **8** *511*; **12** *571*; **16** *696*; **27** *203*; **29** *558*, *562*
Neo-classicism **3** *295*, *296*; **5** *627*, *628*; **6** *129*; **16** *705*, *706*; **22** *736*
Néo-Grec **9** *404*
pavonazzetto **29** VIII2

Italy
marble—cont.
Renaissance **1** *456*, *747*; **3** *138*, *158*, *159*; **4** *738*; **5** *300*, *359*, *361*; **7** *367*; **8** *797*, *798*; **9** *123*, *125*; **11** *27*, *28*, *184*, *203*; **16** *691*, *693*, *694*, *770*, *840*, *842*, *844*; **18** *673*; **19** *560*; **21** *434*, *436*, *437*, *438*, *465*, *692*, *693*; **22** *461*; **24** *286*; **26** *439*, *443*; **27** *769*, *770*, *772*, *773*; **29** *24*
Roman **4** 774; **9** *517*; **26** 887, 889; **27** *22*, *23*, *26*, *32*, *40*; **29** *389*
Romanesque **2** *132*; **3** *237*; **5** *550*; **21** *773*; **26** 576; **30** 777, *777*
12th cent. **7** 918–22; **25** 865
13th cent. **7** *919*, *920*
14th cent. **28** *29*
15th cent. **10** *854*; **20** *303*
16th cent. **3** *924*; **6** *90*; **25** *256*; **32** *648*, *649*
17th cent. **14** I1; **21** *755*
18th cent. **21** *890*
20th cent. **4** *101*
markets **19** 888, 889
marks **20** 441, *446*
marquetry **20** 467, 468
martyria **20** *518*
masks **10** 593; **30** 657
masonry **20** 570, 571; **26** 889; **27** 761; **30** 667
master printers **20** 607
mausolea **7** 325; **20** *864*, 866*; **26** *32*, *33*, *794*
medals **14** 419; **16** 690; **20** 921–2*; **24** 863, *863*
Mannerism **6** *140*
Renaissance **1** *556*; **20** 917–19*, *918*; **26** *399*; **29** *387*
15th cent. **12** *583*
16th cent. **20** *919*, 919–20*; **29** *410*
18th cent. **20** *922*
meeting-houses **32** 224, 228
Megillat **17** 573; **21** 48, *49*
metalwork **16** 741*, 743–4*
Etruscan **10** 587, 593, 624–32*, *625*, *626*, *627*, *628*, *629*, *630*, *631*
Gothic **13** 157, 163*
granulation **10** 587, 631
Romanesque **26** 690*
micrography **21** 476
military scenes **10** 595
mills (industrial) **21** 600
mimesis **13** 138–9
miniatures (manuscript illumination)
Gothic **19** *679*
Jewish art **4** *16*; **27** *226*
justice scenes **4** *274*
Renaissance **2** *697*; **7** *467*; **11** *686*; **20** *657*; **28** *752*; **29** *786*
Romanesque **10** *700*; **22** *11*; **26** *665*
13th cent. **4** *274*
14th cent. **13** *319*, *823*; **20** *696*, *710*
15th cent. **8** *173*; **12** *722*, *734*; **21** *464*; **25** *46*
mints **27** *744*
mirror-cases **10** 636
mirror frames **11** 395
mirror handles **10** 627, 635
mirrors **16** 726; **21** 719; **32** 202, 204
Etruscan **10** 589, 595, *595*, 627–30, *628*, 639
wall **21** 720
mixed-media **20** *352*
modelli **8** *13*
drawings **21** 763, *763*, *766*
relief sculpture **11** *279*
sculpture **21** *769*, *770*
modelling **10** 617, 623

Italy—cont.
models 2 336; 10 590; 16 629, 749*; 27 19
monasteries 21 468, 842; 22 10; 24 285
monuments
equestrian 9 127; 10 440; 14 421; 16 688, 690; 23 754
Gothic 13 94–5
Mannerism 12 573; 30 228
Renaissance 6 13; 9 127; 32 363
Roman 27 10
17th cent. 24 696
funerary 5 128; 31 125
Baroque 27 830; 31 127
Neo-classicism 5 628; 16 706; 22 736
public 22 44, 45; 26 763; 27 23, 26
Rome, ancient 26 900
13th cent. 20 321
19th cent. 13 294
triumphal arches 7 920; 21 520; 22 471, 486; 26 748, 797–8*, 798, 832, 891, 901; 31 351
mosaics 7 275; 11 192; 16 655; 21 899; 32 208
Black and White style 27 61
Byzantine 9 573, 581; 22 161; 26 652–3
Early Christian (c. AD 250-843) 2 243; 3 190; 7 223; 9 573; 16 654, 761; 21 523; 27 68, 782, 782–3
Floral style 27 61
Gothic 13 135, 145
opus signinum 27 61
opus tessellatum 27 61
opus vermiculatum 27 61
Renaissance 22 158
Roman 22 159; 23 623; 25 206, 421, 422; 27 60, 61, 61–2*, 62, 65–7*, 66, 68; 31 62
Romanesque 21 898; 26 679–80, 679, 680, 828
Silhouette style 27 61, 62
5th cent. AD 26 32
6th cent. AD 26 35, 36
12th cent. 32 209
13th cent. 6 105; 27 449; 31 193; 32 210, 211
14th cent. 7 318
mother-of-pearl 16 728
mouldings 22 216, 219, 221
mounts (works on paper and scrolls) 22 237
museums 2 168, 365; 9 14, 23; 13 470; 16 769, 770–76*; 22 356; 27 114–15; 32 343
Etruscan 10 637, 640*
Neo-classicism 16 771–2*, 772; 29 640
Renaissance 16 770–71*; 32 15
sculpture 27 271
15th cent. 13 469
17th cent. 6 360
18th cent. 22 361
musical instruments 22 373; 27 445
narratives 22 522; 24 892
Etruscan 10 593, 611, 611, 624
Gothic 13 129
Renaissance 5 820
Roman 26 792
Nativity groups 22 681
necklaces 17 527
necropoleis 6 353; 23 584
neon 16 708
nestoroi 13 526
niches 9 21
niello 11 86; 16 750*
nude figures 23 291–3
Baroque 1 536; 3 829; 5 406, 860, 863, 866; 11 846; 12 764; 20 376; 26 201, 321; 27 816; 29 563
Etruscan 10 589, 589, 595
Greece, ancient 30 339

Italy
nude figures—cont.
Mannerism 1 670; 3 162; 4 857; 6 145; 7 891; 8 511; 12 672; 20 280; 23 293; 24 201; 27 203, 209; 29 558, 562; 30 33, 319; 31 32
Neo-classicism 3 296; 5 627, 886; 16 705; 22 271
Renaissance 3 157, 665; 4 495, 499; 6 3; 12 656; 14 871; 16 693, 694, 696; 19 676; 21 436, 758; 23 292; 24 523; 25 158, 160; 27 773; 28 701; 29 561; 32 17, 809
Roman 14 443; 25 202; 27 14
Rome, ancient 31 60
13th cent. 16 688
16th cent. 10 477; 11 52, 64; 12 736
18th cent. 29 887
20th cent. 16 707; 20 429; 31 445
nymphaea 13 703
office buildings 16 649, 651; 25 218
oil sketches 12 201; 32 347
oinochoai 10 612
oliphants 16 526; 23 400, 401; 26 698
onyx 12 256, 258; 16 746
opera 30 667
opus sectile 7 919
orangeries 9 21
oratories (i) (chapels) 5 18
orchards 12 110
orders (architecture) 23 485–7
Corinthian 6 358; 23 489; 26 889
Doric 4 648; 6 358; 23 488; 27 761
giant 23 492, 493
Ionic 6 358
Renaissance 6 358
Solomonic 23 488
Tuscan 6 358
organ shutters 23 501; 31 430
orillions 21 566
ornament 23 541, 544
overdoors 9 21; 23 678
overgarments 9 260–61
painting 2 178; 6 1–5*; 7 627; 11 379; 16 652–83*; 19 351; 23 376; 24 3, 4, 5, 7, 7, 8, 8; 30 425
allegorical 1 663
Baroque 12 764; 24 341; 28 39; 30 860
Divisionism 25 567
Mannerism 1 656; 4 857; 12 668; 31 32, 33; 32 221
Renaissance 1 655, 656; 4 494, 495; 9 184; 15 86; 25 898; 27 848; 29 362; 32 14
14th cent. 23 743
16th cent. 11 52; 23 877
17th cent. 4 539; 11 40; 21 89
18th cent. 6 125; 29 889
19th cent. 23 851; 24 345, 346
animal subjects 10 835; 19 634
architectural 2 338, 338–9, 343
18th cent. 26 898
Baroque 5 383; 6 108; 16 668–76*; 26 321
battle 3 387, 388; 22 130
Baroque 19 309
Renaissance 6 2; 31 515
16th cent. 10 762
cabinet pictures 18 871
ceiling
Baroque 3 97; 26 837
Mannerism 32 348
Renaissance 21 20
Roman 27 55
17th cent. 3 57; 30 355
conservation 7 738–9
di sotto in sù 15 136
display 9 14–15, 15; 22 357; 26 775

Italy
painting—cont.
Early Christian (c. AD 250-843) 16 653–4*
Etruscan 12 287; 16 652, 652–3
fêtes champêtres 11 35; 31 71
fresco 7 457–8; 11 761; 13 803; 16 710–11; 20 509, 553; 28 337
Baroque 5 863; 6 28; 7 908; 9 92; 11 9, 24, 53, 681; 13 786; 16 669, 674; 18 733, 735; 27 488; 29 40; 30 372, 858
Benedictine Order 28 702
Carmelite Order 5 778
Early Christian (c. AD 250-843) 6 31, 32
Etruscan 10 617
Franciscan Order 11 709, 710; 12 691, 692, 693; 20 506
Gothic 11 888, 889, 890, 891, 892; 13 132, 135, 136, 144, 145, 145; 20 506, 775; 29 405, 406; 32 II2
Grotesque 31 523
Mannerism 2 494; 7 886; 8 182; 12 283, 755, 756; 15 IV; 21 444, 447; 24 420; 25 222, 223; 26 816; 27 649, 651, 653; 29 741; 30 800; 32 350
Neo-classicism 21 528
Renaissance 2 36, 37, 38, 607, 725; 4 194, 317; 5 816; 6 12, 13; 7 457; 8 504; 9 265; 11 13, 117, 185, 293, 710; 12 550; 13 261; 16 613, 660, 664, 763; 19 444, 450; 20 305, 533, 534; 21 97; 22 413; 24 522, 531, 755, 762, 764, 831, 862; 25 250, 901; 26 184, 457; 27 850; 28 80, 658, 702, 703; 29 360; 31 513, 514; 32 16
Renaissance: Early Renaissance 11 7
Romanesque 1 819; 27 784
13th cent. 2 622, 623, 624; 6 103, 104; 7 315; 20 697, 698, 713; 21 107
14th cent. 1 726, 727; 2 16, 187, 338, 626, 627; 9 260; 11 709; 12 682, 684, 685, 687, 688, 691, 692, 693, 695; 19 665; 20 551; 21 113, 845; 24 VIII1; 28 489, 685, 686; 31 104
15th cent. 1 554; 6 14; 9 262, 263; 12 704; 16 710; 20 554, 555, 558; 26 827; 27 175; 28 682, 687; 33 625
16th cent. 1 17; 3 859; 4 271, 840; 5 455; 11 762; 18 707; 26 727; 27 497; 28 688; 33 716, 717, 719
17th cent. 1 552; 4 813; 11 216, 874; 27 121
18th cent. 4 277; 8 192; 12 528
19th cent. 28 136
frescoes
Renaissance 27 846
Futurism 3 116; 4 200; 11 864; 27 446; 28 507
genre 12 287, 288–9*, 291–2*; 29 375
bambocciate 18 624
Baroque 5 706, 707, 859; 8 143; 12 288, 305; 20 264, 640; 21 701; 30 863
Mannerism 1 670; 22 448; 29 784, 785
Realism (style) 28 705
Renaissance 27 890
Romanticism 8 5
Verismo 16 679
16th cent. 27 622

Italy
painting
genre—cont.
17th cent. 6 347; 21 483; 26 95, 772
18th cent. 6 351; 19 634; 24 706
19th cent. 5 783; 8 136, 137; 10 834; 19 71; 32 197
20th cent. 5 919; 22 84; 28 792; 31 445
glass 12 798
Gothic 13 133, 138–9, 146, 149*, 155; 16 661
Greece, ancient 16 652
grisaille 13 673, 676
hanging 9 14–15, 15
history 14 581–3
Baroque 7 907; 11 15, 287; 20 96; 24 340
Futurism 5 848
Jesuit Order 17 511
Mannerism 4 399
Neo-classicism 12 41; 16 677; 21 132
Realism (style) 6 136
Renaissance 9 96; 10 766; 14 582
Romanticism 3 903; 14 266
15th cent. 20 319
17th cent. 29 254; 30 304; 31 437
18th cent. 5 765; 8 158; 12 40; 24 10, 11; 31 313
19th cent. 3 857; 5 556
hunting scenes 6 38; 19 635; 28 12; 31 515
Islamic 16 525–6
landscape 18 704–5, 707–10*, 711, 712–13; 20 680; 22 414
Baroque 5 861; 9 91; 18 709; 28 220
Italy: 17th cent. 30 60
Mannerism 12 670
Renaissance 18 705
16th cent. 1 18; 18 707
17th cent. 4 487; 7 390, 395, 396, 398; 9 376, 377; 10 159, 160; 25 66; 27 151, 152
18th cent. 4 154; 19 525; 26 324
19th cent. 7 572; 8 716; 11 285
20th cent. 29 10
literary themes
Baroque 6 36
Renaissance 2 228
Romanticism 14 265
14th cent. 6 1
15th cent. 28 70
17th cent. 21 808
Mannerism 12 671; 16 668*; 20 278
marine 7 392; 8 451
miniatures 31 103
murals 16 681, 708; 22 332; 25 652; 28 793
mythological 22 412–14
Baroque 1 535, 536; 4 54; 5 453; 6 126; 7 684; 8 141, 144; 11 680, 846; 12 661; 16 672; 20 265, 376, 496; 26 199, 201; 27 817; 30 857, 859
Mannerism 4 400; 7 891; 12 672; 16 666; 23 293, 377; 24 201; 30 33; 31 34, 35, 36, 39; 32 17
Neo-classicism 17 852; 22 271
Renaissance 4 495, 499; 6 3; 7 322; 9 186; 16 660; 19 676; 24 523, 770; 28 701
Renaissance: High Renaissance 31 429
Rococo 25 3
16th cent. 7 892; 10 477; 12 736

Italy
painting
mythological—cont.
17th cent. 8 99; 12 707; 20 83; 23 750; 27 178; 30 526
18th cent. 3 109; 11 21; 12 22, 39; 20 843; 29 887
panel 13 146
pietàs
Baroque 5 860
Mannerism 7 468, 469; 31 40
Renaissance 3 662; 28 333
15th cent. 5 179; 25 848
quadratura 15 137–40*; 16 714
Baroque 5 280, 652; 7 909; 9 109; 12 199, 663; 16 715; 22 327; 25 415; 27 522; 29 38
Dominican Order 9 109
17th cent. 21 732
religious
Baroque 1 672, 673; 3 33, 95, 353, 381, 713, 737, 834; 4 334, 413; 5 405, 406, 442, 694, 695, 704, 709, 710, 713, 714, 715, 718, 862; 6 27, 33, 110, 114, 337, 338, 339; 7 312, 313, 683, 903; 8 142, 147, 148; 9 76, 77, 89; 10 746; 11 678; 12 306, 307, 589, 662; 13 754, 785, 787; 16 671, 673; 18 731, 732; 19 472, 816; 20 266, 377, 598; 21 526; 22 530; 24 801, 836; 25 562, 564, 643; 26 197, 198, 309, 311, 312, 397; 27 489, 490, 816, 864; 28 473; 29 37, 252, 544, 545; 30 798, 855; 31 791
Camaldolese Order 5 450
Dominican Order 9 107
Early Netherlandish style 17 703
Gothic 3 248, 808; 9 344; 11 381, 892; 12 298, 579, 580; 13 129, 146; 16 826; 19 674, 680, 684; 20 507, 508, 509, 675; 24 XII4; 29 598
Mannerism 3 14, 254, 255, 256, 344, 345, 346, 468; 4 857; 7 776, 887, 888, 890; 11 269, 392; 16 667; 19 383; 20 280; 22 392; 23 574; 24 200; 27 208, 620, 652, 732; 31 6, 8, 9, 11, 12, 37; 32 102, 227, 352, 353
Renaissance 1 818; 2 32, 33, 179, 182, 290; 3 99, 299, 650, 656, 665, 666, 751, 782; 4 336, 496, 497, 653; 5 818, 819, 820; 6 3, 4, 12, 356; 7 320, 321, 564; 9 95; 11 294, 388, 702; 12 552, 708, 711, 753; 13 280; 16 846; 19 182, 185, 442, 443, 448, 895; 20 123, 306, 307, 309, 313, 453, 532, 533, 771; 21 96, 748; 22 108, 133, 522; 23 94; 24 365, 524, 538, 763, 769, 829; 25 157, 161, 162, 251, 569, 897, 900, 903; 26 458; 27 847, 862, 891; 28 85, 331, 334; 29 2, 26; 30 781; 31 444; 32 12, 364, 365, 657; 33 701, 702
Renaissance: Early Renaissance 8 167, 169; 16 662
Renaissance: High Renaissance 31 431, 432
Rococo 9 48
Verismo 22 99, 100
13th cent. 7 815, 816; 12 760; 13 818, 819; 20 407

Italy
painting
religious—cont.
14th cent. **3** *247*; **5** *656*; **7** *337*; **9** *107*; **12** *703*; **15** *94*; **16** *839*; **19** *454*, *667*, *669*, *671*; **23** *91*, *95*, *351*; **24** *31*; **28** *435*, *677*; **31** *105*, *277*; **32** *625*
15th cent. **3** *227*; **4** *506*; **5** *913*; **7** *543*, *925*, *926*; **12** *715*; **20** 51; **24** *781*; **27** *619*
16th cent. **1** *570*, *571*; **3** *317*; **5** *546*, *852*, *853*, *857*; **6** *86*, *362*; **11** *721*; **12** *556*; **13** *293*; **21** *94*; **25** *59*, *149*, *729*; **27** *655*; **28** *83*
17th cent. **2** *619*; **5** *635*; **7** *308*; **10** *157*, *158*, *188*, *189*; **11** *41*; **13** *276*; **19** *452*; **21** *53*; **22** *82*, *83*; **23** *266*, *700*; **24** VII1; **25** *642*; **28** *62*, *379*, *787*; **29** *410*; **30** *303*; **32** *499*
18th cent. **4** *540*; **6** *568*; **7** *310*; **12** *42*; **13** *741*, *742*; **15** *148*; **20** *806*; **24** *704*, *705*; **28** *17*; **31** *314*
19th cent. **23** *853*; **28** *355*, *356*
20th cent. **13** *872*
Renaissance
Early Renaissance **16** 657–63*
High Renaissance **16** 663–8*
restoration **7** 738–9
Roman **16** 653
sacra conversazione **3** *663*; **27** *495*
Mannerism **7** *885*; **12** *673*
Renaissance **3** *303*, *305*, *917*; **5** *307*; **7** *322*; **8** *4*; **9** *100*; **13** *259*; **19** *323*, *441*, *447*, *675*, *711*; **20** *312*; **24** *889*; **28** *700*; **29** *3*
15th cent. **20** *845*
16th cent. **23** *876*
secco **13** 132, 135; **28** *337*, *338*, *339*
social realism **21** *473*
Spazialismo **11** *282*
still-lifes **12** 11; **29** 664, 665, 666, 667, 668–9
Baroque **3** *322*; **16** *675*; **29** *667*
Roman **29** *664*
16th cent. **3** 200; **27** 622
20th cent. **22** *76*
tomb
Etruscan **10** 591, 594, 617–24*, *618*, *619*, *620*, *621*, *622*, *623*; **30** 346; **32** 118, 744
topographical views **11** *214*
16th cent. **4** *271*; **32** *409*
18th cent. **13** *302*; **32** *410*
townscapes **10** *677*; **20** *414*; **31** *248*; **32** *225*
20th cent. **26** *777*
urban life **28** *706*; **33** *612*
vanitas **31** 883
vase **10** 591, 593, *594*, 611–16, *614*, *615*, *616*
vedute **2** 342; **31** 155; **32** 110
16th cent. **9** 181
17th cent. **7** *509*
18th cent. **2** *343*; **5** *595*, *596*, *597*; **13** *743*, *744*; **24** *10*, *11*; **32** *112*
vedute ideate **3** *416*; **13** 347
wall **7** 275; **12** 621
Byzantine **9** 581
Carolingian **5** *798*
Early Christian (*c.* AD 250–843) **6** *70*; **9** *563*; **26** *831*
Etruscan **10** 587, 616–24*, *618*, *619*, *620*, *621*, *622*, *623*; **32** 118, 744
Gothic **13** 144–7*
Jewish art **17** *534*, 557
Ottonian **23** 649–50
Renaissance **32** *805*, 806

Italy
painting
wall—cont.
Roman **9** *563*; **12** *69*; **14** *444*; **25** *204*; **26** *788*; **27** *48*, *49*, *51*, *53*, 53–6, *54*; **32** I2
Romanesque **7** *364*; **26** 650–51, *651*, 652–3, *826*
Romanticism **5** *366*
9th cent. AD **27** 806
14th cent. **6** *467*; **16** *656*
17th cent. **20** *841*
watercolours **11** *190*
13th cent. **9** *258*
18th cent. **8** *160*
20th cent. **16** 679–83*, *680*, *682*
palaces **22** 413; **23** 809
Renaissance **23** 809–10
Roman **26** *895*
see also PALAZZI
palazzi **16** 629, 630; **23** 806, 835–6*
Baroque **1** *622*; **13** *752*; **16** *562*, *644*, *764*; **17** *709*; **20** *45*; **27** *320*; **32** *187*
Gothic **4** *773*, *775*; **13** *64*; **24** *519*; **28** *675*, *683*; **32** *628*
Mannerism **12** *754*; **23** *864*, *865*, *868*; **26** *839*
Palladianism **3** *864*
Razionalismo **26** *15*
Renaissance **1** *562*, *607*; **2** *593*; **3** *16*; **4** *649*, 651; **5** *181*; **7** *518*, *905*; **10** *767*; **16** *629*; **18** *861*; **21** *469*; **23** *810*, *836*; **24** *533*; **26** *820*; **27** *742*, *758*, *760*; **28** *468*; **32** *342*
13th cent. **11** *212*; **31** *237*
14th cent. **32** *218*
15th cent. **27** *189*; **32** *219*
16th cent. **3** *767*; **12** *752*; **13** *649*; **28** *460*
17th cent. **11** *213*; **20** *521*; **27** *194*; **28** *733*
18th cent. **5** *914*; **11** *814*; **22** *388*
19th cent. **3** *50*
20th cent. **3** *327*
paper **10** 381, 728; **24** 48, 51, 55; **31** 258
paperweights **32** 204
papier mâché **12** *814*; **24** 62; **25** III
parchment **24** 107
parks **12** 116–17; **24** 179
parterres de broderie **12** 118
pastiglia **6** 5–6*, *6*; **11** *383*, *384*, *393*; **24** *249*
patchwork **24** 252
paternoster beads **16** 751
patronage **13** 130; **16** 760–65*, 777; **24** 249; **32** 224
pattern books **16** 759; **24** 269, 271
silver **12** 590
textiles **16** 759
pavements **30** 886
pavilions (buildings) **26** *903*
paxes **11** *86*
pearls **16** 751
pectoral crosses **8** *203*
pedestals **9** 21; **24** 316
pendants (jewellery) **10** *635*
perfume burners **9** *520*
pergolas **12** 110, 112
periaktoi **30** 657, 667
periodicals **24** 423, 447–9*; **32** 233
periods
Archaic **10** 587*
Classical **10** 587–8*
Early Iron Age **10** 587*
Etruscan **10** 587–8*
Hellenistic **10** 588*
Iron Age **25** 533
Orientalizing **10** 587*
Villanovan *see* Early Iron Age
peristyles **26** *870*

Italy—cont.
perspective **16** 658; **20** 529; **30** 654, 656, 668
colour **24** 493
linear **24** 486–7
15th cent. **9** 98, 101
pewter **16** 743
picture rails **9** 14
piers (ii) (masonry) **24** 752
pietàs **24** 776–7
pietre dure **14** I1; **16** 746–8*
pigments **1** 588; **10** 617
pilasters **26** 577
pilgrim flasks **16** *736*; **32** *201*
pine **33** 326
pitchers **32** *202*
pithoi **10** 613
plaques **26** 486
Early Christian (*c.* AD 250–843) **16** 686, *686*
Etruscan **10** 593, 620–21, 634–5
16th cent. **21** 529
plaquettes **1** *35*; **16** 689; **21** 783; **25** *19*, 19–21*, *20*
plaster **9** 14, *403*; **12** *268*; **27** *18*, *19*; **29** 829–33*, 843; **31** 523
Byzantine **29** 816–17
Early Christian (*c.* AD 250–843) **29** 816–17
plastics **16** *708*
platters **16** *737*
plinths **9** 23
polychromy **13** *124*; **25** III, V1; **26** *877*; **30** *498*
pools **26** *899*
poplar **33** 326
porcelain **16** 736–9*; **25** 193
blue-and-white ware **4** 176*
hard-paste **16** *737*, *738*
soft-paste **4** 176; **16** *736*, *737*
16th cent. **7** 165
porphyry **27** *43*; **30** 777
portae regiae **30** 656
portals **20** 820; **21** 773; **26** 621; **33** 188
porch **33** 188
Romanesque **24** *858*; **26** *620*
porticos **6** *18*; **25** 265
portraits **20** 509
coins **6** 147
drawings **2** *373*; **10** *521*; **12** *202*; **19** *205*; **21** *449*
engravings **3** *207*; **25** *411*
gem-engraving **12** *257*, 262
group **5** *852*; **17** *704*; **25** *894*
group: 16th cent. **9** *266*
medals **6** *140*; **16** 690; **24** *863*; **29** *408*
painting **2** 180; **5** 822; **16** 660, 665
Abstraction-Création **25** *447*
Baroque **3** *382*, *383*; **4** *292*; **9** *477*, *480*; **12** *308*, *660*; **20** *378*; **23** *321*; **25** *285*; **27** *491*; **29** *42*; **30** *40*
Early Netherlandish style **17** *704*
Etruscan **10** 620
Mannerism **3** *202*; **4** *858*; **5** *843*; **11** *187*, *390*, *391*; **12** *669*; **24** *198*; **31** *14*, *42*
Pittura Metafisica **8** *604*
Renaissance **2** *181*; **3** *100*, *302*, *657*, *659*, *664*; **4** *284*; **5** *128*, *743*, *820*; **9** *263*; **11** *401*, *700*, *704*; **19** *183*, *202*, *711*, *712*; **21** *16*; **22** *109*, *134*; **24** *863*; **25** *466*, *905*; **26** *817*, *818*; **28** *334*; **31** *741*; **32** *11*, *658*
Renaissance: Early Renaissance **16** *659*
Rococo **25** *3*
16th cent. **2** *93*, *374*; **5** *852*; **9** *266*; **23** *878*, *879*; **24** *233*
17th cent. **8** *274*; **29** *33*
18th cent. **12** *560*; **20** 805; **21** *133*; **31** *292*

Italy
portraits
painting—cont.
19th cent. **4** 252, *253*; **5** *555*; **21** *624*; **25** *894*
20th cent. **11** *397*
sculpture **16** 690, 749
Baroque **11** *189*
Etruscan **10** *608*
Gothic **2** *483*
Neo-classicism **3** *295*
relief **12** *542*; **13** *911*
Roman **27** *21*
17th cent. **7** *842*
self-portraits **12** *534*; **27** *150*; **32** *191*
Baroque **12** *308*; **20** *378*
Mannerism **24** *198*
Renaissance **12** *542*; **32** *19*
16th cent. **2** *93*, *373*
18th cent. **21** *133*; **29** *889*
19th cent. **21** *625*
waxes **16** 749
woodcuts **32** *19*
posters **7** *656*; **25** 348
potter's wheels **25** 543
pottery **10** 613–15; **13** 370; **25** 309
alla porcellana **4** 176; **16** 733
a quartieri **16** 734
arlecchini ware **16** 735, *735*
Arretine ware **27** *107*
Black-figure **10** *594*, *614*, 614–15*, *615*
Black-glazed **10** 616*
Bucchero **10** 593, 611–13*, *612*
Candiana ware **16** 395
compendario **16** 735
Etruscan **10** 587, 593, 609–16*; **13** 540–42
Etrusco-Corinthian **10** 613–14*, *614*
Etrusco-Geometric **10** 610–11*, *611*
Gnathia ware **13** 539
Greece, ancient **13** 473, 525–33*, *526*, *527*, *528*, *529*, *531*, *533*, 538
impasto ware **10** *599*, 609–10*, *610*
Istoriato **16** 734, *734*, 735
Italo-Moresque ware **16** 733
latesini ware **16** 735
lustreware **16** 734
Malacena ware **10** 616
Orientalizing style **10** 611*
Ornate style **13** 526
Plain style **13** 526
Polychrome ware **10** 613
Prehistoric **25** 543; **32** *563*
Red-figure **6** 333; **10** 615–16*, *616*; **13** 485, 487, 517, 525–33*, *526*, *527*, *528*, *529*, *531*, *533*; **30** 339
Red ware **10** 613*
relief-blue ware **16** 733, *733*
Roman **6** 333
tin-glazed ware **14** 425
Villanovan culture **32** 562
pouncing **25** 378, 379, *379*
predellas **7** X; **8** *443*; **20** *532*; **25** 462–4, *463*; **26** *456*; **31** 431
printing **8** 37, *37*; **14** 867; **16** 360; **24** 55; **32** 198
print publishers **10** 389; **25** 625
prints **21** *895*; **23** *115*
monotypes **6** 32, *34*
prisons **25** *636*
propaganda **25** 652
proportions (human) **14** *871*, *873*
pulpits **16** *723*; **24** *872*; **25** 723–4
Gothic **25** *724*
Renaissance **20** *114*; **25** *725*
Romanesque **16** 688; **21** *774*; **26** *626*, *627*
12th cent. **21** *536*
pyxides (boxes) **10** *634*
railway stations **21** *521*

Italy—cont.
ramps **12** 115
rapiers **2** *454*
rediscovery **10** 636–8*
religion **10** 588–90*, 591
reliquaries **5** *808*; **9** *520*; **13** 169; **26** *144*; **31** *535*
replicas **2** 141; **7** 562
representation **13** *129*
reservoirs **25** *60*
restoration **4** 247–8; **7** 738–9; **10** 639–40
revetments **10** 593
rings **16** 751
roads **26** 887
rock art **25** 475
rock crystal **3** *817*; **12** *259*; **16** 744–5*, *746*; **26** *485*, 486
rolls **26** 665; **27** 615
romance manuscripts **26** 564*
rond-points **12** 119
roofs **1** 127; **13** 64
rotundas **27** *236*, 236–7
ruffs **9** 266–7
sacrimonti **27** 497–8, *498*; **31** *898*
saints' lives **16** 837
samplers **27** *693*
sanctuaries **25** *421*; **31** *58*
sarcophagi **27** 829–31
Baroque **27** *830*
Early Christian (*c.* AD 250–843) **16** 686
Etruscan **10** 588, 594, *607*
Punic **10** 592
Roman **9** *517*
sard **12** *263*
scabbards **19** *3*
scaenae fissa **30** 656
scaenae frontes **30** *655*
scagliola **28** 28
scena per angolo **30** 668, *668*
schola cantorum **28** *141*
scissors **8** *286*
screens (i) (architectural) **21** *774*; **28** 292, 293; **30** 655, 656; **32** 217
scripts **14** 867; **28** 305, 306, *307*
sculpture **1** 711; **11** 192; **12** 110, 111, 116; **16** 683–709*, 734; **30** 496–8*; **33** 2, *3*
allegorical **4** *621*; **5** *176*; **33** *726*
Baroque **16** *700*
Mannerism **8** *511*; **12** *570*; **20** *279*
Renaissance **5** *359*; **16** *766*; **21** *436*, *437*; **26** *439*
Romanesque **2** *132*
16th cent. **20** *778*
animal subjects **12** *572*
Mannerism **12** *572*
architectural **9** 21; **10** 743, 744
Etruscan **10** 588, 593, 595, 596, *604*
Gothic **5** *430*; **13** *93*; **26** *400*; **32** *227*
Renaissance **11** *201*; **32** *226*
Romanesque **10** 742; **21** *773*
13th cent. **14** 647; **32** *208*
14th cent. **10** *744*
Arte Povera **2** *527*; **16** *708*
Baroque **7** *276*; **16** 697–704*; **20** *47*; **27** *830*
bronze **2** *140*, *141*; **10** 587; **12** *539*; **19** *202*; **27** *830*; **30** 339
Baroque **2** *609*; **5** *533*
Etruscan **10** *605*, *608*; **16** *684*
Futurism **4** *201*; **11** *866*
Mannerism **3** *162*, *469*; **6** *142*, *145*; **12** *572*, *573*; **30** *228*
Renaissance **16** *690*; **27** *448*; **29** *567*; **32** *105*, *360*, *362*, *363*
Roman **14** *443*; **27** *9*, *10*
17th cent. **7** *842*; **24** *696*
20th cent. **16** *707*; **20** *353*, *429*
Cistercian Order **13** 97–8
colossal statues **7** *842*

Italy
sculpture—cont.
display 9 15, 20–22, 22, 23; 11 190; 16 770, 773; 22 361; 26 899
Early Christian (c. AD 250-843) 16 686*
Etruscan 10 587, 589, 603, 604, 606, 639; 16 684; 32 744
Futurism 11 866
Gothic 13 87–92*, 93*, 123–4*; 16 688*
Campania 13 98*
Emilia-Romagna 13 95–6*
Late Gothic 16 692*
Lazio 13 97–8*
Lombardy 13 94–5*
Tuscany 13 93–4*
Umbria 13 96–7*
Veneto 13 95*
Greece, ancient 30 339
korai 10 593
kouroi 10 593
Lombard art 16 686
Mannerism 12 571; 16 695–7*
marble
Baroque 1 711; 3 828, 829; 9 410; 11 18, 189; 20 47, 909; 27 347; 29 563
Etruscan 10 589
Gothic 2 482, 483; 13 94, 96, 97; 20 728; 24 873, 875 26 400
Mannerism 8 511; 16 691, 696; 27 203; 29 558, 562
Neo-Classicism 3 295; 296; 16 705; 22 736
Renaissance 1 747; 3 158; 4 738; 5 359, 361; 7 367; 9 123; 11 27, 203; 16 693, 694, 766, 840; 21 434, 436, 437, 438; 22 32, 461; 26 439; 27 769, 770, 773; 29 24
Roman 27 23, 32; 29 VIII2
13th cent. 2 480
15th cent. 20 303
16th cent. 32 648, 649
18th cent. 21 890
monumental 10 588, 593; 12 539
Mannerism 1 790
Renaissance 16 694; 27 773
mythological
Baroque 3 829; 29 563
Etruscan 10 589
Mannerism 3 162; 6 142, 145; 12 572; 27 203; 29 558, 562
Neo-classicism 5 627; 16 705
Renaissance 2 140, 141; 3 158; 16 693
Roman 14 443; 27 9, 22; 29 389
Neo-classicism 16 704–7*
Néo-Grec 9 404
pietàs 21 434
relief 16 749; 27 23, 26
Baroque 1 629; 5 377; 11 235; 13 815; 19 88; 22 478; 29 29
Carolingian 5 796
Dominican Order 9 106
Etruscan 10 593, 593
Gothic 7 334; 11 200; 16 687; 23 586, 587; 24 869, 870, 874
Lombard art 19 550
Mannerism 12 574
Renaissance 1 456, 748; 3 159, 260, 637, 860; 8 798; 9 125, 130; 11 184, 693; 12 540, 541; 16 689, 692, 842, 844; 19 208, 688; 20 622; 21 693; 24 756; 25 III; 26 327, 443, 444, 446, 766; 30 508
Roman 26 792; 27 38, 40, 43; 31 369
Italy
sculpture
relief—cont.
Romanesque 3 236; 5 550; 11 6; 21 774; 24 194, 195; 26 623, 627; 32 344
13th cent. 9 106
15th cent. 11 896; 22 476
16th cent. 19 556, 557
19th cent. 32 122
religious
Baroque 1 711; 2 609; 3 262, 828, 832; 9 410; 11 18, 280; 16 698; 20 909; 31 790
Gothic 2 482; 20 728; 24 873, 875; 28 680
Gothic: Lombardy 13 94
Mannerism 3 469; 16 696
Renaissance 4 738, 739; 5 361; 9 123, 129; 11 203; 12 539; 16 690, 840; 18 673; 19 560; 20 543, 544, 907; 22 32, 461; 23 90; 26 331; 27 448, 769, 770, 775, 776; 29 561; 32 105, 360, 362
15th cent. 10 854; 18 859
16th cent. 3 496; 6 90; 25 256; 31 787; 32 649
17th cent. 10 800; 21 755
18th cent. 21 890
Renaissance 7 783; 16 688–95*; 30 497, 498
Early Renaissance 16 689–93*
High Renaissance 16 693–5*
Roman 27 14, 18, 19, 21, 32; 29 VIII2
Romanesque 7 455; 16 687–8*; 26 595, 619*, 625–8*, 644*
Abruzzi 26 625*
Emilia-Romagna 26 621*
Lazio 26 624*
Lombardy 26 620*
Tuscany 26 622–4*
Umbria 26 625*
Veneto 26 622*
stone 13 87–92*, 93–8*, 93; 26 619*, 620*, 620, 621*, 622–4*, 625*, 626–8*
terracotta 23 90
tomb
Baroque 1 627; 16 704; 27 347
Gothic 2 480; 13 96, 97
Neo-classicism 22 736
Renaissance 1 747; 3 138; 4 737; 7 367; 8 797; 11 27; 16 841; 21 438; 29 24
14th cent. 22 475
Verismo 9 178, 403
wood 13 123–4*; 26 644*
Renaissance 9 129
15th cent. 20 303
17th cent. 30 228
19th cent. 12 268; 27 207
20th cent. 4 101; 5 279; 16 707–9*
scuole 28 37; 32 226
sets 30 667, 668
settlements 25 473, 502
sgraffito 23 754
shawls 8 37
shell structures 22 806
shelves 9 30
shields 14 405, 410–11, 412, 413
shops 23 621; 26 887
shrines (i) (cult) 13 94; 28 632
signatures 10 629; 16 685; 20 441
silk 11 193; 16 445, 752–4*, 753, 760; 21 600; 27 693; 28 716, 717
bizarre 4 103
chinoiserie 7 167
Gothic 13 197, 197
silver 5 917; 9 30, 520; 11 86; 12 868; 16 690, 741, 741–3*; 20 922; 25 19; 32 212
Etruscan 10 624, 630–32*, 632
Italy—cont.
silver-gilt 5 807; 6 140; 9 520; 16 541, 742, 746; 25 19, 20
Gothic 13 163
silver-stain 13 193
sinopie 28 778
situlae 28 806, 807
spalliere 9 30; 16 711; 29 359–62*, 361, 362
spinets 22 372–3
spires 2 177; 29 414
spolia 26 843
sporting scenes 10 594, 594
sports centres 22 806
sprinklers 32 203
squares (town)
Baroque 3 836
Mannerism 21 454
Neo-classicism 16 648; 31 442
Renaissance 2 593; 11 177
Rococo 16 639
12th cent. 28 675
13th cent. 11 212
16th cent. 27 483
17th cent. 6 18; 31 439
18th cent. 19 685
19th cent. 28 801
stadia 29 489
stage design 30 655, 656–7*, 657, 667–9*, 668
Baroque 25 414
Renaissance 19 195; 28 470
16th cent. 5 184; 27 740
18th cent. 12 25
stage machinery 30 657, 668
stage scenery 30 654, 657
Fortuny cupola 11 326
stained glass 29 504
Gothic 13 192–3*, 193
Romanesque 26 702
13th cent. 2 631
16th cent. 13 827; 29 504
staircases 12 115, 116; 29 521, 525; 32 225, 229
Baroque 26 760, 814; 27 711, 729
18th cent. 31 895
stamping 20 509
statuettes 9 21; 29 568–70*, 572–3*
Baroque 2 610; 16 700
bronze 16 689
Etruscan 10 587
Greece, ancient 30 339
Mannerism 29 569
Renaissance 1 162; 3 861; 25 158; 26 327, 330
Roman 12 68; 25 202
15th cent. 3 636
16th cent. 9 340
steel 2 470, 472
stelae 10 587, 594
stitches 16 759
stone 5 430; 7 516, 517; 13 87–92*, 93–8*, 93; 16 692; 26 619*, 620*, 620, 621*, 622–4*, 625–8*; 32 744
stools 6 388; 10 633
strapwork 32 647
streets 10 602; 25 196
stucco 2 541; 4 776; 16 712, 712, 713, 722; 25 578; 26 400; 29 812, 813, 829–33*, 843; 30 656; 32 193, 550
Baroque 1 626; 16 704; 29 830, 832
Byzantine 29 816–17, 817
Early Christian (c. AD 250-843) 29 816–17, 817
Etruscan 29 814*
Lombard art 16 687*
Mannerism 30 800
Renaissance 29 830
Roman 27 53, 69–72*, 70, 71
stucco bianco 29 812
studies 11 64
studioli 9 11, 14, 21; 16 770; 29 860, 861
Italy—cont.
studios 2 170; 6 98; 10 196; 29 853, 889; 30 121
surveys, photographic 22 27
sword hilts 2 454; 7 835
swords 2 453
synagogues 17 543, 544, 545, 546, 547, 548
tabernacles (ii) (receptacle) 32 215
tables 10 633; 14 426; 16 726
tapestries 20 318, 323; 30 314, 319; 32 205
Mannerism 30 319
14th cent. 16 755–8*, 756
15th cent. 16 711
16th cent. 11 193; 16 757
17th cent. 30 322
18th cent. 30 324
tas 17 569
taste 20 242
tazze 26 485
teapots 16 738
tempera 20 557; 30 425
temples 9 21
Etruscan 2 355, 356; 10 588, 593, 596, 600, 600–601*, 601; 26 886; 30 435
Greece, ancient 16 622; 30 339
podium 23 622; 26 888
Renaissance 4 648
Roman 2 167; 26 793, 887–8, 888, 898; 30 436
temple-theatres 26 888, 888, 889
terraces 12 115, 116
terracotta 1 707; 30 496–8*, 501*
Baroque 11 279; 21 770
Etruscan 1 127; 10 587, 588, 593, 603, 604, 633; 32 119
Greece, ancient 21 342
Mannerism 12 570
Renaissance 3 260; 8 101; 9 124; 20 907; 23 90; 25 V1; 26 331, 443, 444, 445, 446; 30 497, 498, 501, 508
Roman 27 109–10*, 110
16th cent. 3 496; 20 778; 32 649
18th cent. 22 681
textiles 10 635, 635–6*; 16 714, 752–4*
theatre boxes 30 666, 667
theatres 1 125; 12 114, 115, 119; 30 650, 655–6*, 657, 666–7*
Baroque 1 601
Mannerism 30 655
Neo-classicism 3 196; 23 88; 24 758; 28 390
Renaissance 30 654
Roman 26 873, 873, 888–9, 891
16th cent. 27 483–4; 28 32
17th cent. 1 601; 30 666
theories 25 71–2
architectural 1 558–60; 32 638
art
Mannerism 19 546–7
Renaissance 1 557; 32 18–21
15th cent. 6 169; 8 601; 16 658
16th cent. 2 388, 531; 4 198; 6 39; 7 646; 9 74–5; 12 244; 31 906
17th cent. 33 720
18th cent. 21 600
20th cent. 8 182–3
colour 7 627–8
painting 18 708
Mannerism 19 546–7
Renaissance 1 557–8; 19 195–6; 27 790
16th cent. 9 6–7; 24 827
17th cent. 9 7–8; 20 221
perspective 1 113, 557; 19 195, 546
proportions (human) 1 558; 19 546
sculpture 1 558
thermae 1 463; 26 795*, 796
Italy—cont.
threads 11 193
thrones 30 776, 777, 777–8
Baroque 3 832
Etruscan 10 633
Renaissance 30 781
Romanesque 3 237; 16 688
tiles 1 126; 16 422, 735; 27 893; 30 886, 886–7*
tin 10 624
title-pages 2 166; 9 224; 10 389; 31 49; 32 642
tombs 9 125; 16 688; 27 180, 181, 184
arch door 10 597*
Baroque 1 627; 4 621; 16 703; 27 347
caditoia 10 598*
chamber 10 593, 597, 597–9
corbel 10 597*
Etruscan 10 587, 588, 597–9*, 617–24*; 20 863; 30 346
Gothic 13 95–6, 96, 97; 31 3, 4
lunette 10 597*
Renaissance 1 747; 4 737; 7 367; 8 797; 11 27; 16 690, 840, 841; 21 438, 465; 32 361
rock-cut 10 597
Roman 26 877
three-cell 10 598*
tomb-chests 31 121
two-cell 10 598*
wall 31 123, 124, 125, 126–7
13th cent. 2 480, 481
14th cent. 12 303; 22 475; 28 29
15th cent. 4 736; 19 555
16th cent. 27 748, 749
20th cent. 4 101
tondi 4 496; 9 14
topiary 12 109, 110, 114, 115
topographical views 24 841; 31 155*
tortoiseshell 16 748*
towers 5 649
bell-towers 4 855; 8 134; 13 64; 28 675
Gothic 27 751
Neo-classicism 31 442
town halls 13 773; 31 236–7, 237
towns 16 650; 27 4; 31 730
townscapes 31 246, 247–9*
toys 31 258
trade 28 456
armour 10 592
beads 22 648
bronze 2 557; 10 592
ceramics 16 395
chariots 10 591
coins 10 591
copper 10 591
coral 16 750
dress 1 347
Etruscan 10 584–5, 590–92*, 609
faience (i) (glass) 10 590
fans 10 591
feathers 1 250
furniture 25 303, 306
glass 2 557; 3 593; 10 591
iron 10 591
ivory-carvings 10 591
jewellery 10 590, 591, 592
lace 11 649
maiolica 6 333
metalwork 10 591
ostrich eggs 10 590
parasols 10 591
Phoenician 10 590
porcelain 11 610
pottery 10 591, 592; 13 525; 16 417; 25 309
shells 10 590
shoes 10 591
silk 11 645; 16 445; 28 716
silver 10 590
tapestries 3 607
textiles 16 444
tiles 30 880

Italy
trade—cont.
weapons **10** 592
wool **28** 716
travel books **13** 304
trays **11** 388; **22** 413
treatises **8** 609; **27** 894
aesthetics **7** 306
architecture **1** 792; **14** 660; **19** 534; **21** 106; **22** 388; **23** 486, 487, 489, 861; **31** *295*, 295–6*; **32** 550–51, 638
Renaissance **1** 555, 558–60, 568; **3** 850; **7** 863; **11** 71, 72–3, 691; **23** 869; **28** 466, 468–71; **29** 739
15th cent. **16** 629; **22** 44; **32** 639
16th cent. **1** 637; **2** 167–8; **3** 863; **6** 82; **16** 634; **23** 856; **25** 857; **26** 317; **32** 187
17th cent. **13** 753; **23** 870; **28** *31*, 32–3; **32** 594
18th cent. **8** 563; **12** 12, 657; **27** 791; **32** 645
20th cent. **24** 693
armour **11** 270
Byzantine **9** 603
ceramics **6** 17
disegno **9** 142; **23** 879
drainage systems **6** 23
drawing **27** 204; **28** 392
Early Christian (*c.* AD 250-843) **9** 603
engineering **30** 230
engravings **19** 637
epigraphy **12** 656
fortifications **3** 683; **7** 776; **21** 577, 578; **28** 309
fountains **6** 23
gardens **12** 110
hardstones **14** 167
heraldry **7** 780
historiography **3** 98
houses **13** 314
hydraulics **2** 376; **7** 492
iconography **5** 887–8
imitation **5** 526
impresse **9** 142
letters **2** 166
maiolica **24** 733
manuscript illumination **13** 136
metalwork **6** 139, 147, 148
optics **33** 721
orders (chivalry) **32** 507–8
painting **3** 648; **7** 628; **23** 772; **24** 90; **31** 299, 321
Mannerism **19** 546–7
Renaissance **1** 555, 557–8; **16** 778
14th cent. **30** 425
15th cent. **6** 168–9; **7** 627
16th cent. **2** 445–6; **12** 571, 629–30; **23** 839–40
17th cent. **1** 465; **2** 376; **11** 698; **20** 242; **28** 33, 35; **30** 527
18th cent. **7** 177; **12** 720
20th cent. **25** 568
perspective **24** 487, 488, 489, 490; **28** 30; **30** 657, 668
Baroque **25** 416
Renaissance **1** 557
15th cent. **24** 765–6
16th cent. **3** 202; **4** 567, 654; **7** 312; **32** 508
17th cent. **4** 441; **6** 40; **33** 587
proportion **2** 345; **8** 512; **16** 658; **23** 744; **28** 201
Renaissance **29** 738
scenography **33** 721
sculpture **1** 555, 558; **4** 198; **6** 147, 148; **12** 204–5; **28** 509; **31** 302–3*
silver **16** 742
stage design **30** 654, 657, 667
stained glass **11** 892
stones **19** 178
theatres **5** 762

Italy
treatises—cont.
urban planning **22** 78
15th cent. **15** 50
16th cent. **4** 408; **29** 84
tripods **10** *626*, *627*
trompe l'oeil **10** 740; **15** IV; **29** 668; **31** *900*
trophies **31** *369*
trulli **20** 570; **32** *292*, 292
tumuli **10** 598
tympana **11** *6*
type-faces **4** 217; **31** 494
typewriters **15** *826*
typography **31** *494*
typological cycles **31** *500*
universities **13** *630*; **31** *674*, 674
upholstery **31** 682
urban planning **11** *271*; **23** *752*; **31** 712
Etruscan **10** 587, 602; **20** *529*
Roman **27** *4*
Somalia **29** 56
15th cent. **16** 629
16th cent. **27** 482
17th cent. **29** *373*
urns
biconical **10** *610*
Etruscan **10** 588, 593, 594
funerary **7** *176*; **10** 588, 593, *593*, 594, *603*, 609
hut **10** 587, *599*
voting **8** *796*
vases **14** 171
Etruscan **10** 587, 609, 610–16, 631
16th cent. **16** *747*; **21** 529
20th cent. **32** *205*
vaults (ceiling)
barrel **16** 630
rib **13** 51; **26** 578; **32** 92
Roman **26** 796, *878*
sail **22** *806*
trough **32** 94
velvet **16** *753*, 753
vessels **13** 576
vestments (ecclesiastical) **16** *759*
villas **21** 468; **22** 413; **32** 544–51*
Mannerism **20** *545*; **23** *863*, *866*, *867*; **32** *547*, *549*
Neo-classicism **16** *647*, *772*; **20** *393*; **25** *155*
Renaissance **12** 110–12, *278*, *761*; **21** *518*; **24** *530*; **32** *504*, *546*
Roman **28** 496–7; **32** 541, *541*
Veneto **32** 547–8
villa suburbana **16** 633–4
16th cent. **1** *608*; **2** *357*; **5** *683*; **12** *281*; **31** *64*; **32** *548*
19th cent. **5** *385*
vineyards **12** 110
walls **10** 601–2; **26** 887, *902*
walnut **2** 459, 465; **3** *483*, 484; **5** 192; **6** 7, *7*; **11** *383*; **16** *722*, *724*, *725*, *730*; **33** 326
watermarks **32** 908
waterworks **12** 115, 116
waxes **12** *574*; **16** *706*, 749*; **21** *769*; **27** *207*; **33** 2, *3*
weathervanes **33** 8
weaving **10** 635
weights **10** 636
white lead **7** 318
windows **19** *534*; **21** *455*
wings (theatre) **30** 667
women artists **2** 93; **4** 765; **10** 476; **11** 268, 269; **16** 668*, 780
17th cent. **12** 306
wood **1** 709; **8** *215*; **9** *129*, 151–2; **13** 123–4*, *124*; **26** 644*; **27** *12*; **30** *357*, 667, *776*
18th cent. **5** *54*
wood-carvings **6** 6–7*, *7*; **16** *723*; **30** *357*
woodcuts
bird's-eye views **11** *178*

Italy
woodcuts—cont.
chiaroscuro **5** 843–4; **25** VI; **32** 199; **33** *366*, 366–7
Mannerism **33** *356*
Renaissance **12** *656*
15th cent. **4** *196*; **11** *178*; **32** *181*; **33** 350*
16th cent. **28** *214*; **31** 43; **33** 355–7*
17th cent. **26** *415*; **33** 358
wood-engravings **28** *214*
wool **10** 636; **11** *193*
workshops **16** 777; **29** 853
writing **2** 166–7
wrought iron **16** 743, 744
see also ETRUSCAN; VILLANOVAN CULTURE
Itani Hoju
works **17** *324*
Itapé **24** *91*
Franciscan church **24** 94
Itauguá **24** *91*, 100
Museo San Rafael **24** 101
Itaya, Hazan **17** 266
Itazuke **17** 246
Itchō *see* HANABUSA ITCHŌ
I-te, Prince *see* YIDE, Prince
Iten Sōsei **28** 493
Itet **9** 899; **20** 117
Ithaca (NY), Cornell University **2** 382; **17** 435; **29** *678*
Ithaka (Greece) **13** *363*, 488, 600; **16** 782–3*
Sanctuary of the Nymphs **12** 68
Iti **9** 857, 900; **12** 225
I'timad al-Daula **18** 646
Itinerants *see* WANDERERS
Itinerarium imperiis Romanis see TABULA PEURINGERIANA
Itinerary of Einsiedeln **26** 797
It Is: A Magazine for Abstract Art **24** 428
Itjtawy *see* EL-LISHT
Itju **9** 858
Itkine, Sylvain **10** 469
Itō (Japan) **17** 433
Itō (family) **17** 412
Ito, Princess **17** 221
Itō, Chūta **16** 783*; **17** 88
Itō, Motohiko **17** 267
Itō, Sekisui **17** 267
Itō, Shinsui **17** 293, 294; **31** 764
works **17** *294*
Itō, Toyō **16** 783–4*
works **16** *784*; **17** 92
Itō Jakuchū **16** 784–5*; **17** 165, 194; **18** 552
works **16** *785*; **20** 287
Itō Jinsai **17** 236
Itō Tōgai **17** 236
Itri **27** 7
Itsujin Kain *see* TAKAHASHI YŪICHI
Itsuko Hasegawa *see* HASEGAWA, ITSUKO
Itsukushima Shrine **16** 785–7*; **17** *11*, 64*, 160, 219, 325, 326; **28** 638
architecture **16** 786–7*
collections **17** 428
gates **16** *786*
manuscripts **17** 404
masks **17** 392
weapons **2** 450
Itsunen **20** 285, 286
Itsunen Shōyū **16** 787*; **17** 184
Itsuun Kinoshita *see* KINOSHITA ITSUUN
Itsuzan **17** 410
works **17** *410*
Itta **23** 164
Ittagi **15** *294*; **16** 788*
Mahadeva Temple **15** 325, 531
Ittar, Henryk **2** 415
Ittar, Stefano **20** 212
Itten, Arnold **29** 531

Itten, Johannes **3** 824; **16** 788–9*; **22** 380; **29** 875; **30** 135
exhibitions **32** 775
groups and movements **3** 400, 401; **12** 396; **30** 135
methods **7** 630
pupils **2** 381; **23** 357; **29** 577, 696; **31** 361
teachers **14** 694
works **16** *788*; **30** 138; **32** 902
Ittenwiller Château **26** 633
Itu **15** 62
Iturbe (family) **22** 71
Iturbe, José **21** 382
Itúrbide, Agustín de **21** 396
Iturgaiz, Domingo **9** 113
Iturralde, Luis **4** 260
Iturrino, Francisco **16** 789–90*; **24** 829
Itwar 'Ali Khan **15** 380
Itz, G. N. **9** 169
Itzá **6** 579; **21** 203, 251
Itzá Maya **21** 246; **30** 383
Itzlfeldner, Johann Georg **14** 32
Iunet *see* DENDARA
Iunu *see* HELIOPOLIS
Iuput II **9** 887
Iusti, A. W. **31** 652
Iuvenalis, Decimus Iunius *see* JUVENAL
I♀V, Master **20** 800*
IVA *see* INSTITUTO VOCACIONAL DE ARTE (IVA)
Ivachev, I. M. **27** 428
Ivačković, Svetozar **28** 444, 838
Ivailovgrad Villa **26** *906*, 907
Ivaldi, Humberto **16** 790*; **23** 905
pupils **3** 729; **22** 78; **28** 770
works **23** 904
Ivan (*fl* 12th cent. **31** 547
Ivan I Kalita, Grand Duke of Muscovy (*reg* 1325-41) **22** 181, 182
Ivan III, Grand Duke of Muscovy (*reg* 1462-1505) **16** 790*; **27** 371
architecture **11** 116, *116*; **22** 169, 181; **27** 437; **29** 23
Ivan IV, Tsar of Moscow (*reg* 1533-84) **6** 175; **18** 207; **22** 184; **27** 438; **28** 464; **31** 555
cathedrals **22** *184*
Ivan, Johannes **16** 790*; **30** 76, 865
Ivan, Saint **26** 392
Ivan Alexander, King of Bulgaria (*reg* 1331-71) **5** 153; **16** 794; **32** 149
Ivanitsky, A. **3** 88
Ivanjicki, Olja **28** 451
Ivano-Frankovsk
Church of the Birth of the Mother of God **31** 550
Church of the Holy Spirit **31** 552
Ivanoskoye **27** 376
Ivanov, Aleksandr (Andreyevich) **16** 791–2*; **27** 389, 390
collaboration **12** 855
commentaries **25** 736
patrons and collectors **4** 489; **27** 438
pupils **32** 851
works **16** *791*
Ivanov, Andrey **5** 25; **16** 791; **31** 537
Ivanov, Boris **27** 414
Ivanov, Grigory **29** 54
Ivanov, Ivan *see* SHADR, IVAN (DMITRIYEVICH)
Ivanov, Ivan Alexeyevich **21** 127
Ivanov, Ivan Simeonov **31** 911
Ivanov, Mikhail **12** 2
Ivanov, Mina **5** 156
Ivanov, Nikolay **12** 856
Ivanov, Sergey (Vasil'yevich) **16** 792–3*
groups and movements **22** 178; **26** 740; **27** 392
pupils **12** 340; **18** 444
teachers **25** 674
works **16** *793*

Ivanov, Stefan **5** 154; **31** 785
Ivanov, Timothei **20** 924
Ivanov, Viktor **21** 812; **27** 397
Ivanov, Vsevolod **28** 757
Ivanova, Yevgeniya (Aleksandrovna) **27** 418
Ivanov-Alliluyev, Sergey (Kuz'mich) **16** 793*
Ivanović, Katarina **28** 450, 458
works **28** *451*
Ivanović, Ljubomir **19** 324
Ivanovo **5** *144*; **9** *511*; **16** 793–4*; **26** 483
Crkvata **5** 150; **16** 794
furniture **27** 409
manuscripts **5** 152
textiles **27** 431
Ivanovo-Voznesensk Polytechnical Institute **27** 379
Ivanov-Shits, Illarion (Aleksandrovich) **16** 794*; **27** 378
assistants **32** 381
pupils **21** 92
staff **23** 426
works **22** 173
Ivanovski-Karadare, Aleksandar **19** 885
ivans *see* IWANS
Ivan the Great, Grand Duke of Muscovy *see* IVAN III, Grand Duke of Muscovy
Ivan the Terrible, Tsar of Moscow *see* IVAN IV
Ivanyani **5** 146
Iványi Grünwald, Béla **14** 901; **16** 794–5*; **17** 876
groups and movements **22** 434
Ivarson, Ivan **10** 805; **13** 31; **30** 81
Ive, Paul **21** 568, 580
Iveagh, Edward (Cecil) Guinness, 1st Earl of *see* GUINNESS, EDWARD (CECIL), 1st Earl of Iveagh
Iveagh, Rupert Edward Guinness, 2nd Earl of *see* GUINNESS, RUPERT EDWARD, 2nd Earl of Iveagh
Iveagh Bequest *see under* LONDON → museums → Kenwood House
Iveković, Ćiril **4** 460; **8** 176
Iveković, Oton **16** 795*
Iveković, Sanja **8** 179
Ivels Corporation **13** 716
Ivens, Joris **23** 446
Ivens, Petrus Augustinus **3** 599
Iverni, Jacques **16** 795*
Iveropulets, Yoan *see* YOAN IVEROPULETS
Iversen, Kræsten **31** 393
Iverson, Susan **31** 660
Ives, Chauncey **8** 276
Ives, Chauncey B(radley) **16** 796*; **32** 753
Ives, E. R., and Co. **31** 256
Ives, Frederick **24** 670
Ives, James Merritt **8** 276; **19** 485; **23** 883
Ivković, Bogoljub **19** 884
Ivorine *see under* IVORY → types
Ivorite *see under* IVORY → types
Ivorson, Susan **30** 330
ivory **1** 869; **4** 313; **12** 268; **16** 796–800*
conservation **16** 799–800*
dating methods **11** 309
historical and regional traditions
Africa **1** *219*, 292–3*, *293*, 325–8*, *326*, *327*, 350, 351, 352, *356*
Alaska **16** 796; **31** 254, 259
Ancient Near East **1** 868–9*; **14** 353; **30** 774
Austria **2** *801*
Bamileke **3** 145
Belgium **3** 576, *602*, 603–4*, *604*; **29** 575

ivory
historical and regional traditions—cont.
Benin, Kingdom of **1** *219*, 292, 293, *293*, 326, *327*, 327–8, 352; **3** *722*, 723
Buddhism **15** 695
Burma **6** 557
Byzantine **5** 917; **9** *251*, *514*, *521*, *600*
Carolingian **9** 3; **22** *520*
Central Asia, Western **6** 261, *270*, 270–71, *271*
China **6** 557; **7** 18, 19, 107, 128, 130, 132; **10** 777
Cycladic **8** 323*
Cyprus, ancient **8** *350*; **14** 353
Early Christian (*c.* AD 250-843) **9** 3, *514*; **16** 686, *686*
Egypt **16** 497
Egypt, ancient **3** 482; **6** 559; **10** 51, 52, 53, *59*, 59–60*, *775*; **22** *488*; **30** 775; **31** 254, *254*, *265*
England **10** 288, *326*
Fiji **11** *69*
France **5** 917; **6** 558; **9** 3; **11** *588*, 636–7*; **21** *720*; **29** 571, 574; **31** *255*
Germany **2** *45*; **12** 423, *460*, 460–61*; **22** *520*; **23** *661*; **24** *543*, *544*; **26** *146*; **29** 574; **33** *670*
Gothic **21** *720*
Greece **9** *600*
Greece, ancient **6** 388; **12** 247; **13** 390, 435; **16** 798
Bronze Age **14** 353–4*
Helladic **14** 353–4*, *354*
Igbo **1** 292, 293
Indian subcontinent **6** 555, 556, *556*, 557; **15** 450, 549, 693, *693*, 695–7*, *696*, *697*, 724; **21** 717; **25** 303
Indonesia **15** 814
Indus civilization **15** 695
Inuit **31** 254, 259
Iran, ancient **15** 902, *915*
Islamic **6** 556; **16** 487, 497, 500, 503, *506*, *508*; **21** *630*, 718
Italy **1** 707; **5** 192; **16** 686, *686*; **23** *660*; **30** *776*
Japan **17** 371, 398–9, *398*
Kongo **1** 292
Lega **1** 293; **19** *72*
Malaysia **20** 174
Malta (Republic of) **6** 557
Mangbetu **1** 292
Merovingian **21** 164
Morocco **21** *630*
Netherlands, the **29** 571
Nigeria **1** 293, *356*
Norway **23** *229*
Ottoman **16** *508*
Parthian **15** *915*; **24** 217
Pende **24** 359–60
Portugal **25** 303, 305, 314
Prehistoric art **9** 81; **25** 473, 493
Romanesque **26** *146*
Rome, ancient **16** 798; **18** *826*
Scotland **28** 246
Siberia **16** 796, 799
Sierra Leone **1** 241, 293, 326–7, *326*
Spain **6** 558; **16** *506*; **29** *288*, *313*
Sri Lanka **29** 469, 470
Syria **16** 497
Tajikistan **6** *270*
Turkey **1** *729*
Turkmenistan **6** *271*
Urartian **1** *729*
Vietnam **32** 487
Yemen **16** 500
Yoruba **1** 292, 293, 352, *356*; **33** *555*
Zaïre **1** 293; **19** *72*
patinas **7** 102; **19** 73; **24** 258
technical examination **30** 410

ivory—cont.
techniques
carving *see* IVORY-CARVINGS
engraving **25** 491
gilding **16** 797
mass production **16** 799
polychromy **16** 797
staining **16** 797
turning **16** 797, 799
types
boar **16** 796
casque **16** 797
Cellonite **16** 797
elephant **16** 796
Africa **1** 292
China **7** 102, 103
Gothic **13** 171
Japan **17** 399
helmeted hornbill **16** 797; **17** 399
hippopotamus **1** 292; **15** 696; **16** 796
Ivorine **8** 285; **16** 797
Ivorite **16** 797
mammoth **16** 796, *798*, 799; **19** *243*; **25** 490; **32** 679
China **7** 102
France **19** *243*
Germany **32** 679
Siberia **7** 102
morse *see* walrus
narwhal **16** 796; **17** 398
odontolite **16** 796
pig **16** 796
Pyralin **16** 797
synthetic **16** 797
vegetable **16** 797
walrus **2** 82, *82*; **15** 696; **16** 526, 796; **17** 398; **22** 668
warthog **1** 292
whale **16** 796, 797
see also TEETH → types → sperm-whale
Xylonite **16** 797
uses
altarpieces **1** 707; **13** *174*, *177*; **16** 799
altars **29** IX1
amulets **10** 60
anklets **1** 292
armlets **1** 292, *293*; **16** 797
backscratchers **7** 102
bangles **16** 797
baskets **22** 656
beads **3** 440, 441; **25** 473
beakers **7** 102
beds **3** 482
belts **16** 799
book covers **4** IV2; **5** *809*, 809–11; **9** 651; **16** 798; **22** *520*; **23** 660; **26** 695
bowls **7** 103
bows **6** 261
boxes **9** 648, 651; **10** 51, 53; **15** *696*; **16** 797, 798
bracelets **1** 292, 351; **15** 814
breastplates **11** *69*
brush handles **7** 102
brushpots **7** 102
brush-rests **7** 102
bureaux **5** 192
busts **3** *604*; **16** *799*
buttons **16** 799
cabinets (ii) (furniture) **2** *45*; **11** *588*; **12** 421, *460*, 461; **29** 471
caskets **2** *81*; **5** 917; **9** *521*; **10** 52; **15** 696; **16** 524, 525, *525*, 799; **29** 471, *472*
chairs **6** 388, 389; **10** 52; **15** *697*
chess sets **6** 555, 556, *556*, 557, 558; **7** 103; **16** 523, *798*
chests **6** 559; **18** *139*
chryselephantine statues **16** 798
combs (hair) **7** 102; **13** 595; **16** 798, 799; **22** *574*; **25** 734; **29** 471
combs (liturgical) **7** 646, *646*; **9** 648

ivory
uses—cont.
consular diptychs **9** *648*, 650
cosmetics containers **16** 797
crosiers **8** *194*; **13** 176
crosses **26** *697*
crucifixes **3** 604; **13** *171*, *176*; **24** *544*; **26** 698; **29** *288*
cupboards **12** 423
cups **7** 103; **10** *326*
cutlery **1** 326; **16** 799
daggers **16** *506*
devil's work balls **7** 103
diptychs **9** 3, *251*; **18** *826*
discs **7** 102
divination instruments **1** *356*
dolls **17** 371; **31** 259
dominoes **31** 266
doors **9** *600*; **13** 390; **29** 471
earpicks **7** 102
écorchés **9** 706
fans **7** 103; **10** *775*, 777; **16** 799
figurines **16** 797
China **7** 104–6, *105*, *106*
Czech Republic **9** 81
Egypt, ancient **10** *59*, 60
Indian subcontinent **15** 450, 695, 724
Japan **17** *102*
Lega **19** *72*
Prehistoric art **19** *243*; **25** 488, *489*, 490; **32** 679
Urartian **1** *729*
forks **1** 327
furniture **1** 890; **12** 423; **13** 596–7; **15** 693, 696, 697; **16** 798, 799; **25** 303, 305; **29** 470
game-boards **31** *265*
game-pieces **10** 60; **16** 797, 798; **31** 254, 266
gun stocks **20** *853*
hairpins **7** 102
headrests **10** 53
horns **1** 326, 327, 328; **16** 797; **23** 400–402
see also oliphants
inlays **10** 288; **15** *693*; **16** 487, 497, 500, 797, 799; **28** 246; **29** *313*
jewellery **1** 350; **10** 60; **16** 797, 799; **17** 529, 530
keris **20** 174
knife-handles **1** 327; **8** 284, 285; **10** 60; **16** 799
knives **10** 60
labels **10** 60
lacquer **7** 18, 19
lanterns (lights) **16** 799
liturgical objects **16** 799
manuscripts **15** 549
marquetry **12** 423; **16** 797; **20** 466
masks **3** *722*; **24** 359
medallions **22** *895*
medals **16** 799
minbars **21** *630*
mirror-cases **16** 799
mirror frames **16** *527*; **21** 717, 718, 719, 720, *720*
mirror handles **10** 635
mirrors **3** 576; **8** *350*
models **7** 103; **16** 799
mortars (vessels) **7** 103
mosaics **16** 487
musical instruments **10** 60
netsuke **17** 398–9, *398*
oliphants **16** 526, 797; **26** 698
paintings **10** 197; **15** 724; **16** 799
pendants (jewellery) **7** 103, *104*
perfume containers **16** 799
pigments **16** 797
pins **7** 107
plaques **16** 799
Byzantine **9** 647, *650*
Carolingian **5** *811*
Early Christian (*c.* AD 250-843) **16** 686, *686*

ivory
uses
plaques—cont.
Early Christian and Byzantine **9** *514*
Egypt, ancient **22** *488*
Etruscan **10** 634–5
Greece, ancient **13** 595
Indian subcontinent **15** 695
Minoan **21** *681*
Ottonian **23** *660*
Palestine **27** *670*
Romanesque **26** *696*, *699*
powder flasks **16** 799
pyxides (boxes) **1** 326, 327; **9** 648; **10** *634*; **16** 525, 798
regalia **1** 352
reliquaries **9** *647*, 650; **16** 799; **23** 659; **26** *146*
rhyta **6** 270–71, *271*; **15** *915*; **23** *160*; **24** 217
rondelles (sculpture) **25** 493
salts **1** 326, *326*, 327, *327*; **16** 799
scabbards **6** *270*
scientific instruments **16** 799
screens (ii) (furniture) **7** 102
scrimshaw **28** 302
sculpture **1** *219*, 325–8*; **13** 435, 596, 597; **16** 799
relief **23** *229*
seals **7** 102, 128, 130; **12** 247; **13** 595; **16** 798
shrines (i) (cult) **26** 699
situlae **23** 659–60; **28** *805*
snuff bottles **7** 103, 132
spear-throwers **25** 493
spillikins **31** 266
spoons **1** 326, 327, 328; **29** 471
statuettes **16** 799
Austria **2** *801*
Belgium **29** 575
England **10** *267*
France **29** 571, 574
Germany **24** *543*; **29** 574
Gothic **13** 172–4, *173*
Greece, ancient **13** 595–6, *596*
Netherlands, the **29** 571
Ottonian **23** *661*
stools **10** 52
supports **16** 799
sword hilts **15** 696
swords **16** *508*; **33** *555*
tabernacles (ii) (receptacle) **16** 799
tablets **7** 102
tankards **16** 799
tea-services **3** *602*
thrones **30** 774, 775, *776*
tools **25** 493
toys **31** 254, *254*, *255*
trumpets **1** 292
vases **7** 103
veneers **10** 60; **16** 797, 799
watches **7** 443
weapons **15** 696; **16** 503; **29** 469, 471
whistles **24** 359–60
wristrests **7** 102, *103*
writing-tablets **4** 342; **9** 3; **16** 799
Ivory, James **15** 743
Ivory, Thomas (1709-79) **31** 584
Ivory, Thomas (*c.* 1732-86) **16** 37, 800*
patrons and collectors **23** 193
pupils **3** 81; **14** 600; **26** 463
works **2** 617; **9** 297, 317; **16** 8; **23** 247
ivory black **11** 763; **15** 851; **24** 789
ivory-carvers **1** 292
ivory-carvings **16** 797, 799
historical and regional traditions
Achaemenid **1** 872
Afghanistan **1** 195; **3** *501*
Africa **1** 292–3, *293*, *326*, *327*
Akye **1** 515
Alaska **22** *574*
Anatolia, ancient **1** 832

ivory-carvings
historical and regional traditions—cont.
Ancient Near East **1** 866–7, 869–72*, *869*, *870*, *871*, *872*, 890; **16** 797; **24** 336, *336*; **29** *395*; **31** 531
Anglo-Saxon **2** 80–82*, *81*, *82*
Assyrian **1** 871, *871*
Belgium **26** 695
Benin, Kingdom of **1** *293*; **3** 719
Buddhism **7** 104–5, *105*
Burma **5** 256*
Byzantine **9** *521*, *647*, 647–52*, *648*, *650*; **16** 798; **18** 676; **23** 660
Canaanite **5** 557, *557*; **30** 186
Carolingian **4** IV2; **5** *809*, 809–11*, *810*, *811*; **11** 636
Central Asia, Western **6** 269–72*, *270*, *271*; **16** 526*; **23** *160*; **30** *262*
China **7** 101–6*, *103*, *104*, *105*, *106*; **16** 797
Coptic **7** *825*, 825–6*
Côte d'Ivoire **8** 22
Crete
Archaic **8** 154
Minoan **8** 153; **21** 680–82*, *681*
Orientalizing style **8** 154
Cycladic **8** 323*
Cyprus, ancient **8** 323, *350*, 350–51; **24** 643; **27** *608*
Daoism **7** 105–6, *106*
Denmark **8** 752, 753; **13** *171*
Dorset culture **22** 575
Early Christian (*c.* AD 250-843) **9** *647*, 647–52*, *648*; **16** 798
Egypt **7** *825*, 825–6*; **16** *523*, 523–4*
Egypt, ancient **9** 864, 865, *866*; **16** 797
England **16** 799; **19** 638
Anglo-Saxon **2** *81*, 82*
Gothic **13** 176*
Romanesque **7** *646*; **8** *194*; **16** *798*; **23** *539*; **26** *697*, 697–8
19th cent. **16** *799*
Etruscan **1** 872; **10** 593, *634*, 634–5*
France
Carolingian **5** *811*; **11** 636
Gothic **13** 172–6*, *173*, *174*
Ottonian **23** 660
Prehistoric **16** *798*
Romanesque **26** 696–7
13th cent. **16** 799
Germany **16** 799; **29** 520
Carolingian **5** *809*
Gothic **13** 176–7*, *177*
Ottonian **23** 660, *661*; **28** *805*
Palaeolithic **25** *489*
Romanesque **26** 695, *696*; **29** IX1
17th cent. **2** *44*; **20** *853*
Gothic **13** *171*, 171–7*, *173*, *174*, *176*, *177*; **16** 799
Greece, ancient **13** 441, 595–7*, *596*
Bronze Age **14** *353*, *354*
Geometric (*c.* 900–*c.* 700 BC) **13** 442
Hawaii **14** 249
Helladic **14** *353*, *354*
Hittite **1** 870
Iran **16** 526*
Islamic **16** 522–6*, *523*, *525*, *527*, 799
Italy **16** 799
Etruscan **10** 593, *634*, 634–5*
Gothic **13** 176*, *176*
Islamic **16** 525–6*
Ottonian **23** 659–60, *660*
Romanesque **26** 698
Japan **17** *102*
Jordan **24** 336, *336*

ivory-carvings
historical and regional traditions—cont.
Kongo **18** 221–2
Lobi **19** 522
Mende (Sierra Leone) **21** 117
Mesopotamia **1** *871*, *872*
Minoan **8** 153; **21** 680–82*, *681*
Mycenaean **8** 323; **22** 397
Native North Americans **22** 573, 574, *574*, 575, 656
Netherlands, the **13** 176–7*; **16** 799; **22** *895*, 895–6*
Norway **23** *229*, 238
Nubia **27** 101
Ottoman **16** 526*, *527*
Ottonian **23** 659–60*, *660*, *661*; **28** *805*
Phoenician **1** 871, *872*; **16** 573, 798; **24** 643–4*; **25** 734
Phrygian **1** 872
Prehistoric art **16** 797, *798*; **25** 488, 490
Germany **25** *489*
Palaeolithic **25** 491, 493
Punic **25** 734*
Romanesque **7** *646*; **8** *194*; **16** *798*; **23** *539*; **26** 695–9*, *696*, *697*, *699*; **29** IX1
Rome, ancient **27** 100–101*, *101*
Russia **13** 596
Sardinia **25** 734
Sicily **16** 525–6*, 799; **26** 698
Spain **16** 799; **29** 344–5*
Islamic **16** 524–5*, *525*, 799
Punic **25** 734
Romanesque **26** 698–9, *699*
Sri Lanka **29** 471*, *472*, 479
Sumerian **1** *869*
Syria **16** 523–4*, 573
Syria-Palestine **1** *869*, *870*, 871; **5** *557*; **30** 180, 183, 186, 194
Tajikistan **6** *270*; **30** *262*
Tonga (Pacific Islands) **31** 144, *145*
Tunisia **16** 525–6*
Turkey **27** *101*
Turkmenistan **6** *271*; **23** *160*
Urartian **1** 872; **31** 701
Yemen **16** 523–4*
materials
gold leaf **12** 621
inscriptions **16** 524
techniques
painting **16** 525–6
types
Saracenic **16** 525–6
Siculo-Arabic **16** 525–6
Ivory Coast *see* CÔTE D'IVOIRE
Ivory Towers **6** 423
Ivrea **31** 731
Castello di Masino **16** 719
Cathedral **16** 722
Olivetti Plant **10** 749; **11** *63*
Ivriz **1** *821*, 827, 833, 885; **24** 690
rock reliefs **1** *828*
Ivry **30** 505; **31** 735
great tower **6** 52
Notre-Dame-la-Gare **26** 704
Ivry, Baron d' **19** 115; **21** 429
Ivry, Pierre Contant d' *see* CONTANT D'IVRY, PIERRE
Ivry-la-Bataille, St Martin **13** 73
Ivychurch (Kent) **26** 616
Ivy House Works **33** 20
Ivy Leaf group **10** 614
Ivy-Leaf Painter **13** 532
I. W., Master **8** 390
Iwai **17** 364
Iwajuku **17** 19
Iwaki, Sentaro **12** 101
Iwaki City Art Museum **17** 433
Iwakubo Kinemon *see* TOYOTA HOKKEI
Iwami **17** 318
Iwamiya, Takeji **22** 120
Iwamoto, Hiroyuki **16** 811
Iwanami Photographic Library **31** 106
Iwang **30** *806*, 818, 829
Iwano, Ichibei **17** 406
iwans **16** 153, 800–802*
Afghanistan **16** 167
Central Asia, Western **6** *205*; **16** 167
Indian subcontinent **23** 817
Iran **16** 161, 162, 193–4, *801*
Iraq **14** *225*; **16** 142, 153
Islamic **16** 142; **23** 815
Mesopotamia **14** *225*; **21** 291–2
Parthian **15** 912; **21** 291–2; **24** 217
Sasanian **27** 855
Turkey **16** 186
Iwao Uchida *see* UCHIDA, IWAO
Iwasaki, Koyata **17** 429
Iwasaki, Yanosuke **17** 429
Iwasa Matabei **16** 802*; **17** 176
Iwase Samuru *see* KITAO MASANOBU
Iwashimizu Shrine **17** 128
Iwata Nakayama *see* NAKAYAMA, IWATA
Iwato **17** 103
Iwatoya **17** 287
Iwaya Ichiroku **16** 802*; **17** 238
Iwerks, Ubbe **9** 10
Iwkowa **13** 189
Iwo Eleru **23** *129*, 130
Iwŏn **18** 328
Ixart, José **1** 625
Ixchel del Traje Indígena, Museo *see under* GUATEMALA CITY → museums
Ixelles *see* BRUSSELS
Iximché **13** *758*; **16** 803*; **20** *882*
fortifications **21** 599
Museo Arqueológico **13** 769
wall paintings **20** 886
Ixion Painter **13** 531
Ixmiquilpan
Augustinian Monastery **21** 375
S Miguel **21** 375
Ixnard, Pierre Michel d' **16** 803–5*; **29** 751
assistants **27** 623
works **12** 167, 374, 413; **16** *804*; **24** 582
Ixtapa, Hotel Camino Real **14** 788; **21** 382
Ixtapantongo **21** 186, 230
Ixtlán del Río **16** 805*; **21** *193*, *372*
figurines **16** 805
Ixtlilxochitl (*reg c.* 1409-1418) **12** 71
Ixtolinque, Pedro Patiño *see* PATIÑO IXTOLINQUE, PEDRO
Ixworth Cross (Suffolk) **10** 322
Ixworth Thorpe (Suffolk), All Saints **24** 577
Iyasu I, Emperor of Ethiopia (*reg* 1682-1706) **10** 566
İyem, Nuri **16** 805–6*; **31** 454
Iyo **17** 354, 405
Iza, Washington **9** 713; **16** 806*, 834
Izaguirre, Leandro **6** 21; **16** 806*
Izamal **6** 97
Monastery **33** 571
Izapa **16** 806–8*; **20** *882*; **21** *193*, *372*
altars **1** 700
sculpture **20** 885; **21** 218, 219
stelae **29** 619
Stele 5 **16** *807*
Stele 50 **21** 188
Izapan culture **21** 184, 186
Izborsk Fortress **27** 370
Izcue, Elena **24** 509
Izcue, José Augusto de **24** 516
Izdebsky, Vladimir (Alekseyevich) **16** 808*
Izenour, Steven **31** 735; **32** 234
Izer, Zeki Faik **31** 454
Izgirli **16** 372
Izhakevich, I. S. **18** 40
Izhorian **27** 433
Izis **16** 808*
Izkustvo **22** 539
Izmaylov, K. **2** 893; **3** 88
Izmaylovo Glassworks **22** 180; **27** 414
Izmir **16** *104*
architecture **31** 452
Basilica **3** 328; **32** 89
Bikkur Holim synagogue **17** 545, *545*, 551
carpets **31** 455
coins **27** 98
Ege University **31** 456
figurines **13** 581
fortifications **9** 524, 555
inscriptions **13** 605
ketubbot **18** 3
pottery **13** 536
Shalom synagogue **17** 551
Smyrna (New) **9** *512*; **26** *908*; **28** 893*
stelae **13** 427
terracottas **27** 111
textiles **16** 445
Izmit **26** 902
bronzes **27** 91, 92
canal **26** 885
coins **5** 299–300; **9** 636
congregational mosque **16** 222
marble **26** 855
marks
silver **9** 654
masons **26** 907
Nicomedia **9** *512*; **26** *908*
palace **23** 809
tiles **9** *633*
Iznik **9** *512*, 515; **16** *104*, 809–10*
Archaeological Museum **16** 810
architecture **16** 202
ceramics **2** 440; **6** 333; **16** 420
churches **9** 576
Church C *see* Hagios Tryphon
Church of the Dormition **9** 542, 591, 645; **16** 809–10
mosaics **9** 632; **16** *809*
Hagia Sophia **7** 253; **9** 544; **16** 809
Hagios Tryphon **9** 549
Monastery Church of Hyakinthos *see* Church of the Dormition
coins **9** 638
fortifications **9** 555
Green Mosque *see* Yeşil Cami
Hacı Hamza Hamamı **3** 376
madrasa of Süleyman Pasha **16** 810
mosaics **9** 633
mosque of Hacı Özbek **22** 195
Orkhan Gazi Mosque **16** 205, 810; **18** 507
Iznik—cont.
pottery **4** 172, *172*; **6** IV1; **16** 124, 393, 395, 396, 418, *418*, 419, 420–23, *421*, *422*; **19** 717
tiles **16** 221, 248, 249, 604, 610; **21** 506; **29** 18; **30** XIII1
Yeşil Cami **9** 83; **16** 205; **21** 628
Iznik ware *see under* POTTERY → wares
IZO *see under* NARKOMPROS
Izobrazitel'noye iskusstvo **24** 450
Izquierdo, César **25** 455
Izquierdo, Francisco Hurtado *see* HURTADO IZQUIERDO, FRANCISCO
Izquierdo, Isabel **6** 600
Izquierdo, María **16** 811*; **21** 388; **33** 316
Izsó, Miklós **16** 811*
works **14** *895*, 896
Iztapalapa **12** 71
palace of Moctezuma II Xocoyotzin **23** 825
Izue, Hiroshi *see* IZUE, YUTAKA
Izue, Kan *see* IZUE, YUTAKA
Izue, Yutaka **16** 811–12*; **17** 92
Izumi, Seiichi **18** 405; **29** 219
Izumi Shimada *see* SHIMADA, IZUMI
Izumiya Ichibei **31** 765
Izumiyama **17** 241
Izumo
Grand Shrine **16** 812–13*; **17** 60, 62, 98
honden **16** *812*, 812–13
Kamienyastsukiyama tomb **17** 59
potters **17** 104
puppets **17** 408
Izumo no Okuni **17** 329
Izumo taisha *see* IZUMO → Grand Shrine
Izu no Chohachi Museum *see under* MATSUZAKI
Izuru Yamamoto *see* YAMAMOTO, IZURU
Izushi **17** 352
Izyaslav **3** 525
'Izz al-Dawla, Amir (*reg* 967-78) (Buyid) **16** 373
'Izz al-Din ibn Taj al-din Isfahani **6** 246
'Izz al-Din Kayka'us I, Sultan (*reg* 1210-19) (Saljuq of Anatolia) **16** 186; **18** 233; **28** 809
'Izz al-Din Mahmud **1** 97
İzzet Efendi *see* MUSTAFA İZZET
Izzo, J. B. **31** 298

J

Jabach, Everard **4** 807; **11** 661; **15** 158; **16** 814–15*
collections **4** 552; **7** 545; **11** 661, 662
drawings **7** 864; **8** 209; **9** 229, 230; **10** 753; **20** 417; **27** 264
engravings **7** 864
mounts (works on paper and scrolls) **22** 236
paintings **4** 534, 552, 912; **12** 243; **21** 609
writings **9** 211
Jabach, Gerard Michael **10** 753
Jabal Adda **16** 441, 442
Jabal Bani Malik **32** 316
Jabal Barat **32** 318
Jabal Barri **2** 261
Nestorian church **2** 252
Jabaldjari Leura, Tim *see* LEURA (JAPALJARRI), TIM
Jabal Fayfa' **32** 316
Jabal Hafit **2** 248, 266
Jabal Kenzan **2** 261, 265
Jabalkovo **26** 143
Jabalpur, Rani Durgavati Museum **15** 181
Jabal Says **16** 148; **23** 815
Jabaque, Evrard *see* JABACH, EVERARD
Jabbadar, 'Aliquli *see* 'ALIQULI JABBADAR
Jabbaren **1** 343
rock art **1** *373*
Jabbeke **3** *539*
De Vier Winden *see* Permeke Museum
Permeke Museum **24** 458
Jabbul **30** 193
Jabhua Bhil **15** 735
Jablonec nad Nisou **8** 414
Museum **8** 424
Jabłonna **29** 839
Jablonné v Podještědí, St Laurenz **8** 378; **14** 529
Jabłonowska, Anna **25** 139
Jabra, Jabra I. **16** 2
Jabri, Ali **17** 655
Jabrin Fort **23** 436
Jabur, Manhal **21** 301
Jaca **16** 815–16*; **29** *259*
Cathedral **16** 816*; **26** 570, 581, *582*
capitals **26** *605*, 607
crypt **29** 262
sculpture **26** 605, 607
metalwork **26** 689
sculpture **26** 642
jacaranda **2** 465; **4** 720, 721; **29** 315, 319
Jacard, Joseph-Marie *see* JACQUARD, JOSEPH-MARIE
Jaccard, Christian **11** 553
Jachmann, Christine **16** 816*
Jachmund, A. **16** 227, 586; **31** 452
Jáchymov **8** 377, 415
Jack, Richard **33** 679
Jack, Russell **30** 160
Jack, T. C. & E. C. **4** 63
Jäckel, Matěj Václav **16** 816–17*; **25** 432
pupils **14** 515
works **8** 385; **25** 432, 443
Jäckel, Willy **22** 711
jackets **7** 77, 144; **16** 463, 466; **18** 357; **22** *645*
jackfruit-wood **15** 720, 730
Jäckh, Ernst **8** 825
Jack Helen & Brut **11** 101
Jackiewicz, Wiktor **28** 445
Jäckl, Matyás Václav **8** 397
Jack of Diamonds (Bubnovy Valet) **9** 144; **16** 817–18*; **22** 178; **24** 717; **25** 239; **27** 392; **31** 583
exhibitions **17** 764
members **12** 871; **30** 361
Burlyuk, David (Davidovich) **5** 219
Burlyuk, Vladimir (Davidovich) **5** 220
Drevin, Aleksandr (Davidovich) **9** 296
Dymshits-Tolstaya, Sof'ya (Isaakovna) **9** 495
Fal'k, Robert (Rafailovich) **10** 771
Fonvizin, Artur (Vladimirovich) **11** 291
Goncharova, Natal'ya (Sergeyevna) **12** 893
Konchalovsky, Pyotr (Petrovich) **18** 215
Kuprin, Aleksandr (Vasil'yevich) **18** 528
Larionov, Mikhail (Fyodorovich) **18** 792
Lentulov, Aristarkh (Vasil'yevich) **19** 166
Lissitzky, El **19** 474
Malevich, Kazimir (Severinovich) **20** 193
Mashkov, Il'ya (Ivanovich) **20** 548
Osmyorkin, Aleksandr (Aleksandrovich) **23** 605
Survage, Léopold **30** 25
works **31** 519
jack of plates **2** 472
jacks **7** 766
Jacks, Robert **16** 818*
Jackson, Andrew **3** 84; **9** 505
Jackson, A(lexander) Y(oung) **13** 712; **16** 818–19*; **22** 38
groups and movements **5** 566, 567; **13** 711
pupils **30** 753
teachers **5** 67
works **1** 496; **13** *712*
Jackson, Basil Hippisley **16** 821
Jackson, Dan **4** 479
Jackson, Daryl **2** 743; **4** 415; **5** 602; **16** 819*
Jackson, Edward **16** 821
Jackson, F. E. **19** 492
Jackson, George, & Sons **11** 432; **24** 62
Jackson, G. F. **19** 359
Jackson, Gilbert **16** 819*
works **10** 248, *248*
Jackson, H. **28** 483
Jackson, John **16** 819*
patrons and collectors **3** 239; **5** 848; **10** 146
pupils **14** 742
works **23** 687; **25** *609*
Jackson, John Baptist **16** 820*; **32** 815
methods **25** 590
works **10** 178, 278; **13** 301; **25** 622; **32** 815; **33** 359, *359*, 367
Jackson, John Richardson **13** 327; **16** 820*
Jackson, Jonathan **4** 481
Jackson, Linda **2** 768
Jackson, Martha **16** 820*
Jackson, Nathan **22** 581
Jackson, Orlando **10** 333
Jackson, Peter **33** 678
Jackson, Phillip **28** 771
Jackson, Richard *see* WALLACE, RICHARD
Jackson, Samuel **4** 823; **25** 759; **32** 864
Jackson, Thomas **9** 369
Jackson, Thomas Graham **10** 374; **16** 820–21*
collaboration **28** 564
teachers **28** 279
works **23** 688
Jackson, Thomas Theophilus **16** 886
Jackson, T. R. **3** 6
Jackson, W. (*fl* 1856) **26** 337
Jackson, William (*fl* 1698-1714) **4** 373
Jackson, William Henry (1843-1942) **10** 580; **16** 821–2*; **24** 665
works **22** *569*
Jackson & Graham **10** 297; **17** 640; **19** 592
Jackson Photographic Co. **16** 821
Jacmel **14** *54*, 57
Jacob (ii) (family) **3** 578; **4** 302; **19** 11
Jacob (*fl* 1302-7) **16** 822*
Jacob (*d* 1374) **16** 822
Jacob (*fl* 1432-45) **30** 366
Jacob, Abraham bar **17** 537
works **17** *537*
Jacob (ii), Alphonse-George **11** 257; **16** 822; **24** 388
Jacob (ii), François-Honoré-Georges **11** 597; **16** 822
collaboration **8** 107, 648
designers **11** 257; **24** 388
groups and movements **10** 97, 186
patrons and collectors **4** 303, 306, 556; **11** 598; **25** 193
works **11** 597
Jacob (ii), Georges, I (1739-1814) **11** 597; **16** 822*; **24** 151
collaboration **9** 379; **26** 39
groups and movements **9** 5; **10** 643; **22** 738; **26** 85
patrons and collectors **4** 555; **7** 528; **33** 281
works **3** *484*; **6** 390; **11** 580; **17** 639; **29** 305, 315; **30** 783
Jacob (ii), Georges, II (1768-1803) **11** 597; **16** 822
Jacob, Harold **7** 378
Jacob, Louis **4** 514
Jacob, Master **33** 458
Jacob, Max **3** 366; **9** 196; **16** 822–3*
collaboration **18** 577
groups and movements **8** 244; **23** 694; **24** 405; **27** 307
illustrated works **8** 775; **13** 671; **17** 725; **24** 716, 726
productions **31** 832
studio **29** 858
Jacob, Nicholas-Henry **1** 844; **21** 6
Jacob, Pierre *see* TAL-COAT, PIERRE
Jacob, Samuel Swinton **16** 823*
works **1** 648; **4** 58; **15** 403; **16** 871; **19** 775
Jacoba, Countess of Hainault and Holland (1401-36) **13** 159
Jacobazzi, Domenico, Cardinal **26** 802
Jacob Bellaert, Master of **20** 698–9*
Jacob de Littemont *see* LITTEMONT, JACOB DE
Jacob-Desmalter, Alphonse-George *see* JACOB (ii), ALPHONSE-GEORGE
Jacob-Desmalter, François-Honoré-Georges *see* JACOB (ii), FRANÇOIS-HONORÉ-GEORGES
Jacob-Desmalter et Cie **7** 677; **11** 580, 598; **16** 822
Jacobé, Johann **21** 417
Jacobean style **10** 230; **16** 823–4*
houses **10** *230*
portraits **8** *165*; **9** *277*; **19** *583*; **21** *509*
Jacobello d'Antonio **2** 178, 181, 182; **8** 14; **16** 824*; **27** 617, 658
Jacobello del Fiore **16** 662, 824–6*
pupils **8** 166
works **16** *825*, *826*; **32** 189
Jacobello della Chiesa **32** 190
Jacobello di Bonomo **16** 826*
Jacobellus *see* MURIOLUS OF SALERNO
Jacobellus Petrus **7** 922
Jacobethan Revival **16** 823
Jacobi, G. **2** 218
Jacobi, Johann **3** 798; **9** 145; **28** 116
Jacobi, Lotte **16** 827*
Jacobi, Moritz Hermann von **10** 136
Jacobi, Otto **22** 38
Jacobi, Peter **11** 54; **30** 330
Jacobi, R. (*fl* 1940) **24** 798
Jacobi, Ritzi (*b* 1941) **11** 54; **30** 330
Jacobi da Siena, Minuccio *see* MINUCCIO JACOBI DA SIENA
Jacobidis, Georges **8** 602
Jacobite (sect) *see under* CHRISTIANITY → sects
Jacobite glasses *see under* GLASSES → types
Jacob Jansz. van Haarlem **20** 637; **22** 199, 835
Jacob Kettler, Duke of Kurland (*reg* 1641-82) **18** 848
Jacob le Conte **23** 402
Jacob of Sarug **24** 776
Jacob of Strassburg **32** 199; **33** 355
Jacob-Petit **11** 610; **24** 149
workshop **11** *610*
Jacob Riis Projects *see* RIIS, JACOB, PROJECTS
Jacobs, Arnoldo **32** 538
Jacobs, David **29** 98
Jacobs, Hendrick **19** 293
Jacobs, Henk W. M. **29** 117
Jacobs, Henri (François Eugène) **16** 827*
Jacobs, Herbert **33** 404, 405
Jacobs, Hieronimus **3** 605; **8** 204
Jacobs, Isaac **4** 824
Jacobs, Jacob **7** 404; **8** 592; **18** 680; **31** 873
Jacobs, Jane **31** 735
Jacobs, Ken **10** 688
Jacobs, Lazarus **4** 824
Jacobs, Sally **30** 687
Jacobsen, Adrian **22** 676
Jacobsen, Arne (Emil) **16** 827–9*
assistants **21** 821
collaboration **14** 690; **18** 799; **21** 821; **23** 118
groups and movements **8** 729
staff **14** 18; **30** 260
works **8** 728, 729, 745, 746, 752, 803; **16** *828*; **18** 541; **23** 689; **28** 159
Jacobsen, Bent Karl **8** 736
Jacobsen, Carl (Christian Hillmann) **7** 806; **8** 758; **16** 829*; **18** 470; **27** 333
architecture **17** 756
Jacobsen, Carl (Christian Hillmann)—cont.
collections **8** 759
Jacobsen, Egill **7** 488; **8** 736; **16** 829*
Jacobsen, Helge **8** 759
Jacobsen, Holger **16** 830*; **17** 756; **25** 850
Jacobsen, Jacob Christian **14** 543
Jacobsen, Jonna **16** 828
Jacobsen, Niels Hansen **8** 741, 748
Jacobsen, Robert **16** 830*
dealers **26** 193
groups and movements **11** 570
works **8** 741; **16** 58
Jacobsen, Theodore **9** 323; **14** *842*; **17** 877
works **9** *323*
Jacobsen, Thorkild **3** 418; **9** 46
Jacobson, Helge **16** 829
Jacobson, Oscar B. **22** 595
Jacobsthal, E. **6** 280
Jacobsthal, Johann Eduard **25** 856
Jacobsthal, Paul Ferdinand **6** 155, 157; **16** 830*
Jacobsz., Andries **3** 230
Jacobsz., Cornelis **7** 870; **16** 831
Jacobsz., Dirck **7** 868; **16** 831*
works **1** 806; **16** *831*; **22** 837; **31** 881
Jacobsz., Hugo **16** 831–2*; **19** 756
attributions **20** 763
pupils **19** 101, 757; **22** 836
works **22** 836
Jacobsz., Juriaen **16** 832–3*
Jacobsz., Lambert **3** 22; **11** 169; **16** 833*
works **16** *833*
Jacobus (*fl c.* 1360s) **28** 753
Jacobus (*fl* 1440; founder, Sighişoara) **28** 696
Jacobus (*fl* 1440; woodcut dealer, Padua) **33** 350
Jacobus, Master (*fl* 1290s) **31** 384
Jacobus Cairolus **21** 702
Jacobus de Cessolis **6** 557
Jacobus de Venetiis *see* BELLINI, JACOPO
Jacob van Brussel, Abbot of St Bavo **20** 749
Jacob van Maerlant **4** 12; **10** 202; **22** 833; **26** 563
Jacob van Thienen **3** 543; **5** 53; **13** 62
Jacob (Claesz.) van Utrecht **16** 833–4*
works **16** *834*
Jacob von Schweinfurt *see* HAYLMANN, JACOB
Jacoby, Alfred **17** 549
Jacoby, Miklós **14** 298
Jacomart **16** 834*; **31** 815
attributions **26** 267
collaboration **26** 267
patrons and collectors **2** 276; **4** 409
Jacomb-Hood, George Percy **33** 180
Jácome, Manuel Ferreira *see* FERREIRA JÁCOME, MANUEL
Jacome, Master **2** 870
Jácome, Ramiro **9** 713; **16** 806, 834–5*
Jacomet **29** 628
Jacometti, Pietro Paolo **16** 835*
Jacometti, Tarquinio **9** 158; **16** 835
Jacometto Veneziano **16** 835*
Jacomo de Flandria de Angelo **10** 519; **11** 5
Jacomo pittore, Maestro **20** 640
Jacone **27** 851

Jacopi, G. **26** 290
Jacopi, Lorenzo **27** 849
Jacopino Avvocato, Paolo di *see* PAOLO DI JACOPINO AVVOCATO
Jacopino Bavosi **2** 18
Jacopino da Reggio **4** 274; **16** 836*; **20** 681
Jacopino da Tradate **10** 743; **21** 533; **32** 611
Jacopino di Francesco Bavosi **20** 751
Jacopo, Abbot of S Maria degli Angeli (Florence) **22** 800
Jacopo, Insalato di *see* INSALATO DI JACOPO
Jacopo, Mariano del Buono di *see* MARIANO DEL BUONO DI JACOPO
Jacopo, Megliore di *see* MEGLIORE DI JACOPO
Jacopo Arcangelo di Jacopo *see* JACOPO DEL SELLAIO
Jacopo Biondi da Bologna, Cristoforo di *see* CRISTOFORO DI JACOPO BIONDI DA BOLOGNA
Jacopo da Bisticci **32** 384
Jacopo da Camerino **26** 821
Jacopo da Campione **5** 549
Jacopo da Fabriano **24** 731
Jacopo da Faenza **11** 383
  works **11** *382*
Jacopo da Mantova **12** 733
Jacopo (di Paride Parisati) da Montagnana **16** 836*
Jacopo da Pesaro *see* PESARO, JACOPO DA
Jacopo da Pietrasanta *see* PIETRASANTA, JACOPO DA
Jacopo da Pontormo *see* PONTORMO, JACOPO DA
Jacopo d'Avanzi *see* AVANZI, JACOPO
Jacopo da Verona **1** 726, 768; **31** 190
Jacopo da Voragine, Archbishop of Genoa **16** 837–8*
  works **5** 443; **7** 225; **9** 105; **12** 689; **13** 128; **15** 82; **19** 787; **27** 592
Jacopo del Casentino **16** 838–9*; **23** 743
  pupils **29** 404
  works **16** *839*
Jacopo della Fonte *see* JACOPO DELLA QUERCIA
Jacopo della Guercia *see* JACOPO DELLA QUERCIA
Jacopo della Pila **21** 695
Jacopo della Quercia **4** 276; **11** 696; **16** 839–45*; **28** 676
  assistants **10** 853
  attributions **12** 701; **22** 462
  collaboration **11** 696; **27** 765
  competitions **7** 671
  patrons and collectors **3** 743; **8** 50; **28** 677
  teachers **19** 753
  works **1** 490; **4** 280; **11** 254, 341; **12** 716; **13** 96; **16** 691–2, *692, 840, 841, 842, 844*; **20** 844; **27** 829; **28** 681; **31** 121
Jacopo del Meglio *see* COPPI, GIACOMO
Jacopo del Sellaio **16** 846–7*
  patrons and collectors **27** 463
  teachers **19** 444
  works **6** 4; **16** *846*; **29** 361, 362
Jacopo di Antonello *see* JACOBELLO D'ANTONIO
Jacopo di Antonio **12** 713; **16** 847*; **20** 748
Jacopo di Bonapreso Aspettati **4** 274
Jacopo di Cassola **10** 519
Jacopo di Cione *see* CIONE, JACOPO DI
Jacopo di Corso **12** 539
Jacopo di Lello **16** 743
Jacopo di Michele *see* GERA DI PISA
Jacopo di Mino del Pellicciaio *see* GIACOMO DI MINO DEL PELLICCIAIO
Jacopo di Paolo **4** 275, 276, 279; **12** 703; **16** 848*
Jacopo di Pietro d'Angelo *see* JACOPO DELLA QUERCIA
Jacopo di Zuanne **12** 669
Jacopo d'Ognabene, Andrea di *see* ANDREA DI JACOPO D'OGNABENE
Jacopo d'Ognabene, Tallino di *see* TALLINO DI JACOPO D'OGNABENE
Jacopo Filippo d'Argenta **8** 172; **10** 653; **16** 848*
Jacopone da Todi **24** 776
Jacopo Tedesco *see* LAPO
Jacotenango **13** *758*
  church **13** 761
Jacotin, C. **22** 270
Jacoulet, Paul **16** 848–9*
Jacovleff, Alexandre (Yevgeniyevich) *see* YAKOVLEV, ALEKSANDR (YEVGENIYEVICH)
Jacqmain, André **3** 551; **16** 849*; **30** 213
Jacquand, Claudius **16** 849*
  dealers **29** 248
  groups and movements **31** 374
  patrons and collectors **5** 364
  teachers **19** 847
Jacquard, Antoine **16** 849*
Jacquard, Joseph-Marie **2** 838; **11** 647; **16** 849–50*; **19** 416; **30** 548
Jacquard Axminster carpets *see under* CARPETS → types
Jacquard looms *see under* LOOMS → types
Jacquart, Claude **22** 456
Jacquart, Marc **11** 621
Jacque, Charles(-Emile) **16** 850*
  assistants **8** 655
  collaboration **10** 562
  groups and movements **3** 212
  patrons and collectors **12** 147
  personal collection **21** 430
  works **2** 106; **7** 434; **9** 309; **10** 555, 556
  writings **10** 559
Jacque, Emile **16** 850
Jacque, Frédéric **16** 850
Jacque, Léon **16** 850
Jacqueline, Duchess of Bavaria (*reg* 1417–33) **22** 835
Jacquemart, Albert **7** 161; **16** 851
Jacquemart, Henri-Marie-Alfred **28** 346
Jacquemart, Jules (-Ferdinand) **10** 775; **16** 851*
  groups and movements **17** 440
  personal collection **16** 559
  pupils **5** 23
  works **9** 204; **26** 233, *234*; **32** 902
Jacquemart, Nélie (-Barbe-Hyacinthe) **16** 851*
Jacquemart-André, Musée *see under* PARIS → museums
Jacquemart & Bénard **26** 260
Jacquemart de Hesdin **3** 553; **13** 133; **16** 851–2*
  attributions **20** 751
  collaboration **20** 634, 647
  patrons and collectors **31** 837
  works **7** 525; **13** 154; **16** *852*; **18** 704
Jacquemart Pilavaine **8** 208
Jacquemin **27** 240
Jacquemin (de Lenoncourt), Gérard **16** 852–3*
Jacquemin, Rogier *see* JACQUEMIN, GÉRARD
Jacquemon de Nivelle **23** 165
Jacques (ii) *see* BACKER, JACOB DE
Jacques, Charles *see* STERLING, CHARLES
Jacques, Charles-Symphorien **11** 608; **21** 137
Jacques, Cir **10** 735
Jacques (i), François **16** 853
Jacques, John **16** 855*
Jacques, John, & Son **31** 266
Jacques, Maurice **4** 514; **22** 726
Jacques (i), Nicolas **16** 853*; **26** 148
Jacques (i), Pierre **16** 853*
Jacques d'Armagnac, Duc de Nemours *see* NEMOURS, JACQUES D'ARMAGNAC, duc de
Jacques de Baerze **16** 854*
  patrons and collectors **5** 207, 895; **11** 438; **13** 109
  works **1** 710; **3** 567, 568; **4** 841; **8** 892; **11** 439; **13** *109*, 110
Jacques de Besançon **11** 724
Jacques de Besançon, Master of **4** 544; **11** 724; **16** 854; **20** 699*; **31** 845
Jacques de Braibant **5** 548
Jacques de Chartres **26** 43
Jacques de Faveran **12** 738; **22** 505; **29** 263
Jacques de Guise **3** 555; **7** 243; **8** 208
Jacques de Hemricourt **12** 272
Jacques de La Haye **7** 865
Jacques de Litemont **31** 842, 843
Jacques de Lonquon **26** 563
Jacques de Neuilly **8** 891; **17** 460
Jacques d'Estouteville *see* ESTOUTEVILLE, JACQUES D'
Jacques du Châtelier **20** 626
Jacques Dueze *see* JOHN XXII, Pope
Jacques & Hay **5** 575, 579; **16** 855*
Jacques Le Rouge **17** 480
Jacquet, Alain **16** 857*; **20** 913; **28** 300
Jacquet, Alexandre **1** 631; **16** 855
Jacquet, Antoine **16** 855
Jacquet, Germain **16** 855
Jacquet, Jacques **16** 855
Jacquet, J. B. **9** 326
Jacquet, Jean **16** 855
Jacquet, Jules **10** 396
Jacquet, Mathieu (*fl* 1542) **16** 855
Jacquet, Mathieu (1545–*d* after 1611) **16** 855–6*
  attributions **2** 455
  collaboration **13** 825
  patrons and collectors **6** 604
  pupils **4** 524
  works **16** *856*
Jacquet, Nicolas **16** 855
Jacquet, Pierre **16** 855
Jacquet de Grenoble, Matthieu **11** 260; **20** 138
Jacquette, Yvonne **21** 897
Jacqui **17** 522
Jacquier, Emile **6** 601
Jacquietti **24** 846
Jacquin, Nicolas **3** 48
Jacquinet, C. **2** 463, 464
Jacquiot, Ponce **29** 571
Jacquotot, Marie-Victoire **4** 555
Jacquoulet, Paul **17** 293
jade **16** 857–61*, *858*
  historical and regional traditions
    Aztec **16** 859; **21** 252
    Belize **23** 418
    Britain **16** 861
    Burma **16** 858, 861
    Canada **16** 859
    Central Asia **7** 1
    Central Asia, Eastern **16** 860
    Central Asia, Western **6** 272*
    Chile **16** 861
    China **1** 818; **7** 1*, 21, 76, 88, 90, 94, 101, *101*, 106, *107*, 109, 111, 128, 129, 130; **16** 857, 858–9, 860; **22** 466
      Han period (206 BC–AD 220) **7** 81; **20** 236, *236*
      Hongshan culture **7** *2*
      Liangzhu culture **7** 1
jade
  historical and regional traditions
    China—cont.
      Longshan culture **7** 2
      Ming period (1368–1644) **7** 10, *111*
      Prehistoric **7** *2*
      Qing period (1644–1911) **7** 20, 112, 132
      Song period (AD 960–1279) **7** *8*, 110
      Tang period (AD 618–907) **7** 109
      Zhou period (*c.* 1050–256 BC) **3** *686*; **7** *5*, 56, 106, 107, 108; **21** 714
      20th cent. **7** 112
    Colombia **16** 861
    Costa Rica **29** *154*
    Egypt **16** 861
    Egypt, ancient **16** 861
    Germany **16** 861
    Gran Nicoya culture **13** 311–12, *312*
    Guatemala **16** 859; **23** 418
    Honduras **23** 418
    Hongshan culture **7** *2*
    Indian subcontinent **15** 698–9*, 701; **16** 860; **21** 717, *717*
    Iran **16** 528
    Islamic **16** 503, 528, 860; **21** 718
    Italy **16** 861
    Japan **16** 859
    Korea **18** *350, 365, 380*
    Liangzhu culture **7** 1, *1*; **19** 302
    Longshan culture **7** 2
    Maori **16** 859
    Maya **1** 735; **16** III1; **21** 243, 251, 259
    Mesoamerica, Pre-Columbian **16** 858, 859; **21** 240–41, 242, 243, 257, 260, 719
      Aztec **16** 859; **21** 252
      Maya **1** 735; **16** III1; **21** 251, 259
      Olmec **18** *881*; **21** 251
      Zapotec **21** 251
    Mexico **16** III1; **18** *881*
    Mixtec **21** 243, 737
    Mongolia **21** 882
    Mughal **7** 10–11
    Olmec **18** *881*; **21** 242, 251
    Ottoman **16** 528, 860
    Peru **16** 861
    Portugal **16** 861
    Prehistoric art **7** *2*
    Puerto Rico **29** *199*
    Russia **16** 860
    South America, Pre-Columbian **13** 311–12, *312*; **29** *154, 199*
    Spain **16** 861
    Switzerland **16** 861
    Thailand **7** 112
    Toltec **21** 243
    Turkey **16** 860
    Vietnam **32** 487
    Zapotec **21** 251
  patinas **16** 858
  techniques
    abrasion **7** 11; **16** 859
    carving *see* JADE-CARVINGS
    drilling **7** 11
    polishing **16** 859
    qiaose **7** 8
    sawing **7** 11; **16** 859
  types
    albitic jadeite **16** 858
    burnt **16** 858
    calcified **16** 858
    calcined **16** 858
    chicken-bone-white **16** 858
    child *see* river
    chloromelanite **16** 858, 861; **21** 241
    diopside-jadeite **16** 858, 861
    jadeite **16** 857–8, *858*, 860–61
      Aztec **16** 861; **21** 243
      Burma **7** 11; **16** 858, 860–61
jade
  types
    jadeite—cont.
      Celebes **16** 861
      China **7** 1, 11, 132; **16** 860
      Guatemala **16** 861; **21** 241; **29** 152–3
      Japan **16** 861
      Maya **16** 861; **21** 241, 243
      Mesoamerica, Pre-Columbian **16** 861*, *861*; **21** 240, 241, 242, *242*, 243; **22** 158; **23** 418
      Mexico **16** *861*
      New Guinea **16** 861
      Olmec **16** 861; **21** 242, *242*; **23** 418
      South America, Pre-Columbian **29** 152–3, 155
      United States of America **16** 861
    mountain **7** 10
    muscovite **16** 857
    nephrite **16** 857, *858*, 860, 861
      Australia **16** 861
      Brazil **16** 861
      Canada **16** 861
      Central Asia, Eastern **16** 858
      China **7** 1, *7*, 11, 106, 107; **16** 857, *857*, 858, 860, 861
      Indian subcontinent **15** 698, *699*
      Iran **16** *528*
      Islamic **16** 527–8, *528*
      Korea **16** 861
      Maori **16** 861
      Mesoamerica, Pre-Columbian **21** 240, 241
      Native North Americans **16** 861
      New Caledonia **16** 861
      New Guinea **16** 861
      New Zealand **16** 861
      Ottoman **16** 528, *860*
      Poland **16** 861
      Russia **10** *721*
      Siberia **7** 11; **16** 860
      Taiwan **16** 861
      Turkey **16** *860*
      United States of America **16** 861
      Zimbabwe **16** 861
    river **7** 10
  uses
    abrasion **21** 241
    amulets **1** 818; **7** 6, 107
    axes **7** 1, 2
    beads **3** 441; **7** 108; **21** 260
    beds **7** 7
    belthooks **3** *686*; **7** 7, 107
    belts **7** 109, 111
    books **7** 7
    bracelets **7** 109, 111
    burial suits **7** 6; **20** 236, *236*; **22** 466
    candlesticks **10** *721*
    combs (hair) **7** 7, *7*, 109
    cong **7** *1*, 1–2
    crowns **7** 111, *111*; **18** *350*
    cups **7** 6, *9*; **15** *699*; **16** *857*, III1
    discs **7** 2, 81
    flutes (musical instruments) **21** 257
    halberds **7** 3
    headdresses **7** 2
    inkstones **7** 94
    inlays **16** 528
    jewellery **7** 106, 107, 109, 110, 112; **15** 701; **17** 529; **18** *365*; **32** 487
    jugs **16** *528*
    knives **7** 1
    kogoks **18** *365*
    lacquer **7** 20
    lanterns (lights) **16** II2
    masks **16** *861*, III1; **21** 251
    mirror frames **21** 717, *717*, 718
    mirrors **21** 714, 719

jade
uses—cont.
mosaics **21** 243; **22** 158
necklaces **3** 441; **7** 4
norigae **18** *380*
pectoral ornaments **7** *107*
pendants (jewellery) **7** 2, *2*, *5*, 76, *107*, 111; **13** 311, *312*; **29** *154*, *199*
plaques **7** *107*; **16** 528
quivers **16** 528
sceptres **7** 3
seals **7** 128, 129, 130; **21** 882
snuff bottles **7** 132; **16** IV
sword hilts **16** 527, 528
swords **7** 7, 56
tablets **7** 4
tankards **16** *860*
teapots **7** 101, *101*
vases **16** I
vessels
China **7** 3, 6, 9
Indian subcontinent **16** III2
Islamic **16** 527, 528
Ottoman **16** 528
weapons **16** 503, 528
jade-carvers **7** 9
jade-carvings
China **7** 3–11*
Han period (206 BC-AD 220) **7** *6*
Ming period (1368-1644) **7** *9*; **16** III1
Prehistoric **6** 636; **7** *1*, 1–3*
Qing period (1644-1911) **7** *11*, 91; **16** I, II2, IV
Shang period (*c.* 1600-*c.* 1050 BC) **7** *4*
Tang period (AD 618-907) **7** *7*
Zhou period (*c.* 1050-256 BC) **7** 4
Islamic **16** 527–8*
Prehistoric art **7** *1*, 1–3*
jadeite *see under* JADE → types
Jadelot, Nicolas **12** 209
al-Jader, Khalid **16** 2
Jadot de Ville-Issey, Jean-Nicolas **4** 695; **16** 862*
attributions **5** 86
patrons and collectors **3** 613; **13** 922; **14** 11
works **2** 784; **14** 887; **19** 800; **32** 436, 456, 461; **33** 698
jādyakumbha **15** 243*
Jaeckel, Willy **16** 862*; **28** 174
Jaede, F. **29** 600
Jaeger, Astrid **14** 60
Jaeger, Gustave **9** 290
Jaeger, Halvor **14** 60
Jæger, Hans **23** 603; **28** 814
Jægerspris **8** *720*; **16** 863*
Castle **16** 863
Jaén **16** *103*, 863–4*; **29** *258*
Cathedral **16** 863–4; **29** 266, 270, 334, 337; **31** 865–6
metalwork **29** 334, 338
retable **11** 484
sacristy **16** *863*
Convento de las Bernardes **22** 507
metalwork **29** 334
painting **29** 280
Jaenecke, Fritz **10** 105
Jaeren **23** 225
Ja'far (governor of Sicily; 997-1019) **16** 171
Ja'far (*fl* 1412-31) **16** 864*
patrons and collectors **14** 431; **30** 921
pupils **29** 919
teachers **21** 703
works **16** 285
Ja'far (*fl* 1880) **16** 81, 534, 535; **33** 609
Jaffa *see* JOPPA
Jaffé, Arthur, Heliochrome Company **7** 576
Jaffé, Max **7** 576
Jaffe, Norman **17** 549
Jaffer, Wahab **23** 801, 804; **24** 219
Jaffna **16** 864–5*; **29** *440*
architecture **29** 450, 452
fort **16** 864; **21** 572–3, *572*; **29** 452
church **29** 452
Kandaswamy Temple **29** 444
shrines (i) (cult) **29** 448
jagama kilns *see* KILNS → types → climbing
Jagamarra Nelson, Michael *see* NELSON (JAKAMARRA), MICHAEL
Jagan **16** 865*
Jagannath **16** 865
Jagat **15** *279*; **16** 865*
Ambika Temple **15** 273, *273*, 274, 489
reliefs **15** *489*
jagatī **15** 243*
jagatīpīṭhā see PĪTHA
Jagat Singh, Maharaja of Jaipur (*reg* 1803-18) (Rajput) **15** 611
Jagat Singh, Ruler (*reg* 1618-46) (Pahari) **15** *623*
Jagat Singh I, Rana of Mewar (*reg* 1628-52) (Rajput) **15** 385, 491, 740
paintings **15** 598, *603*, 643
Jagat Singh II, Rana of Mewar (*reg* 1734-51) (Rajput) **15** 600
Jagatsukh Shiva Temple **15** 264
Jagdishpur **15** 475; **22** 447
Jagellonica, Katariina, Duchess of Finland *see* CATHERINE, Queen of Sweden
Jager, A. **23** 447
Jäger, Carl **31** 368
Jäger, Franz **2** 785; **13** 200
Jager, Jakob **18** 431
Jäger, János Henrik **5** 82
Jäger, Johann Peter **30** 741
Jäger, Josef **28** 853
Jageshvar **15** 264
Jaggayyapeta **15** 251, 438, 700
Jagger, Charles **3** 373
Jagger, (Charles) Sargeant **16** 865*
works **10** 267; **22** 48, *48*
Jagiellon (House of) **16** 866*; **30** 331
Jagiellon, Anna, Queen of Poland *see* ANNA, Queen of Poland
Jagiellon, Bona, Queen of Poland *see* BONA SFORZA, Queen of Poland
Jagiellon, Catherine, Duchess of Finland *see* CATHERINE, Queen of Sweden
Jagiellon, Elizabeth *see* ELIZABETH, Queen of Poland
Jagiellon, Frederick, Cardinal **20** 395
Jagiellon, Hedwig, Electress of Brandenburg *see* HEDWIG, Electress of Brandenburg
Jagiellon, John I Albrecht *see* JOHN I ALBRECHT, King of Poland
Jagiellon, Louis II, King of Bohemia and Hungary *see* LOUIS II, King of Bohemia and Hungary
Jagiellon, Mary, Queen of Hungary *see* MARY, Queen of Hungary, Regent and Stadholder of the Netherlands
Jagiellon, Sigismund I, King of Poland *see* SIGISMUND I, King of Poland
Jagiellon, Sigismund II Augustus, King of Poland *see* SIGISMUND II AUGUSTUS, King of Poland
Jagiellon, Sophie, Queen of Poland *see* SOPHIE, Queen of Poland
Jagiellon, Vladislav, King of Poland *see* VLADISLAV V JAGIELLON, King of Poland
Jagiellon, Vladislav II, King of Bohemia and Hungary *see* VLADISLAV II, King of Bohemia and Hungary
Jagiellon, Vladislav II, King of Poland *see* VLADISLAV II JAGIELLON, King of Poland
Jagiellon Globe **12** 813
Jagiellonian University *see under* KRAKÓW
Jagmin, Stanisław **25** 123
Jahan Ara **15** 366, 367, 371
Jahan Begam ('Adil Shahi) **4** 52
Jahangir, Cowasji **15** 183
Jahangir, Emperor (*reg* 1605-27) (Mughal) **1** *92*; **2** 235, 236; **7** 717; **8** 848; **15** 371, 375, 410, *587*; **22** 258
albums **1** 582; **15** 547; **21** 703
architecture **1** 502; **10** 828; **13** 882; **15** 363–4, 372; **16** 239; **18** 646; **28** 710
calligraphy **15** 681
carpets **15** 683
coins **15** *688*, 689
collections **15** 740; **16** 122
dress **15** 691
gardens **1** 648; **11** 340; **12** 74; **29** 480
hardstones **15** 698
inscriptions **1** 647
jade **6** 272, 285; **15** 699; **16** 527
jewellery **15** 701, 723
manuscripts **1** 820; **4** 50, 90; **14** 175; **15** 584–7, 740; **16** 295, 345, 356
mirrors **21** 717
paintings **15** 208, 547, 588
'Abd al-Samad **1** 25
Abu'l-Hasan **1** 92
Balchand **3** 91
Bishan Das **4** 91
Daulat **8** 542
Farrukh Beg **10** 817
Ghulam **12** 561
Govardhan (*fl c.* 1596-1640) **13** 235
Hashim **14** 218
Kesu Das **17** 922
Manohar (*fl c.* 1580-1620) **20** 284
Mansur (*fl* 1590-1630) **20** 301
Muhammad 'Ali (i) (*fl c.* 1600-10) **22** 259
Nanha **22** 457
porcelain **6** *918*
portraits **15** 232
weapons **15** 678
Jahangir Album *see under* ALBUMS → individual manuscripts
Jahangirnagar *see* DHAKA
Jahanpanah *see under* DELHI
Jahanshah, Sultan (*reg* 1438-67) (Qaraqoyunlu) **25** 774
Jah Heut **20** 183
al-Jahiz **16** 398
Jahn, Helmut **16** 868*
works **6** *574*, 575; **10** 417; **11** 734; **17** 603; **28** 835
Jahn, Johann Quirin **8** 422, 423, 426; **28** 163
Jahn, O. **13** 542
Jahn, R. (collector) **8** 423
Jahns, Rudolf (*b* 1896; collector) **32** 695
Jahnus, Lt-Col. **11** 886
Jahrbuch der deutschen Bühnenspiele, Das **13** 773
Jahrbuch der kaiserlich königlichen Zentral-Commission zur Erforschung und Erhaltung der Baudenkmale see WIENER JAHRBUCH FÜR KUNST...
Jahrbuch der Königlich Preussischen Kunstsammlungen **24** 423
Jahrbuch der Kunsthistorischen Sammlungen der Allerhöchsten Kaiserhauses **14** 11
Jahrbuch der kunsthistorischen Sammlungen des allerhöchsten Kaiserhauses see JAHRBUCH DER KUNSTHISTORISCHEN SAMMLUNGEN IN WIEN
Jahrbuch der kunsthistorischen Sammlungen in Wien **24** 423, 438
Jahrbuch der Zeitschrift das neue Pathos **24** 427
Jahrbuch des oberösterreichischen Musealvereins **24** 438
Jahrbücher für bildende Kunst see MÜNCHEN JAHRBÜCHER FÜR BILDENDE KUNST
Jahrbücher für Kunstwissenschaft **24** 444
Jahrbuch für Kunst und Kunstpflege in der Schweiz/Annuaire des beaux-arts en Suisse **24** 453
Jahrbuch für Kunstwissenschaft **24** 445
Jahrhunderthalle *see under* WROCŁAW
Jaime, E. **5** 760
Jaime Ortiz, José *see* ORTIZ, JOSÉ JAIME
Jaimes Sánchez, Humberto **16** 868*
Jain, Uttam **17** 600
Jai Nagar *see* JAIPUR
Jaina Island **29** 829; **31** 117
bone-carvings **21** 247
musical instruments **21** 257
pottery **21** 239, *239*
shells **21** 259
Jainism **15** 190, 202, 203–4; **16** 868–70*
art forms and materials
book covers **15** 563–4
bronze **15** 453, 531
domes **9** 86
embroidery **15** 674
gold **15** 564, 616
inks **15** 564
manuscript covers **15** 549
manuscript illumination **16** *869*
Digambara **15** 566, 567, 569
Indian subcontinent **15** 544, 545, 549, 561, 563–9, *565*, 616–17, *617*, 739
Shvetambara **15** 564, 566, 616
manuscripts **15** 226, 549, 563
maps **15** 704
narratives **15** 563, 564
nude figures **23** 290
painting **15** *225*, 563–6, *566*, 674
landscape **15** 565
scroll **15** 617
palm leaves **15** 545, 563–4
paper **15** 564
plaques **15** 226, 443
rock crystal **26** 487
sandstone **15** *442*
sculpture
bronze **15** 453, 531
Indian subcontinent **5** 95; **15** *442*, 442–3*, 453, 467, 497–8, 508, 522, 523, 531; **20** 817
stupas **15** 226; **29** 863, 864
temples **15** 301, 312, 313, *313*, 314, *314*, 528
textiles **15** 565, *566*
iconography **15** 224–6*; **23** 290
patronage **15** 737, 739
sects
Digambara **16** 869
Shvetambara **16** 869
Jaintiapur **30** 162
Jaipur **15** *276*, *285*, 390, *597*; **16** 870–71*
Albert Hall *see* Government Central Museum of Jaipur
architecture **15** 410
art school **15** 542
book arts **15** 610
carpets **15** 682, *683*, 683
Chandra Mahal **15** 611
Jaipur—cont.
chess sets **6** 556
dyeing **15** 671
embroidery **15** 675
enamel **15** 711, 712, 724; **16** 515
furniture **15** 693
Government Central Museum of Jaipur **15** 182, 403; **16** 823, 871
halls **14** 77
houses **15** 390
Jawahar Kala Kendre **7** 883
jewellery **15** 702
Maharaja Sawai Man Singh II Museum **15** 182, 705; **16** 871
maps **15** 705
metalwork **15** 713
observatory **23** *338*, 339
painting **15** 609*, *610*, 610–11*, *611*
pottery **15** 686
silver **15** 707
textiles **15** 673
urban planning **15** *411*
Jai Ram **15** 600
Jaisal, Maharawal of Jaisalmer **16** 871
Jaisalmer **15** *276*; **16** 871*
cenotaphs **15** 491
fortifications **21** 590
houses **32** 323
painting **15** 613
palace **15** 388
Patua ki Haveli **15** *390*
Shri Sambhavanathji Temple **16** 871
temples **15** 314
Jai Singh, Rana of Mewar (*reg* 1680-98) (Rajput) **15** 599
Jai Singh I, Raja of Amer (*reg* 1623-67) (Rajput) **1** 770, 771; **15** 372, 387, 609
Jai Singh II, Maharaja of Jaipur (*reg* 1699-1743) (Rajput) **1** 771; **8** 675; **15** 390, 410, 548; **31** 542, 903
architecture **16** 870; **23** 339
paintings **15** 610
Jaisinghpura **15** 610
Jaisinhapur **15** 455
Jajce **4** *459*
castle **4** 459
Franciscan Monastery **4** 462
St Luke **4** 459
Jajpur **15** 504
jak **29** 470
Jakab, Dezső **18** 212*
Ják Abbey **14** *881*, 883; **16** 871–2*; **26** 594
church **16** *872*
sculpture **14** 892; **26** 638
wall paintings **14** 898
Jakabčic, Michal **28** 853
Jakac, Božidar **28** 860
Jakachū Itō *see* ITŌ JAKACHŪ
Jakamarra Nelson, Michael *see* NELSON (JAKAMARRA), MICHAEL
Jakard, Joseph-Marie *see* Jacquard, Joseph-Marie
Jakarta **15** *753*; **16** 873–4*; **21** 575
architecture **15** 769
Batavian Society for Arts and Sciences building *see* Museums → National Museum
Court of Justice *see* MUSEUMS Fine Arts Museum
exhibitions **15** 808
furniture **15** 813
Gereja Emmanuel **15** 813
Institute for Art Education (Lembaga Kesenian Jakarta) **15** 819
Institut Kesenian Jakarta (IKJ) **15** 819
Istiqlal Mosque **15** 769
Jepang House **15** 772
Koningsplein Palace **15** 769
Lembaga Kesenian Jakarta *see* Institute for Art Education

Jakarta—cont.
museums
Fine Arts Museum **15** 769
Municipal History Museum **29** 239
Museum of Jakarta **15** 769
National Museum **15** 769
Textile Museum **29** 239
National Research Centre for Archaeology **6** 925
painting **15** 807
porcelain **4** 175, 176
Reinier de Klerk House **15** 769
trade **6** 331
Willemskerk **15** 769
Jakawitz **20** 885, 886
Jaki, Robert **19** 885
Jakimow, Igor von **33** 174
Jakob Maximilian, Graf Thurn, Prince-Bishop of Gurk *see* THURN, JAKOB MAXIMILIAN, Graf, Prince-Bishop of Gurk
Jakobson, Roman **7** 660–61
Jakobus di Ser Griffus **7** 329
Jakob von Elchingen *see* ZWITZEL, JAKOB
Jakob von Landshut **16** 874*; **29** 755
Jakoby, Július **28** 853
Jakoby, Miklós **11** 31
Jakopič, Rihard **2** 890; **16** 874*; **28** 860
Jakov, Bishop of Serres **28** 449
Jakovetz, Antal **16** 811
Jakovits, József **10** 650; **14** 896
Jåks, Iver **27** 472
Jaksch, Hans **14** 749; **32** 439
Jaksić, Djura **28** 450
Jakub, Master **31** 353
Jakub of Siena **25** 134
Jakubonis, Gediminas **16** 874–5*; **19** 499
Jakubowicz, Paschalis
works **25** *133*
Jakun **20** 163
Jakunderi Church **12** 322
Jákupsson, Bárdur **10** 813
Jakusai Rokkaku *see* ROKKAKU JAKUSAI
Jakushi Kawamura *see* KAWAMURA JAKUSHI
Jal, Auguste **4** 321; **16** 875*
jāla **15** 243*
Jalabert, Charles (-François) **13** 228; **16** 875–6*
Jalabert, Jean **17** 673
Jalal, Shahid **23** 800, 804
Jalalabad **1** *186*, 204, 206
Jalal al-Din Ahsan, Sultan of Ma'bar (*reg* 1334–*c.* 1339) **15** 358
Jalal al-Din Firuz, Sultan (*reg* 1290-6) (Khalji) **8** 672
Jalal al-Din Muhammad **30** 162
Jalal al-Din Muhammad al-Fakhkhar Shirazi **15** 681
Jalal al-Din Rumi **16** 329
Jalal of Amasya **16** 285
Jalame **9** 644
Jalapa **13** 768; **21** 265
Central de Autobuses **21** 382
Museo de Antropología *see under* Universidad Veracruzana
Museo Arqueológico **21** 397
Universidad Veracruzana
Museo de Antropología **33** 617
Jalasangi **15** 317
Jalatunda **15** 781–2
Jalaun **15** 664
Jalayirid **16** 377, 876*
see also:
AHMAD JALAYIR, Sultan
UWAYS I, Sultan
Jalea, Ion **16** 877*; **26** 716
Jaley, Jean-Louis-Nicolas **16** 877*
Jaley, Louis **16** 877
Jalhay, Eugenio **32** 562
Jalingo **23** *129*
Jalisco **21** 250
figurines **33** 101, 103
Jalisco—cont.
mirrors **21** 718
pottery **5** 660; **21** 237
tombs **21** 216
see also CAPACHA-OPEÑO
Jallier, Noël **11** 265; **13** 224; **16** 877–8*
Jallot, Léon-Albert **11** 601, 602
Jalor
Qila' Mosque **15** 349
Sand Ba'orivari Mosque **15** 349
Tupkhana Mosque **15** 349
Jam **16** *105*
minaret **1** 207; **16** 167, *167*, 248; **21** 627
inscriptions **16** 169
tiles **16** 169
Jama, Matija **2** 890; **28** 860
Jama-Coaque **29** 155
Jamaer, Pierre-Victor **3** 543; **5** 39, 40; **16** 878*
Jamaer, Victor **5** 54
Jamaica **2** 144; **5** 744, *745*; **16** *878*, 878–90*
architecture **16** 882–3*
baskets **16** 882
boxes **16** *889*
carnivals **5** 788; **16** 881, *881*
ceramics **16** 887–8*
collections **16** 889–90*
costumes **16** *881*
court-houses **16** *883*
dealing **16** 889–90*
doorjambs **16** *885*
earthenwares **16** 887, *887*
education (art) **2** 154; **16** 890*
exhibitions **5** 746
furniture **16** 885–7*
gold **16** 888
Guaiacum wood **16** *879*
houses **16** 882, 883
interior decoration **16** 885–7*
jars **16** *887*
lithography **5** 751; **16** *881*
mahogany **16** *884*, 886
marks **16** 889
metalwork **16** 888–9*
museums **16** 890*
painting **2** 149; **16** 883–5*
patronage **16** 889*
pattern books **5** 749
pewter **16** 888; **24** 580
pictographs **16** 880
prints **16** 884
religion **16** 880–81*
sculpture **5** *748*; **16** *879*, 880, 883–5*, *884*
silver **16** *889*
slaves **16** 880
stone **16** *885*
stone-carvings **16** *885*
tortoiseshell **16** 888
trade **16** 886
wood **5** *748*
wood-carvings **16** 882
Jamaica Furniture Co. Ltd **16** 886
Jamaican Art Movement **16** 884
Jamal, A'li **19** 7
Jamal, Ather **23** 801
Jamal al-Din Abu Ishaq **33** 482
Jamāl al-Dīn ibn 'Abdallah al-Mawṣulī Yāqūt al-Musta'ṣimī *see* YAQUT AL-MUSTA'SIMI
Jamalgarhi **5** 94; **15** *264*; **16** 890*; **23** *797*
Jamal of Amasya **16** 285
Jambi **15** *752*, 788, 794, 811
Jámbor, Lajos **14** 890
Jambs, Master of the **13** 104
Jambukola *see* DAMBULLA
James I, King of Aragon (*reg* 1213-76) **13** 67
James I, King of Cyprus (*reg* 1382-98) **8** 363
James I, King of England and Scotland (*reg* 1603-25) **8** *165*; **28** 268; **29** 798*
architecture **10** 360; **17** 634; **19** 568; **28** 225; **29** 797
James I, King of England and Scotland (*reg* 1603-25)—cont.
coins **7** 537
decorative works **30** 662
gardens **6** 96
gems **23** 831
guns **2** 461
illustrated writings **10** 162
manuscripts **20** 171
paintings **4** 847; **9** 724; **14** 547; **31** 889
sculpture **7** 641; **8** 107; **10** 262; **12** 577
sponsorship **21** 509
stage design **17** 637
tapestries **10** 349
James II, King of Aragon (*reg* 1291-1327) **3** 220, 309; **13** 67
James II, King of Great Britain and Ireland (*reg* 1685-8) **2** 473; **12** 591; **29** 804*
architecture **33** 396
furniture **10** 291
interior decoration **32** 358
paintings **8** 495; **12** 280; **18** 144; **19** 122; **32** 143, 379; **33** 260
sculpture **3** 735
James II, King of Mallorca (*reg* 1276-1311) **20** 749; **23** 881; **27** 551
James II, King of Scotland (*reg* 1437-60) **28** 267
James III, King of Scotland (*reg* 1460-88) **7** 179; **28** 233, 268
James IV, King of Scotland (*reg* 1488-1513) **2** 453; **20** *700*; **28** 268; **29** 797–8*
architecture **9** 728; **28** 225; **29** 679
furniture **28** 245
manuscripts **20** 699; **28** 234, 268
paintings **28** 234
James IV of Scotland, Master of **14** 759; **20** 699–700*
patrons and collectors **29** 798
works **20** *700*
James V, King of Scotland (*reg* 1513-42) **9** 728; **28** 268; **29** 679
architecture **28** 225
paintings **28** 234
regalia **28** 260
tapestries **28** 244
woodwork **28** 250
James VI, King of Scotland *see* JAMES I, King of England and Scotland
James, C(harles) H(olloway) **16** 891*
collaboration **33** 382
competitions **7** 668
works **10** 240, *240*; **23** 248; **31** 243
James, C. H., & Bywaters & Roland Pierce **5** 312
James, Charlie **16** 891*; **22** 581
pupils **20** 492
works **16** *891*
James, Edward (Frank Willis) **2** 560; **16** 892*
architecture **5** 925
collections **8** 468; **10** 367
sponsorship **26** 508
James, Francis **19** 589
James, Frederic **27** 475
James, George Abbott **29** 870
James, George Wharton **22** 660, 676
James, Henry (1803-77) **19** 481
James, Henry (1843-1916) **2** 619; **16** 892*
groups and movements **1** 772
works **8** 709; **14** 453; **29** 724
James, H. F. **18** 906
James, Isaac **16** 892*; **29** 713
James, John **16** 893*
collaboration **14** 257
groups and movements **23** 857
works **5** 65; **14** 256, 257
writings **12** 127
James, Joseph **23** 194
James, Maggie Mayo
works **22** *660*
James, M(ontague) R(hodes) **16** 893*; **30** 749
James, P. L. **26** 21
James, Robert **29** 426
James, Shani Rees **32** 786
James, Silas **7** 718
James, Thomas, Bishop of Dol *see* THOMAS JAMES, Bishop of Dol
James Boucher **19** 109
James Cousland **19** 109
James le Palmer **10** 202
James of Kokkinobaphos **9** 605, 617; **12** 71
works **9** *605*
James of St George **16** 894–6*; **22** 211
attributions **5** 373
patrons and collectors **25** 14
works **6** 602; **16** *895*, *896*; **19** 895
Jameson, Anna Brownell **13** 304; **16** 896–7*; **20** 33; **33** 309
Jameson, Charles *see* JAMES, CHARLIE
Jamesone, Andrew **16** 897
Jamesone, George **9** 724; **16** 897–8*; **28** 234
patrons and collectors **25** 281; **28** 268, 269
pupils **33** 409
works **28** 234, *234*
James's Steam Furniture Manufactory **23** 66
Jamestown (VA) **31** 651
church **4** 786
Jamestown Tableau **11** 834
Jamete, Esteban **16** 898*; **29** 289
attributions **8** 253
collaboration **31** 92; **32** 493
patrons and collectors **7** 488
Jamette, Louis **8** 419
Jami, Domenico de *see* AIMO, DOMENICO
Jamieson, Mrs **28** 265
Jamieson & McKay **31** 733
Jamison, Nuala **4** 834
Jamli Temple **15** 292
Jammidoddi **15** 535
Jammu **15** *619*
Jamnagar **15** 671
Jamnitzer (family) **23** 312; **25** 22
Jamnitzer, Abraham **16** 898
Jamnitzer, Albrecht **16** 898
Jamnitzer, Christoph **12** 456; **16** 898, 901–2*
patrons and collectors **8** 413
works **8** 413; **12** 443; **16** *901*; **23** 310; **24** 271; **25** 607
Jamnitzer, Hans, I (*d* 1548/9) **16** 898
Jamnitzer, Hans, II (1539-1603) **16** 898
Jamnitzer, Wenzel, I (1507/8-1585) **2** 455; **12** 456; **16** 898–901*; **18** 574; **23** 312
assistants **33** 727
collaboration **1** 789; **12** 402; **18** 575; **23** 309, 311; **29** 44, 738
illustrated writings **1** 788
patrons and collectors **13** 646, 908, 910; **28** 53; **33** 271
pupils **24** 573; **28** 713
works **7** 835; **12** 443, 446, 456; **16** *899*, *900*; **23** *309*, 540; **28** I1; **29** 571
Jamnitzer, Wenzel, II (1548-72) **16** 898
Jamot, Paul **26** 113
Jamshedpur **15** 411
Jamshoro, Sind University **23** 804
Jamsot **15** 481
Jamuszkiewicz, Jerzy **5** 912
Jamyang Zad Pa **30** 845
Jan (*fl* 1407-39) **6** 363
Jan (*fl* 1511-13) **3** 224
Jan II (Kazimierz), King of Poland *see* JOHN II (CASIMIR), King of Poland
Jan III Sobieski, King of Poland *see* JOHN III SOBIESKI, King of Poland
Janák, Pavel **8** 401; **16** 902*; **25** 429
collaboration **30** 221
groups and movements **7** 182; **8** 373; **12** 834; **13** 711
pupils **25** 143
teachers **18** 405
works **8** 380, 401, 402, *402*, 406, 427; **25** 430, 438
Jana Kiram, Dhanapal **20** 54
Janakiram, P. V. **15** 172
Janakiraman **20** 54
Janáky, István **8** 563; **14** 891; **16** 902–3*
Jananatha-mangalam *see* POLONNARUVA
Janbalat, Sultan (*reg* 1500-01) (Mamluk) **21** 587
Jančić, Olga **28** 453
Janckl, Franz *see* JÄNGGL, FRANZ
Janco, George **24** 405
Janco, Jules **16** 903
Janco, Marcel **16** 567, 571, 903*; **26** 718
groups and movements **3** 113; **8** 433, 434, 436; **9** 758; **20** 877; **22** 921; **23** 25; **31** 503
works **16** 568; **24** 405; **25** 585; **33** 363
Janda, Jacob *see* HANUSZ
Jandial *see under* TAXILA
Jandun, Jean de *see* JEAN DE JANDUN
Jane, Joan Busquets i *see* BUSQUETS I JANE, JOAN
Janeček, Ota **16** 903*
Jänes, Peep **10** 538; **30** 276
Janet *see* CLOUET
Janet, Ange-Louis *see* JANET-LANGE
Janet-Lange **16** 904*
Jänggl, Franz **14** 529; **16** 904*; **24** 808
jaṅghā **15** 243*
Jani, Lukás **14** 906
Janin, Fernand **5** 275
Janin, Jules (Gabriel) **12** 609; **14** 288; **16** 904–5*; **17** 605
Janinet, François **16** 905
Janinet, Jean-François **4** 330; **14** 815; **16** 905–6*; **21** 643
assistants **9** 420
collaboration **8** 791
pupils **8** 790
works **2** 239; **6** *397*; **13** 219, 220; **16** *905*; **25** 619; **33** 292
Janini, Joaquim Pla *see* PLA JANINI, JOAQUIM
Janis, Harriet **16** 906
Janis, Sidney **16** 906*; **22** 189; **31** 665, 667
Janis, Sidney and Harriet
collection *see under* NEW YORK → museums → MOMA (Museum of Modern Art)
Janisch, Jerzy **2** 528
Janitschek, H. **23** 645
Janjevo **28** 456
Janjgir, Vishnu Temple **15** 324
Jan & Jon **23** 222
Jank, Angelo **13** 212; **16** 906*; **22** 331; **28** 143
Jank, Christian **6** 62; **16** 906
Janke, Franc **3** 620
Jankó, János **14** 901
Janković, Dušan **28** 451
Jankovič, Jozef **28** 855
Janković, Nikola **28** 453
Janković, Živorad **28** 445
Jankovich, Miklós **5** 84; **15** 15, 16
Jankowski, Karol **32** 872
Jankowski, Stanislaw **29** 634

Janlet, (Charles-) Emile 3 579; 16 906–7*
pupils 3 44
teachers 3 898
works 3 549, 585
Janlet, Félix 3 898; 16 906
Janlet, Gustave 16 906
Janlet, Max 3 614
Janmot, (Anne-François-) Louis 16 907*
Jannabi
works 23 *642*
Jannau 4 176
Janneau, Guillaume 9 371
Janneck, Franz Christoph 2 795; 4 662; 16 907–8*
Janni, Guglielmo 16 680
Jannings *see* JANYNS
Janniot, Alfred 10 689
Jannot, Henri 11 302, 550; 28 750
Jan of Banská Bystrica, Master 28 851
Jan of Dubava 28 849
Jan of Kraków, Master 27 722
Jan of Lobkovice 8 422
Jan of Opava 8 389; 16 908*
Jan of Pernštejn (i) (*d* 1475) 24 463
Jan of Pernštejn (ii) (*d* 1548) 24 462, 463
Jan of Středa 8 422; 16 908*
works 8 389; 13 151; 16 908
Janoir, Jean 19 848
János 14 904
Janot, Denis 10 725
Janoušek, František 8 393; 16 908*
Janoušek, Vladimír 8 388
Jans, Jean 11 641; 12 828; 22 725
Janscha, Lorenz 2 512
Jansen, A. (*fl* 1619-25) 18 848
Jansen, August (1881-1957) 33 566
Jansen, Cornelius 17 1
Jansen, Frederik 33 162
Jansen, Hendricus 17 1*; 22 850
Jansen, Hermann 3 795; 12 58; 21 796; 31 452; 33 711
Jansen, Jacob 19 595; 30 877
Jansen, J. C. 22 876
Jansen, L. 18 848
Jansen, Michael 21 792
Jansen, Peter 29 58
Jansenism *see under* CHRISTIANITY → sects
Jansenius, Marius 9 479
Jansens, Jean-François 28 845
Janson, Barthel 20 281
Janson, D. J. 23 8
Janson, Horst Woldemar 2 535; 23 8; 31 672
Janson van Ceulen, Cornelis, I *see* JONSON VAN CEULEN, CORNELIS, I
Janssen (family) 4 693
Janssen, Abraham 4 *895*, 915; 17 3–6*
collaboration 4 916; 28 904; 33 181
patrons and collectors 4 559
pupils 26 94, 746; 28 179, 364
reproductive prints by others 17 *598*
teachers 28 899
works 3 559; 17 *4*
Janssen, Ewert 8 725
Janssen, Gerhard 19 336
Janssen, Horst 10 483; 17 6*
Janssen, Karl 8 39; 17 2–3*; 19 94
Janssen, Peter (1844-1908) 14 313; 17 2*; 22 329
Janssen, Peter (*b* 1906) 13 729; 21 76
Janssen, Pieter 33 700
Janssen, Stephen Theodore 10 346
Janssen, Theodor 17 2
Janssen Eijken Sluijters, J. M. 30 16
Janssens, Daniël 2 200
Janssens, François-Joseph 3 613; 17 6–7*; 25 374
Janssens, Hieronymus 17 7*
Janssens, J. (1854-1930) 3 885
Janssens, Jan (1590-1650) 3 559; 5 4; 12 519; 17 7*
Janssens, Jean-Baptiste 17 8
Janssens, Victor Honoré 17 7–8*
Janssens, Wynand 17 8*
collaboration 3 549, 898
pupils 3 44
works 25 64
Jansson (family) 2 696; 20 364
Jansson, Eugène (Fredrik) 17 8–9*
patrons and collectors 30 730
works 11 476, *476*; 17 *8*; 30 80, 81
Jansson, Karl Emanuel 10 127; 17 9*
Jansson, Rune 30 81
Janssone, Jan *see* MERTENS, JAN, THE YOUNGER
Janssonius, Jan 20 364
Jansz., Dirc 22 835
Jansz., Govert 23 112
Jansz., Jan 14 708; 28 76
Jansz., Simon 22 835
Jánszky, Béla 14 890; 17 876; 18 394
Jantas, Jan 32 874
Janthur, Richard 10 695; 21 55; 29 609
Jäntti, Toivo 19 407
Janů, Karel 24 226*
Janunkalniņš, Jūlijs 12 825
Januška, Ipolitas 19 498
Janussan 2 249
Janusz I, Duke of Mazovia (*reg* 1374-1429) 32 868, 879
Jan van Amerongen 20 663
Jan van den Berge 19 260
Jan van den Mijnnesten 20 799
Jan van der Cautheren 19 260
Jan van der Meeren 8 662
Jan van Halderen 2 486; 17 740
Jan van Holland 13 133
Jan van Mergem *see* JEAN DE MARVILLE
Jan van Ruysbroeck 17 9–10*
works 3 543; 5 53; 13 62; 19 260
Jan van Steffeswert 22 857
Jan van Woluwe 3 553
Janvier, Alex (*b* 1935) 22 597
Janvier, Alez (*b* 1948) 22 598
Janvier, Antide 28 194
Jan von Brunswik 26 563
Janvry, Olivier Choppin de *see* CHOPPIN DE JANVRY, OLIVIER
Janyns, Henry 17 10*; 33 248
Janyns, Robert (i) (*fl* 1438-64) 17 10*
Janyns, Robert (ii) (*d* 1506) 17 10*; 19 602; 31 412
Jao Chieh *see* RAO JIE
Jao Tzu-jan *see* RAO ZIRAN
Jaoul, Francesco 10 209
Japaljarri Leura, Tim *see* LEURA (JAPALJARRI), TIM
Japaljarri Sims, Paddy *see* SIMS (JAPALJARRI), PADDY
Japan 17 10–440*, *11*, *241*
abaci (counting frames) 17 399
acacia 17 354
adhesives 17 209
adzes 17 *49*
aesthetics 17 335
aisles 17 65
albums 1 580, 581–2
alcoves 17 *75*, 76
alloys 17 318
hakudō 17 318
irogane 21 330
sawari 17 318
shakudō 17 318; 21 330
shibuichi 17 318
altars 1 703–4*, *704*
aluminium 1 *737*, *738*; 17 213
amber 17 398
animal subjects 17 *45*; *185*
Japan—cont.
antlers 17 297, 401
apartments 21 *317*
appliqué 17 *356*; 30 VII2
archaeology 17 425–7*; 22 148; 23 440
architects 2 317*; 17 51–3*, 65
architecture 17 23, 45–93*, *67*; 31 *79*; 33 539
anti-seismic 17 88, 90
Buddhism 14 773; 17 71–5*
conservation 7 729
Edo period (1600-1868) 17 *77*, *80*, 85
landscape 12 95–101, *97*, *99*, *100*, *101*, *102*
megalithic 21 45
military 17 83–6*; 21 595*
prefabrication 17 50–51, 89
Prehistoric 17 53–6*
restoration 7 729
Shinto 17 74
trabeated construction 31 269
wood 17 45
archives 2 369, 371*
armour 2 448, 449; 17 297, 300, 302, 355, 361–4*, *362*, 375
arrows 17 361
art (imitation of works of) 11 306
art (reproduction of works of) 17 204
art criticism 7 716; 17 437, 439
art history 7 160; 17 345, 439; 33 317–22*
artists' biographies 17 159–60
art market 2 561
art schools 21 59
ashes 17 242, 250–51; 27 699
ashtrays 17 399
asunaro 17 356
auction houses 2 561
auctions 2 561; 17 424
automata 17 373
azaleas 17 367
azurite 17 277; 18 600; 24 790
badges 14 428–9
bamboo 3 144; 17 46, 297, 314, *341*, 358*, 365*, 368, 387, 388, 397, 398, 400, 401, 407; 28 *413*
bamboo-carvings 17 *45*
banners 17 *321*, 363
bark 17 47
baskets 17 358, 365; 31 167
basketwork 17 358*, 359, 365*
bays 17 65
beads 17 385–6; 26 487
beams 17 72
bells 3 626; 17 100, 104, 321; 27 599, 600
Buddhism 17 *322*, 397
dōtaku 17 30, *319*, 319–20
blouses 17 375
bone 4 314
bonsai 17 365–8*, *366*
bookbindings 17 272, *272*
book illustrations 17 186, 270, *271*, 272, 273–4*, 280, 285, 419; 23 *162*
books 17 269–74*, *272*; 22 432
accordion 1 581; 17 220, *272*
botanical 17 274
butterfly 1 581
de luxe 17 271
Edo period (1600-1868) 17 *271*
medical 17 274
sagabon 14 703
Saga books 30 376
stitched-bound 1 582
bookstands 17 301
bottles 17 *256*, *258*, *264*, *265*, *303*
bowls 18 *555*
bows 17 361, 362; 31 167
boxes 14 429, *429*; 17 297, 300, *301*, 302, *305*, 386; 18 *613*
account 17 358
bentō 17 382, *383*
lunchboxes *see* *bentō*
Japan
boxes—cont.
tebako 17 300
writing-boxes: Edo period (1600-1868) 14 *704*
box-wood 17 399
brackets 4 623–5*, *624*; 17 66, 72; 30 913
braids 17 308*, 313
brass 17 276, 370
braziers 17 341
brocades 17 371
bronze 17 100–101*, 110, *110*, 120, 318, 319–20, *323*, *324*, 361, *370*, 396, 397, 409; 22 *497*
Asuka-Hakuhō period (AD *c.* 552-710) 17 *321*
Asuka period (AD *c.* 552-645) 17 *107*
Buddhism 17 *34*, *322*, *375*
Edo period (1600-1868) 17 370
Hakuhō period (AD 645-710) 17 *111*, *112*
Kofun period (*c.* AD 300-710) 17 *320*; 21 716
Nara period (AD 710-94) 17 *113*
Yayoi period (*c.* 300 BC–*c.* AD 300) 17 21, 319, *319*
brushes 5 35; 7 66; 17 208–9, 213*, 226, 227, 235, 315, 368–9*, *369*, 399
brushline 5 35, 36–7, *37*; 17 226
burial chambers 17 *58*, 58–9*, *59*
burial mounds 17 57–9; 18 190
burial practices 17 104
burnishing 17 276
cabinets (ii) (furniture) 5 350; 18 II2
cakes 17 382–3
calligraphers 17 214, 227, 236*
calligraphy 6 772; 11 822; 17 210–40*, *213*, *218*, 219, *230*, *235*, *236*, 341, 342–4*, *343*; 23 *445*
bokuseki 17 342–4, *343*
Buddhism 15 *130*, *131*, *833*; 17 217–21*, *218*, *220*, 229–31*, *230*
Buddhism: Zen 17 *230*
Confucianism 17 236
display 1 581–2; 17 215
Edo period (1600-1868) 17 *216*, *233*; 27 *465*
Gokyōgoku 17 224
Heian period (AD 794-1185) 1 581–2; 17 *212*, *220*, *222*, *223*; 23 445
Hosshōji 11 822, 824; 17 224
Kamakura period (1185-1333) 17 *230*
literati 17 *235*, *236*, *237*
Meiji period (1868-1912) 33 495
Muromachi period (1333-1568) 17 *227*, *228*
Nara period (AD 710-94) 17 *218*
Oie 17 215, 216, 228
Sesonji 11 822, 823; 17 215, 223–4, 226
Shōren'in 17 215, 224, 225–9*, *227*, *228*; 29 66
Shōwa period (1926-89) 17 *239*, *240*
Zen 6 752
Zenga 14 61; 28 408
camellia 17 399
camphor-wood 17 *99*, *109*, 390, 399; 33 325
candles 17 341
candlesticks 17 399
cane 17 365, 401; 21 716
carpenters 17 *49*, 51–2
cartography 20 361–2
cartouches 17 220
carving 17 298, *301*; 18 601
casks 17 *357*
casting 17 99, 101, 320, 321
Japan—cont.
castles 14 551; 17 22, 45, 46, 71, 83–6*, 95–6*, *95*, *96*; 21 595
Edo period (1600-1868) 14 *552*; 17 *85*; 22 *432*
Momoyama period (1568-1600) 21 828; 23 592
catalogues 7 161; 17 428–9, 437–8; 29 85
calligraphy 17 230
celluloid 31 259
censorship 6 175
ceramics 4 70; 17 240–68*, *241*, *247*, 297, 350, 398, 399; 18 601; 21 650; 23 365; 28 495
Edo period (1600-1868) 14 704
Heian period (AD 794-1185) 17 *244*
Kofun period (*c.* AD 300-710) 17 246
Meiji period (1868-1912) 17 378
Nara period (AD 710-94) 17 387
certificates 17 230
chairs 17 384
chapels 2 *7*; 17 *422*
characters (writing) 17 21, 211, 212, 219, 220, 226, 230, 234
charcoal 17 297, 310
chess sets 6 557
chests 17 *302*, 357–8
chests-of-drawers 17 357, 358
chiaroscuro 17 186
chisels 17 48
chopsticks 17 399
chronologies 17 426–7
cinnabar 17 246
civic centres 16 *564*
clay 17 *31*, 98–9*, 240–41*, 242, 371, *372*, 373, 390; 23 822
clocks 7 442*, 447
cloisters 17 66
coal 17 388
coffers 17 301
coffins 17 58, *58*, *426*
coins 7 533; 17 24, 318, 369–71*, *370*
collages 17 223
collections 7 160; 17 421–4*, 425, 427–35*, *430*, *431*; 18 383; 22 359
armour 2 449
Buddhism 17 432
calligraphy 6 752, 772; 17 215, 229, 230, 232
ceramics 17 433
costumes 17 328, 433
curiosities 17 425
dress 17 317
Edo period (1600-1868) 17 237
erotic art 10 487
folk art 17 344
inkstones 17 388
lacquer 17 342
meibutsu 17 428–9
musical instruments 17 396
paintings 6 783, 826; 7 161; 17 229
porcelain 4 174
pottery 18 340
rocks 17 425
rubbings 17 237
seals 17 413–14
Shinto 17 432
vernacular art 17 433
weapons 2 449
Zen 7 161
20th cent. 1 896; 2 561
colophons 7 624–5*; 17 230, *270*
colour 7 632–3*
combs (hair) 17 386
Comic-strip art 7 649
compasses 17 399
competitions 17 334
concrete 17 90
Confucianism 17 236
connoisseurship 7 716*; 17 230, 334, 413–14, 423, 427, 437–40*
calligraphy 17 215, 343
lacquer 17 438

Japan
connoisseurship—cont.
painting **17** 437
conservation **7** 729–30; **17** 138–9*, 208–10*, *209*; **18** 617; **28** 312
consolidants **17** 210
copies **17** 217
copper **7** 813; **17** 47, 276, 277, 318, *362*, 369, 370, 401
copybooks **17** 237
coral **7** 834, 836; **17** 398
cosmetics **17** 332–3*
costumes **17** *314*, 326–8*, *327*, 332*, 333–4
cotton **17** 305, 316–17*, 354, *356*; **30** VII2
Edo period (1600-1868) **17** *317*, 354, *354*, 355
20th cent. **17** *310*
craftsmen and artists **17** 27–30*, 51–3*, *309*, 318, 346, 356, 358, *403*, 418–19
crêpe **17** 313
crests **17** 302
crowns **17** 386
cuirasses **17** *362*
cups **17** *266*, 399
curtains **14** 429
damask **17** 311, 313, 315
dance **17** 333–4
dayflower **17** 277
dealing **2** 561; **17** 424
decanters **17** *387*
desks **17** 300
display of art **1** 777; **17** 335, 342, 367, 423
see also tokonoma
dog-hair **17** 368
dolls **17** 262, 371–3*; **31** 259, 261
daruma **17** 373
gosho **17** 371*, *372*
hina **17** 371*; **31** 260
Ichimatsu **17** 372–3*, *373*
Kamo **17** 372*
kimekomi **17** 372*
kokeshi **17** 372*
Nara **17** 372*
Saga **17** 372*
tsuchibina **17** 373*
dolls' furniture **31** 264
dolls' houses **31** 264
donjons **17** 83, *85*; **20** 835, *835*
doors **9** 162–3*; **17** 47, 155
sliding **11** 862
dormitories **17** 68
dowries **17** 302, *304*, 385
drawings **1** 582
dress **7** 632; **14** 429; **17** *43*, 314, 332, 353–7, 359, 373–7*
drums (musical instruments) **17** *248*, 333
dyeing **17** 308*, *309*, 314
block-resist **17** 308–9*
paste resist **17** 309, 310, *310*, 315
resist **3** 378; **17** 308–10*, 313, 314, 355; **30** 560–61
see also shibori
shibori **17** 309, *311*, *316*
stencil-dyeing **17** 314, 355
stitching **30** 556
stitch-resist **17** 309, 314
tie-dyeing **17** 309, *309*, 314, 316, *317*; **30** 556
wax resist **17** 309; **30** 558
dyes **9** 492; **17** 219, 277, 308*, *309*, 313, 315, 316, 354, 355*; **30** 561
anilines **17** 277
vat **17** *309*
earthenwares **17** *105*, 244, 246, 258, 259*, 262*
Jōmon period (*c*. 10,000–*c*. 300 BC) **17** *104*, *245*
Kofun period (*c*. AD 300-710) **17** *105*
ebony **17** 399
Japan—cont.
education (art) **17** 27–8, 418–21*; **21** 59
architecture **7** 701; **17** 86
Buddhism **17** 419
Christianity **17** 419
conservation **7** 742
Jesuit Order **17** 419
Neo-Confucianism **17** 419
eggshells **18** 604
elm **17** 312
embossing **17** 275
embroidery **14** 429; **17** *306*, 308*, 313, 314, *314*, 315, *316*, 355, *374*; **30** VII2
enamel **17** 242, 256, *263*, 263–4*, 377–9*, *379*, 386; **18** *554*, *555*; **23** *196*
enceintes **22** 431
encyclopedias of art **17** 419
engravings **10** 379; **17** 203
entasis **17** 66
erotic art **10** *485*, 485–6*
etchings **28** 598
ewers **17** *254*
exhibitions **17** 345, 424, 435–7*
calligraphy **17** 239
ōtsue **33** 491
sculpture **17** 135–6, 137–8
20th cent. **17** *436*
ex-votos **17** *25*, 33, 153, *346*, 346–7
fans **3** *144*; **10** 776–7, *777*; **17** 160, 167–8
feathers **10** 848
feldspar **17** 242
felt **10** 873
festivals **18** *549*
fibres **17** 209, 305, 306, 312, 313, 353–4, 355
elm-bark **30** VII2
figurines **17** 262, *263*, *264*, *265*, 348–9*
Jōmon period (*c*. 10,000–*c*. 300 BC) **17** 30, *97*, 103–4, *104*, 371, 629
Prehistoric **17** *102*, 102–4
film sets **31** *82*
firing **17** 242–3
fixatives **17** 210
flags **11** 145–6*, *146*; **14** 429; **17** 363
flasks **17** *252*, *257*
floors **17** 47*, 53
flower arrangements **17** 342, 379–82*, *380*
flowers **17** 341
flutes (musical instruments) **17** 397
folk art **17** 44–5*, *45*, 344–59*, *347*
food **17** 341, 382–3*, *383*
fortifications **17** 46; **21** 595*
frit **17** 242
frontispieces **17** *148*, 219
furnaces **17** 319
furniture **14** 429; **17** 297, 302, 341, 357–8*, 384–5*; **25** 303
gables **17** 48; **20** 835
gamboge **17** 277
game-pieces **17** 386
garden design **12** 95–101*, *96*, *97*, *99*, *100*, *101*; **18** 567
gardens **11** 338; **12** 85*, 95–101*, *96*, *99*, *100*; **17** 337, 340
Buddhism **12** 85; **18** *560*, *562*, *563*
dry-landscape **12** 85, *97*, 98; **18** 556, *560*, *562*, *563*, 564; **31** *400*
sculpture **12** 101
tea **12** 98–9
gates **7** 361*; **16** *786*; **17** 215
gauze **17** 306, 313; **30** 551
gems **17** 387
geomancy **12** 95; **17** 33
gesso **17** 393, *394*
Japan—cont.
gilding **12** 621, 626; **17** *34*, 100, 101, *112*, 319, *321*; **18** 607; **22** *497*
Asuka period (AD *c*. 552-645) **17** *107*
fire **12** 626
Hakuhō period (AD 645-710) **17** 110–12, *111*
Heian **17** 321
Nara period (AD 710-94) **17** *113*
water **12** 626
glass **17** 371, *373*, 385–7*, *387*, 398; **25** 176
crystal **17** 100
Shōwa period (1926-89) **17** 381
glassblowing **17** 386
glazes **17** 242*, 247–9, 252*, 258, 350, 352, 353, *405*; **28** 495
Edo period (1600-1868) **17** 255, 262
Heian period (AD 794-1185) **17** 242, 250–51; **27** 699
Muromachi period (1333-1568) **17** 253
Nara period (AD 710-94) **17** 247, *248*, 250
Shōwa period (1926-89) **17** 266
glues **17** 138, 140, 213, 281, 387, 388
gobaishi **17** 354
gold **17** 220, 297, 298, 313, 318, 319, *334*, 370, 372
Edo period (1600-1868) **10** *777*; **17** *370*
Momoyama period (1568-1600) **17** 370
Muromachi period (1333-1568) **17** *228*, *301*, *362*
Nara period (AD 710-94) **17** 219
Taishō period (1912-26) **17** *305*
gold dust **17** 276
gold leaf **17** 100, *116*, 140, 277, 298, *309*, 314, *314*
gourds **17** 400
government buildings **17** 46, *88*, *92*
granaries **17** 54; **33** 511
granite **17** 102
grasses **17** 365
gromwell **17** 308
guidebooks **13** 812; **17** 274
guilds **7** 624; **17** 52, 311
guns **17** 363
gymnasia **30** *289*
hair **17** 368
cat-hair **17** 368
deer-hair **17** 209, 227
goat-hair **17** 209
hog-hair **17** 209
horsehair **17** *334*
human **17** 371, *373*, 407
rabbit-hair **17** 227, 368
raccoon-hair **17** 368
wolf-hair **17** 368
yak-hair **17** 407
hair ornaments **17** 386
halberds **17** 361, 362
halls **14** 78; **18** 551
honden **23** *597*
shoden *see* sanctuaries
hondō **17** 66, *73*, 73–4, *74*
Modernism **20** *76*
Shōwa period (1926-89) **28** *606*
hammering **17** 320
harnesses **14** *184*, 185*
helmets **17** 300, 302, 362, *362*, 363
hemp **17** 101, 139, 209, 219, 297, 312, 389, 403
heraldry **14** 404, 428–9*, *429*; **17** 302
herbs **17** 365
heritage **14** 452; **18** 556
hinagata-bon *see* pattern-books
Japan—cont.
hinoki (Japanese cypress) **10** 776; **17** 45, 46, 100, 350, 356, 372, 393, *394*, *395*, 399; **23** 598
Heian period (AD 794-1185) **17** 390, 392
Kamakura period (1185-1333) **17** *395*
Muromachi period (1333-1568) **17** *394*
Nara period (AD 710-94) **33** 325
historiography **2** 450; **7** 160; **12** 100; **17** 439*
hōnoki **17** 356
horn **14** 764; **17** 398
horsehair **17** 368
hotels **27** *192*
houses **17** 46, 54–5, 56
farmhouses **17** 81–2, *82*; **18** 173
folk *see minka*
Jōmon period (*c*. 10,000–*c*. 300 BC) **17** 629
machiya **17** 46
minka **17** 46, 81–3*, *82*; **21** 648*
nōka **17** 46
pile dwellings **17** 54, 56
pit dwellings **17** 54, 55, *55*, 56, 384–5
shinden **17** 46, 68–70, *69*, *70*, 71, 384–5
shoin **2** 599; **17** 46, 75–81, *77*, *78*, *79*, *80*, *81*, 335, 385; **18** 563, 564, 565
Shōwa period (1926-89) **16** *784*
sōan **17** 337
teahouses **16** 811–12; **17** 46, 52, 79–81*, 88, 335–6, 337, 340; **18** 565, *566*; **33** 562
Yayoi period (*c*. 300 BC–*c*. AD 300) **17** *55*; **33** 511
housing **18** *41*
human figures **17** 105–6, 158
iconography **17** 30*, 44–5*, 322, 345–50
Buddhism **5** 116, 118; **17** 33–9*, 107, 108, 109, 146–8, 168
bushidō **17** 42*
Confucianism **17** 40–42*
Daoism **17** 39–40*
Neo-Confucianism **17** 41
Prehistoric **17** 30–31*
Shinto **10** 485; **17** 31–3*
Shugendō **17** 42–4*
icons **10** 400; **17** 341
ikat **17** 307–8, 316–17, *317*, *354*, 354–5; **30** 554, 556
ikebana *see* flower arrangements
incense **17** 341
incense burners **17** *265*
indigo **17** 219, 277, 308, *309*, 316, 354; **18** 600; **30** 561
industrial design **15** 826–7*
inks **15** 850; **17** 140, 212–13*, 310, 392
inksticks **17** 213, 227, 387, 388*
inkstones **17** 213, 387–8*
inlays **17** 298*, 386; **18** 603, 604, *613*
inrō **17** 303–4, 398, *400*; **18** I1
inscriptions **17** 107, 230, 234, 321, 348, 369, 391
Buddhism **17** 126
insignia **14** 428
inventories **17** 229
iron **17** 47, 102*, 242, 253, 308, 318, 358
Edo period (1600-1868) **10** *777*; **17** 370
Kofun period (*c*. AD 300-710) **17** 361
Muromachi period (1333-1568) **17** *323*
iron oxide **17** 246
iron sand **17** 358
iron-wood **17** 399
ivory **17** 371, 398–9, *398*
ivory-carvings **17** *102*
jade **16** 859, 861
Japan—cont.
jars **17** *255*, *257*, *263*, *265*; **31** *77*
burial **17** 246, *250*
Edo period (1600-1868) **23** *196*
salt **17** 262
tea **17** 341
jet **17** 398, 399
jingles **17** 396
joinery **17** 45, 50, 384
jugs **17** *264*
kaisho **17** 76–7*, *81*, 173
kaki juice **17** 210
kaolin **17** 263, 351, 392; **28** 312
kasuri *see* ikat
kettles **17** 322, 323, *323*, 341
keyaki **17** 46, 274, 356, 358
kilns **17** 242–3*, 247, 250, 253, 256–7, 350, 353, 373
climbing **17** 255, 351, 352, 811
noborigama **17** *243*, 243, 255
ōgama **17** 254, 259
tunnel **17** 242, 243, *243*, 247, 251, 252, 259, 350
up-draught **17** 243, *243*
kimonos **17** *309*, 310, *311*, 315, *316*, 317, *317*, *327*, 332, 359, 373, 375, 376
kiosks **18** 72*
kiri **17** 358
kirikane **13** 843
kitchens **17** 340
kites **17** 388–90*, *389*
knife-handles **17** 386
knives **17** 399
kondō **17** 66
kudzu **17** 312
lac **17** 357
lacquer **12** 626; **17** 99, 100, 101–2*, *116*, 213, 254, 297–305*, 340–42*, 356–7, 359, *383*, 384, 385, 390, 391, 398, 399, 401, 424; **18** *613*; **21** 650; **28** 495, 600; **31** 167
Buddhism **17** 117, 118
conservation **18** 617
copies **17** 301, 303
dry **17** *299*, 390; **18** 606
Edo period (1600-1868) **14** *429*, *704*; **17** *304*, *357*, 376; **18** I1; **28** 599
filled-in *urushi* **18** 602
gilt-engraved *urushi* **18** 602
guri **18** 601
hari-bori **18** 603
Heian period (AD 794-1185) **17** *300*, 392
hibi-nuri **18** 606
hiramakie **17** 298
ikakeji **17** 298
Japan **17** 297
jogahana-nuri **18** 605
johoji-nuri **18** 606
kamakurabori **17** 298*, 300, *301*; **18** 602
Kamakura period (1185-1333) **17** 227
Kodaiji *makie* **17** 301*
makie **17** 297, 298*, 299–301, *300*, 302, *341*, *385*; **18** II2
marbled *urushi* **18** 602
Meiji period (1868-1912) **28** *600*
Momoyama period (1568-1600) **17** *302*
Muromachi period (1333-1568) **17** *301*
Nanban **17** 301–2*, *302*
Nara period (AD 710-94) **17** *114*, 115–16, *130*, *299*
nashiji **17** 298
Negoroji **17** 356–7
negoro-nuri **17** 297, 300, 303, *303*, 356–7; **18** 606
Shōwa period (1926-89) **17** *136*
Shunkei **17** 356, 357, 358
sprinkled **18** 604
Taishō period (1912-26) **17** *305*
takamakie **17** 298
togidashi makie **17** 298
trompe l'oeil **17** 303

Japan
lacquer—cont.
urushi 18 599, 600, 601, 603, 604, 605, 607, 616, 617
lacquerers 17 300, 304–5, 356
ladders 17 55
ladles 17 341
lampblack 17 213, 387
lamps 17 359
lanterns (lights) 12 98; 17 323, 359
lead 17 242, 247–9, 248, 277, 318, 370, 385, 386
leather 17 297, 313, 355, 362, 362, 363, 365, 376
libraries 17 91; 19 317*, 319, 320
lighters 17 399
limestone 17 242
lime-wood 17 312
lintels 17 47
looms 17 306–8, 328
backstrap 17 306, 307, 354
draw 17 306, 307
high 17 354
Jacquard 17 307, 317
lost-wax casting 17 100–101, 319, 320
lutes 17 396, 397
lye 17 308
madder 17 308
maṇḍalas 17 345–6*
Buddhism 5 117, 117, 119; 17 37, 146
Shinto 17 32, 32, 151–3*, 152, 153; 28 610, 610
Shugendō 17 43–4
manuals
antiquities 30 295
calligraphy 11 823; 15 74; 17 224, 235; 29 902
carpentry 17 51*
drawing 17 419, 847
education (art) 17 273
gardens 12 100
painting 17 185, 189, 273, 419, 439
pottery 17 251; 23 196
ritual objects 17 321
manufacturing 15 826–7*
manuscripts 17 211, 217–21
maple 17 366
maps 32 99
marble 17 137
marbling 17 404; 24 55, I3
marks 17 243–4*, 244; 20 441
masks 17 98, 103, 334, 349, 349–50*, 390–96*, 395
bugaku 17 390, 391–2*
gigaku 17 390, 391*, 391
kyōgen 17 390, 393–4*, 394
nō 17 390, 392–4*, 394
mass production 17 250, 253, 317, 320, 348; 22 667
master printers 20 601
mats 17 336, 339; 31 167
tatami 17 47, 50, 338, 384
mausolea 17 64, 74
mercury 17 101; 21 716
metal 17 318–19*, 381, 384, 387, 398, 399, 401
patinas 24 258
metalwork 17 104, 297, 318–24*, 358*
mokume 21 327*, 327
openwork 17 323
Yayoi period (*c.* 300 BC–*c.* AD 300) 17 30
metalworkers 17 358
mica 17 220, 276, 371
Mingei 17 344
mirror handles 21 716
mirrors 17 319, 320, 320, 322, 323, 324, 386, 387, 399; 21 716*
moats 17 55, 57
monasteries 5 116, 120; 12 97; 17 77, 231
mordants (iii) (dyeing) 17 308, 315

Japan—cont.
mortars (vessels) 17 341
mother-of-pearl 17 277, 298, 299, 300, 300, 398; 18 603, 613
motorbikes 15 826
moulding 17 403
moulds 17 101, 270, 319
mounts (works on paper and scrolls) 17 209–10, 347; 22 233, 234*
mulberry 17 139, 213, 275
museums 17 89, 427, 432–5*, 433, 434; 23 371
High Tech 1 737
modern art 17 436
20th cent. 18 533
musical instruments 17 396–7*
nails 17 45
napkins 17 341
naphthalene 17 388
narratives 17 21, 22, 149–50, 153, 158–9
needlework 17 355–6*
netsuke 7 836; 14 764; 17 23, 98, 386, 398, 398–402*, 399, 400, 402
nozoki karakuri 17 194
nude figures 18 531; 23 290
nuts 17 398
oak 17 354
oils 17 359, 388
okimono 17 323
organs 17 397
ornament 23 553–4*
orpiment 17 277
packaging 17 217
pagodas 5 116, 117; 17 36, 66, 67, 72; 22 499; 23 776*; 29 869
five-element 23 776
miniature 17 270, 321
multi-storeyed 23 776
multi-treasure 23 776
painters 17 28–9, 154, 168–71
painting 1 581–2; 17 99, 139–210*, 342, 423–4; 20 836, 836; 30 559
bamboo 3 144
bird-and-flower 17 165, 184–6, 200
Edo period (1600-1868) 17 164
Kanō school 17 790, 795; 31 253
Momoyama period (1568-1600) 17 786
Buddhism 17 144–50*, 156–7, 158–9, 166, 168–71, 193; 18 223
Asuka-Hakuhō period (AD *c.* 552-710) 17 145
Daigo 18 557
Heian period (AD 794-1185) 17 147, 148
Nara period (AD 710-94) 17 146
Ōbaku 17 183–4*, 189
Pure Land 5 118; 17 38, 147–8
Zen 17 169, 192, 193, 194*
display 17 166, 347
door panel 17 166, 175, 195–6, 208, 210, 790
Edo period (1600-1868) 17 164–5*, 792; 31 200
fan 10 777
flower 23 363
fūzokuga 17 174–6*, 175, 782
genpitsu 17 790
genre 16 802; 17 174*, 175, 176–7*, 783, 794
Edo period (1600-1868) 17 176, 727
Impressionism 18 531
Momoyama period (1568-1600) 17 175, 787
hanging 17 347
Heisei period (1989-) 17 208
ink 2 598; 17 163–4, 168–74*, 341, 423
Buddhism 14 62; 17 38–9, 193

Japan
painting
ink—cont.
Muromachi period (1333-1568) 17 169, 171, 172; 30 466
Neo-Confucianism 17 41
see also Zenga
Jesuit Order 17 182–3
kachōga style 28 587
Kanga 17 166, 794–5
karae 17 156, 162*
kasen'e 17 828–30*, 829
landscape 7 183; 17 200
Buddhism 17 192
Edo period (1600-1868) 14 214; 15 127; 17 191; 33 321, 492
Heian period (AD 794-1185) 17 155
Kamakura period (1185-1333) 17 156
Meiji period (1868-1912) 33 489
Muromachi period (1333-1568) 1 776; 17 780; 31 252
Nanga 30 295; 31 698
Rinpa 27 596
Shinto 17 153
Shōwa period (1926-89) 17 204
marine 17 178, 789
Meiji period (1868-1912) 18 605; 28 600, 600
Momoyama period (1568-1600) 17 163–4*, 319
monochrome 17 38, 163–4
Mori school 22 118, 118
Muromachi period (1333-1568) 17 163*
Nanban 17 22, 181–2*
Nanga 1 582; 17 23, 165, 188–92*, 198–9, 199, 437, 439–40; 18 542; 25 73; 30 29
Edo period (1600-1868) 17 190, 191, 194, 285; 27 596; 33 560
naturalism 17 194*, 195, 195, 197, 197, 200
Nihonga 17 23, 166, 180, 198, 199–202*, 440; 29 904
Meiji period (1868-1912) 17 420; 31 253
Taishō period (1912-26) 17 202, 203; 22 328
oil 17 206
onnae 17 159
otokoe 17 159
ōtsue 17 44, 345, 347, 347–8*
plum blossom 17 190
portraits 11 824; 17 230; 32 896
Rinpa 14 702; 17 23, 165, 166, 177–80*, 178, 180, 194, 293; 23 363, 365, 554; 30 52, 378
screen 17 153, 154–7, 155, 165, 166–7, 178, 208, 210, 780; 28 297
Buddhism 17 145
Edo period (1600-1868) 14 214; 17 197, 309, 789; 23 363, 593
Heian period (AD 794-1185) 17 157
Kamakura period (1185-1333) 17 156
Kanō school 17 181, 182, 728
Momoyama period (1568-1600) 17 175, 181, 784, 786, 787
Muromachi period (1333-1568) 1 776; 17 167; 28 494
Nanban 17 181, 181–2*
Rinpa 27 596
yōfūga 17 183
scroll 13 888; 17 165, 166, 167, 171, 176, 208, 209, 342, 797; 22 118; 28 311; 30 377
Buddhism 5 119; 14 62; 17 149, 150, 158; 22 233

Japan
painting
scroll—cont.
Edo period (1600-1868) 2 210; 14 705; 16 785; 17 216, 347, 438; 20 836; 21 741; 23 384; 32 896; 33 492, 561
Heian period (AD 794-1185) , ; 7 IV2, 3
Meiji period (1868-1912) 17 185
Momoyama period (1568-1600) 17 783
Muromachi period (1333-1568) 17 168, 169, 171; 30 466; 31 197, 252
Nanga 31 698
Rinpa 14 703
Taishō period (1912-26) 17 201; 31 137
Shinto 17 32–3, 151–3*; 28 610–11*
Shōwa period (1926-89) 17 207
Taishō period (1912-26) 17 205
tomb 17 142–4*, 144
townscapes 22 429
ukiyoe 14 577; 16 802; 17 23, 165, 176–7*, 194, 200; 28 311
Edo period (1600-1868) 17 176
wakan 17 781, 794
wall 17 22, 79, 139, 156, 195; 18 190; 20 523; 30 257; 32 804
Yamatoe 14 302; 17 153–61*, 155, 156, 158, 161, 163, 165–8*, 167, 168, 423; 18 396; 28 625
yōfūga 17 181, 182–3*, 186–8*, 187
Yōga 17 23, 202, 203, 203–5*, 204, 420, 440
Zenga 5 120; 14 61; 17 39, 165, 192, 193, 194*; 28 408
20th cent. 17 205–8*
see also HASEGAWA; KANŌ; KITAO, KOSE; MORI; NAGASAKI; SOGA; SUMIYOSHI; TOSA; UNKOKU SCHOOLS
palaces 17 46, 70, 93*, 93; 23 821–3*, 822
Edo period (1600-1868) 17 77, 78, 79, 80
Meiji period (1868-1912) 17 87
palanquins 17 302
pantaloons 17 375
paper 7 114; 17 139, 209, 210, 213–14*, 305, 359*, 371, 388, 390, 392, 402–6*; 22 234; 24 42, 44, 47*, 51, 55, 56; 28 312; 30 541; 31 259
Buddhism 17 219, 220
decorative 24 I3, II1
Edo period (1600-1868) 17 403, 405
fan 10 776
Heian period (AD 794-1185) 10 776; 17 223
Kamakura period (1185-1333) 17 227
Muromachi period (1333-1568) 17 227
rice-paper 17 390; 24 56; 28 619
umbrella 17 359
waterproof 17 359
papercuts 24 56, 57
paper mulberry 17 219, 227, 312, 403; 30 560
paperweights 17 386
papier mâché 17 373, 390; 24 62
parks 12 100
partitions 24 51
fusuma 9 163; 11 862*; 17 45, 404; 27 596; 31 676
patchwork 17 313

Japan—cont.
patronage 17 46, 154, 164, 297, 345, 347, 351, 421–4*; 33 318
Buddhism 17 421–3; 18 213
calligraphy 17 217
lacquer 17 302
pattern books 24 276–7*
calligraphy 17 226, 227, 227, 228, 228, 237
dyeing 24 276
kimonos 24 276–7
textiles 17 264, 354
paulownia 17 371, 390, 391
pavilions (buildings) 18 561; 24 289*
peat 17 398, 399
periodicals 24 436–7*; 30 256
periods
Asuka-Hakuhō period (AD *c.* 552-710) 2 654–5*
Asuka period (AD *c.* 552-645) 2 654; 17 20, 21*
Azuchi-Momoyama period *see* Momoyama period
Edo period (1600-1868) 9 737–8*; 17 20, 22–3*
Hakuhō period (AD 645-710) 2 654
Heian period (AD 794-1185) 14 301–2*; 17 20, 21*
Heisei period (1989-) 14 323*; 17 20
Jōmon period (*c.* 10,000-*c.* 300 BC) 17 20, 426–7, 629–30*; 23 440
Kamakura period (1185-1333) 17 20, 22*, 750*
Kofun period (*c.* AD 300-710) 2 654; 17 20, 57, 426; 18 190*
Meiji period (1868-1912) 17 20; 21 58–9*
Momoyama period (1568-1600) 17 20, 22*; 21 827–8*
Muromachi period (1333-1568) 17 20, 22*; 22 349–50*
Nara period (AD 710-94) 17 20, 21*; 22 503–4*
Prehistoric 17 19–21*, 425; 22 148
Sengoku period (1467-1568) 17 20, 22
Shōwa period (1926-89) 17 20; 28 627*
Taishō period (1912-26) 17 20; 30 241*
Tokugawa period *see* Edo period
Tomb *see* Kofun
Tumulus *see* Kofun
Warring States *see* Sengoku
Yamato *see* Kofun
Yayoi period (*c.* 300 BC-*c.* AD 300) 17 20, 426; 33 511*
persimmon 17 359, 399; 30 560
perspective 17 186; 24 486
pestles 17 341, 352
pewter 17 297, 318
photographic prints 22 445
photography 24 679
pigments 17 140*, 141, 142, 277, 297, 346, 414
blue 17 141
green 17 141
orange 17 141
Prussian blue 17 277, 287, 847
red 17 141
vermilion 17 277, 297
white 17 141
yellow 17 141
pilgrimages 17 345–6*
pillars 17 48, 53, 66
pine 17 109, 366, 366
akamatsu (red pine) 17 46
kuromatsu (black pine) 17 46
pitchers 17 251, 341
planes 17 49, 49–50
plaques 17 215
plastic 17 381; 31 257
plates 17 352, 352–3

Japan—cont.
poetry **1** 581; **17** 154–5, 212, 222, 287; **25** 73
polishing **17** 276
polychromy **17** 99, 100; **25** 175
ponds **12** 95, 96
porcelain **17** 258, 264, *341*, 351–2, 353, 399, 413; **23** 389; **31** 261
blue-and-white ware **4** 174–5*; **17** 263
Edo period (1600-1868) **9** 28; **17** 241, 255, *263*, *264*, *265*, 351
Imari **2** 414; **6** 332; **17** 263; **29** 114
Kakiemon ware **2** 414; **6** 332; **17** *263*, 264, 733*
Kakiemon ware: *see also* Arita → porcelains
kosometsuke **6** 622
Meiji period (1868-1912) **17** 353
Nabeshima **17** 263, 264, 351; **22** 421*
Old Japan ware *see* ARITA → porcelain
Tamura, Kōichi **17** 263–4*
Tenkei **6** 622
portraits **17** 131*, 132*
nisee **13** 213
painting **5** 120; **17** 160–61*, *161*, 168, 184, *335*, 750; **18** *503*
photography **17** *426*; **22** *445*
prints **17** 278, 285
sculpture **17** 36, *130*, 130–32*
self-portraits **28** 494
potters **17** 104, 351
potter's wheels **17** 241–2, 253
pottery **17** 104, 240*, *247*, 247–9*, 250–51*, 252–6*, *252*, 258–63*, *266*, *268*, *269*, *341*, 353
Agano ware **1** 448
Atsumi **17** 260
Bizen **17** 261
Black Oribe ware **17** 255
Black Seto ware **17** 254; **21** 651
Buddhism **17** 252
celadon **2** 211; **17** *266*
Echizen **17** 260
Edo period (1600-1868) **17** 234, *262*, *352*, 399; **23** 196
green-glazed ware **17** 247–9*
Green Oribe ware **17** 255
Haji ware **17** 241, 246–7, *247*, 249, 259, 341
Heian period (AD 794-1185) **17** *251*
Iga **17** 260–61, *261*
Imado **17** 262
Jōmon period (*c.* 10,000–*c.* 300 BC) **17** 30, 244–6*, 629
Karatsu **17** 341, *341*
Kawarake **17** 259
Kenzan ware **17** 244; **23** *366*, 367
Kofun period (*c.* AD 300-710) **17** 246–7*
Koseto ware **17** *252*, 252–3*
Minato **17** 262
Mino Iga ware **17** 255
Nara period (AD 710-94) **17** *248*
Narumi Oribe ware **17** 255
Narushima **17** *257*
Ninsei ware **17** 244
Ōhi ware **25** 869
Omuro ware **17** 244
Ongagawa ware **17** 246
Oribe Black ware **17** 255
Oribe ware **11** 854; **17** 242, *254*, 255, 341; **21** 651
Prehistoric **17** *242*
Raku ware **6** II2; **14** 704; **17** 256, 341; **25** 869*; **28** *410*
Red Oribe ware **17** 255
Satsumon ware **17** 247
Seto **17** 341
Shigaraki **17** *260*, 260–61, 341
shiki **17** 250–51

Japan
pottery—cont.
Shino Oribe ware **17** 255
Shino ware **17** 241, 242, 254, *254*; **21** 651
Shiraiwa **17** *258*
shirashi **17** 259–61*
Sue ware **17** 241, 242, 246, 249–50*, *250*, 251, 258, 259, *426*; **18** 190
Takatori **17** *341*
Tanba **17** 261
three-colour glazed ware **17** 242, 247, 248*, *248*, 250, 251; **23** 389
Tokoname **17** 260
Tsutsumi **17** *257*
two-colour glazed ware **17** 247, 248*, 251
yamachawan **17** 250, 251, 252, 260; **33** 487–8*
Yayoi **17** 246*, *246*
Yayoi period (*c.* 300 BC–*c.* AD 300) **33** 511
Yellow Seto ware **17** 254, *254*; **21** 650
printing **17** 203, 217, 220, *275*, *276*; **25** 588
colour **15** 852; **17** 272, 282–4*, *283*, 285, 286; **30** 50, *51*
Momoyama period (1568-1600) **7** 624
Nara period (AD 710-94) **7** 624
net **17** 276
relief **17** 274
woodblock **7** 624; **17** 185, 272, 597; **20** 601
printing plates **17** 270
printmakers **25** 598
prints **15** 855, 856; **17** 269–96*, *281*, *282*, *283*, *284*
Buddhism **17** 269, *270*
Christianity **17** 271
display **1** 582
Edo period (1600-1868) **17** *269*, *275*, *282*, *284*
inbutsu **17** 270
kasen'e **17** 828–30*
Nara period (AD 710-94) **17** 270–71
shin hanga **17** 279, 294
shunga **10** 485, *485*; **18** *92*
surimono **17** 278, 285, 286–7
Taishō period (1912-26) **17** *294*, *296*
ukiyoe **4** 70; **15** 852, 855; **17** 23, 269, 274, 277, *280*, 280–81*, 283, 286, 290; **23** 290, 594; **31** 764
aizurie **17** 287
benie **17** 282
benizurie **17** 282
Edo period (1600-1868) **2** 7, *9*; **17** 176, *278*, 397, *397*, *415*; **18** *96*; **30** 50, *51*; **31** *766*
hashirae **17** 277, 281
hosoban **17** 277, 281, *283*
Meiji period (1868-1912) **17** 293
ōban **17** 277, *281*, 284, *289*, *291*, *292*; **31** *170*
ōkubie **17** 276, 284; **31** *765*
tane **17** *280*, 281
ukie **17** 282; **31** 169
urushie **17** 281
woodblock **1** 582; **17** 269, 270, 274, *275*, 279, 285–7; **18** *92*; **24** 276–7; **31** *204*
Edo period (1600-1868) **16** *561*; **17** *845*, *847*; **18** *96*, *494*; **22** *231*; **30** *51*; **31** *169*, *170*, *765*, *766*
Kamakura period (1185-1333) **17** *269*, *270*
Meiji period (1868-1912) **17** 293; **33** *539*
Nara period (AD 710-94) **7** 624
20th cent. **17** 293
see also Yokohamae

Japan
prints—cont.
Yokohamae **17** 290; **33** 539, *539*
proportions (architecture) **17** 50
proscenium arches **17** 330
puppets **17** 350, 406–8*, *407*
quivers **17** 361, 363
radios **15** 827, *827*
rafters **17** 66
rami (fibre) **17** 139, 312, 316, *317*, 354
red lead **17** 277
religion **12** 62, 95; **17** 30–31*, 345–50; **28** 607
repoussé **17** 320
representation **17** 284–5
resins **17** 138, 213
restoration **7** 729–30
rice paste **17** 309, 310, *310*, 314, 355, 414
ritual objects **17** 320, 322, *322*
rituals **28** 609
robes **17** 316, 356, *356*, 375, 376; **30** VII2
rock crystal **17** 398; **26** 487
rock reliefs **17** 106
roofs **17** 46, 47*, 48, 51, 54, 66, 259, 337–8; **23** 598, 822; **30** 912–14*
Buddhism **17** 72–3
trussed **30** *913*
ropes **31** 167
rosaries **17** 386
rose-wood **17** 399
saddles **17** 300, 301, 302, 362, 364
safes **17** 358
safflower **17** 277, 282, 308
saggars **17** 253
sakura (Japanese cherry) **17** 47
sakura **17** 399
sanctuaries **16** 74
sandalwood **17** 399
sarcophagi **17** 58, 59*, 106, *106*; **27** 832*
sashes **17** 315–16, 377, 386
satin **17** 311, *311*, 313, 315, *327*
satires **7** 649; **17** 348
saws **17** 48–9, *49*
scabbards **17** 300
sceptres **17** 386
screens (ii) (furniture) **17** 215, *236*, 359; **28** 296, 297
Momoyama period (1568-1600) **17** *376*
shōji **17** 384
scribes **17** 28, 214
scriptoria **17** 211, 214, 218–19
scripts **17** 210–14*, *213*, 217, 226, 234, 238–40*, *239*, *240*
clerical **17** 214, 234
cursive **17** 211, 214, 221, 226, 237
hihaku **17** 213, 219
hihakutai **17** 214
hiragana **17** 211, 212, *212*
kana **17** 157, 211–12*, *223*; **18** 231
katakana **17** 211
literati **17** 234–8, *235*, *236*, *237*
man'yōgana **17** 211
Muromachi period (1333-1568) **7** 624
regular **17** 211, 218, 220, 226
running **17** 211, 226
shakyōtai **17** 211
sōgana **17** 239
scroll cases **28** 312
scroll rollers **17** 386
scrolls **17** 149–50, 153, 157, 219–20, 343; **22** 234; **28** 309, 312
Buddhism **28** 311
conservation **7** 729–30
Edo period (1600-1868) **17** *272*; **29** *925*; **30** *376*
emakimono **17** 21, 22, 153, 750; **25** 72; **28** 610

Japan
scrolls—cont.
handscrolls **17** 139, 149–50, 161, 217, 234, 342–4; **29** *925*
Buddhism **17** 145
Kamakura period (1185-1333) **17** *829*
Muromachi period (1333-1568) **17** *168*
Nara period (AD 710-94) **17** 214; **28** 311
hanging **7** 729–30; **13** *888*; **17** 139, 341, 343; **21** *741*; **22** *118*; **28** 311, *610*
Buddhism **17** 145
Edo period (1600-1868) **2** *210*; **17** *797*; **32** *896*
Heian period (AD 794-1185) **17** *343*
Kamakura period (1185-1333) **17** 159, 161, *230*
Muromachi period (1333-1568) **5** *37*
Muromachi period (1333-1568) **5** *37*
restoration **7** 729–30
sculptors **17** 28*; **31** 676
sculpture **12** 626; **17** 97–139*, 267–8, 299, 341, 422; **25** 175, 176; **31** 676
architectural **17** 98
Asuka period (AD *c.* 552-645) **17** 106–9*, *107*, *109*
bronze **17** 100–101*, 110–12, 120, 320
Asuka-Hakuhō period (AD *c.* 552-710) **17** *34*, *375*
Asuka period (AD *c.* 552-645) **17** *107*
Hakuhō period (AD 645-710) **17** *110*, *112*
Nara period (AD 710-94) **17** *113*
Buddhism **5** 120; **12** 626; **17** 97, 100, 106*, 107, 109, 119, 124, 126–7*, 130–32*, 320
Asuka-Hakuhō period (AD *c.* 552-710) **17** *34*, *375*
Asuka period (AD *c.* 552-645) **17** 106*, *109*; **31** 167
Edo period (1600-1868) **17** *126*
Esoteric **17** 118
Hakuhō period (AD 645-710) **17** *99*, *110*, 110–12*, *111*, *112*
Heian period (AD 794-1185) **17** *116*, 116–21*, *117*, *118*, *120*
Kamakura period (1185-1333) **17** 121–6*, *123*, *125*
Nara period (AD 710-94) **17** 113–16*, *113*, *114*, *130*, *299*; **22** 504
conservation **17** 138–9*
Esoteric **17** 98
Hakuhō period (AD 645-710) **17** *110*
Hakuhō style **17** 97, 107, 110–12*, *111*, *112*
haniwa **17** 30–31, *31*, 104–6, *105*, 425; **18** 190; **23** 157
Heian period (AD 794-1185) **17** 98
marble **17** *137*
Meiji period (1868-1912) **17** 133–4*; **23** 369
monumental **22** *497*
Prehistoric **17** 102*
relief **17** *106*
Shinto **17** 31–2, 98, 127–9*, *128*; **28** 610–11*
Shōwa period (1926-89) **17** *136*
wood **17** 99–100*, *116*, 116–26*, *117*, *118*, *120*, 348*
Edo period (1600-1868) **17** *126*
Hakuhō period (AD 645-710) **17** *99*

Japan
sculpture
wood—cont.
Heian period (AD 794-1185) **17** *128*
Kamakura period (1185-1333) **17** *123*, *125*, 729
Meiji period (1868-1912) **17** *134*
Nara period (AD 710-94) **17** 116
Shōwa period (1926-89) **17** *137*
20th cent. **1** *738*; **17** 135–8
seals **7** 624; **9** 73; **17** 399, 408–14*; **31** 77
Edo period (1600-1868) **15** 129; **17** *410*, *412*; **33** *709*
thread **17** 409
shells **17** 400; **18** 601
shelves **17** *75*, 76, *385*
shingles **17** 47
ships **17** 347
shoes **17** 386
shōji **17** 45, 359; **28** 619*, *619*
shops **17** 357, 358–9; **18** *551*
shrines (i) (cult) **17** 56, 301, 345–7; **28** 638–9*
Buddhism **28** 639
Shinto **16** 72, 74, 812; **17** 46, 60–64*, *62*; **22** *491*; **28** 609–10*, 638–**9**
Edo period (1600-1868) **16** *812*; **17** *61*, *63*
Kamakura period (1185-1333) **20** 833
Yayoi period (*c.* 300 BC–*c.* AD 300) **17** *56*
shuden **17** *76*, 77
signatures **17** 347, 391, 399, 400, 422
signs (markers) **17** 358–9*
silk **17** 139, 161, 209, 305, 306, *307*, 311, *311*, 312, 313, *314*, 315–16, *316*, 317, *362*, 371; **22** 234; **28** 312, 718; **30** 560
silver **17** 219, 220, 297, 298, *305*, 313, 318, 321, 370, 401
Edo period (1600-1868) **10** *777*; **17** *370*
Momoyama period (1568-1600) **17** 370
Muromachi period (1333-1568) **17** *228*, *301*
Nara period (AD 710-94) **17** 369
silver dust **17** 277
silver leaf **17** 140, 277, 298, 314
size **17** 140
sketches **1** 582
skins **17** 305
skirts **17** 375
skyscrapers **17** 90
sledges **17** 59
smelting **17** 318–19*
soda-lime **17** 385
soot **17** 213, 387, 388
soy-beans **17** 310
spearheads **17** 364
spyglasses **17** 399
stage design **17** 325–6*
stages **17** 326, *326*, 329–32*
stamps **17** 309
standards (vexilloid) **11** 152
starch **17** 209
steel **17** 50, 86, 319, 361
stencilling **17** 276, 285, 288, 293, *309*, 309–10*, 313, 314, *314*, 315, 348, 355, 405; **29** 627; **30** 560, 561
stirrups **17** 300, 302, 362, 364
stitches **17** 313, 314, 315, 317
stone **17** 59, 102*, 398, 400
stone-carvings **17** 348–9
stones **17** 366

Japan—cont.
stonewares **17** 249–50, *250, 252, 255, 256, 261*, 262–3*, *263, 268*, 350, 352, 353; **18** *554*; **27** 699; **31** *77*
Edo period (1600-1868) **17** *254, 257, 258*; **18** *555*; **23** *196, 365, 366*
Heian period (AD 794-1185) **17** *251*, 252
storehouses **17** 55; **22** *494*
straw **17** 99, 358, 371, 373
stupas **29** 869*
sugi (Japanese cedar) **17** 47, 356
sundials **17** 399
supports **17** 139–40*; **28** 312
sushi **17** 382
sutra mounds **17** 321
sutras **7** 624; **17** 148, 211, 214, 217–21, 270, 321, 423
sword guards **14** 429
sword ornaments **17** 98
swords **17** 28, 302, 361, 362, 363, 364, 386; **22** 433
syllabaries **17** 211
tablets **17** 230
talismans **17** 399
tankards **17** *264*
tannins **17** 359
tattoos **17** 414–15*, *415*
teabowls **6** II2; **17** *255, 256*, 341, *341*, 342; **28** *410*
teabush-wood **17** 399
tea-caddies **17** *255*, 301, *341*
tea ceremonies **5** 120; **17** 215, 231, 258, 262–3, 301, 322, 323, 334–44*, 351, 358, 383, 424, 428, 438; **28** 410
Buddhism **17** 336
Christianity **17** 341
Edo period (1600-1868) **20** 287
Kamakura period (1185-1333) **17** 382
Momoyama period (1568-1600) **17** 365
Muromachi period (1333-1568) **12** 98; **17** 254, 259; **30** 259
tea-rooms **17** *337*, 337–40*, *338*
tea utensils **17** *341*
teeth **17** 399
televisions **15** 827
temples **14** 429; **17** 94; **23** 596–7
Buddhism **10** 404; **17** 46, 65–8*, *67, 68, 72*, 432; **30** *445*, 445–6*
Edo period (1600-1868) **17** *74*; **20** *286*
Esoteric **18** 222
Heian period (AD 794-1185) **5** *335*; **10** *405*; **17** *71*
Kamakura period (1185-1333) **17** *73, 748*
Nara period (AD 710-94) **22** *490, 503*
Pure Land **30** 445
Shingon **30** 445
Shōtoku **14** *774*
Tendai **30** 445
Zen **17** 748–9; **30** 446
kutai Amidadō **17** 660
mortuary **17** 58
tenements **17** 83
terracotta **17** 47; **30** 509–10*
textiles **12** 621; **17** 235, 297, 305–18*, *309, 316*, 326–7, 353–7*, 386, 390, 392; **29** 627; **30** 559, 560, 561; **31** 260; **33** 511
Edo period (1600-1868) **17** *354*
thatch **17** 47
theatre **17** 324*
bugaku **17** 333–4*, *334*
bunraku **17** 350
gagaku **17** 325
kabuki **17** 328–9*, 332–3*
kyōgen **17** 325, 328
nō **17** 324–5*, *326*, 326–8*; **28** 609
puppet **17** 406
Japan
theatre—cont.
puppets **17** 350
theatres **33** 539
kabuki **17** 329–32*, *330, 331*
nō **17** 325–6*
puppet **17** 406
theories (art) **17** 26, 419
calligraphy **17** 226
painting **17** 439
poetry **17** 26
threads **17** 308; **30** 541
thrones **17** 36–7; **30** 785*
tiles **17** 47, 259, *262*; **23** 822
timber structures **17** 45, 46–7*
tin **17** 318; **21** 716
titles of works of art **31** 53*
tochi (Japanese chestnut) **17** 46
toggles *see netsuke*
tokonoma **17** 47, 80, 343, 367, 435; **28** 311; **31** 77*
tombs **17** *57*, 57–9*; **27** 832; **28** 608; **31** 115
chamber **16** 82
keyhole **17** 57, *57*, 58–9; **23** 157
Kofun period (*c*. AD 300-710) **17** *58, 59*, 142–4*
rock-cut **17** 58
royal **17** 57–8*
tunnel **17** 106
Yayoi period (*c*. 300 BC–*c*. AD 300) **33** 511
tools **17** 47–50*, *49*, 274, 275, *275, 276*
tortoiseshell **17** 398
towers **17** 54, 55, *55*
town halls **31** 242, *243*
towns **17** 97
toys **17** 386; **31** *257*, 258, 259
trade **17** 23–5*, 435; **18** 252
books **17** 186
bronze **17** 318, 319
ceramics **6** 331–2, 914–15*; **17** 22, 259; **28** 496
coins **17** 24
cotton **18** 375
fans **10** 778
furniture **7** 166; **25** 303
glass **17** 385
iron **17** 318
lacquer **7** 16, 166; **17** 298, 301; **18** 612–13*
metalwork **17** 324
mirrors **17** 319, 320, 322; **21** 716
painting **17** 162
paintings **17** 166
paper **24** 49
porcelain **2** 414; **4** 174; **6** 622; **17** 263
Edo period (1600-1868) **4** 175, 176; **6** 331–2, 908; **17** 264; **22** 880
Meiji period (1868-1912) **6** 332
pottery **4** 176; **6** 331; **17** 263; **18** 340
puppets **17** 406
scrolls **28** 311
silk **28** 715
textiles **17** 311, 313, 314, 315
wood **17** 47
trademarks **7** 624
trappings **14** 185*; **17** 386
travel books **17** 273
trays **17** *322*, 383
treatises **17** 26, 415–17*, 425; **23** 347
aesthetics **17** 439
architecture **2** 317; **14** 315; **17** 421
armour **17** 364
calligraphy **17** 224, 226–8, 343; **29** 66, 902
flower arrangements **17** 417
gardens **12** 64, 96–7; **17** 417*
painting **17** 416–17, 791; **27** 865
trees **17** 365
tumuli **17** 57
turntables **17** 241
tusks **17** 398, 399
Japan—cont.
type (movable) **7** 624; **17** 271–2
type-faces **17** 270–71
umbrellas **17** 359
universities **17** *420*
urban planning **17** 84, 93–7*, *93, 94, 95, 96*
varnishes **17** 297, 384
vases **17** *254, 263, 268, 379*; **18** *554*; **28** *413*
velvet **17** 315
vernacular art **17** 265–6, 348–9, 350, 351, 353, *354*, 354, 355, 359
villas **17** *86*
vine **17** 365
walls **17** 47*
walnut **17** 354
wayside monuments **17** 349
weapons **2** 448, 449; **17** 319, 361–4*
weavers **17** 311–12*
weaving **17** 306–8*, 311–12, 317, 354–5*
twill **30** 551
whisks **17** 341, *341*
whistles **17** 399
white mountain cherry **17** 274
willow **17** 372
wind chimes **17** 386
windows **17** 337
wire **17** 99; **31** 260
wisteria **17** 312, 365
women **17** 212
women artists **31** 525; **33** 317–22*
wood **17** 45, 99–100*, 101–2, 348, 356–7*, 371, 384, 387, 398, 407
Edo period (1600-1868) **17** *126, 349*, 372, *407*
Heian period (AD 794-1185) **17** 116, *116, 117, 118, 120, 128*
Kamakura period (1185-1333) **17** 121–6*, *123, 125*, 729
Meiji period (1868-1912) **17** *134*
Nara period (AD 710-94) **17** 116, *391*
Shōwa period (1926-89) **17** *136, 137*
wood-carvers **17** 356
wood-carvings **17** 99–100*, 104, 215, 350, 356; **33** 325
woodcuts **11** *146*; **17** 419; **33** 363
wood-engravings **10** 485, *485*
woodwork **17** 48–50
wool **17** 213, 356
workshops **17** 422
writing **17** 210–29*, *212, 213, 228, 230*, 232–40*, *235, 236, 237, 239, 240*; **28** 625
Kamakura period (1185-1333) **17** *227*
yarn **17** 316
yew **17** 399
zelkova **17** 399
zithers **17** 396, 397, *397*
Japan Advertising Artists Club **14** 160
Japan Creative Print Association (Nihon Sōsaku Hanga Kyōkai) **17** 436
Japanese Abstract Art Club *see* NIHON ABUSUTORAKUTO ĀTO KURABU
Japanese Art Exhibition *see* NITTEN
Japanese Photographic Art Association **11** 811, 826
Japanese Print Association *see* NIHON HANGA KYŌKAI
Japanese Print Club **14** 213
Japan Fine Arts Association *see* NIHON BIJUTSU KYŌKAI
Japan Folk Craft Society *see* NIHON MINGEI KYŌKAI
Japan Graphic Designers Association **17** 752
japanning **18** 610–11*; **23** 790
historical and regional traditions
England **5** 191; **7** 166; **18** 610–11*, 614; **29** 530
France **7** 166; **18** 614
Italy **5** 192
Netherlands, the **7** 166
Portugal **25** 306
types
vernis Martin **18** 599; **32** *337*, 337–8*
uses
bureaux **5** 191, 192; **32** *337*
furniture **24** 61
papier mâché **24** 61
see also LACQUER → types → imitation
Japan Photographers' Society **18** 60
Japan Photographic Association **29** 663
Japan Secession *see* SECESSION (JAPAN)
Japan Society for the Research and Preservation of Arms and Armour **17** 364
Japan wax *see under* WAXES → types
Japan World Exhibition *see* OSAKA → Expo '70
Japar, Salleh **28** 774
Japara **15** 783, 800
Japaridze, U. **12** 327
japonaiserie **17** 440
Japon Artistique **24** 426
Japonisme **4** 70; **7** 165, 168; **17** 440–42*; **33** 137
commentaries **2** 652
England **10** 282; **17** 466; **33** *138*
France **5** 284; **17** *441*
United States of America **33** *138*
Japp, James **28** 253
Jappelli, Giuseppe **17** 442–4*
patrons and collectors **31** 172
works **16** 648, 720, 730; **17** *443*; **23** 753
Jaqmaq, Sultan (*reg* 1438-53) (Mamluk) **16** 259
Jaquard, Joseph-Marie *see* JACQUARD, JOSEPH-MARIE
Jaquerio, Giacomo **14** 422; **16** 710; **17** 444–5*; **31** 443
works **16** *710*
Jaques-Dalcroze, Emile **14** 363
Jaquet, Jean **6** 463; **30** 137
Jaquet, Joseph **14** 42
Jaquet-Droz, Henri-Louis **2** 838
Jaquet-Droz, Pierre **2** 838
Jaquet le Vachier **31** 384
Jaquotot, (Marie-)Victoire **17** 445*
Jara, José **17** 445*; **21** 385
Jara, Roberto Holden *see* HOLDEN JARA, ROBERTO
Jarai **5** 503; **32** 480
Jarai Arap **32** 490
textiles **32** *490*
Jaramillo, Ignacio Gómez *see* GÓMEZ JARAMILLO, IGNACIO
Jaramillo, Manuel Samaniego y *see* SAMANIEGO Y JARAMILLO, MANUEL
Jaray, Tess **4** 790
Jarché, James **17** 445–6*
Jardiel, José Paredes *see* PAREDES JARDIEL, JOSÉ
Jardín **7** 605
Jardin, Karel Du *see* DU JARDIN, KAREL
Jardin, Nicolas-Henri **17** 446*
pupils **14** 201
works **2** 172; **3** 841; **8** 726, 743, *743*; **14** 369; **20** 867; **21** 77; **25** 766
Jardines, Miguel **29** 341
jardinières **22** *880*; **23** *237*
materials **22** *880*
jardins à la française see under GARDENS → types
jardins anglo-chinois see under GARDENS → types
jardins paysagers see under GARDENS → types
Jarema, Maria **17** 446–7*, 802
collaboration **29** 641
groups and movements **18** 429, 433
teachers **9** 394
Jareño y Alarcón, Francisco **17** 447*
works **4** 567; **29** 272, *272*, 355
Jareš, J. **2** 546
Jarl, Birger *see* BIRGER JARL
Jarlath, Saint **31** 402
Jarlshof **28** 223; **32** 533
Jarmo **17** 447*; **21** *267*, 269
figurines **21** 293
houses **21** 280
pottery **21** 305
Järna, Rudolf Steiner school **2** 603
Järnefelt, Eero (Nikolai) **17** 447–8*
works **11** 95; **17** *448*
Jarnuszkiewicz, Jerzy **17** 448*; **25** 116
collaboration **14** 155
pupils **3** 486; **18** 413
works **25** 116
Jarocki, Władysław **12** 602; **24** 441; **29** 641
Jaroměř, Gočáruv department store **8** 379
Jaromir II, Prince of Rügen (*fl* 13th cent.) **29** 744
Jaroš, Tomáš **8** 384, 415, 416
Jarosch, Thoman **24** 331
Jarosław, Jesuit college **25** 140
Jarošvaitė, Ksenija **19** 500
Jaroszynski **32** 879
Jarpa, Onofre **12** 917
Jarrow, Frédéric **19** 769
Jarrow Monastery (Tyne & Wear) **2** 65, 68; **3** 708; **10** 359; **21** 835
glass **10** 315
manuscripts **15** 874
paintings **9** 13
refectory **21** 844
stained glass **2** 83; **29** 501
wall paintings **2** 72
Jarry, Alfred **17** 449*; **27** 240, 260; **33** 361
collaboration **13** 232
productions **4** 325; **28** 484
works **30** 704
illustrated **21** 709; **30** 488
Jarry, Nicolas **17** 449*; **18** 880; **19** 870; **26** 452
jars
historical and regional traditions
Africa **1** 310–11
Belgium **3** 588
Canaanite **30** 185
Chancay **6** 440
China **6** *886*, 888, *888, 899*, 901, *906*; **7** 69, *69, 82*, 144
Crete **21** *665, 668, 669, 670*
Cycladic **8** *312*
Egypt, ancient **6** *329*; **10** *24, 26*, 74
France **20** *471*
Gran Nicoya culture **13** *312*
Islamic **16** 394, 397, *416*
Jamaica **16** *887*
Japan **17** *255, 257, 263, 265*; **31** *77*
Edo period (1600-1868) **23** *196*
Korea **6** III1; **18** *334, 343*
Laos **18** 762
Mexico **21** *392*
Minoan **21** *665, 668, 669, 670*
Native North Americans **22** *601*
Peru **6** *440*
Prehistoric art **18** *334*; **25** 543
Rome, ancient **20** *471*
South Africa **29** *118*
South America, Pre-Columbian **6** *440*; **13** *312*
South-east Asia **29** 232, *232*

jars
historical and regional traditions—cont.
Spain **29** *324*
Syria **16** 397, *416*
Syria-Palestine **30** 185, *197*
United States of America **22** *601*
materials
earthenwares **6** *888*; **16** *887*; **18** *334*
enamel **7** 69, *69*; **23** *196*
glass **7** *82*; **29** *118*
porcelain **6** *899*, *906*, III1; **17** *265*; **18** *343*
pottery
China **7** 144
Egypt, ancient **6** *329*; **10** *24*, *26*
Gran Nicoya culture **13** *312*
Helladic **14** *343*, *345*, *347*
Islamic **16** *416*
Minoan **21** *665*, *668*, *669*, *670*
Rhodes (island) **26** *290*
Syria-Palestine **30** *197*
stone **10** 74
stonewares **6** *886*; **17** *255*, *257*, *263*; **21** *64*; **23** *196*; **31** *77*
types
albarelli **16** *733*
barrel **8** *312*; **14** *343*
bridge-spouted **8** *314*; **21** *668*
burial **17** 246, *250*; **21** 657
canopic *see* CANOPIC JARS
chinas **6** 440, *440*
guan **6** *875*
kendi **6** 875, *875*
leys **6** *875*
Martaban **5** 255*; **6** 332
piriform **14** *345*
salt **17** 262
stirrup **29** 680*
Chimú **29** 176
Cupisnique **29** *177*
Cycladic **8** *314*
Helladic **14** *345*, *347*
Moche (culture) **21** *752*; **29** 176, *176*, *221*
Mycenaean **14** *345*, *347*
Nazca **29** 176
Paracas culture **29** 176
Peru **21** *752*
Rhodes (island) **26** *290*
South America, Pre-Columbian **21** *752*; **29** 176, *176*, *177*, *221*
Tiahuanaco **29** 176
tea **17** 341; **21** *64*
tinajas **29** 322, 323
tinajón **8** 236
tobacco **5** *581*
Jaruru (Tjungarrayi), Charlie **1** 64
Järva-Peetri Church **10** 536
Jarves, Deming **4** 483; **22** 240; **23** 22; **31** 642
Jarves, George D. **22** 240
Jarves, James Jackson **31** 666, 671
Jarves Cassoni, Master of the *see* APOLLONIO DI GIOVANNI (DI TOMASO)
Jarves Collection *see under* NEW HAVEN (CT) → Yale University → Art Gallery
Jarvie, Robert **31** 650
Jarvis, Charles *see* JERVAS, CHARLES
Jarvis, Donald **31** 864
Jarvis, John Wesley **17** 450*
patrons and collectors **12** 645
pupils **15** 857; **23** 629; **25** 818
Jaschik, Álmos **15** 18; **18** 412
Jaschke, Franz **2** 546
Jásd Abbey **26** 638
al-Jashankir
manuscripts **16** *129*
Jasieński, Władysław **18** 398
Jasinski, Stanislas **5** 24
Jasłowski, Tomasz **25** 127
JASMAX Architects **23** 57
jasmine **7** 45
Jasna Góra **25** 128
Chapel of Our Lady of Częstochowa **25** 128
Pauline Monastery Library **25** 121
Jasoku Soga *see* SOGA JASOKU
Jason Vase **26** 486
Jason Works **7** 798
Jasov Abbey **14** 887; **28** *848*
church **28** 849, *850*, 852
paintings **14** 900
sculpture **14** 894; **28** 855
Jaspar, Ernst **9** 764
Jaspar, (Dieudonné) Paul **3** 550; **17** 450*; **28** 583
jasper **14** 167, 168; **16** 859
historical and regional traditions
Ancient Near East **1** *857*
Byzantine **12** 254, *255*
Crete **21** *685*
Egypt, ancient **1** *817*; **10** 38; **12** 246
Greece, ancient **12** 247, *248*
Indian subcontinent **15** *418*
Indus civilization **15** *418*
Islamic **16** *543*
Italy **14** I1
Mesoamerica, Pre-Columbian **21** 241
Minoan **21** *685*
Rome, ancient **12** 251
Russia **27** 428
Syria-Palestine **1** *857*
types
blood **14** 168
Bohemian **14** 168
flowered **14** 168
uses
amulets **1** *817*; **10** 38; **12** 251
cameos **12** *255*
figurines **15** *418*
pietre dure **14** I1
rings **21** *685*
scarabs **12** *248*
seals **1** *857*; **12** 247; **16** *543*; **21** *685*
Jasper, J. E. **29** 241
Jaspers, Gysbrecht **31** 803
Jaspers, Karl **10** 686
Jasper ware *see under* POTTERY → wares
Jaspisporzellan see under POTTERY → wares
al-Jasra House **3** 68
Jasrota **15** *619*
Jasse, Guillaume **31** 842
Jassem Zeini **25** 777
Jastrzębowski, Wojciech **18** 429; **25** 119, 122; **32** 879
Jasulaitis *see* WEST, MARGARET
Jasusch, Anton **28** 853
Jasvant Singh, Prince of Uniara (18th cent.) (Rajput) **15** 607
Jaswant Rao II, Maharaja of Indore (*reg* 1926-48) **4** 662; **27** 322
Jaswant Singh I, Maharaja of Marwar (*reg* 1638--78) (Rajput) **15** 614
Jaswant Singh II, Maharaja of Marwar (*reg* 1873-95) (Rajput) **15** 616
Jászó *see* JASOV
Jat **12** 75; **15** 726
Játiva
crosses **29** 332
paper **16** 351; **24** 48
Pila **16** 130, 131, 246
Jatprolu **15** 540
Jatumpamba **9** 709
Jauch, Joachim Daniel **8** 843; **17** 450–51*; **33** 115
Jauer *see* JAWOR
Jaukh, Joachim Daniel **3** 527
Jaulian *see under* TAXILA
Jaume i Bosch, Miguel **4** 129
Jaunā Kultūras Sabiedrība
Jaunarājs, Olgerts
Jaunpur **15** *261*, 343–4, *360*, 368; **16** *105*; **17** 451*
architecture **15** 195
Atala Mosque **15** 343, *344*; **16** 201; **17** 451; **22** 195
congregational mosque **15** 344
Jhanjhri Mosque **15** 343
Khalis Mukhlis Mosque **15** 343
La'l Darwaza Mosque **15** 344
manuscript illumination **15** 564, 566, 568, 569
Qal'a Mosque **15** 343
Shahi Masjid *see* La'l Darwaza Masjid
Jaunsudrabiņš, Jānis
Jauran **5** 568; **25** 28
Jauss, Hans Robert **26** 62
Jaussely, Léon **17** 451*; **24** 128
pupils **12** 871
works **3** 216; **10** 689; **18** 782; **31** 730
Java **15** *751*, *753*; **29** 226, 235
adzes **29** 227
altars **1** 706
appliqué **15** 792
architecture **15** 762, 769–70*, 772*
Islamic **15** 768–9*
megalithic **21** 45
art history **29** 241
bamboo **15** 772, 809
baskets **15** 809, 810
batik **3** 379, *379*; **9** IV1; **15** 790–92*, *791*, 796; **30** XI
bells **22** 376
boats **15** 810
brick **4** 796
bronze **15** 777, 811; **29** 229
caves **29** 226
ceramics **15** 811
coconuts **15** 810
coins **15** 811
copper **15** 811
cotton **9** IV1; **15** 790, *791*, 792; **30** XI
craftsmen and artists **15** 791
dance **15** 802*
doors **9** 163
drawings **15** 804, 805–6*, 807–8*
dress **15** 792, 812–13*
drums (musical instruments) **15** 817
Pejeng **15** 816
dyeing **15** 790–92, *791*
education (art) **15** 818
fans **10** 778
figurines **15** *783*
gold **15** *783*
gold leaf **15** *798*, 798
gongs **15** 816
guidebooks **13** 812
hardstones **29** 227
headcloths **15** 792
hides **15** *798*, 798
houses **15** 772
iconography **14** 560; **15** 777, 782, 797–8
ikat **15** 792
jewellery **15** 814
limestone **15** *781*
looms **15** 792
manuscript illumination **15** 804, *805*, 805–6*
masks **15** 802*
musical instruments **22** 376
narratives **15** 779, 780
painting **15** 804, 805–6*, 807–8*, *808*, 810
scroll **28** 310
palaces **15** *769*, 775; **30** *9*
palm leaves **15** 772
patronage **15** 798–9; **29** 237
plaster **15** 779
portraits **15** 780
puppets **15** *797*, 797–8, *798*, 801; **29** 234
rattles **15** 817
rice paste **15** 790
rituals **15** 798
Java—cont.
roofs **15** 764, 772
sanctuaries **15** 758–62, *759*, *761*, 764–6, *765*, *766*
sarcophagi **27** 831
sarongs **15** 791; **30** XI
sashes **15** 792
sculpture **14** 561; **15** 776, 777–83*, *781*; **29** 234
bronze **15** 777
Buddhism **15** *778*, 778, 779, *782*
Hinduism **15** 778
relief **15** 779, 780, 781–3
stone **15** 777, *778*, *782*
shrines (i) (cult) **19** *695*; **28** 639
silk **15** 790, 792
spears **15** 818
stone **15** 777, *778*, *782*
stools **30** 785
temples **30** 446
terracotta **15** 772
textiles **15** 758, 790–92*; **29** 239; **30** 558
theatre **15** 797, *801*, 801–2*
shadow **15** *797*, 797–9*, *798*
tin **15** 811
trade **18** 252
ceramics **15** 811
coins **15** 811
porcelain **6** 622
waxes **15** 790
wood **15** 772, *783*
wraps **15** 792
zithers **15** 817
Java Bank **15** 770
Javacheff, Christo *see* CHRISTO AND JEANNE-CLAUDE
Javad al-Imami **15** 143
Javakhishvili, K. I. **12** 320
Javanese **15** 753
Jávea Treasure **15** 60
Javed, Tariq **23** 800
Javed, Zubeda **23** 800
javelins **2** 448
Javier, Vicente **14** 714
Jawahar **15** 627
Jawan Singh, Rana of Mewar (*reg* 1828-38) (Rajput) **15** 601
Jawerth, David **30** 468
al-Jawf Museum **2** 275
Jawhar **5** 395
Jawhar Nasiba (Saljuq of Anatolia) **17** 864
jawi see under SCRIPTS → types
Jawkhdar (family) **32** 315
Jawlensky, Alexei **8** 10; **17** 452, 453*; **28** 78; **33** 77
groups and movements **4** 132, 133, 177; **10** 694; **12** 395; **16** 817; **17** 766; **18** 111; **22** 921; **33** 379
patrons and collectors **20** 880; **33** 45
pupils **31** 416
teachers **2** 890
works **17** *452*
Jawor Church **19** 815
Jawsaq al-Khaqani *see under* SAMARRA' → palaces → Dar al-Khilafa
Jaxa Tympanum **25** *109*
Jay, Adolphe-Marie-François **8** 572; **23** 209; **31** 276
Jay, L.-J. **11** 667
Jay, William **27** 884
Jayabageshvari **22** 759
Jayadeva **15** 228
Jaya Indravarman III, King of Champa (*reg c.* 1139) **6** 428
Jayakarta *see* JAKARTA
Jaya Pandita **21** 882
Jayapura **15** 819
Jayasimha Siddharaja, Ruler (*reg c.* 1093-1145) (Solanki) **8** 432; **24** 251
Jaya Simhavarman II, King of Champa (*reg* 1044) **6** 424
Jayasuria, Anil **3** 419
Jayati **15** 537
Jayavarman II, King of Cambodia (*reg* 802-50) **5** 461, 464; **26** 558
Jayavarman IV, King of Cambodia (*reg* 928-42) **5** 468
Jayavarman V, King of Cambodia (*reg* 968-1001) **2** 55; **5** 471
Jayavarman VII, King of Cambodia (*reg* 1181-1220) **5** 477, *498*
architecture **2** 55, 60; **5** 476–7, 495
hospitals **5** 479
temples **2** 59; **5** 460, 479
terraces **5** 480
inscriptions **30** 581
reliefs **5** 495
Jayavarman VIII, King of Cambodia (*reg* 1243-95) **2** 56
Jayaviravarman, King of Cambodia (*reg* 1002-11) **2** 55
Jayawardene, Swanee **29** 468
Jayendranagari *see under* ANGKOR
al-Jazari
fountains **11** 339
patrons and collectors **16** 379
writings **2** 837
illustrated **16** *298*
on casting **16** 363; **21** 322
on inlays **16** 364
on metalwork **16** 363, 381
translated **15** 573
Jazet, Jean-Pierre-Marie **8** 595; **17** 453*
Jazira culture **21** 269, 305
Jazirat al-Ghanam **2** 267
Jazirat Ibn 'Umar *see* CIZRE
Jaźwiecki, F. **18** 433
Jazz, Paulo **2** 87
al-Jazzar, 'Abd al-Hadi **5** 401; **9** 766; **12** 222*
Jbeil *see* BYBLOS
Jeager-Mewe, Harry **29** 871
Jean, Archbishop of Rouen **9** 708
Jean, Bishop of Beauvais **24** 115
Jean, Bishop of Thérouanne **33** 567
Jean, Duc de Berry *see* BERRY, JEAN I DE VALOIS, Duc de
Jean II, Abbot of Clairvaux **21** 836, 838
Jean, Dreux **3** 555; **4** 921; **17** 454–5*; **20** 680
attributions **4** 841, 842
patrons and collectors **5** 211
pupils **20** 723
works **17** *454*
Jean, Marcel **10** 650; **30** 21
Jean, Roberto **19** 84
Jean, Vincent Joseph *see* CUVILLIÉS, FRANÇOIS DE, I
Jean d'Andeli **27** 249
Jean d'Angers **19** 174
Jean d'Arbois **5** 207; **17** 455*; **21** 463; **29** 597
Jean d'Arras **5** 666; **17** 456*
Jean de Bayeux (*d* 1398; father) **27** 250, 254
Jean de Bayeux (*fl* 1398; son) **27** 254
Jean de Beaumetz **3** 552; **17** 456–9*; **20** 207
collaboration **17** 459
patrons and collectors **5** 207, 208, 895; **6** 393; **11** 531
works **8** 890, 892; **17** *456*; **33** 347
Jean de Benhaud **4** 547
Jean de Boulogne **4** 538
Jean de Bourbon, Abbot of Cluny **7** 476
Jean de Brabant **5** 207
Jean de Brecquessent **5** 666; **17** 457*
Jean de Bruges *see* BOUDOLF, JAN
Jean de Calabre **24** 775
Jean de Cambrai **3** 568; **11** 555; **17** 457*
works **4** 578, 582; **13** 78–9; **31** 837; **33** 28

Jean (Guillaumet) de Chartres 4 546; 7 595; 24 132
works 4 546
Jean de Chastillon 31 841
Jean de Chelles see CHELLES, JEAN DE
Jean de Chetro 16 722
Jean de Cormont 20 778; 31 846
Jean de Coste 31 834
Jean de Courcy 7 241
Jean de Courtecuisse
works 1 654
Jean de Dunois, Bâtard d'Orléans see DUNOIS, JEAN, Comte de
Jean de France, Duc de Berry see BERRY, JEAN I DE VALOIS, Duc de
Jean de Gisors 5 666
Jean de Gros 3 612; 16 69; 20 659
Jean de Hasselt 5 207
Jean de Jandun 13 132
Jean de Jouy 31 841
Jean de la Cloche 7 544
Jean de la Grange, Cardinal 31 840
Jean de la Huerta see JUAN DE LA HUERTA
Jean de Launay 24 132
Jean de Laval 17 458*; 31 844
attributions 20 646, 646
Jean de l'Espine 2 46; 11 512
Jean de Liège (i) (d 1381) 3 455; 11 555; 13 77; 17 458–61*; 19 604; 24 132
collaboration 3 455; 26 43
patrons and collectors 31 835
pupils 19 544
works 13 76; 17 459; 31 129
Jean de Liège (ii) (fl 1381-1403) 3 568; 17 459–60*
patrons and collectors 5 207; 11 438
works 13 126
Jean de Lorraine, Cardinal 27 209
Jean de Loubières 2 862
Jean de Maisoncelles 5 210; 8 893; 17 460*
Jean de Marville 13 172; 17 460*
assistants 28 865
patrons and collectors 5 206, 207; 33 28
works 7 405; 8 890, 892; 20 207; 28 866
Jean de Mauléon, Master of 20 789, 790
Jean de Montmartre 31 834
Jean de Nonancourt 27 252
Jean de Paris see PERRÉAL, JEAN
Jean de Pestinien 17 460
Jean de Planis 26 555
Jean de Prez 14 413
Jean de Rouen (fl c. 1495-1500) 4 544, 546; 17 596
Jean de Rouen (c. 1500-80) see JOÃO DE RUÃO
Jean de Rouppy see JEAN DE CAMBRAI
Jean de St Dié 26 706
Jean de Saint-Romain 24 132; 26 43; 31 835
Jean d'Esserent 5 666
Jean de Sy 13 154
Jean de Sy Bible, Master of the see BOQUETEAUX, MASTER OF THE
Jean de Thioys 5 207
Jean de Thoiry 31 835
Jean de Torvoie 31 384
Jean de Touyl 13 169
works 13 169
Jean de Valenciennes 3 542, 567; 4 925; 17 460–61*; 23 881
Jean d'Oisy 13 62, 100
Jean d'Orbais 17 461*; 26 114
Jean d'Orléans 12 723; 17 461–2*; 20 742
patrons and collectors 31 832, 835, 840
works 17 459
Jean du Clercq 8 524
Jean du Mas, Seigneur de l'Isle 16 854
Jean du Pré 21 730
Jean du Vivier 13 158; 17 461; 31 832, 835, 840
Jean d'Ypres 1 679; 13 125; 23 414
Jeanine, Juan Bautista 23 905
Jean le Bourguignon see CHANGENET, JEAN
Jean le Braellier 11 637; 13 171
Jean le Loup 17 462*; 26 114
Jean le Noir 13 154; 17 462–3*
attributions 31 835
patrons and collectors 31 832, 834, 836, 837
works 13 148; 16 852; 17 462
Jean le Visite 14 422; 20 777
Jean Malouel 5 207
Jean Michel 30 529
Jeanne de Boulogne see BERRY, JEANNE DE VALOIS, Duchesse de
Jeanne d'Evreux see JOANNA OF EVREUX, Queen of Navarre and France
Jeanneret, Charles-Edouard see LE CORBUSIER
Jeanneret, Pierre 7 294; 17 463*; 19 41
collaboration 18 205; 19 46, 50–51; 24 476; 25 663; 27 214
competitions 7 669
groups and movements 25 740
pupils 14 155
works 6 445, 445; 12 276; 15 168; 30 755
Jeannest, Pierre-Emile 21 697
Jean Pépin de Huy 11 555; 13 77; 17 463–4*; 24 132
collaboration 4 608; 5 666
patrons and collectors 5 666, 667
pupils 3 455; 17 458
Jean Rolin, Master of 11 724, 726; 20 626, 699, 700–701*
patrons and collectors 26 555, 556
works 11 726; 20 701
Jeanron, Philippe-Auguste 17 464*; 26 54
jeans 9 491; 20 594
Jean sans Peur, Duc de Bourgogne see JOHN THE FEARLESS, Duke of Burgundy
Jeanselme, Joseph-Pierre-François 16 822
Jean van Brussel see ROOME, JAN VAN
Jean van Valenchine see JEAN DE VALENCIENNES
Jearrad, Robert William 14 786; 25 268
Jeaurat, Edmé 4 512, 514; 17 466; 32 670
Jeaurat, Etienne 17 465–6*
pupils 12 862; 27 530
reproductive prints by others 3 107
works 17 465; 31 704
Jeaurat, Nicolas Henry 17 466
Jeavons, Thomas 25 837
Jebb, Joshua 10 236; 25 637
Jebel Aruda 1 849; 14 13; 17 466*; 21 267, 271; 30 180
architecture 21 281
pottery 21 306
seals 1 862
Jebelet el-Beida 29 613
Jebel Saideh 30 181
Jebuk
sculpture 15 780, 781, 781
Jeckell, Thomas see JECKYLL, THOMAS
Jeckyll, Thomas 17 466–7*
patrons and collectors 1 171; 11 748; 14 132
works 9 29; 10 283; 15 895; 33 139
Jecquier, Emile 6 594; 27 791
Jedburgh (Borders) 28 222
Abbey 23 491; 26 591, 617; 28 223
Jednoróg 10 102; 18 414
Jednota Umelců Výtvarných see UNION OF ARTISTS
Jędrzejów Church 25 105
Jeejheebhoy, Jamshetjee 15 656
Jeffers, A. M. 3 269
Jefferson, Robert 17 516
Jefferson, Thomas 10 401; 17 467–9*; 33 207
archaeology 22 671
architecture
government buildings 7 417; 10 850; 13 237; 18 887; 26 352; 31 591, 591
house 4 787; 22 30; 32 553
libraries 25 266
porticoes 25 266, 267
rotundas 17 468; 27 237
collaboration 2 337; 7 417; 10 850; 26 352
competitions 7 666
excavations 2 299
furniture 25 888
groups and movements 13 610; 22 738; 23 860; 26 735
restorations 13 757
silver 10 851; 23 354
sponsorship 21 615
Jefferson City State Capitol (MO) 3 748, 748
Jeffery, G. 3 638; 10 774
Jeffery & Skiller 33 232
Jeffrey, Allen & Co. 17 469
Jeffrey, George 8 367
Jeffrey, Wise & Co. 17 469
Jeffrey, Wise & Horne 17 469
Jeffrey & Co. 17 469–70*; 27 719; 32 817
designers 8 122, 576, 583; 9 295; 17 640; 30 266; 32 816
production 32 V1
productions 32 812, 816, 817
Jeffreys, Thomas 30 384
Jeffries, Carson 18 809; 29 97
Jeffries, Gloria 5 571
Jeffrys, C. W. 5 566
Jefimija 28 457–8
Jegede, Emmanuel 23 138
Jegenstorf 25 546
Jegenyés, János 15 5
Jegg, Johann Christian 17 470
Jegg, Stephan 2 807, 811, 812; 17 470*
Jegher, Christoffel 2 196; 3 561; 17 470–71*
works 17 471; 27 299; 33 358, 367
Jegher, Jan Christoffel 17 470
Jehan, Dreux see JEAN, DREUX
Jehan de Beauce 6 493, 494
Jehan de Bondolf see BOUDOLF, JAN
Jehan de Gand 3 552
Jehan de Nivelet 12 333
Jehan de Reins 4 546
Jehan de Rouen see JOÃO DE RUÃO
Jehan de Valencia 11 604
Jehan de Vitry 13 126
Jehan Dubrueil 11 726
Jehangir, Cowasji 15 742
Jehan le Frizon 13 171
Jehan le Scelleur 13 171
Jehannin le Conte 7 544
Jehol see CHENGDE
Jéhotte, Louis 11 371; 17 921; 21 369; 31 874
Jeitun see DZHEYTUN
Jejeebhoy, Jamsetjee 4 289
Jekmejeh 27 61
Jekshenbayev, Shibek 18 568
Jekyll, Gertrude 17 471*
collaboration 19 689, 819
works 3 110; 12 140, 141, 222
Jelena, Queen of Serbia (fl c. 1365) 28 448
Jelgava 17 472*; 18 847
Academia Petrina 18 849
Museum 17 472
architecture 18 848
Castle 18 847
Holy Trinity 18 848
Kurland Provincial Museum 18 849
Stavenhagen House 18 851
Villa Medem 18 849
Jelgerhuis, Johannes 17 472*
Jelgerhuis, Rienk 17 472
Jelicich, Stephen 23 67
Jelin, Christoph 33 429
Jelínek (family) 8 386
Jelínek, Alexander 33 255
Jelínek, Julius 23 272
Jelles, E(vert) J(elle) 17 472*
Jellett, Mainie 16 17; 17 472–3*
works 16 17
Jellicoe, Ann 20 894
Jellicoe, Geoffrey (Alan) 6 409; 12 143; 17 473*
Jelling 8 720; 17 473–4*
church 8 721; 26 592
Greater Jelling Stone see King Harald's rune-stone
King Harald's rune-stone 8 719, 737, 758; 17 474, 474; 32 513, 517, 517, 520, 521, 525
metalwork 32 516, 516, 517
royal grave 32 525
wood-carvings 32 521
Jelling style see under VIKING → styles
Jelly, Thomas 3 371
Jelovšek, Franc 17 474*; 28 860
Jelovšek, Kristof Andrej 33 592
Jelski, Jan 3 530
Jelski, Karol' 3 530
Jelski, Kazimier 3 530; 19 497; 27 348
Jeltsema, Frederik Engel 23 908
al-Jem, Maison de Silène 9 562
Jemaa 1 381; 23 129, 179, 181
Jemal, Muetdin-Arabi 27 433
Jemappes 3 591
Jemdet Nasr 1 853, 860; 21 272, 282
Jemec, Andrej 28 861
Jémez (NM) 22 607, 608
Jemmeh, Tell
palace 30 191
Jen 1 328; 22 287
Jena Painter 13 524
Jenewein, Felix 17 474*
Jen Hsiung see REN XIONG
Jen I see REN YI
Jenichen, Balthasar 29 43, 44
Jenins see JANYNS
Jenisch, Philipp 19 779; 33 429
Jen Jen-fa see REN RENFA
Jenkins, Frank Lynn 10 267
Jenkins, James 30 39
Jenkins, John 26 499
Jenkins, (William) Paul 12 795; 16 820; 17 474–5*
Jenkins, Ronald 24 34
Jenkins, Thomas 5 541; 10 328, 365, 366, 637, 642; 13 303; 17 475*; 18 150; 24 570; 27 115; 31 244
dealing 4 894
groups and movements 2 163
paintings 14 598; 31 245
patrons and collectors 25 8
sculpture 4 181, 886; 6 97; 19 531; 24 845; 30 268; 31 60; 33 19
sponsors 1 533
Jenkins, William 23 193
Jenkinson, Alexander 9 726; 28 259
Jenkinson, Robert Banks, 2nd Earl of Liverpool 5 630
Jenkintown (PA), Alverthorpe Gallery 27 166
Jenks, B. 33 152
Jenks, Charles 6 392; 10 285
Jenks, Joseph 31 653
Jenne-jeno 1 222; 21 479, 481
sculpture 1 329
statuettes 21 481
terracottas 1 350; 21 479, 480
Jennens, Charles 10 364; 14 269; 17 476*
Jennens & Bettridge 24 61
Jenner, Walter 4 819
Jenneson, Nicolas 19 800
Jennesson, Jean-Nicolas 14 447; 22 455
Jennewein, Carl Paul 12 615; 20 926
Jenney, Neil 17 476*
Jenney, William Le Baron 17 476–7*
assistants 29 913
collaboration 6 573
groups and movements 6 577
staff 5 273; 14 657; 26 538
works 6 573, 573; 16 55; 28 830, 831; 31 594
Jenney & Mundie 5 274; 6 573; 17 477
Jennings, Humphrey 20 589, 590; 30 22
Jennings, J. D. 17 753
Jennings, R. 8 66
Jennings's Landscape Annual 24 445
Jennys, Richard 17 477*
Jennys, William 17 477*
Jen Po-nien see REN YI
Jen Po-wen see REN BOWEN
Jensdatter, Johanne 23 238
Jensen, Alfred (Julio) 14 633; 17 477–8*
Jensen, Bill 23 50
Jensen, Christian Albrecht 8 734; 17 478–9*
patrons and collectors 14 572
works 11 472; 17 478
Jensen, David 23 450; 33 516
Jensen, Georg (Arthur) 8 751; 17 479*
collaboration 26 546
works 1 762; 8 751, 752, 753, 753; 17 528, 529
Jensen, Gerrit 10 273, 290; 17 479*; 19 592
groups and movements 33 200
patrons and collectors 14 807
works 7 167; 10 291; 20 468
Jensen, Jens 17 479–80*
Jensen, Karl 13 216
Jensen, Knud W. 7 806; 8 758, 759
Jensen, Oluf 8 749
Jensen, Rocky Ka'iouliokahihikolo Ehu 14 251
Jensen, Severin 17 472; 18 849
Jensen, Søren Georg 12 451; 17 479
Jensen, Viggo Møller 8 729
Jensen-Klint, P(eder) V(ilhelm) 17 480*
competitions 3 749
pupils 18 136
works 4 788, 789; 8 727, 728; 18 136; 27 131
Jensen Kolding, Peder 8 739
works 8 740
Jenson (fl 1474-9) 2 186; 4 397
Jenson, Nicolas 17 480–81*; 28 306
patrons and collectors 19 870
works 4 76; 12 734; 31 494, 494; 32 198
Jenson Bible see under BIBLES → types
Jentsch, Adolph 22 450
Jen-tsung, Emperor (Yüan; reg 1312-21) see RENZONG, Emperor
Jenty, C. N. 11 139
Jen Tzu-chao see REN ZIZHAO
Jen Wei-ch'ang see REN XIONG
Jenyns see JANYNS
Jenyns, Lorraine 2 762

Jenyns, (Roger) Soame **17** 481*
Jen Yü *see* REN YU
Jeppesen, Kristian **14** 69, 70–71
Jéquier, Gustave **10** 81, 82, 84
Jerabis *see* CARCHEMISH
Jerablus *see* CARCHEMISH
Jerace, Vincenzo **16** 721
Jeran, Augustin **28** 862
Jerash **17** 655
Antioch-on-the-Chrysorrhoas **12** 337
arch **26** 915; **31** 350
architecture **9** 542, 560
Cathedral complex **12** 338, *339*
columns **26** 882
Gerasa **9** *513*; **12** 337–9*; **26** 914, *915*; **27** 6
mosaics **9** 567, 568
museum **17** 656
nymphaeum **1** 164; **23** 491
pottery **16** 396, 397
Roman circus **7** 342
St John the Baptist **3** 190; **7** 255
Sanctuary of Artemis **26** 918
synagogue **17** 543
Temple of Artemis **12** *337*; **23** 491; **26** 881; **27** 714
Temple of Zeus **26** 918
West Baths **26** 874, 916
Jerba Island **1** *376*; **31** 424, 426; **32** 312
Jerdan, William **21** 265
Jeremiah of Crete **28** 762
Jerez, Julio y Toribio *see* TORIBIO JEREZ, JULIO Y
Jerez de la Frontera
Cartuja **13** 767; **33** 731–2
furniture **29** 316
S Miguel **22** 3–4
jergas see under RUGS → types
Jergušova-Vydarená, Lýdia **28** 856
Jérica **29** 332
Jerichau, Harald **17** 481
Jerichau, Holger Hvitfeldt **17** 481, 482
Jerichau, J(ens) A(dolf) (1816-83) **3** 783; **8** 741; **17** 481–2*
Jerichau, Jens Adolf (1890-1916) **17** 481, 482*
Jerichau Baumann, Elisabeth **17** 481
Jerichow Abbey **12** *360*; **17** 482–3*
church **4** 776; **17** 482–3*, *483*
Jérico(Colombia) **7** 605
Jerico (Israel) **1** 892, 893; **16** *565*; **17** 483–5*, 556; **30** *180*
architecture **30** 191
boxes **5** 557
brick **4** 771
chapel **30** 182
fortifications **21** 552; **30** 185
furniture **1** 890; **5** 557
gardens **12** 70
mud-bricks **30** 190
palace **26** 917
pottery **1** 894; **30** 196
sculpture **25** 175; **30** 181, 188, 192
seals **1** 857
skulls **17** *484*, 484; **30** 181, 182
textiles **1** 881
tombs **5** 557
tower **30** 182
wall paintings **30** 198
walls **17** 484
Jerishe, Tell **24** 634
Jerling, Hans **14** 281
Jerman, Edward **10** 668; **19** 509; **21** 615
Jermyn, Henry, 1st Earl of St Albans **10** 360; **19** 570
Jernberg, August **17** 485*; **30** 79
Jerndorff, August (Andreas) **17** 485*
works **7** *806*
Jerningham, Henry **17** 768
Jerningham, William **29** 515
Jerome, Fra *see* HAWES, JOHN CYRIL
Jérôme, Jean-Paul **5** 568; **25** 28
Jerome, Saint **7** 214; **8** 259; **20** 329
Jerome Bonaparte, King of Westphalia (*reg* 1807-13) **4** *299*, 302; **12** 414; **13** 295; **18** 69, 122; **31** 172
Jérôme de Fiesole **11** 556; **17** 485–6*
works **7** 595
Jérôme de Rouen *see* JERÓNIMO DE RUÃO
Jerome of Ascoli *see* NICHOLAS IV, Pope
Jeromonaku, Kostandin **1** 540
Jeronimites *see* HIERONYMITES
Jerónimo de Ruão **2** 501, 874, 875; **3** 534; **17** 486*
works **31** 179; **32** 157
Jerphanion, Guillaume de **5** 674, 677; **9** 527
Jerpoint Abbey **16** 20
Jerrard, S. J. **17** 897
Jerrems, Carol (Joyce) **17** 486*
Jerrigh, Georg **1** 5
Jerrold, Blanchard **9** 170
Jerrold, Douglas **4** 363; **19** 62
Jersey **25** 329
Jersey, Thomas **23** 780
Jersey Porcelain and Earthenware Co. **1** 772
Jersika **18** 846
Jerusalem **1** *849*; **9** *507*, *513*; **16** *104*, *565*; **17** 486–503*, *487*, *488*, *489*; **23** 847; **26** *915*; **30** *180*
art forms and materials
architecture **9** 542; **16** 207, 208; **20** 227
coats of arms **14** 411
glass **1** 865; **9** 644; **16** 519; **27** 73
icons **9** 622
inscriptions **16** 259
manuscripts **8** 219
maps **20** 362
masonry **16** 180
metalwork **16** 389, 390
mosaics **2** 429; **9** 568; **16** 255
pottery **16** 420
printing **16** 361
tattoos **30** 367
textiles **16** 569
wall paintings **17** 556
Bet-Hakerem **17** 854
Bezalel Academy of Arts and Design **2** 381; **3** 901–2*; **16** 390, 567, 571; **17** 579; **21** 49; **28** 57; **30** 851
ceramics **16** 568; **30** 421
furniture **16** *569*
library **16** 572
metalwork **16** 568
textiles **16** 569
building regulations **2** 325
Calvary *see* CALVARY
Centre for Near Eastern Studies **16** 567
collections **17** 582
Dome of the Rock *see under* Islamic religious buildings
ecclesiastical buildings
Anglican Cathedral **28** 296
Armenian Patriarchate of St James
Cathedral of St James **17** 503
textiles **2** 443
throne of St James the Lesser **16** 499
Treasury **2** 444
Chapel of the Ascension **9** 539; **20** 520
Chapel of the Holy Trinity **9** 549
Jerusalem
ecclesiastical buildings—cont.
Church of the Holy Sepulchre **4** 773; **7** 252, 254; **8** 219; **9** 522, 529, 539, 549; **17** 497–9*, *498*, *499*, 501, 503, 506; **20** 519, 865; **22** 43; **26** 584, 859; **27** 235; **28** 427–9*
Anastasis Rotunda **8** 222; **20** 865
ceiling **9** 654
Golgotha Basilica **3** 329
manuscripts **21** 82
metalwork **6** 173
mosaics **26** 679
sculpture **26** 629
Church of the Nativity **20** *519*
Church of the Resurrection **25** 334
Eleona Church **9** 539, *541*; **20** 519
Kathisma Church **9** 540
Monastery of the Holy Cross **9** 548, *548*; **12** 320, 331
St Anne **17** 503, *503*
St James the Less **9** 540
St Saviour **16** 760
fortifications **17** 553; **21** 587–8
gates
Bab al-Qattanin **20** 228
Chain Gate
sculpture **26** 629
Damascus Gate **21** 588, *588*
Gate of the Cotton Sellers *see* Bab al-Qattanin
Gethsemane **9** 540
guidebooks **13** 812
Haram al-Sharif *see* Temple Mount
Hebrew University
Center for Jewish Art **17** 583
Gottesman Centre for Rare Manuscripts **16** 566
Hadassah Medical Centre **14** 785; **29** 508
library **16** 572
Hezekiah's tunnel **16** 573
Hospital **14** 779; **18** 151; **26** 629
houses **16** 269; **17** 535
Islamic religious buildings
Aqsa Mosque **16** 146, 155, 550; **17** 496–7*, 503; **18** 154; **20** 228; **22** 192, 193, *193*
lighting **16** 364
minbar **16** 490, 491; **21** 630
mosaics **16** 128, 256
wood-carvings **16** 488
Ashrafiyya Madrasa **20** 230
el-Athrun Mosque **26** 628
Dome of the Rock **9** 86; **16** 122, 146–7, *147*; **17** *489*, *495*, 495–6*, 503; **18** 242; **20** 228; **28** 633; **31** 111
arches **2** 292, 294, 296, 297
coffering **7** 527
dome **9** 84; **20** 228
friezes **23** 560
inscriptions **16** 146, 257, 278
metalwork **16** 364, 371
mihrab **21** 505
mosaics **7** 634; **16** 128, 146, 147, 255, 256, 537; **22** 162; **23** 562, 563
stained glass **16** 257
tiles **16** 228
al-Ghawanima minaret **26** 629
madrasa of Is'iridiyya **16** 366, 382
Israel Antiquities Authority Library **16** 572
Jerusalem Foundation **16** 570
Ketef Hinnom **30** 195
Kiryat-Moshe **17** 854
libraries
Jewish National and University Library **17** 582
Schocken Library **17** 582
mausoleum **13** 407
Jerusalem—cont.
museums
Bezalel National Art Museum *see under* Israel Museum
Bible Lands Museum **1** 896; **16** 571; **30** 199
Islamic Museum **16** 558; **17** 497
Israel Museum **16** 566; **17** 493; **20** 299; **22** 366; **23** 176; **27** 225, 226, 715
archives **2** 370
Bezalel National Art Museum **3** 901; **16** 571; **17** 582; **27** 226
Billy Rose Art Garden **28** 314
collections **17** 582
Feuchtwanger Collection **17** 582
Indian collection **15** 743, 744
Islamic collection **16** 558
Jewish collections **30** 199
library **16** 572
Shrine of the Book **17** *492*
Stieglitz Collection **16** 570; **17** 582
Syria-Palestine collection **16** 571
L. A. Mayer Memorial Institute for Islamic Art **16** 558, 571, 572
Museo Nazionale di Arte Ebraica-Italiana **17** 582
Palestine Archaeological Museum *see* Rockefeller Museum
Rockefeller Museum **14** 196; **16** 558; **17** 492; **30** 199
Sir Isaac and Lady Edith Wolfson Museum **17** 582
Ticho House Museum **16** 571
Palace of Herod the Great **14** 465
Rehavia **17** 854
Streichman and Stematsky studio **16** 571
synagogues
Hadassah synagogue **17** 580
Hurva synagogue **17** 552
Ramban synagogue **17** 552
Tif'ereth Yisrael synagogue **17** 552
Talpiot **17** 854
Temple Mount **17** 493–4*, *494*
fountain **20** 230, *231*
mihrab **21** 505
portico **20** 228
Temple **14** 465; **17** 494–5*; **27** 1; **28** 384; **30** 431
Solomonic **16** 147, 572; **17** 532, 538, 539; **30** 191, 431
Tomb of Absalom **20** 864; **31** 109
Tower of David **21** 588
urban planning **30** 190
Yeshivat Porat Joseph Rabbinical College **16** 567
Jerusalem, Latin Kingdom of **17** 499–507*
banners **11** 146
capitals **17** *504*; **22** *705*
castles **17** *505*
churches **17** *503*
coats of arms **14** 406
crosses **17** *502*
icons **9** 627
manuscripts **17** *503*, *506*
mosaics **17** *504*
sculpture **26** 629*
stone **26** 629*
Jervais, Thomas **23** 691; **29** 506
Jervas, Charles **16** 13; **17** 507–8*; **30** 267
collaboration **33** 377
patrons and collectors **4** 611; **21** 348; **30** 267; **32** 824
pupils **11** 906
teachers **18** 146
Jervaulx Abbey (N. Yorks) **26** 381
Jervois, William **21** 581
Jerwan Aqueduct **2** 640; **3** 419; **12** 66; **21** 290; **23** 153; **30** 25
Jerzy, Painter **25** 103
works **25** *103*
Jesenko (family) **28** 862
Jesi, Palazzo della Signoria **11** 691
Jesi, Andrea da **1** 447
Jesi, Lucagnolo da **6** 139
Jespers, Emile **17** 508
Jespers, Floris **2** 197
Jespers, Oscar **3** 573; **17** 508*
groups and movements **5** 44
pupils **8** 846
works **2** 197
(Collins,) Jess **12** 217; **22** 523
works **12** *216*
Jesse Cope **23** 461
Jesse Master **24** 158
Jessen, Gro **23** 241
Jessen, Jes **9** 700
Jessen, Johann Jacob **9** 700
Jessen, P.
works **23** *542*
Jessner, Leopold **30** 686
Jessop, William **2** 242; **4** 802; **7** 693; **9** 58
Jessore **3** *166*; **15** 176
Jessup, Georgia **33** 314
Jessurun de Mesquita, S. **21** 122
Jesuit Order **3** 263; **7** 215; **15** 121; **17** 508–14*
art forms
architecture **7** 566–7; **13** 210, 320; **23** 340
Argentina **2** 394
Austria **2** 781
Belgium **17** 511
Bolivia **4** 259; **17** 513
Brazil **4** 709
France **17** 511
Germany **17** 511
Paraguay **17** 513; **24** 94, 95
Poland **25** 135
enamel **7** 79
furniture **8** 398
painting **4** 261; **8** 178; **12** 389; **17** 182–3, *511*
education (art) **17** 419; **25** 140, 142
iconography **17** 509–10*; **22** 414
patronage **16** 763; **17** 510–12*
regional traditions
Brazil **4** 715, 724; **17** 513
Canada **17** 509
China **6** 627; **17** 513
Indian subcontinent **17** 512
Japan **17** 513
Paraguay **24** 92
Peru **17** 513
Jesurum, Michelangelo **16** 755; **32** 206
Jesurun, John **24** 409
Jésus **24** *91*
Jesuit church **24** 95
Museum **24** 102
Jesus, Agostinho da **4** 722
Jesus, António Luís de **25** 310
Jesus, José Teófilio de **4** 708
Jesús, Manuel Joaquim de **30** 881
Jesus Maria José, Manuel de **24** 395
Jesus of Bethany, Master of **21** 338
jet **12** 268; **17** 514–17*
historical and regional traditions
Britain **25** 518
England **10** 346; **17** *516*, 516–17*
Greece, ancient **1** 816
Japan **17** 398, 399
Peru **21** 718
Prehistoric art **25** 518
Rome, ancient **1** 816; **17** 516
Scotland **17** 516–17*
South America, Pre-Columbian **21** 718
Spain **17** 514–16*, *515*
uses
amulets **1** 816; **17** 514, *515*, 515–16

jet
uses—cont.
beads **3** 441, 442
body ornaments **25** 518
caskets **17** 516
crosses **17** 514, 515
jewellery **10** 346; **17** 516, *516*, 517, 527, 529
mirrors **21** 718
netsuke **17** 398, 399
paxes **17** 515
pilgrim badges **17** 515; **24** 809
rosaries **17** 515
Jetavana Mahavihara **29** 439
Jetelová, Magdalena **8** 388; **17** 517*
Jettel, Eugen **2** 797
Jettmar, Rudolf **11** 320; **17** 517*
Jeuch, Caspar Josef **17** 517–18*
Jeuffroy, Romain-Vincent **12** 221, 264; **17** 518*; **20** 924
Jeune Gravure Contemporaine **8** 63
Jeune Peinture Belge **3** 565; **17** 518*
members **1** 598; **3** 867; **5** 45, 286; **24** 329
Jeune Peinture Belge-Fondation René Lust **17** 518
Jeune Peinture Française **27** 307
Jeurat, Edme Sebastien **6** 570
Jeurat, Etienne
works **2** *703*
Jeurre **21** 150
Jeux, Maître des *see* GAMES, MASTER OF THE
Jevington **32** 529
Jevrić, Olga **28** 453
Jewell, Alvin L. **4** 481
Jewell, R. R. **24** 495
jewellers **19** 596
jewellery **14** 418, 419; **15** 888; **17** 518–30*, *525*
display **9** 27
forms *see* AMULETS; BRACELETS; BROOCHES; CHÂTELAINES; COLLARS; EARRINGS; LOCKETS; NECKLACES; PENDANTS; PINS; RINGS
historical and regional traditions
Achaemenid **1** 118, 875
Afghanistan **1** 205*, 210*
Africa **1** 350–51*
Algeria **16** 532
Anatolia, ancient **1** 834, 836, 876
Ancient Near East **1** 872–4*, *873*, 875–6*, 877
Anglo-Saxon **2** 79*; **26** 303
Antilles, Lesser **2** 152*
Arabia **2** 263–4*
Armenia (Europe) **2** 440–41*
Asante **1** 350
Assyrian **1** 875
Austral Islands **2** 773
Azerbaijan **2** 899–900*
Bali (Indonesia) **15** 814
Bamum **3** 153
Bangladesh **3** 169
Bantu peoples **1** 350, 351
Barbados **2** 152
Baule **1** 350
Belgium **3** 604–5*, *605*
Berber **3** 756, *756*
Bhutan **3** 916
Brazil **4** 723–4*
Britain **17** 526, 528
Buddhism **6** 312*, *312*; **7** 108; **15** 700–701
Bulgaria **5** 160
Burma **5** 250*
Byzantine **9** 652–4*, 657; **17** 519
Cambodia **5** 504, 508
Carolingian **17** 519
Celtic **25** 546
Central Asia, Eastern **6** 312*, *312*
Central Asia, Western **6** 238*, 272–4*; **16** 530–31*
Chile **6** 599*

jewellery
historical and regional traditions—cont.
China **7** 26, 106–10*, *111*, 111–12*, *112*, 145, 836
Creole **11** 759
Crete **8** 153, 154; **21** 657, 658, 682, 683–4*, 686–7*
Croatia **8** 180
Cyprus, ancient **8** 351–2*; **10** 31
Denmark **8** 753
Dominican Republic **5** 752
Early Christian (*c.* AD 250-843) **9** 652–4*
Egypt **9** 652; **16** 515, 529–30*
Egypt, ancient **1** 469; **10** 1, 20*, 28–34*, 38–9, 48, 54, 58, 60; **16** 797
England **10** 344–7*; **17** 516
Anglo-Saxon **2** 79*
Iron Age **25** *545*
16th cent. **17** 522
18th cent. **17** 525
Etruscan **10** 593, 631–2, 635, 636
Finland **11** 108–9*
France , ; **11** 633–5*; **17** 519, 527, II1, 3
French Guiana **11** 759
Fulani **23** 127
Germany **3** 804*; **12** 454, *455*, 455–6*; **17** 530
Gothic **17** 519
Greece, ancient **13** 597–9*, 600–602*; **14** 360
Helladic **14** 356–8*, 360
Hinduism **15** 702
Hong Kong **7** 112
Hopi **22** 615, 629
Hungary **15** 10
Inca **15** 164
India, Republic of **15** 174
Indian subcontinent **15** 423, 699–702*, *703*, 723, 726, 733, 735, 736
Indonesia **15** 814–15*, *815*
Indus civilization **15** 700
Iran **16** 464, 465, 530–31*
Iran, ancient **1** 874–5
Iraq **16** 530–31*
Ireland **16** 33
Islamic **16** 124, 529–33*
Algeria **16** 532
Central Asia, Western **16** 530–31*
Egypt **16** 515, 529–30*
Iran **16** 464, 465, 530–31*
Iraq **16** 530–31*
Kurdistan **16** 531*
Morocco **16** 532
North Africa **16** 529–30*, 532*
Ottoman **16** 531–2*
Spain **16** 515
Syria **16** 529–30*
Tunisia **16** 532
Yemen **16** 532–3*
Italy **10** 593, 631–2, 635, 636; **16** 750–52*; **17** 526
Java **15** 814
Kazakhstan **6** 272, 274; **17** 868
Kenya **1** *256*
Korea **7** 108; **18** *365*, 365–8*
Kuba (iii) (Zaïre) **18** 487
Kurdistan **16** 531*
Kyrgyzstan **6** 272, 274
Laos **18** 775*, 776
Linear Pottery culture **25** 517
Lobi **1** 279
Macedonia (i) (Greece) **19** *881*
Macedonia (ii) (former Yugoslavia) **19** 885–6*
Madagascar **20** 38
Malaysia **20** 180*
Maldives, Republic of **20** 189
Martinique **2** 152
Maya **21** 253, 260
Merovingian **21** 161–2*
Mesoamerica, Pre-Columbian **21** 253, 260; **23** 418

jewellery
historical and regional traditions—cont.
Mesopotamia **1** 873, 875; **21** 303, 304
Mexico **21** 392–3*
Migration period **21** 501, 503
Minoan **8** 153; **21** 657, 658, 682, 683–4*, 686–7*
Mongolia **7** 836; **21** 877–8*
Morocco **3** *756*; **16** 532
Mycenaean **14** 357–8*
Native North Americans **3** 441; **22** 614–16*, *615*, 629*, 642*, 668–9
Navajo **22** 614*, 615*, *615*, 629
Nepal **22** 787–8*, 793
Netherlands, the **17** 521; **22** 896–7*
Newar **22** 788
Nicaragua **23** 83*
Niger **23** 127
Nigeria **15** *119*
North Africa **16** 529–30*, 532*
Norway **23** 238
Nubia **23** 285
Olmec **23** 418
Ostrogothic **23** 624
Ottoman **16** 531–2*
Ottonian **17** 519; **23** 657
Pakistan **23** 803
Parthian **1** 876*; **24** 218
Philippines **24** 625, 626
Phoenician **24** 644*
Poland **25** 127
Portugal **25** 314
Prehistoric **25** 473
Bronze Age **25** 530–31
Iron Age **25** 542, *545*, 545–6*
Linear Pottery culture **25** 517
Palaeolithic **16** 797
Vinča culture **25** 517
Punic **25** 734–5*
Rhodes (island) **13** 597–8
Romania **26** 719–20*
Rome, ancient **10** 34; **12** 456; **27** 101–2*, 103*
Russia **27** 428–9*; **32** 527
Sabah (Malaysia) **20** 180
Sarawak **20** 180
Sardinia **25** 735
Sasanian **1** 876*
Saudi Arabia **27** 877
Scandinavia **32** 516, 528
Scotland **17** 516; **28** *263*, 263–4
Senufo **1** 279
Serbia **28** 456
Somalia **29** 56
Spain **16** 515; **17** 516, 521; **29** 345–6*
Sri Lanka **29** 470, 471–3*, *473*
Sumatra **15** 814, 815
Surinam **30** 16
Sweden **30** 112–13*; **32** 528
Switzerland **17** 526; **25** 547; **30** 148
Syria **16** 529–30*
Syria-Palestine **30** 187
Taiwan **7** 112
Tajikistan **30** 253
Thailand **30** 633–4*
Tibet **7** 836; **30** 839–40*, *840*
Torres Strait Islands **31** 186
Transoxiana **6** 272
Troadic **31** 354–5*
Tuareg **16** 532; **23** 127; **31** 405–6*
Tunisia **16** 532
Turkmenistan **6** 274
Ukraine **31** 562*, *562*
United States of America **31** 654–5*
Urartian **1** 836
Vietnam **32** 487*
Viking **32** 516, 527, 528
Vinča culture **25** 517
Yemen **16** 532–3*
materials
acrylic **17** 530

jewellery
materials—cont.
agate **7** 109, 111; **17** 525, 529
aluminium **17** 530; **18** 775
amber **1** 350, 761, 762; **7** 111
amethyst **10** 29; **17** 524
aquamarines **17** 524
beads **25** 546
bog oak **10** 346; **17** 527
bone **7** 106, 107; **10** 60
brass **1** 350; **20** 180; **30** 839; **31** 562
bronze **1** 350; **6** 274; **7** 107; **13** 600–602; **15** *119*; **25** 547; **30** 633, 839; **31** 562
cameos **17** 525; **28** *263*
ceramics **7** 106; **17** 530
chalcedony **17** 519
chromium **7** 241
chrysoberyl **17** 524
chrysoprase **17** 524
coins **15** 814
copper **1** 350; **6** 274; **7** 112; **9** 652; **10** 29; **21** 253; **31** 562
coq-de-perle **17** 524
coral **1** 350; **7** 111, 836; **17** 529; **21** 877; **30** 839
cornelian **1** *873*; **6** 274; **10** 29; **17** 525, 529
diamonds **3** *605*, 605; **11** 634; **17** 519, 522, 524, 526, 529, II3
emeralds **10** 33; **17** 519, 521
enamel **17** 519, 522–3, 524, 525, 527, 529
China **7** 112
Egypt, ancient **10** 32
France **11** 634; **17** II1
Hungary **15** 10
Islamic **16** 515
Mongolia **21** 877
Prehistoric art **25** 547
Scotland **28** *263*
Ukraine **31** 562, *562*
faience (i) (glass) **1** 877; **10** 29, 48; **21** 683–4; **25** 531
feathers **7** 112; **17** 530; **30** 16
fish **30** 16
garnets **10** 29; **17** 525
gems **6** 273
glass **7** 111; **10** 54, 58; **25** 531, 546
glass paste **16** 33; **17** 524, 525
gold **17** 519, 522, 527
Afghanistan **1** 205
Africa **1** 350
Ancient Near East **1** *873*
Arabia **2** *264*
Central Asia, Western **6** 273, 274
China **7** 106, 107, 112
Early Christian and Byzantine **9** 652–3
Egypt, ancient **10** 28, 29, 30, 33
Finland **11** 108
Germany **21** *502*
Greece, ancient **13** 597–9*
Helladic **14** 357
Indian subcontinent **15** 736
Indonesia **15** 814, *815*
Islamic **16** 529
Korea **18** 366
Mesoamerica, Pre-Columbian **21** 253
Migration period **21** *502*
Minoan **21** 686, 687
Nepal **22** 788
Ottonian **23** 657
Philippines **24** 626
Phoenician **24** 644
Prehistoric **25** 531
Sri Lanka **29** *473*
Troadic **31** 355
Ukraine **31** 562, *562*
Vietnam **32** 487
hardstones **6** 273; **7** 107, 112; **10** 346; **21** 877; **22** *787*
horn **10** 29
inlays **10** 28
inscriptions **6** 274

jewellery
materials—cont.
iron **1** 350; **3** 804*; **12** 454
ivory **1** 350; **10** 60; **16** 797, 799; **17** 529, 530; **32** 487
jade **7** 106, 109, 110, 112; **15** 701; **17** 529; **18** *365*; **32** 487
nephrite **7** 106, 107
jet **10** 346; **17** 516, *516*, 517, 527, 529
lacquer **17** 529
lapis lazuli **1** *873*; **10** 29; **17** 529
malachite **10** 29
marcasite **17** 524, 525; **30** 148
mother-of-pearl **32** 487
niobium **17** 530
nylon **17** 530
onyx **17** 527, 529
opals **17** II1
pearls **17** 519, 522
China **7** 111, 112
Early Christian and Byzantine **9** 653
Egypt, ancient **10** 33
Italy **16** 751
Korea **18** 367
pebbles **28** 264
peridots **17** 524
pinchbeck **17** 525
platinum **17** 529
postcards **17** 530
pottery **7** 107
quartz **7** 111; **25** 314
resins **17** 530
rock crystal **7** 109, 111
rubies **7** 111; **17** 519
sapphires **17** 519, II3
serpentine **10** 29
shells **2** 773; **7** 106, 107; **10** 29; **17** 524; **21** 260; **22** 642; **25** 517; **31** 186
silk **17** 530
silver **17** 522
Afghanistan **1** 210
Africa **1** 350
Belgium **3** *605*
Berber **3** 756
Central Asia, Western **6** 274
China **7** 106, 107, 112
Early Christian and Byzantine **9** 652, 657
Egypt, ancient **10** 29
Islamic **16** 532
Laos **18** 775
Madagascar **20** 38
Minoan **21** 686
Mongolia **21** 877
Native North Americans **22** 614, *615*
Philippines **24** 626
Phoenician **24** 644
Portugal **25** 314
Ukraine **31** 562
Vietnam **32** 487
silver-gilt **7** 112
soapstone **10** 29
steel **10** 345; **17** 525, 530
teeth **7** 106
titanium **17** 530
topaz **17** 519, 524
tortoiseshell **10** 29; **32** 487
toys **17** 530
turquoise **7** 107, 109, 111; **16** 531; **17** 525; **22** *615*; **30** 839
vulcanite **10** 346
wallpaper **17** 530
wampum **3** 441
wire **7** 111
wood **10** 29; **17** 530; **32** 487
zirconium **17** 530
techniques
à l'antique **17** 525
à la sévigné **17** 526
casting **6** 274
chasing **6** 274
filigree **6** 274, *274*; **7** 111, 112; **16** 531

jewellery
techniques—cont.
gilding **6** 274; **17** 524
mass production **17** 526
moulding **15** 423
niello **6** 274
ribbonwork **17** 524
stamping **6** 274
types
archaeological **17** 527, *527*
mourning **17** *516*, 517
jewellery boxes *see under* BOXES → types
jewels *see* GEMS
Jewett, William **32** 778
Jewish art **17** 530–83*
amulets **1** 817; **17** 574
architectural decorations **17** 542
architecture **17** 538–9*, 540–53*, *546*
archives **2** 372
arks **17** 569–70
Bibles **4** 13–18*
bookbindings **17** 566–7*
book illustrations **17** 565–6*
books **17** 537, 565–6*; **29** 62
boxes **17** 572
bronze **17** 574
calligraphy **21** *476*
candlesticks **5** 612
censorship **6** 174
chuppah **17** 575*
circumcision sets **17** 574
codices **27** 226
coins **1** 889
collections **16** 571; **17** 580–82*
curtains **17** 570, 571
display of art **17** *581*
exhibitions **17** *581*
finials (scrolls) **17** 569*, *570*
gold **17** 574
gravestones **17** 555
hadas *see* spice-boxes
Haggadot **14** 34–5*, *35*; **17** *537*, 563, 565–6*
heraldry **14** 410
historiography **17** 583*
houses **17** 552
iconoclasm **6** 175
iconography **9** 517; **17** 533–7*
keter *see* finials
ketubbot **18** 1–3*, *2*; **21** 475
lamps **17** 571–2*, *571*, 573, *573*
leather **17** 566; **20** 327; **26** 557
machzors **17** 563*; **20** 5–6*, *6*
mantles **17** 569, *570*
manuscript illumination **14** *35*; **17** 535, 559–65*, *560*, *564*; **20** *6*
Egypt **4** *14*
France **17** 562–3*
Germany **4** *15*
Italy **17** 564–5*
Portugal **17** 562*
Spain **17** 560–62*, *561*, *562*
13th cent. **20** *122*
manuscripts **1** 70
marble **17** 555
mausolea **17** 553
Megillat **17** 573; **21** 48–9*, *49*
metalwork **25** 128; **31** 563
micrography **21** 475–6*, *476*
minhagim books **21** 636*
miniatures (manuscript illumination) **17** *536*; **19** *624*; **27** *226*
Italy **4** *16*
Spain **4** *16*
mizraḥ **21** 743*, *743*; **24** 57
mosaics **17** 542, 556–9*
museums **17** 580–82*
ossuaries **17** 553
painting **17** 575–80*, *576*, *578*
wall **9** *415*; **17** *534*, 554, 556–9*, *557*, *558*
watercolours **17** *578*
papercuts **21** *743*
pewter **24** 580
religion **17** 531–2*
Jewish art—cont.
rimmonim *see* finials
rings **17** *574*, 574–5*
ritual objects **17** 567–74*, 575*; **24** 580
rolls **26** 557
sandstone **17** *579*
sarcophagi **17** 554
scrolls **20** 327
sculpture **17** 554, *554*, 575–80*, *579*
Seder sets **17** 573*
shivviti **21** 743
shofarot **17** 572
shrines (i) (cult) **17** 538–9
siddurim **28** 664*
silver **5** 612
silver-gilt **17** 574, *574*
spice-boxes **17** 572*, *572*
stamping **17** 566
synagogues **17** 538, 540–52*, *540*, *541*, *544*, *545*, *546*, *548*, *549*, *550*, 568*; **27** *820*; **31** 550
tallit **17** 574
tas **17** 569, *570*
tefillin **17** 574
temples **17** *538*, 538–9
textiles **1** 881; **16** 451
tikim **17** 568*, *568*
title-pages **17** *537*, *577*
tombs **17** 553
Torahs **17** 568*
wood **17** *546*
yad **17** 569, *570*
Jewish Educational Aid Society **17** 578
Jewish Historical and Ethnographical Society **17** 581
Jewitt, Llewellyn **10** 377
Jews **1** 633; **19** 323
Ježek, Pavel **33** 630
Jezersko Church **28** 860
Jezler Silverware Factory **30** 147
Jezorski, Gudbrandur **15** 73
JG, Monogrammist **13** 231
Jhalrapatan **15** 486
Sitaleshvara Mahadeva Temple **15** 485
Jhanda Khan **26** 40
Jhapa-Baijnathpur **22** 758
Jhing ka Nagra **15** 426
Jhodga, Mahadeva Temple **15** 316, *316*
Jhunjhunu **15** 611
Jhusi **15** 423, 455
jia *see under* VESSELS → types
Jiading **7** 59
Jiafau **11** 67
Jiajiang **30** 443
Jian (Fujian) **6** 871, 896
Ji'an (Jiangxi) *see* JIZHOU
Ji'an (Jilin) **18** 328
Changgun Tomb (General's Tomb) **18** 272
Jian (Liaoning) **18** 304
Jian (Xinjiang) **6** 331
Jian'an **6** 901
Jianchuan, Mt Shichong **6** 716
Jiang **6** 663
Jiang Chenying **6** 764
Jiang Jiapu **17** 189
Jiang Jiazhou **7** 123
Jiang Kui **6** 771
Jiangling **6** *615*; **7** 150, 247; **17** 583*
bronzes **6** 854
textiles **7** 46
tombs **17** 583
see also MASHAN; SHAZHONG; TIANXINGGUAN; WANGSHAN; YUTAISHAN
Jiangning **7** 10
Jiang Ren **7** 130
Jiang Rong **33** 536
works **33** *535*
Jiang Song **33** 657
Jianguo factory **6** 912–13
Jiang Yanyang **6** 818
Jiangzhai (Lintong) **6** 684, 835; **15** 51
Jiang Zhaoshen *see* CHIANG CHAO-SHEN
Jiangzhou **7** 94, 95
Jiankang *see under* NANJING
Jianning **7** 101
Jianyang **7** 115
see also JIAN (FUJIAN)
Jianye *see* NANJING
Jianzhang Palace **12** 86
Jianzhen *see* GANJIN
Jianzhou **7** 115
jiao *see under* VESSELS → types
Jiao Bingzhen **6** 818
Jiaohe *see* YARKHOTO
Jiaoshan Island **6** 744, 772
Jiaqing emperor (Qing; *reg* 1796–1820) **6** 684; **7** 85
Jia Sidao **7** 152
Jia Sixie **15** 849
Jiaxiang
que **25** 800
Wu Liang ci **6** 629, 631, 697; **7** 705; **25** 800; **28** 637
reliefs **6** 631, 648, 808
Jiayuguan **6** *614*; **17** 584*; **21** *870*; **28** *719*, 720
fortifications **21** 592
Jiazhuang **7** 14
Jibla **16** *104*, 213
mosque of Arwa bint Ahmad **16** 177–8
courtyard **16** *178*
mihrab **16** 178
Jibladze, A. **12** 320
Ji Buddhism *see under* BUDDHISM → sects
Jibuti *see* DJIBUTI
Jicaque **14** 711, 712
Jicarilla Apache **22** 605, 661, 669
Ji Cheng **12** 64, 88; **33** 496
jichi **7** 31
Jičín **8** 419
Jiddah **3** 168; **6** *623*
Abdulaziz University **27** 876
airport **27** 875
Al Jazirah Mosque *see* Island Mosque
architecture **27** 875, 876
Bayt Nassif **27** 875
fortifications **21** 588
al-Hamra Open Air Museum **27** 876
houses **16** 269, 271; **32** 315, *316*
Island Mosque **27** *876*
King Abdul Aziz International Airport **27** 876
Haj Terminal **1** 495, *495*; **30** 469
King Abdulaziz University Sports Complex **29** 428
mosques **16** 242
Municipality Mosque **27** 876
National Commercial Bank **3** 177; **27** 876; **28** 835
sculpture **27** 876
Sulaiman Palace **27** 876
Jiefangyingzi **7** 36, 37
Jiemon Ouchi *see* OUCHI, JIEMON
Jieqiu *see* KUNCAN
Jieznas **19** *494*
Dominican church **19** 497
Pac Palace **19** 496
Jifei Ruyi *see* SOKUHI NYOITSU
Ji Feng *see* LIU HAISU
Jigalong **1** 43
Jiga Tepe **1** 190
jiggering *see under* CERAMICS → techniques; POTTERY → techniques
jigsaw puzzles **31** 266
Jihei Hara *see* UUKOKR TŌGAN
Jihei Kanō *see* KANŌ, JIHEI
Jihei Ogawa *see* OGAWA, JIHEI
Jihei Sugimura *see* SUGIMURA JIHEI
Jihlava **8** *374*; **17** 584–5*
architecture **8** 379
churches **8** 376
pewter **8** 415
Jihlava—cont.
Regional Museum **17** 585
St Ignatius **8** 382, 383; **17** *585*
sculpture **8** *383*
St James's **8** 382; **17** 584
St Mary **17** 585
textiles **8** 419
Jiita **30** 181
Jike **29** 627
Jikkei **17** 122
Jilani, Abdulwahab **31** 425
al-Jileh **23** 153
Jiloa, Instituto Maestro Gabriel **23** 84
Jiménes, E. León *see* LEÓN JIMÉNES E.
Jiménez, Carlos **14** 803
Jiménez, Diego, II **32** 98
Jiménez, Edith **17** 585–6*; **24** 98, 99, 101
Jiménez, Francisco M. **13** 795; **21** 403
Jiménez, Jorge Bravo *see* BRAVO JIMÉNEZ, JORGE
Jiménez, Luis **18** 831; **27** 872
works **18** *831*
Jiménez, Manuel **29** 341
Jiménez, Max **8** 17; **17** 586*; **25** 826
Jiménez, Miguel *see* XIMÉNES, MIGUEL
Jiménez, P. **18** 784
Jiménez, Pedro **32** 98
Jiménez Aranda, José **3** 869; **17** 586*; **18** 696
Jiménez Bonnefill, Lesmes **8** 16
Jiménez Borja, Arthur **6** 348; **23** 703
Jiménez de Cisneros, Francisco *see* CISNEROS, FRANCISCO JIMÉNEZ DE
Jiménez de Lorca, Andrés **7** 847
Jiménez de Quesada, Gonzalo **4** 233; **7** 600, 603
Jiménez de Singüenza, Francisco **4** 256
Jiménez Donoso, José **17** 586*; **29** 269
collaboration **7** 523; **31** 183
groups and movements **7** 290
teachers **5** 874
works **31** 89
Jiménez la Guardia **8** 16
Jimeno y Carrera, José Antonio **17** 587*
Jimeno y Carrera, Laureano **17** 587
Jimeno y Carrera, Vicente **17** 587
Jimmatsu, Uno **23** 175
Jimyōin Motoharu **17** 224
Jin (family) **7** 16
Jinadevana **15** 528
Ji'nan, Mt Wujing **6** 883
Jinanathapura **29** 439
Ji'nancheng **17** 583
Jin Cheng (1878–1926) **6** 792; **7** 62
Jincheng Sanshen Temple **6** 671–2
Jincun **6** *615*; **17** 587*
bronze **6** 832, 855; **17** *587*
coffin-covers **7** 81
jewellery **7** *107*, 108
tombs **17** 587
Jindřich of Lipá **8** 422
Jindřich of Rožmberk **32** 746
Jindřichův Hradec **8** *374*; **17** 587–8*
Castle **8** 378; **17** 588
church **14** 82
façade decoration **10** 741
furniture **8** 399
metalwork **8** 416
tapestries **8** *420*
textiles **8** 419
Jing, Prince **7** 140
Jingdezhen **6** *615*, 621; **17** 589*
Ceramic Institute **6** 912
ceramics **6** 331, 332, 624, 892, 912; **7** 143; **29** 67
clay **6** 869
enamel **7** 71
Jingdezhen—cont.
glazes **6** 869, 873
houses **6** 687
kilns **6** 324, 871
marks **6** 922, 923
porcelain **4** 173, 174; **6** 622, 872, 875, 894, 897–9, *898*, 901–6, *901*, *902*, 907–10, *908*, *909*, *910*, 912, *912*, 915, 916, 918, 920, 924; **7** 151; **17** 589, *589*; **19** 717; **21** 633; **23** 551, 552
potters **6** 901
Jingdi, Emperor (Han; *reg* 157–141 BC) **6** 883
Jing *gui* **6** 844, *845*
Jing Hao **6** 773; **17** 590–91*
groups and movements **29** 244
works **17** *591*
writings **6** 796; **10** 692
Jing Jun **6** 816; **25** 46
jingles **17** 396
Jingquan **7** 24
jingū *see* JAPAN → shrines (i) (cult)
Jingū, Empress **23** 597
Jingūyama Tomb **17** 59
Jingu yuan **12** 86
Jing xian **7** 115
Jingxing *see* BEIGUTAI; SHIZHUANG
Jingyuan **7** 23
jing zhe zhuang *see* BOOKS → types → accordion books
Jinhua, Wanfo Pagoda **6** 718
Jining, Zhongxue si **7** 99
jinja *see* JAPAN → shrines (i) (cult)
Jinjōji **17** 321
Jinnojō Kanō *see* KANŌ JINNOJŌ
Jin Nong **6** 781, 814; **17** 591–2*
groups and movements **33** 497
pupils **19** 802
works **6** 763, 813; **17** *592*
Jinotega **23** *79*, 83
Jin period (AD 265–420) *see under* CHINA → periods
Jin period (1115–1234) *see under* CHINA → periods
Jin Shaofang **7** 62
Jin Shaotang **7** 62
Jin Shiquan **7** 71
Jinshōji **17** 322
Jinsuke *see* UTAGAWA KUNIMASA
Jintan, Tomb of Zhou Yu
dress **7** 76, *76*
Jinta Temple **6** 708; **30** 443
Jin Temple **30** 443, *444*
Jin Tingbiao **3** 517
Jin Watanabe *see* WATANABE, HITOSHI
Jin xian **6** 695
Jinxiang, Shrine of Zhu Wei **28** 637
Jin Ying **10** 485
Jinyōin Mototaka **17** 809
Jin Yuanyu **7** 62
Jiránek, Miloš **8** 393; **17** 592–3*
Jiricna, Eva **17** 593*
Jiricna, Eva, Architects **17** 593
Jiříková Údolí **23** 264
Jirikovo Udoli glassworks **8** 410
Jiři of Olomouc **24** 108, 109, 462
Jirna-nagara *see* JUNNAR
Jirny Castle **8** 400
Jirō, Yoshihara **23** 595
Jiro Ouchi *see* OUCHI, JIRO
Jiro Takamatsu *see* TAKAMATSU, JIRO
Jiroudek, František **8** 394
Jirō Yoshihara *see* YOSHIHARA, JIRŌ
Jiruft **16** 401
Jirzah **16** 59
Jisaburō Fushimi *see* FUSHIMI JISABURŌ
Jisaidie Cottage Industries **17** 906
Jishō Hachimonjiya *see* HACHIMONJIYA JISHŌ
Jison'in **17** 100
Jitekisai *see* KANŌ NAONOBU

Jitō, Empress 11 821
Jitokusai see HON'AMI KŌETSU
Jitokusō see NISHIKAWA SUKENOBU
Jit Singh, Ruler (reg 1794-1808) (Pahari) 6 405
Jitsu'e 18 222
Jitsuen 17 129
Jitsusaburō Aoki see AOKI, JITSUSABURŌ
Jitsuzō Hinako see HINAKO, JITSUZŌ
jiudie wen script see under SCRIPTS → types
Jiujiang 6 898; 7 10, 71
Jiun Onkō 17 231
Jiun Sonja 17 216, 593–4*
Jiuquan 6 614, 785; 17 594*
see also MT WENSHU
Jiuyan 6 885
Jiva 15 600
Jivan 15 610
works 15 610
Jivarama 30 813, 833
Jívaro 10 848
Jivitagupta, Ruler (reg c. 715-25) (Later Gupta) 15 321
Jiwanshir see:
IBRAHIM KHALIL, Khan
PANAH ALI, Khan
Ji xian 30 798
Dule Temple
Guanyin Pavilion 6 655, 656; 24 289
ewers 7 23
Jiyū Bijutsu Kyōkai (Independent Art Society) 10 102; 14 98; 17 206
Jizang 5 108
Jizan Museum 2 275
Jizhou 6 615; 17 594–5*
kilns 6 871, 873, 892, 896
pottery 6 874, 901
stonewares 17 595
Joachim I, Elector of Brandenburg (reg 1499-1535) 14 648
Joachim II, Elector of Brandenburg (reg 1535-71) 3 805; 14 647, 648, 649–50*
architecture 30 703
metalwork 3 98
paintings 26 314
Joachim, Christian 8 748
Joachim and Anna, Master of 13 114; 22 856
Joachim Frederick, Elector of Brandenburg (reg 1598-1608) 4 666; 7 209
Joachim Murat, King of Naples (reg 1808-15) 4 299; 22 338*
archaeology 25 193
architecture 18 778; 20 901; 22 473
collections 4 412
paintings 13 691; 15 836; 29 658
Joan, Countess of Toulouse (1165-99) 14 408
Joan, Pere (fl 1394-1458) 2 276; 27 516
Joan, Pere (fl 1477-92) see BALLESTER, PEDRO JUÁN
Joan Desi 1 684
Joanikije, Archbishop 29 75
Joanine 4 632; 17 595–6*; 19 775, 776
Joanna, Queen of Castile (reg 1504-16) 13 900; 14 1–2*, 2; 20 659
Joanna I, Queen of Naples (reg 1343-82) 24 36
Joanna II, Queen of Naples (reg 1414-35) 2 17
Joanna II, Queen of Navarre (reg 1328-49) 13 149; 17 463; 23 402, 409; 25 694
Joanna III, Queen of Navarre (reg 1555-72) 4 543
Joanna of Austria, Grand Duchess of Tuscany (1547-78) 3 471; 14 1; 27 704; 32 777
Joanna of Bourbon, Queen of France (d 1378) 20 742
Joanna of Burgundy, Queen of France (1294-1348) 13 158; 31 832
Joanna of Evreux, Queen of Navarre and France (1310-71) 5 667*; 13 148, 148, 175; 25 693; 27 550
architecture 5 666
books 5 666
enamel 13 169
manuscripts 4 370, 394, 764; 11 531; 13 673; 20 742; 23 523; 25 691, 692, 694; 31 835
metalwork 11 614; 13 158
paintings 17 461
reliquaries 26 146
sculpture 10 665
Joanna of France, Duchess of Bourbon (d 1482) 4 544
Joanna of Laval, Duchess of Anjou (fl c. 1456) 2 115; 8 664; 9 4; 11 615, 616; 19 238; 20 735
Joanna of Savoy (fl c. 1320) 25 692, 694
Joanna the Mad see JOANNA, Queen of Castile
Joannes de Caulibus 25 678
Joannes de Ketham 1 840; 21 5, 6
Joannes de Sacrobosco 25 622
Joannes Macarius 12 166
Joannis, Léon de 20 420
Joannon, Eugène 6 594
Joan of Arc, Saint 31 842
João I, King of Portugal see JOHN I, King of Portugal
João II, King of Portugal see JOHN II, King of Portugal
João III, King of Portugal see JOHN III, King of Portugal
João VI, King of Portugal see JOHN VI, King of Portugal
João, Master 3 363; 13 192
João de Ornelas 25 312
João de Ruão 1 766; 17 486, 596*; 20 411; 27 247
assistants 32 147
collaboration 6 44
patrons and collectors 1 679
works 7 531; 14 609; 19 139; 25 301, 724
João Pessoa 4 705
S Antonio 4 709, 710
Joaquim, Leandro 4 716; 11 249; 26 413
Joasaph (1349-1423) 21 343
Joasaph (fl 1545-60) 21 344
Joass, John James 3 532, 533; 33 699
Job (fl 1900) 1 422
works 1 422
Job, Archbishop of Esztergom (reg 1185-1203) 10 545
Job Altarpiece 20 711
Jobard 20 52
Jōbata 30 258
Jobbé-Duval, Félix (Armand Marie) 17 597*
Jobbé-Duval, Frédéric 26 205
Jobin, Bernhard 29 673
Jobling 10 321
Jobst, Heinrich 8 531
Jobst, Kurt 29 120
Jöbstl, Abbot 2 574
Jobun 17 401
Jocelin, Bishop of Glasgow 12 777
Jocelyn, Nathaniel 9 452; 17 597*
Jocelyn, N. & S. S., Co. 17 597
Jocelyn, Simeon 17 597
Jocelyn, Simeon Smith 17 597
Jöchl, Hans 23 706
Jöchl, Lienhard 23 706
Jōchō 5 335; 17 28, 52, 119, 597–8*, 750
groups and movements 17 879
pupils 10 192; 17 98
works 5 119; 11 822; 15 158; 17 21, 98, 100, 116, 117, 119; 18 552
Jocius de Londoniis 7 565
Jocoro 10 153, 153
Jode, Arnold de 4 884; 11 358; 17 599*
Jode, Cornelis de 17 598*
Jode, Gerard de 4 895, 913; 9 64; 17 598*; 25 625
collaboration 12 514; 32 725
printmakers 24 475; 27 501; 32 708; 33 169
works 2 696; 10 174; 25 604; 28 898; 32 711
Jode, Pieter de (i) (1570-1634) 17 598–9*
pupils 17 599
reproductive prints by others 7 557; 23 908
works 5 172; 17 598; 29 431; 32 711
Jode, Pieter de (ii) (1606-74) 17 599*
collaboration 10 391; 22 717
pupils 17 599
works 11 358
Jöde, W. 25 128
Jodensavanne 30 12, 14
Jodh Bai's Palace see under FATEHPUR SIKRI
Jodhpur 15 279; 17 599–600*
dyeing 15 671
Government Museum 17 600
Mahamandir Temple 15 615
Meherangarh Fort 15 388, 616; 17 599–600; 21 590
painting 15 613, 614, 614
palaces 15 388, 390, 693
Sardar Museum 15 182
Umaid Bhavan 14 77
Jōdo Buddhism see under BUDDHISM → sects
Jōdoji 17 131
Jōdodō 17 71, 71, 72
Jōdo Shin Buddhism see under BUDDHISM → sects
Joël 8 22
Joel, Betty 5 841; 10 284; 17 600*
Joel, David 17 600
Joel, Isaac 32 815
Joel ben Simeon 14 34; 17 560, 564, 565, 600*
Joensen, Peder 23 224
Joensen-Mikines, Samuel 10 813
Joes, Gilles 5 210
Joest (von Kalkar), Jan 5 59; 17 600–601*
collaboration 3 41
pupils 7 423
teachers 3 39
works 5 59; 17 601, 740
Joest, Wilhelm 7 584
Jo-fen see YUJIAN
Joffroy, René 32 660
Jogahana 18 605
jogahana-nuri see under LACQUER → types
Jogaila, Grand Duke of Lithuania see VLADISLAV II JAGIELLON, King of Poland
Jogen Araki see ARAKI JOGEN
Jogeshvari Shiva Temple 15 275, 277, 465
Jõgeveste 10 536
monument to Barclay de Tolly 10 539
joggled arches see under ARCHES → types
Jogjakarta see YOGYAKARTA
Joguet, Laurent 4 801
Johan, Jordi 3 221
Johan, Pere see PERE JOHAN
Johan den Meler 4 445
Johani, Andrus 10 540
Johanis de Herbosio see JEAN D'ARBOIS
Johann Emerich of Speier 7 189; 28 306
Johannes (fl 1318-39) 12 356; 29 754
Johannes (fl 1490) 7 471; 17 601–2*
Johannes, Master (fl 1410; illuminator) 1 588
Johannes, Master (fl 1492; wood-carver) 19 111
Johannes Angelus 2 650
Johannes Aquila de Rakerspurga 14 898; 17 602*
Johannesburg 17 602–4*, 603; 29 103, 103
Africana Museum 29 122
architecture 1 319; 29 105
Art Gallery 17 603; 18 727; 19 821; 28 382; 29 121
Bensusan Museum of Photography 29 122
Carlton Centre 29 106
House Rich 29 107
House Stern 29 106
Jan Smuts International Airport 29 121
Jewish Museum 17 582
Polly Street Art Centre 1 433; 28 823; 29 108, 112, 123
School of Art 29 123
South-Western Townships see SOWETO
Standard Bank Foundation Collection of African Art see under University of the Witwatersrand
University of the Witwatersrand 29 123
Art Galleries 14 596; 29 122
Standard Bank Foundation Collection of African Art 29 122
Johannes de Brugis see BOUDOLF, JAN
Johannes de Laibaco see JOHANNES OF LJUBLJANA
Johannes de Modena 1 588
Johannes de Monterchio 18 684
Johannes de Nigellis 12 704
Johannes Fiorentinus 10 546
Johannes Nicolao 7 922
Johannes of Frankfurt 33 355
Johannes of Ljubljana 11 784; 17 604*; 28 860
Johannes of Rosenau 26 711; 28 649
Johannessen, Hans J. 32 512
Johannessen, Kjell S. 23 245
Johannes von Crane 7 593
Johannes von Radkersburg see JOHANNES AQUILA DE RAKERSPURGA
Johannes von Valkenburg 13 151; 17 604*
Johannes von Worms see HANS VON WORMS
Johannis, Andreas see ANDREAS JOHANNIS
Johannishus Slott 33 98
Johann Josès 13 159
Johannot, (Charles-Henri) Alfred 14 853; 17 604–5*; 31 374
Johannot, Charles 17 604
Johannot, François 17 604; 19 482
Johannot, Tony 4 66, 364; 14 853; 17 604–5*; 22 370; 23 522; 29 248; 31 374
Johann Theodor, Bishop of Freising and Liège 8 290
Johann the Steadfast 28 58
Johann von Giltlingen, Abbot of Augsburg 3 472; 12 648
Johann von Gmünd 24 189–91*
assistants 24 191
works 3 336; 11 750, 751
Johann von Hirtz 20 718
Johann von Langenberg 33 458
Johann von Soest 7 721
Johann von Troppau see JAN OF OPAVA
Johann von Wunstorp 3 864
Johann Wilhelm, Elector Palatine see JOHN WILLIAM, Elector Palatine
Johann Wonnecken von Cube 14 433
Johansen, Elise 8 759
Johansen, Felix see RANDEL, FELIX
Johansen, Jakob see WEIDEMANN, JAKOB
Johansen, John M(aclane) 17 605*
Johansen, Karel see IOGANSON, KARL
Johansen, Svend 19 799; 27 643
Johansen, Viggo 17 605–6*
groups and movements 18 470; 28 814
works 17 606
Johanson, Herbert Voldemar 10 537; 30 276
Johansons, Kārlis 26 384
Johansson, Aron 30 73
Johansson, Cyrillus 17 607*
Johansz., Lambert 18 520
Jōhekikyo (1764-1833) see MASUDA KINSAI
Jōhekikyo II (1797-1860) see MASUDA (YAMAGUCHI) GŪSHO
John (9th cent.) 30 718
John (11th-12th cent.; architect) 19 127
John (fl c. 1100; painter) 26 657
John (c. 1345) 24 308
John, Bishop of Genoa 26 576
John, Bishop of Glasgow 12 777
John, Bishop of Mardin (fl 1125-66) 31 436
John, Bishop of Naples 22 483
John, Duke of Finland see JOHN III, King of Sweden
John, Duke of Saxe-Weimar (reg 1572-1605) 33 110
John, Elector of Saxony (reg 1525-32) 8 116; 24 355; 33 110
John, King of Bohemia (reg 1310-46) 19 828*
John, King of Denmark and Norway (reg 1481-1513) 9 427
John, King of England (reg 1199-1216) 7 350; 9 203; 27 249
John, Master (fl 1544-50) 9 274; 17 610*
John I, Duke of Cleves (reg 1448-71) 3 40
John I, Emperor of Byzantium (reg 969-76) 16 582; 26 706
John I, King of Castile-León (reg 1379-90) 24 280
John I, King of Portugal (reg 1385-1433) 2 869, 870*
architecture 3 362; 13 71; 20 325; 28 780
paintings 5 209; 20 207
John I, Margrave of Brandenburg (reg 1220-66) 7 205
John I, Pope (reg 523-26) 26 835
John (-Joseph) I, Prince of Liechtenstein (reg 1805-07; 1813-36) 18 127, 386; 19 338*
John I Albert, King of Poland (reg 1492-1501) 20 395
John II, Duke of Bavaria-Munich (reg 1375-97) 22 305; 33 272
John II, Duke of Bourbon (reg 1456-88) 4 542–4*, 543
collections 31 832
John II, King of Aragon (reg 1458-79) 16 834
John II, King of Castile-León (reg 1406-54) 2 453; 4 784; 5 882; 19 896; 33 117, 118
John II, King of France (reg 1350-64) 13 131; 31 833, 834*
architecture 32 573
coins 7 536

John II, King of France (reg 1350-64)—cont.
manuscripts 4 11, 525; 13 154, 827; 17 462; 20 631, 652
metalwork 13 158
paintings 12 723
John II (Casmir), King of Poland (reg 1648-68) 25 659; 32 7*
architecture 12 745
collections 32 6
gold 20 13
painting 32 875
paintings 31 323
tapestries 25 131
John II, King of Portugal (reg 1481-95) 2 869, 871*; 3 535
John II, Pope (reg 533-35) 7 301; 16 686; 26 824, 829
John II, Prince of Liechtenstein (reg 1858-1929) 10 772; 19 336, 339*
collections 4 209
furniture 19 113
sponsorship 33 723
John II Komnenos, Emperor of Byzantium (reg 1118-43) 9 522; 16 582, 596; 18 211*
architecture 7 228
manuscripts 9 605
military architecture 9 555
John III, Count of Hainault see JOHN III, Duke of Bavaria-Straubing
John III, Duke of Bavaria-Straubing (reg 1417-25) 3 553; 10 705; 18 477; 22 835, 901; 31 448
paintings 22 835
John III, Duke of Brabant see JOHN III, Duke of Bavaria-Straubing
John III, King of Portugal (reg 1521-57) 2 869, 873*; 13 900; 14 698
architecture 2 501; 6 43, 44; 25 291, 317; 30 518; 31 179
decorative works 14 658
furniture 27 823
gold 32 406
painting 25 295, 296
paintings 1 213; 19 655, 656; 27 704
sculpture 14 660
sponsorship 14 660; 27 704
John III, King of Sweden (reg 1568-92)
architecture 24 208; 30 68, 117
castles 4 603; 29 689; 31 460, 692
churches 30 68–9
furniture 30 92
paintings 31 707
reliquaries 30 104
John III, Pope (reg 561-75) 26 799
John III Sobieski, King of Poland see JOHN SOBIESKI, King of Poland
John IV, King of Portugal (reg 1640-56) 4 631, 632, 633*
architecture 32 539
paintings 2 852
John IV, Pope (reg 640-42) 26 822
John IV of Dražice 8 421, 423; 25 430
John IV of Montfort, Duke of Brittany (reg 1341-99) 8 901
John V, King of Portugal (reg 1706-50) 4 631, 635–6*; 13 901; 20 805; 25 317
architecture 7 532; 12 762; 19 776, 777; 20 85, 110; 27 647, 800; 32 422
books 5 364
collections 4 632
decorative works 21 158
education (art) 25 319
furniture 25 306
gardens 5 614
glass 25 311
John V, King of Portugal (reg 1706-50)—cont.
gold 25 313
libraries 17 595
medals 14 106; 20 924
metalwork 16 743
paintings 3 920; 11 289; 25 820; 32 424
sculpture 1 680; 8 858; 17 595; 25 301; 28 79
sponsorship 1 679
John VI, King of Portugal (reg 1816-26) 2 41; 4 631, 637–8*, 716; 25 317
architecture 4 705
barges 3 233, 233
education (art) 4 632, 725
paintings 28 430; 32 426
silver 25 314
John VI Kantakouzenos, Emperor of Byzantium (reg 1347-54) 9 555; 23 831
John VII, Pope (reg 705-08) 17 609*
architecture 26 803
font 26 830
mosaics 22 162
paintings 26 831
John VII Morocharzanios, Patriarch of Constantinople 9 638
John VIII, Pope (reg 872-82) 4 20; 5 803
John VIII Palaeologus, Emperor of Byzantium (reg 1425-48)
John XXII, Pope (reg 1316-34) 17 609–10*
architecture 2 861; 26 755
carpets 5 833
gold 24 36
mosaics 6 106; 26 765
John XXIII, (Anti-) Pope (reg 1410-15) 24 36
John, Augustus (Edwin) 10 374; 17 608–9*; 19 589, 621
catalogues 9 61
groups and movements 5 516; 23 23
house 14 625
patrons and collectors 1 496
personal collection 22 55
pupils 18 667
teachers 4 880; 10 255; 31 146
works 11 437; 17 608; 32 786
John, Friedrich 6 92
John, Gwen(dolen Mary) 17 607–8*; 19 589; 26 513, 515
patrons and collectors 25 823
teachers 10 255; 33 142
works 17 607
John, Jiří 8 394; 17 610*; 28 756
John, Robert, 2nd Lord Carrington 5 194
John, Thomas 17 610
John, William Goscombe 5 732; 17 610–11*
groups and movements 23 35
patrons and collectors 5 732
works 19 606; 20 925; 32 788
John-Adam-Andreas, Prince of Liechtenstein (reg 1684-1712) 19 337*; 29 32
architecture 3 689; 11 130, 886; 12 497; 20 494; 30 455
collections 19 337
drawings 27 195
paintings 11 680, 682
sculpture 20 902; 25 214; 29 30
John Albert I, Duke of Mecklenburg-Schwerin (reg 1503-76) 32 709
John Alexander, King of Bulgaria (reg 1331-71) 9 210, 610
Johnasdóttir, Sigridur 15 73
John Asen II, King of Bulgaria (reg 1218-41) 3 763; 5 162
John Chrysostomos, Saint 9 615, 622
John Cicero, Elector of Brandenburg (reg 1486-99) 14 648
John Clerk of Eldin see CLERK, JOHN (ii)
John Climachus 9 615, 620
John de Bado Aureo 14 406
John de Bello see JOHN OF BATTLE
John de Cyfrewas see JOHN DE SIFERWAS
John de Flandria see JOHN OF ST ALBANS
John de la Bataille see JOHN OF BATTLE
John de Sancto Omero see JOHN OF ST ALBANS
John de Siferwas 17 611–12*
works 17 611
John de Sponlee 33 248, 453
John de Tye 4 237, 238
Johnes, Thomas 12 131; 22 526; 32 783, 787, 791
John-Frederick, Duke of Württemberg (reg 1608-28) 14 865; 28 88
John-Frederick, Elector of Saxony (reg 1532-47) 8 116–17; 12 816; 16 898; 18 444; 33 44
John George, Elector of Brandenburg (reg 1571-98) 3 805; 19 843; 23 252
John-George I, Elector of Saxony (reg 1611-56) 33 110, 110, 113*
altars 17 887
decorative works 33 631
medals 8 444
metalwork 17 888
paintings 9 703
sculpture 14 301
seals 17 888
John-George II, Elector of Saxony (reg 1656-80) 4 507; 12 461; 18 121
John-George III, Elector of Saxony (reg 1680-91) 18 122; 24 460; 27 330
John-George IV, Elector of Saxony (reg 1691-94) 10 857
John Glazier 13 184; 33 238
John le Romeyn 33 547
Johnny Faa brooches see under BROOCHES → types
John of Amiens 26 659
John of Arderne 21 5
John of Austria (1787-1859) 7 832
John of Austria, Governor of the Netherlands (1545-78) 29 741; 32 100
John of Battle 8 197; 17 612*
John of Damascus, Saint 9 617, 622; 19 787
John of Fordun 28 233
John of Gaza 10 129
John of Gloucester 7 420; 19 601, 602; 23 685
John of Kent, Abbot of Fountains 7 353; 11 349
John of Limoges 13 168
John of Luxembourg, King of Bohemia (reg 1310-46) 13 826; 25 430, 439
John of Matha 31 340
John of Mildenhall 7 837
John of Neumarkt see JAN OF STŘEDA
John of Padua 17 612*
John of Pisa 13 169
John of Plano Carpini 21 885
John of St Albans 17 612*; 19 604
John of Salisbury 30 745
John of Tours, Bishop of Wells and Abbot of Bath 3 369
John of Wallingford 24 175
John of Waverley 19 610
John of York, Abbot of Fountains 11 349
Johnová, Helena 8 406
John Reed Club 23 48
Johns, Ambrose Bowden 5 444
Johns, Elizabeth 31 673
Johns, Jasper 17 613–15*; 23 49; 31 608
assistants 18 688
collaboration 20 606, 607; 28 301
dealers 6 23
groups and movements 25 231
methods 10 199; 13 677; 23 784
mixed-media 17 615
paintings 1 89; 2 554; 7 638, VIII1(b); 10 482; 17 613; 18 719
patrons and collectors 6 23; 17 620; 21 135; 28 314; 33 45
personal collection 29 97
prints 10 563; 17 614; 19 492, 493; 21 897; 25 626, 628; 28 52
embossed 10 178
productions 8 270
ready-mades 26 51
sculpture 12 216; 29 671; 31 615
Johns, Joseph 19 394
Johns, R. E. 1 66
Johns, Samuel 19 394
John Schurterre 10 316
Johnsen, Halfdan see EGEDIUS, HALFDAN
Johnsen, Johan 30 78
Johns Hopkins University see under BALTIMORE (MD)
John Skylitzes 7 244; 9 617; 16 455
John Sobieski, King of Poland (reg 1674-96) 17 615–16*; 32 875
architecture 12 34, 224; 18 431; 20 494; 25 98, 135; 32 881
gold 25 127
interior decoration 25 118
paintings 23 447; 25 105, 137; 31 323
sculpture 28 115
stucco 29 839
Johnson (family) 10 261
Johnson 17 616*
Johnson, A. E. 18 888
Johnson, Arthur L. 3 35; 28 771
Johnson, Barbara 30 561
Johnson, Bella 16 888
Johnson, Ben 24 490
Johnson, Cesare 17 622
Johnson, Charles 18 804
Johnson, Cornelius 14 687; 24 296; 26 499
Johnson, C. S. 1 235
Johnson, Daniel 1 444
Johnson, David 17 616–17*; 19 791
Johnson, Donald 16 888
Johnson, (Jonathan) Eastman 17 617–18*; 31 603
collaboration 19 260
groups and movements 9 461
reproductive prints by others 25 450
sponsors 19 259
teachers 8 76
works 17 617; 31 621, 870
Johnson, Ebenezer 14 597
Johnson, Edmond 6 164; 16 32, 33
Johnson, Federico 17 622
Johnson, Frances Benjamin 33 308, 310
Johnson, Francis 22 743
Johnson, Garat, the elder (d 1611) 4 692; 17 616*
groups and movements 10 143
patrons and collectors 1 520
pupils 19 583
Johnson, Garat, the younger (fl 1611-12) 17 616
Johnson, Garrard see JENSEN, GERRIT
Johnson, George Henry 3 35; 13 274; 17 618*; 31 887
Johnson, Giacomo 17 622
Johnson, Henry 10 907
Johnson, Jim 31 737
Johnson, John (1754-1814) 30 502
Johnson, John (1882-1956) 10 421
Johnson, John (b 1939) 2 762
Johnson, John G(raver) (1841-1917) 14 764; 17 618–19*; 24 600
collections 9 200; 16 769; 24 600
paintings 2 180
Johnson, Joseph 1 491; 4 117
Johnson, Joshua 1 440; 12 54; 17 619*
Johnson, Lady Bird 32 888
Johnson, Laura see KNIGHT, LAURA
Johnson, Lester 17 619*
Johnson, Malvin Gray 1 442
Johnson, Mariangela 17 622
Johnson, Michael 2 751
Johnson, Moses (fl 1675-1715) 10 305
Johnson, Moses (1752-1842) 24 40; 28 539
Johnson, Nicholas 8 273; 17 616*
Johnson, Peter see JOHNSON, RICHARD NORMAN
Johnson, Philip (Cortelyou) 14 581; 17 619–21*; 31 672
architecture 14 803; 16 566; 21 422; 31 597
banks 17 621
cathedrals 12 794; 16 56
houses 12 792; 14 802; 24 291
libraries 4 475, 476
museums 12 477; 22 367
office buildings 23 359; 25 359
sculpture garden 28 314
skyscrapers 12 792
synagogues 17 549
theatres 14 200; 30 684
university buildings 4 789; 21 134
collaboration
Burgee, John (Henry) 3 177; 7 385; 19 365; 21 650; 23 43; 25 5; 27 345; 28 835; 31 598
Lipchitz, Jacques 19 438
Mies van der Rohe, Ludwig 21 492; 27 222; 28 834; 33 246
exhibitions 3 271; 14 590
fountains 11 347
groups and movements 25 359
patrons and collectors 21 135
staff 7 895; 27 621
teachers 4 762
Johnson, Ray(mond Edward) 4 110; 7 895; 17 621*; 25 232
Johnson, Riccardo 17 622
Johnson, Richard 15 642, 654; 17 621–2*
albums 1 583
collections 15 744
manuscripts 16 553
paintings 15 741
Johnson, Richard Norman 2 742; 17 622*; 30 161
Johnson, R. J. 23 20; 28 279
Johnson, Robert 20 926
Johnson, Sargent 1 442
Johnson, Stefano, I (fl 1836; grandfather) 17 622
Johnson, Stefano, II (grandson) 17 622
Johnson, Stefano, Stabilimento S.p.A. 17 622*
Johnson, Thomas 7 746; 17 622–3*
Johnson, Tim 1 64; 2 752
Johnson, Tore 17 623*
Johnson, Velia 17 622
Johnson, W. (fl c. 1988) 4 25
Johnson, William (fl 1501-38) 23 686
Johnson, William (fl 20th cent.) 7 159
Johnson, William H. (1901-70) 1 442; 17 623*
works 1 443
Johnson, William T. 27 721
Johnson, Yazzie 22 616

Johnson collection see under PHILADELPHIA (PA) → museums → Museum of Art
Johnson-Marshall, Stirrat 10 241; 26 460, 461*; 28 158
Johnson's Pantascopic see under CAMERAS → types
Johnson van Ceulen, Cornelis, I see JONSON VAN CEULEN, CORNELIS, I
Johnsson, Ivar 30 86
Johnston, David Claypoole 17 623–4*
  works 17 624
Johnston, Edward 17 624–5*; 28 307
  groups and movements 12 631
  pupils 12 631
  works 21 349; 31 497
Johnston, Frances Benjamin 17 625*; 24 671, 673
Johnston, Francis (1760-1829) 17 625*
  works 16 9, 9, 10, 21, 24; 25 268
Johnston, Franz (1888-1949) 5 566; 13 711
Johnston, Henrietta 17 626*
Johnston, James 12 593
Johnston, Johannes 2 105
Johnston, John Dudley
  works 24 652
Johnston, John Taylor 14 396; 19 756
  interior decoration 31 621
Johnston, Joshua see JOHNSON, JOSHUA
Johnston, Lawrence 12 142; 14 512; 31 151
Johnston, Randolph Wardell 3 62
Johnston, Richard 16 24
Johnston, Thomas 4 477; 13 624
Johnston, William L. 17 626*
Johnstone, Brian 2 770
Johnstone, Mrs Butler 22 314
Johnstone, Dorothy 28 239
Johnstone, James, 2nd Marquis Annandale 28 271
Johnstone, Jeanes & Co. 6 484
Johnstone, Marjorie 29 116
Johnstone, William 28 239, 240
John the Fearless, 2nd Duke of Burgundy (reg 1404-19) 3 555; 5 206, 208–9*
  decorative works 7 544
  manuscripts 4 763, 764; 7 525; 19 393; 20 625, 633, 635, 686, 687, 719; 31 290
  paintings 3 639; 5 895; 20 207
  sculpture 7 405; 13 77; 28 866
  tapestries 30 313; 32 823
  wood-carvings 11 438
John the Good, Duke of Burgundy see JOHN II, King of France
John the Good, King of France see JOHN II, King of France
John the Grand Primikerios 9 629
John the Hermit, Saint 8 155
John the Painter 22 79
John the Perfect, King of Portugal see JOHN II, King of Portugal
John Uglješa(, Despot) 9 601
John Uroš Palaiologos see JOASAPH (1349-1423)
John-William, Duke of Jülich (reg 1592-1609) 24 231
John William, Elector Palatine (reg 1690-1716) 33 272, 278, 279–80*
  architecture 9 459; 20 281; 22 918
  collections 9 460
  furniture 31 187
  paintings 12 473, 664; 21 30, 508; 22 721, 846; 33 79
    ceiling 24 341
    display 9 18
    frescoes 3 779
    history 3 681; 29 32
John William, Elector Palatine (reg 1690-1716)
  paintings—cont.
    hunting scenes 33 27
    mythological 7 308; 11 680; 29 789
    religious 19 817; 28 50
    still-lifes 27 454
  sculpture 10 140; 13 725
John William Friso, Stadholder of Friesland 20 458
John Zapolya, King of Hungary (reg 1526-40) 5 86
Jōhōji 17 357; 18 606
johoji-nuri see under LACQUER → types
Johor Baharu 20 162, 169
  Abu Bakar Mosque 20 166
Johow, Margarita 6 600
Joiners' Company 19 592
joinery
  historical and regional traditions
    China 7 31–2, 32, 138, 139–40
    France 11 595
    Japan 17 45, 50, 384
    Toltec 5 408
    United States of America 31 623
  types
    caja-espiga 5 408*
    dovetail 16 487; 33 331
    dowelling 16 487
    kündekâri 16 497
    mortise and tenon 16 487; 33 329–31
    scarfing 16 487
    tongue and groove 16 487
  uses
    architecture 17 45, 50
    furniture 7 31–2, 32; 11 595; 17 384; 33 329–31*
    sculpture 5 408
joining 16 487
joins 5 829–30
Joinville 11 585
  St Laurent
    tomb of Claude de Lorraine, Duc de Guise 3 210
joists 23 257
Jōjin 7 26
Jōjitsu Buddhism see under BUDDHISM → sects
Jōka 17 304
Jōkaku 17 122, 729, 879; 18 195; 31 675
Jokansai Mori see MORI JOKANSAI
Jōkasai 17 304
Jok Bato 20 182
  works 20 182
Jōkei (1155-1213) 17 124, 729
Jōkei (fl 1224-56) 17 131, 392, 879; 22 502
  works 17 125
Jokei Sumiyoshi see SUMIYOSHI JOKEI
Jōkei Tanaka see TANAKA JŌKEI
Jokjakarta see YOGYAKARTA
Jōkō 17 747
Joko, Sankai 24 409
Jokwe see CHOKWE
Jola 12 32
Joli, Antonio 17 626–7*
  patrons and collectors 4 894; 13 301; 30 451
  works 20 63
Joli, Gabriel 4 565
Jolijt, Louis 9 179
Jolin, Einar 17 627*; 30 81; 33 566
Jolineau, Serge 14 58
Jolis, Jehan 2 112
Jolivet 8 161
Joll, Evelyn 1 454
Jollage 29 21
Jollain, Jacques 14 84
Jollain, Nicolas-René 17 627–8*
  works 17 627
Jollat, Mercure 1 842
Jolli, Antonio see JOLI, ANTONIO
Jolli, Carlo Antonio 30 669
Jolliff Studio 2 760
Jollivet, Pierre-Jules 4 528; 11 520, 798; 17 628*
Jolly, Alexander Stewart 2 741; 17 628*
Jolly Koh 20 172
Jølsen, Ragnhild 29 79
Joly, Adrien-Jacques 8 653
Joly, Gabriel 17 628–9*; 27 818; 29 289, 290
Joly, Jules-Jean-Baptiste de 17 629*
Joly, L. 14 486
Jomala Church 11 94; 13 190
Jōman Deme see DEME JŌMAN
Jomantas, Vincas 2 753, 772; 18 64
Jomard, Edmé François 2 155; 8 542; 10 79
Jombert, Charles-Antoine 7 495; 10 206
  works 11 373
Jomei, Emperor (reg 629-641) 23 591
Jomfruens Egede 8 744
Jōmon 17 19, 629
Jōmon culture 17 21
  figurines 17 97
  pottery 17 242, 244–6*
  sculpture 17 97
Jōmon period see under JAPAN → periods
Jonah, Metropolitan 22 170
Jónás, Dávid 17 630*
Jonas, Gena 33 304
Jonas, Joan 17 630*; 24 403; 27 217; 32 420
Jonas, Kurt 19 229
Jonás, Zsigmond 17 630
Jonathan Cape 4 369
Jonchère, Evariste 32 492
Jonchery, Michelin de see MICHELIN DE JONCHERY
Joncquoy, Michel 29 428
Jondhali Baug 15 493
Jones, A. Edward 4 88
Jones, Allen 17 631*; 19 591
  groups and movements 25 231
  patrons and collectors 19 507
  works 10 482; 11 55; 19 492, 493; 25 26, 596
Jones, Arne 7 699; 30 86
Jones, Beatrix see FARRAND, BEATRIX JONES
Jones, Calvert 24 653
Jones, Chilion 11 836; 13 203; 23 632
Jones, David 10 397; 17 631–2*
  groups and movements 12 631; 28 506
  patrons and collectors 5 732
  works 4 366; 32 786, 791, 902
Jones, Dillen 25 293
Jones, Edith Newbold see WHARTON, EDITH
Jones, Edward (fl 1984) 9 43; 28 232
Jones, Edward Richard (fl 1833) 5 265
Jones, Enego see JONES, INIGO
Jones, Evan 2 765
Jones, Frank 22 441
Jones, George (1786-1869) 14 147; 17 630–31*; 28 908
Jones, George Sydney (1864-1927) 2 740; 5 602; 17 632*
Jones, Gerald 2 705
Jones, G. F. 33 192
Jones, G. I.
  works 15 111
Jones, Gordon 7 524
Jones, Harold 10 80
Jones, Helena 2 152
Jones, Horace 4 799; 17 632–3*; 19 318
Jones, Howard 18 63; 29 98
Jones, Hugh 5 562; 31 176
Jones, Inigo 2 314, 314; 10 276; 12 341; 13 299; 17 633–8*; 19 592; 23 362, 859; 28 138
  architecture 2 358, 545; 5 538; 8 45; 10 270
    architectural decorations 23 543
    banqueting houses 3 186; 10 231; 19 618; 30 661; 33 398
    cathedrals 18 855; 19 597, 598
    chimney-pieces 6 604
    choir-screens 28 294; 33 236
    churches 17 636; 23 487
    country houses 23 859, 860; 33 225
    gables 11 876
    galleries (art) 14 805
    galleries (iv) (art) 14 806
    gates 12 340
    houses 32 551
    livery halls 19 509
    palaces 17 635; 33 10
    porticos 25 265
    stables 29 485
    temporary architecture 23 767
    theatres 19 618; 30 661
    town houses 12 306
    urban planning 19 568; 23 492; 27 357; 31 714
  assistants 7 431; 24 752, 753; 33 10
  attributions 12 369; 33 11, 714
  collaboration 6 96; 10 262; 23 678
  decorative works 16 823
  drawings 2 330; 19 249
  furniture 6 390
  groups and movements 10 226; 23 210, 857
  patrons and collectors
    Anne of Denmark, Queen of England and Scotland (1574-1619) 13 623; 29 798
    Boyle, Richard, 3rd Earl of Burlington and 4th Earl of Cork 4 609, 612
    Cecil, Robert, 1st Earl of Salisbury 6 128
    Charles I, King of England and Scotland (reg 1625-49) 29 801
    Churchill, John, 1st Duke of Marlborough 7 286
    Clarke, George 7 378
    Henrietta Maria, Queen of England and Scotland (1609-69) 13 623; 29 797, 803
    James I, King of England and Scotland (reg 1603-25) 10 360; 29 797, 798
    Stuart, Henry (Frederick), Prince of Wales 10 363, 368; 29 798
    Villiers, George, 1st Duke of Buckingham (1592-1628) 32 575
  personal collection 2 330; 23 858, 870; 28 33
  pupils 33 10
  restorations by others 14 172
  stage design 10 247; 12 127; 17 638; 30 662
  weathervanes 33 8
  writings 31 297; 33 11
Jones, Jacobine 5 571
Jones, Jenkin Lloyd 28 728
Jones, J. Langford 20 926
Jones, Joe 29 97
Jones, John (c. 1740-c. 1797) 17 630*; 21 416; 29 675; 31 465
Jones, John (fl early 19th cent.; print publisher) 32 786
Jones, John (1799-1882; collector) 17 639*
Jones, John T.
  works 21 570
Jones, Jonah 32 788
Jones, L. 4 24
Jones, Lois Mailou see MAILOU JONES, LOIS
Jones, Louisa see LOU, MA
Jones, Matilda Sissieretta 3 185
Jones, Olive 23 68
Jones, Owen 15 211; 16 554; 17 639–40*; 25 172
  assistants 22 210
  ceiling decorations 17 640
  chromolithography 26 234
  collaboration 25 172
  exhibitions 15 821; 16 547; 22 59; 24 293, 294; 25 173; 30 504; 33 450
  Grammar of Ornament 1 111; 4 362; 9 295; 10 97, 282, 319; 19 485; 23 546; 24 273; 25 172; 32 415, 864
  Japonisme 13 209
  groups and movements 10 97
  patrons and collectors 9 295
  plans 25 623
  pupils 22 60
  tiles 22 59
  wallpaper 17 469; 32 816
  writings 13 285; 16 143
Jones, Paul Cornwall 20 607
Jones, Peter see PETER JONES
Jones, Phoebe Ageh 28 692
Jones, Pryce 32 790
Jones, Quincey 18 189
Jones, Rebecca Colford 19 346
Jones, Richard, 1st Earl of Ranelagh 9 719
Jones, Robert (fl after 1750) 8 36; 10 356
Jones, Robert (fl after 1808) 4 809
Jones, Robert Edmond 30 687
Jones, Ronald Potter 31 584
Jones, Stanley 19 492; 20 607; 25 628
Jones, Sydney 19 508
Jones, Thomas 13 304; 17 640–41*
  collaboration 22 153
  patrons and collectors 14 486
  teachers 14 611; 19 157; 33 220
  works 17 641; 18 713; 22 686; 32 785
Jones, Ursula 29 220
Jones, W., & Son. 2 758
Jones, Watkin D. 32 787
Jones, W. C. 18 887
Jones, William (1746-94) 16 553; 24 436
Jones, William (fl 1790) 11 242
Jones, William Lorando (c. 1820-90) 32 787
Jones and Willis 29 766
Jones & Baldwin 7 409
Jones & Co. 25 837
Jones-Hogu, Barbara 1 445
  works 1 444
Jones & Kelly 28 284
Jones & Kirkland 5 563
Jones Madonna 7 336
Jong, H. L. de 1 803; 7 328
Jong, Pieter de Josselin de see JOSSELIN DE JONG, PIETER DE
Jonga 1 405
Jonge, Peter van Hecke de see HECKE DE JONGE, PETER VAN
Jongelinck, Niclaes 11 221
Jongeling, Hendrik 22 893
Jongert, Jacob 7 808; 23 450
Jongh, Claude de 10 250; 17 641–2*; 19 583
Jongh, Eddy de 10 176; 15 91, 96
Jongh, Ludolf de 17 642*; 27 230
  teachers 4 53; 23 832
  works 14 709
Jonghe, Clément de 26 166; 29 644
Jonghe, Jean-Baptiste de 17 642*; 23 439; 32 241
Jonghelinck, Jacques 3 569; 17 642, 643*
  patrons and collectors 3 615; 14 5; 17 643
  reproductive prints by others 3 558

Jonghelinck, Jacques—cont.
works **2** 195, 285; **5** 301; **20** 921; **29** 571
Jonghelinck, Niclaes **17** 642, 643*
collections **3** 612, 615; **4** 902, 908; **13** 916
Jonghelinck, Pierre **17** 642
Jong Holland **24** 450
Jongju Pusŏksa **30** 913
Jongkind, Johan Barthold **17** 643–4*; **22** 847
patrons and collectors **7** 528; **30** 375
pupils **21** 862
teachers **8** 539; **14** 42; **16** 66; **28** 72
works **5** 364; **25** 607; **32** 902
Joni, I(cilio) F(ederico) **11** 307, 308; **17** 644*
Jönköping **30** *65*, 106
Jonsborg, Kåre **23** 232, 239
Jonscher, Barbara **2** 502
Jónsdóttir, Kristín **15** 70
Jónsdóttir, Thórunn **15** 72
Jonson, Ben **10** 248; **14** 675; **17** 633, 636, 637; **30** 661, 662
Jonson, George H. **28** 830
Jonson, Nicholas *see* JOHNSON, NICHOLAS
Jonson, Raymond **22** 595
Jonson, Sven **14** 89
Jonson van Ceulen, Cornelis, I (1593-1661) **17** 644–6*; **21** 509
patrons and collectors **14** 178; **20** 141
pupils **27** 360
teachers **12** 514
works **17** *645*
Jonson van Ceulen, Cornelis, II (1634-1715) **17** 646
Jónsson, Ásgrímur **15** 70; **17** 646*
Jonsson, Bo **13** 668
Jónsson, Einar **15** 70; **17** 646*
Jönsson, Erik *see* DAHLBERGH, ERIK
Jónsson, Finnur **4** 807; **8** 569; **15** 70; **17** 646–7*
Jónsson, Rikharður **17** 647
Jonynas, Vytautas Kazimieras **19** 499
Joó, János **15** 18
Joos, Eduard **3** 823
Joosen, Marcel **10** 483
Joosken van Utrecht **19** 172
Joost, Jan *see* JOEST (VON KALCAR), JAN
Joosten, D. J. H. **19** 654
Joostens, Paul **2** 197; **3** 564, 573
Joos van Gent *see* JUSTUS OF GHENT
Jōō Takeno *see* TAKENO JŌŌ
Joppa **16** *104*, *565*; **17** 500, 505; **30** 179
Joraleman, E. E. **5** 126
Jorang Belanga **15** 767
Jordaens, Abraham **17** 647
Jordaens, Hans, I (*c*. 1555-1630) **17** 647*; **22** 844
Jordaens, Hans, II (1581-1635) **17** 647
Jordaens, Hans, III (*c*. 1595-*d* 1643) **5** 352; **11** 720; **17** 647*
Jordaens, Jacob (1593-1678) **2** 196; **3** 576, 613; **17** 648–53*; **19** 381
collaboration **4** 222; **11** 872; **14** 46; **27** 298; **28** 904; **30** 788; **31** 772; **32** 702, 703; **33** 181
drawings **17** *651*
house **3** 546
methods **21** 766
paintings **1** 813; **14** 46; **17** *650*, *652*, *653*; **23** 466; **25** 324
allegorical **1** 658
genre **12** 290
history **14** 584; **22** 843
oil sketches **23** 381
religious **19** 381
watercolour **32** 900
Jordaens, Jacob (1593-1678)—cont.
patrons and collectors
Augustinian hermits **2** 725
Bergeret de Grancourt, (Pierre-) Jacques-Onésyme **3** 776
Brukenthal, Samuel, Baron von **5** 9; **26** 722
Charles I, King of England and Scotland (*reg* 1625–49) **29** 801
De La Gardie, Magnus Gabriel **30** 118
Elizabeth Farnese, Queen of Spain (1692–1766) **4** 559
Francis-Joseph, Prince of Liechtenstein (*reg* 1772–81) **19** 338
Gustav III, King of Sweden (*reg* 1771–92) **30** 118
Habsburg I., Leopold William, Archduke of Austria, Governor of the Netherlands **13** 920
Henrietta Maria, Queen of England and Scotland (1609-69) **23** 208; **29** 803
Koninklijk Museum voor Schone Kunsten (Antwerp) **3** 616
Orléans, Philippe I de Bourbon, 1st Duc d' (1640–1701) **23** 513
Périer, Casimir **24** 418
Saint-Aignan, Paul-Hippolyte de Beavillier, Duc de **27** 524
Snyders, Frans **28** 904
Statens Museum for Kunst (Copenhagen) **8** 758
Thibaudeau, Narcisse-Adolphe, Comte de **30** 727
William VIII, Landgrave of Hesse-Kassel (*reg* 1751–60) **14** 491
pupils **4** 218; **7** 787; **20** 894; **31** 323
reproductive prints by others **4** 283; **12** 851; **17** 599; **18** 879; **22** 717; **25** 221; **32** 700
tapestries **2** 200; **5** 49–50; **17** *649*; **30** 320
teachers **3** 559; **23** 201
Jordaens, Jacob (*b* 1625) **17** 648
Jordaens, Simon **17** 647
Jordan **13** *362*; **16** *104*; **17** 654–6*; **30** 178
architecture **16** 155; **21** 43; **26** 918*
baths **3** 376
boxes **24** 336, *336*
churches **26** 483
dresses **16** *460*
education (art) **17** 654
embroidery **16** *460*
exhibitions **17** 654
galleries (iv) (art) **17** 655
houses **3** 514
inlays **24** 336, *336*
ivory-carvings **24** 336, *336*
limestone **17** *655*
painting **17** 654
palaces **16** *556*
pottery **16** 396, 397; **24** 336
sculpture **17** *655*
stelae **24** *335*
stone-carvings **24** *335*
stucco **29** *819*
synagogues **17** 543
temples **12** *337*
tents **30** 473
see also ANCIENT NEAR EAST; SYRIA-PALESTINE
Jordan I, Prince of Capua *see* CAPUA, JORDAN I, Prince of
Jordan, André **12** 459
Jordán, Armando **4** 262; **17** 656*
Jordán, Domingo Estruch y *see* ESTRUCH Y JORDÁN, DOMINGO
Jordán, Esteban **17** 656*; **29** 290; **31** 822
patrons and collectors **4** 565
works **19** 173
Jordán, Francisco **10** 543
Jordan, Hans **14** 864
Jordan, J. **31** 759
Jordan, Jean-Louis **12** 459
Jordan, J. W. Noel **25** 835
Jordán, Manuel **25** 701
Jordán, Roxanna **25** 703
Jordan, Rudolf **26** 423; **32** 95
Jordan, Thomas **10** 163
Jordanian Art Club *see* NADWA AL-FANN AL-URDUNNIYYA
Jordanów **25** 512
Jordans (Bucks), Friends' Meeting House **11** 785
Jordansmuhl **16** 861
Jordan the Painter **30** 83
Jordasch, Richard L. **24** 281
Jordet, Elljarn **4** 804
works **4** *804*
Jordi, Beat **33** 736
Jordi, Eugen **27** 215
Jordi de Deu **5** 341; **13** 106
Jōrengein **17** 124
Joret, Henry **21** 130
Jörg, Alberlin **14** 117; **28** 182
Jørgensen, Axel **8** 736, 760; **10** 222; **14** 297
Jorgensen, Justus **3** 475; **21** 78
Jørgensen, Torben **8** 750
Jörger von Tollet, Johann Septimius **17** 656*
Jorgji, Haxhi **1** 540
Jörg of Isny **12** 410
Jorg von Ehingen **14** 414
Jörg von Halsbach **12** 365; **17** 657*; **22** 299, 306
Jörg von Polling *see* JÖRG VON HALSBACH
Jorhan, Christian (i) (1727-1804) **7** 212; **12** 405; **17** 657
Jorhan, Christian (ii) (1758-1844) **17** 657
Jorhan, Johann Wenzeslaus **17** 657
Joris, Henry **11** 426, 427; **28** 904
Joris de beeldesnijder **19** 101
Jorisz., David **3** 193; **17** 657*
Jorn, Asger **17** 658–9*
collaboration **9** 189
groups and movements **2** 526; **7** 488, 489; **8** 736; **9** 188
personal collection **8** 759, 760
teachers **19** 83
works **17** *659*; **19** 491; **29** 97
Jornado Mogollon **22** 600
Jornal das belas artes **24** 453
Jornal de belas artes ou Mnemôsine lusitana **24** 453
Jōruiji **17** 659–60*
sculpture **17** *120*
Jorvik *see* YORK
Jorwe culture **15** 247
Joryū Matsui *see* MATSUI, JORYŪ
Jōryū Mihata *see* MIHATA JŌRYŪ
Jos **23** *129*
Museum of Traditional Nigerian Architecture **23** 135
National Museum **23** 139
University **23** 135
Josaphat, Valley of
Tomb of the Virgin **17** 503
José (*fl c*. 18th cent.) **30** 799
José Antonio Echevarria University *see under* HAVANA
Josefa d'Óbidos *see* AYALA (E CABRERA), JOSEFA DE
Josefina, Queen of Sweden and Norway (1807-76) **30** 95, 118
Josefson, Anne Lise **27** 472
Joseph *see* BAUMHAUER, JOSEPH
Joseph, King of Portugal (*reg* 1750-77) **4** *631*, 632, 636*; **19** *893*; **25** 313
architecture **8** 840; **12** 23; **19** 777; **20** 32; **25** 293
gardens **12** 125
Joseph, King of Portugal (*reg* 1750-77)—cont.
paintings **27** 710
plate **3** 122
sculpture **12** 762
silver **11** 619; **12** 357, *357*
Joseph I, Holy Roman Emperor (*reg* 1705-11) **13** *901*; **29** *789*
altarpieces **20** 842
architecture **11** 130; **12** 24
art policies **29** 789
gem-engravings **12** 262
paintings **14** 111
sculpture **30** 851
stage design **3** 488
triumphal arches **10** 445
Joseph II, Holy Roman Emperor (*reg* 1765-90) **5** 614; **14** 508; **24** 299; **32** 436, 456
architecture **2** 785; **5** 41, 82; **25** 155; **32** 436
art policies **22** 357
cameos **24** 734
catalogues **6** 77
furniture **2** 813
interior decoration **2** 807, *807*
paintings **14** 509
silk **8** 419
tapestries **22** 726
Joseph, Antonio **14** 58; **17** 660*
Joseph, Colard **5** 207
Joseph, Jasmin **17** 660*
Joseph, J. G., & Co. **5** 586
Joseph, Peter **10** 258; **17** 661*
Joseph, Richard **19** 703
Joseph, William **16** 885
Joseph Bonaparte, King of Naples and Spain (*reg* 1806-8) **4** *299*, 304*
architecture **16** 645; **22** 474; **32** 566
collections **4** 298
manuscripts **20** 682
paintings **4** 78; **9** 199; **21** 35; **29** 96; **33** 55
works **4** 302
Joseph Chukwu
works **15** *64*
Joseph-Clemens, Elector-Archbishop of Cologne *see* WITTELSBACH, JOSEPH-CLEMENS, Elector-Archbishop of Cologne
Joseph ha-Zarefati **17** 661*, 664
Joseph ibn Hayyim **1** 70; **17** 560, 562, 661*
Josephine, Empress of the French (1763-1814) **4** *299*, 302–4*, *303*; **7** 762; **15** 666; **16** *64*; **24** 149; **31** 478, 856
architecture **10** 186; **11** 257; **24** 388
book illustrations **4** 364
books **26** 73
cameos **12** 264
ceramics **24** 149
collections **4** 298; **26** 733
drawings **31** 149
furniture **6** 517; **10** 187; **11** 597; **25** 193
gem-engravings **3** 687
interior decoration **4** 302
jewellery **11** 635
lace **3** 610
liturgical objects **1** 4
paintings **7** 762; **8** 445, 703; **12** 335; **31** 373, 795
flower **11** 228
genre **6** 517; **14** 482; **18** 867
gouache **19** 399
history **19** 37; **24** 140; **26** 334
mythological **12** 731; **18** 699; **20** 891
portraits **9** 363; **16** 64
religious **22** 338
watercolour **11** 802
sculpture **4** 457; **5** 629, 630, 888; **25** 383
Josephinenhütte **12** 441
Joseph Master **11** 555; **13** 86; **20** 701–2*; **26** 119
attributions **26** *118*
Joseph Sequence, Master of the **3** 554; **19** 350; **20** 702*
Joseph Silks **9** 667
Josephson, Ernst **17** 662–3*; **30** 79
groups and movements **23** 206; **30** 79
patrons and collectors **11** 851
works **11** 474, *474*; **17** *662*
Josephson, Jacob **2** 764
Josephson, John **30** 117
Josephson, Ragnar **30** 120
(Flavius) Josephus **9** 617; **10** 243; **17** 487, 488, 494, 533, 540; **20** 539
Josephus Scotus **5** 779
Joseph-Wenceslas-Lorenz, Prince of Liechtenstein (*reg* 1748-72) **6** 473; **20** 494; **24** 878
Josès, Johann *see* JOHANN JOSÈS
Josetsu **17** 663*; **18** 552
attributions **5** 175
collaboration **13** 887
patrons and collectors **2** 599
pupils **30** 465
works **2** 598; **7** 624; **17** 39, *171*, 171–2
Joshi, Hans Raj **15** 606
Joshi, M. C. **20** 816
Joshimath, Temple of Vasudeva **15** 264
Jōshin Kanō *see* KANŌ JŌSHIN
Joshua ben Abraham ibn Gaon **17** 561, 663–4*
Joshua Roll *see under* ROLLS → individual manuscripts
Joshunsai Yamamoto *see* YAMAMOTO JOSHUNSAI
Josi, Christian **18** 387; **25** 49
Josic, Alexis **2** 660; **5** 608–10*
Josic, Mladen **5** 609
Jósika, Miklós **2** 546
Josimović, Emilijan **3** 621
Josō *see* MIYAZAKI, SEITARO
Josselin, Thérèse **11** 759
Josselin de Jong, Pieter de **17** 664*
Josset de Halle **5** 207
Jossett, Lawrence **10** 398; **21** 418
Josué **22** 248
Josui Sōen **31** 252
Jouarre Abbey **11** *504*; **17** 664–5*; **21** 163, 164
capitals **17** *665*
crypt **11** 509
sculpture **11** 553
Joubert, Canon **2** 51
Joubert, F. **7** 575
Joubert, François **11** 619
Joubert, Gilles **17** 665–6*; **31** 870
collaboration **11** 305
patrons and collectors **4** 554
works **11** 590, 593; **18** I2
Joubert, Jean-Ferdinand **28** 745
Joubert, Mme *see* DROLLING, LOUISE-ADÉONE
Joubert, René **11** 601
Jöuch, Hans **20** 653, 736
Jouderville, Isack (de) **17** 666*; **22** 843; **26** 153
Jouett, Matthew Harris **17** 666*
Jouffroy, François **11** 671; **17** 667*
pupils
Barrias, Louis-Ernest **3** 278
Borrel, Alfred **4** 424
Chaplain, Jules-Clément **6** 461
Cros, (César-Isidore-) Henri **8** 192
Dampt, Jean(-Auguste) **8** 485
Desvergnes, Charles-Jean-Cléophas **8** 818
Falguière, Alexandre **10** 770
Hiolle, Ernest-Eugène **14** 564
Larche, Raoul(-François) **18** 786
Mercié, (Marius-Jean-) Antonin **21** 147
Puech, Denys(-Pierre) **25** 697

Jouffroy, François
pupils—cont.
Ringel d'Illzach, (Jean-) Désiré **26** 408
Saint-Gaudens, Augustus **27** 556
Simões de Almeida, José **28** 748
Soares dos Reis, António **28** 912
Warner, Olin Levi **32** 865
Jouffroy, Jean, Cardinal **24** 732; **32** 384
Jouhanneaud & Dubois **28** 520
Jouhaud, Léon **19** 396
Jouin, Henry(-Auguste) **17** 667*
Joulin, L. **32** 544
Joullain, Charles *see* JOULLAIN, FRANÇOIS-CHARLES
Joullain, François **11** 663; **12** 638; **17** 667–8*; **24** 137
dealing **11** 663
printmakers **33** 44
teachers **12** 638
Joullain, François-Charles **17** 668
Joullain, François-Claude **5** 445
Jounsha **17** 197
Jourdain **3** 275
Jourdain, Abbé (*fl* 1735) **20** 416
Jourdain, Abbot of Mont-Saint-Michel (1192-1212) **22** 40
Jourdain, Bertrand de l'Isle, Bishop of Toulouse **31** 206
Jourdain, Charles-Joseph **23** 521
Jourdain, Francis **11** 584, 601; **17** 668–9*
collaboration **24** 824
groups and movements **11** 602; **31** 581
Jourdain, Frantz (Calixte Raphaël) **7** 528; **17** 668*; **20** 121; **27** 880
collaboration **27** 879, 880
groups and movements **2** 510, 564
works **8** 770; **11** 524, 526; **25** 172, 173; **30** 505
Jourdain, Jules (Paul Louis) **17** 669*
Jourdain de Blaye **30** 313
Jourdan, Adolphe **16** 876
Jourdan, Emile **25** 215
Jouret, Henri *see* JORIS, HENRY
Jour et nuit **20** 878
Journal des amateurs des objects d'art et de curiosité **24** 423
Journal of the American Institute of Architects see ARCHITECTURE: THE AIA JOURNAL
Journal of the Anthropological Institute of Great Britain and Ireland **24** 429
Journal of Archaeology see KOGOHAK
Journal of Architectural Education **24** 434
Journal of the Archives of American Art **24** 433
Journal of Arts and Ideas **24** 436
Journal of the Asiatic Society of Bengal **1** 211; **25** 587
Journal für die Baukunst **24** 444
Journal des beaux-arts et de la littérature **24** 439
Journal belge de l'architecture **24** 439
Journal of the Burma Research Society **24** 437
Journal of Canadian Art History/Annales de l'histoire d'art canadien **24** 430
Journal des cent **31** 214
Journal des dames et des modes (1912-14) **10** 824
Journal des dames et des modes, Le (1797-1839) **10** 823
Journal of Design and Manufactures **24** 422
Journal of Design History **24** 446
Journal of the History of Collections **25** 665
Journal of the IIC Canadian Group **7** 743
Journal of Indian Art **24** 436, 446
Journal of the Indian Society of Oriental Art **18** 437; **24** 436
Journal of the Institute of Architects of New South Wales see ARCHITECTURE AUSTRALIA
journalism *see* PHOTOJOURNALISM; REPORTAGE
Journal of Korea Archaeology see HANGUK KOGOHAKPO
Journal zur Kunstgeschichte und zur allgemeinen Literatur **22** 350; **24** 443
Journal des Luxus und der Moden **12** 413
Journal of the Malaysian Branch of the Royal Asiatic Society **24** 437
Journal de la mode et du goût, Le **10** 823
Journal of the Royal Architecture Institute of Canada/Architecture Canada **24** 430
journals *see* PERIODICALS
Journal of the Siam Society **24** 437
Journal of the Society of Architectural Historians **24** 434
Journal of the Straits Branch of the Royal Asiatic Society see JOURNAL OF THE MALAYSIAN BRANCH OF THE ROYAL ASIATIC SOCIETY
Journal of the Thirties Society **24** 446
Journal of the Warburg and Courtauld Institutes **24** 424, 446
journeymen **19** 532; **20** 560–61, 562, 563
Journu, Bonaventura **4** 391
Joursanvault, Herménégilde Joseph Alexandre Gagnaire, Baron de **25** 670
Jousse, Mathurin **4** 804; **16** 59; **29** 637
Jouve, Paul **4** 48
Jouve, Pierre-Jean **1** 21
Jouveau-Dubreuil, Gabriel (Jules Charles) **15** 211; **17** 669*
collections **15** 744
Jouvenel, Michel, Master of **17** 670
Jouvenel des Ursins (family) **11** 531
Jouvenel des Ursins, Guillaume **17** 670*; **20** 612, 702
Jouvenel des Ursins, Jacques **17** 669–70*
Jouvenel des Ursins, Jean I, Baron de Trainel *see* TRAINEL, JEAN JOUVENEL DES URSINS, Baron de
Jouvenel des Ursins, Jean II, Archbishop of Reims **17** 670*
Jouvenel des Ursins, Marie **17** 670
Jouvenel des Ursins, Master of **20** 626, 702–3*
attributions **8** 664
patrons and collectors **7** 525; **17** 670
works **4** 544; **20** 706
Jouvenel des Ursins, Michel **17** 669
Jouvenet, Jean **14** 83; **17** 670–72*; **27** 248
collaboration **4** 536, 537; **8** 91; **18** 633
groups and movements **27** 286
patrons and collectors **30** 524; **31** 56
pupils **3** 855; **7** 569; **20** 586; **22** 684; **26** 246, 247, 452
reproductive prints by others **2** 709; **9** 362; **18** 47
works **11** 537; **13** 783; **17** *671, 672*; **24** 165
Jouvenet, Laurent **17** 670
Jouvenet, Marie-Madeleine **17** 670; **26** 246
Jouvenet, Noël **20** 897; **26** 246
Jouy, Etienne **12** 153
Jouy, Jean de *see* JEAN DE JOUY
Jouy, Jean Hardouin Mansart de *see* MANSART DE JOUY, JEAN HARDOUIN
Jouy, Joseph-Nicholas **29** 790
Jouy-en-Josas
cotton **8** 36; **11** 649; **23** 331; **30** 562, X1
Jovan **25** 340
Jovan, Metropolitan **9** 630; **28** 447, 448, 449, 457
Jovanović, Anastas **28** 451
Jovanović, Djordje **28** 453
Jovanović, Konstantin **28** 444
Jovanović, Paja **22** 17; **28** 451
Jovanović-Djukin, Dušan **28** 453
Jovánovics, György **14** 897
Jovellanos, Gaspar Melchor de **17** 672–3*; **29** 353
Jövendő **13** 333
Jovinus **26** 121
Jowett Car Company **11** 878
Joy, Albert Bruce **17** 673
Joy, George W(illiam) **17** 673*
Joy, Robert **3** 536
works **3** *536*
Joy, Thomas Musgrave **7** 436; **17** 673*
Joy, William **4** 825; **10** 672, 674; **17** 673–4*; **33** 61
Joya, José **24** 623
Joyant, Jules-Romain **20** 351
Joyant, Maurice **4** 589; **20** 351
Joyce, Bernard **8** 189
Joyce, E. B. **31** 133
Joyce, James **10** 486
Joyce, Thomas A. **5** 581
Joyce, V'Soske **28** 284
Jōzan *see* ISHIKSWA JŌZAN
Jozuus, Pēteris Pauls **12** 825
J & P **29** 581
J.P., Master *see* I.P., MASTER
Jriskulov, Dubanbek **18** 568
Jruchi Gospels *see under* GOSPEL BOOKS → individual manuscripts
J.S., Master *see* SILBER, JONAS
Ju, Charles **23** 514
Ju, Louis **23** 514
Juan, Antonio, Lord of Tous *see* TOUS, ANTONIO JUAN, Lord of
Juan, Archbishop of Aragon **29** 332
Juan, Bishop of Burgos **5** 202
Juan, Peti *see* PETI JUAN
Juana, Regent of Spain (1537-1573) **27** 704
Juan An *see* RUAN AN
Juan de Arqr **5** 205
Juan de Bailles **23** 402
Juan de Balmaseda *see* BALMASEDA, JUAN DE
Juan de Borgoña *see* BORGOÑA, JUAN DE
Juan de Bruxelas **33** 605
Juan de Casanova, Cardinal **8** 140
Juan de Castro el Borgoñón **14** 609
Juan de Colonia *see* COLONIA, JUAN DE
Juan de Flandes **3** 554; **17** 674–5*; **29** 277, 299
patrons and collectors **13** 905
works **17** *675*
Juan de Holanda *see* JOEST (VON KALCAR), JAN
Juan de Horna **29** 333
Juan de Ibarra *see* ALAVA, JUAN DE
Juan de la Cosa **12** 813
Juan de Laguardia **23** 402
Juan de la Huerta **11** 555; **13** 106; **17** 675–6*
attributions **26** 555
collaboration **33** 28
patrons and collectors **5** 210
works **8** 890; **13** 78; **19** 137
Juan de Langres *see* LANGRES, JUAN DE
Juan de Levi **17** 676*; **27** 818
Juan de Segovia (*fl* mid-*15*th cent.; goldsmith) **13** 732
Juan de Segovia (*fl* 1483-8; painter) **21** 125; **31** 88
Juán de Solórzano **20** 493
Juan de Talavera **13** 757
Juan de Tarragona **9** 262; **30** 347
works **9** *261*
Juan de Tournai **29** 289
Juan de Valladolid **29** 333
Juan du Ruisel **23** 402
Juanes, Juan de **20** 9–10*; **31** 815
collaboration **20** 9
patrons and collectors **4** 378, 565, 566; **27** 607
works **20** *10*; **29** 277
Juan Fernandez Islands **6** 589
Juang **15** 734
Juan of Austria **30** 463
Jüan Yuan *see* RUAN YUAN
Juan y Ulloa **8** 303
Juarez, José **17** 676
Juarez, Juan Rodríguez *see* RODRÍGUEZ JUAREZ, JUAN
Juarez, Luis **17** 676*; **21** 383
Juarez, Nicolás Rodríguez *see* RODRÍGUEZ JUAREZ, NICOLÁS
Juárez, Tómas **21** 383
Juárez José **21** 383
Juba II, King of Mauretania (*reg* 25 BC-AD 23) **6** 548; **27** 31
Juban Mansuriyya Madrasa **16** 214
al-Jubayl **27** 875; **32** 316
Jubba **2** *246*
Jabal Umm Silman **2** *269*, 269–70
Jubbadar, 'Aliquli *see* 'ALIQULI JABBADAR
jubé *see* SCREENS (i) (ARCHITECTURAL)
Jubert (family) **13** 79
Ju Boya **7** 101
Jubrías, María Elena **8** 236
Ju Chao **6** 802
Juchipila *see* PEÑOL DE JUCHIPILA
Jucht, Johann Christoph **3** 429
Jüchtzer, Christian Gottlieb **21** 65
Jucker, Karl J. **3** 402; **32** 756
Judah **1** 857; **16** 573
Judaism **15** 204; **16** 453; **28** 915; **30** 431
Judd, Donald **17** 677*; **22** 315; **23** 49; **30** 201
dealers **6** 23
groups and movements **1** 80; **21** 645–6
patrons and collectors **24** 24
works **1** *80*, 738; **16** 58; **31** 615; **33** 364
Jude, Paul **13** 635
Judeideh, Tell **1** 815, 834; **30** 196
Judenburg, Hans von *see* HANS VON JUDENBURG
Judgement of Paris Painter **17** 911
Judgement of Solomon, Master of the **9** 198; **20** 704*
Judi Dagŭ **21** 301
Judin, Samuel **20** 924
Judith de Bretagne **3** 821
Judith Master **24** 158
Judith of Flanders **2** 78; **27** 617*
jue *see under* VESSELS → types
Juel, Annette **8** 756
Juel, Jens (Jørgensen) (1745-1802) **7** 805; **8** 734; **17** 677–8*; **25** 549
pupils **11** 779; **27** 338
reproductive prints by others **7** 410
works **8** 734; **17** *678*
Juel, Niels **8** 725
Juelang **18** 516
Juell, Dagny **22** 291
jufti knots *see under* KNOTS → types
Jugaku, Bunshō **21** 634; **33** 491
Jugarsi **15** 600
Jugda **21** 881
Jugend **2** 562, 565; **12** 394; **14** 576; **16** 906; **24** 444; **29** 847
Jugendgruppe *see* SCHOLLE, DIE
Jugendstil **2** 565; **10** 697; **12** 427–8, 449–50, 456, 463; **14** 576; **26** 374; **32** 446
art forms
architecture **2** *788*; **5** 165; **10** 215; **12** 378; **23** 372; **31** *876*
cartoons (drawings) **18** *130*
ceramics **30** 885
glass **2** 818
metalwork **12** 453–4
painting **2** *797*; **12** 394
Austria **18** *130*
pottery **2** 816
sculpture **2** 803; **12** 407
urban planning **32** *761*
regional traditions
Czech Republic **25** 151; **29** 893
Germany **12** 452
Latvia **12** 825
see also ART NOUVEAU
Jugo **15** 781
Jūgō Gien *see* GIEN JŪGŌ
Jugoslavija *see* YUGOSLAVIA
Jugovec, Oton **28** 860
jugs
historical and regional traditions
Ancient Near East **1** 867
Austria **2** *815*
Belgium **3** 588, 589, *589*
Crete **21** *665*, *666*, *756*
Cycladic **8** *312*, *313*
Cyprus, ancient **8** *344*, 348, *348*
Egypt, ancient **10** *57*
England **10** *302*, *335*; **14** 425; **15** *820*
Etruscan **10** 626
Germany **12** 452; **27** *86*
Greece, ancient **13** 476
Helladic **14** *343*, *344*, *356*
Iran **16** *528*
Iraq **16** 399
Islamic **16** 372, 399, *528*
Italy **10** 626; **12** VIII1
Japan **17** *264*
Minoan **21** *665*, *666*, *756*
Mycenaean **14** *344*, *356*
Netherlands, the **22** *877*, *878*
Rome, ancient **27** *78*, 86, *86*
Thracian **30** 770
materials
bronze **10** 626; **14** *356*; **27** 86, *86*; **30** 770
copper **12** 452
earthenwares **10** *314*
faience (ii) (ceramics) **2** *815*
glass **10** *57*, *335*; **12** VIII1; **27** *78*
gold **16** 372
inscriptions **16** 372
maiolica **22** *877*
nephrite **16** *528*
porcelain **17** *264*
pottery **8** *344*, *348*; **10** *302*; **14** *343*; **15** *820*; **21** *665*, *666*, *756*; **22** *878*
silver **10** *335*; **16** 31, 372
stonewares **3** *589*
types
Bellarmines **6** 333
cream **10** *314*; **16** 31
drinking **10** 302
Harvest **10** 305
knight **10** 302
Toby jugs **33** 341
Jugtown Pottery **31** 639
Jūhakkain, Yūshi Hachimankō **17** 397
Juhan, Duke of Finland *see* JOHN III, King of Sweden
Juhász, Árpád **12** 839
Juhász, László **14** 910
Juhl, Finn **8** 747
Jūichikai (Society of Eleven) **17** 203
Juigalpa Museum **29** 222
Juis, Jean-Marie Delafont de *see* DELAFONT DE JUIS, JEAN-MARIE

Jujol (i Gibert), Josep M(aria) **12** 181, 182; **17** 679*
Jujuy **2** 392, *393*, 394
architecture **2** 394
Cathedral **2** 398
chapels **2** 394
jukeboxes **22** 375
Jukes, Francis **2** 240; **7** 431; **25** 164, 619
Juktas **8** 153
Jukun **17** 679–80*
basketwork **3** 332; **17** 680
brass **1** 382
masks **1** 382; **3** 332; **17** 679–80*; **22** 287
sculpture **1** 382; **17** 679*, *680*
textiles **17** 680
wood **17** 680
wood-carvings **17** 679, *680*
Jula **5** 216
Jules, John *see* DUNAND, JEAN
Juley, Paul **2** 365, 371
Juley, Peter A. **2** 365, 371; **31** 671
Juley, Peter A., Collection *see under* WASHINGTON (DC) → museums → Smithsonian Institute
Julfa *see* ISFAHAN → New Julfa
Juli **4** 261; **17** 513; **24** *498*
Casa Zavala **24** 504
Santa Cruz **24** 504
S Juan Bautista **24** 500
S Pedro Mártir **24** 500, 504
textiles **4** 267
Julia **12** 464
Juliá, Ascensío **13** 252; **17** 681*
Juliá, Eusebio **17** 681*
Julia, Jean-Baptiste **5** 528
Julia Domna **26** 900
Julia Glassworks **3** 418; **25** 125
Julia Gordos **19** 841
Ju Lian **6** 802; **19** 421
Julian, Rodolphe **11** 672; **29** 856; **33** 740
Julian, Stanislas Aignan **7** 161
Julianus, Archbishop of Bosra (*fl* 513) **4** 464
Julianus (*fl* 520; banker) **9** 534
Julianus, Emperor of Rome (*reg* 360–63) **7** 591; **27** 83
Jülich **24** 230
Residenz **24** *230*
Jülich, John-William, Duke of *see* JOHN-WILLIAM, Duke of Jülich
Jülich, William V, Duke of *see* WILLIAM V, Duke of Jülich
Julien **19** 126
Julien, Jean-Antoine **2** 84; **4** 413; **17** 681, 682–3*
works **17** *682*
Julien, Joseph-Laurent **17** 681
Julien, Laurent **17** 681*
Julien, Mathieu **19** 128
Julien, Pierre **17** 683*
collaboration **11** 336
patrons and collectors **4** 555; **11** 561
pupils **10** 509; **25** 647, 798
works **11** 562; **25** 872
Julien, Simon **17** 681*; **20** 202; **26** 57
Julien de Parme *see* JULIEN, JEAN-ANTOINE
Julienne, Jean de **3** 760; **4** 512, 513, 518; **7** 194, 422; **14** 162; **18** 626
Julio Antonio (Rodríguez Hernández) **17** 683*
Juliomagus *see* ANGERS
Juliot (family) **31** 382
Julius (*b* 1939) **29** 98
Julius, Duke of Brunswick-Wolfenbüttel (*reg* 1568–89) **11** 715; **33** 51, 292
Julius I, Pope (*reg* 337–52) **26** 833
Julius II, Pope (*reg* 1503–13) **14** 869; **26** 768–9, *818*; **27** 46, 114, 272–3*
architecture **1** 572; **4** 642, 648; **7** 218; **19** 158; **25** 217; **26** 756
castles **7** 366
churches **4** 649–50; **16** 632; **26** 186, 800, 801, 804, 805
fortifications **25** 216
loggias **27** 737
palaces **4** 648–9; **26** 811
palazzi **27** 737
shrines (i) (cult) **19** 687
urban planning **24** 398; **27** 271
villas **5** 843; **16** 633; **32** 546
collections **16** 763; **26** 768
jewellery **5** 697
paintings **4** 653; **6** 355; **11** 294; **16** 664; **20** 901; **24** 523, 830; **25** 899, 903; **31** 72
frescoes **21** 443; **23** 368; **24** 526; **26** 816, 818
printing **16** 360
sculpture **2** 168, 226; **5** 214; **9** 20; **10** 521; **13** 605; **21** 435; **25** 158; **26** 187, 800, 846; **27** 45, 776; **28** 314
tombs **16** 695; **27** 272
stained glass **13** 827
Julius III, Pope (*reg* 1550–55) **22** 6–7*
architecture **1** 792; **4** 47; **26** 813; **32** 13, 546
churches **32** 505
military **23** 745
villas **32** 504
decorative works **11** 268
medals **6** 360
paintings **8** 504; **30** 800; **32** 13, 16; **33** 716
sculpture **1** 791; **26** 846; **27** 203
Julius style **17** 684*
Jullian de la Fuente, Guillermo **19** 48, 51; **30** 391
Jullien, Adolphe **10** 797
Jullien, Joseph **11** 608; **21** 137
Jullienne, Jean de **17** 684*
patrons and collectors **19** 646
personal collection **19** 369
reproductive prints by others **30** 344
works **7** 778; **8** 209; **11** 539; **18** 692; **24** 255, 256; **31** 306
Julliot, Claude-Antoine **17** 684
Julliot, Claude-François **3** 414; **11** 593, 596; **17** 684*
works **12** 831; **19** 261
Julliot, Philippe-François **17** 684
Jully, Ange-Laurent de La Live de *see* LA LIVE DE JULLY, ANGE-LAURENT DE
Julu **7** 36, 118
Jumayra *see under* DUBAI
Jumbana Designs **1** 64
Jumbey Village **3** 64
Jumeau **31** 261
Jumhouriyya Djibouti *see* DJIBOUTI
Jumièges, Robert of, Bishop of London *see* ROBERT OF JUMIÈGES, Bishop of London
Jumièges Abbey **1** 723; **3** 708, 709; **11** *504*, 653; **17** 684–6*; **21** 835; **26** 585
arches **2** 292, 294
buttresses **5** 319
choir-stalls **13** 126
cloister **7** 453
dormitory **21** 843
gate-house **12** 175
ivory-carvings **26** 696
manuscripts **26** 669
mouldings **22** 215
Notre-Dame **11** 509; **17** *685*, 685–6*, *686*; **26** 586, 597; **30** 728
refectory **21** 844
St Pierre **17** 685*; **26** 586
westwork **33** 108–9
Ju Ming *see* CHU MING
jumpers **18** 158
jumping vaults *see under* VAULTS (CEILING) → types
Jumsai, Sumet **17** 686–7*; **25** 359; **30** 591
Junagadh **15** 348, 349, 450
mosque of Abu'l-Qasim ibn 'Ali al-Idhaji **15** 347
Uparkot **15** 463
Upper Fort *see* Uparkot
Junagadh and Girnar **15** *276*; **17** 687*
Ju'nan **7** 26
Junan Kalijaga, Prince **15** 802
Junayd **16** 318, 876; **17** 687–8*
works **1** 25; **3** 53; **16** 301, 313, 314, 320, *320*
Juncais **25** 511
Juncal, Fábrica do *see* FÁBRICA DO JUNCAL
Junck, Benedetto **8** 136
Juncker, Hans **17** 688–90*
works **2** 591, 592; **17** *689*, *690*
Juncker, Michael **17** 688
Juncker, Zacharias **17** 688*
Junco, Emilio del **25** 823
Juneau, Denis **25** 28
Junek, Leo **9** 672
Jung, Carl Gustav **1** 78; **17** 690*; **33** 680
groups and movements **1** 85
works **22** 416; **25** 684
Jung, Dora **11** 110
Jung, Franz **3** 801; **8** 436; **14** 845
Jung, Gustav **11** 106; **30** 102
Jung, Melchior **30** 102
Jung, Moriz **17** 691*
Jung, Valter **3** 177; **11** 106; **29** 63
Jung/Brannen International **2** 378
Jungala, Uta Uta *see* UTA UTA (JANGALA)
Junge, Johannes **17** 691*
Jungen, Die **28** 340
Junger, Hermann **12** 451, 456; **17** 530; **22** 305
Jünger, Ludwig **22** 860
Jüngere Fridericusgruppe **7** 594–5
Jüngerer, Christoph Murmann der *see* MURMANN DER JÜNGERER, CHRISTOPH
Junge Rheinland **1** 160; **9** 42; **12** 874; **24** 13; **25** 838
Junger Westen **12** 397; **28** 176
Jungfer, Gyula **15** 9
Jungfraujoch **23** 342
Jung Jiddisch group **3** 788
Jung-kwang **18** 312
Jungnickel, Ludwig Heinrich **2** 797; **17** 691–2*; **33** 166
Jung-Stilling, Elise von **18** 851
Jungwierth, Franz Xavier **24** 707
Jungwirth, Josef **17** 897
Juni, Isaac de **17** 693
Juni, Juan de **17** 692–3*; **29** 289, 290
collaboration **24** 712; **31** 163
works **7** 362; **17** 656, *693*; **19** 171; **26** 250; **28** 369; **29** 289, 290; **31** 822
Jun'ichiro, Tanizaki **23** 595
Junij **1** 820
Júnior, José Ferraz de Almeida *see* ALMEIDA JÚNIOR, JOSÉ FERRAZ DE
juniper **25** 304
Juniper Green Workshop **31** 466
juniper resin **32** 1
Junius, Franciscus **9** 8; **10** 204; **17** 693–4*; **22** 911
Junius, Hadrianus **14** 294
Junius Bassus **27** 827
sarcophagus **27** *828*
Junius Manuscript (Oxford, Bodleian Lib., MS. Junius 11) **2** 83
Junk art **16** 58; **17** 694–5*; **23** 334; **29** 539
England **10** 268
Junk art—cont.
United States of America **6** 408; **17** *694*; **26** 27, *27*
Junker, Carl **31** 329
Junker, Hermann **10** 82, 83, 93
Junker, W. **33** 610
Junker von Prag **17** 695*; **20** 564; **27** 145
Jun (Atsushi) Miyagawa *see* MIYAGAWA, JUN (ATSUSHI)
Junna-nagara *see* JUNNAR
Junnar **15** *276*, 553; **17** 695*
Bhuta Lena caves **15** 450
temple **15** 252
Junoy, Josep **8** 436
Junquera, Jerónimo **27** 784
Jun ware *see under* POTTERY → wares
Junweng *see* HUANG CHÜN-PI
Junyent, Olegario **5** 509
Junyent, Sebastiá **29** 308
Junzō Gō *see* GŌ, JUNZŌ
Junzō Sakakura *see* SAKAKURA, JUNZŌ
Junzō Yoshimura *see* YOSHIMURA, JUNZŌ
Jupan, Ludwig **17** 695–6*
works **2** 486; **17** 601, 740, *741*
jupe **24** 40
Ju Peon *see* XU BEIHONG
Jurado, Ximena y *see* XIMENA Y JURADO
Jūraku Castle **21** 828
Juran **6** 773, 790, 820; **17** 696–8*; **23** 582; **29** 67
groups and movements **29** 244
teachers **9** 140
works **6** 761, 789; **17** *697*
Juraszek, Paul **2** 754
Jürchen *see* RUZHEN
Jürgen-Fischer, Klaus **30** 172*
Jürgensen, Peter **17** 547
Juristo, Julio **19** 493
Jurjan *see* GURGAN
al-Jurjani **16** 100
Jurjaniyya *see* KUNYA-URGENCH
Jurkovič, Dušan **8** 401; **17** 698*
Jūrōbei Saitō *see* SAITŌ JŪRŌBEI
Jur pri Bratislave **28** 855
St George **14** 893
Juryfreie **22** 304
Juselius (family) **12** 21
Jushi *see* YARKHOTO
Jūshiya Sōgō **30** 259
Jussieu, Bernard de **32** 373
Jussow, Heinrich Christoph **17** 698–9*
groups and movements **13** 200; **26** 743
patrons and collectors **17** 836
pupils **18** 883
teachers **32** 766
works **9** 456; **12** 413, 414; **13** 200; **17** 836; **20** 867, 868; **27** 323
Juste, Justin de **10** 551
Juste de Gand *see* JUSTUS OF GHENT
juste-milieu style **12** 808, *809*
Justi, Carl **12** 483; **17** 699*
pupils **28** 119
works **7** 471; **12** 873; **29** 358
translated **18** 899
Justice, Thomas **28** 256
justice scenes **17** 699–701*
Belgium **4** *592*; **17** *700*
Germany **3** *40*; **17** 699
Holy Roman Empire (before 1648) **17** 700
Italy **4** *274*
Netherlands, the **17** 699–701
Justin II, Emperor of Byzantium (*reg* 565–78) **26** 143
Justin I, Emperor of Byzantium (*reg* 518–27) **9** 538, *636*
Justinian I, Emperor of Byzantium (*reg* 527–65) **9** 522; **17** 701–2*, 838; **22** *161*; **28** 761
architecture **2** 155; **5** 762, 892; **16** 580–81, 809; **23** 891; **25** 51
aqueducts **9** 560
bridges **9** 560
cathedrals **1** 602; **27** 698
churches
Church of the Holy Apostles (Istanbul) **16** 603
Church of the Nativity (Bethlehem) **9** 540
Hagia Eirene (Istanbul) **16** 600
Hagia Sophia (Istanbul) **2** 135; **9** 513, 654; **16** 592
New St Mary (Jerusalem) **17** 489
SS Sergios and Bakchos (Istanbul) **9** 537; **16** 602
S Vitale (Ravenna) **16** 625
fortifications **9** 554; **26** 909
hospitals **9** 560
military **21** 550
monasteries **28** 761; **31** 434
palaces **16** 581, 607
theatres **16** 582
town walls **23** 145
art policies **5** 135
coins **9** 636; **14** 408
gold **9** 654
icons **9** 623
ivory **9** 648
manuscripts **9** 607; **16** 592
medallions **21** 2
metalwork **1** 694
mosaics **9** 572; **22** 162
silver **9** 654
Justinian I's bridge **9** 560; **17** *702*
Justinian II, Emperor of Byzantium (*reg* 685–95; 705–11) **9** 513, 636, *637*; **16** 582, 607; **17** 701*
architecture **16** 581, 607
coins **9** 636, *636*
fortifications **9** 558
gold **9** 654
metalwork **8** 200
silver **9** 655
Justiniana Prima *see* CARIČIN GRAD
Justinian Codex *see under* CODICES → individual manuscripts
Justinianic Renaissance **9** 606
Justinian Trans-Isthmian Wall **26** 909
Justitz, Alfred **8** 393
Justus of Ghent **3** 553; **14** 870; **17** 702–5*; **21** 96
assistants **3** 844
attributions **3** 844; **8** 501
patrons and collectors **4** 181; **16** 659; **22** 13; **29** 859, 860
works **12** 519; **17** *703*, *704*; **31** 515, 740, *741*, 744
Justyne, Percy William **5** 751
Jutarō Kuroda *see* KURODA, JUTARŌ
jute
historical and regional traditions
Bangladesh **3** 169
China **7** 114
Indian subcontinent **5** 829
uses
canvas **5** 655
carpets **5** 829, 830, 840
felt **10** 872
fibre art **11** 54
paper **7** 114
rugs **27** 317
threads **30** 538
Juvarra (family) **16** 742
Juvarra, Filippo **17** 706–10*
architecture **13** 645
chapels **3** 198
churches **16** 643; **17** *707*, *708*; **20** 320; **25** 266; **27** 486
domes **1** 566

Juvarra, Filippo
architecture—cont.
façades **6** 18; **16** *644*; **17** *709*; **21** 532; **27** 753; **31** 440
hunting-lodges **7** 571; **32** 549
mausolea **20** 866
palaces **29** 304
palazzi **1** 622; **2** 331, 379; **12** 791; **17** *709*; **20** 72; **21** 431; **29** 271, 486
riding houses **26** 363
stables **29** 485
staircases **29** 525
urban planning **31** 441
assistants **5** 907; **26** 519
collaboration **3** 920; **13** 625; **19** 89; **31** 314; **32** 643
dealing **19** 524

Juvarra, Filippo—cont.
furniture **29** 315
groups and movements **3** 266; **16** 643
interior decoration **3** 453; **15** 149
metalwork **9** 158
parks **12** 119
patrons and collectors
Charles-Emanuel III, Duke of Savoy and King of Sardinia (*reg* 1730-73) **28** 17
Elizabeth Farnese, Queen of Spain (1692-1766) **4** 560
John V, King of Portugal (*reg* 1706-50) **4** 635

Juvarra, Filippo
patrons and collectors—cont.
Mary Joanna of Savoy-Nemours, Duchess and Regent of Savoy (1644-1724) **28** 14
Oratorians **23** 473
Ottoboni, Pietro, Cardinal (1667-1740) **23** 637
Philip V, King of Spain (*reg* 1700-24) **4** 558
Victor-Amadeus II, 15th Duke of Savoy (*reg* 1675- 1730) and King of Sardinia (*reg* 1720-30) **16** 716, 764; **28** 16, 17; **31** 444
pupils **4** 560; **27** 486
silver **16** 742

Juvarra, Filippo—cont.
stage design **5** 686; **30** 669
teachers **11** 274, 277
Juvarra, Pietro **16** 742
Juvenal **27** 868
Juvénal des Ursins *see* JOUVENEL DES URSINS
Juvenel, Esther **17** 712
Juvenel, Friedrich **17** 712
Juvenel, Johann **17** 712
Juvenel, Johann Philipp **17** 712
Juvenel, Nicolas, I **11** 819; **17** 711*
Juvenel, Paul, I **17** 711–12*
assistants **33** 130
collaboration **12** 168; **31** 806
groups and movements **9** 446
works **14** 899; **23** 308; **28** 852
ju wood *see* ZELKOVA

Juxon, William, Archbishop of Canterbury **10** 290; **30** 781
Juxtlahuaca **21** 226; **23** 418
Juyan *see* KARAKHOTO
Juybari (family) **16** 235, 236
Juynboll, H. H. **29** 241
Jūzaburō Tsutaya *see* TSUTAYA JŪZABURŌ
Jūzan *see* KUSUMI MORIKAGE
Juzan Maegawa *see* MAEGAWA JUZAN
Juznic, Bohumil **28** 856
Juzo Kagoshima *see* KAGOSHIMA, JUZO
Jwala Ram **15** 628
Jyväskylä **11** *87*
Kortepohja **19** 798–9
theatre **30** 684

K

Kaam **18** 484
Kaan, Arthur **28** 670
Ka-aper *see* SHEIKH EL-BELED
Kaapor **4** 706, 707
Kaas, Wilhelm Friedrich Wolgang von *see* WOLFGANG VON KAAS, WILHELM FRIEDRICH
Kaaz, Carl Ludwig **17** 713*; **23** 410
el-Kab **9** *774*; **17** 713–14*
sacred lake **27** 496
temples **29** 386
Temple of Khasekhemwy **9** 868
Temple of Tuthmosis III **20** 232
tombs **17** *714*
Ahmose (son of Ebana) (Tomb 5) **17** 714
Pahery **9** 823; **17** 714
Reneni **17** 714
Setau **17** 714
town walls **9** 844; **21** 554
Ka'ba *see under* MECCA
Kababish **1** 307
Kabáh **17** 715–16*; **20** *882*, 884; **21** 262, *372*; **23** 826; **31** 779
arches **2** 294
architecture **21** 205
causeway **6** 97, *97*
Codz Poop **17** 715, *715*; **20** 884
Palace of the Masks *see* Codz Poop
Kabakov, Il'ya (Iosifovich) **17** 716*; **27** 397
groups and movements **29** 89
patrons and collectors **8** 10
pupils **5** 142
works **27** *398*
Kabalevsky, Dmitry **24** 818
Kabarda **27** 433
Kabardin **27** 432
Kabardino-Balkaria **27** 433
Kabarnat **6** 379
Kabeiric skyphoi *see under* SKYPHOI → types
Kabeirion **13** 571
sanctuary **13** 370, 513
Kabeirion style pottery *see under* POTTERY → wares
Kabel *see under* TYPE-FACES
Kabel, Adriaen van der *see* CABEL, ADRIAEN VAN DER
Kabilye Berber **1** 317
Kabinettmalerei **13** 188
kabinja see under TYPE-FACES
Kabir **14** 555
Kabnak *see* HAFT TEPE
Kabota **20** 36
Kabotie, Fred **14** 477; **17** 716*; **22** 595, 677
Kabotie, Michael **17** 716; **22** 597, 598
kabuki see under THEATRE → types; THEATRES → types
Kabul **1** *186*, 207; **6** *182*, *623*; **15** *360*; **16** *105*; **17** 716–17*; **22** 258
architecture **1** 208
fort **15** 365
Garden of Fidelity **11** 340; **15** 361
Hindu temple **1** 199
interior decoration **1** 208
metalwork **1** 206
Museum **1** 211; **15** 743; **17** 717
painting **1** 208
Pir Rathan Nath **1** 199
sculpture **1** 198
stone-carvings **1** 208
Wafa Bagh *see* Garden of Fidelity
Kaburagi, Kiyokata **17** 177, 201, 290, 293, 294, 436; **30** 247; **31** 764
Kabushiya *see* MEROË
Kabwe, Paul **33** 603
Kabye **31** 73
Kabyle **5** 145
Kaceli, Sadik **1** 540; **17** 717*
Kaceřov Castle **8** 377
Kachcha Kot *see under* TAXILA
Kachchhapaghata **13** 881
see also:
KIRTTIRAJA, Ruler
MAHIPALA, Ruler
PADMAPALA, Ruler
Kachchhauva **15** 574
Kachelofen, Kunz **19** 111
Kachin **5** 220, 247, 248, 262
kachina dolls *see under* DOLLS → types
kachōga see JAPAN → painting → bird-and-flower
kachōga style **28** 587
Kachrylion **13** 519; **32** 41, 60
Kačina **8** 399
Kačin Castle **8** 379
Kadalik, František **8** 428
Kadamarakalava **15** 534
Shivanandishvara Temple **15** 299, 535
Kadampa Buddhism *see under* BUDDHISM → sects
Kadaň **8** 377, 422
Kádár, Béla **28** 71
Kadau (family) **25** 127
Kadau, Łukasz **25** 127
Kadavu **11** 70
Kadazan **20** 182
Kadet **15** 825
Kadıasker Mustafa İzzet *see* MUSTAFA İZZET
Kadiköy *see* CHALKEDON
Kadirampuram **14** 125
Kadiri **15** 530–31, 539
Lakshmi Narasimhasvami Temple **15** 539
Manjunatha Temple **15** 516, *530*
Kadirli **9** 565
Kadishman, Menashe **17** 717*
Kadiwéu **4** 706
Kadjar *see* QAJAR
Kadlik, František *see* TKADLÍK, FRANTIŠEK
Kadmos Painter **13** 524; **32** 48*, 65
kadoi **13** 475
Kadowaki, Kunio **20** 873
Kadro (family) **1** 540
Kaduna **23** *129*, 135
mosque **23** 134
Kadur **15** 527
Kadwaha **15** 413, 497
monasteries **15** 292
Murayat *see* Shiva Temple
Shiva Temple **15** 292
temples **15** 292
Vaishnava temples **15** 292
Kadyanda **19** 837
Temple **19** 840
Kaédi Library **20** 862
Kaefre *see* CHEPHREN
Kaehler, Heinrich **28** 45
Kaempfer, Engelbert **12** 82; **17** 429
works **16** *265*
Kaendler, Charles **6** 451
Kaendler, Johann Joachim *see* KÄNDLER, JOHANN JOACHIM
Kaepping, Karl **2** 565
Kaeppler, Adrienne L. **23** 738, 739, 740
Kaesbach, Walter **14** 285
Kaesŏng **18** *248*
Manwŏltae Hill Palace **18** 261, 275–6
Museum **18** 383
patronage **18** 258
Sonjuk bridge **18** 280
South Gate **18** 265
State Historical Museum **18** 382
temples **18** 268
tomb of Kongmin **18** 273
Kaessmann, Rutger *see* KASSMANN, RUTGER
Kaesz, Gyula **14** 910
Kaetzaert van Zaer **20** 644
Kafariha, Tepe **1** 195, 196
Kaffa **4** 110; **9** *507*; **17** 717–18*; **31** *546*
Ayvazovsky Picture Gallery **2** 888; **17** 718; **31** 565
Museum of Ethnography **17** 718
Kafir **23** 798
Kafir Kala (Tajikistan, Vakhsh Valley) **6** *182*, 210, 256; **17** 718*; **30** *252*, 440
ossuaries **23** 607
reliefs **6** 276
Kafir Kala (Tajikistan, Sogdiana) **6** 199, 256, 273
Kafir Kot **15** 266
Kafizin **13** 537
Kafka, Bohumil **8** 387; **17** 718–19*; **25** 433
Kafka, Franz **18** 577; **20** 75; **33** 305
Kafka, Paul Ernest **2** 759
Kafrawi, K. El **19** 321
Kafr Ruma **9** 591
kaftans **9** *641*; **16** *446*, 456, 460, 461
Kaftantzoglou, Lysandros **11** 140; **13** 348, 349, 358, 359, 360; **17** 719*
Kaftari **15** 921
Kaga (Japan) **17** 351, 364
Kaga Church (Sweden) **30** 75
Kagaku Murakami *see* MURAKAMI, KAGAKU
Kagami no Ōkimi **22** 501
Kagan, Richard **31** 634
Kåge, Wilhelm **8** 803; **30** 99, 100
Kagel, Mauricio **29** 97
Kagemni **27** 812
tomb **27** *811*
Kagenobu Kanō *see* KANŌ KAGENOBU
Kager, Johann Matthias **17** 719–20*; **18** 42
collaboration **12** 389; **18** 225; **21** 127
patrons and collectors **13** 631
reproductive prints by others **27** 503, 504
works **5** 607; **11** 456; **14** 51; **17** *720*; **18** 533
Kager, Mathias **14** 679
Kagerbauer, Antal **7** 471; **26** 709
Kagetoshi **17** 401
Kâğıthane Palace **16** 226
Kagoshima **17** 18; **27** 873
Kagoshima, Juzō **17** 371
Kagulu **14** 376
Kagulu Kamalungu **14** 376
Kagura **1** 281
Kagyupa Buddhism *see under* BUDDHISM → sects
Kahafajeh Temple **30** 432
Kahana, Aharon **16** 568
Kahane, Anne **5** 571
Kahay **9** 820, 821, 822; **10** 51
Kahei Ōmiya *see* ŌMIYA KAHEI
Kahela **14** 376, 377
Kahemba **1** *401*
Kahl, Gottfried **8** 409
Kähler, Carl Frederik **17** 720
Kahler, Eugen von **4** 132
Kähler, Herman Hans Christian **17** 720
Kähler, Hermann August **8** 748; **17** 720*
Kähler, Joachim Christian Herman **17** 720
Kähler ceramic factory **14** 120
Kahlo (y Calderón), (Magdalena Carmen) Frida **17** 721*; **26** 427; **33** 316
groups and movements **30** 21, 22
pupils **23** 370; **24** 334
works **21** 388, *389*; **33** 316
Kahlo, Guillermo **21** 398
Kahlur **15** 624
Kahn, Albert **17** 721–2*; **33** 254
assistants **20** 460
collaboration **5** 276
staff **32** 851
works **4** 789; **8** 821; **10** 684, 749; **12** 792; **14** 203; **17** *722*; **31** 595, 596, *596*
Kahn, Alphonse **13** 671; **33** 342
Kahn, E(ly)-J(acques) **17** 722–3*; **23** 43; **25** 48
Kahn, Frederick **9** 87
Kahn, Gustave **17** 723*; **19** 36; **22** 746
Kahn, Louis I(sadore) **8** 847; **14** 811; **16** 101; **17** 723–5*; **24** 598
architecture **15** 168; **31** 597
churches **31** 584
government buildings **3** 167, *167*; **13** 239
institutes **1** 473; **27** 721
laboratories **10** 417
libraries **19** 365
museums **17** *724*; **21** 91; **22** 367; **23** 25; **28** 584
synagogues **17** 549
urban planning **31** 735
assistants **24** 697
collaboration **4** 490; **15** 169; **29** 718; **31** 493
groups and movements **5** 56
patrons and collectors **21** 135
pupils **14** 847; **15** 242; **22** 53; **27** 515; **31** 779
staff **32** 234
teachers **8** 152
Kahn, Lydia *see* WINSTON, LYDIA
Kahn, Maurice (*fl* 1900) **17** 777
Kahn, Maurice (*b* 1943) **29** 111
Kahn, Otto H. **9** 200; **12** 615
Kahncrete **32** 801
Kahn & Jacobs **17** 620, 722; **21** 492; **31** 597
Kahn & Stonorov **17** 723
Kahnweiler, Daniel-Henry **2** 225; **6** 80; **9** 465; **10** 680; **11** 165; **16** 823; **17** 725–6*; **18** 864; **19** 66; **20** 208, 285; **24** 144; **25** 626; **27** 162; **29** 605; **33** 362
books **13** 671
collections **24** 720
dealing **11** 664
engravings **4** 674
groups and movements **8** 240, 241, 243, 246
paintings **8** 774; **13** 669; **17** 912; **19** 78, 79; **20** 590; **24** 717
writings **24** 717; **25** 362
Kahnweiler Press **20** 335
Kahnyo Thérèse
works **1** *246*
Kaho'olawe *see* HAWAII
Kahri, Esko **19** 799
Kahukiwa, Robyn **17** 726*; **20** 360
Kahun **9** 823; **10** 74, 759; **18** 647–8
Kahve Assar, Latmos church **8** **9** 550
Kaiapoi **23** *52*
Kaiapoi Woollen Manufactory Co. **23** 73
Kaichirō Nezu *see* NEZU, KAICHIRŌ
Kaifeng **23** 821
ceramics **7** 151
Genyue yuan **12** 87, 88
kilns **6** 891
painting **6** 809
palace **6** 679
rhinoceros statue **7** 99
Shuanglin si **17** 590
urban planning **6** 664
Yuguo Temple
Iron Pagoda **6** 655; **23** 773
Tie ta *see* Iron Pagoda
Kaigetsudō **17** 281
Kaigetsudō Anchi **17** 281, 726–7*
Kaigetsudō Ando **17** 726–7*
groups and movements **17** 726
pupils **17** 726, 727
works **17** 176, 281, *727*
Kaigetsudō Dohan **17** 281, 726, 727*
works **17** *281*
Kaigetsudō Doshin **17** 281, 726
Kaigetsudō Doshu **17** 726
Kaigetsudō Doshū **17** 726
Kaigetsudō school **17** 176, 726–7*
works **17** *727*
Kaigyoku *see* KAIGYOKUSAI MASATSUGU
Kaigyokusai Masatsugu **17** 401
Kaihō Yūsetsu **17** 729
Kaihō Yūshō **17** 164, 727–9*
attributions **17** 787
pupils **14** 704; **21** 742
works **17** *728*
Kaii Higashiyama *see* HIGASHIYAMA, KAII
Kaiji Tsukamoto *see* TSUKAMOTO, KAIJI
Kaikei **17** 729–30*
collaboration **18** 195; **31** 675
groups and movements **17** 879
works **17** 122–4, 129; **18** 557; **22** 497, 499
Kai Kin *see* HOSHIYAMA CHŪJI
Kailasa Temple *see under* ELLORA
Kaimes **21** 551
Kaiming Book Company **10** 885, 886
Kain Itsujin *see* TAKAHASHI YŪICHI
Kainradl, Leo **28** 670
kain songket see under TEXTILES → types
Kaioku Nukina *see* NUKINA KAIOKU
Kaipiainen, Birger **11** 106
Kaiping *see* SHANGDU
Kairak **24** 83
Kairakuen **17** *11*, 730*
Kairos Verlag **23** 121
Kairouan **1** 377; **16** *103*; **17** 730–31*
architecture **16** 219
bridge **16** 156
carpets **1** 378; **16** 486; **17** 731
factories **16** 436
fortifications **21** 585
houses **32** 312
hydraulic works **16** 156
kilims **31** 426

Kairouan—cont.
medina 31 424
mosques 5 893; 16 145
congregational mosque *see* Great Mosque
Great Mosque 1 316, 378; 3 894; 9 86; 16 156, *156*, 219, 243, 248; 17 730–31; 22 193
arches 2 294
Bab Lalla Rihana 16 219, *219*
ceiling 16 493
coffering 7 527
library 1 378
manuscripts 16 356, 357
maqṣūra 16 493; 20 368, *369*
mihrab 16 157; 21 505
minbar 16 488, 493
tiles 1 378; 16 400, 404
tower 21 626
Greek Mosque 21 629
mosque of Muhammad ibn Khairun 16 157
mosque of Sidi' Uqba *see* Great Mosque
mosque of the Sabres *see* Museum of Popular Arts and Traditions
Uqba ibn Nafi' Mosque 16 398
Musée d'Art Islamique 17 731; 20 450
Museum of Popular Arts and Traditions 17 730
scripts 16 282
Sidi 'Abid al-Ghariani *Zāwiya* 16 220, 246
Sidi Sahib *Zāwiya* 16 220
stelae 29 617, 618
stucco 29 820
textiles 31 22
tomb of Abu Zama'a al-Balawi 16 220
tombs 31 111
Kaisar Agha 15 711
Kaisarini 9 546
Kai Sass, Else 8 762
Kaisei 17 125
Kaiseki Noro *see* NORO KAISEKI
Kaisen Oda *see* ODA KAISEN
Kaiser, Eduard 17 731*
Kaiser, Georg 22 339
Kaiser, J. W. 33 266
Kaiser, Karl Georg 8 790
Kaiser, Robert 5 573
Kaiser, Victor *see* KAYSER, VICTOR
Kaiseraugst Treasure 2 721; 9 655; 18 825; 26 862; 27 83, 84
Kaiser Corporation 11 835
Kaiserliche Porzellanmanufactur (Vienna; before 1744) *see* VIENNA PORCELAIN FACTORY (BEFORE 1744)
Kaiserliche Porzellanmanufactur (Vienna; after 1744) 32 449*
modellers 3 899; 19 772
painters 6 92; 8 445; 14 235
production 2 816, *817*; 25 193
Kaisermann, Franz 17 731–2*; 24 822
Kaiserslautern
Kunstgewerbemuseum 29 885
Kaiserstein, Count of 1 669
Kaisheim Monastery 12 372
Kaishin Shinoda *see* SHINODA, KAISHIN
kaisho 17 76–7*, *81*, 173
Kaisuke Tsukamoto *see* TSUKAMOTO KAISUKE
Ka'it Bay *see* QA'ITBAY
Kaivanto, Kimmo 11 97
kaiyū see under GARDENS → types
Kai Yuwen 29 905
Kaizhi, Gyu 18 172
Kaizuri bugyōsho (Shell Polishing Office) 27 470
Kajaia, D. 12 320
Kajander, Ismo 11 97
Kajanus, Gösta 30 368
Kajdy, Lajos 14 910
Kaji 17 233, 234, 732*
Kajikawa (family) 17 304, 399
Kajiki 27 873
Kajima Corporation 17 53; 23 385
Kajita, Hanko 17 293; 18 172; 20 74; 23 390
Kaji Tsunekichi 17 378
Kajiwara, Hisako 17 202
works 17 *202*
Kaj Mosque 16 194
Kájov Church 8 377
Kajruksztis, W. 4 148
Kaka 1 265
Kakabadze, David (Nestorovich) 17 732*
patrons and collectors 12 332
works 12 326, *327*
Kakadu National Park 31 511, *511*
Kakaslomnic *see* VEL'KÁ LOMNICA
Kakatiya 14 130; 17 733*
Kakatiya, Rudradeva *see* RUDRADEVA, Ruler
Kakefuda, Isao 11 826
Kakegamic, Goyce 22 597
Kakei *see* MATSUMURA KEIBUN
Kakheti 12 316, 319, 329
Kakiemon Sakaida (1596-1666) *see* SAKAIDA KAKIEMON
Kakiemon Sakaida, XIV (*b* 1934) 17 267, 733
Kakiemon ware *see under* PORCELAIN → wares
kaki juice 17 210
Kakimoto no Otana 22 497
Kakissa 3 45
kakizotechnos see KALLIMACHOS
Kakongo 1 403; 18 217, 219
Kakooza Wasswa, Katongole *see* WASSWA, KATONGOLE KAKOOZA
Kakō Tsuji *see* TSUJI, KAKŌ
Kakovatos 13 *363*; 14 *332*; 17 733*
faience (i) (glass) 14 358
ivory-carvings 14 353
Tomb A 14 360
Kakrak
wall paintings 1 202, *202*, 203
Kaks, Olle 30 82
kakṣāsana 15 243*
Kakuban 5 119
Kakudia Gopinatha Temple 15 319
Kakudō Tanaka *see* TANAKA KAKUDŌ
Kakugi 17 129
Kakujō 5 334; 15 158; 17 119
Kakukichi 17 132
Kakurei Yamaato *see* YAMAATO KAKUREI
Kakurinji 17 74
Kakusan Shidō 17 747
Kakutei 17 132, 185; 18 60; 28 588
Kakuyū *see* TOBA SŌJŌ
Kakuzō Okakura *see* OKAKURA, TENSHIN
Kalaa, La *see* QAL'AT BANI HAMMAD
Kalaa Bani Hammad *see* QAL'AT BANI HAMMAD
Kalaat Seman *see* QAL'AT SIM'AN
Kalabagura 15 538
Kalabari Ijo 1 257, 291, 294, 300, 342, 343, 347, 350; 15 125–6
dress 1 *348*
sculpture 1 *247*
works 15 *125*
Kalabsha 23 *276*, 286, 287
Kalach, Alberto 21 382
Kalachuri-Chedi calendar *see under* INDIAN SUBCONTINENT → calendars
Kalachuris of Chedi *see* HAIHAYA
Kalachuris of Maharashtra 15 275; 17 733*
Kalacuris of Tripuri *see* HAIHAYA
Kalagi 15 326
Kalahari Studio 29 117
Kalahasti
cotton 15 *673*
gopura 15 335
Kalahastishvara Temple 15 399
textiles 15 673–4; 30 559
Kalaibaland 6 245; 31 701
Kala-i Kafirnigan 6 *182*; 17 734–5*; 30 *252*, 440
sculpture 6 222
temple 17 734–5
wall paintings 6 232; 17 *734*
Kala-i Kakhkakh 5 171–2*; 6 *182*, 277
wall paintings 6 231–2
wood-carvings 6 220, 277
Kala-i Mug 6 *182*, 188; 17 735*; 28 *719*; 30 *252*
manuscripts 6 *189*
paper 24 48
shields 6 230
silk 28 721
textiles 6 249
Kala-i Nofin 6 244
Kalajić, Dragoš 28 451
Kalaly Gyr 6 196
moulds 6 212
ossuaries 23 607
plaster 29 821
sculpture 6 212
Kalaly Gyr I 6 223
Kalaly Gyr II 6 223
Kalamas 8 155
Kalambaka, Church of the Dormition 9 547; 25 335
Kalamis 13 450, 453; 17 735–6*
attributions 2 526, 682
works 2 682; 4 112; 30 286
kalamkārī see under INDIAN SUBCONTINENT → textiles
kalan 6 420, 421, *421*, *422*, 425
Kalan, Tepe 1 211; 14 19; 28 625
stucco 1 196; 29 824
stupas 1 192
wall paintings 1 201
Kalandario, Filippo *see* CALENDARIO, FILIPPO
Kalanga 4 489; 28 621
Kalani'ōpu'u 14 249
Kalanjara 6 444; 15 290, 414; 21 590
K'alant'aryan, Aram 9 471
Kalanti 11 98
church 11 94
Kala Pahar 15 594
Kalapodhi 13 394
Sanctuary of Artemis and Apollo 1 691
Kalapodi 13 600
Kalarrytes 13 358
Kalas 13 552
El Kalas hotel complex 1 320
kalaśa 15 243*
Kalasan 29 865
Kalash 23 798
Kalasin 30 *571*, 576
Kal'at Banī Ḥammād *see* QAL'AT BANI HAMMAD
Kalat Fakra 26 *915*
temple 26 917
Kalauria Bouleuterion 4 530; 14 73
Kalavasos 8 *325*, 333, 356; 13 *362*; 17 736*
Kalavassos-Kopetra Basilica 29 816
Kalaw-Ledesma, Purita 20 274
Kalawun *see* QALA'UN
Kalbak-tay 27 367
Kalb 'Ali 16 509
works 16 *508*
Kalcar, Jan Joest von *see* JOEST (VON KALCAR), JAN
Kalčeski, Risto 19 884
Kal'chenko, Galina N. 31 561
Kalcher, Marton 31 786
Kalckreuth, Eduard Stanislaus, Graf von 17 736; 33 38
Kalckreuth, Leopold (Karl Walter), Graf von 17 736*
groups and movements 28 341
Kalckreuth, Leopold (Karl Walter), Graf von—cont.
pupils 14 623; 21 797; 22 689
Kaldakhvara Church 12 319
Kaldenberg, F. R. 33 42
Kalden Sherab 15 311; 30 832
Kaldeway Press 20 335
Kalebwe 1 406; 29 70, 71
sculpture 29 *69*
Kalehisar 16 411
Kale-i-bogurt fortress 2 899
Kale-i Çanak *see* ÇANAKKALE
Kale-i Sultaniyye *see* ÇANAKKALE
Kalendar Pasha 16 350
Kalenge 1 *401*
Kalenić 22 79; 28 *437*
architectural decorations 22 79
monastery church 9 586; 28 442, 453
wall paintings 22 79, 80; 28 447
Kalents, Armine (Paronyan) 2 432
Kalents, Harut'yun 2 432
Kale Zohak 24 217
Kalf (family) 3 588; 25 845
Kalf, Willem 17 736–7*; 27 230
reproductive prints by others 19 731
teachers 25 363
works 11 445; 17 *737*; 22 843; 29 667, 668; 31 882
Kalff, J. 1 803
Kalgoorlie 2 740
Kalhana 15 265; 30 823
Kalhu *see* NIMRUD
Kalias 24 452
Kalibangan 15 192, 246, *264*; 17 737–9*
altars 15 193
High Mound 17 738*
ivory 15 695
Lower Town 17 738*
masks 15 705
seals 15 421
Kalidasa 15 227, 228
Kalide, (Erdmann) Theodor 17 739*; 26 23
Kalil, Mohammad Omer 29 896
Kalimantan 15 *751*; 30 554
architecture 15 773–4*
baskets 15 810
beadwork 15 814
boats 15 810
ceramics 15 811
drawings 15 807
dress 15 813
hats 15 810
houses 15 773–4*
jars 29 *232*
jewellery 15 814
lutes 15 817
masks 15 804
painting 15 807
rattles 15 817
roofs 15 773
sculpture 15 789
shrines (i) (cult) 28 640
tattoos 15 809
textiles 15 796
Kalin, Boris 14 22
Kalin, Zdenko 14 22
Kalina (Atacama) 29 187
Kalina (French Guiana) *see* GALIBI
Kalina (*fl* late 19th cent.) 8 176
Kalina, Jerzy 17 739*
Kalina, Piotr 25 120
Kalinderu, Ion 26 723, 724
Kalinderu, Nicolae 26 723
Kalinga 24 607, 624, 625, 626, 628, 631
dress 24 *629*
Kaliṅganagara *see* MUKHALINGAM
Kalinga Nippon Buddha Sangha 8 848
Kalinin *see* TVER'
Kalinin, N. S. 17 870
Kalinin, Vyacheslav 27 397
Kaliningrad 17 739–40*; 21 571; 27 *362*
alabaster-carvings 1 519
amber 1 760, 762; 6 558
Castle library 19 314
Cathedral 17 740; 31 501
chess sets 6 558
façades 4 777
metalwork 12 447
Kalınkaya 1 834
Kalinov, Stavri 5 156
Kalinowski, Horst Egon 13 727; 17 818
Kalist Gospels *see under* GOSPEL BOOKS → individual manuscripts
Kalisz
chalice 25 126
Jesuit church 13 162; 25 97
Kalisz, Jacques 2 699
Kaljundi, Tiit 10 538
Kalkar 12 *360*
St Nikolai 7 192; 17 696, 740–41*
altar 2 486; 17 *601*, *741*
Kalkar, Arnt van *see* ARNT VAN KALKAR
Kalkhuran 2 377
tomb of Shaykh Jibra'il 16 230
Kalkutin, Andrey 27 433
Kállai, Ernő 7 771; 10 650
Kallatis *see* MANGALIA
Kállay, Dušay 28 854
Kalleby 25 526, 532
Kallenbach, Kennedy and Furner 11 847; 17 603
Kallenbach, Otto 17 741–2*
Kallergis, Giorgios 22 228
Kallergis, Nikolaos 25 334
Kalliana, Hagioi Joachim and Anna 8 359
Kalliergis, George 30 718
Kallikrates 2 312; 17 742*
attributions 2 680; 13 400
collaboration 2 676; 15 132
works 13 374, 379, 394
Kallimachos 13 453; 17 742*
attributions 2 680
copies 13 *454*
works 2 681; 5 604; 13 409, 454
Kallimaki, Prince 2 869
Kallina, Mór 2 415
Kalling, Mart 30 349
Kallingas, A. G. 21 861
Kallingas, H. A. 21 861
Kallinikos *see* RAQQA
Kallir, Otto 22 189
Kallistratos 10 129
Kallithea *see under* ATHENS
Kallman, McKinnell & Knowles 4 475; 13 239
Kallmann, G. M. 31 243
Kallon 1 480; 17 742*
Kallós, Ede 20 447
Källunge 6 389; 30 75; 32 520
Kallus, Joseph 31 261
Kalm, Pehr 5 574
Kalmak 30 475
Kalman, Jean 30 688
Kalmar 8 722; 30 64, *65*
Castle 30 66, 67, 68, 70, 92, 109, 117; 32 923
Apartment of Erik XIV 30 87
furniture 30 92
interior decoration 29 748; 30 77
stucco 29 840
tapestries 30 114
Cathedral 30 *71*
Grey Hall 18 684
Kalmthout Donation 33 128, *129*
Kalmthout school 14 507; 19 792
Kalmyk 27 432, 433
Kalmyk region 27 433
Kalna 15 *279*; 17 743*
Krishna Chandra Temple 15 396
Lalji Temple 15 396
Pratapeshvara Temple 15 396
Kalnamuiža Church 18 848
Kalnay, Jorge 2 396

Kalniņš, Alfrēds 12 825
Kalniņš, Eduards 3 871; 25 745
Kalnroze, Valdis 25 745
Kalø Castle 4 781
Kalocsa
Cathedral 14 883; 26 638, 687, *687*
collections 15 17
metalwork 26 686
Piarist school 15 17
sculpture 14 895
Kalofer 5 157
Kalokairinos, Minos 18 165
Kalomo District Council Offices 33 602
Kalong
ceramics 30 609, *610*, *611*, 611–12
Kalopanagiotis 8 *325*; 9 *512*; 17 743*
Hagios Herakleidios 8 358
Kalopsida 8 330, 334
Kalo Shop 2 572; 31 650
kalos kagathos 13 413
Kaloyan 4 603; 5 *151*, 162; 9 583
kalpis *see under* HYDRIAI → types
Kalpokas, Petras 17 743–4*; 19 498; 31 854
Kalraet, Abraham van *see* CALRAET, ABRAHAM (PIETERSZ.) VAN
Kalte Kunst *see* COLD ART
Kaltemarckt, Gabriel 18 522
Kaltenhofer, Joel Paul 1 844
Kaltenhofer, Peter 4 760
Kaltenmacher, Jan Michal 8 414
Kalthoeber, Christian Samuel 4 354
Kaluga 17 744*; 27 *363*
Kologrivova House 17 744
Museum of the History of Space Exploration 17 744
Regional Art Museum 17 744; 27 440
Regional Local History Museum 17 744
Kalugumalai 15 305, 416; 24 2
Vettuvankovil cave temple 15 *417*
Kalum 3 45
Kalumburu
body arts 1 *46*
Kalundborg
Castle 8 723, 724
Vor Frue Kirke 4 781; 7 257; 8 723; 26 593, *593*
Kalundsborg Church 12 364
Kaluraz 1 786; 15 919, 921
Kalushin, Boris (Matveyevich) 27 581
Kaluyan 28 809
Kalvach, Rudolf 17 744*; 23 1; 33 166
Kalvoda, Alois 31 792
Kalwaria Zebrzydowska, Crucifixion chapel 25 104
Kalyanavarman, Ruler (*reg* 7th cent.) (Karkota) 15 264
Kalyan Das 15 612
Kalyan Singh, Raja of Kishangarh (*reg* 1797-1848) (Rajput) 15 613
Kalydon 13 *363*; 17 744–5*
couches 13 592
Heroön 14 466; 15 53; 17 745
Sanctuary of Artemis Laphria 1 128; 17 745, *745*
tombs 31 109
town walls 21 557
Kalymnos 9 566
Kalypso 33 307
kalyx kraters *see* KRATERS → types → calyx
Kama 15 632; 22 439
Kamachi 17 262
Kama Dakka 1 197
kamain see under MARKS
Kamakura 17 *11*, 22, 96, 745–50*
calligraphy 17 230
Kamakura—cont.
Engakuji 17 73, 397, 749–50*
Butsunichian 17 229
gardens 12 97
sculpture 17 132
gardens 12 97
Hachimangū Shrine 17 362
Kanagawa Prefectural Museum 17 136, 138
Kanagawa Prefectural Museum of Modern Art 17 89, *89*, 433, 436; 27 597
Kenchōji 17 132, 397, *748*, 748–9*; 25 891
gardens 12 97
Kōtokuin, *Daibutsu* (Great Buddha) 17 24
Meigetsuin 17 132
monasteries 17 231
prints 17 270
sculpture 17 747
Tsurugaoka Hachiman Shrine 17 128
Zuirokusan *see* Engakuji
Zuisenji 17 132
kamakurabori see under LACQUER → types
Kamakura period *see under* JAPAN → periods
Kamal 15 594
Kamal, Aslam 16 288; 23 800
Kamal, Yusuf, Prince 9 766, 768
Kamal al-Din Husayn 16 232
Kamal al-Mulk *see* GHAFFARI, MUHAMMAD
Kamalapuram 14 125
Kaman 15 241, 339
Chaurasi Khamba 15 340
sculpture 15 487, 488
Kamanda 33 598
Kamanets *see* KAMIANIEC
Kamanis (*reg* early 8th cent. BC) 5 729
Kamanokuchi *see under* AKAIKE
Kamara, Kadiato 1 247
Kamares 8 153; 13 *362*; 17 750–51*; 21 *651*
Kamares ware *see under* POTTERY → wares
Kamasan 15 806
Kāmasūtra 10 484
Kamaya 30 287
Kamba 1 246, 252–3; 17 906, 907; 33 598
beadwork 3 442
gourds 1 303
sculpture 17 907
wood-carvings 1 *252*
Kambadahalli 15 301, 528
Kamban 15 227
Kamban, Janus 10 813
Kambara, Tai *see* KANBARA, TAI
Kamberlen, Joseph *see* CAMBERLIN, JOSEPH
Kambli, Johann Melchior 12 424; 29 403
works 12 *425*
Kambuja 5 460
Kamburov, P. 3 527
Kambyses II (*reg* 525-522 BC) 9 *777*
Kamecke, Ernst Bogislav von 28 117
Kameda Bōsai 17 188, 751*
works 17 191, 237, *237*
Kameda Chōkō *see* KAMEDA BŌSAI
Kameda Hōsai *see* KAMEDA BŌSAI
Kamegaoka 17 *11*, 751–2*
figurines 17 103, *104*
pottery 17 245
Kamehameha I, King of Hawaii (*reg* 1810-9) 14 249
Kamei (family) 30 259
Kamei, Tobei 17 295
Kameiros 13 *363*; 26 *289*, 290, 291
faience (i) (glass) 13 *590*
jewellery 13 *598*
Kameiros—cont.
pottery 13 537, *537*
sculpture 26 291, *292*
Kamekura, Yusaku 17 752*; 25 354; 30 286
Kamenets *see* KAMIANIEC 3 525; 4 782; 31 549
Kamenev, L. L. 22 178
Kameneva Mogyla 31 545
Kamenický Šenov 8 410, 411, 425
Kamenka 25 *521*, 522
Kamenka-Buzkaya 31 557
Kamennomostsky dolmens 27 *367*
Kamenny Brod *see* KAMINNYY BRID
Kamenosuke Ogata *see* OGATA, KAMENOSUKE
Kamensetzer, Hans 20 736
Kamensky, Fyodor (Fyodorovich) 27 425
Kamensky, Valentin (Aleksandrovich) 2 99; 17 752–3*; 29 388
Kamensky, Vasily 8 250; 9 145; 18 507; 20 886
Kames, Henry Home, Lord *see* HOME, HENRY, Lord Kames
Kames Brooch 28 263
Kamesuke Kinkodō *see* KINKODŌ KAMESUKE
Kameyama 17 259
Kameyama, Emperor (*reg* 1260-74) 18 558
Kamhof 22 894
Kami, Mutsu no *see* MUTSU NO KAMI
Kamid el-Loz 17 753*; 19 9; 24 643; 30 *180*, 191
Kamieńn, Erasmus *see* KAMYN, ERAZM
Kamień Pomorski Cathedral 4 782; 25 110
Kamigamo Mingei Kyōdan 21 634
Kamigata culture *see* KYOTO; OSAKA
Kamil, Fu'ad 2 511; 5 401; 9 766
al-Kamil, Sultan (*reg* 1218-38) (Ayyubid) 5 403; 16 491
Kamilari 21 659, 679
Kamilaroi 1 49, 56
Kamil of Rohan 8 400
Kami-miharada 17 331, 332
Kamin, Erasmus *see* KAMYN, ERAZM
Kamina 1 *401*
Kaminaljuyú 13 *758*; 17 753–5*; 20 *882*; 21 *193*, 196, 199
bone-carvings 21 248
jade 21 243
pottery 17 753, 755
sculpture 16 806
seals 21 258
shells 21 259
stelae 29 619
Stele 10 21 219
talud-tablero 30 280
temples 30 448
Tomb II 17 *754*
tombs 31 *117*, 118
wall paintings 20 885
Kaminets'-Podil's'ky 2 425; 17 755*; 31 *546*
fortress 31 550
Kamini 8 *304*, 323; 22 698
Kaminnyy Brid 31 562
Kaminoudia *see* SOTIRA
Kamiński, Aleksander 18 413; 24 11; 33 450
Kaminski, Edward 5 169; 11 777
Kaminsky, A. S. 5 333
Kaminsky, Vered 16 569
Kamiya Sōji 14 703
Kamiya Te'yū 33 489
Kamizaka, Sekka 17 293
Kamman Chapra *see* VAISHALI
Kammeraterne 7 805; 30 53
Kammerer, Hans 29 874
Kammerer, Jobst 17 887
Kammerer, Marcel 2 814; 13 330; 14 749; 28 155; 30 755
Kämmer & Reinhardt 31 261
Kammerschreiber, Hans Caspar 33 279
Kamna 28 862
Kamnik Castle 28 858, *858*
Kamo 2 439
Kamo Chō Jōruriji 12 97; 17 68, 120; 30 446
Kamoda, Shōji 17 267
Kamo dolls *see under* DOLLS → types
Kamogo Tomb 17 143
Kamose 1 469
Kamose Stele 9 780, 879; 10 81; 29 615
Kampala 1 *407*
Bahā'ī temple 30 451
Makerere University
Makerere Art Gallery 31 528
Margaret Trowell School of Fine Art 1 432; 17 908; 31 528
Nommo Gallery 1 432; 31 528
Uganda Museum 31 528
Kampen 22 *813*
architecture 22 816
Bovenkerk 22 820
brick 4 778
bronze 22 894
church 22 818
masons' lodges 22 820
Onze Lieve Vrouwekerk 22 820
Oude Raadhuis 22 857
patronage 22 886
St Nicolaaskerk 13 62
textiles 22 899
Kampen, de Stomme van *see* AVERCAMP, HENDRICK (BARENTSZ.)
Kampf, Arthur 11 463; 20 807
Kampf, Avram 17 583
Kampfbund für Deutsche Kultur 22 710
Kampfmeyer, Bernhard 8 824
Kampfmeyer, Hans 8 824; 31 728
Kamphaeng Phet 30 *571*
architecture 30 582
stucco 30 603
Wat Chang Rop 30 584
Wat Kalothai 30 584
Wat Phra Sadet 30 601
Wat Phra Si Iryabot 29 826
Kamphuis, G. 18 126
Kamphuysen, Jan 3 211
Kampia, Hagios Nikolaos 9 547
Kampmann, Christian 17 755
Kampmann, Hack 13 216; 17 755–6*
collaboration 16 829
groups and movements 13 613
pupils 25 850
works 7 804; 8 728
Kampmann, Hans Jørgen 17 755
Kampmann, Jack 10 813
Kampong Ayer 5 11
Kampong Kapor Church 28 772
Kampong Melaka, Malacca Mosque 28 772
Kampong Sumbiling 5 11
Kamprad, Ingmar 20 595
Kampuchea *see* CAMBODIA
Kampung Laut Mosque 20 166
Kampung Peramu Pekan 20 176
Kampyr Kala 6 198
Kamran, Mirza *see* MIRZA KAMRAN
Kamratān 29 241
Kamrowski, Jérome 30 22
Kamsarakan (family) 30 274
Kamsarakan, Nerses, Prince 30 274
Kamsetzer, Jan Chrystian 17 756*; 25 99, 105; 32 871
collaboration 21 158; 32 879
patrons and collectors 25 212
Kamsetzer, Jan Chrystian—cont.
works 7 *416*; 18 693; 23 813; 25 99, 118, 139, 408; 32 879, *880*, 880, 881, *881*
Kamulegeya, Muhammad 31 528
Kamun Temple (North Kyŏngsang) 18 328
Kam'yanets-Podil'sky *see* KAMINETS'-PODIL'S'KY
Kamyn, Benedykt 17 757
Kamyn, Erazm 17 757*; 25 126
Kanachos (i) (*fl* 6th cent. BC) 1 481; 17 757*
Kanachos (ii) (*fl c.* 400 BC) 13 450; 17 757*; 28 712
Kanadej, Jacob 25 130
Kanae, Tanejiro 17 294
Kanae Yamamoto *see* YAMAMOTO, KANAE
Kanaga, Consuela 13 710
Kanagae Sanbei *see* RI SANPEI
Kanagawa
Ennōji 17 125
Kōtokuin 17 125
Kanais 29 386
Kanak 23 17
Kan'ami 17 22
Kanamori Sōwa 17 215, 343; 18 553, 560; 23 196
Kananga 1 *401*
Musée National 33 598
Kanaoka *see* KOSE NO KANAOKA
Kanasara 17 60
Kanashin, Yury 21 812
Kanata 23 632
Kanauj *see* KANNAUJ
Kanawa, Diggeress (Rangituatahi) Te *see* TE KANAWA, DIGGERESS (RANGITUATAHI)
Kanaya Gorosaburō 17 323
Kanayama, Akira 13 866; 17 207
Kanayama Senō 33 709
Kanazawa 17 *11*, 95, 757–8*
Castle 17 758*
ceramics 25 869
Honda Museum 17 757
Hyakumangoku Bunkaen Edo-Mura Museum 17 433; 21 648
Ishikawa Prefectural Museum 17 757
Kanazawa Bijutsu Kōgei Daigaku *see* Kanazawa College of Fine and Industrial Arts
Kanazawa College of Fine and Industrial Arts 17 421
Kasugayama kiln 18 538
Kenrokuen 12 95, 99, *100*; 17 758*
Minzan kilns 18 538
Municipal Nakamura Memorial Art Museum 17 757
Museum for Traditional Products and Crafts 17 757
porcelain 18 538
kanban see JAPAN → signs (markers)
Kanbara, Tai 17 205, 206, 758–9*
Kanbun Master 10 485; 17 280
Kanchanu 15 631
Kănchev, Petăr 5 158
Kanchi *see* KANCHIPURAM
Kanchipuram 15 *294*; 17 759–61*
Devarajasvami Temple *see* Varadarajasvami Temple
Ekambareshvara Temple 15 335, 399; 17 760
Raja-gopura 17 *760*
Kailasanatha Temple 15 304, *305*, 332, 513, 514, 559, 560; 17 759
gopuras 13 3
sculpture 15 513–14
Kamakshi Amman Temple 17 759–60
Rajasimha-Pallaveshvara Temple *see* Kailasanatha Temple
Rajasimheshvara Temple *see* Kailasanatha Temple
sculpture 15 476, *515*, 515–16

Kanchipuram—cont.
  temples 15 332, 514; 23 873; 26 48
  Vaikunthaperumal Temple 15 234, 304; 17 759
  Varadarajasvami Temple 15 335; 17 760–61
    Hundred-pillared Hall see Kalyana Mandapa
    Kalyana Mandapa 17 760, 761
Kandahar 1 186, 211
  citadel 1 190
  fort 15 365
  inscriptions 1 187
  pottery 16 425
Kandalama 29 462
Kanda-Matulu, Tshibumba 33 597
  works 1 430
Kanda-navis see HAYDAR
Kandaules (reg c. late-8th cent. BC) 4 529
Kandava Church 18 848
Kandelaki, N. 12 322
kandhara 15 243*
Kandinsky, Vasily (Vasil'yevich) 3 529; 9 20; 11 315, 547, 550; 12 396; 17 761–7*; 20 381; 22 178, 304, 379; 27 392, 394; 32 328
  dealers 16 906; 20 75
  exhibitions 2 447; 3 801; 20 12
  groups and movements
    Abstract art 1 73, 74, 76
    Abstract Expressionism 1 83
    Abstraction-Création 1 90
    Allied Artists' Association (A.A.A.) 1 666
    anthroposophy 2 138
    Art informel 2 543
    Asnova 2 603
    Bauhaus 3 400, 401, 402, 403; 12 396, 497
    biomorphism 4 74
    Blaue Reiter 4 131–3; 12 395; 22 318
    Blue Four 4 177; 18 111; 28 78
    Cercle et Carré 6 342
    Concrete art 7 698
    Dada 8 434
    Expressionism 10 694
    Inkhuk 15 856, 857
    Jack of Diamonds (Bubnovy Valet) 16 817
    Moderne Kunstkring 21 775
    Narkompros 22 508
    Neue Künstlergenossenschaft (Munich) 22 921
    Neue Künstlervereinigung München (NKVM) 22 921
    Orientalism 23 505
    Phalanx 24 591–2
    Société Anonyme 9 233
    Symbolism (movement) 30 170
    theosophy 30 710, 711
    Valori Plastici 31 852
    World of Art (Mir Iskusstva) 33 380
  house 2 552
  methods 7 630; 28 203
  paintings 17 762, 763, 765, 767; 18 717; 22 380; 32 902
  patrons and collectors
    Art Institute of Chicago 6 575
    Costakis, George 8 10
    Dotremont, Philippe 9 189
    Guggenheim, Solomon R(obert) 13 800
    Koehler, Bernhard (1849-1927) 18 187
    Kuh, Katherine 18 498
    Mattioli, Gianni 20 848
    May, Morton D(avid) 20 880
    Museum of Non-Objective Painting (New York) 1 83
    Neumann, J. B(er) (1887-1961; dealer) 23 7
    Nierendorf, Karl 13 800
    Poortvliet, Marie Tak van 14 295
Kandinsky, Vasily (Vasil'yevich)
  patrons and collectors—cont.
    Rothschild, Philippe de, Baron (1902-88) 27 225
    Städtische Galerie im Lembachhaus (Munich) 22 305
  porcelain 27 413
  prints 9 310; 19 491, 751; 25 624; 29 871; 33 363
  productions 12 497; 24 406
  pupils 2 381; 3 422; 4 60, 104; 10 863; 13 12; 22 318; 26 70; 28 556; 33 254
  studio 29 858
  teachers 2 890
  writings 1 74; 23 569; 28 396
    translated 32 753
Kandler, Charles (Frederick) (fl c. 1727-50) 10 332, 333; 17 768*; 19 593
Kandler, (Charles) Frederick (fl 1735) 17 768
Kändler, Johann Friedrich 2 127
Kändler, Johann Joachim 9 241; 12 434; 17 768–9*
  assistants 9 692
  collaboration 18 82; 21 64
  groups and movements 26 498
  patrons and collectors 8 202; 9 238; 33 115
  works 6 I2; 21 64–5, 65; 23 543; 29 574; 30 219
Kändler, Karl Adolf 18 107
Kando, Ata 33 90
Kandwa Shiva Temple 15 263, 481
Kandy 17 769–70*; 29 440
  Archaeological Museum 17 769
  architecture 29 450–51
  craftsmen and artists 29 469
  Governor's Pavilion 29 453
  jewellery 29 472
  National Museum 17 769; 29 478
  Palace Complex
    Audience Hall 29 477
    Dalada Maligava 5 98; 17 769; 29 451, 451, 477
    King's Harem see National Museum
    King's Palace see Archaeological Museum
    Magul-maduva 29 451
    Temple of the Tooth see Dalada Maligava
  religion 29 442
  sculpture 29 460
  wall paintings 29 465
  weaving 29 476
  wood-carvings 29 477
Kandzta, Grigor 30 305
Kandzta Monastery 30 306
Kane, Herb 14 251
Kane, John 17 770*; 25 5; 30 749
Kane, Julius 2 753; 18 64
Kane, Michael 16 18
Kane, Paul 17 770–71*
  works 5 564, 565
Kanegafuchi Spinning Co. 30 286
Kan'ei no Sanpitsu 17 215, 232, 343; 18 231; 28 619
Kaněk 8 394
Kaneko Kinryō 32 896
Kanem 1 394; 21 597
Kaneria, Raghav 15 173
Kanerva, Aimo (Ilmari) 11 97; 17 771*
Kanesh see KÜLTEPE
Kaneshige, Kōsuke 17 267
Kaneshige, Michiaki 17 267
Kaneshige, Sozan 17 267
Kaneshige, Tōyō 17 266, 267
Kanesuke, Fujiwara no see FUJIWARA NO KANESUKE
Kanezane, Kujō see KUJŌ KANEZANE
kang 6 691; 7 36, 67, 143, 145; 17 772*
Kang, Marquis of 6 842
Kangakai (Painting Appreciation Society) 14 218; 17 200, 793, 798
Kanganaman Wolimbit 24 68
Kangan Kitayama 30 294
Kangar Perlis State Mosque 20 166
Kangavar 15 901, 912; 17 773*
Kanggonaemal 17 773*; 18 286
Kang Hou gui 6 842, 842, 844
Kang-hsi emperor (Ch'ing; reg 1662-1722) see KANGXI EMPEROR
Kang Hŭi 12 93
Kang (ii) Hŭi-an 17 772*; 18 329
  works 17 772; 18 314, 323, 324
Kang (ii) Hŭi-maeng 17 772–3*
Kang Hŭi-ŏn 17 774*; 18 319
Kang Hŭi-u 18 259
Kanghwa Island 18 250, 261
Kangian 17 776
Kangjangjavi
  works 24 72
Kangjin 18 248, 343
  Muwi Temple 18 307, 309
Kang Kuk-chin 18 301
Kangli Naonao 6 754, 755
Kangnŭng
  Hansŏng Temple 18 293
  Hyanggyo academies 30 445
  Sinbŏk Temple 18 293
  Sŏn'gyojang house 18 72, 277
Kangra 15 619
  enamel 15 712
  painting 15 618, 619, 629, 630
  sculpture 15 483
  wool 15 666
Kang Sa-jŏng 7 203
Kang Se-hwang 17 774*; 18 331
  collaboration 14 748; 18 59
  pupils 18 53, 320; 28 759
  teachers 7 203
  works 18 315, 319, 325
Kangsŏ, Yaksu Tomb 18 313
Kang Sŏktŏk 17 772
Kang So Lee 17 774–5*
Kangu Museum 33 598
Kangwŏn Temple 18 311
Kangxi emperor (Qing; reg 1662-1722) 25 783*
  architecture 6 537, 684
  enamel 7 70
  hardstones 7 91
  horn 7 126
  jade 7 10
  paintings 6 39; 7 151; 12 51; 23 581
  porcelain 6 624, 907
  scientific instruments 7 153
Kangyoku see TACHIHARA, NORIGOSHI
Kang Youwei 6 766; 17 775*; 28 553
Kanha 17 775*; 22 457
Kanheri 5 94, 95; 15 276; 17 775–6*
  Cave 3 17 776
  Cave 11 15 277
  Cave 41 15 277
  inscriptions 17 695
  pillars 15 237, 277
  sculpture 15 451, 451
  temples 15 275
Kanibadam 30 252, 252, 253
Kaniet see ANCHORITES
Kaniewski, Xaver Jan 29 86
Kan-i Gil 30 478
Kaninë 1 538
Känischbauer, Johann Baptist 2 819–20; 18 140
Kanishka casket 26 149, 150
Kanishka I, Ruler (reg 1st cent. AD)(Kushana) 5 94; 6 197; 15 446; 24 540; 28 535; 30 17
Kaniski, Hieorhij 3 526
Kaniv
  Cathedral of St George 31 548
  Shevchenko Memorial Museum 18 481; 31 552
Kan Izue see IZUE, YUTAKA
Kanjirō Kawai see KAWAI, KANJIRŌ
Kanji Yō see YŌ, KANJI
Kanjōsō 17 663
Kanka 6 182, 379; 17 776*; 31 781
Kaňka, František Maximilián 14 65; 17 776–7*; 25 548
  attributions 8 398; 23 339
  patrons and collectors 8 426
  pupils 19 807
  works 8 379, 397, 416; 24 108; 25 427, 446
Kaňka, Vít Václav 17 776
Kankali see under MATHURA
Kankanay 24 627, 628
Kankandi 2 890, 894
  Gor'ky Dramatic Theatre 2 894
  urban planning 2 428
Kankan Tani see TANI KANKAN
Kankei 17 125
Kanken 23 445
Kankesanturai 16 864
Kankunde 14 378
Kanmu, Emperor (reg 781-806) 17 69; 18 548; 22 427; 23 592
Kann, Maurice 1 731; 9 467
Kann, Rodolphe 1 731; 9 467; 17 777*
Kannas, Tell see HABUBA KABIRA
Kannauj 15 194, 260, 261, 262, 409, 485; 17 777–8*
  Makran Nagar Temple 15 480
  sculpture 15 218, 478, 479, 479, 480, 480, 481, 481
  wool 15 666
Kannegiesser, Peter 20 714
Kannel, David 33 34
Kannia 13 16
Kannonji 17 115, 131
Kano (Nigeria) 1 386; 14 231; 17 778*; 23 129
  cushion covers 1 218
  dyes 1 250
  Emir's Palace 1 315, 383; 14 233; 23 824
  fortifications 21 597
  Friday Mosque 1 317
  houses 1 284
  patronage 1 242
  regalia 1 242
  textiles 1 249
  town walls 4 793
  University 23 135
  urban planning 23 135
  wall decorations 14 233
  Women's Teacher Training College 23 134
Kanō (family) 17 167, 419, 778–80*, 793; 18 552
  see also KANŌ SCHOOL
Kanō, Jihei 17 429
Kano, Tadao 10 580
Kanō, Tetsuo 33 480
Kanō Einō 17 779, 784
  pupils 17 177; 23 161
  writings 17 166, 416, 439, 782, 788, 797
Kanō Eisen'in 14 778
Kanō Eitoku 2 909; 17 41, 163, 779, 781, 782–6*
  groups and movements 17 794, 796
  patrons and collectors 17 22, 423
  pupils 14 214; 17 727, 786; 31 676
  works 17 40–41, 42, 175, 301, 783, 784, 795, 797; 18 560; 21 828; 23 347; 28 297; 31 253
  workshop 18 558
Kanō Hakkeisei 15 128
Kanō Hideyori 17 779, 782*
  groups and movements 17 794
  works 17 175, 175
Kanō Hōgai 17 779, 792–3*
  groups and movements 17 200, 797–8
  pupils 28 603
  works 31 253
Kanō Ikkei 17 416, 439, 779, 797
Kanō Jikeisai see KANŌ HAKKEISEI
Kanō Jinnojō 17 785
Kanō Jōshin 17 779, 781, 782
Kanō Kagenobu 17 778, 779
Kanokogi, Takeshirō 17 204
Kanō Kōho 17 788
Kanō Kōi 17 175, 779, 787–90*, 793, 797
  collaboration 17 785
  groups and movements 17 796
  pupils 17 790
Kanō Kōshi 17 788
Kanō Kōya 17 788
Kanoldt, Alexander 22 304, 921, 922, 923; 28 169
Kanō Masanobu 17 778, 779, 780*, 795; 18 550
  works 17 780
Kanō Mitsunobu 9 738; 17 163, 779, 785–8*
  assistants 17 788
  collaboration 17 786
  groups and movements 17 794, 796
  pupils 17 788
Kanō Motonubu 12 98; 17 163, 174, 779, 780–82*
  collaboration 31 198
  groups and movements 17 794, 795–6
  pupils 17 727, 782, 786
  works 17 781; 18 560
Kanō Naganobu 17 175, 779, 797
Kanō Naizen 16 802; 17 181, 182, 779, 785, 795, 797
Kanō Naonobu 17 779, 788, 789, 790–91*; 18 537
Kanō Nobumasa 18 537
Kanoria, Gopi Krishna 15 183, 742; 17 793*
Kanō Sadanobu 17 791
Kanō Sanraku 17 779, 784, 786–8*, 793
  attributions 18 557
  groups and movements 17 794, 796
  pupils 17 788
  works 17 181, 181, 786, 787
Kanō Sansetsu 17 779, 788–9*
  collaboration 17 787
  groups and movements 17 796
  works 17 40, 347, 789, 797
Kanō school 7 716; 9 738; 14 215; 17 23, 29, 163, 174, 194, 200, 419, 423–4, 437, 438, 793–8*; 23 347, 594; 30 294; 31 81
  commentaries 17 439
  members 14 214, 218; 17 195, 200, 862
  treatises 17 416*
  works 17 163, 167, 175, 184, 795, 797; 18 559, 564, 565; 22 432
  see also KANŌ (FAMILY)
Kanō Seikō 17 792
Kanō Sesshin see KANŌ YUKINOBU
Kanō Shōei 14 214; 17 779, 781–3*, 794, 796, 797; 18 560; 31 676
Kanō Shōsen'in Tadanobu 14 218; 17 779, 792, 797
Kanō Sōshū 17 779, 785*, 796
Kanō Takanobu (1571-1618) 17 779, 788, 789, 790, 791
Kanō Takanobu (1740-94) 27 595
Kanō Tan'yū 17 165, 419, 779, 782, 784, 789–92*; 18 552; 31 81
  assistants 18 537
  attributions 18 559
  collaboration 18 560; 29 924
  groups and movements 17 796, 797
  patrons and collectors 16 83; 17 423
  pupils 17 792; 18 537; 20 522
  teachers 17 788

Kanō Tan'yū—cont.
works 17 *41*, 41, 42, 234, 236, 438, *438*, *790*; 18 551, 558, 559, 564, 565; 20 286
Kanō Tomonobu 17 198
Kanō Tōun Masunobu 17 *779*, 797
Kanō Tsunenobu 17 419, *779*, 791–2*
collaboration 18 560
works 17 *792*; 18 558
Kanō Yasunobu 17 26, *779*, 791*
collaboration 18 560
pupils 14 129; 17 797
teachers 17 788
writings 17 416, 797
Kanō Yeitan Masanobu *see* FENOLLOSA, ERNEST FRANCISCO
Kanō Yōsen 31 253
Kanō Yoshinobu 17 308
works 17 *309*
Kanō Yukinobu 17 *779*, 792–3*; 18 560; 33 318
Kanō Yūsetsu Munenobu 17 781
Kanpō Yoshikawa *see* YOSHIKAWA, KANPŌ
Kanpur 15 *261*; 17 798*
Lala Bhagat 15 216
Kansa 22 551
Kansai, International Airport 1 496
Kansai Ichikawa *see* ICHIKAWA KANSAI
Kansai Koma *see* KOMA KANSAI
Kansai Koma II *see* KOMA KANSAI II
Kansai Mori *see* MORI KANSAI
Kansas 22 616
Kansas City (KS/MO) 17 *799*, 799–800*; 31 *587*
City Hall 28 830
Country Club Plaza 28 622
Harzfeld Department Store 3 748
Kansas City Power and Light Company building 2 522
Nelson-Atkins Museum of Art 17 800
collections 1 895; 6 735, 826; 7 53, 156; 15 746; 17 434; 28 663
directors 28 663
exhibitions 7 158
Greek collection 13 470
sculpture 27 47
Victoria Hotel 14 787
W. Rockhill Nelson Gallery *see* Nelson-Atkins Museum of Art
Kansetsu Hashimoto *see* HASHIMOTO, KANSETSU
Kanshambi 15 456
Kanshi, Fujiwara no *see* FUJIWARA NO KANSHI
Kan Shikyō 17 410
kanshitsu see LACQUER → types → dry
Kant, Immanuel 1 179; 8 245; 17 740, 800–802*; 26 62
groups and movements 29 890
pupils 14 446
works 1 180; 7 629; 11 315, 319; 26 736
Kantack, Walter 31 654
Kantakouzenoi 9 556
Kantakouzenos, Antonios 21 343
Kantakouzenos, John VI, Emperor of Byzantium *see* JOHN VI KANTAKOUZENOS, Emperor of Byzantium
Kantakouzenos, Manuel, Despot of Morea *see* MANUEL KANTAKOUZENOS, Despot of Morea
Kantara Castle 8 357, 361
Kantchiberd 2 427
Kantei 30 466
Kantemir, Dmitry 26 7
Kan Tenju 17 189, 237
kaṇṭha see ANTARAPAṬṬA
Kantharodei 16 864
kantharoi 17 802*
historical and regional traditions
Crete 21 *658*
Greece, ancient 13 *475*, 477, *477*, 492, 493, 513
Helladic 14 *344*
Minoan 21 *658*
materials
pottery 14 *343*
silver 21 *658*
Kantharos 24 327–8
Kanthos, Telemachos 8 364; 17 802*
Kanthos, Theodotos 21 423
Kantilya 12 252
Kantor, Helene J. 7 186
Kantor, Morris 4 94
Kántor, Sándor 29 61
Kantor, Tadeusz 17 802–3*; 18 429; 25 108
Kantounis, Nikolaos 13 352; 17 803*; 25 6
Kanu 19 72, 74
Kanu, Abu 28 692
Kanukov, E. I. 28 644
Kanuri (people) 1 303; 11 827; 14 231; 23 127, 134
Kanuri (site) 1 305
Kanvinde, Achyut 15 168; 17 803*
Kanyák, Zsófia 15 5
Kanyakubja *see* KANNAUJ
Kanyakubja, Ishana of *see* ISHANA OF KANYAKUBJA
Kanyakumari 15 *294*; 17 803*
Kan Yang *see* GAN YANG
Kanyok 1 403, 405
Kanzan Shimomura *see* SHIMOMURA, KANZAN
Kanzan Yamada *see* YAMADA, KANZAN
Kanzelaltar see under ALTARPIECES → types
Kao Chien-fu *see* GAO JIANFU
Kao Ch'i-feng *see* GAO QIFENG
Kao Ch'i-p'ei *see* GAO QIPEI
Kao Chün *see* GAO JUN
Kao Feng-han *see* GAO FENGHAN
Kao-feng Yüan-miao *see* GAOFENG YUANMIAO
Kaogu 24 435
Kaogu yu wenwu 24 435
Kao Hsiang *se* GAO XIANG
Kao-hsiung Fine Arts Research Association 30 248
Kao I *see* GAO YI
Kao K'an *see* GAO KAN
Kao K'o-kung *see* GAO KEGONG
Kaoku monkyō 17 54
Kaolack 28 405
Kao Lien *see* GAO LIAN
kaolin 4 254; 6 324
historical and regional traditions
Afghanistan 1 202
Africa 1 343
Antilles, Lesser 5 746
Buddhism 1 202; 29 462
China 6 869, 876, 880, 895, 897
France 11 607
Germany 29 574
Japan 17 263, 351, 392; 28 312
Portugal 25 311
Sri Lanka 29 462
uses
bone china 6 326
conservation 7 740
crayons 8 128
dyes 1 343
glazes 6 329
grounds 29 462
masks 17 392
paints 5 746
paper 28 312
pencils 24 353
porcelain 6 325, 869, 895, 897
pottery 6 876, 880
size 28 310
wall paintings 1 202
waxes 33 2
kaolinite 13 535; 25 477
Kao P'ien *see* GAO PIAN
Kaō Ryōzen *see* KAŌ SŌNEN
Kao Shih-ch'i *see* GAO SHIQI
Kaō Sōnen 17 170, 804*; 27 465
Kao-ti, Emperor (Southern Ch'i; *reg* 479-83) GAODI, Emperor
Kao-ti, Emperor (Han; *reg* 202-195 BC) *see* GAODI, Emperor
Kao Ts'en *see* GAO CEN
Kao-tsung, Emperor (Sung; *reg* 1127-62) *see* GAOZONG, Emperor
Kao-tsung, Emperor (Ch'ing; 1736-96) *see* QIANLONG, Emperor
Kao-tsung, Emperor (T'ang; *reg* 649-83) *see* GAOZONG, Emperor
Kaoussié, St Babylas 9 567; 20 520
Kao Yüan-kui *see* GAO YUANGUI
Kapadvanj, Batris Kotha Vav 29 635
Kapara 30 194
Kapelleveld 25 190; 31 875
Kapellus, Adolf 28 670
Kaper Koraon Treasure 9 656; 10 776; 18 826
Kapilavastu 19 790; 22 758
Kapilendradeva, Ruler (*reg c.* 1435-70) (Gajapati) 15 320
kapilī 15 243*
Kapingamarangi 23 723; 25 181, 182
Kapiśā *see* BEGRAM
Kapists 17 804*; 18 429; 25 108, 141
members 8 371; 22 423; 25 373; 32 793
Kapit, Fort Sylvia 21 596
Kapitalistisches Realismus *see* CAPITALIST REALISM
Kapitapita, N. E. 20 161
Kaplický, Josef 25 435
Kaplíř ze Sulevic, Kašpar Zdeněk 25 257
Kapljuč Basilica 6 173
Kapner, G. 28 917
Kapo 16 881, 884, 890; 17 804*
kapok 3 145; 30 538*
Kapolongo 33 598
Kapon 13 874
Kapoor, Anish 7 697; 17 805*; 21 892
Kapor (family) 14 883
Kaposi, Moritz 21 7
Káposztafalvi 14 903
kapota 15 243*
kapotālī 15 243*
Kapova 17 805*; 25 *471*, 475, 477; 27 *362*, 364
Kappata, Stephen 5 761; 33 602
Kappel 7 353
Kappel, Marcus 12 474
Kappel am Albis 30 142
Kappina Mudali 29 477
Kappstein, Karl 21 896
Kaprasová, Ludmila 8 421
Kapren 15 603, 607
watercolours 15 *607*
Kapriany Monastery 21 810, *810*
Kapros 1 795
Kaprow, Allan 17 805–6*; 23 49
collaboration 21 698
groups and movements 10 416; 17 694; 25 231, 647
teachers 24 407
works 15 869; 23 334
Kapsala 8 315
Kapsali *see* CHORA (KYTHERA)
Kap Temple 18 311
Kaptol-Zagreb *see under* ZAGREB
kaptorgas see under CASKETS → types
Kapup, Christof 12 403; 20 88; 25 726
Kap'yŏng 18 352
Kar, Chintamoni 15 172
Kar, Sanat 5 421
Kara 24 85
Kara, Jūrō 33 540
Karabacek, Joseph von 16 548
Karabagi, Kerbelai Sefi Khan 2 893; 28 644
Karabaglar 2 *890*
Karabel 19 840
Basilica 9 537, 590; 19 840
Karabulak 10 896
bronze 6 244
jewellery 6 274
sculpture 6 220
Karaburun 1 118; 10 151; 19 839
wall paintings 10 *151*
Karacaöen 5 677
karacena armour *see under* ARMOUR → types
al-Karacha *see* VILA VIÇOSA
Karachay-Circassian 27 433
Karachayev 27 432
Karachi 6 *623*; 15 *264*; 16 *105*; 17 806*; 23 *797*, 798
Aga Khan Hospital 23 799
American School 23 799
Burmah Shell Headquarters 23 799, *799*
carpets 23 802
Central School of Art 23 802, 803
ceramics 6 330
collections 23 804
enamel 15 712
Finance and Trade Centre 23 799
Institute of Business Administration 23 799
Krokala 17 806
National Council for the Arts 3 170
National Museum of Pakistan 23 804
Pakistan Art Institute 23 803
PIA Squash Complex 17 806
School of Arts and Crafts 23 803
School of Decor 23 803
Society of Contemporary Art Galleries 3 170
tomb of Muhammad ʿAli Jinnah 31 115
University 23 799
Victoria Museum 23 804
Karachin 7 24
Karácsony, László 18 89
Karadağ, Georgian church 9 548
Karadong 6 302
karae mekiki 17 186–7
Karaganda 11 299; 17 *865*, 866
Karageorgevich, Paul, Prince 28 458
Karageorghis, V. 27 608
Karagwe 1 410
Karahisar 16 422
Karahöyük 1 856
Kara'In 1 823
Karaindash 17 836; 21 286; 31 760
Karaiviram 15 516
Karaj, Sulaymaniyya Palace 1 25
Karajá 4 706, 707
Karaka, Emily 17 807*; 20 360
Karakalpak 6 254; 31 *781*; 32 321
Karakhan, Nikolay (Georgievich) 31 783
Karakhoja *see* KHOCHO
Karakhoto 6 *288*, *614*; 17 807*; 30 831
fortifications 21 592
paper 7 114
prints 6 314; 7 118
rolls 7 63
sculpture 6 719
shrines (i) (cult) 28 637
temples 5 110
wall paintings 6 779
writing-tablets 6 741
Karakirgiz 16 451
Karakis, Iosef Yu. 31 552
Karako-Kagi 17 55–6, 246
Karakorum 6 665; 21 *870*, 874, 884, 885
architecture 21 885
tents 30 476
Karakoyunlu *see* QARAQOYUNLU
karakuri ningyō see under PUPPETS → types
Karaliichev, Angel 3 874
Karalius, Gediminas 19 500
Karalyan, Iosif 2 433
Karamama 9 886; 10 36, *36*
Karaman
architecture 16 202
Emir Musa Madrasa 16 204
fortress 21 585
Hatuniye Madrasa 16 204
Ibrahim Bey Imaret 16 204
mosques 16 202
Kara Mehmed Bushatli 1 545
Karamehmedović, Muhamed 4 462
Kara Memi 16 349; 17 807*; 23 641
Karamihailova, Elena 5 154
Karamojong 1 409
Karamono Kyūbei 17 401
Karamtijević, Prvoslav-Pivo 28 451
Kara Mustafa Pasha 16 224
Karamzin, Nikolay 5 25
Karan, Donna 31 655
Karana *see* RIMAH, TELL EL-
Karana 1, Tell 10 507
Karanga 28 620
Karangasem *see* AMLAPURA
Karanis 9 645, 852; 10 758, 759; 26 *921*
sculpture 27 *89*
temple 10 759
Karanog 10 803; 23 284
Karanog Grave 712, Painter of 23 285
Karanović, Bosko 28 451
Karanovo 17 808*; 25 *471*, 498, 499
pottery 17 *808*
Karanovo culture 25 514
Karan Singh, Maharaja of Bikaner (*reg* 1631-69) (Rajput) 15 608
Karantinos, Andreas 25 334
Karantinos, Patroklos 13 349; 17 808*
Karan White Church 28 448
Karapınar Mosque 16 222
Karas, Vjekoslav 8 178; 17 808–9*; 33 593
Karasavina, Tamara 3 119
Karasch 10 720
Karashahr 6 *288*; 28 *719*
roofs 6 295
sculpture 6 298
wall paintings 6 293
Karasharly, S. 2 896
Karasujō *see* MATSUMOTO CASTLE
Karasuk culture 2 101; 27 367; 28 321
metalwork 23 495
rock art 21 882
sculpture 21 883
Karasumaru Mitsuhiro 17 809*
works 17 228, 233, *233*, 343
Karasumaru Sukeyoshi 17 809
Karataş-Semayük 10 150; 19 838
Karatay Han 16 247
Karatay ibn ʿAbdallah 18 234
Karatepe (Turkey) 1 *821*; 17 809–11*; 30 *180*; 31 456
architecture 1 831
inscriptions 1 828, 894
Museum 5 633
reliefs 1 891; 17 *810*; 30 190
sculpture 1 833; 17 *810*, 810–11; 30 187
stupas 29 867
Kara Tepe (Uzbekistan) *see under* TERMEZ
Karatsu 17 *11*, *241*, 258
ceramics 17 240, 256, 811*
kilns 17 255
porcelain 17 255
pottery 17 243, 255, *256*, 262, 351
Tōjinmachi kiln 17 811

Karau **32** 450
Karavan, Dani **16** 567, 570, 571; **17** 812*; **18** 809
Karavelov, Lyuben **5** 163
Karawari **24** 70
karayo see under JAPAN → calligraphy
Karazhusupov brothers **17** 866
karazuri **17** 275–6
Karbabad **3** 69
Karbala'
houses **16** 270
shrine of al-Husayn **16** 90, 159; **22** 322; **28** 633; **31** 110
shrines (i) (cult) **28** 634
Karbowsky, Adrien **9** 382; **12** 830
Karcher, Alusio **20** 323
Karcher, Giovanni **10** 523; **11** 5; **16** 757; **17** 812; **27** 210
Karcher, Luigi **11** 5
Karcher, Nicolas **16** 757; **17** 812*
assistants **11** 5; **27** 210
patrons and collectors **10** 523; **11** 5, 192–3; **20** 323
works **4** 857; **30** 319
workshop **11** *193*; **21** 533
Kardarz **32** 878
Kardorff, Konrad von **5** 924
Kardovsky, Dmitry (Nikolayevich) **17** 812*; **27** 580; **28** 839
pupils
Anisfel'd, Boris (Izrailovich) **2** 108
Grigor'yev, Boris (Dmitriyevich) **13** 654
Kowarski, Felicjan (Szczęsny) **18** 413
Kupreyanov, Nikolay (Nikolayevich) **18** 527
Lentulov, Aristarkh (Vasil'yevich) **19** 166
Ryangina, Serafima (Vasil'yevna) **27** 460
Semashkevich, Roman (Matveyevich) **28** 394
Shmarinov, Dementy (Alekseyevich) **28** 619
Shukhayev, Vasily (Ivanovich) **28** 643
Yakovlev, Aleksandr (Yevgeniyevich) **33** 486
Karega, Ignatas **19** 497
Karel, Hans **8** 413
Karel, Marian **12** 796
Karel, Theodor **23** 450
Karelia **11** *87*; **27** *363*, 434
Karelian **27** 433
Karelianism **11** 95
works **11** *96*
Karelin, Andrey (Osipovich) **9** 51; **17** 813*
Karen **5** 220, 247, 248, 256–7, 258, 262; **29** 229; **30** 571, 623
basketwork **30** 630
dress **5** 250; **30** 623–4*
drums (musical instruments) **30** *637*
jewellery **5** 250; **30** 634
musical instruments **22** 376; **30** 637
weapons **5** 260
Karenen **9** 820
Karer, Antonín *see* KOHER, ANTONÍN
Kåreson, Åsmund **32** 525
Karev, Aleksey **22** 508
Karfík, Vladimír **8** 380; **17** 813*
Kargala **28** 722
Kargaly Diadem **6** 237
Karger, Karl **11** 320
Karger, Mikhail (Konstantinovich) **17** 813–14*
Karghush
pots **6** *243*
Kargilik **28** *719*, 720
Kargopol' **17** 814*; **27** *363*
Kargopoulo **16** 591
Karg Retable **22** 281
Karhu, Cliff **17** 293
Karhula Glassworks **8** 803
Kariba Dam **1** 320
Karim al-Din Erdishah **18** 233
Karim al-Mulk Auhad Khan (*reg c.* 1400-21) **15** 345
Karimata Tomb **17** 144
Karim Khan Zand **17** 830
Karin-Erzerum **2** 442, 443
Karinger, Anton **17** 814*; **28** 860
Karinger, Johann Adam **8** 429
Karinyas **13** 874
Karitzky, Alexander O. **33** 137
Karja **10** *536*
church **10** 536, 538, *538*
Karkal **29** 438
al-Karkh **16** 150, 151
Karkota *see*:
KALYANAVARMAN, Ruler
LALITADIYA MUKTAPIDA, Ruler
MERUVARMAN, Ruler
PRATAPADITYA, Ruler
Karl, Landgrave of Hesse-Kassel *see* CHARLES, Landgrave of Hesse-Kassel
Karl I Ludwig, Elector Palatine *see* CHARLES LUDWIG, Elector Palatine
Karl II, Elector Palatine *see* CHARLES, Elector Palatine
Karl III Philipp, Elector Palatine *see* CHARLES PHILIP, Elector Palatine
Karl IX, King of Sweden (*reg* 1604-11)
architecture **29** 689
crown **30** 112
guns **2** 463, 464
interior decoration **13** 668; **30** 87, *88*
Karl X Gustav, King of Sweden (*reg* 1654-60) **2** 463; **17** 649; **27** 725; **31** 682; **33** 421
Karl XI, King of Sweden (*reg* 1660-97) **11** *468*
decorative works **3** 752
furniture **14** 52; **30** 93
goblets **30** *101*
medals **10** 773
metalwork **30** 105
paintings **3** 509
tapestries **30** 114, 322
Karl XII, King of Sweden (*reg* 1697-1718) **6** 519; **29** 685; **30** 105
Karl XIII, King of Sweden and Norway (*reg* 1809-18) **9** 26; **26** 99
Karl XIV, King of Sweden and Norway (*reg* 1818-44) **17** 814*; **23** 217
architecture **30** 73
interior decoration **23** 231; **30** 90, *90*
metalwork **30** 107
paintings **10** 754, 846; **30** 79
porphyry **30** 113
sculpture **11** 234; **23** 229
Karl XV, King of Sweden (*reg* 1859-72) **7** 156; **29** 690; **30** 79, 90, 96, 117
Karlbeck, Orvar **13** 864; **17** 814–15*; **33** 89
Karlberg Castle **30** 70, 88, 114, 117, 322
Karlby, Bent **32** 817
Karle **15** 194, *276*; **17** 815*, *815*; **21** 847
arches **2** 296, 297; **23** 368
inscriptions **17** 695
pillars **15** 237, 435, 436
sculpture **15** 416, *435*, 435–6*, 450
temple **15** 252, 275
Karl Eugen, Duke of Württemberg *see* CHARLES-EUGENE, Duke of Württemberg
Karl-Friedrich, Margrave of Baden-Durlach *see* CHARLES-FREDERICK, Grand Duke of Baden
Karlgren, (Klas) Bernhard (Johannes) **7** 160; **17** 816*; **33** 89
Karli **5** 94, 95
Karlik **9** 565
Karlinsky, Anton H. **17** 897
Karloukovo **30** 769
Karlovci **28** 450
Karlovo **5** 160
Karlovy Vary **8** *374*; **17** 816*
education (art) **8** 425
glass **8** 410
Hotel Pupp **8** 400
iron **8** 416
pewter **8** 415
St Mary Magdalene **8** 876
Karlsbad *see* KARLOVY VARY
Karlshafen **12** 368
Karlskrona **30** *65*
Marinmuseum **28** 613
Karlskrona Porslinsfabrik **30** 100, 101
Karlsruhe **8** 824; **12** *361*, 471; **17** 816–18*, *817*; **22** 42; **33** 594
architecture **12** 374, 375
Bankhaus Homburger **3** 175
Finanzministerium **12** 376
gardens **12** 105
Hochberg palace **18** 523
museums
Badisches Landesmuseum **17** 816; **30** 332
collections **8** 324; **17** 817
library **12** 481
Gemäldegalerie **18** 523
Hans-Thoma-Museum **30** 739
Prinz-Max-Palais *see* Städtische Galerie
Sammlungsgebäude **17** 817
Staatliche Kunsthalle **17** 817; **22** 363
collections **33** 593, 594
directors **11** 802
library **12** 481
Städtische Galerie **9** 452; **17** 818
painting **12** 394
Polytechnische Schule **33** 40
Schloss **23** 811
Schlossgarten **11** 346
Stadtkirche **33** *39*
synagogue **17** 547, 549; **33** *40*
Technische Hochschule **12** 376; **27** 335
theatre **27** 335
urban planning **12** 368; **33** 38–40
Zentrum für Kunst und Medientechnologie **17** 818
Karlsruhe B9, Painter of **13** 526
Karlsruhe majolica factory **17** 818
Karlsruhe Master **20** 704*, 748; **31** 517
Karlsruhe Passion, Master of the **14** 576; **20** 704–5*
Karlsruhe Secession *see* SECESSION (KARLSRUHE)
Karlstad, Värmlands Museum **17** 607
Karlstadt, Andreas Rudolf Bodenstein von *see* BODENSTEIN VON KARLSTADT, ANDREAS RUDOLF
Karlsteen, Arvid **20** 924; **30** 85
Karlštejn Castle **6** 59; **8** *374*, 376, *376*, 379; **17** 818–21*; **31** 104
Chapel of the Holy Cross **17** 819–20; **27** 551; **30** 705–6, *706*
bars **8** 415
frescoes **17** *820*
paintings **8** 389; **11** 451; **13** *152*, 152
Chapel of the Virgin **13** 128; **17** 819
Great Tower **23** 627
interior decoration **13** 134
Karlštejn Castle—cont.
Luxemburg Genealogy **17** 819; **33** 428
paintings **8** 389; **13** 128, 151; **17** 819–21*; **25** 275; **26** 79
restoration **2** 321
St Catherine's Chapel **13** 187
paintings **17** *819*
stained glass **8** 407
wall paintings **13** *134*; **17** 819
Karlštejn Treasure **8** 412; **19** 829
Karl Theodor, Elector Palatine *see* CHARLES THEODORE, Elector of Bavaria
Karlukovo **5** *144*; **9** *511*; **17** 821*
chapel of St Marina **5** 151; **17** 821
chapel of St Nicholas **17** 821
church **5** 153
Gligora *see* chapel of St Nicholas
Karl Wilhelm, Margrave of Baden-Durlach *see* CHARLES III, Margrave of Baden-Durlach
Karm Abu Girg **9** 848
Karmakar, V. P. **15** 171
Karman, GEG-Versand **23** 360
Kármán, Géza **17** 821*
Karmanski **32** 879
Kármán & Ullmann **17** 821*
Karmapa Buddhism *see under* BUDDHISM → sects
Karmarkar, V. P. **15** 657
Karmi, Dov **16** 565; **17** 821–2
Karmi, Ram **16** 565, 566; **17** 822
Karmi Associates **17** 822
Karmi-Melamede, Ada **17** 822
Karmi-Melzer-Karmi **16** 565; **17** 822
Karmir Blur **1** *821*; **2** *423*; **17** *822*, 822–3*; **31** 700
architecture **1** 831; **17** 822–3
fortress **24** 838; **31** 699
glass **1** 868
jewellery **1** 875; **2** 440
metalwork **2** 441
pottery **2** 439
seals **17** 823
Karmøy **32** 521
Karmravor Church **2** 429
karṇa **15** 243*
Karnadeva, Ruler (*reg* 1064-93) (Solanki) **1** 471
Karnak *see under* THEBES (i) (EGYPT)
Karna Kalachuri, Ruler (*reg c.* 1041-72) (Haihaya) **15** 263, 481
karṇalatā see KARṆARATHA
karṇamalaka see KARṆANDAKA
karṇaṇḍaka **15** 243*
karṇaratha **15** 243*
Karnavati *see* AHMADABAD
Karneia Painter **13** 525
Kärner, Theodor **12** 437
Karnes, Karen **4** 109; **31** 640
karṇprāsāda see DEVAKULIKĀ
Karo, Georg **23** 508
Karo Batak **15** 788; **23** 555
Karok **22** 549, 641, 659, 660, 668, 677
baskets **22** *660*
Karolik, Maxim **12** 608; **17** 823*
Károlyi, Count (*fl* mid 18th cent.) **26** 316
Károlyi, István, Count (*fl* mid 19th cent.) **33** 514
Károlyi, Lajos **13** 333; **33** 514
Károlyi, Sándor **23** 324
Karoridhwaja, Surya Temple **15** 487
Karos *see* KEROS
Karp, Ivan **23** 7
Karp, Raine **30** 276
Karpff, Jean-Jacques **17** 824*
Karphi **13** *362*, 441; **17** 824*; **21** *651*, 664
Karpiński, Zbigniew **17** 824–5*
Karpion **2** 676; **13** 394; **15** 132
Karr, Alphonse **3** 849
Karrana **2** 249
Karrik, Vil'yam *see* CARRICK, WILLIAM
Kars **2** 426; **16** *104*; **17** 825*
architecture **2** 428
Cathedral of the Holy Apostles **2** 434
fortifications **21** 587
Kümbed Cami *see* Church of the Holy Apostles
Museum **17** 825
Kars, Georges **17** 577
Karsen, Eduard **17** 825
Karsen, Kasparus **17** 825*; **22** 848
Karsh, Yousuf **17** 825*; **24** 656
Kar-Shalmaneser *see* TIL BARSIP
Karshi Museum **6** 283; **31** *781*
Karśnicki, Jan **27** 722
Karssen, Kaspar **29** 433
Karsten, Charles **2** 318; **4** 216; **13** 679; **21** 156
Karsten, Herman Thomas **15** 770; **30** 10; **33** 538
Karsten, Ludvig (Peter) **17** 826*
Karsters, Ruben **30** 16
Kart **14** 430
Kartasura **30** 9
Kartell **25** 27
Karteros **1** 794
Karth, Hippolyte **8** 792
Karthaia **17** 874
Karthaus-Prüll Church **14** 81
Kartli *see* IBERIA (GEORGIA)
Kartmin *see* YAYVANTEPE
Kartographische Anstalt Gustav Freytag & Berndt und Artaria **2** 512
Karttunen, Laila **11** 110
Kar Tukulti Ninurta **17** 826*; **21** *267*, 274, 286, 304
architecture **2** 639
wall paintings **21** 308, 309
ziggurat **21** 286; **33** 675
Karuga, Rosemary **17** 907
Karuizawa
Museum of Modern Art **17** 433; **32** 770
Tasaki Museum of Art **14** 161
Karunaratne, H. A. **29** 468
Karunaratne, L. K. **29** 468
Karuppur **15** 672
kārvānsarāy see CARAVANSERAIS
Karyagdy, D. M. **2** 894, 895
Karyes Church *see* MT ATHOS → Church of the Protaton
Karystios **10** 474
Karystos **21** 556; **26** *876*; **27** 15
coins **13** 586
marble **26** 876
Kaş **1** 869; **4** 850; **13** 587; **19** 837
sarcophagi **19** *839*
Kasaba Köyü
congregational mosque **16** 497
Mahmud Bey Mosque **16** 202
K'asagh **2** *423*; **9** *512*; **17** 827*
Church of the Holy Cross **2** 425; **17** 827
Kasai
sculpture **18** *486*; **29** *69*
Kasai Pende **1** 405
Kasamatsu, Shirō **17** 294
Kasan **10** 896
Kasatkin, Nikolay (Alekseyevich) **15** 891; **17** 827*
groups and movements **2** 633; **27** 395
pupils **6** 549; **12** 339; **24** 566
teachers **24** 465
kasba *see* QAṢABA
Kasba Tadla **16** 240
Kaschau *see* KOŠICE
Kaschauer, Jakob **2** 792, 799; **17** 827–8*; **32** 441
assistants **2** 799
works **33** 164
Käsebier, Gertrude (Stanton) **7** 491; **17** 828*; **33** 146
assistants **7** 491
groups and movements **24** 688, 739

Käsebier, Gertrude (Stanton)—cont.
works 24 671, *671*
Kasemann, Rutger *see* KASSMANN, RUTGER
Kasena 5 328
kasen'e painting *see under* JAPAN → painting
kasen'e prints *see under* JAPAN → prints
Kasen Yoshimura *see* YOSHIMURA, KASEN
Kasetsukō *see* KUWAYAMA GYOKUSHŪ
Kasfir, Sidney Littlefield 1 232
Kashaf Rud Basin 15 902
Kashalos, Michael 8 364
Kashan 15 *897*, *901*; 16 *105*; 17 830*
Bagh-i Fin 12 83, *83*; 16 230; 18 71
carpets 15 899; 16 474–5, *475*, 484
cobalt 16 394
cobalt oxides 4 173
kilims 18 49
Maydan Mosque 21 506, 630
mosques 17 830
pottery 4 172; 16 393, *394*, 396, 406, 408, 409, 412, 424, 425, 426
rugs 25 131
textiles 16 449
tiles 16 248, 249
Kashan, Muhammad of *see* MUHAMMAD OF KASHAN
Kashan style pottery *see under* POTTERY → wares
Kashgar 6 *288*, 295, *614*; 17 830–31*; 28 *719*, 720; 30 441
coins 6 309
fortifications 21 592
metalwork 6 314
al-Kashi 16 100
Kashi (China) *see* KASHGAR
Kashi (India) *see* VARANASI
Kashihara 17 83
Kashima, Sada Shrine 16 813
Kashimbila 6 405
Kashina, Nadezhda (Vasil'yevna) 31 783
Kashinara *see* FUJIWARA
Kashirama Dasa 15 227
Kashiwagi Jōtei 17 237
Kashiwara 17 752
Kashkar, Mar Abraham 31 434
Kashmir
architecture 15 264–6
book covers 4 IV1; 16 359
carpets 15 681
embroidery 15 676
enamel 15 712
fans 10 778
fountains 11 340
gardens 11 340; 12 74
goat-hair 16 430
ivory 15 695
lacquer 4 IV1; 18 609
manuscripts 15 548, 650–51, *651*; 16 346; 20 327
maps 15 704
metalwork 15 709
painting 15 650–51
papier mâché 24 62
sculpture 15 458, 482–3*; 30 823–4
shawls 15 665*, *666*, 676, 723
silk 15 661, 662
temples 15 *265*
trade 15 202
manuscripts 16 346
shawls 15 666
woodwork 15 721
wool 15 665, *666*
Kashmiri, Agha Hasher 5 320
Kashta (*reg c.* 770–*c.* 747 BC) 23 281
Kasiā *see* KUSHINAGARA
Kasım Ağa 1 538; 17 831*
Kasimbila 23 *129*
Kasimir I, King of Poland (*reg* 1211–29) 24 698
Kasimir III, King of Poland (*reg* 1333–70) 18 424, 427, 430; 19 835; 24 698–9*
architecture 13 57; 18 424, 430; 19 750; 24 698; 25 93, 95, 134; 27 722; 33 258
metalwork 13 161, 162; 18 429; 25 126, 129
Kasimir IV, King of Poland (*reg* 1446–92) 25 134
Kasimir the Great, King of Poland *see* KASIMIR III, King of Poland
Kasinja, Victor 20 162
Kasiulis, Vytautas 19 499
Kaska 22 546
Kaskipuro, Pentti 11 97; 17 831*
Kasli 27 425
Kasnitzis, Nikiphoros, Magistros 17 840
Kasöil 18 304
Kasongan 30 511
Kasori shell-mound 17 245
Kaspé, Vladimir 17 832*
Kasper, Ludwig 17 832*
Kasper, Ottilie 17 832
Kašperk's chest 8 394
Kasprzycki, Wincenty 17 832*
kasr *see* QAṢR
Kasradze, I. 12 320
Kasr el-Heir *see* QASR AL-HAYR EAST; QASR AL-HAYR WEST
Kassa *see* KOŠICE
Kassabaum, George E. 22 366
Kassai, István *see* STEFAN (*fl* before 1464; *d* before 1499)
Kassák, Lajos 14 896; 15 18; 17 833*, 876; 24 440, 441; 32 447
groups and movements 1 131; 7 771; 8 437; 14 901; 20 103, 104; 22 730; 31 541
patrons and collectors 30 212
works 21 793
writings 1 131
Kassander, King of Macedonia (*reg* 310–297 BC) 13 548, 551; 24 640; 30 716
Kassandra 9 554
Kassandreia 13 561
Kassapa I, King of Sri Lanka (*reg* 479–97) 29 462
Kassel 12 *360*, *361*; 17 833–6*
art forms and materials
ceramics 17 835*
faience (ii) (ceramics) 12 430; 14 491
glass 12 439
hardstones 12 462
lasers 18 809
painting 12 390, 391, 394
pigments 24 792
porcelain 14 492
rock crystal 26 486
silver 12 446
tables 12 *424*
tapestries 30 319
Bildergalerie *see* Neue Galerie
Brüder Grimm Museum 17 834
collections 12 481
Friedrichsplatz 14 492; 31 718
Gemäldegalerie 17 834
Hessisches Landesmuseum 17 835
Königsplatz 31 718
Marmorbad 21 889, 890
Museum Fridericianum 9 455, *455*, 456; 12 374, 475; 14 491; 17 834; 22 361
collections 14 492
Nahl's house 22 *437*
Neue Galerie 17 835
Dokumenta Archiv für die Kunst des 20. Jahrhunderts 2 369, 370
Ottoneum 14 491, 492; 32 339
railway station 25 854
Kassel—cont.
Riesenschloss *see* Wilhelmshöhe → Schloss
Schloss Napoleonshöhe *see* Schloss Wilhelmshöhe
Schloss Wilhelmshöhe 11 345; 12 413, 414; 13 200; 17 698–9, *835*, 835–6*; 20 868; 27 291
collections 14 492
drawings 18 638
Gemäldegalerie Alte Meister 8 887
interior decoration 12 414
Löwenburg 13 200; 17 698; 26 743; 27 323
observatory 14 491; 23 339
paintings 17 651; 18 652; 27 509; 31 71
cabinet pictures 14 492
genre 5 3; 6 346; 8 108; 14 367; 23 611
landscape 26 163, 164
mythological 3 107; 17 6; 18 652; 26 94; 27 292, *292*; 31 780
portraits 14 291; 26 164; 31 42
religious 8 293; 20 628; 25 54; 26 157, 168
still-lifes 28 902
Rondellzimmer 12 413
Staatliche Kunstsammlungen 26 546; 27 46
urban planning 9 455; 17 834, 835; 31 716
William VIII's gallery 9 11
Zwehrenturm 23 340
Kassel *Apollo* 13 453; 14 492
Kasselik (family) 14 889
Kasselik, Ferenc 17 836
Kasselik, Fidél 17 836*
Kassena 1 312
Kassimatas, Antonios I, Patriarch of Constantinople *see* ANTONIOS I KASSIMATAS, Patriarch of Constantinople
Kassis, Hafiz 17 655
Kassite 1 *852*; 3 12; 17 836–7*
architecture 21 286
dress 1 885
furniture 1 869
kudurrus 17 837
palaces 23 806
sculpture 17 *837*; 21 295
seals 1 *861*, 861; 17 836–7
terracotta 17 *837*
ziggurats 2 *236*; 33 675
Kassiteras, Theodotos, Patriarch of Constantinople *see* THEODOTOS KASSITERAS, Patriarch of Constantinople
Kassmann, Rutger 17 837*; 29 747
Kassope 9 151; 13 386, 420; 31 109
Kast, Johann Jakob 28 138
Kastabos, Temple of Hemithea 25 768
Kasteel Ammersoyen 6 53
Kastel Hermitage 14 460
Kastelli 21 692
Kasteyev, Abylkhan 17 867
Kasthamandapa *see under* KATHMANDU
Kastner, Alfred 17 723, 837–8*; 29 718
Kastner, Hans 11 819
Kastner, Jan 8 401
Kastoria 9 *511*; 17 838–41*
Cathedral 9 626
Church of the Holy Apostles 25 336
Hagioi Anargyroi 9 579; 17 840
icons 9 627
wall paintings 17 *839*
Hagion Treis 9 630
Hagios Athanasios Mouzakis 17 840
Hagios Nikolaos Euphraxia 25 334
Kastoria—cont.
Hagios Nikolaos Kasnitzis 9 579; 17 840
Hagios Nikolaos Megaleion 25 334
Hagios Nikolaos Theologina 25 334
Hagios Nikolaos Thomanos 25 336
Hagios Stephanos 9 577; 17 *839*, 839–40
icons 9 601, *601*, 627, 630
Panagia Koumbelidiki 7 256; 17 840
Panagia Navriotissa 17 840
Rasiotissa Church 25 335
Taxiarchis Mitropoleos 9 577; 17 840
Kastraki *see* ASINE
Kastri 8 *304*, 323; 18 570*
bastions 21 551
bronzes 8 323
copper 8 323
fortifications 8 310; 25 522
Kastrop, Bartold 26 1
Kastrophylakas, Georgios 25 334
Kastrup 8 748
Kastrup Glasværker 8 749, 750
Kasturi, Hijas, Associates 20 168, 169
Kasubi Nabalagala 1 309
Kasugayama *see under* KANAZAWA
kasuri see JAPAN → ikat
Kat, Anne-Pierre De *see* DE KAT, ANNE-PIERRE
Katá Bethlen, Princess of Transylvania 14 905
Katachapura 15 538
Katagiri Sadamasa *see* KATAGIRI SEKISHŪ
Katagiri Sekishū 17 344
katagogeia 13 386
kata houses *see* AFRICA → houses
Katajanokka 32 861
katakana see under SCRIPTS → types
Katalog 24 451
Kataluva, Purvarama 29 466
Katane *see* CATANIA
Kataragama 5 97
Katarikawe, Jak 1 430, 431; 17 907, 908
works 1 *432*; 17 *907*
katatexitechnos see KALLIMACHOS
Katayama, Tōkuma 17 87, 88, 841*
works 17 *87*; 31 79
Katayama Naoyoshi 17 411
Katchatrian, A. 9 528
Kate, Herman Frederik Carel ten 8 282; 17 841*
teachers 18 481
works 22 848, *866*
Kate, J. M. H. ten 17 841
Kate, Lambert (Hermansz.) ten 1 808; 22 895; 27 270
Katego 14 376
Katelai 15 718
Katelanos, Frangos 21 345; 22 228; 25 330, 335
Kateřina of Lokšany 8 395
Katerine 13 384
Katha *see* YAZD
Katharina von Lokhorst 20 644
Kathesimbhu 22 771
Kathi 15 176
Kathiawar 15 676
Kat Hing Wai 14 720
Kathmandu 17 841–3*; 22 *753*, 754–5
architecture 22 759
Bagh Durbar 22 764
Bhimsen Stambha 22 764
Central Library 22 796
Dhvaka-bahal 22 763
Hanuman Dhoka Palace 22 765, 768, 785
Itum-bahal 22 763, 774
Jagannatha Temple 22 *762*
Kathmandu—cont.
Janaki Mandir 22 765
Kaiser Mahal 22 765
Kashthamandapa 17 *842*; 22 760, 761
Manjushri-Tol 22 770–71, *771*
manuscripts 15 544
National Museum 22 796
Police Club 22 796
Rastriya Nachghar 22 759
Royal Palace Hotel 22 776
sculpture 22 774, 775, *775*
Singha Durbar 22 765
Taleju temple 22 774
temples 22 761
White Matsyendranatha temple 22 756
Yatkha-bahal 22 774
Kath Mosque 6 211
Katinamakulam, Mahadeva Temple 15 721
Katinas, Linas 19 500
Katinsky, Julio 21 123
Katiram 15 609
Kato, Ariaki 20 269
Katō, Hajime 17 266
Katō, Kiyoyuki 17 267
works 17 *268*
Katō, Kōzō 17 267
Katō, Seizō 17 267
Katō, Shigetaka 17 267
Katō, Tokuro 17 267
Katō Bunrei 30 294
Katoğlu, Oya 33 595
Kato Lefkar, Church of the Archangel Michael 8 358
Kato Panagia Church 9 550
Kato Potamia, Hagios Mamas 22 700
Katō Tamikichi 28 496
Katowice 25 116
State Higher School of Fine Arts 25 142
Kato Zakros 13 *362*; 17 843–4*; 21 *651*
faience (i) (glass) 21 683
ivory-carvings 21 660, 681
palace 17 843–4; 21 651, 658, 663, 691; 23 808
pyxides (vases) 21 656
rhyta 21 659, *663*, 664
sandstone 21 662
stone vessels 21 690
towns 21 664
water supply 21 662
Katranide, Queen of Armenia (*fl c.* 879) 2 435
Katranide, Queen of Armenia (*fl c.* 1001–10) 2 97
Katras 15 321
Katrina, Mary 28 585
Katsamba 21 *651*, 674, 675, 681
Katsev, Vladimir 17 867
Katsina 1 305, *381*; 14 231; 23 *129*
Katsina Ala 1 *386*; 23 *129*, 179, 180
terracottas 1 *221*
Katsman, Yevgeny 2 633
Katsuhiko Narita 21 892
Katsuhiro Yamaguchi *see* YAMAGUCHI, KATSUHIRO
Katsukawa school 17 283–4*, 844*
Katsukawa Shunchō 1 582; 17 278, 284, 285, 844, 845–6*
Katsukawa Shun'ei 17 845*
pupils 17 844
teachers 17 844
works 17 284, *845*
Katsukawa Shungyoku 17 845
Katsukawa Shunjō 17 284
Katsukawa Shunkō (1743–1812) 17 844–5*
groups and movements 17 844
teachers 17 844, 845
works 17 284
Katsukawa Shunkō (*fl* 1800–40) 17 844

Katsukawa Shunkō (*fl* 1806-21) *see* KATSUKAWA SHUNSEN
Katsukawa Shunrō *see* KATSUSHIKA HOKUSAI
Katsukawa Shunsen 17 846*
groups and movements 17 845
teachers 17 844, 845
works 17 284, 286
Katsukawa Shunshō (1726-92) 17 844–6*
collaboration 15 896; 18 95
groups and movements 17 844
pupils 17 844, 845, 846; 28 599
works 17 *176*, 177, 278, 283, *283*, 284
Katsukawa Shunshō (1743-1812) *see* KATSUKAWA SHUNKŌ
Katsukawa Shunsui 17 844
Katsukawa Shuntei 17 286, 844, 845
Katsukawa Shunwa 17 845
Katsukawa Shunzan 17 284
Katsuma Ryūsui 17 410
Katsumasa Nakagawa *see* NAKAGAWA, KATSUMASA
Katsumi Eguchi *see* EGUCHI, KATSUMI
Katsumoto Hosokawa *see* HOSOKAWA KATSUMOTO
Katsuo Takei *see* TAKEI, KATSUO
Katsura Detached Palace *see under* KYOTO → palaces
Katsura Funakoshi *see* FUNAKOSHI, KATSURA
Katsuragi Sanjin *see* JIUN SONJA
Katsura Rikyū 23 823
Katsura Tadaharu 12 100; 31 400
works 31 *400*
Katsurō Yoshida 21 892
Katsushika Hokusai 9 738; 17 177, 846–8*
assistants 33 318
attributions 31 204
collaboration 17 285
exhibitions 17 436; 33 165
paintings 17 177
patrons and collectors 10 487; 11 748; 14 163; 28 670
prints 17 440
albums 17 287
book illustrations 16 84; 17 273, 288, 289, 415
landscape 2 8; 17 271, 287, *847*; 22 231, *231*; 31 53
shunga 10 *485*, 486; 17 280
surimono 17 286, 287
pupils 17 287; 31 253
teachers 17 844
Katsushika Ōi 33 318
Katsu Shikin 17 412, 414, 848*
pupils 17 412
teachers 18 191
works 18 190
Katsutoshi Saito *see* SAITO, KATSUTOSHI
Katsuyama-chō, Ayazuka Tomb 17 59
Katsuzō Satomi *see* SATOMI, KATSUZŌ
Kattakurgan 6 250; 31 784
al-Kattan, Ibrahim 17 654
Kattasay 23 608
Kattutu 14 *232*
Katu 32 487
Katuwas (*reg c.* early 10th-early 9th cent. BC) 5 729
Katz, Alex 8 110; 17 849*; 29 670
Katz, Mané *see* MANÉ-KATZ
Katzenbach 28 299
Katzenellenbogen, Adolf 17 849*
Katzenelnbogischer Willkomm 12 442
Katzheimer, Bernhard 17 849
Katzheimer, Lorenz 20 801
Katzheimer, Wolfgang (*c.* 1430/5-1508) 17 849*; 20 690
Katzheimer, Wolfgang the younger (*fl* 1478-93) 17 849
Kauage, Mathias 23 736, 737
Kaua'i 14 248, 249
see also HAWAII
Kaub, St Trinitatis 9 156
Kaufbeuren 12 455, 456
Gablonzer Schmuckwaren-Industrie 12 456
Kauffer, E(dward Leland) McKnight 7 653; 17 850*; 28 808
groups and movements 8 264; 13 712; 23 438
productions 30 687
works 5 841; 7 653; 25 351, *352*; 29 628; 31 706
Kauffman, (Maria Anna) Angelica (Catharine) 14 585; 17 850–53*; 19 620; 22 480; 26 774; 30 125, 133; 33 308, 721
dealing 30 345
patrons and collectors
Anna Amalia, Duchess of Saxe-Weimar (1739-1807) 33 116
Esterházy, Miklós II, Prince (1765-1833) 10 530
Fries, Moritz, Graf von 11 789
Garrick, David 12 165
George III, King of Great Britain (*reg* 1760-1820) 14 144
Hervey, Frederick Augustus, 4th Earl of Bristol 14 486
Hill, Thomas Noel, 2nd Baron Berwick 14 539
Macklin, Thomas 20 25
Pleydell-Bouverie, Jacob, 2nd Earl of Radnor 25 39
Poniatowski, Stanisław, Prince 25 213
Sanfré, Alexandre de Sousa Holstein, Conde de 29 100
Spinola (family) 29 411
Temple, Henry, 2nd Viscount Palmerston 30 451
Yusupov, Nikolay (Borisovich), Prince (1751- 1831) 33 579
Zamoyski, Stanisław 33 607
personal collection 25 383
reproductive prints by others 3 308; 5 216; 13 220; 18 149; 20 400; 26 231; 27 463; 28 597, 823; 29 675; 32 426
works 7 340; 9 285; 11 *429*, 430, *430*, 471; 17 *851*, *852*; 21 761
Kauffman, Craig 19 702; 27 277; 31 609
Kauffman, Joseph Johann 17 850
Kauffmann, Aage B(asse) G(ustav) von 17 853*
Kauffmann, Hermann 12 394; 17 853*
Kauffmann, Richard (1887-1958; architect) 16 565; 17 853–4*
collaboration 14 686; 26 21
works 30 421
Kauffmann, Yitzchak *see* KAUFFMANN, RICHARD
Kauffmann Doig, Federico 6 523
Kaufman, Herbert 13 727
Kaufmann, Edgar J. 25 5; 33 404
Kaufmann, Isidor 17 576
Kaufmann, Johann Michael 33 240
Kaufmann, K. M. 1 93
Kaufmann, Oszkár 17 854–5*
Kaufmann, Richard von (*fl* 19th cent.; collector) 12 474
Kaufmann, Theodore 22 536
Kaufmann Haggadah *see under* HAGGADOT → individual manuscripts
Kaufmann Mishneh Torah see CODICES → individual manuscripts → *Codex Maimuni*
Kauit 10 12
Kaukab el Hawā *see* BELVOIR CASTLE (ISRAEL)
Kaulak 17 855*; 29 295
Kaulbach, Christian 17 855*
Kaulbach, Friedrich 17 855, 856*; 22 304
Kaulbach, Friedrich August von 14 227; 17 855*
Kaulbach, Hermann 17 855*
Kaulbach, Karl 17 855*
Kaulbach, Philipp Karl Friedrich 17 855*
Kaulbach, (Bernhard) Wilhelm (Eliodorus) 17 855–6*; 22 303
patrons and collectors 25 836
pupils 17 856, 879; 26 245; 29 848; 30 205
teachers 12 394
works 14 587; 32 683
Kaulonia 13 586
Kaunas 17 856*; 19 *494*
A. Žmuidzinavičius Memorial Museum 33 689
Castle 19 495
Cistercian church 19 495
Franciscan Monastery 19 495
House of Perkūnas 4 783
Jesuit church 19 497
M. K. Čiurlionis State Art Museum 7 363; 17 856; 19 499
Pac Palace 19 496
parish church 19 495
St Nicholas 19 495
Kaunda, Alice 20 161
Kaunda, Berlings 20 161
Kaundinya 14 560
Kaunitz, Dominik Andreas, Graf 20 494; 28 836; 33 713
Kaunitz, Max Ulrich, Graf 26 316
Kaunitz-Rietberg, Wenzel Anton, Prince 17 856–7*; 32 444
architecture 14 645; 25 154
catalogues 20 915
collections 2 829
gardens 32 460
paintings 11 680; 19 166; 31 680
sculpture 33 587, 623
sponsorship 14 645
Kaunos 5 741, 743
Kaup, Jakob 3 475
Kaupang 23 219; 32 533
Kaurashi *see* KARACHI
kauri 23 65, *67*
Kaus, Max 17 857*
Kausambi 15 193, *261*, *285*, 409; 17 857*
arches 2 297
fortifications 4 793; 15 248; 21 590
Ghositarama Monastery 15 251, 441
plaques 15 717, 718; 30 510
ring stones 15 423
sculpture 15 424, 426–7, 439, *440*, 455, 480; 30 510
Kausar, Sajjad 18 647
Kauser, József 14 889; 17 858*
Kauser, Lipót 11 34
Kaushany 21 810, *810*, 811
Kautilya 15 194; 21 590; 23 817
Kautokeino 23 *218*
BOARCHs Kulturhus 23 222
Kautsch, Heinrich 20 925
Kautsch, R. 9 528
Kauw, Albrecht (1621-81) 3 823; 8 823; 9 397; 12 389
Kauzer, József 14 524
Kauzlarić, Mladen 17 858*
collaboration 8 766; 12 887
groups and movements 9 672; 15 66
Kavadh I 9 654
Kavajë 1 *537*, 543, 545
Good Friday Church 1 538
Kavajë Glassworks 1 543
Kavak 5 675
Kaván, František 8 393
Kavanagh, J. M. 16 17
Kavčič, Franc *see* CAUCIG, FRANCESCO
Kaveripakkam 15 516
Kaveripattinam 15 *294*, 409; 17 858–9*
Kavertzas, Frangias 25 333
Kavindrarimathana 2 55; 5 462
Kavi Ramabhadriah 15 647
Kaviyur 15 *294*; 17 859*
cave temple 15 306, *521*, 522; 17 859
Mahadeva Temple 15 524, *524*, 721; 17 859
wood-carvings 15 *722*
Kavka, Herald 30 55
Kavlak *see* KAULAK
Kavlashvili, K. 12 320
Kavos, Al'bert (Katarinovich) 3 733; 4 598; 17 859*
Kavos, Tsezar 17 859
Kavousi 4 607; 8 154
Kavvadias, P. 10 432
Kawa 9 *774*; 17 859–60*; 23 *276*, 279, 282
faience (i) (glass) 13 590
inscriptions 23 282
jewellery 23 282
reliefs 30 237
sculpture 23 285; 30 237
shrines (i) (cult) 23 281
stelae 23 282
Temple A 17 859
Temple of Amun 23 281
Temple T 17 859–60
Temple of Tutankhamun 23 280
Kawab 9 859
Kawabata, Minoru 17 860*; 33 562
Kawabata, Ryūshi 17 201
Kawabata Gyokushō 11 821; 17 860
Kawachi *see* CAHUACHI
Kawachi, Seiko 17 296
Kawachi Daijō Ieshige 17 393
Kawada, Kikuji 17 860*
Kawaguchi, Kigai 17 206, 860*
Kawaguchi, Mamoru 30 289
Kawahara Keiga 17 186, 187*; 22 429; 28 670
works 22 *429*
Kawai, Gyokudō 17 433, 860–61*; 33 562
Kawai, Kanjirō 17 861*
collaboration 14 98
groups and movements 17 265; 21 634
patrons and collectors 17 433; 23 371
works 17 265–6; 18 555
Kawai, Kozo 17 87
Kawai, Senro 17 413, 861*
Kawaiisu 22 659
Kawaika-a (AZ)
pottery 22 *604*
Kawai Sen'emon 17 861
Kawait 10 51, 52
Kawajiri, Taiji 17 408
Kawakami Fuhaku 14 37
Kawakami Tōgai 17 198, 419, 420; 30 256
Kawakasi, Kiyoshi 30 256
Kawakatsu, Hata no *see* HATA NO KAWAKATSU
Kawakita, Renshichirō 17 421
Kawakubo, Rei 9 294
Kawamata Tsuneyuki 17 177
Kawamura, Kiyoō 17 204
Kawamura Bunpō 17 273
Kawamura Jakushi 16 787
Kawamura Meikei 17 410
Kawanabe Kyōsai 17 290, 861–2*
pupils 7 701
works 17 200, 216, *216*
Kawanishi, Hiroshi 28 301
Kawara, On 17 862*
Kawara bugyōsho (Office of Tiles) 27 470
Kawaradera 17 67
Kawarake ware *see under* POTTERY → wares
Kawara Mosque 1 316
Kawasaki
Nihon Minkaen 17 331; 21 648
Open Air Museum of Japanese Traditional Houses 17 434
Kawasaki Corp.
motorbikes 15 *826*
Kawasaki Kyosen 17 277
Kawase, Chikushun 17 266
Kawase, Hasui 17 294
Kawase, Shinobu 17 266
Kawashima Textile Mills 30 329
Kawazoe, Noboru 17 90; 21 317; 23 627
Kaw Church 23 288
Kawd am-Sayla 2 263
Kawit 10 66
Kawkab al-Hawā *see* BELVOIR CASTLE (ISRAEL)
Kawm al-Ahmar *see* HIERAKONPOLIS
Kawm al-Gi'eif *see* NAUKRATIS
Kawm Umbū *see* KOM OMBO
Kay, Arthur 26 107
Kay, Dorothy (Moss) 29 108
Kay, James E. De *see* DE KAY, JAMES E.
Kay, Joseph 7 502
Kay, Nathaniel 13 875
Kaya 22 198
Kayabi 4 706
Kayaleh, John 17 654
Kayalıdere 1 *821*, *849*, 894; 17 862–3*; 21 *267*
architecture 1 831
figurines 31 *700*
temple 1 830
Kayalpatnam 15 359
tomb of Shaykh Sam Shahab al-Din 15 359
tomb of Shaykh Sulayman 15 359
Kayama, Matazō 17 180, 202, 863*
Kayan 9 164; 15 773, 774, 804; 20 167, 181, 182
beadwork 4 I2
Kaya ware *see under* POTTERY → wares
Kaybelsky 27 434
Kayck, Daniel 30 884
Kaye, John William 10 580
Kaye, Richard 13 664
Kayenta (AZ) 22 626
Kayes 20 198
Kayiga, Kofi 16 884; 17 863*
Kayim 15 615
Kayışzade osman 22 385
Kaykubadiye 16 186
Kaymaklı 5 673
Kaynarbayev, A. 17 867
Kayō Shirai *see* SHIRAI KAYŌ
Kayragach 10 896
Kayser, Fredrik 23 234
Kayser, Heinrich 17 864–5*
Kayser, J. P., & Sohn 12 453; 22 894; 24 580, 581
works 12 *453*
Kayser, Victor 12 402; 17 863*
Kayseri 16 *104*; 17 864*
carpets 2 439; 16 477, 479; 31 455
Çifte Kümbed 16 185
Çifte Medrese 16 184
congregational mosque 16 222, 497
Döner Kümbed 16 246; 22 323
fortifications 16 186
houses 16 266
Huand Hatun 16 184; 17 864
Khwand Khatun *see* Huand Hatun
Kösk Medrese 16 204
manuscripts 16 329
Sahibiye Madrasa 16 184
Sirçalı Kümbed 16 204
tomb of Ali Cafer 16 204
tombs 16 185
town walls 21 583
Kayserlich Franciscische Akademie der freyen Künste 24 443
Kayser & von Grossheim 9 382; 17 864–5*; 26 190; 28 95
Kayts 16 864
Kayungu 14 376

Kayuweng **18** 484
Kazafranko, Mavro **28** 445
Kazakh (people) **7** 143, 144; **10** 874; **16** 451; **17** 866; **30** 474, 475
Kazakh (Azerbaijan) *see* QAZAKH
Kazakh/Borchaly carpets *see under* CARPETS → types
Kazakhstan **6** 181; **16** *105*; **17** *865*, 865–8*
architecture **17** 866–7*
carpets **17** 867–8
collections **6** 284*
decorative arts **17** 867–8*
historiography **6** 280*
jewellery **6** 272, 274; **17** 868
museums **6** 284*
painting **17** 867*
pendants (jewellery) **17** *868*
sculpture **6** 220; **17** 867*
shrines (i) (cult) **16** *198*
silver **17** *868*; **28** *723*
textiles **17** 867–8*
woodwork **16** *501*
Kazakov, Dimitar **17** 868*
Kazakov, Ivan (Semyonovich) **31** 783
Kazakov, Matvey (Fyodorovich) **17** 869–71*; **27** 375
collaboration **4** 598
patrons and collectors **26** 731
pupils **33** 517
restorations **12** 633
restorations by others **4** 313
teachers **31** 543
works **17** *870*; **22** 171, *172*, 181; **23** 26; **27** 375, 376, 403–4; **31** 486
Kazaks, Jēkabs **17** 871*; **26** 384
Kazakura, Shō **22** 742
Kazan' **17** 871–2*; **27** *362*, *363*, 434
architecture **27** 434
glass factory **27** 403
kremlin **17** *872*
Museum of Fine Arts (Tatarstan) **17** 872; **27** 440
School of Art **27** 434
State Museum of Tartary **6** 285
urban planning **18** 543
Kazan, Emperor (*reg* 984-6) **17** 222
Každharadok, St Nicholas **3** 526
Kazanluk **5** *144*, 145; **25** *471*
tomb **4** 112; **5** 150; **13** 551; **17** 872–3*; **30** *768*, 769, 772
Kazanowski (family) **25** 137
Kazanowski, Adam **32** 869
Kazan Watanabe *see* WATANABE KAZAN
Kazar, Vasile **13** 653; **17** 873*
Kazarma **30** 738
Kazhakuttam, Mahadeva Temple **15** 522
Kazhangorodok *see* KAŽANHARADOK
Kazhukkuta **15** 721
Kazi Kasba *see* VIKRAMPUR
Kazimierz Dolny **17** 873–4*; **25** *92*
Church **17** 873
Przybyła houses **25** 97, *97*
University **24** 699
Kazinczy, Ferenc **14** 901; **20** 439
Kazokas, Leonardas **19** 499
Kazovskij, El **14** 897
Kazuhara Tomb **17** 144
Kazuki, Yasuo **17** 874*
Kazuma Oda *see* ODA, KAZUMA
Kazumasa Ishikawa *see* ISHIKAWA KAZUMASA
Kazumasa Nagai *see* NAGAI, KAZUMASA
Kazumasa Nakagawa *see* NAKAGAWA, KAZUMASA
Kazumasa Yamashita *see* YAMASHITA, KAZUMASA
Kazumasu Nakakawa *see* NAKAKAWA, KAZUMASU
Kazunari Sakamoto *see* SAKAMOTO, KAZUNARI
Kazuo Shinohara *see* SHINOHARA, KAZUO
Kazuo Shiraga *see* SHIRAGA, KAZUO
Kazuo Yagi *see* YAGI, KAZUO
Kazvin *see* QAZVIN
Kazwini *see* ZAKARIYYA' IBN MUHAMMAD AL-QAZWINI
Kazymzade, K. **2** 896, 897, 902
Kea **8** *304*, 305; **13** *363*; **17** 874*
Archaeological Collection **8** 323
figurines **8** 309; **21** 680
gold **8** 322
pottery **8** 309
statuettes **8** 323
stone vessels **8** 317
temple **8** 309
wall paintings **8** 309, 318, 321*; **21** 675
Keall, E. J. **25** 773
Keam, Thomas **22** 676
Kean, Charles **2** 642; **12** 841; **30** 680, 681
Kean, Michael **8** 776
Keana **15** 101
Keane, J. B. **16** 11
Kearn Brothers **16** 886
Kearny, Francis **17** 624; **30** 853
Kearsley, John **24** 596
Keating, George **8** 864
Keating, John **16** 17, 35, 36, 37; **17** 875*
Keating, Tom **11** 306, 307, 309
Keating, William **21** 264
Keaton, Buster **25** 351
Keats, John **13** 304; **22** 111
Keay, Lancelot **19** 506
Keayne, Robert **4** 472
Keban **1** *849*, 895
Keban region **1** *821*; **17** 875*; **21** *267*
Kebar, Karel **31** 135
Kebara **30** 181
Kebo Edan **15** 785
Kebo Iwa **15** 785
Kebran, Church of Gabre'el **10** 566, 569, 572
Kechel, Caspar **27** 228
Keck, Anthony **30** 268; **32** 782
Keck, Charles **32** 109
Keck, George Fred **17** 875–6*
Keck, William **17** 875–6*
Keck & Keck **17** 875–6*
Kecskemét **14** *881*; **31** 541
Church **13** 162
Kecskemét Gallery **14** 890; **20** 447
Kecskemét Studio **15** 2
metalwork **15** 7
Ornate House *see* Kecskemét Gallery
School of Enamel Art **15** 8
Kecskemét colony **13** 333; **16** 795; **17** 876*; **22** 434; **24** 457
members **17** 833
Kecskeméti, W. Péter **15** 6, 7; **17** 876*
Kedah
Zahir Mosque **20** 166
Kedainiai **19** *494*
church **19** 496
Kedaroja **14** 66; **15** 533
Keddy, Kistappa **9** 427
Kederminster Gospels *see under* GOSPEL BOOKS → individual manuscripts
Kedington (Suffolk), SS Peter and Paul **25** 726
Kediri **15** 801
Kedjom Kegu *see* BIG BABANKI
Kedjom Kitingo *see* BABANKI-TUNGO
Kedleston (Derbys), All Saints **10** 265
Kedleston Hall (Derbys) **1** *136*; **7** 339; **8** 281; **9** 16; **10** 233; **25** 192; **31** 351
drawings **9** 30
frames **11** 429, 431
furniture **10** 294, 295; **19** 426
interior decoration **23** 544; **29** 806
paintings **9** 77; **19** 816
Kee, Jenny **2** 768
Keefer, Jeanne **2** 766
keel arches *see under* ARCHES → types
keeled roll mouldings *see under* MOULDINGS → types
Keeler, Rufus **30** 888
keel mouldings *see under* MOULDINGS → types
Keely, Patrick Charles **17** 877*; **18** 629
Keen, Ian
works **1** *45*
Keene, Charles **17** 440, 877*; **32** 903; **33** 369
Keene, Henry **17** 877–8*; **23** 688
collaboration **21** 607; **23** 21
groups and movements **13** 200
works **9** 323; **23** 782
Keene, John **4** 363
Keene, Joseph **9** 317
Keene, Theodosius **17** 877
Keenes cement **1** 516; **29** 812
keeps *see* DONJONS
Keeramalai **16** 864
Keere, Pieter van der **10** 391; **18** 73; **20** 364
Keerel, Jaeckes **32** 709
Keerinckx, Alexander *see* KEIRINCKX, ALEXANDER
Keermiqi **6** 308; **27** 367
Kees & Colburn **31** 464
Keetman, Peter **17** 878*; **29** 608
Kef, Le *see* LE KEF
El Kef, Museum of Popular Arts and Traditions **31** 427
Kefallinia *see* KEPHALLINIA
Kefallinos, Yannis **10** 379; **22** 74
Kefar Bar'am Synagogue **17** *540*, 541
Kefe *see* KAFFA
Kefermarkt Altar **2** 800; **10** 455; **18** 451; **28** 134
Kefermarkt Altar, Master of the **8** 383; **18** 450; **20** 705*
Kefkalesi **1** *821*, 894; **17** 878–9*
citadel **17** 878
fortress **31** 699
reliefs **17** 878–9; **21** 553; **31** 700
sculpture **1** 830, 833
Keflavík, Leifur Eiríksson Terminal **15** *68*, 72
Kefre Beh Church *see* GÜNGÖREN CHURCH
Kefre Zeh *see* ALTINTAŞ
Keftiu **21** 653
Keger, Mathias **22** 919
Kegon Buddhism *see under* BUDDHISM → sects
Kegoshi Tomb **17** 377
Kehr, G. J. **16** 547
Kehren, Josef **26** 256
Kei **17** 729, 879*; **18** 195; **22** 492; **31** 675
works **22** 501
Keibel **27** 584
Keibun Matsumura *see* MATSUMURA KEIBUN
Keien **17** 126
Kei Fujiwara *see* FUJIWARA, KEI
Keifukuin Gyokuei **17** 167
works **17** *168*
Keiga Kawahara *see* KAWAHARA KEIGA
Keiho Takada *see* TAKADA KEIHO
Keiichirō Kume *see* KUME, KEIICHIRŌ
Keikai Kyōkai *see* KYŌKAI KEIKAI
Keikin Hori *see* HORI, KEIKIN
Keil, Alfredo **17** 879*
Keil, Bernhard **17** 879–80*; **22** 843
works **17** *880*
Keil do Amaral, Maria da Silva Pires **30** 882
Keiley, Joseph T. **29** 657
Keilhau, Eberhard *see* KEIL, BERNHARD
Keilhorn, F.
frames **11** *469*
Keiller, Alexander **2** 850, 851
Keim, Adolf Wilhelm **28** 714
Keim, Johann Christian **33** 429
Keiner, Julia **16** 569
Keion Sumiyoshi *see* SUMIYOSHI KEION
Keio University *see under* YOKOHAMA
Keipper, Georg **33** 300
Keir Collection *see under* HAM
Keirinckx, Alexander **17** 880–81*; **22** 843; **25** 68; **28** 235; **32** 724
Keisai Eisen **17** 273, 285, 286, 287, 290
Keisai Masayoshi **17** 273; **18** 96; **28** 598
Kei school **17** 98, 100, 121, 131, 750
Keiseikai **17** 239
Keisen Tomita *see* TOMITA, KEISEN
Keishin **17** 660
Keisho Nakai *see* NAKAI, KEISHO
Keisho Shūzui **28** 493
Keishū **17** 126
Keishun **17** 126
Keisler, Frederick **31** 633
Keisuke Serizawa *see* SERIZAWA, KEISUKE
Kei Suzuki *see* SUZUKI, KEI
Keita Gotoh *see* GOTOH, KEITA
Keith, David **27** 642
Keith, Elizabeth **17** 293
Keith, George, 10th Earl Marischal **8** 12
Keith, James **23** 235
Keith, Robert Murray **11** 817
Keith, Thomas **17** 881*
Keith, William **17** 881*; **29** 536
Keiun *see* OMURA, MINOSUKE
Keizan Ohara *see* OHARA KEIZAN
Keizen **17** 125
Keizō Saji *see* SAJI, KEIZŌ
Keizō Shibusawa *see* SHIBUSAWA, KEIZŌ
Ke Jiusi **6** 805; **7** 151; **17** 881–2*; **30** 49
Kekana, Job **29** 111, 112
Kekchi **3** 621
Kekind, Nilakantheshvara Temple **15** 271, *271*, 488
Kekova Island **9** 537
Keković, Aleksandar **28** 445
Kekushev, Lev (Nikolayevich) **17** 882*; **23** 426; **27** 378
Kel **18** 484
Kelabit **20** 167, 181
Kelang **20** *162*, 169
Sultan Sulaiman Mosque **20** 166
Kelaniya **29** 466
Rajamahavihara **29** 467
Kelantan **3** 379; **20** 172, 173, 176
Kelder, Toon **22** 861
Keldermans (family) **13** 63; **22** 821; **33** 582
Keldermans, Andries, I (*d* 1500) **17** 882, 883*
Keldermans, Andries, III (*fl* 1512-40) **17** 883
Keldermans, Anthonis, I (*d* 1512) **17** 883*
collaboration **17** 883
works **8** 665; **13** 896
Keldermans, Anthonis, II (*d* 1515) **17** 883
Keldermans, Anthonis, IV (*d* 1564) **17** 883
Keldermans, Jan, II (*d* 1445) **3** 542; **17** 882, 883*; **19** 260
Keldermans, Jan, III (*fl* 1450-57) **17** 882
Keldermans, Laureys, I (*fl* 1485-1512) **17** 883
Keldermans, Laureys, II (*d* 1534) **17** 883, 884, 885
Keldermans, Marcelis **17** 883, 884
Keldermans, Matthijs, I (*d* 1479) **17** 882
Keldermans, Matthijs, II (*fl* 1478-1524) **4** 417; **17** 883
Keldermans, Matthijs, III (*fl* 1503-27) **17** 883
Keldermans, Rombout, I (*fl* 1455-75) **17** 882; **19** 260
Keldermans, Rombout, II (1460-1531) **17** 883–5*
collaboration **3** 543; **17** 883
patrons and collectors **13** 906; **22** 822
works **2** 202; **12** 523, *523*; **17** *884*
Keldi Muhammad Sultan **6** 234; **16** 342
Kelébiá **13** 162
Kelekian, Charles Dikran **10** 91
Kelekian, Dikran Garabed **10** 91
Kelekian, Dikran Khan **16** 396, 554
Kelekian, Tigran Khan **2** 444
Kelepha **21** 587
Keler, Georg *see* KELLER, GEORG
Kelermes kurgans **28** 322, *322*
Keleti, Gusztáv **14** 901; **17** 885*
Kelheim **25** 615
Befreiungshalle **6** 171; **33** 282
Kelibia, Church of Felix **9** 570
kelims *see* KILIMS
Kelin, Pyotr **15** 891
Keller, Albert von **5** 215; **17** 885*
Keller, Arthur **14** 751
Keller, Balthasar (Johann) **8** 94; **32** 372
Keller, Ferdinand **16** 795; **33** 429
Keller, Franz **3** 57; **11** 22; **27** 216
Keller, Friedrich (*fl* 1797-1846) **24** 40
Keller, Friedrich von (1840-1914) **28** 111
Keller, Georg **1** 789; **17** 885–6*; **27** 724
Keller, George W. **30** 505
Keller, Gottfried **17** 886*; **33** 736
groups and movements **30** 134
illustrated works **9** 39; **12** 649; **33** 429
Keller, H. **28** 260
works **28** *259*
Keller, Hans **1** 789
Keller, Heinrich, II **17** 886–7*; **30** 137
Keller, Henry G. **26** 477; **33** 703
Keller, Johan Jakob **8** 94; **32** 372
Keller, Johann **27** 636
Keller, Julius **10** 528
Keller, Martin **18** 467
Keller, Rolf **28** 190
Kellerthaler (family) **25** 731
Kellerthaler, Christoph, I (*c.* 1535-1592/1612) **17** 887
Kellerthaler, Christoph, II (*fl* 1587-1639) **17** 887
Kellerthaler, Daniel **17** 887–8*
teachers **17** 887
works **9** 240; **17** *888*
Kellerthaler, Friedrich **17** 887
Kellerthaler, Hans *see* KELLERTHALER, JOHANN II
Kellerthaler, Johann, I (*b* 1530) **17** 887
Kellerthaler, Johann, II (1562-1611) **9** 240; **17** 887*
Kelley, Arthur **1** 29
Kelley, Mike **27** 277
Kelley, Sidney **1** 29
Kellia **7** *819*
cenobitic cells **7** 820
Hagios Antonios **8** 358, 359
monastery complex **7** 820
oratory **7** 820

Kellia—cont.
plates **7** 826
pottery **7** 826
Kellinghausen **8** 748; **12** 431
Kellner, D. B. O. **4** 155
Kelloe (Durham), St Helen **26** 615
Kellogg, E. B.
works **26** *523*
Kellogg, E. C.
works **26** *523*
Kellogg, Martha *see* JACKSON, MARTHA
Kells (Co. Meath) **16** *5*; **17** 888–90*
Broken Cross **17** 889
crosses **15** 876
lace **16** 34
manuscripts **17** 890
Market Cross **17** 889
St Columba's House **17** 888
Tower Cross **17** 888–9, *889*
Unfinished Cross **15** 876; **17** 889
Kells embroidery *see under* EMBROIDERY → types
Kelltendorfer, Christof **28** 167
Kellum, John **17** 890–91*
collaboration **29** 651
works **10** 104; **29** 651
Kelly, C. G. **12** 412
Kelly, Ellsworth **5** 531; **17** 891–2*; **31** 609
dealers **20** 75; **24** 213
groups and movements **1** 79; **25** 361
patrons and collectors **33** 45
works **7** 636; **14** 164, *164*; **17** *892*; **21** 892; **28** 52, 300
Kelly, Florencio **17** 892–3*; **29** 354
Kelly, Gerald **19** 621
Kelly, Isabel **5** 660
Kelly, J. C. **1** 713
Kelly, John (*fl* 1739-59) **16** 26
Kelly, John (*fl* late 20th cent.) **24** 409
Kelly, Juan **17** 892; **29** 354
Kelly, Mary **17** 893*; **33** 313
groups and movements **10** 879, 882
works **10** *881*
Kelly, Oisín (Austin Ernest) **16** 22; **17** 893*; **25** 753
Kelly, Rod (*b* 1952) **10** 337
Kelly, R. Talbot (*fl* 1900) **5** 246
Kelly, Walt **7** 649
Kelmis **4** 688
Kelmscott Press **2** 594; **4** 357, 366; **20** 335; **22** 141, 145–6*; **33** 361, 369
designers **5** 268; **8** 121
works **4** 364; **7** 792; **10** 255; **22** *146*; **24** 107
keloid markings *see* CICATRICES
Kelp, Günter Zamp **14** 237*
Kelpra Studio **5** 726; **10** 258; **20** 606–7; **25** 628; **28** 300
Kels, Franz **12** 409
Kels, Hans **14** 306; **33** 746
Kelso (Borders) **28** 255
Abbey **3** 443; **12** 6; **26** 591, 617; **28** 223
carpets **28** 266
pottery **28** 256–7
bridge **4** 801
Kelson, Kilian **30** 106
works **30** *105*
Kelsterbach **12** 430, 433
Kelt, John **2** 472
Kelterborn, Ludwig Adam **4** 204; **29** 848
Keluk ibn 'Abdallah **16** 127
Kemah *see* ANI
Kemalettin **16** 590; **17** 893–4*
works **16** 227, 586; **23** 639; **31** 452; **32** 108
Kemalpaşa *see* NYMPHAION
Keman, Georges Antoine **11** 362
Kemble, Charles **30** 680
Kemble, Edward Windsor **4** 364
Kemble, John Philip **6** 117; **30** 675, 680
Kemble, Kenneth **2** 401, 837; **17** 694, 894*
Kemeny, Alfréd **7** 771
Kemeny, Zoltan **17** 894*; **30** 140
Kemkaran *see* KHEM KARAN
Kemlin, François **3** 595
Kemmeter, Michael **17** 544
Kemp, Edward **24** 293
Kemp, F(rancis) Bruce **31** 763
Kemp, George M(eikle) **6** 171; **9** 724; **17** 894–5*
Kemp, Henry (Hardie) **23** 327; **31** 763
Kemp, James **23** 72
Kemp, John **29** 594
Kemp, Roger **17** 895*
Kemp, Thomas (*fl* 1850s) **10** 144
Kemp, Thomas Read (*c.* 1781-1844) **4** 809
Kemp, Wolfgang **26** 62–3
Kempe, (Johann) Carl **7** 108, 111, 156; **17** 895*
Kempe, C. E. **7** 410; **29** 507; **33** 193, 239, 550
Kempe, Peter **30** 112
Kempe, Roland **19** 798
Kempe and Tower **4** 826
Kempe Gowda **3** 163
Kempelen, Wolfgang, Baron von **2** 838; **18** 191
Kempen **19** 896
Kempen, Johannes Mattheus van **22** 891, 892; **28** 867
works **22** *891*
Kempen, Van, Begeer & Vos *see* VAN KEMPEN, BEGEER & VOS
Kempeneer, Jan de **16** 867
Kempeneer, Peter de **17** 895–6*
pupils **22** 72; **29** 278
works **5** 49; **17** *896*; **29** 278
Kempeneere, Willem de **16** 867; **30** 317
Kempers, August Johan Bernet *see* BERNET KEMPERS, AUGUST JOHAN
Kempf-Hartenkampf, Gottlieb Theodor von **17** 897*; **28** 670
Kempis, Thomas à **4** 752; **17** 897*; **20** 740
Kempische Akwarellisten **32** 903
Kempley (Glos), St Mary **9** 680; **26** 655; **30** 905
roof **30** *906*
Kempson, Julie Hart Beers **14** 202
Kempster, Christopher **31** 239
works **24** *804*
Kempten, St Lorenz **12** 371; **29** 838
Kempthorne, Sampson **23** 53
Kempton, Reg **23** 70
Kemwer *see* ATHRIBIS
Ken **9** 885
Ken-Amun *see* QENAMUN
Kenar, Antoni **14** 219
Kenchiku zasshi **24** 437
Kendal (Cumbria) **10** 358
Kendall, Edward Hale **12** 643; **23** 41; **25** 327; **28** 831
Kendall, F(ranklin) K(aye) **3** 82; **17** 897–8*; **29** 105
works **4** 155; **5** *662*, 667; **29** 105
Kendall, George **28** 540
Kendall, Henry (*fl* 1847) **28** 156
Kendall, Henry (*fl* 1940s) **17** 492
Kendall, Henry E. (1776-1875) **8** 248; **31** 240; **32** 864
Kendall, John **10** 674; **23** 782
Kendall, Timothy **22** 467
Kendall, William **23** 198
Kenderline, Augustus **5** 569
kendi see under JARS → types
Ken Domon *see* DOMON, KEN
Kendreho **20** 40
Kendrick, George Prentiss **13** 715
Ken'en **10** 192
Kenfack, Pascal **5** 524
Ken Fujiwara *see* FUJIWARA, KEN
Keng Chao-chung *see* GENG ZHAOZHONG
Kengtung **5** 258
Keng Wei *see* GENG WEI
Kenilworth Castle (Warwicks) **6** 50, 56; **10** 227
arches **2** 294
gardens **9** 367; **12** 126, *126*
tapestries **10** 349
Kenji Funaki *see* FUNAKI, KENJI
Kenji Imai *see* IMAI, KENJI
Kenji Yoshida *see* YOSHIDA, KENJI
Kenkadō Kimura *see* KIMURA KENKADŌ
Kenk Boğazi **21** 298
Kenkichi Tomimoto *see* TOMIMOTO, KENKICHI
Kenkō Shōkei **17** 173, 898*; **30** 466
personal collection **1** 776
teachers **1** 776
works **28** 493
Kenkō Yoshida *see* YOSHIDA KENKŌ
Kenmore (VA) **29** 842
Kennard, Henry Martin **10** 91
Kennedy, David, 10th Earl of Cassillis **28** 269
Kennedy, Edward G(uthrie) **17** 898*
Kennedy, Furner, Irvine-Smith and Joubert **11** 847
Kennedy, Garry Neill **5** 569
Kennedy, G. P. **3** 283
Kennedy, James **28** 268
Kennedy, John F. **31** 663; **32** 888
Kennedy, Louis St John **17** 898–9*
Kennedy, Peter **2** 751; **24** 205
Kennedy, Simon **29** 533
Kennedy, Sybil **5** 571
Kennedy, William **12** 779
Kennedy Arts Center *see under* WASHINGTON (DC)
Kennedy Galleries **17** 898
Kennerley *see under* TYPE-FACES
Kennet, W. **19** 818
Kennet, White, Bishop **33** 94
Kennet and Avon Canal **2** 242
Kennet Square (PA), Longwood Gardens **12** 143; **19** 642–3*; **31** *587*
Kennichi Kōhō *see* KŌHŌ KENNICHI
Kennicott Bible, First *see under* BIBLES → individual manuscripts
Kennington, Eric (Henri) **4** 315; **10** 267; **17** 899*
Kenny, Sean **8** 177; **30** 687
Kenpō Shidon **17** 170; **27** 465
Kensett, John Frederick **17** 899*
groups and movements **14** 843; **19** 791; **31** 602
patrons and collectors **7** 840; **32** 829
works **14** 843
Kensett, Thomas **17** 899
Kenshin shodōkai **17** 239
Kenshin Uesugi *see* UESUGI KENSHIN
Kent, Adeline **31** 607
Kent, Edward, Duke of *see* HANOVER, EDWARD, Duke of Kent
Kent, John of, Abbot of Fountains *see* JOHN OF KENT, Abbot of Fountains
Kent, Rockwell **4** 367; **17** 899–900*; **20** 604; **22** 596
Kent, Thomas of *see* THOMAS OF KENT
Kent, Victoria of Saxe-Coburg-Saalfeld, Duchess of *see* SAXE-COBURG-SAALFELD, VICTORIA OF, Duchess of Kent
Kent, William **13** 301; **17** 900–905*
architecture **4** 757; **19** 570; **22** 809; **25** 233; **27** 259; **32** 824
cenotaphs **6** 171
country houses **23** *856*, *859*
domes **9** 84
garden buildings **11** 243; **18** 5; **30** 451
gate lodges **12** 176, *176*
government buildings **13** 237; **17** *903*
hermitages **14** *460*
houses **17** *904*
pavilions **24** 290
porticoes **25** 266
restorations **4** *770*
rotundas **27** 237
stables **29** 486, *486*
assistants **27** 466
barges **3** 232, *232*
collaboration **4** 805; **10** 264; **13** 782; **19** 606; **28** 64; **31** 906
competitions **7** 666
dealing **7** 540
drawings **2** 332; **11** 875; **13** 645; **19** 612
furniture **1** 111; **7** 746; **10** 293, 294, *294*, 295; **12** 333; **17** *902*; **30** 217
gardens **4** 875; **7** 175, 374; **12** 65, 129; **18** 4; **26** 743; **27** 259, *259*; **29** 736
gold **33** 158
groups and movements **13** 198, 199, 200; **22** 738; **23** 858, 859; **26** 735
interior decoration **7** 174; **10** 233, 276, 277; **11** 426; **15** 139; **17** *901*; **19** 612; **23** 543; **24** 316; **25** 191; **27** 494
patrons and collectors **4** 610; **7** 286, 540; **10** 361; **14** 127, 143, 460; **30** 451
prints **25** 630
publications **11** 172
reproductive prints by others **14** 856; **31** 906
sculpture **27** 468; **28** 64
silver **10** 332
teachers **10** 372; **19** 817
writings **2** 314; **4** *612*
Kent & Budden **33** 224
Kenteskalns **18** 846
Kentish tracery *see under* TRACERY types → bar
kentledge **7** 766
Kent Limner *see* PHILLIPS, AMMI
Kenton & Co. **4** 157; **10** 298; **12** 650; **19** 253
Kentridge, William **29** 110, 111
Kentucky **28** 542
Kentucky Dam **31** 596
Kentz, Hans **14** 405
Kenya **1** *214*; **17** 906–8*
aluminium **1** *411*
aprons **1** *297*
architecture **17** 906*
baskets **1** 295, 296
basketwork **1** 296
beads **1** *297*, *350*, *411*
beadwork **3** 442
body arts **1** 288, 344
bracelets **1** 362
burial practices **1** *258*
cedar **1** 307
cement **1** 331
ceramics **17** 906
copper **1** *411*
costumes **1** 255
dress **1** 255, *256*
earrings **1** 351
education (art) **17** 908*
effigies **1** 258, *258*
funerary monuments **1** 331
furniture **30** 57
glass **1** *297*
gourds **3** 442
grasses **1** 307
Kenya—cont.
hairstyles **1** 343
headrests **1** *411*
hides **1** *411*
houses **1** 307, 320
iron **1** *297*
jewellery **1** *256*
museums **17** 908*
necklaces **1** *350*
painting **17** 906–7*, *907*
patronage **17** 908*
pottery **1** 285
rings **1** 362
rock art **1** 374, 375
sculpture **17** 907–8*, *908*
shields **1** *412*
sisal **1** 296
soapstone **17** *908*
textiles **17** 906
tourist art **1** 252, *252*
trade **1** 304
women artists **1** 292
wood **1** *411*, *412*
wood-carvings **1** *252*, 252–3, 292
Ken'ya *see* MIURA TŌTARŌ
Kenyah **20** 182
architecture **15** 773, 774; **20** 167
beadwork **20** 182
canoes **20** 179
doors **9** 164
hats **20** 182
masks **15** 804
tattoos **20** 182
wood-carvings **20** 181, 182
Kenyon, A. W. **8** 810
Kenyon, Kathleen Mary **1** 894; **17** 483, 484, 909*
Kenzan *see* ASHIKAGA YOSHIMOCHI
Kenzan Ogata *see* OGATA KENZAN
Kenzan VI **31** 134
Kenzan ware *see under* POTTERY → wares
Kenzo Okada *see* OKADA, KENZO
Kenzo Takada *see* TAKADA, KENZO
Kenzo Tange *see* TANGE, KENZO
Keonijhar, Jagannatha Temple **15** 395
Keos *see* KEA
Keo Temple **9** 163; **32** 473
Kepes, Gyorgy **5** 122, 531; **7** 434; **17** 876; **18** 62; **19** 843; **21** 795; **28** 887
Kephali Chondrou **21** 664
Kephallinia **13** *363*; **17** 909*; **26** *908*
icons **25** 334
mosaics **27** 61
Kephisodotos (*fl* end 5th cent. BC–*c.* 360 BC) **13** 423, 429, 458; **17** 910*; **25** 458; **27** 31; **29** 781
pupils **25** 455
works **13** *423*
workshop **2** 687
Kephisodotos (*fl c.* early 3rd cent. BC) **25** 455, 457–8*
works **18** 394
Képiró, Franciscus **15** 6
works **15** *6*
Kep i Rodonit Castle **1** 538
Kepler, Johannes **5** 519; **13** 914; **17** 886; **19** 354; **24** 772; **25** 432
Kepoi **4** 110
kepoi see under GARDENS → types
Keppel, Arnold Joost van, 1st Earl of Albemarle **8** 834; **20** 458; **26** 560
Keppel, Commodore **26** *272*
Keppie, John **20** 21
Keppler, Arie **1** 803, 804; **17** 910*
Keppler, Hans **9** 133
Keppler, Joseph **27** 872
Képzőművészek Új Társasága (New Society of Artists) *see* KÚT
Ker, James **28** 261

Kerak 9 737; 17 500, 504, 655
Museum 17 656
Kerak-in-Moab 21 563
Kera Kritsas Church 9 584
Kerald 23 652, 653
Kerameikos Mug 32 66
Kerameikos Painter 13 507
Kerami, Hagios Ioannis 22 700
Keramic Studio see DESIGN
Keramik Hallstatt 2 816; 3 393
Keramik Schleiss 12 822
Keramis Boch Frères 3 591
Keramopoulos 30 702
Keramos Invalidengesellschaft 32 450
Kerandraou 32 280
keratin 31 194
Kerbalai Ahmed 2 893
Kerbalai Mirza 2 893
Kerbel', Lev 27 397
Kerch 4 110; 9 *507*; 17 910–11*; 31 *546*
architecture 4 110, 113
furniture 27 99
metalwork 4 111
pottery 13 542
sarcophagus 4 111
sculpture 4 111
silver 9 653
stelae 4 111
Stele of Dionysios and Aristeides 4 111
Stele of Hellas 4 111
tombs 4 110–11
Stasov Tomb 4 110
Tomb of 1891 4 110
Tomb of 1908 4 110
Tomb of Anthesterios 4 110
Tomb of Demeter 4 110
kerchiefs 16 448; 27 430–31
Kerchove, Josse van der 12 828
Kerch' style 17 911*; 32 56
Kerckhoff, Johan van 22 882
works 22 *881*
Kerckhoven, Barthélmy van den 3 609
Kerckhoven, Jacob van de *see* CASTELLO, GIACOMO DA
Kerckring, Hinrich 16 834
Kerényi, Jenő 14 896
Keres 22 606–8
Keresők *see* SEARCHERS
Kerewa 24 76, 77, 78
skull racks 24 *78*
Kerewe 1 410
Kereyit 30 475
Kerikeri
Kemp House 23 53
Stone Store 23 53
Kerimov, K. 2 894
Kerimov, L. G. 2 898, 899, 902
keris 15 817, *817*; 20 174
historical and regional traditions
Bali (Indonesia) 15 817; 29 239
Indonesia 15 757, 817–18
Islamic 15 757
Malaysia 20 174*
Sabah (Malaysia) 20 174
types
Bugis 15 817, *817*, 818; 20 174
majapahit 20 174
Pattani 20 174
Peninsula 20 174
Straits 20 174
Sulu 20 174; 24 631
Sumatran 15 817; 20 174
sundang see Sulu
see also DAGGERS
Keriya 28 *719*, 720
Kerkenah 32 312
Kerkouane 5 891; 25 732; 31 426
Kerkovius, Ida 12 470; 29 875
Kerkpoort 22 881
Kerkyra *see* CORFU
Kerma 9 *774*; 17 911–12*; 23 *276*, 278, 282
metalwork 9 817, 818
pottery 17 *912*
Kerma culture 10 48; 23 278
Kermadec, Eugène de 17 726, 912*
Kerman *see* KIRMAN
kermes
historical and regional traditions
Byzantine 9 665
Early Christian (*c.* AD 250-843) 9 665
Egypt 16 431
Islamic 16 431
Portugal 25 315
Spain 19 3
uses
dyes 2 83; 9 492, 665; 16 431; 19 3; 25 315
pigments 18 655; 24 796
Kermine 31 *781*, 782
mausoleum of Mir Sayyid Bahram 6 201
Qasim Shaykh *khānaqāh* 6 205
Kern, Achilles 29 60
Kern, Anton 17 912*; 25 3, 443
Kern, Christian 10 528
Kern, Georg *see* BASELITZ, GEORG
Kern, Leonhard 12 460; 17 913*
patrons and collectors 14 650
pupils 24 588
works 12 405; 29 571
Kern, Michael 17 913
Kerney, Michael 25 792
Kernoff, Harry 16 17
kernoi 24 634
Kernstok, Károly 17 913*
groups and movements 10 108; 14 901; 30 211
pupils 2 415; 8 779
works 10 109
writings 10 108
kerography 25 611
Keros 8 *304*, *306*; 13 *363*; 17 913–14*
marble 17 914
Kerouac, Jack 11 728
Kerouälle, Louise-Renée de, Duchess of Portsmouth 21 *497*
Kerr, E. Coe 18 161
Kerr, Kathy 17 593
Kerr, Robert 17 914*
works 8 49, *49*; 16 824
writings 10 236
Kerr, Robert, 1st Earl of Ancram 19 348, 349
Kerr, Robert, 4th Earl and 1st Marquess of Lothian 28 270
Kerr, William, 3rd Earl of Lothian 2 765; 16 898; 28 270
Kerr, William Schomberg Robert, 8th Marquess of Lothian 28 270
Kerr & Binns 33 378
Kerrich, Thomas 29 733
Kerricx, Guillielmus 17 914–15*
pupils 17 915
teachers 25 812
works 3 570
Kerricx, Willem Ignatius 3 571; 17 915*; 32 251
teachers 17 914
works 3 546; 7 703
Kerr & Knight 2 752
Kerry, Charles (Henry) 17 915*
Kerschbaumer, Anton 4 143
Kerseboom, Friedrich 17 915*
Kerseboom, Johann 17 915*; 31 786
Kershaw (SC), Court House 18 887
Kershaw, Thomas 23 789
Kerslake & Mortimer 12 315
Kersting, Georg Friedrich 17 916*; 21 66
works 4 39; 12 294, *414*
Kerstken van Ringenberg 17 741
Kerta 33 537
Kertch 9 655
Kertész, André 17 916–17*; 24 676, 677
works 17 *917*
K'ert'ol, Vrt'anes *see* VRT'ANES K'ERT'OL
Keruru 24 76
Kerver, Jacques 20 455
Kerver, Thielman 4 358
Kerzin, M. 2 903; 3 531
Kesai *see* IKEDA EISEN
Keserű, Ilona 14 902
Keshava Kalan *see* KESU KALAN
Keshav Das 8 848
Keshkarrigan (Co. Leitrim) 6 161
Kesh Raja Shakya 30 53
Késmark *see* KEŽMAROK
Kessel, Ferdinand van 17 917, 920
Kessel, Henry, Graf *see* KESSLER, HARRY, Graf
Kessel, Hieronymus van, II 4 *895*; 11 81; 17 917, 918*
Kessel, Jan van, II (1626-79) 4 894, *895*; 11 227; 17 918, 919–20*
collaboration 17 881; 29 721
patrons and collectors 4 565
personal collection 3 24
pupils 17 920
teachers 27 329
works 5 352; 17 917, *918*, *919*
Kessel, Jan van (1641-80) 17 917, 920*; 22 843; 29 666
Kessel, Jan van, III (1654-1708) 4 *895*; 17 920*
works 17 917
Kessel, Jeroom van, II *see* KESSEL, HIERONYMUS VAN II
Kessel, Willem van *see* WILLEM VAN KESSEL
Kesselhut, Jakob 8 529
Kessell, Mary 28 808
Kessels, Mathieu 17 920–21*; 28 756
Kesselstadt 21 559
Kesslau, Albrecht Friedrich von 17 816; 18 643
Kessler, Franz 22 305
Kessler, Gabriel 17 921
Kessler, George 8 469; 14 802; 17 799
Kessler, Harry, Graf 2 566; 4 366; 8 109; 17 625; 20 121; 22 291; 33 38, 362
Kessler, Josef Anton 25 34
Kessler, Michael 17 921
Kessler, Nikolaus 9 429
Kessler, Raphael 17 921
Kessler, Stephen, I 17 921*
Kessler, William 8 821
Kesslerloch 25 492
Kestel 4 849
Kestelman, Morris 24 839
Kestgen *see* KNÜTGEN
Kesting, Edmund 17 921*
Kestner 31 261
Kestner, (Georg) August (Christian) 17 922*
Kestner-Museum *see under* HANNOVER → museums
Kesu Das 15 581; 17 922–3*
collaboration 20 48
works 17 *922*
Kesu Khurd 22 263; 31 420
Kesu Ram 15 600
Keswick (Cumbria) 10 339
School of Industrial Art 10 344
Keswick Plantation (VA) 1 421
Ket, Dick 17 923*; 22 852
Ketamalla 14 65; 15 533
Ketchum, Morris 33 700
Kete 18 484
masks 1 405; 18 488
wood-carvings 1 403; 18 487
Ketel, Cornelis (Jacobsz.) (*d c.* 1568) 17 923
Ketel, Cornelis (1548-1616) 17 923–4*; 22 841
pupils 8 103; 16 63
teachers 4 148
works 17 *924*; 31 881
Ketel, Cornelis (Cornelisz.) (*fl* 1590s) 8 103
Ketelaar, Johan 15 741
Ketham, Joannes de *see* JOANNES DE KETHAM
Ketmen'-Tyube 6 245
ketone resin *see* RESINS → types → cyclohexanone
Ketterer, Roman Norbert 12 474
Kettering (Northants), SS Peter and Paul 29 413
Kettle, Tilly 15 592, 654; 16 15; 18 1*
teachers 19 157
works 8 265
kettle-hats *see under* HELMETS → types
kettles
historical and regional traditions
Brunei 5 11
Chile 6 599
England 10 341
Germany 15 *823*
Japan 17 322, 323, *323*, 341
United States of America 31 *648*
materials
brass 5 11
copper 10 341
iron 17 *323*
silver 6 599
Kettner, Gerhard 18 1*
Ketton (Northants) 10 227; 29 531
church 29 412
ketubbot 18 1–3*, *2*; 21 475
Ketzel, Ulrich 14 423, III1
devices 7 *177*
Ketzenberger, Balthasar 33 36
Ketzin Paretz Church 13 201
Ketzler, Jörg 10 *162*
Keul, Jacob 10 746
Keul, Jacob, the younger *see* FACHT, JACOB
Keuninck, Kerstiaen de, the elder (1560-1632/3) 18 3–4*
Keuninck, Kerstiaen de, the younger (*d* 1642/3) 18 3
Keuren, F. van 4 24
Keux, Henry Le *see* LE KEUX, HENRY
Keux, John Le *see* LE KEUX, JOHN
Kever, Gerhard 9 72
Kevernburg, Günter of *see* GÜNTER OF KEVERNBURG
Keverwyck, Elizabeth de 12 846
Kevin Roche John Dinkeloo & Associates 26 480
works 26 *480*
kevlar 2 474
Kevorkian, Hagop 16 396; 18 4*
Kevorkian Album *see under* ALBUMS → individual manuscripts
Kew (Surrey)
Dutch House *see* Palace
Palace 4 785, 786; 10 231; 25 804; 30 502
paintings 14 755
Royal Botanic Gardens 4 875; 12 131, 137; 18 4–5*; 24 179; 25 804
collections 1 66
Lodge 25 804; 30 504
Merlin's Cave 11 243
New Room *see* Orangery
Orangery 23 470
Pagoda 6 412; 7 168; 10 233; 23 776
Palm House 5 283; 12 137, 791; 13 619; 16 52; 18 *4*
Queen's Cottage 8 30; 23 398
ruined arch 27 324
Temple of Aeolus 21 893; 27 237
Key, Adriaen (Thomasz.) (*c.* 1544-after 1589) 18 6–7*
works 9 275; 18 *6*
Key, Adriaen (Woutersz.) (*d* before 1542) 18 5*
Key, Cornelis 18 5
Key, Frans 18 5
Key, John 33 412
Key, Lieven de 18 7*; 22 823
attributions 3 741
collaboration 22 823
works 5 543; 13 893, 896; 19 99; 22 *824*
Key, Michiel 18 5
Key, Willem (Adriaensz.) 18 5–6*
pupils 18 6
teachers 7 519; 19 547
works 3 557; 18 5, *6*
Key, Wouter 7 497; 18 5
keyaki 17 46, 274, 356, 358
key design, Greek *see* MEANDER
keyhole arches *see* ARCHES → types → horseshoe
Keyhole carpets *see* CARPETS → types → Bellini
keyhole tombs *see under* TOMBS → types
Key Marco (FL) 18 7*; 22 *544*, 572
Keynes, John Maynard 4 168, 169
Keynooghe, Jan 7 498
Keynsham (Somerset) 4 824
Abbey 4 *465*, 465; 26 617
Keyrincx, Alexander *see* KEIRINCKX, ALEXANDER
keys 11 *625*; 31 *405*
Keys, Eileen 2 761
Keys, Peter H. 28 772
Keyser, Cornelis Dirxz. de 18 8
Keyser, de (family) 3 600
Keyser, Hendrick (Cornelisz.) de, I (1565-1621) 9 760; 18 8–10*; 22 823–4
collaboration 8 496
pupils 10 262; 18 10; 29 594, 713
teachers 4 149
works 1 801, 802; 4 785; 8 496, 666, *666*, 739; 10 668; 18 *8*, 10; 22 858, *859*; 23 464; 29 571; 32 860
workshop 29 594
Keyser, Hendrick de, II (1613-65) 18 8
Keyser, Hendrik de (*fl* late 19th cent.) 19 782
Keyser, Huybrecht de 18 8, 10
Keyser, Louisa *see* DAT SO LA LEE
Keyser, Nicaise De *see* DE KEYSER, NICAISE
Keyser, Pieter (Hendricksz.) de 18 8, 10–11*
attributions 1 802; 18 9
collaboration 18 11
works 1 *802*; 8 665; 22 858
Keyser, Pieter Dirksz. 12 812
Keyser, Raoul de 3 565; 19 756
Keyser, Thomas (Hendricksz.) de 18 8, 10–11*
attributions 25 362; 31 807
collaboration 27 326
patrons and collectors 15 40
pupils 29 714
reproductive prints by others 22 272
teachers 17 924
works 1 813; 3 77; 11 403, *443*; 18 *10*; 22 841, 843
Keyser, Willem (Hendricksz.) de 18 8, 11*
collaboration 22 858
works 1 813; 8 665; 22 858
Keysere, Arend 19 727
Keysere, Johanna de 12 846
Keyssler, Johann Georg 18 12*
keystones 2 292, *292*; 18 12*
Keyt, Edward 27 244
Keyt, George 18 12*; 29 455, 468
groups and movements 4 290; 33 74
works 29 468, *468*
Kezai, Simon 28 326
Kežmarok 28 *848*
architecture 28 849
belfry 28 849
furniture 14 904

Kežmarok—cont.
Lutheran church **28** 850
Thököly Castle **14** 885, 904; **28** 852
Kezthelyi, A. S. **11** 141
Kfar Monash **30** 195
Kgatla **4** 489
Kha **10** 46, 57, 61, 74, 75
Khaba (*reg c.* 2604–*c.* 2600 BC) **9** *776*; **25** 761
Khabarov, Ivan **28** 465
Khabeknet **10** *19*
Khabiboulayev, Zuhan Nurdjanovich **30** 253
Khabura **23** 436
Khabur ware *see under* POTTERY → wares
Khachen, Hovanes **2** 892
Khachen Dorbatly Mausoleum **16** 246
Khadalik **6** 318; **18** 29; **28** 720
Khadda, Muhammad **1** 635; **18** 12*
Khadgayogini *see* VAJRAYOGINI
Khaemhat **1** 770; **9** 902
Khaemwese **9** 843, 860; **27** 813
Khafajeh **1** *849*, 883, 893; **9** 45*; **21** *267*, 303
architecture **21** 282
pottery **21** *307*
stone vessels **2** 272
temple **2** 251; **21** 283
Temple Oval **21** 552
see also DIYALA REGION
Khafreankh **9** 872
Khaghbakian, Grigor
relief sculpture **2** *435*
Khairadih
sculpture **15** 478, *482*
Khairallah **15** 593
Khair Khana **1** 189, 198, 199
Khajanchi, Motichand **15** 183, 742, 748
Khajuraho **15** *261*, *285*
reliefs **15** 227
sculpture **10** 484; **15** 413, 414, *414*, 497
temples **6** 444; **15** 195, 229, 230, 263, 290, 293, 322, 738; **18** 12*; **29** 526
Duladeo Temple **15** 322, 497
Kandariya Mahadeva Temple **14** 77; **15** 290; **18** *13*, 13–15, *14*; **30** 438
Lakshmana Temple **6** 444; **15** 290, 481, 496, *496*
Nilakantha Mahadeva Temple **15** 322
Vishvanatha Temple **15** *289*, 290
Yogini Temple **15** 290
Khakaure *see* SESOSTRIS III
Khakha **1** 414, 415, 418
Khakhar, Bhupen **18** 15–16*
works **15** *170*, 170–71, 748
Khakhuli Monastery **12** 322; **30** 307
church **12** 323; **30** 305
Khakhuli Triptych **9** 660, 661–2*; **12** 328, 329, *329*, 330; **30** 305
Khalaf **16** 524
Khalafov, R. G. **2** 898
Khalchayan **6** *182*, 192; **18** 16*; **30** 440
architecture **6** 198
glass **6** 267
Palace **18** 16
reliefs **6** *187*; **18** *16*
sculpture **6** 214, 215, *215*
wall paintings **6** 224
Khaldé **9** 567
Khaleq, Syed Abdullah **3** 165
Khalid ibn Abu'l-Hayyaj **16** 278
Khalifa, Musa **29** 896
Khalil (*fl* early 15th cent.) **16** 325
Khalil, Sultan (*reg* 1290-94) (Mamluk) **16** 209, 382, 453
Khalil, Sultan (*reg* 1405-9) (Timurid) **30** 489
Khalil, Sultan (*reg* 1478) (Aqqoyunlu) **2** 237; **8** 533; **16** 328, 332; **28** 567; **30** 223
Khalil, Emilienne **9** 768
Khalil, Mohammad O. **20** 609
Khalil, Muhammad Mahmoud **5** 401; **9** 768
Khalil Allah Khan **15** 366
Khalil-Bey **8** 55; **9** 424; **10** 480; **11** 663; **15** 843; **18** 869
Khalili, Nasser David **16** 555
Khalil Pasha **3** 52
Khalji **18** 16–17*
Khalji (Delhi) *see*:
'ALA AL-DIN MUHAMMAD SHAH I, Sultan
JALAL AL-DIN FIRUZ, Sultan
KHIDR KHAN
Khalji (Malwa) *see*:
GHIYATH AL-DIN, Sultan
NASIR AL-DIN SHAH, Sultan
Khalkha **21** 870, 876, 878, 879
dress **21** *876*
Khalkis **13** 586; **14** 339
Khallaweh, Tell **14** 128
Khalykov, G. **2** 896, 902
Kham
Litang Monastery **30** 819
Khambhat **15** 347, 697; **18** 17*
carpets **15** 682
congregational mosque **15** 347
gravestones **15** 308
hardstones **15** 698
Khamdami, Bahram **31** 783
Khamerernebty I **9** 862, 871
Khamerernebty II **22** 398, *399*
Kham-e Zargar **1** 196
Khami **1** *413*, 414, 415
Khamidov, Salimdzhan **27** 425
Kham-Magar *see* MAGAR
Khammash, Ammar **17** 655
Khampti **15** 733
Khan, Fazlur **5** 649; **6** 574; **12** 874; **16** 868; **28** 818, 834
Khan, Keith **13** 877
khānaqāhs **16** 117, 141; **18** 17–18*
Central Asia, Western **6** 211
Egypt **18** 17, *18*
Indian subcontinent **15** 357; **18** 17
Iran **18** 18
Ottoman **16** 265
Tunisia **16** 220
Turkey **16** 265
Yemen **16** 214–15
see also RIBĀṬS
Khandagiri **15** *279*, 437–8*, 503; **18** 18*
Khandalawala, Karl **15** 742
khandaq **21** 546
Khandisi **12** 321
Khandjyan, Grigor **2** 433
Khanenko, Bohdan **20** 705; **31** 565
Khanenko Adoration, Master of the **20** 705*
Khania *see* CHANIA
Khan-i Jahan Junan Shah **8** 673
Khan-i Khanan Farmuli **15** 346
Khani Ruins **1** 305
al-Khanka Mosque **20** 230
Khankendy *see* XANKÄNDI
Khanlarov, T. **2** 894
Khan Mumtaz, Kamil **18** 647
Khanna, Krishen **4** 290; **8** 677; **18** 19*
Khanty **27** 436
Khanykov, N. de **6** 280, 281
Khao Co Hoc **24** 437
Khao Phra Wihan *see* PREAH VIHEAR
Khao Plara
rock art **29** *227*
Khaqan *see* MIRZA BABA
Kharabok, Tell **10** 507
Kharadzhet *see* KANKA
Kharadzhiket **6** 379
Kharagpur Mosque **15** 370
Kharak Bundar **17** 806
Kharaneh *see* QASR KHARANA
Kharashket *see* KANKA
Kharavank' **2** 435
Kharavela **15** 437; **18** 18
Kharayeb **24** 643
Kharga Oasis **7** *819*; **9** 765, *774*; **18** 20*
Khargird **16** *105*, 163
architecture **16** 196
Ghiyathiyya Madrasa **16** 197, *200*, 259; **20** 56, 57
madrasa **16** 199
plaster **16** 200
Kharijite *see under* ISLAM → branches
Kharkiv **28** 838; **31** *546*, 551
architecture **31** 552
carpets **31** 564
ceramics **31** 563
Historical Museum **31** 565
Hospital No. 3 **31** 552
metro **31** 552
painting **31** 559
sculpture **31** 561
Trade Building **31** 551
University **19** 497
urban planning **18** 543
Khar'kov *see* KHARKIV
Kharlamov, Fyodor **28** 837
Kharlamov, V. F. **27** 139
Kharod
Indal Temple **15** 284
Shabarinarayana Temple **15** 284
Kharraqan **2** 292
paintings **21** 506
tombs **4** 791, 792; **16** 163, 164, 165, 248; **23** 558, *559*; **31** 111
Kharro **30** 805, 845, 847
Khartoum **1** *379*; **10** 81; **23** *276*, 290
architecture **29** 895
College of Fine and Applied Art **29** 896, 898
Ethnographic Museum **29** 898
Gordon Memorial College **29** 895
School of Fine Art **1** 433
Governor's House **29** 895
Grand Hotel **29** 895
National Museum **29** 898
Palace **29** 895
printing **16** 361
sphinx of Aspelta **23** 282
Kharuef **1** 770; **9** 882; **10** 83
Khasa
sculpture **22** 775–6, *776*
Khasekhemwy **9** *776*, 855, 866, *867*, 868; **10** 35, 72; **17** 713
Khashabank **2** 892
Khasi **3** 165
Khassaki **21** 506
Khāstī *see* BODHNATH
Khatana **9** 830
Khatchayan *see* KHALCHAYAN
khatchk'ars see under CROSSES → types
Khatim **16** 425
Khatoli **15** 603, 606
Khattat, Hashem al- *see* HASHEM MUHAMMAD AL-BAGHDADI
Khatu **15** 339
architecture **15** 349
Dargah Mosque **15** 349
Shahi Mosque **15** 349
Shrine of Baba Ishaq Maghribi **15** 350, 351
Shrine of Mahmud Qattal **15** 349
Khatun Jan Begum (Qaraqoyunlu) **25** 774; **30** 223
works **30** *224*
Khawam (family) **10** 92
Khawlan **32** 317
Khawlan al-Tiyal **2** 268
Khayachi, Hédi **31** 425
Khayr al-Din Mar'ashi **14** 103
Khazakhstan *see* TEGEA
Khazna, Tell **2** 251
Khecheong **7** 30
Khedel', Jan *see* CHEDZIEL, JAN
Khedrapur *see* KHIDRAPUR
Khedrup Je **13** 885
Kheit Qasim III, Tell **21** 281
houses **14** 128, *128*
khekher frieze **9** 825
Khelaverd **6** *182*, 232; **18** 20*; **30** *252*
khelims *see* KILIMS
Khema **2** 657
Khem Karan **18** 20*
Khemmis **10** 802
Khemus Factory **5** 158
Khendjer **25** 763; **27** 812
Khentika **9** 790
Khentkawes **1** 97; **9** 850; **10** 51
Khent-Min *see* AKHMIM
Kheny **12** 227
Kherahat Temple **15** 262
Kherson **31** 551
Khersones *see* CHERSONESOS
Khersonisos *see* CHERSONISOS
Kheta *see* HITTITE
Khetagurov, Kosta **27** 433
Kheti **9** 823, 824
Khetre, Rao Bahadur **15** 542
Khety II **2** 659; **9** 874
Khety III **9** 844
Khevenhüller, Christoph **14** 573
Khevenhüller, Georg von **2** 779
Khevenhuller, Johann von, Baron **1** 35
Khian **9** 879
Khiching **15** 321, 504
Chandrashekhara Temple **15** 321
Kinchakeshvari Temple **15** 321, *321*
Khidekel, Lazar' **23** 144; **31** 677
Khidrapur, Koppeshvara Temple **15** 317
Khidr Khan (Khalji) **8** 672; **18** 17
Khif al-Zahra **2** 268
Khinnis **3** 418
Khirbat al-Mafjar **16** *104*, 148, *565*; **18** 20–21*; **23** 485, 815
aqueducts **2** 242
audience room **16** 256
baths **2** 295; **3** 376, 378; **16** 142, 148, *149*, 256; **22** 162
façade **16** 243
fountain **11** 340
gardens **12** 77
kiosk **18** 70
mosaics **16** 256
ornament **16** 137
palace **16** 245
sculpture **16** 538
small audience hall **16** 146
stained glass **16** 256
stucco **29** 818, 819, *819*; **31** *573*
Khirbat al-Minya *see* MINYA
Khirbat Bou Hadef **9** 535
Khirbet al-Tall *see* AI
Khirbet ed-Diniyeh **14** 21
grave **14** 22
Khirbet Fahil *see* PELLA (JORDAN)
Khirbet Kerak **30** 197
Khirbet Mouqa **9** 567
Khirbet Susiya **9** 567
Khirbet Tannur **26** *915*
Temple **26** 917
Khirokitia **8** *325*; **13** *362*; **18** 21*
architecture **27** 127; **30** 737
houses **8** 333, *333*
pottery **8** 343
sculpture **8** 337
Khir-Yurt **16** 505
Khisht Tepe **6** 222
Khisl glasswork **28** 862
Khitakhunov, Maris **17** 867
Khitan *see* QIDAN
Khitrovo, A. Z. **26** 735; **27** 439
Khitrovo, B. M. **27** 438
Khiva **6** *182*; **16** *105*; **18** 21–2*; **31** *781*
architecture **16** 235; **31** 782
Bonbonla Mosque **6** 277
caravanserai **16** 238
cenotaph of Sayyid 'Ala' al-Din **16** 249
citadel **23** 820
Khiva—cont.
congregational mosque **6** 277; **16** 159, 491
dress **31** *783*
fortifications **21** 589, 592
Friday Mosque **16** 236, 237
Ichan-Kala State Museum Reserve **6** 283
jewellery **6** 274
Katli Murad Inak Madrasa **6** 208
Khwaja 'ala' al-Din cenotaph **6** 207, *207*
madrasa of Allah Quli **16** 237
madrasa of Muhammad Amin Khan **16** 237; **18** 22
metalwork **6** 241
Museum of Local Lore, History and Economy **18** 21
palaces **23** 820
Tash Hawli Palace **6** 208; **16** 238, *238*; **23** 816; **31** 782; **32** 321
textiles **31** 783
tomb of Pahlavan Mahmud **6** 208; **16** 237
urban planning **16** 264
weapons **6** 262
woodwork **16** 502
Khizan **2** 431
Khizi
kilims **2** *901*, 902
Khlebnikov (company) **22** 180; **27** 421, 426
Khlebnikov, Aleksandr (Vladimirovich) **18** 22*; **27** 409
Khlebnikov, Velimir (Victor Vladimirovich) **12** 893; **18** 22*
collaboration **18** 474
groups and movements **8** 250, 251; **22** 750; **30** 7; **31** 583
productions **18** 474
works **20** 851; **24** 404
illustrated **18** 792; **27** 283; **30** 361
Khlong Thom **30** 632
Khludov, Gerasim **22** 135
Khludov, Nikolay **7** 291
Khmer **5** 457, 459, 460, 463, 502; **14** 561; **18** 23*, 762; **28** 794; **29** 241; **30** 571, 573, 574
altars **1** 706
architecture **30** 578–81*
brick **4** 795
causeways **5** *478*
doors **9** 163
dress **30** 623
face-towers **5** 477
glazes **30** 610
ikat **5** *502*
lintels **30** 599–600
ornament **23** 556
pots **5** *506*; **30** *611*
pottery **30** 610–11*
sanctuaries **5** 477
sandstone **30** *600*
sculpture **5** 486–90; **30** 599–600*
Buddhism **5** 100; **6** 430; **30** *600*
Cambodia **5** 499
Vietnam **6** 430
wood **5** 499
silk **5** *502*
stonewares **5** *506*; **30** 610–11, *611*
stucco **29** 826
temple-mountains **5** 479
temples **2** *58*, 59; **5** *478*; **30** 446
Buddhism **30** *579*, 581
Laos **18** 764*
Thailand **30** 578–81
textiles **5** 502–3*
urban planning **30** 592
wood **5** 499
Khmer Sung **5** 502, 503
Khmer Tam **5** 502
Khmou **32** 489
Khmun *see* HERMOPOLIS MAGNA
Khnopff, Fernand **3** 614; **18** 23–5*
groups and movements **5** 44; **7** 245; **10** 517; **14** 137; **25** 358; **27** 639; **28** 341; **30** 169; **32** 591

Khnopff, Fernand—cont.
teachers 19 66; 21 87
works 3 564, 611; 11 449–50, 450; 18 24; 32 251
Khnumet 10 30, 56
Khnumhotpe 10 50; 27 812
tomb 27 811
Khnumhotpe II 10 65
Khnumhotpe III 9 823, 900; 10 75; 23 532
Khnumnakht 10 10
Kho, Liang Ie 18 25*; 22 876
groups and movements 22 869
works 22 869; 32 756
Khober, Marcin see KOBER, MARCIN
Khobi 12 317, 330
church 12 324
Khocho 5 102; 6 288, 614; 18 26*; 28 720
architecture 6 296
books 6 307
church 6 292, 293
dress 6 310
five towers stupa 29 867
fortifications 6 296
painting 6 304, 305, 310; 30 828
wall 6 293, 294
paper 24 48
prints 6 314
Ruin Q 6 300
Ruin T 6 296
sculpture 6 298, 300
stencilling 6 302
Stupa Y 29 824, 867
tangkas 28 311
Temple A 30 442, 442
Temple Alpha 30 442
Temple B 29 867; 30 475
temples 30 441, 442
Temple Y 4 794; 6 297
textiles 7 48
Khodassievitch, Nadia 19 83
Khodja, Ali 1 635
Khodja obi Garm Sanatorium 30 252
Khodorov Synagogue 17 546, 559
Khodzha Gul'suar 6 217
Khodzhent 6 182; 16 105; 18 26–7*; 30 251, 252
architecture 30 252
ceramics 30 253
Historical and Regional Museum 6 283
jewellery 6 274
Khodzhiev, R. 30 253
Khodzhikov, Khodja 17 867
Khoh 15 214
sculpture 15 469, 469
Khoikhoi 1 417; 29 102
Khoionovskii, I. A. 31 565
Khoisan 1 281, 375
Khojand see KHODZHENT
Khojra 15 322, 323
Khojt-Cenkherijn-aguj 21 882
Khokand see KOKAND
el-Khokha see under THEBES (i) (EGYPT)
Khokhan, Adi Brahma Temple 15 397, 397
Khokhlach 28 325
Khokhov, Aslan-Girey 27 433
Khok Phanom Di, Burial 15 29 228
Kho Liang Ie Associates 18 25
Kholm 31 547, 549
Kholmogorets, Semyon see SPIRIDONOV, SEMYON
Kholmogorov, Aleksey 27 434
Kholmogory 18 27*; 27 363
Kholopov, Aleksandr 27 434
Kholui 27 427
Khomutov, I. 28 747
al-Khonany, Zakaria 9 767
Khong, Krua In 30 616
Khong Lo 32 473
Khon Kaen
National Museum 29 240
textiles 30 621
Khonsheb 9 887
Khonsu 10 53
Khonsumeh 9 860, 861
Khoo Sui-Hoe 20 172
Khoprin see BHAKTAPUR
Khora 6 303; 17 874
Khorasan see KHURASAN
Khor Milkh 1 2 263
Khorog 30 252
Historical and Regional Museum 6 283
Khoroshovo, Church of the Holy Trinity 27 371
Khor Rori 2 246, 263
Khorsabad 1 849, 891, 892, 895; 2 639, 640; 11 732; 18 27–9*, 28; 21 267, 268, 274, 288; 23 806
Adad Temple 21 300
arches 2 297
architecture 2 640; 21 288–90
façade decoration 10 742
glass 1 867
ivory-carvings 1 870; 24 643
metalwork 21 304
Nabu Temple 18 28; 21 300
Palace F 18 28–9
polychromy 25 171
reliefs 1 833; 21 287; 22 510; 31 700
Residence L 18 28
Sargon's palace 1 830; 18 28; 21 288–9, 289, 299–300, 309; 28 611
sculpture 25 650
sculpture 29 395
stucco 29 815
town walls 21 552
ziggurat 25 171; 33 675, 676
Khoshmukhamedov, M. 30 253
Khosh Tepe 1 186
Khosla, Ramesh 23 799
Khosrovanush, Queen of Armenia (fl c. 952-77) 2 434, 444; 14 36; 27 701
Khotan 5 102; 6 288, 614; 18 29*; 28 719, 720
calligraphy 6 307
ceramics 6 309
coins 6 309
furniture 6 311
jade 7 7, 9, 10; 16 860
lapis lazuli 7 89
manuscripts 6 289
Monastery 6 294
painting 6 302, 303–4
palace 6 294
sculpture 6 298
terracotta 6 315
Khot'kovo 1 72
Khotyn' 31 556, 557
Castle 4 783; 31 550
Khoung My 6 418
Khovd-somon 21 882
Khoy 16 230
Khozemyako, P. 1 504
Khramtsov, Vladislav (Mikhailovich) 27 423
Khreis, Khaled 17 655
Khrelyu 26 392
Khromonastiri see CHROMONASTIRI
Khroub, El 23 299
Khruba Srivijaya 6 567
Khrushchov, Nikita 22 726; 27 380
Khrutsky, Ivan (Fomich) see CHRUCKI, JAN
Khryakov, A. F. 32 670
Khryashchev, P. 17 870
Khrychevsky, Vasyl 31 565
Khu Bua 30 571, 576
Dvaravati monument 30 636
reliefs 29 826
sculpture 30 511, 595
Wat Khlong 30 577
Khudainket 6 379
Khuda Quli, Ustad 15 362
Khudozhestvennaya gazeta 27 443
Khudozhestvennaya samodeyatel'nost' 24 451
Khudozhestvennyye sokrovishcha Rossii 27 438, 441
Khudozhestvennyy listok 30 915
khudozhestvennyy zhurnal 27 444
Khudozhnik 24 451
Khudzhand see KHODZHENT
Khuen-Belassi, Count 22 251
Khufu see CHEOPS
Khukhutan 27 436
Khul'buk see HULBUK
Khul'buk see KULBANSHAYID
Khulna 3 166
Art College 3 169
Khumarawayh, Governor (reg 884-96) (Tulunid) 31 421
Khumartash 25 778
Khünischbauer, Johann 25 443
Khuon see KUEN
Khuong My 6 422–3, 428
khura 15 243*
Khurab 15 921
Khurasan 16 105, 373
brass 16 377
bronze 16 370
casting 16 370
cotton 16 428
inkwells 23 562
inscriptions 16 378
manuscript illumination 16 331
metalwork 16 375, 377, 392
shrine of 'Ali Rida 28 633
textiles 16 435, 435
Khurayba 2 268
Khurd, Kesu 30 338
Khurd, Tulsi 30 338
Khurha 24 216
Khurram, Prince see SHAH JAHAN, Emperor
Khurramabad 15 369
Khurremshah ibn Mughith 9 41
Khurshud-banu Natavan 2 896, 901
Khurus-i Jangi 15 898
Khurvin 15 905, 921
Khushala 15 632; 22 439
Khushqadam, Sultan (reg 1461-7) (Mamluk) 16 385, 497; 32 313
Khushqadam ibn 'Abdallah 16 312
manuscripts 16 312
Khushyar, Princess 16 241
Khusnutdinskhodzhayev, Kakim Khodzha 31 783
Khusraw Pasha 5 398
Khuts'k Castle 31 549, 550
Khuzistan 15 902, 903, 915, 920
Khvostov, Oleksander 2 634
Khwabgah 1 194
Khwaja 'Abd al-Hayy see 'ABD AL-HAYY
Khwaja 'Abd al-Ṣamad see 'ABD AL-SAMAD
Khwaja Ahrar 27 673; 30 352
Khwaja 'Ali 16 325; 18 29–30*; 30 921
Khwaja Gida 6 236
Khwaja Hasan 15 371
Khwaja Jahan Muhammad Dust 15 363, 364
Khwaja Khayran 28 633
Khwaja Mu'in 15 699
Khwaja Rukn al-Din Rashid al-Din 'Azizi ibn Abu'l-Husayn al Zanjani 16 374
Khwaja Sa'd Juybari 16 235
Khwaja Siyah Push 16 168
minaret 8 678; 16 166, 169
Khwaja Yaqut 10 493
Khwaja Yusuf 15 676
Khwaju Bridge see under ISFAHAN
Khwandamir 16 196, 198
Khwand Baraka (Mamluk) 16 524; 20 229
Khwarazm 16 105; 31 458
architecture 6 199*
castles 6 199
clay 6 218, 218, 219
columns 6 200
Khwarazm—cont.
cotton 6 249, 250
dress 6 251
earthenwares 16 414
eggs 6 227
gums 6 227
moulds 6 218
ossuaries 6 213, 233; 23 607; 31 76
polychromy 6 219
pottery 6 213, 255, 257, 258, 259
reliefs 6 218, 218–19
sculpture 6 218–19*, 219
silver 6 193, 238
statues 6 212
statuettes 6 275
textiles 31 21
tiles 6 207
vase paintings 6 233
wall paintings 6 223*, 227, 227–8*, 228, 233*
Khwarazmshah, Muhammad see MUHAMMAD, Khwarazmshah
Khydursha 6 254
Kiærskou, Frederik Christian 27 460
Kia Gimen 21 597
Kiam see CH'OE PUK
Kiangan 24 624
Kian Soen 18 558
Kiato 28 712
Ki Baitei 17 190; 20 836
Kibal'chich, T. V. 31 565
Kibal'nikov, Aleksandr 27 285
Kibbutz Ein Harod see EIN HAROD
Kibbutz Ha-Zore'a see HA-ZORE'A
Kibel, Wolf 29 108
Kibitsu Shrine 17 64*
Kibo 1 433
Art Gallery 30 302
Kibria, Muhammad 3 168; 23 799
Kibrik, Yevgeny (Adol'fovich) 18 30*; 25 238; 27 396
Kibris see CYPRUS
Kibriszade Ismail Hakkı Efendi 27 683
Kibwanga, Mwenze 1 432
Kichinosuke Tonomura see TONOMURA, KICHINOSUKE
Kichizaemon Hishikawa see HISHIKAWA KICHIZAEWON
Kichizan see CHŌDENSU MINCHŌ
Kichizan Minchō 17 39, 170
Kick, Simon 9 470; 25 362
Kick, William 7 166; 18 613
Kickert, Conrad 21 852
kick-wheels see under POTTERS' WHEELS → types
Kiczura, Ludwik 25 125
Kidd, Joseph Bartholomew 2 710; 5 750; 16 884
Kidd, William A. 7 530
Kidder, A. V. 17 753
Kidderminster (Hereford & Worcs) 10 225; 18 30*
carpets 5 830, 831; 10 358
see also under CARPETS → types
Town Hall 31 240
Kidd & Kidd 27 474, 475
Kideshka, SS Boris and Gleb 27 369
kid-skin see under SKINS → types
Kidson, Charles 23 62
Kidwell, William 18 31*
works 16 20, 20
Kiedrich, St Valentin 23 502
Kiefer, Anselm 14 589; 18 31–2*
patrons and collectors 2 561; 27 478
works 12 397; 18 31
Kiehtreiber, Albert Conrad see GÜTERSLOH, ALBERT PARIS VON
Kieishi 17 391
Kiel 8 748; 12 468
Kunsthalle 12 476
Nikolaikirche 13 161
Kiel, Beate 14 767
Kiel, Gottfried 14 767
Kielce 25 92, 133
Bishop's Palace 25 97
Cathedral 25 103, 114
Kielland, Kitty (Lange) 18 32*; 23 225
Kielmannseck, Johann Adolf von 23 675
Kien see YANAGISAWA KIEN
Kienbusch, (Karl) Otto von 2 450; 29 515
Kienholz, Edward 9 25; 18 33*; 31 608, 615
collaboration 30 924
groups and movements 7 685; 10 416
patrons and collectors 33 45
works 2 617; 15 869; 19 702; 22 680; 23 334; 31 706
Kienholz, Nancy Reddin 18 33
Kienlin, Adam 12 443
Kien Minagawa see MINAGAWA KIEN
Kiepenheuer & Witsch 23 13
Kier, J. L., & Co. 2 577
Kierkegaard, Søren 8 596; 10 685, 686
Kierstede, Cornelius 31 648
Kies, Symon Jansz. 14 293
Kiesel see KÜSEL
Kieser, Eberhard 14 502
Kiesler, Frederick (John) 7 838; 18 33–4*
collaboration 16 566
groups and movements 10 137; 30 22
works 9 359; 11 526; 13 801; 19 897; 23 48, 49
Kietz, Gustav Adolph 26 378
Kiev 9 507; 18 34–40*; 27 361; 31 545, 546, 551
academy 31 551
architecture 31 546, 547, 548, 551, 552
carpets 31 564
Contracts Building 31 551
Dynamo stadium and restaurant 31 552
Dzerzhinsky Square 31 552
ecclesiastical buildings 27 368; 31 553
Brama Zaborivs'ka 31 552
Cathedral of St Sophia 4 781; 7 261; 9 519; 18 38, 39*; 27 368; 31 547, 553, 554, 555, 560, 561
Holy Doors 31 563
manuscripts 31 555
metropolitan's house 31 551
mosaics 18 37; 22 156, 162; 27 414
parekklesia 24 110
plaques 9 593
sarcophagus of Yaroslav the Wise 9 597; 27 828
wall paintings 9 576
Church of Nikola Pritiska 31 552
Church of Nikolay Naberezhny 31 552
Church of the Mother of God 31 548
Church of the Tithe of the Most Holy Mother of God 27 368, 437; 28 837; 31 547, 553, 554, 560, 561
mosaics 9 561, 645
Desyatinnaya Church see Church of the Tithe of the Most Holy Mother of God
Mikhailovsky Monastery see Monastery of St Michael with the Golden Roofs
Monastery of St Cyril, Church of the Holy Trinity 31 547, 548, 554

Kiev
  ecclesiastical buildings—cont.
    Monastery of St Michael with the Golden Roofs 31 547, 554, 555, 561
      Cathedral of St Michael (1108-13) 27 368; 31 561
      mosaics 31 *554*
      reliefs 31 *560*
    Monastery of the Caves 3 191
    Pecherskaya Lavra 18 39–40*, *40*; 31 547, 550, 554, 555
      Cathedral of the Dormition 27 368; 31 548, 550, 554
      icons 31 557, 558
      Kovnirovsky building 31 552
    St Andrew 18 *36*; 26 8; 31 552
    SS Boris and Gleb 31 546
    St Cyril 27 369
    Trinity Monastery 31 551
    Vladimir Cathedral 31 553
    Vydubetsky Monastery 31 547, 551
      Cathedral of St Michael (1070-88) 27 368
  glass 31 563
  House of Doctors 31 552
  icons 9 626; 25 341; 31 555
  jewellery 31 562, *562*
  Klovsky Palace 31 551
  Lutsk Barracks 31 559
  manuscript illumination 31 555, 556
  metalwork 27 418; 31 562, 563
  metro 31 552
  museums
    Art and Industrial Museum 31 565
    Church and Archaeological Museum 31 565
    City Museum of Antiquities and the Arts 18 38
    Jewish museum 17 581
    Kiev-Pechersky Historical Museum 31 565
    Museum of National Architecture and Life 18 38
    Museum of Russian Art 31 565
    Museum of Ukrainian Art 31 551, 565
    Museum of Western and Oriental Art 6 285; 19 789; 31 565
    St Sophia Historical and Architectural Museum 31 565
    Second State Museum *see* Museum of Western and Oriental Art
  painting 31 559
  Podol 18 35
  Poltava City Council building 31 551
  reliefs 31 561
  sculpture 31 561
  Seminary 31 551
  Ukrainian academy of agriculture 31 552
  University 18 *36*; 19 497; 31 551
  urban planning 9 54
Kievan Gospels *see under* GOSPEL BOOKS → individual manuscripts
Kiev Fraternity School 18 37
Kievo-Mezhgorskaya Factory 27 410
Kieżgajłło-Zawisza (family) 25 131
Kifayut ʿAli 15 376
Kiffa 1 297
Kiga 1 303, 310
Kigai Kawaguchi *see* KAWAGUCHI, KIGAI
Kigali 1 *407*
Kigas Vishnu Temple 15 310
Kihachirō Ōkura *see* ŌKURA, KIHACHIRŌ
Kihago, Abbas 30 301
Kihururu, Edwin 30 301
Kii, Lady 17 154; 33 317
Kiik-Koba 31 545, *546*
Kiitsu Suzuki *see* SUZUKI KIITSU
Kijima, Yasufumi 17 93; 18 40*
Kijkoveral 13 875
Kijō Rokkaku *see* ROKKAKU, KIJŌ
Kijun 18 329
Kikan mizue 24 436
Kikin, P. A. 27 438
Kikkeri, Malleshvara Temple 15 532
Kikkert, Conrad 21 775
Kikkin Bunkai 17 861
Kikō *see* TOYOTA HOKKEI
Kikoïne, Michel 17 577; 18 445; 27 307
Kikomo
  masks 29 *70*
Kikō Mozuna *see* MONTA MOZUNA
Kikongo 8 230; 16 879
Kikuchi, Hobun 17 201; 18 231
Kikuchi Gozan 17 237
Kikugawa Eizan 17 286
Kikuji Kawada *see* KAWADA, KIKUJI
Kikuji Yamashita *see* YAMASHITA, KIKUJI
Kikumaro 17 286
Kikutake, Kiyonori 14 212; 18 41*; 31 734
  groups and movements 17 90; 21 317, 318; 23 627
  staff 16 783; 31 134, 518
  works 17 91; 18 *41*
Kikuyu 1 297, 307, 411; 17 906
  shields 1 *412*
Kilaghari *see* KILOKARI
Kilbowie 28 241
Kilburn 14 544
Kilburn, E(dward) G(eorge) 10 144
Kilburn, William (*fl* 1790) 10 356
  works 8 *36*
Kilburn, William E. (*fl* 1846-62) 19 279; 24 666
Kilchberg Church 33 629
Kilchipura 20 244
Kilclispeen *see* AHENNY
Kildare 16 *5*; 18 42*
  Cathedral (medieval and later)
    tomb of Bishop Wellesley 16 20
  Church (7th cent.) 2 72
Kildare, James Fitzgerald, 20th Earl of *see* FITZGERALD, JAMES, 1st Duke of Leinster
Kildesku, Emil 21 812
Kildrummy Castle (Grampian) 28 224; 31 230
Kilenge 24 84
  headdresses 24 *84*
Kiley, Dan 8 470; 11 347
Kilfane Church (Co. Kilkenny)
  tomb of the Cantwell Knight 16 19, *19*
Kilfenora 16 19
Kilian (family) 2 719; 12 390; 18 47
Kilian, Bartholomäus, I (1548-88) 18 42
Kilian, Bartholomäus, II (1630-96) 18 42, 46*
  works 18 142; 28 127, 149; 33 297
Kilian, Christoph Gustav 18 42
Kilian, Georg 18 42, 46–7*
Kilian, Georg Christoph 3 413; 18 42, 46, 47–8*
  personal collection 18 46
  works 18 *47*; 33 297
  writings 18 44
Kilian, Georg Martin 18 42
Kilian, Jeremias 18 42
Kilian, Johann 29 788
Kilian, Johann Baptist 18 42
Kilian, Johann Jakob 18 42
Kilian, Lucas 2 718; 13 631; 18 42–5*
  collaboration 18 45
  groups and movements 9 446
Kilian, Lucas—cont.
  patrons and collectors 13 631
  teachers 18 42
  works 11 456; 13 847; 14 320, 321; 18 *44*; 27 228; 28 189; 29 431, 748
Kilian, Mang 33 279
Kilian, Paul 18 42
Kilian, Philipp 10 529; 28 149
Kilian, Philipp Andreas (1628-93) 18 42, 45–6*; 33 279
  works 18 *45*
Kilian, Philipp Andreas (1714-59) 18 42
Kilian, Wolfgang 2 718; 18 44–6*
  patrons and collectors 33 274
  pupils 18 46
  teachers 18 42
  works 13 847; 28 149
Kilian, Wolfgang Philipp 18 42
Kılıcar Kilise 5 677; 9 544; 26 483
Kiliç Arslan II, Sultan (*reg* 1156-92) (Saljuq of Anatolia) 16 186
Kilid al-Bahr 21 586
Kilifarevo Monastery 5 152, 153
Kiliman 11 759
kilims 5 829; 18 48–9*
  historic and regional traditions
    Anatolia, ancient 9 490
    Azerbaijan 2 *901*, 901–2
    Bulgaria 5 161
    Iran 18 48, *48*, 49
    Islamic 2 *901*; 16 477, 478
    Kurdistan 18 49
    Morocco 18 49
    Ottoman 16 477, 478; 18 49
    Poland 25 132
    Serbia 28 458
    Tunisia 18 48
    Turkestan (region) 18 49
    Turkey 5 830; 16 477, 478; 18 48, 49
  materials
    camel hair 18 48
    cotton 18 48
    goat-hair 18 48
    silk 18 48, 49
    wool 2 *901*; 18 48, *48*
Kilingeren, Bruno van 29 428
Kilise Deresi Church 9 590
Kiljandend, Elna 2 317
Kilkenny 16 *5*
  Castle 16 22; 26 475
  St Canice's Cathedral 16 7, 13
    tomb of Piers Butler, 8th Earl of Ormonde, and his Wife 16 20
  sculpture 16 20
Kilkenny Design Workshop 16 29
Kilkhampton (Cornwall), St James 24 577
Killarney (Co. Kerry) 16 *5*, 27; 31 335
  Cathedral of St Mary 13 203; 16 11
  Lunatic Asylum 16 11
Killeen, Richard 18 49–50*
  works 23 61, *61*
Killerton (Devon) 6 565
Killick, John Alexander Wentzel 7 788; 14 812; 25 571
Killick, Stephen 2 754
Killigrew, Anne 18 50*
Killigrew, Thomas 9 486; 13 299; 30 673, 674
Killigrew, William 10 305
Killinger, Georg Friedrich 23 313
Killith 31 435, 436
Killke 29 177
Killua Castle (Co. Westmeath) 15 872
Killybegs 5 841
Killymoon Castle (Co. Tyrone) 23 210
Kilmacduagh (Co. Galway) 16 7
Kilmacolm (Strathclyde), Windyhill 20 23–4; 28 270
Kilmarnock (Strathclyde) 5 830; 28 266
  Exchange 28 228
Kilmichael Glassary Bell Shrine 26 689
Kilnasoolagh Church (Co. Clare)
  monument to Sir Donat O'Brien 16 20, *20*
kilns 6 329–30*; 29 499
  historical and regional traditions
    Byzantine 9 633
    China 6 685, 870–72*, *870*, 873, 875, 877, 879, 886, 896
    Cuba (Caribbean) 8 236
    Czech Republic 9 80
    Egypt, ancient 10 22–3
    England 10 301
    Greece, ancient 13 482–3
    Iran 16 409
    Ireland 16 28
    Islamic 16 394, 409
    Japan 17 242–3*, 247, 250, 253, 256–7, 350, 353, 373
    Mesopotamia 21 305
    Netherlands, the 4 778
    Peru 3 364
    Prehistoric art 6 870, 875, 877; 9 80
    South America, Pre-Columbian 3 364
    Yangshao culture 6 870, *870*
  types
    anagama see tunnel
    bonfire 10 301
    clamp 1 305; 4 768, 785; 10 301
    climbing 6 870, 871*, *871*; 17 255, 351, 352, 811
      see also noborigama
    down-draught 4 768; 16 394
    dragon *see* climbing
    drying 6 330
    egg-shaped *see zhenyao*
    electric 16 29
    hebigama see climbing
    Hoffmann 4 768, 787
    horizontal draught 4 768
    jagama see climbing
    long see climbing
    mantou 6 870*, *870*, 892
    muffle 6 329
    noborigama 17 *243*, 243, 255
      see also climbing
    ōgama 17 254, 259
    reducing 16 394
    snake *see* climbing
    step 6 871*
    tunnel 4 768; 17 242, 243, *243*, 247, 251, 252, 259, 350
    up-draught 4 768; 6 870, 873, 876; 10 301; 17 243, *243*
    vertical 16 394
    wood-drying 33 *327*
    zhenyao 6 *871*, 871–2*
Kilokari *see under* DELHI
Kilpatrick, William H. 17 420
Kilpeck Church (Hereford & Worcs) 10 *225*; 18 50*
  sculpture 10 *475*, 476; 26 616
  south door 18 *50*
Kilrimont *see* ST ANDREWS (FIFE)
Kilruddery (Co. Wicklow) 16 24
Kilteel Church (Co. Kildare) 26 618
Kilwa 1 *407*, 410; 16 414; 30 56
  Husuni Kubwa palace 1 315; 23 824
  Museum 30 302
Kim, Tai Soo 14 203
Kim, Vladimir 17 867
Kimball, Fiske 26 491, 735; 31 672
Kimball, Francis H(atch) 18 54*; 22 60; 23 42; 30 505
Kimball, W. W. 3 693
Kimbei Kusakabe *see* KUSAKABE, KIMBEI
Kimbel, Anthony 3 395
Kimbel, Wilhelm 12 426; 18 55*
Kimbel & Friedrichsen 18 55
Kimbell, Kay 31 667
Kimbell Art Museum *see under* FORT WORTH (TX)
Kimberley 29 *103*, 105
  diamonds 29 103
  Kimberley Hall 23 859
  William Humphreys Art Gallery 29 121
Kimbolton Castle (Cambs) 6 60; 12 *7*; 13 200; 21 908; 23 210; 31 860
  paintings 24 340
Kim (ii) Ch'ang-jip 18 51, 52
Kim Ch'ang-su 18 315
Kim Ch'ang-yŏl 18 326
Kim (ii) Ch'ang-yŏp 18 51–2*
Kim Ch'an-yŏng 18 325
Kim Cha-wŏn 18 259
Kim (i) Che 18 50–51*
  attributions 18 51
  groups and movements 18 51
  pupils 33 524
  works 18 *51*, 314, 324
Kim chin-gyu 18 58
Kim Chip 18 50
Kim Chŏng-hŭi 18 55*, 331
  groups and movements 18 59
  paintings 18 52
  personal collection 7 209
  pupils 7 187, 188; 14 817; 18 59, 372; 33 528
  works 18 315, 325
Kim Chŏng-su 18 263, 300
Kim Chŏng-suk 18 301
Kim Chong-yŏng 18 300, 301
Kim Chung-ŏp 18 263
Kim Chun-gŭn 18 321
kimedashi 17 275
kimekomi dolls *see under* DOLLS → types
Kim Hae *see* HOSHIYAMA CHŪJI
Kimhae ware *see under* POTTERY → wares
Kim (iv) Hong-do 17 774; 18 53–4*
  collaboration 33 532
  patrons and collectors 18 259
  personal collection 18 52
  works 18 *54*, 255, 257, 317, *319*, 320
Kim Hŭi-su 18 329
Kim Hu-sin 18 321
Kim Hwa-kyong 18 60
Kim Hwan-gi 18 55–6*, 326
Kim Hyŏn-sŏng 18 56*, 329
Kimiaki Takeuchi *see* TAKEUCHI, KIMIAKI
Kim Ik-hŭi 7 207
Kim In-hu 18 329
Kimizu, Takashi 17 137
Kim Ka-jin 18 331
Kim Ki-ch'ang 18 60
Kim Ki-sung 18 332
Kim Ku (711-91) *see* KIM SAENG
Kim Ku (1488-1534) 18 329
Kim Kwang-su 18 56*
Kim Kwan-ho 18 56–7*, 325
Kim Kwan-p'il 18 56*
Kim Kyŏng-sŭng 18 300, 301
Kim Kyu-jin 18 57*, 325
Kimmeridge coal 17 514
Kimmig, Wolfgang 14 498
Kim Myŏng-guk 18 57–8*, 312, 314
  works 18 *57*
Kim Myŏng-hŭi 18 331
Kim Ok-kyun 18 331
Kimolos 32 294
Kimon 14 456
Kim On-gyŏng 18 328
Kimon of Kleonai 2 676; 12 68; 13 550, 587; 18 58*; 25 44, 176; 30 175
  copies 13 587
  teachers 10 649
kimonos 17 *309*, 310, *311*, 315, *316*, 317, *317*, *327*, 332, 359, 373, 375, 376
Kimpese Museum 33 598
Kim Pokchin 18 300

Kim Po-t'aek **18** 58*
Kim Pu-sik **18** 314
Kim Saeng **18** 58*, 328
Kim Sane **16** 169
tomb of Salar Khalil **16** 166
Kim Sang-hŏn **18** 314
Kim Sang-yong **18** 330
Kim Se-jung **18** 301
Kim Se-yŏn **18** 263
Kim (i) Sik **18** 50, 51*
Kim Si-sŭp **18** 58*
Kim Sŏk-gyong **18** 372
Kim Sŏk-jun **18** 331
Kim (iii) Sŏk-sin **18** 52, 53*
Kim Su-ch'ŏl **18** 59*, 315, 317
Kim Su-chŭng **18** 59*, 330
Kim Su-gŭn **18** 263
works **18** *263*
Kim Tae-sŏk **18** 331
Kim Tae-sŏng **18** 261
Kim Tŏk-myŏng **18** 332
Kim Ton-hŭi **18** 332
Kim Tu-il **18** 300
Kim (iii) Tŭk-sin **18** 52–3*, 320
Kim Tu-ryang **18** 59*, 320
Kim (iii) Ŭng-hwan **18** 52*
Kim Ung-won **18** 331
Kim Ŭn-ho **18** 59–60*, 326; **33** 534
Kimura, Ihei **18** 60*; **22** 445
Kimura, Morikazu **17** 267
Kimura, Shōhachi **13** 315; **18** 87
Kimura Kenkadō **17** 411, 412; **18** 60*; **23** 594
books **18** 542
paintings **17** 424
teachers **15** 126
Kimura Nagamitsu **17** 786
Kimura Yuri *see* YURI
Kim Whanki *see* KIM HWAN-GI
Kim (iv) Yang-gi **18** 53*, 320
Kim Yi-kyung **18** 344
Kim Yong-jin **18** 61*, 325, 332
Kim (ii) Yun-gyŏm **18** 51, 52*
Kim Yu-sin **18** 298
tomb **18** *274*
Kim Yu-sŏng **18** 61*
Kina **17** 262
Kinalua **1** 491; **30** 384
Kincardine, Thomas Bruce, 11th Earl of *see* BRUCE, THOMAS, 7th Earl of Elgin
Kind, George **32** 511
Kinda, František **8** 414
Kinder, John **2** 706; **18** 61*; **23** 57
Kindersley, Richard **19** 606
Kindrochit Brooch **28** 263
Kindt, David (1580-1652) **18** 61–2*
Kindt, David 't (*fl* 1741-70) **18** 62*
works **3** 546, *547*; **33** 179
Kindt, Hieronymus **18** 62
Kindt, Jan **18** 61
Kindt, Louis 't **18** 62
Kineas **1** 190, 487
Kinemon Iwakubo *see* TOYOTA HOKKEI
kinetic art **1** 79; **7** 546, 698; **10** 416; **18** 62–3*
automata **2** 838
dealers **26** 193
exhibitions **1** 448
mobiles **5** 423; **11** *877*; **21** 745
sculpture **18** *63*; **28** 202; **29** 88; **31** 257; **32** 176
Kinetoscope **7** 327
King (family) **10** 265
King, Benjamin **18** 66
King, Bertha *see* EVERARD, BERTHA
King, Brian **16** 22
King, Cecil **16** 18; **18** 64*
King, Charles Bird **18** 64*; **32** 889; **33** 93
King, Charles William **12** 266
King, Clarence **23** 625
King, Daniel **31** 653
King, David H. **19** 766
King, Mrs E. B. *see* BROWNLOW, EMMA
King, Emory **3** 624
King, Gamaliel **17** 890, 891
King, Georgiana Goddard **33** 310
King, Gerry **2** 763
King, Giles **14** 637
King, Grahame **18** 64
King, Inge **2** 753, 766; **18** 64–5*
King, Jaime Litvak *see* LITVAK KING, JAIME
King, James **2** 759
King, Jessie M(arion) **10** 336; **18** 65*; **19** 594
groups and movements **12** 780
works **28** 258
King, John Crookshanks **15** 19
King, Louise **8** 85
King, Oliver, Bishop **3** 369; **32** 378
King, Phillip **10** 375; **18** 65–6*; **19** 591
collaboration **22** 58
groups and movements **1** 80
pupils **20** 27
teachers **10** 268
works **7** 697; **16** 58; **25** 26
King, Samuel **18** 64, 66*
King, Thomas (1741-1804) **10** 265
King, Thomas (*d c.* 1839) **18** 66*
King, Thomas Harper **3** 585; **5** 320; **18** 66–7*
King, William **8** 220
Kingae Sanbei *see* RI SANPEI
Kinga Inoue *see* INOUE KINGA
Kingdon, Jonathan **31** 528
kingindeigawa *see under* LACQUER → types
King John Cup **7** 728, *728*
Kingman, Dong **14** 538
Kingman, Eduardo **9** 713; **18** 67*
Kingoktuk **22** 656
Kingo Tatsuno *see* TATSUNO, KINGO
King René of Anjou, Master of **10** 716; **20** 706–8*
patrons and collectors **2** 114
works **2** *114*; **11** 531; **20** *706*, *707*, 708
King's Company **30** 674
King Scorpion mace head **9** 868, *868*; **14** 514
Kingsfield, Christopher **29** 542
Kingsford, Florence Kate **7** 505
Kingsland, James **14** 200
Kingsley, Charles **4** 363
King's Lynn (Norfolk) **31** 710
Customs House **10** 668
Franciscan church **21** 841
Guildhall of the Holy Trinity **13** 164
St Margaret **26** 589; **28** 294
St Nicholas **9** 152
King's Lynn Cup **10** 322, *323*
King's Psalter *see under* PSALTERS → individual manuscripts
King's Stables **22** 694
King's Stanley (Glos) houses **32** *276*
Kingston (Ont.; Canada) **5** *559*
City Hall **5** 560
Fort Henry **21** 574, 575
fortifications **21** 575
Frontenac County Court House **5** 560
Kingston (Jamaica) **16** *878*
All Saints **16** 889
architecture **16** 882
Bob Marley statue **16** 889
central library **16** 889
Devon House **16** 883, 886, 889
Don Quarrie statue **16** 889
Edna Manley School for the Visual Arts **2** 149, 154; **16** 884, 889, 890
Government House **16** 886
Institute of Jamaica **16** 890
Jamaican Conference Centre **16** 883
Life of Jamaica building **16** 887
Kingston (Jamaica)—cont.
monument to Sir Charles Metcalf **16** 889
National Gallery of Jamaica **5** 746
A. D. Scott Collection **16** 890
collections **12** 917; **16** 889, 890; **27** 280
Cunda collection **16** 888
directors **4** 602
Larry Wirth Collection **16** 890; **17** 804
National Heroes Park
tomb of Norman Manley **16** 889
Norman Manley statue **16** 889
Sir Alexander Bustamante statue **16** 889
University of the West Indies **16** 890
Kingston (Dorset; UK), St James **29** *765*
Kingston, Evelyn Pierrepont, Duke of *see* PIERREPONT, EVELYN, Duke of Kingston
Kingston, George (Strickland) **1** 151; **2** 738; **18** 67*
Kingston Brooch **10** 322
Kingston Down (Kent) **2** 79
Kingston Lacy (Dorset) **3** 178, 179
collections **3** 178, 179; **17** 673
obelisk **10** 90
paintings **10** 510; **20** 588; **26** 301, 364; **29** 543
Kingston Lisle (Oxon), St John the Baptist **9** 155
Kingston-upon-Hull (Humberside) *see* HULL
Kingstown **2** 148
Kings Weston (Avon) **10** 232; **18** 31
King's Works *see* OFFICE OF WORKS
King's yellow *see* ORPIMENT
King William County Court House (VA) **18** 887
king-wood **10** 291; **11** 596; **26** 84
Kinichiro, Ishikawa **30** 246
Kınık *see* XANTHOS
Kininger, Georg **14** 901
Kininger, Vincenz Georg **21** 417; **25** 786; **29** 611
Kininmonth, William **29** 379
Kinizsi, Pál **14** 884
Kinizsi, Mme Pál **14** 899
Kink, Martin **19** 339
Kin Kai *see* HOSHIYAMA CHŪJI
Kinkakuji *see under* KYOTO
Kinkel, Gottfried **28** 916
Kinkodō Kamesuke **18** 554, 555
Kinkoku Yokoi *see* YOKOI KINKOKU
Kinkozan Gen'emon **18** 67
Kinkōzan Kobayashi **18** 67
Kinkozan Sōbei **18** 555
Kinkōzan Zen'emon **18** 67
Kinloss (Grampian) **28** 234
Kinloss, Mary **2** 560
Kinloss Psalter *see under* PSALTERS → individual manuscripts
Kinmei, Emperor (*reg* 531 or 539-571) **2** 654
Kinmel Park (Clwyd) **3** 269; **22** *810*; **25** 804
Kinnaird Castle (Grampian) **22** 190
Kinnal **15** 721
Kinnamos, John **9** 519
Kinnear, C(harles) G(eorge) H(ood) **24** 315*
Kinnear & Peddie **24** 315
Kinneil Castle (Lothian) **28** 244
Kinnema, Johannes
works **11** *447*
Kinnersley, Philip **9** 320
Kinney, Ashley **1** 158
Kinney, Desmond **16** 42
Kinney, O. S. **1** 158
Kinnoul, Thomas Hay, 7th Earl of *see* HAY, THOMAS, 7th Earl of Kinnoul
Kinodoni Art Group **30** 301
Kino-Fot **12** 35; **24** 450
Kinoshita, Hideichirō **17** 206
Kinoshita, Shin **22** 742
Kinoshita Itsuun **17** 189
Kinosuke Ebihara *see* EBIHARA, KINOSUKE
Kinosuke Takeda *see* TAKEDA, KINOSUKE
Ki no Tsurayuki **13** 812; **17** 212, 222, 223, 437
works **17** *213*, *223*
Kinouchi, Yoshi **17** 137
Kinpei Nakamura *see* NAKAMURA, KINPEI
Kinpusenji **17** *11*, 345; **18** 67–8*
Niōmon **18** 68
sutra box **17** 321
Zaōdō **18** 68
kinrande bowls *see under* BOWLS → types
Kinrimund (Fife) *see* ST ANDREWS
Kinross, John **18** 68–9*; **28** 230, 256
Kinross House (Tayside) **28** 226, 246
Kinryō Kaneko *see* KANEKO KINRYŌ
Kinsai Masuda *see* MASUDA KINSAI
Kinsaku Nakane *see* NAKANE, KINSAKU
Kinsarvik **13** 143
Kinsbergen, J. H. van **11** 885
Kinsella, Annie **2** 152
Kinshasa **1** *401*; **29** 69
Académie des Beaux-Arts **33** 596, 597
Bibliothèque Nationale **33** 597
Institut des Musées Nationaux du Zaïre **33** 597, 598
Institut National des Arts **33** 598
Musée National **33** 598
Museum of Indigenous Life **33** 598
National Archives **33** 597
Stanley-Pool School **33** 598
Walloon-Brussels Centre **33** 598
Kinsky (family) **3** 488
Kinsky, Princess **13** 234
Kinský, František Ferdinand **8** 419
Kinský, Josef, Count **8** 409
Kinsman, Edmund **17** 616
Kinsman, Rodney **14** 522
Kinsoen, François-Joseph **18** 69*
Kintō, Fujiwara no *see* FUJIWARA NO KINTŌ
Kintore **1** 56
Kints, Peter **33** 358
Kin-ts'un *see* JINCUN
Kintsune Saionji *see* SAIONJI KINTSUNE
Kintsvisi, St Nicholas **12** *317*, 320, 323; **18** *69*, 69–70*
Kinzaburō Yoshioka *see* TSUKIOKA YOSHITOSHI
Kinzing, Peter **26** 529
kiosk-mosque *see under* MOSQUES → types
kiosks **18** 70–73*
China **18** 72*
Egypt, ancient **9** 830, 831, *831*; **18** 70*
Indian subcontinent **18** 71–2*, *72*
Iran **18** *70*, 71
Islamic **18** 70–71*, *70*
Japan **18** 72*
Korea **18** 72*
North Africa **26** 919
Ottoman **16** *589*; **18** 71
Rome, ancient **26** 919
Spain **18** 71
Syria **18** 70
Turkey **16** *589*
see also BELVEDERES; GAZEBOS; PAVILIONS (BUILDINGS)
Kiowa **22** 62, 551, 562, 592, 595, 616, 629, 643
pectoral ornaments **22** *615*
Kip, Johannes **18** 73*
collaboration **19** 622
works **4** 80, *81*; **5** *751*; **6** 515; **8** 46; **10** 250; **12** 341; **14** *127*; **18** 155; **23** 258
writings **12** 128
Kip, William **18** 73*
Kipling, John Lockwood **4** 288; **15** 407, 656, 741, 747
architecture **14** 148; **28** 748
museum **22** 364
sculpture **4** 289; **15** 542
works **15** 542
Kipling, Rudyard **4** 364; **32** 78
Kipp, Herbert A. **14** 802
Kipp, Karl **31** 653
Kippenberger, Martin **18** 74*
Kiprensky, Orest (Adamovich) **18** 74–6*; **27** 389, 390
exhibitions **32** 724
patrons and collectors **27** 438
works **18** *75*; **27** 579; **29** 778
Kipshidze, D. **12** 329
Kipsigis **1** 307, 411
Kiradu **15** *279*; **18** 76*
Someshvara Temple **15** *312*, 314
Kirakos **31** 177
Kirakos carpets *see under* CARPETS → types
Kirakos Gandzakets'i **23** 355
Király, József **14** 910
Királyfa, Pálffy Castle **14** 887
Kiratas **22** 766
Kirat Dam **16** 198
Kīrāṭkūpa *see* KIRADU
Kirby, John Joshua **11** 908; **14** 144
Kirby, Joshua **24** 490
Kirby, Kent **7** 576
Kirby, R. G. **28** 158
Kirby, Richard **28** 886
Kirby Hall (Northants) **11** 876; **23** 492; **30** 762
Kirby Muxloe Castle (Leics) **4** 770, 779
Kirchbach, Ernst **6** 597; **12** 917
Kirchberg an der Jagst **27** 323
Kirchberg bei Volkach Pilgrimage Church **27** 159
Kirchenschmuck **24** 438
Kircher, Athanasius **18** 76–7*
collections **15** 740; **16** 771; **22** 675
works **24** 55
writings **10** 96; **20** 92
Kircherian collection **27** 46
Kirchheim an der Mindel, Schloss der Fugger **8** 881, *881*; **11** 819; **12** 348
Cedernsaal **6** 604
paintings **17** 711
sculpture **5** 768; **12** 345
Kirchheim Synagogue **17** 544
Kirchhoff, Johann Wilhelm Adolf **14** 864
Kirchinayer, Johannes **8** 111
Kirchmayr, Anton **15** 866
Kirchmeyer, Ferdinand **11** 734
Kirchner, Albert Emil **17** 814; **18** 77*
Kirchner, Dominik **33** 255
Kirchner, Ernst Ludwig **4** 366, 892; **15** 828; **18** 77–82*; **24** 311; **25** 582; **28** 77; **29** 878; **30** 328
drawings **18** *80*; **24** VI; **25** 583
exhibitions **12** 407
frames **11** *464*
groups and movements **4** 132, 891; **10** 694, 695, 696, 841; **12** 395; **14** 284; **16** 817; **27** 213; **28** 124
house **2** 552
methods **6** 471
paintings **10** *694*; **11** 465; **18** *79*, *81*, 717; **22** 331; **31** 705
patrons and collectors **14** 506; **20** 880; **23** 121

Kirchner, Ernst Ludwig—cont.
periodicals 29 871
prints 25 600
drypoints 9 310
lithographs 19 491
posters 25 348
woodcuts 33 363
pupils 27 213
reproductions in embroidery 30 151
sculpture 12 407, 408; 18 *78*
Kirchner, Gregor Wilhelm von 9 146
Kirchner, Heinrich 12 408; 22 267; 29 491
Kirchner, Johann Christian 18 82
Kirchner, Johann Gottlob 17 768; 18 82–3*; 21 64
Kirckstück Church 13 187
Kirdford (W. Sussex), Roundwyck House 23 398
Kirdi
granaries 1 *310*
Kirghiz 1 209; 6 252, 254; 10 874
carpets 1 209
textiles 16 451
Kir-hareseth *see* KERAK
kiri 17 358
Kiriazopoulos, Tasios 25 125
Kiribati 18 83*; 23 *711*
architecture 23 717
armour 3 332; 18 83; 23 735
basketwork 3 332
body ornaments 23 735
canoes 18 83; 23 726
fans 10 779
mats 18 83
meeting-houses 18 83
pandanus 23 735
wood 23 717
kirifuki 17 276
kirikane 13 843
Kirillo-Belozersky Monastery 18 83–4*; 27 *363*, 371
bastion 27 *371*
Cathedral of the Dormition 25 337; 27 371, 385
Kirillov, Averky 22 170
Kirim Temple 18 295
sculpture 18 *295*
Kirinde, Stanley 29 468
Kirish 18 495
Kırışkal 1 824
Kiritsu Industrial and Commercial Company 17 424, 435
Kiriwina Island 24 81
Kirk, Arthur Nevill 4 480
Kirk, John 20 923
Kirk, Joseph 16 21
Kirk, Samuel 31 650
Kirk, Thomas 9 322; 16 21; 25 402
Kirkall, Edward 16 820
Kirkall, Elisha 2 239; 25 619, 622, 664; 33 365
Kirkbride, Diana 3 514; 31 576
Kirkbride, Thomas S. 28 843
Kirkbridge, Thomas 2 658
works 2 *658*
Kirkburn (Humberside)
Grave K3 6 160
Priory 26 614
Kirkby Lonsdale (Cumbria), St Mary 26 614
Kirkcaldy (Fife)
Museum and Art Gallery 28 273
Victoria Hospital 14 783
Kirkcudbright (Dumfries & Galloway) 20 32
Parton Church 28 251
Tolbooth Museum 28 274
Kirkeby, Per 8 736, 741, 761; 18 84*; 21 897
Kırkgöz Han 16 186
Kirkhall, Elisha 10 178
Kirkham Priory (N. Yorks) 14 420; 31 273
Kirkharle 4 874
Kirkhope, John 28 271
Kirkistown (Co. Down) 6 61
Kirkland, Vance 18 84–5*
Kirkleatham (Cleveland), St Cuthbert's 20 866
Kirkleatham Centrepiece 30 299
Kirklees Park (W. Yorks) 4 801
Kirk Michael (Isle of Man) 32 530
Kirkness, D. M. 28 256
Kirkpatrick, Cornwall 31 636
Kirkpatrick, J. H. 2 741
Kirkpatrick, Wallace 31 636
Kirkpatrick, William 15 744
Kirkstall, Dan Alexander of *see* DAN ALEXANDER OF KIRKSTALL
Kirkstall Abbey (W. Yorks) 7 351; 13 43; 21 837, 838; 22 218; 26 590
Kirkstead Abbey (Lincs) 7 351
Kirkuk 3 11
Kirkwall (Orkney)
Cathedral of St Magnus 26 591, 593; 28 224, 251
pulpit 28 251
sculpture 28 241
palace 28 268
Kir-Lareseth *see* KERAK-IN-MOAB
Kirman 15 *897*, *901*, 905; 16 *105*; 18 85*
architecture 16 230
baths 3 377
brass 4 682
carpets 15 899; 16 474, 482, 484
congregational mosque 16 193, 195, 248
felt 10 874
fortifications 21 589
maidan 16 230
metalwork 16 392
pottery 4 172; 16 423
textiles 16 449
wool 16 465
Kirmanshah 15 902
takya of Mu'avin al-Mulk 15 899; 16 234
Kirokugeijutsu no Kai *see* RECORD ART SOCIETY
Kirov 27 434
Museum of History and Arts 19 524; 27 440
Kirovabad *see* GYANJA
Kirovakan *see* VANADZOR
Kirsch, Hugo F. 2 817
Kirschbaum, Engelbert 10 213
Kirschner, Ferdinand 11 134; 25 438; 32 456
Kirschner, Friedrich 19 781
Kirschner, Marie 8 411
Kirschstein, Salli 17 582
Kirşehir
carpets 2 439; 16 477, 478
see also under CARPETS → types
tomb of Aşık Pasha 16 204
tomb of Melik Gazi 9 86; 16 185
Kirsheh, Michel 30 177
Kirshen, Gammili, Trumbo 22 671
Kirstein, Lincoln 18 85*, 594; 22 426
Kīrtidurga 8 767
kīrtimukha 15 243*
Kirti Sri Rajasimha, King of Kandy (*reg* 1747-82) 17 769; 29 461
Kirtland Mormon Temple (OH) 22 126; 30 450
Kirtling (Cambs), All Saints 26 613
Kirtlington Park (Oxon) 10 278; 29 540
Monkey Room 28 776
Kirttiraja, Ruler (*reg c.* 1015-35) (Kachchhapaghata) 15 292
Kirtti Singh, Raja of Gwalior (*reg* 1454-79) (Rajput) 15 386
Kirundu 1 *401*
Kirwan, Laurence 10 81
Kiryonen, A. A. 27 418
Kisaburo Morita *see* MORITA, KISABURO
Kisai Yamada *see* YAMADA, KISAI
Kisangani Museum 33 598
Kisarauskas, Vincas 19 499
Kisbér 15 2
Kisbun Palace 14 885
Kiselevich, L. N. 27 409
Kiselyov, Aleksandr 13 654
Kiselyov, Viktor 32 661
Kisenpur, Chateshvara Temple 15 319
Kisese 2 1 374, *376*
Kisfaludi Strobl, Zsigmond 14 896; 17 876; 18 86*
pupils 21 49; 28 39
Kisfaludy, Károly 14 901
Kish (Mesopotamia) 1 508; 3 11; 18 86*; 21 *267*
architecture 21 291, 292
glass 1 868
ivory-carvings 1 869
musical instruments 1 891
palaces 1 893; 21 284; 23 806; 29 923
pottery 16 397
stone 2 272
stucco 29 816
writing-tablets 21 271
ziggurat 33 675
Kish (Uzbekistan) *see* SHAHR-I SABZ
Kishangarh 15 597, *597*, 611–13*, *613*
Kishangarh Darbar Collection 15 611
Kishi Chikudō 17 200; 18 88
Kishida, Ryūsei 17 421; 18 86–7*
groups and movements 13 315; 17 205
patrons and collectors 23 179
Kishidake kilns 17 811
Kishi Ganku 17 197; 18 87–8*
works 17 *185*
Kishi Gantai 18 88
Kishin Shinoyama *see* SHINOYAMA, KISHIN
Kishinyov *see* CHIŞINĂU
Kishio Suga 21 892
Kishi Renzan 17 198
Kishman Tepe Caravanserai 16 154
Kisho Kurokawa *see* KUROKAWA, KISHO
Kisling, Bogumil 19 497; 27 447
Kisling, Moïse 17 577; 18 88*
groups and movements 11 550
patrons and collectors 9 465
pupils 20 512
Kismárton *see* EISENSTADT
Kismarty-Lechner, Jenő *see* LECHNER, JENŐ
Kiso-Fukushima 17 357
Kisōk 18 312
Kisō Toba *see* TOBA KISŌ
Kiss, August (Karl Eduard) 12 406; 18 89*; 26 23; 33 295
Kiss, Bálint 2 546; 18 89*
Kiss, Istvan 31 519
Kiss, József 10 892; 14 687
Kiss brooch 11 635, 637
Kisselef 26 725
Kissi 13 834; 18 89–91*; 28 690
currency 1 363
divination instruments 1 356
gongs 1 *359*, 360
iconography 1 263
masks 19 310
sculpture 1 *359*
statuettes 18 89–91, *90*
stone 1 292; 18 89–91, *90*
tools 1 *364*, 365
wood 1 *359*
Kissidougou 1 *386*
Museum 13 835
Kissling, Alfred 30 137
Kissling, Richard 18 91*; 28 115; 30 137; 33 736
Kissonerga-Mosphilia 8 *325*, 334, 343
faience (i) (glass) 8 349
figurines 8 337
Kissonerga-Mosphilia—cont.
pottery 8 *329*
vase paintings 8 *343*
Kissonergis, Ioannis 8 364
Kiss & Tell 12 219
works 12 *219*
Kisszeben *see* SABINOV
Kistenfeger, Jakob 22 301
Kistler, Lynton 1 145; 19 492; 20 604; 25 628
Kitade, Fujio 17 267
Kitade, Tōjirō 17 267
Kitagawa, Tamiji 10 505
Kitagawara, Atsushi 1 737
Kitagawa Sōsetsu 17 179; 30 378
Kitagawa Utamaro (1753-1806) 17 281; 18 91–3*
groups and movements 17 797
patrons and collectors 10 487
teachers 10 121
works 1 582; 10 485, 777; 17 177, 273, 276, 277, 280, 285*, 286, 287, 288; 18 *92*; 31 53
Kitagawa Utamaro II (*fl* after 1806) 17 286
Kita Genki 9 74; 17 184; 20 286
Kitain 17 348
Kitaj, R(onald) B(rooks) 17 579; 18 93–4*; 19 591
collaboration 10 258; 20 607
groups and movements 10 258; 25 231
patrons and collectors 19 507
teachers 10 375
works 10 482; 18 *94*; 25 599; 28 300; 32 902
Kitajima Setsuzan 9 73; 14 779; 17 235
works 17 *235*
Kita Kiuemon 17 401
Kita Kyushu *see* KOKURA
Kitakyushu City 17 18
Municipal Central Library 17 *91*, 92; 19 320
Municipal Museum of Art 16 563; 17 433
Kitamuki Dōchin 28 411
Kitamuki Unchiku 17 236
Kitamura, Shigai 17 133
Kitamura Enkin 12 100; 17 417
Kitano, Tsunetomi 17 295; 23 595
Kita no Mandokoro (Asano Nene) 17 785; 23 444
Kitaōji, Rosanjin 17 266; 18 95*
Kitao Masanobu 18 95–6*
collaboration 17 285
teachers 18 96
works 17 285; 18 *96*
illustrated 31 766
Kitao Masayoshi 17 285
Kitao school 18 95
Kitao Shigemasa 18 95–6*
collaboration 17 844
pupils 18 95, 494
works 17 285, 286
Kitashirakawa 17 245
Kita Sōun 17 184
Ki Tasuku *see* URAGAMI GYOKUDŌ
Kitawaki, Noboru 18 96*
Kitayama Kangan *see* KANGAN KITAYAMA
Kitayka, Konstantin 21 811
Kitbugha, Sultan (*reg* 1295-7) (Mamluk) 16 209, 382, 496
Kit-cat club 18 96–7*
Kitchener, Horatio Herbert 10 91; 28 748; 29 895
kitchens 16 141; 17 340; 22 *869*; 26 869
Kitchen Sink school 10 258; 12 296; 18 97–8*; 19 246; 28 880
members 4 693
works 18 *97*; 28 919
Kitchō 23 595
Kite, Jim 1 42
kite brooches *see under* BROOCHES → types
kites
historical and regional traditions
China 7 113*, 114, 147; 17 388
Japan 17 388–90*, *389*
Malaysia 20 180*
Pakistan 23 803
materials
bamboo 7 113, 147; 17 388; 20 180
cane 7 113
cocoons 7 113
cotton 7 113
feathers 7 113
gourds 7 113
hemp 17 389
nuts 7 113
paper 7 113, 114, 147; 17 388; 20 180; 31 258
rice-paper 17 390
silk 7 113
types
whistling 7 113
kithara 22 372
Kithira *see* KYTHERA
Kiti, Panagia Angeloktistos 8 358, *359*; 9 574
mosaics 8 359; 18 825
stucco 29 816
Kitimat (BC) 20 890
Kition 8 *325*, 331; 13 *362*; 18 98–9*; 21 300
bronze 8 353
coins 8 349
copper 8 353
faience (i) (glass) 8 350; 18 *98*; 24 645
ivory-carvings 8 350, 351
mosaics 8 354
rhyta 8 330; 18 *98*
sanctuary 8 335
sarcophagi 8 341
Temple of Astarte 8 335; 18 98
temples 24 641
see also LARNACA; QART HADASHT
Kitka Factory 5 159
Kitman, I. D. 21 812
Kitner, I(eronim) S(evast'yanovich) 18 99*; 25 89; 28 628
Kitō Takai *see* TAKAI KITŌ
Kits, Elmar 10 540
kitsch 15 170, *170*; 18 100–101*, *101*
Kitschelt, August 2 813; 18 101*; 29 722; 32 448
Kitson, Henry Hudson 18 594
Kitsu Bunchō 15 896
Kitsu Bunkō 15 896
Kitsu Mokyo *see* ZŌROKU I
Kitsuzan *see* CHŌDENSU MINCHŌ
Kittel, Johann Anton 7 210; 10 773
Kittel, Johann Josef 7 210; 10 773
Kittelsen, Grete Prytz 23 236, 238
Kittelsen, Theodor Severin 18 101–2*; 33 77
Kittenstein, Cornelis van 1 121; 14 96; 27 508; 32 140
Kittoe 31 904
Kittos 13 484
Kittrich, Josef 8 402; 25 430
Kittrichová, Ema 8 402
Kitulgala, Beli Cave 29 445
Kiuchi Sekitei 17 425
Kiuemon Kita *see* KITA KIUEMON
Kiukok, Ang 24 623
Kiva New, Lloyd *see* NEW, LLOYD KIVA
kivas 1 701; 6 *381*; 18 *102*, 102–3*; 22 566, 567; 28 641
Kivijärvi, Harry (Mikael) 11 101; 18 103*
Kivik 18 103–4*; 25 *470*, 524, 526, 530, 531; 30 *65*
rock art 18 *103*
Kivshenko, Aleksey 31 854
Kiwai 24 76, 77
Kiyev *see* KIEV

Kiyivshchyna, Letskaya Chapel **31** 548
Kiyochika Kobayashi *see* KOBAYASHI, KIYOCHIKA
Kiyoemon **27** 873
Kiyohara Yukinobu *see* KANŌ YUKINOBU
Kiyohide Torii *see* TORII KIYOHIDE
Kiyohira, Fujiwara no *see* FUJIWARA NO KIYOHIRA
Kiyokata Kaburagi *see* KABURAGI, KIYOKATA
Kiyokawa Denjirō *see* KATSUKAWA SHUNKŌ (1743-1812)
Kiyomasu Torii II *see* TORII KIYOMASU II
Kiyomine Torii *see* TORII KIYOMINE
Kiyomitsu Koushi *see* KOUSHI KIYOMITSU
Kiyomitsu Torii I *see* TORII KIYOMITSU I
Kiyomizu (family) **18** 555
Kiyomizu Rokubei **18** 552
Kiyomizu Rokubei I **26** 551
Kiyomizu Rokubei II **26** 551
Kiyomori no Taira *see* TAIRA NO KIYOMORI
Kiyomoto Torii *see* TORII KIYOMOTO
Kiyonaga Torii *see* TORII KIYONAGA
Kiyonobu Torii *see* TORII KIYONOBU
Kiyonori Kikutake *see* KIKUTAKE, KIYONORI
Kiyooka, Roy **5** 569
Kiyōō Kawamura *see* KAWAMURA, KIYŌŌ
Kiyoshige Torii I *see* TORII KIYOSHIGE I
Kiyoshi Goda *see* GODA, KIYOSHI
Kiyoshi Hara *see* HARA, KIYOSHI
Kiyoshi Hasegawa *see* HASEGAWA, KIYOSHI
Kiyoshi Ikebe *see* IKEBE, KIYOSHI
Kiyoshi Kawasaki *see* KAWASAKI, KIYOSHI
Kiyoshi Kobayakawa *see* KOBAYAKAWA, KIYOSHI
Kiyoshi Koishi *see* KOISHI, KIYOSHI
Kiyoshi Seike *see* SEIKE, KIYOSHI
Kiyoshi Unno *see* UNNO, KIYOSHI
Kiyotada Torii I *see under* TORII KIYOTADA I
Kiyoteru Hanada *see* HANADA, KIYOTERU
Kiyoteru Kuroda *see* KURODA, SEIKI
Kiyotomo Torri *see* TORII KIYOTOMO
Kiyotsune Torii *see* TORII KIYOTSUNE
Kiyoyuki Katō *see* KATŌ, KIYOYUKI
Kizaemon Takeda *see* TAKEDA KIZAEMON
Kizhi **18** 104–5*; **27** *363*
  Church of the Transfiguration **18** 104
Kizil **6** *288*, *614*; **18** 105*, 494; **28** *719*, 720
  caves
    Ajatashatru Cave **6** 297
    Cave 17 **6** 293
    Cave 76 **6** 311
    Cave 77 **6** 311
    Cave of Maya II **6** 294
    Cave of Maya III (Cave 224) **6** 292, *292*
    Cave of Preta **6** 296
      roof **6** *295*
    Cave of the Gorge (Cave 181) **6** 292
    Cave of the Red Cupola **6** 310
Kizil
  caves—cont.
    Cave of the Sixteen Sword-Bearers **6** *310*
    Cave with Doves Carrying Rings (Cave 123) **6** 293, 301, 303
    Cave with the Painted Floor **6** 302
    Gorge Cave **6** 303
    Middle Cave (Cave 186) **6** 293
    Painter's Cave (Cave 207) **6** 294, 302
    Treasure Cave (Cave 83) **6** 302, 311
    Western Cave **6** 301, *301*
  craftsmen and artists **6** 294
  manuscripts **6** 306
  Monastery **6** 294
  painting **6** 302
  reliquaries **6** 319
  temples **6** 294–5; **30** 441
  wall paintings **6** 312, 321, 776, 788
  wood-carvings **6** 318
Kızıl Avlu Serapeum **26** 877
Kizil-Ayak **6** 254
Kızılbel **10** 151; **19** 839
Kızıl Çukur, Church of Joachim and Anna **5** 676, *676*; **26** 483
Kizilgarga **18** 495
Kızıltepe Mosque **16** 179
Kızkalesi Fortress **2** 427
Kızlar Hamanai, Narli Kuyu **9** 564
Kizuki ōyashiro *see* IZUMO → Grand Shrine
Kizyl-Arvat **31** 459
Kjaer, Søren **8** 733
Kjaerholm, Hanne **22** 367
Kjærholm, Poul **8** 746
Kjartansson, Ragnar **15** 72
Kjarval, Jóhannes S(veinsson) **18** 105–6*
  works **15** 70, *71*
Kjarval, Sveinn **15** 72
Kjellander, Lars **30** 102
Kjersmeier, Carl **1** 438
Kjestad **26** 647
K. K. Kunst-Erzgiesserei (Vienna) **2** 802; **10** 908
K. K. Linzer Wollzeug- und Tuchfabrik **2** 825
Klaarhamer, Piet J. C. **15** 36; **19** 31; **26** 378
Klabin (family) **27** 307
Klackner, Christian **14** 397
Kladruby Monastery **8** 379; **13** 199, 200
Klagenfurt **2** 780
  Cathedral of St Peter and St Paul **2** 780
  Kreuzberg **27** 500
  Landesmuseum für Kärnten **2** 831
  Landhaus **2** 779, 806
Klagmann, Jean-Baptiste-Jules **11** 42, 622; **26** 191
Klaje, Hans Hermann **2** 502
Klamath **22** 668
Klandūkalns **18** 846
Klapheck, Konrad (Peter Cornelius) **12** 397; **18** 106*
  groups and movements **13** 727; **30** 23
  teachers **12** 875
Klapsi Basilica **9** 538
Klara School **1** 683; **2** 611; **3** 784
Klarenbeek, A. H. E. Pallandt van, Baroness *see* PALLANDT VAN KLARENBEEK, A. H. E., Baroness
Klaros **8** 262; **13** 405; **15** 53; **27** 1; **30** 435
Klarwein, Joseph **17** 493, 822
Klas, Johannes *see* KARLGREN, BERNHARD
Klas, Rinaldo **30** 16
Klassische Moderne **12** 396
Klášterec nad Ohří **8** 405
Klatovy **8** 394, 398
Klauber (family) **2** 719; **8** 838
Klauber, Ignaty **12** 2
Klauber, Johann Baptist **3** 413; **18** 106–7*
Klauber, Joseph Sebastian **3** 413; **18** 106–7*
Klauder, Charles Z. **13** 204
Klauer, Martin Gottlieb **18** 107*
Klauke, Jürgen **18** 107*
Klausenburg *see* CLUJ-NAPOCA
Klausen Church **13** 112
Klauser, Theodor **18** 107–8*
Klaveness, Anton Fredrik **23** 116
Klaxon **24** 435
Klazomenai **13** *363*; **15** 893
  coins **13** 587
  mosaics **13** 559, 560
  pottery **13** 502, 514; **15** 893
  sarcophagi **13** 503; **27** 825; **28** 893
Klazomenian ware *see under* POTTERY → wares
Kldeeti **12** 328, 330
Kleanthes, Stamatis **14** 149; **18** 124
Kleanthes of Corinth **18** 108*
Kleanthis, Stamatis **2** 673; **13** 348, 349, 358, 359
Klearchos of Rhegion **8** 458; **13** 439; **25** 767
Klebe, A. **25** 788
Kleber, Marshall **28** 761
Kleck **3** 525, *525*
Klee, Felix **17** 766
Klee, Paul **3** 824; **6** 588; **9** 460; **11** 309; **12** 396; **18** 108–12*; **25** 583, 584; **29** 872; **30** 125
  cliché-verre **7** 434
  dealers **17** 726; **19** 537
  drawings **9** 217; **18** *111*
    pastel **24** *245*
  exhibitions **32** 775
  groups and movements
    Allianz **1** 666
    anthroposophy **2** 138
    Art informel **2** 543
    Bauhaus **1** 76; **3** 400, 401, 403; **12** 396, 497
    Blaue Reiter **4** 131, 132; **12** 395
    Blue Four **4** 133, 177; **17** 766; **28** 78
    Dada **8** 434
    Moderne Bund **12** 649
    Orientalism **23** 505
    Surrealism **30** 19
    theosophy **30** 711
  house **2** 552
  methods **25** 619; **31** 578
  paintings **18** *112*; **22** 380; **30** 134
  patrons and collectors
    Arensberg (family) **2** 384
    Cooper, Douglas **7** 797
    Dotremont, Philippe **9** 189
    Guggenheim, Solomon R(obert) **13** 800
    Koehler, Bernhard (1849-1927) **18** 187
    Kuh, Katherine **18** 498
    Lefèvre, André **19** 66
    Maitland, Ruth (Esther) **20** 142
    Mattioli, Gianni **20** 848
    Neumann, J. B(er) (1887-1961; dealer) **23** 7
    Neumann, Morton G. **23** 7
    Nierendorf, Karl **23** 121
    Rupf, Hermann and Margrit **27** 343
    Thompson, G(eorge) David **30** 749
    Watson, Peter (Victor William) **32** 912
  periodicals **29** 871
  prints **7** 558
    etchings **18** *109*
    lithographs **19** 491
    monotypes **21** 896
  pupils **2** 381; **4** 60, 104; **10** 863; **22** 113; **28** 556; **29** 696; **33** 254
  studio **29** 858
  watercolours **18** *110*; **32** 902
Klee, Paul—cont.
  works **32** VIII2
  writings **8** 657
Klee, Paul, Stiftung *see under* BERNE → Kunstmuseum
Kleeblatt, Das **14** 388; **18** 501; **32** 924
Kleef *see* CLEVE
Kleen, Lars **30** 87
Klees-Wülbern, J. H. **31** 580
Kleihues, Josef Paul **11** 735; **12** 380; **18** 114*, 456
Klein, Adrian Bernard **18** 62
  works **22** *380*
Klein, Alexander **3** 796; **15** 132; **16** 565; **18** 114*
Klein, Astrid **18** 115*
Klein, Bernat **28** 232
Klein, C. **14** 388
Klein, Calvin **33** 15
Klein, César **18** 115*
  groups and movements **2** 288; **3** 801; **8** 825; **23** 267
Klein, Charles **3** 685
Klein, Franjo **13** 273
Klein, Fred **18** 117
Klein, H. **13** 810
Klein, Jerome **1** 772
Klein, Johann Adam **18** 115–16*
Klein, Josef **8** 386
Klein, Max **18** 116*
Klein, Melanie **25** 683
Klein, Roman (Ivanovich) **18** 116–17*
  assistants **26** 241; **32** 381
  collaboration **24** 400
  restorations by others **23** 426
  works **2** 417; **22** 173; **27** 440; **31** 401
Klein, William **18** 117*; **24** 678
Klein, Yves **9** 20; **11** 570; **18** 117–19*
  dealers **7** 421
  exhibitions **10** 680
  groups and movements **1** 79; **2** 420; **10** 416; **23** 260, 298; **25** 645; **30** 924; **33** 636
  methods **21** 761
  patrons and collectors **21** 135
  works **11** 551; **15** 868; **18** *118*, *119*; **21** 892; **23** 261; **24** 407; **29** 97
Kleinaspergle **6** 155; **12** *361*; **18** 119–20*; **25** *470*
Kleinbauer **4** 24
Kleinberger, François **7** 490
Kleinburg, McMichael Canadian Art Collection **5** 589; **22** 598; **31** 177
Klein & Duclos **30** 679
Kleine Galerie *see* WIENER KUNSTHEFTE
Kleiner, Salomon **18** 120*
  patrons and collectors **28** 146
  works **5** 347, *348*; **9** 18, 28; **11** 135, *135*; **13** 278; **19** 69; **32** 436, 459
Kleinert, Friedrich **20** 923
Kleinhans, Franz **18** 120*
Kleinhues, Josef Paul **25** 359
Kleinmann **20** 603
Kleinmeistern *see* LITTLE MASTERS
Kleiser, Lorentz **30** 327; **31** 659
Kleiss, Wolfram **3** 356
Kleist, Heinrich von **21** 141; **24** 406
Kleisthenes of Sikyon **2** 680; **30** 736
Kleitias **13** 490, 549; **32** 48*
  works **13** 507–8, *508*
Kleiton **33** 461
Kleiva, Per **23** 232
Klek, Jo *see* SEISSEL, JOSEPH
Klem, Théophile **30** 644
Klemens, Jan, Count **9** 324
Klemens, Jozef Božetech **28** 853
Klementz, Dmitri **7** 159
Klemm, Samuel **12** 461
Klemm, Walther **3** 779
Klengel, Johann Christian **9** 239; **18** 120–21*
  pupils **12** 500; **17** 713
  works **12** 392
Klengel, Wolf Caspar von **18** 121–2*
  pupils **32** 752; **33** 114
  works **9** 235; **29** 547; **30** 676
Klengenberg, June
  works **22** *630*
Klenze, (Franz) Leo(pold Karl) von
  architecture **9** 691; **12** 374, 375; **18** 122–5*; **24** 569; **30** 486
    cathedrals **13** 349
    churches **33** 282
    façades **28** 110
    fortifications **15** 835
    gate-houses **28** 186
    government buildings **25** 172; **31** 241
    hermitages **26** 731
    monuments **6** 171; **10** 745; **12** 168, 406; **13** 202, *610*; **22** 42; **25** 268; **33** 282, 295
    museums **2** 695; **9** 25; **27** 440; **33** 282
      Alte Pinakothek (Munich) **7** 871; **9** 12, 17; **12** 379, 476; **18** *124*; **22** *362*, 363
      Glyptothek (Munich) **7** 871; **9** 25; **12** 475; **18** *122*; **22** 362; **25** 267
      Hermitage (St Petersburg) **22** 362; **27** 578
      National Archaeological Museum (Athens) **13** 360
    palaces **8** 290; **11** 128; **22** 308; **23** 546; **33** 282
    theatres **11** 128; **17** 836; **22** 308
    urban planning **2** 673; **22** 300
  frames **11** 461
  groups and movements **13** 607, 610, 612; **22** 738; **26** 190, 704, 743
  patrons and collectors **3** 452; **33** 282
  personal collection **27** 231
  pupils **9** 80; **11** 34; **26** 709
  staff **23** 371
Kleonai, Kimon of *see* KIMON OF KLEONAI
Kleon of Sikyon **2** 160
Kleophon Painter **32** 48–9*
  pupils **13** 522
  teachers **32** 64
  works **13** 490, 522
Kleophrades **13** 520; **32** 49
Kleophrades Painter **13** 511, 519; **32** 49–51*
  works **13** *481*, 520; **32** *50*
Klerk, Michel de **18** 125–7*
  collaboration **18** 436; **21** 58
  groups and movements **1** 814, 815; **10** 698; **18** 436; **22** 868, 875
  works **1** 804, *814*; **4** 788; **18** *126*, 212; **22** 830; **30** 458
Klesecker, Justus *see* GLESKER, JUSTUS
Kletsk *see* KLECK
Klette, Gusztáv *see* KELETI, GUSZTÁV
Klettenhof, Karl Klette von **17** 885
Kletting, Richard **27** 642
Kleuze, Leo von **10** 638
Kleve *see* CLEVE
Klever, Yuly **3** 529
Kleyn, Roman (Ivanovich) *see* KLEIN, ROMAN (IVANOVICH)
Klíč, Karel **2** 119; **18** 127*; **24** 655; **25** 618
Kličevac **25** 528
Klickitat **22** 659
Klieber, Josef **5** 85; **18** 127*
  pupils **10** 702; **12** 842
  works **2** 802; **14** 895
Klijn, C. W. M. **33** 692

Klijnen, Josephus 23 450
Klima, Bohuslav 9 80; 24 291, 332; 25 467
Klimanová-Trizuljaková, Michaela 28 856
Klimaszewski, Kazimierz 32 878
Klimaszewski, Tomasz 32 878
Klimatia-Veltsista
 Church of the Metamorphosis 25 336
 Hagios Demetrios 25 336
Klimburg, M. 6 320
Kliment, Robert Michael 26 441
Klimkeit, Hans-Joachim 6 320
Klimkovics, Béla 18 127–8*
Klimkovics, Ferenc 18 128
Klimkovics, Ignac 18 128
Klimo, Aloyz 28 853
Klimontów Church 25 97; 28 407
Klimov 18 849
Klimsch, Eugen Johann Georg 18 128*
Klimsch, Ferdinand Karl 18 128*
Klimsch, Fritz 18 128–9*
 dealers 5 924
 teachers 28 52
 works 22 712
Klimsch, Karl (1841-1926) 18 128*
Klimsch, Karl Ferdinand (1867-1936) 18 128*
Klimsch, Ludwig 18 128*
Klimsch, Paul 18 128*
Klimt, Ernst 5 792; 18 129; 22 330
Klimt, Georg 11 464
Klimt, Gustav 2 797; 8 596; 9 217; 18 129–32*; 24 438; 32 446
 collaboration 5 792; 17 692
 exhibitions 32 197
 frames 11 464
 groups and movements 2 566, 643, 776; 28 343, 344; 32 446; 33 166
 monuments 18 135
 mosaics 11 320; 12 497; 14 628; 22 163, 378
 paintings 2 *797*; 10 *481*; 11 464; 18 *130*; 25 285
 patrons and collectors 2 829; 10 487; 25 283; 33 284
 prints 10 480; 18 *130*; 19 488; 22 330; 32 *446*
 pupils 23 459
Klimtgruppe 14 749; 17 744; 18 534; 21 365; 28 344
Klinckerfuss, Johannes 26 530
Klinckowstrom, O. W. 11 111
Klindt-Jensen, Ole 32 534
kline see GREECE, ANCIENT → couches
Kline, Franz (Rowe) 18 132–3*
 dealers 16 906
 groups and movements 1 78, 83, 86; 4 110; 23 48; 31 607
 patrons and collectors 9 189; 25 400; 27 277; 28 314
 works 2 839; 11 499; 15 829; 18 *133*; 31 705
Kling, Vincent G(eorge) 18 133–4*
Klingberg, Zina de 23 694
Klingborg, Arne 2 603
Klingen 27 643
Klingenberg *see* ZVÍKOV CASTLE
Klingender, Francis 2 553; 20 528
Klinger, Franz Josef 2 816
Klinger, Johann Gottfried 32 449
Klinger, Julius 25 348
Klinger, Max 10 396; 18 130, 134–6*; 19 112
 groups and movements 28 344
 works 2 240; 4 42; 12 407, 497; 14 628; 18 *135*; 22 330, 371, 378; 25 350
Klinger, Miloslav 33 630
Klingert, Gustav 27 426
Klinghe, Hinrich 11 253
Klinglin 22 436
Klingling (family) 11 736
Klingspor, Karl 9 703
Klingstedt, Karl Gustav 21 642
Klinkenberg, J. C. K. 33 677
Klinkhamer, Jacob F. 13 798
Klinkosch 11 33; 28 188
Klint, Hilma af 30 711
Klint, Kaare (Jensen) 8 761; 18 136–7*; 29 77
 pupils 4 183; 21 791
 works 6 391; 8 728, 746, 756; 17 480; 24 549
Klint, Vibeke 8 756
Klintzsch, Hans 20 88
Klippel, Robert 2 754; 18 137*
Klipstein, August 30 153
klismos see under CHAIRS → types
Klismos chairs *see under* CHAIRS → types
Kljakovic, Jozo 33 592
KLM 19 808; 29 791
Klöcker, David *see* EHRENSTRAHL, DAVID KLÖCKER
Klocker, Hans 2 799; 18 137–8*
Klöde, Silvia 21 67
Klodt, Mikhail (Konstantinovic) (1832-1902) 9 328; 17 447; 27 579
Klodt, Mikhail (Petrovic) (*b* 1835) 27 579
Klodt, Nikolay 31 582
Klodt (von Yurgensburg), Pyotr (Karlovich) 18 138*; 27 390
 collaboration 18 38
 works 27 578; 31 561
Kloet, van der (family) 22 881
Klonówka 25 110
Klontzas, Georgios 25 333
Kloos, Jan Piet 18 138*; 22 832
Kloosterzande Church 22 819
Klopcanows, Aleksanders 29 117
Klopedi 19 234, *234*
Klopp, Nico 19 827
Klöpper 12 196
Klopper, Sandra
 works 33 *725*
Klopstock, Friedrich Gottlieb 11 789
Kloss, Friedrich Theodor 18 798
Klossowski (de Rola), Balthazar, Count *see* BALTHUS
Klossowski, Erich 3 127; 18 138
Klossowski, Pierre 3 127; 18 138–9*
Klösterle porcelain factory 2 817
Klostermann, G. 27 438
Klosterneuburg Abbey 2 *776*, 777, 781, 783
 altarpiece 13 151
 cloister 13 151
 collections 2 829
 enamel 13 168
 manuscript illumination 2 792
 monstrance 2 820
 paintings 2 792; 11 806; 13 *151*
 palace 2 777
 pulpit 2 819; 22 269; 23 97–8, *98*; 25 723; 26 694; 31 284, 499
 sculpture 2 799
 stained glass 13 186
 Stift Lapidarium 13 916
 Stiftsarchiv 1 668
 stucco 29 839
 textiles 2 825
 Treasury 18 *139*, 139–40*
Klosterstrasse cooperative 4 181; 17 832
Kloster-Veilsdorf 30 793
Klotz, Barnardus 18 141
Klotz, Clemens 18 140*; 20 324; 22 711
Klotz, Gustave 29 755
Klotz, Heinrich 25 359
Klotz, Lenz 30 135
Klotz, Matthias 18 140
Klotz, Simon Petrus 18 140*; 19 482
Klotz, Valentijn 13 324; 18 140–41*
Klouček, Celda 25 151
Klovic, Juraj *see* CLOVIO, GIULIO
Klub Młodych Artystow i Naukowcow *see* CLUB OF YOUNG ARTISTS AND SCIENTISTS
Klucis, Gustav 7 770; 18 141*; 27 396; 32 661
 groups and movements 1 75; 7 769; 30 8
 patrons and collectors 8 10
 works 7 769, 770; 24 686; 25 351
Kluge, John 1 66
Kluge Collection 21 621
Klukstad, Jacob Bersveinsson 23 229, 242
Klukwan (AK) 22 *544*
 Whale House 22 *580*, 581
Klumb, Henry 25 701
Klumpke, Anna 4 318
Klungkung 15 775
 Law Courts 15 776
 musical instruments 15 *816*, 817
Klutsis, Gustav (Gustavovich) *see* KLUCIS, GUSTAV
Kluychovka Mausoleum 18 568
Klychev, Izzat Nazarovich 31 459
Klykov, Vyacheslav 27 398
Klymenko, F. 23 262
Klyn, Johannes 7 471
Klyun, Ivan (Vasil'yevich) 18 141*; 22 178; 27 392, 393, 394; 32 661
 groups and movements 8 251; 11 358; 16 818; 28 924; 30 8; 31 583
 patrons and collectors 8 10
Kmentová, Eva 8 388
Kmetty, János 17 876; 18 141–2*
 groups and movements 1 131; 20 103; 30 207
Kmita (family) 33 259
Kmita, Piotr 25 132; 33 259
KMT 14 826
Knab, Michael *see* MICHAEL OF WIENER NEUSTADT
Knabensberg, Hans 4 372
Knabl, Joseph 27 332
Knackfus, M. 19 497
Knackfuss, Hubert
 works 13 *405*
Knaeps, Jean 3 600
Knakfus, Marcin 13 775
Knap of Howar *see under* PAPA WESTRAY
Knapp, Johann 2 796
Knapp, Johann Michael 33 616
Knapp, Stefan 10 347
Knappich, Johann Georg 18 45, 142*
Knapton (Norfolk), SS Peter and Paul 11 253
Knapton, Charles 2 239; 6 117; 18 142; 25 210; 33 367
Knapton, George 18 142–3*
 assistants 1 504
 collaboration 26 345
 patrons and collectors 14 163; 28 924
 pupils 8 26
 works 18 *143*
Knapton, John 18 142; 25 210; 26 30
Knapton, Paul 18 142; 25 210; 26 30
Knaresborough Priory (N. Yorks) 31 340
Knatchbull, Edward 4 845; 7 171
Knaths, Karl 31 490
Knaus, Ludwig 18 143*
 groups and movements 9 460
 patrons and collectors 31 870
 works 9 461; 12 394
Knauth, Susanne K(atherina) *see* LANGER, SUSANNE K(ATHERINA)
Knave of Diamonds *see* JACK OF DIAMONDS
Knazhaya Gora 31 561
Kneale, Bryan 5 215
Knebworth House (Herts) 27 360
kneeling figures *see under* SCULPTURE → types
Kneese de Mello, Eduardo 23 118
Kneib, A. 11 599
Kneiphof *see under* KALININGRAD
Kneller, Godfrey 1 106; 18 144–7*; 19 584
 attributions 8 454
 collaboration 21 891; 33 177, 377
 frames 11 424, *425*, 426
 methods 9 211; 25 279, 281, 282
 patrons and collectors 1 150; 10 361, 658; 11 348; 15 29; 20 910; 23 467; 25 634; 29 58, 804
 pupils 4 70; 14 519; 17 507; 28 835, 869; 30 759; 32 378
 reproductive prints by others 3 476; 13 647; 18 570; 26 231; 28 881; 33 147
 works 8 454; 9 278; 10 249, 345; 18 97, *146*; 25 233; 26 223
Kneller, Johann Zachary 10 249; 18 144
Kneller frames *see under* FRAMES → types
Kneppelhout, Johannes 4 59
Kner Press 18 416
Knerr, Christian 28 852
Knerr, K. 31 353
Knesing, Johann Christian 12 426
Kneuterdijk 9 27
Kneutgen *see* KNÜTGEN
Knewstub, Walter John 27 188
Knezević, Mika 28 452
Kniaseff, Boris 12 894
Knickerbocker Toy Co. 31 261
Knidian Venus see APHRODITE EUPLOIA
Knidos 5 741, 742; 13 *363*; 18 147–8*
 architecture 18 147*
 figurines 13 581
 lamps 13 *603*
 Lion Tomb 6 170; 13 384, 407; 20 863; 31 *108*, 109
 monopteros 21 892
 pottery 27 107
 sculpture 18 147–8*, *148*
Knidos, Eudoxos of *see* EUDOXOS OF KNIDOS
Kniep, Christoph Heinrich 14 17; 28 657
Kniep, Johann 2 796
Knieper, Hans 18 149*
 patrons and collectors 8 732; 14 369; 23 395; 30 320
 works 8 754, *754*, 758; 14 542
Knies, Jan 24 332
knife-daggers 25 540
knife-handles
 historical and regional traditions
  Aztec 22 164
  Egypt, ancient 9 *866*, 867–8; 10 60
  Japan 17 386
  Mesoamerica, Pre-Columbian 21 246, 255; 22 164
  Mixtec 21 255
  Rome, ancient 27 87
  Sierra Leone 1 327
 materials
  amber 8 285
  bone 4 *314*; 8 284, 285
  bronze 27 87
  glass 17 386
  horn 8 285
  Ivorine 8 285
  ivory 1 327; 8 284, 285; 10 60; 16 799
  porcelain 8 285
  silver 8 285
  wood 8 284, 285
  wrought iron 8 284
  xylo 8 285
knife scales 14 763
Knife Sharpeners 21 29
Kniga i Revolyutsiya 24 428
Knight, Charles (Parsons) (1743-*d* after 1826) 3 280; 10 786; 18 149*
 works 8 864; 25 621, 623
Knight, Charles (1791-1873) 14 208; 25 590
Knight, Cyril Roy 23 75
Knight, Daniel Ridgway 31 603
Knight, Denis 3 62
Knight, Eliot 1 444
Knight, Frank 11 808
Knight, Harold 18 149; 23 259
Knight, John Barnard 2 760
Knight, John Prescott 4 845
Knight, Laura 18 149*; 23 259
 groups and movements 23 26
 works 7 434; 10 321
Knight, Mary 4 480
Knight, Richard Payne 13 303, 304; 18 149–50*
 groups and movements 2 163; 12 130, 131; 24 741, 742; 29 890
 house 6 61
 personal collection 5 434; 8 96, 98; 9 230; 10 79, 487; 12 266; 14 270, 279; 22 152; 24 258
 works 22 526; 26 740; 32 554
  illustrated 24 *742*
  on proportion 2 358
Knight, Thomas 9 295
knight jugs *see under* JUGS → types
Knight & Lacey 28 526
Knighton, William 14 145
Knights Hospitaller 18 150–52*
 art forms
  architecture 3 691–2; 6 *52*, 58; 14 126, 779; 17 490; 18 599; 19 566; 20 472; 21 574; 28 428
   Israel 21 564
   Jerusalem, Latin Kingdom of 17 505
   Malta (Republic of) 20 211
   Palestine 3 *691*; 18 *152*
   Rhodes (island) 26 *294*, 294
   Syria 18 421, *422*; 21 564
  ceramics 20 215
  coats of arms 14 410, 420
  coins 18 152
  gold 20 216
  gonfanons 11 *147*
  iconography 18 152*
  icons 26 293, 295
  manuscript illumination 17 506
  metalwork 20 218
  painting 25 563; 26 294–5
  sculpture 26 295
  silver 20 216
 patronage 18 151–2*; 20 219
 regional traditions
  Jerusalem, Latin Kingdom of 17 501, 503
  Malta (Republic of) 20 215
  Portugal 26 516
  Rhodes (city) 26 290
Knights of Calatrava 6 58
Knights of Malta *see* KNIGHTS HOSPITALLER
Knights of St Catherine (Mt Sinai) 7 177
Knights of St John of Jerusalem *see* KNIGHTS HOSPITALLER
Knights of Santiago 6 58
Knights of the Holy Sepulchre (Jerusalem) 7 177
Knights Templar 18 153–4*
 art forms
  architecture 6 58; 7 257; 18 599; 19 566; 28 428
   France 18 *154*
   Israel 21 564
   Jerusalem, Latin Kingdom of 17 503, 505
   Portugal 7 *257*
  banners 11 148
  gonfanons 11 *147*
 iconography 18 153–4
 patronage 18 153–4

Knights Templar—cont.
regional traditions
Jerusalem, Latin Kingdom of **17** 501
Knijff, Jacob **4** 80
Knijff, Leonard
attributions **19** *618*
works **4** 80, *81*; **14** *127*
Knijff, Willem **18** 155
Knijff, Wouter **18** 155*
Kniller, Gottfried *see* KNELLER, GODFREY
Knillinger, Balthasar **14** 893; **31** 353
Knin **8** *174*
basilica **8** 175
Knip, Augustus **18** 156*
Knip, Henriëtta Geertruij **18** 156*
(Ronner-)
Knip, Henriëtte **18** 156, 157*
Knip, Henri Johannes **18** 156–7*
Knip, Josephus Augustus **18** 156–7*
Knip, Mattheus Derk **18** 156*
Knip, Nicolaas Frederick **18** 156*
Knipbergen, François van **7** 673
Knipovitch group pottery *see under* POTTERY → wares
Knipper, Hans *see* KNIEPER, HANS
Knipple & Jaffrey **24** 748
Knirr, Heinrich **1** 141; **22** 113
pupils **1** 724; **14** 302; **18** 108; **19** 283; **22** 689; **23** 528; **32** 753
knitters' guilds *see under* GUILDS → types
knitting **18** 157–8*; **30** 550, 563
historical and regional traditions
Africa **18** 158
Australia **2** 768
Austria **18** 158
China **7** 53; **18** 157
Denmark **8** 753
Egypt **18** 157
Egypt, ancient **18** 157
England **18** 157
France **18** 157
Germany **12** 469; **18** 157, 158
Greece **18** 157
Guyana **18** 158
Iceland **15** 73*; **18** 158
Ireland **18** 158
Islamic **18** 158
Mexico **18** 157
Peru **18** 157; **24** 513
Portugal **18** 157
Russia **18** 158
Scandinavia **18** 158
Scotland **28** 266
South America, Pre-Columbian **18** 157
Spain **18** 157, *157*; **29** 350
Switzerland **18** 157
Turkey **18** 157
Venezuela **18** 158
materials
beads **18** 158
cotton **18** 158
silk **18** 158
wool **18** 158
types
machine **18** 158; **30** 550
peg **30** 550
uses
beadwork **3** 440
caps **18** 157
cushions **18** *157*
fibre art **11** 54
jumpers **18** 158
lace **18** 158
rugs **27** 318
stockings **18** 157
knitting machines **18** 158
knitting needles **18** 157
knives **2** 448; **8** 283–5*
historical and regional traditions
Africa **1** 361
Anglo-Saxon **8** *283*
Belgium **8** *283*
China **7** 1; **23** 495, *495*
knives
historical and regional traditions—cont.
Egypt, ancient **10** 60
France **8** *283*, *284*
Japan **17** 399
Kuba (iii) (Zaïre) **1** 361, 365
Mesoamerica, Pre-Columbian **21** 245
Mongolia **21** 878, 884; **23** 495, *495*
Netherlands, the **8** *283*
Philippines **24** *631*
Prehistoric art **8** 283
Rome, ancient **8** *283*
Shona **28** 621
Zande **33** 610
materials
bronze **23** 495, *495*
gold **28** *651*
ivory **10** 60
jade **7** 1
malachite **23** *495*
netsuke **17** 399
silver **28** *651*
stainless steel **8** 285
steel **8** 284, 285
turquoise **28** *651*
types
folding **8** 283, *283*, *284*, 285
palette *see* PALETTE KNIVES
pocket **8** *284*
throwing **1** 361, *361*
tumi **28** 651, *651*, *652*
Knížák, M. **8** 424
Knobel, Esther **16** 569
Knöbel, Johann Friedrich **3** 527; **33** 115
Knobelsdorff, Georg Wenceslaus von **18** 158–60*
architecture **3** 806; **4** 541; **12** 373
churches **4** 541; **25** 366
palaces **8** 816; **12** 424, 791; **13** 619; **18** *159*; **23** 812; **25** *367*; **27** 324
reconstructions **3** 791
theatres **30** 676
assistants **18** 475; **24** 541
collaboration **11** 459
groups and movements **26** 496, 497
interior decoration **12** 412; **14** 750; **22** 436
patrons and collectors **12** 374; **14** 652; **25** 367, 368
sculpture **9** 687
Knoblauch, Dieter **17** 548, 549
Knoblauch, Edmund **18** 161
Knoblauch, (Carl Heinrich) Eduard **3** 799; **17** 547; **18** 160–61*, 208
Knoblauch, Gustav **18** 161
Knobloch, Johann **13** 267; **33** 18
Knock (Co. Clare) **6** 160
Shrine of Our Lady **28** 632
Knockin (Salop), Top Farm **32** 276
Knocklyon (Co. Dublin), Sanctuary of St Colmcille **7** *269*
Knoder, Hans **4** 759
Knoedler, M., & Co. **1** 454; **2** 559; **5** 589; **7** 377; **11** 774; **14** 47, 117; **18** 161–2*; **21** 90; **31** 664
archives **2** 365, 371
paintings **23** 1; **30** 464
Knoedler, Roland **11** 664; **18** 161
Knoef, Jan **18** 162*
Knoest, Leonard **2** 198; **5** 46
Knöffel, Johann Christoph **9** 238; **18** 162*
collaboration **4** 218; **18** 473; **25** 240
patrons and collectors **29** 912; **33** 115
teachers **19** 642
works **9** 236, 241; **21** 64; **32** 752
Knofler, Heinrich, I (1824-86) **25** 623
Knofler, Heinrich, II (*fl* 1886) **25** 623
Knofler, Rudolf **25** 623
Knole (Kent)
furniture **6** 390; **9** 30; **10** 290, 291; **11** 119; **29** 8, *8*, 804; **30** 217, 781, 783
interior decoration **10** 271
Leicester Gallery **30** 783
paintings **9** 13; **13** 301; **27** 150, 494
sculpture **25** 376
silver **10** 328
staircases **29** 524
tapestries **10** 349
Knoll, Hans **31** 633
Knoll, Quirin **11** 818
Knoll, Willy **14** 523
Knoll Associates *see* KNOLL INTERNATIONAL
Knoller, Franz **18** 162
Knöller, Johann Georg **3** 429
Knoller, Martin **2** 795; **11** 120; **18** 162–3*
collaboration **24** 370, 758
groups and movements **26** 498
pupils **2** 232; **3** 778; **28** 161; **33** 744
teachers **31** 358
works **13** 852; **15** 865; **22** 796
Knoll International **1** 738; **2** 727; **23** 175; **30** 870; **31** 633; **32** 501
Knook, St Margaret **26** 616
Knoop, Jan **2** 464
Knopf, David **11** 224
Knorpelwerk *see* AURICULAR STYLE
Knorr, G. W. **5** 346
Knorr & Hirth **14** 576; **19** 410
Knossos **8** 153, 154; **10** 654; **13** *362*; **18** *163*, 163–8*; **21** *651*, 658, 659, 661, 692
alabaster (gypsum) **1** 517
bronzes **21** *688*
Caravanserai **21** 660, 674
faience (i) (glass) **13** 589; **21** 683, *683*, 684
gardens **12** 67
Hieroglyphic Deposit **21** 685
Hogarth's houses **21** 674
House of the Chancel Screen **21** 664
House of the Frescoes **21** 659, 674, *674*
House of the Ivories **21** 681, 682
House of the Sacrificed Oxen **21** 675
ivory-carvings **21** 660, 681, 682
Ivory Deposit **21** 681
jewellery **13** 597
Little Palace **18** 167
Mavro Spilio tombs **21** 684
North Cemetery **8** 154; **13** 597
North Entrance **21** 675
North-west Fresco Heap **21** 675
paintings **21** 660, 673, 676
Palace of Minos **2** 300; **10** 654; **18** 164–7, *166*; **21** 651, 652, 657, 658, 659, 663, 672, 677, 691; **23** 808
Camp Stool fresco **21** 660, 677, *677*
Central Court **21** 675
Chariot fresco **21** 677
Court of the Stone Spout **21** 660, 675–6, *676*
frescoes **29** 395
Grand Staircase **21** 654, 676
Great East Hall **21** 675
Hall of the Colonnades **21** 677
Hall of the Double Axes **18** 584
Jewel fresco **21** 673, 677
Ladies in Blue fresco **21** 677
Lily Prince relief fresco *see* Priest-King relief fresco
North-west Treasury **21** 675, *688*
paintings **21** 675
Palanquin fresco **21** 677
pottery **18** 167
Knossos
Palace of Minos—cont.
Priest-King relief fresco **21** 659, *660*, 676
Procession fresco **21** 676
reliefs **29** 814
Sacred Dance fresco **21** 677
Sacred Grove and Dance frieze **21** 675
Saffron Gatherer frieze **21** 654, 674
Shrine frieze **21** 675, 677
Shrine of the Double Axes **1** 691; **21** 654
staircase **21** 662; **29** 520, *521*
Throne Room **21** 660, 676, 677
Toreador frescoes **21** 675–6, *676*
vases **18** *168*
Vat Room **21** 684
wall paintings **8** 153; **18** 167; **21** 654, 673, 674, 675, 676, 677
pithoi **18** *167*
plaques **21** 661, 664
pottery **13** 493, 497, 502; **21** 667, 668, *668*, *669*, 670, 671, *672*
Procession fresco **21** 677
Residential Quarters **21** 675
rhyton **21** 664
rock crystal **26** 484
Royal Gaming-board **21** 682
Royal Road **21** 673, 674, 675, 681
Savakis's Bothros **21** 674
sculpture **21** 678
seals **21** 653, 682
South-east House **21** 674
South House **21** 674
South Propylaion **21** 676
stone vessels **21** 690
Temple Repositories **21** 658, 683, *683*, 684, 685
statuettes **21** 653
Temple Tomb **21** 665, *669*, 684, 687
Thirteenth Magazine **21** 675
tombs **21** 659
Town Mosaic **9** 788; **21** 664, 684, 691
towns **21** 664
Unexplored Mansion **21** 674
Villa Dionysus **8** 155
wall paintings **14** 348, 350; **21** 659, 663, 673, 674, 675
walls **21** 662
water supply **21** 662–3
West Entrance **21** 675, 676
writing **18** 167
writing-tablets **6** 479; **14** 333
Knote, Matthias **29** 610
Knotek, V. **31** 353
knot gardens *see under* GARDENS → types
Knothe, Czesław **25** 122
Knothe, Jan **29** 634
Knothe, Matthias **19** 748
knots
asymmetrical **5** 829, *829*; **16** 466
Gördes *see* symmetrical
jufti **5** 829, *829*
Persian *see* asymmetrical
Sehna *see* asymmetrical
single-warp **5** 829, *829*; **16** 466
Spanish *see* single-warp
symmetrical **5** 829, *829*, 835; **16** 466
Turkish *see* symmetrical
Knott, Ralph **19** 576; **31** 242
knotted-pile weaving *see under* WEAVING → types
knotting **21** 877; **30** 550
carpets **5** 828–9, *829*, 831, 832; **14** 65
fibre art **11** 54
lace **18** 588
Knotz, Hans **22** 918; **33** 278
Knowle, Edmund, Abbot of Bristol **4** 825
Knowles, Alison **11** 232; **24** 407
Knowles, Christopher **33** 223
Knowles, Dorothy **5** 569
Knowles, E. F. **31** 243
Knowles, Homer S. **18** 169
Knowles, H. P. **16** 143
Knowles, Isaac Watts **18** 169
Knowles, J. **10** 377
Knowles, James Thomas (i) (1806-84) **18** 168–9*
groups and movements **28** 345
patrons and collectors **28** 781
works **10** 238; **14** 786
Knowles, James Thomas (ii) (1831-1908) **18** 168, 169*; **25** 293
Knowles, Kaye **8** 717
Knowles, Ricardo **3** 64
Knowles, Taylor & Knowles **18** 169*; **31** 638
Knowsley (Merseyside) **29** 835
Knowth (Co. Meath) **16** *5*; **18** *169*, 169–70*; **25** *470*, 508
rock art **25** 509, 510
Knowth East (Co. Meath) **25** 511
Knox, Alistair **2** 742; **18** 170*
Knox, Archibald **9** 295; **18** 170*; **19** 594
groups and movements **6** 164
patrons and collectors **19** 311
works **10** 336, 344
Knox, David **4** 627
Knox, John **12** 776; **19** 875; **20** 32
Knox, Seymour H(orace) **18** 170*
Knox D'Arcy, William *see* D'ARCY, WILLIAM KNOX
Knoxville Court House (IL) **18** 887
Knox Wilson, James *see* WILSON, JAMES KNOX
knucklebones **31** 265, 266
Knudsen, Bent **8** 753
Knudsen, Gerda **23** 226
Knudsen, Knud **24** 664
Knudsen, Nina Sten *see* STEN KNUDSEN, NINA
Knuijt, Maria de **32** 267
Knüpfer, Benedikt **18** 171*
Knüpfer, Nicolaus **4** 487; **29** 587; **32** 683
Knüsel, Martin **30** 143
Knut, King of Denmark and England (*reg* 1019-35) **2** 76; **27** 166
Knut IV, King of Denmark (*reg* 1080-86) **19** 794, 795
Knütgen (family) **12** 429
Knütgen, Anno **18** 171; **28** 671
Knütgen, Bertram **18** 171; **28** 671
Knütgen, Christian **18** 171; **28** 671
Knütgen, Hermann **18** 171
Knütgen, Peter **18** 171; **28** 671
Knütgen, Rutger **18** 171; **28** 671
Knutsen, Knut **18** 171*; **23** 222
Knut the Great *see* KNUT, King of Denmark and England
Knut the Holy, King of Denmark *see* KNUT IV, King of Denmark
Knuytgin *see* KNÜTGEN
Kny, Frederick **33** 13
Knyff, Alfred (Edouard Hyacinthe) de **3** 562; **8** 632–3*
Knyff, Jacob **18** 155*
Knyff, Leonard **18** 155*
collaboration **19** 622
reproductive prints by others **18** 73
works **6** 515; **10** 250
Knysta Church **30** 907
Ko **18** 774
Kōami (family) **17** 29, 303, 304, 424; **31** 81
Kōami Nagashige **17** 304
works **17** *304*
Kōan Ogata *see* OGATA KŌAN
Koati **31** 47
Koba **3** 45
Kobadian **6** 273
Koban **31** 701
Koban culture **27** 366; **28** 321

Kobayakawa, Kiyoshi **17** 295
Kobayashi, Ichizō **17** 429; **23** 595
Kobayashi, Kiyochika **17** 293; **18** 172*
works **17** 290, *292*
Kobayashi, Kokei **18** 172*
groups and movements **17** 201
house **33** 562
pupils **23** 390
works **17** 201, 202
Kobayashi, Masakazu **11** 54
Kobayashi Kinkōzan *see* KINKŌZAN KOBAYASHI
Kobayr, Kat'oghike Church **2** 430
Kobe **17** *11*, 18; **18** 172–3*
Children's Museum **2** 7
City Museum of Nanban Art **17** 429, 433; **18** 173
exhibitions **17** 138
Hakatsuru Fine Art Museum **18** 173
Hyōgo Ceramic Museum **17** 433
Kiyoshi Kōjin Seichōji Temple Tessai Museum **31** 135
Kurokawa Institute of Ancient Cultures **6** 826; **7** 154
Mt Rokko Chapel **2** *7*; **17** 92
Köbel, Jacob **33** 18
Kobeling, Bernd **12** 397
Kobell (i) (family) **20** 282
Kobell (ii), Anna **18** 176, 177*
Kobell (ii), Balthazar **18** 176
Kobell, Egid von **18** 173
Kobell (i), Ferdinand **18** 173–5*; **33** 280
collaboration **18** 175
pupils **18** 175, 523
works **2** 592; **18** *174*
Kobell, Franz (Innocenz Josef von) **14** 135; **18** 173, 175, 176; **33** 280
works **26** *903*
Kobell (ii), Hendrik **18** 176*, 739
Kobell (ii), Jan (Baptista), I (1733-1833) **18** 176*
Kobell (ii), Jan (Baptist), II (1778-1814) **18** 176–7*; **31** 771
Kobell (ii), Jan, III (1800-39) **18** 176, 177*
Kobell, S. **5** 168
Kobell (i), Wilhelm (Alexander Wolfgang) von **18** 173, 175–6*; **33** 280
collaboration **18** 174
copies **18** 115
pupils **14** 322; **23** 9
works **2** 106; **12** 393; **18** *175*
Kōben (1173-1232; monk) *see* MYŌE
Kōben (*fl* 1199-1215; sculptor) **17** 124, 879; **22** 502; **31** 676
Københavns Lervarefabrik **8** 748
Kober, Marcin **18** 177*; **25** 103; **30** 482; **32** 6
Kober, Wacław **18** 177
Koberger, Anton **2** 223; **12** 385; **23** 310; **25** 41, 625
Koberger, Johannes **28** 143
Koberling, Bernd **3** 803; **31** 532
Kobierniki **25** 131
Kobilca, Ivana **18** 177*; **28** 860
Kobizeva, Klavdiya **21** 812
Købke, Christen (Schjellerup) **8** 734, 735; **14** 543; **18** 177–80*
groups and movements **26** 742
patrons and collectors **14** 572
pupils **11** 798
works **11** *472*, 473; **12** 294; **18** *178*, *179*, 715
Koblasa, Jan **8** 388
Koblenz, Peter von *see* PETER VON KOBLENZ
Koblenz, St Kastor **7** 837; **26** 673, *673*; **30** 905
Koblenz Bible *see under* BIBLES → individual manuscripts
Kobliha, František **8** 393; **10** 563; **33** 710
Kōbō Daishi *see* KŪKAI
Kobori, Tomoto **33** 508
Kobori Enshū **12** 99; **18** 180–81*, 564
pupils **30** 258
teachers **11** 855
works **17** 215, 336, 343; **18** 551, 559, 560, 564; **22** 432; **31** 84
writings **17** 428
Kobori Masatsugu **18** 180
Kobro, Katarzyna **18** 181–2*; **29** 794
collaboration **29** 795
groups and movements **1** 76; **2** 409; **4** 148; **7** 772; **25** 108, 116, 422, 423; **30** 8
works **7** *771*
Kobuladze, S. **12** 327
Kobuleti **12** 320
Kobyletskaya, Zinaida **27** 413
Kobyłka **25** 133
Kobystan *see* GOBUSTAN
Kobzdej, Aleksander **18** 182*
Koç (family) **16** 553
Kocamemi, (Ahmet) Zeki **18** 182*; **31** 454
Kočevje Church **28** 859
Koch, Alexander **2** 565; **18** 185*; **24** 427
Koch, August **18** 182
Koch, Bernard **18** 185
Koch, Carl **30** 469
Koch, Ciril Metod **19** 516
Koch, Erduin Julius **32** 751
Koch, Ernest **32** 454
Koch, Gaetano **18** 182, 184*
patrons and collectors **3** 272; **28** 19
works **4** 312; **16** 644, *648*; **24** 692; **26** 762
Koch, Georg **19** 815
Koch, Heinrich **33** 514
Koch, Henrik **30** 210*
Koch, J. **25** 428
Koch, Jacob, II **23** 313; **25** 22
Koch, John A(ugustus) B(ernard) **2** 739; **4** 374; **18** 185*; **21** 75
Koch, Jørgen Hansen **4** 68; **14** 543
Koch, Joseph Anton **2** 796; **18** 182–4*; **30** 133
assistants **11** 236
groups and movements **22** 740
patrons and collectors **7** 871; **30** 766
pupils **14** 766; **25** 550; **26** 358
works **5** 886; **11** *460*, 461; **12** 392; **18** *183*
Koch, Kenneth **26** 431
Koch, M. **33** 30
Koch, Matthias **19** 482
Koch, Mogens **8** 746
Koch, Ödön **30** 139
Koch, Pieter Frans Christian *see* KOCH, PYKE
Koch, Pyke **18** 185–6*; **22** 852; **31** 771
works **22** *852*; **28** 920
Koch, Rudolf **28** 307; **31** 497; **33** 303
Koch, Svend **8** 727
Kochanowski, Jan **33** 606
Kochar, Gevork B. **2** 428; **10** 450; **32** 695
Kochavi, Nora **16** 568
Koch & Bergfeld **12** 449
works **12** *450*
Kocher, Alfred Lawrence **18** 186
Kocher and Frey **18** 186*
Koch-Grünberg, Theodor **10** 580
Kōchi **17** 84, 358
Sekkeiji **17** 124
K'o Chiu-ssu *see* KE JIUSI
Kōcho **18** 195
Kochubey, V. P. **29** 554
Kock, Lucas (Cornelisz.) **7** 497
Kock, Paul de **3** 849
Kocks, Adriaensz. **22** 879, 880
Kocsis, A. **8** 563
Kodachrome *see under* PHOTOGRAPHY → processes
Kōdaiji *makie see under* LACQUER → types
Kodaira, Yoshichika **12** 100
Kodak **8** 579; **15** 822; **24** 648; **28** 256; **30** 390; **33** 58
see also CAMERAS → types; EASTMAN KODAK
Kodály, Zoltán **15** 18
Kodan **22** 758
Kodenji Hayashi *see* HAYASHI, KODENJI
Kodheli, Kel **1** 540
Kodjiamani, Nikos **8** 365
Kodjo, Michel **8** 22
Kodjoyan, Hakob **2** 431, 432
Kodo *see* NAKAMURA, HIROSHI
Kōdō Bijutsu Kyōkai (Action Art Society) **17** 135
Kodōjin Fukuda *see* FUKUDA, KODŌJIN
Kodros Painter **32** 51–2*
Koebner, Marcin *see* KOBER, MARCIN
Koechli, Friedrich **27** 429
Koechlin, Maurice **10** 107
Koechlin, Raymond **13** 171; **16** 559
Koechlin, Schmaltzer & Cie **11** 649
Koeck, Christian **1** 844
Koedijck, Isaak (Jansz.) **18** 186*; **22** 840
Koefoed, Herman **17** 678
Koehler, Bernhard (1849-1927) **18** 186–7*; **20** 381; **29** 872
paintings **20** 11, 12
Koehler, Bernhard (1882-1964) **18** 187
Koehler, Florence **17** 528; **31** 655
Koehler, Otto *see* BALDEN, THEO
Koehler, Sylvester Rosa **21** 895; **24** 431
Koehler, Wilhelm Reinhold Walter **18** 187*
Koekkoek, Barend Cornelis **18** 187–8*
collaboration **23** 590; **32** 241
patrons and collectors **11** 233
pupils **11** 885; **30** 373
works **11** 448; **22** 847
Koekkoek, Hermanus **18** 188; **22** 847, 848
Koekkoek, Johannes Hermanus **18** 187
Koekkoek, Marinus Adrianus **18** 188
Koelderer, Joerg **31** 822
Koeler, Jörg **18** 510
Koelhoff **10** 203
Koella, Johann **21** 408
Koelle, Fritz **22** 712
Koelman, Jan Daniel **18** 188
Koelman, Jan Hendrik **18** 188
Koelman, Johan Philip **4** 159; **14** 42; **18** 188*; **26** 468
Kōen **17** 124, 125
Koen, Terrence **14** 753
Koene, Isaac **17** 920
Koene, Konrad *see* KUENE VON DER HALLEN, KONRAD
Koenen, Matthias **7** 693
Koenig, Friedrich **25** 593
Koenig, Fritz **9** 229, 231; **18** 188–9*
Koenig, Leo **17** 577
Koenig, Pierre **18** 189*
Koenig-Fachsenfeld Collection *see under* STUTTGART → museums
Koenigs, Franz W. **3** 889; **4** 912; **20** 446
Kōen Masuda *see* MASUDA KŌEN
Koenraad, Bishop **22** 817
Koepcke, Arthur **29** 16
Koepell, Matthias **13** 729
Koepf, Hans **2** 834
Koepping, Johann Friedrich **27** 420
Koepping, Karl **22** 291
Koerbecke, Johann **12** 384; **18** 189*
works **19** 530
Koerfer, Jakob **28** 834
Koerten, Joanna **24** 57
works **24** *56*
Koeru **10** *536*
church **10** 536
Koets, Roelof **7** 370
Koetser, David Maurits **30** 153
Kōetsu *see* HON'AMI KŌETSU
Kōetsu Masuda *see* MASUDA KŌETSU
Koffi, Gahou **3** 728
Koffi Mourouffie **8** 23
Kofi, Vincent **12** 509
Kofler-Truniger, E., Collection *see under* LUCERNE
Kofman **33** 313
Kōfu **17** 433
Kofun period *see under* JAPAN → periods
Kō Fuyō **17** 409, 411; **18** 190–91*
collections **17** 414
groups and movements **17** 411–12*
pupils **2** 210; **17** 848; **18** 60; **20** 75; **29** 85; **33** 709
works **17** 237, *412*
Kōga **18** 60; **22** 445; **23** 179; **24** 437
Koga, Harue **18** 191*
groups and movements **17** 206; **30** 22
works **17** *205*, 206
Kogaku Sōkō **18** 560
works **18** *560*
Kogălniceanu, Mihail **5** 73; **26** 722
Kogan, Moisey **22** 921
Kogan, Sh. G. **21** 811
Kōgan Tobari *see* TOBARI, KŌGAN
Koga Seiri **17** 236
Kogei (company) **17** 408
Kōgei **21** 635; **24** 437; **28** 466; **33** 491
Kōgei nyūsu **24** 437
Kō Gentai *see* KŌ TEN'I
Kogi **29** 133; **30** 240, 241
Kōgijae *see* CH'OE PUK
Kogler, Jan Jiří **8** 413
Koglin, Norman **30** 869
Köglsperger, Philip Jakob **11** 125
Kogohak **18** 382
Kogohakpo **18** 382
kogoks **18** 364, 365, *365*, 366
Kogo minsok **18** 382
Kogui **7** 602
Kogŭm sŏhwagwan **18** 57
Kogun **5** 238
Kogŭon *see* KIM SU-CHŬNG
Koguryŏ **18** 382
Koguryŏ ware *see under* POTTERY → wares
Kohán, György **13** 333
Kohar, Andreas **28** 850
Kohayen, Monastery of Debre Maryam **10** 570
Kohayto **1** 513; **10** 565
Koheiji Miura *see* MIURA, KOHEIJI
Kohei Sugiura *see* SUGIURA, KOHEI
Koher, Antonín **8** 413
Kohitsu (family) **17** 439
Kohitsu Ryōsa **17** 439
Koh Ker **2** 55; **5** *458*, 468
Prasat Neang Khmau **5** 486, 487, 501
Prasat Thom **5** 468
sculpture **5** 486
Koh Krieng **5** 484
kohl **1** 344; **10** 67
Kohl, Andreas **17** 656
Kohl, František **8** 386
Kohl, Hieronymus **18** 191–2*
assistants **18** 192
collaboration **18** 505; **23** 195; **25** 548
pupils **18** 191; **25** 548
works **8** 384; **25** 438; **28** 855
Kohl, Ludvík **14** 756
Kohlenberg, Adam **1** 769
Köhler, Bernhard **12** 472
Köhler, David **4** 176, 493
Köhler, F. **29** 435
Köhler, Heinrich Gottlieb **23** 235
Köhler, Johann Heinrich **9** 240
Kohlmann, Etienne **11** 601
Kohlschein, Joseph **10** 396
Kohl-Severa, Johann Friedrich **18** 191–2*
collaboration **18** 505
works **8** 385; **18** 505; **25** 443
Kohn, Adolf **23** 71
Kohn, A. Eugene **18** 193*
Kohn, Gabriel **18** 192*
Kohn, Heinrich **12** 409
Kohn, Jacob **18** 192
Kohn, J. & J. **2** 809, 814; **15** 823; **18** 192*; **30** 755; **32** 448
collaboration **30** 755
Kohn, Josef **18** 192
Kohn, Robert David **17** 547
Kohn Pederson Fox **18** 193*; **21** 650; **23** 43; **28** 835
Kōho Kanō *see* KANŌ KŌHO
Kōhō Kennichi **8** 461
Kohtz, Otto **18** 193*
Ko Hŭi-dong **18** 193–4*, 325
Ko Hung *see* GE HONG
Kohunlich **29** 828
Koichev, P. **5** 149
Kōichi Takita *see* TAKITA, KŌICHI
Koichi Tamura *see* TAMURA, KOICHI
Koide, Narashige **17** 205; **18** 194*
Koidu **28** 691
Koil *see* ALIGARH
Koilani, Ecclesiastical Museum **8** 367
Koili, Hagios Giorgios **8** 358
Koishi, Kiyoshi **18** 194*
Koishiwara **17** *241*, 353
ceramics **30** 259
Japan Handicrafts Museum **21** 635
Nakano **30** 258
Tsutsumi kiln **30** 258
Koitsu Ishiwatari *see* ISHIWATARI, KOITSU
Koizumi Yakumo *see* HEARN, LAFCADIO
Kojève, Alexandre **10** 685
Kojima, Torajirō **17** 429; **23** 371
Kojima, Zensaburō **18** 194*
Kojima, Zentarō **17** 206
Kojima Sōshin **14** 704
Kōjirō Matsukata *see* MATSUKATA, KŌJIRŌ
Koji Rōnen *see* RŌNEN KOJI
Kōjō **17** 119, 121, 221, 597
Kojong, Emperor (*reg* 1864-1907) **6** 448; **7** 208; **18** 57, 300
Kojō Sonoda *see* SONODA, KOJŌ
Kojuharov, Nikola **5** 154
Kōjun Morimoto *see* MORIMOTO, KŌJUN
Kok, Anthony **29** 660
Kok, J. (*fl* 1780s) **5** 322
Kok, J. Jurriaan (1861-1919) **18** 195*; **22** 883
Kō Kaho *see* JIANG JIAPU
Kokamägi, Epp-Maria **10** 540
Kokamthan, Jagadambadevi Temple **15** 316
Kokand **6** *182*; **10** 896; **16** *105*; **18** 195*; **31** *781*
City Museum of Local Lore **6** 283; **18** 195
cotton **6** *250*
Kamal Kai Madrasa **6** 208
palace of Khudoyar Khan **6** 208; **31** 782
textiles **6** 249; **16** 451
woodwork **16** 502
Kōkan Shiba *see* SHIBA KŌKAN
Kokava nad Rimavicou **28** 856
Koka Yamamura *see* YAMAMURA, KOKA

Kōkei (*fl c.* 1151-1200) 17 98, 121, 401; 18 195–6*; 22 492
  assistants 31 675
  collaboration 31 675
  groups and movements 17 879
  pupils 17 729
  works 17 122, 124, 131; 22 492, 497, 502
Kōkei (1648-1705) 22 497
Kokei Kobayashi *see* KOBAYASHI, KOKEI
Kokei Sōchin 17 343
Kokei Tsuruya *see* TSURUYA, KOKEI
Kōkei Yoshimura *see* YOSHIMURA KŌKEI
Kokenhusen *see* KOKNESE
kokeshi *see under* DOLLS → types
Ko Khao 30 578, 598
Kôkhov ha-Yardēn *see* BELVOIR CASTLE (ISRAEL)
Kokka 24 436
Kokkinobaphos Master 9 605, 612
  works 9 *605*
Kokko, Valto 11 107
Kokkola School 11 *90*
Kokla 14 348
Koknese 18 *847*, 847
  Castle 18 847
Kōkō, Emperor (*reg* 884-7) 18 549
Kōkogaku Kyōkai (Archaeology Association) *see* NIHON KŌKOGAKU KYŌKAI
Kokolja, Tripo 18 196*; 22 17
Kokorinov, Aleksandr (Filippovich) 18 196–7*; 27 375; 28 646
  collaboration 27 402; 31 827
  pupils 3 432; 29 551; 33 599
  teachers 31 543
  works 27 575
Kokoschka, Oskar 2 826, 831; 4 366; 12 396; 14 630; 18 197–200*; 27 665; 28 139
  groups and movements 2 553; 9 239; 10 695, 696; 12 395; 14 33; 17 744; 23 2, 505; 33 166
  methods 24 354
  patrons and collectors 2 829; 10 414; 23 121; 28 377
  pupils 23 335; 28 564; 33 427
  teachers 8 428
  works 2 797; 18 *197*, *199*, 442; 19 *485*, 490; 29 871; 32 446
Kokoschka, Václav 8 414
Kokovin (family) 27 428
Kokovin, Yakov (Vasil'yevich) 27 428
Koksijde
  Abbey of Ter Duinen 3 552; 4 778; 13 182
  Fondation Paul Delvaux 8 700
Kokugakai 21 634
Kokugaku (National Learning movement) 17 233
Kokuga sōsaku kyōkai (National Creative Painting Society) 17 135, 201; 22 328; 31 575
Kokugon Engo *see* YUANWU KEQIN
Kokular, Aleksander 25 106, 141; 32 876
kokumon *see under* MARKS
Kokura, Saienba kiln 1 448
Kokusai *see* OZAKI, SOZO
Kokushoku Yōga Ten (Black Western Painting Exhibition) 17 206
Kōkyō Taniguchi *see* TANIGUCHI, KŌKYŌ
Kola-Bankole, (Sebastian) Isola 1 319; 18 200*; 23 135
Kola-Bankole Associates 18 200
Kolacio, Zdenko 33 593
Kolandjiev 8 900
Kolar 5 149
Kolar, Kolaramma Temple 15 529
Kolář, Jiří 8 394; 18 201*; 22 381; 30 23
Kolarević, Ilija 28 453
Kolarov, Georgi 5 159
Kolárovo Church 4 782
Kolb, Anton 3 200; 33 356
Kołbacz Church 4 782
Kolbe, Carl Wilhelm (i) (1759-1835) 8 816; 18 201–2*
  pupils 18 476; 23 410
  works 18 *202*
Kolbe, Carl Wilhelm (ii) (1781-1853) 12 393; 18 201–2*
Kolbe, Christian Friedrich 18 201
Kolbe, Christian Wilhelm 18 201
Kolbe, Etienne Maria 18 201
Kolbe, Georg 12 407; 18 202–3*; 21 491; 31 402
Kolbe, Heinrich Christian 18 201; 26 255
Kolbe, Johann Diederich 18 201
Kolbe, Johann Paul 2 823
Kolberg Cathedral 13 161
Kölbl, Benedikt 2 780
Kolbuszowa
  furniture 25 118, 121, *121*
Kolchan 22 546
Kolcheva, Olya 5 159
Kolchos 32 53
Kölderer, Jörg 2 792; 9 436; 13 902, 903; 20 104
Koldewey, Robert 1 892; 3 9, 10; 4 437
Kolding 8 *720*
  Kunstmuseet Trapholt 8 760
Kolding, Peder Jensen *see* JENSEN KOLDING, PEDER
Kolenze 1 317
Köler, Georg *see* KELLER, GEORG
Köler, Johann 1 148; 10 539, *539*; 18 203*
Kolertal *see* KELLERTHALER
Kolertal, Herman 17 887
Köler-Viliandi, Ivan Petrovich *see* KÖLER, JOHANN
Kolev, Venko 5 159
Kolevica, Petraq 1 539
Koleychuk, Vyacheslav 27 397
Kolff, Jacob van Santen 14 46
Kolhozabad *see* KAFIR KALA
Kolhua *see* VAISHALI
Kolíbal, Stanislav 18 203–4*
  works 8 388, *388*
Kolig, Anton 2 797; 18 204*; 23 2; 33 162
Kolig, Cornelius 2 804
Kolin
  Cathedral 8 376
  Esso power station 8 380; 11 365
  St Bartholomew 8 376, 407; 13 58, 187; 32 821
  Town Hall 8 379
Kolinsky sable 5 32
Kolitz, Louis 18 204*
Koljaka (Hoshi), Kristina 18 204*
Kolk, Gerard van den 25 814
Kolkhozabad 6 221
Koll, Karl 28 840
Kollam *see* QUILON
Kollam calendar *see under* INDIAN SUBCONTINENT → calendars
Kolle, Helmut 31 539
Kollek, Teddy 16 570
Kollektiv Künstlerische Entwicklung/1960 21 67
Köllen, Henrik *see* CÖLLEN, HENRIK
Koller, Broncia 33 166
Koller, Hugo 33 166
Koller, Július 28 853
Köller, Julius Friedrich 4 711; 24 565
Koller, Martin 8 398
Koller, Otto 3 537
Koller, (Johann) Rudolf 18 204–5*; 29 600; 30 134
Kolleri, Valsan 20 54
Kollhof, Hans F. 18 114
Kolli, Nikolay (Dzhemsovich) 18 205*; 23 529; 32 382
Kollie, Jallah 19 310
Kollier, Edwart *see* COLLIER, EDWART
Kölln, Cunrad von *see* KUENE VON DER HALLEN, KONRAD
Kollonitz, Sigismund, Cardinal 12 356
Kollwitz, J. 27 343, 344
Kollwitz, Käthe 10 560; 18 205–6*, *206*; 33 313
  exhibitions 22 430
  groups and movements 2 288; 22 923
  methods 6 471; 8 128
  personal collection 2 370
  works 4 42; 5 758; 10 563; 12 394; 19 491; 25 349, 651, 652, 653; 28 920; 33 363
Kolmården 30 94, 95
Kolmitz, Christoph 14 893
Kolmogorets, Semyon *see* SPIRIDONOV, SEMYON
Kölner Domblatt 13 208
Köln-Lindenthal 25 498, 500, 503
Köln-Müngersdorf Villa 32 544
Koloane, David (Nthubu) 29 109
Kologrivov, Yu. I. 27 438
Koło Klipsa 25 116
Kolokytha, Suzana (Maria) *see* ANTONAKAKIS, SUZANA (MARIA)
Kolombi, Zef 1 540; 15 104; 18 207*
Kolomenskoye 18 207*; 27 *363*
  Church of the Annunciation 4 783
  Church of the Ascension 18 *207*; 27 371
  gardens 12 134
  Kazan' church 9 84
  Tsar's Palace 3 530; 27 *372*, 373, 406
Kolomiiščina 25 502
Kolomna 18 207–8*; 27 *363*, 371, 431
Kolomoki, GA 22 611
Kolonna 1 478*
Kolonyama Pottery Works 19 241
Kolophon 15 893
Koloristerne 7 805; 28 828
Kolossi 8 361
Koloszvári, Tamás 14 898
Kolotes 13 453, 596; 18 208*
  collaboration 13 453; 23 901; 24 594
Kolotes of Teos 13 551
Kolovrat (family) 8 423
Kolowrat, Franz Karl Liebsteinsky, Graf von 23 573; 25 550
Kolowrat, Norbert Leopold, Count 20 494
Kolozsvár *see* CLUJ-NAPOCA
Kolozsvár, George of *see* GEORGE OF KOLOZSVÁR
Kolozsvár, Martin of *see* MARTIN OF KOLOZSVÁR
Kolozsvári, Tamás 5 84
Kolscher, Bernhard 18 161, 208*
Koltai, Ralph 30 687
Koluk ibn ʿAbdallah 18 234
Kölük Şemseddin 17 864
Kolumban Christ Child 20 769
Kolvenaar, Peter 2 199
  works 2 *200*
Kolybnyak, A. 21 812
Kolyvan 27 427, 428
Kom 3 145, 147, 148
Koma (people) 1 330
Koma (family) 17 303, 304, 399
Kom Abu Billo 9 *774*, 842; 18 209*
  stelae 18 *209*
Komada, Isamu 17 402
Komai, Tetsurō 17 296; 18 209*
Komai Genki 17 196; 20 523
Koma Kansai II 17 399; 28 599
Koman, Gezer Ilhan 31 454
Komána 15 3
Koma no Chikazane 17 391
Komar, Vitaly 18 209–10; 27 397
Komar and Melamid 18 209–10*; 29 89
Komárno 28 *848*
  Danubian Museum 28 857
  fortress 28 849
Komárov 8 416
komast cups *see under* CUPS → types
Komast Group 13 507
Komast X Painter *see* KX PAINTER
Komast Y Painter *see* KY PAINTER
Koma tou Yialou Hagia Solomoni 8 358, 359
Komatsu, Hitoshi 17 202
Komatsuken 17 282
Kombolcha 10 576
Komchén 20 881; 21 196
Kōmei Ishikawa *see* ISHIKAWA, KŌMEI
Kom el-Abd 30 701
Kom el-Ahmar, Tomb of Nefersekhem 9 840
Kom el-Asl *see* BACCHIAS
Kom el-Hamman *see* PHILADELPHIA (EGYPT)
Kom el-Nadura 18 20
Kom el-Sultan *see* ABYDOS
Ko-Mende 21 116
Kom-Fut 4 812; 18 536
Kominimung 24 71, 80
Komi region 27 *363*, 433, 434
Komisarjevski, Theodore (London) 7 327
Komissarzhevskaya, Vera 3 87; 29 899
Komissarzhevsky, Fyodor (Moscow) 27 810
Komitas, Catholicos 9 731, 732
Komizo 17 352
Komi-Zyryan 27 433
Komját, Aladár 1 132; 31 541
Komló 14 890
Kom Medinet Ghurab 1 770; 9 851
Kommos 13 *362*; 18 210–11*; 21 *651*
  Building JT 18 *210*
  Building P 21 664
  palace 21 658
  Temple A 18 210
  temples 18 *210*, 210–11
Komnenos (dynasty) 8 155; 9 558; 18 211*
Komnenos, Alexios, Prince 18 211; 22 797
Komnenos, Alexios I, Emperor of Byzantium *see* ALEXIOS I, Emperor of Byzantium
Komnenos, Alexios II, Grand Komnenos *see* ALEXIOS II, Grand Komnenos
Komnenos, Alexios III, Grand Komnenos *see* ALEXIOS III, Grand Komnenos
Komnenos, Isaak 9 579; 16 597, 599
Komnenos, John 16 601
Komnenos, John II, Emperor of Byzantium *see* JOHN II KOMNENOS, Emperor of Byzantium
Komnenos, Manuel I, Emperor of Byzantium *see* MANUEL I, Emperor of Byzantium
Komnenos, Michael I Angelos Doukas, Despot of Epiros *see* MICHAEL I ANGELOS DOUKAS, Despot of Epiros
Komnenos, Michael II, Despot of Epiros *see* MICHAEL II, Despot of Epiros
Komo 1 404, 405
Kom Ombo 2 13; 9 *774*, 896, 897; 18 211–12*
  Temple of Sebek and Haroeris 9 834, 835
  wall paintings 9 805
Komon, Rudy 2 770
Komonen, Markku 11 93
Komor, Marcell 18 212*
Kōmori Dōjin *see* YOKOI KINKOKU
Komor & Jakab 14 890; 18 212*; 20 447
Komos *see* KOMMOS
Komosar, Mirko 4 463
Kompánek, Vladimír 28 855
Kompe, Jan ten *see* COMPE, JAN TEN
Kompong Cham 5 *458*
  Hanchey 5 464
  Kok Preah Theat 5 464
  market 5 482
  sculpture 5 499
Kompong Preah 5 *458*, 464
Kompong Svay, Preah Khan 5 477
  works 5 *497*
Kompong Thom 5 *458*
  Archaeological Museum 29 239
Komter, Auke 18 212–13*; 22 832; 29 484
Kom Ushim *see* KARANIS
Kōmyō, Emperor (*reg* 1336-48) 18 550
Kōmyō, Empress (710-60) 18 213*; 22 496
  architecture 17 422, *422*; 22 496, 502; 33 318
  calligraphy 17 218
  collections 17 432; 22 495
  sculpture 17 114
Kōmyōji 17 306
Kon', Fyodor 22 169; 27 371; 28 892
Kona 17 680
Konakichi, Tachibana no *see* TACHIBANA NO KONAKICHI
Konakovo Factory 27 411
Konan, B. P. 8 22
Konan Hozen *see* EIRAKU HOZEN
Konarak 15 *279*; 18 *214*
  Archaeological Museum 15 182
  sculpture 10 484; 15 *504*, 505; 30 785
  Surya Temple 14 77; 15 216, 229, 230, 319, 320, 504–5, 696; 18 213–14*
  staircase 29 526
  temples 15 309
Koṇārka *see* KONARAK
Konarski, Jan, Bishop 20 395
Konashevich, Vladimir (Mikhaylovich) 18 215*; 27 396
Konate, Abdoulaye 20 199
Konbaung 5 249
  dress 5 *249*
Konbaung, Alaungpaya *see* ALAUNGAPAYA, King
Konch 15 322
Konchalovsky, Pyotr (Petrovich) 18 215*
  groups and movements 12 871; 16 817, 818; 22 178; 27 392, 394
  pupils 18 404, 573; 32 579
Könchok Gyalpo 5 105; 27 600
Kondakov, Nikodim (Pavlovich) 18 215*; 27 443
  pupils 2 880
Kondane 15 *276*; 18 216*
  caves 15 236, *236*
  sculpture 15 435
  temples 15 275
Kondapalle 15 722
Kondaparti 15 538
Kondapur 30 510
Konde 33 598
Kondev, Dimitar 19 884
Kondh 15 734, 735
kondō 17 66
Kondō, Yūzō 17 267

Kondoleon, N. M. 22 698
Kondor, Béla 14 902; 18 216*
Kondotti 15 358
Kondratenko, Ivan (Gavrilovich) 27 378
Kondrat'yev, Pavel (Mikhaylovich) 27 581
Konduri 27 785
Kondzelevich, I. 31 558
Konerirajapuram, Uma-Maheshvara Temple 15 234, 517
Kong 1 316
Kongachoiling Temple 21 875
Kongelige Porcelainsfabrik (Copenhagen) 7 806–7; 8 748, 749; 30 884
designers 8 748, 749; 12 461; 14 391; 18 462; 22 884; 27 413, 643
directors 14 497
porcelain 7 *807*
potters 14 120
Konginkangas farmhouses 32 *288*
Kongju 18 *250*
fortress 18 260
Gold Crown Tomb 18 350
lacquer 18 369
Magok Temple 18 330
Museum 18 382, 383
palace 18 275
Taet ong Temple 5 114
temples 18 267
tomb of King Munyŏng 4 795; 18 *272*, 272, 314, 328, 352, 364
University 18 381
Kongmin 18 216–17*, 273, 316, 329, 391
Kongo 1 393, 395, 425; 2 85; 7 708; 16 880; 18 217–22*
aesthetics 1 236
architecture 1 406
bellows (furnaces) 1 365
cement 1 331
crucifixes 1 *228*, 406
currency 1 363
divination instruments 1 356, 357
emblems 8 231
figurines 1 *275*
funerary monuments 1 331
funerary urns 18 217, *218*
gesture 1 265, 266
glass 1 *233*
gongs 1 360
iconography 1 261
iron 1 *233*
ivory 1 292
ivory-carvings 18 221–2
masks 18 221*
metalwork 18 221
mixed-media 1 301
painting 8 230
patronage 1 241
portraits 1 269
pot-lids 18 222
pottery 1 406
religion 8 230–31
ritual objects 1 241; 18 219–21*, *220*
sculpture 1 263, 274, 322; 2 86
figure 1 *233*, 403; 8 230; 18 *217*, 217–21*, *219*, *220*
stone 18 *217*, *219*
wood 1 *233*; 18 *220*
stone 1 292; 18 *217*, *219*
terracotta 18 *218*
textiles 18 484
wood 1 *233*, *275*; 18 *220*
wood-carvings 18 221–2
writing 8 231
Kongōbuji 5 116–17; 17 *11*, 68, 270, 345; 18 222–4*
collections 17 428
Fudōdo 18 224
paintings 18 *223*
paper 17 404
Kongolo 1 *401*
Kongō Magojirō
works 17 *394*
Kongoussi 1 *381*; 22 198
Kong Rong 14 136
Kongsberg 23 *218*, 220
Church 23 221, 225
silver 23 224
Kong Shangren 8 457; 12 900
Kongsvinger 23 *218*
Fortress 23 220
Konhofer, Konrad 33 301
Koniarek, Jan 28 855
Konica 1 542
Koniecpolski (family) 25 135
Konieczny, Marian 18 430; 25 130
König, Carlo 13 726
König, Franz Niklaus 3 823; 18 224*; 30 133
teachers 11 766
works 8 857, 910
König, Franz Xaver 18 683
König, Friedrich (1774-1833) 25 610
König, Friedrich (*fl* 1900) 28 344
König, Fritz *see* KOENIG, FRITZ
König, Henri 30 138
König, Johann 18 225*
collaboration 12 389
patrons and collectors 13 631
works 12 422, 461; 14 894; 26 713
König, K. (*fl c.* 1910-20) 26 374
König, Karl (1841-1914) 10 870; 20 894; 23 372; 29 777; 30 279; 32 744
König, Leo von 5 924; 28 779
König, Otto 20 891; 25 403; 28 188
König, Tamás 14 890
Königer, Veit 18 225*; 28 862
Königliche Eisengiesserei bei Berlin 3 804; 12 454
Königliche Erzgiesserei (Munich) 10 907
Königliche Porzellanmanufaktur (KPM) (Berlin) 3 804–5; 12 436, 437
porcelain 12 *436*
production 1 763; 12 435
staff 11 894; 21 365; 25 322
Königsberg *see* KALININGRAD
Königsberg Chronicle 2 511
Königsegg-Aulendorf, Graf 16 804
Königsfelden
Altar Frontal 13 151
Monastery 2 824
stained glass 11 712; 13 151, 186; 29 512; 30 125, 130
textiles 2 *823*
Königslutter 7 455; 12 *360*; 26 632
SS Peter and Paul 18 226*
Königswiesen, Mariä Himmelfahrt 2 778; 13 58
Konijnenburg, Willem Adriaan van 14 43; 18 226*; 22 851
Koninck, Daniël 18 228
Koninck, Jacob, I (1614-1690) 18 227, 228*
Koninck, Jacob, II (?1647-1724) 18 228
Koninck, Louis Herman De *see* DE KONINCK, LOUIS HERMAN
Koninck, Philips (de) 3 386; 11 847; 18 227, 228–30*
patrons and collectors 2 382; 4 614; 5 9; 26 722
works 4 873; 18 *229*; 22 843
Koninck, Pieter 18 226
Koninck, Salomon 18 226, 227–8*; 21 791
works 18 *227*
Koning, Cornelis 5 324
Koning, Henrik 23 635
Koningk, Gert 30 276
Koningsbruggen, Rob van 18 230*
Konink, Walenty 25 129
Koninklijke Deventer Tapijtfabriek 7 552; 22 900
Koninklijke Nederlandsche Meubelenfabriek 22 387, 873
Koninklijke Verenigde Tapijtfabriken 23 125
Koninklijk Oudheidkundig Gezelschap (Amsterdam) 1 808
Konishi (family) 23 364; 27 595
Konishi Hirosada 23 594
Konjo 19 72, 74
Konjović, Milán 18 230*; 28 451
Konjuh Church 9 538
Konkowski, Aleksander 7 837
Konnur 15 326
Kōno Bairei 18 231*; 30 260
groups and movements 17 200
pupils 17 860
teachers 17 197
Konoe (family) 17 232; 19 317
Konoe Iehiro 17 233, 344
Konoe Nobutada 14 703; 18 231*
groups and movements 17 215, 232, 343
teachers 30 263
works 17 193, 228, 232
Konoe Sakihisa 17 232, 233, 783
Konohana Society 23 445
Kōnoike Dōoku 17 428
Konopiště Castle 2 321
Konovalov, Yurii N. 19 13
Konozō Nakamura *see* NAKAMURA KONOZŌ
Konrád 28 851
Konrad, Prince-Bishop of Eichstätt (*fl c.* 1714) 11 886
Konrad I, Archbishop of Salzburg (1106-47) 27 660
Konrad I, Bishop of Gurk (*fl* 1127) 13 857
Konrad I, Duke of Mazovia (*reg* 1202-47) 25 119; 26 687
Konrad II, Cardinal Archbishop of Salzburg 2 777
Konrád II, Prince 8 421
Konrad III, Archbishop of Salzburg 27 660
Konrad, Anton 2 450
Konrad of Friesach 18 231*
Konrad of Lindau 2 718
Konrad of Vechta (patron; *fl* 1401-3) 33 71
Konrad von Erling 4 695
Konrad von Heimburg 13 152
Konrad von Hochstaden, Archbishop of Cologne 7 588; 13 48
Konrad von Megenburg 3 879
Konrad von Nürnberg 10 506
Konrad von Schmie 20 859
Konrad von Soest *see* CONRAD VON SOEST
Konrad von Vechta (painter; *fl* 1425-44) 4 418
Konrad von Würzburg 7 242
Konshistorisk tidskrift 24 451
Koński, Jan 25 408
Konso 1 410; 10 577
Konstantinidis, Aris 18 232*
works 13 350, *351*; 14 788
Konstantiniye *see* ISTANBUL → Constantinople
Konstantinoupolis *see* ISTANBUL → Constantinople
Konstantinov, Antip 27 372
Konstantinov, J. 19 883
Konstantinovski, George 19 883
Konstantinovsky, Wladimir *see* ACOSTA, WLADIMIRO
Konstanz 12 *361*; 18 232–3*
enamel 13 169
engravings 10 381
glass 9 646
gold 30 145, 146
houses 32 281
painting 12 384
Petershausen 7 302; 26 684
Rathaus 31 238
reliefs 22 *117*
tapestries 30 311
Konstanz—cont.
Unsere Liebe Frau Cathedral 4 190; 9 680; 10 408; 18 233*; 26 68
altarpieces 12 401
Mauritiuskapelle 13 87
sculpture 13 117
wall paintings 30 129
Zunftstube der Metzger 12 409
Konstanz, Heinrich von *see* HEINRICH VON KONSTANZ
Konstanz Missal *see under* MISSALS → individual manuscripts
Konstförening 29 687
Konsthändverk 24 452
Konsthistorisk tidskrift 24 424
Konstnären 24 451
Konstnärernas riksorganisation (KRO) 29 688
Konstnärsförbund 3 776; 18 449, 801; 23 206, 207; 29 687; 30 79, 81
Konstnärsklubb 29 687
Konstperspektiv 24 451
Konstvärlden 5 776
Kontarinis, Konstantinos 25 334
Kontaris, Frangos 15 890; 21 345; 25 336
Kontaris, Georgios 15 890; 21 345; 25 336
Kontoglou, Fotis 10 379; 13 353; 18 233*; 31 396
Kontuly, Béla 14 159, 901
Kontum 6 431
Konturadjyan, Petros 2 432
Konůpek, Jan 31 792; 33 710
Konya (Turkey) 16 *104*; 18 233–4*
architectural decorations 16 248
architecture 16 183, 186
carpets 16 430, 469, 476
see also under CARPETS → types
Islamic religious buildings
Abdalaziz Mosque 16 183
Alaeddin Mosque 2 437; 16 248; 18 233–4; 22 195
minbar 16 497
spolia 16 183
tomb of Kiliç Arslan II 16 185
Ince Minareli Madrasa 16 184, *184*; 22 323
Ince Minareli Mosque 16 184
Karatay Madrasa 16 184, 248; 23 562
Larende Mosque *see* Sahib Ata Mosque
mosque of Basarabey 16 183
mosque of Erdemşah 16 183
mosque of Haci Ferruh 16 183
mosque of Hoca Hasan 16 184
Sahib Ata Mosque 16 202; 22 323
Şekerfuruş Mosque 16 183
Selimiye Mosque 16 222
Sırçalı Madrasa 16 184
kiosk of Kiliç Arslan II 16 249
manuscripts 16 290, 300, 313, 350
masonry 16 180
miniatures (manuscript illumination) 16 *329*
museums 31 456
Mevlana Museum 16 557; 18 233
Museum of Ceramics 18 234
Seljuk Museum 18 234
palace 16 186, 246, 303
pottery 24 691
tombs 16 185
tomb of Celal al-Din Rumi 16 204
tomb of Fakih Dede 16 204
tomb of Gömeç Hatun 16 186
tomb of Gühertas 16 186
tomb of Şeyh Ahmed 16 185
tomb of Şeyh Aliman 16 185
tomb of Tac ül-Vezir 16 185
town walls 16 245
Konya (artist; Russia) 8 908; 27 400
Konya carpets *see under* CARPETS → types
Konyak 15 733, 734
Konyonkov, Sergey (Timofeyevich) 18 234–5*; 27 392, 394; 32 661
groups and movements 25 649
pupils 22 726
Konyonkov, S. T., Museum of Art *see under* SMOLENSK
Konzak, Ron 29 99
Konzal, Joseph 29 533
Konzova, Antonina 5 159
Konz Villa 26 907
Kooi, Willem Bartel van der 18 235*; 22 848
Koolhaas, Rem 18 235–6*; 22 832; 23 361; 27 231
Kooning, Elaine De *see* DE KOONING, ELAINE
Kooning, Willem De *see* DE KOONING, WILLEM
Koons, Jeff 10 482; 18 236*; 31 609
Koopeksport 31 69
Koopmann, Carl 11 787
Koops, Mathias 24 40
Koort, Jaan 10 539; 18 236*; 33 566
Koos, Victor 25 750, 751
Kooten, L. W. van 22 896; 23 120
Kooymans, Fons 22 877
Kopácsy, József, Archbishop 10 546
Kopar 24 70
Kópavogur, Helgadóttir Museum 14 328
Köpcke, Arthur 8 736
Kopeček, St Kopeček 8 398
Kopecek, Vera 31 660
Koper 28 *858*
Regional Museum 28 863
Kopetzki, Jan *see* KUPECKÝ, JAN
Köpf, Christian von 2 717
Kopf, Willi 2 804
Kophinas 8 153
Kopia 15 694
Köping 13 120
Köpinge Master 18 445
Kopivky 31 562
Kopor'ye Fortress 27 370
Kopp, Georg 11 752
Kopp, Johann Ignaz 23 2
Koppel 18 237*
Köppel 12 510
Koppel, Eva 18 237
Koppel, Henning 7 807; 8 751; 17 479, 529
works 8 *751*
Koppel, Nils 18 237
Koppers, Johan 17 696
Köpping, Karl 18 237*
works 12 441, *441*
Koprivshtitsa 5 *144*
Kableshkov House 5 148
Lizotov House 5 156
Pavlikyanski House 5 147
Kopronymos, Constantine V, Emperor of Byzantium *see* CONSTANTINE V KOPRONYMOS, Emperor of Byzantium
Koprulu Yalisi *see* ANADOLU HISAR
Kops, Jan 23 590
Kops, Willem Philip 11 447
works 22 *865*
Koptos 9 773, *774*, 870; 10 80, 473; 18 237–8*; 26 *921*
figurines 18 *238*
reliefs 9 878, 879, 897
sculpture 27 21
stele 9 897
Kopylkov, Mikhail (Andreyevich) 27 411
Kopyoni 27 367
Kor 21 554

Kōra (family) **17** 52
korai *see under* SCULPTURE → types
Koraïchi, (Mahmoud) Rachid **1** 636; **18** 238*
works **1** 636, *636*
Korais, Adamantios, Library *see under* CHIOS (TOWN)
Korakou (Greece) **21** 46
Korakov (Cyprus), Hagios Mamas **1** 124
Koral, Füreya **31** 455
Koral', V. **3** 527
Koralek, Paul **1** 476*; **9** 323; **16** 12
Koram *see* CHŎN-KI
Kōra Munehiro Bungo **2** 317; **18** 238–9*
Korana **1** 417
Korans **16** 128, 273, 275, 282, 288–91, *289*; **18** 239–42*
historical and regional traditions
Afghanistan **16** *290*
Iran **16** 290
Transoxiana **16** 290
individual manuscripts
Blue Koran **16** 353
Korari Temple **15** 263
Korazim Synagogue **17** 541, 542
Korb, Carl **25** 436
Korb, Flóris Nándor **14** 889
Korb, Hermann **18** 242–3*
collaboration **18** 877
works **5** 30; **19** 315; **33** 51, 53, 292, 293
Korba **25** 733
Korçari, Petro **1** 539; **18** 243*
Korçë **1** *537*, 546
art schools **1** 547
carpets **1** 545
ceramics **1** 543
felt **1** 544
metalwork **1** 543
Mio Museum **21** 699
Mirahori Mosque **1** 538
Museum of Medieval Art **1** 546
Museum of National Education **1** 546
textiles **1** 545
Korçë Glass and Ceramics Factory **1** 543
Korçë Hammer and Sickle Knitwear Combine **1** 545
Korčula **8** 174, *174*
department store **8** 177
St Mark's **8** 180
Korda (Díaz Gutiérrez), Alberto **18** 243*
Korda, Alexander **19** 81
Korda, Vincent **19** 81
Kordyle **9** 556
Korea **18** 245–385*, *248*, *250*
albums **1** 580, 581
alphabets **18** 247; **28** 381
altars **1** 704*, 705; **28** 638
amboyna **33** IV1
animal subjects **18** 51
archaeology **18** 381–2*
architectural decorations **18** 337
architecture **18** 260–82*
brick **18** 264, 266
Buddhism **18** 261, 266–8*
Confucianism **18** 266, 269–71*
landscape **12** 93–5
megalithic **21** 45
military **21** 594*
Prehistoric **18** 260*, 271*
shamanism **18** 268
stone **18** 264, 265, 266
wattle-and-daub **18** 277
wood **18** 264
armour **18** 353–4*
art history **18** 259*
ashes **18** *335*, 340
bamboo **18** 303, 379, 380
banners **18** 308
bark **18** 278
basins **18** 349
beads **18** 364
beds **18** 360
Korea—cont.
bells **3** 626; **18** 346, 347–8
bookcases **18** 362
books **18** 354–6*
bottles **18** *341*
bowers **12** 94
bowls **18** *255*, *336*, *340*, *341*, *342*, 351
boxes **18** 363, *370*, *371*, 380, *602*; **33** IV1
bracelets **18** 366, 367
brackets **4** 623*; **18** *264*, 264–5, *265*; **30** 913
brass **18** *356*, 357, *363*, 378; **33** IV1
brick **4** 795*; **18** 264, 266, 271
bridges **18** *280*, 280–81*
pontoons **18** 281
brocades **18** 373, 380
bronze **18** 249, *287*, 302, 344–7*, *346*, 353, *356*, 378; **21** 715
Buddhism **18** 347–9*, *348*
Prehistoric **18** 297
6th cent. AD **18** *284*
7th cent. AD **5** *114*; **18** *285*
9th cent. AD **18** *364*
13th cent. **18** 349
14th cent. **18** *294*
20th cent. **18** 300, 301
brooches **18** 367
brushes **5** 35; **7** 66; **18** 303
brush handles **18** 303
brushline **5** 35, 37
brushpots **4** *175*; **18** 362
buckles **18** 347, 366
burial mounds **18** 271
calligraphers **18** 258
calligraphy **18** 327–32*, *330*
candlesticks **18** 363
caps **18** 351
caskets **18** 351, 352
ceilings **18** 265
ceramics **17** 351, 352; **18** 257, 332–44*, *338*
chairs **18** 361
chess sets **6** 557
chests **18** 362–3, *363*
chopsticks **18** 380
clay **18** *292*, 295
cobalt **18** 343
coffins **18** 271
coins **7** 533; **18** *356*, 356–7*
collections **18** 382–4*
colour **7** 632; **18** 310–12
combs (hair) **18** 367
concrete **18** 266
containers **18** 362–3
copper **18** 356
copper oxides **18** 339, *340*, 343–4
cotton **18** 358, 374, 375
craftsmen and artists **18** 257–8*, 304
crowns **18** 349, *350*, 350–51
cupboards **18** 362
cups **18** *364*
daggers **18** 345
doors **9** 162*; **18** 276
dress **18** 357–9*, *358*
dyes **18** 379–80
earrings **18** 366, 367, *367*
earth **18** 264
earthenwares **18** 297, 298, 332–3, *333*, *334*, 335, 337, 378
education (art) **18** 258, 380*, 381*
archaeology **18** 381–2
architecture **18** 261
painting **18** 380–81*
embroidery **18** 379*
enamel **17** 377; **18** 359*
engraving **18** 338, 342
ewers **18** *338*
exhibitions **18** 57, 325–6, 384–5*
fans **10** 777; **18** 380
fences **12** 94
fir **18** 361
firing **18** *333*
fortifications **21** 594*
Korea—cont.
fortresses **18** 260, 265, 279; **21** 594
funerary urns **18** 273, 335
furniture **18** 359–63*, *360*
garden design **12** 93–5
gardens **12** 85*, 93–5*, *94*
gates **18** *262*, 279–80*
geomancy **12** 93; **18** 268, 269
gilding **12** 626; **18** *285*, *287*, *294*, *295*, *296*, *364*
gingko **18** 363
glass **18** 266, *364*, 364–5*
glazes **18** *335*, 336, 337, 338, 340
glues **18** 302
gold **18** 249, 339, 349–52*, *350*, 366, *367*, 370
gold leaf **18** 371
gongs **18** 348
granite **18** 264, *280*, *283*, *288*, 298, 302; **23** 775; **29** 869
hair **18** 303
hairpins **18** 367, 368
halberds **18** 345
harnesses **14** 184
heating systems **15** 52
hemp **18** 373
historiography **18** 259*
houses **18** 260, 262, 264, 274*, 276–9*, *277*, *278*
hypocausts **15** 52*
iconography **18** 253–6*, *255*, 316, 375
Buddhism **5** 91; **18** *254*, 254–5, 305–6, 307–9
Confucianism **18** 256
Daoism **18** 255
shamanism **18** 253–4
incense burners **18** *348*, 348–9
inks **15** 850, 852; **18** 303
inlays **18** 338–9, *339*, 341, 344*, *348*, 603
inscriptions **18** 356, *356*
iron **18** 249, 289, *290*, *291*, 352–3*
iron oxide **18** 339, 342, *342*, 343
jackets **18** 357
jade **16** 861; **18** *350*, *365*, *380*
jars **6** III1; **18** *334*, *343*
jewellery **7** 108; **18** *365*, 365–8*, *367*
kiosks **18** 72*
kogoks **18** 364, 365, *365*, 366
kuṇḍikās **18** 349
lacquer **7** 13; **17** 254; **18** 361, 368–71*, *369*, *370*, *371*, *602*
Buddhism **18** 370
urushi **18** 600, 603
lanterns (architecture) **18** 266
lanterns (lights) **18** 363
looms **30** 546
manuals
painting **18** 381
weapons **18** 353
manuscript illumination **18** 304–5, *304*
maps **28** *424*
marbling **18** 339
masks **18** 300, 378, *378*
metal **18** 301, 356
metalwork **18** 344–53*
mirrors **18** 345–6, *346*; **21** 715–16*
mixed-media **18** *326*
mother-of-pearl **18** 370, *370*, *371*, *602*, 603
mounts (works on paper and scrolls) **22** 234
museums **18** 382–3*
musical instruments **22** 376
needles **18** 372
norigae **18** 379, *380*
observatories **23** 339
pagodas **18** *261*; **23** 775*
painters **18** 258
painting **18** 302–27*
animal subjects **14** *724*; **18** *377*; **33** *524*, *527*
bamboo **33** *529*, 579
Korea
painting—cont.
bird-and-flower **18** 315–17*, *316*, *317*, 376
Buddhism **18** 303–12*, *310*, *374*
Sŏn **18** 312
folk **18** 376–7*, *377*
fresco **18** 302
genre **18** 318–21*
6th cent. AD **18** *318*
18th cent. **18** *54*, *319*, *320*
hunting scenes **18** *319*
ink **18** *323*, 323–5, 326; **33** *529*
Buddhism **18** **309*
15th cent. **17** *772*; **18** *316*
16th cent. **18** *51*, *324*
17th cent. **18** *57*, *317*
landscape **18** *313*
7th cent. AD **18** 313–15*
16th cent. **33** *494*, *525*
17th cent. **32** *843*
18th cent. **7** *203*; **18** *315*
literati **18** *323*, 323–5*, *324*
plum blossom **23** *439*
portraits **18** *322*
scroll
Buddhism **18** *305*
Orthodox school **33** *531*
16th cent. **23** *439*; **33** *527*
19th cent. **14** *724*
tomb **18** 302, 318–19
wall **32** 804
20th cent. **18** *326*
palaces **18** 260, 261, 274–6*, *275*, 281; **23** 821*
paper **7** 114; **18** 264, 276, 302, 379, 380; **24** 42, 47
tak **7** 250
patchwork **30** X2
patronage **18** 258–9*
paulownia **18** 361, 363
pavilions (buildings) **12** 94, *94*
pearls **18** 367
pear-wood **18** 361
pine **18** 361
pipes (smoking) **18** 380
plaster **18** 277, 300, 301, 302
poetry **25** 73
ponds **12** 93, *94*
popular art **18** 376–7*
porcelain **6** III1; **18** *255*, 337, 340*, 342–4*, *343*
blue-and-white ware **4** 174*, *175*; **18** 343
portraits **18** 308–9
painting **18** 60, 321–3*, *322*
sculpture **18** 295
self-portraits **18** *322*
pots **18** *333*
potters **17** 255, 262, 351
pottery **18** 249, 335*, 336–7*
black ware **18** 340*
celadon **18** 250, 317, 337–9*, *338*, *340*
Chulmun ware **18** 333*, *333*
green-glazed ware **17** 247
iron-glazed wares **18** 339*
Kaya wares **18** 335*
Kimhae ware **18** 334–5*
Koguryŏ wares **18** 336*
Mumun ware **18** 333–4*, *334*
Paekche wares **18** 336*
Prehistoric **18** 332–5*
Punch'ŏng ware **18** 340–42, *341*, *342*
Silla ware **18** *335*, 335–6*
Wajil ware **18** 334*, *334*
printing **15** 852; **25** 588
woodblock **5** 115; **18** 314, 354–6*
rami (fibre) **18** 358, 372, 373, 374, 375
rattles **18** 346, *346*
religion **18** 252–3*
reliquaries **18** *364*, 364
rings **18** 367, 368
ritual objects **18** *346*, 346–7, 377–8*
robes **18** 357, *358*, *374*, *375*
Korea—cont.
rock art **18** 297
rockets **18** 353
rocks **12** 94
roofs **18** 265, 266, 278; **30** 912–14*, *913*
sarcophagi **27** 832*
schools **18** 269–71, *270*, *271*
screens (ii) (furniture) **18** 315, 362; **28** 297
scripts **18** 327–8
scrolls **18** *315*; **28** 309, 311
sculpture **18** 282–302*
bronze **5** *114*; **18** *284*, *285*, 297, 300, 301, 302
Buddhism **18** 282–96*, *290*
4th cent. AD **12** 626
6th cent. AD **18** *284*
7th cent. AD **5** *114*; **18** *283*, *285*
8th cent. AD **18** *287*, *288*
10th cent. AD **18** *287*, *291*, *292*
14th cent. **18** *294*
16th cent. **18** *295*
monumental **18** 302
Prehistoric **18** 297*
relief **18** *296*, *298*
stone **18** 295, 298–9
wood **18** *292*, *295*, 295, 300, 301
20th cent. **18** *302*
seals **18** 371–2*
sewing **18** 379
shrines (i) (cult) **18** 269; **28** 638*
silk **18** *254*, 302, 305, *315*, 357, 358, 372, 373, *374*, *375*, *380*; **30** X2
silver **18** *348*, 349–52*, *356*, 357, 366, 370
slip **18** 339, 342, 344
soapstone **18** *298*
spinning (textile) **18** 372
spirit poles **18** 300
stadia **18** *264*
stairs **18** 280
stamps **18** 341, *341*
steel **18** 266
stelae **29** 869
stencilling **18** 303
stone **18** 264, 265, 266, 271, 281, 298–9, *299*
16th cent. **18** 295
20th cent. **18** 301
stone-carvings **18** *299*
stonewares **18** 332–3, 335, *335*, 336, *336*, 337–9*, *338*, *339*, 340–42*, *340*, *341*
15th cent. **18** *342*
stucco **18** 277
stupas **18** 266; **29** 868–9*
supports **18** 302
susŏk *see* rocks
swords **18** 345
tables **18** 361, 363
teapots **18** *338*
temples **18** *265*; **30** 444–5*
Buddhism **18** 260, 266–8*, *268*; **30** 444–5
Confucianism **30** 445
terracotta **18** *302*; **30** 509–10*
textiles **18** 372–6*
thatch **18** 266, 278
thrones **30** 785*
tiles **18** 264, 278, 299, *313*, 378
tombs **18** 260, 271–4*, *272*, *274*, 289, 298–300, 316
tortoiseshell **18** *370*
towns **18** 281–2
toys **31** 259
trade **18** 251–2*
bronze **17** 319
ceramics **6** 331, 913–14*; **17** 259; **18** 251, 281
cobalt **18** 343
cotton **18** 375
glass **17** 386
iron **17** 318; **18** 251
mirrors **17** 319; **21** 716

Korea
trade—cont.
painting 17 162
porcelain 4 174; 6 331
pottery 17 249; 18 252, 340
textiles 18 374
type-faces 18 356; 25 588
urban planning 18 281–2*
vases 18 338, 339
walls 12 94
wardrobes 18 362
water droppers 18 338
weapons 18 345, 353–4*
weaving 18 379
willow 18 361, 379
wine-pots 18 338
wood 18 264–5, 264, 266, 271, 277, 281, 292, 295, 295, 300, 301, 378, 379; 23 775
18th cent. 18 296
woodblock 17 270; 18 354, 355
wood-carvings 18 295
wool 18 303
writing 18 330
zelkova 18 361, 363; 33 IV1
zithers 17 396
Korean Archaeological Society see HANGUK KOGOHAGOE
Korean Architecture Experts Association 18 263
Korean Artists' Proletarian Federation (K'apŭ) 18 300
Korean Avant Garde Association 17 775
Korean Folk Village 18 266
Korec 25 123
Korefusa, Fujiwara no see FUJIWARA NO KOREFUSA
Korekore 28 620
Korelicze tapestry workshop 25 131
Koren, Edward 5 759
Koreny', Aleksey 18 385
Koreny', Vasily 3 528; 18 385*
Koreshchenko 12 878
Koressa see KORISSIA
Koretsune no Fujiwara see FUJIWARA NO KORETSUNE
Koreyuki, Fujiwara no see FUJIWARA NO KOREYUKI
Korff, Alexander Hugo Bakker see BAKKER KORFF, ALEXANDER HUGO
Korfi t'Aroniou 22 698
Korfmann, Manfred 31 375
Korgaon Temple 12 827
Korhogo 1 386; 28 421
Museum 8 23
Korhonen, Otto 1 8
Korhonen, Toivo 30 284
Korin, Pavel (Dmitriyevich) 18 385–6*; 27 395
pupils 33 658
works 22 178; 27 439
Korin, Pavel, House-Museum see under PALEKH
Korinfsky, Mikhail 27 376
Kōrin Ogata see OGATA KŌRIN
Korinthos see CORINTH
Korissia 17 874
Koritschan-bei-Gaya 20 593
Korkai 15 200
Korkyra see CORFU
Kormeling, John 32 604
Körmend Castle 13 162
Körmöcbánya see KREMNICA
Korn, Arthur 18 386*
assistants 29 602
groups and movements 20 475; 26 405
pupils 25 571
Korn, Johan Filip 14 543
Körnelein, Johannes 25 49
Kornelimünster Church 5 794; 12 363
Körner, Edmund 10 669; 17 547
Korneychuk, Aleksandr 24 565
Kornhäusel, Joseph 18 386*
patrons and collectors 19 338
Kornhäusel, Joseph—cont.
works 2 784, 785; 4 40; 18 127; 19 55
Kórnik 25 99, 136, 138
Działyński Library 25 142
Museum of the Library of the Polish Academy of Sciences 9 497; 25 139
Kornilov Factory (St Petersburg) 27 582
Kornilov Komel'sky Monastery 25 338
Korniss, Dezső 10 650; 14 902; 18 386–7*; 31 798
Körnlein, Johannes 18 387*
Koro
headdresses 1 386
Korobanov, P. F. 27 439
Korobov, Ivan Kuz'mich 6 562; 27 575; 31 543
Korogo (Papua New Guinea)
masks 24 72
Korogo Church (Georgia) 12 321
Koroibos 13 428
Koroknyai, Ottó 18 387*
Korol', Vladimir 33 585
Korolkiewicz, Łucasz 18 387*; 25 108
Korolyov, Boris (Danilovich) 18 388*; 28 597
Korompay, František Vavřinec 8 392
Koroni 13 538; 32 158
Korope 13 592
Koror see OREOR
Körösfői-Kriesch, Aladár 12 839; 18 388–9*; 22 433
groups and movements 14 901; 15 12
teachers 30 206
works 22 433
Korovia, Hagia Varvara 8 358
Korovin, Konstantin (Alekseyevich) 18 389*; 22 178; 27 391, 442; 30 265; 33 740
collaboration 4 312; 12 878; 27 410
groups and movements 1 71; 12 870; 22 178; 31 582; 33 379
patrons and collectors 22 135; 27 438
productions 20 232
pupils
Cheremnykh, Mikhail (Mikhaylovich) 6 549
Fal'k, Robert (Rafailovich) 10 771
Gerasimov, Aleksandr (Mikhaylovich) 12 339
Gerasimov, Sergey (Vasil'yevich) 12 340
Ioganson, Boris (Vladimirovich) 15 891
Konashevich, Vladimir (Mikhaylovich) 18 215
Korin, Pavel (Dmitriyevich) 18 385
Kravchenko, Aleksey (Il'ich) 18 444
Kuprin, Aleksandr (Vasil'yevich) 18 528
Kuznetsov, Pavel (Varfolomeyevich) 18 542
Larionov, Mikhail (Fyodorovich) 18 792
Mashkov, Il'ya (Ivanovich) 20 548
Morozov, Ivan (Abramovich) (1871-1921) 22 135
Sapunov, Nikolay (Nikolayevich) 27 809
Saryan, Martiros (Sergeyevich) 27 855
Sudeykin, Sergey (Yur'yevich) 29 899
Tatlin, Vladimir (Yevgrafovich) 30 361
Vil'yams, Pyotr (Vladimirovich) 32 579
Korovin, Konstantin (Alekseyevich)
pupils—cont.
Yuon, Konstantin (Fyodorovich) 33 577
sponsors 30 464
Korovin, Sergey (Alekseyevich) 18 389*; 24 465; 25 674
Korpanyuk (family) 31 564
Kořran Chō see CHŌ KŌRAN
Korrodi, Ernesto 18 389–90*
Korsmo, Arne 10 857; 18 390*; 23 222
Körte, A. 13 6
Körte, G. 13 6
Körting & Mathiesson 4 671
Kortrijk 3 539
ceramics 3 588
damask 19 415, 416, 417, 418
guilds 3 579, 587, 598
lace 3 610
linen 19 418
marks 3 601
Onze Lieve Vrouwekerk 3 567, 600
paintings 3 559
sculpture 3 456; 13 100
wall paintings 3 552
Onze Liewe Vrouwhospitaal 13 100
Kortsheli 25 341
Korucutepe 1 824, 826; 17 875
Korunk 24 441
Korunović, Momir 28 444
Koruyu Nishikawa 17 407
Körver, Johann 13 631
korwar 16 43, 43–4
Korwin, Y. 4 27
Koryak 27 436
Korykos 9 512; 18 390–91*
churches 9 537
fortifications 2 427
mosaics 9 565
towers 9 555
Koryŏ 18 391*
Koryŏng 18 341, 351
Tomb 44 18 273
Koryūsai Isoda see ISODA KORYŪSAI
Korzec see KOREC
Korzhev, Gely (Mikhaylovich) 18 392*
Korzukhin, Aleksey (Ivanovich) 18 392*
Korzybski, Alfred 5 169
Kos (island) 13 363; 18 392–4*
castle 18 152
figurines 13 579
Mastichari Basilica 9 590; 32 86
mosaics 27 63
pottery 13 497
Sanctuary of Asklepios 13 405, 418; 18 393, 393–4; 26 910; 27 713
sculpture 18 394*
Kos (town) 18 392; 26 908
Kos, Gojmir Anton 28 861
Kós, Károly 13 889; 18 394–5*
collaboration 14 890; 30 762; 33 699
groups and movements 13 889
Kosa, Emil 19 701
Kosai Hori see HORI, KOSAI
Kosak, Ceno 2 789
Kōsaku Hamada see HAMADA, KŌSAKU
Kosam see KAUSAMBI
Kosan see HWANG KI-NO
Koşap Kale 21 587
Kosárek, Adolf 8 392; 14 235; 18 395*; 25 433
Koşay, Hamit Zubeyr 1 520, 893
Kosch, Károly see KÓS, KÁROLY
Kose (family) 17 154, 419; 18 552
Kosegarten, Gotthard Ludwig Theobul 18 395*
Kōsei 17 124
Kosei Matsui see MATSUI, KOSEI
Koseki
works 17 265
Kōsen see GAOQUAN
Kosenko, A. Y. 9 54
Kose no Hirotaka 17 154
Kose no Kanaoka 17 29, 154; 18 395–6*, 552
Kose no Kinmochi 17 154
Kose no Kintada 17 154
Kose no Yukitada 18 396
Kose school 18 396*
Koseto ware see under POTTERY → wares
Koshelenko, G. A. 6 285
Kōshi Kanō see KANŌ KŌSHI
Kōshirō Onchi see ONCHI, KŌSHIRŌ
Koshka, Fyodor 30 708
Koshkov, Mikhail (Ivanovich) 27 422
Kōshō 17 28, 124, 131, 750, 879; 31 676
works 17 131
Kōshun 17 126, 129
Košice 18 396–7*; 28 848
churches 28 850
Cathedral of St Elizabeth 14 889; 18 396–7*, 397; 28 849, 854
altarpiece 14 893, 899; 28 851
wall paintings 14 898; 28 851
Dominican church 28 849
Protestant church 28 849
St Elizabeth 14 884
copper 15 9
iron 15 9
J. Jakob Gallery 28 857
metalwork 15 5, 7; 28 856
Museum of Eastern Slovakia 28 857
pewter 15 8; 28 856
pottery 28 856
sculpture 28 854
Košice, Gyula 18 397*
groups and movements 2 400, 525
works 2 400; 22 748
Kosikovsky, A. I. 29 554
Kosinski, Blasius 25 90
Kosiński, Józef 33 290
Kositpipat, Chalermchai 30 617
Kosiv 27 411; 31 563
Koskinen, Harro 11 97
Koslov, Petr 7 118; 17 807
Kosmack, Eduard 28 89
Koso 22 659
kosodes see KIMONOS
Kosolapov, Aleksey 29 89
Kosolna 15 2
Kosone Kendō 17 413
Kosŏng 18 352
Och'ŏn Temple 18 308
Kosong Yusu Kwandoin see YI IN-MUN
Koson Ohara see OHARA, KOSON
Koson Temple 23 775
Kosovo 28 437, 454
Mušutište Church 28 446
Kosrae 21 476, 477; 23 711
Kosraf, Wasanē 10 574
Kossak, Jerzy 18 397
Kossak, Juliusz (Fortunat) 18 397–8*; 25 106
pupils 4 670; 13 702; 18 398
Kossak, Lén 18 397
Kossak, Wojciech 18 397, 398–9*
collaboration 10 760; 29 539
works 33 417
Kossatz, Les 2 754, 763
Kossen, Franjo Kos von 17 808
Kössen im Tirol Church 32 822
Kossi, Agbagli 31 74
Kossior, Mateusz 25 103
Kossmann, Rutger see KASSMANN, RUTGER
Kossoff, Leon 18 399*
dealers 19 246
groups and movements 10 258
patrons and collectors 27 478
Kossoff, Leon—cont.
teachers 4 294; 10 257
works 31 706
Kossos, Dmetrios 13 354
Kossos, Ioannis 13 354
Kossov, V. 21 177
Kossuth, Lajos 2 546
Kostabi, Mark 31 609
Kosta Glasbruk 24 58; 30 102–3
Kostaki, Georgy (Dionisovich) see COSTAKIS, GEORGE
Kostalac see KOSTOLAC
Kostandi, Kiriak (Konstyantynovych) 18 399*
pupils 1 731; 4 837; 13 633
works 31 559
Kostandini, Kristo 1 540
Kostanjevica Monastery 28 858, 858
Kostantinov, D. 26 468
Kostas 25 336
Kost Castle 8 376
Kostecki, Stanisław 19 751
Kostelac, Ante Josip von 11 735
Kostelec nad Orlicí Castle 8 379
Koster Farm (IL) 22 570
Kostetsky, Vladimir N. 31 559
Kostka, Ferdiš 28 856
Kostka, Jozef 28 855
Kostolac 28 437, 439
Kostolany Chapel 28 850
Kostroma 18 399–400*; 27 363, 376
Historical and Architectural Museum 18 400
Ipat'yevsky Monastery 27 372, 387
metalwork 27 423
painting 27 386, 387
Kostromskaya 28 322
metalwork 28 320
Kostrzewski, Franciszek 25 107; 30 207
Kostrzewski, J. 4 95
Kostur 5 144
St Stephen 5 146
St Vrachi 5 146, 155
Kostyonki 18 400*; 25 471; 27 363
bone 4 313
carving 27 365
figurines 25 488, 490
marls 25 494
sculpture 27 364
statuettes 27 364
Kostyonki-Avdeyevo period see under PREHISTORIC ART → periods
Kostyonki-Streletskaya period see under PREHISTORIC ART → periods
Kostyrko, Pavel F. 31 552
Kosugi, Misei 17 134, 205
Kosugi, Takehisa 11 232; 29 98
Kōsuke Kaneshige see KANESHIGE, KŌSUKE
Kosuth, Joseph 18 400–401*
collaboration 6 486
groups and movements 2 512; 7 685, 686
patrons and collectors 24 24
pupils 9 72
works 9 227; 22 748
Kos von Kossen, Franjo see KOSSEN, FRANJO KOS VON
Kosyakov, Vasily 23 144
Kőszeg 14 906
Koszta, József 13 333; 18 401*; 30 211
Kosztka, Tivadar see CSONTVÁRY (KOSZTKA), TIVADAR
Kota (i) (India) 15 261, 276, 495, 597; 18 401*
Anand Mahal 15 606
Arjun Mahal 15 606
Bade Devtaji ki Haveli 15 606
Chattar Mahal 15 605

Kota (i) (India)—cont.
  Jhala ki Haveli 15 606
  Kanswa 15 479
  Kanvarpada ka Mahal 15 606
  Lakshmi Bhandar 15 606
  painting 15 603
  palace 15 388, 390
  Raj Mahal 15 606
  sculpture 15 479
  temples 15 270
Kota (ii) (Gabon peoples) 11 878; 18 401–4*
  baskets 18 402
  brass 18 402
  copper 18 402
  masks 18 403–4*
  sculpture 1 323; 18 402*, 402
  spoons 18 404
  stools 18 404
Kota (Indian peoples) 15 736
Kota Baharu 20 162, 175, 176
Kota Bangun 15 776
Kota Batu 5 12
Kota Blater 15 776
Kota Cina 15 811
Kotai Shiva Temple 15 273–4, 274
Kotaji 17 351
Kota Kinabalu 5 10
  Sabah Foundation Headquarters 20 168
Kōtaku Hosoi see HOSOI KŌTAKU
Kotál, Henrik 14 523
Kotalík, Jiří T. 8 426
Kotarbińska, Julia 25 123
Kōtari Jōan 17 792
Kōtarō Mikishi see MIKISHI, KŌTARŌ
Kōtarō Takamura see TAKAMURA, KŌTARŌ
Kotchar, Ervand 2 433, 437; 18 404*
Kotei, Amon 12 508
Kotel 5 161
Kō Ten'i 17 409; 18 404*
  teachers 9 73
  works 17 235, 236, 238
Kotěra, Jan 18 404–5*; 29 893
  assistants 16 902
  collaboration 29 873
  groups and movements 20 254; 28 670
  pupils 3 736; 11 812; 18 445; 23 271; 27 168
  teachers 12 833
  works 4 460; 8 379, 401, 411, 423; 20 254; 23 272; 25 429, 435
Koteshvara 15 463
Kothgasser, Anton 2 818
  works 2 818
kothones 13 475, 477, 513; 18 405*
Kötig, Tibbeke 4 418
Kotík, Pravoslav 8 393
Kotiyagala 29 462, 476
Kotkov, Ernest 31 560
Kotli, Alar 10 538; 30 276, 277
Kotō 17 352
Koto, Gohara 30 246
Kotohira
  gates 7 361
  Konpira-Ōshibai 17 331, 331
Kotohiragu Shrine, Omote Shoin 20 523
Kotokoli 31 73
Kotomin, K. B. 29 554
Kotondo Korii see KORII, KOTONDO
Kotor 22 17
  Cathedral of St Tryphon 22 16, 18; 25 340; 28 453
  palaces 22 16
  St Luke 22 16; 28 445
  St Mary 22 16
  St Paul 22 16
  sculpture 28 452, 453
Kotosh 18 405*; 29 156, 158, 160, 219
  pottery 29 177
  sculpture 29 169
  stirrup jars 29 176
  stucco 29 829
  Temple of the Crossed Hands 1 701; 18 405; 29 159, 165; 30 447
  wall paintings 29 173
Kotrahi
  masks 15 734
Kotrba, V. 8 426
Kotromanić-Tvrtković (family) 4 459
Kotschenreiter, Hugo 3 511
Kotsis, Iván 14 890; 18 405–6*
Kotsubo see KATSUKAWA SHUNKŌ (1743-1812)
Kottarni 22 758
Kotte 29 440
  architecture 29 450
  ivory-carvings 29 471, 472
  Parliament Building 7 613; 29 455, 455–6
  Rajamahavihara 29 461
Kottler, Moses 29 111
Kotukhin, Aleksandr (Vasil'yevich) 23 837
Kotyaion see KÜTAHYA
kotylai 13 475, 476, 477, 496; 18 406*
kotyle kraters see under KRATERS → types
kotyle pyxides 13 477
Kotys 13 570
Koudekerk aan de Rijn Church 22 821
Koudelka, Josef 18 406*; 20 99
Kouklia-Evreti
  hall 8 361
  Tomb 8 8 352, 352
Koukounaries 8 304, 311; 24 204
Koula, Jan, sr (1855-1919) 8 400, 401, 411; 18 434, 462; 23 272; 29 553
  works 8 400
Koula, Jan, jr (1896-1975) 8 402
Koumasa 21 651
  figurines 8 315, 316; 21 656
  gold 21 687
  pottery 21 665
  sculpture 21 656
Koumasa ware see under POTTERY → wares
Koumbi Saleh 1 316, 381
Kōun (fl 1199-1218) 17 124, 879; 31 676
Ko Un (b 1495) 18 406–7*
Koun (857-915) see CH'OE CH'I-WŎN
Koundara Federal Museum 13 835
Kounelakis, Nicolas 18 407*
Kounellis, Jannis 16 682; 18 407*
  collaboration 23 445
  groups and movements 2 527; 10 416; 16 709; 26 778
  works 23 334; 24 408
Kounic (family) 19 807; 28 836
Kōun Takamura see TAKAMURA, KŌUN
Kouřim Church 8 376
Kouřim Lions 26 638
Kourion 8 325; 13 362; 18 407–8*; 26 908
  architecture 8 333
  Baptistery 3 190; 18 408
  basilica 8 357, 359; 9 566; 29 816
  Cathedral 8 357; 11 251; 18 408
  enamel 8 352
  Eustolios complex 8 358; 9 566; 18 408
  House of Achilles 9 566
  marble 8 342
  mosaics 8 354, 355; 18 825; 27 63
  nymphaeum 8 337
  pottery 8 346; 13 496, 497
  Sanctuary of Apollo Hylates 8 336, 342, 353; 18 408
Kourion—cont.
  silver 13 570
  statuettes 8 353
  Temple of Apollo Hylates 8 337
  theatre 8 332, 337
Kourou 11 756, 759
Kouroushis, Nikos 8 364
Kourtir 19 234, 234
Koushi Kiyomitsu 17 393
Kousseri 1 394; 5 525
Koutlidis, Euripides 13 359
Koutlidis Collection see under ATHENS → National Gallery and Alexandros Soutzos Museum
Koutouzis, Nikolaos 13 352; 18 410–11*
Koutsogiannis, A 24 803
Koutsoventis 8 325; 9 512
  St John Chrysostomos 18 411*
  doors 9 599
  Hagia Trias 8 358, 359, 360
  katholikon 8 358
  wall paintings 9 580
Kouwenaar, Gerrit 7 489
Kouwenhorn, Pieter 15 41
Kouyate, Sulemani
  works 1 300
Kovačević, Edo 9 672
Kovačević, Ferdo 18 411*
Kovačić, Mijo 14 596
Kovačić, Viktor 18 411–12*
  collaboration 10 102
  pupils 1 578
  works 8 176, 176; 10 102; 33 593
Kovács, Attila 14 891
Kovács, Gyula 15 2
Kovács, Margit 5 86; 13 888; 15 2; 18 412*
Kovács, Mihály 14 901
Kovács, Zsuzsa 14 910
Kovalenko, D. P. 21 810
Kovalev, Aleksandr A. 31 561
Kovalevo, Church of the Saviour 27 370, 383
Kovalevskaya, Zinaida (Mikhailovna) 31 783
Kovalsky, Sergey 27 581
Kovanda, Matěj 8 386
Kovanda, Václav 8 386
Kovář, Kristián 8 397
Kovář, Zdenek 8 388
Kovařík, František 18 434
Kovel', Cathedral of the Annunciation 31 550
Kövess, András, Bishop of Veszprém 29 922
Kovnir, Stefan D. 18 35, 36, 39; 31 552
kovshy 27 421
Kovtun, Yevgeny (Fyodorovich) 18 412–13*
Kowalski, Alfred (-Wierusz) 18 413*
Kowalski, Grzegorz 17 448; 18 413*; 25 116
Kowalski, Karla 23 500; 30 214
Kowalski, Karol Wierusz 18 413
Kowalski, Piotr 18 63; 22 748
Kowarski, Felicjan (Szczęsny) 18 413–14*
  groups and movements 32 877
  pupils 10 793; 22 423; 30 338
el-Kowm II 30 196
Kowno see KAUNAS
Kōya Kanō see KANŌ KŌYA
Koyama, Shōtarō 2 211; 17 203, 420
Kōyasan see KONGŌBUJI
Koyata 8 411
Koyata Iwasaki see IWASAKI, KOYATA
Koychev, P. 28 838
Koyet, Yuli 27 414
Koy Krylgan Kala 6 182, 196; 18 414, 414–15*; 30 440; 31 781
  architecture 6 199
  mausolea 6 196
Koy Krylgan Kala—cont.
  ossuaries 6 213; 23 607
  sculpture 6 212, 219
  wall paintings 6 223
Ko Yo (island) 30 621
Kōyō (fl 1326-46) 17 126
Kōyō Nakayama see NAKAYAMA KŌYŌ
Kōyū 17 125
Kōyū Fujii see FUJII, KŌYŪ
Kō Yūgai 17 336; 20 287
Koyukon 22 546
Ko Yun-hi 28 311
Koyunoğlu, Arif Hikmet 17 894
Ko Yu-sŏp 18 257
Kozak 29 700
Kozan 21 564
  castle 2 427
Kozani 13 568
Kōzan Makuzu see MAKUZU KŌZAN
Kožarić, Ivan 8 179
Kōzei, Fujiwara no see FUJIWARA NO KŌZEI
Kōzei no Musume 11 823
Kozel, Ana 2 401; 18 415*
Kozelets see KOZOLETS
Koželka, Karel 8 402
Kozhevniki, SS Peter and Paul 27 370
Kozhikode see CALICUT
Kozikowski, Janucz 31 660
Kozikowski, Nancy 31 660
Kozina, Sándor 18 415*
Kozintsev, Grigory 1 573
Kozitskaya, Y. I. 17 870
Koźle 21 571
Kozlinsky, Vladimir 18 507; 33 740
Kozloff, Joyce 18 415*; 19 492
Kozloff, Max 17 583
Kozlov, Gavriil 1 598; 31 536
Kozlov, Petr Kuzmich 21 885; 23 178
Kozlovsky, Mikhail (Ivanovich) 18 415–16*; 27 389, 579
  pupils 24 817
  works 11 345; 24 546; 26 403; 27 402, 403
Kozłowski, Jarosław 18 416*
Kozlowski, Karol 3 527
Koz'ma 25 340
Kozma, Kir 22 17
Kozma, Lajos 18 416*
  works 14 890, 909, 909
kōzo see MULBERRY
Kōzō Katō see KATŌ, KŌZŌ
Kozolets 31 551
  Church of the Birth of the Mother of God 31 561
Kozubowski, Ludwik 7 837
Kozui, Otani see OTANI KOZUI
Kpalla 1 390
Kpa-Mende 21 116
KPM see KÖNIGLICHE PORZELLAN-MANUFAKTUR
Kra, Simon 20 208
Kraak ware see under PORCELAIN → wares
Krabath, György 15 3
Krachkovskaya, V. A. 6 279
Kracker, Johann Lukas 18 417*
  collaboration 18 443
  patrons and collectors 10 531
  works 8 391, 392; 9 754; 14 900; 15 139; 28 852
Kračun, Teodor 28 450
Kraeck, Jan see CARACCA, GIOVANNI
Kraeling, Carl Herman 18 417*
Kraemer, Friedrich Wilhelm 18 417–18*; 29 777
Kraemer, Pfennig & Sieverts 18 417
Kraemer, Sieverts & Partners 18 417
Krafft, David von 3 509; 15 53; 19 796; 30 78
Krafft, Gottfried 12 263
Krafft, Gustave 29 751
Krafft, J.-C. 14 790
Krafft, Lutz 31 567
Krafft, Per, the elder (1724-93) 3 428; 18 418*; 25 105, 212; 30 79
  works 11 471
Krafft, Per, the younger (1777-1863) 18 418; 33 697
Krafft, (Johann) Peter 5 85; 14 901; 18 418–19*
  pupils 10 702; 18 89, 415
  works 14 586; 25 416; 32 456
Krafft, Wilhelmina 18 418
Kraft, Adam 12 401; 13 92; 18 419–20*
  attributions 32 605
  patrons and collectors 15 144
  pupils 20 798
  works 3 508; 18 420; 23 309, 314, 316; 32 605
Kraft, Nikolaus 4 666
Kraft paper see under PAPER → types
Kragujevac National Museum 28 459
Kragulj, Radovan 4 461
Krahe, (Wilhelm) Lambert 18 420–21*; 33 280
  collections 12 474; 24 238
  personal collection 29 889
  writings 6 77
Krahe, Peter Joseph 5 30; 14 151; 18 421
Krahn, Johannes 28 191
Krail, Johann Peter 14 894
Krainburg Altar, Master of the 20 708*
Krairiksh, Piriya 29 243
Kraislav 9 210
Krajcberg, Frans 4 719; 18 421*
Krajewska, Helena 25 108
Krajewski, Juliusz 25 108
Krakau, Aleksandr 3 733
Krakauer, Leopold 16 565, 567; 18 421*; 30 421
Krak de Monreal 16 104; 17 500, 501; 18 421*
Krak des Chevaliers 6 51, 52, 58; 16 104; 17 500, 504; 18 151, 152, 421–3*, 422; 21 564, 587; 30 177
  barbican 3 209
  frescoes 17 505
  Grande Salle 14 74
  walls 8 277
Krake, Holcha 17 623
Kraków 18 423–33*, 424, 426; 25 92, 93, 137
  Academy of Fine Arts 25 140, 141, 142
  art forms and materials
    architecture 25 95, 96, 97, 98, 99
    ceramics 25 123
    enamel 25 128
    furniture 25 119, 120
    gold 25 126, 127
    lithography 25 106
    paper 24 48
    pewter 25 129
    sashes 25 133
    sculpture 25 109, 111, 113; 26 498
    stained glass 13 189
    tiles 25 122
  art schools 25 123, 133
  Cloth Hall 18 425, 426; 25 96, 134; 31 238
  collections 28 673
  colleges 7 566
  Cukiernia Lwowska see Jama Michalika
  Czartoryski Collection 8 372
  ecclesiastical buildings 13 58
    Camaldolite church 25 97
    Church of the Holy Cross 25 101, 129

Kraków
ecclesiastical buildings—cont.
Church on the Rock **25** 115
Convent of the Sisters of St Claire **25** 119
Corpus Christi **13** 189; **25** 114, 115
Dominican church **13** 189; **25** 102
chapel of the Dukes of Zbaraż **25** 97
memorial to Philippo Buonacorsi Kallimach **25** 129
Myszkowski Chapel **25** 97
stained glass **13** *189*
Franciscan church **25** 102, 103, 128
Missionary church **25** 98, 103
Pauline Monastery Library **25** 128
Rotunda of the Virgin **25** 94
St Andrew **25** 134
St Anna **25** 114, 127, *128*
St Catherine **25** 95; **31** 219
St Florian **25** 111
St Gereon **25** 94
St Mary **4** 782, *782*; **13** 162; **18** *426*; **25** 95, 111, 117, 126, 127, 140; **26** 186
altarpiece **1** 710; **13** 117; **25** 134; **29** 726–7, *727*
furniture **25** 120
metalwork **25** 129
stained glass **13** 189
tomb of the Cellari family **25** 113
tomb of Piotr Salamon **25** 129
tomb of Severyn Boner and his Wife Sophie **25** 111
tomb of the Montellupi family **25** 113
St Mary Magdalene **25** 126
SS Peter and Paul **25** 97; **29** 839
metalwork **25** 129
stucco **25** 114
tomb of Bishop Trzebicki **25** 114
St Stephen **25** 129
Wawel Cathedral **4** 782; **13** 57; **18** 430*, *431*, 431*, *574*; **25** 94, 95, 126, 127, 129; **26** 636
banners **11** 149
crypt of St Leonard **18** 430
doors **25** 129
Holy Cross Chapel **18** 431; **25** 344; **31** 557
manuscripts **25** 101
metalwork **25** 129
Monument to Vladislav IV **25** 134
mouldings **22** 220
paintings **25** 102
sculpture **26** 636
Sigismund Bell **16** 867; **25** 129
Sigismund Chapel **18** 432–3*, *433*; **25** 96, 111, 126, 129, 135
stained glass **25** 108
textiles **25** 132
Throne of Piotr Gembicki **25** 120, *120*
tomb of Anna Jagiellon **25** 113
tomb of Bishop Gamrat **25** 113
tomb of Bishop Konarski **25** 113
tomb of Bishop Szyszkowski **25** 114
tomb of Bishop Tomicki **25** 113
tomb of Bishop Zadzik **25** 114
tomb of Bishop Zebrzydowski **25** 113
tomb of Cardinal Frederick Jagiellon **25** 129
tomb of Jadwiga **25** 115, 131
tomb of John Albert **25** 111

Kraków
ecclesiastical buildings
Wawel Cathedral—cont.
tomb of John III Sobieski and his wife **25** 115
tomb of Kasimir III **25** 110
tomb of Kasimir IV **13** 92; **25** 131
tomb of King John Albert **16** 866
tomb of Queen Cecilia **25** 130
tomb of St Stanislas **26** 148
tomb of Sigismund I **25** 113
tomb of Sigismund II Augustus **25** 129
tomb of Sigismund III Vasa **25** 130
tomb of Stanisław Borek **25** 129
tomb of Stephen Bathory **13** *774*
tomb of Thomas Roznowski **25** 129
tomb of Vladislav IV **25** 110, 130
tomb of Vladislav V Jagiellon **25** 110, 113
Treasury **25** 139
Vasa Chapel **18** 431
education (architectural) **25** 142
Florian Tower **7** 359, *359*
guilds **20** 599; **25** 101
High Synagogue **17** 559
Isaac synagogue **17** 559
Jagiellonian University **7** 566; **18** 424; **25** 143; **32** 88
collections **26** 81
Collegium Maius **25** 96
library **25** 142
Museum of Fine Art **25** 139
Jama Michalika **25** *118*, 119
Jewish museum **17** 581
metalwork **13** 162; **18** 429–30*; **25** 126; **26** 686
Museum of Polish Ethnography **25** 140
Museum of Technology and Industry **25** 122, 140; **29** 791
National Museum **18** 428; **25** 139
archives **2** 371
Old synagogue *see* Stora synagogue
Old Town Hall **25** 129
City Council Chamber **25** 120
Pod Baranami Palace **25** 364
Polish Academy of Skills
Commission of Art History **25** 143
library **25** 142
Society of Physicians building **25** 130, *131*
Stora synagogue **17** 543, 545, 548; **25** 129
Town Hall **4** 782
Villa Czermierniki **32** 551
Villa Wala Justowka **32** 551
Wawel Castle **18** 430–31*, *431*; **25** 96, 111; **31** 557
carpets **25** 131
Crown Treasury **25** 139
Deputies' Hall **25** *117*
interior decoration **25** 117–18
Kasimir's Hall **25** 117
Legates' Hall **25** 111
metalwork **25** 129
museum **25** 140
National Art Collections **25** 138
paintings **9** 74
tapestries **16** 867; **25** 131
Kraków Academy (Paris) **25** 141
Kraków group **3** 766; **4** 167; **7** 292; **18** 429, 433–4*
members **17** 446, 447; **23** 273; **29** 641; **30** 342
Kraków Group II **17** 802
Kraków-Sącz **25** 101
Kraków Secession *see* SECESSION (KRAKÓW)

Kraków Workshops (Warsztaty Krakowskie) **8** 371; **18** 429; **25** 119, 122, 133
Krakström, Erik **19** 407
Král, Jaroslav **8** 393
Králíček, Václav **8** 381
Králík, Dušan **28** 855
Králík, Emil **4** 833; **18** 434*, 439; **27** 283
Králik, László **4** 378; **26** 396
Kralj, Franc **18** 434*; **28** 860, 862
Kraljević, Marko **23** 374
Kraljević, Miroslav **8** 178, 181; **18** 434–5*
Kraljevica **8** *174*, 175
Kralovice Castle **8** 378
Kramář, Vincenc **8** 393, 423; **17** 725; **18** 435*
Kramators'k **31** 552
Kramer **32** 136
Kramer, Balthasar **3** 472
Kramer, Bastian **18** 435
Kramer, Christiaan **28** 194
Kramer, Ferdinand **30** 755
Kramer, Friso **18** 435*; **22** 876
Kramer, Hans **10** 220; **18** 435–6*
Kramer, Harry **18** 62, 436*
Kramer, Hilton **17** 694
Kramer, Jacob **32** 701
Kramer, Josef **8** 427
Kramer, Matz **32** 831
Kramer, P(ieter) L(odewijk) **18** 125, 126, 436–7*; **31** 149
collaboration **18** 126; **21** 58
groups and movements **1** 814, 815; **10** 698; **22** 868, 875
teachers **14** 604
works **1** *814*; **4** 788; **18** *437*; **22** 830
Kramer, Simpert **23** 636
Kramm, Christiaan **22** 828
Krammer, Gabriel **18** 437*
collaboration **8** 396
works **3** 576; **29** 747
writings **12** 409
Krampe, Fritz **22** 450
Kramrisch, Stella **15** 211, 558, 748; **18** 437–8*
Kramskoy, Ivan (Nikolayevich) **18** 438*; **27** 390, 391, 442
groups and movements **27** 579; **32** 835, 836
pupils **25** 145; **26** 217; **32** 72; **33** 506
works **8** 766; **18** *438*
Kran *see* WE
Krane **17** 909
Kran family **3** 588; **25** 845
Kranj **28** *858*
museum **28** 863
parish church **28** 858
sculpture **28** 862
Kranjska Gora Church **28** 859
Kranner, Josef Ondřej **25** 428, 441; **33** 687
Kranosel'sk **27** 423
Krans, J.
works **32** *330*
Krantz, Antoni **32** 878
Krantz, David **4** 789
Krantz, Franciszek **32** 878
Krantz, Jan **32** 878
Krantz, Jean-Baptiste **10** 682; **18** 439*
Krantz, Michał **32** 878
Kranz, Josef **18** 439*; **21** 783
Krapf **28** 148
Krapsi, Hagios Nikolaos **25** 336
Krasa, Fr., & Co. **19** 719
Krása, J. **8** 426
Krasauskas, Stasis **18** 439*
Kraševskis, J. **19** 498
Kras group **28** 860
Krasicki, Ignacy **25** 138
Krasil'nikov, Vladilen **27** 381
Krasini, Angelo **5** 161
Krasiński, Jan Dobrogost (Bonaventura) **18** 439–40*; **25** 135; **32** 875

Krasiński, Maciej **14** 819
Krasiński Library and Museum *see under* WARSAW → museums
Kraskovo Church **28** *851*, 851
Krāslava **18** *847*
Cathedral of St Louis **18** 849
Krasnaya Rechka **6** *182*, 195; **18** 440*, *567*; **23** 607
Krasner, Lee **18** 440–41*; **25** 166; **33** 313
dealers **24** 213
groups and movements **1** 83, 772; **31** 607
teachers **14** 633
works **7** 557
Krasniansky, Bernardo **24** 99; **26** 76
Krásno **8** 415
Krasnopevtsev, Dmitry **8** 10; **27** 397
Krasnopol'sky, Otton **3** 527
Krasnorechensk *see* KRASNAYA RECHKA
Krasnovodsk **31** *458*, 459
Krasnow, Peter **19** 702; **31** 607
Krasnoyarsk **27** *362*, 374, 378
Krasnoye Pole, Church of the Nativity **27** 383
Krasnoye Selo **27** 425, 431
Krásný Dvur **8** 379
Krasnyy Gigant Works **27** 417
see also NIKOL'SK GLASSWORKS
Krasov **31** 557
Krassades **2** 160
Krassner, Leonore *see* KRASNER LEE
Krastiņš, Pēteris
Kratchenko, Michel **8** 236
Kratchkovskaya, V. A. **16** 549
Krateros (*fl c.* 320 BC) **19** 169
Krateros (*fl c.* 2nd cent. AD) **17** 909
kraters
historical and regional traditions
Crete **21** *672*
Etruscan **10** *616*
Greece, ancient **13** 474, 476, 477, 478, 492, 504, *527*, *528*, 576, *577*; **32** *660*
Attica **13** *518*, *522*
Chalcidian **13** *515*
Geometric (*c.* 900–*c.* 700 BC) **13** *497*
Neo-Attic **22** *733*
Helladic **14** *345*, *347*
Italy **10** *616*; **13** *527*, *528*
Minoan **21** *672*
Mycenaean **14** *345*, *347*
Philistine **30** *197*
Syria-Palestine **30** *197*
materials
bronze **13** *577*; **32** *660*
marble **22** *733*
pottery **10** *616*; **13** *370*, *473*, *497*, *506*, *508*, *509*, *515*, *518*, *522*, *534*, *540*; **14** *345*, *347*; **21** *672*; **30** *197*
types
bell **3** 672*; **13** *370*, *475*, 476, *531*, 536, *539*
calyx **2** *134*; **5** 448*; **13** *473*, *475*, 476, *518*, *522*, *533*, *534*; **32** 43
column **7** 642*; **13** *475*, 476, 505, *506*, *509*
Corinthian *see* column
kotyle **13** 477, 501
volute **13** *475*, 476, *508*; **32** 693*
Krates of Mallos **12** 813
Kratinos **13** 546, 547
Kratochvíl, Zdeněk **13** 711
Kratohvil, Jovan **28** 453
Krätsch, Matthias **25** 436
Krattner, Karel **22** 393
Kratz, Corinne A.
works **1** *256*
Kratzer, Nicholas **14** 668, 671
Krauer, Wilhelm **14** 287

Kraus, August **12** 407; **18** 441–2*
Kraus, Franz Anton **10** 117; **18** 442*; **33** 455
Kraus, G. M. **10** 103; **33** 37, *37*
Kraus, Hans **11** 586, 587
Kraus, János **3** 224
Kraus, Johann **2** 394; **7** 847; **17** 514; **21** 811
Kraus, Karl **18** 442–3*
Kraus, Samuel **8** 396
Krause, Johann Christian **26** 529
Krause, Johann Wilhelm **10** 537; **30** 349
Krause, Wilhelm **14** 527
Krauss, Albrect **22** 305
Krauss, Franz von **14** 749
Krauss, Johann Anton **9** 754; **14** 894; **18** 443*; **28** 855
Krauss, Johann Ulrich **2** 718; **18** 535
Krauss, Rosalind **25** 362; **31** 673
Kraussin, Johanna Sibylla *see* KÜSEL, JOHANNA SIBYLLA
Krautheimer, Richard **18** 443*
excavations **9** 527
teachers **11** 737
works **9** 528; **15** 91
Krautstrunk see under GLASSES → types
Kravár, Ágnes **20** 151
Kravchenko, Aleksey (Il'ich) **18** 443–4*; **27** 395
Kravsko **8** 405
Krayl, Karl **26** 405
Kraynov, D. A. **30** 350
Krčálová, J. **8** 426
Krebs, Konrad **18** 444*
collaboration **30** 703
patrons and collectors **14** 650
pupils **30** 703
works **3** 805; **12** 367; **31** 166
Krebs, Nathalie **8** 749; **27** 643; **28** 22
Krebs, Rockne **18** 809
Krebs, Thomas **11** 818
Krefeld **12** 469
Deutsches Textilmuseum **12** 464; **29** 240
houses **4** 788
Kaiser Wilhelm Museum **8** 702; **9** 703; **18** 118; **19** 327
Museum Haus Lange **18** 786
pewter **12** *453*
Rathaussaal **17** 2
silk **12** 464
Krefeld, A. van **33** 154
Krefeld-Gellep Cemetry **21** 162
Kregar, Stane **28** 861
Kreibitz *see* CHŘIBSKÁ
Kreis **32** 447
Kreis, Valdemar **8** 759
Kreis, Wilhelm **12** 378; **18** 444–5*
pupils **4** 741
restorations by others **14** 400
staff **14** 284
works **4** 788; **9** 237, 460; **19** 94; **20** 870; **22** 711
Kreischer, Balthasar **28** 830
Kreislinger, Wilhelm **30** 683
Kreissig, Eduard *see* KREYSSIG, EDUARD
Krejcar, Jaromír **18** 445*
groups and movements **7** 772; **8** 829
teachers **18** 405
works **8** 402; **28** 850
Krejčí, Luba **8** 420
Krejčík, J. **30** 221
Kreje, Luba **11** 54
Kreling, August von **9** 691; **17** 879; **29** 388
Krell, Hans **16** 867
Krell, Jodocus **23** 316
Kremberg, Jakob **18** 445*; **23** 635; **30** 84
Krémègne, Pinchus **17** 577; **18** 445*
Kremenets' Castle **31** 549, 550
Kremer, Paul **18** 575

Kremer, Petrus **14** 480
Kremikovtsi **5** *144*; **9** *511*
St George **5** 148; **18** 445–6*; **25** 338, 343
Kremlička, Rudolf **8** 393; **18** 446*; **33** 710
Kremna **26** 913
Kremnica **28** *848*
church **28** 849
furniture **14** 905
lace **15** 12
metalwork **15** 7
pottery **28** 856
stoneware **15** 2
Kremple, John **7** 619
Krems **2** *776*; **18** 3, 446*
Dominican church *see* Historisches Museum
Historisches Museum **2** 791
Kremser Schmidt *see* SCHMIDT, MARTIN JOHANN
Kremsier *see* KROMĚŘÍŽ
Kremsmünster Abbey **2** *776*, 777, 781, 783, 822, 824; **18** 446–7*
church **2** 777
collections **2** 829
ivory-carvings **13** 177
library **19** 316
manuscript illumination **2** 790
observatory **2** 783; **18** *447*; **23** 339
sculpture **2** 801
stucco **29** 838
textiles **2** *824*
Treasury **5** 806; **18** 447*
Krems-Stratzing **25** 490, 494
Kren, Kurt **1** 513; **5** 30; **10** 688; **22** 256
krenai *see* FOUNTAIN HOUSES
Krenek, Ernst **29** 777
Krenides *see* PHILIPPI
Krenov, James **31** 634
Krenz, Alfred **29** 109
Kreševo **4** *459*
Franciscan Monastery **4** 462
Kresilas **13** 453; **18** 448*
competitions **10** 425
copies **24** 418; **27** 39
works **2** 682; **13** 453, 455, 573; **14** 456
Kress, Anton **10** 162
Kress, Max **23** 424
Kress, Samuel H(enry) **2** 560; **7** 782; **18** 448*; **31** 668
collections **32** 890
paintings **9** 467; **31** 664
sculpture **8** 798
Kress Collection *see under* WASHINGTON (DC)→ museums → National Gallery of Art
Kress Cup **24** 573
Kress Foundation **9** 298; **25** 19
Krestlingk, Johann **18** 851
Krestos Dastā, Gabra **1** 433; **10** 573
Kreuger, Nils (Edvard) **18** 448–9*
groups and movements **3** 776; **22** 540; **23** 206
pupils **10** 399
works **30** 80
Kreussen *see* CREUSSEN
Kreutz, Heinz **12** 397; **18** 449*; **25** 786
Kreutzinger, Joseph **14** 901
Kreuzenstein Castle **2** 799
Kreuzfelder, Johann **17** 711
Kreuzlingen, St Ulrich **30** 132
Kreuzwinkel, Master of the **14** 204; **31** 569
Kreva Castle **19** 495
Krey, Andreas **10** 545
Kreymborg, Alfred **8** 435
Kreyssig, Eduard **18** 449*
Kriag, Johannes *see* KRIEG, HANS
Kribbe, Melchior **22** 316
Kricheldorf, Carl **4** 616
Krichevsky, D. L. **12** 234; **23** 144; **27** 578
works **27** *578*
Krichevsky, Fyodor G. **31** 559; **32** 686; **33** 480
Krichevsky, Vasily *see* KRYCHEVS'KY, VASYL'
Krichinsky, Stepan S. **28** 837; **32** 72
Křička, Vavřinc **8** 416
Kricke, Norbert **12** 408; **18** 449–50*
Kriebel, Jürgen **12** 405
Kriebsacius, Friedrich Augustus **9** 236
Kriechbaum (family) **2** 799
Kriechbaum, Johannes **18** 451–2*
Kriechbaum, Martin **18** 450–51*
attributions **20** 705
collaboration **18** 451
pupils **20** 705
works **2** 800; **18** 450
Kriechbaum, Paul **18** 450, 451*
Kriechbaum, Sebastian **2** 800; **18** 450, 452*; **20** 729
Kriechbaum, Stefan **2** 800; **18** 450, 451–2*; **20** 729
(Neunhauser-) Kriechbaum, Ulrich **18** 450*
Krieg, Hans **18** 453*; **25** 104
Kriegbaum, Friedrich **18** 453*
Kriegbaum, Sebastian **14** 664
Kriegck, Johannes *see* KRIEG, HANS
Krieger, Johann Cornelius **12** 135; **18** 453–4*
works **8** 726; **11** 745; **14** 543
Krieghoff, Cornelius (David) **1** 496; **18** 454–5*; **22** 38
patrons and collectors **5** 589
works **5** 565, 575, *575*; **18** *455*
Kriegman, Mitchell **24** 409
Kriegstein, M. **33** 34
Kriehuber, Joseph **19** 339, 486
Krier, Léon **18** 456*; **19** 827; **29** 677; **31** 735
groups and movements **25** 359; **26** 16
patrons and collectors **6** 483
works **2** 361
writings **8** 257
Krier, Rob(ert) **18** 455–6*; **31** 735
groups and movements **25** 359; **26** 16
works **2** 361; **12** 380; **18** 114, *455*; **19** 827
Kriesch, Laura **12** 839; **22** 433
Krig, Johannes *see* KRIEG, HANS
Krig Altarpiece **14** 892; **28** 854
Kriland, Gösta **15** 142
Krim **21** 115
Křimice **33** 160
Krimiller, Pavel **25** 435
Krimmel, John L(ewis) **18** 456*; **31** 602
Krimmer, Eduard (Mikhaylovich) **27** 417
Krimper, Schulim **2** 756, 759; **18** 456–7*
Krims, Les(lie Robert) **18** 457*
Krinsky, Vladimir (Fyodorovich) **18** 457–8*; **32** 661
assistants **28** 747
groups and movements **2** 603, 604; **9** 73; **18** 620; **26** 504
Krio **28** 690
Kripa, F. **28** 452
Kripal **15** 619
works **7** VI1
Kripal Pal, Ruler (*reg* 1694–5) (Pahari) **15** 619
Kripa Ram **15** 615
Kris, Ernst **2** 834; **18** 458*
teachers **28** 115
works **5** 760; **25** 683
Krischanitz, Adolf **2** 789; **28** 344
Krishna I, Ruler (*reg* 758–73) (Rashtrakuta) **10** 148
Krishna III, Ruler (*reg c.* 939–68) (Rashtrakuta) **15** 516
Krishnadasa, Rai **15** 181, 183; **18** 458*
collections **15** 183, 742
Krishna Deva **31** 902
Krishnadeva Raya, Ruler (*reg* 1509–30) (Vijayanagara) **14** 122, 123; **15** 329, 335; **17** 760
Krishnanagar **15** 724
Radha Vallabha Temple **15** 395
sculpture **15** *79*
Krishnapuram Palace **15** 649
Krishnaraja III, Raja (*reg* 1799–1831) (Wodeyar) **15** 649
Krisiko, Kristo **18** 458–9*
Kristall, Bronisław **25** 136
Kristalunie **22** 885
Kristeller, Paul Oskar **18** 459*
Kristensen, Jessie **13** 621
Kristeva, Julia **33** 314
Kristiania *see* OSLO
Kristiania Bohème **22** 289–90
Kristiansand **31** 718
Kristianstad **30** 106
Trefaldighetskyrkan **4** 786; **19** 815
Kristić, Djordje **28** 450
Kristinehamm **31** 718
Kristl, Vlado **8** 179; **10** 667
Kristler, Hans Jacob **18** 459–60*; **30** 69
works **8** 650; **30** 69
Kritias **13** 372
Kritiikin uutiset **24** 452
Kritios **18** 460*
collaboration **2** 685
works **2** 681; **13** 439, *450*, 451
Kritios Boy **13** 422, 449, *449*, 470, 606; **18** 410; **23** 290
Kritische Berichte zur kunstgeschichtlichen Literatur **24** 445
Kritisk Revy **14** 392
Kritsa **18** 460–61*
Panagia Kera **8** 156; **18** 460–61
Krittivasa Ojha **15** 227
Křivánková, Marie **8** 414
Kriva Palanka **19** *882*
Monastery of St Joachim Osogovski **19** 883
Monastery of St John Osogovski **19** 882
Krivaya Luka **28** 325
Křivoklát Castle **2** 321; **8** *374*; **18** 461*
chapel **8** 377
Křivoklát foundry **8** 416
Krivoš, Rudolf **28** 853
Krivoy Rog *see* KRYVY ROG
Krivtsov, I. **22** 181
Kříž, Josef **3** 736; **25** 430
Kříž, Martin **24** 332; **25** 467
Križanke Church **28** 861
Krk **8** *174*, 175
Krmov, Tomislav **19** 885
Krobo **1** 297, 387
Krock, Hendrik **8** 733, 754
Krodel, Martin **18** 461
Krodel, Matthias, I (1550–1605) **18** 461*
Krodel, Matthias, II (*fl* 1590s) **18** 461
Krodel, Wolfgang **8** 118; **18** 461
Kroeber, A. L. **5** 410
Kroeber, Hermann **33** 228
Kroes **15** 756
Kroes, Leonaert **7** 710; **20** 750
Kroess, Johann **18** 462*
Krog, Arnold **7** 807; **8** 748; **18** 462*; **30** 884
Kröger, Jochim **11** 94
Kröger, Jürgen **3** 795
Krogh, Georg Frederik von **23** 221
Krogh, Wilhelm **29** 15
Kroghe, Hinrik van dem *see* HINRIK VAN DEM KROGHE
Kroha, Jiří **18** 462–3*
assistants **18** 439
groups and movements **8** 373
Kroha, Jiří—cont.
pupils **27** 283
works **4** 833; **8** 380, 402, 416
Krohg, Christian **18** 463–5*; **23** 225, 602, 603
collaboration **23** 603
education (art) **23** 244
groups and movements **23** 226; **28** 814
pupils **10** 105; **17** 826; **18** 465; **22** 289
works **11** 474, *474*; **18** *464*; **23** *603*
Krohg, Per (Larsson) **18** 464–5*
collaboration **23** 226
dealers **33** 36
teachers **23** 226
works **23** 226, 603
Krohm, H. **26** 373
Krohn, Pietro **7** 807
Krohne, Gottfried Heinrich **18** 465*
works **12** 373; **26** 355; **32** 466; **33** 36
Krokala *see under* KARACHI
Krokeai **26** *876*
porphyry **26** 876
Krokodil **6** 549; **18** 504
Krolevets **31** 564
Królewiec *see* KALININGRAD
Kroll **10** 211
Kroll, Lucien **3** 551; **18** 465–6*; **23** 500; **31** 868
Kröller-Müller (family) **3** 788
Kröller-Müller, Hélène **18** 466*
architecture **21** 490; **31** 877
collections **4** 743; **22** 906
paintings **12** 861; **19** 31; **22** 905; **30** 760
sculpture **21** 122
Krom, Nicholaas Johannes **3** 825; **4** 445; **18** 466–7*; **19** 542; **29** 873
Kroměříž **8** *374*; **18** 467*
Bishop's Palace **8** 379; **18** 467; **31** 41
collections **8** 422, 423; **15** 158
frescoes **20** 855
paintings **8** 392; **24** 277
Castle *see* Bishop's Palace
school **8** 379
Kromhout, Willem **18** 467–8*; **22** 829
assistants **9** 745
collaboration **33** 676
groups and movements **23** 450
works **1** 803; **22** 830
Krompholcz, Mikuláš **18** 397
Krón, Eugen **28** 853
Kron, Joan **14** 521
Kronberg **11** 735; **28** 142
Kronberg, Johann Schweikard von, Prince-Bishop of Mainz *see* SCHWEIKARD VON KRONBERG, JOHANN, Prince-Bishop of Mainz
Kronberg, Julius (Johan Ferdinand) **18** 468*
Kronborg Castle *see under* HELSINGOR
Krone, Hermann **18** 468–9*
works **24** 663, *667*, 668
Kronenberg (family) **25** 136
Kronenberg, Leopold **25** 138
Kronenberg, Walerian **33** 606
Kröner, (Johann) Christian **18** 469*
Kronewetter, Gábor **5** 84
Kronheim, J. M. **33** 360
Kroniek, De **24** 449
Kronos-Suchos **9** 896
Kronrath, Johann Wilhelm **26** 530
Kronshtadt **27** 375
Krop, Hildo **18** 437; **22** 861, 868, 875, 884
Kropa **28** 862
Kropholler, A(lexander) J(acobus) **18** 469*
collaboration **21** 122; **29** 482; **33** 676
pupils **29** 483*
Kropholler, Margaret *see* STAAL-KROPHOLLER, MARGARET
Kropivnitskaya, Valentina **25** 834
Kropivnitsky, Lev **25** 834
Kropivnitsky, Yevgeny **25** 834; **27** 397
Kropiwnicki, Alfons **7** 837; **12** 212; **32** 871
Kropotkin, Pyotr, Prince **13** 323
Krorayina *see* LOULAN
Kröte, Matz *see* KRODEL, MATTHIAS, I
Kroton **13** 545, 586
Temple of Hera Lakinia **33** 639
Kroupová, Alena **8** 406
Krouwel, Peter **31** 576
Krøyer, P(eder) S(everin) **18** 469–72*
groups and movements **11** 790; **28** 814
patrons and collectors **14** 572
pupils **14** 118, 691; **26** 406, 545; **28** 847; **33** 213
sponsors **8** 758
works **8** 735; **11** *475*, 475–6, *476*, 477; **18** *471*, *472*
Krsek, I. **8** 426
Krsić, B. **28** 451
Kršinić, Frano **8** 179; **18** 472*
assistants **9** 496
groups and movements **9** 672
pupils **3** 86; **9** 496
Krsmanović, Marko **28** 451
Kršnjavi, Izidor **8** 181; **18** 472–3*
Krstanović, Slobodan **4** 462
Krstev, Dičo Zograf **18** 473*; **19** 884
Krstić, Milan **28** 445
Kru **1** 391–2; **8** 21
Krubsacius, Christian Friedrich **18** 473
Krubsacius, Friedrich August **17** 756; **18** 162, 473*; **28** 178
Kruchonykh, Aleksey (Yeliseyevich) **11** 360; **12** 893; **18** 22, 473–4*; **24** 405; **33** 522
collaboration **20** 195
groups and movements **8** 250, 251; **13** 862; **18** 507; **22** 750, 751; **30** 7; **31** 583, 677
productions **20** 193
works **20** 851
illustrated **18** 792; **27** 283; **30** 362
Krug, Erasmus **18** 474
Krug, Hans, I (*d* 1519) **18** 474
Krug, Hans, II (*d* 1529) **18** 474
Krug, Ludwig **18** 474–5*
attributions **12** 225
works **12** 260, 442, 443; **23** 311
Krug, Philipp **8** 445
Krüger, Andreas **18** 475–6*; **25** 367
Krüger, Andreas Ludwig **18** 476*
Krüger, August **13** 30
Kruger, Barbara **18** 476*
groups and movements **7** 686; **10** 882
works **18** 822; **31** 609
Krüger, Dietrich **18** 476*; **33** 131
Kruger, Elsa **10** 700
Krüger, F. A. O. **24** 13
Krüger, Franz **8** 816; **18** 476–7*; **19** 486
pupils **29** 600
teachers **18** 201
works **12** 393
Krüger, Jean Guillaume George **12** 459
Krüger, Karl Ludwig **14** 654
Krüger-Prakhova, Anna **22** 338
Krug Khudozhnikov *see* CIRCLE OF ARTISTS

Kruglikova, Yelizaveta (Sergeyevna) 10 563; 18 477*
Kruibeke, Onze Lieve Vrouwekerk 3 571
Kruiningen, Harry van 22 854
Krujë 1 *537*, 538
castle 1 538
ceramics 1 543
Gjergj Kastrioti Scanderbeg National Museum 1 546
Market Mosque 1 538
metalwork 1 543
sculpture 1 *541*
seraglio 1 539
textiles 1 545
Krum, Boris I Michael, King of Bulgaria *see* BORIS I MICHAEL, King of Bulgaria
Krum, Khan 25 48
Krum, Simeon, Emperor of Bulgaria *see* SIMEON, Emperor of Bulgaria
Krumau *see* ČESKÝ KRUMLOV
Krumau *Madonna* 2 799; 6 363; 12 400; 13 90; 25 431
Krumau Madonna, Master of the 25 54
Krumenauer, Hans der 18 477*
Krumenauer, Stefan 18 478*; 27 660; 32 821; 33 258
Krumlov *see* ČESESKÝ KRUMLOV
Krummacher, Karl 33 383
Krummeck, Elsie 13 716
Krummendieck, Albert, II, Bishop of Lübeck 23 254; 27 125
Krumpel, Helmut 21 84
Krumper, Hans 30 36
Krumperk Castle 28 859
Krumpper, Adam 8 626
Krumpper, Christian 18 480
Krumpper, (Johann) Hans 18 478–80*; 22 302
collaboration 12 346
patrons and collectors 33 275
pupils 28 145; 29 612
works 8 432, 627; 12 346, 369, 404; 18 *478*, *479*; 22 307; 33 274
Krumpper, Livia 18 480; 19 705
Krungthep *see* BANGKOK
Krupa, M. 28 839
Krupnik Gospels *see under* GOSPEL BOOKS → individual manuscripts
Krupp (family) 8 825; 15 747; 31 725
Kruse, E. J. 11 852
Kruse, (Carl) Max 18 480*
Krušedol Monastery 25 339; 28 444
Kruseman, Cornelis 1 808; 18 480–81*; 22 908
pupils 3 86; 4 139; 15 807; 17 841; 18 188, 481; 25 837
works 11 448; 22 849
Kruseman, Jan Adam 18 481*; 22 908
pupils 2 618; 16 573
teachers 18 481
works 22 848; 23 470
Kruseman van Elten, Hendrik 22 847
Kruševac 22 79; 28 *437*, 440
Church of Lazarica 22 79; 28 442, *442*, 453
icons 9 601
Kruševo 19 *882*
Krushenick, Nicholas 20 606
Kruskopf, Pehr Adolf 14 689
Krušná Hora 8 377
Krušovce Chapel 28 851
Krustev, Kiril 5 163
Krusza Zamkowa 25 518
Kruszwica 25 124
collegiate church 25 95
Kruto, Prince 19 745
Kruyder, Herman (Justus) 18 481*; 22 852, 905
Kruzenshtern, Ivan 12 2
Krychev'sky, Vasyl' 18 481–2*; 28 838; 31 551, 552
Krylov, Porfiry (Nikitich) 18 504; 25 352
Krymov, Nikolay (Petrovich) 18 482*; 27 395
groups and movements 4 178; 22 178; 27 392
Krymov, Pyotr 18 482
Krymshamkhalov, Khamzat 27 433
Kryński, K. 4 148; 25 422
Kryster, Holger 14 120
Krystynopol Church 25 105
Kryvy Rog 31 551
Krywult, Aleksander 32 876
Krzemionki 25 515, 516
Krzeszowice 25 99
Krzywda-Polkowski, Franciszek 13 871
Krzywiec, Rudolf 25 123
Krzywobłocki, Aleksander 2 528
Krzyżanowski, Konrad 18 482–3*; 25 107, 108, 141; 32 877
pupils 25 373
Krzyżanowski, Stanisław 10 760
Krzyzanowski, Wacław 18 427
Ksar Akil 30 181
Ksar al-Zit *see* SIAGU
Ksar el-Srhir 16 218
Kseidjke Church 9 591
Ksemahamsagani 15 739
Kshesinskaya, Mathild 12 856
Książ, Schloss Fürstenstein 27 323
Książnice Wielkie Church 25 102
Książ Wielki, Mirow Castle 25 97
Ktesidemos 2 160
Ktesiphon 2 *246*; 15 *901*, 906; 16 2, 371; 18 483*; 21 *267*, 268; 24 215; 27 857; 28 *719*, 721
architecture 21 275, 292
houses 16 153
iwan 2 292; 21 275
Palace *see* Taq-i Kisra
stucco 29 816
Taq-i Kisra 4 792; 12 77; 15 913; 18 483, *483*; 21 275, 292–3; 23 806; 32 89
iwans 16 802
Ktima 8 347
Ktimeni 14 358
Kuala Berang 20 165
Kuala Kangsar 20 *162*
Ubudiah Mosque 20 166
Kuala Lumpur 20 *162*, 169–70; 29 *225*
Bangunan Datu Zainal Building 20 168
Chan See Yuen Temple 20 166
Dayabumi Complex 20 169
Downtown Condominium 20 169
High Court 20 168
Hilton Hotel 20 169
House of Kington Loo 20 169
House of Ng Lu Pat 20 169
Jamek Mosque 20 166
Kompleks Nagaria 20 168
Malay College 20 168
Museum of Asian Art 3 170
National Art Gallery 3 170; 20 172
National Mosque 20 166
National Museum 20 169, 173; 29 240
Negara Mosque 16 242
Parliament House 20 169
Railway Station and Administration buildings 20 168, *168*
Secretariat 20 168
Selangor Club 7 470
Sulaiman Court 20 169
Kuala Selinsing 20 163
Kualo Shiva Temple 15 281
Ku An *see* GU AN
Kuan Ch'iao-ch'ang *see* LAMQUA (i)
Kuang-chou *see* GUANGZHOU
Kuang-han *see* GUANGHAN
Kuang-hsü emperor *see* GUANGXU, Emperor
Kuang-tsung, Emperor *see* GUANGZONG, Emperor
Kuang-wu-ti, Emperor *see* GUANGWUDI, Emperor
Kuan-hsiu *see* GUANXIU
Kuan Lien-ch'ang *see* TINGQUA
Kuan Luk Pat 30 633
Kuan Shan-yüeh *see* GUAN SHANYUE
Kuan Shih-ts'un *see* LAMQUA (ii)
Kuan Tao-sheng *see* GUAN DAOSHENG
Kuan Tso-lin *see* SPOILUM
Kuan T'ung *see* GUAN TONG
Kuan-tzu *see* GUANZI
Kuauá 22 590
Kuba (i) (Azerbaijan) *see* QUBA (i)
Kuba (ii) (Uzbekistan) *see* KUVA
Kuba (iii) (Zaïre) 18 484–9*
anvils 1 365
architecture 18 489*
beads 1 298, 352; 18 *488*
beadwork 3 441
bells 1 360
body arts 1 288
boxes 18 487
chairs 1 366
costumes 3 441
craftsmen and artists 1 *338*; 18 485
cups 18 487, *488*
decorative arts 18 487–8*
divination instruments 1 357
drums (musical instruments) 1 355
figurines 1 *269*
iconography 1 263
interlace 15 882
jewellery 18 487
knives 1 361, 365
masks 1 256, 278, 290, 298, 301, *301*, 334, 336, *336*, 337, 338, *338*, 339, 340, 405; 18 *488*, 488–9*
mixed-media 1 301, *301*
nude figures 18 *486*
ornament 18 487
patronage 1 241, 242
portraits 1 268
photography 10 *579*
sculpture 1 354–5
pottery 1 246
raffia 1 295
regalia 1 352, 354; 18 489
sculpture 1 242, 322, 403; 18 485–7*, *486*
shells 18 *488*
skirts 1 295, 348
textiles 1 295
tools 1 *364*
women 1 340
wood 1 *269*; 18 *486*, *488*
Kuba, Ludvík 2 890; 8 393; 18 489–90*; 25 433
Kubababad 16 186
Kubachi 6 333
metalwork 6 242; 27 423, 425
pottery 4 172; 16 396, 414, 424
silver 27 422
stone-carvings 27 432
Kubachi ware *see under* PORCELAIN → wares
Kubadabad 16 411
palace 16 246, 248
Kuban, Y. 16 599
kubandiz *see* CITADELS
el-Kubaniya Monastery Church of Matias 7 821
Kuban Painter 32 52*
Kubasov, Vladimir 27 380
kubbstol see under CHAIRS → types
Kubelka 15 56
Kubelka, Peter 10 688
Kubera Simha Shakya 30 53
Kubeš, Ludjek 19 883
Kubicka, Małgorzata 26 266
Kubicki, Jakub 18 490*; 25 99; 32 871
groups and movements 13 611
patrons and collectors 25 212
works 23 369; 25 99; 29 839
Kubicki, Stanisław 25 108; 26 266
Kubin, Alfred (Leopold Isidor) 18 490–91*
groups and movements 4 131, 132; 17 763; 22 921; 24 591
patrons and collectors 11 729
personal collection 10 409
works 2 797; 5 758; 8 597; 18 *491*
Kubín, Otokar 8 393; 10 107, 108; 18 491–2*
Kubisch, Christina 29 98
Kubišta, Bohumil 18 492–3*
groups and movements 4 892; 8 250, 393; 10 107; 25 433
works 8 249, 393; 18 *493*
Kubitschek, Juscelino 4 679, 706; 8 8; 23 117
Kublai Khan 1 705; 2 477; 3 516; 7 153; 21 874, 884; 30 825; 33 646
Kübler, Arnold 24 453
Kubler, George 25 291; 29 880; 31 672
Kübler, Werner, II 18 493*
Küblich, Ferdinand 8 752; 30 782
works 30 *782*
Kubly, Felix Wilhelm 18 493*; 22 273
Kubo, Sōtarō 23 595
Kubo Shunman 18 494*
pupils 17 846
teachers 18 96
works 17 285, 287; 18 *494*
Kubota Setsuyō 31 135
Kubotta (Carbajal), Arturo 18 494*
Kubowicz, J. 19 155
Kuča *see* KUCHA
Kuča, Otakar 25 446
Kućanski, Boško 4 462
Kučerová-Zaveská, Hana 8 402
Kucha 6 *288*, 296, *614*; 18 494–5*; 28 *719*
architecture 6 296
calligraphy 6 307
Cave of the Statues (Cave 77) 6 300
dress 6 310
fortifications 6 296
jewellery 6 312
manuscripts 6 320
Monastery 5 102
painting 6 302–3
roofs 6 295
sculpture 6 298, 300
seals 6 *315*
temples 6 290, 296; 30 441
textiles 3 378
tombs 6 289
wall paintings 6 294, 311, 776
Kuchanov, Sergey I. 19 13
Kucharski, Aleksander 4 555; 8 372; 18 495*
Kuchdon Shiva Temple 15 288
Küchel, Johann Jakob Michael 18 495*
groups and movements 26 498
works 3 140; 12 373; 32 466, 467
Kuchi Bandar *see* COCHIN (i) (INDIA)
Kuching 5 *10*; 20 *162*
embroidery 20 176
Fort Margherita *see* Police Museum
High Court 20 168
Police Museum 21 596
Küchler 30 143
Kuchler, Albert 8 735
Küchler, Conrad Heinrich 4 540; 20 924
Kuchuk, Sergey 21 811
Kuchuk Tepe 6 196
Kučukalić, Alija 4 462
Kuçuku, Fatmira 1 543
Kuczinska, Maria 2 762
Kuda Cave 6 15 450
Kudalur, Achutan 20 54
Kudara no Kawanari 17 154
Kudaveli 15 299, 534
Kudělka, Z. 8 426
Kudinov, S. 22 180
Kudo *see* HŎ P'IL
Kudó, Tetsumi 17 207; 18 496*; 22 742
Kudryashov, Ivan 8 10; 28 924
Kudryashov, Oleg 18 496*; 27 397
Kudsia, Begum of Bhopal (*reg* 1820–37) 3 908
kudu see NĀSIKĀ
kuduo 2 589*, *589*
Kudurru 14 21
kudurrus 17 837; 21 276, 295, 302
Kudus 15 *753*, 783
congregational mosque 15 757
kudzu 17 312
Kuefpeck, Leinhart 20 754
Kuefpeck, Margret 20 754
Kuefstein, Count 26 559
Kuehl, Gotthard 9 239
Kuei Fu *see* GUI FU
Kuelap 6 380
Kuen, Franz Anton 8 385; 18 496*
Kuen, Franz Martin 10 215; 18 497*
Kuen, Johann Baptist 3 779; 18 497
Kuen, Johann Georg 10 116; 18 496; 22 61
Kuen, Johann Jakob 18 497
Kuen, Michael 18 496
Kuene von der Hallen, Konrad 18 497*
Kuentz, C. 10 83
Kuepfer, Tony 23 70
Kues, St Nikolausspital 14 781
Kuetner, Samuel 18 849
Kufa 16 *104*; 18 498*; 21 581
cantonments 16 151
maqṣūras 20 368
mosque 16 145; 22 192
palace 16 149; 24 877
pottery 16 398
scripts 16 258, 278
Kufesque *see under* SCRIPTS → types
Kuffarn 28 806
kufic *see under* SCRIPTS → types
kufic-*naskh* script *see* SCRIPTS → types → New Abbasid style
Kufr 9 543
Kuftin, Boris A. 31 319
kuftkārī ware *see under* INDIAN SUBCONTINENT → metalwork
Ku Fu-chen *see* GU FUZHEN
Kuga, Jānis
Kügelgen, Carl Ferdinand von 18 498
Kügelgen, (Franz) Gerhard von 10 539; 11 461; 18 498*; 28 375
Kugler, Franz Theodor 2 532; 12 482; 24 443
pupils 5 189
works 9 682; 23 645; 25 172
illustrated 21 140
translated 9 683; 14 275; 18 897
Kuh, Katherine 18 498–9*
Kuh-i Khwaja 15 *901*; 18 499*
see also GHAGA-SHAHR
Kuh-i-Surh 6 *182*, 220; 18 500*; 30 *252*
sculpture 18 *500*
Kuh-i Tina 10 172
Kuhlefelt-Ekelund, Eva 10 126
Kuhlmann, O. 30 221
Kuhn, Achim 12 454
Kuhn, Ernst 13 724
Kuhn, Fritz 16 60
Kühn, (Carl Christian) Heinrich 18 501*; 24 *739*
groups and movements 14 388; 24 688, 738, 739; 32 924

Kühn, (Carl Christian) Heinrich—cont.
works **24** IX
Kühn, Heinrich Gottlob **21** 65
Kuhn, Johannes **33** 279
Kühn, Justus Engelhardt **18** 501*; **31** 600
Kuhn, Karl **11** 462
works **11** *462*
Kuhn, Walt **2** 447, 633; **23** 47, 701; **31** 605
Kühne, August **25** 403
Kühne, Chrétien **5** 51
Kühne, Hartmut **28** 578
Kühne, Max Hans **19** 111, 705
Kühnel, (Wilhelm) Ernst (Paul) **15** 211; **16** 549, 556; **18** 501*
assistants **10** 645
Kühnel, Pál **10** 546; **14** 888; **23** 747
works **10** *545*
Kuhnen, Johannes **2** 766
Kuhnen, W. **6** 415
Kühnl, Karol **19** 752
Kuhpayeh Friday Mosque **16** 424
Kuhra *see* KURTHA
Ku Hung-chung *see* GU HONGZHONG
Kuhwang, Hwangbok Temple **18** 351
Kui, Deng **31** 67
Kūichi Uchida *see* UCHIDA KŪICHI
Kuijll, Gerard van **14** 731; **31** 772
Kuik, Laurens van **6** 378; **29** 397
Kuindzhi, Arkhip (Ivanovich) **18** 502*; **27** 391
groups and movements **32** 836
pupils **4** 229; **25** 744; **26** 530; **27** 450, 463
Kuitca, Guillermo **2** 401; **18** 502*
Kujačić, Mirko **4** 462; **22** 18
Kujō (family) **17** 789
Kujō Kanezane **22** 496, 501
Kujongdong **18** 273
Kujō Senshi *see* TANOMURA CHIKUDEN
Kūkai **5** 116; **14** 302; **17** 26, 146, 233, 236, 368; **18** 222, 502–4*, *503*, 552
attributions **17** 219
collections **17** 790
groups and movements **27** 519
patrons and collectors **27** 519
works **17** 214, 219, 221, 227, 239, 422
Ku K'ai-chih *see* GU KAIZHI
Kukevičius, Konstantinas **19** 498
Kuki, Ryūichi **17** 204
Kukic, Goran **4** 462
Kukkanur
Kalleshvara Temple **15** 325
Navalinga Temple **15** 301, 527
Kukkapuro, Yrjö **11** 104
Kukkasjärvi, Irma **11** 110
Kukryniksy **5** 759; **18** 504*; **25** 352; **27** 396
Kuks **4** 698, 699; **8** *374*; **18** 504–6*
architecture **8** 379
Church of the Holy Trinity **18** 505, *505*, *506*
Hospital **18** 505–6
Kuku **15** 626
Kukulcán **20** 888
Kukuya **30** 418
Kula **16** 472, 478
Kulakauskas, Telesforas **19** 499
Kułakowska, Maria **25** 131
Kulango **8** 21, 22
Kulashekhara
see also:
KULASHEKHARA ALVAR, King
RAMAVARMA KULASHEKHARA, King
Kulashekhara Alvar, King (*reg c.* 9th cent.) (Kulashekhara) **15** 306, 522
Kulashekharapuram Krishna Temple **15** 523
Kulbanshayid **6** 222
Kulb Church **23** 288
Kul'bin, Nikolay (Ivanovich) **18** 507*; **24** 404
Kuldīga **18** *847*
St Catherine's **18** 848
Kuleshov, Lev **26** 505
Ku Liao-ting *see* GU LIAODING
Kulicke, Robert **11** 499
Kulicki, Karol **6** 366; **25** 127
Kulieša, Mykolas **19** 498
Kul-i Farah **15** *901*, 907
rock reliefs **15** *908*, *917*
Kulík, Tomáš **8** 381
Ku-lin Ch'ing-mou *see* GULIN QINGMOU
Kulisiewicz, Tadeusz **18** 507*
Kulli **15** 246
Kulli culture **15** 245–6, 422
külliye **1** 538; **16** 221; **18** 507–9*, *508*
see also MADRASAS; MOSQUES
Kullrich, Wilhelm **20** 925
Kulm *see* CHEŁMNO
Kulmbach, Hans Süss von **9** 433; **18** 428, 509–12*; **23** 310, 312
attributions **23** 315; **31** 287
collaboration **9** 440; **17** 700
patrons and collectors **25** 364
restorations by others **17** 711
teachers **9** 433; **23** 308
works **12** 386; **13** 188; **14** 572; **18** *510*, *511*; **23** 308, 314, 315, *315*; **27** 256; **29** 504
Kulmbach-Bayreuth, Christian, Margrave of **3** 428
Kulmbach Plassenburg **12** 366
Kul Oba **13** 372, 373; **28** 324
Kul' Olba **4** 111
Kulottunga I, Ruler (*reg* 1070-1120) (Chola) **7** 200
Kulp'o **18** 382
Kültepe **1** *821*, 825–6, 850, 893; **14** 591; **16** *104*; **18** 512–14*, *513*; **21** 269; **31** 456
architecture **1** 824, 826, 830, 831
figurines **1** 825, 832, 835
ivory-carvings **1** 832
metalwork **1** 826
pots **18** *513*
pottery **1** *823*, 824, *837*, 838; **18** 513; **21** 305
seals **1** 826, 856, *859*, 861, 862, 863, 890; **18** 513–14
textiles **1** 880
trade **2** 639
writing-tablets **1** 869
Kulu **15** *619*
enamel **15** 712
houses **15** 720
paintings **15** 618, 620–21*, *621*
wool **15** 666
Kulya, Fackson **33** 602
Kulyab **30** *252*, 252
Kum *see* QUM
Kuma
Cue Saint Dome *see* Kyusendo Forestry Museum
Kyusendo Forestry Museum **17** 93; **18** 40
Kumakichi Kurahashi *see* UTAGAWA TOYOKUNI (1769-1825)
Kumakichi Takahashi *see* TAKAHASHI KUMAKICHI
Kumalo, Sydney (Alex) **1** 433; **18** 514*
pupils **20** 368
works **29** 112, *112*
Kumamoto **12** 100; **17** 18
Kumano shrines **17** 128–9, 345, 346, 428
Kumar **3** 169; **31** 338
Kumar, Ram **4** 290; **8** 677
Kumaragupta, Ruler (*reg c.* 415-55) (Gupta) **5** 95
Kumarajiva **5** 108; **33** 438
Kumar Basu, Nirmal *see* BASU, NIRMAL KUMAR
Kum-arik **6** 300
Kumase **1** 435
Kumashiro Yūhi **17** 184–5, 186, 189; **22** 429; **28** 588; **29** 86
Kumasi **1** *386*; **2** 587
fort **21** 597
metalwork **2** *585*, *587*
National Cultural Centre Museum **12** 510
University of Science and Technology **1** 319
College of Art **12** 510
Kumayri **2** 428, 439
Kumbakonam **15** *294*; **18** 514–15*
Nageshvarasvami **15** 305, 514–15
Sarangapani temple complex **15** 399
Mahamakham tank **15** 399
Tulabhava shrine **15** 399
sculpture **15** 541
temples **15** 399, 519
kumbha **15** 243*
Kumbha, Rana of Mewar (*reg* 1433-68) (Rajput) **7** 175; **15** 386, 491, 597
Kumbharia **15** 314
kumbuk **29** *471*
Kumbum **6** 645; **18** 515*; **30** *806*, 819
kumbum stupas *see under* STUPAS → types
Kŭmch'ŏn **18** 342
Kume **27** 471
Kume, Keiichirō **17** 204; **21** 59
Ku Mei *see* GU MEI
Kumgong, Kumgang Temple **18** 266, 267; **23** 775
Kumidi *see* KAMID EL-LOZ
Kumina **16** 880
Kumi Sugai *see* SUGAI KUMI
Kumkale **21** 586
Kumkapı *see* ISTANBUL
Kumlien, Axel **29** 686
Kumlien, Hjalmar **29** 686
Kumlinge **13** 120
Kumluca **9** 588
Kumma **9** 832
fort **9** 845, 846; **10** 81; **21** 554
Kumoller, Hans **2** 480
Kumordo Cathedral **12** 320, 322
Kumpfe, Georg **17** 835
Kumrahar **15** 423; **24** 264
glass **15** 694
sculpture **15** 423, 452
Kumsŏng *see* KYŎNGJU
Kumtepe **31** 354, 356
Kumtura **6** *614*; **18** 494, 515*; **28** *719*, 720; **30** 441
Nirvana Cave **6** 292
sculpture **6** 298, 300
wall paintings **6** 293
Kumushtakin **4** 464
Kun, A. L. **6** 279
Kun, Hans **10** 406, 865; **14** 322; **18** 515–16; **23** 204; **31** 567
Kun, Kaspar **18** 515, 516; **31** 567
Kuná (Colombia) **9** 165
Kuna (people) **7** 602; **21** 804
dress **21** *804*
Kuna, Henryk **25** 116; **26** 296
Ku Na, King of Chiang Mai (*reg* 1355-85) **30** 604
Kuna, Zdeněk **25** 430
Kuncan **6** 781, 791; **18** 516–17*; **22** 460
collaboration **6** 541
works **6** 792, 813; **18** *517*
Kunckel, Johann **4** 666; **12** 440; **19** 290
Kunckel, Paul **22** 180; **27** 414
Kunda, Style **33** 602
Kundasale **29** 450
Kundavarman (*reg c.* 950-80) (Alupa) **15** 530
kun dga bzang po *see* KUNGA SANGPO
kuṇḍikās **18** 349
Kundmann, Carl **2** 802; **3** 511; **18** 517–18*; **33** 131
Kunduz **1** *186*, 197; **29** 824, 825
Künersberg
faience (ii) (ceramics) **12** 430, *431*
Künes **6** 289, 309
Kunětická Hora **24** 463
Küng, Erhart **18** 518*; **30** 136
works **3** 822; **14** *318*
Kung, King *see* GONG, KING
Kungana **6** 405, 406
Kunga Nyingpo **27** 600
Kunga Sangpo **30** 812
Kungche *see* KIM (iii) TŬK-SIN
Kung Fu *see* GONG FU
Kung Hsien *see* GONG XIAN
K'ung Jung *see* KONG RONG
Kung K'ai *see* GONG KAI
Kungnaesŏng *see* TONG'GOU
Kungnam-chi Pond **18** 260
Kung Pan-Ch'ien *see* GONG XIAN
Kungsan **18** 372
Kungsåra
benches **32** *519*
church **32** 519
K'ung Shang-jen *see* KONG SHANGREN
Kungsholmen Glasbruk **30** 102
works **30** *101*
Kŭng'wŏn *see* KIM (iv), YANG-GI
Kunhuta, Abbess **13** 151
Kunhuta, Abbess, Passional of *see under* PASSONALS → individual manuscripts
Kunichika Toyohara *see* TOYOHARA KUNICHIKA
Kunigunde, Holy Roman Empress (*fl* 11th cent.) **3** 337; **10** 181; **12** 462; **23** 652, 657
Künig von Vach, Hermannus **13** 808
Kunihiko Hayakawa *see* HAYAKAWA, KUNIHIKO
Kunimasa Utagawa *see* UTAGAWA KUNIMASA
Kunimasu Utagawa *see* UTAGAWA KUNIMASU
Kuninaka no Muraji Kimimaro **17** 115; **18** 518*; **22** 497, 498
Kunio Kadowaki *see* KADOWAKI, KUNIO
Kunio Maekawa *see* MAEKAWA, KUNIO
Kunio Yanagita *see* YANAGITA, KUNIO
Kunisada Utagawa I *see* UTAGAWA KUNISADA I
Kunisawa, Shinkurō **2** 578; **17** 198, 420
Kunishirō Mitsutani *see* MITSUTANI, KUNISHIRŌ
Kunitarō Suda *see* SUDA, KUNITARŌ
Kunitomo (family) **17** 363
Kunivin, A. M. **18** 38
Kuniyoshi, Yasuo **18** 518–19*
collaboration **20** 603, 604
patrons and collectors **30** 749
pupils **26** 410
works **19** 492
Kuniyoshi Utagawa *see* UTAGAWA KUNIYOSHI
Kunjara, Prince **30** 589
Kunje *see* CH'OE KYŎNG
Kunming **6** *614*; **18** 519*
Bamboo Temple *see* Qiongzhu si
Dong si *see* East Temple
East Temple **23** 775
Qiongzhu si **6** 723
sculpture **6** 733
West Temple **23** 775
Xi si *see* West Temple
Yunnan Provincial Museum **18** 519
Künnapu, Vilen **10** 538
Kunōji **17** 219
Kunō Tōshōgū Shrine **31** 201
Kunovski, Spase **19** 884, 885
Kunowski, Lothar von **11** 768; **33** 174
Kunozan Tōshōgū Shrine **17** 363
Kunreuth Church **1** 700
Kunst **31** 462*; **32** 593
Kunst, Berend **22** 848
Kunst, Cornelis Cornelisz. **10** 216; **18** 520
Kunst, Pieter Cornelisz. **10** 216; **18** 520*; **19** 101; **20** 801; **25** 725; **27** 256
collaboration **10** 216
teachers **10** 216
works **25** *726*
Kunstavisen **24** 451
Kunstbacksteinfabrik **18** 107
Kunstblatt **24** 421, 443
Kunstblatt, Das **24** 427, 445
kunstbode, De **24** 449
Kunst-Bulletin des schweizerischen Kunstvereins **24** 453
Kunst-Chronik **24** 444
Kunst dem Volk **24** 438
Kunst des Orients **16** 550
Kunstenaars-vereeniging St Lucas **19** 654
Kunst en Kennis **31** 880
Kunstforening (Denmark) **8** 758; **18** 178
Kunst für Alle **24** 312, 423, 444
Kunsthallens Kunstauktioner **8** 759
Kunsthistorici **24** 450
Kunst im Gewerbe **23** 459
Kunst in der Photographie, Die **24** 739
Kunstkammern **5** 351; **9** 14; **18** 520–23*; **22** 355; **29** 861
Austria **2** 812; **9** 14
Belgium **11** *718*
Czech Republic **9** 14
Germany **9** 14; **12** 461, 475; **18** *522*
Poland **25** 137
see also CABINETS (i) (ROOMS); COLLECTIONS → types → curiosities; PAINTING → types → cabinet pictures; STUDIOLI; WUNDERKAMMERN
Kunstkasten see under CABINETS (ii) (FURNITURE) → types
Kunstkroniek **24** 422, 449
Kunstkronijk, De see KUNSTKRONIEK
Künstle, Karl **15** 89
Künstlergenossenschaft (Munich) **7** 855; **22** 303
Künstlergruppe Niederrhein **13** 727
Künstlerhaus **14** 33; **28** 343, 344
members **3** 21, 821; **18** 534; **19** 69, 539; **21** 819; **25** 404
Künstlerische Werkstätte Franz und Emilie Schliess **2** 816, 817; **12** 821; **19** 539
see also VEREINIGTE WIENER UND GMUNDENER KERAMIK
Künstlervereinigung Gruppe 1933 *see* GRUPPE 33
Kunstliefde **21** 851
Kunstmarkt **24** 444
Kunstmuseets årsskrift **24** 424
Kunstnernes Frie Studieskole **8** 760
Kunstnernes Modelskole. (Copenhagen) **7** 805
Kunstnernes Studieskoler. (Copenhagen) **26** 545; **33** 594
Kunst og kultur **24** 452
Kunstschränke see under CABINETS (ii) (FURNITURE) → types
Kunst und Aufbau **24** 439
Kunst und Gewerbe **29** 600
Kunst und Handwerk **24** 427
Kunst und Kirche **24** 438; **33** 73
Kunst und Kunsthandwerk **24** 427, 438
Kunst und Künstler **24** 444; **28** 342
Kunst van Heden *see* ART CONTEMPORAIN
Kunstwart, Der **24** 444

Kunstwerk, Das 24 445
Kunstwerkplaats Amstelhoek 22 874, 883; 24 351
Kunstwollen 2 833
Kuntillet Ajrud 1 881; 16 573; 30 198
K'un-ts'an *see* KUNCAN
Kuntur Wasi 6 521; 18 523*
  sculpture 6 522, 523
  tombs 6 521
  wall paintings 6 523
Kuntz, Carl 11 786; 18 523*
Küntz, Federico de Madrazo y *see* MADRAZO Y KÜNTZ, FEDERICO DE
Küntz, Juan de Madrazo y *see* MADRAZO Y KÜNTZ, JUAN DE
Kuntz, Karl Johann *see* KUNTZ, CARL
Küntz, Luis de Madrazo y *see* MADRAZO Y KÜNTZ, LUIS DE
Küntz, Pedro de Madrazo y *see* MADRAZO Y KÜNTZ, PEDRO DE
Kuntze, Johann Josef 5 613
Kuntze, Tadeusz 18 428, 523–4*; 25 105
Kuntz y Valentini, Antonio 18 524
Kuntz y Valentini, Pedro 18 524
Kununurra 1 43
Kunvaraman 20 54
Kunwi 18 286
Kunwinjku 1 68
Kuny, Domokos 5 85; 15 2
Kunya-Urgench 6 *182*; 16 *105*; 18 524*; 31 *458*
  cenotaph of Najm al-Din Kubra 16 249
  mausoleum of Turabeg Khanum 6 202, 208
  textiles 16 430, 443, 444
  tomb of Najim al-Din Kubra 6 207
Kunz, Otto 9 760
Kunze, E. 23 476
Kunzfeld, Alois 2 832
Kunzō Minami *see* MINAMI, KUNZŌ
Kuo, Prince *see* GUO, prince
Kuo Hsi *see* GUO XI
Kuo Jo-hsü *see* GUO RUOXU
Kuokkala *see* REPINO
Kuo Mo-jo *see* GUO MORUO
Kuon *see* KUEN
Kuo Pai-ch'uan 30 247
Kuo Shou-ching *see* GUO SHOUJING
Kuo Shun *see* GUO SHUN
Kuo Ssu *see* GUO SI
Kupecký, Jan 2 795; 18 524–5*; 28 852
  works 8 391; 12 391
Kupelwieser, Hans 2 804
Kupelwieser, Leopold 24 568; 27 165; 30 210
Kupferman, Moshe 18 525*
Kupka, František 18 525–6*; 22 379
  groups and movements 25 747
    Abstract art 1 73; 8 245
    Abstraction-Création 1 76, 89
    anthroposophy 2 138
    Concrete art 7 698
    Cubism 8 240
    Orphism 23 569, 570
    Puteaux group 25 747
    Symbolism (movement) 30 170
  works 8 393; 11 360; 22 380; 23 *569*; 24 244; 28 920
Kupka, Karel 1 66; 21 482, 733; 33 534
Ku Pon-ung 18 326
Kuppatur 15 241
Kuppelwieser, Leopold 4 438; 14 315; 18 526–7*; 29 611
Küppers, Albert Hermann 18 527*
Kupreyanov, Nikolay (Nikolayevich) 18 527*; 27 394, 396
Kuprin, Aleksandr (Vasil'yevich) 18 528*
  groups and movements 16 817, 818; 22 178; 27 392, 394
  works 22 178
Kupriyanov, Mikhail (Vasil'yevich) 18 504; 25 352
Kurahashi Kumakichi *see* UTAGAWA TOYOKUNI (1769-1825)
Kurakin, Prince 27 430
Kuramata, Shiro 31 576
Kuranganilmuttam Cave Temple 15 507
Kurangun 15 905, 907
Kurashiki 17 *11*; 18 528–9*
  Archaeological Museum 18 528
  City Hall 31 243, *243*
  houses 17 83
  Museum of Folk Art 18 529
  Ninagawa Family Museum 18 529
  Ōhara Museum of Art 17 136, 433; 18 528; 23 371
Kurati Shiva Temple 15 541
Kurayyim, Sayyid 16 241
Kurbanov, Sukhrob Usmanovich 30 253
Kurbanshahid *see* HULBUK
Kurbatov, V. Ya 27 444
Kurbinovo 9 *511*; 19 *882*
  St George 7 221; 9 579; 18 529*; 22 520
  icons 9 627
Kurchan, Juan 2 397; 4 315
Kurcz, Kaspar 18 431
Kurdistan 15 915, 916
  carpets 16 483–4
  filigree 16 531
  gold 16 531
  jewellery 16 531*
  kilims 18 49
  necklaces 16 531
  synagogues 17 550
  turquoise 16 531
Kurdkath *see* KURKAT
Kurds 16 108; 30 470, 473
  tents 30 *472*
Kurebgaseka, William 33 678
Kurel', E. 27 423
Kurelek, William 18 529–30*
Kurennoy, Aleksandr 30 464
Kürer, Jakob *see* KURRER, JAKOB
Kuressaare 10 *536*
  Bishop's Castle 10 536
Kurfürstenhumpen see under GLASSES → types
Kurgan Tepe 30 440
Kurgan-Tyube 30 *252*, 252
KURI (Konstruktiv, Utilitär, Rational, International) 7 771
Kurigalzu 2 236; 17 836
Kuriki, Tatsusuke 17 268
Kurilo Church 5 153
Kurilovo 25 343
Kurimoto 14 37
Kuriyama (family) 17 83
Kurjāns, Pavuls 12 825
Kurkat 6 *182*, 273; 18 530*; 30 *252*
Kurkh 21 298
Kurkihar 15 *279*; 18 530*
  sculpture 15 499, *500*, *501*
Kurkölnisch factory 12 468
Kurland *see* LATVIA
Kurländsische Gesellschaft für Literatur und Kunst 18 849
Kurnas 8 155
Kurnool 15 642
Kurochkin, V. S. 29 631
Kuroda 17 352
Kuroda (family) 17 183
Kuroda, Jutarō 17 205
Kuroda, Kiyoteru *see* KURODA, SEIKI
Kuroda, Seiki 2 11; 11 821; 17 204, 294, 420; 18 193, 530–2*; 21 59
  pupils 14 213; 18 87
Kuroda, Seiki —cont.
  works 18 *531*
Kuroda, Tatsuaki 21 634, 635
Kuroda Mitsuyuki 30 258
Kuroda Nagamasa 30 258
  works 23 *593*
Kuroda Ryozan 23 386
Kuroe 17 356
Kuroishidera 17 118
Kurokawa, Kishō 17 92; 18 532–3*; 30 288; 31 734
  groups and movements 17 90; 21 317, 318; 23 627
  works 3 177; 4 818; 17 90, 92; 18 *533*; 21 *317*; 23 592, 593; 28 834
Kurokawa Harumura 17 439
kuromakie see under LACQUER → types
kuromatsu (black pine) *see under* PINE → types
Kuromuto 17 351
Kurong Batang caves 20 165
Kurosaki, Akira 17 296
Kurosawa, Akira 31 82
Kurpfälzisch factory 12 468
Kurrent, Friedrich 2 287–8, 789; 14 693
Kurrer, Jakob 18 533*; 19 769
el-Kurru 23 *276*
  pyramids 23 282
  tombs 23 281; 25 763
Kursakata 23 *129*, 130
El-Kursi 9 567
Kurspahić, Nermina 4 462
Kuršumlija, St Nicholas 7 261; 28 *437*, 441
Kurteke 6 223
Kurtha Temple 15 262
Kurtiç, Melike 31 455
Kurtović, Ivo 28 445
Kurt Pasha 1 545
Kurtz, Paul 8 752
Kurtz, Rudolf 29 872
Kurtze, Franz 8 16
Kuru 18 530
Kurucutepe 16 411
Kurucz, István D. 13 333
Kuruma, Fode 28 692
Kurumba 1 267, 322; 22 196, 197
Kurume 17 354
Kurunegala 29 *440*, 450
Kurushkada 18 530; 31 701
Kurut 6 222
  congregational mosque 6 277
Kuruvatti, Mallikarjuna Temple 15 324
Kurye, Ch'ŏnun Temple 18 308
Kuryongsanin *see* KIM YONG-JIN
Kurz, Anton 18 446
Kurz, Michael 2 715
Kurz, Otto 2 834; 4 25; 18 458; 28 115
Kurz & Allison 20 604
Kurzin, Mikhail (Ivanovich) 31 783
Kurz & Laufs 12 448
  works 12 *449*
Kurzweil, Max(imilian) 18 533–4*; 28 344, 670
  groups and movements 28 344
Kusa 27 425
Kusa, Lema 33 596, 598
el-Kusair el-Kadim *see* QUESIR
Kusakabe, Kinbei 18 534*; 24 666; 29 663
Kusakabe Meikaku 18 534*
  pupils 17 239
  teachers 33 495
  works 17 238
Kusama, Yayoi 23 298
Kuschke, A. 17 753
Kuseir *see* QUESIR
Küsel (family) 2 719
Küsel, Elias 18 534
Küsel, Johanna Christina 18 534
Küsel, Johanna Sibylla 18 534, 535*
Küsel, Maria Magdalena 18 534
Küsel, Maria Philippina 18 534
Küsel, Mathias (*d* 1664) 18 534
Küsel, Matthäus (1629-*c*.1681) 18 534, 535*
  works 18 142, 535; 28 149
Küsel, Melchior, I (1626-83) 2 718; 18 534, 535*; 21 151, 152
  works 3 416; 20 894; 28 148, 149; 31 574
Küsel, Melchior, II (1674-1738) 18 534
Küsel, Philipp 18 534
Kush *see* NUBIA
Kusha Buddhism *see under* BUDDHISM → sects
Kushana 1 185; 5 94; 6 187, 261; 18 535*; 22 760
  coins 6 263–4; 15 213; 16 890
  furniture 6 311
  sculpture 6 *187*, 215
  seals 6 315
  see also:
    KANISHKA I, Ruler
    VIMA KADPHISES, Ruler
Kushelyov-Bezborodko, N. A., Count 27 439
Kushi, Andrea 1 546
Kushibiki Hachimangū Shrine 17 362
Kushikino 17 318; 27 873
Kushinagara 5 94; 15 220, *261*; 18 536*; 21 847
Kushiro City Museum 22 249
Kushite period *see* EGYPT, ANCIENT → periods → 25th Dynasty; *see also under* NUBIA → periods
Kushite Renaissance 9 888
Kushites 17 *912*
  see also NUBIA
Kushner, Boris (Anisimovich) 15 857; 18 536*
Kushner, Robert 19 492
Kushrabat Caravanserai 16 198
Kuśika *see* KANNAUJ
Kuśinagara *see* KUSHINAGARA
Kuśinārā *see* KUSHINAGARA
Kuskovo 18 536*; 22 177; 27 *363*, 376, 404; 28 593
  gardens 12 134
  Museum of Ceramics and Kuskovo Estate 18 536
Kusmin, Nikolai 10 537
Kusratabad 18 810
kussenkasten see under CUPBOARDS → types
Kussmaul, Adolf 4 39
Küssnacht 30 145
Küster, Friedrich August 33 417
Kustodiyev, Boris (Mikhaylovich) 18 537*; 25 653; 27 580
  groups and movements 2 633; 27 392
  pupils 32 247
  teachers 26 220
  works 27 413
Kusu 14 377
Kusube, Yaichi 17 268
Kusuma Shiva Temple 15 271, 272, 485
Kusumi Morikage 17 792, 797; 18 537*
Kusura 1 856
KÚT (Képzőművészek Új Társasága) 1 796; 8 805; 14 901; 15 14; 20 407
kut see under STELAE → types → funerary
kūṭa 15 243*
Kütahya 9 555
  architecture 16 202
  ceramics 2 440
  church 9 590
  congregational mosque 16 205
  fortress 9 555; 21 585
  Kurşunlu Mosque 16 202
  Pekmez Pazarı Mosque 16 202
  pottery 16 418, 420, 423; 31 455
  Vacidiye Madrasa 16 204
Kütahya—cont.
  Ya'qub Çelebi Madrasa 16 258
Kütahya, Abraham of *see* ABRAHAM OF KÜTAHYA
kutai Amidadō see under TEMPLES → types
Kutaisi 12 320
  Cathedral 12 320
  Memorial to the Glory of Battle 12 *322*, 322
  Museum of History and Ethnography 12 332
Kutal, A. 8 426
Kutani 17 *11*, *241*
  porcelain 17 264; 18 537–8*
Kutateladze, A. 12 327
Kutch *see* KACHCHH
Kutchin 22 546, 631
  works 22 *632*
Kuti, St Thomas 28 445
kūṭina 15 244*
Kutir Nahhunte 1 879
Kutlik, Kirilo 28 451
Kutlug Tepe 1 190
  temple 1 190
Kutná Hora 8 *374*; 18 538–40*
  architecture 8 377
  Cathedral *see* St Barbara
  Hrádek 18 539
  metalwork 8 416
  patronage 8 422
  pewter 8 415
  pottery 8 404
  St Barbara 8 395; 13 58; 18 *539*, 539–40*; 32 90
  Smíšek Chapel 8 390
  St James 8 381, 395; 26 637
Kuttenberg *see* KUTNÁ HORA
Kutter, Joseph 19 827
Kuttia Kondh 15 735
Kuusik, Edgar Johann 10 537; 30 277
  works 10 *537*
Kuva 6 *182*; 10 896; 18 540*; 28 *719*; 31 *781*, 781
  sculpture 6 195; 28 722
Kuvenmas 23 *717*; 24 66
Kuwait 16 *104*; 18 540–41*
  architecture 18 540–41*
  houses 18 540–41
  museums 18 541
  painting 18 541*
  stucco 2 *273*
  water towers 18 541
  see also ARABIA
Kuwait City
  Airport 18 541
  architecture 18 541
  Bayt al-Badr 18 540, 541
  Bayt al-Ghanim 18 541
  Bayt al-Nisf 18 540
  Central Bank 18 541
  Dar al-Athar al-Islamiyya 18 541
  Free Atelier 18 541
  houses 16 270
  Humaydhi collection 18 541
  Ministry of Information building 18 541
  Museum of Islamic Art 16 553, 558, 560
  museums 2 275
  National Museum 15 743; 18 541; 22 366
  Parliament Building 18 541
  Seif Palace 18 541
  State Mosque 16 242; 18 541
Kuwana, Tetsujo 17 413
Kuwayama Gyokushū 18 60, 542*
  teachers 17 190
  writings 17 416, 439
Kūya 13 860; 17 750
Kuybyshev *see* SAMARA
Kuyn, Konrad *see* KUENE VON DER HALLEN, KONRAD
Kuyov Kurgan 6 221; 33 620
Kuyp *see* CUYP
Kuyruk-Tyube 6 220
Kuyumdzhioglu, Arghir 5 157
Küyünjik *see* NINEVEH

Kuz-Balyk *see* BURANA
Kuzma, Dušan **28** 850
Kuzma, Stanislovas **19** 500
Kuz'min, Nikolay **28** 394
Kuzmin, R. I. **12** 173
Kuz'minki Palace **27** 404
Kuznetsk **32** 383
Kuznetsov, A. V. **21** 92; **23** 529
Kuznetsov, I. S. **22** 173
Kuznetsov, Mikhail **22** 180; **27** 410, 413, 414
Kuznetsov, Nikolay **18** 399; **31** 559; **32** 835
Kuznetsov, Pavel (Varfolomeyevich) **3** 529; **18** 542*; **27** 395, 443
 collaboration **11** 358
 groups and movements **4** 178; **11** 358; **22** 178; **25** 649; **27** 392, 394; **33** 379
 patrons and collectors **4** 178; **22** 135; **27** 458
 pupils **3** 692; **31** 459
 teachers **28** 475
Kuznetsov, Vasily **8** 506; **27** 413
Kuznetsova, Lyalya **18** 542–3*; **24** 679
Kuznetsova, Mariya (Dmitriyevna) **27** 422
Kuznetsova, Tamara (Ivanovna) **27** 423
Kuznetsov factory *see* NOVO-GUBFARTREST
Kuz-Ordu *see* BURANA
Kuzyayevo, Novy Factory **22** 180
Kvaran, Karl **15** 70; **18** 543*
Kvarengi, Dzhakomo *see* QUARENGHI, GIACOMO
Kvasov, Aleksey (Vasil'yevich) **13** 653; **18** 543*; **27** 376; **31** 486
Kvasov, Andrey **6** 562; **25** 745; **27** 442; **31** 551
Kvatakhevi Church **12** 320
Kvefjord Altarpiece **13** 120
Kvemo Bolnisi Church **12** 321
Kviknes **23** 221
Kvindelige Kunstskole **8** 760
Kvitnitskaya, Nina **27** 411
Kwa **15** 101, 123
Kwabornament *see* AURICULAR STYLE
Kwach'ŏn **18** 375
Kwakiutl **22** 676
 basketwork **22** 548, 657
 beadwork **22** 640
 carvings **22** 668
 historiography **22** 674
 houses **22** 565
 masks **28** *329*
 painting **17** 770; **22** 588, 589
 sculpture **22** 579
 symbols **22** 632
 totem poles **22** *579*
Kwakwaka'wakw *see* KWAKIUTL
Kwali, Ladi **1** 247; **5** 731; **18** 543–4*
Kwaltangen **22** 198
Kwami **1** 404, 405; **19** 72, 74
Kwamouth **1** *394*, *401*
Kwanajae *see* CHO YŎNG-SŎK
Kwanch'ok Temple **18** 292
Kwanga **24** 68
Kwanghae-gun, King (*reg* 1608–23) **7** 208
Kwangju **18** *248*, *250*
 National Museum **18** 264, 383
 porcelain **18** 342, 343
 tomb of King Chungjong **18** 300
 Tongbu **18** 291
Kwanŭm **18** 342
Kwanyama **1** 351
Kwartalnik architektury i urbanistyki **24** 441
Kwayeb **3** 147
Kwei, Kane **12** 509
 works **12** *509*
Kwele **2** 519; **11** 878
 masks **1** *399*
Kwelien *see* QUELLINUS
Kwese **1** 403, 405
Kwidzyń **4** 783
Kwilu **1** 405
Kwinti **30** 13
Kwirke, Bishop **30** 306
Kwisan, Mirŭk **18** 292, 299, 343
 sculpture **18** *299*
Kwoma **2** 137; **24** 67, 70
 cult houses **24** *67*
Kwŏn Chin-gyu **18** 301
 works **18** *302*
Kwon Soon-hyung **18** 344
Kwŏn Tong-su **18** 331
Kwŏn Ton-in **18** 331, 544*
Kwŏn Yong-jŏng **18** 321
KWY **3** 853; **6** 68; **8** 15
KX Painter **13** 507
Kyaman **1** 515
Kyanzittha, King of Burma (*reg* 1084-1112) (Pagan) **5** 222; **23** 761, 762
kyathoi **13** 513, *513*; **18** 544*
Kyauk-ka **5** 256, 258
Kyaukpyu **5** 247
Kybal, Antonín **8** 420
Kydd, William Shand *see* SHAND KYDD, WILLIAM
Kydna Fort **21** *556*
Kydon **10** 425
Kydonia *see* CHANIA
Kyeser, Konrad **21** 578
Kyeyune, Eli **1** 432
Kyhn, Knud **8** 748
Kyhn, (Peter) Vilhelm (Carl) **18** 544*
 pupils **1** 846; **14** 118; **28** 825, 871
Kyi Thei **5** 248
Kyïv *see* KIEV
Kyje Church **8** 376
Kykko Monastery **8** 367
Kylberg, Carl **30** 81
Kyleakin **12** 635
kylikes **10** 612; **13** *475*, 476, 477; **14** *345*, 346, *358*; **18** 544*; **22** *410*
Kyllenios Painter **13** 508
Kyllmann, Walter **18** 544
Kyllmann & Heyden **3** 794; **18** 544–5*
Kynch Press **29** 641
Kyneton **2** *736*
Kynžvart Castle **8** 379
Kyo Buddhism *see under* BUDDHISM → sects
Kyōden Santō *see* KITAO MASANOBU
kyōgen *see under* THEATRE → types
Kyōgoku (family) **17** 225
Kyōha *see* MARUYAMA-SHIJŌ SCHOOL
Kyohaku *see* SENGAI GIBON
Kyōhei Rai *see* RAI KYŌHEI
Kyōjirō Hagiwara *see* HAGIWARA, KYŌJIRŌ
Kyōkai Keikai **17** 158
Kyōkaku **17** 129
Kyokuzan Hirazawa *see* HIRAZAWA KYOKUZAN
Kyŏmjae *see* CHŎNG SŎN
Kyŏngbong **18** 332
Kyŏngju **18** *248*, 250, *250*, 251, 261, 281, *545*, 545–7*
 bronze **18** 347
 calligraphy **18** 328
 glass **18** 364
 Hwangyong Temple **5** 114; **18** 267–8, 546; **23** 775; **30** 444
 Kamun Temple **23** 775; **30** 444
 lacquer **18** 369
 Mangdŏk **18** 268; **23** 775
 Museum **18** 382, 383
 observatory **23** 339
 palace **18** 545–6
 pottery **18** 336, 341
 Pulguk Temple **12** 94; **15** 855; **18** 261, 266, 268, 331, 364, 546–7; **30** 444
  bridges **18** 280
Kyŏngju
 Pulguk Temple—cont.
  pagoda **23** 775
  Sokka-t'ap Pagoda **18** 265
  Tabo-t'ap pagoda **18** 265; **23** 775
 Punhwang Temple **18** 268
  pagoda **4** 795; **9** 162; **23** 775
 Sach'ŏnwang **5** 115; **18** 268
  pagodas **23** 775
 sculpture **18** 286, 287
 Sŏkchang Temple **33** 493–4
 T'ogwangmyo **18** 369
 tombs **18** 273, 350
  Auspicious Phoenix Tomb **18** 350, 351, 364, 369
  Ch'ŏnmach'ong *see* Heavenly Horse Tomb
  Gold Bell Tomb **3** 626; **18** 350, 359, 364, 367, 369
  Gold Crown Tomb **18** 364, 369
  Great Tomb at Hwangnam *see* Hwangnam, Tomb 98
  Great Tomb of the Southern Emperor *see* Hwangnam, Tomb 98
  Heavenly Horse Tomb **18** 319, 350, 351, 364, 369, 373, 547
  Hoch'ŏnch'ong *see* Lotus Vase Tomb
  Hwangnamdaech'ŏng *see* Hwangnamdong, Tomb 98
  Hwangnamdong, Tomb 98 **18** 367, 547
   glass **18** 251, 364
   gold **18** 350, *350*
   iron **18** 353
   lacquer **18** 369
   silver **18** 351
  Kŭmnyŏngch'ong *see* Gold Bell Tomb
  Kŭmwanch'ong *see* Gold Crown Tomb
  Lotus Vase Tomb **18** 369
  Ornament Tomb **18** 369
  Pubuch'ong *see* Husband and Wife Tomb
  Pubuch'ong Tomb **18** 366, *367*
  Pubu Tomb **18** 273
  Silver Bell Tomb **18** 369
  Singnich'ong *see* Ornament Tomb
  Sŏbongch'ong *see* Tomb of the Auspicious Phoenix
  Tomb 155 *see* Heavenly Horse Tomb
  Tomb of Kim Yu-sin **18** *274*, 298
  Tomb of King Hŭngdŏk **18** 298
  Tomb of King Sinmun **18** 298
  Tomb of King Wŏnsŏng **18** 299
  Tomb of Queen Chindŏk **18** 298
  Ŭnnyŏngch'ong *see* Silver Bell Tomb
 Wŏlsŏng **18** 275
  Anap-chi Pond **12** 93, 94; **18** 250, 261, 275, 300, 336, 361, 369, 370, 546
   calligraphy **18** 328
   king's palace **23** 821
   sculpture **18** *287*, 288, 289
   seals **18** 372
  Kamsan Temple
   sculpture **18** 287, 289
  Kamun Temple **26** 151
   sculpture **18** 286
Kyŏngun *see* KANH HŬI-ŎN
Kyōsai *see* TOYOTA HOKKEI
Kyōsai Kawanabe *see* KAWANABE KYŌSAI
Kyosen **17** 283
Kyosen Kawasaki *see* KAWASAKI KYOSEN
Kyoshū Maegawa *see* MAEGAWA KYOSHŪ
Kyoto **17** *11*, 18, 19, 93, *93*, 95, *241*; **18** 548–67*; **23** 822
 academies and art schools
  Academy of Oriental Culture *see* Tōhō Bunka Gakuin
  Edakumi no tsukasa *see* Imperial Painting Bureau (Edokoro)
  Imperial Painting Bureau (Edokoro) **14** 302; **17** 154, 155, 167, 418, 423; **18** 552; **31** 199, 200
  Kansai Bijutsuin (Kansai Art Academy) **17** 204
  Kyoto City Special School of Painting **17** 420
  Kyōto Furitsu Gagakkō (Kyoto Fu Gagakkō; Kyoto Prefectural School of Painting) **17** 200, 420; **18** 231
  Tōhō Bunka Gakuin (Academy of Oriental Culture) **21** 744
 art forms and materials
  altars **1** *704*
  calligraphy **17** 215, 230, 233, *233*
  ceramics **17** 256; **18** 553–5*, *554*, *555*; **26** 551
  dolls **17** 371, 372
  fans **17** 167
  furniture **17** 358
  glazes **17** 242
  kettles **17** 323
  lacquer **17** 299, 303
  painting **17** 171, 175, 189
  paper **17** 404; **24** 47
  pottery **17** 242, 247, 248, 255, 352; **25** 869
  printing **17** 272
  prints **17** 270, 278, 280
  sculpture **17** 98
  seals **17** 411
  stirrups **17** 364
  textiles **17** 310, 311, 315
  weaving **17** 326
 City Hall **17** 90
 collections **17** 428
 Face House **17** 91
 Floor-loom House **17** 312
 gardens **12** 95–6, *96*, 97, 99
  Heian Shrine gardens **12** 100
  Ryōanji gardens *see under* temples → Ryōanji
 gates **7** 361
  see also Rashomon
 Gion Festival **18** *549*
 Gion Park **17** 233
 Heian (Heiankyō) **14** 301; **17** 21, *94*, 95; **18** 547–9*; **22** 427
 International Conference Hall **7** 668; **17** 90
 Iwakura **17** 248
 Kamigamo **17** 248
 Kanjirō Kawai House *see under* museums
 Kan'yain **17** 404
 kilns **17** 244, 247
 kiosks **18** 72
 Kyoto City University of the Arts **15** 746; **17** 420, 421
 Matsuya **17** 233
 monasteries **17** 231
 museums
  City Art Museum **18** 551
  Fujii Yurinkan Museum **6** 826; **7** 154; **15** 746
  Kanjirō Kawai House **17** 861
  Muncipal Museum of Art *see* City Art Museum
  National Museum **6** 735, 772, 826; **7** 154; **17** 432
  National Museum of Modern Art **17** 433, 436; **20** 147
  Raku Ceramics Museum **17** 433
  Senoku Hakkokan **6** 826, 868; **7** 154
  Sumitomo collection **7** 154
 Nijō Castle **17** 46, 49; **18** 564–5*
  gardens **12** 99; **18** 564–5
  Jōdan no Ma **18** 564
Kyoto
 Nijō Castle—cont.
  lacquer **17** 302
  Ninomaru Palace **17** *78*, 78–9, *79*, *790*, 796; **18** 564–5; **30** 785
  Ōhiroma **17** *77*; **18** 564
  wall paintings **17** 42, 796
 Nishijin district **17** 311, 317
 Omotesenke Headquarters
  Fushin'an tea-room **17** 340
 palaces
  Higashiyama Palace **17** 22, 780
   Agriculture Room **17** 172
   see also temples → Ginkakuji
  Imperial Palace **17** 70, 784; **18** 548–9; **23** 822–3
   Imperial Painting Bureau (Edokoro) *see under* academies and art schools
   paintings **17** 154, 196; **29** 924
   Sentō Gōshō Palace **18** 88
   Shakyō-jo **17** 218
   Shishinden **23** 822, *822*
   Throne Room **17** *70*
  Jurakudai **17** 84, 163, 784; **25** 869
   Ōhiroma **17** 77
   paintings **17** 796
  Katsura Detached Palace (Katsura Rikyū) **17** 45, 47, 49, 80–81; **18** 565–6*; **33** 246
   enamel **17** 378
   gardens **12** 99; **18** 566
   New Palace **17** 80, *80*
   Old Shoin **18** 565
   Shōiken **18** 566
   Shōkintei **18** 565
   verandah **18** *566*
  Muromachi Palace **17** 22, 76
  Shugakuin Detached Palace (Shūgakuin Rikyū) **18** 88, 566–7*
   enamel **17** 378
   gardens **12** 99, *99*
   Middle Villa **17** 80
  Tōfukumonin Palace **29** 925
 pattern books **24** 276
 Rashomon **7** 361
  see also gates
 Sentō Gōshō Palace *see under* palaces → Imperial Palace
 Shisendō (Hall of Poetic Immortals) **17** 234
 shops **18** *551*
 shrines
  Fushimi Inari Shrine **17** 373
  Heian Shrine gardens *see under* gardens
  Hokoku Mausoleum **17** 63
  Iwashimizu Hachiman Shrine **17** 152
  Kamo Shrines **17** 372
   Kamikamo Shrine (Kamo Wakeikazuchi Jinja) **17** 62
   Shimokamo (Kamo Mioya) Shrine **17** 62, *63*
  Kitano Shrine **17** 32, 63, 346
  Matsunōō Shrine **17** 128
  Tōshōgū Shrine **18** 559
  Toyokuni Shrine **28** 611
   Karamon **17** 323
 Shūseidō **23** 298
 Sumiya **17** 83
 sushi **17** 382
 temples **18** 549, 550
  Asukadera **18** 551
  Bujōji **17** 124
  Chion'in **18** 306
  Daigoji **17** 67, 146; **18** 557*
   Enmadō **17** 124
   paintings **17** 196, 197; **18** *557*
   Sanbōin **12** 98; **17** 80, 323; **18** 557–8*
   sculpture **17** 119
   sūtra repository **17** 71, 72
  Daihōonji **17** 124, 125
  Daijōji **17** 197

Kyoto
temples—cont.
Daitokuji **5** 120; **8** 461; **12** 99; **17** 22, 232, 781, 783; **18** 306, 559–61*; **30** 446
architecture **5** 120
calligraphy **17** 215, 342
collections **17** 428
Daisen'in **5** 120; **17** 172, 173; **18** 560, *560*
gardens **12** 98
Jukōin **17** 41, 339
Kohōan **18** 560
Ōbaiin **31** 676
paintings **17** 193, 419
Ryōgen'in **17** 46, 49; **18** 560
Ryūkōin tea-room **17** *337*
Shinjuan **17** *338*, 340; **18** 560; **28** 624
Ginkakuji **12** 98; **18** 562–4*
Dōjinsai **17** *75*, 76, 335
garden **18** *563*, 563–4
Silver Pavilion (Ginkaku) **18** 563; **24** 289
Tōgūdō **2** 599; **17** 76–7; **18** 563
Tokoma **17** 77
see also palaces → Higashiyama Palace
Golden Pavilion Temple *see* Kinkakuji
Hachiokadera *see* Kōryūji
Hatanokimidera *see* Kōryūji
Heitōin **17** 321
Hōjōji **17** 68, 69, 70; **18** 549; **30** 445
Saishōkōin **11** 824; **17** 161
sculpture **17** 597
Hōkaiji **17** 119
Amida Hall **5** 119
Hōkongōin **17** 120
Hosshōji **17** 124
Jingōji **2** 599; **17** 100, 102, 161, *161*
bell **17** 321

Kyoto
temples
Jingōji—cont.
paintings **11** 825
screen **17** 156, *156*
sculpture **17** *117*, 126, 131
Jishiin **17** 99
Jishōji *see* Ginkakuji
Kenchōji **17** 72
Kinkakuji **17** 22; **18** 561*
Golden Pavilion (Kinkaku) **18** 561, *561*; **24** 289
Kiyomizudera **17** *74*, 347
hondō **17** 74
Kōdaiji **17** 785
Kokedera *see* Saihōji
Kōryūji **18** 555–6*
Red Hall (Akado) **18** 556
sculpture **17** 109, *110*, 120
wall paintings **32** 804
Kōzanji **17** 124, 159; **33** 318
Kuramadera **17** 125, 321
Kyōōgokokuji *see* Tōji
Mammoth Hōkōji **17** 74
Mibudera **17** 349, 394
Myōhōin **17** 197
Myōshinji **12** 98; **17** 22
bell **17** 320
Reiun'in **12** 101; **17** 77
Nanzenji **2** 599; **17** *301*; **18** 558–9*
abbot's quarters **18** 558
Konchiin **12** 99; **18** 559
Nanzen'in **18** 558
Tenjūan **18** 558–9
Tōshōgū Shrine *see under* shrines
Ninnaji **17** 119
Nishi Honganji **12** 99; **17** 378, 429
paintings **17** 197
stages **17** 326, *326*
Rengeōin **17** 124
Rinkain **17** 132

Kyoto
temples—cont.
Rokuharamitsuji **17** 100, 131, 132
Rokuonji *see* Kinkakuji
Ryōanji **18** 561–2*
gardens **12** 63, 97; **18** 561–2, *562*
Saifukuji **18** 306
Saihōji **12** 98; **18** 556*
Saiji **17** 65
Seiryōji **17** 119
Shōgoin **17** 131
Shōjiji **17** 126
Shōjuraigōji Guest Pavilion **18** 537
Shōkokuji **2** 598, 599; **17** 22
Shūon'an **17** 132
Silver Pavilion Temple *see* Ginkakuji
Tenryūji **17** 24; **22** 382
Tōfukuji **17** 22, 784
Doshuin **17** 119
gardens **12** 100
paintings **17** 419
Tōji **17** 49, 65, 127, 155, *155*, 428
Higojōkei **17** 125
Mieidō **17** 124, 131
Nandaimon **17** 124
sculpture **17** 118, 122, 128
Uzumasadera *see* Kōryūji
Zenrinji **17** *149*
theatres **17** 330
Urasenke Headquarters
Konnichian tea-room **17** 339; **28** *619*
Yūin tea-room **17** *338*, 339
Week Building **17** 92
Western Camp *see* Nishijin district
Yōmei Bunko **19** 317
Kyō Tsuji *see* TSUJI, KYŌ
Kyōu Hoashi *see* HOASHI KYŌU
Kyōunshi *see* IKKYŪ SŌJUN
KY Painter **13** 507
Kypros *see* CYPRUS
Kypselos **13** 488
Kyras Vrisi *see* ISTHMIA
Kyrenia
Castle **8** 361
Castle Museum **8** 367
Hagia Mavra **8** 359
Hagios Giorgios **8** 358
Kyre Park (Worcs) **10** 270
Kyrgyz **27** 436; **30** 474
Kyrgyzstan **6** 181; **16** *105*; **18** *567*, 567–9*
architecture **18** 568*
bags **18** *569*
bowls **6** *267*
carpets **18** 569
collections **6** 284*
decorative arts **18** 569*
embroidery **18** *569*
glass **6** *267*
historiography **6** 280*
jewellery **6** 272, 274
museums **6** 284*
painting **18** 568–9*
sculpture **6** 220
textiles **18** 569*
wall paintings **6** 232
Kyriakoselia **8** 155
Hagios Nikolaos **8** 156
Kyriotissa *see* PANAGIA TIS KYRAS
Kyrkefalla Church **30** 111
Kyrkenar, Erasmus **2** 472
Kyrmu, I. **21** 812
Kyromos *see* EUROMOS
Kyrrhos, Andronikos of *see* ANDRONIKOS OF KYRRHOS
Kysela, František **8** 373; **13** 711
works **8** *420*
Kysela, Jan **25** 435
Kysela, Ludvík **12** 834; **18** 569–70*; **25** 430
Kystakoz, Arbob Palace **29** 823
Kyte, Francis **18** 570*
Kythera **9** *511*; **13** *363*; **18** 570–71*
Kythnos **8** *304*, 323
Kythrea **8** *325*
aqueduct **8** 356
sculpture **8** 333, 342, 354
Kytson, Lady **13** *239*
Kytson, Thomas **8** 44
Kyū Ei *see* EI, KYŪ
Kyūhaku **17** 304
Kyūichi Takamura *see* TAKAMURA, KYŪICHI
Kyūjō Yamada *see* YAMADA KYŪJŌ
Kyurkchyan, Ruzanna **2** 437
Kyūsai *see* HARAI, SHIN
Kyūshitsuka Kai (Nine Room Society) **17** 206; **20** 834; **27** 594
Kyushu **17** 10, *11*, 18, *241*, 358
Hosshōji **18** 308
pottery **17** 242
sculpture **17** 120
textiles **17** *310*
Kyushuha (Kyushu School) **17** 207
Kyustendil, Dimitrov-Maistora Museum **8** 901; **31** 399
Kyuzeli Gyr **6** *182*, 196
Kyzikos **13** 464, 586, 587
Kyzl-Orda **17** *865*
fort **17** 866
Kyzylcha 6 **6** 196
Kyzyl Tepe **6** 196
Kzyl-Ordin, Historical and Regional Museum **6** 284

L

Laach, Heinrich II, Graf von (*fl* 12th-13th cent) **12** 471
Laag, Heinrich (*b* 1892) **10** 212
Laage, de (family) **20** 732
Laaksonen, Touko *see* TOM OF FINLAND
La Albufereta **15** 59
La Alcudia Church **29** 261
La Aliseda **1** 867; **24** 645
Laan, Adolf van der **21** 368; **25** 736
Laan, Hans van der **28** 594
Laan, Nico van der **28** 594
Laapotti, Jaako **30** 284
Laar, Arnold van der **11** 440
Laar, Gijsbert van **12** 105; **18** 73; **31** 488
works **12** *106*
Laar, Theo van der **21** 789
La Araña **29** 365
Laarmann, Märt **10** 539, 542
Laarne Castle **3** *539*, 552; **18** 572*
Laas, J. C. **4** 81
La Asunción **32** *165*
Cathedral **32** 167
fort of S Rosa **32** 169
Laate, Jenny **22** 608
Laatsch, St Leonhard **28** 134
Laayoun *see* AAIUNA
Labacco, Antonio **18** 572–3*
collaboration **27** 747
teachers **27** 743
works **1** 565; **27** 745
writings **19** 687; **31** 295
Labacco, Mario **18** 573
Labadye, Jean-Baptiste **8** 18
Laban, Rudolph **8** 434; **24** 405
Labande, Léon-Honoré **18** 573*
Labarre, Etienne Eloy de **5** 807
Labarre, Jean de **30** 788
Labas, Aleksandr (Arkadevich) **18** 573–4*; **27** 284, 394; **28** 924
Labastide (pyrenees) **25** 479, 480, 493
Labastide d'Armagnac gate-house **4** 780
La Baume-Latrone **25** 477
Labayen, Joaquín **12** 177; **15** 885
La Bazinière, Bertrand de **4** 534
Labban, Hedi **31** 426
Labbé, Maximiliaan **10** 844; **32** 121
La Bedollière, Emile de **21** 889
Łabędź (family) **25** 134
La Bellière, Tanneguy du Chastel, Vicomte de *see* TANNEGUY DU CHASTEL, 1st Vicomte de La Bellière and Baron de Derval
labels **10** 421; **11** 309; **22** 356
historical and regional traditions
Egypt, ancient **9** 868; **10** 60; **14** 407
Greece, ancient **13** *485*, 488
materials
ivory **10** 60
types
ex libris *see* BOOKPLATES
uses
furniture **20** 442
see also TABLETS
La Bénisson-Dieu **13** 672
Łabenski, Franciszek Xawey **26** 733
Labenwolf, Georg **18** 574, 575*; **23** 309
assistants **33** 434
attributions **8** 739
patrons and collectors **14** 369; **23** 395
pupils **33** 434
Labenwolf, Pankraz **18** 574–5*
collaboration **3** 69; **11** 223; **22** 918; **23** 309; **24** 331; **28** 144; **29** 563
patrons and collectors **16** 866
works **18** *574*; **25** 126; **29** 571
Laber (Blake), Celestine **28** 692
La Berthenoux **26** 599
Labeur, Le **4** 618; **23** 399; **28** 104; **30** 726
Labhardt, Johann Cristoph **12** 462; **14** 491
Labhart, Christoph **12** 261; **26** 486
Labia (family) **16** 752
La Billarderie, Charles-Claude de Flahaut de *see* ANGIVILLER, CHARLES-CLAUDE DE FLAHAUT DE LA BILLARDERIE, Comte d'
La Billarderie d'Angiviller, Comte de *see* ANGIVILLER, CHARLES-CLAUDE DE FLAHAUT DE LA BILLARDERIE, Comte de
Labille-Guiard, Adélaïde **18** 575–7*, *576*; **33** 308
groups and movements **24** 136
works **11** 406
Labino, Dominick **19** 501; **31** 645
Labisi, Paolo **28** 769
Labisi brothers **23** 258
Labisse, Félix **18** 577*; **30** 23
Lábler, Ludvík **18** 538, 539, 540
Labná **18** 577–8*; **20** *882*, 884; **21** *372*; **23** 826
Arch **9** 165; **20** 884; **21** *205*
architecture **21** 205
Palace **18** *578*
Labò, Mario **16** 650; **18** 578*; **21** 422
Laborão, Joaquim José de Barros **1** 679; **18** 578–9*; **25** 301
Laboratorio de Piedras y Mosaico **11** 172; **20** 70, 71; **29** 316
Laboray (family) **2** 704
Laborde, A. de (*fl* late 19th-early 20th cent.) **9** 453
Laborde, Alexandre (-Louis-Joseph) de (1773-1842) **8** 542; **18** 579*
Laborde, Guillermo **3** 214; **8** 806; **10** 509; **29** 26
Laborde, Jean **20** 35
La Borde, Jean-Benjamin de **8** 772; **14** 366
Laborde, Jean-Joseph, Marquis de **11** 595; **18** 579*; **21** 150; **26** 449
Laborde, Léon de, Comte **10** 209; **11** 675; **18** 579; **20** 420
Laborde-Méréville, François (-Louis-Joseph) de **18** 579*; **19** 115
Labores, José March y *see* MARCH Y LABORES, JOSÉ
Labor et Ars **21** 122
Laborio, Pedro **7** 608
Labor Omnia Vincit *see* LOV
Laboureur, Emile **10** 397
Laboureur, Francesco Massimiliano **29** 640
Laboureur, Jean Emile **9** 396
Laboureur, Maximilian **4** 407
Labours of Hercules, Master of the **25** 20
Labours of the Months *see* CALENDARS
Labra, José Maria de **1** 620
Labrador, El **14** 755; **18** 580*
Labraña, Alonso **29** 342
Labrang Tashi Khyl **30** 819
Labraunda **5** 742; **13** *363*; **18** 580*
orders (architecture) **23** 484
Temple of Zeus **13** 414; **25** 768
La Brède **12** 122
La Bretonne, Nicolas E. Restif de *see* RESTIF DE LA BRETONNE, NICOLAS E.
Labronica, Scuola *see* SCUOLA LABRONICA
Labrosse, Paul **22** 37
Labrouste, (Pierre-François)-Henri **3** 465; **11** 323, 359, 520, 521, 671; **18** 580, 581–3*; **24** 221
assistants **2** 14; **14** 512; **19** 116
collaboration **9** 312; **12** 13; **18** 580
groups and movements **13** 607, 612; **24** 173; **28** 345
pupils
Balyan, Nikoğos Bey **3** 130
Balyan, Sarkis Bey
Baudot, (Joseph-Eugène-) Anatole de **3** 394
Boeswillwald, Emile **4** 222
Bossan, Pierre **4** 465
Bouwens van der Boijen, William (Oscar) **4** 597
Galland, P(ierre) V(ictor) **12** 13
Guadet, Julien Azais **13** 732
Lassus, Jean-Baptiste (-Antoine) (1807-57) **18** 816
Lheureux, Louis-Ernest **19** 296
Lienau, Detlef **19** 346
Lisch, Jean-Juste-Gustave **19** 469
Millet, Eugène-Louis **21** 608
teachers **32** 81
works **11** 520, 521, 522, 659; **16** 53, 54; **18** *582*, *583*; **19** 317; **22** 270; **25** 172, 173; **26** 13, 205; **30** 505
Labrouste, Théodore **11** 521; **18** 580–81*
staff **26** 338
teachers **32** 81
works **11** 359, 521
La Bruyère, Jean Baptiste François Graux de *see* GRAUX DE LA BRUYÈRE, JEAN BAPTISTE FRANÇOIS
Labruzzi, Carlo **13** 303; **14** 598; **18** 584*; **25** 213; **28** 271
Labruzzi, Pietro **3** 714; **24** 844
Labruzzi, Tomaso **1** 466
La Buigne, Gace de **31** 834
La Bureba **9** 596; **29** 287
laburnum **7** 442; **20** 467; **28** 252
Labus, Giovanni **8** 523
La Bussola *see* BUSSOLA, LA
Labwe **30** 196
Labyrinthe: Journal des lettres et des arts **24** 453; **28** 820
Labyrinthos: Studi e ricerche sulle arti nei secoli XVIII e XIX **24** 449
labyrinths **12** 105, 114, *118*, 119; **18** 584–6*, *585*
see also MAZES
lac
historical and regional traditions
Egypt **16** 431
Indian subcontinent **15** 667; **16** 431; **21** 717
Iran **16** 449
Islamic **16** 431, 449, 533
Japan **17** 357
uses
brass **4** 684
dyes **9** 492; **15** 667; **16** 431, 449; **18** 607, 655
glazes **12** 623
mirror frames **21** 717
pigments **18** 655; **24** 796–7
La Cabaña **18** 586*; **29** *136*
Lacaille, Nicolas Louis de, Abbé **12** 812
La Calahorra **29** *258*, 299
Castle **18** 586–7*; **29** 264; **32** 147
La Calamine *see* KELMIS
La Calera **3** 919
La Cam, John de **10** 316
Lacambre, Geneviève **22** 688
Lacan, Jacques **10** 480; **18** 587*; **25** 361, 684; **29** 891
La Canea *see* CHANIA
Lacapelle-Biron **24** 148
laçarias e rosas tiles *see under* TILES → types
La Carolina **31** 719
Lacarra and Genond **30** 525
La Case, Nicolas de *see* CASA, NICOLÒ DELLA
Lacasse, Joseph (Fernand) **18** 588*
Lacava, Manuel **29** 343
La Caze, Louis **18** 588*; **20** 498; **26** 500
Lac du Flambeau Museum (WI) **22** 671
lace **18** 588–93*; **30** 549, 563
historical and regional traditions
Armenia (Europe) **2** 443
Australia **2** 768
Austria **18** 158
Belgium **3** 610–11*; **18** 589, 590, 591, 593; **31** 816
Croatia **8** 180
Czech Republic **8** 421*; **18** 593
Denmark **8** 756*
England **10** 355*; **18** 589, 591, 593
France **6** 455; **11** 649–51*, *650*; **18** 590, 591, 593
Germany **11** *461*; **12** 469–70; **18** 158, 590, 593
Hungary **15** 12*
Ireland **16** 34; **18** 593
Italy **16** *754*, 754–5; **18** 589, 590, 593
Lepoglava **8** 180
Maldives, Republic of **20** 189
Malta (Republic of) **20** 218–19
Native North Americans **31** 661
North America **18** 593
Portugal **25** *316*, 317*
Russia **27** 430
Scotland **28** 266
Slovakia **18** 593; **28** 856
Spain **18** 588; **29** 351
Sweden **30** 115*
Switzerland **18** 590; **30** 151–2*
United States of America **31** 661–2*
materials
beads **18** 588, 590
cotton **3** *611*; **18** 588, 590, 593
gold **10** 355; **16** 34; **18** 590, *591*; **30** 151, 542
horsehair **18** 589; **30** 151
linen **11** *650*; **12** 469; **16** *754*; **18** 588, *589*, 590, *592*
metal **30** 540
parchment **18** 588
pearls **18** 590
silk **12** 469; **18** 588, 590
silver **10** 355; **16** 34; **30** 151, 542
straw **30** 151
threads **18** 588, 590; **30** 540, 542
wool **18** 588
techniques
knitting **18** 158
knotting **18** 588
plaiting **18** 589
types
Alençon **18** 589, 591
lace
types—cont.
antique **18** 593
application **3** 610, *611*; **18** 589
Argentan **18** 589, 591
bibila **5** 161; **18** 589
Binche **18** 589, 591
blonde **11** 650; **18** 591
bobbin **18** 589*, 590, 591, 593; **30** 550
Belgium **3** 610, *611*; **18** *589*, *591*, *592*
Bulgaria **5** 161
England **10** 355, *355*
Germany **12** 469
Scotland **28** 266
Brussels **3** 610; **18** 589, 591, 593
burato **18** 588
Carrickmacross (Co. Monaghan) **18** 590, 593
Chantilly (France) **18** 593
chemical **18** 590
Duchesse **18** 589, 593
gros point **18** 589
gros point de Venise **18** 590
hollie point **10** 355; **18** 589
Honiton **18** 593
imitation **12** 463
lacis **18** 588, 590; **30** 549
Belgium **3** *611*
Germany **12** 469
Spain **29** 351
Leavers **18** 590
Lille **18** 589, 591
Limerick **18** 589, 593
machine **18** 589–90*, 591, 593
Belgium **3** 611
England **10** 355
Scotland **28** 266
Malines *see* Mechlin
Mechelen *see* Mechlin
Mechlin **3** 610; **18** 589, 591, 593
medas **18** 588
needle **10** 355; **18** 588–9*, 590–91, 593
Belgium **3** *611*
France **18** *589*
Italy **16** *754*
Venice **32** 205–6
net *see* lacis
pillow *see* bobbin
point d'Angleterre *see* Brussels
point de France **11** 650; **18** 589, 591
point de gaze **18** 589, 593
point de Lierre *see* Limerick
point de neige **18** 589
point de Paris **18** 589, 591
point d'esprit **18** *589*
point net **3** 610; **18** 591
puncetti **18** 589
punto in aria **18** 590
reproduction **18** 593
reticella **18** 590
Schleswig **8** 756
sol **18** 588
tamboured net **28** 266
tape **5** 161; **18** 589, 593
toilé **18** 589
Tønder **8** 756
torchon **18** 589, 590
Valenciennes **3** 610; **11** 650; **18** 589, 591, 593
Venetian **18** 589, 590, 591, 593
vrai drochel **18** 589
uses
coifs (dress) **12** 469
dress **18** *591*, 591
fans **10** 782
frames **11** 461, *461*
hair-nets **12** 469

lace
uses—cont.
shawls **18** 593
sheets **18** *591*
upholstery **18** 591
veils **18** *592*
La Cecca *see* CECCA, LA
La Ceiba **14** *711*, 713
Municipalidad **14** 714
La Celle Church **1** 518
Lacer, C(aius) Julius **26** 884
Lacerba **4** 199; **5** 848; **11** 190, 865, 868; **24** 63, 427; **27** 445
Lacey, Liz **29** 119
Lachaise, Gaston **18** 593–4*; **31** 613
works **18** *594*
La Chaise-Dieu Abbey **11** 654; **26** 601
St Robert **11** 511; **30** 331
La Chalade **7** 353
La Chamba **7** 603
La Champa **29** 214
La Chapelle, J.-O. Pauvert de *see* PAUVERT DE LA CHAPELLE, J.-O.
Lachapelle-aux-Pots **11** 603
La Chapelle-Godefroy Château **22** 682
La Charité-sur-Loire **11** *504*, 606
priory church **18** 595*; **26** 602; **29** 412
La Châtre, Marshal of **11** 639
La Chau, de **23** 520
La Chausse, Michel-Ange de **18** 595*
Lachaussée Château **4** 304
La Chaussée-Tirancourt **25** 508
La Chaux de Fonds
Ecole des Beaux-Arts **30** 127
Villa Fallet **30** 127; **32** 556
Villa Schwob **19** *40*, 40
La Chavignerie, Emile Bellier de *see* BELLIER DE LA CHAVIGNERIE, EMILE
Lache Hilary Haworth Nursery School **28** 158
Lacher, Anton **2** 816
Lacher, Lorenz *see* LECHLER, LORENZ
Lachert, Bohdan **18** 596; **21** 783; **25** 100, 119, 422; **32** 872
Lachert and Szanajca **18** 596*
La Chevreuse, Louis-Marie-François Jacquesson de **11** 297; **31** 393; **33** 43
Lachez, Théodore **7** 693
Lachish **1** *849*; **16** *565*; **18** 596–7*
beads **1** 877
Fosse Temple **18** 596–7
glass **1** 865
level VI temple **18** 597
looms **1** 880
Palace-Fort **17** 553; **18** 597
Residency **17** 553; **18** 597
Solar Shrine **18** 597; **30** 188
town walls **18** 597
vaults (ceiling) **30** 190
Lachmann, Thérèse-Esther-Pauline-Blanche, Marquise de Païva *see* PAÏVA, THÉRÈSE-ESTHER-PAULINE-BLANCHE, Marquise de
Lachnit, Wilhelm **21** 365
La Chorrera **7** 206; **23** *902*; **29** *136*
Lach Truong
metalwork **32** *488*
Łachwa **25** 121
Lacina, Bohdan **8** 394
lacis *see under* LACE → types
La Cité **3** 551
Lack, Antonio Attolini *see* ATTOLINI LACK, ANTONIO
Lacke, Hans **13** 682
Läckö Castle **10** 133; **30** 78, 85, 117; **31** 824
collections **30** 118
Lacković-Croata, Ivan **14** 596
La Clarté **17** 408
Laclede, Pierre **27** 564
Lacloche **17** 529
Laclotte **4** 389
Lacock Abbey (Wilts) **9** 367; **10** 233; **30** *269*
collections **10** 325
Great Hall **8** 48; **10** *234*
Lacock Cup **10** 325
La Cocosa Church **29** 261
Lacoma, Francisco **3** 219
Lacombe, Georges **18** 598*; **22** 421; **28** 484
Lacombe, Jacques **10** 207
Lacombe, Laure **18** 598
Lacombe de Prezel, Honoré **10** 207
La Compañía **29** 212
Laconi **27** 835
Lacordaire, Henri **9** 112
La Coruña **18** 598*; **29** *258*
Castillo de S Antón *see* Museo Histórico Arqueológico
lighthouse **19** 360
Museo Histórico Arqueológico **18** 598; **29** 355
Lacoste, Henri **16** 849
La Cour, Nicholas de **27** 682
Lacour, Pierre (i) (1745-1814) **3** 775; **4** 391; **11** 666, 667
Lacour, Pierre (ii) (1778-1859) **4** 391; **8** 548
Lacourière, Imprimerie **20** 603
Lacourière, Roger **2** 241; **10** 560, 561; **24** 726; **25** 628
La Cour-Marigny **6** 53
La Court van den Voort, Pieter de *see* COURT VAN DEN VOORT, PIETER DE LA
La Couvertoirade **11** *505*; **18** 599*
lacquer **18** 599–617*; **32** 2
conservation **18** 615–17*, *616*
historical and regional traditions
Afghanistan **1** 210
Belgium **3** 583, 585
Bhutan **3** 916
Britain **18** 615
Buddhism **7** 14; **17** *114*, 115–16, *116*, 117, 118, *130*; **18** 768
China **6** 706
Korea **18** 370
Nara period (AD 710-94) **17** *299*
Vietnam **32** 479, *479*, 482
Burma **5** *257*, 257–8*, 261; **18** 600; **30** 618
Cambodia **5** 500
Central Asia, Eastern **6** 306, 313*
China **6** 706, 725, 773; **7** 12–20*, 31, 54, 92, 94, 114, 138, 140; **17** 101, 254; **18** *612*
Han period (206 BC–AD 220) **7** *13*, 95
Ming period (1368-1644) **7** *17*, *18*, 100; **18** II1
Prehistoric **7** 12; **14** 384
Qing period (1644-1911) **7** *19*, *20*, 96
Song period (AD 960-1279) **6** 706; **7** *15*, 25
Tang period (AD 618-907) **7** *14*; **12** 623
Yuan period (1279-1368) **7** *16*
Zhou period (*c.* 1050-256 BC) **7** 107, *139*
England **6** 560; **7** *167*; **18** 615
France **11** 632; **18** I2; **26** *376*
Germany **12** 423
Hinduism **15** 548
Indian subcontinent **4** IV1; **6** 555; **15** 546, 548; **16** 535
Indonesia **3** 331; **15** 813
Iran **16** 533, *534*
Islamic **16** 533–5*, *534*; **26** 303
Italy **18** 614
lacquer
historical and regional traditions—cont.
Japan **12** 626; **17** 99, 100, 101–2*, *116*, 117, 118, 213, 254, 297–305*, 340–42*, 356, *357*, 359, *383*, 384, 385, 390, 391, 398, 399, 401, 424; **18** *613*; **21** 650; **28** 495, 600; **31** 167
Edo period (1600-1868) **14** *429*, *704*; **17** *304*, 376; **18** I1; **28** 599
Heian period (AD 794-1185) **17** *300*, 392
Kamakura period (1185-1333) **17** 227
Meiji period (1868-1912) **28** *600*
Momoyama period (1568-1600) **17** *302*
Muromachi period (1333-1568) **17** *301*
Nara period (AD 710-94) **17** *114*, 115–16, *130*, *299*
Shōwa period (1926-89) **17** *136*
Taishō period (1912-26) **17** *305*
Korea **7** 13; **17** 254; **18** 361, 368–71*, *369*, *370*, *371*, *602*
Laos **18** 768
Maldives, Republic of **20** 189
Netherlands, the **5** 192; **18** 614; **22** 874
Portugal **25** 314
Prehistoric art **7** 12
Russia **18** 614, 615; **23** 837; **27** 427*
Ryūkyū Islands **18** 601; **27** 471, *471*
South Africa **29** 114
Sumatra **15** 810
Thailand **30** 617–19*, *619*, 631, *636*
Turkey **16** 535
United States of America **18** 614, 615
Vietnam **32** 479, *479*, 481, 482*, 489
materials
acrylic **18** 612
ashes **7** 14, 17, 19; **18** 601
azurite **18** 600
bamboo **17** 297; **18** 605
blood **18** 601; **27** 471
bone **7** 19
bronze **18** 605
carbon blacks **18** 608
carnauba wax **33** 1
cellulose **18** 612
ceramics **18** 601, 615
charcoal **17** 297; **18** 604
cinnabar **18** 600
clay **18** 601
copal **18** 609, 611
coral **7** 18, 19
damar **18** 611
dragon's-blood **18** 611
dung **18** 601
eggshells **18** 604; **32** 482
gesso **18** 609
glass **7** 18, 19; **18** 604
gold **7** *14*, 15, 17, 19, 20, 25, 107; **17** 297, 298, *301*, *305*; **18** 370, 604; **30** *619*
gold dust **7** 20; **18** 602, 604, 605, 606, 607
gold leaf **17** 298; **18** 602, 607; **27** 471; **30** 618; **32** 482
hemp **17** 297; **18** 601
indigo **18** 600, 608
inlays **7** 14, *16*; **17** 298; **18** 603–4*, *612*, *613*; **30** *636*; **32** 482
iron salts **18** 600
ivory **7** 18, 19
jade **7** 20
lampblack **18** 600
lacquer
materials—cont.
manila (fibre) **18** 611
mastic **18** 609
mother-of-pearl **7** 15–16, 17–18, 19–20; **17** 298, 299, *300*; **18** 370, *370*, *371*, 603–4, 609; **27** 471, *471*; **32** 482
ochre **18** 600
oils **18** 609
orpiment **18** 600, 608
papier mâché **18** 609, 615
pewter **7** *16*; **17** 297
pigments **17** 297; **18** 600; **32** 482
rice **18** 601
rice paste **18** 609
rosin **18** 609, 611
safflower **18** 600
sandarac **18** 609, 611
sawdust **18** 601
shellac **18** 599, 607, 609, 611
shells **18** 600, 601, 609
silk **7** 19; **18** 601
silver **7** *14*, 25, 107; **17** 297, 298, *301*, *305*; **18** 370, 604
silver dust **18** 604, 605, 606
silver leaf **7** 13; **17** 298; **27** 471
stone **7** 18, 19
textiles **17** 297; **18** 606
tin **18** 605, 615
tortoiseshell **18** *370*
vinyl **18** 612
white lead **18** 600
wood **17** 101; **18** 601, 609
techniques
carving **6** 313; **7** 16–17, 18–19; **17** 298, *301*; **18** 601–3*
gilding **12** 623, 626; **18** 607*
hollow-casting **17** 99, 101
incising **18** 602*
marbling **7** 14, 18, 20
miaojin **7** 15
moulding **18** 606–7*
painting **6** 773; **17** 299; **18** 605–6*, 608–10*
polishing **32** 482
transfer (printing) **32** 482
trompe l'oeil **17** 303
types
Chinkinbori *see* gilt-engraved *urushi*
Coromandel **7** 19
dry **18** 606*
Buddhism **7** 14; **18** 606
Burma **18** 606
China **7** 13, 14; **18** 606
Japan **17** 297, *299*, 390; **18** 606
filled-in *urushi* **18** 602–3*
Burma **5** 257, *257*; **18** 602
China **7** 15, 17, 19; **18** 602
Japan **18** 602
fundame **18** 604*
gilt-engraved *urushi* **18** 602*
China **7** 15, 16, 17, 19; **18** 602
Japan **18** 602
guri **18** 601*
China **7** 15, 16; **18** 601
Japan **18** 601
hari-bori **18** 603*
hibi-nuri **18** 606*
hiramakie **17** 298; **18** 604*
ikakeji **17** 298
imitation **18** 610–11*; **24** 61
see also JAPANNING
imitation carved *urushi* **18** 601–2*
industrial **18** 611–12*
insect **18** 607–10*, 617*
Indian subcontinent **18** 608, 609
Iran **18** 609, *609*
Islamic **18** 608, *609*
Maldives, Republic of **18** 608
Sri Lanka **18** 608
Turkey **18** 609
jogahana-nuri **18** 605–6*
johoji-nuri **18** 606*
kamakurabori **17** 298*, 300, *301*; **18** 602*
lacquer
types—cont.
kingindeigawa **18** 606*
Kodaiji *makie* **17** 301*
kuromakie **18** 605
makie **17** 297, 298*, 299–301, *300*, 302, *341*, *385*; **18** *603*, 604*, *604*, II2
marbled *urushi* **18** 602*
miaojin *see* *kingindeigawa*
monsha-nuri **18** 604*
Nanban **17** 301–2*, *302*
nashiji **17** 298; **18** 605*
Negoroji **17** 356–7
negoro-nuri **17** 297, 300, *303*, 356–7; **18** 606*
qiangjin *see* gilt-engraved *urushi*
qulun *see* *guri*
sai-kai **18** 606*
seshime **18** 600
Shunkei **17** 356, 357, 358
sprinkled **18** 604–5*
tagidashi **18** 605*
takamakie **17** 298; **18** *604*, 605*
tanida-makie **18** 606*
tianqi *see* filled-in *urushi*
tixi *see* *guri*
togidashi makie **17** 298
tsugarunuri *see* marbled *urushi*
urushi **18** 599–607*, 615–17*
Buddhism **18** *607*
Burma **18** 604, 605, 606, *606*, *607*
China **7** 14; **18** 599, 600, 601, *601*, 603, 605, *605*, 606, 607
Japan **18** 599, 600, 601, 603, 604, 605, 607, *616*, 617
Korea **18** 600, 603
Thailand **18** 604
wet inlay **18** 605*
xipi *see* marbled *urushi*
yün *see* filled-in *urushi*
zonseinuri *see* filled-in *urushi*
uses
appliqué **7** 14, 19
armour **6** 306, 313; **7** 13, 14, 54; **17** 297, 300, 302, 376
arrows **6** 313
bamboo **5** 257
baskets **3** 331; **5** *257*; **15** 810
beams **7** 12
beds **7** *167*
betel sets **5** 254; **30** 631
bookbindings **18** *609*
book covers **4** IV1
bookstands **17** 301
bottles **17** *303*
bowls **7** 14, *15*
boxes **7** 13, 14, 15, 16, *16*, *17*, *18*, *19*, *20*, 96, 100; **14** *429*; **17** 297, 300, *301*, 302, *305*, *383*; **18** *370*, *371*, *601*, *602*, *604*, *605*, *612*, *613*
bureaux **18** I2
cabinets (i) (rooms) **5** 349
cabinets (ii) (furniture) **3** 583; **7** 166; **12** 421; **18** II2
calligraphy **17** 213, 227
casks **17** *357*
ceramics **17** 297
chess sets **6** 555
chests **6** 560; **17** *302*; **30** 618
coffers **17** 301
coffins **7** 13
containers **3** 916
cupboards **30** 618
cups **7** 13
desks **5** 192; **17** 300
dowries **17** 302, *304*, 385
filigree **5** 500
furniture **3** 585; **6** 313; **7** 31; **12** 423; **15** 813; **17** 297, 302, 384; **18** 361; **22** 874; **29** 114; **32** 482
goblets **7** 12
gold leaf **7** 15; **18** 371
helmets **17** 300, 302
incense containers **17** *301*
inks **7** 92; **15** 849; **17** 213

lacquer
uses—cont.
inksticks **7** 92
inkstones **7** 94, 95
inlays **5** 500; **7** 12
inrō **17** 303–4; **18** 11
interior decoration **12** 412
jewellery **17** 529
leather **6** 313; **17** 297
lutes **7** *14*
manuscript covers **15** 546, 548
masks **17** 390, 391, 392
metal **5** 257
metalwork **17** 297
mirror-cases **16** *534*
mirror frames **18** *603*
mirrors **7** 14; **21** *721*
musical instruments **7** 14; **32** 489
netsuke **17** 398, 399, 401
painting **7** 13; **23** 837; **28** 600, *600*
palanquins **17** 302
paper **17** 359
papier mâché **7** 114; **24** 61
pottery **6** *881*
saddles **17** 300, 301, 302
scabbards **17** 300
screens (ii) (furniture) **7** 166; **18** *601*
sculpture
Buddhism **18** 606
Burma **18** *607*
Cambodia **5** 500
China **6** 706, 725; **7** 14, 138
Japan **17** 99, 100, 101–2*, *114*, 115–16, *116*, 117, 118, *130*, *136*, 299, *299*
Laos **18** 768
Vietnam **32** 479, *479*
sealants **25** 174
secretaires **26** *376*
shelves **17** *385*
shields **7** 12–13
shrines (i) (cult) **17** 301
snuff-boxes **11** 632
stands **18** *603*
stencilling **28** 298
stirrups **17** 300, 302
swords **17** 302
tea-caddies **17** 301
tea ceremonies **17** 301
trays **27** 471, *471*
varnishes **17** 297
vessels **7** 12; **18** *606*
waxes **33** 1
wood **5** 257; **7** 138, *139*
writing **15** 849; **17** 213; **20** 327
writing-boxes **14** *704*
writing-tablets **20** 327
see also VARNISHES
lacquerers **17** 300, 304–5, 356
lacquer-tree **7** 12, 45
Lacramarca **6** 520
Lacroix *see* VANDERCRUSE, ROGER
Lacroix, A. (*fl* 1869) **6** 582
Lacroix, Adon (*fl* 1919) **8** 435
Lacroix, Charles-François Grenier de **11** 39; **32** 334
Lacroix, Christian **11** 584
La Croix, Guillaume-Frédéric **18** 617–18*
Lacroix, Isaac Jacob **20** 915
La Croix, Jean de **11** 641; **12** 828
Lacroix, Paul **30** 756
La Croix, Pierre Frédéric de **14** 42; **23** 588
La Croix, Susanna de **23** 588
La Croix St Leufroi **26** 669
Lacroux **4** 788
La Cruz, Pablo de *see* CRUZ, PABLO DE LA
La Cruz González, Manuel de *see* GONZÁLEZ, MANUEL DE LA CRUZ
La Cruz y Ríos, Luis de *see* CRUZ Y RÍOS, LUIS DE LA
Lactoid **25** 27
La Cuffle, Pierre de *see* MILAN, PIERRE
lacunae **18** 618*
Lacy, Suzanne **24** 409
Lada, Josef **8** 393
Ladage, Ger **6** 378
Ład Artists' Cooperative **8** 371; **25** 53, 119, 122, 133
Ladatte, François **18** 618*
collaboration **4** 520
competitions **7** 672
patrons and collectors **28** 19
pupils **7** 571
works **16** 702, 704
Ladbrooke, Frederick **18** 619
Ladbrooke, Henry **18** 619
Ladbrooke, John Berney **18** 618, 619; **21** 482
Ladbrooke, Robert (1769-1842) **18** 618–19*; **23** 248; **29** 542; **30** 735
Ladbrooke, Robert (*b* before 1800) **18** 619
Ladby **32** 525
Ląd Church **25** 98
Ladd, John **14** 223
ladders **7** 764; **17** 55; **24** *83*; **25** 479
Laddigam, Nilakantheshvara Temple **13** 3
Ladea, Romul **18** 619*; **26** 716, 726; **32** 669
Ladejinsky, Wolf **15** 743, 744
La Dell, Edwin **19** 492
Ladenburg Benz house **27** 323
Ladendorf, Heinz **15** 92
Ladenspelder, Johann **18** 619*
Ladetti, Francesco *see* LADATTE, FRANÇOIS
Ladheri **13** 882
gate-house **13** 882
al-Ladhiqiyya *see* LATAKIA
Ladi **3** 694
Lâdik **16** 472, 477, 478
carpets **16** *478*
Lâdik carpets *see under* CARPETS → types
Ladislas, King of Bohemia (*reg* 1440-57) **23** 311
Ladislas V, King of Hungary *see* LADISLAS, King of Bohemia
ladles
China **6** *849*; **7** 58
Dan (Africa) **8** 489*
Indian subcontinent **15** 729
Japan **17** 341
Mongolia **21** *884*
L'Admiral, Joanne **25** 623
Ladnun fort **15** 351
Ladommatos, Andreas **8** 365
Ladovsky, Nikolay (Aleksandrovich) **18** 619–20*; **27** 379; **32** 661
assistants **28** 747
collaboration **18** 457
groups and movements **2** 603, 604; **9** 73; **22** 178
pupils **12** 878
works **18** *620*
La Drière, de (family) **3** 599
Ladson, Sarah Reeve *see* GILMOR, ROBERT, Mrs
Lady and the Unicorn tapestries *see* UNICORN HUNT, MASTER OF THE
Lady Artists **33** 309
Lady Barat **2** 259
Lady chapels *see under* CHAPELS → types
Lady Margaret Beaufort's Cup **10** 325
Lady of Brussels **9** 866
Lady of Naples **9** 866
lady's closets *see under* CLOSETS
Lady Waterford Hall (Northumb.) **32** 904
Ladyzhensky, G. A. **18** 399
Laeck, Artus van **1** 161
Laeckman, Martinus **9** 380
Laederach, J. C. **1** 320
Laeffler, Edward **24** 891
Laeken
Notre-Dame **3** 548, *548*; **13** 202
Palais Royal **3** 584, 613; **4** 302; **10** 187
Laem Pho **6** 917; **30** 598
Laenen, Jean-Paul **3** 574
Laer, Pieter (Boddingh) van **18** 622–5*; **26** 772
attributions **4** 486
groups and movements **3** 143; **9** 462; **28** 92
patrons and collectors
Alcalá, 3rd Duque de (1583-1637) **26** 307
Einden, Ferdinand van den **10** 114
Lely, Peter **19** 124
Reynst (family) **26** 283
Roomer, Gaspar **27** 133
Roscioli, Giovanni Maria **27** 160
Simonelli, Niccolò **28** 754
Wouwerman, Philips **33** 391
Zoomer, Jan Pietersz. **33** 700
pupils **6** 346; **9** 380
reproductive prints by others **18** *623*
works **4** 380; **12** 289; **18** *624*; **19** 420; **31** 246
Laer, Roeland van **4** 380; **18** 622
Laermans, Eugène **5** 44; **12** 296; **18** 625*
La Estaquería **22** 706
Laet, de **21** 717
Laet, Johann de **12** 872
Laet, S. De *see* DE LAET, S.
Laethem, Lieven van *see* LIEVEN VAN LATHEM
Laethem-Saint-Martin **8** 785, 809; **10** 696; **18** 626*; **21** 648; **22** 689; **31** 878
painting **3** 564
Laeuger, Max **2** 565; **12** 432
Lafage, Raymond **4** 568; **18** 626*
works **18** *626*; **30** 524
Lafaille, Bernard **30** 468
La Farge, Bancel **18** 628
La Farge, C(hristopher) Grant **14** 317*; **18** 628
La Farge, John **18** 627–8*; **33** 369
assistants **14** 317; **26** 474; **27** 557
groups and movements **1** 171; **17** 440; **23** 47; **30** 868
patrons and collectors **24** 281; **31** 870
pupils **14** 317; **20** 16
teachers **8** 76; **26** 401
works **4** 477; **18** *627*; **26** 338; **29** 508, 516, 871; **31** 644
La Farge, Oliver **7** 645; **18** 881; **22** 674, 679; **31** 145
La Fargue, Jacob Elias **18** 628
La Fargue, Karel **18** 628
La Fargue, Maria Margaretha **18** 628
La Fargue, Paulus (Constantijn) **14** 42; **18** 628–9*; **22** 847
pupils **18** 628
works **31** 247
La Fargue van Nieuwland, Isaack Louis **18** 628
Lafaye, Prosper **11** 580
Lafazanovski, Ilija **19** 885
Lafenestre, Georges **11** 675
La Fère-en-Tardenois Château **6** 506; **11** 514, 656
La Ferrassie **10** 472; **25** 491, 493
La Ferté, Denis-Pierre-Jean Papillon de *see* PAPILLON DE LA FERTÉ, DENIS-PIERRE-JEAN
La Ferté-en-Bray **9** 143
La Ferté-Sénectère, Henri, Maréchal de **8** 785; **18** 837; **19** 33, 696
paintings **18** 840
La Ferté-sur-Grosne **7** 346
La Feuillade, François de, Duc d'Aubusson *see* AUBUSSON, FRANÇOIS, Duc de Roannez, Duc d'
Lafever, Minard **8** 574; **18** 629*
collaboration **12** 26
works **31** 592
illustrated **3** 730; **8** 462
Laffemas, Barthélemy de **11** 645
Laffertée, J. H. **28** 594
Laffón, Carmen **18** 629*
Lafitte, J. W. **7** 529
Lafitte, Louis **8** 828; **25** 193
Lafitte & Desirat **31** 262
La Flamengrie **13** 113
La Florida **4** 260; **29** 159
temple **29** 165
Lafões, Pedro Henrique de Bragança Sousa Tavares Mascarenhos e Silva, Duque de **27** 801
Lafon, Emile **9** 424
Lafond, Charles **30** 569
Lafond, Daniel **11** 766
La Fond, Etienne de **20** 138
La Fond, Jacob de **20** 138
Lafond, Jean **29** 514
La Fontaine, Jean de
works **17** 449
illustrated **4** 364; **5** 884; **6** 384, 547; **9** 407; **10** 725; **18** 783; **32** 502
La Fontaine, Jean de, Musée *see under* CHÂTEAU THIERRY
La Fontaine, Marie-Jo **18** 630*; **32** 421
Lafontaine, P. J. **14** 146
La Font de Saint-Yenne, Etienne **11** 540; **18** 630–31*
Laforesterie, Louis Edmond **14** 58
Laforgue, Adrien **22** 128
Laforgue, Georges **29** 752
Laforgue, Jules **18** 631*
La Fosse, Charles de **18** 631–3*
collaboration **2** 707; **4** 126, 537; **8** 91; **17** 671; **19** 21; **27** 263; **31** 510
groups and movements **27** 286
patrons and collectors **4** 808; **8** 208; **11** 657
pupils **24** 211, 541
works **11** 536; **14** 784; **18** *632*; **21** 907; **24** 165
La Fosse, Louis Rémy de **18** 634*
works **8** 530, *530*; **11** 734
Lafour, Lucien **30** 15
Lafrance, Ambroise-Adhémar **5** 586
Lafranchini, Paul **6** 64; **9** 317; **16** 23, 24; **18** 634*; **29** 835
Lafranchini, Peter-Noel **6** 64; **16** 23, 24; **18** 634
Lafranchini, Philip **6** 64; **9** 317; **16** 23, 24; **18** 634; **29** 835
Lafrensen, Niclas, the elder (1698-1756) **8** 772; **14** 366; **18** 634
Lafrensen, Niclas, the younger (1737-1807) **18** 634–5*
patrons and collectors **10** 478; **31** 362
reproductive prints by others **13** 220; **16** 905; **18** 858
works **21** 643, *644*
Lafrente, Julio **5** 912
Lafréry, Antoine **10** 389; **18** 635*; **26** 229; **27** 606
collaboration **27** 606
patrons and collectors **14** 563
personal collection **3** 448; **30** 746
printmakers **4** 443; **5** 888; **9** 398; **12** 557, 558; **23** 745; **27** 650
works **2** 162, 169, 696; **4** 651; **21** 579; **25** 625, 630; **26** 230, *806*; **32** 111, 112
La Fresnaye, Roger de **18** 635–7*
collaboration **11** 525
groups and movements **2** 225; **8** 240; **9** 361; **20** 431; **23** 569; **25** 747; **28** 347; **29** 899
La Fresnaye, Roger de—cont.
patrons and collectors **19** 282; **20** 524
works **12** 601; **18** *636*; **28** 920
Lafuente, Julio **4** 790; **27** 876
La Fuente de Guarrazar **29** 345
Lafuente Ferrari, Enrique **18** 637*
Lagae, Jules **3** 572; **32** 590
La Galgada **18** 637*; **29** *156*
masonry **29** 162
shells **29** 218
temples **29** 165; **30** 447
textiles **29** 159
Lagana, Guido **23** 81
La Gandara, Antonio de *see* GANDARA, ANTONIO DE LA
Laganello **28** 654
sculpture **28** *654*
La Garde, Jacques de **7** 441
works **7** *441*
La Gardie, De (family) *see* DE LA GARDIE (FAMILY)
La Gardie, Magnus Gabriel De *see* DE LA GARDIE, MAGNUS GABRIEL
Lagarene, Michael Cabaret **10** 347
works **10** *347*
Lagarrigue, Carlos **6** 597
Lagash **18** 638*; **21** *267*
religion **21** 277
sculpture **1** 896; **21** 295, *295*
seals **1** 860
temple **30** 432
trade **21** 268
Lagerfeld, Karl **33** 15
Lagervall-Ringbom, Inga **30** 113
Laget, Denis **11** 553; **19** 848
Laghetto Painter **13** 531
Laghi, Antonín **17** 584
Laghman (Afghanistan) **1** 187
Laghych **2** *890*, 899, 900
Lagi **26** 817
Lagi, Simone **26** 837
Lagich *see* LAGHYCH
La Gleize, Notre-Dame **3** 567; **13** 110
Lagman (Tajikistan) *see* KHELAVERD
Lagneau, Guy **19** 91
Lagneau, Nicolas (*b* 1594) **18** 638
Lagneau, Nicolas (*fl c.* 1600-10) **18** 638*; **20** 455; **26** 470
Lago, Lázaro Pardo *see* PARDO LAGO, LÁZARO
Lago, Silvio *see* FRANCÉS Y SANCHEZ-HERDERO, JOSÉ
Lago d'Orta S Giulio **26** 620
Lagomaggiore, Matteo **4** 811; **12** 281
La Gondola *see* GONDOLA, LA
Lagoon **1** 514–15; **8** 21, 22
La Gorge Meillet **6** 481
Lagos (Nigeria) **18** 638–40*, *639*; **23** *129*
Abayomi Barber School **23** 138
architecture **23** 133, 134, 135
Asele Institute **23** 139
British Petroleum head office **23** 134
Bronze Gallery **23** 139
Centre for Black and African Arts and Civilization **2** 371
Crusader House **23** 135
Didi Museum **18** 640; **23** 139
exhibitions **23** 135
houses **1** 319
Idubor Gallery **23** 139
Liberian Ambassador's residence **23** 135
mosques **1** 317
Municipal Primary School **23** 135
Murtala Muhammed Airport **23** 135
National Art Gallery **18** 640
National Council for Arts and Culture **18** 640; **23** 139
National Gallery of Modern Art **23** 139
National Museum **18** 639; **23** 139

Lagos (Nigeria)—cont.
 Nigerian Museum *see* National Museum
 Nigerian Railway Corporation hospital **23** 135
 Ovuomaroro Studio **23** 136, 138, 139
 painting **23** 136
 parliament buildings **23** 137
 Quintessence Galleries **18** 640
 Red Brick House **18** 640
 St Gregory's College **1** 319; **23** 138
 United Christian Commercial Secondary School **23** 135
 University **1** 319, 432; **23** 135, 138, 139
 West African Airways Corporation building **23** 135
 Yaba College of Technology **18** 640; **23** 137
Lagos (Portugal) **25** 302
 sculpture **25** *302*
Lagoudera, Panagia tou Arakou **8** *325*, 358; **9** *512*; **18** 640*
 icons **9** 626, 627
 wall paintings **8** 359; **9** 580
Lagoy, Marquis de **18** 640–41*
La Grande Chartreuse **5** 893, 894, *894*, 895; **7** 231; **21** 82
Lagrange, Alexis de **9** 340
LaGrange (TX), Fayette County Court House **18** 888
Lagrange, François **11** 759
Lagrange, Jacques **11** 644
La Grange, Jean de, Cardinal **1** 781; **13** 77; **18** 641*
La Grange, Justus de **14** 732
La Graufesenque **27** 107
La Graulière **26** 602
Lagrenée, François **18** 641
Lagrenée, Jean-Jacques **18** 641, 642–3*; **28** 521
 patrons and collectors **11** 540; **32** 719
 pupils **5** 921; **24** 387
 works **32** 374
Lagrenée, Louis (-Jean-François) **18** 641–2*
 patrons and collectors **2** 852; **5** 380; **8** 161; **11** 540; **25** 212
 pupils **4** 59; **18** 642; **19** 278; **24** 583
 reproductive prints by others **4** 331
 teachers **19** 646
 works **11** 411; **18** *642*
La Grèze **25** 485; **26** 133
La Grolais, Jean Villiers de, Cardinal *see* VILLIERS DE LA GROLAIS, JEAN, Cardinal
La Guaira **5** 691; **32** *165*, 169
 Real Compañía Guipuzcoana building **32** 169
Laguardia, Juan de *see* JUAN DE LAGUARDIA
Laguardia, S María de los Reyes **13** 105
Laguens, Julio **5** 378
La Guépière, Jacques de **18** 643
La Guépière, Phillippe de **12** 413; **18** 643*; **19** 780; **26** 257; **29** 874; **33** 429
La Guérinière, François de **24** 212
Laguerre, Louis **18** 644*
 collaboration **30** 759
 patrons and collectors **4** 137; **6** 116, 515; **7** 286; **10** 361
 works **5** 65; **10** 249, 274, *275*; **15** 139; **18** 145, *644*; **30** 872; **32** 358
Laguerre, Mademoiselle **5** 767
Laguna (NM) **22** 607
Laguna, Juanito *see* BERNI, ANTONIO
Laguna de Los Cerros **18** 644–5*; **21** *193*, *372*; **23** 416, 417
 Monument 19 **18** *645*
Lagunillas **32** 177
Lagunita, La *see* LA LAGUNITA
Lagurka **12** 323
Lagut, Irène **3** 120
Lagutenko, Vitaly **25** 323
La Guyane *see* FRENCH GUIANA
lagynoi **13** 476
Lah, Ljubo **4** 461
Laharu **15** 626
Lahauri, Ustad Ahmad **7** 249
Lahay'aman **2** 259
La Haye, Clémence de *see* CLÉMENCE DE LA HAYE
La Haye, Corneille de (1500/10-1575) *see* CORNEILLE DE LYON
La Haye, Corneille de (*b* 1543) *see* CORNEILLE DE LA HAYE
La Haye, Jacques de *see* JACQUES DE LA HAYE
Lahey, Vida **4** 819
Lahham, Rafik **17** 655
La Higuera **29** 364
Lahijan
 mosque **16** 254
 palace **16** 254
La Hire *see* LA HYRE
Lahore **15** 196, *264*, *360*, 363, 409, *619*; **16** *105*; **18** 645–7*; **23** *797*, 798
 Alhamra Arts Council **23** 798, 804
 Allah Bux Academy **23** 804
 Anguri Bagh **23** 799
 architecture **15** 410
 Badshahi Mosque **15** *366*, 367; **22** 195, 259
 Begumpuri Mosque **15** 375
 brocades **15** 662
 carpets **15** 682, 683, *683*; **23** 802
 Central Museum *see* Museum
 Chauburji Gate **15** 366
 Chughtai Museum Trust **7** 249; **23** 804
 coins **16** *513*
 enamel **15** 712
 Faqir Khana Museum **18** 647; **23** 804
 fort **15** 196, 362, 363, 365; **16** 239; **22** 258
 collections **23** 804
 gardens **12** 74
 Hathi Pol gateway **15** 687
 mosaics **15** 375
 fountains **11** 340
 gardens **15** 366
 Gulabi Bagh gateway **15** 375
 halls **14** 77
 Hazuri Bagh Pavilion **15** 375
 High Court **18** 889
 Kala Burj **15** 363
 mansion of Mirza Kamran **15** 362
 Mayo School of Arts *see* National College of Arts
 metalwork **15** 713
 mosque of Dai Anga **15** 375
 mosque of Shahi Begum **15** 363
 mosque of Wazir Khan **15** 366, 374, 687
 Museum **18** 647; **22** 364
 collections **15** 741; **18** 647; **23** 804
 National College of Arts **23** 798, 799, 801, 803
 National Council for the Arts **3** 170
 Open Air Theatre **23** 798
 paintings **15** 544; **20** 284
 Punjab Public Library **23** 800
 Punjab University **23** 799, 803
 sculpture **23** 803
 Shakir 'Ali Museum **1** 638; **23** 804
 Shalimar Bagh **11** 340; **12** 74; **15** 366; **16** 239; **18** *646*
 Society of Contemporary Art Galleries **3** 170
 textiles **15** 664
 tiles **15** 686
 tomb of Anakarli **15** 363
Lahore—cont.
 tomb of Asaf Khan **15** 365, 687
 tomb of Jahangir **15** 364, 686
 tomb of Nur Jahan **15** 364
 tomb of Shaykh Musa Ahangar **15** 374
 Water and Power Development Authority House **23** 799
 weapons **15** 678
 West Pakistan University of Engineering and Technology **23** 798
 wool **15** 665
Lahore Landscape Movement **23** 800
Lahori **15** 629
Lahori Bandar, Thambawaro Mosque **15** 338
Lahrs, Friedrich **17** 740
Lahu **5** 220, 248, 250, 262; **30** 623, 634, 637
 dress **30** 625–6*
 jewellery **5** 250
 pipes (musical) **30** *637*
Lahugala **29** 475
El-Lahun **9** *774*, 822; **10** 758; **18** 647–8*
 pyramid of Sesostris II **9** 850, 877; **10** 759; **18** 647; **25** 763
 tomb of Sithathoriunet **10** 30, 52, 90, 759
 jewellery **10** *30*
 tombs **9** 839
Lahu Na **30** 625, 626
 dress **30** *626*
Lahu Nyi **30** 625, 626
Lahure, Abel **19** 812
Lahu Sheh Leh **30** 625, 626, 637
Lahu Shi **30** 625, 626, 630
La Hyre, Etienne de **18** 648
La Hyre, Laurent de **11** 536; **18** 648–9*
 attributions **3** 759
 collaboration **6** 434
 patrons and collectors **5** 691; **18** 579; **30** 274; **32** 74
 pupils **6** 518; **20** 489
 reproductive prints by others **24** 397, 890; **27** 269
 teachers **18** 662
 works **11** *403*, 534, 641; **18** *648*
La Hyre, Louis de **18** 648
La Hyre, Philippe de **2** 200; **11** 771
Lai, Afong **24** 664
Laib, Conrad **18** 649–50*; **27** 664
 attributions **24** 862
 works **2** 792; **13** 329; **28** 860
Laibach *see* LJUBLJANA
Laibaco, Johannes de *see* JOHANNES OF LJUBLJANA
Laie
 Mormon temple **30** 450
 Polynesian Cultural Centre **23** 737
Laignel, Mathieu **1** 766
Laigue (family) **19** 118
Laiguo **5** 113
Lai-hka **5** *221*, 256, 258
Laiho, Ola **24** 892
Laikmaa, Ants **10** 539
Laikmets **33** 601
Lai-kuo *see* LAIGUO
Lai Lok Kun **20** 169
Lainberger, Simon **18** 650*; **19** 131; **20** 736
 attributions **32** 605
 patrons and collectors **14** 455
 works **32** 605
Laîné, Thomas **11** 405
Laing, Alexander **23** 21
Laing, Charles **30** 516
Laing, David **11** 361; **28** 271, 758; **31** 31
Laing, G. Blair **5** 589
Laing, Gerald **24** 639; **25** 231
Lainger, Antoine **29** 350
Laing of Birkenhead **32** 864
Lainović, Cvetko **22** 18
Laio *see* ALLIO
Laird, Colin **2** 148; **31** 335
Laird, Hugh **28** 271
Laird, Jack **23** 69
laird's houses *see under* HOUSES → types
Lairesse, Gérard de **14** 584; **18** 650–53*; **19** 344; **22** 846
 academy **1** 808
 collaboration **12** 801; **31** 779
 patrons and collectors **21** 348; **23** 466; **29** 7
 pupils **10** 144; **19** 749; **30** 853; **33** 261
 reproductive prints by others **31** 802; **32** 259
 works **1** 659, 802; **14** 45; **18** *651*, *652*; **22** 846
 writings **15** 84; **18** 700; **22** 907; **31** 300
 illustrated **21** 411
Lairesse, Renier de **18** 650
La Isla **29** 187
Laisné, (Jean-) Charles **1** 14; **7** 476; **17** 858; **18** 653*
Lajamanu **1** 64
Lajevardi (family) **15** 900
La Jigua Church **14** 713
Lajim **16** 159; **31** 113
Lajimpat **22** 767, 770
Lajin Beg **30** 784
La Jolla (CA)
 Salk Institute **31** 597
 Sherwood House **7** 619
Lajoüe, Jacques de **18** 653–5*
 copies **26** 499
 patrons and collectors **4** 331
 reproductive prints by others **15** 31; **17** 668
 works **11** 406, 577; **18** *654*; **19** 231; **24** 271; **26** 494; **30** 672
Lajovic, Janez **28** 860
Lajta, Béla **14** 890; **18** 655*
 collaboration **14** 909; **20** 206
 works **14** 890; **31** 797
La Jumelle *see* LE NAIN, MATHIEU
lājvardīna see under POTTERY → wares; TILES → types
Lak **27** 432
La Kalaa *see* QAL'AT BANI HAMMAD
Lakalai **24** 84
lake *see under* PIGMENTS → types
Lake Baykal **27** 427
Lake Bolsena **10** 605
Lake Condah **1** 56
Lake Copais
 figurines **13** *580*
Lakedaimon *see* SPARTA
lake dwellings *see* HOUSES → types → pile dwellings
Lake Forest (IL) **25** 656
Lake Guatavita **22** 266
Lake Hongze, Zu ling **6** 701, 732
Lake Mendocino (CA), Pomo Visitor Center **22** 671
Laken *see* LAEKEN
Lakenham, Henry **4** 692
Lakenheath (Suffolk), St Mary **24** 577
Lake Nojiri **17** 102
 figurines **17** *102*
Lake Nokwé **1** 311
Lake Patzcuaro **21** 203
Lake Placid (NY), Sound-Sculpture Garden **22** 375
lakes **12** 85; **27** 715
Lake Sevan Power Station **2** 428
Lakeside Press **4** 367
Lake Tai **12** 88, 90
Lakhdar, Boujemaa **22** 129
Lakher **15** 205
Lakhish, Tel *see* LACHISH
Lakhmandal Temple **15** 264
Lakhnau *see* LUCKNOW
Lakhnautī *see* GAUR
Laking, Guy **2** 450
Lakkithra **17** 909
Lakkoploutos, Kallias **13** 570
Lakkous **8** 338
Lakkundi
 craftsmen and artists **15** 324
 Jaina temple **15** 531
 Kashivishveshvara Temple **15** 325, 326, 531–2
Lakner, Laszlo **14** 902; **18** 656*
Lakofski, Denise *see* SCOTT BROWN, DENISE
Lakota **22** 556, 557, 562, 616, 636, 650
 pectoral ornaments **22** *616*
Laksanakorn, Kwanchai **17** 686
Lakshmeshvara Someshvara Temple **15** 325, 326
Lakṣmaṇāvatī *see* GAUR
Laktionov, Aleksandr (Ivanovich) **18** 657*; **27** 581; **28** 918
Lal **18** 657–8*
 collaboration **3** 904; **8** 847; **20** 48
 works **15** 584; **18** *657*
Lal, Braj Bashi **17** 738
Lal, Dallu **15** 653
Lal, Fakir Chand **15** 653
Lal, Hulas **15** 653
Lal, Shiva (*fl* 1840-87) **15** 653
Lal, Shiva Dayal (*fl* 1840-80) **15** 653
Lal, Shival (*fl* 1812) **15** 615
Lal, Tuni **15** 653
Lala (people) **33** 602
Lala Bhagat *see under* KANPUR
Lala Deen Dayal *see* DEEN DAYAL, LALA
La Lagunita **27** 607
Lalaing, Antoine de, Count of Hoogstraeten *see* HOOGSTRAETEN, ANTOINE DE LALAING, Count of
Lalaing, Jacques De, Comte *see* DE LALAING, Jacques, Comte
Lala Mustafa Mosque *see under* FAMAGUSTA
Lala Mustafa Pasha **16** 224
La Lance, J.-L. de **31** 721
Lalande, Joseph Jérôme Le Français de *see* LE FRANÇAIS DE LALANDE, JOSEPH JÉRÔME
Lalande, Robert **11** 404
Lalanne **21** 346
Lalanne, Gaston **18** 875
Lalanne, Maxime (-François-Antoine) **18** 658*
 methods **10** 556
 pupils **5** 23
 writings **6** 471; **10** 559, 563
Lala of Cyzicus *see* IAIA OF CYZICUS
lalāṭabimba **15** 244*
Lalauze, Adolphe **5** 131
Lalayan, Ervand **2** 444
Lalbhai, Kasturbhai **15** 742
Lalchand **15** 588
Lale, Etienne de *see* ETIENNE DE LALE
La Lechuga **7** 610
Lalemant *see* LALLEMANT
Lalemant, Hermant **17** 458
Lalewicz, Marian **18** 658*; **32** 872
Laleye, Antoine **3** 728
Lali **30** 418
Laliat, Michel de **3** 456
Lalibela **1** *379*; **26** 483, 484
 churches **1** 379; **10** 565, 567, 568, 576
 Beta Amanu'el **10** 565
 Beta Giyorgis **1** 315; **10** 565, *566*, 576
 Beta Golgota **10** 565, 576, 577
 Beta Maryam **10** 565, 568, 576; **29** 817
 Beta Medhame 'Alem **10** 565
Lalibela, King (*reg* late 12th cent.) **1** 315; **10** 565
Laliberté, Alfred **5** 570; **18** 659*
Lalinde **4** 780
Lalio *see* ALLIO
Lalique, René (Jules) **18** 594, 659*
 collaboration **18** 867

Lalique, René (Jules)—cont.
exhibitions **15** 883
glass **1** 112; **7** 84; **10** 320; **18** *659*
groups and movements **2** 565; **11** 613; **22** 252
jewellery **2** *565*; **10** 195, 346; **11** 635, 637; **12** 869; **17** 528, II1; **23** 547
patrons and collectors **13** 718, 840
pupils **12** 450
Lalique factory **11** 613
Lalitaditya Muktapida, Ruler (*reg c.* 724-60) (Karkota) **15** 265, 482; **20** 481
Lalitagiri **5** 96; **15** 505
Lalitalaya **15** 512
Lalitapur *see* PATAN (ii)
Lalitavajra **30** 845
Lalit Kala (1955-) **24** 436
Lalit Kala Akademi *see under* CALCUTTA; DELHI
Lalit Kala Contemporary (1962-) **24** 429
La Live de Jully, Ange-Laurent de **4** 587; **18** 660*, *660*
architecture **3** 275
collaboration **11** 626
collections **11** 663
decorative works **5** 380
furniture **5** 380; **6** 390; **13** 233; **19** 118
interior decoration **22** 738; **23** 544
paintings **7** 778; **11** 658; **13** 638, 639; **18** 692; **26** 552
sculpture **6** 401; **19** 89; **32** 76
La Llagonne **26** 641
Lallemand, Jean-Baptiste **18** 660–62*
works **7** 474, *476*; **8** *889*; **11** *409*; **18** *661*; **26** *583*; **32** *767*
Lallemant (family) **25** 405
Lallemant, Georges **18** 662–3*; **22** 455; **24** 134; **33** 365
pupils **6** 433; **9** 175; **18** 648; **25** 385
reproductive prints by others **5** 294, *294*; **33** 366
works **6** 433; **11** 641; **18** *663*
Lallemant, Guillaume **18** 662
Lallemant, Jean (*d* 1494; father) **18** 662
Lallemant, Jean (*d* 1533; son) **18** 662*
Lallemant, Jean (*d* 1548; son) **18** 662*
Lallerstedt, Erik (Julius) **18** 663–4*; **30** 74
assistants **2** 476; **23** 615
collaboration **1** 470; **19** 284
staff **20** 437; **30** 2, 459
works **30** 684
Lalli, Stefano **3** 860
Lallié, Jean-François **5** 58
Lalma **1** 196; **14** 19
Lalmai-Mainamati **3** *166*; **15** *279*, 281; **18** 664*
reliefs **15** 719
Salban Vihara **15** 281
sculpture **15** 499
Lalman **15** 629
Lalo, Charles **24** 321; **28** 926
Lalonde, Richard de **7** 746, 747; **29** 683
Laloux, Victor (-Alexandre-Frédéric) **11** 671; **18** 664*; **31** 855
collaboration **4** 597; **15** 849; **22** 508
pupils
Agache, Donat-Alfred **1** 447
André, Emile **2** 13
Astruc, Jules(-Godefroy) **2** 651
Carlu, Jacques **5** 776
Cristino da Silva, Luís (Ribeiro Carvalhosa) **8** 163
Debat-Ponsan, Jacques **8** 589
Ghika-Budeşti, Nicolae **12** 547
Laloux, Victor (-Alexandre-Frédéric)
pupils—cont.
Howe, George **14** 811
Silva, (José) Marques da **28** 731
Terra, (Miguel) Ventura **30** 492
teachers **2** 14
works **3** 464, *465*; **11** 524; **18** *664*; **31** 228, 241
Laloy, Jean-Marie **26** 205
Laloy, Yves **30** 23
Lal Qil'a *see under* DELHI
Laluha, Milan **28** 853
La Luisiana **31** 719
Lam, Dirk de Vries **33** 162
Lam, Wilfredo **1** 425; **8** 233, 236; **18** 665–6*, 834
dealers **7** 421
groups and movements **30** 22, 23
patrons and collectors **20** 832; **23** 85
works **8** 229; **18** *665*, 834, 835; **19** 491
Lama, Agostino **18** 666
Lama, Giovan Bernardo **2** 731
Lama, Giulia **18** 666*
Lama, Victor de la **31** 186
Lamač, Morislav **8** 249, 426
La Madeleine **4** 313; **10** 472
spear-throwers **25** *491*
La Magliana **24** 526
Lamahalot **15** 814
Lamair, Pierre-Alexis de *see* DELAMAIR, PIERRE-ALEXIS
Lamaism *see under* BUDDHISM → branches
Lamaison, Pierre **29** 335
Lamakh, Valery **31** 560
Lamanai **3** 622, *622*; **18** 666–7*; **20** 881, *882*
bone-carvings **21** 248
pyramids **20** 881
Structure N-10-43 **21** 214; **30** 448
temples **30** 448
La Marche **25** 492
La Marche, C.-P. Fyot de *see* FYOT DE LA MARCHE, C.-P.
La Marche, Olivier de *see* OLIVIER DE LA MARCHE
La Mare, Jean de **26** 334
Lamas, Andrés **2** 404
Lamasch, Iosef Carol **4** 680
La Mayanga **29** 173
Lamayuru **15** 311; **30** 833
Lamb, Charles (1860-1942; architect) **31** 728
Lamb, Charles (1893-1964; painter) **16** 17
Lamb, Edward Buckton **10** 238; **14** 190; **18** 667*; **28** 349
Lamb, Henry **5** 516; **11** 774; **18** 667–8*
Lamb, Hugo **28** 604
Lamb, Isaac N. **18** 158
Lamb, James (*fl* 1806) **18** 667
Lamb, James (1843-1900) **3** 893; **33** 565
Lamb, Lynton **4** 369
Lamb, Peniston, 1st Viscount Melbourne **22** 153
Lamb, Thomas (*b* 1938) **5** 580; **15** 408
Lamb, Thomas W. (*fl* 1914-29) **7** 327
Lamb, William **25** 685; **28** 244, 253
Lamb, William Frederick **28** 628–9
Lamb, Winifred **18** 668*
Lamba **1** 307; **31** 73
Lambach **2** *776*
Abbey **2** 781; **3** 710; **18** 668*
church **2** 790
manuscripts **2** 790
metalwork **2** 822
wall paintings **2** 794; **3** *711*; **26** 650, *650*, 659
Lambach *Pietà* **33** 348
Lambaesis **18** 669*
arch **31** 350
fort **21** 559
Lambaesis—cont.
fortress **18** 669; **23** 300; **26** 921
Temple of Aesculapius **26** 867; **30** 436
Lambakis, G. **9** 527
Lamballe, Marie Thérèse Louise de Savoie-Carignan, Princesse de **14** 509
Lambardi, Carlo **18** 669*; **24** 267
Lambardos, Emmanuel **25** 333
Lambarené **1** *394*; **11** 879
Lambart, Bruno **3** 510
Lambax, Michael Wenzel **14** 65*
Lambayeque, Museo Arqueológico Regional Brüning **3** 363
Lambayeque culture **28** 650
Lambdin, George Cochran **17** 823; **18** 670*
Lambdin, James Read **18** 670
Lambeaux, Jef (-Marie-Thomas) **3** 572; **18** 670*
groups and movements **5** 44; **14** 137; **32** 591
works **2** 197; **3** 572; **8** 701; **14** 769
Lambeaux, Jules **18** 670
Lambera, Juan Manuel **25** 700
Lambercy, Philippe **30** 144
Lamberg, Count **28** 69
Lamberger, Simon *see* LAINBERGER, SIMON
Lamberg-Karlovsky, C. C. **33** 482
Lamberg-Sprinzenstein, Anton Franz de Paula, Graf von **2** 829; **18** 670–71*
Lambermont, Bertholet Labeen de **3** 600
Lambert (*fl c.* 1120) **26** 661
Lambert (*fl* 1625) **2** 703
Lambert, André (*b* 1851) **3** 823
Lambert, Andrew (*fl* 1760) **11** 410
Lambert, Catholina **18** 672*
Lambert, Constant **28** 808
Lambert, Elie **12** 889
Lambert, George **18** 672*
assistants **28** 284
collaboration **23** 105, 208
groups and movements **14** 638
patrons and collectors **4** 611; **14** 436; **17** 476; **20** 911
pupils **28** 817
works **10** *250*, 251
Lambert, George W(ashington) **2** 753, 769; **18** 672–3*; **30** 160
groups and movements **8** 2
works **2** 748
Lambert, H. **16** 587
Lambert, James **13** 664
Lambert, Jean (*c.* 1427-91) **31** 843
Lambert, Jean-Baptiste (1608-44) **11** 516, 657; **18** 671*; **19** 262
Lambert, Johann Heinrich **6** 570; **24** 490, 494, 495; **28** 202
Lambert, John (*fl* 1752) **27** 244
Lambert, Lén, Baron **5** 884
Lambert, Marcel **25** 658
Lambert, Maurice **19** 623
Lambert, Nicolas **18** 671*; **19** 248, 268
paintings **19** *248*
Lambert, Paul *see* SAINT PAUL, PAUL
Lambert, Phyllis **5** 574
Lambert, Théodore **11** 601
Lamberti, Bonaventura **3** 712; **13** 277; **18** 674*
Lamberti, Niccolò di Piero **18** 673–4*
collaboration **7** 363
pupils **18** 674; **22** 462
sculpture **16** 692
Cathedral of S Maria del Fiore (Florence) **11** 197, 201; **13** 94; **18** *673*; **22** 461
Orsanmichele (Florence) **11** 204
S Francesco (Bologna) **30** 498
S Marco (Venice) **32** 208
Lamberti, Piero di Niccolò **13** 95; **18** 673, 674*
collaboration **7** 363
patrons and collectors **21** 747
works **27** 830; **32** 208
Lamberti, Stefano **22** 107
Lamberti da Montagnano, Alevisio **22** 182
Lambertini (family) **12** 53
Lambertini, Prospero Lorenzo *see* BENEDICT XIV, Pope
Lambert & Noel **12** 186
Lambert of Saint-Omer **10** 201; **13** 136
works **10** *201*
Lamberton, William **28** 267
Lambertsz., Geraert **8** 739; **18** 9; **22** 858
Lambespringe, Bartholomew **10** 260
Lambeth, Richard **1** 151; **18** 887
Lambeth Apocalypse *see under* APOCALYPSES → individual manuscripts
Lambeth Bible *see under* BIBLES → individual manuscripts
Lambeth pottery **4** 177; **7** 166
Lambini Panagia **8** 156
Lambityeco **18** 675–6*; **21** *193*, 202, *372*; **33** 620
sculpture **18** *675*
stucco **29** 829
talud-tablero **21** 206
Lamboray, Jean-Pierre **19** 827
Lambot, Joseph-Louis **7** 693
Lambotte, Emma **10** 411
Lambourne, Nigel **4** 366
Lambousa **8** 354
Acheiropoiitos **8** 357, 358
Lambousa Treasure *see* LAPITHOS TREASURE
Lambrech, Joos **33** 268
Lambrecht, Arthur **5** 50
Lambrecht, Gottfried **8** 413
Lambrecht, Hans, III **12** 446
Lambrecht, Joost **3** 556
Lambrechtz, Arendt *see* LAMPRECHTS, ARENDT
Lambretta **15** 826
Lambrich, Edmond **28** 921
Lambrinoudakis, V. K. **22** 698
Lambron *see* NAMRUN
Lambrou Myloi **19** 235
Lame, Biagio dalle *see* PUPINI, BIAGIO
Lamego **18** 676*; **25** *288*
Museu Regional **18** 676
Nossa Senhora dos Remédios **26** 254
sculpture **13** 102
Lamego, António da Costa *see* COSTA LAMEGO, ANTÓNIO DA
La Meilleraye, Duc de *see* MAZARIN, Duc de
La Meilleraye, Hortense, Duchesse de *see* MAZARINE, HORTENSE, Duchesse de
lamellaphones **22** 375
lamellar armour *see under* ARMOUR → types
Lamen, Christoffel van der **17** 7
Lamentation, Master of the **25** 101
Lamentation groups **18** 676–7*
Lamerie, Paul de **10** 329, 332; **18** 677*; **19** 593; **29** 432
attributions **33** 158
patrons and collectors **7** 377; **14** 143; **32** 824
teachers **25** 29
works **10** 330, *331*, 332; **14** 857; **19** *594*; **26** 84, 499; **28** *738*
Lamertijn, Passchier **19** 418; **22** 899
La Mésangère, Pierre de **3** 485; **10** 823; **11** 597
Lameyer (y Berenguer), Francisco **18** 678*; **29** 284
Lami, Eugène (-Louis) **8** 616; **18** 678–9*
collaboration **20** 420
groups and movements **26** 500; **31** 374
patrons and collectors **4** 556; **8** 705; **14** 148; **23** 521; **27** 223
sculpture **7** 841
works **10** 781; **18** *678*
Lami, Giovanni **18** 679*
Lami, Stanislas **10** 210
Lamia, Domenico *see* AIMO, DOMENICO
La Mimoserie **11** 495
laminas **10** 625
laminates **3** 685; **28** 256
materials
gold **12** 621
silver **12** 621
uses
chairs **6** 391
furniture **3** 685; **28** 256; **33** 331
gilding **12** 621
panel paintings **24** 4
laminboard **33** 328
Lamine, Jean de **3** 600
Laming-Emperaire, Annette **25** 482, 483
Lamm, Carl Robert **30** 117
Lamm, C. J. **16** 549
Lamme, Arie (1748-1801) **30** 412
Lamme, Arie Johannes (1812-1900) **4** 614; **11** 233; **28** 68
Lamme, Dirk-Ary **28** 68
Lammekens, Philippe **13** 909
Lammens, Bernard **3** 591
Lamo, Alessandro **18** 679–80*
Lamo, Pietro **18** 680*
La Moderna **29** 203
Lamoen, Leopold Joseph van **3** 600
Lam Oi **6** 768
Lamoignon, Chrétien **18** 680
Lamoignon, Chrétien-François **18** 680*
Lamoignon, Guillaume **18** 680*
Lamoignon Hours *see under* BOOKS OF HOURS → individual manuscripts
La Mojarra **29** 620
La Moleta de Cartagena **29** 365
Lamonica, Roberto De *see* DE LAMONICA, ROBERTO
Lamont, James **31** 339
Lamont, T. R. **33** 137
La Montagne, Renaud de **25** 33
La Montaña de La Flor **14** 712
Lamorinière, François **3** 562, 615; **18** 680*
La Mosson **4** 331
La Mota Castle *see under* MEDINA DEL CAMPO
La Mote, Yvonnet de **20** 722
Lamothe, Louis **8** 619, 659; **11** 157; **15** 152; **19** 229; **26** 92; **31** 29
Lamothe, Odon **31** 210
La Mothe Cadillac, Antoine Laumet de **8** 820
La Mothe-Fénelon, François de Salignac de *see* FÉNELON, FRANÇOIS DE SALIGNAC DE LA MOTHE-
La Mothe le Vayer, François de **22** 466
La Motte, Antoine Houdard de *see* HOUDARD DE LA MOTTE, ANTOINE
Lamotte, Denis-François **3** 600
Lamotte, Guillaume-René **3** 600
Lamour, Jacques **3** 599
Lamour, Jean **11** 628; **14** 448; **16** 59; **19** 697; **22** 456; **29** 537
works **22** *455*
Lamourdedieu, Raoul **11** 568; **18** 682*
Lamoureux, Abraham-César **8** 739; **16** 682; **18** 682*; **30** 85
Lamoureux, Charles **8** 71

Lamoureux, Claude 18 682
La Mouthe 25 *470*, 474, 491
rock art 25 *475*
Lamp *see* LAMPI
Lamp, Frederick
works 1 *261*
Lampa 24 *498*
church 24 502
Lampa, Jakob 30 106
Lampang 30 *571*
Wat Pa Fang 30 586
Wat Si Chum 30 586, 618
Wat Si Rong Muang 30 586
lampas weaving *see under* WEAVING → types
lampblack
historical and regional traditions
China 6 736; 7 91, 92; 24 790
England 18 611
Japan 17 213, 387
Rome, ancient 23 785
uses
calligraphy 6 736; 17 213
casts 23 115
crayons 8 128
inks 6 736; 7 91, 92; 15 849, 851, 853; 17 213; 24 790; 25 598
inksticks 7 91, 92; 17 387
japanning 18 611
lacquer 18 600
pigments 15 548; 23 785; 24 789–90
secco paintings 28 338
writing 17 213
Lampe (family) 23 236
Lampecco, Antonio 3 592
Lamperez y Romea, Vicente 8 253; 18 682*
Lampérth, József Nemes *see* NEMES LAMPÉRTH, JÓZSEF
lamp-holders 32 *488*
Lamphun 30 *571*, 576
Wat Kukut 29 866; 30 511, 577
Wat Phra That Haripunchai 29 866; 30 586
Lampi, Franz Xaver 18 682, 683–4*
Lampi, Jan Chrzciciel 25 212
Lampi, Johann Baptist (i) (1751-1830) 18 682–3*; 25 105
patrons and collectors 11 789
pupils 1 728; 4 421; 10 702, 883; 18 683; 32 775
works 2 795; 26 713
Lampi, Johann Baptist (ii) (1775-1837) 18 682, 683*
Lampi, Johann Baptist Matthias Edler von 18 682
Lampi, Matthias 18 682*
Lamport (Northants)
All Saints 20 866
Lamport Hall 8 45; 20 378
collections 10 364
paintings 13 300; 14 810; 19 123
Lamprecht 24 148
Lamprecht, Karl 32 854
Lamprecht, Wilhelm 9 468
Lamprechts, Arendt 2 382; 18 684*; 30 78
lamps 19 364, 366
historical and regional traditions
Byzantine 9 *520*, 656, 657
Central Asia, Western 6 257
China 6 854, 856, 859
Cyprus 13 *603*
Early Christian (*c*. AD 250-843) 9 656
Egypt 16 *520*
Egypt, ancient 13 *603*; 27 104, *104*
France 2 *563*; 11 574
Greece, ancient 13 602*, *603*; 19 364; 27 104, *104*
Indian subcontinent 15 *708*, 708–9, 729
Islamic 14 427; 16 364–5, 394, 397, 421, 422, *520*
Italy 9 *520*; 27 103–4, *104*
lamps
historical and regional traditions—cont.
Japan 17 359
Malta (Republic of) 20 217
Nabataea 22 420
Ottoman 16 421, 422
Pakistan 23 803
Palau 23 833
Palestine 27 104, *104*
Prehistoric art 25 475, 479–80, 491
Punic 25 734
Rhodes (island) 13 *603*
Rome, ancient 19 364; 27 87*, 103–4*, *104*
Sicily 13 *603*
Spain 29 *343*
Syria 16 397, *520*; 27 104
Tunisia 27 104, *104*
Turkey 13 *603*; 16 394
United States of America 30 *868*, 868–9; 31 619
materials
amber 1 762
brass 15 *708*
bronze 6 854, 856, 859; 15 708–9; 27 87*, 105; 29 *343*
enamel 12 IV1
glass 2 *563*; 12 789, IV1; 16 *520*, 521; 30 *868*, 868–9
paper 17 359
pewter 24 581
pottery 6 257; 27 103–5, *104*
silver 9 *520*, 656, 657
silver-gilt 9 *520*
terracotta 13 *603*
types
arc 19 366
Argand 9 13; 19 364; 30 674
electric 19 366
fluorescent 7 736; 19 366
gasoliers 9 13
goose-foot 6 859
halogen 19 366
hanging 17 571–2*, *571*
Hannukah 17 573, *573*
incandescent 19 366
metal halide 7 733
mosque 12 789, IV1; 16 *520*, 521
oil 9 11, 13; 16 394
tungsten 7 733; 19 366
tungsten-halogen 7 733
see also CANDELABRA; CHANDELIERS; LANTERNS (LIGHTS); LIGHTING; SPOTLIGHTS
Lampsacus Treasure 9 655; 18 825
Lampsakos 13 587
Lampsonius, Dominicus 7 500; 9 445; 13 806; 19 548; 22 910; 32 114
lampstands 16 *391*, 391
Lampugnano, Melchiorre 3 782
Lampung 15 *752*, 810, 814; 23 555
hangings 15 *794*
Lamqua (i) (1801-60) 6 624; 13 733, 734*; 19 866
Lamqua (ii) (*fl c*. 1840-70) 13 733, 734, 735*; 14 721
Lamsdorf, A., Count 4 335
Lam Son 32 *468*, 475, 479
Lamu 1 *407*
architectural decorations 1 317
architecture 1 315, 410
doors 30 57
museum 30 56
La Muette Château 5 837; 7 168; 8 813; 19 140; 26 493
Lamunière, Jean-Marc 18 874
Lamy, Peronet 18 684*
works 3 188; 18 *684*; 28 4
Lana, Lodovico 1 103; 18 685*
Lana'i *see* HAWAII
Lanaja, Master of *see* GRAÑEN, BLASCO DE
Lanau, Federico 31 755
Lancaster (House of) 18 685*
Lancaster (Lancs.; UK) 2 150
Ashton Memorial 3 269
Castle 18 887
furniture 10 297
Muses Room 29 835
University Chaplaincy Centre 6 459
Lancaster (MA; USA), Church of Christ 5 *143*
Lancaster (PA; USA) 31 652
Lancaster, Henry VI, King of England *see* HENRY VI, King of England
Lancaster, John of, Duke of Bedford *see* PLANTAGENET, JOHN OF LANCASTER, Duke of Bedford
Lancaster, José de Carvajal y *see* CARVAJAL Y LANCASTER, JOSÉ
Lancaster, Joseph 28 156
Lancaster, Mark 18 687–8*
Lancaster, Osbert 18 688*
Lancaster Canal 2 242
Lance, Adolphe Etienne 18 688*
Lance, David 29 835
Lance, George 18 688–9*
Lance, J.-L. de La *see* LA LANCE, J.-L. DE
Lancefield 2 *736*
Lancefield Pottery 28 257
Lanceley, Colin 2 120, 751; 4 882; 18 689*
Lancellotti (family) 27 194
Lancellotti, Orazio, Cardinal 18 689*
Lancellotti, Scipione, Cardinal 18 689*; 32 693
Lancellotti, Tiberio 18 689
Lancelot Master *see* LATIN 757, MASTER OF
Lancere, Yevgeny 33 379
lances 2 448; 6 305
lancet arches *see under* ARCHES → types
Lancetti, Federico 16 730
lancet windows *see under* WINDOWS → types
Lanchares, Antonio 18 689–90*; 25 168
Lanchester, Elsa 7 483
Lanchester, Henry Jones 18 690
Lanchester, Henry Vaughan 17 600; 18 690*
Lanchester, Stewart & Rickards 3 269; 18 690; 31 241
Lanchester & Rickards 18 690*
competitions 7 668
works 18 890; 23 194; 30 506; 32 784
Lanchi Daolong 17 168
Lanci, Baldassare 18 690–91*; 19 764; 24 491
Lanci, Franciszek Maria 18 691*; 25 99; 30 345; 32 871
Lanci, Marino 18 690
Lanci, Michelangelo 16 547
Lanci, Witold 32 872
Lancia, Bernardo di Luca 18 691
Lancia, Emilio 16 649; 23 263; 25 218
Lancia, Luca 13 909; 18 691*; 19 562
Lancia Motor Co. 32 501
Lanciani (family) 16 776
Lanciani, Rodolfo (Amadeo) 18 691–2*; 26 762; 27 115
Lanciano, Polidoro da *see* POLIDORO DA LANCIANO
Lancillotto di Ludovico 5 672
Lancilotti, Francesco 22 377
Lancisi, Giuseppe Maria 21 831
Lanckaert, Joost Jansz. 19 343
Lanckoroński, Karl Anton Leo Ludwig *see* LANCKOROŃSKI, KAROL
Lanckoroński, Karol 2 829; 18 692*; 25 136, 138; 32 447
Lancour, H. 4 24
Lancret, Jean-Baptiste 30 118
Lancret, Nicolas 11 539; 18 692–3*; 24 135
patrons and collectors
Aumale, Henri-Eugène-Philippe-Louis de Bourbon, Duc d' 23 523
Beringhen, Jacques-Louis, Marquis de Chateau-neuf 3 785
Beurdeley, (Emmanuel-) Alfred (1847-1919) 3 889
Frederick II, King of Prussia (*reg* 1740-86) 3 798; 12 473; 14 652
Péreire (family) 24 396
Périer, Casimir 24 418
Ramsay, John 28 271
Rothschild (family) 27 223
Tessin, Carl Gustav, Count 30 118, 523
Verrue, Jeanne-Baptiste d'Albert de Luynes, Comtesse de 32 368
pupils 8 787
reproductions in porcelain 6 I3
reproductive prints by others 17 668; 18 795; 19 10; 21 800
teachers 12 638
works 2 704; 8 733; 11 34, 36, 407; 12 292; 14 791; 18 *693*; 24 256
Łańcut 18 693–4*; 25 *92*, 136, 138
Castle 18 693–4; 19 752; 25 115, 135
Great Synagogue 17 545
Land, Edwin H. 24 655
Landa, Diego de, Bishop of Yucatán 20 888; 21 185, 190, 258, 262, 264
Landaeta, Antonio José 19 731; 32 180
Landaluze, Víctor Patricio de 18 694*
works 8 233
Land and Building News see BUILDING NEWS
land art 1 80; 9 26; 10 680; 15 869; 18 694–5*, 700; 24 679; 25 646; 28 206
England 10 258; 18 719; 19 625
United States of America 7 *237*; 14 324; 18 *694*; 28 890; 31 615
see also EARTHWORKS
Landau, Georg 32 274
Landauer, Bella C. 10 421
Landauer, Berthold 18 695*; 20 696
Landauer, Fritz 17 548
Landauer, Lukas 25 39
Landauer, Marcus 18 695
Landauer Altarpiece 9 435, 441, 443; 11 455; 18 475; 26 188
Landau-Gutenberger, Gustaw 19 537
Land Dayak *see* BIDAYUH
Landeata, Francisco de 32 177
Landecho 8 15, *15*
Landeck, Armin 9 310; 10 397
Landelle, Charles (-Zacharie) 13 228; 18 695–6*; 28 68
Landells, Ebenezer 11 331
Landenberger, Christian 28 111; 29 875
Lander, H. Clapham 8 810
Landes (France) 32 278
Landes (family) 11 621
Landes, Louis 9 715; 11 621
works 11 *621*
Landesamt für Denkmalpflege 13 810
Landesio, Eugenio 18 696*; 21 385, 397, 404; 32 123
Landfall Press 19 492; 20 609
Landgraff, Hans F. von 28 853
Land group *see* EARTH GROUP
Landi, Angelo 10 799; 18 900
Landi, Antonio Giuseppe (*fl* 1539) 27 740
Landi, Antonio Giuseppe (1713-91) 3 535; 4 711; 18 696*
Landi, Edoardo N. 13 728
Landi, Gaspare 18 697*
collaboration 29 639
patrons and collectors 31 172
pupils 25 62; 30 459
works 5 555; 11 *396*
Landi, Manfredo III, Conte (*d* 1491) 3 384; 26 289
Landi (del Poggio), Neroccio (di Bartolommeo di Benedetto) de' 11 688; 16 662; 18 697–8*
collaboration 16 660
patrons and collectors 6 393; 27 463
works 6 4; 16 *659*; 18 *698*; 20 684; 28 681; 29 362; 32 105
Landing, Haydée 25 702
Landini, Antonio 9 76
Landini, Taddeo 18 698–9*
patrons and collectors 20 839
works 10 909; 16 696; 26 814, 840
Landino, Cristoforo 7 627; 14 868; 18 699*
pupils 32 255
works 2 277; 4 502; 16 780; 20 537; 22 412
illustrated 21 15
Landino, Jacopo di 29 404
Landio, Giovanni 14 885
Lando, Viva di *see* VIVA DI LANDO
Lando di Pietro 13 65, 93, 124; 28 676, 679
Landois, Paul 10 206
Landolf (*fl* 1297) 14 416
Landolfo, Bishop of Turin (*fl* early 11th cent.) 31 447
Landolfo I of Benevento (*reg* 957-82) 10 700
Landolina, Giambattista 28 657
Landolt (family) 30 143
Landolt, Salomon 12 500
Landon, Charles Paul 6 77; 14 395; 18 699–700*; 26 231
Landow, George 10 688
Landowski, Paul Maximilien 11 568
collaboration 10 689; 12 276
pupils 1 132; 3 429; 22 523
works 5 *446*; 6 733
Landozzi, Lando 28 319
Landreau, Marcel 22 441
Landriani, Gaetano 4 247
Landriani, Paolo Camillo 22 81
Landriani, Tommaso 6 357
Landry, Pierre 14 83
LANDSAT (Earth Resources Technology) 2 301
Landsberg, Herrad von, Abbess *see* HERRAD VON LANDSBERG, Abbess
Landsberg, Martin 19 111
Landsberg, Petter 12 634
Landsberg am Lech, St Mariä Himmelfahrt 13 117
sculpture 22 *281*
Wurzbach Altar 12 384
Landsberger, Franz 17 583
Landsbergis-Žemkalnis, Vytautas 19 499
landscape 13 *418*, 418–19; 14 544, *544*; 18 700–701; 24 740, 741
Landscape Annual see JENNINGS'S LANDSCAPE ANNUAL
Landscape Architecture 24 434
landscape architecture *see under* ARCHITECTURE → types
landscape drawings *see under* DRAWINGS → types
landscape gardens *see under* GARDENS → types
landscape painting *see under* PAINTING → types
Landschneck, Ulrich *see* GANTSCHNIGG, ULRICH
Landseer, Anna Maria 18 720
Landseer, Charles 18 720, 721–2*

Landseer, Edwin (Henry) 14 143; 18 720, 722–3*
dealers 1 453; 12 30
groups and movements 26 740
patrons and collectors
Albert, Prince of Saxe-Coburg-Gotha (1819-61) 14 148
Bicknell, Elhanan 4 35
Cavendish, William Spencer, 6th Duke of Devonshire (1790-1858) 6 117
Holloway, Thomas 14 688
Percy, Algernon, 4th Duke of Northumberland 24 390
Russell, John, 6th Duke of Bedford 27 358
Sheepshanks, John 28 576
Tate, Henry 30 359
Victoria, Queen of Great Britain (*reg* 1837- 1901) 10 362; 14 148
Wells, William (i) (1768-1847) 33 65
pupils 19 818
reproductive prints by others 26 232
Atkinson, Thomas Lewis 2 692
Cousins, Samuel 8 69
Finden, William 11 84
Gambart, (Jean Joseph) Ernest (Théodore) 12 30
Graves, Robert 13 327
Hollyer, Frederick 14 688
Jackson, John Richardson 16 820
Landseer, John (George) 18 721
Landseer, Thomas 18 721
Lewis (i), Charles George (1808-80) 19 285
Mottram, Charles 22 208
Periam, George August 24 418
Robinson, John Henry 26 473
Ryall, Henry Thomas 27 460
Tomkins, Charles Algernon 31 137
Tomkins, Charles John 31 138
teachers 11 860; 14 263
works 2 106; 10 252, 334; 18 *722*, *723*; 29 425
Landseer, Emma 18 720
Landseer, George 18 720
Landseer, Henry 1 845; 18 720
Landseer, Jane 18 720
Landseer, Jessica 18 720
Landseer, John (George) 18 720–22*
Landseer, Thomas 18 720, 721–2*; 25 627
collaboration 18 721
works 18 722; 22 208; 25 619
Landshut 12 *361*; 18 723–5*; 33 274
Burg Trausnitz 12 366; 15 137; 20 279
furniture 5 768
Narrentreppe 23 757
paintings 30 34
St Georg 26 634
college of St Ignatius 32 821
coral 7 835
glass 12 439
guns 2 464
Heiliggeistkirche *see* Spitalkirche
Jesuit church 32 821
St Martin 4 777; 18 *724*, 724–5*; 32 91, 92
sculpture 26 646
Spitalkirche 24 751; 32 90, 93
Stadtresidenz 12 366; 14 451; 29 522
Landshut, Jakob von *see* JAKOB VON LANDSHUT
Landshut, Mair von *see* MAIR VON LANDSHUT
Landskrona 11 299
Sports Hall 29 427
Landu 15 756
Landucci, Luca 18 725*
Landuma 1 391; 3 45, 46
Landuyt, Octave 3 573
Landweer, Sonja 22 884
Lane, (Edward) Arthur 16 549; 18 725–6*
Lane, Edward William 14 208; 16 458, 547
Lane, Fitz Hugh 14 843; 18 726–7*; 31 602
groups and movements 18 715; 19 791
patrons and collectors 17 823
works 18 715, *726*; 20 425
Lane, Hugh (Percy) 9 319; 16 17, 36; 18 727*; 29 121
painting 16 35
Lane, Hugh, Gallery *see* DUBLIN → Municipal Gallery of Modern Art
Lane, Jared 17 477
Lane, John 3 446
Lane, Joseph 7 374; 23 782
Lane, Josiah 7 374
Lane, Richard 11 785; 32 904
Lane, Richard James 18 727–8*; 19 484
Lane-Poole, Stanley 16 548
Laneuville, F. 27 563
Laneuville, Jean-Louis 8 557; 18 728*
Lanfranc, Archbishop of Canterbury 7 231
architecture 5 637, 638, 642; 14 75; 26 587; 29 22
capitals 26 615
roods 27 124
Lanfranchi, Carlo Emanuele 18 729*; 28 15
Lanfranchi, Francesco 18 728–9*
Lanfranco (*fl* 1099-1137) 13 813; 18 729*
works 21 771, 772, *772*; 26 578, 595
Lanfranco (*fl* mid-13th cent.) 5 550
Lanfranco, Giovanni 16 670, 672; 18 730–36*; 22 478; 26 773
assistants 3 353; 4 666
attributions 23 874
collaboration 3 32; 4 405; 5 454, 864, 867; 18 689; 24 476; 26 196, 771, 840; 27 817; 30 356; 31 436
patrons and collectors
Aldobrandini (family) 9 175
Collelungo, Clemente Sannesio, Marchese di 27 764
Créquy, Charles de Blanchefort de 19 238
Farnese, Odoardo, Cardinal 10 811
Feilding, Basil, 2nd Earl of Denbigh 10 861
Giori, Angelo, Cardinal 12 680
Jabach, Everard 11 662
Medici, Ferdinando de', Grand Prince of Tuscany (1663–1713) 8 142; 21 30
Monterrey, 6th Conde de 22 21
Patrizi, Costanzo 24 267
Peretti (-Montalto), Alessandro, Cardinal 24 399
Philip IV, King of Spain (*reg* 1621–65) 22 21
Theatine Order 30 649
Urban VIII, Pope (*reg* 1623-44) 3 206; 5 690
pupils 25 562
reproductive prints by others 3 294, 521; 9 176; 18 476
restorations by others 7 916
works 4 405, 406; 5 768; 9 90; 11 81; 15 137–8; 16 670; 18 *731*, *732*, *733*, *735*; 20 841; 22 485; 26 311, 809, 810, 839; 27 486; 30 358
Lanfranco Veris da Milano 32 256*
Lanfrani, Jacopo 13 95; 24 372
Lanfrey, Claude François 23 113
Lang (family) 31 646
Lang, Albert 28 170
Lang, Antal 24 313
Lang, Carlos Alvarado *see* ALVARADO LANG, CARLOS
Lang, Daniel 12 445
Lang, Filip 8 395
Lang, Fritz 11 137; 18 577; 19 234
Lang, Heinrich 22 185
Lang, Herbert
works 1 *343*
Lang, Jack 11 584; 24 145
Lang, János 14 904
Lang, Karl 12 450
Lang, Matthäus 10 220
Lang, Mauritius 28 852
Lang, Thomas 14 834
Langa, Naftal 22 244
Langar 6 185
Langbard, Iosif (Grigor'yevich) 18 737*
collaboration 20 275
works 3 527; 21 696, *696*
Lang Ca 29 230; 32 487
Langdale (family) 10 344; 13 164
Langdale 25 515
Langdale Rosary 27 159
Langdon, Stephen H. 16 85; 18 86
Lange, Adolph 7 448
Lange, Anne-Françoise-Elisabeth 12 730
Lange, Christian (*fl* 1666) 19 418
Lange, Christian Friedrich (1768-1833) 33 228
Lange, Dorothea 18 738*; 24 673; 31 606; 33 310
assistants 12 599
groups and movements 24 685
teachers 33 146
works 25 653; 28 919
Lange, Evert 12 410
works 12 *410*
Lange, Friedrich 19 418
Lange, Gottlieb August 26 111
Lange, Jan (i) *see* JORDAENS, HANS, III
Lange, Jan (ii) *see* BOECKHORST, JAN
Lange, Jens Iversen, Bishop of Århus 8 758; 23 255
Lange, Josef 32 775
Lange, Julius Henrik 8 760, 761; 18 738*
Lange, Konrad 20 925
Lange, Luc *see* LANCIA, LUCA
Lange, Ludwig 13 360; 14 227
Lange, Philip de (*b c.* 1704-66) 8 726
Lange, Philipp (*fl c.* 1910) 21 66
Lange, Zachariasz 25 127
Langeac, Jean de, Bishop of Limoges 19 396
Langeais 6 50, 52, 54
Langelacher, Ignaz 13 852
Langen, Albert 13 841; 14 313
Langenargen Museum 25 744
Langenberg, Johann von *see* JOHANN VON LANGENBERG
Langendijk, Dirk 2 105; 18 738–9*; 22 846
Langendijk, Jan Anthonie 18 739
Langendijk, Pieter 3 211
Langenheim Brothers 20 92
Langenhorst Convent 13 177
Langenhoven, Martinus van 17 649
Langenmantel, Ludwig von 1 141
Langenthal Porcelain Factory 27 724; 30 144
Langenzerdorf, Anton Hanak-Freilichtmuseum 14 130
Langer, Caspar Gottlieb 8 409
Langer, František 8 250; 13 711
Langer, Johann Peter 18 739
Langer, Lea *see* GRUNDIG, LEA
Langer, Peter von 3 155; 14 488
Langer, (Joseph) Robert von 18 739*; 28 375
Langer, Susanne K(atherina) 1 182; 10 691; 18 739–40*
Langerock, Pieter 31 880
Langetti, Giovanni Battista 8 427; 18 740*; 19 706; 32 194
Langford (Oxon) 2 72
St Matthew 26 614; 27 124
Langford, Abraham 7 500; 10 366; 33 94
Langford & Gardiner 23 65
Langgar Mosque 20 166
Langham, St Mary 13 121
Langham Artists' Society 14 800
Langhammer, Arthur 14 694; 21 896
Langhammer, Walter 4 290
Langhans, Carl Ferdinand 3 792; 14 654; 18 741–2*; 20 867; 22 741; 33 417
Langhans, Carl Gotthard 12 642; 18 741*; 33 228
architecture 3 *791*, 792; 4 542; 12 374, 642; 23 490; 28 44, 98
collaboration 33 417
competitions 12 374
groups and movements 13 609
interior decoration 12 413; 18 476; 25 367; 28 44
patrons and collectors 3 806; 12 413; 14 653
pupils 12 641; 18 741; 33 228
Langhemans, Frans 3 570; 4 220; 18 742*; 29 591
Langhof, Christoph 29 428
Langhout, G. J. 29 483
Langinen, Leo 27 434
Langjia zhuang (Linzi) 6 695; 30 509
Langles, Louis-Mathieu 8 542
Langlet, Emil 23 232, 233; 30 73
Langley, Batty 18 742–3*
groups and movements 23 860
works 10 295; 13 645; 23 544; 29 748
writings 13 204; 23 489; 24 275; 30 872; 31 298
Langley, Charles 18 743
Langley, Edward 18 743
Langley, Henry 18 743*
Langley, Langley and Burke 18 743
Langley, Thomas 20 863
Langley, Walter 4 87; 10 335; 18 744*; 23 26
Langley, Warren 2 763, 764; 18 744*
Langley Park (Norfolk) 29 540
Langleys (Essex) 10 271
Langlier 7 778
Langlois, (Jean-) Charles 18 582, 744–5*; 24 19
Langlois, Christian (Jacques) 18 745*; 23 510
Langlois, E. H. 29 514
Langlois, François 10 144; 18 745–6*; 20 416; 25 626; 32 509
printmakers 3 632; 10 761
Langlois, Jacques 11 639
Langlois, Jean 4 391; 19 231; 31 385
Langlois, Lucien-Théophile 21 610
Langlois, Nicolas, the elder (1640-1703) 18 745; 19 210; 32 95
Langlois, Nicolas, the younger (1670-1707) 18 746
Langlois, Pierre (*fl* 1759-81) 16 24; 18 746*; 20 468
Langlois, Pierre-Gabriel (1754-1810) 11 318
Langlumé 13 306; 20 602
Langman, A. 22 174
Langman, Yeleazar (Mykhaylovych) 18 746*
Langnau 30 144
Lango 1 351
Langren, Jacob Floris van *see* FLORIS VAN LANGREN, JACOB
Langres
Cathedral of St Mammès 8 67; 11 639
Musée d'Archéologie 11 667
steel 8 287
Tours de Navarre et d'Orval 21 565
Langres, Juan de 5 203
Langsdorff, Baron de 4 717; 27 319
Lang Shining *see* CASTIGLIONE, GIUSEPPE (i)
Langsner, Jules 14 164
Langton Douglas, Robert *see* DOUGLAS, ROBERT LANGTON
Långtora 26 646
Langu 17 409
language, transrational *see* ZAUM
language and art 19 275; 30 169; 33 284
languages
Afghanistan 1 187–8*; 15 198
Anatolia, ancient 1 854
Babylonian 3 11–12*
Canaanite 5 556
Central Asia, Western 6 184–5*
China 6 737, 764
Coptic 10 1
Egypt, ancient 10 1
Etruscan 10 584, 637; 18 755
Georgia 12 317
Greece, ancient 13 369
Indian subcontinent 15 193, 197–9*
Indonesia 29 226
Iran 16 108
Irian Jaya 16 43
Islamic 16 107–9, 258*
Italy 10 637
Mesoamerica, Pre-Columbian 21 181*, 736, 738; 27 158
Mesopotamia 21 274
Náhuatl 21 262
Papua New Guinea 24 65
Punic 25 *733*
Samoa 27 683
South-east Asia 29 224–6*
Sumerian 1 853
Tibet 30 804
Languedoc, Laurent le 2 464, 465
Languedoc school 26 602
Langus, Matevž 28 860
Langwagen, C. G. 5 30
Langweil 7 157
Langweiler 25 500
Lang & Witchell 8 469
Langworthy, Lawrence 31 651
La Ngyunti Rante 15 818
Lanhas, Fernando 18 746*; 25 300
Lanhydrock House (Cornwall) 10 271; 29 834
Lanier, Nicholas 10 363; 18 747*; 19 582; 29 800
collections 19 124; 20 446; 25 664
paintings 9 480; 12 913
Lanino, Bernardino 18 747–8*; 31 899
Lanino, Gerolamo 18 748
Lanino, Pietro Francesco 18 748
Laniyati 22 614
Lankhorst, Jan 22 895
Lankrink, Prosper Henry 6 116; 18 748*; 25 664
personal collection 9 230; 14 810
works 4 439; 19 123
Lanman, Charles 18 748*
Lanna 6 567
Lanna, Vojtěch 8 423
Lannelier, Etienne 31 839
Lannooy, Chris 22 883
Lannoy (family) 22 64
Lannoy, de 25 671
Lannoy, Marguerite de, Lady of Santes *see* LANNOY, MARGUERITE DE, Lady of Santes
Lannoy, Robert de *see* ROBERT DE LANNOY

Lannuier, Charles-Honoré **18** 748–9*; **31** 619, 628
works **10** 851, 852
Lannuier, Nicolas-Louis-Cyrille **18** 748
lanolin **33** 1
Lanooy, C. J. **1** 734
La Noue, Abbé de **8** 209; **9** 230; **16** 815; **18** 749*; **20** 455
Lanoy, Gaspard **3** 599
Lanqi Daolong *see* RANKEI DŌRYŪ
Lansac, François Emile de **28** 68
Lansbergen, Philips van **32** 232
Lansburgh, G. Albert **3** 83
Lanscroon, Gerard **18** 749*
Lanscroon, Valentin **18** 749
Lansdowne, Francis Fitzmaurice, 3rd Earl of *see* FITZMAURICE, FRANCIS THOMAS, 3rd Earl of Lansdowne
Lansdowne, Henry Fitzmaurice, 5th Marquess of *see* FITZMAURICE, HENRY, 5th Marquess of Lansdowne
Lansdowne, Henry Petty-Fitzmaurice, 3rd Marquess of *see* PETTY-FITZMAURICE, HENRY, Marquess of Lansdowne
Lansdowne, James Fenwick **32** 414
Lansdowne, William Petty, 1st Marquess of *see* PETTY, WILLIAM, 1st Marquess of Lansdowne
Lansdowne Collection *see under* LONDON → British Library
Lansdowne *Herakles* **12** 504; **13** 606; **31** *60*, 60
L'Anse aux Meadows *see* ANSE AUX MEADOWS, L'
Lansere, Nikolay (Yevgen'yevich) **3** 732; **18** 749, 750*; **22** 178
Lansere, Yevgeny (Aleksandrovich) (1848-86) **3** 732; **18** 749*; **27** 390; **28** 459
Lansere, Yevgeny (Yevgen'yevich) (1875-1946) **3** 732; **18** 749–50*; **27** 394, 433; **28** 459
groups and movements **8** 849; **27** 580
works **8** 506
Lansing, A. **14** 513
Łanski, Jan Bogus **32** 880
Lanskoï, Gen. **9** 379
Lanskoy, André **9** 465; **18** 750*; **19** 491; **30** 389
Lantana, Giovanni Battista **5** 328
Lantara, Simon-Mathurin **18** 750–51*; **24** 243
Lantéri, Edouard **18** 751*; **20** 925
collaboration **4** 221
pupils **14** 850; **28** 592; **33** 343
teachers **8** 472
Lanteri, Giacomo **21** 579
Lantern, Master of the **20** 616
Lanterna Lighthouse **19** 360
lantern clocks *see under* CLOCKS → types
Lantern of St Vincent **5** 808; **7** 720
lantern roofs *see under* ROOFS → types
lanterns (architecture) **9** 82; **18** 751*
Islamic **16** 216
Italy **5** *21*
Korea **18** 266
Portugal **10** 664
Spain **16** 216
lanterns (lights)
historical and regional traditions
China **7** 114, 143; **16** II2
Denmark **8** *752*
Egypt, ancient **27** *111*
Japan **12** 98; **17** *323*, 359
Korea **18** 363
Rome, ancient **27** *111*
materials
brass **8** *752*
lanterns (lights)
materials—cont.
bronze **17** *323*
horn **14** 763
ivory **16** 799
jade **16** II2
paper **7** 114
terracotta **27** *111*
lanterns, magic *see* MAGIC LANTERNS
lantern slides *see under* SLIDES → types
Lante Vase **5** 541; **27** 357; **28** 907
Lantgreen, Petrus *see* PETRUS LANTGREEN
Lantian **7** 25
Lantman, George Henri **22** 892
Lantscroon, Gerard *see* LANSCROON, GERARD
Lanu, Olavi **11** 101
Lanuvio *see* LANUVIUM
Lanuvium **10** 617; **26** *886*; **27** 21, 30, 37
sculpture **27** *38*
Lanvin, Jeanne **10** 824; **11** 583
interior decoration **11** *583*
Lanxi Daolong *see* RANKEI DŌRYŪ
Lanyade **22** 614
Lan Ying **18** 751–3*; **33** 657
works **18** *752*
Lanyon, Charles **18** 753–4*
pupils **9** 297; **19** 844; **33** 566
works **3** 536; **9** 323; **16** 11, 25; **18** *753*
Lanyon, John **18** 754
Lanyon, Lynn & Lanyon **9** 366; **18** 754
Lanyon, Peter **3** 373; **18** 754–5*
groups and movements **1** 77, 78; **10** 258; **27** 563
works **28** 300
Lanz, Alfred **30** 137
Lanz, Johann Wilhelm **11** 730, 731; **26** 498
Lanza, Giuseppe, Duca di Camastra *see* CAMASTRA, GIUSEPPE LANZA, Duca di
Lanza, Vincenzo **13** 360
Lanzani, Andrea **2** 795; **18** 755*; **21** 527
teachers **5** 290
works **28** 836
Lanzani, Bernardino **27** 194
Lanzedelly, Joseph **19** 484
Lanzetta, Pablo **4** 234
Lanzhou **28** *719*, 720
Lanzi, Luigi **2** 125, 165; **7** 715; **10** 637, 644; **16** 772; **18** 755–6*
collaboration **3** 701
works **2** 164; **11** 189; **13** 541; **16** 768, 782; **22** 357
Lanzinger, Hubert **12** 396
Lanzy, Sergey **27** 436
Lao **18** 762; **30** 571, 623
Laodameia Painter **9** 248
works **9** *248*
Laodicea *see under* LATAKIA
Lao Khang **30** 619, 620
Laokoon **2** 162, 168, 559; **7** 562, 726; **9** 20, 23; **12** 728; **13** 303, 430, 464, 468, 470, 605; **14** 33, 34; **16** 770; **18** 756*; **23** 291; **25** 45; **26** 187, 286, 292, 846; **27** 8, *8*, 11, 30, 46, 114, 273; **28** 755
copies **3** 157; **11** 661; **26** 768
discovery **7** 562
restoration **7** 739
La Oliva **29** 263
Laon **11** *504*; **18** 756–61*; **31** 709
Cathedral of Notre-Dame **1** 724; **7** 267; **9** 672; **11** 510, 654; **13** 38, 39; **18** 757–9*, *757*, *758*; **30** 729; **32** *569*
bosses **4** 465
buttresses **5** 319
font **11** 253
gargoyles **12** 150
piers (ii) (masonry) **24** 751
Laon
Cathedral of Notre-Dame—cont.
pinnacles **24** 826
portals **18** *759*
sculpture **13** 73–4; **18** 759–60*
spire **29** 412
stained glass **13** 179, *179*; **18** 760–61*; **26** 702, *703*
tracery **31** 271
transept **31** 281
vaults **32** 93
manuscripts **21** 164
Musée Archéologique Municipal **18** 757
St Martin **30** 906
St Vincent **13** 39
Temple Chapel **7** 257; **18** *154*, 154
Laon, Anselm of *see* ANSELM OF LAON
Laon, Colart de *see* COLART DE LAON
Laon Globe **12** 813
Lao-niu Chih-yung *see* LAONIU ZHIYONG
Laoniu Zhiyong **6** 784
Laos **18** 761–77*, *761*; **29** *225*
altars **18** 777
aluminium **18** 775
architectural decorations **18** 766*
architecture **18** 764–7*
belts **18** *776*
betel sets **18** 776*
blouses **18** 772, 773
brocades **18** 771
bronze **18** *768*, 768
candle holders **18** 777
cement **18** 769
ceramics **18** 775*
coins **18** 774, 775*
costumes **18** 774
cupboards **18** 777
cups **18** 776
dance **18** 774–5
doors **9** 163
doorways **18** *766*
dress **18** 770–74*
drums (musical instruments) **22** 376
education (art) **18** 777*
enamel **18** 776
funerary objects **18** 776, 777
furniture **18** 776
gold **18** 770, 776
headdresses **18** 774
houses **18** 764, 766, 767*
iconography
Buddhism **18** 763
ikat **18** 771
jars **18** 762
jewellery **18** 775*, 776
lacquer **18** 768
manuscripts **18** 770
masks **18** *774*, 774–5*
metalwork **18** 776*
molasse **27** 831
monasteries **18** 764–6*, *765*, 767; **19** 737
Buddhism **18** 763
painting **18** 770*
pantaloons **18** 771
puppets **18** 775*
religion **18** 763*
repoussé **18** *776*
rubies **7** 91
sarcophagi **27** 831
sculpture **5** 484; **18** 767–70*
bronze **18** *768*, 768
Buddhism **18** 763, 767, *768*, 770
relief **18** 768–70, *769*
wood **18** 768
shirts **18** 771
shrines (i) (cult) **18** 776
silk **18** 771
silver **18** 775, 776, *776*
skirts **18** 772, 773, 774
stucco **29** 827
stupas **18** 764, 765*
temple offerings **18** 776*
Laos—cont.
temples **18** 764–5*, 767
textiles **18** 770–74*, *773*
theatre **18** 774–5*
thrones **30** 785
trade **7** 91
trays **18** 776
weaving **18** 771
wood **18** 768, *769*, 776–7
wood-carvings **18** 769–70
woodwork **18** 776–7*
see also SOUTH-EAST ASIA
Lao-tzu *see* LAOZI
Laozi **6** 625, 626
Lap, Geert **22** 884
Lapa (de Almeida), Querubim **19** 468; **30** 882
Lapacci, Bartolommeo, Bishop of Cortona **22** 801
Lapadula, Bruno **21** 422
La Pagode **12** 489
Lapai **23** 303
Laparelli, Francesco **18** 152; **20** 211; **21** 580; **31** 720
Lapaty, Mihail **26** 713
La Paz **4** 255, *255*, 260; **18** 777–8*
Academia de Bellas Artes *see* Escuela Superior de Bellas Artes
Academia de Dibujo y Pintura **4** 269
Academia Particular de Pintura **4** 269
Aduana Nacional **4** 260
Alcadía Municipal **4** 260
architecture **4** 259, 260, 267
Banco Central de Bolivia **4** 260
Caja Nacional de Seguro Social **4** 260
Casa Buitrago **4** *260*, 260
Casa del Mariscal Andrés de Santa Cruz *see* S Calixto College
Casa del Repositorio Nacional **4** 259
Casa Kyllman **4** 260
Casa Morales **4** 261
Casa Villaverde **4** 258
Colegio de Ciencias **4** 269
Colegio Militar **4** 260
ecclesiastical buildings
Cathedral **4** 259, 260, 267; **18** *778*
church of the Carmine **4** 266
convent of S Francisco **4** 267
La Merced **4** 259
Monastery of the Tercera Orden Franciscana **4** 259
S Calixto (1882) **4** 259
S Domingo **4** 258
S Francisco **4** 258
Escuela Popular de Dibujo Lineal **4** 269
Escuela Superior de Bellas Artes **4** 265, 269
Estación de Ferrocarril **4** 260
Hospital General **4** 260
Illimani residential block **4** 260
La Papelera **4** 260
La Recoleta **4** 259
Ministerio de Transportes y Comunicación **4** 260
Monument to the National Revolution **4** 260
museums
Casa Museo Núñez del Prado **4** 269
Museo Casa de Murillo **4** 268; **18** 778
Museo Costumbrista Juan de Vargas **4** 269
Museo del Litoral Boliviano **4** 269
Museo Nacional de Arqueología **4** 260, 268
Museo Nacional de Arqueología *see also* Museo Publico
Museo Nacional de Arte **4** 268; **13** 880; **18** 778
La Paz
museums—cont.
Museo Público **4** 268
see also Museo Nacional de Arqueología
Museo Sacro **4** 269
Museo Tambo Quirquincho **4** 268; **18** 778
Núñez del Arco collection **4** 269
Pinacoteca Nacional *see* Museo Nacional de Arte
painting **4** 261, 262, 264
Palacio de Diez de Medina **4** 258
Palacio de Gobierno **4** 259
Palacio Legislativo **4** 260
Plaza Hotel **4** 260
S Calixto College (1830s) **4** 259
S Teresa residential block **4** 260
Teatro Municipal **4** 259, 260
Universidad Boliviana Mayor de S Andrés **4** 260, 269
Escuela de Artes Plásticas **4** 270
La Paz, Manuel Marín de *see* MARÍN DE LA PAZ, MANUEL
La Pegna, Hyacinth **28** 18
La Peña **22** 335
La Peña, Arnau de *see* ARNAU DE LA PEÑA
Laperlier, Laurent **4** 338, 339; **9** 378; **18** 869
La Perrière, Guillaume de (1490-1553) **10** 174; **26** 261
Laperuta, Leopoldo **18** 778*; **22** 474
La Petraia, Villa Medicea **26** 242
Fountain of the Labyrinth **11** 342; **12** 569
frescoes **11** 678; **21** 26
gardens **12** *62*, 115
Lapeyrière, Maximillien, Comte de **24** 418
Lapi, Apollonio **5** 21
Lapi, Geri **16** 759
Lapiccola, Niccolò **18** 779*; **23** 173; **26** 809; **31** 72
Lapicida, Andrea **26** 707; **28** 649
Lapicida, Mikuláš **3** 223
Lapicque, Charles **2** 543; **11** 551, 644; **18** 779*; **26** 193
Lapidge, Samuel **26** 239
Lapidus, Morris **14** 788; **18** 779–80*
La Piedad de Ulldecona **29** 365
Lapierre, Francis **10** 275; **14** 854–7; **31** 682, 683
La Pileta **25** 477, 481
Lapin **8** 51
Lapin, Ivan **20** 147
Lapin, Leonhard **10** 538, 540; **18** 780*
Lapiņš, Gotlībs **12** 825
Lapis, Gaetano **4** 407; **6** 111; **18** 780–81*; **31** 341; **33** 455
lapis gagates *see* JET
lapis lazuli **14** 168; **24** XII2
historical and regional traditions
Afghanistan **1** 185, 850; **14** 168; **24** XII1
Ancient Near East **1** 873, *873*
Byzantine **9** 623; **12** 254
Central Asia, Eastern **6** 302
China **7** 89, 90, 91; **14** I2
Egypt, ancient **10** 28, 29, 38; **12** 246
France **11** *636*
Indian subcontinent **15** 564
Iran, ancient **15** 902; **33** *688*
Islamic **12** 253; **16** *543*
Italy **14** I1; **16** *747*
Mesopotamia **1** 850
Sumerian **31** *696*
uses
amulets **10** 38
beads **3** 441, 442
bowls **33** *688*
carvings **7** 91
ewers **11** *636*
headdresses **1** *873*
icons **9** 623

lapis lazuli
 uses—cont.
  inlays **31** *696*
  jewellery **1** *873*; **10** 29; **17** 529
  pietre dure **14** I1
  pigments **6** 302; **15** 548; **24** 790
  seals **16** *543*
  vases **16** *747*
Lapita culture **23** 710; **29** 50
 pottery **11** 67; **23** 726–8*, *727*; **25** 181; **29** 50; **31** 142, 890
Lapithos **8** *325*, 360, 365
Lapithos-Ayia Anastasia **8** 346
 coins **8** 332
 ivory-carvings **8** 350
 pottery **8** 346
 Tomb 2 **8** *347*
Lápiz **24** 452
La Placa, Pietro **32** 70
Laplagne, Guillaume **9** 768
La Planche, François de **1** 782; **11** 640; **23** 665; **30** 320, 321; **31** 227
Laplanche, Jean-Alexandre **4** 239; **8** 769
 works **8** *769*
La Planche, Raphaël de **11** 640
Lapland **11** *87*; **32** 513
Laplante, Eduardo **18** 781*
La Plata (Argentina)
 Museo Municipal de Bellas Artes **24** 570
 observatory **23** 341
La Plata (Bolivia) *see* SUCRE
Lapo **2** 480, 481; **24** 868, 870, 871
Lapo, Pagno di (1408-70) *see* PAGNO DI LAPO (PORTIGIANI)
Lapo di Bonaccorso **7** 338
Lapo di Corso **19** 673
Lapo di Pagno Portigiani (1448-1511) **23** 772
Lapo di Ricevuto **25** 724
La Pointe, Arnoult de *see* ARNOULT DE NIMÈGUE
La Poretta, Nicolò Sanuti, Conte di **3** 896
La Poretta, Nicolosa Sanuti, Contessa di **3** 896
La Porte, Charles Armand de, Duc de Mazarin *see* MAZARIN, CHARLES ARMAND DE LA PORTE, Duc de
La Porte, de, Canon **17** 672
Laporte, Gilbert **1** 783
La Porte, Henri Horace Roland de *see* ROLAND DE LA PORTE, HENRI HORACE
Laporte, John **21** 901
Laposky, Ben F. **7** 680
Lapostolet, Charles **11** 156
Lapotherie
 works **25** *802*
Lapoujade, Robert **27** 854
Lapp art *see* SAAMI ART
Lappas, Georgios **13** 355
Lappo, Osmo **18** 781*
Lappoli, Giovanni Antonio **18** 781*
Lappoli, Matteo **18** 781
Lapponia Jewellery Ltd **11** 109
Laprade, Albert **18** 782*; **23** 474
 collaboration **17** 451; **28** 464
 works **22** 128
Laprade, Cláudio de **18** 782–3*
 assistants **28** 731
 collaboration **27** 805
 groups and movements **17** 595
 works **7** 532; **18** *783*; **25** 301; **26** 253
Laprade, Pierre **5** 530; **11** 526; **18** 783*; **22** 92; **31** 145
Lapshin, Nikolay **27** 413
La Puná **18** 783–4*; **29** *136*
Lăpuşneanu, Alexandru, Prince **26** 721
Laquan Studio **22** 445
La Quemada **18** 784*; **21** *193*, *372*
 fortifications **21** 599
L'Aquila **16** *620*; **18** 784–6*
 Museo Nazionale d'Abruzzo **18** 785
 S Bernardino **7** 542
 S Maria di Collemaggio **18** *785*
La Quintinie, Jean-Baptiste de **6** 453; **11** 356; **12** 121; **23** 470
Laquy, Willem Joseph **4** 618; **14** 386
Lara, Clever **31** 756
Lara, Enrique Assad *see* ASSAD LARA, ENRIQUE
Lara, Eusebio **30** 872
Lara, Hernán González de *see* GONZÁLEZ DE LARA, HERNÁN
La Rábida monastery **29** 264
Larache **21** 585
La Ramada **29** 140
La Ramée Pertinchamp **31** 442
lararia *see under* SHRINES (i) (CULTS) → types
Lar Ban
 works **5** *247*
larch **33** 324
Larchant, St Mathurin **13** 39
Larche, Raoul (-François) **11** 629; **18** 786*; **29** 575
L'Archevêque, Pierre-Hubert **1** 105; **14** 79; **28** 461, 462; **29** 689; **30** 85
larch turpentine *see* VENICE TURPENTINE
larch-wood **14** *903*
Larco, Jorge **11** 281
Larco, Sebastiano **13** 728
Larco Herrera, Victor, Museo *see* LIMA → museums → Museo Nacional de la Cultura Peruana
Larco Hoyle, Rafael **8** 272; **24** 517; **27** 621
Lardera, Berto **18** 786–7*
Lardi, Vincenzo de' **31** 429
Lardier, F. **11** 291
Laredo (TX) **4** *82*
Laredo, Eladio **21** 82
Laredo, Juan Fernández de *see* FERNÁNDEZ DE LAREDO, JUAN
Laredo, Nuestra Señora de la Asunción **13** 111
Larée, Antoine **27** 239
Laren **1** 650; **18** 149; **21** 853; **26** 468
 painting **22** 850
 Singer Museum **22** 906
Laren school **20** 872; **22** 850; **23** 1
La Reynie, G. N. **20** 455
La Reynière, Laurent Grimod *see* GRIMOD DE LA REYNIÈRE, LAURENT
Largartero **21** 239
Large Cowper *Madonna see* NICCOLINI MADONNA
Large Kantharos in Athens, Painter of the **13** 533, *534*
large regular script *see* SCRIPTS → types → regular, large
large running script *see* SCRIPTS → types → runnning, large
large seal script *see under* SCRIPTS → types
Largillierre, Nicolas de **11** 537; **12** 205; **18** 787–90*
 assistants **26** 385
 collaboration **19** 123; **32** 358
 copies **18** 418
 groups and movements **27** 286
 patrons and collectors
  Académie Royale de Peinture et de Sculpture (Paris) **19** 24; **22** 86
  Aumale, Henri-Eugène-Philippe-Louis de Bourbon, Duc d' **23** 523
  Catherine II, Empress of Russia (*reg* 1762- 96) **8** 210
  Grimaldi (family; Monaco) **21** 830
Largillierre, Nicolas de
 patrons and collectors—cont.
  Hohenzollern, Henry, Prince of Prussia **14** 653
  Houssaye, (François-) Arsène **14** 802
  La Live de Jully, Ange-Laurent de **18** 660
  Titon, Maximilien **31** 56
  Titon du Tillet, Evrard **31** 56
  Vassal de Saint-Hubert, Jean-Antoine-Hubert **32** 74
 pupils **8** 787; **12** 60; **19** 140, 796; **22** 191; **23** 666; **26** 247
 reproductive prints by others **6** 549; **9** 296; **13** 898; **28** 178, 751
 teachers **13** 222
 works **11** 228, 405, 494, 539; **12** 357; **18** *788*, *789*; **24** 134, *134*
Larguía, Jonás **2** 396
Lari **1** 403
Lari, Antonio Maria **18** 790–91*; **24** 533; **28** 675
Lari, Yasmeen **15** 242; **17** 806; **18** 791*; **23** 799
Larice Crepu **10** 613
Larin, Alexandr D. **19** 13
La Rioja (Argentina) **2** 392, *393*, 394
La Rioja (Spain) **29** 290
Larionov, Mikhail (Fyodorovich) **12** 892; **18** 791–4*; **24** 850; **27** 392
 collaboration **18** 474
 exhibitions **3** 802; **23** 438
 groups and movements **12** 893; **28** 597
  Acmeism **1** 121
  Cubism **1** 73
  Cubo-Futurism **8** 251
  Donkey's Tail **9** 144–5; **22** 178
  Golden Fleece (*Zolotoye Runo*) **10** 680; **12** 870, 871
  Jack of Diamonds (Bubnovy Valet) **16** 817
  Neo-primitivism **22** 750
  Post-Impressionism **25** 356
  Rayism **26** 40–41
  Suprematism **30** 7
  Union of Youth **31** 583
  World of Art (Mir Iskusstva) **33** 379
 lithographs **19** 491
 paintings **18** *791*, *792*; **26** *41*; **27** *393*
 patrons and collectors **8** 10; **22** 135
 personal collection **19** 751
 productions **3** 119; **12** 894; **30** 686
 publications **29** 872
Larios, Mauricio Jiménez **10** 154
Laris Partiunu **10** 592
Larissa *see* NIMRUD
La Rive, Pierre-Louis de **18** 794*; **30** 125, 133; **31** 363
La Rivière, Abbé de **11** 574
La Rivière, Etienne de **1** 842
La Rivière, Louis de **19** 21, 267
Lark Hill (Hereford & Worcs) **10** 344
Larkin, Oliver **31** 673
Larkin, William **18** 795*
 attributions **9** *277*
 works **5** 835; **7** 814; **10** 247; **16** 823; **30** 554
Larkins, W. M. **19** 874
Larling (Norfolk) **2** 81
Larmandie, Léonce de, Comte **27** 639
Larmessin, Nicolas de (*fl* 1632) **18** 795
Larmessin, Nicolas de (i) (1632-94) **18** 795*
Larmessin, Nicolas de (ii) (*b c.* 1645-1725) **18** 795
Larmessin, Nicolas de (iii) (1684-1755) **11** 81; **18** 795*
Larmy, René-Marie **29** 348
Larnaca **8** 363, 366
 Hagios Lazaros **8** 358
Larnach Castle **23** 54, 66
larnakes see SARCOPHAGI → historical and regional traditions → Greece, ancient; Minoan; Mycenaean
Larne (Co. Antrim) **16** 28
 St Cedma's **16** 41
La Roche, Pierre de **18** 796*; **27** 279; **30** 68
La Roche, Raoul **19** 41
La Rochefoucauld, Antoine de, Comte **11** 75; **27** 639; **28** 423
La Rochefoucauld, François, Duc de **19** 300
La Rochefoucauld, François I, Duc de **20** 776
La Rochefoucauld, François VI, Duc de **20** 776
La Rochefoucauld Hours *see under* BOOKS OF HOURS → individual manuscripts
La Roche-Guyon **6** 55
Larochette, Jean Pierre **31** 661
 works **1** *146*
La Rocque, Antoine de **6** 473
Larocque, François-Antoine **22** 616
La Roldana *see* ROLDÁN, LUISA
La Romana **9** *114*, 116
 Escuela de Arte y Diseño **9** 119
Laroon, Marcellus **7** 784; **18** 146, 796–7*
La Roque, Antoine de **14** 692; **17** 684; **18** 796*
La Roque, Jean de **18** 796
La Rosa, Vincenzo **2** 879
Larose, Laliberté, Petrucci & Webb **22** 36
Larose, Ludger **11** 322
La Rottière, Jean-Siméon Rousseau de *see* ROUSSEAU DE LA ROTTIÈRE, JEAN-SIMÉON
Laroun, Marcellus **18** 146
Larousse **2** 733
Larpent, Sophus Edmé **23** 243
Larra Churriguera, José de **5** 784; **7** 287
Larra Churriguera, Manuel de **7** 287, 288
Larrad **29** 305
Larraidy, Robert **4** 391
Larraín, Emilio Rodríguez *see* RODRÍGUEZ LARRAÍN, EMILIO
Larraín, Pedro Murtinho *see* MURTINHO LARRAÍN, PEDRO
Larraín Bravo, Ricardo **6** 594
Larraín García-Moreno, Sergio **6** 594; **18** 797*
Larrandi, Master **31** 577
Larravide, Manuel **31** 754
Larraz, Julio **18** 797*, 835
Larrea, Baltasar de **29** 341
Larrea, Juan **24** 339; **29** 220
Larrea, Pedro de **19** 171
Larreur, Barthëlemey **29** 336, 341
Larreur, Juan Tomás **29** 336, 341
Larreur, Tangui **29** 336, 341
Larreur, Yves **29** 336, 341
Larrocha, José **2** 29
Larrtjinga
 works **1** *60*
Larsa **3** 12; **18** 797–8*; **21** *267*
 architecture **4** *771*; **21** 286, 291
 gold **1** 874
 sculpture **18** *798*; **21** 295
 terracottas **21** 552
 trade **21** 268
 ziggurat **33** 675, 676
Larsen, Christine *see* SWANE, CHRISTINE
Larsen, (Carl Frederik) Emanuel **18** 798–9*
Larsen, Helge **2** 766; **18** 799
Larsen, Henning (Gobel) **4** 417; **8** 729; **18** 799*; **30** 260
Larsen, Jack Lenor **31** 657
Larsen, Johannes **8** 735; **24** 549; **33** 595
Larsen, Karl (1897-1977) **19** 799; **27** 643
Larsen and Lewers **18** 799*
Larsen Stevns, Niels **18** 799–800*
Larson, Jean **32** 268
Larson, (Simon) Marcus **18** 800*; **30** 79
 works **30** *80*; **33** 697
Larsson, Anders **13** 668; **18** 801*; **30** 87; **31** 707
Larsson, Carl (Olof) (1853-1919) **18** 801–3*; **30** 79, 80, 81, 90, 114
 groups and movements **29** 774
 patrons and collectors **11** 851; **30** 730
 pupils **11** 142; **33** 186
 teachers **30** 275
 works **10** 563; **11** 476–7, *476*; **18** *802*; **29** 774; **30** *91*
Larter, Richard **2** 751; **18** 803*
Lartigue, Jacques-Henri (-Charles-Auguste) **18** 803*; **24** 671
 works **24** *672*
La Ruche *see* PARIS → La Ruche
La Rue, Jean-Baptiste de **29** 637
Larue, Jean-Denis **28** 524
Larue, Léon-André *see* MANSION
La Rue, Philibert-Benoît de **18** 804*; **24** 212
La Ruelle, Claude de **21** 151
Larwand Mosque **16** 166
La Sablière, Charles-Michel Trudaine de *see* TRUDAINE DE LA SABLIÈRE, CHARLES-MICHEL
La Sablonière, H. de Lussanet de *see* LUSSANET DE LA SABLONIÈRE, H. DE
Lasagna, Gian Pietro **21** 533; **32** 619
La Salette **28** 632
Lasalle, Antoine de **31** 374
La Salle, (Aimé-Charles-) Horace His de *see* HIS DE LA SALLE, (AIMÉ-CHARLES-) HORACE
Lasalle, Philippe de **11** 648; **18** 804–5*; **30** 548
 works **11** 646, *646*, 647; **19** 850; **26** 303
Lasana **29** 189
Lasansky, Mauricio **9** 310; **10** 397; **18** 805*; **20** 605
Las Arboledas, Plaza del Bebedero **12** 143
La Sarraz, St Antoine Chapel **30** 136
Las Bocas **18** 805–6*; **21** *193*, 237, *372*
Lascaris, Constantine **20** 350
Lascaris, Giovanni Giorgio *see* PYRGOTELES (*fl* before 1496; *d* 1531)
Lascaris, Zuan Zorzi *see* PYRGOTELES (*fl* before 1496; *d* 1531)
Lascaris de Castellar, Jean Paul **20** 216
Lascaut, Pierre **26** 778
Lascaux **2** 323; **11** *505*; **18** 806–7*; **25** *470*, 475, 476, 477, 479, 480, 481, 484, 485, 487, 650; **29** 422
 lamps **25** 491
 rock art **18** *807*
 tools **25** 494
 wall paintings **11** 528; **32** 802
Lascaux II **18** 806
Lascelles, Edward (1764-1814) **12** 742
Lascelles, Edward, 1st Earl of Harewood (*d* 1820) **5** 434; **31** 467
Lascelles, Edwin, 1st Baron Harewood **7** 171

Lascelles, Henry, 2nd Earl of Harewood **3** 79
Lascelles, Henry George Charles, 6th Earl of Harewood **4** 403
Lasciac, Antoine **9** 764
Lascio, Pedro di **24** 99
Las Condes **6** 594
Lascurain, Xavier García **32** 558
Lasdun, Denys (Louis) **11** 808; **18** 807–9*; **23** 134, 248; **30** 411
collaboration **22** 719
groups and movements **5** 56; **30** 411
works **2** 337; **5** 513; **10** 242; **19** 578; **30** 684
Lasekan, Akinola **23** 136, 138
Łasek Collegiate Church **25** 96
La Selva de Camp Church **29** 268
Lasem **15** 790
La Serena **6** *590*, 591; **18** 810*
Cathedral **6** 592
Museo de San Francisco **6** 601
La Serre, Puget de **18** 812
La Serreta de Alcoy **15** 60
lasers **14** 689; **18** 809*; **28** 204
conservation **7** 730
printing **25** 345
technical examination **30** 395
typography **31** 498
laser-scanning **26** 236
La Seu d'Urgell **26** 642
Cathedral **26** 581; **29** 263
La Seynie porcelain factory **19** 397
Las Flores **14** 829; **21** 200
Las Haldas **6** 523; **29** 159
Las Higueras **10** 779; **21** 226–7
Lashkar *see* GWALIOR
Lashkari Bazar **1** *186*, 207; **16** *105*, 168; **18** 810*
Centre Palace **16** 167
congregational mosque **16** 166
excavations **16** 550
houses **16** 154
iwans **16** 801
kiosk **18** 71
mausoleum of Ghiyat al-Din Muhammad **29** 825
North Palace **16** 167
palaces **16** 167; **23** 815
pottery **16** 407, 408
South Palace **16** 167, 168
paintings **16** 169, 253, 313
squinches **16** 169
stucco **29** 825
wall paintings **16** 530
Las Huacas **13** 310–11; **29** *136*, 142
La Sierra **29** 140
Lasinio, Carlo **18** 810–11*; **21** 416; **24** 855
works **13** 261; **24** 855, 860; **25** 623
Lasinio, Giovanni Paolo **18** 811; **24** 860
Lasisi, David **23** 736
Lasithi **21** 679
Lasius, Georg **13** 842; **29** 491
Laskar **15** 452
Laskarid (dynasty) **9** 559
Laskaris, Theodore I, Emperor of Byzantium *see* THEODORE I LASKARIS, Emperor of Byzantium
Laskaris, Theodoros II, Emperor of Byzantium *see* THEODOROS II LASKARIS, Emperor of Byzantium
Laske, Joseph **18** 449
Laske, Oskar **2** 797; **14** 33; **32** 446
Lasker-Schüler, Else **29** 872
Łaski, Jan **25** 135
Laskin **3** 889
Laskins, William **22** 375
Las Limas **21** 218
Las Lomitas **29** 202
Lasman, Pieter *see* LASTMAN, PIETER (PIETERSZ.)
Las Marismas del Guadalquivir, Alejandro María Aguado y Ramírez de Estemoz, Marqués de **8** 664; **18** 811*; **26** 722; **29** 353
Las Mercedes (La Cabaña) **29** *136*, *140*
metates **29** *144*
mounds **29** 140
sculpture **9** *679*, 679; **29** 143
stools **9** 679
Las Mesitas **27** 700
Las Monedas **25** 477, 484
Las Navas de Tolosa **16** 215
Las Navas de Tolosa Banner **16** 440
Lasne, Jean **11** 302, 550
Lasne, Michel **18** 811–12*; **20** 415
works **3** 399; **9** 388; **10** 144; **19** 790; **25** 833; **27** 562; **31** 305; **32** 718
Laso (de la Vega de los Ríos), Francisco **18** 812*
works **24** 508, *508*
Laso de la Vega, Pedro, Conde de Arcos *see* ARCOS, PEDRO LASO DE LA VEGA, 1st Conde de
Laso de la Vega de los Ríos, Francisco *see* LASO, FRANCISCO
La Spezia **16** *618*; **18** 812–13*
Laspi Museum **11** 244
Las Remojadas **26** 181
Lassalle-Bordes, Gustave **8** 645
Lassaulx, Johann Claudius von **12** 415; **15** 145; **18** 813*; **27** 335
Lassaulx, Otto van **31** 796
Lassaw, Ibram **1** 83, 772; **18** 813*; **31** 614
Lassay-les-Châteaux **3** 209
Lassels, Richard **13** 298, 299; **18** 814*
Lassen, Christian **1** 211
Lassen, Flemming **16** 827; **21** 821
Lassen, Mogens **8** 728
Lasse of Hungary **21** 524, 533
Lassner, J. **13** 812
Lassnig, Maria **18** 814*; **32** 447
Lassnitz Church **2** 799
Lasso, Francisco **29** 295
Lasso, Giulio **4** 412; **28** 657
Lassurance, Jean **18** 815*; **25** 80
Lassurance, Pierre, I **18** 815*
collaboration **20** 296
groups and movements **26** 492
patrons and collectors **2** 701
works **14** 789
Lassurance, Pierre, II **18** 815
Lassus, Bernard **12** 105
Lassus, J. (*fl* 1940s) **9** 528
Lassus, Jean-Baptiste (-Antoine) (1807-57) **18** 816*; **21** 608; **24** 157; **29** 609
assistants **1** 13
collaboration **4** 222; **12** 155, 312; **13** 824; **32** 594, 596
groups and movements **13** 203, 208
restorations **6** 494
works **11** 521; **24** 152; **25** 172
Last, Clifford **2** 753; **18** 64
Lastanosa (family) **20** 500
Lastanosa, Vicencio Juan de **1** 466; **18** 816–17*; **29** 353
Last Binder of Jean Grolier
works **4** *351*
Lasteyrie, Charles-Philibert de **19** 483; **20** 602; **25** 623
Lasteyrie, Ferdinand de **26** 44; **29** 514
Lasteyrie, Robert de **11** 675
Last Judgement, Master of the **13** 104; **19** 173; **30** 369
Lastman, Claes **18** 817
Lastman, Pieter (Pietersz.) **10** 158; **18** 227, 817–20*
assistants **22** 841; **26** 153
groups and movements **22** 842; **25** 556, 557
patrons and collectors **4** 614
Lastman, Pieter (Pietersz.)—cont.
pupils **19** 348; **26** 152, 175
works **14** 543; **18** *818*, *819*
Lastra, Severiano Sáinz de la *see* SÁINZ DE LA LASTRA, SEVERIANO
Lastra-Signa, Ospedale di Sant'Antonio **14** 781
Lastri, M. **13** 625
Lastricati, Alessandro **18** 820
Lastricati, Zanobi (di Bernardo) **18** 820*; **24** 756
Lasuén, Dionisio **27** 819
Las Vegas (NV) **18** 820–22*; **31** *587*
casinos **18** *821*, 821–2
Liberace Museum **18** 822
Nevada Institute for Contemporary Art **18** 822
Las Ventanas *see* PEÑOL DE JUCHIPILA
Las Victorias **21** 246
Las Villas, Manicanagua **8** 232
Las Viñas, Antonio de *see* WYNGAERDE, ANTHONIS VAN DEN
La Sylve-Bénite **5** 894
Laszczka, Konstanty **18** 822*
pupils **4** 41; **9** 394; **30** 204
works **25** 115
Łaszew Church **25** 96, *96*
Łaszkiewicz, Maria **25** 133
László, Alexander **22** 380
László, Fülöp Elek **18** 822*
Lat **32** 487
latā **15** 244*
Latacunga **9** *709*
Latakia **9** 655; **17** 500; **30** 178
Laodicea **26** *915*
Lataster, Ger(ard) **2** 545; **18** 822–3*; **22** 852, 854
latchets **15** 871
Late Antiquity **18** 823–6*
diptychs **18** *826*; **26** 862
iconography **18** 823–5; **26** 862–3, *863*
icons **18** *825*
manuscript illumination **26** 862, *863*
mosaics **26** 862; **27** 64
portraits **2** 836; **26** 862
relief sculpture **18** *824*
scripts **28** 305
sculpture **18** *824*; **29** 560
Late Cycladic period *see under* CYCLADIC → periods
Late Cypriot period *see under* CYPRUS, ANCIENT → periods
Late Gothic *see under* GOTHIC → styles
Late Helladic period *see under* HELLADIC → periods
Late Metz Group **5** 810
Late Minoan period *see under* MINOAN → periods
La Tène **18** 828*; **25** *470*, 533, 538; **30** *124*
metalwork **6** *153*
swords **6** 157
La Tène culture (*c*. 450-.*c* 50 BC) **6** 152, 154–8*; **16** 830; **18** 828*; **25** 533
bronze **6** *155*, *158*
flagons **6** *155*
metalwork **28** 325
openwork **6** *158*
pottery **25** *543*, 544
scabbards **2** 451; **18** 828
stone-carvings **6** *156*
swords **2** 451; **18** 828
vases **25** *543*
Late Period *see under* EGYPT, ANCIENT → period
Late Predynastic period *see under* EGYPT, ANCIENT → periods
lateral mouldings *see under* MOULDINGS → types
Later Chalukyas *see* CHALUKYAS OF KALYANA
Late Renaissance *see* MANNERISM
Later Gupta *see*:
ADITYASENA, Ruler
JIVITAGUPTA, Ruler
laterite *see under* CLAY → types
Later Ly *see* LY, LATER
Late Roman C pottery *see under* POTTERY → wares
Laterza **16** 735
Laterza Parodi, José **4** 141; **24** 98, 99
Late Shah Jahan Album *see under* ALBUMS → individual manuscripts
latesini ware *see under* POTTERY → wares
latex
moulds **6** 7
paints **23** 784
pigments **28** 338
secco paintings **28** 338
upholstery **31** 687
La Teya Riduni **15** 818
Latgale **18** 849
Latham, James **16** 13; **18** 829*
Latham, Jasper **18** 829*
Latham, John **17** 694; **18** 829–30*; **24** 407
Latham, R. G. **11** 738
Latham, William **28** 204
La Thangue, Henry Herbert **10** 254; **18** 830*; **19** 588; **23** 22
Lathem, Jacob van **13** 905; **19** 350
see also JOSEPH SEQUENCE, MASTER OF THE
Lathem, Lieven van *see* LIEVEN VAN LATHEM
lathes **33** 328
historical and regional traditions
Crete **21** 689
Egypt, ancient **9** 821
Indian subcontinent **6** 556
Italy **20** 90
Minoan **21** 689
uses
amber **1** 761
ceramics **6** 327, *328*
ivory **16** 799; **20** 90
jet **17** 516
La Thieulloye Abbey **5** 666
Lathom House (Lancs) **29** 835
lathomus **20** 559
La Tho Treasure **6** 432
Lathoud, Paul **6** 593
Lathrap, Donald **29** 219
Lathrino, Hagios Georgios **22** 700
Lathrop, Francis **20** 709
Lathrop, Jane *see* STANFORD, JANE
Lathrop Tondo, Master of the **7** 296; **20** 709*; **21** 461
Latif **15** 655
Latifi, Alma **15** 183
Latimer, Clive **8** 583; **10** 299
Latín, Miguel **20** 892
Latin 757, Master of **20** 709–10*
works **20** *710*
latina **15** 244*
Latin America
art history **33** 316–17*
columns
see also ESTÍPITES
craftsmen and artists **18** 830–31*
guidebooks **13** 811
periodicals **24** 434–5*
plaster **29** 841*
stucco **29** 841*
women artists **33** 316–17*
see also SOUTH AMERICA, PRE-COLUMBIAN
Latin Bible *see under* BIBLES → types
Latin crosses *see under* CROSSES → types
Latini, Bruno **1** 654; **10** 202
Latja, Béla, Architectureal Studio **18** 416
Latmos *see* HERAKLEIA UNDER LATMOS
Lato **8** 154
agora **13** 380
prytaneion **25** 675
La Toc **2** 148
La Tolfa group **6** 353; **10** 614
La Tolita **18** 835*; **29** *136*
figurines **18** 835
houses **29** *139*
masks **29** 208, 209
metalwork **29** 211, 212
mounds **29** 139
La Tolita culture **29** 155
Latopolis *see* ESNA
La Torte, Hans de **32** 709
La Tossa de Montbui, S María **26** 580
La Touche, David Digues de *see* DIGUES DE LA TOUCHE, DAVID
La Touche, Gaston **3** 156; **11** 547; **18** 835–6*
Latouche, Henri de (1785-1851; writer) **18** 836*
Latouche, Henri de Louis (*fl* 19th cent.; dealer) *see* LOUIS LATOUCHE, HENRI DE
Latour, Antoine Le Blond de *see* LE BLOND DE LATOUR, ANTOINE
La Tour, Etienne de **18** 836
La Tour, Georges de **18** 836–40*; **19** 696
attributions **20** 640
commentaries **32** 714
groups and movements **30** 456
methods **19** 353
patrons and collectors **5** 356; **26** 348
reproductive prints by others **3** 463
teachers **3** 634
works **11** 309, 403, 534, 661; **12** 289; **18** *838*, *839*, *840*; **19** 800; **25** 150
La Tour, Jacques **5** 564
La Tour, Louis Ovis de **12** 829
La Tour, Maurice-Quentin de **13** 301; **18** 841–3*, *842*; **24** 135
assistants **22** 725
methods **24** 242; **29** 863
patrons and collectors **5** 510; **7** 528; **9** 196; **13** 705
pupils **3** 101; **4** 616; **9** 365; **18** 575; **26** 50; **27** 170
reproductive prints by others **30** 24
sponsors **8** 372
works **9** 216, 224; **11** 408, 460, 539; **18** *842*; **24** 243, V
La Tour d'Aigues, Château **11** 514
La Tour d'Auvergne, Charles-Godefroy de, Prince de Turenne *see* TURENNE, CHARLES-GODEFROY, Prince de
La Tour d'Auvergne, Godefroy-Charles-Henri de, Prince de Turenne *see* TURENNE, GODEFROY-CHARLES-HENRI, Prince de
La Tour d'Auvergne, Louis-Henri de, Comte d'Evreux *see* EVREUX, LOUIS-HENRI DE LA TOUR D'AUVERGNE, Comte d'
La Tour-de-Mare, Notre-Dame-de-Jérusalem **6** 460
La Trappe **7** 348
La Traverse, Charles de **3** 204; **18** 843*; **24** 111
La Trémoille (family) **7** 407
La Trémouille, Marie-Anne de, Princesse des Ursins *see* URSINS, MARIE-ANNE DE LA TRÉMOUILLE, Princesse des
La Trinidad **24** *91*
Jesuit mission church **24** 95
Museum **24** 102
sculpture **24** 97
La Trinità di Cava Abbey **13** 98

Latrobe, Benjamin Henry **18** 843–5*
architecture **10** 850; **31** 591
arsenals **25** 4
banks **3** 175, *175*; **25** 268
cathedrals **3** 128; **7** 258; **10** *850*; **18** *845*
columns **11** 231; **23** 489, 545
country houses **30** 503
government buildings **5** 143; **7** 666; **10** 850; **13** 237, 238, *611*; **17** 468; **18** 887; **25** 267; **30** 761; **32** 892
prisons **17** 467
theatres **27** 349
waterworks **18** *844*; **24** 597; **26** 14; **27** 349
assistants **21** 615
collaboration **33** 195
groups and movements **13** 201, 608, 610; **22** 736, 741; **26** 735
patrons and collectors **24** 602
pupils **29** 769
teachers **7** 502
Latrobe, Henry S. B. **18** 845
Latron **24** 473
La Tronche, Fondation Hébert-d'Uckermann **14** 283
Lattanzi, Luciano **28** 394
Lattanzio da Rimini **3** 667; **5** 913; **18** 846*
Lattanzio di Giovanni **3** 858; **15** 60
Lattanzio di Niccolò **23** 89
latte **20** 411, *412*
latten plate *see under* ALLOYS → types
lattice work **18** 846*; **29** 311
Lattier, Christian **1** 432; **8** 22
works **8** *23*
lattimo *see under* GLASS → types
Lattré, Esaias de **17** 835
Lattré, Jean **12** 812
Lattres, Giovanni **11** 5
Latuada, Serviliano
works **4** *426*
Latvia **18** 846–51*, *847*
artists' biographies **18** 851
bronze
exhibitions **18** 851
houses **26** *383*
insignia **7** 178
painting
palaces **18** *848*
sculpture
Latz, Jean-Pierre **11** 595, 596, 626; **18** 853*; **23** 356
Lau, Marquis Du *see* DU LAU, Marquis
Laube, Eižens **18** 853–4*; **26** 383
Lauber, Diebolt **10** 724; **26** 563
Lauber, László **18** 854*
Lauber & Nyiri **18** 854*
L'Aubespine-Villeroy (family) *see* AUBESPINE-VILLEROY, L' (FAMILY)
Laubisch and Hirth **4** 721
Laubscher, Erik **29** 108
Laubser, Maggie **18** 854*; **29** 108
laubwerk **18** 854*
Lauch, Balthasar **12** 444
Lauch, Christoph **19** 336, 337
Laucheron, Prawat **20** 609
Lau Church **13** 119
Laud, William, Archbishop of Canterbury **15** 594; **18** 854–5*
architecture **23** 687
collections **21** 264
manuscripts **15** 741; **16** 553
paintings **9** 482
Lauda, Jan **3** 391; **8** 387
Laude, Andrea de *see* ANDREA DE LAUDE
Laude, Jean **24** 145
Lauder, Alexander **19** 252
Lauder, Charles James **18** 855
Lauder, James Eckford **18** 855, 856*
Lauder, James Thompson **18** 855*
Lauder, Robert Scott **9** 725; **18** 855–6*; **20** 33; **28** 237, 275
pupils **14** 447; **20** 34; **23** 475; **24** 569
works **11** *431*; **18** *856*; **28** 237, 238
Lauderdale, John Maitland, Duke of *see* MAITLAND, JOHN, 2nd Earl and 1st Duke of Lauderdale
Lauder Old Kirk (Borders) **28** 227
Laudesberg, Herrad of *see* HERRAD OF LAUDESBERG
Laud Machzor *see under* MACHZORS → individual manuscripts
Laudonnière, René de **14** 855
Lauenburg, Heinrich **18** 208
Lauenstein Church **28** 194
Lauenstein glass factory **12** 440
Lauer, Jean-Philippe **10** 81; **27** 811
Lauer, Philippe **2** 592; **18** 856–7*
Lauermann, Josef **25** 445
Laufberger, Ferdinand **18** 129
Laufen, Master of **2** 792
Laufer, Susan **23** 50
Lauffer, Caspar Gottlieb **20** 923; **22** 274; **32** 392
Lauffer, Emil **4** 887
Laugerie-Basse **25** 492, 493
Laugerie-Haute **25** 493
Laughlan Island **24** *64*, 81
Laughlin, Clarence John **18** 857*; **23** 32
Laughlin, Homer **18** 857*; **26** 287; **31** 636, 639
Laughlin, Shakespeare **18** 857
Laughlin Brothers **18** 857
Laughton, Charles **7** 483; **26** 222
Laughton, Elsa *see* LANCHESTER, ELSA
Laugier, Marc-Antoine **11** 515, 518; **18** 858*; **27** 237
groups and movements **22** 734
works **2** 358; **23** 489; **26** 12; **31** 297, 713
Lauingen, St Martin **12** 455
Laukika calendar *see under* INDIAN SUBCONTINENT → calendars → Saptarshi
Laulin, Mikhail S. **27** 428
Laumet de La Mothe Cadillac, Antoine *see* LA MOTHE CADILLAC, ANTOINE LAUMET DE
Launay, Jean de *see* JEAN DE LAUNAY
Launay, Nicolas de (1647-1727) **3** 122; **7** 422; **9** 469; **11** 618, 625; **12** 832
Launay, Nicolas de (1739-92) **11** 368; **18** 858*; **19** 144; **22** 88; **25** 895
Launay, Robert de **12** 336; **18** 635, 858*; **21** 643; **22** 88
Launceston (Tasmania) **2** *736*, 760
Launceston Castle (Cornwall; UK) **6** *55*, 55; **9** 144
Launggyet **2** *281*
shrine **2** *282*
La Unión de Guapiles
metates **29** *142*
Launitz, Eduard Schmidt von der **11** 813
Launitz, Robert E. **8** 124
Launoy, Jean de **27** 882
Laur, Josef **12** 416
Laura, Filippo **4** 609
Laura, Maria **10** 146
Laura Ashley Ltd **32** 790
Laura Caves **1** 41, 61
rock art **1** *41*
Lauragais, Comte de **3** 523; **14** 808
Laura Gonzaga, Duchess of Mantua **2** 610
Laurana, Francesco **11** 556; **18** 859–60*; **28** 656
attributions **11** 896
collaboration **24** 782
Laurana, Francesco—cont.
patrons and collectors **2** 114, 276; **13** 79; **31** 843
pupils **4** 546
works **11** 896; **16** 691; **18** *859*, *860*
Laurana, Luciano **18** 861–2*; **31** 742, 745
assistants **3** 253
collaboration **25** 216
patrons and collectors **12** 906; **16** 630; **22** 13
works **1** 556; **2** 339; **11** 688; **18** *861*; **29** 521; **31** 742, *743*, 744, 745
Laurati *see* LORENZETTI
Lauren, Ralph **33** 15
Laurenberg, Sigismund Seege von **26** 383
Laurence, Luke *see* CROSS, PETER
Laurence, Samuel **7** 709
Laurence Vitraerius **10** 315
Laurencin, Marie **18** 862–3*; **19** 80; **23** 694; **32** 327
collaboration **11** 525
dealers **27** 163
groups and movements **8** 436; **20** 431; **25** 747; **29** 899
Laurens, Henri **11** 568, 569; **18** 863–4*; **24** 144
assistants **7** 555
dealers **17** 725; **27** 162
groups and movements **8** 240, 243, 246; **11** 568; **25** 741; **27** 307
patrons and collectors **19** 66; **20** 203; **23** 169; **32** 568
productions **8** 850
pupils **5** 26; **7** 645; **19** 523
works **18** *863*; **25** 626; **29** 576; **30** 488
Laurens, Jean-Paul **14** 588; **18** 864–6*
pupils
Baca Flor, Carlos **3** 12
Bell, George (Henry Frederick) **3** 628
Bergh, (Sven) Richard **3** 776
Boggio, Emilio **4** 232
Boussingault, Jean-Louis **4** 588
Brandt, Federico **4** 670
Bunny, Rupert (Charles Wulsten) **5** 175
Carneiro, António Teixeira **5** 781
Collier, John **7** 569
Czajkowski, Józef **8** 370
Czigány, Dezső **8** 429
Dărăscu, Nicolae **8** 521
Dunoyer de Segonzac, André (Albert Maris) **9** 396
Flameng, François **11** 156
Gagnon, Clarence (Alphonse) **11** 901
Herter, Albert **31** 659
Jackson, A(lexander) Y(oung) **16** 818
Lartigue, Jacques-Henri (-Charles-Auguste) **18** 803
Lebourg, Albert-Charles **19** 17
Le Fauconnier, Henri **19** 64
Mainssieux, Lucien **20** 126
Martin, Henri (-Jean-Guillaume) (1860-1943) **20** 488
Michelena, Arturo **21** 462; **32** 174
Moreau, Luc-Albert **22** 92
Mucha, Alphonse **22** 251
Pór, Bertalan **25** 245
Prendergast, Maurice (Brazil) **25** 552
Puy, Jean **25** 752
Ressu, Camil **26** 245
Rojas, Cristóbal (*b* 1858) **32** 174
Roy, Pierre (1880-1950) **27** 280
Salas, Tito **32** 174
Shevchenko, Aleksandr (Vasil'yevich) **28** 597
Laurens, Jean-Paul
pupils—cont.
Sousa, Aurélia de **29** 100
Steinhardt, Jacob **29** 609
Steriadi, Jean Al(ex) **29** 638
Taiheiyō Gakai (Pacific Painting Society) **17** 204
Tanner, Henry Ossawa **30** 297
Viana, Eduardo (Afonso) **32** 400
Yasui, Sōtarō **33** 508
teachers **7** 529
works **12** 830; **18** *865*
Laurens, Paul-Albert **3** 88; **10** 435
Laurent **1** 653
Laurent, André **18** 866*
Laurent, Ernest (Joseph) **3** 785; **18** 866–7*
works **18** *866*
Laurent, Girard **11** 640
Laurent, Henri **11** 641; **12** 828
Laurent, Jean-Antoine **4** 303, 305; **18** 867*; **31** 374
Laurent, Juan **18** 867*; **20** 503
Laurent, Michel **22** 36
Laurent, Pierre (1739-1809) **31** 374
Laurent, Pierre (*fl* 1920s) **27** 322
Laurent, Robert **18** 868*; **31** 613; **33** 343
Laurent de Maech **17** 702
Laurent de Premierfait **4** 196
Laurenti, Tommaso **18** 689
Laurentian Library *see under* FLORENCE → ecclesiastical buildings → S Lorenzo
Laurentii *see* LORENZETTI
Laurentii, Lucas **9** 304; **18** 868, 869
Laurentini **16** 748
Laurentius (family) **7** 921, 922; **18** 868–9*; **26** 680
Laurentius (*fl* 1162) **7** 922; **18** 868
Laurentius, Cosmas **7** 920; **18** 868, 869
works **7** *920*
Laurentius, Jacobus **7** 920, 922; **18** 868–9
works **7** *920*
Laurentius de Welize **25** 434
Laurent-Richard **9** 424; **11** 663; **18** 869*
Laurenzano, Aurora Sanseverino, Duchessa di **9** 119; **20** 842
Laurenzano, Niccolò Gaetani, Duca di **9** 119; **27** 201; **32** 580
Laurenziano, Giacomo **25** 257
Laurenziano Codex *see under* CODICES → individual manuscripts
Laureti, Tommaso **18** 869–70*; **26** 770
patrons and collectors **13** 628; **24** 398
reproductive prints by others **30** 803
works **1** 595; **12** 569; **15** 137
Lauréus, Alexander **11** 95; **18** 870*
Laureys, Felix **27** 551
Lauri **6** 440
Lauri, Balthasar **5** 815; **18** 870; **23** 191
Lauri, Filippo **18** 870–71*
collaboration **7** 509; **9** 376, 377; **20** 431
patrons and collectors **6** 129; **7** 418; **16** 82
teachers **5** 815
works **18** *871*
Lauri, Francesco **5** 815; **18** 870
Laurie, Robert **9** 506; **25** 626
Laurie & Whittle **8** 217
Laurin factory **6** 462
Laurinus, Marcus **12** 885
Laurion **13** 372, 568, 570; **30** 770
Lauritzen, Vilhelm (Theodor) **18** 872*
Lauriya Nandangarh **15** *261*, *279*, 423, 453; **18** 872*
Lauron, Marcellus **18** 796
Lauro Padovano **2** 166; **18** 872*; **27** 807
attributions **12** 171
collaboration **3** 667
patrons and collectors **27** 807
works **2** *166*
Laus *see* LENS
Lausanne **18** 873–5*; **26** *908*; **30** *124*
Cathedral of Notre-Dame **9** 672; **13** 41; **18** 874–5*; **30** 125
choir **14** *518*
choir-stalls **7** 191; **30** 136
collections **30** 154
misericords **21** 725
Montfalcon Portal **18** *875*
Painted Portal **18** 874*
sculpture **12** 626; **25** 176; **30** 136
stained glass **29** 511; **30** 130
wall paintings **7** 275
Château de Beaulieu **2** 515
Ecole Cantonale d'Art de Lausanne **30** 156
Galeries du Commerce **30** 885
glass **27** 74
Hôpital de Notre-Dame **30** 127
houses **30** 127
International Centre for Ancient and Modern Tapestry **30** 329, 331
Musée Cantonal des Beaux-Arts **2** 701; **5** 509
Musée Olympique **18** 874
sculpture **30** 136
Théâtre Municipal **3** 76
Lauschmann, Jan **24** 676
Lausell **10** 472
Lausitz culture **21** 551
Lausitz Lodge **2** 480; **12** 209
Laus Julia Corinthiensis *see under* CORINTH
Laussel **11** *505*; **18** 875–6*; **25** *470*, 485
Laut, Carl Gottlob **2** 127
Lautenbach **12** 364
Lautensack, Hanns (Sebald) **18** 876–7*
groups and movements **8** 514
patrons and collectors **10** 531; **13** 908; **33** 271
teachers **14** 837
works **2** 794; **10** 550; **18** 706, *876*; **23** 310; **25** 606
Lautensack, Heinrich **18** 876
Lautensack, Paul **18** 876
Lautenschläger, Karl **30** 685
Lauterbach, Alfred **25** 143
Lauterbach, Heinrich **25** 839
Lauterbach, Johann Balthasar **18** 242, 877*; **33** 53, 292, 293
works **33** *54*
Lauterbach Church **19** 815
Lauterbourg, Philippe Jacques de *see* LOUTHERBOURG, PHILIPPE JACQUES DE
Lauters, Paulus **3** 884; **18** 877–8*; **29** 781; **31** 884
Lauterwasser, Siegfried **29** 608
Lauth, Charles **28** 524
Lautier, Guilherme **25** 814
Lautman, G. **1** 810; **22** 895
Lautréamont, Comte de **8** 466
Lauw Church **13** 110
Lauweriks, J(ohannes) L(udovicus) Mathieu **3** 431; **18** 878*; **22** 829, 874
groups and movements **22** 875; **23** 120
teachers **8** 298
works **14** 31; **22** 860
Lauwers, Balthasar *see* LAURI, BALTHASAR
Lauwers, Conrad **11** 807; **18** 879*
Lauwers, Jacobus **3** 212
Lauwers, Nicolaes **18** 878–9*; **24** 890; **28** 904
Lauzet, A. M. **22** 29
La Vache **25** 492

Lava glass *see under* GLASS → types
Lavagno, Vago di *see* VAGO DI LAVAGNO
Laval, Charles 12 191
Laval, Eugène 11 359
Laval, Jean de *see* JEAN DE LAVAL
Laval, Jeanne de, Duchess of Anjou *see* JOANNA OF LAVAL, Duchess of Anjou
Laval, Louis de *see* LOUIS DE LAVAL
Lavallaye, J. 3 619
Lavallée, Etienne de *see* LAVALLÉE-POUSSIN, ETIENNE DE
La Vallée, Jean De *see* DE LA VALLÉE, JEAN
La Vallée, Simon De *see* DE LA VALLÉE, SIMON
Lavallée-Poussin, Etienne de 18 879*
reproductions in tapestry 3 461
La Vallière, Louis-César de la Baume Le Blanc, Duc de 3 476; 18 880*
La Vallière, Louise de 21 *641*
La Valltorta 29 365
Lavaña, Juan Baptista 30 417
Lavapuri *see* LOPBURI
Lavardin, St Genest 26 599
Lavater, Heinrich 33 737
Lavater, Johann Kaspar 18 880*; 24 661; 30 125, 132
personal collection 2 832; 31 342
works 5 758
illustrated 7 183; 11 860; 28 72
Lavau, André 2 25; 30 238
Lavau, Claude de 19 238
Lavaur, St Alain 4 780
La Vega 9 *114*, 116
Lavega, Francesco 5 650
Laveille, Joseph 27 565
L'Avenant, Jean 5 208; 31 448
lavender oil *see under* OILS → types
Lavenham (Suffolk), SS Peter and Paul 5 319; 10 359; 13 55; 24 576; 28 293
Lavenier, Jean 2 860
Lavenson, Alma 13 710
La Venta 18 881*; 21 *193*, 196, *372*; 23 416–17, 418
Altar 4 1 700, *700*
Altar 5 1 700
architecture 21 209
Ballcourt 3 117
colossal heads 21 219
crosses 21 184
Great Pyramid 30 448
jade 21 242; 22 519
mirrors 21 718
mosaics 21 254
pyramid 25 764
sarcophagus 27 832, *832*
sculpture 18 *881*; 21 218, 219
stelae 23 417
Stele 1 29 619
Stele 2 29 619
Stele 3 29 619
tombs 31 *117*, 118
Laver, Augustus 11 836; 13 203; 23 632; 31 242
La Verna, Chiesa della Stimmate altarpiece 26 *445*
Laverrière, Alphonse 18 874
Lavers, Barraud & Westlake 8 583; 18 881–2*; 29 507
Lavers, Nathaniel Wood 18 881
Lavers & Barraud 5 266; 18 882
Laverstock (Wilts) 10 *225*, 302; 14 545; 18 882*
Lavery, John 3 537; 16 40, 42; 18 882–3*
groups and movements 10 254; 12 779; 19 891
patrons and collectors 16 36, 42
works 9 290, *290*; 16 17; 29 426
Laves, Georg 18 883
Laves, Georg Ludwig Friedrich 6 138; 14 141; 18 883*; 20 869
Laves beams *see under* BEAMS → types
Laviada, Manuel Alvarez 29 295
La Victoire 18 745
La Vid, Monastery of Nuestra Señora de la Vid 29 265
Lavie, Raffie 16 567; 18 883*; 31 747
Lavieille, Eugène 8 539
Lavier, Bertrand 11 553; 18 884*
La Vigne, Antoine de *see* WYNGAERDE, ANTHONIS VAN DEN
Lavigne, Paul Texier *see* TEXIER LAVIGNE, PAUL
Laville, Lionel 2 152
La Villeglé, Jacques Mahé de 8 608; 11 551; 14 52; 23 260
works 23 *260*
Laville-Lerou(l)x, Marie-Guillemine de *see* BENOIST, MARIE-GUILLEMINE
Lavillette, Johann Albrecht 12 462
Lavin, Irving 5 760
Laviña, Matías 24 225
Lavinium 27 9
Lavinsky, Anton 7 769; 32 661
La Virgen Blanca, Master of 13 104; 19 173
works 13 *105*
Laviron, Gabriel 26 53
Lavirotte, Jules (Marie Aimé) 2 564; 8 30; 11 526; 18 884*; 24 128
works 4 48
lavis process *see* WASH MANNER
Lavji Nasarvanji Wadia 4 288
La Voce 11 190
Lavoisier, Antoine-Laurent de 8 *556*
Lavoisier, Marie-Anne Pierette de 8 *556*
La Volpe, Alessandro 28 318
Lavonen, (Antti) Ahti 18 884*
Lavonen, Maija 11 101
Lavongai 24 85
Lavoûte-Chilhac, Sainte-Croix 9 152; 26 641
lavra 18 884*
Lavreince, Nicolas *see* LAFRENSEN, NICOLAS
Lavrenko, Boris 28 918
Lavrenov, Tzanko 18 885*; 25 51
Lavrenov, Tzanko, Museum *see under* PLOVDIV
Lavrent'yev, Zosim 27 434
La Vrillière, Marquise de 8 589
La Vrillière, Louis Phélypeaux de 18 885*
architecture 20 289
collections 11 662
paintings 11 357; 13 786; 20 374; 25 390; 26 198; 31 438
La Vrillière, Phélypeaux de, Archbishop of Bourges 5 167
Lavriv 31 557
St Onufrios 25 344; 31 550, 557
Lavrov *see* LAVRIV
Lavy, Amadeo (Domenico Sotero) 18 885–6*
Lavy, Carlo Michele 18 885
Lavy, (Carlo Domenico) Lorenzo 18 885
Law, Benjamin 2 752
Law, Bob 18 886*; 27 563; 28 804
Law, Jean (*fl* 1756-77) 25 211
Law, John (*fl c.* 1700) 11 881
Law, William 19 357
Law-Code Stele *see* CODE OF HAMMURABI
law courts 13 236; 18 886–90*
Australia 18 887, 888
England 18 886–7, *888*; 29 *766*
France 4 *867*; 9 *337*; 18 887–8
Greece, ancient 13 381
Hong Kong 18 890
law courts—cont.
Indian subcontinent 18 *889*, 889; 20 *53*
South Africa 18 887
United States of America 18 887, 888
Wales 5 *731*
see also COURT-HOUSES
Lawford, Frederick 14 748*
Lawford, H. 6 391
Lawford, St Mary 4 779
Lawford & Heneker 14 748
Lawler, Louise 7 686; 18 890*
Lawlor, John 17 639
lawns 12 109, 121, 122
lawns, decorative *see* COMPARTIMENTS À L'ANGLAISE
Lawrence (KS; USA), Ed Ruhe Collection 20 86
Lawrence (MA; USA), Washington Mills 21 601
Lawrence, Amos 8 843
Lawrence, Andrew *see* LAURENT, ANDRÉ
Lawrence, Cyrus J. 19 756
Lawrence, D. H. 10 482, 486
Lawrence, Henry C. 24 890; 29 515
Lawrence, Jacob 1 443; 4 109; 23 48
Lawrence, James (*fl* 1875) 29 870
Lawrence, James C. (*fl* 1794) 23 38
Lawrence, Simon 25 628
Lawrence, Thomas 3 373; 4 823; 18 890–95*; 19 620; 25 283
assistants 27 226
attributions 1 496
collaboration 8 576
dealing 14 145
drawings 11 789
groups and movements 26 740
methods 24 799; 25 279, 281
patrons and collectors
Angerstein, John Julius 2 51
Bankes, Henry 3 179
Baring, Francis (1740-1810) 3 239
Beisteguy y Benítez, Carlos de 3 522
Berry, Caroline de Bourbon, Duchesse de 4 556
Beurnonville, Etienne-Edmond Martin, Baron de 3 890
Buckner, Richard 5 78
George III, King of Great Britain (*reg* 1760-1820) 14 144
George IV, King of Great Britain (*reg* 1820-30) 14 146
Groult, Camille 13 705
Guinness, Edward (Cecil), 1st Earl of Iveagh 13 836
Huntington, Henry E(dwards) 15 29
Knight, Richard Payne 18 150
Lázaro Galdiano, José 18 900
Leopold I, King of Belgium (*reg* 1831-65) 7 490
Locke, William (1732-1810) 19 531
Rushout, John, 2nd Baron Northwick 27 350
Seymour-Conway, Richard, 4th Marquess of Hertford 28 527
Society of Dilettanti 28 924
personal collection 8 901; 10 366; 30 727
drawings 3 184; 9 229, 755; 10 505; 18 641; 23 634, 690, 777; 33 154, 345
marks 20 446
modelli 12 577; 21 770
mounts 22 236
paintings 14 278
prints 25 631
portraits 14 *147*
pupils 10 645; 14 178; 15 32; 19 285; 21 149
Lawrence, Thomas—cont.
reproductive prints by others 2 234; 4 845; 8 69; 9 148; 14 280; 16 820; 18 149; 19 284; 25 619; 26 473; 28 25, 693; 31 465; 32 856
works 10 249; 11 432; 18 *891*, *892*, *893*, *894*; 32 778
Lawrence Castle (Devon) *see* HALDON BELVEDERE
Lawrence Street porcelain factory 26 500
Lawrie, John 31 466
Lawson, Alexander 33 216
Lawson, Clemclem 31 73
Lawson, Ernest 18 895–6*
groups and movements 10 108; 23 47; 31 605
patrons and collectors 24 638
teachers 31 487
Lawson, G. A. 19 505
Lawson, Robert Arthur 18 896*; 23 54
Lawson Balfour, J. *see* BALFOUR, J. LAWSON
Lawton, James 18 896*
Lax, Robert 7 699
Laxenburg
Blauer Hof 4 663
Franzensburg 2 785, 806, 813; 8 502; 13 200
Haus der Laune 2 808
parish church
pulpit 29 *760*
Layard, Austen Henry 2 576; 3 418; 6 100; 18 896–7*
collections 16 769
excavations 1 895; 21 310
Assur 2 636
Babylon 3 9
Nimrud 1 867, 891, 892; 2 643; 23 148; 30 187
Central Palace of Tilgath-pileser III 21 288, 299; 23 151
Ninurta Temple 21 287; 23 151
North-west Palace of Assurnasirpal II 21 297
South-west Palace of Esarhaddon 21 301
Nineveh 1 895; 2 642; 21 300; 23 152, 154
Nippur 23 158
groups and movements 2 642
personal collection 21 825; 22 102
Layard, G(eorge) S(omes) 18 897*
Laybourne Smith, Louis *see* SMITH, LOUIS LAYBOURNE
Laycock 26 18
Layens, Matheus de *see* MATHEUS DE LAYENS
Layer Marney (Essex)
gate-house 6 59
hall 4 771
St Mary the Virgin 10 261; 30 502
layette baskets *see under* BASKETS → types
lay figures 18 *898*, 898–9*
laying in *see* PAINTING → techniques → dead colouring
laymen *see* LAY FIGURES
Layn, Peter ter 30 531
Laynberger, Simon *see* LAINBERGER, SIMON
Layne, Judy 2 152
Layos 9 596
layouts 31 495
Layraud, Joseph 11 156
Läys, Jean-Pierre 27 563
Layton, Robert 1 68
Lázár, István 14 885
Lazara, de (family) 11 16
Lazara, Giovanni de 18 756
Lazarea Palace 14 885
Lazarev, Viktor (Nikitich) 1 685; 18 899*; 27 444
Lazarević, Stephen, Prince of Serbia *see* STEPHEN, Prince of Serbia
Lazar I, Prince of Serbia (*reg* 1371-89) 22 79; 28 456
Lazaridis, Stefanos 30 687
Lázaro Galdiano, José 18 899–900*; 29 354
Lázaro Galdiano, Museo *see under* MADRID → museums
Lazarov, Ivan 5 156; 18 900*
Lazarov, Nikola 5 149
Lazarroni Andino, Dante 14 715
Lazarus and Tomlin 15 693
Lazcano Castle 13 634; 29 316
Lazellas 10 782
Lazeski, Borko 19 885
Lazi, Adolf 17 878
Lazius, Wolfgang 13 908; 18 877; 19 662; 32 432
Lazo, Agustín 18 900*; 21 388
Lázói, János 1 531; 14 885
Lazosky, Daniel 23 632
Lazrak, Aziz 22 128
lazurite 24 790
Lazzara, Leone de *see* LEONE DE LAZZARA
Lazzari, Dionisio 18 900–901*; 22 477; 32 580
Lazzari, Giacinto 18 900
Lazzari, Jacopo 16 747; 18 900*; 22 477
Lazzari, Ottaviano 18 900
Lazzarini, Antonio 9 47
Lazzarini, Elisabetta 18 901
Lazzarini, Giovanni 23 259
Lazzarini, Gregorio 18 901*; 32 194, 196
patrons and collectors 5 178; 7 779; 27 521
personal collection 8 209
pupils 9 47; 30 855
LC *see* WASHINGTON (DC) → Library of Congress
L.C.C. *see* LONDON COUNTY COUNCIL
Lchashen *see* LTJASHEN
L.Cm., Master *see* L.CZ., MASTER
L.Cz., Master 10 383; 20 800–801*; 25 632
L.D., Master *see* DAVENT, LÉON
L.D. Institute of Indology *see under* AHMABAD
Le, Earlier *see* EARLIER LE
Lea, Broom & Sons 18 30
Lea, Thomas 18 30
Leach *see* PURSAT
Leach, Bernard (Howell) 17 265; 18 344, 901–2*; 31 134
assistants 14 465
collaboration 6 63
forgeries by others 11 307
groups and movements 2 571; 4 110; 10 314; 21 634; 27 563
patrons and collectors 23 371
pupils 5 730; 10 315; 16 888; 25 39
teachers 23 367
works 10 314
Leach, David 10 315; 18 901
Leach, Eric 7 435
Leach, John 14 736
Leach Pottery 18 901; 27 563
lead 18 902–3*
alloys
copper 4 681, 849–54; 17 318; 29 211
silver 17 318
tin 17 318; 21 319; 24 578, 809
see also PEWTER
historical and regional traditions
Africa 1 287
Austria 21 *314*
Byzantine 9 *637*
Central Asia, Western 6 257
China 6 872, 882, 886, 888; 7 81, 100, 632
Egypt 16 415
Egypt, ancient 10 46; 18 902

lead
historical and regional traditions—cont.
England 10 264, 338; 11 253; 18 *903*; 31 *255*
Etruscan 10 624
France 1 *133*; 11 253, 623
Germany 25 *22*
Greece, ancient 13 568; 22 160
Iran, ancient 15 918
Iraq 16 399
Ireland 16 28
Islamic 16 257, 363, 395, 399, 415, 420, 427
Italy 1 *35*; 10 624; 16 743
Japan 17 242, 247–9, *248*, 277, 318, 370, 385, 386
Mesopotamia 18 902; 21 303, 304
North Africa 16 427
Ottoman 16 420
Portugal 25 309
Prehistoric art 25 542
Rome, ancient 27 10
South America, Pre-Columbian 29 211
Spain 16 393
Syria 16 415
Syria-Palestine 21 *331*
technical examination 30 400, 408
techniques
embossing 10 177
uses
architecture 20 560
armatures 18 902
busts 21 *314*
coins 17 370
dyeing 30 559
figurines 21 *331*
fonts (baptismal) 11 253*, 623; 18 902
glass 7 81; 12 781; 17 385, 386
glazes 6 326, 328, 329, 333; 30 874
Central Asia, Western 6 257
China 6 872, 882, 886, 887, 888
Egypt, ancient 10 46
England 10 306
Ireland 16 28
Islamic 16 395, 399, 415, 420, 427
Japan 17 242, 247–9
Portugal 25 309
medals 20 917
monuments 18 *903*
mosaics 13 556, 565; 22 155, 160
paint tubes 23 787
pastiglia 24 248
photography 24 658
pigments 7 632; 24 798–9*
pilgrim badges 18 902; 24 809
plaquettes 1 *35*; 18 902; 25 19, *22*
prints 17 277
roofs 18 902; 27 131
sculpture 1 *133*; 10 264; 18 902–3; 27 10
seals 9 *637*
soldering 7 100; 21 325
stained glass 29 499
toys 31 *255*
windows 16 257
writing 20 328
lead, black *see* GRAPHITE
lead, red *see* RED LEAD
lead, white *see* WHITE LEAD
Leadbeater, Charles Webster 30 710
Leadbetter, John 13 696
Leadbetter, Stiff 14 163
lead chromate 7 241; 24 799
Leader, Benjamin Williams 6 519; 18 903*
lead-glazed ware *see under* POTTERY → wares
lead monoxide 24 798–9
lead nitrate 30 558
lead oxides 6 872; 10 55, 316; 12 439
leadpoints *see under* DRAWINGS → forms
lead salts 32 1
lead sulphate 30 558
lead-tin yellow *see under* PIGMENTS → types
Leaf, June 11 729
leaf and dart *see under* MOULDINGS → types
leaf frames *see under* FRAMES → types
Leafless Group 23 145, 146
Leaf-pattern Book (Munich, Bayer. Nmus., 3604) 4 186, *187*, 187
Leagros group 13 *480*, 511, *511*; 32 27, 52–3*
League of XI 12 394
Leahy, Edward Daniel 23 684
Leaina 2 681
Leak, Jonathon 2 759
Leake, Ralph 10 329
Leake, William Martin 18 903–4*
Leakey, Mary 1 374
Leal, Fernando 18 904*; 21 387, 388, 405; 22 334
Leal, Jorge 19 655
Leal, José do Couto dos Santos *see* COUTO DOS SANTOS LEAL, JOSÉ DO
Leal, Juan de Valdés *see* VALDÉS LEAL, JUAN DE
Leal, Manuel Godinho *see* GODINHO LEAL, MANUEL
Lea Merritt, Anna *see* MERRITT, ANNA LEA
Léandre, Charles-Lucien 18 904*; 19 490
Leaning Tower of Pisa *see* PISA → ecclesiastical buildings → Campanile
lean-to roofs *see under* ROOFS → types
Leão, Carlos Azevedo *see* AZEVEDO LEÃO, CARLOS
Leão, Duarte Núñes de *see* NÚÑES DE LEÃO, DUARTE
Leão, Joaquim de Souza *see* SOUZA LEÃO, JOAQUIM DE
Leão de Tomás 30 799
Leaping Figures, Master of the 26 672; 33 239
works 20 V1
LEAR *see* LIGA DE ESCRITORES Y ARTISTAS REVOLUCIONARIOS
Lear, Edward 16 536; 18 904–6*
groups and movements 23 504
works 4 362, *363*; 18 *905*; 19 484
Leask, Harold 16 38
Leason, Percy 3 475
Leasowes, The (Hereford & Worcs) 10 *225*; 12 130; 18 906*; 29 890
Leathart, James 18 906–7*; 20 493
paintings 4 879; 10 367; 14 849; 19 588; 22 51
leather 7 735; 14 426; 19 1–6*
conservation 19 6*
dating methods 11 309
display 7 732
historical and regional traditions
Afghanistan 12 III; 16 *358*
Africa 1 *218*, 295, 299–300*, *300*, *322*, 349, *349*, *355*, *410*; 3 331; 10 778
Alaska 31 260
Asante 1 *349*
Austria 4 351
Bamana 3 136*
Belgium 3 575, 576, 577, 582, 583; 19 4*
Cambodia 5 *505*
Central Asia 6 305; 20 327
Central Asia, Eastern 6 313
Central Asia, Western 6 251, 261, 262
China 7 50, 54, 63, 122, 147
leather
historical and regional traditions—cont.
Denmark 19 5*
Dogon 1 *322*
Egypt 4 349
Egypt, ancient 6 388; 10 5, 52, 60–62*; 19 2; 20 327; 30 775
England 4 *346*, 349, *350*, 351, *351*, 352, 353–4, *353*; 10 275; 19 *4*, 4–5*
France 4 349, 351, *351*, 352, *353*, 354, *354*, IV3; 11 587; 19 3*
Germany 4 349, 351, 352; 23 254
Hausa 1 *218*, 299; 14 233*
India, Republic of 15 174
Indian subcontinent 15 681, *715*
Indonesia 10 778
Insular art 4 *346*, 349
Inuit 31 260
Islamic 6 557; 12 III; 16 124, 356, *358*, 503, 544, *544*
Italy 4 349, 351, 352, *352*, 353; 19 *3*, 3–4*, 5, 6; 30 657
Japan 17 297, 313, 355, 362, *362*, 363, 365, 376
Jewish art 17 566; 20 327; 26 557
Luba 1 *355*
Maasai 19 860
Malaysia 10 778
Mali 1 *300*
Mande 1 299, 300
Mesoamerica, Pre-Columbian 21 245
Mongolia 21 878*, 883
Native North Americans 22 *654*, 654–5*, 663; 31 260
Netherlands, the 4 352, 353; 19 4*
Niger 23 128
Nigeria 1 *218*, 299
Nubia 10 61
Ottoman 16 544, *544*
Pakistan 23 803
Peru 31 260
Poland 4 352
Portugal 19 4; 25 306
Romanesque 4 *350*, 351
Rome, ancient 19 2; 27 *105*, 105–6*
Scotland 27 *105*
Siberia 31 260
Spain 4 351, 352, 353; 17 566; 19 *2*, 3*, 5; 29 312, *314*
Sudan 1 299
Sweden 19 5*
Tanzania 1 299, *410*
Tuareg 1 299; 23 128; 31 *406*, 406–7*
Turkey 16 544, *544*
Zulu 33 724
materials
alum 10 61; 19 2
dyes 1 299
Japan wax 33 1
lacquer 17 297
technical examination 30 410
techniques
beating 19 *1*
conservation 7 747
cutting 19 *1*, 1–2
drying 19 *1*
dyeing 9 490; 19 2, 3
embossing 10 177; 19 2, *2*
embroidery 1 299
gilding 3 575, 576, 577; 12 621, 623; 19 *1*, 2, 3, *4*, 5
lacquer 6 313
moulding 19 *2*, 2*
painting 22 654, 655
punching 12 623
smoking 22 654
stamping 21 878
stencilling 17 313, 355
stretching 19 1, *1*
leather
techniques—cont.
stuffing 19 1
tanning 19 1; 21 878; 22 654; 27 105
tooling *see* punching
varnishing 3 575; 8 447; 19 *1*
types
bag 19 1
calfskin 19 1; 24 106
see also VELLUM
case *see* bag
cuir-bouilli 5 807; 16 503; 19 2, 4
guadameci 19 3; 29 297, 301
harness 19 1
modelling calfskin 19 1
morocco 19 1
Russia 28 252
scorched 19 2
shagreen 7 447
sole bends 19 1
strap backs *see* harness
upholstery hide 19 1
uses
appliqué 1 299; 21 878
aprons 22 655
armatures 29 813
armour 2 469; 6 305; 7 54; 16 503; 17 362, *362*, 363, 376; 19 2
baskets 1 295; 3 331; 17 365; 22 663
blackjacks 4 109
bookbindings 4 347; 7 63; 17 566
book covers 4 *346*, 349, *350*, *351*, 351–4, *352*, *353*, *354*, IV3; 12 III; 15 549; 16 356, *357*, *358*
books 10 5
bowcases 6 261
caskets 5 918
chairs 3 582, 583; 6 388; 19 5; 25 306; 28 252
chariots 10 61
chess sets 6 557
chests 6 560; 29 312
cords 10 61
costumes 30 654
crosses 5 807
cushion covers 1 *218*
dolls 31 260
doublures 4 349; 16 356
dress 6 251; 10 61; 19 2
dresses 22 655
embroidery 7 50
fans 10 778
footwear 1 349
fringes 1 300
furniture 10 61; 19 5–6*
hangings 19 2, 3, *5*, 5
interior decoration 3 577
leggings 22 654
manuscripts 20 327
masks 22 *545*; 30 657
mats 15 681
panels (wall) 3 575, 576; 19 4
photographs 24 650
puppets 5 *505*; 7 122, 147; 15 *715*; 16 544, *544*
quivers 6 261
robes 22 654, 655
rolls 4 342; 10 5; 26 557
scabbards 19 *3*
screens (ii) (furniture) 19 5; 28 297
scrolls 20 327
sculpture 1 *322*; 15 *172*; 23 254
shields 1 299; 6 262; 19 2; 21 245; 22 *654*
shirts 1 *349*; 22 654
shoes 10 61
skirts 1 *410*; 33 724
staffs 1 *355*
stencilling 24 56
stools 10 52
tankards 19 4
tents 1 307; 10 61
leather
uses—cont.
tepees 22 655
threads 3 440
thrones 30 775
trappings 27 *105*
upholstery 11 587; 19 5; 29 *314*; 31 680
vessels 21 883
watches 7 444, 447
writing 10 5
writing-tablets 4 342
see also HIDES; SKINS
Leaver, James 29 766
Leavers lace *see under* LACE → types
leaves 1 *384*; 6 874; 10 561
Leb, Wolfgang 19 7*
Lebadeia 13 395
oracle of Trophonius 15 53
Temple of Zeus 13 405
Lebanon 13 *362*; 16 *104*; 19 7–9*; 30 178, 179
bone 30 *181*
cedar 30 179
collections 1 896
columns 3 2
fortifications 21 *563*
forts 21 *563*
headdresses 16 459
manuscript illumination 9 619
meander 20 *912*
museums 19 *8*
orders (architecture) 3 2; 23 491
painting 19 7–8
pottery 30 196
sculpture 19 8
temples 3 *3*; 26 *881*
trade 1 896; 9 786
see also ANCIENT NEAR EAST; PHOENICIAN; SYRIA-PALESTINE
Lebanza 26 605
Lebarbier, Elise *see* BRUYÈRE, ELISE
Lebarbier, Henriette 19 9
Lebarbier, Jean-Jacques-François 19 9*
Le Barbier, Louis 21 346; 24 118
Le Barc de Boutteville, Louis 8 715; 19 10*; 22 422
Le Baron Jenney, William *see* JENNEY, WILLIAM LE BARON
Le Bas, Ann 10 398
Le Bas, Benjamin 19 11
Lebas, Jacques-Philippe 19 10–11*; 26 230
assistants 8 542; 22 88
pupils 3 318
Chenu, Pierre 6 547
Eisen, Charles (-Dominique-Joseph) 10 118
Ficquet, Etienne 11 57
Floding, Per Gustaf 11 173
Gaucher, Charles-Etienne 12 178
Helman, Isidore-Stanislas-Henri 14 365
Hoüel, Jean-Pierre-Louis-Laurent 14 799
Laurent, André 18 866
Le Mire, Noël 19 136
Le Veau, Jean-Jacques (-André) 19 268
Longueil, Joseph de 19 641
Major, Thomas 20 144
Numan, Hermanus 23 299
Ravenet, Simon Francis, the elder (1706-74) 26 30
Rehn, Jean Eric 26 98
Strange, Robert 29 747
Vinkeles, Reinier 32 591
Wicar, Jean-Baptiste (-Joseph) 33 153
teachers 30 344
works 4 636; 11 540; 18 751; 21 427; 33 44
Le Bas, James 9 320; 16 32; 19 11*

Lebas, Louis-Hippolyte 19 11*; 32 81
  assistants 12 155
  pupils
    André, Louis-Jules 2 14
    Ballu, Théodore 3 123
    Coquart, Georges-Ernest 7 831
    Durand, Hippolyte-Louis 9 420
    Dutert, Charles-Louis-Ferdinand 9 464
    Gau, Franz Christian 12 178
    Ginain, Paul-René-Léon 12 650
    Gisors, Louis (-Henry-Georges Scellier) de 12 746
    Kubly, Felix Wilhelm 18 493
    Labrouste, (Pierre-François)-Henri 18 581
    Labrouste, Théodore 18 580
    Rohault de Fleury, Charles 26 545
    Van Ysendyck, Jules-Jacques 31 896
    Vaudoyer, Léon 32 81
    Zocher, Jan David, the younger (1791-1870) 33 691
  teachers 24 387
  works 11 520, 525
Lebas, Paul Victor 12 265
Le Bas, William 19 11
Le Bas, William Robert 19 11
Lebasque, Henri 20 75
Le Bastier, Charles 11 633
Lebeau, (Joris Johannes) Chris 19 12*, 417; 22 899, 900
Le Bec Hellouin 26 669
Lebedev, Klavdy 18 482
Lebedev, Mikhail (Ivanovich) 19 12*
Lebedev, Rostislav 29 89
Lebedev, Viktor (Vladimirovich) 19 12–13*, 732; 27 381, 396
Lebedev, Vladimir (Vasil'yevich) 11 358; 19 13*; 27 581
Lebedeva, Mariya 1 453; 27 413
Lebedeva, Sarra (Dmitriyevna) 19 13*; 27 396, 411
Lebedev-Polyansky, Pavel 25 649
Lebedos 15 893
Lebedyn 31 551
Lebeer, L. 3 619
Le Bègue, Jehan 1 588; 15 852
Lebel, Charles Jacques 6 487
Lebel, Jean-Jacques 30 23
Lebena 13 565; 21 656
  Temple of Asklepios 8 154, 155
Lebeña, S Maria 29 262
Lebena ware see under POTTERY → wares
Lebensold, Fred 23 632
Lebenstejn, Jean-Claude 24 145
Lebensztejn, Jan 2 502; 19 13–14*; 25 108; 32 878
Lébény Abbey Church 26 638
Leber, Wolfgang 19 14*
Leberecht, Christian, Baron von Ampach see AMPACH, CHRISTIAN LEBERECHT, Baron von
Leberecht, Karl von 12 263
Leberecht Vogel, Christian see VOGEL (ii), CHRISTIAN LEBERECHT
Lebert, Olga Kaufmann 19 538
lebetes 13 475, 476; 19 14*
lebetes gamikoi 13 475, 478, 479; 19 14*; 32 67
Lebeuf, Abbé 24 154
Lebiš, Ján 28 854
Leblanc, Georges 8 63; 20 604; 25 628
Leblanc, Gustave 21 147
Le Blanc, Horace 4 125; 19 14*; 24 476; 29 623
Leblanc, Jacques-Louis 15 839
Le Blanc, Jean 11 626
Le Blanc, Jean-Bernard 11 561; 19 15*; 26 495
Leblanc, Walter 3 565
Leblanc, William 23 904
Le Blon, Christoph, II 19 15; 21 151, 152
Le Blon, Jacob Christoph 13 837; 19 15*; 26 234
  methods 21 416; 25 590
  pupils 12 208
  works 13 220; 25 622
Le Blon, Michel 19 15–16*
Le Blon, Nicolas 7 464
Le Blond (fl 1784) 23 520
Le Blond (family) 10 761
Le Blond, Alexandre-Jean-Baptiste 19 16–17*
  collaboration 24 546, 821; 27 401
  patrons and collectors 26 730
  works 12 122, 134; 21 474; 24 546; 27 573; 31 318
Leblond, Jacques see LA TOUR, JACQUES
Le Blond, Jean (i) (c. 1594-1666) 19 16*; 27 269
Le Blond, Jean (ii) (c. 1635-1709) 8 845; 19 16*
Leblond, Justus 10 761
Leblond, Nicolas, I 19 16
Le Blond de Latour, Antoine 4 391
Lebo 1 394, 401; 33 609
Leboeuf, Charles-François see NANTEUIL, CHARLES-FRANÇOIS
Lebons, John 23 686; 33 306
Leborgne, Ernesto 31 753
Leborne, Louis 28 388
Lebosse, Henri 26 514
Le Boulou 26 610
Lebourg, Albert-Charles 1 614; 3 888; 9 425; 19 17*
Lebouteiller, Jean 24 155; 26 39
Le Bouteux, Michel 32 372
Le Boutillier, Addison 30 887
Le Braellier, Jean see JEAN LE BRAELLIER
Lebret, Frans 25 269
LeBrethon, Jules 27 556
Le Breton, Gilles 19 18*
  attributions 11 513
  patrons and collectors 6 141; 31 848
  works 11 259, 261, 571; 19 692
Le Breton, Joachim 4 716; 13 295; 24 171
Le Breton, Louis 1 894
Le Breton Collection 22 111
Lebrija
  Nuestra Señora de la Oliva see S María
  S María 5 618
Le Brocquy, Louis 16 18, 35; 19 18–19*, 19
Le Brocquy, Melanie 19 18
Lebrón, Michael 18 834
Le Brouchy 25 749
Le Brument (fl 1783) 27 246
Le Brun 29 376
Le Brun, A. 18 21
Lebrun, André-Jean 3 530; 19 497; 32 579
  patrons and collectors 25 212; 32 876
  pupils 3 530; 21 544; 32 678
  works 25 115; 32 876
Le Brun, Annie 31 250
Lebrun, Benoist 23 509, 510
Le Brun, Charles 5 379; 7 383, 545, 628; 9 8; 11 517, 641, 657; 12 827, 828, 832; 19 19–25*; 20 136, 137, 139; 24 134, 134, 167, 168; 26 842
  architecture 6 508; 11 517; 20 449; 24 162; 29 524; 32 96
    arches 14 83
    screens (i) (architectural) 31 409
  assistants 12 285, 828; 20 480
    Audran, Claude, II (1639-84) 2 707
    Boullogne, Bon 4 535
    Houasse, René-Antoine 14 793
    Houzeau, Jacques 14 804
Le Brun, Charles
  assistants—cont.
    Jouvenet, Jean 17 670
    Marsy, Balthazar & Gaspar(d) 20 480
    Tuby, Jean (-Baptiste) (1635-1700) 31 408
    Verdier, François 32 242
    Vuez, Arnould de 32 737
  collaboration
    Bourdon, Sébastien 4 574
    Le Nôtre, André 12 121
    Le Vau, Louis 6 508; 12 121; 19 267; 23 811; 29 833
    Meulen, Adam Frans van der 21 367, 368
    Monnoyer, Jean-Baptiste 21 890
    Perrault, Claude 23 811; 24 468
    Sève, Gilbert de and Pierre de 28 506
  competitions 7 665
  copies 22 684
  dealing 11 662
  drawings 13 806; 21 764
  furniture 11 588, 617; 30 783
  gardens 20 897
  groups and movements 19 721; 25 398
  interior decoration 5 349; 6 508; 8 252; 9 14, 22; 11 516, 573, 575; 15 138; 19 265; 23 474, 542, 678; 32 96, 369
    stucco 12 725
  monuments 31 408
  paintings 11 575
    allegorical 19 23; 24 134; 32 370
    battle 3 388; 19 20, 22
    ceiling 11 575
    oil sketches 23 381
    portraits 11 534, 536, 537
    religious 19 24; 20 894
    wall 32 370
  patrons and collectors
    Boulle, André-Charles 4 531
    Clève, Corneille van (1646-1732) 7 423
    Colbert, Jean-Baptiste (1619–82) 7 545
    Colebrooke, George 7 552
    Fouquet, Nicolas 11 356, 657
    Girardon, François 12 727
    Henry, Bon-Thomas 14 395
    Hesselin, Louis (-Cauchon) 14 492
    Jabach, Everard 16 815
    John VI, King of Portugal (reg 1816–26) 4 725
    Jouin, Henry(-Auguste) 17 667
    Lambert, Nicolas 18 671
    Louis XIV, King of France (reg 1643-1715) 4 551, 552
    Spencer, Robert, 2nd Earl of Sunderland (1641-1702) 29 381
  prints 18 745
  pupils 5 876; 7 863; 8 883; 9 176, 399; 14 793; 17 915; 18 632, 644; 19 65; 28 743
  reproductions in hardstones 12 264
  reproductions in tapestry 26 260
  reproductive prints by others 10 690; 11 57; 12 832; 25 77; 26 229; 28 756
    Audran, Benoît, I (1661-1721) 2 708, 709
    Audran, Girard 2 708
    Audran, Jean 2 709
    Aveline, Pierre (-Alexandre) (1702-60) 2 853
    Collignon, François 7 569
    Dupuis, Nicolas-Gabriel 9 407
    Gautier-Dagoty, Edouard 12 209
    Genoels, Abraham, II (1640-1723) 12 285
    Habert, Nicolas 13 898
    Huret, Grégoire 15 31
Le Brun, Charles
  reproductive prints by others—cont.
    Kilian, Georg 18 47
    Kilian, Georg Christoph 18 47
    Lasne, Michel 18 812
    Leclerc, Sébastien (i) (1637-1714) 19 33, 33, 34
    Mariette, Jean 20 416
    Masson, Antoine 20 592
    Picart, Bernard (1673-1733) 24 712
    Piles, Roger de 24 805
    Rousselet, Gilles 27 269
    Schuppen, Pierre-Louis van 28 178
    Simon, Pierre (c. 1650-1710) 28 751
    Tardieu, Nicolas-Henry 30 344
    Tocqué, Louis 31 69
  sculpture 11 559; 20 481
    altars 31 409
    garden 12 121; 19 88; 26 91; 32 372
    religious 25 377
    statuettes 29 571
    tombs 31 408
  silver 11 618
  stucco 29 833
  tapestries 4 222; 10 275, 351; 11 641, 643; 12 829, 829; 23 512; 24 470; 30 321, 530
  teachers 24 476
  theories 10 690; 28 206
  writings 1 106; 2 518; 8 612, 788; 12 503; 22 378; 25 396; 31 300
Le Brun, Cornelis see BRUIN, CORNELIS DE
Le Brun, Elisabeth-Louise Vigée see VIGÉE LE BRUN, ELISABETH-LOUISE
Lebrun, François-Martin 7 693
Le Brun, Gabriel 27 269
Le Brun, Jean-Baptiste 31 363; 32 494
Le Brun, Jean-Baptiste-Pierre 2 382; 6 81; 8 542; 11 663; 18 579; 19 25*; 24 137; 27 524
  collaboration 8 792
  collections 7 778
  dealing 11 663
  patrons and collectors 23 778
  works 3 239; 11 32; 12 515; 21 428; 25 888; 32 85
  writings 24 63
Lebrun, Michel 19 649
Le Brun, Napoleon 28 830, 833
Le Brun, Nicolas 13 790; 19 19
Le Brun, Pierre (c. 1703-71; painter) 19 25
Lebrun, Pierre (fl 1740; marchand-mercier) 11 596
Le Brun, Rico 14 512; 19 702; 20 606
Leca, Miguel Mañara Vicentelo de see MAÑARA VICENTELO DE LECA, MIGUEL
Le Camus 20 134
Le Camus, Louis-Denis 19 26*
  attributions 19 26
  patrons and collectors 7 194
  works 7 194; 23 776; 24 122
Le Camus, Paul Duval see DUVAL LE CAMUS, PAUL
Le Camus, Pierre Duval see DUVAL LE CAMUS, PIERRE
Le Camus de Mézières, Nicolas 19 26*; 24 121
  works 2 172; 8 65; 10 668; 19 85; 21 817
  writings 8 613; 23 488
Le Cap 31 721
Le Carbet, Musée Gauguin 2 149
Le Carpentier, Antoine-Mathieu 11 667; 19 27*
  assistants 8 75
  patrons and collectors 7 194
  works 14 448
Le Carpentier, Mathieu 19 27
Lecca, Constantin 1 750; 26 713
Lecce 16 621; 19 27–8*
  architecture 16 640
  Church of the Rosary 16 640
  Il Gesù 1 698
    altar 1 699
  Museo Provinciale 'Sigismondo Castromediano' 16 774; 19 28
  Piazza del Duomo 16 640
  Santa Croce 19 28
  SS Nicola e Cataldo 26 628
Lecce, Matteo da see PÉREZ DE ALESIO, MATEO
Lecco, Accino da see ACCINO DA LECCO
Lecco, Angelo da see ANGELO DA LECCO
Lecelles Church 13 110
Le Centaure see CENTAURE, LE
Lecha, Valero 10 154
Lechaion, St Leonidas 9 538, 589
Le Chaleux, Jacques 24 478
Lechat, H.
  works 13 379
Leche, Gunnar 31 693
Le Chevallier, Etienne 29 750
Lechevallier-Chevignard, Georges 28 525
Lechi (family) 11 33
Lechi, Conte 5 775
Lechleitner, Michael 2 711
Lechler, Lorenz 19 28–9*
  methods 30 430
  works 30 161, 431
  writings 2 345; 10 747; 20 564, 565; 28 497–8, 498
Lechler, Moritz 10 747; 19 29
Lechmere, Kate 26 59
Lechner, Alf 9 121
Lechner, Edmund see LECHNER, ÖDÖN
Lechner, Jenő 19 30–31*
Lechner, Lajos 5 83
Lechner, Ödön 3 412; 15 408; 19 30*; 30 212; 33 710
  collaboration 14 61; 18 655; 20 206; 31 796
  staff 18 212
  works 4 696; 5 83; 14 889, 889; 15 2, 17; 28 850
Lechter, Melchior 12 497; 19 31*
Lechtzin, Stanley 12 866; 31 651
Lechuga, La see LA LECHUGA
Lechwe Trust 33 603
Leck, Bart (Anthonij) van der 19 31–3*
  groups and movements 22 852; 23 505
  patrons and collectors 4 743
  works 19 32
Leckhampstead (Berks), St James 30 533
Leckie, Alex 2 761
Le Clerc, Charles 26 526
Leclerc, Georges-Louis, Comte de Buffon see BUFFON, GEORGES-LOUIS LECLERC, Comte de
Leclerc, Jacques-Sébastien 19 33
Leclerc, Jean (1587-1633) 11 534; 19 35*, 696; 22 455; 24 369; 26 772
  pupils 23 173; 32 102
  teachers 30 660
  works 12 203; 27 817
Leclerc, Jean (c. 1595-c. 1625) 33 669
LeClerc, Jerome 30 324
Leclerc, Louis-Auguste 8 740, 742, 743, 819; 10 110; 19 33
Leclerc, Sébastien (i) (1637-1714) 12 832; 19 33–4*
  collaboration 24 468
  patrons and collectors 23 777; 25 815; 30 727
  pupils 9 370; 24 712
  reproductions in medals 20 854
  reproductive prints by others 18 535

Leclerc, Sébastien (i) (1637-1714)—cont.
works **6** 518; **18** 535; **19** *33*, *34*; **20** 922; **24** *469*
writings **23** 488, 489
Leclerc, Sébastien (ii) (1676-1763) **19** 33, 34–5*
Leclercq, Henri **15** 89
Leclère, (Achille-) François-René **19** 35*
pupils **1** 13; **8** 816; **32** 594
teachers **24** 387
Le Clère, Pierre-Thomas **10** 823
L'Ecluse, Charles de **2** 105
Le Coeur, François **3** 395; **19** 36*
Le Coffre, Benoît **8** 733; **19** 36*
Le Coffre, Claude **19** 36
Lecointe, Charles **1** 642
Lecointe, Jean-François-Joseph **12** 616
Lecointe, Joseph **14** 592, 593
Le Combel **24** 310
Le Comte, Adolf **22** 882; **28** 867
Lecomte, Etienne-Chérubin **24** 388
Lecomte, Félix **8** 650; **30** 515; **32** 77
Le Comte, Florent **6** 78; **19** 36*, 246
Lecomte, Georges **19** 36–7*
Lecomte, Hippolyte **4** 303; **13** 306; **19** 37–8*; **24** 387; **31** 373
Lecomte, Hyacinthe-Aubrey **19** 487
Lecomte, Marcel **30** 20
Lecomte, Pierre **11** 798
Lecomte, Sauveur **20** 489; **21** 368
Lecomte du Nouÿ, André **5** 792; **8** 280; **19** 38; **31** 23
Lecomte du Nouÿ, (Jules) Jean (Antoine) **11** 419; **19** 38*; **23** 504
Leconfield Aprodite **33** 453
Le Cong Thanh **32** 480
works **32** *480*
Le Conte **2** 463
works **2** *463*
Leconte, Etienne-Chérubin **12** 746
Le Coq, Albert von **3** 902; **6** 320; **7** 159; **18** 494; **19** 38*; **31** 438
collections **6** 321
excavations **28** 637; **31** 422; **33** 505
Le Coq, Jean **19** 382
Lecoq de Boisbaudran, Horace **19** 38–9*
pupils **5** 131; **6** 122, 549; **10** 796; **19** 89, 295; **26** 509; **27** 237
works **31** 300
Le Corbusier **7** *294*, 385; **8** 8, 380, 803; **10** 821; **11** 129, 526, 527, 548; **13** 328; **14** 630; **15** 66, 694; **16** 101; **19** 39–52*; **20** 475, 484; **22** 920; **30** 125
architecture **1** 473; **11** 525–6, 659; **14** 362; **15** 887; **24** 129; **27** 129, 379; **29** 874; **30** 468; **31** 236
ecclesiastical buildings **6** *460*, 461, 467; **7** 277, 453, 695; **19** *42*, *46*, 365, *368*; **26** 352
exhibition architecture **10** 684; **11** 526, 584; **12** 380; **19** 80; **21** 782
government buildings **4** *712*; **5** 218; **13** 238; **19** *47*; **26** 414
houses **2** 552; **3** 551, *551*; **15** 891; **19** 367; **24** 815; **25** 740, 741; **30** 127, 128; **32** 556, *556*; **33** 736
Maisons Jaoul **19** *45*
Villa Savoye **12** 792; **24** 752
Villa Schwob **19** *40*
housing **11** 359; **12** 276; **26** 19; **30** 458
Cité de Refuge **12** 792
Cité Frugès **4** 390; **7** 695; **11** 526; **25** 173, 741
Le Corbusier
architecture
housing—cont.
Unité d'Habitation **5** *56*; **7** 295, 695, 696; **11** 527; **19** *45*; **20** 473
law courts **18** 890
museums **6** 382; **20** 834; **22** 365; **28** 823
skyscrapers **28** 833
university buildings **4** 475; **19** *43*
urban planning **4** 233; **6** 445, *445*; **7** 606; **9** 297; **15** 168; **19** *50*; **23** 273; **24** 129; **31** 184, 730, 731
assistants **2** 397; **14** 769; **22** 725; **28** 483
book illustrations **30** 488
collaboration **8** 7
Baungart, Emilio **3** 66
Bodiansky, Vladimir **4** 214
Bonet, Antonio **31** 753
Botta, Mario **4** 490
Braem, René **4** 628
Chowdhury, Eulie **7** 209
Frey, Albert **18** 186
GATEPAC (Grupo de Artistas y Técnos Españoles para el Progreso de la Arquitectura Contemporánea) **3** 217; **12** 177
Harrison and Abramovitz **14** 200
Jeanneret, Pierre **17** 463
Karfík, Vladimír **17** 813
Kolli, Nikolay (Dzhemsovich) **18** 205
Lods, Marcel **19** 535
Moreira, Jorge (Machado) **22** 95
Niemeyer (Soares Filho), Oscar **4** 713; **23** 117, 118
Ozenfant, Amédée **22** 331; **23** 694
Perret, Auguste **24** 474
Pingusson, Georges-Henri **24** 824
Prouvé, Jean **25** 663
Reidy, Affonso Eduardo **26** 109
Roth, Alfred **27** 214
Sakakura, Junzō **27** 597
Savina, Jo(seph) **27** 888
Sert (i López), Josep Lluís **28** 483
Vilar, Antonio Ubaldo **32** 538
Williams, Amancio **33** 203
Yoshizaka, Takamasa **33** 563
competitions **7** 669, 670
dealers **26** 193
drawings **2** 334
furniture **7** 241; **11** 602; **29** 8; **30** 755
groups and movements
Allianz **1** 666
ATBAT **2** 660; **4** 214
Bauhaus **3** 401; **25** 740
Brutalism **5** 55
Cercle et Carré **6** 342
CIAM **7** 293, 296; **11** 526; **13** 798; **21** 782; **30** 128
CIRPAC **7** 343
Cubism **25** 747
Deutscher Werkbund **8** 826; **21** 490
Functionalism **11** 840
International Style **15** 885
Modern Movement **21** 781, 782
Purism **1** 75; **8** 247; **11** 525; **19** 896; **21** 782, 783; **25** 739–40
Rationalism (ii) (style) **26** 15
Union des Artistes Modernes **11** 602; **31** 582
methods **2** 360, *360*; **4** 819; **12** 793; **13** 412; **14** 874; **25** 172; **28** 201
paintings **25** *739*, 741
patrons and collectors **11** 584; **27** 888; **29** 604
personal collection **3** 391
Le Corbusier—cont.
pupils **3** 25; **15** 242; **17** 88, 421
Dávid, Károly **8** 562
Hopwood, Gillian **14** 755
Maekawa, Kunio **20** 76
Matta (Echaurren), Roberto (Antonio Sebastián) **20** 837
Sakakura, Junzō **27** 597
Salmona, Rogelio **7** 606
Sołtan, Jerzy **29** 52
Wogensky, André **30** 684
restorations by others **3** 79
staff **33** 552
Bonet, Antonio **4** 315
Candilis-Josic-Woods **5** 608
Doshi, Balkrishna V(ithaldas) **9** 180
Ginsberg, Jean **12** 652
González de León, Teodoro **12** 920
Heep, (Adolf) Franz **12** 652; **14** 295
Jorn, Asger **17** 658
Komter, Auke **18** 212
Mange, Ernest (Robert de Carvalho) **20** 269
Parent, Claude **24** 111
Perriand, Charlotte **24** 475–6
Sakakura, Junzō **27** 597
Yoshizaka, Takamasa **33** 563
tapestries **3** 462; **11** 644; **30** 329
writings **1** 666; **2** 360–61; **10** 240; **11** 525–6; **31** 300, 730
translated **10** 547; **33** 563
Le Cosquino, Louis **20** 138
Le Coudray-Saint-Omer Church **11** 623
Le Coudray-Salbart **6** 56; **12** 173
lectern desks *see under* DESKS → types
lecterns **7** 282
historical and regional traditions
Belgium **13** 159
Germany **12** 452
Gothic **13** 159
Scotland **28** 251
materials
brass **4** 688
copper **12** 452
Lectionaries
historical and regional traditions
Byzantine **9** 611, 620–21, *621*
Early Christian (*c*. AD 250-843) **9** 611
Turkey **9** *621*
individual manuscripts
Cluny Lectionary (Paris, Bib. N., MS. nouv. acq. lat. 2246) **11** 530; **26** 669
Gospel of Nikephoros Phokas (untraced) **22** 228
Lectionary of Het'um II **2** 444
Lectionary of King Het'um II (Erevan, Matenadaran Inst. Anc. Armen. MSS, MS. 979) **2** 444
Lectionary of St Erentrud (Munich, Bayer. Staatsbib., Clm. 15903) **26** 675, *676*
Lovell Lectionary (London, BL, Harley MS. 7026) **17** 611
Towneley Lectionary (New York, Pub. Lib., MS. 91) **4** 896; **7** 468
see also EVANGELIARIES
Lecuire, Pierre **29** 494
Le Culte rendu au soleil *see* CODICES → individual manuscripts → Aubin Manuscript 20
Lecuona, Juan **2** 401; **19** 53*
Lecurt, Juste *see* CORTE, JOSSE DE
Lécuyer, Antoine, Musée *see under* SAINT-QUENTIN
Le Dai Hanh **32** 486
Le Dantyu, Mikhail **9** 144
Ledbury (Herford & Worcs) **10** 260
Market Hall **31** 239
Leder, Hans **21** 886
Leder, Iosif **26** 708
Lederer, August **2** 829; **18** 130, 131
Lederer, Cristoforo *see* CORIOLANO, CRISTOFORO
Lederer, Erich **28** 89
Lederer, František Xaver **8** 386
Lederer, Hugo **14** 102; **19** 54*; **23** 636; **28** 380; **29** 566
Lederer, Josef **26** 496
Lederle, Carl **23** 272
Ledesma, Blas de **19** 54*; **29** 668
Ledesma, Gabriel Fernández *see* FERNÁNDEZ LEDESMA, GABRIEL
Ledesma, Gaspar de **29** 335
Le Despenser, Francis Dashwood, 15th Baron *see* DASHWOOD, FRANCIS,15th Baron Le Despenser
Ledger, Robert **33** 545
ledger book art **5** 124
Lediņš, Hardijs **33** 378, 379
Lednice **8** *374*; **19** 55*
furniture **2** 813; **8** 400
Schloss Eisgrub **19** 113, 339
sculpture **8** 386
Ledoux, Claude-Nicolas **10** 83; **19** 55–8*; **26** 13
architecture **6** 509; **11** 368, 518; **24** 353
banks **3** 174
cemeteries **6** 166
colleges **3** 873
customs-houses **7** 360; **21** 800; **24** 123
factories **10** 748
hôtels particuliers **3** 463; **14** 789; **24** 120; **29** 833
houses **19** *56*
law courts **18** 887; **24** 353
orders (architecture) **23** 489
pavilions **9** 313; **20** 131; **24** 290
porticos **25** 267
pyramids **25** 766
rotundas **14** 847
staircases **29** 523
theatres **30** *670*, 671
urban planning **31** 713, 714
collaboration **13** 234
commentaries **22** 110
groups and movements **10** 96; **13** 608; **22** 738; **26** 735, 743
patrons and collectors **19** 9; **29** 839
pupils **9** 336; **13** 775
teachers **4** 163; **31** 373
writings **5** 688; **31** 297
Le Doux, Jean Picart *see* PICART LE DOUX, JEAN
Ledoux, Louis **19** 58*
Ledoux, Nicolas **11** 627
Ledra **23** 111
Ledreborg Manor House **8** 754
Ledrede, Richard de, Bishop **16** 13
Ledreux, Louis **11** 883
Le Dreux de la Châtre **7** 677
Ledru, Léon **3** 595
Ledru-Rollin, Alexandre-Auguste **6** 536
Ledsebe, Matěj **8** 427
Ledsham, All Saints **2** 65
Ledu, Qutan Monastery **6** 779
Leduc (family) **20** 854
Leduc (*d c*. 1803) **21** 428
Leduc, Alfred **20** 854
Leduc, Carlos **33** 493
Leduc, Fernand **2** 839; **5** 568; **19** 58*; **25** 28; **26** 76
Le Duc, Gabriel (*d* 1654) **19** 58
Le Duc, Gabriel (1623/5-96) **19** 58–9*, 145
Le Duc, Guillaume **19** 59
Leduc, J. **3** 585
Leduc, Ozias **4** 402; **5** 566; **19** 59*
Ledwich, Edward **13** 693
Lee, Ann **28** 538
Lee, Arthur Hamilton, Viscount Lee of Fareham **11** 308, 309
Lee, Eleanor, Countess of Sussex **25** 282, 283
Lee, Frederick Richard **7** 798
Lee, Henry **12** 514
Lee, Jeremiah **32** 810
Lee, John **5** 514; **10** 168; **19** 59–60*
Lee, Lawrence **29** 508
Lee, Lindy **2** 752
Lee, Philip **31** 652
Lee, Richard (*c*. 1513-1575) **19** 60*; **21** 569; **26** 538
Lee, Richard (*fl c*. 1800) **31** 653
Lee, Russell **19** 60*; **24** 673
Lee, Samuel **10** 330
Lee, Sherman E. **15** 745
Lee, Thomas Stirling **19** 60–61*; **26** 12
Lee, Vernon **19** 61*
Lee, Wesley Duke **4** 719; **19** 61*
Lee, William (*d c*. 1610) **18** 158
Lee, William (*fl* 1753-8) **13** 200
Lee Byng **14** 721, 722
Leech, John **19** 61–2*; **33** 369
collaboration **8** 863
reproductive prints by others **1** 453
works **4** 363; **5** 758
Leech, William John **16** 17; **19** 62*
Leeching **7** 29, 30
Lee Collection *see under* LONDON → Courtauld Institute of Art
Leeds (Kent; UK)
Castle **6** 56; **12** 173; **18** 585; **19** 793; **21** 564
St Nicholas **1** 123
Leeds (W. Yorks; UK)
Corn Exchange **10** 669; **12** 791; **16** *54*
furniture **10** 297
Henry Moore Sculpture Trust Studio **17** 517
Mill Hill Chapel **31** 584
Moot Hall **5** 827
Temple Mill **10** 97
Temple Newsam House **10** 294, 347; **28** 140; **30** 299
candlesticks **5** 612
frames **11** 427
furniture **11** 427; **24** 514
silver **10** 336; **28** *740*
Town Hall **4** 837; **7** 667; **10** 236; **18** 888; **31** 240
Leeds, Francis Osborne, 4th Duke of *see* OSBORNE, FRANCIS, 4th Duke of Leeds
Leeds, Lewis W. **32** 95
Leeds, Thomas Osborne, 1st Duke of *see* OSBORNE, THOMAS, 1st Duke of Leeds
Leeds Union Bank **3** *181*
Leefdael (family) **14** 617; **30** 320
Leeghwater, Adriaensz Symonsz. **19** 63
Leeghwater, Jan Adriaensz. **19** 63*
Lee-Johnson, Eric **19** 63*
Lee Joo For **20** 172
Leek **10** 357
Lee Kang-so *see* KANG SO LEE
Lee Kian Seng **20** 172
Leemans, Gaspard **12** 851
Leemput, Mary van **19** 63
Leemput, Remi van **9** 485; **14** 670; **19** 63*
Leemputten, Cornelis Van *see* VAN LEEMPUTTEN, CORNELIS
Leemputten, Frans Van *see* VAN LEEMPUTTEN, FRANS
Leemputten, Jan-Frans Van *see* VAN LEEMPUTTEN, JAN-FRANS
Leen, Konrad **20** 916
Leen, Nicolaas van der **10** 222
Leenheer, Cornelis de **32** 121
Lee Polyptych, Master of the Lord *see* DOMINICAN EFFIGIES, MASTER OF THE

Leerdam glassworks *see* ROYAL LEERDAM GLASSWORKS
Leersum, Emmy van 22 896
works 22 *896*
Lees, Abraham 33 182
Lees, Derwent 11 774
Lees, Philip 33 182
Lees Court (Kent) 2 545
Leeson, E. W. 14 673
Leeson, Joseph, 1st Earl of Milltown 16 35; 19 63–4*
architecture 6 63; 16 23
paintings 3 276; 16 36; 32 332
Leeson, Joseph Henry 19 64
Leeson, Lorraine 10 879
Leest, Antonij van 19 64*
Leeswood Hall (Clywd) 30 123
Leete, Alfred 25 349
Lee U-fan 21 892
Leeuw, Bert De *see* DE LEEUW, BERT
Leeuw, C. H. van der 4 815; 22 830
Leeuw, Henk de 21 363
Leeuw, Jan de 4 *921*; 13 159
Leeuw, Joseph de 21 362
Leeuw, Willem van der 19 64*
Leeuwarden
Fries Museum 22 906
Gemeentelijk Museum Het Princessehof 7 155; 22 906
Paleis van Justitie 22 828
pewter 22 893
Pier Pander Museum 23 908
silver 22 887, 890
Leeward Islands 2 144; 5 *745*, 749
see also ANTILLES, LESSER
LEF (Left Front of the Arts) 2 578; 7 182; 18 445; 20 887–8; 22 178; 33 599
LEF: Zhurnal levogo fronta isskustv 4 812; 7 291; 24 450; 25 239
Le Falot group 12 277
Le Fauconnier, Henri 19 64–5*
groups and movements 8 240, 243; 9 361; 16 817, 818; 19 78; 21 775; 22 921; 25 747; 31 583
pupils 6 469; 13 681; 25 238; 31 519
Lefébure, August 11 650
Lefébure, Philippe-Auguste 19 261
Le Febure, Thomas 21 640
Le Febvre (family) 3 599; 31 218
Lefebvre 19 382
Lefèbvre, Claude 19 65*
pupils 8 24; 31 378
reproductive prints by others 2 709
works 24 890; 27 845
Lefebvre, François 17 523
Le Febvre, Jacques (1691-1765) 3 599
Lefèbvre, Jacques (*fl* 1947) 2 660
Le Febvre, Jacques, II (1744-1810) 3 600
Lefèbvre, Jean 11 641; 12 828; 19 65, 562
Lefebvre, Jules (-Joseph) 11 546, 672; 19 65–6*
pupils 22 421
Almeida, Belmiro (Barbosa) de 1 678
Benson, Frank W(eston) 3 740
Boutet de Monvel, (Louis-) Maurice 4 589
Dewing, Thomas Wilmer 8 841
Hassam, (Frederick) Childe 14 219
Hitchcock, George 14 589
Khnopff, Fernand 18 23
Marcoussis, Louis 20 399
Maurin, Charles 20 861
Melchers, (Julius) Gari(baldi) 21 76
Metcalf, Willard Leroy 21 342
Moore, George (Augustus) (1852-1933) 22 54
Mucha, Alphonse 22 251
Lefebvre, Jules(-Joseph)
pupils—cont.
Platt, Charles A(dams) 25 32
Rochegrosse, Georges (Antoine Marie) 26 481
Roussel, Ker-Xavier 27 269
Tarbell, Edmund C(harles) 30 343
Le Febvre, Marc, I 3 599
Le Febvre, Piat, I (1684-1728) 3 599
Le Febvre, Piat, II (1722-65) 3 599
Lefebvre, Pierre *see* FEVÈRE, PIETRO
Lefèbvre, Roland 19 65
Le Febvre-Caters *see* LE FEBVRE, JACQUES, II
Lefèvre, André 1 438; 19 66*; 26 107
Lefèvre, Camille 14 724; 21 867
Lefevre, G. J. Shaw 8 830
Lefèvre, Guillaume 8 662; 14 63
Lefèvre, Léon 12 31
Lefèvre, Nicolas 33 357
Lefèvre, Raoul 8 208
Lefèvre, Robert (-Jacques-François) 19 66–7*; 26 93
works 4 616; 19 *67*
Lefèvre d'Etaples, Jacques 14 868
Lefèvre Gallery 12 31
Lefèvre-Pontalis, E. 5 319
Lefèvre-Utile 10 421
Leffler, Heinrich 2 809
L'Effort *see* EFFORT, L'
Lefkandi 13 *363*; 14 *332*; 19 67–8*
architecture 13 409
faience (i) (glass) 13 589
Heroön 14 466; 19 68, *68*
jewellery 13 597
pottery 13 492, 496
sculpture 13 441, *441*
Skoubris tomb 20 13 *600*
Skoubris tomb 59 13 *600*
statuettes 29 567
Toumba building 13 396
Lefkandi I pottery *see under* POTTERY → wares
Lefkara 8 366
Church of the Holy Cross 8 359
Museum 8 367
lefkaritka 8 366
Lefkas *see* LEUKAS
Lefkoniko 8 342
Lefkosia *see* NICOSIA
Lefler, Franz 19 69
Lefler, Heinrich 12 491; 14 33; 19 69*; 28 155
Lefort, Agnes 5 590
Lefort, Martin 13 227; 25 576, 577
Le Fort du Plessy, Claude 2 806; 19 69*; 28 15; 32 456, 459
Le Fort St-André 6 56
Le Foullon, Guillaume Elie 7 778
Le Foyer Schaerbeekois 16 827
Lefranc 7 639
Le Franc, Jean-Jacques, Marquis de Pompignan *see* POMPIGNAN, JEAN-JACQUES LE FRANC, Marquis de
Le Franc, Martin *see* MARTIN LE FRANC
Lefranc, Pierre-Bernard 23 521
Le Français de Lalande, Joseph Jérôme 12 812; 24 38
works 24 *39*
Left Front of the Arts *see* LEF
Left Handed Red 5 276
Lefuel, Alexandre-Henri 19 69
Lefuel, Hector-Martin 5 824; 19 69–70*; 24 221
assistants 12 650; 15 21
groups and movements 28 345
patrons and collectors 23 794
pupils 15 21
works 11 261, 523; 24 163; 32 613
Lega 2 137; 19 72–4*
aesthetics 1 236
craftsmen and artists 1 244
currency 1 363
figurines 1 273; 19 *72*, 73–4
gesture 1 266
ivory 1 293; 19 *72*
masks 1 333, 405; 19 73, *73*, 74
sculpture 1 404; 19 73–4
wood 19 *73*
Lega, Achille 7 779; 16 680
Lega, Silvestro 14 588; 16 678; 19 70–71*
groups and movements 18 715; 19 870, 871; 28 705
patrons and collectors 20 483
teachers 7 344
works 19 *71*
Le Gac, Jean 11 553
Legae, Ezrom (Kyobokano Sebata) 29 109, 112
Le Gaigneur, Louis Constantin 10 297; 26 85
Legalism 6 625
Leganés, 1st Marqués de 13 879*
frames 11 487
furniture 29 303
paintings 27 295; 29 353; 32 706
Legarda, Bernardo de 5 920; 9 712; 19 75*
Légaré, Gédéon 19 75
Légaré, Gilles 11 634; 19 75
Légaré, Joseph 5 590; 19 75*; 25 11
Légaré, Laurent (before 1610-after 1658) 19 75
Légaré, Laurent (*fl* 1692) 19 75
LeGarec, Maurice 7 434
Legarreta, Juan 21 380; 33 493
Legaspi, Cesar 24 622
Legastelois, Jules (-Prosper) 19 75–6*; 20 925
Legay, Marc 18 777
Legazpi, Miguel López de *see* LÓPEZ DE LEGAZPI, MIGUEL
Legé, F. A. 6 457; 12 597
Legeay, Jean-Laurent 19 76*
collaboration 3 645
groups and movements 22 734
patrons and collectors 14 652
pupils 19 232; 32 766
reproductive prints by others 9 390
works 4 541; 20 867
Legègue, Jean 15 85
Legenda aurea *see* GOLDEN LEGEND
Legend of St Barbara, Master of the 3 554; 17 455; 20 710–11*, 781
Legend of St Benedict, Master of the 20 711*
Legend of St Catherine, Master of the 3 554; 20 710, 711*
Legend of St Francis, Master of the 20 712–13*
works 2 624; 13 *145*; 20 *713*; 26 182
Legend of St George, Master of the 20 714*, 718
Legend of St Godelieve, Master of the 20 714*
Legend of St Lucy, Master of the 3 553; 20 714–15*, 758
works 4 921; 20 *715*
Legend of St Mary Magdalene, Master of the 3 641; 20 715–16*, 747
works 20 *716*
Legend of St Ursula, Master of the (i) (*fl c.* 1470-1500; Flemish) 3 553; 20 716–17*
works 4 924; 11 439, *442*
Legend of St Ursula, Master of the (ii) (*fl c.* 1480-1510; German) 12 384; 20 717*
Legend Painting School *see* MORRISSEAU PAINTING SCHOOL
Legendre, J.-G. 24 174
Legendre, Nicolas 11 559; 12 725; 19 76*; 32 96
Legendre-Héral, Jean-François 11 158, 159; 13 806
Legend Scenes, Master of the 20 717*
Leger, Archbishop of Vienne 32 463
Léger, Fernand 7 385; 14 205; 19 76–83*; 23 48, 694; 24 144; 31 607
book illustrations 20 208; 30 488
ceramics 11 607
collaboration 10 687; 11 659; 20 603
dealers 11 165; 16 906; 17 725; 20 75; 27 162, 163
exhibitions 32 775
groups and movements
Artists International Association (AIA) 2 553
Cercle et Carré 6 342
Cubism 8 240, 244, 245, 246; 21 775; 27 307
Jack of Diamonds (Bubnovy Valet) 16 817
Orphism 1 74; 8 240; 23 570
Purism 25 741
Puteaux group 9 361; 25 747
Section d'Or (ii) 28 347
lithographs 19 491
methods 6 471
mosaics 22 163
paintings 8 *244*; 11 419, 420, 548, 551, 582; 19 *77*, *79*, *81*; 32 568
allegorical 19 *82*
genre 12 296
industrial scenes 15 828
murals 5 692; 22 332
still-lifes 29 670
patrons and collectors
Arensberg, Walter and Louise 2 383
a.r. group 2 409
Cooper, Douglas 7 797
Dotremont, Philippe 9 189
Dutilleul, Roger 9 465
Fondation Maeght (Saint-Paul-de-Vence) 20 76; 28 314
Gallatin, A(lbert) E(ugene) 12 15
Guggenheim, Peggy (Marguerite) 13 801
Heemskerck van Beest, Jacoba (Berendina) van 14 295
Kuh, Katherine 18 498
Lefèvre, André 19 66
Masurel, Jean and Geneviève 19 381
Mattioli, Gianni 20 848
Reber, Gottlieb Friedrich 26 59
Rupf, Hermann and Margrit 27 343
Thompson, G(eorge) David 30 749
Winston, Harry Lewis and Lydia 33 254
prints 25 620, 626
productions 3 120; 6 167; 12 497; 25 380; 30 687
pupils 2 528; 4 717; 29 108
Aroch, Arie 2 487
Bærtling, Olle (Bertil Georg) 3 43
Berk, Nurullah 3 785
Brennand, Francisco 4 745
Clark, Lygia 7 376
Clausen, Franciska 7 405
Damian, Horia 8 482
Englund, Lars 10 378
Francis, Sam(uel Lewis) 11 706
Fruhtrunk, Günter 11 807
Grau, Ricardo 13 322
Greco, Alberto 13 339
Hansen, Oskar 14 155
Henri, Florence 14 393
Jorn, Asger 17 658
Kawaguchi, Kigai 17 860
Léger, Fernand
pupils—cont.
Klein, William 18 117
Pepper, Beverly 24 372
Potworowski, (Tadeusz) Piotr 25 373
Reutersward, Carl Fredrik 26 258
Rickey, George (Warren) 26 360
Skúlason, Thorvaldur 28 828
Smart, Jeffrey 28 867
Stankiewicz, Richard 29 539
Tajiri, Shinkichi 30 255
Tarsila 30 348
Tryggvadóttir, Nína 31 393
Veronesi, Luigi 32 358
Włodarski, Marek 33 288
sculpture 14 785
stained glass 29 508
studio 29 858
tapestries 2 704; 11 644; 30 328
Léger, François 8 733, 754; 11 580
Legeret, Jean 12 832
Legeris, Dymenge de *see* DYMENGE DE LEGERIS
Legg, George 30 533
Legg, William 29 532
Legge, Edward 29 548
Legge, William, 2nd Earl of Dartmouth 5 295; 11 910; 33 220
leggings 22 649, 654
Legh, Gerard 14 406
Leghorn *see* LIVORNO
Leghtune, Thomas de *see* THOMAS DE LEGHTUNE
Légion d'Honneur 7 178
legislation, architecture *see* ARCHITECTURE → legislation
legislation, art *see* ART LEGISLATION
legislation, textile *see* TEXTILES → legislation
Legnani, Stefano Maria 7 309; 21 527
Legnica
Haus zum Wachtelkorb 10 738, 741
Prince's Chapel 4 782; 25 95
Legon, Museum of the African Studies Centre 12 510
Legorburo, Gustavo 32 171
Legorreta, Juan 21 403
Legorreta, Ricardo 14 788; 19 84*
collaboration 32 558
works 13 731; 21 381, 382, 397; 22 21; 23 81
Legost, Achille 13 208
Legot, Pablo 5 618; 19 84–5*
Legoupil, André 2 701
Legoupil, Mathieu 2 701; 11 405
Legoux de la Berchère, Jean-Baptiste 25 790
Leg Piekarski 6 162
Legrain, Eugène 5 825; 8 787; 23 794
Legrain, Georges 10 81; 30 691
Le Grain, Jean *see* ZIARNKO, JAN
Legrain, Pierre (-Emile) 11 601; 19 85*; 20 399
collaboration 27 322
patrons and collectors 9 196
works 11 583, *602*, 673
Legraive, Edmond 30 47
Le Grand 22 843
Legrand, Antoine-François 31 373
Legrand, Etienne-François 14 790
Legrand, Gérard 30 23
Le Grand, Henri 18 885
Legrand, Jacques-Guillaume 19 85*
collaboration 3 524; 7 417; 21 817; 24 121
house 21 817
restorations 27 543
works 23 510
writings 9 420
Legrand, José 11 759, 760
Legrand, Louis (1723-1808) 4 330

Legrand, Louis (-Auguste-Mathieu) (1863-1951) **19** 85–6*
Le Grand Andely, Notre-Dame **13** 60
Le Grant, Jacques **30** 529
Legras, Auguste **28** 68
Le Gray, (Jean-Baptiste-) Gustave **19** 86–7*; **24** 657, 659
  pupils **9** 340; **19** 239; **22** 424
  works **19** *87*; **24** 663
Le Grice, Malcolm **10** 688
Legros, Alphonse **8** 891; **10** 266, 374; **19** 89–90*, 891; **21** 418
  assistants **33** 343
  groups and movements **33** 137
  patrons and collectors **15** 894
  pupils **3** 630; **7** 570; **13** 30; **14** 193, 808; **26** 512; **27** 218; **29** 746; **31** 418
  teachers **19** 39
  works **5** 364; **9** 309; **20** 925
Legros, Jean **19** 88, 89*
Legros, Pierre (i) (1629-1714) **19** 87, 88*; **20** 480; **26** 771
  assistants **8** 71
  pupils **19** 88
  works **24** 165; **29** 571, 573
Legros, Pierre (ii) (1666-1719) **19** 87, 88–9*
  assistants **4** 79; **5** 547
  collaboration **15** 121; **30** 704
  methods **21** 765
  patrons and collectors **4** 79; **8** 209; **17** 509, 510
  personal collection **20** 270
  pupils **19** 645
  works **5** 302, 547; **9** 110; **13** 814; **16** 697, 699; **19** *88*; **25** 416; **26** 824
Legros d'Anisy **24** 149
Legrue **8** 776
legs, cabriole *see* CABRIOLE LEGS
Leguay, Etienne **4** 166; **11** 610; **24** 148, 149
  works **24** *149*
Legueult, Raymond-Jean **11** 302; **16** 577; **22** 751; **27** 523; **32** 399
Leh **15** *264*; **19** 90*; **28** *719*, 721; **30** *806*, 819
  architecture **15** 311, 397
  Lechen Pelkar **21** 593
  Maitreya Temple **15** 311
  palace **15** 397; **30** 820
  Peak of Victory Fort **15** 311
  rock art **30** 823
Le Havre **11** *504*, 527; **19** 90–92*, *91*
  docks **9** 58
  Musée des Beaux-Arts **19** 91
  ship-decoration **28** 612
  urban planning **24** 475
Le Hay, Elisabeth-Sophie *see* CHÉRON, ELISABETH-SOPHIE
Le Haze, Jean *see* HAZE, JAN DE
Lehman, Philip **9** 200, 467; **19** 92
Lehman, Robert **3** 725; **8** 682; **9** 467; **19** 92
Lehman collection *see under* NEW YORK → museums → Metropolitan Museum
Lehmann, Arno **2** 816
Lehmann, August Ferdinand **3** 804
Lehmann (von Lewenwaldt), Caspar **8** 407; **12** 786; **14** 171; **19** 92–3*; **25** 435
  attributions **25** 436
  patrons and collectors **13** 914
  works **8** 418; **12** 439, *786*; **25** 436; **26** 486
Lehmann, Christian Frederik **8** 743
Lehmann, E. P. **31** 256
Lehmann, Ernest **20** 187
Lehmann, (Charles Ernest Rodolphe) Henri (Salem) **19** 93*
  pupils **1** 751; **18** 866; **23** 598; **28** 423, 500; **30** 648
Lehmann, (Charles Ernest Rodolphe) Henri (Salem)—cont.
  teachers **15** 839
  works **23** 522
Lehmann, John **22** 751
Lehmann, Karl **9** 528; **19** 93–4*; **31** 672
Lehmann, Leo **19** 93
Lehmann, Rudi **17** 717
Lehmann-Hartleben, Karl *see* LEHMANN, KARL
Lehmann-Haupt, C. F. **31** 158
Lehman *Virgin and Child* **3** 661
Lehmbruck, Wilhelm **12** 407; **19** 94–5*; **22** 48
  assistants **7** 555
  exhibitions **12** 407
  groups and movements **10** 695
  patrons and collectors **10** 414
  teachers **17** 3
  works **9** 310; **12** 407; **19** *95*
Lehmden, Anton **2** 797; **24** 592; **32** 447
Lehnert, Jerzy **25** 115
Lehnert, Johann Georg **8** 386
Le Hongre, Etienne **14** 804; **19** 95–6*
  collaboration **8** 93; **11** 559
  patrons and collectors **4** 551; **7** 699
  pupils **6** 121
  tombs **31** 408
  works **7** 195; **8** *94*; **10** 442; **13** 783; **27** 548; **29** 571; **32** 372
Le Hongrie, Etienne *see* ETIENNE LE HONGRIE
Lehr, John **32** 304
Lehrs, Max **14** 554; **19** 96*, 339
Lehr- und Versuch-Ateliers für Angewandte und Freie Kunst (Munich) **8** 594; **23** 337
Lehtinen, Kauko (Olavi) **11** 97; **19** 96*
Le Huy Mien **32** 482
Lei **24** 535
lei see under VESSELS → types
Leibeg, Justus von **21** 721
Leibl, Wilhelm (Maria Hubertus) **14** 30; **19** 97–8*; **22** 304; **29** 389; **31** 389
  groups and movements **26** 56; **28** 170; **31** 397
  patrons and collectors **31** 397
  pupils **7** 855; **9** 468
  works **12** 394; **19** *97*
Leibniz, Gottfried Wilhelm **14** 469; **18** 243; **33** 53, 293
Leibovitz, Edward **3** 595
Leica *see under* CAMERAS → types
Leicester
  architecture **26** 905
  Bishop Street Church **21** 347
  furniture **33** *157*, 157–8
  Greyfriars' church **1** 518
  Leicestershire Museum and Art Gallery **3** 454
  National Art Slide Library **10** 376
  St Mary de Pré **2** 725
  School of Art **15** 823
  University Engineering Building **10** 242; **12** 793; **13** 239
  White House **29** 843
Leicester, John Fleming, Baron de Tabley **19** 98*
  catalogues **5** 741
  paintings **5** 434; **7** 572; **10** 365; **14** 550; **23** 214; **31** 467; **33** 221
Leicester, Robert Dudley, 1st Earl of *see* DUDLEY, ROBERT, 1st Earl of Leicester
Leicester, Robert Sidney, 2nd Earl of *see* SIDNEY, ROBERT, 2nd Earl of Leicester
Leicester, Simon de Montfort, Earl of *see* MONTFORD, SIMON DE, Earl of Leicester
Leicester, Thomas Coke, 1st Earl of *see* COKE, THOMAS, 1st Earl of Leicester
Leicester Galleries *see under* LONDON → galleries
Lei Chao **6** 718
Lei Cheng Uk **14** 719
Leicher, Felix Ivo **31** 786
Leickert, Charles (Henri Joseph) **19** 99*; **23** 322; **26** 482
Leidecker, Adam **8** 414
Leiden **19** 99–102*; **22** *813*
  art forms and materials
    brick **4** 778
    engravings **22** *355*
    painting **22** 836, 841*; **31** 881
    pewter **22** 893
    stained glass **27** 255
    tapestries **30** 318
    textiles **22** 900
  Castle **22** 822
  cloth hall *see* Stedelijk Museum De Lakenhal
  Gravensteen **18** 886
  guilds **13** 823
  Hooglandse Kerk **19** *100*; **22** 820
  Hortus Botanicus **4** 483; **12** 131, 836; **28** 670
  Kern Institute **15** 744; **32** 677
  Lakenhal *see* Stedelijk Museum de Lakenhal
  Marekerk **2** 385
  monastery of St Hieronymusdal **19** 101
  Pieterskerk **13** 62; **19** 101; **22** 820, 836
    choir-screen **22** 857
    pulpit **25** 725, *726*
    sculpture **13** 100
  Pieterskerkgracht 9 **27** 256, 258
  Rapenburg 65 **33** 262
  Rijksherbarium **28** 670
  Rijksmuseum van Natuurlijke Historie, Geologie en Mineralogie **28** 670
  Rijksmuseum van Oudheden **10** 91, 93; **26** 284; **32** 155
  Rijksmuseum voor Volkenkunde **22** 906
    collections **1** 66; **17** 434, 436, 440; **28** 670; **29** 240, 478; **30** 849
    paintings **22** 795
  Rijksuniversiteit
    collections **19** 102; **22** 905
    library **19** 313; **22** 909
    observatory **23** 339, 340
    Prentenkabinet **14** 875; **29** 548
  Rijnlandshuis **19** 349
  Stadhuis **18** 7; **19** 349; **22** 823, *824*
  Stedelijk Museum de Lakenhal **2** 385; **9** 299; **22** 906
Leiden 'Fine' painters **19** 101, 102–3*; **22** 841
  members **9** 192; **12** 290; **21** 487, 489; **28** 842
  works **9** *192*, *193*
Leiden-Valkenburg **19** 99
Leiderdorp **22** 883
Leidi, Franco **30** 82
Leidrade, Bishop of Lyon **19** 846
Leidse fijnschilders *see* LEIDEN 'FINE' PAINTERS
Leidy, John **31** 634
Leifeng Pagoda **23** 775
Leifrinck, Hans **14** 505
Leifsgade Collective **8** 742
Leigh, George **29** 88
Leigh, James Mathews **10** 373
  pupils
    Burne-Jones, Edward (Coley) **5** 266
    Calderon, Philip Hermogenes **5** 426
    Holiday, Henry (George Alexander) **14** 677
    Houghton, Arthur Boyd **14** 800
Leigh, James Mathews
  pupils—cont.
    Howard (ii), George James, 9th Earl of Carlisle **14** 808
    Marks, Henry Stacy **20** 446
    Osborn, Emily Mary **23** 598
    Wells, Joanna Mary **33** 64
Leigh, John **32** 574
Leigh, Leonard **4** 845
Leigh, St Eadburga **26** 614
Leigh Court Barn (Hereford & Worcs)
  roof **30** *901*
Leigh & Orange **14** 720
Leigh & Sotheby **29** 88
Leigh & S. Sotheby **29** 88
Leighton, Clare **4** 367; **33** 369
Leighton, Frederic **14** 588; **19** 103–4*, 588; **23** 295; **25** 406
  frames **11** *433*
  groups and movements **1** 170; **2** 530; **8** 6; **10** 641; **13** 297; **14** 809; **23** 33, 34, 504
  house **2** 365, 552; **10** 282; **22** 59
  methods **21** 340
  paintings **11** *436*
  patrons and collectors **14** 132; **19** 269, 270, 875; **28** 924; **30** 359
  personal collection **8** 707; **12** 610
  photographed works **14** 688
  pupils **17** 673; **30** 761
  reproductive prints by others **2** 234; **21** 606
  sponsorship **20** 568
  studio **29** 856
  teachers **29** 611
  works **4** 868; **10** 254; **11** 433, 436; **19** *103*; **22** 59, 331, 416; **23** *34*; **29** 575
Leighton, John **17** 440
Leighton, Thomas H. **14** 603; **23** 22
Leighton, William (1808-91) **14** 603
Leighton, William, jr (1833-1911) **14** 603
Leighton, William (1905-90) **24** 496
Leighton Bromswold (Cambs), St Mary **25** 726
Leighton Buzzard (Beds), All Saints **9** 155
Leightone, Thomas de *see* THOMAS DE LEGHTUNE
Leigudun *see* SUIZHOU
Leigu tai Caves *see under* LONGMEN
Leihamer, Abraham **8** 748
Leilan, Tell **19** 104–6*; **21** *267*, 286
  temples **19** *105*, 105–6; **21** 286
  town walls **30** 190
Leimberger, Johann Georg **11** 851
Leiminger, Peter **15** 865; **28** 492
Leinberger, Hans **12** 401; **18** 650; **19** 106–8*, 131
  attributions **20** 796
  groups and movements **8** 514
  patrons and collectors **28** 492
  pupils **8** 682
  works **2** 800; **12** 401, 838; **19** *106*, *108*; **29** 570
Leinberger, Simon *see* LAINBERGER, SIMON
Leinfellner, Heinz **2** 804
Leinie (family) **10** 623
Leiningen, Edward, Prince of **21** *645*
Leiningen, Ernst, Prince of **21** *645*
Leinonen, Karl F. **4** 480; **31** 650
  works **31** *651*
Leins, Christian Friedrich **12** 822; **14** 164; **33** 429, 616
Leinster, James Fitzgerald, 1st Duke of *see* FITZGERALD, JAMES, 1st Duke of Leinster
Leinster, William Robert Fitzgerald, 2nd Duke of *see* FITZGERALD, WILLIAM ROBERT, Duke of Leinster
Leinsweiler, Slevogthof **28** 841
Leiper, William **4** 788; **10** 748; **12** 774; **19** 109*; **27** 636
Leipnik, Joseph ben David **17** 564
Leipzig **12** *360*, *361*; **19** 109–12*
  Akademie für Graphische Künste und Buchgewerbe **19** 112
  Allgemeine Deutsche Kunstgenossenschaft **19** 112
  Altes Gewandhaus **1** 125; **7** 687
  Altes Rathaus **12** 367; **19** *110*
  Battle Monument **22** 47
  botanic garden **4** 483; **12** 133
  Deutsche Bücherei **12** 482
  Deutsches Buchhändlerhaus **26** 190
  exhibitions **10** 678
  galleries (iv) (art) **19** 112
  guilds **19** 111
  Hochschule für Graphik und Buchkunst **12** 481; **19** 112
  Imperial Law Courts **18** 890
  International Fur Fair, 1930 **27** 409
  Konsumverein Leipzig **14** 644
  Künstlerhaus **19** 112
  Leipziger Künstlerverein (1858) **19** 112
  Leipziger Kunstverein (1837) **19** 111
  Market Hall **9** 86
  museums
    Deutsches Buch- und Schriftmuseum **19** 112
    Kunstgewerbemuseum **16** 559; **19** 112
    Museum des Kunsthandwerkes **12** 481; **15** 745; **19** 112
    Museum für Bildende Künste **12** 481; **25** 454
    Museum für Völkerkunde **19** 111; **21** 886; **23** 302
    Staatsgalerie **19** 112; **29** 377
  Neuer Leipziger Kunstverein (1990) **19** 112
  Neues Gewandhaus **7** 687
  painting **12** 391, 392
  paper **24** 55
  Rathaus **26** 190
  Rossplatz **12** 380
  Sächsig-Bayerischer Bahnhof **25** 855, 856
  Thomaskirche **1** 123
  University **12** 442; **19** 112
    Universitätsbibliothek **19** 318
  Verein der Kunstfreunde **19** 112
  Vereinigung für Neue Kunst **19** 112
  Völkerschlachtdenkmal *see* Battle Monument
  Zeichnungs-Mahlerei und Architectur-Akademie **1** 107; **19** 111
Leipzig Cabinet, Master of the **20** 752
Leipziger Kunstblatt **24** 421
Leipzig Machzor *see under* MACHZORS → individual manuscripts
Leiria
  Castle **30** 879
  Cathedral **25** 291, 317
Leiris, Louise **17** 726; **25** 626
Leiris, Michel **17** 726; **20** 75; **21** 709; **24** 144; **30** 18, 20
Leirner, Aldolphe **4** 725
Leirner, Nelson **4** 719
Leiros, Helen **33** 678
Leistikow, Walter **3** 801; **19** 112*
  groups and movements **3** 801; **12** 394; **14** 481; **28** 341, 342; **32** 244
  works **4** 42; **28** *342*

Leistler, Carl **19** 113*; **32** 448
collaboration **30** 754
groups and movements **13** 207
pupils **23** 66; **28** 155
works **2** 808, *809*, 813
Leistler, Matthias **19** 113
Leistler & Son **8** 400
Leistner, O. **4** 26
Leitch, William Leighton **2** 727; **14** 148; **20** 32, 421
Leith, Assembly Rooms **2** 617
Leith, Emmett **14** 689
Leith, (George Esselmont) Gordon **19** 113*
works **17** 603; **29** 105
Leith Academy **28** 232
Leithner **24** 791
Leithner's blue *see under* PIGMENTS → types
Leitl, Alfons **12** 379
Leitner, Franz, Freiherr von **32** 449
Leitrim, Robert Clements, 1st Earl of *see* CLEMENTS, ROBERT, 1st Earl of Leitrim
Leíva Church **7** 604
Leiviskä, Juha **11** 92; **19** 113–14*
Lei Yanmei **7** 117
Lei Yen-mei *see* LEI YANMEI
Leja, Benjamin **30** 113
Lejasdopel **18** 847
Lejeune, Emile **29** 246
Lejeune, Louis-Aimé **25** 718
Lejeune, Louis-François **4** 300; **11** 413
Lejeune, Pierre François **8** 508; **19** 781
Lejjun **21** 560
Lejre **32** 525
Lejuge, Jean **4** 578
Lejwa, Arthur **8** 897
Lejwa, Madeleine **8** 897
Leka (African people) **19** 72, 74
Léka Church (Hungary) **14** 886
Leka Church (Norway) **13** 114
Lekain, Henri-Louis **30** 672
lekanai **19** 114*
lekanides **13** *475*, 478, 513, 536
Lekapenos, Romanos I, Emperor of Byzantium *see* ROMANOS I LEKAPENOS, Emperor of Byzantium
Le Kef **9** *510*
Dar al-Kous **9** 535
Le Keux, Henry **14** 736
Le Keux, John **14** 736
works **5** *512*
Lekeux, Peter
works **30** X3
Lekit Church **2** 891, 892
Leko, Dimitrije **19** 883
Leksand **30** 116
Leksukhum, Santi **29** 242
Lekszycki, Franciszek **18** 428; **25** 104
Lekszycki, Marcin **25** 128
Lekuona, Nicolás de **19** 114*
lekythoi **13** 456, *475*, 478, 491, 507, 535–6; **19** 114*
Lela **5** 328; **22** 196, 197
Lelan, Jozef **3** 579, 587
Leland, John **2** 161, 162; **19** 114*; **26** 67
Leland, Martyn **8** 821
Lelang *see under* NANGNANG
Lelarge, Gaston **4** 233; **7** 606
Lele (Nepal) **22** *753*, 759
Lele (Zaïre) **18** 484, 485
Leleppa **31** 891
Leleu, Jean-François **11** 595; **13** 665; **19** 115*; **26** 303
Leleux, Adolphe **19** 115*; **26** 54
Leleux, Armand **19** 115–16*; **26** 54
Lelie, Adriaan de **11** 448; **12** 620; **19** 116*; **22** 846
Leliendaal Abbey **25** 727
Le Lieur, Jacques **27** 247
works **27** *245*
Lelièvre, Auguste **3** 595
Le Liget **5** 894, 895; **11** 530
Leliman, Jan **19** 116*
Leliman, (Johannes Hendrik) Willem **19** 116–17*
Le Lizo **5** 781
Lelli, Ercole **12** 38, 39; **19** 117*
Lelli, Giovanni Antonio **7** 313; **21** 25; **25** 717
Lello, Jacopo di *see* JACOPO DI LELLO
Le Logis *see under* BRUSSELS
Leloir, Maurice **10** 782
Le Lonay, Charlotte Eleonore **9** 241
Lelong, Paul **3** 125
Lelong, Pierre **31** 340
Le Loquetier, Nicolas **5** 666
Le Lorrain, Charles *see* MELLIN, CHARLES
Le Lorrain, Louis-Joseph **1** 105; **19** 117–18*
collaboration **13** 233; **19** 135, 232
groups and movements **13** 233; **22** 734, 738
methods **10** 198
patrons and collectors **11** 658; **18** 660; **23** 544
pupils **22** 88
works **5** 380, 837; **6** 390; **20** 867
Le Lorrain, Robert **11** 559; **19** 118–19*
assistants **22** 436
pupils **19** 140; **24** 785
teachers **25** 709
works **11** 560; **29** 573
Le Loup, Jean (*fl* 13th cent.) *see* JEAN LE LOUP
Leloup, Jean (*fl* 1954) **29** 764
Leloup, Louis **3** 595
Leloutre, François **24** 148
Leloy, Jean-Charles **28** 523
Lelu **21** 477
Lélu, Pierre **19** 119*
Lely, Peter **10** 249, 273, 361; **19** 119–25*, 583
assistants **13** 618; **18** 748
collaboration **12** 243, 341; **31** 779
copies **12** 600; **19** 63
drawings **6** 116
methods **5** 657; **9** 211; **25** 279, 280, 281
paintings **31** 786
patrons and collectors **12** 473
Bankes (family) **3** 178
Bankes, Ralph **3** 178
Beale, Charles and Mary **3** 444
Brydges, James, 1st Duke of Chandos **5** 65
Butler, Charles (1822-1910) **5** 311
Cosimo III, Grand Duke of Tuscany (*reg* 1670-1723) **21** 29
Cromwell, Oliver **8** 186
Herbert, Philip, 4th Earl of Pembroke and 1st Earl of Montgomery **14** 435
Hyde, Edward, 1st Earl of Clarendon **15** 48
Maitland, John, 2nd Earl and 1st Duke of Lauderdale **20** 141
Pepys, Samuel **24** 373
Percy, Algernon, 10th Earl of Northumberland **24** 390
Somerset, Henry, 1st Duke of Beaufort(, 3rd Marquess of Worcester) (1629-1700) **29** 58
Streeter, Robert (1621-79) **29** 767
personal collection **3** 178; **9** 230; **14** 810; **20** 417, 446; **21** 907; **25** 664; **26** 345; **27** 270; **28** 844; **29** 381
pupils **14** 742; **30** 892; **33** 260
reproductive prints by others **4** 169, 170, 884; **13** 647; **19** 867; **21** 415; **31** 802; **33** 147
Lely, Peter—cont.
works **9** 278; **10** 248, 345; **11** 424, *425*; **17** 524; **19** *120*, *121*, *122*, *123*
Lely frames *see under* FRAMES → types
Lely green *see under* PIGMENTS → types
Lelystad **31** 735
Lema, José Segundo de *see* SEGUNDO DE LEMA, JOSÉ
Lemaire, Auguste **5** 878
Le Maire, Barbara **16** 71
Lemaire, François **20** 922
Lemaire, Hector **8** 811
Lemaire, (Philippe-Joseph-) Henri **19** 125*
Lemaire (de Belges), Jean (1473-after 1515) **3** 397; **14** 502; **19** 126*; **20** 734
patrons and collectors **6** 30
works **20** 733; **25** 405
Lemaire, Jean (1598-1659) **11** 744; **27** 315, 789; **29** 886
Lemaire, Madeleine **3** 888; **18** 862
Lemaire, Philippe *see* LEMER, FELIPE
Lemaire, Pierre **24** 148
Lemaire, R. (*fl* 19th cent.) **3** 620
Lemaire, Rodolphe (*fl* 1728) **6** 333
Lemaître, Guillaume **11** 616; **24** 146
works **24** *146*
Lemaître, Maurice **10** 688
Lemaki **11** 67
Leman, James **4** 103; **7** 167; **10** 357; **28** 717
works **28** *717*
Le Mans **11** *504*; **19** 126–30*
Bibliothèque Municipale **19** 812
Cathedral of St Julien **11** 510; **13** 37; **19** 126–8*, *127*; **26** 45, 570
ambulatory **1** 768
buttresses **5** *318*
mouldings **22** 217, 218
pinnacles **24** 826
sculpture **7** 643; **13** 73; **19** *128*, 128–9*
stained glass **13** 180, 181; **19** 129*; **26** 702; **29** 501, 506, 510
vaults **32** 94
Musée des Beaux-Arts du Locle **11** 665
Notre-Dame-de-la-Couture **19** 129–30*
sculpture **24** *813*
Lemarchand, Charles-Joseph **19** 130
Le Marchand, David **14** 856; **19** 130*; **29** 574
Le Marchand, Guillaume **19** 130
Lemarchand, Louis-Edouard **19** 130*
Lemasle, Dame **19** 849
Le Masle, Michel **6** 434
Le Masson, Louis **28** 521
Lemba **8** *325*, 337; **13** *362*; **19** 131*
Experimental Village **8** 366
Lembang, Villa Isola **15** 770
Lembata **15** 795
Lemberg *see* L'VIV
Lemberger, Georg **18** 650; **19** 111, 131–2*
groups and movements **8** 514
works **19** *132*; **33** 354
Lembessis, Polychronis **13** 352; **19** 132*
Lembke, Johann Philipp *see* LEMKE, JOHANN PHILIPP
Le Mée-sur-Seine, Musée Henri Chapu **6** 468
Le Même, Henry-Jacques **1** 69
Lemeni, Gheorghe **26** 713
Lemer, Felipe **2** 394; **7** 847; **17** 514
Le Mercier, Jacques **4** 391; **19** 133–5*
architecture **6** 507; **11** 657; **26** 346–7
cathedrals **23** 510
châteaux **3** 853
churches **11** 516; **19** *135*; **21** 346; **24** 160; **25** 266
palaces **11** 657; **19** *134*; **24** 118, 161, 162, 165
theatres **30** 658, *658*
assistants **27** 822
attributions **23** 509
collaboration **4** 801
gardens **27** 314
interior decoration **24** 162
patrons and collectors **4** 549; **11** 657; **19** 300; **26** 348; **30** 735
Le Mercier, Nicolas **19** 133; **26** 346
Le Mercier, Pierre **19** 133; **26** 346
Lemercier, Rose-Joseph **19** 488; **20** 603
collaboration **7** 575
methods **25** 615
pupils **14** 135; **20** 603
works **19** 480; **25** 618; **26** 234; **32** *698*
Le-Mesnil-Saint-Denis, Notre-Dame **7** 191
Le Mettay, Pierre-Charles **3** 204; **19** 135*, 232
Lemgo
Hexenbürgermeisterhaus **33** 87
Marienkirche **14** 81
Lemieux, Jean Paul **19** 135–6*
Lemire **29** 750
Le Mire, Antoine-Louis **19** 136
Le Mire, Noël **3** 318; **19** 11, 136*; **20** 584; **22** 88
pupils **3** 318
works **19** 268
Lemire, Sophie **31** 373
Lemke, Johann Philip **5** 9; **19** 137*
works **19** *136*
Lemland Church **11** 94
Lemmen, Georges **19** 137*
groups and movements **10** 517; **19** 792; **22** 746, 747; **32** 591
patrons and collectors **4** 71
Lemmerz, Christian **8** 742
Lemmput, Remi van *see* LEEMPUT, REMI VAN
Lemnos **13** *363*, 547; **31** 355
LeMoal, Guy **5** 217
Le Moal, Jean-Louis **4** 98; **19** 491, 848
Lemogne, Jean-Baptiste **19** 119
Lemoine *see* LEMOYNE
Lemoine, François *see* LEMOYNE, FRANÇOIS
Le Moiturier, Antoine **11** 555; **19** 137–8*
collaboration **33** 28
patrons and collectors **5** 210
works **7** 355; **8** 890; **13** 78; **17** 676; **19** *138*
Lemolieff, Giovanni *see* MORELLI, GIOVANNI (LORENZO)
Lemon, Jacques **19** 492; **20** 609
Lemon, Mark **19** 62
Lemon, William **10** 852
Le Monastier **26** 641
Lemonnier (*fl* late 18th cent.; artist-administrator) **11** 667
Lemonnier (*fl* early 19th cent.; jewellery firm) **17** 526
LeMonnier (*fl c*. 1760; bookbinder)
works **4** *354*
Lemonnier, Camille **5** 44; **7** 245; **21** 369; **28** 921
Lemos, Conde de **19** 139*
Lemos, António Alves Pereira de *see* ALVES PEREIRA DE LEMOS, ANTÓNIO
Lemos, Carlos de Araújo *see* ARAÚJO LEMOS, CARLOS DE
Lemos, Duarte de (3rd Senhor de Trofa, Itales e Pampilhosa) **19** 139*
Lemos, Eugénio **22** 245
Lemos, Fernando **25** 300
Lemos, Francisco da Silva *see* SILVA LEMOS, FRANCISCO DA
Lemot, François-Frédéric, Baron **7** 915; **11** 364; **19** 140*, 846; **25** 417
Le Moulin-Joli **12** 123, 124
Lemoyne (family) **30** 118
Lemoyne, André **19** 130
Lemoyne, François **4** 554; **14** 584; **19** 142–4*
assistants **23** 195
attributions **33** 261
collaboration **25** 2
patrons and collectors **2** 154, 904; **4** 560; **11** 538; **19** 144; **26** 470; **28** 527; **32** 368
pupils **3** 639; **4** 518; **5** 884; **6** 401, 527; **15** 38; **22** 682; **23** 195
reproductive prints by others **5** 884; **19** 261
works **11** 538; **14** 584; **19** *142*; **24** 135
Lemoyne, Jean-Baptiste (i) (1679-1731) **7** 195; **19** 140–41*; **28** 742
Lemoyne, Jean-Baptiste (ii) (1704-78) **11** 561; **19** 140–42*
collaboration **11** 705; **19** 27, 140
competitions **7** 672
patrons and collectors **4** 554; **7** 528; **25** 82; **30** 515, 523
pupils **5** 380; **7** 574; **10** 763; **13** 5; **14** 796; **21** 800; **23** 794; **24** 785
reproductive prints by others **7** 495
works **8** 92; **11** 578; **19** 140, *141*; **30** 499; **32** 372
Lemoyne, Jean-Louis **19** 140*
patrons and collectors **4** 553
pupils **19** 140
works **10** 884; **11** 560
Le Moyne, Jehan **4** 546
Lemoyne, Paul **6** 511; **19** 143*
Lemoyne, Saint-Paul *see* LEMOYNE, PAUL
Le Moyne de Morgues, Jacques **19** 143*
reproductive prints by others **5** 62
works **2** 103; **11** 229; **14** 855; **32** 899
Lempad **15** 809
Lempereur (*fl* 1600s) **25** 377
Lempereur, Catherine-Elisabeth **19** 144
Lempereur, Jean-Baptiste-Denis **19** 144
Lempereur, Jean-Denis, II **8** 542; **19** 143–4*; **29** 487
Lempereur, Louis-Simon **18** 858; **19** 144*
Lempicka, Tamara De *see* DE LEMPICKA, TAMARA
Lemport, Vladimir Sergeyevich **31** 459
Lemput, Remi van *see* LEEMPUT, REMI VAN
Lemsall *see* LIMBAŽI
Lemud, Aimé de **14** 853
Le Muet, Pierre **19** 144–5*
assistants **19** 59
attributions **23** 509
works **5** 344; **7** 773; **11** 516; **19** 59; **20** 896; **24** 160
writings **6** 417; **11** 516, 573; **14** 789; **24** 274; **31** 296
Lemunguier, Lorena **6** 600
Lena, Oscar **29** 309
Lena Church **30** 77
Le Nain, Antoine **11** 535; **19** 146–9*; **22** 85; **24** 167
attributions **20** 627, 678; **21** 463
frames **11** 401
patrons and collectors **4** 636; **32** 85

Le Nain, Antoine—cont.
works 19 *146*, *147*, *148*, *149*
Le Nain, Louis 11 535; 19 146–9*; 22 85; 24 167
attributions 20 627, 678; 21 463
frames 11 402, *403*, 404
patrons and collectors 4 636; 7 194, 778; 15 895; 18 588; 30 727; 32 85; 33 453
reproductive prints by others 19 144
works 12 289; 15 828; 19 *146*, *147*, *148*, *149*
Le Nain, Mathieu 11 535; 19 146–9*; 22 85; 24 167
attributions 20 627, 678; 21 463
frames 11 401
patrons and collectors 4 636; 25 383; 32 85
works 12 289; 19 *146*, *147*, *148*, *149*
Lenardi, Giovanni Battista 3 95; 8 132
Lenartz, Jacob 24 777
Lenbach, Franz von 13 717; 19 150–52*; 22 304; 23 13; 33 38
house 2 552; 28 374
patrons and collectors 20 404; 28 40
pupils 22 433; 28 188
teachers 24 815
works 11 463, *463*; 12 394; 19 *151*
Lenbach, Karl August 19 150
Lenca 14 711
Lencastre, Veríssimo de 2 189
Lenci 31 260
Lenck, Adam *see* LENCKHARDT, ADAM
Lencker, Christoph 2 718; 19 152*
collaboration 32 772
patrons and collectors 8 413; 13 631
works 2 *718*; 25 22
Lencker, Elias 25 22
Lencker, Johannes (*d* 1585) 12 422, 443, 445; 14 52; 33 727
Lencker, Johannes (1573-1637) 12 444, 445; 19 152
Lencker, Zacharias 13 631; 25 22
Lenckhardt, Adam 19 152–3*
Lenckhardt, Nikolaus 19 152
Lendas *see* LEBENA
Lendinara, Cristoforo Canozzi da *see* CANOZZI DA LENDINARA, CRISTOFORO
Lendinara, Lorenzo Canozzi da *see* CANOZZI DA LENDINARA, LORENZO
Lendinara, Pierantonio da *see* PIERANTONIO DA LENDINARA
Lendogno, Zephyrin 11 879
Le Nègre, Pierre 11 626
Lenehan, Andrew 2 758; 19 153*
Lenepveu, Jules-Eugène 19 153–4*
Le Neubourg, St Paul 13 60
Lenfant, Jean 19 154*
works 4 131; 10 *436*; 14 83
L'Enfant, Pierre 24 212
L'Enfant, Pierre-Charles 19 154–5*
groups and movements 22 741
works 5 275; 10 850; 20 19; 31 590, 662, 721; 32 884–6, *885*
Lenger 18 26
Lenginour, Richard 6 561
Lenglart, J. 4 917
Lenglet 8 633
Leng Mei 6 818
Lengnau Synagogue 17 544
Lengola 1 404; 19 72, 74
Lengua 24 93
Lengyel culture 25 498, 500, 513, 516, 517
Lengyel of Arad 26 718
Lenhendrick, Louis 11 620
Leni, Giuliano *see* LENO, GIULIANO
Lenica, Alfred 19 155*
Lenica, Jan 25 354
Lenin, V(ladimir) I(l'ich) 19 155*; 27 394
art policies 25 653; 28 597
sculpture 22 509
Lenin, V. I., Museum *see under* GORKI LENINSKIYE
Leninabad *see* KHODZHENT
Leninakan *see* KUMAYRI
Leningrad *see* ST PETERSBURG
Leningrad Cinephoto Factory 16 793
Leningrad Jewellery Factory 27 423
Leningrad Mirror Factory 27 417
Leningrad Painter 13 521; 32 56
works 13 *481*
Lenis, Giuliano de *see* LENO, GIULIANO
Lenk, Franz 22 923
Lenk, (Kaspar-)Thomas 19 155–6*
Lenk, Torsten 2 451
Lenkart, Leopold 25 128
Lenkas, Pantokrator Cathedral 25 332
Lenker (family) 23 312
Lenker, Christoph *see* LENCKER, CHRISTOPH
Lenkhart, Nicolaus 17 688
Lenkoran 2 *890*; 16 481
Lenmico, Domenico 31 789
Lennard, Thomas Barrett, 17th Baron Dacre 21 607
Lenné, Peter Joseph (*fl* 1789) 19 156
Lenné, Peter Joseph (1789-1866) 14 654, 655; 19 156*; 24 181
collaboration 28 102
pupils 3 794
works 3 793–4; 24 485; 25 367, 368
Lennep, David van 2 25
Lennep, Henry John Van *see* VAN LENNEP, HENRY JOHN
Lenner, Adhémar 25 190
Lennie, Beatrice 5 571
Lennox (family) 11 243
Lennox, (Georgiana) Caroline, Baroness Holland 25 883
Lennox, Charles, 2nd Duke of Richmond and Lennox 19 157*; 24 301
collaboration 22 138
paintings 5 594, 598, 686; 9 486; 32 111
sculpture 4 758
Lennox, Charles, 3rd Duke of Richmond and Lennox 19 157–8*
collections 19 586
education (art) 19 157*, 585
paintings 29 808
sculpture 33 226
Lennox, E(dward) J(ames) 5 561; 19 158*; 31 176
Lennox, J. L. Kincaid 14 108
Lennox, Margaret Stewart, Countess of *see* STEWART, MARGARET, Countess of Lennox
Lennox, Matthew Stewart, 4th Earl of *see* STEWART, MATTHEW, 4th Earl of Lennox
Lennox and Richmond, Charles Stuart, Duke of *see* STUART, CHARLES, Duke of Lennox and Richmond
Lennox Canning, F. 4 155
Leno, Giuliano 19 158–9*; 27 746
Lenoble, Emile 6 462
Le Noir (family) 3 599
Lenoir 11 630
Lenoir, Adélaïde 19 159
Lenoir, Alexandre (-Marie) 3 463; 4 303; 9 209; 11 663, 666, 905; 19 159–60*
personal collection 9 25; 14 876; 23 523; 24 157; 27 548; 29 515
pupils 8 545
works 9 313; 11 665, 675; 27 545
Lenoir, Alexandre-Albert 19 159, 160*
Lenoir, C. 3 578, 585
Le Noir, Jean *see* JEAN LE NOIR
Lenoir, Jean-Jacques 19 510
Lenoir, Louis Stanislas 26 39
Lenoir, Samson-Nicolas 7 356; 8 593; 19 161*
Lenoncourt, Gérard de *see* JACQUEMIN, GÉRARD
Lenoncourt, Robert de, Archbishop of Reims 11 639; 26 113
Lenormand, François 21 830
Lenormand, Louis 9 338; 18 653
Le Normand de Tournehem, Charles-François-Paul 11 670; 19 161*; 20 135
paintings 14 584
sculpture 32 580
Lenormant Statuette 13 453
Lenot, Pascal 32 719
Le Nôtre, André 8 794; 12 64, 118; 19 162–4*; 23 512
châteaux 6 *454*; 11 517, 573; 20 449
collaboration 6 508; 19 265
fountains 11 344
gardens 12 *61*, 120, 121–2; 14 174
Anet 2 28
Chantilly Château 6 454; 12 747; 19 *164*
Gaillon Château 11 905
Saint-Cloud 12 *122*; 23 512; 27 536
Saint-Germain-en-Laye 27 559
Trianon de Porcelaine 26 492; 32 372, 373
Vaux-le-Vicomte 19 *162*; 32 96, 97
Versailles 32 370, 372
groups and movements 19 721
patrons and collectors
Bourbon I., Louis de, le Grand Dauphin (1661-1711) 4 553
Colbert, Jean-Baptiste (1619-83) 7 546
Condé, Louis II de Bourbon, Prince de (1621-86) 6 453
Fouquet, Nicolas 11 356, 657
Henrietta Maria, Queen of England and Scotland (1609-69) 29 803
Louis XIV, King of France (*reg* 1643-1715) 4 551; 32 369, 372
Louvois, Marquis de 19 731; 21 366
personal collection 4 552; 18 840
pupils 12 133, 723; 19 16
sculpture 12 577
urban planning 24 119
Le Nôtre, Jean 19 162; 21 822
Le Nôtre, Pierre 19 162; 21 822
Lenox, James 15 23
Lenox, Walter Scott 19 164–5*; 31 637
Lenox China Co. 19 165; 31 636, 638, 639
Lenox Globe 12 813
Lenproyekt Trust 19 273
Lens, A(ndries) C(ornelis) 3 562; 19 165–6*
pupils 6 151; 11 723
teachers 3 873
works 3 613; 14 479; 19 *166*
writings 3 617
Lens, Andreas 29 774
Lens, Andrew Benjamin 19 165
Lens, Bernard (1681-1740) 8 95; 14 178; 19 165*; 21 642
works 14 *460*
Lens, Bernard, I (1631-1708) 19 165
Lens, Bernard, II (1659-1728) 1 104; 19 165, 583; 21 416; 33 260
Lens, Cornelis 19 165
Lens, Edward 8 95; 19 165
Lens, Jean de 23 512
Lens, John 19 165
Lens, Peter Paul 19 165
Lense *see* LENS
lenses (spectacles) 24 106
lenses (cameras) *see under* PHOTOGRAPHY → materials
Lentate sul Seveso, S Stefano 9 261
Lenteritz, Ernst August
works 21 *66*
Lentia *see* LINZ
Lentini 13 581; 21 556
Basilica del Murgo 28 656
Lentini, Riccardo da *see* RICCARDO DA LENTINI
Lentini-Manfria group 13 530; 28 655; 30 175
Lenton, Holy Trinity 11 252
Lentswe La Oodi Producers Cooperative Society 4 489
Lentulov, Aristarkh (Vasil'yevich) 19 166–7*
groups and movements 16 817; 22 178; 27 392, 394
pupils 3 692
works 8 10
Lentz *see* LENS
Lenuci, Milan 33 593
Lenz, Desiderius (Peter) 32 258
Lenz, Johann Jakob Anton von 33 291
Lenz, Maximilian 28 344
Lenz, Peter 3 890; 22 329
Lenzburg 30 144
Lenzen, H. 31 759
Lenzi (family) 20 533
Lenzi, Bartolommeo 4 32; 22 800
Lenzi, Domenico 20 630
Lenzuoli-Borgia, Rodrigo *see* ALEXANDER VI, Pope
Leo (*fl* 840) 19 169
Leo (*fl* late 9th cent.; official) 28 828
Leo (*fl* early 10th cent.; official) 19 169
Leo (*fl* late 10th cent.; painter) 5 677
Leo I, Pope (*reg* 440-61) 19 167*; 26 801, 803, 820
Leo III, Bishop (*fl* 900) 7 325; 16 761
Leo III, Pope (*reg* 795-816) 14 408; 19 167*; 26 754, 765, 821
Leo III Isaurikos, Emperor of Byzantium (*reg* 717-41) 9 514, 637; 15 75, 80
Leo IV, Pope (*reg* 847-55) 16 761; 26 754, 811, 824
Leo V the Armenian, Emperor of Byzantium (*reg* 813-20) 9 637
Leo VI, Emperor of Byzantium (*reg* 886-912) 9 653; 10 129; 19 887*; 32 213
architecture 9 561; 16 607
coins 9 638
gems 12 254
metalwork 19 886
Leo IX, Pope (*reg* 1049-54) 14 415
Leo X, Pope (*reg* 1513-22) 11 186; 14 869; 16 768; 21 7, *8*, 15–16*, *16*; 25 ; 26 187, 769
archaeology 6 39
architecture 19 158; 26 756; 31 713
churches
Castel Sant' Angelo Chapel (Rome) 21 436, 450
Leo X, Pope (*reg* 1513-22)
architecture
churches—cont.
St Peter's (Vatican, Rome) 12 656; 25 906; 26 805; 27 737, 742
S Lorenzo (Florence) 11 208; 16 695; 21 451
fortifications 27 742
loggias 26 800
military 19 185
triumphal arches 27 739
villas 25 76; 27 734
art policies 2 161, 319
cartoons (drawings) 5 47
coats of arms 14 416
collections 16 763
decorative works 11 704
paintings 1 571; 3 305; 11 661; 12 750; 24 365; 25 899, 902; 27 849; 31 523
frescoes 12 751; 26 817, 818
rock crystal 16 745
sculpture 3 156, 157; 13 605; 26 846
stained glass 13 827
tapestries 16 757; 26 816; 30 315; 32 586
Leo XI, Pope (*reg* 1605) 1 *627*; 3 101; 7 297; 26 834; 29 741; 32 10, 11
Leo XII, Pope (*reg* 1823-29) 2 320, 559; 6 341; 12 738; 25 147
Leo XIII, Pope (*reg* 1878-1903) 24 249; 26 827; 30 210
Leo, Ludwig 19 168*
works 19 *168*
Leo Authentou 18 640
Leoben Church 2 781
Leobersdorf 2 815
Leo Bible *see under* BIBLES → individual manuscripts
Leochares 13 458, 596; 19 169–70*
collaboration 5 64; 19 852
works 2 682; 14 69; 18 148; 23 430, 433
workshop 13 460
Leodebod, Abbot of Saint-Benoît-sur-Loire 27 533
Leodegarius 26 608; 27 752
Leoffler, Leopold 25 106
Leofric Gospels *see under* GOSPEL BOOKS → individual manuscripts
Léogane 31 721
Leombeni, Lorenzo de *see* LEONBRUNO, LORENZO
Leombruno, Lorenzo *see* LEONBRUNO, LORENZO
Leominster, William Fermor, 1st Baron *see* FERMOR, WILLIAM, 1st Baron Leominster
León (Nicaragua) 23 *79*
architecture 23 80
Ateneo 23 85
Basílica de la Asunción 23 80
education (art) 23 85
galleries (iv) (art) 23 85
La Merced 23 80
La Recolección 23 80
museum 29 222
Palacio Departamental 23 80
silver 23 83
Teatro Municipal 23 80
Universidad Nacional Library 23 86
León (Spain) 19 170–78*; 26 *904*; 29 *258*
Cathedral of S María de León 13 51; 19 171–3*, *172*; 23 462; 26 45; 29 263
choir-stalls 13 123
cloisters 13 104
furniture 29 311
high altar 29 270
manuscripts 22 248
metalwork 29 338
misericords 21 725
monstrance 29 333

León (Spain)
Cathedral of S María de León—cont.
mouldings 22 217
Retablo Mayor 11 677
sculpture 13 103, 104, *109*; 19 *173*
stained glass 13 191; 19 173–4*, *174*; 29 502
tomb of Bishop Martín Fernández 13 104
workshop 13 68
embroidery 29 350
ivory-carvings 26 699, *699*
manuscripts 20 330
Monastery of Gradefes 29 311
Monastery of S Marcos 29 289
sculpture 13 104
S Isidoro 19 174*, 175*, *175*; 26 581, 582, 607
Chapel of S Catalina *see* Panteón de los Reyes
crucifixes 29 *288*
crypt 29 262
iconography 26 605
ivory-carvings 26 698
metalwork 26 689
Panteón de los Reyes 19 176*, *177*; 26 656
capitals 26 606
sculpture 19 176–7*; 26 605; 29 288
wall paintings 19 178*; 29 275
Puerta del Cordero 19 *176*; 26 605, 607; 29 288
Puerta del Perdón 26 607
sculpture 19 175–6*; 26 607; 29 288
textiles 16 436
Leon (*fl* late 2nd cent. BC) 17 745
Leon, Archbishop 23 373
León, Adalberto de 13 765
León, Angel Acosta *see* ACOSTA LEÓN, ANGEL
Leon, Anna de
works 22 *336*
León, Enrique Pérez de *see* PÉREZ DE LEÓN, ENRIQUE
León, Fidelio Ponce de *see* PONCE DE LEÓN, FIDELIO
León, Francisco Díaz de *see* DÍAZ DE LEÓN, FRANCISCO
Leon, Giambattista 22 167
León, Juan de 25 877
León, Juan Ponce de *see* PONCE DE LEÓN, JUAN
León, Juan van der Hamen y *see* HAMEN Y LEÓN, JUAN VAN DER
Léon, Omar De *see* DE LÉON, OMAR
León, Pedro de Cieza de *see* CIEZA DE LEÓN, PEDRO DE
León, Rubén Caudra de *see* CAUDRA DE LEÓN, RUBÉN
León, Teodoro González de *see* GONZÁLEZ DE LEÓN, TEODORO
Leonaert *see* BRAMER, LEONARD
Leonard, Master (*fl c.* 1490-1510) 4 254
Leonard, Antonio 19 386
Leonard, Michael 10 483; 12 218
Leonardi, Antonio 24 504
Leonardi, Camillo 16 780; 19 178*
Leonardi, Leoncillo 6 345; 26 777
Leonardi, Vincenzo 25 412
Leonardo (1968) 28 204
Leonardo, Benedetto di *see* MAIANO, BENEDETTO DA
Leonardo, Camillo *see* LEONARDI, CAMILLO
Leonardo, Il (1903-7) 11 190; 24 427
Leonardo, José 24 391
Leonardo, Jusepe 19 178–9*; 29 281
collaboration 26 436
patrons and collectors 32 129
teachers 8 254
Leonardo, Jusepe—cont.
works 19 *179*; 20 *71*
Leonardo: Art, Science and Technology 24 446
Leonardo: International Journal of the Contemporary Artist 24 429
Leonardo Avanzi 24 874
Leonardo (de' Molinari) da Besozzo 19 180*; 21 463
Leonardo da Pavia 32 421
Leonardo da Pisa, Ranieri di 11 747; 20 653
Leonardo da Vinci 7 814; 11 532; 12 214; 16 657, 661, 663, 766; 19 180–98*; 21 525; 22 378; 25 682
academies 1 102; 16 778
acoustics 1 123, *123*
altarpieces 19 *181*
architecture 6 415, 416; 13 210; 16 630; 19 194*; 21 517, 532; 31 712; 33 586
military 3 359; 21 565, 578
assistants 5 688; 19 516
attributions 2 310; 4 304, 307
drawings 26 363
paintings 19 675, 784; 26 279; 32 *364*, 367
sculpture 11 694
automata 2 837
canals 18 662
collaboration 4 284; 6 139; 12 719; 23 744; 25 465, 466; 27 447, 448; 28 532
commentaries 8 563
copies 4 470; 19 187; 20 1
drawings 5 755; 9 220; 14 869; 19 192–3*; 22 686; 23 744; 27 236; 28 201
anatomical 1 *841*; 9 220; 23 292
architectural 2 328; 7 257; 26 187; 29 522
cartoons 5 898; 10 675; 24 53
chalk 6 400; 10 *521*; 19 *186*, *193*
ink 14 871, *871*; 19 *184*, *192*
landscape 18 704
metalpoints 9 216
pastel 24 242
portraits 10 520
silverpoints 19 *191*; 25 558
etchings 10 560
frames 11 377, 384
groups and movements 26 182, 189
methods 21 759; 28 203, 205, 206; 29 53, 437; 32 805
anatomical studies 1 841; 7 783
chiaroscuro 6 569, 570; 30 456
drawing 25 379
painting 3 306; 5 656; 19 352, 354
perspective 24 491, 492; 28 202
proportion 14 871, 873; 28 200, 201
paintings 16 659; 19 187–90*, 191*
animal subjects 2 102
encaustic 7 676; 10 198; 16 663
frescoes 3 387; 7 627; 9 112; 11 186; 14 583; 21 846; 26 187; 31 237
mythological 10 476
portraits 2 225; 9 263, *263*; 17 526; 19 *183*; 25 74
religious 1 711; 12 503; 15 137; 16 663; 19 *182*, *185*, 449; 20 278; 25 162; 26 769; 32 364, 366
secco 28 339
patrons and collectors 10 365; 14 869; 16 763
Alcalá, 3rd Duque de (1583-1637) 26 307
Alexander II, Emperor of Russia (*reg* 1855-81) 26 734
Leonardo da Vinci
patrons and collectors—cont.
Amboise, Charles II d', Comte de Chaumont (1473- (1511) 1 766
Amboise, Georges I d', Cardinal (1460-1510) 1 766
Anne of Brittany, Queen of France (1477-1514) 31 846
Arconati, Galeazzo (Maria), Conte 2 376
Ashburnham, Bertram, 4th Earl of Ashburnham 2 595
Borgia, Cesare, Duca di Valentino 4 411
Borromeo, Federico, Cardinal 4 426
Borromeo, Vitaliano VI, Conte (1620-90) 4 427
Bossi, Giuseppe 4 471
Bouverie, John 4 596
Caprotti, Gian Giacomo 5 689
Charles I, King of England and Scotland (*reg* 1625-49) 10 363; 19 644
Coke, Thomas, 1st Earl of Leicester of the 1st creation (1697-1759) 7 540; 13 301
Condé, Henry II de Bourbon, Prince de (1588-1646) 7 699
Czartoryska, Isabella, Princess (1746-1835) 8 372
Esterházy, Miklós II, Prince (1765-1833) 10 531
Feuchère, Jean-Jacques 11 42
Flinck, Nicolaes Anthonis 11 170
Francis I, King of France (*reg* 1515-47) 10 477; 11 263, 656, 661; 16 695; 31 834, 849
Galeazzo Maria, 5th Duke of Milan (*reg* 1466-76) 21 517
Grimani, Domenico, Cardinal, Patriarch of Aquilea 13 657
Guise, John 13 837
Hamilton, Gavin 14 109
Hammer, Armand 14 117
Howard (i), Thomas, 2nd Earl of Arundel 14 806
Iriarte (family) 16 48
Jabach, Everard 16 814
Josephine, Empress of the French (1763-1814) 4 304
Lely, Peter 19 124
Leoni, Leone 19 203
Leoni, Pompeo 19 203
Ligne, Charles-Joseph-Emmanuel de, Prince (1759-92) 19 369
Louis XII, King of France (*reg* 1498-1515) 31 847
Ludovico (Maria), 7th Duke of Milan (*reg* 1494-99) 28 532
Luini, Aurelio 19 784
Mariette, Jean 20 416
Medici, Ottaviano de' 21 18
Melzi, Francesco 19 784
Mond, Ludwig 21 849
Montagu-Douglas-Scott, Walter Francis, 5th Duke of Buccleuch, 7th Duke of Queensberry 21 908
Musée du Louvre (Paris) 11 665
National Gallery (London) 5 283
Richelieu, Armand-Jean Du Plessis, Cardinal de 11 662; 26 348
Robertet, Florimond de 11 661; 26 454
Robien, Christophe-Paul Gautron, Marquis de 26 469
Roscoe, William 27 161
Rucellai, Bernardo (di Giovanni) 27 307
Rudolf II, Holy Roman Emperor (*reg* 1576- 1612) 13 914
Leonardo da Vinci
patrons and collectors—cont.
Rushout, John, 2nd Baron Northwick 27 350
Saint-Morys, Charles Paul Jean-Baptiste de Bourgevin Vialart de 27 568
Soderini, Piero (di Tommaso) 28 928
Tallard, Marie-Joseph d'Hostun, Duc de 30 274
Thibaudeau, Narcisse-Adolphe, Comte de 30 727
Trivulzio, Gian Giacomo 21 525
Turini, Baldassare 31 448
Vecchietti, Bernardo 32 106
Villiers, George, 1st Duke of Buckingham (1592-1628) 32 575
Vos (ii) Jbzn, Jacob de (1803-82) 32 708
Wellesley, Henry 33 56
William II, King of the Netherlands (*reg* 1840-49) 23 469
performance art 24 404
pupils 4 283; 20 791; 21 99; 25 222
reproductions in stained glass 18 *101*
reproductive prints by others 3 309; 5 412; 9 79; 29 487; 32 689
restorations by others 6 115; 24 343; 26 335; 27 321, 445
sculpture 4 209; 10 441; 16 693, 695; 19 193–4*; 25 158; 29 569; 31 352
stage design 30 656, 657, 659
tapestries 16 755; 26 778
teachers 16 694; 29 853; 32 359, 366
writings 1 662; 2 376; 7 628; 12 695; 14 869; 16 658, 781; 24 472; 31 295
on chiaroscuro 6 569; 19 354
on colour 7 637
on crayons 8 127
on decorum 8 612
on expression 10 690
on *istorie* 16 614
on metalwork 21 323
on painting 4 21; 10 471; 16 658; 21 100; 24 90; 31 299, 321, 768
on perspective 24 379, 380, 487, 492, 493, 494
on pouncing 25 378
on proportion 23 487
on sculpture 31 302
on studios 29 853
translated 10 489; 11 743; 12 203, 490
Leonardo da Vinci *see under* SHIPS → named vessels
Leonardo delle Notti *see* BRAMER, LEONARD
Leonardo di Ser Giovanni (da Firenze) 19 199–200*; 26 442
Leonardo Grazia da Pistoia *see* Grazia de Pistoia, Leonardo
Leonard's Index of Art Auctions 4 23
Leonard Stanley, St Swithin 26 616
Leonardus, Master (*fl* 1408) 26 719
León Bible *see under* BIBLES → individual manuscripts
Leonbruno, Lorenzo 19 200*
León Caldera, Adolfo 23 81
Leoncelli, Filippo 8 427
Leoncillo, Leonardo 11 802
Leoncini, Francesco 3 95
Leone, Andrea di *see* LIONE, ANDREA DI
Leone, Giambattista 26 328
Leone de Lazzara 29 436
Leone di Montecassino *see* LEO OF OSTIA
Leonelli, Antonio (da Crevalcore) *see* ANTONIO (LEONELLI) DA CREVALCORE
Leone Marsicano *see* LEO OF OSTIA
Leone Ostiense *see* LEO OF OSTIA
Leonhardt, Fritz 29 874
Leonhard von Strassburg 2 824
Leonhart, Dorothea 28 300
Leoni, Alessandro 12 722
Leoni, Francesco 32 12
Leoni, Giacomo *see* LEONI, JAMES
Leoni, Ippolito 19 205
Leoni, James 19 204*
collaboration 29 835
groups and movements 23 857
patrons and collectors 30 451
works 2 *356*; 4 787; 10 265; 12 6; 13 645; 27 466; 29 835
writings 31 298
Leoni, Leone 2 716; 19 200–203*; 21 525; 26 769; 29 571
assistants 19 203
attributions 21 533; 31 319
collaboration 10 502; 19 203; 20 66
medals 20 919
patrons and collectors
Anna, d' (family) 2 117
Charles V, Holy Roman Emperor (*reg* 1519-58) 13 907; 16 697
Ercole II, 4th Duke of Ferrara, Modena and Reggio (*reg* 1534-59) 10 523
Gonzaga, Cesare 12 911
Guastalla, Ferrante Gonzaga, Duca da 12 910
Mary of Hungary, Regent of the Netherlands (1505-58) 13 910
Maximilian II, Holy Roman Emperor (*reg* 1564-76) 13 911
Philip II, King of Spain (*reg* 1556-98) 13 922
Sabbioneta, Vespasiano Gonzaga, Duca da 12 911; 27 483
pupils 19 203
restorations by others 2 391
sculpture 16 695
architectural 19 *203*
busts 5 301; 21 II4; 25 282
equestrian monuments 10 441
funerary monuments 21 533
portraits 2 284, 827; 19 *202*; 25 257
statuettes 29 569
Leoni, Ludovico 19 204
Leoni, Ottavio 10 392; 19 204–5*
works 19 *205*; 23 576
Leoni, Pompeo 19 200, 203*; 29 289
collaboration 5 735; 10 502; 19 203; 20 66; 32 730
patrons and collectors 13 910, 922; 27 723
restorations by others 2 391
works 2 285, 391; 10 502, *502*; 11 486; 16 695; 26 250; 29 291
Leonidas 10 649
Leonidas of Naxos 13 386; 23 430
Leonidov, Ivan (Il'ich) 19 206–7*; 27 284, 379
groups and movements 23 590
works 19 *207*; 27 379; 28 834
León Jiménes, E. 9 118, 119
Leonora Gonzaga, Duchess of Urbino 12 278
Leonor of Viseu, Queen of Portugal *see* ELEANOR OF VISEU, Queen of Portugal
Leonov, L. M. 18 482
Leonov, Pavel 27 414
Leonteos 27 111
Leont'ev, Leonid 17 867
Leontinoi *see* LENTINI
Leontios 30 720
Leontios, Abbot of Patmos 24 263
Leontiskos 13 552

Leontopolis *see* YAHUDIYA, TELL EL-
Leontus, Adam **14** 59
Leont'yev, F. **2** 894
Leon't'yev, P. M. **27** 440
León Vieja **23** 80
León y Gama, Antonio **21** 262
Leo of Ostia **8** 800; **19** 207*; **22** 10
Leo of Rožmitál **7** 178
Leopardi, Alessandro **19** 207–8*, 558; **20** 623; **31** 316
collaboration **19** 559
competitions **7** 671; **32** 363
patrons and collectors **19** 663
works **5** 537; **10** 440; **19** *208*; **22** 131; **31** 825; **32** 192
Leopardi, Marcello **12** 889
leopard skins *see under* SKINS → types
leopard teeth *see under* TEETH → types
Leopold, Duke of Lorraine (*reg* 1697-1729)
architecture **4** 224; **16** 862; **19** 696, 800; **22** 453
sculpture **1** 132; **9** 388; **13** 805
tapestries **11** 642; **20** 489; **22** 456; **30** 324
Leopold, Grand Duke of Baden (*reg* 1830-52) **11** 786; **13** 218; **17** 817; **33** 256
Leopold I, Grand Duke of Tuscany *see* LEOPOLD II, Holy Roman Emperor
Leopold I, Holy Roman Emperor (*reg* 1658-1705) **2** 827; **13** *901*, 920–21*; **21** *642*; **32** *442*
amber **1** 762
architecture **5** 264; **12** 24; **13** 845; **28** 162; **32** 442, 456, 460
collections **2** 829, 830; **13** 920
decorative works **20** 852
engravings **10** 445
furniture **20** 852
hardstones **25** 436
metalwork **4** 62
paintings **2** 794; **3** 230; **5** 384; **10** 861; **19** 308; **29** 789; **30** 744
ceiling **25** 813
miniatures **21** 641
mythological **19** 706
portraits **19** 831; **21** 153
still-lifes **23** 447
prints **30** 793
sculpture **11** 130; **26** 25; **28** 193; **29** 788
Leopold I, King of Belgium (*reg* 1831-65) **7** 490*; **28** 756; **33** *110*
architecture **13** 202; **24** 86
paintings **13** 779; **26** 527
Leopold I, Margrave of Austria (*reg* 976-94) **21** 83
Leopold II, Duke of Styria (*reg* 1358-86) **13** *900*; **33** 164
Leopold II, Grand Duke of Tuscany (*reg* 1824-59) **3** 904; **25** 164, 691
Leopold II, Holy Roman Emperor (*reg* 1790-92) **10** 843; **14** 12*
academies **11** 215
art policies **15** 18
catalogues **3** 701
collections **18** 755, 756; **22** 356
decorative works **1** 574
engravings **27** 593
paintings **3** 899; **29** 3; **30** 865; **33** 694
sculpture **29** 403
Leopold II, King of Belgium (*reg* 1865-1909) **7** 490*; **33** *110*
architecture **3** 88, 89, 616; **8** 545; **12** 728; **14** 604, 769
collections **3** 615; **7** 490
paintings **8** 63; **10** 517; **29** 645
urban planning **5** 41
Leopold III, Margrave of Austria (*reg* 1096-1136) **2** 777; **14** 308; **18** 139
Leopold V, Archduke of Austria, Count of Tyrol (*reg* 1625-32) **12** 461; **13** 844, 845; **14** 51; **30** 482
Leopold VI, Duke of Austria (*reg* 1198-1230) **2** 777; **19** 377; **32** 454; **33** 163
Leopold, Henry **1** 158
Leopold, Pic de *see* PIC DE LEOPOLD
Leopold, Rudolf **2** 829
Leopoldski, Wilhelm *see* LEOPOLSKI, WILHELM
Leopoldskron, Schloss **11** 120
Léopoldsville *see* KINSHASA
Leopolski, Wilhelm **19** 208–9*
Léotard, F. **14** 84
Leo the calligrapher **9** 657
Leo the Great *see* LEO I, Pope
Leow, Vincent **28** 774
Lepage, François **27** 563
Lepage, Guillaume-Joseph **11** 596
Lepakshi **15** *294*; **19** 209*
sculpture **15** 539, 540
Virabhadra Temple complex **15** 331, 540, 644–5
paintings **15** *644*
sculpture **15** *540*
wall paintings **15** 543
Lepanto-Monstrance **12** 447
Le Paon, Jean-Baptiste **30** 514
Lepape, Georges **2** 520; **10** 824; **25** 349
works **9** *291*
Le Parc, Julio **19** 209–10*; **21** 746
dealers **26** 193
groups and movements **2** 401; **11** 570; **13** 709; **18** 63; **23** 448, 449
patrons and collectors **23** 85
works **1** 738; **16** 58; **18** *63*
Le Pautre, Adrien **19** 210
Le Pautre, Antoine **19** 210–13*
assistants **4** 887
collaboration **12** 833; **20** 457
groups and movements **24** 169
patrons and collectors **4** 551; **7** 546; **27** 536
pupils **19** 642
works **8** 65; **14** 789; **17** 2; **19** *211*, *212*; **23** 512
writings **23** 493
Le Pautre, Claude **19** 210
Le Pautre, Jacques **19** 210
Le Pautre, Jean (1618-82) **12** 34; **19** 210*; **20** 416
pupils **19** 16, 210; **30** 344
reproductive prints by others **20** 458
works **1** 681; **6** *604*; **7** 569; **8** 455; **9** 28; **11** 573, 576; **18** 745; **19** 225; **24** 271; **29** 610
Le Pautre, Jean (1622-48) **19** 210
Le Pautre, Jean (1648-1735) **19** 210
Le Pautre, Pierre, I (1652-1716) **7** 746; **19** 210, 642; **26** 492; **31** 511
Le Pautre, Pierre, II (1660-1744) **11** 704; **19** 210, 213*; **20** 297
collaboration **20** 298
works **8** 71; **20** 450; **30** 704; **31** *719*
Lepcis Magna *see* LEPTIS MAGNA
Lepe, Mateo de **6** 591
Lepekhin, I. I. **27** 439
Lepel Cointet (family) **17** 685
Lepelletier de la Girardin **12** 725
Lepenski Vir **19** 214*; **25** *471*; **26** *705*; **28** 436, *437*
rock art **25** 495, 512
sculpture **19** 214
Lepère, (Louis) Auguste **19** 214–15*; **20** 603; **33** 369
collaboration **20** 603
groups and movements **17** 441; **33** 369
pupils **24** 884
works **9** 309; **19** *215*; **33** 361, *369*
Lepère, François **19** 214
Lepère, Jean-Baptiste **12** 898; **14** 592; **22** 47
Leperre-Durot **19** 382
Le Perrier, Guillaume (*fl* 14th cent.) **5** 666
Le Pho **32** 482, 483
Lepiani, Juan **24** 509
Lepic, Ludovic (-Napoléon) **8** 623; **10** 556; **19** 215–16*; **21** 896
Lépicié, (François-) Bernard **19** 216*
assistants **3** 107
pupils **19** 216
teachers **19** 646
works **4** 514; **11** 674; **17** 466; **18** 796
writings **6** 77
Lépicié, Nicolas-Bernard **19** 216–18*
patrons and collectors **4** 308; **11** 540; **30** 514
pupils **8** 507; **26** 93; **28** 50; **30** 369; **32** 334
reproductive prints by others **19** 261
works **6** 473; **19** *217*
Lépicié, Renée-Elisabeth **19** 216
Lepidus **27** 96
Lepies (family) **3** 600
L'Epine, Notre-Dame **27** 125
Lépine, Stanislas (-Victor-Edouard) **15** 151, 154; **19** 218*; **30** 375
Lepke **12** 474; **31** 401
Łepkowski, Józef **25** 143
Le Placard **25** 487, 493
Leplae, Charles **3** 573; **5** 44
Leplat, Raymond **33** 115
L'Eplattenier, Charles **19** 39
LePlay, Frédéric **10** 682; **18** 439
works **10** *682*
Le Plessis-Grimoult **6** 52, 53, 56; **12** 173
Lepoglava **8** *174*
Paulist Monastery **8** 178
Lepoittevin, Eugène (-Modeste-Edmond) **19** 218*; **30** 569
Leporskaya, Anna **27** 414
Le Portel **10** 472
Le Portier, Pierre **31** 841
Le Pot, Jean **3** 456
Leppe, Carlos **6** 598
Le Prestre, Blaise **11** 513
Leprestre de Vauban, Sébastien *see* VAUBAN, SÉBASTIEN LEPRESTRE DE
Leprêtre, Pierre **27** 588
Le Prince (family) **3** 460; **19** 218–19*; **27** 247; **29** 504
Le Prince (*fl* 1521) **4** 547
Leprince, Anne-Pierre **19** 219
Leprince, Auguste-Xavier **19** 218, 219*
Le Prince, Engrand **3** 456, 460; **19** 218, 219; **27** 252, 253
Leprince, Gustave **19** 219
Le Prince, Jean **3** 460; **19** 219; **27** 253
Le Prince, Jean-Baptiste **2** 240; **19** 219–20*
collaboration **11** 368
groups and movements **23** 503
methods **10** 559
patrons and collectors **2** 904
pupils **3** 870; **5** 921; **14** 846
reproductive prints by others **6** 563; **14** 366; **18** 858; **19** 268; **27** 571
sponsors **8** 372
works **3** 461; **19** *220*
Le Prince, Nicolas **3** 456, 460; **19** 219
Le Prince, Pierre **19** 219
Leprince, Robert-Léopold **19** 219
Lepsius, Karl Richard **10** 79, 82, 83, 90, 93
Leptis Magna **9** *510*; **19** 220–23*; **26** 853; **27** *5*, 115
amphitheatre **26** 874
arches **26** 868, 920
architecture **26** 854, 875, 885, 921
Arch of Septimius Severus **19** 222; **27** 41, 45; **31** 350
reliefs **19** *223*
baptisteries **3** 191
Basilica **3** 328, *328*; **9** 535; **19** 222, *222*; **23** 491; **26** 868, 883
columns **26** 882, 883
forum **26** 921; **27** 41
Forum of Septimius Severus **23** 485
Hadrianic Baths **19** 221; **26** 872, 919, 921; **27** 4, 67
Hunting Baths **19** *221*, 221–2; **26** 919; **27** 67
markets **11** 328; **19** 888, 889, *889*; **20** 438; **26** 871, 919
mosaics **27** 63
Roman circus **7** 342
sculpture **19** 222–3*
temples **26** 919
temple of the Severan family **26** 867; **30** 436
theatre **26** 919, 921
urban planning **27** 4
leptografia **18** 867; **20** 503
Le Puiset, Hugh of *see* HUGH OF LE PUISET
Le Puy (-en-Vélay) **11** *505*; **19** 223–5*
Cathedral of Notre-Dame **19** 223–5, 895; **26** 585
capitals **19** *224*
Chapelle des Morts **6** 466
doors **9** 152; **11** 623, 624; **12** 209; **16** 135; **26** 641
grilles **11** 624
sculpture **11** 554
jewellery **17** 519
lace **11** 649, 650, 651
Our Lady of France **28** 632
St Michel d'Aiguilhe Chapel **19** 224–5
Lépy, Adrien **22** 456
Le Quesnoy **11** 650; **21** 568
Lequeu, Jean-Jacques **10** 96; **19** 225*; **23** 489; **29** 94
Lequeux, Paul-Eugène **31** 276
Lequien, Justin **28** 500
Lequile, Diego **18** 879
Ler, de *see* ERRI
Lera, Bernardino De *see* DE LERA, BERNARDINO
Lera, Guglielmo De *see* DE LERA, GUGLIELMO
Le Raincy **12** 123; **23** 493
Château **6** 508; **9** 371
Notre-Dame **11** 525, 659; **12** 792; **13** 204; **14** 82; **19** 365; **24** 473, *473*; **29** 508
Lerambert, Henri **11** 639; **13** 878; **19** 225
Lerambert, Louis, II (1620-70) **8** 93; **11** 559; **19** 225*; **30** 660
Lerambert, Simon **19** 225
Lerat, Jacqueline **32** 117
Lerat, Jean **32** 117
Le Ray, Emmanuel **26** 205
Lercari, Nicola, Cardinal **3** 920
Lerch, Franz **32** 447
Lerche, Cornelius **2** 174
Lerchinger, Anton **28** 860
Lerebours **25** 618
Lerena Acevedo, Raúl
works **22** *23*
Leresche, Golay **30** 148
Lergaard (-Nielsen), Niels (Christian) **8** 736; **19** 226*
Le Rheu **3** 226
Leria, Giovanni-Maria **32** 465
Le Riche **32** 374
Lerici, C. M. **10** 638
Le Ricolais, Robert **14** 847
Lérida *see* LLEIDA
Lérins Monastery **11** *505*; **19** 226*
Lerius, Joseph van *see* VAN LERIUS, JOSEPH
Lerma (Spain) **19** 226–7*; **29** *258*
Palacio Ducal **19** *227*
Lerma (family) **2** 391
Lerma, Duquesa de Medinaceli y *see* MEDINACELI Y LERMA, Duquesa de
Lerma, Francisco Gómez de Sandoval y Rojas, Duque de **27** 723–4*
architecture **19** 226–7; **22** 67; **25** 455
gold **29** 336
paintings **5** 735; **27** 289
sculpture **10** 903
Lerma, Francisco José de **32** 172
Lerman, Richard **29** 99
Lermonth Door **28** 250
Lermontov, Mikhail **32** 736
Lerna **13** *363*; **14** *332*; **19** 227–8*, *228*
bastions **21** 551
fortifications **25** 522
House of Tiles **6** 170; **14** 336, 338–9
houses **14** 338
huts **14** 338
pottery **8** 312; **14** 342, 343, 344
seals **14** 336, 359, *359*
walls **14** 338
Lerna IV Patterned ware *see under* POTTERY → wares
Lerner, Abram **14** 575
Lerner, Allan Jay **30** 687
Lerner, Jaime **19** 228*
Leroi-Gourhan, André **19** 229*; **25** 480, 482–3, 485, 490
works **25** *483*, *486*
Le Roith, Harold (Hirsch) **17** 603; **19** 229*; **29** 106
Lerolle, Henry **14** 457; **19** 229–30*
Le Romeyn, John *see* JOHN LE ROMEYN
Le Rond d'Alembert, Jean *see* ALEMBERT, JEAN LE ROND D'
Le Rouge, George-Louis
works **11** *243*; **12** *123*
Le Rouge, Jacques *see* JACQUES LE ROUGE
Leroulx-Delaville, Marie-Guillemine *see* BENOIST, MARIE-GUILLEMINE
Le Roux, Bartholemew **31** 647, 648
Le Roux, Charles **20** 854; **31** 648
Le Roux, C. T. **12** 211; **22** 309–10*
Leroux, Eugène **8** 598
Leroux, (Louis) Hector **19** 230–31*
Le Roux, Jacques **1** 765; **13** 61; **19** 230*; **27** 251
Le Roux, Jean *see* PICARD, JEAN (*fl* mid-16th cent.)
Le Roux, Jean-Baptiste **11** 577; **19** 231*
assistants **4** 455
collaboration **24** 821
works **26** 493
Leroux, Laura **19** 231
Le Roux, Roulland **1** 765, 766; **19** 230*
groups and movements **11** 727
works **1** *766*; **13** 61; **27** 131, 247, 251
Le Roux de Lincy, A.-J.-V. **27** 881
Le Roy **11** 630
Leroy, Amable **9** 370
Leroy, Hugh **5** 571
Leroy, Isidore **8** 792; **32** 812
Leroy, Jean-François **8** 30, 461
Le Roy, Jehan **10** 663
Leroy, Joseph **20** 474
Leroy, Jules **19** 231–2*

Le Roy, Julien-David **11** 520; **19** 232*
 groups and movements **13** 608; **22** 735
 pupils **3** 523; **6** 138; **9** 420; **29** 551; **30** 728; **32** 508
 works **2** 164; **6** 454; **13** 233; **19** 117, 135
 writings **22** 925
Leroy, Léon **20** 603
Leroy, Louis (Joseph) **15** 151; **19** 232*
Le Roy, Marcel **20** 288
Le Roy, Martin **13** 175
Le Roy, Philibert **4** 549; **5** 168; **19** 233*; **32** 369
Leroy, Pierre-François **8** 699; **19** 233*
Le Roy, Simon **7** 466; **11** 265; **13** 226; **22** 448
Leroy de Barde, Alexandre-Isidore **19** 233–4*
Lerski, Helmar **19** 234*
Lersundi, Conde de **1** 523
Lery, Gaspard-Joseph Chaussegros de *see* CHAUSSEGROS DE LERY, GASPARD-JOSEPH
Léry, Jean de **4** 706; **29** 194
Le Sage **29** 668
Lesage, Alain-René **1** 600; **11** 500; **12** 609
Les Andelys *see* CHÂTEAU-GAILLARD
Lesbahy, Philippe **2** 889
Les Baux **1** 736
lesbian art *see* GAY AND LESBIAN ART
Lesbian cymatium moulding *see* MOULDINGS → types → cyma reversa
Lesbian masonry *see under* MASONRY → types
Lesbos **13** *363*; **19** *234*, 234–5*; **26** *908*
 architecture **32** 294
 pottery **13** 491, 497, 502, 571
 Temple of Aphrodite **13** 393
Lesbounit, Robert **15** 895
Les Caisses de St Jean **25** 536
Lescalle, Antoine de **31** 206
Les Cayes **31** *720*
Lescaze, William Edmond **14** 811; **19** 235–6*; **31** 632
 collaboration **3** 177; **24** 598; **28** 629, 833; **31** 597
 groups and movements **15** 885, 886
 works **22** 365; **23** 43; **31** 632
Leschot, Jean-Frédéric **2** 838
Lescluze, Jean de **19** 128
Lescole, Michel **32** 537
Les Combarelles **11** *505*; **19** 236*; **25** *470*, 475
Les Combarelles II **19** 236
Lescot, (Antoinette-Cécile-) Hortense *see* HAUDEBOURT-LESCOT, (ANTOINETTE-CÉCILE-) HORTENSE
Lescot, Pierre **19** 236–7*; **20** 133
 assistants **24** 812
 collaboration **13** 225
 patrons and collectors **6** 506; **19** 134; **31** 849, 850
 works **6** 506; **10** 744; **11** 258, 265, 513, 572, 656; **13** 226, 227; **19** *237*; **24** 159, 161, 468
Lescours, Armand de **6** 138
Lescouvé, François *see* LESCOWÉ, FRANÇOIS
Lescowé, François **14** 83
Lescuyer, Adenet **19** 238*; **20** 756
Lesdiguières, Charles de Blanchefort de Créquy, Duc de *see* CRÉQUY, CHARLES DE BLANCHEFORT DE
Lesdiguières, Duchesse de **27** 530
Lesdiguières, François de Bonne, Duc de **13** 635; **19** 238*; **26** 351
Les Dogues **29** 365
Lese, Benozzo di *see* GOZZOLI, BENOZZO
Les Ecourges **5** 894
Le Secq (des Tournelles), Henri (1818-82) **19** 86, 239*; **24** 663, 668
Le Secq, Henry (*fl* 1900) **19** 239
lesene *see under* PILASTERS → types
Les Eyzies **4** 313
Leshan **6** 707
Le Sidaner, Henri (Eugène Augustin) **19** 239*; **27** 240
Lesire, Paulus **8** 291
Lesja Church **23** 229
Les Jarrans, Ville-du-Pont **32** *280*
Lesker, Ludwig **12** 822
Leskoschek, Axel **28** 476
Leskovac
 Church of the Ascension **25** 343
 Municipal Museum **28** 459
Leskovec Church **28** 859
Leslie, Alfred **10** 688; **11** 729; **16** 820
Leslie, C(harles) R(obert) **11** 860; **19** 239–41*
 groups and movements **26** 500
 patrons and collectors **13** 696; **14** 718; **26** 75; **28** 576; **32** 338; **33** 453
 reproductive prints by others **27** 459
 teachers **33** 93
 works **10** 252; **19** *240*
 writings **10** 377
Leslie, Frank **17** 290
Leslie, George Dunlop **19** 241; **27** 564
Leslie, Robert Charles **19** 241
Leslie, Vernon **3** 624
Leslie, W. S. **14** 120
Leslie Castle (Grampian) **28** 224
Leslie House **32** 245
Les Martres-de-Veyre **27** 107
Les Mournouards **25** 507
Lesney **31** 257
Leşnic **26** 710
Lesnovo Monastery **19** *882*; **28** 449
 Church of the Archangel Michael **28** 442, 447
Le Somptier **8** 657
Les Orphelins d'Auteuil **20** 608
Lesotho **1** *214*; **19** 241–2*; **29** 102
 architecture **19** 241
 education (art) **19** 242
 houses **1** 311
 painting **19** 242
 pottery **19** 241, *242*
 sculpture **19** 242, *242*
 tapestries **19** 241
Lesou **22** 609
Lespagnandelle, Mathieu **5** 379
Lespérance, Pierre **1** 786; **5** 586
Lespicier, Antoine **16** 853; **26** 148
Lespilliez, Carl Albert von **2** 714; **11** 460; **22** 300
Lespinasse, Louis-Nicolas de
 works **24** *122*
L'Espine, Jean de *see* JEAN DE L'ESPINE
Lespingola, François **19** 242–3*; **24** 165
Lespugue **11** *505*; **19** 243*; **25** *470*
 bone-carvings **25** *492*
 figurines **19** *243*; **25** 488, 490
Les-Saintes-Maries-de-la-Mer **26** 603
Lessay Abbey **11** 509; **26** 589, 598; **32** 92
 church **26** 586
Lessayer, Jean **31** 842
Lessel, Fryderyk Albert **33** 607
Lesseline, Pierre de **19** 66
Lessels, John **2** 5; **28** 289
Lesseps, Ferdinand de **9** 765; **11** 622; **23** 902
Lesser, Aleksander **25** 106
Lesser Antilles *see* ANTILLES, LESSER
Lesser Vehicle Buddhism *see* BUDDHISM → branches → Hinayana
Lesseur, Wincenty Fryderyck **23** 530
Lessines **3** 606
Lessing, Carl Friedrich **12** 394; **17** 818; **19** 243–4*
 groups and movements **9** 460; **12** 394; **26** 740
 patrons and collectors **26** 111
 pupils **10** 99; **19** 244
 reproductive prints by others **29** 66
 teachers **14** 838
 works **9** 460; **11** 461, *461*; **14** 587; **22** 329
Lessing, Gotthold Ephraim **1** 660; **10** 401; **19** 245*; **26** 62; **33** 54, 293
 works **1** 179; **23** 108; **24** 91; **26** 224; **31** 768
  illustrated **14** 750; **21** 59
Lessing, Otto **12** 407; **19** 244*; **33** 296
Les Six *see* SIX, LES
el-Lessiya **29** 386
Lessjak, Ida **22** 702
L'Essor *see* ESSOR, L'
Lessore, Emile **10** 312; **33** 22, 452
Lessore, Frederick **19** 246
Lessore, Helen **19** 246*
Lessore, John **19** 246
Lessore, Thérèse **28** 661
L'Estache, Pierre **7** 416
Lestard, Jorge **2** 397
Lesteens (family) **3** 598
Lesteens, Willem **22** 717
Lester, Charles E(dwards) **19** 246*; **31** 671
Lester, Michelle **31** 660
 works **31** *660*
Lester, Richard **14** 511
Lestevenon, Willem Anne **18** 641
Leston, Eduardo **5** 123
Le Strange, Alice **14** 777
Le Strange, Hamon **14** 777
Le Sueur (family) **33** 365
Le Sueur **16** 717
Le Sueur, Antoine **19** 249
Le Sueur, Blaise Nicolas **14** 16
Le Sueur, Cathelin **19** 246
Lesueur, Charles-Alexandre **2** 744; **19** 484
Le Sueur, Eustache **11** 536, 641; **19** 246–9*; **24** 134
 collaboration **19** 21; **24** 253, 476; **25** 70; **26** 566
 patrons and collectors
  Condé, Henry II de Bourbon, Prince de (1588-1646) **7** 699
  Dezallier d'Argenville, Antoine-Joseph **8** 845
  Fieubet, Gaspard de **11** 61
  Girardon, François **12** 727
  Henry, Bon-Thomas **14** 395
  Hesselin, Louis (-Cauchon) **14** 492
  John VI, King of Portugal (*reg* 1816-26) **4** 725
  Lambert, Jean-Baptiste (1608-44) **18** 671
  Lambert, Nicolas **18** 671
  Musée du Louvre (Paris) **11** 666
  Robien, Christophe-Paul Gautron, Marquis de **26** 470
  Tallard, Marie-Joseph d'Hostun, Duc de **30** 274
  Tessin, Carl Gustav, Count **30** 524
  Thibaudeau, Narcisse-Adolphe, Comte de **30** 727
  Vassal de Saint-Hubert, Jean-Antoine-Hubert **32** 74
 pupils **19** 65
Le Sueur, Eustache—cont.
 reproductive prints by others **2** 708; **6** 518; **19** 437; **24** 712; **30** 746
 works **6** 435; **11** 534; **13** 783; **19** *247*, *248*
Le Sueur, Hubert **19** 249–50*, 582
 assistants **3** 875
 patrons and collectors **10** 360; **18** 855, 885; **29** 801; **32** 824
 works **10** 263, *263*, 441; **12** 340; **14** 855; **19** 606; **23** 687; **27** 548; **28** 294; **32** 864
Le Sueur, Jacques Philippe **21** 411
Lesueur, Jean-Baptiste-Cicéron **5** 342; **12** 835; **19** 250*; **26** 190; **31** 896
Le Sueur, Nicolas **25** 619, 622
Le Sueur, Philippe **19** 249
Le Sueur, Pierre **19** 249
Le Sueur, Pierre Etienne **8** 744
Lesueur, Thomas **7** 416
Les Vachons **25** 492
Les XX *see* XX, LES
Les XXX *see* XXX, LES
Lesyngham, Robert **10** 673
Leszczyński, Rafał **13** 774; **25** 138
Leszczyński, Stanislav I, King of Poland *see* STANISLAV I LESZCZYŃSKI, King of Poland
Leszek III, Prince of Lesser Poland and Kraków (*reg* 1279-88)
 seals **14** *410*
Lesznai, Anna **10** 108
Letang, Eugène **29** 913
Letard, Archbishop of Galilee **22** 705
Letarouilly, Paul-Marie **19** 251*
Le Tavernier, Jean **5** 211; **19** 251–2*; **31** 218
 works **3** 555; **19** *252*
Leţcani Round Church **26** 708
Letchworth (Herts) **8** 824; **10** 284; **12** 144, *145*; **14** 809; **24** 185–6, 187; **31** 728
 Art Gallery **26** 10
 Elementary School **28** 158
 First Garden City Heritage Museum **24** 186
 Free Church **23** 194
 furniture **14** 277
Le Tellier, François-Michel, Marquis de Louvois *see* LOUVOIS, Marquis de
Le Tellier, Jean **12** 831
Le Tellier, Louis **12** 831
Le Tellier, Michel **22** 465
Le Tellier, Pierre **19** 252*; **26** 246
Le Temple de Breuil **4** 780
Leth, Hendrik de **27** 271
Leth, Marie Gudme **8** 756
Lethaby, W(illiam) R(ichard) **2** 524; **10** 373–4; **15** 823; **19** 252–3*
 collaboration **5** 340; **11** 499; **12** 650; **25** 633; **26** 316; **28** 563
 groups and movements **2** 569, 575; **9** 739; **10** 239; **23** 498
 patrons and collectors **19** 311
 pupils **12** 314; **14** 252; **31** 348
 works **10** 283; **19** *253*; **29** 748
 writings **2** 360; **9** 527
Lethière, Guillaume **4** 529; **19** 254–5*
 collaboration **4** 36
 groups and movements **24** 387
 pupils **3** 125; **4** 319; **8** 829; **14** 228; **19** 38; **24** 815; **27** 265, 348; **30** 353
 works **19** *255*
Lethieullier, William **10** 79
Lethmaat, Herman **8** 102
Le Thor **26** 604
Le Thoreuil, St Maur-de-Glanfeuil **26** 599
Le Thoronet Abbey **7** 453; **13** 38; **21** 843
Leti **15** *751*, 789
Létin, Jacques de **19** 255*; **31** 382
Letnitsa **19** 255–6*; **25** *471*; **30** 771, 772
Leto, Antonino **28** 317, 657
Leto, Pomponio **19** 256*; **26** 848
Letona, José **5** 355
Letona, Justo **5** 355
Le Tonnelier, Louis-Auguste, Baron de Breteuil *see* BRETEUIL, LOUIS-AUGUSTE LE TONNELIER, Baron de
Letoon **19** 837, 840
Letort, Francis **23** 25
Letourmy, Jean-Baptiste **15** 142; **33** 359
 works **25** *243*
Le Tourneau, M. **9** 527
Lettaford (Devon) **32** 277
Lettera 22 *see under* TYPEWRITERS → models
lettering *see* INSCRIPTIONS
Letterkenny **16** 37
letters **28** 303
 China **6** 740, 742, *742*, 750, 755
 Italy **2** 166–7
Lett-Haines, Arthur **22** 139
Lettice **14** 445
Lettone, Henri **11** 410
Lettré, Emil **12** 450
Lettrisme **13** 890
Letts, Joshua **22** 111
Le Tungard, Guillem **12** 739
Letur **5** 834
Le Tur, Etienne *see* ETIENNE LE TUR
Letyński, Jan **25** 128
Leu, Hans, I (*d* 1507) **19** 256; **20** 641; **33** 736
Leu, Hans, II (*c*. 1490-1531) **19** 256–7*; **30** 131; **33** 736
 works **19** *257*; **30** 131
Leu, Thomas de **10** 392; **19** 257*; **32** 509
 reproductive prints by others **18** 811
 works **5** 172, 814; **9** 388; **25** 816
Leuba, Jeanne **24** 197
Leubingen **25** 523–4, 529
Leubus Monastery **12** 390
Leuchars, St Athernase **28** 267
Leuchtenberg, Eugène de Beauharnais, Duc de **3** 452*; **4** *299*
 architecture **4** 304; **18** 123
 collections **4** 298
 furniture **16** 729; **20** 90
 paintings **1** 141; **4** 470; **29** 658
 sculpture **26** 389
Leuchtenberg, Maria, Duchesse de **9** 403
Leuchtenberg, Maximilian de Beauharnais, Duc de **1** 141; **10** 90; **33** 449
Leufert, Gerd **19** 257*
Leuhusen, Regner **9** 188
Leukadia **13** *363*; **19** 257–8*
 Great Tomb **31** 109
 ivory-carvings **13** 597
 Lyson and Kallicles tomb **13** 546
 paintings **13** 551, 552
 tombs **13** 384, 391, 404, 603; **19** 257–8
 wall paintings **13** *552*
Leukas **13** *363*; **19** 258*; **31** 107
Leukios **27** 689
Leukos Limen (Egypt) *see* QUSEIR
Leukos Limen (Syria) *see* UGARIT
Leunenberger, Werner Otto **30** 135
Leung Kui-ting **14** 722
Leupenius, Johannes **19** 258*; **22** 843
Leupin, Herbert **25** 353
Leupold (family) **12** 430
Leupold, Jacob **4** 804
Leuppi, Leo **1** 666; **19** 541; **30** 135
Leura Tjapaljarri, Tim **19** 258*; **25** 324
Leuring, Dr **30** 760

Leusden, Willem van **19** 258–9*; **21** 789; **22** 854
Leuthner (von Grund), Abraham **6** 526; **8** 873; **19** 259*
Leuthner, Johann Georg **9** 171
Leutkirch im Allgäu Schloss Zeil **12** 410; **14** 50
Leutschau *see* LEVOČA
Leutze, Emanuel (Gottlieb) **19** 259–60*
groups and movements **26** 740
pupils **2** 30; **10** 99; **27** 556; **33** 228
works **11** 463; **14** 587
Leuven **3** *539*; **16** 907; **19** 260–61*
block-books **4** 145
Château of Arenberg **3** 545
colleges **7** 566
Dominican church **3** 552
education (art) **3** 617, 618
faience (ii) (ceramics) **3** 590
Gasthuisberg Hospital **14** *783*, 784
Katholieke Universiteit **3** 619; **27** 291
Lakenhal **13** 99
marks **3** 601
Onze Lieve Vrouw buiten de Muuren *see* Onze Lieve Vrouw van Ginderbuiten
Onze Lieve Vrouw van Ginderbuiten **4** 415–17; **13** 110
St Etienne **27** 256
St Jacobskerk **13** 112; **16** 541
St Michielskerk **3** 546; **14** 488; **25** 727
St Pietersgasthuis **27** 256
St Pieterskerk **3** 542, 566, 612; **13** 10, 62, 63; **15** 85; **26** 186
altarpiece **4** *591*, 591–2; **21** 353
sculpture **13** 112
silver **3** 598
Stadhuis **3** 543; **13** 63; **29** 414; **31** 238, *238*
roof **27** 131
sculpture **13** 100
stained glass **13** 182; **27** 255
tapestries **3** 606
Université Catholique de Louvain Medical Faculty Building *see under* BRUSSELS
Leuwen, Cornelis Cornelisz. van **32** 139
Leuwen Akademie voor Schone Kunsten **19** 260
Leux, Frans *see* LUYCKS, FRANS
Leuzinger **11** 22
Le Va, Barry **25** 645
Le Vacher de Charnois **1** 645; **16** 905
Levada, Villa Marcello **16** 719
Levá fronta **24** 440
Le Vaillant, François **29** 108
Le Val **21** 843
Le Valentin *see* BOULOGNE, VALENTIN DE
Levallois-Perret **10** 106
Le Valois, Nicolas **5** 370
Le Van (family) **32** 481
Levan, King of Kakheti (*reg* 1520–74) **12** 331
Le Van He **32** 483
Levant **30** 179, 186
architecture **30** 184
gem-engraving **16** 573
heraldry **14** 404
metalwork **16** 573; **30** 195
pottery **30** 196
Levantine rock art *see* SPANISH LEVANTINE ROCK ART
Levantino (family) **1** 579
Levanto **6** 380
Levanzo, Grotta dei Genovesi **28** 653
Levard **24** 266
Levasseur (family) **25** 801
Levasseur, Etienne **4** 330; **11** 597; **17** 684; **19** 261*
Levasseur, Eugène **19** 75
Levasseur, François-Noël **19** 261
Le Vasseur, Jean (1622-86) **19** 261
Levasseur, Jean-Baptiste-Antoine **19** 261
Le Vasseur, Jean-Charles **3** 463; **7** 570; **13** 642; **19** 261–2*
Le Vasseur, Jehan **4** 546
Levasseur, Michel **5** 584
Levasseur, Noël **19** 261*
Levasseur, Pierre **19** 261
Levasseur, Pierre-Louis-Noël **19** 261*
Le Vasseur d'Ossimont, Louis **23** 264
Levati, Giuseppe **16** 728
Le Vau, François **11** 517; **19** 262*, 267–8*
groups and movements **24** 169
patrons and collectors **18** 671
works **11** 517; **19** 59, 267
Le Vau, Louis **6** 508; **19** 262–7*; **20** 137; **23** 474
architecture **11** 516; **23** 474
châteaux **6** 508; **9** 176; **11** 573; **19** *266*; **20** 896; **22** 44; **24** 290; **32** 96, *97*, 582
colleges **11** 657; **19** *265*, 315; **23** 493; **24** 118
collonades **11** 657
galleries (iv) (art) **9** 14
hôtels particuliers **4** 756; **9** 353; **11** 657; **14** 789, *790*; **19** *263*, *264*
orangeries **12** 121; **23** 470
palaces **7** 665; **11** 657; **23** 811; **24** 162, 163
porticos **25** 266
stables **29** 485
staircases **29** 524
assistants **12** 725; **13** 790; **23** 474
collaboration **12** 121; **19** 21, 162, 163; **23** 811; **24** 468; **29** 833
competitions **7** 665
gardens **11** 261; **27** 536
groups and movements **19** 721
interior decoration **24** 162
patrons and collectors
Colbert, Jean-Baptiste (1619–83) **7** 546
Fouquet, Nicolas **11** 356, 657
Hesselin, Louis (-Cauchon) **14** 492
Lambert, Jean-Baptiste (1608-44) **18** 671
Lambert, Nicolas **18** 671
Louis XIV, King of France (*reg* 1643-1715) **4** 551; **6** 60; **21** 366; **32** 369, 370, 372
pupils **19** 267
sculpture **20** 481
Le Vaudreuil Castle **31** 834
Levavasseur, Jacques Nicolas **27** 249
Levchenko, Pyotr A. **31** 559
Le Veau, Jean-Jacques (-André) **4** 59; **19** 268*
Le Veau, Louis (*d* 1661) **19** 262*
Le Veau, Louis (1612-70) *see* LE VAU, LOUIS
Le Veau, Victoire-Geneviève **19** 268
Levecq, Jacobus **11** 447; **14** 794
Léveil, Jean **12** 155
Leveilly, Michel **19** 268–9*
works **4** 324, *324*; **5** 8
Level, André **11** 659; **19** 66
levels **13** 411
Leven, David Melville, 3rd Earl of *see* MELVILLE, DAVID, 3rd Earl of Leven
Leven, Hugo **12** 450, 453; **24** 581
Levenclaus, John **33** 637
Levens Hall (Cumbria) **31** 151
Levental', Valery **27** 397
Leventis, A. G., Collection *see under* ATHENS
Levêque, Auguste **19** 269*
Lever, Ashton **23** 740, 741
Lever, Charles **4** 885
Lever, Jill **10** 211
Lever, William Hesketh, 1st Viscount Leverhulme **10** 371; **12** 144; **19** 269–70*; **26** 111; **31** 725
Lever Brothers **5** 175
Leverett, Roger **9** 322
Leverhulme, William Hesketh Lever, 1st Viscount *see* LEVER, WILLIAM HESKETH, Viscount Leverhulme
Levert, Abraham **11** 410
Levert, Antoine *see* LEVERT, ABRAHAM
Leverton, Lancelot **19** 270
Leverton, Thomas **9** 122; **10** 643; **19** 270*
Le Vésinet **12** 120
homes for the aged **11** 359
Ste Marguerite **7** 693
Leveson-Gower, George Granville, 1st Duke of Sutherland **19** 270–71*; **33** 447
paintings **5** 63; **9** 755; **10** 365; **14** 808; **29** 548
Leveson-Gower, George Granville, 2nd Duke of Sutherland **3** 283; **8** 830; **19** 587
Leveson-Gower, Lord Francis *see* EGERTON, FRANCIS, 1st Earl of Ellesmere
Leveson-Gower, Ronald (Charles) *see* GOWER, LORD RONALD
Lévesque, Pierre Charles **10** 207; **32** 898
Levesville, Simon **22** 34
Le Veudre **7** 694
Levi, Carlo **31** 446
Levi, Doro **24** 589
Lévi, Eliphas **8** 244; **30** 168
Levi, Guillén de *see* GUILLÉN DE LEVI
Levi, Joseph de *see* LEVIS, GIUSEPPE DE
Levi, Juan de *see* JUAN DE LEVI
Levi, Rafi **30** 536
Levi, Rino **19** 271–2*
groups and movements **21** 783
staff **8** 181
works **4** 713; **5** 218; **27** 808
Leví, Samuel **22** 254; **31** 86
Lévi, Sylvain **9** 401; **11** 335
Levi Ben Isaac Hijo Caro **20** 122
Levick, Ruby **10** 373
Levicomte, Paul-Frédéric **12** 650
Levide **32** 522
Le Vieil, Guillaume **29** 506
Le Vieil, Pierre **24** 156; **29** 506, 514
Levien, Johann Martin **23** 65
Levieux **7** 778
Levieux, Reynaud **19** 272*
Levieux de Languedoc *see* LEVIEUX, REYNAUD
Le Vignon, Pierre **24** 478
Levi jeans **20** 594
Levi-Montalcini, Gino **16** 649; **23** 764; **31** 443
Levin, Indrik **27** 415
Levin, Renton Howard Wood **23** 259
Levina, L. M. **10** 141
Levine, David **18** 797; **27** 872
Levine, Jack **17** 578; **19** 272*; **27** 872; **31** 606
Levine, Les(lie Leopold) **19** 273*
Levine, Louis **12** 838
Levine, Marilyn **24** 687
Levine, Rahel **3** 799
Levine, Sherrie **19** 273*; **23** 50
groups and movements **7** 686; **25** 360
works **31** 609
Levins, James **16** 28
Levinsky, Ivan **28** 838; **31** 551
Levinsky, P. **28** 838
Levinson, Yevgeny (Adol'fovich) **11** 245; **19** 273–4*; **27** 380, 578
Levinson-Lessing, Vladimir (Frantsevich) **19** 274*
Leviny, Ernest **2** 765; **19** 274*
works **2** 765, *765*
Levi-Provençal, Evariste **16** 549
Le Virloys, Charles François Roland **10** 206
Lévis, Anne-Claude-Philippe de Tubières de Grimoard de Pestels de, Comte de Caylus *see* CAYLUS, Comte de
Levis, Francesco de **19** 274
Levis, Giovanni Battista de **19** 275
Levis, Giuseppe de **19** 274*
Lévis, Marie de **26** 555
Levis, Ottavio de **19** 275
Levis, Paolo de **19** 274
Levis, Servo de **19** 275
Le Visite, Jean *see* JEAN LE VISITE
Lévi-Strauss, Claude **2** 136, 137, 534; **19** 275*; **22** 674
works **29** 787; **30** 22
Levitan, Isaak (Il'ich) **19** 275–7*; **27** 391
groups and movements **33** 379
patrons and collectors **22** 135
productions **20** 232
pupils **27** 809
works **19** *277*; **22** 178; **27** *391*
Levitan, Ye L. **28** 747
Levitan Museum *see under* PLYOS
Levitsky, Dmitry (Grigor'yevich) **19** 278–9*; **27** 388
patrons and collectors **31** 312
works **19** *279*; **27** 579, *579*
Levitsky, Lev (Sergeyevich) **19** 279
Levitsky, Sergey (L'vovich) **19** 279–80*; **24** 669
Levitsky-Nos, Grigory **19** 278
Levitt, Helen **19** 280*; **24** 678
Levkas *see* LEUKAS
Levni **16** 131, 304, 350, 610; **19** 280*
Levoča **19** 280–81*; **28** *848*
architecture **14** 885
Komitat House **28** 850
Minorite church **14** 894
Old Town Hall **28** 849
panel paintings **14** 899
prints **28** 852
St James **14** 883, 893; **28** 854
altarpiece **14** 893, 898; **19** *281*, 281; **28** 851
sculpture **14** 893
tomb of Imre Thurzó **14** 893
tomb of Szaniszló Thurzó **14** 893
wall paintings **14** 898; **28** 851
sculpture **14** 893; **28** 854
Spiš Museum **28** 857
Levoča, Pavel of *see* PAVEL OF LEVOČA
Levon, Anton Christian **11** 108
Levonkla **2** 427
Levrac-Tournières, Robert *see* TOURNIÈRES, ROBERT
Levray, Nicolas **3** 841; **25** 705
Lèvres Nues, Les **20** 414
Levtsky, Dmitri **31** 565
Levuka **11** 70
Lévy, Alfred **20** 145
Levy, Col **2** 761
works **2** *762*
Lévy, Denise **19** 282*; **31** 382
Lévy, Edmond **29** 514
Lévy, Emile **9** 424; **11** 546; **19** 282*
Levy, Emmanuel **17** 580
Levy, H. **30** 411
Lévy, Henri Léopold **11** 546; **19** 282*
Levy, Juan de *see* JUAN DE LEVI
Levy, Julien **7** 873; **13** 12; **30** 22
Levy, Leon **1** 896
Lévy, Leopold **10** 719; **16** 591, 805; **31** 454
Levy, Ludwig **29** 751
Levy, M. **26** 207
Levy, Manuel **9** 311
Lévy, Pierre **19** 281–2*; **31** 382
Levy, Rudolf **19** 283*; **25** 744
Levy, Uriah Phillips **8** 566
Levý, Václav **2** 546; **8** 387; **22** 403
Lévy-Dhurmer, Lucien **19** 283*; **23** 504
Levý Hradec **8** 376
Levyy Front Iskusstv *see* LEF
Lewandowski, Edmund D. **25** 462
Lewenwaldt, Caspar von *see* LEHMANN, CASPAR
Lewerentz, Sigurd **19** 283–4*
collaboration **2** 611; **6** 151; **11** 139; **18** 664
groups and movements **5** 56
teachers **3** 784
works **19** *284*; **30** 75, 684
Lewers, Darani **2** 766; **18** 799
Lewers, Gerald **2** 753; **30** 160
Lewers, Margo **2** 753
Lewes (E. Sussex)
Anne of Cleves House Museum **11** 118
architecture **4** 787
Castle **6** 53, 55; **9** 144
priory of St Pancras **7** 473
Lewes, George Henry **17** 639
Lewes Group **10** 243; **26** 650
Lewicki, L. **18** 433
Lewiczyn Church **25** 105
Lewis, C. Day **26** 360
Lewis (i), Charles (1786-1836) **19** 285
Lewis (i), Charles George (1808-80) **19** 285*; **25** 619
Lewis, (Mary) Edmonia **19** 286*; **33** 309
works **1** 440, *441*
Lewis, Edward G. **27** 565
Lewis, Edward Morland **32** 786
Lewis, Fielding **29** 842
Lewis (ii), Frances **19** 285–6*
Lewis (i), Frederick Christian, the elder (1779-1856) **19** 284*
works **15** *407*
Lewis (i), Frederick Christian, the younger (1813-75) **19** 285*
Lewis (i), George Robert **19** 284*
Lewis, Indian *see* LEWIS (i), FREDERICK CHRISTIAN, THE YOUNGER
Lewis, Ion **33** 136*
Lewis, James **32** 553
Lewis, John (*fl* 1750s) **16** 14
Lewis, John (*fl* 19th cent.) **5** 667
Lewis (i), John Frederick **9** 766; **19** 285*
collaboration **20** 602
collections **15** 742
groups and movements **23** 504
patrons and collectors **11** 331; **33** 251
works **2** 106; **5** 401; **10** 253; **15** 745; **22** 59; **23** *505*
Lewis (i), John Hardwicke **19** 285*
Lewis (i), Lennard **19** 285
Lewis, Lucy M(artin) **19** 286*; **22** 608
Lewis, Meriwether **22** 592
Lewis, Mortimer (William) **19** 286–7*; **23** 36
staff **20** 570
works **2** 738; **18** 887; **30** 158
Lewis, Norman **1** 444
Lewis, Philip **3** 623, 625
Lewis, Roberto (Gerónimo) **19** 287*; **23** 905
pupils **6** 130; **16** 790; **28** 741
works **23** 904, 906
Lewis, Samuel Savage **12** 266
Lewis, Stephen **4** 353
Lewis (ii), Sydney **19** 285–6*
Lewis, Thomas (*fl* 1653-61; bookbinder) **4** 353
Lewis, Thomas C. (*fl* late 19th cent.; organ-builder) **3** 746
Lewis, Thomas Hayter (1818-89; architect) **22** 60
Lewis (i), William **19** 284

Lewis, (Percy) Wyndham **10** 374; **12** 184; **19** 287–8*; **24** 427
 exhibitions **10** 255
 groups and movements **19** 591
  Camden Town Group **5** 516, 517
  Group X **13** 712; **17** 850
  London Group **19** 622, 623
  Omega Workshops **11** 809; **23** 437
  Post-Impressionism **25** 356
  Rebel Art Centre **23** 15; **26** 59, 466
  Vorticism **1** 74; **10** 256; **25** 380; **32** 700, 701, 702
 patrons and collectors **1** 496; **4** 315; **14** 132; **25** 380
 teachers **4** 880; **19** 591; **31** 146
 works **14** 107; **19** *288*, 896; **22** 331; **26** 59; **31** 706
Lewis Chessmen **6** 389, 557; **26** 699
lewises **13** 388
Lewis Painter **13** 523
Lewitt, Jan **25** 353
LeWitt, Sol **19** 288–9*; **30** 201; **31** 609
 collaboration **31** 869
 groups and movements **1** 80; **7** 685; **10** 416; **21** 645, 646
 patrons and collectors **24** 24; **27** 478; **32** 623
 works **1** 738; **10** 558; **16** 58; **19** *289*, 492
Lewthwaite, Jane **14** 275
Lewyn, Gabriel **31** 649
Lewyn, John **19** 289–90*
Lewyn, Walter **19** 290
Lexicon 80 *see under* TYPEWRITERS → models
lexicons *see* DICTIONARIES
Lexikon der Kunst **4** 24
Lexow-Hansen, Søren **23** 230
Leybold, Karl **22** 704
Leybowicz, Herszko **25** 841
Leydel, Peter Joseph **23** 340
Leyden *see* LEIDEN
Leyden, Aertgen van *see* AERTGEN VAN LEYDEN
Leyden, Cornelis, Pieter, Baron van **20** 693; **28** 362
Leyden, Jan van (Anabaptist leader) **1** *592*
Leyden, Jan van (artist) **2** 204
Leyden, Lucas van *see* LUCAS (HUYGHZ.) VAN LEYDEN
Leyden, Pieter Cornelis, Baron van *see* CORNELIS, PIETER, Baron van Leyden
Leyden, Rudolph van **4** 290
Leydenberch, Bruno Ellardsz. van **32** 401
Leydenberch, Cornelis Ellardsz. van **32** 401
Leydendorf, Franz Anton von **18** 175
Leyden jars **24** 651, 653
Leyden Plaque **21** 243
Leydensdorff, Franz Anton **33** 280
Leyen, Anthonie van **4** 38
Leyen, Carl Casper von der, Archbishop of Trier **31** 327
Leyen, Jan van *see* COCK, JAN WELLENS DE
Leyen, von der (family) **12** 464
Leygebe, Gottfried Christian **2** 456; **14** 650; **19** 290*
Leygonier y Haubert, Francisco de **19** 290*
Leykam, Marek **14** 819; **32** 873
Leyland, F(rederick) R(ichard) **19** 290–91*; **33** 143
 decorative works **11** 748
 interior decoration **1** 171; **9** 29; **10** 283; **15** 868; **17** 466
 paintings **5** 266, 267; **10** 367; **22** 51; **25** 555; **27** 187; **33** 139, 144
Leyniers (family) **5** 49; **14** 617; **17** 7; **30** 320, 324
Leyniers, Catherine **16** 867
Leyniers, Daniël, II **5** 50
Leyniers, Everaert **17** 649
Leyniers, Urbaan **5** 50
Leyre, S Salvador **26** 606, 607
Leys, Adam **28** 260
Leys, Henri **3** 615; **14** 587; **18** 680; **19** 291–2*
 assistants **1** 676
 collaboration **8** 592
 patrons and collectors **25** 41
 pupils **8** 592; **14** 384; **29** 682
 teachers **8** 591
 works **2** 197, 204; **3** 562; **19** *291*; **22** 329
Leys, P. **32** 725
Leyster, Judith **13** 895; **19** 292–3*; **21** 813; **22** 840; **33** 308
 teachers **14** 92, 94, 95
 works **11** 225, 447; **19** *292*
Leyten, Johann von der **17** 696
Leytenbach, Joseph Schemerl von *see* SCHEMERL VON LEYTENBACH, JOSEPH
Leython *see* LEIDEN
Leżajsk Church **25** 115, 120
 sculpture **25** *114*
Lezama Leguizamon (family) **28** 884
Lezama Lima, José **8** 233; **25** 272
Lezgin **27** 432
Lezhë **1** *537*, 538
Lézine, A. **13** 841
Leżno **25** 109
Lezoux **27** 107, 108
Lezze, Andrea da **19** 627
Lezze, Giovanni da **19** 627
LF Monogrammist **2** 716
Lhaje Chöchang **30** 829
Lhasa **19** 293–5*; **30** *806*
 coins **30** 837
 dyes **30** 846
 guilds **30** 847
 houses **30** 821
 jewellery **30** 839
 Jokhang Temple **19** 293–4, *294*; **30** 815
  roofs **30** 842
  sculpture **30** 825
  wall paintings **30** 829
  wood-carvings **30** 846
 metalwork **30** 840
 Norbulingka **30** 820, 847
 Potala Palace **5** 105; **19** 294; **21** 593; **30** 813, 820, *820*
  collections **30** 849
  stupas **30** 842
  woodwork **30** 846
 Ramoche **5** 104
 sculpture **30** 822
 textiles **30** 812
 Tibetan Guest House **6** 705
 Tsug Lagkhang *see* Jokhang Temple
Lhatse **30** 818
L'Herbier, Marcel **20** 203
L'Héritier de Brutelle, Charles-Louis **26** 73
L'Hermite, Jean **29** 300
Lhermite, Martin-Etienne **11** 596
Lhermitte, Léon (-Augustin) **19** 39, 295–6*; **22** 330
 works **19** *295*
Lheureux, François **13** 227
Lheureux, Louis-Ernest **19** 296–7*
Lheureux, Pierre **13** 227
Lhota **15** 733
Lhota, Antonín **4** 887
Lhoták, Kamil **8** 394
Lhote, André **14** 205; **16** 17; **19** 297–8*, 325
 assistants **6** 84; **24** 108
 collaboration **8** 482; **13** 836; **14** 486
 groups and movements **8** 240, 246; **28** 347
Lhote, André—cont.
 patrons and collectors **4** 391; **32** 178
 pupils **29** 108
  'Ali, Shakir **1** 637
  Bærtling, Olle (Bertil Georg) **3** 43
  Basaldúa, Héctor **3** 318
  Berk, Nurullah **3** 785
  Berni, Antonio **3** 826
  Bisilliat, Maureen **4** 94
  Black, Dorrit (Foster) **4** 107
  Brennand, Francisco **4** 745
  Butler, Horacio **5** 311
  Camargo, Iberê **5** 451
  Cartier-Bresson, Henri **5** 896
  Castagnino, Juan Carlos **6** 10
  Ciucurencu, Alexandru **7** 362
  Courtin, Pierre (-Louis-Maurice) **8** 63
  Cowley, Grace **2** 749
  De Lempicka, Tamara **8** 662
  Evergood, Philip **10** 661
  Eyüboğlu, Bedri Rahmi **10** 719
  Eyüboğlu, Eren **10** 719
  Gillies, W(illiam) G(eorge) **12** 637
  Grau, Ricardo **13** 322
  Guevara Moreno, Luis **13** 798
  Hone, Evie (Sydney) **14** 718
  Hoyningen-Huene, George **14** 816
  Kawaguchi, Kigai **17** 860
  Kemble, Kenneth **17** 894
  Knudsen, Gerda **23** 226
  Konjović, Milán **18** 230
  Jellett, Mainie **17** 473
  McGuinness, Norah **19** 891
  Mualla, Fikret **22** 251
  Pepper, Beverly **24** 372
  Rickey, George (Warren) **26** 360
  Savva, Christoforos **28** 21
  Schantz, (Karl) Philip (Gunnar) von (*b* 1928) **28** 51
  Schmela, Alfred **28** 120
  Šumanović, Sava **29** 922
  Tarsila **4** 717; **30** 348
  Tollu, Cemal **31** 94
  Villalba, Darío **32** 558
  Weeks, John **33** 24
  Ziapur, Jalil **15** 898
 works **19** *297*
Lhote, François **19** 725
Lhôte, Nestor **10** 82; **20** 418
Lhuillier, Charles **4** 556; **9** 372; **11** 789
li see under VESSELS → types
Li, Chu-tsing **7** 161
Li, J. **6** 924
Liagno, Teodor de *see* NAPOLETANO, FILIPPO
liana **3** *331*
Li An-chung *see* LI ANZHONG
Liancourt **12** 120
Liancourt, Duc de **11** 661; **19** 300*
Liang Boliang *see* LIANG KAI
Liang Ch'ing-biao *see* LIANG QINGBIAO
Liang Fengzi *see* LIANG KAI
Lianghuai **7** 10
Liang Juting *see* LEUNG KUI-TING
Liang Kai **6** 783, 809; **14** 137; **19** 300–301*; **29** 67
 patrons and collectors **17** 172; **30** 465
 works **5** 761; **6** 784; **17** 170; **19** *301*
Liang K'ai *see* LIANG KAI
Liang Qingbiao **2** 124; **7** 153; **30** 49
Liang Sicheng **19** 301–2*; **33** 496
Liang Siyong **7** 159
Liang Ssu-ch'eng *see* LIANG SICHENG
Liang Ssu-yung *see* LIANG SIYONG
Liang Stele **6** 744, *744*
Liangzhou *see* WUWEI
Liangzhu **6** *615*; **19** 302
Liangzhu culture **7** 159; **19** 302*
 jade **7** 1, *1*; **19** 302
 pottery **19** 302
Liani, Francesco **19** 302–3*; **22** 480
Liaño, Felipe de **19** 303*; **27** 706
Liano, Francesco *see* LIANI, FRANCESCO
Lianori, Pietro **21** 462
Lianozovo Circle **25** 834; **27** 397
Li Anzhong **14** 137
Liaoan Qingyu **17** 169
Liao Chi-ch'un **30** 247
 works **30** *247*
Liao Jichun *see* LIAO CHI-CH'UN
Liao period *see under* CHINA → periods
Liardet, John **29** 835
Liatzasolo, Martín Diéz de *see* DIÉZ DE LIATZASOLO, MARTÍN
Liautaud, Georges **14** 58; **19** 304*
Libaerts, Elisius **2** 473
 works **2** *473*
Líbal, D. **8** 426
Libanios (of Antioch) **9** 557; **10** 129; **12** 71
Libation Painter **13** 531
 works **13** *531*
Libau *see* LIEPAJA
Libay, Karol L. **28** 853
Libay, Samuel **28** 856
Libberth, Karol **32** 878
Libbey, Edward Drummond **19** 304; **23** 22; **31** 667
Libbey, William L. **19** 304; **22** 240; **23** 22
Libbey, W. L., & Son Co. **19** 304
Libbey Glass Co. **5** 583; **14** 252; **19** 304*; **20** 593; **23** 22; **31** 644, 667
Libbey-Owens-Ford **12** 854; **19** 304
Libby, W. F. **22** 673
Libby, Willard **2** 303
Libe, Pietro **23** 754
Liběchov Castle **8** 400
libelli **27** 591
Libenice **25** 536
Libenský, Stanislav **8** 411; **23** 271; **25** 423, 435; **33** 630, 631
Libera, Adalberto **16** 649; **19** 304–5*
 collaboration **24** 694; **26** 364
 groups and movements **13** 728; **21** 422; **26** 15, 16
 works **11** 62, 844; **16** 650; **19** *305*; **26** 762
Liberale (Bonfanti) da Verona **19** 305–7*
 attributions **6** 4, *4*; **11** 692; **12** 734
 collaboration **12** 733; **18** 697; **27** 766
 pupils **5** 815; **12** 658; **29** 597; **31** 161
 works **3** 751; **6** 5; **19** *306*
Liberalitas Julia *see* ÉVORA
Liberatore, Niccolò di *see* NICCOLÒ DA FOLIGNO
Liberatore, Niccolò di *see* NICCOLÒ DI LIBERATORE
Liberchies **3** 592
Liberec **8** 381
 education (art) **8** 425, 426
 Museum of Applied Art **8** 424
 textiles **8** 419
Liber Floridus Lamberti **1** 653
Libergier, Hugues **19** 308*; **26** 45, 120
Libergs, Jānis **12** 825; **18** 852
Liber hieroglyphicorum aegyptorum *see under* CODICES → individual manuscripts
Liberi, Marco **19** 308
Liberi, Pietro **16** 675; **19** 308–9*
 assistants **19** 706
 patrons and collectors **8** 427
 works **19** *309*
Liberia **1** *214*, 386; **19** 309–10*
 architecture **19** 310*
Liberia—cont.
 baby-carriers **1** 296
 basketwork **1** 296
 body arts **1** 289
 houses **1** 319
 masks **1** 242–3, 256, 282, 339, 340; **8** *487*, *488*
 museums **19** 310*
 painting **19** 310*
 patronage **1** 242–3; **19** 310*
 portraits **1** 267
 sculpture **19** 310*
 spoons **1** *291*, 368; **8** *489*
 stools **1** 365
 women **1** 247, 340
 wood **1** *291*
 wood-carvings **8** *487*, *489*
Liberikh, Nikolay (Ivanovich) **27** 425
Liberius III, Bishop **27** 827
Liberius, J. **6** 365
Liber linteus **10** 636
Liberman, Alexander **2** 852; **24** 213; **28** 52
Libero, Libero de **26** 777
Liberotti (family) **12** 264
Libert Neven, August *see* NEVEN, AUGUST LIBERT
Liberts, Ludolfs
Liberty, Arthur Lasenby **6** 164; **9** 295; **10** 283, 313; **19** 311*
Liberty & Co. **17** 440; **19** 594, 596; **22** 60
 archives **2** 365
 designers **18** 65
 enamel **10** 347
 interior decoration **10** 283
 jewellery **6** 164; **10** 346; **17** 528; **18** 170
 metalwork **10** 334, 336, 344; **15** 714; **16** 568; **20** 445; **23** 238; **24** 580
 staff **19** 867
 textiles **2** 755; **4** 71; **10** 356; **22** 868
 wallpaper **28** 549, 742
Li Bing *see* LEE BYNG
Libmann, Ivan **27** 584
Libochovice, Prince **5** 701
Libochovice Castle **6** 605
Liboje **28** 862, *863*
Libon (Elia) **23** 429
Libon, Guy **3** 593
Librairie Hachette **6** 491
libraries **2** 364, 365, 366, 367, 368, 533; **4** 25–6, 27; **19** 311–21*; **31** 235
 catalogues *see under* CATALOGUES → types
 historical and regional traditions
  Africa **1** 439*
  Ancient Near East **19** 311*
  Antigua (island) **2** 153
  Antilles, Lesser **2** 153
  Argentina **2** 406*
  Australia **2** 369, 772–3*
  Austria **2** 832–3*; **32** *457*
  Belgium **3** 618–19*
  Benedictine Order **4** 728
  Bolivia **4** 270
  Brazil **4** 728–9*
  Britain **4** 22
  Buddhism **19** 317
  Bulgaria **5** 162–3*
  Burma **5** 232
  Canada **2** 367; **4** 22; **5** 592–3*; **19** *320*
  Chile **6** 600–601*
  China **19** 317*
  Colombia **7** 612
  Czech Republic **8** 425*
  Denmark **8** 761*
  Ecuador **9** 714*
  England **10** 376*; **19** 315; **22** 356; **23** 686
   Baroque **12** *594*; **19** *315*
   Greek Revival **28** *874*
   19th cent. **19** *318*
   20th cent. **33** *218*

libraries
historical and regional traditions—cont.
Finland **10** *219*; **11** 112*
France **11** 673–4*; **13** 153; **18** *582*, *583*
Germany **9** 455; **12** 481–2*; **19** *316*, 318
Gothic **13** 153, 155
Greece **13** 361*
Greece, ancient **19** 311–12*; **26** *909*
Grenada **2** 153
Guadeloupe (country) **2** 153
Guatemala **13** 769*
Hungary **15** 19*
India, Republic of **15** 184*
Indian subcontinent **15** 208, 546; **16** 344
Ireland **16** 38*
Islamic **16** 272; **19** 316–17*
Israel **16** 572*
Italy **2** 365; **8** 601; **14** 867; **16** 776–7*; **21** 468
Mannerism **19** *314*; **21** *452*
17th cent. **4** *426*
Japan **17** *91*; **19** 317*, 320
Mesopotamia **2** 364; **19** 311
Mexico **21** 398*
Netherlands, the **22** 909*
New Zealand **23** 76*
Nicaragua **23** 86*
Norway **23** 244*
Peru **24** 518*
Poland **25** 142*
Portugal **25** 319*
Romania **26** 725*
Rome, ancient **9** 20; **19** 311–12*; **26** *909*, *914*; **27** 30
St Kitts **2** 153
St Lucia **2** 153
St Vincent **2** 153
Scotland **28** 275*
South Africa **29** 121
Spain **29** *272*, 357–8*
Sweden **30** *74*, 119*
Switzerland **30** 156*
Turkey **26** *914*; **31** *453*
United States of America **2** 367; **4** 22, 23, 24; **14** *197*; **31** 666, 670–71*
Gothic Revival **11** *849*
19th cent. **20** *18*
20th cent. **4** *475*; **26** *341*
Uruguay **31** 758–9*
Venezuela **32** 180–81*
types
natural history **4** 484
public **5** 781; **19** 318, 319; **23** *41*; **25** *666*
university **19** 319, 320, 321
library cupboards *see under* CUPBOARDS → types
Library of the Fine Arts **24** 446
Librazhd, Kosharisht cave **1** 539
Libre Esthétique **2** 562, 571; **3** 564; **19** 321–2*; **32** 591
members **3** 614; **5** 44; **19** 137
Carrière, Eugène **5** 880
Cézanne, Paul **6** 371
Claus, Emile **7** 405
Degouve de Nuncques, William **8** 628
Dubois, Paul (-Maurice) (ii) (1859-1938) **9** 326
Ensor, James (Sidney Edouard), Baron **10** 411
Frampton, George (James) **11** 499
Heymans, Adrien Joseph **14** 507
Laermans, Eugène **18** 625
Maus, Octave **20** 862
Mellery, Xavier **21** 86
Morren, George **22** 136
Oleffe, Auguste **23** 399
Rousseau, Victor **27** 268
Signac, Paul **28** 698
Libre Esthétique
members—cont.
Thévenet, Louis **30** 726
Vallgren, Ville **31** 828
Vogels, Guillaume **32** 679
works **14** 604; **31** 888
Libreville **1** *394*; **11** 879
CICIBA building **11** 879
Musée des Arts et Traditions **11** 880
Petit Musée *see* Musée des Arts et Traditions
St Michael of Nkembo **11** 879
sculpture **11** *879*
Libri, Francesco dai **19** 322*
Libri, Girolamo dai **19** 322–3*; **32** 343
collaboration **7** 467; **22** 130
works **19** *323*; **32** 341
Libri, Guglielmo **2** 595
Libri amicorum **12** 273
Libri Carolini **15** 80
Libris, Stefano a *see* STEFANO A LIBRIS
Libro de' disegni **16** 814
Libro della China *see under* CODICES → individual manuscripts
Libro W (untraced) **19** 354
Libsohn, Sol **28** 694
Libštejn, František Karel, Count **8** 409
Libya **1** *214*, 376; **19** 323–4*; **26** *919*
architecture **19** 324
banknotes **3** 182
basilicas (non-ecclesiastical) **3** *328*; **19** *222*
baths **19** *221*
dress **1** 887
finials (scrolls) **17** 569
fortifications **21** *560*
gymnasia **8** *368*
marble **19** *223*
mosaics **27** 63
painting **19** 324
reliefs **19** *223*
rock art **19** 323
skins **19** 3
temples **8** *367*
textiles **19** 324
theatres **27** 485
towns **27** *5*
trade **13** 372
turbans **16** 459
urban planning **27** *5*
Libyan **1** 377; **9** 778, 783, 784; **30** 695
Libyan Palette **9** 868
Lice, Anda **4** 180
Liceaga, Alfonso **32** 558
Licek, Adam Lev **24** 463
licences, export *see* ART LEGISLATION
Ličenoski, Lazar **19** 324–5*, 884
Liceus de Artes e Ofícios *see* CRAFTS AND TRADES SCHOOLS
Li Chao-tao *see* LI ZHAODAO
Lichchhavi **5** 102; **22** 754, 759, 760, 766; **24** 251
see also:
MANADEVA, King
PASHUPRAKHA, King
Li Cheng (919-67) **6** 773, 797, 798, 819; **7** 99; **19** 325–6*; **29** 67
attributions **7** *706*, 707
groups and movements **29** 244; **33** 528
works **6** 789, *797*; **19** *325*; **33** 476
Licheng (Shandong)
Shentong Temple **6** 649; **33** 35
Simen ta **23** 773
Li Chengsou **19** 478
lichens **9** 492*; **18** 656
Licherie, Louis **2** 708; **19** 22; **26** 260
Lichfield (Staffs; UK) **31** 709
Cathedral of St Mary and St Chad **10** 266; **13** 44, 82, 211
ballflower **3** 121
chantry chapels **7** 267
chapter house **6** 466
doors **9** 155
piers (ii) (masonry) **24** 751
restorations **33** 446
screen **28** 295, 296
spire **29** *412*, 413
tombs **31** 131
vaults **32** 94
manuscripts **15** 875
Lichfield School (CA; USA) **28** 159
Lichfield, Patrick **3** 71
Lichfield Gospels *see under* GOSPEL BOOKS → individual manuscripts
Li Chi (1059-1109) **6** 823
Li Chi (1896-1979) **19** 326–7*
excavations **7** 159
works **7** 159
Li Chieh *see* LI JIE
Li Chien-chung *see* LI JIANZHONG
Li Ch'ih *see* LI CHI (1059-1109)
Li Ch'ing-chao *see* LI QINGZHAO
Li Ching-hsün *see* LI JINGXUN
Li Ch'ing-lu *see* LI QINGLU
Li Ching-yu *see* LI JINGYOU
Lichnowsky, Mechtilde von **2** 288
Licht, Hugo **19** 111, 327*; **26** 190; **28** 177
Lichtdruck *see* PRINTING → processes → collotype
Lichtdruck Werkstatt **7** 576
Lichtenau, Frederica, Countess of *see* FREDERICA, Queen of Prussia, Countess Lichtenau
Lichtenberg, Georg Christoph **19** 327*
Lichtenfels, Eduard Peithner von *see* PEITHNER VON LICHTENFELS, EDUARD
Lichtenschopf, Leopold **8** 413
Lichtenstein, Alfred **24** 427
Lichtenstein, Roy **19** 327–9*
dealers **6** 23
groups and movements **23** 49, 261; **25** 232
methods **3** 703; **25** 24
patrons and collectors **24** 24; **33** 45
works **1** 129, *129*; **2** 107; **7** 649; **19** *328*, 492; **25** 620; **28** 52, 300; **29** 671, *671*; **31** 608; **33** 364, *364*
Lichtwark, Alfred **12** 476; **23** 394; **28** 342
Li Chüeh *see* LI JUE
Li Chun (*fl* 605) **4** 800; **6** 644; **29** 905
works **4** *800*
Li Chun (*fl* 12th cent.) **6** 817
Li Chung-jen *see* LI ZHONGREN
Li Chung-sheng **30** 249
Licini, Osvaldo **16** 681; **19** 329–30*; **21** 528
Licinia Sabinilla **27** 91
Licinio (family) **5** 819
Licinio *see* PORDENONE
Licinio, Arrigo **19** 330
Licinio, Bernardino **5** 792; **9** 265; **19** 330*
Licinio, Fabio **19** 330
Licinio, Giulio **2** 716, 793; **19** 330*
works **4** 695; **10** 737, *737*; **28** 852
Licinius, Emperor of Rome (*reg* 307-24) **9** 655; **27** 44
Licinius Murena **27** 30
Licino, Giulio **14** 899
Lick, James **7** 745
Lick, Konrad **11** 731
Lida, St Joseph **3** 527
Li Daoyuan **7** 98
Liddell, Joseph **31** 651
Liddle, Maureen **3** 64
Li Deli **6** 733
Lideřovice **8** 377
Li Deyu **12** 87
Li Di **6** 817; **14** 137; **19** 330–32*
works **19** *331*
Lidický, Karel **8** 387; **30** 162
Lidingö, Carl Millesgården **21** 608; **28** 314
Li Dongyang **6** 772
lidos **19** 332*
see also BATHS; SWIMMING POOLS
lids, basket *see* BASKET LIDS
lids, box *see* BOX LIDS
Lidval, Fyodor (Ivanovich) **19** 332–3*; **27** 404, 578
Lidval, Johann-Friedrich *see* LIDVAL', FYODOR (IVANOVICH)
Lidzbark Warmiński **30** 535
Li E **33** 322
Lie, Emil **23** 230
Lie, Jonas **33** 78
Lie A Fo, John **11** 759
Lieb, Mihály *see* MUNCKÁCSY, MIHÁLY (VON)
Liébana, Beatus of *see* BEATUS OF LIÉBANA
Liebe, Christian Sigismund **5** 345
Liebel, Marianne *see* BRANDT, MARIANNE
Liebenwein, Maximilian **18** 177
Lieberkühn, Christian **12** 447
Liebermann, Carl **18** 655; **24** 796
Liebermann, Leon **28** 892
Liebermann, Max **19** 333–6*; **33** 38
dealers **5** 924
groups and movements **3** 801; **8** 432; **12** 394; **14** 481; **26** 56; **28** 341, 342; **32** 244
patrons and collectors **11** 777; **18** 186; **26** 406; **31** 397
pupils **4** 598; **28** 354
reproductive prints by others **18** 237
teachers **29** 600
works **4** 42; **9** 310; **10** 563; **11** 463; **17** 576, 580; **19** *334*, *335*, 490; **25** 626
Liebermann, Sammy **29** 117; **32** 792
Liebermann Pottery **29** 117
Liebert von Liebenhofen, Benedikt Adam **2** 714
Liebes, Dorothy **11** 54
Liebhardt, Johann Andreas **11** 734
Liebig, H. von, Baron **11** 735
Liebig, Jan **8** 419
Liebig Meat Company **10** 421
Liebler, Otto **1** 67
Liebsteinsky, Franz Karl, Graf von Kolowrat *see* KOLOWRAT, FRANZ KARL LIEBSTEINSKY, Graf von
Liechtenstein (country) **2** *776*; **19** 336, 337, 339–40*
Liechtenstein (House of) **2** 829; **19** 336*; **24** 463
Liechtenstein, Alois (Joseph) I, Prince of *see* ALOIS (JOSEPH) I, Prince of Liechtenstein
Liechtenstein, Alois (Joseph) II, Prince of *see* ALOIS (JOSEPH) II, Prince of Liechtenstein
Liechtenstein, Andrew, Prince of *see* ANDREW, Prince of Liechtenstein
Liechtenstein, Anton-Florian, Prince of *see* ANTON-FLORIAN, Prince of Liechtenstein
Liechtenstein, Charles I, Prince of *see* CHARLES I, Prince of Liechtenstein
Liechtenstein, Charles Eusebius, Prince of *see* CHARLES EUSEBIUS, Prince of Liechtenstein
Liechtenstein, Georg von *see* GEORG VON LIECHTENSTEIN
Liechtenstein, Hans Adam II, Prince of *see* JOHN II, Prince of Liechtenstein
Liechtenstein, Hans von *see* HANS VON LIECHTENSTEIN
Liechtenstein, Hartmann, Prince of *see* HARTMANN, Prince of Liechtenstein
Liechtenstein, Johann Adam (Andreas), Prince *see* JOHN ADAM ANDREAS, Prince of Liechtenstein
Liechtenstein, John (Joseph) I, Prince of *see* JOHN (JOSEPH) I, Prince of Liechtenstein
Liechtenstein, John II, Prince of *see* JOHN II, Prince of Liechtenstein
Liechtenstein, Maria Teresa Felicia, Princess, Comtesse de Soissons *see* SOISSONS, MARIA TERESA FELICIA OF LIECHTENSTEIN, Comtesse de
Liechtenstein, Mary, Princess of *see* MARY, Princess of Liechtenstein
Liechtenstein, Master of the Schloss *see* SCHLOSS LIECHTENSTEIN, MASTER OF THE
Liechtenstein, (Joseph-)Wenceslas (-Lorenz), Prince of *see* (JOSEPH-)WENCESLAS(-LORENZ), Prince of Liechtenstein
Liechtenstein-Castelkorn, Karel von, Bishop of Olmutz **8** 422, 423; **15** 158; **18** 467; **19** 770; **30** 454
Liechtenstein Collection *see under* VADUZ → Burg Vaduz
Liechtenstein foundry **8** 416
Liechtmann, Albrecht **19** 290
Liecke, Joris van **2** 198
Liedberg, Anders **30** 112
Liedekerke, Margaretha I **7** 710
Liedekerke, Margaretha II **7** 710
Liédet, Loyset **4** 921; **19** 340–41*, 727
patrons and collectors **3** 555; **5** 211, 212, 213; **7** 243
works **7** 235; **19** *340*
Liedt, Abraham **11** 446
Lieferinxe, Josse **6** 448; **19** 341–2*; **29** 638
attributions **19** *342*
works **19** *341*
Liefrinck, Cornelis (Johannesz.) (*c.* 1581-1640) **19** 343
Liefrinck, Cornelis, I (*d* before 1545) **19** 343; **33** 353
Liefrinck, Hans, I (?1518-73) **3** 555; **19** 342*; **25** 625; **33** 169
printmakers
Bos, Balthazar van den **4** 442
Collaert, Hans, I (*c.* 1530-81) **7** 555
Huys, Frans **15** 43
Swart (van Groningen), Jan (*c.* 1500-60) **30** 61
Wierix, Jan **33** 169
Wierix, Jerome **33** 169
Liefrinck, Hans, II (*d* 1599) **5** 61; **19** 343
Liefrinck, Mynken **19** 343
Liefrinck, Wilhelmine *see* LIEFRINCK, MYNKEN
Liefrinck, Willem **3** 555; **19** 342; **30** 61
Liège **3** *539*; **19** 343–5*
art forms and materials
architecture **3** 541
armour **2** 471
brass **3** 602, 603; **4** *685*
brick **3** 588
cupboards **12** 423
faience (ii) (ceramics) **3** 590
furniture **3** 583; **19** 344–5*
glass **3** 593, 595

Liège
art forms and materials—cont.
gold **19** 345*
guns **2** 463
ivory **3** 603; **23** 660
ivory-carvings **26** 695, 696
lace **3** 610
leather **19** 4
manuscripts **3** 552; **25** 677; **26** 666, 667
marks **19** 345
metalwork **3** 596
painting **3** 551, 559
pewter **3** 603
sculpture **13** 110, 114; **26** 630–31, 645
silk **9** 664
silver **3** 598, 600, *600*; **19** 345*
stained glass **13** 182
ecclesiastical buildings
Cathedral of St Paul **9** 156; **13** 159
gold **3** 596
reliquaries **5** 213, *213*; **26** 147
Gembloux Abbey **26** 666
Notre-Dame-aux-Fonts **3** 566; **25** 865
St Barthélemy **3** 566; **26** 681
font **7** 383; **11** 252, 253; **25** 865–6; **26** 682
Ste Catherine **26** 147
Sainte-Croix **26** 146
St Jacques **3** 544, 567; **9** 156; **19** 345*
manuscripts **26** 666
sculpture **13** 100
stained glass **29** 512
St Jean **3** 567; **26** 645
St Lambert **5** 213; **26** 147
St Laurent **3** 566; **26** 666, 667
manuscripts **26** *667*
St Martin **13** 62
St Nicolas **13** 114
education (art) **3** 617
Exposition Universelle et Internationale, 1905 **15** 883
fortifications **21** 570, 577, *577*
Galeries Pont d'Avroy **3** 550
guilds **3** 596
Hôtel de Hayme de Bomal *see* museums → Musée d'Armes
Hôtel de la Soër **3** 545
Institut Supérieur d'Architecture Saint-Luc **3** 619
Law Courts **3** 544, 546, 578
museums **3** 616
Musée d'Architecture de la Ville **17** 450
Musée d'Armes **8** 887
Musée Curtius **3** 545, 617; **19** 344
Musée de la Vie Wallone **3** 617, 618; **17** 450
Palais des Princes-Evêques *see* Law Courts
Parc de la Boverie **18** 63
Renommé Public Hall **28** 583
University **8** 700
Liège, Gilles de *see* GILLES DE LIÈGE
Liège, Jean de *see* JEAN DE LIÈGE
Liegeois, Paul **19** 346*
Lieh I *see* LIE YI
Lie-Jørgensen, Thorbjørn **23** 236
Liemaecker, Jacques de **19** 346
Liemaecker, Nicolaas de **3** 559; **19** 346*
Lieman, R. **28** 188
Liénard, Edouard **22** 207
Liénard, Michel-Joseph-Napoléon **13** 680
Liénard, Paul **29** 343
Lienau, Detlef **14** 164; **19** 346*
Liender, Jacobus van **19** 347
Liender, Paulus van **3** 900; **19** 347*; **25** 649; **28** 166
Liender, Pieter Jan van **19** 347
Liendó, Rodrigo Gil de **9** 116
works **9** *116*
Liendo y Salazar, Pedro de **13** 763
Liepāja **18** *847*
Museum of History and Art
St Anne **18** 848
Liepiņa-Skulme, Marta **26** 384
works
Liepiņš, Jānis **26** 384
Lièpvre **26** 633
Lier
Begijnhof **13** 110
embroidery **3** 609
Kluizekerk *see* St Gummaruskerk
St Gummaruskerk **13** 62, 160, 182; **25** 727
Lier, Adolf **8** 432
Lier, Raúl **2** 397
Liere, Joos van **20** 769
Liere, W. J. van **5** 185; **25** 869
Lierner, Pieter de **4** 916
lierne vaults *see under* VAULTS (CEILING) → types
Lies, Joseph (Hubert) **3** 615; **19** 347*
Liesborn, Master of **20** 718*
Liesler, Josef **8** 394
Liessies **11** 530
Lietersdorf, Finny **16** 569
Lieto, Master of **11** 98; **31** 461
works **11** *98*
Liétor **5** 834
Lietuva *see* LITHUANIA
Lieur, Jacques Le *see* LE LIEUR, JACQUES
Lieutaud **5** 380
Lievendale, Abraham van **32** 709
Lieven de Vogeleer *see* VOGHELARIUS, LIVINIUS
Lievens, Jan **3** 798; **5** 326; **19** 347–50*; **22** 841
attributions **18** 228
collaboration **14** 46
patrons and collectors
Becker, Herman (*c.* 1617-78) **3** 475
Charles I, King of England and Scotland (*reg* 1625-49) **29** 801
Frederick Henry, Stadholder of the Netherlands, Prince of Orange (*reg* 1625-47) **23** 465; **26** 157
Frederick William IV, King of Prussia (*reg* 1840-61) **14** 650
Huygens, Constantijn (i) (1596-1687) **15** 40
Snyders, Frans **28** 904
Sparre, Gustaf Adolf **29** 366
Trip, Hendrick and Louys **31** 342
pupils **19** 101; **23** 674
reproductive prints by others **14** 795; **17** 599; **19** 64, 731; **30** 47; **32** 674
teachers **18** 817; **22** 841
works **1** 813; **10** 553; **19** *347*, *348*, *349*; **22** 841, 843; **26** 160; **31** 365; **33** 358
Lievens, Jan Andrea **19** 349; **32** 258
Lieven van der Clite **17** 699
Lieven van Lathem **3** 555; **19** 350*, 727; **20** 747
collaboration **20** 452
patrons and collectors **5** 211, 213; **24** 606
works **4** 842; **19** *350*; **20** 724, 725
workshop **20** 723
Liévin de Stoevere **14** 759
Lièvre, Edouard **6** 519; **11** 600; **19** 295
Lie Yi **6** 816
Liez, Nicolas **19** 827
Liezen-Mayer, Sándor **13** 632; **14** 901; **18** 822; **19** 351*
Li Fangying **33** 497
works **33** *497*
Lifar, Serge **3** 119, 809; **5** 921; **19** 81
Life **4** 586; **20** 99; **24** 677
lifeboat stations **19** *168*
life-drawings *see under* DRAWINGS → types
Life Insurance Corporation of India **3** 163
Life of Lydwina, Master of the **20** 718*
Life of the Virgin, Master of the **7** 583; **12** 384, 385; **20** 718–20*
life-preservers **28** 302
Lifferin, Josse *see* LIEFERINXE, JOSEE
Lifij, Avni **2** 634; **31** 454
Lifshits, Benedikt **33** 486
Lifshitz, Uri **16** 567
lift-ground etchings *see under* ETCHINGS → types
lifts **12** 643; **25** 327; **28** 830; **31** 593
Li Futang *see* LI SHAN
Liga de Escritores y Artistas Revolucionarios (LEAR) **6** 520; **16** 811; **21** 123; **23** 371
Li Gao **6** 817
Ligeia **24** 443
Liger, Louis **12** 122
Ligeti, Antal **14** 901
Ligeti, Miklós **5** 85; **14** 896
Ligeti, Pál **14** 890; **21** 824
light **7** 627, 731; **13** 138; **19** 351–7*, *352*; **24** 379, 646, 647, 669, 788–9; **28** 203; **29** 97
Christianity **26** 700; **28** 203; **29** 500
infra-red **7** 731; **30** 393–4
Islamic **16** 138
ultra-violet **7** 731, 732; **11** 309; **30** 393–4
see also GLORIES; MANDORLAS
Light, C. & R. **10** 299
Light, William **1** 151; **2** 738; **18** 67
works **1** *151*
Light and Space **31** 609
Lightbown, Aspinall & Co. **19** 359*; **32** 812, 816, 817
Lightbown, Henry **19** 359*
Lightbown, James **19** 359*
light bulbs **7** 875; **20** 595
see also FLASH BULBS
lighters **17** 399
Lightfoot, John **6** 118
Lightfoot, Maxwell Gordon **5** 516, 517; **19** 359–60*
Lightfoot, Peter **14** 550
Lighthouse Beaker **27** 78
lighthouses **19** 360–61*
Britain **19** *360*
England **28** 868
lighting **7** 732–3; **9** 11–13; **28** 831
historical and regional traditions
England **9** 13
France **7** 531
Italy **9** *12*; **30** 657, 669
Prehistoric **25** 475, 479–80
types
electric **9** 13; **24** 641, 669; **30** 679, 734
floodlighting **19** 367
gas **30** 679
side **9** 11–13
street **2** 510
top **9** 11–13; **10** 679; **22** 362
England **10** 677; **14** 539
France **23** 778
Rome, ancient **9** 11
top-side **28** 327
uses
architecture **19** 361–8*, *367*
churches **19** 362, *363*, *364*, 365, *368*
cinemas **19** *368*
drawings **7** 732; **9** 232
factories **17** 721
feathers **7** 732
fountains **7** 531
fur **7** 732
leather **7** 732
miniatures (manuscript illumination) **7** 732
museums **19** 365, 367
lighting
uses—cont.
paintings **7** 732; **9** 13
prints **7** 732
textiles **7** 732
theatres **30** 657, 666, 669, 685
wallpaper **7** 732
see also CANDLES; CANDLESTICKS; CHANDELIERS; LAMPS; RUSHLIGHTS
Lightning Brothers **1** *37*, 41; **19** 368–9*
Lightning Ridge **12** 269
Lightoler, Timothy **7** 758
Light-print Press **7** 576
light red *see under* PIGMENTS → types
Liginiac, St Barthélemy **9** 156
Lignamine, Joannes Philippus de **4** 358
Ligne, Charles-Joseph de, Prince (1735-1814) **19** 369
Ligne, Charles-Joseph-Emmanuel de, Prince (1759-92) **19** 369*
architecture **3** 523
collections **26** 732; **33** 116
drawings **3** 310
gardens **6** 563
Ligne, Claude Lamoral II, Prince of (1685-1766) **2** 125
Ligne, Jean De *see* DE LIGNE, JEAN
Ligne, Pierre De *see* DE LIGNE, PIERRE
Lignereux, Martin-Eloi **8** 448; **30** 747
lignite **17** 514; **21** 246; **25** 488, 491, 493
lignum vitae **29** 315
Ligny, di, Viceroy **30** 176
Ligny, Dominique de **22** 466
Ligon, Richard **5** 749
Li Gonglin **6** 780, 809, 818; **10** 692; **19** 369–70*
attributions **6** 819; **12** 52
groups and movements **29** 244
works **6** 780, 783; **19** *370*
Ligor *see* NAKHON SI THAMMARAT
Ligorio, Pirro **2** 161; **10** 524; **12** 115; **19** 370–73*; **26** 783
assistants **10** 524
attributions **4** 286
collaboration **3** 89; **8** 268; **26** 806
excavations **31** 61–2
patrons and collectors **3** 744; **5** 699; **10** 524; **22** 6; **25** 7; **26** 813; **31** 63
works **4** 432, 648; **7** 780; **11** 343; **16** 633; **19** *371*, *372*; **25** 257, 260; **26** 770, 848; **28** 754; **32** 547
Ligozzi, Francesco (*d* before 1635) **19** 374
Ligozzi, Francesco (*fl* 1585-*d* 1641) **19** 374
Ligozzi, Francesco di Mercurio **19** 374
Ligozzi, Giovanni Ermanno **19** 373
Ligozzi, Jacopo **19** 373–4*
collaboration **1** 597
patrons and collectors **2** 103; **4** 549; **11** 188
pupils **12** 169, 648
reproductions in hardstones **11** 191
reproductive prints by others **2** 20; **27** 503
works **11** 192; **14** 11; **16** *737*, 740; **19** *374*
Ligt, Bart van der **9** 62
Li Guangxiu **18** 519
Liguoro (family) **20** 418
Li-Guo school **33** 528
Ligustri, Tarquinio **6** 112; **20** 841
Li Hangzhi **19** 378
Li He **7** 57
Lihir **24** 85
Li Ho *see* LI HE
Li Hong **6** 699, 730
Li Hsien *see* LI XIAN
Li Hsi-sung *see* LI XISONG
Li Hsiung-ts'ai *see* LI XIONGCAI
Li Hua **7** 121
works **7** *121*
Li Hung *see* LI HONG
Liimand, Kaarel **10** 540
Liisberg, Hugo **28** 22
Liiva, Silvi **10** 540
Li Ji *see* LI CHI
Lijialou (Xinzheng) **7** 21; **33** 471–2*
bronzes **33** *471*
Lijiang **30** 847
Li Jianzhong **7** 116
Lijiashan **8** 852, 853; **29** 230
Lijiazhuang, Nanchan Temple **6** 638, 715; **22** 240, 241; **30** 443
Li Jie **2** 317
Li Jih-hua *see* LI RIHUA
Li Jingxun **7** 82, 89, 109
Li Jingyou **7** 24
Lijn, Liliane **18** 63
Lijsternest **3** 579
Li Jue **19** 326
Li Jui-ch'ing *see* LI RUIQING
Li Kan **6** 805, 806, 824; **12** 50; **19** 375*
Li Kao *see* LI GAO
Likarz, Maria **2** 826
Li Keran **19** 375–6*
Likhachov, Dmitry (Sergeyevich) **19** 376–7*
Likhachov, N. P. **27** 439
Likhtenberg, Ya. G. **9** 458; **21** 350
Likić, Stefan **28** 450
Likir **30** 819
Li K'o-jan *see* LI KERAN
Li Kuang-hsiu *see* LI GUANGXIU
Li Kuchan **19** 377*
Līkums, Herberts
Li Kung-lin *see* LI GONGLIN
Lilanga di Nyama, Georges **20** 150
Lilas **24** 129
Lilburn, Douglas **4** 642
L'Ile-Bouchard, St Léonard **26** 599
Lilien, Ephraim **16** 567; **17** 579
Lilienberg, Albert **13** 31
Lilienfeld, Ulrich of *see* ULRICH OF LILIENFELD
Lilienfeld Abbey **2** *776*; **12** 365; **19** *377*, 377–8*
church **2** 777
Lilihan carpets *see under* CARPETS → types
Li Lincan *see* LI LIN-TS'AN
Liling
Ceramic Research Institute **6** 913
porcelain **6** 912, *912*, 913
Li Lin-ts'an **7** 161
Lilio, Andrea *see* LILLI, (GIOVANNI) ANDREA
Li Liufang **19** 378*
Lilius, Jacobus **20** 453
Liljefors, Anders **30** 99
Liljefors, Bruno (Andreas) **11** 142; **19** 379–80*; **30** 730
works **19** *379*
Liljequist, Bertel **19** 408
Lilla Church **26** 639
Lilla Klintegård **32** 523
Lille **11** *504*; **19** 380–83*
carpets **11** 652
Cathedral of Notre Dame de la Treille **7** 668
Centenary Exhibition, 1954 **11** 527
ceramics **19** 382*
citadel **21** 568
education (art) **3** 618
faience (ii) (ceramics) **11** 605
garden city **11** 526
Halle Echevinale **11** 514
lace **3** 610; **11** 650; **18** 589, 591
Métro stations **21** 350

Lille—cont.
museums 11 668
Musée d'Art Moderne du Nord 9 465; 19 381
Musée des Beaux-Arts 11 665, 666; 19 381; 32 920
collections 11 667; 12 568; 19 381; 33 154
Musée Industriel et Commercial 4 130
Musée Wicar 9 229; 22 208
Palais de Justice 18 890
St Sauveur 13 79
tapestries 11 639, 642; 19 382–3*; 30 314
tiles 30 885
University 8 839
Lille, Alain de see ALANUS DE INSULIS
Lille, Ludwik 2 528
Lillebonne 6 54
Lillebonne, Anne de Lorraine-Vaudemont, Princesse de 25 377
Lillehammer
Bys Malerisamling 23 243
Sandvigske Samlinger-Maihaugen 23 243
Lille Toyen Garden City 25 376
Lillhärdal 13 119
Lilli, (Giovanni) Andrea 2 2; 10 810; 19 383–4*
works 19 *383*
Lillie, Joseph Christian 8 743–4, 745
Lilliu, Giovanni 3 311
Lilljekvist, Fredrik 30 73, 74
Lilly, Edmund 19 384*
Lilly, Johann Dietrich 31 27
Li Longmian see LI GONGLIN
Lilongwe 1 *407*
Lilpop, Edward August Karol 9 498
Lilpop, Franciszek 32 872
Lilpop, Karol Jerzy 32 878
Lilpop, Ludwik Mauryc 32 878
Lilstock Chapel 11 252
Li Lung-mien see LI GONGLIN
Lilybaeum 6 70; 25 733; 28 655
Lim 2 442
Lim, Kim 10 268
Lim, William S(iew) W(ai) 19 384*; 28 772
Lima 19 384–8*; 24 497, *498*; 29 *156*; 31 721
Academia Concha 24 517
Academia de Pintura y Dibujo 24 517
Alliance Française 24 515
Allpamérica 24 517
art forms and materials
architecture 24 504, 506
monstrances 24 511
pottery 19 385
retables 26 252
silver 6 599; 24 511
tiles 24 514
trade 19 385
wall paintings 29 173
balconies (houses) 19 385
Biblioteca Nacional 24 518
Casa de Correos 19 387; 24 504
Cementerio General 24 504
Centro Camino Real 24 505
Centro Cívico y Comercial 19 388; 24 505
Centro de Arte 2 371
Centro Qosqo de Arte Nativo 24 517
churches see ecclesiastical buildings
Colegio de Medicina de S Fernando 24 504
Compañía Peruana de Teléfonos building 24 505
Lima—cont.
ecclesiastical buildings 24 502–3
Cathedral of the Assumption 3 470; 20 501; 24 500–501, *501*, 503, *503*
choir-stalls 7 192
Convent of the Immaculate Conception 22 3; 26 252
Corazón de Jesús see Los Huérfanos
Iglesia del Prado 24 511
Jesús María 24 502
La Compañía see S Pedro
La Merced 24 501, 502, 503
Las Nazarenas 19 385; 24 502
Los Huérfanos 19 385; 24 502
Monastery of S Domingo 24 500–501, 502, 506; 30 883
Monastery of S Francisco 24 501, 502, 514; 25 822; 30 883
S Agustín 24 501, 502, 503
S Carlos 24 502
S Domingo 24 501
S Marcelo 19 385
S Pedro 24 501, 504
S Rosa de las Monjas 24 502
S Teresa 24 502
S Tomás 24 502
education (art) 24 517
Escuela de Artes Plásticas 24 517
Escuela de Bellas Artes Corriente Alterna 24 517
Escuela de Dibujo 24 517
Escuela Nacional de Bellas Artes (ENBA) 14 463; 24 517, 518
Escuela Nacional de Ingeniería 19 387; 24 505
Galería Wiese 24 516
Galería y Biblioteca S Marcos 24 515
Garagay 6 522, 523; 19 385; 29 160, 167
Goethe Institute 24 515, 517
Hospital Dos de Mayo see museums → Museo Hospital Dos de Mayo
Hotel Bolívar 24 505
houses 19 385–6
Instituto de Arte Contemporáneo 24 510, 515
Instituto de Raúl Porras Barrenchea 24 518
Instituto Nacional de Cultura 24 517, 518
Instituto Toulouse-Lautrec 24 517
The Llamas statue 24 509
Marrou-Yori houses 24 506
Ministerio de Asuntos Exteriores 19 385, *386*; 24 503
Ministerio de Economía y Finanzas 24 515
Ministerio de Educación 24 515
monument to Jorge Chávez Dartnell 24 509
monument to Manco Cápac 24 509
monument to the 2nd of May 24 509
museums
Colegio de S Pablo 24 516
Galería de Arte Italiano see Museo de Arte Italiano
Museo Amano 24 517
Museo de Arqueología see under Universidad Nacional Mayor de S Marcos
Museo de Arqueología Peruana see Museo Nacional de la Cultura Peruana
Museo Arqueológico Rafael Larco Herrera 29 221
Museo de Arte 10 487; 19 386; 24 504, 515, 516, 517
collections 24 516
library 24 518
Museo de Arte Italiano 24 516
Museo de Arte Popular 24 517
Lima
museums—cont.
Museo del Banco Central de Reserva 24 516
Museo de Historia Nacional 24 516
Museo Histórico Militar 19 386
Museo Hospital Dos de Mayo 19 386; 24 504
Museo de la Nación 24 517
Museo Nacional 24 516
see also Museo de la Cultura Peruana
Museo Nacional de Antropología y Arqueología 29 221
Museo Nacional de Artes see Museo de San Francisco
Museo Nacional de la Cultura Peruana 19 387; 24 516
Instituto Libre de Arte Peruano 27 485
Museo Nacional de Historia 24 518
Museo de Oro del Perú y Armas del Mundo 3 363; 24 517; 28 652; 29 221
Museo Rafael Larco Hoyle 24 517
Museo de San Francisco 24 516
Museo Víctor Larco Herrera see Museo Nacional de la Cultura Peruana
Museo del Virreinato 24 503
Universidad Nacional Mayor de S Marcos
Museo de Arqueología 24 516
Museo Raimondi see Museo de Arqueología
Nacional Consejo para la Restauración y Conservación de Monumentos Históricos 19 387
Palacio Arzobispal 24 505, *505*
Palacio de la Exposición see Museo de Arte
Palacio de Gobierno 19 *387*
Palacio Torre Tagle see Ministerio de Asuntos Exteriores
La Penitencíería 19 386; 24 504
Pontificia Universidad Católica del Perú 24 517
Portada de las Maravillas 24 504
Proyecto Regional del Patrimonio Cultural/UNESCO 24 517
Puente de Piedra 19 385
Quinta de Presa see museums → Museo del Virreinato
Radio El Sol building 24 505
Real Felipe Fort see Museo Histórico Militar
Sociedad de Arquitectos (Peru) 19 387
statue of Admiral Henry Du Petit Thouars 24 509
Taller de Investigaciones Estéticas en el Diseño Andino Contemporáneo (TIEDAC) 24 517
Unidad Vecinal Matute 24 505
Unidad Vecinal No. 3 24 505
Universidad Nacional Mayor de S Marcos 24 518
Viviendas Banco Central de Reserva 24 506
Work statue 24 509
Lima, A. A. Lisboa de see LISBOA DE LIMA, A. A.
Lima, Araújo 23 455
Lima, Attilio Corrêa see CORRÊA LIMA, ATTILIO
Lima, Caetano da Costa see COSTA LIMA, CAETANO DA
Lima, João Araújo see ARAÚJO LIMA, JOÃO
Lima, João Filgueiras see FILGUEIRAS LIMA, JOÃO
Lima, José da Fonseca see FONSECA LIMA, JOSÉ DA
Lima, José Lezama see LEZAMA LIMA, JOSÉ
Lima, José Octávio Corrêa see CORRÊA LIMA, JOSÉ OCTÁVIO
Lima, Santos Pacheco de see SANTOS PACHECO
Lima, Victor Meirelles de see MEIRELLES DE LIMA, VICTOR
Lima Corrêa, Attilio see CORRÊA LIMA, ATTILIO
Lima da Villa Norvada Cerveira (family) 25 821
Limadura see LIMODRA
Limarest, Thomas de 16 31
Lima Sampaio, Joaquim da Costa see COSTA LIMA SAMPAIO, JOAQUIM DA
Limassol
archaeological museum 8 366
Castle 8 361
Cyprus Medieval Museum 8 366
Municipal Art Gallery 8 367
Limatola, Duca di 9 52
Limay, Mme de 8 793
Limbach 30 793
Limbaži 18 *847*, 847
Limbert, Charles P. 31 631
Limborch, Hendrik van 3 42; 14 42; 33 80
Limbour, Georges 17 726; 30 18, 20
Limbourc see LIMBOURG
Limbourg, Arnold de 19 388, 393
Limbourg, de (family)
patrons and collectors 7 597; 11 655, 660; 20 755; 31 832
works 4 395; 9 221, 270; 11 340; 16 838
Limbourg, Herman de 11 531; 13 155; 19 388–93*; 20 207, 333, 703; 31 448
collaboration 20 635
manuscript illumination
Très Riches Heures (Chantilly, Mus. Condé, MS. 65) 31 308–10
Adoration of the Magi 11 *530*
architectural paintings 2 339; 21 549
calendar 5 428; 19 *391*; 31 *838*
Château de Mehun-de-Yèvre 21 *549*
Funeral of Raymond Diocrès 31 *309*
genre 3 596; 30 218
Great Litany Procession 19 *392*
landscape paintings 18 704
Meeting of the Magi 19 *393*
Bible Moralisée (Paris, Bib. N., MS. fr. 166) 19 *389*
patrons and collectors 4 545; 12 287; 13 153; 31 837, 839
Limbourg, Jean de 11 531; 13 155; 19 388–93*; 20 207, 333, 703; 31 448
collaboration 20 635
manuscript illumination
Très Riches Heures (Chantilly, Mus. Condé, MS. 65) 31 308–10
Adoration of the Magi 11 *530*
architectural paintings 2 339; 21 549
calendar 5 428; 19 *391*; 31 *838*
Château de Mehun-de-Yèvre 21 *549*
Funeral of Raymond Diocrès 31 *309*
genre 3 596; 30 218
Great Litany Procession 19 *392*
landscape paintings 18 704
Limbourg, Jean de
manuscript illumination
Très Riches Heures (Chantilly, Mus. Condé, MS. 65)—cont.
Meeting of the Magi 19 *393*
Bible Moralisée (Paris, Bib. N., MS. fr. 166) 19 *389*
patrons and collectors 4 545; 12 287; 13 153; 31 837, 839
Limbourg, Pol de 11 531; 13 155; 19 388–93*; 20 207, 333, 703; 31 448
collaboration 20 635
manuscript illumination
Très Riches Heures (Chantilly, Mus. Condé, MS. 65) 31 308–10
Adoration of the Magi 11 *530*
architectural paintings 2 339; 21 549
calendar 5 428; 19 *391*; 31 *838*
Château de Mehun-de-Yèvre 21 *549*
Funeral of Raymond Diocrès 31 *309*
genre 3 596; 30 218
Great Litany Procession 19 *392*
landscape paintings 18 704
Meeting of the Magi 19 *393*
Bible Moralisée (Paris, Bib. N., MS. fr. 166) 19 *389*
patrons and collectors 4 545; 12 287; 13 153; 31 837, 839
Limburg an der Lahn
Cathedral 12 364; 13 48; 27 130; 31 284, *284*
houses 32 282
Limburg auf der Haardt Abbey 12 *361*; 19 394*; 23 645; 26 573
church 12 363; 26 *573*
Limburg Gospels see under GOSPEL BOOKS → individual manuscripts
Limburg Reliquary 9 658, *658*, 661
lime 29 701
historical and regional traditions
Bhutan 3 914
China 6 873, 881; 7 114
England 10 356
France 33 326
Hungary 14 905
Islamic 29 818
Mesoamerica, Pre-Columbian 21 205
Rome, ancient 11 762; 26 879; 29 812
Syria-Palestine 30 196
uses
arriccio 10 740
brick 4 767
dyeing 10 356; 30 558, 560
frescoes 19 394; 32 802
furniture 14 905
glass 12 781
glazes 6 326, 329, 873, 881, 895
grounds 25 174
paper 7 114
parchment 24 106
plaster 9 562; 11 761, 762; 21 229; 29 846; 30 196
scroll paintings 3 914
size 28 310
stucco 29 812, 818, 845
Limehouse porcelain factory 33 377
Limerick 16 *5*; 19 394*
art school 16 37
Castle 16 8
City Gallery of Art 16 36
furniture 16 25
houses 16 8
Hunt Museum 16 36
lace 16 34; 18 589, 593
Plassey House se Hunt Museum
pottery 16 28
St John's Cathedral 13 165; 16 30

Limerick—cont.
St Mary's Cathedral 16 7, 20, 25; 31 273
urban planning 16 8
Limerick, William Perry, 3rd Earl of see PERRY, WILLIAM, 3rd Earl of Limerick
lime secco see under SECCO PAINTINGS → types
limestone 7 735; 29 700–703*
conservation 7 747
historical and regional traditions
Aegean 8 262
Afghanistan 1 193, 194
Africa 1 305
Akkadian (people) 1 509
Anatolia, ancient 1 833
Ancient Near East 22 511; 29 614
Arabia 2 257
Assyrian 10 742; 21 287; 22 511; 29 701, XI
Austria 2 799, 804; 33 198
Bactria 6 217
Belgium 26 630; 29 701
Buddhism 6 217; 19 638; 29 457; 30 595
Byzantine 9 538, 590–91, 591
Central Asia, Western 6 217
China 12 88; 19 638
Coptic 7 822
Crete 2 879
Cyprus, ancient 8 338, 340, 342
Czech Republic 13 90
Early Christian (c. AD 250-843) 9 538, 590–91
Egypt 7 822
Egypt, ancient 9 773; 27 14; 29 614
Amarna (1353-1333 BC) 9 884; 22 723
Early Dynastic (c. 2925-c. 2575 BC) 1 99; 9 867, 868; 27 824
First Intermediate Period (c. 2130-c. 1938 BC) 9 859, 873
Graeco-Roman (332 BC-AD 395) 13 434
Late Period (664-332 BC) 9 815, 891
Middle Kingdom (c. 1966-c. 1630 BC) 1 793; 10 17
New Kingdom (c. 1539-c. 1075 BC) 9 882; 10 15, 70, 88; 28 34; 29 615; 30 297, 696
Old Kingdom (c. 2575-c. 2130 BC) 9 812*, 814, 815, 858, 863, 872; 10 14; 25 762; 27 824
Predynastic (c. 6000-c. 2925 BC) 1 100; 18 238
Third Intermediate Period (c. 1075-c. 656 BC) 27 825
England 10 224, 227, 262, 674; 25 V2; 26 614, 615; 29 700
Estonia 10 536
Etruscan 10 607
France 4 546, 583; 7 477, 478; 11 290, 554; 25 477; 29 701; 31 211
Germany 8 541; 14 450; 29 700
Gothic 2 799; 10 674; 13 90, 101, 103
Greece, ancient 12 246; 13 387, 393, 395, 434*, 443; 27 14, 825
Hittite 1 833
Hungary 5 86
Iran, ancient 15 914, 914
Italy 10 607
Japan 17 242
Jordan 17 655
Maya 21 213, 260; 29 620
Mesoamerica, Pre-Columbian 21 223; 29 620
Mesopotamia 9 45, 538; 21 273; 29 XI
Minoan 2 879
Netherlands, the 22 117
Ottonian 23 646
limestone
historical and regional traditions—cont.
Palestine 9 538
Parthian 9 414
Portugal 13 101
Prehistoric art 1 194; 25 477, 491, 493, 494; 33 198
Punic 25 733
Romanesque 7 477, 478; 10 227; 11 290, 554; 26 614, 615; 28 727, 728; 31 211
Rome, ancient 26 874, 875, 879; 27 9–10, 13, 14
Ryūkyū Islands 27 470, 471
Sicily 28 654, 654
South America, Pre-Columbian 29 155
Spain 28 727, 728
Sri Lanka 29 457
Sumerian 9 45; 22 159; 31 696
Sweden 13 103
Syria 9 538, 591, 591; 23 894
Syria-Palestine 30 189, 193
Thailand 30 595
Toltec 21 223
Tunisia 27 14
Turkey 9 590–91; 27 14
United States of America 19 437
Zambia 33 603
techniques 25 491
types
alabaster see ALABASTER (LIMESTONE)
andesite (volcanic)
Aztec 21 223
Bolivia 30 796
Greece, ancient 13 387
Indonesia 15 781
Java 15 782
Mesoamerica, Pre-Columbian 21 223
South America, Pre-Columbian 30 796
anorthosite gneiss 9 813*
bleu de Namur 26 630
Colleyweston 27 131
gneiss 1 292; 13 387; 15 510
Mainvault 29 700
marble see MARBLE
Numidian 27 14
Portland stone 20 571; 29 700, 701
Purbeck marble 10 224, 260; 13 136; 29 XII
St Elias 13 387
travertine 10 740
Egypt, ancient 10 72
Etruscan 10 602
Italy 29 701; 31 523
Rome, ancient 26 874; 27 13
Toltec 31 99
uses
arches 26 891
architecture 1 305; 9 538, 773; 10 536; 21 213; 26 874, 875; 27 470; 29 701
busts 22 723
canopic jars 10 14, 15
capitals 7 477; 28 727; 31 211
chacmools 21 223
churches 9 538
cult statues 8 262
dyeing 27 471
effigies 11 290; 25 V2
façade decoration 10 742
figurines 8 338; 9 45; 18 238; 33 198
fonts (baptismal) 9 591
friezes 10 607
gateways 26 891
glazes 17 242
inlays 31 696
lithography 19 480; 25 615
maces 9 868
masonry 20 571
mosaics 22 159; 29 XII
plaster 11 762
limestone
uses—cont.
Portland cement 29 701
pyramids 9 812
relief sculpture
Assyrian 22 511; 29 701
Bactria 6 217
Egypt, ancient 1 100; 9 872, 873, 882, 884; 10 88; 30 696
England 10 674
France 32 397
Germany 8 541
Iran, ancient 15 914
Mesopotamia 21 273; 29 XI
Netherlands, the 22 117
Romanesque 26 614; 28 728
rock reliefs 15 510
sarcophagi 2 879; 10 607; 27 823, 824, 825
scarabs 28 34
sculpture 15 914; 29 701
Afghanistan 1 193, 194
Anatolia, ancient 1 833
Arabia 2 257
architectural 9 590–91
Austria 2 804
China 19 638
Cyprus, ancient 8 340, 340, 342
Czech Republic 13 90
Egypt, ancient 1 793; 9 815, 815, 858, 859, 863, 867; 30 297
England 10 262
France 4 546; 7 478; 11 554
Germany 14 450
Gothic 2 799; 4 583; 13 90
Greece, ancient 13 434*, 443
Hungary 5 86
Indonesia 15 781
Jordan 17 655
Ottonian 23 646
Portugal 13 101
relief 9 891; 25 880; 30 193
Romanesque 26 615
Rome, ancient 27 9–10, 13, 14
Scandinavia 13 103
Sicily 28 654, 654
Sri Lanka 29 457
Thailand 30 595
United States of America 19 437
Zambia 33 603
seals 10 70; 12 246
shabtis 10 17
stelae 1 99, 509; 7 822; 25 733; 29 614, 614, 615, 620; 30 189
tombs 10 262; 11 290; 13 101
tools 25 493
vessels 10 72
walls 26 879
see also POROS
limewater 7 747; 32 488
lime-wood 33 324, 325, 334
historical and regional traditions
Germany 8 627; 10 455, 457; 12 401; 13 316; 19 106; 22 281; 23 887; 26 371; 29 729, 730, 761; 33 31
Gothic 13 316; 22 281; 23 887; 29 727, 729, 730
Hungary 14 903, 903
Japan 17 312
Ottonian 23 648
Poland 29 727
Vietnam 32 488
uses
altarpieces 8 627; 12 401; 19 106; 26 371; 29 727, 730; 33 31
bookcases 14 903
furniture 14 903
inlays 32 488
mirror frames 21 721
panel paintings 24 3
lime-wood
uses—cont.
reliquaries 26 371
sculpture 10 455, 457; 13 316; 22 281; 23 648, 887; 29 729, 761
Lim Hak Tai 28 774
limited editions 19 395–6*; 25 596, 597
Limited Editions Club 4 366, 367
Limmared Glasbruk 30 102
Limnell, E. 10 754
limnings see MINIATURES (ii) (PAINTINGS)
Limniotis, Ioannis 17 840
Limniotis, Theodore 17 840
Limniotis, Theophilos 17 840
Limodra 15 698
Limoges 11 505; 19 396–8*
altarpieces 13 170
candlesticks 5 611
Cathedral of St Etienne 1 767
choir 13 42
manuscripts 26 670
sculpture 13 76
tracing floor 31 275
coins 7 535
enamel 2 569; 4 351; 8 201; 10 194, 195; 11 614, 629, 631; 13 158, 167–8, 168, 170; 14 419; 19 396–7*, 397; 26 691, 692
manuscript illumination 11 529
metalwork 26 681
Musée Municipal 21 166
porcelain 11 607, 609, 610; 19 397–8*
St Martial 3 191; 4 6; 9 569; 26 585, 670
St Michel-aux-Lions 29 414
Limoges-Saint-Saens, (Charles-) Albert d'Arnoux, Comte de see BERTALL
Limon 8 15
Limoncarro 6 523
limonite 1 713; 24 792
Limonum Pictonum see POITIERS
Limosin (family) 19 396
Limosin, Léonard 7 466; 11 629; 19 396, 398*; 22 31; 25 383
works 10 IV1
Limpach, Maximilian Joseph 11 10; 12 590
Limpangaon, Siddheshvara Temple 15 317
Limyra 19 837
cenotaph 6 170
Heroön 13 384, 458; 19 840
shrine 5 904
stoa 19 840
Tomb of Pericles 13 426
Lin, Maya 19 398–9*; 22 49; 31 615; 32 888
Linaiuoli Tabernacle 2 32, 32–4, 33
Lin'an see HANGZHOU
Linar, Rochus Quirinus see LYNAR, ROCHUS QUIRINUS
Linard, Jacques 11 227, 535; 19 399*; 29 668; 31 882
Linard, Lucien 1 21
Linares 6 590
Museo de Arte y Artesanía 6 601
Linares, Francisco 31 89
Linares, Olga 3 278; 14 223; 29 220
Linares, Victor 18 833
Linati (de Prevost), Claudio 19 399*; 21 385, 404
Lin Bu 6 751; 7 66
Lin Ch'ao-ying 30 246
Lincheng kilns see XING KILNS
Linchong 7 30
linchpins see CHARIOT FITTINGS
Linck, Franz Konrad 33 280
Linck, Jean-Antoine 19 399–400*
Linck, Jean-Philippe 19 399
Linck, Johann Konrad 19 399
Linck, Sabaldus 25 132
Linck-Daepp, Margit 30 144
Lincke, François 11 600
Linckh, Jakob 7 502
Lincoln (UK) 10 225; 19 400–406*; 25 470; 26 905
Bishop's Palace 14 422
Castle 6 53; 28 301; 31 710
Cathedral of the Blessed Virgin Mary 1 724; 9 670, 671; 10 359; 13 43, 45, 54, 55; 18 621; 19 401–3*; 26 570, 587, 589
Angel choir 8 261, 610; 10 228; 13 46–7; 19 403–4*
ballflower 3 121
chantry chapels 7 267
chapter house 6 466; 19 403; 20 581
choir-stalls 7 190, 190, 191, 192; 29 413
cloister 22 221
corbels 7 837
dogtooth 9 70
font 11 253; 26 630
furniture 30 778
Judgement Portal 10 261; 13 81; 19 405*, 405; 29 659
Lady Chapel 18 622
Little St Hugh's shrine 3 121
mouldings 22 218
nave 9 670; 19 402, 403
piers (ii) (masonry) 24 751
porch 12 6
restorations 13 200
sacrament house 9 681
St Hugh's choir 2 294; 7 267, 837; 8 184; 9 669; 10 228; 13 45, 45; 19 402–3*; 22 217, 220, 221, 222
sculpture 10 743; 13 82, 83; 19 404–5*, 404, 405; 26 612, 614
shrine 28 630
spires 29 413
stained glass 13 183; 19 406*, 406
stiff-leaf 29 659
Tomb of Christ 9 680
tracery 8 611; 31 271, 273
transept 31 281
vaults 32 92, 93, 94
City and County Museum 19 401
Greyfriars 30 909
houses 14 76
John of Gaunt's Palace 25 711
Law Courts 18 887
manuscripts 26 673
Mencap building 4 790
roofs 30 905
St Mary's Guildhall 19 401
sculpture 19 404–5*
Swanpool Garden Suburb 16 891
town walls 31 710
urban planning 10 226; 27 4
Usher Art Gallery 10 371
Lincoln (NE; USA)
Nebraska State Capitol 31 596, 659
University of Nebraska 22 367
Lincoln, 1st Earl of see CLINTON, EDWARD FIENNES DE, 1st Earl of Lincoln
Lincoln, Abraham 24 661; 26 538; 31 654
Lincoln, Alexander of see ALEXANDER OF LINCOLN
Lincoln, B. 4 26
Lincoln, Gilbert de Gand, Earl of see GAND, GILBERT DE, Earl of Lincoln
Lincoln, Henry Fiennes Clinton, 9th Earl of see CLINTON, HENRY FIENNES, 9th Earl of Lincoln
Lincoln, Mary Todd 9 171; 31 654
Lincoln, Rohaise de Clare, Countess of see CLARE, ROHAISE DE, Countess of Lincoln
Lincoln, Viiu Niiler 30 330

Lincoln College Typicon **9** 641
Lincoln Memorial *see under* WASHINGTON (DC) → monuments and memorials
Lincrusta Walton **32** 812, 816
Lincz, Urban **31** 786
Lind, Edmund G. **3** 128
Lind, E. J. **19** 318
Lind, Jenny **31** 631
Lind, Kari **24** 370
Lind, Ruby **9** 496
Lindahl, Karl **14** 371
Lindauer, Gottfried **23** 59
 works **23** *59*
Lindau Gospels *see under* GOSPEL BOOKS→ individual manuscripts
Lindberg, Alf **30** 81
Lindberg, Erik **20** 926
Lindberg, Gunnar **30** 524
Lindberg, Stig **30** 99, 101
Lindblom, Andreas (Adolf Frederik) **19** 406–7*; **30** 120
Lindblom, Sivert **30** 87
Linde, Andreas **4** 353
Linde, Max **22** 293
Lindeberg, Harrie T. **7** 876
Lindeberg, Karl **30** 102
Lindegaard **23** 243
Lindegren, Agi **30** 73
Lindegren, Yrjö (Lorenzo) **19** 407*
Lindell, Lage Johannes **7** 699; **30** 81
Lindemann, Christian Philipp **15** 34
Lindemayr, Andreas Ferdinand **2** 822
linden *see* LIME-WOOD
Linden, Abraham van der **27** 516
Linden, Gérard van der **8** 831
Linden, Jaspar van der **31** 803
Linden, Wim van der **28** 103
Lindenast (family) **23** 311
Lindenast, Sebastian **19** 407*; **23** 311
Linden-Museum *see under* STUTTGART → museums
Lindenschmidt, Wilhelm von (1829-95) **8** 608; **16** 795; **18** 473; **20** 549
Lindenschmit, Wilhelm (1806-48) **14** 506; **18** 101, 398; **23** 529; **29** 847
Lindenthal, Gustav **4** 803; **23** 41
Linden van Dijk, Philip van der **8** 888
Linder, Autere **11** 111
Linder, Emilie **9** 691
Linder, Hjälmar **11** 111
Linderhof, Schloss *see under* GRASWANGTAL
Linderöd church **8** 731
Lindfors, Lennart **15** 142
Lindgren, Armas (Eliel) **12** 498; **19** 407–8*
 collaboration **19** 643; **27** 473; **30** 277
 pupils **1** 8; **4** 160
 works **10** 537
Lindh, Francesca Mascitti **11** 106
Lindhagen, Albert **29** 686
Lindholm, Berndt (Adolf) **7** 251; **11** 95; **19** 408*
Lindig, Otto **12** 432, 437
 works **12** *432*
Lindisfarne Gospels *see under* GOSPEL BOOKS → individual manuscripts
Lindisfarne Priory (Northumb.) **21** 845
 crosses **2** 69; **8** 196
 gravestones **2** 68
Lindley, John **24** 293
Lindley, William **5** 847
Lindner, Doris **33** 378
Lindner, Emilie **11** 769
Lindner, Richard **19** 409–11*; **29** 613
 works **10** 482; **19** *410*; **29** 420
Lindner GmbH **32** 757
Lindores **28** 234
Lindos **13** *363*; **26** *289*, 290, 291, 294
 Church of the Dormition **26** 295
 Church of the Panagia *see* Church of the Dormition
 governor's residence **26** 294
 Hagios Giorgios Chostos **26** 293
 Hagios Giorgios Pachymachiotes **26** 295
 Hagios Menas **26** 293
 Sanctuary of Athena **13** 418, 600
 sculpture **26** 291
Lindos, Chares of *see* CHARES OF LINDOS
Lindquist, Evan **10** 398
Lindqvist, Selim (Arvid) **11** 92; **19** 411–12*
Lindsay, Alexander (*fl c.* 1636) **28** 261
Lindsay, Alexander (William Crawford), 25th Earl of Crawford and 8th Earl of Balcarres **19** 412–13*
 groups and movements **2** 576
 works **2** 576; **10** 252; **13** 304
 writings **5** 340
Lindsay, Blanche **10** 254
Lindsay, Coutts **9** 19; **10** 254; **19** 413*, 588
Lindsay, David **28** 268
Lindsay, David Alexander Edward, 27th Earl of Crawford and 10th Earl of Balcarres **10** 487
Lindsay, Ian Gordon **15** 892
Lindsay, Jack **19** 413
Lindsay, James Ludovic, 26th Earl of Crawford **19** 736
Lindsay, Jan **25** 213
Lindsay, Norman (Alfred Williams) **19** 413*
Lindsay, Robert, 1st Baron Wantage *see* LOYD-LINDSAY, ROBERT, 1st Baron Wantage
Lindsay War memorial **5** 570
Lindsell (Essex), St Mary **10** 338
Lindsey, Robert Bertie, 4th Earl of *see* BERTIE, ROBERT, 4th Earl and 1st Marquess of Lindsey
Lindsey, Theophilus **31** 583
Lindstedt, Elias **11** 109
Lindstrand, Vicke **30** 102
Lindström, Sune **11** 299; **18** 541
Lindt, Alexis **33** 353
Lindt, John William **10** 580
Lindtmayer, Baschion **19** 414
Lindtmayer, Daniel, II **18** 493; **19** 414*
 works **19** *414*
Lindtmayer, Felix, I **19** 414
Lindtmayer, Felix, II **19** 414*
Lindtner, Maria Susanna **2** 825
Lindum *see* LINCOLN (UK)
Line, John **19** 414
Line, John, & Sons Ltd **19** 414–15*; **28** 549; **32** 813, 817
 works **23** 548; **32** V3
Linea grafica **24** 449
linear perspective *see under* PERSPECTIVE→ types
Linear Pottery culture **25** 498, 500, 503, 513, 514, 515, 517
line block *see under* PRINTING → processes
line-endings **20** 339
Line Islands *see under* KIRIBATI
Línek, Jan **8** 381
linen **19** 415–19*
 historical and regional traditions
  Austria **2** 823, *824*; **32** *388*, *391*
  Belgium **3** *609*; **5** 654; **18** *589*, *592*; **19** 418
  Byzantine **9** 664, 668
  Coptic **7** 826; **16** 431; **30** IV2
linen
 historical and regional traditions—cont.
  Czech Republic **8** 418
  Early Christian (*c.* AD 250-843) **9** 664, 668; **30** 776
  Egypt **9** 247; **16** 432; **30** IV2
   Islamic **16** 431, *433*, 442; **31** 21, *21*
  Egypt, ancient **3** 482; **9** 823–4; **12** *226*; **20** 327; **22** 283; **31** 259
  England **10** 278, 353; **19** 415, 418; **27** 693; **30** *541*
  Etruscan **10** 589, 636
  France **11** *650*; **18** *589*; **19** 418
  Germany **7** 167; **12** 462, 463, 464, *464*, 465, 469; **13** 194; **19** 418; **27** 693
  Gothic **13** 194; **30** *541*; **32** *389*
  Greece, ancient **9** 246, 247
  Hungary **15** 12
  Iceland **15** *74*
  Ireland **5** 654; **16** 33, *34*; **19** 418
  Islamic **16** *137*, 352, 356, 428, 431, 432, *433*, 442, *448*; **31** 21, *21*
  Italy **10** 589, 636; **16** *754*, 760; **19** 418; **27** *693*
  Morocco **16** *448*
  Netherlands, the **19** 418; **22** 899
  Ottoman **16** *137*
  Rhodes (island) **13** *356*
  Romanesque **26** 703
  Rome, ancient **20** 327; **27** 112
  Russia **27** 430
  Scotland **19** 417, 419; **28** 264, *265*, 265–6
  Serbia **28** 456
  Sweden **30** 115
  Switzerland **13** 194
  Turkey **16** *137*
  Venezuela **32** 178
 techniques
  cutwork **18** 588
  drawn-thread work **18** 588
  dyeing **9** 490
  printing **30** 561
 uses
  antependia **2** *823*
  bedding **3** 482
  bookbindings **4** 347; **16** 356
  books **10** 589, 636; **20** 327
  canvas **5** 654
  carpets **5** 831
  chasubles **12** *464*; **32** *388*, *391*
  damask **30** 551
  dolls **31** 259
  dress **9** 246, 247; **28** 717
  embroidery **3** *609*; **9** 668; **10** 181, 353; **12** 462, 463; **13** 194, *356*; **15** 12, *74*; **16** *448*, 760; **27** *693*; **28** 264, *265*; **30** *150*, *541*
  flags **11** 145
  inscriptions **10** 589
  lace **11** *650*; **12** 469; **16** *754*; **18** 588, *589*, 590, *592*
  mummies **22** 283
  napkins **19** 416
  painting **5** 655; **12** *226*; **24** 5
  paper **16** 352; **24** 40
  passementerie **24** 237
  robes **16** 431
  rugs **27** 317
  samplers **27** 693
  satin **30** 551
  shirts **16** *137*
  tablecloths **19** 416
  tapestries **12** 465; **13** 194; **16** *433*; **30** 308, IV2
  threads **12** 463, 464, 469; **30** 537*, 541
  thrones **30** 776
  tiraz **31** 21, *21*
  towels **19** 416
  wall coverings **10** 278
  weaving **12** 463, 464
  wrappings **20** 327
linen—cont.
 see also DAMASK
Line of Habashi, Malik al-Din Firuz Shah *see* MALIK AL-DIN FIRUZ SHAH, Sultan
Line of Ilyas Shah *see*:
 NASIR AL-DIN MAHMUD, Sultan
 SHAMS AL-DIN YUSUF SHAH, Sultan
 SIKANDAR SHAH I, Sultan
Line of Sayyid Husayn Shah, Nusrat Shah *see* NUSRAT SHAH, Sultan
liners *see* SHIPS → named vessels
liner style **24** 266
Lines, Samuel **4** 86
Lines Bros **31** 261
Linfen
 Tiefo si **7** 99
 see also DONGYANG; WEI CUN
Lin Fengmian **7** 149; **14** 722; **19** 419–20*
Lin Feng-mien *see* LIN FENGMIAN
Ling, Arthur **20** 475
liṅga *see under* SCULPTURE → types
Linga Longa **25** 26
Lingapura *see* KOH KER
Lingard, Webster & Co. **7** 434
Lingbao **7** 34
Lingdi, Emperor (Han; *reg* 168-89) **6** 816
Linge, Abraham van **29** 505
Linge, Bernard van **29** 505
Lingel, József **14** 910
Lingelbach, Johannes **19** 420–21*
 attributions **14** 15; **18** 622
 collaboration **3** 494, 501, 762; **14** 499, 504; **22** 208; **27** 329; **33** 178
 groups and movements **3** 143
 patrons and collectors **3** 494
 works **19** *420*
Lingeman, L. **13** 633
Lingeri, Pietro **19** 421*
 collaboration **11** 63; **30** 512, 513
 groups and movements **21** 422; **25** 838; **26** 16
 works **16** 650, 721
Ling *fang yi* **6** 844, *844*
Lingguang dian **6** 815
Lingnan Painters **12** 50
Lingnan school **6** 802; **17** 198; **19** 421–3*
 members **12** 49; **14** 722
 works **19** *422*
Lingshou *see* PINGSHAN
Ling-ti, Emperor *see* LINGDI, Emperor
linguistics **7** 659; **19** 275
Lin Guohua *see* LIN KUO-HUA
Linguzzi, Luciano **17** 622
Linhares, Rodrigo de Sousa Coutinho, 1st Conde de **28** 430; **29** 100
Linhares, Vitorio Maria de Sousa Coutinho, 2nd Conde de **29** 100
Linhart, Evžen **8** 380; **11** 365; **14** 732; **19** 423*
Linhart of Altenberg **6** 363
Linhas Aéreas de Moçambique **22** 245
Linhof *see under* CAMERAS → types
Lin Hsüeh *see* LIN XUE
Linh Thai **6** 430
Lin Huiyin **19** 301
Linien (periodical) **8** 736
Linien I (group) **4** 62, 104; **10** 899; **22** 150; **28** 183
Linien II (group) **7** 805; **8** 736
lining-papers *see under* PAPER → types
Linjan, Pir-i Bakran **3** 894; **16** 194, 244, *244*, 245; **28** 634
 inscriptions **16** 259
 mihrab **21** 506
 stucco **29** 820
Linjeflyg **32** 730
Linjia (Dongxiang) **6** 835; **20** 143
Linji Buddhism *see under* BUDDHISM → sects
Link, O(gle) Winston **19** 423–4*
Linka, Jan Michał **27** 722; **33** 605
Linke, François **5** 193; **24** 317
Linke, Simon **19** 591
Linked Ring **8** 582; **19** 424*; **21** 407; **24** 674
 members **24** 738
  Annan, James Craig **2** 119
  Coburn, Alvin Langdon **7** 491
  Davison, George **8** 579
  Eugene, Frank **10** 649
  Evans, Frederick H(enry) **10** 655
  Gloeden, Wilhelm von **12** 817
  Henneberg, Hugo **14** 388
  Kühn, (Carl Christian) Heinrich **18** 501
  Robinson, Henry Peach **26** 472
  Steichen, Edward J(ean) **29** 601
  Sutcliffe, Frank Meadow **30** 36
  Watzek, Hans (Josef) **32** 924
  White, Clarence H(udson) **33** 146
linking **30** 549
Linköping **19** 424–6*; **30** *65*
 altarpieces **13** 120
 Cathedral of SS Peter and Paul **13** 50; **19** *425*, 425–6*; **30** 67
  monument of Ture Bielke and Margareta Sture **30** 84
 sculpture **13** 102, 103; **30** 83
 jewellery **30** 112
 Östergötlands Länsmuseum **19** 424; **30** 119
 sculpture **30** 83
 University **30** 119
Links Pottery **28** 258
Lin Kuo-hua **30** 244
Lin Lian **6** 801
Lin Liang **19** 426*; **33** 657
Lin Lien *see* LIN LIAN
Linlithgow (Lothian) **28** *222*
 Palace **28** 225, 244, 245, 265, 268
Linnaeus, Carl **4** 484; **10** 101; **12** 135; **14** 692
Linné, Carl von *see* LINNAEUS, CARL
Linnebach, Adolf **30** 685
Linnell, John (i) (1729-96) **4** 845; **19** 592
 assistants **14** 230
 patrons and collectors **7** 659
 works **7** *167*, 659; **10** 279, 295; **11** 431; **16** 24; **18** 614; **30** 268; **31** *685*
Linnell, John (ii) (1792-1882) **7** 548; **19** 426–7*; **20** 593; **30** 747
 books **4** 121
 dealers **12** 30
 engravings **4** 121; **31** 909
 groups and movements **1** 897
 paintings **10** 251; **19** *427*
 patrons and collectors **3** 239; **7** 709; **12** 638; **21** 901
 personal collection **10** 394
 prints **21** 418
 pupils **8** 505; **23** 58
 teachers **31** 909
Linnell, William **10** 295; **19** 426, 592
 works **7** *167*
Linnig, J. T. J. **3** 619
Linnig, Willem **17** 736
Linning, Christian **30** 94
Linnqvist, Hilding **19** 428*; **30** 81
 works **22** 331
Lino, Bartolommeo de *see* BARTOLOMMEO DE LINO
Lino, Raul **19** 428*; **25** 294; **28** 781
linocuts **19** 429–30*; **25** 608
 Aboriginal Australia **1** *65*
 Albania **21** *78*
 Botswana **4** *490*
 Denmark **8** 736

linocuts—cont.
Germany **19** 429, *429*
Namibia **22** 450, *450*
South Africa **29** 110, *111*
Spain **11** *495*
Linossier, Claudius **11** 628
Linotype composition machines **16** 361; **31** 496
Linru **6** 876, 895, 914; **29** 67
Linru ware *see under* POTTERY → wares
Linschoten, Jan Huygen van **10** 162
Linstead, R. P. **24** 792
Linstow, Hans Ditlev Franciscus **13** 693; **19** 430*; **23** 221, 231, 602
Lin Su Laoren *see* YANG SHOUJING
Lint, Hendrik Frans van **32** 112
Lint, Pieter van **7** 466; **19** 430*; **33** 298
Lintas **24** 241
lintels **19** 430*
historical and regional traditions
Cambodia **5** 475
Early Christian (*c.* AD 250-843) **1** *523*
Indian subcontinent **9** 161
Japan **17** 47
Khmer **30** 599–600
Maori **20** *355*
Maya **9** 165
Mesoamerica, Pre-Columbian **9** 165
Thailand **30** 599–600
Turkey **1** *523*
materials
cedar **17** 47
shells **20** *355*
wood **20** *355*
Linthorpe Art Pottery **9** 295; **10** 312
Lin Tinggui **6** 783
Lin T'ing-kuei *see* LIN TINGGUI
Linton **26** 617
Linton, Henry Duff **19** 431
Linton, James Dromgole **19** 430
Linton, Jamie **19** 431
Linton, J. R. **2** 771
Linton, J(ames) W(alter) R(obert) **2** 759, 766; **19** 430–31*; **23** 346; **24** 496
Linton, William James **8** 121; **19** 431*; **25** 611; **33** 369
Lintong **6** *615*; **19** 431–2*
mausoleum complex of Qin Shi Huangdi **6** 648, 696; **19** 431–2
chariots **6** 857
iron **7** 97
terracottas **6** 727, 882; **7** *55*, 56, 160; **19** 431–2, *432*; **30** 509, *509*
Qingshan Temple **7** 23, 24
see also JIANGZHAI
Linwood, Mary **23** 883
Lin Xue **33** 320
Linyiao **7** 94
Lin Yuhao **6** 733
Lin Yu-shan **30** 247
Linz **2** *776*; **19** 433–4*
Cathedral of Maria Empfängnis **2** 787
Hochschule für Künstlerische und Industrielle Gestaltung **2** 831, 833
Landhaus **2** 779, 806; **19** 433
Landstrasse **19** *433*
Mariä Himmelfahrt **2** 824
Martinskirche **2** 777
palace **2** 779
Puchenau Estate **2** 789
St Ignatius **2** 781
St Theresia **2** 789
Schlossmuseum des Oberösterreichischen Landesmuseums **2** 831; **17** 832; **19** 433, 434
Siemens' office building **14** 694
Linz—cont.
Stadtmuseum **10** 640
wool **2** 825
Linz Bros **31** 654
Linz Crucifixion, Master of the **20** 764
Linz Diözesan-Kunstverein **24** 438
Linzhang *see* YECHENG
Linzi **6** 663
see also LANGJIA ZHUANG
Li'o, Lese **23** 737
Liombeni, Lorenzo de *see* LEONBRUNO, LORENZO
Liompardi, Alessandro *see* LEOPARDI, ALESSANDRO
Lion, Jules **1** 440; **23** 32
Lionardo, Agostino **4** 170
Lion Cachet, C(arel) A(dolph) **19** 434*
collaboration **23** 125; **33** 676
groups and movements **22** 875
staff **28** 172
works **33** 260
Lione, Andrea di **3** 388; **10** 762; **19** 434–5*; **22** 21
Lionel Corp. **31** 259
Lionello, 13th Marchese of Ferrara (*reg* 1441-50) **8** 601–2; **10** *518*, 519*; **13** 755
architecture **11** 2; **16** 630; **29** 859
collections **24** 862
interior decoration **11** 4
manuscript illumination **12** 665
medals **20** *918*; **24** 864
paintings **3** 648, 649; **15** 85; **16** 661; **24** 16; **33** 117
sculpture **3** 260
tapestries **11** 5
Lionel of Antwerp **14** 425
Lion Hunt Relief (*c.* 668-627 BC) **1** 892; **23** 154; **29** 423
Lion Hunt Stele (*c.* 4000-*c.* 2900 BC) **21** 271, 293
Lioni, Leone **2** 550
Lionne, Hugues de **19** 264
Lionni, Leo **4** 109
Lion Painter **13** 507
Lion polyptych **19** 683
lions' heads **13** 392, *393*
Lion Silk (10th-11th cent.) **16** 435
Lion-strangler Silk (12th cent.) **9** 666; **16** 436, *437*
Lion Throne **30** 786
Liotard, Jean-Etienne **12** 276; **14** 42; **19** 435–7*; **21** 643; **22** 846; **30** 125
drawings **19** *436*; **30** *132*
groups and movements **23** 503; **31** 363
methods **10** 562; **24** 242; **29** 863
paintings **19** *436*
pupils **3** 101; **33** 594
works **1** 632; **7** 785; **9** 216; **11** 460; **16** 536; **24** 242; **30** 132; **31** 363
Liotard, Jean-Michel **19** 437
Lioyo **33** 598
Lípá (family) **4** 832
Lípa, Oldřich **17** 816
Lipany Church **28** 855
Lipari **13** 582; **14** 333; **29** 703
pottery **13** 539
Lipari group **13** 530; **28** 655
Lipari Painter **13** 531
Liparolo, Girolamo **2** 276
Lipchitz, Jacques **11** 568, 569; **17** 577; **19** 437–8*
collaboration **11** 659; **20** 605
dealers **27** 162
groups and movements **8** 240, 246; **9** 705; **11** 568; **23** 694; **25** 741; **27** 307
house **19** 41
patrons and collectors **20** 203; **23** 169; **26** 489; **28** 167; **30** 749
works **17** 580; **19** *437*
lip cups *see under* CUPS → types
lip-discs **1** 351
Lipharts, von **10** 540
Lipinsky, Sigismondo **24** 840
Lipizer, Luigi **26** 709
Lipkin, M. **23** 391
Lipków **25** 133
textiles **25** *133*
Lipman, Howard W. **19** 439
Lipman, Jean **19** 439
Lipnice Castle **8** 376
Lipovac **22** 79
Lipp, Friedrich **7** 328
Lipp, N. **18** 449
Lippai, János **15** 6
Lippard, Lucy **10** 878; **31** 673
Lipparini, Ludovico **4** 106; **8** 135
Lippay, György, Archbishop of Pozsony **14** 900
Lipper, F. W. **28** 107
Lipper, Wilhelm Ferdinand **12** 413
Lippert, G. **8** 405
Lippert, Józef **13** 888
Lippert, Patricia **19** 827
Lippert, Philipp Daniel **19** 439*
Lippi, Annibale **4** 47
Lippi, Bartolomeo di Giovanni *see* BIGIO, BACCIO
Lippi, Claudio **4** 47; **20** 839
Lippi, Filippino **9** 26; **11** 184; **16** 766; **19** 439, 445–51*; **26** 766
assistants **25** 847
attributions **14** 848; **16** 847
collaboration **3** 15; **12** 551; **24** 523
drawings **6** 139; **9** 216; **19** *449*
groups and movements **26** 186, 187
paintings
frescoes
Brancacci Chapel (S Maria del Carmine, Florence) **4** 658; **16** 837; **20** 534, 554
Carafa Chapel (S Maria sopra Minerva, Rome) **13** 700; **26** 767
Palazzo Vecchio (Florence) **24** 522
Strozzi Chapel (S Maria Novella, Florence) **11** 209; **16** 659; **19** *450*; **20** 279
Villa Medici (Poggio a Caiano) **32** 549
panel
altarpieces **3** 15, 304; **19** 183; **24** 527
religious **3** 845; **19** *447*, *448*
spalliere **29** 362
patrons and collectors
Benson, R(obert) H(enry) **3** 740
Butler, Charles (1822-1910) **5** 311
Carafa, Oliviero, Cardinal **5** 698; **26** 766
Hamilton, Alexander, 10th Duke of Hamilton and 7th Duke of Brandon **14** 107
Kerr, William Schomberg Robert, 8th Marquess of Lothian **28** 270
Lorenzo the Magnificent, Lord of Florence (*reg* 1469-92) **21** 14; **25** 46
Strozzi, Filippo, the elder (1428-91) **29** 782
teachers **4** 493
Lippi, Filippo (di Tommaso) **9** 102; **16** 661; **19** 439–45*; **23** 754; **25** 152
assistants **8** 850; **12** 765
collaboration **2** 130; **12** 713; **20** 642; **24** 537; **25** 9
methods **11** 184
patrons and collectors
Carmelite Order **5** 778
Cosimo, Lord of Florence (*reg* 1434-64) **21** 11
Doria-Pamphili, Alfonso, Prince **9** 175
Eastlake, Charles Lock (1793-1865) **9** 683
Lippi, Filippo (di Tommaso)
patrons and collectors—cont.
Malatesta, Sigismondo Pandolfo **20** 160
Medici, Giovanni (di Cosimo) de' (1421-63) **21** 13
Murray, Charles Fairfax **22** 351
Piero de' Medici, Lord of Florence (*reg* 1464-69) **21** 12
Puccini, Tommaso **25** 691
Rucellai, Giovanni (di Paolo di Messer Paolo) **27** 307
Sanford, John **27** 729
Solly, Edward **29** 46
pupils **4** 493; **5** 782; **16** 847; **19** 445; **20** 623, 642, 679; **24** 537
sculpture **11** 208
works **9** 98; **11** 377, 382, 389; **13** 193; **15** 135; **16** 659; **19** *441*, *442*, *443*, *444*; **25** 450; **27** 495; **29** 665
Lippi, Giovanni *see* BIGIO, NANNI DI BACCIO
Lippi, Juan **29** 315
Lippi, Lorenzo **16** 673; **19** 452*
patrons and collectors **19** 63
pupils **4** 65
teachers **27** 179
works **11** 194; **19** *452*
Lippincott **29** 901
Lippincott, H. Mather **32** 234
Lippincott, Roy (Alston) **19** 453*
collaboration **2** 705; **4** 65
works **2** 705, *706*; **23** 55
Lippi-Pesellino Imitators **20** 752
Lippmann-Lissingen **33** 430
Lippo dalle Madonne *see* LIPPO DI DALMASIO
Lippo di Benivieni **19** 453*; **20** 650
Lippo di Buono **4** 31
Lippo di Corso **11** 698
Lippo di Dalmasio **4** 275; **5** 656; **7** 926; **19** 453–4*
works **5** *656*
Lippo Dini **24** 874
Lippo di Polo, Agnolo di *see* AGNOLO DI LIPPO DI POLO
Lippold, Franz **28** 145
works **28** *145*
Lippold, Richard **19** 454*; **23** 262
Lippo Memmi **3** 247; **19** 454–5*; **20** 506; **21** 108; **24** 854
attributions **3** 247; **19** 453
collaboration **20** 510
paintings **7** 328
patrons and collectors **29** 46
restorations by others **13** 260
works **5** 164; **9** 4, 260, *260*; **19** *454*; **27** 750; **28** 684, 686
Lippo (di) Vanni **13** 149; **19** 455–7*; **28** 684, 686
attributions **28** 683
works **19** *456*; **28** 686
Lipps, Theodor **1** 181; **19** 457*
Lippstadt Marienkirche **14** 81
Lips, Joest *see* LIPSIUS, JUSTUS
Lips, Johann Heinrich **7** 870; **33** 116
Lipshitz, Lippy **29** 111
Lipsius, (Johann Wilhelm) Constantin **9** 237; **19** 457–8*
Lipsius, Justus **17** *598*; **19** 458*
personal collection **15** 85
works **19** 312, 313; **26** 848
Lipskaya, Anna (Aleksandrovna) **27** 417
Lipska-Zworska, Irena **25** 123
Lipton, Seymour **19** 458*; **24** 213
works **18** 301
Liptovská Mara **28** 851
Liptovský Mikuláš **28** *848*
P. M. Bohúň Gallery **28** 857
lipwork **29** 763
Li Qinglu **7** 71
Li Qingzhao **7** 152
Liquan
Jian ling **6** 730
Liquan—cont.
Shun ling **6** 730
Zhao ling **6** 698
Liquitex **23** 787
Li Qun **6** 814
Lira, Genaro Amador *see* AMADOR LIRA, GENARO
Lira, Pedro **5** 188; **6** 597; **13** 9; **19** 458–9*
Lira Gómez, Bernardo **21** 381
Lirangu **33** 609, 610
Liria S Miguel de los Reyes **29** 269
Li Rihua **6** 820
Lironi, Giuseppe **16** 699; **19** 459*; **23** 645
patrons and collectors **7** 897; **23** 577
Li Ruiqing **6** 766, 767; **33** 640
Lisaert, Anton **3** 41
Lisaert, Philip **29** 57
Lisbjerg Altar **11** 465
Lisbjerg Church **8** 738
Lisboa, Antônio Francisco **4** 708, 710, 716, 725; **19** 459, 460–61*
patrons and collectors **4** 727
works **1** 422; **19** *461*; **23** 669; **26** 254, *254*
Lisboa, Inácio Augusto da Silva *see* SILVA LISBOA, INÁCIO AUGUSTO DA
Lisboa, Manoel Francisco **19** 459–60*
pupils **19** 460
works **19** *460*
Lisboa de Lima, A. A. **22** 245
Lisbon **19** 462–9*; **24** 584–5; **25** *288*; **26** *908*
23 Avenida da República **23** 177
2-6 Avenida Luis Bivar **23** 177
Academia de Belas-Artes **25** 293, 298, 302, 317, 319
collections **25** 318
Águas Livres aqueduct **20** 109–10, 402; **25** 292
Águas Livres residential block **25** 294
Arquivo Nacional da Torre do Tombo **25** 319
Arsenal do Exército **1** 466
art forms and materials
architecture **25** 289, 291, 293
books **17** 565
ceramics **6** 331; **19** 467–8*; **30** 881
façades **27** *803*
faience (ii) (ceramics) **19** *468*; **25** 309
glass **25** 311
gold **25** 312, 313
marks **25** 312
metalwork **25** 313; **26** 690
painting **25** 295, 297
pottery **25** 308, 309, 310
Associação Portuguesa de Museologia **25** 319
Aula Regia de Desenho e Figura **25** 317
Avenida Infante Santo **30** 882
Basílica da Estrela **23** 406; **25** 301; **30** 881
Biblioteca Nacional **25** 319
Bull-ring **25** 293
Câmara Municipal **25** 293
Capitólio Concert Hall **25** 294
Centro de Investigação e Pesquisa **25** 319
Cinema Eden **25** 294
Colonial Hospital **20** 909
Court Baroque **25** 292
ecclesiastical buildings
Cathedral **13** 71; **19** *462*; **25** 289, 313
tomb of Lobo Fernandes Pacheco **13** 101
church of the Comendadeiras de Avis **25** 313
Church of the Paulistas **26** 253
Convento da Trinidade **25** 296
Loreto **25** 301

Lisbon
ecclesiastical buildings—cont.
Luz de Carnide Church **25** 296
Madre de Deus **17** 595; **26** 252; **30** 881
Mártires **27** 804
monastery of S Pedro de Alcantara **20** 411
Nossa Senhora da Graça **30** 881
Nossa Senhora das Mercês **23** 405
Nossa Senhora de Jesus *see* Nossa Senhora das Mercês
Nossa Senhora de Pena **17** 595; **19** 523; **26** 253
dos Paulistas *see* S Catarina
Royal Chapel **19** 777
S Antão **25** 291, 306
S Catarina **13** 695; **17** 595; **27** 804–5
S Domingos **25** 306
S Engrácia **2** 188–9, *189*; **25** 292, *292*; **31** 1–2
S Maria della Divina Providenza **13** 750, *751*; **23** 489
S Marta **25** 292
S Roque **25** 291, 313
chapel of S João Batista **16** 743, 760; **19** 777; **25** 292
paintings **25** 296, 297
tiles **30** 880
stained glass **13** 192
S Vicente de Fora **1** 740, *740*; **25** 291; **30** 518, *518*
tiles **30** 880
Xabregas, convent of Madre de Deus **20** 758; **25** 295, 297
see also museums → Museu do Azulejo
Edificio da Casa dos Açores **23** 177
Elevador S Justa **25** 293
Escola de Medicina **4** 387
Estaçao Marítima de Alcântara **25** *299*
French Embassy *see* Santos Palacio
Fundação Calouste Gulbenkian **25** 319
Gares Marítimas **25** 299
guilds **25** 312
Hotel Vitória **25** 294, *294*
Instituto Nacional de Estatística **25** 294
Instituto Superior Técnico **25** 294
kiosks **30** 882
Liceu Camões **25** 294
Marialva palace **27** 801
Metro stations **21** 350; **30** 882
Mitra Palace **2** 188
monument to King Joseph **25** 301
monument to Peter IV **25** 301
museums
Biblioteca e Arquivo Histórico do Ministério das Obras Públicas, Transportes e Comunicações **25** 319
Casa-Museu Fernando de Castro **6** 68
Centro de Arte Moderna **25** 318
Museu das Artes Decorativas **25** 318
Museu do Azulejo **25** 317, 318
see also ecclesiastical buildings → Xabregas, convent of Madre Deus
Museu Calouste Gulbenkian **25** 317
collections **10** 90, 94; **13** 841; **16** 556; **25** 318
periodicals **24** 453
Museu de Etnologia do Ultramar **29** 241
Museu de Marinha **3** 233
Museu Militar **4** 387; **30** 417
Museu Nacional de Arte Contemporânea *see* Museu Nacional do Chiado

Lisbon
museums—cont.
Museu Nacional de Arte Antiga **25** 319
collections **1** 212; **4** 638; **15** 744; **25** 318; **29** 478
Museu Nacional de Arte Contemporânea **4** 388
Museu Nacional do Chiado **4** 638; **25** 318
Museu Nacional dos Coches **25** 318
Museu Nacional do Traje **25** 318
Museu Rafael Bordalo Pinheiro **4** 385
National Gallery for Paintings *see* Museu Nacional de Arte Antiga
Opera do Tejo **4** 636
Paço da Ribeira **4** 635; **19** 777; **25** 297
Paço do Lumiar **30** 881
Palácio da Ajuda **1** 466; **10** 728; **19** 893; **25** 293, 298, 301, 308; **28** 430
metalwork **25** 312
sculpture **18** 578
Palacio Alvor-Pobal *see* Museu Nacional de Arte Antiga
Palacio de Arroios **28** 430
Palácio da Bemposta **25** 313
Palácio do Marquês de Fronteira **12** 124
Palacio das Necessidades **4** 638; **19** 468–9*; **25** 292, 308
Palácio Quintela-Farrobo **11** 249
Parliament Building **4** 387
Passeio Público **27** 803
Praça do Areeiro **25** 294
Praça do Comércio **19** *465*, 777, 893; **25** 293; **27** *800*
façades **25** *186*
Opera House **25** 292
Quinta dos Azulejos **30** 881
Ribeiro da Cunha House **25** 293
Rossio **20** 403
Rossio railway station **25** 293
Royal Palace *see* Paço da Ribeira
Santos Palacio **4** 175
synagogue **25** 294
Teatro do Bairro Alto **25** 297
Teatro Nacional Dona Maria II **4** 387; **19** 533; **25** 293
Teatro S Carlos **8** 9; **25** 293
Terreiro do Paço *see* Praça do Comércio
Triumphal Arch **25** 301
urban planning **12** 55; **14** 662; **19** *465*; **20** 110; **25** 185–6, 294; **27** 800–801; **31** 717
Ventura Terra's house **25** 294
Lisbon Surrealist Group **2** 902; **6** 359; **8** 433; **24** 321
Lisca, Francesco **12** 151
Lisch, Jean-Juste-Gustave **12** 484, 485; **19** 469*
Lischka, Johann Christoph **25** 445
Liselund **8** 30, 744; **12** 135
Lisgoa **16** 28
Li Shan **19** 469–70*; **20** 361; **33** 497
works **19** *469*
Li Shanfu **30** 49
Lishev, Vsevolod **31** 139
Li Shida **19** 470*
Li Shih-chen *see* Li Shizhen
Li Shih-chiao **30** 248
Li Shih-ta *see* Li Shida
Li Shijiao *see* Li Shih-chiao
Li Shimin *see* Taizong (ad 600–649)
Li Shizhen **7** 89
Lishman, Frank **1** 648; **18** 890
Li Shou **6** 699
Lishou, Passd **3** 728
Li Shouli **14** 325

El-Lisht **9** *774*, 780; **10** 94, 758; **19** 470–71*
glass **10** 55
mastaba of Imhotep **19** 471
mastaba of Senebtisi **10** 66; **19** 470
pyramid complex of Ammenemes I **12** 767; **19** 470; **25** 763
mortuary temple of Ammenemes I **9** 877
pyramid complex of Sesostris I **9** 875; **19** 470; **25** 763
pyramid of Sesostris I **9** 877; **19** 470
tomb of Senusertankh **19** 471
tombs **9** 839
Li Shutong **10** 885, 886
Li Si **6** 740, 769; **7** 129
works **6** *739*
Lisieux
Carmelite Convent **26** 148
Cathedral of St Pierre
roof **30** *900*
guns **2** 460, *460*
tiles **30** 885
Lisiewska, Anna Dorothea *see* Therbusch, Anna Dorothea
Lisiewski, Georg **30** 713
Lisitsky, El *see* Lissitzky, El
Lisitsky, Lazar' *see* Lissitzky, El
Li Sixun **6** 789; **19** 298–9*; **30** 288
groups and movements **23** 215
works **19** *299*
Li Sizhen **6** 770
Liška, Jan Kryštof **8** 391; **26** 125; **33** 212
Liska, Jaroslav **25** 467
Lišková, Věra **12** 796
Lislaughtin Abbey (Co. Kerry) **8** 201
crosses **8** *202*
Lisle, G. Barbé-Coquelin de *see* Barbé-Coquelin de Lisle, G.
Lisle, Psalter of Robert de *see under* Psalters → individual manuscripts
Lisle, Robert de **13** 149
L'Isle Adam, Villiers de, Bishop of Beauvais **11** 604
L'Isle d'Abeau **6** 534; **12** 105
L'Isle-en-Dodon Church **4** 780
L'Islet Church (Que.) **5** 585
metalwork **5** *585*
Lismer, Arthur **5** 592; **19** 471*
groups and movements **5** 566, 567; **13** 711; **16** 818
pupils **8** 41
Lismonde, Jules **17** 518
Lismore crosier **26** 688
Lisnicki, Israel ben Mordechai **17** 559
Li Song (*fl c.* 1190-1230) **6** 809
Li Song (*fl* 20th cent.) **7** 113
Lisqui **8** 776
Liss, Anna **19** 471
Liss, Johann (*c.* 1595-1631) **19** 471–3*; **32** 194
commentaries **27** 726
patrons and collectors **4** 125
works **11** 486; **12** 389; **16** 675; **19** *472*
Liss, Johann (*fl* 1622-49) **19** 471
Lissaman, Elizabeth **23** 68
Lissanovich, Boris **22** 776
Lisse, Dirck van der **19** 473–4*; **25** 68
Lissignol, Jean-Abraham **30** 148
Lissitzky, El **3** 529; **7** 770; **17** 576, 577; **19** 474–7*; **24** 450; **27** 394, 405; **30** 128; **31** 677; **32** 412, 661
architecture
skyscrapers **28** 834
assistants **19** 746; **27** 214
collaboration **28** 197
collages **7** 557
exhibitions **3** 802
furniture **27** 409

Lissitzky, El—cont.
groups and movements **1** 76; **10** 415; **15** 856
Abstraction-Création **1** 90
Asnova **2** 603, 604; **18** 620
Bauhaus **3** 401; **12** 407
Constructivism **7** 770; **8** 437
Four Arts Society of Artists **11** 358
Stijl, De **21** 781; **29** 661
Suprematism **1** 75; **30** 8
Unovis **20** 194; **31** 677
World of Art (Mir Iskusstva) **33** 380
patrons and collectors **8** 10
prints **20** 195
pupils **27** 409
title-pages **17** *577*
works **7** 582, 653, 770; **12** 15, 408; **17** 577; **19** *475*, *476*, 491; **22** 331; **24** 686; **25** 351; **32** 902
writings **27** 214
Lissorgues, Guillaume de **11** 514
Li Ssu *see* Li Si
Li Ssu-chen *see* Li Sizhen
Li Ssu-hsün *see* Li Sixun
List, Clemens **30** 754
List, Ferdinand **2** 813
List, Herbert **19** 477–8*
List, Wilhelm **28** 344; **33** 362
Lista, Stanislao **10** 512; **12** 267; **21** 495
Listad, Kristen **23** 229
List Arzubide, Germán **10** 543
list carpets *see under* Carpets → types
Lister, Martin **21** 720
Lister-Lister, William **25** 560
list rugs *see under* Rugs → types
Lisu **5** 262; **30** 623, 634, 637
dress **30** 627–8*
jewellery **5** 250
pipes (musical) **30** *637*
Li Sung *see* Li Song
Liszkowic, Jan **6** 366
works **25** *128*
Li Tang **6** 817; **14** 136; **19** 478–9*
groups and movements **23** 215
pupils **33** 468
works **6** 773, 789, 809; **14** 137; **18** 561; **19** *479*
Li Tao-yüan *see* Li Daoyuan
Litchfield (CT), Mary Perkins Quincy House **7** 619, *619*
Litchfield, Edwin C. **8** 575
Litchfield Manufacturing Co. **24** 62
Li Te-li *see* Li Deli
Litemont, Jacques de *see* Jacques de Litemont
Litér **6** 157
literacy **10** 4–5*
literati **1** 581; **6** 619, 630, 631–2, 636, 637, 787, 823–5; **32** 849
literati calligraphy *see under* Japan → calligraphy
literati painting *see under* Painting → types
literature of art *see* Bibliographies
Literaturnaya Gazeta **28** 917
Li Te-yü *see* Li Deyu
Li Thai, King of Sukhothai (*reg* 1347-68/74?) **30** 584, 601, 602
Lithares **14** 351
litharge **24** 795, 798
Lithgow **2** *736*
Lithgow Pottery **2** 760
Lithografen Printing Co. **3** 784
Lithographie **24** 444
lithography **7** 650; **10** 221; **19** 479–93*; **20** 601; **25** 591, 597, 608, 615–16; **26** 232, 742
historical and regional traditions **17** 441
Australia **2** *744*
Austria **18** *491*; **32** *446*
Brazil **4** 717

lithography
historical and regional traditions—cont.
Britain **4** *363*; **19** *482*, 482–3*; **25** *353*
China **7** 120
Cuba (Caribbean) **8** 233, 234
Czech Republic **19** 894
Denmark **8** 736
Ecuador **9** 714
England **1** 121; **19** *484*, 492; **25** *590*; **31** 910
Estonia **10** 539
France **19** 483*, 486–90, 491; **25** 345, *346*, *347*, *348*, *350*; **31** *214*
Art Nouveau **20** *602*; **22** *252*
Fauvism **19** *491*
Impressionism **20** *260*
Japonisme **17** *441*
Romanticism **8** *640*
19th cent. **3** 775; **4** *750*; **6** 549–50; **8** 545, *545*, *828*; **17** 604; **19** *486*, *487*; **26** *71*; **27** *870*
20th cent. **19** *490*, *513*
Germany **10** 695; **12** 392; **19** 481–2*, 490–91; **25** *349*; **28** 404; **29** 776; **31** *256*
Nazarenes **23** *411*
20th cent. **3** *892*; **14** *571*
Guyana **13** 876
Honduras **14** 716
Indian subcontinent **15** 679, *679*
Iran **16** 342
Islamic **16** 342, 361
Jamaica **5** 751; **16** *881*
Malta (Republic of) **5** 900
Mexico **19** 399; **21** 385, *402*
Netherlands, the **33** *46*
20th cent. **28** *201*
Norway **19** *489*
Panama **23** 904
Poland **25** 106
Russia **25** *351*
South Africa **29** 110, 121
Spain **21** *708*; **29** 283
Surinam **30** 15
Sweden **30** 100
Switzerland **25** *354*
United States of America **1** 145; **17** *614*; **19** 485, 492–3, *493*; **23** 630; **25** *352*, *353*
19th cent. **8** *276*
20th cent. **20** *606*, *608*
Venezuela **32** 173
materials
carbon blacks **19** 480
crayons **8** 128
inks **15** 853, 855
limestone **19** 480; **25** 615
paper **25** 615
presses **19** 480; **24** 650; **25** 592
soap **19** 480
stone **25** *600*
zinc *see* Zincographs
types
chromolithography *see* Chromolithography
offset *see under* Printing → processes
photolithography *see* Photolithography
uses
book illustrations **4** 345, 357, 362, 364, 367
ceramics **6** 328
dolls **31** 262
dolls' furniture **31** 264
dolls' houses **31** 262, 263
game-boards **31** 265
globes **12** 811
medical books **21** 6
porcelain **30** 100
posters **19** 488; **25** 345, *346*, *347*, *348*, *349*, *350*, *351*, *352*, *353*, *354*, 652; **32** *446*
puzzles **31** 267

lithography
uses—cont.
toys 31 255, 256, 258
lithophanes 12 435
lithophones 32 489
lithopone see under PIGMENTS → types
lithotints 25 623
Lithuania 19 494, 494–500*
architecture 4 782, 783; 19 495–7; 25 96, 98
Gothic 13 58; 19 495
brick 4 782, 783
castles 19 495
churches 19 495, 495, 496
collections 19 497, 498
exhibitions 19 498; 26 403; 27 446
insignia 7 178
marble 19 499
painting 19 495, 496, 498
photography 24 679
prints 19 498
sculpture 19 496, 499
stucco 19 496
University 19 497
vaults (ceiling) 19 496
Lithuania, Vitold, Duke of 5 181
Lithuanian Art Society 19 498; 33 688
Lithuanian School of Art 19 498
Liti (Greece) 19 880
Li Ti (c. 1125–c. 1200) see LI DI
Li Tiefu 14 721
Li Tinggui 7 93
Li T'ing-kui see LI TINGGUI
Litlington 14 544, 545
litmus 9 492
Litografía de Iriarte y Compañía 16 48
Litoměřice 25 431
Town Hall 11 876
Litoměřice Altar, Master of the 8 390
Litomyšl Castle 8 374, 378; 19 500*
theatre 8 399
Litovchenko, Ivan S. 31 560
lits à housse see under BEDS → types
Li Tsai see LI ZAI
lits à la polonaise see under BEDS → types
lits de parade see under BEDS → types
lits de repos see COUCHES
lits-en-bateau see under BEDS → types
Litslena 30 76
Li-tsung, Emperor (Sung; reg 1225–64) see LIZONG, Emperor
Litta, Antonio, Duca 32 121
Litta, Giulio, Conte 8 585; 32 121
Litta, Luigi 25 894
Litta, Pompea 20 90
Littell, Emlen T. 7 708; 14 50
Littemont, Jacob de 11 350, 352
littera antiqua see SCRIPTS → types → antique
Littérature 2 279; 4 753; 24 405, 428, 442; 30 17, 18; 31 503
litters 29 237
Little, Arthur 7 619; 19 500*; 28 604
Little, Edward
works 23 738
Little, Francis 33 401, 402
Little, James Edward 23 737
Little, Robert M. 30 684
Little, Thomas 8 830
Little, William 4 482
Little Dunmow (Essex), St Mary's 30 778
Little Haugh Hall (Suffolk) 14 269; 20 33; 30 890
Little Hormead (Herts), St Mary 10 339
Little Master cups see under CUPS → types
Little Masters 1 715; 10 385; 19 501*; 23 310; 24 355
members 3 505; 12 386
works 4 373; 12 420; 25 630
Little Moreton Hall (Ches) 10 230
Little Paxton Church (Cambs) 26 613
Littler, William 10 306, 309; 28 258
Littleton, Edward 30 499
Littleton, Harvey K. 3 595; 19 501*
works 12 795, 795, VII2; 31 645
Littleton, Jesse 19 501
Littleton, South see SOUTH LITTLETON
Little Walsingham (Norfolk)
Friary 21 841
Our Lady of Walsingham 28 630, 632
Littlewood, Joan 25 571
Littmann, Atelie Heilmann 25 409
Littmann, E. 1 512
Littmann, Max 19 501–2*
works 22 301; 29 874; 30 682
Littoria 31 730
Li Tung-yang see LI DONGYANG
liturgical books 13 130, 136
liturgical furnishings 7 277–84*, 280; 25 714
liturgical objects
historical and regional traditions
Byzantine 9 656; 10 437
Early Christian (c. AD 250–843) 9 656
Portugal 25 313
materials
ivory 16 799
pewter 24 580
silver 9 656
Litva see LITHUANIA
Litvak King, Jaime 33 472
Litvinsky, Boris A. 6 213; 9 457; 17 734; 27 599; 30 261; 33 509
Litz, Hans 28 190
Liuan 7 26
Liu An-jen see LIU ANREN
Liu Anren 6 700
Liu Bang see GAODI, Emperor
Liu Ch'i-hsiang 30 248
works 30 248
Liu Chüeh see LIU JUE
Liu Dan 6 816
Liu Daochun 6 804, 822
Liudprand, Bishop of Cremona 19 502*; 29 96
Liu E 6 767
Liu Gongquan 6 748
Liu Guandao 7 37
Liu Guosong see LIU KUO-SONG
Liu Haisu 7 149; 19 502–3*; 28 553
Liu Hai-su see LIU HAISU
Liuhe 7 26
Pagoda 23 773
Liu Hsiang see LIU XIANG
Liu Hsieh see LIU XIE
Liu Hsin-yüan see LIU XINYUAN
Liujiaqu (Shan xian) 7 34
Liu Jue 19 503*
Liu Kang 28 774
Liuksiala 11 108
Liu Kuan-tao see LIU GUANDAO
Liu Kung-ch'üan see LIU GONGQUAN
Liu Kuo-song 14 722; 19 504*; 30 249
Liulige (Hui xian) 6 788
Liulihe (Fangshan) 6 695, 848, 849
Liu Lin 33 67
Liu Pan see LIU HAISU
Liu Pang see GAODI, Emperor
Liu Qixiang see LIU CH'I-HSIANG
Liu Sheng, Prince
armour 7 55, 57
bronze vessels 6 858, 859; 7 81
figurines 6 727
furniture 7 33
glass 7 81
Liu Sheng, Prince—cont.
iron 7 98
jade 7 6
tomb 6 648
Liu Shi 33 320
Liu Songnian 19 504–5*
groups and movements 23 215
works 6 780, 809, 817; 19 504
Liu Sung-nien see LIU SONGNIAN
Liu Tan see LIU DAN
Liu Tao-ch'un see LIU DAOCHUN
Liuthar 20 330
Liuthar Codex see under codices → individual manuscripts
Liuthard 5 804, 810; 7 512; 23 652
Liuthard Group 5 810; 11 636; 13 21
Liu T'i-chih see LIU TIZHI
Liu Tizhi 6 867
Liutoldus monachus 2 791
Liutpirc, Duchess of Bavaria (fl c. 748–777) 18 447
Liu Xiang 33 318
Liu Xie 6 634
Liu Xinyuan 6 867
Liu Yao 17 171; 30 466
Liu Yong 6 764; 19 505*; 33 527
Liu Yu 22 460
Liu Yung see LIU YONG
Liu Zonggu 29 904
Livadia, Panagia tis Kyras 8 358, 359
Livaditti, Niccolò 26 725
Livdal', Fyodor 27 378
live art 24 403
Live de Jully, Ange-Laurent de La see LA LIVE DE JULLY, ANGE-LAURENT DE
Lively Child, Master of the see BAMBINO VISPO, MASTER OF THE
Liven, Martyn A. 29 555
liveries 14 414
Liverloo, de 18 652
Liverloo, Lambert de 11 166
Liverpool (Merseyside) 10 225; 19 505–8*; 24 652
Academy of Arts 19 507
Albert Dock 2 324; 9 59, 59; 32 861
architecture 11 330
Bridewell Studios 19 508
Cathedral of Christ the King 7 258; 8 224; 10 242; 12 591; 19 823
stained glass 29 508
Cathedral of St John 7 664, 670, 813; 8 184
cemetery 31 131
Central Hall 23 194
ceramics 19 508*
clocks 7 448
Crown Street station 25 854
Cunard Building 19 506
dioramas 8 911
docks 9 58, 59
Exchange and Town Hall 10 668; 31 239
gardens 30 749
Halifax Building Society 25 268
Lime Street Station 16 53
Lister Drive Power Station 25 402
Liverpool Museum 4 182; 19 507; 21 265; 28 857
Mansion House 29 565
memorial to the Engine Room Heroes 23 35
Mersey Docks and Harbour Board Offices 19 506
Mersey Docks building 3 269
Merseyside County Museum 22 795
Municipal Buildings 31 240
office buildings 19 506
Oriel Chambers 16 54
painting 19 507
Philharmonic Hall 7 687
Picton Library 19 318
Liverpool (Merseyside)—cont.
porcelain 10 308
pottery 4 177; 10 305
Royal Institution 27 161
Royal Liver Building 19 506
St George's Hall and Assize Courts 7 504, 667, 687; 10 151–2, 236; 18 888; 19 505; 31 240
portico 25 268
sculpture 19 60
St Martin's Cottages 30 458
sculptors 10 265
Society for Promoting the Arts 19 507
Society for the Encouragement of Designing, Drawing and Painting 19 507
Sudley Art Gallery 19 507
Tate Gallery 10 371; 19 508
tiles 30 877
Ullet Road Chapel 31 584
Union Bank see Halifax Building Society
University 1 29; 10 375; 19 507; 30 504
Victoria Buildings 30 458
Walker Art Gallery 10 370; 19 505; 26 12
collections 10 366; 11 330; 19 507; 27 161
Walton Gaol 23 211
warehouses 32 861
White Star Line Offices 28 563
William Brown Library and Museum 19 505
Liverpool, Robert Banks Jenkinson, Earl of see JENKINSON, ROBERT BANKS, 2nd Earl of Liverpool
Liverpool Photographic Society 11 794
Liverseege, Henry 19 508*; 20 239
livery barges see under BARGES → types
livery collars see under COLLARS → types
livery cupboards see under CUPBOARDS → types
livery halls 19 508–10*, 509
see also GUILDHALLS
Lives-sur-Meuse Church 13 114
Livett, R. A. H. 4 214
Livi, José 31 754
Livia 15 135; 26 891; 27 31
Living cross see under CROSSES → types
Living Design see DEZAIN
living painting see PERFORMANCE ART
Livingston (family) 7 702
Livingston, Margery 31 661
Livingstone 1 401
Capital Building 33 602
Museum 33 602
North-Western Hotel 33 602
Livinius Voghelarius see VOGHELARIUS, LIVINIUS
Livino di Giglio 31 429
Livinus Gilii de Burgis 11 5, 192; 16 756
Livno 4 459
basilica 4 459
Franciscan Monastery 4 462
Livois, Marquis de 19 510*
Livonia see ESTONIA; LATVIA
Livorno 16 620; 19 511, 511–12*; 31 718
Bottega d'Arte 28 319
coral 7 835
il Cisternone reservoir 25 60
ketubbot 18 3
Museo Civico Giovanni Fattori 19 512; 25 165
synagogue 17 544, 546, 548
Livre des femmes nobles et renommées, Master of the see CORONATION OF THE VIRGIN, MASTER OF THE
livres d'artiste 4 20; 12 497; 19 512–13*, 513; 26 236; 32 687
see also ARTISTS' BOOKS
Livry, Marquis de 19 56
Livshits, Benedikt (Konstantinovich) 8 250
Livy 3 327; 14 869; 15 84; 20 327; 31 813
Livy, John 3 330
liwan see IWAN
Li Wei 7 27
Li Wenfu 7 60
Li Xian 7 83
Li Xiongcai 19 423
Li Xisong 7 23
Lixus 22 129
Li Yangbing 6 765
Li Yanghu 7 82
Li Yang-ping see LI YANGBING
Li Yangui 8 536
Li Yen-kuei see LI YANGUI
Li Yin 33 496
Liyolo 33 596
Li Yong 6 747
Li Yong-hu see LI YANGHU
Li You 19 326
Li Yu (961–75) 7 120; 33 664
Liyu (Hunyuan) 6 615; 7 22
bronze 6 832, 833, 852, 854; 19 514*
Li Yung see LI YONG
Li Yungchang 2 95
Li Yung-zhang see LI YONGCHANG
Liz, Domingo 9 117
Li Zai 19 514–15*; 31 251
works 19 514
Lizard, John (d 1565) 19 515
Lizard, John (d 1574) 19 515
Lizard, Lewes 19 515*
Lizard, Nicholas, the elder (d 1571) 19 515*
Lizard, Nicholas, the younger (fl 1574) 19 515
Lizard, William 19 515
lizard-skins see under SKINS → types
Lizars, Daniel 19 515
Lizars, John 19 515
Lizars, William Home 19 515*
assistants 20 32
reproductive prints by others 2 710
works 14 243; 28 236
Li Zhaodao 6 789; 19 298, 299–300*; 30 288
attributions 19 298, 299, 299
groups and movements 23 215
Li Zhongren 7 76
Lizinka de Mirbel, Aimée-Zoë 2 723; 4 555; 14 482; 21 644
Lizong, Emperor (Song; reg 1225–64) 6 751; 19 856, 858
Lizzaro 2 608; 21 647
Ljashen 2 440
Ljóri 24 452
Ljøsne, Halvdan 13 726
Ljubižda 28 448
icons 28 447
Ljubljana 9 510; 19 515–16*; 23 490; 26 906; 28 858
Academy of Fine Arts 28 863
Accademia Operosorum 28 859
Bamberg House 28 860
Bishop's Museum 28 863
Cankar, I., Cultural Centre 28 860
Cathedral 28 859, 860
ceramics 28 862
church 28 858
City Hall 28 859
Gallery of Modern Art 19 516; 28 863
glass 28 862
Government Hall 28 859
Gruber House 28 859
mosaics 9 565
Municipal Museum 19 516; 28 863
National Gallery 19 516; 28 863

Ljubljana—cont.
National Museum **19** 516; **28** 863
pottery **28** 862
St James **28** 859
sculpture **28** 862
Strahl Gallery **28** 863
sugar refinery **28** 859
Ursuline church **28** 859
Ljubljana, Johannes of *see* JOHANNES OF LJUBLJANA
Ljubostinja **22** 79; **28** *437*
architectural decorations **22** 79
monastery church **9** 586; **28** 442, 453
wall paintings **22** 79
Ljubović, Ibrahim **4** 461
Ljungstedt, Peter Johan **30** 112
Llach Logostera, Luis **8** 16
Llagonne, La *see* LA LLAGONNE
Llaguno y Amirola, Eugenio **29** 358
Llallagua **4** 267
llama hair *see under* HAIR → types
Llanbadarn Fawr (Dyfed) **32** 784
church **32** 781
High Cross **32** 786
St Padern **26** 617
Llanbeblig Hours *see under* BOOKS OF HOURS → individual manuscripts
Llandaff (S. Glams)
Cathedral of St Peter and St Teilo **1** 738; **26** 617; **32** 781, 787
sculpture **26** 618
tomb of St Dyfrig **26** 618
Llandeilo (Dyfed), St Teilo **15** 875
Llandeilo Fawr (Dyfed) **32** 784
Llandudno (Gwynedd), Mostyn Art Gallery **32** 791
Llanegryn Church (Gwynedd) **32** 786
Llanelli (Dyfed) **31** 710
Llanelli Pottery **32** 789
works **32** *789*
Llanerchaeron (Dyfed) **32** 783
villa **32** 783
Llanes, R. Caballero y *see* CABALLERO Y LLANES, R.
Llanfedw (Glams), Ruperra **32** 782
Llangatock Hours *see under* BOOKS OF HOURS → individual manuscripts
Llangefni (Gwynedd), Oriel Môn **32** 791
Llangoed (Gwynedd) **32** 784
Llanharry (Glams)
pottery **6** *327*
Llanidloes (Powys) **32** 783, 790
Old Market Hall **32** 782
Llano, Francesco *see* LIANI, FRANCESCO
Llano, Marquis del **32** 566
Llano, Teodor de *see* NAPOLETANO, FILIPPO
Llano de Jícaro **18** 645
Llano Grande **21** 217
Llanos, Conde de Los *see* SALAMANCA (Y MAYOL), JOSÉ, Marqués de
Llanos, Fernando **19** 516–17*; **29** 277; **31** 815
Llanos (y) Valdés, Sebastián de **19** 517*; **29** 281
Llano y Dotres, Amalia de, Condesa de Vilches *see* VILCHES, AMALIA DE LLANO Y DOTRES, Condesa de
Llanrhaeadr-yng-Nghinmeirch (Clwyd), St Dyfnog **32** 787, 790
Llanrwst (Gwynedd), Gwydir Chapel **32** 789
Llanthony Priory (Gwent) **10** 228; **22** 222
Llantwit Major (S. Glams) **32** 786
church **32** 781
Llanymynech (Powys) **23** 211
Llarenas, Carlos Gómez de *see* GÓMEZ DE LLARENAS, CARLOS
Llauró, Juan **2** 397
Lledó **29** 321
Lleida **16** *103*; **29** *259*
Cathedral of S María *see* Seu Vella
sculpture **13** 105
Seo Antigua *see* Seu Vella
Seu Vella **13** 50, 106; **19** 517–18*; **29** 263
paintings **13** 150; **29** 275
sculpture **13** 106; **26** 610
textiles **30** 331
S Llorenç **13** 106
textiles **16** 436
Lleó, Gaspar **29** 337
Lleo, Javier Goerlich *see* GOERLICH LLEO, JAVIER
Lleopart, Pere **29** 337
Llewellyn, William **25** 835
Llewellyn Park (NJ) **25** 656; **31** 592
Nicholls-McKim House **31** 592
Llewelyn, Emma Thomasina **19** 519
Llewelyn, John Dillwyn **19** 518–19*
Llewelyn, Thereza Mary **19** 519
Llewelyn-Davies, Richard **19** 519*
works **14** *783*, 784
Llibre Vert **2** 476
Llimona, José **29** 295
Llonye, Antonio **13** 192
Llopart, Bernat **29** 332
Llorens, Antonio **31** 755
Llorens, Cristóbal **20** 10
Llorens, Tomas **10** 443
Lloret, Rosa **6** 600
Lloyd, A. L. **2** 553
Lloyd, Edward **3** 129
Lloyd, H. **31** 241
Lloyd, Mrs Hugh *see* MOSER (i), MARY
Lloyd, Hydie **19** 520
Lloyd, John **3** 476
Lloyd, Marshall B. **33** 158
Lloyd, Nathaniel **31** 151
Lloyd, Seton (Howard Frederick) **19** 519–20*
excavations
Agrab, Tell **9** 46
Bavian **3** 418
Beycesultan **3** 898
Eridu **1** 894; **10** 460
Harran **14** 192
Kayalıdere **17** 862
Ubaid, Tell al- **31** 509
Lloyd George, David **32** 789
Lloyd Jones (family) **33** 400
Lloyd-Jones, Hermia **2** 761
Lloyd Manufacturing Co. Ltd. **33** 158
Lloyds **31** 368
Lloyds, Frederick **30** 681
Lluch-Dalena, Julie **24** 620
Llull, Bernat **3** 218
Llwynypia (Mid Glams), Scotch Houses **32** 783
Llyn Cerrig Bach (Gwynedd) **6** 161
Llywelyn Fawr, Prince **32** 781, 786
Lmbat Church **2** 429
Lnáré Castle **8** 398
L.N.E.R. **25** 351
Lo, K. S. **7** 154
loams **6** 325
Loanen, Jean de **19** 238
loan exhibitions *see under* EXHIBITIONS → types
Loarre
Castle **19** 520–21*; **26** 581; **29** *259*, 263
church **19** *520*, 520–21; **26** 607
parish church **26** 642
Loarte, Alejandro de **19** 521*
Loaysa, García de, Archbishop of Toledo **27** 706
Loayza **8** 302
Loayza, Vicente **4** 259
Lob, J. M. **22** 883
Lobamba, National Museum of Swaziland **30** 63
Lobanov-Rostovsky, A. B. **27** 439
Lobb, Joel **6** 515; **11** 424
Lobbes
Abbey **3** 552; **26** 666
St Ursmer **13** 211; **33** 107
Lobbes Bible *see under* BIBLES → individual manuscripts
lobby-tables *see under* TABLES → types
Lobech, Albert **23** 235
Lobedu **1** 414
Löbenicht *see* KALININGRAD
Lobenigk, Egidius **33** 670
Lobermann, Harald **23** 307
Lobi **1** 383; **8** 21, 23; **19** 521–2*
architecture **19** 522*
collections **19** 521
figurines **1** 272, *272*
gesture **1** 264, 265, 266
granaries **1** 310
ivory-carvings **19** 522
jewellery **1** 279
sculpture **8** 22; **19** 521–2*
shrines (i) (cult) **19** *522*
wood **1** *272*
wood-carvings **19** 522
Lobineau **10** 867
Lobkovic (family) **8** 395, 423; **19** 807; **25** 432
Lobkovic, Benigna Kateřina z **25** 443
Lobkovic, Ferdinand August **25** 257
Lobkovic, Vaclav Eusebius **25** 257
Lobkowitz, Christoph Popel von *see* POPEL VON LOBKOWITZ, CHRISTOPH
Lobkowitz, Ferdinand Filip, Prince **5** 598
Lobkowitz, Juan Caramuel de *see* CARAMUEL DE LOBKOWITZ, JUAN
Lobmeyr, J. & L. **2** 818; **17** 691; **19** 522–3*
designers **2** 818; **14** 25, 628; **25** 404, 435, 674; **29** 722
works **8** 410, 411; **19** *523*
Lobmeyr, Josef (1792-1855) **2** 818; **19** 522
Lobmeyr, Josef, jr (1829-1917) **2** 818; **19** 522
Lobmeyr, Ludwig **2** 818; **15** 4; **19** 522
Lobming, Ernst von *see* ERNST VON LOBMING
Lobo
tools **1** *364*
Lobo, António **19** 523*
Lobo, Baltasar **10** 822; **19** 523*; **29** 296; **32** 568
Lobo, Filipe **3** 534; **19** 524*
Lobo, Francisco Xavier **19** 523
Lobo, Silvestre de Faria **4** 637; **19** 524*; **25** 814; **26** 254
Łoboda, Zygmunt **25** 409
Lobos, Alfredo **6** 597
Lobo Sevilla, Gonzalo **14** 716
Lobovikov, Sergey (Aleksandrovich) **19** 524*
Locarno **27** 75; **30** *124*, 144
glass **27** *76*
Locarno Beach **29** 743
Locatelli, Marchese **29** 381
Locatelli, Andrea **19** 524–5*; **26** 774
collaboration **1** 796; **20** 394
patrons and collectors **4** 560
pupils **21** 831; **24** 9
works **17** 708; **18** 710; **19** *525*; **28** 16
Locatelli, Bartolomeo **21** 831
Locatelli, Giovanni Francesco **19** 524
Locatelli, J. B. **27** 197
Locci, Augustyn **17** 615; **25** 98; **28** 115; **32** 7, 881
works **32** *870*
Locelso, Angel **7** 848
Lochard, Archibald **14** 60
Lochard, Colbert de, Baron **14** 58, 60
Lochee, Camperdown Works **28** 228
Lochen, Karl
works **11** *474*
Lo Chen-yü *see* LUO ZHENYU
Locher, Carl **10** 563; **28** 814
Locher, Leonhard **30** 143
Locher, Robert Evans **8** 708
Löcherer, Alois **19** 525*
Loches **11** *504*; **19** 525–7*
Château **6** 55, 57; **8** 278; **19** 526*
staircases **29** 521
tomb of Agnès Sorel **11** 555; **13** 79
La Trinité **19** 527*
St Ours **19** 526*, *527*; **26** 586, 599
sculpture **13** 79
Lochhead, Kenneth **4** 169; **5** 569
Lochis, Guglielmo, Conte **5** 872
Loch Leven Castle (Tayside) **28** 265
Lochner, Kunz **2** 473; **16** 867; **23** 307
Lochner, Stefan **7** 583; **13** 156; **19** 527–30*
cleaned by others **5** 59
patrons and collectors **32** 823
reproductive prints by others **20** 622
works **11** 452; **12** 384, *384*, 455; **19** *528*, *529*; **29** 665
Lochon, René **28** 506
Lochorst, van (family) **10** 216
Lochstoer, Niels **18** 614
Lock, Adam **4** 825; **33** 60, 62
Lock, John **10** 401
Lock, Josef Michael **12** 450
Lock, Matthias (*fl* 1720) **19** 530
Lock, Matthias (*c*. 1710-65) **19** 531
Lock, Matthias (*fl* 1769) **10** 294; **19** 530–31*
works **7** 746; **10** 294; **12** *626*; **23** 543; **24** 273; **26** 499
Locke, Alain **1** 235, 441
Locke, Donald **13** 877
Locke, Henry Hover **15** 656; **29** 272
Locke, John **13** 300
Locke, Joseph **23** 22
Locke, William (1732-1810) **19** 531*
collections **17** 475
interior decoration **3** 277
panoramas **24** 18
sculpture **12** 577; **32** 106
Locke, William (20th cent.) **12** 55
lockets **15** 726; **17** *522*, 524, 527
Lockey, Nicholas **19** 532
Lockey, Rowland **19** 531–2*; **21** 766
Lockhart, Betty *see* JOEL, BETTY
Lockhart, John Gibson **18** *856*
Lockhart River **1** 44
Lockhorst *see* LOKHORST
Lockleys **32** 541
Locko Park **9** 306
locks
historical and regional traditions
Bamana **3** *132*
Bijogo **4** 55
Britain **20** 442
England **10** 342
Germany **12** 454; **16** *59*
Spain **29** 340, *340*
Tuareg **31** *405*
United States of America **15** 822; **20** 593
materials
iron **16** 59
steel **16** *59*; **29** *340*
wood **3** *132*
Lockwood, Frederick & Roe **31** 266
Lockwood, Henry Francis **4** 837; **23** 194; **27** 641
Lockwood, LeGrand **19** 346
Lockwood, Thomas, and Sons **7** 529
Lockwood, Thomas Meakin **6** 561
works **6** *561*
Lockwood-Greene Co. **21** 601
Lockwood & Mawson **10** 237, 669
Lockyer, Charles **32** 240
Lockyer, James **7** 469
Locmariaquer **5** 780
Grand Menhir Brisé **25** 505
Locré-Russinger **24** 148, 149
Locri *see* LOKROI EPIZEPHYRIOI
Locri Painter **13** 530
Lőcse *see* LEVOČA
Locsin, Leandro
works **20** *274*
locus amoenus **18** 701
see also under GARDENS → types
locust-beans **1** 305
locust gum *see under* GUMS → types
Lod **16** 247; **17** 500
Diospolis **9** *513*
St George **9** 539
Lodai **21** 881
works **21** *881*
Löddeköpinge, *Grubenhäuser* **32** 533
Lodehat, Peder Jensen, Bishop of Roskilde **8** 724
loden **2** 823
Lodensanis, Angelo de *see* ANGELO DE LODENSANIS
Loder, J. C. von **1** 845
Loder, Matthäus **2** 796
Löderup Church **26** 639
lodestone **7** 133
Lo De Vaca **29** 139
Lodewijk, Philip **16** 575
Lodewijk van Bodeghem *see* LOYS VAN BODEGHEM
Lodewijk van Gruuthuse *see* LOUIS DE GRUUTHUSE
Lodge, Edmund **27** 459
Lodge, Henry Cabot **29** 870
Lodge, Jean **10** 398
Lodge, T. A. **18** 690
Lodge, William **33** 545
Lodgebook of Wolfgang Rixner and Jerg Reiter *see under* SKETCHBOOKS → individual manuscripts →Vienna Sketchbook
lodgebooks **19** 532*
lodges **3** 185; **24** *275*
Native North Americans **22** 569, 570, 572
United States of America **22** 569, 570, 572
lodges, gate *see* GATE LODGES
lodges, masons' *see* MASONS' LODGES
Lodi (India) **8** 673–4; **19** 533*
see also SIKANDER SHAH II, Sultan
Lodi (Italy)
Church of the Incoronata **3** 385
Fondazione Cosway **8** 21
pottery **16** 735
Lodi, Callisto da *see* PIAZZA, CALLISTO
Lodi, Carlo **3** 466, 869; **20** 497
Lodi, Fortunato **4** 638; **19** 533*; **25** 293
Lodi, Giovanni Agostino da *see* GIOVANNI AGOSTINO DA LODI
Lodi, Giovanni da *see* BATTAGGIO, GIOVANNI DI DOMENICO
Lodi, M. C. da **30** 656
Lodoli, Carlo (Cristoforo Ignazio Antonio) **19** 533–5*; **21** 106; **26** 13
works **19** *534*; **31** 296
Lodovico da Forlì **11** 383
Lodovico di Angelo **3** 858; **15** 60
Lodrino **30** 145
Lods, Marcel **19** 535–6*
collaboration **2** 660; **3** 450; **4** 57, 214; **26** 19; **28** 809; **30** 468

Lods, Marcel—cont.
pupils 26 192
staff 25 663
works 11 526; 23 122; 31 731
Lods, Pierre 1 432; 7 708; 28 406; 33 596
Lo Duca 10 486
Łódź 19 536–7*; 25 92
architecture 25 99
Central Museum of Textiles 19 536; 25 133
Museum of Art 2 409; 18 182; 19 537; 25 140
Museum Sztuki 24 682
Poznański palace 19 536
State Higher School of Fine Arts 25 142
textiles 25 133
Lodzeysky, K. I. 21 813
Loe, Joe 29 871
Loeb, Frits 31 576
Loeb, Pierre 1 438; 19 537*
Loeber, Lou 19 537*; 22 852
Loebnitz, Jules-Paul 24 148; 28 349
Loeb Tripod C 10 626, 626
Loedewich, Meister see JUPAN, LUDWIG
Loefftz, Ludwig von 18 101
Loehr, Max 6 840; 7 160, 161; 19 537–8*
Loemans, A. 7 556
Loeschke, Georg 11 854
Loeser, Charles Alexander 9 231; 19 538*; 29 604
Loeser, Frederick 19 538
Loeser Madonna, Master of the 19 668
loess 16 859
Loesser, Frank 30 687
Loe Thai, King of Sukhothai (reg 1298-1347) 30 584
Loeulliard, Octave 17 527
Loevestein Castle 22 822
Loew, Elias see LOWE, ELIAS AVERY
Loewe, Adolf 7 837
Loewe, Frederick 30 687
Loewensberg, Verena 1 666; 30 135; 33 737
Loewenstein, Rudolph 25 683
Loewenthal, Isadore 25 891
Loewy, Raymond (Fernand) 8 802; 15 824, 825; 19 538*
works 19 897; 20 594
Löffelbach 9 557
Löffelhardt, Heinrich 12 437; 32 757
Löffelholz Altar, Master of the 25 40
Löffler, Bela 17 547
Löffler, Bertold 2 816, 817; 19 538–9*; 25 404; 32 450
groups and movements 17 744; 33 166
pupils 17 691
works 12 821
Löffler, Gregor 6 171; 15 865
Löffler, Peter see LEIMINGER, PETER
Löffler, Sándor 17 547
Löfftz, Ferdinand 29 847
Löfftz, Ludwig von 7 855; 14 506; 16 906; 20 455; 21 37; 29 578
Löfgren, E. J. 3 821
Lofrano, Michele 16 743
Löfsta 30 71, 72
Loftus, William Kennett 1 892; 18 797; 21 301; 23 154; 30 27; 31 759
Logan, George 28 256
Logan, Juan 1 444
log cabins 31 589
Logelain, Henri 19 539*
loges 20 369
log forks 11 118
Loggan, David 19 539–40*
collaboration 33 147
pupils 31 871; 33 147
Loggan, David—cont.
works 7 566; 23 690
loggias 9 14, 21; 12 110; 19 540*, 634; 25 907
see also GALLERIES (ii) (CORRIDORS)
Loghem, Johannes Bernardus van 2 318; 19 540*; 23 450
Logina, Zenta
Logo, Oto 28 453
logograms 1 853
logos 15 824; 28 488; 31 497
Logostera, Luis Llach see LLACH LOGOSTERA, LUIS
Logosthetis, Anetis 1 513
Logroño 29 333
S María del Palacio 26 642
logs 1 48–9
Logteren, Ignatius van 19 540–41*; 22 859
Logteren, Jan van (fl c. 1685-c. 1709) 19 540
Logteren, Jan van (1709-45) 19 541*; 22 826, 859
Løgumkloster 4 781; 13 50
church 8 730
log-wood 9 491; 18 656; 25 315
Lohanipur 15 225, 423
Lohaus, Bernd 3 574; 23 906
Lohenstein, Daniel Caspar von 26 25
Lohja Church 11 94
Lohne 25 511
Lohr, Anthonius 10 458
Löhr, Henrik Michael 29 762
Lohrmann, F. A.
works 12 223
Lohse, Richard Paul 19 541–2*
dealers 26 193
groups and movements 1 79, 666; 7 546, 547; 30 135; 33 737
works 19 541
Lohuizen, T. K. van 1 804
Lohuizen-de Leeuw, Johanna Engelberta van 19 542*
Lohwasser, Kurt 20 607
Loiani, Giacomo di Giovanni d'Antonio see GIACOMO DI GIOVANNI D'ANTONIO LOIANI
Loi Malraux 2 324
Loimi 30 626, 627
Lóios Church 30 881
Loir, Alexis, I (1640-1713) 11 618; 12 832; 19 543*; 24 147
works 11 588
Loir, Alexis, II (1689-1775) 14 84
Loir, Alexis, III (1712-85) 19 543*
Loir, Marianne 19 543*
Loir, Nicolas-Pierre 13 783; 19 542*; 31 378
Loire Studio
works 29 499
Lois, Jacob 4 614; 19 543*; 27 230
Lois, Viktor 14 897
Loiseau, Georges 2 699
Loiseau, Gustave 19 544*; 25 215
Loiseau and Tribel 2 700
Loisel, Robert 17 459; 19 544*; 25 637; 26 43; 31 840
Loisia 27 91
Lois-Paul Originals 23 670
Loja 9 709
Universidad Técnica Particular de Loja 9 715
Lojacono, Francesco 28 317
Lojsta
church 13 190
hall 14 73
Løjt Church 8 730
Lojze, Aloysius see SPAZZAPAN, LUIGI DI GIUSTO
Loka Mahadevi, Queen (fl 1745) (Chalukyas of Badami) 15 526
Loket 8 379, 405
Lokhorst (family) 20 644, 786; 28 216, 218
Lokhorst, Dirk van 33 72
Lokhorst, Herman 22 837
Lokhorst, Katharina von see KATHARINA VON LOKHORST
Lokhovinin, Yury (Nikolayevich) 27 581
Łokietkowa Madonna 25 110
Lokman 16 347, 348
Loko, El 31 74
Lokono 13 874
Lokroi Epizephyrioi 6 170; 13 362, 582; 16 621; 19 544*
figurines 13 579, 580
sculpture 13 450; 21 342
temple 1 128
Lokros 1 646
Lokšany, Kateřina of see KATEŘINA OF LOKŠANY
Lola, Francesco 21 462
Lolei 5 481
Loleit, L. A. 21 92
Lolin (family) 19 627
Lolland-Falster Kunstmuseum see under MARIBO
Lolli, Stefano 10 811
Lollia Paulina, Empress of Rome (fl c. 37-41 AD) 27 103
Lolo 7 45; 32 489
Loloma, Charles 22 616
Loltun 21 231
Loma 1 263, 390; 19 310
masks 1 390
Loma Alta 31 812
Loma del Aguacate 30 866
Lomaheftewa, Linda 22 599
Loma Negra 32 418
Loma Rica 29 191
Lomas de Olmedo 29 202
pottery 29 202
Lomazzo, Giovanni Paolo 19 545–7*; 21 525; 22 378
personal collection 11 64
pupils 11 64
works 7 783; 19 545
writings 8 612; 9 7, 445; 12 287, 503, 571; 16 614, 781; 18 700; 19 354; 20 281; 22 374, 413, 414; 24 493; 31 299, 768
translated 9 8; 14 547; 23 690, 748; 31 300
Lombard, Alfred 24 266
Lombard, Jean 1 497
works 11 515
Lombard, Lambert 19 547–8*; 29 885
collaboration 13 28
education (art) 19 344
groups and movements 26 728
patrons and collectors 2 382; 20 395; 28 904
pupils 11 220; 12 884; 18 5; 23 200
reproductive prints by others 4 442; 7 499, 555, 799; 14 505
works 3 545, 554, 555; 19 345, 548
writings 9 445
Lombard, Peter (fl late 12th cent.) 13 130; 26 660, 664
works 7 514
Lombard, Pierre (c. 1613–82) see LOMBART, PIERRE
Lombard, Raymond the see RAYMOND THE LOMBARD
Lombard art 19 548–50*
coins 7 533
initials (manuscript) 19 549
interlace 19 550*
manuscripts 19 549*
marble 19 550
reliefs 19 549–50*, 550
sculpture 16 686
stucco 16 687*
Lombardelli, Giovanni Battista 26 818
Lombardi, Alfonso 11 4; 19 551*
collaboration 4 280
patrons and collectors 1 555; 6 41; 13 906
works 11 4; 16 749; 29 561; 30 498
Lombardi, Antonio 19 687
Lombardi, Franco 21 533
Lombardi, Gaetano 31 442
Lombardi, Martino 3 55
Lombardi, Niccolò 19 551; 29 561
Lombardi, Pietro 3 55; 11 346
Lombardi-Baldi 9 683
Lombardini, Bartolomeo 30 887
Lombardino, il see LOMBARDO, CRISTOFORO
Lombardo (family) 28 436; 29 853; 31 316; 32 192
Lombardo, Alfonso 3 495
Lombardo, Antonio (c. 1458-?1516) 11 4; 19 551, 553, 555, 556, 559*; 20 623; 27 888; 32 192
collaboration 16 693; 19 208, 556; 32 192; 33 633
patrons and collectors 10 522; 16 693
works 5 537; 16 693; 19 551, 554; 29 569
Lombardo, Antonio (c. 1564-1608/10) 5 415; 9 158; 19 552
collaboration 19 560; 32 249
Lombardo, Antonio (fl 1806) 22 481
Lombardo, Aurelio 19 552, 559–60*
collaboration 19 560
pupils 5 414
works 5 414; 19 560
Lombardo, Cristoforo 3 137; 19 561*
assistants 28 460
collaboration 3 138; 4 280; 12 761
works 1 462; 3 137; 21 517, 532, 533; 24 287
Lombardo, Giovanni Girolamo 19 552
Lombardo, Girolamo 19 552, 560*
collaboration 9 158; 19 560
pupils 5 414
works 19 559, 560
Lombardo, Guglielmo 9 158
Lombardo, il see RAGGI, (ERCOLE) ANTONIO
Lombardo, Ludovico 9 158; 19 552, 560
Lombardo, Martino 31 316
Lombardo, Paolo 19 552
Lombardo, Pietro (c. 1435-1515) 16 630; 19 551, 552–5*, 558; 32 192, 409
architecture 32 184
cathedrals 19 558
churches 3 663; 9 86; 19 554, 555; 32 185
façades 19 555; 32 185, 226
palaces 3 201; 32 218, 219, 219
screens (i) (architectural) 28 293; 32 224
assistants 19 555
attributions 19 663
collaboration 3 253; 7 517; 19 558; 32 225, 228
patrons and collectors 4 739; 19 663; 21 747
pupils 19 559; 21 632
sculpture 19 551; 32 217
tombs 3 201; 16 693; 31 125, 126, 316; 32 215
workshop 30 722
Lombardo, Pietro (d before 1608) 19 552
Lombardo, Sante 19 552, 560–61*; 32 160
Lombardo, Tommaso 18 691; 19 560, 562*
Lombardo, Tullio (c. 1455-1532) 16 689; 19 551, 553, 554, 555–60*; 20 623; 32 192
collaboration 4 739; 16 693; 19 559; 29 370
patrons and collectors 10 521; 21 747; 33 633
pupils 4 738
Lombardo, Tullio (c. 1455-1532)—cont.
works 5 537; 11 711; 16 693; 19 551, 554, 555, 556, 557, 559; 27 304; 32 192, 216, 225, 226, 545
Lombardo, Tullio (fl mid-16th cent.) 19 552
works 32 228
Lombardo della Seta 5 871; 27 789
Lombardo di Guido 19 765
Lombards 21 500, 501
Lombart, Pierre 7 431; 19 562*
Lombe, John 10 748
Lombe, Thomas 21 600
Lombez Cathedral 4 780; 11 623
Lombok 15 751, 795, 809
Lombroso 25 686
Lomé 1 386
Musée National 31 74
sculpture 31 74
Lome, Jehan 13 107; 19 562*; 23 901
Lomellini (family) 2 127; 3 34, 393; 6 34; 9 480; 11 53
Lomellini, Antonio 4 620; 28 461
Lomellini, Baldassarre 4 620; 20 902
Lomellini, Battista 2 179
Lomellini, Francesco 11 897; 25 254
Lomellini Triptych 2 179; 10 747
Lomellino, Giacomo 3 922
Lomellino, Nicolosio 6 24
Lomellino, Sofonisba see ANGUISSOLA, SOFONISBA
Lomello
Baptistery 7 256; 16 625
S Maria 26 577–8, 578
Lomello, Giovanni 16 739
Lomen Church 29 580
Loménie, Louis-Henri de see BRIENNE, LOUIS-HENRI, Comte de
Lomersheim, Walter von see WALTER VON LOMERSHEIM
Lomi, Alessandro 9 79
Lomi, Aurelio 11 52; 16 674; 24 860; 26 396
Lomi, Giovanni 28 319
Lomi, Giovanni Battista di Bartolomeo 12 304
Lommé, Guy 11 629
Lomme, Janin see LOME, JEHAN
Lommellini, Battista 10 709
Lomnica Monastery (Bosnia) 4 461; 25 339; 28 450
St George 25 343
Lomnicka Altarpiece (Slovakia) 28 854
Lomonosov 19 562–3*; 26 403; 27 363, 373
Chinese Palace 27 402, 415
gardens 12 134
paintings 9 18
pavilion 27 402
Lomonosov, Mikhail (Vasil'yevich) 19 563*; 27 415, 582; 28 646
Lomonosov Porcelain Factory (St Petersburg) 1 148; 8 506; 27 411–16*, 582
designers 6 529; 12 461; 20 850; 27 413, 414; 30 8; 31 677
production 1 453; 27 412, 413, 414, 414
Lomonosov University see under MOSCOW
Lomozzo, Giovanni Paolo 10 690
Lomp see LAMPI
Łomża Cathedral 25 126, 131
Lonad 15 277
Lonar Daityasudana 15 316
Lonate, Antonio da 33 634
Lonay, Charlotte Eleonore Le see LE LONAY, CHARLOTTE ELEONORE
Londerseel, A(ha)ssuerus van 5 62; 19 564

Londerseel, Johannes van (1578–1625) **19** 563–4*
copies **8** 663
teachers **5** 62
works **14** 706; **27** 885; **32** 588
Londerseel, Johannes van (*fl* 1654) **19** 564
Londicer, Ernst Wilhelm **10** 539
Londinium *see* LONDON
London **2** 66; **10** 223, *225*; **19** 564–624*, *565*, *569*; **25** *470*; **26** *905*; **31** 585, 709, 710, 711, *716*, 723, *732*
academies and art schools **1** 104; **19** 583–4, 591
Architectural Association **10** 240, 374; **17** 914; **32** 95
Camberwell School of Art **10** 375
Central School of Arts and Crafts **2** 569; **10** 373–4; **11** 499; **15** 823
Euston Road School *see* EUSTON ROAD SCHOOL
Government School of Art for Females **10** 374
Government School of Design **10** 252, 362, 372–3; **15** 821
Great Queen Street Academy **10** 249, 371; **18** 146; **19** 584
National Art Training School *see* Royal College of Art
Richmond House Gallery *see under* houses → Richmond House
Royal Academy of Arts **1** 104, 106, 108; **5** 531; **6** 79; **9** 12, 13, 16; **10** 233, 249, 264, 361, 362, 374, 480, 678, 806–7; **12** 599; **14** 142, 144, 269, 599; **18** 895, 899; **19** 584, 585, 586, 588, *589*, 590, 619–22*, *620*; **20** 599; **21** 759; **22** 739; **24** 91; **28** 574, 924; **33** 192, 521
collections **8** 264; **9** 1
competitions **7** 667, 676
exhibitions **7** 157, 563, 677; **9** 1, 12; **10** 365, 367, 677–8, *678*, 680, 681; **15** 747, 923; **16** 560; **17** 436; **19** 620, 621–2; **24** 683
library **10** 376
lighting **9** 13
sculpture **9** 306
see also houses → Burlington House
Royal Academy Schools **10** 372, 374; **19** 619, 621
Royal College of Art **10** 337, 373, 374, 375; **11** 360; **19** 591, 621
directors **25** 406
St John's Wood School of Art **10** 373
St Martin's Lane Academy **1** 106; **6** 554; **10** 249, 361, 368, 372; **14** 269, 856; **19** 584, 585; **31** 869
St Martin's School of Art **10** 375; **19** 591
School for Promoting Practical Design **10** 373
School of Design **2** 524; **7** 831; **8** 802; **19** 594
Slade School of Fine Art **1** 108; **7** 547; **10** 374, 375; **19** 591, 621; **21** 761
see also Government School of Design
Society of Arts (London) **10** 374
Westminster School of Art **10** 374
Adelaide House **10** 98, 240
Adelphi **1** 138; **3** 285; **10** 643
Airport *see* HEATHROW → Airport
Albany **6** 412
London—cont.
Albert Hall *see* Royal Albert Hall
Albert Memorial *see under* monuments and memorials
Albion Mill (Blackfriars) **33** 444
Alliance Assurance Office **23** 359
apartment blocks **2** 216
Highpoint blocks **15** 886
Highpoint One (Highgate) **10** 241; **19** 747
Highpoint Two (Highgate) **5** 905, *905*
Kensal House Flats **11** *808*
Landsbury Estate (Poplar) **19** 577
Lawn Road Flats (Hampstead) **2** 216; **7** 482, *483*
Lillington Gardens Estate **19** 578
Palace Green (Kensington) **2** 216
Prince's Mansions **2** 216
Prince Teck Buildings **2** 216
Queen Anne Mansions **2** 216; **28** 830
Arcadia Works **10** 98
architecture (legislation) **19** 569–70
art forms and materials
alabaster-carvings **1** 517
amber **1** 761
architecture **2** 67; **22** 529; **23** 860; **26** 743
brick **19** 567
armour **2** 472
bells **3** *627*
bookbindings **4** *350*, 351, 352; **12** 628
brass **10** 339; **19** 594
brasses **4** 692
caricatures **5** 755
carpets **10** 357
ceramics **19** 595*
chairs **19** 592
chandeliers **6** *443*
clocks **7** *443*, *445*, 448; **31** 624
coats of arms **14** 425
coins **19** *581*
cotton **10** 356
dress **9** 286
earthenwares **19** 595
embroidery **13** 195; **23** 460
enamel **13** 170; **14** 419; **19** 596
engravings **10** 393; **29** 675
felt **10** 875
figurines **27** 111
furniture **10** 290, 297, 299; **19** 591–3*, *593*; **20** 468
gem-engraving **12** 263
glass **10** *315*; **19** 595*; **27** 74
gold **19** 593–4
guns **2** *466*
harness-mounts **6** 161
helmets **6** 161
heraldry **14** 409
iron **19** 595
japanning **19** 592
jewellery **10** 345; **17** 523, 526
knives **8** 284
lace **10** 355
leather **19** 5; **27** 105
manuscripts **4** 372; **13** 140; **20** 332
marks **7** 30; **20** 444, *444*
metalwork **3** 597; **6** 160; **10** 323, 324; **14** 418; **19** 593–5*
mezzotints **21** 417
miniatures (manuscript illumination) **13** *141*
mosaics **19** 579
murals **22** 333
musical instruments **20** VIII1
objects of vertu **19** 595–6*
panoramas **24** 17, 18, *18*, *19*
papier mâché **24** 62
pattern books **24** 274
pewter **10** 344; **19** 594; **24** 579, *579*
plaques **32** 521
London
art forms and materials—cont.
porcelain **19** 595
railings **16** 59
scissors **8** 286
sculpture **13** 84; **19** 579, *579*; **26** 615
seals **19** *580*
signs (markers) **32** 324, *324*, *325*
silk **10** 356; **28** 716, 717, *717*
silver **10** 324, 331, 334; **19** 593–4, *594*
spoons **8** *284*
stonewares **19** 595
swords **6** 160
tapestries **10** 275; **19** 596*
tea-caddies **28** *737*
textiles **6** 624; **9** 283; **13** 195
tiles **30** 877
trappings **6** 161
wallpaper **10** 278
watches **7** *444*
art market **2** 559, 560–61; **15** 888; **19** 582, 584–5, 587; **29** 375
Astor House **11** 499
auction houses **2** 559; **19** 583, 584
auctions **2** 706
banks
Bank of England **3** 174; **7** 666; **10** 234; **19** 571, 576; **22** 741; **26** 13; **28** 905–6
architectural decorations **30** 503
Consols Office **5** 905
model **2** 337
Old Dividend Office **5** 905; **28** *906*
Stock Office **28** 905–6
Birkbeck Bank **30** 506
Coutts' Bank (Strand) **19** 578; **32** 818
London and Westminster Bank **10** 235
Midland Bank (Poultry) **3** 177
National Westminster Bank (Bishopsgate) **3** 176; **12** 599
National Westminster Bank Tower **19** 578; **28** 376
Barbican Centre **6** *409*, 410; **19** 578
Baynard's Castle *see under* palaces
Bear Garden **29** 489
Bedford Park **1** 146; **10** 239; **12** 144; **19** 574; **23** 547; **25** 805, *805*; **31** 725
Belgravia **8** 248–9
Bevis Marks synagogue **17** 544
Boundary Street (Bethnal Green) **19** 575; **30** 458
bridges
Blackfriars Bridge **4** 801; **19** 572
Hungerford Bridge **19** *574*
London Bridge (destr. 1831) **4** 800, 801; **19** 566
Roman bridge **19** 565
Southwark Bridge **4** 802; **26** 206
Strand Bridge *see* Waterloo Bridge (destr. 1937)
Tower Bridge **4** 799; **17** 633
Waterloo Bridge (destr. 1937) **4** 801; **19** 576
Westminster Bridge (destr. 1854) **19** 572
Brinsley Ford Collection **29** 38
British Architectural Library **10** 376
British Institution **18** 150
collections **3** 184
exhibitions **6** 80; **10** 365, 677, 678, 679; **19** 586
British Library **10** 376; **19** 318, 321; **33** 218, *218*
catalogues **4** 23
collections **2** 371; **10** 376; **11** 140; **13** 664; **27** 225; **32** 379
London
British Library—cont.
Cotton collection **8** 38; **19** 409; **20** 43
Egerton Collection **9** 755; **21** 82
Lansdowne Collection **33** 94
manuscripts **1** 23; **2** 371, 596; **20** 43; **22** 795; **25** 893; **32** 852
Oriental and India Office collections **1** 583; **2** 306; **15** 184, 741, 744; **16** 449, 555, 556; **17** 622; **22** 795
printed ephemera **10** 421
prints **10** 422
Reading Room *see under* museums → British Museum
Royal Collection **2** 559; **19** 727, 792
Thompson collection **30** 749
British Medical Association building *see* Zimbabwe House
Broadcasting House (BBC) **7** 483
Broadgate office development **19** 367, 578
Brockwell Park Lido **19** 332
Brunswick Centre **14** 613; **19** 578
building regulations **5** 135
Burlington Fine Arts Club **6** 80; **26** 473
exhibitions **10** 94; **15** 747; **16** 559
Bush Lane House **16** 56
Cadena Café **23** 438
Canary Wharf **19** 578; **24** *343*; **25** 656, *656*; **28** 834
Canterbury Hall **30** 679
Carlton House *see under* houses
Castrol House **10** 242
cemeteries
Highgate Cemetery **6** 166; **10** 97; **20** 869
Kensal Green Cemetery **6** 166; **10** 97; **20** 869; **31** 131
St James's Cemetery *see* Highgate Cemetery
West Norwood Cemetery **31** 131
Central Criminal Court **18** 890
Central Hall (Westminster) **23** 194
Centre Point Tower **19** 577
Cheapside Cross *see under* monuments and memorials
churches *see* ecclesiastical buildings
Churchill Gardens **7** 670
cinemas
Astoria Cinema **7** 327; **22** 60
Carlton Cinema **7** 327
Electric Cinema **7** 327
Gaumont State Cinema (Kilburn) **19** 576
Granada Cinema (Tooting) **7** 328
Odeon Cinema (Leicester Square) **7** 328
Citadel *see under* government buildings
Clapham Common **18** 73
clubs
Albion Hotel **7** 469
Army and Navy Club **7** 470
Athenaeum Club **3** 244; **7** 469
Boodle's **7** 469
Brooks's Club **7** 469; **28** 924
Carlton Club **7** 470
Constitutional Club **7** 470
Crockford's Club **33** 447
Junior Carlton Club **7** 470
Junior Constitutional Club **7** 470
National Liberal Club **7** 470
Reform Club **7** *469*, 470, 667; **8** 65; **10** 236; **26** 190; **30** 503
Royal Automobile Club **7** 470; **9** 739
Savile Club **3** 244
Senior United Services Club **7** 469
Travellers' Club **7** 667; **26** 190
United Services Club **7** 469
London
clubs—cont.
University Club **7** 469
White's **7** 469
Coal Exchange **10** 669; **16** 52
collections **10** 487; **17** 582; **19** 582, 588
Commonwealth Institute **5** 746
Conservation Unit of the Museums & Galleries Commission **7** 742, 744
Conway Library *see under* Courtauld Institute
County Hall **19** 576; **31** 242
Courtauld Institute of Art **8** 62; **19** 591
archives **2** 371
collections **7** 579; **8** 62; **10** 367; **12** 33; **19** 590
Conway Library **10** 376; **12** 146
Garrison Collection **12** 165
Lee Collection **20** 658
Princes Gate Collection **28** 377
Witt Library **10** 376; **11** 305
Covent Garden **2** 324; **19** 568, 578; **23** 492; **27** 357; **29** 485; **31** 714
craftsmen and artists **10** 289; **19** 583, 591
Crossness Sewage Works **10** 236
Crystal Palace *see under* exhibitions → Great Exhibition, 1851
Cumberland Terrace **22** *528*
Cutty Sark see under SHIPS → named vessels
Daily Express Building **10** 240
Design Centre **8** 804
Diorama **8** 449, 911, *911*
Docklands **4** 790; **9** 59; **19** 578
docks **9** 59; **19** 573
Blackwall Dock **9** 58
East India Docks **7** 693; **9** 58
Howland Great Wet Dock **9** 58
London Dock **9** 58
St Katharine's Dock **2** 324; **9** 58; **19** 573, 578; **27** 129
Tobacco Dock **2** 324; **16** 52
West India Dock **9** 58
Doughty St **19** *571*
drainage systems **3** 430
ecclesiastical buildings **19** 569
Abbey of St Mary Graces **7** 350; **19** 566
All Hallows (London Wall) **8** *493*
All Hallows Barking **19** 566
All Hallows the Great **28** 295
All Saints (Fulham)
monument to John, Viscont Mordaunt **10** *264*
All Saints (Margaret Street) **4** 787; **5** *314*, 314–15; **7** 277; **10** 237; **13** 203; **14** 746; **25** 173; **28** 295; **30** 503
Brompton Oratory **23** 473–4
Charterhouse **5** 895; **19** 568; **21** 841
Christ Church (Spitalfields) **10** 232; **14** 256–7
Christ Church (Streatham) **10** 238; **25** 173
City Road Chapel *see* Wesley's Chapel
Essex Hall **31** 583
Franciscan church **21** 842; **32** 828
Hanover Chapel **7** 503
Holy Trinity Priory **19** 566, 567
Metropolitan Tabernacle (Newington Butts) **23** 194
Priory of St John of Jerusalem **19** 566
see also museums → Museum of the Order of St John
St Alban (Wood Street) **19** 566
St Alfege (Greenwich) *see under* GREENWICH
St Andrew Undershaft **19** 566

London
ecclesiastical buildings—cont.
St Anne (Limehouse) **14** 256
St Augustine (Kilburn) **28** 295
St Benet (Paul's Wharf) **4** 786
St Bride (Fleet Street) **10** 232; **19** 566
St Clement Danes **10** 232
St Cyprian (Clarence Gate) **28** *295*
St Dunstan-in-the-East **29** 414
St Ethelburga **19** 566
St Etheldreda (Ely Place) **8** 611; **10** 325; **19** 567; **31** 273
St George (Bloomsbury) **10** 232; **14** 257; **20** 866
St George-in-the-East **14** 256, *256*
St George's Roman Catholic Cathedral **31** 271
St Helen (Bishopsgate) **19** 566
St James (Clerkenwell) *see* St Mary's Nunnery (Clerkenwell)
St James (Piccadilly) **10** 329
St John (Smith Square) **2** 307; **10** 232
St John's Chapel *see under* Tower of London
St Katherine by the Tower **21** *724*
St Katherine Cree **13** 211
St Luke (Chelsea) **10** 235
St Magnus the Martyr (London Bridge) **25** 727
St Margaret Lothbury **28** 295
St Martin-in-the-Fields **10** 232; **12** *593*, 594
model **2** 337
pews **24** 577
portico **25** 266
St Mary-le-Bow **19** 566
St Mary-le-Strand **2** 337; **10** 232
St Mary Magdalen (Bermondsey Street) **10** 323
St Mary Overie *see* St Saviour and St Mary (Southwark)
St Mary's Nunnery (Clerkenwell) **19** 566
St Mary Woolnoth **10** 327; **14** 257; **25** 727
St Matthew (Brixton) **20** 868
St Michael (Cornhill) **24** 576
St Pancras **30** 503
St Pancras New Church **5** 905; **10** 235; **25** 268
St Paul (Clapham) **10** 263
St Paul (Covent Garden) **2** 358; **17** 635, *636*; **19** 568; **23** 487; **25** 265
weathervane **33** 8
St Paul (Deptford) **2** 307; **10** 232, *232*
St Paul's Cathedral (Old; destr. 1666) **8** 610; **10** 228, 232; **13** 46; **17** 635–6; **18** 622; **19** 564, 566, 569, 579, 582, 597–8*, *597*; **25** 885
arches **2** 294
commentaries **9** 375
monuments **32** 529
portico **25** 265
restoration **19** 598*
sculpture **13** 82
spire **29** 413
stone-carvings **26** 409, *409*
weathervane **33** 8
St Paul's Cathedral **7** 258; **10** 249; **19** 569, 588, 597*, 598–9*, *599*; **23** 210, 857; **29** 708; **33** 393, *395*, 395–6, 399
chairs **14** 522
choir-stalls **7** 192
crypt **8** 224
dome **2** 292; **4** 786; **9** 82, 84, 86; **15** V; **20** 567, 580, *580*
frescoes **15** 139
metalwork **10** 327, 342
model **2** 336

London
ecclesiastical buildings
St Paul's Cathedral —cont.
monument to Arthur Wellesley, 1st Duke of Wellington **7** 673; **10** 265; **19** *600*; **27** 831; **29** 646–7
monument to Horatio Nelson, 1st Viscount Nelson **27** 831
monument to John Donne **29** *714*
monument to Ralph Abercromby **33** *100*
monument to Reginald Heber, Bishop of Calcutta **6** *456*
mosaics **22** 163; **26** 354
portico **25** 266
screens (i) (architectural) **10** 342
sculpture **4** 79; **10** 262; **19** 599–600*
tombs **31** 130
St Peter (Cornhill) **33** 8
St Peter (Vauxhall) **24** *307*, 307
St Saviour (Eltham) **10** 240
St Saviour and St Mary (Southwark) **10** 260, 288; **19** 566, 567; **32** 92
St Sophia's Greek Orthodox Cathedral **5** 340
St Stephen's Chapel *see under* Palace of Westminster (Old)
St Stephen Walbrook **7** 258, 277; **10** 232; **33** 394, *394*
Syon Abbey *see* SYON ABBEY (MIDDX)
Temple Church **7** 257; **14** 82; **18** 154; **22** 218; **23** 212; **26** 616
choir **22** 218
Tottenham Court Road Tabernacle **23** 193
Unitarian Church *see* Essex Hall
Wesley's Chapel (City Road) **21** 347, *347*; **23** 193
Westminster Abbey **2** 64, 67; **10** 227, 228, 359; **13** 43, 45, 46, 53, 142, 199; **19** 564, 582, 600–602*, *601*, *609*; **23** 211, 368, 462; **26** 45, 587
bosses **4** 465; **29** 659
capitals **26** 615
carvings **8** 856, *857*
Chapter House **6** 465, 467; **10** 245, *259*; **13** 128, 152, 153; **14** 424; **19** 604; **30** 877
choir **13** *46*
choir-stalls **7** 191
cloister **7** 455; **19** 602*
coats of arms **12** 273
Coronation Chair of Edward I **10** 287; **30** 779, *780*
enamel **13** 168
Feretory pavement **7** 275; **24** 783
galilees **12** 6
gargoyles **12** 150
Great Pavement **29** XII
Henry V's Chapel **13** *84*, 84, 85; **19** 604; **26** 79
Henry VII's Chapel **6** 460; **10** 228; **13** 55; **14** 424; **19** 602, *602*; **24** 466; **33** 446
Henry VII's Chapel: arches **2** 296
Henry VII's Chapel: bosses **4** 465
Henry VII's Chapel: choir-stalls **7** 192
Henry VII's Chapel: pinnacles **24** 826
Henry VII's Chapel: sculpture **10** 261; **13** 84; **19** 604
Henry VII's Chapel: tracery **31** *272*
Henry VII's Chapel: vaults **20** 579; **32** 89
Lady Chapel **18** 621; **19** 602

London
ecclesiastical buildings
Westminster Abbey—cont.
marble **7** 921
memorial to Dr Hugo Chamberlen **28** *64*
memorial to Henry Fawcett **23** 34
misericords **21** 725
monument to Admiral Sir Thomas Hardy **19** *606*
monument to General James Wolfe **33** 227, *227*
monument to Henry Ireton **10** 263
monument to Henry Priestman **4** 79
monument to John Campbell, 2nd Duke of Argyll and Greenwich **27** 243
monument to John Ernest Grabe **4** *79*
monument to Joseph and Lady Elizabeth Nightingale **27** 243–4, *244*; **31** 128
monument to Philip de Saumarez **31** 127, *128*
monument to William Murray **10** *265*
mouldings **22** 220
paintings **19** 606–7*, *607*
piers **24** 751
rood **27** 124
sculpture **7** 275; **10** 259, 262, 263, 264, 265; **13** 80, 81; **19** 603–6*, *603*; **26** 611
shields **14** 407, 419
shrine of St Edward the Confessor *see* tomb of St Edward the Confessor
stained glass **13** 183; **14** 422
stiff-leaf **29** 659
tie-bars **30** 853
tiles **30** 501
tomb of Aveline, Countess of Lancaster **19** *605*
tomb of Edmund Crouchback, Earl of Lancaster **14** 420; **33** 28
tomb of Edward III **25** 276
tomb of Eleanor of Castile **9** 155; **10** 338, 339; **13** 164; **31** 164
tomb of General William Hargrave **31** 129
tomb of Henry III **10** 338; **31** 164
tomb of Henry VII and Elizabeth of York **10** 270, 360; **16** 695; **31** 189–90, *190*
tomb of Henry VIII **3** 646
tomb of Margaret Beaufort **31** 189
tomb of Philippa of Hainault **13** 83; **31** 129
tomb of Princess Sophia **8** 107
tomb of Richard II and Anne of Bohemia **10** 359; **12** 626
tomb of St Edward the Confessor **24** 783; **28** 630
tomb of Sir Isaac Newton **22** 45, *46*
tomb of William de Valance, Earl of Pembroke **14** 420
tombs **7** 303; **8** 611; **10** 260; **22** 44; **31** 127, 129
tracery **8** 610; **31** 273
vaults **32** 92
wall paintings **10** 245
waxworks **33** 3
weathervane **33** 8
Westminster Retable **10** 245; **11** 420, *421*; **13** 138, *138*, 139, 141; **19** 606–7
Westminster Cathedral **2** 749; **3** *746*, 746–7; **4** 788; **5** 340; **9** 739; **10** 325
Architects' Room **3** 747
Chapel of St Andrew **30** 782

London
ecclesiastical buildings
Westminster Cathedral—cont.
ciborium **7** 304
Westminster Central Hall **21** 347
Westminster Chapel (Buckingham Gate) **23** 194
Whitefield's Tabernacle **21** 347
The Economist Building **5** 56; **19** 577; **28** *890*
education (art) **19** 583, 621
Eleanor crosses *see* monuments and memorials → Charing Cross; Cheapside Cross
Embankment Place **19** 578, *578*
Eros see monuments and memorials → Shaftesbury Memorial
Euston Road **19** 572
exhibitions **10** 677, 678; **15** 883; **19** 586–7, 589–90, *590*
British Empire Exhibition, 1924 *see under* WEMBLEY
Festival of Britain, 1951 **1** 736; **8** 804
Great Exhibition, 1851 **7** 549; **8** 802; **10** 281, 335, 343, 362, 678, 681; **14** 449; **15** 724, 821, 883; **19** 573; **33** 449
Crystal Palace **7** 744; **10** 235, 236, 319, 679, 681; **12** 791; **15** 883, *884*; **16** 53; **23** 814; **24** 293; **25** 173; **26** 17, *17*; **32** 415
Crystal Palace: Alhambra Court **22** 59; **30** 504
Crystal Palace: Belgian Section **25** VIII1
Crystal Palace: Byzantine and Early Christian Court **5** 340
Crystal Palace: decoration **17** 639
Crystal Palace: Medieval Court **13** 207; **25** *715*, 716
Crystal Palace: Nineveh Court **2** 642
Crystal Palace: Sydenham reconstruction **2** 642; **10** 97; **24** 179, 293–4, *294*; **33** 450
Ideal Home Exhibition, 1908 **10** 284
International Exhibition, 1862 **10** 282, 682; **15** 883
Olympia **30** 686
factories **19** 576
Festival of Britain, 1951 *see under* exhibitions
Financial Times Printing Works **10** 242
Finsbury Health Centre **10** 241; **19** 747, *747*
Forster House **27** 130
fortifications **19** 565–6; **21** 569
see also walls
Foundation for Ephemera Studies **10** 421
galleries **19** 588, 589–90
Baillie Gallery **30** 850
Grafton Gallery **10** 679, 680; **19** 589, *590*
Grosvenor Gallery **9** 19; **10** 254, 679; **19** 413
Hayward Gallery **19** 577
exhibitions **15** 748; **16** 560; **23** 741; **24** 683
Historic and Biblical Galleries **19** 588
Leicester Galleries **10** 362, 367
Mayor Gallery **31** 673
Milton Gallery **19** 588
New Gallery **10** 679; **19** 413
Paul Cassirer Gallery **26** 405
Saatchi Gallery **9** 19
Shakespeare Gallery **19** 588
Whitechapel Art Gallery **7** 640; **22** 365; **31** 249
exhibitions **15** 748; **22** 332

London—cont.
General Cemetery of All Souls *see* cemeteries → Kensal Green Cemetery
General Post Office (St Martin-le-Grand) **13** 610; **25** 268
Glass House Studios **10** 321; **29** 507, 858
Goldsmith's College **19** 591
government buildings
Citadel **21** 548
Colonial Office **9** 705
Foreign Office **9** 705; **10** 236; **13** 238; **19** 573; **26** 190
Home Office **9** 705
Horse Guards **23** 859
India Office **9** 705; **19** 573; **26** 190; **31** 477; **33** 450
India Office Library *see* British Library → Oriental and India Office collections
Ministry of Defence **3** 269; **9** 739; **23** 34
New Government Offices **7** 667; **20** 572
see also Treasury Chambers
New Scotland Yard (Norman Shaw North and South buildings) **25** 804
Privy Council, Whitehall **28** *908*; **32** 814
wallpaper **32** *815*
Royal Arsenal **2** 502
Somerset House (Old) *see under* palaces
Somerset House **5** 767; **6** 412–13; **7** 339; **10** 233, 275, 361; **13** 238; **19** 591, 621; **22** 739; **23** 362
exhibitions **10** 677
furniture **10** 291
gardens **12** 126
Great Room **9** 12; **10** 677; **19** 586, *587*, 621
paintings **17** 851
porcelain **9** 28
sculpture **3** *26*; **6** 323
Treasury Building **13** *237*, 238
Treasury Chambers **5** 66
see also New Government Offices
War Office *see* Ministry of Defence
Woolwich Arsenal *see* Royal Arsenal
Great Queen Street **25** 654
Greenwich *see* GREENWICH
Grosvenor Estate **8** 266–7
Guildhall **8** 494; **13** 824; **15** 406; **19** 566, *567*; **31** 235, 239
Library **10** 422; **19** 318
guilds **10** 289; **13** 822; **19** 580–81, 592
masons' **20** 561
pewterers' **24** 579
see also livery companies; livery halls
Hampstead Garden Suburb **12** 144; **19** 576; **24** 185, 186; **31** 728
Free Church **23** 194
Reynolds Close **24** *186*
Hanover Square Rooms **1** 125; **7** 687
Hanseatic Steelyard **19** *568*
Harrington Gardens **12** *315*
Hays Wharf **10** 240
Herbrand Street **30** *457*
Herne Hill **4** 35
Hoover Factory (Perivale) **10** 749; **19** 576
hospitals
Bedlam (Royal Bethlehem Hospital) **2** 657, 658; **7** 666; **14** 743, 784
Chelsea Hospital *see* Royal Hospital
Christ's Hospital **19** 583
Elsing Spital **19** 566

London
hospitals—cont.
Foundling Hospital **4** 886; **10** 361, 368; **14** 272, 841; **18** 672; **19** 585
collections **14** 519; **20** 911; **32** 778; **33** 220
paintings **10** 677; **11** 907; **14** 269, 784
Guy's Hospital **2** 658; **8** 64
Herbert Hospital **14** 783
Hospital of St Katharine by the Tower **19** 566
Hospital of St Mary of Bethlehem **19** 566
Hospital of St Mary without Bishopsgate **19** 566
Hospital of St Thomas of Acre **19** 566
Priory Hospital of St Mary's within Cripplegate *see* Elsing Spital
Royal Bethlehem Hospital *see* Bedlam
Royal Hospital **10** 232, 360; **15** 139; **33** 397
Royal Naval Hospital *see under* GREENWICH
St Bartholomew's Hospital and Priory **14** 785; **19** 566, 568
St Luke's Hospital **2** 658
St Thomas's Hospital **10** 236; **14** 783, 785
Savoy Hospital **14** 781
Westminster Hospital **14** 783
hotels
Albion Hotel *see under* clubs
Charing Cross Hotel **30** 503
Dorchester Hotel **13** 615
Great Western Hotel **14** 786; **26** 190
Grosvenor Hotel **10** 238; **14** 786; **28** 345
Le Méridien *see* Piccadilly Hotel
Midland Hotel **7** 667; **14** 786
Piccadilly Hotel **3** 269; **10** 239
Ritz Hotel **9** 739; **14** 787; **16** 55
St Pancras Station Hotel **10** 237; **13** 204
Savoy Hotel **14** 786
Strand Palace Hotel **10** 98
Waldorf Hotel **9** 739
House of Commons *see under* Palace of Westminster
House of Lords *see under* Palace of Westminster
houses **19** 566–7, 568, 577; **32** 555
Apsley House *see under* museums
Arundel House **10** 363; **11** 140; **14** 805
Ashburnham House **10** 275
Barn Elms **13** 634; **18** 97
Bedford House **15** 165
44 Berkeley Square **17** *904*
Bridgewater House **13** 219
Burlington House **4** *610*; **19** 621
paintings **17** 851; **24** 341; **26** 321, *322*
see also academies → Royal Academy of Art
Carlton House **10** 279, 361; **14** 145; **28** 592; **33** 48
armour **9** 31
Blue Velvet Room **9** 17
Crimson Drawing Room **30** XIV2
furniture **5** 192; **10** 296; **30** 783
interior decoration **10** 277, 279; **11** 432; **26** 84
Plate Closet **9** 30
porcelain **9** 29
sculpture **7** 480
silver **9** 30
16 Carlton House Terrace **17** *640*
Chelsea Manor House **28** 844

London
houses—cont.
Chesterfield House **10** 276; **26** 499
Chiswick House *see* CHISWICK HOUSE (MIDDX)
Clarendon House **8** 46; **15** 47; **25** 454
Cleveland House **19** 270
Crosby Place **19** 567
Cumberland House **10** 643
Debenham House **30** 507
Denmark House *see* palaces → Somerset House (Old)
Derby House **7** 659; **15** 165
Devonshire House **6** 116, 117; **10** 364
Dorchester House **29** 646, *647*
10 Downing Street **13** 238
Duchess Street (Thomas Hope's house) **9** 12, 24, 29; **10** 96–7, *97*
Dudley House **9** 17
Durham House **14** 435
6 Ellerdale Road **25** 804
Grosvenor House **9** 17; **13** 696
Ham House *see under* RICHMOND (SURREY; UK)
18 Harrington Gardens **25** 805
39 Harrington Gardens **30** 504
Hertford House *see* museums → Wallace Collection
Holland House **7** 431; **10** 290; **11** 362; **30** 506; **32** 551
Home House **10** 233, 643; **30** 503
Kenwood House *see under* museums
Lancaster House **33** 447
Lansdowne House **7** 339, 416
Leicester House **10** 293
Leighton House *see under* museums
Lindsey House **14** 50; **19** 568; **23** 492, 857
Linley Sambourne House *see under* museums
Lowther Lodge *see* Royal Geographical Society
Marlborough House **7** 286; **10** 292, 370; **12** 306
Museum of Manufactures *see* museums → Victoria and Albert Museum
Museum of Ornamental Art *see* museums → Victoria and Albert Museum
staircase **18** 644
Melbourne House *see* Albany
Montagu House (Bloomsbury) **10** 368, 369; **14** 743; **21** 907; **27** 263
collections **10** 364
paintings **18** 633
Montagu House (Whitehall) **4** 893
Norfolk House **4** 758; **12** 626
Northumberland House **5** 349; **10** 277; **33** 226
Nottingham House *see* palaces → Kensington Palace
Osterley Park House *see* OSTERLEY PARK HOUSE (MIDDX)
8 Palace Gate **25** 805
10 Palace Gate **7** 482
1 Palace Green **25** 804; **33** 12
2 Palace Green **22** 743
7 Park Street *see* 14 Queen Anne's Gate
Pembroke House **23** 857
20 Portman Square *see* Home House
49 Prince's Gate **9** 29; **10** 283; **17** 466
14 Queen Anne's Gate **9** 13
170 Queens Gate **22** 743
Richmond House **10** 372; **19** 585; **23** 857; **33** 226

London
houses—cont.
5 Royal Adelphi Terrace **7** 172
22 St James's Place **26** 541
20 St James's Square **10** 279; **26** 463
Spencer House **29** 381
furniture **29** 381
interior decoration **11** 428; **25** 192; **29** 806
Painted Room **22** *737*, 738; **23** 544
Stafford House *see* Lancaster House
18 Stafford Terrace *see* museums → Linley Sambourne House
Strawberry Hill *see under* TWICKENHAM (MIDDX)
Sutton House (Hackney) **10** 272
Syon House *see* SYON HOUSE (MIDDX)
35 Tite Street **25** 805
44 Tite Street **12** *840*; **25** 805
Tower House **5** 195, 196
Wade House **23** 856
White House (Tite St) **10** 238
York House (Pall Mall) *see* Cumberland House
York House (Stable Yard) *see* Lancaster House
York House (Strand) **9** 477; **32** 575
York Place *see* palaces → Whitehall Palace
Houses of Parliament *see* Palace of Westminster
housing **19** 574, 576, 578
Hungerford Market **11** 361; **16** 52
Imperial Assurance Co. building **19** 573
Imperial Institute **7** 559
India Office Library *see* British Library → Oriental and Indian Office collections
Inner London Education Authority **3** 170
Inns of Court **14** 420, 422
Barnard's Inn **19** 567
Gray's Inn **19** 567
Lincoln's Inn **19** 567; **22** 330
Middle Temple **19** 567
Institute of Archaeology **7** 742
Institute of British Architects *see* Royal Institute of British Architects
Institute of Chartered Accountants **3** 269, 532–3, *533*; **7** 668; **9** 739; **23** 34
jewellers **19** 596
Kodak Building **9** 740
Law Courts **7** 667; **10** 237; **13** 203; **14** 420; **18** *888*, 889; **27** 131; **29** 766, *766*
model **2** 337
Leadenhall Market **19** 566
Leicester Square Panorama **24** 18, *19*
livery companies **3** 233; **14** 422; **19** 583
Barbers' Company **10** 326
Carpenters' Company **10** 287; **19** 592
Clothworkers' Company **10** 329
Fishmongers' Company **10** 332
Goldsmiths' Company **10** 325, 328, 330, 337; **19** 594, *594*, 595; **28** 262; **33** 50
collections **10** 326, 327
Joiners' Company **19** 592
Painter-Stainers' Company **4** 880; **8** 106; **10** 371; **19** 583
Pewterers' Company **10** 330, 340
Vintners' Company **10** 325
Worshipful Company of Glass Sellers **10** 316
see also guilds; livery halls

London—cont.
livery halls **19** 508
Apothecaries Hall **19** 510
Barber Surgeons' Hall **14** 670; **19** 509, 510
Brewers' Hall **19** 510
Draper's Hall **19** 567
Fishmongers' Hall **19** 509, *509*
Goldsmiths' Hall (Dowgate Hill) **7** 30; **19** 510
Goldsmiths' Hall (Foster Lane) **2** 545; **19** 509
Grocers' Hall **25** 813
Leathersellers' Hall **10** 231
Mercers' Hall **19** 509, 510
Merchant Taylor's Hall **19** 509, 510, 567
Saddlers' Hall **19** 510
Skinners' Hall **19** 510
Society of Apothecaries greenhouse **13** 619
Vintners's Hall **19** 510
see also guilds; livery companies
Lloyd's Building **10** 242, 669; **12** 794; **16** 55; **19** 578; **23** 360; **26** 540, *540*; **28** 835
lighting **19** 367
Lloyd's Registry of Shipping **11** 499; **23** 34
Lord Mayor's Show **23** 766
Lord's Cricket Ground **29** 426
Mound Stand **29** 490
Madame Tussaud's **15** 134; **33** 4
Mansion House **7** 666; **8** 492; **10** 233; **14** 391; **19** 571
markets **31** 711
Millbank **30** 458
Millbank Estate **7** 667
Millbank Penitentiary **25** 637; **28** 875
Montfichet's Tower **19** 566
monuments and memorials
Albert Memorial **6** 171; **10** 266; **11** 238, *238*; **13** 204; **18** *903*, 903; **22** 47, 163; **24** 605
Cenotaph **2** 360, 362; **6** 171; **19** 822; **22** 48
Charing Cross **8** 197
Cheapside Cross **8** 197
Cleopatra's Needle **14** 331; **23** 331; **29** 709, 712
Constitution Arch **22** 47; **31** 351
Marble Arch **10** 745; **31** 351, *351*
memorial to Edith Cavell **23** 35
Monument (Great Fire) **14** 742
monument to Charles I **10** 441; **19** 250
monument to Charles James Fox **29** 565
monument to Major-General Charles George Gordon **23** 34
monument to Richard Cœur de Lion *see under* Palace of Westminster
monument to Sir John Franklin **23** *172*
Nelson's Column **7** 673, *673*; **10** 265; **22** 47
Queen Victoria Memorial **23** 34; **29** 566, *566*
Royal Artillery Memorial **22** 48, *48*
Shaftesbury Memorial **1** 737; **6** 9; **10** 266; **12** *610*, 611; **22** 48; **23** 34
Moorgate **31** 710
museums
Apsley House **9** 13, 17, 19; **20** 900; **26** 500; **33** 55
frames **11** 432
gems **5** 679
paintings **4** 304, 306, 330, 566, 914; **5** 271; **9** 211; **10** 158; **14** 147, 503; **19** 67; **20** 78; **28** 8; **33** 189, 190
porcelain **12** 435; **22** 741
sculpture **4** 301; **22** 741; **23** 295

London
museums
Apsley House—cont.
silver **25** 314; **28** 429, 431; **29** 732
sketches **24** 583
Waterloo Gallery **10** 280
Architectural Museum **8** 34; **28** 279
Bethnal Green Museum **28** 528
see also Victoria and Albert Museum
British Museum **2** 165, 332, 560; **10** *234*, 235, 362, 369, 745; **13** 610; **18** 523; **19** 573; **21** 907; **22** 356, 362; **25** 235; **28** 872, 873; **33** 100, 218
Aboriginal collection **1** 66, 67
African collection **1** 437, 439
Anatolian collection **1** 839
Ancient Near East collection **1** 855, 892, 895
Arabian collection **2** 275
Assyrian collection **18** 896
Bhutanese collection **3** 916
Blacas Collection **23** 36
bronze **6** 868
Calvert Collection **31** 355
cameos **27** 878
catalogues **6** 78; **7** 161; **9** 60; **25** 238, 377
Central Asian collection **6** 321
ceramics **3** 812; **6** 925; **10** 649; **12** 839; **16** 395
Chinese collection **1** 150; **6** 735; **7** 155, 158
clocks **7** 439
coins **1** 211
collections **1** 839; **2** 559; **6** 826; **10** 368, 487; **11** 738; **14** 114, 178; **18** 893, 895; **22** 739; **24** 240, 478; **25** 412; **29** 48, 88; **31** 694; **33** 345
conservation workshop **17** *209*
Crace Collection **8** 106
Cycladic collection **8** 324
directors **25** 236
Dodgson collection **9** 61
drawings **7** 839; **9** 229, 230, 738; **10** 479; **24** 846; **26** 177, 246, 473; **27** 641; **33** 154
Duveen Gallery (1933-62) **9** 25
Edward VII Galleries **5** 270; **30** 241
Egyptian collection **10** 71, 79, 90, 92
Elgin Room (*c.* 1839) **9** 25
engravings **4** 884; **28** 25; **32** 795
etchings **27** 271
Etruscan collection **10** 637, 640
exhibitions **6** 322; **13** 864; **15** 748
fans **10** 782; **28** 168
Franks Collection **10** 347
gems **12** 266; **14** 808; **20** 389
Greek collection **8** 366; **13** 468, 469, 470, 541, 542, 605, 606; **14** 70; **22** 340
Harris collection **14** 196
Hull Grundy Collection **6** 20
Indian collection **1** 753; **8** 269; **15** 744
Iranian collection **15** 922
Islamic collection **16** 554, 555
Japanese collection **17** 431, 434, 440, 441
jewellery **6** 20; **13** 718
King's Library **28** *874*, 874
Knight collection **18** 150
Korean collection **18** 308, 383
lighting **9** 13
manuscripts *see under* British Library
medals **20** 921
Mesoamerican collection **21** 264, 265

London
museums
British Museum—cont.
Mesopotamian collection **21** 301, 310
Mexican gallery **12** 921
mounts (works on paper and scrolls) **22** 238
musical instruments **22** 376
Nineveh Gallery **2** 642
paintings **8** 570; **15** 742; **22** 795; **31** 234, 475
pithoi **18** 165
plaquettes **25** 18
portico **25** 267
pottery **3** 243; **13** 555
printing plates **8** 867
prints **8** 218, 264, 886; **10** 422; **17** 851; **20** 421; **25** 631; **26** 177; **28** 25, 575
Reading Room **16** 54; **19** *318*; **28** 871
regalia **2** 585
reproductions **26** 227
restorations **7** 729
Roman collection **27** 58, 115
sculpture **7** 502, 788; **9** 25; **10** 365; **15** 741; **18** 904; **21** 266; **27** 244
silver **31** 317
Sloane Collection **1** 437; **7** 87; **28** 844
Slovakian collection **28** 857
South American collection **29** 221
South Pacific collection **23** 739; **28** 921
Sri Lankan collection **29** 478
Stein Collection **6** 317, 318
Syria-Palestine collection **30** 198, 199
textiles **7** 54
Tibetan collection **30** 849
Townley Collection **27** 46; **31** 245
watercolours **10** 478
West Gallery **9** 468
wood-engravings **4** 869
writing-tablets **19** 311
see also Museum of Mankind
Bullock's London Museum and Panthenion **5** 169; **19** 233; **21** 265, *265*; **23** 740
collections **22** 340, 675
Design Museum **7** 725; **8** 805
Dulwich Picture Gallery **4** 576; **9** 12, 17, 19; **10** 234, 369; **22** 362; **24** 805; **28** 908; **30** 749
collections **10** 366; **19** 588, 621; **22** 351
Mausoleum of Sir Peter Francis Bourgeois **20** 868; **22** 362
East India Company Museum **1** 211; **10** 898; **15** 744; **16** 555
Egyptian Hall **5** 169; **10** 97; **21** 265, *265*
exhibitions **10** 94, 679; **19** 587
see also Bullock's London Museum and Panthenion
European Museum **6** 79
Geffrye Museum **7** 482
Geological Museum **28** 844
Holophusicon **23** 741
Horniman Museum **3** 630; **30** 506; **31** 250
collections **22** 376; **29** 240
exhibitions **21** 886
Imperial War Museum **23** 568
Institute of Contemporary Arts (ICA) **9** 297; **19** 590; **24** 369; **26** 49; **32** 912
Jewish Museum **17** 581
Kenwood House **1** 137; **10** 233
chimney-pieces **6** 605
collections **30** 451
interior decoration **1** 111
Iveagh Bequest **13** 836*

London
museums
Kenwood House—cont.
library **1** *138*
paintings **8** 123; **9** 482; **10** 367, 785; **11** 909, 910, 912; **13** 718; **17** 641; **23** 613; **26** 169; **27** 119
Leighton House **2** 365; **22** 59; **23** 504
Arab Hall **5** 422; **10** 282; **30** 504
Leverian Museum **22** 675; **23** 740
Linley Sambourne House **10** *283*
London Transport Museum **10** 422
Museum Minervae **10** 371
Museum of Anatomy and Curiosities **33** 3
Museum of Economic Geology **24** 364
Museum of London **10** 422; **18** 899
Museum of Mankind **1** 437; **24** 364
collections **28** 581; **29** 240
exhibitions **1** 437, 438
see also British Museum
Museum of Manufactures *see* Victoria and Albert Museum
Museum of the Order of St John **20** 217
see also ecclesiastical buildings → Priory of St John of Jerusalem
National Gallery **2** 560; **3** 284; **10** 362, 369; **13** 610; **19** 573, 621; **22** 358, 362; **24** 364; **33** 192
Aders collection **1** 154
Angerstein collection **2** 559; **10** 365; **18** 893
Banks collection **3** 184
Beaumont collection **3** 455
Beckford collection **3** 477
Beit collection **3** 522
Carr collection **6** 77
catalogues **6** 78; **8** 571; **12** 925; **27** 351
cleaning **7** 727; **22** 58
collections **5** 848; **8** 172, 582; **9** 683; **10** 366; **14** 107; **16** 773; **18** 727; **19** 271, 588, 624; **22** 296; **26** 473
conservation and restoration **32** 748
directors **4** 602; **5** 283; **8** 571; **9** 682; **10** 362; **16** 768; **25** 407
display **9** 19; **10** 371
Duveen collection **9** 467
extension (1982) **7** 670
extension (1987-91) *see* Sainsbury Wing
Howard collection **14** 807, 809
Layard collection **18** 897
library **10** 376
lighting **9** 13
Maitland collection **20** 142
Micro Gallery **2** 534
Mond collection **21** 849
Peel collection **24** 322
Phillips collection **24** 638
Rogers collection **26** 541
Rushout collection **27** 350
Sainsbury Wing **9** 19; **10** 242, 371; **19** 591; **27** 524; **32** 236
Salting collection **27** 642
Solly collection **29** 46
Vernon Collection **30** 359; **32** 338
Woodburn collection **33** 345
National Gallery, Millbank *see* Tate Gallery
National Gallery of British Art *see* Tate Gallery

London
museums—cont.
National Maritime Museum *see under* GREENWICH
National Portrait Gallery **9** 467; **10** 370, 371
collections **10** 907; **18** 145; **32** 338, 923
directors **28** 54
Natural History Museum **10** 266, 371; **13** 204; **19** 573; **22** 363; **30** 504; **32** *905*, 905
collections **3** 183; **28** 844
Percival David Foundation of Chinese Art *see under* University of London
Petrie Museum *see under* University College
Science Museum **14** 149
collections **22** 390; **30** 271
conservation **7** 742
Wellcome Museum of the History of Medicine **33** 55
Sir John Soane's Museum **2** *550*, 552; **9** 12, 13, 23; **10** 234, 279; **14** 810; **19** 588; **28** 907–8; **30** 503
collections **1** 140; **2** 337; **3** 184; **8** 495; **10** 369; **24** 240
drawings **25** 35
Monk's Parlour **28** *908*
sculpture **9** 24–5; **13** 213; **27** 468
South Kensington Museum *see* Victoria and Albert Museum
Tate Gallery **9** 468; **10** 362, 370–71; **11** 360; **14** 809; **25** 235
archives **2** 364, 371; **7** 376
Clore Gallery **9** 19; **10** 242, 371; **19** 591; **22** 367; **29** 678; **31** 475
collections **19** 590, 735; **21** 606; **26** 96; **27** 222; **29** 383; **30** 359; **31** 475; **32** 338, 923
exhibitions **22** 332; **33** 151
library **10** 376
Restaurant **5** 688; **33** 145
screenprinting **28** 300
sculpture **22** 57
Theatre Museum **10** 422
Victoria and Albert Museum **7** 549; **8** 802; **10** 281; **11** 360; **14** 149; **15** 821; **19** 594; **22** 363; **30** 162, 503, *504*; **33** 9
architectural decorations **9** 306; **10** 266; **33** 515
archives **2** 371
Bhutanese collection **3** 916
Boilerhouse **8** 805
Casts Court **7** 831
catalogues **26** 473
ceramics **6** 925; **10** 649; **16** 395; **32** 800
Chinese collection **1** 150; **7** 62, 155
collections **2** 475; **3** 812; **5** 536; **10** 755; **11** 663; **14** 525; **15** 741, 742; **17** 582; **22** 278
directors **20** 27
display **9** 19, 25
doors **9** 158
drawings **26** 246; **29** 55; **31** 348
drawing schools **1** 107
Dutch Kitchen **25** 406; **30** XII
exhibitions **7** 157; **15** 747, 748; **16** 559, 560; **17** 436
furniture **8** 34; **17** 639; **19** 531
Grill Room *see* Dutch Kitchen
Handley-Read collection **14** 132
holograms **14** 690
Indian collection **2** 306; **15** 183, 687, 744
interior decoration **3** 857
Ionides Collection **15** 895
ironwork **9** 156

London
museums
Victoria and Albert Museum—cont.
Islamic collection **16** 554, 556
Japanese collection **17** 434, 441
jewellery **6** 20
lighting **9** 13
manuscripts **15** 741; **24** 478
marbles **12** 577
metalwork **11** 307
murals **22** 331
musical instruments **22** 376
National Art Library **4** 22; **10** 376, 422; **25** 372; **33** 8
Norfolk House Music Room *see under* houses → Norfolk House
Northumberland House Glass Drawing Room *see under* houses → Northumberland House
oil sketches **5** 765
paintings **10** 370, 371; **15** 741, 742; **22** 112, 795; **32** 338; **33** 685
photographs **14** 251; **24** 682
Plaster Court **26** 226
portraits **19** 775
posters **14** 174
pottery **3** 243; **28** 168
prints **8** 886; **10** 422, 487
reliefs **9** 182
roof **11** 360
Salting collection **27** 641; **29** 416
Samsung gallery of Korean art **18** 383
sculpture **6** 735; **11** 499; **12** 608; **22** 795
Sheepshanks Gallery **11** 360; **28** 575
South-east Asian collection **29** 240
Sri Lankan collection **29** 478
staff **26** 473
stained glass **29** 516
tangkas **4** 883
tapestries **30** 332
textiles **7** 53
see also Bethnal Green Museum
Wallace Collection **5** 379; **12** 489; **19** 261; **28** 527, 528
armour **7** 579; **8** 639; **9** 31
catalogues **21** 817
collections **4** 322; **10** 371; **20** 875; **21** 413; **23** 126; **27** 143; **28** 527
decorative works **13** 234
furniture **1** 110; **4** 532; **5** 379; **7** 658; **12** 185; **13** 665; **16** 748; **20** 468; **21** 817; **26** 303; **31** 870
guns **2** 462, 464
miniatures **21** 643, 644; **24** 554
mirrors **28** 776
painting (genre) **21** 68
paintings (allegorical) **25** 382
paintings (architectural) **11** 720; **14** 503; **23** 613; **33** 267
paintings (*fêtes champêtres*) **11** 36
paintings (*fêtes galantes*) **24** 256; **32** 85, 916
paintings (genre) **19** 646; **30** 462; **32** 915, 917, 918
paintings (landscape) **27** 297
paintings (literary themes) **8** 640, 705
paintings (mythological) **2** 722; **9** 480, 486; **20** 891; **23** 634; **25** 671
paintings (portraits) **4** 304; **9** 367, 480; **14** 95; **26** 168; **32** 702
paintings (religious) **4** 304; **6** 434, 436
paintings (still-lifes) **14** 290

London
museums
Wallace Collection—cont.
porcelain **26** 303; **27** 139
pottery **12** 429
sculpture **6** 121; **9** 451; **28** 11
statuettes **5** 380
weapons **2** 455, 467; **9** 31
Wellcome Museum of the History of Medicine *see under* Science Museum
Wellington Museum *see* Apsley House
William Morris Gallery and Brangwyn Gift **20** 26; **22** 141
collections **4** 673
National Art Library *see under* museums → Victoria and Albert Museum
New Cavendish Street **30** 502
New Exchange **11** 876
Newgate Gaol **8** 493–4, *494*; **10** 233; **19** 571, 576; **20** 572
New Road *see* Euston Road
New Zealand Chambers **25** 804
Norman Shaw North and South buildings *see* government buildings → New Scotland Yard (Norman Shaw North and South buildings)
Notting Hill Carnival **5** 788
Nour Collection **16** 555
Old Bailey **3** 269; **5** 293; **10** 239; **29** 843
Old St Pancras Road **30** 457
Palace of Westminster (Old; destr. 1834) **12** 6; **13** 237; **19** 564, *608*, 608–10*, *609*, 612–13*; **28** 909
almonry **19** 609
capitals **26** 616
carpets **10** 270
cloisters **19** 608
collections **10** 363
conduit **19** 609
Court of Augmentations **19** 609
Court of Requests *see* White Hall
gate-house **19** 609
Great Hall **14** 75; **30** 779
Great Palace **19** 609–10
House of Lords **10** 349; **30** 318; **32** 732
interior decoration **29** 298
Jewel Tower **19** 608, 610
King's Bridge **19** 609
Law Courts **19** 613
Lesser Hall *see* White Hall
New Hall *see* White Hall
Office of the Clerk of the King's Works **19** 609
Painted Chamber **6** 407; **10** 245; **13** 128, 141, 142; **14** 421; **19** 610, *611*, 611–12
mouldings **11** 420
shields **14** 415
paintings **13** 128, 134, 139; **19** *611*, 611–12*
Palace of the Princes of Wales **19** 610
Privy Palace **19** 609, 610
Queen's Chamber **10** 269; **19** 610
Queen's Chapel **19** 610
St Stephen's Chapel **5** 890; **6** 459; **8** 611; **10** 245; **13** 46, 53–4; **14** 421; **19** 608, 609, 610, 612; **21** 423; **24** 465; **31** 273
crypt **22** 219
paintings **13** 134, 152
vaults **32** 90, 94
see also Palace of Westminster → St Mary Undercroft
Scala Regia **19** 613, *613*
Speaker's House **19** 613
Star Chamber **19** 609
Stone Building **19** 612, 613
Upper Exchequer **19** 609

London
Palace of Westminster (Old; destr. 1834) —cont.
water-gate 19 609
Westminster Hall 10 227; 14 454; 18 886; 19 608, *609*, 609–10, 612, 613; 23 809; 30 901
capitals 26 612
corbels 7 837
roof 30 900, *900*, 909
sculpture 13 82, 83, 84
White Hall 19 608, 610
workshops 29 852
Palace of Westminster 3 282; 7 667, 676; 10 235, 236, *237*, 281, 297, 362; 13 203, 237; 14 420; 16 52; 19 608*, 613–15*; 23 546, 814; 25 714–15; 26 743; 32 415
Big Ben 7 448; 21 322
collections 19 615
Commons Corridor
wall paintings 19 614
frescoes 14 436
House of Commons 1 125; 7 676; 10 291; 19 613–14, 615
House of Lords 4 672; 7 676; 19 613–14, *614*
frescoes 2 446; 20 28
metalwork 10 343
stained glass 28 248
Test Roll 26 558
throne 30 783
wall paintings 19 614
interior decoration 9 475
Law Courts 19 615
monument to Richard Cœur de Lion 10 442
Moses Room 19 614
murals 10 252
New Palace Yard 19 615
Peers' Corridor 19 614
Peers' Robing Room *see* Moses Room
Poets' Hall 19 614
Prince's Chamber 19 614
Queen's Robing Room 10 252; 19 614
Royal Gallery 19 614; 20 28
St Mary Undercroft 19 615
see also Palace of Westminster (Old) → St Stephen's Chapel
sculpture 10 265; 19 614
tiles 30 503, 877
Upper Waiting Hall *see* Poets' Hall
wall paintings 19 614
wallpaper 32 816
Westminster Hall (after 1834) 19 615
palaces
Baynard's Castle 19 566, 567
Bridewell Palace 19 567
Buckingham Palace 4 170; 5 877, 905; 14 145, 148; 23 814, 857; 30 503
drawings 10 368
furniture 5 767; 17 666
hangings 16 760
interior decoration 10 279; 26 85
paintings 8 443; 9 27; 14 146, 147; 24 23; 26 160; 27 296
paintings (genre) 14 146, 147
paintings (history) 14 146, 586
paintings (landscape) 8 296, 297; 24 256; 27 294
paintings (mythological) 14 146
Pavilion 9 475; 10 252
plate 8 149; 25 712
porcelain 4 848
portraits 8 493; 9 480, 481, 482, 486; 11 910, 912; 14 146; 19 649; 23 618; 24 636; 25 883; 26 157, 163
staircase hall 18 644

London
palaces
Buckingham Palace—cont.
summer-house 27 173
vases 9 399
Eltham Palace *see under* ELTHAM (KENT)
Kensington Palace 10 275, 277, 360; 33 199
clocks 1 784; 7 446
frescoes 15 139
furniture 10 291, 292, 294; 17 479
gardens 19 622; 33 199, 257
interior decoration 17 901; 33 100
New Green House *see* Orangery
Orangery 12 791; 14 254; 23 470, *471*
paintings 3 54; 8 454; 28 902, *903*; 29 804
Presence Chamber 22 738
Queen's Closet 21 640
sculpture 7 298; 27 466
Lambeth Palace 6 60
Roman Governor's palace 19 565
St James's Palace 12 127; 19 568
bronzes 30 515
collections 10 363; 19 582
paintings 2 446; 10 368; 14 147, 148
Queen's Chapel 17 634–5
sculpture 19 250
Somerset House (Old) 7 431; 10 231; 19 250, 621
Whitehall Palace 10 229, 360; 14 76; 19 564, 568, 582, 610, 617–18*, *618*; 33 306, 398
Banqueting House 1 658; 3 186; 8 45; 10 231, 248, 249, 360; 12 790; 14 730; 17 470, 634, *635*; 19 582, 618; 29 798; 30 660
Chapel Royal 19 617
Cockpit 19 618
collections 10 363; 15 150; 19 582
drawings 9 26, 27
furniture 10 288, 291
gardens 12 114
gate-house 12 176
Great Hall 14 75; 19 617
Holbein Gate 19 617
interior decoration 3 646
King Street Gate 19 617
Long Gallery 19 617
Matted Gallery *see* Long Gallery
Privy Council Building 19 618
Privy Garden 19 617
Privy Lodging Rooms 9 16; 19 582
Privy Stairs 19 617
theatre 30 661
wall paintings 14 670
Pantheon 7 666, 687; 19 571; 30 674
parks and gardens
Chelsea Physic Garden 4 483; 12 137; 29 564
Danvers House (Chelsea) 12 127
Green Park 19 586; 24 179
Hyde Park 18 73; 24 179
Kew Gardens *see* KEW → Royal Botanical Gardens
New Spring Gardens *see* Vauxhall Gardens
Parliament Hill Fields 19 332
pleasure gardens 19 618, *619*
Regent's Park 19 574; 22 527, 741; 25 655
Park Square East 8 911, *911*
Park Village 22 527; 32 554
terraces 10 234; 22 527
Royal Horticultural Society's Gardens 12 139

London
parks and gardens—cont.
St James's Park 12 106; 23 776; 24 179; 33 257
Tradescants' Garden (Lambeth) 12 127; 19 582
Vauxhall Gardens *see* Vauxhall Gardens
Victoria Tower Gardens 26 512
Park Village *see under* parks and gardens → Regent's Park
patronage 13 128
Pentonville Model Prison 10 236; 25 637
Piccadilly 10 360
Piccadilly Circus 4 *158*
Pimlico Housing 25 399
Pioneer Health Centre, Peckham 10 241
Poet's Gallery 19 588
Pont Street 30 504
pottery 10 302, 303–4, *304*, 305
power stations
Bankside Power Station 28 *282*
Battersea Power Station 10 241; 25 403, *403*
Lots Road Power Station 25 402
St John's Wood Power Station 25 402
Prudential Assurance Building 30 504
public houses
Balmoral Castle 25 688
Bride of Denmark 25 689
Central 25 688
Connaught Tavern 25 688
Eagle 25 688
Galleons Hotel 25 688
King's Head pub, Tooting 19 576
Prince Albert 25 688
Princess Louise 25 688
Red Lion 25 688, *688*
Rising Sun 25 688
Salisbury 25 688
Ship *see* Central
Tabard Inn 25 688
Public Records Office 2 367
Queen Elizabeth Hall 10 242; 19 577
Queens Hall 7 687
Regent Street 19 574, *576*; 22 528; 25 655
RIBA *see* Royal Institute of British Architects
Richmond Terrace 23 359
Robin Hood Gardens 30 391
Roehampton Housing Estate *see under* ROEHAMPTON
Roman basilica (Cornhill) 19 565
Roman fort 19 565
Royal Albert Hall 1 798; 7 687; 10 266; 11 360; 16 54; 30 503
Royal College of Music 22 376
Royal College of Physicians 5 303; 7 503
Royal Commonwealth Society 1 439
Royal Courts of Justice *see* Law Courts
Royal Exchange 7 667; 8 65; 10 263, 668; 19 568, 569, 582; 33 8
portico 25 268
sculpture 5 293; 23 253
Royal Festival Hall 1 126; 7 687; 10 242; 19 577, *577*
Royal Fine Arts Commission 10 362
Royal Geographical Society 1 439; 25 804; 30 504
Royal Institute of British Architects (RIBA) 2 314, 315; 7 670; 10 235, 240, 374; 33 382
collections 7 776; 25 165; 28 894
competitions 7 667; 28 488
directors 9 122

London—cont.
Royal Naval College *see* GREENWICH → Royal Naval Hospital
Royal Panopticon of Science and Art 22 60
Royal Society of Arts building 1 *139*
St Bride Printing Library 10 422
schools 26 476
Berger Road School 28 158
Bonner Street School 25 804; 28 *157*, 158
Borstall Wood School 28 158
Charterhouse School Chapel 28 156
City of London Boys' School 19 567
Dulwich College 5 900; 13 618; 30 503
Eel Brook Common School 25 804
Fairlawn Primary and Junior School 28 159
Freemen's Orphan School 14 391
Johnson Street School 28 157
Quintin Kynaston School 4 790
St Giles-in-the-Fields National School 28 157
St Martin's-in-the-Fields Northern District School 28 157
St Paul's School 28 156
Sir John Cass School 26 473
Westminster School 28 156
sculptors 10 262
shops 3 464
Harrods 8 770; 30 507
John Lewis Partnership 1 738
Morgan & Sanders Co. 19 *593*
Peter Jones Department Store 19 576, *576*
Selfridges 3 423; 8 770; 11 628; 19 576
South Bank Arts Centre 19 577
spears 25 *540*, 541
Spicer Street 30 457
squares
Bedford Square 19 571–2; 20 572; 31 714
Bloomsbury Square 31 714
Cadogan Square 30 504
Cavendish Square 19 570
Columbia Square 30 457
Fitzroy Square 19 571
Grosvenor Square 10 233; 19 570, *570*
Hanover Square 19 570
King Square 31 714
Lincoln's Inn Fields 19 568; 25 655
Portland Place 19 571
Red Lion Square 25 655
St James's Square 10 360; 19 571; 31 714
Trafalgar Square 19 575
Staple Inn 19 567
stations
Cannon Street railway station 25 856
Charing Cross railway station 10 266; 19 *574*; 25 856
Euston railway station 16 52; 19 575; 25 854, 855
King's Cross railway station 25 856
Paddington railway station 10 236; 12 791; 16 53; 19 575; 25 *856*, 857; 28 248
St Pancras railway station 3 246; 16 54, *54*; 19 575; 25 856; 30 27
Arnos Grove underground station 21 349
Blackfriars underground station 21 349
Holland Park underground station 21 349

London
stations—cont.
Kennington underground station 21 349
Moorgate underground station 21 349
St James's Park underground station 10 439
South Kensington underground station 21 349
railway stations 19 575
underground 10 240; 14 674; 15 824; 19 575; 21 349
Streatham Street 30 457
studios 29 856, 858
Sun Fire and Life Assurance Office 19 573
Temple Bar 5 293
Temple of Mithras 19 565, 579; 27 105
sculpture 19 *579*
Thames embankments 3 430; 19 *574*, 575
theatres 30 660, 677
Adelphi 19 571
Alhambra 22 59; 30 679
Blackfriars Theatre 30 661
Cockpit Theatre 30 661, 674
Coliseum 2 294; 30 678
Covent Garden Theatre 30 674
Dorset Garden Theatre 30 673, 674
Drury Lane Theatre 30 673, 674, 675
East London 30 679
Fortune Theatre 30 661, 662
Globe Theatre 30 *661*, 662
Goodman's Fields Theatre 30 673
Half Moon Theatre 30 685
Hippodrome 29 489
Hope Theatre 30 662
King's Theatre 30 674
Lincoln's Inn Fields Theatre 30 673, 674
Little Theatre 30 673
National Theatre *see* Royal National Theatre
New London Theatre 8 177; 30 687
Old Vic Theatre 7 483
Olympic Theatre 30 681
Princess's Theatre 30 680
Queen's Theatre 30 673, 675
Rose Theatre 30 661, 662
Royal Lyceum 30 680, 682
Royal National Theatre 10 242; 19 578; 30 684
Royal Opera House (destr. 1855) 30 677
Royal Opera House (1858) 30 680
Royalty Theatre *see* East London
Swan Theatre 30 661, 662, *662*
Theatre (Shoreditch) 30 661, 662
Theatre Royal (Bridges Street) 30 673, 674
Theatre Royal (Covent Garden; 1809-56) 13 610; 28 *873*; 30 673, 679, 681
Theatre Royal (Covent Garden; from 1856) *see* Royal Opera House
Theatre Royal (Drury Lane) 8 911; 30 677, 679, 680
Tivoli Music Hall 30 679
Vere Street Theatre 30 673
Time-Life Building 10 745
Tooks Court 4 786
Tower of London 6 49, 51, 54, 56; 10 359; 14 75; 19 615–17*, *616*; 21 563, 564; 31 710
Beauchamp Tower 19 616
Bell Tower 19 615
Bloody Tower 12 174; 19 616
Byward Tower 10 245; 13 153; 19 616

London
Tower of London—cont.
Coldharbour Gate 19 615
collections 19 582; 26 78
Cradle Tower 19 616
Great Storehouse 19 617
Jewel House 22 717
keep 33 198
Legge's Mount Battery 19 617
Lieutenant's Lodgings *see* Queen's House
Lion Tower 3 209; 19 616
Middle Tower 19 616
New Armouries 19 617
Queen's Chamber 10 269
Queen's House 19 616
Royal Armouries 2 449
St John's Chapel 2 295; 19 615, *617*; 26 615
St Peter ad Vincula 13 121; 19 615, 616
St Thomas's Tower 19 616
Wakefield Tower 6 54; 12 174; 19 615
Waterloo Barracks 19 617
White Tower 6 52, 54; 10 227; 19 564, 566, 615
workshops 29 852
town halls
Deptford Town Hall 31 241
Hampstead Town Hall 31 240
Poplar Town Hall 31 243
St George's Town Hall (Tower Hamlets) 22 *333*
trade 19 592
Unilever House 19 576
University College 13 610; 33 192
collections 11 164
exhibitions 10 94
Petrie Museum 10 71, 90, 92; 24 561
portico 25 268
University of London 10 375; 14 674
collections 3 244; 10 367
Percival David Foundation of Chinese Art 6 925; 7 155; 8 564; 14 155
urban planning 19 574–5; 27 3; 31 714, 716, 724, 725, 730, 738
US Embassy 8 278
Vauxhall Gardens 10 249; 12 106, 293; 14 269; 19 585, 618–19*; 27 *278*
Grand Walk 19 *619*
paintings 10 785
Rotunda 19 619
sculpture 29 564
vestry halls 7 668; 31 240
Victoria Embankment *see under* Thames embankments
villas 32 556
walls 29 712; 31 710
see also fortifications
Warburg Institute 6 502; 8 62; 28 23; 32 854–5*; 33 243
archives 2 371
library 4 22; 28 23
warehouses 32 861
water supply 30 26
Watkin's Folly 11 242
Wellcome Institute Library 10 422; 33 55
Westminster Palace *see* Palace of Westminster
West Pumping Station 7 813
Wolseley showroom 10 240
York Buildings 7 687
Zimbabwe House 10 437–9; 14 *674*
Zoo 10 241; 33 698
Elephant House 7 695
Gorilla House 33 699
Mappin Terraces 33 699
Penguin Pool 7 695, 698; 33 700
Reptile House 33 698
Snowdon Aviary 33 700
London, George 19 622*; 33 257
assistants 4 805; 30 123
London, George—cont.
patrons and collectors 6 116, 128, 515; 14 127
works 5 65; 6 65, 66; 12 128; 23 467
London, Gregory of *see* GREGORY OF LONDON
London, Midland and Scottish Railway Company 14 397; 19 519; 20 491
London, William 23 251
London and Birmingham Railway 15 830
London Artists' Association 1 454; 3 631; 4 168
London Bulletin 24 428
London Carpenters Company 22 717
London County Council (L.C.C.) 10 241, 242; 19 572, 575, 576, 577; 20 491; 30 458
Architects' Department 22 743
architecture 19 *577*
Londonderry
Altnagelvin Hospital 16 40
Faughan Valley School 16 40
Tower Museum 16 42
Londonderry, Robert Stewart, 2nd Marquess of *see* STEWART, ROBERT, 2nd Marquess of Londonderry
London Dock Co. 19 573
London F484, Painter of 10 615
London Gallery Bulletin 30 22
London Group 4 168; 5 517; 10 256; 19 591, 622–3*; 24 228; 31 706
members 8 265
Agar, Eileen 1 449
Bell, Vanessa 3 631
Bevan, Robert (Polhill) 3 894
Coldstream, William (Menzies) 7 547
Dismorr, Jessica 9 9
Epstein, Jacob 10 439
Ginner, Charles (Isaac) 12 652
Gotlib, Henryk 13 212
Grant, Duncan (James Corrowr) 13 314
Hamnett, Nina 14 120
Hitchens, Ivon 14 590
Hodgkins, Frances (Mary) 14 613
Lamb, Henry 18 668
Manley, Edna 20 276
Nash, John (1893-1977) 22 525
Piper, John 24 839
Potworowski, (Tadeusz) Piotr 25 373
Ratcliffe, William (Whitehead) 26 10
Richards, Ceri 26 335
Smith, Matthew (Arnold Bracy) 28 884
works 1 454
Londoniis, Jocius de *see* JOCIUS DE LONDONIIS
London Impressionists 29 595
London Jason, Master of the 22 835
London Metropolitan Railways 21 349
London Miscellany (London, BL, Add. MS. 11639) 17 563; 19 623–4*, *624*
London Passenger Transport Board 15 824; 25 350, 351
London Passional, Master of the 20 662, 663
London Pliny Master 12 171; 32 198
London Press Exchange 7 652
London Salon 24 739
London Satyr, Master of the 12 247
works 12 *247*
London Secession *see* SECESSION (LONDON)
London situla *see* BASILEWSKI SITULA
London Stereoscopic Company 23 447; 24 657
London Throne of Mercy, Master of the 2 792
London Transport 17 625; 19 485; 26 39
London Underground Railways 7 652, 653; 17 850; 31 706
Londsdale, H. W. 29 797
Lonedo di Lugo, Villa Godi-Malinverni 23 862, *863*; 32 547
Long, Amelia, Lady Farnborough 12 742; 14 877; 19 624–5*
Long, Birch Burdette 25 446
Long, Charles 4 845
Long, Charles, 1st Baron Farnborough 5 631; 19 599, 624*; 28 370
dealing 14 145
paintings 10 365
Long, Edward 16 880, 886
Long, Edwin (Longsden) 7 406; 14 688; 19 625*
Long, John 31 652
Long, Richard 4 823; 19 591, 625–6*
groups and movements 1 80; 10 258, 269
works 18 694, 695; 19 493, *625*
Long, Robert Cary, sr (1770-1833) 19 626; 31 666
Long, Robert Cary, jr (*c.* 1810-49) 19 626*; 25 268
Long, Stephen 33 184
Long, Sydney 2 748; 19 626–7*
long and short masonry *see under* MASONRY → types
long and short stitch *see under* STITCHES
Longanikos 9 556
Longarone Church 7 258
long barrows *see under* BARROWS → types
Longcang Temple Stele *see under* LONGXING TEMPLE
longcase clocks *see under* CLOCKS → types
Longchamp Castle 3 578
Longchang Monastery 33 318
Long Count *see under* MAYA
Longdon-on-Tern (Salop) 2 242
Longfellow, Henry Wadsworth 8 528; 10 99; 14 699
Longfish, George 22 599
Longford, Thomas Pakenham, 2nd Earl of *see* PAKENHAM, THOMAS, 2nd Earl of Longford
Longford Castle (Wilts) 32 540
collections 25 39
furniture 16 60
paintings 14 114, 666; 21 355
Longhena, Baldassare 19 627–30*; 32 410
collaboration 7 900
patrons and collectors 5 778; 7 861; 24 537
works 7 258; 16 641, *641*, 702; 19 *628*, *629*; 20 585; 28 31; 32 160, 186, 187, *187*, 188, 195, 215, 216, 217, 229, *229*
Longhena, Melchisedech 19 627
Longhi (ii), Alessandro 19 634, 636*; 32 194
patrons and collectors 21 849; 27 864
teachers 23 175
Longhi, Alessio 5 180; 15 866
Longhi (iii), Barbara 19 631*; 33 308
Longhi (iii), Francesco 19 631*
Longhi, Giuseppe 2 233; 19 636–7*; 21 624, 824
Longhi (iii), Luca 19 631*
assistants 19 631
pupils 19 631
Longhi (i), Martino, I (1534-91) 19 631–2*
assistants 19 806; 20 542
attributions 13 628
collaboration 11 78; 25 227
patrons and collectors 11 740; 13 628; 24 398
pupils 25 226
works 1 721; 3 644; 16 635; 26 814, 831, 834; 31 236
Longhi (i), Martino, II (1602-60) 19 631, 632–4*
works 19 *634*; 24 371
Longhi (i), Onorio 19 631, 632*
collaboration 25 227
pupils 19 632
Longhi (ii), Pietro 19 634–6*; 32 194
patrons and collectors 7 895
pupils 19 636
reproductive prints by others 3 308; 10 770; 19 636; 24 894
works 7 787; 11 395, *395*; 12 292; 16 676; 19 *634*, *635*; 32 194
Longhi, Roberto 7 715, 782; 19 637*; 24 448; 28 319
works 2 517; 6 125; 16 782
Longhi, Silla 4 280; 19 638*
Long House (NC) 32 303
longhouses *see under* HOUSES → types
Longhurst, A. H. 22 428
Longhurst, Margaret (Helen) 19 638*; 20 26
Longin 4 461; 25 339, 343; 28 450
works 25 *339*
Longines 7 448
Longinus 29 889
Long & Kees 21 649
Long Kesh, Maze prison 7 679
long kilns *see* KILNS → types → dragon
Longleat (Wilts) 3 185; 8 44; 10 143; 13 240; 19 362; 20 893; 24 290; 28 648, *648*, 894; 30 794
banqueting houses 10 324
collections 33 375
coral 31 285
gardens 12 128; 19 622
gazebo 12 222
interior decoration 8 106; 13 702
leather 19 5
models 2 336
paintings 17 915; 24 637; 29 424; 32 244
plaster 29 834
tapestries 10 349
Longleat Breviary *see under* BREVIARIES → individual manuscripts
Longman, Evelyn Beatrice 3 30
Long Man of Wilmington (E. Sussex) 14 *544*, 544
Longmate, B. 28 557
Long Melford (Suffolk)
Holy Trinity Church 1 518; 10 359; 13 55, *55*; 24 465
Kentwell Hall 4 790
Longmen 5 108; 6 *615*; 7 151; 19 638–40*; 33 34
Binyang Cave 6 710; 19 639
sculpture 19 *638*
Cave 4 6 713
Cave 20 6 713
caves 6 650, 743, 772; 30 443
Fengxian Temple 6 713
sculpture 19 *639*
Guyang Caves 6 709
Leigu tai Caves 6 715
sculpture 6 708, 709, *710*; 7 161; 33 318
Longo *see* LONGHI (i)
Longo, Robert 19 640*; 24 409; 25 360; 27 478
works 20 *608*
Longobardi, Nicolo 12 814
Longoni 27 192
Longoni, Emilio 13 714; 28 354
Longos Vales, S João 26 611
Longperier, Adrien de 21 264
Long-petal bowls *see under* BOWLS → types
long-pile rugs *see under* RUGS → types
Longpont Abbey 20 578
Longpré, Marchand & Goudreau 22 36
Longquan
ceramics 6 331, 914, 917; 29 67
Jinmiao Stupa 6 781
kilns 6 871, 893, 899
porcelain 6 894
pottery 6 622, 873, 874
Longquan ware *see under* POTTERY → wares
Longroy, Louis De Soissons, Viscomte d'Ostel, Baron *see* DE SOISSONS, LOUIS, Viscomte d'Ostel
Longshan 6 *615*; 19 640*
jewellery 7 106
pottery 6 878; 19 640
Longshan culture 7 159
hardstones 7 107
jade 7 2
pottery 6 869, 877, *878*, 878
Longstaff, John (Campbell) 19 641*
Longstaff, Will 2 748
Long Thien Shih 20 172
Longthorpe Tower (Cambs) 10 *225*; 13 128; 19 641*
wall paintings 13 *128*
Longton (Staffs) 29 495
Longton Hall Porcelain Factory 6 605; 9 368, 369; 10 308, 309; 28 258; 29 495
Longuda 1 303, 328, 381
Longueau 11 526
Longueil, Joseph de 19 11, 641–2*; 33 196
Longueil, René de, Marquis de Maisons 11 657; 13 790; 19 642*; 20 290; 23 523
Longuelune, Zacharias 9 236; 19 642*; 25 135
assistants 18 162
collaboration 4 218; 9 29; 25 240
patrons and collectors 33 114, 115
pupils 18 473
works 5 348; 9 235, 236; 12 373; 21 64
Longueuil, René de 23 460
Longueville, Anne, Duchesse de 32 509
Longueville, Catherine de Gonzague, Duchesse de 4 865
Longueville, François, Duc de 13 254
Longus 4 360; 10 129; 23 514
Longwood Foundation 19 643
Longworth, Nicholas 1 440; 25 400; 31 662
Longwy, Claude de, Cardinal 25 570
Lonhy, Antoine de *see* ANTOINE DE LONHY
Loni, Alessandro *see* LOMI, ALESSANDRO
Lonigo, Rocca Pisani 27 237; 28 30, *31*; 32 548
Lonis, Giuseppe Antonio 27 836
Lonlay L'Abbaye 26 597
Lönn, Wivi 19 643*
collaboration 19 408; 30 277
works 10 537; 30 284
Lönnberg, William 23 266
Lönnrot, Elias 22 540
Lonquon, Jacques de *see* JACQUES DE LONQUON
Lonsdale, James Lowther, 1st Earl of *see* LOWTHER, JAMES, 1st Earl of Lonsdale

Lonsdale, William Lowther, 1st Earl of see LOWTHER, WILLIAM, 1st Earl of Lonsdale
Lonsing, François-Louis 4 391; 19 643*
Lontor, Fort Hollandia 21 596, 596
Loo, (Charles-)Amédée (-Philippe) van 11 261, 643; 19 337, 644, 645, 649*; 25 368
Loo, Andreas de 19 644*
Loo, Arent van 12 523
Loo, Carle van see VANLOO, CARLE
Loo, (Jules-)César (-Denis) van 8 703; 19 644, 649*; 28 19
Loo, C. T. 15 744
Loo, François van (1708-32) 19 644
Loo, Frans van (fl 1607-35) 32 254
Loo, Georges Hulin de see HULIN DE LOO, GEORGES
Loo, Jacob van 11 402; 19 644–5*; 22 720
Loo, Jan van (b 1585) 19 644
Loo, Jean-Baptiste van (1684-1745) 1 504; 19 644, 645–9*
collaboration 24 212
house 1 497
patrons and collectors 4 611; 14 485
pupils 8 499; 9 398; 19 647, 649; 31 306
reproductive prints by others 18 795
teachers 19 817
works 19 644
Loo, Jean van (fl 1682-94) 19 644
Loo, Joseph 19 644
Loo, Kington 20 169
Loo, Louis-Abraham van 19 644, 645
Loo, Louis-Michel van 11 670; 19 647–9*; 24 168; 29 282
assistants 21 80; 31 229
patrons and collectors 4 558, 559; 5 902; 25 287
pupils 1 105; 11 173; 23 202; 24 222
reproductive prints by others 21 815
teachers 19 645
works 8 866; 11 407, 408, 410, 472; 19 644, 648
Loo, van (family) 20 417
Loofs, Adam 14 42; 22 865, 888, 897
works 22 888
looking-glasses see MIRRORS
Loomis, L. H. 19 649
Loomis, Roger Sherman 19 649–50*
loom pulleys 5 258*
looms 10 636; 30 309, 543, 544–6
draw
China 30 547
historical and regional traditions
Africa 1 250, 294, 294
Ancient Near East 1 880
Bali (Indonesia) 15 793
Belgium 3 605
Brazil 4 724
Cameroon 1 294
Central Asia, Western 6 253
China 7 43–4
Egypt, ancient 9 824, 824; 10 75
Etruscan 10 635, 636
France 2 838; 16 850
Hausa 14 231
Inca 15 163
Indonesia 15 792, 793, 794
Ireland 16 34
Italy 10 635, 636
Japan 17 306–8, 328
Java 15 792
Madagascar 1 294
Malaysia 20 175, 176
looms
historical and regional traditions—cont.
Mesoamerica, Pre-Columbian 21 261
Native North Americans 22 622
Navajo 30 545
Nigeria 1 246, 294
Sri Lanka 29 476
Sumatra 15 794
Tibet 30 837, 845
Vietnam 32 489
Zaire 1 294, 294
types
backstrap 21 261; 30 544*
Bhutan 3 915
Egypt, ancient 30 544
Guatemala 13 766
Japan 17 306, 307, 354
Malaysia 20 176
South America, Pre-Columbian 29 135
Vietnam 32 490
band 30 545*
box 30 544–5*
card 7 43
draw 16 849; 19 415; 30 546–8*, 547
Central Asia, Western 6 248
China 7 44, 44, 52; 30 547
England 30 547
Indian subcontinent 30 547
Japan 17 306, 307
Netherlands, the 19 416
high 17 354
high-warp 30 309, 309
horizontal ground 30 544*, 544
inkle 30 545, 545
Jacquard 2 825; 5 831; 16 849–50; 19 416; 30 548–9*
China 7 53
England 10 357
Ireland 16 33
Japan 17 307, 317
low-warp 30 309, 309
pedal 3 915
power 5 831–2, 840
shaft 19 415–16
steam 5 831
treadle 13 766; 16 850; 30 546*
vertical 30 545*
warp-weighted 30 545–6*, 546
Loon, Johan van 22 884
Loon, Maurits N. van 22 341
Loon, Theodoor van 3 559; 19 650–51*
works 19 650, 651
Loon, van (family) 21 813
looping 3 332; 29 179; 30 549
Loos Church 11 616
Loos, Adolf 2 815; 19 650–53*; 24 440
collaboration 10 102; 11 727; 18 33; 32 439
groups and movements 2 567, 776; 21 779; 26 14, 15
pupils 8 617; 33 284
translated writings 28 548
works 2 788, 789, 810; 4 833; 8 402; 10 102; 11 526; 18 192; 19 522, 652, 653; 23 490, 548; 25 54; 28 833; 32 438, 555
writings 11 525
Loos, Daniel Friedrich 19 654*
Loos, Gottfried Bernhard 19 654; 32 682
Loosdorf Church 2 780
Loosduinen Church 4 778, 778; 22 819
Looten, Emmanuel 20 815
Looten, Jan 13 647
Lootsman (family) 33 358
lootwit see under PIGMENTS → types
Loover, Ago-Himm 10 538; 30 276
Looy, Jacobus van 19 654*; 22 908
groups and movements 22 850; 32 392; 33 266
Looy, Jacobus van—cont.
teachers 1 650
Lopadion 9 555
Lopburi 30 571
Ban Chao Phraya Wichayen 30 575
coins 30 632
National Museum 30 590
palaces 23 823; 29 827; 30 575, 588
Phra Narai Ratchaniwet Lopburi 30 575
Phra Prang Sam Yot 29 826; 30 581
sculpture 30 594, 606
Sondet Phrai Narai Maharat Museum 29 240
Suttha Winitchai see National Museum
Wat Khao Samoa Khon 30 594
Wat Phra Si Ratana Mahathat 30 587
Lope de Vega, Félix 5 739; 19 139, 709; 30 664
Lope el Barbicano 23 402
Loperráez Corvalán, Juan 12 33
Loperuelo, Johan de 3 810
Lopes, António Teixeira see TEIXEIRA LOPES, ANTÓNIO
Lopes, Cristóvão 19 656*; 25 296
Lopes, Domingos 12 888; 25 306
Lopes, Fernão 2 874
Lopes, Francisco 5 421
Lopes, Gregório 19 654–6*; 25 295; 26 253
collaboration 1 213; 2 874; 11 65
pupils 19 656
works 19 655; 25 296
Lopes, José Joaquim Teixeira see TEIXEIRA LOPES, JOSÉ JOAQUIM
Lopes, Mateus 27 117
Lopes, Sebastião 19 656*
López (Spain; glass-making family) 29 331
López (Spain; metal-working family) 29 343
López (Paraguay; ruling family) 24 102
López (fl 1950s) 24 96
Lopez, Aaron 31 249
López, Alfonso 11 662; 31 526
Lopéz, Benigno 24 96
López, Bernardo 4 378
López, Cándido 2 399; 19 656–7*
López, Carlos Antonio 24 95, 100
López, Cristóbal 19 664
López, Diana 21 229
López, Domingo 18 833
López, Felipe 10 504
López, Francisco (1552-1629) 10 483; 24 23
López, Francisco Solano see SOLANO LÓPEZ, FRANCISCO
Lopez, Gaspare 21 31
López, Graciela Carrillo de see CARRILLO DE LÓPEZ, GRACIELA
López, Ignacio see LÓPEZ, NACHO
López, J. 14 403
López, José 11 493; 29 305, 315, 316
Lopez, Josep Lluís Sert i see SERT I LOPEZ, JOSEP LLUÍS
López, José Sáez y see SÁEZ Y LÓPEZ, JOSÉ
López, Juan 19 172, 173
López, Juan Carlos 2 397
López, Juan Manuel 7 847
López, Juan Pedro 32 166, 172
works 32 173
Lopez, Millito 18 833
López, Nacho 19 657*
López, Pedro 16 863
Lopez, Raymond 24 130
Lopéz, Venancio 24 96
López Aguado, Antonio 19 657; 20 64; 29 272
López Aguado, Martín 4 567; 19 657*
López Anaya, Fernando 2 399
López Antay, Joaquín 24 499, 511
López Bueno, Diego 19 657*; 29 268
López Callejas, Manuel 14 716
Lopez Carmona, Fernando 5 603; 22 69
López Caro, Francisco 4 211
works 4 211
López-Castro, Leandro de Saralegui y see SARALEGUI Y LÓPEZ-CASTRO, LEANDRO DE
López Cepero, Manuel 19 658*; 29 354
López Criado, Cecilio 22 68
López de Arbaiza, Diego 17 514
López de Arenas, Diego 14 469; 19 658*; 29 357, 637
López de Arteaga, Sebastian 19 658*; 21 383
López de Ayala, Diego 20 2
López de Cárdenas, Garci 2 409
López de Castro, Francisco 4 261
López de Cogolludo, Diego 21 262
López del Campo, Rafael 25 702
López de Legazpi, Miguel 21 596; 24 611, 612
López de los Ríos, José 4 261
López de Loyola, Iñigo see IGNATIUS LOYOLA, Saint
López de Medrano, Manuel 29 336
López de Medrano, Pedro 29 336
Lopez de Mendoza, Iñigo, 1st Marqués de Mondéjar see MONDÉJAR, IÑIGO LOPEZ DE MENDOZA, 1st Marqués de
López de Rojas, Eufrasio 16 863, 864
López de Victoria 25 701
López Enguidanos, José 19 659
López Enguidanos (y Perles), Tomás 19 659*; 31 816
López Enguidanos, Vicente 19 659
López García, Antonio 19 659*; 20 68; 29 287, 297
López Loza, Luis 19 659*
López Martínez, Fernando 21 381
López Méndez, Luis Alfredo 19 659*; 32 175
López Otero, Manuel 20 64
López Palomino, Antonio 29 337
López Rodezno, Arturo 14 715, 716
López Romero (family) 29 331
López Salaberri, José 20 64
López Soler, Ramón 2 62
López-Torres, Domingo 11 886
López y Piquer, Bernardo 19 659
López y Piquer, Luis 19 659
López y Portaña, Vicente 19 659–60*; 31 816
patrons and collectors 18 899
reproductive prints by others 1 776; 12 33
works 5 453; 19 660; 22 328; 29 283, 306
Łopieński 32 878
Lo P'ing see LUO PING
Lop Nor (lake) 6 289, 309
Lopnor (site) 7 114
Lopokhova, Lydia 3 119
Loppem
Castle of Caloen (1856) 3 578, 585; 13 208
Château (gothic) 13 182
Lop Sanpra 6 317
Lopukhina, Mariya
works 4 421
Łopuszna Church 25 101
Lora, Eduardo Muñoz see MUÑOZ LORA, EDUARDO
Lora, Francesco della 11 713
Lora, Silvano 9 117, 119
Lorago see LURAGO
Loraine, William 4 874
Loran, Paul 12 333
L'Orange, Hans P(ieter) 19 660*; 23 245
Lorangère, Quentin de see QUENTIN DE LORANGÈRE
Lorca, Andrés Jiménez de see JIMÉNEZ DE LORCA, ANDRÉS
Lorca, Federico García 1 573; 2 30; 8 465; 19 660–61*; 29 286
Lorca, S Patricio 29 266
Lorch 2 776; 12 455
Lorch, Melchior see LORCK, MELCHIOR
Lörcher, Alfred 12 408; 19 661*
Lorck, Melchior 8 758; 19 661–2*; 30 478
patrons and collectors 9 556; 23 395
works 4 80; 8 732, 732; 16 585; 19 662; 33 354
Lord, Austin W. 23 904
Lord, David 27 613
Lord, James Brown 19 766
Lord, P. 1 207
Lord, Samuel Hall 2 151
Lord, Thomas 25 268
Lord, Wilfred 16 887
Lord Chamberlain's Men 30 661
Lord Chen's Spirit Road 6 741
Lord Lee Polyptych, Master of the see DOMINICAN EFFIGIES, MASTER OF THE
Lord of Asine 14 352
Lordon, Jean-Abel 19 254
Lorecký, Jiří 8 395
Loredan (family) 5 819
Loredan, Andrea di Nicolo 2 162; 7 517; 19 663; 29 738
Loredan, Leonardo, Doge of Venice (reg 1501-21) 3 664; 6 85; 19 663*
Loredano, Giovanni Francesco 9 489
Lorell, Lucien 27 205
Lorena, Niccolò da see CORDIER, NICOLAS
Lorenese, Claudio see POUSSIN, CLAUDE
Lorent, Jakob August 19 663–4*
Lorente Germán, Bernardo 19 664*
Lorentzen, Christian August 11 779; 17 478; 18 178; 23 225; 27 144; 29 696
Lorentzen, Vilhelm Birkedal 8 761
Lorentzon, (Anders) Waldemar 14 89
Lorenz, Bente 33 602
Lorenz, Bente, Ceramic Studio 33 603
Lorenz, Gerhard 31 568
Lorenz, Johann 4 833
Lorenz, W. Philipp, Graf von Daun 20 842
Lorenzale y Sugrañes, Claudio 11 324; 29 283
Lorenzana, Francisco Antonio da, Cardinal 29 348; 31 89
Lorenzana, Luis de 23 489
Lorenzetti, Ambrogio 19 664, 668–72*; 20 510; 28 676, 684
attributions 1 621; 4 30; 9 348; 27 859
collaboration 9 346, 349; 19 666
methods 13 139
patrons and collectors 28 676
restorations by others 4 493
works 1 653; 2 339; 5 164; 6 466; 9 260; 10 738; 13 149; 16 657, 762; 18 703; 19 669, 670, 671; 26 182; 28 681, 684, 685–6, 686; 31 154, 703
Lorenzetti, Pietro 12 567; 19 664–8*; 20 510; 28 676
altarpieces 5 164
attributions 9 348; 20 776
collaboration 9 346, 349
methods 13 139
patrons and collectors 7 905; 29 46

Lorenzetti, Pietro—cont.
pupils **3** 917
restorations by others **16** 847
works **2** 389, *626*, 626–7; **6** 466; **9** 261; **10** 780; **12** 287; **13** 138, 149; **16** 657, 710; **19** *665*, *667*; **25** 183, 463; **28** 681
Lorenzetto *see* LOTTI, LORENZO
Lorenzi, Antonio **31** 320
Lorenzi, Battista (di Domenico) **6** 147; **19** 672*; **27** 648
Lorenzi, Francesco **18** 683; **24** 894; **30** 862
Lorenzi, Stoldo (di Gino) **19** 672–3*; **24** 855
collaboration **6** 147; **11** 279
patrons and collectors **7** 541
works **11** 215; **16** 696
Lorenzini, Giovanni Antonio **21** 30
Lorenzino da Bologna *see* SABATINI, LORENZO
Lorenzo (*fl* 1471) **20** 323
Lorenzo I de' Medici, Lord of Florence *see* LORENZO THE MAGNIFICENT, Lord of Florence
Lorenzo II de' Medici, Lord of Florence *see* LORENZO DE' MEDICI, Lord of Florence and Duke of Urbino
Lorenzo, Antonio di *see* ANTONIO DI LORENZO
Lorenzo, Antonio di Niccolò di *see* ANTONIO DI NICCOLÒ DI LORENZO
Lorenzo, Bicci di *see* BICCI DI LORENZO
Lorenzo, Diosdado **24** 622
Lorenzo, Fiorenzo di *see* FIORENZO DI LORENZO (DI CECCO DI PASCOLO)
Lorenzo, Gregorio di *see* GREGORIO DI LORENZO
Lorenzo, Juan **29** 336
Lorenzo Costa di Ottavio *see* COSTA DI OTTAVIO, LORENZO
Lorenzo da Bologna **19** 673*; **28** 293; **30** 731; **32** 409
Lorenzo d'Ambrogio
patrons and collectors **12** 701
Lorenzo d'Andrea d'Oerigo *see* LORENZO DI CREDI
Lorenzo da Viterbo **24** 830; **32** 628
Lorenzo de' Medici, Lord of Florence and Duke of Urbino (*reg* 1513-19) **16** *763*; **21** *8*, 18*
manuscripts **31** 845
paintings **3** 306; **11** 661
Lorenzo di Bastiano Zucchetti **4** 859
Lorenzo di Bicci **4** 30, 31; **7** 338; **19** 412, 673–5*; **22** 797
attributions **4** 30; **22** 798
works **19** *674*
Lorenzo di Credi **11** 217; **19** 675–7*; **29** 853
attributions **32** 367
collaboration **32** 364
forgeries by others **3** 357
methods **18** 898
patrons and collectors **4** 307; **5** 537; **20** 482; **27** 350; **33** 594
pupils **1** 454; **29** 14; **31** 205
restorations **6** 14
teachers **32** 366
works **10** 476; **11** 197; **19** 188, *675*, *676*, 752; **32** 365, 366
writings **3** 306
Lorenzo di Niccolò (di Martino) **6** 2; **11** 380; **19** 678*; **29** 405, 406
Lorenzo di Odrisio **16** 725
Lorenzo di Pietro di Giovanni *see* VECCHIETTA
Lorenzo di Turino **31** 450
Lorenzo Monaco **5** 451; **13** 149; **16** 661; **19** 678–83*
collaboration **3** 300
drawings **25** 557
methods **7** 627
patrons and collectors **5** 537; **6** 393; **12** 33; **29** 781; **30** 766
pupils **20** 621, 787
teachers **28** 752
works **2** 34; **5** 450; **7** II1; **19** *679*, *680*, *681*
Lorenzoni, Peter Anton **2** 795; **18** 682
Lorenzo the Magnificent, Lord of Florence (*reg* 1469-92) **9** 102; **11** 178; **14** 869; **21** 7, *8*, 13–14*; **25** 151; **26** 848; **32** *11*
architecture **11** 178; **25** 451; **27** 733, 734, 736; **31** 674; **32** 545
art policies **1** 102; **2** 523
bronzes **20** 847
collections **7** 561; **16** 770, 778; **18** 521; **24** 278
decorative works **32** 364
education (art) **16** 778
gems **12** 257, 265
hardstones **14** 169, 170; **16** 746
interior decoration **11** 384
manuscripts **7** 540; **11** 296, 686; **20** 413
medals **3** 859; **13** 730
paintings **4** 502; **19** 447; **24** 522, 523; **25** 46; **28** 702
frescoes **4** 494; **12** 551
patronage **11** 186
porcelain **4** 176
pottery **13** 541
sculpture **3** 861; **9** 125; **11** 661; **12** 111; **21** 21; **25** 157; **27** 830; **31** 188
sponsorship **4** 496–8; **11** 56; **19** 445; **21** 433
writings **15** 50
Lorenzo Veneziano **19** 683–4*
patrons and collectors **28** 29
works **4** 275; **11** 382; **16** 657; **19** *684*
Lorenzo Zaragoza **19** 684*
Lorenz von Bibra, Prince Bishop of Würzburg **26** 371, 372
Loret, François *see* LORETE, FRANCISCO
Loret, Jean **22** 466
Loret, Victor **10** 80
Lorete, Francisco **19** 685*
Loreti, David **23** 873
Loreti, Mario **22** 805
Loreto **16** *620*; **19** 685–9*
Palazzo Apostolico **19** 688–9*
Piazza della Madonna **19** *685*
S Maria di Loreto **19** *685*, 686*, *686*, 687*; **28** 630
architecture **19** 686–7*
frescoes **27** *121*
paintings **19** 688
Santa Casa **19** 685, 687–8*
doors **9** 158
paintings **15** 136
Sacristy of S Giovanni **28** 701
sculpture **4** 650; **19** *560*, *688*; **26** 137; **27** 777
sculpture **5** 415
Lorge, Maréchal de **20** 295
lorgnettes **17** 526
Lorich, Thilo von *see* THILO VON LORICH
Lorichs, Melchior *see* LORCK, MELCHIOR
Lorient **31** 718
Naval Arsenal **30** 467
Lorillard, Pierre **24** 300; **25** 571
Lorillon, Pierre-Benoit **4** 42
Lorimer, Hew **19** 689; **28** 244
Lorimer, John Henry **19** 689
Lorimer, Robert S(toddart) **19** 689*
collaboration **26** 460; **28** 256; **29** 843
Lorimer, Robert S(toddart)—cont.
groups and movements **28** 289
pupils **23** 170; **26** 99
teachers **2** 5; **4** 215
works **9** 724, 727; **28** 230, 249, 250, 255, 256, 263
Lorimer and Matthew **26** 460
Lorimier, Henriette **4** 303; **31** 373
Loring, Frances N(orma) **5** 570, 573; **19** 689–90*
Loring, John **30** 867
Loring, Sanford **30** 505
Lorini, Bonaiuto **23** 882
Lorino, Giuliano di Jacopo **12** 713
Loriot, Louis-Adam **6** 396
Loris-Melikov (family) **5** 333
Loriyan Tangai **15** *264*, 446; **19** 690*; **23** *797*
Lorjou, Bernard **14** 701
Lorme, Anthonie de **2** 341, 342; **23** 832; **27** 230
L'Orme, Charles de **11** 662; **18** 811; **20** 455
L'Orme, Jean de, I (*fl c.* 1514-30; father) **19** 690
L'Orme, Jean de, II (*fl* 1549; son) **19** 690
L'Orme, Philibert de **2** 313; **19** 690–94*; **20** 133
architecture **11** 513–14; **19** *691*
architectural decorations **6** 142
arsenals **2** 502
bridges **6** 546
chapels **6** 506; **19** *691*; **32** 582
châteaux **2** *27*, 27–8; **4** 780; **6** 506, *545*; **11** 572; **19** *692*; **27** 559, *559*
columns **11** 231
monuments **27** 547
orders (architecture) **23** 488, 492
palaces **19** *694*
roofs **30** 901, 911
staircases **9** 354; **11** 260; **29** 523
tombs **4** 337; **27** 547; **31** 351
assistants **21** 345
attributions **9** 350
gardens **12** 120
interior decoration **6** 506
patrons and collectors **8** 856; **11** 656; **31** 850
reproductive prints by others **20** 457
writings **2** 28, 336, 357; **23** 487, 489; **29** 637; **31** 296
Lorme, Pierre de *see* DELORME, PIERRE
Lorne, Francis **30** 242
Loro Jonggrang **14** 561; **15** *753*, 755, 758, 762, 765; **19** 695–6*; **30** 446
Candi Brahma **15** 780
Candi Vishnu **15** 780
reliefs **23** 556
sculpture **3** 379; **15** 778, 779, 780
Temple of Brahma **19** *695*
Temple of Shiva **19** *695*
Temple of Vishnu **19** *695*
Lorrain, Charles Le *see* MELLIN, CHARLES
Lorrain, Claude *see* CLAUDE LORRAIN
Lorrain, Jean **4** 507
Lorrain, Louis-Joseph Le **2** 704
Lorrain, Nicolas François **26** 772
Lorraine (House of) **18** 840; **19** 696–7*
Lorraine, Duchy of **19** 709
Lorraine, Anthony, Duke of *see* ANTHONY, Duke of Lorraine
Lorraine, Catherine de Bourbon, Duchess of *see* CATHERINE DE BOURBON, Duchess of Lorraine
Lorraine, Charles Alexander, Prince of, Governor of the Netherlands **3** 613
architecture **2** 122; **3** 547; **5** 40; **8** 840; **10** 837; **16** 862
Lorraine, Charles Alexander, Prince of, Governor of the Netherlands—cont.
furniture **26** 529
gems **32** 8
glass **3** 594
paintings **19** 165
sculpture **2** 125; **8** 699; **10** 899; **12** 835; **30** 283
silver **3** 599
sponsorship **19** 643; **32** 252
Lorraine, Charles de, Duc d'Aumale *see* AUMALE, CHARLES DE LORRAINE, Duc d'
Lorraine, Charles III, Duke of *see* CHARLES III, Duke of Lorraine
Lorraine, Charles IV, Duke of *see* CHARLES IV, Duke of Lorraine
Lorraine, Claude de (*fl c.* 1640; patron) **17** 449
Lorraine, Francis, Duke of *see* FRANCIS I, Holy Roman Emperor
Lorraine, François de, 2nd Duc de Guise *see* GUISE, FRANÇOIS DE LORRAINE, 2nd Duc de
Lorraine, Henri de, Bishop of Reims **26** 113
Lorraine, Henry, Duke of *see* HENRY, Duke of Lorraine
Lorraine, Henry II, Duke of *see* HENRY II, Duke of Lorraine
Lorraine, Jean-Baptiste de **20** 914
Lorraine, Jean de, Cardinal *see* JEAN DE LORRAINE, Cardinal
Lorraine, Leopold, Duke of *see* LEOPOLD, Duke of Lorraine
Lorraine, Nicole, Duchess of *see* NICOLE, Duchess of Lorraine
Lorraine, Philippe de **23** 515
Lorraine, René II (of Vaudemont), Duke of *see* RENÉ II (OF VAUDEMONT), Duke of Lorraine
Lorraine, Stanislav Leszczyński, Grand Duke of *see* STANISLAV I LESZCZYŃSKI, King of Poland
Lorraine cross *see* CROSSES → types → Papal
Lorraine method *see under* GLASS → techniques
Lorraine-Vaudemont, Anne de, Princesse de Lillebonne *see* LILLEBONNE, ANNE DE LORRAINE-VAUDEMONT, Princesse de
Lorris, Guillaume de *see* GUILLAUME DE LORRIS
lorry paintings *see under* PAINTING → forms
Lorsch Abbey **5** 794; **7** 262; **12** *361*, 471; **13** 18; **19** 697–8*; **21** 835
cloister **5** 795; **7** 453
gate-house *see* Torhalle
manuscript illumination **5** 801, 803
manuscripts **20** 330
outer crypt **5** 795
sculpture **5** 796
stained glass **29** 501, 516
Torhalle **12** 175, 363; **19** 698, *698*; **23** 485; **26** 573; **31** 350
arches **2** 296
corbels **7** 837
masonry **20** 572
sculpture **5** 796
stripwork **29** 776
wall paintings **5** 798
wall paintings **12** 382
westwork **5** 795; **7** 264; **12** 363
Lorsch Codex Aureus *see under* CODICES → individual manuscripts
Lorsch Gospels *see under* GOSPEL BOOKS → individual manuscripts
Lorsica **12** 285
Lort, Ross A. **20** 30
Lortet **25** 493
Lorvão
Monastery **25** 317
S Maria **25** 295
Lory, F. B. P. **15** 742
Lory, (Mathias) Gabriel **3** 823; **19** 699*
Lory, Gabriel Ludwig **1** 31; **3** 823; **19** 699
Lorymer, Henry **4** 692
Lorymer, John **4** 692
Los, Pierre de **13** 196; **19** 382
Losada, Diego de **5** 691
Losada, Manuel **9** 696
Los Angeles (CA) **19** 699–703*; **31** *587*
Aerospace Museum **1** 737; **12** *236*
American Institute of Architects (A.I.A.) **19** 700
architecture **5** 173
Atlantic Richfield Building **30** 507
Bradbury Building **33** 452
City Hall **19** *700*
County Arboretum **9** 685
County Museum of Art **22** 359
collections **6** 735; **7** 156; **12** 504; **14** 117, 296; **15** 742, 743, 746; **16** 557; **17** 434, 436; **19** 703; **20** 142; **22** 795; **28** 167; **29** 241, 478; **30** 332, 849
drawings **9** 231
exhibitions **15** 748
Greek collection **13** 470
Modern and Contemporary Art Department **19** 702
paintings **15** 743
Pavilion for Japanese Art **12** 855
sculpture **22** 795; **27** 47
Craft and Folk Art Museum **19** 703
Electric Theater **7** 327
Health House *see* Lovell House
Hebrew Union College Skirball Museum **17** 581
Lovell House **23** *10*; **25** 741
Loyola University **1** 737
Memorial Colosseum **29** 489
Metro stations **21** 350
Museum of Contemporary Art **1** 737; **12** 236; **16** 775; **19** 702; **22** 360, 367; **33** 45
collections **19** 703; **24** 24; **27** 277; **28** 167
Natural History Museum of Los Angeles County **19** 703
Otis House **7** 619
Pacific Asia Museum **19** 702
Pacific Design Center **12** 794
Pantages Theatre **2** 522
Samson Tire Company building **2** 643
Tail o' the Pup hot-dog stand **18** 73
Union Passenger Terminal **25** 857
University of California
Dickson Art Center **20** 142
Museum of Cultural History **1** 437, 440; **11** 827; **23** 738
sculpture garden **28** 315
urban planning **19** 699, 700
Walter Luther Dodge House **12** *632*
Watts Towers **11** 243; **16** 892; **23** 334; **26** 508
Los Arcos **29** 335
Lo Savio, Francesco **16** 682, 709; **19** 704*; **26** 778
Los Cerritos **20** 885
Los Certales workshop **29** 321
Loschbur **19** 826
Löschenkohl, Hieronymus **25** 673
Loscher, Sebastian **5** 200; **8** 541; **11** 818; **12** 401; **15** 144; **20** 104
Loschi, Bernardino **24** 833
Los Disidentes *see* DISIDENTES, LOS

Loseley House (Surrey) **6** 604
chimney-piece **6** *604*
Losenko, Anton (Pavlovich) **19** 704*; **27** 388, 389, 442; **28** 646
pupils **28** 823
teachers **2** 410
works **27** 579
Losenstein, Hans Wilhelm von **28** 50
Losenstein, Wolfgang Sigmund von **19** 92
Loser, Gabriel **27** 555
Los Esteros **3** 65
Losey, Joseph **14** 511
Los Frailes **1** 464
Los Grajos **29** 365
Losinga, Herbert de **23** 250
Losinga, Robert de, Bishop of Hereford **26** 590
Löslein, Peter **32** 198
Los Llanos, Conde de *see* SALAMANCA (Y MAYOL), JOSÉ, Marqués de
Los Millares **19** 704–5*; **21** 551; **25** *470*; **29** *259*
fortifications **25** 503, 522
Los Naranjos **29** 138, 139
Los Negros **24** 82
Lösner, Carl **19** 113
Los Novísimos *see* NOVÍSIMOS, LOS
Losonczi, Antal **15** 6
Lo Spagnoletto *see* RIBERA, JUSEPE DE
Los Reyes **21** 718
Los Reyes Acozac **21** 192
Los Ríos **29** 152
Lossangoye **11** 879
Lossing, Benson J. **8** 528
Lössnig **19** 111
Lossonczy, Tamás **10** 650; **14** 902
Lossow, William **19** 111, 705*
Lossow & Kühne **18** 140
Lossow & Viehweger **19** 705*
Los Tapiales **21** 192
Loštice **8** 404
lost-wax casting **19** 705*; **21** *321*, 321–2
historical and regional traditions
Africa **1** 288
Asante **2** 589
Bhutan **3** 914
Central Asia, Eastern **6** 313
Champa **6** 428
China **6** 833, 834, 855, 865; **7** 99; **8** 853
Cyprus, ancient **8** 339, 353
Dian culture **8** 853
Egypt, ancient **9** 817, 818; **10** 36, 56
England **12** 612; **19** 60
Greece, ancient **13** 435, 437–8, 571, 572, 575; **21** 321
Indian subcontinent **15** 727, 735
Indonesia **15** 816
Iran, ancient **15** 904, 918
Islamic **16** 363
Japan **17** 100–101, 319, 320
Mesopotamia **21** 293, 303
Nepal **22** *774*, *775*, 789
Nigeria **15** 117
Prehistoric art **8** 339; **25** 524
Rome, ancient **27** 17
Sinú **28** *781*
South America, Pre-Columbian **29** 211–12
Syria-Palestine **30** 183
Tibet **30** 823
Vietnam **6** 428
uses
brass **15** 735
bronze **4** 850, 851, 852, 854; **6** 833, 834, 855, 865; **8** 339; **13** 575; **17** 100, 320; **27** 17
glass **10** 56; **12** 782
gold **12** 865; **28** *781*
iron **7** 99
metalwork **16** 363
lost-wax casting
uses—cont.
musical instruments **15** 816
sculpture **22** *775*
silver **28** 739
Losy (family) **19** 807
Lotario dei Conti di Segni *see* INNOCENT III, Pope
Lote, Stephen **5** 645; **33** 523
Loten, H. Stanley **18** 666; **20** 382
Loth, Johann Carl **2** 794; **19** 706–7*; **32** 194
collaboration **6** 29; **10** 757
patrons and collectors **8** 427; **21** 30
pupils **14** 65; **27** 233; **28** 378; **29** 789; **33** 48
reproductive prints by others **18** 45
teachers **27** 817
works **2** 795; **19** 705, *706*
Loth, Johann Ulrich **19** 705–6*; **22** 302
pupils **19** 706; **25** 672; **29** 400
works **12** 390
Loth, Libia *see* KRUMPPER, LIBIA
Loth, Matthias **22** 302
Loth, Ulrich **18** 480
Loth, Wilhelm **19** 707–8*; **30** 172
Lothair I, Emperor (*reg* 840-55) **5** 800, 802, 803; **20** 330
Lothair II, King of Lotharingia (*reg* 855-69) **5** 811; **12** 255; **19** 709
Lothair III, Holy Roman Emperor (*reg* 1125-37) **19** 708*
architecture **18** 226
Lothair III of Supplinburg *see* LOTHAIR III, Holy Roman Emperor
Lothair Cross **1** 4; **8** 201; **12** 256; **23** 657; **26** 145
Lothair Crystal **3** 812; **9** 155; **11** 737; **12** 255, *256*; **26** 485
Lothair Gospels *see under* GOSPEL BOOKS → individual manuscripts
Lothair Seal **12** 255
Lothal **15** 192, 246, *276*, 408; **19** 708*
figurines **15** 421
Lothar *see* LOTHAIR
Lothar, Eli **30** 20
Lothar Franz, Prince Bishop and Elector of Mainz **4** 890; **33** 65
Lotharingen, Karel Alexander of, Prince **4** 924
Lotharingia **19** 709*
Lotherton Hall (W. Yorks) **24** 62
Lothian, Marquesses of **28** 270
Lothrop, Samuel K. **13** 290, 310; **24** 89; **28** 799; **29** 220, 222; **32** 153, 238
Lotin, François **22** 466
Lotiron, Robert **22** 751
Lotter, Abraham **2** 718
Lotter, Andreas **25** 443
Lotter, Gerhardus **19** 709; **29** 119
Lotter, Hieronymus **19** 110, 843; **33** 113
works **19** *110*
Lotter, Johannes Casparus **19** 709
Lotter, Matthias **19** 709*; **29** 119
Lotter, Melchior **19** 111, 131
Lotter, Michael (1494-1529) **19** 131
Lotter, Michael (*d c.* 1555) **19** 131
Lotter, Willem Godfried **19** 709
Lotti, Cosimo **19** 709–10*
attributions **24** 25
patrons and collectors **33** 579
works **12** 124; **20** 71; **23** 405; **30** 664
Lotti, Lorenzo **19** 710*
collaboration **4** 47
patrons and collectors **16** 770; **31** 825
pupils **4** 47; **22** 15
works **6** 583; **32** 362
Lottino, Dionigi d'Andrea di Bernardo di *see* DIONIGI D'ANDREA DI BERNARDO DI LOTTINO
Lottman, Adam **33** 88
Lotto, Lorenzo **3** 771; **4** 99; **16** 667; **19** 710–15*
attributions **27** 634
collaboration **22** 107; **27** 778
frames **11** 377
intarsia **3** 643, 773; **16** 725; **20** 467; **25** 570
interior decoration **19** 687
methods **21** 758
paintings **2** 2; **11** 36; **16** 470; **19** 689, *711*, *713*; **27** 496
altarpieces **2** 1; **11** 382
frescoes **9** *265*, 266
portraits **2** 162, 558; **14** 869; **19** *711*, *712*; **21** 632; **24** 537; **32** 191
patrons and collectors
Benda, Gustav **3** 703
Benson, R(obert) H(enry) **3** 740
Canino, Lucien Bonaparte, Prince of (1775-1840) **4** 304
Carrara, Giacomo, Conte **5** 872
Charles II, King of England and Scotland (*reg* 1660-85) **26** 283; **29** 804
Herbert, Thomas, 8th Earl of Pembroke **14** 436
Jabach, Everard **16** 815
Julius II, Pope (*reg* 1503-13) **27** 273
Rospigliosi-Pallavicini, Giuseppe **23** 873
Serra, Giovan Francesco, Marqués di Cassano **28** 479
Skippe, John **28** 819
Solly, Edward **29** 46
Tarnowski, Jan Feliks, Count and Waleria **30** 345
Uffelen, Lucas van **31** 526
pupils **3** 644
reproductive prints by others **9** 466
restorations by others **20** 375; **21** 825
teachers **3** 667
Lotto carpets *see under* CARPETS → types
Lott's Bricks Ltd **31** 258
Lotufo, Xenon **4** 714; **23** 118
lotus **19** 716–17*, *717*; **23** 550
Lotus flower and crosslined ware *see under* POTTERY → wares
Lotus International **24** 449
Lotus Jewel **11** 635
Lotus Sutra **17** 729
Lotus tile factory **23** 120
Lotz, Károly **5** 85; **14** 901; **19** 717–18*
collaboration **8** 585; **30** 641
pupils **2** 415; **18** 388, 822
works **14** 315; **28** 118
Lotz, Wolfgang **14** 505; **19** 718*
Lötz-Gerstner, Susanne **19** 718
Lötz Witwe **2** 818; **8** 411; **12** 788; **19** 522, 718–19*
designers **2** 818; **14** 628; **25** 404, 674
production **12** VI3
Lou, Ma **16** 887
Loubchansky, Marcelle **2** 545; **11** 551; **30** 23
Loubières, Jean de *see* JEAN DE LOUBIÈRES
Loubon, Emile **7** 762; **13** 821; **20** 473
Lou Ching *see* LOU JING
Louco (Boaventura da Silva Filho) **22** 441
Loud, Gordon **1** 893; **18** 28; **21** 47
Louda, Jan **8** 381
Loudon, Jane **12** 64
Loudon, John Claudius **7** 744; **19** 719–20*; **24** 179
assistants **18** 667
Loudon, John Claudius—cont.
works **7** 744; **12** 137; **13** 619; **32** 554
writings **2** 758; **6** 166; **10** 298; **12** 64
illustrated **7** 789
Loudun **9** 144; **11** 650
Lough, John Graham **19** 720*; **23** 21
Lough Crew (Co. Meath) **6** 161; **16** *5*; **19** 720–21*; **25** *470*, 508, 510
Lough Cutra Castle (Co. Galway) **16** 10
Lough Erne Shrine **15** 872
Lough Gur (Co. Limerick) **25** 503
Loughnashade **22** 694
Loughrea Cathedral (Co. Galway) **6** 164
Louhisaari Manor House **11** 90
Louis, 2nd Duke of Savoy (*reg* 1434-65) **12** 721; **18** 684; **28** 1
Louis, King of Spain (*reg* 1724) **4** *557*; **14** *793*
Louis, Prince of Taranto and King of Naples (*reg* 1342-55) **23** 506
Louis de Bourbon, Duc d'Orléans *see* ORLÉANS, LOUIS DE BOURBON, Duc d'
Louis I, Count of Provence *see* LOUIS I, Duke of Anjou, King of Naples, Sicily and Jerusalem
Louis I, Duke of Anjou (*reg* 1356-84), titular King of Naples, Sicily and Jerusalem **2** 49, 108–9, 111–13*; **3** 361, 606; **11** 655, 660; **12** 257; **14** 75; **31** 832, *833*, 834
collections **13** 158
enamel **13** 169
gold **13** 863
hardstones **11** 635
manuscript illumination **13** 153
metalwork **2** *112*
tapestries **4** 525; **13** 128, 154; **30** 312
Louis I, Duke of Bourbon (*reg* 1327-41) **4** *543*; **27** 550
Louis I, Emperor *see* LOUIS THE PIOUS, Emperor
Louis I, King of Hungary and Poland (*reg* 1342-82) **2** 110–11*
architecture **32** 614
manuscripts **14** 898
metalwork **13** 161, 162
Louis I, King of Naples *see* LOUIS I, Duke of Anjou, King of Naples, Sicily and Jerusalem
Louis I, Prince of Monaco (*reg* 1662-1701) **21** 830
Louis I de Valois, Duke of Orléans (*reg* 1392-1407) **31** *833*, 841–2*
architecture **14** 74; **26** 43; **31** 832
decorative works **7** 544
paintings **17** 461
sculpture **17** 459
tapestries **3** 362; **30** 313
Louis II, Count of Blois (*reg* 1342-46) **12** 723
Louis II, Count of Flanders (*reg* 1346-84) **14** *413*; **19** 721*
coins **7** 536; **14** 413
decorative works **4** 841
manuscript illumination **13** 154
paintings **3** 552; **5** 207
sculpture **3** 455; **13** 77; **16** 854
Louis II, Count of Provence *see* LOUIS II, Duke of Anjou, King of Naples, Sicily and Jerusalem
Louis II, Duke of Anjou, King of Naples, Sicily and Jerusalem (*reg* 1384-1417) **2** 49, 51, 111, 113*; **20** 755
manuscripts **2** 113; **31** 290
Louis II, Duke of Bourbon (*reg* 1356-1410) **14** 417
Louis II, King of Bohemia and Hungary (*reg* 1516-26) **2** 109; **13** *900*; **16** 866, 867*; **18** 461
architecture **25** 134; **26** 367
Louis III, Duke of Anjou (*reg* 1417-34) **2** 113
Louis VI, King of France (*reg* 1108-37) **11** 147; **27** 558
Louis VII, King of France (*reg* 1137-80) **11** 655
Louis IX, King of France (*reg* 1226-70) **2** 222, 632; **5** 664–5*; **11** 654
altars **1** 697
architecture **5** 663; **13** 42
castles **2** 48
chapels **6** 459; **11** 655; **24** 156; **27** 550, 558
châteaux **32** 581
churches **11** 654; **27** 541
fortifications **1** 483; **5** 726; **17** 505
monasteries **5** 664, 895
towns **1** 483
coins **7** 535
enamel **13** 168
interior decoration **13** 128
jewellery **11** 634; **14** 418
manuscripts **11** 530; **17** 505; **26** 677; **27** 565
paintings **27** 449
stained glass **6** 498; **11** 530; **29** 501, 512
tents **30** 470
Louis XI, King of France (*reg* 1461-83) **28** 268; **31** *833*, 843*
architecture **8** 889; **20** 133
books **5** 213
liturgical objects **1** 5
manuscripts **4** 569; **17** 458; **20** 727
paintings **4** 569; **5** 127; **11** 355; **31** 832
silk **11** 645
tomb **7** 595
Louis XII, King of France (*reg* 1498-1515) **4** *572*; **31** *833*, 846–7*
architecture **4** 155, 780; **6** 504; **8** 889; **12** 656; **19** 230; **24** 116
decorative works **2** 14
manuscripts **3** 614; **4** 76, 570; **19** 726; **20** 744; **27** 247; **31** 413, 834
paintings **1** 766; **4** 569; **7** 462; **11** 660, 661; **19** 185; **24** 471; **31** 846
sculpture **3** 706, 742; **11** 556; **20** 906; **27** 546; **32** 603
Louis XIII, King of France (*reg* 1610-43) **4** 542, *543*, 549*; **6** *443*; **14** 394; **20** 138
architecture **6** 60; **11** 260; **19** 134, 144, 233; **22** 34; **23** 811; **26** 348; **27** 246; **30** 344; **32** 369
art policies **11** 651
books **14** 616
churches **2** 419
coins **7** 537
collections **19** 779; **26** 349
fountains **6** 96
gardens **19** 162
guns **2** 460, *460*, 461
maps **5** 438
paintings **3** 449; **9** 387; **11** 661; **18** 840; **26** 349; **29** 623; **30** 530; **31** 908; **32** 509, 717
mythological **25** 390
portraits **3** 449; **6** 434; **10** 144
religious **18** 837; **26** 348
topographical **11** 357
sculpture **27** 821
tapestries **3** 207, 613; **26** 778, 838
toys **31** 255
Louis XIII style **11** 587*
cabinets (ii) (furniture) **11** *587*
frames **11** *401*, 401–2, *402*, *403*

Louis XIV, King of France (reg 1643-1715) 3 833; 4 542, 543, 549–52*, 550, 557; 8 820; 9 280; 12 828; 19 21; 20 132, 134; 22 465; 26 387
architecture 11 657; 19 59, 264; 24 467
chapels 20 866
churches 20 294; 24 155
fortifications 20 473; 29 750
hospitals 24 163
ice-houses 15 68
military 31 217
palaces 19 212, 262; 20 134–5
Fontainebleau Château 11 260–61
Marly Château 14 460; 20 449
Meudon Château 21 366
Palais du Louvre 3 833; 6 508; 7 665; 23 811; 24 162, 468; 25 861
Saint-Germain-en-Laye Château 20 294; 27 559
Versailles Château 6 60, 508; 11 508, 517; 19 721; 23 811; 29 524; 32 369–70, 372
Vincennes Château 19 264
art policies 1 101; 11 517, 651, 657; 24 169
carpets 11 652
ceramics 24 148
collections 7 561; 11 662; 16 814–15; 22 536; 24 258
competitions 26 842
copies 3 203
costumes 30 660
decorative works 3 633; 8 252; 11 305; 25 70; 28 776
drawings 9 229, 230; 19 730; 28 742
dress 9 277, 280
embroidery 11 648; 16 714
enamel 11 630
engravings 6 518; 9 296; 10 390, 392; 19 16; 25 77; 28 751; 30 746
etchings 25 629
fountains 11 344
furniture 1 110; 4 532; 8 68; 11 588; 12 874; 20 139, 442; 28 298; 30 783; 31 682, 683
gardens 12 105, 121; 19 163; 32 371–2
gems 3 48; 9 12; 11 635; 12 261, 266
glass 11 612
gold 7 565
guns 2 463, 465, 466; 3 752
hardstones 9 28; 11 635; 12 830, 831; 14 171
interior decoration 10 489; 11 574–5, 576; 19 265; 27 263
ivory 11 637; 23 460
jewellery 11 634
lacquer 18 613
manuscripts 17 449
medals 4 807; 6 553; 10 773; 13 681; 26 532
mirrors 21 720
paintings 4 125, 126, 222, 535; 6 433; 8 525; 9 87; 12 664, 677; 19 19, 23, 164, 542; 20 896; 21 496; 22 536; 24 134, 805, 828; 25 326; 26 349; 32 7
allegorical 11 166
animal 8 812
battle 20 489
botanical 26 452; 32 372
cabinet pictures 1 536
decoration 6 437
flower 23 447
genre 31 223
hunting scenes 2 105; 8 811
landscape 9 87, 703
miniatures 24 554
mythological 20 375
portraits 3 449; 5 416; 21 497; 25 635; 26 386
religious 4 807; 19 65; 27 789
Louis XIV, King of France (reg 1643-1715)—cont.
patronage 26 492
prints 20 455; 24 397; 25 631; 28 742
reliefs 31 341
sculpture 4 36; 6 518; 7 562; 12 725; 14 174; 19 76, 95; 25 706; 26 91; 32 369
bronzes 12 577
copies 2 163; 19 213; 32 395
equestrian monuments 3 833; 12 726
garden 7 422; 8 70; 19 95, 225; 25 706; 29 564; 31 408
silk 11 645
silver 3 122; 7 565; 8 68; 11 618; 19 543
sponsorship 8 94
tapestries 1 782; 3 460; 11 48, 641, 642; 12 285, 827, 829, 829; 21 366, 367, 367; 23 512
Louis XIV Revival style 29 307
Louis XIV style 11 356, 575; 19 262, 721–2*; 33 447
cabinets (ii) (furniture) 11 588
commodes 11 589
frames 11 402–4, 403
furniture 11 587–90*
squares (town) 11 517
Louis XV, King of France (reg 1715-74) 4 542, 543, 553–4*; 11 881; 20 135
architecture 11 882–3; 24 121; 32 510
academies 11 518; 24 122
churches 24 165
factories 10 748; 19 56
maisons de plaisance 8 33; 20 131
palaces 7 677; 25 363; 32 369, 370, 373, 374
squares (town) 7 665
braziers 9 398
bronze 11 626
ceramics 6 333
clocks 5 379
collections 10 487
decorative works 28 790
drawings 20 587
education (art) 24 168
engravings 9 469; 11 540
frames 11 407, 410
furniture 5 192, 379; 7 657; 11 626; 17 666; 18 I2; 26 420
gardens 32 372, 373
gems 11 634; 12 262; 13 771
gold 11 620
interior decoration 32 240
medals 9 469; 20 921
metalwork 2 722; 9 399
paintings 4 516–17; 10 478; 22 682; 24 211
allegorical 19 142
animal subjects 8 814; 23 667
battle 18 804
ceiling 11 538
genre 18 693
history 14 585
hunting scenes 2 105; 4 513; 8 811; 19 646
mythological 8 92
portraits 9 302; 22 685
religious 32 670
topographical 23 693; 24 135; 32 331, 332, 684
pastels 19 797
patronage 11 657–8; 26 491
porcelain 6 454; 9 398; 11 609; 28 521; 30 219; 32 582, 583
prints 3 395
productions 12 638
sculpture 1 133, 665; 4 509, 510; 11 335, 705; 19 140, 141, 213; 24 785; 28 462; 31 56; 32 76
silver 3 122; 11 619
tapestries 3 461; 4 514; 22 683; 26 247; 29 424
teachers 10 909
Louis XV style 12 638; 19 722–3*
architecture 11 517; 14 448; 22 454
frames 11 406, 407
interior decoration 19 722
Louis XVI, King of France (reg 1774-92) 4 542, 543, 554*; 11 540; 19 397; 20 135
architecture 7 195, 677; 11 261; 19 91; 24 122, 177; 32 370
art policies 11 658
ceramics 28 521
collections 20 417
decorative works 11 305; 24 176
drawings 14 799
furniture 3 715; 11 595, 627; 12 898; 25 578; 26 376, 530
gardens 25 872; 26 449; 32 372
gems 4 874
guns 2 467
metalwork 13 234
miniatures (paintings) 21 643; 29 255
paintings 4 616; 8 556, 763; 13 641; 19 25, 247; 23 778; 24 584; 26 449; 30 46; 32 430
patronage 26 491
porcelain 11 609; 28 522
pottery 8 763
tapestries 31 373
Louis XVI style 19 724*
architecture 11 518
frames 11 408, 409
furniture 6 I3; 8 235, 235; 19 723
interior decoration 19 723
Louis XVIII, King of France (reg 1814-24) 4 542, 543, 555–6*; 14 482; 21 903
architecture 24 163; 32 370
art policies 24 171
ceramics 10 97
collections 7 374; 10 90
engravings 22 88
furniture 11 598; 29 683
gardens 32 372
glass 3 13
paintings 2 722; 9 209; 12 335; 13 791; 14 657; 19 67, 219
flower 8 445
frescoes 27 58
history 6 519; 12 158; 18 576
literary themes 15 839
miniatures 21 644
portraits 13 793
religious 12 206; 14 482
still-lifes 31 824
watercolours 19 233
porcelain 11 610
prints 8 867
sculpture 27 547; 32 236
sponsorship 11 658
Louis, A. J. 24 824
Louis, Jacob see LOUYS, JACOB
Louis, Johann Jakob 19 781
Louis, Louis-Nicolas see LOUIS, VICTOR
Louis, Morris 19 724–5*; 31 609
dealers 16 820
groups and movements 1 79; 25 361; 32 890, 894
methods 7 631; 25 24
patrons and collectors 1 71
works 1 129, 130; 7 636; 19 725
Louis, Séraphine see SÉRAPHINE
Louis, Victor 19 725–6*; 25 99, 118, 212
attributions 23 509
collaboration 3 844; 5 380; 25 577; 32 879
restorations by others 8 593
works 4 389; 6 509; 11 518; 13 733; 16 52; 19 726; 23 519; 24 120, 176; 25 121, 212; 30 670, 671, 674, 677
Louisa-Henrietta, Electress of Brandenburg (1627-67) 5 347; 19 349
Louisa Maria Gonzaga, Queen of Poland (1611-67) 32 875
Louisa Ulrica, Queen of Sweden (1720-82) 6 473; 14 17, 648, 692*; 30 94
architecture 13 668; 29 691
furniture 3 414; 14 230; 30 94
interior decoration 26 99
paintings 4 516; 14 543; 30 118
sponsorship 26 99
Louis Bonaparte, King of Holland (reg 1806-10) 4 299, 305*
architecture 1 802, 813; 22 828
collections 4 298; 22 903, 906
interior decoration 22 866
paintings 1 808; 13 308; 17 472
sculpture 14 29
Louisbourg 21 573
Louis de Beauvau 20 706, 707
Louis de Châtillon, Count of Blois see LOUIS II, Count of Blois
Louis de Gruuthuse 19 726–7*
books 31 846
manuscripts 3 555, 612, 614; 4 921; 19 350; 20 618; 32 728
works 4 922
Louis de Laval 4 395, 547; 7 597; 22 30
Louis de Luxembourg 20 707
Louis de Mâle, Count of Flanders see LOUIS II, Count of Flanders
Louise, Queen of Spain (1751-1819) 28 593
Louise Elizabeth, Duchess of Parma (1727-59) 7 309; 9 324; 18 853
Louise of Mecklenburg-Strelitz, Queen of Prussia (1776-1810) 28 42
furniture 3 485; 12 426, 427
interior decoration 12 414; 28 97
paintings 5 286; 26 258
Louisiade Archipelago 24 64, 64, 81
Louisiana Museum see under HUMLEBÆK
Louisiana Purchase International Exposition, 1904 see under ST LOUIS (MO)
Louisiana revy 24 451
Lou Island 24 82, 83
Louis Latouche, Henri de 24 883
Louis-Napoleon, Emperor of the French see NAPOLEON III, Emperor of the French
Louis of Anjou, King of Poland see LOUIS II, King of Bohemia and Hungary
Louis-Philippe, King of the French (reg 1830-48) 23 511, 511, 520–21*, 521; 27 319; 28 67
architecture 11 256, 523; 12 746; 19 726; 32 370, 373, 374
censorship 6 175
collections 13 252, 309
drawings 5 439; 11 60
furniture 13 680; 19 130
gardens 24 120
glass 3 13
mausolea 20 868
obelisks 23 330
paintings 3 112; 10 679; 14 489; 16 64, 849; 24 396, 402; 29 535; 30 385
battle 8 641; 18 678; 32 336
genre 26 452
history 8 829; 11 666; 14 482; 16 65; 17 628; 18 867; 20 59, 420; 24 736
landscape 8 864
marine 13 779
miniatures 21 644
mythological 24 736
portraits 14 277; 15 842; 33 256
religious 15 841
prints 7 579
satires 27 871
sculpture 3 313; 7 421; 22 465; 25 418; 27 311
silver 6 535; 11 619
Louis-Philippe, King of the French (reg 1830-48)—cont.
stained glass 28 523
Louis Poulsen-Nyt see LP-NYT
Louis Revival 10 281, 282
Louis the German (reg 876-82) 5 803, 805; 26 85; 33 734
Louis the Great, King of Hungary and Poland see LOUIS I, King of Hungary and Poland
Louis the Pious, Emperor (reg 814-40) 5 779, 797, 810; 7 246; 11 732; 14 100
Louis the Younger 19 697
Louisville (KY) 30 505
J. B. Speed Art Museum 12 229
Jefferson County Court House 18 887
Lou Jing 28 493
Louka Monastery 8 386; 20 856
Loukas the younger 14 776
Loukianos see LUCIAN OF SAMOSATA
Loukopoulos, Clearchos 13 355; 19 727*
Loulan 6 288, 614; 19 727*; 28 719, 720
architecture 6 297
carpets 5 833
forts 6 296
furniture 6 311, 313
lacquer 6 313
paintings 6 776
silk 6 290
stupa 29 867
textiles 3 378; 6 290, 316, 317; 7 46, 53
wood-carvings 6 319
writing-tablets 6 289
Louny 8 377, 422; 18 405
Loup, Jean le see JEAN LE LOUP
Loupot, Charles 25 353
Lourdes 25 490
basilica of Our Lady 28 632
basilica of St Pius X 7 695
Lourdet, Simon 5 836; 11 652; 27 894
Loureiro, Artur José de Sousa 14 307; 19 727–8*
Lourenço, Martim 2 871; 10 664
Loures
Nossa Senhora da Conceição 17 595
Palacio de Correio-Mór 29 841
Quinta dos Arcebispos 2 188
Santo Antão do Tojal 1 680
Lourinhã, Master of 5 775; 19 655; 20 719*; 25 295
louteria 13 538
Louth (Lincs), St James 29 413
Louthe (family) 20 452
Louthe Hours see under BOOKS OF HOURS → individual manuscripts
Louthe Master 20 452
Loutherbourg, Philippe Jacques de 19 728–30*
collaboration 12 640; 33 14
copies 21 170
dealing 14 145
groups and movements 26 740; 29 891
paintings
industrial scenes 18 III2
patrons and collectors 5 733; 8 87, 161; 9 31; 19 98; 20 26; 25 364; 27 350
pupils 4 576; 33 291
reproductive prints by others 2 238; 14 536; 18 720; 20 914; 29 491; 32 621
teachers 5 908
works 2 240; 3 389, 476; 4 601; 10 105; 15 828; 18 713; 19 729; 20 424; 24 18; 30 675, 680
Loutherbourg, Philipp Jakob 19 728

Loutherburg, Johann Rudolf 19 730*
loutrophoroi 13 456, 475, 478, 529; 19 730*
Louvain see LEUVEN
Louvain, Lambert II, Comte de 5 38
Louvain-la-Neuve, Université Catholique de Louvain Medical Faculty Building see under BRUSSELS
Louveciennes Château 4 248; 6 509; 20 131
paintings 10 479; 32 429
Pavillon 22 111; 24 290
Salon en cul-de-four 11 368
Salon Ovale 13 234
sculpture 1 665; 23 795
Louvet, Albert 12 728
Louvier, Antoine Georges 18 884; 19 847
Louviers, Notre-Dame 11 155; 13 60
façade 13 60
sculpture 13 79, 110
tracery 11 154
Louvois, Anne de Souvré, Marquise de 19 731
Louvois, Marquis de 4 550; 6 417; 12 828; 19 730–31*; 20 134, 139, 295
architecture 4 888; 21 366
art policies 11 517
paintings 18 633, 840; 32 738
sculpture 12 726
sponsorship 11 536
tapestries 12 285
Louvre, Musée du see PARIS → Louvre (Musée du Louvre, 1793-)
Louvre Annunciation, Master of the 4 621
Louvre Centauromachy, Painter of the 13 523
Louvre F314, Painter of 32 53
Louvre F6, Painter of 13 508; 32 54
Louvre G433, Painter of 32 65
Louvre MNB1148, Painter of 13 529
Louw, Chrisna 29 117
Louw, Hendrik Jacobus 19 731
Louw, Pieter 6 88
Louw, Wynand Hendrik 19 731; 29 105
Louw & Louw 5 668; 19 731
Louys, Jacob 19 731*
LOV (Labor omnia vincit) 22 868, 876
Lovatelli, Comtesse 18 866, 867
Lovčičky 25 521, 522
Love, Iris C. 18 147, 148
Love, Jim 14 803
Love, Nicholas 25 678
Lovech (Bulgaria) 5 147, 148
Lovek (Cambodia) 5 458, 481
Lovelace, Jacob 7 445
Lovelace, Richard 13 299
Lovell, George H. 29 117
Lovell, James 13 637
Lovell, Lord John 17 611
Lovell, Philip 23 9
Lovell-Smith, Rata 7 211
Løvenøns cup 14 387
Love of Art see KUNSTLIEFDE
Lovera, Francisco 32 173
Lovera, Juan 5 691; 19 731–2*; 32 173, 180
Lovera, Pedro 30 16
Lovere, Gianfrancesco Capoferri di see CAPOFERRI DI LOVERE, GIANFRANCESCO
love-seats 29 8
Lovets 30 772
Lovett, Mildred 2 760
Lovett Pearce, Edward see PEARCE, EDWARD LOVETT
Loveyko, Iosif (Ignat'yevich) 19 732*
Loviisa 11 91, 103
Loving, Alvin 1 444
loving-cups see under CUPS → types
Lovisa, Domenico 19 732*; 33 721
Low, David (Alexander Cecil) 5 758; 19 732–3*
Low, J. and J. G., Art Tile Works 13 715; 30 887
Löw, Johannes 33 46
Low, John Gardner 30 887
Low, Mary Fairchild Macmonnies 20 31
lowboys see under TABLES → types
Low Countries see BELGIUM; NETHERLANDS, THE
Lowder, Rose 10 689
Löwe, Alexander 32 449
Lowe, Allan 2 760
Lowe, Alton 3 62, 63
Lowe, Elias Avery 19 733*
Lowe, Gareth 16 806
Lowe, James 9 390
Lowe, William Drury see DRURY LOWE (HOLDEN), WILLIAM (i)
Loweish & Moorhouse 24 296
Lowell (MA) 21 601; 31 656
Lowell, Guy 19 733*
works 4 475; 22 365
Lowell, John 4 477; 10 90; 12 809
Löwen see LEUVEN
Löwen, Axel von 11 90
Löwenburg Church 13 200
Lowendal, Ulrich-Frédéric 3 645
Lowenfeld, Henry-Michel Hegu de, Baron see HEGU DE LOWENFELD, HENRY-MICHEL, Baron
Lowenfeld, Viktor 31 670
Löwenfinck, Adam Friedrich von 3 429; 14 606; 19 733–4*
Löwenfinck, Christian Wilhelm 19 734
Lowengrund, Margaret 19 492
Löwensprung, Paul 20 641, 728
Löwenstam, Leopold 19 734*
Löwenstern, Baron von 32 676
lower case 31 495
lower crypts see under CRYPTS → types
Lower Kazimierz see KAZIMIERZ DOLNY
Lower Keo Temple see KEO TEMPLE, LOWER
Lowes, Matthew 10 526
Lowestoft (Suffolk) 4 789
Lowestoft porcelain factory 10 308, 309; 19 734*; 20 441
Low Ham 13 211; 27 60
Lowick (Northants), St Peter 1 518; 13 84
Łowicz
Cistercian church 25 115
collegiate church 25 104
Lowie, Robert H. 10 94; 27 47
Lowie, Robert H., Museum of Anthropology see under BERKELEY (CA) → University of California
Lowndes, Mary 29 858
low power microscopy see under TECHNICAL EXAMINATION → types
Lowry, John 7 758
Lowry, L(aurence) S(tephen) 19 734–5*; 20 239, 240; 21 601; 29 426
Lowry-Corry, Armar, 1st Earl of Belmore 16 24
Lowry-Corry, Armar, 2nd Earl of Belmore 16 24, 27
Lowther, James, 1st Earl of Lonsdale 3 74
Lowther, John 30 278; 33 177
Lowther, William, 1st Earl of Lonsdale 19 735*
Lowther, William, 3rd Baronet of Marske 19 735*
Lowther Castle (Cumbria) 28 874
Lowther Cross (Northumb.) 2 69
Low Tiles 4 482
low-warp looms see under LOOMS → types
Loxin, Jamet 16 898
Loy, Hans 20 796
Loyalty Islands 23 17, 18
Lo-yang see LUOYANG
Loyd, Samuel Jones, 1st Baron Overstone 3 239; 19 735–6*; 32 377
Loyd-Lindsay, Harriet, Baroness Wantage 19 736
Loyd-Lindsay, Robert, 1st Baron Wantage 19 736
Loyer, Toussaint 29 93
Loyet, Gerard 19 736*
patrons and collectors 3 596; 5 213; 13 159; 26 147
works 5 213
Loyola 19 736*; 29 259
Sanctuary of St Ignatius Loyola 19 736
Loyola, Ignatius, Saint see IGNATIUS LOYOLA, SAINT
Loypeau, Etienne 20 719
Loys, Jacob see LOIS, JACOB
Loys, Jean-Louis de 18 873
Loys van Bodeghem 4 869; 13 905
works 4 869
Loza, Luis López see LÓPEZ LOZA, LUIS
Lozano, David 24 509
Lozano, Francesc de Paula del Villar i see VILLAR I LOZANO, FRANCESC DE PAULA DEL
Lozano, Jose Honorato 24 622
works 24 621
Lozano, Manuel Rodríguez see RODRÍGUEZ LOZANO, MANUEL
Lozano, Pedro 6 596
Lozano Sanchis, Francisco 31 816
Loża Wolnomalarska see FREEPAINTERS' LODGE
Loża Wolnomularska see FREEMASONS' LODGE
Lozi 1 296; 33 602
Lozingot, Serge 19 491; 20 608
Łoziński, Jerzy 25 143
Lozowick, Louis 1 772; 17 578; 19 492; 20 604, 605; 25 461
Lozza, Raúl 2 400, 604; 24 386
Lozza, Rembrandt 24 386
LP-Nyt 14 392
LSD 25 681
Ltjashen 2 423; 6 479; 19 736–7*; 25 471
Lu, Duke of 25 818
Lua 30 571
Luacchagira 8 767
Luanda 1 401
architecture 2 85; 25 294
Igreja de Jesus 2 85
Museu Nacional de Antropologia 2 87
Nossa Senhora da Nazaré 2 85
Nossa Senhora do Carmo 2 85
Nossa Senhora dos Remédios 2 85
trade 1 249
Luangiua 25 181
bark 25 182
sculpture 25 182
tattoos 25 182
weaving 25 182
Luang Prabang 18 761; 19 737, 737–8*; 29 225
houses 18 767
National Museum 18 764, 766–7, 769, 770, 777; 23 823
Royal Palace see National Museum
textiles 18 771
That Mak Mo 18 768, 776
Vat Mai 18 764, 765, 766, 766, 769, 777
Vat Pa Hwak 18 770
Vat Pa Ke 9 163; 18 766, 769, 770
Luang Prabang—cont.
Vat Pa Khan 18 769
Vat Phan Luong 18 766
Vat Sen 18 777
Vat Visun 18 762, 764, 765, 768
sculpture 18 769
Vat Xieng Thong 18 764, 765, 765, 766, 768
Chapel of the Royal Funerary Chariot 18 769
mosaics 18 770
paintings 18 770
sculpture 18 770
Wat Nang 9 163
Luano see LUGANO
Luarasi, Skënder (Kristo) 1 539
Luba 14 375; 19 738–44*; 29 68
architecture 1 406
axes 19 740*
baskets 19 741*
beads 1 325
cups 19 741*
divination instruments 1 357; 19 742, 742–3*
drums (musical instruments) 19 741*
emblems 19 741–2*
fibres 1 355
gesture 1 266
headrests 19 743*, 744
iconography 19 738–9*
leather 1 355
masks 1 405; 19 742
musical instruments 19 744
pendants (jewellery) 1 350; 19 743–4*
regalia 1 354, 355
sculpture 1 323, 324, 325, 403; 19 742, 742–3*, 743
spears 19 740*
staffs 1 354, 355; 19 740*
stands 19 740–41
stools 19 740*, 740
tools 1 364
women 19 739*
wood 1 325, 355; 19 740, 742, 743, 744
wood-carvings 14 378
Luba (Eastern) 1 403
Luba(-Hemba) 1 405, 406
staffs 1 402
Luba (Kasai) 1 360, 403
Luba(-Shaba) 29 70
Luba (Shankadi) 1 403
Luba (Upemba) 1 403
Lubaantún 21 256
Lubaki, Albert 33 596
Lubalin, Herb 4 369
Lu Ban 7 113
Luban, Milch Chemical Factory 10 697; 21 780; 25 69
Lu Ban Hap 5 483
Lubańska, Zofia see STRYJEŃSKA, ZOFIA
Lubarda, Petar 19 745*; 22 18; 28 451
Lubartów Church 25 98
Lübben, Eilhard 13 630, 631
Lubbock, J. G. 10 561
Lubbock, John 2 299
Lübeck 12 360; 19 745–6*
altarpieces 8 730; 13 120
amber 1 761
architecture 32 282
Burgtor 4 777
Cathedral 23 254; 27 125
bells 26 686
brasses 4 693, 693
crucifix 8 214; 25 176
metalwork 13 161
sculpture 12 403; 13 118
tomb of Heinrich of Bokholt 13 160
chapel of the Heilig-Geist-Spital 14 780
coins 7 536
cupboards 12 423
embroidery 10 181; 12 462
flagons 12 444
Lübeck—cont.
glass 16 520
guilds 24 579
Holsteintor 29 414
Holstentor 4 777, 777
houses 4 777
Jakobikirche 14 81
Marienkirche 4 777; 12 365; 13 49, 56, 161, 186; 14 81; 19 745, 746*; 23 255–6; 32 93
Hutterock brass 4 693
metalwork 25 129
Museum Behnhaus 19 746; 26 98
painting 12 384, 385; 13 151
pewter 12 452
Rathaus 13 161; 19 746; 31 238
paintings 33 209
war cabinet room 10 662; 12 409
St Annen-Kloster see Rathaus
Sankt-Annen-Museum 19 746
sculpture 13 85, 118
silver 12 443
stained glass 13 186, 187
tapestries 12 468
warehouses 32 861
wood-carvings 11 98
Lübeck Bible see under BIBLES → individual manuscripts
Lübeck Bible, Master of the 20 719*
Lübeck Briefkapelle, Master of the 20 186
Lubeke, Johan 22 870
Lubennikov, Ivan Leonidovich 18 569
Lü Benzhong 25 72
Lubersac, Marquis de 23 795
Luberti Augustini factory 9 298
Lubetkin, Berthold 19 746–7*
collaboration 12 652
groups and movements 10 241; 20 475; 30 411
staff 8 256
works 19 747
Lubiąż Abbey 19 747–8*; 25 92, 101, 110
Abbot's Palace 19 748, 748
Lubieniecki, Krzysztof 19 749*
Lubieniecki, Teodor (Bogdan) 19 748, 749*
Łubieński, Kazimierz 25 135
Lubieński, Władysław 30 213
Lubin, Jacques 9 718
Lubiniecki, Christoffel 25 822
Lubinski, Rudolf 19 749*; 25 12; 33 593
Lubinus, Eilhard see LÜBBEN, EILHARD
Lübke, Wilhelm 14 80; 19 749*; 24 423
lubki see under PRINTS → types
Lublin 9 507; 19 750*; 25 92, 135
architecture 25 97, 98, 99
bronze 25 129
Castle 3 528; 19 750; 31 557
Dominican church 25 105
furniture 25 119
metalwork 25 126
synagogue 17 545
Lublinský, Martin Antonín 8 391
lubok see LUBKI
Lubomirska, Aleksandra 25 364
Lubomirska, Elżbieta 33 722
Lubomirska, Isabella 25 136, 138
Lubomirski (family) 12 34; 25 97, 121, 135, 137
Lubomirski, Andrzej 25 138
Lubomirski, Henryk 19 751, 752*; 25 136
Lubomirski, Izabella 19 751
Lubomirski, Jerzy 19 751; 25 136
Lubomirski, Sebastian 19 751
Lubomirski, Stanisław 19 751*
architecture 18 693; 25 135; 32 870; 33 259
interior decoration 10 768

Lubomirski, Stanisław Herakliusz 19 751, 752*; 32 875
architecture 25 135; 32 880
Lubortow 31 718
Lubumbashi 1 *401*; 29 69
Académie des Arts 1 431
Académie des Beaux-Arts 1 431
Le Hangar 33 596
Léopold II Museum *see* Musée National
Musée National 29 764; 33 598
Lubynski, Rudolf *see* LUBINSKI, RUDOLF
Luc, Comte de 19 261
Luc, Frère *see* FRANÇOIS, CLAUDE
Luca, Giulio De *see* DE LUCA, GIULIO
Luca da San Colombano 22 799
Luca di Borgo *see* PACIOLI, LUCA
Luca di Firenze 31 905
Luca di Giovanni da Siena 19 752–3*
Luca di Randazzo, Ruggero de *see* RUGGERO DE LUCA DI RANDAZZO
Luca di Tommè 19 753–4*
collaboration 7 329, 330; 23 95
works 19 *753*; 28 686
Lucae, Richard 19 754–5*
assistants 19 327; 32 801
pupils 14 631; 20 386
works 3 794; 11 734; 14 594
Lucan, Richard Bingham, 2nd Earl of *see* BINGHAM, RICHARD, 2nd Earl of Lucan
Lucano 13 817
Lucardi, M. 22 891
Lucas, Bill 30 160; 31 792
Lucas, Charles Thomas 19 574
Lucas, Colin Anderson 7 712–13; 31 673
Lucas, David 7 755; 21 417; 25 600, 627; 26 232
works 21 *417*
Lucas, Diogo Castro *see* CASTRO LUCAS, DIOGO
Lucas, Fielding 14 536; 19 755
Lucas, Francisco (*fl* 1577) 28 307
Lucas, François (1736-1813) 5 528; 17 466; 19 755*
Lucas, Geoffrey 18 690
Lucas, George A(loysius) 2 858; 19 755–6*
Lucas, G. T. 32 866
Lucas, John Robert 4 824
Lucas, Lloyd & Co. 7 712
Lucas, Louis Désiré 32 415
Lucas, Paul 10 79, 82
Lucas, Pierre 19 755
Lucas, Richard Cockle 4 209
Lucas, Ruth 30 160
Lucas, Samuel 11 785
Lucas, Seymour 30 680
Lucas, Thomas 19 574
Lucas, W. 24 777
Lucas de Burgos 14 609
Lucas de Montigny, Jean-Robert-Nicolas 19 756*
Lucas & Niemeyer 13 898; 14 484
Lucas (y) Padilla, Eugenio *see* LUCAS VELÁZQUEZ, EUGENIO
Lucassen, Reinier 3 565; 19 756*; 22 853
Lucas (Huyghz.) van Leyden 10 384, 386; 13 28; 16 832; 19 756–62*
attributions 1 167; 23 883
catalogues 3 310; 6 78
methods 31 578
patrons and collectors 14 682
Alexander II, Emperor of Russia (*reg* 1855-81) 26 734
Arenberg, Engelbert-Marie, 9th Duke of 2 382
Becker, Herman (*c.* 1617-78) 3 475
Gondi, Bartolomeo 12 897
Herbert, Thomas, 8th Earl of Pembroke 14 436
Lucas (Huyghz.) van Leyden
patrons and collectors—cont.
Imhoff, Willibald 15 145
Marolles, Michel de 20 455
Nys, Daniel 23 326
Rudolf II, Holy Roman Emperor (*reg* 1576- 1612) 22 272
Ryerson, Martin A(ntoine) 27 463
Schrieck, Otto Marseus van 28 169
Snyders, Frans 28 904
Stedelijk Museum de Lakenhal (Leiden) 22 906
Tallard, Marie-Joseph d'Hostun, Duc de 30 274
Verstolk van Soelen, Jan Gijsbert, Baron 32 377
Wicar, Jean-Baptiste (-Joseph) 33 154
prints 6 76; 26 162
reproductive prints by others 9 79; 11 794; 13 222; 14 709; 17 599; 22 272, 723; 28 80
teachers 10 216; 16 832; 18 520; 19 101; 22 836
works 1 782; 9 221; 10 549; 11 441; 12 288, 912; 16 614; 19 101, *757*, *758*, *760*, *761*; 25 604, 605, 618; 27 256, 257; 33 355
Lucas Velázquez, Eugenio 13 252; 19 762–3*; 20 67; 29 284
works 19 *763*
Lucas Villamil, Eugenio 19 762
Lucas Villamil, Julián 19 762
Lucasz., Jan 14 291
Lucatelli, Gioran Petro 6 97
Lucatelli, Pietro 11 24
Lucayan 3 61
Lucayo 3 58
Lucca 16 *620*; 19 762–6*, *764*; 31 709
academy 1 104
art forms and materials
coins 7 535
furniture 16 727
glass 16 740
lacquer 18 614
manuscripts 16 655
sculpture 16 691–2*; 26 623
silk 12 284; 16 752; 19 765*; 28 716
tiles 30 886
velvet 16 753
wrought iron 16 744
Biblioteca Statale di Lucca 20 494
Cathedral of S Martino 13 65, 813; 16 625; 19 765–6*, *766*
capitals 26 623
crucifix 8 213
façade 2 290
Labyrinth 18 584
rood 27 124
sculpture 16 692; 26 624
tomb of Ilaria del Carretto 16 840, *841*; 27 829; 31 121
tomb of Pietro da Noceto 7 *367*
Museo e Pinacoteca Nazionale 19 765
Museo Nazionale di Villa Guinigi 19 765
Palazzo Mansi 29 32
Palazzo Micheletti 23 836
Palazzo Pubblico 30 527
S Frediano 2 723, 724
font 26 619
fountain 26 *623*
sculpture 26 623
Trenta Chapel 16 841–2
S Michele in Foro 16 625; 26 624
S Salvatore 26 623
Villa Gattajola 23 126
walls 19 764
Lucca, Fernando da 19 497
Lucca, Maria Luisa, Duchessa di *see* MARIA LUISA, Queen of Etruria
Lucca, Nanni da *see* NANNI DA LUCCA
Lucca di Piero 32 366
Lucca *Madonna* 23 470
Lucca manuscript *see* COMPOSITIONES VARIAE
Lucchese *see* LUCHESE
Lucchese, il (1606-75) *see* RICCHI, PIETRO
Lucchese, il (1638-1709) *see* FRANCHI, ANTONIO (i)
Lucchesi, Matteo 24 841
Lucchesi, Urbano 5 378
Lucchi, Giuseppe Antonio 31 72
Lucchini, Patrick 2 447
Lucchino, Lord of Milan (*reg* 1339-49) 24 193
Luccichenti, Amedeo 22 77
Luce 5 364
Luce, Clarence Sumner 19 766*
Luce, Gordon (Hannington) 5 237; 19 766–7*; 29 241
Luce, Henry 4 586
Luce, Maximilien 19 767–8*
dealers 19 10
groups and movements 22 745
works 13 323; 15 828; 19 489, 490, *767*
Lucebert 7 489; 19 768*; 22 852, 854
Lucena, Hospital de S Juan de Dios 14 782
Lucena, Víctor 19 768*; 32 176
Lučenec 28 856
Lucenti, Ambrogio 19 768
Lucenti, Girolamo 1 631; 14 105; 19 768*
Luceram Church 11 615
Lucerne 19 769*
art market 30 153
Central Library 11 770
ceramics 30 143
chronicles 7 244
E. Kofler-Truniger Collection 22 203
Galerie Fischer 30 153
glass 30 145
Hofkirche 30 131, 136
Jesuitenkirche 30 132
Kunstgewerbeschule 30 156
Lion of Lucerne 22 47
painting 30 135
Picasso-Sammlung 30 153
Ritter'scher Palast 30 126
Spreuerbrücke 30 131
stage design 30 653
Weinmarkt 30 665
Lucerne Chronicle (Lucerne, Zentbib., fol. S.23) 30 130
Lucha 31 719
Lu Chai 6 543
Lu Chao-lin *see* LU ZHAOLIN
Luchese (family) 12 370
Luchese, Alberto 19 769
Luchese, Bartolomeo 29 838
Luchese, Carlo Domenico 29 838
Luchese, Giovanni 2 780; 4 58; 15 866; 19 769*
Luchese, Philiberto 19 770*; 30 454
assistants 30 454
patrons and collectors 10 529; 13 919; 14 893; 32 456
works 2 781, 782; 14 886; 18 467; 30 455
Lu Chi (261-303) *see* LU JI
Lü Chi (*c.* 1420-1504) *see* LÜ JI
Luchi, Giuseppe Antonio 23 173
Luchian, Ştefan 19 770*; 26 715
patrons and collectors 26 723
works 26 *715*
Lu Ch'ien *see* LU QIAN
Lu-chien, King *see* LUJIAN, KING
Lu Chih *see* LU ZHI
Luchini, Domenico 26 317
Luchino, Vincenzo 26 806
Luchino di Giovanni Belbello *see* BELBELLO DA PAVIA
Luchizm see RAYISM
Luchsperger, Lorenz 2 800; 19 770–71*; 33 164
Luciani, Sebastiano *see* SEBASTIANO DEL PIOMBO
Lucian of Samosata 14 870; 19 771–2*; 26 925; 27 28
works 2 518; 13 808; 27 18, 27; 31 768
Lucier, Alvin 29 98
Lucile 9 291
Lucillus 27 53
Lucini, Antonio Francesco 19 772*
Lucini, Francesco Teodoro Arese 23 829
Lucini, Girolamo *see* LUCENTI, GIROLAMO
Lucite 25 23
Lucius 27 52
Lucius, Jakob, I (*c.* 1530-1597) 19 772*
Lucius, Jakob, II (*d* 1616) 19 772
Lucius Munmius 32 539
Lück, Carl Gottlieb 11 731; 14 606
Luck, Isaac 23 54
Lück, Johann Friedrich 11 731; 14 606
Luck, Johann Jacob 4 746
Lücke, Carl August, I (*fl* 1688) 19 772
Lücke, Carl August, II (*c.* 1703-80) 19 772, 773*
Lücke, Christian Gottlob 19 772
Lücke, Ernst Friedrich 19 772
Lücke, Johann Christian Ludwig (von) 12 460; 19 772–3*
pupils 31 342
works 29 574
Lücke, Johann Friedrich, I (*fl* 1720-38) 19 772
Lücke, Johann Friedrich, II (1729-97) 19 772; 33 280
Lücke, Karl Gottlieb 19 772; 33 280
Luckenbooth brooches *see under* BROOCHES → types
Luckhardt, Hans 3 795; 19 168, 773*; 26 405
Luckhardt, Wassili 3 795; 12 380; 19 168, 773*; 26 405
Luckman, Charles, & Associates 4 475
Lucknow 15 *261*, 588, 592, 593; 19 774–5*
architecture 15 376–8
Bara Imambara 15 376
Baoli Palace 15 376
Rumi Darvaza 7 361; 15 376, *377*
Turkish Gate *see* Rumi Darvaza
carpets 15 684
Chattar Manzils 15 377, *378*
Chaulakhi Palace 15 377
cikan 15 676
congregational mosque 15 377
Constantia 15 377, 402; 19 *774*
Daulat Khana 15 376
embroidery 15 675
enamel 15 712
Farhad Baksh 15 376
Great Imambara *see* Bara Imambara
houses 15 376–7
Kaiserbagh Palace 15 181
La Martinière *see* Constantia
Machchi Bhavan 15 376
Martinière, La *see* Constantia
metalwork 15 713, 714, 724; 21 330
models 15 724
paintings 15 654–5*
Sikandar Bagh 15 377
State Museum 15 181; 19 775
weapons 15 678
Lúčky 28 851
Lúčky, Master of 28 851
Lucky Bean Farm 29 117
Luco de Jiloca 29 337
Luçon Cathedral 13 211
Luçon Master 20 719*
Lucotte 31 256
Lucotte, J. R. 11 620
Lucretia Master 25 20
Lucretius 10 657
Lucrezia Borgia, Duchess of Ferrara (1480-1519) 4 409, 411*; 10 *518*
paintings 20 904, 905; 24 342
paxes 11 699
Lucullus(, Lucius Licinius)
architecture 22 469, 475; 26 856
paintings 24 283
sculpture 2 416; 4 112; 13 469; 17 735; 27 29
Lucullus, M(arcus) 4 112
Lucumi 33 553
Lucus Feroniae
Temple of Feronia 27 6
Villa of Volusii 27 61
Lucy, Charles 10 887; 19 775*
Lucy, George Hammond *see* HAMMOND LUCY, GEORGE
Lucy, Thomas 18 795
Luda, William de *see* WILLIAM DE LUDA
Lü Dalin 6 867; 7 158
Lüdecke, Carl 18 741
Ludegar, Abbot of Altzella 11 749
Luder, Jan 20 923
Luder, Josef 7 471
Ludhiana 15 665
Lüdicke, Carl Friedrich 30 884
Lüdinghausen, St Felizitas 9 680
Ludius 9 185; 18 701; 25 44; 26 862; 27 52
Ludlow, Edmund 33 10
Ludlow Castle (Salop) 6 53; 12 173
Ludolf, Duke of Swabia (*reg* 949-54) 7 904; 29 873, 875
Ludolphus of Saxony 4 145
Ludorf, Henry J. 14 850
Ludovica 28 677
Ludovice, António 20 85
Ludovice, João Frederico 12 54; 19 775–7*
assistants 23 757
collaboration 18 782, 783; 23 405, 757
patrons and collectors 4 635, 636
pupils 19 524
works 10 663; 19 *776*; 20 85, *85*; 23 757; 25 292, 313, 317; 32 422
Ludovice, João Pedro 19 777
Ludovico (Maria), 7th Duke of Milan (*reg* 1494-99) 10 *518*; 28 529, 531–2*
architecture 3 236; 4 645, 646; 16 630, 778; 19 194; 21 517; 27 736; 29 23, 24
decorative works 31 432
gems 16 751
gold 5 696
hardstones 16 746
jewellery 5 697
manuscripts 4 76; 20 618
paintings 4 643; 19 183; 20 741; 25 466; 26 187; 31 432
sculpture 10 522; 16 694; 25 158; 29 24
urban planning 5 701
Ludovico II, 2nd Marchese of Mantua (*reg* 1444-78) 12 903, *904*, 905–6*; 24 861; 29 568
architecture 1 556, 564; 10 784; 11 204; 16 630; 20 319; 21 466
manuscript illumination 13 833
medals 20 322
paintings 3 99; 6 14; 12 905; 16 661; 20 309, 310
sculpture 9 130
tapestries 5 46
Ludovico, Lancillotto di *see* LANCILLOTTO DI LUDOVICO

Ludovico, Maestro 32 200
Ludovico d'Angulo 2 650
Ludovico de Castellani 11 4
Ludovico il Moro see LUDOVICO (MARIA), 7th Duke of Milan
Ludovisi (family)
architecture 26 748
collections 26 773; 27 46, 114
decorative works 3 744
paintings 27 623; 30 41
sculpture 2 168; 13 470; 23 353; 27 42
Ludovisi, Alessandro see GREGORY XV, Pope
Ludovisi, Ignazio Boncompagni 4 312
Ludovisi, Ludovico, Cardinal 19 778, 779*; 26 758
architecture 1 628; 13 321
collections 26 847
crucifixes 1 625
gardens 11 741
paintings 19 778; 26 307; 32 509
sculpture 1 626; 4 406; 6 360; 29 562
Ludovisi, Niccolò 22 21; 29 352
Ludovisi, Ugo Boncampagni, Prince of Piombino see PIOMBINO, UGO BONCAMPAGNI LUDOVISI, Prince of
Ludovisi Gaul group 2 169; 24 414, 414
Ludovisi Herakles 1 450
Ludovisi Hermaphrodite 21 27
Ludovisi Mars 2 169; 3 830
Ludovisi Throne 13 451, 452, 470; 19 544
Ludwig I, Duke of Bavaria (reg 1183-1231) 18 723
Ludwig I, Grand Duke of Hesse (reg 1806-30) 2 319; 21 821; 29 516
Ludwig I, King of Bavaria (reg 1825-48) 8 897; 15 144; 33 273, 281–3*
architecture 9 25; 11 128; 12 167, 168; 13 202, 610; 14 87; 18 122, 123, 125; 22 300, 308; 25 193; 32 555, 683; 33 673
museums 22 362, 363
collections 10 93; 12 474, 475; 27 115
dealing 9 690
drawings 8 898
paintings 1 141; 2 30; 4 242; 7 871; 8 503; 10 446; 12 393; 14 586; 17 855; 18 176; 22 303; 27 231–2; 29 658, 776
encaustic 10 199
murals 22 328
wall 28 136
pottery 13 542
sculpture 3 155; 13 470; 14 87; 22 272; 28 184, 186; 30 137; 32 759; 33 160
allegorical 26 23
busts 7 211; 12 406; 28 44; 30 854; 33 296
monuments 26 378
mythological 5 629, 631; 30 764
stained glass 29 506
Ludwig II, Duke of Upper Bavaria and Count Palatine of the Rhine (reg 1253-94) 22 297; 33 272
Ludwig II, King of Bavaria (reg 1864-86) 22 306; 33 273, 281, 283*
architecture 5 340; 6 62; 9 80; 12 376; 13 209, 705; 23 546; 32 684
embroidery 12 463
interior decoration 12 416
objects of vertu 22 306
paintings 3 702; 5 342
sculpture 32 758; 33 726
stucco 29 843
Ludwig III, Grand Duke of Hesse (reg 1848-77) 3 475
Ludwig III, Landgrave of Thuringia (reg 1172-90) 32 882
Ludwig IV, Count of Württemberg (reg 1419-50) 4 187
Ludwig IV, Duke of Bavaria (reg 1294-1347) and Holy Roman Emperor (reg 1314-1347) 22 298; 33 270–72*, 272
Ludwig IV, Elector Palatine (reg 1410-36) 33 272
Ludwig V, Elector Palatine (reg 1436-49) 14 305; 19 29
Ludwig VI, Duke of Württemberg (reg 1568-93) 3 491; 20 858; 31 311; 33 429, 711
Ludwig VI, Elector Palatine (reg 1508-44) 4 760
Ludwig VII, Count Palatine of the Rhine (1576-83) 1 788
Ludwig VII, Duke of Bavaria-Ingolstadt (reg 1413-43) 31 841
Ludwig VIII, Landgrave of Hesse-Darmstadt (reg 1739-68) 28 351
Ludwig IX, Landgrave of Hesse (1768-90) 32 767
Ludwig X, Duke of Bavaria-Landshut (reg 1516-45) 1 170; 3 507, 507; 14 451; 18 724; 26 76; 33 85
Ludwig X, Landgrave of Hesse-Darmstadt see LUDWIG I, Grand Duke of Hesse
Ludwig, Bernhard 2 814; 32 448
Ludwig, Carl 7 251
Ludwig, Irene 7 585
Ludwig, Johann Friedrich see LUDOVICE, JOÃO FREDERICO
Ludwig, Peter (Ernst Rudolf Georg) 5 354; 7 585; 12 474; 19 779*
Ludwig der Springer, Landgrave of Thuringia (fl 11th cent.) 32 882
Ludwigsburg 12 361, 471; 19 779–81*; 31 719
faience (ii) (ceramics) 12 430
Monrepos 13 200, 200
porcelain 19 780–81*
Schloss 5 349; 12 372, 412; 19 779, 780, 780; 26 495; 33 429
Opera House 33 429
paintings 24 277
stucco 12 404
urban planning 12 368, 372
Ludwigsburg porcelain manufactory 3 899; 12 433, 435; 26 498; 29 73; 33 429
Ludwigshaven 31 724
Ludwig the Bavarian, Holy Roman Emperor see LUDWIG IV, Duke of Bavaria and Holy Roman Emperor
Ludwig the Bearded, Duke of Bavaria see LUDWIG VII, Duke of Bavaria
Ludwig the Severe see LUDWIG II, Duke of Bavaria and Count Palatine of the Rhine
Ludwig-William, Margrave of Baden-Baden (reg 1677-1707) 26 547; 27 196
Lueg, Konrad 12 397; 26 355
Luese, Kamba 33 596
Lü Fengzi 28 553
Lufft, Hans 4 864; 8 120; 20 791
Lufi, Anton (Mati) 1 539; 19 781*
Lufrio, Juan Bautista 27 819
Luft (family) 30 311
Lufthansa 12 480
Lufwa 33 598
Lugagnano, Raffaello Rossi da see ROSSI DA LUGAGNANO, RAFFAELLO
Lugano 19 781–5*; 30 124
Banca del Gottardo 30 129
Cathedral of S Lorenzo 30 126
Crédit Suisse 30 152
Lugano—cont.
Museo Civico di Belle Arti 19 782
S Maria degli Angioli 19 784–5; 30 131
Swiss Volksbank 30 152
Villa Ciani see Museo Civico di Belle Arti
Lugano, Petrus Italus da see PETRUS ITALUS DA LUGANO
Lugano, Tommaso da see LOMBARDO, TOMMASO
Lugar, Robert 28 288, 758; 32 554, 784
Lugardon, Jean Léonard 21 485
Lugardon, Léonard 21 135
Lugato, Pietro 7 862
Lugau, Meinert Mill 10 748
Lugdunum see under LYON
Lugdunum Convenarum see SAINT-BERTRAND-DE-COMMINGES
Lugeon, Raphael 18 875
Luginbühl, Bernhard 3 824; 9 121; 19 782*; 30 140, 924
Lugné-Poe, Aurélien-François 4 325; 22 422; 30 682, 685; 32 739
Lugo 29 292
Cathedral of S María 29 263, 271, 341
choir-stalls 29 292
Hospital Real 29 341
S Martín Pinario 29 341
Lugo, Emil 28 104
Lugo, Genaro 25 455
Lugo Albarracín, Pedro de 7 607
Lugossy, László fe 14 902
Lugossy, Maria 15 5; 20 926
Lugt, Frits (Johannes) 19 782–3*
pupils 1 722
works 4 24; 6 81; 9 229; 10 212; 20 446; 22 910; 25 664
illustrated 6 77
Lugt, Gerrit van der 22 874
Lugt Collection see under PARIS → Institut Néerlandais
Luhillier, Alberto Ruz 23 838
Luhn, Joachim 12 390; 19 783*
Luhrs, Jorge 6 594
Lu Hsiu-ching see LU XIUJING
Lu Hsün see LU XUN
Luick see LÜCKE
Luidl, Gabriel 22 302; 29 760
Luik see LIÈGE
Luika Niembo 14 377
Luini, Aurelio 19 784; 31 746
Luini, Bernardino 19 783–6*; 21 525; 30 131
attributions 7 303; 29 26
methods 6 470
patrons and collectors
Benson, R(obert) H(enry) 3 740
Borromeo, Federico, Cardinal 4 426; 16 771
Borromeo, Vitaliano VI, Conte (1620-90) 4 427
Canino, Lucien Bonaparte, Prince of (1775-1840) 4 304
Carr, William Holwell 5 848
Monti, Cesare, Archbishop of Milan 22 26
Poldi Pezzoli, Gian Giacomo 25 144
Proby, William, 5th Earl of Carysfort 25 639
Sanfré, Alexandre de Sousa Holstein, Conde de 29 100
Settala, Manfredo 28 496
Valenti Gonzaga, Silvio, Cardinal 12 914
works 19 191, 781, 785; 21 534; 30 125
Luini, Giuseppe Antonio 30 125
Luis 13 192
Luis, Fernando 25 209
Luís, King of Portugal (reg 1861-89) 3 361; 4 631; 29 343
Luís, Salvador 26 52
Luiseno see MISSION
Lui Shou-kwan 7 208; 14 722; 19 786*, 866; 33 323
Luisiana, La see LA LUISIANA
Luisinich, Mateo 26 252
Luís João di Portogallo 25 295
Luiz, Washington 9 335
Luján, Emiliano 4 265
Lujan, Marina 22 595
Luján Pérez, José 29 294
Lu Ji (AD 261-303) 7 114
Lü Ji 6 801; 19 786–7*; 33 657
works 6 801
Lujian, King (d 1568) 6 732
Luk 30 806, 812
Luk, George 28 919
Lukács, György 1 183; 10 108; 20 527; 24 440; 28 926
Lukacs, Kato 14 910
Lukange, W. 31 528
Lukasbrüder 22 426, 703–4; 24 588; 26 738; 32 444
collections 26 406
members 14 488; 23 410, 675; 28 46
works 24 587
see also NAZARENES
Lukasbund 2 796; 24 588; 32 677; 33 255
see also NAZARENES
Luka Vrublets'ka 31 545
Luke, Saint 19 787–9*; 28 449
works 9 622; 19 788; 22 228
Luke, Alexandra 23 791
Luke Master 26 667
Lukić, Živojin 28 453
Lukin, Mikhail 27 436
Lukin, William 10 330
Lukini, Giovanni F. 29 555
Lukke see LÜCKE
Lukomsky, Georgy (Kreskent'yevich) 12 875; 19 789*; 22 506; 27 444
Lukovit 30 772
Luks, George (Benjamin) 14 393; 19 789*; 31 605
groups and movements 2 596, 597; 10 108; 12 769; 23 47
patrons and collectors 24 638
pupils 27 212
works 7 648; 21 897; 31 605
Luksch, Richard 2 803; 14 785; 20 152; 28 344
Luksch-Makovsky, Yelena (Konstantinovna) see MAKOVSKAYA-LUKSH, YELENA (KONSTANTINOVNA)
Lukutin (family) 24 62; 27 427
Lukwakongo
masks 19 73
Lula 1 403
Lula, Henryk 25 123
Lula, Johannes 28 649
Luleburgaz
complex of Sokollu 16 224
mosque of Sokollu Mehmed Pasha 16 222
Lulier, Claude 3 873; 4 755
Lullin, Aimé 4 162
Lullingstone (Kent) 9 510
chapel 9 535
villa 10 226; 26 861
Lullington (E. Sussex), All Saints 26 616
Lullubi 15 916
Lully, Jean-Baptiste 20 458; 30 671, 672
Lu'lu' see BADR AL-DIN LU'LU'
Lulua
tools 1 364
Luluabourg see KANANGA
Lulumbamba, Pucará de see PUCARÁ DE RUMICUCHO
Luluwa 1 256, 405
Lumague, Barthélémy 19 790
Lumague, Carlo see LUMAGUE, CHARLES
Lumague, Charles 19 790
Lumague, Marc-Antoine (i) (d 1619) 19 790
Lumague, Marc-Antoine (ii) (1566-1655) 19 790
Lumbee 22 555
Lumbini 5 94; 15 220, 261; 19 790*; 22 753, 758
Lumbo 11 878, 879
Lumbreras, Luis G. 6 523; 29 219
lum chests see under CHESTS → types
Lumi 24 70
Lumiares, Manuel de Moura y Corte Real, Conde de see CASTEL RODRIGO, MANUEL, 2nd Marqués de
Lumière, Auguste 7 327; 24 648, 670
Lumière, Louis 7 327; 24 648, 670
Lumikangas, Pentti 11 97; 19 790–91*
Luminais, Evariste 20 117
luminance 19 351, 352, 356, 791*
Gothic 13 135
Luminism (i) (USA) 12 606; 14 276, 843; 18 715, 726, 726; 19 355, 791*; 27 635; 31 602
works 14 276
Luminism (ii) (Belgium and the Netherlands) 19 791–2*
see also NEO-IMPRESSIONISM
luminosity see LUMINANCE
Lumitron Ltd 33 50
Lumley, John, 1st Baron Lumley 19 792–3*
collections 11 140
furniture 10 293
gardens 12 126; 23 198
paintings 10 363, 666; 14 806; 21 368
Lumley, John Savile 22 730
Lumley, Richard, 1st Earl of Scarborough 19 570; 30 278
Lumley Castle (Durham) 21 549; 29 835
Lummus, William 27 613
Lumsden, E. S. 28 239
Lumumba, Omowale 13 877
Luna (family) 29 323
pottery 29 324
Luna (Italy) 16 620; 19 793*; 26 886; 27 13, 29
marble 16 623; 26 854, 875
quarries 27 10
Luna, Álvaro de 13 69, 106; 14 134, 578; 19 793; 31 92
Luna, Antonio Rodríguez see RODRÍGUEZ LUNA, ANTONIO
Luna, Delfina 5 355
Luna, Fernando de Rojas see ROJAS LUNA, FERNANDO DE
Luna, Francisco de 31 865, 866
Luna, François 24 148
Luna, Maria de, Duquesa de Infantado see INFANTADO, MARIA DE LUNA, Duquesa de
Luna, Master of the see JUAN DE SEGOVIA
Luna, Miguel 28 520
Luna, Pedro 6 597; 13 9
Lunacharsky, Anatoly (Vasil'yevich) 19 794*; 20 887; 27 444
groups and movements 4 231; 22 508
works 6 529
Lunar, Emerio (Darío) 19 794*
Lunardi, Camillo see LEONARDO, CAMILLO
Luna Victoria, Francisco Javier de, Bishop of Panama City 23 906
Luna ware see under POTTERY → wares
Luna y Novicio, Juan 20 274; 24 622
Luna y Saldaña, Bernardo de Rojas see ROJAS (LUNA Y SALDAÑA), BERNARDO DE

lunchboxes *see* BOXES → types → bentō
Lund **19** 794–6*; **30** *65*
architecture **32** 533
Archiv for Dekorattiv Konst **2** 371
Cathedral of St Laurentius **4** 141; **8** 721, 723, 758; **9** 427; **12** 47; **19** 794*, *795*; **26** 592; **30** 66
altarpiece **13** 120
architecture **19** 794–5*
choir-stalls **8** 738
doors **26** 691
manuscripts **26** 675
sculpture **8** 738; **19** 795–6*, *796*; **26** 620, 639; **30** 83
church **26** 592
University **30** 119
wood-carvings **32** 517
Lund, Benjamin **4** 824; **33** 377
Lund, F(rederick) C(hristian) **8** 754; **14** 542
Lund, Frederik (Ludvig) Konow **19** 796*
Lund, Hakon **8** 761
Lund, J(ohan) L(udvig Gebhard) **8** 734, 735; **9** 297; **19** 797; **29** 72; **30** 852
Lund, Johan **23** 236
Lund, Kjell (Arve) **19** 798*
Lunda **1** 313, 328, 405; **7** 195–6; **24** 358; **30** 509; **33** 482
Lundberg, Bertil **15** 142
Lundberg, Erik **30** 120
Lundberg, Gustaf **19** 796–7*; **30** 78, 79
patrons and collectors **30** 524
pupils **14** 79
works **11** 471
Lundberg, Jon **23** 222
Lundbohms, Sixten **30** 81
Lundbye, Johan Thomas **8** 735; **14** 572; **19** 797*; **30** 766
Lunde, Einar **23** 243
Lunde, Rolf **23** 230
Lundeberg, Helen **19** 702; **31** 607
Lunde Church **26** 639
Lundelius, Anders **30** 95
Lundelius, Anders Wilhelm **30** 95
Lundell, C. L. **5** 411
Lunden, Arnold **5** 351; **27** 301
Lundgreen, Konrad Daniel **25** 128; **28** 105
Lundgren, Olof Robert **11** 108
Lundie, Edwin H. **21** 649, 650
Lundin, Ingeborg **30** 103
Lund & Kallmorgen **14** 644
Lund & Miller **10** 308, 309
Lundø Crucifix **10** 322, 338; **26** 687
Lundquist, Evert **19** 797–8*; **30** 81
Lundquist, Oliver **27** 476
Lund & Slaatto **19** 798*; **23** 222, 602
Lundsten, Bengt **19** 798–9*; **26** 261
Lundstrøm, Vilhelm (Henry) **8** 736; **19** 799*; **27** 643
Lundt, Just Nicolaus **27** 584
Lundu-Mbo **1** 396, 399
Lundy, Andrew **28** 234
Lundy, Victor A. **30** 469
Luneau de Boisjermain **13** 325
Lüneburg **12** *360*; **19** 799*
gold **12** 442, 443
iron **12** 454
metalwork **12** 444; **23** 659; **26** 683
pewter **12** 452
Rathaus **12** 446, 467; **13** 187; **17** 700
St Johanniskirche **1** 695; **14** 81
St Michael **20** 681
St Nikolai **13** 111
stained glass **13** 186
tapestries **12** 467
Lunenburg **5** 578
lunes **20** *579*, 580
lunettes **2** 292; **9** 11; **19** 799*
lunette tombs *see under* TOMBS → types
Lunetti, Stefano **2** 697; **4** 197
Lunéville **11** *504*; **19** 800–801*
ceramics **19** 801*
Château **4** *224*; **19** 5, *800*
faience (ii) (ceramics) **11** 606
pottery **11** 606
St Jacques **14** 82, *82*
tapestries **11** 642
Lunghi *see* LONGHI (i)
Lunghi, Silla *see* LONGHI, SILLA
Lung-men *see* LONGMEN
Lungo *see* LONGHI (i)
Lungren, Fernand Harvey **19** 802*
Lung-shan *see* LONGSHAN
Luni *see* LUNA
Lunois, Alexandre **19** 489, 490
works **19** *490*
Luns, Huib **28** 595
Luntz, Viktor **2** 787
Luny, Thomas **3** 61; **19** 802*; **20** 424
Luo **1** 299; **17** 906, 907
Luong Xuan Nhi **32** 482
Luo Ping **6** 811; **19** 802–3*
groups and movements **2** 96; **33** 497
teachers **17** 592
works **6** 813; **19** *802*
Luoyang **5** 108; **6** *615*, 695, 850; **12** 86; **19** 803–4*; **29** 905
Baima Temple **5** 107; **6** 666, 728; **33** 318
bronzes **6** 842, 845, 847
Dule yuan **12** 87
figurines **7** *55*
Guanlin miao **6** 724, 729, 730; **7** 99
jars **6** *888*
lacquer **7** 14
mirrors **6** 863
paintings **6** 808
palace **6** 679
pottery **6** 882, 888
sarcophagi **6** 808; **27** 832
sculpture **6** 733
temples **6** 626, 667, 671
Tomb 61 **6** 629, 788
tomb of Bu Qianqiu **6** 697, 785
tombs **4** *794*
urban planning **6** 664
wall paintings **6** 778
White Horse Temple *see* Baima Temple
see also CHENGZHOU
Luo Zhenyu **6** 767, 867; **19** 804*
Lupaca **2** 386; **31** 46–7
Lupardo de Benincasa **3** 808
Luparello, Girolamo *see* LIPAROLO, GIROLAMO
Lupas, Ana **19** 804*
Lupaş, Eva **26** 722
Lüpertz, Markus **17** 818; **19** 805*
groups and movements **3** 803; **12** 397; **31** 532
house **18** 114
works **12** *397*, 408
Lupi, Bonifacio **27** 789
Lupi, Miguel Ângelo **19** 805*
pupils **4** 385, 639; **17** 879; **26** 130
works **29** 101
Lupi, Raimondino de' **1** 725
Lupiae *see* LECCE
Lupicini, Antonio **21** 579
Lupi di Soragni, Bonifacio *see* BONIFACIO LUPI DI SORAGNI
Luplau, Anton Carl **7** 806; **11** 852
Lupo di Francesco **12** 709; **13** 105; **31** 3
Lupshinsky, O. **28** 838
Lupton, Thomas Goff **10** 394; **19** 806*; **21** 417; **31** 470
Lupu, Vasile, Prince **31** 23
Lu Qian **22** 460
Luque **24** *91*
Franciscan church **24** 94
Luque, Javier de **32** 630
Luquet **21** 430
Luquet, G. H. **6** 586; **24** 696
Luquet, Jules **5** 364
Luquez, Pedro António **12** 762
Luraas, Thomas **23** 242
Luraghi, Giovanni Battista **29** 837
Luraghi, Giovanni Martino **1** 668
Luragho *see* LURAGO
Lurago (ii) (family) **12** 370
Lurago (ii), Anselmo Martino **19** 806, 807*
groups and movements **26** 496
works **8** 379, 427; **25** 438, 445
Lurago (ii), Carlo **19** 806, 807*
collaboration **23** 573
works **8** 378, 385; **12** 370, *371*; **19** 259; **20** 814; **25** 426, 427
Lurago (ii), Domenico Antonio **19** 806
Lurago (ii), Francesco Anselmo **19** 806
Lurago (i), Giovanni **12** 281; **19** 806*
Lurago (ii), Giovanni Antonio **19** 806
Lurago (i), Rocco **19** 806*
Lurasi, Skënder (Kristo) **19** 738*
Lurçat, André (Emile Lucien) **7** *294*; **19** 809*
collaboration **32** 439
groups and movements **11** 526; **15** 885
pupils **6** 534
staff **5** 608; **12** 652; **29** 718
works **11** 526; **23** 122; **30** 755
Lurçat, Jean **13** 681; **19** 808*; **30** 149, 328
collaboration **9** 374; **11** 635, 659
pupils **1** 145
tapestries **19** *808*
works **2** 704; **3** 462; **11** 644; **12** 830; **30** 329
Lurçat, Jean, Atelier-Musée *see under* TOURS-SAINT-LAURENT
Lurçat, Jean, Musée *see under* ANGERS
Lurcy, Georges **24** 183
lurex **30** 542
Luria, Isaac **17** 551
Lurie, Yael **31** 661
Lurie-Larochette studio **31** 661
Luristan **15** *897*, *901*, 904, 905, 907; **19** 809–12*
bronze **1** 894, 896; **15** 902, 904, 905, 907, 919, 922; **19** *810*, 811–12, *811*
bronzes
forgeries **1** 896
metalwork **15** 919
Luritja **1** 52, 56
Lurøy **12** 135
lurs *see* HORNS
Lürsen, Joan B. **5** 132
Lurye, Artur **33** 486
Lusaka **1** 319, *401*
Bank of Zambia **33** 602
British South Africa Company **33** 602
Cathedral of the Holy Cross **33** 602
Evelyn Hone College **33** 603
Findeco House **33** 602
Lusaka Club **33** 602
Meridian Bank HQ **33** 602
Mpapa Gallery **33** 603
Mulungushi International Conference Centre **33** 603
National Assembly Building **33** 602
State House **33** 602
tourist art **1** 247
Town School **33** 602
University of Zambia **1** 319; **33** 602
Zintu Museum **33** 603
Lusanna, L. **21** 471
Luschan, F. von **33** 684
Luschner, Michael **3** 221
Luscombe Castle (Devon) **6** 61; **7** 172, 744; **10** 234
Lushai **15** 732
Lushan **6** 729
tomb of Fan Min **25** 800
Lu Shen **6** 760; **7** 10
Lu Shih-i *see* LU SHIYI
Lu Shiyi **30** 246
Lushnje Museum **18** 459
Lü Shoukun *see* LUI SHOU-KWAN
Lusieri, Giovanni Battista **4** 889; **13** 304; **22** 480
Lusieri, Tito **5** 541; **30** 451
Lusignan **14** 411
Château **21** 549
Lusignan, Henry I, King of Cyprus *see* HENRY I, King of Cyprus
Lusignan, Hugh II, King of Cyprus *see* HUGH II, King of Cyprus
Lusignan, Hugh IV, King of Cyprus *see* HUGH IV, King of Cyprus
Lusignan, Hugues de, Cardinal **20** 786
Lusignan, Peter II, King of Cyprus *see* PETER II, King of Cyprus
Lusitânia factory **30** 882
Lusitano, Francisco Vieira *see* VIEIRA LUSITANO, FRANCISCO
Lusk, Doris **7** 211
Luss **29** 843
Lussanet de la Sablonière, H. de **8** 670
Lussier, Denis **11** 880
Lusson, Adrien-Louis **12** 178; **19** 812–13*
Lusson, Antoine **29** 506
Lust, René **17** 518
Lustige Blätter **26** 715
Lustleigh, St John **28** 294
lustre **1** 613; **6** 336; **14** 425; **19** 352
lustre glass *see under* GLASS → types
lustre painting **2** 569
lustre tiles *see under* TILES → types
lustreware *see under* POTTERY → wares
Lustrum Press **12** 599
Lusty, W., & Sons Ltd **33** 158
Łuszczkiewicz, Władysław
pupils
Grottger, Artur **13** 702
Kossak, Wojciech **18** 398
Leopolski, Wilhelm **19** 208
Malczewski, Jacek **20** 187
Mehoffer, Józef **21** 51
Stanisławski, Jan (Grzegorz) **29** 538
Wyspiański, Stanisław **33** 455
works **25** 143
Lü Ta-lin *see* LÜ DALIN
Lu Tanwei **6** 635, 788, 808, 816
Lu T'an-wei *see* LU TANWEI
Lutbetkin, Berthold **5** 905
works **5** *905*
luteolin **9** 491; **24** 799
lutes **22** 374, 376
Ancient Near East **1** 891
China **6** 788; **7** *14*; **17** 396; **22** 376
Egypt, ancient **10** 65
Japan **17** 396, 397
Sumatra **15** 817
Tibet **30** 844
Vietnam **32** 489
Lutetia Parisiorum *see* PARIS
Lutf'Ali Ghulam **16** 509
Lutf 'Ali Khan **16** 341; **19** 813*
Lutfullin, Akhmet **27** 434
works **27** *435*
Lutgen, Véronique **3** 595
Lüth, Oskar **12** 649
LUTH complex **20** 169
Luthelmus **20** 683
Luther, Martin **2** 725; **7** 215, 258, 269, 277; **10** 450; **14** 868; **19** 813–14*
collections **8** 115
Luther, Martin—cont.
works **2** 223; **15** 80
illustrated **4** 864; **8** 115, 120; **20** 791; **25** 650
on altars **1** 700
on painting **10** 738
Luther, Robert **8** 270
Lutheranism *see under* CHRISTIANITY → sects
Lutherbourg, Philippe Jacques de *see* LOUTHERBOURG, PHILIPPE JACQUES DE
Lüthi, Bernhard **30** 135
Lüthi, Urs **19** 815–16*; **24** 408; **30** 135
Lüthy, Oskar **8** 434; **22** 921; **30** 134
Luti, Benedetto **16** 672; **19** 816–17*; **20** 213; **26** 774
assistants **24** 9
drawings **7** 418
patrons and collectors **1** 532; **23** 874
personal collection **9** 229
pupils **1** 733; **3** 713, 816, 920; **8** 12, 132; **17** 900; **32** 424
works **3** 920; **19** *816*; **23** 352; **25** 297
Luti, Bernardino **5** 812
luting *see under* POTTERY → techniques
Lutjens, Helmuth **26** 405
Lütke, Franz **29** 751
Lütken, Per **8** 750; **12** 795
works **8** *750*
Lutma, Jacob **19** 817
Lutma, Johannes (i) (?1589-1669) **1** 165; **19** 817*; **22** 871
groups and movements **2** 732
works **1** 811; **22** 887, 894; **24** 271
Lutma, Johannes (ii) (1624-89) **19** 817–18*; **22** 888; **25** *731*
methods **25** 731
works **8** 130
Lutma frames *see under* FRAMES → types
Luton (Beds)
congregational mosque **4** 790
St Mary **11** 254
Luton Hoo (Beds) **3** 809; **29** 796; **33** 84
Lutowski, Alberto **32** 169
Luts'k **31** 557
Castle **31** 549, 550
Lutsk Gospels *see under* GOSPEL BOOKS → individual manuscripts
Lutterell, Edward **2** 597
Lutterotti, Otto von **2** 834
Luttersson, Petur **15** 72
Lutti, Benedetto **8** 209; **19** 645
Lüttich *see* LIÈGE
Lüttich, Johann Christian **33** 36
Luttrell, A. E. **23** 55
Luttrell, Edward **19** 818*
Luttrell, Geoffrey **19** 818
Luttrell, Sydney **23** 55
Luttrell Psalter *see under* PSALTERS → individual manuscripts
Luttringer, Andreas **14** 893; **28** 855
lutuan *see* PHILIPPINES → betel sets
Lutyens, Charles Henry Augustus **19** 818
Lutyens, Edwin (Landseer) **15** 411; **17** 471; **19** 818–24*; **23** 814; **31** 729; **32** 773
architecture **8** 675–6; **9** 35; **10** 240
banks **3** 177
castles **6** *62*
cathedrals **19** 506
cenotaphs **2** 362; **6** 171; **20** 238; **22** 48
churches **8** 676; **23** 194
country houses **8** 49; **19** *821*
crypts **8** 224
galleries (iv) (art) **17** 603
gazebos **12** 222

Lutyens, Edwin (Landseer)
architecture—cont.
houses 3 630; 5 925; 15 693; 23 398, 820; 25 268; 29 527; 32 325
monuments 2 362; 7 613; 16 12; 19 823
public houses 25 689
urban planning 6 167; 12 144; 15 404, 542; 19 822
assistants 3 82; 16 891; 19 113
collaboration 12 140; 17 471; 24 186
furniture 30 783
gardens 12 75, 76, 141; 19 820
groups and movements 2 575; 3 269; 9 739; 22 743
methods 2 360
models 2 337
patrons and collectors 6 62; 13 697; 16 892; 17 471; 18 727
staff 13 844; 14 196; 19 519; 21 2; 28 622; 29 379
teachers 12 316
Lutz, Georg 19 825
Lutz, Hans 4 286; 19 825*
Lutz, Peter 19 825
Lützelburger, Hans 14 667; 19 825*; 33 354
Lützeler, Heinrich 10 211
Lütze-Museum see SINDELFINGEN → Galerie der Stadt Sindelfingen
Lützow, Karl von 19 749
Lu Tzu-kang see LU ZIGANG
Luup, Rein 30 277
Luve, William 10 672
Luwa 33 482
Luwian 1 827, 828, 855; 17 810
Lux, Franz Julius 25 54
Lux, Géza 10 544; 14 890
Lux, Jan Jiří 8 413
Lux, Joseph 14 788
Luxembourg (city) 19 826
Centre Européen 19 827
Citadelle du Saint Esprit 19 827
Marché aux Poissons 19 826
Musée de l'Etat 19 827
Musée J. P. Pescatore 19 827
Notre-Dame 19 826
Palais Grand-ducal 19 826
Pont Adolphe 4 802
Rocher du Bock 19 826
St Michael 19 826
sculpture 13 114
Luxembourg (country) 12 361; 19 825–7*
architecture 19 826–7
castles 19 826
manuscripts 9 698
miniatures (manuscript illumination) 9 698
scriptoria 9 698, 698
Luxembourg (House of) 19 827*
Luxembourg, Bonne de see BONNE DE LUXEMBOURG
Luxembourg, Cathrine of see CATHRINE OF LUXEMBOURG
Luxembourg, Charles, Count of see CHARLES IV, Holy Roman Emperor
Luxembourg, John, King of Bohemia see JOHN, King of Bohemia
Luxembourg, Louis de see LOUIS DE LUXEMBOURG
Luxembourg, Thiebaut de see THIEBAUT DE LUXEMBOURG
Luxembourg, Wenceslas, Holy Roman Emperor see WENCESLAS, Holy Roman Emperor
Luxembourg-Martigues, Master of 9 466
Luxembourg Palace see PARIS → Palais du Luxembourg
Luxemburg see LUXEMBOURG
Luxenstein, Frans von see LUYCKX, FRANS
Luxeuil 11 529; 19 549
Lu Xiujing 6 785
Luxor see under THEBES (i) (Egypt)
Lu Xun 7 121, 149; 10 886; 14 826; 19 831*
Luyando, Ochoa de 8 231
Luyck, Hans van 13 664; 32 708; 33 169
Luyckx, Frans 3 560; 13 919; 19 831*; 25 221
Luyken, Casper 19 832
Luyken, Jan 10 175, 176; 19 832*; 27 271
Luynes, Albert, Duc de 11 659; 12 809; 15 842, 844; 28 746
Luynes, Jeanne-Baptiste d'Albert de, Comtesse de Verrue see VERRUE, JEANNE-BAPTISTE, Comtesse de
Luynes, Marie Charles Louis d'Albert, Duc de Chevreuse see CHEVREUSE, MARIE CHARLES LOUIS D'ALBERT, Duc de
Luynes, Victor, Duc de 4 798; 5 779; 11 159; 16 851; 27 311
Luytge, Lambert von 20 692
Lu Yugang 7 71
Lu Yü-kang see LU YUGANG
Luyun, Ibn see IBN LUYUN
Luz, Arturo 24 620, 622
Lužany 8 400
Luzán y Martínez, José 3 424; 13 241; 20 501
Luzarches, Robert de see ROBERT DE LUZARCHES
Luzern see LUCERNE
Luzhany
Church of the Dormition 31 557
Lu Zhaolin 6 761
Lu Zhi 19 832–3*; 32 848
works 19 833; 33 437
Luzi, Filippo 3 95
Lu Zigang 7 9, 90
works 7 90
Luzio, Alessandro 19 833–4*
Luzira Hill 1 407, 408
Lužnice 23 264
Luzon 24 607, 609
barkcloth 24 623
basketwork 24 628, 628
body ornaments 24 625
containers 24 626–7
dress 24 628, 629
furniture 24 629
tattoos 24 626
weaving 24 623, 624
wood-carvings 24 618
Luzzatto, Israel David 17 572
Luzzi, Luigi 14 416
Luzzo, Giovanni Pietro 28 81
Luzzo, Lorenzo 10 877; 19 834–5*; 28 81
L'viv 2 425; 19 835–6*; 25 135, 138
art forms and materials
alabaster (gypsum) 25 113, 114
architecture 25 97, 99; 31 550, 551, 552
bronze 25 129
furniture 25 119
glass 31 563
icons 25 341
jewellery 31 562
lithography 25 106
metalwork 25 126, 127; 31 563
painting 25 104
sculpture 25 115; 26 498; 31 561
wall paintings 31 556
art school 25 123
Brotherhood building 31 551
ecclesiastical buildings
Armenian Cathedral 2 427; 31 557, 561
Bernardine Monastery 31 552, 553
Boimi chapel 19 836; 25 113
L'viv
ecclesiastical buildings—cont.
Cathedral of St George 25 105, 113; 31 552, 561
Cathedral of the Dormition 31 552
Chapel of the Three Saints 31 552
Corpus Christi 19 836; 25 98
Dominican church see Corpus Christi
St Elizabeth 31 553
St Nicholas 25 115
Uniat Cathedral 25 98
education (architectural) 25 142
Jewish museum 17 581
Kornyakta tower 31 551
Museum of Ukrainian Art 14 819
museums 25 140
Ossolineum see Ossoliński Library
Ossoliński Library 25 142
Picture Gallery 19 836; 31 565
Polytechnic Institute 19 836
School of Architecture 19 836
synagogue 17 545
L'vov see L'VIV
L'vov, Nikolay (Aleksandrovich) 12 134; 19 837*
assistants 21 127
works 3 527; 12 173; 27 375, 377
Lwalwa 1 256, 405
Lwena 7 195–6, 198–9*; 33 602
beads 7 198
body arts 1 342
fibres 7 198
masks 1 405; 7 198, 198
pots 1 328
pottery 7 198–9
sculpture 1 403
terracotta 30 509
wood 7 198
wood-carvings 7 198
Lwiro Museum 33 598
Lwów see L'VIV
Ly (Later) 32 472, 486
Lyagman 6 274
Lyalevich, Marian-Lyudovik 24 400
Lyalin, Alexander 20 925
Lyallpur 15 411
Lyangajö Church 8 738
Lyatifov, Abuzar 2 901
Lyautey, Hubert 22 128; 25 658
Lybaert, Théophile 11 448
Lybke, Harry 3 803
Lychnidos see OHRID
Lycia 1 821; 9 512; 13 363; 19 837–40*; 26 852
reliefs 19 839
sarcophagi 19 839
sculpture 13 458; 33 459
tombs 19 838–40, 839
see also TURKEY
Lycian Sarcophagus 13 458; 28 668
Lycopolis see ASYUT
Lycra 30 543
Lycurgus Painter 13 526, 529
Lyda Castle 19 495
Lydda see LOD
Lyddington (Leics), Bede House 10 271
Lyde, Lionel 26 264
Lydeman, Simon Gustaf 11 108
Lydén, Edwin 11 96; 20 148
Lydenburg 1 222, 329, 413, 418
terracotta 1 222
Lydgate, John 7 242; 18 686
Lydia 1 821; 13 363; 19 840–41*; 26 852
coins 1 888; 7 532; 19 841
dies (ii) (stamps) 7 532
dress 1 887
marbling 19 841, 841
pottery 13 504; 19 841
skyphoi 19 841
synagogues 19 841
temples 19 841
Lydia—cont.
tombs 19 841; 31 108
writing 19 840
lydion 13 478
Lydney 27 2
Lydos 13 484; 32 53–4*
works 13 508, 509
lye 17 308; 30 428
Lye, Len 10 688; 19 842*; 29 98
Lye Church 13 190
Lyell, Charles 2 299
Lyell, Michael, Associates 31 584
Lyen, Jacques-François de 18 795; 19 216
Lyen, Robert 10 674
Lyeon see SMET, LEON DE
Lyfing, Archbishop of York 2 77
Lygyt 27 432
Lyialichi Palace 31 564
Lykaon Painter 13 522
Lykios 2 682; 19 842*; 22 402
Lykosoura, Temple of Despoina 1 128; 13 464; 21 45–6
Lykourgos 2 680, 681
Lykourgos Cup 9 520, 645; 18 825; 27 76; 30 398
Lyle, C. 33 310
Lyle, John M(acIntosh) 5 562, 573; 19 842*; 31 176
Lylge, Dirck 18 436
Lyman, Fenton & Co. 31 636
works 31 636
Lyman, John (Goodwin) 5 568; 19 842–3*; 22 38
Lyman, Theodore 31 691
Lymburner, Francis 30 160
Lyna, Frédéric 8 650
Lynar, Rochus Quirinus 8 816; 19 843*
Lynch, Lady (fl late 17th cent.) 16 888
Lynch, Mme (fl 1850-60) 24 96
Lynch, Kevin 19 843*; 31 735
Lynch, Thomas 16 888
Lynche, J. 15 83
Lyncker, Anton 22 882
Lyndhurst, St Michael and All Angels 28 295
Lyndon, Donlyn 22 52
Lynds, Elam 25 637
Lyne 28 251
Lynen, Amédée Ernest 10 517
Lynes, George Platt 12 216; 19 844*
works 19 844
Lyngdal Church 23 224
Lynge, Hans 13 620
works 13 620
Lyngenfjord 11 109
Lyngwode, William 33 238
Ly Nhan Tong 32 472
Lynn, Vivian 19 844*
Lynn, William Henry 3 536; 9 366; 18 754; 19 844–5*
Lyns (family) 3 598
Lynsted (Kent)
houses 32 277
SS Peter and Paul 10 262
Lyon 11 505; 19 845–51*, 847; 26 905; 31 714, 724
Abbey of the Dames de St Pierre see museums → Musée des Beaux-Arts
art forms and materials
chess sets 6 558
coral 7 835
embroidery 11 648
faience (ii) (ceramics) 11 604, 604; 19 849*
glass 27 74
gold 11 616
lace 11 649, 650
medals 20 919, 920
metalwork 11 624
pewter 11 624, 628
sashes 25 133
silk 11 644, 645, 645, 646, 646, 647; 19 849–50*; 28 716, 717, 718; 32 391
Lyon
art forms and materials—cont.
tapestries 12 412
textiles 28 564
Bourse 10 669
Cathedral of St Jean 13 41; 19 850–51*; 26 908
Bourbon Chapel 11 511
sculpture 19 851*
stained glass 13 180; 26 702
conservatory 7 745
Ecole de Dessin 11 671
Espace Lyonnais d'Art Contemporain 19 848
festivals 23 768
Folklore Gallery 19 848
Galerie du Griffon 19 848
Gier aqueduct 19 845
Hôtel Bulliod 11 513
Hôtel-Dieu 29 91, 91
Hôtel de Gadagne see Musée Historique de Lyon
Hôtel de Ville 4 36, 128; 7 665
Loge du Change 10 668; 29 91, 92
Lugdunum 12 70; 19 845*; 27 62, 107
Lutrin, Le 19 848
Lyon-Perrache railway station 6 377
Mont d'Or channel 27 7
monument to Louis XIV 10 442
museums 11 668
Musée d'Art et d'Industrie 19 848
see also Musée Historique des Tissus
Musée des Arts Décoratifs 9 379; 19 848; 30 332
Musée des Beaux-Arts 2 881; 4 128; 6 537; 11 666; 14 577; 19 846, 848, 848, 849; 25 750
collections 2 232; 3 785; 19 847
Musée Saint Pierre Art Contemporain 19 849
Salon de la Fleur 19 847
Musée de la Civilisation Gallo-Romaine 19 848; 33 628
Musée Guimet 13 833; 15 744
Musée Historique de Lyon 19 848
Musée Historique des Tissus 11 647; 19 848; 29 240; 30 332
Musée de la Marionette 29 240
Musée Saint Pierre Art Contemporain see under Musée des Beaux-Arts
Musées de Peinture et Sculpture 13 806
Nouveau Musée 19 848
Notre Dame de Fourvière 7 304
Oeil Ecouté, L' 19 848
paintings 11 229; 27 56; 29 669
Palais des Beaux-Arts see museums → Musée des Beaux-Arts
Palais de Justice 11 522; 18 888
Palais St Pierre see museums → Musée des Beaux-Arts
Pont St Esprit 4 801
Porte St-Clair 29 91
Roman theatre 23 349; 26 873, 905
Royal Mint 32 864
St Just 24 36; 26 908
Salon de la Fleur see under museums → Musée des Beaux-Arts
Sanctuary of the Three Gauls 27 2
Temple de Paradis 14 855
Théâtre 29 91–2; 30 670
tiles 30 885
University 11 676
urban planning 27 3
water pipes 27 7

Lyon, Corneille de *see* CORNEILLE DE LYON
Lyon, Cottier & Co. **2** 756
Lyon, Danny **19** 851–2*
Lyon, Gustave **1** 125
Lyon, John Lamb **2** 755
Lyon, Thomas **5** 418
Lyon Bible *see under* BIBLES → individual manuscripts
Lyonet, Pieter **22** 905
Lyons **11** 748
Lyons, Israel and Ellis **13** 239; **29** 677
Lyons, J., & Co. **3** 814
Lyon school **26** 264
Lyons House **16** 14
Lyotard, Jean-François **29** 891
Lyre Bird Press **1** 147
lyre clocks *see under* CLOCKS → types
lyres **1** 890–91; **10** 65; **22** 372
Lyrical Abstraction *see* ABSTRACTION, LYRICAL
Lys, Johann *see* LISS, JOHANN
Lysakerkretsen **10** 458; **23** 226; **29** 78
Lyseas Stele **13** 544
Lysenko, Mikhail G. **31** 561
Lysenko, Mykola **24** 565
Lysi **8** 357
Lysimacheia **25** 178
Lysimachos, King of Thrace (*reg* 306-81) **10** 422; **13** 405, 588; **16** 809; **24** 410
coins **13** *588*
Lysippides Painter **23** 146; **32** 31, 54*
collaboration **32** 31
works **13** 510, 518
Lysippos (*fl c.* 370-300 BC) **1** 613; **13** 429, 430, 439, 440, 461, 467; **19** 852–4*; **28** 712
attributions **13** *459*
Lysippos (*fl c.* 370-300 BC)—cont.
collaboration **19** 169
copies **15** *92*
groups and movements **33** 461
patrons and collectors **13** 605
pupils **10** 653
works **1** 652; **7** 853; **8** 697; **13** 423, 462, 573; **14** 443; **19** *853*, 854; **26** 292; **27** 30; **29** 567
workshop **13** 459
Lysippus the younger (*fl c* 1470-84) **8** 164; **19** 854*; **20** 918
Lysistratos **13** 438, 603; **19** 854*; **27** 18
Lyskovo **27** 430
Lysle, Anthony de **10** 316
works **10** *315*
Lysons, Daniel **29** 733
Lysons, Samuel **4** 826; **13** 693
Lystrup **8** 725
Lystsovo **22** 180
Lytens, Gysbrecht **5** 351
Lyth, Harald **30** 82
Ly Thai Tong **32** 472
Lytham (Lancs), Park Street Church **21** 347
Ly Thanh Tong **32** 472, 474
Lythgoe, Albert **10** 94
Lythrankomi, Panagia Kanakaria **5** 676; **8** *325*, 358, 359; **9** *512*, 573; **19** 855*
Lytlington, Nicholas, Abbot of Westminster **19** 602; **21** 730
Lytras, Nikiforos **19** 855*
education (art) **13** 360
pupils **1** 690; **12** 2; **24** 20
works **13** 352
Lytras, Nikolaos **13** 353
Lyttelton **23** *52*, 64
Timeball Station **23** 54
Lyttelton, George, 1st Earl of Lyttelton **13** 608
Lyttleton, George, 1st Baron Lyttleton **29** 806
Lytton, Edward Bulwer, 1st Baron Lytton **8** 106
Lytton, Edward Robert, 2nd Baron and 1st Earl of Lytton **12** 75; **23** 692
Lyttos **8** 155
Lyubitel' *see* ETTINGER, PAVEL (DAVYDOVICH)
Lyubomil **31** 549
Lyutibrod **5** *144*
basilica **5** 155
Lyutin **27** 428
Lyveden (Northants) **10** 302; **19** 855*
Lyveden New Bield **32** 551
Lyversberg, Jakob Johann **20** 720
Lyversberg Passion, Master of the **12** 384; **20** 718, 720*

M

M59 **7** 805
MA **1** 131; **17** 833; **20** 103–4*; **24** 440; **31** 541; **32** 447
contributors **8** 437; **20** 833
Maa **32** 487, 490
Ma'abad, Tell al- *see* UBAID, TELL AL-
Maadi **9** 850
Maagden van den Hoek **22** 898
Ma al-'Aynayn, Shaykh **33** 98
Ma'ali ibn Salam **16** 490
Ma'almin Hadadi **33** 98
Maaltebrugge **3** 885
Ma'anyan **15** 773
Maa-Palaeokastro Archaeological Museum **8** 366
Maar, Dora **24** 722
Maar, Karl von **31** 785
Ma'arrat an Nu'man **9** 646
mosque **21** 627
Maarten van Rode **5** 54
Maas, Arnoldo **25** 701
Maas, Dirk **3** 759, 762; **12** 801; **19** 858–9*
Maas, Godfried **17** 915
Maas, Günter **29** 97
Maas, Paul **5** 44
Maas, V. F. **28** 838
Maasai **3** 442; **10** 580; **17** 906; **19** 859–61*; **30** 300
architecture **1** 306, 411
beads **1** 297
beadwork **3** 442; **19** *859*, 859–60
body arts **1** 254, 297, 344
colour **19** 860
feathers **10** 848
hairstyles **1** 343
leather **19** 860
metalwork **19** 860
metalworkers **1** 286
poles **1** 306
rock art **19** 861
shields **1** 362, 411
spears **1** 362
trade **1** 249
Maasdijk, A. H. R. van **6** 378; **33** 162
Maaseik **3** 601
St Katharinakerk **2** 83; **10** 181, 353
Måås-Fjetterström, Marta **30** 328
Maaskant, Hugh Aart **19** 861*; **22** 832; **30** 871
assistants **31** 867
collaboration **13** 685
works **1** 804
Maastricht **19** 861–4*; **22** *813*, 908
art forms and materials
brass **3** 603
earthenwares **22** 882
glass **3** 593; **22** 884
guns **2** 464
manuscripts **26** 563
roofs **30** 907
sculpture **22** 855; **26** 630, 631
silk **9** 664
stained glass **27** 255
Bonnefanten Museum **19** 862
churches
Dominican church **22** 821
Franciscan church **22** 821
Onze Lieve Vrouw **22** 816, *816*, 817
capitals **22** 855
sculpture **26** 631
westwork **22** 816
St Janskerk **13** 62, 100; **22** 819, 821
St Mathiaskerk **22** 821
St Servatius **19** 862–3*; **22** 817
capitals **22** 855
Maastricht
churches
St Servatius—cont.
choir-screen **26** 631
portal **22** 855
reliquaries **10** *115*
sculpture **10** 115; **13** 98, 110; **19** 863*, *863*; **26** *630*, 631
shrine of St Servatius **26** 683; **28** 630
Treasury **9** 657; **19** 863–4*
westwork **33** 109, *109*
St Servatius
reliquaries **26** 145
town walls **22** 822
Maastricht Dioscuri Silk **9** 667
Maaten, Jacob Jan van der **22** 847
Maatkare *see* HATSHEPSUT
Ma'bar **15** 681
Mabaruma style pottery *see under* POTTERY → wares
Mabasa, Noria **19** 864*; **29** 113
Mabe, Manabu **4** 719; **19** 864*
Mabel of Bury St Edmunds **23** 460
Mabille, Pierre **30** 21, 23
Mabillon, Jean **19** 864–5*; **23** 828
Mabuse *see* GOSSART, JAN
Mabuseus *see* RÉGNIER, NICOLAS
MAC (Muebles de Acero Curvado) **29** 321
MAC *see* MOVIMENTO ARTE CONCRETA
MAC *see* MUSEUMS ASSOCIATION OF THE CARIBBEAN
Macadré, Nicolas **12** 903
Macael **27** 13; **29** 702
Macagnino (da Siena), Angelo (di Pietro) del *see* ANGELO (DI PIETRO) DEL MACAGNINO (DA SIENA)
MacAgy, Jermayne **21** 134
Macaire, Abbot of Saint-Benoît-sur-Loire **27** 534
Macalister, Molly (Morell) **2** 706; **19** 865*
works **23** 62, 63, *63*
Maçan **5** 673
Macanari Murai *see* MURAI, MACANARI
Maçan-Avcılar
Cistern Church **5** 678
tombs **5** 676
Macao **6** *614*, *623*; **19** 865–6*
architecture **25** 294
chess sets **6** 557
S Paulo **19** *866*; **25** 292
trade **6** 557, 624
Macaracas Polychrome pottery *see under* POTTERY → wares
Macaray Cathedral **32** 177
Macario Chonverso, Fra **12** 711
Macarius, Joannes *see* JOANNES MACARIUS
Macarthur, William **32** 249
Macartney, Mervyn **2** 575; **9** 739; **12** 650
Macazaga, Antonio de **29** 337
Macazaga, José Ignacio de **20** 501; **29** 337
Macazana Church **12** 827
Macbeth, Ann **28** 258, 265
Macbeth, Norman **19** 868
Macbeth, Robert Walker **19** 868*
MacBryde, Robert **7** 639; **19** 868*
groups and movements **22** 751
works **19** 492; **28** 240
Maccabaeus, Jonathan **17** 487
Maccabaeus, Simon **17** 487
MacCabe, Eamon **29** 426
Maccari, Cesare **14** 479; **19** 687, 869*; **24** 218; **28** 689
Maccari, Mino **16** 680
mac Carrthach, Cormac, King of Desmond (*d* 1138) **5** 915
MacCarthy, Coeur de Lion **5** 570
MacCarthy, Desmond **4** 168; **25** 355
MacCarthy, Hamilton **5** 570
MacCarthy-Reagh, Justin, Count **19** 870*
MacCartney, Mervyn **22** 743
Maccaruzzi, Bernardino **25** 144; **32** 229
Macchi, Gustavo **27** 788
macchia **19** 871; **23** 852
Macchiaioli **2** 106; **11** 190; **16** 678; **18** 715; **19** 870–71*; **26** 56; **32** 197, 257
collections **19** 512; **20** 482, 483
commentaries **20** 483
members **4** 252; **6** 129; **10** 834; **19** 70; **28** 704; **32** 108
Macchietti, Girolamo (di Francesco di Mariotto) **6** 111; **16** 664; **19** 871–2*; **24** 239
Macció, Rómulo **2** 401; **19** 872*
Macclesfield (Ches) **10** 357; **28** 717
St Alban **28** 295
MacColl, Dugald Sutherland **19** 872*; **20** 27
Maccoy, Guy **28** 299
MacDiarmid, Hugh **28** 240
Macdonald, Alexander **1** 30; **28** 273
MacDonald, Alexander, 2nd Baron MacDonald **12** 635
Macdonald, Duncan **5** 581
Macdonald, Edward C. **5** 581
Macdonald, Frances (Eliza) **2** 562; **11** 358; **12** 776, 777, 780; **19** 875–6*; **20** 22, 31; **23** 17; **28** 238, 275
groups and movements **12** 780
Macdonald, George **14** 850; **27** 726
MacDonald, J(ames) E(dward) H(ervey) **5** 573; **19** 877*
groups and movements **5** 566; **13** 711; **16** 818; **23** 791
works **5** 573
Macdonald, Jock **4** 63; **5** 567, 568; **19** 877–8*; **31** 864
MacDonald, John **15** 745; **18** 743
Macdonald, J(ames) W(illiamson) G(alloway) *see* MACDONALD, JOCK
Macdonald, Lawrence **19** 878*; **28** 242
MacDonald, Malcolm **7** 155
Macdonald, Margaret **2** 562; **12** 777; **19** 875–7*; **20** 22, 31; **23** 17
exhibitions **33** 165
groups and movements **11** 358; **12** 780; **28** 275
works **19** *876*; **20** 23; **28** 238
Macdonald, Robert Henry **27** 173
Macdonald-Wright, Stanton **19** 702, 878–9*; **30** 173; **31** 607
groups and movements **1** 74; **23** 570; **27** 360
works **31** 490
writings **33** 412
MacDowell, Patrick **3** 537; **19** 879*
Macdowell, Susan Hannah **9** 501
Mace, Arthur **10** 80, 81
Macé, Jean **11** 587; **20** 467
works **11** *587*
Macé, Robert, II **25** 17
Macedo, João Rodrigues de *see* RODRIGUES DE MACEDO, JOÃO
Macedo, Manuel de **19** 879*; **27** 141
Macedonia (i) (Greece) **13** *363*; **19** 879–81*; **26** *852*
beads **13** 602
coins **13** 587–8
icons **9** 624
jewellery **19** *881*
malachite **23** 785
mosaics **13** 561
neck rings **13** 601
painting **13** 546
pendants (jewellery) **13** 602
pins **13** 600
rock crystal **26** 485
tombs **15** 53; **31** 109
vaults (ceiling) **15** 53
wood-carvings **13** *357*
see also GREECE, ANCIENT
Macedonia (ii) (former Yugoslavia) **19** 881–6*, *882*; **33** 571
architecture **16** 228; **19** 882–3*
cathedrals **23** *373*
churches **19** *883*
collections **19** 886*
decorative arts **19** 885–6*
embroidery **19** 885*
icons **9** *628*
jewellery **19** 885–6*
monasteries **19** 882–3
museums **19** 886*
painting **19** *884*, 884–5*
paintings
wall **19** 884; **23** 373, *374*
prints **19** 885*
screens (i) (architectural) **19** *884*; **28** *291*
sculpture **19** *884*, 885*
textiles **19** 885*
Macedonian dynasty **8** 155; **19** 886*
see also:
BASIL I, Emperor of Byzantium
BASIL II BULGARROCTONOS, Emperor of Byzantium
CONSTANTINE IX MONOMACHOS, Emperor of Byzantium
CONSTANTINE VII PORPHYROGENITOS, Emperor of Byzantium
LEO VI, Emperor of Byzantium
ROMANOS II, Emperor of Byzantium
Macedonian Renaissance **5** 677; **9** 606
Macedonian tombs *see under* TOMBS → types
maceheads (tools) *see* MATTOIRS
maceheads (weapons) *see* MACES
Maceió **4** *705*
Museu da Polícia **4** 708
Maček, Gregor **19** 516; **28** 859
macella **19** 888–9*, *889*; **26** 867, 871
Greece **19** 888; **26** 910
North Africa **19** 889, *889*; **26** 919
see also MARKETS
MacEntyre, Eduardo **2** 401, 525; **19** 890*
Macerata
Accademia di Belle Arti *see* Palazzo Buonaccorsi
architecture **16** 644
Isola di Cessapalombo **2** 291
Palazzo Buonaccorsi **3** 109; **5** 178; **29** 40
S Filippo **7** 781
Macerata—cont.
S Giovanni **27** 160
S Maria delle Vergini **1** 637
S Paolo **3** 249
maces **2** 448
historical and regional traditions
Central Asia, Western **6** 261
Cuba (Caribbean) **8** 237, *237*
Egypt, ancient **9** 868, *868*; **10** 40; **21** 554
Iran **16** *504*, *506*, 509
Islamic **16** *504*, 505, *506*, 508, 509
Moche (culture) **29** 205
Ottoman **16** 508
Scotland **28** 260
South America, Pre-Columbian **29** 205
Transoxiana **16** *506*
materials
brass **16** *506*
bronze **16** *504*
cast iron **16** *504*
limestone **9** *868*
silver **8** *237*
Macfarlane **13** 619; **26** 18
MacFarlane, David Huron **23** 631; **27** 173
MacGaffey, Wyatt **1** 233
MacGeagh, John **16** 39
MacGibbon, David **28** 289
Macgill, David **28** 243
Macgillivray, James Pittendrigh **28** 243
MacGlynn, Matthew **9** 113
MacGonigal, Maurice **9** *319*; **16** 17, 37
Macgregor, W(illiam) Y(ork) **19** 891*
groups and movements **12** 779; **28** 238
personal collection **10** 91
pupils **14** 397; **32** 834
works **28** 238
Mach, David **19** 892*
Machadinho (family) **13** 695
Machado, Alvaro **19** 892*
Machado, Cirilo Wolkmar **5** 903; **25** 319
Machado, José **29** 272
Machado, Manuel **28** 731
Machado da Silva Castro e Vasconcelos, Félix **19** 892*
Machado de Castro, Joaquim **19** 892–3*; **25** 310
patrons and collectors **32** 539
teachers **12** 763
works **19** *893*; **25** 186, 301; **27** 803
Machaerus **17** 556
Machairas Monastery **8** 359
Machalilla **29** 138
Machang **6** *615*, 629, 773; **19** 894*
Machang culture **6** 876, 877
Machati, Gratiadio *see* AGUCCHI, GIOVANNI BATTISTA
Machaut, Guillaume de *see* GUILLAUME DE MACHAUT
Machaut d'Arnouville, Jean-Baptiste **11** 609; **18** 804; **20** 135; **26** 420
Machek, Antonín **8** 392; **14** 586; **19** 894*; **25** 433
Machemma's Kop **1** 414
Macherey, Pierre **2** 537
Macherino, Ottaviano **20** 242
Machern, Ritterburg **27** *323*, 323, 324
Machete, El **13** 796
Machhilipatanam **15** 684
textiles **15** 669, *669*, 673

Machiavelli, Niccolò (di Bernardo dei) 2 550; 10 413; 11 893; 14 867; 19 183; 27 740
Machiavelli, Zanobi (di Jacopo di Piero) 19 894–5*
works 19 895
Ma-chia-yao see MAJIAYAO
machicolation 6 56–7; 8 278; 9 554, 556; 12 174; 19 895–6*, 896; 21 546
Machida, Hara House 17 91
Machim, Master 13 125; 25 304
Machin, Arnold 33 23
machine aesthetic 10 256; 19 896–7*; 20 594
machine embroidery see under EMBROIDERY → types
machine knitting see under KNITTING → types
machine lace see under LACE → types
machine production 20 593
machine-readable format see MARC FORMAT
machinery, construction see CONSTRUCTION MACHINERY
machines 15 822
machine weaving see under WEAVING → types
Machin factory 10 310
machiya see under HOUSES → types
Mächler, Martin 31 729
Machlup, Karl 17 855
Machmadim (Precious Ones) 17 577
Machnaka 26 915
temple 26 917
Macho, Victorio 19 897*; 29 295; 31 90
Machonin, O. 8 381
Machonin, V. 8 381; 25 430
Machoninová, V. 25 430
Mächselkircher, Gabriel see MÄLESSKIRCHER, GABRIEL
Mächtig, Hermann 20 1*
Ma Ch'üan see MA QUAN
Machuca, Luis 20 2
Machuca, M. 31 823
Machuca, Manuel Timoteo de Vargas see VARGAS MACHUCA, MANUEL TIMOTEO DE
Machuca, Pedro 10 535; 20 1–3*; 29 278
collaboration 25 148
groups and movements 25 31
patrons and collectors 13 288, 906
works 6 72; 11 484, 485; 13 287; 20 2; 29 266
Machuda, Pedro 14 474
Machu Picchu 15 161, 162; 20 3–5*, 3, 4; 29 156, 219
architecture 20 3–5; 29 166
doors 9 166
fortress 15 162
Intihuatana 1 701
observatory 23 338
Semicircular Temple
altar 1 701
Sun Dial shrine 28 640, 641
temple 29 166
Machy, Pierre-Antoine de 20 5*; 22 87; 23 517
works 8 791; 13 220
machzors 17 563*; 20 5–6*
individual manuscripts
Amsterdam Machzor (Amsterdam, Joods Hist. Mus.) 20 5
Catalan Machzor (Jerusalem, Jew N. & U. Lib., heb. 8o 6527) 21 475, 476
Darmstadt Machzor 17 563
Dresden/Wrocław Machzor (Dresden, Sächs. Landesbib. Cod. A45a; U. Wrocław, MS. Or. I, 1) 17 563; 20 6
machzors
individual manuscripts—cont.
Laud Machzor (Oxford, Bodleian Lib., MS. Laud Or. 321) 17 563; 20 5, 6
Leipzig Machzor (Leipzig, Karl-Marx-Ubib., MS. V1102) 17 535, 563; 20 6
Michael Machzor (Oxford, Bodleian Lib., Mich. MS. 617, 627) 20 5
Tripartite Machzor (Budapest, Lib. Hung. Acad. Sci.; London, BL; Oxford, Bodleian Lib.) 20 6
Worms Machzor (Jerusalem, Jew. N. & U. Lib., Heb. MS. 40781) 20 6
Maci, Jacques 25 694
Maciachini, Carlo 20 6*; 21 521
Macías (family) 26 425
Macías, Juan 24 612
Maciej see NOWICKI, MATTHEW
Maciej, Abbot of Tyniec 25 126
Maciejowski, Samuel, Bishop 18 425
Maciejowski Bible see under BIBLES → individual manuscripts
Maciet 11 674
Macijauskas, Aleksandras 20 7*
Macintosh, George 28 266
Macintosh, Henry 30 16
MacIntosh, William 2 308
Macintyre, James, & Co. Ltd 22 50
Maçip, Vicente 20 9–10*; 29 277; 31 815
works 20 9, 10
Maciunas, George 1 34; 11 232; 24 407; 29 16
MacIver, Loren 20 10*, 832
Mack, Georg 25 621
Mack, Heinz 12 397; 13 727; 20 10–11*; 33 636
Mack, Ludwig Hirschfeld see HIRSCHFELD-MACK, LUDWIG
Mackay, Charles 8 218
Mackay, David 20 516*; 29 309
Mackay, Donald 4 367
Mackay, Ernest J. H. 6 449; 15 418, 419; 18 86; 21 792
MacKay, Tony see EXUMA
Macke, August (Robert Ludwig) 20 11–12*; 22 379
exhibitions 32 775
groups and movements 1 74; 4 131, 132; 8 434; 10 695; 12 395; 16 817; 17 764; 23 505
patrons and collectors 4 324; 10 414; 18 187
works 12 395; 20 12; 22 379; 29 871
Mackelvie, James 23 75
Mackenna, Benjamín Vicuña see VICUÑA MACKENNA, BENJAMÍN
MacKenna, Fernando Díaz see DÍAZ MACKENNA, FERNANDO
Mackennal, (Edgar) Bertram 2 752; 20 13*
works 2 753; 5 419
Mackennal, John Simpson 2 752
MacKennell, Bertram 5 66
MacKenney, Thomas L. 18 64
Mackensen, Andrzej, I (c. 1596-1677/8) 4 43; 20 13*; 25 127
Mackensen, Andrzej, II (1660/1-after 1701) 20 14*; 25 127
Mackensen, Fritz 20 14*
groups and movements 26 394; 33 382
pupils 21 784; 33 383
works 33 383
Mackenzie, Alexander (d 1827) 20 14
Mackenzie, Alexander George Robertson (1879-1963) 9 739; 20 15*
Mackenzie, Alexander Marshall (1848-1933) 1 30; 9 739; 20 14–15*
Mackenzie, Colin 1 753
Mackenzie, D. 18 165
Mackenzie, David (fl 1830-42) 20 14
Mackenzie, David (1832-75) 20 14
Mackenzie, Emma see LANDSEER, EMMA
Mackenzie, Frederick 1 121; 9 19
MacKenzie, I. A. 29 97
Mackenzie, John 33 566*
Mackenzie, Robert Tait 5 570
Mackenzie, Thomas 20 14*
MacKenzie, Warren 28 300
Mackenzie, William MacDonald 20 14*
Mackeprang, Carl Mouritz Cold 8 762
Mackevičius, Jonas 19 498
Mackey, Carol J. 6 441
Mackey, John W. 31 650
Mackh, Fanz 2 823
Mackie, Charles 28 238
Mackie, George 4 369
MacKie & Kamrath 14 802
Mackinac Island (MI), Grand Hotel 14 787; 25 268
Mackinstosh Virgin and Child 26 541
Mackintosh, Charles Rennie 12 776; 19 876; 20 20–25*
architecture 12 775; 20 22, 23, 24; 28 228, 229
calligraphy 2 333
collaboration 19 876–7; 20 31
competitions 7 668
drawings 2 333
exhibitions 33 165
furniture 3 485; 6 391, 391; 12 780; 28 255, 256, 666
groups and movements 9 739
Arts and Crafts Movement 2 571; 28 289
Four, The 11 358; 19 875–6; 25 347; 28 275
Glasgow style 2 562; 6 164; 12 780; 23 547
house 28 273
interior decoration 28 249
metalwork 8 284; 16 60; 28 262
paintings 28 238
patrons and collectors 12 777; 14 132; 28 270; 32 834
stained glass 29 508
textiles 20 25
Macklin, Charles (c. 1700-97; actor) 30 675
Macklin, Charles (fl 1790s; print publisher) 26 277
Macklin, Thomas 14 599; 19 588, 730; 20 25–6*; 25 626
book illustrations 14 115; 33 95
paintings 23 452; 26 388; 31 308
printmakers 4 845; 5 171; 18 720; 28 558, 573; 29 732
prints 28 597
writings 29 676
Mackmurdo, A(rthur) H(eygate) 15 142; 20 26*; 24 426
groups and movements 2 562; 6 322; 10 298; 12 780; 21 779
staff 14 764
works 7 559; 14 281; 23 547; 28 298
Macknight, Charles Horatio 32 308
Macknight, W. Dodge 11 141
Macky, John 32 824
Maclagan, Eric (Robert Dalrymple) 20 26–7*
Maclaine Pont, Henri 15 770
Maclaren, Archibald 5 265
MacLaren, James 28 228
MacLaren, James M(arjoribanks) 20 27*; 28 230
Maclaren, Walter 10 641
Maclaurin, Oudot de 3 275; 28 486
Maclean, Peter 2 758
Maclean, Will 28 240
Macleay, Alexander 32 249
MacLeish, E. 10 419
Maclise, Daniel 15 821; 20 28–9*
collaboration 8 863
groups and movements 26 740
patrons and collectors 14 148; 32 338; 33 251
reproductive prints by others 29 691
works 14 587; 16 16; 19 614; 20 29; 22 328
Maclise, Joseph 1 844
MacLow, Jackson 11 232; 24 407
Maclure, Samuel 20 30*; 32 414
collaboration 5 572; 26 21; 32 414
groups and movements 32 414
works 5 562; 31 863
Maclure & Macdonald
works 12 774
Macmillan 4 363; 13 648, 811
Macmillan, Alexander 27 727
MacMillan, Andy 7 530
Macmillan, Kenneth 23 183; 30 688
Macmillan, Malcolm 32 54
MacMillan, Robert Senseman 30 226
Macmillan Painter 13 500; 32 54–5*
works 13 500, 500, 549
MacMonnies, Frederick William 4 477; 20 30–31*; 24 281; 31 612
MacMorran, Donald 22 743
MacMurray, William 7 838
MacNair, (James) Herbert 12 776; 19 876; 20 31–2*
collaboration 19 876; 20 23
groups and movements 2 562; 11 358; 12 780; 19 875–6; 20 22; 28 275
patrons and collectors 12 777
pupils 19 359
Macnee, Daniel 12 776; 20 32*
MacNeil, Hermon Atkins 15 47; 31 612
MacNicol, Bessie 20 32*; 28 238
Macomboa, Manuel Alves 20 32*
Macomer, S Maria di Corte 27 836
Mâcon
Cathedral 26 602
Musée Municipal des Ursulines 5 296
Maconde see MAKONDE
MacOrlan, Pierre 3 366
Macpherson, Joseph 8 83
MacPherson, Margaret (Rose) see PRESTON, MARGARET (ROSE)
Macpherson, R. 28 772
Macpherson, Robert 20 32–3*; 24 664
Macquarie, Lachlan, Governor 2 738; 13 622
Macquer, Pierre-Joseph 28 521
MacRae, Elmer 2 633
macramé 18 588; 29 350; 30 550
Macready, William Charles 30 680
Macregol Gospels see under GOSPEL BOOKS → individual manuscripts
Macret 4 524
Macridy, Théodor 1 520
Macrikeuy see HEBDOMON
Macrino d'Alba see ALBA, MACRINO D'
Macrinus, Emperor of Rome (reg 217-8) 27 41
Macro, Cox 14 269; 20 33*; 30 890
Macrobius, Ambrosius 1 652; 10 201; 22 412
MacTaggart, William 12 637
Mactaris 26 919; 31 427
Arch of Trajan 26 920; 31 350
Macuilxóchitl 8 460
see also DAINZÚ
maculatures see under PRINTS → types
Mačve, Milić od 28 451
MacWhirter, John 18 856; 20 34*
Macy, Everette 10 91
Macy, George 4 366
Mácza, Iogann Lyudvigovich see MATSA, IVAN LYUDVIGOVICH
Mácza, János Lyudvigovich see MATSA, IVAN LYUDVIGOVICH
Mączyński, Franciszek 27 722; 29 792
Madaba 9 513, 542
mosaics 9 567, 568; 17 656
museum 17 656
Madaba Map 9 568; 17 488, 489
Madagascar 1 214; 20 35–40*
architecture 21 43
bellows (furnaces) 1 287
body arts 20 38–9*
boxes 20 39
cement 1 331
cenotaphs 20 36, 37–8
charms 20 38–9
coins 20 39
furniture 20 40*
gilding 20 39
jewellery 20 38
looms 1 294
marquetry 20 36
mats 20 39
metalwork 20 36
monoliths 20 37
monuments 1 331
obelisks 20 37
portraits 1 269
raffia 1 293; 20 40
sashes 20 39
sculpture 20 36–8*, 38
shrouds 20 38
silk 1 293; 20 38, 39
silver 20 38
spoons 20 39
staffs 20 40
textiles 20 36, 38*, 40, 40
tombs 20 36
weaving 1 246, 293, 294; 20 36
wood 20 38, 40
wood-carvings 20 36–8, 37
wool 1 293
Mada'in Salih 2 246, 268; 27 877
architecture 22 419
Qasr al-Bint 2 250
sculpture 22 419
stelae 2 255
tombs 2 249–50
Madak 24 85
Madaleno, Juan Sordo see SORDO MADALENO, JUAN
Madamud
heads of Sesostris III 28 492, 492
houses 9 851
lintel of Sesostris III 9 878; 28 491
sacred lake 27 496
temples 9 829, 830
Temple of Montu 9 830–31, 878; 10 81
Temple of Sebekhotpe I 9 878
Madam Wei see WEI FUREN
Madan 27 470
Madanpur 15 290
Madara 5 144, 146, 155; 26 906
villa 5 145; 26 907
Madarász, Viktor 14 901; 20 41–2*
works 14 588; 20 42
Madauros 26 872, 919
Madavela 29 465
Rajamahavihara
wall paintings 29 466
Maddaloni, Diomede Carafa, Duca di 25 563
Maddaloni, Duca di 25 55
Madden, Frederic 20 42–3*
Madden, Samuel 15 28; 16 25
madder
historical and regional traditions
Byzantine 9 665
Central Asia, Western 6 253; 16 485
Early Christian (c. AD 250-843) 9 665

madder
historical and regional traditions—cont.
Egypt 16 431
Indian subcontinent 15 667
Iran 16 449
Islamic 16 431, 438, 449, 473, 485
Japan 17 308
Scotland 28 266
Yemen 16 438
uses
dyes 9 491*, 492, 493; 10 872; 30 559, 561
Anglo-Saxon 2 83
Central Asia, Western 6 253
Early Christian and Byzantine 9 665
Indian subcontinent 15 667
Islamic 16 431, 438, 449, 473, 485
Japan 17 308
Scotland 28 266
pigments 18 655, 656; 24 796
Maddison, C. A. 2 742
Maddock, Bea (Louise) 20 43*
Maddox, Allen 23 61
Maddox, Conroy 4 87; 30 22
Maddox, George 5 282
Maddox, Richard Leach 24 647, 651
Madebe, Adam 33 679
Madeghe, Job Andrew 30 301
Madeira 25 287
architecture 25 290, 292, 294
tiles 30 879
Mademoiselle 18 476
Maden 10 340
Maden Şehir 4 66, 67
Church no. 7 4 67
Mader, Christoph 29 760, 761
Mader, Johann Christoph 32 453
Mader, Xavier 9 370
Mader Frères 8 792
Maderna, Giovanni Battista 8 426
Maderna, Pietro 19 55
Maderni, Giovanni Manfredo 27 553
Madernieks, Jūlijs 12 825; 18 850, 852
Maderno, Carlo 11 270; 16 641; 20 43–6*
architecture 11 273; 32 692
aqueducts 4 405; 30 344
churches 3 835; 4 404, 428; 16 635, 637; 20 *44*; 21 455; 25 861; 26 807, *807*; 32 692
columns 4 405
crypts 8 224
palazzi 4 405; 11 273; 16 638; 18 689; 20 *45*; 26 836, 840
theatres 11 *740*, 741
villas 25 260
assistants 4 427, 428
attributions 26 840
collaboration 4 405, 428; 6 22; 11 272; 13 321; 25 227; 32 9
engineering 11 *272*
fountains 4 405, 646; 11 741
groups and movements 3 264
patrons and collectors
Barberini (family) (17th cent.) 3 205; 16 *764*
Borghese, Scipione, Cardinal 32 9
Clement VIII, Pope (*reg* 1592-1605) 1 595; 32 547
Giustiniani (i), Vincenzo, Marchese 12 764
Montalto, Alessandro, Cardinal 30 649
Paul V, Pope (*reg* 1605-21) 16 637
Peretti (-Montalto), Alessandro, Cardinal 3 56; 24 399
Rocca Sinibaldi, Asdrubale Mattei, Duca di 20 840
Salviati (family) 27 648
Maderno, Carlo
patrons and collectors—cont.
Urban VIII, Pope (*reg* 1623-44) 3 207
pupils 2 849; 30 453
Maderno, Stefano 20 46–8*
collaboration 4 405; 29 559
patrons and collectors 1 595; 7 418; 28 529
works 20 *47*; 26 840
Madé Wianta 15 809
Madeyski, Antoni 18 692; 25 115
Madge, Charles 20 589, 590
Madhhur, Tell 14 128
Madhi, Guri 1 540
Madhloom, Tariq 21 300
Madho Singh I, Maharaja of Jaipur (*reg* 1750-68) (Rajput) 15 610; 16 871
Madhubani 15 730
Madhu Kalan 20 48–9*; 31 420
Madhu Khurd 20 48–9*
Madhupura *see* MATHURA
Madhur, Tell 21 281
Madhu Singh
works 15 *623*
Madhyamika Buddhism *see under* BUDDHISM → sects
Madi, Hussein 19 8
Madigan, Colin (Frederick) 20 49*
Madin, J. H. D. 4 86
Madin, John, Design Group 19 320
al-Madīna *see* MEDINA
al-MadīnaT al-Munawwara *see* MEDINA
Madinat al-Salam *see* BAGHDAD
Madinat al-Zahra' 16 *103*, *187*, 187–8; 20 49–51*; 29 *258*, 262; 32 125
Alcázar 16 187; 20 *50*; 23 815
aqueducts 2 242
ceilings 2 528
coffering 7 527
congregational mosque 30 882
excavations 16 550
fountains 16 *368*
gardens 12 79
gates 16 246
ivory 16 525
ivory-carvings 16 121, 524
kiosk 18 71
majlis al-sharqī 16 493; 20 49–50
metalwork 16 368, 369
mosaics 16 256
pottery 16 397, 403–4
Salón Rico *see majlis al-sharqī*
sculpture 16 246; 29 288
wall paintings 16 253; 29 275
Madingo 28 690
Madisia, Joseph 33 245
Madison, James 31 642
Madi Temple *see* MT MADI (MINLE) 5 108
Madjah ilmu-ilmu sastra Indonesia 24 437
Madjalah untuk ilmu bahasa imlu bumi dan kebudajaan 24 437
Madkheda, Surya Temple 15 288
Madley (Hereford & Worcs), Church of the Nativity of the Virgin 9 155; 24 577
Madola 29 330
Madonna Cagnola, Master of the 7 898
Madonna dell'Acqua 20 755
Madonna di S Biagio 16 633; 27 *739*, 739–40
Madonna di S Luca 16 641
Madonna in the Nimbus, Master of the *see* LONDON THRONE OF MERCY, MASTER OF THE
Madonna of Montserrat 25 432
Madonna of the Alberetti 7 775
Madonna of the Seven Sorrows, Master of the *see* ISENBRANDT, ADRIAEN
Madonnas, Master of the Beautiful *see* BEAUTIFUL MADONNAS, Master of the
Madonneri 20 51–2*; 25 331
Madou, Jean-Baptiste 3 562; 20 52*
Madoura pottery 24 724, 726; 29 329
Madox Brown, Ford *see* BROWN, FORD MADOX
Madras 15 *294*; 20 52–4*
Adyar Club 7 470
architecture 2 428; 15 403, 411
art school 15 542
Assembly Rooms 2 618
Banqueting Hall 15 402; 29 526
Board of Revenue 15 403
Connemara Public Library 15 184
curtains 2 442
fortifications 21 591
Fort St George 15 411; 20 52–3; 21 574
Government College of Arts and Crafts *see* School of Industrial Art
Government House 12 75
Government Museum and National Art Gallery *see* State Museum of Tamil Nadu
ivory 15 696
jewellery 15 702, *703*
Kothari Building 15 169
Law Courts 18 889; 20 *53*
Madras Art School 15 656
Madras Club 7 470
models 15 724
Museum of Basic Technology 11 778
Orr and Sons 15 723
paintings 15 652
prints 15 177
St Andrew 15 402
St George's Cathedral 15 402, 542
St Mary 31 115
School of Industrial Art 20 54
silk 15 662
silver 15 707, 708
State Museum of Tamil Nadu 1 753; 15 182, 184; 20 53
temples 15 406
textiles 15 664, 669, 723
University Senate House 15 403
Victoria Technical Institute Museum 20 53
madrasas 16 141, 158, 246; 20 54–7*
Central Asia, Western 5 137; 6 201, *205*, 211; 16 237
Egypt 5 396; 16 175–6; 20 55, 56
Indian subcontinent 15 *341*, *357*
Iran 16 163, 197; 20 54, 55, 57
Iraq 3 *52*; 16 180
Morocco 16 218; 20 *56*, 57
North Africa 16 215
Ottoman 16 222, 223–4, 265, 810
Syria 4 464; 16 180, *181*; 20 56
Tunisia 16 219
Turkey 10 493; 16 *184*, 184–5, *185*, 202–4, 223–4; 20 56, 57; 27 632
Beylik 16 204
Ottoman 16 222, 265, 810
Saljuqs of Anatolia 16 184
Yemen 16 214
see also KÜLLIYE; MOSQUES
Madrassi, Luca 19 271
Madrazo (family) 8 630
Madrazo, Federico de 27 156
Madrazo, Mariano Fortuny y *see* FORTUNY Y MADRAZO, MARIANO
Madrazo Garreta, Raimundo 8 718; 11 326; 20 57, 60*
Madrazo Garreta, Ricardo 20 57
Madrazo y Agudo, José de 18 524; 20 57–8*, *58*, 67
assistants 26 517
dealing 4 378
Madrazo y Agudo, José de—cont.
patrons and collectors 4 566
personal collection 4 565; 29 354
pupils 1 600; 4 328; 12 744; 20 58
works 29 283
Madrazo y Küntz, Federico de 11 326; 18 524; 20 57, 58–60*, 67; 24 452; 29 284, 357
collaboration 24 422
patrons and collectors 18 899; 23 627
pupils 4 328; 12 744; 20 60, 860; 23 415
works 20 *59*; 24 105
writings 29 283
Madrazo y Küntz, Juan de 20 57
Madrazo y Küntz, Luis de 20 57
Madrazo y Küntz, Pedro de 20 57, 59, 60*
Madre de Deus, Master of the 1 213
Madre de Dios, Alberto de la 10 535; 19 227; 29 269
Madrid 16 *103*; 20 60–73*; 29 *258*
academies and art schools 1 104, 105, 106
Academia Breve de Crítica de Arte 23 572; 33 583
Academia de Ciencias *see* museums → Museo del Prado
Academia de S Lucas 29 357
Escuela Superior de Arquitectura 29 357
Junta de Ampliación de Estudios 29 357
Real Academia de Bellas Artes de S Fernando 4 558; 20 67; 23 413; 24 351; 29 271, 282, 293, 357
collections 12 839; 29 357
directors 3 424; 5 902; 29 283, 284
Museo *see* museums → Museo de la Real Academia de Bellas Artes de S Fernando
Real Escuela de Platería 20 69, 501; 29 337
Alcázar 29 267
Great Hall 13 922
paintings 13 922; 19 179
Salón de los Espejos 32 131–2
Salón Dorado 26 436
sculpture 14 8
Wunderkammer 13 922
art forms and materials
architecture 20 62
carpets 5 835
engravings 20 *66*
fountains 29 293
gold 29 333, 335
hardstones 20 70*
interior decoration 29 306
ivory-carvings 16 524, 525
metalwork 20 69*; 29 334, 335, 336, 337, *338*, 341, 342
painting 20 66; 29 279, 281–2, 284
porcelain 20 69–70*
sculpture 20 66–7, *68*; 29 290, 292
stage machinery 30 664
tapestries 29 301
Asilo Santamarca 27 781; 29 354
Atocha Station 29 272
Ayuntamiento 29 269, 270
Banco de España (Paseo del Prado) 29 272
Banco Hispano-Americano 1 591
Bankinter building 29 274
Bar Chicote 29 321
Biblioteca Nacional 4 379; 29 357
see also museums → Biblioteca Nacional y Museo Arqueológico Nacional
Buen Retiro *see under* palaces
Calcografía Nacional 3 426
Carrion-Capitol 29 273, 309, 321
Madrid—cont.
Casa de Campo 12 124; 20 842; 29 291
Casa de las Flores 29 273
Casino del Círculo de Bellas Artes 29 273
Centro Cultural de la Villa de Madrid 20 68
Centro Nacional de Información Artística Arqueológica y Etnológica 2 371
churches *see* ecclesiastical buildings
Club de Campo 29 321
collections 9 18
Congreso de los Diputados 25 225; 29 294
Consejo Superior de Investigaciones Científicas 29 309, 357
craftsmen and artists 29 315
dealing 29 354
ecclesiastical buildings
Capilla del Obispo 26 249
Cathedral of La Almudena 29 272
pro-cathedral of S Isidro el Real 3 418; 29 269
Colegio Imperial Church *see* pro-cathedral of S Isidro el Real
Las Comendadoras de Santiago 29 269
Convento de la Encarnación 6 *71*; 29 841; 30 883
church 29 269
Convento de las Descalzas Reales 14 5; 30 883
Capilla del Milagro 11 491
Chapel of Our Lady of Guadalupe 14 478
collections 20 68
Salón de los Reyes 14 5
tapestries 3 558; 13 917; 30 331; 31 501
Convento de la Visitación 5 766
Fuente el Saz parish church 11 491
Montserrat (Spain) 29 270
Las Salesas Reales 29 271
collections 20 68
tomb of Barbara of Braganza 29 293
tomb of Ferdinand IV 29 293
S Antonio de la Florida 29 342
S Antonio de los Portugueses o Alemanes 11 491
S Bárbara *see* Salesas Reales
S Francisco el Grande 26 309; 29 295
S Isabel 29 350
SS Justo y Pastor 29 271
S Marcos 26 519; 29 271
S Plácido 11 491
S Tomás 9 110
education (art) 20 *66*
equestrian statue of Philip IV 10 441; 29 291
exhibitions
Concurso de Muebles para Viviendas Económicas, 1961 29 322
Exposición de Minería, 1883 29 272
Fundación Alberto 1 573
Fundación Banco Exterior de España 20 68
Fundación Juan March 20 68; 33 690
Gabinete de Historia Natural *see* museums → Museo del Prado
Galería Juana Mordó 20 68
Galería Theo 20 68
Gimnasio Maravillas 29 274
government buildings
Cárcel de Corte *see* Ministerio de Asuntos Exteriores
Ministerio de Agricultura 29 272
Ministerio del Aire 29 273

Madrid
government buildings—cont.
Ministerio de Asuntos Exteriores **29** 269
Ministerio de Fomento *see* Ministerio de Agricultura
Ministerio de Guerra **29** 344
Palacio de Correos y Communicaciones **23** 827; **29** 273
Palacio de las Cortes **25** 419; **26** 308; **29** 284
guilds **29** 315, 334
Hospital de Maudes **29** 273
Institución Libre de Enseñanza **29** 357
Instituto de Estudios Islámicos **29** 358
Instituto de Estudios Madrileños **29** 358
Instituto Nacional de Previsión **29** 321
Instituto Valencia de Don Juan *see under* museums
Jardín Botánico **7** 608; **9** 712; **12** 125
museums
Biblioteca Nacional y Museo Arqueológico Nacional **4** 567; **17** 447; **29** 272, *272*, 355
sculpture **1** 591; **29** 295
see also Biblioteca Nacional; Museo Arqueológico Nacional
Centro de Arte Reina Sofía **20** 68; **29** 358
Fundación Casa de Alba **20** 68; **29** 355
Instituto Valencia de Don Juan **29** 358
Museo de América **20** 68; **29** 220, 221
Museo Antropológico González Vázquez *see* Museo Nacional de Etnología
Museo Arqueológico Nacional **20** 68; **29** 356, 357
catalogues **21** 82
collections **25** 409; **27** 607; **29** 220; **30** 883
directors **21** 82
see also Biblioteca Nacional y Museo Arqueológico Nacional
Museo de Arte Contemporáneo **20** 68
Museo de Arte Moderno **20** 60; **22** 365
Museo Cajal **25** 879
Museo Cerralbo **20** 68; **29** 355
Museo de Ciencias Naturales *see* Museo del Prado
Museo Español de Arte Contemporáneo **29** 357
Museo Lázaro Galdiano **5** 529; **18** 900; **20** 68; **29** 354
Museo Municipal **29** 270
Museo Nacional *see* Museo del Prado
Museo Nacional de Arte del Siglo XIX **20** 68
Museo Nacional de Artes Decorativas **29** 357
Museo Nacional de Ciencias Naturales **31** 188
Museo Nacional de Etnología **8** 239; **29** 241
Museo del Prado **4** 557, 562; **20** 67, 68; **22** 358; **29** 272; **32** 563, 565, *565*
architectural sculpture **3** 199; **29** 294, *294*
busts **13** 275
collections **4** 566; **21** 35; **29** 354, 355
directors **12** 744; **20** 58; **24** 722; **27** 704; **29** 284
exhibitions **5** 746
Galería de la Reina **5** 411

Madrid
museums
Museo del Prado—cont.
Greek collection **13** 470
library **29** 357
metalwork **29** 352
paintings **5** 509; **11** 304; **13** 917; **20** 900; **29** 352, 354
sculpture **27** 46, 646
Museo de la Real Academia de Bellas Artes de S Fernando **29** 355
Museo Real de Pintura y Escultura *see* Museo del Prado
Museo de Reproducciones Artísticas **21** 82
Museo Thyssen-Bornemisza **20** 68; **30** 795
Museo de la Trinidad *see* Museo del Prado
Prado *see* Museo del Prado
Real Museo de Pintura y Escultura *see* Museo del Prado
Observatorio Astronómico **32** 566, *566*
palaces
Alcázar **7** 746; **8** 79; **29** 267, 300; **30** 664
Armoury **13** 922
collections **13** 862
Galería del Príncipe **5** 526
interior decoration **29** 302–3
paintings **5** 411, 873; **32** 130
Salón de los Espejos **21** 732
Salón Dorado **26** 436
Salón Nuevo **5** 737; **14** 7; **19** 178
tiles **30** 883
Buen Retiro **5** 844; **8** *32*; **20** 70–71*, *71*; **23** 405; **29** 269; **30** 664; **32** 551
Casón Felipe IV **20** 66; **31** 790
frescoes **12** 663
gardens **12** 124
hermitages **14** 460
interior decoration **29** 303
metalwork **29** 336
paintings **4** 486; **6** 30; **7** 394, 395; **9** 16; **12** 587; **18** 734; **19** 434; **20** 71; **22** 472; **29** 45, 352
Salón de Reinos **5** 411, 738; **6** 25; **14** 8, 583; **19** 178; **20** 125; **24** 391; **32** 128, 568; **33** 731
sculpture **24** 394; **29** 291
tapestries **9** 30
see also FÁBRICA DEL BUEN RETIRO; LABORATORIO DE PIEDRAS Y MOSAICO; Parque del Retiro
Palacio de Anglada **29** 306
Palacio de Bibliotecas y Museos *see* museums → Biblioteca Nacional y Museo Arqueológico Nacional
Palacio Goyeneche **32** 564
Palacio Lassala **29** 306
Palacio de Linares **29** 306
Palacio de Liria **1** 528; **29** 20
Palacio Moncloa **20** 77
Palacio de Oriente *see* Palacio Real
Palacio de Parcent **29** 306, 308
Palacio Real **4** 558; **20** 71–3*, *72*; **27** 481, 487; **29** 271
Alcázar *see* Alcázar
Antecámara del Gasparini **21** 133
architectural sculpture **23** 413; **29** 293
Armería Real **2** 449; **9** 31; **20** 73; **24** 840
Capilla Real **2** *278*; **29** 271, 341, 343, 348
carpets **29** 347

Madrid
palaces
Palacio Real—cont.
Cuarto de la Reina *see* Gran Comedor
frescoes **3** 424, *425*; **12** 587, *588*, 924, *924*; **15** 139; **29** 283
furniture **29** 321, 342, 343
Gabinete de la Porcelana *see* Sala de Porcelana
Gran Comedor **21** 133
interior decoration **29** 304, *304*
Mesoamerican collection **21** 265
metalwork **29** 336, 341, *343*
paintings **4** 562; **5** 907; **6** 25; **20** 77, 900; **28** 903; **29** 283
paintings (ceiling) **30** 860
Sala de Porcelana **4** 564; **5** 348; **20** 69
Saleta de Gasparini **21** 133
Salón de Carlos III **29** 306
Salón de Columnas **4** 561; **29** 318
Salón del Trono **29** 304, 315
Salón Gasparini **29** 316
sculpture **1** 149; **6** 68; **24** 840; **29** 20
tapestries **23** 525
textiles **29** 348, *348*
Throne Room *see* Salón del Trono
Palacio de Recoletos **27** 607
Palacio de Santoña **29** 306–7
Palacio del Senado *see* Government Buildings → Palacio de las Cortes
Palacio de Sonora **29** 306
Palacio de Villahermosa *see* museums → Museo Thyssen-Bornemisza
Palacio de Vista Alegre **27** 607
Paraninfo Auditorium **29** 283
Parliament Building *see* government buildings → Palacio de las Cortes
Parque del Retiro **20** 64
monument to Alfonso XII **1** 591
monument to Benito Pérez Galdós **29** 295
sculpture **29** 295
Velázquez Pavilion **29** 272; **30** 506
Paseo della Castellana **6** 602
Patrimonio Nacional **30** 331
Plaza de la Villa **20** *63*
Plaza del Dos de Mayo **29** *20*
Plaza de Oriente **16** 700
Plaza Mayor **20** 63, *63*; **29** 267, 269; **31** 718
Prado *see* museums → Museo del Prado
Puente de Toledo **29** 270
Puerta de Alcalá **27** 480, *481*; **29** 271, 293
Puerta de Toledo **29** 272
Quinta del Sordo **13** 249
Real Calcografía *see* Real Establecimiento Litográfico
Real Establecimiento Litográfico **20** 58; **29** 283
Real Fábrica de Platería *see* REAL FÁBRICA DE PLATERÍA
Sindicatos building **29** 273
theatres
Cruz Theatre **30** 663
Príncipe Theatre **30** 663
Teatro Real **29** 272
Torres Blancas **29** 274
university campus **29** 273
urban planning **14** 476; **20** 61–3, *63*, *65*; **22** 67–8; **31** 714
El Viso district **29** 273
Zarzuela racecourse **7** 696; **29** 273
Madrid, Antonio **23** 905

Madrid, José de **29** 334
works **29** *335*
Madrid, Nicolás de **10** 501
Madrid Alcalá-Zamora, María de la Salud *see* SALUD MADRID ALCALÁ-ZAMORA, MARÍA DE LA
Madrid Codex (Madrid, Mus. América, Iventory no. 70300) *see under* CODICES → individual manuscripts
Madrid Codex (Madrid, Bib. N., MS. 8936) *see under* SKETCHBOOKS → individual manuscripts
Madrid Puteal **33** 56, *57*
Madrid Skylitzes **9** 617
Madrigal, S Nicolás **29** 263
Madrigal, Ayerdi de **9** 710; **17** 514
Madrigal, Gil de **9** 710; **17** 514
Madruzzo, Cristoforo, Cardinal **32** 114
Madsen, Karl **8** 761; **11** 790; **13** 216; **28** 814
Mád Synagogue **17** 544
Madura **15** 801, 809, 810
Madurai **15** *294*, 533; **20** 73–4*
architecture **15** 398
bronze **15** 708
dyeing **15** 671
gopuras **13** 5; **15** 398
ivory **15** 696
metalwork **15** 709
Minakshi Sundareshvara Temple **15** 233, 398, *398*, 506, 646; **20** 73–4, *74*; **24** 2
Museum **15** 697
sculpture **15** *519*, 519–20
palace of Tirumalai Nayaka **20** 74
Qadi Taj al-Din Mosque **15** 359
sculpture **15** 541
Subrahmanya Temple **15** 559
textiles **15** 667, 673
tomb of 'Ala al-Din Udauji **15** 359
wall paintings **15** 646
Madurell i Marimón, Josep María **20** 74*
Madurese **15** 753
Madurov, Fyodor **27** 435
madyalatā **15** 244*
Madyski, Antoni **18** 430
Madżarski, Jan **25** 841; **28** 864
Madżarski, Leon **28** 864
maeander *see* MEANDER
Maecenas **31** 58
Maech, Laurent de *see* LAURENT DE MAECH
Mae-ch'ang **33** 523
Maecht, Hendrick de **30** 318; **32** 732
Maecht, Philippe de **10** 349; **22** 153
Maeda (family) **17** 179, 304, 423, 430, 757, 758; **30** 378
Maeda, Asensio de **19** 657; **28** 513; **29** 268
Maeda, Juan de **13** 283
Maeda, Kentaro **16** 848
Maeda, Seison **14** 568; **17** 201, 436; **20** 74–5*
Maeda Nariyasu **17** 758
Maeda Shōun **17** 378
Maeda Toshiharu **18** 537
Maeda Toshiie **17** 758
Maeda Toshitsune **17** 303
Maeder, François **19** 242
Maegawa Juzan **20** 75
Maegawa Kyoshū **17** 412, 414, 415; **18** 191; **20** 75*
Maegawa Yūrin **20** 75
Maeght, Adrien **20** 75; **25** 626
Maeght, Aimé **19** 491; **20** 75–6*
Maeght, Fondation *see under* SAINT-PAUL-DE-VENCE
Maeght, Marguerite **20** 75
Maeght van Gent, De **2** 201
Maeglin, Rudolf **13** 726
Maehle, Ole **23** 226

Mae Hong Son, Wat Phra That Doi Kong Mu **30** 586
Maejuk-hŏn *see* YI YŎNG
Maekawa, Kunio **17** 88, 89; **19** 51; **20** 76–7*
collaboration **27** 597; **33** 563
staff **23** 627; **30** 288
works **17** 89, 90; **20** *76*; **22** 365
Maekawa, Senpan **17** 295
Maekawa Gorei **20** 837
Maelbecke, Nicholas van *see* NICHOLAS VAN MAELBECKE
Maeler, Arnold de *see* ARNOLD DE MAELER
Mael fsu (Mac Bratdan Ui Echan) **7** 458; **20** 77*
Maella, Mariano Salvador (*fl* 1739; father) **20** 77
Maella, Mariano Salvador (1739-1819; son) **4** 564; **20** 77–8*; **29** 283; **31** 816
assistants **5** 452
collaboration **3** 424; **12** 651
patrons and collectors **4** 563, 566; **12** 839
pupils **12** 924
works **10** 504; **24** 108; **27** 753; **31** 90
Maelre, Pieter de *see* PIETER DE MAELRE
Maelwael, Herman (*fl* 1382-*c.* 1400) **31** 448
Maelwael, Herman (*fl c.* 1400-1416) *see* LIMBOURG, HERMAN DE
Maelwael, Jean (*b c.* 1365-1415; uncle) *see* MALOUEL, JEAN
Maelwael, Jean (*d* 1416; nephew) *see* LIMBOURG, JEAN DE
Maelwael, Pol *see* LIMBOURG, POL DE
Maelwael, Willem **20** 207; **31** 448
Maenad Silk **9** 667
Maenan (Gwynedd) **32** 788, *788*
Maeneard, Allen *see* MAYNARD, ALAN
Maerlant, Jacob van *see* JACOB VAN MAERLANT
Maes, Dirk *see* MAAS, DIRK
Maes, Eugène R. **25** 269
Maes, Evert Crijnsz. van der **22** 844
Maes, Godfried **3** 559
Maes, J. **3** 884
Maes, Karel **3** 399, 564, 587; **7** 770
Maes, Léo **3** 592
Maes, Nicolaes **9** 169; **20** 78–81*
attributions **10** 734
patrons and collectors **1** 731; **2** 382; **19** 624; **31** 342; **32** 377
teachers **22** 843, 845
works **5** 447; **11** *443*, 444, 447; **20** *79*, *80*
Maes, Tideman **13** 113
Maesan
tombs **18** 272
Maes Howe **20** *81*, 81–2*; **25** *470*, 505, 508; **28** *222*, 223
Maeso, Angel **29** 306, 318
works **29** *318*
Maestri, Adriano di Giovanni de' *see* ADRIANO FIORENTINO
Maestro, Matías **24** 504
Maesu *see* CHO HŬI-RYONG
Maeta, Kanji **27** 506
Maeterlinck, Maurice **3** 563; **9** 196; **20** 370; **21** 648; **30** 169, 685; **32** 258
Maewo **31** 890
Maewŏl-tang *see* KIM SI-SŬP
Maeyer, Marcel (de) **20** 82*
Mafai, Mario **20** 82*; **26** 777
groups and movements **16** 681; **21** 87; **25** 910; **26** 777; **28** 212, 319
works **26** 777, *777*
al-Mafarrukhi **12** 81
Mafeis, Maffeo de *see* MAFFEO DE MAFEIS

Ma Fen **19** 856
Mafezzoli, Giovanni **16** 730
Maffei, Francesco **20** 82–4*
works **10** 495; **20** *83*
Maffei, Francesco (*fl* 1515) **10** 766
Maffei, Giacomo **20** 82
Maffei, Girolamo **10** 766
Maffei, Paolo Alessandro **2** 164; **20** 84*; **26** 230
Maffei, Raffaele **20** 84*
Maffei, Scipione **20** 85*; **24** 240; **32** 343
architecture **25** 191
collaboration **30** 857
works **27** 762
illustrated **33** 721
Maffei, (Francesco) Scipione **2** 165
Maffeo, Matteo di Giovanello di *see* GATTAPONE
Maffeo de Mafeis **20** 323
Maffioli, Giovanni Giacomo **32** 602
Maffiolo da Carrara, Alberto **8** 134; **20** 302; **24** 286
Maffiolo da Cremona **33** 624
Mafra **25** *288*
palace-convent **12** 762–3; **19** *776*, 776–7; **20** 85–6*; **25** 292, 317
Basilica **20** *85*; **21** 831
Capela do Santo Cristo **12** *762*
library **19** 316
paintings **25** 298; **28** 430
sculpture **8** 858; **25** 301
Mafraq **16** 369
Magagnini, Gaetano **27** 190
Magalashvili, K. **12** 326
Magalhães, Duarte José de **10** 729
Magalhães, Gregório de **4** 709
Magan *see* OMAN
Magana, David **3** 624
Magaña, Mardonio **21** 389
Magani, Mick **20** 86*
Maganza (family) **20** 82
Maganza, Alessandro **20** 86*; **32** 411
Maganza, Giambattista **28** 214; **32** 406
Magar **22** 757, 789
masks **22** *788*
Magas, B. **8** 177
Magasin Anglais *see* NICHOLLS & PLINCKE
Magasin des modes nouvelles françaises et anglaises, Le *see* JOURNAL DE LA MODE ET DU GOÛT, LE
Magasin pittoresque **6** 491; **32** 82
Magazine for Abstract Art, A **24** 433
Magazine of Art **24** 423, 431, 432, 433, 446
magazines **14** 690; **17** 526; **32** 82
Magazzino di mobilia o sieno modelli di mobili di ogni genere **24** 447
Magdal
church **9** 543
Qarqaphta **31** 434
Magdalen, Queen of Denmark and Norway (1700-70) **8** 753
La Magdalena **32** 564
Magdalenenberg **25** 538
Magdalenian period *see under* PREHISTORIC ART → periods
Magdalen Legend, Master of the **3** 554; **14** 379
Magdalen Master **20** 720*
works **9** *258*, 259; **11** 380
Magdeburg **12** *360*; **20** 87–9*
bronze **9** 153; **25** 137; **26** 684
Cathedral of SS Mauritius and Katharina **12** 399; **13** 48; **20** 87–8*, *87*
altar **1** 695
cloisters **10** 740
pulpit **25** 726
Rider **13** 87
sculpture **7** 643; **12** 399, 403; **13** 86, 87; **20** 88–9*, *89*
Magdeburg
Cathedral of SS Mauritius and Katharina—cont.
tomb of Archbishop Friedrich of Wettin **26** 684
tomb of Archbishop Wichmann **26** 684
tomb of Ernst von Sachsen **13** 160
Tonsur chapel **32** 89
faience (ii) (ceramics) **12** 430
iron **12** 454
metalwork **26** 683
parks **24** 181
sculpture **13** 85; **25** 110
UFA-Schauberg Cinema **7** 328
Wilhelm-Pieck-Allee **12** 380
Mage, Pierre **2** 704
Magellan, Ferdinand **24** 611
magenta *see under* PIGMENTS → types
Magenta, Giovanni Ambrogio *see* MAZENTA, GIOVANNI AMBROGIO
Magerin, Clara **30** 161
Mages, Joseph **9** 177
Magg, Ferdinand **13** 852
Maggenberg, Peter
works **23** *500*
Maggi, Baldassare **17** 588; **20** 89–90*
patrons and collectors **14** 818
works **6** 363; **17** 588; **27** 285
Maggi, Giacomo Antonio de' **6** 363
Maggi, Giovanni **2** 105; **32** 203
Maggi, Girolamo **21** 578
Maggi, Pietro **8** 526
Maggiolini, Carlo Francesco **20** 90*
Maggiolini, Giuseppe **20** 90*; **21** 527
collaboration **1** 575
pupils **16** 730
works **7** 659; **16** 719, 728, 729; **20** 468
Maggioni **7** *294*
Maggiore, Dionigi **20** 90
Maggiore, Giovanni Ambrogio **20** 90*
Maggiotto, Domenico **20** 91*; **24** 707
Maggiotto, Francesco **14** 264; **20** 91*; **32** 689
works **32** 689
Magha **15** 227
Magharat Abloun **28** 667
Maghera Monastery **26** 618
al-Maghribi, Taher **19** 324
maghribi scripts *see under* SCRIPTS → types
Maghzaliyah **2** 639; **21** 269, 280
Mägi, Konrad **10** 539; **20** 91*; **33** 566
magic lanterns **20** 91–2*
Magic Realism **5** 671; **15** 49; **20** 93*; **22** *852*; **25** 6
Magi da Bassano, Annibale **10** 767
Magilp *see* MEGILP
Magimel, Albert **15** 842
Magimel, Philippe-Antoine **10** 347
Magini, Carlo **29** 669
Maginnis, Charles D(onagh) **20** 93*
Maginnis, Hayden **23** 362
Maginot Line **21** 577
Magischer Realismus *see* NEUE SACHLICHKEIT
magistrates' courts *see* LAW COURTS
Magistretti, Vico **12** 59; **19** 6
magistri Comacini **20** 559
Magistris, Giovanni Andrea de **20** 93
Magistris, Giovanni Francesco de **20** 93
Magistris, Simone de **20** 93*
Magistros, Grigor **2** 436
Magius **22** 248; **27** 763; **29** 275
Magius, Stephanus *see* STEPHANUS MAGIUS
Maglakeli, Mikael **12** 323
Maglia, Michele **23** 644; **29** 831; **30** 704
Magliabechi, Antonio **21** 29
Magliabechiano, Anonimo **10** 730; **16** 781; **20** 93–4*; **26** 767
Magliano **10** 589, 620
Maglič **28** 440
Mağlova Aqueduct **16** 225
Magna **23** 787
Magna Carta **10** 141
Magna Mahumeria **21** 564
Magnani, Giovanni Battista **20** 94*; **33** 585
Magnani, Lorenzo **30** 803
Magnani, Paolo **8** 159; **21** 539
Magnanini, Magnanino **28** 62
Magna paint *see under* PAINTS → types
Magnasco, Alessandro **20** 95–6*; **21** 527
collaboration **21** 30; **26** 323
patrons and collectors **5** 9
works **11** 489; **12** 292; **16** 674; **20** *96*; **23** 444
Magnasco, Lissandrino *see* MAGNASCO, ALESSANDRO
Magnasco, Stefano **6** 29; **20** 94–5*
Magne, Auguste-Josephe **20** 97*
Magne, Lucien **1** 14; **20** 97*
Magne, Pierre **20** 97
Magnelli, Alberto (Giovanni Cesare) **11** 191; **16** 681; **20** 97*
dealers **26** 193
groups and movements **11** 551
works **10** 822; **11** 398; **16** 680, *680*; **19** 491
Magnelli, Alessandro **20** 97
Magnencio **6** 177
Magnentius, Emperor of Rome (*reg* 350-53) **9** 635
Magner, Alejandro **7** 488
Magnesia ad Sipylum *see* MANISA
Magnesia on the Maeander **9** *512*; **13** *362*, *363*; **20** 98*
Altar of Artemis **13** 426
fortifications **9** 554
heroön of Themistokles **14** 466
pottery **8** 312
Sanctuary of Artemis Leukophryene **1** 692; **13** 417; **27** 714; **29** 681
Temple of Artemis **1** 128; **13** 380, 405, 408; **15** 894; **20** 98; **23** 482
frieze **13** 426
magnesite **15** *914*
magnesium **7** 80, 82; **21** 320; **29** 813
magnesium flash powder **24** 651, 669
magnesium silicate **6** 335
magnesium wire **24** 651, 669
magnetic surveys *see under* SURVEYS → types
magnetite **21** 195, 241, 718; **24** 790
Magni, Cesare **20** 98*
Magni, G. B.
works **28** *338*
Magni, Giuseppe **9** 14
Magni, Pietro **16** 706; **20** 99*; **30** 215
Magniac Miniatures **19** 697
Magnier, Laurent **19** 76
magnificentia **26** 925
Magnin, André **11** 158, 159
Magnin, Maurice **8** 891
Magnin, Musée *see under* DIJON
Magnitogorsk **11** 299; **21** 622
Magno, Olao **2** 103
Magnoncourt **25** 383
Magnone, Carlo **27** 489
Magnum **8** 568; **14** 100; **17** 623; **19** 851; **20** 99*; **28** 670
members
Bischof, Werner **4** 90
Brake, Brian **4** 642
Capa, Robert **5** 659
Magnum
members—cont.
Cartier-Bresson, Henri **5** 897
Chim **6** 603
Erwitt, Elliott **10** 493
Freed, Leonard **11** 747
Koudelka, Josef **18** 406
Meiselas, Susan **21** 61
Salgado, Sebastião **27** 616
Magnus III, King of Norway (*reg* 1093-1103) **29** 578
Magnus III, King of Sweden (*reg* 1275-90) **19** 424
Magnus IV, King of Sweden (*reg* 1319-65) **31** 794
Magnus, Albertus *see* ALBERTUS MAGNUS
Magnus, Johann Bernhard **11** 731
Magnus, Olaus *see* Mansson, Olaf
Magnussen, Erik **7** 807; **13** 9
Magnusson, Anne **24** 409
Magnusson, Gunnar **15** 72
Magny, Alexis **8** 130
Magny-en-Vexin, St Martin
tomb of Nicholas III de Neufville de Villeroy and Madeleine de l'Aubespine **16** *856*
Mago, Pran Nath **8** 677
Magobei **23** 366
Magojirō Kongō *see* Kongō Magojirō
Magomedova, Mamana (Omapovna) **27** 423
Ma Gongxian **19** 856
Magonigle, Harold van Buren **17** 799; **20** 18, 870
Magor, Liz **5** 572
Magosa *see* FAMAGUSTA
Magosaburō Ōhara *see* ŌHARA, MAGOSABURŌ
Magosuke Fugetsu *see* FUGETSU MAGOSUKE
Magoula **29** 368
Magré, Giovanni di *see* GIOVANNI DI MAGRÉ
Magre, Maurice **6** 167
Magri, Gaetano **22** 486
Magris, Alessandro **30** 3
Magris, Roberto **30** 3
Magritte, Paul **20** 101
Magritte, René (-François-Ghislain) **20** 100–103*; **21** 176
commentaries **20** 414
groups and movements **5** 44, 45; **20** 93; **25** 6; **30** 20, 21
methods **24** 490
patrons and collectors **7** 812; **21** 135; **24** 369; **28** 273
works **3** 564; **7** 831; **10** 482; **11** 420, 450; **20** *101*, *102*; **29** 670; **31** *51*, 52
Magro, Antonio **29** 337
Magro, Eduardo Adaro *see* ADARO MAGRO, EDUARDO
Magro, Guglielmo del *see* GIRALDI, GUGLIELMO
MA group **20** 103–4*
members **1** 131; **4** 441; **13** 840; **18** 142; **20** 849; **21** 793; **24** 417
Magsaysay-Ho, Anita **24** 622
Magt, Leonhard **12** 838; **20** 104*; **29** 571
Magubane, Peter **20** 104*; **24** 679
maguey **21** 249
Maguindanao **24** 628
Maguire, Brian **16** 18
Maguire, H. C. **25** 714
Măgureni **26** 708
church **26** 712
Magyar Aktivizmus *see* HUNGARIAN ACTIVISM
Magyar epitőművészet **24** 441
Magyar iparművészet **14** *909*; **24** 440
Magyar irás **24** 441
Magyar nemzeti galeria évkönyve **24** 441
Magyar nemzeti galeria közleményei **24** 441
Magyars **21** 500, 501
Mahabalipuram **15** 541
Mahaban **20** 820
Mahabat Khan **24** 540
Mahadba **16** 486
Mahadeva **15** 531; **16** 788
Mahafaly **1** 269; **20** 35, 36, 37, 39, 40
wood-carvings **20** *37*
Mahajan **15** 177
Mahakuta **3** 34; **15** 293, 298, 302, 526
Mahakuteshvara temple **15** 295
Mallikarjuna temple **15** 295
Naganatha Temple **15** 325
Maham Anga **8** 675
Mahan **16** *105*; **20** 105*
shrine of Ni'matallah Vali **16** 230
Mahanadi **15** 299
Mahant Ghasi Dass Memorial Museum *see under* RAIPUR
Maharai **15** 615
Maharaja Fateh Singh Museum *see under* VADODARA
Mahares Bourdj Tonga, *ribāṭ* **16** 156
Maharosei **5** 484
Maharosei Harihara **5** 484
el-Maharraqa **9** 897
Mahasanghika Buddhism *see under* BUDDHISM → sects
Maha Sarakham **30** 635
Mahasena, King of Sri Lanka (*reg* 4th cent.) **25** 169
Maha Singh **15** 373
el-Mahasna **9** 850; **10** 59
Mahasthan **15** 253, 452
Mahasthangarh **15** 499
Mahatittha *see* MANTAI
Mahaut, Comtesse d'Artois *see* ARTOIS, MAHAUT, Comtesse d'
Mahavira **16** 869
Mahayana Buddhism *see under* BUDDHISM → sects
Mahdaoui, Nja **20** 105*
works **31** *425*, 426
al-Mahdi, Caliph (*reg* 775-85) (Abbasid) **16** 170; **17** 496; **20** 914; **21** 32; **26** 47
Mahdia **13** *362*; **16** *103*, 170; **20** 105*
bronzes **13** 574, *574*
Burj al-Kabir **21** 585
candelabra **5** 604, *604*
congregational mosque **16** 170, *170*; **20** 105; **21** 626
fortifications **21** 582
gates **16** 246
medina **31** 424
palace **16** 170
pottery **16** 403
sculpture **27** 29
textiles **16** 436
Mahdi 'Abbas **16** 500
Mahdia shipwreck **20** 105–6*; **22** 733
Mahdists **1** 295
Mahé de La Villeglé, Jacques *see* LA VILLEGLÉ, JACQUES MAHÉ DE
Mahelot, Laurent **30** 659
Mahendra, Ruler (*reg* 870-95) (Nolamba) **23** 182
Mahendradatta **15** 784
Mahendravadi Cave Temple **15** 507
Mahendravarman I, Ruler (*reg c.* 570-630) (Pallava) **15** 234, 738
architecture **15** 302; **20** 223; **23** 872
sculpture **15** 506, 507, 508
Maher, George W(ashington) **20** 106*; **28** 728
groups and movements **2** 572; **6** 578; **25** 446
Maher, Karel **21** 875
Maheré, Ewald **27** 665

Mahesh **20** 106*; **21** 726, 727
works **15** 626, *626*
Ma Hezhi **20** 107–8*
works **6** 809; **20** *107*; **33** *319*
Mahier, Edith **22** 595
Mahieu, Thomas **4** 352
Mahiloŭ **3** *525*
Cathedral of St Joseph **3** 527
Church of the Epiphany **3** 526
Church of the Saviour **3** 526
House of Soviets **3** 527
Palace of Hieorhij Kaniski **3** 526
St Stanislav **3** 528
theatre **3** 527
Mahinda (Maurya) **5** 94, 97
Mahipala, Ruler (*reg c.* 1093-1105) (Kachchhapaghata) **15** 292
Mahishadal **15** 227
Mahiṣūru *see* MYSORE
Mahiyangana **29** 464
Mahjam **16** 213
mosque **16** 178
Mahlangu *see* NDZUNDZA
Mahlangu, Esther **22** 713
Mahlangu, Judas **29** 110
Mahlau, Alfred **17** 6
Mahler, Bernard **32** 198
Mahler, Gustav **19** 69
mahlsticks **20** *108*, 108–9*; **23** 377
Mahmatlar **1** 522, 834
Mah Meri **20** 181, 183
Mahmood, Sultan **23** 804; **24** 219
Mahmoud al-ʿAli and Partners **16** 1
Mahmoud Khan **15** 898
Mahmud (*fl* 16th cent.) **28** 568
Mahmud, Ruler (*reg* 998-1030) (Ghaznavid) **12** 512*; **15** 79; **26** 40
architecture **12** 511; **16** 167; **18** 810
manuscripts **16** 302
paintings **16** 253
sculpture **16** 245
tents **30** 477
Mahmud I, Sultan (*reg* 1730-54) (Ottoman) **11** 626; **16** 226, 498, 595, 610
Mahmud II, Sultan (*reg* 1808-39) (Ottoman) **23** 638, 643–4*
architecture **16** 227; **18** 509
dress **16** 461
manuscripts **22** 385
Mahmudabad **15** 348, 349
Mahmud al-Hafiz al-Husayni **30** 919, 920
Mahmud al-Kurdi **32** 160, 161
works **32** *161*
Mahmud Bigara, Sultan (*reg* 1458-1511) (Sultans of Gujarat) **15** 348–9; **17** 687; **27** 842
Mahmud Efendi **27** 683
Mahmud Gawan **4** 35
Mahmud ibn al-Isfahani **2** 380
Mahmud ibn Muhammad of Herat **16** 376
Mahmud ibn Murtaza al-Husayni **16** 324; **30** 921
Mahmud ibn Sunqur **16** 367, 376
works **16** *376*; **21** II
Mahmud ibn ʿUthman al-Irbili **29** 553
Mahmud ibn Yahya ibn al-Hasan al-Kashi **30** 919
Mahmud Khan **16** 536
Mahmud Mirza **16** 287
Mahmud Muzahhib **6** 235; **15** 585; **16** 343; **20** 109*
Mahmud Shah I, Sultan (*reg* 1436-69) (Khalji) **6** 444; **20** 250
Mahmud Shah ibn Muhammad **16** 501
Mähnensphinx **29** 394
Ma Ho-chih *see* MA HEZHI
Mahodayapura *see* KANNAUJ
Mahodayapuram **15** 306
Kizhtali Shiva Temple **15** 522
mahogany **33** 335
historical and regional traditions
Australia **2** *758*
Barbados **2** 151
Brazil **4** 721
Britain **7** 445
Canada **5** 578, *578*
Caribbean Islands **5** 752
Czech Republic **8** 399
England **5** 191, 192; **10** 292, 293, 297
France **7** 658; **11** 595, 597, 598, *598*
Germany **3** *485*; **12** 425, *426*, 426
Guatemala **13** *767*
Hungary **14** 907
Ireland **16** 23, 26, *26*, *27*
Jamaica **16** *884*, 886
Netherlands, the **5** 191
Portugal **25** 305, 307
Russia **27** *583*
Scotland **28** 252, *253*
Spain **29** *313*, 314
Surinam **30** 16
Sweden **30** *95*
United States of America **31** 625, *626*; **33** II2
uses
beds **3** 485, *485*
bookcases **31** *626*, *628*
bureaux **5** 191, 192; **27** *583*; **31** *626*, *628*
cabinets (ii) (furniture) **30** *95*
chairs **2** *758*; **6** 390; **11** 595; **28** *253*
chests-of-drawers **31** *627*
clocks **7** 445
commodes **7** 658
desks **11** *598*; **29** *313*, 314; **33** II2
dolls' furniture **31** 264
furniture **11** 851
Brazil **4** 721
Canada **5** 578
Caribbean Islands **5** 752
Czech Republic **8** 399
England **10** 292, 293, 297
France **11** 598
Germany **12** 425, 426
Hungary **14** 907
Ireland **16** 26
Jamaica **16** 886
Scotland **28** 252
United States of America **31** 625
mirror frames **21** 721
sculpture **3** *574*; **13** *767*; **16** *884*
supports **24** 3
tables **5** *578*; **16** *26*, *27*
veneers **12** *426*
writing-desks **11** 597
Maholi **15** 442
Mahoma de Palacios **29** 299
Mahon, Denis **25** 362, 664
Mahoney, Edward **23** 53
Mahoney, Maurice **23** 56
Mahoney, M. E. **32** 866
Mahoney, Thomas **2** 705; **23** 54
Mahongwe **18** 401, 402, 403
Mahon Harbour, Lazaretto **14** 782
Mahony, Marion *see* GRIFFIN, MARION MAHONY
Mahood, Marguerite **2** 760
Mahperi Khwand Khatun (Saljuq of Anatolia) **17** 864
Mahua **15** *285*
larger Shiva Temple **15** 286–7, *287*, 494
sculpture **15** 478
smaller Shiva Temple **15** 286, *286*
temples **15** 262
Ma Huan **4** 173; **6** 622
Mahudi **15** 463
Mahumana, Mankeu **22** 244
Mahurā *see* MATHURA
Mahy, Emile **17** 518
Mahyar **16** 232
MAI (Masters of Analytical Art) **12** 804; **18** 30
Maia, Antonio **4** 719; **20** 109*
Maia, Manuel da **20** 85, 109–10*
collaboration **25** 186, 292; **27** 800
works **19** 464; **25** 185; **31** 717; **32** 422
Maiano, Benedetto da **20** 110–11, 113–15*
architecture **2** 390; **11** 178
architectural decorations **16** *629*
chapels **27** 751
ciboria (ii) (structure) **27** 751
palaces **23** 809
attributions **29** 782
ceilings **11** 211
collaboration **20** 113
frames **11** 382
furniture **16** 724
intarsia **31** 744
patrons and collectors **14** 904; **29** 782
restorations by others **19** 677
sculpture **11** 28; **26** 187
busts **11** 198
relief **1** 711; **11** 206; **20** *114*; **25** 724; **26** 137
religious **8** 799
tombs **11** 209; **19** 450; **20** 124; **27** 184
teachers **11** 705
Maiano, da (family) **11** 206
Maiano, Giacomo del **11** 384
Maiano, Giovanni da, I (1439-78) **20** 110–11, 113
Maiano, Giovanni da, II (1486-1542) **20** 111, 116*
patrons and collectors **16** 695; **33** 306
works **10** 260, 261; **19** 617; **31** 191
Maiano, Giuliano da **20** 110–14*; **28** 70
architecture
cathedrals **20** *112*
chapels **20** 114
churches **19** 686; **27** 751
gates **2** 277; **22** *471*
palazzi **16** 629; **22** 471; **26** 445; **28** 675; **31** 744
urban planning **2** 277
villas **32** 545
attributions **5** 22; **24** 278
collaboration **3** 99; **9** 148; **11** 86, 382, 705; **12** 549; **20** 114; **22** 800, 802; **32** 360
frames **11** 382, 384, 389
intarsia **11** 86; **16** 724
patrons and collectors **2** 277; **22** 470, 471; **24** 299; **29** 782
pietre dure **16** 724
sculpture **22** 801
teachers **11** 705
woodwork **11** 211
Maiano, Leonardo d'Antonio da **20** 110–11
Maiao **28** 921
Maibud **15** 899
Maichelbeck, Franz Maria Joseph Anton **2** 717
maidans **16** 230, *231*
Maidbronn Church
sculpture **26** *372*
Maidburg, Franz **2** 118; **7** 590
Maiden Castle (Dorset) **2** 300; **10** *225*; **18** 584, 585; **20** 116–17*; **21** 549, 551, 552; **25** *470*, 536
Maidenhead Viaduct (Berks) **32** 398
Maidstone (Kent), Whatman Turkey Mill **24** 45
Maidu **22** 549
basketwork **22** 659
beadwork **22** 641
feathers **22** 652
tourist art **22** 668
Maiduguri **23** *129*
University **23** 135
Maidum **9** *774*; **10** 80; **20** 117*
Onion pyramid **20** 863
pottery **10** *25*
pyramid of Huni **2** 296; **20** 117, 863; **25** 762
pyramid of Sneferu **9** 779; **31** 107
reliefs **9** 871, 872
tombs **9** 838
Neferma'at and Itet **9** 872, 899; **10** 47; **20** *117*, 117
Rehotpe and Nofret **20** 117
Maidum Geese **9** 899; **20** 117, *117*
Maiel, John *see* MAYELLE, JEAN
Maier, Michael **10** 174
Maigelein see under GLASSES → types
Maignan, Albert (-Pierre-René) **20** 117–18*; **22** 93
Maignan, Emmanuel **24** 491
Maigre **5** 58
Maihar Shiva Temple **15** 290
Maiherpri **10** 80; **20** 118*
Maihingen *Pietà* **33** 349
Maiji shan *see* MT MAIJI
Maikop *see* MAYKOP
Mai La **12** 49
mail-and-plate armour *see under* ARMOUR → types
Mailardi, Angelus **7** 922
mail art *see* CORRESPONDENCE ART
Maile, George **29** 677
Mailītis, Ivars
Maillard, J. D. **19** 488
Maillard, Robert **23** 8
Maillardet, Henri **2** 838
Maillardet, Jacques-Rodolphe **2** 838
Maillardet, Jean-David **2** 838
Maillardet, Julien-Auguste **2** 838
Maillart, Diogène **32** 738
Maillart, Robert **7** 694; **20** 118–19*; **31** 465
works **4** 803; **7** 696; **20** *119*; **32** 861
Maille, Michel *see* MAGLIA, MICHELE
Maillé-Brézé, Clémence de *see* CONDÉ, CLÉMENCE, Princesse de
Maillet, Benoît de **10** 79
Maillet, Jacques-Léonard **20** 119*; **28** 345
Maillol, Aristide (-Joseph-Bonaventure) **7** 385; **11** 567, 568, 569; **20** 119–21*; **30** 326
collaboration **5** 216
dealers **32** 686
groups and movements **22** 421; **23** 260
patrons and collectors **19** 282
pupils **12** 665; **29** 491, 718
works **11** 648; **19** 491; **20** *120*; **23** 296; **26** *419*; **30** 500
Maillot, Théodore **29** 610
Maillou, Jean-Baptiste **5** 560; **20** 121*; **25** 802
Maillou, Joseph **20** 121
Mailly, Garnier de **8** 888
Mailly, Jean de **16** 837; **33** 627
Mailly, Mlle de **11** 593
Mailly, Simon de **11** 532; **20** 122*
Mailly-le-Camp **6** 160
Mailou Jones, Lois **1** 425
works **1** *426*
Maiman, Theodore H. **18** 809
Maimonides, Moses **17** 532; **20** 122
Maimonides manuscripts **20** 122*, *122*
Ma'in (Jordan) **9** *513*, 543
Acropolis Church **9** 568
Maʿin (Yemen) **2** *246*, 268
temple of ʿAthtar **2** 253, 255
Mainaladevi **8** 848
Mainamati *see* LALMAI-MAINAMATI
Main à Plume, La **30** 22
Mainardi, Antonio **3** 636
Mainardi, Bastiano **12** 548; **20** 123–4*; **27** 751
collaboration **12** 554, 555
works **20** *123*; **27** 751
Mainardi, Cristoforo **8** 172
Mainardi, Sebastiano *see* MAINARDI, BASTIANO
Mainardi, Vanni **22** 680
Mainardi Missal *see under* MISSALS → individual manuscripts
Mainau Island Castle **30** 536
Mainbocher **9** 293
Maincourt, Renaud de *see* RENAUD DE MAINCOURT
Maincy tapestry factory **11** 356, 641; **12** 828; **19** 21; **30** 321
Maindron, Ernest **19** 488; **25** 345
Maindron, Etienne-Hippolyte **11** 564; **20** 124–5*
Maine, Charles I d'Anjou, Comte de **17** 458
Maine, Charles II d'Anjou, Comte de *see* CHARLES III, Count of Provence
Maine, Georges Clémensin du *see* CLÉMENSIN DU MAINE, GEORGES
Maine, Jonathan **6** 128; **10** 275; **11** 424
Maine, Louis Auguste de Bourbon, Duc de **4** 225; **8** 32; **21** 823; **31** 378
Maine, Louise-Bénédicte de Bourbon-Condé, Duchesse de **11** 606; **14** 846; **25** 377
Maine, Thom **2** 552
Maineri, Gian Francesco de' **11** 4
Mainersberg, Anton II von, Abbot of Admont **1** 160
Maingaud, Martin **12** 391
Maini, Andrea **23** 636
Maini, Giovanni Battista **6** 67; **20** 125*
collaboration **3** 920; **11** 345; **22** 45; **27** 646
patrons and collectors **4** 635; **7** 897
pupils **7** 571; **12** 762; **29** 403
teachers **27** 347
works **4** 622; **10** 744
Maini, Michele **11** 27
Mainland Polychrome style pottery *see under* POTTERY → wares
Mainneville Church **13** 77
Maino, Giacomo del **16** 725
Maino, Juan Bautista **20** 125–6*; **29** 280
collaboration **23** 201
patrons and collectors **14** 7; **32** 129
pupils **26** 434
works **9** 110; **20** *126*; **31** 89
Mainoni, Luigi **31** 172
Mainssieux, Lucien **20** 126*
Mainstone, R. F. **9** 528
Maintenant **24** 427
Maintenon **2** 242
Château **12** 122
Maintenon, Françoise d'Aubigné, Marquise de **17** 672; **25** 71
Mainvault **13** 100
Mainwaring, Daniel **32** 787
Mainwaring, Henry **13** 301
Mainz **12** *361*; **20** 126–9*; **26** *905*
Cathedral of St Martin und St Stephan **9** 86; **12** 471; **13** 47; **20** 127–8*, *128*; **26** 570, 575, 620
Benno Cross **27** 124
chancels **12** 364
doors **4** 688; **9** 153; **23** 658; **26** 684
Gotthard Chapel **14** 81; **26** 574
metalwork **13** 161
sculpture **13** 86; **20** 128–9*, *129*
tombs **31** 123

Mainz
Cathedral of St Martin und St Stephan—cont.
Treasury **26** 646
coins **14** 419
Deutschhaus **30** 536
furniture **5** 192
Jüdisches Museum **17** 581
Jupiter Column **26** 885
Kaufhaus **20** 129*
manuscript illumination **5** 803; **23** 654, 655
Martinsburg **12** 424
Mittelrheinisches Landesmuseum **19** 99
paper **10** 381
Römisch-Germanisches Zentralmuseum **27** 115
St Stephen **14** 81
silver **12** 446
SS Peter und Ignaz **7** 303
tapestries **12** 467
terracottas **27** 110
textiles **27** 112
tiles **30** 884
University **1** 439
urban planning **18** 449
Mainz Golden Gospels *see under* GOSPEL BOOKS → individual manuscripts
Mainz Psalter *see under* PSALTERS → types
Maioli, Thomas **14** 616
maiolica **6** 333; **20** 130*
historical and regional traditions
Central Asia, Western **6** 207
Finland **11** 105
France **30** 885
Guatemala **13** 768
Islamic **16** 250, 418
Italy **6** 333, I1; **14** 425; **16** 732–6*, *733*, *734*, *735*; **30** 886, *886*; **31** *742*, 747
Netherlands, the **22** *877*, 878–9; **30** 878
Sicily **16** 735, 736
Spain **16** 418
Tunisia **16** 250
uses
jugs **22** *877*
tiles **30** 875, *886*, 886
see also POTTERY → wares → majolica; tin-glazed
Mair, Alexander **1** 789
Mair, Hans **14** 663
Mair, Hector **4** 760
Mair, Johann Ulrich *see* MAYR, JOHANN ULRICH
Mair, Paulus **10** 454
Mair, Paulus Hector **33** 34
Mairet, Ethel **2** 571
Mairovich, Zvi **23** 25
Mair von Landshut **14** 663; **20** 130*; **25** 632; **33** 349
Mais, Hilary **2** 754
Maiser von Berg, Agnes *see* MAISER VON BERG, ENGELIN
Maiser von Berg, Engelin **22** 188
Maisières, M. Thibault de *see* THIBAULT DE MAISIÈRES, M.
Maison, Marquis **8** 599; **9** 378
Maison, Rudolf **20** 130*; **33** 283
Maison Carrée *see under* NÎMES
Maisoncelles, Jean de *see* JEAN DE MAISONCELLES
Maison Cubiste **19** 78; **20** 431
Maison Dominique **11** 601
Maison du Roi **20** 131–9*
Bâtiments du Roi **2** 53, 314; **3** 451; **20** 132–6*, 139; **29** 92
collections **2** 904
Garde Meuble de la Couronne **20** 138–9*
Menus Plaisirs du Roi **4** 550; **20** 137–8*, 139; **22** 88; **28** 845
Maison Henry **11** 647
Maison-Lafitte Château **29** 523
Maison Moderne, La **11** 241
Maisonneuve, Paul de Chomedey, Sieur de **22** 35
Maison Poirer et Remon
works **30** XV
Maisons, René de Longueil, Marquis de *see* LONGUEIL, RENÉ DE, Marquis de Maisons
Maisons Château **6** 507–8; **11** 516, 657; **12** 121; **20** 290–91
courtyard **20** *291*
sculpture **11** 562
Maisons de la Culture **20** 208
maisons de plaisance **20** 131*
Maisons d'hier et d'aujourd'hui/De Woonstede door de Eeuwen Heen **24** 439
Maissonier, André **2** 660
Maistora, Vladimir Dimitrov *see* DIMITROV-MAISTORA, VLADIMIR
Maistre, (Le)Roy (Leveson Laurent Joseph) de **2** 749, 759; **4** 143; **20** 139–40*
groups and movements **2** 756
works **4** 882
Maitani, Lorenzo **13** 93; **20** 140*
attributions **13** 124; **23** 586, 587–8
collaboration **2** 41
works **10** 743; **13** 96; **16** 688; **23** 292, 585; **28** 679
Maitec, Ovidiu **20** 141*
Maitland, Alexander **28** 272
Maitland, Dick **8** 248
Maitland, John, 2nd Earl and 1st Duke of Lauderdale **4** 890; **10** 897; **11** *424*; **20** 141–2*; **33** 177
Maitland, Paul **19** 589
Maitland, Ruth (Esther) **20** 142*
Maitland, Walter McClymonds **20** 142
Maitland, William Fuller **20** 142*
Mai Trang Thu **32** 482
Maître à la Chandelle *see* CANDLELIGHT MASTER
Maître François *see* FRANÇOIS, MAÎTRE
Maitreya Buddhism *see under* BUDDHISM → sects
Maiuri, Amadeo **26** 290
Maius, Jehan *see* VERMEYEN, JAN CORNELISZ.
Mai Van Hien **32** 482
Maiwand **1** 190
Mai Xianyang *see* MAK, ANTONIO
Majani, Augusto **31** 268
Majano, da *see* MAIANO, DA
Majapahit **14** 560; **29** 236; **32** 485
majapahit keris see under KERIS → types
Majault **1** 898; **6** 121; **10** 198
Majer, Giovanni **21** 532
Majer, Jeremias *see* MEYER, JEREMIAH
Majerník, Cyprián **28** 853
Majeroni, T. **8** 267
Majerský, Ladislav **28** 855
Majestatis **26** 639
Majewski, Hilary **19** 536–7
Majhoor **15** 483
Majiabang (Jiaxing) **6** 685, 878
Majiabang culture **6** 877, 878
Majiayao **6** *615*, 629, 773; **20** 142–3*
Majiayao culture **6** 835, 876–7; **20** 143*
pottery **20** *143*
Majid, Abdul **23** 804
Majnun of Herat **16** 277
Majo, Bartolomeo di **27** 728
Majolikamanufaktur (Karlsruhe) **12** 432
Major, Isaac **27** 885; **29** 649
Major, Máté **14** 890; **20** 143–4*
Major, Thomas **11** 908; **13** 324; **18** 866; **20** 144*
Major, Wantue **19** 310
Majorana, Cristoforo **1** 127; **20** 144*
Majorca *see* MALLORCA
Majorel, Denise **11** 644
Majorelle, Auguste **20** 145
Majorelle, J. S. Henry de **29** 308
Majorelle, Jules **20** 145
Majorelle, Louis **11** 600; **20** 145*
assistants **25** 663
collaboration **27** 879
exhibitions **15** 883
groups and movements **2** 564; **12** 19; **22** 456
house **20** 470
works **5** 193; **6** 391; **8** 544; **11** 582, *600*; **20** 469
Majumdar, Hamendranath **15** 657
Majumdar, N. G. **6** 449
Majumdar, Nirode **5** 420
Majuro **23** 735
majuscule script *see under* SCRIPTS → types
Mak, Antonio **14** 722
Makach-Kala, Soviet House **29** 529
Makah **22** 565, 578–9; **23** 695
works **22** *578*
Makala **33** 598
Makambo **11** 879
Makamo, Sansão **22** 244
Makan **1** 887
Makaraka **33** 610
Makarandanagar, Kutlupur **17** 777
Makaravank' **2** 436
church **2** 435
Makarewicz, Julian **27** 722
Makarije **9** 630; **22** 16; **28** 450
Makarios, Patriarch of Antioch **23** 142
Makarios Choumnos **30** 725
Makarios the Painter **22** 79
Makaronas **24** 337
Makart, Hans **2** 797; **14** 588; **20** 145–6*
collaboration **29** 885
groups and movements **23** 503
patrons and collectors **18** 692
pupils **18** 387; **28** 183
studio **12** 416
teachers **12** 394; **24** 815
works **2** *796*; **20** *146*; **22** 711; **31** 241; **32** 445
Makassar *see* UJUNG PANDANG
Makeig-Jones, Susannah Margaretta (Daisy) **33** 22
Mäkelä, Juno **27** 633
Makepeace, John **6** 392; **10** 300
Makeš, Branislav **28** 452
make-up *see* COSMETICS
Makhachkala **27** 433
Makhayev, Mikhail (Ivanovich) **20** 146–7*; **27** 389, 420
works **26** *8*
Makhsusabad *see* MURSHIDABAD
Makhsus Khan **15** 368, 378
Makhtar *see* MACTARIS
Maki, Fumihiko **17** 53; **20** 147*; **30** 288
groups and movements **17** 90; **21** 317, 318; **23** 627
works **1** 737, *737*; **17** 91, 92; **27** 731
Maki, Haku **17** 296
makie see under LACQUER → types
Makigawa, Akio **2** 754
Makigawa, Carlier **2** 766
Maki Kagaku **17** 410
Mäkilä, Otto **11** 96; **20** 148*
Makiniemi, Elissa **1** 10
Maki Ryōko **17** 237; **20** 148*
Makiya, Mohamed (Saleh) **3** 52; **16** 1, 242; **18** 541; **20** 148–9*
Makiyevskaya, Tat'yana (Solomonovna) **27** 426
Makka *see* MECCA
Makkum **22** 881; **30** 878, 879, 883
Makolis, Peter **9** 240
MAKONA **20** 151
Makonde (Mozambique) **1** 428; **20** 149–50*; **22** 244
caricatures **5** 761
carving **1** 428
masks **1** 256, 409; **5** 761; **20** 149, 150
patronage **20** 149
pots **1** 369
sculpture **1** 410; **20** 149, 150, *150*; **30** 301
tourist art **1** 253, *253*
wood **20** *150*
wood-carvings **1** 253, *253*; **20** 149
Makonde (Tanzania) **20** 149
Makotai Tirukkulashekharapuram Krishna Temple **15** 522
Makoto Suzuki *see* SUZUKI, MAKOTO
Makouria **23** *276*, 287, 288
Makovecz, Imre **20** 150–51*; **23** 500
works **14** 891
Makovets **20** 151*; **22** 178; **27** 394
members **6** 530; **11** 291; **28** 597
Makovskaya-Luksh, Yelena (Konstantinovna) **20** 151, 152*
Makovsky, Konstantin (Yegorovich) **20** 151–2*; **27** 579
Makovsky, Nikolay **20** 151
Makovsky, Sergey (Konstantinovich) **20** 151, 152*
groups and movements **27** 444
works **32** 724; **33** 379
illustrated **33** 486
Makovský, Vincenc **8** 387, 388; **20** 153*; **25** 433
Makovsky, Vladimir (Yegorovich) **20** 151, 152*; **27** 442
groups and movements **27** 579
pupils **2** 417; **6** 547; **12** 877; **20** 222; **27** 284; **31** 854; **32** 686
teachers **33** 622
Makovsky, Yegor (Ivanovich) **20** 151*
Makowski, Tadeusz **20** 153*
Makowski, Tomasz **19** 496; **25** 840
Makowski, Zbigniew **20** 153*
Makowsky, Z. S. **24** 697
Makoza **1** 269
Makramat Khan **15** 365, 366
Makre, Zéphérin **8** 22
Makrisz, Agamemnon **14** 896
Makromalis, Andrew **33** 602
Makron **13** 520, 523; **32** 55*
Makrychori, Hagios Demetrios **9** 584
Makryiannis, Yannis **13** 359
Maks, Cornelis Johannes **20** 153–4*
Maksimov, Ignat **27** 387
Maksimov, Vasily (Maksimovich) **20** 154–5*; **22** 394; **27** 391; **31** 553
works **20** *154*
Maksimović, Stojan **28** 445
Makua **20** 149
Makua-Lomwe **22** 243
Makuc, Vladimir **28** 861
Ma Kui **19** 856
Ma Kun-hu **18** 321
Makusi **13** 874, 875, 877
Makuzu Kōzan **17** 399
Malabaila, Luigi, Conte di Canale *see* CANALE, LUIGI MALABAILA, Conte di
Malabar **15** 652
Malaca *see* MÁLAGA
Malacarne, Bartolomeo **32** 411
Malacca **15** 200; **20** 155–6*, *162*, 169, 170; **29** *225*
48 and 50 Jalan Tun Cheng Lok **20** 181
A Famosa **20** 168; **21** 595
architecture **21** 45
ceramics **20** 179
Chan Museum **20** 156
Cheng Hoon Teng Temple **20** 156, 166
Malacca—cont.
coins **20** 179
fortifications **21** 595
Historical Museum **20** 155
houses **20** 167
Kampung Hulu Malacca Mosque **20** 166
Kampung Keling Mosque **20** 166
palace of Sultan Mansur Shah *see* State Museum
Peringgit Mosque **20** 166
roofs **20** 167
Santiago Gate **21** 595
Sri Poyotha Vinayagar Moorthi Temple **20** 156
State Museum **20** 155; **29** 240
Terengkera Mosque **20** 166, *166*
Town Hall **20** 168
wood-carvings **20** 181
Malacena ware *see under* POTTERY → wares
malachite **14** 168
historical and regional traditions
Africa **1** 287
Central Asia, Eastern **24** 793
China **6** 830; **7** 88, 91, 107, 632; **21** 714; **23** *495*
Egypt, ancient **10** 29; **24** 793
Greece, ancient **13** 536
Macedonia (i) (Greece) **23** 785
Mesoamerica, Pre-Columbian **1** 713; **22** 158
Mongolia **23** *495*
Rome, ancient **23** 785
Russia **14** *172*; **27** 428
uses
belthooks **7** 107
carvings **7** 91
inlays **7** 88
jewellery **10** 29
knives **23** *495*
mirrors **21** 714
mosaics **22** 158
pigments **7** 632; **11** 763; **13** 536; **23** 785; **24** 793
urns **14** *172*
vessels **7** 88
malachite green *see under* PIGMENTS → types
Małachowski, Jacek **25** 130
Malachowski, Ricardo, the elder **19** 387; **24** 505
Malachowski, Ricardo, the younger **19** 388
Małachowski, Stanisław **18** 490, 691
Malachy, Archbishop of Armagh **21** 87
Malade, Etienne **29** 758
Málaga (Spain) **16** *103*; **20** 156–8*; **29** *258*
Alcazaba **12** 79; **16** 189; **20** 156, *157*
architecture **16** 216
Castillo de Gibralfaro **20** *157*
Cathedral **7** 192; **20** 157; **29** 266
ceramics **20** 157–8; **30** *397*, 406
citadel **16** 215
earthenwares **16** *419*
factories **16** 436
fortifications **21** 584, 585
ivory-carvings **25** 734
metalwork **16** 368
Museo Provincial de Bellas Artes **27** 478
painting **29** 280
pottery **6** 333; **16** 411, 418; **22** 256; **29** 323, 324
Málaga (Peru) **19** 388
Malagasy Republic *see* MADAGASCAR
Málaga windows *see under* WINDOWS → types
Malagis, Vladimir **7** 341
Malagoli, Giovan Battista **16** 744
Malaguzzi-Valeri, Francesco **20** 158*
Malahide Castle (Co. Dublin) **22** 136

Malain **27** 85
Malaine, Joseph-Louis **33** 711
Malaise, Charles **18** 877
Malaita **23** 734; **29** 50
Malaka *see* MÁLAGA
Malakal **1** *379*
Malakar **3** 169
Malakate, Frangiskos **13** 354; **20** 158*
Malakate, Jacob **13** 354; **20** 158*
Malakate, Yacoumis *see* MALAKATE, JACOB
Malake **11** 70
Malakhov, Mikhail **33** 518
Malakula **31** 890, 891
Malalas, John **3** 2
Malamažajka, Murovanka church **3** 526
Malang **15** 780
malangan **24** 85, *85*
Malangatana Valente Ngwenya **1** 431; **22** 244, 245
works **22** *244*
Malangawa **1** 42
Malangi **15** 531
Malangi, David **1** 61; **20** 158*
Malang Santos, Mauro **24** 623
Malani, Nalini **4** 291; **15** 171; **20** 159*
Malantic, Antonio **20** 274; **24** 622
Malan Yavoh *see* YAVOH, MALAN
Malaparte, Curzio **19** 305
Mālaqa *see* MÁLAGA (SPAIN)
Mälardal school **11** 94; **20** 159*; **27** 165; **30** 76
Mälaren **13** 167
Malaspina, Argentina **28** 928
Malatesta (family) **3** 359; **12** 537; **24** 247
Malatesta, Carlo **20** 159
Malatesta, Elisabetta **11** 690
Malatesta, Galeotto Roberto **20** 159
Malatesta, Novello **8** 172; **19** 313; **20** 159, 160*
Malatesta, Pandolfo III **4** 747; **12** 299; **20** 159; **23** 319; **24** 559
Malatesta, Paola *see* GONZAGA, PAOLA
Malatesta, Sigismondo Pandolfo **20** 159–60*; **26** 398
architecture **1** 556, 561; **24** 247; **26** 398; **31** 351
medals **20** 917
paintings **16** 661; **24** 760
reliefs **26** 442
sculpture **1** 456; **26** 400, *400*
works **24** *762*
Malatesta Romano **4** 20
Malatya
architecture **1** 824, 830
Arslantepe **1** *821*, *849*; **2** 503–5*; **21** *267*
congregational mosque **16** 497
Great Mosque **16** 183
manuscripts **9** 620, 621
metalwork **1** 824
rock reliefs **1** *829*, 829
sculpture **1** 827, 828, 833
seals **1** 824, 856; **2** 504
swords **1** 824, 834
wall paintings **1** 839; **2** 504
Malaussena, Luis **32** 567
Malaval, Robert **20** 160*
Malaviya, Madan **31** 903
Malawi **1** *214*; **20** 160–62*
granite **20** *161*
houses **1** 320
rock art **1** 374, 375
sculpture **20** *161*
snuff-boxes **1** 367
Malay **5** 10; **15** 753; **20** 163, 174; **29** 105, 120, 440
Malaya Pereshchepina **9** 655
Malaysia **20** 162–84*, *162*; **29** *225*
architecture **20** 165–6*, 167–9*; **21** 45
bamboo **20** 180
bamboo-carvings **20** 183
Malaysia—cont.
baskets **3** 332; **4** I2; **20** 182
basketwork **20** 183
batik **3** 379; **20** 176
beadwork **3** 442; **4** I2; **20** 182
betel sets **20** 175*
boats **20** 179*
brass **20** 173, 174, 175
brick **20** 166
bronze **20** 175
buckles **20** 180
cane **4** I2; **20** 182
ceramics **20** 179*
chess sets **6** 557
churches **20** 155
coins **20** 179–80*
colophons **20** *171*
costumes **20** 177*
cotton **20** *175*
domes **9** 86
doors **9** 164
dress **20** 180*
dyeing **20** 176
earrings **20** 180
education (art) **20** 184*
embroidery **20** 176
fans **10** 778
gilding **20** 176
gold **20** 173, 174, 175, 176, 179
gold leaf **20** 176
gravestones **20** 170
gum arabic **20** 176
hair ornaments **20** 180
hats **20** 182
headcloths **20** *175*, 176, 180
houses **20** 167–8
ikat **20** 176; **30** 554
inscriptions **20** 170
iron **20** 174; **29** 228
ivory **20** 174
jewellery **20** 180*
keris **20** 174*
kites **20** 180*
leather **10** 778
looms **20** 175, 176
manuscript illumination **20** *171*, 171–2*
manuscripts **20** 171
masks **20** 177*
mats **20** 182
menhirs **20** 170
metalwork **20** 173*
mosques **20** 165, 166, *166*
painting **20** 171*, 172*, 182, *182*
palm leaves **20** 167
paper **20** 180
periodicals **24** 437
pewter **20** 173
puppets **20** 178*, *178*
railway stations **20** *168*
religion **20** 164–5*
roofs **20** 167
sarongs **20** 180
scripts **20** 171
sculpture **20** 170–71*
shells **4** I2
silk **20** 175
silver **20** 173, 174, 175, 180
spears **20** 174
steel **20** 174
stone **20** 166
temples **20** 156
textiles **20** 175–6*, 182
theatre **20** 177–8*, *178*
threads **20** 176
thrones **30** 785
tin **16** 393; **20** 179, 180
trade **6** 557; **29** 230
ceramics **6** 331; **20** 179
tin **16** 393
tunics **20** 180
urban planning **20** 169–70*
wall decorations **3** 442
waxes **20** 176
weaving **20** 175–6
wood **20** 166, 167, 174
wood-carvings **20** 170, 181*, 182–3
Malaysia—cont.
see also SABAH; SARAWAK; SOUTH-EAST ASIA
Mal'berg, V. K. **27** 443
Malbeste, G.
works **9** *283*
Malbin, Lydia Winston *see* WINSTON, LYDIA
Malbone, Edward Greene **20** 184*; **21** 644
Malborch, Jacob van **22** 898
Malborghetto **31** 350
Malbork Castle **4** 783; **6** 57; **20** *185*, 185–6*; **25** *92*; **30** 534, 535; **32** 93
Grand Master's Palace **19** 895; **20** 186
Winter Refectory **21** 846
Malchair, J(ohn) B(aptist) **10** 374; **11** 83; **20** 186*; **23** 690; **28** 819
Malcolm III, King of Scotland (*reg* 1058-93) **9** 722
Malcolm, John **26** 473
Malcolm, Robert **5** 581
Malcom, J. W. **9** 230
Malcomson (family) **22** 282
Malcontenta di Mira, Villa Foscari **23** 866; **32** 548
Malcz, Karol Filip **20** 186*; **25** 128; **32** 878
Malczewski, Jacek **18** 428; **20** 187–8*; **25** 141
patrons and collectors **18** 692
pupils **10** 102
works **20** *188*; **25** 107
Maldarelli, Federico **21** 495
Maldives, Republic of **20** 188–9*
architecture **20** 188–9
coral **20** 188
houses **20** 188–9
jewellery **20** 189
lace **20** 189
lacquer **18** 608; **20** 189
mats **20** 189
metalwork **20** 189
stone-carvings **20** 189
textiles **20** 189
Maldonado **31** *751*
Museo S Fernando **31** 758
S Fernando **31** 753
Maldonado, Antonio **25** 702
Maldonado, Estuardo **9** 713
Maldonado, José Luis Pérez *see* PÉREZ MALDONADO, JOSÉ LUIS
Maldonado, Juan **18** 833
Maldonado, Juan Díaz de *see* DÍAZ DE MALDONADO, JUAN
Maldonado, Rocio **33** 316
Maldonado, Tomás **12** 480; **20** 189*
groups and movements **2** 400, 525, 546, 604
pupils **13** 338
Maldonado. Antonio **26** 426
Male **20** 188
Hukuru Miskit **20** 189
National Museum **20** 189
Mâle, Emile **2** 532; **11** 676; **20** 189–90*
pupils **29** 642; **30** 514
works **15** 89
Mâle, Louis de, Count of Flanders *see* LOUIS II, Count of Flanders and Duke of Brabant
malea see under SHELLS → types
Male Agrippa **23** 892
Maleas, Konstantinos **13** 353; **19** 727
Malebouche *see* VILLATE, PERE
Małecki, Władysław **25** 107
Malepart Beaucourt, François *see* BEAUCOURT, FRANÇOIS MALEPART
Malequin, Laurencin **2** 112
Maler, Blasius **12** 494
Maler, Christian **20** 190, 923
Maler, Hans (1448-91/2) *see* MOLLER, HANS
Maler, Hans (*fl* 1477-98) **18** 137
Maler, Hans (*c.* 1480-*c.* 1526-9) **20** 190–91*
patrons and collectors **1** 731; **13** 908
works **12** 384; **20** *191*
Maler, Hans (*d* 1587) *see* KNIEPER, HANS
Maler, Leopold **13** 725
Maler, Teobert **7** 484; **21** 263; **24** 743; **33** 510
Maler, Thomas **1** 711
Maler, Valentin **1** 789; **16** 901; **20** 190
Maler, Wenzel **20** 190
Malerba, Gian Emilio **23** 263
Maler-Journal **12** 822
Malermi Bible *see under* BIBLES → types
Maler Müller *see* MÜLLER, (JOHANN) FRIEDRICH
Maleshevskaya, Yevgeniya **21** 811
Maleskircher, Gabriel *see* MÄLESSKIRCHER, GABRIEL
Malespine, Emile **19** 848
Mälesskircher, Gabriel **20** 191–2*, 772
works **20** *192*
Malet, Gilles **31** 835
Malet de Graville, Louis **7** 599
Malevich, Kazimir (Severinovich) **3** 529; **19** 474–5; **20** 192–5*; **22** 178; **26** 356; **27** 392, 394, 442; **31** 677; **32** 412
assistants **31** 520
collaboration **18** 474, 507; **23** 169
groups and movements **8** 251
Abstract art **1** 74, 76
Abstraction-Création **1** 90
anthroposophy **2** 138
Asnova **2** 603
Concrete art **7** 698
Cubo-Futurism **8** 250
Donkey's Tail **9** 144, 145
Inkhuk **15** 856, 857
Jack of Diamonds (Bubnovy Valet) **16** 817
Narkompros **22** 508
Neo-primitivism **22** 750
Suprematism **1** 75; **16** 818; **30** 6–8; **31** 519
theosophy **30** 711
Union of Youth **31** 583
Unovis **31** 677; **33** 522
methods **28** 202
paintings **20** *193*, *194*
patrons and collectors **8** 10; **27** 714
productions **18** 474; **20** 851, 887; **24** 405
pupils **18** 141; **19** 746; **23** 144; **27** 284
works **7** 557; **11** 360; **19** 491; **20** 851; **21** 891; **27** 413; **28** 396; **30** *9*
writings **27** 283
Malewotkuk *see* CHAUNCEY, FLORENCE NUPOK
Malfatti, Anita **4** 717; **28** 394; **30** 348; **32** 855; **33** 316
Malfi **6** 57
Malfray, Charles **10** 581; **11** 568, 569; **20** 196*; **29** 496
Malgrange Château **6** 508; **11** 518, 642
Malharro, Martín **2** 399
Malhata, Tell **1** 868
Malhoa, José **4** 386, 629; **20** 196–8*; **23** 211; **25** 299
Mali **1** *214*, 380; **20** 198–200*
archaeology **21** 480–81
architectural decorations **1** 317
architecture **1** 260, 312, 315; **20** 198*
basketwork **1** 296
blankets **11** *829*, 829–30
bogolanfini **20** 198, *199*
chronologies **21** 480
collections **21** 478
compounds **1** 312
Mali—cont.
cotton **11** 830; **20** *199*
craftsmen and artists **1** *300*
dating methods **21** 479–80
doors **9** 164
dyeing **20** 198, *199*
embroidery **20** 198
ethnography **21** 480
figurines **1** 273, *281*
gongs **1** 360
granaries **1** 310
houses **1** 317; **20** 198
human figures **21** 479, *479*
iconography **1** 280
leather **1** *300*
masks **1** 229; **9** *68*; **20** 199
medical centres **1** *320*
meeting-houses **1** *309*, 310
mosques **1** *316*, 317; **20** 198
mounds **21** 478
mud **20** 198
mud-bricks **20** 198
painting **20** 199*, *200*
paints **20** 198
regalia **3** 132
sculpture **1** *262*, 274; **20** 199*
shrines (i) (cult) **1** 261
signs (markers) **20** *200*
statuettes **21** 478–81
terracotta **1** 285; **21** 478–81, *479*
textiles **20** 198–9*, *199*
trade **1** 251
weaving **11** 829–30
women **1** 247
wood **1** *262*, *281*; **9** *68*, 164
wool **11** *829*, 829–30
see also MIDDLE NIGER CULTURE
Malia *see* MALLIA
Maliavine, Philippe *see* MALYAVIN, FILIPP (ANDREYEVICH)
Malibu (CA), J. Paul Getty Museum **7** 386; **12** 504; **19** 703; **25** 194; **31** 667, 669; **32** 556
collections **2** 561, 600; **11** 308; **12** 266; **13** 470, 606; **15** 888
conservation **7** 744
drawings **9** 231
Greek collection **13** 470
paintings **16** 769
sculpture **27** 46
Malibu Painter **32** 37
Malich, Karel **8** 388
Malichos II **24** 556
Malicka-Zamorska, Anna **25** 123
Maligavila **29** 448
Mali Grad, Church of the Councils **9** 601
Malik, Jahanzeb **23** 801
Malik al-Din Firuz Shah, Sultan (*reg* 1486-9) (Line of Habashi) **15** 352
al-Malik al-Zahir Ghazi, Sultan (*reg* 1186-1216) (Ayyubid) **16** 180
Malik Ayaz **9** 40
Malik Daylami **16** 335
Malik Ibrahim (Tughluq) **17** 451
Malik Kafur **32** 535
Malik Muhammad, Ruler (*reg* 1134-42) (Danishmendid) **17** 864
Malikshah, Sultan (*reg* 1072-92) (Saljuq) **12** 81; **16** 161; **21** 169
Malik-Verlag **13** 698
Ma Lin **19** 856, 857–8*
works **19** *858*
Malina, Frank Joseph **18** 62, 63; **28** 204
Malinalco **20** 200–201*; **21** *193*, *372*
architecture **21** 208
doors **9** 166
drums (musical instruments) **21** 257
stucco **29** 829
wall paintings **21** 230
Malinas, Juan de **19** 173
Malinconico, Andrea **20** 411
Mălîncrav Church **14** 898; **26** 710
Malindi **1** 315, *407*; **30** 57

Malines see MELCHELEN
Malines, Egidio da see VLIETE, GILLIS VAN DEN
Malines Bible see under BIBLES → individual manuscripts
Malini 15 619
Malinke 1 246, 385; 3 132; 8 21; 13 834
- currency 1 363
- dress 1 348
- iconography 1 261
- masks 1 256
- textiles 20 198

Malinovsky, A. I. 9 54
Malinovsky, Aleksandr (Aleksandrovich) see BOGDANOV, ALEKSANDR (ALEKSANDROVICH)
Malinowski, Bronislaw 2 137; 11 840
Malinowski, J. 25 422
Maliński, Pawel 25 141; 29 86; 30 359
Malínský, Josef 8 386
Malipiero, Caterino 32 205
Malipiero, Girolamo 4 828
Malipiero, Pasquale, Doge of Venice (reg 1457-62) 4 176
Malitis, Inese 11 54
Malitis, Ivars 11 54
Malizard, André 19 535
Malkasten 9 460; 14 217; 19 259
Malkchiev, G. 8 900
Malkhed 26 4
- Kali Mosque 15 358

Malkin, Samuel 10 303
Malkine, Georges 30 18, 19, 20
Malko Tŭrnovo 16 447
Malla 24 251
- see also:
- BHUPATINDRA, King
- PRATAPA MALLA, King
- SIDDHINARASIMHA, King
- SRI NIVASA, King
- YOGANARENDRA, King

Mallaha, Ain see AIN MALLAHA
Mallakam 16 864
al-Mallakh, Kamal 10 81; 12 767
Mallam Mikaila 23 824
Malla period see under NEPAL → periods
Mallarmé, Stéphane 8 596; 20 201–2*
- collaboration 26 72
- groups and movements 30 168; 32 591
- works 2 616; 8 596
  - illustrated 4 366; 7 702; 20 257, 518, 829, 829; 28 819; 30 488

Mallay, A. 19 224
Mallaya, N. V. 15 212
Malle, Louis 18 117
Malleny House 22 531
Maller, Wolffgang 26 105
Malleret, Louis 23 343
Mallery, Karel van 12 15
Málles Venosta, S Benedetto 16 618; 20 202*
- reliefs 5 796, 796
- wall paintings 5 796, 798, 798

Mallet 31 442
Mallet, Alain Manesson
- works 2 884

Mallet, Jean-Baptiste 20 202*
- groups and movements 31 373
- patrons and collectors 8 868
- works 14 396

Mallet, Maurice 20 203
mallets 9 814, 815, 821
Mallet-Stevens, Robert 20 203*
- collaboration 5 776; 13 798; 17 668; 24 824; 25 663
- groups and movements 11 526; 31 581
- patrons and collectors 11 584; 23 169
- works 10 137; 11 525, 526, 602; 19 80; 24 129

Mallett, Col. 12 650
Malleyn, Gerrit 28 165
Mallia 13 362; 20 203–4*; 21 651
- basketwork 21 658
- Chrysolakkos tomb 21 664
- gold 21 687, 687
- ivory-carvings 21 680, 682
- jewellery 21 658, 687
- palace 8 153; 20 203, 204; 21 651, 657, 658, 663, 691; 23 808
- pottery 21 667
- sandstone 21 662
- Sealmaker's House 21 680
- seals 21 682, 685
- terracotta 29 395
- towns 21 664
- vases 21 658
- vessels 21 689

Mallia, Jean-Baptiste 14 285
Malling, Peter 8 727
M'Allister, George 9 321
Mallmann, Marie-Thérèse de 15 211
Mallo, Cristino 20 204*; 29 295
Mallo, Maruja 20 204–5*; 29 286
Mall of America 28 623
Mallon 10 91; 12 510
Mallorca 29 259
- architecture 32 291
- castles 3 106
- embroidery 29 349, 350
- furniture 29 317
- interior decoration 29 305
- metalwork 29 332
- pottery 16 411
- trade 30 875

Mallorca, Contanza, Queen of see CONSTANZA, Queen of Mallorca
Mallorca, James II, King of see JAMES II, King of Mallorca
Mallorytown Glass Works 5 582
Mallos, Krates of see KRATES OF MALLOS
Mallowan, Max (Edgar Lucien) 4 640; 6 386; 20 205*; 23 152
- excavations 1 867, 894; 2 491; 21 298; 23 149, 151

Mallows, Charles Edward 2 691
malls see SHOPPING CENTRES
Mallý, Gustáv 28 853
Malmaison, Château National 4 303; 10 186; 11 257, 257, 519; 19 399; 22 740; 24 140; 25 193
- interior decoration 4 302–3; 11 579; 13 702
- paintings 4 300, 303; 19 37; 26 334; 32 584
- Salon Doré 12 334
- sculpture 3 452; 4 457; 7 421
- silk 19 850

Malmanger, Magne 23 245
Malmberg, Bror Carl 13 30
Mal'mberg, Vladimir 32 600
Malmborg, Jonas 30 119
Malmédy Abbey 7 265
Malmesbury, William of see WILLIAM OF MALMESBURY
Malmesbury Abbey (Wilts) 10 225, 228; 20 205*; 26 618
- sculpture 26 617

Malmö 20 206*; 30 65
- jewellery 30 112
- Malmöhus 20 206
- metalwork 32 524
- Museum 14 537
- painting 30 80
- St Peter's 4 781; 8 723; 13 56; 20 206*; 30 66
- stadium 29 489
- theatre 30 684

Malmqvist, Sune 30 75
Malmsten, Carl 30 92, 96
- works 30 96

Malmström, (Daniel Hermann) August 18 468
Malmström, Johan August 20 206*
- works 30 79, 96, 98, 98

Málnai, Béla 20 206–7*
Malnaia, Guccio di see GUCCIO DI MANNAIA
Malo 31 892
Malo, Vincent 32 76
Maloh 20 173
Maloisel, Emile François 12 830
Malombra, Pietro 27 655
Malomeřice 6 158
- metalwork 6 158

Malomozheykov see MALAMAŽAJKA
Malon, Charles Henry de 19 268
Malone, Brent 3 62, 63, 64
- works 3 62

Malone, Wyannie, Historical Museum see under HOPE TOWN
Malonyai, Dezső 14 890; 21 4
Maloof, Sam 31 634
Malosso, il see TROTTI, GIOVANNI BATTISTA
Malot Temple 15 266
Malouel, Herman see LIMBOURG, HERMAN DE
Malouel, Jean (uncle) 13 156; 19 388; 20 207*
- assistants 3 639
- collaboration 4 841; 28 866
- patrons and collectors 5 208, 209, 895; 11 531; 13 153; 31 841
- works 3 640; 8 890, 893; 13 131; 20 207; 31 142

Malouel, Jean (nephew) see LIMBOURG, JEAN DE
Malouel, Pol see LIMBOURG, POL DE
Malpaga Castle 4 776
Malpartida de Caçeres, Museo Vostell 32 714
Malpizzi, Bernardo 2 20
malqaf see WIND CATCHERS
Malqata see under THEBES (i) (EGYPT)
Malraux, (Georges-) André 3 128; 11 527, 659, 668, 673; 16 808; 17 726; 20 208*; 24 145, 163, 453; 28 820
- lithographs 10 838
- paintings 20 591
- writings 10 838; 26 237

Mals see MÁLLES VENOSTA
Mälsåker Palace 29 840; 30 65, 70, 93
Malsch, Karol Filip see MALCZ, KAROL FILIP
Malsisar 15 611
Mal'ta (Siberia) 20 209*; 25 471, 488; 27 362
- architecture 27 365
- beads 27 365
- sculpture 27 364
- statuettes 27 364

Malta (Republic of) 16 103; 20 209–19*
- architecture 20 210–12*, 212; 21 43
  - military 21 574, 580
- blacksmiths 20 218
- bookcases 20 215
- catacombs 6 70
- ceramics 20 215*
- chairs 20 215
- chess sets 6 557
- chests 20 215, 215
- Church of the Virgin Damaskene 26 293
- clocks 20 215
- coffeepots 20 217
- coffers 20 215
- coins 18 152
- cotton 20 218
- craftsmen and artists 20 216*
- deal (wood) 20 215
- ecuelles 20 217
- filigree 20 216*
- fortifications 21 574, 580
- founders 20 218
- furniture 20 215*
- gates 20 217
- glass 20 215–16*

Malta (Republic of)—cont.
- gold 20 216–17*
- goldsmiths 20 216*
- hospitals 20 216
- iron 20 218
- ivory 6 557
- lace 20 218–19
- lamps 20 217
- lithography 5 900
- marks 20 216
- metalwork 20 211, 216*, 218*
- miradors 12 222
- museums 20 219*
- painting 20 213*; 25 563
- patronage 20 219*
- postage stamps 25 329
- pottery 20 209
- printing 16 361
- rock art 25 509, 510, 510
- sculpture 20 209–10, 210, 213–14*, 214; 25 512
  - relief 20 210
- silver 20 216–17*, 217
- stone 20 210
- tables 20 215
- teapots 20 217
- temples 20 210; 30 433–4
- textiles 20 218–19*
- trade
  - ceramics 10 592
- trays 20 217
- vernacular art 32 328
- windows 20 218
- wood 20 214
- wood-carvings 20 215
- wrought iron 20 218

Malta, Knights of see KNIGHTS HOSPITALLER
Maltai 20 219–20*; 21 267, 278
- rock reliefs 2 640; 21 277, 278, 300; 23 153

Máltás, Hugó 14 889
Maltepe see BRYAS
Malterer Hanging 12 463
Maltes, Antoni 29 335
Maltese, Francesco 20 220*; 29 667
Maltese cross see under CROSSES → types
Malthe, Rasmus Secher 16 829
Malthesius, B. 2 546
Malton 17 516
Malton, James 13 204; 16 16; 20 220
- works 6 64

Malton, Perry 11 424
Malton, Thomas, the elder (1726-1801) 20 220
Malton, Thomas, the younger (1748-1804) 20 220–21*
- pupils 24 86; 31 466
- works 24 490, 490; 31 155

Malton, Thomas Watson-Wentworth, 1st Earl of see WATSON-WENTWORTH, THOMAS, 1st Earl of Malton
Malton, William de see WILLIAM DE MALTON
Maltravers, James Howard (i), Lord see HOWARD (i), JAMES, Lord Maltravers
Mal'tsov (family) 27 403, 416
Mal'tsov, Akin 27 415
Mal'tsov, Aleksandr 27 415
Mal'tsov, Ivan (Sergeyevich) 27 416
Mal'tsov, Sergey (Ivanovich) 27 416
Mal'tsov, Vasily 27 415
Mal'tsov Glass Factory 27 415
Maluk 18 484
Maluku 15 751, 789, 810
Maluquer, Josep Ma Sostres see SOSTRES MALUQUER, JOSEP MA
Malussena, Antonio 32 170
Malvagna Triptych 5 625; 7 712
Malvasia, Carlo Cesare, Conte 4 277; 12 559; 20 221*
- dealing 21 28

Malvasia, Carlo Cesare, Conte—cont.
- patrons and collectors 10 446
- personal collection 8 141, 209; 9 230
- works 3 98; 4 282; 16 781; 23 497
- writings 33 615

Malvezzi, Matteo 28 658
Malvezzi Angelelli, Massimiliano, Marchese 3 295
Malvito, Tommaso 5 698; 18 860; 20 418; 22 471, 476, 477
Malwa culture 15 247
Malwael, Jean see MALOUEL, JEAN
Maly, Andrey 27 211
Maly, Petrok 22 169
Malyan, Tall'i 1 894; 10 132, 133; 15 901, 902, 904, 905, 909, 910; 20 222*
- Anshan 1 849, 850; 10 132
- painting 15 922
- palace 23 807

Malyavin, Filipp (Andreyevich) 20 222*; 27 392; 33 379
Maly Theatre 17 812
Malyutin, Sergey (Vasil'yevich) 20 222–3*; 27 408, 410
- groups and movements 2 633; 27 392; 33 379
- patrons and collectors 27 438
- pupils 6 549; 18 215, 385
- sponsors 30 464
- works 22 173; 30 265

Mama 1 382
Māmačā, Taddasa 10 577
Mamadai
- wall paintings 32 803

Mamaia International Hotel 26 709
Mamaladze, S. 12 327
Mamallapuram 15 294, 303; 20 223–5*
- Adi Varaha Mandapam 15 234, 511, 512, 559, 738
- Archaeological Museum 15 182
- Arjuna Ratha 15 303, 304
- Bhima Ratha 15 303
- Dharmaraja Mandapam 15 512; 20 224
- Dharmaraja Ratha 15 303, 304, 511, 512, 513
- Draupadi Ratha 15 303, 304, 512
- Ganesha Ratha 15 304, 512
- Kotikal Mandapam 15 512; 20 224
- Mahishasuramardini Mandapam 15 512, 513
  - reliefs 20 224
- metalwork 4 853
- Nakula-Sahadeva Ratha 15 303
- Pandava Rathas 15 303–4; 20 224
- Rajasimheshvara see KAILASANATHA TEMPLE
- Ramanuja Mandapam 15 512
- rock reliefs 15 218, 416, 507, 509–13, 510
- sculpture 15 179, 509
- Shore Temple 15 304, 304
- shrines (i) (cult) 2 362; 15 239
- temples 15 509, 514, 519; 20 224–5*; 23 873; 30 437

Mamandur 15 303, 508
- North cave 15 507
- South cave 15 507

Mamane Dheri 15 446
- sculpture 15 446

Mamani, Paulino 24 500
Mamay al-Sayfi 32 313
Mambetullayev, M. 18 22
Mambeyev, Sabur 17 867
Mambila 1 265, 266, 322, 328, 360; 22 287
Mambo Graphics 2 768
- textiles 2 768

Mambo Mutota 1 308
Mambo Screenprinters
- textiles 2 768

Mambwe 14 376, 377, 378

Mamchenko, Vyacheslav 27 434
Mamedbeyli, N. 22 446
Mamedov, Mamed 31 459
Mamedov, T. 2 895
Mamedova, D. M. 2 899
Mamerot, Sébastien 7 597
Mamhead 10 142
Mamikon 2 436
Mamikonian, Vahan see VAHAN MAMIKONIAN, Prince of Armenia
Mamistra see MISIS
Mamluk 20 225–6*
Mamluk (Egypt and Syria) 16 112, 116; 20 225, 226–8*
  architectural decorations 20 227
  architecture 16 143; 20 227
  basins 20 228
  carpets 20 227; 28 716
  fountains 20 231
  heraldry 14 427
  inscriptions 20 227
  mosques 20 226
  silk 28 716
  textiles 20 227
  tombs 20 226, 227
  see also:
    BARQUQ, Sultan
    BARSBAY, Sultan
    BAYBARS I, Sultan
    BAYBARS II, Sultan
    FARAJ, Sultan
    HAJJI, Sultan
    HASAN, Sultan
    JANBALAT, Sultan
    JAQMAQ, Sultan
    KHALIL, Sultan
    KHUSHQADAM, Sultan
    KHWAND BARAKA
    KITBUGHA, Sultan
    AL-MANSUR HUSAM AL-DIN LAJIN, Sultan
    MU'AYYAD SHAYKH, Sultan
    AL-NASIR MUHAMMAD, Sultan
    QA'ITBAY, Sultan
    QALA'UN, Sultan
    QANSUH AL-GHAWRI, Sultan
    SHA'BAN I, Sultan
    SHABAN II, Sultan
    TUMAN BAY I, Sultan
Mamluk (Indian subcontinent) 8 671; 20 225, 226*; 21 587
  see also:
    GHIYATH AL-DIN BALBAN, Sultan
    ILTUMISH, Sultan
    MU'IZZ AL-DIN KAY-QUBADH, Sultan
    QUTB AL-DIN AYBAK, Sultan
Mamluk carpets see under CARPETS → types
Mamluk Revival 16 241, 545
Mammadov (family) 2 899
Mammadova, A. 2 902
Mammen 32 517, 524, 525
  axes 32 517
Mammen, Jeanne 3 803; 12 215
  works 12 215
Mammen style see under VIKING → styles
mammisi see under TEMPLES → types
Mämmo, Warqu 10 574
Mamne 12 328
Mamontov, Savva (Ivanovich) 1 71; 20 232*; 22 178; 27 438; 28 474
  architecture 18 389
  collections 27 439
  groups and movements 19 276
  murals 22 331
  paintings 32 736
  productions 32 73, 736
Mamontova, Yelizaveta 20 232; 25 146
Mamoru Yamada see YAMADA, MAMORU
Mampukuji see UJI → Manpukuji
Mamuang Son Ton 30 621
al-Ma'mun, Caliph (reg 813-33) (Abbasid) 16 272, 432, 511; 17 496; 23 338
Ma'mun al-Bata'ihi 16 174
Mamurra, L. Vitruvius 32 632
Mamurt Kale 14 73
Mamvaniraja 1 760
Man 24 429
Man, Cornelis de 2 342; 6 558; 8 667; 22 844
Man, Edward Horace 10 580
Man, Felix H(ans) 19 492; 20 232–3*
Man, Jan de 13 255
Mana 11 756
  houses 11 757
Manabi 30 786
Mañach, Pedro 24 713
Manadeva I, King (reg c. 464-505) (Lichchhavi) 4 213; 6 449; 27 755
Manaean 15 905
Managua 23 79
  Acahualinca Museum 29 222
  Avenida Bolivar 23 84
  Ayuntamiento 23 80
  Banco de América 23 80
  Banco Central de Nicaragua 23 80, 84, 86
  Biblioteca Nacional 23 86
  Centro de Convenciones Olaf Palme 23 85
  education (art) 23 85
  Escuela Nacional de Bellas Artes 23 85
  galleries (iv) (art) 23 85
  Hotel Intercontinental 23 80
  Instituto Boanerges Cerrato see under Museo Julio Cortázar del Arte Moderno
  Instituto Nacional de Cultura 23 86
  La Colonia supermarket 23 84
  Mercado Central 23 80
  Mercados Municipales 23 80
  Museo de Antropología 23 85
  Museo del Arte de las Américas 23 85
    see also Teatro Nacional de Rubén Darío
  Museo de la Historia de la Revolución 23 85
  Museo Julio Cortázar del Arte Moderno de América Latina 23 85, 86
  Museo Las Ruinas 23 85
  Museo Nacional 23 84; 29 222
  New Cathedral 21 382; 23 81, 81
  Old Cathedral 23 80
  Palacio de Casa Presidencial 23 80
  Palacio de Comunicaciones 23 80
  Palacio Nacional 23 80
  Parque Central 23 80
  S María de los Angeles 23 84
  Teatro Nacional de Rubén Darío 23 80
    see also Museo del Arte de las Américas
  Telcor Building 22 335; 23 84
  Universidad Centroamericana 23 86
  Universidad Nacional Autónoma de Nicaragua 23 86
  Velásquez Park 23 84
Manaigo, Silvestro 24 703
Manaki, Milton 19 884
Manaku 15 619, 629; 20 233*; 22 438; 23 908
Manala 22 712
Manali 15 705
Manalt, Antonio Viladomat y see VILADOMAT Y MANALT, ANTONIO
Manama
  architecture 3 68
  Bahrain National Museum 3 68, 69
  Beit Al Qur'an 3 69
Manama—cont.
  exhibitions 3 68
  metalwork 3 69
  museums 2 275
Manam Island 24 69
Manansala, Vicente 24 622, 623
Manara, Baldassare 20 233–4*
Manara, Giuliano 20 233
Manara, Sebastiano 20 233
Mañara Vicentelo de Leca, Miguel 20 234*; 28 515, 520; 31 810
Manaresi, Ugo 12 545
Manas 2 601
Manasa 6 207
Manasar 15 463
  sculpture 15 463
Manasija 28 437, 440, 447
  monastery church 9 586; 22 79; 28 442, 453
  wall paintings 22 79, 79–80
Manasse Codex see under CODICES → individual manuscripts
Manasser, Daniel 18 45
Manasses 26 660
Manastir see BITOLJ
Mănastireni-Bika Church 25 341
Manastyrski, V. 31 565
Manaure, Mateo 20 234*; 32 568
Manaylo, F. F. 31 560
Manbhum 15 664
Manca, P. A. 27 836
Mancadan, Jacobus Sibrandi 20 234–5*
  works 20 235
Mance, D. 8 177
Mancel, Bernard 11 32
Mancheng 6 615, 648; 7 150; 20 235–6*
  bronze 6 832
  bronzes 6 727, 834, 858, 858, 859
  glass 7 81
  incense burners 6 785
  jade 7 6; 20 236
  tombs 6 697
    tomb of Dou Wan 6 858, 859, 859
    tomb of Liu Sheng 6 859; 7 33, 55, 57, 81
Manchester (Jamaica), Marlborough 5 749; 16 882
Manchester (Greater Manchester; UK) 10 225; 20 236–40*; 31 723
  Albert Memorial 23 172
  Amoskeag Millyard 10 749
  Art Museum see City Art Gallery
  Assize Court 7 667; 18 888
  Cathedral of St Mary, St Denys and St George 7 192
  Central Library 19 319
  City Art Gallery 3 281; 10 369; 14 391; 15 744; 20 237, 239
  Cornerhouse 20 239
  dioramas 8 911
  Edgar Wood Centre 23 194
  exchange 10 669
  Friends' Meeting House 11 785
  furniture 10 297
  glass 10 320
  Liverpool Road station 25 854
  Manchester Museum 1 66
  Manchester School of Art 10 373
  mills (industrial) 21 601
  monument to Arthur Wellesley, 1st Duke of Wellington 23 171
  National Art-Treasures Exhibition, 1857 6 80; 9 31; 10 679, 755; 20 238, 239; 32 864
    Great Hall 10 679
  Royal Institution see City Art Gallery
  Royal Manchester Institution see City Art Gallery
  Royal Peel Park Museum see SALFORD → Musem and Art Gallery
  St Augustine 4 215
  St Paul's, Didsbury 21 347
Manchester (Greater Manchester; UK)—cont.
  School of Design 8 802
  silk 10 357
  Town Hall 5 303; 7 667; 10 237, 362; 20 237, 237; 31 240, 240, 241
  Unitarian Chapel, Upper Brook Street 23 194
  University 10 375
    John Rylands Library 16 557; 29 380
    Museum 29 221
    Whitworth Art Gallery 20 239
  urban planning 31 738
Manchester, Charles Montagu, 1st Duke of see MONTAGU, CHARLES, 4th Earl and 1st Duke of Manchester
Manchester, Robert Montagu, 3rd Duke of see MONTAGU, ROBERT, 3rd Duke of Manchester
Manchester, William Montagu, 2nd Duke of see MONTAGU, WILLIAM, 2nd Duke of Manchester
Manchester-by-the-Sea (MA), Kragsyde 25 806, 806
Manchester Gospels see under GOSPEL BOOKS → individual manuscripts
Manchester Madonna 21 442
Manchete, Museu see under RIO DE JANEIRO → museums
Manching 21 551
  bronze 25 541
  metalwork 6 157, 158
  pottery 25 544
  settlements 25 536
Manch'ong 18 345
Manchu 6 309
Manci, Vincenzo 28 433
Manciano 10 626
Manciewicz, Alice Sedgwick see WERNHER, ALICE SEDGWICK
mañcikā 15 244*
Mancinelli, Giuseppe 5 431, 527; 6 136; 8 463, 716; 22 97, 480
Mancini (family) 25 862
Mancini, Antonio 16 678; 20 154, 240*; 22 480
  groups and movements 32 256, 257
Mancini, Domenico 20 240–41*; 28 332; 31 32
Mancini, Francesco 16 672; 20 241*
  pupils 6 124, 125; 7 915; 18 779
  teachers 7 309
Mancini, Francesco Maria 20 240
Mancini, Giacomo 8 785
Mancini, Giovanni 26 766
Mancini, Giulio 9 7, 14; 16 781; 18 708; 20 242–3*
Mancini, Lorenzo 20 240
Mancini, Paolo 20 240
Mancini Mazarin, Filippo Giuliano 20 240
Mancini-Mazarin, Louis-Jules-Barbon, Duc de Nivernais see NIVERNAIS, LOUIS-JULES-BARBON, Duc de
Mancoba, Ernest (Methuen Ngungunyana) 10 899; 20 243*; 29 111, 112
Manco Inca Yupanqui (reg 1533-45) 23 414
Man Curta, Rainaldo de see RENAUD DE MAINCOURT
Manda 1 315
Mandagappattu 15 507
  cave temple 15 507
Manda Island 1 407
Mandala Collaborative 2 378
Mandalaeshvara see MUNDESHVARI
Mandalagiri see MEDIRIGIRIYA
maṇḍalas
  Buddhism 5 90
    Esoteric 5 96
    Indian subcontinent 5 96; 26 139
    Japan 5 117, 117, 119; 17 37, 146
    Pure Land 5 119
    Shingon 5 117, 117
    Tibet 5 104, 104
  Indian subcontinent 5 96; 26 139
  Japan 17 345–6*
    Buddhism 5 117, 117, 119; 17 37, 146
    Shinto 17 32, 32, 151–3*, 152, 153; 28 610, 610
    Shugendō 17 43–4
  Shinto 17 32, 32, 151–3*, 152, 153; 28 610, 610
  Shugendō 17 43–4
  Tantra 5 96
  Tibet 5 104, 104; 22 234
Mandalay 1 753; 5 221; 20 243*; 29 225
  architecture 5 237, 238
  coins 5 255
  Eindaw-ya 5 234
  glass 5 256
  ivory-carvings 5 256
  Kim-wun-min-gyi Palace 23 823
  lacquer 5 258
  palace 5 235–6; 23 823
  puppets 5 253
  sculpture 5 241, 242
  Shwe-In-Bin 5 241
  Shwe-nan-daw 5 236, 236, 241, 241
  State Museum 29 239
  textiles 5 248
  Theehathana Throne 5 261, 261
  wood-carvings 5 261, 261
Mandan 22 551, 584, 649, 650
Mandan Robe 22 592, 592
maṇḍapa 15 244*
Mandapadurga see MANDU
Mandapeshvara 15 277
Mandar, Charles-François 24 174
Mandara Mountains
  granaries 1 310
Mandasor 15 276, 285, 474–5; 20 244*
Mandaya 24 626, 631
Mande 1 229, 385, 425; 5 216; 8 21; 13 835; 14 55; 20 244*
  architecture 1 422
  compounds 1 312
  currency 1 363
  embroidery 1 300
  leather 1 299, 300
  metalworkers 1 286
  mythology 1 282
  sculpture 1 386
Mandelberg, Johan Edvard 1 31; 7 410; 8 734, 743
Mandelbrot, Benoît 28 204
  works 28 204
Mandelshtam, A. M. 30 261
Mandel'shtam, Osip 1 121
Mandepeshvara 15 275
Mander, Karel van, I (1548-1606) 1 104; 20 244–9*; 22 839; 25 625
  attributions 22 273
  collaboration 7 710; 12 530; 16 63; 29 428
  groups and movements 13 895; 26 728
  patrons and collectors 14 93; 23 112
  pupils 14 91, 95; 25 362
  reproductive prints by others 9 79
  teachers 14 296
  translated writings 27 726
  works 6 78; 7 814; 15 82; 20 247, 248, 249; 22 907, 910

Mander, Karel van, I (1548-1606)—cont.
writings 2 531; 9 443, 445; 13 708, 895; 14 584, 868; 22 835; 23 680; 31 300
illustrated 20 245
Mander, Karel van, II (1579-1623) 8 667, 754; 14 542; 20 244; 22 897; 23 396; 30 320
Mander, Karel van, III (1610-70) 20 249*
patrons and collectors 23 396
personal collection 8 758
reproductive prints by others 10 761; 14 25
works 8 733; 18 700; 20 244
Mänderlein, Hieronymus 24 295
Manderston (Borders) 22 744; 28 230
Mandessi-Bell, David 5 523
Mandeville, John 7 165; 31 289
works 31 290
Mandhatar 15 512
Mandi 15 619, 620, 633–4*
Palace Library 15 634
Parashara Temple 15 310, 310
Trilokinatha Temple 15 309
Mandian 15 483
Mandibamora Temple 15 292
Mandijn, Jan 3 554; 20 249–50*
pupils 22 199; 29 428
works 2 194; 20 750
Mandingo 12 32; 16 880
Mandinka 21 597
Mandiola, Fernando 6 600
Mandjuwi see GURRAWIWI, MANDJUWI
Mändl, (Michael) Bernhard 2 801; 20 250*; 27 664; 30 793
Mandor 15 459, 491
Fort 15 485
Mandori 3 45
mandorlas 20 250*
see also LIGHT
maṇḍovara 15 244*
Mandra Antine-Thiesi 2 52
Mandragora 30 22
Mandredini, Luigi 20 924
Mandrot, Hélène de 7 292, 294; 19 42; 20 148; 21 782
Mandu 15 285, 354, 360, 372; 16 105; 20 250–51*
Andheri Ba'oli 15 355
architecture 15 195, 354–5*; 16 201
Ashrafi Mahal 15 355
Baz Bahadur Palace 15 355
Champa Ba'oli 15 355
congregational mosque 15 354
Da'i ka Mahal 15 355
fort 15 354–5
fortifications 21 591
Gada Shah Dukkan 15 355
Hindola Mahal 15 355; 23 818
Jahaz Mahal 15 354, 355; 23 818; 29 825
Jali Mahal 15 355
manuscript illumination 15 564, 566, 567–8, 569, 573, 573, 739
manuscripts 16 330
Mosque of Dilawar Khan 15 354
Mosque of Malik Mughith 15 354
Nil Kanth 15 372
Rupmati Pavilion 15 355
Shah Gada's house 15 372
Ship Palace see Jahaz Mahal
Taikhana 15 355
Tauli Mahal 15 372
tiles 15 686
tomb of Hushang Shah Ghuri 15 355; 20 251
tomb of Mahmud Khalji 15 372
Ujala Ba'oli 15 355
Mandylion of Edessa 9 548, 622, 658; 20 251*; 26 141
Mandyn, Jan see MANDIJN, JAN
Mane, John see MAIANO, GIOVANNI DA, II
Man-eater 28 320
manège see RIDING HOUSES
Mané-Katz 17 577; 20 251–2*
Manenti, Paolo 26 809
Maner 15 369
Manerbe 11 604
Manerbio 6 159
Manerius Bible see under BIBLES → individual manuscripts
Mánes, Amálie 20 252
Mánes, Antonín 20 252*; 25 433
pupils 14 247
teachers 25 358
works 8 392
Mánes, Antonína 20 252
Mánes, Josef 8 423; 20 252–3*
groups and movements 2 546; 25 433
teachers 31 64
works 8 375, 392, 400; 17 544; 25 433
Manes, Pablo Curatella see CURATELLA MANES, PABLO
Manès, P. C. 11 568
Mánes, Quido 20 252
Mánes, Václav 20 252
Manesse, Rüdiger 33 736
Manessier, Alfred 11 551; 20 253–4*
collaboration 4 98
groups and movements 2 543, 544; 10 581; 30 231
teachers 4 98
works 19 491
Mánes Union of Artists 2 546; 20 254*
members 2 546
Aleš, Mikoláš 1 604
Benš, Adolf 3 736
Černý, František M(aria) 6 345
Filla, Emil 11 79
Fragner, Jaroslav 11 365
Fuchs, Bohuslav 11 812
Janeček, Ota 16 903
Janoušek, František 16 908
Jiránek, Miloš 17 592
Jurkovič, Dušan 17 698
Krejcar, Jaromír 18 445
Kroha, Jiří 18 462
Muzika, František 22 393
Novotný, Otakar 23 271
Roškot, Kamil 27 169
Slavíček, Antonín 28 836
Špála, Václav 29 359
Štursa, Jan 29 873
Sucharda, Stanislav 29 893
Švabinský, Max 30 52
Žák, Ladislav 33 599
periodicals 24 440
teachers 16 908
see also SECESSION (PRAGUE)
Manet, Edouard 2 652; 10 797; 11 508, 547, 659; 19 92; 20 254–62*; 22 119; 23 295; 24 140
collaboration 20 201
commentaries 30 216; 33 696
dealers 9 424; 28 744
exhibitions 10 680; 24 140, 142
groups and movements 2 530
Impressionism 15 151, 152, 153, 154
Post-Impressionism 25 356
Realism (style) 26 55
Secession (Vienna) 28 344
Second Empire style 28 345, 346
Société Nationale des Beaux-Arts 20 498
methods 11 545; 12 295; 19 353; 24 243, 495
paintings 6 439; 7 675; 8 596; 9 245; 11 38; 21 776; 31 704
fêtes champêtres 20 255
flower 20 257
genre 20 259
history 14 588; 24 667
marine 20 426
Manet, Edouard
paintings—cont.
nude figures 8 596; 10 480; 11 37, 415; 12 295; 23 295; 26 56
portraits 9 673; 11 417, 544; 25 660; 26 723
sporting scenes 2 107; 29 426
still-lifes 29 669
patrons and collectors
Alte Nationalgalerie 31 397
Bellio, Georges de 3 671; 26 722
Bührle, Emil Georg 5 132
Burrell, William (1861-1958) 5 278
Cadart, Alfred 5 364
Caillebotte, Gustave 5 391
Camondo, Isaac de, Comte 5 530
Cone, Claribel and Etta 7 702
Courtauld, Samuel (1876-1947) 8 62; 10 367
Dale, Chester 8 463
Davies, Gwendoline and Margaret 5 732
Degas, (Hilaire-Germain-) Edgar 8 622
Duret, (Jules-Emmanuel) Théodore 9 448
Faure, Jean-Baptiste 10 837
Frick, Henry Clay 11 774
Haus der Kunst 31 397
Havemeyer, Louisine (Waldron) 14 244
Haviland, Charles 14 246
Lane, Hugh (Percy) 18 727
Liebermann, Max 19 334
Lucas, George A(loysius) 19 756
May, Ernest (1845-1925) 20 878
Moore, George (Augustus) (1852-1933) 22 54
Moreau-Nélaton, Etienne 22 94
Morozov, Ivan (Abramovich) (1871-1921) 22 135
Musée du Luxembourg 24 142
Museo Nacional de Bellas Artes (Buenos Aires) 2 404
Museum of Modern Egyptian Art 9 768
Palmer, Bertha Honoré 23 882
Polignac, Winnaretta, Princesse Edmond de 25 150
Pope, Alfred Atmore 25 234
Reber, Gottlieb Friedrich 26 59
Rouart, Henri(-Stanislas) 27 238
Tavernier, Adolphe-Eugène 30 375
personal collection 13 879; 17 440
posters 25 345
prints 2 240; 3 392; 5 364; 19 488; 20 260, 602; 25 607
pupils 12 915
reproductive prints by others 32 577
studio 29 856
teachers 8 76; 15 152
Manetho 9 775
Manětín 8 386
Manětin Hradec 25 546
Manetti, Alessandro 19 512
Manetti, Antonio (di Tuccio) (1423-97) 16 781; 20 262–3*; 27 183
Manetti, Antonio (1805-87) 16 730
Manetti, Antonio di Ciaccheri 20 263–4*
works 1 565; 11 204, 210, 382, 384; 12 906
Manetti, Domenico 20 265; 28 688
Manetti, Giuseppe 5 363
Manetti, Lorenzo 19 442
Manetti, Rutilio 20 264*
attributions 20 738
collaboration 31 885
works 20 264; 24 860; 28 688
Manevich, Abram A. 31 559
Manfredi (family) 16 733
Manfredi, Bartolomeo (fl 1473) 20 319
Manfredi, Bartolomeo (1580-1620) 16 670; 20 265–7*
attributions 26 94
groups and movements 30 456
patrons and collectors 10 525; 12 906
pupils 26 94
teachers 5 719
works 20 265, 266; 31 223
Manfredi, Carlo II, Lord of Faenza 29 387
Manfredi, Clarice 3 868
Manfredi, Emilio 20 497
Manfredi, Manfredo 26 762; 33 469
Manfredi degli Embriachi, Lorenzo d'Antonio di Messer see EMBRIACHI, LORENZO D'ANTONIO DI MESSER MANFREDI DEGLI
Manfredini, Achille 27 788
Manfredini, Francesco 16 729
Manfredini, Luigi 16 729
Manfredino da Como 24 732
Manfredino (d'Alberto) da Pistoia 20 267*
Manfrini, Enrico 9 159; 17 622; 28 681
Manfron, Giulio 4 398
Mang, Heinrich 20 693
Mangaasi 25 181; 31 890
Mangaia 7 790, 791
Mangal 15 610
works 15 610
Mangala, A. G. 11 879
Mangalesha, Ruler (reg 597/8-609/10) (Chalukyas of Badami) 6 404
Mangalia 4 110, 112
manganese
historical and regional traditions
Central Asia, Western 6 207
China 6 869
Egypt, ancient 10 55
Iran 16 402
Iraq 16 400
Islamic 16 248, 394, 400, 402
Turkey 16 248
uses
glass 10 55; 30 407
glazes 6 869; 16 394, 402, 407
pottery 16 400
manganese black see under PIGMENTS → types
manganese blue see under PIGMENTS → types
manganese brown see under PIGMENTS → types
manganese dioxide 4 767; 10 740; 16 248; 24 790; 25 175, 477; 32 200, 201
manganese oxide 6 872; 24 792
manganese purple see under PIGMENTS → types
manganese violet see under PIGMENTS → types
Mangard, Adolfo Best 22 334
Mangareva 31 403
human figures 31 403, 404
see also GAMBIER ISLANDS
Mangasarov, Sh. 2 896
Mangbetu 20 267–9*
architecture 1 406; 20 268
arrows 1 362
beds 1 366
body arts 1 342, 343, 344
ceramics 1 329
hairstyles 1 343, 343
halls 20 268
harps 1 359
ivory 1 292
meeting-houses 1 310
painting 1 425
pots 1 328, 329
pottery 1 406
sculpture 1 404, 404
wood 1 404
Mange, Ernest (Robert de Carvalho) 20 269*
Mangeant, Adolphe 25 173
Mangeot, Jean 4 547
Manger, Heinrich Ludwig 14 652; 19 76
Mangetsudō Okumura see OKUMURA MANGETSUDŌ
Manggyu 15 311
Mangi see CHŎNGJO, KING
Mangiarotti, Angelo 16 650; 20 269*
Mangijm, Jan 15 42
Mangin, Charles 20 270
Mangin, Joseph François 19 873; 20 270*; 23 38
Mangione, Salvatore see SALVO
Manglard, Adrien 14 190; 20 270*; 21 896; 32 331
Manglieu Abbey 30 907
Manglisi Church 12 319
Mangnang 30 806, 831
Mango, Cyril 9 528
Mangold, Franz Joseph 31 395
Mangold, Robert (Peter) 2 241; 20 270*; 31 609
Mangold, Sylvia Plimack 20 270–71*
Mangoldt, Franz Joseph 19 748; 33 417
Mangona, Niccolò 4 502
Mangone, Fabio 4 426; 5 328; 26 318; 30 802
Mangone, Giovanni 20 271*, 587
Mangones, Albert 14 57; 20 271*
Mangrai, King of Chiang Mai (1296-1318) 6 566, 567; 21 595
Mangrol 15 347
Chishtiwala Mosque 15 347
congregational mosque 15 347
Mangualde Misericórdia 17 596
Mangueiras 20 372
Manguin, Henri (-Charles) 20 271–2*
groups and movements 10 839, 840, 841; 25 356
patrons and collectors 29 604
works 20 272
Manguin, P. 23 794
Manguma, Cornelius 33 679
Mangup 20 273*; 31 546
Mangyan 24 624
Manhal Jabur 21 290
Manheim,(PA) 29 654; 31 642
Mani (Greece) 29 702
Hagios Panteleimon 9 577
St Prokopios 9 575
Mani, Ioyan see NOEL, MAXINE
Maniago, Silvestro 31 356
Manichaeism
Central Asia, Eastern 6 291*
Central Asia, Western 6 195*
China 6 626
dress 6 311
iconography 6 293
manuscripts 6 305, 306
painting 6 305
scripts 6 308
temples 30 442
manière criblée see ENGRAVINGS → types → dotted prints
manière de lavis see WASH MANNER; see also under PRINTS → techniques
Manifattura Cantagalli 11 190
Manifattura di Signa 11 190
Manifesto della Pittura Murale 5 849
manifestos 4 27
Manifold, John 13 783
Manifold, Peter 13 783
Manigault, Gabriel 10 850
Manihiki 7 790
Manihira see MINNERIYA VAVA
Mani i Roig, Carlos 12 182
Manika 14 360
Manikyala
reliquaries 26 151
manila (fibre) 18 611; 24 40

Manila (Philippines) **20** 273–4*; **24** *607*
Academia de Dibujo (1823) **24** 621, 632
Academia de Dibujo y Pintura (1850) *see* University of the Philippines → College of Fine Arts
Army and Navy Club **24** 614
Ateneo Art Gallery **20** 274
Caloocan Rotunda **24** 619
coins **24** 626
Cultural Center of the Philippines **20** 274, *274*; **24** 623
embroidery **29** 350
fortifications **21** 596; **24** 617
Luz Gallery **20** 274
Manila Hotel **24** 614
Metropolitan Cathedral of S Agustín **24** 612–13*
Metropolitan Theater **24** 615
museums
Ayala Museum **20** 274
Lopez Museum **20** 274
Metropolitan Museum of Art **20** 274
National Museum of the Philippines **20** 274; **29** 240
Philippine Art Gallery **20** 274
Philippine General Hospital **24** 614
Philippine Normal School **24** 614
S Agustín **24** 611, 612*, *612*
S Domingo **24** 627
University of Santo Tomás School of Fine Arts **24** 622, 632
University of the Philippines **24** 619
College of Fine Arts **24** 622, 632
urban planning **24** 616–17
Manili, Jacomo **2** 163
Manilla, Manuel **21** 386
Manì Monastery (Mexico) **33** 571
Manin (family) **17** 512
Maningrida **1** 58; **20** 470
Manini, Luigi **20** 275*; **25** 293
Maninka *see* MALINKE
maniples **9** 642; **32** 388*
Manipur **15** 685, 727
Manipur Naga **15** 732
Manique, D. I. de Pina *see* PINA MANIQUE, D. I. DE
Manique do Intendente Palace **25** 293
Manirampa, Antoine **5** 285
Manisa **16** *104*; **19** 840, 841
architecture **16** 202
complex of Murad III **16** 224
congregational mosque **16** 202, *203*, 497
Hafsa Sultan Mosque **16** 223
Manises **29** 323, 324, 325, 327, 328
pottery **29** *324*
tiles **30** XIII3
Manishtushu (*reg* 2269-2255 BC) **1** 509*; **23** 153
Manizales **7** *601*, 605
Museum **7** 612
Manizer, Matvey (Genrikhovich) **20** 275; **27** 394
collaboration **19** 274; **27** 285
pupils **2** 903
works **31** 561
Manjaco **1** 253, 424; **13** 835
Manjeshwar Temple **15** 523
Manji Inoue *see* INOUE, MANJI
Manjui **24** 93
Man Jyoti Shakya **30** 53
Mankes, Jan **20** 275*; **22** 854
Mankeshvara, Mahadeva Temple **15** 317
Mankheda, Surya Temple **15** 495
Mańkowski, Simon **23** 113
Mańkowski, Tadeusz **25** 143
Mankuwar **15** 456
Manley, Edna **16** 890; **20** 276*
assistants **14** 858
patrons and collectors **16** 890
Manley, Edna—cont.
pupils **5** 541
works **5** 754; **16** 884, *884*, 889
Manley, Marion I. **30** 684
Manley, W. B. **15** 742
Manlich, Heinrich, I **2** 718
Manlich, Johann Heinrich **2** 718
Mann, Alexander **20** 276*
Mann, George R. **9** 699–700*; **10** 146
Mann, Gothar **21** 575
Mann, Hans **8** 123
Mann, Harrington **29** 508
Mann, Heinrich **8** 596
Mann, Horace **10** 366; **14** 598, 848; **20** 276–7*
Mann, James (*fl* before 1853) **20** 276
Mann, James Gow (1897-1962) **2** 450
Mann, John **23** 737
Mann, Thomas **8** 596, 597; **10** 413, 894; **14** 314; **18** 490; **28** 54
Mannaia **13** 775
Mannaia, Gheri di *see* GHERI DI MANNAIA
Mannaia, Giacomo di *see* GIACOMO DI MANNAIA
Mannaia, Guccio di *see* GUCCIO DI MANNAIA
Mannaia, Montigiano di *see* MONTIGIANO DI MANNAIA
Mannaia, Pino di *see* PINO DI MANNAIA
Mannellini, Bernardino **6** 147
mannequins **18** 899
Mannerheim, A. **11** 111
Mannerism **20** 277–81*; **33** 418
art forms
allegories **30** *319*
altarpieces
Denmark **11** *467*
Italy **1** *710*; **12** *673*; **31** *38*
Mexico **21** *383*
altars **33** *738*
architecture (general)
France **11** 514
Italy **16** 634–5*; **20** 279, 280
Netherlands, the **18** 7; **22** 823–4
architecture (chapels) **19** *836*
architecture (churches)
Italy **16** *636*; **23** *869*; **30** *802*; **32** *214*
Portugal **10** *664*
architecture (colleges) **5** *512*
architecture (houses) **8** *377*
architecture (libraries) **19** *314*; **21** *452*
architecture (mints) **27** *744*
architecture (palazzi) **12** *754*; **23** *864*, *865*, *868*; **26** *839*
architecture (squares) **21** *454*
architecture (theatres) **30** *656*
architecture (town halls)
Germany **14** *678*, *679*
Netherlands, the **8** *666*; **22** *824*
architecture (villas)
Italy **20** *545*; **23** *863*, *866*, *867*; **32** *547*, *549*
ceilings **32** *404*
daggers **1** *593*
drawings
Belgium **29** *742*
France **5** *814*
Italy **6** *141*; **9** *218*; **12** *755*; **19** *545*; **23** *575*; **24** *199*; **27** *209*; **32** *354*
Netherlands, the **4** *152*; **14** *292*; **22** *840*
Portugal **32** *157*
engravings **11** *264*; **14** 293; **22** *272*; **32** *725*
erotic art **11** *267*
etchings **5** *437*, *438*
ewers **32** *401*
fountains **1** *791*; **11** *341*; **12** *347*
Mannerism
art forms—cont.
frames **11** 373, 389–92*, *390*, *391*, *392*, *400*, 400–401*, 467–8*, *484*, 484–5*, *489*
gardens **6** 95
gates **16** *634*
interior decoration **12** *410*
medals **6** *140*
metalwork **6** *143*; **23** *540*; **32** *400*
modelli **21** *769*
monuments **4** *338*
monuments (equestrian) **12** *573*; **30** *228*
nude figures **20** *280*; **23** 293; **33** *418*
Belgium **3** *24*
Czech Republic **1** *5*
France **20** *673*
Germany **3** *103*; **14** *320*
Italy **1** *670*; **3** *162*; **6** *145*; **7** *891*; **8** *511*; **12** *672*; **24** *201*; **27** *203*, *209*; **29** *558*, *562*; **30** *33*, *319*; **31** *32*
Netherlands, the **4** *151*; **22** *272*, *846*
oil sketches **32** *347*
ornament **23** 539–41*
painting (general)
France **11** 260
Germany **3** *103*
Italy **12** *671*; **16** 668*
Portugal **25** 296
Spain **3** 845; **29** 277–8
painting (allegorical) **1** *6*; **29** *429*
Belgium **21** *358*
Italy **1** *656*; **4** *857*; **12** *668*; **31** *32*, *33*; **32** *221*
painting (architectural) **32** *726*
painting (ceiling) **32** *348*
painting (epitaphs) **8** *390*
painting (*fêtes champêtres*) **11** *35*
painting (fresco)
France **16** 877
Italy **2** *494*; **7** *886*; **8** *182*; **12** *283*, *755*, *756*; **15** IV; **21** *444*, *447*; **24** *420*; **25** *222*, *223*; **26** *816*; **27** *649*, *651*, *653*; **29** *741*; **30** *800*; **32** *350*
painting (genre)
France **11** *533*
Italy **1** *670*; **22** *448*; **29** *784*, *785*
painting (history) **4** *399*; **13** *342*; **30** *35*
painting (landscape) **12** *670*; **31** *50*, *805*
painting (mythological)
Czech Republic **1** *5*; **29** *429*
France **9** *328*; **20** *673*
Germany **14** *320*
Italy **4** *400*; **7** *891*; **12** *672*; **16** *666*; **23** *293*, *377*; **24** *201*; **30** *33*; **31** *34*, *35*, *36*, *39*; **32** *17*
Netherlands, the **4** *151*
painting (*pietàs*) **7** *468*; **31** *40*
painting (religious) **18** *663*
Belgium **3** *24*; **7** *414*; **17** *896*
Czech Republic **29** *430*
France **3** *399*
Germany **8** *882*
Italy **3** *14*, *254*, *255*, *256*, *344*, *345*, *346*, *468*; **4** *857*; **7** *776*, *887*, *888*, *890*; **11** *269*, *392*; **16** *667*; **19** *383*; **20** *280*; **22** *392*; **23** *574*; **24** *200*; **27** *208*, *620*, *652*, *732*; **31** *6*, *8*, *9*, *11*, *12*, *37*; **32** *102*, *227*, *352*, *353*
Netherlands, the **14** *293*; **33** *418*
Spain **7** *225*; **13** *340*, *343*; **23** *705*; **31** *347*
Mannerism
art forms—cont.
painting (*sacra conversazione*) **7** *885*; **12** *673*
painting (topographical) **13** *344*
portraits (painting)
France **7** *465*; **11** *267*; **25** *282*
Italy **3** *202*; **4** *858*; **5** *843*; **11** *187*, *390*, *391*; **12** *669*; **24** *198*; **31** *14*, *42*
Netherlands, the **17** *924*
Spain **13** *343*, *922*
portraits (sculpture) **6** *144*
sculpture (general)
France **11** *558*
Italy **12** *571*; **16** 695–7*
sculpture (allegorical) **12** *570*
Germany **18** *478*
Italy **8** *511*; **20** *279*
sculpture (animal subjects) **12** *572*
sculpture (monumental) **1** *790*
sculpture (mythological)
Czech Republic **32** *731*
Italy **3** *162*; **6** *142*, *145*; **12** *572*; **27** *203*; **29** *558*, *562*
sculpture (relief) **12** *574*; **24** *814*; **33** *739*
sculpture (religious)
France **24** *813*
Germany **12** *346*; **26** *104*
Italy **3** *469*; **16** *696*
Spain **3** *846*
sculpture (statuettes) **29** *569*
sculpture (tomb) **16** *856*; **18** *479*
stucco **30** *800*
tapestries **8** *67*; **30** *319*
terracotta **12** *570*
tombs **4** *147*; **13** *774*; **16** *856*
windows **21** *455*
woodcuts **2** *136*; **4** *864*; **33** *356*
regional traditions
Germany **12** 410
Italy **20** 278–9; **25** 221
Netherlands, the **20** 281
Portugal **32** 156, 157
Spain **10** 534
treatises **31** 299
see also ARTISAN MANNERISM
Mannerist Workshop **13** 521*; **32** 56*, 57, 61
Manners (family) **17** 633
Manners, Charles, 4th Duke of Rutland **5** 337; **10** 146; **26** 277, 280
Manners, Elizabeth, Duchess of Rutland **33** 447
Manners, John, 1st Duke and 9th Earl of Rutland (1638-1711) **7** 298; **10** 328
Manners, John, 8th Earl of Rutland (1604-79) **24** 753; **33** 10
Manners, John, Marquess of Granby **24** *366*
Manners, Roger, 5th Earl of Rutland **1** 520
Manners, Violet, Duchess of Rutland **4** 127
Mannes, Leopold **24** 653
Mannesmann **8** 825
Mannessier, Alfred **7** 592
Mannheim **12** *361*; **20** 281–2*, *282*
Academia Theodoro Palatina **33** 280
City Art Museum **20** 282
gallery **33** 280
garden city **8** 824
Kleines Haus **30** 684
Nationaltheater **30** 684
observatory **23** 339
St Sebastian **26** 498
Schloss **18** 420; **20** 281–2
Städtische Kunsthalle **4** 64; **18** 523
Städtisches Reiss-Museum **31** 380
urban planning **12** 368; **31** 719
Zeichnungsakademie **18** 107; **33** 280
Mannheim, Charles **27** 224
Mannin, James **16** 25, 26, 37
Manning, Charles **3** 26
Manning, Eleanor **20** 282*
Manning, Henry Edward, Cardinal Archbishop **3** 745, 746; **7** 479
Manning, May **17** 472
Manning, S. (*fl* 1871)
works **6** *395*
Manning, Samuel (1788-1842) **3** 26
Männistö Church **11** 92
Männl, Jakob **19** 337
Männlich, Daniel **28** 116
Mannlich, Johann Christian von **20** 282–3*; **26** 232; **33** 281
patrons and collectors **33** 281
pupils **14** 303
teachers **4** 513
works **19** 482; **29** 776
writings **1** 845
Mannlich, Johann Heinrich **12** 445
works **12** *445*
Mannlich, Konrad **20** 282
Manno, Antonio **20** 283*
Manno, Francesco **20** 283; **26** 840
Manno, Vincenzo **20** 283
Manno, Yasuyuki **23** 595
Mannocchi, Giuseppe **1** 140
Manno di Benincasa **16** 723
Mannozzi, Giovanni *see* GIOVANNI DI SAN GIOVANNI
Mano **1** 390; **8** 486, 490
Manohar (*fl c.* 1580-1620) **3** 320; **15** 228, 584, 586; **20** 284*
patrons and collectors **15** 745
works **16** 345; **17** 512; **20** *284*
Manohor (*fl c.* 1640-50) **15** 598
Manole, Master **8** 280
Manolo **11** 569; **17** 725; **20** 285*
groups and movements **19** 92; **20** 68; **23** 260; **30** 3
works **29** 295
Manolov, Zdravko **5** 159
Manomètre **19** 848; **24** 442
Manoncour, Charles Sonnini de *see* SONNINI DE MANONCOUR, CHARLES
Manono **27** 683
Manoogian, Alex **2** 444
Manoogian, Marie **2** 444
manor houses *see under* HOUSES → types
Manos del Uruguay **31** 757
Manou Degala Mosque **1** 317
Manousakis, Georgios **8** 157
Manowe, David **4** 489
Manoy, N. **3** 585
Manpukuji *see under* UJI
Man Ray **6** 558; **8** 435; **19** 476, 702; **20** 203, 287–8*; **21** 607; **23** 48; **24** 144, 654, 657, 676, 678; **30** 21; **31** 605
assemblages **2** 616
assistants **1** 23; **4** 669
cliché-verre **7** 434
collaboration **8** 435; **9** 358; **10** 164, 687; **14** 237, 816
dealers **7** 421; **19** 537
films **10** 687; **18** 577
groups and movements **8** 433, 435, 438, 439; **28** 920, 925; **30** 17, 19
methods **30** 20
mobiles **18** 62; **21** 745
paintings **30** 19
patrons and collectors **7** 812; **21** 135
performance art **24** 406
personal collection **23** 741
photographs **7** 655; **8** 435; **9** 293; **25** 283
pupils **30** 216
rayographs **20** *288*; **30** 19
sculpture **8** 435; **26** 51; **29** 12, 670; **31** 613
Manresa
Baptistery **32** 619
glass **29** 330

Manresa—cont.
S María de la Seu 9 262; 11 480, 481; 13 67; 16 759; 26 249
Manrique, Jorge 30 664
Manrique, Juan Hurtado *see* HURTADO MANRIQUE, JUAN
Manrique, Luis 14 505
Manrique, Miguel 23 157
Manrique de Lara, Bishop 19 171
Mans, Le *see* LE MANS
Mansa Musa 30 914
Mansard, Pierre 31 305
mansard roofs *see under* ROOFS → types
Mansart, Absalon 20 288
Mansart, François 11 880; 20 288–93*; 24 221; 27 128
architecture 20 866
châteaux 6 507; 11 516; 12 120
Balleroy 29 523, *523*; 32 551
Blois 4 155; 13 825; 20 *290*
Coulommiers Château 4 865
Maisons Château 5 323, 349; 6 507; 20 *291*; 29 523
churches 7 303; 9 84; 11 657; 19 134; 20 *289*, *292*; 24 160; 25 266
hôtels particuliers 13 783; 14 789; 19 262
assistants 20 293; 26 91; 27 821
patrons and collectors 11 657; 18 885; 19 642; 20 895; 23 794; 25 390
pupils 19 162
Mansart, Jules Hardouin 3 867; 4 550; 11 881; 12 829; 19 163; 20 134, 136, 139, 288, 293–8*; 23 512; 24 *164*
architecture 2 419; 7 422; 20 134, 473
chapels 20 *297*
châteaux 12 791; 19 211; 20 *295*, 449; 23 512; 27 559; 32 370, *373*
chimney-pieces 9 325
churches 4 225; 19 696; 20 *294*; 22 453, 455; 24 164
ciboria (ii) (structure) 7 303
colonnades 11 657
façades 8 889; 20 *296*
hospitals 4 888; 14 782, 784
hotels 19 846
hunting-lodges 33 281
orangeries 12 121; 23 470
palaces 22 453; 26 113
pavilions (buildings) 20 450
riding houses 26 363
roofs 27 130
school buildings 2 *724*
screens (i) (architectural) 31 409
squares (town) 11 *517*, 517, 518; 21 371; 23 493; 24 118, *119*; 31 717
stables 29 485
temples 7 778
assistants 2 701; 4 224; 7 876; 8 31; 11 881; 18 815
attributions 23 512
collaboration 2 868; 5 167; 19 163; 23 474
gardens 20 450; 27 536; 32 372, 373
groups and movements 3 266; 26 492
interior decoration 5 349; 6 508; 9 22; 11 577; 23 678
patrons and collectors
Augustinian Canons 2 725
Bourbon I., Louis de, le Grand Dauphin (1661-1711) 4 553; 21 366
Colbert, Jacques-Nicolas, Archbishop of Rouen 11 905
Condé, Louis-Henri de Bourbon, Prince de 6 453
Fieubet, Gaspard de 11 61
Louis XIV, King of France (*reg* 1643-1715) 4 551; 6 60; 11 657; 19 212; 32 369, 372
Mansart, Jules Hardouin
patrons and collectors—cont.
Louvois, Marquis de 19 731
Orléans, Philippe I de Bourbon, 1st Duc d' (1640-1701) 27 536
personal collection 7 876; 20 293
pupils 19 16; 23 457; 24 820
sculpture 20 897; 32 373
Mansart de Jouy, Jean Hardouin 20 288
Mansart de Sagonne, Jacques Hardouin 20 288, 298*; 24 821
Mansdale, Jan van, I 5 43; 17 700, 882
Manse, Jacques de 6 453
Mansehra 23 798
Mansel, Jean 3 555; 7 241; 19 340; 20 451; 22 895
Mansel, Master of 3 555; 5 211; 20 686, 721*
Mansel, Thomas, 2nd Baron Mansel of Margam 11 *427*
Mansell, Robert 4 824; 9 726; 10 316; 19 595; 28 259
Mansell, Thomas 32 784
Mansel Talbot, Thomas *see* TALBOT, THOMAS MANSEL
Mansen, Matthias 29 556
Mansenius 30 659
Manser Muser 23 824
Mansfeld, Al(fred) 17 493; 20 299*; 22 366
collaboration 16 565, 566
Mansfeld, Detlef Jürgen 12 443
Mansfeld, Peter Ernst von Mansfeld, Graf von 19 826; 28 898
Mansfeld-Fondi garden palace *see* PALAIS SCHWARZENBERG
Mansfield (Notts) 31 239
Bancroft Lane Primary School *see* Intake Farm Primary School
Intake Farm Primary School 28 158
Mansfield, Isaac 12 594
Mansfield, Janet 2 761
Mansfield, John 29 58
Mansfield, William Murray, 1st Earl of *see* MURRAY, WILLIAM, 1st Earl of Mansfield
Manship, Paul (Howard) 8 82; 18 594; 20 299*
groups and movements 2 642; 7 875
pupils 22 446
works 20 926; 22 49
Manshiya 10 55
al-Manshura 6 915, 917; 15 307, 695
Mansi 27 436
Mansi, Battista, Marchese 20 721
Mansi, Lodovico 3 8
Mansi Magdalene, Master of the 20 721*
Man Singh, Maharaja of Marwar (*reg* 1803-43) (Rajput) 15 615
Man Singh, Raja of Amer (*reg* 1590-1614)(Rajput) 1 770; 15 385; 32 732
architecture 15 363, 368, 369, *369*, 371
paintings 15 609
Man Singh Tomar, Raja of Gwalior (*reg* 1486-1516) (Rajput) 13 881, 882; 15 386, 391
Mansion 13 306; 21 644
Mansion, Colard 3 555; 4 357, 921; 19 727; 20 631, 659; 23 680
mansions 30 653
Belgium 3 *547*
Bhutan 3 913
England 30 653, 662
France 30 653, *653*
Greece 32 *294*
Ireland 12 6
Russia 28 *579*, 580
Spain 30 663
mansions—cont.
United States of America 17 891; 22 539, *539*
Manso, Luis 29 334
Manso de Velasco, José 19 385
Manson, James Bolivar 5 516
Manson, William 7 233
Mansone (family) 26 698
Mansoor (family) 10 87, 92
Mansour, Joyce 5 449
Mansoura (Algeria) 21 584
congregational mosque 16 218
palace 16 218
Mansoura (Cyprus) 8 354
Mansouroff, Paul *see* MANSUROV, PAVEL (ANDREYEVICH)
Månsson, Filip 22 331
Mansson, Olaf 20 299*
Mansueti, Giovanni (di Niccolò) 18 846; 20 300*; 32 190
collaboration 3 656
patrons and collectors 7 775
works 32 224, 226
Mansur (*fl* 1590-1630) 15 584; 20 300–301*
works 15 585, *585*; 16 345; 17 775; 20 *301*
al-Mansur, Caliph (*reg* 754-75) (Abbasid) 23 562
architecture 3 51; 16 150, 170; 21 582; 26 2
fortifications 18 498
mosques 16 152, 189; 17 496; 20 914
palaces 23 815
mosaics 16 256
al-Mansur, Caliph (*reg* 946-53) (Fatimid) 10 832; 17 731
al-Mansur (*d* 1002) 7 843, 846; 16 246, 493
Mansur, Hajra Zuberi 23 801
al-Mansur al-Husayn, Imam (*reg* 1727-48) (Zaydi) 16 500
Mansur Bihbihani 16 321
al-Mansur Husam al-Din Lajin, Sultan (*reg* 1297-99) (Mamluk) 5 402; 16 496
al-Mansuriyya Palace 10 832; 16 170, 250; 23 815
coins 16 *512*
ivory-carvings 16 525
pottery 16 403
stained glass 16 256
stucco 16 246
Mansurov, Pavel (Andreyevich) 15 857; 20 301*
Mansurov, Ya. 31 782
al-Manṣūr Sayf al-Dīn Qalā'ūn al-Alfī *see* QALA'UN
Mansur Shah, Sultan of Malacca (*reg* 1458-77) 20 155
Mansur Tepe 6 223, 224
Mant, Charles 7 173; 15 393, 403, *404*; 31 793
Manta 3 65; 29 133, *136*, 139
Mantai 20 302*; 29 *440*
architecture 29 448
ceramics 6 330, 917
mantas *see* BLANKETS
Mantegani, Jose 31 756
Mantegazza, Antonio 1 747, 748; 20 302–3*; 24 286; 29 24
works 20 *303*; 24 *286*
Mantegazza, Cristoforo 1 747; 20 302–3*; 24 285, 286
Mantegna, Andrea 3 648, 649; 14 869; 16 614, 667; 20 304–15*, 322; 25 9; 26 765; 33 689
architecture 18 862; 20 322
assistants 3 531
attributions 3 667; 4 336; 11 308; 20 661; 25 557; 33 703
collaboration 32 654
copies 5 286
dealers 7 234
dealing 10 521
drawings 10 130; 20 321; 25 557
frames 11 382
Mantegna, Andrea—cont.
groups and movements 26 187
house 2 547
manuscript illumination 13 834; 32 198
methods 5 654, 656, 657; 9 11; 10 198; 24 487; 28 813
paintings 5 300; 14 869; 16 659, 662
allegorical 1 *655*
altarpieces 26 185
capriccios 5 685
ceiling 15 136
frescoes 9 262; 15 *136*; 20 *305*; 25 9
history 1 656; 8 4; 14 582; 16 660
portraits 7 784; 12 907
religious 10 476; 11 487; 13 676; 16 659; 20 *306*, *307*, *309*, *312*, *313*; 27 495
patrons and collectors 14 128; 16 763
Albarelli, Giovanni 5 432
Amboise, Charles II d', Comte de Chaumont (1473- (1511) 1 767
Amboise, Georges I d', Cardinal (1460-1510) 1 766
André, Edouard (*b* 1827) 16 851
Baring, Thomas (ii) (1799-1873) 3 239
Bembo, Pietro, Cardinal 3 698
Boulle, André-Charles 4 531
Brudenell, George, 4th Earl of Cardigan and 1st Duke of Montagu 4 893
Butler, Charles (1822-1910) 5 311
Charles I, King of England and Scotland (*reg* 1625-49) 5 844; 10 363; 29 801
Coningham, William 7 709
Cromwell, Oliver 8 186
Fesch, Joseph, Cardinal 11 32
Francesco II, 4th Marchese of Mantua (*reg* 1484-1519) 12 908
Gonzaga (family) 20 318
Hawkins, John Heywood (1803-77) 14 252
Innocent VIII, Pope (*reg* 1484-92) 15 861
Isabella d'Este, Marchesa di Mantua (1474-1539) 1 656; 7 891; 10 520; 14 870; 16 659, 770; 22 412; 29 860
Knight, Richard Payne 18 150
Lorenzo the Magnificent, Lord of Florence (*reg* 1469-92) 16 770
Ludovico II, 2nd Marchese of Mantua (*reg* 1444-78) 12 903, 906
Mond, Ludwig 21 849
Museu de Arte de São Paulo 4 726
Richelieu, Armand-Jean Du Plessis, Cardinal de 11 662
Salamanca (y Mayol), José, Marqués de 27 607
Skippe, John 28 819
Solly, Edward 29 46
Thibaudeau, Narcisse-Adolphe, Comte de 30 727
Valenti Gonzaga, Silvio, Cardinal 12 914
Vincenzo I, 4th Duke of Mantua (*reg* 1587- 1612) 2 558
Wright, John Michael 33 409
prints 19 395; 24 248; 25 600, 632
drypoints 9 308
engravings 10 384; 26 228; 32 199
mythological 25 605
religious 8 838
Mantegna, Andrea—cont.
pupils 4 642; 19 200; 20 628; 21 904
reproductive prints by others 2 20; 5 888; 8 220; 12 698, *698*; 18 619
restorations by others 13 229; 24 343
sculpture 10 784
stage design 30 656
tapestries 20 323
teachers 23 754; 29 436
Mantegot, Xavier 11 602
Mantello, Bartolomeo 22 167
mantelpieces *see* CHIMNEY-PIECES
Manteño culture 20 316–17*; 27 610
chairs 20 316–17, *317*; 29 145
hardstones 29 155
pottery 13 735
sculpture 20 316–17; 29 127, 145, 193
stelae 29 145, 620
stone 20 *317*; 29 145
towns 1 464
Mantenois, Elisabeth 27 593
Manteola, Flora 2 397
Mantes 11 *504*
Musée Maximilien Luce 19 768
Notre-Dame 5 319; 9 672; 13 39, 73; 20 317*
Manthani, Gautameshvara Temple 15 328
Mantiklos Apollo 13 442, *443*; 29 567
Mantilla, Francisco de Burgos *see* BURGOS MANTILLA, FRANCISCO DE
Mantinea 13 428, 461; 21 556, 557
bouleuterion 4 530
Temple of Poseidon Hippios 13 389
Mantirolli, Giovanni 24 390
Mantle of King Roger 23 844
mantles 7 179
historical and regional traditions
Byzantine 9 639, 643
Central Asia 10 873
Colombia 29 152
Early Christian (*c.* AD 250-843) 9 639, 643
Indonesia 15 *795*
Ireland 16 33
Islamic 16 459
Italy 17 569
Jewish art 17 569
Peru 24 *513*
Poland 17 *570*
Rome, ancient 9 251
South America, Pre-Columbian 29 152
materials
cotton 15 *795*
felt 10 873
wool 16 33; 24 *513*
Mantota *see* MANTAI
mantou kilns *see under* KILNS → types
Mantova, Jacopo da *see* JACOPO DA MANTOVA
Mantovani, Alessandro 5 616
Mantovano *see* CELLI, CAMILLO
Mantovano, Marcello *see* VENUSTI, MARCELLO
Mantovano, Rinaldo *see* RINALDO MANTOVANO
Mantrayana Buddhism *see under* BUDDHISM → branches
Mänttä, Serlachius Art Museum 11 112
Mantua 10 585; 16 *618*; 20 317–23*, *320*
art forms
books 14 35; 17 565
engravings 10 383
furniture 16 726
Haggadot 17 565
ketubbot 18 3
medals 20 918

Mantua
art forms—cont.
painting **16** 667
paintings **16** 661
plaquettes **25** 19
sculpture **16** 688
tapestries **16** 755, 757; **20** 323*; **30** 319
Bertani's house **3** *850*
Burgo Paper Mill **30** 468
Casa Giocosa **28** 156
Casa Pippi **12** 757; **20** 572
Castello di S Giorgio **2** 140
Cathedral of S Pietro **3** 850; **11** 616
convent of S Orsola **32** 403
Giardino dei Semplici **4** 483
imprese **15** 150
monument to Virgil **20** *321*
Nova Domus **11** 40, 41
Palazzo d'Arco **10** 766–7
Palazzo Cavriani **3** 437
Palazzo Ducale **3** 849–50; **8** 81; **12** 756–7, 906; **20** 320; **27** 289
Appartamento delle Metamorfosi **32** *404*
Camera degli Sposi **15** *136*, 136; **16** 659; **20** 310–11*; **24** 487; **26** 185
Camera Picta *see* Camera degli Sposi
Camerino d'Alabastro **29** 860
Castello di S Giorgio **4** 776; **10** 520–21; **20** 309–10, 312*; **24** 523
Studiolo (before 1522) **1** 656; **2** 140; **8** 4; **9** 21; **14** 870; **16** 660; **22** 412
collections **20** 322
Corte Nuovo
Camera di Apollo **8** 5
Camera di Giove **8** 5
Camera di Nettuno **8** 5
Loggie dei Frutti **8** 5
Sala dei Capitani **8** 5
Sala di Manto **8** 5
Corte Vecchia **16** 770
Studiolo (after 1522) **7** 891; **11** 40; **29** 860
Cortile della Cavalleriza **23** 488, *488*
frescoes **24** 863
Galleria degli Antichi **1** 552
Galleria della Mostra **11** 40; **16** 771
Grotta Isabelliana **10** 521
interior decoration **16** 712
paintings **12** 913; **22** 130; **29** 738
Sala dei Fiumi **12** 26
Sala di Troia **12** *756*
Saleta Lanzeloti **16** 711
Scala Santa **12** 912
Scalcheria **19** 200
sculpture **27** 46
Studiolo of Isabella d'Este **16** 711; **26** 349
Wunderkammer **12** 912
Palazzo di Giustizia **32** 403
Palazzo Guerrieri Gonzaga *see* Palazzo di Giustizia
Palazzo del Te **12** *754*, 754–6, 909; **13** 700; **16** 633, 635; **20** 280; **22** 413; **23** 492, 539, 836; **32** 546
Appartamento della Grotta **13** 703, *703*
frescoes **1** 657; **10** 477
interior decoration **16** 712
orders (architecture) **23** 488, *488*
paintings **16** 667; **23** 680
Sala dei Cavalli **20** 279
Sala dei Giganti **12** 756; **15** 137; **27** 323; **32** *810*
Sala del Fregio **15** 150
Sala di Psyche **12** *755*, 755–6
Sala di Troia **25** 72
stucco **25** 578; **29** 830
Palazzo Vescovato **3** 437
Mantua—cont.
patronage **16** 763
Reggia dei Gonzaga *see* Palazzo Ducale
S Andrea **1** *565*, 565–7, *566*, *567*; **2** 355; **16** 630; **22** 378; **23** 492; **26** 186
campanile **4** 775
coffering **7** 527
portico **25** 265
vaults **32** 88
S Barbara **3** 850
S Francesco **31** 104–5
S Sebastiano **1** *564*, 564–5; **2** 355; **7** 257; **16** 629, 630
Teatro Scientifico **30** 667
Mantuano, Dionisio **14** 472
Mantuan Vase **12** 265
Mantz, Werner **20** 323–4*
Manu **24** 82
Manua **27** 683
Manuae **7** 790
manuals **9** 37
historical and regional traditions
Burma **5** 263
Islamic **16** 100
individual manuscripts
Regius MS. (London, BL, Bibl. Reg. 17 AI) **20** 562
types
aesthetics **21** 127
antiquities **30** 295
architecture **3** 863; **6** 638, 640, 643; **10** 205, 208; **15** 249, 403, 409
Belgium **26** 192
China **4** 623
England **22** 211; **23** 860
France **2** 869; **5** 167; **9** 350; **19** 26
Germany **3** 410; **4** 203; **22** 61; **33** 297
Indian subcontinent **15** 237, 242, 312, 315
Italy **1** 607; **24** 25
Poland **25** 142
Portugal **28** 433
Sri Lanka **29** 446
United States of America **23** 860; **31** 591
astronomy **5** 800, 801
bricklaying **10** 208
building **10** 205, 208
Britain **12** 333
Germany **19** 532
Rome, ancient **26** 884
calligraphy **10** 389
China **6** 767; **32** 839
Japan **11** 823; **15** 74; **17** 224, 235; **29** 902
carpentry **10** 208
France **19** 26
Japan **17** 51*
United States of America **3** 730
collections **9** 229; **11** 307
colour **26** 69
connoisseurship **7** 715
drawing **10** 374; **11** 51; **17** 419, 847; **31** 359
education (art) **17** 273
etching **10** 551, 562, 563; **18** 658
fortifications **21** 594
gardens **12** 64, 126, 130
Byzantine **12** 71
England **12** 647
France **8** 846; **12** 118, 122
Italy **12** 115
Japan **12** 100
Netherlands, the **12** 132
Rome, ancient **12** 68
glass **4** 666
heraldry **14** 406
hieroglyphs **22** 414
iconography **1** 658; **10** 174; **15** 82–4*, 87, 89
Christianity **15** 82*
England **2** 709
Indian subcontinent **15** 749
Italy **4** 521; **26** *415*, 415–16
manuals
types
iconography—cont.
Netherlands, the **20** 246
icons **29** 778
interior decoration **23** 789
jade collecting **7** 8
jewellery **29** 473
libraries **19** 313
manuscript **20** 324–5*, 367
manuscript illumination **8** 588
marbling **24** 55
mining **8** 823
mythology **22** 412, 414
ornament **2** 709
painting **10** 199
China **6** 803, 806, 824; **7** 120, 148; **15** 854; **17** 189; **19** 478; **22** 461; **32** 839
England **3** 228; **19** 818; **31** 480
France **24** 806; **28** 485
Germany **22** 923
Gothic **13** 133, 137
Greece **8** 910
Indian subcontinent **15** 550
Italy **21** 74
Japan **17** 185, 189, 273, 419, 439
Korea **18** 381
Netherlands, the **18** 653; **20** 244
Post-Byzantine **25** 330, 340
Serbia **25** 340
Spain **10** 651
Tibet **28** 543
United States of America **26** 467
see also MANUSCRIPTS
papers **7** *116*, 117
perspective **9** 352; **24** 495
photography **24** 656, 658; **26** 472
pottery **17** 251; **23** 196; **29** 475
print collecting **9** 466
printing **4** 217, 468; **25** 622; **31** 495
prints **20** 807
proportions (human) **14** 872
ritual objects **17** 321
scenery **30** 681
screenprinting **28** 299
sculpture **6** 706; **15** 415; **25** 177; **28** 543
seals **33** 663
tapestries **10** 211
textiles **27** 471
theatre design **27** 482
topography **13** 810–11
typography **11** 359; **31** 495, *495*
urban planning **24** 186
weapons **18** 353; **29** 468
writing **22** 920; **28** 307
see also TREATISES
Manuata **15** 784
Manucci, Niccolo **15** 652, 741; **21** 717
Manucharova, Nina D. **31** 552
Manuchihr II, Shirvanshah (*reg* 1120-49) (Shirvanshahs) **3** 87; **21** 584
Manuchihr Khan *see* MUHAMMAD, Shah (*reg* 1834-48)
Manuel (*fl* 915-21) **1** 452; **2** 426, 444
Manuel (family) *see* DEUTSCH
Manuel I, Emperor of Byzantium (*reg* 1143-80) **3** 882; **9** 519, 555, 576, 657; **16** 582, 607; **18** 211; **33** 153
Manuel I, King of Portugal (*reg* 1495-1521) **2** 869, 871–2*; **6** 622
altarpieces **5** 775
architecture **2** 500; **3** *362*, 363, 534, 535; **4** 245; **6** 43; **10** 900; **19** 463; **20** 325; **25** 317; **28** 499, 780; **31** 101, 179
books **26** 516
gold **3** 534; **25** 312; **32** 406
Manuel I, King of Portugal (*reg* 1495-1521)—cont.
manuscripts **2** 697; **11** 296; **14** 658, 659; **25** 295
paintings **1** 213; **11** 65; **14** 395; **19** 654; **25** 295, 296
porcelain **6** 622
sculpture **6** 451, 452
Manuel II, Grand Komnenos **31** 304
Manuel II, King of Portugal (*reg* 1908-10) **32** 540
Manuel II Palaeologos, Emperor of Byzantium (*reg* 1391-1425) **10** 130
Manuel, Herman *see* LIMBOURG, HERMAN DE
Manuel, Jean *see* LIMBOURG, JEAN DE
Manuel, João **27** 704
Manuel, Manuel de Moura, Bishop of Miranda do Douro *see* MOURA MANUEL, MANUEL DE, Bishop of Miranda do Douro
Manuel, Pol *see* LIMBOURG, POL DE
Manuel Chrysoloras **10** 130; **12** 303; **14** 867
Manuel de Sousa *see* CIPRIANO DA CRUZ
Manuel Eugenikos **9** 586
Manuel Frères **27** 205
Manueline style **2** 500; **7** 531; **14** 579; **20** 325–6*; **25** 288, 290, 304
aqueducts **10** *165*
architecture **25** 290–91*
chapels **3** *362*
churches **4** *245*
cloisters **10** 900; **25** *290*
metalwork **32** 406
monstrances **32** *406*
sculpture **13** 102
towers **3** *534*
Manuel Kantakouzenos, Despot of Morea **22** 408
Manuel Panselinos **9** 584; **22** 228; **24** 59; **30** 718
attributions **9** *584*
manufactories *see* FACTORIES
Manufacture de Cristaux et Emaux de la Reine **11** 612
Manufacture Royal de faïence de terre blanche purifiée **23** 510
Manufacture Royale Daubisson *see* AUBUSSON TAPESTRY FACTORY
Manufacture Royale des Glaces de France **11** 612
Manufacture Royale des Gobelins *see* GOBELINS
Manufacture Royale des Meubles de la Couronne *see* GOBELINS
Manufacture Royale des Terres d'Angleterre **24** 148
Manufacture Royale des Vernis Martin **19** 723; **32** 337*
manufacturing **15** 820–27*; **20** 593
see also INDUSTRIAL DESIGN
Manuha, King (*reg c.* 1056) (Mon) **5** 257
Manuilova, Olga Maksimillianovna **18** 568
Manuk, P. C. **15** 183, 742
Manulf, Bishop of Maastricht **19** 862
Manus **24** 82, 83
manuscript covers **15** 544, 546, 548, 549; **20** *328*
see also BOOK COVERS
manuscript illumination **4** 344; **5** *779*; **14** 423–4; **20** 336–42*, 347–9*; **22** 520
conservation **20** 349*
historical and regional traditions
Afghanistan **1** 208*; **16** *122*, *290*, *552*
Africa **1** *380*
Anglo-Saxon **2** 72, 74–8*, *76*; **10** 242–3*; **20** II; **25** 676
manuscript illumination
historical and regional traditions—cont.
Armenia (Europe) **2** 425, 430–31*, *431*
Austria **2** 790–91*, 792*; **26** 674–5*
Azerbaijan **2** *896*
Aztec **21** 182, 234–5; **22** *518*
Bali (Indonesia) **15** 804
Belarus' **3** 527
Belgium **3** 552*, 555*
Cistercian Order **7** *348*
Early Netherlandish style **3** *727*; **5** *429*; **9** *271*; **12** *524*; **20** *682*, *725*; **31** *449*
Romanesque **26** 666–8*
14th cent. **9** *269*
Britain **26** *863*
Buddhism
China **6** 782*
Indian subcontinent **5** *92*, 96, *96*; **15** 544, *545*, 549, 563, 570–71, 739
Korea **18** 304–5, *304*
Sri Lanka **29** 462
Thailand **30** 613–14, *614*
Tibet **30** 827, 828, 830, 836, *836*
Bulgaria **5** 152–3*
Burma **5** 244–6*
Byzantine **9** 602–3*, 604–18*, 619–21*, 622; **17** 664; **19** 356; **20** 340; **21** *138*; **22** 519; **24** 177, *178*
Egypt **9** 619
England **9** *603*
Greece **9** *607*, *609*, *611*, *614*, *615*; **28** *764*
Lebanon **9** 619
Mesopotamia **9** 619
Syria **9** 619
Turkey **9** *621*
9th cent. AD **7** *181*
Cambodia **5** 501
Carolingian **5** 800–805*; **13** *20*; **19** 827; **20** *337*; **31** 773, *773*
commentaries **18** 187
France **9** 686; **31** *226*
Germany **12** *381*, 382
Catalonia **4** 764
Central Asia, Western **6** 233*, 234–5*, *235*, 236*; **30** *922*
Islamic **16** 252, 321–7*, 342–3*
Uzbekistan **6** *234*
China **6** 782*
Christianity **16** 455
Cistercian Order **7** *348*, 351–2*
Coptic **7** 823–4*
Croatia **8** 177
Crusaders **21** 83
Czech Republic **13** 137, 151; **31** *290*
Early Christian (*c.* AD 250-843) **9** 602–3*, 604–18*, 619–21*, 622; **19** 356; **22** 519
Egypt **9** 619
England **9** *603*
Italy **16** 654
Lebanon **9** 619
Mesopotamia **9** 619
Syria **9** 619
Egypt **4** *14*; **7** 823–4*; **9** 619; **16** *129*, 305–6*, 310–12*
England **15** 874–6; **28** 233
Anglo-Saxon **2** 74–8*, *76*; **10** 242–3*; **20** II; **25** 676
Arts and Crafts Movement **20** *335*
Early Christian (*c.* AD 250-843) **9** *603*
Gothic **4** *237*; **7** *231*; **13** *130*, *131*, 136, 138, 140, 141–2, 147–8, 152; **17** 611, *611*; **18** *703*; **20** *348*; **24** *175*; **25** *677*; **33** *200*
Insular art **15** *874*

manuscript illumination
historical and regional traditions
England—cont.
Romanesque 5 428; 10 243–4*; 26 670–73*, 677*; 27 528; 33 233
15th cent. 19 727
Ethiopia 1 380; 10 567, 568–9*, 569, 570
France 5 804–5; 13 673; 28 233
Carolingian 5 804; 9 686; 31 226
Gothic 4 10; 7 242, 243; 13 136, 138, 140, 140, 141–2, 142, 148, 148–9*, 153–5, 674; 17 462; 20 332, 647; 26 562; 31 836
Gothic: Channel style 13 142
Gothic: Late Gothic 19 389, 392, 394
Gothic: Transitional style 31 285
Jewish art 17 562–3*
Late Antiquity 26 863
Romanesque 10 201; 26 668–70*, 677*; 27 247
Style au fonds d'or 13 136
14th cent. 13 827; 25 692, 693
15th cent. 4 371; 7 598, 599; 11 353, 354; 17 454; 19 350; 20 756; 31 388
Georgia 12 317, 322–3*, 324–5*, 325
Germany
Carolingian 12 381, 382
Gorze, Order of 13 19
Gothic 4 11; 10 723; 13 137, 140, 142, 151
Jewish art 4 15
Ottonian 20 754
Romanesque 26 673–4*, 675*; 33 293
15th cent. 20 324
Gorze, Order of 13 19
Gothic 4 13; 9 268, 269, 270; 13 128, 129–30*, 136–8*; 24 179
Austria 2 792*
Catalonia 4 764
Czech Republic 13 137, 151
England 4 237; 7 231; 13 130, 131, 136, 138, 140, 141, 147–9, 152; 17 611, 611, 612; 18 703; 20 348; 24 175; 25 677; 33 200
France 4 10; 7 242, 243; 13 133, 136, 138, 140, 140, 141–2, 142, 148, 148–9*, 153–5, 674; 17 462; 20 332, 647; 26 562; 31 836
France: Late Gothic 19 389, 392, 394
France: Transitional style 31 285
Germany 4 11; 10 723; 13 137, 140, 142, 151
Italy 12 666; 13 133, 137, 149; 18 684; 20 331, 650
Netherlands, the 22 833
Spain 13 144; 29 275, 852
Style au fonds d'or 13 136
Switzerland 13 151; 30 130*
Greece 9 607, 609, 611, 614, 615; 28 764
Hinduism 15 545, 566, 567, 616
Indian subcontinent 15 228–9, 230, 549–50, 563–9*, 570–71*, 647, 739
Assam 15 548
Bengal 15 570, 571, 634
Bihar 15 570–71*
Buddhism 5 92, 96, 96; 15 544, 545, 549, 563, 568, 569, 570–71, 739
Candāyana 15 576, 576–7*
Caurapañcāśikā 15 574–6*, 575
Deogarh 15 227, 548
Gujarat 15 564, 616–17*, 617

manuscript illumination
historical and regional traditions
Indian subcontinent—cont.
Hinduism 15 545, 566, 567, 616
Islamic 15 571, 571–4*, 572, 573, 739–40; 16 330–31*, 344–6*
Jainism 15 544, 545, 549, 561, 563–9, 565, 616–17, 617, 739; 16 869
Kashmir 15 650–51*, 651
Kota 15 606
Mamluk 15 571–2
Mughal 15 230, 545–7, 546, 549, 579–84*, 583, 586, 740
Mughal: 16th cent. 1 26; 15 577, 579, 582, 583, 586; 21 727; 22 517
Mughal: 17th cent. 15 585
Mysore 15 649
Orissa 15 547, 570, 636, 636
Pala 15 545
Rajasthan 15 564
Rajput 15 227, 548
11th cent. 22 517
16th cent. 15 690
17th cent. 15 648
Indonesia 15 804, 805
Insular art 15 873–6*, 876; 17 889–90; 20 339; 28 233
Iran 4 49; 16 124, 290, 292–3, 295, 302–3, 313–17*, 315, 316, 317, 318–29*, 331–40*, 341–2*; 18 609; 22 515
Iraq 16 114, 307–10*, 313–17*, 318–21*, 327–9*
Ireland 15 873–4, 875; 16 12–13; 17 889–90
Islamic 7 437; 16 128, 131–2, 136, 288–99*, 300–301*, 302–4*, 305*, 310*, 331*, 455; 22 515–16
Afghanistan 1 208*; 16 122, 289, 290, 552
Azerbaijan 2 896
Central Asia, Western 16 252, 321–7*, 342–3*
Egypt 16 129, 305–6*, 310–12*
Indian subcontinent 15 571, 571–4*, 572, 573, 739–40; 16 330–31*, 344–6*
Iran 4 49; 16 124, 290, 292–3, 295, 302–3, 313–17*, 315, 316, 317, 318–29*, 331–40*, 341–2*; 18 609; 22 515
Iraq 16 114, 307–10*, 313–17*, 318–21*, 327–9*
Morocco 16 302
North Africa 16 306–7*
Ottoman 16 118, 304, 329–30, 346–51*; 23 642; 30 478
Spain 16 302, 306–7*
Syria 16 307–12*, 311
Transoxiana 16 290
Turkey 12 84; 16 118, 304, 307–10*, 329–30*, 346–51*; 23 642
14th cent. 16 298
Italy 14 424; 32 197–8
Early Christian (c. AD 250-843) 16 654
Gothic 12 666; 13 133, 137, 149; 18 684; 20 331, 650
Jewish art 17 564–5*
Renaissance 4 19; 13 834; 20 III; 27 807
Romanesque 26 664–6*
12th cent. 16 655
14th cent. 1 640; 8 614; 14 432; 15 93; 31 500
15th cent. 3 532; 19 306
Jainism 16 869
Digambara 15 566, 567, 569
Indian subcontinent 15 544, 545, 549, 561, 563–9, 565, 616–17, 617, 739

manuscript illumination
historical and regional traditions
Jainism—cont.
Shvetambara 15 564, 566, 616
Java 15 804, 805, 805–6*
Jewish art 4 14; 14 35; 17 535, 559–65*, 560, 561, 562, 564; 20 6, 122
Germany 4 15
Korea 18 304–5, 304
Lebanon 9 619
Malaysia 20 171, 171–2*
Maya 21 182, 183, 184
Merovingian 21 164–5*
Mesoamerica, Pre-Columbian 21 184, 233–5*, 737, 738; 22 518
Mesopotamia 9 619
Mixtec 21 234–5, 737, 738
Mixteca-Puebla 21 182
Morocco 16 300
Mughal 1 26
Nepal 15 570; 22 778, 778–80*, 780, 786
Netherlands, the 12 523–5; 22 833, 833–5*
North Africa 16 306–7*
Ottoman 16 118, 304, 329–30, 346–51*; 23 642; 30 478
Ottonian 19 827; 20 754; 23 651–5*
Poland 25 137
Portugal 17 562*; 25 295
Romanesque 19 351; 26 658–77*
Austria 2 790–91*; 26 674–5*
Belgium 26 666–8*
England 5 428; 10 243–4*; 26 670–73*, 677*; 27 528; 33 233
France 10 201; 26 668–70*, 677*; 27 247
Germany 26 673–4*, 675*
Italy 26 664–6*
Spain 26 675–6*
Transitional style 26 677*
Romania 26 711
Rome, ancient 26 862, 863
Russia 27 385
Scotland 15 875; 28 233–4
Serbia 28 449–50*
Slovakia 28 851
Spain 14 423; 23 683; 29 275, 297
Gothic 13 144; 29 275, 852
Islamic 16 302, 306–7*
Jewish art 17 560–62*, 561, 562
Romanesque 26 675–6*
10th cent. AD 27 763
13th cent. 9 259
Sri Lanka 29 462, 465
Sweden 30 77
Switzerland 12 272; 13 151; 30 130*
Syria 9 619; 16 307–12*, 311
Thailand 30 613–14*, 614
Tibet 30 827, 828, 830, 832, 835, 836, 836
Transoxiana 16 290
Turkey
Byzantine 9 621
Islamic 12 84; 16 118, 304, 307–10*, 329–30*, 346–51*; 23 642
Ottoman 16 118, 304, 329–30, 346–51*; 23 642
Ukraine 31 555–6*, 557–8*
Uzbekistan 5 138; 6 234
Wales 15 875
historiography see under HISTORIOGRAPHY → types
materials
albumen 13 136; 20 347
gold 9 606; 13 136; 15 564, 616; 16 292–3, 311; 19 351; 20 336; 30 836

manuscript illumination
materials—cont.
gold leaf 19 356; 20 347
gums 13 136, 843
inks 13 136; 15 852, 855; 20 347
pigments 16 330; 21 233
red lead 24 796
silver leaf 20 347
techniques
colouring 13 138–9
gilding 12 621, 623, 625; 13 136
grisaille paintings 13 148, 148, 673*, 674
highlighting 13 138–9
incidere 13 138
modelling 6 569
uses
Bibles 4 3–7*, 13–17
chronicles 12 272
coats of arms 12 272
genealogies 12 272
Gospel books 13 20
Psalters 25 676–8
rolls 12 272
see also BOOKS OF ARMS; BORDERS, (MANUSCRIPT); DROLLERIES; HEADPIECES (MANUSCRIPTS); INITIALS, (MANUSCRIPT); MINIATURES (MANUSCRIPT ILLUMINATION)
manuscript manuals see under MANUALS → types
manuscripts 7 513–14; 20 326–36*
forms see APOCALYPSES; BENEDICTIONALS; BIBLES; BOOKS OF HOURS; BREVIARIES; CODICES; EVANGELIARIES; GOSPEL BOOKS; MISSALS; PONTIFICALS; PRAYERBOOKS; PSALTERS; ROLLS; SACRAMENTARIES
historical and regional traditions
Anglo-Saxon 20 330
Azerbaijan 2 895
Aztec 20 327; 21 233, 234, 235
Belgium 12 272
Benedictine Order 3 709
Buddhism 6 303, 306; 7 114; 17 211; 30 836
Japan 17 217
Bulgaria 5 162
Burma 5 251
Byzantine 9 602–3*, 604–18*, 619–21*; 17 664
France 9 603
North Africa 9 603
Spain 9 603
Carolingian 5 800–805*; 20 330; 28 303
Central Asia, Eastern 6 306*, 314
Buddhism 6 303
Manichaeism 6 305
Central Asia, Western 6 189; 16 321, 342
China 6 740, 741; 7 62–3*, 114
Cyprus 8 363; 9 605
Dominican Order 9 109*
Early Christian (c. AD 250-843) 9 602–3*, 604–18*, 619–21*
France 9 603
North Africa 9 603
Spain 9 603
Egypt, ancient 20 327
England 12 272
France 5 800, 804–5; 9 603; 12 272
Germany 12 272
Gothic 20 331*; 28 306
Greece, ancient 13 369
Hinduism 15 544, 548, 549
Iceland 15 69
Indian subcontinent 15 208, 544–9*, 563–6*, 749; 20 327
Hinduism 15 544, 548, 549
Islamic 15 545*
Jainism 15 226, 549, 563
Kashmir 15 548

manuscripts
historical and regional traditions
Indian subcontinent—cont.
Mughal 16 304, 344
Pahari 15 547
Pala 15 570
poṭhī 15 547
Rajput 15 547
Indonesia 20 327
Insular art 28 304
Iran 16 290, 296, 302–3, 304, 321; 30 919
Islamic 16 271–9*, 280–84*, 285–99*, 300–301*, 302–12*, 313–17*, 318–40*, 341–3*, 344–62*; 18 242; 33 504
Indian subcontinent 15 545*
Iran 16 290, 302–3
Malaysia 20 171
Morocco 27 506
Ottoman 16 304
Transoxiana 16 290
Turkey 16 304
Italy
Byzantine 9 605
Early Christian (c. AD 250-843) 9 605
Jainism 15 226, 549, 563
Japan 17 211, 217–21
Jewish art 1 70
Laos 18 770
Lombard art 19 549*
Luxembourg (country) 9 698
Malaysia 20 171
Manichaeism 6 305, 306
Maya 20 327, 886; 21 233, 234
Mesoamerica, Pre-Columbian 20 886; 21 233–5*, 266
Aztec 21 233, 234, 235
Maya 21 233, 234
Mixtec 21 233, 234
Toltec 21 233
Mixtec 21 233, 234
Nepal 22 777, 778
Netherlands, the 12 272; 29 666
North Africa 9 603
Ottoman 16 304; 23 639–40
Ottonian 20 330
Palestine 9 605, 617
Pictish art 28 233
Romanesque 14 398; 20 330–31*
Rome, ancient 20 329
Scotland 28 233–4
Sogdiana 6 189; 7 114
Spain 9 603; 20 330
Sri Lanka 20 328; 29 442, 478
Switzerland 5 805
Tajikistan 6 189
Tibet 6 306; 30 835–6*, 845
Toltec 21 233
Transoxiana 16 290, 304
Turkey 16 304
materials
aloe 15 549
bamboo 7 62–3; 20 327, 327
bark 15 544, 548, 549; 20 327; 21 233
copper 22 778
cotton 21 234
deerskin 21 233
gold 9 611, 618
gold leaf 9 617
hides 21 234
ivory 15 549
leather 20 327
metal 15 549
palm leaves 5 96, 245*; 15 544, 545, 547, 548, 561, 563–4, 570, 636, 851; 20 327, 328; 22 777, 778; 29 442; 30 613
paper 7 63; 15 545, 549, 564; 16 275, 351–4; 20 327, 329; 22 779; 30 613
papyrus 16 275
parchment 7 513; 16 274, 351; 20 329; 24 106, 107
silk 7 63

manuscripts
 materials—cont.
  silver 9 612
  skins 21 234
  styluses 29 883
  textiles 15 549; 20 327
  wood 7 62–3; 30 835
 see also BOOKS; CALLIGRAPHY; CODICES; INSCRIPTIONS; MANUSCRIPTS; ROLLS; ROMANCE (MANUSCRIPTS); SCRIPTS; TABLETS; WRITING
Manuscrit de Veletri *see under* CODICES → individual manuscripts
Manuscrit du cacique *see under* CODICES → individual manuscripts
Manus Island 24 64, *64*, 82–3*
 wood-carvings 24 *83*
Manutius, Aldus 5 535; 14 867; 20 350*; 32 198, 199
 collaboration 12 656
 pupils 24 833
 works 4 358; 15 50; 28 306; 31 494; 32 160
Manuzio, Paolo 5 684; 24 24; 33 718
Manwaring, Robert 8 528; 10 295; 20 350*; 22 320
Manwŏl Palace 23 821
Manyakheta *see* MALKHED
Manygoats, Betty 22 605
Manyika 28 620
Mányoki, Adám 20 350–51*; 25 105; 28 852; 33 115
 patrons and collectors 14 900; 28 856
 works 14 *900*
Manzano, Alonso de 2 868
Manz Church 1 315
Manzi, Michele 20 351
Manzier, Matvey (Genrikhovich) 20 275*
Manzi-Joyant 20 351*; 27 238; 31 214
Manzikert 9 *512*
Manzini, Convent of the Holy Paraclete 29 112
Manzini, Giovanni
 works 3 *771*
Manzo, Fausto Rodríguez *see* RODRÍGUEZ MANZO, FAUSTO
Manzo (y Jaramillo), José (María) 20 351–2*; 21 378, 385; 25 696, 697
Manzolini, Giovanni 19 117
Manzolini Morandi, Anna 25 893
Manzoni, Alessandro 10 835; 12 901
Manzoni, Giacomo *see* MANZÙ, GIACOMO
Manzoni, Herbert 4 86
Manzoni, Piero 6 21; 20 352*; 21 528
 groups and movements 1 79; 2 526; 23 298
 works 16 682, *682*, 709; 20 *352*; 21 892; 24 407; 26 51
 writings 6 21
Manzù, Giacomo 20 352–4*; 21 528; 24 448
 collaboration 20 808
 groups and movements 7 894; 13 872; 16 681
 pupils 6 582; 12 851
 works 9 159, *159*; 16 709; 20 *353*; 26 810; 27 665
Manzuoli, Tommaso (d'Antonio) *see* SAN FRIANO, MASO DA
Manzuolo, Alberto 28 61
Ma'on Synagogue 9 567; 17 542, 558
Maoqinggou 23 496
Maori 20 354–60*; 23 51, 710
 architectural decorations 20 *355*, *356*
 architecture 20 355–6; 23 53–4, 715, 717
Maori—cont.
 baskets 3 331
 body ornaments 23 720, 735
 bone 4 314
 canoes 10 848; 20 356–7; 23 724–5, *725*; 28 611
 carving 20 355–6
 cloaks 20 *357*, *358*
 clubs (weapons) 23 *734*
 collections 23 75
 decorative motifs 32 829
 education (art) 23 75
 erotic art 10 474
 feathers 10 848; 23 720
 flax 3 331
 forgeries 23 737, 738, *738*
 greenstone 23 *734*
 jade 16 859, 861
 lintels 20 *355*
 obsidian 29 703
 pendants (jewellery) 23 720
 periods
  Classic Phase *see* Flowering Phase
  Contact and Transition 20 355
  Flowering Phase 20 355
  Growth Phase 20 354
  Nga Kakano *see* Seeding Phase
  Seeding Phase 20 354
  Te Huringa *see* Contact and Transition
  Te Puawaitanga *see* Flowering Phase
  Te Tupunga *see* Growth Phase
  Transition *see* Contact and Transition
 portraits 23 59, *59*
 sculpture 20 *360*; 23 62, 63, 731
 shells 28 581
 stone 23 715
 tattoos 20 358; 23 713, 719; 30 366, *367*
 textiles 20 357–8
 weapons 23 734
 wood 23 717
 wood-carvings 20 *355*, *356*; 23 *731*
Mao suits 7 78
Mao Tse-tung *see* MAO ZEDONG
Maoxinggou 3 686
Mao Zedong 6 619, 636, 768; 7 149; 20 360–61*; 25 329
Ma'oz Hayyim Synagogue 17 542, 556, 558
Mapa Quinatzín 21 235; 23 825
Mapa Sigüenza 21 235
Mapa Tloltzin 21 235
Mapeo 6 406
Ma-Pe-Wi *see* HERRERA, VELINO
maple 33 324
 historical and regional traditions
  England 2 465; 10 297
  France 2 465
  Germany 5 *191*; 12 426
  Hungary 14 905
  Japan 17 366
  Native North Americans 3 331
  Shakers 28 *542*
  United States of America 28 *542*
 uses
  baskets 3 331
  bonsai 17 366
  bureaux 5 *191*
  chairs 28 *542*
  furniture 10 297; 14 905
  gun stocks 2 465
  veneers 12 426
Mapledurham House (Oxon) 25 634
Maples 10 297; 22 744
Maples Arce, Manuel 10 543
Mapoch *see* NDZUNDZA
mappae 9 641, 642
Mappae clavicula 13 138; 20 324, 367*
mappaemundi see under MAPS → types
Mappin, John Newton 24 569
mapping pens *see under* PENS → types
Mapplethorpe, Robert 12 218; 20 367–8*
 works 6 176; 7 327; 10 483; 12 218; 23 297
maps 2 300, 649, 695–6; 4 80; 20 361–7*; 26 221, 224; 28 206
 historical and regional traditions
  Austria 14 573
  Aztec 20 362
  Colombia 7 609
  Egypt, ancient 10 62–3*; 20 361
  England 30 *318*
  Eskimo 20 362
  France 20 367
  Germany 2 *695*; 20 *365*
  Greece, ancient 20 362
  Hungary 10 472
  Indian subcontinent 15 703–5*, *704*
  Ireland 9 *314*
  Italy 16 *584*; 20 363, *366*
  Jainism 15 704
  Japan 32 99
  Korea 28 *424*
  Maya 20 362; 21 234
  Mesoamerica, Pre-Columbian 21 234, 235
  Mesopotamia 20 361
  Native North Americans 20 362
  Netherlands, the 20 364
  Rome, ancient 20 362
  South Africa 29 121
  Spain 20 363; 33 454
  Sri Lanka 32 99
  Sweden 20 299
  United States of America 11 331
 materials
  parchment 20 363
  silk 31 *153*
  tapestries 20 366*
 technical examination 30 395
 techniques
  engravings 10 389
  printing 20 363–5
 types
  mappae mundi 20 362, *363*
  portolan charts 20 363
  sea charts 20 362–3
  T-in-O maps 20 *362*, 362
  topographical 31 151–3*, *153*
  wall 20 365–6*
 see also ATLASES; CARTOGRAPHY; GLOBES; TOPOGRAPHY
Mapua, Tomas 24 615, 632
Mapuche 6 589, 599, 600; 29 132
 works 6 *599*
Mapungubwe 1 *413*; 13 335
 beads 1 297
 sculpture 1 415, 418
 walls 1 414
Maputo 1 *413*; 22 245
 Casa de Ferro 22 245
 Centro de Estudos Culturais 22 245
 Escola de Artes Visuais 22 245
 Hotel Clube 22 245
 Mercado Municipal 22 245
 Museu de Arte 22 245
 railway station 22 245
 Smiling Lions Apartments 13 *781*
 University 22 245
Maqabelein 30 196
al-Maqdisi 16 155; 18 21
Maqhubela, Louis Khela 1 433; 20 368*; 29 108
al-Maqqari 16 246, 306, 369, 386
al-Maqrizi 9 161; 16 252, 382, 385, 456, 542, 547
 writings 16 209, 441, 514
Maqsud 16 326
Maqsud of Kashan 16 474
maqṣūras 16 121, 130, *188*, 188, 487; 20 368–70*, *369*
Ma Quan 33 321
Maquenoise glass works 3 593
maquettes *see* MODELLI → types → sculpture
MAR *see* MOVIMENTO DELL'ARCHITETTURA RAZIONALE
Mar, Alexander Stewart, Earl of *see* STEWART, ALEXANDER, Earl of Mar
Mar, John Erskine, Earl of *see* ERSKINE, JOHN, 6th and 11th Earl of Mar
Mař, N. 9 471
Mara, Pol 3 565
Marabitti, (Francesco) Ignazio 20 370*
Marabitti, Lorenzo 20 370
Marabitti, Pietro 20 370
Maracá 4 *705*, 706, 722
Maracaibo 32 *165*, 170
 castle of S Carlos 32 169
 Prison 32 170
Maracanda *see* SAMARKAND
Maracay 32 *165*
Maradiaga, Balta Zar de 14 713
marae see PLATFORMS
Maragall (i Gorina), Joan 7 373; 20 370*
Maragha 16 *104*, *105*; 20 370–71*
 architecture 16 193
 Ghaffariyya tomb 22 321
 Gunbad-i Kabud 4 792
 Gunbad-i Surkh 4 792; 16 163, 165
 manuscripts 16 299, 314, 358, 545
 observatory 16 193; 20 371; 23 338
 Red Tomb *see* Gunbad-i Surkh
 tombs 16 248; 20 370
Maragliano, Antonio Maria 20 371*; 24 835
Maragliano, Giovanni Battista 20 371
Maragues, Pere 3 221
Mar Aha 31 434
Maraino, Innocenzo 23 369
Marais, Jean 11 584
Marai Shiva Temple 15 290
Marajó 4 *705*, 722; 20 371–2*
 pottery 4 706; 20 *372*; 29 192, 193, *193*
Marajoará 20 372; 29 128, 193, *193*
 terracotta 20 *372*
Mařák, Julius (Eduard) 8 392; 14 235; 20 372–3*; 25 433; 28 836
Maramasike 29 50
Maran, Olav 10 540
Maranao
 architecture 24 610
 boats 24 625
 containers 24 627, 628
 furniture 24 629
 metalwork 24 627
 sculpture 24 618
 weapons 24 631
Marand
 caravanserai 16 193
 mosque 16 162
Marangou, L. 1 795
Maranjan, Tepe 1 196, 197
Maraş 1 827, 833; 17 499; 29 614
 fortress 2 427
Marascalchi, Pietro de' 20 373*
Marash 2 443
Marasi, Costantino 16 747
Marasi, Mario 16 747
Marastoni, Giacomo 2 546; 5 85; 15 18; 19 717; 33 669
Marat, Jean-Paul 11 *541*
Maratha 31 903
Maratha, Rani Bhawani *see* RANI BHAWANI
Marathon 13 *363*; 20 373*
 gateways 26 909
 sculpture 13 470
 tombs 31 108
 tumuli 6 170
Marathon, Bay of 13 460
Marathovouno Basilica 8 357; 29 816
Mařatka, Josef 8 387
Maratta, Carlo *see* MARATTI, CARLO
Maratta, Carlo, frames *see under* FRAMES → types
Maratta, Hardesty 14 393
Maratti, Carlo 1 102; 3 674; 9 8; 15 862; 20 373–9*; 26 774, 842; 27 491
 architecture 23 353
 assistants 22 313; 28 163
 attributions 25 644
 collaboration 4 154; 5 770; 6 585; 18 871; 20 431; 23 874; 28 379; 30 284
 drawings 2 170; 25 644; 27 193
 furniture 16 726
 groups and movements 13 297
 models 9 706
 paintings 16 672; 23 352; 26 810, 840; 27 878
  allegorical 1 659
  frescoes 11 741; 27 489
  mythological 20 *376*
  portraits 20 *378*; 27 172
  religious 20 *377*
 patrons and collectors
  Albani, Alessandro, Cardinal 1 533
  Algarotti, Francesco 1 633
  Altieri (family) 1 728
  Altieri, Angelo 1 728
  Barberini, Antonio, Cardinal 3 208
  Boyle, Richard, 3rd Earl of Burlington and 4th Earl of Cork 4 610; 13 301
  Bracciano, Livio Odescalchi, Duca di 23 353
  Carpio, Gaspar de Haro y Guzmán, 7th Marqués del 5 845
  Cecil, John, 5th Earl of Exeter 6 129; 10 364; 13 299
  Clement XI, Pope (*reg* 1700-21) 1 532
  Clerk, John, 2nd Baronet of Penicuik (1679-1755) 7 418
  Elizabeth Farnese, Queen of Spain (1692-1766) 4 560
  Ensenada, Marqués de 10 406
  Falconieri, Paolo Francesco (1626-96) 10 769
  Ferdinando I, Grand Duke of Tuscany (*reg* 1587-1609) 21 30
  Hoare (i), Henry the elder (1677-1724) 14 598
  Isham, Thomas 13 300; 16 82
  Jennens, Charles 17 476
  Jesuit Order 17 509
  La Vrillière, Louis Phélypeaux de 18 885
  Massimo, Camillo (Carlo), Cardinal 20 588; 26 773
  Mead, Richard 20 910
  Medinaceli, Luís de la Cerda Fernández de Córdoba Folch de Cardona y Aragón, 9th Duque de (1660-1711) 21 35
  Orléans, Philippe II de Bourbon, 2nd Duc d' (1674-1723) 23 516
  Paliano and Castiglione, Lorenzo Onofrio Colonna, Duke of 7 622
  Pallavicini, Nicolò Maria (*d* 1759) 23 874
  Philip V, King of Spain (*reg* 1700-24) 4 558
  Polignac, Melchior de, Cardinal 25 150
  Rospigliosi, Jacopo, Cardinal 27 171
  Saint-Aignan, Paul-Hippolyte de Beauvillier, Duc de 27 524

Maratti, Carlo
patrons and collectors—cont.
Seiter, Daniel **28** 379
Spencer, Robert, 2nd Earl of Sunderland (1641-1702) **29** 381
Tallard, Marie-Joseph d'Hostun, Duc de **30** 274
Vassal de Saint-Hubert, Jean-Antoine-Hubert **32** 75
Victor-Amadeus II, 15th Duke of Savoy (*reg* 1675- 1730) and King of Sardinia (*reg* 1720-30) **28** 16
Walpole, Robert, 1st Earl of Orford (1676-1745) **32** 824
personal collection **25** 645; **29** 352
pupils
Altomonte, Martino **1** 732
Asam, Cosmas Damian **2** 580
Audran, Girard **2** 708
Badaracco, Giovanni Raffaello **3** 34
Balestra, Antonio **3** 108
Calandrucci, Giacinto **5** 413
Carlone (i), Giovanni Andrea, II (1639-97) **5** 770
Chiari, Giuseppe Bartolomeo **6** 568
Frey, Johann Jakob, I (1681-1752) **11** 770
Howard, Hugh **14** 810
Huber, Johann-Rudolf **14** 834
Le Blon, Jacob Christoph **19** 15
Masucci, Agostino **20** 805
Parodi, Domenico (1672-1742) **24** 203
Parrocel, Pierre **24** 211
Passeri, Giuseppe **24** 238
Pesci, Girolamo **24** 537
Piola, Paolo Gerolamo **23** 874; **24** 837
Procaccini, Andrea **4** 560; **25** 644
Redi, Tommaso **26** 69
Werner, Joseph, II (1637-1710) **33** 82
reproductive prints by others
Clouwet, Albert **7** 466
Dorigny, Nicolas **2** *170*; **9** 176
Frey, Johann Jakob, I (1681-1752) **11** 770
Masson, Antoine **20** 592
Picart, Etienne **24** 712
Poilly, François de **25** 77
Simon, Pierre (*c.* 1650-1710) **28** 751
Smith, John (i) (*c.* 1654-*c.* 1742) **28** 881
Tardieu, Nicolas-Henry **30** 344
sculpture **15** 861; **21** 889; **27** 346
teachers **27** 487
Maraval **31** *330*
Church of the Purification of Our Lady **31** 335
Maravi **20** 161
Maravijayottungavarman, Shri **22** 427
Mar Awgen **31** 435, 436
church **9** 543
Marawi **29** 898
Aga Khan Museum of Islamic Arts **29** 240
Marbach, Gotthard Oswald **26** 256
Marbach, Ueli **33** 736
Marbain, Sheila **20** 609
Mar Barsauna Monastery **9** 619
Marbatan **5** 255
marble **7** 735; **29** 701–2*
historical and regional traditions
Afghanistan **1** 198–9
African American art **1** *441*
Austria **5** *628*; **29** *789*; **30** *889*; **32** *442*; **33** *623*
Babylonian **3** *12*
Belgium **3** *417*, *571*, 583; **9** *413*
Black Sea Colonies **4** *111*, *113*
Brazil **4** *720*

marble
historical and regional traditions—cont.
Buddhism **6** 706
Byzantine **7** *221*; **9** 587, *587*, 588, *592*, *593*, *595*, *598*; **27** 827
Crete **8** 155
Carolingian **5** 794, *796*
China **1** *702*; **3** *520*; **6** 706; **7** *57*
Crete **8** 155
Croatia **23** *93*
Cycladic **8** *315*, *316*, 317*, *317*; **29** 701
Cyprus, ancient **8** 340, 342; **27** *609*
Denmark **11** *219*
Dominican Order **9** *106*
Early Christian (*c.* AD 250-843) **9** 587, 588; **27** 827, *828*
Egypt **29** *618*
Egypt, ancient **9** *895*; **13** *465*; **27** 14
England **10** 224, 262, 288, 293; **13** 44
Arts and Crafts Movement **11** *256*
Baroque **10** *264*; **24** *753*
Baroque Revival **22** *28*
Neo-classicism **5** *629*; **8** *587*; **10** *265*; **11** *164*
Rococo **27** *244*
Roman **19** *579*
12th cent. **31** *122*
13th cent. **29** XII
15th cent. **10** *260*
16th cent. **10** *262*
18th cent. **3** *184*; **4** *79*; **10** *293*; **19** *606*; **27** *468*; **28** *64*; **29** *564*; **33** *227*
19th cent. **3** *78*; **6** *456*, *457*; **12** *598*; **19** *600*; **23** *190*; **33** *100*
20th cent. **29** *566*
Etruscan **10** 589, *589*, 602
Finland **11** *99*
France **7** 657; **11** 589, 592; **31** 122
Baroque **2** *91*; **3** *833*; **12** *725*, *726*; **24** *785*, *786*; **25** *706*; **28** *846*; **29** *563*
Baroque Revival **5** *879*
Cubism **33** *590*
Mannerism **24** *813*
Merovingian **17** *665*
Neo-classicism **4** *301*; **6** *517*; **8** *566*; **10** *764*; **11** *561*
Renaissance **7** *596*; **11** *557*
Rococo **8** *70*, *71*; **28** *845*
Romanesque **31** *209*
16th cent. **4** *338*; **11** *503*, *898*; **24** *133*; **27** *547*
17th cent. **8** *94*
18th cent. **4** *510*; **7** *450*; **19** *141*; **23** *795*
19th cent. **5** *304*, *826*; **6** *468*; **7** *163*; **11** *564*
20th cent. **2** *491*; **4** *660*; **20** *120*
Germany
Baroque **12** 423
Gothic **12** *400*
Neo-classicism **9** *691*
Rococo **1** *712*
18th cent. **28** *42*, *43*
19th cent. **9** *692*; **14** *526*
Gothic **2** *482*, *483*; **7** *334*; **13** 44, *94*, *96*, *97*, *108*; **20** *728*; **23** *587*; **24** *869*, *870*, *872*, *873*, *875*; **32** *227*
Germany **12** *400*
Greece **29** *702*
Greece, ancient **13** 387, 388, 389, 393, *422*, *423*, 427, 433, 434*, 436, 438, *457*, 592; **25** *179*; **27** 825; **29** 701–2
Archaic **8** *688*, *695*, *870*; **18** *244*, *409*, *410*; **22** 699, *699*; **27** 688, *689*

marble
historical and regional traditions
Greece, ancient—cont.
Archaic, Early **13** 445
Archaic, Late **10** *449*; **13** *447*, *448*, *449*; **18** *244*
Archaic, Middle **13** *446*
Classical **2** 679
Classical, Early **1** *480*; **8** *697*; **13** *425*, *426*, *452*
Classical, High **8** 262, *689*; **10** *139*, *434*; **13** *428*, *454*, *455*, *456*, *458*; **23** *433*; **25** *576*; **29** *616*
Classical, Late **13** *459*; **19** *853*; **23** *291*
Geometric (*c.* 900-*c.* 700 BC) **12** 246
Hellenistic **13** *371*; **24** *414*; **27** *692*
Hellenistic, High **22** *514*
Hellenistic, Late **13** *466*
Neo-Attic **22** *733*
Roman **5** *604*; **26** 875; **27** 14
Turkey **14** *69*, *70*
5th cent. BC **23** *432*; **24** *205*
6th cent. BC **29** *368*
Honduras **29** *153*
Hungary **14** *895*
India, Republic of **15** 174
Indian subcontinent **15** 340, 354; **16** 239
Islamic **15** 354
Egypt **29** *618*
Indian subcontinent **15** 340; **16** 239
Ottoman **16** 221
Syria **21** *505*
Turkey **16** 221
Italy **25** 865; **26** 887, 889; **31** 523
Baroque **1** *627*, *629*, *630*, *711*; **3** *262*, *828*, *829*; **4** *406*, *621*; **5** *302*, *377*; **9** *410*; **11** *18*, *189*, *235*, *280*; **13** *815*; **16** *698*; **19** *88*; **20** *47*, *902*, *909*; **26** *773*; **27** *830*; **29** *563*; **31** *790*; **32** *195*
Carolingian **5** *796*
Dominican Order **9** *106*
Etruscan **10** 589, *589*
Gothic **2** *482*, *483*; **7** *334*; **13** *94*, *96*, *97*; **16** *687*; **20** *728*; **23** *587*; **24** *869*, *870*, *872*, *873*, *875*; **26** *400*; **28** *680*; **31** *3*, *4*; **32** *227*
Lombard art **19** *550*
Mannerism **1** *790*, *791*; **8** *511*; **12** *571*; **16** *696*; **27** *203*; **29** *558*, *562*
Neo-classicism **3** *295*, *296*; **5** *627*, *628*; **6** *129*; **16** *705*, *706*; **22** *736*
Néo-Grec **9** *404*
Renaissance **1** *456*, *747*; **3** *138*, *158*, *159*; **4** *738*; **5** *300*, *359*, *361*; **7** *367*; **8** *797*, *798*; **9** *123*, *125*; **11** *27*, *28*, *184*, *203*; **16** *691*, *693*, *694*, *766*, *840*, *842*, *844*; **18** *673*; **19** *560*; **21** *434*, *436*, *437*, *438*, *465*, *692*, *693*; **22** *461*; **24** *286*; **26** *439*, *443*; **27** *769*, *770*, *772*, *773*; **29** *24*
Roman **4** 774; **9** *517*; **27** *22*, *23*, *26*, *32*, *40*; **29** *389*
Romanesque **2** *132*; **3** *237*; **5** *550*; **21** *773*; **26** 576; **30** 777, *777*
13th cent. **7** *919*, *920*
14th cent. **14** I1; **28** *29*
15th cent. **7** 918–22; **10** *854*; **20** *303*
16th cent. **3** *924*; **6** *90*; **25** *256*; **32** *648*, *649*
17th cent. **21** *755*
18th cent. **21** *890*

marble
historical and regional traditions
Italy—cont.
20th cent. **4** *101*
Japan **17** *137*
Jewish art **17** 555
Libya **19** *223*
Lithuania **19** *499*
Lombard art **19** *550*
Mesopotamia **3** *12*; **31** *760*
Nigeria **23** *138*
Numidia **23** 300
Ottoman **16** 221
Peru **24** *510*
Phrygian **9** 72
Poland **4** *147*; **25** 114, 118
Portugal **1** *742*; **28** *913*
Romanesque **2** *132*; **3** *237*; **5** *550*; **21** *773*; **26** 576; **31** *209*
Rome, ancient **5** 298, 604; **25** 44–5; **26** 854–5, *858*, 864, 865, 875–7*, *876*, 878, 885, 911–12, 925; **27** 45, 826; **29** 702; **30** 436
Antonine **5** *299*; **8** 342; **27** *17*, *40*
Augustan **26** 889; **27** 10, 13–14, *32*, *41*, *42*
Black Sea Colonies **4** *113*
Crete **8** 155
England **19** *579*
Greece, ancient **5** *604*
Hadrianic **27** *37*, *38*
Italy **9** *517*; **27** *21*, *22*, *23*, *26*
Julio-Claudian **27** *33*; **29** *389*
Libya **19** *223*
Republican **2** *169*; **13** *462*; **19** *853*; **23** *291*; **25** *178*; **26** 887, 889; **27** *8*, 12–13, 15, 29
Turkey **2** *220*; **10** *428*
Russia **27** *389*
Serbia **28** *453*
Sicily **21** *900*
South America, Pre-Columbian **29** *153*
Spain **10** *783*; **13** *108*; **20** *68*; **23** *629*; **29** *20*, 291, *294*, *296*; **32** *618*
Sumerian **31** *760*
Sweden **5** *303*; **28** *462*
Syria **21** *505*
Tunisia **27** 14
Turkey
Byzantine **9** *587*, *592*, *593*
Greece, ancient **8** *870*; **14** *69*, *70*
Islamic **16** 221
Ottoman **16** 221
Roman **2** *220*; **10** *428*; **27** 14
Ukraine **31** 561
United States of America **1** *441*; **25** *401*
Vietnam **32** 477
Visigothic **32** *618*
patinas **11** 309; **24** 258
technical examination **30** 400, 405, *406*
techniques
painting **5** 336
staining **5** 336
types
africano see Marmor luculleum
Aquitanian marble **29** 702
bardiglio **26** 875
brecciated **28** 28
Carrara **27** 13, 826, *826*
see also under CARRARA
cipollino **26** 876
Docimian **27** 13
see also under DOKIMEION
giallo antico **23** 300; **26** 876; **29** 702
Marmor luculleum **29** 702
marmor lunensium **26** 875, 876
onyx-marble *see* ALABASTER (LIMESTONE)

marble
types—cont.
Parian **8** 457; **27** 13, 825; **29** 701
see also under PAROS
pavonazzetto **26** 875, 876; **29** 702, VIII2
Pentelic **23** *536*; **26** 876; **27** 13; **30** 405
see also under MT PENTELIKON
Phrygian **27** 13
Prokonnesian **9** *589*, *593*; **26** 876
see also under PROKONNESOS **9** *593*
Rosso antico **29** 702
Thasian **26** 877; **27** 13
see also under THASOS (ISLAND)
verde antico **26** 877; **29** 702
uses
acroteria **1** 128
altarpieces **1** *711*, *712*; **7** *334*; **11** *28*; **13** *815*; **20** *728*; **24** *286*
altars **1** 698, *702*; **27** *23*; **32** *195*
ambos **7** *919*
arches **7** *920*
architecture **16** 221, 239; **26** 854, 875–7*, 885, 889; **32** 477
architraves **9** *592*
arcosolia **9** *593*
boats **3** *520*
busts **5** 298, *826*
Austria **29** *789*; **30** *889*; **32** *442*; **33** *623*
England **6** *457*; **23** *190*; **24** *753*
France **3** *833*; **5** *304*; **7** *163*; **19** *141*
Italy **1** *630*; **3** *924*; **4** *406*; **5** *300*, *302*; **6** *129*; **20** *902*; **21** *692*; **26** *773*; **32** *648*
Rome, ancient **5** *299*; **27** *37*, *41*
Sweden **5** *303*
cabinets (ii) (furniture) **12** 423
candelabra **5** 604, *604*
candlesticks **7** *919*
capitals **9** *589*; **17** *665*; **21** *900*; **26** *876*, 877
chess sets **6** 555
chimney-pieces **29** *647*
churches **9** 588; **13** 44
columns **21** *900*; **26** 877, 925
commodes **7** 657, *658*; **11** 592
effigies **11** *898*; **29** *24*; **31** 122
façade decoration **4** 774; **25** 865
façades **27** *772*
figurines **8** *315*, *316*
fonts (baptismal) **11** *256*
friezes **13** *426*; **27** *26*
furniture **3** 583; **13** 592
gravestones **17** 555
grilles **16** 256
icons **7** *221*
inlays **10** 288; **12** 423; **15** 340, 354
kraters **22** *733*
masonry **20** 570
metopes **23** *432*
mihrabs **21** *505*
monuments
Belgium **9** *413*
England **4** *79*; **6** *456*; **19** *600*, *606*; **28** *64*; **29** *566*; **33** *100*, *227*
France **4** *338*
Italy **5** *628*; **16** *706*
Rome, ancient **27** *23*, *26*
mosaics **22** 154; **29** XII
pavements **26** 875
pietre dure **14** I1
plaster **11** 762; **31** 523
pulpits **21** *774*; **24** *872*
relief sculpture
Black Sea Colonies **4** *111*
Byzantine **7** *221*; **9** *595*, *598*
Carolingian **5** *796*
Dominican Order **9** *106*
England **8** *587*

marble
uses
relief sculpture—cont.
France 11 557; 31 209
Germany 28 43
Gothic 23 587; 24 869, 870
Greece, ancient 13 371, 428, 447, 455, 456, 458; 22 514; 29 368
Italy: Baroque 1 629; 5 377; 11 235; 13 815; 19 88
Italy: Gothic 7 334; 16 687; 23 587; 24 869, 870
Italy: Lombard art 19 550
Italy: Renaissance 1 456; 3 159; 8 798; 9 125; 11 184; 16 842, 844; 19 557; 21 693; 26 443
Italy: Romanesque 5 550
Romanesque 5 550
Rome, ancient 9 517; 19 223; 26 858; 27 23, 26, 33, 38, 40, 42
Serbia 28 453
Spain 32 618
Turkey 2 220
revetments 5 794; 26 876
sarcophagi 9 517; 23 536; 26 854–5; 27 42, 825, 826, 826, 827, 828; 28 668; 31 561
screens (i) (architectural) 21 774
sculpture 7 57; 8 457; 13 463; 27 692; 29 559
Afghanistan 1 198–9
African American art 1 441
architectural 2 679; 9 588; 13 425; 29 294
Austria 5 628
Belgium 3 417, 571
Belgium: Baroque 9 413
Black Sea Colonies 4 113
Brazil 4 720
Byzantine 9 587, 587
China 6 706
Croatia 23 93
Cyprus, ancient 8 340, 342; 27 609
Denmark 11 219; 30 764, 765
Early Christian (c. AD 250-843) 9 587
Egypt, ancient 9 895; 13 465
England 3 78
England: Baroque 10 264; 22 28
England: Neo-classicism 5 629; 10 265; 11 163
England: Rococo 27 244
England: Roman 19 579
England: 16th cent. 10 262
England: 18th cent. 3 184; 4 79; 27 468; 28 64; 29 564
England: 19th cent. 6 456; 12 598
Etruscan 10 589, 589
Finland 11 99
France 1 766; 2 91; 4 660; 8 94; 20 120; 25 418; 29 563
France: Baroque 12 725, 726; 24 785, 786; 25 706; 28 846
France: Baroque Revival 5 879
France: Cubism 33 590
France: Mannerism 24 813
France: Neo-classicism 4 301; 6 517; 8 566; 10 764; 11 561
France: Renaissance 7 596
France: Rococo 8 71; 28 845
France: 16th cent. 11 503; 24 133; 27 547
France: 18th cent. 4 510; 7 450; 23 795
France: 19th cent. 6 468; 11 564
France: 20th cent 2 491
Germany 1 712
Germany: Gothic 12 400

marble
uses
sculpture—cont.
Germany: Neo-classicism 9 691
Germany: 18th cent. 28 42
Germany: 19th cent. 9 692; 14 526
Gothic 13 94, 96, 97, 108; 20 728; 26 400
Gothic: Italy 2 482, 483; 24 873, 875
Greece, ancient 1 480; 8 262, 688, 689, 695, 697, 870; 10 434, 449; 13 422, 423, 433, 434*, 436, 438, 445, 446, 448, 449, 452, 454, 459, 466; 14 69, 70; 18 244, 409, 410; 19 853; 22 699, 699; 23 291, 433; 24 205, 414; 25 179, 576; 27 688, 689
Hungary 14 895
Ireland 14 500
Italy 10 589
Italy: Baroque 1 627, 711; 3 262, 828, 829; 9 410; 11 18, 189, 280; 16 698; 20 47, 909; 27 347, 830; 29 563; 31 790
Italy: Etruscan 10 589
Italy: Gothic 2 482, 483; 13 94, 96, 97; 20 728; 24 873, 875; 26 400; 28 680; 32 227
Italy: Mannerism 1 790, 791; 8 511; 12 571; 16 696; 22 203; 29 558, 562
Italy: Neo-Classicism 3 295, 296; 5 627; 16 705; 22 736
Italy: Renaissance 1 747; 3 138, 158; 4 738; 5 359, 361; 7 367; 9 123; 11 27, 203; 16 691, 693, 694, 766, 840; 18 673; 19 560; 21 434, 436, 437, 438; 22 32, 461; 26 439; 27 769, 770, 773; 29 24
Italy: Roman 27 21, 22, 32; 29 389, VIII2
Italy: Romanesque 2 132; 21 773
Italy: 15th cent. 10 854; 20 303; 26 400
Italy: 16th cent. 6 90; 25 256; 32 649
Italy: 17th cent. 21 755
Italy: 18th cent. 21 890
Japan 17 137
Lithuania 19 499
Mesopotamia 31 760
monumental 27 33
Nigeria 23 138
Peru 24 510
Poland 25 114
Portugal 1 742; 28 913
Roman 8 342
Romanesque 21 773
Rome, ancient 2 169; 13 462; 19 853; 23 291; 25 44–5, 178; 26 854; 27 8, 10, 12–14, 15, 17, 29, 32, 45
Rome, ancient: Black Sea colonies 4 113
Rome, ancient: Italy 27 21, 23; 29 VIII2
Rome, ancient: Republican 19 579
Rome, ancient: Turkey 10 428
Russia 27 389
Spain 13 108; 20 68; 23 629; 29 20, 291, 296
Sumerian 31 760
Sweden 28 462
Turkey 8 870; 9 587; 10 428; 14 69, 70
United States of America 1 441; 25 401
seals 12 246

marble
uses—cont.
shrines (i) (cult) 13 94
statuettes 29 567
stelae 3 12; 13 427, 457; 29 616, 618
stucco 29 812
tables 10 293, 293; 11 589
temples 26 865, 887; 30 436
thrones 3 237; 13 452; 30 777, 777
tiles 13 387, 390
tombs
England 10 260, 262, 262; 31 122
Finland 11 99
France 8 94; 12 726; 16 856
Gothic 13 96, 97, 108
Italy 1 627, 747; 2 480; 4 101, 621; 5 628; 7 367; 8 797; 16 841; 19 555; 21 465; 27 347; 28 29; 31 3, 4
Poland 4 147
Spain 10 783
vases 29 153
veneers 26 875
marbled urushi see under LACQUER → types
Marblehead Pottery 3 50; 4 482
production 4 482
Marble Madonnas, Master of the 11 51; 20 721–2*
works 13 99, 99
marble powder 28 339; 29 818
marblers 20 559
marbling
historical and regional traditions
Ancient Near East 1 865
China 7 14, 18, 20; 24 55
England 23 790; 24 55
Germany 12 413; 24 55
Iran 24 55
Islamic 16 353, 353
Japan 17 404; 24 55, I3
Korea 18 339
Lydia 19 841, 841
Mesopotamia 1 865
Ottoman 24 55
Turkey 24 55
uses
glass 1 865
lacquer 7 14, 18, 20
painting 23 789–90, 790
paper 16 353, 353; 17 404; 24 55*, 56, I3
pottery 18 339; 19 841, 841
Marbodus 17 519
Marburg 12 361
Bildarchiv Foto 2 366, 369, 370; 14 99; 15 97
collections 12 482
earthenwares 12 431
Elisabethkirche 9 156; 12 365; 13 49, 49, 161, 185, 186; 14 80, 81, 82; 17 696; 20 379–80*, 379; 30 536
altarpiece 1 709
piers (ii) (masonry) 24 751
roof 30 907
sculpture 20 380*
shrine of St Elizabeth 12 442; 28 630
spire 29 414
stained glass 29 502
tomb of Grand Master Konrad von Thüringen 30 535
tapestries 12 467
Marburger Index 2 367, 369; 4 27; 31 671
Marburger Jahrbuch für Kunstwissenschaft 24 445
Marby Carpet 16 470
Marc, Franz (Moriz Wilhelm) 3 478; 20 380–82*; 32 328
exhibitions 32 775

Marc, Franz (Moriz Wilhelm)—cont.
groups and movements 1 74; 4 131–3; 10 694; 12 395; 16 817; 17 763, 764; 20 12; 21 775; 22 304, 318, 921; 24 585
patrons and collectors 10 414; 11 729; 14 295, 506; 18 187; 22 305
works 2 107; 4 132; 20 381; 29 871; 33 363
Marcacci, Bishop of Arezzo 3 750
Marcahuamachuco 20 382–3*; 29 156
architecture 29 163
masonry 29 162
Marçais, Georges 16 548; 20 383*
Marçal de Sas, Andrés 20 383–4*; 29 276
collaboration 23 109; 24 455
works 20 384
Marcantellis, Rafael de see RAFAEL DE MARCANTELLIS
Marcantonio Romano 2 184
Marca-Relli, Conrad 8 636; 20 384*
marcasite 17 524, 525; 22 158; 30 148
Marcassus, Nicolas-Joseph, Baron de Puymaurin see PUYMAURIN, NICOLAS-JOSEPH MARCASSUS, Baron de
Marcavalle 31 45
Marcel, Etienne 11 655
Marcelino de Souza Aguiar, Francisco 4 712
Marcel-Lenoir 11 419; 20 385*
Marcelli, Federigo Niccola, Count 11 194; 16 758; 30 327
Marcellini, Carlo Andrea 11 18, 322; 20 385*
Marcellinus, Ammianus 7 621; 28 324
Marcello 20 385–6*; 28 346; 30 137
Marcello, Jacopo 2 114; 12 733; 20 308
Marcellus II, Pope (reg 1555) 1 722; 20 649; 32 504
Marcette, H. 2 511
MARC format 2 367
March (Cambs), St Wendreda 13 55
March, Ernst 33 296
March (i), Esteban 7 689; 20 386*
March, Giovanni 28 319
March, Horacio 2 400
March, Lionel 20 491
March (i), Miguel 20 386*
March (ii), Otto 20 386*; 30 678
March, Vernon 23 631
March (ii), Werner 1 798; 3 796; 20 387*; 29 489
Marchal, Henri 2 56, 57, 59
Marchand 26 191
Marchand, André 20 387*
Marchand, Esteban 26 519; 27 753
Marchand, François 4 337; 27 547
Marchand, Jean (Hippolyte) 20 387*
Marchand, Jean-José 2 544; 20 815
Marchand, J(ean) Omer 20 388*; 22 36; 23 632
Marchand, Nicolas-Jean 7 658; 17 666
marchands-amateurs 20 388*
marchands-merciers 20 388–9*; 24 150
Marchant, Guy 33 350
Marchant, Jehan 3 609
Marchant, Nathaniel 12 263; 20 389*
patrons and collectors 3 179
works 1 756; 9 1; 12 263, 263; 20 389
Marchant, William 13 337
Marchat, Philipp 12 468

Marche, C.-P. Fyot de La see FYOT DE LA MARCHE, C.-P.
Marche, La see LA MARCHE
Marche, Olivier de la see OLIVIER DE LA MARCHE
Marche-en-Famenne 13 114
Marchelli, Rolando 23 874
Marchena 29 334
Marchese, Saverio, Count 20 219
Marchese, Vincenzo 21 538
Marchesi, Antonio di Giorgio 11 28
Marchesi, Giuseppe 11 679; 20 390*
Marchesi, Luigi 31 901
Marchesi, Pompeo 16 705; 20 390–91*
pupils 22 28
works 5 385; 20 390; 21 533; 32 456
Marchesi da Settignano, Antonio 11 691; 22 487
Marchesini, Alessandro 7 779, 780; 18 47; 20 391*
Marchetti (family) 20 842
Marchetti, Antonio 7 650
Marchetti, Augusto 8 463
Marchetti, Domenico 5 412
Marchetti, Giovan Battista 4 748
Marchetti, Giovanni Matteo, Bishop of Arezzo 9 230; 26 246
Marchetti, Pietro 30 459
Marchi, Francesco de 14 5; 21 579; 24 825
Marchi, Giuseppe (i) (1694-1705) 20 391*
Marchi, Giuseppe (Filippo Liberati) (ii) (1721-1808) 20 391–2*; 26 277
Marchi, Mario 22 805
Marchi, Salvator 25 418
Marchi, Virgilio 11 868–9; 16 648
Marchiani, Francesco Paolo 21 472
Marchi da Crema, Agostino de' 7 926, 927
Marchiennes Abbey 26 668
Marchiis, Pantaleone de 3 695
Marchini, Giovanni Francesco 27 611
Marchino 22 716
Marchionne 26 624
Marchionni, Carlo 2 174; 20 392–3*
collaboration 3 920
groups and movements 22 735
patrons and collectors 1 533; 9 23; 16 772; 23 577; 25 8; 26 840
works 2 2; 16 644, 717, 772; 20 393; 22 361; 24 290; 26 808, 841; 27 324; 29 833; 32 553
Marchionni, Edoardo 11 192
Marchionni, Filippo 2 2; 20 393
Marchiori, Giovanni 11 902; 20 394*; 32 195
Marchis, Alessio de 20 394*
Marchis, Eugenio de 20 394
Marchitt, Paratene Moko Puorongo 20 809*
March y Labores, José 21 704; 31 750
Marci see MARSY
Marcia 33 307
Marcialis, Giuseppina 27 686
Marcianopolis see DEVNJA
Marcibányi, István 15 15
Marcier, Emeric 4 719; 9 49
Marcii (family) 9 198
Marcil, Tancrède 2 839
Marcillat, Guillaume de see GUILLAUME DE MARCILLAT
Marcille, Camille 11 663
Marcille, Eudoxe 11 663
Marciniec, Andrzej 20 395
Marciniec, Marcin 18 430; 20 395*; 25 126
Marciniec, Stanisław 20 395

Marcin of Bylica 25 139
Marcius Quadratus, P. 9 198
Marck, Erard de la, Prince-Bishop and Cardinal of Liège 3 596; 20 395*, 658
architecture 3 544
paintings 19 547
Marcks, Gerhard 12 437; 20 395–6*
groups and movements 2 288; 3 400, 402; 8 826
works 12 408, 432, 437; 14 102; 20 396; 21 67
Marco, Buono di see BUONO DI MARCO
Marco, Giovanni di see GIOVANNI DAL PONTE
Marco, Guy 13 877
Marco, Maestro 5 656
Marco, Santiago 29 308, 309
Marco (di) Costanzo see MARCO (DI) COSTANZO
Marco da Carona 13 318; 32 611
Marco da Firenze 2 17
Marco da Montepulciano 4 32
Marco del Buono di Marco 2 228; 4 32
Marco dell'Avogaro 4 20
Marco di Berlinghiero 3 808*
Marco di Martino da Venezia 20 784
Marco di Pietro da Troia 1 604
Marco di Ruggero see ZOPPO, MARCO
Marcolini, Camillo, Graf von 21 65
Marcolini, Francesco 4 828; 15 83; 27 654; 32 199
Marcon, Giovanni 16 738; 23 263
Marcone 6 139
Marconi, Ferrante 20 396
Marconi, Francesco 20 396
Marconi, Giovanni Battista 20 396
Marconi, Guglielmo 23 295
Marconi, Henryk 20 396–7*; 32 871
collaboration 20 397
house 20 397
works 25 99, 675
Marconi, Jan 20 398; 32 872
Marconi, Karol 20 396; 32 876
Marconi, Leandro (1763-1837) 20 396
Marconi, Leandro Jan (Ludwik) (1834-1919) 20 396, 397*
Marconi, Leonard (1836-99) 20 396
Marconi, Rocco 3 667; 20 398*
Marconi, Władysław 3 527; 20 396, 397–8*; 32 872
Marcopoli (family) 1 895
Marcopoli, Paolo 1 895
Marco Romano 13 95; 20 398*
Marcos, Jorge G. 26 52
Marcotte (family) 28 746
Marcotte, Mme 15 843
Marcotte d'Argenteuil, Charles 15 837
Marcou, François 2 463
Marcoussis, Louis 2 409; 8 240; 19 85; 20 399*; 28 347
Marcoussis Church 13 78; 17 457
Marcovaldo, Coppo di see COPPO DI MARCOVALDO
Marco Veneto 20 398
Marcovich, Cecilia 13 338
Marcu, Duiliu 20 400*; 26 709
Marcuard, Robert Samuel 20 400*
Marcus, Aage 8 761
Marcus, Elli 7 407
Marcus, Gert 30 86
Marcus, Jacob Ernst 20 400*; 32 592
Marcus, Scharon 31 660
Marcus, Steven 10 486
Marcus Agrippa 13 469
Marcus Aurelius, Emperor of Rome (reg 161-80) 2 729–30*; 27 10, 15
architecture 31 350
coins 27 97
sculpture 16 761; 27 39, 40, 40, 45
Marcus Claudius Marcellus 28 654
Marcuse, William 20 527
Marcuson, Thelma 29 117
Marcy see MARSY
Marczibányi, Antal 20 400
Marczibányi, Imre 20 400
Marczibányi, István 20 400
Marczyński, Adam 18 433; 20 401*
Mardakan 2 890; 16 105; 20 401*
fortifications 2 892
fortress 2 892
Mardall, Cyril 33 552
Mardan 20 401–2*
Hoti-Mardan 15 264; 23 797
Mardefeld, Baron von 12 60
Mardel, Carlos 20 402–3*
assistants 27 803
collaboration 25 186; 27 801
pupils 27 803
works 11 19; 19 464; 20 402; 25 185, 186, 293; 27 803; 31 717
Mardell, Károly see MARDEL, CARLOS
Mar del Plata 2 393
House over the Brook 2 397; 33 203
multisports complex 2 397
Villa Ortiz Basualdo 28 482
Marden, Brice 20 403*; 31 609
groups and movements 1 81
patrons and collectors 21 135; 24 24
works 21 892; 32 902
Mardersteig, Hans 20 403–4*
Mardi Gras 5 784
see also CARNIVALS
Mardikh, Tell see EBLA
Mardin 9 512
Church of the Forty Martyrs 9 621
fortifications 31 434
manuscripts 9 619, 621
palace 16 182
Mardones, Héctor 6 594
Mardrus, Joseph-Charles-Victor 9 135
Marduel, Jean-Baptiste, Abbé 6 401
Marduk-apla-iddina II 1 886
Marduk-nadin-ahhe 1 886
Marduk-zakir-shumi I 1 886
Mare, André 11 601; 19 78; 29 899; 32 578
carpets 5 841
collaboration 9 361; 11 525, 582; 25 747; 32 576
furniture 11 601, 602
groups and movements 2 521, 522; 25 747
reproductive prints by others 32 577
Mare, J. de
works 1 809
Mare, John 20 404*
Maré, Rolf de 3 120; 22 350
Maréchal, Charles-Raphaël 7 575
Maréchal, Jacques-Philippe 12 914
Maréchal, Paul 17 523
Maréchal de Metz 29 507
Marées, Hans (Reinhard) von 8 816; 20 404–6*
collaboration 14 525; 22 329
groups and movements 25 357; 26 735
patrons and collectors 19 151; 28 40; 31 397
teachers 29 600
works 12 394; 20 405
Marega, Charles 5 571; 32 414
Marell, Jakob 11 165, 225, 226; 12 389; 20 406*; 29 666
pupils 21 153
Mar Elyan Monastery Church 9 599
Marenda (family) 11 394
Marengo, Bosco 25 8
Marengo Hoard 27 15
Mare-Richart, Florent de la 19 562
Marès (family) 3 585
Marès, B. 3 885
Marés, Frederic 29 354
Marescalchi, Ferdinando 12 584
Marescalchi, Pietro de' see MARASCALCHI, PIETRO DE'
Marescalco, Il see BUONCONSIGLIO, GIOVANNI
Marescotti, Bartolomeo 26 197
Marescotti, Giulio 10 524
Márévár 14 893
Marey, Etienne-Jules 20 406*; 24 649, 653, 669
Márffy, Ödön 10 108; 14 901; 20 406–7*
Marfino, Panin House 5 333
Marg 4 290; 24 436
Mar Gabriel 31 435
Margain, Carlos 18 784
Margall, Francisco Pi i see PI I MARGALL, FRANCISCO
Margam (W. Glam.) 32 780
Abbey 6 465; 32 784
cross 32 786
Orangery 32 782
Margaret, Countess of Cleves (fl 1140) 26 561
Margaret, Duchess of Burgundy see MARGARET OF BAVARIA, Duchess of Burgundy
Margaret, Queen of Italy (1902-29) 10 782
Margaret, Queen of Scotland see MARGARET OF SCOTLAND, Saint
Margaret II, Queen of Denmark (reg 1972-) 8 755; 12 830
Margaretenhöhe 31 725
Margaret of Anjou, Queen of England (1430-82) 20 772; 24 775; 32 828
Margaret of Austria, Duchess of Florence see MARGARET OF AUSTRIA, Duchess of Parma and Regent of the Netherlands
Margaret of Austria, Duchess of Parma and Regent of the Netherlands (1522-86) 7 468; 14 2, 5–6*; 32 506
Margaret of Austria, Duchess of Savoy and Regent of the Netherlands (1480-1530) 13 900, 904–5*, 909
architecture 4 869; 11 604, 875; 13 59; 24 472
cartoons (drawings) 23 526
collections 3 615
decorative works 14 759
furniture 8 107
manuscripts 3 188, 614; 4 76; 8 208; 13 659; 14 759
paintings 3 200, 201, 554, 612; 4 446; 7 710; 13 26, 908, 909; 14 759; 21 101; 22 200; 23 524; 27 132; 28 803; 31 413; 32 271
sculpture 3 451; 21 71–2; 31 189
stained glass 20 752; 26 744
tapestries 1 165; 3 606, 607; 10 222; 23 525; 24 15; 27 132; 30 317; 31 219
tombs 7 595
Margaret of Austria, Queen of Spain (1584-1611) 13 900, 901; 14 2, 6–7*
gold 29 335
Margaret of Bavaria, Duchess of Burgundy (1363-1423) 5 209
Margaret of Brabant, Countess of Flanders (1310-82) 4 525; 8 662
Margaret of Burgundy, Queen of France (d 1315) 14 780
Margaret of Cleves, Duchess of Bavaria (fl 1358-1404) 22 835, 901
Margaret of Cleves, Master of 22 835
Margaret of Denmark (fl 1470) 28 268
Margaret of Flanders, Duchess of Burgundy (1350-1405)
altarpieces 16 854
architecture 5 207
crosses 11 615; 13 158
furniture 17 459
manuscripts 5 208
paintings 4 842; 20 207
tapestries 4 841; 5 208
Margaret of Orléans, Comtesse d'Etampes see ETAMPES, MARGARET OF ORLÉANS, Comtesse d'
Margaret of Orléans, Master of 7 525; 20 722–3*
works 20 613, 723
Margaret of Parma see MARGARET OF AUSTRIA, Duchess of Parma and Regent of the Netherlands
Margaret of Provence, Queen of France (1221-95) 11 634
Margaret of Scotland, Saint 2 78; 28 233, 267
Margaret of Spain, Holy Roman Empress (1651-73) 30 455
Margaret of York, Duchess of Burgundy (1446-1503) 8 524; 20 452, 724, 726
crowns 1 5; 10 323
manuscripts 2 223; 3 555; 5 213; 20 723, 724
paintings 17 455
Margaret Tudor, Queen of Scotland (1489-1541) 20 699; 28 234, 268; 29 798
Margarit, Joan 7 884
Margarita 32 165, 166
Margarito d'Arezzo 20 407–8*
works 1 708; 11 379; 20 407
Margas, Jacob 2 304
Margas, Samuel 10 330
Margat Castle 6 58; 17 500, 505, 505; 18 152; 21 564, 587
Margate Pier 24 748
Margdis see MARDIN
Marggraf, Georg 22 536
Marggraff, Rudolf 22 296
Margherita Gonzaga, Duchess of Ferrara (d 1618) 24 252, 863; 32 403
Marghinotti, Giovanni 27 836
Margi 8 329
Margilan 31 781, 783
Marginal Psalters see under PSALTERS → types
Margineni Monastery 26 720
margins see BORDERS (MANUSCRIPT)
Margo, Boris 7 558; 10 178; 24 213
Margold, Emanuel 3 422
Margounios, Michael see MAXIMOS OF CYTHERA
Margraf, Christoph 13 914
Margrav, Georg 2 105
Marguerite de Hornes 26 745; 29 512
Marguerite de Lannoy, Lady of Santes 3 615
Marguerite de Valois, Duchess of Savoy (1523-74) 6 360; 28 4
Marguerite de Verdun 3 361
Marguerite of Foix, Duchess of Brittany 4 828
Margueron, Jean 18 797; 20 408
Margum see ORAŠJE
Mar Hananiya see under DEIR ZAFARAN
Marhia see DEORI KALAN
Marhkhera, Vishnu Temple 15 323
Mari 1 849; 20 408–10*; 21 267, 286; 30 178, 180
architecture 21 286
archives 25 777
beads 21 272
dress 1 883
faience (i) (glass) 1 878
ivory-carvings 1 869, 869
jewellery 1 877
mosaics 1 889
Palace of the Rulers 1 893; 20 409; 21 285, 285; 23 806; 29 395; 30 197
wall paintings 30 198
Palace of Zimri-Lim see Palace of the Rulers
sculpture 1 891; 20 410; 21 294, 295
seals 1 862
stone vessels 2 272
Temple of Dagan 21 286, 287; 30 191
textiles 1 880
trade 30 179
wall paintings 12 66; 21 308; 23 532; 30 197
writing-tablets 19 311
Mari, Ascanio de' 6 147; 12 4
Mari, Enzo 2 528; 18 63
María 29 331
Maria 15 734
Maria, Queen of Portugal (1482-1517) 14 658
Maria I, Queen of Portugal (reg 1777-1816) 4 631, 632, 637*
architecture 5 375; 23 406
furniture 2 41
paintings 3 382; 10 509; 28 429
Maria II, Queen of Portugal (reg 1826; 1834-53) 4 631, 638*; 33 110
education (art) 4 632
furniture 25 308
Maria, D. (dos Cacos) 5 421
Maria, Ercolino de 26 201
Maria, Francesco di 10 803; 20 411*; 22 479; 29 37
Maria, Mario De se DE MARIA, MARIO
Maria, Nicola De see DE MARIA, NICOLA
Maria, Petrus de see PETRUS DE MARIA
Maria, Walter De see DE MARIA, WALTER
Maria Alexandrovna, Empress of Russia (1824-80) 14 768; 26 734
Maria Amalia, Electress of Bavaria (fl 1727) 11 124
Maria Amalia, Queen of Spain (1724-60) 4 562; 5 348; 27 201; 29 315
Maria Anna Josepha, Queen of Portugal (1683-1754) 13 901
Maria Anna of Spain, Holy Roman Empress (d 1642) 19 770
María Bárbara, Queen of Spain (fl 1746-59) 4 560, 631
Maria Bianca Sforza, Holy Roman Empress (1472-1510) 4 76; 10 456; 13 905; 25 466; 33 118
Mariaca Dietrich, María Luisa see PACHECO, MARÍA LUISA
Mariaca Pando, Julio (fl 1947) 4 260; 23 706
Maria Carolina, Queen of Naples (1752-1814) 14 17
Maria Christina of Austria, Queen of Spain (1858-1929) 20 58; 27 156, 767; 29 321, 354
Maria Christina of Sicily, Queen of Spain (1806-78) 25 225
Maria Dávila Arnalte 20 493
Maria de Almenar 16 437
Maria de las Mercedes, Queen of Spain (1860-78) 29 343, 344
Maria de Luna, Queen of Aragon (d 1406) 29 332

Maria de Molina, Queen of Castile (*d* 1321) 31 822
Maria de Rapiza 26 825
Maria Despoina of the Mongols 16 599
Maria di Bologna 20 323
Maria Eleanora, Queen of Sweden (1599-1655) 10 133; 30 112
Maria Francisca (Isabel), Queen of Portugal (1646-83) 4 *631*, 632, 634*; 28 *2*
Maria Fyodorovna, Empress of Russia (1759-1828) 9 399; 10 722
  architecture 24 291
  furniture 5 767; 8 448; 27 583, *583*
  gem-engraving 12 263
  interior decoration 27 404
  metalwork 27 424
  porcelain 28 521
  sculpture 4 248
  tapestries 22 726
Maria Glavas Tarchaneiotes 16 602
María Isabel de Braganza, Queen of Spain (1789-1848) 1 *742*
Maria Kulm 32 822
Maria Laach Monastery 12 471; 26 633; 27 129
  church 12 364
Marialba Church 29 261
Maria Leszczyńska, Queen of France (1703-68) 31 *69*
  architecture 21 699
  clocks 5 379
  drawings 7 495
  furniture 11 592, 596; 26 420
  interior decoration 4 554; 11 881; 32 240
  paintings 22 685, *685*
  silver 8 68
Maria-Louisa of Parma, Queen of Spain (1751-1819) 3 595; 29 316
Maria Ludovica, Empress of Austria (1787-1816) 2 808
Maria Luisa, Duchess of Lucca, Queen of Etruria (1782-1824) 4 566; 23 259
Maria Luisa Gabriela of Savoy, Queen of Spain (1688-1714) 4 *557*
Marialva, 5th Marqués de 20 411*; 28 430, 780
Marialva, Pedro José de Coutinho, 4th Marquês de 27 801
Maria Maddalena of Habsburg, Grand Duchess of Tuscany (1589-1631) 7 311; 12 308; 24 113; 30 *40*
Mariamin 27 64
Mariana (Brazil) 4 *705*
  Cathedral 4 710
  Museu Arquidiocesano 4 727
  Nossa Senhora da Ascensão *see* Cathedral
Mariana (Greece), Docheiariou Monastery 9 556
Mariana Islands 20 411–12*; 23 *711*, 715
  latte 20 411, *412*
Mariani, Camillo 20 412*
  assistants 21 754
  collaboration 4 405; 26 823
  patrons and collectors 1 595
  pupils 21 754; 27 767, 815
Mariani, Carlo Maria 7 385; 16 683
Mariani, Jacopo 33 15
Mariani, Pompeo 3 920; 21 896
Mariani Associates 13 763
Marianka Church 14 894; 28 855
Mariannhill Mission 29 123
Mariano 8 236; 20 413*
Mariano, Pellegrino di *see* PELLEGRINO DI MARIANO
Mariano del Buono 26 326
Mariano del Buono di Jacopo 2 697; 4 197; 12 734; 20 413*; 26 326
Mariano Filho, José 4 712, 725
Marianos 17 557
Mariánské Lázně 8 416
Maria of Bavaria, Archduchess of Austria (*fl* 1564) 13 329
Maria of Navarre, Queen of Aragon (*fl* 1342) 3 339
Maria of Savoy, Duchess of Milan (*d* 1447) 3 531; 20 783
Mariapfarr 2 790
Maria Pia, Queen of Portugal (1847-1911) 4 629; 5 902
Maria Schlaf Altar, Master of the 18 497
Mariátegui, Francisco Javier de 24 225
Maria-Theresa, Queen of France (1638-83) 4 *543*, *557*; 6 437; 19 542; 20 860; 23 173, 460; 28 506
Maria-Theresa, Queen of Hungary (*reg* 1741-80) and Bohemia (*reg* 1743-80), Holy Roman Empress 13 899, *901*, 922*; 14 508; 24 758
  architecture 8 840; 14 11; 15 865; 25 437, 438; 26 316, 496; 31 787; 32 460
  collections 2 830
  drawings 4 663; 12 273
  furniture 2 811; 19 69
  gems 12 262; 28 790
  gold 2 820, *820*
  interior decoration 2 *806*, 807
  paintings 3 382; 14 111; 15 741, 745; 16 553; 20 456, 856; 33 694
  porcelain 32 449
  prints 24 240
  sculpture 2 802; 19 337; 21 819
  silk 8 419
  sponsorship 10 899
  urban planning 31 329
Mariatrost Church 2 783
Máriavölgy *see* MARIANKA
Mariawald 29 503, 512
Maria Wörth Winterkirche 2 790
Mariazell Wallfahrtskirche 2 824
Marib 2 *246*, 247, 252; 16 *104*; 33 520
  Awwam Temple 2 253, 259
    sculpture 2 *258*
  Mahram Bilqis *see* Awwam Temple
  mosque of Sulayman ibn Dawud 16 177
  walls 2 250
Maribo
  Cathedral 8 723
  Lolland-Falster Kunstmuseum 8 759
Maribor 28 *858*
  Art Gallery 28 863
  church 28 858
  Regional Museum 28 863
Marić, Jovo 22 18
Maricá, Casa de Câmara 4 711
Marichal, Carlos 25 701
Maridadi Fabrics 17 906
Marie 30 20
Marie (*fl* 1312) 5 667
Marie, Christophe 11 656; 24 118
Marie, Grand Duchess of Mecklenburg-Strelitz (*fl* 1820) 31 579
Marie-Amélie, Queen of France (1782-1866) 15 841, 842
Marie-Antoinette, Queen of France (1755-93) 4 542, *543*, 555*; 14 508
  architecture 8 461; 11 658; 21 699; 22 740; 25 872; 27 536
  decorative works 3 523; 11 305; 24 811; 26 182; 30 747
  drawings 26 73
  embroidery 11 648
Marie-Antoinette, Queen of France (1755-93)—cont.
  furniture 5 192, 350; 9 379; 10 643; 11 590, 595, 627, *627*; 13 840; 19 *723*; 21 817; 26 376; 28 194, 527; 30 783; 31 480; 33 48
  gardens 32 369, 373–4
  interior decoration 2 245; 13 701; 19 *723*
  metalwork 13 234
  paintings 9 365; 22 191; 31 824; 32 495
  porcelain 18 643; 28 521, *522*
  sculpture 5 888; 17 683
  silk 19 850
  vases 9 399
Marieberg Factory 25 460; 30 97, 98, 99–100, 106
  marks 20 441
  works 30 *99*
Mariedal Castle 30 69
Mariedal Factory 11 106
Marie de Bourbon, Duchess of Württemberg *see* ORLÉANS, MARIE(-CHRISTINE-CAROLINE-ADÉLAÏDE-FRANÇOISE-LÉOPOLDINE), Princesse d'
Marie de France 10 724; 26 561
Marie de Gueldre, Master of 22 835
Marie de Medici, Queen of France (1573-1642) 4 542, *543*, 548–9*; 21 *9*
  aqueducts 2 242
  architecture 4 864, 865, *866*; 11 656; 24 118, 165; 26 348; 27 246; 30 735
  drawings 13 786
  furniture 11 587
  hardstones 11 29
  interior decoration 9 363; 11 573; 12 898
  paintings 8 483; 12 306; 25 383; 26 348; 27 823
    ceiling 22 190
    flower 11 225
    history 3 613; 4 53; 9 762; 11 661, 662, 666; 20 854; 24 165
    mythological 12 913
    portraits 14 730
    religious 6 433, 434; 22 190; 26 198
  sculpture 3 853; 4 547; 10 441; 11 503
  stucco 29 833
  toys 31 255
Mariefred 30 111
Marie Galante
  Chateau Murat 2 148; 5 749
  Eco Museum 2 154
Marie-Louise, Empress of the French, later Duchess of Parma (*reg* 1815-47) 11 635
  architecture 3 887
  decorative works 5 889
  furniture 25 672; 30 747
  gem-engravings 22 103
  metalwork 23 354
  paintings 7 306; 8 445
Marie Louise d'Orléans, Queen of Spain (1662-89) 17 524
Mariemont Château (Belgium) 3 545, 613; 13 910; 17 711
  Musée Royal de Mariemont 3 616
Mariemont (OH; USA) 7 326
Mariën, Marcel 3 565, 573; 20 414*
  groups and movements 30 23
Marienberg Health Centre (Surinam) 30 15
Marienburg (Poland) *see* MALBORK CASTLE
Marienburg, Schloss (Germany) *see* SCHLOSS MARIENBURG
Marienfeld Abbey 18 189
Marienpoel 19 101; 22 836
Marienstatt Abbey 12 365, 400
  church 13 116
Marienwalde 4 666
Marieschi, Michele Giovanni 20 414–15*; 31 155
  attributions 3 676
  methods 5 519
  patrons and collectors 28 173
  reproductive prints by others 5 55; 12 582
  works 11 395; 20 *414*; 31 248; 32 112; 33 691
Marietta (GA), J. H. Boston House 7 619
Mariette (family) 10 390; 25 626; 26 229
  collections 32 74
  drawings 5 445; 10 753
Mariette, (François-)Auguste (-Ferdinand) 5 401; 9 768, 843; 10 79, 82, 90, 92, 93; 20 418*; 27 593
  excavations
    Dendara 8 710
    Edfu 9 719
    Karnak 30 691
    Saqqara 27 811, 813
    Sheikh el-Beled 28 577
    Tanis 30 296
  exhibitions 10 94
Mariette, François 21 121
Mariette, Jean 20 415, 416*
  personal collection 19 369
  pupils 19 216
  works 4 163, 455, 532; 24 821; 31 321
  writings 6 563
Mariette, Pierre (i) (1596-1657) 10 144; 20 415*; 25 77
  printmakers 3 632; 25 77; 27 269
Mariette, Pierre (ii) (1634-1716) 10 144; 18 745; 19 210; 20 415–16*; 24 805; 25 77
  collections 30 727
  dealing 11 662
  pupils 7 864
Mariette, Pierre-Jean 6 81; 11 662; 20 388, 415, 416–17*, *417*, 457; 24 137; 25 631
  collaboration 19 143
  drawings 5 866; 8 209; 9 230; 16 815; 19 89, 143; 29 487
  engravings 4 635
  mounts (works on paper and scrolls) 22 236
  paintings 9 416, 418; 26 452
  personal collection 18 626; 20 446; 23 855; 25 664; 30 424
  printmakers 10 761
  writings 4 509, 766; 6 81; 7 714; 8 209; 11 675; 25 395
Mariette, Pierre-Joseph 20 416
Mariga, Joram 33 679
Marigliano, Giovanni 20 418–19*
  assistants 2 730
  collaboration 22 477
  pupils 2 731; 5 358
  works 1 698; 29 583
Marignolle, Church of Le Campora 19 446–7
Marignolli, Giovanni 17 819
Marignolli, Lorenzo 5 131
Marigny, Enguerran de 9 707, 708; 13 76
Marigny, Jean de, Bishop of Beauvais 3 460; 26 453
Marigny, Jean Girardot de *see* GIRARDOT DE MARIGNY, JEAN
Marigny, Marquis de 7 495; 20 135, 137; 25 81–2*
  architecture 3 645; 11 658; 24 166; 25 363; 29 92; 32 767, 768
  collections 17 668
  drawings 4 518
  education (art) 12 334
  furniture 3 414; 12 159; 23 356
  metalwork 13 234
Marigny, Marquis de—cont.
  paintings 3 203, 395; 11 367, 540; 13 640, 641; 14 585; 19 217
  sculpture 1 665; 19 140
  sponsorship 32 766
  tapestries 22 726
Mariinsko Gospels *see under* GOSPEL BOOKS → individual manuscripts
Marijnissen, R. 3 619
Marika, Banduk 1 65; 20 419*
Marika, Bayngul 20 419
Marika, Dhuwarrwarr 20 419
Marika, Mawalan 1 61; 20 419*
  pupils 20 419; 21 733
Marika, Wandjuk 20 419*
Marilhat, Prosper (-Georges-Antoine) 20 419–21*
  groups and movements 23 504
  teachers 27 143
  works 11 233; 20 *420*; 23 522
Marillier, Clément-Pierre 20 421*
  groups and movements 31 373
  reproductive prints by others 4 331; 9 365; 13 220; 16 905; 32 502
  works 27 530
Marimar 8 232
Marimekko 11 110
Marimo, José María Madurell i *see* MADURELL I MARIMÓN, JOSEP MARÍA
Marín, Augusto 18 832; 25 701, 702
Marín, Hugo 6 598
Marin, John 10 397; 20 421–2*; 23 47
  exhibitions 31 490
  groups and movements 28 925
  patrons and collectors 26 488; 29 655, 657; 31 605
  teachers 2 130
  works 11 499
Marin, Joseph-Charles 20 422*
  patrons and collectors 6 511
  pupils 11 364
  works 29 573; 30 499
Marin, Pierre 11 799
Marina (*fl* 464-5) 12 339
Marina, Princess (*fl* 1429) 31 748
Marina del Rey (CA), Getty Conservation Institute (GCI) 7 742, 743–4
Marinali (family) 32 195
Marinali, Angelo 20 422, 423*
Marinali, Francesco (1609-after 1655) 20 422*
Marinali, Francesco, the younger (1647-after 1717) 20 422*
Marinali, Orazio 20 422–3*
  pupils 2 801
  works 16 702; 22 387, 388
Marinari, Onorio 4 65; 9 78; 11 874
Marinatos, Spiridon (Nikolaos) 20 423*
  excavations 1 794; 2 415; 8 320; 17 909; 30 711; 32 78
Marind-Anim 31 185
Marin de la Châtaigneraie, Denis *see* CHÂTAIGNERAIE, DENIS MARIN DE LA
Marín de la Paz, Manuel 7 609
marine archaeology *see under* ARCHAEOLOGY → types
marine drawings *see under* DRAWINGS → types
Marin-Epagnier 18 828
marine paintings *see under* PAINTING → types
marine ply 31 283
Marine Style Master 21 670
  works 21 *670*
Marine Style pottery *see under* POTTERY → wares
Marinetti, Angelo *see* MARINETTI, (EMILIO) FILIPPO TOMMASO
Marinetti, Antonio 24 894; 27 864
Marinetti, Benedetta 25 *447*

Marinetti, Carlo *see* MARINETTI, (EMILIO) FILLIPO TOMMASO
Marinetti, (Emilio) Filippo Tommaso **1** 21; **11** 190; **16** 680; **20** 426–8*; **24** 448; **25** 108; **26** 59
collaboration **7** 557
exhibitions **10** 255
groups and movements
Aeropittura **1** 166; **8** 771
Cubism **8** 247
Fascism **10** 821
Futurism **4** 200; **5** 848; **11** 862, 863, 865, 867, 868, 869; **19** 330; **21** 527
patrons and collectors **33** 254
productions **31** 832
works **8** 771; **11** 80; **16** 679, 681; **20** 336, *427*; **23** 15; **24** 404; **31** 300
writings **11** 525
Maring **24** 75
Maring and Ladd **30** 753
Marinha Academia **25** 293
Marinha Grande **25** 311
Marinho, Adhemar **32** 624
Marinho, Roberto **4** 726; **26** 414
Marinho, Roberto, Fundação *see under* RIO DE JANEIRO → museums
Marini, Alejandro **5** 365
Marini, Angelo **21** 533; **24** 287
Marini, Antonio **11** 189; **26** 323
Marini, Francesco **16** 730
Marini, Giacinto **26** 242
Marini, Leonardo **16** 719; **28** 18
Marini, Marino **10** 638; **11** 191; **20** 428–9*; **21** 528; **24** 448
patrons and collectors **7** 782, 797; **26** 489
pupils **3** 94; **17** 517; **26** 67; **30** 286
works **16** 708, 709; **19** 491; **20** *429*
Marinica Pottery **2** 152
Marinid **16** 114; **20** 430*
architecture **21** 73, 584
see also:
ABU 'INAN FARIS, Ruler
ABU'L-HASAN 'ALI I, Ruler
ABU SA'ID 'UTHMAN, Ruler
ABU YA'QUB YUSUF, Ruler
ABU YUSUF YA'QUB, Ruler
Marinis, Angelo de **10** 744
Marinković, Vojislav **28** 452
Marino, Domenico di **12** 664
Marino, Giambattista **20** 430–31*
collections **25** 385
drawings **8** 139; **20** 588; **25** 385, 386; **28** 62
paintings **28** 220
pupils **9** 174
writings **25** 385
Marino, Giovan Battista *see* MARINO, GIAMBATTISTA
Marino, João **4** 725
Marino Casino (Ireland) **6** *411*, 412; **16** 8, 21, 24
gardens **12** 131
Marino (Italy) **10** *583*, *599*
Mithraeum **27** 48
Marinoni, Jakob **32** 436, 458
Marinori, Baldassare **16** 738
Marinot, Maurice **20** 431*
patrons and collectors **19** 282
works **11** 582, *612*, 613; **12** 795
Marinov, Nikola **5** 154
Marinus *see* GOES, MARINUS ROBYN VAN DER
Marinus van Reymerswaele *see* REYMERSWAELE, MARINUS VAN
Mario dei Fiori **18** 871; **20** 431–2*
collaboration **20** 375; **21** 54
patrons and collectors **6** 585; **7** 622
pupils **4** 65
works **11** 227; **16** 726, 727
Marion **8** *325*, 348
coins **8** 332
gravestones **8** 341
Marion—cont.
pottery **13** 538
Marion, Salomon **5** 585
marionettes *see under* PUPPETS → types
Mariotti, Carlo Spiridione **3** 714
Mariotti, Giovanni Battista **3** 109
Mariotti, Vicenzo Maria **11** 329; **32** 615
Mariotto, Giambattista **21** 72
Mariotto de Pesaro **16** 724
Mariotto di Francesco **10** 877
Mariotto di Nardo **11** 698; **20** 432*
Mariotto di Pace **11** 118
Maripasoula **11** *756*
Mari Republic **27** *363*, 434
Maris, Jacob(us Hendricus) **20** 432, 433–5*
groups and movements **14** 43, 46, 47; **22** 849
patrons and collectors **4** 588, 589; **28** 271
pupils **4** 203; **20** 435; **33** 743
reproductive prints by others **33** 677
teachers **21** 58
works **11** 448; **20** *433*
Maris, Matthijs **20** 432, 434–5*; **22** 905
groups and movements **14** 43, 46, 47; **22** 849
patrons and collectors **9** 305; **11** 301; **28** 271
pupils **20** 435
reproductive prints by others **33** 677
works **20** 433; **22** 849
Maris, Simon Willem **20** 435
Maris, Willem **20** 433, 435*
groups and movements **14** 46, 47; **20** 871; **22** 849
patrons and collectors **28** 271
pupils **4** 740
reproductive prints by others **33** 677
teachers **20** 434
works **2** 106; **20** *435*
Mariscal, Alonso **20** 436
Mariscal, Enrique **20** 436
Mariscal, Federico **20** 436; **21** 378, 379, 380, 403
Mariscal, Javier **29** 322
Mariscal, Nicolás **20** 436; **21** 378, 379
Mariscalchi, Pietro de' *see* MARASCALCHI, PIETRO DE'
Marischal, George Keith, 10th Earl of *see* KEITH, GEORGE, 10th Earl Marischal
Marischal, Mary Erskine, Countess *see* ERSKINE, MARY, Countess Marischal
Marismas del Guadalquivir, Marqués de Las *see* LAS MARISMAS DEL GUADALQUIVIR, Marqués de
Marisol (Escobar) **20** 436*, 607; **25** 232; **32** 175; **33** 316
Marissa **27** 57
Marissal, Philippe-Charles **26** 284
māristan **16** 143
Maristany, Hiram **18** 833
Maritain, Jacques **1** 182; **20** 436–7*
Maritsa, St Nikola **5** 148
Mariupol' Museum **27** 440
Marius(, C.) **11** 150; **26** 856
Marius, G(erharda) H(ermina) **20** 437*
Marius Pictor *see* DE MARIA, MAARIO
Mariuspolski, Vyacheslav **28** 918
Marjanović, Rista **28** 451
Marjinashvili, Kito **1** 507
Mark, St Mark's (Somerset) **24** 576
Mark, Edward Walhous **7** 609
Mark, William **2** 766; **20** 437*
Marka **1** 385; **3** 132; **5** 216
Markanda, Mahadeva Temple **15** 324
Markandi **15** 492
Markandeshvara Temple **15** 493
Mark Antony **27** 28, 30, 96; **32** 632
Markapuram **15** 540
Markaryan, S. **2** 894
Marke Castle **3** 578
Markelius, Sven (Gottfrid) **20** 437–8*; **30** 92, 96
groups and movements **8** 8; **15** 885
teachers **18** 663
works **30** 75
Marken **22** 898
Markenfield Hall (N. Yorks) **12** 176
Marker, Jamshed **23** 804
Marker, Minoo **23** 804
market crosses *see under* CROSSES → types
markets **10** 667; **20** 438*; **31** 235, 711
Bulgaria **5** 148
Central Asia, Western **16** *237*, 238
Egypt **10** *831*
England **11** 330
France **3** *125*
Greece, ancient **19** 888; **20** 438
Islamic **16** 141, 260–61, 262, 430; **20** 438; **31** 235
Central Asia, Western **16** *237*, 238
Egypt **10** *831*
Ottoman **16** 266
Turkey **16** 266
Italy **19** 888, 889
Ottoman **16** 266
Rome, ancient **19** 888; **20** 438; **26** 867, 871
Turkey **16** 266; **19** 889
Venezuela **32** 169
see also AGORA; EXCHANGES; FORA; MACELLA
Markets of Trajan *see under* ROME → fora → Forum of Trajan
Markham, Frank **5** 591
Markham, J. H. **18** 73
Markham Pottery **31** 639
Markiani **1** 795
Markianos Kyris **9** 591
Markichev, Ivan (Vasil'yevich) **23** 837
Markiewiczowa, Anastazja **25** 131
Märkische Elektrizitätswerke **25** 402
Märklin **31** 256, 265
works **31** *256*
Märklin, Konrad *see* MERKLIN, KONRAD
Marklund, Bror **30** 86
Markó, András **20** 438, 439*; **28** 318
Markó, Ferenc **20** 438, 439–40*
Markó, Károly (i) (1791-1860) **14** 901; **15** 14; **20** 438, 439*
exhibitions **2** 546
pupils **18** 696; **20** 439; **28** 318
staff **14** 315
Markó, Károly (ii) (1822-91) **20** 438, 439*
groups and movements **28** 318
works **28** 318
Markon **27** 440
Markos, Georgios **25** 336
Markov
Monastery **19** 882; **28** 447
St Demetrius **9** 553
Markov, Aleksey (Tarasovich) **12** 490; **18** 203, 392; **22** 394
Markov, Andrija **8** 180
Markov, Viktor (Ivanovich) **27** 425
Markov, Vladimir (Ivanovich) **20** 440*; **31** 583
Markova, Alicia **3** 119
Markovits, Mária **15** 12
marks **20** 440–46*
artists' *see* MONOGRAMS; SIGNATURES, ARTISTS'
marks—cont.
ceramics **11** 308; **20** 441–2*
Cambodia **5** 506
China **6** *922*, 922–3*, *923*; **20** 441
France **20** 441
Greece, ancient **13** 487, 488
Iran **16** 424
Islamic **16** 424
Italy **20** 441
Japan **17** 243–4*, *244*; **20** 441
Mesopotamia **20** 441
Netherlands, the **22** 879, 881
Rome, ancient **6** 333; **20** 441; **27** 106
collectors' **10** 212; **19** 782; **20** 445–6*, *446*; **25** 631, 664
see also PROVENANCE
enamel **7** 69; **12** 152
furniture **20** 442*
Australia **2** 758
Britain **20** 442
France **20** 442
Portugal **25** 307
United States of America **20** 442
glass **7** *84*, 86; **12** 440
gold **12** 865; **20** 444
heraki **17** 243*
kamain **17** 243, 244*
kokumon **17** 243–4*, *244*
masons' **20** 440–41*; **31** 547
metalwork **11** 308; **20** 443–5*
Argentina **2** 402
Australia **2** 766
Austria **20** *444*
Belgium **3** 596, 600–601, 603; **20** *443*, *444*
Brazil **4** 724
Britain **20** 443, 445
Byzantine **20** 443
China **20** 444
Czech Republic **8** 414, 415
Denmark **8** 750, 751
England **10** 325, 328, 330, 331; **20** 443, 444, *444*
Finland **11** 108
France **11** 613; **13** 158; **20** 443, 444
Germany **12** 442
Gothic **13** 157, 158, 165
Guatemala **13** 767
Indian subcontinent **15** 707
Indonesia **15** 813
Ireland **16** 32; **20** 444, *444*
Jamaica **16** 889
Malta (Republic of) **20** 216
Mexico **21** 393
Netherlands, the **22** 887, 890, 894
New Zealand **23** 71
Nicaragua **23** 83
Norway **23** 236
Portugal **25** 312, 313
Rome, ancient **20** 443; **27** 80
Russia **20** 444; **22** 179; **27** 419, 420, 422
Scotland **20** 444; **28** 260, 262
South Africa **29** 120–21*
Spain **13** 165; **20** 444; **29** 332, 333, 335, 336, 337
Sweden **30** 104, 108, 110
Switzerland **30** 146, 147
United States of America **20** 443
Venezuela **32** 177
ormolu **20** 445
pewter **20** 445
England **20** 445
Germany **20** 445
Hungary **15** 8
Netherlands, the **22** 893
United States of America **31** 652
platinum **20** 445
porcelain **6** 903
silver **20** 443
Burma **5** 259
Byzantine **9** 654
China **7** 30
Early Christian (*c.* AD 250-843) **9** 654
marks
silver—cont.
Hungary **15** 5
Norway **23** 236
tapestries **30** 317
see also TRADEMARKS
Marks, Henry Stacy **7** 410; **18** 882; **20** 446*; **25** 398
collaboration **12** 840
groups and movements **10** 254; **27** 564
works **23** *547*; **24** 641
Marks, Sammy **25** 566
Marks & Spencer **10** 300
Marks Tey (Essex), St Andrew **11** 252
Márkus, Géza **14** 890; **20** 447*; **29** 398
Markus, Louis Casimir Ladislas *see* MARCOUSSIS, LOUIS
Markus Böblinger *see* BÖBLINGER, MARX
Markus von Esselingen *see* BÖBLINGER, MARX
Markyate, Christina of *see* CHRISTINA OF MARKYATE
marl **25** 488
Marlbork Castle **13** 57
Marlborough, Charles Spencer, 3rd Duke of *see* SPENCER, CHARLES, 3rd Duke of Marlborough
Marlborough, George Spencer, 4th Duke of *see* SPENCER, GEORGE, 4th Duke of Marlborough
Marlborough, Henrietta Churchill, Duchess of *see* CHURCHILL, HENRIETTA, Duchess of Marlborough
Marlborough, John Churchill, 1st Duke of *see* CHURCHILL, JOHN, 1st Duke of Marlborough
Marlborough, Sarah Churchill, Duchess of *see* CHURCHILL, SARAH, Duchess of Marlborough
marl clay *see under* CLAY → types
Marle, Félix Del *see* DEL MARLE, FÉLIX
Marle, (Valentin) Raymond (Silvan) van **15** 90; **20** 447*; **22** 911
Marlfield embroidery *see under* EMBROIDERY → types
Marlia, Villa Reale **12** 119; **31** 73
Marliani, Fabrizio, Cardinal **25** 465
Marliani, Giovanni Bartolomeo **20** 447*
works **2** 162; **26** 848
Marliano, Ambrogio da *see* AMBROGIO DA MARLIANO
Marlie, Renée-Elisabeth *see* LÉPICIÉ, RENÉE-ELISABETH
Marlik **1** 786; **15** *901*, 902, 905, 907, 921; **20** 447–9*
glass **1** 866, *866*
gold **20** *448*
jewellery **1** 875; **20** 448
metalwork **15** 919; **20** 448
pottery **1** *786*; **20** 448
sculpture **15** 914
tombs **1** 894; **20** 448
Marlois, Samuel **21** 580
Marlot, Guillaume **8** 534
Marlow, William **14** 144; **20** 449*; **26** 774; **28** 285; **32** 111
Marlowe, Christopher **30** 662
marls **6** 325; **25** 488, 493
Marly Château **6** 508; **20** 296, *449*, 449–50*; **23** 493
Chambre de la Reine **17** 627
façade decoration **10** 737
furniture **11** 592
gardens **6** 121; **7** 422; **8** 70–71, 94; **11** 559; **12** 121, 123; **20** 450
sculpture **11** 156, 754; **28** 845; **29** 564
Grand Salon **26** 492

Marly Château—cont.
Hermitage 14 460
interior decoration 3 621; 7 168; 27 263; 28 776
paintings 4 537; 8 91, 812; 9 87; 18 632; 20 489; 23 667; 24 211; 30 343
Pavillon du Roi 20 295
sculpture 3 258; 11 559; 25 377; 29 572
Marly Table 26 376
Marmara see PROKONNESOS
Marmaraereğlisi see PERINTHOS
Marmaria see DELPHI
Mar'mariya 9 774
figurines 9 865
Marmashen Monastery 2 423, 426, 427
Mar Mattai 9 621
Marmey, Jacques 20 450*
Marmi, Giacinto Maria 9 15; 21 30
Marmier, Hugues 25 570
Marmion, Edmond
works 10 272
Marmion, Jean 20 450
Marmion, Simon 3 555; 20 450–53*; 25 668
collaboration 20 659
patrons and collectors 5 211, 213; 8 208
pupils 25 668
works 7 243; 11 440; 13 675; 20 451, 452, 721, 724, 725; 21 638
Marmitta, Francesco 20 453–4*
works 20 453
Marmitta, Ludovico 20 454
Marmolejo, Pedro de Villegas see VILLEGAS MARMOLEJO, PEDRO DE
Marmoles Vasallo 25 703
Marmontel, Antoine-François 4 655; 18 869
Marmontel, Jean-François 6 528; 20 497; 24 787
marmorarii Romani see COSMATI
marmor claudianus see under GRANITE → types
Marmor luculleum see under MARBLE → types
marmor lunensium see under MARBLE → types
Marmorstein, Martin see MUNKACSI, MARTIN
marmor troadense see under GRANITE → types
Marmottan, Jules 20 454
Marmottan, Paul 20 454*
Marmoucha 16 486
Mar Moussa al-Habachi 7 273
Marmoutier Abbey 26 599
Marmoutier Sacramentary see under SACRAMENTARIES → individual manuscripts
Mar Musa Church 9 543
Marne-la-Vallée 6 534; 13 716; 24 131
Les Espaces d'Abraxas 2 361; 4 227, 228; 11 528; 25 359
Marneuf, Antoine-André 28 520
Marney, Henry, 1st Baron 31 417
Marney, John, 2nd Baron 31 417
Marnez, Louis 2 565
Marnix, J. de, Graaf 10 491
Marnix, Marie de 1 584
Marochetti, Carlo 20 454–5*
groups and movements 26 742
patrons and collectors 3 179; 14 148
pupils 23 126
works 10 266, 442; 16 706; 17 798; 18 723; 31 131, 132, 446
Maroger, Jacques 9 374; 20 476
Maroggia, Tommaso da see RODARI, TOMMASO
Marold, Luděk 20 455*
Marolles, Michel de 10 757; 11 674; 20 455–6*
personal collection 4 552; 6 78; 9 230; 10 390; 11 662; 18 638; 20 855; 25 631
Marolois, Samuel 14 709; 29 649; 32 725
Maron, Anton von 20 456*; 21 131; 26 842
patrons and collectors 7 758; 14 486
pupils 3 778; 28 892
teachers 21 132
Marone, F. 14 904
Marone, Pietro Paolo 4 18
Marone, Roberto see RAFFAELLO DA BRESCIA
Marone & Artigas 2 542
Maroneia 13 567
Maroni 8 353
Maronite see under CHRISTIANITY → sects
Maroon 5 754; 16 879, 880, 882
Marosvasárhely see TÎRGU-MUREŞ
Marot, Daniel, I (c. 1661-1752) 10 275, 276; 19 540; 20 457, 458–60*; 22 826, 872, 888
architectural decorations 1 110
architecture 1 802; 14 39, 46, 495; 25 324
assistants 20 460
attributions 14 295
collaboration 3 418; 8 834; 26 560
decorative works 18 854
engravings 5 347; 9 28; 24 160
fountains 11 345
frames 11 374
furniture 3 484; 5 347, 349; 7 746; 9 28
gardens 12 132, 132; 14 127, 495; 23 467; 29 8; 31 488
groups and movements 33 199
interior decoration 4 159; 7 166; 10 273, 291; 14 856; 20 459; 21 907; 22 864; 23 542, 542; 29 837; 31 683
ivory-carvings 22 896
metalwork 7 167
paintings 9 14
patrons and collectors 4 177; 14 855; 22 826, 864; 23 466, 467
pattern books 24 273, 274
tiles 23 467; 30 878
tombs 14 44
writings 25 324
Marot, Daniel, II (1695-1769) 20 457, 460*
Marot, Girard 20 456
Marot, Jean (fl 1507) 4 571
works 4 572
Marot, Jean, I (1619-79) 20 456, 457–8*
collaboration 28 742
engravings 14 394; 19 145
châteaux 4 865; 19 133; 20 457; 26 347
churches 4 866
hôtels particuliers 4 756; 14 790; 19 59, 133, 211, 300
interior decoration 11 573
topographical 8 455
pupils 20 458
Marot, Jean, II (fl 1686-1702) 20 457
Marot, Jean-Baptiste 20 456
Maróthy, Győző 14 890
Maróthy, Kálmán 26 396
Maróti, Géza (Rintel) 4 185; 15 4; 20 460*
Maroto, Diego 19 385; 20 460*; 24 502, 503
Marotta, Gino 26 778
Maroua 1 394; 5 525
marouflage 20 461*
Marpadas 25 426
Marperger, Paul Jacob 10 205
Marples, George 14 545
Marpole 29 743
Marpole Image 29 743
Marq, Charles 6 386; 26 113; 29 508
Marqab see MARGAT CASTLE
Marqasi see MARAŞ
Marquand, Alan 31 671
Marquand, Henry G(urdon) 19 104; 20 461*; 31 667
Marquart, Bartholomaus 2 458
Marque, Albert 11 568; 20 461*
Marquelet, Robert 20 138
Marques, Agostinho 20 461–2*; 25 306
Marques, Agustín Esteve y see ESTEVE Y MARQUES, AGUSTÍN
Marques (Lucas), Diogo 20 462*
Marqués, El Viso del, Palace see VISO DEL MARQUÉS PALACE
Marqués, Francisco Domingo y see DOMINGO Y MARQUÉS, FRANCISCO
Marquesas Islands 20 462–3*; 23 711
architecture 20 462
body ornaments 23 720
canoes 23 725
carving 20 463
fans 10 779
feathers 23 720
forgeries 23 737, 738
hair 23 720
headdresses 23 720
human figures 20 463
paddles 23 724
pendants (jewellery) 23 720
platforms 23 715
sculpture 23 731
stilts (walking) 20 463
tattoos 20 462; 23 719, 719
weapons 23 734
wood-carvings 20 463
Marques da Silva, (José) see SILVA, (JOSÉ), Marques da
Marques de Figueiredo, Manuel 20 464
Marques de Oliveira, João 20 463–4*; 25 298; 29 100
Marquês do Herval Building 32 258
Marques dos Santos, Francisco 4 725
Marques dos Santos, Joaquim 20 464*
Marques Pereira da Silva, Teodoro 10 155
Marqueste, Laurent-Honoré 10 771; 11 567
Marquet, Albert 4 391; 5 529; 11 549; 20 464–5*; 22 91
attributions 5 528
collaboration 29 329
groups and movements 10 840, 841; 25 356
methods 24 349
patrons and collectors 10 885; 26 723; 28 569
works 20 465
Marquet, Jaime 4 563
Marquet-Krause, Judith 1 476
marquetry 20 465–9*
historical and regional traditions
Belgium 20 467
Catalonia 29 320–21
Egypt 16 490
Egypt, ancient 20 466
England 20 467, 468, 468, VIII1
Finland 11 103
France 5 192; 11 588, 589, 589, 590, 596; 20 467, 468, 469, 469, VII
Germany 5 191; 12 423, 424, 425; 20 467
Hungary 14 904
Indian subcontinent 20 VIII2
Islamic 16 487, 490; 20 VIII3
Italy 20 467, 468
Madagascar 20 36
marquetry
historical and regional traditions—cont.
Netherlands, the 5 192; 20 467; 22 872
Peru 33 332
Poland 25 121
Portugal 20 468; 25 306, 307
Spain 20 VIII3
Sweden 20 468
Syria 16 490
United States of America 20 468, 469
materials
adhesives 20 466
bog oak 20 466
bog yew 20 466
bone 20 466
box-wood 12 423
brass 20 466
copper 20 VII
ebony 20 466
glues 20 466
gold dust 20 466
hare-wood 20 466
holly 20 466
horn 20 466
inks 20 466
ivory 12 423; 16 797; 20 466
laburnum 20 467
miniatures (paintings) 20 466
mother-of-pearl 12 424, 425; 20 466; 22 205; 33 332
olive-wood 20 467
pewter 12 423; 20 466
rose-wood 25 307; 33 332
satin-wood 25 307
shells 20 466
silver dust 20 466
sycamore 20 466
tortoiseshell 20 466; 33 332
tulip-wood 25 307
veneers 20 465, 466, 467, 468
walnut 20 467
wood 16 487, 490; 20 466, 468
techniques
cutting 20 466
engraving 20 466, 468
pouncing 20 466
scorching 20 466
types
boullework 20 466; 31 195; 33 333
Belgium 3 585
England 10 297; 20 468
France 11 596; 20 467
Germany 12 422; 29 60
floral 20 467, 468, 469
France 11 596
Netherlands, the 20 467
oyster-work 20 467
Tunbridge ware 20 469
Wrangelschrank 12 421; 20 467
uses
armoires 20 VII
bureaux 5 191, 192; 11 103
cabinets 20 VIII2
cabinets (ii) (furniture) 11 588, 589; 20 467, 468
chests-of-drawers 20 469
commodes 11 589
cupboards 8 271
desks 5 192
doors 9 160
furniture 11 590, 596; 12 420; 20 467; 33 332
musical instruments 20 VIII1
sideboards 25 121
writing-boxes 20 VIII3
Márquez, Laura 24 99
Márquez, Lorenzo 29 334
Marquéz, Luis 21 398
Marquez, Pedro 33 472
Márquez Miranda, F. 29 202
Marqui, José del Pozo y see POZO Y MARQUI, JOSÉ DEL
Marquí, Santiago 12 57; 13 761, 770
Marquina, Angel 29 338
Marquina, Ignacio 7 201; 21 228; 30 452
Marquina, Juan de 13 283
Marquina y Bueno, Rafael 19 387; 24 505
Marquis, Richard 2 764
Marr, Carl 17 692
Marr, N. 2 98, 444; 6 280; 33 521
Marr, Nikolay (Yakovlevich) 12 331
Marradi, Master of 6 4
Marrakesh 1 376; 16 103, 190; 20 469–70*
Abtan House 22 128
architecture 1 315; 16 190, 240; 22 128; 27 506
Badi' Palace 16 240; 23 816
Barudiyyin cupola 22 323
fortifications 21 583
Haheqdesh synagogue 17 551
Hotel Tichka 22 128
Islamic religious buildings
'Ali ibn Yusuf Mosque 16 494
Almoravid mosque 21 629
Bab Dukkala Mosque 16 240
Ben Yusuf Madrasa 16 240, 246; 20 57, 470; 23 562
Tanka Masjid see TAKA MOSQUE
Berrima Mosque 16 240
Booksellers Mosque see Kutubiyya Mosque
congregational mosque 16 190
Kasba Mosque 16 191, 250
Kutubiyya Mosque 16 190–91, 250; 20 470; 21 629; 23 485
capitals 16 191
ceiling 2 529
ceilings 16 494
maqṣūra 20 368
minaret 21 626, 626
minbar 16 493, 494, 525; 21 630; 23 560
stucco 29 818
minbars 21 629
Muwassin Mosque 16 240
Qubbat Barudiyyin 16 244; 20 470
shrine of Sidi Bel 'Abbas al-Sabti 16 240
shrine of Sidi Ben Sulayman al-Jazuli 16 240
kasba 16 240
manuscripts 16 357
Sa'di necropolis 16 240, 240
shrine of Sidi Bel 'Abbas al-Sabti 16 244
stained glass 16 257
Marrakesh Studio 29 117
Marralwanga, Peter (Djakku) 1 67; 20 470–71*
Marrast, Joseph 22 128
Marré, Carlos 2 397
Marrel Frères 11 621
Marrellus, Jakob see MARELL, JAKOB
Marrina, Lorenzo 20 745; 24 732
Marriott, Alvin 16 884, 887, 889; 20 471*
Marriott, Gordon 28 691
Marris, Robert 8 832
Marrow, James Henry 15 91
Marrugal, José de la Vega see VEGA MARRUGAL, JOSÉ DE LA
Marryat 29 536
Marsal, Mariano (José Bernardo) Fortuny y see FORTUNY Y MARSAL, MARIANO (JOSÉ BERNARDO)
Marsala see LILYBAEUM
Marsalaer, Jodoco Ricke de 9 710
Marsalle, L. de see KIRCHNER, ERNST LUDWIG
Marsa Susa 7 820; 9 557
Marschack, Alexander 25 489
Marschall, Rudolph 20 925
Marsden, A. M. 8 717

Marsden, May **2** 772
Marseille **9** *510*; **11** *505*, 657; **20** 471–5*; **25** *470*; **26** *908*; **31** 724
  architecture **26** 904
  Canebière, La **20** *474*
  caskets **5** 918
  Cathedral **9** 569; **11** 521, 522; **25** 173; **28** 346; **32** 82–3, *83*
    Baptistery **9** 533
  Centre d'Etude et de Documentation sur l'Image (CEDDCI) **2** 370
  ceramics **20** 474*
  coins **13** 585, 586
  coral **7** 834
  cotton **11** 649
  docks **9** 58
  faience (ii) (ceramics) **11** 605, 606; **19** 723
  Hospice de la Charité **25** 709
  Jardin des Vestiges **20** 472
  jars **20** *471*
  Massalia **20** 472*
  monasteries **7** 230
  museums **11** 668
    Musée des Arts et Traditions Populaires du Terroir Marsellais **2** 370
    Musée des Beaux-Arts **11** 665, 666; **20** 473; **22** 357
    Musée Borély **2** 275; **27** 142
    Musée des Docks Romains **20** 472
    Musée de la Marine et de l'Economie de Marseille **20** 472
  Palais Longchamp *see* Musée des Beaux-Arts
  Palais Longchamps **25** 750
  porcelain **11** 609
  Porte d'Aix **11** 564
  pottery **14** 498; **25** 543
  quilting **25** 821
  sacred grove **27** 1
  St Victor **20** 475*; **26** 596, 603; **27** 828
  sculpture **11** 556
  silk **11** 644, 646
  Stock Exchange *see* Musée de la Marine et de l'Economie de Marseille
  trade **10** 592
  Unité d'Habitation **2** 361; **5** 56; **7** 295, 695, 696; **11** 359, 527, 659; **19** 44–6
  urban planning **24** 352–3
  water supply **2** 243
Marseille, Olivier de *see* OLLIVIER, JEAN-PHILIPPE-AUGUSTIN
Marselis, Christoph **25** 29
Mar Sergius **31** 434
Marseus van Schrieck, Otto *see* SCHRIECK, OTTO MARSEUS VAN
MARS Group **10** 241; **13** 688; **20** 475*; **33** 552
  members **2** 578; **7** 294, 482, 712; **11** 808; **12** 871; **14** 222; **28** 548; **29** 927
  urban planning **1** 29
  works **31** 731
Marsh, Alice **20** 476
Marsh, Dwight Whitney **1** 895
Marsh, Edward (Howard) **20** 476*
Marsh, Fred Dana **20** 476
Marsh, Narcissus, Archbishop **26** 475
Marsh, Reginald **10** 397; **20** 476*; **31** 606
  collaboration **20** 603, 604
  groups and movements **1** 773
  pupils **19** 328; **26** 426
  teachers **21** 606
  works **31** 663
Marshak, Samuil **12** 804; **19** 13
Marshal, Alexander **20** 476*
Marshall (family) **12** 174
Marshall, A. S. **9** 310
Marshall, Ben(jamin) **20** 477*
  patrons and collectors **14** 146; **21** 91; **33** 150
  pupils **10** 907
  works **2** 106; **10** 250; **29** 424
Marshall, Benyon and Bage **21** 601
Marshall, Edward **4** 693; **5** 263; **10** 262, 263; **20** 477*
Marshall, James **4** 789
Marshall, John (1876-1958; archaeologist) **14** 162; **15** 211; **20** 477–8*
  excavations **15** 747; **21** 792; **27** 708; **30** 378
  works **30** 380
Marshall, John A. (*fl* 1906; architect) **3** 746
Marshall, Joshua **10** 263; **20** 477*
Marshall, Lambert **20** 477*
Marshall, Peter **24** 18
Marshall, Peter Paul **14** 809; **22** 143
Marshall, William **4** 600; **20** 478*; **27** 187
Marshall, William Calder **20** 478–9*; **29** 646
  teachers **3** 79
  works **9** 1; **10** 266; **28** 243
Marshall, William E. **27** 461
Marshall, W. K. **5** 513
Marshall Islands **20** 479*; **23** *711*
  canoes **20** 479; **23** 726
  fans **10** 779
  maps **31** 152
  plaiting **20** 479
  tattoos **23** 723
  weaving **20** 479
Marsh Court **12** 141
Marshidabad **15** 662
Marsh & Jones **3** 893
Marsigli, Filippo **22** 97
Marsigli, Fino **26** 459
Marsili, Luigi **8** 159; **33** 615
Marsiliana d'Albegna **10** 604, 631
Marsio-Aalto, Aino **1** 10; **8** 803
Marske, William Lowther, 3rd Baronet of *see* LOWTHER, WILLIAM, 3rd Baronet of Marske
Mars orange *see under* PIGMENTS → types
Marsoulas **25** 475, 478, 479, 484
Mars red *see under* PIGMENTS → types
Marston House (Somerset) **30** 123
Marstrand, Wilhelm (Nicolai) **7** 805; **20** 480*
  patrons and collectors **14** 572; **30** 766
  pupils **1** 845; **4** 142; **18** 469; **33** 594
  works **4** 142; **9** 701; **27** 168
Marsum **22** *813*
Marsum Church **22** 819
Marsvin (family) **20** 632
Marsvinsholm **30** 92
Mars violet *see under* PIGMENTS → types
Marsy, Balthazar **20** 480–81
  collaboration **12** 725; **25** 79; **26** 91
  sculpture **4** 551; **11** 559; **29** 571, 833; **31** 408; **32** 372
Marsy, François Marie de **10** 206
Marsy, Gaspar(d) (1624-81) **4** 807; **11** 156; **20** 480–81
  collaboration **11** 156; **12** 725; **25** 79; **26** 91; **31** 408
  sculpture **4** 551; **7** 546; **11** 559; **29** 572, 833; **31** 408; **32** 372
Marsy, Gérard **29** 571
Marsy, Jaspard (1600-74) **20** 480
Marsyas **27** 46
Marsyas Painter **17** 911; **32** 56*
  works **9** 249; **13** 524, *524*
Mars yellow *see under* PIGMENTS → types
Marsyglle, Antonio **29** 347
Martaban jars *see under* JARS → types
Martanda **15** *264*; **20** 481*
  Surya Temple **15** 216, 265; **20** 481
Marteau, François **20** 922
Marteau, Georges **16** 549
Marteau, Giles de **2** 467
Marteau, Louis **8** 372; **25** 212
Martebo Church **13** 103
  reliefs **13** *103*
Marteinsdóttir, Steinunn **15** 72
Martel, B. U. *see* UITZ, BÉLA
Martel, Geoffrey II, Count of Anjou *see* GEOFFREY II MARTEL, Count of Anjou
Märtel, Hermann **25** 550
Martel, Jan **11** 568
Martel, Joël **11** 568
Martellange, Etienne **20** 482*; **24** 104
  assistants **31** 462
  patrons and collectors **17** 511; **29** 886
  pupils **19** 210; **31** 462
  works **2** *859*; **4** 578; **8** 775; **11** 516; **19** 846; **23** 510
Martelli (family) **19** 443; **20** 482*
Martelli, Diego **16** 678; **19** 870, 871; **20** 482–3*; **24** 448
Martelli, Giovan Francesco **27** 771
Martelli, Giuseppe **11** 189
Martelli, M. **25** 245
Martelli, Roberto **20** 482
Martelli *David* **16** 614; **33** 159
Mårten **26** 639
Märten, Lü **33** 308
Marten, Miloš **4** 700
Martenot, Jean-Baptiste **26** 205
Martens, Baertge **25** *276*, 277
Martens, Conrad **2** 745; **4** 882; **20** 483*; **30** 160; **31** 754
Martens, Friederich von **20** 483–4*; **24** 654, 659
Martens, Gustav **31** 580
Martens, Joseph **7** 606
Marth, Juraj **28** 856
Martha Washington chairs *see under* CHAIRS → types
Martí, Francesc **29** 332
Martí, Josep **20** 501; **29** 337
Martí, Marcel **3** 220
Martial **2** 558; **4** 343; **26** 557, 924
Martialis, Marcus Valerius *see* MARTIAL
Martial Potémont, Adolphe (-Théodore-Jules) **20** 484*
Martí Alsina, Ramón **20** 484*; **29** 284, 306
  groups and movements **24** 829
  pupils **32** 97
  works **3** 219
Martianus Mineus Felix Capella **1** 652; **22** 412
Martienssen, Rex (Distin) **10** 825; **20** 484*
  groups and movements **1** 319; **29** 106
  pupils **19** 229
  works **17** 603; **29** 106
  writings **20** 8
Marties, Colinet de *see* COLINET DE MARTIES
Martigny, Fondation Pierre Gianadda **30** 152
Martigny, V.-G. **3** 620
Martigues, Musée d'Art et Archéologie **33** 674
Martikainen-Ypäm, Martta **2** 317
Martin (Slovakia)
  church **14** 898
  Slovak National Museum **28** 857
  Turčiec Gallery **28** 857
Martin (ii) (family)
  groups and movements **2** 569, 570
Martin (*fl* late 12th cent.) **2** 842
Martin (ii) (family) **19** 595
  works **10** 312, *312*
Martín, Master (*fl* 1227-34) **31** 91
Martin, Master (*fl* late 13th cent.) **10** 515
Martin (*fl* early 18th cent.) **1** 665
Martin, King of Aragon (*reg* 1395-1410) **4** 764; **25** 58; **30** 313, 779
Martin V, Pope **7** 218, 620*
  architecture **26** 755, 765
  metalwork **26** 766
  mitres **12** 543
  paintings **12** 299, 302; **20** 535, 556; **26** 765
Martin, Agnes (Bernice) **1** 81; **20** 486–7*; **24** 213; **31** 483, 609
Martin, Albert C. **19** 700
  works **19** *700*
Martín, Alberto Manrique **7** 605, 606
Martin, Albin **2** 706; **23** 58
Martin, Arthur **29** 514
Martin, August **23** 502
Martin, Carl (*b* 1951) **13** 877
Martin, Charles (*fl* 1927) **18** 631
Martin, Charles Douglas **20** 485*
Martin, Claude **15** 376, 377, 402, 654, 741; **16** 553
Martin, Darwin **33** 401
Martin, David **20** 487*; **25** 883; **28** 235
Martin, Edgar **28** 121, 122
Martin, Edward **6** 128
Martin, Edwin Bruce **20** 485*
Martin (iii), Elias **20** 484–5*
  assistants **20** 485
  patrons and collectors **8** 161; **31** 362
  pupils **10** 100
  teachers **11** 113
  works **29** 676; **30** 79, 80
Martin, Emile **3** 314
Martin, Etienne *see* ETIENNE-MARTIN
Martin, Etienne-Edmond, Baron de Beurnonville *see* BEURNONVILLE, ETIENNE-EDMOND MARTIN, Baron de
Martin (i), Etienne-François **32** 337
Martin (i), Etienne-Simon **18** 610, 611, 614; **32** 337, 338
Martin, Firmin **17** 644
Martín, Francisco (*fl* 1590) **7** 362
Martin, François (*fl* 1674) **25** 211
Martin, François Auguste **20** 472
Martin, Fredrik (Robert) (1868-1933) **2** 437; **16** 549, 554, 559; **20** 487*
  collaboration **16** 548
  collections **16** 559, 560
Martin, Georg **30** 370
Martin, Glenn, Aircraft **17** 722
Martin (i), Guillaume **18** 610, 611, 614; **32** 337
Martin (i), Guillaume-Jean **32** 337
Martin, Helen **22** 140
Martin, Henri (-Jean-Guillaume) (1860-1943) **20** 387, 487–8*; **22** 330
Martin, Henri (*fl* 1909-29) **26** 478
Martin, Homer Dodge **20** 488*
Martin, Jan (*fl* 1769-91) **32** 878
Martin, Jean (*d* 1553) **20** 488–9*; **21** 368; **32** 641
Martin (i), Jean-Alexandre **32** 337
Martin, Jean-Baptiste (1659-1753) **12** 832; **20** 489*; **22** 456
  collaboration **1** 664; **11** 642
  works **8** 24; **11** *642*; **30** 672; **32** *373*
  illustrated **13** 225
Martin, Jean-Baptiste (*d* after 1741) **20** 489
Martin, Jesse **23** 336
Martin (iii), Johann Fredric (1755-1816) **20** 485*; **30** 79, 80
Martin, John **20** 489–91*; **23** 21; **25** 686
  groups and movements **10** 97; **26** 741; **29** 891
Martin, John—cont.
  patrons and collectors **13** 637; **19** 98; **25** 41
  pupils **28** 389
  reproductive prints by others **22** 208
  works **7** 924; **15** *407*, 828; **20** *490*; **21** 417
Martin, Joseph **9** 320
Martin, Josiah **23** 59
Martín, Juan **27** 765
Martin (i), Julien **18** 610, 611, 614; **32** 337
Martin (iii), Kenneth **20** 485–6*; **30** 201
  groups and movements **18** 62, 63
  works **21** 746
Martin, Laurin Hovey
  works **4** *480*
Martin, (John) Leslie **10** 241; **11** 877; **19** 519; **20** 491*; **33** 218
  collaboration **19** 321; **23** 103; **28** 158
  staff **14** 613; **33** 218
  works **1** 126; **4** 789; **5** 513; **7** 687; **10** 242; **14** 863; **19** 577, *577*; **23** 689; **25** 318; **26** 460
  writings **7** 772
Martín, Luis Quinquela *see* QUINQUELA MARTÍN, LUIS
Martin, Mandy **2** 752
Martin, Maria (*d* 1863) **2** 710
Martin (iii), Mary (1907-69) **20** 485, 486*; **30** 201
Martin, Milo **30** 138
Martin, Moses **28** 225; **29** 679
Martin, Mungo **16** 891; **20** 492*; **22** 581, 589; **32** 414
  works **20** *492*
Martin, Noel **5** 531
Martin, Olof **30** 94
Martin, Paul (Augustus) **20** 492*; **24** 671
Martin, Père **5** 441; **15** 154; **24** 883; **30** 354
Martin, Pierre-Denis **12** 832; **20** 489
  works **20** *449*
Martin, Pierre-Lucien
  works **4** *354*
Martin, Raymond **14** 229
Martin (i), Robert (1706-65) **18** 610, 611, 614; **32** 337
Martin, Robert (*fl* 1758-96) **3** 330
Martin, Robert-Henri
  works **8** *902*
Martin, Robert Wallace **20** 485*
Martin, Ron **5** 569
Martin, Rose **23** 235
Martin, Sébastian **26** 349
Martin, T. Mower **32** 414
Martín, Vicente **12** 29
Martin, von **28** 917
Martin, Walter Fraser **20** 485*
Martin, William **4** 85; **6** 408
Martincourt, Etienne **11** 625, 627; **26** 376
  works **11** *627*
Martindale, Andrew **2** 536
Martindale, Colin **25** 684
Martindale, John **5** 580; **12** 45
Martín de Bruselas **14** 135
Martín de Oñate *see* OÑATE, MARTÍN DE
Martín de Santiago **9** 112; **12** 619; **29** 265
Martin des Batailles *see* MARTIN, JEAN-BAPTISTE (1659-1735)
Martin des Gobelins *see* MARTIN, PIERRE-DENIS
Martín de Solórzano **2** 278, 863, 865; **14** 578; **20** 493*
  patrons and collectors **9** 112
Martín de Soria **27** 818
Martineau, Robert Braithwaite **11** 434; **20** 493*
Martinelli (family) **32** 435

Martinelli, Anton Erhard
20 493–4*
works 6 363; 11 31; 14 886; 26 708; 32 434
Martinelli, Domenico 2 782; 20 494–5*; 32 435
assistants 5 295; 11 886
collaboration 19 337
patrons and collectors 8 378; 28 836
teachers 11 274
works 11 135; 12 748; 14 190; 25 427; 26 316
Martinelli, Ezio 18 301
Martinelli, Fioravante 20 495*; 26 849; 31 536
Martinelli, Francesco 1 669; 10 529; 14 886
Martinelli, Giovanni 16 673; 20 495–6*
works 20 *496*
Martinelli, Giovanni Battista 4 695; 28 850
Martinelli, Manlio 28 319
Martinelli, Niccolo *see* TROMETTA
Martinelli, Vincenzo 3 869; 10 199; 20 497*
Martinengo, Ascanio 7 646
Martinengo, Ludovico
works 3 *302*
Martinengo, Pedro 2 284
Martinengo-Colleoni, Alessandro, Conte 19 711
Martinet, François-Nicolas 20 497*, 584
works 27 *541*
Martinet, Louis 6 79; 9 423; 11 663; 20 497–8*; 24 141
paintings 10 680
Martinet, Thérèse 20 497
Martinetti 20 497
Martinetti, Francesco 10 639
Martínez, Our Lady of Fatima 2 397
Martínez, Alonso 28 516
Martínez, Celestino 31 229; 32 180
Martinez, Crescencio 20 498; 22 594
Martinez, Crisostomo 1 842
Martínez, Daniel 20 499
Martínez, Domingo 20 499*, 860; 25 460; 29 282; 31 195
Martínez, Eduardo 3 123
Martínez, Eduardo Rosales *see* ROSALES MARTÍNEZ, EDUARDO
Martínez, Federico 7 559
Martinez, Felix 24 622
Martínez, Fernando 7 606; 14 714
Martínez, Fernando López *see* LÓPEZ MARTÍNEZ, FERNANDO
Martínez, Ginés 22 73
Martínez, Jeronimo (*fl* 1790-1826) 2 402
Martínez, Jerónimo Jusepe Bautista (*fl* 17th cent.) 20 500
Martinez, J. J. 4 365
Martínez, José Luzán y *see* LUZÁN Y MARTÍNEZ, JOSÉ
Martinez, José María 26 298; 27 783
Martinez, Julian (1885-1943; painter on ceramics) 20 498–9; 22 606
works 20 *498*
Martínez, Julio (*fl* early 20th cent.; painter) 25 701
Martínez (y Lurbe), Jusepe 13 863; 20 499–500*
works 20 *500*
Martínez, Leoncio 21 902
Martinez, Maria 20 498–9; 22 606, 668, 677
works 20 *498*
Martínez, María Cadilla de *see* CADILLA DE MARTÍNEZ, MARÍA
Martínez, Oliverio 20 500*; 23 335; 33 728
Martinez, Popovi Da 20 499
Martínez, Raúl 8 234; 25 354
works 8 *234*
Martínez, Rubén 10 154
Martinez, Santana 20 499
Martínez, Sebastián 12 59; 20 501, 502
Martínez, Selmo 24 99
Martínez, Silvestre Pérez y *see* PÉREZ Y MARTÍNEZ, SILVESTRE
Martínez Altés, Gabriel 23 194
Martínez Barrio, Antonio (*fl* 1750; father) 20 501
Martínez Barrio, Antonio (1750-98; son) 20 69, 501*; 29 337
Martínez Cañas, María 18 835
Martínez Carrión, Jesús 21 386
Martínez Compañon, Baltasar Jaime, Bishop of Trujillo 29 218, 220
Martínez de Aranda, Ginés 29 637
Martínez de Arce, Diego 27 644
Martínez de Arrona, Juan 20 501*; 23 178; 24 501, 506
Martínez de Burueva, Roi 13 104
Martínez de Compañon y Bujanda, Baltazar Jaime 6 441
Martínez de Hebert, Pedro *see* HEBERT, PEDRO
Martínez de Hoyos, Ricardo 20 501*
Martínez del Mazo, Juan Bautista *see* MAZO, JUAN BAUTISTA MARTÍNEZ DEL
Martínez del Rio, Pablo 31 65
Martinez de Montanchez, Alonso 22 241
Martínez de Oviedo, Diego 20 501–2*; 24 506
Martínez de Salas, Cristóbal, Bishop of Panama 23 905
Martínez de Velazco, Juan 23 369
Martinez Díaz, Marcelo *see* DÍAZ, MARCELO MARTINEZ
Martinez Gutierrez, Juan 6 594; 20 502*
Martínez Montañés, Juan *see* MONTAÑÉS, JUAN MARTÍNEZ
Martínez Pedro, Luis 8 236; 20 502*
Martínez Pérez, Sebastián 2 174; 20 502*
Martínez-Richiez, Luichy 9 117, 118
Martínez-Rivas (family) 28 884
Martínez Sánchez, José 18 867; 20 502–3*
Martín Fierro 2 400; 24 435; 25 459
Martinho 12 760
Martinho de Portugal, Primate of India 14 659
Martini 23 169
Martini, Alberto 20 503*; 24 708
Martini, Andreas 23 507
Martini, Arturo 10 638; 16 680; 20 503*; 31 316
groups and movements 11 866; 25 6; 31 852
pupils 21 704
works 16 *707*, 708; 23 754; 30 500
Martini, Cristofano di Michele *see* ROBETTA
Martini, Donato 20 510
Martini, Ferdinando 7 782; 20 503*
Martini, Francesco 18 849
Martini, Francesco (Maurizio) di Giorgio *see* FRANCESCO (MAURIZIO) DI GIORGIO MARTINI
Martini, Giovanna 28 677
Martini, Giovanni 31 523
Martini, Giuseppe 31 73
Martini, Luca 19 672; 24 756
Martini, Ndoc (Andon) 1 540; 15 104; 20 504*
Martini, Pietro Antonio 10 677; 24 168
works 10 *678*, *823*; 24 135, *169*
Martini, Simone 13 139, 146, 155; 14 421, 868; 16 657; 19 454; 20 504–11*, 649; 25 138; 28 676, 684
attributions 2 632; 9 348; 13 192; 28 681
collaboration 9 349; 19 454, 666
frames 11 380, 381, *381*, 387
methods 7 627; 12 501, 625; 13 136, 139; 25 731; 32 805
paintings 11 711; 28 686
altarpieces 1 709; 5 164; 8 892; 9 4; 20 *507*; 24 854; 25 183, 463
frescoes 2 627, *627*, 861; 13 135, 149; 16 762; 20 *506*; 22 476; 28 684–5, *685*, 686; 32 II2
miniatures (manuscript illumination) 13 133
portraits 13 131
religious 2 860; 13 *146*, 150; 20 *508*, *509*; 25 679
patrons and collectors 12 304; 13 150–51; 23 575; 24 559; 27 359
pupils 3 247; 12 696
reproductions in tapestry 16 756
underdrawings 2 862; 29 596
workshop 12 625; 13 146
Martinioni, Giustiniano 27 774; 32 196
Martinique 2 144, 149; 5 *745*
basketwork 2 145
body ornaments 5 747
carnivals 2 146
galleries (iv) (art) 2 153
jewellery 2 152
pottery 5 747
trade 31 338
see also ANTILLES, LESSER; WINDWARD ISLANDS
Martinis, Dalibor 8 179
Martin Le Franc 18 684
Martin *le jeune* *see* MARTIN, PIERRE-DENIS
Martino 3 699
Martino, Francesco di Giorgio 22 487
Martinó, José Antonio Torres *see* TORRES MARTINÓ, JOSÉ ANTONIO
Martino, Moro di *see* CODUSSI, MAURO
Martino da Modena 6 102; 8 173; 12 666
Martino da Udine *see* PELLEGRINO DA SAN DANIELE
Martino da Venezia 20 784
Martino da Verona 1 726
Martino di Bartolomeo 16 845; 28 687; 29 406
Martin of Braga
works 1 *654*
Martin of Kolozsvár 13 160; 14 892; 20 492–3*; 26 710, 719
Martin of Tours, Saint 21 834
Martinolo, Cristoforo 31 901
Martinoski, Nikola 19 884, 885; 20 512*
Martinotti 16 731
Martinozzi, Ludovico 1 622
Martin Periz de Estella *see* PERIZ DE ESTELLA, MARTIN
Martins, Isabel 22 245
Martins, João 10 812
Martins, Leandro 4 721
Martins, Manuel Alves *see* ALVES MARTINS, MANUEL
Martins, Maria 4 718; 21 855
Martinus 25 434
Martinus Magnus 16 871
Martinus 'opifex' 2 792; 20 512*
Martinus Polonus 13 627
Martinuzzi, Carlo 19 516
Martin van Rode 13 161
Martiny, Philip 24 281; 33 42
Martire d'Anghiera, Pietro 32 147
Martirosyan, Harut'yun Artashes 20 512*
Martis, Antoine 2 148
Marton (Lincs), St Margaret 20 571
Márton, Ludovít 28 856
Martorana, Gioacchino 10 488; 20 513*
Martorana, Pietro 20 513*; 23 843
Martorel, María 2 401; 20 513*
Martorell, Antonio 14 697; 20 513*
Martorell, Bernat 3 218; 20 513–15*; 25 879; 29 276
attributions 11 480; 20 767
works 3 221; 9 264; 20 *514*, *515*
Martorell, Bohigas, Mackay 20 516–17*
collaboration 26 333
works 3 217; 20 *516*; 24 291
Martorell, Francesc 29 337
Martorell, Joanot 26 563
Martorell (Codina), Josep (Maria) 13 725; 20 516*; 29 309
Martorell i Montells, Joan 12 179
Martoriello, Gaetano 25 56
Martos, Francisco de Paula *see* PAULA MARTOS, FRANCISCO DE
Martos, Ivan (Petrovich) 20 517–18*; 27 389, 390, 579
assistants 18 74
pupils 3 530
works 22 172; 23 353; 24 546; 27 *389*; 31 561
Martszen, Jan 2 614; 23 191, 788; 25 369; 32 140
Marttanda Varma, King of Travancore (*reg* 1729-58) 31 288
Martu *see* AMORITE
Martuni 2 439
Martvili 12 *317*, 330
church 7 256; 12 319, 330
Cross 12 328
Marty, Alexandre 11 631; 19 396
Marty, André 19 215, 489; 20 603; 25 626; 29 628
printmakers 2 733; 15 58; 25 623; 33 198
Marty, André Edouard 10 824
Martyn 14 445
Martyn, Ferenc 10 650; 14 902; 20 518*
Martyn, Thomas 10 364
Martynov, Ivan 27 414
Martynov, N. A. 32 78
Martynovka 9 655
Martyrdom of St Erasmus, Master of the 8 118
Martyrdom of St Lucy, Master of the *see* FIGDOR DEPOSITION, MASTER OF THE
Martyrdom of SS Crispin and Crispinian, Master of 20 711
Martyrdom of the Ten Thousand, Master of the 3 555; 20 628
martyria 17 *489*, *495*; 20 518–20*, 865
Byzantine 8 155; 9 528
Crete 8 155
Early Christian (*c.* AD 250-843) 7 254–5; 9 528, 534, 535; 20 518, *518*, *519*; 28 629
Germany 9 534
Islamic 17 *489*, *495*
Italy 20 *518*
North Africa 9 535
Palestine 20 *519*
Rome, ancient 26 908
Martyrologies 27 591; 28 487
Martyrology of St-Germain-des-Prés 13 141
Martyropolis *see under* SILVAN
Marubashira 15 108
Marubi, Pietro 15 103
Marucelli (family) 26 321
Marucelli, Francesco 14 366
Marucelli, Paolo *see* MARUSCELLI, PAOLO
Marucelli, Valerio 22 448
Marudi, Fort Hose 21 596
Marukumayama 17 59
Marullo, Cesare, Archbishop of Palermo 23 843
Marullo, Giuseppe 28 367; 29 544
Marum, Egbert van 5 322
Maruscelli, Giovanni Stefano 24 860
Maruscelli, Paolo 20 520–21*
collaboration 13 321; 21 823; 29 251
works 4 431, 434; 20 *521*; 24 520; 29 250
Marushchenko, A. A. 23 159
Marussig, Piero 20 521–2*; 21 528; 23 263
Maruyama, Banka 17 204
Maruyama, Daiu 17 413
Maruyama, Kinya 30 392
Maruyama, Ryōshū 17 413
Maruyama Ōkyo 9 737; 17 165, 194; 20 522–3*
attributions 31 204
collaboration 26 551
groups and movements 17 194–6, 797
pupils 18 552; 20 837; 22 429
works 17 *195*; 20 *523*; 22 118; 28 297
writings 17 417
Maruyama Ōzui 17 196; 20 523
Maruyama school 18 87; 20 523, 836
works 20 *523*
Maruyama-Shijō school 1 582; 9 737; 17 194–200*, 285; 20 523, 837; 22 118; 23 386
works 17 *195*, *197*
Marv *see* MERV (TURKMENISTAN)
Marvánek, O. 33 710
Marvazi 21 885
Marvel, Claude 20 406
Marville, Charles 20 523–4*
works 15 843; 24 663, *665*; 31 156
Marville, Jean de *see* JEAN DE MARVILLE
Marvis, Gautier de, Bishop of Tournai *see* GAUTIER DE MARVIS, Bishop of Tournai
Marvy, Louis 8 655; 10 562
Marw *see* MERV (TURKMENISTAN)
Marwan II, Caliph (*reg* 744-50) (Umayyad) 14 192; 16 434, 436; 31 22
Marwan Ewer 16 367, 369
Marwar 15 *360*, 674
Marx, Enid 24 55
Marx, Erich 12 474; 20 524*
Marx, Florene 20 524
Marx, Karl 15 99; 20 524–7; 21 777; 27 591; 28 925–6
Marx, Louis, and Co. 31 256
Marx, Roberto Burle *see* BURLE MARX, ROBERTO
Marx, Roger 20 351, 524*
Marx, Samuel A(braham) 20 524*; 26 472
Marx Böblinger *see* BÖBLINGER, MARX
Marxdorf *see* GARNCARSKO
Marxer, Franz Anton 12 356
Marxism 15 99; 20 524–8*; 21 778; 28 926–7
China 7 149, 160
theories (art) 2 536; 6 768; 14 234
Marx von Esselingen *see* BÖBLINGER, MARX
Mary *see* MERV (TURKMENISTAN)
Mary, Countess of Champagne (1145-98) 26 561
Mary, Duchess of Burgundy *see* MARY OF BURGUNDY, Empress
Mary, Duchess of Guelders (*fl* early 15th cent.) 22 901

Mary, Princess of Liechtenstein (1850-78) 8 652
Mary, Queen of Hannover (1818-1907) 13 202
Mary, Queen of Hungary *see* MARY OF HUNGARY, Regent of the Netherlands
Mary, Queen of Scotland (*reg* 1542-67) 15 150; 20 612; 28 234, 244, 263
Mary I, Queen of England (*reg* 1553-58) 10 666; 11 140; 13 147; 19 515; 22 *64*; 24 36; 25 677, 807; 30 411
Mary I, Queen of Portugal *see* MARIA I, Queen of Portugal
Mary II, Queen of England and Scotland (*reg* 1688-94) 23 463, *463*, 467–8*
  architecture 10 232, 360; 14 126; 33 199, 397, 398
  barges 3 232
  ceramics 9 28; 33 199
  decorative works 5 918
  furniture 17 479; 22 865
  gardens 12 128
  gold 22 897
  interior decoration 4 232; 10 274; 14 855; 20 *459*
  metalwork 10 342, *342*; 30 871
  paintings 18 144; 26 394
  porcelain 5 347; 7 166
  pottery 4 177
  tiles 30 878
Marya Fyodorovna of Württemberg, Empress of Russia *see* MARIA FYODOROVNA OF WÜRTTEMBERG, Empress of Russia
Maryan Basilica 5 155
Mary Anne of Austria, Queen of Spain (1634-96) 13 *901*; 14 *2*, 10*; 20 899; 29 336
  architecture 19 736
  drawings 3 17
Mary Casimira, Queen of Poland (1641-1766) 12 34; 25 135
Mary Catherine, Princess of Monaco (*d* 1813) 4 848
Mary Christina, Duchess and Regent of Savoy *see* CHRISTINA, Duchess and Regent of Savoy
Mary Christina of Naples, Duchess of Savoy and Queen of Sardinia (1779-1849) 5 616
Maryculter (Grampian) 31 736, *737*
Mary de Bohun, Queen of England (1369-94) 4 238
Marye, Georges 16 559
Marye, P. Thornton 2 694
Mary Joanna of Savoy-Nemours, Duchess and Regent of Savoy (1644-1724) 1 103; 13 752; 28 *2*, 13–14*
Mary of Anjou, Queen of France (1404-63) 32 744
Mary of Austria, Queen of Bohemia and Hungary *see* MARY OF HUNGARY, Regent of the Netherlands
Mary of Burgundy, Holy Roman Empress (1457-82) 5 206, 214*; 13 *900*; 17 10; 20 723, 724, *724*, 726, 727; 32 729
Mary of Burgundy, Master of 3 725; 12 519; 20 723–7*
  collaboration 20 452
  groups and movements 12 525
  patrons and collectors 5 213; 22 535
  pupils 20 737
  works 4 371; 11 224; 15 140; 20 *724*, *725*, *726*; 29 666
Mary of Cleves, Duchess of Orléans (1426-86) 2 14; 11 355; 31 842
Mary of Guise, Queen of Scotland (1515-60) 29 679
Mary of Hungary, Queen of Naples (?1257-1323) 2 109
Mary of Hungary, Regent of the Netherlands (1505-58) 13 *900*, 908–10*, 922; 14 382; 16 867; 20 *191*; 21 ; 28 313
  architecture 3 545, 613; 9 329
  manuscripts 3 188; 7 467
  metalwork 5 52
  paintings 3 554; 4 400; 20 753; 22 64; 23 524; 27 704; 31 39; 32 271; 33 118
  sculpture 18 691
  stained glass 13 *909*
  tapestries 7 520; 10 222; 30 317; 32 272
Mary of Modena, Queen of England (1658-1718) 24 36
Mary of Teck, Queen of Great Britain (1867-1953) 3 232; 10 782; 14 523; 22 51, 312
Mar Yohannen Tayaya 31 434
Mary Rose *see under* SHIPS → named vessels
Mary's Family, Master of 25 103
Mary Stuart cup 25 383
Marzabotto 10 *583*, 585, 587, 639; 16 *618*; 20 528–9*, *529*; 26 869
  altars 1 692
  houses 10 *598*, 599
  trade 10 592
  urban planning 10 602
Marzan, Penhap 32 279
Marzano, Milka 31 754
Marzell, Jakob *see* MARELL, JAKOB
Marzi, Erzio 11 194
Marzi, Nicolò de *see* DESMARZ, NICOLAUS
Marziale, Marco 3 667; 20 529*; 25 857
Marziani, Giovanni Domenico 26 837
Marziano da Tortona 32 611
Marzocco, Il 11 190
Mar Zutra 17 550
Mas, Bartomeu 3 222
Mas, Jean du, Vicomte de La Bellière *see* LA BELLIÈRE, JEAN DU MAS, Vicomte de
Masaaki Horie *see* HORIE, MASAAKI
Masaccio 11 184; 13 155; 14 869; 16 661; 20 529–38*; 28 69
  assistants 2 19; 28 70
  attributions 5 541; 14 848; 18 584; 20 553, 556; 26 827
  collaboration 2 339; 11 185; 20 553, 554–6
  methods 19 354; 21 763; 24 487; 32 805
  paintings 16 660, 661
    frescoes 20 *533*, *534*
      Brancacci Chapel 5 *778*; 7 627; 11 *185*; 16 659, 837; 19 446; 22 521
      S Maria Novella 7 527; 11 209, 381; 15 135; 26 183; 31 124
    panel 20 *531*, *532*, *533*, 556; 24 855
  patrons and collectors 2 514; 4 658; 5 778; 7 218, 620; 14 870; 26 765; 27 307
  plaquettes 25 19, *19*
  reproductive prints by others 13 303; 24 252
  studio 29 853
  teachers 20 553
Masaccio di Bartolommeo *see* MASO DI BARTOLOMMEO
Masada 17 556; 20 539–40*; 21 559; 26 *915*; 27 112
  synagogue 17 541
Masaharta 9 887
Masahira Yamada *see* YAMADA, MASAHIRA
Masahisa Fukase *see* FUKASE, MASAHISA
Masai *see* MAASAI
Masajid, Temple of Almaqah 2 252, 253
Masaji Yoshida *see* YOSHIDA, MASAJI
Masaki, Takayuki 23 595
Masaki Art Museum *see under* OSAKA → museums
Masakiyo Nakai *see* NAKAI YAMATO MASAKIYO
Masako, Empress (*fl* 1611) 17 179
Masakuzo Horiuchi *see* HORIUCHI, MASAKUZO
Masamochi Ishikawa *see* ISHIKAWA MASAMOCHI
Masamoto Hosokawa *see* HOSOKAWA MASAMOTO
Masamoto Nakai *see* NAKAI MASAMOTO
Masamune Date *see* DATE MASAMUNE
Masamu Yanase *see* YANASE, MASAMU
Masan 18 281
Masana, Josep 20 540*
Masanao 17 400
Masanja, John 30 301
Masanobu Heinouchi *see* HEINOUCHI MASANOBU
Masanobu Kanō *see* KANŌ SHŌSEN'IN TADANOBU
Masanobu Kitao *see* KITAO MASANOBU
Masanobu Okumura *see* OKUMURA MASANOBU
Masanobu Tanaka *see* TANAKA MASANOBU
Masanzana, Augustinus de Ramellis de 4 756
Masao, Horino 24 674
Masaon Shiva Temple 15 290
Masao Tsuruoka *see* TSURUOKA, MASAO
Masar, Mattheo de 3 615
al-Ma'sara 9 812
Masarh 15 423
Maşathöyük 1 *821*, 826; 20 540–41*
  architecture 1 830
  palace 1 831, 839, 894; 20 *540*; 23 806
Masato, Otaka 21 318
Masatomo Fukurai *see* FUKURAI MASATOMO
Masato Otaka *see* OTAKA, MASATO
Masatoshi *see* NAKAGAWA, KATSUMASA
Masatoshi Toda *see* TODA, MASATOSHI
Masatsugu Kaigyokusai *see* KAIGYOKUSAI MASATSUGU
Masatsugu Kobori *see* KOBORI MASATSUGU
Masaya 23 85
Masaya, Antonio Sarria de *see* SARRIA DE MASAYA, ANTONIO
Masaya, Pedro Ortiz de *see* ORTIZ DE MASAYA, PEDRO
Masayoshi Keisai *see* KEISAI MASAYOSHI
Masayoshi Kitao *see* KITAO MASAYOSHI
Masazo Fuji *see* FUJI, MASAZO
Mascacotta, Il *see* GRECO, GENNARO
Mascagni, Donato Arsenio 2 793; 14 361, 645; 19 374; 27 664
Mascagni, Paolo 1 844, 845; 21 6
Mascaraque (family) 29 343
Mascardi, Augustini 12 16
Mascarene (family) 7 702
Mascarenhas, Fernando 12 124
Mascarin, Mario 30 144
Mascarino, Ottavio dei Nonni *see* MASCHERINO, OTTAVIANO
Mascarons 20 541*
  see also GROTESQUE
Masch, Jacob *see* MASCHIUS, JACOB
Mascherino, Giulio 20 541
Mascherino, Ottaviano 20 541–2*
  patrons and collectors 13 628; 24 399; 26 814
  works 4 812; 11 277; 20 *541*; 22 5; 26 840
Mascherone *see* GARGOYLES
Maschinenfabrik Escher, Wyss & Co. 10 496
Maschio, Lattanzio 10 526
Maschius, Jacob 23 224
Masci, Girolamo *see* NICHOLAS IV, Pope
Masciotta, Michelangelo 10 211
Mascó, Diego de Vich y *see* VICH Y MASCÓ, DIEGO DE
Mascoli Altar, Master of the 13 95; 20 728*
  works 20 *728*
Mascret, Achille 6 535
Mas d'Azil 11 *505*; 20 542*; 25 *470*
  batons 25 493
  contours découpés 25 493
  rock art 25 495
Mas d'en Josep
  rock art 29 *365*
Masegne, dalle (family) 32 190
Masegne, Jacobello dalle 13 95; 20 543–5*
  altarpieces 1 709; 4 275; 25 183
  architecture 12 903; 20 318
  sculpture 13 96; 20 *543*; 21 533; 32 208
Masegne, Pierpaolo dalle 13 95; 20 543–5*, 728
  altarpieces 1 709; 4 275; 25 183
  architecture 12 903; 20 318
  sculpture 13 96; 20 *543*, *544*; 21 533; 32 208
Masella, Antonio 2 395; 5 122
  works 2 *395*
Masen, Jacob 10 174
Maser, Villa Barbaro 3 202; 16 *618*, 634; 20 279, *545*, 545–6*; 23 865–6; 27 236, *236*; 32 350–51, 548
  Chapel of the Redeemer 20 546
  frescoes 15 137, IV; 16 667; 32 550
  overdoors 23 678
  paintings 9 265; 13 676; 15 87; 18 708; 32 806
  Sala Olimpo 32 *350*
Masereel, Frans 3 564; 4 366; 5 163, 651; 20 547*; 33 363
Maseru
  National Museum 19 242
  Protestant church 19 241
Masey, Francis (Edward) 3 81; 4 155; 5 667; 20 547–8*; 29 105
Masey, Philip 20 547
Masey & Uren 7 328
Masfen, Tāddasa 10 574
Mashamoun, Salih Abdou 29 897
Mashan (Jiangling), Tomb 1 7 140
Mashco 24 100
Mashel ha-Kadmoni 21 176–7*
Mashhad 4 172; 6 *182*; 15 *897*, 898; 16 *105*; 20 548*
  architecture 16 196, 231
  caravanserai 16 230
  carpets 15 899; 16 484
  congregational mosque 16 197, 200
  houses 16 269
  Imam Riza Shrine Museum 12 834; 15 900; 16 557
  inscriptions 16 232
  manuscripts 16 331, 334, 335, 337
  musalla 16 232; 22 354
  pottery 16 414, 423
  shrine of Imam Riza 1 97; 16 197, 230, 231, 232, 234, 249, 414; 21 506; 22 194; 28 IV1; 31 110
  shrines (i) (cult) 28 634
  textiles 16 449
Mashhad—cont.
  tombs 16 163
    tomb of 'Ali ibn Musa 6 172
    tomb of 'Ali Rida 28 633, 634
    tomb of Khwaja Rabi' 16 230
Mashhad-i Misriyan 16 161; 29 822
Ma Shi 19 514
Mashiko 17 *241*, 353; 21 635
  Mashimizu Zōroku 17 399
Ma Shirong 19 856
Mashkov, Il'ya (Ivanovich) 20 548–9*; 27 443; 32 661
  groups and movements 12 871; 16 817, 818; 22 508; 27 392, 394; 31 583
  pupils 10 771; 22 268; 23 605; 28 715; 29 19, 632; 33 588
Mashman Bros Pottery 2 760
Ma Shou-chen *see* MA SHOUZHEN
Ma Shouzhen 33 320
mashrabiyya 16 132, 494
Masi, Bernardino 11 194
Masi, Giovanni 2 32
Masi, Leonardo 7 337
Mašić, Nikola 8 178; 20 549*; 33 593
Masić, Slobodan 28 452
Masikoro 20 35
Masilelea, Elizabeth 22 *713*
Mašín, J. 8 426
Masini, Alessandro 11 21
Masini, Bartolomeo di Giovanni 3 300
Mas i Vila, Josep 3 215
masjid *see* MOSQUES
Masjid-i Solaiman 1 *849*, 887; 10 171; 15 908; 24 218
  rock reliefs 10 *171*
Maska, Karel 25 467
Maskana 20 549–50*; 30 *180*
  Balis 16 *104*; 20 550*
  Emar 1 *849*, 863; 14 591; 20 549*
  faience (i) (glass) 1 878
  glass 1 865
  minaret 16 180
  pottery 16 406
  terracottas 20 *550*
  trade 30 179
Maskell, Alfred 19 424
Maskhuta, Tell el- 9 *774*, 849; 10 80; 20 550–51*
Maski 15 421
masking tape 24 53
Maskit 16 569
Mask of Agamemnon 14 *355*
masks 5 297–8
  historical and regional traditions
    Aboriginal Australia 1 44, 61
    Africa 1 *237*, *239*, 256*, *268*, *273*, 273–4, 278–9, *279*, 290, 296, 298, 301, *301*, 333–40*, *335*, *336*, *337*, *338*, *339*, *341*, 341–2*, 382, 384, 389–90, *390*, *399*, *405*, 405–6, 409–10, 423*
      Bwa 1 *384*
      Chamba (ii) (Africa) 6 *406*
      Islamic 1 229
      Mossi 1 *384*
      Nigeria 1 *241*
      Western Equatoria 1 398–9
      Yoruba 1 *241*
    Alaska 22 *545*, *573*
    Angola 1 296; 7 *198*
    Antilles, Lesser 2 147
    Aztec 21 250, 251–2; 22 164
    Baga 1 256, 279, 391; 3 46–7*
    Bali (Indonesia) 15 802–4*, *803*
    Bamana 1 256, 279, 301, 340, 341; 3 134–6*, *135*, *136*
    Bamileke 1 278, 298; 3 148, *149*
    Bamum 1 339, *339*; 3 153*
    Bangwa 1 324; 3 171–2*
    Bantu peoples 1 333
    Baule 1 279, 324, 392; 3 405–6
    Bembe 1 256, 405; 19 74
    Benin, Kingdom of 3 *722*

masks
historical and regional traditions—cont.
Benin Republic **1** *337*; **3** 728
Bermuda **2** 146
Bijogo **1** 391; **4** *55*, 55–6*
Bobo **1** 279, 341; **4** 192–4*, *193*; **5** 217
Buddhism **17** 394, 395
Burkina Faso **1** *341*, 342; **4** *193*; **5** 217; **22** *197*
Burma **5** 251*, *252*
Bwa **1** 290, *384*; **5** 217, 328–30*
Cambodia **5** 504, *504*
Cameroon **1** 259*, *279*, *339*, 399; **6** *406*
Canada **20** *492*
Caribbean Islands **5** 748
Chamba (ii) (Africa) **1** 382; **6** 405–6, *406*; **22** 287
Chimú **29** 209
Chokwe **1** 256, 405; **2** 85; **7** 196, 197*
Colombia **7** 603
Congo, Republic of **1** *399*
Côte d'Ivoire **1** 229, 256, 339; **13** *860*
Dan (Africa) **1** 236, 243, 333, 338, 339, 340, 390; **8** 486–8*, *487*, *488*; **19** 310
Dogon **1** 290, 339, 342; **9** 67–8*, *68*
Dominican Republic **2** 146
Edo (Africa) **1** 290, *335*, 337; **9** 734–5, 736
Egypt, ancient **5** 298; **10** 68
Ejagham **1** 273; **10** *122*, 122–3*
Eskimo **22** *545*, *573*, 575
Etruscan **10** 593
Fang **10** 791–2*
Gabon **1** 399, *399*; **11** 878
Gambia, The **12** 32
Germany **28** *111*
Ghana **1** 342
Greece, ancient **13** 438, 582*
Guinea **1** 336, *336*
Guro **1** 236, 392; **13** 859–60*, *860*
Gurunsi **5** 217, 328–30*
Hausa **1** 342
Helladic **14** 338, *355*
Hemba **1** 405; **14** 378
Hopi **22** *583*
Ibibio **1** 256, 273–4, *273*; **15** 61–2*, *62*
Idoma **1** 383; **15** 101–2, *102*
Ife (kingdom of) **15** *104*
Igalu **15** 108–9*
Igbo **1** 256, 273, 274, 290, 301, 338, 341, 342; **15** 110–13*
Ijo **15** 124
Inca **29** 209
Indian subcontinent **15** 705–6*, 731, *734*, 734–5
Indonesia **15** 802–4*, *803*
Islamic **1** 229
Italy **10** 593; **30** 657
Japan **17** 98, 103, *334*, 349*, *349*, 390–96*, *395*
Java **15** 802*
Jukun **1** 382; **3** 332; **17** 679–80*; **22** 287
Kissi **19** 310
Kongo **18** 221*
Korea **18** 300, 378, *378*
Kota (ii) (Gabon peoples) **18** 403–4*
Kuba (iii) (Zaïre) **1** 256, 278, 290, 298, 301, *301*, 334, 336, *336*, 337, 338, *338*, 339, 340, 405; **18** *488*, 488–9*
Laos **18** *774*, 774–5*
Lega **1** 333, 405; **19** 73, *73*, 74
Liberia **1** 242–3, 256, 282, 339, 340; **8** *487*, *488*
Luba **1** 405; **19** 742
Lwena **1** 405; **7** 198, *198*
Makonde (Mozambique) **1** 256, 409; **5** 761; **20** 149, 150

masks
historical and regional traditions—cont.
Malaysia **20** 177*
Mali **1** 229; **9** *68*; **20** 199
Maya **16** II1; **20** 881; **21** 250, 251, *251*
Mende (Sierra Leone) **1** *237*, 256, 282, *282*, 334, 336, 337, 340; **19** 309; **21** *115*, 115–17*, *117*
Mesoamerica, Pre-Columbian **16** *861*, II1; **21** 241, *242*, *243*, 247, 250–52*, *251*, 254, 255, *255*, 266, IV1; **22** 158, 164
Mexico **16** *861*; **21** *255*, IV1
Pre-Columbian **16** II1
Micronesia, Federated States of **21** 477
Mixtec **21** 251, 255, *255*, 737
Moche (culture) **29** 208–9
Mossi **1** 290, 334, *384*; **5** 217; **22** 196–7*, *197*
Mumuye **1** 382; **22** 286–7*, *287*
Mycenaean **14** 338, *355*
Native North Americans **16** *891*; **22** 545, 563, 573, *573*, 575, 578, *578*, 579, 613, 663, *664*, 665
Alaska **22** *545*
Hopi **22** *583*
United States of America **22** *558*
Nazca **29** 208
Nepal **22** *788*, 788–9*
Nevis **2** 146
New Caledonia **23** 19, *19*
Nigeria **1** *239*, *268*, 273, *273*, 282, 290, *335*, 342; **10** *122*; **15** *62*, *102*, *104*, *111*
Yoruba **1** *241*
Nupe **1** 383; **23** 303
Olmec **21** 250–51, 254
Papua New Guinea **24** 71–2, *72*, *77*, 77–8*, 80, 84, 85, *85*, 86
Pende **1** 256, 290, 333, 405; **24** *358*, 358–9*
Peru **29** 208–9, *209*
Puerto Rico **25** 699
Punic **25** 733
St Kitts **2** 146
Santa Cruz Islands **27** 779
São Tomé and Príncipe **27** 809
Scandinavia **32** 520–21*
Senufo **1** 241, 279, 301, 338, 341; **28** 420–21*, *421*, *422*
Shinto **17** 390, 394, 395
Sicán culture **28** 651
Sierra Leone **1** *237*, 256, 282, *282*, 340
Songye **1** 405, 406; **29** 69, *70*, 70–71*
South America, Pre-Columbian **28** 651; **29** 208–10*, *209*
Sri Lanka **29** 473–4*
Sumatra **15** 804
Syria-Palestine **30** 182
Tairona **29** 193
Teke **1** 290; **30** 419–20, *420*
Thailand **30** 629, *629*
Tibet **30** 839
Torres Strait Islands **31** *185*, 185–6
Trinidad and Tobago **31** 332
United States of America **22** *558*
Viking **32** 520–21*
Yaka **1** 240, 256, 261, 290, 405; **33** 482, 483–5, *484*
Yoruba **1** *239*, 241, *241*, 282, 290, 334, 336, *337*, 340, 341, 423; **5** 761; **15** *104*; **33** 557*
Zaïre **1** 261, *301*, *336*, *338*, *405*; **18** *488*; **19** *73*; **29** *70*; **33** *484*
Zambia **1** 296
Zapotec **21** 251

masks—cont.
materials
basalt **21** 251
basketwork **1** 296; **3** 332; **24** 71
beads **1** 298; **3** *149*; **7** *198*; **18** *488*
blackstone **21** 251
bone **21** 247
camphor-wood **17** 390
clay **17** 390; **21** 250; **29** *209*
copper **3** *722*; **15** *104*
coral **21** 251
cornhusks **22** 663
cypress **17** 390, 392, 393, *394*, *395*
dung **29** *209*
feathers **1** *405*
fibres **1** *405*; **7** *198*; **28** *422*
gesso **17** 393, *394*
gold **14** *355*; **17** *334*; **28** 651
greenstone **21** 251
hair **15** 734; **17** *334*
horn **3** *135*
inks **17** 392
inscriptions **17** 391
ivory **3** *722*; **24** 359
jade **16** *861*, II1; **21** 251
kaolin **17** 392
lacquer **17** 390, 391, 392
leather **22** *545*; **30** 657
leaves **1** *384*
metal **22** 613
mixed-media **1** 301, *301*
mosaics **21** 251, *255*
mother-of-pearl **21** 251
nuts **24** 84
obsidian **21** 251, 254
onyx **21** 251
painting **1** 289
paper **15** 706; **17** 390, 392
papier mâché **17** 390
paulownia **17** 390, 391
plaster **10** 68
pyrite **21** 251
quills **3** *135*
raffia **1** 336; **3** *149*; **24** *358*
shells **18** *488*; **21** 251
skins **10** 122, *122*; **21** 252
skulls **24** 84
stone **5** 748
stucco **20** 881
terracotta **13** 582*; **15** *734*
textiles **17** 390, 392
tortoiseshell **31** 185, *185*
turquoise **21** 251, 737, IV1; **22** 158
wood
Africa **1** *399*
Asante **1** *390*
Bamana **3** *135*
Bobo **4** 192
Dan (Africa) **8** *487*
Dogon **9** *68*
Ejagham **10** *122*, 122–3
Fang **10** *791*
Gabon **1** *399*
Guro **13** *860*
Ibibio **1** *273*
Indian subcontinent **15** 706
Japan **17** 349, *349*, *391*
Jukun **17** 680
Korea **18** *378*
Kuba (iii) (Zaïre) **18** *488*
Lega **19** *73*
Lwena **7** *198*
Mende (Sierra Leone) **1** *282*; **21** *115*, *117*
Mossi **1** *384*; **22** *197*
Native North Americans **16** *891*; **22** *545*, *573*, *578*, *664*
Nepal **22** *788*
New Caledonia **23** *19*
Papua New Guinea **24** *72*
Pende **24** *358*
Senufo **28** *421*, *422*
techniques
gilding **30** 654

masks—cont.
types
bugaku **17** 390, 391–2*
death-masks *see* DEATH-MASKS
face **3** 406
gigaku **17** 390, 391*, *391*
Goli **3** 406
helmet **3** 405–6; **10** *791*; **15** *108*, 108–9
kyōgen **17** 390, 393–4, *394*
nō **17** 390, 392–4*, *394*
plank **5** *329*, 329*, *330*
uses
carnivals **5** 785, 787
Maslać, D. **28** 838
Maslama ibn 'Abdallah **20** 49
Masle, Michel Le *see* LE MASLE, MICHEL
Maslenkov, I. L. **9** 54
Maslennikov, Yakov **27** 420
Masłowski, Stanisław **25** 107
Masnago, Alessandro **12** 259, 260
Masnago, Giovanni Antonio **12** 259
Masniković, Nikola **28** 452
Maso, Antonio di *see* ANTONIO DI MASO
Masó, Luis Bonifás y *see* BONIFÁS Y MASÓ, LUIS
Maso, Pace di *see* PACE DI MASO
Masoabi, Martin **19** 242
Maso di Banco **13** 149; **20** 551–2*
attributions **12** 681
patrons and collectors **2** 110
teachers **8** 443
works **2** 479; **11** 888; **16** 655, 837; **20** *551*; **22** 486
Maso di Bartolommeo **9** 129; **20** 552*; **21** 466; **24** 232; **31** 740
assistants **24** 232
collaboration **9** 157; **11** 198; **26** 444
patrons and collectors **20** 160; **22** 13
works **5** 19, 782; **16** 630; **21** 469; **25** 450; **29** 568; **31** 739
Maso di Cristofano **20** 553
Masó i Valentí, Rafael **20** 552–3*
Masolino (da Panicale) **16** 661; **20** 553–8*
assistants **32** 103
attributions **8** 682; **20** 531, 536; **26** 827, *827*
collaboration **2** 339; **9** 98; **11** 185; **20** 530, 531, 534–5
copies **18** 584
patrons and collectors **4** 658; **7** 620; **26** 765, 766
works **16** 659; **19** 446; **20** 536, *554*, *555*, *557*, *558*; **24** 539; **26** 183
Mason, Ada **25** 39
Mason, Alice (Bradford) Trumbull **20** 568*
Mason, Charles James **10** 307; **29** 495
Mason, C. J. & Co. **10** 310
Mason, George **20** 570
Mason (ii), George C(hamplin), sr (1820–94) **20** 568*
Mason (ii), George C(hamplin), jr (1850–1924) **20** 568*
Mason, George D. **14** 787
Mason, George Heming **10** 641; **19** 868; **20** 568–9*
Mason, Gilbert **4** 87
Mason, Helen **23** 69
Mason, Hilda **10** 462
Mason, J. Alden **28** 799
Mason, James **17** 640
Mason, Jan **29** 591
Mason, John **19** 702
Mason, Joseph **2** 710
Mason, Josiah **10** 143
Mason, Judith **29** 109
Mason, Miles **10** 309, 310
Mason, Otis **22** 673
Mason, Peter the *see* PETER THE MASON

Mason, Phillip **1** 445
Mason, Ralph **4** 478
Mason, Raymond **19** 246; **20** 569*
Mason, Thomson **5** 77
Mason, W. **24** 494
Mason, William(1725–97) **9** 199; **12** 131; **20** 569*
collaboration **14** 163
patrons and collectors **33** 20
works **4** 787; **12** 130
Mason, William (1810–97) **7** 410; **20** 570*; **23** 53, 54
works **2** 705; **23** 54
Mason City (IA), City National Bank **3** 176
Masone, Giovanni *see* MAZONE, GIOVANNI
Mason & Hamlin **9** 684
Masoni, Gaetano **32** 362
Mason & Parker **31** 263
Mason & Rice **17** 721; **25** 268
masonry **1** 156; **20** 570–84*
conservation **4** 797
historical and regional traditions
Anglo-Saxon **2** 64, 65
Byzantine **9** 553
Cambodia **5** 482
Central Asia, Western **16** 160
Early Christian (*c*. AD 250–843) **9** 553
Egypt, ancient **9** 850; **20** 570
England **10** 226
France **29** *636*
Georgia **12** 318
Germany **28** 129
Greece, ancient **13** 387, *395*, 396, 397, 400, 403; **20** 570
Inca **15** 163; **29** 163–4*, *164*
Iran **16** 160
Islamic **16** 160, 186; **20** 570
Mesoamerica, Pre-Columbian **20** 570; **21** 205; **24** 367
Mexico **24** 367
Norway **23** 219
Peru **14** *827*
Prehistoric art **25** 507
Romanesque **26** 569
Rome, ancient **20** 570; **26** 877–8
South America, Pre-Columbian **14** *827*; **23** 415; **29** 162*, *162*, 163–4*, *164*
Turkey **16** 186
materials
brick **16** 160; **20** 560, 573
clamps **13** 388
dowels **13** 388
flint **20** 570, 571
marble **20** 570
mortars (building) **20** 573, 574
Portland stone **20** 571
stone **20** 559, 560, 573, 574
types
ablaq **2** 888; **16** 182; **33** 614
ashlar **20** 571*, 572
Egypt, ancient **20** 571
England **10** 227
Germany **26** 574
Helladic **22** *396*
Italy **30** 667
Mesoamerica, Pre-Columbian **31** 310
Mexico **31** 310
Mycenaean **22** *396*
Olmec **31** 310
Peru **14** *827*
Romanesque **26** 574
Rome, ancient **26** 874, 904, 911, *912*
South America, Pre-Columbian **14** *827*
Spain **25** 410
Syria-Palestine **30** 180, 190, 192
Turkey **26** *912*
broken ashlar **13** 388
cloisonné **20** 571*
Byzantine **4** 773; **9** 547, *551*; **20** 571
Greece **4** 773; **9** 547, *551*

masonry
types
cloisonné—cont.
Serbia 4 773
Turkey 4 773
Cyclopean 20 571*; 21 39
Anatolia, ancient 1 826, *831*
Etruscan 20 571
Greece, ancient 20 571
Hittite 1 826, *831*
Inca 15 163
Rome, ancient 20 571; 26 874; 27 7
Diamond Point 20 572
dressed 9 779; 20 571*, 572
dry-stone 1 305; 20 570, 571*
Arabia 2 248
Bolivia 4 256
Egypt, ancient 20 571
England 20 571
Greece, ancient 20 571
Italy 20 570, 571
Syria-Palestine 30 182
Zimbabwe 1 305; 13 334, 336
flushwork 20 571*
galleting 20 571*
headers 13 388
herringbone 20 571*
interlaced 16 180
isodomic 13 388
Lesbian 13 388
long-and-short 20 571
long and short work 20 571–2*
opus Africanum 20 572*
opus incertum 4 782, 783; 20 572*; 26 874, 879, *879*
opus mixtum 4 773; 20 572; 26 877; 27 368
opus pseudisodomum 25 410
opus quadratum 26 874
opus quasi-reticulatum 26 879, 887
opus reticulatum 4 772; 8 856; 20 572*; 26 874, *875*, 877, 879, *879*, 889
opus spicatum 4 782
opus testaceum 20 572*; 26 877, 879, *879*
parpend stones 13 388
polygonal *see* Cyclopean
pseudo-isodomic 13 388
rubble 20 571, 572*; 26 879
England 20 572
Maya 21 213
Rome, ancient 20 572; 26 877, 911, *912*
Turkey 26 *912*
rustication 20 572*; 27 447*
Greece, ancient 20 572
Italy 27 761
Rome, ancient 26 874, 892, *892*
spolia 20 572*; 27 323
Byzantine 4 773
Carolingian 5 794
Indian subcontinent 15 307
Islamic 16 131, 141, 221, 243
Ottoman 16 221
Turkey 16 221
striped *see ablaq*
vermiculation 20 572*; 32 272*
uses
arches 20 *574*, 574–5*, *583*
architecture 5 482
buttresses 20 581–2*, *582*
domes 20 *579*, 579–80*
piers (ii) (masonry) 20 576*
spires 20 581*
theatres 30 667
tiles 13 757
tombs 25 507
towers 20 576
tracery 31 270
vaults (ceiling) 20 576–9*, *577*, *583*
walls 20 574, 576*; 21 205
see also ARCHITECTURE
Masonry, Constitutions of *see* CONSTITUTIONS OF MASONRY
masons 2 362; 20 559–67*, 573; 28 497; 30 430–31
Anglo-Saxon 2 64
England 19 532; 20 560–61*, 562*
France 19 532
Germany 19 532; 20 561, 562–3*
Greece, ancient 13 394–5*
Inca 15 163
Romanesque 26 595
Rome, ancient 26 884–5*
masons (master) 20 559, 561
England 19 532; 20 561; 22 211
Germany 19 532; 20 563
Inca 29 135
South America, Pre-Columbian 29 135
masons' guilds *see under* GUILDS → types
masons' lodges 13 823; 20 560, 561–3*; 29 851
England 19 532; 20 561
France 19 532
Germany 3 399; 19 532; 20 562–3
masons' marks *see under* MARKS
Masood, Jamila 23 801
Ma Sostres Maluquer, Josep *see* SOSTRES MALUQUER, JOSEP MA
masoun 20 559
Maspero, Gaston 10 80, 82, 84; 20 418; 30 691
Masquelier 19 382; 30 885
Masqueliers, Jacqueline 5 51
Masquerier, John James 31 465
Masreliez, Jean Baptiste 30 89, 95
Masreliez, Louis Adrien
groups and movements 13 864
patrons and collectors 30 89, 95
pupils 33 98
works 11 471; 23 890; 29 689; 30 *89*, 95
Masriera 29 346
Masriera, Luis 29 346
Masriera & Campins 29 344
Masriera i Rosés, Lluis 29 307
Masriera y Vila, Victor 29 344
Masrur 15 *264*, 265, 483; 20 584*; 30 437
Massa, Duc de 8 817
Massa, Donato 7 458; 16 736
Massa, Giuseppe 7 458; 22 486
Massa, Isaac 14 94
Massa, Lafranco 5 693
Massachusetts 31 625
Massaciuccoli 27 67
Massad group 29 626
Massa Fermana Altarpiece 8 168
Massagli, Pietro 16 729
Massaio, Piero del *see* PIERO DEL MASSAIO
Massala 11 879
works 11 *879*
Massalia *see under* MARSEILLE
Massalski, Ignacy, Bishop of Vilnius 13 775; 25 136
Massa Marittima 10 *583*, 624, 626; 13 93
Cathedral of S Cerbone 11 254
metalwork 10 *625*
Massangano Fortress 2 86
Massani, Giovanni Antonio 1 465; 5 755, 760, 865
Massard, Alexandre (-Pierre-Jean-Baptiste) 20 585
Massard, (Jean-Baptiste-) Félix 20 585
Massard, Horace 20 585
Massard, Jean 20 584–5*
works 10 *118*; 13 642
Massard, Jean-Baptiste (-Louis) 20 585
Massard, Jules-Louis 20 585
Massard, (Jean-Marie-Raphaël-) Léopold 20 585
Massard, (Jean-Baptiste-Raphaël-) Urbain 20 585
Massarello 28 684
Massarenti, Marcello 32 829
Massari, Giorgio 20 585–6*; 32 410
collaboration 22 121
patrons and collectors 26 286
works 16 646; 32 188, 229, 549
Massari, Lucio 4 830; 20 586*; 28 395
Massari, Stefano 20 585
Massario, Pietro del 11 179
Massaro, Antonio del *see* PASTURA, IL
Massaro, Matteo dal 14 171
Massawwarat el-Sufra 23 *276*
Great Enclosure 23 283, 284
temples 23 283, 284, *284*
mass concrete *see under* CONCRETE → types
Masse, Bob 25 353
Massé, Jean-Baptiste (1687-1767; artist) 20 586–7*
assistants 31 69
pupils 14 815; 19 435
reproductive prints by others 2 853; 9 407
works 20 *417*; 21 643
Massé, Jean-Baptiste (*fl* 1728; soldier) 4 709
Massei, Girolamo 3 101
Massella, Antonio 22 313
Masséot, Abaquesne 27 248
Masses, The 5 759; 27 872
Massey, Geoffrey 10 458; 31 864
Massey, (Charles) Vincent 5 589, 590; 20 587*; 31 910
Massi, Giovanni Antonio 31 341
Massianus 6 173
massicot (lead-monoxide yellow) 24 798–9
massicot see PIGMENTS → types → lead-tin yellow
Massié (family) 11 609
Massié, André 19 397
Massié, Joseph 11 609; 19 397
Massier, Clément 19 283
Massie-Taylor, Guy 28 693
massif occidental see WESTWORKS
Massignon, Louis 10 804; 16 100; 31 543
Massignon, Pierre-Henry-Ferdinand *see* ROCHE, PIERRE
Massilia *see* MARSEILLE
Massilla, Gregorio 5 415
Massim 24 64, *64*, 81–2*
canoes 23 726
wood-carvings 24 *81*
Massimi, Camillo, Cardinal 3 294; 9 409; 26 773
Massimi, Massimo 24 239
(Ercole) Massimiliano, 8th Duke of Milan (*reg* 1512-15) 4 76; 6 357; 13 659; 20 791; 28 533*
Massimo (family) 11 820
Massimo, Angelo 20 271, 587
Massimo, Camillo (Carlo), Cardinal 1 728; 20 587, 588*; 25 394
paintings 21 624
Massimo, Carlo, Marchese 7 870; 20 588; 22 704; 23 676; 28 135
Massimo, Domenico 20 587
Massimo, Fabrizio 20 587
Massimo, Fabrizio Camillo IV 20 588
Massimo, Francesco 20 588
Massimo, Francesco Camillo VII 20 588
Massimo, Luca 20 587
Massimo, Marc'Antonio 27 780
Massimo, Massimo 20 587
Massimo, Pietro (*d* 1489) 20 587
Massimo, Pietro (*d* 1544) 20 587; 24 533
Massimo Altarpiece 23 107
Massin, Juliette 8 628
Massin, Olive 17 527
Massina, Pino da *see* JACOBELLO D'ANTONIO
Massine, Léonide 3 119; 26 531; 30 390
collaboration 6 385; 19 81; 20 591; 24 405, 718
Massinelli 21 824
Massingberd, Burrell 17 900
Massingham, John (i) (*fl* 1409-50) 13 84; 20 588–9*
Massingham, John (ii) (*fl* 1438-78) 20 589*
Massinguitana 1 332; 22 244
Massironi, Manfredo 13 728
mass media 20 29–30
Mass Moving 3 574
Massó, Rafael 3 216; 23 260
Mass Observation 10 257, 652; 20 589–90*; 24 674
works 20 *589*; 28 919; 29 385
Mass of St Gregory, Master of the 20 728*
Massol, Joseph 29 750, 755
Masson 19 490
Masson, André 11 550; 20 590–91*; 31 607
collaboration 17 463; 20 603, 605
dealers 17 726; 19 537
groups and movements 1 75; 21 341; 24 144
Art informel 2 543
Surrealism 30 18, 19, 20, 21
patrons and collectors 7 797; 11 659; 12 15; 19 66; 27 343
teachers 14 271
works 2 839, *839*; 3 462; 9 310; 11 549; 19 491; 20 *591*; 22 416; 27 854; 28 52, 820; 31 504
Masson, Antoine 13 898; 20 592*
Masson, Charles 1 204, 211; 13 841; 14 19, 162; 28 535
Masson, Francis 11 229
Masson, Louis Le *see* LE MASSON, LOUIS
Masson, Luis León 20 592*
Masson, Madeleine 13 898
Masson, Maurice 19 381
Masson, M. Ye. 1 504; 2 882; 17 776; 23 159; 30 489
Massone, Giovanni *see* MAZONE, GIOVANNI
Masson & Ramée 25 874
Massot, Firmin 12 277; 20 592*; 30 133
Massot, Pernette 20 592
Massot, Pierre de 8 439
Massou, François-Benoît 30 705
Massoudy, Hassan 16 1, 288; 20 592–3*
mass production 7 651; 8 801; 14 690; 15 820–27; 19 896; 20 593–5*; 26 51, 743
historical and regional traditions
Britain 20 593, *595*
Buddhism 6 314; 15 448; 17 320
Central Asia, Eastern 6 314
Czech Republic 20 593
Hong Kong 22 667
Inca 29 135
Indian subcontinent 4 793; 15 448
Japan 17 250, 253, 317, 320, 348; 22 667
Mesopotamia 21 271
Native North Americans 22 667, 668
Netherlands, the 22 892
Scandinavia 32 524
Scotland 28 255
South America, Pre-Columbian 29 135
Switzerland 7 448
United States of America 3 114; 20 593, *594*; 31 619, 656
Viking 32 524
uses
banners 6 314
brick 4 771, 793
cars 20 *594*
chairs 20 *595*
mass production
uses—cont.
clocks 7 447
furniture 28 255
glass 31 643
ivory-carvings 16 799
jewellery 17 526
posters 25 345
pottery 17 250, 253; 21 271
sculpture 3 114; 15 448; 17 320
textiles 17 317; 21 600; 31 656
tiles 30 877, 882, 887
wall paintings 6 314
watches 7 447, 448
Massys, Cornelis 3 554, 556; 18 619; 21 352, 359–60*
reproductive prints by others 15 43
teachers 21 352
works 9 271; 18 706; 31 414
Massys, Jan 3 554; 21 352, 357–9*
patrons and collectors 22 127; 28 904; 32 7
teachers 21 352
works 17 700; 21 *357*, *358*
Massys, Joost 13 63; 21 352
Massys, Quinten *see* METSYS, QUINTEN
Mast, Jan van der 8 150
mastabas *see under* TOMBS → types
Mastai-Ferretti, Giovanni *see* PIUS IX, Pope
Mastaing, St Martin 32 92
Mastara 2 *423*; 9 *512*; 20 596–7*
St Hovhannes 2 426; 20 596
Mastbaum, Jules E. 24 601; 26 511
Mastelletta 9 111; 20 597–8*; 31 307
works 20 *598*
Mastera Analyticheskogo Iskusstva *see* MAI
Master Drawings 24 183, 433
Master Impression 6 450; 21 654, 691
Masterkova, Lidiya 27 397
master masons *see* MASONS (MASTER)
Master of the Rocks Noble Occupations Pebble 16 IV
masterpieces 2 523, 557; 20 598–600*
master printers 20 600–610*
masters (anonymous) 20 611*
Masters, A. H. 23 212
Masters, Charles Harcourt 3 371
Masters, Edgar Lee 29 746
Masters of Analytical Art *see* MAI
Masters of the New East 31 783
Masters Plaque 26 694
Master Temple *see* THAY TEMPLE
master theorem *see* THEORIES → masonry
mastic 20 804–5*; 26 243
architecture 4 787
fixatives 11 142
glazes 12 803
grounds 10 548
japanning 18 610
lacquer 18 609
secco paintings 28 339
varnishes 32 1, 2, 3
masticot see PIGMENTS → types → lead-tin yellow
Mastini *see* AMASTINI
Mastini, Angelo Tesei 1 756
Mastino II, Lord of Verona (1308-51) 28 29; 32 345
mastos cups *see under* CUPS → types
Mastrantonio, Antonio 18 859
Mastrilli, F. M., Marchese 13 541
Mastrodonato, Luigi 16 731
Mastroianni, Domenico 20 805
Mastroianni, Umberto 20 805*
masts 7 765, 766
Masturzio, Marzio 10 762

Masucci, Agostino **13** 301; **16** 672; **20** 213, 805–6*; **26** 842
- collaboration **20** 377
- patrons and collectors **1** 533; **3** 707, 708; **4** 560; **7** 898; **28** 18
- pupils **2** 125; **4** 491; **8** 474; **14** 108; **25** 410; **33** 692
- works **20** *806*; **24** 238; **26** 840; **28** 489

Masucci, Lorenzo **20** 806
Mas'ud I, Ruler (*reg* 1031-41)(Ghaznavid) **12** 511; **18** 810; **30** 784
Mas'ud I, Sultan (*reg* 1116-56) (Saljuq of Anatolia) **18** 233
Mas'ud III, Sultan (*reg* 1099-1115) (Ghaznavid) **12** 512; **16** 166, 167
Masuda, Takashi **17** 424, 429
Masuda (Yamaguchi) Gūsho **17** 413; **20** 806, 807*
Masuda Kinsai **17** 412, 413; **20** 806–7*
Masuda Kōen **20** 806, 807
Masuda Kōetsu **20** 806
al-Mas'udi **16** 252, 303, 304, 538
Masulipatam *see* MACHHILIPATANAM
Masuo Ikeda *see* IKEDA, MASUO
Masurel, Geneviève **9** 465; **19** 381
Masurel, Jean **9** 465; **11** 664; **19** 381
Maswanganyi, Johannes **29** 104, 113
Masyaf **16** *104*; **20** 807*
Masyutyn, Vasyl' (Mykolayevych) **20** 807*
Maszkowski, Jan Kanty **13** 702; **18** 398
Mat (India) **15** 444, 690, 737; **20** 817
- sculpture **15** *444*

MAT (company) **29** 419
Mata, Andrés de **21** 375
Mata, Arturo Soria y *see* SORIA Y MATA, ARTURO
Mata, Jerónimo de la **29** 335
Mata, Miguel **13** 868
Mata, S. **31** 823
Matabei Iwasa *see* IWASA MATABEI
Matacapan **21** 197
Mataco **24** 100
Matadi Museum **33** 598
Mataemon Ono *see* ONO MATAEMON
Matagalpa **23** *79*, 83
Matal, Bohumír **8** 394
Matale **29** 450
Mataloni, Giovanni **25** 348
Matamala i Pinyol, Lorenzo **12** 182
Matamba, S Maria **2** 86
Matanchén Bay **21** 197
Matankor **24** 82, 83
- works **24** *83*

Matanzas **8** *228*, 238
Matara **1** 513; **10** 576; **29** *440*
- fortress **29** 452
- Ruhuna University **29** 456

Mataram, Puri Kanginan **15** 776
Matarana, Bartolomé **26** 306
Matarazzo Sobrinho, Francisco **4** 726, 727
Mataré, Ewald **1** 5; **20** 807–8*
- exhibitions **12** 407
- pupils **3** 891; **14** 26; **21** 71
- works **12** 407; **20** *808*; **33** 364

Mataró **29** 330
Matas, Antonín **9** 303
Matas, Juan **9** 267
Matas, Niccola **11** 182, 205; **16** 646; **20** 808–9*; **25** 172
Matawi *see* MATUARIËR
Matazō Kayama *see* KAYAMA, MATAZŌ
Matba'at al-Ma'arif **16** 361
Matcham, Frank **20** 809*
- works **2** 294; **3** 537; **15** 408; **19** 576; **22** 60; **30** 678, 679, *679*

Matchbox Toys **31** 257
Matchitt, Paratene Moko Puorongo **20** 359, 809; **23** 63
matchlocks *see under* GUNS → types
Mate, Vasyl' V. **20** 807; **28** 570
Mateescu, Patriciu **26** 719
Matějček, Antonín **4** 134; **8** 426
Matejić, Church of the Assumption **9** 526, 553; **19** 884
Matejka, Peter **28** 853
Matejko, Jan **18** 428; **20** 809–11*; **25** 141
- assistants **21** 51
- patrons and collectors **25** 139
- pupils **13** 215; **20** 187; **21** 51; **25** 673; **33** 450, 455
- works **14** 588; **20** *810*; **25** 106, 140; **32** *297*; **33** 455

Matejovce **28** 854
- church **14** 899; **28** 851

Matejovce, Master of **28** 851
Matemera, Bernard
- works **33** *679*

Mateo **5** 911; **20** 811*; **26** 608; **29** 288
- works **13** 103; **27** 794

Mateo, Julio **20** 811*
Matera, Giovanni Antonio **22** 680
Materna, Pietro **5** 701
Maternovy, Ivan Stepanovich *see* MATTARNOVY, GEORG JOHANN
mates **31** 756
Mates, Joan **20** 811–12*; **27** 836
Mates, Jorge **20** 812
Matet, Maurice **11** 601
Mateusz, Painter **25** 105
Matha, John of *see* JOHN OF MATHA
Matham, Adriaen **14** 375; **20** 812
Matham, Jacob **10** 387; **13** 895; **20** 812*
- collaboration **13** 896
- pupils **29** 246; **32** 140
- reproductive prints by others **5** 325
- teachers **12** 879
- works **4** 151; **6** 48; **12** 881, 882, 884; **20** 247; **22** 839; **29** 428; **32** 588, 723; **33** 181, 358

Matham, Jan **20** 812; **25** 625
Matham, Theodor **20** 812
Mathaus, Master **17** 740
Matheis, Georg *see* MATTHEUS, GEORG
mathematical books **4** 360
mathematics **1** 104; **28** 212
Mather, Frank Jewitt **3** 270
Mather, J. B. **2** 771
Mather, John **14** 307
Mather, Margarethe **33** 104
Mather, Richard **4** *476*
Matheron Diptych **9** 4; **11** 799
Mathers and Haldenby **31** 176
Máthes, J. N. **10** 545
Matheson, Elizabeth **23** 68
Matheson, Robert (1807-82) **9** 724
Matheson, Robert M(ichael) (1887-1935) **31** 245*
Matheson & Co. **13** 734
Matheus, Georg *see* MATTHEUS, GEORG
Matheus de Layens **20** 812–13*
- collaboration **17** 10
- works **3** 543, *543*; **13** 63; **19** 260

Mathew, Tobie **20** 813*
Mathews, Arthur F. **2** 572; **11** 498
Mathews, Lucia **2** 572
Mathews, Robert **1** 67
Mathews, Ryan & Partners **28** 232
Mathews, T. F. **9** 528
Mathey, Jean Baptiste **8** 422; **20** 813–14*
- works **8** 378; **20** *814*; **23** 573; **25** 426, *428*, 438, 445

Mathian factory **28** 863
Mathias of Arras **13** 89; **20** 814–15*; **25** 430
- patrons and collectors **19** 828
- works **8** 376; **20** 441; **24** 190; **25** 439; **29** 522

Mathie, William **9** 727; **28** 252
Mathieu, Daniel **33** 36
Mathieu, Georg *see* MATTHEUS, GEORG
Mathieu, Georg David *see* MATTHIEU, GEORG DAVID
Mathieu, Georges **11** 551; **20** 815–16*
- collaboration **14** 160
- groups and movements **1** 78; **2** 515, 543, 544; **26** 414; **30** 231
- patrons and collectors **9** 189
- works **3** 462; **20** *816*

Mathieu, H. **3** 601
Mathieu, Jean (*fl* 1618-46) **18** 795
Mathieu, Jean (1749-1815) **8** 660
Mathieu d'Arras *see* MATHIAS OF ARRAS
Mathieu de Vendôme, Abbot of Saint-Denis **27** 550
Mathijsen, F. E. **30** 15
Mathilda, Countess of Toulouse (*fl* 11th cent.) **31** 207
Mathilda, Duchess of Saxony (*fl* 10th cent.) **25** 803
Mathilde, Abbess **23** 659
Mathildenhöhe **7** 346; **12** 428
Mathilde of Portugal, Countess of Flanders (*d* 1218) **14** 409
Mathonère, Nicolas de **21** 151
Mathonière, Alain de **33** 357
Mathonnière, Denis de **5** 814
Mathsson, Bruno **30** 96
Mathulā *see* MATHURA
Mathura **8** 269; **15** 194, *261*, 262, *360*, 409, 452, 737; **20** 816–20*; **29** 439
- Bhuteshar **15** 442
- Chamunda Tila **15** 457
- figurines **15** 717, 718
- Government Museum **15** 181; **20** 820
- ivory **15** 695
- Kankali Tila
  - plaques **15** 443
  - sculpture **15** *442*, 443, 444; **20** 820
  - stupa **20** 817; **29** 864
- Katra Mound **15** 440; **20** 818
  - sculpture **15** *440*
- Maholi **15** 445
- Palikhera **15** 445
- pillars **15** 442
- plaques **15** 444, 717, 718
- Potra Kund **15** 481
- Rajghat **15** 442
- reliefs **15** 248, 249, 250, 252, 442, 444, 452, 456
- ring stones **15** 423
- Saptarshi Tila **15** 439
- Saptasamundri Well **15** 443
- Sardar Bazaar **15** 445
- Sat Samundri Well **15** 443
- sculpture **5** 94–5; **7** 793; **10** 484; **15** 218, 220, 229, 231, 414, 416, 424, 426, 427, *428*, 428, 439, 440, *440*, 441, 442, 443, 444–5, 449, 451, 454, 455, 456, 457, *457*, 458, 479, 480, 494, 677; **20** *819*; **30** 784
- Serai Azampur **15** 441
- stupas **15** 226
- Swamighat **15** 253
- tablets **15** 226
- *toraṇa* **31** 160

Mathurins *see* TRINITARIANS
Mathys, Pieter **4** 846
Mati **30** 812
Matías, Alonso **29** 291
Matías Francés **29** 265
Maticska, Jenő **22** 434
Maties, Gert **29** 110
Matifat **5** 825
Matifou **9** 570
Matilda, Countess Palatine of Württemberg (1419-82) **20** 660
Matilda, Duchess of Saxony and Bavaria (*fl* 1160) **26** 675, 685
Matilda, Queen of England (*d* 1083) **5** 372; **7** 473
Matilda of Canossa, Countess of Tuscany (*fl c.* 1045-1115) **20** 820–21*; **21** 771, 773; **24** 695; **26** 579
Matilda of Flanders (*fl* 1053) **5** 369; **33** 198
Matilla, Pedro de **7** 287, 524; **9** 112
Matilo **19** 99
al-Matira **16** 151
Matisse, Henri (Emile Benoît) **7** 385; **10** 840; **11** 307, 547; **20** 464, 821–32*; **23** 694; **24** 142, 144; **25** 582, 584; **31** 605
- architectural decorations **6** 460; **9** 112; **11** 551
- book illustrations **4** 366; **28** 819, 820; **29** 628; **30** 488; **31** 504
- collaboration **11** 659; **20** 464, 603; **29** 508
- dealers **13** 826; **17** 725; **19** 537; **20** 75, 832; **27** 163; **29** 655; **32** 686
- drawings **9** 213, 217, 226; **20** *825*, *829*
- exhibitions **2** 447; **3** 826; **27** 163; **28** 808; **31** 490
- frames **11** 419
- groups and movements **10** 839, 840–41; **15** 156; **16** 817; **22** 747; **23** 505; **25** 356; **32** 668
- interior decoration **14** 31
- methods **7** 630, 631; **23** 379; **24** 349, 490
- mosaics **22** 163
- paintings **8** 596; **11** 547, 549; **20** *827*, *828*; **23** *379*; **24** *382*, 383, *384*
  - *fêtes champêtres* **11** 39
  - landscape **18** 717
  - nude figures **20** *823*; **23** 296
  - still-lifes **29** 670
- patrons and collectors **11** 659; **20** 193; **25** 629; **27** 439; **28** 273; **30** 361
  - Arensberg, Walter and Louise **2** 383
  - Barnes, Albert C. **3** 251
  - Bliss, Lillie P(lummer) **4** 142
  - Chrysler, Walter P(ercy) **7** 245
  - Cone, Claribel and Etta **7** 702
  - Cooper, Douglas **7** 797
  - Delektorskaya, Lidiya **27** 440
  - Dominican Order **11** 659
  - Fénéon, Félix **10** 885
  - Hirshhorn, Joseph H(erman) **14** 575
  - Maitland, Ruth (Esther) **20** 142
  - Marx, Sam and Florene **20** 524
  - Moll, Oskar **21** 820
  - Morozov, Ivan (Abramovich) (1871-1921) **22** 136
  - Musée Matisse **2** 370
  - National Gallery of Modern Art (Edinburgh) **27** 333
  - Ōhara, Magosaburō **23** 371
  - Paul VI, Pope (*reg* 1963-78) **24** 278
  - Quinn, John **25** 823
  - Robinson, Edward G(oldenberg) **26** 472
  - Rockefeller, Abby Aldrich **26** 488
  - Rump, Johannes **30** 533
  - Schreiber, Taft and Rita Bloch **28** 167
  - Shchukin, Sergey (Ivanovich) **22** 331; **28** 569
  - Soby, James Thrall **28** 914
  - Stein, Leo **29** 604
  - Stein, Michael and Sarah **29** 604
  - Stieglitz, Alfred **31** 605
  - Tetzen-Lund, Christian **30** 532
  - Walter-Guillaume Collection **13** 826
  - Zambaccian, K. H. **26** 723

Matisse, Henri (Emile Benoît)—cont.
- personal collection **1** 438; **10** 842
- posters **25** 350
- prints **19** 429, 491; **21** 896; **28** 299; **33** 362
- pupils **10** 399; **12** 10; **19** 283; **33** 566
  - Grünewald, Isaac (Hirsche) **13** 719
  - Heiberg, Jean (Hjalmar Dahl) **14** 302
  - Hjertén, Sigrid (Maria) **14** 594
  - Jolin, Einar **17** 627
  - Karsten, Ludvig (Peter) **17** 826
  - Krohg, Per (Larsson) **18** 465
  - Maurer, Alfred H(enry) **20** 860
  - Nakakawa, Kazumasu **17** 206
  - Revold, Axel (Julius) **26** 265
  - Sørensen, Henrik (Ingvar) **23** 226; **29** 78
  - Stefánsson, Jón **29** 599
  - Stein, Sarah **29** 604
  - Steinhardt, Jacob **29** 609
  - Survage, Léopold **30** 25
  - Tscharner, Johann (Wilhelm Jan) von **31** 396
- reproductive prints by others **32** 577
- sculpture **20** *828*; **26** 133; **29** 576
- stage design **3** 120
- stained glass **26** 140; **29** *509*, 513
- studio **29** 858
- tapestries **2** 704; **3** 462; **30** 328, 329
- teachers **22** 91

Matisse, Musée *see under* NICE
Matisse, Pierre **20** 832*; **30** 22, 291
Matiushin, Mikhail *see* MATYUSHIN, MIKHAIL (VASIL'YEVICH)
Matiz, Francisco Javier **7** 608
matizando **6** 569
Matjeka-Felden **2** 831
Matka Monastery, Church of the Councils **25** 343
Matkov, Franko **25** 340
Matlazinca **5** 433
Matmar **9** 849
Matmata **1** 304, *376*, 377; **31** 424
Matome, Neo **4** 489
Maton, Bartholomeus **19** 102
Matons, Joan **29** 337
Matopo Hills, Cyrene Mission **1** 431; **33** 678, 680
Matos, Belchior de **30** 416
Matos, Fernandes de **4** 710
Matos, Francisco de **20** 832; **25** 309; **30** 880
Matos, Francisco Vieira de *see* VIEIRA LUSITANO, FRANCISCO
Matos, Marçal de **1** 586; **20** 832; **30** 880
Matos, Ramiro **9** 118
Matosinhos, Quinta do Viso **22** 534
Matos Moctezuma, Eduardo **21** 230
Matozinhos *see* CONGONHAS DO CAMPO
Matrakçı Nasuh *see* NASUH, MATRAKÇI
matrices **16** *506*
Matricula de Tributos **21** 251
Matṛvishnu, Ruler (*reg c.* 485) (Huna) **10** 444; **15** 473
Matryoshka see under DOLLS → types
mats
- historical and regional traditions
  - Africa **1** 296, 306, 308, 366
  - Ancient Near East **1** 879
  - Brunei **5** 13
  - Central Asia **10** 873
  - China **7** 146
  - Egypt, ancient **3** 482; **30** 433
  - Fiji **11** 69; **23** 713; **27** 235
  - Indian subcontinent **15** 727
  - Indonesia **15** 809, 810

mats
historical and regional traditions—cont.
Islamic **16** 262
Japan **17** 336, 339; **31** 167
Kiribati **18** 83
Madagascar **20** 39
Malaysia **20** 182
Maldives, Republic of **20** 189
Native North Americans **22** 657, *657*, 662
Pacific Islands **23** 713
Samoa **23** 735
Somalia **1** 296
Sri Lanka **29** 470
Swahili **30** 57
Tokelau **31** 75
Tonga (Pacific Islands) **23** 735; **31** 143
Tuareg **31** 407
Vanuatu **31** 892
materials
bamboo **7** 146; **15** 809
bark **22** 662
basketwork **1** 296
calligraphy **15** 727
cane **15** 809; **20** 182
embroidery **15** 681
felt **10** 873
grasses **15** 809
leather **15** 681
palm leaves **15** 809
pandanus **15** 809
types
tatami **17** 47, 50, 338, 384
see also RUGS
Matsa, Ivan (Lyudvigovich) **20** 833*; **27** 444; **32** 695
Matsch, Franz von **5** 792; **18** 129; **19** 538; **22** 330; **25** 673
Matschinsky, Martin **20** 833
Matschinsky-Denninghof **12** 408; **20** 833*
Matschinsky-Denninghof, Brigitte **20** 833; **33** 635
Matskhvarishi **12** *317*, 323, 325, 326
Ma Tsuan *see* MA ZUAN
Matsubara, Juzō **22** 445
Matsubayashi, Tsuronoske **25** 39
Matsuda, Gonroku **17** 305
works **17** *305*
Matsudaira **16** 812
Matsudaira Fumai **17** 342, 344, 428, 438; **20** 834
Matsudaira Harusato *see* MARSUDAIRA FUMAI
Matsudaira Morimura **17** 429
Matsudaira Naomasa **20** 834, 835
Matsudaira Nobutsuna **9** 73
Matsudaira Sadanobu **17** 344, 414; **30** 294
Matsudaira Yorishige **18** 553
Matsue **17** *11*; **20** 833–4*
Kamosu Shrine **16** 813; **17** 62; **20** 833
Manai Shrine **16** 813
Matsue Yamada *see* YAMADA, MATSUE
Matsugatani
pottery **17** *250*
Matsui, Hiromichi **13** 629
Matsui, Joryū **17** 240
Matsui, Kosei **17** 267
Matsui, Yoshiuke **33** 480
Matsukata, Kōjirō **17** 429; **20** 834*; **32** 394
Matsumoto **17** *11*
Castle **20** 834–6*, *835*; **27** 129
ceramics **14** 36
metalworkers **17** 358
Ukiyoe Museum **28** 605
Matsumoto, Hikohichirō **17** 426
Matsumoto, Isami **17** 266
Matsumoto, Sachiko **20** 834
Matsumoto, Shunsuke **17** 207; **20** 834*
Matsumura Goshun **17** 165, 196, 830; **20** 836–7*; **23** 594
collaboration **17** 196; **18** 87
groups and movements **17** 194
pupils **23** 386
teachers **33** 562
works **17** 196–7, *197*; **20** *836*
Matsumura Keibun **17** 197; **20** 837*; **23** 594
Matsunaga, Yasuzaemon **17** 429
Matsunōō Shrine
sculpture **17** *128*
Matsuo, Saigorō **11** 811
Matsuo Bashō **9** 738; **14** 129
Matsuoka, Hisashi **17** 203
Matsuoka, Seijirō **15** 746
Matsura (Japan) **17** 263, 351, 811
Matsusaburō Yokoyama *see* YOKOYAMA, MATSUSABURŌ
Matsushita Useki **17** 235, 237, 410
Matsuu Ono *see* ONO MATSUU
Matsuura (family) **17** 423, 429
Matsuura Screens **17** 175
Matsuura Seiken **17** 409
Matsuura Seizan **17** 177
Matsuya *see under* KYOTO
Matsuya Hisamasa **17** 429
Matsuyama **17** 18
Matsuzaki, Izu no Chohachi Museum **16** 84
Matsys, Cornelis *see* MASSYS, CORNELIS
Matsys, Quentin *see* METSYS, QUINTEN
Matt, Paul **32** 789
Matta, Dora **6** 600
Matta, José Antonio **29** 841
Matta (Echaurren), Roberto (Antonio Sebastián) **6** 598; **16** 681; **20** 837–8*; **25** 584
groups and movements **30** 22, 23
methods **8** 128
patrons and collectors **7** 812, 842; **20** 832; **23** 85
works **20** *838*; **28** 299
Mattäi, Friedrich **32** 119
Mattarnovy, Georg Johann **20** 839*
works **6** 572; **23** 339; **27** 373, 574, 585; **31** 318
Mattarnovy, Johann Christian **20** 839
Mattarnovy, Philip Georg **20** 839
matt board *see under* BOARDS
Matte, Rebeca **6** 597; **20** 839*
Mattei (family)
architecture **4** 47
collections **26** 847; **32** 612
sculpture **4** 886; **7** 437
Mattei, Alessandro **20** 839
Mattei, Asdrubale, Duca di Rocca Sinibaldi *see* ROCCA SINIBALDI, ASDRUBALE MATTEI, Duca di
Mattei, Ciriaco *see* ROCCA SINIBALDI, CIRIACO MATTEI, Duca di
Mattei, Francesco **3** 920
Mattei, Giacomo **20** 839
Mattei, Giovanni Battista **24** 371
Mattei, Girolamo, Cardinal **20** 839, 840
Mattei, Giuseppe, Duca **25** 664
Mattei, Ludovico, Duca di Paganica *see* PAGANICA, LUDOVICO MATTEI, Duca di
Mattei, Michele **11** 41
Mattei, Muzio **20** 839
Mattei, Paolo **20** 839, 840
Mattei *Ceres* **20** 840
Matteini, Teodoro **5** 378; **14** 264
Matteis, Paolo de **20** 841–3*; **22** 479
collaboration **13** 347
patrons and collectors **7** 796; **23** 577
pupils **3** 816; **24** 397; **27** 845
teachers **20** 411
works **20** *841*, *843*
Mattel Co. **31** 261
Matteo **28** 436
Matteo, Ansano di *see* SANO DI MATTEO
Matteo, Bernardo di *see* ROSSELLINO, BERNARDO
Matteo, Giorgio di *see* GIORGIO DA SEBENICO
Matteo, Jacopo **33** 716
Matteo, Lorenzo **6** 46
Matteo, Pasquino di *see* PASQUINO (DI MATTEO) DA MONTEPULCIANO
Matteo, Sano di *see* SANO DI MATTEO
Matteo, Turino di *see* TURINO DI MATTEO
Matteo (di Pietro di Giovanni di Ser Bernardo) da Gualdo **20** 844*
Matteo da Bologna **23** 586
Matteo da Bologna, Michele di *see* MICHELE DI MATTEO DA BOLOGNA
Matteo da Campione **5** 551
Matteo d'Acquasparta, Cardinal **13** 775
Matteo da Milano **20** 618, 844*
Matteo da Pistoia **32** 4
Matteo da Viterbo *see* GIOVANETTI (DA VITERBO), MATTEO
Matteo di Giovanello di Maffeo *see* GATTAPONE
Matteo di Giovanni **16** 662; **20** 844–6*
attributions **12** 716
collaboration **12** 716
patrons and collectors **28** 676, 677
pupils **8** 100
works **11** 383; **16** 750; **20** 684, *845*
workshop **24** 760
Matteo di Nuccio Vagnoli *see* NUTI, MATTEO
Matteo di Pacino **12** 702
Matteo di Ser Cambio **17** 564
Matteo Giovanetti (da Viterbo) *see* GIOVANETTI (DA VITERBO), MATTEO
Matteo Italus **18** 431
Mattern, Carl Maximillian **12** 423
Mattern, Hermann **14** 118
matter painting **1** 77; **2** 543; **20** 846*; **22** 313; **30** 335
Matteson, Tompkins Harrison **2** 858; **20** 846*; **32** 108
Mattet, Charles **5** 57
Matte' Trucco, Giacomo **7** 694; **20** 846*
Matteus, Arnold **30** 349
Matthaei, Johann Gottlieb **21** 65
Matthaei, Leni **12** 470
Mattheuer, Wolfgang **19** 112; **20** 847*
Mattheuer-Neustaedt, Ursula **19** 112
Mattheus, Georg **20** 847*
Mattheus Beblinger *see* BÖBLINGER, MATTHÄUS
Matthew (*fl* 1430-40; bricklayer) **30** 366
Matthew, Metropolitan (*fl* 15th cent.) **22** 405
Matthew, John Fraser **26** 99, 460
Matthew, Nathaniel **2** 462
Matthew, Robert (Hogg) **1** 126; **10** 241; **20** 491; **26** 460–61*
staff **33** 218
Matthew, Tobie *see* MATHEW, TOBIE
Matthew of Edessa **2** 97
Matthews, James **20** 14; **28** 289
Matthews, Martha **31** 661
Matthews, Thomas **32** 792
Matthey, Jean Baptiste **8** 426
Matthiae, Paolo **1** 894; **9** 693
Matthias, Archduke of Austria *see* MATTHIAS, Holy Roman Emperor
Matthias, Holy Roman Emperor (*reg* 1612-19) **2** 613; **13** *847*, *900*, *901*, 916*
architecture **11** 77
collections **13** 915
engravings **27** 504
gems **12** 266
hardstones **21** 726
metalwork **8** 413; **32** 771
paintings **1** 6; **2** 793; **13** 847; **31** 803, 804
regalia **32** 458
sculpture **1** 36
Matthias Corvinus, King of Hungary (*reg* 1458-90) **3** 211; **4** 694; **20** 847–8*; **28** 848, 849
architecture **5** 86; **7** 471; **11** 116; **14** 880, 884; **17** 601; **30** 206; **32** 614
book covers **4** 352
collections **15** 15
enamel **15** 10
furniture **14** 903, 904
gardens **12** 114
gold **5** 697
manuscripts **2** 697; **4** 197, 764; **5** 84; **7** 246; **11** 295, 296; **13** 319; **20** 413, 729; **27** 176
sculpture **12** 700; **21** 14; **32** 364
tapestries **13** 196, 634
Matthias Flask **10** 528
Matthieu, Anna Rosina **20** 848
Matthieu, David **20** 848
Matthieu, Emil **20** 607
Matthieu, Georg David **20** 848*
Matthijsen, J. **8** 150
Matthys de Waeyer **19** 260
Matti, Severino M. **29** 897
Mattia, Alphonse **4** 479; **31** 634
Mattia, Prince **20** 909
Mattia di Giovanni **28** 687
Mattielli, Lorenzo **2** 801, 819; **8** 386; **9** 238; **19** 642; **32** 443, 456, 458
Mattioli (family) **12** 671
Mattioli, Carlo **20** 848*
Mattioli, Lodovico **13** 330; **20** 848–9*; **23** 497
Mattioli, Pietro Andrea **12** 114, 133; **14** 433
Mattioli Rossi, Laura *see* ROSSI, LAURA MATTIOLI
Máttis Teutsch, János **14** 896; **20** 849*; **26** 716
groups and movements **1** 131; **14** 901; **20** 103
Matto, Francisco **30** 275; **31** 758
Mattocks, R. H. **1** 29
mattoirs **20** 849*; **25** 612
Mattoni, Andreas **17** 816
Mattox, Charles **18** 63; **29** 97
Matt-painted ware *see under* POTTERY → wares
mattresses **3** 482
Matuariër **30** 13
Matulka, Jan **8** 896; **28** 875
Maturanzio, Francesco **24** 525
Maturino da Firenze **25** 148; **31** 448; **32** 407
Matuschek, Franz **14** 749
Matuschka **12** 472
Matusevich, Naum **27** 381
Matute, Mariano Ormuza y *see* ORMUZA Y MATUTE, MARIANO
Matvejs, Voldemārs Hans *see* MARKOV, VLADIMIR (IVANOVICH)
Matveyev, Aleksandr (Terent'yevich) **20** 849–50*; **27** 392, 394, 396, 413
groups and movements **11** 358; **22** 508; **27** 395
pupils **2** 99; **33** 601
Matveyev, Andrey **20** 850*; **27** 388, 442; **29** 778
works **27** 401
Matveyev, A. S. **27** 438
Matveyev, Colonel **6** 281
Matveyev, Fyodor (Mikhaylovich) **20** 850*
Matveyev, V. **3** 531
Maty *see* WUVULU
Maty, Matthew **27** 244
Matyushin, Mikhail (Vasil'yevich) **13** 862; **20** 850–52*; **22** 380; **27** 394, 580; **31** 763
collaboration **18** 507
groups and movements **13** 862; **15** 857; **30** 7; **31** 583
productions **18** 474; **20** 193
pupils **27** 284
teachers **33** 740
works **20** *851*
Matz, O. H. **18** 888
Matza, Iogann (Lyudvigovich) *see* MATSA, IVAN (LYUDVIGOVICH)
Matzendorf **30** 144
Matzenkopf, Franz **2** 456
Maubert, Alexandre **11** 369
Maubeuge **19** 809
Ste Aldegonde **11** 615; **13** 159
St Pierre **26** 147
Maubeuge, Thomas de *see* THOMAS DE MAUBEUGE
Maubuisson
Abbey **5** 666
tomb of Charles IV and Joanna of Evreux **17** 458
tomb of Charles V **13** 76
barn **30** 908
Mauch, Carl **13** 334
Mauch, Daniel **20** 852*
Maucher, (Johann) Christoph **1** 762; **20** 852*; **28** 183
Maucher, Johann Georg **20** 852
Maucher, Johann Michael **12** 460; **20** 852–3*
works **20** *853*; **28** 183
Mauchline ware **28** 264
Mauclair, Camille **19** 10; **20** 853*
Mauclerc, Pierre, Comte de Dreux *see* DREUX, PIERRE MAUCLERC, Comte de
Maucó, José Manuel **14** 479
Maud, Queen of Norway (1869-1938) **23** 236
Maude, Clementina, Viscountess Hawarden *see* HAWARDEN, CLEMENTINA, Viscountess
Mauder, Josef **4** 59
Maudslay, Alfred Percival **2** 300; **16** 803; **17** 753; **21** 263, 264; **25** 825; **33** 510
Mauduit, Louise-Marie-Jeanne **14** 482
Maueha, Kuai **23** 736
Mauer **27** 90
Pilgrimage Church **2** 800; **18** 451; **20** 729
Mauer, Otto **32** 447
Mauer, Rudolph **18** 205
Mauer Altar, Master of the **20** 729*
Mäuerl, Anton Wilhelm **23** 313
Mauersmünster **12** 364
Maues, King (*reg c.* 90-80 BC) (Shaka) **3** 32; **15** 213
Maufangejo, John **29** 110
Maufe, Edward (Brantwood) **4** 790; **20** 853–4*
Maufra, Maxime (-Camille-Louis) **3** 366; **9** 425; **19** 10; **20** 854*; **25** 215
Maugard, Adolfo Best **21** 397
Mauger, Jean **8** 533; **11** 637; **20** 854*, 922
Maugeri, Concetto **11** 314
Maugerville, Christ Church **5** 561
Maugham, Syrie **10** 284
Maugis, Claude, Abbé **20** 455, 854–5*
Maui *see* HAWAII
Mauke **7** 790
Maukhari *see*:
SARVAVARMAN, Ruler

Maukhari—cont.
see: SURYAVARMAN, Prince UDAYASENA, Ruler
Maukhari, Harsha see HARSHA
Maukhari, Suryavarman I see SURYAVARMAN, Prince
Maulana Dust 15 578
Maulana Khalil Tonki 15 681
Maulana Shakibi Imami 15 594
Maulbertsch, Anton 20 855
Maulbertsch, Franz Anton 2 796; 11 122; 20 855–8*; 26 713; 30 212
paintings
altarpieces 2 795; 7 471; 13 888
frescoes 14 900; 15 139; 32 444
Bishop's Palace (Kroměříž) 8 392; 18 467
Carmelite Church (Székesfehérvár) 30 207
Heiligenkreuz-Gutenbrunn Church 2 *795*
Hofburg (Vienna) 32 457
Lyceum (Eger) 9 754
Palace of the Primates (Bratislava) 4 695
Strahov Monastery (Prague) 8 391; 25 445
Sümeg Church 29 922
Trenčianské Bohuslavice Castle 28 852, *852*
Vác Cathedral 31 786
history 20 *857*
oil sketches 20 *856*; 23 381
patrons and collectors 10 531
pupils 33 256
Maulbronn Abbey 12 *361*; 20 858–9*; 21 839; 32 93
chapter house 6 464; 13 57; 20 *859*
church 12 364; 20 858; 27 125
doors 9 156
gate-house 12 174
monks' refectory 20 859, *859*
mouldings 22 217
Maulde, Wallez Chapel 13 113
Maulden, Bruce Mausoleum 5 293
Maule, James, 4th Earl of Panmure 28 252
Maule, William Ramsay, Lord Panmure 17 673; 24 636
Maulpertsch, Franz Anton see MAULBERTSCH, FRANZ ANTON
Maumbury Rings (Dorset) 10 473
Maun 1 *413*
Mauna Kea
Beach Hotel 14 788
Observatory 23 342
Maunay 11 584
Maunier, V. Galli 10 92
Maunoury, Eugenio 8 61
Maunsell, G., & Partners 4 803
Maunsell Structural Plastics 4 804
Maupassant, Guy de 18 783; 29 612
Mauperché, Henri 1 664; 18 671; 20 860*
Maupertuis Château 6 509
Maupin, Simon 19 846; 32 574
works 19 *847*
Maupiti 28 921
Maur, Bishop of Kraków 18 429
Maurand, Jérôme 12 84
Maura y Montaner, Bartolomé 20 860*
Maurel see MOREL
Maurel Studios 20 609
Maurer, Alfred H(enry) 20 860–61*
dealing 3 251
pupils 23 675
works 2 447; 3 251; 31 490
Maurer, Hubert
pupils
Altini, Eustatie 1 728
Amerling, Friedrich von 1 774
Daffinger, Moritz Michael 8 445
Fendi, Peter 10 883
Maurer, Hubert
pupils—cont.
Lampi, Johann Baptist (ii) (1775-1837) 18 683
Pforr, Franz 24 586
Scheffer von Leonhardshoff, Johann (Evangelist) 28 68
Waldmüller, Ferdinand Georg 32 775
Maurer, Ingo
works 12 *418*
Maurer, Jakob 33 424
Maurer, Kristoffel see MURER, CHRISTOPH
Maurer, Louis 8 276
works 8 *276*
Mauretania 1 297, 305, 376; 26 *852*
Mauri (family) 29 422
Mauri, Emilio 4 670; 5 354; 21 902
Mauriac 26 602
Maurice, Bishop of Burgos 13 103
Maurice, Elector of Saxony (*reg* 1547-53) 8 120; 9 235; 26 127; 32 830, 831
Maurice, Emperor of Byzantium (*reg* 582-602) 9 654; 16 581
Maurice, Landgrave of Hesse-Kassel (*reg* 1592-1627) 8 895; 14 491*; 17 835; 28 357; 32 339
Maurice, Stadholder of the Netherlands, Prince of Orange (*reg* 1584-1625) 23 462, *463*, 464*
architecture 14 38
armour 2 473
drawings 12 530
gardens 12 131, 530
paintings 12 532; 33 167
textiles 22 899
Maurice, Charles 8 705
Maurice, F. D. 28 916
Maurice de Sully, Bishop of Paris 11 654
Maurier, George du see DU MAURIER, GEORGE (LOUIS PALMELLA BUSSON)
Maurin, Charles 20 603, 861*; 31 830
Maurisan, Louis 11 408
Mauritania 1 *214*; 20 861–2*
architecture 20 861–2
collections 20 862
Mauritania 22 129
Mauritius 1 *214*; 21 573, 574
Mauro, Alessandro 30 669, 676
Mauro, Antonio 3 863
Mauro, Bono 6 359
Mauro, Domenico 10 812; 30 669, 676
Mauro, Ernesto di 8 275; 26 478
Mauro, Gaspare 30 669, 676
Mauro, Lucio 26 848
Mauro di Codussis see CODUSSI, MAURO
Mauroner, José 2 404
Mauroux, Philippon 19 341
Maurs Church 26 641
Maurus (*fl c.* 1070) 26 698
Maurus (*fl* 14th cent.) 31 359
Maurus, Hrabanus See RABANUS MAURUS, Abbot
Maurus of Amalfi 9 154
Maurya 15 275; 20 862*
see also:
ASHOKA, Ruler
CHANDRAGUPTA, Ruler
DASHARATHA, Ruler
MAHINDA
Maus, Octave 3 614, *614*; 11 298; 20 862*
groups and movements 2 562; 3 563, 564; 5 44; 19 321–2, 792; 22 746; 26 96; 32 591
mausolea 6 165; 20 863–70*; 22 362–3
historical and regional traditions
Afghanistan 16 166
Austria 2 781; 13 *329*
mausolea
historical and regional traditions—cont.
Byzantine 9 556–7
Central Asia, Western 5 137, 139
Islamic 6 201, *206*; 16 *140*, *159*, 159–60, 166, 197
Samanid 16 159, *159*
Turkmenistan 21 *169*
China 6 697, 698, 699
Early Christian (*c.* AD 250-843) 7 325; 9 530, 556–7; 20 865*
Egypt 9 *765*; 16 175, 207, *209*
Egypt, ancient 20 863*
England 20 866*, 867–8*
Baroque 14 *258*
Greek Revival 20 *868*
Neo-classicism 20 *867*; 33 *444*
France 20 *864*, 867*, 868–9*
Germany 20 867*, 868*
Gothic 13 71
Greece, ancient 13 407; 14 *71*
Indian subcontinent 6 165; 15 *383*; 27 858, *858*
Iran 15 *898*; 16 159–60, 194, *194*, 197, 230
Iraq 16 159, 181
Islamic 16 130, 158, 246; 27 681
Afghanistan 16 166
Central Asia, Western 5 137, 139; 6 201, *206*; 16 *140*, *159*, 159–60, 166, 197
Egypt 16 175, 207, *209*
Iran 15 *898*; 16 159–60, 194, *194*, 197, 230
Iraq 16 181
Syria 16 181, 207
Turkey 16 204
Italy 7 325; 20 *864*, 866*; 26 *32*, *33*, *794*
Japan 17 *64*, 74
Jewish art 17 553
Palestine 17 553
Poland 25 135
Portugal 13 71
Rome, ancient 20 863–5*, *864*; 26 *794*
Russia 20 *870*
Syria 16 181, 207
Turkey 14 *71*; 16 204; 31 *452*
Turkmenistan 21 *169*
United States of America 20 *869*
materials
brick 6 *206*
tiles 16 *140*
see also CEMETERIES; CENOTAPHS; TOMBS
Mausolos, Satrap of Caria (*reg* 377-352 BC) 5 741; 14 *70*; 20 871*
architecture 13 407; 14 68, 69–72; 21 556; 31 109
Maussabré, Jacques 11 352
Mauter, Conrad 11 593
Mautern 2 776
Mauthausen, Monument to the Fallen Italians 16 650
Mautner-Markhof, Edith 33 166
mauve see under PIGMENTS → types
Mauve, Anton 14 43; 20 871–2*; 22 850
groups and movements 14 43, 46, 47; 20 435; 22 849
patrons and collectors 4 588; 11 301; 28 271
pupils 12 857; 32 393; 33 677
teachers 32 375
works 2 106; 11 448; 20 *872*
Mauve, Anton Rudolf 20 872
mauvine 9 493
Mauzaisse, Jean-Baptiste 20 873*
Mavatupuram 16 864
Mave, S María la Real 13 123
Mavelikara 15 521
Maverick, Andrew 20 873
Maverick, Peter 5 916; 9 418; 20 873
Maverick, Peter Rushton 20 873*
Maverick, Samuel 20 873
Mavignier, Almir 4 719; 33 636
Mavinakere 29 438
Mavinga 33 596, 598
Mavisbank 28 227, 269; 32 553
Mavlyanov, Ashurbay 30 253
MAVO 17 206; 20 873–4*; 22 339
Mavo 22 339
Mavr, Radislav 9 210
Mavrina, Tat'yana 27 396
Mavrocordat, Constantin 5 72; 26 708, 722
Mavrocordat, Nicolae 5 72; 26 708, 722
Mavrodiev, Zdravko 5 161
Mavroïdi, Christine 31 398
Mavros 25 340
Maw, John Hornby 10 311
Mawaki 6 586
Mawallock 12 142
Mawangdui 6 *615*; 7 150; 20 874*
bamboo 7 58
banners 6 812; 28 310
books 20 874
bronzes 6 834
dress 7 *75*
figurines 7 140
lacquer 7 13, *13*
manuscripts 7 63
paintings 6 773; 20 874
screens (ii) (furniture) 28 296
textiles 6 627; 7 46
tombs 6 697
Tomb 1 6 629, 648, 788
banners 6 773, 808
caskets 6 629
coffins 6 773
dress 7 75
furniture 7 33, 34
Tomb 3 31 152
Maw & Co. 8 122, 583; 10 312; 30 876, 877; 33 343
Mawlana Muhammad 28 811
Mawley Hall (Salop) 10 277
Mawṣil see MOSUL
Mawson, David 10 861
Mawson, Douglas 15 31
Mawson, Richard 26 21; 27 641
Mawson, Samuel Moses 20 875*; 28 527
Mawson, Thomas Hayton 2 691; 5 776; 12 141; 32 414
Mawson, William 26 21
Max, Anton 20 875
Max, Mme Charles 4 *253*
Max, Colombus Josef 20 875
Max, Corneille 20 875
Max, Emanuel 8 387; 20 875*; 25 432
Max, Gabriel (Cornelius) 12 394; 20 875–6*; 28 188
Max, Heinrich 20 875
Max, Josef Calasanza 8 387; 20 875; 25 432
Max, Josef Franz 20 875
Maxence, Edgard 20 876*
Maxentius, Emperor of Rome (*reg* 306-12) 16 761; 23 809; 26 782, 796, 902
palaces 9 556
Ma-Xia school 14 137; 19 478; 33 462
Maximian, Archbishop of Ravenna 9 649; 20 876*; 25 720; 30 776
thrones 30 *776*
Maximianus, Emperor of Rome (*reg* 286-305 AD) 21 514; 27 *43*
Maximilian, Archduke of Austria, Count of Tyrol (*reg* 1612-18) 12 347; 13 *900*, *901*, 916*; 18 139; 24 573
paintings 31 806
sponsorship 17 918
Maximilian I, Duke of Bavaria (*reg* 1598-1651) and Elector of Bavaria (*reg* 1623-51) 2 827; 33 *272*, *273*, 275*
architecture 9 12; 12 238; 22 305, 307; 28 109, 145
brass 12 838
cabinets (ii) (furniture) 2 *45*
collections 9 443, 446
decorative works 2 43
furniture 2 44; 12 460; 28 144
interior decoration 18 479
ivory-carvings 12 460
metalwork 12 446
paintings 9 443; 14 381; 17 711; 19 705; 27 291
plaquettes 25 22
sculpture 1 36; 2 44, 45
sponsorship 25 672
tapestries 5 606, *606*; 10 222; 12 467; 30 319
Maximilian I, Holy Roman Emperor (*reg* 1493-1519) 13 899, *900*, 902–4*, *903*; 15 865
architecture 12 471; 15 863, 864
armour 2 470, 471; 15 866, 867
book illustrations 12 385
books 4 76; 25 621
cartoons (drawings) 23 526
coats of arms 14 420
coins 6 102; 25 466
collections 9 435–6
drawings 1 714, 719
flags 11 149
furniture 32 448
jewellery 11 818
liturgical objects 1 5
manuscripts 8 114; 20 690, 727, 736–7, *737*; 32 759
orders (chivalry) 7 179
paintings 1 719; 2 871; 3 200; 12 387; 20 190; 26 105; 28 492
portraits 25 466
sculpture 2 800; 10 456; 13 822; 15 866; 29 571
silver 18 139
stained glass 23 315
swords 2 453
tapestries 31 219
textiles 2 824
woodcuts 5 199, *199*; 19 342, 825; 22 723; 29 433; 33 353, 365
Maximilian I, King of Bavaria (*reg* 1799-1825) 13 918; 14 488; 22 309; 23 354; 28 186
Maximilian I Joseph, King of Bavaria (*reg* 1806-25) 33 *273*
architecture 14 449; 22 308; 27 623
drawings 29 776
paintings 8 899; 18 176; 20 283; 29 658
watercolours 18 115
Maximilian II, Holy Roman Emperor (*reg* 1564-76) 13 *900*, 910–11*, *911*
architecture 2 778; 29 375; 31 23; 32 434, 456
coins 20 190
collections 29 738; 32 442
drawings 29 738
fountains 16 900; 28 53
frescoes 29 428
gardens 12 115
hardstones 21 726
manuscripts 14 619
medals 1 35; 8 790
metalwork 16 899
paintings 1 141; 11 270; 18 877; 33 428
palaces 10 889
sculpture 8 384; 12 570, 576; 18 575; 21 903; 22 857; 23 309, *309*
silver 16 899
sponsorship 29 739
swords 2 454, *454*

Maximilian II, King of Bavaria (*reg* 1848-64) **12** 415; **22** 303; **25** 789; **33** *273*
architecture **5** 217; **9** 704; **13** 202, 798; **22** 300; **32** 684
paintings **3** 514; **4** 205; **11** 244; **17** 856; **18** 739; **28** 195
sculpture **28** 186
Maximilian II Emanuel, Elector of Bavaria (*reg* 1679-1706; 1715-26) **33** *273*, 276–7*
architecture **4** 225; **8** 31; **9** 746; **11** 124; **12** 371, 723; **22** 307, 308; **23** 776; **28** 109; **32** 603; **33** 713
bronze **11** 626
decorative works **28** 162
drawings (pastel) **32** 659
furniture **12** 424
gardens **8** 794
ivory **29** 520
paintings **13** 845; **32** 706; **33** 296
sculpture **9** 336; **13** 679, 680; **19** 88; **29** 759
silver **3** 122; **24** 147
sponsorship **3** 779; **8** 288
tapestries **3** 388; **12** 467; **30** 324
Maximilian III Joseph, Elector of Bavaria (*reg* 1745-77) **33** *273*, 278*
architecture **8** 290; **12** 26; **22** 307; **26** 495
art policies **10** 860
interior decoration **22** 309
ivory-carvings **12** 460
paintings **14** 757
porcelain **23** 324
sculpture **21** 313; **31** 358
textiles **12** *463*
Maximilian IV Joseph, Elector of Bavaria *see* MAXIMILIAN I JOSEPH, King of Bavaria
Maximilian, Alexander **29** 377
Maximilian, Master of the Older Prayerbook of *see* OLDER PRAYERBOOK OF MAXIMILIAN, MASTER OF THE
Maximilian-Master *see* OLDER PRAYERBOOK OF MAXIMILIAN, MASTER OF THE
Maximilian of Habsburg, Emperor of Mexico (*reg* 1864-7) **14** 11
architecture **13** 202; **21** 402; **31** 329
art policies **21** 265
collections **2** 830; **10** 92, 93; **21** 249
paintings **14** 315; **26** 60
Maximilian Schoolbooks, Master of the **20** 729*
Maximinus, Emperor of Rome (*reg* 235-38 AD) **7** 246; **27** 41
Maximinus II Daïa **9** 897
Maximos (*fl c.* 1560; painter) **21** 344
Maximos, Bishop of Cythera (*fl c.* 1600) **8** 910
Ma Xingzu **19** 856
Maxman, Susan (Abel) **20** 876–7*
Max-Planck-Institut **2** 369
Maxwell, Edward **5** 562; **6** 513; **20** 877*; **31** 863
Maxwell, Edward John **20** 877
Maxwell, Edward R. **20** 877
Maxwell, James Clerk **22** 745; **24** 647
Maxwell, John **28** 240
Maxwell, John Grenfell **10** 91
Maxwell, William Stirling- *see* STIRLING-MAXWELL, WILLIAM
Maxwell, William Sutherland **5** 562; **20** 877*
Maxy, Max Herman **20** 877*; **26** 716, 719
May, Cliff **20** 877–8*
May, Edward John **10** 239; **25** 805; **30** 504
May, Ernest (1845-1925) **4** 374; **7** 293, *294*; **20** 878*
May, Ernst (1886-1970) **1** 319; **8** 824; **20** 878–9*; **24** 186; **31** 730
collaboration **28** 179
groups and movements **15** 885; **26** 405
staff **19** 746; **29** 531
teachers **11** 129
works **12** 378, 380; **20** *879*; **26** *18*, 19; **28** 122
May, Georg, II **26** 720
May, Hugh **12** 591; **20** 879–80*
assistants **23** 253
groups and movements **23** 210
patrons and collectors **10** 360; **29** 804; **33** 249
works **4** 786; **10** 273; **32** 358; **33** 396
May, Jakob **11** 844
May, Max **8** 189
May, Morton D(avid) **20** 880*
May, Octavio **19** 849
May, Phil(ip William) **2** 747; **20** 880–81*
May, Saidie Alder **17** 477
May, Stephen de
works **30** *333*
Maya **1** 14, 706; **3** 621, 622; **4** 295; **6** 579; **7** 483; **13** 759; **16** 806; **17** 753; **18** 666; **20** 881–8*, *882*; **21** 177, 181, 198, 199, 200, 202–3, 242, 700; **22** 8; **23** 837; **25** 825; **27** 780, 786; **28** 26; **30** 872; **31** 145, 778; **33** 588
altars **1** 700; **28** 640
archaeology **2** 300
arches **2** 294; **21** *205*, 213
architecture **3** 623; **7** 484; **20** 881, 883, 884; **21** 207, *214*, *215*, 700; **24** *744*; **31** *778*, 778
military **21** 598, 599
polychromy **21** 213
armour **21** 246, 247
arrows **21** 246
astrology **21** 207
astronomy **21** 215–16; **31** 778
axes **21** 246
ballcourts **3** 117, *118*; **6** 579; **20** *883*, 886; **30** 254
beads **21** 259
blow guns **21** 246
bone **4** 314
bone-carvings **21** 247–8
bows **21** 246
brick **4** 796; **7** 645
calendars **1** 14; **6** 579; **9** 498; **20** 883, 885; **21** 234; **22** 444; **27** 786; **31** 778
canals **9** 741
caskets **21** 259
causeways **6** 97, *97*; **21** 213
ceramics **1** 706; **20** 884, 886
chronologies **21** 191–2; **31** 507
cinnabar **21** 259
clubs (weapons) **21** 246
collections **13** 769
colour **7** 635, 636; **21** 183
cosmologies **21** *184*, 215, *215*
cotton **21** 246
craftsmen and artists **21** 190
crypts **23** 838
diorite **21** *251*
doors **9** 165–6, *166*
drums (musical instruments) **21** 257
erotic art **10** 474
facings **21** 213
fans **10** 779
feathers **21** 249
figurines **21** *239*, 247, 251, 256
finials (architectural) **21** 207
flutes (musical instruments) **22** 375
forgeries **21** 266
fortifications **21** 598, 599
friezes **31** 778
fuchsite **21** 243, 251
gardens **12** 71
gold **16** 803; **21** *253*
Maya—cont.
greenstone **21** 251, *251*
haematite **21** 718
hardstones **29** 153
headdresses **21** 249
hieroglyphs **17** 753; **20** 883; **22** 443; **27** 607
historiography **21** 234
houses **21** 208; **32** 307
iconography **21** *184*, 187, 189, 190
incense burners **20** 884
inscriptions **20** 883, 884; **21** 264; **24** 743
jade **1** 735; **16** 861, II1; **21** 241, 243, 251, 259
jewellery **21** 253, 260
limestone **21** 213, 260; **29** *620*
lintels **9** 165
Long Count **20** 885; **21** 191–2, 199; **29** 619
manuscript illumination **21** 182, 183, *184*
manuscripts **20** 327, 886; **21** 233, 234
maps **20** 362; **21** 234
masks **16** II1; **20** 881; **21** 250, 251, *251*
masonry **21** 213
metalwork **21** 252
military scenes **21** 247
mirrors **21** 718
monoliths **5** 412
mosaics **17** *715*; **21** 243, 254; **22** 164; **31** 778
musical instruments **21** 256, 257
narratives **22** 518
necklaces **21** 259
observatories **23** 338
obsidian **20** 881; **21** 251
ocarinas **21** 257
ornament **23** 565
painting
fresco **21** 251
vase **21** 190
wall **4** 295–6, *296*; **7** 636, I1; **20** 881, 886; **21** 259; **26** *411*, 411–12; **27** 786; **31** 507
palaces **17** *715*; **18** *578*; **20** 883; **21** *204*, *208*, 214; **23** 825, *825*, 826, 837; **28** 26, *26*
pendants (jewellery) **21** 243, 247
pigments **7** 636
plaster **29** 828–9
platforms **20** 881
portraits **25** *825*
pottery **20** 883; **21** 237, 239, *239*, 240
Fine Orange ware **6** 580; **17** 755; **20** 884; **28** 373
fine paste pottery **28** 373
Pabellón Modelled-carved ware **28** 373
Plumbate ware **6** 580; **17** 755
Thin Orange ware **17** 755
Tiquisate Ware **17** 755
Usulután ware **17** 753; **20** 881
pyramids **6** 579; **20** 881; **21** 212–16*, *214*, *215*; **24** *744*; **25** 764, 765; **30** *254*
pyrite **21** 718
quetzal **21** 249
rediscovery **21** 262, 263
religion **21** 183, 184, *184*, 186, 190
roads **7** 484
rock art **22** *444*
roofs **21** 205; **27** 128
sanctuaries **23** 838
sarcophagi **27** 823, 832
scripts **21** 233
cursive **23** 838
hieroglyphic **17** 753; **20** 883; **22** 443; **26** *411*
sculpture **1** 735; **4** 296–7; **17** 753; **21** 218, 254; **24** 743; **25** 825; **33** 511
Chacula style **27** 158
colossal heads **22** 8–9
Maya
sculpture—cont.
figure **4** 296–7; **5** *394*; **16** 807–8; **27** 780
monumental **1** 14–15; **16** 806–8; **20** 885; **22** 8–9; **25** *825*, 825–6; **28** *373*
relief **5** *394*; **7** *801*; **16** 807–8; **21** 217, 266; **23** *839*; **27** 607, 780
seals **21** 258
shells **21** 251, 259–60
shrines (i) (cult) **28** 640
skulls **21** 248
spear-throwers **21** 246
staircases **29** 527
stelae **5** 412; **7** *801*; **16** *807*, 807–8; **20** 883; **21** 266; **24** 743; **25** 825; **27** 780; **28** *373*; **29** 620, *620*
stucco **20** 881; **21** 266; **23** *839*; **29** *828*, 828–9
tablets **21** 243
talud-tablero **30** 280, *280*
temples **6** *580*; **20** 884, 885; **21** 212–16*, *214*, *215*; **24** *744*; **30** *448*, 448–9, *449*, *872*; **31** *420*; **33** *510*
textiles **13** 766, *766*; **21** 259
tombs **17** *754*; **20** 885; **21** 213; **26** *411*, 411–12; **31** 117, 118
trade **29** 214
travel books **21** 262
trumpets **21** 260
vases **20** 883; **21** 257, 266
vaults (ceiling) **21** 205, 207; **23** 838
vaults (tombs) **20** 885
walls **21** 205
weapons **21** 246, 247
whistles **21** 257
wood-carvings **33** 325
writing **20** 883, 885; **27** 607
Maya (*fl c.* 1320 BC) **27** 812
Maya, Raymundo Ottoni de Castro *see* OTTONI DE CASTRO MAYA, RAYMUNDO
Mayaklik-Tarishlak **18** 29
Mayakovsky, Vladimir (Vladimirovich) **20** 886–8*; **24** 405, 450; **27** 394
collaboration **26** 505; **29** 632
groups and movements **1** 453; **8** 250; **18** 536; **22** 508, 750; **31** 583, 677
posters **25** 351
productions **21** 410; **24** 405; **33** 486
works **4** 812; **20** *887*; **24** 404; **30** 362
illustrated **4** 100; **6** 530; **18** 793; **19** 476; **20** 195; **22** 50
Mayall, John **20** 888
Mayall, John Jabez Edwin **20** 888*
Mayapán **20** *882*, 888–9*; **21** *193*, 200, 203, 244, *372*; **23** 826
architecture **20** 884
fortifications **21** 599
pottery **21** 240
stucco **29** 829
May Art Club **30** 249
Mayat, Vladimir (Matveyevich) **27** 378
Maybeck, Bernard (Ralph) **10** 683; **20** 889*; **27** 730
Mayburger, Josef **27** 662
Maydell, Friedrich Ludvig von **10** 539
Maydūm *see* MAIDUM
Mayelle, Jean **28** 268
Mayemba **33** 596
Mayen Villa **32** 541, 542
Mayer (family) **7** 210
Mayer, A. **28** 628
Mayer, A(ugust) L(iebmann) **20** 890*; **21** 478; **24** 445
Mayer, Albert (1897-1981) **6** 445; **19** 46; **20** 890*; **23** 273
Mayer, Albrecht (*fl* 16th cent.) **11** 838
Mayer, B. H. **20** 891
Mayer, (Marie-Françoise-) Constance **11** 672; **20** 890–91*; **25** 671
works **20** *891*
Mayer, Demeter **33** 434
Mayer, Franz (*fl* 1905) **21** 395
Mayer, Franz Ferdinand (*fl* 1745-70) **14** 235
Mayer, Hans **28** 96
Mayer, Heinrich **30** 790; **32** 821
Mayer, J. **25** 430
Mayer, J., & Co. **26** 374
Mayer, Jan Oldřich **8** 385
Mayer, Johann Ernst **28** 142
Mayer, Johann Prokop **33** 434
Mayer, Johann Tobias **12** 813
Mayer, Joseph **12** 266
Mayer, Józef Jan **25** 105
Mayer, Karl **13** 215
Mayer, Leon Arie **16** 550, 571
Mayer, Louis (1810-66) **22** 908
Mayer, Louis (*b* 1870) *see* VAUXCELLES, LOUIS
Mayer, Mathias Johannes **12** 824
Mayer, Matteo *see* BENEDETTI, ELPIDIO
Mayer, Ottila **18** 510
Mayer, Ralph **10** 212
Mayer, Rudolf **20** 891–2*
Mayer, Theodor M. **28** 96
Mayer Club **2** 546
Mayerhofer & Klinkosch **2** 821
Mayerhofer von Grünbühel, Karl Franz Xaver **32** 449
Mayerhoffer, András (1725-85) **4** 695; **14** 887; **20** 892
Mayerhoffer, Andreas (1690-1771) **5** 81; **10** 545; **20** 892*; **28** 850
Mayerhoffer, János **14** 887; **20** 892; **28** 850
Mayerhöffer, Johann Wolfgang **2** 127
Mayern, Franz von **32** 437
Mayerne, Théodore Turquet de *see* TURQUET DE MAYERNE, THÉODORE
Mayer van den Bergh, Fritz **2** 196
Mayer van den Bergh, Henriette **2** 196
Mayer van den Bergh Museum *see under* ANTWERP → museums
Mayer & Zie **29** 507
Mayeul, Abbot of Cluny **7** 474; **21** 836
Mayhew, Henry **7** 659; **8** 218; **24** 672
Mayhew, Horace **8** 218
Mayhew, John **7** 659, 746; **8** 529; **11** 119; **15** 164–5; **20** 350, 468
Mayhew, Mark **28** 299
Mayhew, Richard **1** 444
Mayhew-Young, Joanne **23** 50
Mayipulo **11** 759
Mayito **20** 892*
Maykop **20** 892–3*; **25** *471*; **27** *362*, 409; **28** 321
Maymont, Paul **11** 527, 778; **20** 893*
Maymurru, Banapana **1** 67; **20** 893
Maymurru, Bumiti **20** 893
Maymurru, Naminapu **20** 893
Maymurru, Nanyin **20** 893
Maymurru, Narritjin **1** 61; **20** 893*
works **1** 51, *51*, 67
Maymurru, Nyapililngu **20** 893
Mayn, John de la *see* MAIANO, BENEDETTO DA, II
Maynal, Georges **26** 556
Maynard, Abbot of Mont-Saint-Michel **22** 39
Maynard, Alan **20** 893*; **28** 894
Maynard, George **27** 557
Maynard, Hannah **10** 580
Maynard, Lesley **1** 40, 68
Maynard, Richard **10** 580
works **22** *564*

Maynard of Gunnersbury, John 33 10
Mayne, Roger 20 894*; 31 706
Mayner, Alexander 29 299
Mayno, Giovanni Angelo del 11 13
Maynooth (Co. Kildare) 6 164
College of St Patrick 16 11
Mayo, Daphne 2 753; 4 819
Mayo, Juan de *see* VERMEYEN, JAN CORNELISZ
Mayo, Walter 1 29
Mayo Belwa 23 *129*
Mayocc 13 229
Mayol, Bartolomé 25 701
Mayol, Salvador 3 219
Mayor, David 10 99
Mayor, Freddy 7 797
Mayorga Collection 22 73
Mayr, Hans (Matthias) (1643-1718) 10 529; 32 822
Mayr, Hans (*b* 1677) 32 822
Mayr, Johann (1677-1731) 11 124
Mayr, Johann Ulrich (1630-1704) 12 390; 18 45; 20 894*; 22 843; 33 83
Mayr, Josef Georg 14 18
Mayreder, Julius 20 894, 895*
Mayreder, Karl 20 894–5*; 32 744
Mayreder, Keil, List GmbH 20 895
Mayreder, Rudolf 20 895
May Salon 5 903
Maysar 2 *246*, 264, 271, 272
Mays of Notre Dame de Paris 20 894*
Maystorov, Nikolay 20 895*
Maysuradze, Grigol 12 326
Ma Yuan 3 517; 14 137; 19 856–7*
attributions 19 857
groups and movements 19 478; 23 215; 33 462, 463
patrons and collectors 1 581; 30 465
works 6 773, 783, 789, 809, 817; 19 *857*
Ma Yuanyu 33 321
Ma Yueguan 33 496
Ma Yüeh-kuan *see* MA YUEGUAN
Ma Yüeh-lu *see* MA YUELU
Ma Yuelu 33 496
Mayumi Miyawaki *see* MIYAWAKI, MAYUMI
Mayuyama, Ryūsendō 17 431
Maywald, Benjamin 8 409
Maywald, Johann Gottfried 8 409
Mayyafariqin *see* SILVAN
Maza, Jacopo d'Andrea del 11 28
Mazairac, Pierre 22 877; 31 576
Mazairac & Boonzaaijer 31 576
Mazalić, Djoko 4 461
Mazamieu, Jean 18 805
Mazapan Ware *see under* POTTERY → wares
Mazarakata 17 909
Mazaramboz monstrance 29 334
Mazarin (family) 14 435
Mazarin, Duchesse de 3 414; 5 767; 9 379; 13 234; 19 231
Mazarin, Charles Armand de La Porte, Duc de 19 267; 20 896; 21 346
Mazarin, Hortense, Duchesse de 20 896
Mazarin, Jules, Cardinal 11 657; 20 895–7*; 22 465
architecture 3 706; 6 508; 19 264, 633; 20 290; 24 118; 32 582
books 13 866; 19 315
carpets 31 478
collections 7 544, 545; 9 22, 387; 11 661, 662; 19 779
dealing 11 662
decorative works 3 633; 30 659
engravings 7 494
furniture 7 166; 11 587; 12 832
gems 11 634
hardstones 11 636
Mazarin, Jules, Cardinal—cont.
interior decoration 10 489; 11 573
paintings 3 211, 745; 4 552; 6 435; 13 656; 16 814; 26 566
sculpture 9 22, 409; 26 348
silver 11 617
triumphal arches 19 21
Mazarin, Louise-Jeanne de Dufort, Duchesse de 5 767; 20 897*
Mazarin, Michel, Archbishop 1 497
Mazarin Bible *see under* BIBLES → individual manuscripts
Mazarin bureaux *see under* BUREAUX → types
Mazarini, Giulio, Cardinal *see* MAZARIN, JULES, Cardinal
Mazar-i Sharif 3 113; 16 268; 28 634
mausoleum of Muhammad Bosharo 6 207
Mazarović, Antun 22 17
Mazar Tagh 21 592
Mazaruni River Penal Settlement 13 875
Mazatec 21 736
Mazdean 9 731
Mazebedi, Bolaane Jack 4 489
Mazel, Ruvim Moiseyevich 31 459
Mazeline, Pierre 15 34; 20 897*; 22 34
Mazenta, Giovanni Ambrogio 3 249; 20 898*
collaboration 3 250
works 16 641; 30 803; 31 180
Mazer, Carl Peter 20 898*
Mazerolle, Alexis Joseph 12 830
Mazerolles, Philippe de *see* PHILIPPE DE MAZEROLLES
mazers 25 885; 28 261
mazes 18 584–6*
historical and regional traditions
Africa 21 597
France 12 123
Mesoamerica, Pre-Columbian 18 586*
Native North Americans 18 586*
Nigeria 21 597
South America, Pre-Columbian 18 586*
types
garden 18 585*
turf 18 585*
see also LABYRINTHS
Mazetti, Carpoforo 29 831
Mazev, Petar 19 884; 20 898–9*
Mazi 13 534
Temple of Athena 13 460; 24 319
Maziarska, Jadwiga 25 108
Mazi Dağ *see* ṬUR 'ABDIN
Mazière, P. 24 165
Mazin, Jean 8 64
Mazloum, Shafiq 27 876
Mazmanyan, M. 2 428
Mazo (family)
works 20 *900*
Mazo, Juan Bautista Martínez del 20 899–900*; 32 131
attributions 19 179; 20 *71*
teachers 32 135
works 20 *900*; 25 39; 27 *818*
Mazois, Charles-François 4 106; 20 901*
Mazois, F. M. 12 178
Mazone, Giacomo 20 901
Mazone, Giovanni 20 901–2*; 27 272
assistants 7 898
works 7 899; 28 461
Mazovia, Anastasia, Duchess of *see* ANASTASIA, Duchess of Mazovia
Mazovia, Konrad I, Duke of *see* KONRAD I, Duke of Mazovia
Ma Zuan 7 52
Mazuecos, P. 31 823
Mazur, Michael 21 897
Mazuras, Petras 19 500
Mazuré, Miguel Rodrigo 24 505
Mazurkiewicz, Alfons 25 108
Mazza, Camillo 1 631; 20 902
Mazza, Giovanni 27 196
Mazza, Giuseppe 20 902–3*
collaboration 29 32
patrons and collectors 7 779; 12 559; 19 337; 29 372
pupils 7 898; 24 834
works 16 699; 20 *902*; 30 496, 498; 32 216
Mazza, Tommaso del 1 709; 11 892
works 1 *709*
Mazzacurati, Marino 20 82; 26 777; 28 319
Mazzafirri, Michele 20 903*
Mazzaforte, Pietro 23 89
Mazzanti, Ludovico 18 523; 20 903–4*
works 20 *904*
Mazzarella, Bernardino 14 716
Mazzaroppi, Marco 22 12
Mazzei, Girolamo 22 805
Mazzocchio, Giacomo 1 572; 11 839
Mazzola, Alessandro 3 487
Mazzola, Bartolomeo, II 20 904
Mazzola, Filippo 3 667; 20 904; 24 197
Mazzola, Girolamo Francesco Maria *see* PARMIGIANINO
Mazzola, Michele 20 904; 24 197
Mazzola, Pier' Ilario 3 486; 20 904; 24 197, 199
Mazzola Bedoli, Girolamo *see* BEDOLI, GIROLAMO MAZZOLA
Mazzolino, Ludovico 11 3; 20 796, 904–5*
Mazzon, Galliano 22 242
Mazzoneschi, Vicente 1 675
Mazzoni, Angiolo 11 869; 20 905*; 26 762
Mazzoni, Cesare Giuseppe 10 446
Mazzoni, Giovanni *see* MAZONE, GIOVANNI
Mazzoni, Giulio 9 14
Mazzoni, Guido 20 905–7*; 31 189
patrons and collectors 31 413, 845, 847
works 2 277; 11 556; 18 677; 20 *907*; 24 133; 27 546; 30 496, 498
Mazzoni, Sebastiano 20 908*; 32 194
attributions 5 407; 6 126
pupils 6 137
works 19 308
Mazzotti factory 7 865
Mazzucchelli, Pier Francesco *see* MORAZZONE
Mazzucchetti, Alessandro 31 442
Mazzucco, Tiberio 11 114
Mazzuchelli, Gian Maria 26 564
Mazzuchetti, Alessandro 6 323; 25 856
Mazzucotelli, Alessandro 20 908*
collaboration 24 851; 25 793
works 16 744; 21 527; 29 59
Mazzucotelli-Engelmann 20 908
Mazzuoli 7 584
Mazzuoli, Bartolomeo 20 909
Mazzuoli, Dionysio 20 909
Mazzuoli, Giovanni Antonio 20 909, 910*
Mazzuoli, Giuseppe (*c.* 1536-89) 4 334; 10 524
Mazzuoli, Giuseppe (1644-1725) 3 838; 11 4; 20 909–10*
collaboration 6 585; 29 830
patrons and collectors 1 532; 23 874; 27 172
works 5 377; 16 699; 20 214, *909*; 26 817; 28 681
Mbagani 1 403
Mbala 1 357, 403
works 1 *403*
Mbama 1 *394*; 30 420
Mbandaka 1 *401*
Museum 33 598
Mbanefo, Arthur 18 640
Mbangwé *see* BANGWA
M'banza Congo *see* SÃO SALVADOR
Mbari Art Club 1 429; 23 136, 139
mbari houses *see under* HOUSES → types
Mbatha, Azaria 20 910*; 28 602; 29 110
works 9 427; 29 *111*
Mbeko 1 403
Mbella, Francis 5 524
Mbembe 1 360; 10 122, 124; 30 418
Mbengi 18 484
M'Bengue, Gora 28 406
works 28 *406*
Mbeudjang 3 147
works 1 *277*
Mbigou 11 879
Mbitim 33 610
MBM *see* MARTORELL, BOHIGAS, MACKAY
Mbole 1 256, 405; 19 72, 74
Mboma 1 403, 406
Mbomio Nsue, Leandro 10 440
Mbope 18 485
Mbop Mabiinc ma Kyen, King (*reg c.* 1940) 10 *579*
Mbughuni, Louis 30 301
Mbukushu 4 489
Mbunda 1 403
Mbundu *see* OVIMBUNDU
Mbuno, Kivuthi 17 907
Mbuti pygmies 1 306; 19 72
Mbyá 24 92, 93
McAfee, Phoebe 31 661
McAlpine, Lord 1 66
McAlpine, Alistair 7 788
McAlpine, Malcolm 33 205
McArdell, James 19 867*; 21 416; 26 231
pupils 11 139; 32 910
works 14 132; 21 148; 26 272, 278; 33 217
McArthur, John 19 867*; 31 593; 32 828
McArthur, Warren 31 654
McBean, Angus 19 867–8*
McBey, James 1 30; 28 238
McBirney, David 3 641
McBride, Will 32 680
McCahon, Colin (John) 2 706; 19 868–9*; 23 60
teachers 11 59
works 23 60, *60*
McCain, Ward 29 99
McCance, William 28 239
McCardell, Claire 9 294
McCarten, Edward 33 343
McCarter, Henry Bainbridge 8 708; 24 600
McCarter, John Young 19 869
McCarter Nairne 5 562; 19 869*; 31 863, 864
McCarthy, Fred 1 66, 68
works 1 *43*
McCarthy, J(ames) J(oseph) 7 718; 9 369; 16 11; 19 869–70*
McCarthy, Sophie 10 315
McCaw, Terence (John) 29 108
McCay, Winsor 5 759
McClair, Denis 12 134
McClay, Robert 25 353
McCloskey, Alberta 19 701
McCloy, Eveline 16 41
McClymonds, Ruth (Esther) *see* MAITLAND, RUTH (ESTHER)
McCobb, Paul 21 363
McCollum, Allan 19 873*
McComb, John, sr (1732-1811) 19 873
McComb, John, jr (1763-1853) 10 850; 19 873*; 20 270; 23 38
McCombie, Hamilton 6 527
McConkey, Kenneth 22 688
McConnel, Henry 20 238; 31 472
McConnel, R. 28 228
McConnel, Smith & Johnson 2 742; 17 622
McConnell, Carl 2 761
McConnochie, James 5 195
McCord Museum *see under* MONTREAL → McGill University
McCoubrey, John 31 672
McCowat, R. L. 26 107
McCown, Theodore D. 20 382
McCracken, Francis 8 827
McCracken, John 25 26
McCredie, A. L. 24 296
McCredie, G. 24 296
McCubbin, Frederick 2 746; 19 873–4*; 21 76
groups and movements 2 746; 14 306–7; 29 767; 30 39
pupils 21 77; 25 560, 884
works 2 746; 19 *874*
McCubbin, Louis 19 874; 29 243
McCullin, Don(ald) 19 874–5*
McCulloch, George 19 270, 875*
McCulloch, Horatio 12 776; 19 875*; 20 32; 28 236
McCulloch, Hugh, & Co. 12 197
McCullough, Conde B. 4 803
McCutcheon, Osborn 3 368*
McDermott, Edith 16 41
McDonald, Andrew 31 141
McDonald, Anthony B. 7 436
McDonald, William P.
works 31 *638*
McDurnan Gospels Binder 4 352
McElcheren, William 5 571
McEllen, Angus 25 685
McElney, Brian S. 7 155
McEntee, Jervis 19 889–90*
McEvan, Juan Bautista 5 886
McEvoy, Ambrose 10 374; 19 890*; 23 23
McEwan, James, & Co. 2 758
McEwan, William 28 271
McEwen, Frank 1 429; 33 679
McEwen, Jean (Albert) 5 568; 19 890*
McGaw, William Frederick 19 158
McGill, Alexander 4 890; 28 880
McGill University *see under* MONTREAL
McGluie, Margaret 16 888
McGoldrick, Hubert 31 229
McGrath, Raymond 19 890–91*
assistants 6 551; 23 679
groups and movements 10 241
staff 13 709
works 10 284; 31 *274*
McGraw-Hill 13 811; 15 886
McGregor, John 5 876
McGuffie, Jessie 11 113
McGuinness, Norah 19 891*
McGuire, Edward 16 18
McGurn, Logan, Duncan & Opfer 28 231
McHale, John 15 166
McHenry, James 4 44
McHorse, Christine 22 605
McIlvaine, J. Gilbert 10 718
McIlworth, Thomas 20 7*
McInnes, William 12 777
McIntire, Samuel 10 850; 20 7–8*; 31 610
attributions 27 613
collaboration 10 852; 27 613
patrons and collectors 17 823
works 2 618; 10 851; 27 613; 31 591, 628
McIntosh, R. J. 1 330
McIntosh, S. K. 1 330
McIntosh, W(illiam) Gordon 20 8*, 484
groups and movements 1 319; 29 106
works 25 566; 29 106
McIntosh, William 28 255
McIntosh Brooks, W. *see* BROOKS, W. MCINTOSH

McIntyre **2** 756
McIntyre, Dione **20** 8
McIntyre, (Robert) Peter **2** 742; **4** 415; **20** 8*
McIntyre, Robert H. **20** 8
McIver, D. Randall **33** 373
McIvor & Allan **28** 256
McKay, Arthur **4** 169; **5** 569
McKay, Ian **8** 85; **30** 161
McKean, John Thomas Chalmers **20** 13
McKean & Fairweather **5** 561; **20** 13*
McKee, Eva **16** 41
McKelvey, Frank **3** 537; **16** 36
McKendry, James **16** 42
McKenna, James **16** 22
McKenna, Stephen **7** 385
McKenzie, Colin **28** 261
McKenzie, Robert Tait **20** 15*
McKenzie, Voorhees & Gmelin **32** 797
McKie, Judi Kensley **31** 634
McKim, Charles Follen **5** 275; **7** 357; **8** 544; **11** 143; **20** 15–20*, 31
  architecture **5** 275; **7** 619; **22** 111; **32** 894
  assistants **3** 30; **26** 338
McKim, Mead & White **2** 315; **4** 479; **5** 274; **13** 757; **20** 15–19*; **31** 622
  architecture **4** 474; **23** 40; **25** 666; **30** 505
    apartments **2** 216; **23** 41
    banks **3** 176; **5** 562; **22** 36; **23** 38
    clubs (meeting places) **7** 470
    concert halls **1** 122; **7** 687
    exhibition architecture **10** 683; **29** 845
    hotels **8** 232
    houses **3** 128, *128*; **14** 788; **20** *17*; **25** 234; **31** 593, 594
    libraries **1** 23; **13** 757; **19** 318; **20** *18*; **27** 840
    monuments **4** 477
    museums **21** *649*, 650; **23** 40; **31** 598
    office buildings **14** 223; **17** 799
    power stations **25** 402
    railway stations **23** 40; **25** 268, 857; **31** 595
    town halls **31** 242
    university buildings **13** 2; **20** *19*
  collaboration **19** 766; **30** 385
  groups and movements **7** 619; **25** 806; **28** 604
  patrons and collectors **23** 32
  pupils **3** 269
  staff
    Atterbury, Grosvenor **2** 698
    Atwood, Charles B(owler) **2** 699
    Bacon, Henry **3** 30
    Carrère, John Merven **5** 875
    Gilbert, Cass **12** 613
    Hamlin, A(lfred) D(wight) F(oster) **14** 115
    Harmon, Arthur Loomis **28** 628
    Harrison, Wallace K(irkman) (1895-1981; architect) **14** 199
    Hoppin, Francis L(aurens) V(inton) **14** 753
    Swartwout, Egerton **30** 62
    Warren, Whitney **32** 866
    Wheelwright, Edmund M(arch) **33** 135
    Whidden, William M(arcy) **33** 136
McKinley, W. N. **32** 792
McKinnell, N. M. **31** 243
McKinnon, John
  works **27** *883*
McKnight, Gordon **16** 40
McLanahan, M. Hawley **14** 787; **25** 573
McLaren, Henry Duncan, 2nd Baron Aberconway **4** 216
McLaren, John **27** 730
McLaren, Norman **10** 688
McLaren, Sidney **16** 884; **20** 27*
McLaughlin, James W. **7** 326
McLaughlin, John **19** 702; **31** 607
McLaughlin, M(ary) Louise **27** 132; **31** 638
McLaughlin, Samuel
  works **11** *837*
McLay, Roger **2** 759
McLean, Bruce **20** 27–8*
  groups and movements **10** 258, 269
  productions **30** 688
  works **24** 409; **28** 240
McLean, James Stanley **5** 589
McLean, Richard **24** 686
McLean, Thomas **22** 208
McLean, W. H. **17** 492
McLellan, Archibald **12** 777; **28** 271
McLenan, John **2** 858
McLeod, Duncan **15** 380, 402
  works **15** *402*
McLoughlin Bros **31** 255, 258, 263, 267
McLuhan, (Herbert) Marshall **20** 29–30*; **24** 743
McLure, David **28** 240
McMaster, Gerald **22** 598
McMeekin, Ivan **2** 761
McMichael, Robert **5** 589
McMichael, Signe **5** 589
McMichael Canadian Art Collection *see under* KLEINBURG
McMillan, James **5** 275
McMillan Commission **20** 19
McMillen, Louis Albert **30** 226
McMillen, Michael **19** 703
McMinn, R. M. H. **1** 845
McMullan, J. V. **8** 899
McMullan Carpet **15** 683
McNab, Iain **9** 310
McNab, Theo **16** 18
McNair, J. F. A. **28** 772
McNally, Joseph **28** 775
McNeil, George **19** 492; **33** 223
McNeil, Hermon Atkins **33** 184
McNeill, Dorothy **17** *608*
McNeill, John **3** 430
McNicoll, Carol **10** 315
McNight Kauffer, E(dward Leland) *see* KAUFFER, E(DWARD LELAND) MCKNIGHT
McPherson, Craig **24** 490
McPherson, Ron **20** 607
McQueen **25** 627
  drawings **25** *627*
McQueen, John **11** 54; **30** 331
McRae, George **2** 740
McSwiny, Owen
  book illustrations **4** 514
  paintings **5** 686; **19** 157; **22** 115
    Canaletto **5** 594
    Creti, Donato **8** 159
    Imperiali (1679-1740) **15** 148
    Monti, Francesco **22** 27
    Piazzetta, Giovanni Battista **24** 704
    Pittoni, Giambattista **25** 2
    Ricci, Marco **26** 323
    Ricci, Sebastiano **26** 322
McTaggart, William (1835-1910) **20** 33–4*; **28** 240
  dealers **26** 107
  groups and movements **32** 903
  patrons and collectors **28** 269, 273
  pupils **26** 108
  teachers **18** 856
  works **28** 238
McTaggart, William (1903-81) **28** 240
McWilliam, F(rederick) E(dward) **16** 40; **20** 34*
Mdaburu **1** *407*
  doors **30** *57*
Mdina **20** 218
  Cathedral **20** 214, 215
  Cathedral Museum **20** 219
Meacham, George F. **4** 473
Mead, Henry **31** 637
Mead, John Clement **23** 340
Mead, Larkin **20** 16; **31** 611
Mead, Margaret **10** 580
Mead, Ray **23** 791
Mead, Richard **15** 29; **20** 910–11*
  books **29** 88
  collections **10** 364, 372
  drawings **9** 230
  manuscripts **21** 6
  paintings **3** 259; **18** 147; **32** 917
Mead, S. M. **20** 354
Mead, William Rutherford **20** 15–20*
Meade, Constance **10** 421
Meade, Martin Johnson **17** 823
Meade Brothers **24** 660
Meadmore, Clement **2** 756; **20** 911*
  groups and movements **30** 160
  works **4** 882
Meadow, Richard **14** 162
Meadows, Algur Hurtle **20** 911*
Meadows, Bernard (William) **11** 793; **13** 629; **20** 911–12*; **22** 58
Meadows, Elizabeth, Sculpture Garden *see under* DALLAS (TX) → Southern Methodist University
Meadows, (Joseph) Kenny **7** 924; **20** 912*
Meadows, Samuel D. **28** 772
Meadows-Taylor, Philip
  works **21** *44*
Meal, Jabez *see* MAYALL, JOHN JABEZ EDWIN
meander **13** 391; **20** 912*, *912*
Meano, Vittorio **2** 396; **5** 123
  works **2** *396*; **5** *122*
Meare (Somerset) **6** 161
Mearne, Charles **4** 353
Mearne, Samuel **4** 353
  works **4** *353*
Mears, Frank **6** 387
Meason, Gilbert Laing **32** 554
measurements **2** 349, 350; **20** 564–6; **28** 497–8
  Cycladic **13** 411
  Egypt, ancient **13** 411
  Greece, ancient **13** 386, *410*, 410–15*, *411*, *413*, *414*
  Indian subcontinent **15** 210
  Islamic **16** 143
  Rome, ancient **26** 867, 924–5
measures **1** 363–4; **12** 453; **28** 262
  baluster measures **28** 262
  tappit hens **24** 580; **28** 262, *262*
Measures, Harry B. **21** 349
measuring instruments **13** 411–12; **30** 26
Meath, John Brabazon, 10th Earl of *see* BRABAZON, JOHN, 10th Earl of Meath
meatplates *see* PLATES
Meatyard, Ralph Eugene **20** 912*
Méaulle, F.
  works **12** *157*
Meaux
  Abbey **7** 351, 353; **21** 164
  Bishop's Palace **11** 654
  Cathedral of St Etienne **13** 38, 42; **30** 907
Meaux, Adam of *see* ADAM OF MEAUX
Meaux, Jacques de **30** 88
Meaux, Jean de **5** 667
Meazi, Ambrogio **18** 431
Mebart, Michael **3** 428
Mebel Corporation **5** 158
Mebel Factory **5** 158
Mebes, Paul **2** 288; **3** 796; **20** 912–13*
Mebon *see under* ANGKOR
Mecamor **2** 439
Mécano **8** 437; **9** 62; **24** 428, 449; **29** 661
Mecarino, Domenico *see* BECCAFUMI, DOMENICO (DI GIOVANNI DI PACE)
Mec art **16** 857; **20** 913*; **27** 214
Mecca **2** *246*, 247; **6** *623*; **16** *104*, 110, 211, 453, 454; **20** 913–14*
  aqueducts **16** 225
  architecture **16** 207; **20** 230; **27** 875, 876; **32** 315
  guidebooks **13** 811, 812
  ḥaram **16** 245
  Holy Mosque **27** 876
  houses **16** 271
  Ka'ba **16** 88, *89*, 128, 141, 144, 366, 371, 379, 429; **20** 913–14; **28** 632
    mosaics **16** 255, 256
    textiles **16** 431, 438, 441
  Masjid al-Haram **16** 229; **21** 626, 628; **22** 191
  mosaics **16** 255
  printing **16** 361, *361*
  Umm al-Qura University **27** 876
  water supply **2** 242
  Zamzam **16** 256
Meccano Ltd **31** 264
mechanical tufting **5** 832
Mechanicus, Athenaeus *see* ATHENAEUS MECHANICUS
Mechau, Jacob Wilhelm **23** 410; **26** 128
Mechel, Christian von **6** 77; **12** 475; **20** 914–15*; **22** 357
  dealing **31** 342
  engravings **13** 871
  works **22** *356*
  writings **9** 18
Mechelen **3** *539*; **20** 915*
  art forms and materials
    alabaster-carvings **1** 517
    brass **3** 603
    bronze **3** 603
    cabinets (ii) (furniture) **3** 585
    embroidery **3** 609
    furniture **3** 584, 585
    lace **3** 610; **18** 589, 591, 593
    leather **19** 4
    marks **3** 601; **20** 915
    painting **3** 612
    pewter **3** 603
    sculpture **3** 569, 570; **13** 112
    silver **3** 598
    stained glass **13** 182
    statuettes **29** 571
    tapestries **3** 606, *607*; **30** 326
    textiles **25** 315
  Begijnhof **3** 545
    altarpiece **3** *504*
  De Zalm *see* Museum of Decorative Arts
  guilds **3** 596
  Hof van Buysleden *see* Stadsmuseum Hof van Buysleden
  Law Courts **3** 544; **11** 875
  metalwork **13** 159
  Museum of Decorative Arts **3** 544
  St Rombouts Cathedral **3** 542; **13** 61, *61*, 62
    altar **10** 844–5
    pulpit **25** 727
    sculpture **13** 100
    spire **29** 414
  Savoy Palace *see* Law Courts
  Schepenhuis **17** 700
  Stadhuis **13** 63; **23** 528
  Stadsmuseum Hof van Buysleden **3** 544; **28** 41
Mechelen, Henricus van *see* BROECK, HENDRIK VAN DEN
Mecherchar **23** 832
Mecherino, Domenico *see* BECCAFUMI, DOMENICO (DI GIOVANNI DI PACE)
Mechlin lace *see under* LACE → types
Mechtild, Saint **24** 776
Meckenem, Ida van **10** 383
Meckenem, Israhel van (i) (*fl* *c*.1457-*c*. 1465) **3** 555; **10** 383; **20** 915–16*; **25** 607, 624
  attributions **20** 628
  pupils **20** 916
  works **29** 311; **30** 529
Meckenem, Israhel van (ii) (*c*. 1440/45 -1503) **10** 383; **20** 915, 916*; **25** 625
  collaboration **32** 727
  works **12** 385; **17** 741; **20** *916*; **22** 203; **25** 605
Mecklenburg **4** 776; **13** 161
Mecklenburg, Johann Albrecht I, Herzog von **4** 667
Mecklenburg, Ulrich III, Herzog von **4** 667; **31** 889
Mecklenburg-Schwerin, Charles-Leopold, Duke of *see* CHARLES-LEOPOLD, Duke of Mecklenburg-Schwerin
Mecklenburg-Schwerin, Frederick, Duke of *see* FREDERICK, Duke of Mecklenburg-Schwerin
Mecklenburg-Schwerin, Frederick-Franz I, Grand Duke of *see* FREDERICK-FRANZ I, Grand Duke of Mecklenburg-Schwerin
Mecklenburg-Schwerin, Frederick-Franz II, Grand Duke of *see* FREDERICK-FRANZ II, Grand Duke of Mecklenburg-Schwerin
Mecklenburg-Schwerin, John Albert I, Duke of *see* JOHN ALBERT I, Duke of Mecklenburg-Schwerin
Mecklenburg-Schwerin, Paul-Frederick, Grand Duke of *see* PAUL-FREDERICK, Grand Duke of Mecklenburg-Schwerin
Mecklenburg-Strelitz, Charlotte Sophia of *see* CHARLOTTE, Queen of Great Britain
Mecklenburg-Strelitz, Louise, Duchess of *see* LOUISE OF MECKLENBURG-STRELITZ, Queen of Prussia
Mecklenburg-Strelitz, Marie, Grand Duchess of *see* MARIE, Grand Duchess of Mecklenburg-Strelitz
Mecquenem, Roland de **7** 187
Meda, Giuseppe **2** 373; **21** 525; **32** 612
Medaglia **17** 622
Médaillier de Mérovée **11** 599, *599*
Medak Fort **15** 541
Medallion, Master of the **20** 629
medallion portraits *see under* PORTRAITS → media
medallions
  historical and regional traditions
    Byzantine **7** *763*; **21** 2
    Greece, ancient **13** 599
    Islamic **16** 372–3
    Netherlands, the **22** *895*
    Romania **26** *715*
    Rome, ancient **21** 1–2*, *2*, *3*; **27** *96*
    Syria **16** 538
  materials
    bronze **21** 1
    copper **26** *714*
    enamel **33** *114*
    glass paste **28** *242*
    gold **7** *763*; **13** 599; **21** 1; **27** *96*
    ivory **22** *895*
  see also COINS; MEDALS
Medallion style **8** 235, *235*
medallion windows *see under* WINDOWS → types
medals **7** 178; **14** 419; **20** 917–27*
  display **9** 27
  historical and regional traditions
    Belgium **20** 921
    Britain **20** 923–4*, 925
    England **14** 487; **20** 921*, *924*; **28** *749*; **33** 455

medals
historical and regional traditions—cont.
France 14 419; 20 920*, *922*, 922–3*, 924, 925; 32 864
Germany 20 920*, *920*, 923*, 926, *926*; 26 127; 28 190
Italy 14 419; 16 690; 24 863
Mannerism 6 *140*
Renaissance 1 *556*; 20 917–19*, *918*; 24 *863*; 26 *399*; 29 *387*
15th cent. 12 *583*
16th cent. 20 *919*, 919–20*; 29 *410*
18th cent. 20 *922*
Netherlands, the 20 921*, 923*
New Zealand 23 *72*
Poland 25 127
United States of America 7 *875*; 20 926
materials
brass 20 917
bronze 1 *556*; 7 *875*; 16 690; 20 917; 23 *72*; 24 *863*; 29 *387*, *408*, *409*
cameos 16 690
copper 20 *922*
glass 20 926
gold 12 *583*; 16 690; 20 917; 28 *749*
hardstones 16 690
inscriptions 20 917
ivory 16 799
lead 20 917
silver 16 690; 20 917, *922*
silver-gilt 6 *140*
techniques
casting 20 917, 921
hammering *see* striking
moulding 20 917
striking 20 917, 921
see also COINS; MEDALLIONS
Medamahanuvara 29 450
Médard Gospels *see under* GOSPEL BOOKS → individual manuscripts
medas see under LACE → types
Medd, Henry (Alexander Nesbitt) 5 419; 8 676; 19 822; 21 2–3*
Mede, Cuthy 20 161
Mededelingen van de Koninklijke Vlaamse Academie voor wetenschappen, letteren en schone kunsten van België, Klasse voor schone kunsten 24 439
Medeiros (Anaya), Gustavo 4 260–61; 18 778; 21 3*
works 4 *260*
Medek, Mikoláš 8 394
Medellín 7 *601*, 606; 21 3–4*
art market 7 611
Banco de la República 7 606
Church of Veracruz 7 605
Gobernación de Antioquia 7 606
Instituto Pedagógico 7 606
Museo de Antioquia Francisco Antonio Zea 7 612; 21 4
Museo de Arte Moderno 7 612; 21 4
Museo Etnológico Miguel Angel Builes 21 4
Palacio Nacional 7 606
Teatro Junín-Europa Hotel 21 4
Villa Nueva Cathedral 7 605
Medellín Zenil, Alfonso 18 645; 27 756; 31 310
Medem, Count von 18 851
Medemblik Castle 22 822
Mederdra 20 861
library 20 862
medersas see MADRASAS
Medes 1 115, *852*; 15 900, 905–6, 907; 21 4*
architecture 15 910
dress 1 886
metalwork 15 919
rock reliefs 15 916
Medford (MA) 4 482
Medford, Richard, Bishop of Salisbury 17 611
Medgidia 30 770
Medgyaszay, István 14 890; 21 4*
Medgyessy, Ferenc 14 896; 21 4–5*, 49; 29 61
Medhane Alem Church 1 315
media 21 36*
Mediala group 28 451
Mediana 9 557
Median Wall 21 291, 552
Medias 13 523
Mediaş 26 707, 719
church 14 899
St Margaret 26 707, 711, 712
Medias Painter
works 13 *523*, 523–4
Medibli
wall decorations 1 *246*
medical books 1 844, 845; 17 274; 21 5–7*, *6*; 26 661; 28 206
see also ANATOMICAL STUDIES
medical centres 1 *320*
Medici (family) 11 177; 21 7, *8*, *9*; 25 59
academy 14 868
architectural decorations 12 710
architecture 11 178, 185, 322; 21 467
churches 5 22; 11 206, 207, 208; 16 763; 27 320; 32 106
military 3 17; 30 229
palazzi 11 179; 16 630; 20 521; 32 14
temporary 32 15
villas 3 173
cameos 9 124
carpets 16 472, *472*
ceramics 5 376
coats of arms 14 410
collections 6 76; 9 14, *15*; 10 487; 14 12; 16 764, 765; 22 355, 356; 27 114; 32 359
drawings 11 721
fountains 11 342
frescoes 32 500
furniture 16 727
gardens 12 115
gold 2 367; 10 751; 16 742
imprese 15 149; 29 740
ivory-carvings 20 90
jewellery 32 106
manuscripts 2 697; 11 296; 20 333, 689; 26 325
mosaics 21 255
oil sketches 23 381
pageants 13 280
paintings 3 615; 4 493; 16 658; 19 374, 443; 20 536; 22 447; 25 221; 32 14, 22
altarpieces 9 14; 19 678
battle 31 514, 516
deschi da parto 11 388
frescoes 1 671; 22 414; 27 178
landscape 18 709
portraits 1 671; 3 745; 9 15; 30 40
religious 2 34; 6 112; 8 275; 10 713; 19 441; 25 222
still-lifes 4 66; 12 170
porcelain 6 923; 11 191; 16 395; 20 441
portraits 1 5
pottery 13 541
rock crystal 21 529
ruin buildings 27 323
sculpture 2 168; 7 562; 11 234; 12 568, 575, 576, 577; 16 689; 24 460; 27 46; 30 227, 495; 32 105, 361
allegorical 12 569
animal subjects 12 572
busts 6 149; 8 798
friezes 9 125
modelli 12 576
reliefs 8 799
restorations 5 359
statuettes 29 572
tombs 16 694; 25 283
Medici (family)—cont.
silver 2 367
spalliere 29 360
stables 29 485
statuettes 3 860; 29 569
tapestries 11 193, 194; 16 714; 25 223; 30 314, 319, 331
weapons 9 31
Medici, Alessandro de', Cardinal *see* LEO XI, Pope
Medici, Alessandro de', Duke of Florence *see* ALESSANDRO, Duke of Florence
Medici, Anna Maria Luisa de', Electress Palatine *see* ANNA MARIA LUISA, Electress Palatine
Medici, Carlo de', Cardinal 1 113; 21 *9*, 25*
architecture 11 181; 20 521, *521*
paintings 3 96; 4 53, 813; 7 394; 8 275; 10 188; 27 851; 32 500
sculpture 11 26
Medici, Catherine de', Queen of France *see* CATHERINE DE' MEDICI, Queen of France
Medici, Claudia de', Countess of Tyrol *see* CLAUDIA DE' MEDICI, Countess of Tyrol
Medici, Cosimo de', Lord of Florence *see* COSIMO, Lord of Florence
Medici, Cosimo I de', Grand Duke of Tuscany *see* COSIMO I, Grand Duke of Tuscany
Medici, Cosimo II de', Grand Duke of Tuscany *see* COSIMO II, Grand Duke of Tuscany
Medici, Cosimo III de', Grand Duke of Tuscany *see* COSIMO III, Grand Duke of Tuscany
Medici, Donato de', Bishop of Pistoia 11 686; 32 365
Médici, Eduardo 2 401; 21 32*
Medici, Eleonora de', Duchess of Mantua *see* ELEONORA DE' MEDICI, Duchess of Mantua
Medici, Eleonora de', Grand Duchess of Tuscany *see* ELEONORA OF TOLEDO, Grand Duchess of Tuscany
Medici, Ferdinando de', Cardinal (1548-1609) *see* FERDINANDO I, Grand Duke of Tuscany
Medici, Ferdinando de', Grand Prince of Tuscany (1663-1713) 21 *9*, 30*
exhibitions 10 676
medals 29 30
paintings 5 920; 8 141, 142; 11 188, 697, 743, 873; 12 527; 20 95; 21 54; 26 321, 397; 27 851
sculpture 11 322; 33 726
Medici, Ferdinando I de', Grand Duke of Tuscany *see* FERDINANDO I, Grand Duke of Tuscany
Medici, Ferdinando II de', Grand Duke of Tuscany *see* FERDINANDO II, Grand Duke of Tuscany
Medici, Francesco I de', Grand Duke of Tuscany *see* FRANCESCO I, Grand Duke of Tuscany
Medici, Francesco Maria de', Cardinal (1660-1711) 7 898; 11 188; 12 528; 16 770; 22 288; 26 242
Medici, Gian Gastone de', Grand Duke of Tuscany *see* GIAN GASTONE, Grand Duke of Tuscany
Medici, Gian Giacomo de' 29 738
Medici, Giovanni Angelo de' *see* PIUS IV, Pope
Medici, Giovanni Carlo de', Cardinal (1611-63) 21 *9*, 26–7*
architecture 30 229
Medici, Giovanni Carlo de', Cardinal (1611-63)—cont.
paintings 1 535; 9 78; 11 188, 679; 21 27; 27 150
sculpture 23 265
Medici, Giovanni (di Cosimo) de' (1421-63) 13 196; 21 *8*, 13*
architecture 32 545
books 32 384
paintings 19 443
sculpture 8 797
tapestries 19 382
Medici, Giovanni de' (*fl* 1545) 4 *858*
Medici, Giovanni de' (1566-1621) 21 *8*, 24*; 23 140
architecture 11 208; 21 24
paintings 7 311
works 16 778; 19 511; 24 853
Medici, Giovanni de', Cardinal (1475-1521) *see* LEO X, Pope
Medici, Giovanni di Averado de' (1360-1429) 21 7–10*, *8*
architecture 5 17; 11 206
Medici, Giuliano de', Duc de Nemours *see* NEMOURS, GIULIANO DE' MEDICI, Duc de
Medici, Giulio de', Cardinal *see* CLEMENT VII, Pope
Medici, Ippolito de', Cardinal 5 *843*; 21 18–19*
gems 3 817
paintings 32 10
sculpture 19 551
Medici, Isabella de' 27 204
Medici, Jacopo Filippo de' *see* JACOPO FILIPPO D'ARGENTA
Medici, Laudomia de' 2 697; 4 197
Medici, Leopoldo de', Cardinal 11 *189*; 21 *9*, 27–8*
collections 10 769; 11 188; 16 771; 20 221; 21 27
drawings 3 97, 306; 6 362; 7 911; 9 229; 10 190, 746; 25 59; 27 851; 29 410
frames 11 392, *392*
miniatures (paintings) 9 27
paintings 4 455; 9 76; 16 767; 24 834; 27 178; 28 8, 433; 29 683; 30 42; 33 264
prints 25 631
Medici, Lorenzino de' 27 740
Medici, Lorenzo de' (*d* 1440) 2 34; 12 542; 21 10, 11
Medici, Lorenzo de', Lord of Florence *see* LORENZO THE MAGNIFICENT, Lord of Florence
Medici, Lorenzo de', Lord of Florence and Duke of Urbino *see* LORENZO DE' MEDICI, Lord of Florence and Duke of Urbino
Medici, Lorenzo de' (1599-1648) 21 *8*, 25–6*
architecture 25 76; 32 692
drawings 25 216
paintings 4 54; 8 498; 11 678; 13 787
Medici, Lorenzo di Galeotto de' 29 3
Medici, Lorenzo di Pierfrancesco de' 4 496; 11 56; 21 *8*, 15*; 25 151
Medici, Lucrezia de' (*fl* 1475) 12 734
Medici, Lucrezia de' (*fl* 16th cent.) 20 *919*
Medici, Maria Maddalena de', Duchess of Tuscany *see* MARIA MADDALENA, Duchess of Tuscany
Medici, Marie de, Queen of France *see* MARIE DE MEDICI, Queen of France
Medici, Mattias de' 7 902; 21 *9*, 27*, 53
Medici, Niccolò di Vieri de' 26 442
Medici, Ottaviano de' 21 18*; 27 850; 32 10, 11
Medici, Pierfrancesco de' 21 15
Medici, Piero de' (*fl c.* 1630) 9 76
Medici, Piero de', Lord of Florence *see* PIERO DE' MEDICI, Lord of Florence
Medici, Violante Beatrice 11 698, 743
Medici, Vittoria de', Grand Duchess of Tuscany *see* VITTORIA DELLA ROVERE, Grand Duchess of Tuscany
Medici Bank 11 192; 16 755
Medici *Madonna* 21 439
Medicine Hat 4 789
Medici Society 7 576; 21 32*; 26 235, 236
Medici Tapestry Factory *see* ARAZZERIA MEDICEA, (FLORENCE)
Medici tondo 28 702, 703
Medici Vase 19 397; 28 522
Medici Venus *see* VENUS DE' MEDICI
Mediesu Aurit Palace 14 885
Medieval art *see*:
ANGLO-SAXON; BYZANTINE; CAROLINGIAN; EARLY CHRISTIAN; GOTHIC; INSULAR ART; LOMBARD ART; MEROVINGIAN; OSTROGOTHIC; OTTONIAN ROMANESQUE; VIKING; VISIGOTHIC
Medina 2 *246*, 247; 16 *104*; 21 32–3*
aqueducts 16 225
architecture 16 208; 20 230; 32 315
Castilo de la Mota 19 896
congregational mosque 16 146; 18 242; 22 354
fortifications 21 588
House of the Prophet 6 171; 16 144, *145*, 146, 211, 229, 496; 20 230; 21 32–3, *33*; 22 192; 27 876; 28 633
maqṣūra 20 368
mihrab 16 278; 21 504
minbar 21 629
tomb of Muhammad 22 192
tower 21 626
houses 16 263, 271
mosaics 16 255
Mosque of the Prophet *see* House of the Prophet
mosques 16 242
printing 16 361
water supply 2 242
Medina, Bartolomé de 21 392
Medina, Eduardo Reyna *see* REYNA MEDINA, EDUARDO
Medina, Efren 25 455
Medina, Elizabeth 22 607
Medina, John (Baptist de) (1659-1710) 9 724; 21 34*; 28 235
methods 25 280, 281
patrons and collectors 7 417; 28 269
pupils 1 488; 14 259
works 4 359; 28 234
Medina, John (*d* 1764) 21 34
Medina, José Miguel 24 516
Medina, Juan de (*fl c.* 1660) 32 168
Medina, Marcellus 22 607
Medina, Pedro de 8 231
Medina, Santos 23 82, 85
Medina, Stuart Robles de *see* ROBLES DE MEDINA, STUART
Medina, Trinidad 22 607
Medina Alcoton *see* ECIJA
Medina Azzahra *see* MADINAT AL-ZAHRA'
Medina Barba, Diego González de *see* GONZÁLEZ DE MEDINA BARBA, DIEGO
Medinaceli, 8th Duque de 21 34

Medinaceli, 15th Duquesa de **28** 519
Medinaceli, Juan de la Cerda II, Duque de **32** 100
Medinaceli, Luis de la Cerda, Duque de (*fl* 1492-5) **32** 100
Medinaceli, Luís de la Cerda Fernández de Córdoba Folch de Cardona y Aragón, 9th Duque de (1660-1711) **21** 34–5*, 124
Medinaceli, Luís de la Soledad Fernández de Córdoba y Figueroa de la Cerda, 13th Duque de **21** 35*
Medinaceli, Nicolas Maria Fernández de Córdoba y Figueroa de la Cerda, 10th Duque de **21** 35
Medinaceli y Lerma, Duquesa de **21** 35
Medina de las Torres, Ramiro Nuñez de Guzmán, Duque de **19** 434; **21** 35–6*; **22** 472; **26** 310–11; **29** 353
Medina del Campo
 Hospital de Simon Ruiz **13** 106
 La Mota Castle **4** 784; **6** 58; **18** *681*, 681–2*; **29** *258*
 Palace of the Dueñas **32** 116
 S Antolín **29** 265
Medina de Pomar, Hospital de la Vera Cruz **29** 333
Medina de Rioseco
 Monastery of S Francisco **29** 290
 S María del Mediavilla **17** 692; **26** 250
Medina-Sidonia, Duque de **26** 527
Medina y Peñas, Sabino de **21** 36*
Medinet 15 Mayo **9** 765
Medinet Ashara Ramadan **9** 765
Medinet el-Faiyum **7** 825; **10** 758, 760
 congregational mosque **10** 758
 Temple of Sebek **10** 759
Medinet el-Obour **9** 765
Medinet el-Sadat **9** 765
Medinet Habu *see under* THEBES (i) (EGYPT)
Medinet Madi **9** 830; **10** 759
Medininkai **19** *494*
 Castle **19** 495
Mediolanensis, Bernardinus **19** 784
Mediolano, Franciscus de Castello Italico de *see* FRANCISCUS DE CASTELLO ITALICO DE MEDIOLANO
Mediolanum Santonum *see* SAINTES
Mediouna **16** 486
Medirigiriya **25** 169; **29** 459
Medis, Maria *see* GAZZARD, MAREA
Méditateurs, Les *see* PRIMITIFS, LES
Médium **30** 23
Medjidov, G. **2** 894; **22** 446
Medland & Son **23** 194
Medley, John **33** 212, 213
Medley, Robert **21** 36*; **24** 839
Medma **13** 579, 580
Mednieks, Kriš *see* ZAĻKANS, TEODORS
Mednyánszky, László **14** 901; **21** 37*; **28** 853; **30** 211
Medoro, Angelino **4** 264; **7** 607; **21** 37*; **24** 506; **31** 427
Medović, Celestin Mato **18** 473; **21** 37–8*
Medrano (family) **29** 348
Medrano, Giovanni Antonio **4** 562; **5** 614; **22** 473; **30** 667
Medrano, José Velázquez de *see* VELÁZQUEZ DE MEDRANO, JOSÉ
Medrano, Manuel López de *see* LÓPEZ DE MEDRANO, MANUEL
Medrano, Pedro de Mena y *see* MENA (Y MEDRANO), PEDRO DE
Medrano, Pedro López de *see* LÓPEZ DE MEDRANO, PEDRO
Medrano, Sebastián Fernández de *see* FERNÁNDEZ DE MEDRANO, SEBASTIÁN
Medrea, Cornel **21** 38*; **26** 726
 pupils **15** 132; **32** 662
 works **26** 716
medreses see MADRASAS
Medulić, Andrija *see* SCHIAVONE, ANDREA
Medum *see* MAIDUM
Meduna, Giambattista **27** 791; **28** 390
Meduna, Tommaso **28** 390
Medunetsky, Konstantin (Konstantinovich) **7** 768; **21** 38*; **29** 626
Medusa cameo **7** 834
Meduwael, Jan **3** 615
Medvedev, Grigory **27** 434
Medvinsky, Dina **6** 600
Medzhibozh **31** 550
Medzilaborce **28** *848*
 Warhol Museum **28** 857
Mee, Anne **21** 644
Meecle, Hennequin de *see* BROECK, HENDRIK VAN DEN
Meegeren, Han van **21** 38–9*; **32** 906
 patrons and collectors **3** 889
 works **2** 835; **4** 732; **11** 306, *306*, 307, 309, 310; **32** 269
Meehan, James **30** 158
Meek, Caroll **31** 672
Meeker, Dean **7** 558
Me'ekkudi, Yohannes Church **10** 573
Meeks, Arone Raymond **1** 65
Meeks, John **13** 209
Meeks, Joseph, & Sons **3** 685; **13** 209; **31** 628, 629
Meel, Raul **10** 540
Meem, John Gaw **22** 568
Meens, Adrian van **7** 493
Meer, H. van **22** 832
Meerbergen, Rudolf **3** 565
Meeren, Jan van der *see* JAN VAN DER MEEREN
Meerman, Gerard **21** 39*
Meerman, Johan **21** 39*; **33** 106
Meermanno-Westreenianum, Rijksmuseum *see under* HAGUE, THE → museums
Meersburg, Neues Schloss **2** 234
Meerssen Church **22** 821
Meertens, Victor **2** 754
Meerut **8** 673
Meer van Haarlem, van der *see* VERMEER VAN HAARLEM
Meerwein, Emil **14** 87
Meesen, Félix da Costa *see* COSTA MEESEN, FÉLIX DA
Meester, Willem **29** 7
Mée-sur-Seine, Le *see* LE MÉE-SUR-SEINE
meeting halls *see under* HALLS → types
meeting-houses
 Africa **1** 310, *314*
 Britain **23** 193
 Côte d'Ivoire **1** 310
 Dogon **1** 310, *314*
 Igbo **1** 310; **15** 116
 Indonesia **15** *771*
 Italy **32** 224, 228
 Kiribati **18** 83
 Mali **1** *309*, 310
 Mangbetu **1** 310
 Nigeria **1** 310
 Palau **23** 833, *833*
 Senufo **1** 310
 Sumatra **15** *771*
 United States of America **23** 193; **31** 589
 Wales **32** 783
 Zaïre **1** 310
 see also ASSEMBLY ROOMS; TOWN HALLS
Meetkerke Church **13** 113
Mefesh, Tell **30** 196
Meftah, Muhammad ben **31** 426
 works **31** *426*
megaletoscopio see under PHOTOGRAPHY → instrument
megalithic architecture *see under* ARCHITECTURE → types
megalithic tombs *see under* TOMBS → types
megalographia **27** 53, 57
Megalopolis **13** *363*; **21** 45–6*
 Stoa of Philip **29** 681
 theatre **21** 45
 Thersilion **13** 381; **14** 73; **21** 45
 town walls **21** 556
megaphones
 Bembe **1** 360
 Congo, Republic of **1** 360
 Sierra Leone **1** 360
 Sudan **1** 360
 Zaïre **1** 360
Megara (Greece)
 bouleuterion **14** 466
 fountain **13** 382
 graves **13** 383
 Long Walls **21** 556
 mosaics **13** 562
 St Ierotheos monastery **9** 579
 town walls **21** 556
megara (buildings) **21** 46*
 Greece, ancient **13** 382–3, *382*, 397; **25** 500
 Helladic **14** 338, 340; **21** *46*, 46
 Mycenaean **14** 338, 340; **23** 808
 Phrygian **13** *7*
 Turkey **13** *7*
Megara, Eupalinos of *see* EUPALINOS OF MEGARA
Megara Hyblaea **13** 419; **21** 556
 figurines **13** 579
 pottery **13** 502; **28** 654
 sculpture **28** 654
 vases **10** 612
Megarian bowls *see under* BOWLS → types
megaron houses *see* HOUSES → types → megara
Megasthenes **15** 194, 248, 690, 720; **24** 264
Megat Iskandar Shah (Paramesvara), Sultan of Malacca (*reg c.* 1400) **20** 155
Megaw, A. H. S. **9** 527, 528; **28** 828
Mège collection **13** 173
Mège Diptych, Master of the **13** 175
Megenburg, Konrad von *see* KONRAD VON MEGENBURG
Meggen, von (family) **30** 311
Meggers, Betty **7** 206; **20** 371
Megginch **9** 202; **28** 229
Meghen, Peter **31** 750
Megiddo **1** 892, 893; **16** *565*, 573; **21** 47–8*; **30** *180*
 architecture **30** 192
 fortifications **16** 573; **17** 553; **21** 553
 glass **1** 865, 867
 ivory-carvings **1** 870; **5** 557, *557*; **21** 47–8; **22** 511; **24** 643; **30** 186
 musical instruments **1** 891
 palaces **17** 552, 553; **30** 186, 191
 pottery **21** 48; **24** 634; **30** *197*
 rhyta **24** 634
 sanctuary **30** 191
 sculpture **30** 185
 seals **1** 857
 temples **5** 557; **30** 184, 185, 188, 191
 urban planning **30** 190
Megillat **17** 573; **21** 48–9*, *49*
megilp **21** 49*; **23** 784; **32** 1, 3
Meglinger, Kaspar **30** 131
Meglio, Jacopo del *see* COPPI, GIACOMO
Megliore di Jacopo **21** 82
Megyeri, Barna **14** 896; **21** 49–50*
Mehdi, Eqbal **23** 801
Mehdia **21** 585
Mehdi ʿAli Mirza **17** 806; **23** 798
Méhes, László **14** 902
Méhes, Lóránd **14** 897
Mehetia **28** 921
Méheut, Mathurin **28** 525
Mehi **15** 246
Mehkek, Martin **14** 596
Mehl, Ewa **25** 123
Mehmed, Prince (Ottoman) **16** 355
Mehmed I, Sultan (*reg* 1403-21) (Ottoman) **5** 282; **9** 729; **16** 206, 266
Mehmed II, Sultan (*reg* 1544-81) (Ottoman) **8** 14; **9** 634; **16** 222, 224, 595; **18** 509; **23** 638, 640*
 architecture **9** 729; **16** 584, 603, 604, 608; **18** 71; **19** 317
  military **16** 206; **21** 585–6
 bridges **9** 730
 drawings **3** 651, 655
 dress **16** 445
 manuscripts **16** 272, 330, 348, 552
 maps **20** 366
 paintings **16** 536
 sculpture **3** 636
Mehmed III, Sultan (*reg* 1595-1603) (Ottoman) **3** 53; **16** 348, 350; **23** 642
Mehmed V Reşad, Sultan (*reg* 1909-18) (Ottoman) **16** 611
Mehmed Ağa **1** 538; **16** 221, 223; **18** 509; **21** 50*
 collaboration **28** 768
 works **16** 499, 605; **30** 784
Mehmed Çelebi, Kara *see* KARA MEMI
Mehmed Dedezade **10** 494
Mehmed Esad Yesari *see* ESAD YESARI
Mehmed Hilmi **22** 385
Mehmed Hulusi **21** 51
Mehmed ibn Ilyas **16** 349
Mehmed-i Siyah *see* KARA MEMI
Mehmed of Bosnia **16** 388; **21** 50*
Mehmed Pasha *see* SOKOLLU MEHMED PASHA
Mehmed Rasim **16** 353; **21** 50*
Mehmed Şefik **21** 50*; **22** 385
Mehmed Şevki **21** 51*; **23** 391
Mehmood, Khalid **23** 800
Mehoffer, Józef **18** 428; **21** 51–2*; **24** 441
 collaboration **33** 455, 456
 pupils **7** 292; **8** 431; **20** 153; **22** 423; **33** 264
 teachers **20** 810
 works **11** 773; **21** *52*; **25** 107
Mehrauli *see under* DELHI
Mehrenan **1** *849*; **10** 172
Mehrgarh **15** 245, 421, *421*
Mehring, Bruno **30** 370
Mehring, Howard **32** 894
Mehring, Walter **8** 436
Mehta, Jaimini **21** 732
Mehta, N. C. **15** 183, 742
Mehta, N. C., Collection *see under* AHMADABAD → museums → Sanskar Kendra Municipal Museum
Mehta, Tyeb **4** 290; **15** 169; **21** 52–3*
Mehu **9** 899
Mehun-sur-Yèvre **31** 836
 Castle **13** 59; **21** 549, *549*
 Notre-Dame **1** 768
Mehus, Livio **11** 188; **21** 53–4*
 patrons and collectors **21** 27, 30; **27** 205
 pupils **11** 743; **26** 242
 works **21** *53*
Mei, Bernardino **21** 54*
 collaboration **18** 871; **20** 431
 patrons and collectors **6** 585
 works **28** 688
meibutsu collections *see under* COLLECTIONS → types
Mei Ch'ing *see* MEI QING
Meicholas, P. Neko **3** 62
Mei Chong **2** 96; **21** 60
Mei Ch'ung *see* MEI CHONG
Meid, Hans **21** 66
Meidias Painter **10** 592; **32** 56–7*
 attributions **32** 29
 collaboration **32** 41
 works **9** 248; **13** 551
Meidner, Ludwig (Baruch) **3** 802; **12** 395; **17** 578; **21** 54–6*; **24** 427
 groups and movements **2** 288; **10** 695; **23** 267; **24** 585; **29** 609
 works **15** 828; **21** *55*; **31** 705
Meier, Jeremias *see* MEYER, JEREMIAH
Meier, J. P. **31** 256
Meier, Melchior **21** 56*
Meier, Peter **9** 759
Meier, Richard (Alan) **3** 217; **21** 56–7*
 groups and movements **23** 50
 staff **29** 642
 works **1** 737; **2** 694, *694*; **11** 735; **19** 703; **22** 367; **31** 598
Meier, Sigrid **30** 330
Meier-Denninghof, Brigitte *see* MATSCHINSKY-DENNINGHOF, BRIGITTE
Meier-Graefe, Julius **2** 532; **21** 57*; **24** 427; **25** 350
 ceramics **11** 83
 furniture **3** 586
 groups and movements **2** 288, 565; **22** 291; **25** 357; **28** 342
 works **4** 42
Meier-Graefe and Bodenhausen **22** 292
Mei Geng **2** 96; **21** 60
Meiger von Werde, Hans *see* HAMMER, HANS
Meigh, Charles **13** 207
Meighan, Clement W. **1** 751; **2** 904
Meigin Hiraga *see* HIRAGA, MEIGIN
Meigle Museum **24** 738
Meigs, Montgomery (Cunningham) **21** 58*
 collaboration **32** 828
 works **4** 802; **16** 54; **30** 505; **32** 892, *893*
Meigyokusai *see* HIRAGA, MEIGIN
Meij, J(ohan) M(elchior) van der **21** 58*
 collaboration **18** 126, 436
 groups and movements **1** 814, 815; **10** 698; **18** 436
 pupils **29** 531
 works **1** 804, *804*
Meijer, Christoffel **18** 739
Meijer, D. C. **23** 447
Meijer, Hendrik **2** 229
Meijer, Jacob de **3** 769
Meijer, (Johan Hendrik) Louis **21** 58*; **22** 847, 848
 assistants **20** 434
 works **20** 433
Meiji, Emperor (*reg* 1867-1912) **12** 100; **31** 136
Meiji Bijutsukai (Meiji Fine Arts Society) **2** 578; **17** 204, 435; **18** 531
 see also TAIHEIYO GAIKAI (PACIFIC PAINTING SOCIETY)
Meiji-Mura Museum **17** 331
Meiji period *see under* JAPAN → periods
Meijt, Konrad *see* MEIT, CONRAT
Meikaku Kusakabe *see* KUSAKABE, MEIKAKU
Meikei **17** 402
Mei Keng *see* MEI GENG
Meil, Johann Christoph **21** 59
Meil, Johann Wilhelm **14** 750; **21** 59*
Meillant **1** 767; **11** 511

Meilleraye, Charles Armand de la Porte, Duc de see MAZARIN, CHARLES ARMAND DE LA PORTE, Duc de
Meilleraye, Hortense, Duchesse de La see MAZARIN, HORTENSE, Duchesse de
Mein, James (1759-1830) 28 255
Mein, James (fl c. 1830-51) 28 255
Meinardus, Dietrich 3 423
Meinecke, Michael 16 549
Meinwerk, Bishop of Paderborn 12 471; 14 74; 23 647, 748; 28 428
meiping see under VASES → types
Mei Qing 2 96; 6 818; 21 60*
Meir 9 774; 10 45, 77; 21 60–61*
dress 10 45
tombs 9 899
Pepyankh (A2) 21 61
Senbi (B1) 9 877; 21 61
Ukhhotpe (B2) 21 60, 61; 24 88
Ukhhotpe (C1) 21 61
wall paintings 9 804, 811
Meira 29 263
Meire, Gerard van der see GERARD VAN DER MEIRE
Meireles, Cildo 4 720
Meirelles de Lima, Victor 4 717; 21 61*
patrons and collectors 4 726
pupils 1 681; 32 613
Meïr Jaffé 17 533, 566
Meiron Synagogue 17 541, 542
Meise, Bouchout Castle 30 47
Meisei 29 547
Meiselas, Susan 21 61*
Meisenbach, Georg 25 617
Meishan, San Su Ci 28 638
Meisho, Empress of Japan 18 559
Meishu 24 435
Meishu shilun 24 435
Meiss, Millard 21 61*; 31 672
Meissen 12 360, 361; 21 62–4*
Albrechtsburg 2 480; 12 366; 13 58, 58; 21 64
Great Hall 32 88
porcelain 33 112
staircase 29 522, 522
Cathedral of St Johannes der Täufer and St Donatus 21 62–3*
brasses 4 693
Fürstenkapelle 32 92
sculpture 13 86, 87
Tomb of Frederick I 13 160
tombs 13 160
sculpture 8 384
Meissen, Agnes of see AGNES OF MEISSEN
Meissen, Otto the Rich, Markgraf von 19 110
Meissen Porcelain Factory 3 804; 4 493; 6 923–4; 9 238; 12 433, 434, 435, 436, 437; 21 63–7*
collections 4 639; 7 528; 12 412; 25 138; 33 110, 112, 114, 115
designers 12 436
Eberlein, Johann Friedrich 9 692
Höroldt, Johann Gregorius 14 766
Hunger, Christoph Conrad 30 97
Kändler, Johann Joachim 12 434; 17 768
Kirchner, Johann Gottlob 18 82
Lücke, Johann Christian Ludwig (von) 12 461; 19 772
Lücke, Johann Friedrich, II (1729-97) 19 772
Lücke, Karl Gottlieb 19 772
Meyer, Friedrich Elias 3 805
Niemeyer, Adelbert 12 437
Permoser, Balthasar 24 460
Riemerschmid, Richard 26 374
Scheurich, Paul 12 437
Schindler, Philipp Ernst, II (1723-93) 2 823
Meissen Porcelain Factory designers—cont.
Van de Velde, Henry 8 802
Wersin, Wolfgang von 33 84
directors 5 7
marks 20 441
painters 14 235; 17 916; 19 439, 733
production 4 176–7; 6 332, 333; 7 166; 9 29; 12 433; 18 615; 21 63; 22 880; 30 219
bells 3 627
chess sets 6 558, 558
coffee-services 21 65
dolls 31 261
figurines 6 12; 9 29; 26 498
fireplaces 9 240
Jaspisporzellan 6 332; 21 64
sword grips 2 456
table services 12 434, 435
tiles 30 506, 885
vases 21 66
teachers 26 358
Meissner, Johann Heinrich 21 68*
Meissonier, Charles 21 69
Meissonier, (Jean-Louis-) Ernest 11 663; 21 68–9*; 28 345; 29 609; 33 369
collaboration 6 545
dealers 2 858
groups and movements 26 54
patrons and collectors
Aumale, Henri-Eugène-Philippe-Louis de Bourbon, Duc d' 23 523
Chauchard, Hippolyte-Alfred 6 516
Delessert, (Jules-Paul-) Benjamin (1773-1847) 8 664
Morny, Charles-Auguste, Duc de 22 127
Orléans, Ferdinand-Philippe (-Louis-Charles- Henri) de Bourbon, 7th Duc d' (1810-42) 23 522
Petit, Francis 24 551
Seymour-Conway, Richard, 4th Marquess of Hertford 28 527
Stanford, Leland and Jane 29 536
Stewart, Alexander Turney 29 651
Vanderbilt, William Henry 31 870
pupils 8 819; 17 841; 21 81
reproductive prints by others 4 126, 242, 625
studio 29 856
teachers 7 529
works 3 389; 4 364; 9 245; 11 37, 545; 14 587, 588; 21 69; 31 704
Meissonnier, Etienne 21 69
Meissonnier, Gérôme 28 345
Meissonnier, Juste-Aurèle 6 509; 16 742; 20 137; 21 69–70*; 23 543; 24 271; 30 219; 32 876
copies 26 499
groups and movements 19 723
patrons and collectors 11 631; 25 138; 32 535
reproductive prints by others 6 527; 15 31
works 7 168; 10 332; 11 374, 406, 577, 619, 632; 12 410; 13 701; 21 70; 25 121; 26 477, 493, 493
Meister, Jakob Heinrich 13 663
Meister, Simon 29 66
Meisterlin, Sigismund
works 2 713
Meistermann, Georg 7 592; 17 818; 21 70–71*; 29 508
Meistratzheim Cemetery Chapel 26 633
Meiszner, Elias Albertus 15 813
Meit, Conrat 3 612; 12 401; 21 71–3*
attributions 24 807
Meit, Conrat—cont.
collaboration 27 132
patrons and collectors 13 905; 33 112
sculpture 21 72
works 2 800; 3 569; 4 870; 23 293; 29 570
Meitinger, Joseph 9 183
Meitner, Laszlo 4 719
Meixmoron, Charles de 22 456
Meixner, Johann 14 895; 16 811
Meizan, Yabu 23 595
Mejía, Emiliano 5 435
Mejía, Radhamés 9 118
Mejorada, Marqués de 21 73*
Mekchakov, I. 25 170
Mekeren, Jan van 21 73*
works 20 467, 467
Meketre
models 9 820, 823, 824, 825, 850, 851; 10 81
reliefs 9 877; 10 46
statuettes 10 16, 16
Mekhandzhiyski, Dimitǎr 5 158
el-Mekki, Hatem 31 425, 426
Meknès 16 103; 21 73–4*; 23 816
architecture 16 240; 22 128
Bu 'Inaniyya Madrasa 16 495
ceramics 22 129
Dar Jamaï Museum 21 74; 22 129
fortifications 21 585
Kasba 1 527
Lalla 'Awda Mosque 16 240
madrasas 20 57
palace 16 240
pottery 16 427
El Mekta 1 376, 377
Mektepini 2 261
Mel, Dayananda de 29 468
Melaka see MALACCA
Melamid, Aleksandr 18 209–10; 27 397
melamine see FORMICA
Melana, Antonio 17 588; 20 89, 90
Melanau 20 164, 182, 183
Melanchthon, Philipp 8 120; 9 443; 10 534; 14 868
Melandri, Achille 29 58
Melanes 22 699
Melanesia see:
FIJI; IRIAN JAYA; NEW CALEDONIA; NEW GUINEA; PACIFIC ISLANDS; PAPUA NEW GUINEA; SANTA CRUZ ISLANDS; SOLOMON ISLANDS; VANUATU
Melani, Alfredo 21 74*
Melani, Francesco 24 855
Melani, Giuseppe 24 855
melanin 9 491; 15 852
melanite 17 514
Melano 24 868; 28 678
Melano, Ernesto 13 202; 21 74–5*
Melanous
stelae 18 209
Melanthios (fl early 5th cent. BC; poet) 13 548
Melanthios (fl late 4th cent. BC; painter) 13 549, 551; 21 75*; 23 900
collaboration 2 217
Melantrich, Jiří 8 395
Melazo 10 576
temple 10 564
Melba, Nellie 25 884
Melbārzdis, Kārlis 25 745
Melber, Abraham 8 384
Melbourne (Australia) 1 37; 2 736, 769; 21 75–6*
9 by 5 Exhibition 2 746
architecture 2 738, 739, 742; 4 374, 789
Caroline House 4 882
Centennial International Exhibition, 1888-9 15 883
ceramics 2 760
1 Collins Street 2 743
120 Collins Street 2 743
Eaglemont 29 767
Melbourne (Australia)—cont.
Exhibition Building 2 739, 739
exhibitions 2 762
furniture 2 759
Government House 2 738, 758
Heide Park Art Gallery 26 74
houses 4 788
ICI House 2 742; 15 887
Independent Church see Uniting Church
Institute of Technology 2 763
Jewish museum 17 582
Labassa 4 374
Mandeville Hall 2 755
Melbourne Club 2 738; 7 470
Melbourne International Exhibition, 1880-81 5 393; 15 883
memorial to Burke and Wills 2 752
Mercy Hospital 2 742
Monash University 2 763; 29 509
Museum of Modern Art and Design 26 74
National Gallery of Victoria 2 769, 772; 10 876; 11 756; 13 709; 21 76; 22 358
Art School 2 770, 771
collections 1 66; 2 770; 4 623; 6 563; 7 154; 15 746; 18 65; 19 641; 29 768; 33 264
Great Hall 2 763, 763
National Museum of Victoria 1 66; 17 434
Olderfleet building 2 739
Olympic Swimming Pool 2 742
painting 2 746
Parliament House 2 738, 752; 20 13
Princess Theatre 2 739
Public Library see State Library of Victoria
Rialto building 2 739
Rippon Lea 4 788; 12 142
Royal Melbourne Institute of Technology 2 772
St James Old Cathedral 2 738
St Patrick's Cathedral 2 738; 32 858, 858
St Paul's Cathedral 28 296
Sanitarium Health Food Building 2 741
Sniders & Abrahams Warehouse 2 740
State Cinema 7 328
State Library of Victoria 2 738, 740, 769, 770, 772
Supreme Court 18 888
Treasury Building 2 738
Uniting Church 2 738, 763
University of Melbourne 2 769, 772; 18 65; 29 509
Victorian Arts Centre 2 742; 21 76
Victorian Zoological Gardens 2 763
Wardlow 4 374
Wesleyan Church (1872) 2 738
Wesley Church (1858) 2 738
Melbourne (Derbys; UK)
church 9 670
Melbourne Hall 3 83; 10 342; 13 228; 15 44; 18 902
Melbourne, Donald 28 549
Melbourne, Peniston Lamb, 1st Viscount see LAMB, PENISTON, 1st Viscount Melbourne
Melbourne Altarpiece 20 660, 711, 716
Melbury House (Dorset) 14 538; 23 105
Melbye, (Daniel Herman) Anton 21 76*
Melbye, Fritz Georg 24 879; 32 173
Melbye, Vilhelm 18 800
Melcem, Gerhard von 9 241
Melcher, Gaspare Otto 30 135
Melcher, Mihály 15 5
Melchers, (Julius) Gari(baldi) 8 820; 21 76–7*
Melchers, Gari, Memorial Gallery see under FALMOUTH (VA)
Melchers, Julius Theodore 8 820; 21 76
Melchert, Jim 31 640
Melchet Park 15 406
Melchior, Johann Peter 11 731; 12 434; 14 606; 23 325; 33 280
Melchiorre da Montalbano 13 98
Melchisedek 12 331; 22 251
Melcombe, George Bubb Dodington, 1st Baron see DODINGTON, GEORGE BUBB, 1st Baron Melcombe
Meldahl, Ferdinand 8 760; 14 543; 21 77*
pupils 17 755
teachers 14 497
works 7 802; 8 726, 727; 10 112; 17 446
Meldemann, Nikolaus 29 719
Melderis, Emīls 26 384
Meldgaard, Jørgen 19 812
Meldolla, Andrea see SCHIAVONE, ANDREA
Meldorf Church 4 776
Meldrum, (Duncan) Max 2 749, 771; 3 475; 21 77–8*
Meldrum, Percy 29 634
Mele 25 181
Mele, Pandi 1 540; 21 78*
works 21 78
Meleager Painter 13 524
Meleda 9 510
Mele da Stigliano 21 78–9*
Meleghino, Jacopo 10 808, 809; 11 740; 21 79*
Melehi, Mohammed 3 625; 21 79*; 22 129
Meléndez, Francisco Antonio 21 80*; 23 413; 29 357
Meléndez, Luis 21 80–81*; 29 283
patrons and collectors 4 378, 563
works 11 493, 493, 494; 21 80; 29 668
Meléndez, Miguel Jacinto 5 435; 21 79–80*; 29 282
Melendez Contreras, José 18 832; 25 702
Melensky, Andrey I. 18 36; 31 551
Meler, Johan den see JOHAN DEN MELER
Melero, Miguel 2 289
Meletius, Bishop of Antioch 2 159
Meleto, Evangelista di Pian di see EVANGELISTA DI PIAN DI MELETO
Meletos Painter 32 28
Meletovo
Church of the Assumption 25 342
Church of the Dormition 27 370
Melfi 12 174
Melfi, Roger of see ROGER OF MELFI
Melfort, John Drummond, Duke of see DRUMMOND, JOHN, Duke of Melfort
Melfort necklace 17 516
Melgar, Diego de 32 126, 135
Melgar, José 31 310
Melgar de Fernemental Church 14 82
Melhoun, Johann Gottfried 4 176
Meli, G. 17 809
Mélick, J. 12 13
Mélida y Alinari, Arturo 5 202; 21 81–2*
works 31 90
Mélida y Alinari, Enrique 21 81*
Mélida y Alinari, José Ramón 21 81, 82*
Melidoni, Maria 33 635
Melie 21 555
Méliès, Georges 10 686
Melighino, Jacopo 32 503
Melijn, Mattheus 3 598

Melikian-Chirvani, A. S. **16** 549
Meli Lupi (family) **4** 456
Melioli, Bartolommeo **12** 908; **20** 322, 918
Meliore **1** 709; **21** 82*
Meliš, Juraj **28** 855
Melisende, Queen of Jerusalem (*fl* 1131-61) **17** 502–3; **21** 82
  manuscripts **17** *506*
Melisende Psalter *see under* PSALTERS → individual manuscripts
Melissi, Agostino **4** 54
Melitene *see* MALATYA
Melitopol **28** 324
Melk Abbey **2** *776*, 783, 825, 828; **3** 777; **7** 254; **21** *83*, 83–4*
  church **12** 497; **21** 84*; **25** 448
  Colman Monstrance **2** 820
  Cross *see* MELK CROSS
  interior decoration **2** 806
  library **19** 316
  paintings **2** 794, *794*, 795; **27** *234*
  reliquaries **13** 901
  sculpture **2** 801
  stucco **29** 839
Melk Cross **2** 819; **13** 901
Mel'khisedekov, E. **2** 894
Melkites **7** 818
Mellaart, James **1** 894; **6** 73; **14** 14
Mellan, Claude **9** 410; **21** 85*
  methods **10** 392
  patrons and collectors **3** 745; **20** 455; **24** 330; **30** 524
  pupils **19** 154
  works **4** 746; **11** 401, 534; **19** 790; **20** 456; **21** *85*; **28** *6*; **32** 716
Melle (France) **26** 600
Melle (Johannes Oldeboerrigter) **10** 483
Mellein, Henri **31** 842
Mellem Reyen **23** *218*
Meller, Simon **13** 638; **14** 901
Meller, Vadym **2** 634
Mellerio, André **19** 488; **20** 601; **21** 86*
Mellerstain House (Borders)
  Library **28** 246, 247, *247*
  paintings **1** 488; **22** 531
  Round Drawing Room **28** 247
Mellery, Xavier **21** 86–7*
  groups and movements **5** 44; **14** 137; **32** 591
  pupils **18** 23
  teachers **28** 756
  works **3** 564; **21** *87*
Melli, Karl **27** 412
Melli, Roberto **11** 398; **21** 87*; **28** 319; **31** 852
Mellier & Co. **22** 744
Mellifont Abbey (Co. Louth) **7** 353; **16** *5*, 7; **21** 87–9*, *88*; **26** 592
  mouldings **22** 217
  silver **16** 30
  tiles **30** 877
Mellin, Charles **19** 696; **21** 89–90*; **22** 455; **26** 772
  works **21** *89*
Mellin, Roland **11** 108
Melling, Antoine-Ignace **4** 555
Mellini, Giovan Garzia, Cardinal **1** *630*; **12** 706
Mellini, Pietro **20** 114
Mellink, M. **10** 150
Mellis, Margaret **27** 563
Mello, Eduardo Kneese de *see* KNEESE DE MELLO, EDUARDO
Mello, Guy de, Bishop of Auxerre *see* GUY DE MELLO, Bishop of Auxerre
Mello, Heitor de **21** 90*
Mello, Icaro de Castro *see* CASTRO MELLO, ICARO DE
Mello di Gubbio **22** 727
Mello e Castro, João de Almeida e *see* ALMEIDA E MELLO E CASTRO, JOÃO DE
Mellom Kravik **23** 219
Mellon (family) **25** 5
Mellon, Andrew W(illiam) **2** 560; **9** 467; **18** 161; **21** 90*; **31** 662
  collections **9** 298; **10** 367; **31** 667; **32** 890
  museums **33** 159
  paintings **8** 210; **9** 467; **18** 161; **31** 664
Mellon, Paul **1** 23; **21** 90–91*; **24** 183; **29** 366
  paintings **1** 454
Mellon *Christ Child* **8** 798
Mellone, Carlo Francesco **5** 327; **21** 533
Mellor, David **10** 337; **19** 594; **21** 91*; **28** 576
Mellor, Meigs & Howe **14** 811
Mellor & Meigs **14** 811
Mells (Somerset), Manor House **24** 16
Melngailis, Emilis **12** 825
Mělnice Church (Czech Republic) **8** 377
Mělnik (Bulgaria) **5** *144*; **8** *374*
  St Nikola **5** 147, 148, 151; **7** 261
Mel'nikov, Avraam (Ivanovich) **21** 91–2*
  works **3** 527; **7** 174; **21** 810; **23** 353; **27** 211, 376, 428; **28** 892
Mel'nikov, Konstantin (Stepanovich) **11** 526; **12** 876; **21** 92–3*; **32** 661
  collaboration **19** 746
  groups and movements **2** 604; **21** 782
  house **2** 552
  pupils **19** 732
  works **10** 684; **21** *93*; **22** 173, 174; **27** 379
Mel'nikov, S. P. **2** 417
Melo, Duarte de **32** 147
Melo, Jaime de, 3rd Duque de Cadaval *see* CADAVAL, JAIME DE MELO, 3rd Duque de
Melo, João de (*fl* early 17th cent.) **12** 892
Melo, João de Almada e (1703-86) *see* ALMADA E MELO, JOÃO
Melo, Nuno Alvares Pereira de, Duque de Cadaval *see* CADAVAL, NUNO ALVARES PEREIRA DE MELO, Duque de
Melo, Pedro Américo de *see* AMÉRICO DE (FIGUEIREDO E) MELO, PEDRO
Melo, Rodrigo de **5** 364
Melo, Sebastião José de Carvalho e, 1st Marquês de Pombal *see* POMBAL, SEBASTIÃO JOSÉ DE CARVALHO E MELO, 1st Marquês de
Melocco, Miklós **14** 897
Melo da Stigliano *see* MELE DA STIGLIANO
Melodos, Romanos *see* ROMANOS MELODOS
melon domes *see under* DOMES → types
Melone, Altobello (da) **8** 135; **21** 93–4*
  attributions **26** 726
  collaboration **3** 697; **4** 195
  works **21** *94*
Meloni, Francesco Antonio **9** 30
Melos **8** *304*, 305, 308, 324; **13** *363*; **21** 94–5*
  collections **8** 323
  figurines **14** *352*
  fortifications **21** 556
  gems **12** 247
  jewellery **13** 597, 598
  obsidian **8** 153, 305; **14** 332; **21** 652; **29** 703
  pottery **8** 309; **13** 497, 502
  sculpture **13** 450
    relief **13** 582
  stone vessels **8** 317
Melos—cont.
  vase paintings **8** 309
  wall paintings **8** 318, 320–21*; **21** 674
Melo shells *see under* SHELLS → types
Melotte, Sébastien **18** 873
Melotti, Fausto **21** 95–6*
  collaboration **23** 169
  teachers **33** 183
  works **10** 822; **16** 708; **21** 533
Melozzo da Forlì **21** 96–8*; **26** 765; **31** 740
  attributions **17** 705
  collaboration **2** 184; **23** 889
  groups and movements **26** 187
  patrons and collectors **27** 271, 272; **28** 530
  pupils **10** 765
  restorations by others **29** 892
  works **15** 136; **16** 659; **19** 313, 687, 788; **21** *96*, *97*; **23** 889
Melper, Isaak **22** 305; **33** 271
Melrose (LA; USA), Melrose Plantation House **1** 440
Melrose Abbey (Borders) **7** 350; **12** 6; **13** 56; **21** 838, 839; **28** 267
Melsonbury (Yorks) **6** 162
Melter, Jean de **19** 382
Melton, William de, Archbishop of York **3** 895; **33** 548, 549
Mel'tser, Roman (Fyodorovich) **21** 98–9*; **31** 565
Meltwitz, Hans **12** 365; **21** 99*
Meluel, Jean *see* MALOUEL, JEAN
Meluhha **15** 902
Melun-Sénart **24** 131
Melville, Arthur **12** 779; **19** 109; **21** 99*; **23** 504; **28** 238
Melville, David **31** 651
Melville, David, 3rd Earl of Leven **21** 34; **28** 269
Melville, George, 1st Earl of Melville **10** 291
Melville, Henry Dundas, 1st Viscount *see* DUNDAS, HENRY, 1st Viscount Melville
Melville, Herman **28** 302
Melville, H. S **31** 185
Melville, John **4** 87
Melville House (Fife) **28** 246
Melville state bed **24** 237; **28** 252; **31** 682
Melvin, James **12** 875
Melvin, Robert Grieve **19** 109
Melzer, Moriz **3** 801
Melzer, Robert Friedrich *see* MEL'TSER, ROMAN (Fyodorovich)
Melzer, Z. **17** 822
Melzi, Francesco **19** 186; **21** 99–100*
  personal collection **19** 187; **23** 523
  works **19** 191, 784
  writings **19** 195
Melzi d'Eril, Francesco **7** 662
Même, Pierre-Jules **2** 99
memento mori **21** 100*
  see also PAINTING → types → *vanitas*
Memhardt, Johann Gregor **3** 789, 790; **5** 347; **14** 650; **25** 366
  works **3** *789*
Memi, Kara *see* KARA MEMI
Memlinc, Hans *see* MEMLING, HANS
Memling, Hans **3** 553; **4** 918, 920; **21** 100–105*; **22** 836; **33** 8
  attributions **2** 178
  frames **11** 439, 441
  methods **25** 281
  paintings **16** 470
    altarpieces **12** 223
      diptychs **9** 4; **21** *104*
      triptychs **19** 530; **21** *101*, *103*
    portraits **9** 271
    religious **11** *440*, 440; **18** 704; **21** *102*
Memling, Hans
  paintings—cont.
    still-lifes **29** *665*, 666
  patrons and collectors
    Aders, Carl **1** 154
    Altman, Benjamin **1** 731
    Bembo, Pietro, Cardinal **3** 698
    Beurnonville, Etienne-Edmond Martin, Baron de **3** 890
    Boisserée, Melchior and Sulpiz **4** 242
    Brukenthal, Samuel, Baron von **5** 9; **26** 722
    Burrell, William (1861-1958) **5** 278
    Clark, Robert Sterling **7** 377
    Ertborn, Florent (Joseph) van **10** 491
    Grimani, Domenico, Cardinal, Patriarch of Aquilea **13** 657
    Isabella I, Queen of Castile-León (*reg* 1474-1504) **2** 278
    Lehman, Philip **19** 92
    Museu de Arte de São Paulo **4** 726
    Nieuwenhove, Maarten van **29** 504
    Pius V, Pope (*reg* 1566-72) **25** 8
    Portinari, Tommaso **25** 269
    St Janshospitaal, Bruges **14** 784
    Straus, Percy Selden **29** 763
    Tani, Angelo di Jacopo **3** 612; **30** 294
    Thyssen-Bornemisza, Heinrich, Baron von **30** 795
    Vrelant, Willem (Backer van) **32** 729
  pupils **28** 803
  teachers **5** 43; **33** 126
Memling carpets *see under* CARPETS → types
Memmelsdorf, Schloss Seehof **32** 675
Memmi, Lippo *see* LIPPO MEMMI
Memmi, Tederigho *see* TEDERIGHO MEMMI
Memmingen **12** 384
Memminger, Levinus **33** 300
Memmo, Andrea (1670-1754) **6** 351
Memmo, Andrea (1729-93) **21** 106–7*
  architecture **6** 340
  collections **27** 864
  teachers **19** 534
  works **5** 626; **19** 534; **31** 296
Memmo, Giulio, Bishop of Verona **3** 648
Memmo di Filippuccio **19** 454; **20** 510; **21** 107–8*; **24** 854
  works **21** *107*; **27** 750
Memnon, Colossi of *see under* THEBES (i) (EGYPT)
Memória, Archimedes **8** 7; **21** 90
memorial posts **15** 730
memorials *see* MONUMENTS; TOMBS
memorials, war *see* WAR MEMORIALS
memorial stones **17** *474*; **32** 517, *517*, 518, *518*, 521–5*, *522*, *523*, *524*
  see also MONUMENTS
Memorie enciclopediche romane sulle belle arti, antichità ecc. **24** 447
Memorie per le belle arti **24** 422, 447
Memorie romane di antichità e di belle arti **24** 447
Mémorin, Guillaume **4** 544
Memphis (Egypt) **7** *819*; **9** 773, *774*, 778, 779, 782, 887, 891; **10** 33, 76, 77, 78; **21** *108*, 108–9*; **23** 281
  Abu al-Hol **9** 863
  Alabaster Sphinx **9** 813
  bone-carvings **7** 825
  casts **10** 68
  coffins **10** 12
  faience (i) (glass) **10** 48
Memphis (Egypt)—cont.
  forts **9** 848
  furniture **10** 50
  houses **9** 852
  mummies **22** 286
  necropolis **9** 843; **10** 18; **22** 716
  Palace of Apries **9** 849, 852; **23** 807
  palace of Merneptah **23** 807
  pottery **10** 24
  sculpture **9** 854, 855, 863, 869, 872, 877, 884, 886; **10** 33; **14** 758; **21** *109*
    reliefs **9** 887, 891; **10** *69*
  statue of Petosiris **9** 895
  temples **9** 831; **30** 237
  tombs **9** 899
Memphis Furniture **13** 326; **25** 27
Memphis group **15** 826; **22** 869, 877; **29** 90; **31** 633
Memphis State University (TE; USA) **28** 693
Men **3** 523; **10** 57
Mena (y Escalante), Alonso de **21** 109*
  collaboration **26** 552
  pupils **21** 109; **26** 552
  teachers **23** 343
  works **13** 284; **24** 506
Mena, Juan Pascual de **4** 562; **21** 110–11*; **24** 225; **31** 95
  collaboration **29** 293
  patrons and collectors **4** 564
  works **29** 293
Mena (y Medrano), Pedro de **21** 109–10*; **29** 292
  collaboration **22** 68
  teachers **21** 109
  works **5** 620; **20** 157; **29** 291; **31** 89
Menabuoi, Giusto (di Giovanni) de' **13** 149; **21** 111–13*; **23** 753
  works **5** 871; **16** 655; **21** *112*, *113*
Ménage, Gilles **3** 261
Ménageot, Augustin **21** 113
Ménageot, François-Guillaume **21** 113–14*; **26** 737; **30** 672
menageries **24** 179; **33** 698
  see also ZOOS
Menander (*fl* 279 BC) **6** 248; **13** 547
Menander (*reg c.* 155-130 BC) (Indo-Greek)
  coins **15** *688*
Ménard, (Marie Auguste Emile) René **3** 156; **14** 486; **18** 537; **21** 114*
Ménard, René-Joseph **21** 114
Menars, Abel-François Poisson de Vandières, Marquis de *see* MARIGNY, Marquis de
Ménars Château **19** 140
Menascé, James **10** 91
Mencaglia, Giulio **11** 81
Menchaca, Miguel de los Angeles **24** 502
Mencia de Mendoza, Marquesa *see* NASSAU-BREDA, MENCIA DE MENDOZA, Countess of
Mencius **6** 625, 634
Mencl, V. **8** 426
Mende (Greece) **19** 880
Mende (Sierra Leone) **1** 391; **21** 114–17*; **28** 690
  aesthetics **1** 236
  body arts **1** 342, 344
  Cathedral **13** 211
  divination instruments **1** 356
  feathers **10** 848
  figurines **21** 117
  hairstyles **1** 343
  headdresses **1** 236
  horns **21** 117
  iconography **1** 263
  ivory-carvings **21** 117
  masks **1** *237*, 256, 282, *282*, 334, 336, 337, 340; **19** 309; **21** *115*, 115–17*, *117*
  sculpture **21** 117*

Mende (Sierra Leone)—cont.
statuettes **18** 90
textiles **21** 117
women **1** 236, 247, 340
wood **1** *282*; **21** *115*, *117*
wood-carvings **21** 114
Mende, Durandus of *see* DURANDUS OF MENDE
Mende, Valér **18** 394; **21** 118*
Mendel, Samuel **20** 238; **21** 604
Mendel Art Gallery *see under* SASKATOON
Mendelowitz, Daniel **8** 870
Mendelsohn, Erich **3** 795, 902; **7** 695; **16** 565; **21** 118–21*
assistants **23** 679
collaboration **6** 551; **20** 324
competitions **7** 670
groups and movements **2** 288; **3** 801; **10** 241, 697; **15** 885, 886; **21** 781, 782; **23** 498; **26** 405
patrons and collectors **16** 570
staff **8** 814; **10** 857; **18** 386; **23** 9
teachers **11** 129
works **1** 738; **2** 337; **4** 788; **7** 328, 695; **8** 770; **12** 378; **17** 492, 549, *549*; **21** *119*, *120*; **23** 695; **25** 367, 402; **29** 874; **30** 685; **33** 417
Mendelson, Marc **3** 565; **5** 45; **17** 518; **20** 846
Mendelssohn, Felix **7** 687
Mendelssohn, Moses **1** 660; **21** 59, 121*; **23** 108
Mendes **9** *774*; **13** 560, 566–7; **21** 121–2*
Mendes, Jácome **4** 634; **25** 292
Mendes Belisario, Isaac **5** 751; **16** 882, 884
works **16** *881*
Mendes Coutinho, António **10** 812; **32** 616
Mendes da Costa, Joseph **21** 122*; **22** 860
works **3** 432; **22** 860, 861
Mendes da Rocha, Carlo **27** 808
Mendes da Rocha, Paulo (Archias) **4** 714; **21** 123*; **33** 185
Mendes de Vasconcelos, Hernani **4** 713; **23** 117
works **4** *712*
Mendez, Alejandro **3** 278
Méndez, J. **21** 81
Méndez, Leopoldo **10** 543; **21** 123*, 388; **30** 275; **33** 490
Méndez, Luis Alfredo López *see* LÓPEZ MÉNDEZ, LUIS ALFREDO
Méndez, Ramón Torres *see* TORRES MÉNDEZ, RAMÓN
Méndez, Vicente **32** 180
Méndez Castillo, Consuelo **18** 832
Méndez de Haro y Guzmán, Catalina, Duquesa de Alba *see* ALBA, CATALINA MÉNDEZ DE HARO Y GUZMÁN, Duquesa de
Méndez de Haro y Guzmán, Luis, Marqués de Carpio *see* CARPIO, LUIS MÉNDEZ DE HARO Y GUZMÁN, 6th Marqués de
Méndez Gonzalez, Diego **10** 822
Mendieta, Ana **21** 123–4*
Mendis, Solias **29** 467
Mendive, Manuel **8** 229, 234
Mendivil, Hilario **24** 499
Mendívil, Luis Aladrén y *see* ALADRÉN Y MENDÍVIL, LUIS
Mendizábal, Benjamín **24** 509
Mendizabal, José Antonio **32** 558
Mendonça, Francisco de Almada e *see* ALMADA E MENDONÇA, FRANCISCO DE
Mendoza (Argentina) **2** 392, *393*, 394
Mendoza (family) **14** 410; **31** 88
Mendoza, Alsonso de **18** 777
Mendoza, Antonio de **21** 233
Mendoza, Cerro de la Gloria **31** 754
Mendoza, Diego Hurtado de, Cardinal *see* HURTADO DE MENDOZA, DIEGO, Cardinal
Mendoza, Gregorio Hurtado de *see* HURTADO DE MENDOZA, GREGORIO
Mendoza, Iñigo López de, Conde de Tendilla *see* TENDILLA, IÑIGO LÓPEZ DE MENDOZA, Conde de
Mendoza, Iñigo López de, Marqués de Santillana *see* SANTILLANA, IÑIGO LÓPEZ DE MENDOZA, Marqués de
Mendoza, José Salazar y *see* SALAZAR Y MENDOZA, JOSÉ
Mendoza, Mencía de (*fl* 1482) **5** 203
Mendoza, Mencía de, Marquesa de Canete (*fl* 1530s) *see* NASSAU, MENCÍA DE MENDOZA, Countess of
Mendoza, Pedro de (*fl* 1536) **2** 392, 394
Mendoza, Pedro González de (1428-95) *see* GONZÁLEZ DE MENDOZA, PEDRO, Cardinal
Mendoza, Pedro Salazar de, *see* SALAZAR DE MENDOZA, PEDRO
Mendoza, Rodrigo Díaz de Vivar y, 1st Marqués del Zenete (1464–1523) *see* ZENETE, RODRIGO DÍAZ DE VIVAR Y MENDOZA, 1st Marqués del
Mendoza, Tony **18** 835
Mendoza-Infantado (family) **13** 756
Mendoza-Infantado, Diego de Hurtado de Mendoza, Conde de **28** 675
Mendoza-Infantado, Iñigo López de Mendoza II, 2nd Duque de **21** 124
Mendoza-Infantado, Rodrigo Diaz de Vivar, Duque de, 1st Marqués del Zenete (*fl* 1738) **13** 634; **29** 316
Mendoza y Moreno, Francisco de Paula **21** 126*
Mendoza y Sandoval, Gregorio Mariá de Silva, Duque del Infantado y Pastrana *see* INFANTADO Y PASTRANA, GREGORIO MARIÁ DE SILVA MENDOZA Y SANDOVAL, Duque del
Mendut **29** 865
Mène, Pierre-Jules **5** 392; **11** 629; **12** 30; **21** 126–7*; **33** 3
Meneghetti, Lodovico **13** 629
Meneghini, Agostino **17** 442
Menekrates **2** 229; **13** 384
Menelaos (*fl* 1st cent. AD) **27** 27
Menelas, Adam (Adamovich) **5** 521; **21** 127*; **25** 746; **27** 377
works **24** 546; **27** 377, 577
Menelau, João **14** 658
Menelaus **8** 3
Menelik II, Emperor of Ethiopia (*reg* 1889-1913) **1** 315; **10** 573, 577
Meneller, Caspar **12** 238; **21** 127*; **32** 772
Menen **3** 598
Menéndez, Gonzalo **26** 689
Menéndez de Avilés, Pedro *see* AVILÉS, PEDRO MENÉNDEZ DE
Menéndez y Pelayo, Marcelino **21** 127–8*
Menéres, Clara **25** 302
Menes **9** *776*, 778; **21** 108
Menescardi, Giustino **30** 862
Meneses **29** 344
Meneses, Antonio Luis de *see* MARIALVA, 1st Marquês de
Meneses, Francisco Andrés **5** 691; **32** 168
works **32** *168*
Meneses, Jorge de **17** 596
Meneses, Luís Pereira de, Visconde **21** 128*
Meneses, Olegario **32** 169
Meneses, Rodrigo Aires de Sá e, Marquês de Fontes *see* FONTES E ABRANTES, Marquês de
Meneses, Visconde de **4** 638
Meneses Osorio, Francisco **21** 129*
Menestrier, Claude-François **10** 176; **23** 770; **24** 467; **32** 574
works **23** *770*
Menez **21** 129*; **25** 300
Menez de Sylva, Amedeo **28** 531
Menezes, José de, Bishop of the Algarve **1** 679
Menezes, Luiz da Cunha *see* CUNHA MENEZES, LUIZ DA
Menezes, Muoka Mutiso *see* MUTISO, DAVID
Menezes Coutinho e Vasconcelos, Fernando de **19** 655
Menganti, Alessandro **5** 856
Mengari, Carlo **3** 868
Mengaroni, Ferruccio **24** 535
Mengazzino *see* SANTI, DOMENICO
Meng Chengshun **6** 542
Mengel, Erik C. **8** 759
Mengelberg, Egidius **4** 114; **21** 129
Mengelberg, Heinrich Otto **21** 129
Mengelberg, (Friedrich) Wilhelm **21** 129*; **30** 485
Mengen **24** 84
Menger, J. P. **27** 282
Mengersdorf, Ernst von, Bishop of Bamberg **33** 434
Meng Haoran Suzhou Jade **16** IV
Menghini, Nicolò **26** 771
Mengi Berti al-Haj al-Ahlati **18** 233
Mengin, Antonio **20** 924
Mengin, Sigisbert **11** 642; **22** 456
Mengli Giray I, Khan (*reg* 1466-74; 1475-6; 1478-1514) (Giray Khans) **3** 84
Mengli Giray II, Khan (*reg* 1724-30; 1737-40) (Giray Khans) **31** 564
Mengolini family **3** 868
Mengoni, Giuseppe **21** 129–30*; **26** 190
works **16** 647; **21** *130*, 520
Mengozzi, Girolamo **13** 740; **15** 139
Mengozzi-Colonna, Girolamo **16** 719; **30** 856, 857
Mengs, Anna Maria **12** 925; **21** 131; **27** 645
Mengs, Anton Raphael **4** 564; **10** 406; **12** 391; **17** 575, 892; **20** 67; **21** 130, 131–4*, *132*; **26** 774, 842; **29** 283
assistants **3** 424, 426; **6** 47, 111; **12** 923; **14** 16
attributions **20** 456
collaboration **5** 908; **20** 456; **31** 679; **33** 241
dealing **4** 564; **29** 354
groups and movements **10** 96; **22** 735
paintings
allegorical **16** 717, 772; **20** 72, 73; **23** 295; **26** 774, 841
mythological **25** 192
portraits **11** 410, 494
religious **5** 914; **15** 139
patrons and collectors **7** 412
Albani, Alessandro, Cardinal **1** 533; **16** 677
Augustus III, King of Poland (*reg* 1733-63) **33** 115
Borbón y Braganza, Sebastián Gabriel **4** 378
Brudenell, John, Marquess Monthermer and Baron Montagu **4** 894
Charles III, King of Spain (*reg* 1759-88) **4** 562
Charles IV, King of Spain (*reg* 1788-1808) **4** 565
Mengs, Anton Raphael
patrons and collectors—cont.
Clement XIII, Pope (*reg* 1758-69) **26** 286
Corcoran, William Wilson **7** 840
Cowper, George Nassau Clavering, 3rd Earl **8** 83
Harrach, Ernst Guido, Graf von **14** 190
Hoare (i), Henry the younger (1705-85) **14** 598
Iriarte, Bernardo de **16** 48
Maria Amalia, Queen of Spain (1724-60) **4** 562; **22** 479
Pius VI, Pope (*reg* 1775-80) **25** 8
Poniatowski, Stanisław, Prince **25** 213
Robinson, Thomas, 2nd Baron Grantham **26** 475
Smithson (Percy), Hugh, 1st Duke and 2nd Earl of Northumberland **1** 533
Stanislav II Poniatowski, King of Poland (*reg* 1764-95) **25** 212
Swymmer, Anthony Langley **27** 356
Tarnowski, Jan Feliks, Count and Waleria **30** 345
Williams-Wynn, Watkin, 4th Baronet, of Wynnstay (1749-89) **32** 790; **33** 209
Yusupov, Nikolay (Borisovich), Prince (1751- 1831) **33** 579
personal collection **6** 97; **11** 8
pupils **20** 456
Als, Peder **1** 686
Brompton, Richard **4** 845
Byres, James **5** 336
Casanova, Giovanni Battista **5** 908
Ceán Bermúdez, Juan Agustín **6** 123
Follin, Bartolomeo **11** 241
Guibal, Nicolas **13** 805
Quarenghi, Giacomo **25** 790
Rehberg, Friedrich **26** 98
West, Benjamin **33** 91
Zick (ii), Januarius **33** 671
reproductive prints by others **8** 267; **32** 99
teachers **7** 682
writings **2** 171, 889; **9** 18; **13** 468; **31** 300
Mengs, Ismael Israel **21** 130; **33** 115
Mengs, Juliane Charlotte **21** 130
Mengs, Theresia Concordia **13** 301; **20** 456; **21** 130, 131*
Mengshoel, Hans Christian **23** 234
Meng Tian **13** 333
Meng T'ien *see* MENG TIAN
Mengu, Khan (*reg* 1251-60) (Great Khans) **21** 874, 881
Mengucci, Giovanni Francesco **18** 733
Mengujak, Ahmad Shah *see* AHMAD SHAH MENGUJAK
menhirs **20** 170; **21** 40, 134*; **23** 833; **25** 498, 504–5*
see also MEGALITHS; MONOLITHS
menhirs (statue) *see under* SCULPTURE → types
Meni **22** 509
Menia, Il **3** 385; **17** 626
Menichini, Giuliano **26** 306
Menidi **14** 354
Menier **10** 421; **27** 879
Meniko **8** 335
Menil, de (family) **14** 802
Menil, Dominique de **21** 134–5*; **27** 222
Menil, John de **21** 134–5*; **27** 222
Menil Collection *see under* HOUSTON (TX)
Menin, Ludovico **28** 391
Menini, Felipe **8** 267
Meninsky, Bernard **11** 784; **14** 718; **17** 631; **24** 241; **26** 334
Menkauhor (*reg c.* 2396-*c.* 2388 BC) **9** *776*
Menkaure *see* MYCERINUS
Menkemaborg **22** 865
Menkès, Sigmund **17** 577
Menkheperraseneb **9** 822, 902
Menkheperre *see* TUTHMOSIS III
Menkov, Mikhail **30** 8
Menla Döndrup Gyatso **30** 848
Menn, Barthélemy **12** 277; **21** 135–6*
assistants **28** 750
pupils **3** 291, 391; **5** 265; **6** 66; **14** 614
works **21** *136*; **30** 134
Menn, Christian **4** 804
Menna **9** 840, 902; **21** 136*; **29** 664
Mennecy, Château de Villeroy **16** 855
Mennecy Porcelain Factory **11** 608; **21** 136–7*; **30** 97, 100
production **11** *608*
Mennicken (family) **3** 589; **12** 429
Mennicken, Baldem **3** 588; **25** 845
Mennicken, Jan Baldems **3** 588; **25** 845
Mennicken, Jan Emens **12** 429; **21** 137*; **25** 845
works **3** 588, *589*
Menniti, Mario *see* MINNITI, MARIO
Men of the Year 1909 *see* YOUNG ONES
Menologion of Basil II (Rome, Vatican, Bib. Apostolica, MS. Vat. gr. 1613) **9** 252, 616, 640; **16** 589; **21** 137–8*, *138*; **24** 23
Menominee **17** 770; **22** 552, 562, 627, 673
Menon, Anjolie **8** 677
Menon, V. K. Krishna, Museum *see under* CALICUT
Menon Painter *see* PSIAX
Menorca **21** 574; **29** *259*, 316–17
architecture **3** *105*
Menou, De **3** 461; **11** 652
Menours, Jacques de **4** 605
Menpes, Mortimer **9** 309; **21** 138*; **33** 141, 180
Mensah, Cietta **19** 310
Mensa Isiaca **3** 698; **10** 95
Menshikov, Aleksandr (Danilovich), Prince **12** 134; **19** 562; **27** 401; **28** 41
architecture **27** *574*
Mente, Giovan de *see* MONT, HANS
Mentessi, Giuseppe **21** 139*; **25** 567
Mentewab, Empress of Ethiopia (*reg* 1730-55) **10** 566
Mentijn, Simon **22** 850
Mentmore Towers (Bucks) **2** 324; **10** 142; **19** 231; **24** 821
paintings **3** 302; **5** 884
Mentuemhet **9** 841, 889, *889*, 891, 892; **21** 139*
paintings **9** 805
Mentuhotpe (scribe) **9** 858, 859
Mentuhotpe (family) **2** 422
Mentuhotpe I (*reg c.* 2008-*c.* 1957 BC) **9** *776*
Mentuhotpe II (*reg c.* 1957-*c.* 1945 BC) **9** *776*
chapel **8** 711
mortuary temple (Deir el-Bahri) **9** 779; **10** 80, 94; **30** 688
garden **12** 67
wall paintings **9** 811, 874, 900
statues **9** 874
Mentuhotpe II, mortuary temple of *see under* THEBES (i) (EGYPT) → mortuary temples
Mentuhotpe III (*reg c.* 1945-*c.* 1938 BC **2** 422; **9** *776*, 831, 874
Mentuhotpe VII **9** 879

Mentuhotpe-aa **9** 873
Mentzaina Basilica **9** 547
Menua, King of Urartu (*reg c.* 810-786 BC) **31** 699
Menua Canal **31** 700
menuisiers **21** 139*
Menumorut, Voivode of Wallachia **26** 706
Menuny **10** 66
Menus Plaisirs du Roi *see under* MAISON DU ROI
Menut-Alophe, Marie-Alexandre **13** 306
Menville, Vincenzo **20** 218
Menyhért, Miklós **13** 889
Menyő *see* MINEU
Menzel, Adolph (Friedrich Erdmann von) **21** 139–43*; **33** 369
groups and movements **26** 56; **32** 243
patrons and collectors **19** 335; **26** 406; **31** 397
works **3** 799–800, *800*; **4** 365; **9** 217, 225, *226*; **10** 555; **11** 463; **12** 393, 853; **14** 588; **15** 828, 829; **19** 486; **21** *140*, *141*; **31** 704
Menzel, Carl Erdmann **21** 139
Menzel, Dorothy **15** 67
Menzel, G. S. **8** 409
Menzel, Wolfgang **10** 211
Menzies & Son
works **11** *437*
Menzio, Francesco **31** 446
Menzocchi da Forlì, Francesco **24** 536; **27** 273
Méobecq
sculpture **26** 599
Meo da Caprino **21** 143–4*
works **31** 439, 447, *447*
Meo da Settignano *see* MEO DA CAPRINO
Meo (di Guido) da Siena **21** 144–5*
works **21** *145*
Meo di Pietro **28** 687
Meo Fiorentino *see* MEO DA CAPRINO
Meotoiwa **28** 638
Meque, Louis **33** 679
Méquesse **25** 771
Mequinez *see* MEKNÈS
Meram
congregational mosque **16** 202
Hasbey Hammam **16** 204
Merano, Francesco **11** 53
Merano, Giovanni Battista **21** 145–6*
teachers **6** 29; **11** 14, 53
works **24** 836
Mérard, Pierre **21** 146*
Merault, Pierre **19** 225
Mercadal, Fernando García *see* GARCÍA MERCADAL, FERNANDO
Mercadante, Lorenzo **21** 146–7*
works **12** 739; **13** 107, 108; **28** 518; **29** 289
Mercadé i Queralt, Jaume **23** 260; **29** 308, 346
Mercado, Antonieta Rivas *see* RIVAS MERCADO, ANTONIETA
Mercado, Antonio Rivas *see* RIVAS MERCADO, ANTONIO
Mercado, Conrado **24** 620
Mercado, Melchor María **4** 262, 268; **21** 147*
Mercado, Pedro del **29** 335
Mercandetti, Tommaso **20** 924
Mercatellis, Raphael de, Abbot of St Bavo **3** 555
Mercati, Michele **10** 119
Mercati, Venturino **19** 307
Mercator, Arnold **7** 581, 583
Mercator, Gerard **10** 389
atlases **2** 695, *695*; **12** 820; **20** 364
globes **12** 812, 814
manuals **28** 307
Mercator, Gerard—cont.
maps **4** 360; **14** 708
Merced Rada, José de la **32** 173
Mercer, Alexander Cavalie **5** 564
Mercer, Henry Chapman **30** 887
Mercereau, Alexandre **1** 21; **8** 243, 244; **25** 747
mercerization *see under* COTTON → techniques
Merchant, Ismail **15** 743
merchants **6** 620; **13** 486
Merchant Taylors' Company **3** 233
Merchem **6** 55, 56
Castle **6** 53
Mercié, (Marius-Jean-) Antonin **11** 563, 565; **12** 488; **21** 147*
pupils
Brancusi, Constantin **4** 659
Frampton, George (James) **11** 499
Laszczka, Konstanty **18** 822
MacMonnies, Frederick William **20** 30
Morlon, Pierre-Alexandre **22** 125
Nikoladze, Yakov **23** 143
Nikolov, Andrey **23** 143
Pomeroy, Frederick William **25** 187
Sandoz, Edouard-Marcel **27** 724
Simões de Almeida, José **28** 748
teachers **10** 771; **17** 667
works **11** 563; **26** 353
Mercier (family) **8** 63
Mercier, A. **18** 236
Mercier, Charlotte **21** 149
Mercier, Dorothy **21** 149
Mercier, François **11** 770
Mercier, J.-M. **19** 153
Mercier, Philip **21** 147–9*; **33** 545
patrons and collectors **14** 143
reproductive prints by others **21** 416
works **7** 785; **10** 785; **11** 37; **12** 294; **21** *148*
Mercier, Pierre **3** 804; **12** 468; **21** 147; **30** 322
Mercier, Pierre-Philippe *see* MERCIER, PHILIP
Mercimekli **9** 543
Mar Lazarus **31** 435
Mar Symeon **31** 435
Merck, Johann Heinrich **9** 443
Merckel, C. A. **28** 51
Merckell, Konrad *see* MERKLIN, KONRAD
Merckem Castle (Belgium) **6** 53
Merckerghem Castle (France) **6** 53
Mercks, Petrus Paulus *see* MERCX, PETER PAUL
Mercoeur, Duc de **8** 902
Mercogliano, Pacello da *see* PACELLO DA MERCOGLIANO
Mercouri, Melina **2** 555
Mercure de France, Le **12** 208; **13** 232; **18** 796; **24** 426, 427
Mercuri, Paolo **4** 123
Mercuriale, Girolamo **19** 373
Mercurius *see* JOHN II, Pope
mercury **17** 101; **21** 716, 718
gilding **6** 328; **9** 663; **12** 623, 624*, 869–70; **17** 101; **21** 331; **22** 774
mirrors **21** 716, 718, 720
photography **24** 650
soldering **21** 325
mercury iodide **24** 796
Mercx, Peter Paul **21** 149*
Mercy *see* MARSY
Mère, Clément **2** 521; **11** 601
Merecinus, Petrus *see* HEYDEN, PIETER VAN DER
Meredith, John **5** 569
Meredith, Louisa Ann **21** 149*
Merega, Yevgeny **21** 811
Merello, Rubaldo **16** 678
Meremetçi *see* MUSTAFA AĞA
Merenda **24** 204
Merengo, Enrigo **7** 650
Merenre (*reg c.* 2256-*c.* 2246 BC) **9** *776*, 870; **10** 35, *35*; **27** 812
Mereret **10** 30
Mereri **9** 874
Mereruka **21** 149–50*
drawings **9** 904
furniture **10** 51
inscriptions **10** 83
models **9** 822
reliefs **9** 673, 790; **10** 65
tomb **20** 596; **27** *811*, 812
wall paintings **9** 808, *817*, 817
Meresankh III **9** 789, 870; **10** 43, 50, 51
Meretta, Gustav **18** 467; **21** 150*; **23** 424
Meretyn, Bernard **19** 836; **25** 98, 364; **31** 552
Merevale Hall (Warwicks) **4** 439
Méréville **6** 171; **11** *504*; **12** 123; **21** 150*; **26** 449
Mereworth Castle (Kent) **10** 233, 278; **23** 858, *858*; **27** 237; **32** 553
East Pavilion **11** 243
portico **25** 266
Mergelpe Castle **22** 822
Mergem, Jan van *see* JEAN DE MARVILLE
Mergenov, Erkin **17** 867
Merguelte, José González *see* GONZÁLEZ MERGUELTE, JOSÉ
Mergui **5** 255
Merhautova, A. **8** 426
Merhing, Howard **32** 890
Meriamlık, St Thekla **9** 537
Merian (family) **17** 886; **21** *153*
Merian, Caspar **4** 756; **21** 151, 152; **29** 644
works **33** *50*
Merian, Maria Sibilla **21** 151, 153–4*; **23** 308
works **2** 105; **11** 229; **21** *154*; **30** 15, *15*
Merian, Matthäus (i) (1593-1650) **11** 735; **14** 502; **21** 151–2*, 580
assistants **14** 683
collaboration **4** 746
patrons and collectors **33** 274
prints **12** 390; **22** 249; **29** 59, 577; **30** 132; **31** 154
Cologne **7** 583
Lausanne **18** 873
Münchenstein **21** *152*
Nuremberg **33** 295
Paris **22** *298*
Schloss Ambras (Innsbruck) **15** *867*
Schwalbach **21** 711
publications **17** 565
pupils **18** 46, 535; **21** 152, 406
reproductive prints by others **4** 468; **18** 534; **30** *221*
works **24** 118
writings **13** 809
Merian, Matthäus (ii) (1621-87) **21** 151, 152–3*
pupils **21** 407; **33** 82
works **3** *789*; **12** 390; **14** 669; **21** *153*; **33** 287
Merica, Petrus a *see* HEYDEN, PIETER VAN DER
Méricourt **29** 900
Mérida (Spain) **27** 57
Alcazaba **16** 157; **21** 582
amphitheatre **1** 797; **26** 904
aqueduct **2** 242; **27** 7
Augusta Emerita **2** 721–2*; **26** *908*; **29** *259*
bridge **4** 800
forum **27** 31
glass **27** 74
House of the Amphitheatre **27** 52
House of the Mithraeum **27** 63
houses **26** 904
Museo Nacional de Arte Romano **2** 722; **21** 861; **22** 368; **29** 274, 355
Mérida (Spain)—cont.
Roman circus **7** 342
S Eulalia **29** 261
theatre **26** 904, 905; **30** 652
Mérida (Mexico) **21** 154–5*, 265, *372*
Casa de Montejo **21** 376; **33** 571
Cathedral of S Ildefonso **21** 154, 375; **33** 571
Church of the Third Order of the Jesuits **33** 571
Monastery **33** 571
Museo Regional de Antropología de Yucatán **21** 155
Palacio Cantón *see* Museo Regional de Antropología de Yucatán
S Cristóbal **33** 571
Universidad del Mayab **21** 382
Mérida (Venezuela) **32** *165*
painting **32** 173
rugs **32** 177, *177*
textiles **32** 178
Mérida, Carlos **13** 765; **21** 155*, 388, 390
collaboration **24** 9
patrons and collectors **13** 769
works **22** 334
Mérida, Jose **24** 500
Meriden Britannia Co. **31** 650
Meriden Gravure **7** 576; **26** 236
Merigliano, Giovanni *see* MARIGLIANO, GIOVANNI
Merimar **17** 550
Merimda **9** 849
Merimée, Léonor **12** 158
Mérimée, Prosper **11** 521, 672; **23** 148
Měřín, St John the Baptist **26** 638
Merina **20** 35, 36, 38, 40
jewellery **20** *39*
Merindole, Jules **22** 73
Mering, Everhard Oswald von **7** 584
Merini, Cosimo **8** 204
Merino, Emilio Boix *see* BOIX MERINO, EMILIO
Merino, Francisco **21** 156*; **28** 516; **29** 334; **31** 90
Merino, Ignacio **21** 156*; **22** 20; **24** 508, 516, 517
Merino wool *see under* WOOL → types
Merion Station (PA), Barnes Foundation **3** 251–2; **12** 769; **13** 826; **19** 438
Merioola Group **23** 336
Merisi, Fermo **5** 702
Merisi, Michelangelo *see* CARAVAGGIO, MICHELANGELO MERISI DA
Merivale, John Herman **31** 233
Merk, Gottfried **22** 306
Merka **9** 868
Merkel, Leo **6** 363
Merkelbach, Ben(jamin) **21** 156*
groups and movements **2** 318
staff **4** 216
works **10** 163; **13** 679; **30** 871
Merkelbach, Reinhold **26** 374
Merkelbach & Karsten **21** 156
Merken, L. W. van **32** 591
Merkinė **19** *494*
church **19** 495
Merklein, Juan Andrés **3** 424
Merklin, Konrad **21** 157*
Merkulov, Pyotr **3** 527
Merkur **24** 443
Merkurov, Sergey (Dmitriyevich) **2** 437; **21** 157*; **27** 394, 396; **33** 518
Merle, Comte de **23** 778
Merle, Hugues **13** 228
Merle, Jacques van **24** 890
Merleau-Ponty, Maurice **1** 182; **10** 686; **21** 157–8*
Merlemont Church **30** 907
Merlen, Jacobus van **11** 155
Merlen, Theodor van, I (*c.* 1600-59) **22** 717; **28** 506
Merlen, Theodor van, II (1609-72) **7** 466
Merli, Carlo Giuseppe *see* MERLO, CARLO GIUSEPPE
Merli, J. **19** 497
Merlimond, Oliver de *see* OLIVER DE MERLIMOND
Merlin, Henry Beaufoy **2** 745; **3** 427
Merlin, Thomas **11** 618; **24** 146
Merlina, Nadezhda **27** 431
Merling & Mertens **25** 857
Merlini, Cosimo **21** 158
Merlini, Domenico **21** 158*; **32** 871
assistants **17** 756; **18** 490
collaboration **32** 879
patrons and collectors **25** 211, 212; **32** 880–81
works **23** 813; **25** 99; **29** 839, 912; **32** *880*
Merlini, Giovanbattista **23** 265
Merlini, Lorenzo **12** 6; **21** 158–9*
Merlini, Marc Antonio **12** 6; **23** 265
Merlino, Dionis **28** 859
Merlino, Guido di *see* GUIDO DI MERLINO
Merlo, Carlo Giuseppe **21** 159*, 519, 532
Merlo, de (family) **13** 763
Merlo, Giraldo de **13** 732; **21** 159*; **31** 89
Merlo, Pedro Francisco de **21** 159
Merlo, Tomás de (1694-1739) **2** 143; **13** 769; **21** 159*
Merlo, Tomás de la Vega *see* (1659-1749) VEGA MERLO, TOMÁS DE LA
merlons **8** 138; **21** 546
Merlzioun, Walter **29** 679
Mermesha **9** 879
Merneith **27** 810
Merneptah (*reg c.* 1213-*c.* 1204 BC) **9** *777*, 805; **10** 80; **16** 572
architecture **12** 227; **14** 462; **23** 807
Merodach-Baladan, King of Babylon (*reg* 721-711 BC) **3** *12*
Mérode, Comte de **3** 600
Merode, Hendrik van **22** *200*
Mérode, Master of **20** 669, 730*
Mérode Altarpiece **11** 438; **19** 354, 356; **31** 50, 154, 246
Mérode Cup **10** 195; **13** 170
Mérode-Westerloo, Marquis de **25** 53
Meroë **21** 160–61*; **23** *276*, 282
ceramics **23** 284
collections **29** 898
palaces **21** 160; **23** 283
pyramid of Natakhamani **23** 284
pyramids **9** 842; **25** 763
Roman bath *see* water sanctuary
sculpture **4** 851
temples **21** 160; **23** 281
Begarawiya North 7 **23** 284
Begarawiya North 19 **23** 284
Begarawiya North 22 **23** 284
Begarawiya North 32 **23** 284
M292 **23** 284
mortuary temples **23** 284
Temple of Apedemak **21** *160*; **23** 283
Temple of Isis **23** 283
Temple M195 **23** 283
Temple M250 **23** 283
tombs **23** 281, 282, 283
tomb of Queen Amaniskakheto **23** 285
water sanctuary **23** 283
Meroitic period *see under* NUBIA → periods
Meronas **8** 156
Merovingian **21** 161–5*
amber **1** 761

Merovingian—cont.
architecture **11** 509*; **21** 163*; **25** 85, 88
baptisteries **25** *86*
cameos **21** *162*
capitals **17** *665*
chalices **21** *163*
coins **7** 533; **21** 162
dress **9** 252–3*
enamel **21** *163*
fibulae **21** *162*
filigree **21** *162*, *163*
garnets **21** 162, *162*
glass **21** 163
gold **21** *162*, *163*
gravestones **21** *164*
initials (manuscript) **15** 847
ivory **21** 164
jewellery **21** 161–2*
manuscript illumination **21** 164–5*
metalwork **21** 161–3*
miniatures (manuscript illumination) **31** *48*
ornament **23** 536
patens **21** *163*
reliquaries **26** 144–5*
rock crystal **26** 485
sarcophagi **21** 163–4*
sculpture **21** 163–4*
stone-carvings **21** *164*
title-pages **31** 48, *48*
wood-carvings **21** 164
see also FRANKISH ART
Merport, I. **30** 352
Merrett, Christopher **10** 316
Merrick, Paul **31** 864
Merrifield, Mary Philadelphia **21** 165*; **22** 329; **32** 806; **33** 309
Merrild, Knud **19** 702; **31** 607
Merrill, John O(gden) **28** 817–18*
Merrin Head **8** 314
Merritt, Anna Lea **21** 165*; **31** 250
Merritt, George **8** 575
Merritt, Henry **21** 165
Merrymount *see under* TYPE-FACES
Merrymount Press **2** 572; **31** 680
Merrythought cups *see under* CUPS → types
Mersch **19** 826
Mersch, Passcier van der **20** 692; **21** 102
Merse, Pál Szinyei *see* SZINYEI MERSE, PÁL
Merseburg **12** 412; **26** 632
Cathedral **26** 632
memorial to Rudolf of Swabia **12** 399, *399*; **26** 684; **31** 122
palace of Henry I **23** 649
Mersham-le-Hatch (Kent) **7** 171, 172; **11** 119, 430
Mersin **1** *821*, 824, *849*, 893; **21** 166*
architecture **1** 824, 830
bronze **1** 824
Mersinaki **8** 342
Merson, Charles-Olivier **21** 166
Merson, Luc Olivier **14** 853; **21** 166–7*
groups and movements **23** 504
pupils **2** 700; **4** 588; **8** 521; **9** 396; **12** 878; **20** 387; **25** 752
Mersy *see* MARSY
Merta
congregational mosque **15** 372
'idgāhs **15** 372
Mertens, Charles **21** 167*; **32** 259
Mertens, D. **10** 415
Mertens, Hennen **13** 22
Mertens, Herman Frederik **31** 576
Mertens, Jan, the elder (*fl c.* 1473–1509) **21** 167
Mertens, Jan, the younger (1470–1527) **2** 204, 206; **4** *895*; **21** 167*
attributions **20** 612
pupils **2** 540; **7** 518
teachers **13** 22
Mertens, Jan (*fl c.* 1620) **25** 127
Mertens-Schaaffhausen, Sybille **12** 266
Merthyr Tydfil (Mid Glams) **32** *780*
Cyfarthfa Castle **32** 784
Cyfarthfa ironworks **32** 783
The Triangle **32** 783
Mertijn, Jacques de Riva **10** 222
Mértola
Castle **25** 311
congregational mosque **4** 784
Merton (Surrey) **10** 356
St Mary's Priory **33** 6
seals **33** *5*
Merton, Samuel **19** 11
Merton Abbey Studio **10** 351; **19** 596; **22** 144; **30** 326, 327, 328
Mertoun **25** 68
Mertz, Albert **8** 736
Merula, Carlo Giuseppe *see* MERLO, CARLO GIUSEPPE
Meruvarman, Ruler (*reg c.* 700) (Karkota) **6** 566
Merv (Turkmenistan) **6** *182*, 201, 209; **15** *901*; **16** *105*; **21** 167–70*; **28** *719*, 721; **31** 457, *458*
Abdallahkhan-kala **21** 167, 169
architecture **6** 210; **16** 161; **31** 459; **32** 321
Bairamalikhan-kala **21** 167, 169
citadel **6** 210
coins **16** 512
congregational mosque **6** 211
Erk-kala **21** 167, 168, *168*
fortifications **6** 196; **21** 584, 591
governors' palace **16** 163
Gyaur-kala **6** 223; **21** 167, 168; **23** 607
houses **16** 154, 269
madrasas **20** 55
mausoleum of Sultan Sanjar **6** 202; **16** 163, 164; **21** *169*, 169–70*; **31** 111, 112
plaster **29** 822
metalwork **6** 238, 239; **16** 373
palace **23** 815
pottery **6** 258; **16** 400, 425
sculpture **6** 275
stelae **29** 618
stucco **29** 821
Sultan-kala **21** 167, 168, 169; **29** 822
terracottas **6** 275
textiles **16** 433; **31** 21
urban planning **16** 264
Merv (Uzbekistan) **6** 196
Merveilleux, Charles-Frédéric **25** 820
Mervile, Jehan de *see* JEAN DE MARVILLE
Merville, Friedrich **21** 170
Merville, Karl Georg **21** 170*; **32** 454
Merville, Maria Anna *see* TORRICELLA, MARIA ANNA
Merwart, Paul **30** 16
Mer-wer *see* MEIR
Méry, Vincent **31** 130
Meryaa **9** 874
Merymose **10** 13
Meryon, Charles **21** 170–71*
collaboration **20** 603
groups and movements **26** 742
patrons and collectors **5** 284; **19** 239
works **9** 204; **10** 555, 556; **21** *171*; **31** 156
Meryptah **9** 860
Meryre **9** *898*
tomb **9** *840*
Meryre, Prince (*fl* 1075–656) **2** 690
Meryre I **9** 805
Meryre II **9** 826; **33** 246
Mèry-sur-Oise **33** 131
Merytamun **10** 10
Merytaten, Princess **23** 788
Merz **2** 552; **8** 437; **21** 171*; **28** 196–8
works **28** *197*
Merz **19** 476; **21** 171; **24** 428; **28** 197
Merz, Gerhard **12** 472
Merz, Hans **21** 67
Merz, Joseph Anton **3** 779; **14** 694
Merz, Mario **21** 171–2*; **30** 201
collaboration **21** 172
groups and movements **2** 527; **10** 416; **16** 709
works **2** *527*; **16** *708*; **22** 748
Merz, Marisa **21** 171, 172*
Merz & McLellan **25** 403
Merz-Werbezentrale **28** 197
Mes **27** 812
Mesa, Alonso de **23** 905
Mesa, Blas de **13** 763; **14** 714
Mesa, Gregorio **27** 819
Mesa, José de **4** 269, 270
Mesa, Juan de **21** 173*
pupils **26** 302
works **21** *173*; **22** 3; **23** 625; **29** 291
Mesa-Bains, Amalia **33** 316
Mesakin Nuba **23** 275
Mésangère, Pierre de La *see* LA MÉSANGÈRE, PIERRE DE
Mesara **8** 153; **13** *362*; **21** 173–4*, *651*
faience (i) (glass) **21** 683, 684
gold **21** 686, 687
ivory-carvings **21** 680
pottery **21** 667
seals **21** 682, 684, 691
tombs **21** 664
vessels **21** 689
Mesarites, Nikolaos *see* NIKOLAOS MESARITES
Mesa Rodríguez, Oscar **21** 4
Mesastris, Pierantonio *see* MEZZASTRIS, PIERANTONIO
Mesa Verde (CO) **1** 820; **21** 174*; **22** *544*, 566
Cliff Palace **21** *174*
Mesdag, H(endrik) W(illem) **11** 885; **21** 175–6*
groups and movements **14** 47; **20** 435, 871
personal collection **4** 588; **22** 906
pupils **14** 589
teachers **26** 528
works **11** 448; **14** 43, *43*; **21** *175*; **22** 849; **24** 19
Mesdag, H(endrik) W(illem), Rijksmuseum *see under* HAGUE, THE → museums
Mesdag, Sientje *see* HOUTEN, SIENTJE VAN
Mesdag-van Houten, Sientje *see* HOUTEN, SIENTJE VAN
Mesehti **10** 16, *40*
Mesembria *see* NESEBĂR
Mesens, E(douard-)L(éon-)T(héodore) **3** 565; **20** 101, 414; **21** 176*
groups and movements **30** 20, 22
Mesha **9** 737
Meshad Hashavyahu **13** 499
Mesha Stele **17** 655
Meshed *see* MASHHAD
Meshkov, Vasily Nikitich **31** 571; **32** 579
Mesita A **27** 700
Mesita B
sculpture **27** *700*
Mesitas, Las *see* LAS MESITAS
Mesius, Quintinus *see* METSYS, QUINTEN
Meskalamdug **21** 303
Mesken *see* MASKANA
Meskendir
SS Peter and Paul **5** 676
St Stephan **5** 676
Meskene *see* BALIS
Meskla, Church of Our Saviour Christ **8** 156; **9** 584
Mesmakher, Maksimilian (Yegorovich) **21** 177*
Mesme, Jean-Antoine de **4** 225
Mesnard, Albert **22** 36
Mesnier du Ponsard, Raul **25** 293
Mesnil, Elie **20** 914
Mesnil, Oscar du, Baron **12** 267
Mesny, Barthélemy **22** 456
Mesoamerica, Pre-Columbian **21** 177–266*, *178*, *193*; **33** 101
actinolite **21** 241
adobe **4** 796
alloys **21** 253
altars **1** *700*, 700–701*; **25** 764; **31** 505
alum **21** 261
amazonite **21** 241
amber **1** 761
amethyst **21** 241
amphiboles **21** 241
amphibolite **21** 241
amulets **21** 243, 248
aprons **21** 249
aragonite **21** 241, *243*
archaeology **21** 263
arches **21** *205*
architecture **7** 484; **21** 204–12*, *210*, *214*, *215*, 216*, 700
Classic (*c.* AD 250–*c.* 900) **21** 216–17*
Guatemala **24** *744*
Huastec **14** 829
Maya **20** 881; **21** 212–16*
Mexico **30** *483*; **31** *778*
military **21** *598*, 598–9*
Olmec **23** 416–18
Pre-Classic (*c.* 2000 BC–*c.* AD 250) **21** 216*
rock-cut **21** 208
Toltec **31** 98–9
West Mexico **33** 102
armour **21** 244–7, *245*
arrowheads **21** 192
arrows **21** 245, 246
art history **2** 533; **21** 262–3*
astronomy **31** 778
axes **21** *242*, 246; **23** 418
azurite **1** 713
ballcourts **3** 117–18*, *118*; **5** 408; **6** 579; **20** *883*; **21** 187; **27** 756; **30** 254
bamboo **10** *779*; **21** 241
basalt **21** *188*, *218*, 251; **23** *417*; **30** *341*
baths **3** 378*
batik **21** 261
beads **21** 243, 259, 260
bells **21** 254, 256
beryl **22** 158
blackstone **21** 251
bloodstone (chalcedony) **21** 241
blow guns **21** 245, 246
body arts **21** 258
body ornaments **21** 248
bone **4** 314; **21** 256, 257
bone-carvings **21** 247–8*
bowls **21** *240*
bows **21** 245, 246
brick **4** 796*; **7** 645
bronze **21** 245
calendars **1** 14; **6** 579; **9** 498; **22** 444; **23** 338; **27** 786; **31** 778
Aztec **21** *224*, 234, 265
Maya **21** 234
Mixtec **21** 234
canals **9** 741
cane **21** 249
caricatures **5** 761*
cartography **21** 235
caskets **21** 259
catalogues **21** 265
catechisms **21** 233
causeways **6** 96–7*, *97*
caves **22** 443
celts **18** *881*; **21** 242, 266
ceramics **1** 706; **21** 181, 195, 266, 737
West Mexico **33** 102, *102*
chacmools **28** 640
Mesoamerica, Pre-Columbian—cont.
chalcedony **21** 192, 241, 243
chert **1** 713; **21** 192, 246
chronicles **21** 235
chronologies **21** *191*, 191–2*, 262, 263; **31** 507
cinnabar **1** 713; **21** 250, 259
clay **21** *193*, 250; **26** *181*; **33** 617, *619*
clubs (weapons) **21** 245, 246
coatepantlis **7** *481*, 481–2*
collections **21** 262*, 264–5*, *265*, 266; **26** 426
colour **7** 635–6*; **21** 183
copies **21** 266
copper **21** 245, 253, 256, 259
copperas **21** 261
coral **7** 836; **21** 251, 260
cosmologies **21** 183–4*, *184*, 209
cotton **21** 234, 246, 249, 261
craftsmen and artists **21** 190–91*, *190*, 195, 198, 236, 238, 249
crypts **23** 838
daguerreotypes **21** 263
darts **21** 245, 246
dating methods **21** 266
diorite **21** 243, *251*
doors **9** 165–6*, *166*
dress **21** *261*, 261–2*
drills **21** 241
drums (musical instruments) **21** 256–7*, *257*
dyeing **21** 261, *261*
dyes **9** 492; **21** 249, 261
ear-spools **21** 260
earthenwares **21** 236
earthworks **21** 204
embroidery **21** 261
emery **21** 241, 259
encyclopedias **21** 233
erotic art **10** 474
ethnic groups **21** 181*
exchange **21** 181–2*
exhibitions **21** 264–5*, *265*
fans **10** *779*, 779–80*; **21** 250
feathers **10** *779*; **21** 245, 249–50*, *250*, 261
duck **21** 249
quetzal **10** 848
figurines **21** 195, 235*, 236–40, 242, 250; **30** 511–12
Aztec **21** 243
Huastec **14** 830–31
Maya **21** *239*, 247, 251, 256
Mexico **8** 255; **18** *881*; **21** *218*, *238*, *239*; **33** *619*
Olmec **18** *881*; **21** 241; **23** 418
Palaeolithic **21** *194*
Pre-Classic (*c.* 2000 BC–*c.* AD 250) **21** *218*
Remojadas **26** 181
West Mexico **21** 196, *236*; **33** *102*
Zapotec **33** *619*
finials (architectural) **21** 207*
flint **21** 259
flutes (musical instruments) **21** 257*
forgeries **21** 266*
fortifications **21** 208*, *598*, 598–9*; **24** 367
friezes **31** 99, *99*, 778
fuchsite **21** 241, 243, 251
fur **21** 261
galena **1** 713
games **21** 187
gardens **12** 71*
garnets **22** 164
genealogies **21** 235
glues **21** 249
gold **12** 866; **16** 803; **21** 250, 252, *253*, 253; **22** 158
Maya **21** *253*, 253
gold leaf **21** 246
gourds **21** 256
greenstone **21** *185*, 240–41, 242, 251, *251*, 257; **23** 418
guilds **21** 249

Mesoamerica, Pre-Columbian—cont.
haematite **1** 713; **21** 241, 719
halls of columns **33** 101
hardstones **1** 713; **21** 218, 240–44*
hatchets **21** 245
headdresses **21** 246, 249, 250
helmets **21** 245; **22** 164
hides **21** 234
hieroglyphs **17** 753; **21** 219; **22** 443; **27** 607
historiography **21** 234
houses **21** 204, 207–8*; **32** 305
human figures **21** 218
humming-bird feathers **21** 249
iconoclasm **23** 417–18
iconography **21** 182–3*, 184–6*, 187–90*, 218, 373–4, *374*; **29** 133
Maya **21** *184*
Mixteca-Puebla **21** 739
ideograms **21** 248
ikat **21** 261
ilmenite **21** 241, 718
inscriptions **21** 264; **24** 743; **29** 620
jade **16** 858, 859; **21** 240–41, 242, 257, 260, 719
Aztec **16** 859; **21** 243, 252
chloromelanite **21** 241
jadeite **16** 861*, *861*; **21** 240, 241, *242*; **22** 158
Maya **1** 735; **16** II1; **21** 243, 251, 259
Mixtec **21** 243
nephrite **21** 240, 241
Olmec **18** *881*; **21** 242, 251; **23** 418
Zapotec **21** 251
jasper **21** 241
jewellery **21** 253, 260; **23** 418
joinery **5** 408
knife-handles **21** 246, 255; **22** 164
knives **21** 245
labyrinths **18** 586*
languages **21** 181*, 262, 736, 738; **27** 158
leather **21** 245
lignite **21** 246
lime **21** 205
limestone **21** *223*; **29** *620*
limonite **1** 713
lintels **9** 165
looms **21** 261
magnetite **21** 195, 241, 718
maguey **21** 249
malachite **1** 713; **22** 158
manuscript illumination **21** *184*, 233–5*, 737, *738*; **22** *518*
manuscripts **20** 886; **21** 233–5*, 266
maps **21** 234, 235
marcasite **22** 158
masks **16** *861*; **21** 241, *242*, *243*, 247, 250–52*, *251*, 254, 255, *255*, 266, IV1; **22** 158, 164
Maya **16** II1
masonry **20** 570; **21** 205; **24** 367; **31** 310
mazes **18** 586*
metadiorite **21** 241, 242
metalwork **21** 200, 252–4*, *253*; **33** 103
metalworkers **21** 252
Mexican onyx **21** 241
mines **1** 713
miniatures (manuscript illumination) **21** *234*
mirror frames **21** *719*
mirrors **21** 195, 241, 718–19*, *719*
mitres **21** 249
Mixtec **26** 487
monoliths **5** 412
monuments **18** *645*; **21** 209
mosaics **21** 241, 251–2, 254–6*, 737, IV1; **22** 158, 164*; **31** 778
Aztec **21** 244, 248, 255
Mesoamerica, Pre-Columbian mosaics—cont.
Maya **17** *715*; **21** 243, 254
Mexico **17** *715*; **21** *255*
Mixtec **21** *255*, *734*
Olmec **21** 254
mother-of-pearl **21** 251; **22** 158, 164, 205
mouldings **21** 206
mounds **23** 417
mud **21** 226
museums **21** 264–5*
musical instruments **21** 236, 247, 248, 256*, 257
narratives **22** 517–19*, *518*
necklaces **21** 259, 260
observatories **23** 338
obsidian **21** 181, 192, 195, 198, 245, 246, 251, 254, 718, 719, *719*; **22** 158, 164; **29** 703
ocarinas **21** 257
onyx **21** 251
ornament **23** 564–5*
painting
fresco **21** 226*, *228*, 229, *230*, 251
tomb **21** *230*
wall **21** 226–32*, *229*, *230*, 260; **27** 786; **32** 803*
Huastec **14** 831; **21** 227
Maya **4** 295–6, *296*; **7** I1; **21** 259; **26** *411*, 411–12; **31** 507
Maya region **21** 231–2*
Mexico **4** *296*; **5** *357*; **26** *411*; **30** *484*
Mixtec **21** 231
Olmec **21** 226
Zapotec **21** 230–31*
palaces **21** 204, *207*; **23** 825–6*, *825*
Maya **17** *715*; **18** *578*; **21** *204*, *208*; **23** 837; **28** 26, *26*
Mexico **17** *715*; **18** *578*; **28** *26*
Mixtec **21** *734*
palettes **21** 241
paper **21** 233, 245, 249, *250*, 266
parapets **21** 206, *207*
patronage **21** 191
pectoral ornaments **21** 266
pendants (jewellery) **21** 241
Huastec **21** 260
Maya **21** 243, 247
Mixtec **21** 243
Olmec **21** 242
Toltec **21** 243, 260
periods **23** 416
Archaic (before *c.* 2000 BC) **21** *191*, 192–4*
Classic (*c.* AD 250-*c.* 900) **21** *191*, 192, 197–8*, 200*
Classic, Early (*c.* AD 250-*c.* 600) **21** *191*
Classic, Late (*c.* AD 600-*c.* 900) **21** *191*
Palaeolithic **21** 192*
Post-Classic (*c.* AD 900-1521) **21** *191*, 192, 200*, 202*
Post-Classic, Early (*c.* AD 900-*c.* 1200) **21** *191*
Post-Classic, Late (*c.* 1200-1521) **21** *191*
Pre-Classic (*c.* 2000 BC-*c.* AD 250) **21** *191*, 192, 194–5*
Pre-Classic, Early (*c.* 2000-*c.* 1000 BC) **21** *191*
Pre-Classic, Late (*c.* 300 BC-*c.* AD 250) **21** *191*
Pre-Classic, Middle (*c.* 1000-*c.* 300 BC) **21** *191*
Prehistoric **25** 468
photography **21** 263
pigments **21** 226, 233, 241
black **7** 636
blue **7** 636
blue-green **7** 636
red **7** 636
white **7** 636
Mesoamerica, Pre-Columbian pigments—cont.
yellow **7** 636
plaster **21** 226, 229; **29** 828–9*
platforms **25** 764
see also pyramids
porphyry **21** *244*
portraits **18** *675*; **21** *222*; **25** *825*
pottery **21** 235*, 236–40*, 249, 256, 257
Aztatlán **2** 904
Aztec **21** 266
Aztec ware **21** 240
Capacha-Opeño **5** 660, *660*
Codex style **21** 239
Coyotlatelco ware **21** 239
Fine Orange ware **6** 580; **17** 755; **21** 240; **28** 373
fine paste pottery **28** 373
Fortress White-on-Red Style **20** 886
Huastec **14** 831
Maya **21** *239*
Mazapan ware **20** 886; **21** 239
Mexico **2** 904; **7** 250; **21** *238*, *239*, *240*
Mixtec **21** *240*
Olmec **23** 418
Pabellón Modelled-carved ware **28** 373
Plumbate ware **6** 580; **17** 755; **20** 886; **21** 239
pox **33** 102
Red ware **18** 667
Thin Orange ware **17** 755; **21** 238
tipo códice **21** 737
Tiquisate Ware **17** 755
Usulután ware **17** 753; **21** 237
West Mexico **21** *236*
prase **21** 241
pyramids **6** 579; **21** 197, *211*, *214*, *215*; **25** 760, 764–5*, *765*; **30** 279–80, *453*; **31** 116
Guatemala **24** *744*
Mexico **7** 201, *201*; **30** *254*; **31** *65*
see also platforms
pyrite **21** 241, 251, 718, 719
quartz **21** 241; **22** 158
quartz sand **21** 241
quetzal **21** 249
ramps **25** 764
rattles **21** 256
rediscovery **21** 262–3*
reliefs **21** 219*
religion **21** 182–6*, *184*, 187–90*
roads **6** 96; **7** 484
rock art
carving **22** 443–4
painting **21** 192, 226*, 230; **22** 443–4, *444*
rock crystal **1** 713; **21** 241, 243; **26** 487
roofs **21** 205, 206–7*
sanctuaries **23** 838
sandstone **14** 830, *830*; **21** 719; **27** *832*
sarcophagi **27** *832*, 832–3*
saws **21** 241
scripts **21** 233*; **25** 468
Aztec **21** 233
cursive **23** 838
hieroglyphic **17** 753; **22** 443; **26** *411*
Maya **21** 233
sculpture **1** 735; **17** 753; **21** *185*, *188*; **24** 743; **33** 617, 618
Aztec **21** *400*
chacmools **21** 223, *223*
Chacula style **27** 158
clay **21** 236
colossal heads **21** 219; **22** 8–9; **23** *417*
colossal statues **21** 218
figure **4** 296–7; **5** *394*; **21** *244*; **27** 780
Huastec **14** *830*, 830–31
Mesoamerica, Pre-Columbian sculpture—cont.
Maya **4** 296–7; **21** 254; **33** 511
Maya region **21** 219–20*, 221–2*, *222*, 225*
Mexico **5** *409*; **14** *830*; **30** *341*; **33** *618*
monumental **21** 196, 217–18*, 236
Classic (*c.* AD 250-*c.* 900) **21** 220–22*
Maya **1** 14–15; **22** 8–9; **25** *825*, 825–6; **28** *373*
Olmec **18** *645*; **21** 195; **23** 416–18
Post-Classic (*c.* AD 900-1521) **21** 222–5*
Pre-Classic (*c.* 2000 BC-*c.* AD 250) **21** 218–20*
Zapotec **21** 195
relief **21** 198–9, *206*; **25** 764; **27** 780
Aztec **2** *906*, *907*
Honduras **7** *801*
Maya **6** *394*; **7** *801*; **21** 266; **23** *839*; **27** 607
Mexico **2** *907*; **8** *460*; **23** *839*; **33** *473*
Zapotec **8** *460*
Remojadas **26** *181*
stone **30** 340–41; **33** *103*
Tarascan **30** 340–41, *341*
Toltec **5** *409*; **31** 99
seals **21** 258*
cylinder **21** 258
Huastec **21** *258*
Mexico **21** *258*
stamp **21** 258, *258*
Toltec **21** *258*
serpentine **18** *881*; **21** 241
shells **21** 246, 251, 257, 259–60*, 719; **22** 158
busycon **21** 259
clam **21** 259
conch **14** 831; **21** 260
oliva **21** 259
oyster (thorny) **21** 259
strombus **21** 259
shields **14** 411; **21** 245, 246, 249, *250*, 255; **22** 164
shrines (i) (cult) **28** 640–41*
signatures **21** 249
silica **21** 241
silver **21** 253
skins **21** 234, 245, 252, 257, 261
deerskin **21** 233
skull racks **1** 701; **21** 188; **31** 505–6*, *506*; **33** 101
skulls **21** 248; **31** 505–6
slate **21** 718, 719
slings **21** 245
spearheads **21** 192, 245
spears **21** 245
spear-throwers **21** 245, 246
spindles **21** 236
squares (town) **21** 195
staircases **29** 527*, *527*
stairs **21** 206*; **25** 764, 765
stamps **21** 236
standards (vexilloid) **11** *152*, 152–3
stelae **24** 743; **25** 825; **27** 780; **29** 619–20*
Classic (*c.* AD 250-*c.* 900) **21** *220*
Honduras **7** *801*
Maya **5** 412; **7** *801*; **16** *807*; **21** 266; **28** *373*; **29** *620*
Mexico **16** *807*
Pre-Classic (*c.* 2000 BC-*c.* AD 250) **21** 219
stone **2** *907*; **8** *460*; **21** 206; **30** 340–41; **33** *103*
stone-carvings
Aztec **2** *906*; **21** *223*, *224*
Classic (*c.* AD 250-*c.* 900) **21** *221*
Maya region **21** *221*
Olmec **6** *393*; **18** 645; **23** 418
Zapotec **22** *8*
Mesoamerica, Pre-Columbian—cont.
stucco **18** *675*; **21** *222*, 266; **23** *839*; **29** *828*, 828–9*
swords **21** 245
tablets **21** 243
talud-tablero **21** 205–6*, *206*; **30** 279–80*, *280*
tempera **21** 226*
temples **6** *580*; **21** *211*, *214*, *215*; **25** 764; **30** 448–9*
Aztec **30** *453*
Guatemala **24** *744*
Maya **30** *448*, *449*, *872*; **31** *420*; **33** *510*
Mexico **30** *448*, *449*, *453*, *872*; **31** *420*; **33** *510*
terracotta **14** 830–31; **21** 256; **30** 511–12*; **33** *618*
textiles **21** 181–2, 259, 260–62*, *261*
thrones **30** 786*
tombs **25** 764; **31** *117*, 117–18*
Guatemala **17** *754*
Maya **17** *754*; **26** *411*, 411–12
shaft **21** 197, 216; **33** 101, 102
Zapotec **18** 675–6
tools **21** 190, 195, 247
tortoiseshell **21** 256
tourist art **21** 249
toys **21** 236
trade **21** 181–2*, 195
copper **22** 612
mirrors **21** 718
traps **21** 245
travel books **21** 262
trumpets **21** 257*, 260
turquoise **21** 241, 246, 251, 252, 254, 255–6, 737, IV1; **22** 158, 164; **33** 103
Mexico **1** 713
urns **21** 266
vases **21** 266
vaults (ceiling) **23** 838
walls **21** 205, 255
water supply **21** 208*
weapons **21** 244–7*, *245*
weaving **21** 261
whistles **21** 257
wood **21** *719*
writing **21** 737; **25** 468; **27** 607
yácatas **31** *504*
Mesogeia Painter **13** 500; **32** 64
Mesopotam, St Nicholas **1** 538
Mesopotamia **1** 507, *849*; **2** *246*, 638; **9** *512*, *513*; **15** 904; **21** 266–310*, *267*; **26** *852*
alabaster (gypsum) **1** 516; **9** *45*; **21** *293*, *297*; **28** 21, *22*
ambos **1** 764
amulets **1** *856*
archaeology **2** 299, 300
architectural decorations **4** 771, *771*
architecture **12** 212; **21** 280–81*, 283–7*
Byzantine **9** 538–41*, 542–3*
Early Christian (*c.* AD 250-843) **9** 538–41*, 542*
Halaf culture **30** 737
military **14** 21; **21** 552*
Neo-Assyrian (*c.* 883-*c.* 612 BC) **21** 287–90*, *289*
Neo-Babylonian (*c.* 627-539 BC) **21** 291*
Parthian **21** 291–2*
Samarra (*c.* 5500-*c.* 5000 BC) **21** *280*
Sasanian **21** 292–3*
Ubaid (*c.* 5th millennium BC) **21** *280*
Uruk (*c.* 4000-*c.* 2900 BC) **21** 281–2*
arsenic **21** 304
baptisteries **9** 541
basalt **21** *296*
beads **1** 850, 873, 877
bitumen **21** 283
blackstone **1** *856*

Mesopotamia—cont.
bone **4** 313
brick **4** *771*, 771–2, *772*
bricklaying **3** *10*
bronze **21** *276*, 296, 298, 303, 304; **30** *28*
building regulations **5** 134, *134*
bullae **21** 271
burial practices **21** 269
casting **12** 782
chariots **6** 478
chronologies **1** *852*, 853; **21** 272, 275; **25** 472
churches **9** 538–41*, 542–3*; **31** *435*
clay **1** 853; **20** 326
coffins **21** 304
collections **21** 310*; **31** 827
copper **21** 270, 303–4
arsenical **21** 304
cotton **16** 428
courtyards **8** 64
cream stone **1** *856*
diorite **21** 294; **29** X2; **30** *423*
doors **21** 296
drapery, sculpture **21** 294
dress **1** 883–4, *884*
engraving **10** 381
entasis **21** *283*; **31** 695
erotic art **10** 473, *473*
exhibitions **21** 310*
façade decoration **10** 742*
faience (i) (glass) **21** 308
figurines **7** *186*; **21** 276, 277, 293*, 295; **28** *22*
eye idols **4** 641, *641*; **21** 272
Sumerian **9** *45*
firing **4** 771
fortifications **21** 552*
friezes **11** *792*
furniture **21** 304
glass **1** 864–5*, 866, *867*, 868*; **12** 782, 785, 787
millefiori **12** 788
mosaic **1** 865
glazes **6** 333; **21** 308
gold **1** 874, 875; **12** 864, 867; **21** 303, 304
gypsum **9** *45*; **21** 296
hardstones **14** 169
houses **21** 280–81, 284, 287
tripartite **14** 128, *128*
human figures **2** *504*; **21** 296
huts **16** 801
iconography **15** 916; **21** 276–9*
inlays **1** 865
inscriptions **2** 299; **4** 771; **21** 276–7, 297
Neo-Assyrian (*c*. 883-*c*. 612 BC) **1** *854*
iron **21** 269, 304
irrigation systems **7** 185; **21** 269
ivory-carvings **1** *871*, *872*
iwans **14** *225*; **21** 291–2
jewellery **1** 873, 875; **21** 303, 304
kilns **16** 394; **21** 305
kudurrus **21** 276, 295, 302
languages **21** 274
lapis lazuli **1** 850
lead **18** 902; **21** 303, 304
libraries **2** 364; **19** 311
limestone **9** *45*, 538; **21** *273*; **29** XI
lost-wax casting **21** 293, 303
manuscript illumination **9** 619
maps **20** 361; **31** 152
marble **3** *12*; **31** *760*
marbling **1** 865
marks **20** 441
metalwork **9** 539; **21** 302–4*
monuments **21** 296
moulds **1** 865
mud-bricks **10** 742; **21** 269, 271, 280, 283; **23** 806; **30** 383
museums **21** 310*
musical instruments **22** 372
narratives **21** 293
niches **31** *434*
obelisks **21** 296
Mesopotamia—cont.
observatories **23** 338
painting
fresco **32** 803
secco **21** 308
vase **21** *307*
wall **21** 271, 308*, 309*, *309*; **32** 802–3*
palaces **21** 272, *285*, 285–6, 291; **23** 806*
pendants (jewellery) **1** 855
periods **21** 268*, 272–5*
Akkadian (*c*. 2340-*c*. 2113 BC) **1** *852*
Assyrian (*c*. 883-*c*. 612 BC) **1** *852*
Babylonian (*c*. 747-*c*. 539 BC) **1** *852*
Early Dynastic (*c*. 2900-*c*. 2340 BC) **1** *852*; **21** 272
Halaf (*c*. 5500-*c*. 4500 BC) **1** *852*
Hassuna (*c*. 6000-*c*. 5000 BC) **1** *852*
Hellenistic **21** 275
Historic **21** 272*
Isin-Larsa **21** 273*
Islamic **1** *852*
Jemdet Nasr **21** 272
Middle Assyrian (*c*. 1363-*c*. 1157 BC) **1** *852*; **21** 274*
Neo-Assyrian (*c*. 883-*c*. 612 BC) **21** 274*
Neo-Babylonian (*c*. 627-539 BC) **21** 274*
Neolithic **10** *506*
Old Assyrian **21** 273–4*
Old Babylonian (*c*. early 19th cent.-*c*. 1595 BC) **1** *852*; **21** 273*
Prehistoric **21** 268*
proto-Hassuna (before *c*. 6000 BC) **1** *852*
Samarra (*c*. 5500-*c*. 5000 BC) **1** *852*
Susiana **7** 186
Third Dynasty of Ur *see* Ur III
Ubaid (*c*. 5th millennium BC) **1** *852*
Ur III (*c*. 2112-*c*. 2004 BC) **1** *852*; **21** 273
Uruk (*c*. 4000-*c*. 2900 BC) **1** *852*; **21** 270–72*
pictographs **21** 282
pigments **21** 308
plaques **1** 865; **10** *473*; **21** *276*
pots **21** *307*
potter's wheels **21** 270, 306
pottery **6** 333; **16** 398; **21** 269, 271, 305–8*, *306*
blue-and-white ware **4** 172
Halaf pottery **21** 269–70, *305*, 305–6; **30** 183; **33** 505
Islamic **16** 401
Khabur ware **21** 308
Ninevite 5 ware **21** 307
Nuzi ware **21** 308; **23** 322
Samarra' **27** *677*
Scarlet ware **21** 306, *307*
Susa A **1** 894
Susiana **7** 186
Uruk (*c*. 4000-*c*. 2900 BC) **21** 306
rediscovery **1** 892
red lead **16** 393
reeds **20** 326
religion **21** 276–9*
rock reliefs **20** 219; **21** 276, *278*, 296
rolls **20** *326*
roofs **9** 539; **21** 283, 287
ruin mounds **21** 268
sarcophagi **27** 825
scripts **25** 467
alphabetic **3** 12; **21** 274
cuneiform **1** 850, 853–4; **2** 299; **31** 827
sculpture **4** 641; **21** 271, 293–6*, 298, 302*
architectural **10** 742*; **21** 296
bronze **30** *28*
Mesopotamia
sculpture—cont.
cult statues **8** 261
Elamite **30** *28*
Kassite **17** *837*
relief **21** 293, 296–302*, 308; **26** 133–4
Assyrian **2** *641*; **21** *297*; **29** XI
Early Dynastic (*c*. 2900-*c*. 2340 BC) **21** *273*
Elamite **10** *133*
2nd cent. AD **14** *226*
Sumerian **18** *798*; **29** X2; **30** *423*; **31** *760*
Uruk (*c*. 4000-*c*. 2900 BC) **4** *641*
seals **12** 212; **21** 269, 272, 274, 275, 278; **28** 783
cylinder **1** 850, 856, 858, *859*, *860*, 860–62, *861*; **4** 641; **21** 271, *271*, 276, *277*, 310
seal amulets **1** *856*
stamp **1** 855, *856*, 858; **4** 641
shells **1** 869
shrines (i) (cult) **33** 675, 676
silver **21** 303, *303*, 304
skins **1** 883
soapstone **21** *295*
statuettes **21** *295*
steel **21** 304
stelae **21** 271, *296*, 296; **29** 613–14
Babylonian **3** *12*
commemorative **21** 276
Elamite **10** *133*
stone **9** 538
styluses **20** 326
surveyors **30** 25
tauf **21** 280
temenoi **21** 283
temples **4** *772*; **19** *105*; **21** 281, 282, 283, 285, 286, 287, 291; **30** 431, *432*
terracotta **17** *837*
terracottas **21** 295, 302
textiles **1** 881
tin **21** 304
tokens **1** 853; **21** 271
tombs **31** 107*
tools **21** 304
trade **21** 268, 273; **30** 179
bowls **15** 902
ceramics **6** 330
copper **2** 265
lapis lazuli **15** 902; **21** 272
pottery **6** 333; **16** 397, 401
wood **2** 248
urban planning **21** 281
vases **1** *867*; **21** *293*, *303*
vaults (ceiling) **21** 275, 284–5; **23** 806; **32** 89
villages **21** 269
walls **21** 271, 291, 552; **30** 383
weapons **21** 304
wood **9** 539
writing **1** 853–4; **10** 1; **20** *326*, 326; **21** 268, 271; **25** 467; **31** 827
writing-tablets **1** 853, 868; **2** 364; **19** 311; **20** 326, *326*, 327; **21** 271, 282; **23** 322; **31** 827
ziggurats **21** *283*, 283–4, 286; **23** 338; **33** 675–6*
see also ANCIENT NEAR EAST; IRAQ
Mespelbrunn, Julius Echter von, Prince-Bishop of Würzburg *see* ECHTER VON MESPELBRUNN, JULIUS, Prince-Bishop of Würzburg
Mesquita, Jessurum de **22** 854
Mesquita, Joana Eufrásia de **23** 454
Mesquita, Jõao de **5** 903
Mesquita de Melo, Antonio de **22** 534
Messa **19** 234, *234*
Temple of Aphrodite **13** 379
Messageot, Lucille **25** 581
Messager, Annette **11** 553, 571; **21** 310–11*
groups and movements **10** 879
works **24** 145
Messager, Jean **20** 415
Messager des sciences et des arts du Royaume des Pays-Bas **24** 422
Messagier, Jean **3** 462; **21** 311*
Messel, Alfred **21** 311*
assistants **18** 655
groups and movements **2** 565
works **3** 795, 807; **8** 770, 816; **12** 376, *377*; **14** 632
Messel, Oliver **5** 531; **21** 312*; **30** 687
assistants **31** 139
productions **30** 688
works **2** 151
Messel Collection *see under* CAMBRIDGE → Fitzwilliam Museum
Messene **13** *363*, 403; **21** 312*
Arkadian Gate **7** 358
coins **13** 587
town walls **21** 312*, *312*, 556, 557
Messenger **13** 619
Messengère, Pierre La *see* LA MESSENGÈRE, PIERRE
Messenia **14** 337; **31** 108
Messenta, Francesco **5** 774
Messer, Thomas **2** 525
Messerer, Boris **27** 397
Messerer, Wilhelm **2** 834
Messer Manfredi degli Embriachi, Lorenzo d'Antonio di *see* EMBRIACHI, LORENZO D'ANTONIO DI MESSER MANFREDI DEGLI
Messerschmidt **9** 241
Messerschmidt, Franz Xaver **21** 313–14*
assistants **11** 123
patrons and collectors **13** 922; **19** 337
works **2** 802; **4** 695; **14** 894; **21** *314*; **28** 836, 855; **32** 444
Messerschmidt, Johann Adam **21** 313
Messey, Guidone **16** 69
Messick, Ben **19** 701
Messil, Gabriel **2** 401; **21** 314*
Messina
Cathedral of S Maria **16** 742; **30** 905
Church of the Candelora **28** 656
coral **16** 750
Fountain of Neptune **11** 342
Fountain of Orion **11** 342; **22** 33
gold **16** 742
Jesuit college **7** 566
manuscripts **26** 665
Nativity groups **22** 680
Palazzo Ruffo **27** 316
S Maria Alamanna **26** 628
S Maria Annunziata **28** 657; **30** 649
Messina, Antonello da *see* ANTONELLO DA MESSINA
Messina, Francesco **16** 709; **24** 278; **26** 810; **31** 132
Messina, Pietro da *see* SALIBA, PIETRO DE
Messinger, Henry **4** 478
Messkirch, Master of *see* STRÜB, PETER (*d* ?1540)
Messkirch Palace **12** 369
Messmacher, Miguel **7** 201
Messmer, Tomo **28** 450
Messmore, Carmen **18** 161
Mestdach, Salomon **22** 839
Mestia, Museum of History and Ethnography **12** 332
mestica **13** 708
mestiche see under PAINT CONTAINERS
Mestiechkin **30** 421
Mestizo (Baroque) **21** 314–15*
Bolivia **4** 258, 261–2
churches **2** *386*
Mestizo (Baroque)—cont.
Cuba (Caribbean) **8** 231
metalwork **24** 511
Nicaragua **23** 81
portals **4** *258*
sculpture **4** 264
Meston, A. L. **22** 229
Mestral, O. **19** 86; **24** 663
Mestre **32** 182
Mestre, Enric **29** 329
Mestre, Héctor **21** 380
Mestre, Manuel **21** 382
Mestre, Roy de *see* MAISTRE, (LE)ROY (LEVESON LAURENT JOSEPH) DE
Mestre Bonga *see* AFONSO, MATONDO
Mestres, José Oriol **31** 829
Mestres, Josep Fontseré i *see* FONTSERÉ I MESTRES, JOSEP
Mestres Esplugas, José Oriol **3** 220; **12** 165; **21** 315*
Meštrović, Ivan **8** 181; **21** 315–16*; **25** 12; **28** 855
collaboration **30** 482
patrons and collectors **8** 181; **29** 419
pupils **3** 86
works **8** 179; **21** *316*; **26** 723; **28** 459; **33** 592
Meštrović, Matko **23** 262
Mestrozzi, Paul **2** 825
Mestrozzi, Vitalis **2** 825
Meszaros, Andor **20** 926
Mészáros, László **14** 896; **21** 316*
Meszaros, Michael **20** 926
Mészöly, Géza **21** 317*
Meta **13** 217; **24** 428
Metabolism **17** 90; **18** 41, 532; **19** 897; **21** 317–18*; **23** 627; **30** 290; **31** 734
architecture **13** 351; **21** *317*
members **20** 147
metacinnabar *see under* PIGMENTS → types
metadiorite **21** 241, 242
Metagenes **2** 312; **10** 430; **13** 394, 408
metal **21** 318–36*
historical and regional traditions
Africa **1** 286–8*, *322*
Anatolia, ancient **21** 302
Australia **2** 739
Belgium **3** 610
Buddhism **15** 499, *500*, *501*; **22** 768–9, 771, 773
Byzantine **9** 668
Central Asia **6** 305
China **6** 726; **7** 31
Dogon **1** *322*
Early Christian (*c*. AD 250-843) **9** 668
Egypt, ancient **30** 775
France **11** 602; **27** 879; **30** 542
Germany **12** 463; **30** 542
Haiti **14** 58
Hinduism **22** 772–3
Hungary **15** 11, 12
Inca **21** 718
India, Republic of **15** 175
Indian subcontinent **6** 556; **15** 499, *500*, *501*, 505, 549, 729–30
Indonesia **15** 795
Iran, ancient **21** 302
Islamic **9** 160; **16** 443
Japan **17** 318–19*, 381, 384, 387, 398, 399, 401
Korea **18** 301, 356
Native North Americans **22** 612–14
Nepal **22** 768–9*, 771–3*
Niger **1** 287
Oman **21** 302
Peru **24** 512
Portugal **25** 305
South America, Pre-Columbian **21** 718
Spain **1** 743; **29** *349*

metal
historical and regional traditions—cont.
Sumatra **15** 795
Tanzania **1** 287
Togo **1** 287
United States of America **30** 542
Zambia **1** 287
Zimbabwe **1** 287
noble *see* GOLD; PLATINUM; SILVER
patinas **21** 329–30*; **24** 258
technical examination **21** *319*; **30** 395, 397, *408*, 408–9*
techniques
casting **21** 320–22*; **29** 211–12
joining **21** 324–5*
moulding **21** 320
uses
arcades **1** 743
architecture **2** 194; **27** 879
armour **6** 305
belts **6** 244
blades **8** 283
book covers **12** 442
bowls **6** 245
braids **30** 540
ceilings **2** 739
chess sets **6** 555, 556, 557
diptychs **9** 3
dolls' furniture **31** 264
doors **9** 160
embroidery **3** 610; **30** 540
flower arrangements **17** 381
furniture **3** *587*; **7** 31; **11** 602; **17** 384; **25** 305; **31** 633
hats **22** 613
headbands **22** 613
inkstones **17** 387
lace **30** 540
manuscripts **15** 549
masks **22** 613
mirrors **21** 718, 719
netsuke **17** 398, 399, 401
pens **24** 349–50*
polychromy **5** 332; **13** 393
prints **11** 173
rattles **22** 613
ritual objects **15** 729–30
sculpture **10** 702
Africa **1** *322*
China **6** 726
Egypt, ancient **10** 35–7*
Haiti **14** 58
Indian subcontinent **15** 499, *500*, *501*, 505
Korea **18** 301
Nepal **22** 768–9*, 771–3*, 774–6*
threads **18** 48, 588, 590; **30** 540–42*
Belgium **3** 610
Byzantine **9** 668
Germany **12** 462, 463, 467, 469
Hungary **15** 11, 12
Iran **18** 49
Islamic **16** 443
Italy **11** *193*
Peru **24** 512
Spain **29** *349*
thrones **30** 775
toners **24** 647
toys **31** 258
trays **6** 245
type-faces **18** 356
vessels **2** 899; **10** 37–8*; **13** 574–7*; **27** 418, *425*
wallpaper **32** 816
weaving **12** 463
writing **20** 328–9
yarn **15** 795
metalcuts **21** 337–9*, *338*; **24** 246; **25** 597, 608, 610
Metalen Pot **22** 879
works **22** *880*
metal-ground textiles *see under* TEXTILES → types
metal halide lamps *see under* LAMPS → types
metallo-chromes **10** 135
metalpoints *see under* DRAWINGS → forms
metalsmiths' guilds *see under* GUILDS → types
metalwork **14** 417; **21** 322–36*
cleaning **21** 334–6
conservation **21** 333–6*, *334*
display **9** 29–30*
historical and regional traditions
Achaemenid **1** 117, 118, *118*; **15** 919
Afghanistan **1** 205–7*
Africa **1** 287, 400
Akkadian (people) **1** 509–10
Albania **1** 543–4*
Anatolia, ancient **1** 826, 827, 835–6*, *836*
Phrygian **1** 836*
Prehistoric **1** 824–5, 834–5*, *835*
Urartian **1** 836*
Ancient Near East **1** 853
Anglo-Saxon **2** 79–80*; **30** 44
Antilles, Lesser **2** 152*
Arabia **2** 264–6*, *265*
Armenia (Europe) **2** 441–2*
Assyrian **15** 919
Australia **2** 764–6*
Austria **2** 819–22*; **27** 663
Azerbaijan **2** 899–900*; **16** 378
Aztec **2** 908
Bangladesh **3** 169
Belgium **3** 596–8*, 601–3*; **26** 682–3*
Gothic **13** 159–60*
Benin, Kingdom of **23** 131–2
Bhutan **3** *914*
Black Sea Colonies **4** 111
Bosnia **4** 462
Brunei **5** 11–12*
Buddhism **1** 206; **6** 313; **21** 878–9, *879*; **30** 841–3, *849*
Bulgaria **5** 155, *160*, 160–61*
Byzantine **9** 539, 654*
Cambodia **5** 507*, 508*
Cameroon **1** 400
Caribbean Islands **5** 752
Carolingian **5** 805–9*; **23** *538*
Celtic **6** *153*, 155–6, 157–8, 159–60; **27** 663
Central Asia, Eastern **6** 313–14*
Central Asia, Western **6** 236–47*
Islamic **16** 370*, 377
Timurid **16** 377
Champa **6** 432*
Chavín culture **29** 214–15
Chimú **6** 606–7*
Cistercian Order **7** 353
Costa Rica **9** 679–80
Côte d'Ivoire **8** 22
Crete **8** 154; **21** 652, 658, 659–60, 686–7*, 688*
Cuba (Caribbean) **8** 237–8*
Cycladic **8** 307–8, 321–3*
Cyprus **8** 363, 365*; **13** 359
Cyprus, ancient **8** 352–4*, *354*
Czech Republic **8** 411*, 415–16*; **13** 161
Denmark **8** 750–52*; **13** 167; **32** 515
Dogon **9** 69*
Early Christian (*c*. AD 250-843) **9** 539, 654*
Ecuador **9** 710
Egypt **9** 766–7
Islamic **16** 369*, 382–6*, 389–90*
Mamluk **16** 382
Ottoman **16** 386
Egypt, ancient **9** 816–18*, *817*, *818*; **10** 34*, 35–8*
Elamite **15** 919
England **10** 322–30*, 331–7*, 338–44*; **28** 576
Anglo-Saxon **2** 79–80*
Gothic **13** 163–5*
Romanesque **10** 338; **26** 687–8*, *688*
metalwork
historical and regional traditions—cont.
Etruscan **10** 587, 593, 624–32*, *626*, *627*, *630*, *631*
Fang **10** 792
Finland **11** 107–8*
France **11** 613*, 623–5*, 628–9*, *629*
Gothic **13** 157, 158–9*
Romanesque **7** 720; **26** 681–2*
Georgia **12** 328–30*
Germany **12** 442*, 451–4*, *452*, *453*, *454*
Celtic **6** 155
Gothic **13** 160–61*
Renaissance **33** *18*
Ghana **16** 383
Gothic **13** 135, 157*
Belgium **13** 159–60*
Czech Republic **13** 161
Denmark **13** 167
England **13** 163–5*
France **13** 157, 158–9*
Germany **13** 160–61*
Holy Roman Empire (before 1648) **13** 160–61*
Hungary **13** 161–2*
Ireland **13** 164, 165
Italy **13** 157, 163*
Netherlands, the **13** 159–60*
Norway **13** 167
Poland **13** 162*
Portugal **13** 166*
Scandinavia **13** 166–7*
Scotland **13** 164, 165
Spain **13** 165*, *165*
Sweden **13** 167
Gran Chiriquí culture **13** 291
Greece **13** 358–9*
Greece, ancient **13** 391, 393, 568*, 574–7*, *575*, *576*, *577*; **26** 544
Hausa **1** 247; **14** 233
Helladic **14** 354*
Herzegovina **4** 462
Hittite **1** 827
Holy Roman Empire (before 1648) **13** 160–61*; **26** 683–6*
Hopi **22** 614
Hungary **13** 161–2*; **15** 5–9*; **26** 687, *687*
Iceland **15** 73*
Ife (kingdom of) **23** 131
Inca **15** 164*; **29** 133, 210, 211
Indian subcontinent **15** 706*, 708–14*, 727, 732
Bengal **15** 709
Bidri ware **15** 713–14, *714*, 724; **21** 326
Islamic **15** 709
Kashmir **15** 709
kuftkāri ware **21** 330
Maratha period **15** 709
Rajput **15** 709
Insular art **15** 871–3*, *873*
Iran **15** 899; **16** 368, 369*, 370*, 372, 373–8*, 390–91*, 392*
Timurid **16** 377
Iran, ancient **1** *118*; **15** 904, 918–20*; **26** 544
Iraq **16** 369*, 379*, 380–82*
Ireland **13** 164, 165; **15** *873*; **26** 688–9*
Gothic **13** 164
Islamic **14** 427; **16** 135, 363–8*, 371–3*, 387*
Azerbaijan **16** 378
Central Asia, Eastern **6** 314
Central Asia, Western **16** 370*, 377
Egypt **16** 369*, 382–6*, 389–90*
Ghana **16** 383
Indian subcontinent **15** 709
Iran **16** 368, 369*, 370*, 372, 373–8*, 390–91*, 392*
Iraq **16** 369*, 379*, 380–82*
Khurasan **16** 377, 392
metalwork
historical and regional traditions
Islamic—cont.
Morocco **16** 386–7
North Africa **16** 386–7*
Ottoman **16** 386, 387–9*
Spain **16** 386–7*; **20** 51
Syria **14** *427*; **16** 367, 369*, 379*, 380*, 381–6*, 389–90*
Turkey **16** 378, 379, 387–9*
Veneto-Saracenic **32** 160–62*, *161*
Israel **16** 568–9*
Israelite **30** 195
Italy **16** 741*, 743–4*
Etruscan **10** 587, 593, 624–32*, *625*, *626*, *627*, *628*, *629*, *630*, *631*
Gothic **13** 157, 163*
Romanesque **26** 690*
Jamaica **16** 888–9*
Japan **17** 104, 297, 318–24*, 358*
mokume **21** 327*, *327*
Yayoi period (*c*. 300 BC-*c*. AD 300) **17** 30
Jewish art **25** 128; **31** 563
Karasuk culture **23** 495
Khurasan **16** 377, 392
Knights Hospitaller **20** 218
Kongo **18** 221
Korea **18** 344*
Laos **18** 776*
La Tène culture (*c*. 450-*c* 50 BC) **28** 325
Levant **16** 573; **30** 195
Maasai **19** 860
Madagascar **20** 36
Malaysia **20** 173*
Maldives, Republic of **20** 189
Malta (Republic of) **20** 211, 216*, 218*
Maya **21** 252
Medes **15** 919
Merovingian **21** 161–3*
Mesoamerica, Pre-Columbian **21** 200, 252–4*, *253*
Maya region **21** 252–3
West Mexico **21** 254; **33** 103
Mesopotamia **9** 539; **21** 302–4*
Mexico **21** 254
Migration period **21** 503
Minoan **21** 652, 686*, 688*
Early Minoan (*c*. 3500/3000-*c*. 2050 BC) **21** 686–7*
Late Minoan (*c*. 1600-*c*. 1050 BC) **21** 659–60, 687*
Middle Minoan (*c*. 2050-*c*. 1600 BC) **21** 658, 687*
Mixtec **21** 254, 737
Mixteca-Puebla **21** 254
Moche (culture) **21** 332; **29** 215
Mongolia **21** 878–9*, *879*; **23** 495
Morocco **16** 386–7
Muisca **29** 212
Nabataea **22** 421
Native North Americans **22** 612–16*, *613*, *617*, 617–18*
Navajo **22** 614
Nepal **22** 774–6*, 789–90*, *790*, 793
Netherlands, the **22** 885*, 890–92*, 893–5*
Gothic **13** 159–60*
New Zealand **23** 70*, 72–3*
North Africa **16** 386–7*
Norway **13** 167; **15** 873; **23** 236*, 237*, *237*
Nuba **23** 275
Nubia **10** 38
Nupe **23** 303*, *303*
Old Copper culture **22** 617
Ottoman **16** 386, 387–9*
Ottonian **23** 656–9*
Pakistan **23** 803
Palestine **9** 539
metalwork
historical and regional traditions—cont.
Paracas culture **29** 214
Parthian **15** 919
Peru **24** 500, 511–12*
Philippines **24** 627–8*
Philistine **24** 635–6*; **30** 195
Phoenician **20** 211; **24** 644*; **30** 196
Phrygian **1** 836
Pictish art **27** 569
Poland **25** 125–8*, *127*, *128*, 129–30*
Gothic **13** 162*
Romanesque **26** 687
17th cent. **25** *130*
Portugal **13** 166*; **26** 690*
Prehistoric art
Afghanistan **1** 205–6*
Anatolia, ancient **1** 824–5, 826, 834–6*, *835*
Bronze Age **25** 518, 524–7*
Iron Age **25** 535, 539–42*
Japan **17** 30
Neolithic **25** 516–17*
Punic **25** 734*
Romanesque **26** 681*, 686–7*
Belgium **26** 682–3*
England **10** 338; **26** 687–8*, *688*
France **7** 720; **26** 681–2*
Holy Roman Empire (before 1648) **26** 683–6*
Hungary **26** 687, *687*
Ireland **26** 688–9*
Italy **26** 690*
Poland **26** 687
Portugal **26** 690*
Scandinavia **26** 690–91*
Scotland **26** 689*
Spain **26** 689*
Romania **26** 719–20*
Rome, ancient **27** 79–84*, 93–4*
Russia **27** 418*, 424*, 425–6*; **28** *320*, *322*
Sarmatian **28** 321, 324
Sasanian **6** 238; **15** 920
Scandinavia **13** 166–7*; **32** 513, 515, 516, 524*
Romanesque **26** 690–91*
Scotland **13** 164, 165; **26** 689*; **28** 260–63*, *262*
Scythian **6** 237; **15** 919; **28** *320*, 321, *322*, 322–4
Serbia **28** 454–6*
Shona **28** 621
Siberia **28** 321, 322, 324–6
Sicán culture **28** 651–2; **29** 210
Sinú **29** 211, 213
Slovakia **28** 856*
Slovenia **28** 862–3
Sogdiana **6** 238–41*
Somalia **29** 56
Songye **29** 69
South Africa **29** 119–21*
South America, Pre-Columbian **29** 127, 135, 210–15*
Chavín culture **29** 214–15
Costa Rica **9** 679–80
Inca **29** 133
Sicán culture **28** 651–2
Veraguas culture **32** 238
Spain **25** 734; **29** 332–44*, *338*
Gothic **13** *165*, 165–6*
Islamic **16** 368–9*, 386–7*; **20** 51
Romanesque **26** 689*
Sri Lanka **29** 474–5*
Swahili **30** 57
Sweden **30** 104–11*
Gothic **13** 167
Switzerland **6** 157; **30** 145–7*
Syria
Byzantine **9** 539
Early Christian (*c*. AD 250-843) **9** 539
Islamic **14** *427*; **16** 367, 369*, 379*, 380*, 381–6*, 389–90*

metalwork
 historical and regional traditions
  Syria—cont.
   Mamluk 16 382
   Ottoman 16 386
  Syria-Palestine 30 180, 183, *183*, 186, 187, 194–6*
  Tairona 29 213
  Tarascan 21 254; 30 341
  Thailand 30 635–6*
  Thracian 26 544
  Tibet 30 808, 812, 840–43*, *849*
  Trinidad and Tobago 2 146
  Tuareg 31 405*, *405*
  Turkey 16 378, 379, 387–9*
  Ukraine 31 562–3*
  United States of America 31 646–7*, 648–9*, 651–4*
  Urartian 1 835, 836, *836*; 2 441; 15 919; 31 700–701
  Veraguas culture 32 238
  Vicús culture 29 215
  Vietnam 6 432*; 32 487–8*
  Viking 32 513, 515, 516, 524*
  Visigothic 32 618*
  Wales 32 789*
  West Mexico 33 103
  Yemen 2 *265*
 marks *see under* MARKS
 materials
  bitumen 4 688
  enamel 3 596; 25 547
  inlays 16 364, 375–6, 377, 378, 379, 381–2; 21 328–9*
  inscriptions 16 135, 367–8, 377, 378, 381, 383, 386, 390, 391
  lacquer 5 257; 17 297
  niello 21 329
  tools 21 *323*, *326*
  wire 11 76
 techniques
  carving 21 326*
  casting 16 363
  chasing 21 326
  damascening *see* DAMASCENING
  dhokra 15 727, *727*
  electroplating *see* ELECTROPLATING
  embossing 21 878
  engraving 16 364, 377, 378; 21 326
  filigree *see* FILIGREE
  gilding 12 627*
  granulation 21 328*
   Ancient Near East 1 874
   China 7 108, 109, *109*
   Egypt, ancient 10 30
   Etruscan 10 587, 631
   Italy 10 587, 631
  hammering 6 830; 9 818; 21 322–3*, *324*; 29 211
  incising 16 364
  lost-wax casting 16 363
  mokume 21 *327*
  moulding 9 818
  niello 30 635–6
  openwork 6 *158*; 11 76; 17 *323*; 18 776
  patrix-working 30 770
  pattern welding 2 451; 21 *327*, 327–8*
  piercing 16 364; 21 327*
  plating 21 330–32*
  polishing 9 818
  polychromy 21 327–8*
  punching 16 364; 21 326
  raising 16 363; 21 323, *324*
  repoussé 30 635
  riveting 21 324*
  rolling 21 323
  scribing 21 326, *326*
  sinking 16 363; 21 323
  soldering 9 818; 21 324–5*
  spinning (metalwork) 21 323
  stamping 21 327*
  welding 21 325*
  wirework 11 76; 21 328*
metalwork—cont.
 types
  toreutic 30 767, 768–73*, *770*, *771*; 31 166*
metalworkers 1 246, 286; 17 358; 21 252
metamorphism 21 340–41*
Metapán 10 153, *153*
metaphor 10 691; 26 221
Metaphrastian Menologion 9 616
Metapontion 13 *362*, 401; 16 *621*; 21 341–2*
 coins 13 586, 587
 ekklesiasteria 21 341
 figurines 13 579
 frieze 21 *342*
 pottery 13 525
 sculpture 21 342*
 Temple of Apollo 10 414
 Temple of Hera 10 414
 theatre 21 341
Metapontum *see* METAPONTION
Metastasio, Pietro 13 802; 24 733
Metata 18 570
metates 29 141–4*
 Costa Rica 9 *678*, 678–9; 29 142, *142*, *144*
 Gran Nicoya culture 13 310–11; 29 *141*, 142
 Panama 29 144; 32 *239*
 Veraguas culture 32 238–9, *239*
Metaxata 17 909
Métayer 32 913
Metayer, Louis 22 888, 897
 works 22 *889*
Metayer, Philippe 22 888
 works 22 *889*
Metcalf, Willard Leroy 4 478; 7 875; 21 342–3*; 30 452; 31 603
Metcalfe, Percy 20 926; 21 343*
Met de Bles, Herri *see* BLES, HERRI MET DE
Metelák, Alois 8 411; 33 630
Metelák, Antonín 23 272
Metelák, Luboš 17 816
Metelák, Milan 23 272
Metelli, Orneore 22 441
Metellino, Giovan Battista 21 529
Metellus Baliaricus, (Quintus) Caecilius 23 880
Meteora 7 229; 8 157; 9 *511*, 524; 21 343–5*; 26 483
 architecture 21 344
 churches 9 526, 622
 Great Meteoron 21 343; 25 334, 335
 Holy Trinity Monastery 21 343
 icons 21 345
 Monastery of the Presentation of Christ in the Temple 21 343
 Roussanos Monastery 21 343, *343*; 25 335
 St Nicholas Anapafsas Monastery 21 343; 25 335
 St Stephen's Monastery 21 343
 Stavronikita Monastery 25 335
 Varlaam Monastery 21 343; 25 335, 336
 wall paintings 21 344–5; 25 331, 333
 Ypsilotera Monastery 21 345
Metepec 29 901
Métevier, Joseph 29 833
Meteyard, Sidney Harold 4 87
Metezeau (family) 27 547
Métezeau, Clément, I (*d c.* 1545) 21 345
Métezeau, Clément, II (1581-1652) 21 345, 346*
 collaboration 30 735
 patrons and collectors 4 548; 19 134
 works 12 913; 31 719
Métezeau, Guillaume 21 346
Métezeau, Jean 21 345
Métezeau, Louis (1559-1615) 20 133; 21 345–6*
 attributions 9 353
Métezeau, Louis (1559-1615)—cont.
 patrons and collectors 4 548
 works 11 514; 24 161; 29 917
Métezeau, Louis, II (*b* after 1579) 21 346
Métezeau, Thibaut 21 345
Metge, Guillermo 3 218, 221
Methan 15 272
Methey, André 11 606; 27 240
Methi 15 316
 triple temple 15 316
Methley, Joan 29 116
Methodios, Patriarch of Constantinople 9 638
Methodism *see under* CHRISTIANITY → sects
Methuen, Paul (1672-1757) 4 845; 7 486; 17 623; 21 348*
Methuen, Paul (1723-94) 21 348
methylene chloride 12 629
Methymna 19 234, *234*
Metis 22 546, 555, 638
Metlakatla 22 657
Metlin, N. 18 400
Metochites, Theodore *see* THEODORE METOCHITES
Metope group 10 611
Metope Painter 13 529
metopes 10 742; 11 790; 13 377, *378*, 390, 391, 392, 393, 398, 425–6, 432*, 445, 446–7; 21 348*; 23 478
 Classical, High 13 *425*
 5th cent. BC 23 *432*
Metope style 14 338
Metoyer (family) 1 440
Metrass, Francisco 21 348–9*
Metrodoros 13 549; 26 764
Metrological Relief 13 411
metrology *see* MEASUREMENTS, ARCHITECTURAL; SURVEYING
Metron 16 650
Metropoli, Michele 20 216
Metropolitan Board of Works (London) 3 430; 19 572
Metropolitan Electric Tramway Company 33 204
Metropolitan ware *see under* POTTERY → wares
Metro stations 19 575; 21 *349*, 349–50*; 31 176
 see also RAILWAY STATIONS
Metsch, Johann Friedrich 3 429
Mets Mazra 2 436
Metsovaara, Marjatta 11 110
Metsovo, Averoff Gallery 13 359
Metsu, Gabriel 19 101; 21 350–52*; 22 843; 29 375
 groups and movements 22 841
 patrons and collectors
  Angran, Louis-Auguste, Vicomte de Fontpertuis 2 90
  Arenberg, Auguste-Marie-Raymond, 6th Duke of 2 382
  Boilly, Louis-Léopold 4 241
  Braamcamp, Gerrit 4 618
  Bryan, Michael 5 63
  Catherine II, Empress of Russia (*reg* 1762-96) 26 732
  Detuit (family) 9 466
  Fagel (family) 10 754
  Fesch, Joseph, Cardinal 11 32
  Gildermeester, Jan (Jansz.) (1744-99) 12 620
  Josephine, Empress of the French (1763-1814) 4 304
  Marguard, Henry G(urdon) 20 461
  Peel, Robert 24 322
  Sparre, Gustaf Adolf 29 366
  Tronchin, François 31 362
  William V, Stadholder of the Netherlands, Prince of Orange (*reg* 1751–95) 23 469
 pupils 22 383
 teachers 9 194; 22 841; 29 587
 works 7 784; 11 444; 12 290, 292; 21 *351*
Metsue, Jacques 21 350
Metsys (family) 3 603
Metsys, Quinten 2 206; 3 554; 19 260; 21 352–9*
 attributions 13 160; 20 721
 collaboration 21 359; 24 260, 261
 methods 12 625
 patrons and collectors 11 65
  Borbón y Braganza, Sebastián Gabriel 4 379
  Duarte, Diego 9 311
  Elizabeth I, Queen of England (*reg* 1558- 1603) 10 363
  Erasmus (of Rotterdam), Desiderius 10 445; 14 869
  Geest, Cornelis van der 12 233
  Gillis, Pieter 3 612
  Mead, Richard 20 910
  Vincenzo I, 4th Duke of Mantua (*reg* 1587- 1612) 12 912
 pupils 20 721, 731
 reproductive prints by others 27 503
 works 2 194, *195*; 3 554, 596, 597; 10 445, 713; 11 440, 441, *441*; 12 287; 20 921; 21 *353*, *354*, *355*, *356*
Mettay, Pierre-Joseph 19 641
Metten, Jean de 11 642
Mettenleiter, Johann Michael 25 789
Metten Monastery 12 369
Metternich, Franz Arnold von, Prince-Bishop of Paderborn 28 105
Metternich, Franz Wolff, Graf von 7 194
Metternich, Klemens von, Prince 6 519; 18 115
Metternich, Melanie, Princess 8 445
Mettis *see* METZ
Mettoy 31 257
Mettray, penal colony 25 637
Metz 5 793; 11 *504*; 19 709; 21 360–62*; 31 713
 Abbey 3 709
 Cathedral of St Etienne 4 *165*; 7 265; 13 59; 21 360–62*, *361*
  stained glass 21 362; 29 508
  textiles 26 703
 Fort Gambetta 21 576
 gems 12 255
 glass 11 611
 ivory 23 660
 ivory-carvings 5 810; 22 *520*
 manuscripts 5 803; 11 653; 20 330
 metalwork 11 614
 Musée d'Art et d'Histoire 7 878
 Notre-Dame-la-Ronde 21 361, 362
 Palais de Justice 18 886
 rock crystal 5 811
 roofs 30 907
 Ste Marie *see* Notre-Dame-la-Ronde
 St Pierre-aux-Nonnains 4 780; 7 263; 11 553; 21 163
 sculpture 5 *806*; 12 398
 theatre 30 670
Metz, Guillebert de *see* GUILLEBERT DE METZ
Metz, Master of Guillebert de *see* GUILLEBERT DE METZ, MASTER OF
Metz & Co. 1 811; 21 362–3*; 22 868, 876; 26 379
 designers 4 844; 24 351
Metzel, Olaf 3 803
Metzelaar, Johan Frederik 19 116
Metzelaar, W. C. 13 798
Metzendorf, Georg 17 853
Metzger, Eduard 28 398
Metzger, Friedrich 25 436
Metzger, Fritz 19 769
Metzger, Gustav 2 837; 21 363*
Metzger, Louise 28 692
Metz Group, Late *see* LATE METZ GROUP
Metzinger, Jean 21 363–4*
 collaboration 12 806
 dealers 27 162
 exhibitions 32 775
 groups and movements 2 225; 8 240, 241, 244, 246; 9 361; 12 805; 16 818; 19 78; 21 775; 22 747; 23 569, 570; 25 747; 28 347
 patrons and collectors 2 383
 pupils 6 469; 9 9; 25 238; 31 519
 reproductive prints by others 32 577
 works 11 582; 21 *364*
  translated 20 851
 writings 25 747; 31 300
Metzinger, Valentin Janez 21 365*; 28 860
Metzkes, Harald 21 365*
Metzner, Franz 2 803; 21 365*
 assistants 25 403; 29 549
 groups and movements 28 344
 pupils 1 550
Metzner Museum *see under* BERLIN (GERMANY) → museums
Metz Pontifical *see under* PONTIFICALS → individual manuscripts
Metzsch, Johann Friedrich 14 235
Metzstein, Isi 7 530
meuble à deux corps *see* BUFFETS
Meucci, Vincenzo 3 101; 4 491; 11 20, 194; 16 674; 21 31
Meuccio, Giovanni di Contaldino di *see* GIOVANNI DI CONTALDINO DI MEUCCIO
Meudon
 Château 4 553; 21 366–7*; 25 71
  Cabinet du Dauphin 26 492
  gardens 12 122
  paintings 3 856; 4 537; 8 91, 812; 21 368
 Musée Rodin 26 509
 Studio-House 9 64
Meudon-la-Forêt 25 375
Meulebeeck, Andries 4 522
Meulemans, Adriaan 28 164
Meulen, Adam Frans van der 21 367–8*
 collaboration 4 220; 12 828; 18 742; 19 22; 20 489
 patrons and collectors 4 552; 25 815; 33 196
 reproductive prints by others 4 521; 8 544
 teachers 28 898
 works 2 496, *497*; 3 388; 7 195; 12 832; 21 *366*, *367*; 27 *559*
Meulen, Andries van der 33 268
Meulen, Claes Pietersz. van der 21 368
Meulen, Cornelis van der 14 739; 30 78
Meulen, Jan van der *see* MOLANUS, JOHANNES
Meulen, Laurent van der 11 404
Meulen, Pierre van der *see* PIERRE VAN DER MEULEN
Meulen, Sieuwert van der 21 368*
Meulen, Steven van der 9 367; 11 140; 19 793; 21 368–9*; 30 77
Meulengracht, Jakob (Adriansz.) van 8 733
Meunier, (Jules-) Arthur *see* VIERENDEEL, (JULES-)ARTHUR
Meunier, Constantin 19 260; 21 369–70*
 groups and movements 3 156; 5 44; 7 245; 19 321; 26 57, 96; 28 921
 pupils 17 669
 teachers 11 371; 22 697
 works 3 563, 572, *573*; 12 296; 15 830; 21 *370*

Meunier, Etienne 11 595
Meunier, Henri 25 347
Meunier, Jean-Baptiste 21 369
Meunier, Louis 28 742
Meunier, N. 29 719
Meurant, Ferdinand 2 764
Meurice, Jean-Michel 11 553
Meuron, Albert de 12 810; 21 370
Meuron, Charles-Daniel de 30 155, 728
Meuron, Louise de 19 699
Meuron, Maximilien de 21 370*; 22 920; 30 133
Meuron, Pierre de 30 129
Meurs, Cornelis van 22 916
Meursault Leprodarium 14 781
Meursius, Johannes 22 717
Meusel, Johann Georg 24 421
Meuse region *see* BELGIUM
Meusnes, St Vincent 26 585, 586
Meusnier, Georges *see* ROBERT, KARL
Meuszyński, J. 21 288, 299
Meuvaines 26 598
Meux, Valerie 10 91
Mévisto, Jules 15 58
Mevlevi Order 16 461
Mevorakh, Tel 1 865
Mevorakh ben Yoseph
  manuscripts 4 *14*
Mew, Frederick 31 240
Mewar *see* DEOGARH
Mewe *see* GNIEW
Mewès, Charles Frédéric 14 787; 21 371*
Mewès & Davis 21 371*
  groups and movements 9 739
  works 7 470; 14 787; 16 55
Mewton, Geoffrey 13 709
Mexborough, John Savile, 1st Earl of *see* SAVILE, JOHN, 1st Earl of Mexborough
Mexborough, John Savile, 2nd Earl of *see* SAVILE, JOHN, 2nd Earl of Mexborough
Mexica 21 201, 398
Mexican onyx 21 241
  see also ARAGONITE
Mexican Renaissance 25 653
Mexico 21 177, *178*, *193*, 371–405*, *372*
  academies 21 404
  altars 1 *700*
  amber 1 761
  aqueducts 2 242
  arches 21 376
  architectural decorations 25 II1
  architecture 21 374–82*
    Augustinian Canons 21 375
    Dominican Order 21 375
    Franciscan Order 21 373, 375; 33 571
    Pre-Columbian 30 *483*; 31 *778*
    United States of America 18 832
    vernacular 32 306, 307
    20th cent. 7 *695*
  archives 2 371*
  art history 33 316
  basalt 21 *218*; 23 *417*; 30 *341*
  bells 21 254
  bowls 21 *240*
  bronze 21 *384*
  carnivals 5 787
  catalogues 21 265
  cathedrals 21 375–6, *376*, *377*; 25 *696*
  causeways 6 *97*
  celts 18 *881*; 21 242
  chairs 21 *391*
  chalices 21 *393*
  chapels 21 376
  churches 5 *603*; 25 II1; 31 *65*
  clay 21 *193*; 26 *181*; 33 617, *619*
  coatepantlis 7 *481*
  coins 7 537
  collections 10 487; 21 264, 265, 394–7*
  colleges 21 *381*
  columns 21 377
Mexico—cont.
  concrete 4 185; 7 *695*
  copper 21 254
  courtyards 21 *401*
  craftsmen and artists 18 831–2*
  dealing 21 394–6*
  dolls 31 259, 261
  dolls' houses 31 264
  doors 9 *166*
  drawings 21 384
  dress 21 394
  dyeing 9 492
  dyes 21 394
  earthenwares 21 *392*
  education (art) 21 397–8*, 404
  embroidery 21 *394*
  enamel 28 *784*
  engravings 10 393; 21 385; 24 418; 25 *321*; 27 872
  erotic art 10 474
  fibreglass 18 *831*
  figurines 8 255; 18 *881*; 21 *194*, *218*; 33 *619*
    Pre-Columbian 21 *238*, *239*
  filigree 21 254
  fonts (baptismal) 21 *374*
  fortifications 24 367
  friezes 31 *99*
  furniture 21 391*
  glass 21 392*
  gold 21 392–3*
  guidebooks 13 811
  guilds 21 382, 397
  Happenings 21 390
  houses 32 305
  iconography 18 831–2; 21 373–4; 26 426
  interior decoration 21 391*
  jade 16 II1; 18 *881*
  jadeite 16 *861*
  jars 21 *392*
  jewellery 21 392–3*
  knitting 18 157
  libraries 21 398*
  lithography 19 399; 21 385, *402*
  marks 21 393
  masks 16 *861*; 21 *255*
    Pre-Columbian 16 II1; 21 IV1
  masonry 24 367; 31 310
  metalwork 21 254
  miniatures (manuscript illumination) 21 *234*
  monasteries 21 375; 33 571
  monuments 18 *645*
  mosaics 17 *715*; 21 *255*, *734*; 22 163; 23 *370*
    Pre-Columbian 21 IV1
  museums 21 *380*, 396–7*, 404
  nude figures 18 *831*
  painting 21 382–90*, *389*
    easel 21 388*
    history 21 *386*
    landscape 32 *123*
    murals 7 841; 10 866; 15 830; 21 387–8*, 405, *405*; 22 *334*, 334–5*; 25 653; 27 872
      20th cent. 23 *567*; 26 426, *428*, 429; 28 *785*
    wall 4 *296*; 5 *357*; 22 163; 26 *411*; 30 *484*; 32 807
      Pre-Columbian 7 I1
    20th cent. 30 *282*
  palaces 17 *715*; 18 *578*; 21 *734*; 23 *825*; 28 *26*
  paper 24 48
  papercuts 24 56
  parks 24 *182*
  patronage 21 394–6*
  performance art 21 390
  photoarchives 5 910; 21 398*
  photography 24 *676*
  polychromy 25 II1
  portraits 10 393; 18 *675*
  pottery 21 392*; 31 261
    blue-and-white ware 4 175–6*
    Capacha-Opeño 5 660, *660*
    Pre-Columbian 2 904; 7 250; 21 *238*, *239*, *240*
Mexico
  pottery—cont.
    Talavera de Puebla ware 4 175; 21 392
    tin-glazed ware 21 392, *392*
  prints 21 382, 386, 388*, *390*
  propaganda 25 653
  pyramids 7 *201*, 201; 30 *254*, *453*; 31 *65*
  reproductions 26 227
  retables 21 383, *383*
  rock crystal 21 393
  rugs 27 316
  sandstone 14 *830*; 27 *832*
  sarapes 21 394
  sarcophagi 27 *832*
  satires 27 872
  sculpture 21 383*, 384, 385–7*, 389*, 390; 29 901, *901*
    bronze 21 *384*
    colossal heads 23 *417*
    equestrian monuments 21 *384*
    monumental 18 *645*; 21 386
    Pre-Columbian 5 *409*; 14 *830*; 21 *400*; 26 *181*; 30 *341*; 33 *618*
    relief 2 *907*; 8 *460*; 23 *839*; 33 *473*
  seals 21 *258*
  serpentine 18 *881*
  shell structures 7 *695*
  shelters 33 571
  silver 7 537; 21 392–3*; 28 737
  silver-gilt 21 *393*
  skull racks 31 *506*
  stables 3 *273*
  staircases 29 *527*
  stelae 16 *807*
  stoles (secular) 21 394
  stone 2 *907*; 8 *460*; 21 *400*
  stone-carvings 2 *906*; 6 *393*; 18 645; 21 *374*
  stucco 18 *675*; 23 *839*
  sugar 29 901, *901*
  temples 30 *448*, *449*, *453*, *872*; 31 *420*; 33 *510*
  terracotta 33 *618*
  textiles 21 394*, *394*
  theatres 13 *730*; 21 *379*; 23 208
  tiles 25 II1
  trade 5 842; 21 252, 254; 32 180
  treatises 13 868
  trompe l'oeil 10 737
  tunics 21 *394*
  turquoise 21 IV1
  urban planning 21 375
  women artists 33 316
  wood-engravings 21 388
  yácatas 31 *504*
Mexico, West *see* WEST MEXICO
Mexico City 21 *372*, 375, 398–406*; 31 721
  Academia de las Nobles Artes de San Carlos *see* Academia Nacional de Bellas Artes
  Academia Nacional de Bellas Artes 21 384, 385, 396, 397, 398, 404
  Aduana 21 377
  airport 23 370
  apartments 21 380
  Archivo General de la Nación 21 398
  art forms and materials
    architecture 21 376
    bone-carvings 21 248
    glass 21 392
    marks 21 393
    metalwork 21 392
    mosaics 22 164
    painting 21 384
    retables 21 383, 397
    sculpture 21 183
    silver 21 393
    silver-gilt 21 *393*
  Ayuntamiento 21 377
  Aztec Stadium 29 489
  Biblioteca Nacional 21 398
  Bolivar Amphitheatre 25 653
Mexico City—cont.
  Bolsa de Valores 21 381
  Casa Bosque de las Lomas 21 381
  Casa Diego Rivera 21 379
  Centro Cultural de Arte Contemporáneo 21 397, 406
  Centro del Espacio Escultório 21 390
  Centro Escolar Revolución 21 380
  Chapultepec Castle 21 249; 28 784
  Ciudad Universitaria 21 380; 28 786
    collections 21 396
    cosmic ray laboratory 7 696; 28 583
    library 21 388
    murals 22 334
  Colegio de México 21 381, *381*, 398
  ecclesiastical buildings
    Augustinian church 21 383
    Basilica de Guadalupe 21 393
    Cathedral (destr.) 21 375
    Cathedral of México 2 375; 21 375, *376*, 378, *399*
      Chapel of the Kings 21 377, 383
      choir-stalls 21 383
      cípres 21 393
      retable 21 383
      Sagrario Chapel 21 *376*, 377; 26 518
      sculpture 21 384
    Church of La Profesa 21 377
    Church of the Miraculous Virgin *see* Church of the Virgin of the Miraculous Medal
    Church of the Virgin of the Miraculous Medal 5 *603*; 21 380
    College of SS Pedro y Pablo 21 376, 387; 22 20, *334*
    Franciscan Monastery 21 373
    Jesús María 21 376
    La Concepción 21 376
    Loreto Church 21 378
    S Domingo 21 375
    S Ildefonso *see* Escuela Nacional Preparatoria
    S Jerónimo 21 376
    S Juan de Dios 21 377
    S Teresa la Antigua 21 377
  Edificio Central de Correos 21 378
  Edificio Comercial 21 380
  Edificio Parque Reforma 21 381
  Electricians' Union Building 28 784
    murals 1 129; 28 785, *785*
  Escuela Benito Juárez 21 379
  Escuela de Talla Directa y Escultura 21 389, 397
  Escuela Nacional de Artes Plásticas 21 398
  Escuela Nacional de Bellas Artes *see* Academia Nacional de Bellas Artes
  Escuela Nacional de Maestros 21 380
  Escuela Nacional Preparatoria 17 513; 21 376, 377, 387
    murals 6 488; 7 841; 22 334
  Escuela Técnica 21 380
  Estado Olímpico 21 380
  Gymnasium Gustavo Díaz Ordaz 21 381
  Hernández studio 21 381
  Hospital de la Raza 14 785
  Hospital para Tuberculosos 21 379
  Hotel Camino Real 21 381
  Hotel de México 28 784
  Instituto de Higiene y Granja Sanitaria 21 379
  Instituto de Investigaciones Estéticas 2 371; 21 398, 406
Mexico City—cont.
  Instituto Nacional de Antropología e Historia (INAH) 13 811; 21 398
  Instituto Nacional de Bellas Artes 21 395, 398, 406
  Jardines del Pedregal de San Angel 21 381
  Jaysour Building 21 380
  Las Arboledas 21 381
  Mercado El Volador 21 378
  Metro stations 21 350
  Ministerio del Patrimonio Nacional 30 282
  Ministry of Public Education 21 387, 389
  monuments
    equestrian statue of Charles IV 21 384, *384*
    Monument to Independence 21 378
    Monument to the Revolution 20 500
  museums
    Galería de Arte Mexicano 21 406
    Galería de Historia Mexicana 25 878
    Museo de Arte Moderno 21 406; 25 878
      collections 21 396
      directors 10 497
      library 21 398
    Museo de Arte Popular 22 20
    Museo Diego Rivera de Anahuacalli 21 395
    Museo El Eco 12 843; 21 381, 396
    Museo Franz Mayer 21 396
    Museo Nacional 21 396
    Museo Nacional de Antropología 5 910; 6 520; 8 65; 21 265, 380, *380*, 396; 22 366; 25 878
      Mesoamerican collection 21 265
      murals 7 877
    Museo Nacional de Arte 7 784; 10 487; 21 378, 396, 398
    Museo Nacional de Historia 21 396
    Museo Rufino Tamayo 21 397, 406
  Music Conservatory *see* Ministerio del Patrimonio Nacional
  New Chapultepec Park 24 181, *182*
  O'Gorman House 21 379
  Pabellón de Rayos Cósmicos 21 380
  Palacio de Bellas Artes 4 184; 15 4; 21 378, 379, *379*; 26 427
    murals 30 282
  Palacio de Justicia Federal 21 382
  Palacio de la Minería 21 378, *401*
  Palacio Nacional 10 727; 21 265, 387, *405*; 27 872
  Pasaje Jacaranda store 21 380
  Penitenciaría 21 378
  Plaza de la Constitución 21 *402*
  Plaza Mayor 21 265
  Real Seminario de Minería *see* Palacio de la Minería
  Registro Publico de la Propriedad 21 380
  Restaurante Xochimilco 7 *695*, 696
  San Cristóbal estate 3 *273*
  Secretaría de Comunicaciones *see* museums → Museo Nacional de Arte
  Secretaría de Educación Pública 6 488; 26 426
  Secretaría de Salubridad y Assistencia 21 379
  Secretaría de Trabajo y Previsión Social 21 380

Mexico City—cont.
Sindicato Mexicano de Electricistas **21** 380
Supreme Court **25** 653
Teatro de los Insurgentes **22** 164
Teatro de Santa Ana *see* Teatro Nacional
Teatro Nacional *see* Palacio de Bellas Artes
Tlatelolco *see* TLATELOLCO
Torre Latino Americana **15** 887; **21** 380
Universidad Iberoamericana **21** 398
Universidad Nacional Autónoma de México **10** 497; **19** 321; **21** 398; **23** *370*
Universidad Pedagógica **21** 381
urban planning **21** 400–401
see also TENOCHTITLÁN
Mey, J(ohann) M(elichior) van der *see* MEIJ, J(OHANN) M(ELCHIOR) VAN DER
Meybod **16** 426
Meybusch, Anton **20** 924; **21** 406*
Meydam, Floris **22** 885
Meyer (family) (15th cent.; patrons) **30** 311
Meyer (family) (18th cent.; glass-makers) **30** 143
Meyer, Adolf (1881-1929) **3** 511; **13** 687; **21** 407*
collaboration **4** 788; **10** 749; **12** 379, 792; **13** 687, 689
competitions **7** 669
groups and movements **10** 697; **21** 780, 781, 782; **26** 15, 405
staff **14** 295
Meyer, Adolf (Gayne) de, Baron (1868-1949) **21** 407*
groups and movements **24** 688
pupils **21** 157
Meyer, Agnes Ernst **1** 438; **11** 748; **29** 656
Meyer, Alfred **25** 236
Meyer, Ben **33** 407
Meyer, Caspar **12** 334
Meyer, C. De *see* DE MEYER, C.
Meyer, Christian **27** 407, 583
Meyer, Conrad **21** 407*; **30** 132; **33** 736
pupils **14** 834; **29** 644
teachers **21** 152, 406
works **21** 406
Meyer, Cornelis **33** 268
Meyer, Dietrich Theodor, I (1572-1658) **21** 151, 406, 407
Meyer, Dietrich Theodor, II (1651-1733) **21** 406
Meyer, Else **21** 55
Meyer, Ernst **8** 734
Meyer, Felix **5** 168; **30** 132
Meyer, Florence *see* BLUMENTHAL, FLORENCE
Meyer, Frederick H. **23** 35
Meyer, Friedrich Elias **3** 805
Meyer, F. X. **2** 829
Meyer, Georg **12** 453
Meyer, Grethe **7** 807; **8** 749; **21** 791
Meyer, Gustav **3** 794; **19** 156; **20** 1
Meyer, Hannes **11** 526; **21** 408*
assistants **33** 41
competitions **7** 669, 670
groups and movements **1** 76; **3** 403; **7** 293; **11** 841; **12** 378; **15** 886; **30** 275
pupils **8** 814; **28** 556
works **11** *841*; **28** 122; **30** 127
Meyer, Hans *see* HAMMER, HANS
Meyer, (Hans) Heinrich (1760-1832; painter) **21** 408–9*
patrons and collectors **12** 853; **33** 116
pupils **14** 655; **25** 550; **33** 37
works **14** 285
writings **33** 117
Meyer, Heinrich (1802-77) **5** 168
Meyer, Hendrick de (*fl* 1641-83) **11** 446; **27** 230
Meyer, Hendrik (*fl* 1792) **10** 562
Meyer, Henry (*c.* 1782-1847; engraver) **29** 677
Meyer, Jacob **14** 667, *667*
Meyer, Jeremiah **21** 409*, 644; **33** 685
Meyer, Johannes, I (1614-66) **21** 406
Meyer, Johannes, II (1655-1712) **21** 406
Meyer, Johann Heinrich **14** 303
Meyer, Johann Hermann **14** 606
Meyer, Johann Jakob **4** 215
Meyer, Joseph **27** 555
Meyer, Kh. F. **3** 733
Meyer, Oscar **2** 399
Meyer, Pedro **21** 409*; **24** 679
Meyer, Rasmus **23** 243
Meyer, Richard **24** 455
Meyer, Rudolf **17** 886; **21** 152, 406–7*
Meyer, Wilhelm **25** 566; **29** 106
Meyer Altarpiece **10** 752; **14** 667, *667*, 668
Meyer-Amden, (Friedrich) Otto **3** 824; **21** 409–10*; **30** 134
Meyerbeer **27** 315
Meyer de Haan, Jacob (Isaac) **12** 191; **21** 410*; **25** 215
Meyere, van (family) **4** 692
Meyer-Esslinger, Hans-Jakob **28** 120
Meyer glassworks **17** 816
Meyerheim, Paul **12** 196
Meyerhold, Vsevolod (Emil'yevich) **18** 507; **21** 410*; **25** 239; **30** 682, 686
collaboration **2** 122
productions **2** 62; **29** 899; **30** 684
Balaganchik **27** 809
Boris Godunov **12** 878
Der Schal der Colombine **27** 810
Die Hochzert der Sobeide **2** 108
Hedda Gabler **21** 545
Klop **26** 505
Magnanimous Cuckold **7** 769
Misteriya-Buffa **20** 194; **33** 486
Schluck und Jau **31** 572
Smert Tarelkina **29** 632
Tristan und Isolde **28** 596
Meyeringh, Aelbert **9** 462; **21** 411*
Meyeringh, Frederik **21** 411
Meyerkhol'd, Karl Theodore Kasimir *see* MEYERHOLD, VSEVOLOD
Meyer-Lévy, Claude **17** 548
Meyerowitz, Joel **21** 411*
Meyers, Isidore **3** 562; **8** 62; **14** 507
Meyers, Jacques **22** 905
Meyerson, Andrey **27** 381
Meyer von Schauensee, Franz Josef **11** 770
Meyer zum Pfeil, Niklaus **30** 149
Meyjes, Christian Bernardus Posthumus *see* POSTHUMUS MEYJES, CHRISTIAN BERNARDUS
Meyn, Peter **8** 727
Meynal, Bertrand de *see* BERTRAND DE MEYNAL
Meynardier, H. **7** 745
Meynell, Francis **22** 117
Meynier, Charles **21** 411–12*
works **1** 28; **21** *412*
Meyr, Johann **23** 264
Meyr, Johann Ulrich *see* MAYR, JOHANN ULRICH
Meyr, Josef **23** 264
Meyran, Jean-Baptiste-Forentin-Gabriel de, Marquis de Lagoy *see* LAGOY, Marquis de
Meyriat **5** 894
Meyrick, Samuel Rush **21** 412–13*
armour **2** 450; **7** 579; **8** 639; **9** 31; **28** 528
interior decoration **10** 280
Meyring, Heinrich **32** 195
Meyssens, Johannes **4** 38; **17** 599; **18** 879; **22** 910; **24** 890; **25** 221; **28** 904; **33** 262
Meyt, Konrad *see* MEIT, CONRAT
Meytens, Martin I *see* MIJTENS, MARTIN I
Meytens, Martin van, II (1695-1770) **19** 337; **21** 508, 511–12*; **32** 444
patrons and collectors **28** 18
pupils **8** 809; **14** 49; **23** 359
works **2** 795; **32** *443*
Mez
works **13** *270*
Mez, François de, Cardinal **33** 287
Meza, Guillermo **30** 22
Mezadah *see* MASADA
Mezas, J. E. **30** 16
Mezei, A'rpád **10** 650
Mezei, Gábor **20** 151
Mezek **5** 145; **6** 158
Mezentsev, Boris **9** 458; **25** 89
Mezer, Franciszek de **25** 123
Mezer, Michał de **25** 123
Mezey, Lajos **30** 209
Mezherichev, Sergey **28** 567
Mezhirech'ye *see* MIZHRICHCHYA
Mezhirich *see* MIZHRICHCHYA
Mézières **13** 211
Mézières, Nicolas Le Camus de *see* LE CAMUS DE MÉZIÈRES, NICOLAS
Mezières, Philippe de *see* PHILIPPE DE MEZIÈRES
Mezin-Mezhirich period *see under* PREHISTORIC ART → periods
Mezőcsát **15** 1
Mezőtur **15** 1
Mezquida, Gaspar Homar i *see* HOMAR I MEZQUIDA, GASPAR
Mezr'eh **9** 543
Mezurashizuka Tomb **17** 143
Mezyn **21** 413*; **25** *471*, 489, 490, 493; **31** *546*
Mezzabarba, Ambrogio **32** 157
Mezzabarba, Gerolamo **32** 157
Mezzabarba, Giuseppe **32** 157
mezza-maiolica *see under* POTTERY → wares
Mezzanganica, Cherubino **20** 90
mezzanine **21** 413*
Mezzarisa, Antonio **21** 413
Mezzarisa, Francesco di Antonio **10** 751; **21** 413*
Mezzarisa, Giovanni **21** 413
Mezzarota, Lodovico Scarampi, Cardinal **8** 164
Mezzastris, Bernardino **21** 414
Mezzastris, Pierantonio **11** 711; **21** 414*
mezzotints **2** 239; **10** 393, 394; **21** 414–18*; **25** 597, 614, 619; **26** 231; **28** 671
historical and regional traditions
Austria **21** 414
England **10** 252; **19** 818; **21** 415, 416–17; **31** 465
19th cent. **21** *417*; **28** 25
France **21** 416
Germany **21** 414, 415, *415*
Ireland **16** 24; **21** 416
Netherlands, the **21** 414, 415; **31** 797
United States of America **4** 477; **21** 416; **31** 599
materials
grounds **13** 706
rockers *see* ROCKERS
steel **28** 25
uses
book illustrations **4** 359
MFI **10** 300
Mfinu **1** 403
Mg Gyi **5** 246
MGM **13** 709
M'Gombo **2** 87
Miaczyński, Ignacy **25** 138
Miagao, S Tomàs de Villanueva **24** 611, 614*
Mialhe, Federico **18** 781
Miami (FL) **21** 421–2*; **31** *587*
Art Deco district **21** 421–2
Breakwater Hotel **21** *421*
Cuban Museum of Arts and Culture **21** 422
Fontainebleau-Hilton Hotel **14** 788
Ring Theater **30** 684
University of Miami **29** 397
Vizcaya **12** 143; **21** 421
Miami (North American people) **22** 552
Mi-an Hsien-chieh *see* MI'AN XIANJIE
Miani, Hieronymus **8** 733
Mi'an Xianjie **6** 752
Mianyang, Ping Yang que **6** 649; **25** 800, *800*
Mian Zorawar Singh, Ruler (*reg c.* 1740) (Pahari) **15** 631
Miao **3** 379; **7** 45, 144
Miaodigou (Shan xian) **6** *615*; **21** 422
ceramics **6** 629
paintings **6** 773
pottery **6** 875, 876
Miaodigou culture **21** 422*
Miaofeng **6** 645
miaojin see LACQUER → types → *kingindeigawa*
MIAR **13** 728; **16** 721; **21** 422*; **26** 15
members **19** 304; **26** 364; **27** 853
works **16** 649
Miari (family) **5** 55
Miaux **11** 645
Miazzi, Giovanni **25** 561
MIBI (Mouvement International pour un Bauhaus Imaginiste) **2** 526; **7** 759; **17** 658
Mibu Suiseki **17** 413
mica
historical and regional traditions
China **7** 116
Indian subcontinent **15** 724
Japan **17** 220, 276, 371
Nigeria **1** 284
Prehistoric art **25** 477
uses
dolls **17** 371
grounds **25** 174
houses **1** 284
painting **15** 653, 724
paper **7** 116
printing **17** 220
prints **15** 855; **17** 276
rock art **25** 477
sculpture **17** 99
wallpaper **32** 811, 812
Micali Painter **10** 615
works **10** *594*, *615*
Mica Moraine **11** 92
Micault (family) **32** 272
Miccinelli, Francesco
works **16** *773*
Micele Agnolo di Papi **22** 800
Michael (*fl c.* 1295) **2** 646; **9** 584; **19** 884
Michael (*fl* late 14th cent.) **25** 442
Michael (*fl* late 16th cent.) **25** 336
Michael I, Emperor of Byzantium (*reg* 811-13) **9** 657
Michael I Angelos Doukas, Despot of Epiros (*reg* 1204-14) **2** 508
Michael II, Despot of Epiros (*reg* 1236-71) **2** 508, 509; **9** 550
Michael II, Voivode of Wallachia (*reg* 1593-1601) **26** 722
Michael III, Emperor of Byzantium (*reg* 842-67) **9** 657; **16** 607
Michael IV the Paphlagonian, Emperor of Byzantium (*reg* 1034-41) **9** 638; **16** 582
Michael VII Dukas, Emperor of Byzantium (*reg* 1071-8) **9** *662*
Michael VIII Palaiologos, Emperor of Byzantium (*reg* 1259-82) **9** *636*, 638; **16** 583–4; **23** 830
Michael (Feodorovich), Tsar of Russia (*reg* 1613-45) **7** 172; **18** 459; **27** 428
metalwork **27** *419*
Michael, Master **13** 49; **22** 116
Michael, Johann Georg **12** 132; **31** 488
Michael, Romae **4** 443
Michael Choniates **2** 689
Michaelermeister **2** 799
Michael Glavas Tarchaneiotes **9** 550, 585; **23** 830
Michaelides, Neoptolemos A. **8** 364; **21** 423*
Michaelis, Adolf **21** 423*
Michaelis, Max **5** 668; **18** 727; **29** 122
Michaelis Collection *see under* CAPE TOWN → Old Town House
Michael Keroularios, Patriarch of Constantinople **9** 638
Michael Machzor *see under* MACHZORS → individual manuscripts
Michael of Canterbury **8** 198; **19** 581; **21** 423*
works **10** 163; **19** 598, 602, 610
Michael of Wiener Neustadt **21** 424*; **32** 452, 454; **33** 164
Michaels, Jan **8** 663
Michael Scotus **22** 412
Michaelsen, Johan Carl Christian **23** 231
Michael the Brave, Voivode of Wallachia *see* MICHAEL II, Voivode of Wallachia
Michael the Syrian **9** 619
Michael von Freiburg **24** 191*; **29** 754
Michael von Gmünd *see* MICHAEL VON FREIBURG
Michael Wiśniowecki, King of Poland (*reg* 1669-73) **12** 34; **25** 128; **31** 323
Michailescu, Corneliu **20** 877; **21** 424*; **26** 716
Michalak, Antoni **10** 871
Michališki Church **3** 530
Michallon, Achille (Etna) **3** 855; **7** 877; **21** 424–5*; **31** 817
Michallon, Claude **21** 424
Michał of Działdowo **25** 102
Michal of Trnava **28** 851
Michałowicz z Urzędowa, Jan **18** 425; **21** 425*; **25** 113
pupils **3** 918
teachers **22** 168
works **2** 415; **32** 874
Michałowski, Kazimierz **2** 690
Michałowski, Piotr **18** 428; **21** 425–7*; **25** 106
works **21** *426*
Michals, Duane (Steven) **21** 427*
Michau, Théobald **21** 427*
Michaud, Marcel **10** 581; **19** 848; **29** 496
Michaux, André **11** 551; **26** 73
Michaux, Henri **21** 427–8*
dealers **7** 842
groups and movements **1** 78; **2** 515, 543; **11** 551; **24** 144; **30** 231
methods **24** 242
patrons and collectors **7** 842
works **2** *544*; **19** 491
Michel, Alfonso **21** 428*
Michel, André (-Paul-Charles) **8** 50; **9** 453; **21** 428*; **32** 643
Michel, Carl **12** 449
Michel, Claude *see* CLODION
Michel, Ferdinand **10** 93
Michel, Georges **21** 428–30*
collaboration **8** 703; **30** 63

Michel, Georges—cont.
groups and movements **26** 741
works **11** 543; **18** 714; **21** *429*
Michel, Jean (*fl* 1723) **16** 803
Michel, Jean (*fl* 1730-53) **3** 107
Michel, Jean-Baptiste **29** 676
Michel, Jorge **2** 401; **5** 123; **21** 430*
Michel, Marius **4** 354
Michel, Monsù *see* MATTEI, MICHELE
Michel, Pierre (1723-95) *see* IXNARD, PIERRE MICHEL D'
Michel, Pierre (1728-1809) **24** 108
Michel, Robert (i) (1720-86) **21** 430*
collaboration **29** 293
patrons and collectors **4** 562
pupils **1** 462
works **20** 73; **24** 108
Michel, Robert (ii) (1897-1988) **3** 779; **21** 430–31*
Michel, Sigisbert-François **1** 132
Michel, Thomas **1** 132
Michela, Costanzo **21** 431*
Michelangelo (Buonarroti) **1** 102; **3** 742; **7** 382, 783; **9** 7; **11** 187, 217; **12** 214; **14** 869, 870; **15** 80; **16** 661, 663, 689, 693, 766, 778; **21** 19, 432–61*; **22** 378, 413; **25** 296; **26** 769; **28** 201, 676; **31** 188
architecture **2** 294; **5** 700; **11** 179; **16** 634; **21** 450–56*; **25** 171, 258; **26** 756, 902; **31** 825
architectural decorations **11** 186; **14** 416; **23** 539
ceilings **16** 724
chapels **11** 178; **25** 258; **31** 524
churches
St Peter's (Vatican, Rome) **4** 404, 649; **7** 258; **9** 86; **16** 632, 637; **23** 492; **25** 265; **26** 187, 756, 805–6, *806*
S Lorenzo (Florence) **5** 17, *17*; **7** 527; **10** 744; **11** 208; **20** 278–9, 865; **21** 16; **25** 265
S Maria degli Angeli (Rome) **16** 644; **26** 844
competitions **7** 664
domes **9** 82
fortifications **10** 809
gateways **7** 359; **16** *634*
libraries **19** *314*; **21** *452*, *454*; **29** 523; **30** 357, *357*
models **2** 335, 336
orders (architecture) **23** 488, 492
palazzi
Campidoglio palazzi (Rome; Conservatori, Nuovo, Senatorio) **13** 813; **23** 810, 836
Palazzo Farnese (Rome) **16** 633; **23** 810, *810*; **26** 838, *839*; **27** 745
urban planning **21** *455*; **25** 258; **26** 813; **31** 237, 712
assistants **22** 166
Alghisi, Galasso **1** 636
Bramante, Donato **4** 648
Bugiardini, Giuliano (di Piero di Simone) **5** 129
Cosini, Silvio **7** 918
Duca, Giacomo del **9** 338
Ferrucci, Andrea di Piero (di Marco) **11** 28
Gagini, Antonello **11** 898
Granacci, Francesco **13** 280
Montelupo, Baccio da **22** 15
Montelupo, Raffaello da **22** 15
Montorsoli, Giovanni Angelo **22** 32
Sangallo, Bastiano da **27** 740
Sangallo, Francesco da **27** 747
Toledo, Juan Bautista de **13** 922; **31** 93
Michelangelo (Buonarroti)—cont.
attributions **4** 886; **7** 332; **10** 751; **12** 607; **19** 672; **21** 770; **22** 21; **26** 363; **27** 204; **28** 5; **31** 55
collaboration **5** 129; **13** 281; **14** 171; **19** 551; **22** 15; **27** 179; **28** 331, 333, 335; **32** 504
commentaries **2** 558; **7** 701–2; **25** 74; **31** 95
copies **3** 845; **4** 47; **29** 568
dealers **16** 766
drawings **9** 220; **21** 431–2*, 758; **24** 756; **32** 237
cartoons **3** 387; **16** 614, 663; **25** 223
military scenes **7** 676; **11** 186; **14** 583; **19** 184
patrons and collectors **28** 928
chalk **6** 400; **9** 11; **21** *449*
models **21** 765
presentation **12** *214*; **25** 557, 558, *558*
reproductions in hardstones **12** 258
tomb projects **9** 181
frames **11** 388, 391
groups and movements **3** 262; **26** 182
house **8** 187
imprese **15** 150
methods **18** 898; **28** 205
architecture **7** 692; **21** 458*
drawings **5** 898; **21** 758
painting **5** 614; **19** 352; **21** 457–8*; **32** 805, *806*
sculpture **16** 749; **21** 456–7*, 768
paintings and frescoes **21** 442–8*
Doni Tondo **16** 663
mythological **10** 476
Palazzo Vecchio (Florence) **31** 237
Pauline Chapel (Rome, Vatican) **21** *447*; **33** 719
Sistine Chapel (Rome, Vatican)
conservation **32** *809*
Last Judgement **5** 699; **8** 505, 612; **16** 614; **23** 293; **24** 521; **26** 286, 816, *816*
Sistine Ceiling **4** 648; **12** 503; **13** 676; **15** 137; **20** 279; **21** *444*; **22** 521; **23** 292; **26** 189, 816; **31** 501
patrons and collectors **16** 763; **18** 895; **27** 270
Alcalá, 3rd Duque de (1583-1637) **26** 307
Alfonso I, 3rd Duke of Ferrara, Modena and Reggio (*reg* 1505-34) **10** 522
Altoviti, Bindo **1** 735
Beaumont, George (Howland) **3** 454
Bird, Francis **4** 79
Bouverie, John **4** 596
Catherine de' Medici, Queen of France (1519-89) **10** 441
Charles I, King of England and Scotland (*reg* 1625-49) **2** 558
Christina, Queen of Sweden (*reg* 1632-54) **32** 8
Clement VII, Pope (*reg* 1523-34) **19** 313; **21** 17
Colonna, Vittoria **7** 623
Cosimo III, Grand Duke of Tuscany (*reg* 1670-1723) **10** 769
Crozat, Pierre **8** 209
Dimsdale, Thomas **8** 907
Doni, Agnolo **9** 142
Faesch, Johann Jakob **10** 753
Fountaine, Andrew (1676–1753) **11** 348
Francesco I, Grand Duke of Tuscany (*reg* 1574-87) **5** 183
Francis I, King of France (*reg* 1515-47) **10** 477; **23** 855; **31** 849
Michelangelo (Buonarroti)
patrons and collectors—cont.
Franco, (Giovanni) Battista **11** 721
Galli, Jacopo **9** 21; **12** 21
Grimani, Domenico, Cardinal, Patriarch of Aquilea **13** 657
Hoffmann, Lorenz **6** 76
Holanda, Francisco de **14** 660
Howard, Hugh **14** 810
Howard (i), Thomas, 2nd Earl of Arundel **14** 806; **24** 572
Isabella d'Este, Marchesa di Mantua (1474-1539) **10** 521
Jabach, Everard **16** 815
John III, King of Portugal (*reg* 1521-57) **14** 660
Julius II, Pope (*reg* 1503-13) **7** 218; **16** 664; **26** 768; **27** 272, 273; **28** 314
Julius III, Pope (*reg* 1550-55) **22** 6
Knight, Richard Payne **18** 150
Lagoy, Marquis de **18** 641
Lawrence, Thomas **18** 895
Leoni, Leone **19** 203
Ligne, Charles-Joseph-Emmanuel de, Prince (1759-92) **19** 369
Loeser, Charles Alexander **19** 538
Macpherson, Robert **20** 33
Mariette, Pierre-Jean **20** 417
Medici, Lorenzo di Pierfrancesco de' **21** 15
Montmorency, Anne, Duc de, Constable of France **6** 453; **22** 31
Museo Nazionale del Bargello **16** 774
National Gallery (London) **4** 602
Nollekens, Joseph **30** 496
Nys, Daniel **23** 326
Orsini, Fulvio **23** 577
Ottley, William Young **23** 634
Paul III, Pope (*reg* 1534-50) **10** 808, 809; **16** 665; **26** 769, 800
Paul IV, Pope (*reg* 1555-59) **6** 175
Pius III, Pope (*reg* 1503) **24** 732
Pius IV, Pope (*reg* 1559-66) **25** 7
Reynolds, Joshua **26** 280
Riario, Raffaele (Sansoni), Cardinal **26** 299
Richelieu, Armand-Jean Du Plessis, Cardinal de **26** 348
Robertet, Florimond de **11** 661; **26** 454
Robinson, John Charles **26** 473
Röver, Valerius **27** 270
Rubens, Peter Paul **25** 664
Seilern, Antoine, Count **28** 377
Soderini, Piero (di Tommaso) **28** 928
Taddei, Taddeo **30** 231
Tallard, Marie-Joseph d'Hostun, Duc de **30** 274
Thibaudeau, Narcisse-Adolphe, Comte de **30** 727
Valori, Baccio **31** 851
Vasari, Giorgio (1511-74) **32** 22
Vecchietti, Bernardo **32** 106
Wellesley, Henry **33** 56
William II, King of the Netherlands (*reg* 1840-49) **23** 469; **33** 345
Wright, John Michael **33** 409
personal collection **28** 436
photographed works **26** 236
pupils **3** 19; **9** 338; **10** 812
reproductive prints by others
Alberti, Cherubino **1** 551
Barbiere, Domenico del **3** 211
Beatrizet, Nicolas **3** 448; **26** 174
Biard, Pierre (ii) (1592-1661) **3** 925
Bos, Cornelis **10** *477*
Michelangelo (Buonarroti)
reproductive prints by others—cont.
Cartaro, Mario **5** 888
Casa, Nicolò della **5** 906
Cunego, Domenico **8** 267
Dupérac, Etienne **9** 398
Ghisi, Giorgio **12** 558
Jode, Gerard de **17** 598
Le Mercier, Jacques **19** 133
Lorck, Melchior **19** 661
Musi, Agostino dei **22** 369
Raimondi, Marcantonio **10** 385; **25** 858
Rota, Martino **27** 212
Ruscheweyh, Ferdinand **27** 346
Scultori, Adamo **28** 316
Vico, Enea **32** 412
Volpato, Giovanni **32** 689
restorations by others **3** 688; **7** 627; **27** 321; **31** 894
sculpture **3** 157; **7** 842; **16** 694–5*; **21** 432–41*; **26** 187
allegorical **23** 293
crucifixes **8** 215
monuments
David **1** 456; **7** 383; **10** 476; **16** *694*, 774; **18** 725; **22** 44; **23** 292; **24** 527; **27** 739; **29** 561
Marcus Aurelius pedestal **2** 168; **29** 565
mythological **29** 561
portraits **4** 280
reliefs **11** 217; **25** 152; **26** 137; **31** 142
religious **3** 706; **4** 920; **16** 694, 695
Piccolomini Altar **4** 737; **28** 677, 681; **31** 189
Pietà (St Peter's) **1** 711; **21** *434*; **24** 777; **26** 809
Rondanini *Pietà* **16** 775
shrine of St Dominic **4** 276, 278; **23** 89
tomb projects **14** 870; **26** 186
Gian Giacomo de' Medici **16** 697
Giuliano de' Medici, Duc de Nemours and Lorenzo de' Medici, Duke of Urbino **11** 208; **21** *438*; **25** 283; **27** 830; **31** 320
Julius II, Pope (*reg* 1503-13) **4** 649; **5** 166; **13** 703; **16** 696; **19** 159; **21** *436*, *437*; **25** 682; **26** *235*
studio **29** 853
teachers **12** 554
writings **1** 102, 640; **11** 56, 200, 770; **21** 538; **24** 90
Michelangelo delle Battaglie *see* CERQUOZZI, MICHELANGELO
Michelangelo di Pietro **20** 709; **21** 461*
Michelangelo di Viviano **3** 156
Michel de Gand **31** 218
Michel de Ungaria **24** 16
Michele, Bartolo di *see* BARTOLO DI MICHELE
Michele, Felice di *see* FELICE DI MICHELE
Michele da Calcina *see* MICHELE DI MATTEO DA BOLOGNA
Michele da Firenze **10** 519; **13** 95; **21** 461*; **30** 497
Michele da Fornace *see* MICHELE DI MATTEO DA BOLOGNA
Michele dai Unii *see* PANNONIO, MICHELE
Michele da Parma *see* ROCCA, MICHELE
Michele d'Aria **11** 897; **27** 546; **29** 411; **32** 603
Michele di Bartolommeo **23** 754; **29** 436
Michele di Giovanni da Fiesole **31** 743
Michele di Matteo da Bologna **4** 275; **16** 848; **21** 461–2*
Michele di Niccolaio *see* MICHELE DA FIRENZE
Michele di Niccolò detto Scalcagna *see* MICHELE DA FIRENZE
Michelena, Arturo **21** 462*
works **32** 174, *174*, 178
Michelena, Bernabé **31** 755
Michelena, Juan Antonio **21** 462; **32** 174
Michele Squilli, Benedetto di *see* SQUILLI, BENEDETTO DI MICHELE
Michelet **4** 546
Michelet, Jules **11** 675
Michelet, Raoul *see* UBAC, RAOUL
Michelham Priory (E.Sussex) **6** 603
Micheli, Guglielmo **21** 786
Micheli, Parrasio **21** 462*
Micheli, Pietro Adamo de' **12** 906; **20** 322
Micheli, Vincenzo **10** 761; **17** 547
Michelin **13** 811
Michelin, Jean (*b* before 1616-70) **21** 462–3*, 640
Michelin, Jean (1629-96) **21** 463
Michelin de Jonchery **31** 384
Michelino (*fl* 15th cent.) **9** 95
Michelino, Domenico di *see* DOMENICO DI MICHELINO
Michelino (de, Molinari) da Besozzo **1** 588; **21** 463–4*
assistants **19** 180
attributions **21** 533; **24** 779
collaboration **16** 824
works **12** 287; **21** *464*
Michell, Mathew **27** 279
Michelozzi, Corrado **28** 319
Michelozzi, Giovanni Battista **5** 360
Michelozzi, Girolamo **4** 408
Michelozzi, Michelozzo **16** 763
Michelozzo di Bartolomeo **11** 178; **12** 111, 544; **20** 264; **21** 464–70*; **26** 766
architecture **2** 39; **5** 21; **11** 196; **21** 13
architectural decorations **21** 12
bastions **9** 330
churches **1** 556; **7** 257; **11** 178, 204; **21** *470*; **27** 733
courtyards **3** 173; **8** 65; **21** *469*; **31** 237
forts **8** 175
libraries **16** 630; **21** *468*; **23** 319; **32** 214
orders (architecture) **23** 486
palazzi **3** 174; **5** 22; **11** 178; **16** 629; **20** 111; **23** 809, *836*; **31** 173
porticos **5** 361
staircases **29** 521
villas **28** 283; **32** 545
assistants **2** 17; **23** 772; **29** 568
attributions **5** 17; **11** 210; **20** 264; **31** 55; **32** 545
collaboration **9** 124, 125, 129, 157; **11** 185, 198; **12** 710; **20** 552; **22** 476; **25** 450; **26** 444; **27** 830
patrons and collectors
Cosimo, Lord of Florence (*reg* 1434-64) **11** 206; **19** 313; **21** 10, 11; **23** 835
Medici (family) **9** 112; **11** 207; **16** 630
Piero de' Medici, Lord of Florence (*reg* 1464-69) **28** 490
pupils **27** 180
sculpture **16** 689, 690, 742; **21** 10
altars **5** 128
tabernacles (ii) (receptacle) **21** 12
tombs **21** *465*
Michels, J. W. **17** 753
Michelsberg culture **25** 504

Michelsen, Anton **8** 751
Michelsen, Hans **17** 814; **21** 471*; **23** 229
Michelucci, Giovanni **21** 471–2*
collaboration **11** 182; **16** 650; **24** 694
groups and movements **26** 16
patrons and collectors **7** 782
works **7** 258; **16** 650; **25** 855
Michener, James **17** 431
Michetti, Francesco Paolo **16** 678; **21** 472–3*; **32** 256, 257
works **21** *473*
Michetti, Niccolò **21** 473–5*; **23** 637
assistants **6** 571
patrons and collectors **10** 769; **23** 637, 874; **27** 172
pupils **21** 475
works **10** 537; **11** 277; **12** 9; **19** 17; **24** 546; **25** 322; **30** 277; **33** 633
Michiaki Kaneshige *see* KANESHIGE, MICHIAKI
Michie, James Beattie **26** 74
Michie, James Coutts **19** 875
Michiel (family) **32** 615
Michiel (*fl* 1412) **13** 111
Michiel, Master *see* SITTOW, MICHEL
Michiel, Marcantonio **7** 714; **21** 474–5*; **23** 355; **32** 193
works **3** 659; **16** 767, 781; **18** 707; **21** 632
Michiel, Pietro **23** 751
Michiel, Pietro Antonio **13** 338
Michieli, Andrea *see* VICENTINO, ANDREA
Michieli, G. **9** 159
Michieli, Parrasio *see* MICHELI, PARRASIO
Michieli, Salvi di *see* SALVI DI MICHIELI
Michiel van der Borch **22** 833
Michigan Central Railroad **32** 866
Michigan City Public Library (IN) **19** 320
Michikaze *see* ONO NO MICHIKAZE
Michilini, Sergio **23** 84
Michinaga, Fujiwara no *see* FUJIWARA NO MICHINAGA
Michitada Funaki *see* FUNAKI, MICHITADA
Michiyo, Tachibana no *see* TACHIBANA NO MICHIYO
Michizane, Sugawara no *see* SUGAWARA NO MICHIZANE
Michl, Martin **10** 531
Michle **8** 382
Michna, Count **5** 701; **8** 875
Michoacán **21** 249
Augustinian Monastery **21** 375
furniture **21** 391
Museo Michoacáno **21** 396
sculpture **21** 217, 225; **29** *901*
statuettes **10** 474
Michon, King of Koguryo (*reg* 300-331 AD) **18** 353
Mich'u, King of Silla (*reg* 262-84 AD) **18** 364, 367
Michurin, Ivan (Fyodorovich) **21** 475*
collaboration **27** 374; **31** 552
pupils **31** 543
works **22** 171; **27** 374; **28** 465
Mičić, Ljubomir **8** 437
Micker, Barent **33** 24
Micker, Jan Christiaensz. **4** 80; **33** 24, 25
Micklethwaite, J. T. **2** 64; **28** 279
Miclescu, P. E. **20** 400
Micmac **22** 556, 647, 650, 651, 670, 674
microcrystalline wax *see under* WAXES → types
microfiches **2** 367; **31** 671
microforms **2** 364; **26** 236, *236*
micrography **21** 475–6*, *476*
see also CALLIGRAPHY; CARMINA FIGURATA
microliths **29** 445
micro-mosaics *see* ICONS → historical and regional traditions → Byzantine; Early Christian
Micronesia *see* KIRIBATI; KOSRAE; MARIANA ISLANDS; MARSHALL ISLANDS; MICRONESIA, FEDERATED STATES OF; NAURU; PACIFIC ISLANDS; PALAU
Micronesia, Federated States of **21** 476–7*
dress **23** 723
fibres **21** *477*
gateways **23** *716*
masks **21** 477
sashes **21** *477*
stone **23** *716*
tattoos **21** 477
tourist art **21** 477
weaving **21** 477
microscopes **11** 309; **24** 655; **28** 210, 211, *212*
microscopy *see under* TECHNICAL EXAMINATION → types
Micu, Efrem **26** 713
Micus, Eduard **30** 172*
Midas **24** 690
Midas City *see* YAZILIKAYA (ii) (PHRYGIAN)
Middachten **12** 132
Castle **22** 822, 826
Middelaer, Daniel de **8** 464
Middelburg (Belgium) **4** 113
Middelburg (Netherlands) **13** 159
Abbey *see* Zeeuws Museum
brass **3** 603
glass **22** 884
Koorkerk **22** 819
Munck's house **22** 295
Nieuwe Kerk Organ **22** *373*
Oostkerk **9** 299
painting **22** 839*
Provincial Registry **8** 670
tapestries **30** 318
Town Hall **13** 63; **22** 822; **33** 582
warehouses **32** 861
Zeeuws Museum **32** 732
Middelburg Tapestries **30** 318; **32** 732
Middeldorf, Helmut **12** 397
Middeldorf, Ulrich **21** 478*; **24** 25
Middelfart Church **8** 723
Middelthun, Julius Olavus **21** 478*
pupils **10** 105; **18** 101, 463; **22** 289; **33** 77
works **23** 229
Middendorf, E. W. **23** 703
Middiman, Samuel **28** 883
Middlebourg, Comte de **24** 821
Middle Caicos Island **3** 59
Middle Cycladic period *see under* CYCLADIC → periods
Middle Cypriot period *see under* CYPRUS, ANCIENT → periods
Middleditch, Edward **18** 97, 98; **28** 880
Middleham Pendant **13** 170
Middle Helladic period *see under* HELLADIC → periods
Middle Kingdom *see under* EGYPT, ANCIENT → periods
Middle Minoan period *see under* MINOAN → periods
Middle Niger cultures **21** 478–81*
archaeology **21** 480–81*
chronologies **21** 480*
collections **21** 478
dating methods **21** 479–80*
ethnography **21** 480*
human figures **21** *479*, 479*
mounds **21** 478*
statuettes **21** 478–81*
terracotta **21** 478–81*, *479*; **30** 509
Middlesbrough (Cleveland)
Tees Bridge **4** 800
Town Hall **31** 240
Transporter Bridge **4** 800
Middleton (Cumbria; UK)
Cross B **32** 529
Middleton (CT; USA) **31** 651
Middleton, Ann **21** 482
Middleton, Charles (1756-before 1818) **23** 782
Middleton, Charles (1799-1867) *see* MONCK, CHARLES
Middleton, Colin **16** 40
Middleton, Conyers **32** 825
Middleton, Henry **12** 136
gardens **12** *136*
Middleton, Henry Willoughby, 6th Baron *see* WILLOUGHBY, HENRY, 6th Baron Middleton
Middleton, John (*fl* 19th cent.; architect) **26** 316
Middleton, John (*d* 1848; painter; father) **21** 482
Middleton, John (1827-56; painter; son) **18** 619; **21** 482*; **23** 249
Middleton, J. R. **5** 246
Middleton, William **3** 283; **19** 11
Middleton & Bailey **3** 280
Middleton Place (SC) **12** 62, 136, *136*
Middleton Towers (Norfolk) **4** 779
Middletown (RI)
F. W. Andrew House **7** 619
Jacob Cram House **29** 653; **31** 593
Middot **17** 494
Midea **8** 712; **14** 339, 340, 354
Midewiwin Grand Medicine Society **22** 563
mi'dhana **21** 625
Midian **27** 877
Midianites **2** 268
Midjawmidjaw, Jimmy **21** 482*
Midland Great Western Railway Company **22** 282
Midlands black ware *see under* POTTERY → wares
Midland Scripture Crosses **8** 196
Midlands yellow ware *see under* POTTERY → wares
Midow, Claus **4** 667
Mi Duc **6** *418*, 422
MIDVA *see* MOBLES I DECORACIÓN DE LA VIVIENDA ACTUAL
Miechów Monastery Church **25** 114
Miel, Jan **21** 482–3*; **31** 443
collaboration **2** 43; **7** 509; **27** 489, 643
groups and movements **3** 143
patrons and collectors **28** 11, 12
works **11** *394*; **21** *483*; **28** *12*; **30** 527; **32** 101
Mielatz, Karl Friedrich Wilhelm **21** 896
Mielich, Hans **2** 455; **21** 484–5*; **22** 299, 302; **28** 188
assistants **28** 188
patrons and collectors **12** 387; **33** 271, 275
works **9** 750; **21** *484*
writings **12** 455
Mielich, Wolfgang **21** 484; **26** 76; **28** 161
Miélot, Jean **3** 555; **8** 208; **19** 252
Mielziner, Jo **5** 531; **30** 684, 687
Mielżyński (family) **25** 139
Mielżyński, Maksymilian **17** 756; **18** 741
Mielżyński, Seweryn Józef Stanisław **21** 485*; **25** 138
Mien **30** 623, 634, 639
dress **30** 625*, *625*
MIENK **10** 108
Mierevelt, Jan van **8** 665; **21** 486
Mierevelt, Michiel (Jansz.) van **8** 665, 667; **21** 485–6*, 509
patrons and collectors **5** 9; **15** 40; **22** 127; **29** 797, 799; **33** 279
pupils **8** 665; **22** 94; **23** 831; **26** 38; **32** 673
reproductive prints by others **4** 282; **8** 664; **10** 393; **22** 272
teachers **4** 148
works **5** 764; **11** 446; **21** *486*
Mierevelt, Pieter van **21** 486
Mieris, Dirck (Bastiaensz.) van **21** 486
Mieris, Frans (Bastiaensz.) van (*c.* 1576-before 1625) **21** 486
Mieris, Frans van, the elder (1635-1681) **19** *101*; **21** 486–9*; **22** 843; **29** 375
attributions **32** 683
groups and movements **19** 102; **22** 841
patrons and collectors **21** 29
pupils **22** 50
reproductive prints by others **21** 800
teachers **9** 194; **19** 101; **30** 425
works **11** 459; **15** *96*; **21** *487*, 488, *488*
Mieris, Frans van, the younger (1689-1763) **19** *101*, 102; **21** 486, 489–90*; **22** 841, 846
groups and movements **19** 102
patrons and collectors **23** 469
teachers **21** 489
works **12** 290
Mieris, Jan (Bastiaensz.) van (*c.* 1586-1650) **21** 486
Mieris, Jan van (1660-90) **19** 102; **21** 486, 488; **22** 841, 846
groups and movements **19** 102
Mieris, Johannes van *see* MIERIS, JAN VAN (1660-90)
Mieris, Willem (Fransz.) van (*c.* 1600-1656) **21** 486, 487
Mieris, Willem van (1662-1747) **19** *101*; **21** 486, 488–9*; **22** 50, 841
attributions **21** 488
groups and movements **19** 102
patrons and collectors **5** 65; **11** 141; **23** 468; **29** 366
teachers **21** 488
works **21** *489*
Mieroszewski, Krzysztof **18** 693; **19** 751
Miers, Henry **5** 591
Mies, François de, Cardinal *see* MEZ, FRANÇOIS DE, Cardinal
Miesbach, Alois **32** 437
Miesnieks, Kārlis
Miessner, Michał **25** 127
Miestchaninoff **19** 41
Mies van der Rohe, Ludwig **2** 397; **3** 512; **4** 61; **5** 573; **7** 385; **8** 803; **17** 722; **21** 490–94*; **29** 321; **31** 633
architecture **3** 796; **4** 789; **16** 55
apartments **31** *597*
banks **3** 177
exhibition architecture **3** 216; **10** 684; **15** 883; **21** *491*; **29** 273
government buildings **3** 513
halls **21** *492*
houses **2** 360; **4** 788; **8** 380, *380*, *826*; **18** 786; **21** *493*; **31** 597
housing **8** 821; **29** 874; **30** 458
models **2** 337
museums **3** 797; **12** 380, 477; **14** 803; **22** 366
office buildings **6** 574; **23** 43, 359
plans **4** 143
roofs **27** 129
shopping centres **5** 573
skyscrapers **1** 736; **3** 128; **12** 792; **28** 834; **31** 597
villas **4** 833; **32** 556
assistants **14** 524; **31** 754
Mies van der Rohe, Ludwig— cont.
collaboration **13** 266; **14** 524; **17** 620; **24** 188; **27** 222; **31** 176; **33** 246
commentaries **17** 620
drawings **2** *333*, 334
exhibitions **12** 417
furniture **8** 402; **12** 428; **26** 226; **29** 321; **30** 218, 755, 784
groups and movements **3** 795; **10** 698; **25** 741
Bauhaus **3** 403; **12** 378
CIAM **7** 293
Deutscher Werkbund **8** 826; **21** 782
Elementarism **10** 137
Modern Movement **15** 885, 887
Rationalism (ii) (style) **26** 15
Ring, Der **21** 782; **26** 405
methods **2** 360; **12** 792
patrons and collectors **11** 735
pupils **12** 873
staff **27** 621
Mieszko I, Prince of Poland (*d* 992) **12** 823; **25** 408
Mieth, Adolph **25** 648
Miethke, H. O. **2** 829
Mietsch **11** 760
Mieza *see* LEUKADIA
Mifflin (family) **1** 184
Mifflin, Thomas **31** 642
Mi Fu **6** 748, 749, 750, 760, 771, 789, 816, 818; **7** 129, 141, 152; **10** 692; **12** 87; **21** 418–20*; **30** 49
attributions **21** *419*; **32** 837
groups and movements **14** 825; **29** 244; **33** 528
patrons and collectors **6** 772
personal collection **7** *96*
works **1** 581; **6** *750*; **7** 115
writings **6** 749–50, 754, 771, 819, 823
Migadis, Ioannis **8** 157
Migahara, Takehara Art Museum **17** 138
Mig Aran Church **26** 642
Migazzi, Christoph Anton, Cardinal **5** 614; **31** 786
Migdol *see* HEIR, TELL EL-
migdols *see* TOWERS → types → watch → Syria-Palestine
Migeon, Gaston **16** 548, 559
Migéon, Pierre, I (*b c.* 1670) **21** 494
Migéon, Pierre, II (1701-58) **4** 524; **21** 494*; **24** 150
works **11** 591, *592*
Migéon, Pierre, III (1733-75) **21** 494
Migge, Leberecht **21** 494–5*
Migjeni Artistic Products Enterprise **12** 862; **31** 20
Migliara, Giovanni **21** 495*, 527; **31** 445; **32** 114
Migliara, Teodolinda **21** 495
Migliaro, Vincenzo **21** 495*
Miglioranza, Giovanni **32** 411
Migliore, Ferdinando Leopoldo del **21** 495–6*
Migliore, Pietro di *see* PIETRO DI MIGLIORE
Migliore, Zanobi di *see* ZANOBI DI MIGLIORE
Migliorini, Ferdinando **11** 636; **12** 830
Migliorini, Orazio **11** 636; **12** 830
Migliorisi, Ricardo **21** 496*; **24** 99
groups and movements **22** 743; **24** 99
works **24** 101
Migliorotti, Atalante **10** 522
Migna, Andrea del **12** 897
Mignard, Nicolas **2** 860; **21** 496–7*; **25** 461; **31** 382
patrons and collectors **7** 546; **19** 731
reproductive prints by others **20** 592; **25** 77

Mignard, Nicolas—cont.
works **11** *402*; **24** 161; **32** 573
Mignard, Paul **12** 391; **22** 302; **33** 276
Mignard, Pierre, I **2** 860; **11** 534, 537; **12** 828; **21** 496, 497–8*; **23** 512; **24** 134, 167; **31** 382
collaboration **9** 372
copies **18** 418
groups and movements **24** 169; **27** 287
methods **21** 764
patrons and collectors **4** 552
Asse, (Louis-)Auguste **2** 614
Aumale, Henri-Eugène-Philippe-Louis de Bourbon, Duc d' **23** 523
Beringhen, Jacques-Louis, Marquis de Chateau-neuf **3** 785
Bourbon I., Louis de, le Grand Dauphin (1661-1711) **4** 553
Grimaldi (family; Monaco) **21** 830
Houssaye, (François-) Arsène **14** 802
Louis XIV, King of France (*reg* 1643-1715) **4** 552
Orléans, Philippe I de Bourbon, 1st Duc d' (1640-1701) **23** 513; **27** 536
Tallard, Marie-Joseph d'Hostun, Duc de **30** 274
Trinitarians **31** 340
personal collection **5** 866; **7** 864
pupils **7** 863; **10** 909; **25** 77; **32** 670
reproductions in tapestry **12** 829
reproductive prints by others **2** 708; **11** 57; **13** 898; **25** 77; **28** 178, 751
works **7** 415; **9** 278; **11** 536; **21** *497*, *498*; **23** 512; **24** 160
Mignard d'Avignon *see* MIGNARD, NICOLAS
Mignard le Romain *see* MIGNARD, PIERRE, I
Mignault, Claude **10** 174
Migne, Jacques Paul **10** 209
Migneco, Giuseppe **7** 894; **21** 528
Mignon **16** 53
Mignon, Abraham **11** 225, 227, 229; **12** 389; **14** 289; **22** 844; **27** 270; **29** 667
Mignon, Jean **10** 551; **11** 264, 532; **21** 499*
Mignon, Léon **21** 499*
works **21** *499*
Mignoni, Fernando **13** 725
Mignot **31** 256
Mignot, David **12** 446
Mignot, Jean **2** 351; **20** 567; **21** 530
Mignot, Victor **25** 347
Migom **26** 526
Migration period **21** 499–503*
buckles **21** *503*
enamel **21** *502*, 503
fibulae **21** *502*
filigree **21** 503
gravestones **21** *502*
jewellery **21** 501, 503
metalwork **21** 503
ornament **23** 536–7
stone-carvings **21** *502*
styles **21** 502, *502*
Migros Genossenschaftsbund **30** 153
Miguel, Antonio **3** 7
Miguel, Carlos de **29** 322
Miguel, Juan Antonio
works **29** *348*
Miguel, Pedro **29** 334
Miguel Juan de San Leocadio **24** 27
Migumo Senshō **17** 412
Mihailich, Győző **14** 865
Mihailidis, Polyvios **31** 819
Mihailo, King of Duklja (Serbia; *reg* 1077-81) **28** 445
Mihailov, Nikola **5** 154; **21** 503–4*
Mihailović, Milorad-Bata **28** 451
Mihailovo **5** 152
Mihajlović, Josif **19** 883
Mihalcheva, Irina **5** 163
Mihalidis, Polyvios **13** 349
Mihalik, Dániel **30** 211
Mihály, Mikes **15** 3
works **15** *3*
Mihály, Rezső **12** 839
Mihály Hesz, János *see* HESZ, JÁNOS MIHÁLY
Mihanović, Robert Frangeš **8** 178
Mihata Jōryū **17** 197
Mihelič, Franc **28** 861
Mihelič, Milan **28** 860
Mihevc, Edo **19** 516
Mihin, Djouman **8** 23
Mihindusaya **29** 475
Mihintale **5** 97; **21** 504*; **29** *440*
monasteries **29** 446
sculpture **29** 457
wall paintings **29** 464
Mihira Bhoja, Ruler (*reg c.* 836-85) (Gurjara-Pratihara) **15** 288
Mihmandust **16** 163
mihrabs **16** 100, 130, 141, 146; **21** 504–6*, *505*; **22** 192
historical and regional traditions
Afghanistan **16** *163*
Central Asia, Western **16** 161, 245, *492*, 492
Egypt **16** *176*, 176; **21** 505–6
Indian subcontinent **15** 338, 351; **21** 506
Iran **16** 161, *244*, 249, 492; **21** 506; **29** *820*
Morocco **16** *240*
Saudi Arabia **21** 32
Spain **16** 188, *188*
Sudan **21** 505
Syria **1** *603*; **21** 505, *505*
Tajikistan **16** *492*
Turkey **21** 506
Yemen **16** 178
materials
marble **21** *505*
stucco **16** *163*, *244*, 245; **21** 506; **29** *820*
tiles **5** *282*; **16** 249; **21** 506
wood **16** *492*, 492; **21** 505
Mihr 'Ali **21** 506–7*
pupils **1** 471; **12** 507
works **16** 522, 534, 535, *536*; **25** 770; **30** 415
Mihr Chand **15** 208
Mihrimah Sultan **23** 641; **28** 767
mosque **28** *767*
Mihr Narseh **27** 854
Mihu de la Crişul Alb **21** 507*; **26** 710
Mij, Hieronymus van der **19** 102; **21** 489
Mijae *see* NAM KU-MAN
Mijares, Carlos **21** 381
Mijares, José (Maria) **18** 834; **21** 507*
Mijares, José Manuel **32** 567
Mijares, Manuel **32** 567
Mijares, Rafael **5** 603; **21** 380, 381; **22** 366
works **21** *380*
Mijares de Solorzano, Juan Javier **32** 179
Mijarez, Rafael **25** 878
Mijić, Karlo **4** 461
Mijikenda **1** 258, 292; **17** 906
works **1** *258*
Mijliyya **3** 376
Mijn, Agatha van der **21** 507
Mijn, Andreas van der **21** 508
Mijn, Cornelia van der **21** 507
Mijn, Frans van der **21** 508*; **22** 846; **23** 468
Mijn, George van der **21** 508*; **22** 846
Mijn, Gerard van der **21** 507
Mijn, Heroman van der **21** 507, 508*; **22** 846
Mijn, Robert van der **21** 508
Mijnnesten, Jan van den *see* JAN VAN DEN MIJNNESTEN
Mijtens, Aert **21** 508
Mijtens, Daniel, I (*c.* 1590-*c.* 1647) **10** 248; **21** 508, 509–10*; **22** 844; **30** 517
collaboration **29** 592
copies **14** 777; **28** 234
patrons and collectors **14** 435; **29** 803; **32** 575
pupils **21** 510
reproductive prints by others **8** 665
works **2** 163; **9** 22; **10** 363; **16** 823; **17** 645; **19** *583*; **21** *509*
Mijtens, Daniel, II (1644-88) **21** 508
Mijtens, Isaac **21** 508, 509
Mijtens, Jan **14** 41; **21** 508, 509–10*; **22** 844
teachers **21** 509
works **21** *510*
Mijtens, Martin, I (1648-1736) **5** 9; **11** 123; **21** 508, 510–11*
pupils **21** 511
works **21** *511*; **30** 78
Mijtens, Martin van, II *see* MEYTENS, MARTIN VAN, II
Mijuláš Gallic reliquary **28** 856
Mikarew style pottery *see under* POTTERY → wares
Mikashavidze, T. **12** 320
Mik'ayelyan, Mik'ayel **2** 436
Mikelić, Jovan **28** 459
Mikėnas, Juozas **16** 874; **19** 498, 499
Mikeshin, Mikhail (Osipovich) **21** 512*
collaboration **23** 450; **30** 915
works **18** 38; **23** 271; **27** 390, 578; **31** 561
Miketti, Nikola *see* MICHETTI, NICCOLÒ
Mikhailishki *see* MICHALIŠKI
Mikhalovsky, B. G. **31** 551
Mikhalyov, Andrey Nikolayevich **18** 568
Mikhaylin, Ivan **27** 434
Mikhaylov, Andrey (Alekseyevich) **4** 598; **21** 512*; **27** 198
Mikhaylovsky Cross **31** 563
Miki, Tomio **17** 207; **21** 512–13*; **22** 742
Mikio Ōsako *see* ŌSAKO, MIKIO
Mikishi, Kōtarō **17** 206
Miki Suizan *see* SUIZAN, MIKI
Mikkiades **2** 308
Mikko, Leppo **10** 540
Mikl, Josef **2** 797
Miklashevsky Factory **27** 412
Miklos, Gustave **26** 486
Miknās *see* MEKNÈS
Mikohidari **17** 224
Mikołaj **32** 878
Mikon **13** 522; **21** 513*; **25** 177; **32** 60
attributions **23** 901
works **13** 545, 548; **14** 466
Míkonos *see* MYKONOS
Mikov, Vasil **17** 808
Mikovíny, Samuel **28** 853
Mikre Vigla **22** 698
Mikuláš **3** 223; **18** 396
Mikulčice **8** 375, 388
Mikulić, Mario **4** 461
Mikulov
Jewish museum **17** 581
Loreto Church **8** 386
synagogue **17** 545
Mikulski, Kazimierz **18** 429
Mikus, Sándor **14** 896
Milà, Alfonso **7** 884*
Milagres, Joaquim Rodrigues *see* RODRIGUES MILAGRES, JOAQUIM
Milagro-Quevedo **21** 513*; **29** 152; **31** 118
Milà i Fontenals, Manuel **21** 127
Milà i Fontenals, Pablo **12** 179; **29** 283
Mila Mergi **21** 299
Milan **9** *510*; **16** *616*, *618*; **21** 514–38*, *514*
academies **1** 104
Accademia Ambrosiana *see* Accademia del Disegno
Accademia di Belle Arti di Brera **4** 470; **22** 26; **26** 319
collections **11** 396, 798; **16** 772, 773
library **16** 776
Pinacoteca **2** 233; **3** 355, 452; **4** 470; **8** 172; **16** 774, 775; **19** 786; **22** 357
Pinacoteca: directors **3** 857
Accademia del Disegno **1** 103; **4** 426; **21** 526; **26** 245; **28** 34
see also Biblioteca Ambrosiana
Accademia Leonardi Vinci **1** 102; **16** 778
Accademia di S Luca **16** 779
apartment blocks
Ca' Brutta **16** 649; **22** 393; **23** 263, 264
Casa Borletti **16** 649
Casa della Meridiana **16** 649
Casa Ferrario **16** 648
Casa Marmont **16** 650; **23** 263
Gallaratese 2 **25** 359; **26** 16; **30** 455
Arco della Pace **16** 647, 705; **21** *520*
Arco del Sempione *see* Arco della Pace
Arena **1** 798
art forms and materials
architecture **16** 646; **26** 577
armour **2** 469, 471, *472*
books **14** 433
coins **7** 535
embroidery **13** 195; **16** 760
engravings **10** 383
furniture **16** 724, 730
hardstones **14** 171; **16** 746, 747
ivory **23** 659–60
lace **16** 754; **18** 589, 590
maiolica **21** 529*
manuscripts **26** 564
medals **20** 919
metalwork **16** 742
mosaics **9** 571; **22** 161
painting **13** 149; **16** 661; **23** 649; **29** 301
rock crystal **16** 745; **21** 529*; **26** 486
sculpture **16** 688, 697*, 700–701*
silk **13** 197; **16** 752, 753; **28** 716
stained glass **13** 182
tapestries **16** 755, 756, 757, 758; **30** 328
Atrium of Porto Marengo **16** 647
Biblioteca Ambrosiana **4** 426, *426*; **19** 313
collections **2** 376; **6** 146, 381; **16** 771
Pinacoteca Ambrosiana **3** 857; **4** 426; **9** 229
see also academies → Accademia del Disegno
Biblioteca d'Arte *see under* Castello Sforzesco
Biblioteca Nazionale **16** 776
Casa degli Omenoni **19** 201–3, *203*
Casa di Riposo per i Musicisti Giuseppe Verdi **4** *246*
Casa Fontana-Silvestri **4** 643; **31** 268, 269
Casa Panigarola-Prinetti **4** 643
Casa Prina **2** 233
Casa Sannazzaro *see* Casa Prina
Casa Silvestri *see* Casa Fontana-Silvestri
Milan—cont.
Castello Sforzesco **3** 439, 695; **14** 421; **16** 647, 775; **21** *515*
Accademia Leonardi Vinci *see under* academies
Achille Bertarelli collection **16** 776, 777
Biblioteca d'Arte **16** 776
Cortile della Rocchetta **4** 643
drawings **19** 632; **20** 494; **26** 318
dress **16** 760
furniture **20** 468
manuscripts **19** 322
medals **2** 117
Missals **12** 666
monument to Bernabò Visconti **13** 94
paintings **5** 308, 405, 406; **19** 785; **20** 312; **27** 445; **28** 531, 532; **29** 26; **31** 5
Sala della Balla **5** 307
Sala delle Asse **19** 183, 189; **28** 532
sculpture **1** 747; **12** 709; **16** 688; **26** 620; **32** 610
tapestries **30** 332
chronicles **7** 243
Cimitero Monumentale **4** *101*; **31** 131
Civico Archivio Fotografico **16** 777
Collegio Borromeo **30** 801
Collegio Elvetico **26** *319*
ecclesiastical buildings
basilica **9** 531
Canonica **30** 801
Cathedral of Maria Nascente **1** 748; **4** 774; **7** 265; **13** 65, 199, 210; **16** 627, 647; **19** 561; **20** 566–7, 573; **21** 529–32*, *530*, *531*, 534*; **25** 155; **26** 317; **28** 460; **29** 24; **30** 801–2
altars **7** 263
candelabrum **26** 686
choir-screen **26** 620
competitions **4** 746
confessio **8** 224
Cross of Bishop Aribert **26** 690
doors **9** 159
ivory-carvings **13** 172; **23** 659, 660; **28** 805
paintings **5** *550*; **21** *526*; **25** 643
sculpture **3** 138; **4** 655; **5** 182; **10** 743, 744; **13** 95; **16** 697, 701; **21** 532–3*
stained glass **13** 193; **29** 504, 505
Treasury **21** 533–4*
Trivulzio candelabrum **1** 653; **21** 533
weathervane **33** 8
Oratory of the Fabbrico *see* S Maria Annunziata
S Alessandro **3** 249
S Ambrogio **7** 302; **8** 260; **9** 86, 532; **16** 625, 630; **21** 534–5*, *535*, 840
Canonica **4** 646; **23** 488
chapel of S Vittore **8** 261; **9** 571
collections **28** 805
corbels **7** 837
doors **9** 151; **16** 686
Doric Cloister **4** 646
furniture **30** 776
Golden Altar **5** 807, *807*; **8** 259; **9** 668; **21** 536; **22** 520; **26** 144
Ionic Cloister **4** 646
pulpit **21** 536, *536*; **25** 723; **26** 620
sarcophagus **9** 596; **27** 827
sculpture **5** 796; **21** 535–6*; **26** 619, 620
stucco **29** 818, 831
vaults **26** 578; **32** 94

Milan
ecclesiastical buildings
S Ambrogio—cont.
wall paintings 23 649
S Angelo
paintings 5 *546*
S Antonio Abate 16 747
SS Apostoli *see* S Nazaro Maggiore
SS Barnaba e Paolo 1 608; 3 249
S Carlo al Corso 7 258; 16 647; 29 833
S Carlo Borromeo 16 742
S Eustorgio
monument to Giovanni Stefano Brivio 27 830
Portinari Chapel 11 *293*; 16 630
shrine of St Peter Martyr 13 *94*, 94
S Fedele 30 802, *802*
S Francesco di Paola 16 641
S Francesco Grande 16 562
S Giorgio al Palazzo
altarpiece 19 *785*
S Giovanni in Conca 9 531; 14 421
S Giuseppe 1 164; 16 641; 26 317–18, *318*
S Gottardo in Corte 13 65; 16 688; 32 609, 610
S Lorenzo 3 355, *355*; 7 255, *255*; 9 525, 531; 16 624; 20 572; 21 536–7*, *537*; 27 235
chapel of S Aquilino 3 189; 7 272; 9 571; 32 88
mosaics 16 654; 21 *523*
S Marco 19 545
Foppa Chapel 19 *545*
paintings 25 *642*
S Maria Annunziata 21 534
S Maria di Brera
sculpture 13 94
S Maria delle Grazie 4 645–6, 774; 9 86, 112; 16 630; 21 *516*; 30 501
Last Supper fresco 15 137; 19 189; 21 846; 22 378; 26 187; 27 445; 32 805
S Maria della Passione 8 148; 16 747; 23 320
S Maria presso S Celso 1 608; 11 279–80; 16 634
sculpture 11 *280*
S Maria presso S Satiro 4 *644*, 644–5; 7 256; 16 630; 30 501
S Maurizio 23 659
S Nazaro Maggiore 4 654; 7 252; 9 531; 31 280
S Satiro 15 137
S Simpliciano 2 292; 7 252; 9 531, *532*; 20 572; 21 537–8*; 31 280
S Tecla 9 529, 531, *531*; 21 537*
Baptistery 3 189; 7 255
S Vincenzo in Prato 26 577
S Vittore al Corpo 29 831
Swiss parish church 23 320
exhibitions
6th Triennale 16 650
Esposizione Internazionale del Sempione, 1906 15 883
Galleria Azimut 6 21
Galleria Bardi 24 484
Galleria Il Milione 6 582; 16 721; 19 421; 24 484
Galleria Pesaro 28 792
Galleria Schwarz 28 188
Galleria Vittorio Emanuele II 2 290; 12 792; 16 54, 647; 21 130, *130*; 29 833
guilds 21 523–4*
IBM Building 16 651
INA-Casa housing project 16 650
Instituto Marchiondi 16 650
Martesana Canal 2 242
Mattioli collection 11 398
Milan—cont.
Medici Bank 3 173; 11 292; 16 630
Monte Amiata 16 651
Montecatini building 16 650
monuments
monument to Bernabò Visconti *see under* Castello Sforzesco
monument to the Cinque Giornate 13 *294*; 16 706
Monument to the Victims of the Concentration Camps 3 438–9
Pertini monument 16 651
Mostra dell'Aeronautico Italiano 16 650
museums
Galleria d'Arte Moderna 13 715
Museo di Arte e di Etnologia Estremo-Orientale 29 240
Museo Civico di Storia Naturale 4 484; 6 352; 28 496
Museo Marino Marini 20 429
Museo dell'Opera del Duomo 16 774
Museo Poldi Pezzoli 3 857; 16 774; 25 143–4; 30 332
Museo Settala *see* Museo Civico di Storia Naturale
Palazzo Bagatti Valsecchi 3 49, 50, *50*
Pinacoteca Ambrosiana *see under* Biblioteca Ambrosiana
Pinacoteca di Brera *see under* academies → Accademia di Belle Arti di Brera
Olivetti Building 1 736
Ospedale Maggiore 7 257; 11 72, *72*; 14 781; 16 630; 30 501
courtyard 8 64
Lazaretto 14 782
palazzi
Palazzo Archinto 30 856
Palazzo Arciducale *see* Palazzo Reale
Palazzo Arcivescovile 22 26; 30 801
courtyard 21 *519*
Palazzo dell'Arte 28 793
Palazzo Bagatti Valsecchi *see under* museums
Palazzo Belgioioso *see* Villa Reale
Palazzo Berri-Meregalli 16 648
Palazzo Borromeo 32 611
Palazzo di Brera *see* academies → Accademia di Belle Arti di Brera
Palazzo Busca 3 856
Palazzo Casati 30 856
Palazzo Castiglioni 16 721; 25 793
Palazzo Clerici 16 716; 29 832
frescoes 15 138; 16 674, *674*
Palazzo Cusani 27 *320*, 321
Palazzo Diotti 29 832
Palazzo Ducale *see* Palazzo Reale
Palazzo Fidia 16 649
Palazzo dei Giureconsulenti 28 *460*, 460
Palazzo di Giustizia 22 332
Palazzo Litta 2 233; 29 832
Palazzo Lucini-Passalacqua 2 233
Palazzo Marino 1 607–8, *608*; 16 647
Palazzo Moriggia 31 268
Palazzo Negroni-Prata 31 268
Palazzo Pertusati 16 647
Palazzo Radice-Fossati 29 832
Palazzo della Ragione 18 886
Palazzo Reale 16 646, 719, 728
frescoes 14 267; 31 268
paintings 2 233; 16 677
Sala dei Senatori 5 289
stucco 29 833
Palazzo del Senato *see* Collegio Elvetico
Milan
palazzi—cont.
Palazzo Serbelloni 31 268
Palazzo Visconti 32 609–10
Piazza del Duomo 16 647
Piazza de' Mercanti 4 643
Pirelli Building 7 696; 16 650; 22 806; 25 *218*; 28 834
Politecnico di Milano 16 651
Porta Romana 26 619, 620
Settala collection *see* museums → Museo Civico di Storia Naturale
Società Ceramica 9 58
S Siro Stadium 29 489
Stazione Centrale 16 648; 21 *521*; 25 857
Teatro alla Scala 16 646; 24 758, *758*; 30 667
Teatro Patriottico 2 233
Teatro S Erasmo 30 684
Torre Velasca 3 *438*; 15 887; 16 650, *651*
Università Cattolica del Sacro Cuore 16 650; 22 394; 23 263
urban planning 2 174–5; 3 195; 5 385; 16 647; 29 486
Villa Belgioioso *see* Villa Reale
Villa Crivelli 16 719
Villa di Monza 16 719
Villa Gonzaga *see* Villa Simonetta
Villa Reale 16 646, 719; 25 154, *155*
Villa Simonetta 12 *761*; 21 *518*
Milan, Pierre 10 388; 11 532; 21 538*
assistants 4 615
groups and movements 11 264
works 11 *264*; 27 209, 210; 30 735
Milan Adoration, Master of the *see* BEER, JAN DE
Milanés, Martín 32 147
Milanes, Paolo Stella *see* STELLA MILANESE, PAOLO
Milanese Madonna *see under* COLOGNE → churches → Cathedral of St Peter and St Maria
Milanesi, Carlo 6 148; 21 538
Milanesi, Gaetano 10 730; 16 782; 21 538*; 25 74
Milanesi, N. 13 680
Milan Gregory 9 614
Milan Hours *see* BOOKS OF HOURS → individual manuscripts → Turin-Milan Hours
Milani, Aureliano 16 670; 21 538–9*
pupils 12 658; 20 390
teachers 24 227
works 21 *539*; 28 489
Milani, Giulio Cesare 21 539
Milani, Luigi Adriano 16 774
Milano, Amadio da *see* AMADIO DA MILANO
Milano, Ambrogio da *see* BAROCCI, AMBROGIO (D'ANTONIO)
Milano, Carlo da *see* BRACCESCO, CARLO
Milano, Filippo Veris da *see* FILIPPO VERIS DA MILANO
Milano, Francesco Canova da (1497-1543) 22 370
Milano, Francesco da (*fl* 1377-88) *see* FRANCESCO DA MILANO
Milano, Giovanni Antonio di 30 799
Milano, Giovanni da *see* GIOVANNI DA MILANO
Milano, Lanfranco Veris da *see* LANFRANCO VERIS DA MILANO
Milano, Matteo da *see* MATTEO DA MILANO
Milano, Pietro di Martino da *see* PIETRO DI MARTINO DA MILANO
Milano, Venturino Mercanti da *see* VENTURINO MERCANTI DA MILANO
Milano, Zuan de *see* RUBINO, GIOVANNI
Milanov, Yordan 5 149; 28 838
Milan Situla 28 805
Milant, Jean 19 492; 20 609
Milâs 5 742–3; 29 702
carpets 16 472, 478
see also under CARPETS → types
congregational mosque 16 202
Great Mosque 16 202
sculpture 13 459
tomb 5 742–3; 31 109
Milashevsky, V. A. 28 394
Milazzese 25 522
Milborne Port (Somerset), St John the Evangelist 2 67; 26 616
Milchschranken 5 579
Milcx, Philips 1 161
Milde, Ary de 8 668; 22 879
Milde, Carl Julius 4 39; 21 540*
Milde Furniture Factory 31 20
Mildenhall (Suffolk) 10 *225*
Mildenhall Great Dish 18 825; 21 540, I2; 27 *84*
Mildenhall Treasure 9 655; 21 540*; 26 *905*; 27 83, 84
Mildeová-Paličková, Emilie 8 421
Mildert, Antoon van 21 541
Mildert, Cornelis van 2 202; 3 570
Mildert, Hans van 3 570; 21 541*
collaboration 21 765; 23 460
dealing 3 615
works 7 500
Mildmay, Bingham 32 377
Mildmay, Walter 5 511
Mildner, Johann Joseph 2 818; 8 409
Mildorfer, Josef Ignaz 21 541*
patrons and collectors 10 529
teachers 31 358
works 11 31; 14 900
Mildorfer, Michael Ignaz 21 541*
Mildura 2 754
Miled, Tarak ben 31 424
Milembwe 29 70
Milemete, Walter of *see* WALTER OF MILEMETE
Miles *see* SOLON, MARC-LOUIS-EMANUEL
Miles, Bishop of Nanteuil 3 458
Miles, (George) Frank 12 840; 21 541; 25 805
Miles, Philip John 21 541*
Mileševa 9 *511*; 21 541–2*; 28 *437*
Church of the Ascension 9 582; 25 343; 28 441, 445, 452
Monastery 28 440
milestones 27 6
Milet, Jean *see* FRANCISQUE
Milet, Pierre-François 11 410
Milet d'Auxerre 2 109
Milet le Cavelier 31 839
Mileto 31 717
SS Trinità 16 626
Miletos 9 *512*; 13 *363*, *381*, 502; 15 893; 21 542–3*; 26 883, *908*
agora 13 380, *381*; 24 456; 26 912; 29 681
architecture 15 893, 894; 26 911, 913
bath-gymnasium 26 912
Baths of Faustina 3 374; 26 *912*
bouleuteria 13 405
bouleuterion 4 530, *530*; 13 381, 390, *405*, 407; 14 73; 21 543; 23 349, 484
Cape Monodendri 1 692
East Stoa 13 406
figurines 13 578
fortifications 9 554; 21 555, 556, 558
gymnasium 3 375; 23 828
Harbour Stoa 13 406
heroön 14 466
North Agora 19 888; 20 438
nymphaeum 27 6
Miletos—cont.
palace 9 557
pottery 13 497, 503; 16 420
protomes 13 582
Sacred Gate 7 358
sculpture 18 245; 27 46
stoa 13 381; 27 714
stone 13 387
Temple of Asklepios 9 590
theatre 21 543, *543*
trade 14 337
urban planning 13 419, 420; 14 564; 26 913
Miletsky, A. M. 9 54
Miletus, Hecataeus of *see* HECATAEUS OF MILETUS
Miletus ware *see under* POTTERY → wares
Milev, Ivan 5 155, 163; 21 543–4*
Milevsko 8 412
St Giles 8 376
Milewski, Ignacy Korwin 12 604
Milford Haven (Dyfed) 21 569; 32 782
Milford Haven, George Mountbatten, 2nd Marquess of *see* MOUNTBATTEN, GEORGE LOUIS VICTOR HENRY SERGE, 2nd Marquess of Milford Haven
Milháltz, Pal 30 207
Milhau, John 4 228
Milhaud, Darius 18 864; 20 387, 591
collaboration 6 167; 7 508; 9 373; 19 81, 83
groups and movements 8 438
patrons and collectors 16 892
Milhomme, François-Dominique-Aimé 21 544*
pupils 19 125
Milián, Raúl 21 544*
miliaresoi see under COINS → types
Milić, Periša 28 453
Miličević, Kosta 28 451
Milik 31 557
Milik, Olga 19 885
Milingimbi 1 60, 66
Milinis, Ignaty 12 654; 27 379
works 12 *654*
Milioti, Nikolay (Dmitriyevich) 4 178; 21 544–5*; 27 458; 33 379
Milioti, Vasily (Dmitriyevich) 4 178; 21 545*; 27 458
military architecture *see under* ARCHITECTURE → types
military decorations and awards *see* MEDALS
military drums *see under* DRUMS → types
military scenes 3 387–90*
Etruscan 10 595
France 12 *349*; 24 *256*
Greece, ancient 13 493
Italy 10 595
Maya 21 247
Poland 25 *107*
Spain 32 *129*
United States of America 24 *666*
see also PAINTING → types → battle
Miliutin, Stephen Uroš II, King of Serbia *see* STEPHEN UROŠ II MILIUTIN, King of Serbia
Milizia, Francesco 19 535; 21 600*; 30 667
works 2 358; 3 262; 31 296
Miljuš, Branko 28 452
milk 30 560
brass 4 684
crayons 8 127
plaster 29 813
secco paintings 28 338, 339
stucco 29 813
milk glass *see* GLASS → types → *lattimo*
milkpails *see* BUCKETS
Mill, Edward 21 347

Millais, John Everett **8** 828; **10** 362; **19** 269, 507, 588; **21** 601–4*
assistants **29** 47
book illustrations **4** 363
collaboration **15** 26
dealers **12** 30
groups and movements **10** 253; **17** 440; **25** 554, 555, 556; **26** 56; **27** 185
methods **18** 899
patrons and collectors
City Art Gallery (Manchester) **20** 239
Combe, Thomas and Martha **7** 647
Grosvenor, Hugh Lupus, 1st Duke of Westminster **13** 697
Holloway, Thomas **14** 688
Leathart, James **18** 907
Lever, William Hesketh, 1st Viscount Leverhulme **19** 270
Plint, T(homas) E(dward) **25** 41
Proby, William, 5th Earl of Carysfort **25** 639
Stephens, F(rederic) G(eorge) **29** 633
Tate, Henry **30** 359
Tennant, Charles **30** 464
Windus, B(enjamin) G(odfrey) **33** 251
pupils **17** 673
reproductive prints by others **2** 692; **3** 245; **6** 519; **12** 30; **19** 868; **28** 748
works **4** 868; **9** 289; **10** 253, 420, *420*; **11** 433, 434, 436; **21** *601*, *602*; **25** *555*; **27** *351*; **28** 664
Millan, Carlos B(arjas) **21** 604*; **27** 308
Millan, Ignacio **29** 343
Millán, Pedro **13** 108; **21** 604–5*
Millar, Anne **13** 303
Millar, James **4** 86
Millar, Liam **16** 18
Millar, Pedro **6** 598
Millard, George **33** 403
Millardet, Charles **26** 205
Millares, Los *see* LOS MILLARES
Millares, Manolo **21** 605*
dealers **7** 842
groups and movements **2** 545; **29** 286
patrons and collectors **7** 842; **20** 832
works **29** 286
Millauer, Abraham **32** 822
Millbank, Albert *see* BELLEROCHE, ALBERT (GUSTAVUS) DE, Count
millboard *see under* BOARDS
Millburn (NJ), B'nai Israel Synagogue **10** 890; **17** 549, 580
Millé (family) **3** 599
Mille, Cecil B. De *see* DE MILLE, CECIL B.
Mille, Giovanni **11** 5; **31** 431, 432
Millech, Knud **8** 761
Milledonne, Antonio **31** 13
millefiori see under GLASS → types
millefleurs see under CARPETS → types; TAPESTRIES → types
Miller **20** 744
Miller, Abraham **31** 637
Miller, Albrecht **12** 446
Miller, Alfred Jacob **21** 605*
patrons and collectors **12** 618; **32** 829
pupils **33** 371
works **33** 184
Miller, Andrew **16** 15; **18** 829
Miller, Arthur **30** 687
Miller, Barse **19** 701
Miller, David (father) **16** 882
Miller, David (son) **16** 882
Miller, Dorothy C(anning) **21** 606*
Miller, Ellen **31** 658
Miller, Ferdinand von, the elder (1813-87) **12** 406; **28** 186
Miller, Ferdinand von (1842-1929) **7** 326
Miller, Fritz von **12** 449
Miller, George C. **3** 681; **19** 492; **20** 604; **25** 628
Miller, Godfrey (Clive) **18** 689; **21** 606*
Miller, Hans Rudolf **14** 899
Miller, Henry **4** 691; **16** 808
Miller, Herman, Inc.
designers **9** 502; **22** 728; **23** 175; **26** 545; **31** 632, 633
production **15** 825; **31** 633
chairs **15** *825*; **20** 595; **31** *632*, 633
furniture **23** 360
Miller, H. McRae **5** 571
Miller, Jacob **12** 445
Miller, James **12** 774; **28** 230, 231
Miller, John **33** 251
Miller, John, & Partners **7** 640
Miller, John Douglas **8** 579; **21** 606*
Miller, John Frederick **15** 892
Miller, John Harmsworth **7** 639–40
Miller, John Paul **12** 867; **31** 655
Miller, Kenneth Hayes **21** 606–7*
pupils **3** 31; **4** 93; **14** 751; **18** 518; **20** 476; **23** 12; **24** 362
Miller, Lee **12** 871; **21** 607*; **24** 369, 657
groups and movements **30** 20
works **24** *656*
Miller, Lilian B. **31** 673
Miller, Philip **10** 101
Miller, Ruprecht **30** 112
Miller, Samuel **32** 904
Miller, Sanderson **21** 607–8*; **23** 21
collaboration **4** 875
groups and movements **13** 199
works **7** 291; **8** 48; **10** 233, *234*; **12** 130, *130*, 176; **13** 645; **17** 878; **18** 886; **27** 323
Miller, Thomas **9** 757
Miller, Wilhelm (*fl* 1914) **25** 446
Miller, William (1796-1882) **10** 396
Miller, William H. (*fl c.* 1944) **25** 25
Miller, Wolfgang **33** 274
Millerd, Jacob
works **4** *820*
Miller-Parker, Agnes **4** 367
Millers, Emīls *see* MELDERIS, EMĪLS
Miller von Aichlolz (family) **2** 829
Milles, Carl (Wilhelm Emil) **21** 608*; **27** 474; **30** 86
pupils **27** 475; **30** 54
works **13** 31; **30** *87*
Millet, Aimé **18** 751; **21** 608*; **25** 207
Millet, Etienne **24** 103
Millet, Eugène-Louis **18** 816; **21** 608*; **27** 560
Millet, Francis Davis **1** 22; **27** 557
works **27** *557*
Millet, Francisque **11** 536; **21** 609–10*
collaboration **9** 87
patrons and collectors **5** 278; **30** 451
reproductions on porcelain **14** 323
works **21** *609*
Millet, Gabriel **21** 610*; **28** 439
excavations **9** 528
pupils **17** 732; **26** 332; **33** 479
works **9** 527, 528
Millet, Jean **21** 609
Millet, Jean Charles **11** 309
Millet, Jean-François (1642-79) *see* MILLET, FRANCISQUE
Millet, Jean-François (1814-75) **11** 545, 671; **21** 610–13*
cliché-verre **7** 434
forgeries by others **11** 308
groups and movements **3** 212; **22** 687; **26** 54; **28** 921
Millet, Jean-François (1814-75)—cont.
patrons and collectors
Boussod, Valadon & Cie **4** 589
Bruyas, Alfred **5** 57
Camondo, Isaac de, Comte **5** 530
Chauchard, Hippolyte-Alfred **6** 516
Cognacq, (Théodore-) Ernest **7** 528
Dugléré, Adolphe **9** 378
Forbes, James Staats **11** 301
Havemeyer, Louisine (Waldron) **14** 244
Ionides, Alexander Constantine **15** 895
Laurent-Richard **18** 869
Le Secq (des Tournelles), Henri (1818-82) **19** 239
National Museum of Wales (Cardiff) **5** 732
Shaw, Quincy Adams **28** 560
Tret'yakov, Pavel (Mikhaylovich) **31** 312
Vanderbilt, William Henry **31** 870
Wyndham, George O'Brien, 3rd Earl of Egremont **33** 453
personal collection **17** 440; **27** 266
pupils **20** 145
reproductive prints by others **4** 625; **6** 519; **31** 830
works **7** 433; **8** 618; **11** 309, 415, *415*, 774; **12** 294; **18** 715; **21** *611*, *612*; **24** 551; **25** *600*; **28** 919
Millet, Joseph **21** 609
Millet, Kate **10** 483; **12** 217
Millet, Roger **3** 226
Milley, Dom
works **21** *837*
Mill Green (Essex) **10** 301, 302
Millich, Nicolaas **21** 614*
patrons and collectors **14** 288
works **29** 690; **30** 85, *93*
Millies, Jacob **32** 592
Milliet, Mme. **8** 73
Millin de Grandmaison, Aubin-Louis **8** 471; **10** 208; **21** 614*
Millin Du Perreux, Alexandre **4** 303; **31** 373
Millingen, A. van **9** 527
Millington, Edward **10** 366; **19** 583; **21** 614*
Millmore, Martin **31** 611
Millon, René **30** 483
mills (industrial) **21** 600–601*
England **10** 748; **16** 52; **21** 600–601
Italy **21** 600
Scotland **28** 228
United States of America **10** 748; **21** 601
Mills, Alexander W. **10** 669
Mills, Clark **31** 610, 611
Mills, Edward David **4** 790
Mills, H. N., & Cie **3** 602
Mills, J(ohn) Saxon **21** 614–15*
Mills, Mark
works **29** *35*
Mills, Peter **2** 545; **19** 509; **21** 615*; **32** 551
Mills, Robert **14** 246; **21** 615–19*
collaboration **33** 195
groups and movements **13** 611
teachers **18** 845
works **3** 128; **6** 486; **10** 850; **18** 887; **21** *617*, *618*; **25** 4; **26** 353; **31** 591, 662; **32** 886
Mills, Roger **2** 150
Mills, Russell **10** 403
Millstatt Abbey **2** 790, 798
cloister **7** 455
sculpture **26** 634, *634*
Millstone Grits *see under* SANDSTONE → types
Milltown, Joseph Leeson, 1st Earl of *see* LEESON, JOSEPH, 1st Earl of Milltown
Milltwitz, Bartłomiej **25** 104
Milman, Adolph **14** 676
Milmore, Martin **11** 756
Milne, David B(rown) **21** 619–20*
patrons and collectors **5** 589
works **1** 496; **5** 567, *567*
Milner, Edward **4** 216; **24** 293; **25** 402
Milner, John **21** 620*; **24** 598
Milner, William (*fl* 1710) **5** 827
Milner, William (*fl* 1864) **18** 667
Milner-White, Eric **33** 545
Milnes, Richard Moncton, 1st Baron Houghton **10** 487
Milo, Jean **2** 510, 545; **5** 45; **17** 518
Milo, Konrad **8** 433
Mil'oneg, Pyotr **18** 35; **31** 547
Milon of Solos **13** 552
Milos *see* MELOS
Milosavljević, Pedja **28** 451
Miloslavsky, F. S. **22** 170; **27** 438
Miłosław **25** 138
Miloš Obrenović, Prince of Serbia (*reg* 1815-39; 58-60) **3** 620; **28** 438
Milot **14** *54*
Citadelle de la Ferrière **14** 57
Palais de Sans Souci **14** 57, *57*, 60
Milovanović, Djordje **28** 450
Milovanović, Milan **19** 324; **28** 451
Milovuk, Josif **28** 451
Milow, Keith **21** 620*
Milpurrurru, George **21** 620–21*
Milroy, Lisa **21** 621*
Miltiades **13** 489
Milton (MA)
John Denny House **25** 806
Museum of the American China Trade **7** 30
Milton, John (1608-74) **4** 359, 366; **13** 299; **21** 640
Milton, John (1759-1805) **21** 621*
Milton, Joseph Damer, 1st Baron *see* DAMER, JOSEPH, 1st Earl of Dorchester
Milton, Peter **10** 398, 558
Milton, Thomas **2** 597; **16** 15
Milton and Richards **19** 310
Milton Bradley **31** 260, 266, 267
Milton Bryan Church (Beds) **10** 286
Milton Dyer, J. **7** 428
Milton Keynes (Beds) **19** 519; **31** 733
Milton Lockhart (Strathclyde) **28** 288
Milton Park (Cambs) **32** 797
Miltos, Alberto **24** 99
Mil'tsy, Nikolayev Monastery **31** 550
Milučký, Ferdinand **28** 850
Milunič, Vlado **8** 381
Milunović, Milo **21** 621*; **22** 18; **28** 451
Milunović, Nikola-Kolja **28** 454
Milvus, F. *see* KYTE, FRANCIS
Milwaukee Art Museum (WI), Richard and Anna Flagg Collection **14** 60
Milyutin, Nikolay (Aleksandrovich) **21** 621–2*; **27** 379; **31** 730
Milzetti, Francesco, Conte **12** 584
Mimar see ARKITEKT
al-Mi'mar, Mahmud Fahmi **9** 764
Mimara, Ante **8** 180
Mimault, Bernardin **10** 836
Mimaut, Jean François **10** 91
Mimbres **22** 560, 602–3; **23** 565
pottery **22** *603*
Mimbros Associates **22** 671
Mimeograph **28** 299
Mimerel, Jacques **4** 36
mimesis **13** 467–8; **14** 99; **15** 93; **21** 622*; **30** 163; **33** 462
Gothic **13** 128, 138–9
mimesis—cont.
Greece, ancient **1** 175; **2** 413; **25** 32
Italy **13** 138–9
see also ILLUSIONISM; REALISM; REPRESENTATION
Mimey, Maximiliano **19** 386; **24** 504
Mimi, Fuad **17** 655
Mimic Master **13** 103
Mimigernaford **22** 315
Mimkakhani ibn Muhammad Amin **6** 208
Mimmenhausen **12** 405
Mimoserie, La *see* LA MIMOSERIE
Mimura, Chikusei **17** 414
Mimura Baizan **17** 412
Mina (India) **1** 770; **15** 726
Mina (Togo) **31** 73
Mina (*fl* 1594) **26** 712
al-Mina (Lebanon)
Burj al-Siba' **21** 587
fortifications **21** 587
al-Mina (Syria) **1** *849*; **13** *362*, 372; **21** 622–3*
excavations **33** 373
faience (i) (glass) **1** 878
pottery **1** 877; **16** 397; **21** 623; **30** 197
Mina, Marqués de la **3** 215
Minagawa Kien **17** 196, 236, 414; **20** 837
minā'i see under TILES → types
Minai, Ali **2** 902
Minaj **1** 540
Minakshi Sudareshvara Temple *see under* MADURAI
Minami, Hisakazu *see* HISAKAZU MINAMI
Minami, Kunzō **17** 205
Minamoto (family) **17** 154
Minamoto Nagaharu **32** 840
Minamoto no Kaneyuki **17** 222
Minamoto no Morofusa **5** 334
Minamoto no Sanetomo, Shogun (*reg* 1205-19) **31** 675
Minamoto no Yoritomo, Shogun (*reg* 1192-99) **14** 566; **17** *161*, 746; **22** 496
Minamoto no Yoriyoshi **17** 746
Minamoto Shitagō **17** 388
Minangkabau **15** *752*, 753, 807; **20** 163
architecture **15** *771*, 771–2
jewellery **15** 814
keris **20** 174
textiles **15** 794, 813
Minard, Louis-François-Martial **3** 547; **21** 623*
house **3** 578
personal collection **3** 585
teachers **26** 526
Minardi, Bruno **16** 651
Minardi, Tommaso **21** 623–5*, *625*; **26** 776
collaboration **23** 829
groups and movements **3** 921; **16** 677; **25** 741; **26** 735
pupils **5** 900; **7** 408; **8** 522, 786; **21** 61; **24** 866; **25** 741
Minardus **12** 704
Minare *see* PINARA
minarets **16** 100, 130, 138, 141, 142, 158, 223; **21** 625–8*
Afghanistan **16** 166, *167*
Central Asia, Western **6** 201; **16** 160, 166, 237; **18** 22
China **6** *677*
Egypt **16** 175, *212*; **21** 627
Indian subcontinent **8** *672*
Iran **16** 160, 163, 164, 165, 194; **21** *627*
Iraq **16** 180; **21** *626*
Morocco **16** 190; **21** *626*
North Africa **16** 190
Ottoman **16** 223; **21** 628
Spain **21** 626
Syria **16** 180; **21** 627
Turkey **16** 202, 223; **21** 628

minarets—cont.
Uzbekistan 5 140
Yemen 16 178, 215
Minar-i Chakri 1 192
Minarro da Canosa 21 78
Mináry, Pál 17 855
Minas Gerais 7 538
Minato, Gherardo di Giovanni da *see* GHERARDO DI GIOVANNI DA MINATO
Minato ware *see under* POTTERY → wares
Minaux, André 21 628–9*
Minaya, Pedro Díaz *see* DÍAZ MINAYA, PEDRO
minbars 16 130, 487, 516; 21 629–30*; 22 192; 30 784
historical and regional traditions
Egypt 16 496–7; 21 629
Indian subcontinent 15 340; 21 630
Iran 21 630
Morocco 11 50; 16 493, 495; 21 630
North Africa 16 493–4
Spain 16 493
Syria 16 496–7; 21 629
Turkey 16 498; 21 630
materials
ivory 21 630
stone 21 630
wood 16 487, 493, 493–4, 495, 496–7, 498; 21 629–30, 630
see also PULPITS
Minbin, King (*reg* 1531-53) (Myohaung) 2 280
Minc, Salek 24 496
Mincham, Jeff 2 762
Min Chen *see* MIN ZHEN
Minchioni, Giuseppe 22 481
Minchō Chōdenso *see* CHŌDENSU MINCHŌ
Minchō Kichizan *see* KICHIZAN MINCHŌ
Minchou *see* FUZHOU
Mincu, Ion 5 72; 21 630–31*; 26 709, 726
Mind, Georg 11 766
Mindanao 24 607, 628
architecture 24 625
basketwork 24 628
body ornaments 24 625, 626
containers 24 627
dress 24 628
grave markers 24 630
houses 24 611
metalwork 24 627
weapons 24 631
weaving 24 623, 624
Mindata 2 369
Mindaugas, Grand Duke of Lithuania (*reg c.* 1265-63) 19 495
Mindelheim 12 403; 25 540
Minden
Cathedral 13 49; 14 80, 81; 26 684; 27 131
copper 12 452
metalwork 23 659; 26 683
Minderhout, Antoon van 21 631
Minderhout, Hendrik van 3 561; 9 745; 21 631*
Minderhout, Willem August van 21 631
Mindlin, Henrique E(phim) 4 713; 21 631*
Mindlin Associates 4 713
Mindon, King of Burma (*reg* 1853-78) 5 246, 255; 20 243
Mindoro 24 607, 624, 627, 630
Minella, Pietro di Tommaso del *see* PIETRO DI TOMMASO DEL MINELLA
Minello (de' Bardi), Antonio (di Giovanni) 21 632*; 32 192
collaboration 21 632
works 4 739; 21 474
Minello, Giovanni 21 632
Minello (de Bardi), Giovanni d'Antonio 21 632*; 23 754
assistants 27 304
attributions 19 556
pupils 22 167; 27 304
works 2 609; 16 693; 23 756
Mineo Okabe *see* OKABE, MINEO
mineral green *see* MALACHITE
mineral tannage *see under* TANNING
Minerbetti, Bernardo 32 14
Minerbi, Arrigo 21 533
Miner's coat 12 461
Minerva Giustiniana 12 764
Minerva romana, La 24 448
Minerve 1 694
mines 1 713
Mines Royal Societie 10 339
Mineu 14 885
Minev (family) 31 393
Minev, Peter 31 393
Minfeng *see* NIYA
Mingachevir 2 890, 894, 898; 21 633*; 25 471
Mingdi, Emperor (Han; *reg* AD 57-75) 6 815, 816; 7 152
Mingdi, Emperor (Eastern Jin; *reg* AD 323-6) 6 776
Mingdi, Emperor (Liu Song; *reg* AD 465-73) 6 816
Ming dynasty *see*:
HONGWU EMPEROR
XUANDE EMPEROR
YONGLE EMPEROR
see also CHINA → periods → Ming period
Mingei 17 295, 344, 353; 21 634–5*; 23 371; 31 134
Minghetti, Angelo 4 278
Minghetti, Prospero 11 283
Ming-oi 5 102; 28 720
sculpture 29 823
wall paintings 5 102
Ming-ti, Emperor *see* MINGDI, Emperor
Ming Tombs *see under* CHANGPING
Minguet, Juan 32 563
El Minguillo 25 508
Mingun 5 221, 234, 253
Hsin-byu-me 5 234
Minguzzi, Luciano 21 533, 636; 24 278; 26 810
minhagim books 21 636*
Minh Mang (monk) 32 479
Minh Mang, Emperor (*reg* 1820-41) 32 488
Min Hyŏng-sik 18 331
Mini, Antonio 21 449
Miniato, Giovanni *see* GIOVANNI MINIATO
Miniato, Nanni *see* GIOVANNI MINIATO
miniature cameras *see under* CAMERAS → types
miniature pagodas *see under* PAGODAS → types
Miniature Print Society 25 629
miniatures (manuscript illumination) 2 649, 650; 4 344; 14 413; 20 337–43*; 21 636–8*
historical and regional traditions
Afghanistan 16 324, 326; 20 VI
Albania 1 539
Anglo-Saxon 2 75, 77; 3 710
Austria 2 790; 26 676
Belgium
Early Netherlandish style 4 370; 5 211; 13 660; 14 389; 19 252, 340; 20 659, 682, 687, 700, 725, 726
Ottonian 3 552
Romanesque 26 667
15th cent. 21 638; 32 729
16th cent. 14 760
Benedictine Order 3 710
Bulgaria 5 153
Burma 5 245, 246
miniatures (manuscript illumination)
historical and regional traditions—cont.
Byzantine 4 4; 9 605, 620; 20 I
Greece 9 607, 609, 611, 614, 615
Turkey 7 228; 9 621
Ukraine 31 556, 558
6th cent. AD 27 174; 32 462
Carolingian 2 221; 4 5; 5 801, 804; 9 253; 11 151; 21 637; 30 166
Central Asia, Western 16 343
Coptic 7 824
Czech Republic 33 71
Early Christian (*c.* AD 250-843) 4 4
Egypt 7 824; 16 306, 312
England 33 90
Anglo-Saxon 2 75, 77; 3 710
Benedictine Order 3 710
Gothic 2 222; 3 879; 4 372; 13 130, 141, 147; 14 415; 21 729; 25 807; 28 66
Romanesque 4 6; 5 288; 10 244; 26 670, 671, 672
Ethiopia 10 570
France
Carolingian 5 804
Gothic 2 313; 3 643; 5 207; 7 765; 11 530; 13 140, 153, 154; 14 414; 16 852; 20 340, 342, 637, 706, 707, IV; 28 487
Gothic: Late Gothic 24 116; 31 309
Renaissance 20 334; 25 405
Romanesque 26 668, 677
13th cent. 14 725
14th cent. 4 525
15th cent. 2 114; 4 763; 6 463; 7 235; 11 725; 20 452, 562, 625, 626, 629, 633, 634, 646, 701, 723, 735; 31 838
16th cent. 24 472; 30 529
Germany
Gothic 3 472; 33 589
Ottonian 20 V2; 23 653, 654, 655; 26 78
Romanesque 26 673, 674, 675
15th cent. 2 713
Gothic 12 107, 109; 13 130; 21 637; 33 308
Czech Republic 33 71
England 2 222; 3 879; 4 372; 13 130, 141, 147; 14 415; 21 729; 25 807; 28 66
France 2 313; 3 643; 5 207; 7 765; 11 530; 13 140, 153, 154; 14 414; 16 852; 20 340, 342, 637, 706, 707, IV; 28 487
France: Late Gothic 24 116; 31 309
Germany 3 472; 33 589
Italy 19 679
Switzerland 3 188
Greece 9 607, 609, 611, 614, 615
Indian subcontinent *see* INDIAN SUBCONTINENT → painting
Insular art 4 343; 15 874; 17 890; 21 637
Ireland 16 13
Iran 16 319, 328, 336, 338, 341; 18 70; 30 477
Safavid 16 301, 302, 333
Timurid 16 322, 325
Iraq 16 308, 309, 320
Ireland 16 13; 17 890
Insular art 4 343
Islamic 16 293
Afghanistan 16 324, 326; 20 VI
Central Asia, Western 16 343
Egypt 16 306, 312
miniatures (manuscript illumination)
historical and regional traditions
Islamic—cont.
Iran 16 301, 302, 319, 322, 325, 328, 333, 336, 338, 341; 18 70; 30 477
Iraq 16 308, 309, 320
Ottoman 16 348, 349, 446, 454
Turkey 16 329, 348, 349, 446, 454
Italy
Gothic 19 679
Jewish art 4 16; 27 226
Renaissance 2 697; 7 469; 11 686; 20 657; 28 752; 29 786
Romanesque 10 700; 22 11; 26 664, 665
13th cent. 4 274
14th cent. 13 319, 823; 20 696, 710
15th cent. 8 173; 12 722, 734; 21 464; 25 46
Jewish art 17 536; 19 624; 27 226
Italy 4 16
Spain 4 16
Luxembourg (country) 9 698
Merovingian 31 48
Mesoamerica, Pre-Columbian 21 234
Mexico 21 234
Netherlands, the
Early Netherlandish style 5 443; 12 524; 20 343, 643, 644, 662
15th cent. 20 737
Ottoman 16 348, 349, 446, 454
Ottonian 3 552; 9 698; 20 V2; 23 653, 654, 655; 26 78
Poland 25 101
Romanesque 21 637
Austria 2 790; 26 676
Belgium 26 667
England 4 6; 5 288; 10 244; 26 670, 671, 672
France 26 668, 677
Germany 26 673, 674, 675
Italy 10 700; 22 11; 26 664, 665
Spain 26 676
Serbia 28 449
Spain 4 16; 17 536; 26 676
Switzerland 3 188; 20 560
Tibet 30 835
Turkey 16 446
Byzantine 7 228; 9 621
Islamic 16 329, 348, 349, 454
Ottoman 16 348, 349, 446, 454
Ukraine 31 556, 556, 558
lighting 7 732
materials
red lead 24 796
techniques
gilding 12 625
see also DROLLERIES
miniatures (paintings) 7 178; 17 526; 19 396; 21 636–45*; 24 659
display 9 26, 27–8*
historical and regional traditions
Argentina 2 398
Central Asia, Eastern 6 305
England 10 246; 14 761, 855; 21 639, 640, 643, 644
16th cent. 14 545, 546; 30 412
France 21 638, 641, 642, 643–4
Renaissance 7 463
Germany 21 640
Baroque 21 640
17th cent. 11 803
Indian subcontinent 15 724
Italy 31 103
Sweden 21 644; 28 68
Switzerland 21 641
miniatures (paintings)—cont.
materials
brushes 5 32, 34
enamel 14 855; 17 522
gums 13 843
ivory 16 799
Sweden 21 641
uses
marquetry 20 466
Miniature style pottery *see under* POTTERY → wares
miniaturization 15 827; 22 668
Minik, Domingo Perez *see* PEREZ MINIK, DOMINGO
Minimalism 1 78, 80; 9 360; 20 403; 21 645–7*; 23 30; 24 595; 25 645
art forms
installations 15 868, 869
painting 31 609
sculpture 2 12; 19 289; 21 646
collections 6 23; 21 135; 24 24
regional traditions
England 10 258, 268; 18 886
United States of America 2 12; 13 272; 17 677; 22 140; 29 621
Minim Friars 32 157
Miniño, José 9 119
Minio, Guido *see* LIZZARO
Minio, Tiziano 2 608; 6 89; 8 796; 16 697; 19 560; 21 647*; 23 754
Minissi, Franco 22 367
Minis Tell 16 406
Ministry of Education Art Exhibiton *see* BUNTEN
minium *see under* PIGMENTS → types
miniver *see under* HAIR → types
Minjares, Juan de 14 474
Minjung misul (Mass Art) movement 18 327
minka *see under* HOUSES → types
Minkō Tachibana *see* TACHIBANA MINKŌ
Minko Tanaka *see* TANAKA MINKO
Minkus, Mikhail 12 243
Min Kyožng-gap 18 326
Minne, George 21 648*
groups and movements 2 516; 3 564; 18 626; 28 344; 32 591
works 3 572
Minne, Joris 2 197; 20 547
Minneapolis (MN) 21 649–50*; 31 587
American Indian Center 22 670
Bovey Johnson Building 32 861
Institute of Arts 6 868; 13 470; 21 649, 650; 30 332
jewellery 31 655
Southdale Center 28 623
University of Minnesota
Frederick R. Weisman Museum of Art 33 45
Northwest Architectural Archives 21 650
Walker Art Center 3 252; 21 650
warehouses 32 861
Minnebroer, Frans *see* CRABBE (VAN ESPLEGHEM), FRANS
Minneburg tapestries 30 311
Minneriya Vava 25 169
Minnis, Eddie 3 62
Minnis, Nicole 3 62
Minniti, Mario 20 213; 21 650*
Minns, B. E. 14 397
Minnucci, Gaetano 13 728; 19 304; 23 753; 26 15
Mino 17 11, 241
ceramics 17 256; 21 650–51*
porcelain 17 264
pottery 17 242, 243, 252, 253–5*, 254, 351; 33 487
Mino, Master 28 684, 686
Minoa *see* MONEMVASIA
Minoan 8 153; 21 651–92*, 651; 26 290
alabaster (gypsum) 1 517
altars 1 691*

Minoan—cont.
archaeology **2** 300; **4** 607; **10** 654
architecture **8** 153; **18** *210*; **21** 658–9, 661–5*
bathtubs **21** 667
beads **21** 687
bone **21** 681
bone-carvings **21** 680*
bronze **2** 451; **4** 850; **8** 153; **21** *679*, 679–80, 688*, *688*
caves **8** 153
cemeteries **2** 304–5; **8** 153
chalices **21** *665*
chlorite **21** *656*
chronologies **21** 655*, *655*
collections **21** 691–2*
columns **23** 477
combs (hair) **21** 682
cups **21** *688*
Vapheio **21** 659, *688*; **26** 134
diadems **21** 686
ewers **21** *688*
ex-votos **2** 415
faience (i) (glass) **8** 153; **14** 358; **21** 682*, 683–4*
Middle Minoan (*c.* 2050–*c.* 1600 BC) **21** 658, *683*
figurines **21** 678–80, 681*, 683*
Early Minoan (*c.* 3500/3000–*c.* 2050 BC) **21** 656
Late Minoan (*c.* 1600–*c.* 1050 BC) **21** *679*, *680*
Middle Minoan (*c.* 2050–*c.* 1600 BC) **21** 657–8, 679, *683*
filigree **21** 687
flasks **21** *670*
forgeries **21** 690–91*
friezes **21** 675*
goblets **21** *669*, 671
gold **8** 153; **21** 686*, *686*, 688*, *688*
Early Minoan (*c.* 3500/3000–*c.* 2050 BC) **21** 686–7*
Late Minoan (*c.* 1600–*c.* 1050 BC) **21** 687*
Middle Minoan (*c.* 2050–*c.* 1600 BC) **21** 687*, *687*
houses **8** 153; **21** 655–6, *662*, 664*
iconography **21** 653–4*, 677
inlays **21** 682*, 684*
iron **2** 451
ivory-carvings **8** 153; **21** 680–82*
Late Minoan (*c.* 1600–*c.* 1050 BC) **21** *681*
jars
bridge-spouted **21** *668*
burial **21** 657
Late Minoan (*c.* 1600–*c.* 1050 BC) **21** *669*, *670*
Middle Minoan (*c.* 2050–*c.* 1600 BC) **21** *665*, *668*
jasper **21** *685*
jewellery **8** 153; **21** 682, 683–4*, 686*
Early Minoan (*c.* 3500/3000–*c.* 2050 BC) **21** 657, 686–7*
Late Minoan (*c.* 1600–*c.* 1050 BC) **21** 687*
Middle Minoan (*c.* 2050–*c.* 1600 BC) **21** 658, 687*
jugs **21** *665*, *666*, *756*
kantharoi **21** *658*
kraters **21** *672*
lathes **21** 689
limestone **2** *879*
metalwork **21** 652, 686*, 688*
Early Minoan (*c.* 3500/3000–*c.* 2050 BC) **21** 686–7*
Late Minoan (*c.* 1600–*c.* 1050 BC) **21** 659–60, 687*
Middle Minoan (*c.* 2050–*c.* 1600 BC) **21** 658, 687*
miniature paintings *see* friezes
museums **21** 691–2*
obsidian **21** *689*
painting
floor **21** 660
fresco **2** *879*

Minoan
painting—cont.
wall **8** 153; **21** 659, 672–7*; **32** 803
Late Minoan (*c.* 1600–*c.* 1050 BC) **21** 659, 660, *660*, *674*, *676*, *677*
Middle Minoan (*c.* 2050–*c.* 1600 BC) **21** 657
palaces **8** 153; **20** *203*; **21** 651, 657, 661, 663–4*; **23** 808
palmettes **23** 888
pendants (jewellery) **21** 687, *687*
periods
Early Minoan (*c.* 3500/3000–*c.* 2050 BC) **21** 655–7*, *655*
Final Neolithic (*c.* 3800–*c.* 3500/3000 BC) **21** *655*
Late Minoan (*c.* 1600–*c.* 1050 BC) **21** *655*, 658–61*
Late Neolithic (*c.* 4500–*c.* 3800 BC) **21** *655*
Middle Minoan (*c.* 2050–*c.* 1600 BC) **21** *655*, 657–8*
Sub-Minoan (*c.* 1050–*c.* 1000 BC) **21** *655*
pithoi **18** *167*; **21** 671
plaques **21** *681*
potter's wheels **21** 667
pottery **8** 153; **14** 338; **21** 665*, *756*; **24** *591*; **26** 290
Abstract style **21** 670
Alternating style **21** 671
Ayios Onouphrios I ware **21** 666
Ayios Onouphrios II ware **21** 666, *666*
Barbotine ware **21** 667
Close style **21** *669*, 672
Early Minoan (*c.* 3500/3000–*c.* 2050 BC) **21** *665*, 666–7*, *666*
Final Neolithic (*c.* 3800–*c.* 3500/3000 BC) **21** 665–6*
Fine Grey ware **21** 666
Floral style **21** *669*, 670
Kamares ware **17** 751; **21** 657, *665*, 668, *668*
Koumasa ware **21** *665*, 666
Late Minoan (*c.* 1600–*c.* 1050 BC) **21** 661, 668–72*, *669*, *670*, *672*
Lebena ware **21** 666
Marine style **21** *669*, 670, *670*
Middle Minoan (*c.* 2050–*c.* 1600 BC) **21** 657, *665*, 667–8*, *668*
Open style **21** 672
Palace style **21** *669*, 671
Plain style **21** 672
Post-Kamares ware **21** 668
Pyrgos ware **21** *665*, 666
Scored ware **21** 666
Special Palatial tradition **21** *669*, *670*, 670–71
Tortoiseshell Ripple ware **21** 668
Vasiliki ware **21** 666–7
White-on-dark ware **21** *665*, 667
pyxides (vases) **21** *656*
religion **21** 653–4*
rhyta **21** 668, *669*
rings **21** *685*, *686*
rock crystal **26** 484–5
sanctuaries **8** 153; **18** 164
sarcophagi **2** *879*; **21** 657; **27** 825
scripts **1** 855
sculpture **8** 153; **21** 678–80*
bronze **21** *679*, 679–80
Early Minoan (*c.* 3500/3000–*c.* 2050 BC) **21** 656, 678–9*
Late Minoan (*c.* 1600–*c.* 1050 BC) **21** 659, *679*, 679–80*
Middle Minoan (*c.* 2050–*c.* 1600 BC) **21** 657–8, 679*, 680
Neolithic **21** 678–9*
relief **21** *663*; **26** 134
seals **8** 153; **21** 682, 684–6*
Early Minoan (*c.* 3500/3000–*c.* 2050 BC) **21** 656–7

Minoan
seals—cont.
Middle Minoan (*c.* 2050–*c.* 1600 BC) **21** 658
Popular group **21** 686
ring **21** *685*, *686*
stamp **21** *684*
Talismanic group **21** 686
serpentine **21** *690*
shrines (i) (cult) **21** *663*, 663–4*
silver **21** *658*, 686–7*, 688*
soapstone **18** *168*
staircases **29** *521*
stone **21** 656, 659, 689–90
stone-carvings **8** 153
stone vessels **21** 656, 659, 689–90*
stucco **29** 814
swords **2** 451
temples **2** 305
terracotta **21** *680*; **27** 825
tombs **18** 164; **21** 664–5*; **31** 107
chamber **21** 659
Early Minoan (*c.* 3500/3000–*c.* 2050 BC) **21** 656
Late Minoan (*c.* 1600–*c.* 1050 BC) **21** 659
Middle Minoan (*c.* 2050–*c.* 1600 BC) **21** 657
tholos **21** 656; **30** 738
tools **8** 153
towns **21** 664*
trade **8** 306, 313, 317; **9** 787; **21** 652–3*
vases **18** *168*; **21** *689*, *690*
walls **21** 662
weapons **8** 153; **21** 688*
writing **18** 167
see also CRETE
Mino da Fiesole **21** 692–5*; **26** 766
attributions **4** 737; **10** 542
collaboration **4** 737; **12** 699; **24** 232, 278; **26** 767
patrons and collectors **9** 298; **21** 13; **27** 271; **29** 782
pupils **20** 721
teachers **8** 799
works **5** 300, *300*; **9** 125; **16** 690, 691; **21** *693*; **24** 28; **26** 809, 816; **31** 173
Mino del Pellicciaio, Giacomo di *see* GIACOMO DI MINO DEL PELLICCIAIO
Mino del Reame **10** 542; **21** 693, 694, 695*; **24** 28
Mino del Regno *see* MINO DEL REAME
Mino di Giovanni *see* MINO DA FIESOLE
Mino Ige ware *see under* POTTERY → wares
Mino Parcis da Siena **12** 567
Minoprio, Charles **30** 740
Minoprio & Spencely **18** 541
Minor, Robert (1884-1952) **27** 872
Minor, Robert C. (1840-1904) **10** 114
Minorca *see* MENORCA
Minoresses *see* CLARESSANS
Minorites *see* FRANCISCAN ORDER
Minorsky, V. F. **6** 281
Minoru Kawabata *see* KAWABATA, MINORU
Minoru Nakahara *see* NAKAHARA, MINORU
Minoru Takeyama *see* TAKEYAMA, MINORU
Minoru Yamasaki & Associates **23** 43
Minos, Palace of *see under* KNOSSOS
Minosuke Omura *see* OMURA, MINOSUKE
Minotaure **1** 744; **10** 164; **24** 428, 442, 720; **28** 820; **30** 21, 488
Minotaurgruppen **14** 865; **15** 142; **21** 696*; **22** 729; **30** 52
Minovici, Dr **6** 342
Minozzi, Flaminio **12** 40

Minshall, Peter **31** 336
Minshull, Charles Howard **9** 200
Minsk **3** 525, *525*; **21** 696–7*
Archbishop's Residence **3** 527
Belarus Art Museum **2** 903; **21** 697
Central Post Office **3** 527
church archaeological museum **3** 527
Church of the Dormition **3** 527
Dominican church **3** 526
Francysk Skaryna Prospect **3** 527
Government Building **3** 527, 531; **21** *696*
Karl Marx statue **3** 531
Katravycki House **3** 527
Lenin Prospect *see* Francysk Skaryna Prospect
monument to O. Krasnopol'sky **3** 531
State Bank **3** 527
T. Lekert statue **3** 531
urban planning **18** 737
Minster Jug **13** 207
Minster Lovell Jewels **10** 322
Minta, Lassine **1** 317
Mintchine, Abraham **17** 577
Minto Album *see under* ALBUMS → individual manuscripts
Minton, Herbert **10** 311; **21** 697; **25** 715
ceramics **13** 207; **25** 716
collaboration **15** 821
encaustic tiles **10** 311; **19** 614; **25** 715, 716; **30** 503, 877
patrons and collectors **30** 504
tea-services **7** 548
Minton, Hollins & Co. **10** 311; **28** 881; **30** 162
Minton, (Francis) John **21** 697*
groups and movements **18** 718; **22** 751
works **4** 369; **19** 415; **22** *752*
Minton, Thomas (1766-1836) **21** 697
Minton, Thomas Webb (1791-1870) **21** 697
Minton Ceramic Factory **10** 313; **15** 821; **21** 697*
designers **5** 878; **9** 295; **10** 312; **28** 881; **29** 51; **33** 449
production **10** 310, 312
bone china **10** 310
chess sets **6** 558
creamware **10** 307
encaustic tiles **4** 769; **30** 876
imitation Sèvres ware **10** 311; **26** 227, 501
majolica **10** 311; **20** 143; **26** 191; **29** 496; **33** 450
pâte-sur-pâte **10** 312; **24** 149
terracotta **30** 503
mints **25** 245; **27** *744*
Minturnae **26** 887
Minucci, Gaetano **16** 649
Minuccio Jacobi da Siena **24** 36
works **24** *36*
Minujín, Marta **2** 401; **21** 698*
Minulescu, Ion **3** 88
Minusca, Gabriel del Barco y *see* BARCO Y MINUSCA, GABRIEL DE
minuscule script *see under* SCRIPTS → types
Minutolo Master **13** 150
Minya **16** 148, 256; **23** 815
El Minya art school **9** 768
Mi-nyag
dress **30** *838*
Minyan ware *see under* POTTERY → wares
Minyazagyi, King (*reg* 1593-1612) (Myohaung) **2** 281
Min Yŏng-hwan **21** 698*
Min Yŏng-ik **18** 325, 331; **21** 698*
Min Yong-ki **18** 344
Minzan **23** 367
Minze-Minkoe, Marcellin **11** 879
Min Zhen **33** 497

Mio, Giovanni de *see* DEMIO, GIOVANNI
Mio, Vangjush **1** 540; **21** 698–9*
Miollis, François de **15** 837
Mionnet, M. **1** 210
Miotti (family) **3** 593; **32** 203
glass **32** *203*
Miotti, Antonio **10** 316
Miqne-Ekron, Tell **24** 634
Mique, Richard **19** 801; **21** 699*; **32** 374
collaboration **3** 124, 852; **11** 658; **32** 374
patrons and collectors **4** 554, 555; **8** 461; **27** 536; **29** 537; **32** 374
pupils **30** 728
works **11** 261; **21** 893; **22** *454*; **27** 536; **32** 374
Mique, Simon **21** 699
Mir (i Trinxet), Joaquím **5** 509; **21** 699–700*; **29** 285, 309
groups and movements **24** 829
Mir, Vicente Rivera y *see* RIVERA Y MIR, VICENTE
Mira, Ricardo **8** 232
Mira (Italy), Villa Vernier-Contarini-Zen **9** 489
Mirabel, Eva **22** 595
Mirabel, Marqués de **33** 578
Mirabella Eclano, Collegiata **26** 665
Mirabello di Salincorno *see* CAVALORI, MIRABEL (D'ANTONIO DI PACINO)
Mirabent Gatell, Josep **23** 194; **29** 306
Mir Abu'l-Qasim **8** 847
Miracle of the Apostles, Master of the **1** 167
Miracles of the Mariazell, Master of the **20** 717
Mirador **5** 411; **13** *758*; **20** 881, 882, *882*; **21** *193*, 196, 700*
Burial 16 **21** 248
Burial 29 **21** 247
Danta temple **21** 214
El Tigre Temple **21** 214
rock art **29** 195
stelae **29** 619
temples **30** 448
Miradori, Luigi **21** 700–702*
works **21** *701*
miradors **12** 222
see also WINDOWS
Miraflores **5** 201
Charterhouse **28** 724–5
choir-stalls **13** 123
retables **26** 249
tomb of John II of Castile and Isabella of Portugal **13** 108; **28** *724*
tomb of the Infante Alfonso **13** 108
metalwork **29** 333
Miraflores Triptych **23** 470; **33** 118, *119*, 119–20, 124, 127
Mir Afzal *see* AFZAL
Mirahmadov, Mirdadash **2** 900
Miraiha Bijutsu Kyōkai (Futurist Art Society) **17** 205; **20** 873
Mirailhet, Jean **21** 702*
Mirak **16** 326; **21** 702*
patrons and collectors **1** 645
pupils **4** 49
works **16** 292, 326
Mirak Husayn Yazdi **16** 390
Mirak Mirza Ghiyath **8** 679; **15** 362
Mirak Sayyid Ghiyath **15** 361, 362
Miralheti, Johes *see* MIRAILHET, JEAN
Mir ʿAli Herati
works **15** *586*
Mir ʿAli Husayni Haravi **1** 208; **16** 343; **21** 702–3*
pupils **21** 722
works **16** 286, 345, 358

Mir ʿAli ibn Hasan al-Sultani **16** 876
Mir ʿAli ibn Hasan al-Tabrizi al-Sultani *see* MIR ʿALI TABRIZI
Mir ʿAli ibn Ilyas Tabrizi **16** 313
Mir ʿAli Ilyas **21** 703
Mīr ʿAlī Shīr *see* ʿALISHIR NAVAʾI
Mir ʿAli Tabrizi **15** 586; **16** 276, 285; **21** 703*
Miramar (Peru) **29** 133
Miramar Brickworks **23** 68
Miramare collections *see under* VIENNA → museums → Kunsthistorisches Museum
Miran **5** 102; **6** *288*, *614*; **21** 703–4*; **28** *719*, 720
  armour **6** 306; **7** 57
  fortifications **21** 592
  lacquer **6** 313; **7** 14
  M. III stupa **21** 703
  M. V stupa **6** 302; **21** 703
  sculpture **6** 298
  stupas **6** 297; **29** 867
  wall paintings **6** 294, 301, 302, 321
Miranda (Venezuela) **32** *165*
  S Lucia **32** 177
Miranda, Condes de **5** 201, 411
Miranda, Fernando **21** 704*
Miranda, F. Márquez *see* MÁRQUEZ MIRANDA, F.
Miranda, Francesco (*fl* 1432) **23** 843
Miranda, Francisco (?19th cent.) **21** 704
Miranda, Juan Carreño de *see* CARREÑO DE MIRANDA, JUAN
Miranda, Juan García de *see* GARCÍA DE MIRANDA, JUAN
Miranda, Marta **6** 600
Miranda do Douro Cathedral **25** 291
Mirande, Raymond **4** 391
Mirandola, Duca di **5** 281
Mirandola, Antonio **13** 785
Mirandola, Giovanni Pico della *see* PICO DELLA MIRANDOLA, GIOVANNI
Mirandola, Lodovico Pico della, Cardinal *see* PICO DELLA MIRANDOLA, LODOVICO, Cardinal
Mirandola, Lucretia Quistelli della **33** 308
Mirandola, Niccolò Cavallerino della *see* CAVALLERINO DELLA MIRANDOLA, NICCOLÒ
Mirandola Castle **31** 429
Mirandolese, il **4** 46
Miranshah, Sultan (*reg* 1404-9) (Timurid) **30** 917
Miranui Mill **23** 73
Miravet **18** 153
Mirbabayev, A.K. **18** 530
Mirbach, Ernst von **31** 284
Mir Baqi **2** 881
Mirbeau, Octave **10** 480; **12** 191; **30** 290
Mirbel, Aimée-Zoë Lizinka de *see* LIZINKA DE MIRBEL, AIMÉE-ZOË
Mir Castle **3** 526; **4** 783
Mircea I, Voivode of Wallachia (*reg* 1386-94; 1397-1418) **26** 706, 707, 710
Mircea V, Voivode of Wallachia (*reg* 1545-52; 1552-54) **5** 72; **26** 707
Mircea the Old, Voivode of Wallachia *see* MIRCEA I, Voivode of Wallachia
Mir Chand **15** 592
Mir Chaqmaq **33** 512
Mirdita, Tush **1** 544
Mirdjavadov, M. **2** 897
Mire, Antoine-Louis Le *see* LE MIRE, ANTOINE-LOUIS
Miré, Georges de **1** 439
Mire, Noël Le *see* LE MIRE, NOËL
Mirea, G. D. **7** 361; **13** 650
Mirecourt **11** 651
Mirei Shigemori *see* SHIGEMORI, MIREI
Mirepoix, Mme de **11** 593
Miret, Eduoardo Torroja *see* TORROJA (MIRET), EDUARDO
Mirgissa fort **9** 844, 846; **10** 81; **12** 67; **21** 554, 555
Mir Hindu Beg **15** 361
Mirhkani, Hasan **15** 899
Mirhkani, Husayn **15** 899
Miri, Lodovico **13** 701
Miri, Muhammad Said **19** 7
Mirian III, King of Iberia (*reg* 284-361) **12** 318
Miricinus, Petrus *see* HEYDEN, PIETER VAN DER
Mirigliano, Giovanni *see* MARIGLIANO, GIOVANNI
Mir ʿImad **15** 681; **16** 286, 287; **21** 704*
Mir Iskusstva (periodical) **3** 692; **4** 60, 156; **8** 849; **27** 443, 580; **29** 61; **33** 487
  see also WORLD OF ART
Mir Iskusstva (group) *see* WORLD OF ART
Mir Jaʿfar ʿAli Khan, Nawab of Bengal (*reg* 1757-60; 1764-5) **15** 702, 711
Mirjan **16** 193, 876
Mirkadim *see* VIKRAMPUR
Mir Kalan Khan **15** 592
Mir Khwand **16** 196
Mirko (Basaldella) **1** 446; **11** 191; **21** 704*; **26** 777
Mirliton, Le **29** 612
Mirmala Shanmughalingam **20** 172
Mir Muhammad **16** 236
Mir Muhammed Yusuf *see* MUHAMMAD YUSUF
Mir Musavvir **21** 704–5*, 722
  collaboration **2** 235
  patrons and collectors **27** 514
  works **15** 578; **16** 333, 334
Miró, Joan **3** 219; **10** 822; **21** 705–10*; **25** 582; **27** 478; **29** 285, 286; **33** 744
  book illustrations **4** 753; **20** 75; **30** 488; **31** 504
  collaboration **2** 542; **10** 467; **20** 603, 605; **29** 329
  collages **6** 9; **7** 557; **25** 599
  commentaries **20** 75
  dealers **19** 537; **20** 75, 832
  drawings **9** 213
  exhibitions **11** 569; **28** 920; **29** 286
  groups and movements **3** 120
    Abstract art **1** 75
    biomorphism **4** 74
    Ecole de Paris **9** 705
    metamorphism **21** 341
    Noucentisme **23** 260
    Surrealism **2** 839; **11** 549, 550; **30** 18, 19, 20
  methods **11** 495; **25** 619, 686
  paintings **18** 717; **21** *706*, *707*
  patrons and collectors
    Arensberg, Walter and Louise **2** 384
    Cooper, Douglas **7** 797
    Dotremont, Philippe **9** 189
    Farsi, Mohammed Said **27** 876
    Fondation Maeght (Saint-Paul-de-Vence) **20** 76; **28** 314
    Gallatin, A(lbert) E(ugene) **12** 15
    Lefèvre, André **19** 66
    Maitland, Ruth (Esther) **20** 142
    Marx, Sam and Florene **20** 524
    Neumann, Morton G. **23** 7
    Penrose, Roland **24** 369
    Soby, James Thrall **28** 914
    Thompson, G(eorge) David **30** 749
    Winston, Harry Lewis and Lydia **33** 254
Miró, Joan—cont.
  posters **25** 350
  prints **5** *725*, 726; **19** 491; **21** *708*, 897; **25** 626; **28** 299; **33** 362
  productions **8** 850
  sculpture **11** 568; **21** *709*; **29** 295, 296
  studio **28** 483
  tapestries **11** 644; **12** 830; **30** 328
Miró, Joaquim de **30** 3
Miró, Miguel **21** 705
Miroballo, Giovanni **24** 782
Mirobriga (Portugal) **7** 342
Mirobriga Vettonum (Spain) *see* CIUDAD RODRIGO
Miroffsky, Wenzeslaus **8** 289; **11** 458
Mirola, Girolamo **3** 859
Mironenko, Vladimir **27** 398
Mironov, A. **23** 615
Miropolsky, Leonty **19** 279
Miropolsky-Lang, A. **5** 69
Miró Quesada Garland, Luis **19** 387; **24** 505
Miroshnichenko, Yu. **30** 352
Miroslav, Prince of Hum **28** 449
Mirou, Antoine **11** 731; **21** 710–11*
Mirpur Khas **15** 719
Mir Qasim **16** 236
Mirri, L.
  works **26** *788*
mirror cabinets *see under* CABINETS (i) (ROOM) → types
mirror-cases **2** *112*; **10** 636; **16** *534*
mirror frames **18** *603*
  Aztec **21** 719, *719*
  Czech Republic **21** 721
  England **21** 721
  France
    Gothic **21** *720*
  Germany **21** 721
  Gothic **21** *720*
  Indian subcontinent **21** 717, *717*
  Islamic **16** *527*; **21** 718
  Italy **11** 395
  Mesoamerica, Pre-Columbian **21** *719*
  Ottoman **16** *527*
  Rome, ancient **21** 713
  Sweden **30** 90
mirror handles **10** 627, 635; **21** 712, 716
  Italy **10** 635
mirrors **9** 12–13; **12** 791; **21** 711–22*
  historical and regional traditions
    Africa **1** *219*
    Ancient Near East **21** 711*
    Aztec **21** 719, *719*
    Bali (Indonesia) **15** 812
    Belgium **3** 576, *576*
    Benin, Kingdom of **1** *219*
    Celtic **6** *153*, 161
    China **6** 862–3, *863*; **21** 714–15*
      Han period (206 BC–AD 220) **6** 858, 859–60
      Liao period (AD 907-1125) **6** 864
      Shang period (*c.* 1600–*c.* 1050 BC) **4** 855
      Song period (AD 960-1279) **6** 864
      Tang period (AD 618-907) **6** 863–4, *864*; **7** 14
      Zhou period (*c.* 1050-256 BC) **6** 854, 855
    Cyprus, ancient **8** *350*
    Dian culture **21** 714
    Egypt **21** 718, *718*
    Egypt, ancient **10** 38, 67; **21** 711*, *713*
    England **6** *153*, 161; **10** 276; **21** 720
    Etruscan **10** 589, 595, *595*, 627–30, *628*, 639; **21** *712*, 712–13*
mirrors
  historical and regional traditions—cont.
    France **9** 12; **11** 589; **21** *720*, 720; **26** 492
    Germany **12** 412, *424*
    Gothic **21** *720*
    Greece, ancient **13** 577*; **21** 711–12*
    Inca **21** 718
    India, Republic of **15** *176*
    Indian subcontinent **21** 716–17*, *717*, 718
    Iran **16** 257; **21** 717–18
    Ireland **16** 26, 30
    Islamic **16** 365; **21** 717–18*, *718*
      Iran **16** 257
    Italy **16** 726; **21** 719; **32** 202, 204
      Etruscan **10** 589, 595, *595*, 627–30, *628*, 639
    Japan **17** 319, *320*, 322, 323, *324*, 386, 387, 399; **21** 716*
      Kofun **17** 320
    Korea **18** 345–6, *346*; **21** 715–16*
    Maya **21** 718
    Mesoamerica, Pre-Columbian **21** 195, 241, 718–19*, *719*
    Mycenaean **21** 711
    Native North Americans **21** 718
    Olmec **21** 241, 718
    Ottoman **21** 718
    Panama **21** 718
    Peru **21** 718
    Prehistoric art **28** 806
    Rome, ancient **4** 855; **21** 713*
    South America, Pre-Columbian **21** 718*; **29** 134
    Spain **29** 302
    Sweden **30** 95
    Syria **21** 717, *718*
    Tibet **30** 840–41, *841*
    Turkey **21** 717
    United States of America **31** 624, 626–7, 629
  materials
    bronze **21** *712*, 714
      Celtic **6** 161
      China **4** 855; **6** 854, 855, 858, 859–61, 862–4, *863*, *864*; **7** 14; **21** 714, *715*
      Egypt, ancient **21** 711, *713*
      England **6** 161
      Greece, ancient **21** 712, *712*
      Indian subcontinent **21** 716
      Islamic **21** 717
      Italy **10** *595*, *628*; **21** 712
      Japan **17** 319, *320*, *324*; **21** 716
      Korea **18** 345–6, *346*; **21** 715
      Roman **21** 713
      Tibet **30** *841*
    cast iron **21** 715
    copper **21** 712, 714, 717
    earthenwares **21** 714
    glass **3** 576; **7** *87*; **12** 789; **17** 386, 387; **21** 713, 714, 718, 719, 720; **32** 202
    gold **21** 714, 715, *718*
    haematite **21** 718, 719
    ilmenite **21** 241, 718
    inlays **30** *841*
    inscriptions **6** 863
    iron **21** 714, 719
    ivory **3** 576; **8** *350*
    jade **21** 714, 719
    jet **21** 718
    lacquer **7** 14; **21** *721*
    magnetite **21** 195, 718
    malachite **21** 714
    mercury **21** 716, 718, 720
    metal **21** 718, 719
    mother-of-pearl **7** 14; **21** 715
    obsidian **21** 718, 719, *719*
    pyrite **21** 241, 718, 719
    rock crystal **21** 717, *717*, 719
    sandstone **21** 719
    shells **7** 14; **21** 715, 719
    silver **21** 711, 713, *713*, 714, 715, *718*; **28** 738
mirrors
  materials—cont.
    silver nitrate **21** 721
    slate **21** 718, 719
    steel **3** 576; **21** *718*
    stone **21** 718
    tin **21** 716, 720
    turquoise **21** 714
    wood **3** 576; **21** 713
  techniques
    gilding **6** 863; **21** *721*
    inlays **6** 863
  types
    back-painted **7** 87, *87*
    box **13** 577; **21** 712, *712*
    hand **13** 577; **21** 711, *712*, 713, *713*
    pier-glasses **9** 30; **21** 721; **31** 627
    stand **21** 712, *712*
    TLV mirrors **6** 860–61, 862; **21** 714, *715*
    trumeau **31** 393*
    wall **21** 713, 720
  uses
    architectural decorations **16** 257; **21** 718
    bed hangings **15** *176*
    embroidery **21** 717
    inlays **5** 256
    interior decoration **5** 349*; **12** 412; **21** 717
    netsuke **17** 399
    photography **24** 660
    sculpture **1** *219*
    towers **15** 812
mirror stands *see under* STANDS → types
Mir Sanʿi **27** 506
Mir Sayyid Ahmad **1** 583; **16** 551; **21** 722*
Mir Sayyid ʿAli **16** 344; **21** 705, 722–3*
  patrons and collectors **16** 344; **27** 514
  works **15** 578, 579, *579*; **16** *125*, 333; **30** 480
Mirshade **6** 212
Mir tapestry workshop **25** 131
Mir-Ubaydulla **18** 195
Miryam Zamani **15** 363; **18** 646
Miryang **18** 341
  Yŏngnam-ru Pavilion **12** 95
Mirys, Augustyn de **19** 497; **25** 105
Mirza, Bashir **23** 801
Mirza ʿAbd al-Rahim **15** 681
Mirza ʿAli **16** 333, 335; **21** 723*; **29** 920
Mirza ʿAziz Koka Muhammad Khan ʿAzam **15** 595; **16** 345
  manuscripts **15** *595*
Mirza Baba **16** 341; **21** 723–4*
  patrons and collectors **25** 770
  works **16** 341, *341*, 522, 534, 535, 539; **30** 415
Mirza Bek Kala **6** 275
Mirzaganj, Masjidbari **15** 352
Mirza Ghiyath Beg **1** 460
Mirza Hasan **28** 27
Mirza Kadym Irevani **2** 895
Mir Zakah **1** 204
Mirza Kamran **15** 362, 578; **18** 646
  works **15** *578*
Mirza Kuchik Khan **16** 287
Mirza Mahdi Khan Astarabadi **22** 260
Mirza Muhammad Haydar (Mughal) **15** 578
Mirza Muhammad Khan, Ruler of Baku (*reg c.* 1720) **20** 401
Mirzamuratov, M. **18** 22
Mirzapur **16** 485
Mirza Riza Khan *see* RICHARD, JULES
Mīr Zayn al-ʿĀbidīn Tabrīzī *see* ZAYN AL-ʿABIDIN
Mirzoyam *see* ZHAMBYL
Misano *see* MARZABOTTO
Misao Yokoyama *see* YOKOYAMA, MISAO

Misato, Ueshiba Tomb
  sculpture **17** *31*
Miscellanea d'arte see RIVISTA D'ARTE
Miscellaneen artistischen Inhalts **24** 443
Miscević, Radovan **28** 823
Mi school **33** 528
Misei Kosugi *see* KOSUGI, MISEI
Miseno, Piscina Mirabilis **7** 354
mis-en-page **21** 724*
Miserden (Glos), St Andrew **10** 262
Misereor **5** 524
Misericordia, Master of the **11** 891
misericords **16** 25; **21** *724*, 724–5*; **28** 250
Miseroni (family) **12** 260; **14** 171; **16** 745; **21** 529; **25** 436
  patrons and collectors **13** 914
  works **8** 407; **26** 486
Miseroni, Alessandro **8** 417; **21** 726; **25** 435
Miseroni, Ambrogio Matteo **21** 725
Miseroni, Dionisio **8** 417; **13** 919; **21** 726; **22** 204; **25** 435; **28** *827*
  works **25** *436*
Miseroni, Ferdinand Eusebius **8** 417; **21** 726; **25** 436
Miseroni, Gasparo **16** 746; **21** 725–6*
Miseroni, Giovanni Ambrogio **8** 417; **21** 726; **25** 435
Miseroni, Girolamo **21** 725–6*
Miseroni, Ottavio **8** 417, 418; **12** 259, 260; **14** 168; **21** 726*; **25** 432, 435
  works **14** II1; **21** *726*
Mišević, Radenko **4** 461
Mishen' *see* DONKEY'S TAIL
Mishihase *see* AINU
Mishima, Pasadena Heights **17** 91; **18** *41*
Mishima, Yukio **33** 540
Mishima ware *see under* POTTERY → wares
Mishmi **15** 733
Mishosai Ippo *see* IPPO MISHOSAI
Mishrifa *see* QATNA
Misis **9** 565; **17** 500, 559
Miskana *see* MASKANA
Miskin **20** 106; **21** 726–8*
  collaboration **8** 847
  works **21** *727*
Miskito **14** 712
Mis'ko, Emmanuil P. **31** 561
Miskolc **14** *881*; **15** 2
  Cistercian church **14** 887
  Reformed Church **14** 904
  Technical University of Heavy Industry **14** 891
Miskolci, Bálint **15** 7
Mislata **29** 324
Misle, Carlos Eduardo **32** 181
Mislej, Luka **26** 441
Mi Son **6** *418*, 419, 420, 421, 422, 424; **21** 728*; **29** *225*; **32** *468*
  A1 **6** 422, 423, *423*
    reliefs **29** IX2
    sculpture **6** 428, 429, *429*
  A2 **6** 421
  canopies (ii) (textile coverings) **6** 433
  E1 **6** 420–21, 427
    sculpture **6** 427
    tiles **6** 432
  E4 **6** 429
  F1 **6** 421
  G1 **6** 430
  gold **6** 432
  H1 **6** 430
  sanctuary **6** 418
  sculpture **6** 427
Misonne, Léonard **24** 739
Misr *see* CAIRO
miśraka **15** 244*
Misrian **32** 321
Misridas **15** 615
Miss, Mary **18** 695; **21** 728*; **31** 615
Missaglia (family) **2** 471
Missal of Borso d'Este, Master of the **12** 665
  works **12** *666*
Missals **4** 3; **13** 130; **21** 728–30*; **28** 486, 487
  individual manuscripts
    Arcimboldi Missal (Milan, Bib. Capitolare, MS. II.D.I.13) **20** 844
    Barozzi Missal (Padua, Bib. Capitolare, Inc. N. 260) **4** 397
    Bobbio Missal (Paris, Bib. N., MS, lat. 13246) **21** 729
    Coronation Missal of Gian Galeazzo Visconti (Milan, Bib. Capitolare S Ambrosiana, MS. 6) **2** 123
    Frisingen Missal (untraced) **4** 759
    Greiffenklau Missal (Baltimore, MD, Walters A. G., MS. W. 174) **20** 644, 786
    Hahn Missal (Budapest, N. Széchényi Lib., Cod. Lat. 94) **28** 851
    Hasenburk Missal (Vienna, Österreich. Nbib., Cod. 1844) **13** 153
    Hildesheim Missal (private coll.) **31** 499
    Hoya Missal (Münster, Ubib., MS. 41) **20** 786
    Konstanz Missal (untraced) **4** 759
    Lytlington Missal (London, Westminster Abbey, MS. 37) **4** 238; **21** *729*, 730
    Mainardi Missal (Cremona, Bib. Stat. & Lib. Civ., MS. 188) **22** 716
    Missal della Rovere (New York, Pierpont Morgan Lib., MS. 306; Turin, Archv Stato, MS. J.b.II. 2,3,4) **20** 657, *657*
    Missale Hallense (Aschaffenburg, Hofbib., MS. 10) **12** 816
    Missal of Arnold van Rummen (Brussels, Bib. Royale Albert 1er, MS. 9217) **3** 553
    Missal of Barbara of Brandenburg (Mantua, Mus. Dioc.) **3** 531
    Missal of Borso d'Este (Modena, Bib. Estense, MS. lat. 239) **12** *666*
    Missal of Cardinal Bertrand de Deux (Rome, Vatican, Bib. Apostolica, MS. Cap. 63B) **2** 18; **20** 696
    Missal of Cardinal Ferry (Siena, Bibl. Com. Intronati, MS. XVI) **32** 729
    Missal of Clement VII (Paris, Bib. N., MS. lat. 848) **7** 525
    Missal of Henry of Chichester (Manchester, John Rylands U. Lib., MS. lat. 24) **13** 138, 140
    Missal of Jacques de Beaune (Paris, Bib. N., MS. lat. 886) **4** 571
    Missal of Jean des Martins (untraced) **25** 795
    Missal of Louis de Mâle (Brussels, Bib. Royale Albert 1er, MS. 1217) **19** 721
    Missal of Richard Chambellan (Paris, Bib. N., MS. lat. 879) **20** 638
    Missal of Robert of Jumièges (Rouen, Bib. Mun., MS. Y.6) **2** 77, *77*; **33** 232
    Missal of Sainte-Chapelle (Lyon, Bib. Mun., MS. 5122) **17** 463
Missals
  individual manuscripts—cont.
    Missal of S Tecla (Milan, Bib. Capitolare Met., MS. II, D.I.2) **2** 123
    Missal of the Bishops of Paris (Paris, Bib. Arsenal, MS. 621) **20** 625, 626
    Missal of the Madonna del Monte (Varese, Mus. S Maria del Monte) **25** 465
    Nouailher Missal (Poitiers, Cathedral Treasury) **30** 529
    Rovere Missal *see* Missal della Rovere
    Saint-Denis Missal (London, V & A, MS. 1346-1891) **4** 394, *394*; **13** 154, 827
    Sherborne Missal (London, BL, Loan MS. 83) **13** 153; **17** 611–12, *611*; **31** 500
    Stowe Missal **7** 458
  see also SACRAMENTARIES
Misshitsuga (Secret Room Painting) **17** 207
Mission **22** 550, 658, 666, 668
Missionary style **4** 709
Mission furniture **2** 572
Mission Héliographique *see under* COMMISSION DES MONUMENTS HISTORIQUES
Mission Revival **7** 619
Mississauga City Hall **5** 563
Misson **8** 776
Misson, Maximilian **5** 345
Missoni, Ottavio **30** 887
Missorium of Theodosios **27** 84
Missouri **22** 551
Mist, John **4** 805
Mistail, Peterskirche **5** 798
Misto Mame Woodwork Combine **1** 543; **31** 20
Mistral, Frédéric **5** 265
Mistras *see* MYSTRAS
Mistrovice **8** 410
Mistruzzi, Aurelio **21** 730*
Mistuhiro Ōhara *see* ŌHARA MITSUHIRO
Misu (1152-1220) *see* YI IN-NO
Misu (1592-1682) *see* HŎ MOK
Misul charyo **18** 383
Mita **17** 264
Mitan, James **11** 84
Mitannian **1** *852*; **2** 661; **21** 730–31*
  architecture **21** 286
  dress **1** 885
  friezes **15** 33
  glass **1** 865; **15** 33
  pottery **15** 33
  seals **1** 862, *862*, 877; **15** 33; **21** 730, *731*; **23** 322
  writing-tablets **1** 853
  see also HURRIAN
Mitaoli Temple **15** 290, 292
Mitaraka **11** 760
Mitau *see* JELGAVA
Mitau Service **27** 584
Mitava *see* JELGAVA
Mitcham Methodist Church (Surrey) **21** 347
Mitchell, Alfred R. **27** 721
Mitchell, C. **23** 20
Mitchell, David Scott **2** 771
Mitchell, Donald G. **7** 619
Mitchell, Ehrman B. **7** 670; **21** 732*
Mitchell, Fred **4** 602
Mitchell, Horner **12** 500
Mitchell, Joan **1** 88; **9** 189; **16** 820; **21** 731*
Mitchell, Julia **31** 661
Mitchell, Norris **13** 876
Mitchell, Robert **24** 18
  works **24** *19*
Mitchell, Russell **14** 223
Mitchell, Samuel Latham **22** 649
Mitchell, (Arthur George) Sydney **2** 5; **21** 731–2*; **28** 229
Mitchell, Thomas L. **2** 738; **19** 286
Mitchell/Giurgola **13** 648; **21** 732*; **24** 598
  works **2** 743
Mitchell/Giurgola & Thorp **5** 602
  works **5** *602*
Mitchell Carson Associates **3** 61
Mitchom, Morris **31** 260
Mité, Charles **11** 642; **22** 456
Mitelberg, Tim Louis **5** 759
Mitelli, Agostino (Stanzani) (1609-60) **8** 280; **20** 66; **21** 732*
  assistants **5** 873
  collaboration **4** 277; **7** 622; **21** 26
  patrons and collectors **3** 90; **10** 526; **32** 131
  reproductive prints by others **21** 732
  works **2** 849; **11** 214; **15** 138; **16** 714, *715*; **20** 72
Mitelli, Agostino (*c*. 1671-96) **21** 733
Mitelli, Giuseppe Maria **21** 732–3*; **32** 356
Mit Faris, Statue of Ammenemes III **9** 875
Mitford-Barberton, Ivan **5** 668; **29** 111
Mithila **15** 726
Mithinari **1** 42; **21** 733*
Mithradatkirt *see* NISA
Mithraea **26** 859, 867; **30** 436
Mithridates I (*reg* 171-138 BC) **23** 159; **24** 215
Mithridates I Kallinikos, King of Commagene (*reg c*. 100-*c*. 70 BC) **22** 731, 732; **24** 217
Mithridates II (*reg* 123-88 BC) **1** *888*; **4** 94
Mithridates III, King of Pontus (*reg c*. 250-*c*. 185 BC) **5** 298
Mithridates VI Eupator the Great, King of Pontus (*reg* 121-63 BC) **4** 686, *686*; **12** 248; **13** 589
Mitiaro **7** 790
Mitilíni *see* LESBOS
Mitima, Jorge de la Cruz **9** 710
Mitjana, Rafael **2** 133
Mitjans, F. **20** 516
Mitki **27** 581
Mitla **21** *193*, 200, 202, *372*, 733–4*
  architecture **21** 202
  fortifications **21** 599
  Hall of Columns **21** 204; **23** 565
  lintels **9** 166
  mosaics **21** 255; **22** 158, 164
  Palace of Columns **21** *734*
  palaces **21** 733–4, 737; **23** 825; **33** 620
  tombs **31** 118
  wall paintings **21** 226, 231
Mitlyansky, Daniil **27** 397
Mitoko **1** 404; **19** 72, 74
Mitoraj, Igor **3** 366; **21** 528
Mitov, Boris **5** 154
Mitra, Debala **26** 20
Mit Rahina **25** 874
mitres **9** 643; **14** 404; **21** 249; **32** 387, *389*, 390*
Mitrić, Nebojša **28** 454
Mitrofan **8** 908
Mitrofanović, Georgije **4** 461; **22** 17, 228; **24** 308; **25** 339–40, 344; **28** 450
Mitrofanović, Jovan **4** 461
Mitropolis Basilica **8** 155
Mitrović, Mihajlo **28** 445
Mitrovský (family) **24** 463
Mitsakis, Nikolaos **13** 349; **21** 735*; **23** 901; **24** 803
Mitsu, Ai **20** 834
Mitsubishi Corporation **10** 833
Mitsuharu **17** 400
Mitsuhige, Fujiwara no *see* FUJIWARA NO MITSUHIGE
Mitsuhiro
  works **17** *400*
Mitsuhiro Karasumaru *see* KARASUMARU MITSUHIRO
Mitsui (family) **17** 414
Mitsui Bussan **17** 435
Mitsui Shinna **17** 235, 237, 410, 751
Mitsukuni Tokugawa *see* TOKUGAWA MITSUKUNI
Mitsu(?) Mitsuyori *see* KANŌ SANKAKU
Mitsumochi Tosa *see* TOSA MITSUMOCHI
Mitsumoto Tosa *see* TOSA MITSUMOTO
Mitsunari Tosa *see* TOSA MITSUNARI
Mitsunobu Kanō *see* KANŌ MITSUNOBU
Mitsunobu Tosa *see* TOSA MITSUNOBU
Mitsunori Tosa *see* TOSA MITSUNORI
Mitsuoki Takahashi *see* TAKAHASHI DŌHACHI
Mitsuoki Tosa *see* TOSA MITSUOKI
Mitsuru Ishibashi *see* ISHIBASHI, MITSURU
Mitsusuke Tosa *see* TOSA MITSUSUKE
Mitsutani, Kunishirō **17** 204
Mitsuyasu Deme Yūkan *see* DEME YŪKAN MITSUYASU
Mitsuyoshi Tosa *see* TOSA MITSUYOSHI
Mitsuyuki Kuroda *see* KURODA MITSUYUKI
Mittagong **2** *736*
  Clubbe Hall **30** 161
Mittal (family) **15** 742
Mitteilungen der Gesellschaft für vervielfältigende Kunst **24** 438
Mitteilungen der Kaiserlich-Königlichen Zentral-commission für Erforschung und Erhalting der Baudenkmale see ÖSTERREICHISCHE ZEITSCHRIFT FÜR DENKMALPFLEGE
Mitteilungen des kaiserlich-königlichen Österreichischen Museums für Kunst und Industrie **24** 438
Mitteilungen des Kunsthistorischen Instituts in Florenz **24** 445
Mitteilungen für christliche Kunst **24** 438
Mittelhaus **10** 211
Mittel'man, B. Ya. **12** 877
Mittelzell Minster *see under* REICHENAU
Mitterand, François **7** 670; **11** 508, 659, 660; **24** 145
  installations **24** 145
  interior decoration **11** 584; **29** 546
  museums **11** 660, 668
Mitterer, Hermann Josef **14** 135; **19** 480, 482
Mittey, Joseph **28** 181
Mitthila **15** 174, *175*
Mitti, Masiye **33** 603
Mittleheim, St Ägidius **9** 156
Mittmann, Johann Nicolaus **11** 731
Mittwoch, Eugen **27** 846
Miturich, Pyotr (Vasil'yevich) **21** 735*; **27** 284, 394, 396; **32** 661
  groups and movements **11** 358
  works **8** 10
Miuphalaung, King (*reg* 1571-93) (Myohaung) **2** 281
Miura, Koheiji **17** 266
  works **17** *266*
Miura Gomon **17** 189
Miura Kenya **23** 367
Miura Tōtarō **17** 399
Miville, Jakob Christophe **3** 336; **21** 735–6*; **30** 133

Miwa **17** 401
Miwa, Sigeru **25** 354
Miwa Chūbei Toshisada *see* MIWA KYŪSETSTU
Miwa Kyūsetsu I **14** 37
Miwa Miyayama **17** 104
Mi Wan-chung *see* MI WANZHONG
Mi Wani Sabi **11** 760
Mi Wanzhong **6** 761
Miwok **22** 549, 641, 652
 regalia **22** *549*
Mixco Viejo **21** 599; **25** 765
mixed-media **1** 300–302*, *301*; **18** *119*, *326*; **20** *352*; **29** *622*
Mi xian **6** *615*; **21** 736*
 paintings **6** 808
 tombs **6** 648; **21** 736*
 wall paintings **7** 33, 34
mixiang see under BARK → types
Mixtec **21** 177, 202, 736–8*; **33** 481, 618
 amethyst **21** 737
 amulets **21** 243, 248
 bone **21** 737
 bone-carvings **21** 248
 bowls **21** *240*
 calendars **21** 234, 253, *253*
 drums (musical instruments) **21** 256, *257*
 gold **21** *253*, 737
 gongs **21** 737
 hardstones **21** 243
 ideograms **21** 248
 jade **21** 243, 737
 knife-handles **21** 255
 manuscript illumination **21** 234–5, 737, *738*
 manuscripts **21** 233, 234
 masks **21** 251, 255, *255*, 737
 metalwork **21** 254, 737
 mosaics **21** 251, 254–6, *255*, *734*, 737
 obsidian **21** 737
 painting **21** 231*, 737
 palaces **21** *734*; **23** 825
 pectoral ornaments **21** *253*
 pendants (jewellery) **21** 243
 pottery **21** 238, 239, *240*, 737
 pyramids **25** *765*
 religion **21** 183, 188
 rock crystal **21** 737; **26** 487
 sculpture **21** 737
 shields **21** 255, 737
 spear-throwers **21** 737
 tombs **31** 118
 turquoise **21** 251, 255–6, 737
 walls **21** 255
 wood-carvings **21** 737
 writing **21** 737
Mixteca-Puebla **20** 886; **21** 202, 737, 738, 739–40*
 codices **21** *739*
 colour **21** 183
 iconography **21** 186, *739*, 739
 manuscript illumination **21** 182
 metalwork **21** 254
 pottery **21** 239
 religion **21** 184, 186
Mixtec Codices **21** 202
Miyagawa, Jun (Atsushi) **21** 741*
Miyagawa Chōki **21** 742
Miyagawa Chōshun **21** 741–2*
 works **17** 177; **21** *741*
Miyagawa Chōsui **21** 742
Miyagawa Isshō **21** 742
Miyagi, Museum of Art **27** 873
Miyake, Chūichi **21** 635
Miyake, Issei **9** 294
Miyake, Yonekichi **17** 426
Miyake Sekian **17** 236
Miyako (island) **27** 469, 471
Miyako (Kyoto) *see* KYOTO
Miyamoto Musashi Niten **21** 742*
Miyamotoya kiln **18** 538
Miyan Bhuwa **8** 674
Miyani Temple **15** 267
Miyasaka Hakuryū **17** 401
Miyasaki, George **19** 492
Miyashita, Zenji **17** 268
Miyatev, Krustyu **5** 163
Miyawaki, Kazuo **21** 742
Miyawaki, Mayumi **2** 363; **17** 91; **21** 742*; **30** 260
Miyazaki, Seitaro **17** 402
Miyazaki, Yūzen **17** 732
Miyazaki Tominosuke **23** 367
Miyazaki Yūzensai **17** 315
Miyazu, Kono Shrine **16** 74
Mi Youren **6** 750; **21** 420*
 groups and movements **29** 244
 works **6** 819; **21** 420; **25** 72
Mizdakhkan **6** 207
Mizhrichchya **25** 473, 489, 493
 Monastery **31** 550
Mizmaze (Hants) **18** 585
mizraḥ **21** 743*, *743*; **24** 57
Mizudoro Tomb **17** 59
Mizue see KIKAN MIZUE
Mizuno, Seiichi **7** 161; **21** 744*
Mizuno, Toshikata **17** 293
M Jewel **10** 344
MKhAT (Moscow Art Theatre) **3** 734; **28** 757
Mkrtchyan, Karo **2** 433
Mladá Boleslav **8** 415
Mladenović, Branko **28** 449
M'lefaat **2** 639
Mleiha **2** *246*, 249
 bronze **2** 265
 coins **2** 261, *262*
 fortress **2** 251
 glass **2** 263
 metalwork **2** 266
 pottery **2** 267, 268
 vessels **2** 273
 wine sets **2** 265
Mlitchetsi, Grigor **2** 431
Mlk'e, Queen (*fl* 990-1020) **13** 21
Młodożeniec, Jan **25** 108
MLTW **22** 52
Mmabatho Government Secretariat Building **29** 107
Mmani **1** 391; **3** 45, 47
Mndoyants, Ashot **1** 126; **22** 175; **25** 89, 323
Mnesiades **13** 484
Mnesikles **2** 677; **13** 394, 554; **21** 744*
Mnichovo Hradiště Abbey **22** 216
Mniszcz, M. **28** 170
Mniszech, Michał Wandalin **25** 138, 139, 140
Mniszech Collection **25** 138
Mnodoyants, Ashot **25** 323
Moab **1** *849*, 857; **9** 737*; **30** 179, 189
Moabite Stone *see* MESHA STELE
Moal, Jean-Louis Le *see* LE MOAL, JEAN-LOUIS
el-Moalla **9** *774*; **21** 744–5*
 sculpture **9** 873
 tomb of Ankhtifi **9** 874, 899–900
 wall paintings **21** *745*
Moarves, S Pedro **26** 609
moats **12** 174, 176; **17** 55, 57
Moba **31** 73
mobiles **2** 838; **21** 745–6*
 Constructivism **11** *877*
 United States of America **5** 423; **21** *746*; **31** 613
Mobil Oil Company **6** 176; **12** 510; **23** 273; **28** 488
Möbius, Helga **29** 877
Mobles i Decoración de la Vivienda Actual (MIDVA) **29** 321
Mob Shop **23** 896
Moca **9** *114*, 116
Moçambique *see* MOZAMBIQUE
mocárabes see MQARNAS
Mocatta, David **25** 855; **32** 864
moccasins **3** 441; **22** 648, 649, 651, 654
Moce **11** 69
Mocenigo, Alvise I, Doge of Venice (*reg* 1570-77) **21** 747; **27** 347
Mocenigo, Alvise IV, Doge of Venice (*reg* 1763-79) **21** 747
Mocenigo, Giovanni, Doge of Venice (*reg* 1478-85) **21** 747
Mocenigo, Leonardo **21** 747
Mocenigo, Pietro, Doge of Venice (*reg* 1474-6) **21** 747
Mocenigo, Polisena **16** 752
Mocenigo, Tommaso, Doge of Venice **21** 747
Mocetto, Girolamo **10** 385; **21** 748*
 collaboration **10** 765; **22** 130
 teachers **3** 667
 works **21** *748*
Mocha **6** *590*, 592
Mochal'sky, Dmitry **27** 889
Moche (culture) **21** 749–54*; **23** 897; **29** 127, 160–61, 218
 adobe **4** 796
 altars **1** 701
 architecture **21** 749; **29** 163
 body ornaments **29** 218
 bowls **29** *134*
 caricatures **5** 761
 ceramics **29** *221*
 collections **10** 487
 craftsmen and artists **29** *134*
 erotic art **10** 474
 fans **10** 780
 feathers **29** 207
 figurines **29** 134
 gilding **29** 212
 graves **21** 749
 hardstones **29** 186
 human figures **29** *176*
 iconography **29** 133, 134
 jars **21** *752*; **29** 176, *176*, *221*
 maces **29** 205
 masks **29** 208–9
 metalwork **21** 332; **29** 215
 mud-bricks **21** 749
 musical instruments **29** 216
 painting
  wall **29** 173, *173*, *174*
 plaster **29** 829
 portraits **21** 752–3
 pottery **5** 761; **21** *752*, 752–4*, *753*; **23** 565; **29** *134*, 135, 177, *216*, 221
 pyramids **21** *750*, 750–52*; **28** 652
 religion **29** 130–31
 rock art **6** 520
 sculpture **29** 171
 shells **23** 897; **29** 218
 spear-throwers **29** 204–5
 stucco **29** 829
 textiles **29** 135, 180
 tombs **31** 118, *119*
Moche (site) **29** *156*
 Huaca de la Luna **21** 750–51*; **29** 173
  wall paintings **21** 751; **29** *174*
 Huaca del Sol **21** *750*, 750–51*; **29** 160, 165, 218; **30** 447
 Platform of the Moon **23** 826
Mochi, Francesco (1580-1654) **21** 754–5*
 collaboration **4** 405
 patrons and collectors **3** 205
 teachers **20** 412
 works **3** 830; **4** 254; **9** 410; **10** 441; **16** 697–8, *698*; **21** *755*; **24** 695, *696*; **26** 809
Mochi, Francesco (1603-49) **21** 755
Mochi, Juan **6** 597; **12** 917
Mochi, Orazio **21** 755–6*
Mochi, Stefano **21** 755
Mochica *see* MOCHE
Mochizuki Gyokusen **18** 231
Mochizuki Riunsai **17** 381
Mochlos **8** 153, 155, 308; **13** *362*; **21** *651*, 756*
 faience (i) (glass) **21** 683, 684
 fortifications **8** 155
 gold **8** 322; **21** 686
 ivory-carvings **21** 680
Mochlos—cont.
 jewellery **21** 657
 jugs **21** *756*
 pottery **21** *665*, 667
 pyxides (vases) **21** 656, *656*
 seals **21** 682
 stone vessels **21** 689
 tombs **21** 656, 664, 756
 towns **21** 664
Mochudi **4** 490
Mock, Johann Samuel **21** 756–7*; **25** 105; **33** 115
mock castles *see under* CASTLES → types
Möckel, Ludwig **9** 237
Mocker, Josef
 pupils **21** 757*
 works **2** 321; **8** 379; **17** 819; **18** 540; **25** 425, 428, 429, 438, 441, 444, 445; **30** 221
mock-velvet *see under* VELVET → types
Moco **5** 753
Mocquet, Jean **20** 138
Modanino, Paganino *see* MAZZONI, GUIDO
Modebild und Grafik-Design **9** 703
Model, Lisette **2** 289; **11** 87; **21** 762*; **24** 685; **33** 15
model books *see* PATTERN-BOOKS
model houses *see under* HOUSES → types
Modelled Alligator ware *see under* POTTERY → wares
modelli **8** *13*; **21** 762–71*; **23** 380
 materials
  armatures **21** 769
  clay **21** 768
  terracotta **11** *279*; **21** 768, *770*; **30** 495
  waxes **21** 768, *769*, *771*; **33** 2
 types
  drawings **21** 762–7*, *763*, *764*, *765*, *766*
  painting *see* OIL SKETCHES
  sculpture **4** 618; **11** *279*; **13** 438–9*; **20** 370; **21** 767–71*, *769*, *770*, *771*; **27** 18–19*, *19*; **29** 705, *705*
modelling **6** 569; **24** *376*, 378, 382
 historical and regional traditions
  Etruscan **10** 617, 623
  Gothic **13** 139
  Greece, ancient **2** 227
  Italy **10** 617, 623
 uses
  manuscript illumination **6** 569
  painting **6** 569; **10** 617; **13** 139; **19** 352
  wall paintings **10** 623
 see also CANGIANTI; CHIAROSCURO
modelling calfskin *see under* LEATHER → types
Modello, Paolo del *see* BALDINI, PIETRO PAOLO
models **2** 335; **8** 911; **19** 354
 historical and regional traditions
  China **6** *883*, 883–4, 889; **7** 103
  Cyprus, ancient **8** *307*
  Egypt, ancient **9** *823*
  Etruscan **10** *590*
  Indian subcontinent **15** 724
  Italy **10** *590*; **16** 749*
  Prehistoric art **8** *307*
 materials
  bronze **10** *590*
  earthenware **6** *686*, *883*, 889
  ivory **7** 103; **16** 799
  plaster **4** *568*
  pottery **6** *686*, 883–4
  terracotta **24** *374*
  waxes **16** 749
 types
  anatomical **28** 205
   see also ECORCHÉS
models
 types—cont.
  architectural **2** 335–8*; **12** 182; **20** 576; **29** *607*
   Canada **7** *858*
   China **6** 648, 686, *686*; **23** 821
   Egypt, ancient **9** *849*, 850, *851*
   England **2** 336, *337*; **23** 687
   Ethiopia **1** *513*
   France **2** 337
   Germany **12** *366*; **14** 513
   Greece, ancient **13** 376, 395, 409–10*; **24** *374*
   Italy **2** 336; **16** 629
   South America, Pre-Columbian **29** *139*
   Spain **14** *475*
   Switzerland **29** *607*
   Syria-Palestine **10** *173*
   United States of America **2** *552*
   see also PROPORTIONS (ARCHITECTURE)
  artists' **7** 149; **21** 757–61*; **25** 274
  ceramics **3** 591
Model T Ford *see under* CARS → models
Modena **16** *618*; **21** 771–4*
 academy **1** 103
 ark **17** 570
 Beccherie **1** 17
 Biblioteca Estense **16** 776
 Biblioteca Luigi Poletti **16** 776
 Cataldo Cemetery **16** 651
 Cathedral of S Geminiano **5** 549; **16** 625, 687; **18** 729; **21** 771–2*, *772*; **26** 570, 578–9, *579*, 595; **33** 187
  crypt **8** 224
  Porta dei Principi **26** 621; **33** 188
  sculpture **10** 476; **21** 772–4*, *773*, *774*; **26** 619, 620, 621; **30** 498
 Galleria e Museo Estense **5** 553; **23** 333
 paintings **18** 708
 Palazzo Comunale **15** 87
 Palazzo Ducale **2** 849; **10** 524; **11** 682
  frescoes **16** *715*
 Palazzo d'Este *see* Palazzo Ducale
 Palazzo Pubblico **1** 17
 San Cataldo Cemetery **25** 359; **26** 16; **30** 455
 tapestries **16** 755
Modena, Barnaba da *see* BARNABA DA MODENA
Modena, Bartolomeo da *see* BARTOLOMEO DA MODENA
Modena, Giovanni da *see* GIOVANNI DA MODENA
Modena, Gulielmo da *see* WILIGELMO
Modena, Martino da *see* MARTINO DA MODENA
Modena, Nicoletto da *see* NICOLETTO DA MODENA
Modena, Tomaso da *see* TOMASO DA MODENA
Modena Hours, Master of the *see* TOMASINO DA VIMERCATE
Modena Triptych **13** 339
Moderati, Francesco **23** 577
Modern Architects Group **28** 444
Modern Architectural Research Group *see* MARS GROUP
Modern Art **26** 536
Modern Art Circle (Malta) **20** 213
Modern art circle (Netherlands) *see* MODERNE KUNSTKRING
Modern Artists Association *see* HYŎNDAE MISULGA HYŎPHOE
Modern Artists in America **24** 433
modern art museums *see under* COLLECTIONS → types; MUSEUMS → types

Modern Art Society **21** 32
modern cursive script *see under* SCRIPTS → types
Moderne Architektur **2** 567
Moderne Bauformen **12** 416; **24** 444
Moderne Bund **2** 488; **17** 764; **30** 134
Moderne Kunst **2** 197; **24** 324
Moderne Kunstkring **1** 809; **9** 135; **17** 764; **19** 65; **21** 363, 775*, 852; **28** 864; **29** 660
exhibitions **12** 502
members **12** 806; **14** 295; **31** 149
Moderner Bund **12** 649
moderne Stil, Der **24** 427
Modern Gothic style **31** 630
Moderni **12** 31
Modernism **7** 615; **11** 315, 360, 835; **20** 258; **21** 775–8*, 851; **24** 743; **25** 582; **31** 582
art forms
architecture
Africa **1** 319
Australia **2** 741
Austria **2** 788–9
Bolivia **4** 260–61
Brazil **4** *712*, 712–14, *713*
Canada **5** 562–3, *563*
Chile **18** 797
Czech Republic **8** *380*; **18** 405
Denmark **16** *828*
England **6** *551*; **7** *483*; **11** *808*; **19** *747*
Finland **26** 260; **29** 769
France **11** 526; **19** *42*, *43*, *46*, *368*; **24** *131*; **28** *483*
Germany **3** *292*; **10** 684; **13** 687; **26** 405
Greece **13** 349, *350*; **21** 735
Ireland **16** *11*, 12
Israel **26** 20
Italy **11** 869; **19** 304, *305*; **25** *218*; **26** 14
Japan **17** 86, 88–90; **20** *76*
Mexico **5** *603*; **21** 379–81, *380*; **32** 558
Poland **25** 100; **29** 52
Switzerland **19** *40*; **22** 185, 187; **29** 602, *603*
United States of America **10** *120*; **23** *10*; **27** *314*; **28** *96*
Uruguay **31** 753
book illustrations **11** *82*
drawings **22** *56*
interior decoration **19** *45*
painting **2** 748; **31** 605
Belgium **3** 563–4, *563*
Brazil **4** *718*
Cuba (Caribbean) **32** 416
India, Republic of **15** 169
Ireland **16** *17*
sculpture **8** 178; **22** *57*; **25** 582
urban planning **19** *50*
collections **7** 561
commentaries **13** 616
regional traditions
Australia **29** 634
Belgium **3** 563–4
Brazil **4** 717–19*, 727
Finland **11** 100
Germany **33** 384
Netherlands, the **29** 660
Uruguay **30** 275
see also INTERNATIONAL STYLE; MODERN MOVEMENT
Modernisme **2** 562; **3** 219; **29** 308
architecture **3** 216; **12** 179, 180, *181*, *182*; **29** 272–3
ceramics **29** 329
furniture **29** 319–21
mosaics **22** *158*
Modernismo **12** 180; **29** 308
Moderniste Illustré **2** 732
modernity **21** 775, 777–9*
Modern Line **8** 236
Modern Movement **7** 698; **8** 803; **10** 749; **15** 824; **20** 595; **21** 775, 779–83*; **29** 530
art forms
architecture **7** 293; **8** 247; **25** 741; **26** 14
Argentina **32** 600
Austria **19** *652*
Belgium **3** *550*
Brazil **23** *118*, *119*; **26** *110*
Croatia **15** 66
Dominican Republic **9** *117*
England **7** 712
France **12** *160*; **19** *653*
Germany **21** *491*, *780*, *783*; **23** *394*
Netherlands, the **4** *815*; **21** *781*; **31** *868*
Switzerland **30** *128*
United States of America **2** *551*; **5** *649*; **21** *492*, *493*; **23** *272*, *360*
ceramics **10** 313
mixed-media **18** *119*
painting **9** *63*; **18** *118*
sculpture **29** 873
silver **10** 337, *337*
regional traditions
Austria **32** 439
Cuba (Caribbean) **25** 823
England **10** 239, 241, 313
France **21** 782
Germany **13** 687; **21** 491, 780–81
Ireland **28** 284
Italy **30** 512
Netherlands, the **21** 781–2
Scotland **20** 24
Switzerland **27** 853
United States of America **17** 875
see also INTERNATIONAL STYLE; MODERNISM
Moderno **21** 783–4*
attributions **12** 31
patrons and collectors **6** 393
works **20** 918; **25** 20, *20*
Modern Painters **24** 429
Modern Sculpture Group *see* SHŪDAN GENDAI CHŌKOKU
Modern style see ART NOUVEAU
Modersohn, Otto **20** 14; **21** 784; **26** 394; **33** 382, 383
Modersohn-Becker, Paula **21** 784–5*; **33** 313
groups and movements **10** 694; **26** 394; **33** 382, 383
patrons and collectors **14** 506, 622
works **12** 395; **21** *785*
Modersohn-Becker, Paula, Haus *see under* BREMEN
Modes, Les **10** 823
Modesne, le *see* BELLIN (OF MODENA), NICHOLAS
Modeste, Rod **22** 589
Modestus, Patriarch **17** 498
Modhera **21** 785*
Surya Temple **15** 216, 314, 489; **21** 785; **29** 526
torana **31** 161
Modica **16** 640
Modigliani, Amedeo **3** 366; **16** 679, 680; **17** 577; **19** 512; **21** 786–8*; **23** 296; **25** 582
dealers **13** 826; **33** 36, 627
exhibitions **28** 808
forgeries by others **11** 307
groups and movements **9** 705; **11** 550
patrons and collectors
Barnes, Albert C. **3** 251
Cooper, Douglas **7** 797
Dale, Chester **8** 463
Dutilleul, Roger **9** 465
Guggenheim, Solomon R(obert) **13** 800
Maitland, Ruth (Esther) **20** 142
Masurel, Jean and Geneviève **19** 381
Modigliani, Amedeo
patrons and collectors—cont.
Mattioli, Gianni **20** 848
Sainsbury, Robert and Lisa **27** 524
Walter-Guillaume Collection **13** 826
personal collection **1** 438
studio **29** 858
works **21** *787*, *788*
modillions **21** 788*; **26** 865
Modjeski, Ralph **8** 152
Modler, Johann Baptist **11** 125
Modler workshop **31** 512
Mödlhammer, E. **14** 298
Modoc **22** 641, 659, 668
Modor **15** 2
Modorov, Fyodor **27** 889
Modotti, Tina **21** 788*
Modoura *see* MADURAI
Modra, Slovenska Majolika factory **28** 856
modules **12** 872; **13** 412*; **14** 86; **15** 210
Modulor system **2** *360*, 360–61; **29** 52
Modum **23** 225
Moe, Jörgen **22** 540
Moe, Terje **18** 390
Moedano, Hugo **8** 255; **18** 784
Moelaert, Jacob **20** 81
Moelder, Charles de **10** 329
Moeller, Ferdinand **12** 474
Moel y Gaer **25** 535
Moenkopi **22** 567
Moerdijk, Gerard **19** 113, 731; **25** 566; **29** 105
Moerdrecht, Otto van *see* OTTO VAN MOERDRECHT
Moerenhout, Joseph Jodocus **21** 58; **28** 72
Moerentoft, Jan *see* MORETUS, JAN
Moerman (family) **3** 598
Moerman, Albert Edouard **8** 765
Moerman, Jan (*fl* 1608) **15** 84
Moerman, Joannes (*fl* 1670–7) works **3** *599*
Moerner, Wilhelm von **3** 794
Moeschal, Jacques **5** 45
Moesgård **32** 533
Moesman, Johannes (Hendrikus) **21** 789*; **22** 852
Moest, Walter **3** 797
Moeyaert, Claes (Cornelisz.) **21** 789–91*
groups and movements **22** 842; **25** 556, 557
patrons and collectors **14** 370
pupils **3** 757; **18** 227; **25** 369; **33** 25, 26
reproductive prints by others **23** 191
works **21** *790*; **25** 369
Moffard, Jean **18** 640
Moffard, Robert **18** 640
Moffat, John **2** 755
Moffat, Sandy **9** 725
Moffat, William Lambie **31** 240
Moffatt, Tracey **1** 65
Moffatt, William Bonythorn **7** 667; **28** 277; **29** 764
Mofou **1** 310
Mogadishu **1** 315, *379*; **6** *623*; **29** 56, *56*
architecture **1** 379
National Museum of Somalia **29** 57
palace **1** 308
Mogador *see* ESSAOUIRA
Mogalli, Cosimo **21** 30; **30** 40
Mogao *see* DUNHUANG
Mogasa **14** 376
Mogensen, Børge (Vestergaard) **8** 746, 747, 803; **21** 791*
Moger, Rafael **23** 160
Moggi, Ferdinando Bonaventura **6** 39
Moggridge, Hal **7** 644
Mogh **3** 165
Moghul *see* MUGHAL
Moghulpura Engineering College *see* LAHORE → West Pakistan University of Engineering and Technology
Mogiła *see* NOWA HUTA
Mogila, Pyotr, Metropolitan of Kiev **18** 39
Mogilas **17** 840
Mogilev *see* MAHILOŬ
Mogilno Abbey **25** 95
Mogollon **22** 550, 554
architecture **22** 566
jewellery **22** 642
pottery **22** 600–601, 603, *603*
rock art **22** 559
textiles **22** 622
Mogontiacum **20** 127
Mogrobejo, Nemesio **29** 295
Moguer, Convento de S Clara **13** 123; **22** 255; **29** 311
Mogul *see* MUGHAL
Mogulrajapuram Cave 4 **15** 477
Mohács **14** *881*; **15** 1
mohair *see under* HAIR → types
Mohalyi, Yolanda **4** 719
Mohamed, Raza **30** 301
Mohammad, Nasiruddin **23** 801
Mohammad, Sardar **23** 800, 801
Mohammad Kaleem Khan **23** 801
Mohammad Reza, Shah *see* MUHAMMAD RIZA, Shah
Mohammed Hoessein Enas **20** 172
Mohammedia Palace of Justice **1** 319
Mohan **15** 605
Mohangarh **6** 444; **15** 290
Mohapi, Ts'itso **19** 242
Mohave **22** 605, 668
Mohawk **16** 61; **22** 552, 612, 665
Mohedano, Antonio **21** 791*; **23** 156; **26** 307
Mohelnice Church **8** 376
Mohenjo-daro **15** 192, 193, 246–7, *264*, *276*, 408; **21** 792*; **23** *797*, 798
Archaeological Museum **23** 804
architecture **4** 793
figurines **15** 213, *412*, 415, 418–20, *419*, 421–2
gems **12** 252
Granary **15** 246
Great Bath **15** 246, *246*
ivory **15** 695
Museum **23** 799
needles **15** 674
sculpture **4** 853; **15** 417, 699, 706
seals **15** 420; **30** 784
stone vessels **2** 272
textiles **15** 658
Moh Klan **30** 578
Mohlitz, Philippe **10** 398
Mohn, Gottlob Samuel **2** 818
Mohn, Samuel **2** 818
Moholy, Lucia **21** 792*; **24** 676
Moholy-Nagy, László **3** 802; **5** 531; **6** 576; **7** 772; **17** 876; **21** 792–5*; **28** 197
architectural models **2** 335
collaboration **20** 104
exhibitions **3** 802; **19** 477; **20** 475
films **10** 687
groups and movements
Abstract art **1** 75, 77
Abstraction-Création **1** 90
Activists (Aktivizmus) **1** 131
American Abstract Artists **1** 772
Bauhaus **3** 401, 402, 403; **12** 407, 497; **25** 350
CIAM **7** 294
Constructivism **7** 771; **12** 396
Dada **8** 437
kinetic art **18** 62
MA group **20** 103
Photo League **24** 685
lithographs **19** 491
methods **24** 657
paintings **21** *795*
Moholy-Nagy, László—cont.
patrons and collectors **13** 800
photograms **24** 654, *654*
photographs **24** 676
photomontages **20** 104; **24** 686
prints **29** 872; **33** 363
productions **19** 81
pupils **3** 93; **4** 60; **10** 863; **14** 393; **28** 887; **32** 756
sculpture **2** 838; **19** 355; **21** *794*; **25** 25
staff **20** 837
writings **13** 727; **17** 833; **18** 111; **19** 848; **24** 441
Mohr, Christian **21** 796*
Mohra Moradu *see under* TAXILA
Mohrbutter, Alfred **12** 468
Möhring, Bruno **21** 796*
staff **19** 283
works **11** 727
Mohs, Friedrich **14** 167
Moh Wee Teck **28** 773
Moille, Damiano **2** 166
Moilliet, Louis (René) **21** 796–7*; **30** 134
Moillon, Isaac **21** 797
Moillon, Louise **11** 535; **21** 797*
patrons and collectors **29** 803
works **11** *535*; **29** 668
Moillon, Nicolas **21** 797
Moine, Antoine-Marie **11** 564; **21** 797–8*
Moinichen, Jacob Henriksen **8** 752
Moinville, François-Nicolas-Henry Racine, Baron de **11** 242; **26** 257, 743
Moira, Gerald Edward Lobb **3** 269; **22** 331; **31** 584
moiré **21** 798*
Moiret, Ödön **14** 896
Mois, Rolan **13** 862
Moiseiwitsch, Tanya **1** 125
Moiseyenko, Yevsey (Yevseyevich) **27** 397, 581
Moissac **11** *505*, 529
St Pierre **7** 232; **21** 798–800*; **26** 584
cloister **7** *232*, 453, 454; **21** 798–9; **26** 602
manuscript illumination **11** 653
porch **26** 602
portal **11** 554
reliefs **21** *798*
sculpture **7** 642, *642*; **11** 554; **13** 125, *126*; **21** 798–800; **26** 596, 597, 641
tower porch portal **7** 642; **21** *799*, 799–800
Moisset, Jean *see* MONTAUBON, JEAN
Moissi, Alexander **19** 653
Moissieff, Leon S. **4** 803
Moitessier, Mme **25** *279*
Moitte (family) **13** 640
Moitte, Alexandre **21** 800
Moitte, Elisabeth-Mélanie **21** 800
Moitte, François-Auguste **21** 800
Moitte, Jean-Baptist-Philibert **21** 800
Moitte, Jean-Guillaume **21** 800–801*
collaboration **3** 852
patrons and collectors **2** 722; **11** 561
pupils **12** 177
reproductive prints by others **16** 905
works **8** 867; **11** 562, 621; **27** 548; **30** 499
Moitte, Pierre-Etienne **15** 38; **21** 800*
Moitte, Rose-Angélique **21** 800
Moja, Frederico **21** 495
Mojados, Miguel **29** 335
Moje, Klaus **2** 764; **21** 801*
Mojeque **6** 523
Moje-Wohlgemuth, Isgard **12** 441; **21** 801

moji see BUDDHISM → art → calligraphy → Chan
Mojna Church 26 707, 718
Mojonier Studio 33 104
Mojos 29 192
Mojović, Dragan 28 452
Mo Ju-chung *see* MO RUZHONG
Mokan Singh, Raja of Kishangarh (*reg* 1838-41) (Rajput) 15 613
Mokanyane, Samuel 19 242
 works 19 *242*
Moke 33 597
 works 33 *596*
Mokh, Mikhail 27 414
Mokhlablur 2 439
Mokitimi, Meshu 19 242
Moknine 1 *376*; 31 426
Mokolo 5 525
Mokpo 18 382
Mokuan Reien 21 801*
 works 17 169, *169*
Mokuan Shōtō 17 234, 409; 20 286; 21 801–3*
 groups and movements 17 231
 works 21 *802*, *803*
Mokubei Aoki *see* AOKI MOKUBEI
Mokugo *see* ASAI, CHŪ
Mokujiki Myōman *see* MYŌMAN MOKUJIKI
mokume see under JAPAN → metalwork
Mokusu *see* MOZI (1596-1657)
Mokvi Gospels *see under* GOSPEL BOOKS → individual manuscripts
Mol, Jacobs Smits Museum 28 891
Mol, H. W. 33 323
Mol, Joannes de 22 882
 works 22 *882*
Mol, Leo 5 571
Mol, Natalis de 3 599
Mol, Pieter Laurens 21 803*
Mol, Pieter van 5 792; 21 803–4*; 33 298
Mol, Robert van 21 804
Mola, Antonio 10 521; 16 712
Mola (i), Gasparo 12 405; 20 919; 21 804–5*
 pupils 6 553; 21 805
 works 20 921; 30 228
Mola (i), Gasparo Morone 14 105; 21 805*
Mola (ii), Giacomo 21 805*
Mola (ii), Giovanni Battista 6 23; 21 805*; 23 898, 900
Mola, Paulo 16 712
Mola (ii), Pier Francesco 21 805, 806–8*
 collaboration 6 585
 patrons and collectors 5 792, 848; 7 622; 21 35; 23 898, 900; 24 225
 pupils 11 305; 12 525
 reproductive prints by others 7 466; 19 10
 teachers 1 535
 works 5 756; 9 222; 21 *807*, *808*; 26 840; 30 527
Mola, Piero 10 521
Molanus, Johannes 4 20; 7 276; 21 809*
 works 8 612; 15 89; 18 704
Mola Ram 15 627
Molares, Per Afán de Ribera (i), 6th Conde de *see* ALCALÁ, 1st Duque de
Molaroni, Eliseo 24 535
Molaroni, Telesforo 24 535
Molart, Michel 20 922
molas 21 804*, *804*
molasse 27 831
Mölckh, Josef Adam von *see* MÖLK, JOSEF ADAM VON
Mold (Clwyd) 25 525
 Leeswood Park 32 789
 metalwork 25 *525*
 St Mary's 32 782
Moldakhmetov, Asanbek 18 568
Moldavia *see* MOLDOVA
Moldavian vaults *see under* VAULTS (CEILING) → types
Mold Cape 12 869
Moldenschardt, H. H. 18 114
Molder, Jan de 21 809*
Moldova 21 *810*, 810–13*; 26 *705*
 architecture 21 810–11*
 batons 25 493
 book illustrations 21 812*
 figurines 25 489
 heraldry 14 411
 painting 21 811–12*
 portraits 21 *812*
 sculpture 21 811–12*
Moldoviţa Monastery 26 717
 thrones 26 *717*
Molé, Claude 20 744
Mole, F. J. 2 765
Molé family 6 563
Molenaer, Bartholomeus 21 813
Molenaer, Cornelis 7 708
Molenaer, Jan Jansz. 21 814
Molenaer, Jan Miense 13 895; 19 293; 21 813–14*
 collaboration 19 293
 patrons and collectors 19 338
 pupils 22 840
 works 1 659; 21 *814*
Molenaer, Klaes 21 813; 27 329
Molenberg, Alberto 2 604
Molepolole 4 490
Molero, Miguel 29 348
Molerov, Dimitar Vishanov 3 186
Molerov, Georgi Simeonov 3 186
Molerov, Simeon Dimitrov 3 186
moles 26 864
Moles, Pedro Pascual 14 85; 21 815*
Moleta de Cartagena, La *see* LA MOLETA DE CARTAGENA
Molezún, Ramón Vázquez *see* VÁZQUEZ MOLEZÚN, RAMÓN
Molfetta, Cathedral of the Assumption 26 580
Molfetta, Ferrante Gonzaga, Duca di *see* GUASTALLA, FERRANTE GONZAGA, Duca da
Molholt, Pat 1 13
Moli, Gasparo *see* MOLA (i), GASPARO
Molière 4 360; 5 884; 27 868; 30 669, 671; 31 165
Molière, Marinus Jan Granpré *see* GRANPRÉ MOLIÈRE, MARINUS JAN
Molière-Bardin, François 23 510
Molijn, Pieter (de) *see* MOLYN, PIETER (DE)
Molijn Dzn, François Adriaan 3 769
Molin, Johan Peter 21 815*; 30 86
Molina, Antonio de 26 548
Molina, Fernando 19 704
Molina, Francisco Daniel 21 229, 815–16*
Molina, Gonzalo Argote de *see* ARGOTE DE MOLINA, GONZALO
Molina, Pedro Antonio de 24 503
Molina i Casamajó, Francesc 3 215
Molinari, Antonio 21 816*; 22 39; 24 703; 32 194; 33 608
Molinari, Giovanni (1633-87) 21 816
Molinari, Giovanni Domenico (1721-93) 31 447
Molinari, Guido 21 816*; 22 39
 groups and movements 25 28
 works 5 568, *568*
Molinari, Leonardo de' *see* LEONARDO (DE' MOLINARI) DA BESOZZO
Molineau, J 22 25
Molinet, Claude Du *see* DU MOLINET, CLAUDE
Molineux, Emery 12 814; 14 708
Molineux, John 4 481
Molinier, Auguste 21 816
Molinier, Emile 16 555; 21 816–17*
Molinier, Pierre 10 482; 30 23
Molino, Domenico 25 889; 32 223
Molino, Fernando García del *see* GARCÍA DEL MOLINO, FERNANDO
Molinos, Jacques 3 524; 19 85; 21 817*; 24 121
Molinos Jesuit Mission 2 394
Molins de Rey 29 330
Molisson, de *see* MONTLUÇON, DE
Molitor, Bernard 10 186; 11 593, 597; 21 817*
Mölk, Josef Adam 21 817–18*
Mölk, Mathias 21 817
Molkenboer, Antoon 21 818; 22 850
Molkenboer, Theo(dorus Henricus Antonius Adolf) 21 818*
Moll, Anton Cassian 21 818
Moll, Balthasar Ferdinand 21 818–19*; 28 855
 assistants 32 758
 patrons and collectors 13 922; 19 337
 pupils 9 171; 21 313; 25 648
 teachers 9 147
 works 2 802; 15 865
Moll, Carl 2 829; 21 819*; 32 445
 groups and movements 2 797; 28 343, 344; 32 446
 works 33 166, 362
Moll, Didier 23 635
Moll, Johann Nikolaus 2 802; 21 818; 25 33
Moll, Margarete 25 744
Moll, Nikolaus 15 865; 21 818*; 31 358
Moll, Oskar 21 819–20*; 25 744
Moll, Virgil 33 738
Mollakurgan 6 193; 23 607, 608
Mollari, Antonio 31 329
Mollarts (family) 25 443
Mollem, David van 8 149, 150; 33 676
Möllenborg, Gustaf 30 107, 108, 113
Møller (family) 23 236
Möller, Anton, I 21 820*; 25 104
 works 12 389; 31 196; 33 354
Moller, Bertil 11 467
Møller, C(hristian) F(rederik) 21 820–21*
 collaboration 11 139; 29 77, 601
 groups and movements 8 728
 staff 11 793
 works 8 728, *728*
Møller, Erik 16 827; 21 821*
Möller, Fabian 25 120
Møller, Georg (*fl* 1889-96) 18 237
Moller, Georg (1784-1852) 21 821–2*
 pupils 28 142; 29 491
 teachers 33 40
 works 8 530–31, *531*
 writings 2 319
Möller, Göran 30 109
Möller, Hans 8 112
Möller, Istvan 14 880
Møller, Lars 13 620
Moller, Lize 6 600
Möllerberg, Nils 30 86
Mollerum, Diedrich 11 94
Mollet (family) 8 794
Mollet, André 12 135; 21 822*
 patrons and collectors 12 127; 29 803
 works 23 465; 26 392
 writings 12 64
Mollet, André-Armand 21 822, 823
Mollet, Armand-Claude 11 518; 21 822, 823*; 24 120
 patrons and collectors 8 32
Mollet, Charles 21 823
Mollet, Claude (*d* 1644) 21 822
Mollet, Claude (*c.* 1564-*c.* 1649) 12 64, 120; 21 822
Mollet, Jacques 21 822
Mollet, Noël 21 822
Mollet, Pierre 21 822
Mollett, John William 10 209
Molli, Benedetto 20 521; 21 823*
Molli, Clemente 19 628, 630; 25 114, 130; 32 7, 874
Mollijns, Jan 3 555
Mollinedo y Angulo, Manuel de 8 302; 24 502, 507
Mollinger, G. A. 28 270
Mollino, Carlo 8 803; 16 732; 21 824*
 pupils 22 747
 works 16 721, *721*
Mollino, Eugenio 21 824
Mollner, Peter 2 784
Mollo (Vienna) 10 530
Mollo culture 31 47
Molmenti, Pompeo 25 824; 29 885; 33 611
Molnár, Farkas 14 890; 21 824*
 collaboration 2 416
 groups and movements 14 890; 15 886
 works 30 683
Molnár, Pál C. 14 901
Molnár, Sándor 14 902
Molnár, Wolfgang *see* MOLNÁR, FARKAS
Molner, Dietrich 11 254
Molo, Gasparo *see* MOLA (i), GASPARO
Moloka'i *see* HAWAII
Molotov *see* PERM'
Molpir 25 535
Molsheim 21 *162*
 Holy Trinity Church 12 368
 Jesuit church 12 369
 St George 13 211
Molteni, Enrico Gasi *see* SIGNORINI, TELEMACO
Molteni, Giuseppe 6 115; 21 824–5*; 22 102, 296
Moltke, Adam Gottlob, Count 8 760; 21 825*
 architecture 10 111
 collections 8 758
 gardens 17 446
 interior decoration 29 841
 paintings 32 428
Moltke, Helmuth von 16 587
Moltke Mansion *see under* COPENHAGEN → Amalienborg Palace
Molto, Carlos Arniches 31 193
Molvig, Jon 21 825*
molybdate orange *see under* PIGMENTS → types
molybdate red *see under* PIGMENTS → types
Molyn, Pieter (de) 13 895; 21 825–7*
 collaboration 14 94
 patrons and collectors 21 485
 pupils 4 381; 10 660; 17 7
 reproductive prints by others 28 79; 32 140
 works 9 222; 18 710; 21 *826*; 22 840
Molyneux, Charles-William, 3rd Earl of Sefton 2 127
Molyneux, Emery *see* MOLINEUX, EMERY
Molyneux, Robert 24 188
Molyneux, William 26 475
Molyneux Carpet 10 276
Moly-Sabata 12 806
Molyvann, Vann 5 482–3
 works 5 *482*
Molzahn, Johannes 32 775
Molzbich, St Tiburtius 2 798
Mölzlagl, Simon *see* JUNG, MORIZ
Momal, Jacques-François 8 123
Mombaers, Corneille 3 589; 5 50
Mombaers, Philippe 3 589; 5 50
 works 3 *590*
Mombasa 1 *407*; 30 57
 Fort Jesus 1 318; 21 572, 597
Momchilov, Petko 5 149; 28 838
Momi *see* VERE
Momik 2 436; 8 198; 23 202; 30 360
Momil 29 134
Momma, Joseph 10 195
Mommers, Hendrick 19 858; 22 840
Mommsen, Theodor 12 873
Momontov, Savva 27 410
Momoyama Castle 17 22; 21 828
Momoyama period *see under* JAPAN → periods
Mömpelgard 33 360
 St Martin 12 370; 28 *88*
Mömpelgard, Georg I von, Graf 11 838
Mömpelgarder altar 11 838
Momper, Bartolomeus de 15 43; 21 828
Momper, Frans de 20 142; 21 828, 830*
Momper, Gaspard 21 828
Momper, Jan de, I (*fl* 1512-16) 21 828
Momper, Jan de, II (*fl* 1603) 21 828
Momper, Josse de, I (1516-59) 21 828
Momper, Josse de, II (1564-1635) 21 828–30*
 collaboration 3 108; 4 913, 915; 11 718; 17 647; 28 358; 32 724
 patrons and collectors 3 613; 14 807
 reproductive prints by others 7 556
 works 3 560; 4 905; 5 352; 20 424; 21 *829*; 29 375
Momper, Philips de, I (*fl* 1622-34) 21 828
Momper, Philips de, II (*fl* 1622- *d* 1675) 21 828
Mompere, Bartolomeus de 3 558
Mompós 7 *601*, 603, 604
 S Barbara 7 605
Mompox *see* MOMPÓS
Mon 5 99, 222, 223, 240, 258; 29 231; 30 571
 architecture 5 225
 ceramics 5 254
 coins 5 255
 sculpture 5 238*
 stucco 29 826
Mona, Domenico 28 38
Monache 22 659
 baskets 22 *659*
Monaco 21 830*
 archives 18 573
 art legislation 2 560
 Cathedral of St Nicholas 21 830
 collections 15 888
 Palais Grimaldi 11 16; 21 830
 Stade Louis II 29 490
Monaco, Giacomo 21 831
Monaco, Guglielmo (lo) *see* GUGLIELMO (LO) MONACO
Monaco, Lorenzo *see* LORENZO MONACO
Monaco, Pietro 8 193; 21 830–31*; 27 719
Mónaco, Primaldo 2 604
Monaco, Vincenzo 22 77
Monagri, Panagia Amasgou 8 358
Monagrillo 7 506; 29 *136*, 138
Monahan, Gordon 29 99
Monaldeschi, Tramo, Bishop of Orvieto 31 534
Monaldi, Carlo 20 125; 21 831*
 patrons and collectors 4 635; 7 897; 25 301
 pupils 1 679
 works 20 86
Monaldi, Jakub 21 831*; 32 876
 patrons and collectors 25 212
 pupils 32 678
 works 25 115

Monaldi, Paolo **2** 27; **3** 199; **21** 831–2*; **27** 172
Mona Lisa *see* GIOCONDO, LISA DEL
Mon'ami **17** 380
Monamy, Peter **4** 862; **20** 424; **21** 832*; **30** 58
Monanni, Monanno **1** 673
MONARK **11** 92
Monasterboice (Co. Louth) **16** *5*; **21** 832*
crosses **8** 196; **15** 876; **21** 832
Muiredach's Cross **15** 877, *877*; **16** 19; **21** 832
sculpture **15** 877
West Cross **21** 832
monasteries
historical and regional traditions
2 364, 372; **7** 227–32*, 262; **19** 312–13; **20** 559; **21** 833*, 843–6*; **31** 708, 710
Africa **1** 314–15
Anglo-Saxon **2** 66
Armenia (Europe) **2** *427*; **12** *235*; **14** *36*; **30** *360*
Augustinian Canons **21** 840
Austria **2** *777*; **19** *377*; **21** *83*
Benedictine Order **3** 708, 709; **21** 835–6*, *836*, *839*, *840*
Bhutan **3** 913; **21** 848*
Brigittine Order **21** 840
Buddhism **21** 846–8*
Bhutan **21** 848*
Cambodia **5** 481
Central Asia **5** 102
Central Asia, Eastern **6** 294, 296
China **7** 25
Gelugpa **5** 105
Indian subcontinent **1** 499; **21** 847*; **22** 447
Japan **5** 116, 120; **12** 97
Japan: Zen **17** 77, 231
Laos **18** 763, 764–6*, *765*
Mongolia **21** *874*, 875
Nepal **5** 103; **21** 847*; **22** 763, *763*, *764*, 765–6
Thailand **2** *886*; **29** *910*; **30** 574–5, 582, 585–6, *586*, 587–8, *588*
Tibet **5** 105; **21** 847–8*; **27** 695; **30** *351*, 808, *817*, 818, 828
Zen **5** 120
Bulgaria **5** 147
Burma **5** 227, 232*, *232*, 234–5*, *236*
Byzantine **7** 227–30*; **9** 514, 522, 524, 561, 576; **21** 834
Cappadocia **5** *675*
Egypt **28** 761
Greece **22** *226*, *227*
Ukraine **18** *40*
Cambodia **5** 462, 481, 501
Cappadocia **5** 675*, *675*
Carolingian **5** 794–5, 800; **19** *698*
Carthusian Order **5** *894*; **21** 840–41*, *841*
Central Asia **5** 102
Central Asia, Eastern **6** 294, 296
China **7** 25
Cistercian Order **21** 836–9*
Czech Republic **32** *746*
England **11** *349*, *350*; **21** *833*; **26** *380*
France **21** *837*, *838*
Gothic **11** *349*, *350*; **26** *380*; **32** *746*
Ireland **16** *7*; **21** *88*
Portugal **1** *590*
Romanesque **21** *88*
Cluniac Order **7** *476*
Coptic **7** 820; **27** 813
Cyprus **3** *638*
Czech Republic **27** *797*; **32** *746*
Denmark **8** 721
Dominican Order **21** 841–2*, *842*
monasteries
historical and regional traditions—cont.
Early Christian (*c.* AD 250-843) **9** 522, 524, 561; **25** *771*
Egypt **21** 833; **27** 813; **28** 761, *761*
England **9** 374–5; **10** 229, 259; **21** 834–5, 839, 841
Benedictine Order **3** 708; **21** 836, *839*, *840*
Carthusian Order **21** *841*
Cistercian Order **11** *349*, *350*; **21** *833*; **26** *380*
Dominican Order **21** *842*
Gothic **5** *638*; **11** *349*, *350*; **26** *380*
Romanesque **33** *551*
Ethiopia **1** 314–15
France **13** 210
Benedictine Order **3** 708; **21** *836*
Carthusian Order **5** *894*
Cistercian Order **21** *837*, *838*
Cluniac Order **7** *476*
Gothic **11** 510; **21** *844*; **22** *40*
Romanesque **7** *476*; **26** *583*; **27** *560*
12th cent. **7** *372*
18th cent. **7** *774*
Franciscan Order **21** 841–2*; **33** 571
Georgia **8** *567*; **12** *239*; **30** 305
Germany **12** 369, 372, 471
Baroque **23** *5*
Benedictine Order **3** 709
Carolingian **19** *698*
Gothic **7** *206*
Gilbertine Order **21** 840
Gothic
Cistercian Order **11** *349*, *350*; **26** *380*; **32** *746*
Czech Republic **32** *746*
England **5** *638*; **11** *349*, *350*; **26** *380*
France **11** 510; **21** *844*; **22** *40*
Germany **7** *206*
Portugal **1** *590*
Greece **21** 343, *343*; **22** *226*, *227*
Indian subcontinent **1** 499; **15** 311; **21** 847*; **22** 447
Ireland **16** *7*; **21** *88*, 834
Italy **21** *468*, 842; **22** *10*; **24** *285*
Japan
Buddhism **5** 116, 120; **12** 97
Buddhism: Zen **17** 77, 231
Laos **18** 763, 764–6*, *765*, 767; **19** 737
Macedonia (ii) (former Yugoslavia) **19** 882–3
Mexico **21** 375; **33** 571
Mongolia **21** *874*, 875
Nepal **5** 103; **21** 847*; **22** 760, 763, *763*, *764*, 765–6, 792
North Africa **21** 834
Palestine **21** 833
Poland **29** *792*; **32** *749*
Portugal **1** *590*; **7** *531*; **31** *179*
Romanesque **26** 570
Austria **19** *377*
Cistercian Order **21** *88*
Cluniac Order **7** *476*
England **33** *551*
France **7** *476*; **26** *583*; **27** *560*
Ireland **21** *88*
Poland **29** *792*; **32** *749*
Russia **10** *889*; **28** *465*; **32** *149*, *667*
Scotland **8** 550
Serbia **28** 440
Spain **10** *499*, *500*
Sri Lanka **29** 446–8*
Sweden **7** 703
Switzerland **10** *116*; **22** *61*
Syria **21** 834; **25** *771*
Thailand **2** *886*; **29** *910*; **30** 574–5, 582, 585–6, *586*, 587–8, *588*
monasteries
historical and regional traditions—cont.
Tibet **5** 105; **21** 847–8*; **27** 695; **30** *351*, 808, 813–14, *817*, 818, 819, 820, 828
Ukraine **18** *40*
types
fortified **12** 174–5; **22** 226; **27** 371, *371*
see also RIBĀṬS
see also PRIORIES; SACRIMONTI
Monasterio, Andrés de **28** 368
Monasterio, Luis Ortiz *see* ORTIZ MONASTERIO, LUIS
Monasterios, Rafael **21** 832–3*; **32** 175
Monastery of Begadeus **31** 434
Monastery of Buenavista **14** 517
Monastery of Dorotheus **9** 543
Monastery of Hagion Panton Hagios Prodromos **25** 331
wall paintings **25** *330*
Monastery of Kusquam **1** 315
Monastery of St Andrew **22** 79
Monastery of St Anthony **7** *819*, 823
Monastery of St Catherine *see under* MT SINAI
Monastery of St George of Choziba **9** 549
Monastery of St Gerasimus **9** 549
Monastery of St John **7** 820
Monastery of St Simeon the Stylite *see under* SAMANDAĞI
Monastery of S María de Pedralbes **13** 191
Monastery of the Syrians *see under* WADI NATRUN
Monastery of Zebinus **31** 434
Monastier, Le *see* LE MONASTIER
Monastir (Macedonia) *see* BITOLJ
Monastir (Tunisia) **31** 424
congregational mosque **16** 157
Museum **31** 427
ribāṭs **16** 156
tombs **31** 111
Monatshefte für Kunstwissenschaft **24** 444
Monbushō Bijutsu Tenrankai *see* BUNTEN
Moncada **29** 330
Moncalieri, Castello **16** 719
Moncalvo **16** 730
Moncalvo, il **8** 147; **21** 848–9*; **28** 6
works **23** 830
Moncarapacho, Nossa Senhora da Graça **24** 804
Monceau, Guy de, Abbot of Saint-Denis *see* GUY DE MONCEAU, Abbot of Saint-Denis
Monceau, H. L. Duhamel du *see* DUHAMEL DU MONCEAU, H. L.
Monceaux-en-Brie Château **19** 693
Mönchengladbach
St Vitus-Münster **13** 142; **31** 499
Städtisches Museum Abteiberg **12** 380, 498; **14** 685; **22** 368, *368*
Moncheux **13** 125
Moncino, Michele **3** 90
Monck, Charles **9** 55
Monck, George, 1st Duke of Albemarle **3** 244
Moncloa, Francisco **24** 515
Moncloa porcelain factory **20** 70
Monconys, Gaspard de **25** 413
Moncornet, Balthazar **19** 154
Moncrieff Glassworks **10** 320; **28** 260
Moncunill (i Perellada), Lluís **21** 849*
Mončys, Antanas **19** 499
Mond, Alfred Moritz **21** 850*
Mond, Ludwig **21** 849–50*; **26** 358
Mond, Robert **2** 689; **5** 74; **10** 87
Monda, Jean **26** 718
Mondavio **3** 359
Mond *Crucifixion* **21** 849; **25** 897, *897*, 898
Mondéjar, Iñigo Lopez de Mendoza, 1st Marqués de **13** 634; **21** 124
Mondéjar, Monastery of S Antonio **29** 264
Mondella, Galeazzo *see* MODERNO
Mondella, Giambattista **21** 784
Mondella, Girolamo **21** 783
Mondo, Domenico **5** 914; **21** 850*; **22** 479
Mondon, François **17** 666
Mondon, Jean **11** 577; **24** 271; **26** 494, 499
Mondoñedo Cathedral **29** 263
Mondoubleau great tower **6** 52
Mondragone Head **27** 37
Mondriaan, Frits **14** 43; **21** 851
Mondriaan, Willem Frederik **21** 851
Mondrian, Piet(er Cornelis) **1** 77; **7** 772; **11** 550, 885; **19** 476, 477, 591; **21** 775, 850–57*; **22** 849, 851; **23** 48, 124; **24** 144, 428; **31** 607
exhibitions **28** 920
groups and movements **1** 90
Abstract art **1** 73, 74
Abstraction-Création **1** 90
American Abstract Artists **1** 772
anthroposophy **2** 138
Cercle et Carré **6** 342
Concrete art **7** 698
Cubism **21** 775
Divisionism **28** 864
environmental art **10** 416
Luminism (ii) (Belgium and the Netherlands) **19** 792
Moderne Kunstkring **21** 775
Stijl, De **1** 76; **29** 660–61
theosophy **1** 74–5; **30** 170, 710, 711
methods **7** 630
patrons and collectors **2** 409; **4** 743; **12** 15; **14** 295; **22** 906; **28** 167; **30** 749; **33** 254
pupils **14** 294
teachers **14** 43
works **9** 19; **11** 360, 450; **18** 717; **21** *852*, *853*, *854*, *856*; **22** 331, 749, *749*, 851; **28** 396; **31** 705
writings **19** 848
Mondsee, Master of **20** 730*
Mondsee Abbey **2** 776; **13** 799
altarpieces **20** 730
manuscripts **2** 790; **25** 676
sculpture **2** 801
wall paintings **2** 794
Mone, Jean **3** 544, 569, 612; **21** 857–8*
collaboration **23** 494
patrons and collectors **13** 905, 906
pupils **11** 219
works **3** 569; **14** 63; **21** *858*
Monedas, Las *see* LAS MONEDAS
Monegro, Juan Bautista de **5** 902; **21** 858–9; **29** 267
patrons and collectors **6** 44
works **2** 868; **10** 503, 535; **29** 290; **31** 89, 92
Monegro, Pedro **31** 180
Monel metal *see under* ALLOYS → types
Monemvasia **9** *511*; **21** *859*, 859–61*
architecture **9** 524
Church of the Hodegetria *see* Hagia Sophia
Hagia Sophia **9** 547; **21** 860, *860*
houses **9** 561
icons **9** 629
Moneo (Vellés), (José) Rafael **21** 861*
teachers **27** 511
works **22** 368; **29** 274, 355
Moner, Francesco Muntaner *see* MUNTANER MONER, FRANCESCO
Moner, Gaspar Benasar *see* BENASAR MONER, GASPAR
Moner, José Muntaner *see* MUNTANER MONER, JOSÉ
Moner, Juan Muntaner *see* MUNTANER MONER, JUAN
Monestiroli, Antonio **16** 651
Monet, (Oscar-)
Claude **7** 674; **9** 768; **11** 547, 667; **21** 861–8*; **24** 142; **27** 238; **30** 290
dealers **3** 826; **4** 589; **9** 424, 425; **26** 107; **27** 163
exhibitions **10** 680; **19** 589
groups and movements **8** 621; **24** 591
Impressionism **15** 151, 152, 153, 154, 155; **28** 344
Post-Impressionism **25** 357
World of Art (Mir Iskusstva) **33** 379
XX, Les **32** 591
house **2** 552
methods **7** 629, 630; **9** 673; **13** 709; **24** 495
paintings **2** 342; **9** 287, *288*; **11** 417, 418; **19** 355; **27** 248
architectural **21** *865*
fêtes champêtres **11** 37
landscape **15** *151*; **18** 715, 716, 717; **21** *866*; **31** 51
marine **20** 426
portraits **9** *288*
still-lifes **29** 669
tondi **31** 142
townscapes **31** 156, 157, 704
urban life , ; **15** VI2; **21** *863*, *864*; **23** III, IV
patrons and collectors
Barnes, Albert C. **3** 251; **12** 769
Bazille, (Jean-)Frédéric **3** 435
Bellio, Georges de **3** 671; **26** 722
Bührle, Emil Georg **5** 132
Cadart, Alfred & Luquet, Jules **5** 364
Caillebotte, Gustave **5** 391
Camondo, Isaac de, Comte **5** 530
Clark, Robert Sterling **7** 377
Cognacq, (Théodore-) Ernest **7** 528
Courtauld, Samuel (1876-1947) **8** 62
Davies, Gwendoline and Margaret **5** 732
Drummond, George A(lexander) (1827-1910) **9** 305
Durand-Ruel, Paul (Marie Joseph) **28** 744
Duret, (Jules-Emmanuel) Théodore **9** 448
Ephrussi, Charles **10** 432
Faure, Jean-Baptiste **10** 837
FitzGerald, Desmond **11** 141
Ford, Henry, II (*b* 1917) **24** 183
Frick, Henry Clay **11** 774
Hammer, Armand **14** 117
Havemeyer, Louisine (Waldron) **14** 244
Havemeyer, Louisine and Henry **14** 244
Haviland, Charles **14** 246
Houssaye, (François-) Arsène **14** 802
Khalil Museum **5** 401
Lambert, Catholina **18** 672
Liebermann, Max **19** 334
May, Ernest (1845-1925) **20** 878
Mellon, Paul **21** 91
MOMA (Museum of Modern Art, New York) **31** 667
Moore, George (Augustus) (1852-1933) **22** 54
Moreau-Nélaton, Etienne **22** 93

Monet, (Oscar-)Claude
patrons and collectors—cont.
Morozov, Ivan (Abramovich) (1871-1921) **22** 135, 136
Musée des Beaux Arts (Le Havre) **19** 92
Ōhara, Magosaburō **23** 371
Palmer, Bertha Honoré **23** 882
Phillips, Duncan **24** 638
Polignac, Winnaretta, Princesse Edmond de **25** 150
Pope, Alfred Atmore **25** 234
Robinson, Edward G(oldenberg) **26** 472
Shchukin, Sergey (Ivanovich) **28** 569; **30** 361
Tavernier, Adolphe-Eugène **30** 375
Tschudi, Hugo von **31** 397
Vever, Henri **32** 394
Whitney, John Hay **33** 150
Wrightsman, Charles B(ierer) **33** 416
personal collection **6** 366; **17** 440
pupils **22** 431
sponsorship **3** 435
studio **29** 857
teachers **12** 810
Monet, Jan *see* MONE, JEAN
Moneto, Domenico Canevale de *see* CANEVALE DE MONETO, DOMENICO
Monetus **3** 188
money *see* BANKNOTES; COINS
Money, John **9** 504, 505
Money, Timothy **7** 485
Moneypenny, George **33** 232
Moneypenny Breviary *see under* BREVIARIES → individual manuscripts
Monferrand, (Henri Louis) August Ricard **23** 168
Monferrat, William VI, Margrave of *see* WILLIAM VI, Margrave of Monferrat
Monfort **21** 564
Monforte del Cid **15** 59
Monforte de Lemos
Colegio del Cardenal **29** 268
Monastery **29** 269
Monfort y Asensi, Manuel **21** 868–9*; **33** 470
Monfreid, (Georges-)Daniel de **10** 841; **12** 191, 193; **21** 869*
Mongan, Agnes **27** 493; **33** 310
Mongardini, Pietro **5** 699
Mongch'on **18** 281
Monge, Gaspard, Comte de Péluse **21** 568, 869*; **24** 494; **28** 202; **29** 637
writings **11** 518
Monge, Joaquim **26** 254
works **26** *253*
Monge, José María Barrantes *see* BARRANTES MONGE, JOSÉ MARÍA
Monghyr **15** 678
Mongin, Pierre-Antoine **19** 37, 483
Mongis, Pierre **19** 849
Mongkut, King (Rama IV; *reg* 1851-68) (chakri) **30** 588, 589, 590, 593, 632
Mongo **1** 360
works **1** *364*
Mongol **5** 112; **6** 190; **7** 77, 143; **14** 184; **15** 901; **16** 116; **21** 870–71, 875, 877, 880–81, 885; **23** 816
ceramics **6** 331
coins **14** 428
dress **7** 77
tents **30** *477*
Mongolia **6** 616; **21** 869–86*, *870*
altars **1** 705*
amber **3** 441
appliqué **21** 878
archaeology **21** 885–6*
Mongolia—cont.
architecture **21** 873–5*
armour **21** 875*
art history **21** 884–5*
banners **21** 877
beadwork **3** 441
boleros **21** 878
book covers **21** 876
book illustrations **21** 876
books **21** 875–6*
boots **21** 878
bowcases **21** 875, 878
bows **21** 875
boxes **21** 878
braids **21** 876, 877
brass **21** 882
bridles **21** 878
bronze **21** 882; **23** 495, *495*, 496, *496*
bronzes **21** 885
cards **21** 881
carving **21** 878, 879–80
cases (bags) **21** 878
clasps **21** 877, 878
coats **21** 876
collections **21** 886*
copper **21** 878
coral **3** 441; **7** 836, *836*; **21** 877
craftsmen and artists **21** 878–9
daggers **23** 495
doors **21** 883
drawings **21** *881*
dress **21** 876–7*
drums (musical instruments) **21** 879
earrings **21** 877
embossing **21** 878
embroidery **21** 876, 877*
enamel **21** 877
exhibitions **21** 886*
felt **10** 873, 875; **21** 877
fiddles **21** 879
flasks **21** 878
furniture **21** 883
gold **7** 21; **21** 882, 884
hair ornaments **21** 877
hardstones **21** 875, 877
headbands **21** 878
headdresses **3** 441; **7** *836*; **21** 877, 878
heating systems **15** 52
heraldry **14** 404
historiography **21** 884–5*
houses **6** 692
hypocausts **15** 52
iconography **5** 91; **21** 872–3*, 880
inks **15** 850
inscriptions **21** 883
iron **21** 882
jade **21** 882
jewellery **7** 836; **21** 877–8*
knives **21** 878, 884; **23** 495, *495*
knotting **21** 877
ladles **21** *884*
leather **21** 878*, 883
malachite **23** *495*
metalwork **21** 878–9*, *879*; **23** 495
monasteries **21** *874*, 875
mortars (vessels) **21** 883
museums **21** 886*
musical instruments **21** 879–80*
painting **21** *873*, 880–81*, *880*
scroll **21** 880, *880*
palm leaves **21** 876
paper **21** 875
patronage **21** 884*
pendants (jewellery) **21** 878
plaques **23** 496, *496*
printing plates **21** 875
prints **21** 875, 884
quilting **21** 877; **25** 820
quivers **21** 875, 878
religion **21** 872*
rings **21** 875, 877
rock art **21** 881–2*
saddles **21** 878
scripts **5** 106; **6** 308; **21** 882–3*
Mongolia—cont.
sculpture **21** 883*
Animal style **21** 883
Buddhism **21** 880, 883*
Urga school **21** 883
seals **21** 882*
shabracks **21** 878
shrines (i) (cult) **28** 637
silk **21** *876*, 877
silver **7** *836*; **21** 876, 877, 878, 882, 884
snuff bottles **21** 884
stamping **21** 878
standards (vexilloid) **23** 496, *496*
steel **21** 878
stelae **21** 882, 883
stitches **21** 877
swords **21** 878
tangkas **21** *880*
tanning **21** 878
temples **30** *442*
tents **21** 873, 883, 884–5; **30** 473–6*
textiles **21** 876
threads **21** 877
towns **21** 871*
trade **21** 871–2*
tunics **21** 876, *876*
turquoise **3** 441; **7** *836*
undercutting **21** 878
vessels **21** 883
waistcoats **21** 876
weapons **21** 875*
wood **21** 883–4*
wood-carvings **21** 883, *884*
woodwork **21** 883–4*, *884*
wreaths **21** 878
writing **21** 875
Mongolian script *see under* SCRIPTS → types
Mongolkure **6** 309
Mongpa **15** 721
Mongrain, Claude **22** 39
Monguí **7** 604
Monheim, Bernhard **7** 586
Monheim, Bird and Proudfoot **27** 642
Moni, Louis de **8** 887; **19** 102
Moni, Virgin Drosiani **9** 575; **22** 700
Monicart, Jean-Baptiste de **6** 563; **11** 171
Mónico, Lilí del **4** 141; **24** 98
Monicx van Montvoort, Cornelis Sybertsz. **31** 807
Monier, Joseph **7** 693
Monier, Pierre **11** 674
Monif, Khan **15** 742
Monigetti, Ippolit (Antonovich) **15** 19; **21** 887*; **22** 173; **29** 778
Monimbó **23** 85
Moninckx, Cornelis **9** 760
Moninckx, Pieter **15** 41
Monington, Walter **12** 800
Moninks, Cornelis **14** 44
Moñino, José *see* FLORIDABLANCA, Conde de
Monisdze, Ioann **12** 328
Moniteur des architectes **18** 688; **24** 442; **28** 463
Moniteur des arts see REVUE D'ART
Monjo, Enrico **29** 886
Monjós **29** 330
Monk, Meredith **24** 407
Monk bond *see under* BONDING
Monkey Beaker **13** 170
Monkhouse, William **33** 545
Monkstown Church (Co. Dublin) **16** 10
Monk stretcher bond *see under* BONDING
Monkton House (W. Sussex) **16** 892
Monkton Old Hall (Dyfed) **32** 782
Monkwearmouth Abbey (Tyne & Wear) **2** 65, 68; **3** 708; **9** 13; **10** *225*; **21** 835, 887–8*
crosses **2** 68
furniture **30** 776
Monkwearmouth Abbey (Tyne & Wear)—cont.
glass **10** 315
manuscripts **15** 874
St Peter's **2** 68; **21** *887*, 887–8
sculpture **2** 68; **10** 259
stained glass **2** 83
wall paintings **2** 72
Monlione, Carlo di *see* CARLO DI MONLIONE
Monlong, Pierre **2** 466; **14** 856
works **2** *466*
Monmouth (Gwent) **32** *780*
St Mary **10** 338
Shirehall **32** 782
Monmouth, Geoffrey of *see* GEOFFREY OF MONMOUTH
Monmouth and Buccleuch, James Scott, Duke of *see* SCOTT, JAMES, Duke of Monmouth and Buccleuch
Monmouth Crucifix **10** 338
Monneret de Villard, Ugo **16** 548; **21** 888*
Monnet, Charles **3** 318; **14** 366; **22** 88
works **24** *176*
Monnet, Gianni **16** 681; **22** 242
Monnet, Jean **30** 680
Monnickendam Church **22** 821
Monnickes, Hendrik *see* MUNNICHHOEVEN, HENDRIK
Monnier **4** 354
Monnier, Henry (Bonaventure) **5** 758; **21** 889*; **27** 871
Monnier, Marcel **10** 580
Monnington, Thomas **14** 193; **25** 556
Monnington, W. T. **19** 621
Monnot, Alessandro **21** 890
Monnot, Pierre-Etienne **21** 889–90*; **26** 771
collaboration **20** 378
patrons and collectors **2** 577; **6** 129; **11** 304; **14** 491; **17** 834; **23** 353; **30** 267
pupils **6** 97
works **6** *129*; **20** 379; **21** *890*; **23** 353; **24** 35; **26** 810
Monnoyer, Antoine **21** 891
Monnoyer, Jean-Baptiste **11** 535, 641; **12** 832; **19** 381; **21** 890–91*
collaboration **3** 621; **12** 828; **18** 633; **21** 907; **27** 263
patrons and collectors **18** 693
pupils **3** 621; **32** 94
teachers **4** 756
works **3** 461; **7** 167; **11** 227, 642; **21** *891*; **29** 667, 668; **32** 94
Monochrome movement *see* MONOK'ŬROM MOVEMENT
monochrome painting *see under* PAINTING → types
Monochrome ware *see under* POTTERY → wares
Monod, Eloi **11** 613
Monod, Gabriel **18** 856
Monogissa **25** 180
Monogrammist NH *see* HOGENBERG, NICOLAS
monograms **2** 733; **10** 205, 208, 210, 212; **14** 404; **16** 425; **24** 6, *6*, 674
see also SIGNATURES
Monoha **17** 207; **21** 892*; **27** 594
Monok'ŭrom (Monochrome) movement **18** 326
Monolith **30** 491
Monolithos **26** *289*, 294
monoliths
Madagascar **20** 37
Maya **5** 412
Mesoamerica, Pre-Columbian **5** 412
Olmec **23** 417
Prehistoric art **21** 40, 134
Tibet **30** 816
see also MEGALITHS; MENHIRS
Monom **32** 487
Monomotapa, King of Great Zimbabwe **1** 308
Monongye, Preston **22** 616
Monophysitism *see under* CHRISTIANITY → sects
Monópoli
Cathedral **26** 627
S Maria degli Amalfitani **26** 627
Monópoli, Reginaldo Piramo da *see* PIRAMO DA MONÓPOLI, REGINALDO
monoprints *see under* PRINTS → types
monopteroi **21** 892–3*, *893*; **30** 736
Monory, Jacques **11** 552; **21** 893–4*
Monosiet, Pierre **14** 60; **21** 894*
Monosilio, Salvatore **26** 809
Monot, Martin-Claude **32** 77
Monotype composition machines **31** 496
Monotype Corporation **13** 649; **22** 117; **31** 494, 498; **33** 304
monotypes *see under* PRINTS → types
Monreal, Krak de *see* KRAK DE MONREAL
Monreale **9** *510*; **16** *621*
Cathedral of S Maria Nuova **14** 240; **16** 172, 627, 762; **21** 897*, *898*; **26** 579, 628; **28** 655
cloister **7** 453, 455; **21** *899*, *900*
corbels **7** 837
doors **3** 240; **4** 297; **9** 154
mosaics **9** 581, 645; **16** 655; **21** 897–9*, *898*; **22** 156, 162; **26** 653, *679*, 680
mouldings **22** 216
sculpture **21** 900–901*; **26** 628
tombs (royal) **26** 628
wall paintings **22** 520
Nativity groups **22** 680
throne **30** 779
Monrealese, Il *see* NOVELLI, PIETRO
Monro, Alexander **26** 742; **32** 415
Monro, John **21** 901
Monro, Nicholas **10** 268; **25** 231
Monro, Thomas **8** 842; **21** 901*; **32** 903
Drawing Academy **8** 27, 163; **11** 703; **12** 741; **15** 24; **31** 908
drawings **8** 98; **15** 24
pupils **31** 467
watercolours **14** 279
Monroe, James **3** 84; **5** 143; **31** 642
Monro Turner, (Annie) Helen (Nairn) *see* TURNER, (ANNIE) HELEN (NAIRN) MONRO
Monrovia **1** *386*
Capitol **19** 310
Cuttington University College **19** 310
Ducor Palace Hotel **19** 310
Executive Mansion **19** 310
Hotel Africa **19** 310
National Legislative Hall *see* National Museum
National Museum **19** 310
Supreme Court **19** 310
True Whig Party Headquarters **19** 310
University of Liberia **19** 310
Mons **3** *539*; **21** 901–2*
Castle **3** 552; **26** 648
convent of Sacré-Coeur **13** 112
education (art) **3** 617
guilds **3** 596
marks **3** 601; **21** 901
pewter **3** 603
Ste Waudru **3** 543, *543*; **9** 329; **13** 62
sculpture **3** 569
stained glass **13** 183; **26** *745*
St Nicolas en Havré **11** 250
sculpture **13** 113
silver **3** 598, 599, 600

Mons—cont.
stage machinery **30** 654
Mons, Jean Joseph Du *see* DU MONS, JEAN JOSEPH
Monsaldy, A. M. **26** 333
Monsaldy, Antoine **4** 834
Monsanto, Antonio Edmundo **5** 354; **21** 902*; **32** 175
Mons Claudianus **9** 813; **26** 876, *876*; **27** 112
monsh-nuri see under LACQUER → types
Monsiau (family) **29** 834
Monsiau, Nicolas-André **20** 421; **21** 902–3*
works **21** *902*
Monsignori, Francesco *see* BONSIGNORI, FRANCESCO
Monson, W. H. **31** 797
Mons Porphyrites **26** *876*
porphyry **9** 813; **26** 855, 876; **29** 702
Mons Regalus *see* KRAK DE MONREAL
Monstier, Etienne du **1** 766
monstral blue *see* PIGMENTS → types → phthalocyanine blue
monstrances **1** 697; **7** 299
historical and regional traditions
Belgium **3** 598, *599*
Canada **5** *585*
Colombia **7** 610
France **26** 493
Germany **12** 442, 447
Gothic **13** 162; **29** *333*
Peru **24** 511
Poland **13** 162
Portugal **25** 312; **32** *406*
Spain **2** 390; **11** 713; **29** *333*
Switzerland **30** 145
materials
coral **7** 835
emeralds **7** 610
gold **5** *585*; **29** *333*; **32** *406*
silver **3** *599*
Monsú **29** 136, 150
Mont, Déodat van der *see* MONTE, DEODAAT DEL
Mont, Guilliam vander **3** 598
Mont, Hans **13** 910; **20** 244; **21** 903*; **29** 430
collaboration **29** 428
works **5** 79
Mont, J. de **32** 706
Mont, Louis Du *see* DU MONT, LOUIS
Mont, Pol de *see* DE MONT, POL
Mont, Raoul du, Abbot of Mont-Saint-Michel *see* RAOUL DU MONT, Abbot of Mont-Saint-Michel
Monta, Guilermo de la *see* GUILERMO DE LA MONTA
Montabert, Jacques Nicolas Paillot de *see* PAILLOT DE MONTABERT, JACQUES NICOLAS
Montacada, Ot de *see* OT DE MONTACADA
Montacute **24** 290
montages *see* ASSEMBLAGES
Montagna, Bartolomeo **21** 904–6*
attributions **6** 5; **26** 726
pupils **3** 342; **5** 179; **7** 320; **11** 235
works **8** 855; **11** 385; **21** *904*, *905*; **32** 225, 409
Montagna, Benedetto **21** 904, 906–7*; **24** 248
Montagnac, Jean de **2** 860; **15** 85; **32** 574
Montagnais **22** 546, 647, 648
Montagnana
Villa Pisani *see* Villa Placco
Villa Placco **32** 647
Montagnana, Jacopo da *see* JACOPO (DI PARIDE PARISATI) DA MONTAGNANA
Montagnano, Alevisio Lamberti da *see* LAMBERTI DA MONTAGNANO, ALEVISIO
Montagna Spaccata **27** 6
Montagne, Matthieu de *see* PLATTENBERG, MATTHIEU VAN
Montagne, Nicolas de Platte *see* PLATTE MONTAGNE, NICOLAS DE
Montagne, Renaud de La *see* LA MONTAGNE, RENAUD DE
Montagny, Jean-Pierre **20** 925
Montagny-Sainte-Félicité **13** 211
Montagu, Charles, 1st Earl of Halifax **21** 348; **30** 267
Montagu, Charles, 4th Earl and 1st Duke of Manchester **13** 200; **21** 908*; **26** 323
architecture **12** 6; **31** 860
frescoes **15** 139
paintings **5** 765; **24** 340; **32** 111
Montagu, Edward Wortley **10** 79
Montagu, Elizabeth, Duchess of Buccleuch **4** 333, 894; **29** 806
Montagu, George Brudenell, 1st Duke of *see* BRUDENELL, GEORGE, 4th Earl of Cardigan and 1st Duke of Montagu
Montagu, John, 2nd Duke of Montagu **4** 806, 893
Montagu, John, 4th Earl of Sandwich **10** 79
Montagu, John, Lord Brudenell *see* MONTAGU, JOHN, Marquess of Monthermer
Montagu, John, Marquess of Monthermer **3** *382*
Montagu, Mary Brudenell, Duchess of *see* BRUDENELL, MARY, Countess of Cardigan and Duchess of Montagu
Montagu, Mary Wortley **12** 84; **25** 279
Montagu, Ralph, 1st Duke of Montagu **21** 907*
architecture **14** 743, 856
decorative works **21** 891
glass **14** 856
interior decoration **14** 856; **27** 263
paintings **6** 554; **18** 632
tapestries **10** 275, 350; **22** 154
Montagu, Robert, 3rd Duke of Manchester **29** 31
Montagu, Willam, 2nd Duke of Manchester **29** 31
Montagu-Douglas-Scott, Walter Francis, 5th Duke of Buccleuch, 7th Duke of Queensberry **14** 252; **21** 908*; **25** 631; **29** 549
Montagu-Douglas-Scott, Walter Francis John, 9th Duke of Buccleuch and 11th Duke of Queensbury **17** 479
Montagu-Dunk, George, 2nd Earl of Halifax **10** 368
Montague, William **8** 495
Montaiglon, Anatole de Courde, Comte de **11** 675; **21** 908*
Montaigne, Matthieu de *see* Plattenberg, Matthieu van
Montaigne, Michel de **11** 187; **14** 868; **25** 452; **32** 551
Montaigu, Bertrand de *see* BERTRAND DE MONTAIGU
Montaigu, Domenico **3** 204
Montaigu, Eustorge de, Archbishop of Nicosia **23** 111
Montalambert, Charles Forbes René, Comte de **5** 369; **13** 201; **21** 909*
Montalambert, Marc René **3** 360
Montalbani, Ovidio **21** 909*
Montalbano, Leonardo **28** 657
Montalbano, Melchiorre da *see* MELCHIORRE DA MONTALBANO
Montal Château **29** 522
Montalcini, Gino Levi **21** 422
Montald, Constant **3** 564; **6** 91; **20** 590; **22** 1*; **31** 502
Montalegre, Josef von **29** 422
Montalembert, Marc-René de **21** 571, 581
works **21** *571*
Montallegro *see under* TYPE-FACES
Montalto (family) **31** 901
Montalto, Alessandro, Cardinal **5** 870; **11** 194; **12** 912; **29** 563; **30** 516
Montalto, Antonio Pérez de *see* PÉREZ DE MONTALTO, ANTONIO
Montalvo, Diego de **11** 490
Montalvo, Ramirez di *see* RAMIREZ DI MONTALVO
Monta Mozuna Atelier **22** 249
Monta Mozune Mobile Molgue **22** 249
Montanari (family) **31** 262
Montanaro, Antonio **3** 385
Montaner, Bartolomé Maura y *see* MAURA Y MONTANER, BARTOLOMÉ
Montaner, Luís Doménech i *see* DOMÉNECH I MONTANER, LUÍS
Montaner, Pere Pau i *see* PAU I MONTANER, PERE
Montaner Castle **4** 780
Montañés, Juan Martínez **22** 1–4*; **23** 301; **28** 515; **29** 344
assistants **21** 173
attributions **14** 714
collaboration **2** 291; **5** 619
patrons and collectors **14** 6
teachers **26** 549
works **4** 264; **9** 110, *110*; **22** *2*, *3*, *4*; **24** 506; **26** 252; **29** 291
Montañez Ortiz, Ralph **2** 837; **18** 833
Montani (*fl c.* 1871) **23** 644
Montani, Gabriele **16** 904; **32** 435
Montani, Tommaso **22** 422, 423
Montano, Benito Arias *see* ARIAS MONTANO, BENITO
Montano, Giovanni Battista **22** 4–5*; **28** 908; **29** 80
Montano, Marcelo de **29** 335
Montano d'Arezzo **13** 150
Montans **27** 107
montan wax *see under* WAXES → types
Montanyà, Lluís **8** 465
Montargis
Musée Girodet **12** 733
St Louis **3** 249
Montarsis (family) **2** 92
Montauban
Cathedral **1** 712; **15** 839
paintings **15** *840*
faience (ii) (ceramics) **11** 605
houses **4** 780
Musée Ingres **2** 370; **10** 479; **15** 841, 842, 843
Montaubon, Jean **26** 348; **27** 314
Montauron, Pierre Puget de *see* PUGET DE MONTAURON, PIERRE
Montausier, Charles, Duc de Sainte-Maure *see* SAINTE-MAURE, CHARLES MONTAUSIER, Duc de
Montauti, Antonio **7** 897; **22** 5*; **29** 572
Montbazon **6** 52
Mont Bego **25** 532
Montbéliard *see* MÖMPELGARD
Mont Beuvray **21** 551; **25** 536, 541, 544, 547
Montboissier, François-Claude de **5** 380; **24** 11; **32** 332
Montbouy **25** 545; **27** 12
Montbrun, Comte de **19** 233
Montceaux Château **4** 864–5; **12** 120
Montceaux-l'Etoile **26** 602
Montclair Lekythos **13** 509
Montcut, Antoine de **21** 72
Mont-Dauphin **21** 568
Monte, Antonio del, Cardinal **22** 6; **27** 739, 770
Monte, Baldovino del **1** 792; **22** 6
Monte, del (family) **22** 6
Monte, Deodaat del **22** 7*
patrons and collectors **33** 279
teachers **27** 298
works **3** 559
Monte, Francesco Maria Bourbon del, Cardinal *see* BOURBON DEL MONTE, FRANCESCO MARIA, Cardinal
Monte, Giovanni Maria Ciocchi del, Cardinal *see* JULIUS III, Pope
Monte, Guidobaldo Bourbon del *see* BOURBON DEL MONTE, GUIDOBALDO
Monte, Paolo de **22** 167
Monte, Piero del **18** 686
Monte, Rainieri del **30** 517
Monte Abatone cycle **10** 614
Monte Acuto, Villa Blasi Foglietti **13** 281
Monteagudo **12** 80
Monte Albán **21** *193*, 196, 197, 198–9, 263, *372*, 737; **22** 7–8*; **33** 618, 619–20
Ballcourt **3** 117
Burial XIV-10 **21** 251
houses **21** 208
musical instruments **21** 256
paintings **21** 226, 230–31*
pipes (smoking) **21** 189
pottery **21** 237
pyramids **25** 764
reliefs **21** 219
religion **21** 186
sculpture **21** 185
stairs **21** 206
stelae **21** 221; **29** 619
stone-carvings **22** *8*
stucco **29** 829
System IV **25** *765*
talud-tablero **30** 280
Temple J **23** 338
tombs **21** 202, 230–31; **31** *117*, 118
Tomb 7 **21** 243, 248, *253*, 253–4, 737; **31** 116, 118; **33** 620
fans **10** 779
Tomb 72 **21** 231
Tomb 104 **7** 636; **21** 230; **31** 118
Tomb 105 **7** 636; **21** 230, *230*; **31** 118
Tomb 112 **21** 230
Tomb 123 **21** 231
urns **21** 238
Montealbán, Francisco de **14** 475, 476
Monte Alto **13** *758*; **20** *882*; **22** 8–9*
Monte Andranone **25** 733
Montebelo, Marquês de *see* MACHADO DA SILVA CASTRO E VASCONCELOS, FÉLIX
Monte Berico, Basilica **16** 702
Monte Bibele **6** 157
Monte Carlo **2** 561
Casino **21** 830
Montecarlo, Bastiano da *see* BASTIANO DA MONTECARLO
Monte Carmelo, Jesuíno do **4** 716
Montecassino **22** 11*
Montecassino, Alberic of *see* ALBERIC OF MONTECASSINO
Montecassino, Amatus of *see* AMATUS OF MONTECASSINO
Monte Cassino, Giovanni da *see* GIOVANNI DA MONTE CASSINO
Montecassino Abbey **3** 708, 709; **16** *620*, 626; **22** 9–12*, *10*; **26** 580, 625
arches **2** 295, 298
architecture **16** 762; **22** 9–10*
basilica **22** 10
chapter house **6** 464, 466
collections **27** 617
education (art) **16** 777
Montecassino Abbey—cont.
manuscripts **10** 201; **16** 654; **20** 331; **22** *11*, 12*; **26** 661, *664*, 665; **27** 591; **28** 25; **32** 638
Monastery **8** 800–801
mosaics **7** 275; **22** 162, 163; **26** 679
opus sectile **7** 920
rolls **10** 700
Monte Castillo **6** 46, 47
Montecatini company **25** 218
Montecatini-Lombardi, Sebastiano **3** 305
Montecatini Terme **16** 646
Montecchio Maggiore, Villa Cordellina **32** 549
Montecino, Sergio **6** 598
Montecuccoli, Prince **3** 488
Montecuccoli, Raimondo **24** 227
Montefalco, S Francesco **11** 712; **13** 260; **14** 517
Montefeltro, Antonio **13** 772
Montefeltro, Federigo II da, Duke of Urbino *see* FEDERIGO II, 1st Duke of Urbino
Montefeltro, Guidobaldo I da, Duke of Urbino *see* GUIDOBALDO I, 2nd Duke of Urbino
Montefeltro Altarpiece **7** 527
Montefiore, Gentile (Partino) da, Cardinal *see* GENTILE (PARTINO) DA MONTEFIORE, Cardinal
Montefiore, Moses **17** 491
Montefiorentino polyptych **32** 657
Monteforte, Nicola da *see* NICOLA DA MONTEFORTE
Montefortino **6** 157
Montefuscolo, Ricardo di *see* RICARDO DI MONTEFUSCOLO
Montegaldella, Villa Lampertico **20** 423
Monte Giordano, Palazzo Taverna **23** 575
Montego Bay **16** *878*, 889
Monteguragazza **10** 605, 639
Monte Iato **28** 654
Monteiro, António Augusto de Carvalho *see* CARVALHO MONTEIRO, ANTÓNIO AUGUSTO DE
Monteiro, José Luís **19** 892; **22** 13–14*; **23** 177; **25** 293
Monteiro, Pardal **22** 14*; **25** 294
Monteiro, Vicente do Rego *see* REGO MONTEIRO, VICENTE DO
Monteiro da Cruz, André **8** 163
monteiths **22** 14*; **31** *647*
Montejo, Francisco de, II **21** 154; **33** 571
Montelatici, Francesco *see* CECCO BRAVO
Monteleón, Duque de (*fl* 17th cent.) **24** 401
Monteleone **10** *583*, 626; **22** 156
Monte Leone, Duca di (*fl* late 18th cent.) **10** 488
Monteleone Chariot **6** *481*; **10** 587, 605, 626
Montelius, Oscar **2** 299, 300; **25** 519
Montellano, Duque de **27** 768
Montelli, Giuseppe, Archbishop of Florence **11** 20
Montells, Joan Martorell i *see* MARTORELL I MONTELLS, JOAN
Montelupo **16** *620*, 734, 735; **22** 14–15*
maiolica **16** *735*
Montelupo, Baccio da **22** 15*
attributions **8** 799
collaboration **4** 739
pupils **22** 15
works **8** 799; **25** 690
Montelupo, Raffaello da **22** 15–16*; **27** 758
assistants **7** 331; **9** 181

Montelupo, Raffaello da—cont.
collaboration 19 688; 21 439; 27 777
patrons and collectors 10 808, 809
works 19 688, *688*; 21 16, 439; 24 757
writings 16 781
Montemar, Conde de 12 547
Montemayor, Diego de 22 20
Montemayor, Fernando de 28 709
Montemezzano, Francesco 9 14; 32 354
Montemór-o-Novo 25 308
Montenard, Frédéric 25 751
Montenari, Augusta 31 262
Montenay, Georgette de 10 175; 33 289
Montenegro 22 16–19*, *17*; 33 571
architecture 22 16*; 32 293
cathedrals 22 *18*
chests 22 19
collections 22 19*
corn 31 260
decorative arts 22 18–19*
dolls 31 260
museums 22 19*
painting 22 16*, 17–18*, *19*
prints 22 16–17*, 18*
textiles 22 19
Montenegro, Baldomero Yela *see* YELA MONTENEGRO, BALDOMERO
Montenegro (Nervo), Roberto 21 386, 397, 405; 22 19–20*; 25 653
collaboration 10 906
groups and movements 21 387; 30 22
teachers 2 62
works 22 334, *334*
Monteneri, Alessandro 16 730
Monte Oliveto Altarpiece 11 384; 19 680; 28 *702*; 29 404–5, 406
Monte Oliveto Maggiore 7 457; 25 275; 29 1–2
frescoes 7 *457*
Monte Oliveto Master 9 349
Monte Prama 27 835
Montepulciano
Cathedral 21 467; 27 830
altarpiece 30 *232*
S Biagio 23 486
Montepulciano, Cardinal 29 290
Montepulciano, Domenico Savino da *see* SAVINO DA MONTEPULCIANO, DOMENICO
Montepulciano, Marco da *see* MARCO DA MONTEPULCIANO
Montepulciano, Pasquino (di Matteo) da *see* PASQUINO (DI MATTEO) DA MONTEPULCIANO
Montepulciano, Pietro di Domenico da *see* PIETRO DI DOMENICO DA MONTEPULCIANO
Monterchio, Johannes de *see* JOHANNES DE MONTERCHIO
Montereau 11 606
Monterey (CA), St John's Episcopal Church 28 604
Montero, Beatriz 23 905
Montero, Luis 22 20*; 24 508, 516, 517
Monteros 2 403
Monterrey 21 *372*; 22 20–21*
Centro Cultural Alfa 21 397
collections 21 395
glass 21 392
Museo de Arte Contemporáneo 19 84; 21 397; 22 21
Museo Marco 21 382
Museo de Monterrey 22 21
Monterrey, Juan, 7th Conde de 5 40; 11 872; 21 149
Monterrey, Manuel de Acevedo y Zúñiga, 6th Conde de 1 528; 22 21*
paintings 7 832; 14 755; 18 734, 736; 26 310; 29 353
sculpture 10 800
tapestries 12 285
Montes, Fernando 4 264
Montes, Sebastian de Ochoa *see* OCHOA MONTES, SEBASTIAN DE
Monte Sallia 6 30
Monte San Giusto, S Maria della Pietà
altarpiece 19 *713*
Monte San Savino, S Maria di Vertighe 1 709
Montesantangelo
Cathedral 26 626
S Giovanni in Tumba 26 627
S Maria Maggiore 26 628
S Michele 30 777
Montes de Oca, Confucio 14 715
Monte Senario 28 489
Monte Sinay potteries 25 310
Montesinos, Rafael 9 104
Monte Sirai 25 733
Montésiste, Laurent *see* GAUSSON, LÉO
Montespan 25 476, 477
Montespan, Marquise de 19 163, 212; 31 378
Montesquieu(, Baron de) (1689-1755) 7 *450*; 8 595; 19 *141*; 22 21–2*
Montesquiou, Marquis de (*fl* 1765) 19 56
Montesquiou (-Fezensac), Robert, Comte de (1855-1921) 4 127; 14 363; 22 22*
Montesson, Marquise de *see* ORLÉANS, CHARLOTTE-JEANNE DE BOURBON, Duchesse d'
Montessori, Maria 31 254
Montet, Pierre 5 331; 30 296
Montevarchi, Roberto da *see* ROBERTO DA MONTEVARCHI
Monteverde, Giulio 20 839; 22 22–3*; 31 131
Monteverdi, Achille 3 814
Monteverdi, Claudio 12 911
Montevergine Abbey 13 98; 26 625; 30 777
Monte Verità 28 352
Montevideo 22 23–4*; 31 751, *751*, 752
Aduana 22 *23*
Alliance Française 31 759
architecture 31 753, 754
Banco de la República 22 *23*
Biblioteca Artigas-Washington 31 759
Biblioteca del Instituto Cultural Anglo-Uruguayo 31 759
Biblioteca Municipal del Museo de Historia del Arte 31 759
Biblioteca Nacional del Uruguay 31 759
Cabildo 31 753
Cathedral 31 753, 756
Cementerio del Norte 31 754
Central railway station 31 753
Centro de Diseño Industrial 31 759
Centro Médico 31 753
Clínica Médica 31 753
Escuela Nacional de Artes y Oficios 31 756, 758
Escuela Nacional de Bellas Artes 31 756, 759
Estadio Centenario 31 753
French Embassy 31 759
Hospital Policial 31 754
houses 22 23–4
Instituto Italiano de Cultura 31 759
Intendencia Municipal de Montevideo 31 759
Montevideo—cont.
Jardin Zoológico Municipal 31 758
Mario Peyssé-Reyes House 31 754
Ministry of Education and Culture 31 759
museums
Archivo y Museo Histórico Nacional 31 757
Museo de Arte Contemporáneo 31 758
Museo de Arte Precolombino y Colonial 31 758
Museo Histórico Nacional 31 758
Museo Juan Zorrilla de San Martin 31 758
Museo Municipal de Historia del Arte 31 759
Museo Municipal Juan Manuel Blanes 31 758
Museo Nacional 31 757
Museo Nacional de Artes Plásticas 22 24; 31 759
Museo Nacional de Bellas Artes 31 757–8
Museo Nacional de Historia Natural 31 757
Museo Torres García 31 758, 759
Notariado building 31 754
Old Government House 31 *753*
Palacio Municipal 31 753
Palacio Salvo 28 834
Plaza Independencia 31 753
Plaza Virgilio 31 756
Statue of Liberty 31 754
Teatro Solís 31 753
Umberto I Hospital 31 753
Universidad Católica 31 759
Universidad de la República 31 759
Universidad del Trabajo del Uruguay 31 756
Universidad de Montevideo 31 753
Uruguay Club 31 753
Montfalcon, Aymo von, Bishop of Lausanne 18 874
Montfalcon, Sebastian von, Bishop of Lausanne 18 874
Montfaucon, Bernard de 22 24*
personal collection 10 83
works 2 164; 10 78, 79, 96; 11 674; 15 84; 17 464; 22 415; 26 230, 307; 27 *543*, 544, 545, 549
Montferland Castle 22 822
Montferrand, (Henri Louis) August Ricard de 22 25*; 27 377, 408, 576, 577, 584; 28 642; 33 599
works 16 53; 27 *576*, *577*
Montferrand, Benoît de *see* BENOÎT DE MONTFERRAND
Montfoort, Anthonie van *see* BLOCKLANDT, ANTHONIE
Montford, Horace 22 25
Montford, Paul Raphael 2 753; 8 445; 22 25–6*
works 5 66; 19 606
Montfort, Benito 21 868
Montfort, John IV of, Duke of Brittany *see* JOHN IV OF MONTFORT, Duke of Brittany
Montfort, Nicolas-Alexandre Salins de *see* SALINS DE MONTFORT, NICOLAS-ALEXANDRE
Montfort, Rotrou V, Comte de 19 129
Montfort, Simon de, Earl of Leicester 11 148
Montfort, Willem van *see* WILLEM VAN MONTFORT, Burggraf
Montfort Castle 6 58; 17 505; 22 822; 30 535
Montforte *Adoration* 3 596; 12 846, *846*
Montfort Hours *see under* BOOKS OF HOURS → individual manuscripts
Montgaroult 26 598
Montgeron, Château de Rottembourg 21 864
Montgeron, Louis-Basile Carré de *see* CARRÉ DE MONTGERON, LOUIS-BASILE
Montgomerie, Hector 33 678
Montgomerie, Hugh, 12th Earl of Eglinton 23 105
Montgomerie, James 28 259
Montgomerie, Oldfield, Kirby 33 602
Montgomery (Powys), St Nicholas 32 787
Montgomery, James 10 145
Montgomery, Philip Herbert, 1st Earl of *see* HERBERT, PHILIP, 4th Earl of Pembroke & 1st Earl of Montgomery
Montguró, Pau 13 726
Montheillet, Pierre 19 848
Monthelon, Antoine Ferrand de *see* FERRAND DE MONTHELON, ANTOINE
Montherlant, Henri de 8 811; 14 457; 20 830; 22 92
Monthermer, John Montagu, Marquess of *see* MONTAGU, JOHN, Marquess of Monthermer
Monthey 30 *124*, 145
Monthly Bulletin 24 446
Monthureux-sur-Saône 13 125
Monti 16 731
Monti, Alessandro 8 149
Monti, Cesare, Archbishop of Milan 21 526; 22 26*
Monti, Francesco 22 26–7*; 28 18; 29 33
Monti, Gaetano 2 232; 21 533; 22 27
Monti, G. F. 22 82
Monti, Giovanni Giacomo 7 357; 10 526, 527
Monti, Paolo 3 764; 22 27*
Monti, Raffaelle 3 79; 10 311; 22 27–8*; 25 156
works 22 *28*
Monticelli, Adolphe (-Joseph-Thomas) 20 473; 22 28–30*; 33 674
patrons and collectors 18 672; 24 638; 28 271, 272; 33 180
works 22 *29*
Monticelli, Angelo Michele 10 446
Monticelli, Giuseppe 28 318
Monticelli, S Pietro 13 124
Monticello *see* SHADWELL (VA), MONTICELLO
Montiel, Ramona *see* BERNI, ANTONIO
Montier-en-Der, Notre-Dame 13 38; 26 586
Montigiano di Mannaia 13 775
Montigny, Adriaan de 8 208
Montigny, Jean-Robert-Nicolas Lucas de *see* LUCAS DE MONTIGNY, JEAN-ROBERT-NICOLAS
Montigny, Jenny 19 792
Montigny, L. de 20 914
Montigny, Philippe-Claude 11 593, 596, 597; 17 684
Montigny, Trudaine de *see* TRUDAINE DE MONTIGNY
Montigny de Clarges, Cornelis de 22 841; 31 882
Montilla, Manuel 9 118
Montini, Bartolomeo 7 322
Montini, Giovanni Battista, Cardinal *see* PAUL VI, Pope
Montino della Rosa, Scipione 24 198
Montioni, Jacopo 6 568
Montirac, Pierre Selva de, Cardinal of Pamplona *see* SELVA DE MONTIRAC, PIERRE, Cardinal of Pamplona
Montiroli, Giovanni 5 616
Montirone, Villa Lechi 15 139; 16 719
Montjoie! 24 442
Montjoie, Arnaud de *see* ARNAUD DE MONTJOIE
montjoie crosses *see under* CROSSES → types
Montjosieu, Louis de 10 198
Mont Lassois 25 543
Mont-Louis 21 568; 31 718
Montluçon, Jacquelin Raoul de 7 597; 22 30–31
Montluçon, Jean Raoul de 22 30–31*
Montlyard, Jean de 18 811
Montmajour
Abbey 6 54; 26 603
cloister 26 *604*
St Pierre 26 603
Montmartel, Jean Pâris de 24 786
Montmartre, Jean de *see* JEAN DE MONTMARTRE
Montmaurin Villa 26 907, *908*
Montmorency, Prince de 19 56
Montmorency, Princesse de 19 56
Montmorency, Anne, Duc de, Constable of France 10 ; 22 31*
architecture 5 166; 6 415, 453; 9 706; 11 656; 14 855
art policies 11 656
ceramics 11 268; 14 425; 23 849
collections 19 398
gardens 6 453
interior decoration 11 265
metalwork 11 617
paintings 1 19; 6 76; 27 209
pottery 11 604
sculpture 13 226; 26 348
Montmorency, Henri I de (1534-1614) 6 453
Montmorency, Henri II de (*d* 1632) 6 453
Montmorency, Madeleine of Savoy, Duchesse de 25 577
Montmorency, Master of 29 512
Montmorency-Laval, Bishop of Metz 3 13
Montmorency-Laval, François de, Bishop of Québec 5 592; 22 37
Montmorency-Luxembourg, Christian-Louis de, Prince of Tingry *see* TINGRY, CHRISTIAN-LOUIS, Prince of
Montmorillon 26 653
Octagone 7 643
Montmoulin, Olivier de 18 667
Montmusard Château 2 337; 6 509
Montoire 11 530
Montor, Jean-Alexis-François Artaud de *see* ARTAUD DE MONTOR, JEAN-ALEXIS-FRANÇOIS
Montorfano, Abramo (di Alberto) da 22 31
Montorfano, Alberto (di Abraam) da 22 31
Montorfano, Alberto (di Giovanni Donato) da 22 32
Montorfano, Bernardino da 22 32
Montorfano, Giovanni da 22 31
Montorfano, Giovanni Donato (di Alberto) da 5 307; 22 31
Montorfano, Paolino da 22 31
Montorfano, Vincenzo (di Alberto) da 22 32
Montorgeuil, G. 15 58
Montorsoli, Giovanni Angelo 2 162; 11 216; 12 116; 18 756; 22 32–3*; 28 490, 657
collaboration 1 789; 21 439
patrons and collectors 9 172
pupils 6 147
works 2 226; 11 342; 12 283; 22 *32*

Montoya, Alfredo **22** 594
Montoya, Eudora **22** 607
Montoya, Florentino **22** 606
Montoya, Geronimo Cruz *see* CRUZ MONTOYA, GERONIMO
Montoya, Maria *see* MARTINEZ, MARIA
Montoya, Martina **22** 606
Montoya, Pedro de, Bishop of Burgo de Osma *see* PEDRO DE MONTOYA, Bishop of Burgo de Osma
Montoyer, Louis (Joseph) **3** 547; **22** 33*
patrons and collectors **3** 613
works **2** 785, 808; **3** 274; **5** 40; **13** 832; **19** 260; **32** 457
Montparnasse, Grupo *see* GRUPO DE MONTPARNASSE
Montpellier **11** *505*; **22** 33–5*, *34*
Antigone complex **2** 361
Aqueduc St Clément **2** 242
botanic garden **4** 483
Cathedral of St Pierre **13** 211
Collège des Ecossais **12** 229
enamel **13** 169
faience (ii) (ceramics) **11** 605
marks **20** 443, 444
Musée Atger **22** 35
Musée Fabre **5** 58; **10** 726, 727; **11** 665, 666; **22** 35
silk **11** 644
verdigris **24** 793
Montpensier (family) **4** 544
Montpensier, Anne-Marie-Louise de Bourbon, Duchesse de **7** 195; **8** 90; **18** 633; **19** 95
Montpensier, Antoine-Marie-Philippe-Louis de Bourbon, Duc de **23** *511*, 523*; **24** 59; **28** 516, 519; **29** 343
Montpensier, Louis I, Comte de **27** 551
Montpensier, Luisa Fernanda de Bourbon, Duchesse de **10** *513*
Montpéreaux, Dubois de *see* DUBOIS DE MONTPÉREAUX
Montplaisir factory **5** 51
Montrastruc
ivory-carvings **16** *798*
Montreal **5** *559*, 561; **22** 35–9*, *37*
Art Association of Montreal Gallery *see* Museum of Fine Arts
Bank of Montreal **5** 562
Banque du Peuple **24** 471
Boer War memorial **5** 570
Bonsecours Market **11** 292
Centre Canadien d'Architecture **5** 574, 592; **24** 683
Christ Church Cathedral **5** 585
collections **5** 589
Cormier House **5** 562, 573, *573*
Ecole des Beaux-Arts **5** 592
Ecole du Meubles **5** 592
education (art) **5** 592
Expo 67 **5** 562, 573; **10** 685, *685*; **15** 883
American pavilion **5** 562
German Pavilion **30** 469
Habitat '67 **5** 562, *563*, 573; **10** 685; **26** 17; **27** 515
Indian Pavilion **22** 597
US Pavilion **12** *311*; **25** 24; **29** 250
furniture **22** 39*
Hôtel de Ville **5** 561
interior decoration **5** 574, 576
International Exhibition, 1967 *see* Expo '67
La Cité **32** 108
McGill University
Blackader-Lauterman Library of Architecture and Art **5** 592
McCord Museum **23** 257
Redpath Museum **5** 590
Union Building **5** 572
Mechanics Institute **5** 590
Metro stations **21** 350
Montreal—cont.
Mt Royal cemetery **20** 869
Mt Royal Park **24** 179
Museum of Fine Arts **5** 591; **20** 877; **27** 515
collections **5** 589; **15** 746
decorative arts **22** 111
exhibitions **5** 582
library **5** 592
Museum of the Geological Survey of Canada **5** 590
New York Life Insurance Co. **5** 562
Notre-Dame **5** 561; **9** 156; **13** 202
Olympic Stadium **29** 489
Place Ville Marie **5** 562
Post Office **24** 471
Protestant Church *see* Christ Church Cathedral
St Sulpician Seminary **12** 136
silver **5** 584
Universal and International Exhibition, 1967 *see* Expo '67
Université de Montréal **7** *858*, 859
Victoria Bridge **4** 802
Montréal, Krak de *see* KRAK DE MONREAL
Montreal Cottons Ltd **9** 390
Montréal-Séeviac **9** 568
Montresor, John **33** 442
Montresor, Michelangelo **3** 179
Montreuil **11** 631
St Sauve **8** 194
Montreuil, Eudes de *see* EUDES DE MONTREUIL
Montreuil, Nicolas de **30** 659
Montreuil, Pierre de *see* PIERRE DE MONTREUIL
Montreuil, Raoul de *see* RAOUL DE MONTREUIL
Montreuil-Bellay **3** 209
Château **10** 476
Pavilion **15** 140
Montroeuil-au-Bois Church **13** 113
Montrose (Tayside) **28** 254
Sunnyside Royal Hospital **25** 685
Montrose, James Graham, 1st Duke of *see* GRAHAM, JAMES, 1st Duke of Montrose
Montrose Panels **28** 250
Montross, Newman E. **32** 796
Montrouge, Atelier de *see* ATELIER DE MONTROUGE
Montrouge Château **18** 880
Mont-Saint-Eloi **2** 723
Mont-Saint-Michel Abbey **3** 709, 710; **11** *504*; **21** 839; **22** 39–41*, *40*; **32** 94
cloister **7** 455
dormitory **21** 843
manuscripts **26** 663, 669
piers (ii) (masonry) **24** 750
Mont-Saint-Quentin Château **11** 585
Mont-Saint-Vincent **26** 601
Montsalvy Church **26** 641
Montserrat (Leeward Islands) **2** 144; **5** *745*
body ornaments **5** 747
museums **2** 153
National Museum **2** 153
pottery **5** 747
see also ANTILLES, LESSER; LEEWARD ISLANDS
Montserrat (Spain)
Black Madonna **26** 140
Monastery **26** 642; **29** 290, 344
S Cecilia **26** 580
Montserrat, José **29** 344
Mont-St-Michel Sacramentary *see under* SACRAMENTARIES → individual manuscripts
Montt, Alberto Cruz *see* CRUZ MONTT, ALBERTO
Montufar **4** 261
Montúfar, Francisco **13** 763
Montvallier, Jean-Baptiste Suzanne Buquet de **6** 454
monumental crosses *see under* CROSSES → types
monumental sculpture *see under* SCULPTURE → forms
Monumental style pottery *see under* POTTERY → wares
Monumenten en Landschappen **24** 439
Monumenti antichi inediti ovvero notizie sulle antichità e belle arti di Roma **24** 447
Monumenti inediti **24** 447
monuments
historical and regional traditions
Anglo-Saxon **10** 259
Austria **10** *908*
Czech Republic **22** 403
France
16th cent. **4** *338*
Georgia **12** 322
Germany **12** 407, 472
India, Republic of **15** 183
Mesoamerica, Pre-Columbian **18** *645*
Mesopotamia **21** 296
Mexico **18** *645*
Olmec **18** *645*
Phrygian **24** *689*
Prehistoric art **14** 387
see also TRILITHONS
Rome, ancient **26** 860, 864, 867, 911; **27** 39, 41, 43
Russia **22** *179*
Scandinavia **32** 521–2*
Spain **25** *225*
Turkey **24** *689*
United States of America **31** *611*
Viking **32** 521–2*, 525
materials
bronze **10** 440
Austria **10** *908*
England **3** *26*; **10** *266*; **19** *600*; **23** *172*; **27** *467*
France **26** *112*; **27** *822*
Germany **12** *399*
Italy **32** *363*
Italy: Mannerism **12** *573*; **30** *228*
Italy: 17th cent. **24** *696*
Rome, ancient **27** *10*
cast iron **22** *860*
copper **3** *290*
lead **18** *903*
marble
Belgium **9** *413*
England **4** *79*; **6** *456*; **19** *600*, *606*; **28** *64*; **29** *566*; **33** *100*, *227*
France **4** *338*
Italy **5** *628*; **16** *706*
Rome, ancient **27** *23*, *26*
sandstone **27** *867*
wood **10** 440
types
equestrian **10** 440–42*; **14** 421, 869; **29** 564–5
Austria **13** 315; **33** 624
Czech Republic **25** *434*
Denmark **10** *110*
Ecuador **9** *711*
England **27** *467*
France **10** 442
Germany **3** *142*, *798*; **26** *23*; **32** 832
Gothic **13** 94–5
Indian subcontinent **15** 735
Italy **9** 127; **10** 440; **14** 421; **16** 688, 690; **23** 754
Italy: Gothic **13** 94–5
Italy: Mannerism **12** *573*; **30** *228*
Italy: Renaissance **6** *13*; **9** *127*; **32** *363*
Italy: Roman **27** *10*
Italy: 17th cent. **24** *696*
Mexico **21** *384*
monuments
types
equestrian—cont.
Norway **23** 230
Portugal **19** 893
Rome, ancient **10** 440*; **27** *10*, 12, 29, 30, 35, 39
Russia **10** *442*
funerary **20** 863
Belgium **3** *571*; **9** *413*
Cambodia **5** 461
China **6** 725–33*
Coptic **7** 820*
Côte d'Ivoire **1** 331
Egypt **7** 820*
England: Baroque **10** *264*
England: Neo-classicism **10** *265*; **11** *163*
England: 16th cent. **10** 261–2
England: 17th cent. **29** *714*
England: 18th cent. **19** *606*; **22** 45, *46*; **27** *467*; **28** *64*; **31** *128*; **33** *227*
England: 19th cent. **6** *456*; **19** *600*; **33** *100*
Finland **11** 99, *99*
France **7** *596*; **27** *822*; **28** *846*; **31** *132*
Germany **12** *399*, 471
Ghana **1** 331
Greece, ancient **13** 371, 383–4*, *384*; **20** 863
Ibibio **1** 331
Ireland **14** *500*; **16** *20*, 21
Italy: Baroque **27** *830*; **31** *127*
Italy: Neo-Classicism **5** *628*; **16** *706*; **22** *736*
Italy: Renaissance **5** *128*; **31** *125*
Kenya **1** 331
Kongo **1** 331
Madagascar **1** 331
Netherlands, the **18** *8*
Nigeria **1** 331
Ottonian **12** *399*
Poland **25** 134, 135
Rome, ancient **27** 25–6*, 31
Spain **10** *502*
Sweden **30** 84, *84*
Zaïre **1** 331
see also TOMBS
hero stones **15** 231; **27** 866–8*
historic *see* HERITAGE (ARCHITECTURE)
hogback **32** 529, 530
public **22** 41–9*; **29** 563–6
Achaemenid **22** 42
Austria **2** *803*; **20** *390*
Byzantine **22** 43*
Denmark **18** 682
Early Christian (*c.* AD 250-843) **22** 43*
Egypt, ancient **22** 42*
England: Neo-classicism **3** *26*
England: 18th cent. **4** 79, *79*; **7** *340*
England: 19th cent. **7** *673*; **10** *266*; **18** *903*; **23** *172*
England: 20th cent. **22** *48*; **29** *566*
France **1** *497*; **8** *473*; **11** *561*; **22** 45–7; **24** *124*; **26** *112*
Germany **7** *381*
Gothic **22** 44*
Greece, ancient **22** 42–3*
Italy **13** *294*; **22** 44, *45*; **26** *763*; **27** *23*, *26*
Italy: Roman **26** *900*
Italy: 13th cent. **20** *321*
Netherlands, the **22** *860*
Ottonian **7** *381*; **22** 43, *43*
Poland **32** 7
Rome, ancient **22** 43*; **26** *900*; **27** *23*, 23–5*, *26*
Russia **32** *685*
Slovenia **28** 862
Switzerland **5** *446*
United States of America **3** *290*; **21** *618*, 619
monuments
types—cont.
sacred **21** 209
satī stones **27** 866–8*, *867*
triumphal arches **23** 767; **31** 349*, 350–52*
England **31** *351*
France **2** 286–7, *287*; **24** *469*; **26** 112; **31** 351
Germany **3** *791*
Hungary **31** 787
Italy **7** *920*; **21** *520*; **22** *471*, *486*; **26** *748*, 797–8*, *798*, *832*, *891*, *901*; **31** 351
North Africa **26** 920, *920*
Rome, ancient **2** 297; **10** 742; **22** 43; **26** 135, 863, 864, 868; **27** 24, 25; **31** 349–50*
Rome, ancient: Augustan **26** 890; **27** 32
Rome, ancient: Constantinian **26** 797–8*, 903; **27** 43–4, *44*
Rome, ancient: Flavian **26** 895
Rome, ancient: France **2** 286–7, *287*; **27** 31
Rome, ancient: Italy **3** 715; **26** *748*, *798*, *891*, *901*; **31** *349*
Rome, ancient: North Africa **26** 920, *920*
Rome, ancient: Republican **27** 29
Rome, ancient: Tetrarchs **27** 43
Rome, ancient: Trajanic **26** 897
Russia **4** *598*
wayside **17** 349
see also MEMORIAL STONES
Monuments, Fine Arts and Archives Service **12** 477
Monvaërni **19** 396
Monvel, (Louis-) Maurice Boutet de *see* BOUTET DE MONVEL, (LOUIS-)MAURICE
Monville, de **10** 884
Monvoisin, Raymond **5** 365; **6** 596, 597; **21** 156
Monymusk (Grampian) **28** 869
Monywa **5** *221*, 247
Monza **19** 549
Casa Elettrica **16** 649
Cathedral **1** 696; **13** 65
crosses **8** 203
crowns **26** 79
metalwork **5** 807
reliquaries **5** 807; **26** 144
Teodolindo Chapel **9** 262; **33** 624–5, *625*
Treasury **16** 770; **22** 519
fans **10** 776
park **16** 647
Villa Reale **1** *574*; **2** 232; **16** 646; **23** 263
Villa Regio-Ducale *see* VILLA REALE
Monza, Antonio de **29** 311
Monzaemon Chikamatsu *see* CHIKAMATSU MONZAEMON
Monzie, Gabrielle de **19** 42
Monziès, Louis **5** 131
Monzo, Elís Tormo y *see* TORMO Y MONZO, ELÍS
Monzo, Osvaldo **22** 49*
Monzóin **29** 335
Moodie (*fl* 19th cent.) **5** 282
Moodie, Donald **9** 725
Moodie, Thomas Anderson **14** 193
Moody, Dwight Lyman **7** 216; **29** 913
Moody, Ronald **5** 754; **16** 884; **22** 49*
works **5** *753*
Moody, William **5** 839; **33** 226
Mooijen, P. A. J. **15** 769
Mookerjee, Ajit **15** 748
Mookherjea, Sailoz **30** 58
Mookiah, T. R. P. **20** 54
Mooleyser, Willem **22** 885

Moon, Francis G. 10 378
Moon, Jeremy 28 805
Moon, Mick 21 897
Moon, Milton 2 761
Moone (Co. Kildare) 15 877; 16 19
  stone-carvings 15 876
Moonens, Laurent 1 431; 33 598
Mooney, David 31 661
Mooney, James 10 580
Moon of Bali drum 29 229
moonstones 29 443, 443
Moor, Alexander de 12 519
Moor, Cesar de 12 519, 520
Moor, Dmitry (Stakhiyevich) 22 49–50*; 27 394
Moor, Frans de 12 519; 23 665
Moor, Johann 30 276
Moor, Karel de 21 488; 22 50*, 846
  groups and movements 19 102
  teachers 21 488; 30 425
  works 19 349
Moor, Karel Isaac de 22 50
Moora, Harri 22 50*
Moor Abbey (Co. Cork) 16 20
Moorcroft, Walter 22 51
Moorcroft, William (c. 1765-1825) 1 210; 15 665
Moorcroft, William (1872-1945) 10 313; 22 50–51*
Moore, Albert Joseph 11 435; 15 895; 22 51–2*; 33 545
  groups and movements 1 170; 23 504; 33 139
  patrons and collectors 14 132; 18 907; 30 359
  teachers 10 373
  works 9 290; 10 254; 11 376, 433, 435; 19 588; 22 52, 416; 23 547; 24 641
Moore, Andrew 10 328
Moore, Bernard 2 570
Moore, Charles 25 556
Moore, Charles, Marquess of Drogheda 2 598
Moore, Charles W(illard) 22 52–3*; 23 490
  groups and movements 25 359
  works 11 345, 347; 22 53; 25 174; 27 730; 31 598
Moore, Christopher 9 322
Moore, Clement C. 25 449
Moore, David (Murray) 22 53–4*
Moore, Edward 18 640
Moore, Edward Chandler 16 554; 30 867; 31 650
Moore, Edwin 22 51
Moore, Esther Mary 10 373
Moore, Garrett 28 844
Moore, George (fl 1850s) 18 168
Moore, George (Augustus) (1852-1933) 22 54*
Moore, Henry (1831-95) 20 424; 22 51
Moore, Henry (Spencer) (1898-1986) 2 560; 10 267, 375; 14 452; 22 54–8*; 23 296; 25 582; 27 876
  altars 33 394
  assistants 5 789; 18 65; 20 833, 911; 24 205
  collaboration 14 674; 20 603, 607; 33 75, 552
  collograph 25 618
  dealers 18 161
  drawings 9 216, II2; 22 56; 32 902
  groups and movements 2 553; 4 75; 19 591, 623; 22 751; 28 506; 30 22; 31 673
  lithographs 19 492
  methods 8 128
  patrons and collectors 7 376; 9 716; 10 91, 362; 13 629; 14 575; 15 36; 27 524; 28 315
  personal collection 31 177
  porcelain 12 437
  prints 7 576, 576; 25 628
Moore, Henry (Spencer) (1898-1986)—cont.
  pupils 2 753; 32 423
  screenprinting 28 299
  sculpture 9 25; 22 57; 28 314, 315
    alabaster (gypsum) 1 520
    architectural 10 745
    bronze 25 26
    clay 30 500
    concrete 7 696
    lead 18 903
    monumental 22 49
    reliefs 4 790
    statuettes 29 576
  studio 29 859
  tapestries 10 352
  teachers 27 219
  textiles 9 293
Moore, James, sr (1670-1726) 4 138; 10 276, 292; 17 902
  works 10 292
Moore, James, jr (c. 1690-d before 1734) 10 294
Moore, James (1762-99) 8 584; 12 741; 18 721
Moore, John Bradford 22 626, 676
Moore, John C. (fl 1850s; manufacturer) 30 867
Moore, John Collingham (1829-80; painter) 22 51
Moore, John D. 7 619
Moore, Joseph 4 87; 27 878
Moore, Leslie T. 22 59
Moore, Lyndon, Turnbull, Whitaker see MLTW
Moore, Morris J. 22 58*
Moore, Philip 13 877
  works 13 877
Moore, Robert 33 678
Moore, S. 33 310
Moore, Temple (Lushington) 14 743; 22 58–9*
  pupils 28 281, 282
  works 14 501
Moore, Thomas (c. 1700-88) 2 877; 5 838, 839; 10 279, 358
Moore, Thomas (1779-1852) 14 263, 399; 20 28
Moore, William (fl 1785-1814) 16 27
Moore, William (1790-1851) 22 51
Moore, William (1817-1909) 22 51
Moorea 28 921
Moore Abbey (Co. Clare) 16 10
Moore-McCormack lines 20 10
Moores, John 19 507
Moores, Peter 19 507
Moorfields carpet factory 10 279, 358
Mooriaen, Jan-Baptist 31 807
Moorish style 17 640; 22 59–61*, 60, 256
Moorman, Charlotte 23 777; 27 215; 28 829; 29 99
Moor Park (Herts) 1 784; 7 339; 10 278; 12 127
  overdoors 23 678
  Tea Pavilion 24 290
Moortele, Anan van den 14 784
Moortgat, Anton 7 248
Moortgat-Correns, Ursula 7 248
Moos, Hermine 18 198
Moos, Johann Kaspar 8 790
Moos, Max von 30 135, 747
Moosbrugger (family) 30 137
Moosbrugger, Caspar 22 61–2*; 33 41
  works 10 116, 116; 13 713; 22 61; 30 126, 126; 32 822
Moosburg an der Isar, St Castulus 26 634
  altarpiece 12 401; 19 106, 106–7
  epitaph to Sigismund Pucher 10 436, 436
moose-hair see under HAIR → types
Mootwingee 1 37; 22 62*
Mootzka, Waldo 22 595
Mooy, Cornelis (Pietersz.) 27 230
Mopan 3 621
Mopelia 28 921
Mopin & Co. 4 214
Mopope, Stephen 22 62–3*, 595; 28 742
  works 22 63
MOPP see OPPENHEIMER, MAX
Mopsuestia see MISIS
Mopti 1 381; 11 829
  congregational mosque 1 317; 4 793
  Medical Assistance Clinic 1 320, 320; 20 198
Moqeke see MOXEKE
moquette carpets see under CARPETS → types
Mor (van Dashorst), Antonis 9 269; 22 63–6*
  methods 25 280
  patrons and collectors
    Alba, Fernando Alvárez de Toledo, Gran-Duque de, Governor of the Netherlands 1 528
    Alcalá, 3rd Duque de (1583-1637) 26 307
    Catherine of Austria, Queen of Portugal (1507-78) 2 874
    Charles V, Holy Roman Emperor (reg 1519-58) 33 578
    De la Gardie, Magnus Gabriel 30 118
    Fitzalan, Henry, 12th Earl of Arundel 11 140
    Mary of Hungary, Regent of the Netherlands (1505-58) 3 612
    Pernštejn (family) 24 462
    Philip II, King of Spain (reg 1556-98) 13 922
    Philip IV, King of Spain (reg 1621-65) 32 127
  pupils 27 704
  teachers 22 837; 23 188; 31 771
  works 3 557; 9 267, 274, 275; 11 454; 22 64, 66; 25 280
Mor, Paulus 2 716
Mor, Tell 1 880; 24 635
Mora (India) 15 428; 20 817
Mora (Sweden)
  brass 30 111
  jewellery 30 113
  paintings 30 116
  Zorn Museum 30 91, 119; 33 705
Mora (ii), Bernardo de 21 109; 22 68–9*; 29 292
Mora (ii), de (family) 13 284
Mora (ii), Diego de 22 69; 26 421
Mora (y Palomar), Enrique de la 5 603; 21 380; 22 69–70*
Mora (i), Francisco de 14 474; 22 66–7*
  attributions 14 476
  collaboration 10 903; 25 455
  patrons and collectors 14 6; 27 723
  teachers 14 476
  works 2 864, 865; 10 501, 535; 14 473, 474; 19 226, 227, 227; 20 62, 63, 72; 21 159; 24 108; 25 291; 29 268, 300; 30 518; 32 116
Mora, Gabriel 29 428
Mora, George 2 770
Mora, Jerónimo de 24 23
Mora (ii), José de 9 407; 22 68, 69; 26 421
Mora, José Rincón see RINCÓN MORA, JOSÉ
Mora (i), Juan Gómez de 22 66, 67–8*
  assistants 5 725
  methods 21 765
  patrons and collectors 14 6, 7; 29 269
  restorations by others 20 62
  teachers 14 477
Mora (i), Juan Gómez de—cont.
  works 1 587; 2 284; 5 725; 10 501, 535; 14 473, 476; 19 226, 227; 20 63, 72; 21 159; 27 603; 29 269; 31 93, 718; 32 551
Mora, Lola 2 399
Morača Monastery 22 17; 25 340
  icons 22 17
  St Luke 25 340; 28 441, 452
  wall paintings 22 16; 25 344; 28 450
Morach, Otto 8 434; 22 921; 30 134
Moradabad 15 409
Moradillo, Francisco 4 561
Moradillo de Sedano church 26 609
Morado, José Chavez see CHAVEZ MORADO, JOSÉ
Moragas, Miguel 29 308, 309, 322
Moragas, Tomás 2 62; 27 350
Moragas Gallissa, Antoni de 13 726; 20 516
Moraglia, Giacomo 19 782; 21 520; 22 70*
Moraglia, Pietro 22 70
Mora González, Juan 8 17
Moragues, Pere 22 70–71*
  collaboration 8 817
  groups and movements 3 217
  patrons and collectors 2 276; 29 332
  works 13 106, 165
Morais, Cristóvão de 2 874; 14 5; 22 71*; 25 296
Morais, Graça 25 300
Morais de Silva Ramos, Manuel de 10 729
Morakau 24 66
Moral, Enrique del 21 380; 22 71*
  collaboration 23 578; 24 9
  works 21 380, 403
Moral, Francisco del 19 178
Moral, Lesmes Fernández del see FERNÁNDEZ DEL MORAL, LESMES
Morales 24 96
Morales, Andrés de 29 340
Morales, Antón de 5 724
Morales, Armando 22 72*; 23 81, 85
Morales, Benito de 30 517
Morales, Carlos 7 607
Morales, Dario 7 610
Morales, Eulalio 4 259
Morales, Ignacio Diaz see DIAZ MORALES, IGNACIO
Morales, José Gil de Castro y see CASTRO (Y MORALES), JOSÉ GIL DE
Morales, Juan de 28 331
Morales, Juan Luis 8 233
Morales, Leonardo 8 232; 25 823
Morales, Lucio Correa see CORREA MORALES, LUCIO
Morales, Luisa Raphaela 31 808
Morales, Luis de 22 72–3*
  patrons and collectors 1 690; 10 806; 17 673; 23 11; 26 306
  works 22 72; 29 278
Morales, Rafael Colón see COLÓN MORALES, RAFAEL
Morales de los Ríos (y Goncía), Adolfo 1 523; 4 712, 726; 22 73–4*
Morales Schildt, Mona 30 103
Moralis, Yannis 13 353; 22 74*
moral rights 2 554
Moralys, Christophele 22 71
Moran, Edward 22 74; 24 304
Moran, John 22 74
Moran, Mary Nimmo 9 309; 20 604; 22 74
Moran, Peter 21 896; 22 74
Moran, Thomas 22 74–5*; 31 603; 33 185
  collaboration 16 821
Moran, Thomas—cont.
  groups and movements 14 843; 25 629
  patrons and collectors 12 618
  reproductive prints by others 19 485; 25 450
  works 9 309; 20 604; 22 75; 33 185
Morand (family) 11 628
Morand, Eugène 4 765
Morand, Jean Antoine 19 846; 29 93
Morand, Paul (d 1854) 5 585
Morandi, Anna Manzolini see MANZOLINI MORANDI, ANNA
Morandi, Antonio see TERRIBILIA, ANTONIO
Morandi, Bernardino 30 515
Morandi, Francesco see TERRIBILIA, FRANCESCO
Morandi, Giorgio 4 278; 16 680; 22 75–7*
  groups and movements 11 866; 25 6; 31 852
  patrons and collectors 7 782; 20 848; 32 178
  pupils 12 772; 19 329
  works 22 76; 29 670
Morandi, Giovanni 30 515
Morandi, Giovanni Maria 6 584; 20 431, 841; 27 205; 29 399; 33 714
Morandi, Riccardo 7 696; 22 77*
  collaboration 23 117, 119
  works 12 282; 16 650
Morandini (da Poppi), Francesco see POPPI
Morando, Bernardo 19 835; 22 78*
  patrons and collectors 33 606
  works 25 97; 31 718; 33 605
Morando, Francesco 10 765
Morando, Paolo see CAVAZOLLA, PAOLO
Morani, Fortunato 22 78
Morani, Vincenzo 22 78*
Morano, Moggi di 16 774
Morano, Moggi di, collection see TURIN → Accademia Albertina di Belle Arti
Mora Noli, José Guillermo 22 78*
Morant 10 297
Morant, Adam 1 765
Morant, Conrad 29 750
Morant, Edward 4 845
Morant, Jehan 1 765
Morant Bay 16 878, 889
Morante, Pedro Diaz see DIAZ MORANTE, PEDRO
Moranzone (family) 13 124
Moranzone, Francesco 12 580
Morar 13 883
Moras, Abraham Peyrenc de see PEYRENC DE MORAS, ABRAHAM
Moratalla, Church of the Assumption 29 267
Morates, Carios 4 234
Moratilla, Francisco 29 338
Moratti, Francesco 20 378; 24 35
Morava 9 586; 22 79–80*
  architecture 22 79*
  painting 22 79, 79–80*
  sculpture 28 453
Moravia see CZECH REPUBLIC
Moravia, Přemysl, Margrave of see PŘEMYSL, Margrave of Moravia
Moravian Brethren see under CHRISTIANITY → sects
Moravian Pottery and Tile Works 30 887
Moravská Třebová 8 383
Moravský Krumlov Castle 8 378; 22 331
Morawaka 29 474
Moray, Francis Stuart, 10th Earl of see STUART, FRANCIS, 10th Earl of Moray
Morazini 8 427

Morazzone 6 340; 16 674; 22 81–3*; 27 499
attributions 5 405; 8 149
collaboration 25 644; 31 899
patrons and collectors 21 526; 22 26; 28 7, 496
pupils 5 405
works 15 138; 22 82, 83; 24 695; 31 899, 900
Morbelli, Angelo 9 40; 16 678; 22 83–5*
dealers 13 714
groups and movements 22 747
teachers 5 918
works 22 84
morbidezza 6 570; 22 85*
Morbio Inferiore School 30 129
Mörby Castle 30 69
morceaux de réception 20 599; 22 85–6*
Mørch, Dea Trier 8 736
Morciano (d'Addosio), Duca di 31 789
Morco, Bernardino di Giacomo da 27 748
mordants (i) (acid) 10 548–9; 22 86*
Dutch see POTASSIUM CHLORIDE
see also ACIDS
mordants (ii) (gilding) 7 245–6; 12 622, 625; 22 86*
mordants (iii) (dyeing) 22 86*
historical and regional traditions
Indian subcontinent 15 667, 668, 672, 673
Japan 17 308, 315
materials
alum 9 665; 15 667, 668; 21 261; 30 559
ashes 15 667
copperas 21 261
iron 9 490; 15 667, 668; 17 308; 30 559
lye 17 308
uses
dyes 9 490, 491, 493; 15 667, 672; 17 308; 30 559
photography 24 647
Mordvinia 27 434, 435
Mordvinov, Aleksandr 6 526
Mordvinov, Arkady 12 879; 23 426; 32 695
Mordvinov, I. A. 22 171
More (family) 21 766
More, The (Herts) 33 306
Moré, Gustave 9 117
Moré, Humberto 9 714
More, Jacob 22 86*
patrons and collectors 8 83; 14 486
teachers 27 334
works 13 304; 25 883; 28 236
More, Thomas 14 868; 22 87*; 25 277
personal collection 10 445; 14 869; 21 355; 25 227
works 12 109; 31 297
More, William
works 6 604
Moréas, Jean 30 168
Moreau (family) 6 455
Moreau, Adolphe 22 93
Moreau, Antoine-Jean 24 893
Moreau, Auguste 5 320; 22 92
Moreau, Charlemagne 23 850
Moreau, Charles 8 661
Moreau, Gustave 11 546; 22 88–91*; 24 142
groups and movements 25 356; 30 168, 170; 33 379
personal collection 2 552
pupils 10 840
Bonhomme, Léon (-Félix-Georges) 4 319
Camoin, Charles 5 528
Evenepoel, Henri (-Jacques-Edouard) 10 658
Flandrin, Jules 11 160
Moreau, Gustave
pupils—cont.
Guérin, Charles (-François-Prosper) 13 789
Manguin, Henri (-Charles) 20 271
Marquet, Albert 20 464
Matisse, Henri (Emile Benoît) 20 821
Maxence, Edgard 20 876
Pallady, Theodor 23 872
Piot, René 24 838
Renan, (Cornelis) Ary 26 191
Rouault, Georges (Henri) 27 239, 639
Valtat, Louis 31 853
reproductions in tapestry 12 830
reproductive prints by others 4 625
works 8 596; 10 480; 11 419, 547; 22 90, 91, 416; 32 902
Moreau, Gustave, Musée see under PARIS → museums
Moreau, Hippolyte 8 789
Moreau, Jean 31 842
Moreau, Jean-Baptiste 22 92
Moreau, Jean-Charles-Alexandre 20 867
Moreau (i), Jean-Michel 19 11; 20 137; 22 87, 88*; 24 135
groups and movements 31 373
patrons and collectors 30 727
reproductive prints by others 9 283, 365; 12 179, 516; 13 871; 14 365; 19 136; 28 754
works 3 318; 9 283–4; 10 823, 823; 24 63, 137
Moreau, John see MOROW, JOHN (fl c. 1400)
Moreau, Karl 22 91–2*
assistants 14 524
patrons and collectors 10 530
works 2 785; 3 175; 14 888
Moreau (i), Louis-Gabriel 22 87–8*; 24 136
works 9 217; 22 87
Moreau, Luc-Albert 5 530; 13 790; 19 491; 22 92*, 751
Moreau, Marie 27 537; 28 42
Moreau, Marie-Edmée 30 352
Moreau, Mathurin 22 92–3*
Moreau, Nikolaus 11 461
Moreau, Robert 22 93*
Moreau-Desproux, Pierre-Louis 6 396; 22 93*; 23 517; 30 670
Moreau-Nélaton, Etienne 22 93–4*
paintings 6 516; 24 883
writings 4 589; 11 674; 25 52
Moreau-Vauthier, August 11 637
Moreel, Willem 21 103
Moreelse, Benjamin (Pauwelsz.) 22 95
Moreelse, Hendrick (Pauwelsz.) 22 94
Moreelse, Johannes (Pauwelsz.) 22 95
Moreelse, Paulus (Jansz.) 22 94–5*; 31 771
groups and movements 22 843; 31 772
pupils 3 7
reproductive prints by others 26 542
works 1 658, 659; 22 95; 33 367
Moreelse, Willem 22 95
Moreira, Jorge (Machado) 22 95*
collaboration 4 712; 8 7; 23 117; 26 109
works 4 712, 713
Morel, Auguste 8 57
Morel, Bartolomé 28 518; 29 338; 32 100
Morel, Carlos 2 399; 22 96–7*
Morel, Jacques 11 555; 13 79; 19 137; 22 95
Morel, Jean-Marie 12 124
Morel, Jean-Valentin 11 622, 631; 28 520
Morel, Maurice 27 241
Morel, Nicholas 10 297; 28 348
Morel, Pierre 2 860; 22 95, 96*
Morel, Yoryi 9 117, 119
Morel & Cie 26 191
Morel d'Arleux, Louis-Marie-Joseph 24 387
Morel de Vindé, Charles Gilbert 23 777
Morelia 21 265
Cathedral 21 376, 377
College of S Francisco Xavier 21 376
College of S Nicolás 21 376
Convent of Las Rosas 21 376
Morell, Gerhard 8 758, 759
Morell, José Arburo (y) see ARBURO (Y) MORELL, JOSÉ
Morella 29 332
S María la Mayor 13 106
Morel-Ladeuil, Léonard 4 88; 10 143
Morellensalz see under PIGMENTS → types
Morellet, François 11 571; 22 97*
dealers 26 193
groups and movements 11 551; 13 709, 710; 18 63; 23 448, 449
works 22 748
Morelli, Alessio 10 316
Morelli, Benedetto 5 854
Morelli, Carlo 22 103
Morelli, Cosimo 1 575; 31 800
Morelli, Domenico (Soldiero) 16 678; 22 97–100*, 480
groups and movements 19 870; 28 317; 32 257
pupils 5 431; 8 463; 10 512; 21 472, 495; 31 100
works 16 677; 22 99, 100; 30 358
Morelli, Francesco 3 53
Morelli, Fulgenzio 22 103
Morelli, Gioacchino 22 103
Morelli, Giovanni (Lorenzo) 2 532; 11 190; 12 483; 16 769; 21 825; 22 101, 101–2*, 296; 25 143; 26 570
collaboration 6 100; 16 769; 18 897
collections 5 872
pupils 26 358
writings 7 714; 11 798; 24 423
on attributions 11 307; 16 782; 32 27
translated 18 897
Morelli, Giovanni Battista 1 631
Morelli, Guido 2 560
Morelli, Lazzaro 2 594; 22 103*
collaboration 26 810
pupils 12 680
works 26 810
Morelli, Nicola 16 752; 22 103*
works 12 264, 264
Morelli, Pier Antonio 32 615
Morello, Carlo 13 748; 28 12
Morelos Augustinian Monastery 21 375
Morel & Seddon 25 712; 28 348; 33 250
Moremi, Victor 4 489
Morenbout, Gerard 2 871
Moreni, Domenico 2 125
Moreni, Mattia 13 727
Moreno, Anibal 7 607
Moreno, Blás 9 112
Moreno, Custodio Teodoro 24 225; 32 566
Moreno, Francisco de Paula Mendoza y see MENDOZA Y MORENO, FRANCISCO DE PAULA
Moreno, José 22 103–4*; 29 45
Moreno, Juan 32 616
Moreno, Luis Guevara see GUEVARA MORENO, LUIS
Moreno, M. 21 396
Moreno, Manuel Gómez see GÓMEZ MORENO, MANUEL
Moreno, Rodrigo 26 549
Moreno, Servando Cabrera see CABRERA MORENO, SERVANDO
Moreno, Shirley 33 313
Moreno Capdevila, Francisco 22 104*
Moreno Carbonero, José 13 668; 27 781
Moreno Villa, José 22 104*; 24 334
Morera, L. 23 410
Moreruela Abbey 22 218; 29 263
S María 13 50
Mores, Jakob 2 455; 8 739; 14 102
Moresqui, Antonio 4 566
Moret, Henry 25 215
Moret, Jacqueline Varde de Bueil, Comtesse de 9 387
Moreto, Il see SOMAZZI, GIOVANNI
Moreton, Anson 2 759
Moreton, Henry, 2nd Earl of Ducie 30 533
Moreton, John 2 759
Moreton Valence (Glos), St Stephen 26 616
Moretti, Carlo Brentano 33 276
Moretti, Cristoforo 22 104–5*; 24 861
Moretti, Egidio 14 805
Moretti, Gaetano 22 105*
assistants 12 653
collaboration 24 851
teachers 4 247
works 20 908; 22 24; 24 516
Moretti, Giambattista 5 55; 27 720
Moretti, Gino 6 322
Moretti, Giuseppe (fl 1770s) 1 598; 12 914; 26 320
Moretti, Giuseppe (1869-1935) 25 5
Moretti, Luigi 5 562; 16 649; 19 305; 22 36, 106*
Moretti, Mattia 23 845
Moretti, Roberto 12 795
Moretti, Vincenzo 32 204
Moretto (da Brescia) 4 748; 22 106–9*; 28 388
attributions 22 133
collaboration 22 133; 26 727
copies 3 56
patrons and collectors 27 350
pupils 22 132
works 16 667; 21 525; 22 108, 109
Moretto da Bergamo see CODUSSI, MAURO
Moretus, Balthasar 4 359; 21 765; 25 17, 627; 27 291, 299
works 4 360
Moretus, Jan 25 17
Moretus-Plantin, Edward 25 17
Moreux, Jean-Charles 22 110*
Morey, Charles Rufus 3 270; 15 96; 22 110*; 31 672
Morey, Pere 23 881
Morez, Mary 22 597
Morf, David 30 127; 33 734
Morfontaine 6 171
Morgan (family) 32 782
Morgan, Lady 33 309
Morgan, Barbara 4 109; 24 685
Morgan, Charles Octavius Swinnerton 20 444
Morgan, Edwin D. 23 32
Morgan, F(rederick) Cleveland 22 111*
Morgan, Henry de 10 94
Morgan, Jacques de 1 892; 10 82; 14 513; 22 488
excavations 1 894; 10 80; 18 211; 30 27
Morgan, James (fl 1806-34) 8 911; 25 711
Morgan, James (early 20th century) 11 901
Morgan, James, sr (before 1750-84) 22 111*; 31 635
Morgan, James, jr (1756-1822) 22 111
Morgan, J. P. (1867-1943) 13 616; 22 112
Morgan, J(ohn) Pierpont (1837-1913) 1 454; 2 560; 3 174; 9 451; 11 774; 13 616; 18 161; 22 111*
architecture 20 19
books 31 680
carpets 8 899
collections 9 200; 10 367; 11 774; 12 474; 16 554; 28 384; 31 667; 33 182
drawings 9 229; 22 351
paintings 7 490; 9 467; 31 664
photography 8 280
porcelain 26 487
sculpture 15 30
Morgan, Julia 6 63; 14 279; 22 112*
Morgan, M. H.
works 2 355
Morgan, Norma 1 444
Morgan, Octavius 11 738
Morgan, Sally 1 65
Morgan, Thomas A. 17 626
Morgan, Walls & Clements 2 643; 30 507
Morgan, William 10 397
Morgan, William (Frend) De see DE MORGAN, WILLIAM (FREND)
Morgan 453, Master of 1 782
Morgan Carpet 15 682
Morgan Ciborium 10 322; 26 694
Morgan Infancy Cycle, Master of the 22 835
Morgan Leaf, Master of the 10 244; 26 677; 33 240
works 33 239
Morgan & Sanders Co. 19 592, 593; 27 139
Morgantina
agora 28 654
architecture 28 654
figurines 13 580, 581
House of Ganymede 22 155, 160
macellum 19 888
mosaics 13 559, 561, 566
Morgenblatt 24 443
Morgenstern, Carl 12 394
Morgenstern, Christian (Ernst Bernhard) 22 112–13*
Morgenthaler, Ernst 22 113*
Morghen, Antonio 22 113
Morghen, Filippo 22 113
Morghen, Giovanni Elia 22 113
Morghen, Guglielmo 22 113
Morghen, Raphael 10 394; 22 113*
assistants 18 810
collaboration 2 40; 32 689
teachers 30 865
works 16 677; 26 230
Morgner, Wilhelm 10 695; 12 395; 22 114*
Morgue, Olivier 25 25
Morgues, Jacques Le Moyne de see LE MOYNE DE MORGUES, JACQUES
Morgunov, Alexey 9 144, 145
Mōri (family) 14 37; 17 427, 429; 31 677
boxes 14 429
Mori, Camilo 6 597; 22 114*
Mori, F. 1 370, 372
Mori, Nobuo Mitzutani see MITZUTANI MORI, NOBUO
Mori, Ōgai 31 81
Mori, Osamu 12 101; 17 660
Mori, Togaku 17 267
Mori, Yoshitoshi 17 293, 296; 22 114–15*
Moria 19 234, 235
Moriamé, E. Soil de see SOIL DE MORIAMÉ, E.
Mori Arinori 17 420
Moriarty, Mervyn 2 772
Moriatsu Hayashi see HAYASHI MORIATSU
Morice, Charles 12 192; 22 421
Morice, Humphry 22 115*

Morice, Leopold 11 565
Morice, William 22 115
Móricz, Zsigmond 10 894
Morienval, Notre Dame 11 *504*; 13 36; 22 115*
capitals 22 *115*
Morie Ogiwara *see* OGIWARA, MORIE
Morier, David 14 143
Morigia, Camillo 31 740, 800
Morigia, Giacomo Antonio 3 249
Morigia, Paolo 12 11
Moriguchi, Kako 14 452
Mori Ippo 22 119
Morija Museum and Archives 19 242
Mori Jokansai 22 118
Morikage *see* KUSUMI MORIKAGE
Mori Kansai 17 196, 200; 22 119
Morikawa Toen 17 372
Morikazu Kimura *see* KIMURA, MORIKAZU
Morikuni Tachibana *see* TACHIBANA MORIKUNI
Morillon, Antoine 22 116*
Morimond Abbey 2 791; 7 351
Morimoto, Kōjun 17 428
Morimura Matsudaira *see* MATSUDAIRA MORIMURA
Morin, Claude 11 613
Morin, Gustave 19 17; 29 58
Morin, Jean 10 392; 22 116*
teachers 6 436
works 6 435; 10 144; 11 358; 25 33
Morin, Mathurin 33 274
Morin, Paul 1 786
Morinck, Hans 22 116–17*
works 8 629; 12 404; 22 *117*
Moringer, Hans 32 821
Morini, Francesco 11 397
Morini, Jorge 2 397
Morino, Hiroaki 17 267, 268
Morioka 17 355
morions *see under* HELMETS → types
Moriori 6 514
rock art 6 *514*
Mori Ransai 17 186; 18 87
Mori school 17 196; 22 118
works 22 *118*
Morise, Max 30 17, 19, 20
Mōri Shigetaka 14 37
Mori Shūhō 22 118
Morison, Alexander 21 7
Morison, George Pitt 24 496
Morison, George Shattuck 4 803
Morison, Julia 23 62
Morison, Richard 14 670
Morison, Stanley (Arthur) 22 117–18*
typography 33 304
works 12 631; 31 494, 498
writings 31 498
Morison, William Leslie 23 62
Mori Sosen 22 118–19*; 23 594
works 10 777; 17 196; 22 *118*
Morisot, Berthe (-Marie-Pauline) 19 589; 22 119–20*; 31 820
dealers 4 589
groups and movements 8 621; 15 151, 152, 154, 155
patrons and collectors 22 54; 26 722
teachers 7 880; 13 806; 20 256
works 9 309; 11 417; 18 716; 22 *119*
Morisot, Edma 22 119
Morisset, Gérard 5 558; 22 120*
Morisset, James 10 348; 19 596
works 2 *457*
Morita, Kisaburo 17 402
works 17 *402*
Morita, Shiryū 17 240
works 17 *240*
Morita, Sunao 11 811
Mōri Terumoto 14 36, 568; 16 786; 17 784; 31 676
Mori Tetsuzan 17 196; 20 523; 22 118, 119
Moritim 29 867
Moritz, Andreas 12 450, 451
works 12 *451*
Moritz, Bernhard 16 557; 27 846
Moritz, Karl (*fl c.* 1900) 7 582; 18 140
Moritz, Karl Philipp (1756-93) 1 660; 5 885; 32 751
Moritz Rugendas, Johann *see* RUGENDAS, JOHANN MORITZ
Moriuji Ashina *see* ASHINA MORIUJI
Morixe, Hector 32 538
Moriyama, Daido 22 120*
Moriyama, Raymond 22 120–21*
works 5 563; 19 320, *320*; 31 176
Moriyoshi Naganuma *see* NAGANUMA, MORIYOSHI
Morizet, André 24 129
Morken 21 162
Morlaiter, Giovan Maria 22 121*; 32 195
Morlaiter, Gregorio (*fl* before 1699) 22 121
Morlaiter, Gregorio (1738-84) 22 121
Morlaiter, Michelangelo 1 784; 20 91
Morland, George 22 122–4*
groups and movements 26 740
patrons and collectors 3 366; 19 270
pupils 7 572; 28 370
reproductive prints by others 8 864; 9 464; 12 187; 21 417; 26 231; 28 882; 29 675; 31 137
works 2 105; 12 293, 294; 22 122, *123*
Morland, Henry 22 122–3*
Morland, Henry Robert 10 786; 22 122*
Morland, J. S. 5 668
Morland, Maria 22 122*
Morlanes (family) 27 818
Morlanes, Gil de (i) (*c.* 1450-*c.* 1515) 22 124*
works 22 124; 29 265
Morlanes, Gil de (ii) (*fl* 1515-47) 22 124*
collaboration 17 628; 22 124
works 22 124; 26 249
Morlaye, Guillaume 4 615
Morley, David 32 789
Morley, Harry 10 397
Morley, James 9 473; 10 305
Morley, Malcolm 22 124–5*; 24 686; 29 437
Morley, Sylvanus G. 5 411; 6 488; 21 263; 31 507
Morley, Sylvanus G., Museo Arqueologico *see under* TIKAL PARK
Morley Town Hall (W. Yorks) 31 241
Morlon, Pierre-Alexandre 22 125*
Morlotti, Ennio 22 125*
groups and movements 11 802; 13 727; 16 681; 21 528
Mormons *see under* CHRISTIANITY → sects
Mornaix, Sallandrouze de la *see* SALLANDROUZE DE LA MORNAIX
Mörner, (Carl) Stellan (Gabriel) 14 89
Morne Sion 2 152
Morny, Charles-Auguste, Duc de 16 851; 22 126–7*
collections 16 851; 20 498
paintings 21 69
Moro 1 312
Moro, Alvise 2 88; 5 744
Moro, Antonio *see* MOR (VAN DASHORST), ANTONIS
Moro, Battista dell' Angolo del *see* ANGOLO DEL MORO, BATTISTA DELL'
Moro, César 21 388; 30 21, 22
Moro, Cristoforo, Doge of Venice (*reg* 1462-71) 22 127*
architecture 19 553
manuscripts 11 722
sculpture 26 438
silver 16 741
Moro, dell'Angolo del *see* ANGOLO DEL MORO, DELL'
Moro, Giacomo Antonio 27 767
Moro, Giovanni 31 163
Moro, Giulio dell' Angolo del *see* ANGOLO DEL MORO, GIULIO DELL'
Moro, il *see* TORBIDO, FRANCESCO (DI MARCO INDIA)
Moro, Lorenzo del 11 20, 194
Moro, Luigi Del *see* DEL MORO, LUIGI
Moro, Marco dell' Angolo del *see* ANGOLO DEL MORO, MARCO DELL'
Moro, Peter 19 519; 23 259; 26 460; 28 159
Moro, Raúl Salinas *see* SALINAS MORO, RAÚL
Moro, Ventura di *see* VENTURA DI MORO
Moroccan Association of Plastic Arts 21 79; 22 129
Morocco 1 *214*, 376, 527; 16 *103*; 22 127–30*
adobe 1 305
arches 16 190
architectural decorations 16 190, 191, 250
architecture 16 217–19*, 239–41*; 22 128
'Alawi 16 220, 239–41
Almohad 16 187, 190–91*
Almoravid 16 187
Islamic 16 157–8*, 187*, 190–91*
Marinid 16 217, 250
megalithic 21 43
military 16 240; 21 585
Sa'di 16 239–41
vernacular 32 309–11*, *310*
Wattasid 16 217
Zayyanid 16 217
bookbindings 1 682; 12 628
book covers 12 628
bracelets 16 532
brass 4 *687*
buckets 4 *687*
capitals 16 191
carpets 16 486, *487*
chandeliers 16 386–7
collections 16 448
coral 7 834
courtyards 16 *218*
domes 16 190
earthenwares 16 427
embroidery 16 448, *448*
enamel 16 *504*
felt 10 875
fibulae 16 532
fortifications 1 311; 21 585
gardens 12 78
gateways 21 *584*
gilding 12 628
gold 1 682
grilles 16 257
guidebooks 13 812
hats 16 459
headscarves 16 459
helmets 16 *504*
houses 16 218–19
iron 16 *504*
ivory 21 *630*
jewellery 3 *756*; 16 532
kilims 18 49
lamps 17 572
linen 16 *448*
madrasas 16 218; 20 *56*, 57
manuscript illumination 16 *300*
maqsūras 20 369
metalwork 16 386–7
mihrabs 16 *240*
Morocco—cont.
minarets 16 190; 21 *626*
minbars 11 50; 16 *493*, 495; 21 *630*
mosques 11 *50*; 16 190–91, *191*, 217–18, 240, *240*; 22 *128*
Marinid 16 257
Sa'di 16 257
T-plan 16 240
necklaces 16 532
painting 22 128–9
palaces 16 240; 23 816
pigments 16 448
pottery 16 412, 418, 427
robes 16 459
saddle-bags 3 *755*
sashes 16 429
sculpture 22 129
shields 16 505
silk 16 429, *448*
stained glass 16 257
stelae 29 618
stone 1 305
stucco 16 190, 257
synagogues 17 551
tents 30 473
textiles 16 447–8
tiles 16 250
tombs 16 240, *240*
trade 16 427
vaults (ceiling) 16 190
weaving 3 *755*; 16 429
wood 16 *493*; 21 *630*
woodwork 16 494
wool 3 *755*
see also NORTH AFRICA
Morocco, Alberto 28 239
Morocco Binder 4 352
Morocco City *see* MARRAKESH
morocco leather *see under* LEATHER → types
Morocharzanios, John VII, Patriarch of Constantinople *see* JOHN VII MOROCHARZANIOS, Patriarch of Constantinople
Morocho, Francisco 9 710
Moro di Martino *see* CODUSSI, MAURO
Morofusa Hishikawa *see* HISHIKAWA MOROFUSA
Morogues Church 13 79, 125
Moroiso 17 245
Morokuzo Shukin 17 792
Moromichi, Fujiwara no *see* FUJIWARA NO MOROMICHI
Morón, Pedro Pablo 24 401
Moroncelli, Amanzio 12 812
Morondava 20 36
Morone, Domenico 22 130*
collaboration 10 765
patrons and collectors 8 147; 12 908
pupils 21 904; 22 130
works 20 318, *319*; 32 343
Morone, Francesco 22 130–31*; 32 343
collaboration 19 322; 22 130
pupils 6 112
works 6 113
Morone Mola, Gasparo *see* MOLA (i), GASPARO MORONE
Moroney, Martin 2 760
Moroni, Andrea 22 131–2*
works 3 771; 22 *132*; 31 825
Moroni, Giovanni Battista 4 748; 22 132–4*
teachers 22 109
works 3 771; 9 265, 266; 11 389; 15 121; 16 667; 22 *133*, *134*; 31 898
Moronobu Hishikawa *see* HISHIKAWA MORONOBU
Moroshige Furuyama *see* FURUYAMA MOROSHIGE
Morosini (family) 25 334
Morosini, Alvise 19 629
Morosini, Bernardo 3 343
Morosini, Francesco di Pietro 8 156
Morosini, Gianfrancesco 19 629
Morosini, Vincenzo 31 *14*
Morosov, Ivan (Abramovich) *see* MOROZOV, IVAN (ABRAMOVICH)
Morot, Aimé 3 630; 8 125; 23 872
Moroufie, Koffi 1 332
Morow, John (*fl c.* 1400) 22 135*
Morow, John (1795-1844) *see* KEMP, GEORGE M(EIKLE)
Morozov 27 584
Morozov, A. V. 28 579
Morozov, I. (*fl* 1926) 27 409
Morozov, Ivan (Abramovich) (1871-1921) 22 135–6*
collections 11 659; 27 439; 30 361
murals 22 331
paintings 17 725; 20 193, 826; 27 441
sculpture 20 121
Morozov, Mikhail 22 135
Morozov, S. T. 28 579; 32 736
Morozov collection *see under* MOSCOW → museums → Pushkin Museum of Fine Arts
Morozzi, Massimo 2 373
Morpeth County Hall (Northumb.) 4 789
Morphey, Garret 22 136*
works 16 13, *14*
morphology 12 853; 30 748–9
Morphosis 2 552
Morphou 8 350
Museum of Archaeology and Natural History 8 367
St Mammas 8 362
Morphy, Howard 1 68; 2 137
works 1 *51*, *60*
Morpurgo 22 731
Morrel, Jakob *see* MARELL, JAKOB
Morrell, Ottoline 12 493
Morren, George 2 197; 19 792; 22 136–7*
Morrice, James Wilson 22 38, 137–8*
groups and movements 5 566, 593
patrons and collectors 5 589
works 22 *138*
Morricone, Luigi 18 392
Morris (family) 18 749
Morris, Cedric (Lockwood) 11 764; 22 139–40*; 32 786
Morris, Charles 1 182
Morris, Christianne 14 68
Morris, David 16 568
Morris, Edmund 5 593
Morris, Francis Orpen 4 369
Morris, George 4 332
Morris, Herbert & Co. 28 250, 256
Morris, James 33 207
Morris, James Shepherd 28 231
Morris, Joshua 10 351; 19 596
Morris, Ken 31 335
works 5 *788*
Morris, Lydia Thompson 15 745
Morris, Margaret 8 792
Morris, Marshall, Faulkner & Co. 10 298; 13 209; 22 141, 142–4; 25 555; 33 11
designers 4 879; 5 266; 8 706; 22 51; 27 187
furniture 22 *143*
interior decoration 11 331
stained glass 5 731; 6 439; 29 507, *513*
Morris, May 10 354
Morris, Michelle 31 660
Morris, Robert (*fl* 1660-70) 10 291; 31 681
Morris, Robert (*c.* 1701-54) 22 138, 139*; 32 553
groups and movements 23 860
Morris, Robert (1734-1806) 19 154; 25 655
Morris, Robert (*b* 1931) 22 140*; 23 49
collaboration 3 717

Morris, Robert (b 1931)—cont.
dealers 6 23
groups and movements 1 80; 7 685; 21 645, 646; 25 645, 646–7
patrons and collectors 24 24; 32 623
pupils 2 878; 29 73
works 10 875; 18 695; 24 407; 29 13; 31 615
Morris, Roger 22 138–9*
architecture 4 801; 12 176; 19 157; 29 861
castles 1 134, 135; 28 227
villas 27 131; 32 553, 553
collaboration 5 540
gardens 33 226
groups and movements 13 200
Morris, Talwin 12 780
Morris, Tim(othy William) 22 140–41*; 29 117
works 29 117
Morris, William 1 107, 171; 2 321, 524; 10 255; 15 211, 747; 19 596; 22 141–6*; 23 546; 28 916; 30 559
assistants 4 672
book illustrations 4 364, 366; 22 146
books 22 111; 33 55
chimney-pieces 6 605
collaboration 5 268
furniture 5 196; 6 391; 10 298; 22 143; 32 415; 33 332
groups and movements
Art Nouveau 2 562
Arts and Crafts Movement 2 569, 570, 571; 8 802; 13 209; 15 823; 23 498; 24 426; 29 858
Art Workers' Guild 2 575; 10 373
Japonisme 17 440
Modern Movement 21 779
Pre-Raphaelitism 25 555
Queen Anne Revival 25 804
house 2 365, 552; 10 235, 320; 28 664
interior decoration 9 29; 10 282; 15 895; 22 22; 23 36
manuscripts 20 335, 335
metalwork 10 343
paintings 10 254; 22 329; 27 186
patrons and collectors 4 71; 14 809; 25 41; 27 719
personal collection 14 849
prints 14 580; 33 361, 369
pupils 29 507
scripts 28 307
stained glass 4 810; 22 143; 23 690; 29 516; 33 239
teachers 29 765; 33 11
textiles
carpets 5 840–41
embroidery 10 182, 354
printed 8 36; 9 IV2; 10 356; 22 144; 28 717; 30 562
tapestries 10 351; 28 266; 30 326, 333
wallpaper 1 111
writings 8 121; 18 65; 22 351
Morris, William, Gallery and Brangwyn Gift see under LONDON → museums
Morris, William Richard, Lord Nuffield 23 684
Morris-Aubry 14 803
Morris chairs see under CHAIRS → types
Morris & Co. 3 741; 10 282; 22 141, 142; 25 555, 556; 28 561; 29 48
embroidery 10 354
interior decoration 2 756
stained glass 14 850; 28 348; 29 766, VI2
tapestry 30 326
textiles 9 IV2
tiles 30 879
Morris & Co.—cont.
wallpaper 17 469; 32 812, 816
Morrison 7 754
Morrison, Alfred 17 640; 22 148
Morrison, Andrew 31 633
Morrison, George (b 1919) 22 596, 599
Morrison, George (1862-1920) 7 154
Morrison, Ian 2 149, 151
Morrison, James 22 147–8*
Morrison, Jaspar 6 392
Morrison, John 22 147
Morrison, Mabel 22 148
Morrison, Richard 22 147*
pupils 22 147
works 6 64; 9 323; 16 9, 24
Morrison, William 28 259
Morrison, William Vitruvius 8 586; 22 147*
collaboration 16 9
works 16 9, 10, 24
Morrison & Co. 9 727; 28 256
Morrison Irwin, Harriet see IRWIN, HARRIET MORRISON
Morrison Triptych, Master of the 3 554; 20 731*; 22 148
Morrisseau, Norval 22 148*, 597
collaboration 22 597
groups and movements 22 666
works 22 666
Morrisseau Painting School 22 666
Morris Singer Foundry 13 877
Morris & Steedman 28 231
Morriston 32 782
Morritt, J. B. S. 13 303
Morro d'Alba 3 359
Morrow, Dwight D. 26 427
Morrow, Irving 27 730
Morrow, Stanley 4 627
Mors, Gustave 28 319
Morschel, Jürgen 13 267
Morse, Edward Sylvester 17 426, 629; 22 148*
excavations 17 244; 23 440
personal collection 17 431
works 17 425; 23 440
Morse, Samuel F(inley) B(reese) 4 477; 17 597; 22 149–50*; 24 659; 31 669
patrons and collectors 14 718; 26 75
pupils 4 627; 11 58; 15 30; 23 765
teachers 1 674; 33 93
works 22 149
Morsegno, Carlo Pietro 5 8; 19 269
Morsel, Jakob see MARELL, JAKOB
morses 14 419
Morstadt, Vincenc 8 405
Mortaigne (family) 31 227
Mortaigne, Nicolas 31 227
Mortaigne, Pasquier 31 227
Mortain reliquary 10 322
Mortara, S Lorenzo 13 64
mortars (building)
historical and regional traditions
Byzantine 4 773
Greece, ancient 13 403, 404
Indian subcontinent 15 351
Iran, ancient 15 912
Islamic 15 351; 16 268
Peru 19 386
Rome, ancient 26 879, 911, 912
Turkey 22 159; 26 912
materials
albumen 19 386
gypsum 15 912; 16 268
technical examination 30 409
uses
architecture 4 767; 16 268
frescoes 11 762, 764
masonry 20 573, 574
mosaics 22 156, 159, 165
plaster 29 812
stucco 29 812
mortars (vessels)
historical and regional traditions
Caribbean Islands 29 133
mortars (vessels)
historical and regional traditions—cont.
Chavín culture 29 133
China 7 103
Ecuador 29 133
Germany 12 452
Japan 17 341
Mongolia 21 883
Prehistoric art 25 477
South America, Pre-Columbian 29 133
Venda 1 417
materials
copper 12 452
ivory 7 103
uses
rock art 25 477
tea ceremonies 17 341
Morte da Feltro 9 142
Mortelècque 24 149
Mortemart, Duchesse de 7 168
Mortensen, Karl 27 413
Mortensen, Kevin 2 772
Mortensen, Richard 8 736; 22 150–51*
collaboration 8 755
groups and movements 4 62; 8 736; 11 570
works 22 151; 26 193
Mortensen, William 13 710
Morten the Painter 8 730
mortice and tenon joinery see under JOINERY → types
Mortier 12 814
Mortier, Antoine 3 565; 5 45; 17 518
Mortier, Etienne 7 460
Mortier, P.
works 24 535
Mortillet, Gabriel de 25 474
Mortimer, Francis J. 24 738, 739
Mortimer, Ian 25 628
Mortimer, John (fl 1820s) 29 723
Mortimer, John (1912-71) 28 244
Mortimer, John Hamilton 14 586; 22 151–3*
collaboration 17 640; 33 133
groups and movements 26 737; 29 891
patrons and collectors 18 150; 27 277
reproductive prints by others 3 309
teachers 14 841; 19 157
works 10 249; 22 152
Mortimer, Raymond 22 751
Mortimer, Roger 22 151
Mortimer & Hunt 29 723
Mortlake Tapestry Factory 2 199, 558; 8 186; 10 275, 349–51; 21 907; 22 153–4*; 29 800; 30 319, 322
designers 4 182; 7 431
directors 23 884
production 10 350
Mortlock 30 161
Mortlock Islands 21 477; 23 730
Morto da Feltre 19 834; 28 928
Morton, Alastair 7 772
Morton, Alexander 5 841; 28 266
Morton, Alexander, & Co. 18 65; 23 17
Morton, Douglas 4 169; 5 569
Morton, Francis 26 18
Morton, George 27 565
Morton, Ree 22 154*
Morton, Scott, & Co. 28 250, 256
Morton, William Scott 28 256
Morton-Sundour Fabric Co. 32 835
mortuary temples see TEMPLES → types
Morububna, Martin 23 736; 24 82
Mo Ruzhong 6 760; 9 136
Morveau, Guyton de 23 786
Morville, Comte de 8 92
Morwood, Michael 1 68
Moryson, Fynes 13 298
Mosa 22 884
Mosae Trajectum see MAASTRICHT
mosaic glass see under GLASS → types
mosaic gold 12 623
mosaicists 29 87
mosaics 22 154–65*
conservation 22 165*
historical and regional traditions
Africa 1 377–8
Algeria 27 63
Ancient Near East 1 889–90*; 27 64
Arabia 16 256
Armenia (Europe) 2 429
Assyrian 1 889–90*; 2 640
Aztec 2 908; 21 244, 248, 255; 22 164
Britain 27 62; 32 542
Byzantine 9 526, 561–2*, 563–4*, 570–81*, 582–6*, 623, 627, 630, 645; 12 71; 15 II3; 19 351, 356; 22 161–2, 163, 165
Crete 8 155
Cyprus 9 566–7*, 580
Egypt 28 763
Greece 7 170; 9 565–6*, 572, 577–9, 585, 630; 22 162; 30 721, 723
Italy 9 573, 581; 22 161; 26 652–3
North Africa 9 569–70*
Palestine 9 567–8*, 574
Sicily 9 581
Syria 9 567, 567–8*
Turkey 2 158; 7 220; 9 564, 564–5*, 577, 583; 16 594, 598, 601, 809; 21 III2; 22 157
Ukraine 18 37, 38–9; 31 554
Carolingian 5 799*; 12 485
Catalonia 21 IV2; 22 158, 164
Central Asia, Western 6 208; 16 199, 248
Crete 8 155
Cyprus
Byzantine 9 566–7*, 580
Early Christian (c. AD 250-843) 8 358–9*; 9 566–7*
Roman 8 333; 24 60
6th cent. AD 8 359
Cyprus, ancient 8 333, 354–5*, 355; 27 63
Early Christian (c. AD 250-843) 7 271, 271, 272; 9 561–4*, 568–9*, 570–75*, 645; 19 356; 22 161–2; 26 782
commentaries 33 215
Cyprus 8 358–9*; 9 566–7*
England 9 568
Greece 7 278; 9 565–6*, 572
Italy 2 243; 3 190; 7 223; 9 573; 16 654, 761; 21 523; 27 68, 782, 782–3
North Africa 9 569–70*
Palestine 9 567–8*, 574
Spain 6 177
Syria 9 567, 567–8*
Tunisia 9 569
Turkey 2 158; 9 564, 564–5*
Egypt 28 763
Egypt, ancient 1 617; 22 159
England 9 568; 29 XII
France 12 485; 26 681; 27 62; 32 542
Georgia 12 322–3*
Germany 21 III1; 26 681; 27 62; 30 506
Gothic 13 134–5, 145
Greece 7 170, 278; 9 565–6*, 572, 577–9, 585, 630; 22 162; 30 721, 723
Greece, ancient 8 691; 13 383, 556–61*, 557, 558, 559, 560, 562–7*, 562, 563, 564, 566; 22 159–60; 24 411
Floral style 13 558, 561, 562, 563, 563–4
mosaics
historical and regional traditions
Greece, ancient—cont.
Roman 27 63
4th cent. BC 23 435
Indian subcontinent 15 374–5
Iran 16 195, 199, 248, 249
Islamic 16 248, 250, 255*, 259, 466, 487; 22 154, 162
Central Asia, Western 16 199, 248
Indian subcontinent 15 375
Iran 16 195, 199–200, 248, 249
Ottoman 16 199
Spain 16 216
Syria 16 146, 148, 255
Tunisia 16 256
Turkey 16 199
Italy 7 275; 11 192; 16 655; 21 899; 32 208
Black and White style 27 61
Byzantine 9 573, 581; 22 161; 26 652–3
Early Christian (c. AD 250-843) 2 243; 3 190; 7 223; 9 573; 16 654, 761; 21 523; 27 68, 782, 782–3
Floral style 27 61
Gothic 13 135, 145
Renaissance 22 158
Roman 22 159; 23 623; 25 206, 421, 422; 27 60, 61, 61–2*, 62, 65–7*, 66, 68; 31 62
Romanesque 21 898; 26 679–80, 679, 680, 828
Silhouette style 27 61, 62
5th cent. AD 26 32
6th cent. AD 26 35, 36
12th cent. 32 209
13th cent. 6 105; 27 449; 31 193; 32 210, 211
14th cent. 7 318
Jewish art 17 542, 556–9*
Maya 17 715; 21 243, 254; 22 164; 31 778
Mesoamerica, Pre-Columbian 21 241, 251–2, 254–6*, 737, IV1; 22 158, 164*
Aztec 21 244, 255
Maya 17 715; 21 243, 254; 31 778
Mexico 17 715; 21 255
Mixtec 21 255, 734
Olmec 21 254
Mexico 17 715; 21 255, 734, IV1; 22 163; 23 370
Mixtec 21 251, 254–6, 255, 734, 737
North Africa 9 569–70*; 27 63; 32 542
Olmec 21 251, 254
Ottoman 16 199, 260
Palestine 3 882; 22 162
Byzantine 9 567–8*, 574
Early Christian (c. AD 250-843) 9 567–8*, 574
Jewish art 17 557–8*
Roman 27 63
6th cent. AD 17 488
Parthian 24 218
Phrygian 1 890*
Punic 25 732
Romanesque 22 163; 26 679, 679–81*
France 26 681
Germany 26 681
Italy 21 898; 26 679–80, 679, 680, 828
Sicily 6 133; 23 844, 846; 26 679, 680
Rome, ancient 13 559; 22 155, 160–61; 23 622; 26 691, 861; 27 58–61*, 62–5*, 67–8*; 30 408; 31 254; 32 542
Africa 1 377–8
Algeria 27 63
Ancient Near East 27 64

mosaics
historical and regional traditions
Rome, ancient—cont.
Black and White style **23** *623*; **27** 59, 60, 61
Britain **27** 62; **32** 542
Crete **8** 155
Cyprus **8** 333, 354–5, *355*; **24** *60*
Cyprus, ancient **27** 63
Egypt **1** *617*
First Style **29** 665
Floral style **27** 61
France **27** 62; **32** 542
Germany **21** III1; **27** 62
Greece, ancient **27** 63
Italy **22** *159*; **23** *623*; **25** *206*, 421, *422*; **27** 60, *61*, 61–2*, *62*, 65–7*, *66*, *68*; **31** *62*
Late Antiquity **26** 862; **27** 64
Monochrome style *see* Black and White Style
Multiple Décor style **27** 62
North Africa **27** 63; **32** 542
Palestine **27** 63
Rainbow style **27** 64
Sicily **24** 700, 701–2, *702*; **27** 63
Silhouette style **27** 61, *62*
Spain **27** 63
Syria **2** *157*; **27** *64*, 64, *65*
Tunisia **1** *377*; **32** *543*
Sicily **22** 162, 163
Byzantine **9** 581
Roman **24** 700, 701–2, *702*; **27** 63
Romanesque **6** *133*; **23** *844*, *846*; **26** *679*, 680
South America, Pre-Columbian **29** 217, 218
Spain **6** 177; **16** 216; **27** 63; **30** 882
Sumerian **22** 158
Syria **16** 147, *255*, 256; **22** 162
Abbasid **16** 256
Byzantine **9** *567*, 567–8*
Early Christian (*c*. AD 250-843) **9** *567*, 567–8*
Islamic **16** 146, 148
Roman **2** *157*; **27** 64, *64*, *65*
Umayyad **16** 255
Tunisia **1** *377*; **9** *569*; **16** 256; **32** *543*
Turkey
Early Christian and Byzantine **2** *158*; **7** *220*; **9** *564*, 564–5*, *577*, *583*; **16** *598*, *601*, *809*; **21** III2; **22** *157*
Islamic **16** 199
Ukraine **18** *37*, 38–9; **31** 553–4*, *554*
United States of America **19** 878; **22** 336
Vietnam **32** 481
materials
beryl **22** 158
bone **16** 487; **21** 248
brick **2** 640
cartoons (drawings) **13** 556
ceramics **32** 481
clamps **22** 165
copper **22** 159
enamel **22** 154
faience (ii) (ceramics) **16** 248
frames **11** 374
garnets **22** 158, 164
glass **9** 562, 645; **12** 622, 789, 790; **16** 255, 256; **22** 155, 156; **27** 66
glass paste **22** 154, 163
gold **19** 351; **22** 155, 156, 158, 161, 162
gold leaf **9** 645; **12** 622; **22** 155
hardstones **22** 154
ivory **16** 487
jade **21** 243
jadeite **22** 158
lead **13** 556, 565; **22** 155, 160

mosaics
materials—cont.
limestone **22** 159
malachite **22** 158
marble **22** 154; **29** XII
marcasite **22** 158
mortars (building) **22** 156, 159, 165
mother-of-pearl **16** 256; **22** 154, 158, 164
nails **22** 156, 165
obsidian **22** 158, 164
onyx **29** XII
paper **24** 57
pebbles **13** 556, *557*, *560*, *562*, 562–6*, *563*, *564*; **22** 154, 159–60; **23** *435*
plaster **9** 562
Purbeck marble **29** XII
quartz **22** 158
scagliola **28** 28
shells **22** 154, 158, 159; **29** 217, 218
silver **22** 155
silver leaf **12** 622
sinopie **13** 556
stone **9** 562; **13** 556; **16** 255, 256; **22** 154, 155, 159
templates **13** 556
terracotta **13** 556, 565; **22** 154, 155, 158, 160
tiles **6** 208; **16** 195, 199, 216, 248, *249*, 250, 259; **22** 159; **30** 506, 882
tin **22** 155
turquoise **21** 254, 255–6, 737, IV1; **22** 154, 158, 164; **29** 217
reuse **26** 691
technical examination **30** 409
techniques
cartoons (drawings) **22** 156, 163
sinopie **22** 156; **28** 778
trompe l'oeil **22** 160
types
emblemata **22** 155, *155*, 160; **27** 59, 60
micro-mosaics *see* ICONS → historical and regional traditions → Byzantine; Early Christian
opus musivum **27** 58–9, 65
opus sectile *see* OPUS SECTILE
opus signinum **27** 59, 61
opus tessellatum **13** 556; **27** 58–9, 61
opus vermiculatum **22** 155, 160; **27** 59, 61
pavimenta punica **25** 732
portative *see* ICONS → historical and regional traditions → Byzantine; Early Christian
uses
apses **22** 161
architectural decorations **15** 374–5; **16** 199, 248, 250, 255*, *255*; **22** 158
architecture **16** 216; **22** *164*
carpets **16** 466
churches *see under* CHURCHES → decoration
emblems **26** 750
fountains **27** *66*
icons **9** 623, 627, 630, *630*; **15** II3; **28** *763*
inscriptions **27** 61
knife-handles **21** 255
masks **21** 251, *255*
mosques **16** 147
murals **22** 333, 336
palaces **17** *715*
sculpture **11** 192; **21** 254
shields **21** 255
toys **31** 254
wall paintings **22** 163
walls **21** 255
woodwork **16** 487
Mosan *see* BELGIUM
Mosbach **12** 430
Mosbacher, Alois **32** 447

Mosca, Francesco **22** 166*; **24** 855
Mosca, Francesco di Simone **22** 166
Mosca, Giovanni Maria *see* MOSCA PADOVANO, GIOVANNI MARIA
Mosca, Simone **22** 166*
assistants **22** 15
collaboration **22** 15
patrons and collectors **10** 808
works **22** 16, 166
Mosca Moschino, Simone **4** 287; **22** 166*
Moscano di Fabriano **6** 157
Mosca Padovano, Giovanni Maria **18** 425; **22** 167–8*; **23** 754; **25** 113; **32** 192
attributions **27** 304
patrons and collectors **16** 868
pupils **3** 918; **21** 425
teachers **21** 632
works **18** 425, *425*; **19** 496; **22** *167*; **25** 113; **30** 345
Moscarda, Cira **5** 739; **21** 496; **24** 102
Moscardo, Lodovico **5** 345; **32** 343
Moschini, il *see* MOSCA, SIMONE
Moschini, Piero **16** 730
Moschini, Zanobi **11** 297
Moschino, il *see* MOSCA, FRANCESCO
Moschopoulos, Nikephoros, Metropolitan **22** 405
Moscoso, Jaime Andrade *see* ANDRADE (MOSCOSO), JAIME
Moscoso, Victor **25** 353
works **25** *353*
Moscoso y Guzmán, Joaquín Ventura Osorio de, 10th Conde de Altamira *see* ALTAMIRA, JOAQUÍN V. O. MOSCOSO Y GUZMÁN, 10th Conde de
Moscoso y Guzmán, Vicente Joaquín Osorio, 11th Conde de Altamira *see* ALTAMIRA, VICENTE JOAQUÍN O. MOSCOSO Y GUZMÁN, 11th Conde de
Moscovitz, Shalom *see* SAFED, SHALOM VON
Moscow **2** 425; **22** 168–84*; **27** *362*, *363*, 370, 371, 372, 373, 378; **29** 529
academies and art schools
Academy of Arts of the USSR **22** 179; **27** 443
Academy of Sciences **27** 439
Moscow School of Painting, Sculpture and Architecture **22** 178
New Russian Academy **21** 92
School of Contemporary Art **27** 443
School of Painting, Sculpture and Architecture **27** 442
Stroganov School of Applied Art **22** 178; **29** 778
Stroganov School of Technical Drawing *see* Stroganov School of Applied Art
V. I. Surikov Art Institute **27** 443
apartments **27** 381
Armoury *see under* Kremlin
art forms and materials
architecture **2** 428; **17** 869–71; **27** 374, 375, 376, 377–8
ceramics **22** 180*
chess sets **6** 558
cotton **8** 37
enamel **10** IV3; **27** 426
furniture **27** 409
glass **22** 180*; **27** 415, *416*
gold **22** 179–80*; **27** *419*
icons **25** 337; **27** 384–5
lace **27** 430
manuscripts **27** 385
metalwork **27** 418, 420, 421, 422
painting **22** *176*, *177*; **27** 383, 385, 386, 387, 394

Moscow
art forms and materials—cont.
panoramas **24** 19
paper **24** 48
printing **8** 37
silver **22** 179–80*
textiles **27** 400, 430, 431
tiles **30** 884
art market **2** 560
Bersenevskaya Embankment residential complex **15** 890
Bluebird Café (Sinyaya ptitsa) **18** 209
Café Pittoresque **10** 415; **26** 504; **31** 519; **33** 486
City Hall *see* museums → Central Lenin Museum
clubs
Dynamo Club **27** 379
English Club *see* museums → Central Museum of the Revolution
Nobles' Club **27** 404
Rusakov Workers' Club **2** 604; **21** *93*
Zil Club **15** 886
Zuyev Club **12** *877*
ecclesiastical buildings
Andronikov Monastery **27** 371
Cathedral of the Saviour **27** 304
see also museums → Andrey Rublyov Museum of Ancient Russian Art
Cathedral of the Annunciation *see under* Kremlin
Cathedral of the Archangel Michael *see under* Kremlin
Cathedral of the Dormition *see under* Kremlin
Cathedral of the Miracle of the Archangel Michael *see under* Kremlin → Chudovo Monastery
Cathedral of the Protective Veil **27** 371; **30** 884
Chudovo Monastery *see under* Kremlin
Church of Christ the Redeemer **27** 377; **28** 837
Church of the Archangel Gabriel **27** 373, *374*; **33** 621
Church of the Deposition of the Robe *see under* Kremlin
Church of the Georgian Mother of God **27** 386
Church of the Resurrection **27** 372
Don Monastery **3** 530; **27** 373
Martha and Mary Mission Convent **28** *837*
New Convent of the Virgin **22** *170*
Smolensk Cathedral **3** 530; **25** 342; **27** 372, 385
New Monastery of the Saviour **27** 372, 374
Cathedral **25** 342
Novodevichy Convent *see* New Convent of the Virgin
Patriarch's Sacristy **27** 440
St Basil's Cathedral **4** 783; **7** 256; **22** 184*, *184*
St John the Warrior **27** 373
St Lazarus *see under* Kremlin
Simonov Monastery **3** 530
Trinity Church **25** 342
Zaikonospassky Monastery Cathedral of Our Saviour **27** 373
education (art) **27** 442
exhibitions **27** 284
All-Russian Agricultural Exhibition, 1937
Azerbaijani SSR Pavilion **2** 899
All-Russian Exhibition of Art and Industry, 1882 **27** 421

Moscow—cont.
government and state buildings
Frunze Military Academy **27** 380
Gosbank **27** 379; **29** 529
Gostorg building **22** *174*
House of Unions *see* clubs → Nobles' Club
Intourist Building **27** 380, *380*; **29** 529
Ministry of Trade *see* Gostorg building
Narkomfin **12** *654*; **21** 622; **27** 379
Palace of Culture **27** 379
Palace of the Soviets **7** 670; **29** 529, 530
Palace of Youth **27** 381
Pravda complex **12** 876; **27** 379
RSFSR House of Soviets **27** 381
Senate *see under* Kremlin
State Bank *see* Gosbank
Tsentrosoyuz building **27** 379
Young Pioneer Palace **27** 380
hospitals
Dostoyevsky Hospital **21** 157
First Memorial Hospital *see* Golitsyn Hospital
Foundling Hospital **27** 402
Golitsyn Hospital **17** 869, *870*; **27** 375
Mariya Hospital *see* Dostoyevsky Hospital
Military Hospital **27** 375
Second City Hospital **27** 376
hotels
Hotel Metropol **12** 878
Hotel Moskva **18** 750; **27** 409; **29** 529
Leningrad Hotel **25** 170
houses
17 Aleksey Tolstoy St **32** 736
Demidov House **27** 403
M. P. Gagarin House **27** 401
Khrushchov House *see* museums → Pushkin Museum of Fine Arts
Lopukhin House *see* museums → Tolstoy Museum
Lunin House *see* museums → Museum of Oriental Art
Mel'nikov's House **27** 379
Z. G. Morozova Mansion
Imperial Art and Industrial Institute *see* academies and art schools → Stroganov School of Applied Art **27** 404
Pashkov House *see* Russian State Library
Razumovsky House *see* museums → Central Museum of the Revolution
Ryabushinsky House **27** 404, *404*
V. M. Vasnetsov House *see under* museums
institutes
All-Union Scientific Research Restoration Institute
collections **6** 285
Architecture Institute **27** 443
Imperial Art and Industrial Institute *see* academies and art schools → Stroganov School of Applied Art
Institute of Archaeology of the Russian Academy of Sciences **6** 285
Institute of Architects **27** 409
Institute of Scientific Information on the Social Sciences **27** 381
Khwarazm Expedition Institute of Ethnology and Ethnic Anthropology **6** 285, 286
Lazarian Institute **2** 445

Moscow
institutes—cont.
V. I. Surikov Art Institute *see under* academies and art schools
Textile Institute **27** 379
International Trade Centre **27** 405
Kitay-gorod **27** 371
Kremlin **1** *599*; **22** 169, 180–81*, *181*; **31** 140
Armoury **6** 284; **27** 377, 386–7, 440, 441, 442
bell-tower of Ivan the Great **22** *169*; **27** 371
Cathedral of the Annunciation **4** 783; **22** *183*, 183–4*; **27** 371, 384, 385, 438
iconostasis **7** *279*; **9** 601
icons **7** 261; **9** 630; **30** 708, V3
wall paintings **25** 342
Cathedral of the Archangel Michael **22** *182*, 182–3*; **25** 342; **27** 371, 386
reliquaries **26** 149
Cathedral of the Dormition **4** 783; **11** 116, *116*; **22** 181–2*; **27** 371, 383, 386, 438; **31** 555
icons **8** *909*; **25** 337; **27** 382
reliquaries **26** 149
wall paintings **25** 342
Chudovo Monastery
Cathedral of the Miracle of the Archangel Michael **25** 342
Church of the Deposition of the Robe **25** 338, 342; **27** 371
collections **10** 326
enamel **27** 426
Faceted Palace **27** 371, 400
fortifications **27** 371
Golden Chamber **27** 385
Granovitaya Palace *see* Faceted Palace
Great Kremlin Palace **27** 377
hardstones **27** 427
icons **25** 338
jewellery **27** 429
lace **27** 430
Meeting Hall **21** 157
metalwork **10** 325
Museum of the Moscow Kremlin **22** 179
Palace of Congresses **1** 126; **27** 380, 410
St Lazarus **27** 370
Senate **17** 869; **27** 374, 375
Sverdlov Hall **27** 403
silver **9** 30; **10** 324, 329
Terem Palace **27** 372, *399*, 400
Tsar Bell **3** 627; **21** 322
Lenin Mausoleum **20** 870, *870*; **27** 379; **29** 529; **31** 132
Lomonosov University **5** 334; **17** 869; **22** *175*; **27** 376, 380, 409, 443; **29** 530
Museum of Fine Art **27** 440
Menshikov Tower *see* ecclesiastical buildings → Church of the Archangel Gabriel
Metro stations **21** 350
monuments **22** *179*
Moscow Arts Society *see* academies and art schools → Moscow School of Painting and Sculpture
Municipal Primary School, Bol'shaya Pirogovskaya Street **6** 529
museums
Aleksey Viktorovich Shchusev State Research and Scientific Museum of Russian Architecture **22** 179; **27** 441; **28** 572
Alexander III Museum of Fine Arts *see* Pushkin Museum of Fine Arts

Moscow
museums—cont.
All-Russian Museum of Decorative, Applied and Folk Art **27** 441
Andrey Rublyov Museum of Ancient Russian Art **22** 179
see also ecclesiastical buildings → Andronikov Monastery
Anna Golubkina Museum **12** 887
Armoury *see under* Kremlin
Ars Asiatica *see* Museum of Oriental Art
Bakhrushin State Central Theatre Museum **27** 439, 440
Central Lenin Museum **22** 173
Central Museum of the Revolution **4** 312; **12** 633
First Museum of Modern Western European Painting **27** 441
see also Museum of Modern Western Art; Pushkin Museum of Fine Art
Historical Museum **5** 276; **22** 173, *173*; **28** 596; **32** 73
collections **6** 284; **22** 178; **27** 406
directors **33** 583
library **4** 312
Museum of Fine Art *see under* Lomonosov University
Museum of Folk Art **27** 441
Museum of Icons and Painting *see* Tret'yakov State Gallery
Museum of Modern Western Art **12** 340; **22** 136; **27** 441
see also First Museum of Modern Western European Painting; Second Museum of Modern Western European Painting; Pushkin Museum of Fine Art
Museum of Oriental Art **12** 633; **27** 441
collections **6** 284; **7** 156; **15** 742, 745; **21** 886; **29** 241; **31** 783
exhibitions **6** 286; **22** 179
Museum of Photographic Art **24** 682
Museum of Private Collections *see under* Pushkin Museum of Fine Art
Museum of the Academy of Building and Architecture **27** 441
Museum of the Moscow Kremlin *see under* Kremlin
Museum of V. Tropinin and the Moscow Artists of his Time **31** 370
Polytechnical Museum **21** 887; **22** 173
Pushkin Museum of Fine Arts **13** 654; **18** 116; **22** 178; **27** 444; **31** 401
archives **2** 371
collections **6** 284; **10** 90; **11** 664; **26** 241; **27** 441; **28** 669
exhibitions **22** 179
Morozov collection **22** 136; **30** 491
Museum of Private Collections **27** 440, 441
see also First Museum of Modern Western European Painting; Museum of Modern Western Art; Second Museum of Modern Western European Painting
Rumyantsev Museum **19** 498; **27** 439, 440, 441
see also Russian State Library
Russian Museum **25** 736

Moscow
museums—cont.
Second Museum of Modern Western European Painting **27** 441
see also Museum of Modern Western Art; Pushkin Museum of Fine Art
State Museum of Icons and Painting *see* Tret'yakov State Gallery
Tolstoy Museum **13** 654
Tret'yakov State Gallery **31** 311–12; **32** 74
Botkin collection **4** 489
Central Asian collection **6** 284
collections **9** 747; **27** 439, 440, 441
Costakis collection **8** 10
directors **15** 891
exhibitions **22** 179
Morozov collection **22** 135
Ostroukhov collection **23** 624
Sidorov collection **28** 669
V. M. Vasnetsov House-Museum **32** 74
Nikitskiye Gates **21** 157
Northern River Terminal **29** 529
Novy Arbat Street **27** 380
palaces **27** 374
Annenhof **26** 7
Faceted Palace *see under* Kremlin
Granovitaya Palace *see* Kremlin → Faceted Palace
Lefort Palace **27** 373, 401
Palace of the Troyekurovs **27** 373
Peter Palace **22** *172*
Petrovsky Palace *see* Peter Palace
Summer Palace *see* Annenhof
Terem Palace *see under* Kremlin
Printing Office (Pechatny dvor) **22** 177
Prospekt Kalinina *see* Novy Arbat Street
Public History Library **25** 342
Russian State Library **3** *433*; **19** 319; **27** 375; **29** 529; **31** 401
see also museums → Rumyantsev Museum
squares
Red Square **27** 376
Theatre Square **27** 376
Victory Square **4** *598*
stations
Kazan Railway Station **18** 750; **28** *571*; **33** 607
Kropotkinskaya station **21** 350
Metro stations **21** 349, 350
Palace of the Soviets station *see* Kropotkinskaya station
theatres **30** 684
Bol'shoy Theatre **13** 654; **27** 464
Central Children's Music Theatre **27** 381
Red Army Theatre **27** 409
Taganka Theatre **27** 381
Upper Trading Rows **27** 376
urban planning **4** 598–9; **9** 73; **16** 790; **27** 379, 380; **31** 715, 723, 730
Utro Rossii Printing House **27** *377*, 378
Vesenkha skyscraper **2** 604
Moscow Art Society **27** 438, 442
Moscow Art Theatre **27** 404; **30** 685
Moscow Bank **28** 570
Moscow City P. M. and S. M. Tret'yakov Art Gallery *see* MOSCOW → museums → Tret'yakov State Gallery
Moscow Fellowship of Artists **33** 607
Moscow Jewellery Works **27** 423
Moscow Painters **22** 178

Moscow Private Russian Opera **28** 757
Moscow Society of Architects **22** 178
Moscow Society of Art Lovers **27** 442
Moscow Union of Artist-Sculptors **30** 491
Moscron, Pieter **4** 161
Moscufo, S Maria del Lago **26** 625
Mose **9** 825
Moseley, H. **24** 826
Moseley, Mrs Henry *see* CHALON, MARIA A.
Moseley, Michael E. **6** 441
Moser (i), George Michael **10** 372; **19** 596; **22** 185*
groups and movements **19** 585
pupils **14** 144; **22** 185
works **5** 611; **10** 332, *332*, 345, 348
Moser (ii), Johann **22** 185
Moser, Johann Michael **2** 816; **27** 665
Moser, Joseph **2** 820; **18** 140
Moser (ii), Karl **22** 185, 186*; **30** 127
collaboration **3** 175
groups and movements **7** 293
pupils **14** 24; **19** 235; **22** 186; **27** 214; **28** 122; **29** 602
staff **27** 657; **29** 531
works **3** 335; **18** 192; **22** *186*; **30** 127, 128; **33** 735
Moser, Kolo(man) **2** 814, 826; **14** 628; **15** 823; **22** 187–8*; **24** 438; **28** 343; **32** 446
drawings **2** 797
furniture **8** 802; **32** 448
glass **2** 818
groups and movements **2** 567, 571; **8** 802; **28** 343, 344, 670; **32** 449; **33** 165–6
interior decoration **14** 785
jewellery **17** 528
metalwork **2** 822; **8** 802; **33** *165*
mother-of-pearl **22** 205
porcelain **2** 817; **32** 450
pottery **2** 816
pupils **11** 320; **14** 25; **18** 490
silver **2** 821
stained glass **11** 320
textiles **2** *826*
Moser (ii), Lorenz **22** 185
Moser, Ludwig **8** 411; **17** 816; **19** 12
Moser, Lukas **13** 187; **22** 188–9*
pupils **1** 120
works **12** 384; **22** *188*; **26** 184
Moser (i), Mary **14** 145; **19** 620; **22** 185*; **33** 308
Moser (ii), Robert **22** 185–6*
Moser (ii), Werner (Max) **7** *294*; **22** 185, 186–7*; **30** 128
collaboration **14** 24; **27** 214; **29** 603
groups and movements **15** 885
works **4** 790; **29** *603*; **30** *128*
Moser, Wilfrid **30** 135
Moser Glassworks **8** 411
Moses, Anna Mary *see* MOSES, GRANDMA
Moses, Ed **19** 492; **33** 45
Moses, Grandma **16** 906; **22** 189*, 441
Moses, Henry **26** 231
works **26** *232*
Moses, (James) Kivetoruk **22** 189–90*
Moses, Robert **10** 183; **23** 43
Moses Khorenatsi'i **12** 154
Mosesyan, A. G. **2** 902
Mosfil'm Studio **16** 793
Mosgiel **23** *52*
Mosgiel Woollen Factory Co. **23** 73
moshavim **17** 854

Moshchevaya Balka **6** 248, 249; **9** 663, 668; **16** 505
kaftans **9** *641*
Moshett, Hubert **13** 876
Moshev, Arkady **27** 434
Moshi **1** *407*
Sanaa Zetu **30** 302
Mo Shih-lung *see* MO SHILONG
Mo Shilong **6** 760, 820; **23** 215; **29** 243; **32** 848
Moshinskaya, Vanda I. **31** 764
Mosini, G. A. *see* MASSANI, GIOVANNI ANTONIO
Mosini, Giovanni Atanasio *see* MASSANI, GIOVANNI ANTONIO
Mosinyi, Keeme **4** 489
Mosjö **26** 647; **30** 83
Mosko, Sokrat (Llaqi) **1** 539; **22** 190*
Mosko Company **3** 63
Moskorzew Church **25** 129
Moskos, Ilias **25** 334
Moskos, Leo **9** 205
Moskov Dol Church **5** 150
Moskovsky khudozhnik **24** 451
Moskovsky yuvelir **27** 425
Moskovtchenko, Michel **19** 848
Moskovy Company **27** 430
Mosley, Catherine **20** 609
Mosman, John **28** 260
Mosman, William **22** 190*; **28** 235
Mośna Church **13** 189
Mosnier, Jacques **22** 190
Mosnier, Jean (*fl* 1600; father) **22** 190
Mosnier, Jean (1600–54; son) **22** 190*
Mosnier, Jean-Laurent **22** 191*
Mosnier, Michel **22** 190
Mosnier, Nicolas **22** 191
Mosnier, Pierre **19** 118; **22** 190–91*; **25** 637
Mosolov, F. S. **27** 439
Mosphilia *see* KISSONERGA-MOSPHILIA
mosques **11** 339; **16** 128, 141, 144, 145, 146, 158, 241–3, 246, 487; **20** 368; **22** 191–6*
historical and regional traditions
Afghanistan **16** 166
Africa **1** 229, *316*, 316–17
Albania **1** 538, *542*
Algeria **16** 190, 217–18
Arabia **16** 229
Bosnia **4** *460*
Bulgaria **5** 148
Caribbean Islands **5** 755
Central Asia, Western **6** 202, 211; **16** 153–4, 159, 166, 236–7
Timurid **30** *918*
China **6** 676–7*
Egypt **5** 401, *404*; **16** *155*, *173*, 173–5, *174*, 209, *210*, *212*
Fulani **1** 317
Greece **2** *672*; **30** 716
Hausa **1** 316
Indian subcontinent **1** *502*; **15** *48*, 207, *344*, *350*, *379*; **16** 239
Bengal **15** *353*
Kerala **15** *359*
Mughal **8** *679*; **15** *361*, *366*
8th cent. AD **15** *307*, 338–40
12th cent. **15** *339*
14th cent. **15** *345*, 351
15th cent. **1** *472*; **15** *348*
18th cent. **15** *379*
Indonesia **15** 757, 768–9
Iran **15** 338; **16** 142, 153–4, *154*, 159, 161–3, *164*, 193–4, 196–7, 198, 234, *234*; **30** *224*
Timurid **30** 919
14th cent. **33** *512*
15th cent. **16** *77*
17th cent. **16** *78*
Iraq **16** 151, *151*, 152, 179–80; **27** 680
Malaysia **20** 165, 166, *166*

mosques
historical and regional traditions—cont.
Mali **1** *316*, 317; **20** 198
Morocco **11** *50*; **16** 190–91, *191*, 217–18, 240, *240*; **22** *128*
Marinid **16** 257
Sa'di **16** 257
Nigeria **1** 316
North Africa **16** 190, 493
Ottoman **16** 142, 228, 257
Arabia **16** 229
Turkey **9** *730*; **16** 205–6, *206*, 221–4, *223*, *224*, 226, 265, 266, 605; **22** *195*
Philippines **24** 611
Qatar **16** *242*
Saudi Arabia **21** 32, *33*; **27** *876*
Singapore **28** 772
South Africa **9** 427; **29** 105
Spain **7** *845*; **16** 157–8, 188
Sudan **1** 284, 316
Syria **8** 479–80, *480*; **16** *148*, 179–80
Tunisia **16** *156*, 156–7, *170*, 219
Turkey **2** 437; **5** *282*; **16** *179*, 183–4, 202, *203*, *206*, 497
Islamic **9** *526*
Ottoman **9** *730*; **16** 205–6, 221–4, *223*, *224*, 226, 265, 266, 605; **22** *195*
16th cent. **28** *766*, *767*, *768*
Uzbekistan **5** *139*
Yemen **16** 177, *178*, *214*
materials
brick **20** 166
concrete **5** 755
domes **16** 130, 161–2, 221, 222–3
mosaics **16** 147
mud **5** 755
mud-bricks **1** 284
stone **20** 166
wood **5** 755; **16** 202, 222; **20** 166
types
Arab-type mosques *see* hypostyle
basilica **16** 183, 202
circular **16** 145
congregational **16** 130, 260, 262, 266
Central Asia, Western **6** 201
Iran **33** 624
Ottoman **16** 221
Turkey **16** 221
courtyard **16** 153–4, 177
domed **16** 213–14; **22** *195*, 195–6*
festival *see musalla*
four-iwan **22** 194–5*
Central Asia, Western **16** 162–3
Indian subcontinent **22** 195
Iran **16** 162–3; **22** 194, *194*
hypostyle **16** 145; **22** 192–4*
Central Asia, Western **16** 159
Iran **16** 159
Ottoman **16** 202
Palestine **22** *193*
Syria **16** 146–8
Turkey **16** 183, 202
'idgāhs **15** 340, 343; **22** 353
see also musalla
kiosk-mosque **16** 162
multi-unit **16** 205
musalla **16** 152, 163; **22** 353–4*
see also 'idgāhs
namāzgāh see musalla
single-domed square **16** 183, 202, 205
single-unit **16** 222
T-plan **16** 205–6, 240, 810
see also KÜLLIYE; MADRASAS
moss **32** 286
Moss, Boniface **9** 55; **20** 489
moss agate *see under* AGATE → types
Mössbauer spectroscopy *see under* TECHNICAL EXAMINATION → types
Mosscher, Jacob van **23** 611, 613
Mosse, Bartholomew **33** 95
Mosse, Dr **16** 26
Mosselman, Paul **17** 457
Mosset, Olivier **5** 193; **11** 552, 553; **21** 892; **30** 135
Mossi **1** 383; **5** 216; **22** 196–9*
brass **5** 217, *217*; **22** 197
dolls **22** 198*, *198*; **31** 259
figurines **1** 273
masks **1** 290, 334, *384*; **5** 217; **22** 196–7*, *197*
sculpture **1** 383; **22** *197*, 197–8*
textiles **22** 199*
tools **1** *364*
wood **1** *384*; **22** *197*, 198, *198*
wood-carvings **1** 291; **22** 197, 198–9*
Mossman, John **28** 242
Mössmer, Josef **4** 838; **10** 702; **12** 185
Mossop, William **22** 199*
Mossop, William Stephen **22** 199*
Most **8** 407, 422
Church of the Assumption **8** 377; **13** 58; **32** 821
Mostaert, Frans **22** 199; **29** 428
Mostaert, Gillis **3** 554; **22** 199, 201*
collaboration **4** 912; **7** 428; **8** 464
patrons and collectors **3** 613; **28** 358
pupils **7** 710
reproductive prints by others **33** 169
teachers **4** 839; **20** 249
works **11** 442
Mostaert, Jan (Jansz.) **3** 554; **12** 233; **22** 199–201*
attributions **12** 232; **16** 69; **20** 637
patrons and collectors **13** 905
works **11** 441; **22** *200*, 835
Mostaert, Nicolas **32** 674
Mostafa, Ahmed Youssef **12** 767
Mostar **4** *459*, 462
architecture **4** 460
bridge **4** 801; **16** 228
cemetery **4** 462
Orthodox church **25** 340
Vučjaković Mosque **4** 460; **16** 222
Mosti, Ippolito **6** 141
Mosto, Cosimo da **3** 351
Mosto, Ottavio **8** 385
Mostyn, Augusta **32** 791
Mostyn ewer and basin **3** 597; **29** 747
Mostyn Salt **10** 326
Mosui *see* KARAKHOTO
Mosul **16** *104*, 379; **22** 202*
architecture **16** 182; **32** 314
craftsmen and artists **16** 380
education (art) **16** 2
fortifications **21** 588
houses **16** 269, 270
madrasas **20** 55
manuscripts **9** 620; **16** *114*, 307, 308, 516
markets **16** 261
mausoleum of Imam 'Awn al-Din **16** 381
metalwork **16** 367, 379, 380
miniatures (manuscript illumination) **16** *308*
mosques
al-'Amadiyya Mosque **3** 894; **16** 491
Nabi Jirjis **16** 491
Nur al-Din Zangi **16** 179
Shaykh 'Abbas Mosque **16** 228
Mosul Museum **21** 310
palace of Badr al-Din Lu'lu' **16** 182
printing **16** 361
shrine of Imam 'Awn al-Din **16** 181; **22** 322
Mosul—cont.
shrine of Imam Yahya ibn al-Qasim **16** 181
shrines (i) (cult) **28** 634
textiles **16** 430, 443
urban planning **16** 261
Mosul school **9** 621
Mosvik **13** 119, 121
sculpture **13** *121*
Mosyn, Michiel **9** 742
Moszyński, August Fryderyk **22** 202*; **25** 140, 142; **32** 879
Mota **12** 891
Mota, António Augusto da Costa *see* COSTA MOTA, ANTÓNIO AUGUSTO DA
Mota, La, Castle *see under* MEDINA DEL CAMPO
Motamedi, N. **33** 688
Motau, Julian **29** 109, 110
Mota Udai Singh, Raja **15** *580*
Mote, Yvonnet de La *see* LA MOTE, YVONNET DE
Motecuhzoma II (*reg* 1502–20) **12** 71; **21** 191, 250, 255, 264; **23** 825
motels *see* HOTELS
Mote of Urr **28** 224
Motesiczky, Marie-Louise (von) **22** 202–3*
Mothe, Jean-Baptiste-Michel Vallen de la *see* VALLEN DE LA MOTTE, JEAN-BAPTISTE-MICHEL
Mothebe, Rantefe **4** 489
Mothe-Fénelon, François de Salignac de La *see* FÉNELON, FRANÇOIS DE SALIGNAC DE LA MOTHE-
Mothe le Vayer, François de La *see* LA MOTHE LE VAYER, FRANÇOIS DE
mother-of-pearl **22** 203–5*
historical and regional traditions
Austria **22** *204*
Aztec **22** 164
Burma **20** 327
China **7** 14, 15–16, *16*, 17–18, 19–20, 101; **18** *601*, 603, *612*; **21** 715
England **10** 288; **24** *62*
France **4** *601*; **11** 632; **28** I2
Germany **12** 424, *425*, 450
Indian subcontinent **6** 556
Islamic **9** 160; **16** 256, 499, 500
Italy **16** *728*
Japan **17** 277, 298, 299, 300, *300*, 398; **18** 603, *613*
Korea **18** 370, *370*, *371*, *602*, 603
Mesoamerica, Pre-Columbian **21** 251; **22** 158, 164, 205
Ottoman **9** 160; **16** 499
Pacific Islands **23** 720; **28** II2
Parthian **24** 218
Peru **33** *332*
Russia **27** *423*
Ryūkyū Islands **27** 471, *471*
Solomon Islands **28** II2
South-east Asia **22** 205
Thailand **30** 636*, *636*
Vietnam **32** 482, 487, 488*, 489
Yemen **16** 500
techniques
carving **22** 203–4
uses
body ornaments **23** 720
boxes **4** *601*; **18** *602*; **28** I2
cabinets (ii) (furniture) **16** *728*
canoes **28** 611
chains **12** 450
chess sets **6** 556
commodes **12** 424, *425*
doors **9** 160
inlays **7** 15–16, *16*, 17–18, 19–20, 101; **10** 288; **16** 499, 500; **18** *612*, *613*; **24** 218; **30** 636*, *636*; **32** 488
jewellery **32** 487
mother-of-pearl
uses—cont.
lacquer **7** 15–16, 17–18, 19–20; **17** 298, 299, *300*; **18** *369*, 370, *370*, *371*, 603–4, 609; **27** 471, *471*; **32** 482
marquetry **12** 424, *425*; **20** 466; **22** 205; **33** *332*
masks **21** 251
mirrors **7** 14; **21** 715
mosaics **16** 256; **22** 154, 158, 164
musical instruments **7** 14; **32** 489
netsuke **17** 398
papier mâché **22** 205; **24** 61
pendants (jewellery) **27** *423*
prints **17** 277
saddles **17** 300
screens (ii) (furniture) **18** *601*
shields **28** II2
snuff-boxes **11** 632
standishes **29** 535
statuettes **10** *267*
tabernacles (ii) (receptacle) **22** *204*
trays **24** *62*
writing **20** 327
see also SHELLS
Motheron, Alexandre **31** 227
Motheron, Sébastien **31** 227
Motherwell, Robert **4** 27; **11** 729; **22** 205–7*; **23** 48
collaboration **20** 605, 606, 607
dealers **16** 906; **18** 162
groups and movements **1** 78; **4** 109; **29** 534; **30** 22; **31** 607
patrons and collectors **9** 189; **13** 801; **26** 489; **27** 225, 277
studio **6** 476
works **4** 75; **7** 557; **11** 499; **19** 493, *493*; **21** 897; **22** *206*; **25** 619; **28** 52
Mothes, O.
works **12** *415*
motifs **15** 94
Moti Jheel Congregational mosque **15** 379
Motilone **7** 602
Motjuoadi, Andrew (Tshidiso) **29** 109, 110
works **29** *109*
Motley, Archibald **1** 442; **6** 576
Motohiko Itō *see* ITŌ, MOTOHIKO
Motohira, Fujiwara no *see* FUJIWARA NO MOTOHIRA
Motokiyo Zeami **17** 22, 325, 367, 395
Motolinia, Father *see* BENAVENTE, TORIBIO DE
Motomitsu, Fujiwara no *see* FUJIWARA NO MOTOMITSU
Motonaga, Sadamasa **13** 866; **17** 207
Motonubu Kanō *see* KANŌ MOTONUBU
motorbikes **15** *826*
motor-cars *see* CARS
motors (electric) **7** 766, 767
Motoška, Miroslav **28** 855
Mototaka Jinyōin *see* JINYŌIN MOTOTAKA
Mototoshi no Fujiwara *see* FUJIWARA NO MOTOTOSHI
Motouji Ashikaga *see* ASHIKAGA MOTOUJI
Motovilov, Georgy **25** 170
Motoyashiki **21** 651; **27** 873
Motraye, Aubrey de la **32** 378
Motrico **29** 272
Motschmann, Charles **31** 262
Motsurin *see* SHŌTŌ BOKUSAI
Motsusi, Mpho **19** 242
Motswai, Tommy **29** 110
Mott, Hay & Anderson **4** 800
Motta **27** 788
Motta, Camillo **11** 42
Motta, Fabrizio Carini *see* CARINI MOTTA, FABRIZIO
Motta, Flavio **21** 123
Motta, Raffaello *see* REGGIO, RAFFAELLINO DA
Mottahedah & Co. **26** 227
Motte, Antoine Houdard de la *see* HOUDARD DE LA MOTTE, ANTOINE
Motte, Charles-Etienne **8** 828; **13** 252; **20** 602
Motte, Jean-Baptiste-Michel Vallen de la *see* VALLEN DE LA MOTTE, JEAN-BAPTISTE-MICHEL DE LA
Motte, Yvonnet de la *see* YVONNET DE LA MOTTE
motte-and-bailey castles *see under* CASTLES → types
mottes **3** 427; **21** 547, 550, 562–3
Mottez, Louis **22** 207
Mottez, Victor (-Louis) **19** 381; **22** 207–8*, 329
Mottis, Cristoforo de **22** 31
Mottley, John **2** 151
Mottram, Charles **22** 208*
Motul **5** 412
Motya **25** 732; **28** 655
houses **25** 732
mosaics **13** 562
sculpture **25** 733
town walls **25** 733
Motya Charioteer **28** 654
Motzfelt, Benny **23** 236
El Mouassat **9** 570
Mouat **28** 270
Moubray, Robert **9** 727; **28** 252
Moubray, Rowan & Hicks **2** 758
Mouchel, Bon Du *see* DU MOUCHEL, BON
Moucheron, Frederik de **17** 666; **22** 208*
collaboration **28** 74; **32** 145
copies **3** 873
pupils **22** 208
teachers **2** 615; **9** 463
Moucheron, Isaac de **22** 208–9*
collaboration **32** 259; **33** 262
groups and movements **9** 462
patrons and collectors **19** 735
reproductive prints by others **12** 515
works **14** 295; **22** *209*, 847
Moucheron, Pierre de **9** *275*
Mouchette, Mme **29** 243
mouchettes *see under* TRACERY → types
Mouchy, Louis-Philippe **8** 791; **11** 561; **22** 210*; **24** 787
Moudarres, Fateh **22** 210*
works **30** 177, *178*
Moudon, St Etienne **21** 725
Moufarrege, Nicolas **12** 218
Mouflart, François **4** 391
Mouflon wool *see under* WOOL → types
Mouhot, Henri **2** 56; **5** 460
Mou I *see* MOU YI
Mouilleron, Adolphe **1** 650; **14** 116; **26** 232
works **26** *233*
Mouka *see* MUTISO, DAVID
Moukhtar, Mahmoud *see* MUKHTAR, MAHMUD
Moulaloukou **11** 879
Moulay Idris **15** 103
Mould, Jacob Wrey **19** 386; **22** 60, 210–11*; **23** 40; **32** 95
moulded piers *see under* PIERS (ii) (MASONRY) → types
moulding
historical and regional traditions
China **6** 882, 883, 888, 893
Egypt **16** *403*, 403, 415
Islamic **16** 394, *403*, 403, 415
Japan **17** 403
Rome, ancient **12** 783; **27** 17–18*
Syria **16** 415
Turkey **4** 771

moulding—cont.
types
open moulding **21** 320
piece moulding **21** 321
two-piece moulding **21** 320–21
uses
adobe **4** 767
brick **4** 767, *768*, 771; **6** 882
bronze **4** 852; **6** 830–32, *831*, 838–9; **17** 101, 319
ceramics **6** 327–8, *327*, 336
coins **32** 486
earthenwares **6** 888
figurines **6** 887; **13** 578
forgeries **15** 750
glass **12** 782, 783*, *783*; **31** 643
Ancient Near East **1** 865
Egypt, ancient **10** 56, 57
England **10** 320, 321
Greece, ancient **13** 594
Islamic **16** 517
inksticks **7** 92
iron **7** 97, 98
jewellery **15** 423
lacquer **18** 606–7*
leather **19** *2*, 2*
medals **20** 917
metal **21** 320
metalwork **9** 818
paper **17** 403
pewter **24** 578
porcelain **6** *895*, 895
pottery **1** 285; **6** 333, 874, 883, 889; **10** 303; **16** 394, *403*, 403, 415; **31** 636
presses **12** 783
printing plates **17** 270
relief sculpture **6** 218
sculpture **1** 198; **6** 298; **27** 17–18*
stonewares **6** 893, 899
stucco **29** 813, 825
terracotta **6** 275
tiles **6** 772
vases **13** 480
waxes **33** 2
mouldings **22** 211–22*, *212*, *213*, *214*; **23** 477
historical and regional traditions
Anglo-Saxon **2** 67
Austria **22** 211, 217
Cistercian Order **22** 214, 216, 217, 218, 220, 222
Czech Republic **22** 216, 217, 219, 220, 221, 222
England **22** 211, 213–22
France **22** 211, 215, 216–22
Germany **22** 211, 219, 220, 221, 222
Gothic **22** 211, 213–15, 216–22*
Decorated style **22** 215, 219, 220, 221
Flamboyant style **22** 215, 219, 220, 221
Perpendicular style **22** 219, 220, 221, 222
Rayonnant style **22** 217, 219, 220, 221, 222
Sondergotik **22** 219
Greece, ancient **13** 389, 391–2*, *392*, 393, *393*, 394, 399; **20** 912; **22** 211
Indian subcontinent **15** *241*, 312, 317, 326
Iraq **16** 182
Ireland **22** 217
Islamic **15** *241*; **16** 182
Italy **22** 216, 219, 221
Mesoamerica, Pre-Columbian **21** 206
Netherlands, the **22** 219, 220, 221
Baroque **23** *542*
Norway **22** 217
Poland **22** 211
Romanesque **22** 211, 213–16*, 218, 220; **26** 569
Rome, ancient **22** 211, 215
Scotland **22** 216
mouldings
historical and regional traditions—cont.
Spain **22** 216, 217, 218, 219, 221
Syria **16** 182
materials
brick **4** 769
papier mâché **24** 62
templates **28** 497
zinc **22** 211
types
angle **22** 213
angle-fillet **22** 213*, *214*, 216, 218, 220, 222
see also chamfered mitre; spiked hollow
angle roll **22** 213*, *213*, 215, 216, 217–18
astragal **3** 439; **13** 392
Attic **22** *213*, 216, 218, 221
axial **22** 213, 215, 216, 217, 218, 220
bead **22** 213*, *213*, *214*, 221
bead and reel **3** 439*, *439*; **13** 392, *393*
beak **22** 213*, *214*, 216, 217, 218
see also beaked roll
beaked half roll *see* beak
beaked ogee keel **22** 213, *214*, 217
beaked roll **22** 213*, *214*, 217
beaked roll-and-fillet **22** 213, *214*, 215
bell **22** *213*, 222
bowtell *see* bead; roll
cable *see* ROPEWORK
casement **22** 213*, *214*, 221
see also wave
cavetto *see* hollow chamfer
chamfer **22** 211, 213*, *213*, 214, *214*, 215, 216, 220–21, 222
see also chamfered mitre; hollow chamfer; sunk chamfer
chamfered mitre **22** 213*, *214*, 220, 221
channelled roll *see* grooved roll
chisel-nosed *see* angle-fillet
coarse keel mould **22** 215
concave mouldings *see* hollow mouldings
convex lip **22** 213
cupid's bow **22** 214
cyma **8** 324*
cyma recta **8** 324; **22** *213*, 218; **23** 478, 479, 480
Greece, ancient **13** 392, *393*
cyma reversa **8** 324; **10** 431; **13** 392, *393*
demi-roll-and-fillet **22** *214*, 215, 220
double hollow base **22** *213*, 216
double ogee **22** 214*, *214*, 219, 220
see also ogee
double roll **22** *214*
edge roll *see* angle roll
egg and dart **9** 757*; **23** 478
Greece, ancient **8** 869; **9** 757, *757*; **13** 392, *392*, 393, *393*
Rome, ancient **9** 757
Turkey **8** 869
egg and tongue *see* egg and dart
face roll **22** 214*, 216
fillet **11** 80*; **22** 214*, *214*, 215, 217, 218, 219, 220, 221; **23** 478
England **10** 278
Greece, ancient **13** 377, 392, *393*
see also angle-fillet
filleted roll *see* roll-and-fillet
fillet moulding *see* roll-and-fillet
free-standing fillet **22** 214*
grooved roll **22** 214*, *214*, 217
half pear **22** 215
half-roll **22** 214
half roll-and-fillet *see* quadrant
mouldings
types—cont.
hawksbeak **13** 392, 393
hollow **9** 70; **22** 213, *213*, 214*, *214*, 217, 218, 221
hollow and bead **22** 218
hollow and roll **22** 221
hollow chamfer **9** 825; **22** *213*, 214*, *214*, 216, 220–21
hollow quirk
hollow roll **22** 214*
hood **22** 218
hook *see* beak
horn *see* beak
keel **22** 214*, *214*, 216–17, 218, 219
keeled roll *see* keel
lateral **22** 213, 217, 218
leaf and dart **13** 392, *392*, 393, *393*
Lesbian cymatium *see* cyma recta
little bowtell *see* bead
nib *see* ogee keel
ogee **8** 324; **22** 214*, *214*, 215, 220, 221; **23** 368
ogee casement *see* wave
ogee keel **22** 214*, *214*, 215, 216, 217, 218, 219*
see also beaked roll; pear
ovolo **13** 392; **23** 683*
see also quadrant
peaked *see* beak
pear **22** 215*
plain chamfer *see* chamfer
pointed *see* keel
pointed bowtell *see* keel
polygonal termination *see* chamfered mitre
quadrant **22** 211, *214*, 215*
see also ovolo
quarter-round moulding *see* quadrant
quirk **22** *213*, 215*, 216
quirked roll *see* angle roll
roll **22** 213, *213*, 214, *214*, 215–16*, 217, 218, 220; **26** 558
see also angle roll; bead; beaked roll; face roll; grooved roll; keel; pear; scroll; soffit roll
roll-and-fillet **22** 214, *214*, 215*, 216, 217, 218, 219*, 220, 221
see also pear; quadrant
roll-and-triple-fillet **22** 215
rounded ogee keel **22** 215
scroll **22** *214*, 215*, 222
semicircular hollow **22** 214*, *214*, 217, 221
sharp fillet *see* keel
side-filleted **22** 215
soffit **22** 213, 215, 217, 218, 220
soffit roll **22** 215*, 216, 218
spiked hollow **22** *214*, 215*, 221
sunk chamfer **22** 211, *214*, 215*
sunken semi-circle *see* semicircular hollow
three-quarter hollow **22** 214*, *214*, 221
tongue-shaped member **22** 213
torus **22** 215; **31** 196*
triple roll **22** *213*, *214*, 218, 221
water-holding **22** *213*, 218
wave **22** 211, *214*, 215*, 220
see also casement
uses
abaci (capitals) **22** 213, *213*
Early Gothic **22** 218
Late Gothic **22** 220, 222
Romanesque **22** 216
arcades **22** 215, 218
arches **22** 212, *212*, 213, *213*, 214, 215, 216, 217, 218, 219, 220, 222
architecture **16** 182
bases **22** 213, *213*, 214, 215, 216, 218–19, 221–2
capitals **22** *213*, 215, 216, 218–19, 221–2
mouldings
uses—cont.
dating methods **22** 212
frames **24** 4
glass **31** *643*
mullions **22** 213, *213*, 219, 220, 221
piers (ii) (masonry) **22** 214, 216, 217, 218, 219, 220, 221
portals **22** 216, 219, 222
ribs **22** 211, 212, 213, *213*, 214, 215, 216, 217, 218*, 219, 220, 221
tracery **22** 220
vaults (ceiling) **22** 217, 218, 221
window-frames **22** 221
windows **22** 216
mouldings combs **22** 212
moulds **6** 7–8*
historical and regional traditions
Afghanistan **1** 198; **29** 825
Africa **1** 285
Ancient Near East **1** 865
Buddhism **1** 198; **6** 298, *298*
Central Asia, Eastern **6** 298, *298*
Central Asia, Western **6** 218, 275
China **6** 887; **7** 97, 98; **21** 320
Han period (206 BC–AD 220) **6** 874
Shang period (*c.* 1600–*c.* 1050 BC) **6** 830–32, *831*, 838–9
Song period (AD 960–1279) **6** *895*, 895
Tang period (AD 618–907) **6** 889; **7** 92
Yuan period (1279–1368) **6** 899
Zhou period (*c.* 1050–256 BC) **6** *833*; **14** *800*
Cyprus, ancient **8** 340
Egypt, ancient **9** 818; **10** 56, 57
England **10** 303, 306
Greece, ancient **13** 480, 539, 578, 594
Indian subcontinent **15** 423, 750; **29** 825
Islamic **16** 352, 517
Japan **17** 101, 270, 319
Khwarazm **6** 218
Mesopotamia **1** 865
Prehistoric art **25** 530
Punic **25** 733, 734
Rome, ancient **27** 17, 18
Spain **19** *2*; **25** 734
Syria-Palestine **30** *195*
Vietnam **32** 486
materials
alabaster (gypsum) **6** 327
cast iron **7** 97; **21** 320
clay **6** 7, 327, 832–3, *833*; **7** 98; **21** 320; **27** 17
copper **7** 92
fibreglass **11** 55
gelatin **6** 7; **21** 321
latex **6** 7
plaster **6** *8*, 327, *327*; **21** 321; **27** 17; **33** 2
plaster of Paris **6** 7; **10** 306
rubber **21** 321
sand **21** 320
soapstone **30** *195*
stone **25** 530
talc **25** 530
terracotta **6** *298*; **25** 734
waxes **6** 7
wood **7** 92
uses
conservation **6** 336
paper **16** 352
Moulijn, S. **6** 378
Moulin, Denis du *see* DENIS DU MOULIN
Moulin, Joel **25** 638
Moulin, Pierre **11** 596
Moulin, Raymonde **28** 926
Moulinier, Marie **11** 644
Moulin-Joli, Le *see* LE MOULIN-JOLI
Moulins **8** 286, 287; **11** 531
Lycée, tomb of Henri, Duc de Montmorency **2** *91*
Musée de Moulins **4** 545
Pavillon d'Anne *see* Musée de Moulins
Sacré-Coeur **11** 521; **13** 203
Moulins, Francis Du *see* DU MOULINS, FRANCIS
Moulins, Guiart des *see* GUIART DES MOULINS
Moulins, Master of **3** 554; **14** 502; **20** 731–4*; **25** 570
patrons and collectors **2** 840; **4** 242, 544, 546; **23** 355; **31** 845, 846
works **11** 531; **20** *731*, *733*; **31** 344
Moulins, Regnault de *see* REGNAULT DE MOULINS
Moulins Triptych **20** *731*, 731–2; **31** 344
Moulmein **5** *221*, 256, 261
Moulthrop, Reuben **22** 222*
mounds
Indonesia **15** 754
Mali **21** 478
Middle Niger cultures **21** 478*
Native North Americans **14** 746; **22** 572, 671–2
Olmec **23** 417
South America, Pre-Columbian **29** 139
United States of America **22** 572, 671–2
mounds, burial *see* BURIAL MOUNDS
mounds, reliquary *see* STUPAS
Moundville (AL) **10** *656*; **22** 560; **30** 449
Mount, Henry **22** 223
Mount, Nicholas **2** 763, 764
Mount, William Sidney **22** 222–4*; **31** 602
patrons and collectors **12** 645; **26** 75; **29** 870
works **12** 294; **22** *223*; **31** 602
Mt Abu **15** *279*; **22** 224–5*
Dilwara **9** 86; **15** 490; **22** 224–5*
Adinatha Temple **15** 314
Luna Vasahi Temple **15** *313*, 314
Vimala Vasahi Temple **15** 314
sculpture **15** 414, 485
temples **16** 869; **20** 570; **24** 102
Mt Admirable *see* SAMANDAĞI
Mt Allan **1** 64
Mt Atago **17** 387
Mt Athos **7** 228; **8** 157; **9** *511*, 524; **22** 225–9*
architecture **9** 561; **22** 226–7*
Chilandar Monastery **9** 552, 627; **28** 440, 447, 448
chapel of St Tryphon **25** 340
icons **9** 601, 628, 629; **25** 340; **28** 450
katholikon **9** 526
liturgical furnishings **28** 458
manuscript illumination **28** 449, *449*
metalwork **28** 455
screens (i) (architectural) **9** 601
textiles **28** 458
vestments (ecclesiastical) **28** 457
wall paintings **25** 344; **28** 446
Church of the Protaton **9** 584; **25** 334
doors **9** *600*
icons **9** 628; **25** 333
screens (i) (architectural) **9** 600
wall paintings **9** *584*
collections **9** 523, 622
Dionysiou Monastery **7** 222; **22** *226*
icons **25** 333
manuscripts **9** 622
reliquaries **26** 149
wall paintings **25** 335

Mt Athos—cont.
Esphigmenou Monastery **9** 630; **15** 77; **28** 450
fortifications **9** 556
Great Lavra Monastery **21** 834; **32** 94
chapel of Hagios Nikolaos **25** 335
icons **9** 623, 628, 629, 630
katholikon **9** 546, 547
Koukouzelissa Chapel **25** 336
manuscripts **9** 658
parekklesia **24** 110
plaques **9** 593
refectory **21** 844
wall paintings **25** 335, *335*
icons **9** 623, 625, 627, 628; **22** 228*
Iviron Monastery **9** 546, 547; **12** 320, 331
icons **9** 628; **25** 333
Koutloumousiou Monastery **25** 335
manuscript illumination **22** 228*
mosaics **22** 227*
Pantokrator Monastery **25** 333; **28** 457
Pavlos Monastery **25** 335
Philotheou Monastery **25** 335
sculpture **22** 228–9*
Stavronikita Monastery **9** 630; **10** 437; **25** 333
Vatopedi Monastery **9** 546, 547, 556
chapel of Hagios Demetrios **25** 336
icons **9** 628, 629, 630, *630*
manuscripts **4** 4, *4*
metalwork **28** 455
refectory **22** *227*
wall paintings **25** 335
wall paintings **22** 227–8*; **25** 331, 333
Xenophontos Monastery **7** 222; **25** 335
Mt Athos painters' guide **8** 910; **32** 804
Mt Bao **6** 700
Song Liu ling **6** 700
Mt Baoding **6** 717, 718–19, 723
Mt Baohua, Huiju Temple
altar **5** *112*
Mt Bei **6** 716, 718
Mt Cameron West **1** *37*, 41; **22** 229*
Mt Carmel **30** 191
Mt Deo Ngang **6** 426
Mt Dongting, Zijin Temple **6** 718
Mt Ebal **16** 572
Mt Elgon **1** 408
Mt Fang, Yunju Temple **23** 773
Mt Fubo *see under* GUILIN
Mt Fuji **17** *11*; **22** 230–31*, *231*; **28** 638
Mt Garizim, Church of the Theotokos **7** 255; **20** 520; **26** 574
Mt Girnar **15** 314
Amera Mata **15** 349
Mt Grace Priory **21** 840, 841, *841*
Mt Grenfell **1** *37*; **22** 231–2*
Mt Gu, Yongquan Temple **11** 870
Mt Guh, Church of Abune Yem'ata **10** 570
Mt Hamilton (CA), Lick Observatory **23** 341, 342
Mt Heng
Beiyue miao **6** 724
Nanyue miao **6** 724
Temple of the Northern Peak *see* Beiyue miao
Temple of the Southern Peak *see* Nanyue miao
Mt Hiei *see* ŌTSU → Enryakuji
Mt Holly (NJ), Historic Burlington County Prison Museum **21** 616
Mt Hua **6** 724
Cuiyun guan **6** 673
Mt Hua—cont.
temples **6** 673
Yuchuan yuan **6** 673
Yuntai guan **6** 673
Yunü Shrine **6** 673
Mt Hymettos **13** 387; **29** 702
Mt Iouktas **1** 691
Mt Irvine, Museum of Tobago History **31** 339
Mt Izla *see* ṬUR 'ABDIN
Mt Ještěd **8** 381
Mt Kishidake **17** 243
Mt Kongwang (Lianyungang) **5** 107; **6** 707
Mt Kosara **4** 462
Mt Kōya *see* KONGŌBUJI
Mt Kynthos **8** *304*, 310
Mt Lazaros **9** 554
Mt Longhu **6** 673
Shangqing guan **6** 673
Tianshi Mansion **6** 673
Mt Lu **12** 93
Cao tang **12** 87
Mt Madi (Minle) **6** 708; **30** 443
Mt Maiji **6** *615*, 710, 711; **22** 239*; **23** 550; **28** *719*, 720; **30** 443
caves **6** 777
Mt Masius *see* ṬUR 'ABDIN
Mt Mug *see* KALA-I MUG
Mt Nam **18** 250, 288
sculpture **18** *283*
Mt Nebo Chapel **9** 542
Mt Odae
Sangwŏn Temple **3** 626; **18** 347
Wŏlchong Temple **18** 329
Mt Olympos **7** 228
Mt Otowa **17** 250
Mt Palomar Observatory (CA) **23** 342
Mt Penteli, Rododafni **13** 349
Mt Pentelikon **26** *876*; **27** 13
marble **2** 157; **13** 387; **26** 855, 875, 876; **27** 826; **29** 702
see also under MARBLE → types
Mt Qingcheng **6** 540, 674
Changdao guan **6** 674
Mt Qoror, Beta Maryam **10** 568, 576
Mt Rushmore National Memorial **22** 49
Mt Shangfang, Yunti Temple **6** 721
Mt She *see under* NANJING
Mt Shichong *see under* JIANCHUAN
Mt Shisun *see under* QIONGLAI
Mt Shoan Church **27** 432
Mt Sinai **8** 157
manuscripts **9** 619
Monastery of St Catherine **7** *819*, 823; **9** *507*, 524, 538, 539, 540, 554, 615; **12** 331; **21** 834; **23** *505*; **28** 760, 761–2*, *761*; **33** 49
collections **9** 622
doors **9** 599, 600
icons **7** 823, 824; **8** 212; **9** 3, 4, 623–4, *624*, 625, *625*, 626, *626*, 627, 628, 629; **12** 625; **18** 824, *825*; **25** 183, 333, 334; **28** *762*, 762–3*, *763*
Katholikon **9** 574, *574*
manuscripts **9** 620; **28** *764*, 764–5
mosaics **22** 162
Moses Cross **8** 199
paintings **17** 505, 506
roof **30** 903, 905
templon **28** 291
tie-bars **9** 599
see also SINAI
Mt Song **8** 712
Chuzu an **6** 654
Fawang Temple **6** 668
Shaolin Temple **6** 669; **8** 713; **23** 773
pagoda **23** *774*
Patriarch's Hall **6** 669
Songyue Temple **4** 794; **6** 649, *650*, 668
Mt Song—cont.
stupa **29** 868
temples **5** 108
Zhongyue miao **6** 673, 724; **7** 99
Main Hall **6** 673
Sanshen Hall **6** 674
sculpture **6** *724*
Mt Stuart **2** 5; **28** 230
Mt Tai **30** 443
altars **1** 702
Dongyue miao **6** 724
sculpture **6** 724
Temple of the Eastern Peak *see* Dongyue miao
Temple of the Jade Emperor **6** 673
temples **6** 673
Mt Takao **17** 387
Mt Tepsey **28** 325
Mt Tianlong **6** 714; **7** 161; **22** 239–40*; **30** 443
Cave 2 **7** 34
Cave 13 **6** 714
Cave 17 **6** 714
sculpture **6** *714*
cave temple **23** 214
Mt Tiantai
Guoqing Temple **6** 669, *670*
Maitreya Hall **6** 670
Precious Hall of the Great Hero **6** 670
Yuhua Hall **6** 670
Mt Tianti **30** 443
Mt Tuo **6** 712
Mt Ushida **18** 499
Mt Vernon (VA) **12** 136; **29** 842
Pope-Leighey House **33** *405*
Small Dining-Room **29** *842*
Mt Wanshou **12** 89
Mt Washington Glass Works **5** 583; **22** 240*; **31** 644
Mt Wenshu (Jiuquan) **6** 708; **17** 594; **30** 443
temple **5** 108
wall paintings **6** 778
Mt Wilson (CA) Observatory **23** 342
Mt Wudang
Golden Hall **6** 645, 673
Nanyai gong **6** 673
temples **6** 673
Zixiao gong **6** 673
Mt Wutai **6** *615*; **22** 240, 241*; **30** 443
Foguang Temple **6** *652*, 653, 656, 667, 715, 716; **9** 162; **14** 78; **22** 241; **23** 773; **30** 443
brackets **4** 623
Buddha Hall **6** 668
Main Hall **14** 78
Manjushri Hall **6** 643, 719
roof **30** 913
wall paintings **6** 778
Great Xiantong Temple **6** 645
Nanchan Temple **6** 652, 668
pagodas **23** 773
sculpture **6** 715
Tayuan Temple **29** 868
Temple of Nanchan **1** 702
Xuantong Temple **6** 661
Mt Xi *see under* GUILIN
Mt Xiangtang **6** 711–12; **30** 443
Cave 5 **6** 712
Cave 7 **6** 712
cave temple **23** 214
Mt Xiaoshi *see* MT SONG
Mt Xiaotang **28** 637
Mt Xumi **6** 712
Mt Yen Tu Monastery **32** 473
Mt Zheng *see under* DANLENG, MT ZHENG
Mt Zhonglong
sculpture **6** *716*
Mt Zijin *see under* NANJING
Mountain, Charles **14** 862, 863
mountain blue *see under* PIGMENTS → types
mountain green *see* MALACHITE
mountain jade *see under* JADE → types
Mountain mahogany *see* OBSIDIAN
Mountain people **22** 546
mountains, artificial *see* ARTIFICIAL MOUNTAINS
Mountainville (NY), Storm King Art Center **28** 315, 820
Mountbatten, George Louis Victor Henry Serge, 2nd Marquess of Milford Haven **10** 487
Mountbatten, Louis, Earl Mountbatten **17** 600
Mountbatten, Philip, Duke of Edinburgh *see* PHILIP, Prince, Duke of Edinburgh
mount board *see under* BOARDS
Mountenay, Edward **14** 857
Mountford, C. P. **1** 66, 67, 68; **20** 419
Mountford, E(dward) W(illiam) **22** 229–30*
collaboration **25** 187
groups and movements **3** 269
works **10** 239; **18** 890; **29** 843; **31** 240
Mountford, Thomas **29** 419
Mountfort, Benjamin Woolfield **22** 230*
staff **28** 326
works **7** 210; **23** 53, 54
mounting *see* MOUNTS
Mountjoy, Joseph B. **2** 904
Mountmarin **12** 70
Mountmellick embroidery *see under* EMBROIDERY → types
mounts **22** 232*
mounts (furniture) **11** *589*, 590
mounts (guns) **2** *460*
mounts (icons) **9** 622, 625
mounts (porcelain) **9** 28, 29
mounts (works on paper and scrolls) **22** 232–8*, *238*
historical and regional traditions
Buddhism **22** *233*
China **1** 580; **22** 233–4*
Indian subcontinent **22** 235–6*
Islamic **22** *235*, 235–6*
Japan **17** 209–10, 347; **22** *233*, 234*
Korea **22** 234
Ottoman **22** *235*
Tibet **22** 234*, *234*
Italy **22** *237*
materials
canvas **22** 236
cardboard **22** 233, 236
hinges **22** 238
paper **22** 234
silk **22** 233, 234
uses
calligraphy **1** 580
drawings **9** 26, 232–3; **22** 236
painting **1** 580; **22** *234*
photography **24** 674
prints **9** 26
scrolls **22** 233, *233*, 234
Mounts, Paul **18** 639
Mounychia **24** 327–8
Mour, Jean-Baptiste van **16** 536; **23** 503
Moura, Cristóbal de **30** 518
Moura Manuel, Manuel de, Bishop of Miranda do Douro **18** 782
Moura Teles, Rodrigo de, Archbishop of Braga **4** 629; **25** 301; **32** 537
Moura y Corte Real, Manuel de *see* CASTEL RODRIGO, MANUEL, 2nd Marqués de
Moure, Francisco de (*c.* 1576–1636) **22** 241*; **29** 292
Moure, Francisco de (*fl* 1630s) **22** 241
Mourgue, Olivier **11** 584
Mouriatada **21** 46
Mourik, D. van **1** 126
Mourlot, Fernand **19** 491, 492; **20** 603; **24** 726; **25** 350; **26** 236
mourners *see* WEEPERS
Mourne Textiles **16** 42
Mourning Athena **13** 427
mourning jewellery *see under* JEWELLERY → type
Mourning Women, Sarcophagus of the **28** 668, *668*
Mournouards, Les *see* LES MOURNOUARDS
Mouron, Adolphe Jean-Marie *see* CASSANDRE
Mousa **21** 552; **22** 241–2*; **25** *470*; **28** *222*, 223
Mouscron, Alexander **21** 435
mouse oracles **3** *407*, 407
Moushovitsa Mogila **30** 770
Mousquet, Léon **4** 391
Moussages **26** 641
Mousseau, Jean-Paul **2** 839; **5** 568
Moussinac, Jeanne **9** 196
Moussinac, Léon **9** 196
Mousterian period *see under* PREHISTORIC ART → periods
Moustiers **4** 177; **7** 166; **11** *505*, 605; **22** 242*
Mouthe, La *see* LA MOUTHE
mouthpieces **8** 352
Moutier-Grandval Bible *see under* BIBLES → individual manuscripts
Moûtiers-Saint-Jean **7** 456; **26** 602
Moutiers-Saint-Jean, Master of **2** 841
Moutoullas, Church of the Councils **9** 627
Moutoussamy-Ashe, Jeanne **33** 310
Moutsopoulos, N. **25** 559
Mouve Artists Society **30** 248
Mouveau, Georges **11** 601
Mouvement International pour un Bauhaus Imaginiste *see* MIBI
Mouwerijn (family) **20** 666
Mou Yi **7** 37
Mouyondzi **1** *394*; **3** *694*
Mouzakis, Stoia **17** 838, 840
Mouzakis, Theodore **17** 838, 840
Mouzin, Lecat & Cie. **3** 591
Mouzon **10** 875
movable type *see* TYPE (MOVABLE)
movement **18** 62
movement, depiction of **8** 698; **9** 721; **14** 263; **20** 406; **22** *389*, 389, 390; **23** 295; **24** 649, 651, 653, 669, *670*; **29** 426
Movement group **27** 397
Movimento arte concreta (MAC) **1** 79; **16** 681; **22** 242*; **29** 31; **31** 446
Movimento dell'Architettura Razionale (MAR) **16** 649; **19** 304; **23** 764; **26** 15
Movimento di Comunità **25** 792
Movimento Italiano per l'Architettura Moderna *see* MIAR
Movimento nucleare *see* ARTE NUCLEARE
Movimento Spaziale **9** 201
Movimiento Nacional **25** 652
moving pictures *see* EIDOPHUSOKA; FILMS
movingui **33** 325
Mowanjum **1** 44
Moxeque **1** 701; **29** 170; **30** 447
temple **29** 165
Moxon, Edward **4** 363; **10** 254; **21** 602; **27** 186; **32** 502
Moxon, Joseph **31** 495
Moxos and La Plata, Master of **4** 262
Moya, Antonio García *see* GARCÍA MOYA, ANTONIO
Moya, Hidalgo **25** 399
Moya, Juan Pérez de *see* PÉREZ DE MOYA, JUAN
Moya, Luis (1904–90) **29** 273

Moya, Luis de (*fl* 1531) **9** 116
 works **9** *116*
Moyen, de (family) **30** 317
Moyen, Jehan **20** 138
Moyker, Heinrich, Abbot **20** 764
Moylough (Co. Sligo) **15** 872
Moymier, Charles **20** 138
Moynan, Richard **16** 17
Moynat, Jean **11** 632; **20** 138
Moyne, Jehan Le *see* LE MOYNE, JEHAN
Moyne de Morgues, Jacques Le *see* LE MOYNE DE MORGUES, JACQUES
Moynet, Jean-Pierre **30** 682
Moynihan, Rodrigo **10** 652; **22** 243*; **23** 333
Moyon **22** 243*
Moyreau **28** 776
Moyreau, Jean **33** 391
Moyser, James **23** 780
Moyses of Altenburg **21** 63
Mozac, St Pierre
 capitals **26** *601*, 601
 enamel **26** 692
 metalwork **11** 614
 sculpture **26** 601
Mozac Silk **9** 252, *252*, 666
Mozambique **22** 243–5*
 apartments **13** *781*
 architecture **21** 572; **22** 245*
 collections **22** 245*
 fortifications **21** 572
 forts **21** *572*
 houses **1** 320
 painting **22** *244*, 244–5*
 pots **1** 369
 sculpture **22** 244*
 trade **1** 249
Mozarabic **22** 246–8*
 architecture **6** *135*; **22** 246–8, *247*; **29** 262
 manuscript illumination **22** 248
 see also MUDÉJAR
Mozart, Anton **2** 374; **22** 248–9*
 collaboration **14** 51; **32** 771
 patrons and collectors **13** 631
 works **2** *716*; **12** 461; **22** *249*
Mozart, Christoph, II **22** 248
Mozart, Wolfgang Amadeus **10** 97; **25** 787
Mozat **7** 456
Mozi (*c.* 480-397 BC) **6** 634; **7** 113
Mozi (1596-1657) **17** 409
Mozia *see* MOTYA
Mozin, Jean-Baptiste **11** 641; **12** 828
 works **21** *367*
Mozo, el *see* OVIEDO (Y DE LA BANDERA), JUAN DE
Mozo, Juan el *see* BADAJOZ, JUAN DE (ii)
Mozuizi (Wuwei) **7** 66
Mozumabad **15** 609
Mozuna, Kikō **15** 408; **22** 249*
mozzettas **32** 390*
Mozzi, Lorenza dei **23** 95
Mpahehlele, Ezekial **1** 429
M R., Master *see* REICHLICH, MARX
Mrauk U *see* MYOHAUNG
Mraz, Franjo **14** 595, 596
Mrazek, Bohdan **30** 330
Mrazek, Wilhelm **2** 834
Mren
 church **2** 425, 429, 434; **7** 256
 sculpture **2** 434
Mrigasthali **22** *753*, 767; **24** 226
 sculpture **22** *768*
Mrkusich, Milan **22** 249–50*; **23** 60, 61, 67
Mrnjavčević, Andrija **28** 447
Mrohaung *see* MYOHAUNG
Mrštík, Vilém **4** 700
MS, Master **14** 899; **20** 801; **28** 851
 works **14** *898*
Msangi, Francis **1** 433; **30** 301
 works **30** *301*
Msecké Žehrovice **6** 158
 sculpture **6** *158*
Mshatta **16** *104*, 149; **17** 656; **22** 250*; **23** 815
 architecture **16** 146
 palace **4** 791; **16** *556*; **24** 877
  façade **16** 243
  sculpture **16** 245
MS. Poitiers 30, Master of *see* ADELAIDE OF SAVOY, MASTER OF
Mstera Jewellery Factory **27** 423
Mstera Museum **27** 441
Mstislav Vladimirovich, Prince **6** 552; **23** 267, 270
Mstiž Gospels *see under* GOSPEL BOOKS → individual manuscripts
Mstyora **27** 427
Mthawanji, R. S., and Associates **20** 161
mtho gling *see* THOLING
Mtoko **1** *413*
Mtskheta **12** *317*, 318; **22** 250–51*
 Cathedral of Sveti-Tskhoveli **12** 320
  sculpture **12** 322
  wall paintings **12** 324
 Cathedral of the Life-creating Pillar **22** 251
 Church of Samtavro **12** 320
 large church of Jvari **7** 256; **12** *318*, 319, 321; **22** *251*
 metalwork **12** 328
 pottery **12** 330
 small church of Jvari **12** 319, 323
 Svetitskhoveli *see* Cathedral of the Life-creating Pillar
Mtuli, Pitika **30** 63
Mu, King (Zhou) (1027-256 BC) **6** 769
Mu, King (*reg* 600-41) **18** 275
Mua **23** 715
Muafangejo, John **22** 450; **33** 245
 works **22** *450*
Mualla, Fikret **22** 251*; **31** 454
al-Mu'allah *see* EL-MOALLA
Muallaka **17** 551
Muang Khorakhapura, Prasat Non Khu **30** 579
Muang Phra Rot **30** 579
Muang Thai *see* THAILAND
mua noi ruoc *see* PUPPETS → types → water puppets
Muan Xingtao *see* MOKUAN SHŌTŌ
Muar, Jamek Mosque **20** 166
Muara Jambi **15** 757, 766, 811
Muara Takus **4** 796; **15** *752*, 766
Mu'awiya, Caliph (*reg* 661-680) (Umayyad) **16** 145; **20** 368; **21** 629; **23** 815
Mu'ayyad al-Din al-'Urdi **20** 371
Mu'ayyad Da'ud **16** 441
Mu'ayyad Shaykh, Sultan (*reg* 1412-21)(Mamluk) **9** 160; **16** 92, 211; **20** 229
al-Mu'azzam Sharaf al-Din, Sultan, (*reg* Damascus 1218-27) (Ayyubid) **16** 259; **17** 497; **18** 421
Mubarak, 'Ali **9** 764
Mubarakabad *see under* DELHI
Mubarak al-Daula **15** *652*
Mubarakpur *see under* DELHI
Mubarakshah ibn Ahmad al-Dimishqi al-Suyufi **16** 284
Mubarakshah ibn Qutb Tabrizi **16** 283; **33** 482
Mubarat al-Makki
 works **29** *618*
Mucavele, Estevão **22** 245
Mucchi, Anton Maria **8** 267
Muccio di Rinaldo **28** 684
Mucha, Alphonse **22** 251–3*; **25** 433; **32** 817
 assistants **25** 548
 carpets **8** 419
 collaboration **25** 151
Mucha, Alphonse—cont.
 furniture **8** 401
 groups and movements **2** 565; **8** 393
 jewellery **11** 635
 paintings **22** 331
 posters **11** 419; **22** *252*
 prints **19** 490
 pupils **14** 397
 sculpture **29** 575
 teachers **33** 142
 works **25** 345, 346, 623
Muchalls **28** 226
Muchanga, Abdias **22** 245
Muche, Georg **22** 253–4*; **29** 872
 groups and movements **3** 400, 401, 403; **12** 470
 pupils **31** 361
 works **13** 689
Mu Chen **8** 458
Much Hadham (Herts) **9** 25; **28** 314
 Henry Moore Foundation **22** 57
Mu-ch'i *see* MUQI
Much Marcle (Hereford & Worcs) **10** 260
 St Bartholomew **10** 262
Muchtar, But **15** 808
Much Wenlock Abbey (Salop) **21** 838; **26** 613
 sculpture **26** *614*
Mucianus, Gaius Licinius **13** 807
Mucius(, C.) **26** 856, 925
Mücke, Heinrich Anton **5** 290; **12** 394
Mücke, Heinrich Karl **22** 329; **26** 423
Mücke, J. Franz **25** 824
Mücke-Melder **8** 402
Mucur **16** 472, 477, 478
Mucur carpets *see under* CARPETS → types
mud
 historical and regional traditions
  Africa **1** 284–5*, 295, 305, 307, 330–31*, 409; **9** 164
  Bamana **1** 285
  Caribbean Islands **5** 755
  Chimú **6** *607*
  Ghana **1** 284; **9** 164
  Hamar **1** 285
  Igbo **1** 331
  Indian subcontinent **15** 548
  Linear Pottery culture **25** 500
  Mali **20** 198
  Mesoamerica, Pre-Columbian **21** 226
  Ndebele **1** 284, 285
  Peru **6** *607*
  Prehistoric art **25** 493, 498, 499
  South America, Pre-Columbian **6** *607*
  Sudan **1** 285
  Yemen **33** *519*
  Zaïre **1** 285
 uses
  architecture **1** 305; **15** 909; **25** 498, 499, 500
  beds **1** 285
  body arts **1** 285, 409
  brick **2** 362
  doors **9** 164
  dyes **1** 295
  frescoes **21** 226
  friezes **6** *441*, *607*
  grounds **21** 226
  hairstyles **1** 285
  houses **33** *519*
  mosques **5** 755
  paints **1** 285; **20** 198, *199*
  sculpture **1** 330–31*
  secco paintings **15** 548
  temples **5** 755
  textiles **1** 285
  writing-tablets **20** 327
Mudabber, Muhammad **15** 898
Mudabidri **15** 336
 Basadi **15** 561
 Chandranatha Basti **15** 336
Mudabidri—cont.
 Chauter Palace **15** 533
Mudali, Kappina *see* KAPPINA MUDALI
Mudarra, Juan de Nápoles *see* NÁPOLES MUDARRA, JUAN DE
Mudarris, Fātiḥ *see* MOUDARRES, FATEH
mud-bricks
 historical and regional traditions
  Afghanistan **16** 168
  Africa **4** 792, *792*
  Anatolia, ancient **1** 823
  Ancient Near East **4** 772; **23** 806
  Babylonian **10** 742
  Central Asia, Western **6** 195, 199; **16** 168, 199–200
  Egypt **4** 772
  Egypt, ancient **2** 296; **4** 792; **9** 775, 824–5, 844, 850; **23** 807; **30** 433
  Greece, ancient **4** 772; **13** 376, 389, 394
  Hausa **4** 793
  India, Republic of **15** 169
  Iran **16** 199
  Iran, ancient **28** 537
  Iraq **16** 150
  Islamic **4** 791; **16** 140
   Afghanistan **16** 168
   Central Asia, Western **16** 168, 199–200
   Iran **16** 199
   Iraq **16** 150
   Ottoman **16** 266
   Turkey **16** 266
  Mali **20** 198
  Mesopotamia **10** 742; **21** 269, 271, 280, 283; **23** 806; **30** 383
  Moche (culture) **21** 749
  Ottoman **16** 266
  Rome, ancient **26** 877
  Sogdiana **6** 199
  Sudan **1** 284
  Syria **30** *177*
  Syria-Palestine **30** 182, 190
  Tokharistan **6** 199
  Turkey **16** 266
  Zambia **4** 792, *792*
 uses
  arches **2** 296
  architecture **4** 793; **6** 195, 199; **9** 775, 824–5, 850; **15** 169; **16** 140, 150, 199–200; **21** 283, 749; **30** *177*
  façade decoration **10** 742
  houses **4** *792*; **13** 396; **16** 266; **20** 198; **21** 280; **26** 877
  mosques **1** 284
  palaces **23** 806, 807
  ramparts **4** 772
  temples **9** 844; **13** 376; **30** 433
  vaults (ceiling) **23** 806; **28** 537, *537*
  walls **21** 271
Mudéjar **22** 254–6*; **31** 86
 art forms **13** 68; **14** 578
  architecture **13** 68; **22** *255*; **29** 263–4
  bookbindings **17** 566
  brick **13** 68
  castles **7** *491*
  ceilings **2** 528; **19** 658
  furniture **29** 311
  interior decoration **29** 297
  panelling **9** 710
  pottery **7** XI2
  textiles **16** 440
  towers **13** 68
 regional traditions
  Colombia **7** 603
  Cuba (Caribbean) **8** 231
 see also MOZARABIC
Mudéjar revival **22** 59, 256*
Mudéjar roofs *see under* ROOFS → types
Mudie, Edward **20** 493
Mudie, James **8** 770; **9** 303; **20** 924
Mudist, Peeter **10** 540
Mudjur *see* MUCUR
Mudo, El *see* NAVARRETE, JUAN FERNÁNDEZ DE
Mudon **5** 247
Mudroch, Ján **28** 853
Mudukutore, Mallikarjunasvami Temple **15** 649
Mudurnu
 houses **32** *319*
 Yıldırım Bayezid Mosque **16** 205
Muduva **15** 734
Muebles de Acero Curvado *see* MAC
Muehl, Otto **22** 256–7*
 collaboration **5** 31; **28** 192
 groups and movements **1** 513; **5** 30; **28** 344; **32** 447
 works **10** 483; **24** 408
Muel **29** 326, 327, 328
Muelenbroec, Willem **20** 721; **21** 352
Müelich, Hans (1516-73) *see* MIELICH, HANS
Müelich, Hans (*d* 1613) **33** 274
Muelich, Wolfgang *see* MIELICH, WOLFGANG
Mueller, Ferdinand, Baron von **21** 75
Mueller, Herman Carl **30** 887
Mueller, Maschka **25** 600
Mueller, Otto **22** 257–8*
 groups and movements **4** 892; **10** 694; **12** 395; **18** 77
 patrons and collectors **11** 729
 pupils **5** 452; **11** 776; **13** 870
 works **19** 491; **22** *257*; **25** 600
Mueller, Paul **1** 158
Muet, Pierre le *see* LE MUET, PIERRE
Muette, La *see* LA MUETTE
Muffati, Raffaele **22** 481
Muffel (family) **10** 444
Muffel, Jakob **9** *439*
Muffel, Nikolaus **25** 40
Muffet, Thomas **2** 103
Muff-Ford, John **4** 155; **29** 123
muffle kilns *see under* KILNS → types
muff technique *see* GLASS → techniques → Lorraine method
Mug, Mount *see* KALA-I MUG
Mugaguren, Juan de **28** 369
Mugahid, Sultan **16** 213
Mugaku Sogen *see* WUXUE ZUYUAN
Mugardos **29** 272
Mugello, Guido di Piero da *see* ANGELICO, FRA
Mugeni Church **26** 710
Mugford, William **24** 621
Muggeridge, Edward James *see* MUYBRIDGE, EADWEARD
Mughal **16** 121; **22** 258–9*
 architecture **8** 679; **12** 204; **16** 239
 art policies **16** 100
 ceramics **6** 918
 chess sets **6** 556
 domes **9** 84
 gems **12** 253
 jade **7** 10–11; **16** 860
 jewellery **17** II2
 mirrors **21** *717*
 mosques **8** *679*
 reliefs **23** 803
 screens (i) (architectural) **23** 803
 tents **30** *472*
 textiles **3** 168; **10** I2
 tombs **1** *459*; **8** *679*
 trade **7** 10–11
 see also:
  AKBAR, Emperor
  AURANGZEB, Emperor
  A'ZAM SHAH, Emperor
  AZIM, Emperor
  BABUR, Emperor
  BAHADUR SHAH I, Emperor
  BAHADUR SHAH II, Emperor

Mughal
see also:—cont.
FARRUKHSIYAR, Emperor
FATEHPURI BEGUM
HUMAYUN, Emperor
JAHANGIR, Emperor
MIRZA MUHAMMAD HAYDAR
MUHAMMAD HAKIM
MUHAMMAD SHAH, Emperor
NUR JAHAN, Empress
SHAH 'ALAM II, Emperor
SHAH JAHAN, Emperor
see also under INDIAN SUBCONTINENT
al-Mughira 7 845; 16 524
Mughni Gospels see under GOSPEL BOOKS → individual manuscripts
Muğla 16 202
Mugnai, Carlo 22 481
Mugnai, Francesco 12 462
Mugnai, Giovanni 16 747; 22 481
Mugri 14 22; 20 899
mugs 20 594
historical and regional traditions
China 6 920; 7 29, 29
England 10 303, 304
Greece, ancient 13 476, 537
materials
pewter 24 580
porcelain 6 920
pottery 10 303; 13 537
silver 7 29, 29
stoneware 10 304
Mug Tepe 31 701
Mugur-Sargol 27 367
Mugurza, Pedro 10 822
Mugye 18 271, 353
Muhammad (fl 1313-14) 4 100
Muhammad, Khwarazmshah (reg 1200-20) 5 137; 14 427
Muhammad, Prophet 15 81; 16 110–11*, 539; 18 239; 22 354
architecture 16 144; 21 629; 22 192; 27 698
Muhammad, Shah (reg 1834-48) (Qajar) 16 81, 539
Muhammad I, Amir (reg 852-86) (Umayyad) 7 845; 20 60, 71
Muhammad I, Ruler (reg 1358-75) (Bahmani) 3 66; 15 678
Muhammad I, Sultan (reg 1230-72) (Nasrid) 13 282, 285; 22 534
Muhammad II, Sultan (reg 1272-1302) (Nasrid) 13 282, 286; 20 156; 22 535
Muhammad III, Sultan (reg 1320-28) (Nasrid) 13 287; 16 386; 22 535
metalwork 16 387
Muhammad III, Sultan (reg 1757-90) ('Alawi) 1 527; 16 240; 20 470; 21 74, 585
Muhammad V, Sultan (reg 1354-9; 1362-91) (Nasrid) 11 340; 13 282, 287, 289; 16 253; 22 535
Muhammad VII, Sultan (reg 1395-1407) (Nasrid) 13 287, 288
Muhammad XI, Sultan (reg 1482-92) (Nasrid) 2 452; 16 386; 22 535
Muhammad, Sami 18 541
Muhammad 'Adil Shah, Ruler (reg 1626-56) ('Adil Shahi) 15 639–40
Muhammad Afzal 15 591
Muhammad Ahmad (the Madhi) (reg 1881-5) 23 290
Muhammad al-Haravi 27 513
Muhammad al-Husayni al-Imami 15 143
Muhammad 'Ali (i) (fl c. 1600-10) 22 259*
Muhammad 'Ali (ii) (fl 1645-60) 5 399; 22 259*
Muhammad 'Ali (ibn Muhammad Zaman) (fl 1772) 22 264
Muhammad 'Ali (fl early 19th cent.) 15 681
Muhammad 'Ali, Pasha (reg 1805-48) (Muhammad 'Ali's Line) 5 405; 9 765; 10 85, 91; 16 361, 547; 23 330
architecture 8 18
Muhammad 'Ali al-Fadli 14 217
Muhammad 'Ali al-Mashhadi ibn Malik Husayn al-Isfahani see MUHAMMAD 'ALI (ii) (1645-60)
Muhammad 'Ali Inoyaton 6 258
Muhammad 'Ali Shah, Nawab of Avadh (reg 1837-42) 8 269; 15 377
Muhammad 'Ali's Line see:
'ABBAS I, Pasha
'ABBAS II, Khedive
FAROUQ I, King
ISMA'IL, Khedive
MUHAMMAD 'ALI, Pasha
TAWFIQ, Khedive
Muhammad al-Muhtasib al-Najjari 16 380
Muhammad al-Qasab 31 584
Muhammad al-Salih 16 399
Muhammad al-'Urdi 12 812
Muhammad al-Washsha' 16 455–6
Muhammad 'Amin 15 588; 16 345
Muhammad Amin al-Rushdi 14 217
Muhammad Amin Bukhari 16 343
Muhammad Baqir (i) (fl 1820s) see BAQIR
Muhammad Baqir (ii) (fl 1750s-60s) 1 638; 12 506; 15 681; 22 259–60*
Muhammad bin 'Umar Syaikh Farid 20 172
works 20 171
Muhammad Darvish 6 236
Muhammad Faqirallah Khan 15 590
Muhammad Ghaffari see GHAFFARI, MUHAMMAD
Muhammad Hadi 1 638; 16 341
Muhammad Hakim (Mughal) 10 817
Muhammad Hasan Afshar 16 561; 22 260*
Muhammad Hasan Khan 1 25; 16 535; 22 260*
Muhammad Husayn Kashmiri 15 681
Muhammad Husni 14 217
Muhammadi 14 431; 16 132; 22 260–61*; 26 434
Muhammad ibn 'Abd al-Wahid 16 374
works 16 366
Muhammad ibn Abi Tahir 1 97–8*; 21 506
Muhammad ibn Abi Talib al-Badri 16 308
Muhammad ibn Abu Bakr 2 891
Muhammad ibn 'Ali 16 496
Muhammad ibn al-Zayn 22 261*
works 16 366, 382, 383, 384; 21 718
Muhammad ibn Atsiz al-Sarakhsi 21 169
Muhammad ibn Aybak ibn 'Abdallah 1 473
Muhammad ibn Fattuh (fl 1212-27; Spain) 16 386
Muhammad ibn Fattuh (fl 1252; Spain) 16 386
Muhammad ibn Fatuh (fl 13th cent.; Egypt) 16 381
Muhammad ibn Hasan al-Mawsili 16 382
Muhammad ibn Hawlan al-Dimishqi 18 233
Muhammad ibn Khayrun al-Ma'afari 17 731
Muhammad ibn Khutlukh 16 381
Muhammad ibn Mahmud 6 208
Muhammad ibn Mahmud Shah Khayyam 1 24
Muhammad ibn Mu'ayyad al-Urdi 20 371
Muhammad ibn Mubadir 20 229
Muhammad ibn Muhammad 16 409
Muhammad ibn Muhammad ibn 'Ali 16 299
Muhammad ibn Muhammad ibn 'Uthman al-Tusi 18 234
Muhammad ibn Sa'id Abi'l-Fath 'Abd al-Wahid 16 308
Muhammad ibn Sam see GHIYATH AL-DIN MUHAMMAD IBN SAM, Sultan
Muhammad ibn Shams al-Din al-Ghuri 30 923
Muhammad ibn Sunqur 16 382
Muhammad ibn Sunqur al-Baghdadi 16 382, 389
works 16 383, 389
Muhammad ibn Tughluq, Sultan (reg 1325-51) (Tughluq) 8 672–3; 15 341, 355, 716; 31 416
Muhammad ibn Yusuf al-Tabrizi (fl 14th cent.) 6 208
Muhammad ibn Yusuf ibn 'Uthman al-Hisnkayfi (fl 1206) 16 307
Muhammad ibn Zayyan 16 525
Muhammad ibn Ziyad, Ruler (reg c. 820) (Ziyadid) 33 583
Muhammad Ibrahim (ibn Hajji Yusuf) 22 264
Muhammad Isma'il 16 81–2*, 534
Muhammadiyya, Mosque of Kucha-Mir 16 492; 28 634
Muhammad Ja'far 16 516; 22 261*
Muhammad Juki, Prince (Timurid) 16 324, 344, 552; 18 30; 30 917
Muhammad Karim Khan, Ruler (reg 1750-79) (Zand) 12 82; 16 233, 535, 539; 21 589; 28 616
architecture 16 234
Muhammad Kazim (fl late 19th cent.) 16 81, 516, 534
Muhammad Khan (fl c. 1630-40) 15 590
Muhammad Khan (fl 1651) 15 640
Muhammad Muhassib 10 92
Muhammad Muhsin 16 232
Muhammad Mu'in Khan, Khan-i Khanan 15 368
Muhammad Mundi 31 584
Muhammad Muqim 6 236
Muhammad Murad Samarqandi 6 236; 16 342, 343
works 6 235
Muhammad of Kashan 16 424
Muhammad-Paolo Zaman 22 263
Muhammad Qasim (Tabrīzī) 16 339; 22 261–3*
Muhammad Quli Qutb Shah, Ruler (reg 1580-1612) (Qutb Shahi) 15 48; 25 831
Muhammad Qutb Shah, Ruler (reg 1612-26) (Qutb Shahi) 15 48, 641
Muhammad Rashid Pasha
metalwork 16 508
Muhammad Riza, Shah (reg 1941-79) (Pahlavi) 13 798; 15 899; 16 539
Muhammad Riza 'Abbasi 16 79
Muhammad Riza al-Imami 16 232, 425
Muhammad Riza Isfahani 12 82
Muhammad Sadiq 22 262*; 28 617; 33 609
teachers 1 638
works 16 341, 534, 534, 535
Muhammad Sadykkori 6 208
Muhammad Salih 6 205
Muhammad Shafi' 22 262*; 26 433
Muḥammad Shafīq see MEHMED ŞEFIK
Muhammad Shah, Emperor (reg 1719-48) (Mughal) 15 590–92, 591
Muhammad Shah, Sultan (reg 1442-51) (Sultans of Gujarat) 27 842
Muhammad Sharif 1 26; 15 208, 681; 16 343; 22 262–3*
works 6 236; 16 343
Muhammad Sharif Khan 15 368
Muhammad Sharif Kirmani 16 482
Muḥammad Shawqī see MEHMED ŞEVKI
Muhammad Shaybani, Khan (reg 1500-10) (Shaybanid) 4 49; 16 235; 27 677; 28 565
Muhammad Shirin (fl c. 1825-50) 16 535; 22 263*
Muhammad Siyah Qalam 28 811
Muhammad Sultan 27 675
Muhammad Taqi 28 566
Muhammad Yousif (b 1954) 31 585
Muhammad Yusuf 16 339; 22 263*
Muhammad Zaman 22 263–4*
pupils 1 638
works 16 333, 338, 340, 341, 464, 533
Muhanna, Fawaz 17 654
muḥaqqaq see under SCRIPTS → types
Muharraq 3 68
House of Ahmad Siyadi 3 68
House of Shaykh 'Isa 3 68
Muhezzeh 9 543
Muhibb 'Ali 4 49; 16 335
Muhibbi see SÜLEYMAN THE MAGNIFICENT, Sultan
Mühl, Otto see MUEHL, OTTO
Mühlen, Rudolf Julius von Zur see ZUR MÜHLEN, RUDOLF JULIUS VON
Mühlenen, Max von 9 759; 29 534
Mühlhausen 12 360, 361; 22 264–5*
St Maria 22 264–5*; 30 535
sculpture 13 89; 22 264
Mühll, Robert von der 7 294
Muhona 14 376, 377, 378
Muhsinzade Abdullah 22 385
Muidebled 11 598
Muidebled, Jean-Baptiste Joseph 7 778
Muiden 22 813, 884
Castle 22 265, 265–6*, 822
Muiderkring 4 868
Muijs, Robert 7 662
Mu'in 16 339; 22 266*
teachers 26 434
works 16 127, 132, 339, 517, 533
Mu'in Khan 15 363
Muir 5 282
Muiredach 21 832
Muiredach's Cross see under MONASTERBOICE
Muisca 22 266*; 29 132
figurines 22 266
gold 29 211
metalwork 29 212
pottery 29 150
sculpture 29 146
textiles 29 152
Muizen 3 541
Muižule, Malda
al-Mu'izz, Caliph (reg 953-75) (Fatimid) 5 395; 16 512, 525
Mu'izz al-Din Kay-Qubadh, Sultan (reg 1287-90) (Mamluk of Delhi) 12 73
Mu'izz al-Din Mubarak Shah, Sultan (reg 1421-34) (Sayyid) 8 673; 28 27
Mu'izzi see MAMLUK (Indian subcontinent)
al-Mu'izz ibn Badis, Ruler (reg 1016-62) (Zirid) 16 272; 33 686
architecture 16 493; 17 730; 20 368
writings 16 277, 352, 353, 356, 357; 24 45
on inks 15 851, 852
Mujadžić, Omer 4 461; 9 672
Mujahid, Khan (reg c. 1435-67) (Dandani) 15 350
Mujezinović, Ismar 4 461
Mujezinović, Ismet 4 461
Mujica, Manuel 32 170, 171
Mujica Gallo, Manuel 24 515
Mujica Gallo, Miguel 24 517
Mujur see MUCUR
Muka 5 10
Mukachevo see under MUNKÁCS
Mukai, Masaya 22 249
Mukaiharamachi 17 249
al-Mukalla 16 271
Mukandara see DARRA
Mukandgarh 15 611
Mukan Fumon 18 558
Mukarovsky, Jan 28 396
Mukayyar, Tell el see UR
Mukela, Progress 33 602
Mukengo 33 598
Mukerjea, Sailoz 8 677
Mukhalingam 15 279, 294, 534; 22 266–7*
Madhukeshvara Temple 15 282, 536; 22 267
sculpture 15 536
sculpture 15 536, 537
Someshvara Temple 15 282, 537
sculpture 15 537
Mukhammedov, Telman 31 783
Mukharramov, M. 27 425
Mukherjee, Benode Behari 15 657; 22 267*; 29 891
Mukherjee, Meera 15 172; 22 267–8*
Mukhina, Vera (Ignat'yevna) 22 178, 268*; 27 396
collaboration 10 700
groups and movements 11 358; 27 395
works 15 890; 27 395, 417; 28 534
Mukhitdinov, Albek 18 568
Mukhitdinov, Kh. 27 599
Mukhomory 29 89
Mukhtar, Mahmud 9 766, 768; 22 268–9*
groups and movements 9 766; 22 431
patrons and collectors 5 401
pupils 19 8
works 9 766, 766
Mukhuba, Nelson 29 104, 113
Muki Dōja see ZŌROKU V
Mukosaddari Monastery see KANDZTA MONASTERY
Mūksala group
Mūkukalns 18 846
Mukund 22 269*
Mukundarra 15 460
Mulas, Ugo 22 269*
mulberry
Brazil 4 721
China 7 64, 114–15
Islamic 16 429
Japan 17 139, 213, 275
mulberry, paper see PAPER MULBERRY
Mulberry Press 20 609
Mulcahy, Michael 16 18
Mul-Chic
stucco 29 829
wall paintings 21 231, 246
Muldenfaltenstil 22 269–70*; 31 284
Mulder, Ries 15 818
Mule 13 120
Mulgrave, Henry Phipps, 1st Earl of see PHIPPS, HENRY, 1st Earl of Mulgrave
Mulgrave Castle 26 153
mulḥam see SILK → types → half-silk
Mülheim (family)
crests 14 412
Mülheimer Freiheit 9 72; 12 397; 31 356
Mulholland, Andrew 16 25

Mulhouse 30 458
cotton 8 37; 11 649; 30 562
St Stephen 31 501
Town Hall 10 738
Muli, Joseph 33 679
Mülich, Hektor
works 2 *713*
Mulier, Pieter (*c.* 1615-70) 22 840; 28 92; 32 673
Mulier, Pieter (1637-1701) 16 562
Mulinaretto 21 145
Mulinari, Stefano 2 239
Mulken, Arnould van 3 544; 19 345
Mulkirigala 29 466
Lower Temple 29 466
Mull, C., & Co. 10 580
Mulla ʿAla al-Mulk Tuni 15 366
Mulla Bihzad 6 236
Mullaghmast (Co. Kildare) 15 872
Mullali Tepe 6 195
Mulla Muhammad Tabrizi 21 704
Mulla Sadiq *see* MUHAMMAD SADIQ
Mulla Simla Congregational Mosque 15 352
Müllauer, Thomas 33 294
Mullearne Dairy (Perth) 8 461
Muller 6 489
Müller (family) 3 595; 19 801
Muller, Adam 8 735
Müller, Albert 18 81; 27 213*; 30 135, 138
Müller, Albin 8 531
Müller, Andreas 18 128
Müller, C. F. 25 856
Muller, Charles-Louis 4 306; 8 618; 11 545
Müller, Christian Benjamin 10 857
Muller, Christina 27 *503*
Müller, Constantin, Abbot of Alt-Birnau 3 6
Müller, Daniel 19 826
Müller, Elias 23 271
Muller, Emile 5 363; 22 270–71*; 27 879; 30 504, 505
Müller, Ernst 14 606
Müller, Ferdinand 30 144
Müller, Frantz Heinrich 7 806
Muller, Frederik 19 782
Müller, (Johann) Friedrich 22 271–2*
works 22 *271*
Müller, Gabriel 18 525
Muller, Georges Michel 29 750
Müller, Hans 3 797; 19 168
Muller, Harmen Jansz. 14 294; 22 272
Müller, Heinrich 17 817
Müller, Heinrich Anton 25 685
Müller, Hélène *see* KRÖLLER-MÜLLER, HÉLÈNE
Müller, H. F. 1 687
Muller, Jan (Harmensz.) 4 152; 10 387, 392; 12 879; 13 847; 22 272–3*; 25 626; 29 377
works 1 662; 22 *272*; 27 299
Muller, Jan (Ewoutsz.) 33 355
Müller, Johann
works 4 *345*
Müller, Johann Adam 2 580
Müller, Johann Friedrich Wilhelm 22 273
Müller, Johann Georg 23 225
Müller, Johann Georg Wilhelm 2 786; 22 273*; 32 437
Müller, Johann Gottfried 27 411
Müller, Johann Gotthard von 22 273*
works 33 *37*
Müller, Johann Heinrich 21 821
Müller, Johann Sebastian 19 619; 32 778
works 19 *619*
Müller, Josef Felix 30 135, 140
Müller, Karl 18 204; 31 583, 637
Müller, Kozma 33 592
Müller, Leopold Carl 2 797; 3 20; 17 897; 18 533; 23 504; 24 568; 32 445
Müller, Louis 22 271; 29 751
Müller, M. 12 498
Müller, Marcus 2 812
Müller, Matthias
works 2 *813*
Müller, Michael 8 408
Müller, N. 26 506; 28 917
Müller, Nikolaus 30 146
Müller, Otto *see* MUELLER, OTTO
Müller, Paul 33 279
Muller, Peter (Neil) 2 742; 22 273–4*; 30 161
Müller, Philipp Heinrich 2 718; 20 923; 22 274*
Müller, Philipp L. 5 346
Müller, Richard 13 697; 28 70
Müller, Robert 22 274*; 30 140
Müller, Siegfried 11 852
Müller, Siegismund 20 894
Müller, Sophus 32 534
Müller, Theodor 3 602
Müller, Victor 12 394
Müller, Wilhelm 12 450
Müller, William James 22 274–5*
groups and movements 4 823; 23 504; 32 903
pupils 8 84
works 25 837
Müller, Wouter 20 923
Müller-Brockman, Josef 7 656; 25 352
Müller-Helwig, Alen 12 468
Müllerová, Augusta 8 402
mullers 22 270*
Müller-Wiener, Wolfgang 1 93
Müller-Wulkow, Walter 13 274
Mullet, Arthur B. 9 705
Mullett, Alfred B(ult) 22 275*
groups and movements 26 190, 704; 28 345
works 27 565; 31 593; 32 886
Mullgardt, Louis C(hristian) 22 275–6*; 27 731
Mullineux, Timothy 16 31
Mullins, George 16 14
mullions 22 213, *213*, 219, 220, 221
Müllner, Josef 2 803
Müllner, Paul 33 112
Mullo Akhmad Domullo 18 195
Mullock, J. F. 32 785
Mullokandov, M. 14 578
Mullooly, Joseph 26 824
mulls 28 264
Mulongoya, Pili-Pili 1 432
works 1 *432*
Mulot 19 657
Mulpas, Victor 16 849
Mulraj II, Maharawal of Jaisalmer 16 871
Mulready, A(ugustus) E(dwin) 8 121; 22 276, 278–9*
Mulready, Michael 22 276
Mulready, William (1786-1863) 22 276–8*
dealers 1 453
patrons and collectors 14 147; 28 575; 32 338
reproductive prints by others 10 378; 11 362; 26 473
teachers 11 860; 31 909
works 10 252; 16 16; 22 *277*
Mulready, William (1805-78) 22 276
Multan 15 *264*; 16 *105*; 22 279*; 23 *797*
architecture 15 337–8; 16 201; 22 279
enamel 15 712
leather 23 803
metalwork 15 713
Mosque of Khalid ibn Walid 15 337
pottery 23 802
textiles 15 664; 23 802
tiles 15 686, 687
Multan—cont.
tomb of Khalid ibn Walid 16 168
tomb of Rukn al-Din ʿAlam 15 *337*, 337–8, 686; 16 201; 31 112
tomb of Shadna Shahid 15 337
tomb of Shah Yusuf Gardizi 15 307, 337
tomb of Shams al-Din Tabrizi 15 337
tomb of Shaykh Baha' al-Haqq Zakariya 15 337
Multiflex housing system 8 232; 27 621
multimedia 22 279*
multiple art 26 235
multiple cameras *see under* PHOTOGRAPHY → processes
Multiple Décor style *see under* ROME, ANCIENT → mosaics
multiple exposures *see under* PHOTOGRAPHY → processes
Multiples 19 395; 26 51
multi-purpose mosque *see* MOSQUES → types → T-plan
multi-storeyed pagodas *see under* PAGODAS → types
multi-treasure pagodas *see under* PAGODAS → types
multi-unit mosques *see under* MOSQUES → types
Multscher, Hans 13 187; 22 280–82*; 31 566
attributions 20 770
groups and movements 26 184
paintings 29 665
patrons and collectors 12 843
reliquaries 13 160
sculpture 13 91, 117; 19 831; 31 570
altarpieces 2 799; 12 384; 22 *281*; 31 570
palmesels 23 887, *887*
relief 22 *280*
religious 12 401; 13 *91*; 31 569
workshop 13 117
Multscher, Heinrich 22 280
Mulvaney, Charles, & Co. 9 320
Mulvany, D. J. 31 133
Mulvany, G. 16 38
Mulvany, John Skipton 22 282*
Mulvey, Laura 10 689
Mumadona, Countess 13 831
Mumba, Eddie 33 603
Mumbai *see* BOMBAY
mumbira 22 375
Mumford, Lewis 19 896; 20 890; 22 282–3*; 31 672
Muʾmina Khatun 22 445
Muʾmin Jahangiri 15 699
mummies
Egypt, ancient 1 342; 9 842–3; 10 14*; 20 327; 22 283–6*, *284*, *285*; 24 792
Nubia 1 342
South America, Pre-Columbian 29 132
see also CORN-MUMMIES
mummiform figures *see* SCULPTURE → types → chrysaliform figures
Mummius, L. 2 413; 23 431
mummy-boards 10 11, 12, 13
mummy cases 10 *9*, 12, 13–14*, *197*, 197; 22 285; 25 276; 28 *667*
see also SARCOPHAGI
mummy masks 10 11, 13–14*; 22 284
mummy portraits *see under* PORTRAITS → types
Mumtaz, Kamil Khan 23 799
Mumun ware *see under* POTTERY → wares
Mumuye 22 286–7*
ceramics 22 287*
masks 1 382; 22 286–7*, *287*
sculpture 1 382; 22 287*
Muna 4 193
Muna al-Khaja 31 585
Munakata, Shikō 17 293; 22 287–8*
exhibitions 17 436
groups and movements 21 634
patrons and collectors 17 433; 23 371; 25 629
works 17 293, 295–6; 19 492; 33 363
Munari, Bruno 22 288*
groups and movements 1 166; 11 867; 16 681; 18 62, 63; 22 242
works 2 528, 838; 7 656, *656*; 10 135; 21 746; 29 97
Munari, Cristoforo 22 288–9*; 29 668; 31 883
Munbaqa 30 197
Munch, Edvard 3 801; 10 693; 22 289–94*, *293*; 29 878
collaboration 20 603
exhibitions 4 71; 8 393; 13 711; 27 731
groups and movements 25 357; 28 342; 30 169
paintings 8 596; 10 693; 11 *474*; 22 *290*; 23 226
genre 22 *292*
landscape 11 474
murals 22 330, 331; 23 603
nude figures 23 297
patrons and collectors 22 135; 23 7, 243; 30 730
personal collection 23 243
prints 23 227
drypoints 9 310
lithographs 19 489, *489*; 25 596, 626
woodcuts 22 *293*; 25 624; 33 362
sponsorship 22 701
Munch, Eggert 23 224
Munch, Jacob 3 111
Munch, Peter Andreas 22 540
Munchaev, R. M. 33 504
Munchak Tepe 18 530
München, Heinrich von *see* HEINRICH VON MÜNCHEN
Münchener Jahrbuch der bildenden Kunst (Munich: 1842-6) 24 443
Münch-Khe, Willi 21 66
Münchner Gobelin-Manufaktur 30 331
Münchner Jahrbuch der bildenden Kunst (Munich: 1906-23; 1924-39; 1950-) 24 445
Münchner Künstlergenossenschaft 28 340, 341
Mun-ch'ŏng *see* BUNSEI
Munch'ung *see* NAM KU-MAN
Munck, Jan de 22 295*
Munday, Richard 14 197; 22 295–6*
Münden, S Blasiikirche 11 253
Mundeshvari Shiva Temple 15 260–61, 478
al-Mundhir (*reg* 569-82) (Ghassarid) 27 344
Mundie, William B. 17 477
Mundigak 1 185, *186*, 189; 6 185
figurines 1 188
palace 1 *189*, 190, *191*
sculpture 1 193–4, *194*
Mundine, Djon Scott 1 64
Mündler, Otto 7 714; 16 768; 21 824; 22 296*
dealing 9 683
paintings 9 378, 683
works 6 100
Munduruců 4 707; 10 848
Mundus AG 18 192; 30 755
Mundy, Francis 11 428
Mundy, Henry 28 805
Mundy, J. S.
works 7 *766*
Mundy, Peter 22 235
Muñeca 5 411
Munehiro *see* KŌRA MUNEHIRO BUNGO
Munemaro Ishiguro *see* ISHIGURO, MUNEMARO
Munemichi Yanagi *see* YANAGI, MUNEMICHI
Munet, Melchior 29 93
Munetada Himi *see* HIMI MUNETADA
Muneyoshi Yanagi *see* YANAGI, MUNEYOSHI
Munezane *see* HATA CHITEI
Munge, Mutisya 17 907
Mungenast (family) 19 827
Munggenast, Franz 2 783; 22 297
Munggenast, Joseph 13 217; 22 296–7*
collaboration 25 449
patrons and collectors 31 510
works 2 783; 14 260; 21 83; 29 611
Munggenast, Matthias 22 297
Munggenast, Sigismund 22 297
Munhata 30 196
Munhwa yusan 18 382
Munia Elvira, Queen of Navarre (*fl c.* 1066) 11 801
Muñiátegui, Juan de 5 427
Munich 12 *361*; 22 297–309*, *300*
Akademie der Bildenden Künste 1 106; 22 303
art forms and materials
altarpieces 12 391
architecture 12 374
bookbindings 17 567
embroidery 12 *463*
façade decoration 10 737
frescoes 12 391
furniture 12 423, 426, 427
glass 12 439, 440
gold 12 451; 22 305*
guns 2 *458*
interior decoration 12 416
ivory-carvings 12 460
jewellery 12 455
metalwork 12 449
mirror frames 21 721
objects of vertu 22 306*
painting 12 389, 390, 393, 394; 22 *304*
pewter 12 452
reliquaries 12 447
sculpture 12 403, 405, 406; 22 *303*
silver 12 446, 449; 22 305*
tapestries 12 467; 22 306*; 30 319, 324
art market 12 474
Bahnhof 25 856
Bau der Anatomie 19 502
Café Fürstenhof 29 843
cemetery 31 131
churches
Allerheiligen-Hofkirche 26 704
Augustinian church *see* museums → Deutsches Jagd- und Fischerei Museum
Cathedral 10 *702*
Dreifaltigskeitkirche 32 603
Frauenkirche 4 777; 12 365, 367; 22 306*; 32 821
stained glass 29 504
tomb of Ludwig IV 12 404
Heiliggeistkirche 12 372; 14 82
Ludwigskirche 7 872; 12 *167*, 167–8; 27 336
St Anna am Lehel 11 124, *125*; 12 372
St Johann Nepomuk 2 582, *584*; 8 216; 23 543; 26 497; 29 838
altar 1 699
St Kajetan 3 229, *229*; 12 370; 33 276
St Michael 12 368, 471; 32 821; 33 274
altarpieces 12 389
sculpture 12 346, *346*, 402
tomb of Wilhelm V 12 404

Munich
 churches—cont.
  Theatinerkirche see St Kajetan
 Dessauerhaus 23 9
 Dörner Institut 9 440; 22 304
 education (art) 12 451, 479
 Elvira photographic studio 2 566, 566; 12 376; 29 843
 Englischer Garten 12 106, 134; 24 180; 28 213
  Chinese Tower 7 168; 12 373
 exhibitions 10 678
 fortifications 33 270
 government buildings 31 241
  Bayerisches Verkehrsministerium 7 694
  Hauptpostamt 25 172; 29 761
  Hauptwache 13 852
  Law Courts 18 890; 30 734
  Mint 12 366
  Parliament Building 22 300
  Salinengebäude 27 336
 guilds 22 305
 Hall of Fame see Ruhmeshalle
 Hofgarten 4 375; 27 231–2
  Hofgartengalerie see under museums
 Kunstverein 22 303; 29 416, 658
 libraries and archives
  Bayerisches Hauptarchiv 2 370
  Bayerische Staatsbibliothek 12 167, 168, 376; 19 314, 317; 27 336
   collections 12 482; 15 745; 33 271
  Bibliothek des Zentralinstituts für Kunstgeschichte 2 366, 370; 12 481
  Residenzbibliothek see Bayerische Staatsbibliothek
 Ludwigstrasse 18 123
 Marstall 33 271
 Maximilianeum see government buildings → Parliament Building
 museums
  Alte Pinakothek 2 560; 9 12, 17; 12 375, 475, 476, 477; 18 123–4, 124; 22 305, 363; 33 282
   catalogues 8 897; 22 296
   collections 4 242; 22 300, 303
   directors 11 244
   frescoes 7 871
   restoration 12 379
   Rubens Gallery 22 362
   sculpture 28 186
   see also Gemäldegalerie
  Bayerisches Nationalmuseum 12 476; 14 227; 19 152; 22 303, 363; 28 374
   collections 29 516; 30 332; 33 84
  Bayerisches Staatsgemäldesammlung see Haus der Kunst → Staatsgalerie Moderner Kunst
  Bayerische Verwaltung der Staatlichen Schlösser, Gärten und Seen 30 331
  Deutsches Jagd- und Fischerei-Museum 22 298
  Deutsches Museum 7 694; 23 342; 28 374
  Gemäldegalerie 8 897; 18 739
   see also Alte Pinakothek
  Glyptothek 3 155; 7 871, 872; 12 375, 475–6, 477; 13 218, 610; 14 87; 18 122, 122–3; 22 300, 362; 23 9, 371; 26 377; 28 186; 33 282
   collections 22 303
   directors 11 854
   display 9 25
   Greek collection 13 469, 470
   portico 25 267
   Roman collection 10 637, 638; 27 45, 46, 115
   Roman sculpture 22 272

Munich
 museums—cont.
  Haus der Kunst 12 379, 477; 22 301, 304, 305, 710, 710–11; 31 368
   Staatsgalerie Moderner Kunst 11 729; 22 305; 31 397; 33 271
  Hofgartengalerie 9 177
  Jüdisches Museum 17 581
  Kunstausstellungsgebäude see Staatliche Antikensammlungen
  Kunstausstellungs-Gebaüde see Staatliche Antikensammlung
  Lenbachhaus Museum see Städtische Galerie im Lenbachhaus
  Moderne Gallerie Heinrich Thannhauser 12 474
  Neue Pinakothek 12 380, 475, 477; 22 300, 363; 27 232; 32 683; 33 282
   collections 22 303, 304; 33 282
  Pinakothek see Alte Pinakothek; Neue Pinakothek
  Residenzmuseum see Residenz
  Schack-Galerie 26 190; 28 40
  Staatliche Antikensammlungen 13 555; 22 300; 27 46; 28 341; 33 282, 673
  Staatliche Münzsammlung 33 271
  Staatliche Sammlung Ägyptischer Kunst 10 91, 93
  Staatliches Museum für Völkerkunde 1 67; 2 275; 15 745; 28 670
  Staatsgalerie Moderner Kunst see under Haus der Kunst
  Städtische Galerie im Lenbachhaus 18 187, 491; 19 152; 22 304; 28 374
  Villa Stuck 2 365, 550; 29 847
 Odeon 7 687
 Odeonsplatz 18 123
 Olympiapark 12 380; 29 489; 30 469, 469
 palaces
  Avco-Palais 23 546
  Herzog-Karl-Theodor-Palais 23 546
  Herzog-Max-Palais see Herzog-Karl-Theodor-Palais
  Leuchtenbergpalais 12 375
  Palais Törring see under Government buildings → Hauptpostamt
  Preysing Palais 9 746, 747
  Residenz see Residenz
  Schloss Nymphenburg 3 229; 9 746; 12 371, 372, 410; 22 308–9*, 309; 23 811
   Amalienburg pavilion 8 289, 289, 880; 12 411; 26 497; 29 838; 30 878; 33 682, 682
   Badenburg pavilion 1 784
   Borgo delle Ninfé 33 276
   gardens 4 375; 12 133; 13 679; 26 497
   Magdalenenklause 13 199, 704
   Monopteros 25 172
   Pagodenburg 12 373; 23 776
   paintings 3 514; 13 845
   Schönheitsgalerie 29 658
 Propyläen 13 610
 Ratjen Foundation 19 478
 Residenz 3 229; 8 288–9; 9 746; 12 369, 372, 477; 22 306–8*; 26 496; 33 274, 275, 282
  Ahnengalerie 11 457; 29 838
  altars 1 697
  Antiquarium 2 162; 9 22, 750; 22 739; 29 738, 739; 33 271, 274
   interior decoration 12 367
   paintings 9 133; 30 35
   sculpture 12 475
  ciborium 7 302

Munich
 Residenz—cont.
  clocks 16 900
  Dutch Cabinet 33 276
  Festsaalbau 28 137
  frames 11 458
  frescoes 28 186
  gardens 12 346
  Green Gallery 9 17
  Grottenhof 13 703; 27 610; 30 35
  Herkulessaal 33 81
  house-altar of Albert V 10 194
  interior decoration 12 410, 411; 18 479; 22 307; 33 682
  Kunstkammer 9 14; 12 446; 13 680; 18 521; 33 271, 274
  metalwork 5 808; 8 412; 12 457; 16 900; 18 479
  murals 22 328
  paintings 3 507; 5 200, 606–7, 877; 28 148; 30 35; 33 608
  Porcelain Room 5 348, 349
  Residenztheater 8 290, 290, 880; 29 811; 30 676
  rock crystal 16 541
  St Georgssaal 33 271
  sculpture 5 768, 769
  silver 30 35
  Steinzimmer 29 612
  stucco 29 838, 843
  tapestries 12 467
  wall paintings 10 199; 28 136–7
 Ruhmeshalle 12 375; 13 610
 theatres
  Künstlertheater 30 682
  Prinzregententheater 30 682
  Residenztheater see under Residenz
  Salvatorplatz Komödienhaus 30 676
  Schauspielhaus 26 374
 town halls
  Altes Rathaus 13 316
  Rathaus 12 376; 13 161; 31 237
 University 7 527
 urban planning 11 128; 12 605; 31 735
 Villa Schülein 8 533
 Villa Stuck see under museums
 Wittelsbach Fountain 14 526
 Zoo 33 700
Munich, Lucas, Abbot of St Bavo 4 161
Munich, Painter of 13 516
Munich 892, Painter of 10 615
Munich 2335, Painter of 13 524
Munich Arrest of Christ, Master of the 4 594; 20 734*
Munich Golden Legend, Master of the 20 626, 734–5*
 works 4 371; 17 669; 20 735
Munich green see PIGMENTS → types → emerald green
Münichhoven, Hendrik see MUNNICHHOEVEN, HENDRIK
Munich Psalter see under PSALTERS → individual manuscripts
Munich Treasure 9 655
al-Munif (family) 2 316
Mun Ik-chŏm 18 374
Mun'im Khan 17 451
Munir 22 263
Munir, Hisham 16 1
Muniz Sodré, Niomar 4 726
Munjang see SŎNG SE-CH'ANG
Munjŏng, Queen (fl 1545) 7 208
Munka 17 833
Munkács 15 9; 22 310*
 Castle 31 549, 550
 Mukachevo 31 546
Munkacsi, Martin 22 310*
Munkácsy, Mihály (von) 14 588, 901; 22 310–11*; 30 210
 assistants 26 419
 groups and movements 9 461
 pupils 18 387; 20 276; 31 537
 reproductive prints by others 18 237

Munkácsy, Mihály (von)—cont.
 works 11 581; 20 146; 22 311
Munka Kor 15 18
Munka Kört 17 833
Munkbrarup Church 11 252
Munkkiniemi-Haaga 27 474
Munktorp 13 120
Munmu, King (reg 661-81) 18 275
Mun Myŏng-dae 18 259
Munn, Nancy 1 56, 68
Munn, Paul Sandby 12 742; 21 901
Munné, Enrique 3 826
Munnekus, Hendrik see MUNNICHHOEVEN, HENDRIK
Münnerstadt Church 1 710
Munnesvaram 29 448
Munni Begum (Nawabs of Bengal) 15 379
Münnich, Aladár 13 889; 14 890
Münnich, Christopher von Burckhardt, Count 10 461
Munnichhoeven, Hendrik 22 311–12*; 30 78, 117
Munniks, Hendrik see MUNNICHHOEVEN, HENDRIK
Munnings, Alfred (James) 1 108; 2 107; 19 621; 22 312*; 23 249; 29 426
Munnings, I. F. 24 265
Munnings, Sir Alfred, Art Museum see under DEDHAM (ESSEX)
Munns, Henry Turner 4 86
Munnuswamy 20 54
Muñoz, Blas 31 89
Muñoz, Evaristo 7 689
Muñoz, Fernão 22 312*; 23 414; 31 102
Muñoz, Gerónimo Fures y see FURES Y MUÑOZ, GERÓNIMO
Muñoz, Lucio 22 313*
Muñoz, Osmín 10 154
Muñoz, Sebastián 7 524; 22 313*
Muñoz (family), Vega y see VEGA Y MUÑOZ (FAMILY)
Muñoz, Vicente 2 394; 7 847; 22 313*
Muñoz Degrain, Antonio 22 313–14*; 24 829
Muñoz de Ugena, Manuel 29 316
Muñoz García, Antonio 21 380
Muñoz Lora, Eduardo 7 603, 603
Muñoz Suárez, David 21 381; 22 314*; 25 878; 31 186
Múñoz Tebar, Jesús 32 170
Múñoz Tebar, Luis 32 170
Munro, Alexander 22 314*; 28 243
Munro (of Novar), H(ugh) A(ndrew) J(ohnstone) 22 314–15*; 31 472
Munro, J. A. R. 27 608
Munro, Thomas 1 230
Münsingen 25 538
Mun Sŏ-go 18 300
Munsŏng see YI (i) I
Munstead Wood 12 140
Münster (Germany) 12 360; 22 315–16*
 Cathedral of St Paulus 13 48, 684; 22 315–16*; 32 94
  monument to Heidenreich von Lethmathe see Stephanus altar
  sculpture 13 683, 684; 22 315
  Stephanus altar 13 683
  Treasury 32 727
 Erbdrostenhof 28 106
 façades 4 777
 Rathaus 31 238
 St Mauritz 23 647; 26 632
 Schloss 12 413
 Stadtmuseum 12 238
 Überwasserkirche 22 316*
 University 2 382
 Westfälisches Landesmuseum 32 727
Münster (Switzerland) see MÜSTAIR
Münster, Bernt von 30 84
Münster, Sebastian 5 448; 8 823

Munsterbilsen Quadriga Silk 9 667
Münstereifel 30 905
Munsterhjelm, (Magnus) Hjalmar 11 95; 22 316–17*
Münsterlingen Monastery Church 32 822
Münsterman, Claus 22 317
Münsterman, Johan 22 317
Münsterman, Ludwig 12 405; 22 317*
Münsteuer Chapel 32 821
Muntaner, Juan 22 317
Muntaner Moner, Francesco 22 317
Muntaner Moner, José 22 317
Muntaner Moner, Juan 22 318
Muntaner y Diez de Armendariz, Lorenzo María 22 318
Muntaner Yupe, Lorenzo 22 317
al-Muntasir, Caliph (reg 861-2) (Abbasid) 16 434
al-Muntasir, Ruler (reg 1434-5) (Hafsid) 16 219, 220
Muntaya, Pere Pau 29 305
Munteanu, Lažar 26 723
Münter, Gabriele 17 761–4; 22 318*; 29 872
 groups and movements 4 131, 132; 12 395; 16 817; 22 921; 24 591
 patrons and collectors 22 305
 works 29 871
Munthe, Alf 19 428
Munthe, Gerhard (Peter Frantz Wilhelm) 18 464; 22 318–19*; 23 239; 30 326
 groups and movements 22 540; 23 226, 232
 works 11 476, 478; 23 233–4
Munthe, Holm (Hansen) 22 319*; 23 221
Munthe, J(ohan) W(ilhelm) N(ormann) 22 319–20*
Munthe, Ludvig 22 318, 320*
Munthe-Kaas, Herman 4 123; 23 234
Muntok 15 794
Munts, O. R. 32 381
Munts, Viktor O. 2 894; 22 174; 27 313
Muntu, Mode 33 596
Muntyan, Yury (Afanas'yevich) 27 417
Müntz, Eugène 22 320*
Müntz, Johann Heinrich 10 199; 22 320*
 groups and movements 13 199
 works 22 59; 32 825
Muntz metal see under ALLOYS → types
Munyŏng, King of Paekche (reg 501-23) 4 795; 18 249, 260, 272, 349, 352, 361, 364, 366, 369, 383, 384; 21 716
 tomb 18 272
Münze, Walter 14 323
Münzer, Adolf 16 906
Münzer, Hieronymus 28 518
Muona, Toini 11 105, 106
Muong 32 489
Muong Chawa see LUANG PRABANG
Muong Sing Buddha 18 768
Muoto 24 452
al-Muqaddasi 6 320; 13 811; 16 369, 370; 23 561
muqarbas see MUQARNAS
muqarnas (architecture) 9 161; 16 138, 142, 158; 22 321–5*; 26 139
 Algeria 16 170, 190
 Central Asia, Western 6 202; 16 161, 169
 Egypt 16 176; 22 321–2, 323, 324
 Iran 16 161, 164, 169, 194, 233; 22 321, 322
 Iraq 22 322
 Sicily 22 324
 Spain 16 216, 494; 22 324

muqarnas (architecture)—cont.
Syria **22** 322–3
Turkey **22** 323, *323*
Yemen **16** 215
see also under CAPITALS → types; DOMES → types; VAULTS → types
Muqarnas (periodical) **16** 550; **24** 433
Muqi **14** 137; **22** 325–6*
patrons and collectors **2** 599; **17** 428; **30** 465
works **5** 120; **6** 773, 784, *785*, 789, 804; **18** 560; **22** *325*
al-Muqtadir, Caliph (*reg* 908-32) (Abbasid) **16** 432, 456
Mur, Dalmau de, Archbishop *see* DALMAU DE MUR, Archbishop
Mur, Ramón de *see* RAMÓN DE MUR
Mur, Tomás **13** 764
Mura, Francesco de **16** 673; **22** 326–7*, 479
collaboration **8** 856
patrons and collectors **2** 727; **4** 562; **28** 18
pupils **3** 225
tapestries **22** 481; **31** 447
teachers **29** 43
works **20** 213; **22** *327*; **31** 444
Murad (*fl c.* 1630-40) **15** 588, 590
Murad (*fl c.* 1700-20) **15** 609
Murad I, Sultan (*reg* 1360-89) (Ottoman) **5** 282; **9** 729; **16** 810; **18** 509
Murad II, Sultan (*reg* 1421-44; 1446-51) (Ottoman) **5** 282; **9** 729; **16** 205, 378; **25** 51
Murad III, Sultan (*reg* 1574-95) (Ottoman) **15** 16; **20** 284; **23** 638, *642*, 642–3*
albums **7** 717
architecture **16** 224, 602, 610; **21** 50
carpets **16** 473
collections **16** 122
gardens **12** 84
manuscripts **16** 301, 348, 349, 350; **22** 235
patronage **16** 123
sculpture **16** 91
sponsorship **23** 641
treatises **16** 277
Murad IV, Sultan (*reg* 1623-40) (Ottoman) **16** 225, 499, 610
architecture **16** *225*
Murad Daylami **16** 337
Muradia **31** 426
Murad Khan **15** 369
Muradogly, Ashraf **2** 897
Muradov, Shirin **29** 823; **31** 782
Muradyan, Sargis **2** 433
Murai, Macanari **17** 293
Murak, Teresa **22** 327–8*
Murakami, Emperor (*reg* 946-67) **18** 548; **23** 445
Murakami, Kagaku **17** 201; **22** 328*
Murakami, Saburō **13** 866; **17** 207
Murakhver, Vladimir (Semyonovich) **27** 417
Muralidharan **20** 54
Muralli **10** 190
murals **11** 54; **22** 328–36*; **28** 337, 339
historical and regional traditions
Afghanistan **1** *209*
Argentina **22** 335*
Austria **2** *798*
Belgium **3** 588
Bolivia **4** 263; **22** 335*
Britain **22** 330–31, 332, 333, *333*
Canada **22** 335
Chile **22** 335*
England **22** 333
Fascism **25** 652
France **22** 329, 330, *330*, 333
Germany **22** *328*, 329, 330, 332, 333
murals
historical and regional traditions—cont.
Honduras **14** 715
Ibibio **15** 64
Israel **16** 568
Italy **16** *681*; **22** 332; **25** 652; **28** 793
20th cent. **16** 708
Mexico **7** 841; **10** 866; **15** 830; **21** 387–8*, 405, *405*; **22** *334*, 334–5*; **25** 653; **26** *428*; **27** 872
20th cent. **23** *567*; **26** 426, 429; **28** *785*
Netherlands, the **22** 332, 333
Nicaragua **22** 335*
Portugal **22** 333; **25** *299*
Sri Lanka **29** *468*
Union of Soviet Socialist Republics **22** 332
United States of America **15** 830; **22** 335–6*, *336*; **25** 653, 654; **26** *427*; **31** 606
19th cent. **1** *22*
20th cent. **3** *748*; **19** 878; **23** *566*
materials
acrylic **22** 336
ceramics **16** 568
concrete **22** 336
enamel **22** 333
faience (ii) (ceramics) **3** 588
mosaics **22** 163, 333, 336
steel **22** 336
terracotta **22** 333
see also FRESCOES; SECCO PAINTINGS; WALL PAINTINGS
Muralto **26** 635
S Vittore **26** 635
mural towers *see under* TOWERS → types
Muráň **28** 856
Murano (Venice) **32** 182, 186
archives **32** 204
glass **7** 84, 86; **10** 316; **12** 786, VIII1, VIII3; **16** 740; **20** 215; **21** 719; **24** 57; **32** 200–205, *201*, *202*, *203*, *205*
mirrors **21** 720
monastery of S Mattia **7** 189
Museo Vetrario di Murano **6** 443; **7** 895; **32** 204
Palazzetto Corner **24** 339
Palazzo Trevisiano **32** 349
paperweights **24** 57
S Pietro Martire
paintings **3** *659*
SS Maria e Donato **4** 774; **16** 625
vases **32** *205*
Murano (family) **11** 383
Murano, Andrea da *see* ANDREA DA MURANO
Murano, Tōgo **17** 90; **22** 336–7*; **23** 592
Murano Cappellini **28** 35
Murano & Mori **22** 336
Murant, Emanuel **33** 26, 391
Muraro, Michelangelo **22** 337*
Murasaki Shikibu **12** 96; **14** 302; **17** 157, 212, 221, 224, 371, 375, 437
Murase Kōtei **17** 236
Murase Taiichi *see* MURASE TAIITSU
Murase Taiitsu **17** 188; **22** 337–8*
works **17** 198, *199*, 238
Murashko, Nikolay (Ivanovich) **18** 38, 482; **24** 818; **31** 559; **33** 607
Murashko, Oleksandr **22** 338*; **31** 559
Muraste **10** *536*, 538
Murat III, Sultan *see* MURAD III, Sultan
Murat, Caroline, Queen of Naples *see* CAROLINE MURAT, Queen of Naples
Murat, Joachim, King of Naples *see* JOACHIM MURAT, King of Naples
Murata, Hiroshi **20** 609
Murata, Hirozo **30** 329
Murata, Yutaka **10** 685
Murata Shukō **18** 550; **22** 338–9*
works **17** 335, 342, 423; **18** 563
Muratori, Ludovico Antonio **2** 310; **7** 678; **21** 520
Muratori, Saverio **16** 650; **25** 792
Muratori, Teresa **29** 33
Muratov, Pavel (Pavlovich) **22** 339*; **27** 444
Muratov, Vladimir (Sergeyevich) **27** 418
Muratowicz, Sefer **16** 553; **32** 6
Murayama, Kaita **23** 179
Murayama, Ryūhei **17** 429
Murayama, Tomoyoshi **17** 206; **20** 873, 874; **22** 339*
Murch, Walter **24** 213
Murcia
Cathedral **29** 265, 266, 271, 336, 337
metalwork **16** 386
pottery **16** 411, *411*, 412; **29** 323
Murcutt, Glenn (Marcus) **2** 743; **22** 339–40*
Murdac, Henry, Abbot of Fountains, Archbishop of York **7** 351
Murdoch, J. S. **24** 296
Murdoch, Keith **2** 769
Murdoch, Peter **6** 392; **8** 804
Murdoch Smith, Robert **22** 340*
ceramics **16** 395, 426
dealing **16** 554
tiles **1** 642
Murdock, William **19** 366; **28** 831
Murdolo, Emilio **13** 871
Murena, Carlo **24** 757, 885; **31** 895
Murer, Christoph **22** 340–41*
works **22** *341*
Murer, Eugène **15** 154; **24** 883
Murer, Heinrich **21** 406
Murer, Jakob, Abbot **14** 50
Murer, Jos **22** 340; **33** 736
Murer, Paul **29** 750
Murer, Peter **28** 138
Muretto de Sant, Lorenzo de *see* SENES, LORENZO
Mureybet **21** *267*, 269; **22** 341*; **30** *180*
houses **21** 280
pottery **21** 269, 305; **30** 196
skulls **30** 181
statues **30** 182
wall paintings **30** 197
Murghab **30** *252*
Murguía **16** 48
Muri **30** 126
ceramics **30** 143
Klosterkirche **3** 886; **26** 635; **30** 136
statuettes **27** 91, *91*
Muria **15** 734
Müridoğlu, Zühtü **3** 194; **22** 342*; **31** 454
Muriel, Luis **26** 522
Murik **24** 71
Murillo, Bartolomé Esteban **20** 234; **22** 342–8*; **28** 515, 520
attributions **13** 730; **18** 840; **19** 25; **21** 348
collaboration **16** 48; **24** 822
methods **29** 281
paintings **11** 494
genre **10** 785; **11** 488; **12** 290; **22** *343*, *347*
religious **5** 367; **6** 467; **9** 110; **11** 488; **14** 784; **20** 234; **22** *344*; **24** 506; **28** 520; **31** 810
patrons and collectors **28** 515
Akademie der Bildenden Künste, Vienna **2** 831
Alexander I, Emperor of Russia (*reg* 1801-25) **26** 733
Murillo, Bartolomé Esteban
patrons and collectors—cont.
Augustinian hermits **2** 726
Beit, Otto (John) **3** 522
Bonnemaison, Ferréol de **4** 330
Borbón y Braganza, Sebastián Gabriel **4** 378
Bourbon II., Luis Antonio, Infante of Spain **4** 565
Brudenell, George, 4th Earl of Cardigan and 1st Duke of Montagu **4** 893
Bryan, Michael **5** 63
Calonne, Charles-Alexandre de **5** 439
Capuchins **5** 690, 691
Carraquiri, Nazario **5** 871
Catherine II, Empress of Russia (*reg* 1762- 96) **26** 733
Charles III, King of Spain (*reg* 1759-88) **17** 893
Charles IV, King of Spain (*reg* 1788-1808) **4** 565
Conti, Louis-François de Bourbon, Prince de (1717-76) **7** 778
Dennistoun, James **8** 763
Dugléré, Adolphe **9** 378
Elizabeth Farnese, Queen of Spain (1692-1766) **4** 559
Ensenada, Marqués de **10** 406
Esterházy, Pál, Prince (1786-1866) **10** 530
Farinelli, Carlo Broschi **10** 806
Ferdinand VII, King of Spain (*reg* 1808; 1814-33) **4** 566
Ford, Richard **11** 304
Gaignat, Louis-Jean **11** 902
Galliera, Maria de Ferrari, Duchessa di **4** 811
Gideon, Sampson **12** 601
Gillott, Joseph **12** 638
Godoy, Juan Silvano **24** 101
Godoy (y Alvárez de Faria), Manuel, Príncipe de la Paz **12** 839
Guzmán, Ambrosio Ignacio Spínola y, Archbishop of Seville **13** 880
Hohenzollern, Henry, Prince of Prussia **14** 653
Iriarte (family) **16** 48
Joseph Bonaparte, King of Naples and Spain (*reg* 1806-8) **4** 304
Jovellanos, Gaspar Melchor de **17** 673
Las Marismas del Guadalquivir, Alejandro María Aguado y Ramírez de Estemoz, Marqués de **18** 811
López Cepero, Manuel **19** 658
Louis-Philippe, King of the French (*reg* 1830-48) **30** 385
Loyd, Samuel Jones, 1st Baron Overstone **19** 736
Mañara Vicentelo de Leca, Miguel **20** 234
Mauroner, José **2** 404
Miles, Philip John **21** 541
Montpensier, Antoine-Marie-Philippe-Louis de Bourbon, Duc de **23** 523
Munro (of Novar), H(ugh) A(ndrew) J(ohnstone) **22** 314
Musée des Beaux Arts (Le Havre) **19** 92
Museo Provincial (Cádiz) **5** 368
National Gallery of Art (Washington, DC) **1** 454
Neve (y Chaves), Justino de **23** 11
Omazur, Nicolas **23** 437
Péreire (family) **24** 396
Pollok House **28** 273
Pourtalès-Gorgier, James-Alexandre, Comte de **25** 383
Murillo, Bartolomé Esteban
patrons and collectors—cont.
Salamanca (y Mayol), José, Marqués de **27** 607
Santiago, Fernando Augustín Rodríguez de los Rís, 2nd Marqués de **27** 793
Santiago, Francisco Esteban Rodríguez de los Ríos, 1st Marqués de **27** 792–3
Seymour-Conway, Richard, 4th Marquess of Hertford **20** 875; **28** 527
Soult (Jean de Dieu), Maréchal **29** 96
Standish, Frank Hall **29** 535
Tallard, Marie-Joseph d'Hostun, Duc de **30** 274
Verrue, Jeanne-Baptiste d'Albert de Luynes, Comtesse de **32** 368
Wilson, Andrew **33** 216
Wyndham, George O'Brien, 3rd Earl of Egremont **33** 453
pupils **21** 129
reproductive prints by others **10** 533; **12** 28, 33; **19** 659; **20** 5, 144; **26** 473; **28** 389
teachers **6** 48
Murillo, Enrique **21** 382
Murillo, Geraldo *see* ATL, DR
Murillo, Museo Casa de *see under* LA PAZ → museums
Murillo, Rosario **23** 86
Murin'an **12** 100
Muriolus of Salerno **4** 274
Murius Castle **19** 495
Murkvichka **21** 503
Murlo *see* POGGIO CIVITATE
Murmann, Christoph **10** 436; **11** 819; **22** 725
Murmann, Ferdinand **33** 275
Murmann, Jakob, I **17** 863
Murmann der Jüngerer, Christoph **21** 127
Murner, Thomas **9** 442; **20** 793
Muro, José Antonio Fernández *see* FERNÁNDEZ MURO, JOSÉ ANTONIO
Murōji **17** *11*, 68; **22** 348–9*
Murom **22** 349*
Muromachi Palace *see under* KYOTO
Muromachi period *see under* JAPAN → periods
Murphy **6** 94
Murphy, Anna Brownell *see* JAMESON, ANNA BROWNELL
Murphy, C. F., Associates **1** 495; **16** 868; **21** 492; **24** 457
Murphy, Denis **16** 896
Murphy, Dudley **10** 687
Murphy, Edmund **25** 402
Murphy, Fiona **2** 762
Murphy, Gerald **3** 120; **22** 350*; **29** 670
Murphy, Henry George **10** 337
works **10** *337*
Murphy, James Cavanah **13** 204; **16** 547; **22** 59
Murphy, J(ohn) Francis **22** 350*; **31** 141
Murphy, John **2** 742; **4** 415; **20** 8
Murphy, Maud **8** 463
Murphy, Phyllis **2** 742; **4** 415; **20** 8
Murphy, Seamus **16** 22
Murphy/Jahn **9** 427; **16** 868; **28** 835; **29** 106
Murphy & McGill **14** 115
Murphy Radio **25** 400
Murr, Christoph Gottlieb von **9** 443; **22** 350*; **24** 443
works **4** 21; **18** 47; **25** 454
Murr, Johan Baptist, Abbot of Marienberg **14** 694
Murray **30** 161
Murray, Miss **18** *894*
Murray, Alexander **22** 639

Murray, Charles (Oliver) 22 351*
Murray, Charles Fairfax 5 269; 9 229; 22 111, 351*
Murray, David, 2nd Lord Balvaird 18 814
Murray, Elizabeth (1940-) 22 351–2*
Murray, Elizabeth, Countess of Dysart (*fl* 1600s) 19 121
Murray, Frank Stuart 8 568
Murray, George 3 533
Murray, J. 28 349
Murray, James (*d* 1634) 28 225
Murray, James (*d c.* 1730) 17 768
Murray, James, 2nd Duke of Atholl (*d* 1674) 7 409; 17 623; 28 252
Murray, John (?1768-1827) 33 322–3
Murray, John (1778-1843) 13 304, 810; 22 352; 24 637
Murray, John (1808-92) 6 100; 11 304; 13 810, 811; 22 352*
Murray, John, 4th Duke of Atholl (*d* 1830) 5 169; 10 145
Murray, Keith Day Pearce 7 713; 10 313, 320
Murray, Kenneth 1 432; 23 136, 139
Murray, Pearce 33 23
Murray, Robert 5 571
Murray, Thomas 22 352*; 26 394
Murray, Ward and Partners 7 713
Murray, William (1785-1849) 16 9
Murray, William, 1st Earl of Dysart (*d* 1674) 20 142
Murray, William, 1st Earl of Mansfield (*fl c.* 1756-93) 1 137; 25 882; 28 271
Murray, William, 3rd Earl of Mansfield (*b* 1777) 2 692
Murray, William, 6th Earl of Dysart (1739-1821) 7 750
Murray, William George 9 297; 17 625
Murray, William Grant 32 792
Murray, William Staite 10 314, 375; 22 352–3*
Murray Writing-Cabinet 10 294
Murrer, Johann 25 549
Murrey, Thomas *see* MURRAY, THOMAS
Murrovalle, Giovanni da *see* GIOVANNI DA MURROVALLE
Murrumbeena Pottery 4 605; 24 387
Murrumurru, Dick *see* NGULAYNGULAY, DICK
Murshid 16 337
Murshidabad 3 *166*; 15 370, 592, 662
art forms
architecture 15 378–80*
carpets 15 684
enamel 15 711
furniture 15 693
ivory 15 697, 724
metalwork 15 724
painting 15 634, *635*, *652*, 652–3*, 724
textiles 15 671
Islamic religious buildings
Chhote Chowk ki Masjid 15 380
Chowk Mosque 15 379, *379*
congregational mosque *see* Katra Mosque
Husayniya 15 380
imambara 15 380
Katra Mosque 15 378
Miyan Halal Mosque 15 380
mosque of Farhat Allah Khan 15 380
Moti Jheel Mosque 15 379
Phuti Mosque 15 378
Qadam Sharif complex 15 380
Safed mosque 15 379
Zarad mosque 15 379
Medina 15 379
palace 15 380, 402, *402*
Murshid Quli Jafar Khan, Nawab of Bengal (*reg* 1703-26) 15 378
Murtaza Quli Bukhari 15 595
Murten 30 126
Murthly Hours *see under* BOOKS OF HOURS → individual manuscripts
Murti 15 253
Murtić, Edo 8 179; 22 353*
Murtinho Larraín, Pedro 6 594
Murtuk 6 294
Muru, Selwyn 20 359; 22 353*
works 20 *360*
Murumbi, Joseph 17 908
murus gallicus see under ARCHITECTURE → techniques
Murut 20 182, 183
Murville, Maurice Couve de, Archbishop of Birmingham *see* COUVE DE MURVILLE, MAURICE, Archbishop of Birmingham
Muryōji 17 196; 22 430
Muryŏng, King (*reg* 501-23) 18 297
Murza, G. 2 428
Mus, Paul 15 211; 22 353*
Musabayev, Mulchtar (Nabiyevich) 31 783
Musaion 24 440
musallas see under MOSQUES → types
Musan 18 352
Musanagar 15 424, 427
Musango, Francis 31 528
Musashi *see* MIYAMOTO MUSASHI NITEN
Muşaşir 31 699
shrine of Haldi 1 830
temple 31 700
Musawwarat el-Sufra *see* MASSAWARAT EL-SUFRA
Musa Yola 14 233
works 14 *232*
Muscat 2 *246*
Armed Forces Museum 23 436
Atelier for Fine Arts 23 436
Bayt Nadir 23 436
fort 23 436
metalwork 23 436
museums 2 275
Omani French Museum 23 436
Muscat, Jörg 13 904
works 2 *800*
Muscat and Oman *see* OMAN
Müsch, Leo 3 423
Muschenheim, William 25 48
Muschik, Johann 24 592
Muscogee Creek (OK) 22 671
muscovite *see under* JADE → types
Muscovite Empire style *see* EMPIRE STYLE → regional traditions → Moscow
Muse, Isaac Lane 14 203
musea see NYMPHAEA
Museée Central des Arts *see under* PARIS → Musée Napoléon
Musées et monuments de France 32 643
Musegai *see* KUSUMI MORIKAGE
museiarii 22 154
Museifneh 10 507
Muselli, Giacomo 32 343
Muselli, Vincent 8 775
Museo 24 452
museology 2 368
musettes 22 374
Museum (Germany) 24 443
Museum (Spain) 24 452
Museum: artistic collections in the USSR see MUZEY: KHUDOZHESTVENNYYE SOBRANIYA SSSR
Museum: Blätter für bildende Kunst 24 421
Museum Archivists' Newsletter 2 366
museum board *see under* BOARDS
Museum der Gegenwart 24 445
Museum etruscum 10 637
Museumleven 24 440
Museum Press 26 536
museums 2 298, 364, 365, 366, 368, 369, 534, 557, 559–60, 561; 4 22; 7 561, 563; 8 911; 9 11, 13, 25; 10 675; 15 888; 18 522; 20 208; 22 354–68*, *355*; 25 818; 28 820; 29 859; 31 235
catalogues *see under* CATALOGUES → types
historical and regional traditions
Aboriginal Australia 1 66–7*
Afghanistan 1 211–12*
Africa 1 437*
Albania 1 545–6*
Algeria 1 636
Anatolia, ancient 1 839*
Antigua (island) 2 153, 154
Antilles, Lesser 2 153–4*
Arabia 2 275*
Argentina 2 403–5*; 7 *847*
Armenia (Europe) 2 444–5*
Athens 13 360*
Australia 2 369, 770–71*; 22 360
Austria 2 *786*, 826, 830–31*; 9 19; 15 867; 22 356, *356*
Bahamas, the 3 64*
Bangladesh 3 169–70*
Barbados 2 153
Belgium 3 616–17*
Belize 3 624–5*
Bolivia 4 268–9*
Bosnia 4 462–3*
Brazil 4 719, 726–7*, 728; 27 *808*
Neo-classicism 13 *296*
Britain 2 601; 22 364; 29 426
Bulgaria 5 162–3*
Burkina Faso 5 217*
Canada 5 590–91*; 10 *459*; 31 177
Central Asia, Eastern 6 320–21*
Central Asia, Western 6 282–5*
Chile 6 600–601*
China 6 772; 7 154–6*
Colombia 7 611–12*
Côte d'Ivoire 8 23
Crete 8 157; 21 691–2*
Croatia 8 180–81*
Cuba (Caribbean) 8 238–9*
Cycladic 8 323–4*
Cyprus 8 366–7*
Czech Republic 8 424*
Denmark 4 *68*; 8 746, 759–60*; 22 *366*
Dominica 2 153, 154
Dominican Republic 9 *117*, 119*
Ecuador 9 714*
Egypt 9 768*; 10 80; 16 557
Egypt, ancient 10 85, 92–4*
England 9 13, 25, 30; 10 368–71*; 22 356, 362; 30 *504*
Greek Revival 7 *504*; 10 *234*; 28 *874*
19th cent. 4 *86*; 9 30; 22 362; 23 259; 32 *905*
Eritrea 10 577–8*
Estonia 10 540*
Ethiopia 10 577–8*
Etruscan 10 637, 640*
Finland 11 112*; 14 *373*
France 2 366; 3 873; 6 77; 9 25; 11 664–8*; 19 *848*; 22 357–8, *358*, 359, 362; 24 138
Baroque 24 *163*
Modernism 24 *131*; 28 *483*
18th cent. 20 139
19th cent. 5 *536*; 11 301–2; 23 126; 32 *82*
20th cent. 20 208; 24 *127*
Georgia 12 332*
Germany 3 807; 12 374, 475–7*; 14 492; 22 358, 362; 31 *736*
Baroque 25 *240*
Greek Revival 18 *122*
Nazism 22 *710*
museums
historical and regional traditions
Germany—cont.
Neo-classicism 12 *375*
Renaissance Revival 18 *124*
16th cent. 33 274
18th cent. 9 455, *455*; 14 491
19th cent. 22 *362*
20th cent. 7 *386*, *585*; 11 *736*; 12 *498*; 22 *368*
Greece 7 *852*
Greece, ancient 13 469–71*, 604*; 22 354
Grenada 2 153
Guadeloupe (country) 2 154
Guatemala 13 769–70*
Guinea-Bissau 1 440
Haiti 14 60
Helladic 14 360–61*
Herzegovina 4 462–3*
Honduras 14 716–17
Hungary 15 16–17*
India, Republic of 7 *882*; 15 180*, 184
Indian subcontinent 15 743–6*; 22 364, *364*
Iran 15 899–900*; 16 557
Iran, ancient 15 922*
Ireland 16 *10*, 36–7*
Islamic 16 555–8*
Israel 16 571*; 17 *492*, 582*
Italy 2 168, 365; 9 14–15, 23; 13 470; 16 769, 770–76*; 22 356; 27 114–15; 32 343
Etruscan 10 637, 640*
Neo-classicism 16 771–2*, *772*; 29 *640*
Renaissance 16 770–71*; 32 *15*
15th cent. 13 469
17th cent. 6 360
18th cent. 22 *361*
Jamaica 16 890*
Japan 17 *89*, 427, 432–5*, *433*, *434*; 23 371
High Tech 1 *737*
20th cent. 18 *533*
Jewish art 17 580–82*
Kazakhstan 6 284*
Kenya 17 908*
Korea 18 382–3*
Kuwait 18 541
Kyrgyzstan 6 284*
Lebanon 19 *8*
Liberia 19 310*
Macedonia (ii) (former Yugoslavia) 19 886*
Malta (Republic of) 20 219*
Mesoamerica, Pre-Columbian 21 264–5*
Mesopotamia 21 310*
Mexico 21 *380*, 396–7*
Minoan 21 691–2*
Mongolia 21 886*
Montenegro 22 19*
Montserrat (Leeward Islands) 2 153
Native North Americans 22 360, 675–8*
Nazism 22 *710*
Nepal 22 795*, 796*
Netherlands, the 14 *40*; 22 *829*, 906–7*; 30 568
Nevis 2 154
New Zealand 23 74–5*
Nicaragua 23 85*
Nigeria 1 440; 23 139*
Northern Ireland 16 *39*, 42*
Norway 23 *222*, 243*, 602
Ottoman 16 557
Pacific Islands 23 737, 739–40*
Pakistan 23 804*
Panama 23 906
Paraguay 24 101–2*
Peru 24 516–17*
Poland 25 139–40*
Portugal 25 318–19*
Puerto Rico 25 703–4*
Romania 26 724–5*
museums
historical and regional traditions—cont.
Rome, ancient 26 782; 27 45–7*, 114–16*
Russia 6 284–5; 27 439–41*
19th cent. 22 *173*
20th cent. 20 194; 22 508; 27 *381*
St Kitts 2 153, 154
St Lucia 2 153
St Vincent 2 154
Saudi Arabia 2 275
Scotland 28 *231*, 272–4*
Senegal 1 440; 28 406*
Serbia 28 458–9*
Slovakia 28 857
Slovenia 28 863*
South Africa 29 121–2*
South America, Pre-Columbian 29 220–21*, 222*
South-east Asia 29 239–41*
Spain 29 *272*, 332, 354–6*; 32 *565*
Sri Lanka 29 478–9*
Sudan 29 898
Surinam 30 17
Sweden 30 118–19*
Switzerland 30 154–5*
Syria-Palestine 30 198–9*
Taiwan 30 *245*
Tajikistan 6 283*
Tanzania 30 302*
Tibet 30 849*, 850
Trinidad and Tobago 31 339–40*
Troadic 31 355–6*
Tunisia 31 426–7*
Turkey 1 839; 16 557; 31 456
Turkmenistan 6 283–4*
Ukraine 31 565*
United Arab Emirates 2 275; 31 585*
United States of America 2 368, 369; 4 23; 6 772; 15 745–6; 17 434–5; 22 359*, 360, 365; 26 *480*; 27 613; 28 *328*; 31 662, 665–9*, 670–71; 32 753, 889, *889*
Jewish art 17 581–2*
Neo-classicism 7 *429*; 21 *649*
Romanesque Revival 26 *213*
20th cent. 2 *694*; 8 *821*; 12 *236*; 17 *724*; 22 *365*; 24 *325*
Uruguay 31 757–8*
Uzbekistan 6 283*
Venezuela 32 179–80*
Wales 32 791*
Zaïre 33 598*
Zambia 33 603*
Zimbabwe 1 440
lighting 19 365, 367; 28 327
types
applied art 22 363
art 21 404
arts and crafts 22 363
decorative arts 32 446
design 8 802
modern art 7 561; 12 15; 17 436
natural history 2 710; 4 484; 21 147; 30 154
sculpture 27 271
see also COLLECTIONS; GALLERIES (iv) (ART)
see also GALLERIES (iv) (ART)
Museums Association (England) 10 370
Museums Association of the Caribbean (MAC) 2 154
Museumsnytt 24 452
Musfeld, Ernst Max 13 726
Musfik, Mihri 16 537
Mushailov, Mushail 27 433
Musharrahat 16 153
Mushatta *see* MSHATTA
Mushenge Museum 33 598
Mushfiq 15 593, 594, 595
Mushki, Tall-i 15 918

Mush Monastery **2** 436
Musi, Agostino dei **10** 385; **22** 369*; **27** 207
  collaboration **8** 765
  engravings **20** 1
  pupils **28** 316
  reproductive prints by others **12** 203; **16** 778
  teachers **25** 860
  works **1** 102; **7** 425; **11** 217; **13** 700; **16** 778; **25** 607; **27** 848; **28** 467
Musi, Giulio de' **1** 841
music (printed) **22** 369–71*, *370*
Mušič, Marko **28** 860
Music, Sead **4** 462
Musić, Zoran Anton **19** 491; **22** 371*; **28** 861
musical boxes *see under* BOXES → types
musical instruments **22** 371–7*, *377*
  historical and regional traditions
    Africa **1** 302, 358–60*, *359*; **22** 375
    Ancient Near East **1** 890–91*
    Aztec **21** 248
    Buddhism **17** 396; **21** 879; **30** 843
    Burma **5** 253*, 256–7*, 258–9*, *259*
    Cambodia **5** 508–9*
    Chimú **29** 216
    China **6** 829*; **7** 14; **22** 376
    Dogon **1** 358
    Egypt, ancient **10** 60, 64–5*; **22** 372
    Etruscan **10** 619
    Fang **1** 358
    Gabon **1** 358
    Inca **15** 164; **29** 216
    Indian subcontinent **22** 376
    Indonesia **15** 816–17*; **22** 376
    Islamic **16** 498
    Italy **22** 373; **27** 445
    Japan **17** 396–7*
    Java **22** 376
    Korea **22** 376
    Luba **19** 744
    Maya **21** 256, 257
    Mesoamerica, Pre-Columbian **21** 236, 247, 248, 256*
    Mesopotamia **22** 372
    Moche (culture) **29** 216
    Mongolia **21** 879–80*
    Nazca **29** 216
    Ottoman **16** 498
    Papua New Guinea **24** 68*, 79
    Philippines **24** 630*
    Puerto Rico **25** 703
    Senufo **1** 360
    Shinto **17** 396
    Sinú **29** 217
    South America, Pre-Columbian **29** 215–17*
    Tairona **29** 217
    Tanzania **1** 358
    Thailand **30** 636–7*
    Tibet **30** 843–4*
    Trinidad and Tobago **31** 331
    Uganda **31** 528
    Vanuatu **31** 892–3*
    Venezuela **32** *166*, 167
    Vicús culture **29** 215–16
    Vietnam **32** 489*
    Zaïre **1** *359*
    Zambia **1** 358
    Zande **1** *359*; **33** 610
  materials
    bone **21** 247, 248, 256
    box-wood **33** I2
    brass **22** 375
    bronze **6** 829*
    gourds **1** 302
    ivory **10** 60
    lacquer **7** 14; **32** 489
    mother-of-pearl **7** 14; **32** 489
    skins **21** 257
    stone **32** 489
musical instruments materials—cont.
    tortoiseshell **21** 256; **31** 195
    wood **1** *359*; **5** *259*
  techniques
    lost-wax casting **15** 816
musical notation **5** 381–2; **22** 369–71, *370*
musical scores **7** 685; **14** 675
music and art **2** 354–6; **9** 20; **22** 377–81*, *380*
music-halls **30** 679
Müşik, Mihri **31** 455
Musil, Alois **16** 549; **25** 830
Musin-Pushkin, A. I. **27** 439
Musin-Pushkin, L. A. **27** 439
Musitu, Lorenzo de la Hidalga y *see* HIDALGA (Y MUSITU), LORENZO DE LA
musivarii see MUSEIARII
musk **7** 91; **15** 850
Muskar Church **9** 590; **19** 840
Muskau **12** 134, *360*; **22** 381–2*; **25** 696
  gardens **12** 105
  stonewares **12** 428, 430
Muskebi **5** 741
Muskogean **22** 552
Muskogee (OK), Bacone Junior College **22** 595
Muslim (*d* 875) **16** 86
Muslim (*fl c.* 1000) **16** 404; **22** 382*
Muslim ibn Quraysh *see* SHARAF AL-DAWLA MUSLIM, Ruler
muslin **15** 660–61; **16** 430
Musman, E. B. **25** 689
Musoke, Theresa **17** 907, 908
Musō Sōseki **12** 98; **17** 169, 747, 749; **22** 382–3*
  patrons and collectors **17** 343
  works **18** 556
Musquara Mosque **16** 226
Musqueam **29** 743
Muss, Charles **20** 489
Musscher, Michiel van **22** 383*
  patrons and collectors **3** 239
  pupils **10** 144
  teachers **21** 350; **23** 609; **30** 425
Musseau, Richard **14** 855; **22** 888
mussel shells *see under* SHELLS → types
Mussen, Matthijs **28** 904; **30** 463
Musset, Alfred de **6** 489
Mussikiysky, Grigory **27** 426
Mussill, William **10** 312
Mussini, Cesare **22** 383; **25** 74
Mussini, Luigi **11** 189; **22** 383–4*
  groups and movements **16** 677; **25** 741
  pupils **11** 697; **19** 70
  works **24** 218
Mussini-Franchi, Luisa **22** 384
Mussini-Piaggio, Luigia **22** 384
Musso, Boniface *see* MOSS, BONIFACE
Musso, Charles *see* MUSS, CHARLES
Musso, Niccolò **22** 384*
Mussolini, Benito **10** 820; **12** 843
  architecture **16** 650; **24** 693, 694; **26** 762
  murals **22** 332; **25** 652
  sculpture **16** 708
Musson, Matthijs **8** 125; **14** 467; **19** 430; **25** 841
Mustafa II, Sultan, (*reg* 1695-1703) (Ottoman) **14** 27
Mustafa III, Sultan, (*reg* 1757-74) (Ottoman) **10** 494
Mustafa IV, Sultan (*reg* 1807-8) (Ottoman) **22** 385
Mustafa, Ghulam **23** 800
Mustafa Ağa (*d c.* 1665) **16** 223; **22** 384*
Mustafa Aga ibn Farhad Pasa (*fl c.* 1574-*c.* 1595)
  works **7** *626*
Mustafa Agha Ayat (*fl c.* 1881) **10** 91
Mustafa ʿAli **7** 717; **16** 127, 350
  writings **16** 277, 356
Mustafa al-Imami **15** 143
Mustafa Darir **16** 458
  works **16** *349*
Mustafa Dede Shaykhzada **16** 285
Mustafa Fadil **16** 553
Mustafa İzzet **16** 595; **21** 50; **22** 384–5*
Mustafa Izzet Yesarizade **10** 494; **16** 287
Mustafa Pasha Vlora **1** 545
Mustafa Raqim **16** 287; **22** 385*
Mustafa Vasıf **22** 384
Mustafayev, R. **2** 897
Müstair **30** *124*
  St Johann **5** 797–8; **22** 385*; **26** 653, 657
al-Mustaʿli, Caliph (*reg* 1094-1101) (Fatimid) **16** 432; **31** 21
al-Mustansir, Caliph (*reg* 1036-94) (Fatimid) **10** 832; **16** 490; **17** 497; **31** 22
al-Mustansir, Caliph (*reg* 1226-42) (Abbasid) **16** 180, 309, 491; **20** 55
Mustapha Kemal *see* ATATÜRK, KEMAL
Mustaqimzade **16** 277
mustard **4** 684
al-Mustaʿsim, Caliph (*reg* 1242-58) (Abbasid) **16** 309
  metalwork **16** *506*
Musterbuch **2** 791
Müstereiffel, Romanisches Haus **32** 281
Mustique **2** 151
Mustoe, W. R.
  works **12** *76*
Musume, Kozei no *see* KŌZEI NO MUSUME
Musya Bahal **21** 847
Muszyński, Tomasz **25** 105
Mutakkil-Nusku (*reg* 1113 BC) **23** 153
Muʿtamad Khan **15** 373
al-Muʿtamid, Ruler (*reg* 1069-91) (Abbadid) **12** 80; **28** 510, 511
Mutasa, David **33** 679
al-Muʿtasim, Caliph (*reg* 833-42) (Abbasid) **16** 151, 252, 256, 400, 511; **27** 678
al-Mutawakkil, Caliph (*reg* 847-61) (Abbasid) **12** 77; **16** 152; **21** 32, 626; **27** 680; **30** 477
al-Mutawakkil, Great Mosque of *see under* SAMARRAʿ
al-Mutawakkil, Imam (*reg* 1716-27) (Zaydi) **16** 500
Muʿtazilism *see under* ISLAM → branches
Muteba **33** 598
Mutesa, King of Baganda (*reg* 1852-84) **1** 309
Mutesellim, Tell el- *see* MEGIDDO
Muther, Richard **22** 385*; **26** 394; **27** 444
Mütherich, Florentine **18** 187
Muthesius, Hermann **12** 378, 479; **20** 594; **21** 779; **22** 386*, 450
  collaboration **9** 237; **28** 177
  groups and movements **2** 321, 565, 566, 571; **8** 824–5; **21** 781; **23** 498
  pupils **32** 759
  works **3** 795; **8** 824; **12** 416; **14** 362
  writings **10** 283
Muthu Vijayaraghunatha Sethupati, Ruler (*reg* 1710-20) **15** 647
Muti (family) **7** 393; **19** 735
al-Muti, Caliph (*reg* 946-74) (Abbasid) **16** 432
Muti, Carlo **25** 259
Muti, G. B. **8** 139
Muti, Orazio **28** 4
Muti, Vincenzo, Marchese **21** 89
Mutina *see* MODENA
Mutis, José Celestino **7** 612; **9** 712
Mutiso, David **1** 319; **22** 386–7*
Mutone, Carlo **29** 831
Mutschele, Johann Martinus **12** 431
Mutschler, Carlfried **14** 306
Mutsu, Marju **10** 540
Mutsu no Kami **21** 716
Muttenz, Siedlung Freidorf **30** 127
Mutter Ey *see* EY, JOHANNA
Mutters, H(ermanus) P(ieter) **14** 44; **22** 387*, 873
Mutton, William **10** 325
Muttoni, Francesco **11** 745; **22** 387–8*
  works **4** 611; **22** *388*; **32** 410
Muttoni, Pietro *see* VECCHIA, PIETRO DELLA
Muttoni Collection **32** 102
Muttra (Oman) **23** 436
Muttra (India) *see* MATHURA
Mutual Improvement Group (Grupa Samokształceniowa) **33** 416
Mutualista Previsión y Seguridad **9** 714
mutules **11** 790; **13** 377, *378*, 393; **22** 389*; **23** 478
Mutu Pîrvu *see* PÎRVU, MUTU
Mützner, Samys **19** 659
Művészet **24** 440
Művészettörténeti értesítő **24** 425, 441
Művészi ipar **24** 440
Muxima **2** 86
Muybridge, Eadweard **22** 389–90*; **24** 649, 653, 665, 669; **29** 536
  assistants **2** 130
  collaboration **21** 761
  works **2** 107; **7** 576; **22** *389*; **23** 295; **24** *670*; **29** 426
Muyden, Alfred van **7** 896; **22** 390
Muyden, Evert van **22** 390*
Muys, Nicolaas **28** 165
Muysen, Gielis van **32** 725
al-Muzaffar, Sultan (*reg*1250-95) (Rasulid) **16** 214
Muzaffar Al-Din, Shah (*reg* 1896-1907) (Qajar) **15** 897; **30** 415
Muzaffar al'Din Mahmud ibn Yaghıbasan **17** 864
Muzaffar ʿAli **4** 49; **22** 390–91*
  patrons and collectors **27** 513
  pupils **27** 506; **28** 811
  works **16** 333, 335, 337
Muzaffargah **15** 338
Muzaffar ibn Hibatallah al-Mufaddal al-Burujirdi **28** 809
al-Muzaffar ibn Muzaffar al-Tusi **2** 646
Muzaffarid **18** 85; **22** 391*
Muzaffarid, Shah Shujaʿ, Amir *see* SHAH SHUJAʿ, Amir
Muzard, José **6** 594
Muzell-Stosch, Wilhelm **29** 724
Muzey **27** 441
Muzey: Khudozhestvennyye sobraniya SSSR **27** 441
Muzeynoye delo **27** 441
Muzeynoye delo v SSSR **27** 441
Mu Zhi *see* DU MU
Muziano, Girolamo **22** 391–3*; **26** 770, 841
  collaboration **8** 181
  patrons and collectors **4** 567; **13** 628; **17** 509; **20** 840; **31** 63
  pupils **22** 715
  reproductive prints by others **3** 448; **6** 381; **7** 899; **27** 502; **30** 804; **32** 560
  works **16** 665; **18** 708; **22** *392*; **25** 606; **26** 809, 817, 823
Muzii, Muzio **4** 333
Muzika, František **8** 393; **22** 393*; **25** 433
Muzio, Giovanni **22** 393–4*; **28** 793
  collaboration **23** 263; **25** 218; **28** 792
Muzio, Giovanni—cont.
  groups and movements **23** 264
  pupils **31** 436
  works **10** 820, *821*, 822; **16** 649, 650, 731; **23** 263; **28** 793
Muzio, Virginio **22** 393
Muzondo, Joseph **33** 679
Muzubiza **17** 408
Muzzarelli, Giulia **5** 843
Muzziolo, Giovanni **22** 803
MVDV, Monogrammist *see* MICHAEL, MASTER
M'Vemba **2** 87
M. V. Lomonosov Artistic Carving Factory **18** 27
Mvula, Dervis **33** 602
Mwamba, Lutanda **33** 602
Mwamuka, Vernon **33** 678
Mwanza **1** *407*
  Sukuma Museum **30** 302
Mwata Yamvo **7** 195
Mweemba, Patrick **33** 602
Mwenze **33** 596
Mwera, Tiona **20** 161
Myachin, Church of the Annunciation **27** 370
Myagkova, Lyudmila (Mikhaylovna) **27** 417
Myan ma *see* BURMA
Myasoyedov, Grigory (Grigor'yevich) **22** 394*; **27** 579; **32** 835
Myatlev (family) **27** 439, 441
Myauk U *see* MYOHAUNG
Mycenae **2** 299; **8** 153; **13** *363*; **14** *332*; **22** 394–8*
  acropolis **14** 354, 359
  art forms and materials
    beads **14** *357*
    bronzes **14** 356
    collections **14** 361
    daggers **22** *397*
    faience (i) (glass) **14** 358, *358*, 359
    furniture **14** 354
    gold **12** 868; **29** 395
    ivory-carvings **14** *353*, 354, *354*
    jewellery **14** 357; **22** 397
    metalwork **21** 329; **22** 397
    pottery **4** 172; **14** 341
    reliefs **13** 444
    sculpture **14** 333, 351–2, *352*, 353
    swords **2** 451
    wall paintings **14** 348, 349, *349*, *350*
  citadel **22** *395*, 396–7*
  Citadel House **14** 350, 359
  cult centre **14** 334, *349*, 350
    altar **1** 691
    wall paintings **14** 349
  excavations **28** 114
  fortifications **14** 340
  Grave Circle A **31** 108
    daggers **14** 355
    gold **14** 355
    Grave III **14** 355
    Grave IV **14** 355
    Grave V **14** 355, 360
    metalwork **14** 355, *355*
  Grave Circle B **31** 108
    Grave Gamma **14** 355
    Grave Omikron **14** 356
    metalwork **14** 355
    swords **14** 356
  House M **21** 46
  House of Shields **14** 353, 354, 358, *358*
  House of the Oil Merchant **14** 349, 350
  House of the Warrior Vase **21** 46
  houses **22** 396
  Lion Gate **7** 358; **14** 340, 353; **21** 549; **22** 395, *396*; **23** 478; **26** 134
  megara (buildings) **14** 340; **21** 46
  North Terrace **14** 359
  palace **14** 340; **22** 397; **23** 808
    megaron **14** 350; **21** 46, *46*

Mycenae
palace—cont.
wall paintings **14** 350
Ramp House **14** 348, 349
shaft graves **14** 337, 352, 353, 358; **21** 659; **22** 396, 397
tombs **2** 296; **14** 337; **30** 738; **31** 108
chamber **22** 395, 397
Chamber Tomb 102 **14** 359
Chamber Tomb 517 **14** 359
Chamber Tomb 529 **14** 358, 359
cist **13** 383
Cyclopean Tomb **30** 738
tholos tombs **14** 340–41; **22** 395
Tomb of Klytemnestra **30** 738
Treasury of Atreus **9** 85; **14** 338, *340*, 340–41, 353; **27** 127; **30** 738, *738*; **31** 108; **32** 88
Tsountas's House **14** *350*; **21** 46
wall paintings **14** 334
walls **14** 340; **20** 571
West House **21** 46; **22** 396
Mycenaean **14** 337; **22** 394, 398*; **26** 290
alabastra **14** *344*
altars **1** 691*
amber **1** 761
arches **2** 294, 296*
architecture **4** 772; **14** 338, 339–41*; **29** 367
armour **4** *851*; **14** 356
arrowheads **14** 356
beads **14** 357, *357*
bowls **14** *345*, *347*
brick **4** 772
bronze **2** 451; **4** 849, 850, *851*; **14** 356*, *356*; **22** *397*
cenotaphs **6** 170
chronologies **14** *334*, 334–5*
citadels **14** 340
columns **14** 340
cups **14** *344*, 344, 355
Vapheio **14** 337; **26** 134
daggers **14** 355; **22** *397*
domes **9** 85
doorways **14** 340
dromoi **14** *340*
faience (i) (glass) **14** *358*, 358–9*
figurines **14** 352, *352*
forgeries **14** 360
fortifications **14** 340
gateways **22** *396*
glass **1** 865
goblets **14** 338, *344*
gold **14** 355*, *355*, 357, *357*
iconography **14** 333–4*
inlays **22** *397*
ivory-carvings **8** 323; **22** 397
jars **14** *345*, *347*
jewellery **14** 357–8*
jugs **14** *344*, *356*
kraters **14** *345*, *347*
kylikes **14** *345*
masks **14** 338, *355*
masonry **22** *396*
Mycenaean—cont.
megara (buildings) **14** 338, 340; **23** 808
mirrors **21** 711
painting **14** 338, 340; **32** 803
palaces **14** 338, *339*, 340; **23** 808; **31** *25*, 25–6
pithoi **14** 341, *344*
plaster **14** *352*
pottery **1** 826; **8** 346; **13** 491; **14** 337–8, 341, 344–7*, *344*, *345*, *347*; **26** 290
pyxides (vases) **14** *345*
religion **14** 333–4*
rhyta **14** 355
sarcophagi **27** 825
sculpture **14** 351–3*, *352*; **26** 134
seals **14** 338, 358
settlements **14** 340
silver **14** 355*
spearheads **14** 356
stelae **14** 338
swords **2** 451; **14** 356
terracotta **14** *352*; **27** 825
tombs **14** 340–41
tholos **14** 338, *340*, 340; **23** 476; **30** *738*, 738; **31** 107
trade **14** 333*
vaults (ceiling) **32** 88
walls **14** 340
Mycenaean period *see* HELLADIC → periods → Late Helladic IIIC
Mycerinus (*reg c.* 2490–*c.* 2472 BC) **9** *776*, 869; **22** 398–9*
architecture **9** 813, 826, 850, *850*; **25** 762
dress **10** *43*
pyramid **10** 79; **20** 863
sculpture **9** 858, 862, 870, 871; **10** 84; **22** *399*
temple **10** 72
Myconius **14** 665, 667
Myddleton (family) **32** 787, 790
Mydzhum **31** 701
Myene **11** 878
Myers, Abraham **23** 71
Myers, A. N., & Co. **31** 266
Myers, Barton **31** 176
Myers, Bernard Samuel **10** 213
Myers, Christopher **9** 323
Myers, Elijah E. **22** 398*; **26** 353
Myers, George **19** 574; **25** 713, 715, 716
Myers, George Hewitt **16** 555, 557; **22** 400*
Myers, Graham **9** 323; **23** 340
Myers, Jerome **2** 597, 633
Myers, Myer **31** 649
Myers, Oliver **15** 105
Myers, Virginia **10** 398
Myers, W(illiam) J(oseph) **10** 90, 92
Myerscough-Walker, Raymond **2** 333
Myinkaba *see* PAGAN
Myjak, Adam **25** 116
Mykolaïv
Magistrates Court **31** 551
Mykonos **8** *304*; **12** 68; **13** 499
Hotel Xenia **13** 350, *351*
Myladdi **16** 864
mylar **7** 432
Mylasa *see* MILÂS
Mylius, Brødrene **23** 237
Mylius, Jan Fryderyk **25** 106
Mylius, Karl Jonas **4** 182; **14** 786; **17** 853; **28** 46
Mylius & Bluntschli **30** 733
Mylne, Alexander **28** 242
Mylne, Janet **22** 400
Mylne, John, I (*d* 1621) **22** 400; **28** 242
Mylne, John, II (*d* 1657) **22** 400; **28** 225, 242
Mylne, John, III (1621-67) **22** 400; **28** 242
Mylne, Robert, I (1633-1710) **4** 889; **22** 400; **28** 225, 246, 880
Mylne, Robert, the younger (1733-1811) **22** 400–401*
competitions **7** 666
pupils **7** 791
works **1** 125; **3** 536, *536*; **4** 540; **7** 687; **9** 728, *728*; **28** 228; **31** 860
Mylne, Thomas (*d* 1763) **22** 400
Mylne, William, I (1662-1728) **22** 400
Mylne, William, II (1734-90) **22** 400
Mylne, William (*fl* 1811-42) **22** 401
Mylne, William (1817-90) **22** 401
Myl'nikov, Andrey **27** 397, 581
Mylopotamos **18** 570
Mymensingh **3** *166*
figurines **15** *726*
weaving **3** 168
Zainul Abedin Sangrahasala **3** 170
Myn, van der *see* MIJN, VAN DER
Mynard, Giovanni **26** 779
Mynheer, Govert *see* JANSZ., GOVERT
Mynona **3** 672
Myōan Eisai **17** 746
Myochin **17** 364
Myōchō Shūhō *see* DAITŌ KOKUSHI
Myōe **17** 159, 729
Myōen **10** 192; **17** 121, 122
Myohaung **2** *281*; **5** *221*; **21** 595; **29** *225*
Archaeological Museum **5** 239, 241
architecture **2** 280–81
coins **5** 255
Htuk-kaw-thein **5** 241
Lin-ban-pyauk **5** 234
palaces **5** 235
sculpture **5** 241
Myohaung—cont.
Shitthaung **2** 280–81; **5** 241
Teza-rama **5** 234
Thakya-man-aung **5** 234
see also:
MINBIN, King
MINYAZAGYI, King
MIUPHALAUNG, King
NARAPATIGYI, King
SANDAWIZAYA, King
Myōhōin **17** 124
Myōjō *see* FUJIWARA NO TEIKA
Myōmanji **29** 869
Myōman Mokujiki **5** 120; **17** 127, 348; **22** 401*
Myŏng-hyŏn **18** 321
Myous **15** 893
Myra (Turkey) **9** *512*; **19** 837; **22** 401*
Hagios Nikolaos **7** 252, 261, 279, 301; **9** 542, 590
tombs **19** 838, 840; **31** 109
Myra, Abraham **11** 94
Myrbach, Felician von **8** 419; **28** 344
Myrina **13** *363*
figurines **12** 286; **13** 581, *581*
terracottas **13** 582; **27** 111
Myriokephala
Katholikon **9** 578
Panagia **8** 155, 156
Myrmekion **4** 110
myrobalans **4** 684
Myroffski, Wenzeslaus **12** 411
Myron of Eleutherai **13** 422, 430, 440, 453; **22** 402*; **27** 689
attributions **2** 526, 682
copies **2** 685; **6** 9; **13** *422*; **27** 46
forgeries by others **11** 307
pupils **19** 842
teachers **1** 450
works **1** 481; **2** 682; **13** 450, 454, 467, 470, 573; **23** 291; **29** 423; **31** 49
myrrh *see under* RESINS → types
Myrsilos, King of Lydia *see* KANDAULES, King of Lydia
Myrtia Monastery **25** 334, 335
Myrtos **8** 153; **13** *362*; **21** *651*; **22** 402–3*
Mys **2** 682; **13** 545, 570; **24** 206, 593
Myshkin **22** 181
Mysian granite *see under* GRANITE → types
Myslbek, Josef Václav **22** 403–4*; **25** 433
pupils **17** 718; **18** 472; **29** 873, 893
works **8** 381, 387; **22** *404*; **25** 433, *434*
Myson **32** 57*
pupils **32** 56, 62
works **13** 520
workshop **13** 521
Mysore **15** *294*; **22** 404*
Ambavilas Palace **22** 404
ivory **15** 696
Lalitamahal Palace **29** 526
metalwork **15** 709
sculpture **7** *616*
temples **15** 405
Venkataramanasvami Temple **15** 649
Mystras **9** *511*, 515; **22** 405–9*
architecture **9** 524
churches **9** 526
Church of the Peribleptos **7** 221; **9** 586; **22** 408*
Evangelistria Church **22** 408*
fortifications **9** 555
Hagia Sophia **22** 408*
Hagios Demetrios **9** 551, 583; **22** 405–6*, *406*
houses **9** 561
Little Palace **9** 556
Metropolis *see* Hagios Demetrios
Monastery of the Brontochion **22** 406–8*
Church of the Aphentiko *see* Church of the Hodegetria
Church of the Hodegetria **7** 230, 253; **9** 551, *552*, 585–6; **22** 406–8
wall paintings **22** *407*
Hagioi Theodoroi **9** 547, 551; **22** 406
Palace of the Despots **9** 524, 559; **22** 405
Pantanassa **7** 253; **9** 551, 586; **22** 408–9*, *409*
Peribleptos Monastery **9** 556
pottery **9** 631
wall paintings **22** 520
Myszków (family) **25** 135
Myszkowski (family) **13** 774
Myszkowski, Piotr, Bishop **13** 774
mythological drawings *see under* DRAWINGS → types
mythological painting *see under* PAINTING → types
mythology **10** 206; **22** 411–12*
Akan **1** 281
Greece, ancient **22** 410–11
Guinea **1** 281
Islamic **16** 137
Mande **1** 282
Zaïre **1** 282
Mytilene **19** 234–5, *234*; **21** 556
belts **9** 653, *653*
coins **13** 586
mosaics **27** 63
Mytilene Treasure **9** 655
Mytilidae shells *see under* SHELLS → types
Myudui, A. K. **27** 198
Myyrmäki Church **11** 92
Myzithras *see* MYSTRAS
MZ, Master **20** 691, 801*

N

N(eutron) A(ctivation) A(nalysis) *see under* TECHNICAL EXAMINATION → types
Na'aba, Nazir **30** 177
Naachtún **5** 411
Naaldwijk **22** 831
Raadhuis **8** 669
Naantali **11** 109
Brigittine convent **11** 94
Na'aran **9** 567; **17** 535, 542
Naarden **21** 570; **22** 418*, *813*
Nabakhtevi Church **12** 324
Nabarrayal, Lofty **22** 418*
Nabataea **1** *849*; **2** *246*; **22** 418–21*; **24** 556
architectural decorations **22** 419
architecture **22** 418–19*; **26** 917–18*
basalt **22** *419*
bowls **22** *420*
busts **24** *557*
capitals **22** 419
ceramics **22** 420*, *420*
coins **1** 889; **2** 261; **22** 420
dress **16** 454
figurines **22** 420
hydraulic works **22** 419; **24** 556
lamps **22** 420
metalwork **22** 421
pottery **27** 108
sculpture **22** *419*, 419–20*
stone **24** *557*
tombs **2** 249–50, *250*; **24** *558*
see also ANCIENT NEAR EAST; ARABIA; SYRIA- PALESTINE
Nabatu *see* NABATAEA
Nabesha, Tell **10** 80
Nabeshima (family) **22** 421
Nabeshima ware *see under* PORCELAIN → wares
Nabeta **17** 106
Nabeul **1** *376*; **16** 427; **31** 426
Archaeological Museum **31** 427
nymphaeum **22** 154; **27** 60, 63
Nabha **9** 543
Nabi-ogly, I. **3** 88
Nabis **10** 693; **11** 547; **12** 870; **22** 421–2*; **30** 169, 174
collections **8** 715; **18** 598; **22** 538; **32** 686
dealers **19** 10; **24** 143
members **8** 715; **15** 888; **19** 489; **20** 603
Bonnard, Pierre **4** 325
Denis, Maurice **8** 714
Ibels, Henri-Gabriel **15** 58
Lacombe, Georges **18** 598
Maillol, Aristide (-Joseph-Bonaventure) **20** 120
Ranson, Paul **25** 893
Rippl-Rónai, József **26** 419
Roussel, Ker-Xavier **27** 269
Sérusier, (Louis) Paul (Henri) **28** 484, 485
Vallotton, Félix (-Emile-Jean) **31** 830
Verkade, Jan **32** 258
Vuillard, Edouard **32** 738
paintings **12** 296; **31** *830*
Nabisco-RJR **31** 661
Nablus **16** 208; **17** 500
Nabokov, Nicolas **30** 390
Nabonidus **1** 886; **2** 254, 298; **28** 782; **31** 695
Nabopolassar **21** 274, 291; **28** 782
Nabratein Synagogue **17** 541, 542
Nabu-apla-iddina **1** 886
Nabuco, Joaquim, Fundação **4** 729
Nacascolo **29** *136*
Naccherino, Michelangelo **22** 422–3*, 477
collaboration **3** 828; **5** 525; **18** 900
pupils **11** 84
works **16** 703
Nachgotik *see* GOTHIC → styles → Late Gothic
Nachna **15** *279*, *285*; **22** 423*
Kumramath Temple **15** 473
Mahadeva Temple **15** 214, 289, 473
Parvati Temple **15** 237, *254*, 255, *416*, 472; **22** 423
reliefs **15** 227
sculpture **15** 470, 473, 475
Nachtegale, Pieter **7** 238
Nachtigall, Johannes **7** 471; **26** 713, 718
Nachtlicht, Leo **14** 399
Nacht-Samborski, (Stefan) Artur **17** 804; **22** 423*; **25** 108
Nachtweh, Johan Hendrik Conrad **2** 487
Naci, Elif **31** 454
Naciaceno Quiróz, Gregorio **14** 713
works **14** *713*
Nacional de Vivienda **9** 118
Nada, Hamid **5** 401; **9** 766, 768
Nadagopal, S. **20** 54
Nadaillac, Comtesse de **3** 396
Nadal, Geronimo **33** 169
Nadal, J. **17** 509
Nadal, Torcuato Tasso y *see* TASSO Y NADAL, TORCUATO
Nad 'Ali Minaret **16** 166
Nadar **15** 154; **22** 424–5*; **24** 661, 669
groups and movements **28** 346
works **22** *424*; **24** 669
Nadar, Paul **22** 425
Nádasdy (family) **14** 899; **15** 13, 15
Nádasdy, Ferenc **14** 899; **15** 15
Nádasdy, László, Bishop of Csanád **30** 206
Nadauld **6** 116
Nadel, Otto **32** 439
Nadelman, Elie **22** 425–6*; **32** 328
exhibitions **31** 490
patrons and collectors **29** 655
works **9** 310; **22** *426*; **31** 613
naderugi houses *see* AFRICA → houses
Nadhr Muhammad Khan **16** 236, 238
Nadiad, Gokulnathji Temple **15** 394–5
Nad-i Ali **1** 190
al-Nadim (*fl* 10th cent.) **16** 356
Nadim (*fl* late 16th cent.) **15** 594
Nadira Begum (Mughal) **15** 590
Nadir Shah, Ruler (*reg* 1736-47) (Afsharid)
architecture **20** 548
crowns **16** 539
enamel **15** 710
gold **15** 707
manuscripts **16** 346
paintings **16** 535
tents **30** 480
thrones **30** 784
trappings **16** 539
Nádler, István **14** 902
Nadorp, Franz (Johann Heinrich) **22** 426*
Nadr Bi Arlat **16** 236
Nadr Divan Begi Arlat **5** 138; **6** 205; **27** 673
Nadroga **11** 70
Nadslav, St Procopius **13** 187
nadun **29** 470
Nadwa al-fann al-urdunniyya (Jordanian Art Club) **17** 654
Naedong **18** 272
Naef, Albert **6** 602
Naef, J. **30** 128
Naei **18** 252
Naeri Tomb 1 **18** 313
Naeser, Frederik **23** 221
Naeshirogawa **17** 352, 353; **27** 873
Naesmyth, Michael **22** 530
Naessens, Maurits **3** 614
Næstved
Herlufsholm School **13** 171, *171*, 172
Næstved & District Museum **17** 720
St Peter's **4** 781; **8** 723
Skovkloster, Abbey Church **8** 722
Naet, J. **10** 662
Nafara Senufo **28** 420, 421
Näfveqvarn ironworks **30** 110
Naga (people) **3** 332; **5** 220, 262; **15** 721, 732–4*
sculpture **15** *733*
textiles **15** 671
Naga (Philippines), University of Nueva Caceres Museum **29** 240
Nagadipa *see* JAFFNA
Nagahama **17** 363
Nagahashi Tōgen **20** 807
Nagahide **17** 288
Nagahiro, Toshio **7** 161
Nagai, Kazumasa **10** 178
Nagai Rantei **17** 401
Nagai Shōgen **17** 410
Nagaizumi-cho, Musée Bernard Buffet **5** 125
Nag' al-Dayr *see* NAG EL-DEIR
Nagamachi Shuzan *see* SHUZAN NAGAMACHI
Nagamangala, Saumyakeshvara Temple **15** 328
Nagamasa Kuroda *see* KURODA NAGAMASA
Nagamma **16** 864
Nagamo, Tesshi **17** 324
Naganika, Queen (*fl c.* 1st cent. BC) (Satavahana) **17** 695
Naganuma, Moriyoshi **17** 133
Nagaoka **17** *11*, *93*, 95; **22** 426–7*
Nagaokakyō *see* NAGAOKA
nāgapāśa **15** 244*
Nagappattinam **15** *294*; **22** 427*
University **29** 231
Nagarajayashri **2** 59
Nagaral **15** 526
Naganatha Temple **15** 295
Nagaram **15** 454
Nagara Svarga, Chumbot, Princess of **30** 617
Nagardhan **15** 463
Nagardukas Castle **19** 495
Nagare, Masayuki **12** 101
Nagari **15** 286, 460
temple **15** 251
Nagari Das *see* SAVANT SINGH, Raja of Kishangarh
Nagarjunakonda **15** *294*, 737; **22** 427–8*
apsidal temples **15** 252
Archaeological Museum **22** 428
ivory **15** 695
pillars **27** 867
reliefs **15** 248
sculpture **15** 220, 233, 453–4, 537
stucco **29** 824
Nagarjuni **3** 194–5*; **15** *279*
Nagarkovil **15** 541
nāgaśākhā *see* ŚĀKHĀ
Nagasaki **17** *11*, 18; **22** 428–9*
Deshima **22** *429*
kites **17** 389
Memorial Building **17** 90
prints **17** 285–6*
seals **17** 410–11*
Sōfukuji **17** 75
trade **6** 331
Nagasaki school **17** 165, 181, 183–8*; **28** 588
members **16** 787
works **17** *187*
Nagasawa, Hidetoshi **28** 657
Nagasawa Rosetsu **17** 165, 196; **22** 429–30*
collaboration **17** 196
teachers **20** 523
works **17** 196
nāga sculpture *see under* SCULPTURE → types
Nagassi **1** 315
Nagata Tōsenshi **17** 411
Nagatman
shields **24** *70*
Nagato **17** 318
Fukawa **14** 37
Nagatoki Hōjō *see* HŌJŌ NAGATOKI, Shogunal Regent
Nagaur
Akadwali Mosque **15** 351
Akbari Mosque **15** 351, 371
architecture **15** 349–50
Chowk ki Mosque **15** 371
congregational mosque *see* Akbari Mosque
Ek Minar ki Mosque **15** 350
Firuz Khani Mosque, shrine of Bare Pir Sahib **15** 351
Khānaqāh al-Tarikin
Buland Darwaza **15** 338, 349
Mosque of Makhdum Husayn Chishti **15** 349
paintings **15** 615
Shams Khan Mosque **15** 350, *350*
Shams Khan Tala'o **15** 350
Nagazare Tomb **17** 143
Nagda **10** 127*; **15** *276*, 695
Sas-Bahu temples **15** 274, 489
Nagel, J. **30** 15
Nagel, L. **13** 811
Nagel, Otto **21** 365; **22** 430*, 923
Nagel, Peter **33** 627
Nagel, Tile **4** 418
Nag-el-Deir **9** *774*; **10** 38, 80; **22** 430–31*
dress **10** 45
reliefs **9** 874
tomb of Tjamerery **22** 431
Nagele **13** 685
Nägeli, Hans Jakob **33** 737
Nageoires, Jan des *see* VINNE, JAN VINCENTSZ. VAN DER
Nag Hammadi **7** *819*
Nag Hammadi Codices *see under* CODICES → individual manuscripts
Naghi, Muhammad **5** 401; **9** 766; **22** 431*
Naglas factory **28** 863
Nagle, Ron **31** 640
Nagle, William **7** 378
Nagler, G(ustav) K(aspar) **2** 23; **10** 208, 210; **22** 431*
Nagler, Johanna *see* EHRENREICH, JOHANNA
Nagnajit **15** 209
Nagnoor Shiva Temple **15** 328
Nagobaru **17** 352
Nagore **15** 359
shrine of Hadrat Qadir Wali **15** 359
Nagori, Abdul Rahim **23** 801
Nagorni, Miodrag **28** 451
Nagoshi (family) **17** 323
Nagoshi Yaemon **17** 323
Nagoshi Yashichirō Zensei **17** 323
Nagoya **17** 18, 84, 95, 97, 355; **22** 431–3*
Atsuta Shrine **17** 392
Castle **17** 175; **22** 431, 432, *432*
Jōraku Palace **17** 796
Hōsa Library **22** 432
houses **17** 83
kilns **17** 247
Ofuke kiln **28** 495
painting **17** 189
prints **17** 278
stirrups **17** 364
Taisō **22** 432
Tokugawa Art Museum **6** 826; **17** 429, 432; **18** 532; **22** 433
collections **7** 154
Nagpur **4** 853
Bhonda Mahadev Mandir **15** 405
Central Museum **15** 182
Dikshabhumi **15** 406
Nagu **13** 190
Naguib **22** 245
Nagulapadu **15** 538
Nagy, Antal **14** 910
Nagy, Ervin **20** 151
Nagy, István **13** 333; **22** 433*
Nagy, Károly **14** 910
Nagy, Sándor **12** 839; **15** 12; **22** 433*
groups and movements **12** 839; **14** 901; **15** 12
house **21** 4
teachers **30** 206
works **12** 839; **15** 4
Nagybánya colony **14** 901; **15** 18; **17** 876; **22** 434*; **30** 212
members
Bernáth, Aurél **3** 820
Csók, István **8** 225
Czóbel, Béla **8** 431
Ferenczy, Károly **10** 892
Galimberti, Sándor **12** 10
Galimberti, Valéria **12** 10
Hollósy, Simon **14** 687
Huszár, Vilmos **15** 36
Iványi Grünwald, Béla **16** 794
Máttis Teutsch, János **20** 849
Paizs Goebel, Jenő **23** 794
Perlrott Csaba, Vilmos **24** 457
Réti, István **26** 256
paintings **10** *892*
see also BAIA MARE
Nagyganna, Esterházy Mausoleum **14** 895
Nagy Mihaly, K.
works **15** *2*
Nagyszeben *see* SIBIU
Nagyszentmiklós Treasure **11** 145; **22** 434–5*, *435*; **26** *705*
Nagyszombat *see* TRNAVA
Nagytállyá **13** 162
Nagyugróc **14** 908
Nagyvárad *see* ORADEA
Nagyvázsony
castle **14** 884
church **14** 894
Naha
Enkakuji **27** 470
Japan Handicrafts Museum **21** 635
pottery **27** 470
Royal Palace **27** 470
Tsuboya **17** 262, 353; **27** 470

Naha, Helen 22 609
Nahalal 17 854
Nahal Hemar 1 881; 30 181, 182
Nahal Mishmar 30 180
copper 4 850; 30 183, 188, 194–5
metalwork 30 183
sculpture 30 183
textiles 1 881
Nahal Oren 30 181
Nahapet of Urfa, Katholikos (reg 1691-1705) 10 449
Nahariya 30 180
glass 27 79
metalwork 30 195, 195
Nahavand 16 530
al-Nahhariya 27 593
Nahl, Charles Christian 23 904
Nahl, Johann August (der Ältere) (1710-81) 14 492; 22 436–7*
collaboration 11 459; 18 160
house 17 834
patrons and collectors 14 492, 652; 25 368
works 3 806; 12 412, 424, 424; 14 750; 22 437
Nahl, Johann August (der Jüngere) (1752-1825) 22 436
Nahl, Johann Samuel 22 436
Nahl, Samuel 22 436
Nahman, Maurice 10 92
Nahohai, Josephine 22 608
Nahohai, Milford 22 608
Nahohai, Randy 22 608
Nahohai, Rowena 22 609
Nahr el-Kelb 21 301; 29 614
Nahua 14 711; 21 738
Nahuange 30 240
Náhuatl 21 262
Na Hye-sŏk 18 325
Naidu, Redappa 20 54
Naiki (1598-1670) see SUMIYOSHI JOKEI
Naiki (1631-1705) see SUMIYOSHI GUKEI
Naiki (1755-1811) see SUMIYOSHI HIROYUKI
Naikoku Kaiga Kyōshinkai (National Competitive Painting Exhibitions) 17 204*
Nailor, Gerald 22 595
nails
historical and regional traditions
Central Asia, Western 6 217
Greece, ancient 9 151
Islamic 16 500
Japan 17 45
Parthian 6 217
Rome, ancient 9 151
Yemen 16 500
uses
architecture 17 45
conservation 22 165
display of art 9 14
doors 9 151
mosaics 22 156, 165
panel paintings 24 5
sculpture 6 217
Nailsea Glasshouse 4 824
Naimero 21 113
Na'in 15 897; 16 105; 22 437–8*
carpets 15 899
congregational mosque 3 894; 4 791; 16 159, 160; 22 437–8; 29 819
maqṣūra 20 369
mihrab 21 506
mihrabs 16 161
minbar 16 501
palace 16 230, 253; 22 438
pottery 15 899; 16 426
Nainativu 16 864
Nainggolan
sarcophagi 27 831
Nainsukh 15 232, 740; 20 233; 22 438–9*; 23 908
works 15 619, 629, 630, 631, 631–2; 22 438
writings 15 629
Nair, Rajsekaran 20 54
Nairainpur 15 322
Nairn 28 250
Nairn, James M(cLachlan) 22 439*; 23 59; 33 58
Nairne, George Colvill 19 869
Nairobi 1 407, 429
City Park 24 181
Gallery Watatu 17 908
Goethe Institute 1 432
Kenyatta Conference Centre 17 906
Law Courts 17 906
National Archives 17 908
National Museum 17 908
Paa-ya-Paa Art Gallery 1 433; 17 908
painting 1 432
Naish, Thomas 27 626
Naish, William
works 27 625
Naismith, Mungo 28 242
Naissant, Claude 26 704
Naissus see NIŠ
Naitō, Shin 17 135
Naitō Sensuke 17 401
naive art 22 439–42*
painting
Antilles, Lesser 2 150
Croatia 22 441
France 27 261, 262
Grenada 2 150
Nicaragua 23 82
collections 12 54
regional traditions
Croatia 22 441
France 27 260
see also PSYCHOTIC ART
Naiveu, Matthijs 19 102; 22 442*
Naiwyncx, Herman 22 443*
Naizen Kanō see KANŌ NAIZEN
Najaf 28 634
mausoleum of 'Ali 16 159; 21 506; 28 633, 633; 31 110
Najaf 'Ali 1 638; 16 81*, 534
Najafehabad 21 300
Nájera 29 333
S María la Real 26 689
tomb of Doña Blanca 26 608
Nájera, Andrés de see ANDRÉS DE NÁJERA
Nájera, Carlota de Santamarca y Donato, Duquesa de 27 781
Nājī, Muḥammad see NAGHI, MOHAMMED
Najibabad 15 409
Najima Castle 31 677
al-Najjar, Ibrahim 19 7
Najm al-Din 'Umar 16 380
Najmányii, László 14 896
Najran 2 246
houses 27 875; 32 316
museum 2 275
rock art 2 270
town walls 2 250
Naj Tunich 13 758; 20 882; 22 443–4*
rock art 22 444
Nakabayashi Chikkei 17 192
Nakabayashi Chikutō 17 191, 417, 439; 22 432; 33 322, 489
works 17 191
Nakabayashi Gochiku 17 238
Nakagawa, Hachirō 17 204
Nakagawa, Katsumasa (fl 1980s) 17 402
Nakagawa, Kazumasa (1893-1991) 13 315; 18 87
Nakagusuku 27 470
Nakahara (family) 17 154
Nakahara, Minoru 17 206
Nakahara, Teijirō 17 134; 22 444*; 23 369
Nakahira, Takuma 22 120
Nakai (family) 17 52
Nakai, Keisho 17 413, 414
Nakai Chikuzan 17 236
Nakaide see under SHIGARAKI
Nakai Masamoto 18 564
Nakai Riken 17 236
Nakai Yamato Masakiyo 18 238; 31 202
Nakajima, Hiroshi 17 266
Nakajima, Ken 12 101
Nakajima Ise 17 846
Nakajima Raishō 17 198; 18 231
Nakakawa, Kazumasu 17 206
Nakamura (family) 17 414
Nakamura, Fusetsu 17 204
Nakamura, Hiroshi 17 402
Nakamura, Kazuo 5 568; 23 791
Nakamura, Kinpei 17 267
Nakamura, Randai 17 413, 861
Nakamura, Ranseki 17 413
Nakamura, Seijurō 17 203
Nakamura, Tsune 17 205; 22 444*
Nakamura Hōchū 17 180; 23 594
Nakamura Konozō 31 204
Nakamura Kuranosuke 17 179; 23 363
Nakamura Suichiku 17 413
Nakanai 24 84
Nakane, Kinsaku 12 101
Nakanishi, Natsuyuki 14 568; 17 207; 30 256
Nakanishi, Toshio 17 206
Nakapapula Caves 1 304
Nakapenkem see MARTIN, MUNGO
Nakarius, Sameer 26 425
Nakashima, George 31 633, 634
Nakasone 17 364
Nakayama 17 298
Nakayama, Bunpo 17 381
Nakayama, Iwata 18 60; 22 444–5*
works 22 445
Nakayama Kōyō 17 416, 439
Nakazawa, Hiromitsu 17 204
Nakazawa Setsujō 16 802
Nakbe 29 619
Nakhchyvan 2 890, 894; 16 105; 22 445–6*
architecture 2 892
Armenian Museum 2 445
jewellery 2 900
mausoleum of Mu'mina Khatun 2 892
mausoleum of Yusuf ibn Kusayr 2 892
Musical Dramatic Theatre 2 894
pottery 2 898
tiles 2 898
Nakhichevan see NAKHCHYVAN
Nakhite 9 543
Nakhlat al-Hamra
sculpture 2 259, 259
Nakhon Pathom 30 571, 635
Chedi Chula Pathon 30 595
coins 30 631
Phra Pathom Chedi 30 576, 576, 601
royal palace 30 590
sculpture 30 595
stupa 30 590
urban planning 30 592
Wat Na Phra Men 30 594
Nakhon Ratchasima 30 571, 576
San Phra Narai 30 579
Wat Sala Loi 30 446, 511
Nakhon Si Thammarat 20 179
enamel 30 632
Ho Phra Phuttha Sihing 30 606
metalwork 30 635
niello 30 635
Wat Mahathat 30 583
Nakht 9 879, 902, 905; 12 67; 22 446*
Nakhtankh 10 10
Nakhterheb 9 860
Nakhti 2 659
Nakhuda Mithqal 15 358
Nakian, Reuben 22 446*
Nakijin 27 470
Nakipari 12 323, 326
Nakkaş, Osman see OSMAN
nakkashane 16 346
Nakkaş Hasan see HASAN, NAKKAŞ
Nakodar
tomb of Haji Jamal 15 374, 375
tomb of Muhammad Mumin 15 374
Nakoku Hidai see HIDAI, NAKOKU
Nakonech 31 557
Nakp'a see YI (ii) KYŎNG-YUN
Nakrason 19 841
Naksal 22 771
Nakşi, Ahmed see AHMED NAKŞÎ
Naksŏ see YUN TŎK-HŬI
Nakum, Temple N 21 214
Nalanda (India) 4 853; 5 95, 226; 15 279, 476; 21 847; 22 447*
Archaeological Museum 15 181
manuscript illumination 15 570
plaques 30 510
sculpture 15 499, 500, 501
Site 3 15 280
stucco 29 824
Temple 2 15 281
Temple 3 15 500
temples 15 322
tiles 15 686
Nalanda Image-House (Sri Lanka) 29 448
Nalbandyan, Ar'penik 2 432
Nalbandyan, Dmitry 2 432
Nal'chik Fortress 27 433
Naldini, Giovan Battista 22 447–8*
collaboration 3 101; 25 241; 32 14; 33 722
patrons and collectors 12 897
pupils 3 101; 8 274; 24 239
teachers 25 224
works 21 22; 22 448; 26 813
Naldini, Lorenzo 11 265; 13 226; 22 448*
Naldini, Paolo see BALDINI, PIETRO PAOLO
Naldo (da Norcia), Niccolò di see NICCOLÒ DI NALDO (DA NORCIA)
Nalepinskaya-Boychuk, Sofiya A. 2 634; 4 605
Naletale 1 305
Naliboki Glassworks 22 449*; 25 124; 31 760
glass 25 125
Nalik 24 85
Nalimov (family) 27 428
Nalimov, Gavriil (Firsevich) 27 428
Nallur 16 864
Nalo, Joe 23 736
Nalu 1 336, 391; 3 45, 46, 47
works 1 391
Nalya 1 406
Nama 22 457
Namakkal 15 294; 22 449*
Naman 22 457
Namangan Museum 6 283
al-Namara 16 278
Namatjira, Albert 1 63, 67; 2 750; 22 449*
Namau 24 76, 77, 78
namāzgāhs see MOSQUES → types → musallas
Namazga Tepe 6 185, 195; 31 458
pottery 6 255
statuettes 6 275
Namch'ang see KIM HYŎN-SŎNG
Nam Dinh 32 468
Pho Minh (Thap) Temple 32 473
Thap Temple see Pho Minh Temple
Namen see NAMUR
Nämforsen 25 532
Namibia 1 214; 22 450*
architecture 22 450
caves 1 304
linocuts 22 450, 450
rock art 27 695–6
Namikawa, Sōsuke 17 378
Namikawa, Yasuyuki 17 378
works 17 379
Namingha, Dan 22 599
Namio Egami see EGAMI, NAMIO
Nam Ku-man 22 451*
Nam Kye-u 18 317; 22 451*
Namora, Fernando 26 243
Namord ware see under POTTERY → wares
Nampeya, Willie 20 161
works 20 161
Nampeyo 22 452*
works 22 451, 609
Namponan, Angus
works 1 62
Nampula, Museu de 22 245
Namri see KIM TU-RYANG
Namrun Castle 2 427
Nam Sach Kilns 32 484
Namsong 18 345
Namudlyg 6 379
Namuka-i-Lau 11 69
Namukolo, London Missionary Society Church 33 602
Namur 3 539; 22 452*
brass 3 602, 603
Cathedral of St Aubin 3 547
faience (ii) (ceramics) 3 590
fonts (baptismal) 11 253
fortifications 21 570, 577
furniture 22 452*
glass 3 593, 595
gold 22 452*
guilds 3 596
Hastière-par-delà Abbey 26 574; 31 281
church 3 552
marks 3 601
Musée d'Armes et d'Histoire Militaire du Comte de Namur 29 240
Musée Groesbeeck-de-Croix 3 594, 595
Musée de l'Hôtel de Croix 19 233
pewter 3 603
St Loup 3 546
sculpture 26 630
silver 3 598; 22 452*
Trésor Hugo d'Oignies 13 159, 159; 14 854
Namur Triptych 11 614
Namuth, Hans 22 452*
Namwala, Mbeza local government complex 33 602
Namwon
Kwanghan-ru Temple 12 94
Silsang Temple 18 289, 290
Nan 30 571
boats 30 631
ceramics 30 609, 610
urban planning 30 592
Wat Phumin 30 616, 620
Nan, Prince of 30 590
Nana-Benz 31 73
Nanaghat 15 737
Nanak, Guru 2 881; 14 555; 28 711
Nanak Ram 15 613
Nanay 27 436
Nanban see under JAPAN → lacquer; painting
Nanbata, Tatsuoki 17 207
Nanboku Tōzaian see TŌZAIAN NANBOKU
Nanbō Sōkei 17 438
Nanbu 17 355, 358
Nanchang 7 133
house of Zhu Da 6 687
Nancheng 7 111
Nancré, Marquis de 23 514
Nancy 11 504; 22 453–6*; 31 719
Cathedral 11 614; 24 255
Church of the Cordeliers
Chapelle Ronde 20 866
Hémicycle 22 454
Hôtel de Ville 14 448
Musée des Beaux-Arts 11 665, 666; 13 306; 30 332
Musée de l'Ecole de Nancy 29 516; 31 829
Musée Historique Lorrain 5 439
painting 11 533
Palais du Gouvernement 22 454

Nancy—cont.
Place Stanislas **11** 628; **16** 59; **22** *455*; **31** 718
Primatiale *see* Cathedral
tapestries **11** 642; **22** 456*; **30** 324
urban planning **14** 447–8
Villa Majorelle **32** 555
Nancy, Ecole de *see* ECOLE DE NANCY
Nand **15** 443
Nanda **27** 593–4*
Nandagopal, S. **15** 173; **20** 54
works **15** *173*
Nandan, P. S. **20** 54
Nandangarh *see* LAURIYA NANDANGARH
Nandchand **15** 475, 495
Nandi **15** 301, 531; **23** 182
Arunachaleshvara Temple **15** 529
Bhoganandishvara Temple **15** 529
sculpture **15** 529
Nandikundi, Ramalingeshvara Temple **15** 328, 537
Nandivardhana *see* NAGARDHAN
Nandivarman II Pallavamalla, Ruler (*reg* 731-96) (Pallava) **15** 234, 304
Nanev, M. **8** 900
Nanga see under JAPAN → painting
Nangaku Watanabe *see* WATANABE NANGAKU
Nangazizi **20** 267, *268*
Nanggan-kŏsa *see* YI YŎNG
Nanggok *see* KIM (iv), YANG-GI
Nangnang **7** 108
furniture **7** 34
lacquer **7** 13
Lelang **18** *248*, *250*
mirrors **21** 715
sculpture **18** 299
Tomb 194 **18** 366
Tomb 200 **18** 366
Tomb of the Painted Basket **7** 33, 34
tomb of Wang Xu **18** 366, 373
Nangulay, Dick *see* NGULAYNGULAY, DICK
Nanha **4** 90; **15** 586; **22** 457*
collaboration **31** 420
works **15** 587
Nanhua Temple **6** 718
Nani **25** 383
Nani, Antonio **28** 4
Naniwa *see under* OSAKA
Nanjing **6** *615*; **7** 151; **22** 457–61*
albums **1** *580*
altars **1** 702
bamboo **7** 60
books **7** *64*
Central University **7** 149
coins **7** 73
gardens **12** 89
Great Sacrifice Hall **1** 702
Imperial Palace **6** 732, *732*
jade **7** 7
Jiangsu Provincial Museum **7** 154
Jiankang **6** 537
lacquer **6** 624; **7** 18
Liangjiang Higher Normal School **7** 149
Linggu Temple
Beamless Hall **6** 645, 661
Mt She **22** 458
Qixia Temple **22** *459*
Mt Zijin **22** 459
Museum **6** 772
painting **22** 459–61, *460*
prints **7** 119
sculpture **6** 729, 732
Sun Yatsen mausoleum **6** 705, 733
textiles **6** 624
tomb of Song Sheng **6** 905
tomb of Wang Xingzu **7** 10
tombs **6** 698
town walls **6** 661
Nanjing—cont.
urban planning **6** 664, 665
walls **22** 458
Xiao ling **6** 702, 732
Xishanqiao **6** 808, 812
Nanjing school **17** 189; **22** 459–61*
members **12** 899
works **12** *900*; **22** *460*
Nankai Gion *see* GION NANKAI
Nankei *see* ZŌROKU III
Nanking *see* NANJING
Nanking Cargo **6** 921
Nankok *see* CHŎNG SŎN
Nankou **13** 334
Juyongguan **5** 112; **6** 731; **13** 334; **33** 570
Naňková, V. **8** 426
Nan Madol **21** 477; **23** 715, *716*
Nanni, Castorlo di *see* CASTORLO DI NANNI
Nanni, Giovanni (1432-1502) *see* ANNIO OF VITERBO
Nanni, Giovanni (1487-1564) *see* UDINE, GIOVANNI DA
Nanni, Jacopo di Notar **28** 745
Nanni, Ser Ricciardo di *see* RICCIARDO DI NANNI, SER
Nanni da Lucca **27** 765
Nanni di Baccio Bigio *see* BIGIO, NANNI DI BACCIO
Nanni di Banco **22** 461–2*
attributions **11** *184*; **12** 701; **22** 462
collaboration **22** 462
groups and movements **26** 183
pupils **26** 442
sculpture **11** 184; **16** 658, 690; **22** 44
reliefs **11** 197; **16** 689
religious
Cathedral of S Maria del Fiore (Florence) **10** 743; **11** 197, 198, 201; **16** 689; **18** 673
Orsanmichele (Florence) **1** 110; **11** 204; **16** 689; **22** *461*; **26** 183
Nanni di Bartolo **13** 95; **22** 462–3*
attributions **5** 176
collaboration **9** 129; **11** 201
works **11** 201; **16** 689, 692
Nanni di Pietro *see* GIOVANNI DI PIETRO (DI GIOVANNI) (ii)
Nanninga, Jaap **14** 43; **22** 464*, 852
Nanpo Ōta *see* ŌTA NANPO
Nanpō Sōkei **17** 415
Nansei Shōtō *see* RYŪKYŪ ISLANDS
Nansen, Fridtjof **9** 751; **33** 78
Nanshangeng (Ningcheng) **7** 21
nanshuga see JAPAN → painting → *Nanga*
Nantaungmya, King of Burma (*fl* 13th cent.) **23** 763
Nantei Nishimura *see* NISHIMURA NANTEI
Nanteos **32** 782
Nantes **11** *504*; **22** 464*; **31** 714
architecture **8** 216–17
Cathedral of St Pierre **13** 59, 211
monument to Francis II, Duke of Brittany and his wife Marguerite de Foix **7** *596*; **11** 555, 556
cotton **8** 36; **11** 649; **30** 562
fortress **19** 895
Magasins Decré **27** 881
Musée des Beaux-Arts **5** 356; **8** 217; **11** 665, 666
Passage Pommeraye **20** 438
Pirmil **8** 902
urban planning **8** 216–17; **32** 511
Nantes, Hugo **31** 756
Nanteuil, Célestin François **4** 365; **8** 618; **11** 500; **14** 288, 853
Nanteuil, Charles-François **22** 465*
Nanteuil, Robert **20** 416; **22** 465–6*
collaboration **9** 718; **33** 669
methods **10** 392
patrons and collectors **20** 455; **21** 28; **32** 377
pupils **10** 757; **28** 178, 751
works **4** 359; **9** 22; **10** 144; **11** 534; **20** 456, *896*; **22** *465*; **25** 606; **26** 229
Nantgarw porcelain factory **4** 65; **5** 732; **7** 481; **32** 789
Nanto *see* NARA
Nanto, Francesco de **12** 735; **22** 466*
Nantong **7** 113
Nantucket Island (MA), Trubeck-Wislocki Houses **31** 598
Nantwich (Ches), St Mary **7** 192; **29** 507
Nanu, N. **26** 720
Nanumanga **31** 484
Nanumea **31** 484
nan wood **7** 31
Nanyn, Pierre **13** 227
Nanyue **22** 466*
Naogram *see* RANIGAT
Naojirō Harada *see* HARADA, NAOJIRŌ
Naokata Ueda *see* UEDA, NAOKATA
Naomasa Matsudaira *see* MATSUDAIRA NAOMASA
Naong (1320-77) **18** 295
Naong (1578-1607) *see* YI CHŎNG (ii)
Naonobu Kanō *see* KANŌ NAONOBU
Naonov, D., Factory **27** 410
Naopano, Ambika Temple **15** 310
naophorous statues *see under* SCULPTURE → types
naos **22** 467*
Naotake Odano *see* ODANO NAOTAKE
Naousa **13** 552
Năpăruş, Georgeta **22** 467*
Napata **1** 867; **9** *774*; **22** 467*; **23** *276*, 281, 282
architecture **23** 281
pyramids **9** 842; **25** 763
temples **30** 237
Napatan period *see under* NUBIA → periods
Nape, Comte de **8** 703
naphtha **33** 335
naphthalene **17** 388
Napier **22** 467–9*, *468*; **23** 52, *52*
architecture **23** 56
Hawke's Bay Museum **22** 468
Napier, John **30** 687
Napier, Robert (1791-1876) **26** 473
Napier, Robert Cornelis, 1st Baron Napier of Magdala (1810-90) **8** 526
Napier Waller, Mervyn *see* WALLER, MERVYN NAPIER
Napir Asu, Queen **10** 132
napkins **17** 341; **19** 416, *416*, 417; **28** 265–6
Naples **2** 277; **9** *510*; **13** 298, *362*; **16** *616*, *621*; **22** 469–87*, *470*; **26** *886*
academies
Accademia di Belle Arti **1** 105, 107; **23** 852
Pontano Academy **1** 127
art forms and materials
altarpieces **13** *146*
architecture **9** 120; **10** 209
coats of arms **14** 410
coins **7** 535, 537
coral **7** 834, 835; **16** 750
embroidery **16** 714, 760
enamel **13** 170
figurines **13** 581
frames **11** *394*
furniture **16** 723, 729, 730
gold **16** 742
Naples
art forms and materials—cont.
guns **2** 464, 466, 467
hardstones **16** 747; **22** 481–2*
jewellery **16** 751; **17** 526
lamps **27** 104
manuscripts **15** *93*; **26** 564; **31** 49
marble **29** 702
marks **22** 482
metalwork **13** 163
mosaics **22** 161
Nativity groups **22** 680; **29** 573
painting **9** 120; **12** 289; **13** 150–51; **16** 661; **29** 375, *544*
Baroque **16** 672–3
still-lifes **29** 667, 668
porcelain **11** 610; **22** 482*
pottery **16** 733, 735; **27** 106
printing **28** 664
rapiers **2** 456
rock crystal **16** 745
sculpture **9** 120; **16** 688, 703–4*
silk **16** 753
silver **16** 742
statuettes **29** 573
stucco **29** 831
tapestries **16** 755, 758; **22** 481*; **30** 324
thrones **30** 776
tortoiseshell **16** 748
Capodimonte *see* CAPODIMONTE
Castelnuovo **21** 566, *566*; **22** 486–7*
doors **9** 157
paintings **13** 150
tapestry workshop **22** 481
Triumphal Arch **2** 276; **16** 67; **22** *476*, *486*, 487; **24** 28, 782; **31** 351
catacombs **22** 482–3*
Catacomb of S Gaudioso **6** 70; **22** 482
Catacomb of S Gennaro **6** 69, *70*, 70; **9** 572; **22** 482
chronicles **7** 243
collections **1** 766; **13** 470
display of art **9** 18
ecclesiastical buildings
Cathedral of S Gennaro
altarpiece **22** *478*
Cappella del Tesoro **9** 158; **16** 743; **18** 736; **26** *311*
Cappella di S Gennaro *see* Cappella del Tesoro
ciborium **7** 303
sculpture **13** 98
Succorpo **5** 698
throne **30** 779
tomb of Archbishop Filippo Minutolo **13** 98
tomb of Charles II **13** 98
Certosa di S Martino **5** 894; **16** 640, 748; **22** 484–6*; **26** 500; **29** 543–4, *544*
Chiostro Grande **10** *800*; **16** 703; **22** *485*
frescoes **29** 253
paintings **5** *695*; **12** *663*; **18** 734
sculpture **31** 789
Church of Monteoliveto **27** 184–5
altar **1** 698
altarpieces **1** 711; **22** *477*
sculpture **18** 677; **20** *907*; **30** 496, 498
Church of the Annunziata **16** 645; **22** *327*; **27** 728
Church of the Pietà dei Turchini
monument to Francesco Rocco **31** 788
Concezione a Montecalvario *see* S Maria della Concezione
Gesù delle Monache **31** 788
Gesù Nuovo **17** 511
frescoes **29** *40*
sculpture **16** 703
Naples
ecclesiastical buildings—cont.
La Nunziatella *see* Church of the Annunziata
Monastery of S Giovanni Battista *see* Istituto di Belle Arti
S Angelo a Nilo
tomb of Cardinal Rinaldo Brancaccio **21** *465*, 467; **27** 830
S Anna dei Lombardi *see* Church of Monteoliveto
SS Apostoli **9** 411; **11** 81; **18** 735–6
paintings **18** *735*
S Chiara **2** 110; **13** 63; **16** 736
Chiostro delle Clarisse **7** 458
tomb of Robert I **13** 98
S Domenico Maggiore **13** 63
S Francesco di Paola **16** 646; **22** *473*
S Gennaro extra moenia **9** 533; **16** 624, 742, 743
S Giorgio Maggiore **9** 533; **16** 624
S Giovanni a Carbonara **30** 886
S Giovanni in Fonte Baptistery **9** 571
S Lorenzo Maggiore **13** 52, 63; **22** *483*, 483–4*
mosaics **9** 569
paintings **7** *543*
tomb of Ludovico Aldomorisco **13** 98
tombs **31** 124
S Maria della Concezione **16** 640
S Maria Donnaregina **13** 63; **16** 657; **31** *4*
frescoes **6** 106
tomb of Mary of Hungary **22** *475*
wall paintings **13** 146
S Maria Egiziaca **10** *801*
S Maria Incoronata **23** 351
S Maria la Nova
Cappella delle Grazie **31** 789
S Maria Maggiore **20** *557*
S Maria della Pietà dei Sangro
Sansevero Chapel **16** 703–4
Sansevero Chapel: tomb of Caetani **16** 703, *703*
S Maria della Sanità **23** 319
S Paolo Maggiore **16** 748; **29** *38*; **30** 648
sculpture **31** *790*
S Pietro a Maiella **13** 63
S Restituta **9** 533
Baptistery **3** 191
Chapel of S Maria del Principio **26** 626
Foro Carolino *see* Piazza Dante
Galleria Umberto I **26** 478
gardens **12** 115
housing
Albergo dei Poveri **11** 815–16
Cesate housing project **16** 650
Mangiagalli workers' housing project **16** 650
Istituto di Belle Arti **1** 745
Largo di Palazzo *see* Piazza del Plebiscito
museums
Museo Archeologico Nazionale **2** 165; **14** 444; **27** 115
collections **10** 808; **13** 605; **14** 445–6; **25** 191; **27** 115
paintings **27** 58
sculpture **27** 46
Museo Artistico delle Ceramiche **11** 70
Museo Artistico Industriale **11** 70; **22** 100; **23** 852
Museo Borbonico *see* Museo Archeologico Nazionale
Museo Civico Gaetano Filangieri **11** 70; **16** 774

Naples
museums—cont.
Museo Diego d'Aragona Pignatelli Cortes **31** 818
Museo e Galleria Nazionali di Capodimonte *see under* CAPODIMONTE
Museo Nazionale di S Martino **4** 412; **21** 472
Neapolis **8** 263; **22** 469*
Odeion **23** 349
Olivetti factory **16** 650
palazzi
2-6, Via della Sanità *see* Palazzo Sanfelice
Palazzo Arcivescovile **18** 736
Palazzo della Borsa **10** 512; **13** 795
Palazzo Cassacalenda *see* CAPODIMONTE → Palazzo Reale di Capodimonte
Palazzo Cellammare **11** 136
Palazzo Cuomo **11** 70; **16** 629
Palazzo Maddaloni **11** 136
Palazzo Mattei **25** 55
Palazzo Reale
doors **9** 157
frescoes **19** 434; **29** 41
furniture **16** 730
paintings **4** 323; **5** 555, 695; **22** 326; **23** 851
sculpture **12** 267
Stanza del Belvedere **12** 587
Palazzo Reale di Capodimonte *see under* CAPODIMONTE
Palazzo Sanfelice **16** 640
Palazzo della Sapienza **31** 674
Palazzo Serra di Cassano **27** *729*
Palazzo dei Vecchi Studi *see* museums → Museo Archeologico Nazionale
Palazzo di Vico S Maria Apparente **29** 39
patronage **16** 762
Piazza Dante **16** 645
Piazza del Plebiscito **3** 920–21
Pio Monte della Misericordia **5** *694*
Poggio Reale **9** 148; **12** 110; **20** 112–13; **32** 545
Porta Capuana **22** *471*
Stazione Centrale **29** 833
Teatro S Carlo **23** 87, *88*; **30** 667
tunnel **27** 6
urban planning **1** 745; **31** 714, 717
Villa Acton *see* museums → Museo Diego d'Aragona Pignatelli Cortes
Villa Floridiana **23** 87
Naples Hydriskai, Painter of the **32** 40
Naples Painter **13** 523
Naples yellow *see under* PIGMENTS → types
Napoca *see* CLUJ-NAPOCA
Napoléon, Musée *see under* PARIS → museums
Napoleon I, Emperor of the French (*reg* 1804-14) **4** 298–302*, *299*, *301*; **11** 658; **12** *264*
archaeology **10** 79, 82, 97; **23** 503
architecture **11** 256, 257–8; **24** 387; **29** 736; **32** 508
cathedrals **5** 327; **16** 647; **21** 532
châteaux **7** 677; **10** 186; **21** 367; **25** 872; **27** 536; **32** 370, 372, 373
monasteries **27** 543
pavilions (buildings) **32** 374
triumphal arches **6** 397; **28** 390
urban planning **5** 399; **16** 647; **19** 91; **26** 743
art policies **10** 93, 678; **11** 538; **22** 357, 358; **24** 139
barges **3** 233
bronze **26** 39
cameos **12** 264; **22** 103
Napoleon I, Emperor of the French (*reg* 1804-14)—cont.
carpets **2** 704; **11** 652; **27** 896
ceramics **10** 97
collections **27** 115; **30** 118
decorative works **20** 70
display of art **9** 13
drawings **3** 97
education (art) **28** 595
enamel **11** 630
engravings **10** 394
fountains **6** 139
furniture **4** 883; **5** 169; **6** 390; **11** 597; **16** 822; **20** 138; **30** 747
gems **11** 635
gold **24** 147
guns **2** 467
interior decoration **11** 261
jewellery **11** 635
lace **3** 610; **5** 51; **18** 591
orders (chivalry) **7** 178
ornament **23** 544
paintings **3** 853; **4** 733; **8** 559–60; **9** 18; **24** 138, 140; **25** 651; **26** 53; **27** 271; **32** 356
allegorical **24** 478
battle **4** 234; **12** 335; **30** 369
decorative **16** 64; **20** 283
flower **11** 228
history **3** 750; **13** 691; **14** 390; **21** 903; **27** 485
portraits **3** 735; **8** 558; **9** 363; **21** 507; **24** 478
porcelain **11** 609; **28** 523
regalia **26** *81*
sculpture **3** 775; **4** 404, 406, 407, 798; **7** 562; **11** 562; **16** 705, 768; **22** 47
silk **11** 646
silver **2** 722; **4** 42; **11** 621; **23** 354
snuff-boxes **11** 633
standards (vexilloid) **11** 151
stucco **29** 834
tapestries **12** 830
Napoleon II, King of Rome *see* REICHSTADT, NAPOLEON II BONAPARTE, Herzog von, King of Rome
Napoléon III, Musée *see under* PARIS → museums
Napoleon III, Emperor of France (*reg* 1852-70) **4** *299*, 306–7*, *307*; **14** 42, 802; **30** 608
archaeology **26** 785
architecture
castles **6** 51
châteaux **13** 202, 208
churches **17** 491
military **19** 91
palaces **24** 163
theatres **11** 261; **19** 69
urban planning **7** 841; **11** 143, 523, 659; **14** 593; **28** 346
art policies **4** 298; **11** 508, 672
cameos **12** 265
ceramics **12** 487
collections **5** 536; **10** 637; **11** 667
exhibitions **10** 680; **24** 172
furniture **3** 889; **11** 599; **13** 680
hardstones **11** 636
interior decoration **3** 877
jewellery **17** 526
museums **11** 667
paintings
allegorical **5** 342; **7** 879; **10** 480; **12** 10
animal subjects **32** 375
genre **3** 259; **14** 607; **18** 696; **21** 69
history **13** 779; **33** 581
landscape **8** 616; **18** 177
military **8** 883; **24** 816
religious **25** 211
photographs **19** 86; **22** 723
porcelain **28** 524
pottery **13** 542
Napoleon III, Emperor of France (*reg* 1852-70)—cont.
sculpture **6** 515; **7** 421, 841; **11** 753; **20** 385; **21** 608; **22** 47; **24** 554; **28** 632
relief **26** 791
urban planning **14** 238
Napoleoni, Carlo Antonio **6** 97
Nápoles Mudarra, Juan de **29** 334
Napoletano, Filippo **11** 188; **22** 478, 487*
attributions **30** 356
collaboration **12** 706; **28** 388
patrons and collectors **3** 745; **6** 586; **21** 25; **27** 205
works **18** 709
Napoletano, Francesco *see* FRANCESCO NAPOLETANO
Napoli, Aloise da **30** 514
Napoli, Giovanna da *see* MARIGLIANO, GIOVANNI
Napoli, Michele De *see* DE NAPOLI, MICHELE
Napoli, Tommaso Maria **16** 640; **32** 549
Napoli nobilissima **24** 2, 448
Napolitain, Pierre *see* PIERRE NAPOLITAIN
Nappel'baum, Moisey (Solomonovich) **22** 488*
Napper, Henry **28** 742
Napredåk Factory **5** 158
Náprstek, V. **8** 424
Náprstek Museum of Asian, African and American Culture *see under* PRAGUE → museums
Naprudnoye, St Trifon **27** 371
Napuka Island **31** 403
see also TUAMOTU ISLANDS
Naqa
temples **23** 282, 283, 284
Naqada **9** 773, *774*, 866; **10** 59, 80; **22** 488–9*
ivory-carvings **9** 779
pottery **10** *26*
tomb of Neithhotpe **14** 407; **20** 596; **22** 488, *488*, 509
Naqada I *see under* EGYPT, ANCIENT → periods
Naqada II *see under* EGYPT, ANCIENT → periods
Naqada III *see under* EGYPT, ANCIENT → periods
Naqsh, Jamil **22** 489*; **23** 800
al-Naqshabandi, Munib **30** 177
Naqshi **16** 355
Naqsh-i Rustam **15** 905, 906, 907, 908, 916; **24** 482; **27** 856
fire altar **33** *708*
inscriptions **6** 186, 379
Ka'ba-i Zardusht **33** 707, *707*
rock art **33** 707
sculpture **1** 117
tomb of Darius I **15** 912, 915; **22** 42
Nara **17** *11*, 19, 21; **22** 489–504*
Akishinodera **17** 101, 346
art forms and materials
calligraphy **17** 214
inksticks **17** 388
pottery **17** 242
prints **17** 270
scriptoria **17** 211
sculpture **17** 115
collections **17** 428
Daianji **17** 68, 93, 94, 114, 248; **22** 500–501*
sculpture **17** 116
Daidairi *see* Heijō Palace
Daikandaiji *see* Daianji
Darumadera **17** 132
Eizanji **17** 66, 321
Enjōji **17** 121
Hakusandō **17** 62
Kasugadō **17** 62
Gangōji **17** 65, 94, 114
Gokurakubō **17** 125, 131
gardens **12** 95
Nara—cont.
gates **7** 361
Hannyaji **17** 125
Heijō **17** 93, *93*, *94*, 94–5; **22** 489–92*
temples **22** 491–2
Heijō Palace **17** 52, 247, 382; **22** 492*; **23** 822
Hokkeji **17** *118*, 139
Hōkongōin **17** 120
Hōryūji *see under* IKARUGA
Ichijōin **17** 79
Kasuga Grand Shrine **17** 51, *61*, 62, 347, 372; **22** *491*, 492–4*; **28** 638
armour **17** 362
collections **17** 428
honden **22** 493
maṇḍalas **17** 151, 152
masks **17** 392
paintings **5** *117*
paper **17** 404
Kawaradera **17** 217, 247
kilns **17** 247
Kōfukuji **17** 67, 94, 98, 101, 114, 299, *299*, 325, 347; **22** *490*, 501–2
bell **17** 320, 321
Hokuendō **17** 122, 124, 131
kondō **17** 73
Nan'endō **17** 131
North Octagonal Hall **17** 117
prints **17** 270, *270*
sculpture **17** 22, 114, *114*, 119, 121, 122, 124, 598; **22** 501–2
West Main Hall **18** 213
Konbuin **17** 115
Kuramadera **17** *125*
National Museum **17** 432; **33** 563
Office of Needleworkers **17** 311
Okadera **17** 130
Palace Dyeing Office **17** 311
Raigōji **17** 131
Saidaiji **17** 94, 125; **33** 318
reliquary **17** 322
sculpture **17** 115
Shinyakushiji **17** 66; **18** 213; **22** 502*; **33** 318
Shōrinji **17** 102, 115
Shōsōin **7** 152; **17** 66; **20** 361; **22** *494*, 494–5*
brushes **17** 368
ceramics **6** 914
collections **7** 154; **17** 419, 428, 432; **22** 495, 504; **28** 620, 721
crowns **7** 108
dress **17** 374
enamel **17** 377
felt **10** 873
furniture **7** 35; **17** 384
glass **17** 385, 386
horn **7** 124
lacquer **7** 13; **17** 299; **18** 369, 612; **23** 551
masks **17** 391, 392, 395; **28** 722
metalwork **17** 320
musical instruments **17** 396; **22** 376
paper **17** 403
pottery **17** 248, *248*
screens (ii) (furniture) **28** 297
silk **28** 721
textiles **3** 378; **7** 52; **17** 306, 307, 309, 312, 313; **28** 715
Taimadera **17** 66, 67, 99, 101; **30** 913
ex-votos **17** 346
Tamukeyama Shrine **17** 392
Teiraku Art Gallery **17** 414
temples **30** 445
Tōdaiji **5** 116; **17** 21, 46, 52, 67, 68, 94, 349, 422; **22** *495*, 495–9*
belfry **17** 72
Chūshōin **17** 124
collections **17** 211, 428; **18** 213; **22** 504
Nara
Tōdaiji—cont.
Daibutsu (Great Buddha) **17** 98, 113, 114–15, 127, 320, 422; **22** 496*, 497*, *497*
Daibutsuden (Great Buddha Hall) **17** 45, 71, 74, 122; **18** 213; **22** 498
hardstones **7** 90
Hokkedō **17** 65, 99, 101, 115, *422*; **22** 498
hondō **14** 78
lacquer **17** 299
masks **17** 391, 392
musical instruments **17** 397
Nandaimon **17** 71, 122, *123*, 124; **22** 499
Sangatsudō *see* Hokkedō
screen paintings **17** 154
scriptoria **17** 218
sculpture **17** 22, 115, 117, 121, 122, 124, 125, 126, 129, 130
Shōsōin **17** 23
Tegaimon **7** 361; **22** 498
tiles **17** 260
Tōkondō **17** 124
Tōtō **17** 124
Tōshōdaiji **17** 66, 98, 99, 101; **22** 502–3*, *503*
brackets **4** 625
collections **17** 428
Daibutsu (Great Buddha) **17** 115
Great South Gate **4** 625
hondō **14** 78
kondō **17** 73; **22** 502–3
Main Hall **17** 115, 117
Mieidō **17** 130
sculpture **17** 113, 115, 116, 117, 130, *130*
urban planning **17** 52
Wakakusa **17** 65
Weaving Office **17** 311
writing **17** 214
Yakushiji **2** 655; **17** 67, 68, 94, 101, 127, *146*; **22** 499–500*
East Pagoda **22** *499*
sculpture **6** 835; **17** *113*, 114, 128
Yamato Bunkakan **18** 306, 383, 384
Nara busshi *see* KEI
Nara dolls *see under* DOLLS → types
Narahara, Ikko **14** 779; **22** 503*; **31** 106
Narahara Shrine, *sūtra* repository **17** 321
Narai **15** 446; **17** 97
Narai, King of Ayutthaya (*reg* 1656-88) **4** 796; **30** 575, 588, 611
Naraina
Mujahid Khan Mosque **15** 350
Mustafa Sar **15** 350
Naram-Sin (*reg* 2254-2218 BC) **1** 508, 509–10*, 884; **29** 614
stelae **1** *509*
Naranco *see under* OVIEDO
Naranjo (Argentina) **29** 202
El Naranjo (Mexico) **21** 188
Naranjo-Morse, Nora **22** 606
Narannag **15** 265
Bhutesha Temple **15** 265
Jyeshthesha Temple **15** 265
Narapatigyi, King (*reg* 1638-45) (Myohaung) **2** 281
Narapatisithu, King of Burma (*reg* 1170-3) (Pagan) **5** 222
Nara period *see under* JAPAN → periods
Narashige Koide *see* KOIDE, NARASHIGE
Narasimha I, Ruler (*reg c.* 1156-73) (Hoysala) **14** 816
Narasimha I, Ruler (*reg* 1238-64) (Eastern Ganga) **15** 504; **18** 213

Narasimhavarman I Mahamalla, Ruler (*reg c.* AD 630-68) (Pallava) **15** 303, 509, 510, 511, 738; **20** 223, 225
Narasimhavarman II Rajasimha, Ruler (*reg* 690-728) (Pallava) **15** 304, 513, 514; **20** 223; **23** 873
Narasinghnath, Narasinhanatha Temple **15** 320
Narasmangalam **15** 528, 529
Ramalingeshvara Temple **15** 528, 529
Narasobba **1** 485; **15** 526
works **15** *527*
Narastan **15** 265
Shiva Temple **15** 265
Narayan, Akittam **20** 54
Narayana **15** 228
Narayanpur **15** 317, 498
Narbet, Jacques **30** 127
Narbona, Juan de **2** 28
Narbonne **11** *505*; **22** 504–6*; **26** *908*
Cathedral of St Just **8** 789; **13** 43; **22** *504*, 504–6*; **26** 46; **32** 821
altars **1** 697
choir **22** *505*
mouldings **22** 219, 222
paintings **23** 516
tracing floor **31** 275, *275*
Clos de la Lombarde **27** *56*
gravestones **17** 554
Roman capitolium **26** 904
St Paul-Serge **9** 680
silk **11** 646
wall paintings **27** 56
Narbonne, Eugène **5** 125
Narbonne, Master of the Parement de *see* PAREMENT DE NARBONNE, MASTER OF THE
Narborough Hall (Norfolk) **29** 88
Narbut, Georgy (Ivanovych) **12** 875; **22** 506*; **33** 740
Narbut, Yegor (Ivanovich) *see* NARBUT, GEORGY (IVANOVICH)
Narce **10** 611
Narciso, Cicero Alves *see* ALVES NARCISO, CICERO
Nardi, Angelo **19** 179; **22** 507*
patrons and collectors **2** 291; **14** 6, 8
works **1** 587; **20** 72
Nardini, Famiano **26** 849; **31** 787
Nardini, Francesco **16** 725
Nardis, de' (family) **18** 785
Nardo, Mariotto di *see* MARIOTTO DI NARDO
Nardo di Cione *see* CIONE, NARDO DI
Nardo Rapicano *see* RAPICANO, NARDO
Nardo Romano **2** 184
Narendratitya, Prince **30** 581
Naresar **15** 323
architecture **15** 322
sculpture **15** 495, 497
temples **15** 287, 322
Naresuan, King of Ayutthaya (*reg* 1590-1605) **2** 885
Narford Hall (Norfolk) **11** 348; **24** 341
Narga, Sellasé Church **10** 566, 572
Narhatta **15** 476
Nari, Sebastiano **8** 134
Narice, Francesco **22** 507–8*
Narimanbekov, T. F. **2** 897
Nariño **29** 152
Narishkine *see* NARYSHKIN
Narita, Shinshōji **17** 47
Narjoux, André **4** 597; **18** 664; **22** 508
Narjoux, Félix **22** 508*
Närke, Skjernsunds Slott **33** 98
Narkiss, Bezalel **17** 583
Narkiss, Mordechai **16** 571; **17** 582, 583
Narkissos/Hyakinthos **25** 179
Narkompros **3** 734; **10** 446; **18** 536; **20** 887; **22** 508–9*
Glavprofobr **28** 642
IZO (Department of Fine Arts) **1** 731; **4** 811; **9** 495; **11** 870; **17** 764; **18** 141, 388; **20** 194; **22** 508–9; **25** 239; **26** 504; **27** 283, 443; **28** 642; **30** 362; **31** 519
members **5** 69; **25** 735; **26** 70
TEO (Department of Theatre) **21** 410
Narmer **9** *776*, 867; **21** 108; **22** 509–10*
maces **9** 868
Narmer Palette **9** 778, 868; **11** *150*; **22** *509*, 510; **23** 848
discovery **10** 80; **14** 514
reliefs **9** 797, 808, 844, 864, 868; **10** 37, 42; **14** 407; **23** 848
Narnaul **15** *360*, 363
Jal Mahal **15** 363
mansion of Rai Mukhund Das **15** 372
tomb of Ibrahim Sur **15** 362
Narni
Augustan Bridge **13** 300
Cathedral of S Giovenale **16** 625
Narni, Erasmo da *see* GATTAMELATA
Narodnyy Komissariat Prosveschcheniya *see* NARKOMPROS
narratives **22** 510–23*
Ancient Near East **22** 510–11*, *511*
Assyrian **22** *511*
Aztec **22** *518*, 519
Buddhism
China **6** 788
Indian subcontinent **15** 442, 448; **22** 516*
Indonesia **15** 779
Japan **17** 149–50
Java **15** 779
Byzantine **9** 609–10; **22** 519–20*
Cambodia **5** 487, 490–92, *492*, 495–6
Cappadocia **22** 520
Carolingian **22** *520*
China **6** 777, 779, 788
Christianity **2** 3; **13** *129*
Early Christian (*c.* AD 250-843) **9** 609–10; **22** 519–20*
Egypt, ancient **9** 799, 865, 882; **22** *512*, 512–13*; **28** 494
England **22** *523*
Etruscan **10** 593, 611, *611*, 624
Gothic **13** 128, 129, *129*
Greece, ancient **13** 464, 472, 493; **22** 513–14*, *514*
Classical, Early **13** 451
Hinduism
Cambodia **5** 487
Indian subcontinent **22** 516–17*
Indian subcontinent: Vaishnavism **15** 226–8*
Indonesia **15** 780
Java **15** 780
Indian subcontinent **15** 228–9*; **22** 516–17*
Buddhism **15** 442, 448; **22** 516*
Hinduism **15** 226–8*; **22** 516–17*
Islamic **22** 517*
Jainism **15** 563, 564
Mughal **22** *517*
Indonesia **15** 779, 780
Iran **22** *515*
Islamic **22** *515*, 515–16*, 517*
Italy **22** *522*; **24** 892
Etruscan **10** 593, 611, *611*, 624
Gothic **13** *129*
Renaissance **5** *820*
Roman **26** 792
Jainism **15** 563, 564
Japan **17** 21, 22, 149–50, 153, 158–9
Java **15** 779, 780
narratives—cont.
Maya **22** 518
Mesoamerica, Pre-Columbian **22** 517–19*, *518*
Mesopotamia **21** 293
Olmec **22** 519
Palau **23** 833, *833*
Peru **22** 518
Romanesque **22** 520
Rome, ancient **22** 514*; **26** 792, 861
Scandinavia **32** 521–3*, *522*, *523*
Scotland **23** *476*
South America, Pre-Columbian **22** 517–19*
Sweden **32** *522*, *523*
United States of America **12** *216*
Viking **32** 521*, *522*, 522–4*, *523*
Narses **29** 421
Narses III, Katholikos (*reg* 641-61) **30** 305
Narshakhi **6** 248; **31** 897
Narshima Murthy, P. L. **20** 54
Narsingharh *see* NARSYANG SHAHAR
Narsyang Shahar **15** 602
Narthang **5** 105; **21** 846; **30** *806*, 814, 845
narthex **22** 523*
Narttamalai, Vijayalaya Cholishvara Temple **15** 559
Narubutal **24** 82
Narumi **17** 316, 355
Narushima ware *see under* POTTERY → wares
Naruto **17** 390
Narva **10** *536*, 537
Regional Museum **10** 541
Town Hall **10** 537
Narváez, Alonso de **7** 607
Narváez, Francisco **22** 523–4*; **32** 175, 568
Narwal **24** 82
Narwar **15** 292
narwhal tusks *see under* TUSKS → types
Narykov, Stefan **29** 54
Naryshkin, Lev (Kirillovich), Prince **27** 372
Naryshkin, Prince (*fl* 1866) **3** 277
Naryshkin Baroque **5** 141; **27** 372–3
Naryshkine collection **24** 552
NASA **19** 538
Nasca *see* NAZCA
Naschberger, Gerhard **9** 72
Nasello, Francesco **31** 432
Nash, Arthur J. **30** 868
Nash, David **22** 525*; **32** 788
Nash, Douglas **30** 869
Nash, Frederick **7** 924
Nash, Garry **23** 70
Nash, John (1752-1835) **10** 374, 375; **22** 525–9*
architecture
architectural decorations **14** 681; **30** 503
banks **19** 578
castles **6** 61
cathedrals **27** 538
clubs (meeting places) **7** 469
conservatories **7** 744
country houses **7** 791; **8** 30, 48; **16** 10; **22** *526*
dairies **8** 461
houses **2** 540; **3** 79; **8** 30; **22** *528*
pavilions **4** 809, *809*; **9** 84; **10** 297; **22** 59
temporary architecture **23** 776
triumphal arches **31** 351, *351*
urban planning **4** 822; **14** 173; **19** *573*, 574; **25** 655, 656; **26** 743; **31** 724
villas **8** 30; **32** 554
assistants **5** 282; **25** 710
collaboration **10** 234–5; **26** 238
groups and movements **10** 234; **22** 740, 741; **23** 210; **26** 85, 735, 743
Nash, John (1752-1835)—cont.
illustrated writings **25** 710
interior decoration **9** 17; **23** 678, *679*
patrons and collectors **10** 361; **14** 145, 539; **15** 407; **32** 783
pupils **13** 622; **24** 364
restorations by others **12** 926
teachers **30** 386
Nash, John (1893-1977) **22** 525*
groups and movements **8** 264; **19** 622
patrons and collectors **20** 476
works **4** 366; **8** 911; **18** 718
Nash, Joseph **8** 400; **14** 148
works **24** *294*
Nash, Leslie **30** 869
Nash, Paul **10** 375; **22** 524–5*
groups and movements **19** 591; **22** 751; **23** 23; **25** 556; **30** 22; **31** 673
patrons and collectors **20** 476; **28** 273
pupils **3** 420; **26** 39
teachers **19** 591
works **4** 366; **10** 257, 284, 321; **18** 718; **19** 492; **22** *525*; **29** 628; **32** 902
al-Nashar, Abd al-Rahman **9** 766
Nashe naslediye **24** 451; **27** 444
Nash Hill (Wilts) **10** 301
Nashid, Sabry **9** 766
Nashid, Samir **9** 766
nashiji see under LACQUER → types
Nashio **17** 404
Nashq *see* AL-BAYDA'
Nashville (TN)
Fisk University **1** 442; **29** 657
Tennessee State Capitol **13** 611; **29** *771*
Nasi, Vicente **7** 606
Našice **8** *174*
Pajačević Palace **8** 176
Nasik **5** 94, 95; **15** 257, *276*; **21** 847; **22** 529*
Cave 3 **15** 451; **21** *847*
Cave 19 **15** 275
Guatamiputra Cave *see* Cave 3
maps **15** 705
sculpture **15** 435*, 450–51
temples **15** 252, 275
textiles **15** 664
nāsikā (window motif) **15** 244*
Nāsikka *see* NASIK
Nasilai **11** 70
Nasimovich, Nikolay (Fyodorovich) *see* CHUZHAK, NIKOLAY (FYODOROVICH)
Nasini, Antonio **22** 529
Nasini, Apollonio **22** 530
Nasini, Francesco **22** 529
Nasini, Giuseppe Nicola **22** 529–32*
pupils **22** 532
works **22** *530*; **28** 688
Nasir (family) **32** 315
al-Nasir, Caliph (*reg* 1180-1225) (Abbasid) **3** 52; **16** 182; **22** 322; **27** 681
al-Nāṣira *see* NAZARETH
Nasir al-Din, Shah (*reg* 1848-96) (Qajar) **16** 466; **25** 770*
architecture
military **21** 589
mosques **16** 234; **25** 830
museums **30** 415
palaces **16** 234, 235; **30** 415
urban planning **30** 414–15
gardens **12** 83
manuscripts **16** 298, 307, 341
paintings **16** 535
portraits **16** 81, 561
regalia **16** 539
al-Nāṣir al-Dīn Faraj *see* FARAJ
Nāṣir al-Dīn Ḥasan *see* HASAN
Nasir al-Din Haydar, Nawab of Avadh (*reg* 1827-37) **15** 377
Nasir al-Din Mahmud, Ruler (*reg* 1201-22) (Artuqid) **16** 379
Nasir al-Din Mahmud, Sultan (*reg* 1442-60) (Line of Ilyas Shah) **15** 352
al-Nāṣir al-Dīn Muḥammad ibn Qalā'ūn *see* AL-NASIR MUHAMMAD
Nasir al-Din Shah, Sultan (*reg* 1500-11) (Khalji) **15** 355, 573, 739; **16** 359; **20** 251
Nasir al-Din Tusi **16** 193; **23** 338
Naṣir-i Efkâr **2** 634; **31** 454
Nasir-i Khusraw **13** 811; **16** 432, 541; **17** 490
al-Nasir Muhammad, Sultan (*reg* 1294-5; 1299-1309; 1309-40) (Mamluk) **14** 428; **16** 209, 382, 383, 490, 496; **20** 56, 228–9*
architecture **5** 397, 403, 404; **16** 209
metalwork **16** 382, 389, *389*; **20** *228*; **23** 557
screens (i) (architectural) **16** *496*
textiles **16** 441
Nasiruddin **15** 598
Naskapi **22** 546, 631, 638, 648, 656, 670, 673
naskh script *see under* SCRIPTS → types
Näskott **13** 119
Nasmyth, Alexander **22** 530, 531–2*; **26** 774; **28** 235; **30** 680
pupils **13** 314; **26** 467; **28** 78; **30** 752; **32** 910; **33** 204, 216
reproductive prints by others **19** 515
teachers **25** 883; **27** 334; **28** 274
works **9** 725, *726*; **28** 236
Nasmyth, Anne **22** 530
Nasmyth, Barbara **22** 530
Nasmyth, Charlotte **22** 530
Nasmyth, Elizabeth **22** 530
Nasmyth, James **21** 896; **22** 530
Nasmyth, Jane **22** 530
Nasmyth, Margaret **22** 530
Nasmyth, Patrick **22** 530, 532*; **28** 236
Nasmyth, Peter *see* NASMYTH, PATRICK
Nason, Joseph **28** 831
Nason, Pieter **9** 380
Na Songkhla (family) **30** 590
Nasoni, Nicolau **22** 532–4*
collaboration **7** 522
works **18** 676; **22** *533*; **23** 453; **25** 293; **27** 805; **28** 732; **31** 2
Nasonovskaya, Pavla (Alekseyevna) **27** 422
Nasr, Abu *see* ABU NASR
Nasr, Sultan (*reg* 1308-13) (Nasrid) **13** 287
Nasr al-Din Mutatabbib *see* NASRULLAH AL-TABIB
Nasrallah Imami **15** 143
Nasrid **16** 114; **22** 534–5*
architecture **13** 281
coats of arms **14** 428
palaces **13** 285; **23** 815
see also:
ISMA'IL, Sultan
MUHAMMAD I, Sultan
MUHAMMAD II, Sultan
MUHAMMAD III, Sultan
MUHAMMAD V, Sultan
MUHAMMAD VII, Sultan
MUHAMMAD XI, Sultan
NASR, Sultan
YUSUF I, Sultan
YUSUF III, Sultan
Nasrid chairs *see under* CHAIRS → types
Nasrullah al-Tabib **16** 283
Nassaro, Matteo del **11** 634, 635; **12** 258, 259; **17** 520
Nassa shells *see under* SHELLS → types
Nassau (Bahamas) **3** *59*, 60
architecture **3** 61

Nassau (Bahamas)—cont.
Bahamas Historical Society Museum 3 64
Bahamia Museum 3 64
Balcony House 3 61, 63
Central Bank of the Bahamas 3 61
College of the Bahamas 3 65
Deanery 3 63
Fort Charlotte 3 60
Fort Fincastle 3 60
Fort Montague 3 60
Government House 3 61
Government Offices 3 61
Jacaranda House 3 *61*, 61
Legislative Council Chamber 3 61
National Archives 3 64
National Insurance Board Headquarters 3 61
Oakes House 3 61
Pompey Museum 3 64
Post Office 3 61
Public Library and Museum 3 60, 61, 64
Russell's Academy of Fine Arts 3 64
St Andrew's 3 61
St Matthew's 3 61
Supreme Court 3 61
Nassau (Cook Islands) 7 790
Nassau (Germany)
Schloss 12 415
Steinischer Hof 15 145
Nassau, Englebrecht II, Count of 11 224; 22 535*
manuscripts 20 724, 726, 727, 749; 26 563; 29 666
stained glass 26 745
Nassau, Hendrik III, Count of 22 535*, 902
architecture 4 732; 17 884; 22 823
paintings 3 554; 4 446; 32 586
sculpture 21 71
tapestries 23 464, 465
Nassau, Mencía de Mendoza, Countess of 3 612
paintings 3 554; 4 448, 452; 13 27; 28 803
sculpture 31 815
tapestries 23 525
Nassau-Dietz, Albertina of Orange Nassau, Princess of 23 *463*
Nassau-Dietz, Ernst Casimir, Count of 12 233
Nassau-Dietz, John William Friso, Prince of Orange, Prince of *see* ORANGE, JOHN WILLIAM FRISO, Prince of, Prince of Nassau-Dietz
Nassau-Dietz, Sophia Hedwig, Countess of 1 *658*
Nassau-Dietz, William Frederick of Orange, Prince of 16 832
Nassau-Dillenburg, William, Count of 23 *463*
Nassau-Idstein, Johann, Graf von 29 725
Nassau-Odijk, Willem Adriaan, Count of 20 458; 26 560
architecture 26 560
Nassau-Saarbrücken, Johann III, Count of 14 86
Nassau-Siegen, Johan Maurits, Count of 2 105, 696; 4 715; 14 39; 22 535–6*
architecture 5 345, 542; 22 824
collections 22 904
paintings 4 656, 724; 9 702–3; 25 326
sculpture 9 760; 25 327
tapestries 12 829
Nassau Tile Factory, The 3 63
Nassau-Weilburg, Charles Christian, Prince (*reg* 1753-88) 14 39; 30 62
Nasser, Frederico 4 728
al-Nasser, Gamal 'Abd 10 91
Nasser Sabah al-Ahmad al-Sabah, Shaykh (al-Sabah) 16 553; 18 541
Nasser Youssef 3 69
Nassini, Giuseppe Nicola 1 532
Nassols, Narciso 23 369
Nast 11 610; 24 148, 149
Nast, Thomas 22 536–7*
works 5 759; 25 651, 652; 27 872
nasta'līq script *see under* SCRIPTS → types
Nastalus 2 646
works 2 *647*
Nastyukov 9 51
Nasuh Matrakçı 22 537*
works 12 84; 16 304, 347
Natá 23 *902*
church 23 903, 904, 906
Natakhamani, King of Kush (*reg c.* 1st cent. AD) 22 467
Natal 4 *705*
Reis Magos 4 709
Natali, Francesco 12 528
Natali, Giovanni
works 16 *718*
Natali, Giovanni Battista 11 10
Natali, Giuseppe 24 9
Natali, Renato 28 319
Natalini, Adolfo 16 651; 30 3, 4*
Natalis, Hieronymus 7 120
Natalis, Michel 1 787; 22 717
Natanson, Adam 32 740
Natanson, Alexandre 22 422, 425, 537; 32 740
Natanson, Alfred 22 425, 537
Natanson, Thadée 22 422, 425, 537–8*; 32 740
Natanz 16 *105*; 22 538*
congregational mosque 4 791; 16 159, 160; 21 506
funerary complex of 'Abd al-Samad 16 194, 195, *195*; 24 877; 28 634
muqarnas (architecture) 22 322
stucco 29 820
inscriptions 16 232
khānaqāh 18 18
minaret 21 628
Natchez (MS) 20 869; 22 538–9*; 31 *587*
Natchez National Historical Park 22 539
Rosalie mansion 22 *539*
Natchez (people) 30 449
Natchitoches (LA) 1 422
Nater 29 553
Nates, Juan de 10 535; 14 476; 29 268; 31 822, 823
Nathan, Ernesto 26 762
Nathan bar Simeon ha-Levi 20 122
works 20 *122*
Nathanson, Mendel Levin 9 701
Nathdwara 15 599, 674, 730
Nat-hluang-kyuang 29 826
National Art Collections Fund 10 367; 19 872; 26 512
National Art Council of Tanzania 30 301
National Artists Equity Association 32 890
National Art Slide Library *see under* LEICESTER
National Art Society of Bulgaria 5 163; 22 539–40*
members 21 544; 23 16, 335; 28 820; 31 399, 785; 33 599
National Board of Antiquities (Finland) 11 112
National Buildings Record 29 926
National Capital Development Commission 5 602
national catalogues *see under* CATALOGUES → type
National Competition 10 373
National Competitive Painting Exhibitions *see* NAIKOKU KAIGA KYŌSHINKAI
National Cottage Industries Corporation (NCIC) 30 301
National Council for Culture, Arts and Letters 18 541
National Course of Instruction 10 373
Nationale Maatschappij voor Goedkope Woningen 3 551
National Endowment for the Arts (NEA) 25 703; 31 663; 32 890
National Endowment for the Humanities 25 703
National Furniture Company 11 584
National Heritage Memorial Fund 14 452, 453
National Hungarian Fine Art Society 2 547
National Learning movement *see* KOKUGAKU (NATIONAL LEARNING MOVEMENT)
Nationalmuseum bulletin 24 451
National Park Services (NPS) 14 452
National Print Council 25 629
National Romanticism 22 540–41*; 33 705
art forms
architecture
Finland 19 643; 22 541
Norway 22 541
Sweden 30 74; 32 765
painting
Finland 17 *448*; 29 63
Hungary 14 901
Sweden 22 *541*; 23 *206*
regional traditions
Denmark 29 72; 32 270
Finland 11 100; 12 20, 498; 14 89; 23 498
Norway 13 776
Sweden 22 540
National Serigraphic Society 28 465
National Socialism *see* NAZISM
National Society of Friends of Art (Prague) 25 433
National Theatre Generation 8 392
National Trust 9 19
Native American Artists Association 22 667
Native North American collection 22 552
Native North Americans 5 63; 17 770; 22 541–679*, *544*, *552*, *555*; 31 588
adobe 22 567
aesthetics 22 561–2
altars 1 701*
amber 1 761
amulets 22 573, 652
anthropology 2 137; 22 673–4
antlers 14 *746*
appliqué 22 648, 654
aprons 22 655
archaeology 22 671–3*, *672*
architecture 21 597–8*; 22 563–5*, 566–73*, *571*, 670–71*
arm-bands 22 651
art (works of) 22 665
art history 2 533; 22 674
art legislation 22 667, 670
art market 22 660–61, 665, 666–70*
ash 3 331
asymmetry 22 562
authenticity 22 667
bags 22 627, *643*, 645–6, *646*, 662
baleen 22 656
banners 22 655
bark 22 *547*, 648, 651, 656, 657, 663
cedar 3 331
basket lids 22 657
Native North Americans—cont.
baskets 3 331, 332, *332*; 8 *537*; 22 *641*, 652, 655–7*, 658–63*, *659*, *660*, *662*, *663*
basketwork 22 655–7*, *657*, 658–63*, 666, 668, 669
beads 3 331; 22 648, 654, 655, 656
beadwork 3 440, 441, 442; 4 I1; 22 637–40*, *639*, *640*, 641–4*, *641*, *642*, *643*, 655, 665
belts 3 441; 22 *651*, 652, 653
bird's feet 22 655
blankets 22 *547*, *623*, 652, 669, 673
body arts 22 628*, 630, 631, 633, 635*, 636–7
body ornaments 22 628*, 629*, 630, 632, 633, 635*, 636–7
bone 4 314; 22 668
bone-carvings 22 573, 575
bottles 22 661
bowls 22 586, *603*, *604*
mush 22 *659*
Weeden Island culture 22 *612*
bracelets 22 613, 614, 651
breech-cloths 22 654
burial mounds 1 153; 22 570, 571–2, *571*; 31 116*
cane 22 662
canoes 22 563
caps 22 658
carving 22 573–82*, 585–6*
catalogues 22 679
catlinite 22 584, *585*
cedar 9 165; 22 563
ceramics 22 562, 563
ceremonial objects 22 668, 669
charms 22 652
chronologies 22 672
churches 22 567
cloaks 22 652
clubs (weapons) 22 586
coats 22 651
collections 22 360, 562, 565, 648, 660, 667, 668, 669, 673, 675–8*
ethnographic art 22 666
colour 22 561
combs (hair) 22 574, *574*
containers 22 651, 654
copper 14 *746*; 22 612, 613, *613*, *617*, 617–18*; 29 *415*
copyright 22 666
cornhusks 22 647, 663
cosmologies 22 556–7
costumes 22 *583*
cotton 22 622–3
cotton-wood 3 331; 22 *583*
cradles (i) (cots) 22 651
craftsmen and artists 22 561, 562, 563, 661, 665, 666, 667
currency 3 441
daggers 22 613
dating methods 22 672
display of art 22 360
dolls 22 574, 582–4, *583*, 669; 31 259, 260
doors 9 165*
drawings 14 *814*; 22 592
dress 3 441; 22 623, 628–31*, 632*, *632*, 633*, 634*, *635*, 635–7*, *637*, *640*, *642*, 648, 649, 650; 28 *546*
dresses 22 655
dyes 22 619–20, 648, 649, 661
earrings 22 614
earthworks 21 597; 22 570–72, *571*
education (art) 22 594
effigies 1 *153*
embroidery 22 *623*, 644*, 645–7*, *645*, 648
false 22 *646*, *647*, 657, 658, 663, *663*
see also QUILLWORK
ethnographic art 8 280; 22 666
exchange 22 562, 565
exhibitions 22 595, 598, 674, 677, 678–9*
Native North Americans—cont.
fans 10 780*; 22 654
feathers 3 331; 10 847, 848; 22 *549*, *583*, 652–4*, *653*; 31 260
ferns 3 331
fetishes 22 669
figurines 22 573, 582, *669*
forgeries 22 668
fortifications 21 597–8*
fringes 22 644, 655
fur 22 551, 656
games 31 266
garters 22 *651*
glazes 22 604
gnomons 22 572
grasses 3 331, *332*; 22 570, 647, 655, 656, 663; 31 260
beargrass 3 331
guilds 22 650, 666
haematite 21 718
hair
horsehair 22 649; 31 260
human hair 31 260
moose-hair 22 647, 650, 663
mountain goat-hair 22 619, 620
hair ornaments 22 649
hairstyles 22 628*, 631
harnesses 14 185; 22 *650*
hats 22 613, *659*
hazel 3 331
headbands 22 613, 652
headdresses 22 652, 653, *653*; 28 II1
headpieces (body ornament) 22 652
helmets 14 *746*
hemlock 22 563
heraldry 22 562
hickory 3 331
hides 22 592, 654–5*
buffalo 22 *592*, 654, *654*, 655
elk 22 655
historiography 22 673–4*
houses 21 *174*; 22 *567*, 570, 572–3
hogan 22 568
pithouses 22 566
plank 22 563–5, *564*
pueblo 22 566, *567*
wikiup 22 567
human figures 1 *153*
iconography 22 559–61*, 665
igloos 9 165
insignia 22 652
interior decoration 22 *580*
investment 22 668
iron 22 612, 613
ivory 22 668
ivory-carvings 22 573, 574, *574*, 575, 656
jackets 22 *645*
jars 22 *601*
jewellery 3 441; 22 614–16*, *615*, 629*, 642*, 668–9
kivas 1 701; 6 *381*; 18 *102*, 102–3*; 22 566, 567; 28 641
labyrinths 18 586*
lace 31 661
leather 22 *654*, 654–5*, 663; 31 260
leggings 22 649, 654
lodges 22 569, 570, 572
looms 22 622
maple 3 331
maps 20 362; 31 152
masks 16 *891*; 22 545, 563, 573, *573*, 575, 578, *578*, 579, 613, 663, *664*, 665
Alaska 22 *545*
Hopi 22 *583*
United States of America 22 *558*
mass production 22 667, 668
mats 22 657, *657*, 662
mazes 18 586*
metal 22 612–14
metalwork 22 612–16*, *613*, *617*, 617–18*

Native North Americans—cont.
miniaturization **22** 668
mirrors **21** 718
moccasins **3** 441; **22** 648, 649, 651, 654
mounds **14** 746; **22** 572, 671–2
museums **22** 360, 675–8*
necklaces **22** 613, 651, *651*
nephrite **16** 861
oak **3** 331
ornament **23** 564–5*
painting **14** *477*; **22** *63*, 560*, 587–99*, *588*, *594*
battle **22** *592*
Canada **22** 597–8*, *666*
genre **3** *500*
sand **22** 558, 590–91*, *591*
United States of America **22** 593–7*
watercolour **14** *811*; **22** *596*, *599*
paints **22** 587
parkas **22** *630*
patronage **22** 675–8*
pectoral ornaments **22** *616*
pendants (jewellery) **22** 614
periods **22** 553
photography **10** 580
pictographs **13** 332, *332*
pigments **22** *545*, 561; **27** 727
red **22** 561
pine-needles **22** 663
pipe-bags **22** 649
pipes (smoking) **22** 584–5, *585*, 586, *586*, 651, 653, 668
pipestone **1** *153*
pitchers **22** *602*
plaques **29** *415*
poles **22** *564*
polychromy **22** 665
portraits **8** *537*; **10** *578*
posts **22** 572
pottery **20** *498*; **22** 600–612*, *603*, *607*, 666, 668
Gila Polychrome ware **22** 604
Salado Polychrome ware **22** 604
Sikyatki Polychrome ware **22** 604, *604*
Sikyatki style **22** 562
Weeden Island culture **22** *611*, *612*
White Mountain Redware **22** 604
20th cent. **22** *451*
pouches **4** I1; **22** *557*, *647*, *649*, 651
pyrite **21** 718
quills **22** 644, 648–9*, 651, 652
bird **22** 647, 648, 649
porcupine **22** 647, 648, 649, *650*, 651
quillwork **22** 647–52*, *650*, 654, 655, 656
17th cent. **22** *651*
19th cent. **22** *649*
quivers **22** 652
rattles **22** 613
red-wood **22** 563
regalia **22** *549*, 653, 654
religion **22** 556–9*, *557*, *558*
repoussé **29** *415*
ribbons **22** 654
ritual objects **14** 747; **22** 575
robes **22** 618–21*, *619*, *621*, 654, 655
rock art **22** 549, 559–60*, 581–2, 589–90*, 592
carving **22** 575
painting **13** 332, *332*; **27** 727
roots **3** 331; **22** 656
rugs **22** 669; **30** VIII2
rushes **3** 331
sarapes **22** *625*
sashes **22** 627, 651
scalps **22** 652
screenprinting **22** 589
sculpture **22** 573–86*
sedges **3** 331
shell middens **18** 7

Native North Americans—cont.
shells **22** 637–40*, 641–2*, *641*, 644*; **28** 582
abalone **28** II1
shields **22** *562*, 653, 654, *654*
shirts **22** 636, 648, 649, 654
shrines (i) (cult) **28** 641*
silk **22** *645*
silver **22** 614, *615*, 668–9
sinew **3** 440
skins **22** 654–5*
bird **22** 653
deerskin **22** 654, *654*; **31** 260
sheepskin **22** 654
skirts **22** 652
soapstone **22** 668
souvenirs **22** 668
spinning (textile) **22** 619, 620–21
spruce **22** 563
stamps **22** 662, 663
stone **21** 718
stone-carvings **22** 573
sumac **3** 331
tattoos **22** 630, 631; **30** 366
temples **22** 572; **30** 449–50*, *450*
tepees **9** 165; **22** 568–9, *569*, 570, 653, 655
textiles **22** 562, 618–28*, *625*, 663
tombs **22** 571
topknots **22** 652
totem poles **22** *579*, 668
tourist art **22** 575, 651, 655, 656, 658, 660, 667–70*, *669*; **31** 259
towns **5** 386
trade
beadwork **3** 441
copper **22** 612
fur **22** 546, 551, 556, 613
metal **22** 613
trappings **14** 185; **22** *639*
traps **22** 656
trays **22** 656, 658
turquoise **22** *615*, 668–9
urns **22** *611*
vernacular art **22** 666
villages **22** *552*
water pots **22** *608*
weapons **22** 573
weaving **22** 620*, 621–2*, 623–4, 627, 665
wickerwork **22** 663
willow **3** 331; **22** 656, *662*, 663
wire **3** 331
wood **16** *891*; **22** *578*, 582, 586, 662, 663, *664*
wood-carvings **11** *321*; **22** *564*, 573, *573*, 575, *577*, *580*; **28** *329*; **33** 325
wool **22** *547*, *623*; **30** VIII2
yarn **22** 655
yucca **3** 331, *332*; **22** 661
see also Alaska; Canada; Usa
Native Soil movement **7** 249
Nativity groups **22** 679–81*, *681*
NATO (Narrative Architecture Today) **7** 482
Natoire, Charles-Joseph **22** 682–3*
patrons and collectors **13** 665; **18** 693; **19** 752; **20** 417; **25** 150; **32** 898
personal collection **13** 665
pupils **8** 792; **9** 301; **13** 639, 805; **20** 282; **24** 772; **25** 882; **32** 427
reproductive prints by others **2** 853; **24** 480
teachers **19** 143; **32** 670
works **3** 461; **4** 408; **7** 677; **11** 538, 577, 578; **14** 791; **19** 142, 231; **22** *683*; **24** 135, *136*; **26** 494; **32** 900
Natoire, Florent **22** 682
Natori, Shunsen **17** 295
Natori, Yōnosuke **9** 121; **18** 60
natron **16** 431; **22** 283
Natsume, Sōseki **17** 294; **31** 81
Natsuo *see* Fushimi Jisaburō
Natter, Heinrich **15** 865; **33** 736
Natter, Johann Lorenz **12** 262; **20** 924; **22** 683–4*

Natter, Lorenz **12** 263
Natthu **15** 608
Nattier, Jean-Baptiste **11** 405; **22** 684*
Nattier, Jean-Marc **11** 657; **22** 684–5*; **24** 135
attributions **19** 543
collaboration **9** 362
patrons and collectors **7** 528; **13** 705; **23** 517; **28** 527; **30** 524
pupils **3** 101; **31** 69
reproductive prints by others **3** 463; **12** 179; **19** 216
works **11** *457*, 539; **22** *685*; **23** 295; **25** 882; **31** 69
Nattier, Marc **22** 684
Nattier, Marie **22** 684
Natufians **30** 181, 192
works **30** *181*
natural dyes *see under* Dyes → types
natural history *see under* Collections → types; Libraries → types; Museums → types
natural history books **4** 363; **6** 87
naturalism **8** 910; **22** 685–8*; **26** 53
art forms
painting **9** *717*; **19** *334*
theatre **30** 685
regional traditions
Byzantine **9** 520–21*
Early Christian (*c.* AD 250-843) **9** 520–21*
England **22** 686
France **6** 9; **12** 234; **22** 687–8*, *688*
Germany **19** 334
Gothic **13** 128–9*
Indian subcontinent **15** 206
Italy **32** 256
Netherlands, the **22** 686
Rome, ancient **22** 686
Naturalists **28** 344
naturamas **7** 924
Naturns, S Procolo **5** 798; **8** 836
Natusch & Sons **22** 468
Natzler, Gertrude **31** 640
Natzler, Otto **31** 640
Nau, John-Antoine **20** 830
Nauclerio, Giambattista **13** 802; **23** 576
Nauclerus, Simon **5** 817; **29** 840
Naudé, Gabriel **19** 313
Naudé, Hugo **29** 108, 110
Nauders **2** 790
Naudet, Mlle **21** 426
Naudet, Paul-Antoine **25** 600
Naudet, Thomas **7** 762
Naudin, Bernard **14** 499; **19** 807
Nauen, Heinrich **10** 695; **20** 808; **21** 70; **22** 689*
Nauheim, Sigmund **17** 581
Naujoks, H. **29** 435
Naukratis **9** *774*, 788; **10** 80; **13** *362*, 372; **22** 689–90*
faience (i) (glass) **13** 590
fortress **9** 849
pottery **13** 485, 486, 487, 504, 512, 537, 542; **32** 57
statuette **22** *690*
Naukratis Painter **13** 512; **32** 57–8*, 66
Naukydes **13** 453, 596; **22** 690*; **25** 179
works **2** 682; **13** 454; **25** 179
Naum, Saint **23** 373
Nauman, Bruce **14** 690; **22** 690–91*
dealers **6** 23
groups and movements **10** 416
productions **8** 270
works **6** 9; **22** 748; **24** 403, 408; **32** 420
Naumann, Friedrich **8** 825
Naumann, Johann Christoph von **8** 843; **9** 241

Naumburg **12** *360*, *361*; **22** 691–3*
Cathedral of SS Peter and Paul **22** 691*
bosses **22** *693*
crucifix **8** 214, *214*
liturgical furnishings **22** 693
rood **27** 125
rood screen **13** 87; **28** 293
sculpture **7** 643; **9** *257*, 258; **12** 399, 471; **13** 86, 87, 143; **20** 736; **22** 44, *692*, 692–3*; **26** 182
stained glass **13** 186
Naumburg, Elkanah **17** 571
Naumburg Master **20** 735–6*
works **8** 214, *214*; **22** 692, *692*
workshop **20** 129; **21** 63
Naumkeag *see* Salem (MA)
Naumov, Aleksandr **17** 753
Naumov, Pavel **3** 809
Naumovski, Vangel **19** 885
Nauna Island **24** 82
Naupara **22** 79
Nauri Decree **29** 616
Nauru **22** 693–4*; **23** *711*
Nausharo **15** 246
Nausicaa Painter **13** 521; **32** 56
nautilus cups *see under* Cups → types
nautilus shells *see under* Shells → types
Nautré
works **25** *84*
Nauwelaerts, Nicolaas **2** 199
Nauwjnx, Herman *see* Naiwyncx, Herman
Nava, Cesare **4** 842; **22** 105
Nava, Francisco García *see* García Nava, Francisco
Navagero, Andrea **20** 350
Navahrudak **3** *525*; **9** 646; **16** 520; **27** 414
fortress **3** 526
SS Boris and Gleb **3** 526
Navajo **12** 647; **22** 550, 554, 556, 557, 558, 563, 567, 568, 661–2, 665, 666, 668, 669, 670, 674, 676, 677, 694*
blankets **22** 624–5; **27** 317
dress **22** 634, *635*
iconoclasm **15** 78
jewellery **22** 614*, 615*, *615*, 629
looms **30** 545
metalwork **22** 614
pottery **22** 605, 677
rugs **5** 829; **22** 626; **27** 317; **30** VIII2
sand painting **18** 586; **22** 560, 591*
sarapes **22** *625*
silver **22** 614, *615*
textiles **22** *625*
turquoise **22** *615*
weaving **22** 624–6
Navakas, Mindaugas **19** 500
Naval Binder **4** 353
Navan (Co. Meath) **15** 873
Nava Nakorn **17** 686
Navan Fort **16** *5*; **22** 694*; **25** *470*
Navaretta, C. **33** 310
Navarre, Henri **10** 422; **11** 569
Navarre, Peter of *see* Peter of Navarre
Navarrete, Juan Fernández de **20** 65; **22** 694–5*; **29** 280
patrons and collectors **13** 922
works **10** 502, 503; **22** *695*; **29** 278; **33** 118
writings **29** 301
Navarro, Elizalde **24** 620
Navarro, Emídio **4** 45; **25** 319
Navarro, Gilberto Aceves *see* Aceves Navarro, Gilberto
Navarro, José de **1** 620
Navarro, Juan **29** 339
Navarro, Julio **14** 716
Navarro, Luis Díez *see* Díez Navarro , Luis

Navarro Baldeweg, Juan **29** 274
Navarro de los Arcos, Luis Antonio **26** 553
Navarro y Cañizares, Miguel **14** 479
Navas, Jorge **23** 81
Navasie, Joy **22** 609
Nave, Adalberto (della) **24** 196; **31** 181
Nave, Bartolomeo della **10** 861; **13** 919; **22** 696*
nave chancels *see* Schola cantorum
Navenby (Lincs), St Peter **13** 82
Naver, Kim **8** 756
naves **22** 695*
Navesi, Giovanni di Rafaello **28** 682
Navez, François-Joseph **3** 562; **5** 44; **22** 696–7*
pupils **8** 628; **18** 481; **21** 369; **25** 261; **28** 891; **29** 645, 781
teachers **8** 560; **11** 724
works **5** 43; **22** *696*
Navia, Antonio **14** 464
Navier, Claude-Louis-Marie-Henri **5** 649
navigation charts *see* Maps → types → sea charts
Navigius **27** 107
Naville, Edouard **10** 80, 82, 90; **14** 403; **20** 550; **30** 693; **33** 481
Naville, Pierre **30** 17, 19
Navjot, Altaf **4** 291
Navoi *see* Kermine
Navplion **14** *332*
Archaeological Museum **2** 602; **8** 712; **14** 361
Navrátil, Jan **8** 401
Navrátil, Josef Matěj **22** 697*; **25** 433
works **8** 392, 400; **22** 329
Navvab, M. M. **2** 896, 901
Nawab of Murshidabad **14** 186
Nawabs of Avadh *see*:
Asaf al-Daula, Nawab
Ghazi al-Din Haydar, Nawab
Muhammad ʿAli Sha, Nawab
Nasir al-Din Haydar, Nawab
Shujaʿ al-Daula, Nawab
Wajid ʿAli Shah, Nawab
Nawabs of Bengal *see*:
ʿAlivardi Khan Mahabat Jang Ghazi, Nawab
ʿAzim al-Nisa Begum
Feridun Jah, Nawab
Mir Jaʿfar ʿAli Khan, Nawab
Munni Begum
Murshid Quli Jafar Khan, Nawab
Sarfaraz Khan, Nawab
Shahamat Jang
Suraj al-Daula, Nawab
Nawalgarh **15** 611
Nawar, Ahmad **9** 766
Nawaria **25** 115
Nawash, Ahmad **17** 655
Nawe, Francis **7** 441
Nawidemak, Queen (early 1st cent.) **23** 283
Naworth Castle (Cumbria) **11** 140; **21** 369
Naxian Colossos **22** 700
Naxos (Greece) **8** *304*; **9** *511*; **13** *363*; **22** 698–700*; **32** *158*
acropolis **22** 699
architecture **22** *698*, 698–9*; **32** 159
bronzes **8** 323
churches **22** 700
coins **13** 586
collections **13** 359
emery **29** 706
figurines **13** 579, 580
fortifications **22** 699
gold **8** 322
graves **13** 383
jars **8** 313

Naxos (Greece)—cont.
marble 8 314; 13 387, 434, 436; 22 699, *699*; 29 701
metalwork 8 322
models 8 306
Monastery of Kaloritsa
Church of the Nativity 22 700
Museum 8 323
pottery 13 492, 502
sculpture 13 436, 445, 447; 18 409; 22 699–700*
korai 18 245
kouroi 13 445; 22 699, *699*
vases 10 612
Naxos (Sicily) 13 594; 28 654
Naxos Museum Master 8 315
Nay, Ernst Wilhelm 22 701–2*
groups and movements 12 397; 14 624
patrons and collectors 11 729
works 19 491; 22 *701*
Naya, Carlo 22 702*
Nayagarh 15 635
Nayaka 17 769; 22 702–3*; 30 641
see also:
ACYUTAPPA, Ruler
TIRUMALAI, Ruler
VIJAYARANGA CHOKKANATHA, Ruler
Nayarit
figurines 33 101, 103
mirrors 21 719
models 32 305
pottery 21 237; 22 519
tombs 21 250
Nayatola 15 452
Nayin *see* NA'IN
Nayler, George 12 272
Naylor, John 12 598
Naylor, Richard 12 598; 29 870
Nayral, Jacques 8 244
Nayriz Mosque 16 801
Nayshābūr *see* NISHAPUR
Nay-ta-hut *see* YAHUDIYA, TELL EL-
Naywinck, Harman *see* NAIWYNCX, HERMAN
Nazarenes 2 796; 6 535; 7 726; 11 462; 12 479; 14 839; 15 54; 16 677; 18 183; 22 328, 703–4*; 23 572; 26 738, 776
collections 3 291; 30 766
members 7 870; 11 802; 12 392–3; 14 580; 23 412, 675; 24 234; 25 872; 26 128; 28 68, 135; 31 428; 32 119
methods 32 806
works 12 *392*; 23 *411*, *676*; 28 *136*
see also LUKASBRÜDER; LUKASBUND
Nazarenko, Tat'yana 27 397
Nazareth (Israel) 9 *513*; 16 *565*; 22 704–5*; 26 629
Cathedral of the Annunciation 17 502, 504; 22 705*, *705*
capitals 17 *504*
Nazareth (PA; USA) 22 80
Nazari, Bartolomeo 3 308; 6 91; 10 770; 24 865
Nazarov, Ye. S. 22 171
Nazca 5 388–9; 22 706–9*; 24 *498*; 29 127, 135, *156*, 160
altars 1 701
dress 29 182
feathers 29 207
gourds 13 229
jars 29 176
masks 29 208
musical instruments 29 216
pottery 22 706–7*, *707*; 29 133, 175
religion 29 134
rock art 22 707, *708*
S Javier 24 503
S José 24 503
textiles 29 180
Nazca lines 18 586; 22 707–9*, *708*
Nazerat *see* NAZARETH (ISRAEL)
Nazianzus, Gregory of *see* GREGORY OF NAZIANZUS
Nazif, Mehmed 2 883
Nazir, Mohammad 23 800
Nazism 22 709–12*
architecture 12 379, 605; 22 711*; 29 378; 31 368
art policies 2 560; 10 413
censorship 6 176
iconography 22 711
museums 22 *710*
painting 22 711*
posters 25 352, 652, *652*
propaganda 25 652, *652*
satires 27 872
sculpture 12 408; 22 711–12
Nazli, Queen of Egypt (*fl c.* 1940 BC) 10 92
Nazzano Painter 7 366; 10 615
Nazzoni, Niccoló *see* NASONI, NICOLAU
Nbaka 1 359
Ncheke, Leetsang 19 242
NCIC *see* NATIONAL COTTAGE INDUSTRIES CORPORATION
Ndabagoye, Richard 31 528
N'Dahla Gorge 1 40, 41
Ndaleni Teachers' Training College 29 123
Ndambomo 18 401
Ndamvu 33 596, 598
Ndandarika, Locardia 33 679
Ndasa
houses 4 *792*
Ndassa (people) 11 878; 18 401
Ndau 28 620
NDB, Monogrammist 33 367
Nde 10 123
Ndebele 22 712–13*; 28 621; 33 678
aprons 1 418
architectural decorations 1 313, *313*
architecture 1 414
basketwork 1 296
beads 1 297, 298; 22 712, *713*
beadwork 1 262, 418, 419; 3 442
blankets 1 348
body arts 1 285
dolls 1 419
dress 22 712, *713*; 29 104
fences 1 311
headdresses 1 349
houses 1 *313*
mud 1 284, 285
necklaces 1 351
painting 1 425
pigments 22 713
staffs 1 417
textiles 29 104
wall paintings 1 289; 22 712–13
Ndembo, Peter Paul 30 301
Ndembu 1 256, 266
Ndengese 1 403; 18 484
Ndiama Obube House 15 *114*
N'Diaye, Iba 1 432; 28 405, 406
N'Diaye, Serigne 28 406
N'Djamena 1 *394*; 6 382
Musée National Tchadien 6 382
Ndjuka 11 759
Ndlovu, Ndebe (David) 33 679
Ndoki 15 109
Ndola 1 *401*
Falcon Hotel 33 602
Ndudzu, Barnabas 33 679
Ndundu 1 *407*
Ndzundza 22 712
NEA *see* NATIONAL ENDOWMENT FOR THE ARTS
Nea Anchialos 9 *511*, 565; 22 713–14*
Basilica A 7 301; 9 *529*, 538
Basilica C 9 590
NEAC *see* NEW ENGLISH ART CLUB
Nead, Lynda 10 378; 33 312
Neagle, John 22 714*; 23 630; 24 600
Neagoe Basarab, Voivode of Wallachia (*reg* 1512-21) 8 279; 26 707, 712, 722; 31 23
Nea Ionia 13 383
Neal, Ellen Newman 16 891
Neale, James (*b* 1739/40) 10 307, 309
Neale, Thomas 19 570
Nealkes 13 552
Neamţ
church 4 783; 26 707
fort 26 707
Neanderthals 25 472, 473
Nea Nikomedia 19 880; 22 715*; 25 *471*, 498
architecture 25 499, *499*
Neapolis (Italy) *see under* NAPLES
Neapolis (Tunisia) *see under* NABEUL
Neapolis (Ukraine) 22 715*; 31 *546*
Nearchos 13 484, 490, 508; 32 58*
Neatby, William J. 19 415
Neatkarīgo Mākslinieku Vienība
Neave, Stacey Arthur 33 224
Neave, Thomas 29 515
Nebaj 21 243
Nebamun (Captain of Troops; TT 90) 9 825
wall paintings 9 *807*, 902; 32 11
Nebamun (Pharoh's head sculptor; TT 181) 9 789, 820, 821, 839; 10 52
Nebamun (unknown tomb) 9 810, 902
wall paintings 9 *901*
Nebankh
amulets 1 *817*
Nebbia, Cesare 22 715–16*
collaboration 8 181; 13 795; 19 383; 26 809
patrons and collectors 1 595; 13 628; 26 836
works 22 393; 24 399; 26 809
Nebbia, Ugo 11 868; 27 788
Nebbia de Castellazzo Bormida, Galeotto 20 901
Nebehay, Gustav 2 829; 11 62
Nebel, Karl 21 385
Nebelongs, Johan Henrik 23 221, 232, 233
Nebemakhet 10 51
Nebet 27 812
tomb 27 *811*
Nebhepetre *see* MENTUHOTPE I
Nebit-Dag 31 *458*, 459
Nebi Yunus *see* NINEVEH
Nebka 9 *776*
Nebmaatre *see* AMENOPHIS III
Nebo 17 656
Nebot, Balthasar 22 716*; 29 862
Nebot, Francesc de Paula *see* PAULA NEBOT, FRANCESC DE
Nebridio da Cremona 22 716*
Nebtawyre *see* MENTUHOTPE III
Nebuchadnezzar II (*reg* 604-562 BC) 1 115; 4 769
architecture 3 10, 11; 25 171
military architecture 21 291, 552; 31 695
sculpture 21 304
urban planning 21 274, 291
Nechanice, Hradek u Nechanic 8 400; 14 190
Nechayeva, V. E. 21 812
Nechayev-Mal'tsev, I. S. 27 440
Nechodoma, Antonín 25 701
Necho I (*reg* 672-664 BC) 9 *777*
Necho II (*reg* 610-595 BC) 9 *777*
Nechtain 20 77
Nechton, King of the Picts (*reg* 706-24) 15 871
neck amphorae *see under* AMPHORAE → types
Neckelmann, Skjold 29 751
Necker *see* HAWAII
Necker, Anne-Louise-Germaine *see* STAËL(-HOLSTEIN), (ANNE-LOUISE-GERMAINE), Mme de
Necker, Jost, Abbot of Salem 12 816
Necker, Jost de *see* NEGKER, JOST DE
neck gables *see under* GABLES → types
Neckham, Alexander of *see* ALBRICUS
necking *see* CINCTURES (COLUMNS)
necklaces 17 519, 520, 526, 527, 529
historical and regional traditions
Aboriginal Australia 1 53
Africa 1 350, *350*
Ancient Near East 1 *873*
Brazil 4 707
Buddhism 22 *787*
Byzantine 9 653, *653*
Caribbean Islands 5 748
Central Asia, Eastern 6 312
China 7 4, *107*, 109, 111
Cyprus, ancient 8 338
Denmark 8 *753*
Early Christian (*c.* AD 250-843) 9 653, *653*
Egypt 9 *653*
Egypt, ancient 10 *31*, 47
England 17 *528*, *529*; 20 *389*; 25 *545*
France 11 *634*
Greece, ancient 13 599
Iran 16 531
Islamic 16 531, 532, 533, *533*
Italy 17 *527*
Kenya 1 *350*
Kurdistan 16 531
Maya 21 259
Mesoamerica, Pre-Columbian 21 259, 260
Morocco 16 532
Native North Americans 22 613, 651, *651*
Ndebele 1 351
Nepal 22 *787*, 787–8
Ottoman 16 532
Pakistan 23 803
Portugal 25 *314*
Prehistoric art 25 545, *545*
Punic 25 735
Rome, ancient 27 102, *103*
South America, Pre-Columbian 29 217
Sweden 30 *113*
Tasmania 1 53
Troad 31 *376*
Turkey 31 *376*
Yemen 16 531, *533*
materials
acrylic 17 *529*
agate 7 4
amber 1 761, 762; 8 *753*
amethyst 17 *528*
aquamarines 9 *653*
beads 1 *350*; 25 545
beadwork 3 442
brass 1 350
cameos 17 *527*
chrysolite 17 *528*
copper 22 613
coral 3 442
cornelian 20 *389*
diamonds 11 *634*; 17 524
enamel 11 *634*
garnets 27 *103*
glass 7 *109*; 16 *533*
gold 17 *527*, *529*
Byzantine 9 *653*
China 7 *107*, 111
Egypt, ancient 10 *31*
England 20 *389*
Greece, ancient 13 599
Islamic 16 531
Rome, ancient 27 *103*
Sweden 30 *113*
Troad 31 *376*
iron 22 613
jade 3 441; 7 4
opals 7 *109*
necklaces
materials—cont.
pearls 7 *107*, 111; 9 *653*; 11 *634*
quartz 25 *314*
quills 22 651, *651*
reeds 1 53
rock crystal 7 4; 27 *103*
sapphires 7 *109*; 11 *634*; 27 *103*
shells 21 259, 260; 29 217
silver 8 *753*; 16 *533*; 25 *314*
neckrests 24 79
neck rings
historical and regional traditions
Celtic 6 155, 157, *157*, 158, 161; 12 *867*
England 6 161
Germany 6 155, *157*
Greece, ancient 13 601
Ireland 12 *867*
Prehistoric art 25 542, 545, 546
Switzerland 6 155
materials
gold 6 *157*, 158; 12 *867*
see also COLLARS
necks (capitals) 23 478
Necmeddin Okyay 16 354
necropoleis 6 166; 22 716*
historical and regional traditions
Egypt, ancient 9 779; 12 *766*; 22 716
Etruscan 6 *353*; 22 716; 23 *584*
Italy 6 *353*; 23 *584*
types
animal 5 70; 9 842–3*, *843*; 22 285–6
see also CEMETERIES; MAUSOLEA; TOMBS
Necropolis (Peru) 24 89
Nectanebo I (*reg* 380-362 BC) 9 *778*, 843, 892; 10 68; 30 296, 690
Nectanebo II (*reg* 360-343 BC) 9 *778*
architecture 2 657; 3 508; 18 238; 24 602; 28 810
reliefs 9 892, 894
sculpture 9 861
Nedabylice, Petr Straka von *see* STRAKA VON NEDABYLICE, PETR
Nedeham, James 7 420; 22 717*; 23 362
works 10 229; 19 616
Neder, Michael 2 796; 4 39
Nederlandsche Etsclub 10 563; 33 266
Nederlandsche Handel Maatschappij 1 802; 3 432; 21 122
Nederlandsche Vereeniging voor Ambachts- en Nijverheidskunst (VANK) 1 809
Nederlandse Informele Groep *see* INFORMELEN
Nederlands kunsthistorisch jaarboek 24 449, 450
Nedjemankh 9 866
Nedkov, Mikhayl 5 159
Nedkova, Vera 23 16
Nedo, M. F. 19 257
Nédroma 1 636; 21 629
mosque 16 190
minbar 16 493
Nedyalko 25 338, 339
Nedzingė Church 19 497
Needham, (Noel) Joseph (Terence Montgomery) 22 717*
Needham Market (Suffolk), St John the Baptist 13 55
needle lace *see under* LACE → types
needle-painting *see under* EMBROIDERY → types
needlepoint lace *see under* LACE → types
needles 18 372; 30 366
needlework
historical and regional traditions
England 21 721

needlework
historical and regional traditions—cont.
Japan **17** 355*
United States of America **31** 657–8*
materials
wool **17** 356
uses
carpets **5** 830–31*
fibre art **11** 54
mirror frames **21** 721
see also EMBROIDERY; SEWING
Neef, Sebastien de *see* NEVE, SEBASTIEN DE
Neeffs, Jacob **22** 717*; **30** 788
Neefs, E. **3** 619
Neefs, Jacques *see* NEEFFS, JACOB
Neefs, Ludovicus **22** 718*
Neefs, Pieter (i) (?1578-1656/61) **11** 720; **22** 718*
collaboration **2** 341; **11** 718, 720; **22** 718; **32** 724
works **2** 341; **3** 560; **11** *409*
Neefs, Pieter (ii) (1620-after 1675) **22** 718*
collaboration **2** 341; **7** 833; **11** 718
works **2** 341
Neel, Alice (Hartley) **10** 403, 484; **22** 718–19*
Neel, Edric **22** 719*
Neeld, Joseph **1** 454; **3** 79; **22** 719*
Neer, Aert van der **22** 719–20*
patrons and collectors **4** 304, 893; **5** 682; **10** 753; **14** 163; **22** 127; **29** 796
pupils **22** 720
works **11** 445; **22** 843; **29** 374
Neer, Eglon (Hendrick) van der **22** 719, 720–21*, 846
patrons and collectors **22** 846; **30** 274; **33** 280
pupils **33** 79
reproductive prints by others **6** 547
works **22** *721*
Neer, Jacobus van der **28** 868
Neer, Johannes van der **22** 719
Neeracher, Matthias **30** 144; **33** 737
Neerman, Marc **3** 551
Nees, Joseph **19** 781; **33** 737
Nefer and Kahay **9** 820, 821, 822, 838; **10** 51; **27** 812
tomb **27** *811*
Neferenpet **9** 840, 904; **27** 812
Neferhetepes **1** 95
Neferirkare (*reg c.* 2446-*c.* 2426 BC) **1** 96; **9** *776*, 779; **25** 763
Neferkare Peftjau'awybast **9** 887
Neferma'at **9** 899; **10** 47; **20** 117
tomb **20** *117*
Nefersekhem **9** 840
Nefertari, Queen (*fl c.* 1280 BC) **1** 96; **10** 83; **22** 722*; **23** 279; **25** 875; **31** 107
dress **10** *43*
wall paintings **9** 903
Nefertiti, Queen (*reg c.* 1353-*c.* 1335 BC) **9** *884*; **22** 722–3*, *723*
busts **5** 298; **9** 884; **10** 93
dress **10** 43
reliefs **9** 884; **23** 280
sculpture **1** 505; **9** 883, 884; **30** 794
tomb **10** 80
Neferu **9** 876; **10** 66
Neff, Carl Timoleon von **10** 539
Neff, Timofey Andreyevich **22** 394
Nefrure **9** 857, 880
nefs **11** *616*; **22** 694, 722*
Nefyodov, Stepan (Dmitriyevich) *see* ER'ZYA, STEPAN (DMITRIYEVICH)
Negahban, Ezat O. **1** 894; **20** 448
Negara Brunei Darussalam *see* BRUNEI
Negargar Husayni, Mansur *see* HUSAYNI, MANSUR NEGARGAR
Negges, Johann Simon **21** 149
Negker, Jost de **2** 718; **22** 723*
collaboration **5** 199; **33** 353
patrons and collectors **11** 818
works **33** 355, 365
Negmatov, N. **18** 26, 530; **31** 702
Negorodera **17** 314
Negoroji lacquer *see under* LACQUER → types
negoro-nuri see under LACQUER → types
Negoro Sōkyū **17** 401
Negotin Regional Museum **28** 458
Negrar, Villa Rizzardi **12** 119
Nègre, Charles **22** 723–4*; **24** 668
teachers **19** 86
works **22** *724*
Negreiros, (José Sobral de) Almada *see* ALMADA NEGREIROS(, JOSÉ SOBRAL DE)
Negreiros, José Manuel da Costa *see* COSTA NEGREIROS, JOSÉ MANUEL
Negreiros, Manuel da Costa *see* COSTA NEGREIROS, MANUAL DA
Nègrepelisse **32** 685
Negret, Edgar **22** 724*
patrons and collectors **7** 612; **25** 233
works **4** 234; **7** 609
Negret, Museo *see under* POPAYÁN
Negretti & Zambra **23** 447
Negri, Pietro **8** 427; **25** 227
Negrin, Henriette **11** 326
Negri Sembilan **21** 45
Negrito **20** 183; **24** 623
Negro di Sanfront, Ercole **31** 440
Negroli (family) **2** 472
Negroli, Filippo **13** 906
works **2** *472*
Negroli, Gian Paolo **28** 4
Negroni (family) **4** 886
Negroponte, Antonio da *see* FALIER, ANTONIO
Negroponte, New Navarino **21** 586
Negros, Los *see* LOS NEGROS
Negulici, Ion **26** 713
Negunza Cathedral **2** 86
Neher, Bernhard **8** 41
Neher, Caspar **30** 687
Neher, Ludwig **17** 853
Nehmitz, Michael **21** 64
Nehou, Louis Lucas de **23** 470
Nehru, Jawaharlal **12** 76; **20** 890
Neidhardt, Juraj **4** 460; **8** 177; **22** 725*
Neidhart, Christoph **22** 725
Neidhart, Wolfgang, II (1575-1632) **22** 725*
Neidhardt, Wolfgang, III (1597-1653) **22** 725
Neijn, Pieter de **23** 191; **32** 137
Neikon **27** 73
Neilos **21** 343
Neilson, Daniel-Marie **22** 726
Neilson, Jacques **22** 725–6*
Neilson, John **17** 468
Neilston (Strathclyde), Gateside Cotton Mill **28** 228
Neiman, Jochim **11** 94
Neiqiu kilns *see* XING KILNS
Neirab **30** 194, 196
Neish Owen Rowland & Roy **24** 188
Neisser, Albert **10** 463
Neithardt, Matthis Gothardt *see* GRÜNEWALD, MATTHIAS
Neithhotpe **14** 407; **20** 596; **22** 488, 509
tomb **22** *488*
Neizvestny, Ernst **8** 10; **22** 726*; **27** 397
Nejeloff *see* NEYELOV
Nekheb *see* EL-KAB
Nekhen *see* HIERAKONPOLIS
Nekrasov, Konstantin **15** 742, 745
Nekresi
basilica **12** 318
Church of the Virgin **25** 344
Nektarius **25** 340, 344
Nel, Karel **29** 110
Nelahozeves Castle **8** 378, 390, 395; **24** 462
Nélaton, Camille **22** 93; **24** 148
Nelevda, Galina A. **31** 560
Nelfert **9** 856
Nel Gómez, Pedro **7** 609; **21** 4; **22** 727*
Nellemose, Knud **8** 741
Nelli (family) **11** 206
Nelli, Bastiano di Giovanni **29** 496
Nelli, Fabio **31** 823
Nelli, Martino **22** 727
Nelli (di Nello), Ottaviano (di Martino) **22** 727*; **31** 740
attributions **27** 619
patrons and collectors **2** 725
Nelli, Pietro **1** 709; **23** 95
works **1** *709*
Nelli, Plautilla **3** 306; **11** 875; **22** 727*; **24** 27; **33** 308
Nelli, Suor Pulisena *see* NELLI, PLAUTILLA
Nelli, Tommaso **22** 727
Nello di Betto **28** 686
Nello di Mino de' Tolomei **19** 454
Nelme, Anthony **22** 727–8*
works **5** 365; **10** 329; **14** 856
Nelme, Francis **22** 728
Nelson **23** 51, *52*
ceramics **23** 70
Provincial Council Chambers **23** 54
silk **23** 74
wool **23** 73
Nelson, B. **18** 784
Nelson, George **22** 728*; **31** 633
Nelson, Harold H. **10** 83
Nelson, Horatio, 1st Viscount Nelson **6** 408; **33** 378
Nelson, James **14** 748*
Nelson, N. C. **21** 885
Nelson (Jupurrurla), Paddy
works **1** *63*
Nelson, Paul (Daniel) **4** 214; **22** 728–9*
Nelson, Thomas, & Sons **31** 465
Nelson-Atkins Museum of Art *see under* KANSAS CITY (KS/MO)
Nelson Brick and Pipe Co. **23** 69
Nelson-Matter **13** 297
Nelson Tjakamarra, Michael **1** 64; **22** 729*
Nemanjić, Stephen Nemanja, King of Serbia *see* STEPHEN NEMANJA, Grand Župan of Serbia
Nemanjić, Stephen Uroš I, King of Serbia *see* STEPHEN UROŠ I, King of Serbia
Nemanjić, Stephen Vladislav, King of Serbia *see* STEPHEN VLADISLAV, King of Serbia
Nemanjich, Stephen Radoslav, King of Serbia *see* STEPHEN RADOSLAV, King of Serbia
Nemanjich, Stephen Uroš IV Dušan, Emperor of Serbia *see* STEPHEN UROŠ IV DUŠAN, Emperor of Serbia
Nemausus *see under* NÎMES
Nemawar Temple **15** 292
Nemazal, Šimon **8** 404
Nembe **15** 126
Němcová, Božena **20** 253
Nemea **13** *363*; **22** 729*
stadium **13** 403, 418; **29** 488
Temple of Zeus **10** 415; **13** 379, 401, 418; **22** 729
hypogea **15** 52
Němec, Josef Ladislav **8** 414, 416
Němec, Václav **8** 414
Nemencha **16** 486
Nemes, Endre **21** 696; **22** 729–30*; **30** 81
Nemes Lampérth, József **22** 730*
collaboration **18** 142
groups and movements **1** 131; **14** 901; **18** 142; **20** 103
Nemetacum *see* ARRAS
Németh, József **13** 333
Németlipcse *see* PARTIZÁNSKÁ ĽUPČA
Nemi **16** *620*; **22** 730–31*; **26** *886*
Museo delle Navi **22** 731
sacred grove **27** 1
Sanctuary of Diana **10** 606; **22** 730–31
statuettes **27** 85
Nemirovich-Danchenko, Vladimir **9** 747; **28** 757; **31** 572
Nemours, Musée de la Préhistoire de l'Ile-de-France **28** 757
Nemours, Charles-Amédée of Savoy, Duc de **28** *2*
Nemours, Giuliano de' Medici, Duc de **4** 494; **20** 844; **21** *8*, 18*; **32** 364
architecture **19** 185; **26** 756
heraldry **5** 913
sculpture **3** 156; **27** 830
Nemours, Jacques d'Armagnac, Duc de (1433-77) **11** 726; **16** 853–4*
books **4** 545
manuscripts **11** 355
Nemours, Jacques de (1591-1637) **4** 549; **32** 369, 371
Nemours, Louis de Bourbon, Duc de **18** 678; **28** 523
Nemours, Philip of Savoy, Duc de **28** *2*
Nemrik **2** 639; **10** 506, *506*
Nemrut Dağ **1** *821*; **13** *362*; **22** 731–2*
colossal statues **22** *731*
sculpture **1** 833; **13** 466
Nemukhin, Vladimir **8** 10; **27** 397
Nenadović, Hadži Ruvim **28** 450
Nenbutsuji Stupa **29** 869
Nendö **27** 778
body ornaments **27** *779*
headdresses **27** *779*
wood-carvings **27** 779
Nendrum Abbey (Co. Down) **21** 834
Nene, George **33** 678
Nenets **27** 436
Nenkheftka **11** 306
Nennig Villa **26** 870, *905*, 906
Nennius **14** 408
Nénot, Henri-Paul **12** 276; **22** 732–3*
collaboration **3** 465; **19** 43
works **23** 342
Nenov, Ivan **5** 163; **22** 733*; **23** 16
Nenumbo
pottery **23** *727*
Neo-Antique styles **8** *746*
Neoartes **2** 528
see also ARTES (POLAND)
Neo-Assyrian period *see under* MESOPOTAMIA → periods
Neo-Attic **22** 733*; **27** 29, 31
kraters **22** *733*
neo-Baroque *see* BAROQUE REVIVAL
Neo-Buddhism *see* BUDDHISM → sects → Ambedkar
Neo-classicism **7** 383–5; **10** 401; **22** 734–42*; **23** 498; **24** 841
art forms
architecture (general) **10** 95; **12** 374
Belgium **3** 547
Bolivia **4** 259–60*
Brazil **4** 711
Britain **8** 105
England **10** 151; **19** 505
France **11** 518; **19** 725
Germany **12** 374–5
Greece **13** 348–9
Neo-classicism
art forms
architecture (general)—cont.
Guatemala **13** 761
Ireland **16** 8
Italy **16** 643–8*, 771–2*; **31** 442
Netherlands, the **22** 827
Poland **25** 99; **33** 722
Portugal **12** 889
Romania **26** 708
Russia **27** 375
Spain **29** 271–2; **32** 564
Sri Lanka **29** 453
United States of America **17** 467; **31** 591
Wales **5** 731
architecture (anatomy theatres) **22** *739*
architecture (banks) **28** *906*
architecture (bridges) **27** *715*
architecture (cafés) **17** *443*; **24** *553*
architecture (cathedrals)
Bolivia **18** *778*
Canada **5** *559*
Nicaragua **23** *81*
Russia **27** *577*; **29** *552*; **32** *698*
architecture (châteaux) **4** *224*; **11** *257*, *883*; **19** *800*; **32** *767*
architecture (churches)
Denmark **14** *153*
England **8** *493*
France **6** *397*; **26** *13*; **29** *93*
Germany **16** *804*; **33** *39*
Italy **31** *800*
Portugal **4** *629*
Scotland **30** *751*
United States of America **5** *143*; **24** *209*
architecture (clubs) **29** *770*
architecture (courtyards) **21** *401*
architecture (domes) **2** *177*
architecture (exchanges) **27** *375*; **29** *92*; **30** 748
architecture (façades) **17** *443*; **25** *186*
architecture (galleries) **16** *773*
architecture (gateways) **2** *786*; **24** *886*; **27** *481*
architecture (government buildings)
Chile **6** *593*
Denmark **14** *152*
England **28** *909*
Finland **10** *218*
France **2** *172*
Germany **3** *793*
Ireland **9** *316*
Russia **33** *600*
United States of America **26** *352*; **31** *591*
architecture (hospitals) **29** *91*
architecture (houses)
England **1** *136*; **2** *550*; **17** *904*; **28** *907*; **30** *386*
France **19** *56*, *57*
Ireland **6** *411*
Netherlands, the **22** *827*
architecture (law courts) **9** *337*
architecture (libraries) **10** *219*
architecture (mausolea) **20** 866, *867*; **33** *444*
architecture (museums) **22** 361
Brazil **13** *296*
Germany **12** *375*
Italy **16** *772*; **29** *640*
United States of America **7** *429*; **21** *649*
architecture (office buildings) **1** *139*
architecture (opera houses) **11** *882*
architecture (palaces) **23** 812–13*
Germany **23** *813*; **28** *101*
Poland **32** *881*
Portugal **23** *453*
Russia **5** *520*
architecture (rotundas) **17** *468*

Neo-classicism
art forms—cont.
architecture (schools) 28 100
architecture (spires) 2 177
architecture (squares) 16 648; 31 442
architecture (synagogues) 33 40
architecture (theatres)
France 19 726; 32 768
Germany 28 99
Italy 3 196; 23 88; 24 758; 28 390
Mexico 13 730
Poland 32 871
Russia 27 199
architecture (universities) 30 72
architecture (villas)
Germany 28 102
Italy 16 647, 772; 20 393; 25 155
Sweden 2 611
architecture (water towers) 22 34
cotton 23 545
doors 1 574
drawings 7 340; 12 585; 17 468
frames
England 11 428–31*, 430
France 11 409–11*
Germany 11 460
Italy 11 396, 396–7*
Scandinavia 11 471–2*
Spain 11 493, 493–4*
Sweden 11 471
furniture 12 831
England 10 293; 17 902
Hungary 14 907
Italy 24 845
Russia 27 407, 408, 408
Scotland 28 254
South Africa 29 115
United States of America 31 628
interior decoration 10 95
England 1 138; 17 901; 22 737
France 11 579
Ireland 16 24, 24
Netherlands, the 22 865, 866
Russia 27 402–4, 403; 29 839
Scotland 9 723
United States of America 31 618
metalwork 10 333; 27 420
monuments (equestrian) 21 384; 33 624
monuments (funerary)
Belgium 3 571
England 11 163
Greece 13 354
Indian subcontinent 5 418
Ireland 14 500; 16 21
Italy 5 628; 16 706; 22 736
monuments (public) 3 26; 11 561; 22 36, 45–7*
nude figures 23 295
Denmark 1 32; 29 541
England 5 629
France 4 301; 6 517; 12 730; 14 798; 24 172, 736
Germany 8 509
Italy 3 296; 5 627, 886; 16 705; 22 271
Portugal 27 615
Spain 29 294
Sweden 28 462
United States of America 25 401
oil sketches 23 381
ornament 23 544–5*
painting (general)
Germany 12 391–2*
Malta (Republic of) 20 213
Spain 29 283
Switzerland 30 132–3*
painting (allegorical) 7 384; 32 429
painting (fresco) 14 154; 21 528
painting (genre) 32 428

Neo-classicism
art forms—cont.
painting (history)
Belgium 19 166
Denmark 8 734
England 10 402
France 8 554, 555, 556, 559; 11 541, 900; 12 732; 13 792; 15 846; 19 255; 22 735; 24 172, 381, 583
Italy 12 41; 16 677, 677; 21 132
painting (literary themes) 3 286
painting (mythological) 22 415
Belgium 26 285
France 12 730; 13 794; 24 736
Germany 26 128
Italy 17 851; 22 271
Portugal 27 615
painting (religious) 27 580
portraits (painting)
France 8 556, 558; 19 67; 23 520; 26 81; 32 585
Germany 31 27
Russia 27 579
portraits (sculpture) 3 295
sarcophagi 27 831
screens (i) (architectural) 28 294
sculpture (general)
Germany 12 406
Italy 5 625; 16 704–7*
Portugal 1 466
Spain 1 741; 6 67; 29 20
Sweden 30 86
United States of America 31 610–11
sculpture (allegorical)
Denmark 29 541; 30 764
France 4 301; 27 311
Portugal 1 741
Spain 1 742; 29 20
United States of America 25 401
sculpture (architectural)
France 8 566
Spain 29 294
sculpture (busts) 5 302*
Austria 33 623
France 14 797
Germany 12 406
Italy 6 129
Sweden 5 303
sculpture (monumental)
Austria 2 802, 803
France 25 418
United States of America 31 611
sculpture (mythological)
Denmark 30 765
England 5 629
France 6 517; 10 764; 14 798
Germany 4 376; 8 509; 9 691
Italy 5 627, 630; 16 705
Sweden 28 462
sculpture (relief) 8 587; 27 310, 389
sculpture (religious)
England 11 164
Italy 16 773
sculpture (tomb) 31 130
Austria 5 628
Belgium 3 571
England 10 265; 22 46
Ireland 14 500
Italy 22 736
staircases 6 412; 19 613
urban planning 22 34
collections 5 419; 22 361
commentaries 9 336
regional traditions
Bolivia 4 262
Brazil 8 10
Chile 6 592
Denmark 8 740
England 10 235; 11 162; 28 924
France 11 256; 18 713; 21 114; 29 90; 32 430
Germany 12 413, 643; 28 43

Neo-classicism
regional traditions—cont.
Guatemala 12 57
Honduras 14 713
Indian subcontinent 4 288
Ireland 14 500; 26 475
Italy 2 233; 20 805; 30 520
Lithuania 19 497
Mexico 21 377–8, 384–5
Nepal 22 765
Poland 25 93, 124
Portugal 1 752, 753
Rome, ancient 27 31
Russia 18 196; 30 748
Sardinia 27 836
Scotland 25 36
Spain 19 657; 21 815; 25 225; 27 480; 29 337
Sweden 13 864–5; 30 89; 33 86
Switzerland 10 496
Union of Soviet Socialist Republics 29 529
United States of America 10 851
Uruguay 31 753, 754
treatises 19 9
see also: CONSULATE STYLE; DIRECTOIRE STYLE; EMPIRE STYLE; ETRUSCAN STYLE; FEDERAL STYLE; GOÛT GREC; GREEK REVIVAL; PALLADIANISM; POMPEIAN REVIVAL; REGENCY STYLE
neo-colonial style 2 903
Neo-Concrete group 4 719; 23 382; 33 317
Neo-Confucianism
calligraphy 17 234
censorship 6 175
China 5 111; 6 626*
education (art) 17 419
iconography 17 41, 41
Japan 17 188, 215
painting 17 41
Neo-cubism 7 881; 22 749
see also NEO-PLASTICISM; STIJL, DE
neo-Dada 7 685; 25 231; 31 615
Neo-Dadaism Organizers 2 282; 21 513; 22 742–3*
Neo-Expressionism 10 696; 28 174
Neofiguración 22 743*; 24 99
Neo-Geo 1 81
Neo-Georgian 9 739; 10 240; 12 333; 22 743–4*
architecture 22 743*
neo-Gothic *see* GOTHIC REVIVAL
Néo-Grec 12 271, 486; 22 744–5*
art forms
architecture 25 173; 26 111
painting 24 58
sculpture 9 404
regional traditions
France 22 744; 24 126; 31 372
United States of America 22 744; 31 630
Neo-Hittite 1 828, 833, 852, 855, 857
Néo-Humanisme 3 753; 30 389
Neo-Impressionism 14 264; 15 156, 828; 19 355, 767; 22 745–7*; 30 168
art forms
drawings 28 503
frames 11 375
nude figures 28 503
painting 9 40
France 9 40; 19 767; 22 746; 28 501, 502, 698
Netherlands, the 21 852
collections 18 466; 19 10
commentaries 1 142, 613; 10 885; 19 37
exhibitions 8 715; 12 870; 24 142
regional traditions
Belgium 32 591
England 11 160

Neo-Impressionism
regional traditions—cont.
France 8 204; 9 324; 24 552, 880–81; 28 502
Netherlands, the 19 792; 21 852
see also DIVISIONISM; LUMINISM (ii) (BELGIUM AND THE NETHERLANDS); POINTILLISM
Neo-Liberty 15 887; 16 650–51*, 651; 22 747*
Neo-Mexicanism 21 390
Neo-Moorish style 1 634
neon 16 708; 19 366; 22 747–8*, 748
NÉON 24 428; 30 23
Neon, Bishop of Ravenna 3 189; 26 33
Neophit of Rila 5 162
Neophytos (*fl* early 13th cent.) 3 21
Neophytos (*fl* early 16th cent.) 25 335
Neo-plasticism 1 75; 7 630; 10 416; 21 781, 851; 22 749*
collections 21 135
France 10 904
Netherlands, the 22 749; 32 695
Uruguay 31 755
see also NEO-CUBISM; NIEUWE BEELDING
Neo-Platonism 1 178, 654, 655–6, 657; 14 867; 22 412–13, 749–50*
Neo-primitivism 9 144–5; 22 750–51*
members 18 792, 793; 27 392; 28 597
painting 18 791, 792
works 27 393
Néo-Réalisme 22 92, 751*
Neorealismus see NEUE SACHLICHKEIT
Neo-Romanticism 19 591; 22 751–2*; 26 743
drawings 22 752
furniture 8 235
members 7 639; 10 258; 18 718; 19 868; 21 697; 30 389; 32 85, 912
painting 28 825
Neo-Russian *see* OLD RUSSIAN REVIVAL
Neo-Sudanese style 20 198
Neo-Tantric art 15 170
Neotia (family) 22 795
Neo-Tudor 22 752*
Nepal 22 753–96*, 753
albums 22 786, 795
alloys 22 787
architecture 22 758, 759–66*, 792–3
bahāl 22 763, 763, 764
bahīl 22 763
banners 22 778, 780–83, 782
bone 4 314
book illustrations 22 786, 786–7, 795
brackets 22 774, 792–3, 793
brass 4 687; 22 789
caityas 22 760; 29 867
carpets 22 791
collections 22 795*, 796*
manuscripts 22 795
paintings 22 795
copper 22 769, 772, 774, 774, 775, 776, 777, 778, 789
cotton 22 791, 791
craftsmen and artists 22 789, 790, 794, 794–5
dharmaśālās 22 760, 792
dress 22 787*
ethnic arts 22 794–5*
exhibitions 22 795
figurines 22 790
fountains 22 759–60
gilding 22 755, 772, 774, 774, 775, 776
gold 12 867; 22 788
guilds 22 789
gūṭhīs 22 769

Nepal—cont.
hair 22 791
hangings *see* banners
hardstones 22 787
houses 22 766
iconography 22 755–6*, 757*
Buddhism 5 103; 22 756–7*
Hinduism 22 756*
Tantra 5 103
jewellery 22 787–8*, 793
linga shrines *see* shrines
lost-wax casting 22 774, 774–5, 775, 789–90
manuscript illumination 15 570; 22 778–80*, 786
13th cent. 22 778
15th cent. 22 780
manuscripts 22 777, 778
masks 22 788, 788–9*
meeting halls 17 842
metal 22 768–9*, 771–3*
metalwork 22 774–6*, 789–90*, 790, 793
monasteries 5 103; 21 847*; 22 760, 763, 763, 764, 765–6, 792
museums 22 795*, 796*
necklaces 22 787, 787–8
nettles 22 791
pagodas *see degas*
painting 22 777–83*, 784–7*
Buddhism 22 782
scroll 22 784
wall 22 785; 30 833
palaces 22 765, 765, 792
palm leaves 22 777, 778
paper 22 779
patronage 22 769
paubhās 22 778, 780–83, 782
periods
Malla period 22 754–5
Transitional period 22 754
pillars 22 759
portraits 22 755
pottery 22 758
religion 22 755–7*
repoussé 22 755, 775, 775
ritual objects 22 757
rock crystal 26 487
roofs 22 792–3
sal 22 793
scrolls 22 784, 784–5*
tangkas 28 309
sculpture 22 758, 766*, 768–70*, 771–3*, 776–7*, 793–4, 795, 796; 30 825
Buddhism 22 758, 758–9, 768–9, 769, 770, 771, 771, 773, 777
Hinduism 5 121; 6 449; 22 767, 767–8, 768, 770, 770, 771, 772, 772–3
Malla period 22 773–6*, 774, 775, 776
metal 22 774–6*, 775, 776
stone 6 449; 22 758, 758–9, 766–8*, 767, 768, 770, 770–71*, 771, 773–4*
wood 22 774
shrines (i) (cult) 22 759, 760, 793
silver 22 777
statuettes 22 774
stone 6 449; 22 758, 758–9, 766–8*, 767, 768, 770, 770–71*, 771, 773–4*
struts *see* brackets
stupas 5 103; 22 760; 29 867–8*
temples 22 760, 761–4, 762, 792
degas 22 761, 761–3, 762
śikhara 22 763–4
16th cent. 22 761
17th cent. 22 762
terracotta 22 758, 790*
textiles 22 791, 791–2*
tourist art 22 777, 777, 789
vihāras 22 792
windows 22 792
wood 17 842; 22 774*, 788

Nepal—cont.
  wood-carvings **22** 774, 792–4*, *793*; **23** 907
  wool **22** 791
  see also INDIAN SUBCONTINENT
Nepal Association of Fine Arts **22** 785
Nepauer, Máté **5** 81
Nepean **23** 632
Nepherites I (*reg* 399-393 BC) **9** *778*; **21** 122
Nepherites II (*reg* 380 BC) **9** *778*
nephrite *see under* JADE → types
Nepo, Ernst **15** 865
Nepomuceno Gómez, Juan **7** 612
Nepomucký Palliardi, Ignác **25** 445
Nepraš, Karel **8** 388
Nepuyos **31** 331
Nepveu, (Eugène-Charles-) Frédéric **11** 413; **14** 756; **23** 520
Nequam, Alexander **10** 202
Nerazik, Ye. Ye. **31** 157
Nerazzini Pietà **21** 730
Nerdrum, Odd **23** 227
Neresheim Abbey **12** *361*; **22** 796*
  church **12** 372; **22** 796; **23** 5, *5*; **26** 498; **32** 823
  library **19** 316
Nereus Painter **32** 34
Nerezi **9** *511*, 631; **19** *882*
  St Andreas **25** 343
  St Panteleimon **9** 547, 576, 579; **19** 882; **22** 797*; **24** 110; **25** 343
  icons **28** 291
  plaques **9** 593
  wall paintings **22** 520
Nerger, Christian **8** 739
Neri, Antonio, Abbot **10** 316; **16** 740
Neri, Filippo, Saint *see* FILIPPO NERI, Saint
Neribtum *see* ISCHALI
Neri da Rimini **22** 797*
Neri di Bicci **4** 30; **11** 375; **22** 797–802*
  assistants **4** 505
  collaboration **11** 382; **20** 748
  patrons and collectors **29** 782
  pupils **9** 148; **12** 765; **27** 174
  works **4** 31, 32; **11** 192, 711; **20** 111, 113, 115; **22** *798*, *799*, *800*
  writings **16** 661
Neri di Fioravante **11** 203
Neri di Goro **13** 15
Nering, Johann Arnold **22** 803*
  collaboration **25** 366
  patrons and collectors **14** 651
  works **2** 502; **3** 790, 805, 806; **4** 218; **28** 116
Nering Bögel factory **22** 895
Nerinuki **17** 311
Nerio **4** 274; **22** 803*
Nerio, Andrea di *see* ANDREA DI NERIO
Nerio, Ugolino di *see* UGOLINO DI NERIO
Nerio di Binduccio **19** 453
Neri Razzanti, Pietro de' **12** 257
Nerita shells *see under* SHELLS → types
Nerli, G(irolamo) P(ieri) B(allati) **14** 612; **22** 803–4*; **23** 59
Nerli, Tanai de' **22** 800
Nerlinger, Oskar **22** 923; **29** 872
Nerman, B. **22** 50
Nerman, Ejnar **33** 566
Nero, Emperor of Rome (*reg* 54-68) **13** 369; **22** 804*; **29** 749
  architecture **26** 856, 891, 892
    amphitheatres **1** 797
    baths **26** 751
    concrete **26** 879
    domes **7** 692; **9** 83
    macella **19** 888; **26** 871
    nymphaea **27** 66
Nero, Emperor of Rome (*reg* 54-68)
  architecture—cont.
    palaces
      Domus Aurea **16** 623, 760; **23** 808; **26** 788, 869, 880, 884, *893*
      Domus Transitoria **26** 786
    villas **26** 892
  art policies **5** 134
  coins **25** 650; **27** 96, *96*
  lighting **9** 11
  mosaics **27** 59
  paintings **5** 655
  porticos **26** 782
  sculpture **8** 695; **9** 20; **25** 43; **26** 764; **27** 15, 21, 28, 32, 33; **33** 636
  stucco **27** 70
Neroccio de' Landi *see* LANDI (DEL POGGIO), NEROCCIO (DI BARTOLOMMEO DI BENEDETTO) DE'
Neroda, Georgy **9** 458
Neroni (family) **11** 206
Neroni, Bartolommeo (di Sebastiano) **22** 804–5*; **28** 675; **29** 2
  patrons and collectors **28** 676
  works **7** 457
Neroni, Diotisalvi **21** 693
Nerpio **29** 364
Nerquis Hall **32** 782
Nerses II, King of Armenia (*reg* 538-57) **2** 601
Nerses III, King (*reg* 641-61) **2** 444; **33** 740
Nersisian, Grigor **13** 22
Nersisian, Stephan **2** 431
Neruda, Pablo **29** 455; **31** 160
Nerva, Emperor of Rome (*reg* 96-98) **26** 784
Nerval, Gérard de **13** 653; **20** 399
Nervander, Emil **11** 113
Nerve, Damianus de **2** 455
Nerven, Cornelis van **2** 122
Nervi **30** 328
Nervi, Antonio **22** 805, 806
Nervi, Mario **22** 805
Nervi, Pier Luigi **7** 696; **22** 805–6*
  architecture **5** 562; **16** 650; **29** 250; **30** 468
    exhibition centres **28** 583; **31** 443; **33** 627
    office buildings **25** *218*
    railway stations **22** 474
    sports centres **22** *806*; **28** 583; **29** 427
    stadia **11** 182; **29** 489
  collaboration **3** 682; **11** 527; **19** 305; **22** 106; **23** 117; **24** 130, 695; **25** 218; **28** 375, 834; **33** 627
  engineering **7** 696
  patrons and collectors **16** 765; **24** 279
  pupils **12** 873
Nervi, Vittorio **22** 805
Nervi & Bartolia **22** 805
Nervi & Nebbiosi **22** 805
Nervo, Roberto Montenegro *see* MONTENEGRO (NERVO), ROBERTO
Nery, Eduardo **25** 300
Nery, Ismael **4** 718; **22** 806–7*
Nes **13** 143; **23** *218*, 224; **26** 639
Nesa *see* KÜLTEPE
Nesactium **9** *510*; **28** 807
  Cathedral **9** 529
Nesar **30** 818
Nesbitt, Lowell **10** 483
Nesch, (Emil) Rolf **22** 807–8*
  works **7** 558; **9** 310; **10** 178, 557, *557*; **23** 227; **25** 599, 620
Nesebăr **4** 110; **5** *144*, 145; **9** *511*; **22** 808*
  architecture **9** 551
  Church of the Weeping Virgin **5** 154
Nesebăr—cont.
  coins **4** 112
  icons **25** 338, 339
  Old Metropolis **5** 146
  Pantokrator **5** 147; **9** 552
  pottery **4** 112
  St John Aleitourgetos **5** 147; **9** 526, 552
  St John the Baptist **5** 146–7, 151; **25** 339
  St Paraskeva **5** 147
  St Stephen **5** 146, 153, 154; **25** 343
  sculpture **5** 155
  walls **4** 113
Neset **9** 866
Neseus of Thasos **33** 639
Nesfield, Markham **22** 808*
Nesfield, W(illiam) E(den) **22** 808, 809–10*; **28** 561
  assistants **4** 884; **5** 65
  collaboration **5** 421
  groups and movements **3** 269; **10** 238; **22** 752; **23** 398; **25** 804
  teachers **27** 657
  works **10** 282; **18** 5; **22** 51, *810*; **23** 398; **28** 298; **30** 504
Nesfield, William Andrews **22** 808–9*
  collaboration **14** 548
  works **1** 734; **6** 66; **12** 139
Nesgun **12** 323
Nesiotes **18** 460*
  collaboration **2** 685
  works **2** 681; **13** 439, *450*, 450, 451
Nesitanebtasheru **9** 906
  papyrus **9** *905*
  shabtis **10** *17*
Nesjar, Carl **24** 726
Nesković, Nikola **28** 450
Nesle, Louis Ferdinand de **19** 800; **32** 461
Nesle, Raoul de *see* RAOUL DE NESLE
Nesles, Louis de Mailly, Marquis de **3** 752
Nesles-la-Vallée Church **13** 41
Nespakashuty **9** 859
Nespanetjerenpere **22** *284*
Nesptah **9** 855
Ness, Rupert **22** 810–11*; **23** 636
Nessa *see* NISA
Nessana **9** 543
Nesselthaler, Andreas **2** 795; **31** 679
Nessenthaler, Elias **15** 166; **28** 852
Nesshu **24** 555
Nessi, Ricardo Baroja y *see* BAROJA Y NESSI, RICARDO
Nesterov, Church of the Nativity **31** 552
Nesterov, Mikhail (Vasil'yevich) **18** 38; **22** 811*; **27** 391, 395
  collaboration **28** 572
  groups and movements **1** 71; **20** 232; **32** 836; **33** 379
  teachers **24** 465
  works **22** 178
Nestesrova, Natal'ya **27** 397
Nestfell, Johann Georg **12** 411
nesting dolls *see* DOLLS → types → *Matryoshka*
Nestlé **19** 808
Nestor **18** 37
Nestor, Palace of *see under* PYLOS
Nestora *see* KAKOVATOS
Nestorianism *see under* CHRISTIANITY → branches
Nestorian script *see under* SCRIPTS → types
nestoroi **13** *526*
Nestorović, Bogdan **19** 883
Nestorović, Nikola **28** 444
Nestor's cup **14** 355
Nesvedov, Boris **21** 811
Nesvizh *see* NIASVIŽ
Nesymin **18** 238
Net **7** 788
Net, G. van 't **26** 542
Nethang **30** 818
Netherlands, Southern *see* BELGIUM
Netherlands, the **22** 812–916*, *813*; **29** 441
  acacia **33** IV2
  academies **22** 907*
  alabaster (gypsum) **3** *456*; **21** *858*; **22** *858*; **29** 571
  allegories of art **21** *760*
  altarpieces **1** 710
    Beguines **3** *503*
    diptychs **9** 4; **20** *636*
    Flügelaltar **1** 709
    Gothic **13** 110–11, *114*
    polyptychs **31** 344
    triptychs **4** *446*, *447*, *448*; **10** *217*; **19** *761*; **20** *656*; **31** 344
    16th cent. **4** *149*
  altars **1** 699; **21** *858*
  aluminium **22** *896*
  amber **1** 761
  anatomical studies **1** *843*
  apartments **1** *814*; **19** 116; **22** *831*
  Apocalypses **4** *144*
  aquatints **25** *50*
  architecture **4** 785–6; **22** 815–32*
    brick **4** 777–8*
    Cistercian Order **4** 777
    Dutch Classicism **22** 824
    Gothic **13** 61–3*; **22** 819–21*
    Mannerism **22** 823–4
    military **21** 569–70*, 572–3*
    Neo-classicism **22** 827
    Premonstratensian Canons **4** 777
    Renaissance **4** 732; **22** 822–3*
    Romanesque **22** 816–18*
    South Africa **29** 102
    Sri Lanka **29** 452–3*
    United States of America **31** 589
    vernacular **32** 283–5*
  archives **2** 371*
  arks **17** 570
  armour **2** 473
  art (illustrations of works of) **6** 77
  art criticism **13** 3
  art history **20** 245–6, 437; **22** 909–11*; **30** 756
  artists' biographies **10** 208; **13** 2–3; **22** 910*
    18th cent. **14** 794; **33** 131
    19th cent. **32** 713
  art market **2** 558; **29** 374–5
  art policies **29** 862
  atlases **2** 696
  auction houses **7** 562
  auctions **2** 558, 706
  avenues **12** 131, 132
  basins **22** *881*, 890
  baskets **22** 890
  batik **22** 900
  beakers **22** 884, 886, 890
  beds **3** 484; **22** 865, 870, 871
  bird's-eye views **4** 80
  block-books **4** 143, 144–6*, *144*, *145*
  bonding **4** 778
  bookbindings **4** 348, 349; **24** 51
  book covers **4** 350, 352, 353, 354
    Gothic **13** *159*
  book design **8** 779
  book illustrations **4** 359; **20** 631
  books **8** 666
  Books of Hours **4** 370; **24** 809; **29** 666
  borders (manuscript) **4** 395
  bottles **22** 884
  bowls **22** 890
  boxes **22** *894*, 897*
  bracelets **22** *896*
  brass **13** 159–60; **22** *894*, 894–5*
  brick **4** 777–8*, *778*, 785–6; **8** 299
  bronze **13** 159–60; **22** 894–5*
  bureaux **5** 191
Netherlands, the—cont.
  busts **22** *859*
  cabinets (i) (rooms) **5** 347, 349
  cabinets (ii) (furniture) **20** *467*; **22** 873, *873*; **33** IV2
    bureaux-cabinets **5** 191
  canals **12** 132; **31** *770*
  cane **33** 157
  capitals **19** *863*
  caps **9** 271
  caricatures **5** 756
  carpets **22** 900*
  caskets **22** 890, *890*
  cast iron **22** *860*, 894
  castles **17** *884*; **22** 822
  catalogues **28** 882
    auction **6** 80; **14** 622
    museum **29** 592
    prints **14** 688
  cathedrals **13** *62*; **28** *595*
  ceramics **3** 589; **22** 865, 877–84*
  chairs **22** 870, *875*; **29** 763
    boarded seats **6** 390
    bucket seat **22** 876
    fauteuils **6** 390
    Sri Lanka **29** *471*
    20th cent. **22** *868*; **26** *378*
  chandeliers **6** 443; **9** 13
  chasubles **32** 392
  chests **6** 560; **22** 870
  chimney-pieces **23** *188*
  chintz **22** 899
  chromium steel **22** *875*
  churches **2** *192*
    Cistercian Order **4** *778*
    Gothic **1** *812*; **13** *61*; **19** *100*; **22** *820*
    Gothic Revival **8** *299*
    Romanesque **19** 862; **22** *816*, *818*
  ciboria (i) (vessels) **7** 300
  clasps **4** 350, 355; **22** 896
  clay **22** 877
  cloaks **9** 274
  clocks **7** 441, 442, 446
  coats of arms **12** 272
  coffeepots **22** *891*
  coins **7** 536, 537, 538, 539; **29** 469
  collections **6** 77; **22** 904–7*
    paintings **7** 562, 563
    prints **14** 563
    royal **9** 27
    17th cent. **7** 561
    20th cent. **4** 743
  commercial art **7** 655
  commodes **22** *873*, *874*
  copper **14** 293; **22** 894–5*
  cornices **23** *542*
  costumes **30** 665
  cotton **8** 36
  craftsmen and artists **10** 245; **14** 855
  cupboards **8** 271; **22** 871, 872, *872*
  cups **22** 886, *886*, 887, 889, *889*
  damask **19** 416, *416*; **22** 899, *900*
  dealers **2** 558; **7** 562
  dealing **22** 904–6*
  department stores **18** *437*
  desks **5** 192
  dictionaries of art **10** 208
  display of art **1** *809*; **9** 15, 22
  dolls **31** 259
  dolls' furniture **31** 264
  dolls' houses **31** 262
  drawings **9** 221
    allegorical **31** *148*
    animal subjects **26** *162*
    architectural **4** *440*; **12** 132; **27** *509*
    chalk
      Baroque **26** *162*
      Romanticism **32** *694*
      Symbolism (movement) **31** *148*
      16th cent. **28** 218
      17th cent. **9** *456*; **26** *194*
    genre **13** *257*

Netherlands, the
drawings—cont.
ink
Baroque **9** *222*; **24** *349*
Mannerism **22** *840*
15th cent. **20** *694*
16th cent. **20** *247*, *248*; **30** *62*; **33** *252*
17th cent. **4** *96*; **5** *324*; **12** *531*; **23** *612*
landscape
Mannerism **4** *152*; **14** *292*
17th cent. **3** *759*; **4** *734*; **10** *514*; **15** *41*; **27** *518*; **31** *806*; **32** *140*, *622*, *900*
marine **29** *720*; **32** *141*, *734*
metalpoints **21** 340
mythological **20** *248*
Renaissance **16** *770*
topographical **5** *542*; **9** 149; **16** *585*; **28** *74*
16th cent. **26** *900*
17th cent. **2** *856*
dress **9** 269, 277*, 278–9*
dressers **22** 870, *870*
drypoints **9** *307*, 308, *308*; **20** *693*; **28** *361*
dyeing **30** 558
earthenwares **22** 877–8, 882, 883
ebony **11** *443*, 444; **22** *872*, *891*, *892*
education (art) **19** 116; **22** 907–8*
ceramics **23** 121
emblem books **6** 88
emblems **10** *175*
embossing **22** 888, *889*
embroidery **22** 897–9*
blackwork **22** 898
crewelwork **22** 898
Gothic **13** 196
needle-painting **22** 898, *898*
whitework **22** 898
enamel **10** 195; **28** *739*
engraving **22** *885*
stippling **12** *786*; **22** 885
engravings **10** 391, 392; **20** 631; **22** 884–5
dotted prints **9** 190
Mannerism **14** 293; **15** *90*; **22** *272*
Renaissance **19** *758*, *763*
16th cent. **10** *388*; **12** *531*, *882*; **15** *96*; **25** *612*
17th cent. **10** *175*, *478*; **13** *223*, *893*; **18** *623*; **24** *235*; **29** *247*; **32** *699*
19th cent. **1** *809*
erotic art **10** *478*, 483
etchings **10** 549–50*, 553*
Baroque **26** *165*
lift-ground **28** 358
17th cent. **5** *325*; **10** *553*; **11** 794; **25** *606*; **28** *361*
18th cent. **25** *50*
ewers **22** *881*, 890
exchanges **10** *668*; **22** *830*
exhibitions **1** 808; **14** 42
façade decoration **10** 745
factories **4** *815*
faience (ii) (ceramics) **22** 879–80, 881–2
fans **10** 781
fireplaces **22** 862
flagons **22** 893, *893*
fortifications **7** 521; **21** 569–70*, *570*, 572–3; **22** 822
Sri Lanka **21** 572
forts **21** *572*; **29** 452
fountains **12** 131
frames **11** 373, 438–50*, *440*, *441*, *443*, *447*; **23** *542*
frontispieces **22** *355*
furniture **22** 869–77*, *872*, *873*, *874*, *876*; **33** 157
Indonesia **15** 813*
Sri Lanka **29** 470
gables **1** 801, *802*; **11** 875–6; **32** 588
galleries (iv) (art) **9** 15, 22
Netherlands, the—cont.
garden design **12** *106*, 131–2, *132*
gardens **12** 104, 131–2*, *132*; **33** 691
gilding **11** *440*, *441*, *443*
glass **12** *786*; **22** 884–5*, *885*
glasses **12** *786*; **22** 884, 885, *885*
glass holders **1** *811*; **22** 887, 889
glazes **12** 803
gold **13** *159*; **22** 885–92*, *889*, 897*
government buildings **9** *368*
gowns **9** 275
graves **25** 508
grottoes **12** 530
guidebooks **13** 810
guilds **22** 886, 894
embroiderers' **22** 898
furniture-makers **22** 870
painters' **1** 104; **22** 907
pewterers' **22** 893
guns **2** 464
Haggadot **17** *537*
halls **14** *45*
hangings **20** 365
Hausmalers **14** 235
historiography **22** 909–11*
hospitals **4** *57*; **19** 116
hotels **23** *671*
houses **2** *193*; **4** 786
country **22** *827*
farmhouses **32** 283–5, *284*
Modern Movement **21** *781*
Régence style **22** *826*
Renaissance **1** *802*
South Africa **29** 104
teahouses **12** 132
town **5** *542*
17th cent. **32** *589*
housing
Amsterdam school (*fl* 1915-30) **1** *804*
Delft School (ii) (20th cent.) **8** *670*
Expressionism **18** *126*
Functionalism **23** *664*
20th cent. **10** *715*
Huguenots **14** 855
humanism **14** 868
illusionism **15** 139
indigo **8** 36
inks **15** 852
intarsia **22** 871
interior decoration **22** 862–9*, *868*, *869*; **31** *683*
Biedermeier **22** *866*
Neo-classicism **22** *865*
15th cent. **22** *863*
17th cent. **20** *459*; **22** *864*
investment **7** 562
iron **13** 160; **22** 894*
ivory **29** 571
ivory-carvings **13** 176–7*; **16** 799; **22** *895*, 895–6*
japanning **7** 166
jardinières **22** *880*
jewellery **17** 521; **22** 896–7*
jugs **22** *877*, *878*
justice scenes **17** 699–701
kilns **4** 778
kitchens **22** *869*
knives **8** *283*
lacquer **5** 192; **18** 614; **22** 874
leather **4** 352, 353; **19** 4*
libraries **22** 909*
limestone **22** *117*
linen **19** 418; **22** 899
lithography **28** *201*; **33** *46*
looms **19** 416
mahogany **5** 191
maiolica **22** *877*, 878–9; **30** 878
manuals
etching **10** 562
gardens **12** 132
iconography **20** 246
painting **18** 653; **20** 244
manuscript illumination **12** 523–5; **22** *833*, 833–5*
Netherlands, the—cont.
manuscripts **12** 272; **29** 666
hunting scenes **20** *343*
maps **20** 364
marks
ceramics **22** 879, 881
metalwork **22** 887, 890, 894
pewter **22** 893
marquetry **5** 192; **20** 467, *467*; **22** 872
mass production **22** 892
medallions **22** *895*
medals **20** 921*, 923*
metalcuts **21** 337
metalwork **22** 885*, 890–92*, 893–5*
Gothic **13** 159–60*
mezzotints **21** 414, 415; **31** 797
miniatures (manuscript illumination)
Early Netherlandish style **5** *443*; **20** *343*, *643*, *644*, *662*
15th cent. **20** *737*
misericords **21** 725
mock velvet **22** 899
monuments **18** *8*; **22** *860*
mouldings **22** 219, 220, 221; **23** *542*
museums **14** *40*; **22** *829*, 906–7*; **30** 568
naturalism **22** 686
nude figures **12** 530; **23** 294
Baroque **1** *657*; **26** *158*
Mannerism **4** *151*; **22** *272*, *846*; **33** *418*
Renaissance **13** *26*; **19** *758*
16th cent. **7** *868*; **13** 25; **20** *248*, *249*
17th cent. **12** *884*; **20** *245*; **31** *780*
oak **8** 271; **13** *114*; **22** *856*, *872*; **25** *726*; **33** IV2
objects of vertu **22** 895–6*, 897*
office buildings **3** *787*; **14** *484*
olive-wood **33** IV2
orangeries **12** 132
orders (architecture) **23** 492
orphreys **22** 898
painting **14** 423; **19** 356; **22** 832–54*; **23** 376; **24** 3, 4, *6*, 8; **30** 394
Abstract art **22** *853*
Abstraction-Création **21** *854*
allegorical
Baroque **1** *657*, *658*; **11** *170*; **14** *617*; **33** *80*
Early Netherlandish style **4** *450*, *451*
16th cent. **22** *838*
17th cent. **15** *96*
18th cent. **19** *101*
animal subjects **14** *707*
architectural **2** 341–2*
Neo-Impressionism **21** *852*
Post-Impressionism **12** *861*
17th cent. **2** *341*; **14** *504*, *796*; **22** *844*; **27** *510*; **29** 592; **33** *267*
19th cent. **4** *444*
battle **3** *388*; **33** *390*
17th cent. **11** *447*
19th cent. **22** *849*
Beguines **3** *504*
bird's-eye views **1** *800*
cabinet pictures **5** 351; **6** 77; **9** 15, *16*
conversation pieces **7** *510*, 784; **19** 644
Cubism **21** *853*
di sotto in sù **14** *729*
display **9** 15
Fauvism **22** *851*
flower **11** 225–7; **22** 848
17th cent. **4** *467*; **11** *226*, *227*; **27** 885
18th cent. **11** *228*; **15** 46, *46*; **22** *847*; **23** *589*; **29** *668*
Netherlands, the
painting—cont.
genre **7** 562; **12** 287, 289, 290–91*; **14** 733; **15** 96; **22** 848*
Baroque **14** *91*; **26** *164*, *171*
Early Netherlandish style **31** *703*
Impressionism **22** *850*
Leiden 'Fine' painters **9** *192*
Magic Realism **22** *852*
Post-Impressionism **7** III1
Renaissance **19** *760*
15th cent. **20** 637
16th cent. **1** 168, *169*
17th cent. **3** *8*; **4** *381*, *382*; **5** *3*, *5*; **9** *471*; **12** *291*; **14** *728*, *733*, *734*, *739*; **15** *96*; **19** *292*; **20** *79*; **21** *351*, *814*; **22** *721*, *916*; **23** *344*, *611*, *614*, *831*; **25** *797*; **26** *746*; **28** *93*, *207*; **29** *586*, *589*, *855*; **32** *262*, *264*, *265*, *587*; **33** *176*
18th cent. **21** *489*; **31** *366*, *367*
19th cent. **1** *651*; **12** *857*; **16** *574*
hanging **9** 15
history **14** 584; **22** 848–9*
Baroque **4** *250*; **22** *842*
17th cent. **10** *659*; **18** *652*, *819*
hunting scenes
17th cent. **14** *710*
landscape **7** 562; **18** 704, 705, 706–7*, 708, 710–11*; **22** 847*; **32** *672*
Baroque **26** *159*
Mannerism **31** *805*
Post-Impressionism **12** *859*
17th cent. **2** *615*, *855*; **3** *758*; **4** *380*, *488*; **5** *681*; **8** *294*, *295*, *296*, *297*; **9** *463*; **10** *661*; **12** *801*; **13** *256*; **14** *15*, *601*, *602*; **18** *229*, *711*, III1; **20** *235*; **21** *826*; **23** *614*; **25** *67*, *370*, *755*, *756*; **26** *543*; **27** *325*, *326*, *327*, *328*, *455*, *457*; **28** *359*, *360*; **32** *137*, *138*, *145*, *907*; **33** *179*
18th cent. **22** *209*
19th cent. **20** *433*, *435*; **22** 848; **26** *528*
literary themes **4** *657*
Mannerism **33** *418*
marine **20** 424*; **29** 375
17th cent. **3** *85*; **5** *680*; **20** *425*; **23** *200*; **25** *247*; **32** *142*, *143*, *671*, 732, *733*; **33** *25*, *194*
Modern Movement **9** *63*
murals **22** 332, 333
mythological
Baroque **26** *158*
Mannerism **4** *151*
Renaissance **13** *26*
16th cent. **7** *867*, *868*
17th cent. **4** *703*; **12** *884*; **18** *651*, *818*; **27** *517*; **29** *587*; **31** *780*; **32** *261*
Neo-plasticism **22** *749*
Post-Impressionism **7** *674*
religious
Baroque **3** *23*; **4** *52*; **8** *292*; **11** *169*; **12** *241*; **19** *347*, *348*; **21** *790*; **23** II; **25** *230*; **26** *154*; **33** *262*
Early Netherlandish style **4** *449*, *841*; **12** *231*, *232*; **20** *773*; **23** *672*; **28** *804*
Gothic **20** *782*
Mannerism **14** *293*
Renaissance **13** *24*, *25*; **28** *216*, *217*
16th cent. **1** *167*; **3** *230*; **7** *869*; **14** *379*, *380*
Netherlands, the
painting
religious—cont.
17th cent. **4** *377*, *735*; **5** *2*, *4*; **8** *104*; **9** *300*, *380*, *742*, *743*; **10** *733*; **14** *727*, *731*; **16** *833*; **18** *227*; **20** *249*; **25** *758*; **28** *180*, *365*; **29** *588*, *697*
Renaissance **16** *834*; **22** 836–8*
still-lifes **7** 562; **29** 664, 666–7
17th cent. **1** *165*; **2** *644*; **3** 900; **7** *370*, *800*; **9** *489*; **13** 914; **14** *286*, *290*; **17** *737*; **29** *666*; **33** *27*
18th cent. **27** *454*; **29** *668*
topographical **1** *585*
townscapes **31** *247*
17th cent. **3** *761*; **8** *667*
urban life **31** *703*
17th cent. **19** *420*
vanitas **3** *77*; **31** 881–2*, *882*, *883*
vedute **33** *269*
watercolours **22** *866*; **28** *166*; **32** *271*
14th cent. **7** 627
15th cent. **22** 834–6*
17th cent. **3** *495*; **10** *732*; **21** *486*, *487*, *488*
19th cent. **20** *872*; **21** *175*
20th cent. **2** *230*; **7** *489*; **19** *32*
palaces **14** *38*
panels (wall) **19** 4
panoramas **14** *43*
paper **10** 381; **24** 40, 48, 51
parchment **24** 107
parterres (i) (gardens) **12** 132
parterres de broderie **12** 132
patronage **22** 886, 900–903*; **32** 267
pattern books (garden) **12** 105, *106*, 131, 133
pavilions (buildings) **12** *106*, 131
periodicals **22** 911–15*; **24** 449–50*
perspective **24** 486, 490, 492
pewter **1** 810; **12** 453; **22** *893*, 893–4*; **24** 578, 580
photoarchives **22** 909*
photographic prints **2** 618
photography **22** 853
photolithography **2** 619
plaques **16** 799
plaquettes **25** 21
plastics **22** 876, *877*
polychromy **13** *115*
pommels (guns) **2** 464
pools **12** 132
porcelain **6** 333; **22** 882, *882*, 883
eggshell **22** *883*, 883
19th cent. **18** 195
porticos **12** 748
portraits
double **10** 709
drawings **12** *880*; **13** *27*; **26** *156*, *167*
engravings **10** 392
etchings **19** *349*; **26** *160*
full-length **10** 709
group **1** 806, *807*; **4** 592; **13** 26, *895*; **14** *93*; **17** *924*; **26** 369–70
Baroque **1** *658*; **26** *169*
Renaissance **22** *837*
16th cent. **9** *275*
17th cent. **14** *41*
painting **18** *10*; **22** 848*
Baroque **1** **658*, *807*; **4** *251*; **13** *895*; **14** *92*; **22** *846*; **23** I; **25** *276*; **26** *163*, *169*; **28** *50*
Early Netherlandish style **7** *239*
Mannerism **17** *924*
Post-Impressionism **12** *858*
Renaissance **22** *66*, *837*
16th cent. **9** *275*; **16** *831*; **18** *6*; **22** *200*

Netherlands, the
portraits
painting—cont.
17th cent. **3** *77*; **9** *193*; **14** *41*, *139*, *289*, *374*; **18** 10; **20** *80*; **21** *510*; **22** *95*; **23** *675*; **24** *357*, *377*; **32** *263*, *376*
18th cent. **19** *101*
self-portraits **22** *846*; **25** *731*
Baroque **26** *160*
17th cent. **3** *77*; **9** *193*
tronie **26** 152, 154
posters **7** 655, *655*; **25** 347, 348
potters **3** 589
pottery
blue-and-white ware **4** 176*; **7** 166; **8** *668*
creamware **22** 881, 882
Delftware **4** 176; **6** 333; **7** 166, *166*; **8** *668*; **22** *878*, 879–80, *880*, *881*, 881–3; **29** 114
Hollands porceleyn **22** 879
Pingsdorf ware **22** 877
tin-glazed ware **30** *876*
predellas **25** 464
printing **8** 36, 666; **22** 899–900; **30** 561
print publishers **25** 625
prints **2** 558; **22** 854*
monotypes **3** 495
punched **25** 731, *731*
15th cent. **20** 802
pulpits **25** *726*
quarries **26** 630
quilting **22** 898
roundels **27** 255, 256, 257, *257*
samplers **27** 694
sandstone **22** *855*; **23** *188*
sarcophagi **27** *99*
satin-wood **5** 192
schools **11** *840*
scissors **8** *286*
sculptors **10** 261
sculpture **12** 132; **22** 854–62*
architectural **10** 745
display **9** 15, 22
Gothic **13** 98–101*, 109–15*
group **16** 799
mythological **22** *858*
relief **22** *117*, *855*
religious **22** *856*
Gothic **3** *456*; **13** *114*, *115*
Renaissance **16** 695
Romanesque **26** 630–31*, 644–5*
stone **13** 98–101*; **26** 630–31*
wood **13** 109–15*, *115*; **26** 644–5*
20th cent. **22** *861*
shutters (window) **9** 12
signatures **22** 894
silk **22** 899
silver **3** 598; **13** 159; **22** 885–92*, *886*, *888*, *890*, *891*, *892*; **28** *739*
Indonesia **15** 813*
silver-gilt **1** *811*; **32** *400*
snuff-boxes **22** 897
speculation **7** 562
spires **13** 62–3
spoons **28** *739*
stained glass **2** 485; **8** 102, *103*; **14** *737*; **27** *257*
stamps **22** 887
statuettes **29** 571*
stone **13** 98–101*; **26** 630–31*
stonewares **22** 877
stucco **22** 866; **29** 837*
studios **26** *171*; **29** 854, *855*
symbolism (critical term) **15** 94
synagogues **17** 544, 545, 548, 549
tables **22** *868*, 870
tankards **22** 893
tapestries **22** 862, 897*; **30** 317, 320
Gothic **13** 196
Renaissance **13** *907*
tazze **22** 886
teapots **22** *891*
Netherlands, the—cont.
tea-services **22** *892*
textiles **22** 864, 897–900*, *898*; **30** 561
Romanesque **26** 703
theatres **30** 665*, 676
theories (art) **18** 226
theories (painting) **14** 740–41
tiles **22** 878, 880–81; **25** 303; **30** *876*, 878–9*, *879*, XIII2
title-pages **17** *537*; **20** *245*
topographical views **31** 154–5*
towels **19** *416*
towers **13** *62*, 62–3
town halls **31** *239*
Dutch Classicism **22** *825*
Mannerism **8** *666*; **22** *824*
Modern Movement **31** *868*
17th cent. **4** *702*; **13** *893*
towns
fortified **21** 570, *570*
garden cities **1** 803; **13** 312, 321, 632; **17** 910
new **31** 735
townscapes **31** 154–5, 246–7*
trade **1** 799; **6** 624
brick **3** 588; **4** 778
ceramics **6** 331–2; **31** 338
chintz **22** 899
faience (ii) (ceramics) **25** 309
furniture **15** 693; **19** 592
glass **7** 87; **16** 522
Indian subcontinent **15** 201
iron **17** 318
lace **3** 610
lacquer **18** 613
manuscripts **16** 553
paintings **23** 224
paper **24** 48
porcelain **4** 175, 176; **6** 332, 622, 918; **22** 878, 879
pottery **4** 173; **6** 333
tapestries **3** 607; **29** 350
textiles **7** 53; **17** 315
tiles **25** 303; **30** 884
treatises
architecture **8** 496; **22** 823
painting **20** 245–6; **31** 300
trompe l'oeil **11** 440; **14** *740*; **29** 668
tufa **4** 778
tureens **22** *882*, *888*
tympana **26** *630*
typography **31** 494
upholstery **22** 866; **31** *683*
urban planning **9** 746; **14** 39; **31** 737
Brazil **4** 704, 710
13th cent. **3** 504
20th cent. **13** 313
vases **8** *668*; **22** *883*
vaults (ceiling) **8** 299; **22** *819*
veneers **8** 271; **22** *872*, *873*; **33** IV2
verre églomisé **5** 192
video art **22** 853
wagons **30** 665
wallpaper **32** 813
walnut **8** 271
weaving **22** 899–900*
westworks **33** *109*
white lead **24** 797
wicker **33** 157
wig stands **7** *166*
willow **33** 157
windows **9** 12
women **3** 504
wood **13** 109–15*, *115*; **22** *870*, *876*; **26** 644–5*
woodcuts **2** *136*; **4** *144*, *145*; **33** *168*, 349–50*, 354–5*, 358*
chiaroscuro **12** *883*; **33** 367
workshops **28** 218
wrought iron **22** 895
see also BELGIUM
Netherlands Antilles *see* ANTILLES, NETHERLANDS
Netherton, Samuel **33** 158
Nether Wallop (Hants), St Andrew **2** 67, 72, *73*; **10** 243
N. E. Thing Co. **5** 569
Netjerykhet *see* DJOSER
net lace *see* LACE → types → lacis
Netley **7** 350
Neto **22** 245
Neto, Estevão Gonçalves *see* GONÇALVES NETO, ESTEVÃO
Neto, Guilhermo Zamoner *see* ZAMONER NETO, GUILHERMO
Neto, Manuel Chong *see* CHONG NETO, MANUEL
Neto, Mario Cravo *see* CRAVO NETO, MARIO
Neto, Vicente Ferreira de Castro *see* FERREIRA DE CASTRO NETO, VICENTE
net prints *see under* PRINTS → types
nets **10** 355; **18** 589
Netsch, Walter **28** 818
Netscher, Caspar **14** 41; **22** 845, 915–16*
copies **33** 594
patrons and collectors **23** 469; **24** 322; **32** 368
reproductive prints by others **8** 481; **33** 196
teachers **4** 383
works **7** 784; **22** 844, *916*
Netscher, Constantijn **22** 916
Netscher, Johann **22** 915
Netscher, Theodorus **22** 916
netsuke **7** 836; **14** 764; **17** 23, 98, 386, 398–402*, *398*, *399*, *400*, *402*; **31** 195
see also TOGGLES
Nette, Johann Friedrich **19** 779; **33** 429
works **19** *780*
Netti, Francesco **22** 916–17*
netting *see* LACE → types → lacis
netting, knotless *see* LOOPING, CROSSED
Nettlecombe Chalice **10** 325
Nettlecombe Paten **10** 325
Nettleford, John Sutton **4** 86
nettles **1** 493; **3** 915; **22** 791; **30** 538
Netto, Luiz Forte *see* FORTE NETTO, LUIZ
Nettos Painter **13** 501; **32** 58–9*
works **9** 246; **13** 506, *507*
Nettuno Fortress **3** 359; **21** 566
net vaults *see under* VAULTS (CEILING) → types
Netzer, Hubert **4** 741; **22** 917*
Neu, Hans **3** 870
Neu, Wenzel **11** 832
Neuber, Johann Christian **2** 823; **9** 240; **12** 458, 461
works **12** *458*
Neuberger, Roy R. **22** 917*
Neuberg Stiftskirche Mariae Himmelfahrt **2** 777
Neubirnau Pilgrimage Church **11** 44, *45*; **12** 372, 404; **26** 498
Neubrandenburg
Marienkirche **13** 56; **14** 81
Treptower Tor **4** 777
Neuburg, Eleanor of, Holy Roman Empress *see* ELEANOR OF WITTELSBACH, Holy Roman Empress
Neuburg, Philipp Ludwig, Count Palatine of **9** 133; **33** *272*, 279
Neuburg, Philip William, Count Palatine of *see* PHILIP WILLIAM, Elector Palatine
Neuburg, Wolfgang William, Count Palatine of **33** *272*, 278, 279*
architecture **9** 459
paintings **27** 291
sculpture **26** 522
Neuburg an der Donau **12** *361*; **22** 917–19*
façade decoration **10** 741
Neuburg an der Donau—cont.
Jesuitenkirche **12** 368, 370; **32** 821
Rathaus **12** 370
St Maria **22** 918–19
Schloss **22** 918, *918*
chapel **19** 814
Neucha **32** 879
Neuchâtel **22** 919–20*; **30** *124*
Collegiate Church of Notre-Dame **26** 635
cenotaph of the Comtes de Neuchâtel **22** *919*
Hôtel de Ville **30** 127
Maison des Halles **30** 126
marks **20** *444*
Musée d'Art et d'Histoire **3** 20; **14** 281; **21** 370; **22** 920
Musée des Beaux-Arts *see* Musée d'Art et d'Histoire
Musée d'Ethnographie **3** 916; **30** 155
Palace Hall **26** 575
Neu-Dachau **22** 304
Neudeck factory **5** 305
Neudeck Schloss **12** 348
Neudörfer, Johann **22** 920*, *924*
Neue bildende Kunst **24** 445
Neue Graphik **25** 352
Neue Gruppe (Berlin) **21** 365
Neue Gruppe (Munich) **22** 305
Neue Jugend **3** 801; **14** 845
neue Kunst, Die **24** 427
Neue Künstlergenossenschaft (Munich) **22** 305
Neue Künstlervereinigung München (NKVM) **22** 304, 921*
members **16** 817; **17** 763
Girieud, Pierre (Paul) **12** 729
Izdebsky, Vladimir (Alekseyevich) **16** 808
Jawlensky, Alexei **17** 452
Kandinsky, Vasily (Vasil'yevich) **17** 762
Kubin, Alfred (Leopold Isidor) **18** 491
Le Fauconnier, Henri **19** 64
Macke, August (Robert Ludwig) **20** 12
Marc, Franz (Moriz Wilhelm) **20** 381
Münter, Gabriele **22** 318
Werefkin, Marianne (von) **33** 77
Neue Leben **22** 921–2*
members **2** 489; **8** 434; **9** 758; **16** 903; **28** 352
Neue Miscellaneen artistischen Inhalts für Künstler und Kunstliebhaber **24** 421
Neuenberg Priory **12** 382
Neuenburg, Johann von Freiburg, Graf von **10** 407
Neuenkirchen, Porphyrius von *see* PORPHYRIUS VON NEUENKIRCHEN
Neuenschwander, Eduard **33** 736
Neuenstadt **30** 143
Neue Pathos see JAHRBUCH DER ZEITSCHRIFT DAS NEUE PATHOS
Neuerberg, Norman **7** 386
Neuer Büchersaal der schönen Wissenschaften und freyen Künste **24** 443
Neue Reklame Gestaltung **11** 299
Neue Sachlichkeit **3** 802; **9** 239; **22** 922–3*; **25** 741
members **3** 479; **9** 41; **25** 838, 842; **26** 195; **28** 40, 113
works **3** *802*; **9** *42*; **12** 396, *396*; **13** *698*; **22** *922*; **28** 920
Neues Bauen **8** 826; **21** 782; **30** 127–8
members **2** 513; **3** 795; **9** 60; **25** 839; **27** 215; **28** 122; **30** 128
works **14** 24; **21** 782
see also NIEUWE BOUWEN
Neues Deutsches Museum **24** 443; **28** 108
Neue Sezession *see* SEZESSION (NEUE)
Neues Journal zur Literatur und Kunstgeschichte **22** 350
Neueste aus der anmuthigen Gelehrsamkeit, Das **24** 443
Neue Teutsche, Der **24** 443
Neue Wilden **3** 17, 803; **10** 696; **12** 397; **27** 398; **32** 447
Neufahrer, Ludwig **18** 575; **22** 923–4*
Neuf-Brisach **21** 568
Porte de Strasbourg **21** 549
Neufchâtel, Charles de, Bishop of Besançon *see* CHARLES DE NEUFCHÂTEL, Bishop of Besançon
Neufchatel, Colyn van *see* NIEUWCASTEL, Colyn van
Neufchatel, Nicolas **22** 924–5*
attributions **20** 790
patrons and collectors **22** 920
pupils **17** 711
works **22** *924*; **23** 308
Neufeld, Inge *see* KING, INGE
Neufeld, Joseph **14** 785; **30** 421
Neufert, Ernst **12** 380
Neufforge, Jean-François de **3** 546; **22** 925*
collaboration **13** 233; **19** 232
groups and movements **22** 738
reproductive prints by others **9** 390
works **7** 747; **29** 91; **32** 554
writings **20** 867; **23** 544
Neufville, François-Louis de, Marquis de Villeroy *see* VILLEROY, FRANÇOIS-LOUIS DE NEUFVILLE, Marquis de
Neufville, Nicolas de, Maréchal de Villeroi *see* VILLEROI, NICOLAS DE NEUFVILLE, Maréchal de
Neufville de Villeroi, Camille de, Archbishop of Lyon **32** 574*
Neufville de Villeroy (family) **16** 855, 856
Neugablonz-Kaufbeuren *see* KAUFBEUREN
Neugeboren, Heinrich **22** 381
Neuhaus, Friedrich **3** 794; **25** 856
Neuhaus, Jans **15** 809
Neuhaus, Max **29** 98
Neuhaus, Rolf **15** 809
Neuhaus, Werner **27** 213
Neuhofer, Jeremias **12** 469
Neuhuys, (Johannes) Albert **14** 47; **22** 850; **23** 1*
Neuilly, Jacques de *see* JACQUES DE NEUILLY
Neuilly-sur-Seine
bridge **4** 801
chapel of St Ferdinand **11** 520
Folie Saint-James **3** 524; **13** 705
mairie **31** 241
Maisons Jaoul **19** *45*
Neukastel *see* LEINSWEILER → Slevogthof
Neukunst **23** 1
Neukunstgruppe **23** 1–2*
members **10** 756; **13** 867; **17** 744; **18** 204; **28** 88; **33** 162
Neukünstler *see* NEUKUNSTGRUPPE
Neumagen **12** 463
Neumann **1** 687
Neumann, Alfred **16** 566
works **16** *566*
Neumann, Balthasar **4** 225; **12** 373; **23** 2–6*; **33** 277, 431
altars **2** 843
architecture **33** 430, 432, *432*
castles **5** 8; **32** 120
churches **4** 324; **12** 372; **23** *5*; **32** 823
Jesuit Church (Mainz) **30** 741
Monastery of St Michael (Bamberg) **3** 140
Münsterschwarzbach Abbey Church **14** 695, 696

Neumann, Balthasar
architecture
churches—cont.
Neresheim Abbey 22 796
SS Nicolas and Elisabeth (Cheb) 6 526
St Paulin (Trier) 31 325
Schloss Brühl Church 5 8
Vierzehnheiligen 7 254; 23 543; 32 *467*
palaces 4 890; 23 *4*, 811; 29 838; 30 858
staircases 12 371; 23 *3*; 29 525; 33 *433*
collaboration 8 875; 14 530; 18 495
groups and movements 26 495, 498
interior decoration 12 413; 27 610, 611
models 2 336
patrons and collectors 3 140; 13 631; 17 512; 18 495; 26 422; 28 146; 32 466
pupils 14 540; 28 105, 381
reproductive prints by others 33 *431*
Neumann, Ernst 29 638
Neumann, Franz Ignaz Michael von 20 128; 23 6; 29 392
Neumann, Gustav von 19 339
Neumann, J. (*fl* after 1945; art historian) 8 426
Neumann, J. B(er) (1887-1961; dealer) 3 479, 801; 11 729; 23 7*; 25 626; 29 609
Neumann, Krzysztof 25 127
Neumann, Morton G. 23 7*
Neumann, Osha
works 22 *336*
Neumann, R. 32 155
Neumann, Wilhelm 13 717
Neumarkt, John of *see* JAN OF STŘEDA
Neumayer, Erwin 15 552
Neunhertz, Georg Wilhelm *see* NEUNHERTZ, JERZY WILHELM
Neunhertz, Jerzy Wilhelm 23 7–8*; 25 445
Neurath, Otto 27 714
Neurath, Walter 23 8*
Neureuther, Eugen (Napoleon) 23 8–9*
works 12 853; 23 *8*
Neureuther, Gottfried von 23 9; 25 829
Neureuther, Ludwig 23 8
Neuri 28 320
Neurone, Giovanni Battista 12 668
Neurone, Pietro 12 668
Neuschwanstein, Schloss *see under* SCHWANGAU
Neuserre (*reg c.* 2416-*c.* 2392 BC) 9 *776*
altars 1 691
architecture 9 779
pyramids 1 96; 25 *761*, 763
temples 1 90–91, *91*, 97; 9 830; 30 433
tombs 1 96
gold 10 66
reliefs 9 860
sculpture 9 869; 30 691
Neuss 12 364
Clemens-Sels-Museum 8 631
Dreikönigekirche 29 508
Neustaedt, Ursula *see* MATTHAUER-NEUSTAEDT, URSULA
Neustein, Joshua 16 568
Neustift Convent 23 707–8
Neustück, Maximilian 14 488
Neusüss, Floris M(ichael) 23 9*
Neutra, Dion 23 10
Neutra, Richard (Josef) 10 150; 11 526; 23 9–10*; 31 596, 632
collaboration 1 490; 2 383; 14 118
Neutra, Richard (Josef)—cont.
groups and movements 15 885; 21 783; 25 741
pupils 14 194
staff 6 365; 29 81
works 2 789; 19 701; 23 *10*; 28 488; 29 643; 31 730
Neutral 22 552, 612
neutron activation analysis *see under* TECHNICAL EXAMINATION → types
Neu Ulm, St John the Baptist 4 *235*
Neuville, Alphonse (Marie-Adolphe) de 23 10–11*
collaboration 8 819
works 3 389, 390; 6 489
Neuvy-Saint-Sepulchre 9 680; 26 599
St Etienne 9 156
Neuwelt *see* NOVÝ SVĚT
Neuwiller-sur-Saverne, SS Peter and Paul 29 752
Neuwirth, J. 8 426
Nevali Çori 1 823, 832
Nevalon 26 659
Nevan, Eugen 28 853
Nevasa 15 718
Neve, Felipe de 19 699
Neve, Frans van der 23 11*
Neve (y Chaves), Justino de 23 11*, 437; 28 515
Neve, P. 4 229
Neve, Richard 10 205
Neve, Sebastien de 10 717; 23 11–12*
Neve, Simon de 32 242
Nevele, Lucas van 5 47
Nevelson, Louise 23 12–13*; 30 329
collaboration 20 605, 606
patrons and collectors 19 439
teachers 14 633
works 6 460; 19 492; 23 *12*, 334; 31 614
Neven, August Libert 23 13
Neven DuMont 23 13*
Neven DuMont, Alfred (1868-1940) 23 13
Neven DuMont, Alfred (*b* 1927) 23 13
Neven DuMont, Josef 23 13
Neven DuMont, Kurt 23 13
Neven DuMont, Reinhold 23 13
Nevern, Great Cross 32 786
Nevers 11 *504*, *505*; 23 13–15*
ceramics 23 13–14*
faience (ii) (ceramics) 11 605
glass 11 611
pottery 4 177; 7 166
St Etienne 23 *14*, 14–15*; 26 586
St Sauveur 26 602
sculpture 26 602
tiles 30 885
Nevers, Duc de 20 896
Nevers, Carlo I Gonzaga, Duc de *see* CARLO I, 8th Duke of Mantua
Nevers, Carlo II Gonzaga, Duc de *see* CARLO II, 9th Duke of Mantua
Nevers, Guillaume, Comte de 23 14
Nevers, Jette 8 756
Nevers, Ludovico Gonzaga, Duc de 11 604
Neves Carvalho, Zulmiro de 4 629; 25 302
Neveu, Matthijs *see* NAIVEU, MATTHIJS
Neveux, Pol 26 113
Nevile, Thomas 5 511
Nevill, Henry, 2nd Earl of Abergavenny 6 408
Neville (family) 20 735
Neville, George 24 62
Neville, Ralph, 6th Baron Neville 19 290
Neville Hours *see under* BOOKS OF HOURS → individual manuscripts
Nevinson, Christopher (Richard Wynne) 10 374; 23 15–16*; 24 427
groups and movements 8 264; 10 255, 256; 11 865; 19 622; 32 701
patrons and collectors 1 496
works 11 *437*; 19 492; 26 59; 29 426, *427*
Nevirnum *see* NEVERS
Nevis 2 144; 5 *745*
carnivals 2 147; 5 788
ceramics 2 152
costumes 2 *146*
Hamilton House Museum 2 154
masks 2 146
museums 2 154
pottery 2 152
see also ANTILLES, LESSER; LEEWARD ISLANDS
Nevis Pottery 2 152
Nevjestić, Virgilije 4 462
Nevole, Jan 28 444
Nevryov, Nikolay (Vasil'yevich) 23 16*; 27 390
groups and movements 20 232; 22 178
pupils 31 571
teachers 33 622
Nevşehir *see* MUSHQARA
Nevşehirli Ibrahim Pasha *see* IBRAHIM PASHA
Nevsky Pickwickians 8 849; 33 379
Nev'yansk 27 374
Nevy-en-Sullias 6 159
New, Edmund Hort
works 4 *87*
New, Keith 4 826; 29 508
New, Lloyd Kiva 22 597
New Abbasid style script *see under* SCRIPTS → types
New Abbey (Dumfries & Galloway), Shambellie House Museum of Costume 28 274
New Age 25 380
New Amsterdam (Guyana) 13 *873*
National Insurance Scheme Building 13 876
New Amsterdam (USA) *see* NEW YORK
Newar 22 754, 761, 780, 785, 787; 23 16*; 24 251; 30 807, 812, 839, 840
collections 22 795
manuscripts 22 795
paintings 22 795
jewellery 22 788
manuscript illumination 22 786
metalwork 22 *790*
Newark (Notts; UK)
Ossington Coffee Tavern 25 688
St Mary Magdalen 29 413
Town Hall 2 617
Newark (NJ; USA)
International Airport 1 495
Newark Museum 22 795
collections 15 745; 30 849, 850; 31 659
sculpture 22 795
Shelton collection 30 850
New Art (Arta Noua) 3 88
New Art Club 12 777
New Art Examiner 24 429, 433
New Art History 2 533, 538
New Artists' Society 22 733; 23 16*, 335
New Art Work Society *see* SHIN SEISAKU KYŌKAI
New Association of Fine Artists 18 142
Newbattle (Lothian)
Abbey 4 182
church 28 251
Newbattle House 28 270
New Bauhaus 8 803
Newberry, Francis H. 12 780
Newberry, Percy 10 80, 82
Newberry Cave 22 582
Newbery, Francis H. 12 777; 23 17; 28 238, 270, 275
Newbery, Jessie 12 780; 23 17*; 28 265
Newbold Jones, Edith *see* WHARTON, EDITH
Newbould, Frank 7 653; 25 351
New Bremen Glassmanufactory 1 769; 10 852; 31 642
Newbridge House (Co. Dublin) 16 27
New Britain 24 64, *64*, 65, 83–4*
canoes 23 725
headdresses 24 *84*
masks 24 80
rock art 23 729
weapons 23 734
wood-carvings 23 732
New Brutalism 5 56–7; 23 17*; 28 889
office buildings 28 *890*
New Buckenham 6 54
New Bunten *see* SHIN BUNTEN
Newburgh Priory (N. Yorks) 17 623; 29 31, 714
Newbury, Abbot of Bristol 4 825
Newburyport Court-House (MA) 18 886
Newby, Frank 25 571
Newby Hall (N. Yorks) 9 30; 23 860; 33 20
furniture 7 172; 11 119
paintings 26 475; 33 20
sculpture 6 98; 9 12; 10 365; 33 19
tapestries 33 19
New Calcutta School 15 747
New Caledonia 23 17–19*, *711*; 25 181
architecture 23 17–18
axes 23 19
canoes 23 725
finials (architectural) 23 18, *18*
forgeries 23 737
masks 23 19, *19*
nephrite 16 861
pottery 23 728
rock art 23 729, 730
sculpture 23 17–18, 731
shells 28 581
weapons 23 734
wood 23 *18*, *19*
see also POLYNESIAN OUTLIERS
New Canaan (CT), Glass House 12 792; 24 291; 31 597
Newcastle, Henry Pelham-Clinton-Hope, 8th Duke of *see* PELHAM-CLINTON-HOPE, HENRY, 8th Duke of Newcastle
Newcastle, John Holles, 1st Duke of *see* HOLLES, JOHN, 1st Duke of Newcastle
Newcastle, Thomas Pelham-Holles, 1st Duke of *see* PELHAM-HOLLES, THOMAS, Marquess of Clare and 1st Duke of Newcastle
Newcastle (Australia)
Christ Church Cathedral 2 766
court-house 18 887
Newcastle Region Art Gallery 2 771
steel 2 740
University
Students' Union 30 161
Newcastle (Nevis) 2 152
Newcastle upon Tyne (Tyne & Wear; UK) 10 *225*; 23 19–21*, *20*; 31 724
architecture 9 55
Black Gate 12 173
Castle 10 227
Castle Chapel 26 615
Cathedral of St Nicholas 29 413
enamel 10 318
furniture 10 297
Newcastle upon Tyne (Tyne & Wear; UK)—cont.
glass 10 317, 318
Laing Art Gallery 23 21
law courts 18 886
Lightfoot Centre 29 427
murals 22 333
Swing Bridge 4 799
town walls 31 710
trade 5 580
University Hatton Gallery 28 198
viaducts 32 398
New Chinese-style Painting Movement 6 774
Newcombe, William 32 414
Newcomb-Macklin Co. 11 498
frames 11 *498*
Newcomb Pottery 23 32; 31 638, 639
New Culture Society *see* JAUNĀ KULTŪRAS SABIEDRĪBA
New Culture Studio 23 138
New Dachau school 14 694
Newdegate, Richard 19 124
New Delhi *see under* DELHI
Newdigate, Roger 23 21–2*
architecture 17 877, 878
collaboration 21 607
decorative works 24 845
paintings 8 832
sculpture 23 690
Newdigate Candelabrum 14 109
New Dutch Waterline 21 570
New Earswick (N. Yorks) 11 785; 24 185; 27 279
New Ebenezer (GA) 31 721
New Empiricism 5 56; 23 22*
New England Glass Co. 4 483; 19 304; 22 240; 23 22*; 31 642
production 10 852; 24 57; 31 642, 644
staff 14 603
New English Art Club 3 631; 5 516; 6 79; 10 254; 19 591, 621; 23 22–3*; 27 359; 29 768
collections 26 12
members 23 26, 568
Bevan, Robert (Polhill) 3 894
Bone, (David) Muirhead 4 315
Brabazon, Hercules Brabazon 4 619
Brown, Frederick 4 880
Clausen, George 7 406
Coldstream, William (Menzies) 7 547
Conder, Charles (Edward) 7 701
Forbes, Stanhope (Alexander) 11 300
Gotch, Thomas Cooper 13 30
Hamnett, Nina 14 120
John, Augustus (Edwin) 17 608
La Thangue, Henry Herbert 18 830
Lee, Thomas Stirling 19 61
Lowry, L(aurence) S(tephen) 19 734
MacColl, Dugald Sutherland 19 872
Mann, Alexander 20 276
McEvoy, Ambrose 19 890
Orpen, William (Newenham Montague) 23 568
Osborne, Walter Frederick 23 599
Pissarro, Lucien 24 884
Roussel, Theodore (Casimir) (1847-1926) 27 269
Sickert, Walter Richard 28 659
Steer, Philip Wilson 29 595
Swynnerton, Annie Louisa 30 157
Thomas, James Havard 30 744
Tonks, Henry 31 146
Tuke, Henry Scott 31 418
Walker, Ethel 32 794
Walton, E(dward) A(rthur) 32 834
Newenham, Frederick 25 635

Newenham Abbey (Devon) **7** 350
Newent (Glos), St Mary **2** 70
New Era Western Painting Exhibition *see* SHINJIDAI YŌGA TEN
New Generation **18** 65
New Georgia Islands **29** 49
New Gourna *see under* THEBES (i) (EGYPT)
Newgrange (Co. Meath) **16** *5*; **21** 42; **23** 23–4*, *24*; **25** *470*, 508
jewellery **27** 103
rock art **25** 509, *509*, 510
New Graz Architecture *see* GRAZ SCHOOL
New Group (South Africa) **25** 566; **29** 108
New Group (Yeniler Grubu; Turkey) **16** 805; **31** 454
New Guinea
architecture **23** 715
barkcloth **23** 713
canoes **23** 724, 725
erotic art **10** 474
feathers **10** 848
jade **16** 861
photography **10** 580
rock art **23** 728
weapons **23** 734
see also IRIAN JAYA; PAPUA NEW GUINEA
New Guinea, Western *see* IRIAN JAYA
Newhailes (Lothian) **25** 882; **28** 226, *226*
Newhall, Beaumont **24** 683
New Hall Factory **4** 177, 824; **10** 309, 310; **29** 495
Newhall House (Lothian) **5** 885
New Hanover **24** 85
New Harmony (IN)
church **31** 597
maze **18** 585
New Haven (CT) **23** 24–5*; **31** *587*
architecture **4** 788
Collegiate School of Connecticut *see* Yale University
David S. Ingalls Hockey Rink *see under* Yale University
Grove Street Cemetery **31** 592
Peabody Museum of Natural History *see under* Yale University
Temple Street Car Park **7** 695
Yale University **14** 139; **23** 25
Art Gallery **5** 56; **7** 30; **14** 139; **17** 723–4; **22** 917; **30** 62; **31** 493
collections **6** 826; **9** 758; **10** 94
Jarves Collection **2** 228; **7** 336
Beinecke Rare Book and Manuscript Library **19** 320; **23** *176*; **28** 314
collections **9** 231, 233; **17** 435; **28** 920; **31** 666
David S. Ingalls Hockey Rink **29** 489, *490*; **30** 468
Kline Science Center **4** 789
library **4** 23
Peabody Museum of Natural History **13** 897; **21** 265
School of Art and Architecture **27** *314*
School of the Fine Arts **33** 42
Sterling Memorial Library **19** 319
Trumbull Gallery **31** 392, 666
Yale Center for British Art **17** 725; **21** 91; **22** 367
collections **3** 129; **8** 886; **9** 231
Yale University Stadium **1** 798; **29** 489
New Hebrides *see* VANUATU
New Horizons **16** 567, *567*, 568; **17** 579; **23** 25*
members **2** 487; **8** 515; **16** 571, 903; **18** 525; **29** 626, 769; **33** 620
New Humanism **5** 56; **25** 653
New Hungarian Quarterly **24** 441
New Iddo
masks **1** *268*
New Image *see* NIEUWE BEELDING
New Ireland **24** 64, *64*, 65, 85–6*
exchange **23** 741
masks **24** *85*
sculpture **23** 732, *732*
New Japanese Art Exhibition *see* SHIN BUNTEN
New Jerusalem Monastery **3** 530; **23** 25–6*; **27** *363*, 372, 438
New Julfa *see under* ISFAHAN
New Kalabsha **23** 280
New Kingdom *see under* EGYPT, ANCIENT → periods
New Lanark (Strathclyde) **28** 228; **31** 725
Newland (Glos), All Saints **9** 269
Newland, Abbot of Bristol **4** 825
New Lebanon (NY) **28** 541, 542
Meeting House **28** 539
Newlyn school **4** 86, 657; **10** 254; **12** 166, 296; **18** 149, 717, 744; **20** 425; **23** 22, 26*
collections **26** 12
members **11** 299, 300; **13** 30; **22** 139, 312; **31** 418
works **10** *255*; **11** *300*
Newman, Mrs **4** 99
Newman, Arnold (Abner) **23** 26*
Newman, Barnett **5** 569; **23** 27–30*; **27** 731; **31** 608
collaboration **20** 606
dealers **18** 161; **24** 213
groups and movements **1** 78, 83, 85, 86, 87; **13** 214; **21** 646; **23** 48; **29** 534, 891; **31** 607
methods **7** 631
patrons and collectors **21** 135; **33** 45
works **7** 636, III2; **14** 164; **17** 580; **23** *29*; **31** 52
Newman, Frank E. **28** 879
Newman, John Henry, Cardinal **7** 479; **23** 30*, 472
architecture **9** 338
groups and movements **5** 340
Newman, O.
works **7** *295*
Newman, Robert B. **10** 417
Newman, Robert Loftin **23** 31*
Newman, Smith & Greenhough **23** 56
Newman, Smith & Newman
prints **32** *722*
Newman, William Herman **5** 586
Newman, Woodman & Harris **28** 879
New Mardol, Temple of Mhalsa **12** 827
Newmarket (Suffolk) **29** 424
National Horseracing Museum **29** 426
Newminster, Robert of *see* ROBERT OF NEWMINSTER
New Moscow *see* NOVAYA MOSKVA
New Negro movement *see* HARLEM RENAISSANCE
Newnham Croft (Cambs) **6** 160
Newnham-on-Severn (Glos), St Peter **26** 617
New Orleans (LA) **23** 31–2*; **31** *587*
Contemporary Art Center **23** 32
Cornstalk Hotel **16** 54
Delgado Museum *see* Museum of Art
Gellier House **12** 26
Louisiana Superdome **16** 55
Mardi Gras **5** 788
New Orleans (LA)—cont.
Museum of Art **23** 32; **29** 222
Piazza d'Italia **11** *345*, 347; **25** 359
Pontalba Building **23** *31*
Public Library **19** 320
railings **16** 54
St Charles Hotel **14** 786
St Charles Theatre **15** 408
St Louis Cemetery **6** 166
Tulane University
Middle American Research Institute **29** 222
New Paphos *see* PAPHOS, NEW
New Path **24** 431
New Photography **18** 194
New Plymouth **23** 51, *52*
Govett-Brewster Art Gallery **19** 842
Taranaki Museum **23** 737
Newport (Gwent; UK) **32** *780*
INMOS Microprocessor Factory **10** 749; **32** 783
Museum and Art Gallery **32** 791
St Woolos **26** 618
Tredegar House **32** 782
Newport (Isle of Wight; UK)
St Thomas **25** 726
Newport (RI; USA) **23** 32–3*; **31** *587*
Casino **25** 806
furniture **5** 192; **31** 625, 626, *626*
Historic Hill **2** 325
houses **3** 464
interior decoration **31** 617
Isaac Bell jr House **20** *17*; **28** 604; **31** 593
J. N. A. Griswold House **15** *22*; **29** 653
Newport Historical Society Museum **23** 33
Redwood Library and Athenaeum **14** 197, *197*; **23** 860; **31** 590
Robinson House **7** 619
silver **31** 648
Taylor House **31** 594
The Breakers **23** *33*; **25** 806; **31** 622
The Elms **24** 821
Touro synagogue **17** 545
Trinity Church **7** 270
William Watts Sherman House **18** *627*; **25** 806
Newport Beach (CA), Lovell Beach House **21** 782; **28** *96*
Newport News (VA), Mariners' Museum **15** 30
Newport Pottery **7** 434; **10** 313
Newport Restoration Foundation **23** 33
New Providence **3** *59*, 63
Newquay Methodist Church (Cornwall) **21** 347
New Realism **22** 381
New River Company **22** 401
Newry **16** 28
Newsam, Albert **15** 857
Newsam, Bartholemew **7** 441
New Scottish Group **10** 898; **12** 777; **28** 240
New Sculpture (UK) **3** 367; **10** 266; **11** 303; **12** 610, *610*, *611*; **13** 29; **17** 611; **19** 104; **23** 33–5*, *34*; **29** 575; **30** 761
relief sculpture **3** *367*
sculpture **30** *762*
statuettes **10** *267*; **11** *303*; **25** IV; **29** *575*
New Sculpture Group (USA) **29** 900
New Seville **16** 882
New Seville Carvings **5** 750; **16** 883, 885, *885*
New Society of Fine Artists *see* KÚT
New Society of Painters (NOZh) **22** 178
Newsom, John J. **23** 35
Newsom, Joseph Cather **9** 685; **23** 35
Newsom, Noble **23** 35
Newsom, Samuel **9** 685; **23** 35
Newsom, Sidney B. **23** 35
Newsom, Thomas D. **23** 35
New South Wales Government Architect **23** 36*
newspapers **2** 372; **6** 491; **8** 545; **11** 54; **13** 306
Newstead (Notts)
Abbey **26** 590
leather **27** 105, *105*
metalwork **27** 94
New Style I script *see under* SCRIPTS → types → New Abbasid style
New Testaments **9** 608–11*; **27** 173
individual manuscripts *see under* BIBLES → individual manuscripts
see also GOSPEL BOOKS; GOSPEL LECTIONARIES
Newton, Adam **8** 45
Newton, Charles (Thomas) **8** 869; **23** 36*
collaboration **22** 340; **25** 722
excavations **14** 68, 69, 70; **18** 147
Newton, Dudley **29** 653; **31** 593
Newton, Ernest **23** 36*; **25** 688; **26** 316; **28** 563
collaboration **25** 633
groups and movements **2** 575; **9** 739; **10** 239; **22** 743
works **23** 398
Newton, Francis **10** 81
Newton, Gilbert Stuart **14** 718; **23** 37*; **26** 75; **32** 338
Newton, Harry Robert **29** 919
Newton, Helmut **23** 37*; **24** 656
Newton, Isaac **4** 360; **7** 628; **10** 401; **19** 354; **24** 376; **28** 203
Newton, Peter **29** 514
Newton, Richard **5** 756
Newton, William (*d* 1643) **25** 654
Newton, William (1730–98) **23** 20; **25** 727; **29** 806
Newton House (Dyfed) **32** 788
New Topographics **3** 129; **23** 37*
Newtown (Y Drenewydd; Powys) **32** *780*, 783, 790
new towns *see under* TOWNS → types
New Vision Group **10** 833; **16** 2
New Wave **17** 91
New Wing Group **31** 454
New Wiśnicz **19** 751
New York **23** 37–50*; **25** 359; **31** *587*, 588, 724, *724*, *729*
42nd Street **22** 748
academies and art schools
American Academy of Arts and Letters **15** 30
American Academy of Fine Arts **23** 46
Beaux-Arts Institute of Design **32** 867
Columbian Academy of Painting **26** 466, 467
National Academy of Design **1** 106, 108; **2** 365; **6** 79; **22** 150; **23** 46, 50; **31** 669
exhibitions **7** 677
School of Visual Arts **25** 353
airports
Idlewild Airport *see* John F. Kennedy Airport
John F. Kennedy Airport
Pan-American Airways hangar **30** 468
Trans World Airlines Terminal **1** 495; **7** 696; **27** *128*, 129; **30** 853; **31** 597
La Guardia Airport **4** 863
Queens Airport **1** 495
apartment blocks
998 Fifth Avenue **2** 216
Alwyn Court **30** 507
New York
apartment blocks—cont.
Apthorp Building **7** 436
Dakota Apartments **2** 216
Stuyvesant Building **2** 216
Armory **2** 502
art forms and materials
architecture **31** 589
brick **4** 786
dioramas **8** 911
frames **11** 498
furniture **31** *621*, 623, 625, 626, 628, 631
glass **31** 642
graffiti **13** 270
interior decoration **31** 616, 617, 621
medals **20** 924
pewter **31** 651
portraits **23** 45–6
pottery **31** 634
sewing-machines **15** *821*
silver **31** 616, 646, 647, 648, 649
tapestries **30** 327; **31** 659, 661
wallpaper **32** 815
art market **2** 561; **20** 199; **31** 607, 608, 665
auction houses **2** 561
Battery **12** 136
Bettmann Archive **2** 364, 372
bridges
Brooklyn Bridge **4** 803; **16** 54; **23** *42*; **26** 524; **31** 594
George Washington Bridge **4** 803; **29** 250
Hell Gate Bridge **4** 803
Williamsburg Bridge **24** *674*
Bronx Developmental Center **1** 737
Bronx Zoo **33** 700
Brooklyn Carnival **5** 788
building regulations **5** 136
Burns Archive **24** 683
Carnegie Hall **7** 687, *688*
Cayman Gallery *see* museums → Museum of Contemporary Hispanic Art
cemeteries **20** 869
Greenwood Cemetery **6** 166; **31** 131
churches
Blessed Sacrement **31** 659
Cathedral of St John the Divine **7** 277; **8** *110*; **13** 757; **14** 317; **31** 595
crockets **8** 184
stained glass **29** 508
tapestries **26** 778
Cathedral of the Immaculate Conception **17** 877
Chapel of the Intercession **12** *927*
Church of the Pilgrims **31** *691*
Grace Episcopal Church **26** 212
Holy Trinity Episcopal Church **4** 788
Madison Square Presbyterian Church **30** 505
Riverside and Park Avenue Baptist Church **29** 515
St George's Episcopal Church **10** 103–4
St Patrick's Cathedral **7** 254; **13** 203; **26** *214*, 214
St Paul the Apostle **24** 281, *281*
St Peter's Lutheran Church
Erol Beker Chapel of the Good Shepherd **6** 460
St Thomas's **31** 595
Trinity Church, Wall Street **7** 254; **13** 203; **31** 592, 688, 689, *690*
Village Community Church **25** 267
cinemas
Roxy Cinema **7** 327
Strand Theater **7** 327
clubs
Century Club **7** 470

New York
clubs—cont.
Columbia Club 7 470
Harvard Club 7 470
Knickerbocker Club 7 470
Metropolitan Club 7 470
Montauk Club 30 505
University Club 7 470
Yacht Club 7 *470*, 470
Columbia Presbyterian Medical Center 14 783
Columbia University
Avery Architectural Memorial Library 2 367, 858; 4 23; 14 115; 29 871
library 4 23
Cooper Union Building 16 54
see also museums → Cooper-Hewitt Museum
Cornell Medical Center 14 783
Department of Cultural Affairs *see* museums → Huntington Hartford Art Gallery
exhibitions
Armory Show, 1913 2 311, 383, 447*, 633; 3 681; 8 571; 10 680; 17 725; 21 776; 23 *47*, 47–8; 25 553, 823; 31 588, 664; 33 516
commentaries 23 701
paintings 1 746; 2 383; 5 529, 567, 763; 8 577, 774; 9 355; 14 751; 17 764; 18 862; 24 223, 362, 709, 717; 27 462; 29 670; 31 605, 880; 32 798; 33 703
sculpture 4 660; 9 361; 22 425
Exhibition of the Industry of All Nations, 1853-4 15 883
Exhibitions of Independent Artists 10 680
World's Fair, 1939-40 8 802; 10 684; 15 883, 885; 27 422
Brazilian Pavilion 4 *713*; 15 886
Finnish Pavilion 1 *9*
Polish Pavilion 14 819
Works Progress Administration Pavilion 13 865
World's Fair, 1953 16 560
Factory, The 29 859
Federal Hall 25 267; 31 652
foundations
Alexis Gritchenko Foundation 14 819
Harmon Foundation 1 442
Rockefeller Foundation 22 677
galleries 23 46
291 Gallery 29 655–6; 31 605, 664; 32 798
An American Place 29 657
Art of this Century Gallery 23 *49*; 31 607, 665
Intimate Gallery 29 657
Macbeth Galleries 10 680
Madison Gallery 31 664
Nordness Gallery 3 170
Sidney Janis Gallery 16 906; 31 665
Gay Artists Alliance Building 12 218
Grant's Tomb 20 869, *869*
Great Iron Store 17 891
Gritchenko, Alexis, Foundation *see* foundations → Alexis Gritchenko Foundation
Halls of Justice 31 592
Harlem Community Art Center 23 48; 27 882
Haughwout Building 12 221; 23 *39*; 28 830; 31 592, *592*
hotels
American Hotel 14 787
Astor House 14 786, 787
Fifth Avenue Hotel 14 787
Helmsley Palace Hotel 14 788
Hotel Everett 14 787
Hotel Netherland 14 787

New York
hotels—cont.
Manhattan Hotel 31 659
Marriott Marquis Hotel 14 788
McAlpin Hotel 31 659
Park Avenue Hotel 17 891
St Regis Hotel 24 210
Waldorf-Astoria Hotel 14 788
houses 3 464; 4 786
Alfred Corning Clark House 11 144
Andrew Carnegie Residence 3 6
see also museums → Cooper-Hewitt Museum
Arden House 31 659
Frick Mansion *see under* museums → Frick Collection
Hamilton Fish House 15 408
John D. Rockefeller House
Moorish Smoking Room 22 60
675-9 St Mark's Avenue, Brooklyn 23 *40*
Stevens Mansion 8 *574*
Villard House 31 594
iconography 15 828
institutes
American Institute of Architects (A.I.A.) 2 315; 10 103, 104; 23 39; 31 691; 32 95
Institute of Architecture and Urban Studies 10 120
Iranian Institute 16 560
Leo Baeck Institute 2 372
Interborough Rapid Transit Company power station 25 402
Jacob K. Javits Convention Center 29 250
Jacques Marchais Center 30 821
Jewish Art Center 17 578
Jewish Theological Seminary 17 581
Lesbian and Gay Community Center 12 218
libraries
Avery Architectural Memorial Library *see under* Columbia University
Pierpont Morgan Library 22 111
catalogues 26 325
collections 9 231; 13 616; 22 112, 351; 24 846; 26 177
Public Library 19 319; 23 *41*
catalogues 4 22, 23, 26
collections 2 4, 858; 10 422; 16 557; 17 434
Schomberg Library 9 200
Woodside Library 4 863
Lincoln Plaza 11 347
Madison Square Garden 1 798; 30 505; 33 8
Masonic Mecca Temple 16 143
museums 31 666
American Museum of Natural History 1 437; 22 211, 673
collections 1 439; 9 719; 21 265; 22 673, 675, 679; 29 221, 222, 241
exhibitions 27 47
Asia House Galleries *see* Asia Society Galleries
Asia Society Galleries
collections 15 743
exhibitions 3 916; 15 747
Barnum's American Museum 31 666
Brooklyn Museum 13 757; 22 359; 23 46
architecture 31 598
archives 2 372
collections 7 156; 10 84, 90, 94; 15 745; 16 557; 18 4; 22 675, 795; 29 222; 31 616, 666; 33 193
exhibitions 10 94
Greek collection 13 470
Moorish Smoking Room *see under* houses → John D. Rockefeller House
Center of African Art 1 438, 440

New York
museums—cont.
Cloisters, The 9 25; 26 487–8
collections 3 250; 27 568; 29 516
Cooper-Hewitt Museum 14 174; 23 50; 31 668; 32 890
collections 12 585
directors 9 401
drawings 9 231
see also Cooper Union Building; houses → Andrew Carnegie Residence
Frick Collection 2 560; 11 774*; 23 48; 31 668
catalogues 6 78
collections 13 343; 23 369; 25 138; 31 480
Fragonard Room 11 369
gardens 12 143
Gallery of Fine Arts 26 75; 29 870
Guggenheim Museum *see* Solomon R. Guggenheim Museum
Hispanic Society of America Museum 15 30
library 29 83
Huntington Hartford Art Gallery 29 716
International Center of Photography 23 50
Isamu Noguchi Museum 23 177; 28 314
Jewish Museum 17 567, 581; 23 50
Kronos Collection 15 743
Metropolitan Museum of Art 1 731; 2 560; 10 81; 11 809; 14 616; 15 23, 30; 17 899; 18 523; 20 461; 22 210, 359, 366; 23 46, 50; 31 666, 667, 670; 32 95
African collection 1 437, 439; 9 64
American Wing 2 618; 31 632
Ancient Near East collection 1 896
archives 2 371
armour 2 450
Art Deco collection 2 522
Astor Court 12 93
Bache collection 3 18
Bliss collection 4 142
carpets 8 899; 16 554
ceramics 6 925
Chinese collection 6 735, 826; 7 156
collections 31 616
Crosby Brown Collection 22 376
Cycladic collection 8 324
Cypriot collection 8 366
doors 9 158
drawings 5 866; 9 231
Egyptian collection 10 83, 90, 91, 94
Etruscan collection 10 639, 640
exhibitions 1 438; 4 168; 6 322; 10 94; 15 748; 16 559; 24 683; 27 47
Francis W. Little House 31 *622*
Garbisch collection 12 54
Greek collection 13 470, 606
Hammer collection 14 117
Havemeyer collection 14 244; 18 672; 23 156
Indian collection 15 745
Iranian collection 15 922
Islamic collection 16 554, 557
ivory 1 114
Japanese collection 17 434
Kann collection 17 777
Korean collection 18 384
Lehman collection 13 745; 19 92
library 4 22

New York
museums
Metropolitan Museum of Art—cont.
Manney Parlour 31 620, *620*
Mesoamerican collection 21 310
Neuberger collection 22 917
north wing 26 480, *480*
paintings 2 560, 858; 4 318; 22 112; 29 651
periodicals 24 433
photographs 24 682, 683; 28 624; 31 875
pottery 13 542, 555
Powel Room 31 617, *618*
prints 10 422
reproductions 26 227
Robert Goldwater Library 1 440
Rockefeller collection 1 439; 26 489
Roman collection 27 46, 58, 115
rugs 16 554
Sala del Alcovo 29 831
sculpture 19 454
Seager Collection 21 692
Sicán collection 3 363
South American collection 29 221
South-east Asian collection 29 241
stained glass 29 516
Stieglitz Collection 29 657
Swiss Period Room 11 456
tapestries 30 332
terracotta 30 496
Textile Study Room 7 53
Untermeyer Collection 24 22
Wentworth Room 31 *616*, 617
Wilkinson collection 33 193
Wrightsman Galleries 33 416
see also Cloisters, The
MOMA (Museum of Modern Art) 2 560; 4 142; 14 396; 18 85; 22 360, 365; 23 48; 24 343; 26 488; 28 914; 29 716; 31 667, 668, 670
Abby Aldrich Rockefeller sculpture garden court 1 491; 17 620; 28 315
archives 2 371
ceramics 31 639
collections 8 804; 21 606; 26 489; 29 643
Department of Photography 1 143
directors 3 271; 30 120
exhibitions 15 885; 17 620; 22 677; 23 741; 24 683
frames 11 499
furniture 31 632
library 4 23
Native North American collection 22 679
paintings 7 245; 8 238; 9 200; 14 751; 17 620; 20 195, 524, 838; 24 715; 29 605
photographs 2 663; 21 788; 24 682
sculpture 12 922; 19 454; 30 140; 31 613
Sicán collection 28 652
Sidney and Harriet Janis collection 16 906
Museo del Barrio 18 833; 23 49
Museum for African Art 1 437
Museum of Contemporary Hispanic Art 18 833; 23 50
Museum of Holography 14 690
Museum of Living Art 12 15; 31 667
Museum of Natural History 32 95
Museum of Non-Objective Painting 13 800; 23 48; 31 607

New York
museums—cont.
Museum of Primitive Art 1 439; 26 489
Museum of the American Indian
collections 3 738; 15 30; 21 265; 22 673, 675; 29 222
exhibitions 22 678
Museum of the City of New York 23 49
New Museum of Contemporary Art 23 50
New York Gallery of the Fine Arts *see* New-York Historical Society
New-York Historical Society 31 666
collections 2 710; 10 94, 422; 23 46; 26 75, 539
New York Museum 24 304
Riverside Museum 5 746
Roerich Museum 7 838; 26 531
Society of St Tammany 31 666
Solomon R. Guggenheim Museum 9 19; 13 800, 801; 19 396; 22 367; 23 43, 48, 49; 24 548; 30 120; 31 668; 33 405
architecture 31 596
collections 21 710; 23 121; 26 58
Studio Museum 23 50
Whitney Museum of American Art 3 747; 4 762; 13 326; 22 366; 23 43, 48; 31 663, 668
collections 13 1; 14 752; 19 439; 22 917; 24 683
directors 13 1
exhibitions 13 327; 24 683
Yeshivah University Museum 17 582
National City Bank 3 177
National Park Bank 3 176, *176*
New School for Social Research 3 747; 31 702
New-York Historical Society *see under* museums
New York University
Museum of Living Art *see under* museums
parks and gardens
Brooklyn Botanic Garden
Ernest F. Coe Collection 17 368
Central Park 7 430; 23 420; 24 179, *180*; 31 725
bandstand 22 60
Belvedere Castle 11 243
Bethesda Foundation 29 583
Cleopatra's Needle 14 331; 23 331; 29 712
Gothic Dairy 11 243
New York Botanical Garden
Enid A. Haupt Conservatory 7 745
Paley Park 11 347
Prospect Park 23 *420*
Post Office 31 593
prisons
Auburn Prison 25 637
Sing Sing Prison 25 637
Produce Exchange 28 830; 30 505
Radio City Music Hall *see under* skyscrapers → Rockefeller Center
Sherman Monument 22 48
shops
Arnold Constable 30 741
Barney's 32 501
Bloomingdales 32 501
Gimbel's 30 507
Laing Stores 16 54
Lord & Taylor 2 522
Macy's 8 770
Saks Fifth Avenue 32 501
shrine of Keteri Tekakwitha 28 632

New York—cont.
shrine of St Elizabeth Ann Seton **28** 632
shrine of St Frances Xavier Cabrini **28** 632
skyscrapers **3** 464; **23** 41; **28** 831, 833; **31** 595
American Radiator Building **30** 507, *507*
American Surety Building **28** 831
AT&T building **7** 386; **23** 359; **25** *359*; **28** 835; **31** 598
Bank of Tokyo *see* American Surety Building
Battery Park City **23** *44*
Bayard Condict Building **30** 505, *506*
Celadon building **30** 505
Central Bank Building **28** 831
Chase Manhattan Bank **3** 177; **31** 597, 665
sculpture garden **28** 314
Chrysler Building **2** 522; **16** 56; **23** 359; **28** 833, *833*; **31** 596, 855
Daily News Building **14** *735*; **28** 833
Empire State Building **7** 766; **14** 563; **23** 359; **28** 629, *629*, 833; **31** 596
Equitable Life Assurance Company Building **12** 643; **25** 327; **28** 831; **31** 593
Flat Iron Building **16** 55; **30** 507
Fred F. French Building **2** 643
Gillender Building **28** 831
Goelet Building **2** 522
Heron Tower **28** 835
IBM Building
sculpture garden **28** 314
Knickerbocker Trust Company **3** 176
Lever House **5** 175; **12** 792; **15** *887*; **23** 359; **28** 818, 834; **31** 597
Manhattan Life Insurance Co. Building **28** 830
Manufacturers' Hanover Trust **3** 177
McGraw-Hill Building **5** *136*; **28** 833
Metropolitan Life Insurance Building **28** 833
Municipal Building **31** 242
New York Tribune Building **28** 831; **31** 593
Park Row building **26** 468
RCA Building *see under* Rockefeller Center
Rockefeller Center **7** 838; **14** 199; **26** *488*; **31** 662
murals **25** 653
Prometheus Fountain **20** 299; **22** 49
Radio City Music Hall **1** 738; **2** 522; **30** 678
RCA Building **28** 833
Seagram Building **12** 792; **23** 359; **28** 834; **31** 597; **33** 246
Four Seasons Restaurant **9** 20; **27** 222
Singer Building **11** 144; **28** 833; **31** 595
Sony Building *see* AT&T building
Tower Building **28** 830, 831
United Nations Secretariat building **8** 278; **13** 238, *238*; **14** 200; **15** 887
tapestries **30** 328
Woolworth Building **12** *614*, 614–15; **16** 55; **27** 129; **28** 833; **30** 507; **31** 595
World Financial Center **23** *44*
World Trade Center **23** *44*; **27** 216; **28** 834
New York—cont.
stations
Grand Central Terminal **3** 464, 693; **31** 728; **32** 866–7
Metro stations **21** 349
Pennsylvania Station **25** 268, 857; **31** 595
Statue of Liberty **3** 290, *290*; **6** 500; **20** 31; **22** 42, 47; **29** 566
Studio Building **15** 21; **29** 857
studios **29** 858
synagogues **31** 649
Shearith Israel synagogue **17** 548
Temple Emanu-El (destr. 1901) **22** 60
Temple Emanu-El (1929) **17** 547, 582
tenements **30** 458
Clark Tenements **30** 458
theatres **30** 677
Casino Theater **18** 54; **22** 60
Metropolitan Opera House **30** 684
State Theater **30** 684
Vivian Beaumont Repertory Theater **30** 684
Ziegfeld Theater **30** 684
United State Warehouse Corporation Grain Elevator **13** 274
urban planning **31** 723, 724, 729
US Army Warehouse **32** 861
US Custom House **12** 614
water supply **2** 242
New York and New England Railway **31** 464
New York Ballet Society **8** 270
New York *Centauromachy*, Painter of the **13** 524
New York Central Railroad **32** 866
New York Correspondence School of Art **7** 895; **17** 621
New York Dada **8** 435; **24** 428
New York Etchers Club **25** 629
New York Evening Journal **3** 680
New York Five **23** 50–51*
members **10** 120; **13** 325, 883; **14** 325; **21** 56; **26** 16
New York Kouros **13** 606
New York Life Insurance Co. **14** 223; **20** 18; **31** 659
New York Magazine **12** 772
New York Photogravure Company **7** 575
New York Rubber Co. **31** 260
New York school **1** 78; **11** 729; **13** 11, 12; **14** 175; **22** 206
members **13** 214
works **11** *730*
New York situla *see* PIERPONT MORGAN SITULA
New York State College of Ceramics **31** 669
New York Terra Cotta Company **30** 505
New York Times **24** 425
New York Water Color Society **14** 536; **33** 43
New Zealand **23** 51–76*, *52*, *711*
adobe **32** 308
architecture **23** 53–7*, *56*, 717
Art Deco **22** *468*
vernacular **32** 307–9*
archives **2** 371*
bronze **23** 63, *63*, *67*, *72*; **33** *374*
ceramics **23** 68–70*
chapels **23** *56*
churches **23** 53, *53*
collections **23** 74–5*
corrugated iron **32** 308
cups **23** *71*
curtain walls **23** 56
dyeing **23** 74
earthenwares **23** *69*
education (art) **23** 75*
flax **23** 73*, 712
furniture **23** 65–8*
glass **23** 56, 70*
New Zealand—cont.
gold **23** 70–72*
greenstone *see* nephrite
interior decoration **23** 63–5*, *64*
kauri **23** 65, *67*
libraries **23** 76*
marks **23** 71
medals **23** *72*
metalwork **23** 70*, 72–3*
museums **23** 74–5*
nephrite **16** 861
oak **23** *67*
painting **23** 57–62*
landscape **23** *60*
watercolours **23** 57, 58
20th cent. **7** *210*; **23** *61*
patronage **23** 74–5*
periodicals **24** 437–8*
photoarchives **23** 76
photography **23** 57
pisé de terre **32** 308
portraits **23** *59*; **33** *374*
pottery **23** *68*
railway stations **23** *55*
rimu **23** 67
rock art **23** 728–9
scrimshaw **28** 302
sculpture **23** 62–3*, *63*; **33** *374*
secretaires **23** *66*
silk **23** 74*
silver **23** 70–72*, *71*
spinning (textile) **23** 74
tables **23** *67*
tapestries **23** *74*
textiles **23** 73–4*
timber structures **23** 54
universities **2** *706*
weaving **23** 74
wood **23** *53*, 717
wool **23** 73–4*, *74*
see also MAORI
New Zealand Company **23** 51, 57
New Zealand Glass and Pottery Co. **23** 70
New Zealand Glassware Co. **23** 70
New Zealand Insulators *see* TEMUKA POTTERY
New Zealand Railways
pottery **23** *68*
New Zealand Woollen Manufactory Co. **23** 73
Nexemperger, Giovanni *see* NIESENBERGER, HANS
Nexon **13** 168
reliquary of St Ferreolus **11** 623
Next Interiors **10** 315
Ney, Marshal **22** 103
Neye, Carl **21** 820
Neyelov (family) **25** 746
Neyelov, Il'ya (Vasil'yevich) **12** 134; **23** 76*; **25** 746; **26** 403; **27** 579; **31** 828
Neyelov, Peter (Vasil'yevich) **25** 746
Neyelov, P. I. **18** 36; **31** 551
Neyelov, Vasily (Ivanovich) **12** 134; **23** 76*; **25** 746
Neyra, Pedro Domínguez *see* DOMÍNGUEZ NEYRA, PEDRO
Neyt, Herman de **23** 76*
dealing **3** 615
Neyts, Gillis **23** 77*
Nezahuacóyotl, King of Tetzcoco (*reg* 1431-72) **12** 71; **30** 531
Nezahua'pilli
works **21** *261*
Nezhin *see* NIZHYN
Nezhnie, Muriel **31** 661
Nezó, João Carlos **27** 809
Nez Perce **22** 649, 669
Nezu, Kaichirō **17** 429
Nezval, Viteslav **30** 22
Ngaang Lobsang Gyatso *see* DALAI LAMA, 5th
Ngaba **21** 593
Ngada **9** 164; **15** 814; **23** 554
Ngaju **1** 817; **15** 789; **20** 181
Ngan, Wayne **32** 414
Ngangalala
sculpture **1** *45*
Ngangela **1** 403
Nganjmira, Robin
works **1** *59*
Nganjuk **15** 801
Ngao, Wat Huad **30** 586
Ngaruwahia, Turangawaewae Marae **23** 63
Ngata, Apirana **30** 238
Ngatane, Ephraim (Mojalefa) **29** 108
Ngati Tarawhai, Tene Waitere of *see* WAITERE, TENE
Ngbaka **1** 351, 404, 405
Ngbandi **1** 256, 360, 404, 405
Ngeaur **23** 832
Ngecha **17** 907
Ngelima **1** 311, 406
Ngende **18** 484
Ngenga **30** 418
Ngengele **19** 72
Ng Eng Teng **28** 774
Ngere *see* WE
Ngeruklabel **23** 832
Nggala **24** 67
Nghi Ve Tomb **21** 595
Ng Kah Onn, Patrick **20** 172
Ngnetchopa, Jean-Baptiste **5** 524
N'Gom, Alexis **28** 406
Ngombe **1** 360, 406; **18** 484
Ngongo **18** 484
Ngoni **20** 161
Ngor *see* NOR
Ngove **11** 878
Ngozi **5** 285
Ngulayngulay, Dick **23** 77*
Ngulmarrmarr **21** 620
Ngumba **10** 787, 789–90
works **1** *397*
Ngungulu **30** 418
Nguni **1** 281; **22** 712; **29** 104; **33** 678, 723, 724
architecture **1** 308, 414
beadwork **1** 298, 419
dolls **1** 419
staffs **1** 417
Nguu **1** 273, 418
Nguyen, Minh Mang *see* MINH MANG, Emperor
Nguyen Dang (family) **32** 481
Nguyen Gia Tri **32** 482, 483
Nguyen Hoang, Ruler of Hue (*reg* 1558-1613) **14** 844
Nguyen Kim **32** 488
Nguyen Sang **32** 483, 484
Nguyen Si Ngoc **32** 482
Nguyen Trung **32** 483
Nguyen Tu Nghiem **32** 482, 483
works **32** *484*
Ngwa **15** 111
Ngwane **33** 723
Ng Yiu-chung **14** 722
Ngynamau **33** 596
N.H., Master **8** 67
Nhan van **32** 483
Nharo San *see* SAN
Nha Trang **6** *418*; **23** 77*; **29** *225*
Po Nagar **6** 418, *418*, 419, 420, 421, 423; **23** 77
sculpture **6** 427
tiles **6** 432
Vo Canh stele **23** 77
Nhieu textiles *see under* TEXTILES → types
Niagara Falls (Ont.; Canada) **5** *559*
Art Gallery and Museum **5** 590
Niagara Falls (NY; USA) **9** 505; **31** *602*
Native American Cultural Center **22** 671
suspension bridge **26** *523*, 524; **30** 467
Niagara-on-the-Lake (Ont.), St Andrew **4** 787
Niamey **1** *386*
cotton **23** *128*
Niamey—cont.
Handicrafts Centre and Cultural Activities Centre **23** 128
Musée National du Niger **23** 128
Niankhkhnum **10** 50; **27** 812
tomb **27** *811*
Niankhpepi **9** 838
Niankhra **9** 859
Nian Xiyao **6** 40, 908; **17** 589
Nias **15** *751*
altars **1** 706
architecture **15** 756
drums (musical instruments) **15** 817
houses **15** 774–5
jewellery **15** 814
ornament **23** 555
sarcophagi **27** 831; **31** 115
sculpture **15** 776, 788–9
textiles **15** 795
Niasviž **3** *525*, 526
Jesuit church **3** 526, 528; **19** 496; **25** 97
Jesuit college **25** 140
Radziwiłł Palace **19** 496
Niaux **6** 469; **11** *505*; **23** 77–8*; **25** *470*, 476, 477, 484, 487
rock art **25** *478*
Nibbrig, F(erdinand) Hart **14** 294; **23** 78*
Nibby, Antonio **8** 616; **23** 78–9*; **29** 640
collaboration **12** 244
works **26** 785
nib mouldings *see under* MOULDINGS → types
nibs *see* PENS
Nicaea *see* IZNIK
Nicaise, Saint **26** 114
Nicander **9** 618
Nicaragua **21** 177; **23** *79*, 79–86*; **29** 123
architecture **23** 80–81*
bowls **23** *83*
cathedrals **23** 80, *81*
collections **23** 84–5*
dealing **23** 84–5*
education (art) **23** 85–6*
exhibitions **23** 84
galleries (iv) (art) **23** 84
gold **23** 83*
jewellery **23** 83*
libraries **23** 86*
marks **23** 83
museums **23** 85*
painting **22** 335*; **23** 81–2*
naive art **23** *82*
patronage **23** 84*
pottery **23** 82–3*, *83*
sculpture **23** 81; **29** 145
silver **23** 83*
Nicasio, Alberto **2** 399
Niccolaio (Niccolò detto Scalcagna), Michele di *see* MICHELE DA FIRENZE
Niccoli, Niccolò **14** 867; **16** 658; **23** 86*
collections **21** 468
manuscripts **21** 10
works **16** 614
Niccolini, Antonio **23** 87–8*
collaboration **8** 806
patrons and collectors **22** 473, 474
works **12** 657; **16** 730; **23** *88*
Niccolini, Fausto **23** 88
Niccolini, Filippo (1586-1666) **23** 87
Niccolini, Filippo (1655-1738) **23** 87
Niccolini, Giovanni **3** 161; **23** 87*
Niccolini *Madonna* **23** 87
Niccolò II, 10th Marchese of Ferrara (*reg* 1361-88) **3** 298; **10** 517–18*, *518*; **11** 2
Niccolò III, 12th Marchese of Ferrara (*reg* 1393-1441) **10** 517–19*, *518*; **13** 754
architecture **11** 2

Niccolò III, 12th Marchese of Ferrara (*reg* 1393-1441)—cont.
dress 31 429
manuscripts 3 531
paintings 1 554; 3 648
tapestries 11 5; 16 756
Niccolò (*fl c.* 1106-40) *see* Nicholaus
Niccolò (*fl* 1365) 23 94
Niccolò, Andrea di *see* Andrea di Niccolò
Niccolò, Arrigo di *see* Arrigo di Niccolò
Niccolò, Domenico di *see* Domenico di Niccolò
Niccolò, Francesco di *see* Francesco di Niccolò
Niccolò, Giovanni 17 182, 513
Niccolò, Giovanni di *see* Giovanni di Niccolò
Niccolò (di Martino), Lorenzo di *see* Lorenzo di Niccolò (di Martino)
Niccolò Alunno di Alife 23 505
Niccolò Aretino *see* Spinelli, Niccolò
Niccolò da Foligno 21 414; 23 89*
Niccolò da Gubbio 24 781
Niccolò da Lorena *see* Cordier, Nicolas
Niccolò da Padova, Battista di *see* Battista di Niccolò da Padova
Niccolò da Prato, Cardinal 9 348
Niccolò da Ragusa *see* Niccolò dell'Arca
Niccolò da Siena 23 93
Niccolò da Uzzano 4 31
Niccolò da Varallo 11 292
Niccolò del Cavallo *see* Baroncelli, Niccolò
Niccolò dell'Arca 4 276; 23 89–90*
works 4 278; 18 677; 21 433; 23 *90*; 24 868; 30 498
Niccolò di Bartolomeo da Foggia *see* Nicola di Bartolomeo da Foggia
Niccolò di Buonaccorso 23 90–91*
works 23 *91*
Niccolò di Forzore Spinelli *see* Spinelli, Niccolò di Forzore
Niccolò di Giacomo da Bologna 4 274; 16 848; 20 695; 23 91–2*
works 2 18; 23 *92*
Niccolò di Giovanni Fiorentino 23 92–3*; 31 359
attributions 4 736
collaboration 1 604; 31 359
works 8 175, 178; 12 668; 14 885; 23 *93*
Niccolò di Goro 22 801
Niccolò di Lutero, Battista di *see* Dossi, Battista
Niccolò di Lutero, Giovanni di *see* Dossi, Dosso
Niccolò di Naldo (da Norcia) 3 707; 23 93*
Niccolò di Paolo 28 687
Niccolò di Pietro 13 95; 23 94*; 33 614
attributions 32 205
works 23 *94*
Niccolò di Pietro Gerini 13 149; 23 94–5*; 29 406
collaboration 7 338; 19 678; 24 849
patrons and collectors 8 535; 11 892
pupils 19 678
works 11 380; 23 *95*
Niccolò di Segna 5 164; 9 306; 28 365
Niccolò di ser Sozzo 13 149; 19 753; 23 95–6*
Niccolò di Ulisse 23 93
Niccolò Fiorentino *see* Spinelli, Niccolò di Forzore
Niccolò Pisano 23 96*
Nice
carnivals 5 787
Musée des Beaux-Arts 6 550
Musée Matisse 2 370; 20 831
Musée National Marc Chagall 2 370
Musée National Message Biblique Marc Chagall 6 386
observatory 23 342, *342*
Villa des Arènes *see* Musée Matisse
Nice, R. van 9 527
Nicephoros I, Emperor of Byzantium (*reg* 802-11) *see* Nikephoros I, Emperor of Byzantium
Nicephoros Ischyrios 2 602
Niceron, François 24 491
Nice Style 20 27
Nicetas Choniates 13 808
Nichegoki group 8 437
niches
historical and regional traditions
Central Asia, Western 16 161
Early Christian (*c.* AD 250-843) 31 *434*
England 10 263; 13 82
Gothic 13 82
Iran 16 161
Islamic 16 161
Italy 9 21
Mesopotamia 31 *434*
Rome, ancient 22 161; 26 923, *923*
Turkey 26 *923*; 31 *434*
materials
brick 4 769
types
conch 7 688*
nicchione 23 86*
uses
altarpieces 28 133
display of art 9 21
urns 9 29
Nichinan, Cultural Centre 7 695
Nichini *see* Anichini
Nichiren 5 90, 119; 17 22, 747
Nichiren Buddhism *see under* Buddhism → sects
Nichirō 17 747
Nichokuan Soga *see* Soga Nichokuan
Nichol, Oliver de *see* Oliver de Nichol
Nicholas (*fl c.* 1100) 26 657
Nicholas (*fl* 17th cent.) 21 345
Nicholas, Archbishop of Bari (*fl* after 1050) 3 234
Nicholas, Archbishop of Ohrid (*fl* 1346-50) 23 374; 28 448
Nicholas I, Emperor of Russia (*reg* 1825-55) 12 606; 18 124; 26 733–4*; 27 439, 579; 31 461; 33 669
architecture 3 733; 21 127; 31 140
paintings 1 650; 5 69; 7 896; 11 783; 13 779; 28 509
porphyry 30 113
sculpture 27 831; 30 459
stained glass 29 515
Nicholas II, Emperor of Russia (*reg* 1894-1917) 8 531; 10 722; 21 98; 25 648; 26 734–5*; 30 367
paintings 11 156
Nicholas III, Pope (*reg* 1277-81) 23 575, 576*
architecture 26 811
gold 9 657
sculpture 7 923
Nicholas IV, Pope (*reg* 1288-92) 2 632; 23 96*
architecture 26 821, 832
enamel 10 194; 13 169
metalwork 2 632; 13 163, 775
mosaics 26 765; 31 192
painting 13 144, 145
Nicholas V, Pope (*reg* 1447-55) 1 560; 23 96–7*; 26 765
architecture 12 112; 16 630, 631; 24 399
churches 4 650; 16 631; 26 755, 800, 801, 804, 835
palaces 26 755, 811
urban planning 24 398; 26 756; 27 271
books 14 867
frescoes 2 37
gold 24 36
paintings 32 655
sculpture 24 28
tapestries 26 778
Nicholas, Benjamin 3 624
Nicholas, Peter 32 788
Nicholas Abbey 5 749
Nicolás de Southampton *see* Nicolás de Antona
Nicholas of Cusa 2 354; 4 752; 12 812; 14 867; 19 356
Nicholas of Strasbourg 20 564
Nicholas of Verdun 23 97–100*
attributions 1 653; 7 591
paintings 13 *151*
pupils 14 854
works 2 792, 819; 3 567; 7 583; 13 151, 168; 18 139; 22 269; 23 *98*, *99*; 26 146, 683, 694; 31 217, 499
Nicholas van Maelbecke 10 710
Nicholas von Ybbs 13 186
Nicholas Wurmser of Strasbourg *see* Wurmser of Strasbourg, Nicholas
Nicholaus 11 3; 13 804; 23 101*; 26 619, 620, 621, 622; 32 343
patrons and collectors 19 708; 20 820
teachers 33 188
works 11 5; 16 687; 18 226; 24 695; 26 595; 32 342, *344*, 344
workshop 18 226
Nicholaus von Stettin (*fl* 1392) 11 253
Nicholl, Andrew 3 537; 16 16; 23 102*
Nicholl, S. J. 29 695
Nicholl, William 23 102
Nichollò de Bari *see* Niccolò dell'Arca
Nicholls, Henry 4 476
Nicholls, Joseph *see* Nickolls, Joseph
Nicholls, Thomas 5 194; 17 610; 29 797; 31 131
Nicholls, Walter 5 336
Nicholls & Plincke 27 420, 584
Nicholo da Fiorenza *see* Baroncelli, Niccolò
Nichols, Daniel Cubitt 24 560
Nichols, George Ward 15 859
Nichols, J. C., Company 17 799; 28 622
Nichols, John (*fl* 1822; publisher) 14 280
Nichols, John (*fl* 19th cent.; architect) 27 613
Nichols, Maria Longworth 27 132; 31 638
Nichols, Rose Standish 7 876
Nicholson, Annabel 10 688
Nicholson, Ben 11 877; 14 401; 23 103–4*; 32 328
groups and movements 19 591
7 & 5 Society 10 257; 28 506
Abstraction-Création 1 90
Constructivism 7 772
Cubism 8 246
St Ives group 1 77; 27 563
Unit One 10 258; 31 673
patrons and collectors 9 716; 13 629; 28 274
pupils 18 754
teachers 19 591
works 10 *257*; 23 *104*; 27 *562*
writings 7 772
Nicholson, Charles 12 926
Nicholson, Christopher 5 924
Nicholson, Francis (*fl* 1688-98) 2 120–21; 31 721; 33 206
Nicholson, Francis (1753-1844) 23 104–5*; 32 903
patrons and collectors 14 598
works 29 735
Nicholson, Grace 3 737, 738; 14 510; 22 660
Nicholson, J. 31 239
Nicholson, James 5 514
Nicholson, Michael Angelo 23 105; 26 85
Nicholson, Peter 10 208; 12 773; 23 105*; 26 85; 30 741
Nicholson, Richard 33 545
Nicholson, W. A. (*fl* early 19th cent.) 31 239
Nicholson, William (1781-1844) 22 530
works 32 *501*
Nicholson, William (Newzam Prior) (1872-1949) 23 102*, 259; 33 369
collaboration 25 674
pupils 8 109
teachers 14 454
works 4 364; 25 245, 347; 33 361
Nicholson, Winifred 23 102–3*; 27 317; 28 506
Nichoria, House IV.1 13 396, *396*
nickel 3 *402*; 21 319
Nickel, Hanns 14 573
nickel-brass 7 539
Nickele, Isaac van 2 342
Nickelen, Jan van 33 280
nickel-silver 10 135
Nicker, Jan *see* Nicquet, Jan
Nickerie 30 *12*, 15
Nickolls, Joseph 23 105*
Nickolls, Trevor 1 65; 23 105–6*
Nickson & Borys 10 131; 15 56
Niclausse, Paul 11 568, 569
Nicodemus 23 106*; 26 469
collaboration 26 469
works 26 534, 625
Nicodim, Ion 23 106*; 26 721
Nicol, A. W. 2 318
Nicol, Erskine 23 106–7*; 28 237, 238
Nicol, Miranda Burney 28 691, 692, 693
Nicola *see* Nicolaus
Nicola, Norberto 4 724
Nicola da Guardiagrele *see* Gallucci, Nicola
Nicola da Monteforte 13 98
Nicola de Apulia *see* Pisano (i), Nicola
Nicola di Bartolomeo da Foggia 13 98; 23 107*; 25 724
Nicola di Gabriele Sbraghe *see* Sbraghe, Nicola di Gabriele
Nicola di Maestro Antonio (di Ancona) 23 107–8*
Nicolae of Cluj 26 710
Nicolai, Elias 23 108*; 26 712; 28 649
Nicolai, (Christoph) Friedrich 3 799; 23 108*; 24 443
Nicolai, Georg Hermann 19 457; 23 108*
Nicolai, Nicolas, I *see* Juvenal, Nicolas, I
Nicolaï-Chaillet, Cora 22 869
Nicolaides, Kimon 23 12
Nicolao, Giovanni *see* Niccolò, Giovanni
Nicolao, Johannes *see* Johannes Nicolao
Nicolao da Noceto 7 296
Nicolao Florentino *see* Delli, Niccolò
Nicolas, Abbot 27 254
Nicolas, Mathurin 33 357
Nicolas, Nicholas Harris 3 421
Nicolas d'Amiens *see* Dipre, Nicolas
Nicolás de Antona 13 106
Nicolás de Biedma, Bishop of Jaén 16 863
Nicolas de Bonaventure 20 566; 21 530
Nicolas de Chaume 5 666
Nicolas de Moustier 20 645
Nicolas d'Ypres *see* Dipre, Nicolas
Nicolás Fiorentino *see* Delli, Dello
Nicola *talapiera* 11 712
Nicolau, Pere 23 109*; 29 276
collaboration 20 383
pupils 24 455
works 9 108; 20 383
Nicolaus (*b* 1138) 23 109*
Nicolaus (*fl* 1347) 28 860
Nicolaus Claus 25 434
Nicolaus de Angelo 23 109*; 26 624
collaboration 32 75
works 26 624, 821
Nicolaus de Apulia *see* Niccolò dell'Arca
Nicolaus Glaser 25 434
Nicolaus le Rouge *see* La Fosse, Louis Rémy de
Nicolay, Président de 20 295
Nicolay, L. de 11 111
Nicolay, Nicolas de 8 549; 19 64
Nicole, Duchess of Lorraine (*fl* 1640) 17 449
Nicole, Nicolas 23 110*
Nicoletti, Franesco 5 552
Nicoletto da Modena 23 110*; 25 625
works 13 700; 16 750; 29 311, 747
Nicoletto Rosex *see* Nicoletto da Modena
Nicoli, Carlo 13 764
Nicolin, Pierluigi 13 629
Nicolino di Giovanni da Campione 5 551
Nicoll, Archibald 23 60; 33 24
Nicolle, Emile-Frédéric 9 354; 32 576
Nicolle, Joseph 9 312; 28 524
Nicolò Coccari da Firenze 3 261
Nicolò da Cesena 3 858
Nicolò da Venezia 21 533
Nicolò da Voltri 3 249; 23 110–11*; 28 656
Nicolò de Marzi *see* Desmarz, Nicolaus
Nicolò di Francia 20 323
Nicolò di Lombarduccio *see* Corso, Nicolò (di Lombarduccio)
Nicolò of Zadar 24 29
Nicolo Rugina Greco da Corfu 32 160
Nicolson, Harold 12 142; 27 494
Nicolson, Robin 8 256
Nicolson, William 28 237
Nicoluccio d'Antonio 22 799
Nicomachi 9 3
Nicomachorum-Symmachorum Diptych 9 647, 649; 18 825
Nicomedes 10 415
Nicomedia *see under* Izmit
Nicopolis-ad-Istrum 5 145, 155; 18 243; 26 *906*
agora 26 907
Nicosia 8 *325*, 361; 23 111–12*; 32 *158*
Arabahmet Mosque 8 364
Archbishop Makarios III Foundation Cultural Centre Byzantine Museum 8 367
Bank of Cyprus Museum of the History of Cypriot Coinage 8 367
bastion 3 359
Bedesten 8 362
Cathedral of St Sophia 8 361, 362; 23 111–12*, *112*
Cyprus Jewellers Museum 8 367

Nicosia—cont.
  Cyprus Museum **8** 366
  Cyprus State Art Gallery **8** 367; **11** 334
  Dominican Monastery **8** 361
  Ethnological Museum **8** 364, 367
  Famagusta Gate
    Municipal Cultural Centre **8** 367
  Folk Art Collection **8** 366
  fortifications **21** 550, 565; **32** 159
  Hagios Ioannis **8** 364
  Hagios Loukas **9** 627
  House of the Dragoman
    Hadjigeorgakis Kornessios *see* Ethnological Museum
  interior decoration **8** 365
  Lapidary Museum **8** 367
  Leventis Municipal Museum **8** 367
  Mansion of Dervish Pasha **8** 367
  metalwork **8** 365
  Mevlevi Tekke **8** 367
  Municipal Art Centre **8** 367
  Palazzo Pubblico **14** 420
  Panagia Chrysaliniotissa **9** 623, 627, 629
  Panagia Hodegetria *see* Bedesten
  Popular Bank Cultural Centre **8** 367
  Selimye Mosque *see* Cathedral of St Sophia
  silver **8** 365
  textiles **8** 366
Nicot, L.-H. **11** 568
Nicquet, Jacques **23** 112–13; **26** 283
Nicquet, Jan **23** 112*; **26** 283
Niculiţel **26** 719
  church **26** 706
Niculoso (Pisano), Francisco **16** 734; **29** 325; **30** 880, 882
Nicz-Borowiak, Maria **4** 148; **25** 422
Niczky, Rolf **24** 591
Nidaros *see* TRONDHEIM
Nidau, Rudolph of Neuchâtel, Count of **24** 36
Nidda, Heiliggeistkirche **19** 815
Niddry **31** 230
Niderviller **11** *504*; **29** 573
  ceramics **23** 113*
  faience (ii) (ceramics) **11** 606
  porcelain **11** 607, 609
Ni Duan **6** 817
Nieborów **23** 113*; **25** *92*, 138
  furniture **25** 121
  gardens **12** 134
  palace **23** 113
Nieborów faience factory **23** 113; **25** 123
Nieborowski (family) **23** 113
Niebuhr, Carsten **1** 895; **16** 547; **23** 114*; **33** 520
Niederaltaich Monastery **12** 371
Niederdollendorf **21** 164
  stone-carvings **21** *164*
Niederdonven **19** 826
Niederer, Roberto **30** 145
Niederhaslach Abbey **13** 180
Niederhäusern, Auguste de **23** 114*; **30** 138
Niedermayr, Johann Josef **2** 816; **32** 449
Niedermayr, Matthias **32** 449
Niedermoser, Otto **2** 810, 815
Niederrotweil Altarpiece **20** 796–7
Niederwildungen Altarpiece **7** *722*, 722–3, *723*, 724; **19** 528, 529
Niederzier **6** 160
Niegeman, Johan **18** 25, 435; **22** 869
Niehaus, Charles H. **3** 31; **33** 42
Niehus, Walter **33** 736
niello **12** 869; **23** 114–15; **28** 740
  historical and regional traditions
    Anglo-Saxon **2** *80*; **10** 322, 381
    Austria **21** I3
    Byzantine **10** 381
niello
  historical and regional traditions—cont.
    Central Asia, Western **6** 274
    Denmark **32** *516*
    Egypt, ancient **9** 818; **10** 381
    England **2** *80*; **10** 322
    Greece, ancient **10** 381
    Islamic **16** 364
    Italy **11** *86*; **16** 750*
    Phoenician **5** 332
    Rome, ancient **10** 381; **27** 102
    Russia **27** 419, 420, 421, 422
    Scandinavia **32** *516*
    Syria-Palestine **30** 195
    Ukraine **31** 562
    Viking **32** *516*
  technical examination **30** 409
  uses
    brooches **2** *80*
    cups **32** *516*
    jewellery **6** 274
    metalwork **21** 329
    paxes **11** *86*
    teapots **21** I3
niello prints *see under* PRINTS → types
Nielsen, Ejnar (August) **14** 297; **23** 116*
Nielsen, Elmar Moltke **11** 793
Nielsen, Fabby K. J.
  works **1** *409*
Nielsen, Harald **17** 479
Nielsen, Jais **8** 736, 748
Nielsen, Jørn **13** 850
Nielsen, Kai **23** 116*
  house **3** 749
  works **8** 741, *741*; **24** 549
Nielsen, Orla Juul **8** 749
Nieman, Leroy **18** 822
Niemann, George **18** 517
Niembo **14** 376, 377, 378
Niemcewicz, Count **13** 690
Niemen Glassworks **25** 124
Niemeyer, Adelbert **12** 437
Niemeyer, Erna **9** 758
Niemeyer (Soares Filho), Oscar **8** 8; **23** 117–20*; **32** 855
  architecture **4** 713, 714; **5** 218; **12** 380; **18** 786; **24** 291
    arts centres **19** 91
    cathedrals **12** 793, *794*; **19** 365
    churches **23** *118*
    exhibition architecture **4** *713*
    government buildings **4** *712*, 714; **13** 238; **23** *119*
    museums **26** 414
    pavilions **7** 258
    public buildings **4** 679, 726; **7** 696; **27** 808
    university buildings **16** 566
  collaboration **4** 214, 713; **5** 218; **8** 7; **11** 75; **12** 665, 793; **14** 200; **22** 95; **25** 663; **26** 109, 414; **31** 398
  furniture **4** 721
  groups and movements **15** 886
  pupils **26** 286
  staff **28** 374
Niemeyer-Holstein, Otto **23** 120*
Nien Hsi-yao *see* NIAN XIYAO
Nienhuis, Bert **18** 878; **22** 883, 896; **23** 120–21*
Nienhuis, Lambertus *see* NIENHUIS, BERT
Niépce, Claude **23** 121
Niépce, Isidore **8** 450
Niépce, (Joseph) Nicéphore **5** 519; **23** 121*; **24** 646, 655, 658; **25** 617, 618
  attributions **12** 486
  methods **10** 558
  works **8** 450
Niépce de Saint-Victor, Claude Abel Félix **24** 651
Nieper, Ludwig **27** 141
Niepołomice Church **25** 134
Nieremberg, Fray **2** 398
Nieremberg, Juan Eusebio **17** 470, 471
Nierendorf, Karl **13** 800; **23** 7, 121*
Niermans, Edouard (1904-84) **23** 122*
Niermans, Edouard Jean (1859-1928) **13** 798; **23** 121–2*; **28** 867
Niermans, Jean (Karl) **23** 122*
Niesenberger, Hans **11** 750; **13** 329; **21** 532; **23** 122–3*
Niesołowski, Tymon **11** 317
Niesse **21** 571
Niestlé, Jean Bloé **4** 132
Niestronno **25** 119
Nieto, Alonso **7** 492; **18** 681
Nieto, Leonardo Alenza y *see* ALENZA Y NIETO, LEONARDO
Nietzsche, Friedrich (Wilhelm) **1** 181; **8** 596; **23** 123*
  works **1** 174; **2** 517
Nietzschmann, János **9** 754
Nieuenhuys, Christian-Johannes **7** 490
Nieuhoff, Jan **23** 776; **25** 10; **26** 492
Nieukercke, Loys van **3** 598
Nieukerken, J. J. van **3** 431
Nieulandt, Adriaen van **18** 227; **22** 841; **23** 124*
  patrons and collectors **14** 370; **28** 358
  works **14** 543
Nieulandt, Jacob van **23** 124
Nieulandt, Willem van, I (1560-1626) **17** 3; **22** 841; **23** 124
Nieulandt, Willem van, II (1584-?1635) **23** 124*, 191; **27** 885
Nieumegue, Artus van Ort de *see* ARNOULT DE NIMÈGUE
Nieuwcastel, Colyn van **7** 519
Nieuwe Beelding **10** 696; **21** 852, 853, 854, 855; **22** 749, 875; **23** 124–5*; **29** 660
  see also NEO-PLASTICISM; STIJL, DE
Nieuwe Bouwen **1** 804; **4** 814; **30** 871
  see also NEUES BAUEN
Nieuwe Groep **1** 510
Nieuwe Kunst **2** 567; **8** 894; **10** 119; **18** 878; **22** 867, 875; **33** 260
  furniture **22** *874*
  woodcuts **23** 125
  see also ART NOUVEAU; RATIONALISM (i)
Nieuwelaar, Aldo van den **22** 877; **31** 576
  works **22** *876*
Nieuwenhove, Maarten van **21** *104*; **29** 504
Nieuwenhuis, T W **23** 125*
  collaboration **19** 434
  groups and movements **21** 122; **22** 875
  works **22** 899, *900*; **33** 260
Nieuwenhuuys (*fl* early 19th cent.) **29** 46
Nieuwenhuys, Constant Anton *see* CONSTANT
Nieuwenhuys, Jan **7** 489; **27** 137
Nieuwenkamp, Wijnand Otto Jan **23** 125–6*
Nieuwerkerke(, Alfred-Emilien O'Hara), Comte de **4** 306; **11** 672; **14** 394; **23** 126*
  education (art) **24** 171
  personal collection **9** 326; **12** 487; **28** 528
  works **14** 42
Nieuwe School voor Beeldende Kunsten **30** 17
Nieuwe Zakelijkheid **22** 868, 875
  see also HAGUE SCHOOL (ARCHITECTURE)
Nieuwland, Isaak Louis La Fargue van *see* LA FARGUE VAN NIEUWLAND, ISAAK LOUIS
Nieuwmoer, Onze Lieve Vrouw **7** 703
Nieuwpoort, Onze Lieve Vrouw **17** 700
Nievergalt von Worms, Nikolaus **20** 693
Niewenhuys, C. J. **24** 322
Niewiadomski, Eligiusz **25** 141
Nif *see* NYMPHAION
Nifo, Agostino **23** 127*
Nifo Medici (family) **29** 39
Nifont, Bishop of Pskov **25** 679
Niftrik, J. G. van **1** 803
Nigar **1** 202
Nigari *see* HAYDAR RA'IS
Niğde
  Ak Medrese **2** 295; **16** 204
  Alâeddin Mosque **16** 183, 247
  Museum **1** 114
  Şah Mosque **16** 202
  Sungur Bey Mosque **16** 202, 247
  tents **30** *474*
  tomb of Hüdavend Hatun **16** 204; **31** *114*
Nigelli, Gottlieb **2** 784
Nigellis, Johannes de *see* JOHANNES DE NIGELLIS
Niger **1** *214*, 380; **23** 127–8*
  architecture **23** 127
  bells **1** 360
  body arts **1** 288
  ceramics **1** 330
  cotton **23** *128*
  fans **10** 779
  gourds **11** 828, *828*
  granaries **1** 263
  jewellery **23** 127
  leather **23** 128
  metal **1** 287
  sculpture **1** 330
  skins **1** *307*
  tents **1** *307*
  textiles **23** 128
  wood **23** 127
Niger, Franciscus *see* FRANCISCUS NIGER
Nigeria **1** *214*, 380, 429–30; **23** 128–39*, *129*
  adobe **1** 305
  appliqué **1** 299
  architectural decorations **1** *318*
  architecture **1** *250*; **23** 134–5*
  archives **2** 371*
  art history **2** 530
  baskets **1** 296; **3** 331
  beadwork **4** I3
  body arts **1** 288, *289*
  bowls **1** *356*; **4** *854*
  brass **15** *106*
  bronze **4** 854, *854*; **15** 118, *118*, *119*
  cement **1** 331; **23** 137–8
  ceramics **1** 328
  chests **33** III2
  collections **23** 139*
  columns **1** 261
  concrete **1** 319; **23** *138*
  copper **1** 287; **15** *104*, *105*, 117–18, *119*; **23** 131
  costumes **1** *268*, 269–70, *270*; **15** *111*
  cotton **1** *218*, *229*; **9** III2
  craftsmen and artists **1** *243*, *244*, *286*, *303*
  crowns **1** *353*
  cushion covers **1** *218*
  dancewands **33** *556*
  divination instruments **1** *356*
  doors **1** *427*; **9** 164, *164*
  dress **1** *348*; **14** *231*
  dyeing **3** 379; **9** III2; **11** 828; **30** 558
  dyes **1** *250*
  earth **9** 164
  education (art) **1** 432; **23** 138–9*
  embroidery **1** *229*; **14** *231*
  engraving **1** *302*, *303*
  etchings **1** *429*
  20th cent. **23** *136*
Nigeria—cont.
  exhibitions **23** 135, 139*
  fan-holders **15** *119*
  figurines **1** *270*, 273
  funerary objects **1** 258
  galleries (iv) (art) **23** 139
  gongs **1** 360
  gourds **1** *248*, 302, *302*, 303, *303*; **11** 828
  gowns **23** 302
  hats **1** 348
  headdresses **9** *734*
  houses **1** 284, 305, *318*; **15** *114*
  human figures **15** 106, *106*, *118*; **23** *180*, 180–81
  iconography **1** 261
  indigo **1** *250*
  iroko-wood **33** III2
  iron **23** 130, 180
  ivory **1** 293, *356*
  jewellery **15** *119*
  leather **1** *218*, 299
  looms **1** 246, 294
  lost-wax casting **15** 117
  marble **23** *138*
  masks **1** *239*, *268*, 273, *273*, 282, 290, *335*, 342; **10** *122*; **15** *62*, *102*
    Igbo **15** *111*
    Yoruba **1** *241*; **15** *104*
  mazes **21** 597
  meeting-houses **1** 310
  mica **1** 284
  monuments **1** 331
  mosques **1** 316
  museums **1** 440; **23** 139*
  painting **23** 135–7*, *137*
  palaces **1** 314; **23** 824
  patronage **23** 139*
  pendants (jewellery) **15** *118*
  pipes (smoking) **1** 368
  portraits **1** 267, 268
  pots **1** 369, *369*
  pottery **1** *286*; **15** *120*; **23** 130
  prints **23** 136
  regalia **1** *242*, *353*
  religion **1** 230
  robes **1** *353*
  rock art **23** 130
  roofs **1** 320
  scarification **1** 254, *255*, 345, *345*
  sculpture **1** *247*, 281, 331; **4** I3; **15** *63*, *64*; **23** 137–8*
    equestrian **1** 280
    figure **15** *112*, *113*, *115*; **23** *132*, *133*
    marble **23** *138*
    wood **15** *113*, *115*
    Yoruba **15** 105*, *105*, *106*, 106–7*, *107*
    20th cent. **23** *138*
  shells **3** 331
  shrines (i) (cult) **1** 289; **9** *736*
  silk **1** 293
  soapstone **23** *133*
  steel **1** *247*
  stencilling **30** 561
  stone **1** 292
  stone-carvings **15** 107
  swords **33** *555*
  tattoos **1** 346
  temples **1** 309
  terracotta **1** *221*; **15** *107*; **23** *132*, 179–81, *180*, *181*; **30** *508*
  textiles **1** 349; **15** *64*; **23** 131; **30** 561
  tin **4** 854; **15** 118
  trays **1** *356*
  tunics **1** *229*
  urban planning **23** 135
  wall decorations **14** *232*
  weaving **1** 246, 293, 294
  wood **1** *270*, *273*, *356*, *427*; **9** 164, *164*; **15** *113*, *115*
  wood-carvings **9** *734*, *735*, *736*
  writing **8** 231
  see also BENIN, KINGDOM OF; EDO (AFRICA)
Nigeria Magazine **24** 430

Nigerian Institute of Architects 10 131
Nigerian Railway Corporation 1 319; 10 131
Nigetti, Giovanni 28 734
Nigetti, Matteo 23 139–40*
collaboration 23 880
patrons and collectors 21 25
works 11 181, 205, 208; 16 641, 745; 21 24
Nigg, Josef 2 817
Nightingale, Florence 10 236; 14 783; 33 385
Night Society see YORU NO KAI
Nigris, Giuseppe De see DE NIGRIS, GIUSEPPE
Nigro, Mario 22 242
nigrum optimum see VINE BLACK
Niguarda, Francesco da see FRANCESCO DA NIGUARDA
Niha 26 915
Temple A 26 866, 917; 30 436
Nihal Chand 15 612–13
works 15 613
Nihavend
seals 1 856
Nihoa see HAWAII
Nihon Abusutorakuto Āto Kurabu (Japanese Abstract Art Club) 14 213; 17 207, 860
Nihon Andepandan Ten (Japanese Independent Exhibition) 17 135
Nihon Bijutsu Kyōkai (Japan Fine Arts Association) 17 200
see also RYŪCHIKAI
Nihon bijutsu nenkan 24 437
Nihon Bijutsu Tenrankai see NITTEN
Nihon Bonsai Association 17 367
Nihon Hanga Kyōkai (Japanese Print Association) 17 436
Nihon Jinruigakki (Anthropological Association of Japan) 17 426
Nihon Kōkogaku Kyōkai (Association for Japanese Archaeology) 17 426, 427
Nihon Kokusai Bijutsu Ten (Japanese International Art Exhibition) 17 135
Nihon Mingei Kyōkai (Japan Folk Craft Society) 17 265; 21 634, 635
Nihon shodō bijutsuin 17 239
Nihon shogeiin 17 239
Nihon Sōsaku Hanga Kyōkai see JAPAN CREATIVE PRINT ASSOCIATION
Ni'ihau see HAWAII
Nijenbeek 22 822
Nijenrode, Geertruyt van 23 188
Nijinska, Bronislava 3 119
Nijinsky, Vaslav 3 119
Nijland, Dirk (Hidde) 15 36; 22 854; 23 140*
Nijmegen 22 813
architecture 26 905
furniture 27 94
glass 22 884; 27 78
pewter 22 893
St Stevenskerk 22 821
silver 22 887
town walls 22 822
Valkhof Castle 22 822
Nijmegen, Arnold of see ARNOULT DE NIMÈGUE
Nijmegen, Arnt see ARNOULT DE NIMÈGUE
Nijmegen, Dionys van 23 140; 33 262
Nijmegen, Elias van 23 140; 33 262
Nijmegen, Gerard van 23 140–41*
Nijmegen, Gideon van 23 140
Nijmegen, Herbert van 23 140
Nijmegen, Tobias van 23 140
Nijō (family) 17 225; 23 366
Nijō Castle see under KYOTO
Nijs, Pieter 29 79
Nijvel, Engelbrecht van 13 896
Nikaia see IZNIK
Nikaidō Michimori 17 747
Nikakai (Second Division Society) 17 134, 135, 137, 205, 206, 207, 436; 18 194; 20 834; 23 141*, 384; 27 594; 30 241; 33 488, 552
members 11 337; 27 597; 31 74, 82; 33 508
Nikandre Kore 8 688; 13 434, 444, 445; 18 244; 22 700
Nikandre of Naxos 13 445
Nike Balustrade 13 457
Nikel, Lea 16 571
Nikelszky, Géza 15 2
Nike of Delos 8 688; 13 445
Nike of Paionios 13 434, 470
Nike of Samothrace 2 171; 13 464, 470, 605; 23 141*; 26 292; 27 692, 692
Nikephoros (fl after 1065) 16 810
Nikephoros I, Emperor of Byzantium (reg 802-11 AD) 2 509; 9 637
Nikephoros III Botaniates, Emperor of Byzantium (reg 1078-81) 12 254
Nikephoros II Phokas, Emperor of Byzantium (reg 963-69) 7 221; 9 658; 22 156, 225, 228, 229
Nikeratos 24 414
Niketas, Patriarch (fl 768/9) 16 593
Niketas (fl late 10th cent.) 9 607
Niketas (fl 1075-9) 9 593
Niketas Choniates 9 617
Nikias (fl 420-400 BC) 32 59
Nikias (fl 350-300 BC) 13 554; 23 141–2*
patrons and collectors 13 555
teachers 13 551
works 13 546, 546, 548–9
Nikias of Athens (fl c. 417 BC) 8 689
Nikias Painter (fl c. 420-400 BC) 13 434, 524; 32 59*
Nikiforov', I. 27 427
Nikitin, Gury 23 142*; 25 338; 27 387
Nikitin, Ivan (Nikitich) 23 142–3*; 27 388
patrons and collectors 31 312
works 27 388, 401
Nikitin, Pyotr Romanovich 17 744, 869; 27 375; 31 486
Nikitin, Roman 23 142
Nikitniki, Church of the Trinity 27 372
Nikka 15 626, 632; 22 439
Nikka Tanaka see TANAKA NIKKA
Nikkelen, Jan van 14 491
Nikken Sekkei Ltd 9 765; 33 490
Nikkō
Daiyuin 17 74
Futarasan Shrine 31 202
Tōshōgū Shrine 17 11, 45, 46, 49, 52, 63, 64; 28 611; 31 201–3*
enamel 17 378
haiden 31 203
honden 31 202–3
ishinoma 31 203
lacquer 17 302
metalwork 17 323
paintings 17 796
Yōmeimon 17 52; 31 203
Niklas, Josef 30 221; 33 162
Nikogesyan, Nikolay 2 437
Nikokles 24 59
Nikokrates of Kolonos 13 570
Nikola (fl 1306-7) 25 639
Nikola (fl 1752) 5 160
Nikoladze, Vasily 23 143
Nikoladze, Yakov 12 322; 23 143*
Nikola Firentinac see NICCOLÒ DI GIOVANNI FIORENTINO
Nikolais, Alwin 30 688
Nikolaos (fl late 16th cent.) 25 336
Nikolaos (fl 1692-1741) 21 345
Nikolaos Mesarites 10 129; 16 603
Nikolayev see MYKOLAÏV
Nikolayev, Aleksandr (Vasilyevich) 31 783
Nikolayev, B. see TERNOVETS, BORIS (NIKOLAYEVICH)
Nikolayev, Ivan 27 379
Nikolayev, V. N. 18 40
Nikolayeva, Suzanna Mar Yelena 8 437
Nikolić, Dobrilo 28 452
Nikolides 8 334
Nikoljski, Aleksandar 19 883
Nikolla 1 540
Nikolla, Llazar 1 541; 23 143*
Nikolov, Andrey 5 156; 23 143*
Nikolov, Nikola 5 150
Nikol'sk Glassworks 27 415, 416, 417
glass 27 415
see also KRASNYY GIGANT WORKS
Nikolsky, Aleksandr (Sergeyevich) 12 234; 23 144*; 27 578; 30 8
Nikol'sky, D. J. 23 391
Nikomachos of Thebes 2 413; 13 545, 551, 554; 23 144*; 32 250
pupils 24 640
works 2 682; 13 548, 551
Nikon, Abbot of Sergiyev Posad (d 1422) 8 506
Nikon, Patriarch of Moscow and All Russia (reg 1652-66) 23 25; 27 372, 438
Nikonor, Pavel 27 397
Nikopolis 9 511; 23 144–5*; 26 908
aqueducts 26 910
architecture 26 908
Basilica A 7 278; 9 538, 566, 590; 12 71
Basilica of Doumetios see Basilica A
fortifications 9 554; 26 909
marble 26 855
mosaics 9 565
nymphaeum 26 910
odeion 23 350
temples 26 911
Nikopolis ad Istrum see NICOPOLIS AD ISTRUM
Nikortsminda 12 317
church 7 274; 12 320, 321, 321–2
Nikos 20 913
Nikosthenes (potter; fl c. 550-505 BC) 13 487, 519; 23 145–6*; 32 40, 60
works 13 535; 32 40
Nikosthenes Painter (painter; fl c. 550 BC) 10 591; 13 510, 519; 23 146
collaboration 32 53
patrons and collectors 23 829
pupils 32 60
workshop 10 612
Nikoxenos Painter 13 511
Nikritin, Solomon 8 10; 26 70
Niksar
architecture 16 183, 202
tomb of Hacı Cikirik 16 186
Yaghıbasan Madrasa 16 184
Nikšić 22 17
Nikulainen, Tuula 10 875
Nilambenuvara 29 450
Nilavarei 16 864
Nile (Australia), Clarendon House 2 738
Nile clay see under CLAY → types
Nile mosaic 18 701; 25 421, 422
Nilson, Andreas 23 146
Nilson, Johann Esaias 2 719; 14 695; 23 146*
works 10 103; 11 458; 12 391; 14 695; 21 512; 24 272
Nilson, Rosina Barbara 23 146
Nilssen, Georg 22 894
Nilsson, Axel 19 428; 30 81
Nilsson, Gladys 6 577
Nilsson, Gösta Adrian 30 81
Nilsson, Johannes 30 116
Nilsson, Karl-Gustaf 30 82
Nilsson, Kristian 30 113
Nilsson, Sten Åke 30 120
Nilsson, Vera 30 81
Nilsson, Wiwen 30 108, 113
Nilus, Pyotr A. 31 559
nim 15 721
Nimaatsed 9 870
Ni Malle, Gravina see O'MALLEY, GRAVINA
Nimani, Shyqri 28 452
Ni'matallah ibn Muhammad al-Bawwab 16 198
Nimègue, Arnoult de see ARNOULT DE NIMÈGUE
Nîmes 11 505; 23 146–8*; 26 908
amphitheatre 1 797; 23 147; 26 904, 905; 29 521
castellum urbanum 27 6
Cathedral of Notre-Dame and St Castor 26 603
gates 7 358; 26 904
lace 11 650
Maison Carrée 23 147, 148; 24 352; 25 265; 26 858, 866, 883, 885, 907; 30 435, 436
staircase 29 520
Nemausus 23 147*
Palais de Justice 18 888
Pont du Gard 2 242, 297; 4 800; 6 178, 178; 13 303; 23 148*; 24 750; 26 449; 27 7; 32 398
Porte d'Auguste 23 147
silk 11 644, 646; 28 716
Temple of Diana 26 883
textiles 28 564
town walls 26 904
Nimmons, George C. 6 578; 25 446
Nimnia Khera 15 262
Shiva Temple 15 263
Nimri, Kuram 17 655
Nimrud 1 849, 891, 895; 2 639; 16 2; 18 896; 21 267, 268, 275, 304; 23 148–51*
1950 Building 2 640
architecture 2 640, 641; 21 274, 287–8, 290
Neo-Assyrian (c. 883-c. 612 BC) 23 149–51*
arsenal see Fort Shalmaneser
Black Obelisk see BLACK OBELISK
bowls 24 644
brass 4 682
bronze 30 187
Burnt Temple 2 640
Central Palace of Tiglath-pileser III 21 288, 299; 23 151
citadel 23 149
coins 13 587
façade decoration 10 742
figurines 13 579
Fort Shalmaneser 1 867, 872; 2 640; 21 288, 298; 23 150, 150–51
glass 1 867, 867, 868; 10 591; 24 645
gold 30 187
Governor's Palace 2 640
harnesses 14 179
ivory-carvings 1 870–71, 871, 890; 10 591; 24 643; 29 395
jewellery 1 875; 24 218
Kidmuru Temple 21 288
marble 29 702
metalwork 13 359; 21 304
Nabu Temple 2 640, 641; 21 288; 23 151
Ninurta Temple 21 287, 288, 297, 298; 23 150
Nimrud—cont.
North-west Palace of Assurnasirpal II 1 879, 895; 21 287, 296–7; 23 149–50
ivory-carvings 15 881
palmettes 23 888
reliefs 1 517; 23 888
sculpture 21 297
reliefs 1 891, 895; 6 478; 22 510; 29 701, XI
rock crystal 26 485
sculpture 21 298, 310; 29 395
Sharrat-niphi Temple 21 288, 297
South-east palace 2 640
South-west Palace of Esarhaddon 21 290, 297, 299, 301
Town Wall Palace of Assurbanipal 21 290
TW 53 houses 23 151
wall paintings 21 309
White Obelisk see WHITE OBELISK
writing-tablets 4 342
ziggurat 2 640; 33 675
Nims, Charles F. 10 83
Nimsameur, Chalood 30 608
Nimy 3 590, 591; 27 85
Nin 8 174
Church of the Holy Cross 8 175
Treasury 8 180
Nin, Buck 18 529
Ninaber van Eyben, Bruno 22 877
Nin'ami Dōhachi (1740-1804) 17 262; 18 554, 555
works 18 555
Nin'ami Dōhachi (1783-1855) see TAKAHASHI DŌHACHI
Nindirí Museum 29 222
Nindowari 15 245
Ninetjer 9 776; 27 811
Nineveh 1 508, 509, 849, 891, 892, 895; 2 639; 10 133; 16 2; 18 896–7; 21 267, 268, 275, 303, 304, 309; 23 152–4*, 152, 154
Adad Temple 2 640
architecture 2 639, 640, 641; 21 274, 290
arsenal 21 290; 23 154
Assur Temple 2 639
canals 2 241; 3 418
copper 2 639
façade decoration 10 742
Garden Party relief see GARDEN PARTY RELIEF
gardens 12 66; 21 291
glass 1 865, 867, 868
helmet 16 504
Ishtar Temple 2 639, 640; 21 288, 298; 23 153
Küyünjik 1 892, 895; 23 152, 153, 154
palace 1 892
Lion Hunt Relief see LION HUNT RELIEF
metalwork 1 510
Nabu Temple 2 640; 21 288
Nebi Yunus 21 290; 23 152, 153, 154, 154
Nergal Gate 21 300
North Palace of Assurbanipal 2 641; 19 311; 21 290, 301
Palace without Rival 21 287; 23 154
pottery 1 894; 21 307; 23 152
reliefs 1 516, 891; 2 641, 641; 22 510, 511; 29 923; 30 774
religion 21 277
sculpture 21 294, 298, 301, 310
bronze 4 850
Sin and Shamash Temple 2 639
South-west Palace of Sennacherib 18 597; 21 290, 300, 301–2
reliefs 9 85
writing-tablets 19 311
stucco 29 815
ziggurat 2 639

Ninevite 5 ware *see under* POTTERY → wares
Ningbo **6** 624, 885; **7** 42
Ningguo **7** 115
Ning-tsung, Emperor (Sung; *reg* 1195-1224) *see* NINGZONG, Emperor
Ningxiang **6** *615*; **23** 155*
bells **6** 841
bronzes **6** 832; **23** *155*
metalwork **23** 155
ningyō jōruri see under THEATRES → types
Ningzong, Emperor (Song; *reg* 1195-1224) **19** 856, 858; **33** 462
Ninham, Henry **23** 155–6*
Ninh Phuc Temple *see* BUT THAP TEMPLE
Nini, Domenico **23** 156
Nini, Giovanni Battista **23** 156*
Ninigo atoll **24** *64*, 82
Ninkai **17** 410
Ninmyō, Emperor (*reg* 833-50) **17** 391
Niño, Andrés **10** 153
Niño, Carmelo **23** 156*
Niño, Luis **4** 261; **25** 365
works **4** *262*
Niño de Guevara, Fernando, Cardinal **13** *343*; **23** 156*
Niño de Guevara, Juan **23** 157*
Ninotsminda **12** *317*
Cathedral **12** 319
Georgian church **2** 426
Ninove, Onze Lieve Vrouw **7** 703, *703*
Ninsei Nonomura *see* NONOMURA NINSEI
Ninsei ware *see under* POTTERY → wares
Ninshō **17** 747
Ninski, Grgur **21** *316*
Nintoku, Emperor (*reg c.* 400-450) **18** 190; **23** 157, 591; **27** 832
Nio **17** 364
Niobe Group **2** 168; **3** 701; **14** 12; **16** 772; **21** 23; **23** 157–8*; **26** 845; **27** 46
Niobid Painter **32** 59–60*
copies **13** 541
pupils **32** 64
works **9** 248; **13** *473*, 522, *522*
niobium **17** 530
Niochori, Church of the Eisodia **9** 629
Niogret, Camille **19** 848
niombos **1** 259, *260*
Niō Mōsho **17** 410
Niono, Great Mosque **1** 317
Nioro du Sahel **20** 198
Niort **6** 53
Musée des Beaux-Arts **11** 665
Niotis **8** 316
Nio Unga **10** 463
Nipa **22** 767
Niphon *see* NEOPHYTOS
Niphon, Patriarch **30** 724, 725
Nippon *see* NIHON
Nippon Design Centre (Tokyo) **17** 752; **30** 286
Nippon Kōbō *see* PUBLISHING ON DESIGN, INC.
Nippur **1** *849*, 892; **20** 361; **21** *267*, 271; **23** 158*
architecture **21** 292
figurines **15** 421
Inanna Temple **21** 281, 285
pottery **21** 306
religion **21** 277
sculpture **21** 294
stone vessels **2** 272
Temple of Inanna **29** *923*
writing-tablets **1** 895
ziggurat **33** 675
Niqmaddu **1** 857
Niqmepa **2** 661
Niquinohomo
galleries (iv) (art) **23** 85
Niqula Masabiki **16** 361
Nirand, Pichai **30** 617
works **30** *617*
Nirenstein-Kallir, Otto **2** 829
Nirim Synagogue **17** 542
Nirmand **15** 309
Shiva Temple **15** 310
Nirou Khani **8** 153; **21** *651*
ivory-carvings **21** 682
villa **21** 664
wall paintings **21** 674
Nirvana Buddhism *see under* BUDDHISM → sects
Niš **9** 565, 654; **28** 439
National Museum **28** 458
Nisa **1** 887; **5** 742; **6** *182*, 198–9; **15** *901*, 906, 915; **16** *105*; **23** 159–60*; **24** 215, 216; **30** 440; **31** *458*
architectural decorations **6** 206
architecture **6** 196
bouleuterion **4** 530
congregational mosque **16** 163
glass **6** 269
ivory **23** 160
ivory-carvings **1** 195; **6** 271
library **19** 312
mausoleum **24** 216
palace **6** 206
rhyta **6** 270, *271*; **23** *160*
Round Hall **6** 198, 217; **24** 216
sculpture **6** 217
sculpture **6** 213–14; **23** 159
seals **23** 159; **24** 218
silver **6** 237
Square Hall **6** 198, *198*; **23** 159, 807; **24** *216*, 216
sculpture **6** 217
Square House **6** 199; **24** 216
statuettes **24** 217
Tower **6** 199; **24** 216
wall paintings **6** 223
Nisaia Alexandropolis *see* NISA
Nisar, Qudsia Azmat **23** 800
Nisard, Désiré **8** 596
Nisart, Pere **23** 160*, 881
Nisbet, Robert **23** 160
Nisbet, Thomas (1776-1850) **5** 578; **23** 160*
works **5** 575, 578, *578*
Nisbet, Thomas (1810-45) **23** 160
Nisbet, William Hamilton **25** 664; **28** 271
nisee portraits *see under* PORTRAITS → types
Nisenan **22** 549, 641
Nish **9** 655
Nishapur **15** 899; **16** *105*, 365; **23** 160–61*
ceramics **6** 915
chess sets **6** 556
coins **6** 266; **16** 512, *512*
glass **16** 518
houses **16** 154, 160
jewellery **16** 530, *530*
kilns **16** 394
maces **16** 505
madrasas **20** 54, 55
metalwork **16** 370, 373
muqarnas (architecture) **22** 321
niches **16** 161
pottery **16** 135, 397, 400, 401–2, *402*, 408, 414, *414*, 505; **23** 558, 562
Qanat Tepe **16** 253
rock crystal **16** 540
Sabz Pushan **16** 253
stucco **16** 160
Tepe Madrasa **16** 160, 253
textiles **31** 21
veils **16** 456
Vineyard Tepe **16** 253
wall paintings **16** 253, 530
weapons **16** *504*, *506*
Nishapur Ewer **16** 369
Nishat Bagh **12** 74
Nishga **22** 547
Nishi, Kikuji **11** 811
Nishi Honganji *see under* KYOTO
Nishikawa, Yasushi **17** 240
Nishikawa Koruyu *see* KORUYU NISHIKAWA
Nishikawa Shundō **17** 238, 240
Nishikawa Sukenobu **18** 552; **23** 161–2*
pupils **30** 50
works **17** 177, 273, 282*; **23** *162*; **24** 276
writings **17** 417
Nishiki (family) **17** 311
nishiki see under TEXTILES → types
Nishimiyama Tomb **17** 249
Nishimochida kiln **27** 873
Nishimura Dōnin **17** 323
Nishimurai **17** 287
Nishimurai Yohachi **17** 287
Nishimura Myakuan **23** 367
Nishimura Nantei **17** 196
works **17** *269*
Nishimura Ryōzen **10** 117
Nishimura Shigenaga **16** 83; **17** 282; **30** 50
Nishimura Shigenobu *see* ISHIKAWA TOYONOBU
Nishimura Sōshirō **17** 262
Nishino, Shotaro **17** 402
Nishiwaki, Okanoyama Graphic Art Museum **22** 367
Nishiyama Hoen **20** 837; **23** 594
Nishizawa, Luis **23** 162*
Nisibis **9** *512*, *513*
architecture **9** 543
Baptistery **9** 541
Cathedral **9** 539, 543
colonnades **26** 918
manuscripts **9** 619; **31** 436
Nispert (family) **8** 77
Niss, Thorvald Simon **23** 162*
Nissanka Malla, King Sri Lanka (*reg* 1187-96) **25** 169; **29** 459
Nissan Motor Manufactory (UK) **15** 827
Nisse Church **22** 821
Nissen, A. I. **28** 628
Nissen, Henrik **22** 319
Nissky, Georgy (Grigor'yevich) **27** 396
Nissl, Franz Xaver **14** 834
Nitado, Everardo **26** 10
Niten *see* MIYAMOTO MUSASHI NITEN
Niterói **4** *705*
Museu Antonio Parreiras **4** 727; **24** 206
Nithart, Mathis Gothart *see* GRÜNEWALD, MATTHIAS
Nitinaht **22** 565
Nitocris **10** 13
Nitot, Etienne **11** 635
Nitot, F. R. **11** 635
Nitovikla **8** 334
Nitra **13** 162; **28** *848*
Andrej Bagar Theatre **28** 850
Castle **28** 849
Cathedral **14** 900; **28** 848, 849
church **28** 849
Great Seminary **28** 850
jewellery **25** 517
Piarist church **14** 887
Piarist school **15** 17
university campus **28** 850
nitre **4** 687
nitric acid **10** 192, 548, 560
Nitrobriges **6** 160
nitrocellulose **1** 155
Ni Tsan *see* NI ZAN
Nitsch, Hermann **2** 698; **23** 162–3*
collaboration **27** 216
groups and movements **1** 513; **2** 798; **5** 30; **22** 256; **28** 344; **32** 447
works **10** 483; **24** 408
Nitsche, Walter **11** 852
Nitszchké, Oscar **4** 214
Nitta Yoshisada **17** 748
Nitten (Japanese Art Exhibition) **17** 135, 207, 435, *436*
Nittis, Giuseppe De *see* DE NITTIS, GIUSEPPE
Ni Tuan *see* NI DUAN
Nitzchké, Oscar **22** 728
Niue **23** 163–4*, *711*
Niulakita **31** 484
Niure, Erik **5** 817
Niuron, Peter **8** 816
Niurone, Bernardo **24** 207
Niutao **31** 484
Nivå, Nivaagaards Malerisamling **8** 758, 759
Nivelles **3** *539*
architecture **3** 541
Notre-Dame **7** 262
Ste Gertrude **3** 541; **14** 74; **23** *164*, 164–5*; **26** 574; **28** 631
sculpture **3** 566; **13** 100; **26** 631
wall paintings **3** 552
westwork **33** 109
St Paul **7** 262
St Pierre **7** 262
sculpture **3** 570
Nivelles, Girart of *see* GIRART OF NIVELLES
Nivelon **4** 391
Nivernais, Louis-Jules-Barbon Mancini-Mazarin, Duc de **17** 683; **20** 240
Nivinsky, Ignaty (Ignat'yevich) **32** 661
Nivison, Josephine Verstille **14** 751
nīvrapaṭṭikā **15** 244*
Niwaki **17** 351
Nixon, Francis **10** 356
Nixon, Job **27** 278
Nixon, Nicholas **23** 37
Niya **6** *288*, *614*; **23** 165*; **28** *719*, 720
architecture **6** 296
armour **6** 306
ceramics **6** 309
furniture **6** 311
lacquer **6** 313
seals **6** 314
silk **6** 290
textiles **6** 302, 317; **7** 48
writing-tablets **6** 289
Niyeminen, Fol'ke **27** 434
Niza Fiorentinus **14** 904
Nizamabad **23** 803
Nizam al-Din Shami **16** 196
Nizam al-Mulk **16** 162, 163; **20** 54, 369
Nizami **7** 634; **10** 486; **15** 572; **21** 704; **30** 338
works **16** *301*
Nizam Shahi **23** 165*
see also HUSAYN NIZAM SHAH I, Ruler
Ni Zan **6** 754, 755, 773, 790, 824; **7** 151; **21** 633; **23** 165–8*, 582; **30** 49; **33** 439
collaboration **17** 882
groups and movements **14** 822; **25** 73; **29** 244; **32** 845
paintings **6** 812
patrons and collectors **32** 838
works **1** 581; **6** 790, 805, *812*; **23** *166*, *167*; **33** 570
writings **6** 819, 824
Nizet, Denis **3** 594
Nizet, Jacques **3** 594
Nizet glassworks **3** 593
Nizharadze, Z. **12** 327
Nizhny Dzhulat
church **27** 432
congregational mosque **27** 432
Nizhny Novgorod **23** 168*; **27** *363*, 434
All-Russian Exhibition **30** 467
Art Museum **27** 440
Church of the Birth of the Mother of God **27** 373; **29** 779
embroidery **27** 430
fortress **27** 371
House of Soviets **27** 379
metalwork **27** 424
Nizhny Novgorod—cont.
painting **27** 386
sculpture **27** 382
Nizhny Tagil **27** 424
Nizhyn **31** 562, 563
All Saints **31** 553
Nizip **9** 548
Nizwa **21** 588; **23** 436
Nizzoli, Giuseppe Di *see* DI NIZZOLI, GIUSEPPE
Nizzoli, Marcello **8** 803; **15** 826; **23** 168–9*
works **1** 736; **16** 650; **25** 351
Njabi **11** 878
Njau, Elimo **1** 433; **17** 908
Njenga, Edward **17** 908
Njinawanga **1** 44
Njoya, Ibrahim **3** 152, 153
works **3** *153*
Njoya, King of Bamum (*reg* 1887-1924) **1** 242, *352*; **3** 151, 152
Nkanu **1** 403, 405; **18** 217, 221; **33** 485
NKF **33** 743
Nkotsi, Tony **29** 109
Nkrumah, Kwame **14** 511
Nkusu, Albert **33** 596
Nkuvu **14** 376, 377, 378
NKVM *see* NEUE KÜNSTLERVEREINIGUNG MÜNCHEN
N(uclear) M(agnetic) R(esonance spetrometry) *see under* TECHNICAL EXAMINATION → types
Nnagenda, Francis **1** 433; **17** 908; **31** 528
Nnam **10** 123
sculpture **10** *123*
nō see under THEATRE → types
Noa, Amalia Cletos *see* CLETOS NOA, AMALIA
Noa, Asunción Cletos *see* CLETOS NOA, ASUNCIÓN
Noa, Juan Cletos *see* CLETOS NOA, JUAN
Noa, Magdalena Cletos *see* CLETOS NOA, MAGDALENA
Noailles, Cardinal de **4** 587
Noailles, Adrien-Maurice, Duc de **18** 815; **19** 115; **24** 211
Noailles, Charles de, Vicomte **23** 169*
architecture **20** 203
films **7** 508
furniture **26** 38
gardens **13** 798
interior decoration **9** 63; **10** 137; **11** 584
sculpture **18** 864
Noailles, Marie-Laure de, Vicomtesse **7** 508; **23** 169*
Noakes, Michael **11** 437
Noakowski, Stanisław **23** 169–70*; **25** 100
Nōami Shinnō *see* SHINNŌ NŌAMI
Noanama **7** 602
Noanori Hori *see* HORI NAONORI
Nobatia **23** *276*, 285, 287, 288
Nobbe, Walter **14** 43
Nobbs, Percy (Erskine) **5** 562, 572; **23** 170*
Nobel, Emmanuel **19** 332
Nobel, Ole **8** 727
Nobile, Pietro
works **2** 785, 787, *788*; **5** 385; **13** 330; **28** 859; **32** 437, 457
Nobili, Roberto de' **17** 512
Nobili, Salvatore **26** 827
Nobilior, Marcus Fulvius **10** 675
Nobis, Balcer **25** 121
Noble, James Campbell **21** 99
Noble, Juan **14** 662
Noble, Matthew **20** 237; **23** 171–2*
works **23** *172*; **31** 241
Noble, Mrs Saxton **4** 127
noble metals *see* GOLD; PLATINUM; SILVER

Noblesse, François 28 742
Noblet, Martin 23 172*
noborigama see under KILNS → types
Nobumasa Kanō *see* KANŌ NOBUMASA
Nobunaga Oda *see* ODA NOBUNAGA
Nobuo Sekine 21 892
Noburu Kitawaki *see* KITAWAKI, NOBURU
Nobutada Konoe *see* KONOE NOBUTADA
Nobutsuna Matsudaira *see* MATSUDAIRA NOBUTSUNA
Nobuyoshi Araki *see* ARAKI, NOBUYOSHI
Nobuzane, Fujiwara no *see* FUJIWARA NO NOBUZANE
Nocchi, Bernardino 23 173*; 31 72
Nocchi, Pietro 23 173
Nocchieri, Francesco Maria 32 8
Nocé 23 516
Noceto, Nicolao da *see* NICOLAO DA NOCETO
Nochistlán 21 393
Nochlin, Linda 2 538; 31 673; 33 310, 312, 313
Nocq, Henry 6 489
Nocret, Jean 22 191; 23 173*; 25 461
  patrons and collectors 23 513
  works 23 512; 29 803
Nocret, Jean-Charles 23 173
Nocte 15 732
Noda, Tetsuya 17 293, 296; 23 173*
  works 17 *296*
nodding arches *see under* ARCHES → types
Nodernskiöld, Gustaf 22 676
Nodet, Henri 18 599
Nodier, Charles
  collaboration 5 392; 8 867; 11 521; 30 385
  groups and movements 25 581
  illustrated works
   Ciceri, Eugène 7 304
   Dauzats, Adrien 8 548
   Huet, Paul 14 848
   Isabey, (Louis-)Eugène (-Gabriel) 16 65
   Johannot, Alfred and Tony 17 605
   Prassinos, Mario 25 450
   Steinlen, Théophile-Alexandre 4 365
   Viollet-le-Duc, Eugène-Emmanuel 32 594
Noé, Amédée-Charles-Henry de, Comte *see* CHAM
Noé, Luis Felipe 2 401; 19 872; 23 174*
Noé, Manuel 29 334
Noël 24 266
Noël, Alexandre-Jean 31 156; 32 334
Noél, Carlos 2 405
Noel, Charles, 1st Earl of Gainsborough 4 596
Noël, Georges 23 174*
Noel, Gerald 29 533
Noël, Jules 5 131; 20 117
Noél, Martín 2 396, 405
Noel, Maxine 22 598
Noel, Miriam 33 403
Noël, Peter Paul Joseph 26 83
Noel, Tony 31 241
Noels, Joseph Matthias de 7 584
Noero, Jo 29 107
Noewielle, Noe de 17 647
Noferi, Giovanni Antonio 22 481
Noffke, W. E. 23 632
Nofret 9 870; 20 117
Nofretere *see* NEFERTARI
Nofri, Andrea 2 17
Nogal, S Salvador 26 607
Nogales, Avelino 4 262; 23 174*
  pupils 13 880
  works 4 262; 7 493
Nogales, Pedro 7 493
Nogari, Giuseppe 13 300; 23 174–5*
  patrons and collectors 28 18; 30 523
  pupils 19 636
  reproductive prints by others 6 91
Nogari, Paris 1 595; 26 818
Nogata
  Takuma kiln 30 258
  Uchigaiso 1 448; 30 258
Nogay 30 476
Nogent, Guibert de *see* GUIBERT DE NOGENT
Nogent-le-Rotru 6 52
Nöggi, Ludwig 2 606
nogging *see under* BRICKLAYING → types
Noguchi, Isamu 4 75; 12 101; 17 136; 23 175–7*; 31 633
  bridges 14 568
  collaboration 8 270
  exhibitions 17 436
  fountains 3 177; 11 347
  gardens 26 42
  productions 30 688
  sculpture 14 203; 31 613
  sculpture gardens 14 803; 16 571; 20 299; 23 *176*; 28 314
Noguchi, Isamu, Museum *see under* NEW YORK → museums
Noguchi, Sono 17 371
Noguchi, Yatarō 17 206
Noguchi Shōhin 17 188, 199
Nogué, Miguel 4 260
Nogueira, Miguel (José) 23 177*
Nogueira, (Rolando de) Sá *see* SÁ NOGUEIRA(, ROLANDO DE)
Nogueira da Silva, Francisco Augusto 23 177*
Noguera, Eduardo 8 255; 30 452; 33 472
Noguera, Pedro (de) 7 192; 23 178*; 24 506
Nogués i Casas, Francesc Xavier 29 329
Noh 15 426, 449
Nohpat 6 97
Nohta Shiva Temple 15 290
Noi: Rivista d'arte futurista 24 448; 25 447
Noiers, Geoffrey of *see* GEOFFREY OF NOIERS
Noigandres 7 698
Nointel, Charles-Henri-François Olier, Marquis de 13 608; 23 178*; 32 914
Noin Ula 21 *870*, 885; 23 178–9*
  embroidery 10 181
  felt 10 873; 21 877
  metalwork 21 878
  textiles 7 46
  Tumulus 6 7 46
Noir, Jean le *see* JEAN LE NOIR
Noir, Le (family) *see* LE NOIR (FAMILY)
Noirlac Abbey 21 *844*, 845
Noise 24 443
Noisiel-sur-Marne, Menier Chocolate Factory 4 788; 10 748; 16 54; 30 504
Noisot, Claude 27 312
Noisy-le-Roy 13 703
Noizet, Gaspard 21 581
Nojima, Yasuzō 11 811; 18 60; 22 445; 23 179*
Nojiri, Lake 17 21
Nok 1 *386*, 436; 23 129, *129*, 179–81*
  beads 1 297
  collections 23 180
  hairstyles 1 343
  metalwork 23 130
  scarification 1 344
Nok—cont.
  sculpture 1 258, 274, 329, 330; 23 130
  terracotta 1 221, *221*, 258, 342, 350; 21 481; 23 *180*, *181*; 30 508
nōka see under HOUSES → types
Noke, Charles 9 201
Nokes Collection 28 693
Nokonzok 1 191
Nola 10 585; 13 475
Nola, Giovanni da *see* MARIGLIANO, GIOVANNI
Nolamba 23 181–2*
  see also:
   ANNIGA, Ruler
   AYYAPA, Ruler
   DIVAMBIKA
   MAHENDRA, Ruler
Nolan, François-Joseph 20 473
Nolan, Sidney (Robert) 23 182–3*
  patrons and collectors 2 769; 4 882
  works 2 749, *750*; 23 *183*
Nolan amphorae *see under* AMPHORAE → types
Noland, Kenneth 23 183–5*; 31 609
  collaboration 20 608
  groups and movements 1 79; 4 110; 25 361; 32 890, 894
  patrons and collectors 23 7
  teachers 1 549; 29 534
  works 1 130; 5 569; 7 636; 14 164; 23 *184*
Nolasco, Pedro 7 709
Nolde, Emil 23 185–7*
  groups and movements 4 132, 892; 10 694, 695, 841; 28 124
  patrons and collectors 11 729; 14 506; 20 880
  pupils 33 427
  works 9 310; 10 695, *695*; 11 230; 12 395, 396, 450; 18 717, IV2; 19 491; 23 *186*, *187*; 25 582, 619; 29 871; 32 902; 33 363
Nole, Andris de 21 765
Nole, Colijn de 22 857; 23 187–8*
  works 23 *188*
Nole, Colyns de 19 349
Nole, Guillaume de 23 187
Nole, Jacob Colijn de 22 857; 23 188*
Nole, Jean de 21 765
Nole, Robert de 21 765
Nole, Willem (Colijn) de 22 95; 23 188
Nolen, John T. 7 326; 20 282; 26 353
Nolfo, Domenico 10 488
Noli, Guillermo Mora 23 905
Noli, José Guillermo Mora *see* MORA NOLI, JOSÉ GUILLERMO
Noli, S Paragorio 26 576
Nölken, Franz 4 892
Noll, Anthoni 8 822
Noll, Marcel 30 17, 19
Nolle, Karl 7 576
Nollekens, Jan (*b* 1695) 23 189
Nollekens, Jan Baptiste (*b* 1665) 23 189
Nollekens, Joseph 5 751; 10 372; 23 189–90*
  collaboration 24 846
  copies 3 79
  patrons and collectors 6 94; 8 475; 10 361, 487; 12 165; 27 357; 32 790; 33 19, 209
  personal collection 12 577; 21 770; 30 496
  teachers 19 157
  works 1 665; 5 302, 303; 10 264, 265, 475; 19 606; 21 770; 23 *190*; 24 844; 32 787
Nollekens, Joseph Francis 23 189*
  patrons and collectors 30 451; 32 912; 33 453
Nolli, Carlo 24 757
Nolli, Giovanni Battista 23 190–91*; 32 429
  works 11 *271*; 26 *757*
Nolli, Johann 28 862
Nolpe, Pieter 23 191*; 25 369
Nomé, François de 3 271; 11 534; 19 696; 23 191–2*
  patrons and collectors 27 205
  works 5 686
Nomellini, Plinio 16 678; 23 192*
  groups and movements 9 41; 22 747
  pupils 32 405
  teachers 10 835
nomismates *see under* COINS → types
Nomura, Izaburō 23 628
Nomura, Shiro 17 317
Nomura Collection *see under* SAKURA → National Museum of Japanese History
Nomuri, K. 18 259
Nonancourt, Jean de *see* JEAN DE NONANCOURT
Nonantola Abbey 16 *618*; 20 820; 23 193*
  sculpture 26 621
  West Porch 23 193
Nonconformist chapels *see under* ENGLAND → chapels
Nonda 14 376
Nonell (i Monturiol), Isidre 3 219; 5 509; 23 194–5*; 29 285
Nonesuch Palace *see* NONSUCH PALACE (SURREY)
Nonesuch Press 4 366; 17 850; 22 117; 26 39
Non-Figurative Artists' Association 22 39
non finito 23 195*
Nong Chae Sao 30 591
Nongp'o 18 365
Nong Song Hong, Wat Su Bua Kaeo 30 *615*, 616
Nonius Balbus, M. 14 439
Nonkō Tanaka *see* TANAKA DŌNYŪ
Nonnberg Altarpiece, Master of the 29 730
Nonnberg Gospels *see under* GOSPEL BOOKS → individual manuscripts
Nonnebakken 8 721; 32 532
Nonnenmacher, Bernhard 29 755
Nonnenmacher, Georg 23 195
Nonnenmacher, Josef František 23 195
Nonnenmacher, Marek 23 195*
  collaboration 18 191; 25 548
  works 8 397
Nonnesuche Palace *see* NONSUCH PALACE (SURREY)
Nonni, Ottavio dei *see* MASCHERINO, OTTAVIANO
Nonnotte, Donat 23 195–6*
  assistants 7 640
  pupils 14 389
  reproductive prints by others 18 858
Nonnotte, Jean 23 195
Nono, Luigi 32 110, 197
Nono, Urbano 20 503
Nonoalca 31 97
Nonoguchi Ryūho 17 400
Nonomura Ninsei (*fl c.* 1648-90) 17 258; 23 196*, 367
  works 17 242, 244, 256; 18 553–4; 23 *196*
Nonomura Ninsei (*fl* 1699) 23 196, 366
Nonotte, Donat 7 162; 9 301; 19 35
Nonpareil *see under* TYPE-FACES
Nonsuch chests *see under* CHESTS → types
Non-Such Flint Glassworks 4 824
Nonsuch Palace (Surrey) 6 59; 10 *225*, 229, 231, 360; 11 140; 19 568; 23 *197*, 197–9*; 29 835
  carvings 3 646
  collections 11 140
  Diana Fountain 11 342
  gardens 12 114, 126; 23 198–9*
  Grove of Diana 12 126
Nonthaburi 30 590
Nooijer, Paul(us) de 23 199*
Nooms, Reinier 23 199–200*
  copies 21 170
  patrons and collectors 7 194; 14 375
  reproductive prints by others 21 171
  works 20 424; 22 843; 23 *200*; 31 246
Noordendorp, J. E. G. 27 116
Noordewolde Church 22 819
Noordt, Jan 33 700
Noordwijk, Anna van 22 200
Noordwijkerhout, Vakantiehuis De Vonk 23 663
Noor-Eesti *see* YOUNG ESTONIA
Noormarkku Villa Mairea 1 9; 32 556
Noort, Adam van 23 200, 201*
  pupils 3 107; 17 648; 27 288; 32 722
  works 23 *201*
Noort, Juan de 5 679; 23 201–2*; 29 424
Noort, Lambert van 23 200–201*
  collaboration 8 102
  groups and movements 26 728
  pupils 23 201
  reproductive prints by others 14 505
  works 27 256
Noort, Willem van 22 857
Noorwits, Pieter Arentsz. *see* ARENTSZ, NOORWITS PIETER
Noot, Philippe Evrard Vander, Count of Everberg *see* EVERBERG, PHILIPPE EVRARD VANDER NOOT, Count of, Bishop of Ghent
Noot, T. van der 29 399
Nootka *see* NUU-CHAH-NULTH
Nopiloa 21 238
Noquart, Girard 31 381
Nora 25 733
  shrine 24 642
Noraduz 8 198
Norat, Felix Bonilla *see* BONILLA NORAT, FELIX
Noravank' 2 *423*; 23 202*
  Church of the Forerunner 2 434; 23 202
  Church of the Mother of God 2 434, 435
  Fagel (family)
  gavit' 2 435
  khatchk'ars 2 436
Norba 26 887
Norberg, Jonal 19 361
Norberg-Schulz, Christian 18 390; 23 245
Norbert, Saint, Archbishop of Magdeburg 25 551
Norbertines *see* PREMONSTRATENSIAN CANONS
Norbert of Xanten *see* NORBERT, Saint
Norblin 32 878
Norblin, Adam 25 128
Norblin, Ludwik 25 128
Norblin de la Gourdaine, Aleksander Jan 23 203
Norblin de la Gourdaine, Jan Piotr 8 372; 23 202–3*
  pupils 23 530; 27 446
  works 2 414; 9 308; 23 *203*; 25 106
Norblin de la Gourdaine, Sebastian 2 142; 23 203

Norbo, Pietro di Domenico di *see* PIETRO DI DOMENICO DI NORBO
Norbury (Derbys), St Mary
  tombs of the Fitzherbert family 13 84
Norbury Park (Surrey) 3 277; 10 278; 24 18
Norchia 10 598
Norcross, O. W. 26 340
Norcross Brothers 26 340, 342
Nord, Comte du *see* PAUL, Emperor of Russia
Nord, Comtesse du *see* MARIA FYODOROVNA OF WÜRTTEMBERG, Empress of Russia
Nordau, Max 8 596; 10 413
Nordbeck, Peter 5 586
Norden, Frederik Ludwig 10 79, 82, 83, 96; 31 481
Norden, John 18 73
Nordenberg, Bengt 23 203–4*; 30 79
  patrons and collectors 11 851
  works 33 697
Nordentche Steingut Fabrik 30 885
Nordgard Marstein
  storehouses 23 *219*
Nordhagen, Johan 23 227; 29 15
Nordheim, Arne 14 229
Nordin, Lorens 30 94
Nordiska Kompaniet 3 784
Nordisk Konservatorforbund 7 744
Nordkirchen Castle 24 740
Nördlingen 12 *361*; 23 204–5*
  painting 12 385
  Rathaus 28 *59*
  St Georg 10 408; 12 342; 23 204–5*, *205*
Nordlingen, Marie 25 661
Nördlingen, Master of 12 342; 20 653, 736*
Nördlingen, Trünklin of *see* TRÜNKLIN OF NÖRDLINGEN
Nordman, Maria 24 24; 31 609
Nordmand, Peder Andersen *see* ANDERSEN NORDMAND, PEDER
Nordoy, Amariel 10 813
Nordström, Folke 30 120
Nordström, Karl (Fredrik) 23 205–7*; 30 79, 80
  groups and movements 3 776; 22 540; 29 774; 30 79
  patrons and collectors 30 730
  pupils 10 399
  works 23 *206*; 30 80
Nordström, Lars-Gunnar 11 97; 23 207*
Nordström, Patrick 8 748
Nord-Sud 13 670; 24 442
Noreña, Miguel 21 386; 23 207*
  collaboration 7 783
  pupils 7 783; 13 795
  works 21 403
Norfolk (VA)
  Chrysler Museum 7 245; 12 54
  Norfolk Museum of Arts and Sciences *see* Chrysler Museum
Norfolk, Charles Howard, 10th Duke of *see* HOWARD, CHARLES, 10th Duke of Norfolk
Norfolk, Henry Fitzalan Howard, 1st Duke of *see* HOWARD, HENRY FITZALAN, 1st Duke of Norfolk
Norfolk, Henry Howard, 6th Duke of *see* HOWARD, HENRY, 6th Duke of Norfolk
Norfolk, Thomas Howard, 8th Duke of *see* HOWARD, THOMAS, 8th Duke of Norfolk
Norfolk Triptych 11 438
Nørgaard, Bjørn 8 741, 755, 761; 12 830
Norgate, Edward 8 127; 23 207–8*
  works 9 8; 18 705, 706; 21 640; 23 787; 32 898
Nori, Pietro 20 124
Norie (family) 9 724
Norie, George 23 208
Norie, Helen 23 208
Norie, James (1684-1757; father) 7 418; 23 208*; 28 236, 274
Norie, James (1711-36; son) 23 208
Norie, Robert 23 208*; 27 333
Noriega 21 221
Noriega, Domingo 13 770
Noriega, José 21 378; 23 208–9*
norigae 18 379, *380*
Norigoshi Tachihara *see* TACHIHARA, NORIGOSHI
Norinaga, Fujiwara no *see* FUJIWARA NO NORINAGA
Noritaka Asakawa *see* ASAKAWA, HAKKYŌ
Nørlund 8 725
Norman 9 255
  thrones 30 777, 779
  see also:
    ROGER BORSA, Duke of Apulia
    ROGER II, King of Naples & Sicily
    TANCRED, Prince of Antioch
    WILLIAM I, King of England, Duke of Normandy
    WILLIAM II, King of Naples and Sicily
Norman, A. C. 20 168
Norman, A. V. B. 2 450
Norman, Carl 30 111
Normán, Juán 28 518
Normanby Park (Lincs) 28 874
Normand, Alfred Nicolas 4 308; 23 209*
  groups and movements 22 744; 28 345
  patrons and collectors 4 308; 11 580
  works 11 *581*; 25 193; 26 205
Normand, Charles (-Pierre-Joseph) 23 209*
  collaboration 3 463
  pupils 5 23
  works 21 114
  writings 23 487
Normand, Charles Nicolas 23 209
Normand, Jacob Jensen 8 752
Normand, Louis Eléonor 23 209
Normand, Paul 23 209
Normand, Svend, Bishop of Roskilde 8 721, 722
Normand de Tournehem, Charles-François (-Paul) Le *see* LE NORMAND DE TOURNEHEM, CHARLES-FRANÇOIS(-PAUL)
Normandeau, Pierre 5 571
Normandie 2 522
Normandy 21 563
Normandy, Charles, Duc de *see* BERRY, CHARLES DE VALOIS, Duc de
Norman MacKenzie Art Gallery *see under* REGINA → University
Norman Revival 6 61; 23 209–11*; 27 336
  castles 23 *210*
  see also ROMANESQUE REVIVAL
Norman slab glass *see under* GLASS → types
Norman style *see under* ROMANESQUE → styles
Normanton Park (Leics) 32 540
Nor Monastery 30 812, 814, 825, 832
Norn, Otto 8 761
Norniella, Angel 8 237
Noro Kaiseki 17 189, 190; 18 60
Noronha, Manuel de, Bishop of Lamego 18 676
Noronha, Manuel Pereira da Costa *see* PEREIRA DA COSTA NORONHA, MANUEL
Noronha Leme Cernache, Jerónimo de Távora e *see* TÁVORA E NORONHA LEME CERNACHE, JERÓNIMO DE
Norpertus Seal 12 255
Norra Vånga Church 13 119
Norreys (family) 7 283
Norreys, Thomas 33 60, 62
Norrie, James 28 269
Norrie, Susan 2 752
Norrie's Law 24 737
Norris, John 11 423
  frames 11 *424*
Norris, John S. 27 884
Norrköping 31 718
  jewellery 30 112
  Löfstad Slott 11 901
  Norrköpings Konstmuseum 30 119
Norrman, Gottfried L. 2 693
Norrmén, Herman 23 326
Norrström, Carl Hjalmar 30 110
  works 30 *110*
Norsk Billedvev 23 239
Norske Husflidsforening 23 239
Norske Kompagni 23 235
Norşuntepe 1 824, 839; 17 875
Norte, Manuel Joaquim 23 211–12*; 25 294
Norten, Enrique 21 382
North (family) 31 652
North, Alexander 2 740; 23 212*
North, Benjamin, & Sons 14 523
North, Edward 19 568
North, Francis, 1st Earl of Guilford 33 158
North, Frederick, 5th Earl of Guilford 23 212*
North, James 26 239
North, John William 24 832; 32 795
North, Marianne 30 171
North, Robert 12 510
North, Roger 19 124; 23 212–13*; 25 632, 664
North Africa
  aqueducts 26 919
  architecture 9 535; 16 190*; 26 919–22*
  balneae 26 919
  baptisteries 9 535
  baskets 3 331
  baths 26 872
  belts 16 530
  book covers 16 357
  caldaria 26 919, 920
  calligraphy 16 *281*
  caps 16 459
  carpets 16 473, 485–7*
  ceilings 2 528–9
  churches 9 533, 535*
  clay 1 368
  coins 7 532; 16 512, 513
  cotton 8 35
  dress 16 456–7, 458–60*
  earthenwares 16 427
  gardens 12 78
  glazes 16 427
  grasses 3 331
  houses 26 870, 920
  inscriptions 16 512, 513
  jewellery 16 529–30*, 532*
  kiosks 26 919
  lead 16 427
  macella 19 889, *889*; 26 919
  madrasas 16 215
  manuscripts 9 603; 16 306–7*
  martyria 9 535
  masonry 20 572
  metalwork 16 386–7*
  minarets 16 190
  minbars 16 493–4
  monasteries 21 834
  monuments 26 920, *920*
  mosaics 9 569–70*; 27 63; 32 542
  mosques 16 190, 493
North Africa—cont.
  orchestras 26 *920*
  painting 10 197; 27 57
  piers (ii) (masonry) 16 190
  pigments 16 427
  pipes (smoking) 1 367
  pottery 16 403–4, 411–12*, 418–19*, 427–8*
  scaenae 26 *920*
  scripts 16 *281*
  silk 16 447–8; 28 715
  silver 16 532
  stelae 29 613
  strapwork 16 487
  temples 26 *866*, 919
  textiles 16 436–7*, 439–40*, 447–8*
  theatres 26 919, *920*, 921; 30 652
  thermae 26 919
  tiles 16 427
  trade 16 368, 395, 448
  turbans 16 456–7, 459
  urban planning 26 921
  villas 26 870
  weaving 16 440, 447–8
  wood 29 618
  woodwork 16 492–5*
  wraps 16 459
North America
  architecture 21 573–4, 575–6*
  auditoria 1 125
  fortifications 21 573–4, 575–6
  lace 18 593
  periods
    Prehistoric 25 468
  photography 10 580
  quilts 25 821
  trade
    silk 28 717
  verandahs 32 240
  see also CANADA; USA
Northampton (UK)
  architecture 10 226
  County Hall 31 242
  Cross 17 612
  New Ways 10 241; 21 782
  royal palace 2 65
  sculptors 10 265
  Town Hall 12 840; 31 241
Northampton (MA; USA), Smith College 22 917; 31 393
Northampton, 7th Earl of *see* COMPTON, CHARLES
Northampton, Elizabeth de Bohun, Countess of *see* BOHUN, ELIZABETH DE, Countess of Northampton
Northampton, Spencer Joshua Compton, 2nd Marquess of *see* COMPTON, SPENCER JOSHUA, 2nd Marquess of Northampton
Northampton, William Compton, 1st Earl of *see* COMPTON, WILLIAM, 1st Earl of Northampton
Northampton group pottery *see under* POTTERY → wares
North British Glassworks 28 260
North British Pottery 28 257
Northbrook, Francis Baring, 1st Lord *see* BARING, FRANCIS, 1st Lord Northbrook
Northbrook, Thomas George Baring, 1st Earl of *see* BARING, THOMAS GEORGE, 1st Earl of Northbrook
North Cadbury (Somerset), St Michael 24 577
North Cerney (Glos), All Saints 25 725
Northcote, James 23 213–14*
  collaboration 26 273, 277
  patrons and collectors 3 239; 4 607; 19 98
  reproductive prints by others 12 187
  works 4 607; 12 293; 23 *214*; 25 282
  writings 14 272
North Cray (Lincs) 10 292
North Elmham (Norfolk) 2 66
North Elmham Censer 10 338
Northern and Southern Dynasties *see under* CHINA → periods
Northern Art Workers' Guild 33 342
Northern Athapaskan 22 648
Northern Bank 18 754
Northern Black Polished ware *see under* POTTERY → wares
Northern Ch'i period *see under* CHINA → periods
Northern Chou period *see under* CHINA → periods
Northern Ireland 16 *5*, 38–42*; 31 585, *585*
  air-conditioning 3 537
  architecture 3 536; 16 39–40*
  collections 16 42*
  dealing 16 42*
  decorative arts 16 41–2*
  education (art) 16 42*
  glass 3 536
  iron 3 536
  menhirs 25 505
  museums 16 *39*, 42*
  opera houses 30 *679*
  painting 16 *40*, 40–41*
  periodicals 16 42
  sculpture 16 40–41*
  stained glass 16 *41*
  synagogues 17 548
  workhouses 3 *536*
Northern Master 2 622
Northern niello craft collective *see* SEVERNAYA CHERN' CRAFT COLLECTIVE
Northern Ojibwa 22 648
Northern Painted ware *see* POTTERY → wares → Red-on-white ware
Northern Qi period *see under* CHINA → periods
Northern Railway Company 26 314
Northern Rhodesia *see* ZAMBIA
Northern school 6 820, 824; 7 148; 17 188; 19 299; 23 215–16*
Northern song period *see under* CHINA → periods
Northern Wei period *see under* CHINA → periods
Northern Zhou period *see under* CHINA → periods
Northey (family) 31 646
North Hatley (Que), Bradley House 5 563
Northington (Hants), Grange Park 8 48; 13 610, *610*; 25 267; 33 192
North-International 24 451
North Kazi Kasba *see* VIKRAMPUR
Northleach (Glos), SS Peter and Paul 13 55
North Leigh Villa (Oxon) 32 542
North Luffenham (Leics), The Pastures 32 *721*
Northoff 14 25
North Rona Lighthouse 19 361
North & Scoullar 23 66
North Soto *see* SOTHO (NORTH)
Northumberland, Algernon Percy, 10th Earl of *see* PERCY, ALGERNON, 10th Earl of Northumberland
Northumberland, Algernon Percy, 4th Duke of *see* PERCY, ALGERNON, 4th Duke of Northumberland
Northumberland, Henry Percy, 9th Earl of *see* PERCY, HENRY, 9th Earl of Northumberland
Northumberland, Hugh Smithson, 1st Duke of *see* SMITHSON (PERCY), HUGH, 1st Duke of Northumberland

Northumberland, John Dudley, 1st Duke of *see* DUDLEY, JOHN, 1st Duke of Northumberland
Northumbria, Earl of **33** 550
Northwest Printmakers **25** 629
Northwich School **28** 158
Northwick, George Rushout Bowles, 3rd Baron *see* BOWLES, GEORGE RUSHOUT, 3rd Baron Northwick
Northwick, John Rushout, 2nd Baron *see* RUSHOUT, JOHN, 2nd Baron Northwick
Northwick Park (Glos) **27** 350
Northwold, Bishop of Ely **9** 670; **10** 167
Northwood (Middx), Frithwood House **9** 739
Northwood, J. & J. **33** 13
Northwood, John **5** 730; **10** 320; **26** 227; **27** 74; **33** 13
Norton, Charles Eliot **4** 477; **23** 216–17*; **31** 669
Norton, Christopher **5** 337
Norton, John (1823-1904) **28** 279
Norton, John (1877-1934) **8** 777
Norton (Hereford & Worcs), St Egwin **26** 613
Norton (Cleveland), St Mary **2** 66
Norton Company **2** 698
Norton Hall (Glos) **19** 454
Norum **26** 639
Norvada Cerveira, Lima da Villa *see* LIMA DA VILLA NORVADA CERVEIRA
Norville, Alexandre de *see* PRZEZDZIECKI, ALEKSANDER (NARCYZ KAROL)
Norwalk (CT) **31** 634
Norway **23** 217–45*, *218*
  academies **23** 602
  altarpieces **11** 465; **13** 143, *144*
    triptychs **23** 224
  amber **1** 761
  antependia **11** *466*; **13** 135, 143, *144*; **23** 223–4
  archaeology **23** 227
  architecture **4** 781; **23** 218–19*, 220–22*
    Gothic **31** 363
    Romanesque **26** 593*
    vernacular **32** 286–9*
    Viking **23** 219
    wood **32** 286–7
  archives **2** 369
  art history **23** 244–5*
  art legislation **23** 243
  art schools **23** 603
  banknotes **3** 180, *181*
  brick **4** 781
  bridges **4** *804*
  bronze **3** 783; **23** *230*; **32** *497*, *515*
  brooches **32** *514*
  capitals **23** 228; **31** *750*
  carpets **5** 829
  ceramics **23** 234–5*
  chairs **6** 389; **23** 234
    ergonomic **23** *233*
    kubbstol **6** 389
    post seats **6** *389*
  churches **23** 219, 220
    stave **23** 217, 219, 228; **29** *579*, 579, *580*, 580–81; **30** 894
    Viking **32** 532
  coins **7** 537
  collections **23** 242–3*
  competitions **3** 783
  concrete **4** *804*
  coverlets **23** 240
  cupboards **11** *240*
  dealing **23** 242–3*
  doors **9** 156
  education (art) **23** 222, 227, 244*
  enamel **10** *194*
  etchings **10** *557*
  exhibitions **23** 602
  faience (ii) (ceramics) **23** *234*, 234–5
Norway—cont.
  farmhouses **32** *287*
  frames **11** 465–6, *466*, *472*, *474*
  furniture **23** *233*, 233–4*
  gardens **12** 135, *135*
  glass **23** 221, 235–6*
  goblets **10** *194*
  gold **23** 236
  guilds **23** 236
  halls **3** *774*
  hangings **23** *239*, 240
  harness-mounts **32** *515*
  heritage **23** 243
  historiography **23** 244–5*
  hospitals **23** 221
  hotels **23** 221
  houses **23** 219
    farmhouses **32** 286, 287–8
    Grubenhäuser **32** 532
    summer-houses **23** *220*
  interior decoration **23** 231–2*, *232*
  iron **9** 156; **23** 237
  ivory **23** *229*
  ivory-carvings **23** *229*, 238
  jardinières **23** *237*
  jewellery **23** 238
  libraries **19** 318; **23** 244*
  lithography **19** *489*
  marks **23** 236
  masonry **23** 219
  memorial stones **32** *518*, 521
  metalwork **13** 167; **15** 873; **23** 236*, 237*, *237*
  monuments **23** 230
  moss **32** 286
  mouldings **22** 217
  museums **23** *222*, 243*, 602
  nude figures **14** *506*; **32** *497*
  oak **13** *119*
  objects of vertu **23** 238*
  painting **23** 223–7*
    genre **22** *290*; **23** *603*; **33** *78*
    Gothic **13** 143; **23** 223
    history **23** *225*, *226*
    landscape **8** *452*; **23** 224; **28** *825*
    marine **3** *112*
    oil **23** 224, 375
    panel **13** 135, 143
    religious **13** *144*; **29** *78*
    Romanesque **23** 223
    Symbolism (movement) **22** *292*
    wall **23** *223*
    19th cent. **9** *751*
  parterres (i) (gardens) **12** *135*
  patronage **23** 242–3*
  periodicals **24** 452*
  pewter **23** 237
  photography **22** *293*
  pine **6** *389*
  polychromy **13** *119*
  porcelain **23** 235
  portals **29** 580–81
  portraits **14** *506*; **18** *464*; **21** 478
  prints **23** 227
  rock art **25** 495
  rosemaling **23** 231, *232*, 242*
  rugs **5** 829
  rune-stones **23** 227
  sanatoria **23** 221
  sculpture **14** 229; **21** 478; **23** 227–31*
    allegorical **23** *230*
    bronze **3** 783; **32** *497*
    Gothic **13** 102, *119*, 119
    relief **23** *229*
    Romanesque **26** 639*, 644; **29** 580; **31** *364*
    stone **26** 639
  shields **23** 223
  silver **23** 236*, *237*, 238; **32** *514*
  soapstone **13** 102; **31** *364*
  stained glass **13** 190
  stone **26** 639*
  stone-carvings **32** *518*
  stonewares **23** 235
  storehouses **23** *219*
  stoves **23** 237
  tables **23** 233
Norway—cont.
  tankards **23** 236
  tapestries **23** 238–9*, *239*, 240, *240*, 241
  textiles **23** 238–41*; **32** 523
  theories (art) **13** 726
  tiles **30** 884*
  timber structures **32** 287
  town halls **23** *602*
  towns **14** 97; **23** 222; **25** 376; **31** 718
  trade
    paintings **23** 224
  tureens **23** *234*
  tusks **6** 389
  urban planning **23** 220
  vernacular art **23** 238, 241–2*
  villas **23** 602
  windows **23** 221
  wood **23** 219, *219*, 220, 221; **31** *750*; **32** 286–7
  wood-carvings **11** *240*; **23** *228*, 229, 241–2, *600*
    Viking **31** *749*
  woodcuts **22** *293*
  wool **5** 829; **23** *239*
  see also SCANDINAVIA; VIKING
Norwich (Norfolk) **10** *225*; **23** 245–51*; **31** 710
  art forms and materials
    architecture **23** *246*, 250*
    brasses **4** 692
    carpets **5** 835; **10** 357
    manuscript illumination **13** 147
    painting **18** 715; **23** *249*
    pottery **10** 300, 301, 303
    silk **10** 357
    stained glass **13** 184; **29** 503
    textiles **28** 564, 565, *565*
  art schools **10** 373
  Assembly Rooms **2** 617
  Castle **6** 54, 55; **26** 613
  Castle Museum **20** 33; **23** 249
  Churchman House **23** *247*
  City Hall **7** 668; **10** 240, *240*; **31** 243
  Cow Tower **4** 779
  ecclesiastical buildings
    Cathedral of the Holy Trinity **1** 723, 724; **4** 465; **21** 839; **23** *250*, 250–51*; **26** 588
      ambulatory **1** 768
      clock **7** 438
      cloister **7** 454, 455, 456
      Despencer Retable **11** 421, *421*; **13** 139
      doors **9** 152
      gate-house **12** 175
      Prior's Door **7** *456*
      sculpture **23** 251*; **26** 612, 613
      spire **29** 412, 413
      tracery **31** 271
      vaults **32** 92
    Dominican friary **21** 842, *842*
    Octagon Chapel **23** 193; **31** 584
    St Mary Coslany **2** 296
    St Michael Coslany **32** 93
    St Peter Mancroft **13** 184; **23** 251*; **24** 465
  Guildhall **14** 76
  houses **14** 76
  Music House **14** 76; **29** 22
  Norfolk and Norwich Museum *see* Castle Museum
  Old Meeting **23** 193
  Pickerell House **14** 76
  Sainsbury Centre for the Visual Arts *see under* University of East Anglia
  St Andrew's Hall **14** 316
  sculptors **10** 265
  Stranger's Hall **14** 76
  town walls **4** 778; **31** 710
  undercrofts **23** 247
Norwich (Norfolk)—cont.
  University of East Anglia
    Sainsbury Centre for the Visual Arts **1** 440, 737; **7** 808; **10** 371; **11** 332; **14** 521; **22** 366; **23** 249, 742; **27** 524; **29** 250, *250*
Norwich Grocers **30** 653
Norwid, Cyprian Kamil **25** 119
Norwid's Group *see* Group of Five
Norwisz., Pieter Arentsz. *see* ARENTSZ. NOORWITS, PIETER
Nosadella, il *see* BEZZI, GIOVANNI FRANCESCO
Nōsayama **17** 352
Nosecký, Siard **8** 427; **25** 445
Nosenzo **20** 428
Noseret, Luis Fernández *see* FERNÁNDEZ NOSERET, LUIS
Noshiro **17** 357
Noskowiak, Sonya **13** 710
Noso-dong Tomb 15 **18** 367
Nossa Senhora, Feliciano de, Bishop of Lamego **18** 676
Nosseni, Giovanni Maria **5** 76; **23** 252–3*
  attributions **9** 235
  collaboration **9** 238; **12** 403; **28** 60; **32** 833
  patrons and collectors **28** 60; **33** 113
  reproductive prints by others **17** 887
  works **5** 768; **9** 235; **12** 405, 461; **23** *252*; **32** 731
Nost, Gerard van **23** 253
Nost, John van (i) (*d* 1729) **3** 570; **23** 253*
  assistants **5** 827
  collaboration **25** 813
  patrons and collectors **13** 645
  works **4** 79; **10** 263, 264; **18** 902; **23** 782; **30** 451
Nost, John van (ii) (*d* 1787) **9** 322; **16** 21; **23** 253–4*; **28** 64
Nost, van (family) **27** 259
Nostell Priory (W. Yorks) **7** 171; **30** 123; **32** 818
  frames **11** 430, 431
  furniture **7** 172, 659; **9** 29; **11** 119
  paintings **21** 766
  plaster **29** 835
  sculpture **33** 449
Nøstetangen Glassverk **23** 235
Nostic (family) **8** 395
Nostic, Count **5** 701
Nostitz, Christoph Wenzel von, Graf **29** 811
Nostre, André Le *see* LE NÔTRE, ANDRÉ
Nøstvik, K. H. **17** 906
No Su-hyŏn **18** 326; **25** 760; **33** 534
Nota **13** 267
notebooks *see under* BOOKS → forms
Notenberg, Eleanora *see* GURO, YELENA (GENRIKHOVNA)
Noter, Jean-Baptiste De *see* DE NOTER, JEAN-BAPTISTE
Noter, Pierre-François De *see* DE NOTER, PIERRE-FRANÇOIS
Noterman, Emanuel **29** 682
Notger, Prince-Bishop of Liège **3** 603; **19** 343; **26** 695
Noticiero Universal, El **29** 87
Notizblatt des Architekten-Vereins **18** 161; **24** 444
Notke, Bernt **12** 401; **23** 254–6*
  pupils **14** 303
  sculpture **4** 692; **11** 98; **12** 384; **13** 118
    altarpieces **8** 738, 758; **10** 538; **13** 120; **23** *254*, *255*; **29** 687; **30** 83, 276
    crucifixes **8** 214; **25** 176; **27** 125
    statuettes **12** 442
  workshop **8** 731
Notman, Charles **23** 257
Notman, George **23** 257
Notman, John **23** 256–7*
  groups and movements **13** 203; **26** 190
  staff **11** 848
  works **24** 597; **25** 4; **26** 353; **32** 555
Notman, William (1826-91) **5** 565; **22** 38; **23** 257*
  staff **11** 742
  works **24** 668
Notman, William McFarlane (1857-1913) **23** 257
Notman Photographic Studios **22** 38; **32** 795, 910
Notmark Church **8** 722
Noto **11** 899; **16** *621*; **23** 257–8*; **28** 657; **31** 717
  architecture **16** 640
  Municipio **28** 769
  Palazzo Ducezio *see* Municipio
Nôtre, Le *see* LE NÔTRE
Notre-Dame-de-Hal *see under* HAL
Notre-Dame de Lyre **26** 669
Notre-Dame de Pontaut **7** 455
Notre-Dame-de-Tronoën **13** 79
Notre-Dame-de-Vaux **7** 643
Notre-Dame du Bonsecours **3** 288
Nötsch school **2** 797; **33** 162
Notsi **24** 85
Notsjö Porcelain Factory **11** 105
Nott, Eliphalet **25** 371
Nott, George **18** 183
Nottingham **10** *225*; **23** 258–9*
  alabaster (gypsum) **8** 738
  alabaster-carvings **1** 518, 519; **23** 258
  Boots Wets Factory **10** 241; **12** 792; **33** *205*
  Castle **6** 407
  Castle Museum **6** 60; **22** 731; **23** 259
  lace **10** 355
  law courts **18** 886
  Park Estate **23** *259*
  pottery **10** 302, 306
  Royal Concert Hall **1** 126
  sculpture **13** 84
  tiles **30** *876*
  University Art Gallery **23** 259
Nottingham ware *see under* POTTERY → wares
Nottolini, Lorenzo **19** 765; **23** 259*
Nottum **20** 281
No Two Horns **22** 585
Notzing, Jakob Schrenck von *see* SHRENCK VON NOTZING, JAKOB
Nouailher Missal *see under* MISSALS → individual manuscripts
Nouakchott **1** *376*; **20** 861, 862
  central library **20** 862
  Hospital **20** 862
Noucentisme **23** 260*, 572; **29** 285, 308; **30** 3
  architecture **3** 216
  painting **3** *219*
  Spain **7** 373
Noue, Abbé de La *see* LA NOUE, ABBÉ DE
Nougé, Paul **20** 101; **30** 20, 22
Nouhuys, Jan van **22** 892
Nour, Amir I. M. **1** 433; **29** 897
  works **29** *897*
Nour, Zaki **10** 81
Nour Collection *see under* LONDON
Nourisson, René **21** 797; **29** 668
Nourriche, Guillaume de *see* GUILLAUME DE NOURRICHE
Nouruz **1** 786
Nousianinen Cathedral **13** 120
Nouveau, Hierosme de **19** 268

Nouveau Réalisme **2** 617; **7** 895; **8** 608; **10** 416; **17** 694; **22** 279; **23** 260–61*; **24** 145; **25** 232; **26** 46, 51; **27** 587
collections **14** 48
commentaries **8** 609
members **2** 420; **7** 421; **14** 52; **18** 117, 119; **27** 214; **29** 419; **30** 924
works **6** 354, *354*; **15** 868; **23** *260*
Nouveaux Plasticiens, Les **25** 28
Nouvel, Jean **11** 528; **12** 381; **23** 261–2*; **24** 131
Nouvelle Génération, Salon de la *see* SALON DE LA NOUVELLE GÉNÉRATION
Nouvelle revue française **12** 600
Nouvelles de l'estampe **1** 154
Nouvelle Tendance **1** 79, 745; **13** 710; **23** 262*; **24** 733
members **13** 267
Nouveua, Jérôme de **19** 248
Nouwijnx, Herman *see* NAIWYNCX, HERMAN
Nouÿ, Jean Lecomte du *see* LECOMTE DU NOUŸ, (JULES) JEAN (ANTOINE)
Nova, Pacino da *see* PACINO DA NOVA
Nová Bystřice Monastery **8** 378
Novac, Traian **18** 619
Novaesium **21** 559
fortress **26** 905
Nova Gorica **28** 860
Novais, Manuel Fernandes *see* FERNANDES NOVAIS, MANUEL
Novais, Mario **25** 319
Novak **28** 455
Novak, Barbara **31** 672
Novák, Břetislav **33** 630
Novák, Emanuel **8** 414, 416
Novák, Ignác **8** 414
Novak, J. V. **8** 423
Novak, Karel **29** 898
Novák, L. **8** 426
Novakivsky, Aleksey Kh. **31** 559
Novakivs'ky, Oleksa **23** 262*
Novaković, Dimitrije **28** 451
Novaković, Ivo **22** 18; **28** 838
Novalesa **16** 722
Abbey Church **26** 653
Novalis **20** 370
Nova Pavlica **22** 79
Novara **9** *510*; **27** 76
Baptistery **9** 533
Cathedral **23** 649
Novara, Bartolino da *see* BARTOLINO DA NOVARA
Novarank' Monastery **9** 733
Novarina, Maurice **11** 256, 527
Nova Scotia Glass Co. **5** 583
glass **5** *583*
Nova Štifta Church **28** 859
Novate, S Fedelino **23** 649
Novator photography club **18** 22
Novaya Moskva **12** 876
Nova Zemblaya shipwreck **10** 389
Nove (Italy) **16** *618*; **23** 262–3*
Nove (family) **31** 141, 142
Novecentismo **16** 648*; **23** 263*
Novecento Italiano **5** 919; **10** 820; **11** 843; **16** 680; **21** 528; **22** 393; **23** 263–4*; **25** 6, 652; **28** 793; **31** 268
members **16** 708
Campigli, Massimo **5** 548
Ghiglia, Oscar **12** 546
Licini, Osvaldo **19** 329
Marini, Marino **20** 428
Marussig, Piero **20** 522
Oppi, Ubaldo **23** 459
Ponti, Gio(vanni) **25** 218
Rosai, Ottone **27** 156
Sarfatti, Margherita **27** 839
Severini, Gino **28** 508
Sironi, Mario **28** 792
Wildt, Adolfo **33** 183
Nové Hrady **8** *374*, 410; **23** 264*
Noveliers, Salomon **9** 480
Novellara, Conte di **8** 159
Novellara, Duca di **5** 281
Novellara, Alfonso Gonzaga, Lord of **3** 56; **8** 4; **9** *266*
Novelli, Antonio **21** 26, 27; **23** 264–5*; **24** 894
Novelli, Francesco **27** 720
Novelli, Gastone **7** 782
Novelli, Giambattista **5** 902
Novelli, Paolo **23** 265*
Novelli, Pietro **20** 213; **23** 265–6*; **28** 657
pupils **20** 91
works **23** *266*; **24** 697
Novelli, Pietro Antonio **1** 784; **4** 362; **12** 582; **23** 265
Novello, Giovan Battista **8** 483
November Group (Finland) **11** 96; **23** 266*; **27** 633
Novembergruppe (Germany) **3** 795, 801; **10** 697; **14** 175; **21** 490; **23** 266–7*; **25** 375
members **3** 647; **9** 86, 758; **10** 862; **11** 768; **18** 115; **19** 773; **21** 781, 782; **25** 842; **28** 113, 352; **33** 210
Bartning, Otto **3** 292
Felixmüller, Conrad **10** 870
Heckel, Erich **14** 285
Hilberseimer, Ludwig (Karl) **14** 524
Mataré, Ewald **20** 807
Maxy, Max Herman **20** 877
Meidner, Ludwig (Baruch) **21** 55
Pechstein, (Hermann) Max **24** 312
Taut, Max **30** 371
Nové Město nad Metuji **8** 377
castle **8** 401, 402
Nové Město nad Váhom **28** 849
Noventa Padovana, Villa Giovanelli **30** 348
Nove porcelain factory **16** 738
porcelain **16** *738*
Noverre, Jean Georges **30** 672
Noves **25** *470*
Novet, Brisson **9** 2
Novgorod **9** *507*; **23** 267–71*; **27** 361, *363*
chess sets **6** 557
ecclesiastical buildings **25** *342*; **27** 368, 370
Cathedral of St Nicholas the Wonder-worker **27** 370, 381
Church of the Dormition on Volotovo Field **25** 337
Church of the Entry into Jerusalem **27** 383
Church of the Saviour **27** 370, 382
Church of the Transfiguration **9** 586; **23** *269*; **27** 370, 383
paintings **30** *708*, 708
Monastery of St George *see* Yur'yev Monastery
Peobrazhenskaya *see* Church of the Transfiguration
St Anthony Monastery Cathedral **27** 381
St Nicholas the White **27** 370
St Paraskeva Pyatnitsa **23** 268; **27** 370
St Sergius **25** 342
St Theodore Stratilates **27** 370, *370*, 383
Yur'yev Monastery
Cathedral of St George **7** 261; **23** *268*; **27** 370
icons **31** 555
manuscripts **31** 556
embroidery **27** 430
filigree **27** 418
icons **25** 337, 342; **27** 382, 383–4, *384*
Novgorod—cont.
Kremlin **23** 270–71*
Cathedral of St Sophia **7** 261; **9** 153; **23** *270*, 270; **25** 110, 129, 337; **26** 684, 687; **27** 368, 381
manuscripts **27** 385
metalwork **27** 418
painting **27** 381–2, 383
town walls **27** 370
Novgorodova, Eleonora A. **21** 885
Novgorod school **32** 662
works **25** *337*
Novgorod-Seversky **31** 548, 551
Church of the Transfiguration of the Saviour **31** 553
Novi Beograd *see* BELGRADE → New Belgrade
Novicio, Juan Luna y *see* LUNA Y NOVICIO, JUAN
Novi Grad **8** *174*
fortifications **8** 175
Novikov, Feliks **27** 380
Novikov, Maksim (Yevstatyevich) **31** 783
Novi Marof **8** *174*
Januševac Manor House **8** 176
Noviodunum *see* SOISSONS
Noviodunum Aeduorum *see* NEVERS
Novios Plautios **10** 629; **26** 860
works **10** *629*
Novi Pazar **28** *437*
Altun-alem Mosque **28** 444
St George **28** 441
St Peter **28** 439, 457
Novi Sad **28** *437*, 444
Gallery of the Serbian Cultural Association **28** 458
National Theatre **28** 445
Pavle Beljanski Gallery **28** 459
Vojvodina Sports and Business Centre **28** 445
Novísimos, Los **5** 739; **24** 99
Novissima **24** 448
Novitsky, Pavel **32** 661
Novius Blesamus **27** 28
Nóvoa, Fernando Casas y *see* CASAS Y NÓVOA, FERNANDO
Novoa, Glexis **8** 234
Novo Brdo **28** *437*, 440, 457
St Nicholas **9** 601
Novocherkassk, Grekov House-Museum **13** 633
Novocherkassk Hoard **28** *325*
Novogrudok *see* NAVAHRUDAK
Novo-Gubfartrest **6** 529
Novo Hopovo Monastery Church **28** 444
Novo Mesto **28** *858*
museum **28** 863
Novosibirsk House of Soviets **27** 379
Novosielski, Michael **30** 674
Novosiltseva, Barbara Yermolayevna **26** *551*
Novosti **28** 643
Novotný, Antonín **8** 405
Novotny, Fritz **2** 834; **29** 795
Novotný, Otakar **8** 401; **23** 271*
groups and movements **8** 373
teachers **18** 405
works **8** 379, 401; **20** 254
Novruzshakh **6** 199
Novy, Aleviz **3** 84; **22** 169, 182; **27** 371
works **22** *182*
Nový Bor **8** *374*, 411; **23** 271*
Museum **8** 424
Nový Jáchymov **8** 416
Nový Svět **8** *374*; **23** 271–2*
glass **8** 409, 410
staff **4** 41
Novyy LEF **4** 812; **20** 887; **24** 450
Nowa Huta Abbey **4** 782; **25** 95
Nowak, Ernst **30** 851
Nowak, Willi **10** 107, 108; **13** 711; **22** 729
Nowakowski, Waldemar **17** 579
works **17** *578*
Nowicki, Matthew **19** 46; **23** 272–3*
works **6** 445; **20** 890; **23** *272*; **29** 489
Nowohratsky-Kollowrath, Count **10** 531
Nowosielski, Jerzy **18** 429; **23** 273*
Nowy Sącz **25** 119
Noye, Sebastiaan van **3** 544, 545
Noyes, Eliot (Fette) **3** 538; **23** 273*; **28** 488
Noyette, De *see* DE NOYETTE
Noyon
Cathedral of Notre-Dame **1** 723; **9** 672; **11** 510; **13** 37, 38; **26** 44; **30** 729
bosses **4** 465
library **19** 313
reliquaries **26** 148
transepts **13** 39; **31** 281
manuscript illumination **13** 141
No Yŏng **18** 306; **23** 274*
N Painter **13** 501
Npepe **1** 403
NPS *see* NATIONAL PARK SERVICES
Nri Museum **23** 139
Nsei **3** 147
Nselle **10** 123
Nsheng **18** 489
sculpture **18** *486*
Nshryhb **14** 224
Nsibidi **8** 231
Nso **3** 145, 147, 148
Nsru **14** 224
Nsukka **15** 116; **23** *129*, 136
Ntendu, Tshyela **33** 596
Nthako, 'Mathabo **19** 242
Ntiro, Sam **1** 433; **30** 301
Ntwane **1** 414, 417, 418, 419
dolls **1** *420*
Nuaillé-sur-Boutonne Church **26** 600
Nuba **1** 378; **23** 274–5*
aesthetics **1** 237
basketwork **23** 275
body arts **1** 288, 344, *344*; **23** 274–5, *275*; **26** 221, 222; **29** 895
compounds **1** 312
craftsmen and artists **1** 245
gourds **23** 275
granaries **23** 275
hairstyles **1** 343
huts **23** 275
metalwork **23** 275
ochre **23** 274
pottery **23** 275
Nubia **7** *819*; **9** *507*, *774*; **23** 275–90*, *276*
architectural decorations **1** 317
architecture **21** 554–5; **29** 895; **32** 314
ceramics **23** 284–5, 289
churches **23** 287–8
collections **10** 93; **29** 898
crowns **23** 286, *286*
dress **1** 887
epigraphy **10** 83
exhibitions **10** 94
faience (i) (glass) **10** 48
fortifications **21** 554–5
fortresses **9** 844, 847; **21** 554–5, *555*; **23** 278
gold **9** 817
hardstones **23** *286*
ivory-carvings **27** 101
jewellery **23** 285
leather **10** 61
liturgical furnishings **7** 280
Lower Nubia **23** *276*, 285
metalwork **10** 38
mummies **1** 342
painting **10** 803; **23** 284, 288–9, *289*
Nubia—cont.
periods
Ballana (*c.* AD 360–*c.* 550) **23** 285–6*
Christian (*c.* AD 550–*c.* 1500) **23** 287–9*, *289*
Islamic **23** 289–90*
Kushite (*c.* 1075 BC–AD 360) **22** 467; **23** 281*
Meroitic (*c.* 300 BC–*c.* AD 360) **23** 282–5*, *284*
Napatan (*c.* 1075–*c.* 300 BC) **23** 281*, 282*
pottery **17** *912*; **23** 277, 285, 286
pyramids **23** 281, 282; **25** 760
rediscovery **10** 81*
schist **21** *160*
sculpture
architectural **23** 288
ba statues **23** 283
Prehistoric **23** *278*, *279*
relief **9** 881; **23** 281
Graeco-Roman (332 BC–AD 395) **9** 896
Meroitic (*c.* 300 BC–*c.* AD 360) **23** *284*
silver **23** 286, *286*
stelae **29** 615
stone-carvings **21** *160*
tablets **21** *160*
Tanqasi culture **23** 285
tattoos **1** 346
temples **23** 279
tombs **23** 279, 282
trade **9** 786
Upper Nubia **23** *276*, 285
see also KUSHITES
Nubians *see* BANDE NOIRE
Nubkheperre Inyotef **9** 878, 879; **10** 10, 56
Ñucchu **4** 260
Nucci, Allegretto *see* NUZI, ALLEGRETTO
Nuccio Vagnoli, Matteo di *see* NUTI, MATTEO
Nuchulus (Giovanni) **7** 318
Nuclear magnetic resonance spectrometry *see under* TECHNICAL EXAMINATION → types
Núcleo Bernardelli **4** 718; **8** 433
Nude, Jan **13** 101, 114; **22** 855
nude figures **8** 612; **14** 869; **23** 290–97*; **25** 276
Australia **4** *606*
Austria **10** *481*, *894*; **33** *198*
Azerbaijan **2** 897
Belgium **32** 151
Baroque **17** *650*; **25** *273*; **27** *288*, *292*, *293*
Early Netherlandish style **12** *847*
Mannerism **3** *24*
Renaissance **33** *170*
Surrealism **8** *700*
17th cent. **3** *108*; **33** *388*
Britain **23** 295
Chicano **18** *831*
Christianity **23** 291
Czech Republic **1** *5*; **33** *435*
Denmark **1** *32*; **8** *736*; **29** *541*
Dogon **9** *66*, *67*
Egypt, ancient **27** *89*
England **10** 265
Neo-classicism **5** *629*
New Sculpture (UK) **11** *303*
New Sculpture **23** *34*
New Sculpture (UK) **29** *575*
18th cent. **3** *184*
19th cent. **3** *78*; **8** *122*; **10** *646*; **12** *598*; **22** *52*
20th cent. **4** *670*
Etruscan **10** 589, *589*, 595
France **23**, 294–5
Baroque **12** *725*; **25** *706*; **29** *572*
Cubism **9** *355*
Impressionism **23** *296*
Mannerism **1** *17*

nude figures
France—cont.
Neo-classicism 4 301; 6 517; 12 730; 14 798; 24 172, 736
Neo-Impressionism 28 503
Orientalism 6 501; 15 844
Realism (style) 26 56
Rococo 4 515, 516; 17 627; 23 294; 25 275; 28 845; 29 573
Rococo Revival 11 545
Surrealism 30 292
16th cent. 11 503
18th cent. 4 510; 10 726; 23 795; 26 93
19th cent. 4 528; 5 342, 825; 26 509, 510
20th cent. 20 120, 825, 828
Germany 23 294
Baroque 23 309
Expressionism 22 257
Gothic 10 455; 26 370
Mannerism 3 103; 14 320
Neo-classicism 8 509
Neue Sachlichkeit 22 922
Renaissance 3 102; 11 223; 12 402; 29 557
Surrealism 3 672
16th cent. 3 200; 21 72
17th cent. 11 803; 24 543
19th cent. 7 856; 9 692; 14 526; 20 405
20th cent. 19 95; 20 396, 808
Gothic 10 455; 26 370
Greece, ancient 13 422, 449, 459, 459, 463; 18 148, 409, 410; 19 853; 22 699; 23 290–91*, 291; 24 328, 414; 25 456, 456; 26 297; 30 339
Classical 25 178, 179
Classical, High 13 429, 453
Hellenistic 25 179
Hellenistic, Late 13 466
Hinduism 15 218
Indian subcontinent 15 218; 20 818; 23 290
Iran 23 290
Italy 23 291–3
Baroque 1 535, 536; 3 829; 5 406, 860, 863, 866; 11 846; 12 764; 20 376; 26 201, 321; 27 816; 29 563
Etruscan 10 589, 589, 595
Greece, ancient 30 339
Mannerism 1 670; 3 162; 4 857; 6 145; 7 891; 8 511; 12 672; 20 280; 23 293; 24 201; 27 203, 209; 29 558, 562; 30 33, 319; 31 32
Neo-classicism 3 296; 5 627, 886; 16 705; 22 271
Renaissance 3 157, 665; 4 495, 499; 6 3; 12 656; 14 871; 16 693, 694, 696; 19 676; 21 436, 758; 23 292; 24 523; 25 158, 160; 27 773; 28 701; 29 561; 32 17, 809
Roman 14 443; 25 202; 27 14; 31 60
13th cent. 16 688
16th cent. 10 477; 11 52, 64; 12 736
18th cent. 29 887
20th cent. 16 707; 20 429; 31 445
Jainism 23 290
Japan 18 531; 23 290
Kuba (iii) (Zaïre) 18 486
Mexico 18 831
Netherlands, the 12 530; 23 294
Baroque 1 657; 26 158
Mannerism 4 151; 22 272, 846; 33 418
Renaissance 13 26; 19 758
16th cent. 7 868; 13 25; 20 248, 249
17th cent. 12 884; 20 245; 31 780
Norway 14 506; 32 497
nude figures—cont.
Portugal 27 615; 28 913
Prehistoric art 33 198
Renaissance 11 223
Rome, ancient 23 291; 29 562
Egypt 27 89
Greece, ancient 25 178
Italy 14 443; 25 202; 27 8, 14; 31 60
Republican 2 169; 19 853; 23 291; 29 561
Russia 28 475
Sogdiana 18 500
Spain 27 157; 29 294; 32 131, 132
Sweden 17 662; 28 462; 30 86
Switzerland 12 798; 19 414
Tajikistan 18 500
United States of America 18 594; 23 297; 26 430
Mexico 18 831
Neo-classicism 25 401
19th cent. 26 401, 401; 31 604
20th cent. 19 844
Zaïre 18 486
see also EROTIC ART; HUMAN FIGURES
nu en straks, Van 24 439
Nuer 1 237, 409, 411
Nuerhashi see NURHACHI
Nuestra Señora de Atocha 7 610
Nuestra Señora de Benavides, Tomb of Rodrigo González Girón 13 104
Nuestra Señora de la Concepción Treasure 29 345
Nuestra Señora de la Salceda 27 498
Nueva Baztán 29 331
Nueva Figuración group 2 401; 26 216
Nueva Forma 21 861
Nueva Generaciõn 29 287
Nueva Gerona 8 228, 237
Nueva Presencia 3 625
Nueva Visión 20 189
Nuevo Baztán 29 270
S Francisco Javier 7 288
Nuevo Espacialismo 11 371
Nuevo León, Instituto Tecnológico de Monterrey 21 381
Nuevo Realismo 3 826
Nuffield, W. R. Morris, Lord see MORRIS, W. R., Lord Nuffield
Nugent, Thomas 6 148; 13 298
Nuggihalli, Sadashiva temple 15 328
Nuguria 25 181
Nui 31 484
Ñuiñe 21 737
Nui Thanh 32 480
Nukha 2 900
Nukina Kaioku 17 412; 23 298*
groups and movements 17 237
works 17 216, 238
Nu Kuay 18 774
Nukufetau 31 484
Nukuhiva 20 462; 23 719
see also MARQUESAS ISLANDS
Nukulaelae 31 484
Nukuma 24 67
Nukumanu 25 181
sculpture 25 182
tattoos 25 182
weaving 25 182
Nukunonu 31 75
Nukuoro 23 723; 25 181
sculpture 23 730; 25 181, 182, 182
tattoos 25 182
weaving 25 182
Nukus 31 781
Karakalpakiya Museum of Art 6 283; 31 783
Karkalpakia State Regional Museum 6 283
museums 6 282
Nul 1 79; 22 852; 23 298*
members 2 422; 8 668; 9 168; 28 159
Nulamba see NOLAMBA
Nule 27 835
Nüll, Eduard Van der see VAN DER NÜLL, EDUARD
Numan, Hermanus 23 299*
Numan factory 9 298
Numankadić, Edin 4 461
Numantia 21 559
Number Ten Architectural Group 5 563
Numidia 23 299–300*; 26 852
limestone 27 14
marble 23 300
tombs 23 299
see also ALGERIA; TUNISIA
Numidian limestone see under LIMESTONE → types
Numisius, P. 14 440
numismatics 16 547; 24 848
Numizmatika i Epigrafika 6 279
Numkena, Dennis 22 671
Nuna 5 328; 22 196, 197
Nunakuma Shrine 17 326
Nuncques, William Degouve de see DEGOUVE DE NUNCQUES, WILLIAM
Nuneaton (Warwicks) 10 225; 23 300*
Chilvers Coton 23 300
Nuneham, George Simon Harcourt, Viscount see HARCOURT, GEORGE SIMON, 2nd Earl Harcourt
Nuneham, Simon Harcourt, 2nd Earl see HARCOURT, SIMON, 1st Earl Harcourt of Stanton Harcourt
Nuneham Park (Oxon) 3 201, 655; 14 163; 20 569
Nunes, Adelino 25 880; 28 729
Nunes, Alberto 26 130
Nunes, Domingos 26 253
Nuñes, Francisco 29 341
Nuñes, Julián Juan García see GARCÍA NUÑES, JULIÁN JUAN
Nunes, Pedro 3 218; 23 300*
Nunes Tinoco, João see TINOCO, JOÃO NUNES
Nunes Tinoco, Pedro see TINOCO, PEDRO NUNES
Núñez, Agustín 24 297
Nuñez, Domingo Vicente 32 176
Núñez, Elsa 9 117
Nuñez, José Corona see CORONA NUÑEZ, JOSÉ
Núñez, Max 6 595; 19 388
Nuñez, Orso 21 381
Núñez, Oscar 2 604
Núñez de Arce, Gaspar 21 81
Núñez de Balboa, Vasco 23 902
Núñez del Arco collection see under LA PAZ → museums
Núñez de Leão, Duarte 25 309
Núñez Delgado, Gaspar 23 300–301*; 29 344
Núñez del Prado, Casa Museo see under LA PAZ → museums
Núñez del Prado, José 4 259; 18 777
Núñez del Prado, Marina 4 265; 18 778; 23 301*
patrons and collectors 4 269
works 4 265, 265
Núñez del Prado, Nilda 4 269
Núñez de Villavicencio, Pedro 23 301*; 29 280
Nuñez Soler, Ignacio 23 301–2*; 24 99, 101
Nuñez Ureta, Teodoro 23 302*; 24 510, 515
Nŭnghogwan see YI IN-SANG
Nŭngsan 18 272
Nunilo, Queen of Asturias (fl 910) 23 682
Nunn, Pamela Gerrish 10 378
Nunnenmacher, Markus see NONNENMACHER, MAREK
Nunney (Somerset) 19 895
Nunnez, Fabrica see COXE, PETER
Nuño-MacGregor-de Buen 21 382
Nunuma 5 328
Nunziata, Antonio Toto del see TOTO DEL NUNZIATA, ANTONIO
Nunzio 16 709
Nuoffer (family) 30 143
Nuova Città, La 21 472
Nuova Secessione Artistica Italiana see FRONTE NUOVA DELLE ARTI
Nuove Tendenze 6 571; 10 493; 11 868; 21 781; 27 788
Nupe 9 733; 14 231; 23 302–3*
brass 23 303, 303*
craftsmen and artists 23 302
doors 1 383, 383; 9 164; 23 303
ewers 23 303
fortifications 21 597
gowns 23 302
guilds 23 302
masks 1 383; 23 303
metalwork 23 303*, 303
patronage 1 241, 242
pots 1 369, 369
sculpture 1 281
textiles 23 302*
tourist art 23 303
vessels 23 303
wood 1 383; 9 164
wood-carvings 23 303*
Nuppenbecher see under GLASSES → types
Nurabad 13 882
nuraghi 21 547
Corsica 21 551
Sardinia 3 311; 21 551; 23 304–5*, 304, 808; 25 522; 27 835
see also TOWERS → types → fortified
Nur al-Din, Ruler (reg 1146–74) (Zangid) 1 602, 603; 8 477; 14 98; 16 180, 181, 259, 490; 17 497; 21 629; 22 322; 33 614
Nurali, Byashim 31 459
Nurata 31 783
Nurbanu Valide Sultan 28 768
Nure 15 609
Nurek 6 237; 30 252, 252
Nuremberg 8 824; 12 361, 471; 23 304, 305, 305–17*, 307; 27 316
art forms and materials
armour 2 471
brass 3 603; 4 688, 692; 12 452, 452; 23 312–13
bronze 13 160, 160; 23 314; 29 570–71
ceramics 23 313*
chess sets 6 557
chests 16 59, 60
clocks 7 439
cupboards 12 421, 421
cups 24 573
dolls' houses 31 262
dress 9 273
enamel 14 235
façade decoration 10 737
faience (ii) (ceramics) 12 430; 14 235; 30 883
frames 11 455
furniture 5 350; 7 166; 33 332
gem-engraving 12 260
glass 12 439; 23 313*
gold 12 442, 443, 451; 23 310–12*; 25 137; 30 112
ivory 12 460; 33 669–71, 670
jewellery 12 455
maps 20 365
marks 12 442; 20 444; 23 311, 312, 313
medals 20 920, 923
Nuremberg
art forms and materials—cont.
metalwork 12 446, 452, 454; 13 160, 161; 23 310*, 312–13*; 25 126, 129
musical instruments 22 375
objects of vertu 28 11
painting 12 385, 389, 390, 391; 13 151; 17 699; 23 308*
glass 12 798
paper 24 55
pattern books 24 271
pewter 12 452, 453; 23 313; 24 578, 579
plaquettes 25 22
printing 17 521
prints 23 310*; 25 625
sculpture 12 399, 400, 402, 403; 13 85, 117; 23 308–9*
shells 22 204
silver 23 310–12*, 311
snuff-boxes 12 457
stained glass 27 255; 29 504
tapestries 12 465, 466, 466, 467, 468; 13 196; 23 314*; 30 312, 312, 319, 328
tiles 30 884
toys 10 135; 31 255
watches 7 441
weights 23 313
Burg 12 364; 29 434
Margarethenkapelle 14 81
craftsmen and artists 12 472; 23 307–8; 25 624
ecclesiastical buildings 23 305–6
Dominikanerkirche 12 466
Frauenkirche 12 365; 13 89; 14 81
Rochuskapelle 15 144
St Jacob 30 536
St Lorenz 12 365; 18 827, 828; 23 316, 316–17*; 32 821
paintings 27 159
rood 27 125
sacrament house 18 419
sculpture 9 680, 681; 29 729
stained glass 13 188; 29 504
textiles 30 331
St Martha 13 187
St Sebaldus 12 365; 13 187; 23 314*, 314
Bamberg window 29 504
clock 7 439
crucifix 8 215
piers (ii) (masonry) 24 751
Schreyer-Landauer Monument 18 420
sculpture 12 401
Sebaldus Tomb 13 160; 29 570–71; 32 607, 607
stained glass 23 315, 315–16*; 29 504
textiles 30 312, 331
Volckamer Donation 29 727
education (art) 12 478, 479
exhibitions 10 678
fountains
Apollo Fountain 11 223, 223–4; 29 563
Fountain of the Virtues 12 403
Neptune Fountain 28 193
Putto Fountain 24 331
Schöner Brunnen 11 341, 341
guilds 13 822; 24 579
Handelskammer 11 47
heraldry 14 409
houses 23 306–7; 32 282
Albrecht-Dürer-Haus see under museums
Fembohaus see under museums
Hirschvogelhaus 12 367
Pellerhaus 12 368; 33 294, 294
Tucherhaus 12 367; 17 711; 28 60
libraries
Bibliothek des Germanischen Nationalmuseums see under museums → Germanisches Nationalmuseum

Nuremberg
libraries—cont.
Stadtarchiv **2** 366
Stadtbibliothek Nuremberg **19** 314
museums
Albrecht-Dürer-Haus **23** 339
Fembohaus
Hirsvogelsaal **12** 409
Germanisches Nationalmuseum **3** 878; **10** 515; **12** 476; **27** 315
Bibliothek des Germanischen Nationalmuseums **12** 481
collections **2** 365, 370; **9** 156; **29** 516; **30** 332
exhibitions **16** 901
musical instruments **22** 376
Gewerbemuseum **29** 600
Stadtmuseum *see* Fembohaus
Rathaus **12** 370; **23** 317*, *317*; **31** 236; **33** 295
paintings **17** 699, 711, 712
wall paintings **33** 130
Schembart Carnival **5** 785
Teutsche Academie der Edlen Bau-, Bild- und Malerey-Künste **12** 478
theatres **30** 665
Tucher-Schlösschen *see* houses → Tucherhaus
Nuremberg, Frederick VI, Burgrave of *see* FREDERICK I, Elector of Brandenburg
Nuremberg Chronicle **31** 495
Nuremberg Faience Factory **23** 313
Nuremberg Hours *see under* BOOKS OF HOURS → individual manuscripts
Nuremberg Little Masters **12** 422; **19** 501; **20** 799
Nuremberg Madonna **18** 512
Nurhachi **6** 684; **7** 71
Nuri **23** *276*
church **23** 287
tombs **23** 281, 282; **25** 763
Taharqa (Nuri 1) **10** 18; **30** 237
Nuri İyem *see* İYEM, NURI
Nuristani **1** 188, 209, 210
Nuritdinov, Sirodzhiddin **30** 253
Nur Jahan, Empress (1517-1645) (Mughal) **1** 458, 460; **15** 364; **18** 646; **29** 480
Nurmesniemi, Antti **11** 104
Nurmesniemi, Vuokko **11** 110
Nurminen, Kerttu **11** 107
Nur Muhammad Tajikhan **16** 238
Nurmukhammetov, Rashid **27** 434
Nürnberg, Albrecht von *see* ALBRECHT VON NÜRNBERG
Nürnberger Gobelin-Manufaktur **23** 314
Nurpur **15** *619*
enamel **15** 712
paintings **7** VI1; **15** *623*, 623–4*
nursery gardens *see under* GARDENS → types
Nurse's Koran **16** 281
Nursling (Hants), Grove Place **10** 271
Nürtingen, Sammlung Domnick **9** 121
Nurymov, Makhtumkuly **31** 459
Nusay *see* NISA
Nusaybin *see* NISIBIS
Nusberg, Lev **27** 397
Nushabad Congregational Mosque **16** 250
Nush-i Jan, Tepe **15** *901*, 911; **21** 4; **23** 318*, *318*
altar **33** 707
architecture **15** 905
jewellery **1** 875
vaults (ceiling) **28** 537
Nusink & Co. **33** 323
Nušl, Jan **8** 414, 416
Nusrat Shah, Sultan (*reg* 1519-31) (Line of Sayyid Husayn Shah) **12** 204; **15** 574
Nuss, Fritz **23** 319*
Nussbaum, Felix **3** 802; **17** 579
Nussdorf, Hans von *see* HANS VON NUSSDORF
Nutan **2** 378
Nutclauss, Ambrosius **19** 835
Nuti, Curio **28** 318
Nuti, Matteo **3** 359; **19** 313; **20** 160; **23** 319*
nuts
historical and regional traditions
Africa **1** 296
China **7** 113
Indonesia **15** 812
Torres Strait Islands **31** 186
types
corozo **17** 398
palm **16** 797
parinarium **24** 84
uses
beads **1** 296
ex-votos **15** 812
headdresses **31** 186
kites **7** 113
masks **24** 84
netsuke **17** 398
scrimshaw **28** 302
Nutt, Haller **11** 361
Nutt, James **6** 577; **31** 609
Nuttall Group **21** 233, 235
Nutting, Wallace **31** 632
Nützel, Johan **30** 105
Nuu-chah-nuulth **22** 548
dress **22** 632
houses **22** 565
painting **22** *588*, 588–9
roofs **22** 565
sculpture **22** 578–9
tourist art **22** 668
Nuu-chah-nuulth (Northern) **22** 565
Nuutajärvi Glassworks **11** 105, 106, 107
Nuvolo, Giuseppe **23** 319*
Nuvolone, Carlo (*fl* 1650-1700) **23** 320
Nuvolone, Carlo Francesco (1609-62) **23** 319, 320–21*
works **23** *321*
Nuvolone, Giuseppe **23** 320, 321*
collaboration **23** 320
patrons and collectors **28** 12
Nuvolone, Michelangelo **4** 456
Nuvolone, Panfilo **23** 319, 320*
pupils **4** 456; **5** 289; **23** 320
al-Nuwayri **16** 441
Nuxalk **22** 548, 564, 579, 588, 632, 668
Nuyen, Wijnand(us Johannes Josephus) **14** 42; **23** 321–2*
pupils **19** 99; **26** 482
works **14** 42; **22** 848
Nuyts, Cornelis **23** *675*
Nuyts, Jean-Joseph **3** 584
Nuzal **27** 432
Nuzi **1** *849*; **21** *267*; **23** 322*
glass **1** 864, 865
Ishtar Temple **21** 285
palace **21** 285, 730; **23** 888
seals **1** 863; **4** 641; **21** 274, *731*
terracotta **1** 877
wall paintings **21** 308
writing-tablets **19** 311
Nuzi, Allegretto **23** 322–4*; **25** 691
works **23** *323*
Nuzi ware *see under* POTTERY → wares
Nuzstil **2** 567
Nuzzi, Mario *see* MARIO DEI FIORI
Nwe Daung **5** 257
Nwoko, Demas **15** 57; **23** 136, 137, 138, 139
Ny Abstraktion **8** 736, 742
Nyakabiga **5** 285
Nyama, Georges Lilanga di *see* LILANGA DI NYAMA, GEORGES
Nyamwezi **1** 249, 411
Nyanga **1** 282, 404; **19** 74; **22** 375
Nyanhongo, Agnes **33** 679
Nyári (family) **13** 162
Nyarko **1** 224
Nyarma **15** 311
Nyasa **1** 311
Nyasaland, British *see* MALAWI
Nyberg, Niels **23** 237
Nyblom, Carl Rupert **30** 119
Ny Carlsbergfond **4** 790; **8** 758, 760; **14** 543
Nydala **13** 50
Nydam **27** 93
Nye, Edmund **31** 422
Nyék Villa **14** 885
Nyendwa, Dickson **33** 603
Nyholm, Erik **7** 489
Nyilasy, Sándor **13** 333
Nyindu **1** 404, 405
Nyírbátor **14** *881*, 904; **23** 324*
bell-towers **14** 886
Calvinist church **14** 884, *886*
Minorite church **14** 894
St George *see* Calvinist church
Nyíregyháza, Collection of Greek Orthodox Art **15** 17
Nyiri, István **18** 854*
Nyitra *see* NITRA
Nyköping **30** 111
Nylen, Arend van **23** 665
Nylén, Erik **13** 848
nylon **5** 33; **30** 542
brushes **5** 33
etchings **10** 561
fibre art **11** 54
jewellery **17** 530
pens **24** 350
Nylund, Felix **11** 100
Nylund, Gunnar **28** 22; **30** 99, 101
Nymaatre *see* AMMENEMES III
Nyman, Gunnel **11** 106
Nyman, Olle **19** 798; **30** 81
Nyman, Roman **33** 566
Nymburk **8** 376
church **4** 782
crematorium **8** 380; **11** 47
Nymburský, Jakub **8** 395
Nymølle Fajancefabrik **8** 749
Nymølle Kobbermølle **8** 751
nymphaea **11** 339; **12** 69; **23** 324*; **27** 29, 65–6
Greece, ancient **26** 910
Italy **13** 703
Rome, ancient **26** 910
see also GROTTOES
Nymphaeum (Turkey) *see* KARABEL
Nymphaion (Bulgaria) **4** 110; **9** 524
palace **9** 559
tomb **4** 111
Nymphenburg Palace *see* MUNICH→ Schloss Nymphenburg
Nymphenburg Porcelain Factory **6** 924; **12** 433, 434, 437; **22** 300; **23** 324–5*; **26** 498
designers **5** 305; **12** 434; **33** 278
directors **12** 167; **23** 9
marks **20** 441
painters **14** 322–3
porcelain **12** *433*
Nyoitsu Sokuhi *see* SOKUHI NYOITSU
Nyolcak *see* EIGHT, THE (iii)
Nyoman Gunarsa **15** 809
Nyon **30** 144
Nyongo ya Chintu **14** 378
Nyon'in Kōya *see* MURŌJI
Nyor Diaple
masks **8** *487*, *488*
wood-carvings **1** *291*
Nypoort, Justus van der **28** 852
Nyrén, Carl **30** 75; **31** 693
Nyrop, Martin **23** 325*
works **7** 804, *804*; **8** 727, 745; **31** 242
Nys, Daniel **5** 764; **10** 363; **13** 299; **23** 325–6*; **24** 572; **29** 800
paintings **12** 913; **29** 799
Nys, J. F. **17** 599
Nys, Johannis **31** 648
Nysa (Poland), St James **4** 782
Nysa (Turkmenistan) *see* NISA
Nysø **8** 725
Nyssa **19** 841
Nystad **11** 106
Nyström, Erik **13** 864
Nyström, (Carl) Gustaf **23** 326*
works **14** 371; **23** 326; **31** 461
Nyts, Aegidius *see* NEYTS, GILLIS
Nyugat **24** 440
Nyundo **27** 458
Nzabi **1** 393
N'Zerekore **1** *386*
Local Museum **13** 835
NZIA Journal **24** 438
Nziku **30** 418
Nzima **1** 503
Nzinga Mvemba Alfonso I, King of Kongo (*reg* 1509-41) **1** 406; **2** 86

O

O, François, Marquis d' 20 133
Ó, Manuel do 26 254
Ó, Sebastião do 26 254
O'ahu see HAWAII
oak 33 324, 335
historical and regional traditions
Belgium 3 575, 577, 578, 580, 580, 581, 582, 583, 585, 586; 25 727
Catalonia 29 320
Czech Republic 8 399, 400
Denmark 11 467
England 10 274, 277, 286, 286, 288, 289, 293, 297, 298; 13 121; 18 610
Finland 11 98
France 5 192; 8 271; 11 585, 589
Germany 6 559; 12 423, 425; 13 118; 33 326
Gothic 3 580, 581; 6 559; 13 114, 118, 119, 121, 135; 25 726
Holy Roman Empire (before 1648) 13 118
Japan 17 354
Native North Americans 3 331
Netherlands, the 8 271; 13 114; 22 856, 872; 25 726; 33 IV2
New Zealand 23 67
Norway 13 119
Portugal 25 303
Scotland 6 391; 11 850; 28 251, 251
United States of America 31 624
types
Amur cork 7 45
yellow 7 115
uses
altarpieces 11 467
armoires 8 271; 11 589
baskets 3 331
beds 10 289
buffets 11 589
bureaux 5 192
cabinets (ii) (furniture) 3 581; 22 873; 33 IV2
chairs 6 391; 8 400; 11 850; 29 320
chests 6 559; 10 286
chests-of-drawers 3 583
choir-stalls 7 190; 13 118
coffers 3 580
cradles (i) (cots) 8 107
cupboards 8 271; 22 872; 28 251; 31 624
desks 3 586
doors 3 575; 9 157
dyes 7 45, 115; 17 354
floors 3 577; 10 273
furniture
Belgium 3 580, 582, 583, 585
Czech Republic 8 399
England 10 286, 288, 293, 297, 298
France 11 585
Germany 12 425
japanning 18 610
panel paintings 13 135; 24 3, 4, 5, 6
parquetry 3 578
pigments 18 656
pulpits 25 726, 727; 28 251
sculpture 13 114, 119, 121; 22 856; 24 776
sideboards 3 585
supports 30 5
tables 11 589; 12 423; 23 67
oak, bog see BOG OAK
oak apples see GALL-NUTS
Oakden, Percy 2 738; 23 327*; 30 516; 31 763
Oakeshott, Ewart 2 450
Oakey, Charles 11 424
Oakey, Maria see DEWING, MARIA OAKEY
oak galls see GALL-NUTS
Oakham (Leics) 14 75
Oakland (CA)
bridge 4 803
Fiberworks Center for the Textile Arts 30 330
Museum 26 480; 28 314
Oakland Six 31 607
Oak Park (IL)
Frank Lloyd Wright House 2 551; 31 595
Unity Temple 31 584; 33 402, 403
Oak Ridge (TN) 28 817
Oaksey Church (Wilts) 10 476
Oamaru 23 52
Bank of New South Wales 23 54
Bank of Otago 23 54
Woollen Mill 23 73
Oates, David 4 640; 7 185
Oates, Joan 4 640; 7 185
Oatlands Park (Surrey) 10 229, 363; 28 581
Oatley, George 4 823
Oaxaca 21 195, 198, 265, 372; 23 327*
Cathedral 21 375
collections 21 395
Dominican Monastery 21 375
furniture 21 391
Instituto de Artes Gráficas de Oaxaca 21 397; 31 93
jadeite 21 242
La Coyotera 31 505
manuscript illumination 21 234
masks 21 251
mirrors 21 718
Museo del Arte Contemporáneo 21 397
Museo de Arte Prehispánico 23 327; 30 282
Museo Regional de Oaxaca 21 396
S Domingo 29 841
silk 21 394
OBAC see ORGANIZATION OF BLACK AMEERICAN CULTURE
Oba Eresoyen, King (fl 18th cent.) 3 722
Obaid Srour 31 585
Ōbaku Buddhism see under BUDDHISM → sects
Ōbaku no Sanpitsu 15 832; 17 231, 234; 20 286; 21 801; 29 19
Ōbakuzan see UJI → Manpukuji
Obaldía, Isabel de 23 905
Obama, Hagadera 17 118
Obamba 11 878; 18 401, 403
sculpture 18 402
Oban 28 241, 260
ōban see under PRINTS → types → ukiyoe
Obari 17 407
Obata 14 37
Obata, Gyo 22 366
Oba Uke Shrine 15 112
Obberghen, Antonis van 12 224; 14 369; 23 328*; 29 593
patrons and collectors 23 395
works 4 781, 786; 12 224; 23 328; 31 196
Obedineniye Sovremennikh Arkhitektorov see OSA (Association of Contemporary Architects)
Obeid, Tell al- see UBAID, TELL AL-
Obelar, Pedro Domínguez de see DOMÍNGUEZ DE OBELAR, PEDRO
obelisks 23 329–31*
historical and regional traditions
Bulgaria 5 156
Egypt, ancient 2 362; 7 813; 9 813, 825; 23 329–30*, 330, 331
Madagascar 20 37
Mesopotamia 21 296
Rome, ancient 23 330*
South America, Pre-Columbian 29 131
materials
copper 7 813
granite 9 813, 825; 23 329, 330, 331; 29 131
Ober, Artur (Lavrent'yevich) 27 425
Oberaden 30 772
Oberaltaich Abbey Church 12 370
Oberammergau, Linderhof 5 349
Oberberg, Antonis van see OBBERGHEN, ANTONIS VAN
Oberberg, Hercules von 8 725; 23 396
Oberehnheim Stadtkirche 13 188
Oberelchingen Monastery 12 372
Öberg, Thure 11 105
Oberhausen, Ludwig Institut für Kunst der DDR 19 779
Oberhessen, Münzenberg 7 303
Oberholzer, Obie 9 427
Oberhölzer, Philip 8 413
Oberhuber, Oswald 2 797, 804; 28 344; 32 447
Oberkampf, Christophe-Philippe 8 36; 11 649; 23 331*; 30 562
works 7 167; 14 792; 19 11; 30 X1
Über Kunst und Alterum 24 443
Oberländer, Marek 2 502; 25 108
Oberleutensdorf 8 419
Oberlin (OH)
Allen Memorial Art Museum 29 584
Oberlin College 9 231; 17 435
Obermaier, Hugo 33 197
Oberman, Anthony 22 848
Obermarchtal Monastery Church 12 371; 29 838; 32 821, 822
Obermeyer 33 167
Obermillner, Martha see SCHERZHAUSER, MARTHA
Obermillner, Thomas 23 331–2*
works 2 815, 815; 27 665
Obermuschelstil 23 332*
Oberndorf 29 779
Oberndorffer, Oswald 20 614
Oberpleis, St Pankratius 26 633
Oberried Altarpiece 14 666
Oberschleissheim, Schloss Schleissheim 12 361, 369, 372; 26 495; 28 109–10*
Altes Schloss 28 109
gardens 8 794; 12 133; 26 497
Lustheim 12 371; 28 109
Nativity groups 22 680
Neues Schloss 3 514; 9 746; 12 371, 410; 28 109–10, 110
collections 9 18; 25 675
stucco 29 838
Viktoriensaal 9 336; 12 411
Oberschleissheim, Schloss Schleissheim—cont.
paintings 1 796; 3 514; 4 54; 5 908; 9 198; 13 845; 17 918; 19 817; 24 341; 27 291, 725; 28 38
Oberstein, Ivo 8 381
Oberwesel 12 400
Unsere Liebe Frau 1 709; 13 116
Oberwinterthur, St Arbogast 30 129
Óbidos 25 318
Misericórdia 26 253
S Maria
tomb of Isabel de Souza 25 301
tomb of João de Noronha 25 301
Óbidos, Josefa d' see AYALA (E CABRERA), JOSEFA DE
Obigarm 30 252
school 30 252
Obin, Philomé 14 58, 60; 23 332*
Obiols, Josep 29 309
Obiri Rock see UBIRR
Obizzi (family) 15 87
Obizzi, Gasparo 23 332; 25 18
Obizzi, Pio Enea, I (1525-89) 23 332
Obizzi, Pio Enea, II (1592-1674) 23 332
Obizzi, Tomaso degli, Marchese 23 332–3*
Obizzo Alidosio d'Imola see IMOLA, OBIZZO ALIDOSIO D'
Obizzo I, Marchese of Ferrara (reg 1264-93) 11 2
Obizzo II, Marchese of Ferrara (reg 1317-52) 11 3
Objective abstraction 22 243; 23 333*
Objective Reality Group see BYTIYE
Object School see MONOHA
objects of vertu
Australia 2 764–6*
Belgium 3 603*
Czech Republic 8 416*
Denmark 8 752–3*
England 10 344*
France 11 629*
Germany 12 455*
Hungary 15 10*
Ireland 16 33*
Netherlands, the 22 895–6*, 897*
Norway 23 238*
Portugal 25 314*
Russia 10 721; 27 426*
Scotland 28 263–4*
Spain 29 344–6*
Sweden 30 112–14*
Switzerland 30 148*
Objektiv 24 451
objets de luxe see under COLLECTIONS → types
Objets et Mondes 24 430
objets trouvés 2 615; 7 557; 23 333–5*; 26 51
France 23 334
United States of America 31 608, 614
Oblate, Master of 8 212
Oblation 24 619
Oblik 4 680; 20 512
Obmas 2 603
Obminsky, Tadyeush 28 838
Obmokhu see SOCIETY OF YOUNG ARTISTS
Obnorsk 25 337
Obolensky, A., Prince 27 416
Oboli, Jacques 19 137
Ōbora shell-mounds 17 246
Obori kiln 17 258
Obořiště, St Joseph 8 378; 15 139
Obrazopisov (family) 27 685
Obrazopisov, Nikola 27 686
Obraztsov, Vladimir Vitalyevich 18 568
Obre 5 313
Obregón, Alejandro 23 335*
works 7 609, 610, 611
Obregón, José María 21 385
Obregón, Roberto 23 335*
Obregón Santacilia, Carlos 21 379, 403; 23 335*
collaboration 20 500
works 21 379
Obrera Mataronense, La 12 180
Obreshkov, Bencho 5 163; 23 16, 335*
Obri-Chambra Shiva Temple 15 627
O'Brien, Catherine 31 229
O'Brien, Dermod 16 17
O'Brien, George 23 58
O'Brien, Justin (Maurice) 23 336*; 30 160
O'Brien, Lucius R(ichard) 5 566; 19 791; 23 336*
O'Brien Publicity Co. 32 770
Obrisset, Jean 14 856
Obrist, Hermann 8 594; 22 304; 23 336–7*
groups and movements 2 565–6; 8 825; 10 215; 12 416; 24 279; 26 374; 28 341
house 24 13
pupils 18 77; 28 126
works 12 463; 23 337; 30 138
Obrocki, Jan 19 836; 25 115; 26 498
Ó Brolchán, Donald 15 892; 28 241
Obrovsky, Jakub 22 393
Obrtel, Vít 8 380; 11 365; 14 732; 19 423
Obsequies of St Francis, Master of the 2 624
observatories 23 337–42*
Austria 18 447
Britain 21 42
Central Asia, Western 16 198
China 23 338
France 23 339, 342
Germany 14 491; 21 119
Inca 23 338
Indian subcontinent 23 338, 339
Iran 16 193
Islamic 16 193, 198; 23 338
Jesuit Order 23 340
Korea 23 339
Maya 23 338
Mesoamerica, Pre-Columbian 23 338
Mesopotamia 23 338
Prehistoric art 21 42
South America, Pre-Columbian 23 338
Spain 32 566
United States of America 23 341, 341
Zapotec 23 338
observatory clocks see under CLOCKS → types
Obshchestvo arkhitektorov 3 409
Obshchestvo khudozhnikov-stankovistov (OST) see SOCIETY OF EASEL PAINTERS
obsidian 12 780; 17 514; 29 702–3*
historical and regional traditions
Aztec 21 719; 22 164
Crete 21 689

obsidian
historical and regional traditions—cont.
Cycladic **8** 305; **21** 94
Ethiopia **29** 702
Maori **29** 703
Maya **20** 881; **21** 251
Mesoamerica, Pre-Columbian **21** 181, 192, 195, 198, 245, 246, 251, 254, 718, 719; **22** 158, 164; **29** 703
Minoan **21** *689*
Mixtec **21** 737
Prehistoric art **25** 515
South America, Pre-Columbian **29** 155
Toltec **31** 98
West Mexico **21** 718
uses
arrowheads **21** 192
masks **21** 251, 254
mirrors **21** 718, 719, *719*
mosaics **22** 158, 164
spearheads **21** 192, 245
swords **21** 245
tools **21** 195; **25** 515
vases **21** *689*
Obstal, Gerard van *see* OPSTAL, GERARD VAN
Óbuda *see* BUDAPEST
Obukhovichi **31** 564
Oburdon **6** 277; **16** 491
obverse **23** 342*; **26** 66
Oca, Confucio Montes de *see* MONTES DE OCA CONFUCIO
Ocampo, Andrés de **14** 714; **21** 109; **23** 342–3*
Ocampo, Francisco de **14** 714; **23** 343
Ocampo, Galo **24** 613, 622
Ocampo, Hernando **24** 622, 623
Ocampo, Miguel **2** 401, 546; **23** 343*
Ocampo, Salvador de **21** 383
Ocampo, Sebastián de **21** 383
Ocaña, Artemio **24** 509
Ocaña, Diego de **8** 302
Ocaranza, Manuel (Egidio) **23** 343*
ocarinas **21** 257; **29** 217
O'Carroll, Donough, King of Uriel *see* DONOUGH O'CARROLL, King of Uriel
O'Carryd, Thomas **13** 165; **16** 30
Occhi Ammiccanti, Master of the **11** 8
Occhi Spalancati, Master of the **11** 8
Occidental Petroleum **14** 117
Occo, Pompeius **1** 806; **16** *831*
Occultism **8** 244
Oceania *see* ABORIGINAL AUSTRALIA; PACIFIC ISLANDS
Oc Eo **23** 343–4*; **29** *225*; **32** *468*
Ocggl, Wilhelm *see* EGCKL, WILHELM
Ochiauri, I. **12** 329
Ochier, Jean-Baptiste **7** 476
Ochiltree Stalls **28** 250
Ochiltrie, John **28** 266
Öchkel, Wilhelm *see* EGCKL, WILHELM
Ochoa, Eugenio de **20** 59; **24** 422, 452; **29** 283
Ochoa Montes, Sebastian de **32** 176
Ochomogo **29** 205
Ocho Rios **16** *878*
ochre
historical and regional traditions
Central Asia, Western **16** 248
China **6** 874; **7** 632
Iran **16** 248
Islamic **16** 248
Rome, ancient **27** 51
types
brown **24** 792
ochre
types—cont.
red **11** 763; **18** 600; **23** 274; **24** 795*; **25** 477
Nuba **23** 274
Sri Lanka **29** 463
yellow **9** 623; **11** 763; **12** 622; **23** 274; **24** 798*
Byzantine **9** 623
Greece, ancient **13** 536
Nuba **23** 274
Sri Lanka **29** 463
uses
gilding **24** 56
lacquer **18** 600
mordants (ii) (gilding) **12** 622
pigments **7** 632; **9** 623; **11** 763; **13** 536; **23** 274; **24** 792*, 795*, 798*
pottery **6** 874
tiles **16** 248
Ochrona zabytków **24** 441
Ochs, Jakob **21** 494
Öchsel, Jörg **24** 807
Ochsenfurt, Hans Paur van *see* PAUR VAN OCHSENFURT, HANS
Ochsenhausen Monastery **12** 369
Ochsner, Albert J. **14** 783
Ochtervelt, Jacob **23** 344–5*; **27** 230
reproductive prints by others **12** 209
teachers **3** 759
works **7** 784; **11** 446; **14** 732; **23** *344*
Ochungo Buluma, Mordechai *see* BULUMA, MORDECHAI OCHUNGO
Očko, Jan **8** 389, 422
Ocktha-Ecklesia **30** 306
church **12** 323
wall paintings **30** 305
OCLC (Ohio College Library Center) **4** 23
Ocna Sibiului Church **26** 710
Ocón, René **10** 154
O'Connell, Daniel **16** 28
O'Connell, Eilis **16** 22
O'Connell, Michael **2** 756
O'Connor, Andrew **16** 21; **33** 150
O'Connor, Bunty **31** 339
O'Connor, G. **16** 27
works **16** *27*
O'Connor, James Arthur **16** 16; **23** 345*
O'Connor, John (1830-89) **30** 681; **31** 156
O'Connor, John (*b* 1913) **4** 367
O'Connor, Johnson **20** 282
O'Connor, Kate (Laetitia) **23** 346*; **24** 496
O'Connor, Michael **9** 321
O'Connor, Patrick **9** 427
O'Connor, Turlough, King of Connaught *see* TURLOUGH O'CONNOR, King of Ireland
O'Conor, Roderic (Anthony) **16** 17; **23** 346*; **25** 215
Ocós culture **7** 207
Ocotillo **22** 567
Ocotlan **27** 499
Ocros style pottery *see under* POTTERY → wares
Ócsa **14** *881*
Calvinist church **14** 883, 898
octastyle **23** 346*
Octavien, François (*c.* 1652-1722) **23** 346
Octavien, François (*c.* 1682-1740) **23** 346–7*
works **11** *407*
October group (Finland) **17** 771
octopartite vaults *see under* VAULTS (CEILING) → types
Octopus Cup **8** 712
Ocucaje **29** 179, 180
Ó Cuinn, Mael-Sechlainn **28** 241
oculi **9** 11; **23** 347*; **26** 880
al-Oda **9** 565
Oda, Archbishop of Canterbury **5** 643
Oda, Kazuma **17** 293
Oda Kaisen **31** 135
O'Daly, Raymond **24** 409
O'Daly, Tomas **25** 700
Oda Nobunaga **17** 783; **18** 550; **23** 347*, 592
architecture **2** 908; **16** 73; **17** 40, 84; **18** 550, 551; **21** 827; **23** 554
assistants **28** 411
collections **17** 428
metalwork **17** 323
paintings **2** 909; **17** 22, 423, 796
standards (vexilloid) **11** 152
Odano Naotake **17** 165; **23** 347*
teachers **14** 565; **27** 865
works **17** 186; **27** 866
Odasi, Giovanni *see* ODAZZI, GIOVANNI
Oda Uraku **14** 704; **17** 336, 340
Odawara, Matsunaga Memorial Hall **15** 746
Odazzi, Giovanni **23** 347–8*
attributions **20** 903
collaboration **3** 920; **8** 12
works **26** 827
Odbert of St Bertin **2** 76; **23** 348*
Odda **13** 143
Odder Church **8** 738
Oddi, Mauro **24** 196
Oddi, Muzio **19** 764; **23** 348–9*; **27** 274; **31** 740
Oddie, Walter M. **14** 396
O'Dea, Cornelius **16** 30
odeia **23** 349–50*
Greece, ancient **13** 386; **23** 349, *350*; **26** 910; **27** 712
Rome, ancient **23** 349–50; **26** 874, 910; **27** 712
see also CONCERT HALLS
Odell, W. J. **19** 415
Ödenburg *see* SOPRON
Odense **8** *720*
Blangstedgård **8** 729
Cathedral of St Knud **4** 781; **8** 723, 725, 738
altarpiece **13** 120
Franciscan church **13** 120
Fynske Kunstakademi **8** 761
Fyns Kunstmuseum **8** 760
H. C. Andersens Hus **18** 800
Museum for Fotokunst **8** 760, 761
sculpture **8** 738
University **8** 729
Odenwald, Michael **2** 734
Odenwald-Limes **26** 906
Oderfeld, Henryk **30** 199
Odericus Romanus *see* PIETRO DI ODERISIO
Oderigo, Lorenzo d'Andrea d' *see* LORENZO DI CREDI
Oderisi, Roberto d' **23** 350–51*
works **23** *351*
Oderisii, Petrus *see* PIETRO DI ODERISIO
Oderisio, Pietro di *see* PIETRO DI ODERISIO
Oderisio da Gubbio **4** 273
Oderisius (family) **7** 922
Oderisius, Abbot of Montecasino **4** 763; **19** 207; **26** 665
Oderisius of Benevento **9** 154; **23** 352*
Oderisius Stephani **24** 783
Odescalchi (family) **5** 711; **19** 816; **23** 516; **30** 118
Odescalchi, Baldassare d'Erba **23** 352, 353; **24** 10
Odescalchi, Benedetto, Cardinal *see* INNOCENT XI, Pope
Odescalchi, Livio, Duca di Bracciano *see* BRACCIANO, LIVIO ODESCALCHI, Duca di
Odescalchi, Tommaso **23** 352
Odescalchi *Dioscuri* **23** 353
Odessa **21** *810*; **23** 353–4*; **27** 376; **31** *546*, 719
Archaeological Museum **23** 354
architecture **31** 551
Art Museum **18** 399; **23** 354
Art School **23** 354
Jewish Museum **17** 581
Khadzhibei Estuary **31** 559
Museum of Local History **23** 354
Museum of Western and Oriental Art **23** 354
Opera and Ballet Theatre **23** *354*
painting **31** 559
sculpture **31** 561
Vorontsov palace **31** 564
Odessos *see* VARNA
Odevaere, Joseph-Denis **23** 354*
competitions **25** 638
teachers **8** 560
works **3** 562; **30** 46
Odier, E. A. **32** 829
Odieuvre, Michel **3** 107, 318; **11** 57, 81; **33** 195
Odiham Hunting Lodge (Hants) **10** *285*
Odilo, Abbot of Cluny **6** 464; **7** 474; **21** 836
Odin, Jacquemart de *see* JACQUEMART DE HESDIN
Odinayev, Valimad **30** 253
Odiot **24** 147
Odiot, Charles-Nicolas **11** 621; **23** 355, 778
Odiot, Jean Baptiste Claude **11** 621; **22** 889; **23** 354–5*
collaboration **32** 458
groups and movements **10** 186
patrons and collectors **4** 302, 303
personal collection **2** 722
pupils **12** 221
works **11** 621; **24** 147, 388; **27** 641
Odjig, Daphne **22** 597
Odo (Japan) **17** 352
Odo, Abbot of Cluny (*reg* 1423-56/7) **7** 476
Odo, Bishop of Bayeux (1030-97) **3** 426; **11** 654
Odo I, Duke of Burgundy (*reg* 1079-1102) **7** 355
Odo II, Count of Champagne (*reg* 996-1037) and Count of Blois (*reg* 1004-37) **25** 667
Odo II, Duke of Burgundy (*reg* 1143-62) **8** 888
Odoacar **11** 146
Odoardo, 5th Duke of Parma and Piacenza **10** 808
Odo Clement, Abbot of Cluny (*fl* 1229-45) **27** 541
Odolric, Abbot of Conques **7** 718
Odoni, Alvise **9** 28; **23** 355
Odoni, Andrea **14** 869; **19** *712*; **23** 355*
collections **32** 193
frescoes **12** 736
paintings **12** 676; **27** 891
sculpture **2** 558; **21** 632
Odoni Altarpiece **8** 166, 171
O'Donnell, James **5** 561; **13** 202; **22** 36
O'Donovan, William **27** 557
odontolite *see under* IVORY → types
Odo of Metz **1** 2
Odorhei, Roman Catholic College **26** 724
Odorico, Isidore **26** 205
Odoric of Pordenone **16** 193; **31** 289
Odoricus *see* PIETRO DI ODERISIO
Odriozola, Francisco Ibero y *see* IBERO Y ODRIOZOLA, FRANCISCO
Odrisio, Lorenzo di *see* LORENZO DI ODRISIO
Odrowąż, Iwo, Bishop of Kraków **27** 722
Odù **24** 430
Odua, Ikem **18** 640
Oduber, Ciro **23** 905
Odumann, Joël Ola Wouwou *see* JOËL
Odundo, Magdalene **17** 906
Oduya, Fred **17** 907
O'Dwyer, Kevin **16** 32
Odzun **2** *423*, 425; **9** *512*; **23** 355–6*
church **2** 425, 434; **23** *355*, 355–6
sculpture **2** 434
stelae **2** 435; **23** 356
Oe, Hiroshi **17** 93; **23** 356*
Oe, Shintarō **23** 356
Oea *see* TRIPOLI
Oeben (family) **11** 408
Oeben, Jean-François **8** 638; **23** 356–7*
collaboration **5** 767; **9** 399; **11** 305
groups and movements **19** 723
patrons and collectors **4** 554; **7** 528, 658; **17** 639
pupils **26** 375
works **5** 192, *192*, 380; **7** 658; **11** 591, *591*, 592; **20** 468
Oeben, Simon **14** 230; **17** 666; **26** 375
Oechs, Joseph **18** 851
Oechslin, Johann Jakob **30** 137
oeci **13** 382; **23** 357*
Oedtl (family) **25** 448
Oedtl, Christian Alexander **13** 661
Oefele, Ignaz **8** 897; **13** 258
Oegckl, Wilhelm *see* EGCKL, WILHELM
Ōe Genpo **17** 414
Oegg, Johann Georg **2** 822; **14** 297; **33** 432, 434
works **2** *822*
Oehlensläger, Adam **22** 540
Oehme, Ernst Ferdinand **12** 393
Oehme, Erwin **23** 872
Oeil, L' **24** 429, 442
oeil-de-boeuf windows *see under* WINDOWS → types
Oeiras
Quinta Pombal **13** 695; **20** *402*; **30** 881
S Julião da Barra **25** 291
Oelde, Ambrosius von **13** 684
Oelefe, Francesco **4** 154
Oelsner, Gustav **16** 591
Oelze, Richard **23** 357–8*; **30** 21
works **23** *357*
Ōe no Asatsuna **17** 222; **23** 445
Ōe no Chikamichi **22** 497, 500
oenochoai *see* OINOCHOAI
Oenpelli **1** 51, 58; **22** 418
Oenslager, Donald **5** 531
Oerder, Frans (David) **25** 566; **29** 108, 110
Oeri, Hans Peter **30** 147
works **30** *146*
Oerley, Robert **2** 814; **23** 358*
Oernster, Emanuel Gottlieb **12** 447
Oertl, Jan **23** 271
O(ptical) E(mission) S(pectrometry) *see under* TECHNICAL EXAMINATION → types
Oeser, Adam Friedrich **19** 111; **23** 358–9*
patrons and collectors **33** 116
pupils **11** 817; **12** 853; **26** 98, 127
teachers **4** 695
works **12** 392; **19** 110
writings **12** 413
Oeskus *see* GIGEN
œsophage **30** 20
Oesterlen, Dieter **12** 379, 380
Oesterly, Carl **3** 288
Oesterreicher, Matthias **23** 855
Oetingen-Wallerstein, Ludwig von, Prince **14** 148
Oettingen-Schrattenhofen **12** 430, 431

Oettinger, Johan Friedrich von 18 851
Oettner, Andreas Philipp 11 731; 19 780
Oeuf de Naples ruby, L' 11 634
oeuvre catalogues see under CATALOGUES → types
Oey, Jan van 22 857
Ofakim Hadashim see NEW HORIZONS
O'Fallon, James 33 13
O'Farrell, Jasper 27 729
Ofek, Avraham 16 567; 17 579
Öfele, Franz Ignaz 1 579
Ofellius Ferus, C. 27 27
Offa, King of Mercia (reg 757-96) 7 534; 19 566
Offamilio, Gualtiero, Bishop of Palermo 23 841, 842
Offenbach, Jacques 6 549
Offenburg, Heinrich von 14 285
offering bowls see under BOWLS → types
offering tables 1 507; 29 664
office buildings 23 359–61*
Belgium 14 771
Catalonia 7 511
Chile 6 595
England 10 233, 235; 19 506
Greek Revival 7 503
Neo-classicism 1 139
New Brutalism 28 890
Post-modernism 19 578
19th cent. 3 533; 28 563
20th cent. 14 674; 19 506; 26 540
France 11 527; 14 388
Germany 18 417
Greece 9 207
Italy 16 649, 651; 25 218
Netherlands, the 3 787; 14 484
Pakistan 23 799
Scotland 12 775
United States of America 15 887; 23 360
19th cent. 6 573; 11 848; 27 138; 31 592
Office for Metropolitan Architecture (OMA) 18 236; 22 832; 23 361*
office landscaping see BUROLANDSCHAFT
Office Lectionaries 28 487
Office of Buildings (St Petersburg) 27 442
Office of Tiles see KAWARA BUGYŌSHO
Office of Works 10 229, 232, 360; 19 617; 23 361–2*
Officina Bodini 20 404
Officina Goltziana 12 885
Officina Plantiniana 33 168
Offley, Hugh 10 288
Offner, Richard 23 362*
assistants 29 613
pupils 12 165; 21 61
sponsors 29 763
works 31 671
offset see COUNTERPROOFS
offset printing see under PRINTING → processes
Ofir, Arie 16 568
ōgama see under KILNS → types
Ogasawara (family) 1 448
Ogata (family) 17 180
Ogata, Gekkō 17 290, 293; 18 172
Ogata, Kamenosuke 17 205, 206; 20 873
Ogata Ihachi 23 367
Ogata Kenzan 9 738; 17 179, 258; 23 196, 363, 364–7*, 554; 27 596
personal collection 23 196
pupils 18 901
works 17 244; 18 554; 23 365, 366
writings 17 418; 23 196
Ogata Kōan 23 592
Ogata Kōrin 9 738; 17 165, 177, 179; 23 363–7*, 554; 27 595
collaboration 17 303; 18 554; 23 366
commentaries 27 596
groups and movements 17 797
patrons and collectors 11 748; 27 595
works 10 777; 14 551; 17 166, 311; 23 363, 365, 367
Ogata Shūhei 18 555
Ogata Sōhaku 14 703, 704; 23 362
Ogata Sōken 14 704; 23 363
Ogawa, Gesshū 11 811
Ogawa, Jihei 12 100; 18 551
Ogawa Haritsu 17 303
Ogawa Isshin see ISSHIN, OGAWA
Ogawa Sadanobu see KANŌ KŌI
Ogbe 9 734
Ogden, William B. 31 887
Ogedei, Khan (reg 1227-41) (Great Khans) 21 874; 30 470
ogee 23 368*; 31 271
ogee arches see under ARCHES → types
ogee mouldings see under MOULDINGS → types
Ogen, Gedula 16 568
Oggiono, Marco d' 23 368*
collaboration 4 284
patrons and collectors 1 766; 22 26, 31
Ogier, Louisa Perina see COURTAULD, LOUISA PERINA
Ogier de Gombauld, Jean 25 461
Ogilby, John 3 244; 7 431; 10 725; 14 684
works 3 245
Ogilvie, Elizabeth 28 240
Ogilvie, Will 7 648
Ōgimachi, Emperor (reg 1557-86) 17 784
Ogiński, Michał Kazimierz, Prince 23 368–9*; 25 136
architecture 3 526
furniture 25 121
interior decoration 23 113
paintings 27 446
Ogiński, Michał Kleofas 25 136
Ogishima, Yasuji 17 135
ogive 23 369*
Ogiwara, Morie 17 134; 21 59; 23 369*
Oglakhty 27 367
Oglala (SD), Lakota College 22 671
Ogle, Tom 11 101
Oglethorpe, James 27 883; 31 721
Ognabene, Andrea di Jacopo d' see ANDREA DI JACOPO D'OGNABENE
Ognabene, Tallino di Jacopo d' see TALLINO DI JACOPO D'OGNABENE
Ognibene of Lonigo 12 907
Ögödey Khan 30 476
Ogol, Master of 9 66
Ogoni 15 65
O'Gorman, Cecil 23 370
O'Gorman, Juan 14 715; 23 369–70*
collaboration 24 402
groups and movements 15 886; 33 493
works 19 321; 21 379, 380, 388, 403; 22 158, 164, 334–5; 23 370
Ogotemmêli 9 65, 66
Oguchi, Shugyō 17 239
Ogunquit 18 868
Ogura Collection see under TOKYO → museums → National Museum
Oguri Sōkei 23 371
Oguri Sōritsu 23 371
Oguri Sōtan 17 29, 780; 23 371*
pupils 17 795
teachers 30 466
Ogwa Palace 9 735
Ogyū Sorai 17 236, 419; 33 491
Ohafia 15 109, 111, 114
Ohanessian, David 30 507
Ōhara (family) 18 528
O'Hara, Alfred-Emilien, Comte de Nieuwerkerke see NIEUWERKERKE(, ALFRED-EMILIEN O'HARA), Comte de
O'Hara, Frank 1 88; 14 203; 20 606; 26 431
Ohara, Hōun 17 381
Ohara, Koson 17 293
Ōhara, Magosaburō 18 528; 21 635; 23 371
Ōhara, Sōichirō 17 430; 18 528; 23 371
Ohara, Unshin 17 381
Ohara Keizan 17 186
Ōhara Mitsuhiro 17 401; 31 199
Ōhara Museum of Art see under KURASHIKI
Ōhashi 27 600
Ohbayashi 17 53
O'Hedian, Archbishop 5 916
Ohettoint 22 63; 28 741, 742
O'Higginiano y de Bellas Artes, Museo see under TALCA
O'Higgins, Bernardo 6 592; 27 791
O'Higgins, Pablo 21 388; 23 371*; 30 275
Ōhiroma 17 77–9*
Ōhi ware see under POTTERY → wares
Ohlmüller, (Joseph) Daniel 13 202; 23 371–2*; 33 282, 673
Ohly, Friedrich 10 176
Öhman, Johan 30 95
Ohmann, Béla 14 896
Ohmann, Friedrich 23 372*
assistants 10 102
collaboration 25 548
pupils 24 309; 33 172
staff 18 421; 29 777
works 2 787, 788; 8 379; 23 813; 25 151; 32 457
Ohnsorg, Kurt 32 450
Ohr, George E. 31 638
Ohrid 5 146; 9 511; 19 882; 23 372–4*
basilica 19 882
Bogorodica Bolnička see Virgin of the Hospital
Cathedral (5th cent.) 23 372
Cathedral of St Sophia (11th cent.) 5 146, 155; 7 253, 272, 279; 9 547, 551; 19 882, 884; 23 373, 373–4; 24 110
templon 28 291
wall paintings 9 579; 22 520
Dom Roveva see National Museum
Hagia Sophia see Cathedral of St Sophia
icons 19 884; 25 340; 28 455, 458
Imaret Mosque 7 256
manuscripts 5 152, 162
Monastery of St Naum 19 882, 883; 25 340
National Museum 19 886; 23 373
Retirement Home 19 883
St Clement 5 155; 9 551; 19 882; 23 373, 374
icons 9 628, 629
wall paintings 9 584; 23 374
St John Kaneo 19 882
St Nicholas Bolnički see St Nicholas of the Hospital
St Nicholas of the Hospital 9 600; 19 884; 25 343; 28 447
St Panteleimon 5 146; 7 256; 19 882
Virgin of the Hospital 28 447
Virgin Peribleptos see St Clement
wall paintings 19 884; 25 343
Öhrmark, Erik 30 95
Ohrmuschelstil see AURICULAR STYLE
Öhrström, Edvin 30 86, 102
Ohtake, Ruy 4 714; 21 123
Ohtake, Tomie 4 719
Ohthere 2 82
Oibō 17 243
Oie see under JAPAN → calligraphy
Oignies, Hugo d' see HUGO D'OIGNIES
Oignies Priory 14 854
oignon watches see under WATCHES → types
Ōi Katsushika see KATSUSHIKA ŌI
oikoi see OECI
Oil and Grease Company 28 488
oil black 17 213
oil-drums 14 58
oil gilding see under GILDING → types
oiling 24 258
oil lamps see under LAMPS → types
Oilli, Robert d' (fl 1070-1119) 23 685
Oilli, Robert d', II (fl 1129) 23 685
oil paintings 7 562; 18 706; 23 375–9*; 30 5
historical and regional traditions
Austria 8 445
Germany 23 375
Greece 9 206
Indian subcontinent 5 419
Iran 16 535–6*
Islamic 16 535–7*
Italy 2 178; 23 376
Japan 17 206
Netherlands, the 23 376
New Zealand 23 57
Norway 23 224, 375
Ottoman 16 536–7*
Turkey 16 535, 536–7*
materials
brushes 23 376, 379
canvas 23 376
glazes 2 178; 23 375
grounds 13 708; 23 377, 378
oils 23 375, 376, 377
turpentine 23 375, 377
varnishes 8 447; 24 569
techniques
modelling 6 569
see also OIL SKETCHES;
see also under PAINTING → historical and regional traditions
oil paints see under PAINTS → types
oil pastels see PASTELS
oil pigment process see under PHOTOGRAPHY → processes
oils 24 789
historical and regional traditions
Africa 1 305
Gothic 13 134
Japan 17 388
Prehistoric art 25 477
Sudan 1 305
Syria-Palestine 30 180
types
Castor 10 196; 23 379
drying 7 747; 10 548; 12 803; 13 706; 23 379–80*, 783, 784; 25 174; 28 653; 30 427
hempseed 23 379
lavender 10 192; 23 377; 29 53
linseed 8 127, 128; 10 560; 12 622; 18 611; 23 375, 379, 783, 785, 792; 24 55; 25 598; 29 813; 32 1
Kashmir 18 609
13th cent. 13 135
15th cent. 23 376; 29 712
16th cent. 23 376; 28 339
19th cent. 23 786
olive 8 127; 10 560
perilla 17 359; 23 379
pinenut 23 379
poppyseed 18 611; 23 375, 379, 783, 792
rapeseed 17 388
safflower 23 783
sesame 17 388; 18 609
oils
types—cont.
spike see lavender
stand 23 792, 793
tobaccoseed 23 379
tung 7 92; 17 388; 23 379
walnut 13 135; 23 375, 376, 379, 783; 25 598
yew 17 388
uses
architecture 29 712
binders 25 477
brick 1 305
brushes 5 34
ceramics 6 329
consolidants 7 747
crayons 8 127, 128
emeralds 12 270
enamel 10 192
etchings 10 560
glazes 2 178; 12 803
grounds 10 548; 13 706–7*, 708
inks 15 849, 851, 853; 25 598
inksticks 17 388
lacquer 18 609
painting
encaustic 10 196
oil 23 375, 376, 377
panel 13 135
secco 28 339*, 340
paints 23 380, 785, 786
paper 24 55
parchment 24 106
plaster 29 813
sealants 25 174
tattoos 30 366
tempera 30 427
varnishes 32 1
vernis Martin 18 611
waxes 33 2
oil sketches 1 106; 23 380–82*
Belgium 23 381
Baroque 8 127; 22 415
17th cent. 8 878, 879; 32 115
19th cent. 32 853
Czech Republic 20 856
England 13 676
Italy 12 201; 32 347
Russia 25 145
Spain 12 588
see also OIL PAINTINGS
oil tannage see under TANNING
oil transfers see under PHOTOGRAPHY → processes; DRAWINGS → techniques
Oiman (family) 12 429
Oiniadai 13 386
baths 3 374
Oinoanda 27 7
oinochoai 13 476; 23 382*
historical and regional traditions
China 6 875
Etruscan 10 612
Greece, ancient 13 436, 488, 491, 507, 569, 569
Orientalizing style 13 503
Italy 10 612
materials
pottery 10 612; 13 436, 488, 503
silver 13 569
Oinoe 21 556
Oī no Mikado Tsunetaka
works 17 405
Oinonen, Mikko 11 96; 28 427
Oinophile Painter 23 145
ointment pots see under POTS → types
Oirat 21 870, 877
Oiron Château 6 506; 11 265, 726; 13 224
frescoes 16 877
Oirschot Church 22 821, 856
Oisy, Jean d' see JEAN D'OISY
Ōita, Sueda Art Gallery 14 161
Ōita, Torao 17 430
Oiticica, Hélio 4 719; 23 382*; 26 414
Oiwake 17 347

Oiwayama 27 600
Oíza, Francisco Javier Sáenz de *see* SÁENZ DE OÍZA, FRANCISCO JAVIER
Ōizumi-cho
 sculpture 17 *105*
Öja Church 13 119; 27 124, 125; 30 83
Ojai (CA), Pratt House 13 *618*
Ojców, Pieskowa Skała Castle 24 586
Ojeda, Gustavo 23 382*
Ojetti, Ugo 11 190; 16 775; 23 382*; 24 448
Ojibwa 17 770; 22 546, 551, 552
 architecture 22 671
 beadwork 22 639
 collections 22 675
 embroidery 22 *647*
 quillwork 22 649, 650, 651
 religion 22 556, 558
 sculpture 22 584, *585*
 shamanism 28 547
 textiles 22 627; 31 661
Ōjin, Emperor (*reg c.* 4th-5th cent.) 23 591
Ojio Yūshō 17 417
Ojojona 14 *711*
 Museo Pablo Zelaya Sierra 14 715
Oka, Shikanosuke 17 207; 23 383*
Okabe, Mineo 17 266
Ōkabe, Sōfū 17 240
Okabe Mataemon 2 908
Okada, Amina 15 748
Okada, Kenzō 17 268; 23 384–5*; 24 213
Okada, Mikichi 7 154
Okada, Saburōsuke 14 213; 17 204; 21 59
Okada, Shin'ichi 18 890; 23 385*
Okada, Takahiko 22 120
Okada, Tetsuo 20 874
Okada Beisanjin 23 383*, 594, 595
 pupils 23 383
 works 17 190
Okada Hankō 23 383–4*, 594
 works 17 191; 23 *384*
Okado, Kenzo 28 314
Ōkajima Rinsai 2 7
Okakura, Kakuzō *see* OKAKURA, TENSHIN
Okakura, Tenshin 17 133, 138, 200, 204, 420, 431, 435, 798; 23 385*; 28 603; 31 81
 groups and movements 21 59; 27 596
 pupils 14 577; 33 541
 teachers 17 200, 420
 works 17 108, 336; 23 554
Okamoto, Ippei 23 385
Okamoto, Shinjirō 17 207
Okamoto, Tarō 17 207; 23 385–6*
Okamoto Masafusa 17 288
Okamoto Toyohiko 20 837; 23 386*
 pupils 17 197
 works 17 197
Okamoto Yūkoku 22 118
Okano Heiemon 17 372
Okanoyama Graphic Art Museum *see under* NISHIWAKI
Okas, Jüri 10 538, 540
Okawachi 17 264
Ōkawauchiyama 22 421
Okayama 17 *11*, 84; 23 386–7*
 Hayashibara Museum of Art 23 386
 Kōrakuen 12 99; 23 386–7*
 Orient Museum 23 385, 386
 pottery 17 260
 Prefectural Museum 23 386
 Tsukinowa 17 308
Okcho 18 382
Okediji, Moyo
 works 7 I2
O'Keeffe, Georgia 23 47, 387–8*; 29 656; 31 605, 606
 exhibitions 31 490
O'Keeffe, Georgia—cont.
 groups and movements 10 880; 23 48; 25 461
 patrons and collectors 26 488; 29 655, 657
 personal collection 22 677
 teachers 6 500
 works 18 718; 23 *388*
Okehampton (Devon) 6 55
Okeke, Uche 1 245, 432; 15 57; 23 136, 137, 139
Okelele 9 734
Okello, Gard 31 528
O'Kelly, Aloysius 16 17
Oke-Padi
 doors 1 *427*
Okhitovich, Mikhail 3 287; 27 379
Okhotsk 17 247
Okiek 1 255
 beadwork 1 *256*
Okigbo, Godwin 15 56
Okigwi 15 116
Ōkimi, Kagami no *see* KAGAMI NO ŌKIMI
okimono see under STATUETTES → types
Okinawa 17 18, 353, 354, 355; 27 469
 Oceanic Cultural Museum 30 286
 stonewares 17 262
 textiles 17 310, *317*; 27 470, 471; 30 559
Okinawan 17 19
Okinojima 17 320
Ōkinoshima 17 *11*, 60; 23 388–9*
okir see under SCULPTURE → types
Okisada Asaoka *see* ASAOKA OKISADA
Okkura Kakuzō 17 793
Okladnikov, Aleksey (Pavlovich) 21 885; 23 389*
Okobo 15 62
Okoh, Theodosia 12 508
Količné 28 851
Okpe 9 734
Okpella 1 236
 masks 1 268, *268*, 270, *270*, 290; 9 734, 735
Okpolo-Enwe 9 737
Okra Glass 10 321
Okrika 15 126
Okrouhlá 23 264
Oksan *see* YI (i) U
Oksapmin 24 73, 74
Oktobergruppe (Germany) 21 407
Oktyabr group (Russia) 15 122; 18 746; 20 833; 28 643; 31 542
Oku 3 147, 148
Oku-Ampofo 12 509
ōkubie see under PRINTS → types → *ukiyoe*
Ōkubo Shibutsu 17 237
Okubo Tadanobu 30 51, *51*
Oku Bunmei 17 195, 196, 417
Okuda Eisen 17 258; 23 389–90*
 pupils 30 255
 works 17 286; 18 554
Okuhara Seiko 12 215; 17 199; 23 390*
Okuhara Seisui 23 390
Ōkuma, Ujihirō 17 133, 134
Okumura, Togyū 23 390*
Okumura Genroku 23 391
Okumura Mangetsudō 23 391
Okumura Masafusa 23 391
Okumura Masanobu 17 281; 23 390–91*
 pupils 17 282
 works 1 582; 17 166, 281, 282
Okumura Toshinobu 17 282; 23 391
Okumuraya 23 391
Okuni 1 331
Ōkuni, Hakusai 17 324
Okunyo culture 27 366
Ōkura, Kihachirō 17 429
Okushko, Vladimir 21 811
Öküz'İn 1 823
Öküz Mehmed 1 474
Okvik 22 546, 574
Okyay, Necmeddin 23 391*; 27 683; 31 454
Ōkyo Maruyama *see* MARUYAMA ŌKYO
O Kyŏng-sok 18 331
O Kyu-il 18 372
Ol', Andrey (Andreyevich) 23 391–2*; 24 546
Olaf III Kyrre, King of Norway (*reg* 1066-93) 3 773; 31 363, 364
Ólafsson, Sigurjón 15 70; 23 392*
Ólafsson, Sigurjón, Museum *see under* Reykjavik → museums
Olaf Tryggvesson, King of Norway (*reg c.* AD 995-1000) 31 363
Olaguíbel, Juan 23 392*
Olaktún 21 231
olambrillas tiles *see under* TILES → types
Olamosquin (family) 32 620
Olanda, Luca d' 11 5
Øland Church 8 722; 30 *65*
Olaniyi Davis, Nike *see* DAVIS, NIKE OLANIYI
Olasz, Antal 15 3
Olatunde, Asiru 15 57
Olaus Magnus *see* MANSSON, OLAF
Olavide, Pablo de 28 513
Olavinlinna Castle 11 89
Olayinka *see* NICOL, MIRANDA BURNEY
Olazábal, Santiago Rodríguez *see* RODRÍGUEZ OLAZÁBAL, SANTIAGO
Olba 13 *362*; 23 392–3*; 26 *908*
 Temple of Zeus 23 392
Olbia (Greece) *see* OL'VIYA
Olbia (Sardinia) 6 271
Olbiades 13 546
Ołbin Abbey 4 782; 25 109, 134; 26 636–7
 portal 26 *636*
 St Michael 25 109; 26 637
 tympanum 25 *109*
Olbrich, Joseph Maria 2 788, 814, 826; 23 393–4*
 architecture 8 379, 531; 12 378; 25 173; 30 506
  department stores 9 460
  exhibition architecture 2 566, 788, *788*; 10 683; 14 622; 21 779; 29 843; 32 438, 446; 33 284
  galleries (art) 22 365
  roofs 27 131
  towers 8 531; 10 697; 21 779; 23 *394*
  villas 3 68
 collaboration 22 187; 32 761
 furniture 12 428
 groups and movements
  Darmstädter Künstler-Kolonie 2 566; 8 531; 12 416
  Deutscher Werkbund 21 780
  Secession (Vienna) 2 567, 776; 28 343, 344; 32 762
  Siebenerklub 3 398; 28 670
 interior decoration 15 883
 silver 12 450
 textiles 8 419; 12 463
 tiles 30 885
Olcott, Lucy 24 457
Oldach, Julius 12 394; 23 394*
Old Alwa *see* ALODIA
Old Babylonian period *see under* MESOPOTAMIA → periods
Old Balkh *see* BALKH
Old Bering Sea culture 22 546, 574
Old Brick Church (VA) 31 589
Old Colony Railroad 26 342
Old Copper culture 22 617
Old Dongola 23 *276*, 287
 Church of Stone Pavement 23 287
 Cruciform Church 23 287
 episcopal church 23 288
Old Dongola—cont.
 excavations 23 287
 Old Church 23 287
 sculpture 23 288
 wall paintings 23 288
Olde, Hans 21 796
Oldeland, Hendrik 5 172
Oldenbourg, Rudolf 23 395*
Oldenburg (House of) 3 111; 8 746; 11 220; 23 395*; 32 765
Oldenburg, Anton Günther, Count of *see* ANTON GÜNTHER, Count of Oldenburg
Oldenburg, Caroline Mathilda, Queen of Denmark *see* CAROLINE MATHILDA, Queen of Denmark and Norway
Oldenburg, Christian I, King of Denmark *see* CHRISTIAN I, King of Denmark
Oldenburg, Christian II, King of Denmark and Norway *see* CHRISTIAN II, King of Denmark and Norway
Oldenburg, Christian IV, King of Denmark and Norway *see* CHRISTIAN IV, King of Denmark and Norway
Oldenburg, Christian VII, King of Denmark *see* CHRISTIAN VII, King of Denmark
Oldenburg, Christian IX, King of Denmark *see* CHRISTIAN IX, King of Denmark
Oldenburg, Christina of Saxony, Queen of Denmark *see* CHRISTINA OF SAXONY, Queen of Denmark
Oldenburg, Claes (Thure) 22 315; 23 397–8*
 collaboration 20 605, 607
 groups and movements 10 416; 23 49; 25 231, 232
 patrons and collectors 24 24, 601; 28 315
 works 6 577; 10 482; 15 868, *868*, 869; 22 49; 23 *397*; 24 407; 25 25, 26; 28 52; 29 12, 671; 31 615, 706
Oldenburg, Frederick, Prince 1 33; 14 151
Oldenburg, Frederick I, King of Denmark *see* FREDERICK I, King of Denmark
Oldenburg, Frederick II, King of Denmark and Norway *see* FREDERICK II, King of Denmark and Norway
Oldenburg, Frederick VI, King of Denmark and Norway *see* FREDERICK VI, King of Denmark and Norway
Oldenburg, Frederick VII, King of Denmark *see* FREDERICK VII, King of Denmark
Oldenburg, Fritz 14 644
Oldenburg, George, Prince of Denmark *see* GEORGE, Prince, Duke of Cumberland
Oldenburg, John, King of Denmark and Norway *see* JOHN, King of Denmark and Norway
Oldenburg, Peter Friedrich Ludwig, Duke of 14 153; 31 28
Oldenburg, Rudolf 10 580
Ol'denburg, Sergey F. 6 279, 321
Oldenburg, Sophie Amalie, Queen of Denmark *see* SOPHIE AMALIE, Queen of Denmark
Oldenburg, Ulrica, Queen of Sweden *see* ULRICA, Queen of Sweden
Oldenburg, Valdemar Christian, Prince of Denmark 30 *41*
Oldenburg Schloss 12 494
Old English style 10 *238*, 238–9; 22 809; 23 398*; 28 561; 32 277
Older Prayerbook of Maximilian *see under* PRAYERBOOKS → individual manuscripts
Older Prayerbook of Maximilian, Master of the 3 725; 20 693, 737*
 works 20 *737*
Oldfield, Edmund 2 576
Oldfield, Peter 33 678
Oldfield and Denn 20 161
Old German painting *see* GOTHIC → styles → Late Gothic
Old Goa *see* GOA VELHA
Old Hall 33 50
Old Hall Earthenware Co. 9 295
Oldham, James 17 468
Oldham (Lancs), Town Hall 31 241
Old Hittite ware *see under* POTTERY → wares
Old Japan ware *see* ARITA → porcelain
Old Jar Pottery 29 117
Old Kingdom *see under* EGYPT, ANCIENT → periods
Old Lyme 14 220
Oldman, W. O. 1 438; 23 742
Old Master Drawings 24 183
Old Masters 7 563; 24 138
Old Nectar 12 142
Old Norse Revival 23 231
Old Oyo 1 *386*; 33 553
Old Paphos *see* PAPHOS, OLD
Old Radnor 11 252
Old Red sandstone *see under* SANDSTONE → types
Oldřichov 8 410
Oldřiš Castle 8 381
 St John the Baptist 26 637
Old Russian 27 361; 31 545
 architecture 27 368, 369, 443
 see also RUS'; UKRAINE
Old Russian Revival 27 377, 421; 32 73
Old Sarum (Wilts) 27 624*, *624*
 Castle 26 616
 Cathedral of the Blessed Virgin Mary 3 443; 26 617
  sculpture 26 616, *617*
 chapter house 6 466
 church 26 590
 sculpture 26 643
 textiles 26 703
Old Syrian style 1 862
Old Testaments 9 611–14*
 individual manuscripts *see under* BIBLES → individual manuscripts
 see also PSALTERS; TORAHS
Oldtown 16 8
Old Turkic scripts *see* SCRIPTS → types → Uygur
Old Uppsala *see* GAMLA UPPSALA
old Vienna school *see* ALT-WIENER SCHOOL
Old Warden (Beds), St Leonard 7 353
Old Windsor (Berks), Royal Palace 2 83
Old Woodstock Manor (Oxon) 12 128
Olé, António (*b* 1951) 2 87
Olé, António (*b* 1963) *see* ALVIM, FERNANDO
Ole, Eduard 10 539, 542
Olearius, Adam 6 280; 12 811
Oleffe, Auguste 23 398–9*
 groups and movements 2 516; 4 618; 19 539; 28 104
 sponsorship 8 630
 works 3 564
Oleggio, Giovanni da *see* GIOVANNI DA OLEGGIO
Olekova, Zdravka 5 159
Olendorf, Christopher 25 129
Oleneostrovski Mogilnik 25 496
Ölenhainz, Friedrich 19 338
Oleni Island
 carvings 27 365, *365*

Olenin, A. N. 27 439
oleographs 23 399*
Olery, Guillaume 16 854
Olerys, Joseph 22 242
Olesen, C., A/S 21 791
Olesen, Ebbe 8 730, 731
works 8 *731*
Oleškevicius, Juozapas *see* ALAŠKEVIČ, JOZEP
Oleśnicki, Zbigniew, Cardinal 23 399*; 25 95, 134
Oleszczynski, Władysław 25 115
Oleszko, Pat 24 409
Olga, Queen (*c.* 957) 9 657
Olgiati, Giovanni Maria 28 533
Olgiati, Rudolf 28 190
Olgyay, Aladár 23 399*
Olgyay, Ferenc 30 211
Olgyay, Viktor (1870-1929) 1 16; 23 399
Olgyay, Viktor (1910-70) 23 399*
Olgyay & Olgyay 23 399*
Oliaros *see* ANTIPAROS
Oliba, Abbot of Saint-Michel-de-Cuxa 27 568
Olica, Achille Bonito 16 683
Olie, Jacob 23 400*
Olier, Isaac d' 16 31
Olier, Jean-Jacques 19 21
Olieslaegher, Jan d', I (1621-80) 12 519, 520; 23 665
Olieslaegher, Jan d', II (1657-1712) 12 520
Olifantsfontein 29 *103*, 116
Olinda 4 *705*; 23 400*
architecture 4 709
Misericórdia 26 254–5
Museu de Arte Contemporânea de Pernambuco 4 727; 23 400
Museu de Arte Sacra 23 400
Museu da Moeda 23 669
silver 4 723
Oliphant, Ebenezer 28 261
Oliphant, Lawrence 28 261
oliphants 16 797; 22 372; 23 400–402*
Islamic 16 526
Italy 16 526; 23 400, *401*; 26 698
Romanesque 23 *401*; 26 698
Sicily 26 698
see also HORNS
Olisey Grechin 23 402*
Olite Castle 13 68; 23 402–3*, *403*; 29 *259*
Olitski, Jules 23 403–4*; 31 609
groups and movements 25 361
works 1 130; 5 569; 7 636
Oliv, M. S. 27 439
Oliv, Ye. P. 27 439
Oliva *see* LA OLIVA
oliva *see under* SHELLS → types
Oliva, Abbot of Ripoll 26 417, 689
Oliva, Antoni 29 332
Oliva, Conde de la *see* CALDERÓN, RODRIGO
Oliva, Giovanni Paolo 12 198; 25 413; 26 824
Oliva, Giovanni Pietro 2 105
Oliva, Jusepe 29 326
Oliva, Ladislav 23 271; 33 630
Olivares 4 261
Olivares, Conde-Duque de 23 404–5*; 30 417
architecture 5 725; 20 70; 29 270
books 1 528
furniture 29 303
gold 29 336
Olive, Agnes 5 582
Oliveira, Antônio Manuel de 4 720
Oliveira, Augusto Gomes de *see* GOMES (DE OLIVEIRA), AUGUSTO
Oliveira, Francisco de Paula e *see* PAULA E OLIVEIRA, FRANCISCO DE
Oliveira, João, Marques de *see* MARQUES DE OLIVEIRA, JOÃO
Oliveira, Joaquim de (*fl* 1760-70) 23 405*
Oliveira, Joaquim José de (*fl* 1869-81) 10 729
Oliveira, Mateus Vicente de 23 405–6*
collaboration 25 293
palaces 25 814
patrons and collectors 4 637
works 12 125; 20 403; 23 *405*; 26 471
Oliveira, Nathan 8 871; 19 492; 20 606; 23 406*
Oliveira, Raimundo de 4 719
Oliveira Bernardes, António de *see* BERNARDES, ANTÓNIO DE OLIVEIRA
Oliveira Bernardes, Inácio de *see* BERNARDES, INÁCIO DE OLIVEIRA
Oliveira Bernardes, Policarpo de *see* BERNARDES, POLICARPO DE OLIVEIRA
Oliveira do Hospital Church 13 102
Oliveira Passos, Francisco de 4 712
Olivença, S Madalena 17 595
olive oil *see under* OILS → types
Oliver, Basil 25 689
Oliver, Bronwyn 2 754
Oliver, Despot 28 447
Oliver, Isaac 14 547; 23 406–9*
assistants 23 409
collaboration 12 514
groups and movements 10 142
patrons and collectors 4 609; 18 795; 19 124; 20 910
pupils 17 637
reproductive prints by others 29 799
teachers 14 546, 547
works 8 828; 10 246; 14 855; 21 639; 23 *407*, *408*, 409; 32 899
Oliver, Jesus 18 832
Oliver, John (*fl* 1346-50) 23 374
Oliver, John (*c.* 1616-1701) 21 615
Oliver, Jovan 28 442
Oliver, Juan (*fl* 1330-32) 23 409*
works 13 149, *150*; 21 845; 29 275, *276*
Oliver, Juan de (*fl* 1550) 8 237
Oliver, Peter 21 640; 23 406, 409*
copies 12 600
patrons and collectors 19 124
personal collection 23 408
pupils 7 795
works 14 855; 21 639; 23 408; 32 899
Oliver, Pierre 14 855
Oliver, Reneth 3 623
Oliver, Thomas 23 20
Olivera y Vidal, Vidal 24 516
Oliver & Boyd 20 34
Oliver de Merlimond 26 616
Oliver de Nichol 9 320
Oliveri, G. M. 23 169
Oliveria, Manuel Dias de *see* DIAS DE OLIVEIRA, MANUEL
Oliveros, Arturo 5 660
Olivet, Ramón 23 410*
Olivetan Master 20 783
Olivetan Order 3 709
Olivetti 12 480
architecture 2 727; 8 256; 11 63
furniture 29 90
posters 7 656; 25 351
type-faces 5 921
typewriters 8 803; 15 826, *826*; 29 89
Olivetti, Adriano 3 438, 439; 11 63; 16 650; 23 169; 25 792; 31 730
olive-wood 3 585; 7 442; 11 596; 33 IV2
Olivier (French family) 32 863
Olivier (*fl* 12th cent.) 26 659
Olivier, Alexandre 23 412*; 26 95
Olivier, Aubin 8 67; 23 412
Olivier, (Johann Heinrich) Ferdinand 8 816; 23 410–11*; 33 282
collaboration 23 410
groups and movements 2 796; 22 704
teachers 18 201
works 12 393; 19 486; 23 *411*
Olivier, Friedrich (Woldemar) 8 816; 23 412*; 33 282
collaboration 22 308
groups and movements 12 393
teachers 18 201
Olivier, Gilbert 23 412
Olivier, Heinrich 8 816; 18 201; 23 410*
Olivier, Thomas 8 548
Olivier de Barlay 5 46
Olivier de Coëtivy 20 650
Olivier de Gand *see* OLIVIER OF GHENT
Olivier de la Marche 20 656, 763
Olivier de Marseille *see* OLLIVIER, JEAN-PHILIPPE-AUGUSTIN
Olivieri, Giovanni Domenico 6 67; 23 412–13*; 29 292, 357
collaboration 27 644; 29 293
patrons and collectors 4 558; 5 902
Olivieri, Juan Domingo *see* OLIVIERI, GIOVANNI DOMENICO
Olivieri, Leonardo 22 479, 486
Olivieri, Maffeo 4 748; 20 918; 23 413*; 29 569
Olivieri, Pietro Paolo 1 595; 23 413–14*; 29 559; 31 787
Olivier of Ghent 23 414*
collaboration 13 125; 22 312
patrons and collectors 1 679; 2 871
works 31 102
olivine 16 857
Olivuccio di Ceccarello 3 301
Oliwa Cathedral, Tomb of the Koss Family 25 114
Olkion *see* VULCI
Olkusz Church 25 102, 129
Ollanda, Alberto da 30 34
Ollanda, d' *see* HOLANDA, DE
Ollantaytambo 15 *161*, 163; 23 414–15*; 29 *156*
architecture 29 162
temple 29 167
Ollemans, Frieda 4 155
Ollendorff 2 733
Oller (y Cestero), Francisco 23 415*; 25 701, 704
Oller, Museo *see under* BAMAYON
Oller, Pere 3 218; 7 373; 23 415–16*; 29 289
collaboration 13 106
works 3 221; 11 482; 12 739
Ollers, Edwin 30 102
Ollila, Yrjö 11 96; 28 427
Olliver 24 148
Ollivier (family) 11 604; 22 35
Ollivier, Jean-Philippe-Augustin 23 416*
Ollivier, Michel-Barthélémy 7 778; 23 416*
Ollivier, Pierre 23 406
Olmec 1 700; 18 805, 881; 21 195, 196, 209, 242; 23 416–18*; 27 756; 31 310; 33 101, 618
altars 23 417
architecture 23 416–18; 27 756
axes 21 *242*; 23 418
ballcourts 3 117; 23 417; 27 756
basalt 21 *218*; 23 417, *417*
caricatures 5 761
celts 18 *881*; 21 242; 23 418
craftsmen and artists 21 190
drains 23 417
earthworks 21 209
figurines 18 *881*; 21 *218*; 23 417, 418
forgeries 21 266
greenstone 21 *185*; 23 418
Olmec—cont.
hardstones 21 241; 29 154
human figures 21 218
iconoclasm 23 417–18
jade 16 861; 18 *881*; 21 *242*, 242, 251; 23 418
jadeite 21 242
jewellery 23 418
masks 21 250–51, 254
masonry 31 310
mirrors 21 241, 718
monoliths 23 417
monuments 18 *645*
mosaics 21 251, 254
mounds 23 417
narratives 22 519
pendants (jewellery) 21 242
polychromy 23 418
ponds 23 417
portraits 23 417
pottery 21 237; 23 418
religion 21 183
rock art 21 226*
sandstone 27 *832*
sarcophagi 27 832, *832*
sculpture 5 408; 21 *185*, 217
colossal heads 21 219; 23 417, *417*
colossal statues 21 209
monumental 18 *645*; 23 416–18
Pre-Classic (*c.* 2000 BC–*c.* AD 250) 21 218–19*
seals 21 258
serpentine 18 *881*
shells 21 260
squares (town) 23 417
stages 23 417
stelae 21 219; 23 417; 29 619
stone 21 218
stone-carvings 5 761; 6 393, *394*; 18 645; 23 418
temples 30 448
tombs 31 117
trumpets 21 260
wall paintings 21 226; 23 418
weapons 21 246
Olmedo, Monastery of La Mejorada 15 835
Olmer, L. J. 16 426
Olmo, Giovanni dell' 30 517
Olmo, José del 7 287; 20 72; 23 419*; 29 269
Olmo, Manuel del 23 419; 29 269
Olmos, José 9 712; 19 75
Olmsted, F. L., & Co. 23 422
Olmsted, Frederick Law (1822-1903) 5 274, 275; 20 16; 23 419–23*; 26 340; 29 536; 31 725; 32 414
collaboration 6 573; 12 614; 23 39; 24 179; 26 340, 342; 27 730; 32 95; 33 263
house 10 186
pupils 10 141
works 2 694; 4 475; 5 274; 7 357, 429; 22 36; 23 32, *420*, *421*, *422*; 26 338; 27 730; 31 352, 728; 32 892
Olmsted, Frederick Law, jr (1870-1957) 2 698; 23 422, 423; 28 327
Olmsted, John Charles 2 698; 23 32, 422, 423; 28 327
Olmsted, Olmsted & Eliot 10 142; 23 422; 33 407
works 23 *422*
Olmsted, Vaux & Co. 23 421
Olmsted & Olmsted 33 407
Olmsted & Vaux 23 421
works 23 *420*
Olmütz *see* OLOMOUC
Olmützer, Hans *see* HANUŠ Z OLOMOUCE
Ołobok 25 110
O'Lochlainn, Colm 16 18
Olodiama 15 123
Olofsson, Hans 30 104
Olofsson, Pierre Sager 7 699; 30 81
Olofsson, Urian 23 424*
Olofström 30 110
metalwork 30 *110*
Olomouc 8 *374*; 23 424–5*, *425*
Archbishop's Palace 15 158
architecture 8 377
Cathedral 8 376, 379
education (art) 8 425
Hradisko Monastery 8 391
palace 26 637
St Mary of the Snows 8 391
St Maurice 8 383
Olomouc, Jiří of *see* JIŘÍ OF OLOMOUC
Olomouce, Hanuš z *see* HANUŠ Z OLOMOUCE
Olot
Casa Solà 11 493
Casa Ventós 11 493
Ca Trinxerias 29 305
furniture 29 315
sculpture 29 294
S Esteban 26 251
Olous 8 155
Olowe 9 165
works 9 *164*; 33 *554*
olpai 13 476
Olpai cycle 10 614
Ołpiny 25 103
Olpoe 31 892
Olrik, Dagmar 8 755
Olrikes, Lutke 12 443, 444
Olry-Roederer, Léon 13 325
Olsen, Cathinca 8 748
Olsen, Charles 24 407
Olsen, Hans Pauli 10 813
Olsen, John 2 750, 762; 23 425–6*
groups and movements 30 160
pupils 2 120; 18 689
works 2 *751*
Olsen, Kjell Erik Killi 23 227
Olsen, Michel 23 238
Olsen, Theodor 33 50
Ol'shevsky, Vladimir (Nikolayevich) 27 411
Olshger, Kaufmann & Hostettler 19 319
Olson, Axel 14 89
Olson, Charles 4 109; 8 270
Olson, Erik (Arthur) 14 89
Olssen 32 879
Olsson, Hagar 1 12
Olsson, Julius 27 562
Olszanica 25 500
Olsztyn 25 116; 30 535
Oltar-Jevsky, W. K. *see* OLTARZHEVSKY, VYACHESLAV (KONSTANINOVICH)
Oltarzhevsky, Vyacheslav (Konstantinovich) 22 173; 23 426*; 24 400; 26 241
Olteni 26 719
Oltos 32 60*
attributions 23 145
works 13 472, 490, 519
Olufsen Schutte, Hans 8 733
Olugebefola, Ademola 1 445
Olumuyiwa, Oluwole (Olusegun) 23 135, 426–7*
works 1 319; 23 135
Oluwole Olumuyiwa & Associates 23 426
Olvi, Henrik 10 542
Olvia *see* Ol'viya
Ol'viya 4 110; 23 427*; 25 *471*; 31 *546*
coins 13 586
ivory 15 *915*
mosaics 13 559, 565
sculpture 4 111
Olycan (family) 14 94
Olympia 13 *363*
Olympia (Greece) 13 *362*; 23 427–33*, *428*; 26 *908*
Altis 26 909
Archaeological Museum 1 159; 13 469, 470, 606
art forms and materials
acroteria 1 128

Olympia (Greece)
art forms and materials—cont.
antefixes **2** *131*
architecture **23** 427–30*
armour **13** 584
bracelets **13** 601
bronzes **10** 625; **13** 571, 572
chests **13** 488
fibulae **10** 591
figurines **13** 571
glass **13** 594
gold **13** 568
helmets **10** 585
jewellery **13** 600
metalwork **10** 591; **21** 322
pins **13** *600*
pottery **13** 512, 534
sculpture **13** 430, 453, 454, 459, 462; **23** 431*, 432–3*, *433*; **26** 292
bronze **4** 851; **13** 441, 448
chryselephantine statues **13** 435
baths **3** 374; **13** 386; **15** 51
bouleuterion **4** 530
Byzantium Treasury **13** 418
collections **14** 361
Echo Stoa **29** 681
excavations **13** 606; **14** 655
exedra **10** 671
Gela Treasury **13** 418; **15** 881; **30** *493*, 494; **31** 294
gymnasium **10** 670; **13** 406, 886; **23** 828; **24** 456
Heroön **13** 386
Leonidaion **13** 373, 386; **30** *493*, 494
Megarian Treasury **13** 380, 418; **30** *493*, 494; **31** 294
Nymphaion of Herodes Atticus **26** 857, 910
monopteros **21** 893
Pelopion **14** 466; **23** 429
Philippeion **13** 373, 390, 435; **23** 430; **27** 235; **30** 435, 737
prytaneion **25** 675
Sanctuary of Hera **23** 429; **27** 1
Temple of Hera **13** 377, *377*, 389, 397, 398, 445, 592; **23** 481; **24** 456; **31** 269
acroteria **1** 127; **23** *429*
pilasters **24** 805
Sanctuary of Zeus **10** 591; **13** 416, 417, 419; **27** 713
altar **1** 691; **27** 713
bouleuterion **13** 381
Temple of Zeus **13** 373, 374, 378, 387, 391, 469, 560, 565; **22** 160; **23** 429, *432*, 481; **24** 204; **30** 435; **31** 269
acroteria **1** 127; **13** 440
façade decoration **10** 742
metopes **13** 425
pediments **13** 425; **24** 318
proportions **2** 351
reliefs **13** 431, 432, *432*; **22** 513
sculpture **13** 438, 450, 451; **22** 411; **23** 431–2*, 793
workshop **13** 371
Selinus Treasury **13** 418; **31** 294
Sikyonian Treasury **13** 418; **31** 294
stadium **2** 297; **13** 403, 418; **29** 487, 488, *488*
Sybaris Treasury **31** 294
Syracuse Treasury **13** 418; **31** 294
Temple of Eileithyia
heroön of Sosipolis **14** 467
treasuries **13** 418; **23** 429; **27** 712; **31** 294
Zeus statue **7** 245; **8** 262; **13** 370, 371, 374, 392, 393, 594, 596; **24** 594; **29** 396; **31** 294
Zeus throne **6** 388; **10** 585
Olympia (artist) **33** 307
Olympia & York **25** 657
works **25** *656*
Olympic Games **23** 427, 428, 430, 431; **27** 712; **29** 423, 427, 489
Olympos **19** 837
Olynthos **13** *363*; **19** 880; **23** 433–5*, *434*
aqueducts **13** 381
architecture **23** *434*
bouleuterion **4** 530; **14** 73
cenotaph **6** 170
cisterns **7** 354
doors **9** 151
figurines **13** 579
houses **13** 382, *382*, 383, 556, 603
mosaics **13** 383, 556, 557, *557*, 559, *560*, 561, 562–3; **22** 155, 159, 513; **23** 435*, *435*
paintings **13** 394, 548
pendants (jewellery) **13** *600*
pottery **13** 534, 536
urban planning **13** 420, 421
Villa of Good Fortune **13** 559, *560*, 563
Olynthos 5.141, Painter of **13** 534
Olynthos 5.156, Painter of **13** 534
Ölzant, Franz Xaver **2** 804
Ol'zhichi **31** 547
Olzignano, Baldassare **3** 636
OMA *see* OFFICE FOR METROPOLITAN ARCHITECTURE
Øm Abbey **8** 722
Omagua **24** 514; **29** 194
Omaha (people) **22** 551, 653, 673
Omaha (NE) **32** 861
Deere and Co. Warehouse **32** 861, *861*
O'Mahoney, T. E. **5** 602
OMAKhRR *see* ASSOCIATION OF AKHRR YOUTH
O'Malley, Gravina **16** 30
O'Malley, Tony **16** 18
Oman **15** 902; **23** 435–7*
architecture **23** 436*
metal **21** 302
porcelain **4** 173
rock art **2** 270
trade
copper **2** 265
porcelain **6** 622
weapons **16** 503
see also ARABIA
Omani Society of Fine Arts **23** 436
Omare, Flora **17** 908
el-Omari **9** 849
Omarov, Omar **27** 433
Omazur, Nicolas **4** 210; **23** 437*
(Rh)ombos **13** 445
Ombreval **32** 574
Ŏm Ch'i-uk **18** 321
Omčikus, Petar **28** 451
Omdurman **1** *379*; **23** *276*; **29** 895
architecture **23** 290
Niliem Mosque **1** 317
trade **1** 249
O'Meara, Frank **16** 17; **23** 437*
Omega Workshops **3** 631; **4** 168; **10** 284; **11** 809; **13** 313; **18** 793; **23** 437–8*; **29** 508
carpets **5** *840*, 841
craftsmen and artists **10** 256; **32** 753
exhibitions **10** 255
members **10** 547; **14** 107, 120; **19** 287; **26** 59, 466
murals **22** 331
Omenagara *see* JUNNAR
Ometepe Island **29** *136*, 148, 220
Omi **17** 354
Omi, Wokake no *see* WOKAKE NO OMI
Ōmi Izeki (family) **17** 393
Ōmiwa **17** 58, 60
Ōmiya Kahei **17** 401
Ommeganck, Balthasar-Paul **17** 642; **23** 438–9*; **26** 83; **32** 241
works **23** *438*
Ommeren, Harold van **30** 15
Omobona Painter **32** 37
Omodei, Luigi, Cardinal **4** 667; **25** 386, 388
Omondi, Lincoln **17** 907
Ŏ Mong-nyong **23** 439–40*
works **18** 324; **23** *439*
omophoria **9** 642, 643, *643*
see also PALLIA (LITURGICAL)
Omoregie, Ekhator **3** 719, *719*
Ōmori **17** *11*
Ōmori shell-mound **17** 244, 425, 629; **22** 148; **23** 440*
Omorkulov, Mirza **18** 568
Ō Mōsho *see* NIŌ MŌSHO
Omphalion **23** 141
Omri **27** 670
Oms, Vincente **23** 440
Omsk **27** *362*, 375
Oms y Canet, Manuel **23** 440*
Oms y Canet, Vicente **23** 440*
Omura, Minosuke **17** 402
O'Murchadha, Domhnall **16** 22, 37
Omuro ware *see under* POTTERY → wares
O'Murphy, Louise **25** *275*
Omurtag, Khan **25** 48
On *see* HELIOPOLIS
Ona **2** 394
Onabolu, Aina **1** 432; **23** 135–6
Onabrakpeya, Bruce **32** 86
Oña Cathedral **16** 437
Onafhankelijken, De **1** 810; **3** 704; **18** 185; **21** 789; **31** 149; **33** 210
Onasias **13** 545, 550
Onassis, Aristotle **24** 826
Onat, Emin **16** 591; **23** 440–41*; **31** 452
works **31** *452*
Onat, Hikmet **2** 634; **16** 805; **31** 454
Onatas **1** 481; **13** 450; **23** 441*
Oñate, Condes de **23** 156
Oñate, Juan de **32** 176
Oñate, Martín de **29** 333
Oñate University **31** 674
Oñate y de Villamediana, Conde de **23** 441*
Once, Grupo de los *see* GRUPO DE LOS ONCE
Onchi, Kōshirō **23** 441–2*
collaboration **17** 295
exhibitions **17** 436
groups and movements **17** 295
works **17** 293; **33** 363
Onckelbag, Gerrit **31** 648
Ondashi **17** 298
Onder den St Maarten **28** 867
Ondumbo **11** 878
Ondür Gegen *see* ZANABAZAR
O'Neale, Lila **14** 510; **22** 677
One Art Group **14** 722
Ōne Deme (family) **17** 393
One-dimension group **16** 2
Onega region **23** 442*; **25** *471*; **27** *363*, 365
one-handler cups *see under* CUPS → types
Oneida **16** 61; **22** 552, 612
O'Neil, Henry Nelson **23** 442*
groups and movements **7** 436; **9** 756; **10** 254
reproductive prints by others **8** 549
O'Neill, Eugene **30** 687
O'Neill, George Bernard **8** 121; **23** 442*
O'Neill, Henry **5** 577
one-man exhibitions *see under* EXHIBITIONS → types
One-Off **10** 300
one-piece amphorae *see under* AMPHORAE → types
Onesimos **13** 520; **32** 60–61*
collaboration **32** 39
pupils **32** 36
works **9** *247*; **13** 520
Onesos **13** 371
Onetti, Juan Carlos **30** 275
Ongagawa ware *see under* POTTERY → wares
Ongania, Ferdinando **23** 442–3*; **24** 25
Ongaro, Michele *see* PANNONIO, MICHELE
Ongesa, Elkana **17** 908
works **17** *908*
Ongtong Java **29** 50, 51
Onias **33** 481
onion domes *see under* DOMES → types
Onis, Federico de **25** 358
Onishi (family) **17** 323
Ōnishi Chinnen **17** 196, 273
Onishi Gyorai collection **6** 745
Ōnishi Suigetsu **17** 196; **20** 836
Onitsha **23** *129*
Onizuka Tomb **17** 144
Onjōji *see under* ŌTSU
On Kawara *see* KAWARA, ON
Onkō Sonja *see* JIUN SONJA
on-line catalogues *see* CATALOGUES → types → computer
onnae see under JAPAN → painting
Onnes, Harm Kamerlingh **29** 397
Önningeby group **33** 96
Ono, Chikkyō **17** 201
Ono, Hyakuren **17** 239, 240
Ono, Tadashige **17** 295
Ono, Yoko **11** 232; **24** 403, 407
Onobrakpeya, Bruce **1** 432; **15** 57; **18** 640; **23** 136, 138, 139
works **23** *136*
Onoe Shimizu *see* SHIMIZU ONOE
Onofrei, Dimitrie **13** 653
Onofri, Crescenzio **23** 444*
collaboration **21** 30
teachers **9** 378
works **7** 621
Onofrio, Andrea de *see* ANDREA DA FIRENZE (ii)
Onofrio di Giordano della Cava **8** 175; **9** 330, 331
Onofrio di Pietro **20** 113
Ono Gadō **23** 444–5*
Onogi, Gaku **17** 293, 296
onomastica **10** 63
Ono Mataemon **17** 400
Onondaga (people) **16** 61; **22** 552, 612
Onondaga Pottery Co. **8** 82; **31** 639
Ono no Imoko **17** 380
Ono no Michikaze **11** 824; **17** 215; **23** 445*
groups and movements **17** 221, 227
works **11** 823; **17** 155, 215, 221–2, 227; **23** *445*
Onoratou *see under* CONSTANTINOPOLE
Ono Shō **33** 709
Onossorius de Blondi **2** 817
Onouphrios **25** 336, 343
Ōno Yasumaro **17** 214
Onsi, Omar **17** 654; **19** 8
Ons Industrieel Erfgoed **24** 439
Ønslev, Karise **4** 781
Onslow, Denzil **3** 244
Onslow-Ford, Gordon **30** 22
Onta **17** *241*, 352, 353
ceramics **21** 635; **30** 259
Ontani, Luigi **16** 682; **23** 445–6*; **24** 408
Ontari, Luigi **16** 709
Ontario College of Art *see under* TORONTO
Ontario Craft **24** 431
Ontario Potters Association **5** 582
Ontario Society of Artists (Toronto) **5** 566, 591, 592
Onteniente **29** 332
Onufri **1** 540
Ōnuma Chinzan **23** 390
Onus, Lin **1** 65; **23** 446*
works **1** 42, *65*
Onwin, Glen **28** 240
Onythe House **13** 382
onyx **14** 167
historical and regional traditions
China **7** *89*, 90
onyx
historical and regional traditions—cont.
England **10** *345*; **29** XII
France **12** *262*
Islamic **16** *543*
Italy **12** *256*, *258*; **16** *746*
Mesoamerica, Pre-Columbian **21** 251
Pakistan **23** 803
Rome, ancient **12** 251; **14** II2
Switzerland **17** *520*
uses
amulets **12** 251
cameos **12** *256*, *258*, *262*; **14** II2; **16** *746*; **17** *520*
jewellery **17** 527, 529
masks **21** 251
mosaics **29** XII
pendants (jewellery) **10** *345*
rhyta **7** *89*
seals **16** *543*
onyx-marble *see* ALABASTER (LIMESTONE)
Onze Kunst **24** 439
Ooidonk Château **3** 545
Ōoka Shunboku **16** 784; **17** 416; **18** 60; **23** 594
Ōoka Unpō **2** 7
Oolen, Adriaen van **14** 707
Ooli **18** 484, 485
O On-hu **18** 328
Oort, Adam van *see* NOORT, ADAM VAN
Oort, Lambert van *see* NOORT, LAMBERT VAN
Oort, van (family) **22** 881
Oorthuys, Cas(parus Bernardus) **23** 446*
Oortmans-De la Court, Petronella **21** 489
Oosschot, Kees **22** 860
Oost, Dominique Joseph van **23** 447
Oost, Frans van **23** 446
Oost, Jacob van, I (1603-71) **23** 446–7*
works **3** 559, 560; **23** *447*
Oost, Jacob van, II (1639-1713) **23** 447
Oost, Pieter van **3** 542; **4** 924, 925
Oosterbeek **1** 650; **11** 885; **14** 46; **20** 433, 434, 435, 871
painting **4** 59
Oosterblokker Church **22** 821
Oosterhuis, Pieter **23** 447*
Oosterland, Hendrick Steengracht van *see* STEENGRACHT VAN OOSTERLAND, HENDRICK
Oosterlingh, Jan Gerritsz. **14** 42
Oosterwijck, Maria van **1** 166; **23** 447–8*; **29** 667
Oosthuizen Church **22** 821
Oosting, Jeanne Bieruma *see* BIERUMA OOSTING, JEANNE
Oostkapelle, Johan Steengracht van *see* STEENGRACHT VAN OOSTKAPELLE, JOHAN
Oostsanen, Jacob Cornelisz. van *see* CORNELISZ. VAN OOSTSANEN, JACOB
Oostvoorne Castle **22** 822
Ootacamund, Botanic Garden **12** 76
Ootam **28** 897
Ootmarsum Church **22** 818
Opaku Ware II, Asantehene (*reg* 1731-42) **2** 587
opalescent enamels *see under* ENAMELS → types
Opaliński (family) **4** 295
Opałka, Roman **23** 448*; **24** 24
opals **7** *109*; **12** 252, 268, 269, I; **17** II1
Opa Oranmiyan **15** 107
opaque enamel *see under* ENAMEL → types

Op art 1 79; 2 208; 7 546, 631, 637, 698; 18 62; 19 355; 23 448–9*; 24 376; 26 193
exhibitions 16 820
regional traditions
England 10 258; 23 *449*
France 32 9
United States of America , ; 7 VIII2(c); 25 228
Opatów Collegiate Church 25 95, 113, 129
tomb of Ludwik Szydłowiecki 25 113
Opava 8 376
Silesian Museum 8 424
Opava, Jan of *see* JAN OF OPAVA
Opazo, Rodolfo 6 598; 23 450*
Opbergen, Antonis van *see* OBBERGHEN, ANTONIS VAN
Opbouw, De 22 868; 23 450*
members 2 318; 4 815; 9 746; 13 685; 19 540; 21 781; 29 531
Opbouwen 3 551
Opdahl, Jakob *see* WEIDEMANN, JAKOB
Opekushin, Aleksandr (Mikhaylovich) 22 178; 23 450*; 27 390, 578
Opel 15 824, 825
Open Air Art Schools *see* ESCUELAS DE PINTURA AL AIRE LIBRE
Open Air group *see* AR LIVRE GROUP
Openbaar kunstbezit in Vlaanderen 24 439
open-bite etchings *see under* ETCHINGS → types
Open Form 17 448; 18 413
opening bridges *see under* BRIDGES → types
open-mould casting *see under* CASTING → types
open moulding *see under* MOULDING → types
Open-mouthed Boys, Master of the 20 737–8*; 27 817
El Opeño 21 *372*; 33 102
ceramics 33 101
pottery 5 660
tombs 5 661; 21 216; 31 *117*, 118
see also CAPACHA-OPEÑO
open-spandrel arch bridges *see under* BRIDGES → types
open-weave *see under* TEXTILES → types
openwork 23 451*
see also under METALWORK → techniques; WOODWORK → techniques
opera 30 667; 32 490, 491
Opera, Giovanni dell' *see* BANDINI, GIOVANNI
opera houses
acoustics 1 124–5*
Argentina 5 *122*
Australia 31 *777*
Austria 15 864
Czechoslovakia 29 422
France 11 *882*; 12 *156*, *157*
Germany 33 429
Northern Ireland 30 *679*
see also CONCERT HALLS; THEATRES
operator's cabs 7 766, 767
Opere, Giovanni delle *see* GIOVANNI DELLE OPERE
Opfido, Federico 4 721
Ophey, Walter 10 695
Ophir 14 523
Ophorn, Johann von 12 467
Opie, John 10 369; 19 591; 23 451–2*
patrons and collectors 3 239; 19 98, 271
pupils 30 751
reproductive prints by others 28 882; 30 384
works 23 *451*
Opie, Robert 10 422; 11 569
Opificio delle Pietre Dure (Florence) 16 746, 748; 21 24; 22 482
designers 11 29, 192; 33 691
directors 11 192, 234
library 16 777
production 5 350; 11 191; 14 171, I1; 16 724, 727, 745
opisthodomoi 8 154; 13 376, *376*; 23 452*
Greece, ancient 13 398
opium weights *see* WEIGHTS
Opiza Monastery 9 84; 12 321; 30 305
Opizari, Beka 23 452*; 30 305
works 12 328
Opizari, Beshken 12 328; 23 452*
works 12 328
Oplinter, St Genoveva 13 99, 110
Oplinter Cross 3 552
Oplontis, Villa of Poppaea 12 69; 26 869; 27 50, 54, 58
Opmerker, De 25 355
Opobo 15 65
Opochka Fortress 27 370
Opočno Castle 3 97; 8 378; 14 756
Opole 25 119
Oporinus, Johannes 14 439; 32 199, 681
Oporto 23 452–5*, *453*; 25 *288*; 33 149
Academia de Belas-Artes 25 293, 298, 317, 319
collections 25 318
Armazéns Nascimento 25 294
art forms and materials
architecture 25 291
ceramics 23 454–5*; 30 881
faience (ii) (ceramics) 25 310
gold 25 312
marks 25 312
metalwork 25 313
pottery 25 310
sculpture 13 102
silk 25 315
Casa de Cerralves *see* Museu Nacional de Arte Moderna
churches
Cathedral 17 595; 22 533; 25 289, 313
retables 26 253; 27 805
sculpture 26 611
Góis Church 13 125
Nossa Senhora da Carmo 26 254
Nossa Senhora da Vitória 26 254
S Bento da Vitória 2 286; 26 253
S Francisco 23 *453*; 26 253, 254
S Ippolito 26 148
S Lourenço 25 291
S Pedro dos Clérigos 22 533, *533*; 25 293
Factory House 25 293
monument to Peter IV 25 301
Museum of Ethnography and History 18 746
Museu Nacional de Arte Moderna 25 318
Museu Nacional de Soares dos Reis 25 318; 28 913; 33 149
Palácio da Bolsa 23 *453*; 25 293
Palácio de Cristal 25 293
Ponte Dona Maria I 25 293
Prison 25 293
Relação law courts 25 293
Rua de S João 25 293
S Antonio Hospital 25 293
S Bento station 30 882
Vila da Feira market 25 294
Oposhnya 27 411; 31 563
Opovo 25 499
OPOYAZ 4 811
Oppé, A(dolph) Paul 10 367; 23 455*
Oppenheim, Katharinenkirche 13 56, *57*; 22 221; 31 271
Oppenheim, Adeline 13 832
Oppenheim, Dennis 23 49, 455–6*; 28 397; 29 98
works 18 694, 695; 24 403, 408
Oppenheim, Max von (*fl* 1911-29; archaeologist) 14 63
Oppenheim, Meret 3 824; 11 568; 23 456*; 30 139
groups and movements 17 694; 30 21
works 2 617; 23 334; 29 12, 670
Oppenheim, Moritz Daniel 17 575
Oppenheimer, Henry 9 229, 231
Oppenheimer, Max (1885-1945; artist) 8 434; 23 456–7*; 32 446
Oppenord, André 19 261
Oppenord, Gilles-Marie 11 405; 12 747; 23 457–9*, 514, 516
groups and movements 26 493
patrons and collectors 8 208; 11 631
pupils 4 163
reproductive prints by others 12 727; 15 31; 17 668
works 11 577, 589, 754; 12 410; 19 118; 23 *458*, 517; 24 271; 26 84, 492
Oppenordt, Alexandre-Jean 4 552
Oppert, Jules 18 86
Oppervelt, van (family) 3 600
Oppe-Sundby Church 4 781
Oppi, Ubaldo 16 680; 23 263, 459*
oppida see TOWNS → historical and regional traditions → Celtic; Prehistoric art
oppida period *see under* CELTIC → periods
Oppitz, József 15 4
Oppitz, M. 25 435
Oppler, Edwin 17 547; 23 459*
collaboration 14 229, 301
works 12 415
Opponenterna 3 776; 17 662; 18 449; 23 206; 30 79
Oppositions 24 434
Oppurg Church 7 304
Oprescu, George 26 723, 724
Opsomer, Isidore, Baron 23 459–60*
Opstal, Gérard van 3 570; 11 587; 23 460*
collaboration 19 21; 27 821
patrons and collectors 14 492; 18 671
pupils 20 480
works 3 604; 19 642; 29 833
Opsvik, Petter 23 234
optical discs 31 671
optical emission spectrometry (OES) *see under* TECHNICAL EXAMINATION → types
optical instruments 28 210
optical microscopy *see under* TECHNICAL EXAMINATION → types
optics 24 375–7, 485, 658; 28 202
Optsal, Kaspar van 27 133
opus 13 467
Opus 5 3 62
opus Africanum masonry *see under* MASONRY → types
opus anglicanum see under EMBROIDERY → types
opus francigenum see under GOTHIC → styles
opus incertum masonry *see under* MASONRY → types
Opus International 24 442
opus interrasile see under FILIGREE → types
opus mixtum masonry *see under* MASONRY → types
opus musivum see under MOSAICS → types
opus pseudisodomum see under MASONRY → types
opus quadratum see under MASONRY → types
opus quasi-reticulatum masonry *see under* MASONRY → types
opus reticulatum masonry *see under* MASONRY → types
opus sectile
Byzantine 16 *596*
England 29 XII
Italy 7 919
Rome, ancient 14 170; 26 875; 27 47, 59, 60; 32 543
Turkey 16 *596*
opus signinum see under MOSAICS → types
opus spicatum masonry *see under* MASONRY → types
opus tectorium see under ROME, ANCIENT → stucco
opus tessellatum see under MOSAICS → types
opus testaceum masonry *see under* MASONRY → types
opus teutonicum see under EMBROIDERY → types
opus topiarium 31 150
opus veneticum see under FILIGREE → types
opus vermiculatum see under MOSAICS → types
Opzoomer, Simon 22 848
Oquendo 4 262, 269; 29 894
oracle bones 2 *208*; 4 *313*; 6 625, 735, 737–8, *738*, 767, 836; 19 804
oracle bone script *see under* SCRIPTS → types
Oracsek, Ignác 10 545; 14 887; 23 462*
Oradea 26 *705*
architecture 26 708
Cathedral 26 706, 707, 710, 713
Criş County Museum 26 724
Episcopal Palace 14 892; 26 708
fortifications 26 708
interior decoration 26 718
Jesuit college 26 708
metalwork 15 5
paintings 14 898
Premonstratensian church 26 708
Town Hall 26 709
Orage, A. R. 25 380
Oraibi, Old (AZ) 22 567
Őraljaboldogfalva *see* SÎNTĂMĂRIA-ORLEA
Oran (Algeria) 1 634
Demaeght Museum 1 636
Orán (Argentina)
Hospital Regional S Vicente de Paul 2 397
parish church 2 402
Orang Asli 20 181, 183
Orang Bukit 3 440
works 3 *441*
orange *see under* PIGMENTS → types
Orange (France) 13 303
Arausio 2 286–7*; 27 3
Arch of Tiberius 2 286–7, *287*; 10 742; 11 151; 26 868, 882; 27 34, 45; 31 349
coffering 7 527
Brangwynmuseum 4 673
cotton 11 649
sculpture 11 553
silk 11 644
theatre 2 287; 26 873, 904, 905; 30 652, *652*
Orange (NJ; USA), Holy Face Shrine 28 632
Orange, Hans P(ieter) L' *see* L'ORANGE, HANS P(IETER)
Orange, Philiberte of Chalons, Princess of 21 72
Orange, William Frederick of, Prince of Nassau-Dietz *see* NASSAU-DIETZ, WILLIAM-FREDERICK OF ORANGE, Prince of
orange mineral *see under* PIGMENTS → types
Orange Nassau (House of) 23 462–4*, *463*; 32 231
architecture 5 542
collections 22 906
paintings 14 729; 28 362
Orange Nassau, Albertina of, Princess of Nassau-Dietz *see* NASSAU-DIETZ, ALBERTINA, Princess of
Orange Nassau, Amalia van Solms, Princess of Orange *see* AMALIA VON SOLMS, Princess of Orange
Orange Nassau, Frederick Henry, Stadholder *see* FREDERICK HENRY, Stadholder of the Netherlands,Prince of Orange
Orange Nassau, Henrietta Catherina, Princess of *see* ANHALT-DESSAU, HENRIETTA CATHERINA, Princess
Orange Nassau, John William Friso, Prince of Orange, Prince of Nassau-Dietz *see* ORANGE, JOHN WILLIAM FRISO, Prince of, Prince of Nassau-Dietz
Orange Nassau, Louisa Henrietta *see* LOUISA HENRIETTA, Electress of Brandenburg
Orange Nassau, Louise-Henrietta, Electress of Brandenburg *see* LOUISE-HENRIETTA, Electress of Brandenburg
Orange Nassau, Marianne, Princess of *see* HOHENZOLLERN, MARIANNE OF ORANGE NASSAU, Princess of Prussia
Orange Nassau, Mary II, Queen of England and Scotland *see* MARY II, Queen of England and Scotland
Orange Nassau, Mary Stuart, Princess (1631-61) 23 *463*
Orange Nassau, Wilhelmina, Queen of the Netherlands *see* WILHELMINA, Queen of the Netherlands
Orange Nassau, William I, King of the Netherlands *see* WILLIAM I, King of the Netherlands
Orange Nassau, William I, Prince, Stadholder of the Netherlands *see* WILLIAM THE SILENT, Stadholder of the Netherlands, Prince of Orange
Orange Nassau, William II, King of the Netherlands *see* WILLIAM II, King of the Netherlands
Orange Nassau, William III, King of England *see* WILLIAM III, King of England
Orange Nassau, William III, King of the Netherlands *see* WILLIAM III, King of the Netherlands
Orange Nassau, William III, Stadholder of the Netherlands *see* WILLIAM III, King of England
Orange Nassau, William IV, Stadholder of the Netherlands, Prince of Orange *see* WILLIAM IV,Stadholder of the Netherlands
Orange Nassau, William V, Stadholder of the Netherlands *see* WILLIAM V, Stadholder of the Netherlands, Prince of Orange
Orange Nassau-Dietz, John William Friso, Prince of 23 *463*
orangeries 7 744; 9 21; 12 132, 791; 23 470–71*, *471*; 27 285
see also CONSERVATORIES; GREENHOUSES
Orang Laut *see* JAKUN
Orango Grande 4 56
Orang Ulu 20 167
Oranienbaum *see* LOMONOSOV

Oranienburg, Schloss *see* SCHLOSS ORANIENBURG
Oransky, P. V. **33** 518
orants **23** 471*
Oraon **15** 205
oraria *see* STOLES (ECCLESIASTICAL)
Oraschek, Ignác **5** 86
Orăscu, Alexandru **5** 72; **23** 471–2*; **26** 709, 726
works **15** 56
Orašje **28** 439
Oraska, Arthur A. **18** 114
Orator see ARRINGATORE
Oratorians **11** 78; **23** 472–4*
churches **23** *473*
iconography **23** 472–3*
patronage **23** 473–4*
oratories (i) (chapels) **23** 474*
Ireland **12** 14
Islamic **16** 141
Italy **5** *18*
oratories (ii) *see* ORATORIANS → churches
Orava **28** *848*
Castle **28** 849, 852
tomb of György Thurzó **14** 893, 899
Orazi, Manuel **25** 623
Orazio di Paolo **16** 848
Orbais, Jean d' *see* JEAN D'ORBAIS
Orbais Abbey Church **13** 39, 180, 181; **26** 702
Orban, Desiderius **23** 425
Orbán, Dezső **10** 108
Orbán, Katalin **15** 2
Orb and Cross, Master of the **2** 471
Orbay, François d' **4** 551; **23** 474*, 512
attributions **23** 512
collaboration **19** 267; **20** 296
groups and movements **24** 169
pupils **19** 231
works **2** 869; **16** 855; **24** 122; **30** 669
Orbeli, I. A. **6** 280
Ōrbelian, Liparit **23** 202
Ōrbelian, Smbat **23** 202
Ōrbelian, Step'anos **30** 360
Ōrbelian, Tarsayich' **23** 202
Orbetello **13** 541
Orbetto, L' *see* TURCHI, ALESSANDRO
Orbœklunde **4** 781
orbs **26** 81*
Orcagna *see* CIONE, ANDREA DI
Orccha **21** 590; **23** 818
Orchar, James Guthrie **28** 269
Orchar Collection *see under* BROUGHTY FERRY (TAYSIDE); DUNDEE (TAYSIDE) → McManus Galleries
Orchard, Jenny **2** 762
Orchard, John **19** 604, 605
Orchard, William **23** 474–5*, 686
orchards **12** 110
Orchardson, William Quiller **23** 475–6*
collaboration **20** 34
groups and movements **22** 744
patrons and collectors **19** 270
teachers **18** 856
works **10** 254; **12** 296; **23** *476*; **28** 237, 238
Orchardson-Mazrui, Elizabeth **17** 908
orchestras **13** *385*, 385–6; **23** 475*; **26** *920*; **30** 650, 651, 652
Orchha **15** 373, 392
Chaturbuj Temple **15** 393
Jahangir Mandir **15** *391*, 393
orchid fibres *see under* FIBRES → types
orchil *see under* DYES → types
Orchoë *see* URUK
Orchomenos **13** *363*; **14** *332*; **23** 475–7*
bouleuterion **4** 530
Orchomenos—cont.
cemetery **23** 476
Church of the Dormition **9** 592, 593; **28** 828
granaries **14** 339
palaces **23** 476–7
Skripou **9** *511*; **28** 828*
temple **13** 389
Treasury of Minyas **14** 341, 353; **23** 476; **30** 738; **31** 108
wall paintings **14** 348, 350, 351
Orcival, Notre-Dame **26** 585, 601
Orco Azapa, Eladio **24** 500
Orda, Napoleon **3** 529
Ordal **29** 330
Ordericus Vitalis **9** 256
Order of Christ **23** 414
Order of Crato **26** 516
Order of Friars Minor *see* FRANCISCAN ORDER
Order of Poor Clares **11** 707; **25** 229–30*
altarpieces **25** *229*
Order of Preachers *see* DOMINICAN ORDER
Order of St George **7** 178
Order of St John *see* KNIGHTS HOSPITALLER
Order of St Louis **7** 178
Order of St Michael **7** 178
Order of St Michael of France **7** 179
Order of Strict Observance **7** 348
see also CISTERCIAN ORDER
Order of the Annunciation of Savoy **7** 178
Order of the Band **7** 177
Order of the Blessed Virgin Mary of Mt Carmel *see* CARMELITE ORDER
Order of the Collar **7** 178
Order of the Elephant **7** *178*
Order of the Garter **7** 177, 178, *178*, 179; **33** 248
Order of the Golden Fleece **3** 609, *609*; **7** 178, 179, *179*; **13** 196
Order of the Holy Ghost **7** 178
Order of the Holy Saviour *see* BRIGITTINE ORDER
Order of the Holy Trinity for the Redemption of Captives *see* TRINITARIANS
Order of the Knights of the Cross with the Red Star *see* PRAGUE → ecclesiastical buildings → St Francis
Order of the Star **31** 834
Order of the Starry Cross **7** 178
Order of the Thistle **7** 179
orders (architecture) **22** 211; **23** 477–93*
historical and regional traditions
Belgium **3** 544
France **24** *170*; **31** *297*
Germany **23** 490
Gothic **23** 489
Greece, ancient **13** 377, 396, 398*, 404, 407, 408, 412, 424; **23** 429, 477; **27** 690
Ionic **27** 687, *688*
Turkey **18** 580
Islamic **16** 241
Italy **6** *358*; **23** 485–7
Romanesque **23** 485
Rome, ancient **23** 477; **26** 863, 865, 924
Russia **22** 182
Seleucid **28** 384
Spain **8** 79
Turkey **18** 580; **23** 392
18th cent. **18** 857–8
types
Aiolic **13** 398; **23** 481
Composite **1** 559; **11** 791; **23** *479*, 480*, 483, *486*, 487; **26** 863, 893
Rome, ancient **23** 477, 480
orders (architecture)
types—cont.
Corinthian **7** 502, 746; **11** 791; **13** 384, 408; **15** 132; **23** 478–80*, *479*, 482–3*, 484, *486*, 487, 491
Greece **13** 387
Greece, ancient **13** 387, 391, 401, 405, 415, 416; **23** 477, 482, 534
Italy **6** *358*; **23** *489*; **26** 889
Lebanon **3** 2
Rome, ancient **23** 480, 482–3, *483*; **26** 865, 875, 889; **30** 436
Seleucid **28** 384
Turkey **23** 392
Doric **11** 790; **13** 389, 393, 408, 409; **23** 429, 477–8*, 481*, 483, 484, *486*, 487
France **2** 173
Greece, ancient **2** 676, *677*; **7** 851; **13** 377, *378*, 387, 388, 389, 390, 391, 393, 398, 401, 405, 406, 408, 415, 416; **23** 429, 477, 478, *479*, 481, *481*, 533
Italy **4** 648; **6** *358*; **23** *488*; **27** 761
Rome, ancient **23** 478, *479*, 481
giant **23** 477, 491*, 492–3*
England **23** 491, 492
France **5** 166; **19** 693; **23** 492, 493
Italy **23** 492, *493*
Lebanon **23** 491
Netherlands, the **23** 492
Rome, ancient **23** 491
Spain **23** 492
Syria **23** 491
Hierosolymitan **23** 489
Ionic **7** 502; **11** 790–91; **13** 408, 409; **23** 478*, *479*, 481–2*, 483, 484, *486*, 487; **27** 687
Greece, ancient **8** 692; **13** 377, 387, 388, 389, 391–2, 393, *393*, 398–400, *399*, 401, 402, 405, 408, 415, 416; **15** 893; **19** 232; **23** 477, 481, *482*, 533; **27** *688*
Italy **6** *358*
Rome, ancient **23** 478, 482
Solomonic **23** 488, *488*
Tuscan **6** *358*; **11** 791; **23** 477, *479*, 480*, 483, *486*, 487
see also under COLUMNS → types
orders (chivalry) **7** 177–9*, *177*, *179*; **14** 414
Denmark **7** *178*
England **7** *178*
Holy Roman Empire (before 1648) **7** 178
Portugal **7** 179
Russia **7** 178
orders (religious) *see*: BENEDICTINE; CARMELITE; CARTHUSIAN; CISTERCIAN; CLUNIAC; DOMINICAN; FRANCISCAN; JESUIT; THEATINE ORDERS
orders (knighthood) *see* KNIGHTS HOSPITALLER; KNIGHTS TEMPLAR; TEUTONIC ORDER
Ordinaire, Marcel **8** 57
ordinatio **20** 565; **26** 924
ordination halls **5** 232
Ordini, Master of the **12** 567
Ordini, Pietro Benvenuti dagli *see* BENVENUTI DAGLI ORDINI, PIETRO
Ordish, Rowland M. **25** 857; **30** 27
works **16** *54*
Ordnance Survey of the British Isles **30** 26
Ord och bild **24** 451
Ordona *see* HERDONIA
Ordóñez, Bartolomé **23** 494*; **29** 289
assistants **21** 857
collaboration **28** 725
works **3** 218, 221; **7** 345; **10** 784; **13** 283; **22** 477; **29** 311
Ordóñez, David **23** 494*
Ordóñez, Fernando Alvárez *see* ALVÁREZ ORDÓÑEZ, FERNANDO
Ordóñez, Joaquín Alvárez *see* ALVÁREZ ORDÓÑEZ, JOAQUÍN
Ordoñez, Juan de **2** 386
Ordoñez, Luisina **25** 701
Ordoño I, King of León (*reg* 850–66) **19** 170
Ordoño II, King of León (*reg* 910–25) **19** 171; **20** 330
Ordos (people) **21** 870
Ordos (style)
bronze **23** *495*, 495–6, *496*; **28** 603
gold **7** 21
jewellery **7** 108
metalwork **6** 313; **23** 495–6*
Ordu-Balik Palace **21** 874
Orduna, Fructuoso **29** 295
Ordzhonikidze *see* VLADIKAVKAZ
Orea, Juan de **13** 284; **14** 474; **29** 266
Örebro
castle **30** 92
Nikolaikyrkan **13** 102
Rosta housing estate **30** 75
Town Hall **30** 73
orecchioni see ORILLIONS
Ořechovka **8** 380
Øregaard Grammar School **8** 728
oreikhalkos **4** 681–2
O'Reilly, Alejandro **25** 700
O'Reilly, A. W. F. **16** 36
Orel **27** 411
Orell, Joseph **21** 407
Orellana, Francisco (Domínguez) Chávez y *see* CHÁVEZ Y ARELLANA, FRANCISCO (DOMÍNGUEZ) CHÁVEZ Y
Orellana, Gastón **13** 725
Orellana, Marcos Antonio de **32** 248
Orellano, Blas de **24** 502
Orelli, Antonio Baldassare **23** 497*; **30** 132
Orelli, Giuseppe Antonio Felice **23** 497; **30** 132
Oren-kala **2** 896
Oreno, Casino Borromeo **18** 704
Orense
Cathedral **13** 69; **26** 642; **29** 263, 335
Santuario de las Ermitas **27** 498
sculpture **29** 292
Oreor **23** 832, 833
Meeting House **23** *833*
Orestes **28** 481
Oretti, Marcello **19** 117; **23** 497*
Orfa *see* URFA
Orfelin, Jakov **28** 450
Orfelin, Pedro **13** 863
Orfelin, Zaharije **28** 450
Orford (Suffolk) **10** 227
keep **6** 55; **8** 138; **9** 144
Orford, George Walpole, 3rd Earl of *see* WALPOLE, GEORGE, 3rd Earl of Orford
Orford, Horace (William) Walpole, 4th Earl of *see* WALPOLE, HORACE (WILLIAM), 4th Earl of Orford
Orford, Robert Walpole, 1st Earl of *see* WALPOLE, ROBERT, 1st Earl of Orford
Orford, Robert Walpole, 2nd Earl of *see* WALPOLE, ROBERT, 2nd Earl of Orford
Orgagna *see* CIONE, ANDREA DI
Organ, Brian **29** 438
organ altars *see under* ALTARS → types
organ clocks *see under* CLOCKS → types
organdy **16** 430
Organ für christliche Kunst **13** 204
Organi, Filippino degli **21** 532, 533
organic analysis *see under* TECHNICAL EXAMINATION → types
organic architecture **12** 378; **23** 498–500*
Germany **11** 841; **14** 175; **23** *499*
United States of America **11** 840; **33** 402
Organización Paiz **13** 768, 769
Organization of Black American Culture (OBAC) **1** 445
organs **17** 397; **22** 372, *373*, 373–4; **32** *832*
organ shutters **22** *373*; **23** *500*, 500–502*, *501*; **31** *430*
Orgaz **29** 337
Orgemont, Pierre d' **6** 453
Orgeyev **21** *810*, 812
church **21** 810
Orgues, Hugues d', Archbishop of Rouen *see* HUGUES D'ORGUES, Archbishop of Rouen
Ørholms **8** 751
Oriani, Defendente **20** 908
Oriani, Pippo **1** 166
Oribe Black ware *see under* POTTERY → wares
Oribe Furuta *see* FURUTA ORIBE
Oribe ware *see under* POTTERY → wares
Orient, Josef **4** 662; **10** 896
Oriental alabaster *see* ALABASTER (LIMESTONE)
Oriental Art **24** 425
Oriental Ceramic Society **7** 157; **17** 431
Orientalism **7** 165, 168, 615; **11** 800; **16** 143; **23** 502–5*; **24** 667; **25** 582; **31** 480
art forms
furniture **33** 155
nude figures **6** *501*; **15** *844*; **23** 504
painting **1** 634
Austria **2** *796*
England **23** *505*
France **6** *501*; **7** *760*, II2; **15** *844*; **20** *420*, 420–21; **26** *92*; **32** VII2
miniatures **21** *644*
photography **30** 569
villas **4** *809*
Orientalizing style
amphorae **13** *501*, *503*
aryballoi **13** *499*, *500*
earrings **13** *598*
metalwork **10** 591
oinochoai **13** *503*
painting **13** *550*
pottery **10** 591
Crete **13** 498, 504
Cycladic **13** 498, 502
Cyprus, ancient **8** 347
Etruscan **10** 611*
Greece, ancient **13** 368, 471, 472, 496, 498–501*, 502–4*, 553*
Lakonia **13** 498
sculpture **13** 442
origami **24** 57
Origenes **8** 233
original works of art *see* ART (ORIGINAL WORKS OF)
Orihuela
Cathedral **29** 337
University **31** 674
orillions **21** 547, 566, *566*
Orimina, Cristoforo **23** 505–6*
works **2** 110; **23** *506*
workshop **23** 351
Orimina, Pietro **23** 505
Orio, Baltasar de Echave *see* ECHAVE ORIO, BALTASAR DE

Oriola, Maria Berna, Gräfin von **4** 205
Orioli, Pietro **11** 842; **20** 684
Oriolo, Giovanni (di Giuliano) da *see* GIOVANNI (DI GIULIANO) DA ORIOLO
Oriolo, Giovanni Pietro da *see* GIOVANNI PIETRO DA ORIOLO
Oriol y Bernadet, José **10** 543
Orive, María Cristina **10** 747; **23** 506–7*
Oriximiná **27** 785
Orizaba, Convent of S José **21** 378
Orizzonte *see* BLOEMEN, JAN FRANS VAN
Örjan the painter **23** 507*
Orkhan, Sultan (*reg* 1324-60) (Ottoman) **5** 281; **16** 206, 810; **23** 638
Orkhon Turks **27** 436
Orkney, George Hamilton, 1st Earl of *see* HAMILTON, GEORGE, 1st Earl of Orkney
Orkney, Patrick Stewart, 2nd Earl of *see* STEWART, PATRICK, 2nd Earl of Orkney
Orkney, William Sinclair, 3rd Earl of *see* SINCLAIR, WILLIAM, 3rd Earl of Orkney
Orkney Islands
architecture **25** 503
baskets **3** 332
chairs **28** 256; **29** 763
heraldry **14** 409
stone-carvings **25** 513
tombs **25** 507
Orlandi, Deodato *see* DEODATO (DI) ORLANDI
Orlandi, Pellegrino Antonio **23** 507*
works **4** 21, 89; **10** 205; **11** 675; **13** 746
Orlandi, Stefano **1** 597; **4** 46, 277; **7** 926
works **4** *277*
Orlandini, Mirko **3** 592
Orlando (family) **4** 277
Orlando, Bernardo **28** 6
Orlando, Felipe **23** 507–8*
Orlandos, Anastasios **9** 528; **23** 508*
Orlat **6** 270
Orléans (France) **11** *504*; **23** 508–11*, *509*
architecture **26** 585
Cathedral of Ste Cécile **23** 510–11*
Cathedral of Sainte Croix **13** 49, 59, 199, 210, 211; **26** 585
ambulatory **1** 767
buttresses **5** 319
restoration **2** 319
tracing floor **31** 275
transept **31** 281
Hôtel des Créneaux **11** 512; **31** 238
hôtels particuliers **23** 508–9
Hôtel de la Vieille Intendance **11** 656
Hôtel de Ville *see* Hôtel des Créneaux
manuscripts **5** 803; **11** 653
Musée des Beaux-Arts **2** 142; **8** 793
paper **24** 55
porcelain **23** 510*
St Aignan **7** 266; **13** 59, 60; **26** 585, 599
ambulatory **1** 767
crypt **8** 224
silk **11** 645
Town Hall *see* Hôtel des Creneaux
urban planning **23** 509–10
woodcuts **25** *243*; **33** 359
Orléans (Bourbon House of) **23** 511*, *511*
architecture **25** 404
Orléans (Bourbon House of)—cont.
paintings **5** 63; **10** 678; **11** 663; **14** 808, 877; **32** 774
sculpture **8** 617
Orléans (Valois House of) **11** 655
Orléans, Anne-Marie-Louise de Bourbon, Duchesse de Montpensier *see* MONTPENSIER, ANNE-MARIE-LOUISE DE BOURBON, Duchesse de
Orléans, Antoine de Bourbon **23** 523
Orléans, Antoine-Marie-Philippe-Louis de Bourbon, Duc de Montpensier *see* MONTPENSIER, ANTOINE-MARIE-PHILIPPE-LOUIS DE BOURBON, Duc de
Orléans, Arnulph van **23** 679
Orléans, Charles de Valois, Duke of *see* CHARLES, Duke of Orléans
Orléans, Charlotte-Jeanne de Bourbon, Duchesse d' **4** 847; **23** 518
Orléans, Elisabeth-Charlotte de Bourbon, Duchesse d' **23** *511*, 513*; **33** *272*
collections **23** 512
gems **12** 266
medals **32** 368
Orléans, Elisabeth-Marguerite d', Duchesse de Guise *see* GUISE, ELISABETH-MARGUERITE D'ORLÉANS, Duchesse de
Orléans, Evrard d' *see* EVRARD D'ORLÉANS
Orléans, Ferdinand-Philippe (-Louis-Charles-Henri) de Bourbon, 7th Duc d' (1810-42) **23** *511*, 521–2*
architecture **11** 258
paintings **7** 878; **8** 599, 616, 640, 641; **11** 233; **14** 480; **15** 836, 841; **26** 451; **27** 266; **30** 353; **33** 674
porcelain **28** 523
sculpture **3** 314; **11** 565
Orléans, François d' *see* FRANÇOIS D'ORLÉANS
Orléans, (Jean Baptiste) Gaston de Bourbon, Duc d' (1608-60) **4** *543*, 887; **12** 261, 266; **19** 233; **31** 321
architecture **4** 155–6; **20** 289
gardens **19** 162
paintings **9** 387; **11** 661; **26** 452
Orléans, Girard d' *see* GIRARD D'ORLÉANS
Orléans, Hélène-Louise-Elisabeth de Bourbon, Duchesse d' **11** 663; **23** 522
Orléans, Henrietta Anne de Bourbon, Duchesse d' **23** 515
Orléans, Henri-Eugène-Philippe-Louis de Bourbon, Duc d'Aumale *see* AUMALE, HENRI-EUGÈNE-PHILIPPE-LOUIS DE BOURBON, Duc d'
Orléans, Jean d' *see* JEAN D'ORLÉANS
Orléans, Jean de Dunois, Bâtard d' *see* DUNOIS, JEAN, Comte de, Bâtard d'Orléans
Orléans, Jean-Philippe de Bourbon, Chevalier d' **22** 685; **23** 517; **25** 895
Orléans, Louis de Bourbon, 3rd Duc d' (1703-52) **23** *511*, 516–17*
architecture **21** 549
gems **8** 209
paintings **8** 813
Orléans, Louis de Bourbon, Duc de Nemours *see* NEMOURS, LOUIS DE BOURBON, Duc de
Orléans, Louis I de Valois, Duke of *see* LOUIS I DE VALOIS, Duke of Orléans
Orléans, Louis-Philippe-Albert de Bourbon, Comte de Paris *see* PARIS, LOUIS-PHILIPPE-ALBERT DE BOURBON, Comte de
Orléans, Louis-Philippe de Bourbon, 4th Duc d' (1725-85) **5** 779; **14** 798; **23** *511*, 517–18*; **24** 773; **31** 870
architecture **4** 847; **5** 888; **7** 773
drawings **27** 531
furniture **9** 324
paintings **18** 579
porcelain **3** 591
sculpture **23** 795
Orléans, Louis-Philippe de Bourbon, 6th Duc d' (1773-1850) *see* LOUIS-PHILIPPE, King of the French
Orléans, Louis-Philippe-Joseph de Bourbon, 5th Duc d' (1747-93) **2** 559; **8** 87; **23** *511*, 518–20*, *520*; **31** 220
collections **11** 663; **19** 587
engravings **14** 366
gems **8** 209
paintings **19** 25
Orléans, Margaret of, Comtesse d'Etampes *see* ETAMPES, MARGARET OF ORLÉANS, Comtesse d'
Orléans, Marie (-Christine-Caroline-Adélaïde-Françoise-Léopoldine) de Bourbon, Princesse d' **23** 511, *511*, 520, 522*
furniture **3** 585
groups and movements **31** 374
paintings **3** 241
teachers **28** 68
works **31** 346
Orléans, Marie-Adelaïde de Bourbon, Abbess of Chelles **24** 148
Orléans, Marie Isabelle d', Comtesse de Paris *see* PARIS, MARIE ISABELLE D', Comtesse de
Orléans, Marie Louise d', Queen of Spain *see* MARIE LOUISE D'ORLÉANS, Queen of Spain
Orléans, Philippe-Egalité, Duc d' *see* ORLÉANS, LOUIS-PHILIPPE-JOSEPH DE BOURBON, Duc d'
Orléans, Philippe I de Bourbon, 1st Duc d' (1640-1701) **4** *543*; **12** 874; **23** 511–15*, *511*; **33** *272*
architecture **19** 210; **27** 536
collections **23** 515
gardens **19** 163; **27** 536
glass **11** 612
interior decoration **27** 263
paintings **4** 245, 756; **8** 90
sponsorship **27** 536
Orléans, Philippe II de Bourbon, 2nd Duc d' (1674-1723) **11** 657; **23** 511, *511*, 514–16*
architecture **23** 457
book illustrations **4** 360
collections **10** 487; **11** 662
decorative works **30** 781
engravings **31** 69
furniture **7** 657; **26** *84*
gems **11** 634; **29** 724
gold **11** 631
interior decoration **26** 83, 84
paintings **2** 418; **8** 91, 92, 474; **9** 12; **10** 365, 478; **11** 404; **15** 47; **19** 817; **22** 684; **26** 386; **27** 789; **32** 8, 919
miniatures **21** 642
religious **26** 424
reproductive prints by others **2** 709
Orléans, Robert-Philippe-Louis-Eugène-Ferdinand de Bourbon, Duc de Chartres *see* CHARTRES, ROBERT-PHILIPPE-L.-E.-F. DE BOURBON, Duc de
Orléans *Madonna* **8** 664
Orleans Triptych, Master of the **13** 170
Orléansville *see* ECH CHELIFF
Orlers, Jan Jansz. **22** 841; **25** 369
Orley (i) (family) **33** 306
Orley (i), Barent van *see* ORLEY (i), BERNARD VAN
Orley (i), Bernard van **17** 895; **21** 124; **23** 523, 524–7*; **27** 256; **29** 504
attributions **5** 47; **10** 349
collaboration **24** 15
groups and movements **26** 728
methods **31** 578
paintings
glass **8** 86
patrons and collectors
Boisserée, Melchior and Sulpiz **4** 243
Margaret of Austria, Duchess of Parma and Regent of the Netherlands (1522-86) **3** 612; **13** 905
Mary of Hungary, Regent of the Netherlands (1505-58) **3** 613; **13** 909, 910; **16** 867
Nassau, Hendrik III, Count of **22** 535
Nassau, Mencía de Mendoza, Countess of **3** 612
Przezdziecki, Aleksarder (Narcyz Karol) **25** 675
Robien, Christophe-Paul Gautron, Marquis de **26** 470
pupils **5** 43; **7** 519; **12** 513
tapestries **13** 906
works **1** 165; **3** 387, 554; **5** 47, 53; **12** 513; **13** *909*; **23** 294, 465, *525*, *527*, 667; **29** 504; **30** 315
Orley (i), Everard van **23** 523, 524
Orley (ii), Jan van **23** 528*
collaboration **23** 528
works **5** 50; **10** 351; **23** 528
Orley (ii), Pieter van **23** 528
Orley (ii), Richard van **23** 528*
Orley (i), Valentin van **23** 523, 524*
pupils **23** 524
Orliac, Jean d' **14** 32
Orlier, Jean d' **28** 150
Orlier Altarpiece **28** *150*, 150–51
Orlik, Emil **23** 528–9*
groups and movements **28** 344
pupils **13** 697; **14** 604, 832; **31** 910
works **17** *276*; **33** 362
Orlik Hermitage
SS Peter and Paul **25** 343
Orlina, Ramon **24** 620
Orlitsa Hermitage, SS Peter and Paul **5** 148, 153
Orloff, Chana **11** 569; **13** 328; **17** 577; **23** 529*
Orloff Service **11** 620; **27** 584
Orlopp & Kusener **8** 469
Orlov **27** 439
Orlov, Aleksey **10** 461
Orlov, Boris **27** 398; **29** 89
Orlov, Dmitry (Stakhiyevich) *see* MOOR, DMITRY (STAKHIYEVICH)
Orlov, Georgy (Mikhaylovich) **23** 529–30*; **32** 382
Orlov, Grigory (Grigoryevich), Count **5** 530; **10** 461; **12** 173; **26** 403, 532
Orlov, Ivan (Dmitriyevich) **27** 425
works **27** *425*
Orlov, Mikhail **27** 416
Orlov, Sergey **27** 435
Orlova, Chana *see* ORLOFF, CHANA
Orlovsky, Aleksandr (Osipovich) **8** 372; **23** *530*, 530–31*; **25** 106
Orlovsky, Boris (Ivanovich) **23** 531*; **27** 390
Orlovsky, Vladimir D. **31** 559
Orlowski, Hans **4** 732
Orly **7** 694; **11** 525, 771
airship hangars **11** *771*
Ormani, Maria **16** 780
Ormanni, Antonio **24** 732
Orme, Daniel **22** 123
Orme, Edward **25** 164; **29** 676
Orme, Philibert de l' *see* L'ORME, PHILIBERT DE
Ormea, Willem **33** 194, 195
Ormesby Psalter *see under* PSALTERS → individual manuscripts
ormolu **23** 531*
historical and regional traditions
Britain **7** *445*
France **11** 590; **23** 531
Russia **27** *424*
marks *see under* MARKS
techniques
gilding **12** 627
uses
candlesticks **27** *424*
clocks **7** *445*
mounts (furniture) **11** 590
mounts (porcelain) **9** 29
statuettes **29** 572
Ormond, Richard **10** 213
Ormonde, James Butler, 1st Duke of *see* BUTLER, JAMES, 1st Duke of Ormonde
Ormonde, James Butler, 1st Marquess of *see* BUTLER, JAMES, 1st Marquess of Ormonde
Ormonde, Pierce Butler, 8th Earl of *see* BUTLER, PIERCE, 8th Earl of Ormonde
Ormonde, Thomas Butler, 10th Earl of *see* BUTLER, THOMAS, 10th Earl of Ormonde
Ormonde and Ossory, James Butler, 12th Earl of *see* BUTLER, JAMES, 1st Duke of Ormonde
Ormonde School **23** 531*
Ormophoklisia, Hagios Georgios **9** 601, 627
Ormsbee, Caleb **13** 617
Ormside Bowl **2** 79; **10** 322
Ormus, Sigmund **26** 724
Ormuz *see* HORMUZ
Ormuza y Matute, Mariano **7** 605; **8** 16
ornament **23** 531–65*; **25** 472
Ancient Near East **23** 532–3*
Anglo-Saxon **23** 537
Buddhism **23** 550–51, 553, 555–6
Burma **23** 556
Byzantine **9** 618, 619, 620, 621
Carolingian **23** 537
China **23** 549–52*
Early Christian (*c.* AD 250-843) **9** 618
Egypt **16** *129*
Egypt, ancient **9** 810–11*; **23** 532–3*
England **23** 541, 542–4, 545, 546
France **23** 542, 543, 544
Georgia **12** 318
Greece, ancient **23** 533–5*
Hinduism **23** 555–6
Indonesia **23** 554–5
Insular art **23** 537
Islamic **16** *129*, 132–3, 134, 146; **23** 556–63*
Italy **23** 541, 544
Japan **23** 553–4*
Khmer **23** 556
Kuba (iii) (Zaïre) **18** 487
Maya **23** 565
Merovingian **23** 536
Mesoamerica, Pre-Columbian **23** 564–5*
Migration period **23** 536–7
Native North Americans **23** 564–5*
Romanesque **23** 538
Rome, ancient **23** 533–5*
Scandinavia **32** 519–21*, 523–4*

ornament—cont.
South America, Pre-Columbian 23 564–5*
South-east Asia 23 554–6*
Thailand 23 555
Viking 23 537–8; 32 519–21*
Ornano, Alphonse d', Maréchal 4 390
Ornans, Musée Maison Natale de Gustave Courbet 8 60
Ornäs 30 67
Ornate style pottery see under POTTERY → wares
Ornelas, João de see JOÃO DE ORNELAS
Ornes see URNES
ornithological books 4 362
Örnster, Zygmunt 25 127
or nué see under EMBROIDERY → types
Oroglas 25 23, 27; 26 244
Oromo 1 378; 10 564
Oron 15 61, 62, 63
National Museum 15 65; 23 139
portraits 1 267
Orongo 9 674, 675
sculpture 9 675
Oronsay Cross 28 241
Oropa 27 498
Oropesa see COCHABAMBA
Oropesa, Condes de 33 577
Oropos 13 363
Sanctuary of Amphiaraios
water-clock 13 382
stoa 13 414
Theatre 13 385, 386, 406; 30 651
O'Rorke, Brian 6 409
Orosi 8 15; 9 678, 679
church 8 16
Orosius (fl early 5th cent.) 7 241
Orosius Master (fl c. 1390-1430) 20 634
Oroszvár see RUSOVCE
Orotava, Botanic Garden 12 125
O'Rourke, Dearbhforgaill 7 353
O'Rourke, Jeremiah 24 281
works 24 281
Orović, Savo 22 18
Orozco, José Clemente 14 589; 21 387, 388, 390, 397, 405; 23 565–8*; 25 653; 31 702
collaboration 24 8
groups and movements 21 387
patrons and collectors 21 395; 26 488
restorations by others 8 861
teachers 10 727
works 13 730, 731; 14 785; 15 830; 21 380; 22 334; 23 566, 567; 25 653; 27 868, 872; 28 920
Orozco Romero, Carlos 1 115; 23 568*
Orpen, William (Newenham Montague) 10 374; 16 17, 37; 23 568*
groups and movements 23 23
patrons and collectors 1 496; 4 315; 16 35, 36
pupils 7 377; 9 53; 17 875; 18 667
teachers 4 880; 10 255
works 9 2, 2
Orpheus and Orion, Master of the 25 20
Orpheus Legend, Master of the 25 19
Orphism 1 74; 2 225; 7 630; 8 240, 244, 245, 656; 19 355; 23 569–70*
painting 23 569
orphreys 22 898
orpiment
historical and regional traditions
Buddhism 29 462
China 7 632
Japan 17 277
Rome, ancient 23 785
Sri Lanka 29 462
orpiment—cont.
uses
inks 15 852
lacquer 18 600, 608
pigments 7 632; 17 277; 23 785; 24 798*; 29 462
Orp-le-Grand Church 13 110
Orquesta, La 16 48
Orr, Eric 19 702
Orr, P., & Sons 15 702
works 15 703
Orrefors Glasbruk 8 803; 10 320; 12 795; 24 58; 30 65, 99
designers 30 100, 102, 103
staff 14 65
vases 30 103
Orrego, Alberto 6 597
Orrente, Pedro 23 570–72*; 31 815
patrons and collectors 5 844, 871; 27 724
pupils 20 386
works 23 571; 31 89
Orrery, Charles Boyle, 4th Earl of see BOYLE, CHARLES, 4th Earl of Orrery
Orri 27 834
orrice 24 237
Orrock, James 19 269
Orrouer, d' (family) 24 821
Orrouer, Paul de Grivel, Comte d' 4 455
Orry, Jean 23 572
Orry, Philibert, Comte de Vignory see VIGNORY, PHILIBERT ORRY, Comte de
Orry de Fulvy, Jean-Henri-Louis 2 704; 11 608; 32 582
Ors, Eugenio d' 23 572*; 29 286
groups and movements 3 216; 10 822; 11 302; 23 260
works 33 583, 744
Orsanmichele see under FLORENCE → ecclesiastical buildings
Orsati, Antonio 29 922
Orsay, Alfred, Comte d' 9 287
Orsay, Pierre-Marie-Gaspard Grimod, Comte d' 13 665*; 19 115
decorative works 5 380
drawings 5 445
furniture 26 376
paintings 30 865
sculpture 8 650
Orsel, (André-Jacques-) Victor 23 572–3*
pupils 3 867; 16 907
reproductive prints by others 3 867
teachers 19 847
works 11 415, 462
Orseolo, Pietro I, Doge of Venice (reg 976-8) 32 206, 213
Orseolo, Pietro II, Doge of Venice (reg 991-1008) 31 162
Orsha Gospels see under GOSPEL BOOKS → individual manuscripts
Orshanka Gospels see under GOSPEL BOOKS → individual manuscripts
Orsi, Achille D' see D'ORSI, ACHILLE
Orsi, Bernardino 23 573
Orsi, Giovanni Battista 23 573; 25 443
Orsi, Giovanni Domenico 6 526; 23 573*
works 8 378; 18 539; 25 445
Orsi, Lelio 23 573–5*
attributions 3 56
pupils 26 89
works 10 737; 23 574, 575; 29 363
Orsi, Prospero 20 841
Orsi, Tranquillo 5 378
Orsini (family)
architecture 6 354; 8 156; 23 576; 26 747, 755
Orsini (family)—cont.
archives 2 367
collections 16 762
paintings 1 731; 13 754; 26 765; 29 37
Orsini, Princess 29 303
Orsini, Alfonsina 1 570
Orsini, Antonio 31 430
Orsini, Clarice 11 686
Orsini, Corradino 23 575
Orsini, Domenico, Cardinal (1719-89) 3 920; 8 12
Orsini, Fulvio 5 684, 789; 10 810; 23 577*; 26 838
collections 12 266; 13 341; 23 575
publications 1 468
Orsini, Gentil Virginio 2 184
Orsini, Gianfrancesco, Conte di Pitigliano see PITIGLIANO, GIANFRANCESCO ORSINI, Conte di
Orsini, Giordano, Cardinal 20 556; 23 575; 26 766
Orsini, Giorgio see GIORGIO DA SEBENICO
Orsini, Giovanni Domenico de see ORSI, GIOVANNI DOMENICO
Orsini, Giovanni Gaetano see NICHOLAS III, Pope
Orsini, Napoleone, Cardinal 2 625; 12 697; 19 665; 23 575
Orsini, Nicolò, Conte di Pitigliano see PITIGLIANO, NICOLÒ ORSINI, Conte di
Orsini, Paolo Giordano I, Duca di Bracciano see BRACCIANO, PAOLO GIORDANO I ORSINI, Duca di
Orsini, Paolo Giordano II, Duca di Bracciano see BRACCIANO, PAOLO GIORDANO II ORSINI, Duca di
Orsini, Pierfrancesco, Cardinal see BENEDICT XIII, Pope
Orsini, Pier Francesco Vicino, Duca di Bomarzo see BOMARZO, PIER FRANCESCO VICINO ORSINI, Duca di
Orsini, Virginio 1 162; 11 691
Orsini Madonna 16 67; 26 808
Orsini polyptych 23 575; 25 183
Orsino, Pier Francesco 22 166
Ors i Rovira, Eugeni see ORS, EUGENIO D'
Ørskov, Willy 8 741
Orso, Filippo 2 455
Orsolini, Carlo 5 686; 24 894
Orsolino, Giovanni Pietro 12 281; 19 806; 24 287
Orsolino, Jacopo 24 287
Orsolino, Pietro 14 886
Orsolino, Tommaso 11 17
Ország, Lili 23 577–8*
works 14 902, 902
Országos Magyar Képzőművészeti Társulat see NATIONAL HUNGARIAN FINE ART SOCIETY
Országos Magyar Szépművészeti Múzeum evkönyvei 24 441
Orta 27 498
sacromonte 23 320
Ortaca Church 31 435
Ortahisar
Ali Reis Street Church 5 678
architecture 5 673
St Theodore 5 677
Tavşanlı Kilise 5 676, 677
Ortaköy Church 5 678
Orte 10 617
Ortega, Carlos 31 186
Ortega, Enrique Rodríguez see RODRÍGUEZ ORTEGA, ENRIQUE
Ortega, Gilberto Hernández see HERNÁNDEZ ORTEGA, GILBERTO
Ortega, Josē 29 286
Ortega, Martín Rico y see RICO Y ORTEGA, MARTÍN
Ortega, Nufro 32 100
Ortega Flores, Salvador 21 380; 23 578*; 24 9
Ortega y Gasset, José 20 204; 23 578–9*
Ortelius, Abraham 9 64; 10 389; 23 579*
albums 14 620
paintings 4 908
works 2 696; 14 643; 17 598; 25 606; 30 417
writings 13 808
Ortenberg, Gabriel of Salamanca, Graf von 2 778, 779; 25 248
Ortenberg Altar, Master of the 20 738*
Ortenblad Filho, Rodolpho 4 725
Ortensi, Girolamo d'Andrea degli 25 451
orthochromatic plates see under PHOTOGRAPHIC PLATES → types
orthoclase 14 167
Orthodox Caliphs see:
ABU BAKR, Caliph
'ALI IBN ABU TAHIB, Caliph
'UMAR, Caliph
'UTHMAN, Caliph
Orthodox church see under CHRISTIANITY → branches
Orthodox school 6 791, 820; 23 579–81*; 29 244
members 32 837, 839, 843; 33 426, 652
works 23 580; 33 531
orthodoxy in art 23 581–2*
orthographic perspective see under PERSPECTIVE → types
orthostats
Anatolia, ancient 1 831; 33 685
Canaanite 30 186
France 12 211
Greece, ancient 13 376, 388
Prehistoric art 12 211
Syria-Palestine 30 185, 190
Orth Schloss
furniture 2 812
Ortie, Jehan de l' 3 397; 31 218
Ortigão, José Duarte Ramalho see RAMALHO ORTIGÃO, JOSÉ DUARTE
Ortiz (fl 1971) 19 388
Ortiz, Blas 23 582*
Ortiz, Diego 4 264
Ortiz, José 7 605; 21 4
Ortiz, José Jaime 9 711; 25 829
Ortiz, Manuel Angeles see ANGELES ORTIZ, MANUEL
Ortiz, Ralph Montañez see MONTAÑEZ ORTIZ, RALPH
Ortiz, Vicente Urrabieta y see URRABIETA Y ORTIZ, VICENTE
Ortiz de Castro, José Damián 21 378
Ortiz de Masaya, Pedro 23 81
Ortiz de Vargas, Luis 21 110
Ortiz de Vilhegas, Diogo, Bishop 32 616
Ortiz de Villajos, Agustín 23 582*
Ortiz de Villajos, Manuel 23 582
Ortiz de Zárate, Julio 22 114
Ortiz de Zárate, Manuel 6 597; 22 114
Ortiz de Zúñiga, Diego 2 409; 25 30
Ortiz Echagüe, José 23 582*
Ortiz Monasterio, Luis 21 380; 23 583*; 24 8
Ortkens, Aert see ARNOULT DE NIMÈGUE
Ortner, Laurids 14 237–8*
Ortobello 29 250
Ortolani (family) 16 738
Ortolani, Ludovico 16 738; 32 398
Ortolani, Mario 12 309
Ortolano 11 4; 23 583*
Orton Church (Cumbria) 10 286
Orton Waterville, St Mary 25 726
Ortt, Johan 14 707
Ortukid see ARTUQID
Ortvad, Erik 7 488
Ortwein 32 879
Ōrudo Manuribā see under SHŌBO
Orukallu see WARANGAL
Orup, Bengt 15 142
Oruro 4 255, 255
art school 4 270
Ciudad Universitaria 4 261; 21 3
Museo de la Casa de la Cultura 4 269
Palais Concert Theatre 4 260
silver 4 255
Orvieto 10 583; 16 620; 23 583–8*
Archivo dell'Opera de Duomo 21 538
Belvedere Temple 10 601, 601, 603
bronze 10 627
Cannicella Necropolis 1 692; 10 588, 589
Cathedral of the Assumption 7 918; 13 52, 53, 65; 16 627; 20 140; 23 585, 585–6*; 27 758
altar 1 695
Cappella di S Brizio 13 700; 28 702–3, 703
Chapel of the Assumption see Cappella di S Brizio
choir-stalls 13 124
crucifixes 13 124
frescoes 16 613
furniture 16 723
metalwork 13 163
mosaics 7 275; 22 156, 157, 163
paintings 1 840; 9 263
pinnacles 24 826
pulpits 16 723
railings 16 743
reliefs 23 292; 26 136
reliquaries 26 146
reliquary of the Santo Corporale 13 169; 31 534, 535
sculpture 10 197, 743; 13 96; 16 688; 23 586, 586–8*, 587
woodwork 16 723
ceramics 14 425
Crocefisso del Tufo necropolis 10 598; 22 716; 23 584
cult statues 8 263
Golini Tomb I 10 620, 623
Museo dell'Opera del Duomo 16 774; 23 584
Palazzo del Capitano del Popolo 23 584
pottery 10 613; 16 732
Sanctuary of Voltumna 10 585
sculpture 10 605, 625; 27 29
S Domenico
tomb of Cardinal Guillaume de Braye 2 481; 13 96, 97
S Francesco 13 124
S Lorenzo de Arari 7 302
S Margarita 16 520
Torre del Moro 4 776
vase paintings 10 615
vases 10 612
Volsinii Veteres 10 583, 585, 601, 602; 23 583–4*
wall paintings 10 617
Orvieto, Angelo da see ANGELO DA ORVIETO
Orvieto, Giovenale da 26 826
Orvieto, Teodorico da, Cardinal see TEODORICO DA ORVIETO, Cardinal
Orvieto group 10 615; 23 584
Orvola, Heikki 11 107
Orwell, George 8 613; 20 590
Or Yehud, Museum of Iraqi Jewry 17 582
Oryol Gun 31 563
Orzel Pottery 23 68
Os, Georgius (Jacobus Johannes) van 22 848; 23 590*
collaboration 23 590
works 11 228

Os, Jan van **12** 620; **14** 42; **23** 588–90*
pupils **23** 588, 590
teachers **28** 165
works **11** 228; **23** *589*; **29** 668
Os, Maria Margaretha van **23** 588
Os, Pieter Frederik van **2** 106; **20** 871; **23** 588
Os, Pieter Gerardus van **22** 847, 848; **23** 588–90*; **32** 375
collaboration **23** 590; **28** 72
pupils **3** 769
OSA (Association of Contemporary Architects) **7** 770; **22** 178; **23** 590*; **27** 378
members **32** 661
Barshch, Mikhail (Osipovich) **3** 287
Ginzburg, Moysey (Yakovlevich) **12** 654
Golosov, Il'ya (Aleksandrovich) **12** 877
Golosov, Pantaleymon (Aleksandrovich) **12** 876
Gol'ts, Georgy (Pavlovich) **12** 878
Leonidov, Ivan (Il'ich) **19** 206
Milyutin, Nikolay (Aleksandrovich) **21** 622
Nikolsky, Aleksandr (Sergeyevich) **23** 144
Orlov, Georgy (Mikhaylovich) **23** 529
Vesnin, Aleksandr (Aleksandrovich) **32** 382
Osafune **4** 103
Osage **22** 551, 616
Osahozuka **17** 58
Osaka **17** *11*, 18, 93, 95; **23** 591–8*
Arahakadera *see* Shitennōji
Azuma House **17** 92
books **23** 594
bunraku **17** 350
calligraphers **17** 236, 237
calligraphy **17** 214
Castle **17** 45, 52, 84, 163, 784; **21** 828; **23** 592, *593*
Kigane no Chashitsu **28** 411
metalwork **17** 323
paintings **17** 796
Yamazato no Chatei **28** 411
coins **17** 371
Expo '70 **10** 685; **15** 883; **17** 90; **23** 593
Fuji Pavilion **25** 24
US Pavilion **30** 469
furniture **17** 358
glass **17** 386
houses **17** 83
Ishiyama **23** 592
Ishiyama Honganji **17** 93, 781
Japan World Exhibition *see* Expo '70
Kanshinji **17** 102
Keiden'in *see* Shitennōji
Kongoji **17** 166
Kōryōsan Keiden'in *see* Shitennōji
Mitsudera *see* Shitennōji
museums
Castle Museum of Art **17** 181
Fujita Museum of Art **6** 826; **7** 154; **23** 595
Itsuo Art Museum
aizurie **23** 595
Izumi Metropolitan Kubo so Memorial Art Gallery **23** 595
Manno Museum **23** 595
Masaki Art Museum **23** 595
collections **15** 746
Municipal Museum of Art **6** 735, 772, 826; **17** 429; **23** 595
collections **7** 154
Museum of Oriental Ceramics **17** 433; **18** 383; **23** 595
National Museum of Art **17** 433; **23** 593
Osaka museums—cont.
National Museum of Ethnology **1** 67; **3** 916; **18** 532; **23** 593; **29** 241
Nihon Mingeikan (Japan Folk Art Museum) **21** 635; **23** 593
Ryōkuchi open-air museum **23** 593
Yuki Art Museum **23** 595
Nanban Culture Hall **17** 181, 433
Naniwa **17** 93, *93*; **23** 591–2*
Naniwa Daiji *see* Shitennōji
Naniwa Nagara Toyosaki no Miya **23** 591
pattern books **24** 276
printing **7** 624; **17** 272
prints **17** 278, 288–9; **23** 594
puppets **17** 407
seals **17** 410*
Shitennōji **17** 65, 67; **23** 595–7*, *596*; **30** 445
collections **15** 746
fans **17** 160
masks **17** 392
paintings **17** 157; **28** 625
Sumiyoshi Shrine **17** 60; **23** *597*, 597–8*
Office of Painting **29** 924
Sumiyoshi Taisha *see* Sumiyoshi Shrine
swords **17** 364
tea ceremonies **23** 594
Tennōji *see* Shitennōji
theatres **17** 330
Tsuboi Hachiman Shrine **17** 129
Osaka Art Society **23** 595
Ōsako, Mikio **17** 267
Osamu Ishiyama *see* ISHIYAMA, OSAMU
Osamu Mōri *see* MŌRI, OSAMU
Osamu Suzuki *see* SUZUKI, OSAMU
Osan **18** 297, 333
Osato kiln **27** 873
Ōsawa Nagayuji **27** 596
Osbert, Alphonse **23** 598*; **27** 639
Osborn, Emily Mary **23** 598–9*
Osborn, Frederic J. **14** 809
Osborne, Arthur **30** 887
Osborne, Charles Francis **32** 95
Osborne, Francis, 4th Duke of Leeds **5** 597
Osborne, Harold **10** 212
Osborne, John **15** 406
Osborne, J. W. **19** 481
Osborne, Thomas, 1st Duke of Leeds **30** 278
Osborne, Walter Frederick **16** 37; **23** 599*
patrons and collectors **16** 36
pupils **19** 62
works **16** *16*, 17
Osborne, William **23** 599
Osborne House (Isle of Wight) **2** 541; **3** 689; **14** 148; **28** 255; **33** 145
Durbar Room **14** 148; **15** 407
interior decoration **9** 475
sculpture **4** 220; **9** 25; **11** 238; **33** 449
tiles **30** 504
Oscae, Jerónimo Aguesca *see* AGUESCA, JERÓNIMO
Oscar Frederik Wilhelm Olaf Gustaf Adolf, King of Sweden *see* GUSTAV VI ADOLF, King of Sweden
Oscar I, King of Sweden and Norway (*reg* 1844-59) **10** 754; **23** 221, 232, 233; **30** 95, 107
Oscar II, King of Sweden (*reg* 1872-1907) **29** 690
Oscott (Hants), St Mary's College **11** 432; **28** 156
Oscott Psalter *see under* PSALTERS → individual manuscripts
Osdel, John Mills Van *see* VAN OSDEL, JOHN MILLS
Oseberg grave **23** *218*, 219, 233, 240, 599–600*; **32** 515, 525, 534
burial chamber **30** 904
cart **32** 523
figureheads **28** *612*
furniture **30** 779
sculpture **23** *228*
Shetelig's sledge **32** 521
ships **23** 227–8
silk **9** 668
tapestries **32** 523
wood-carvings **23** 600*, *600*; **28** 611; **32** 513, 515, 520, 521, 525
Oseberg style *see under* VIKING → styles
O Se-ch'ang **18** 331
Osei Bonsu, Asantehene (*reg* 1800-24)
works **2** *591*
Osei Tutu, Asantehene (*reg* 1697-1731) **2** 585, 587
Osek Monastery **8** 376, 407
Osenbruck, Andreas **8** 413; **12** 259; **32** 458
Öser, Christoph Erhard **18** 107
Osera **29** 263
Osgood, Charles **27** 613
Osgood, Jere **4** 479; **31** 634
Osh **18** *567*
Historical and Regional Museum **6** 284
theatre **18** 568
Oshchepkov, Vitaly (Petrovich) **27** 425
O'Shea (family) **10** 266; **16** 21
O'Shea, James **8** 586; **23** 600
O'Shea, John **8** 586; **23** 600
O'Shea, Mary Lynn **31** 661
Oshima Island, Meteorological Station **17** 88
Oshita, Tojirō **17** 204
Oshkeli, Grigor **30** 306
Oshki Church **7** 279; **9** 84; **12** 319; **30** 305, 306, *306*
sculpture **12** 322
wall paintings **12** 323
Oshogbo **1** 282, 331, 332, 429; **23** *129*
painting **23** 136
temples **1** 309
workshops **1** 428, 429; **23** 136, 138
Osian **15** *276*; **23** 600–601*
doors **9** *161*
sculpture **15** 486
temples **15** 216, 270, 275
Hari-Hara Temple 1 **15** *269*, 270
Hari-Hara Temple 2 **15** 486
Hari-Hara Temple 3 **15** 486
Mahavira Temple **15** 270, 486
Pipla Devi Temple **15** 487
Surya Temple 1 **15** 270, 486
Surya Temple 3 **15** 486
Temple 7 *see* Surya Temple 1
Vishnu Temple 2 **15** 487
Osiander, Lucas **8** 882
osier **3** 331
Osijek **8** *174*
Archaeological Museum **8** 180
barracks **8** 175
Gallery of Fine Arts **8** 181
Osiński, Antoni **19** 836; **25** 115; **26** 498
works **25** *114*
Osipov, Daniil **27** 419
Osipov, Valery **15** 831
Osir, Paulo Rossi **4** 722
Osirarte **4** 722
Osirid statues *see under* SCULPTURE → types
Osiris-beds **10** 20*
Osiris Stone **10** 638
Osis, Jānis
Oskan, Yervant **31** 454
Öşk Church *see* OSHKI CHURCH
Osler, F. & C., Glasshouse **10** 319; **12** 789; **17** 640
Oslinyy Khvost *see* DONKEY'S TAIL
Oslinyy Khvost i Mishen' **9** 145
Oslo **23** *218*, 219, 220, 601–3*; **31** 718
Akershus Castle **23** 219, 220, 231
Andersen, David, workshop **23** 236
architecture **23** 221
Art Association *see* Kunstforening
Baerum Town Hall **14** 229
Bank of Norway **23** 222
'Bazaar' market stalls **23** 221
Cathedral **13** 102; **23** 220; **26** 593
ceilings **23** 231
Church of Our Saviour **23** 229
City Hall **23** 226, 230, 232, *602*; **25** 376–7; **31** 243
frescoes **18** 465
community centre **23** 222
Gamle Aker Church **23** 219; **26** 593
Government Building *see* Regjeringsbygning
Henie-Onstad Kunstsenter *see under* HØVIKODDEN
Historisk-Filosofiske Fakultetsbibliotek *see under* Universitet
House of Artists **23** 222
Ila housing development **23** 222
jewellery **23** 238
June Square **1** 12–13
Kongelige Tegne- og Kunstskole **23** 227, 244, 602
Kunstforening **23** 225, 602
marks **23** 236
metalwork **23** 236
monument to King Karl Johan **3** 783
museums
Bymuseum **23** 243
Historisk Museum **5** 165; **23** 221, *222*
Kunstindustrimuseum **23** 235, 239, 243, 602
Munch-Museum **22** 294; **23** 243, 603
Museum for Samtidskunst **23** 243, 603; **24** 452
Nasjonalgalleri **23** 225, 602
collections **8** 453; **23** 226, 243
Norske Folkemuseum **23** 243
Universitetets Oldsakamling *see under* Universitet
Vigeland-Museum **23** 222, 243, 603
Vigeland-Park **23** 230; **28** 314; **32** 498*
National Library of Norway *see* Universitet → Universitetsbibliotek
Nationaltheater **23** 221
New Crematorium **23** 226
Norwegian University Press building **23** 222
paintings **23** 223
Parkveien 29 **23** 602
Parkveien 31 **23** 602
Police Headquarters **23** 222
Regjeringsbygning **23** 221
Restaurant Skansen **23** 222
Royal Palace **23** 231
Royal School of Art and Crafts *see* Kongelige Tegne- og Kunstskole
St Olav's Priory **4** 781
School of Craft and Applied Arts *see* Statens Håndverks- og Kunstindustriskole
sculpture **13** 119
Seamen's School **23** 226
silver **23** 236
Slott **23** 221
Slottspark **23** 230
Statens Håndverks- og Kunstindustriskole **23** 241, 244
Oslo—cont.
Statens Kunstakademi **23** 244, 603
stone-carvings **32** 518
Storting **23** 232, 233
Tostrup, Jacob, workshop **23** 236
Town Hall *see* City Hall
trade **23** 242
Universitet **23** 221, 231
Aula **23** 226
Historisk-Filosofiske Fakultetsbibliotek **23** 244
Universitetsbibliotek **23** 244
Universitetets Oldsaksamling **23** 243
urban planning **5** 165; **31** 717
walls **23** 220
wood-carvings **32** 517
Osłonki **25** 500, 516, 518
Osma *see* EIGHT, THE (i)
Osma Cathedral **9** 105
Osmak, Vasily A. **31** 552
Osman **23** 604*
collaboration **16** 347, 348
patrons and collectors **16** 347, 348
pupils **14** 208
Osman III, Sultan *see* 'UTHMAN III
Osman, Ahmed (sculptor) **9** 766, 768
Osman, Ahmed ben (painter) **31** 425
Osman, Louis **12** 866; **17** 530
works **12** *866*
Osman Hamdi **16** 536, 557, 591; **23** 604*
education (art) **16** 590
works **16** 537, *537*; **31** 453, 456
Osmanlı *see* OTTOMAN
Osmanli ressamlar cemiyeti *see* ASSOCIATION OF OTTOMAN PAINTERS
Osmanov, Abdinaj **18** 568
Osmanpur, Gayebi Mosque **30** 162
Osmington **14** 544
Osmond, Comtesse d' **11** 598
Osmond, Jean-Baptiste **23** 604
Osmond, Robert (1713-89) **11** 627; **23** 604–5*
Osmond, Robert (*fl c.* 1900-50) **4** 373
Osmyorkin, Aleksandr (Aleksandrovich) **23** 605*; **27** 394; **32** 661
Osnabrück
Cathedral of St Johanniskirche **6** 557; **11** 253, 614; **14** 81; **26** 684
chess sets **6** 557
Rathaus **17** 700
Osnago, Francesco **3** 783
Osogbo **10** 779; **33** 556
Osona, Francisco de *see* FRANCISCO DE OSONA
Osona, Rodrigo de *see* RODRIGO DE OSONA
Osor **8** *174*, 175
Osorio, Bishop **12** 56
Osorio, Carlos **18** 833
Osorio, Francisco Meneses *see* MENESES OSORIO, FRANCISCO
Osorio, Jerónimo de **7** 493
Osorio, Pepón **18** 834
Osorkon kings **5** 70
Osorkon I (*reg c.* 989-*c.* 973 BC) **9** *777*
Osorkon II (*reg c.* 929-*c.* 914 BC) **9** *777*; **10** 32
Osorkon III (*reg c.* 888-*c.* 860 BC) **9** *777*, 886; **30** 296
Osorkon IV (*reg* 777-749 BC) **9** 886, 887
Osorkon V (*reg c.* 730 BC) **9** *777*
Osorno **6** *590*, 591
Osostowicz, S. **18** 433
Ospel, Anton **23** 605–6*
Ospina, Marco **7** 609
Ospina, Nadín **7** 610

Ospino **32** *165*
church **32** 168
Osrey Pottery **2** 760
Osric **3** 369
Ossaye, Roberto **13** 765; **23** 606*
Ossenovo Basilica **5** 155
Osserijn, Gert **8** 755
Osservanza, Master of the **1** 621; **20** 738–40*
attributions **1** 622; **4** 30; **27** 862
works **20** *739*; **27** 765
Osses **32** 280
Ossetia **27** 433
Osslund, Helmer **30** 81
Ossoliński (family) **25** 97, 137
Ossoliński, Jerzy **4** 43; **25** 135; **28** 407; **32** 869
Ossoliński, Józef Kajetan, Count **17** 832; **25** 136, 138
Ossoliński, Józef Maksymilian **19** 752
Ossoliński, Krzysztof **25** 118, 135; **28** 407
Ossorio, Alfonso **24** 213
Ossorio, Juan Antonio **31** 229
Ossorio y Bernard, Manuel **23** 606*
Ossovsky, Pyotr **27** 397
ossuaries
historical and regional traditions
Central Asia, Western **6** 193, *213*, 233, 276; **23** 606–9*, *608*
Jewish art **17** 553
Khwarazm **6** *213*, 233; **23** 607
Punic **25** 733
Sogdiana **6** 193; **23** 607
Syria-Palestine **30** 183
Uzbekistan **6** *213*; **31** *76*
Zoroastrianism **6** 193; **23** 606–9*, *608*
materials
plaster **31** *76*
pottery **6** *213*
terracotta **6** 276
Os Surrealistas **25** 300
Osswald, E. Otto **29** 874
OST *see* SOCIETY OF EASEL PAINTERS
Ost, Peter *see* OSTEN, PETER
Ost, van *see* NOST, VAN
Ostade, Adriaen van **13** 894, 895; **22** 893; **23** 609–14*; **29** 375
attributions **23** 614
patrons and collectors
Angran, Louis-Auguste, Vicomte de Fontpertuis **2** 90
Arenberg, Prosper-Louis, 7th Duke of, Duke of Arschot **2** 382
Aved, Jacques (-André-Joseph) **2** 852
Boymans, F(rans) J(acob) O(tto) **4** 614
Braamcamp, Gerrit **4** 618
Catherine II, Empress of Russia (*reg* 1762- 96) **26** 733
Feitama, Sybrand, the younger (1694–1758) **10** 864
George IV, King of Great Britain (*reg* 1820-30) **14** 146
Gildemeester, Jan (Jansz.) (1744-99) **12** 620
Gol van Franckenstein (family) **12** 876
Guinness, Edward (Cecil), 1st Earl of Iveagh **13** 836
Peel, Robert (1788-1850) **24** 322
Röver, Valerius **27** 270
Souza, Madame de **22** 126
Sparre, Gustaf Adolf **29** 366
Verstolk van Soelen, Jan Gijsbert, Baron **32** 377, 707
Vos (ii) Wzn, Jacob de **32** 707
personal collection **23** 614
pupils **3** 494; **9** 456; **22** 383; **29** 585
reproductive prints by others **6** 527, 547; **8** 542; **19** 731; **30** 47
Ostade, Adriaen van—cont.
teachers **14** 95; **22** 840
works **9** 221, 457; **12** 290; **14** 95; **23** *611*, *612*, 613; **29** *855*
Ostade, Isack van **23** 609, 612–14*
patrons and collectors **11** 789; **24** 322
reproductive prints by others **33** 196
teachers **23** 609
works **9** 457; **23** *614*
Ostankino **22** 177; **23** 615*; **27** *363*, 376
Palace-Museum of Serf Art **23** 615; **27** 404
Östberg, Ragnar **3** 784; **23** 615–16*
assistants **2** 611
competitions **7** 668
groups and movements **13** 204; **22** 541
pupils **2** 611; **19** 283
teachers **7** 379
works **29** 686; **30** 74; **31** 242, *242*, 693
Ostel, Louis De Soissons, Viscomte d' *see* DE SOISSONS, LOUIS, Viscomte d'Ostel, Baron Longroy
Ostell, John **5** 561; **23** 616*; **24** 470
Osten, Hildegard **12** 468
Osten, Peter **8** 529; **23** 616–17*
Ostend **3** 565
Provinciaal Museum voor Moderne Kunst **3** 616
Ostend Company **6** 332
Ostendorf, Friedrich **23** 617*; **30** 899
pupils **14** 524; **25** 675
works **17** 817; **30** 903
Ostendorfer, Hans, I (*d* 1524) **22** 302
Ostendorfer, Hans, II (*d* 1570) **28** 188
Ostendorfer, Michael **8** 514; **23** 617–18*
works **23** *617*; **33** 354
Østerbrofabriken **8** 748
Östergötland, John, Duke of **30** 104
Osterhofen Abbey Church **2** 581–2; **12** 372; **29** 838; **32** 822
Osterkamp, Peggy **11** 55
Osterlamb, Jonas **15** 8
Osterley Park House (Middx) **1** 137; **3** 173; **7** 339; **8** 48; **9** 17; **10** 643; **24** 317; **25** 192
carpets **5** 839; **9** 31
cartoons (drawings) **19** 9
Eating Room **5** 687
Etruscan Dressing Room **10** 637, *643*; **13** 702; **22** 738; **23** 544
furniture **7** 659; **9** 29; **10** 295, 353, *354*; **11** 119, *119*; **15** 165; **19** 426; **20** 468
interior decoration **10** 276, 279
paintings **9** 482
portico **25** 266
tapestries **4** 514; **9** 30; **10** 351; **11** 643
Österlin, Anders **7** 489; **14** 865; **15** 142; **30** 81
Osterling, Frederick **30** 507
Österlövsta Church **30** 865
Ostermann, d' **29** 432
Österreichische Kunst *see* KUNST DEM VOLK
Österreichische Kunst Chronik **24** 423
Österreichische Künstverein **11** 33
Österreichischer Künstlerverein **17** 814
Österreichischer Werkbund **2** 789, 803; **7** 368; **8** 428; **11** 727; **25** 404
Österreichische Zeitschrift für Denkmalpflege **24** 438
Österreichs Bau- und Werkkunst **24** 438
Osterspey, Jakob **11** 731
Ostertag, Heinrich Jonas
works **2** *714*
Ostervald, J(ean) F(rédéric) d' **4** 85, 321; **5** 439; **11** 60
Osthaus, Karl Ernst **2** 288; **3** 511; **8** 825; **14** 30; **21** 648; **30** 760; **31** 876
Ostia **16** *620*; **20** 362; **23** 618–23*, *619*; **26** 856, *886*
architecture **16** 623; **26** 750, 887, 891–2, 896, 900
Basilica of Pammachius **9** 532
bastions **3** 359, *360*
baths **23** 620–21
Baths of Neptune **23** 620; **26** 872; **27** 62, *62*
Baths of the Drivers **23** 621
Baths of the Seven Sages **27** 67
Baths of Via dei Vigili **27** 61
Forum Baths **23** 620; **26** 872
Casa a Giardino **15** 869
Caseggiato degli Aurighi **15** 869
Episcopio **6** 355
granaries **26** 883
harbours **26** 854, 892
Horrea Epagathiana et Epaphroditiana **23** 621; **26** 878; **32** 860
Horrea of Hortensius **26** 891
houses **23** 620
Garden Houses **26** 869
House of Bacchus and Ariadne **23** *623*; **27** 61
House of Cupid and Psyche **23** 620; **26** 883; **27** 59
House of Diana **23** 620, *621*
House of the Charioteers **27** 55; **32** 87
House of the Hierodules **27** 55
House of the Muses **27** 55
House of the Painted Vaults **27** *55*
Insula delle Volte Dipinte **15** 869
insulae **15** 869–70, *870*; **16** 623; **23** 620; **26** 863, 868, 869, 900
insula of Serapis **26** 869
lighthouse **19** 360
macellum **19** 888
masonry **20** 571, 572; **26** 877, 878
mosaics **2** 348; **22** 160; **23** 622–3*, *623*; **26** 750; **27** 60, 67
Palazzo Imperiale **27** 67
Piazzale delle Corporazioni **23** 622
reliefs **22** 154
Roman capitolium **23** 621, *622*
sarcophagi **9** 594
S Aurea **25** *216*
sculpture **27** 37
shops **26** 871
synagogue **17** 543
Temple of Mithras **22** 161
Temple of Rome and Augustus **26** 891; **27** 22, 31
temples **23** 621; **26** 900
theatre **30** 652
tombs **7** 642; **31** 110
Via Laurentina
Tomb 18 **27** 69
wall paintings **16** 653; **26** 857; **27** 55–6, 58
warehouses **23** 621
Ostia, Leo of *see* LEO OF OSTIA
Ostiglia, Antonio da **21** 632
Ostionoid culture **25** 699; **29** 200*
Ostlund, Egon **14** 89
Ostmantown *see* DUBLIN
Ostmar, Tommy **30** 82
Ostolle **10** 782
Ostor, P. *see* MÉSZÁROS, LÁSZLÓ
Ostorp, Dirik **14** 102
Ostra *see* OSTROH
ostraca **9** *810*, *903*, 904; **10** 5; **23** 623*; **30** 701
Östra Herrestad Church **26** 639
Ostrava
architecture **8** 380
bridge **8** 379
textiles **8** 419
Östra Vram **13** 119
ostrea see under SHELLS → types
Østre Starup church **8** 737; **26** 640
ostrich feathers *see under* FEATHERS → types
Ostrogothic **7** 533; **8** 527; **23** 623–4*
Ostrogoths **21** 501
Ostrogradsky, A. A. **28** 837
Ostroh **23** 624*; **31** *546*
chapel of St George **31** 548
Museum of Local History **23** 624
Ostromir **31** 556
Ostromir Gospels *see under* GOSPEL BOOKS → individual manuscripts
Ostroukhov, Il'ya (Semyonovich) **22** 178; **23** 624*; **27** 439, 441
Ostroumova-Lebedeva, Anna (Petrovna) **23** 624*; **27** 394
groups and movements **27** 580; **33** 379
pupils **18** 527; **32** 247
teachers **33** 740
Ostrov nad Oslavou, Convent of St John the Baptist **8** 403; **26** 637
Ostrovsky, Aleksandr (Nikolayevich) **17** 812; **18** 482, 537; **32** 73
Ostrovul Mare **26** 711
Ostrówek **25** 119
Ostrów Lednicki, Piast residence **25** 94
Ostrowski, Antoni **30** 213
Ostrowski, Tomasz **18** 490
Ostwald, Wilhelm **7** 630
Ostyor, St Michael **31** 554
Ōsui Gyofu *see* MARAYAMA ŌKYO
O'Sullivan, Timothy **23** 624–5*; **24** 665, 667; **31** 602
collaboration **4** 627
works **24** *666*, 667
Osuna **23** 625–6*; **29** *258*
convent of the Encarnación **30** 883
reliefs **15** 60
sculpture **15** 59, 60
S Juan Bautista **23** 625, *625*
University **31** 674
Osuna, Duques de **3** 700; **13** 242; **21** 125; **29** 353, 354
Osuna, 3rd Duque de (1574-1624) **23** 626*
paintings **26** 310
Osuna, Duquesa de (1752-1834) **23** 626–7*
architecture **19** 657
paintings **13** 242
sculpture **3** 199
Osuna, 9th Duque de (1755-1807) **10** 134; **13** 242; **23** 626*
Osuna, Pedro de Alcántara Téllez Girón, 11th Duque de (1810-44) **19** 657
OSVAG **18** 750
Osvald, Master **23** 627*; **25** 431
attributions **19** 829
works **17** 821; **25** 440
Oswaggo, Joel **17** 907, 908
Oswald, Archbishop of York **2** 66, 75–6
Ōta (family) **17** 414
Ōta, Seizō **17** 430
Ōta Dōkan **31** 78, 83
Ōtagaki Rengetsu **17** 234; **23** 627*; **33** 322
Ōtaguro, Motō **11** 826
Ōta Gyūichi **2** 909
Otaka, Masato **17** 90; **20** 147; **21** 317; **23** 627–8*
Otake, Koichi **30** 392
Otaki Rangiatea Church **23** 53, *53*
Otami **24** 56
Ōta Nanpo **17** 417
Ōtani **17** 347
Ōtani, Kōzui, Count **2** 645; **23** 628*
collections **7** 154; **17** 429
excavations **18** 383
personal collection **6** 321
Ōtani, Sachio **7** 668; **17** 90; **23** 628*; **33** 509
Ōtani, Shirō **17** 267
Ōtani, Tokuan **17** 414
Otanidera **17** 102
Otaniemi, Institute of Technology **4** 790; **11** 92, *93*
Otasević, Dušan **28** 451
Ot Danum **15** 774
Ot de Montacada **3** 339
Oteiza (Embil), Jorge (de) **23** 628–9*; **29** 296
groups and movements **8** 538
patrons and collectors **9** 113
pupils **22** 724
works **23** *629*; **24** 511
Otemar, Jacques d' **1** 21
Otero, Alejandro **23** 629*; **32** 176
Otero, Manuel **18** 833
Otero, Nestor **18** 833
Otero, Raúl **8** 232
Otero & Aguirre **23** 629*
Otero Goñi, Hermenegildo **23** 629
Otersen, Johann Conrad **14** 103
Oteyza, Victor **24** 622
Otgar, Archbishop of Mainz **5** 779
Othelric **26** 639
Othem **30** 76
Otho, Emperor of Rome (*reg* 69 AD) **27** 34
Otilo, Duke of Bavaria (*reg* 737-48) **2** 776
Otis, Bass **23** 629–30*; **24** 600
Otis, Elisha Graves **28** 830
Otis, Fessenden Natt **23** 904
Otis, Harrison Gray **4** 472; **5** 143
Otlet, Paul **4** 577; **31** 888; **32** 380
Otley (W. Yorks), All Saints **2** 71
Oto **22** 551
Oto, Antid *see* TROTSKY, LEON
otokoe see under JAPAN → painting
Otomanguean **21** 736
Otomani culture **25** 528
pottery **25** *528*
Otomo Gekko **17** 185
Ōtomo no Yatō, Prince **23** 443
Ōtomo Sōrin **17** 781
Ōtoneri **17** 311
O'Toole, Gillachrist **31** 402
Otovala **9** 709
Otranto
Cathedral of Annunziata **7** 275; **26** 627, *680*, 681
mosaics **22** 163
painting **20** 51
Otranto, Giacomo Bellanti di Terra d' *see* GIACOMO BELLANTI DI TERRA D'OTRANTO
Otrar **6** *182*; **16** *105*; **17** *865*; **23** 630*
architecture **32** 321
jewellery **6** 274
Otskheli, P. **12** 327
Ōtsu **17** 93, *93*, 347
Enryakuji **10** 404–6*; **17** *11*, 33, 68
Daishidō **17** 131
Great Lecture Hall **10** *405*
Konpon Chūdō **10** 405
maṇḍalas **17** 151
pagoda **23** 776
prints **17** 270
Saitō **10** 404, 406
Sakamoto **10** 404
sutra box **17** 321
Tōtō **10** 404, 405
Yokawa **10** 404, 406
Hie Shrine **17** 63
Jimon *see* Onjōji
Miidera *see* Onjōji

Ōtsu—cont.
Onjōji **17** *11*; **23** 443–4*
collections **17** 428
Kōjōin **17** *76*, 77; **23** 444
kondō **10** 406; **23** 444
sculpture **17** 131
Zenjindō **23** 443
palace **17** 93
ōtsue see under JAPAN → painting
Ōtsuka Tomb (Fukuoka)
painting **17** 142, 143, *144*
Otsup, Pyotr (Adol'fovich) **23** 630*
Ott, Carlos **7** 670; **11** 528; **24** 132; **30** 684
Ott, David **11** 818
Ott, Joseph **31** 637
Ott, Michał **18** 430
Otta, J. **8** 401
Ottaviani, Giovanni
works **13** *669*
Ottaviani, Giuseppe **31** 315
Ottaviano (di Antonio) di Duccio **1** 456; **26** 400
Ottavio, 2nd Duke of Parma (*reg* 1550-86) **3** 706; **14** *2*
architecture **11** 318; **23** 745; **24** 695; **32** 506
medals **4** 340
paintings **3** 487, 859
sculpture **12** 571; **22** 166
wood-carvings **16** 726
Ottavio, Lorenzo Costa di *see* COSTA DI OTTAVIO, LORENZO
Ottavio da Campione **5** 549
Ottavio dei Nonni *see* MASCHERINO, OTTAVIANO
Ottawa **5** *559*; **13** 338; **23** 630–32*, *631*
Bank of Nova Scotia **5** 573
Canadian Conservation Institute **7** 744
Château Laurier **6** 513
Totem Pole Room **14** 676
Confederation Square **23** 631
Fitzroy Fenwick Collection **25** 238
Houses of Parliament *see* PARLIAMENT BUILDINGS
monument to Alexander Mackenzie **5** 570
monument to Queen Victoria **5** 570
monument to Sir George-Etienne Cartier **5** 570
monument to Sir John A. Macdonald **5** 570
museums
Canadian War Museum **1** 496
National Archives of Canada **2** 364, 365, 370; **7** 648; **8** 81
National Arts Centre **5** 573; **23** 632
National Gallery of Canada **5** 588, 590, 591; **22** 358; **23** 632; **27** 515
archives **2** 370
catalogues **25** 238
collections **1** 496; **5** 589, 590, 591; **8** 81; **20** 587; **24** 338, 682
Croscup Room **5** 575
directors **7** 648
drawings **9** 231
exhibitions **5** 591
library **5** 592
National Museum of Man **27** 515; **29** 241
Victoria Museum **23** 631
Nurses' National memorial **5** 570
Parliament Buildings **5** 561, 572; **11** *837*; **13** 203, 237; **23** *631*, 632*
railway station **5** 562
Royal Canadian Academy of Arts **5** 566, 590, 592
Ottawa (people) **22** 552, 627, 651
Ott & Brewer **1** 171; **4** 863; **19** 165; **31** 637
porcelain **31** *637*
Otte, Johann Nicolaus **8** 748
Otte, Stachius *see* OTTO, STATIUS
Ottenbach, Ambrosius **21** 62
Ottenheimer, Stern & Reichert **28** 96
Otten-Husly, (Hans) Jacob **1** 808; **22** 827, 907; **23** 633*; **32** 465
collaboration **32** 465
pupils **32** 465
works **1** 802; **22** 827
Otterlo
Rijksmuseum Kröller-Müller **8** 632; **18** 466; **29** 791; **31** 877
collections **4** 743; **12** 861; **22** 906; **23** 901; **25** 827
sculpture garden **28** *315*, 316
St Hubertus Hunting Lodge **22** 867
Ottery St Mary (Devon) **8** 611; **32** 92
Ottheinrich, Count Palatine *see* OTTO HENRY, Elector Palatine
Ottieri della Ciaia (family) **1** 621
Ottin, Auguste-Louis-Marie **23** 633*
Ottin, Léon-Auguste **23** 633
Ötting, Alt **7** 466
Öttingen, Johann von **10** 865
Öttingen-Wallerstein (family) **4** 377
Öttingen-Wallerstein, Blasius, Abbot of Hirsau **4** 377
Ottinger, George **27** 642
Ottino, Pasquale **5** 32; **23** 633–4*
Ottley, William Young **13** 302, 304; **18** 895; **23** 634*
drawings **9** 26; **14** 875; **28** 474; **33** 154
engravings **19** 284
mounts (works on paper and scrolls) **22** 236
paintings **10** 366; **31** 532; **32** 774
publications **3** 309
Ottmarsheim **27** 236
church **6** 459; **7** 256; **12** 363
Ottmer, Karl Theodor **3** 792; **5** 30
Otto (*fl c.* 1302) **31** 122
Otto, Saint, Bishop of Bamberg **3** 140
Otto I, Duke of Brunswick and Lüneberg (*d* 1252) **33** 50
Otto I, Holy Roman Emperor (*reg* 936-73) **28** 24*
architecture **12** 363; **20** 87
churches **33** 107
coins **7** 534
manuscripts **33** 90
regalia **26** 80; **32** 458
seals **7** 383
Otto II, Count of Habsburg (*fl* 11th cent.) **13** 899
Otto II, Duke of Lüneburg (*reg c.* 1277-1330) **6** 138
Otto II, Holy Roman Emperor (*reg* 973-83) **28** 24*
architecture **2** 191
ivory-carvings **9** 650
manuscripts **7** 246
situlae **28** 805
Otto III, Holy Roman Emperor (*reg* 983-1002) **28** 24–5*
gold **12** 823
liturgical objects **1** 4
manuscripts **12** 254; **13** 20, 21; **23** *653*, 654; **28** 146
paintings **23** 649
regalia **26** 80
silk **9** 666
situlae **28** 805
textiles **30** 552
Otto III, Margrave of Brandenburg (*reg* 1266-1308) **7** 205
Otto IV, Holy Roman Emperor (*reg* 1198-1218) **5** 29; **14** 411; **23** 99; **33** 50
Otto, Frei **23** 635*
assistants **18** 455
collaboration **3** 510; **12** 380; **29** 489
groups and movements **11** 778; **23** 500
works **10** 685, *685*; **25** 24; **29** 428; **30** 468–9, *469*; **33** 700
Otto, Rolf G. **11** 304
Otto, Statius **23** 635*; **30** 84
collaboration **18** 445
patrons and collectors **23** 396
works **8** 739
Otto, Waldemar **23** 635–6*
Ottobeuren **12** *361*; **23** 636*
Benedictine Monastery **12** 372; **22** 810; **33** 681
frescoes **1** *785*; **15** 139
Klosterkirche **7** 192, 211–12; **10** 859, *859*; **11** *126*, 127; **12** 372, 404; **26** 498
library **19** 316, *316*
Ottoboni (family) **3** 708; **5** 819; **16** 764
Ottoboni, Antonio, Prince **19** 524
Ottoboni, Pietro, Cardinal (1667-1740) **23** 637*
architecture **17** 706; **27** 348
paintings **5** 907; **6** 568; **7** 682; **8** 91, 143, 563; **9** 47; **12** 586; **17** 900; **19** 525, 816; **26** 331, 774; **31** 306
frescoes **6** 350
patronage **26** 773
sculpture **27** 193
tapestries **26** 778
Otto-Dorn, K. **27** 344
Otto Henry, Elector Palatine (*reg* 1556-9) **14** 451; **18** 575; **33** *272*, 278*
architecture **12** 367; **14** 305
manuscripts **12** 494
paintings **4** 207; **11** 33; **19** 814
sculpture **22** 918
tapestries **12** 495
Ottoman **16** 117–19; **23** 637–43*
amethyst **16** *507*
aqueducts **16** 224
arches **2** 295
architects **2** 316; **16** 220–21
architectural decorations **16** 221
architecture **16** 143, 199, 201, 220–21*, 227–9*; **23** 638–9
Albania **16** 228
Algeria **16** 229
Arabia **16** 229
Bosnia **16** 228
Cyprus **8** 364
Egypt **16** 229
Empire style **16** 227
Macedonia (ii) (former Yugoslavia) **16** 228; **19** 882–3
military **16** 206; **21** 585–7, *586*
Orientalism **16** 227
stone **16** 266
Syria **16** *228*, 228–9
Tunisia **16** 229
Turkey **16** 205–7*, 226, 227, 265–7*, 604
wood **16** 222
Yemen **16** 229
armour **16** 507–9*
art policies **16** 100
axes **16** 508
barracks **16** 225
baths **16** 224
bazaars **16** 206
belts **16** 462
belvederes **16** 266
book covers **16** 359
books **16** 360
bowls **16** *421*
bows **16** 508
bracelets **16** 532
brass **16** *388*
brick **16** 207
bridges **4** 801; **16** 207, 225
calligraphers **16** 285
calligraphy **14** 27; **22** *235*
Ottoman—cont.
candlesticks **16** *388*
canteens **16** *542*
caps **16** 462
caravanserais **16** 206, 224, 228, 266
carpets **5** II; **28** 716
Bellini **16** 471
Crivelli **16** 471
Gördes **16** 478
Kirşehir **16** 478
Lâdik **16** *478*, 478
Large-pattern Holbein **16** 471
Lotto **16** 471, *471*
Memling **16** 471
Milâs **16** 478
Mucur **16** 478
prayer rugs **16** *478*
Small-pattern Holbein **16** 471
Transylvanian **16** 472
Turkey **16** 470–72*, *471*, 476–9*
Ushak **16** 471–2
ceramics **16** 419–23*
chains **16** 532
chasing **16** *388*
chests **16** *499*
citadels **16** 266
coats **16** 462
coins **16** *513*, 514
collections **16** 122, 445, 552
cotton **16** 445, 462
courtyards **16** 221
craftsmen and artists **16** 346, 387
daggers **16** 509
diplomatic gifts **16** 445
domes **16** 205, 221, 222–3
semi-dome **9** 84; **23** 641
doors **9** 160
doublures **16** 356
dress **16** 454, 462–3*
Algeria **16** 458
Egypt **16** 458
Hungary **16** 463
Tunisia **16** 458
Turkey **16** 460–62, *462*
dresses **16** *460*, 461, 462
dyes **16** 477
education (art) **16** 536
embroidery **16** *460*
emeralds **16** *542*
enamel **16** 516
façades **16** 221
flint **16** 420
fortifications **21** 585–7, *586*
fortresses **16** 228
fountains **16** 225, *226*, 265
frit **16** 420, *421*
Islamic **16** 419, 421, *422*
furniture **16** 498
glass **16** 221, 522
glazes **16** 420
gold **16** *507*, *508*, 532, *860*
Turkey **16** *513*, *542*
grilles **16** 257
guilds **16** 445
guns **16** 508–9
gun stocks **16** 499
hair **16** 445
hats **16** 462
headdresses **16** 454, 461
helmets **16** *504*, 507, *507*
heraldry **14** 428
houses **16** 228, 266, *266*, 271
imarets **16** 224
incising **16** *388*
inlays **16** 499, 528
inscriptions **16** 260, 810
Turkey **16** *137*, 514
iron **16** *504*, *507*
ivory **16** *508*, 526
ivory-carvings **16** 526*, *527*
jade **16** 528, 860, *860*
jewellery **16** 531–2*
kaftans **16** *446*, 460, 461
khānaqāhs **16** 265
kilims **16** 477, 478; **18** 49
kiosks **16** *589*; **18** 71
külliye **16** 221; **18** 507–9*, *508*
lamps **16** 421, 422
Ottoman—cont.
lead **16** 420
leather **16** 544, *544*
linen **16** *137*
loges **20** 369
maces **16** 508
madrasas **16** 810
Turkey **16** 222, 223–4, 265
manuscript illumination **30** *478*
Turkey **16** *118*, 304, 329–30, 346–51*; **23** *642*
manuscripts **16** 304; **23** 639–40
marble **16** 221
marbling **24** 55
markets **16** 266
masonry **16** 221
metalwork **16** 386, 387–9*
minarets **16** 223; **21** 628
miniatures (manuscript illumination) **16** *348*, *349*, *446*, *454*
mirror frames **16** *527*
mirrors **21** 718
mosaics **16** 199, 260
mosques **16** 142, 228, 257
Arabia **16** 229
congregational mosques **16** 221
domed **22** *195*, 195–6
hypostyle **16** 202
multi-unit **16** 205
single-domed square **16** 205
single-unit **16** 222
T-plan **16** 205–6, 810
Turkey **9** *730*; **16** 205–6, *206*, 221–4, *223*, *224*, 226, 265, 266, 605; **22** *195*
mother-of-pearl **9** 160; **16** 499
mounts (works on paper and scrolls) **22** *235*
mud-bricks **16** 266
museums **16** 557
musical instruments **16** 498
nakkashane **16** 346
necklaces **16** 532
painting **16** 221, *537*
oil **16** 536–7*
wall **16** 254
palaces **16** 225, 227, 266; **23** 816
paper **24** 55
papier mâché **16** 359
patronage **16** 122, 133
pavilions (buildings) **16** *225*; **23** *638*
pigments **16** 420, 421
plans **16** 143
plaques **16** 528
plates **16** *422*
polychromy **23** 643
porcelain **16** 423
porticos **16** 222
pottery **16** 419; **23** 643
blue-and-white ware **4** 172, *172*; **16** 420
Damascus ware **16** 420
Golden Horn ware **16** 420, 421
Islamic **16** *421*, *422*
Iznik ware **16** 124
Miletus ware **16** 420
printing **16** 360
puppets **16** 544, *544*
quartz **16** 420
quivers **16** 528
regalia **16** 539
robes **16** 460
rock crystal **16** 542, *542*
rubies **16** *507*, *542*
rugs **23** 643
sabres **16** 508
sashes **16** 461, 462
saz **16** 349
scabbards **16** *508*
schools **16** 229, 265
scripts **16** 285
serge **16** 445
shadow theatre **16** 544–5
shields **16** 507
shirts **16** *137*, 460
shoes **16** 452, 461
shops **16** 266

Ottoman—cont.
signatures **16** 508
silk **16** 430, 445, 446, *446*, 462, 508; **23** *639*; **28** 716
silver-gilt **23** *639*
slip **16** 420, 422
stained glass **16** 257
steel **16** 507, *508*, 508
stelae **29** 618
stone **16** 266
streets **16** 206, *266*
stucco **16** 257
sword hilts **16** 528
swords **16** 508, *508*, 509
talismans **16** *137*
tankards **16** *860*
tents **30** 478–80*
textiles **16** 121, 444–7*; **23** *639*
tiles **16** 206, 221, 260, 419, 420, 421, 422, 423, 604; **23** 643
cuerda seca **16** 199
tin **16** 420
tombs **16** 206
topographical illustrations **16** 347
tortoiseshell **16** 499
trade
carpets **16** 470, 476, 479
ceramics **16** 419
glass **16** 221, 257
guns **16** 508
porcelain **16** 124
pottery **16** 420
silk **16** 430, 445; **28** 716
textiles **16** 448, 463
treatises **16** 221
trousers **16** 460, 461, 462
tughras **14** 428; **16** 514; **31** 416–17*
tunics **16** 461
turquoise **16** *507*
underclothes **16** 461
uniforms **16** 461
urban planning **16** 265–7*
velvet **16** 446; **23** *560*
veneers **16** 499
walnut **16** *499*
weapons **16** 507–9*, 528
weaving **16** 476–7, 478–9
wicker **16** 507
windows **16** 257
women artists **16** 476
wood **9** 160; **16** 222
woodwork **16** 498–9*, *499*
wool **5** II; **16** 445, *471*, *478*
see also:
ABDÜLAZIZ, Sultan
ABDÜLHAMID I, Sultan
ABDÜLHAMID II, Sultan
ABDÜLMECID, Prince
ABDÜLMECID I, Sultan
AHMED I, Sultan
AHMED III, Sultan
BAYEZID, Prince
BAYEZID II, Sultan
FATMA SULTAN
HÜRREM SULTAN
MAHMUD I, Sultan
MAHMUD II, Sultan
MEHMED II, Sultan
MEHMED III, Sultan
MEHMED V REŞAD, Sultan
MURAD III, Sultan
MUSTAFA II, Sultan
MUSTAFA III, Sultan
ORKHAN, Sultan
ŞEHZADE MUSTAFA
SELIM I, Sultan
SELIM II, Sultan
SELIM III, Sultan
SÜLEYMAN THE MAGNIFICENT, Sultan
'UTHMAN, Sultan
'UTHMAN III, Sultan
see also TURKEY
Ottoman Baroque **16** 225–7
ottomans (furniture) **31** *632*
Ottonelli, Giovanni Domenico **15** 82
Ottoni, Lorenzo **15** 862; **23** 644–5*
collaboration **26** 810; **30** 704
pupils **5** 525
works **24** 35; **30** 704
Ottonian **13** 202, 207; **23** 645–61*; **29** 546
antependia **23** 657, *657*
arches **2** 294, 295
architecture **12** 363–4*; **23** 645*; **26** 571
bells **23** 658
book covers **4** III, IV2; **23** 660
book illustrations **12** 382
borders (manuscript) **20** 338
brass **23** 658
bronze **7** *381*; **9** *153*; **12** *399*; **23** 657–9*, *658*
candelabra **23** 659
canon tables **5** 624; **6** 564
chandeliers **23** 659
churches **14** *533*, *534*
clasps **23** *658*
crowns **23** 656
crucifixes **7** 590; **8** *213*; **12** 399; **23** 647–8, 659
domes **9** 84
doors **9** *153*; **23** 657, 658, *658*
enamel **4** III
Evangeliaries **23** 652
fonts (baptismal) **23** 659
gems **4** III; **26** *145*
gold **4** III; **22** *43*; **23** 647, 656–7*, *657*, *658*; **26** *145*
Gospel books **13** 20; **23** 652
iron **23** 658
ivory-carvings **23** 659–60*, *660*, *661*; **28** *805*
jewellery **17** 519; **23** 657
limestone **23** 646
lime-wood **23** *648*
manuscript illumination **19** 827; **20** *754*; **23** 651–5*
manuscripts **20** 330
metalwork **23** 656–9*
miniatures (manuscript illumination) **3** *552*; **9** *698*; **20** V2; **23** *653*, *654*, *655*; **26** *78*
monuments **7** *381*; **12** *399*; **22** 43, *43*
painting **12** 382; **23** 649*
wall **23** 649–51*, *650*; **26** 101
patronage **12** 471
piers (ii) (masonry) **24** 749, 750
plaques **23** *660*
regalia **26** *78*
reliquaries **7** 720; **22** *43*; **23** 656, 659; **26** *145*, 145–6*
rock crystal **26** 485
sandstone **23** 646, *647*
scripts **28** 305
sculpture **7** *381*, 590; **12** 399; **23** 646*, *647*, *648*
stone **23** 646–7*
wood **23** 647–9*
shrines (ii) (altarpieces) **23** 656
silver **22** *43*; **23** 647, 656–7*
situlae **23** 659–60; **28** *805*
statuettes **23** *661*
stone **23** 646–7
stucco **23** 646, *647*
swords **23** 658
title-pages **31** 48
westworks **33** *108*
wood **23** 647–9
Ottoni de Castro Maya, Raymundo **4** 725, 726, 727
Ottoni de Castro Maya, Raymundo, Fundação *see under* RIO DE JANEIRO
Otto of Deuil, Abbot of Saint-Denis **29** 511
Otto of Freising **7** 241; **26** 662
Otto of Wittelsbach, King of Greece (*reg* 1832–62) **12** 168; **14** 149, 654; **15** 144; **18** 124; **28** 102
Otto Pittori Italiani **1** 446
Otto the Child *see* OTTO I, Duke of Brunswick and Lüneberg
Otto the Great, Holy Roman Emperor *see* OTTO I, Holy Roman Emperor
Otto the Strict, Duke of Lüneburg *see* OTTO II, Duke of Lüneburg
Otto van Moerdrecht **20** 740
Otto van Moerdrecht, Master of **20** 740*; **22** 835
Otumfuo Nana Opuko Ware II **1** *388*
O'Tunney (family) **16** 20; **23** 661*
Otuo **9** 734
Otzaki Magoula **21** 46; **25** 500
Otzen, Johannes **3** 794; **13** 677; **23** 661–2*; **32** 421
Ouagadougou **1** *381*
brass **5** 217
Centre National des Arts **5** 217, *217*
Institut Français de l'Afrique Noire (IFAN) **5** 217
Oualata **1** 317, *376*; **20** 861
library **20** 862
Ouborg, Pieter **14** 43; **22** 852; **23** 662*
works **22** *853*
Ōuchi (family) **31** 251
Ouchi, Jiemon **17** 402
Ouchi, Jiro **17** 402
Ouchi Yoshihiro **17** 173
Oud, Hans **23** 664
Oud, J(acobus) J(ohannes) P(ieter) **11** 129; **13** 328; **19** 476; **21** 362; **23** 662–4*; **27** 230
collaboration **9** 62; **25** 845
groups and movements **3** 401; **8** 826; **15** 885; **21** 781, 782; **22** 868; **23** 450; **26** 15; **29** 397, 660
personal collection **9** 62
works **22** 830, 831; **23** *664*
Oudain, Jacquemart de *see* JACQUEMART DE HESDIN
Oudancour **11** 661
Oudegem **26** 645
Oudenaarde **3** *539*
guilds **3** 598
Halle **17** 700
marks **3** 601
Onze Lieve Vrouwekerk **3** 542; **13** 41
Stadhuis **3** 543, *544*; **17** 699; **31** 238
tapestries **3** 606; **23** 665*; **30** 314, 317, 320
Oudenhoven, Jacob van **32** 232
Oudenrogge, Johannes **4** 740
Ouderaa, Pierre Jean van der *see* VAN DER OUDERAA, PIERRE JEAN
Ouder Amstel **22** 882
Ouderkerk Jewish cemetery **17** 555
Oudewater Church **22** 820
Oud Holland **1** 722; **22** 910; **24** 424, 449
Oudiné, Eugène (-André) **6** 461; **12** 178; **23** 666*; **25** 214
Oudinot, Achille-François **22** 119
Oud Loosdrecht
porcelain **22** 882, *882*
Oudna **27** 67
baths **9** 562
Oudry, Jacques **23** 666
Oudry, Jacques-Charles **23** 669
Oudry, Jean-Baptiste **11** 657; **12** 830; **23** 666–9*; **24** 137; **29** 424; **30** 323
collaboration **6** 121; **10** 842
patrons and collectors
Azincourt, Barthélémy-Augustin Blondel d' **2** 904
Brukenthal, Samuel, Baron von **5** 9
Caffiéri, Philippe (ii) (1714–74) **5** 380
Oudry, Jean-Baptiste
patrons and collectors—cont.
Camondo, Moïse de, Comte **5** 530
Creutz, Gustav Filip **8** 161
La Live de Jully, Ange-Laurent de **18** 660
Lancret, Nicolas **18** 693
Louis XV, King of France (*reg* 1715–74) **4** 554
Seymour-Conway, Richard, 4th Marquess of Hertford **28** 527
Tessin, Carl Gustav, Count **30** 118, 524
Trudaine de Montigny, Jean-Charles-Philibert **31** 390
Verrue, Jeanne-Baptiste d'Albert de Luynes, Comtesse de **32** 368
pupils **14** 845; **26** 552
reproductions in tapestry **12** 830; **14** 543
reproductive prints by others **2** 853; **5** 884; **6** 527, 547; **9** 407; **19** 10, 144; **21** 800
tapestries **4** 514
teachers **18** 790
works **2** 105; **3** 461; **10** 726; **11** 470, 539, *539*, 577, 643; **14** 791; **15** 140; **21** 825; **23** *667*, *668*; **24** 135, *135*; **29** 668; **30** 114, 323
writings **24** 494
El Oued **1** 304, 305, 315, *376*, 636
Oued Athmenia, Baths of Pompeianus **3** 375
'Oueili, Tell el- **21** 270, 280, 306
brick **4** *771*
Ouezon City, University Museum of Anthropology **29** 240
Ougarit *see* UGARIT
Ougete *see* HUGETE
Oug Sadam **5** 483
Oujda Baths **16** 218
Oukaïmeden **22** 129
Oulad Naïl **16** 487
Ouless, Walter William **25** 868
Oulton, Therese **21** 897
Oulu **11** 103
Cathedral **11** 94
St Thomas **19** 114
Oumançoff, Véra **17** 608
Oŭn **18** 366
Ŏŭndong **18** 297
Ōura, Shūzo **20** 873
Ouradou, François Maurice **8** 372; **18** 428
Ouranoupolis, Pyrgos Prosphoriou **9** 556
Ouri
masks **5** *330*
Ouro Prêto **4** 704, *705*; **23** 669*
Casa de Câmera *see* Museu da Inconfidência
Casa dos Contos **4** 710
Museu da Inconfidência **4** 710, 727, 728
Nossa Senhora do Carmo **26** 254
Nossa Senhora do Pilar **4** 710
Nossa Senhora do Rosário dos Pretos **4** 710
S Efigênia **19** *460*
S Francisco de Assis da Penitência **4** 716, *716*; **19** 460; **26** 255
Ours, Yves des **19** 800
Ourscamp Abbey **11** 624; **13** 49
Infirmary **14** 780
Oury, Jules *see* MARCEL-LENOIR
Ouseley, Gore **16** 554; **22** 261
Ouseley, William **16** 342, 554; **27** 854
Ouspensky, Peter *see* USPENSKY, PYOTR (DEM'YANOVICH)
Outcalt, Richard Felton **7** 648
Outerbridge, Paul (Everard) **23** 669–70*; **24** 676
collaboration **14** 816
teachers **33** 146
outer crypts *see* CRYPTS → types
Outer Mongolia *see* MONGOLIA
outline engraving *see under* ENGRAVINGS → types
outlines **24** 380–81
outrigger canoes *see under* CANOES → types
Outryve, Louis-Emmanuel van **30** 46
Outshoorn, Cornelis **23** 670–71*
groups and movements **26** 190
works **1** 803; **14** 786; **22** 828; **23** *671*
Outsider art **2** 515
outworks **9** 555; **12** 174; **21** 547, 557, 558
Ouvea **25** 181
Ouwater, Albert van **10** 713; **22** 835; **23** 671–3*
attributions **4** 590; **20** 734
pupils **12** 230, 231
works **23** *672*
Ouwater, Isaak **22** 846; **23** 673*; **31** 247
Ou-yang Hsiu *see* OUYANG XIU
Ou-yang Hsün *see* OUYANG XUN
Ouyang Xiu **23** 673–4*; **30** 29
writings **6** 770–71, 787, 823
Ouyang Xun **6** 745–6; **7** 73; **23** 674*
patrons and collectors **30** 251; **32** 836
works **7** 290
Ovalle, R. **21** 396
Ovambo **1** 414, 416
Ovando, Nicolas de **9** 116
Ovčarovo **25** 501
Ovcharenko, Ye. **30** 55
Ovchinnikov (firm) **22** 180; **27** 421, 422, 426
Ovchinnikov, Pavel **27** 426
Ovchinnikov, Vladimir **27** 581
Ove Arup & Partners **10** 833; **14** 521; **26** 332
works **14** *522*
Övedskloster **30** 71
Ovens, Jürgen **22** 843; **23** 674–5*
works **1** 813; **12** 390; **23** *675*
Overbeck, Friedrich **23** 675–7*; **26** 776
collaboration **7** 870; **28** 46
groups and movements **3** 921; **12** 392, 393, 479; **14** 580; **16** 677; **22** 703, 704; **24** 587; **25** 741; **32** 677
patrons and collectors **3** 291; **7** 870; **20** 588; **30** 766
pupils **8** 790; **12** 29; **21** 128
reproductions in stained glass **29** 506
reproductive prints by others **27** 346
teachers **32** 751
works **11** *460*, 461, 462; **12** *392*; **22** 328; **23** *676*; **30** 358
Overbeck, Fritz **26** 394; **33** 382
Overbeke, Adriaen van **2** 204; **23** 678*
teachers **21** 352
Overbeke, Pauwels van
works **2** *191*
Overbeke, Willem van **12** 846
Overberg, Antonis van *see* OBBERGHEN, ANTONIS VAN
overdoors **9** 21; **14** 791; **23** 678–9*, *679*
overdyeing *see under* DYEING → techniques
Overend, (Acheson) Best **2** 741; **4** 415; **23** 679*
Överenhörna Church **30** 92
overgarments **9** 260–61
overglaze decoration *see under* CERAMICS; EARTHENWARES; PORCELAIN; POTTERY → techniques
overlaying *see under* GLASS → techniques

overmantels 14 791; 16 23
Överselö 13 120
Overstone, Samuel Jones Loyd, 1st Baron see LOYD, SAMUEL JONES, 1st Baron Overstone
Overstraeten, Henri Désiré Louis Van see VAN OVERSTRAETEN, HENRI DÉSIRÉ LOUIS
Overstraeten, Jan van 7 413
Overstreet, Joe 1 445
Overton, John 24 753
Overton, Philip 14 637
Ovetum see OVIEDO
Ovey, Richard 10 356
Ovid 4 360, 362; 15 84; 23 679–80*
works 15 82; 18 701; 22 412, 413
illustrated 22 414
on coral 7 834
on dress 9 249
translated 5 887; 20 245
Ovide, François 13 295
Oviedo 23 681–3*; 29 258
architecture 2 652–3
churches
Cathedral of S Salvador 23 681–2*, 682; 29 265, 275
Arca Santa 23 683; 26 689
Cámara Santa 2 653; 23 682*; 26 605, 609, 642
crosses 8 201
Cross of Angels 2 654; 23 682
Cross of Victory 2 654; 5 808; 23 682
crypt of S Leocadia 29 261
metalwork 26 689
Nicodemo cross 26 689
retables 13 123
sculpture 13 104; 29 292
textiles 16 436
Treasury 23 682–3*
S María de Naranco 2 653, 653; 29 261, 262, 287; 32 88
Santullano see S Julían de los Prados
S Julián de los Prados 2 652, 653; 24 750; 29 261, 275
S Miguel de Lillo 2 653; 5 319; 29 287
S Pedro de Nora 2 652
S Tirso 2 653; 29 261
manuscripts 20 330
Naranco palace 2 653
University 31 674
Oviedo, Diego Martínez de see MARTÍNEZ DE OVIEDO, DIEGO
Oviedo, Francisca de 26 414
Oviedo, Gonzalez de 14 56
Oviedo, Juan de (fl before 1580) 22 2; 23 683
Oviedo (y de la Bandera), Juan de (1565-1623) 22 2; 23 683*; 29 268
patrons and collectors 26 307; 28 519
works 28 513; 29 355
Oviedo, Lorenzo de 23 683*
Oviedo, Luis de 27 724
Oviedo, Martín de 4 257; 29 893
Oviedo, Pedro Díaz de see DÍAZ DE OVIEDO, PEDRO
Oviedo, Ramón 9 118
Ovile Annunciation, Master of the 12 716
Ovile Master 5 164
Ovimbundu 7 195–6, 199–200*
body arts 1 342
sculpture 1 403; 7 199, 199–200
wood 7 199
Ovis de La Tour, Louis see LA TOUR, LOUIS OVIS
Ovissi, Nasser 15 898
Ovnatanyan see HOVNAT'ANIAN
ovolo see under MOULDINGS → types
Ovruch 31 548
St Basil 31 548
Ovsov, Andrey 27 426
Ovtcharov, Vladimir 5 161
Ow, (Andreas) Meinrad von see AW, (ANDREAS) MEINRAD VON
Owari Tokugawa (family) 22 432
Owatonna (MN), National Farmers Bank 3 176; 29 916
Owen, Jacob 16 9; 18 753
Owen, Richard 32 784
Owen, Robert 31 725
works 31 725
Owen, Robert Dale 26 212
Owen, S. 26 76
Owen, William (1769-1825) 23 683–4*
Owen, William (1780-1831) 32 789
Owens, Bill (Elmo) 23 684*
Owens, Michael Joseph 19 304
Owens Bottle Machine Co. 19 304
Owens-Illinois Inc. 19 304
Owerri 1 314; 15 115, 116; 23 129
Owers, David 20 491
Owidzka, Jolante 25 133
Owings, Nathaniel A(lexander) 28 817*
Owiti, Herzbon 1 433
Owo 23 129, 132; 33 555
headdresses 9 734
sculpture 1 329; 23 132
sword 33 555
OWO 29 547
Owusu-Dartey 12 508
oxalic acid 30 537, 559
Oxburgh Hall (Norfolk) 4 779; 10 359; 12 176; 28 301
Oxenhall St Anne (Glos) 26 688
Oxenstierna (family) 4 180; 30 69
Oxenstierna, Axel 30 70, 92; 33 186
Oxenstierna, Bengt 11 242
Oxenstierna, Bengt Jönsson 27 165
Oxford 10 225; 23 684–91*; 31 710
art forms and materials
architecture 7 378–9
bookbindings 4 349, 351, 351
coats of arms 14 420
glass 16 520
manuscripts 13 130; 20 332; 28 233; 32 637
papier mâché 24 62
stained glass 23 689
Blackwell's Bookshop 3 420
Botanical Gardens 4 483; 12 127
churches see ecclesiastical buildings
collections 23 689–90
colleges 7 565, 566, 567; 10 230; 14 418; 23 686–9
All Souls College 10 232; 13 199; 14 255, 255; 18 687
chapel 13 184
enamel 13 168
gate-house 12 175
sculpture 13 84
Balliol College 13 329
Chapel 29 505
Brasenose College 13 210
Cardinal College see Christ Church
Christ Church 13 210; 23 686; 30 662
catalogues 6 78; 28 560
collections 10 362, 365; 11 364; 13 837; 26 363
Peckwater Quadrangle 23 857
Tom Quad 8 65
Tom Tower 13 199
tracery 31 271
Corpus Christi College
collections 10 325
gate-house 12 175
gold 10 325
Exeter College
Chapel 29 507
Jesus College 7 647
Keble College 4 769, 787; 5 316, 316; 25 173
Chapel 10 238
Oxford
colleges
Keble College—cont.
collections 7 647
Lincoln College 11 167
Chapel 29 505
Magdalen College 10 266; 13 84
Chapel 29 506
Merton College 10 287; 13 142
Chapel 13 183
library 23 686
roof 30 907
stained glass 10 245
New College 7 566, 566; 10 359; 23 691*; 28 302; 33 202
Chapel 24 465; 29 506
collections 9 28; 10 325, 344
gate-house 12 175
sculpture 13 84
stained glass 13 183; 23 691*
vaults 32 93
Oriel College 7 565
Queen's College 7 565; 10 323
Chapel 29 505
Queen's Hall see Queen's College
Ruskin School of Drawing and Fine Art 23 690; 27 354
St Bernard's College see St John's College
St Edmund Hall 14 77
library 23 685
St John's College 7 350; 18 855
Canterbury Quadrangle 8 65; 23 687, 687
University College
Chapel 29 505
Wadham College
Chapel 29 505, 506
3 Cornmarket 10 271
craftsmen and artists 13 133
Divinity School see under university buildings
ecclesiastical buildings
Christ Church Cathedral 23 491, 685, 685; 32 92
restoration 2 321
spire 29 413
stained glass 29 505, 507, VI2
see also St Frideswide
Osney Abbey 23 685
St Ebbe 3 443
St Frideswide 3 443; 23 685
see also Christ Church Cathedral
St Mary 23 685; 29 413
St Michael at the Northgate 2 67; 23 685
St Peter in the East see colleges → St Edmund Hall → library
fortifications 21 569
see also town walls
Grand Pont 23 685
Griffith Institute 10 83, 92
Holywell Music Room 7 687
libraries 19 313, 314
Bodleian Library 10 376; 13 225; 15 594; 19 315, 319
catalogues 32 852
collections 5 623; 9 195; 10 421; 15 741, 744; 16 557; 23 690
manuscripts 17 694
Schools Quadrangle 23 686
Duke Humphrey's library see under university buildings → Divinity School
Law Library 10 242
Radcliffe Camera 9 86; 10 233, 295, 342; 12 594; 19 314; 20 572; 27 237; 29 540
model 2 336
museums
Ashmolean Museum 2 275; 3 466; 7 504, 504; 10 370; 13 613; 19 810; 22 362; 23 688, 689, 690
Anatolian collection 1 839
Oxford
museums
Ashmolean Museum—cont.
Ancient Near East collection 1 855
Beazley Collection 3 466
ceramics 6 925
Chinese collection 7 155
collections 2 601; 10 368, 654, 658; 11 323; 22 356; 26 130; 31 276
Cycladic collection 8 324
drawings 5 846, 866; 9 195, 229; 12 594; 18 641, 895; 20 186; 24 183, 247; 26 405, 473; 27 354; 33 345
Egyptian collection 8 570; 10 71, 79, 83, 92
Evans Collection 18 165
gems 12 266; 14 807
Greek collection 13 605
Indian collection 15 744, 748
Islamic collection 16 557
manuscripts 24 478
Mesopotamian collection 21 310
Minoan collection 21 692
Native North American collection 22 675
paintings 7 647; 8 166; 11 364; 24 882, 885; 33 685
plaquettes 25 18
portico 25 267
pottery 3 243; 13 542
sculpture 6 457; 7 788; 9 25; 22 795; 27 46
staff 10 654
Syria-Palestine collection 30 198
see also Old Ashmolean Building; Taylorian Institution
Museum of Natural History see University Museum
Old Ashmolean Building 2 601
see also Ashmolean Museum
Oxford Museum see University Museum
Pitt Rivers Museum 1 437
collections 1 66, 439; 22 679; 23 738; 29 48
Native North American collection 22 675
South-east Asian collection 29 240
University Galleries see Ashmolean Museum
University Museum 8 586; 10 266, 370; 16 54; 22 363; 23 600; 27 351
Oxford Union Society 5 266; 10 254; 22 142
Radcliffe Camera see under libraries
Radcliffe Observatory 23 340; 30 502
Taylorian Institution 7 504, 504; 13 613; 22 362; 23 689; 30 386
drawings 30 386
see also museums → Ashmolean Museum
town walls 31 710
see also fortifications
University 10 242; 31 674
collections 3 466; 6 446; 10 658; 23 22; 27 352; 33 154
manuscripts 18 686
Schools Quadrangle see under libraries → Bodleian Library
university buildings
Clarendon Building 10 232; 14 254; 23 688
Divinity School 23 686; 24 466, 466
Duke Humphrey's library 19 313; 23 686
sculpture 13 84, 85
Oxford
university buildings—cont.
Sheldonian Theatre 10 232; 23 687, 688; 29 767; 30 673; 33 393
interior decoration 10 249
University Museum see under museums
Oxford, Edward Harley, 2nd Earl of see HARLEY, EDWARD, 2nd Earl of Oxford
Oxford, Robert Harley, 1st Earl of see HARLEY, ROBERT, 1st Earl of Oxford
Oxford, Thomas of see THOMAS OF OXFORD
Oxford and Cambridge Magazine, The 24 426
Oxford Art Journal 24 446
Oxford Lectern Bible see under BIBLES → types
Oxford University Press 4 368
oxgall 23 792; 24 55; 32 898
ox-hair see under HAIR → types
ox-horn see under HORN → types
Oxmantown see DUBLIN
Oxpemul 5 411
Oxtotitlán 23 418
paintings 30 786
rock art 21 226
wall paintings 21 226
Oxus Treasure 1 118, 205, 206, 875, 876; 6 212, 237, 273, 285, 480; 11 738; 15 908; 23 691–2*
coins 1 203
see also TAKHT-I KUBAD
Oxwich Brooch 10 344
Oxylithos, Church of the Dormition 9 584
oxymel process see under PHOTOGRAPHY → processes
Oxyrhynchus see under EL-BAHNASA
Oya 29 263
Ōyamazaki, Myōkian
Taian tea-room 17 46, 338, 339; 28 412
Oyamazumi Shrine 2 450
Oyarzún, Rodulfo 6 594
Oych (Verneyken), Heinrich 32 339
Øye Church 29 580
Oye-Ekiti 1 431
Oyelami, Muraina 23 136
Oyly, Charles D' see D'OYLY, CHARLES
Oyo 23 131, 132
Oyo Yoruba 1 345
Oyster Bay (NY), Laurelton Hall 30 869
oyster shells see under SHELLS → types
oyster-work see under MARQUETRY → types
Øystese, Vik Museum 32 512
O Yun 18 327
Ōyu stone circles 17 11, 629; 23 693*
Öz, İlban 16 611
Ozaani Church 12 330
Ozaki, Sozo 17 401
Ozanne, Nicolas(-Marie) 23 693*
Ozanne, Pierre 23 693
Ozemblowski, Jozef 19 498
Ozene see UJJAIN
Ozenfant, Amédée 11 525, 548; 19 40; 23 693–5*
collaboration 22 331; 26 44
groups and movements 1 75; 4 109; 6 342; 8 247; 21 782; 25 739–40, 741
house 2 552; 19 41
patrons and collectors 2 409
pupils 2 574; 5 882; 12 613; 13 1; 14 393; 26 360
studio 25 740, 741
works 11 420; 19 80, 896; 23 694; 24 143, 144
writings 3 391; 31 300

Ozenfant, Jean **23** 694
Ozette **22** *544*, 578; **23** 695*
Ożga, Abbot of Tyniec **25** 126
Özgüç, Nimet **1** 114, 893
Özgüç, Tahsin **1** 728, 893; **18** 512
Ozhegov, A. I. **24** 458
Ozieri **27** 834
Ozieri, Master of **27** 836
Özkan, Huseyin **31** 454
Ozmo, Danijel **4** 461; **28** 451
ozokerite *see under* WAXES → types
Özsoy, Ihsan **1** 132; **22** 342; **31** 454
Ōzui Maruyama *see* MARUYAMA ŌZUI
Ozu Shrine **17** 129
Ozyazıcı, Halim **2** 883; **23** 695–6*; **31** 454

P

P, Master **2** 469
Pa **5** 328
Paál, László **14** 901; **23** 697*
Paalen, Wolfgang **21** 388; **23** 697–8*
  groups and movements **30** 21, 22
  teachers **14** 633
Paan **30** 609, 610
Paar *see* PARRI
Paas, John **26** 75
Paas-Aleksandrovna, Yuta (Ioxannesovna) **27** 426
Paaschen, (Hans) Henryk van *see* PASSE, (HANS) HENRYK VAN
Pääsuke, Tiit **10** 540
Paatelainen, Raili *see* PIETILÄ, RAILI
Paatenemheb *see* HOREMHEB
Pabel, Hilmar **23** 698*
Pabellón Modelled-carved ware *see under* POTTERY → wares
Pabenham, Simon **17** 612
Pablo, Master **31** 88
Pablo, Luis de **1** 610
Pablo, Severino Flavier *see* FLAVIER PABLO, SEVERINO
Pablo di San Leocadio *see* PAOLO DA SAN LEOCADIO
Pabst, Daniel **24** 602
Pabst, Theo **27** 315
Pabst von Ohain, Gottfried **21** 63
Pac (family) **19** 496; **25** 135
Pac, Ludwik **20** 396; **25** 136
Pacák, Jiří František **8** 386; **18** 505
Pacal, Lord **23** 838; **27** 823, 833; **30** 449
  masks **16** II1
  sarcophagus **21** *221*
Pacard, Alexis **25** 172
Pacasmayo Shrine **29** 130
Pacassi, Nikolaus **23** 698*
  attributions **5** 86
  groups and movements **26** 496
  works **2** 784, 806; **4** 695; **5** 349; **8** 379; **14** 887; **19** 807; **25** 438; **32** 456, 457, 460, 461
Pacatnamú **30** 447
Pacauds, Jean Baudouin des *see* BAUDOUIN DES PACAUDS, JEAN
Paccaicasa **29** 168
Paccard, Alexis **2** 14
Paccard, André **16** 550
Paccassi, Nikolaus *see* PACASSI, NIKOLAUS
Pacchia, Girolamo del **4** 749; **11** 388, *388*; **24** 831; **29** 3
Pacchiarotti, Giacomo **11** 842; **23** 698*; **24** 831
Pacchiarotti, Girolamo *see* PACHEROT, JÉRÔME
Pacchioni, Francesco **3** 89
Paccinelli, Venanzio **27** 447
Pacciotto, Francesco *see* PACIOTTO, FRANCESCO
Pace, Buonaccorso di *see* BUONACCORSO DI PACE
Pace, George **5** 731
Pace, Giovan Battista (*b c.* 1640-45) **23** 701
Pace, Giovanni Battista Ranieri del (*fl* 1704-19) *see* RANIERI DEL PACE, GIOVANNI BATTISTA
Pace, John Henry **2** 764
Pace, Luigi da **6** 583; **22** 163
Pace, Mariotto di *see* MARIOTTO DI PACE
Pacea, Ion **23** 699*
Pace Associates **21** 492
  works **21** *492*
Pacecco **23** 699–700*; **27** 205; **29** 544; **32** 624
  works **23** *700*
Pace da Lugo **11** 712
Pace del Campidoglio, Michele **21** 35; **23** 701*
Pace di Bartolo **2** 628
Pace di Maso **21** 97, 98
Pace di Valentino **7** 817
Pacello da Mercogliano **4** 155; **11** 905; **12** 110, 112; **20** 133; **31** 845
Pacenza, Onofrio **2** 400
Pacetti, Camillo **23** 701*
  patrons and collectors **16** 705
  works **5** 385; **20** 390; **21** 533
Pacetti, Vincenzo **23** 701*; **31** 679
  collaboration **2** 612
  patrons and collectors **25** 8
  works **4** 407; **12** 583
Pacey, P. **4** 28
Pach, Walter **2** 447; **23** 47, 701–2*; **25** 823
  groups and movements **2** 633; **25** 747; **28** 925
Pachacamac **2** 300; **15** *161*; **23** *702*, 702–3*; **28** 651; **29** *156*, 218; **30** 447
  architecture **29** 162
  doors **9** 166
  pottery **14** 828; **23** 703
  Temple of Pachacamac **23** 703
  Temple of the Sun **23** 703; **29** 167
  textiles **29** 181
  wall paintings **29** 172
Pachacutec Yupanqui (*reg* 1438-71) **8** 300, 301; **15** 162
Pachacuti **29** 167
Pachamama **30** 447
Pachatata **30** 447
Pacheco **14** 829; **29** *156*, 205
Pacheco, Bishop of Málaga (*fl* 1581) **3** 7
Pacheco, Ana-Maria **23** 704*
Pacheco, Armando **4** 263
Pacheco, Castro **31** 415
Pacheco, Duarte **19** 467; **25** 294
Pacheco, Fernando Castro *see* CASTRO PACHECO, FERNANDO
Pacheco, Francisco (*b* 1535) **28** 515
Pacheco, Francisco (1564-1654) **1** 104; **23** 704–6*; **28** 515; **29** 279, 280; **32** 126; **33** 728
  collaboration **32** 99
  patrons and collectors **26** 307; **28** 519
  pupils **4** 211; **5** 618; **32** 125
  works **2** 411; **6** 365, 467; **19** 303; **22** 1, 2; **23** *705*; **29** 276, 278
  writings **4** 209; **10** 191; **13** 708; **15** 82; **20** 109; **29** 357, 358
Pacheco, Francisco, Archbishop of Burgos **7** 362
Pacheco, Juan, Marqués de Villena *see* VILLENA, JUAN PACHECO, Marqués de
Pacheco, Juan Vicente de Güemes *see* GÜEMES, PACHECO, JUAN VICENTE DE
Pacheco, María Luisa **4** 263; **23** 706*; **33** 317
Pacheco, Pedro de Alcántara Téllez Girón y *see* OSUNA, 9th Duque de
Pacheco, Santos *see* SANTOS PACHECO
Pacheco Altamirano, Alba Arturo **6** 601
Pacheia Ammos **21** 657
Pacher, Friedrich **23** 706–7*
  collaboration **23** 707
  pupils **26** 105
  works **4** 286; **15** 146
Pacher, Hans **23** 707, 708
Pacher, Leonhard **23** 707
Pacher, Michael **2** 792, 799; **23** 706–9*
  assistants **23** 706
  attributions **20** 705; **27** 664
  groups and movements **26** 186
  pupils **18** 137; **26** 105
  works **1** 710; **2** 799; **4** 286; **11** 452; **12** 385, 401; **23** *707*, *708*, *709*; **26** 186; **28** 134
  workshop **13** 117
Pacherot, Jérôme **23** 709*
  collaboration **3** 868; **7** 595
  patrons and collectors **1** 766; **11** 399
Pachkhanwalla, Pilloo **4** 291
Pachomios, Abbot of Mystras (*fl c.* 1310-22) **22** 407
Pachomius, Saint (*c.* 290-346 AD) **7** 227; **9** 643; **21** 833
Pachoras *see* FARAS
Pachote, Francesco *see* PACIOTTO, FRANCESCO
Pächt, Otto **2** 833, 834; **11** 315; **15** 91; **26** 63; **28** 115, 916
Pachta, Count of **1** 669
Pachuca **21** 393
  Fototeca del Instituto Nacional de Antropología e Historia **5** 910
  Instituto Nacional de Antropología e Historia (INAH) **21** 398
Paciência, João **24** 395
Pacific Arts Association **23** 740
Pacific Fine Art Society (Taiheiyō Bijutsukai) **17** 435
Pacific Islands **23** 709–42*, *711*
  adzes **23** 712, *712*
  aesthetics **23** 713–14*, *714*
  architecture **23** 715–18*, *736*
  armour **23** 735
  art (works of) **23** 713
  art history **2** 533; **23** 738–9*
  barkcloth **23** 713
  basalt **23** *712*
  body arts **23** 718–20*, 721–2*, *722*, 723*
  body ornaments **23** 719*, 723
  canoes **23** 723–6*, *725*, *726*
  clubs (weapons) **23** *734*
  collections **7** 562; **23** 739–40*, 741–2*
  cords **23** 712–13
  craftsmen and artists **23** 718, 724
  dealing **23** 741–2*
  dress **23** 723
  education (art) **23** 736
  exhibitions **23** 740–41*
  fans **10** 779*
  feathers **23** 720, 721
  flax **23** 712
  forgeries **23** 737–8*
  gateways **23** *716*
  greenstone **23** *734*
  hair **23** 720
  headdresses **23** 720, 721*
  heritage **23** 737
  historiography **23** 738–9*
  houses **23** *717*
  mats **23** 713
  mother-of-pearl **23** 720; **28** II2
  museums **23** 737, 739–40*
  paddles **23** 724
  painting **23** 721–2*, 723
  pandanus **23** 712
Pacific Islands—cont.
  pendants (jewellery) **23** 720
  periods
    Prehistoric **25** 468
  platforms **23** 715
  pottery **23** *727*
  rock art **23** 728–30*, *730*
  scarification **23** 721
  sculpture **23** 730–33*, *732*
  sennit **23** 712, *712*
  shells **23** 721*; **28** 581
  shields **23** 734; **28** II2
  stone **23** 715*, *716*
  tattoos **23** 713, 718–19*, *719*, 722*, 723
  textiles **23** 723
  tourist art **23** 735–6
  turmeric **23** 723
  weapons **23** 733–5*
  whale teeth **23** 720
  wigs **23** 721
  wood **23** 712, *712*, 715–18*, *717*, *732*
  wood-carvings **23** *731*; **33** 325
Pacific Painting Society *see* TAIHEIYŌ GAKAI
Pacific Palisades (CA), 203 Chautauqua Boulevard **9** 503
Pacific Stone Company **7** 693
Pacificus **32** 340
Pacilli, Pietro **27** 357; **31** 244
Pacini, P. **3** 301
Pacini, Sante **3** 750; **5** 451
Pacino, Francesco di **11** 192, 193
Pacino, Matteo di *see* MATTEO DI PACINO
Pacino da Nova **3** 773
Pacino di Bonaguida **23** 742–4*
  pupils **20** 641, 658
  works **11** 379, 710; **23** *743*
Pacio da Firenze **22** 476
Pacioli, Luca **9** 434; **21** 517; **22** 378; **23** 744*
  works **2** 167, 345, 356; **19** 451; **24** 765; **28** 201
  illustrated **19** 182
Paciotto, Francesco **10** 535; **14** 5; **21** 570; **23** 745–6*; **29** 267
  patrons and collectors **14** 5; **28** 4; **31** 439
  works **2** 192; **10** 498; **14** 473; **19** 764; **23** *745*; **24** 695; **28** 308; **31** 94
Pacitan **30** 10
Paciurea, Dimitrie **23** 746*
  patrons and collectors **26** 723
  pupils **2** 52; **16** 49, 877; **18** 619
  works **26** 715, 716
Packages Limited **23** 804
packaging **15** 825; **17** 217; **24** 52*
Packard, Harry **17** 431
Packard Motor Car Company **17** 721; **31** 596
Packeny, Jan Domenik **8** 414
Packh, János **23** 747*
  works **10** 545, *545*, 546
Packington Hall (Warwicks) **22** 738; **25** 192–3
  interior decoration **10** 277; **11** 83–4
  paintings **32** 592
  Pompeian Gallery **10** 644; **11** 83; **25** *193*
  wall paintings **10** 199
Packl, János **14** 888
Packneny, Jan **8** 413
Paco **24** 616
Paço, Afonso do **32** 562
Paço, Janaq **23** 747*
  works **1** 541, *541*
Paco de Oca **12** 125
Paço de Sousa, Monastery of S Salvador **25** 289, 300
Paco do Calhariz **12** 125
Pacon, Henri **23** 747*
Pacopampa **6** 521, 523
Pactius, Thomas **19** 526
Pactumeius Rufinus, L. Cuspius **24** 413
Pacuvius **25** 44; **27** 52
Pacyków **25** 123
Paczółzowice Church **25** 129
Padalacqua **9** 331
Padalka, Ivan I. **2** 634; **4** 605
Padamsee, Akbar **4** 290, 291; **23** 747–8*
Padam Singh, Ruler of Ghanerao (*reg* 1720-42) (Rajput) **15** 615
Padang Lawas **4** 796; **15** *752*, 766–7, 787–8
padauk **33** 325
Padaung **5** 250
Padaviya **29** 448
paddles **1** 365; **23** 724; **31** 491
Padegs, Kārlis
Padellaio, Rosso **28** 678
Padeloup **4** 354
Pader, Hilaire **23** 748*
Pader, Tobias **22** 302
Paderborn **12** *360*; **23** 748–9*
  Bishop's Palace **14** 74
  Cathedral of St Maria, St Kilian und St Liborius **5** 794; **14** 81; **23** 749*
    alabaster-carvings **1** 519
    altar **26** 683
    sculpture **13** 682
    spire **29** 412
    wall paintings **5** 797
  chapel of St Bartholomew **23** 647
  collegiate church of Busdorf **7** 256; **9** 680
  Franciscan church **24** 562
Paderborn Altar **26** 651
Padhaoli **15** 289
Padilla, Juan de **21** 393
Padilla, Rafael Rodriguez *see* RODRIGUEZ PADILLA, RAFAEL
Padilla, Ricardo **21** 382
padmakośa *see* KARNARATHA
Padmanabhapuram Palace **15** 524, 649, 721; **23** 817
Padmapala, Ruler (*reg c.* 1085-93) (Kachchhapaghata) **15** 292
Padmavati *see* PAWAYA
Padova, Battista di Niccolò da *see* BATTISTA DI NICCOLÒ DA PADOVA
Padova, Giovanni Antonio da *see* PÁDUA, JOÃO ANTÓNIO BELLINI DE
Padovanino **16** 675; **23** 749–51*; **32** 194
  pupils **5** 782, 845; **19** 308; **32** 102
  works **23** *750*
Padovano, Alessandro **23** 751*
Padovano, Benedetto *see* BORDON, BENEDETTO
Padovano, Gasparo *see* GASPARO PADOVANO
Padovano, Gerolamo *see* GEROLAMO PADOVANO
Padovano, Giovanni *see* RUBINO, GIOVANNI
Padovano, Giuseppe *see* GIUSEPPE PADOVANO
Padovano, Gualtiero dall'Arzere **30** 33
Padovano, Il *see* LEONI, OTTAVIO
Padovano, Jan Maria *see* MOSCA PADOVANO, GIOVANNI MARIA

Padovano, Lauro *see* LAURO PADOVANO
Padovini, Alexander *see* PADUANO, ALEXANDER
Padre Piedra, Monument 1 **29** 619
Padrlík, Arnošt **8** 394
Padrta, Jiří **8** 249
pads **25** 477
see also DABBERS
Padua **13** 298; **16** *618*; **23** 751–7*, *753*; **26** *886*
Anatomical Theatre **1** 797
architecture **23** *752*
botanic garden **4** 483, *483*
bronze **10** 528
Caffè Pedrocchi **16** 648, 720; **17** *443*, 443–4
Casa Vitaliani **14** 869
caskets **5** 918
ceramics **23** 754*
colleges **7** 566
Cornaro House *see* Palazzo Giustiniani
ecclesiastical buildings
Arena Chapel **3** 173; **4** 774, 775; **6** 460; **13** 135; **16** 837; **23** *756*, 756–7*; **26** 182; **29** 665
altar **16** 688
furniture **16** 723
gilding **12** 621
paintings (frescoes) **4** 493; **5** 443; **6** 1; **12** *682*, *684*, *685*, *687*, *688*, 688–90; **13** 145, 673; **15** 135; **16** 655; **18** 676; **19** 353; **22** 521; **23** 756; **24** VIII1; **32** 805
sculpture **13** 95; **24** *873*
shields **14** 415
Baptistery **21** 112–13, *113*
Cappella degli Scrovegni *see* Arena Chapel
Cappella di S Giacomo *see* S Felice
Cathedral of S Maria Assunta **13** 133; **16** 726
Eremitani **2** 725; **15** 136
Cappella del Mantegna *see* Ovetari Chapel
frescoes **2** 725; **13** 747
Ovetari Chapel **16** 659; **20** 304–7*, *305*; **25** 9
sculpture **13** 95
tomb of Benavides **1** 790–91
Oratorio di S Giorgio **1** 725–6, *726*; **9** *260*, 261
Il Santo **4** 774, 775; **9** 127, 159; **11** 711, 712; **13** 52; **16** 627; **23** 754–6*, *755*; **26** 136, 185
altar **11** 711; **16** 693
altarpiece **1** 711
Belludi Chapel **21** 113
Cappella della Croce **16** 747
Cappella dell'Arca di S Antonio **19** *556*, 556–7
chapter house **6** 466
choir-screen **3** 636, *637*
crucifix **8** 215
monument to Pietro Bembo **31** *125*, 127
Paschal candlestick **26** 328–9, *329*
sculpture **13** 95; **16** 693, 697; **21** 632
Treasury **12** 260
Scrovegni Chapel *see* Arena Chapel
S Felice **1** 725
S Francesco
monument to Pietro Roccabonella **16** 693
S Giovanni **7** 672
S Giustina **3** 709; **22** 131; **31** 825
altar **16** 747
altarpiece **20** 307
sculpture **13** 95; **26** 622
woodwork **16** 723, 726
S Maria Gloriosa dei Frari **16** 692
Padua
ecclesiastical buildings—cont.
S Maria Mater Domini *see* Il Santo
S Nicolò
Frigimelica Chapel **28** 84
SS Sacramento **16** 747
glass **16** 740
Loggia Cornaro **30** 655
maiolica **16** 732, 734, 735
manuscripts **23** 754; **26** 564; **31** 49
medals **20** 919
monument to Gattamelata **9** *127*; **10** 440; **22** 44; **26** 185; **29** 565
Museo Civico **4** 247; **16** 776
Orto Botanico **12** 115; **22** 131
painting **16** 661, 662
Palazzo del Bò **22** 131, *132*
Palazzo Carrara **16** 710
chapel *see* Sala dell'Accademia
Sala dei Giganti **1** 725; **24** 559
Sala dell'Accademia **13** 747
Sala Vivorum Illustrium *see* Sala dei Giganti
Palazzo Giustiniani **10** 767, *767*
Palazzo Mantova-Benavides **3** 700
Palazzo Municipale **22** 131
Palazzo del Podestà *see* Palazzo Municipale
Palazzo della Ragione **13** 64; **18** 886
frescoes **2** 650
interior decoration **17** 442
monument to Lucrezia Dondi degli Obizzi **1** 669
Palazzo Strozzi **1** 789
Piazza del Duomo **28** *801*
Piazza degli Eremitani **28** *801*
Piazza Santo **16** 690
porcelain **16** 737
pottery **16** 395
Prato della Valle **5** 626
Reggia **5** 871
sculpture **16** 688, 692–3
Scuola del Carmine **5** 535
Scuola del Santo **9** 264; **23** 754
studium **16** 778
textiles **26** 855
Torre di Ezzelino **4** 776
Torre di Ponte Molin **4** 776
Università degli Studi **3** 700; **26** 779
urban planning **23** 753
Villa Emo Capodilista **16** 719
Pádua, João Antônio Bellini de **23** 757*
Padua, John of *see* JOHN OF PADUA
Padua, Paul **22** 711
Paduano, Alexander **11** 819; **23** 757*; **30** 34; **33** 81
works **15** 137; **20** 279
Padula, Attilio la **22** 805
Paduli, Duca di **12** 657
Padura, Miguel **18** 835
Paduraru, Neculai **23** 757–8*
Padwey, Johannes de *see* JOHN OF PADUA
Padyenaset **10** 68
Pae, Kru Khong **30** 616
Paechtown, Putlands Cottage **32** 308
Paegun bridge **18** 280
Paekche **17** 214
Paekche ware *see under* POTTERY → wares
Pae Kil-gi **18** 332
Paekka **18** 304; **23** 758*
Paek Kwang-hun **18** 329
Paek Nak-son **18** 365
Paek Ŭn-bae **18** 321
Paele, Georg van den *see* GEORG VAN DER PAELE
Paelinck, Joseph **3** 562; **23** 758*
Paen, Willem **22** 418
Paepe, Gillis de **23** 665
Paepe, Simon de **23** 665
Paerels, Willem **3** 564; **4** 618; **23** 399; **28** 104
Paes, Domingo de **15** 702
Paeschen, Hans von **4** 781; **14** 369
Paesschen, (Hans) Henryk van *see* PASSE, (HANS) HENRYK VAN
Paestum **13** 303, *362*; **16** *621*; **23** 481, 758–60*; **26** *886*
Basilica *see* Sanctuary of Hera → Temple of Hera
coins **13** 586
Corinthian-Doric temple **3** 439, *439*
figurines **13** 579, 581
Heroön **6** 170
ivory-carvings **10** 635
macellum **19** 889
metalwork **13** 576
Museo Archeologico **13** 470
pottery **13** 532
Sanctuary of Hera **23** *759*, 759
Temple of Hera **13** *377*, 378, 397, 398; **16** 622; **30** 435
entasis **10** 414, 415
proportions **2** 351
roof **30** 903
Temple of Athena **10** 414; **13** 378; **16** 622; **23** 481, *481*, 759
Temple of Poseidon **11** 231; **13** 414; **23** 481
Tomb of the Diver **13** 544, 555; **23** 759
wall paintings **13** *543*; **16** 653
town walls **21** 556
wall paintings **18** 701
Paez **7** 602
Páez **19** 388
Páez, José Antonio **32** 180
Páez, José de **32** 173
Páez, Juan Espinosa *see* ESPINOSA PÁEZ, JUAN
Paez Villaro, Carlos **31** 754
Paffe, Louis **11** 626
Pafnutie *see* PÎRVU, MUTU
Pag **8** 180
Pagaczewski, Julian **25** 143
Pagan **2** *281*; **5** *221*, 222, 223, 225; **23** 760–64*, *760*; **29** 224, *225*; **30** 446
Abe-yadana **5** 243
Ananda **5** 222, 226, 227, 228, 229, 230, 254; **23** 762*, *762*
plaques **5** 239
sculpture **5** 240, 243
stelae **5** 239
Ananda Ok-kyaung **5** 244
Archaeological Museum **5** 240; **29** 239
architecture **5** 225–32, 237; **29** 237
brick **4** 796
coins **5** 255
Dhamma-yan-gyi **5** 228, 232
Dhamma-yazika **5** 222, 226, 231
Gadaw-palin **5** 222, 228, 229
Gu-ni, North **5** 228
Gu-ni, South **5** 228
Hpet-leik, East **5** 231, 239, 243
Hpet-leik, West **5** 231, 232, 239, 243
Hpyat-sa **5** 231, 232
Hsu-taung-pyit **5** 232
Hti-lo-min-lo **5** 228, 229; **23** *763*, 763–4*
Kyakku-ohn-min **5** 229
lacquer **5** *257*, 258, 263
Le-myet-hna **5** 232
Loka-hteik-pan **5** 230, 243, *243*
Mingala-zedi **5** 222, 231, *231*; **28** 639; **29** 866
plaques **5** 239
Min-o-chantha **5** 227
Monastery 1111 **5** 232
Monastery 1112 **5** 232
Monastery 449 **5** *232*
Mye-bon-tha **5** 228, 230
Pagan—cont.
Naga-yon **5** 226, 227, 228, 229; **23** 761–2*; **29** 866
plaques **5** 243
stelae **5** 239
Nan-hpaya **5** 240
Nat-hlaung-kyaung **5** 228, 240
Nga-kywe-na-daung **5** 231
Pahto-tha-mya **5** 228, 243
painting **29** 231
wall **5** 242*
Paya-thon-zu **5** 227
Pe-natha **5** 227
Pitaka-taik **5** 232
Sapada **5** 231
sculpture **5** 239–40*, *240*; **18** *607*
Sein-nyet Ama **5** 227
Sein-nyet Nyi-ma **5** 227, 232
Setana-gyi **5** 231
Shin-pahto **5** 231
shrines (i) (cult) **28** 640
Shwe-gu-gyi **5** 226, 230
Shwe-hsan **5** 231
Shwe-hsan-daw **5** 240
Shwe-zigon **5** 223, 226, 230, 231, 240, 261; **23** 761*; **29** 866
plaques **5** 239, 243
Somin-gyi **5** 231, 232
Stupa 495 **5** 231
Stupa 1754 **5** 231
Stupa 1982 **5** 231
stupas **29** 866
Sula-mani **5** 222, 228, 229, 230, 244
tablets **5** 242
Temple 1359 **5** 228
Temple 1756 **5** 230
Temple 1790 **5** 228
Temple 1843 **5** 229, *229*
Temple 1844 **5** 229, *229*, 230
Temple 1845 **5** 229, *229*
Temple 1846 **5** 229, 230
Temple 1847 **5** 229, 230
Temple 1890 **5** 230
Temple 2070 **5** *227*
Temple 315 **5** 242
terracotta **30** 511
Thabeik-hmauk **5** 228
That-byin-nyu **5** 226, 229, 253; **23** 762–3*; **29** 866
That-tei-gu **5** 228
Thein-hwet-ohn-min **5** 229
Thein-mazi **5** 228
Thissa-wadi **5** 229
Upali Thein **5** 232
Wetkyi-in
Kubyauk-gyi **5** 228, *228*, 230, 243, 244
Kubyauk-ngè **5** 232
Wuthana-daw Temple 357 **5** 230
Zedi-she **5** 231
Pagan (Burmese dynasty) *see*: ANAWRAHTA, King KYANZITTHA, King NARAPATISITHU, King
Pagan, Blaise de **21** 567
Paganello, Ramo di *see* RAMO DI PAGANELLO
Pagani, Gregorio **23** 764*; **31** 55
patrons and collectors **32** 106
pupils **1** 671; **27** 177
works **27** 177
Pagani, Paolo **18** 467; **24** 339
Pagani, Pietro **29** 840
Paganica, Ludovico Mattei, Duca di **1** 792; **20** 839
Paganico, S Michele **8** 836
Paganini, Alessandro de **2** 223
Paganini, Niccolò **8** *565*
Paganini, Paganino de' **16** 360
Pagano, Francesco **22** 479; **24** 27; **31** 815
Pagano, Giuseppe **10** 822; **23** 764*
collaboration **16** 649, 650; **24** 484, 694
groups and movements **21** 422; **26** 15
works **16** 649, 650; **26** 762; **31** 443
Pagano, Salvatore **16** 731
Pagano della Fede, Matteo **25** 889
Pagaruyung Palace **23** 824
P'agat **5** 238
Page, Master **7** 190
Page, Benjamin **3** 84
Page, Gregory **15** 47
Page, Hilary **31** 259
Page, James **1** *109*, 111; **24** 273
Page, Karen **10** 875
Page, Robert **10** 265
Page, Russell **12** 143; **17** 473
works **12** *143*
Page, William **23** 765*
pupils **4** 627
works **23** *765*
Page and Steel **31** 176
pageants **23** 765–71*, *768*, *770*
pageant wagons *see under* WAGONS → types
Page beneath the Cross, Master of the **20** 666
Page & Park **28** 232
Pagès, Bernard **11** 552, 570; **30** 6
works **11** *570*
Paget, Charles, 6th Marquess of Anglesea **5** 688
Paget, Violet *see* LEE, VERNON
Page-Turner, Gregory **3** 383
Paggi, Giovanni Battista **23** 771–2*
assistants **10** 786
patrons and collectors **4** 811; **9** 173, 174; **15** 148
pupils **3** 736; **5** 769; **6** 32; **11** 52; **25** 62; **28** 219
Pagine d'arte **24** 448
Paglia, Giuseppe **26** 794
Pagliaccetti, Raffaello **16** 707
Pagliarini, Giovanni **4** 252
Pagliarolo, Domenico **8** 173
Paglicci **25** 492
Pagni, Raffaello **5** 360; **24** 855
Pagni da Pescia, Benedetto **11** 193
Pagnini, Sante **3** 304
Pagno di Antonio di Berti da Settignano **24** 731
Pagno di Lapo (Portigiani) **9** 129; **23** 772*
collaboration **11** 254; **27** 179
patrons and collectors **3** 743
works **4** 271; **21** 469
Pagno Portigiani, Lapo di *see* LAPO DI PAGNO PORTIGIANI
pagodas **23** 772–6*
historical and regional traditions
Burma **23** 772
China **6** *645*, 649, *650*, 654, 656, *658*, 666, 668; **7** 98, 99; **19** 303; **23** 772–5*
Esoteric **5** 117
Indian subcontinent **23** 772
Japan **5** 116, 117; **17** 36, 66, 67, *72*; **22** *499*; **23** 776*; **29** 869
Korea **18** *261*; **23** 775*
Nepal *see* DEGAS
Shingon **23** 776
Tendai **23** 776
materials
brick **6** 668
cast iron **7** 98
granite **23** 775
stone **6** 668; **18** *261*
wood **19** 303; **23** 775
types
close-eave **23** 773, *774*
five-element **23** 776
flower **23** 773
miniature **17** 270, 321; **23** 775
multi-storeyed **23** 776
multi-treasure **23** 776
pavilion **23** 773, *774*
storeyed pavilion **23** 773, *774*
stupa *see* STUPAS → types → pagoda-stupas
Pagoda Table **1** 890
pagoda tree **7** 45
Pagoh, Tomb of Alauddin Riayat Syah **20** 165
Pagomenos, Ioannis **8** 156

Pagot, François-Narcisse 23 509
Paguenin 8 684
Pahang 20 162, 163, 179
 Sultan Abu Bakar Museum 29 240
Pahari (Basohli) see:
 AMRIT PAL, Ruler
 KRIPAL PAL, Ruler
Pahari (Bilaspur) see:
 DIP CHAND, Ruler
Pahari (Chamba) see:
 BHURI SINGH, Ruler
 CHARAT SINGH, Ruler
 JIT SINGH, Ruler
 PRITHVI SINGH, Ruler
 RAJ SINGH, Ruler
 SHRI SINGH, Ruler
 UMED SINGH, Ruler
Pahari (Guler) see:
 BALDEV SINGH, Ruler
 DILIP SINGH, Ruler
Pahari (Jasrota) see:
 BALWANT SINGH, Prince
 MIAN ZORAWAR SINGH, Ruler
Pahari (Kangra) see:
 SANSAR CHAND, Maharaja
Pahari (Kulu) see:
 BAHADUR SINGH, Ruler
 PRITAM SINGH, Ruler
 SIDDHA PAL SINGH, Ruler
 TEDHI SINGH, Ruler
Pahari (Mandi) see:
 BAN SEN, Ruler
 SIDH SEN, Ruler
Pahari (Nurpur) see:
 JAGAT SINGH, Ruler
Pahari style painting see under INDIAN SUBCONTINENT → painting
Paharpur 15 279, 281; 16 101; 23 776–7*
 manuscripts 5 96
 reliefs 15 227, 719
 sculpture 15 413, 499
 Somapura Vihara 15 281, 571
 stucco 29 824
 temples 15 256
Pahery 9 823; 17 714, 714
Pahlava, Gondophares see GONDOPHARES, Ruler
Pahlavi see:
 FARAH, Empress
 MUHAMMAD RIZA, Shah
 RIZA, Shah
Pahlawuni, Abgharip 2 97
Pahlawuni, Grigor 2 97
Pahr see PARRI
Pahr, Franciscus 12 135; 31 692
Paiania, Vorres Museum of Greek Art 13 359
Pai Chü-i see BAI JUYI
Paignon-Dijonval 8 901; 23 777*; 33 345
Paik, Nam June 23 777–8*
 collaboration 27 215
 groups and movements 11 232; 18 63
 patrons and collectors 14 48
 works 10 688; 24 407; 29 97, 98; 32 420
Paillard, Victor 5 878; 11 42
Paillart 6 161
Pailleron, Edouard 27 839
Paillet, Alexandre-Joseph 6 81; 8 653; 11 663; 23 778*
 collaboration 23 778
 dealing 11 663
Paillet, Charles 23 778*
Paillet, Eugene 3 753
Paillet, Fernando 23 778–9*
Paillot de Montabert, Jacques-Nicolas 10 199; 23 779*; 25 581; 31 300
Pailós, Manuel 30 275
Pai Lo-t'ien see BAI LUOTIAN
pailou 23 779–80*, 780
Pailthorpe, Grace 30 22
Pai-ma see BAIMA
Paimio chairs see under CHAIRS → types
Paimio Sanatorium 11 92, 104; 14 783; 15 886, 886
Pain, George Richard 16 10
Pain, James (1779-1877) 16 10
Pain, John 23 780
Paine, James (1717-89) 23 780–82*
 assistants 30 59
 patrons and collectors 2 576; 6 117, 515; 8 281; 22 153; 24 390
 personal collection 7 171
 works 10 233; 11 39; 17 476; 20 867, 868; 23 781; 29 835
Paine, James (1745-1829) 23 782
Painshill Park (Surrey) 10 225; 12 130; 23 782*
Painsun, Louis-Simon 9 71
Paintbox see MALKASTEN
paintboxes 23 788–9*
paint containers 9 791; 23 787–8*
 bladders 4 113; 23 787, 787
 bottles 23 787
 mestiche 11 763
 paint tubes 23 378, 787, 787–8
 shells 23 787
 syringes 23 787, 787
painted enamel see under ENAMEL → techniques
Painted Grey ware see under POTTERY → wares
Painted Stoa see under ATHENS → Agora
Painter, Hal 31 661
Painter-Graveurs of America 25 629
painters
 historical and regional traditions
  England 5 656
  Greece, ancient 13 547–9
  Inca 29 135
  Indian subcontinent 15 207, 550*
  Japan 17 28–9, 154, 168–71
  Korea 18 258
  Romanesque 26 656–7*
  South America, Pre-Columbian 29 135
 types
  drapery 9 211–12*
Painters' Atelier 22 178
Painters Eleven 5 292, 568, 571; 23 790–91*; 31 177
 members 19 878; 27 121; 31 231
Painters' Guild 16 780
painters' guilds see under GUILDS → types
painters' palettes see under PALETTES → types
Painter-Stainers' Company see under LONDON → livery companies
Painter-Stainer's Cup 10 336
painting 14 869; 15 562
 cleaning 7 727; 29 53; 32 4
 collections see under COLLECTIONS → types
 conservation 5 657–8*; 7 727, 737–9*, 738; 17 209; 24 569
  China 1 580
  Italy 7 738–9
  Japan 17 208–10
 display 7 562; 9 11–20*; 19 351; 22 355, 356; 25 279
  Austria 9 19; 14 191; 22 356
  Belgium 9 15–16, 22
  China 1 580–81
  England 9 16–17, 17, 18–19, 26; 10 678
  France 9 14, 18, 22; 10 676; 24 139
  Germany 9 18; 22 362
  Greece, ancient 7 561; 9 13
  Italy 9 14–15, 15; 22 357; 26 775
  Japan 1 581–2; 17 166, 347
  Netherlands, the 9 15
  Rome, ancient 9 13
painting
 display—cont.
  Russia 9 18
  Spain 9 15, 18
  see also hanging
 education see under EDUCATION (ART) → types
 forms
  acrylic 1 129–30*
   Aboriginal Australia 1 63, 63–4, 64
   Africa 1 432
   England 6 94
   Germany 25 153
   Spain 25 851
   United States of America 1 129; 7 680; 19 702; 32 862
   Zaïre 1 432
  bark 1 50–51*, 51, 58, 59, 59–60, 61, 63; 10 474
  cave see CAVE ART
  ceiling
   Austria 25 56; 26 24
   England 17 851
   France 9 417; 19 248
   Indian subcontinent 15 562, 645
   Italy 3 57, 97; 21 20; 26 837; 27 55; 30 355; 32 348
   Rome, ancient 27 55
   Scotland 28 234, 244, 245
   Tibet 15 562
  door panel 17 166, 175, 195–6, 208, 210, 790
  easel 7 562; 9 673, 674*; 21 388*; 29 665
  encaustic see ENCAUSTIC PAINTINGS
  finger 12 50, 51
  floor
   Bangladesh 3 169
   China 14 826
   Crete 21 660
   Egypt, ancient 9 898
   Islamic 16 251
   Minoan 21 660
   Rome, ancient 27 47
   Syria 16 251
  fresco see FRESCOES
  glass 8 911; 12 797–8*; 15 806
   Austria 12 798
   Belgium 32 151
   Germany 12 798
   Indian subcontinent 16 522
   Iran 16 522
   Islamic 16 522*
   Italy 12 798
   Rome, ancient 12 798
   Senegal 28 405–6*, 406
   Switzerland 12 798; 22 341
   Syria 12 798
  gouache 5 277; 33 379
  ink 15 850, 854
   Bangladesh 3 168
   Buddhism 14 62; 17 38–9; 18 *309
   China 15 853, 854; 17 168
   China: Ming period (1368-1644) 15 854; 19 514, 833; 28 587; 30 294; 33 478
   China: Song period (AD 960-1279) 20 107; 33 651
   China: 20th cent. 14 821, 826
   Japan 2 598; 17 163–4, 168–74*, 341, 423
   Japan: Buddhism 14 62; 17 38–9, 193
   Japan: Muromachi period (1333-1568) 17 169, 171, 172; 30 466
   Korea 18 323, 323–5, 326; 33 529
   Korea: 15th cent. 17 772; 18 316
   Korea: 16th cent. 18 51, 324
   Korea: 17th cent. 18 57, 317
   Korea: Buddhism 18 *309
   Neo-Confucianism 17 41
painting
 forms—cont.
  lorry 1 208; 2 146; 28 691, 692
  murals see MURALS
  oil see OIL PAINTINGS
  panel see PANEL PAINTINGS
  panorama see PANORAMAS
  sand 18 586; 22 558, 560, 590–91*, 592
  screen
   Buddhism 17 145
   China 28 296, 311
   conservation 17 210
   Edo period (1600-1868) 14 214; 17 309
   France 28 298
   Japan 17 153, 154–7, 155, 165, 166–7, 178, 208, 210, 780; 28 297
   Japan: Buddhism 17 145
   Japan: Edo period (1600-1868) 17 197, 789; 23 363, 593
   Japan: Heian period (AD 794-1185) 17 157
   Japan: Kamakura period (1185-1333) 17 156
   Japan: Kanō school 17 181, 182, 728
   Japan: Momoyama period (1568-1600) 17 175, 784, 786, 787
   Japan: Muromachi period (1333-1568) 1 776; 17 167; 28 494
   Japan: Nanban 17 181, 181–2*
   Japan: Rinpa 27 596
   Japan: yōfūga 17 183
  scroll 3 914, 915; 33 666
   Bangladesh 3 169
   Bhutan 3 914
   Buddhism: China 22 325
   Buddhism: Japan 5 119; 14 62; 17 149, 150, 158; 22 233
   Buddhism: Korea 18 305
   Buddhism: Mongolia 21 880
   Buddhism: Nepal 22 784
   Buddhism: Pure Land 5 119
   Buddhism: Tibet 30 829, 830, 831, 833, 834
   Central Asia, Eastern 6 306
   China: Confucianism 7 705
   China: Ming period (1368-1644) 6 807; 9 137, 381; 11 855; 15 854; 25 785; 32 841; 33 436, 438, 659
   China: Nanjing school 12 900
   China: Northern Song period (AD 960-1127) 33 650
   China: Qing period (1644-1911) 2 96; 6 543, 621; 7 624; 8 518, 520; 12 90; 14 723, 825; 17 592; 18 752; 19 469, 802; 21 802, 803; 22 460; 23 580; 25 73; 28 590; 32 844, 845; 33 643
   China: Song period (AD 960-1279) 6 784; 17 697; 19 301, 331, 370, 504; 20 107; 22 325; 33 319, 501, 647, 651
   China: Southern school 9 141; 13 738; 21 419
   China: Tang period (AD 618-907) 13 838; 14 136; 19 299; 32 849; 33 499, 662
   China: 11th cent. 12 87
   China: Yuan period (1279-1368) 6 805, 806; 7 IV1; 14 822, 823; 23 166, 167; 26 211; 32 846; 33 440
   China: 20th cent. 25 781
   Confucianism 7 705
   conservation 15 856
   Edo period (1600-1868) 17 216; 23 384
   India, Republic of 15 175
   Indian subcontinent 15 563, 643; 28 309, 311–12
painting
 forms
  scroll—cont.
   Indian subcontinent: Jainism 15 617
   Indian subcontinent: Nayaka 15 647
   Indonesia 15 801, 801
   Jainism 15 617
   Japan 17 165, 166, 167, 171, 176, 208, 209, 342; 28 311
   Japan: Buddhism 5 119; 14 62; 17 149, 150, 158; 22 233
   Japan: Edo period (1600-1868) 2 210; 14 703, 705; 16 785; 17 347, 438; 21 741; 32 896; 33 492, 561
   Japan: Heian period (AD 794-1185), ; 7 IV2, 3
   Japan: Kanō school 17 797
   Japan: Meiji period (1868-1912) 17 185
   Japan: Momoyama period (1568-1600) 17 783
   Japan: Muromachi period (1333-1568) 17 168, 169, 171; 30 466; 31 197, 252
   Japan: Nanga 31 698
   Japan: Taishō period (1912-26) 17 201; 31 137
   Java 28 310
   Korea 14 724; 23 439; 33 527, 531
   Korea: Buddhism 18 305
   Mongolia 21 880, 880
   Nepal 22 784
   Tibet 30 829, 831, 833, 834
  secco see SECCO PAINTINGS
  silicate 28 714*
  tomb
   Achaemenid 1 118
   Anatolia, ancient 1 118
   Bulgaria 5 150
   conservation 10 618
   Egypt, ancient 9 790, 791, 897, 898–903; 27 57; 32 802
   Etruscan 10 591, 594, 617–24*, 618, 619, 620, 621, 622, 623; 30 346; 32 118, 744
   Japan 17 142–4*, 144
   Korea 18 302, 318–19
   Mesoamerica, Pre-Columbian 21 230
   Rome, ancient 27 48–9, 57
   Zapotec 21 230
   see also WALL PAINTINGS
  vase
   Central Asia, Western 6 233
   Crete 8 154
   Cycladic 8 309; 30 712
   Cyprus, ancient 8 343–5*, 344, 347–9*
   Cyprus, ancient: Bronze Age 8 345, 345–6*
   Cyprus, ancient: Cypro-Archaic I 8 348
   Cyprus, ancient: Cypro-Geometric (c. 1050 -c. 750 BC) 8 346–7*
   Cyprus, ancient: Cypro-Geometric I 8 346, 347
   Cyprus, ancient: Cypro-Geometric III 8 347
   Cyprus, ancient: Prehistoric 8 343*, 343
   Etruscan 7 366; 10 591, 593, 594, 611–16, 614, 615, 616
   Greece, ancient 3 466; 9 247, 248; 10 591; 12 286; 13 485, 489, 583; 14 407; 16 830; 22 410, 410, 411, 513; 31 254; 32 26–7*
   Greece, ancient: 5th cent. BC 2 134; 32 44
   Greece, ancient: Attica 13 517–19*, 517, 518, 519, 520, 522, 523, 591; 29 396
   Khwarazm 6 233
   Maya 21 190

painting
forms
vase—cont.
Mesopotamia 21 *307*
Prehistoric art 8 *343*, 343*
wall *see* WALL PAINTINGS
watercolours *see* WATERCOLOURS
hanging 7 562; 9 11, 12–20*, *15*, *17*, *26*, 27; 17 347; 22 357, 358–9
see also display
historical and regional traditions
Aboriginal Australia 1 60–61, 63–4*; 2 752; 3 331
Afghanistan 1 208*
Africa 1 303, 380, 399–400, 425*, 430–31
United States of America 1 *426*
20th cent. 7 I2
African American art 1 *445*
Albania 1 539–41*
Algeria 1 634–6
Anglo-Saxon 2 72*, 74*
Angola 2 86–7*
Argentina 2 398–401*, *399*
Armenia (Europe) 2 429*, 431–3*
Australia 2 743–7*, 752*
Abstract art 2 *751*
20th cent. 4 *606*
Austria 2 790–92*, 796–8*, 817
Baroque 2 794–6*
Gothic 2 791–2*
Jugendstil 32 446
Renaissance 2 793–4*
Romanesque 2 790*
19th cent. 18 419
20th cent. 25 *864*
Azerbaijan 2 895–7*
Aztec 2 907*
Bactria 6 216; 28 722
Bahamas, the 3 61–3*, *62*
Bahrain 3 68–9*
Bali (Indonesia) 15 804, 806*, 807, 808–9*, 810, 812, *812*
Bangladesh 3 168*, *169*
Belarus' 3 527–30*
Belgium 3 551–62*, 564–5*, 596–7
Expressionism 24 *459*
Modernism 3 *563*
Surrealism 8 *700*; 20 *101*, *102*; 31 *51*
Symbolism (movement) 11 *450*; 18 *24*
19th cent. 3 562–4*; 10 *410*
Belize 3 623–4*
Benin Republic 3 *729*
Bolivia 4 261–4*
Bosnia 4 460–62*
Brazil 4 715*, 716–20*
Buddhism
Bhutan 3 914–15*
Central Asia 5 102
Central Asia, Eastern 6 302
China 6 776–85*, *780*, *781*; 9 *393*
Heian period (AD 794-1185) 17 *147*
Indian subcontinent 15 570, *570*
Japan 17 144–50*, 156–7, 158–9, 166, 168–71
Japan: Asuka-Hakuhō period (*c.* 552-710) 17 *151*
Japan: Daigo 18 *557*
Japan: Esoteric 18 *223*
Japan: Heian period (AD 794-1185) 17 *148*
Japan: Nara period (AD 710-94) 17 *146*
Japan: Ōbaku 17 183–4*
Japan: Pure Land 5 *118*; 17 38, 147–8
Japan: Zen 17 *169*, 194*
Korea 18 303–12*, *310*, *374*

painting
historical and regional traditions
Buddhism—cont.
Mongolia 21 *873*, *880*, 880–81*
Nepal 22 *782*
Sakyapa 30 832
Sri Lanka 29 466
Thailand 30 612–13*, *613*, *617*
Tibet 5 *104*; 30 *810*, 827–35*
Bulgaria 5 150–51*, 152–5*
Burma 5 242*, 246–7*; 18 605
Byzantine 9 561*, 621–30; 19 351, 356
Bulgaria 5 152
Cambodia 5 501–2*
Cameroon 5 523–4*
Canada 5 564–7*, 568–9*
Native North Americans 22 597–8*, *666*
19th cent. 5 *575*
20th cent. 5 *567*, *568*, *569*, *846*; 13 *712*; 22 *38*
Caribbean Islands 5 750–52*
Carolingian 5 797*; 12 381–2
Catalonia 5 *909*
Central African Republic 6 *179*
Central Asia 5 102
Central Asia, Eastern 6 301–5*, 314
Central Asia, Western 6 216, 222*, 230; 16 160
Chile 5 188; 6 595–9*
China 1 580–81; 6 631, 638, 735, 772*, 773–82*, 785–92*, 795–814*, 821–5*, 826*; 7 13, 157, 158, 632; 10 777; 25 72; 30 559
Blue-and-green style 6 789
Buddhism 6 776–85*, *780*, *781*; 9 *393*
Communism 6 *774*, 774–5, 811
Confucianism 6 803, 807, 808; 7 632
Daoism 6 785–7*, *786*, 823, 824
export 6 624
Han period (206 BC-AD 220) 6 633–4, 636
Ming period (1368-1644) 6 *802*, *810*; 19 857; 33 *420*
Northern and Southern Dynasties (AD 310-589) 6 887
Northern school 19 299
Prehistoric 6 773, 876
Qing period (1644-1911) 6 *40*; 18 605; 28 *554*
Song period (AD 960-1279) 1 580; 6 *800*; 7 *36*; 10 776; 19 857, *857*, *858*
Southern school (China) 7 632
Tang period (AD 618-907) 6 *809*, 888; 30 288
20th cent. 6 *775*; 19 *422*; 33 *641*
Christianity 10 568–73*
Cistercian Order 7 352
Colombia 7 601, 607*, 608–10*, *610*
Communism 6 *774*, 774–5, 811
Confucianism 6 803, 807, 808; 7 632
Coptic 7 822–4*
Costa Rica 8 *17*, 17–18*
Côte d'Ivoire 8 22
Crete 8 156; 25 330
Croatia 8 177–9*
Cuba (Caribbean) 8 229, 233–4*, *234*; 18 *665*, *834*
Cyprus 8 364–5*; 25 330
Czech Republic 8 388–94*
Futurism 18 *493*
Gothic 13 151–2*; 30 706
Orphism 23 *569*
Realism (style) 8 *392*
Romanesque 8 388

painting
historical and regional traditions
Czech Republic—cont.
Surrealism 8 *393*
Daoism 6 785–7*, *786*, 823, 824
Denmark 8 729–31*, 732–7*
Symbolism (movement) 33 *214*
19th cent. 26 *525*
20th cent. 8 *736*; 17 *659*; 22 *151*; 24 *316*
Dominica 2 149
Dominican Republic 9 117–18*, *118*
Early Christian (*c.* AD 250-843) 9 561*, 621–4; 16 653–4*; 19 356
Ecuador 9 712–14*
Egypt 7 822–4*; 9 765–6*
Egypt, ancient 9 897–903*, *898*; 10 5, 26; 12 *226*
El Salvador 10 154
England 5 656; 10 242–55*, 256–8*; 23 *790*; 33 *331*
Abstract art 24 *229*
Anglo-Saxon 2 72*
Constructivism 10 *257*
Cubism 23 *104*
Gothic 13 147*, 152–3*
Japonisme 33 *138*
Jewish art 17 *576*, 577–8*
Op art 23 *449*
Post-Impressionism 10 *256*; 19 *590*
Vorticism 32 *701*
18th cent. 11 *859*
19th cent. 8 *440*; 26 *69*
20th cent. 3 *28*; 4 *293*; 10 *258*; 14 *612*; 19 *288*; 22 *523*, *525*; 27 *562*
Eritrea 10 567–74*
Estonia 10 538–40*, *540*
Ethiopia 10 567–74*, *571*, *573*, *575*
Etruscan 12 287; 16 *652*, 652–3
Faroe Islands 10 813*
Finland 11 93–7*, *97*; 12 *20*
France 11 528*, 529–31*, 533–53*; 24 *720*
Abstract art 1 *74*; 8 *657*; 9 *334*; 12 *806*; 14 *206*; 20 *816*, *831*; 25 *148*; 32 *577*; 33 *305*
Abstraction-Création 1 *89*
Cubism 4 *676*, *677*; 8 *244*; 9 *355*; 12 *806*; 13 *670*; 18 *636*; 19 *77*; 21 *364*; 24 *719*
Dada 8 *435*; 11 *549*; 24 *709*
Gothic 11 530–31*; 13 147*, 153–5*
Impressionism 9 *288*
Jewish art 17 577*
juste-milieu style 12 *809*
Modern Movement 18 *118*
naive art 27 *262*
Orientalism 20 *420*
Pittura Metafisica 8 *603*
Post-Impressionism 7 *675*; 25 *357*
Purism 23 *694*; 24 *144*; 25 *739*
Realism (style) 19 *381*
Romanesque 11 529–30*
Surrealism 4 *700*; 10 *467*, *469*; 30 *20*, *292*
Symbolism (movement) 30 *170*
Synthetism 28 *484*
Tachism 20 *816*
19th cent. 24 *138*, *139*, *713*
20th cent. 3 *127*; 8 *604*, *774*; 9 *335*; 10 *533*; 11 *546*, *550*; 19 *79*, *81*; 20 *591*; 21 *706*, *707*; 24 *224*, *715*, *718*, *721*, *723*; 27 *239*; 31 *775*
Gabon 11 879*
Georgia 12 323–4*, 325–8*

painting
historical and regional traditions—cont.
Germany 12 381–7*, 389–94*, 395–7*
Abstract art 17 *763*, *765*, *767*; 22 *379*, *701*
Art informel 12 397
Baroque 12 389–90*
Carolingian 12 381–2
Dada 8 *434*; 12 395
Expressionism 3 *478*; 10 *694*; 12 *395*, 395; 22 *257*; 23 *187*; 24 *311*
Gothic 12 383*; 13 151
Gothic: Early Gothic 12 382–3
Gothic: Late Gothic 12 385*
Gothic: Zackenstil 13 142–3
Jesuit Order 12 389
Jewish art 17 578–9*
Mannerism 3 *103*
Nazism 22 711*
Neo-classicism 12 391
Neue Sachlichkeit 3 *802*; 12 396
Ottonian 12 382
Realism (style) 12 393–4; 19 *97*
Renaissance 12 385–7*
Rococo 12 390–91*
Romanesque 12 382
Romanticism 12 393
Socialist Realism 12 397
19th cent. 20 *405*
20th cent. 3 *324*, *803*; 12 *397*, *398*; 14 *327*, *623*; 20 *12*; 23 *357*; 25 *841*; 26 *355*; 28 *177*; 32 *695*
Ghana 12 *508*, 508–9*
Gothic 13 126–30*, 132–9*, 143–4*
Austria 2 791–2*
Channel style 13 140–42*
Croatia 8 178
Czech Republic 13 151–2*; 30 706
England 13 147*, 152–3*
France 11 530–31*; 13 *142*, 147*, 153–5*
Germany 12 382–3*, 385*; 13 142–3, 151
Holy Roman Empire (before 1648) 13 142–3*, 151–2*
Iceland 13 143
International Gothic 13 155–6*
Italy 13 133, 138, 146, 149*, 155; 16 661
Late Gothic 23 256
Norway 13 143; 23 223
Poland 25 101, *102*
Scandinavia 13 143*
Spain 13 143–4*, 149–50*; 29 275–6
Transitional style 13 139–40*
Greece 13 351–3*
Greece, ancient 2 217; 13 375*, 545–7*, 592; 16 652; 25 44; 30 715
Archaic 13 545*, 549–53*
Classical 13 550–51*
Geometric (*c.* 900-*c.* 700 BC) 13 549–50*
Hellenistic 13 *544*, 551–3*
Orientalizing style 13 549–53*, *550*
Guatemala 10 154; 13 760, 763–6*, *765*
Guyana 13 876–7*
Haiti 1 425*; 14 58*, *59*
Herzegovina 4 460–62*
Hinduism 14 *556*, *559*; 15 *79*, *217*, 599, *602*, *622*, *628*, *633*, *673*, 674
Hivaoa 12 *193*
Holy Roman Empire (before 1648) 13 142–3*, 151–2*
Honduras 14 714–16*
Hong Kong 14 721–2*
Hungary 14 898–902*
Expressionism 8 *806*

painting
historical and regional traditions
Hungary—cont.
Great Plains painting 13 332–3*
20th cent. 8 *226*; 14 *902*
Iceland 13 143; 15 69–71*
Inca 15 162
India, Republic of 15 *79*, 169–71*, 175, 178
Indian subcontinent 7 *616*; 15 206, 228, 230, 543*, 548*, 549–51*, 553*, 577*, 634*, 643, 656–8*, 673–4*; 28 309; 30 559–60
Andhra Pradesh 15 647–8, *650*, 650
Bengal 15 635*, *635*
Bihar 15 *570*
Bilaspur 15 624*
Buddhism 15 570, *570*
Bundi (Rajasthan) 15 603–7*
Chamba (i) (India) 15 625–7*, *626*
Company painting 2 306; 5 419; 8 676; 15 651–5*, *654*, 724
Deccan 15 637–42*, 643*
Deogarh 15 597–601*, *599*, *600*, *601*, 643
Garhwal 15 627–8*, *628*
Golconda 15 640–42*
Gujarat 15 565
Guler 15 *217*, 628–9*, *629*
Hinduism 14 *556*, *559*; 15 *217*, 599, *602*, *622*, *628*, *633*, *673*, 674
Islamic 12 *74*
Jainism 15 *225*, 563–6, *566*, 674
Jammu 15 *630*, 630–31*
Jasrota 15 *631*, 631–2*
Kachchh 15 617–18*, *618*
Kangra 15 *217*, *632*, 632–3*
Kashmir 15 650–51
Kerala 15 650
Kishangarh 15 611–13*, *613*
Kota 15 605–6
Kulu 15 620–21*, *621*
Malwa 15 597, *602*, 602–3*, *603*
Mandi 15 *633*, 633–4*
Mankot 15 621–2*, *622*
Maratha period 15 647
Marwar 15 613–16*, *614*
Mughal 15 575, 577–8*, 584–7*, 588–93*
Mughal: 16th cent. 1 *26*; 10 *816*, *818*; 15 *231*, *578*, *716*; 17 *922*
Mughal: 17th cent. 12 *74*; 13 *235*; 14 *217*; 18 *657*
Mughal: 18th cent. 15 *591*; 22 *438*
Mughal: Sub-imperial 15 593–7*, *594*, *596*
Mysore 15 649
Nurpur 15 *623*, 623–4*
Orissa 15 635–6*
Pahari 7 VI1; 14 611; 15 618–19*, *620*, 620–22*, *621*, *623*, 623–4*, 625–9*, *626*, *629*, *630*, 630–34*, *631*, *632*; 22 *438*
Punjab 10 485
Rajasthan 7 VI2; 10 485; 15 596, 597–601*, *599*, *600*, *601*, *608*, 608–16*, *610*, *611*, *613*, *614*, 617–18*, *618*, 740
Rajput 15 211, 597–601, 603–7*, *608*, 608–11*, *610*, *611*, 613–16*, *613*, 617–18*, *618*, 643
Shekhavati 15 609*, 611*
Timurid 15 638
15th cent. 15 569
16th cent. 15 574–6*, *575*

painting
historical and regional traditions
Indian subcontinent—cont.
18th cent. **15** 648
19th cent. **5** _420_
20th cent. **15** _656_
Indonesia **15** 804–9*, _807_, _808_
Iran **15** 898–9*; **16** 160, 331, 337; **21** 507
15th cent. **7** V
17th cent. **16** _464_
Iran, ancient **15** 922*
Iraq **16** 1–2, 434
Ireland **16** 12–18*, _17_
Islamic **16** 250*, 487, _537_
Algeria **1** 634
Central Asia, Western **16** 160
Indian subcontinent **12** _74_
Iran **7** V; **16** 160, 331, 337, _464_
Iraq **16** 434
Italy **16** 525–6
Ottoman **16** 221, _537_
Sicily **16** 525–6
Turkey **16** 221, 497
Israel **16** 567*, _567_; **17** 579–80*
Italy **6** 1–5*; **7** 627; **16** 652–7*, 676–8*
Baroque **16** 668–76*
Early Christian (_c._ AD 250–843) **16** 653–4*
Etruscan **12** 287; **16** _652_, 652–3
Futurism **3** _116_; **4** _200_; **11** _868_; **27** _446_; **28** _507_
Gothic **13** 133, 138, 146, 149*, 155; **16** 661
Greece, ancient **16** 652
Islamic **16** 525–6
Mannerism **12** _671_; **16** 668*
Renaissance **16** 657–68*
Roman **16** 653
social realism **21** _473_
Spazialismo **11** _282_
13th cent. **9** _258_
18th cent. **8** _160_
20th cent. **16** 679–83*, _680_, _682_
Jainism **15** _225_, 563–6, _566_, 674
Jamaica **16** 883–5*
Japan **1** 581–2; **10** 777; **17** 99, 139–40*, 144–50*, 163*, 181*, 183*, 198*, 208–10, 342; **30** 559
Buddhism **17** 144–50*, _146_, _147_, _148_, _151_, 156–7, 158–9, 166, 168–71; **18** _223_
Buddhism: Daigo **18** _557_
Buddhism: Ōbaku **17** 183–4*
Buddhism: Pure Land **5** _118_; **17** 38, 147–8
Buddhism: Zen **17** _169_, 194*
Edo period (1600–1868) **17** 164–5*, _792_; **31** _200_
fūzokuga **17** 174–6*, _175_, 782
genpitsu **17** 790
Heisei period (1989-) **17** _208_
Jesuit Order **17** 182–3
Kanga **17** 166, 794
karae **17** 156, 162*
kasen'e **17** 828–30*, _829_
Meiji period (1868-1912) **18** 605; **28** 600, _600_
Momoyama period (1568-1600) **17** 163–4*, 319
Muromachi period (1333-1568) **17** 163*
Nanban **17** 22, 181–2*
Nanga **17** 23, 165, 188–92*, 198–9, _199_, 437, 439–40; **18** 542; **25** 73; **30** 29
Nanga: Edo period (1600-1868) **17** _190_, _191_, 194, 285; **27** 596; **33** 560
naturalism **17** 194–8*, _195_, _197_
Nihonga **17** 23, 166, 180, 198, 199–202*, 440; **31** 253
Nihonga: Meiji period (1868-1912) **17** 420; **31** 253
painting
historical and regional traditions
Japan—cont.
Nihonga: Taishō period (1912-26) **17** _201_, _202_; **22** 328
onnae **17** 159
otokoe **17** 159
ōtsue **17** 44, 345, _347_, 347–8*
Rinpa **14** 702; **17** 23, 165, 166, 177–80*, _178_, _180_, 194, 293; **23** 363, 365, 554; **30** 52, 378
Shinto **17** 32–3, 151–3*; **28** 610–11*
Shōwa period (1926-89) **17** _206_, _207_
Taishō period (1912-26) **17** _205_
ukiyoe **14** 577; **16** 802; **17** 23, 165, _176_, 194, 200; **28** 311
wakan **17** _781_, 794
Yamatoe **14** 302; **17** 153–61*, _155_, _156_, _158_, _161_, 163, 165–8*, _167_, _168_, 423; **18** 396; **28** 625
yōfūga **17** 181, 182–3*, 186–8*, _187_
Yōga **17** 23, 202, _203_, 203–5*, _204_, 420, 440
Zenga **5** 120; **14** 61; **17** 39, 165, _192_, _193_, 194*; **28** 408
20th cent. **17** 205–8*
Java **15** 804, 805–6*, 807–8*, _808_, 810
Jesuit Order **4** 261; **8** 178; **12** 389; **17** 182–3
Jewish art **17** 575–80*, _578_
Jordan **17** 654
Kazakhstan **17** 867*
Kenya **17** 906–7*, _907_
Korea **18** 302–3*, 315–17*, 318–27*
Buddhism **18** 303–12*, _310_, _374_
20th cent. **18** _326_
Kuwait **18** 541*
Kyrgyzstan **18** 568–9*
Laos **18** 770*
Latvia
Lebanon **19** 7–8
Lesotho **19** 242
Liberia **19** 310*
Libya **19** 324
Lithuania **19** 496, _498_
Macedonia (i) (Greece) **13** 546
Macedonia (ii) (former Yugoslavia) **19** _884_, 884–5*
Malaysia **20** 171*, 172*, 182
Mali **20** 199*
Malta (Republic of) **20** 213*; **25** 563
Mangbetu **1** 425
Manichaeism **6** 305
Mexico **21** 385–90*, _389_
Moldova **21** 811–12*
Mongolia **21** _873_, 880–81*, _880_
Montenegro **22** 16*, 17–18*, _19_
Morocco **22** 128–9
Mozambique **22** _244_, 244–5*
Native North Americans **14** _477_; **22** _63_, 560*, 587–99*, _588_, _594_
Canada **22** 597–8*, _666_
United States of America **22** 593–7*
Nazism **22** 711*
Ndebele **1** 425
Nepal **22** 777–8*, 779–83*, _782_, 784–7*
Netherlands, the **22** 832–4*, 839–45*, 846–54*; **30** 394
Abstract art **22** _853_
Abstraction-Création **21** _854_
Cubism **21** _853_
Modern Movement **9** _63_
Neo-plasticism **22** _749_
Post-Impressionism **7** _674_
Renaissance **22** 836–8*
painting
historical and regional traditions
Netherlands, the—cont.
14th cent. **7** 627
15th cent. **22** 834–6*
17th cent. **3** _495_
19th cent. **20** _872_
20th cent. **2** _230_; **7** _489_; **19** _32_
New Zealand **23** 57–62*, _61_
Nicaragua **23** 81–2*
Nigeria **23** 135–7*
Northern Ireland **16** _40_, 40–41*
Norway **23** 223–7*
Gothic **13** 143; **23** 223
Romanesque **23** 223
Symbolism (movement) **22** _292_
19th cent. **9** _751_
Op art ,
Ottoman **16** 221, _537_
Ottonian **12** 382; **23** 649*
Pacific Islands **23** 721–2*, 723
Pakistan **23** 799–801*, _801_
Panama **23** 904–5*, _905_
Papua New Guinea **23** 721–2*
Paraguay **24** 97*, 98–100*
Pauline Order **8** 178
Peru **24** 506–11*
Philippines **24** 620–23*
Poland **9** 74; **25** 101–3*, 104–6*, 107–8*
Constructivism **29** _794_
Gothic **25** 101, _102_
Symbolism (movement) **21** _52_; **24** _12_
Portugal **25** 295–300*, 511
Post-Byzantine **8** 156; **25** 330
Prehistoric art **25** 491, 493*, 514
China **6** 773
Neolithic **25** 509*, 511
Portugal **25** 511
Sardinia **27** 834
Puerto Rico **18** _833_; **25** 701–2*
Qatar **25** 776–7*
Romanesque **26** 648*
Austria **2** 790*
Czech Republic **8** 388
France **11** 529–30*
Germany **12** 382
Norway **23** 223
Spain **29** 275; **30** 368
Romania **26** 710–11*, 712–13*, 714*, _715_, 715–16*
Rome, ancient **16** 653; **25** 43–4; **26** 860; **27** 16, 78*
Russia **23** 837; **27** 381–2*, 387*, 388–93*, 394–8*
Abstract art **12** _895_
Cubo-Futurism **20** _193_
Expressionism **27** _396_
Futurism **12** _893_
Jewish art **17** 576–7*
Post-Byzantine **25** 330
Rayism **26** _41_
Realism (style) **26** _218_, _219_
Socialist Realism **28** _918_
Suprematism **19** _476_; **20** _194_; **25** _239_; **26** _504_; **30** _7_
19th cent. **19** _277_; **32** _736_
20th cent. **6** _385_; **10** _699_; **20** _851_; **27** _433_
Ryūkyū Islands **27** 470*
St Vincent **2** 149
Sardinia **27** 834, 836
Scandinavia **13** 143*
Scotland **28** 233–40*, _239_
Senegal **28** 405*
Serbia **28** 445*, 450–52*
Shakers **28** 540–41*
Shinto **17** 32–3, 151–3*; **28** 610–11*
Sicily **16** 525–6
Sierra Leone **28** 691–2*, _692_
Singapore **28** 774*
Slovakia **28** 850–54*
Slovenia **28** 860–61*
Sogdiana **6** 230; **28** 722
painting
historical and regional traditions—cont.
South Africa **29** 107*, 110*
Spain **29** 274–8*, 282–5*
Art informel **30** _336_
Baroque **29** 278–82*
Gothic **13** 149–50*; **29** 275–6
Noucentisme **3** _219_
Romanesque **29** 275; **30** 368
Surrealism **8** _466_, _467_; **9** _293_
16th cent. **3** 844
19th cent. **19** _763_
20th cent. **13** _6_; **29** 285–7*, _287_
Sri Lanka **29** 466–8*, _467_, 479
Sudan **29** 896–7*
Sumatra **15** 804
Surinam **30** 15–16*
Sweden **30** 75–80*, 81–2*
19th cent. **17** _8_
20th cent. **30** _82_
Switzerland **30** 129*
Abstract art **1** _77_; **18** _112_
Baroque **30** 132*
Neo-classicism **30** 132–3*
Renaissance **30** 131*
Rococo **30** 132*
Romanticism **30** 133–4*
Symbolism (movement) **30** 134*
16th cent. **14** _438_
20th cent. **16** _788_; **19** _541_; **30** _134_, 134–5*
Syria **30** _178_
Taiwan **30** 246–50*, _249_
Tajikistan **30** 252–3*
Tanzania **30** 301*
Teke **30** 420*
Thailand **30** 612*, 613–14*, 616–17*
Buddhism **30** 612–14*, _613_, _617_
Tibet **5** _104_; **22** _234_, 785; **30** _810_, 827–35*
Trinidad and Tobago **2** 149; **31** 335–6*, _337_
Tunisia **31** 424–6*
Turkey **16** 221, 497, _537_; **31** 453*
Turkmenistan **31** 459*
Uganda **31** 528*
Ukraine **31** 553*, 554–6*, 557–8*
20th cent. **4** 605; **31** _559_
United Arab Emirates **31** 584–5*
United States of America **31** 599–610*
Abstract art **1** _549_; **2** _857_; **8** _635_, _871_; **17** _892_; **21** _856_; **26** _126_; **31** _605_
Abstract Expressionism **1** _86_, _87_; **8** _634_; **11** _730_; **13** _215_; **14** _633_; **18** _133_; **22** _206_; **23** _29_; **27** _220_, _221_; **29** _663_
African American art **1** _445_
Cuba (Caribbean) **18** _834_
Japonisme **33** _138_
Jewish art **17** 578*, _578_
Native North Americans **22** 593–7*
Op art **7** VIII2(c)
Photorealism **24** _687_
Pop art **7** VII2(b), VIII1(b); **12** _217_; **19** _328_
Post-modernism **25** _360_
Post-painterly Abstraction **19** _725_
Precisionism **25** _462_
Puerto Rico **18** _833_
Realism (style) **23** _297_
Surrealism **20** _838_
19th cent. **22** _672_
painting
historical and regional traditions
United States of America—cont.
20th cent. **1** _426_, _773_; **2** _596_; **8** _578_, _709_, _903_; **13** _12_, _865_; **17** _615_; **18** _94_; **19** _410_; **21** _795_; **25** _166_; **26** _29_; **30** _173_; **31** _68_, _606_
Uruguay **31** 754–6*
Uzbekistan **31** 782–3*
Venetian Empire **32** 159–60
Venezuela **32** 172–6*, _175_
Vietnam **32** 481*, 482–4*, _484_, 488
Wales **32** 784–6*
Zaïre **1** 430; **33** 595*, _596_, _597_
Zambia **33** 602–3*
Zimbabwe **33** 678
historiography _see under_ HISTORIOGRAPHY → types
lighting **7** 732; **9** 13
materials
bark **15** 806
beetles **15** 618
canvas **5** 653, 655–7*
copper **7** 814*
cotton **5** 501
emulsions **10** 191
frames **9** 14; **11** 372
gesso **6** 779; **13** 139
glass (inlay) **13** 139
glass (support) _see_ forms → glass
glazes **12** 802; **24** 789
glues **17** 140; **18** 302
gold **7** 627; **13** 139; **18** 770; **19** 351, 352
gold leaf **17** 140
grounds **13** 706–9
hands **25** 478
hides **22** 592, _592_
inks **15** _850_, 853–4*; **17** 140
inlays **32** 488
inscriptions **6** 774, 777, 805
ivory **15** 724
lacquer **7** 13; **23** 837; **28** 600, _600_
linen **5** 655
mica **15** 653, 724
mounts (works on paper and scrolls) **1** 580; **22** _234_
pads **25** 477
paper **5** 501; **15** 806; **17** 209; **24** 49–50*
parchment **24** 106, 107
pastiglia **13** 139
pens **10** 5
pigments **9** 623; **13** 137; **17** 140*, 142, 346
plaster **9** 623
plastic **25** 24–5*
projectors **24** 668
silk **5** 501, 656; **6** 773; **17** 139, 161, 209; **18** 305; **19** _857_, _858_
silver **17** 319
silver leaf **17** 140
size **17** 140
tempera **8** _823_
textiles **15** 599
tin **13** 139
varnishes **2** 217; **32** 2–3, _4_
washes **15** 854
waxes **33** 5*
wood **15** 806
restoration **7** 737–9*, _738_; **17** 209–10; **24** 569; **28** 340
schools _see_ COLLECTIONS → types → classified; SCHOOLS OF PAINTING
status **1** 102, 662–3*
technical examination **2** 835; **30** 393, 395, 397, 400, 409–10*
techniques
alla prima **20** 258
cartoons (drawings) **5** 898
dead colouring **8** 585*

painting
techniques—cont.
enlarging 24 668
faux boix 23 789
faux marbre 23 789
frottis *see* FROTTIS
gilding 12 624–5*; 13 139
graining 23 789–90
hand prints 25 478
hatching 13 138
highlighting 13 138
incising 13 139
inlays 13 139
laying in *see* dead colouring
linen 12 226
marbling 23 789–90, 790
modelling 13 139; 19 352
punching 12 625; 13 139; 25 730, 730–31*
relining 5 657; 26 142*
sgraffito 13 139
spatter painting 30 90
spraying 25 478
stencilling 18 303
stippling 6 569; 23 789
transfer (conservation) 31 281–3*
verre églomisé 13 139
theories *see under* THEORIES (ART)
types
action *see* ACTION PAINTING
allegorical
Austria: Baroque 1 659; 5 774; 29 790
Austria: Expressionism 28 90
Austria: Jugendstil 2 797; 18 130
Austria: 18th cent. 25 56
Belgium 1 663
Belgium: Baroque 17 4, 652
Belgium: Mannerism 21 358
Belgium: Renaissance 4 898, 899, 901, 902, 903, 906, 907; 11 222
Belgium: 16th cent. 11 221; 25 381
Belgium: 17th cent. 4 912; 17 919; 32 704
Bulgaria 5 154
Croatia 8 179
Czech Republic 1 6; 29 429
England: Baroque 26 322
England: Pre-Raphaelitism 5 267; 15 25, 27
England: 16th cent. 15 81
England: 19th cent. 32 922
England: 20th cent. 29 384
France: Baroque 4 125; 19 23
France: Fauvism 20 823
France: Neo-classicism 7 384; 32 429
France: Realism 8 53
France: Rococo 11 539; 19 142
France: Romanticism 1 660; 15 88
France: Symbolism (movement) 5 880
France: 19th cent. 20 891
France: 20th cent 19 82
Germany: Expressionism 3 480
Germany: Neue Sachlichkeit 12 396
Germany: Renaissance 8 117
Germany: Rococo 1 785
Germany: Romanticism 11 781; 22 379
Germany: 16th cent. 19 132
Germany: 17th cent. 32 230
Germany: 19th cent. 23 676; 29 847
Holy Roman Empire (before 1648) 1 6
Hungary 8 780
Italy 1 663
Italy: Baroque 12 764; 24 341; 26 321; 28 39; 30 860

painting
types
allegorical—cont.
Italy: Divisionism 25 567
Italy: Mannerism 1 656; 4 857; 12 668; 31 32, 33; 32 221
Italy: Renaissance 1 655, 656; 4 494, 495; 9 184; 15 86; 25 898; 27 848; 29 362; 32 14
Italy: 14th cent. 19 670; 23 743
Italy: 16th cent. 11 52; 23 877
Italy: 17th cent. 4 539; 11 40; 21 89
Italy: 18th cent. 6 125; 29 889
Italy: 19th cent. 23 851; 24 345, 346
Netherlands, the: Baroque 1 657, 658; 11 170; 14 617; 33 80
Netherlands, the: Early Netherlandish style 4 450, 451
Netherlands, the: 16th cent. 22 838
Netherlands, the: 17th cent. 15 96
Netherlands, the: 18th cent. 19 101
Poland 4 148; 20 188; 27 451
Portugal 25 298
Russia 18 792; 32 246
Spain 12 924; 24 392
Sweden 30 78
Switzerland 14 615; 24 564
United States of America 33 93
all-over 1 673*
see also drip
animal subjects *see* ANIMAL SUBJECTS
architectural 2 338–43*; 10 739
Belgium 2 340–41*; 14 785; 32 726
Brazil 30 348; 32 690
China 6 687
Denmark 27 144
England 2 339; 28 648
France: Impressionism 21 865
France: Romanticism 8 449
France: Troubadour style 13 309
France: 18th cent. 26 448, 449
Germany 4 136; 14 664
Italy 2 338, 338–9, 343; 26 898
Netherlands, the 2 341–2*
Netherlands, the: Neo-Impressionism 21 852
Netherlands, the: Post-Impressionism 12 861
Netherlands, the: 17th cent. 2 341; 14 504, 796; 22 844; 27 510; 29 592; 33 267
Netherlands, the: 19th cent. 4 444
see also CAPRICCIOS; *vedute*
bamboo
China 6 802, 803–4, 805, 806, 807, 807, 818, 820, 823, 823; 33 75, 653, 654
Japan 3 144
Korea 33 529, 579
battle 3 387–90*
Belgium 32 722
England 3 389–90, 390
France: Baroque 19 20, 22
France: 19th cent. 11 370; 21 412
France: 20th cent 8 605
Germany 12 388
Indian subcontinent 15 589
Italy 3 387, 388; 22 130
Italy: Baroque 19 309
Italy: Renaissance 6 2; 31 515
Italy: 16th cent. 10 762
Native North Americans 22 592

painting
types
battle—cont.
Netherlands, the 3 388; 11 447; 22 849; 33 390
Spain 5 737
Sweden 19 136
Venezuela 32 178
see also MILITARY SCENES
bird-and-flower
China 6 798, 799, 801, 802, 803, 804
Japan 17 165, 184–6, 200
Japan: Edo period (1600-1868) 17 164
Japan: Kanō school 17 790, 795; 31 253
Japan: Momoyama period (1568-1600) 17 786
Korea 18 315–17*, 376
Korea: 15th cent. 18 316
Korea: 17th cent. 18 317
bodegones 4 209–12*, 210, 211; 12 289; 32 126
boundary 32 851
cabinet pictures 1 663; 5 345, 351–4*; 12 291; 18 522
Belgium 5 351–3; 9 15–16
Belgium: 17th cent. 3 108; 5 351, 353; 11 442, 718; 30 463
Czech Republic 5 352
France 24 138
Italy 18 871
Netherlands, the 5 351; 6 77; 9 15, 16
United States of America 22 149
camaïeu see GRISAILLE PAINTINGS
colour field 1 78; 7 631, 636*; 13 616; 21 776; 23 7, 30; 27 219; 31 52
England 10 258
Pakistan 23 799
South Africa 29 109
United States of America , ; 1 86; 7 III2, VII2(d); 23 184, 404; 31 608, 608
see also ABSTRACT EXPRESSIONISM
conversation pieces 7 784–7*; 33 217
Belgium 3 561; 22 864
England 7 784, 785–7*; 10 249; 21 148, 149; 33 695
England: Rococo 33 694
England: 18th cent. 7 785, 786; 10 277
France 30 XIV1
Netherlands, the 7 510, 784; 19 644
Portugal 28 431
United States of America 24 302
court
China 6 635–6, 789, 790, 797, 799, 800, 801, 803, 810, 814–18*, 815
drapery 9 211–12*; 25 281
drip 1 673; 14 633
see also all-over
fancy pictures 10 785–6*, 786; 12 294; 21 149; 26 276
fêtes champêtres 11 34–9*, 35, 38; 18 693; 20 255; 31 71
fêtes galantes 11 34, 36–7, 37, 368; 12 292, 638; 18 711; 22 85; 26 83; 32 914, 915, 915–17, 916
flower 11 224–30*; 14 626; 29 666, 668
Belgium 4 915; 28 364; 29 665
Buddhism 6 804
China 6 631, 803, 804, 805, 806, 807, 818
China: Buddhism 6 804
China: Daoism 6 804

painting
types
flower—cont.
China: Ming period (1368-1644) 12 49; 33 320
China: Qing period (1644-1911) 28 759; 33 576
China: Yuan period (1279-1368) 6 806
China: 20th cent. 14 821
France 11 228, 229, 230; 20 257; 26 73; 29 256
Japan 23 363
Netherlands, the 11 225–7; 22 848
Netherlands, the: 17th cent. 4 467; 11 226, 227; 27 885
Netherlands, the: 18th cent. 11 228; 15 46, 46; 22 847; 23 589; 29 668
Rome, ancient 27 49
Spain 29 668
see also plum blossom; still-lifes
folk 18 376–7*, 377
four-colour 2 217; 13 535, 535
genre 12 286–96*; 26 740; 33 313
Africa 1 432
African American art 1 443
Antilles, Lesser 2 150
Australia 19 874; 26 465
Belgium 3 560, 562; 12 290*, 296
Belgium: Early Netherlandish style 9 272
Belgium: Renaissance 4 904; 7 428; 21 354
Belgium: 16th cent. 3 557, 887
Belgium: 17th cent. 4 871, 872; 8 108; 26 391; 30 461, 462; 32 712, 723
Belgium: 19th cent. 8 591; 19 291; 21 370
Brazil 4 718
Canada 18 454
Czech Republic 29 649
Denmark: Baroque 17 880
Denmark: Biedermeier 18 178
Denmark: Romanticism 3 705
Denmark: 19th cent. 8 734; 17 606; 18 471, 472; 26 407
England 10 250; 12 291, 292–4*
England: Impressionism 29 595
England: Pre-Raphaelitism 4 877, 878; 10 253; 21 601
England: Rococo 13 324
England: social realism 11 74
England: 18th cent. 12 293; 22 123; 24 366; 33 413
England: 19th cent. 1 677; 9 756; 10 255; 11 796; 22 277; 27 841; 31 30; 32 795
England: 20th cent. 5 517; 12 644; 18 97; 28 659, 660
Finland 9 717; 10 128
France 12 289*, 291, 292*, 294*
France: Barbizon school 21 611, 612
France: Baroque 11 535; 19 146, 147, 148, 149
France: Fauvism 9 134
France: Impressionism 8 622; 9 289; 11 298; 15 153, VIII; 20 259; 24 879; 26 208, 209
France: Mannerism 11 533
France: Neo-classicism 32 428
France: Néo-Grec 24 58
France: Neo-Impressionism 22 746; 28 502, 698
France: Orientalism 7 760, II2; 15 844
France: Post-Impressionism 6 370; 31 213, 215, 216

painting
types
genre—cont.
France: Realism 4 339, 754; 8 51, 52, 54, 56; 12 295; 26 54, 56
France: Rococo 4 514; 17 627; 31 380
France: 17th cent. 18 839; 19 247
France: 18th cent. 6 473, 474; 8 500; 12 638; 13 639, 640, 641; 17 465; 19 217, 220; 23 788; 32 921
France: 19th cent. 2 142; 3 434; 5 441; 8 448, 599; 9 286; 19 295; 21 69; 25 750, 751; 26 451; 32 739, 740, 742
France: 20th cent 4 326, 327; 9 373; 20 827; 29 493
Germany 12 294
Germany: Baroque 12 390
Germany: Biedermeier 28 196
Germany: Expressionism 14 284
Germany: Gothic 12 108
Germany: Neue Sachlichkeit 9 42; 22 922
Germany: Romanticism 30 167
Germany: 19th cent. 12 415; 19 334; 22 304; 29 416; 30 740; 33 383
Germany: 20th cent. 21 785; 28 840
Gothic 12 108
Greece 13 352
Greece, ancient 12 286–7*
Hungary: 19th cent. 30 209
India, Republic of 15 170
Italy 12 287, 288–9*, 291–2*; 29 375
Italy: *bambocciate* 18 624
Italy: Baroque 5 706, 707, 859; 8 143; 12 288, 305; 20 264, 640; 21 701; 30 863
Italy: Mannerism 1 670; 22 448; 29 784, 785
Italy: Realism (style) 28 705
Italy: Renaissance 27 890
Italy: Romanticism 8 5
Italy: *Verismo* 16 679
Italy: 16th cent. 27 622
Italy: 17th cent. 6 347; 21 483; 26 95, 772
Italy: 18th cent. 6 351; 19 634; 24 706
Italy: 19th cent. 5 783; 8 136, 137; 10 834; 19 71; 32 197
Italy: 20th cent. 5 919; 22 84; 28 792; 31 445
Japan 16 802; 17 174*, 176–7*, 783, 794
Japan: Edo period (1600-1868) 17 176, 727
Japan: Impressionism 18 531
Japan: Momoyama period (1568-1600) 17 175, 787
Korea 18 318–21*
Korea: 6th cent. 18 318
Korea: 18th cent. 18 54, 319, 320
Mexico 30 282
Native North Americans 3 500
Netherlands, the 7 562; 12 287, 289, 290–91*; 14 733; 15 96; 22 848*
Netherlands, the: Baroque 14 91; 26 164, 171
Netherlands, the: Early Netherlandish style 31 703
Netherlands, the: Fauvism 22 851
Netherlands, the: Impressionism 22 850
Netherlands, the: Leiden Fine Painters 9 192

painting
types
genre—cont.
Netherlands, the: Magic Realism **22** *852*
Netherlands, the: Post-Impressionism **7** III1
Netherlands, the: Renaissance **19** *760*
Netherlands, the: 15th cent. **20** 637
Netherlands, the: 16th cent. **1** 168, *169*
Netherlands, the: 17th cent. **3** *8*; **4** *381, 382*; **5** *3, 5*; **9** *471*; **12** *291*; **14** *728, 733, 734, 739*; **15** *96*; **19** *292*; **20** *79*; **21** *351, 487, 488, 814*; **22** 721, *916*; **23** *344, 611, 614, 831*; **25** *797*; **26** *746*; **28** *93, 207*; **29** *586, 589, 855*; **32** *262, 264, 265, 587*; **33** *176*
Netherlands, the: 18th cent. **21** *489*; **31** *366, 367*
Netherlands, the: 19th cent. **1** *651*; **12** *857*; **16** *574*; **21** *175*
Norway **22** *290*; **23** *603*; **33** *78*
Poland **25** *64*
Portugal **4** *387*; **28** *736*
Rome, ancient **12** 287*
Russia: Critical Realism **24** *464*
Russia: Neo-primitivism **27** *393*
Russia: 19th cent. **10** *856*; **20** *154*; **32** *163*
Scotland **9** *725*; **28** *237, 277*; **33** *189*
Spain **12** 289–90*
Spain: 17th cent. **22** *343, 347*
Spain: 18th cent. **24** *112*
Spain: 19th cent. **11** *325*; **27** *157*; **29** *84*, 284, *284*
Sweden: 17th cent. **10** 100
Turkey **31** *455*
Uganda **1** *432*
United States of America **12** 294, 296; **31** 602
United States of America: African American art **1** *443*
United States of America: Barbizon school **15** *20*
United States of America: 18th cent. **25** *453*
United States of America: 19th cent. **4** *72*; **6** *499*; **17** *617*; **22** *223*; **26** *180*; **31** *604*; **32** *327*; **33** *184*
United States of America: 20th cent. **14** *752*; **25** *553*
Uruguay **31** *755*
Vietnam **32** *481*
grisaille *see* GRISAILLE PAINTINGS
hard-edge **1** 79; **14** 164*; **21** 776; **23** 30
Australia **32** 909
England **10** 258
Germany **12** 397
United States of America **14** *164*; **23** 184; **25** 361; **31** 608
United States of America: 20th cent. **23** *185*
history **1** 104; **10** 690; **14** 581–9*; **24** 741; **26** 737, 740
Albania **1** *540*
Australia **2** *750*; **9** 464
Austria **2** *796*; **20** *857*; **26** *559*; **32** *443*
Belgium **3** *559*; **9** *197*; **19** *166*; **26** 740; **33** *171*
China **33** *474, 499*
Czech Republic **13** *134*
Denmark **8** 734
England **10** 249–50; **14** 585

painting
types
history—cont.
England: Neo-classicism **10** *402*
England: Romanticism **17** *576*
England: Troubadour style **4** *322*
England: 18th cent. **23** *214, 451*
England: 19th cent. **15** *884*
France **2** 53; **3** 451; **11** 538*, 540*; **14** 583, 584–5; **24** 138; **25** 638; **31** 373
France: Baroque **14** *583*; **24** *212*
France: Neo-classicism **8** *555, 559*; **11** *541, 900*; **12** *732*; **13** *792*; **15** *846*; **19** *255*; **22** *735*; **24** *172, 381, 583*
France: Orientalism **26** *92*
France: Realism **14** *587*
France: Rococo **14** *585*
France: Romanticism **8** *643*; **12** *352*; **13** *690*; **26** 737, 738–40
France: Troubadour style **26** *265*
France: 15th cent. **11** *353*
France: 16th cent. **9** *276*
France: 17th cent. **4** *574*; **8** *784*; **18** *648*; **19** 246; **24** *476*; **29** *623*
France: 18th cent. **4** *744*; **9** 209; **13** *643*; **18** *642*; **21** *902*; **26** *424*; **30** *46*; **32** *670*
France: 19th cent. **3** *396*; **8** *76, 654*; **11** *546*; **14** *311*; **15** *840*; **16** *66*; **18** *865*; **21** *761*; **24** *816*; **28** *67*; **32** *336*
France: 20th cent **8** *714*; **24** *143*
Germany **12** 472
Germany: Mannerism **30** *35*
Germany: Realism (style) **21** *140, 141*
Germany: 16th cent. **33** *85*
Germany: 17th cent. **2** *716*
Germany: 19th cent. **11** *46*; **24** *587*; **26** 740
Hieronymites **14** *516*
Hungary **3** *703*; **15** 13; **20** *42*; **30** *205*
Ireland **20** *29*
Italy **14** 581–3
Italy: Baroque **5** *383*; **7** *907*; **11** *15, 287*; **20** *96*; **24** *340*
Italy: Futurism **5** *848*
Italy: Jesuit Order **17** *511*
Italy: Mannerism **4** *399*
Italy: Neo-Classicism **12** *41*; **16** *677*; **21** *132*
Italy: Realism (style) **6** *136*
Italy: Renaissance **9** *96*; **10** *766*; **14** *582*
Italy: Romanticism **3** *903*; **14** *266*
Italy: 15th cent. **20** *319*
Italy: 17th cent. **29** *254*; **30** *304*; **31** *437*
Italy: 18th cent. **5** *765*; **8** *158*; **12** *40*; **24** *10, 11*; **31** *313*
Italy: 19th cent. **3** *857*; **5** *556*
Jesuit Order **17** *511*
Jewish art **17** *576*
Mexico **21** *386*
Netherlands, the **14** 584; **22** 848–9*
Netherlands, the: Baroque **4** *250*; **22** *842*
Netherlands, the: 17th cent. **10** *659*; **18** *652, 819*
Norway **23** *225, 226*
Poland **20** *810*
Rome, ancient **27** 39
Russia: 19th cent. **5** *25, 68*; **16** *793*; **27** *390*; **32** *73*

painting
types
history—cont.
Russia: 20th cent. **27** *435*
Scotland **33** *190*
Spain **27** 157
Spain: Baroque **19** *179*; **26** *437*
Spain: Cubism **14** *588*
Spain: Mannerism **13** *342*
Spain: 17th cent. **5** *874*; **14** *516*; **20** *126*
Spain: 19th cent. **11** *324*; **13** *246*; **27** *156*; **29** 284
United States of America **31** 600
United States of America: Romanticism **26** 740
United States of America: 18th cent. **7** *811*; **31** *392*; **33** *92*
United States of America: 19th cent. **31** *872*
Venezuela **32** *174*
see also ISTORIE
landscape **1** 107; **6** 785–6; **8** 910–11; **9** 35–6; **15** 828–9; **18** 700–719*; **19** *325*; **22** 686; **26** 736, 740–42
Africa **1** *430*
Armenia (Europe) **2** *432*
Australia **2** 745–6, 747–8
Australia: Impressionism **2** *746*
Australia: 19th cent. **2** *745*; **13** *784*; **29** *767*
Australia: 20th cent. **2** *748*; **23** *183*
Austria **32** *445, 776*
Belgium **3** 558, 562; **18** 711*
Belgium: Baroque **27** *297*
Belgium: Mannerism **31** *50*
Belgium: Renaissance **4** *140, 903*
Belgium: 16th cent. **7** *497, 711*; **12** *171*; **18** *706*; **24** 259, *260*, 262, *262*, VIII2; **31** *804*
Belgium: 17th cent. **11** *357*; **21** *829*; **31** *522*; **33** *182*
Belgium: 18th cent. **23** *438*
Bolivia: 20th cent. **4** *263*
Brazil **22** 840; **25** *326*; **26** *413*
Britain **26** 740–41
Buddhism **6** *784*; **17** *192*
Byzantine **18** 703*
Cambodia **5** 502
Canada **5** 564; **14** *195*; **30** *754*; **33** *14*
Chile **6** *597*
China **6** 632, 773, 787–92*, 795–8*; **7** 150; **28** 311
China: Buddhism **6** *784*
China: Confucianism **7** *706*
China: Daoism **6** 785–6
China: Five Dynasties (AD 907-60) **17** *591*
China: Ming period (1368-1644) **6** *791, 825*; **8** *459*; **9** *137, 138*; **11** *855*; **15** *854*; **19** *514, 833*; **25** *785*; **28** *587*; **30** *48*; **33** *68, 69, 70*, 642, *650*
China: Northern Song period (AD 960-1127) **19** *479*
China: Qing period (1644-1911) **2** *96*; **7** *624*; **8** *518, 520*; **12** *90*; **14** *723, 825, 831*; **18** *517, 752*; **28** *590*; **32** *838, 839, 844*; **33** *426*
China: Song period (AD 960-1279) **9** 139; **10** *795*; **13** *855*; **17** *697*; **19** *504*; **33** *476*
China: Southern school **21** *419*
China: Southern Song period (1127-1279) **19** 478
China: Tang period (AD 618-907) **19** 298, *299*

painting
types
landscape—cont.
China: Yuan period (1279-1368) **6** *790, 797, 819*; **7** IV1; **32** *846*; **33** *440*
China: Zhe school **33** *656*
Confucianism **7** *706*
Denmark **18** *179*, 715; **26** 742; **28** *824*
Ecuador **9** 713
Egypt, ancient **9** 809*
England **10** 250–52*; **12** 294–5*; **18** 711–15
England: Gothic **18** *703*
England: Impressionism **7** *700*
England: Orientalism **23** *505*
England: Romanticism **18** *714*; **26** 740, *741*
England: 17th cent. **27** *264*
England: 18th cent. **3** *276*; **8** *97, 98*; **10** *250*; **11** *910*; **18** *712*; **19** *729*; **27** *716*; **29** *890*; **31** *233*; **33** *221, 415, 715*
England: 19th cent. **7** *749, 752, 755, 756*; **8** *185, 842*; **11** *300*; **18** *905*; **19** *427*; **23** *249*; **26** *238*; **29** *878*; **31** *469, 474*; **32** *857*
Etruscan **18** 701
Finland **11** *96*, 96; **17** *448*
France **18** 704, 708, 711–14
France: Art informel **10** *838*
France: Baroque **24** *211*
France: Fauvism **10** *840*; **32** *668*
France: Gothic **5** 428; **13** 154
France: Impressionism **12** *188*; **15** *151*; **21** *866*; **22** *119*; **24** *880, 881*; **28** *795*
France: naive art **27** *261*
France: Pointillism **18** *716*
France: Post-Impressionism **6** *368*
France: 15th cent. **20** 452
France: 17th cent. **21** *609*; **24** *254*; **25** *393*
France: 18th cent. **9** 416; **18** *661*; **31** *817*
France: 19th cent. **3** *212*; **7** *878, 879*; **8** *539, 859*; **11** *501*, 543–4*; **14** *189, 847*; **18** *713*; **21** *429*; **26** 741; **27** *266*; **31** *387, 479*
France: 20th cent **20** *272*
Georgia **12** *327*
Germany **1** 714; **18** 77, 714
Germany: Baroque **28** *148*
Germany: Expressionism **3** *477*; **18** *81*, IV2
Germany: Renaissance **1** 715–16
Germany: Romanticism **4** *135*; **11** *779, 780, 782*; **12** *393*; **26** *359*, 742
Germany: 18th cent. **18** *174*
Germany: 19th cent. **4** *206*; **8** *898*; **18** *183*; **26** 741; **27** *232*
Germany: 20th cent. **17** *762*; **18** *31*; **28** *125, 342*
Gothic **5** 428; **13** 154; **18** *703*
Greece, ancient **8** 704; **18** 701
Honduras **14** *715*
Iceland **15** *71*; **30** *757*
Indian subcontinent **15** 565, 566
Ireland **16** 14, *15*
Islamic **16** 136
Italy **18** 704–5, 707–10*, 711, 712–13; **20** 680; **22** 414
Italy: Baroque **5** *861*; **9** *91*; **18** *709*; **28** *220*
Italy: Mannerism **12** *670*
Italy: Renaissance **18** *705*
Italy: 16th cent. **1** *18*; **18** *707*

painting
types
landscape—cont.
Italy: 17th cent. **4** *487*; **7** *390, 395, 396, 398*; **9** *376, 377*; **10** *159, 160*; **25** *66*; **27** *151, 152*; **30** *60*
Italy: 18th cent. **4** *154*; **19** *525*; **26** *324*
Italy: 19th cent. **7** *572*; **8** *716*; **11** *285*
Italy: 20th cent. **29** *10*
Jainism **15** 565
Japan **7** 183; **17** 200
Japan: Buddhism **17** *193*
Japan: Edo period (1600-1868) **14** *214*; **15** *127*; **17** *191*; **33** *321, 492*
Japan: Heian period (AD 794-1185) **17** *155*
Japan: Kamakura period (1185-1333) **17** *156*
Japan: Meiji period (1868-1912) **33** *489*
Japan: Muromachi period (1333-1568) **1** *776*; **17** *780*; **31** *252*
Japan: *Nanga* **30** *295*; **31** *698*
Japan: *Rinpa* **27** *596*
Japan: Shinto **17** *153*
Japan: Showa period (1926-89) **17** *204*
Korea **18** *313*
Korea: 7th cent. **18** 313–15*
Korea: 16th cent. **18** *51*; **33** *494, 525*
Korea: 17th cent. **32** *843*
Korea: 18th cent. **7** *203*; **18** *315*
Mexico: 19th cent. **32** *123*
Netherlands, the **7** 562; **18** 704, 705, 706–7*, 708, 710–11*; **22** 847*; **32** *672*
Netherlands, the: Baroque **26** *159*
Netherlands, the: Mannerism **31** *805*
Netherlands, the: Post-Impressionism **12** *859*
Netherlands, the: 17th cent. **2** *615, 855*; **3** *758*; **4** *380, 488*; **5** *681*; **8** *294, 295, 296, 297*; **9** *463*; **10** *661*; **12** *801*; **13** *256*; **14** *15, 601, 602*; **18** *229, 711*, III1; **20** *235*; **21** *826*; **23** *614*; **25** *67, 370, 755, 756*; **26** *543*; **27** *325, 326, 327, 328, 455, 457*; **28** *359, 360*; **32** *137, 138, 145, 907*; **33** *179*
Netherlands, the: 18th cent. **22** *209*
Netherlands, the: 19th cent. **20** *433, 435*; **22** *848*; **26** *528*
New Zealand **7** *210*; **23** *60*
Norway **8** *452*; **23** 224; **28** *825*
Poland **25** 107; **29** *538*; **32** *877*
Rome, ancient **18** 700, 701–3, *702*; **26** 862; **27** 48, 50, 53
Russia **25** 145; **27** *391*
Scotland **28** 235–6
Shinto **17** *153*
Slovenia **28** *861*
Spain: Baroque **32** *131*
Spain: Romanticism **24** *403*
Spain: 17th cent. **7** 559
Spain: 19th cent. **29** 284–5, *285*
Sweden **30** 79; **31** 707
Sweden: National Romanticism **22** *541*; **23** *206*
Sweden: 19th cent. **30** *80*
Switzerland **30** 133, *133*; **33** 287, *291*
Taiwan **30** *248*
Trinidad and Tobago **22** *138*

painting
types
landscape—cont.
United States of America 18 715, 718, 719; 31 601, 602, 603
United States of America: Luminism 14 276
United States of America: Romanticism 26 742
United States of America: 19th cent. 1 674; 2 710; 4 44; 7 285, 550; 8 191; 9 419; 12 606; 15 859; 18 IV1; 22 75; 28 560; 31 487, 602
United States of America: 20th cent. 18 718
Venezuela 32 175
Zaïre 1 430
see also PANORAMAS; PLEIN-AIR; vedute
literary themes
Belgium 9 479
Denmark 1 33
England: Neo-classicism 3 286
England: Pre-Raphaelitism 5 268; 14 850; 25 555; 27 187
England: Rococo 14 636
England: 18th cent. 11 860, 861; 12 646; 14 520; 17 641; 31 871
England: 19th cent. 19 103, 240, 507; 29 732
France 26 739; 27 143; 32 510
France: Romanticism 8 639
Italy: Baroque 6 36
Italy: Renaissance 2 228
Italy: Romanticism 14 265
Italy: 14th cent. 6 1
Italy: 15th cent. 28 70
Italy: 17th cent. 21 808
Netherlands, the 4 657
Poland 21 426
United States of America 31 601
literati
China 6 631, 783, 788, 789, 790, 795, 797, 798, 824; 7 147
China: Ming period (1368-1644) 6 806, 820; 7 148
China: Qing period (1644-1911) 6 818
China: Song period (AD 960-1279) 6 636, 773–4, 783, 804, 812, 823; 30 30
China: Yuan period (1279-1368) 6 805, 819
China: 20th cent. 25 781
Japan see JAPAN → painting → Nanga
Korea 18 323, 323–5*, 324
marine 18 700; 20 423–6*
Belgium 9 745; 24 323
Denmark 9 701
Egypt, ancient 20 424
England 20 424–5*
England: 18th cent. 14 610
England: 19th cent. 4 757; 29 535; 31 468, 472
France 20 426*
France: 18th cent. 24 811; 32 333, 684
France: 19th cent. 4 523
Germany 10 862
Greece, ancient 20 424
Italy 7 392; 8 451
Japan 17 178, 789
Netherlands, the 20 424*; 29 375
Netherlands, the: 17th cent. 3 85; 5 680; 20 425; 23 200; 25 247; 32 142, 143, 671, 732, 733; 33 25, 194
Norway 3 112
United States of America 20 425–6*

painting
types
marine—cont.
United States of America: 19th cent. 18 726; 26 336; 27 462
monochrome 21 891–2*
Buddhism 6 785
China 6 784, 785, 789, 796, 801, 802, 803, 804–6, 805, 806, 807, 818
Japan 17 38, 163–4
see also GRISAILLE PAINTINGS
mythological 22 410–11*, 412–14*, 415–16*
Austria 29 401
Belgium: Baroque 17 650; 25 273; 27 292, 293
Belgium: Neo-classicism 26 285
Belgium: 16th cent. 11 221
Belgium: 17th cent. 3 108; 25 809; 30 788; 33 388
Czech Republic 1 5; 29 429
Denmark: 18th cent. 1 32
England: Aesthetic Movement 11 436
England: Baroque 19 120
England: Pre-Raphaelitism 29 48
England: 18th cent. 11 911
England: 19th cent. 8 122; 22 52
France: Baroque 4 535, 537; 17 672; 32 717
France: Mannerism 1 17; 9 328
France: Neo-classicism 12 730; 13 794; 24 736
France: Rococo 3 855; 4 515, 516; 11 367; 22 683; 23 294
France: Rococo Revival 11 545
France: Romanticism 8 642
France: 17th cent. 18 632; 19 246; 21 498; 25 387, 390, 392
France: 18th cent. 14 84, 85; 24 136; 26 93
France: 19th cent. 1 641; 4 528; 5 342; 18 713
Germany: Baroque 27 228; 28 147
Germany: Mannerism 14 320
Germany: Neo-classicism 26 128
Germany: 17th cent. 27 886
Germany: 19th cent. 4 204; 7 856
Greece, ancient 13 545
Italy 22 412–14
Italy: Baroque 1 535, 536; 4 54; 5 453; 6 126; 7 684; 8 141, 144; 11 680, 846; 12 661; 16 672; 20 265, 376, 496; 26 199, 201; 27 817; 30 857, 859
Italy: Mannerism 4 400; 7 891; 12 672; 16 666; 23 293, 377; 24 201; 30 33; 31 34, 35, 36, 39; 32 17
Italy: Neo-Classicism 17 852; 22 271
Italy: Renaissance 4 495, 499; 6 3; 7 322; 9 186; 16 660; 19 676; 24 523, 770; 28 701; 31 429
Italy: Rococo 25 3
Italy: 16th cent. 7 892; 10 477; 12 736
Italy: 17th cent. 8 99; 12 707; 20 83; 23 750; 27 178; 30 526
Italy: 18th cent. 3 109; 11 21; 12 22, 39; 20 843; 29 887
Netherlands, the: Baroque 26 158

painting
types
mythological—cont.
Netherlands, the: Mannerism 4 151
Netherlands, the: Renaissance 13 26
Netherlands, the: 16th cent. 7 867, 868
Netherlands, the: 17th cent. 4 703; 12 884; 18 651, 818; 27 517; 29 587; 31 780; 32 261
Portugal 27 615; 32 425
Rome, ancient 26 860, 861
Spain 32 132, 133
Sweden 17 662
Switzerland 8 823; 17 682
United States of America 14 492; 32 109
plum blossom
China 6 802, 803, 804–5, 805, 806, 807, 818; 32 847; 33 493
Japan 17 190
Korea 23 439
see also flower
Poonah see POONAH PAINTING
portraits see under PORTRAITS → media
quadratura 5 653; 15 135
Austria 1 659; 15 139
Brazil 4 716; 26 412
Dominican Order 9 109
Italy 15 137–40*; 16 714
Italy: Baroque 5 280, 652; 7 909; 9 109; 12 199, 663; 16 715; 22 327; 25 415; 27 522; 29 38
Italy: Dominican Order 9 109
Italy: 17th cent. 21 732
see also DI SOTTO IN SÙ; TROMPE L'OEIL
religious 19 680
Austria: Baroque 1 732
Austria: Gothic 13 151
Austria: Renaissance 14 836
Austria: 16th cent. 26 106
Austria: 18th cent. 27 234
Beguines 3 504
Belgium: Antwerp Mannerism 3 492
Belgium: Baroque 4 914; 8 126; 9 478, 488; 19 650, 651; 27 288, 295, 296
Belgium: Early Netherlandish style 3 553; 4 593, 594, 595; 8 25, 524, 552; 10 706, 709, 710; 11 440; 12 846, 848, 849; 15 95; 16 70; 20 660, 715, 716, 780; 22 863; 25 281; 29 692; 33 121, 123, 125, 129
Belgium: Expressionism 3 565
Belgium: Mannerism 3 24; 7 414; 17 896
Belgium: Renaissance 2 195; 3 554; 7 519; 11 221; 19 548; 20 665; 21 357; 25 668
Belgium: 16th cent. 4 911; 23 201, 378; 24 VIII2; 32 114, 710
Belgium: 17th cent. 4 219; 11 719; 25 810; 32 755
Belgium: 19th cent. 22 696
Bolivia: 18th cent. 4 262
Camaldolese Order 5 450
Crete 20 51, 51
Czech Republic: Gothic 13 152; 17 819; 25 431; 30 706
Czech Republic: Mannerism 29 430
Czech Republic: 14th cent. 20 774
Czech Republic: 18th cent. 25 448
Dominican Order 9 107

painting
types
religious—cont.
Dominican Republic 9 115
England: Gothic 13 138
England: Pre-Raphaelitism 11 785; 21 602
England: Romanticism 20 490
England: 19th cent. 8 491; 9 474; 10 646; 25 407
England: 20th cent. 29 383
France: Baroque 6 434; 8 90; 11 534; 17 671; 19 24; 25 708; 32 715, 718
France: Gothic 3 640; 11 399; 25 794
France: Mannerism 3 399; 18 663
France: Orientalism 6 501
France: Rococo 19 647
France: Symbolism (movement) 12 190; 22 90
France: 14th cent. 17 456
France: 15th cent. 11 351, 800; 20 613, 651
France: 16th cent. 19 341, 342
France: 17th cent. 4 128; 7 864; 9 175; 11 166; 18 838, 840; 24 VII2; 25 391; 30 354
France: 18th cent. 8 795; 9 208; 10 726; 24 773; 26 247; 28 743
France: 19th cent. 3 358; 4 527; 12 158
France: 20th cent 13 714
Franciscan Order 11 710
Germany: Baroque 19 706; 27 227
Germany: Expressionism 23 186
Germany: Gothic 11 715; 12 384; 14 455; 20 765; 26 507
Germany: High Renaissance 26 188
Germany: Mannerism 8 882
Germany: Renaissance 1 717, 718; 5 59; 8 113; 9 432; 13 723; 17 601; 28 48, 189
Germany: Romanticism 11 462
Germany: 15th cent. 12 409; 16 71; 19 529; 20 654; 25 40; 28 150, 151, 171
Germany: 16th cent. 3 473; 26 11
Germany: 17th cent. 17 720; 22 249
Germany: 18th cent. 12 411
Germany: 19th cent. 23 676; 28 135; 31 538
Gothic: Austria 13 151
Gothic: Czech Republic 13 152; 17 819; 25 431; 30 706
Gothic: England 13 138
Gothic: France 3 640; 11 399; 25 794
Gothic: Germany 11 715; 12 384; 14 455; 20 765; 26 507
Gothic: Hungary 14 898
Gothic: Italy 9 344; 11 382, 892; 12 298, 579; 13 129, 146; 16 826; 19 674, 680, 684; 20 507, 508, 509, 675; 24 XII4; 29 598
Gothic: Netherlands, the 20 782
Gothic: Norway 13 144
Gothic: Spain 29 277
Gothic: Switzerland 30 130
Greece 20 51
Holy Roman Empire (before 1648) 13 847
Hungary 14 898
Ireland 14 718

painting
types
religious—cont.
Italy: Baroque 1 672, 673; 3 33, 95, 353, 381, 713, 737, 834; 4 334, 413; 5 405, 406, 442, 694, 695, 704, 709, 710, 713, 714, 715, 718, 862; 6 27, 33, 108, 110, 114, 337, 338, 339; 7 312, 313, 683, 903; 8 142, 147, 148; 9 76, 77, 89; 10 746; 11 678; 12 306, 307, 589, 662; 13 754, 785, 787; 16 671, 673; 18 731, 732; 19 472, 816; 20 266, 377, 598; 21 526; 22 530; 24 801, 836; 25 562, 564, 643; 26 197, 198, 309, 311, 312, 397; 27 489, 490, 816, 864; 28 473; 29 37, 252, 544, 545; 30 798, 863; 31 791
Italy: Camaldolese Order 5 450
Italy: Dominican Order 9 107
Italy: Early Netherlandish style 17 703
Italy: Early Renaissance 3 99; 8 167, 169; 24 538
Italy: Gothic 3 248, 808; 9 344; 11 381, 892; 12 298; 13 129, 146; 16 826; 19 674, 684; 20 507, 508, 509, 675; 24 XII4; 29 598
Italy: Gothic (Late) 12 579, 580
Italy: Mannerism 3 14, 254, 255, 256, 344, 345, 346, 468; 4 857; 7 776, 887, 888, 890; 11 269, 392; 16 667; 19 383; 20 280; 22 392; 23 574; 24 200; 27 208, 620, 652, 732; 31 6, 8, 9, 11, 12, 37; 32 102, 227, 352, 353
Italy: Renaissance 1 818; 2 32, 33, 179, 182, 290; 3 299, 650, 656, 665, 666, 751, 782; 4 336, 496, 497, 653; 5 818, 819, 820; 6 3, 4, 12, 356; 7 320, 321, 564; 9 95; 11 294, 388, 702; 12 552, 708, 711, 753; 13 280; 16 662, 846; 19 182, 185, 442, 443, 448, 895; 20 123, 306, 307, 309, 313, 453, 532, 533, 771; 21 96, 748; 22 108, 133, 522; 23 94; 24 365, 524, 763, 769, 829; 25 157, 161, 162, 251, 569, 897, 900, 903; 26 458; 27 847, 862, 891; 28 85, 331, 334; 29 2, 26; 30 781; 31 431, 432, 444; 32 12, 364, 365, 657; 33 701, 702
Italy: Rococo 9 48
Italy: Verismo 22 99, 100
Italy: 13th cent. 7 815, 816; 12 760; 13 818, 819; 20 407
Italy: 14th cent. 3 247; 5 656; 7 337; 9 107; 12 703; 15 94; 16 839; 19 454, 667, 669, 671; 23 91, 95, 351; 24 31; 28 435, 677; 31 105, 277; 32 625
Italy: 15th cent. 3 227; 4 506; 5 913; 7 543, 925, 926; 12 715; 20 51; 24 781; 27 619
Italy: 16th cent. 1 570, 571; 3 317; 5 546, 852, 853, 857; 6 86, 362; 11 721; 12 556; 13 293; 21 94; 25 59, 149, 729; 27 655; 28 83

painting
types
religious—cont.
Italy: 17th cent. **2** *619*; **5** *635*; **7** *308*; **10** *157*, *158*, *188*, *189*; **11** *41*; **13** *276*; **19** *452*; **21** *53*; **22** *82*, *83*; **23** *266*, *700*; **24** VII1; **25** *642*; **26** *311*; **28** *62*, *379*, *787*; **29** *410*; **30** *303*; **32** *499*
Italy: 18th cent. **4** *540*; **6** *568*; **7** *310*; **12** *42*; **13** *741*, *742*; **15** *148*; **20** *806*; **24** *704*, *705*; **28** *17*; **31** *314*
Italy: 19th cent. **23** *853*; **28** *355*, *356*
Italy: 20th cent. **13** *872*
Netherlands, the: Baroque **3** *23*; **4** *52*; **8** *292*; **11** *169*; **12** *241*; **19** *347*, *348*; **21** *790*; **23** II; **25** *230*; **26** *154*; **33** *262*
Netherlands, the: Beguines **3** *504*
Netherlands, the: Early Netherlandish style **4** *449*, *841*; **12** *231*, *232*; **20** *773*; **23** *672*; **28** *804*
Netherlands, the: Late Gothic **20** *782*
Netherlands, the: Mannerism **14** *293*; **33** *418*
Netherlands, the: Renaissance **13** *24*, *25*; **16** *834*; **28** *216*, *217*
Netherlands, the: 16th cent. **1** *167*; **3** *230*; **7** *869*; **14** *379*, *380*
Netherlands, the: 17th cent. **4** *377*, *735*; **5** *2*, *4*; **8** *104*; **9** *300*, *380*, *742*, *743*; **10** *733*; **14** *727*, *731*; **16** *833*; **18** *227*; **20** *249*; **25** *758*; **28** *180*, *365*; **29** *588*, *697*
Norway **13** *144*; **29** *78*
Poland: 14th cent. **8** *430*
Poland: 16th cent. **25** *103*
Poland: 17th cent. **25** *104*
Portugal: Baroque **32** *424*
Portugal: 15th cent. **12** *890*, *891*
Portugal: 16th cent. **10** *901*
Portugal: 19th cent. **19** *655*
Portugal: 18th cent. **25** *297*
Russia **16** *791*; **22** *176*, *177*; **27** *580*
Sicily **28** *656*
Spain: Baroque **5** *526*, *618*, *619*; **7** *522*; **11** *710*; **12** *58*; **20** *617*; **22** *695*; **26** *435*, *436*; **29** *280*, *281*, *282*; **31** *809*; **32** *127*; **33** *729*, *731*
Spain: Franciscan Order **11** *710*
Spain: Gothic **29** *277*
Spain: Hispano-Flemish style **8** *872*
Spain: Mannerism **7** *225*; **13** *340*, *343*; **23** *705*; **31** *347*
Spain: Renaissance **20** *10*; **29** *278*
Spain: 14th cent. **9** *261*
Spain: 15th cent. **9** *264*; **20** *384*; **29** *298*
Spain: 16th cent. **5** *736*
Spain: 17th cent. **2** *878*; **5** *738*; **6** *365*; **7** *559*; **10** *510*; **14** *470*, *471*; **20** *500*; **22** *344*; **23** *571*; **26** *300*, *301*
Switzerland **11** *788*; **21** *136*; **30** *130*; **33** *287*
Venezuela **32** *173*
see also ALTARPIECES; ICONS; PREDELLAS; *sacra conversazione*
rose *see* ROSEMALING

painting
types—cont.
sacra conversazione **3** *663*; **9** *99*; **27** 494–6*
Belgium **4** *162*; **23** *447*
Italy: Mannerism **7** *885*; **12** *673*
Italy: Renaissance **3** *303*, *305*, *917*; **5** *307*; **7** *322*; **8** *4*; **13** *259*; **19** *323*, *441*, *447*, *675*, *711*; **20** *312*; **24** *889*; **27** *495*; **28** *700*; **29** *3*
Italy: 15th cent. **20** *845*
Italy: 16th cent. **23** *876*
seascapes *see* marine
still-lifes **11** 224; **15** 140; **29** 663–71*; **31** 880
Belarus' **3** *529*
Belgium **11** *871*; **28** *902*; **29** *665*; **33** *537*
Byzantine **29** 665
Czech Republic **11** *79*
Early Christian (*c.* AD 250–843) **29** 665
Egypt, ancient **29** 664
France **29** 664, 668
France: Cubism **29** *670*
France: Post-Impressionism **6** *369*; **29** *669*
France: 17th cent. **11** *535*; **21** *891*
France: 18th cent. **6** *472*, *475*; **8** *812*, *813*; **11** *539*; **24** *135*; **30** 836
29 *669*
France: 19th cent. **22** *29*
Germany **29** 664
Greece, ancient **29** 664–5
Italy **12** 11; **29** 664, 665, 666, 667, 668–9
Italy: Baroque **3** *322*; **16** *675*; **29** *667*
Italy: Roman **29** *664*
Italy: 16th cent. **3** 200; **27** 622
Italy: 20th cent. **22** *76*
Netherlands, the **7** 562; **29** 664, 666–7
Netherlands, the: 17th cent. **1** *165*; **2** *644*; **3** 900; **7** *370*, *800*; **9** *489*; **13** 914; **14** *286*, *290*; **17** *737*; **29** *666*; **33** *27*
Netherlands, the: 18th cent. **27** *454*; **29** *668*
Portugal **29** 668
Rome, ancient **26** 861–2, *862*; **27** 50; **29** *664*, 665
Spain **29** 664, 667–8
Spain: Baroque **33** *730*
Spain: 16th cent. **25** 419; **27** 706
Spain: 17th cent. **14** *104*; **27** *707*
Spain: 18th cent. **21** *80*
Sweden **30** 78
Taiwan **30** *247*
United States of America **29** 669, 670, *671*; **31** 603
see also flower; *vanitas*
Theorem *see* POONAH PAINTING
topographical **24** 17; **32** *410*
England **28** *285*; **31** *155*
France **27** *559*; **31** *156*
Italy **11** *214*; **13** *302*; **32** *409*
Netherlands, the **1** *585*
Spain **13** *344*; **20** *63*, *71*
see also BIRD'S-EYE VIEWS; TOWNSCAPE; *vedute*
townscapes *see* TOWNSCAPES
vanitas **3** 77; **8** 595; **11** 225; **15** 140; **18** 64; **29** 667; **31** 880–83*
Belgium **4** *917*
France **31** 883
Germany **29** *725*
Italy **31** 883
Netherlands, the **3** *77*; **31** 881–2*, *882*, *883*
Spain **31** *810*, 883

painting
types
vanitas—cont.
see also MEMENTO MORI; still-lifes
vedute **5** 378; **18** 700, 711; **32** 110–14*
England **5** *599*
Germany **4** *663*
Italy **2** 342; **31** 155; **32** 110
Italy: 16th cent. **9** 181
Italy: 17th cent. **7** *509*
Italy: 18th cent. **2** *343*; **5** *595*, *596*, *597*; **13** *743*, *744*; **24** *10*, *11*; **32** *112*
Netherlands, the **33** *269*
Switzerland **30** 133
see also topographical
vedute ideate **3** 415, *416*; **13** 347; **32** 111
see also CAPRICCIOS
uses
altarpieces **9** 3–5
architectural decorations **16** 221
architecture **6** 638; **15** 548, 806, *807*; **16** 160, 250*
banners **30** 612–13, *613*
baskets **3** 331
boats **15** 810
body arts **23** 721–2, *722*, 723
bone **25** 493
book covers **4** *353*; **15** 563–4; **30** 836
cabinets (i) (rooms) **5** 346
cassoni **6** 1–5*, *1*, *2*, *3*, *4*
ceramics **6** 772, 773; **8** 312
cloisters **7** 456–8*
coffins **15** *812*
cotton **15** *673*, 674
crucifixes **8** 211–12*
cult statues **8** 262
doors **17** 155
earthenwares **6** 874, 888
enamel *see under* ENAMEL → techniques
façade decoration **10** 735*, *736*, *737*, *739*
faience (ii) (ceramics) **14** 235
fans **6** 791; **10** 776, 777; **17** 160
furniture **13** 592; **23** 790; **24** 258; **33** 331–2
glass **12** 788*; **14** 235; **27** 78*; **32** 202
gold leaf **12** 623
gourds **1** 303
interior decoration **23** 789–90*, *790*; **30** 90
ivory-carvings **16** 525–6
lacquer **6** 773; **17** 299; **18** 605–6*, 608–10*
leather **22** 654, 655
marble **5** 336
masks **1** 290
pebbles **25** 493
plaques **25** 493
porcelain **2** 817; **10** *309*, 309–10
portraits *see under* PORTRAITS → media
pottery **6** 874, 876, 887; **10** 26; **13** 535–6; **25** 514; **29** 176–7
rock art *see under* ROCK ART → techniques
rock crystal **26** 484
screens (ii) (furniture) *see under* forms → screen
scrolls *see under* forms → scroll
sculpture **6** 216, 725; **7** *616*; **14** *352*; **15** *79*, 548; **17** 99; **25** 175*; **27** 16
shields **23** 223
ships **5** 530–31, *531*; **10** 197; **28** 611–14
stained glass **29** 498–9*
stelae **13** *544*
stone **25** 493
tables **33** *331*
tea ceremonies **17** 342

painting
uses—cont.
textiles **5** *104*; **6** 303; **15** 548, 565, *566*, 636, 673–4*, 806, 807; **16** 434; **17** 313, 314; **30** 559–60*
tiles **30** 874
towers **15** 812
wallpaper **32** 810–11*
wood **33** 335
woodwork **16** 487, 497
see also MANUSCRIPT ILLUMINATION; OIL SKETCHES; *see also under* MANUALS → types; TREATISES → types
Painting and Calligraphy Arts group *see* SŎHWA MISULHOE
Painting Appreciation Society *see* KANGAKAI
painting media **23** 791–3*
painting-needle *see under* EMBROIDERY → types
Painting Society of New Talent *see* SHINJIN GAKAI
paints **23** 782–8*, 791–3*
historical and regional traditions
Africa **1** 285, 288–90*
Antilles, Lesser **5** 746
Bhutan **3** 914
Central Asia, Western **6** 222
Egypt, ancient **10** 47
France **18** 118
Greece, ancient **13** 544
Mali **20** 198
Native North Americans **22** 587
Prehistoric art **23** 783*; **25** 477–9*, *478*
South America, Pre-Columbian **29** 176–7
Spain **29** 349
materials
acrylic **1** 129, 130; **25** 24–5
albumen **23** 783; **32** 898
alcohol **32** 898
alkyds **23** 793
binders **18** 118; **23** 782
bitumen **4** 103
casein **5** 912; **9** 39; **32** 898
chalk **3** 914
charcoal **5** 746
consolidants **7** 747
copal **23** 784
dextrin **32** 898
egg yolks **32** 898
feldspar **25** 477
flour **32** 898
frit **10** 47
gelatin **23** 792
gin **23** 792
glues **3** 914; **9** 39
glycerin **32** 898
gouache **32** 900
gum arabic **23** 783, 792; **32** 898
gums **13** 843; **23** 783
gum tragacanth **23** 792; **32** 898
kaolin **5** 746
latex **23** 784
linseed oil **23** 786
megilp **21** 49; **23** 784
mud **1** 285; **20** 198, *199*
oils **5** 33, 34; **23** 380, 785
oxgall **23** 792; **32** 898
pigments **23** 782; **24** 788
red lead **24** 796; **31** 282
resins **23** 784, 787
rice paste **32** 898
seeds **13** 874
silica gel **23** 793
size **32** 898
solvents **23** 792; **29** 53
starch **32** 898
talc **25** 477
tallow **23** 378
turmeric **23** 723
turpentine **23** 785, 792, 793
varnishes **32** 3
waxes **23** 378, 784; **33** 1, 5
white lead **31** 282

paints—cont.
patinas **11** 309
technical examination **30** 396, 402
types
acrylic emulsion *see* POLYMER COLOUR
alkyd **23** 784*; **25** 24
bladder colours **4** 113*
bodycolour *see* gouache
day-glo **25** 681
distemper **9** 39*; **23** 783*; **32** 811
Duco **1** 129; **25** 24
emulsion **10** 191; **23** 783
Glyptal **1** 129
gouache **9** 217, 898; **13** 219*; **23** 783; **32** 899
Magna **1** 129; **25** 24
oil **23** 783–4*, 792
oil-modified alkyd **23** 787
peinture à la colle see distemper
polymer colour **10** 191; **23** 783, 787, 792; **25** 25, 181*
poster **13** 219; **15** 855
powder **24** 647
Rhoplex **1** 129
tempera *see* TEMPERA
vinyl **23** 783
watercolour **9** 217; **13** 843; **23** 783*, 792; **32** 812, 898*
watercolour cakes **23** 787
uses
appliqué **29** 349
body arts **1** 288–9, *289*, 343–4, *344*; **10** 66; **13** 874
cliché-verre **7** 432
frescoes **11** 763–4
panel paintings **24** 6
photography **24** 647
plaster **29** 813
rock art **25** 477
screenprints **15** 855
sculpture **25** 477
shrines (i) (cult) **1** 289
stucco **29** 813
transfer (conservation) **31** 282
wallpaper **32** 811, 812, 813, 815, 818
waxes **33** 2
paint tubes *see under* PAINT CONTAINERS
Paionios of Ephesos **8** 869; **10** 431
Paionios of Mende **13** 423; **23** 793*
attributions **23** 432
works **13** 440, 454; **23** 432, *433*
pair-case watches *see under* WATCHES → types
Pair-non-Pair **25** 475, 485
Pair Painter **13** 501
Pairpoint, Thomas Joseph **13** 9
Pairpoint Manufacturing Co. **22** 240
País, El **31** 758
Pais, Gualdim **31** 101
Paischeff, John **11** 104
Pais da Silva, J. H. **25** 320
Paisley (Strathclyde)
art schools **28** 275
church **28** 288
mills (industrial) **28** 228
Neilson Institute **28** 228
shawls **28** 266
textiles **28** 564
Paisley pattern **28** 564
Paisy **8** 908
Paitava
sculpture **1** 196, *196*
Paiute **22** 550, 582, 659, 660, 662
Paiute (Northern) **22** 549, 633, 641
Paiute (Southern) **22** 549, 633
Paiute (Owens Valley) **22** 549
Paiute, Mono Lake **22** 641
baskets **22** *660*
Paiva, José Francisco de **23** 793–4*; **25** 307

Païva, Thérèse-Esther-Pauline-Blanche, Marquise de **5** 879; **8** 653; **23** 794*; **26** 190
Paix, Pierre de *see* PIERRE DE PAIX
Paizs Goebel, Jenő **23** 794*
Pajatén *see* GRAN PAJATÉN
Pajot, Antoine-Louis **11** 627
Pajou, Augustin **11** 627; **23** 794–6*
 collaboration **32** 766
 house **32** 767
 patrons and collectors **11** 561; **31** 56; **32** 719
 pupils **3** 463; **4** 457; **8** 508, 523, 791; **9** 389; **12** 334; **26** 551; **30** 747
 teachers **19** 142
 works **10** 764; **11** 342, 562; **12** 159; **13** 226; **23** *795*; **24** 149; **27** 558, 659; **30** 499
Pajou, Jacques-Augustin **23** 796
Pajou, Martin **23** 794
P'aju, Yŏngmi **18** 293
Pak **24** 82, 83
Pak Che-ga **23** 796*
Pak Chi-wŏn **23** 796*
Pak Chong-bae **18** 301
Pakenham, Thomas, 2nd Earl of Longford **16** 27
Pakenham Hall *see* TULLYNALLY CASTLE
Pakhan-gyi **5** 233
Pakhomov, Aleksey **7** 341; **27** 396
Pak In-jun **18** 263
Pakistan **15** 185; **16** *105*; **23** 797–805*, *797*
 archaeology **23** 804–5
 architecture **16** 166–9*; **21** 43; **23** 798–9*
 art legislation **23** 804–5*
 awnings **23** 803
 basketwork **23** 802
 body arts **23** 803
 bronze **23** *802*
 calligraphy **23** 800, *801*
 carpets **23** 802*
 ceramics **23** 802–3
 coins **16** *513*
 collections **23** 804*
 colleges **24** *540*
 education (art) **23** 798, 803–4*
 embroidery **23** 802
 epigraphy **16** 166
 forgeries **15** 750
 gardens **18** *646*
 gold **16** *513*; **23** 803
 government buildings **16** *93*
 henna **23** 803
 inscriptions **16** 166
 jewellery **23** 803
 kites **23** 803
 lamps **23** 803
 leather **23** 803
 metalwork **23** 803
 museums **23** 804*
 necklaces **23** 803
 office buildings **23** *799*
 onyx **23** 803
 painting **23** 799–801*, *801*
  portraits **23** *800*
 paper **23** 803
 papier mâché **23** 803
 rugs **23** 802
 schist **5** *308*, *309*
 screens (i) (architectural) **23** 803
 scripts **16** 166
 sculpture **23** 801–2*
  bronze **23** *802*
  relief **5** *308*, *309*; **23** 803
 shisham **23** 803
 shoes **23** 803
 shrines (i) (cult) **30** *380*
 silver **23** 803
 stone **23** 803
 terracotta **16** 166
 textiles **23** 802*
 tombs **23** 803
 trappings **23** 803
 wood **23** 803
Pakistan—cont.
 see also INDIAN SUBCONTINENT
Pakistan Burmah Shell **17** 806
Pakistan Environmental Planning and Architectural Consultants **23** 799
Pak Kil-ryong **18** 263, 264
Pak Kyu-su **23** 796*
Pakot *see* POKOT
Pakourianos, Grigorios **9** 523
Pak P'aeng-nyŏn **18** 329
Pakpak Batak **15** 788
Pakpatan, Shrine of Shaykh 'Ala' al-Din **15** 337
Pak P'yŏng-ŭi *see* KIYOEMON
pakṣabhadra **15** 244*
Pak Saeng-gwang **18** 326
 works **18** *326*
Pakse **18** 767, 771–2
Pak Sŏ-bo *see* PARK SEO BO
Pak Sŏg-wŏn **18** 301
Pak Su-gŭn **18** 326; **23** 805*
Pak Sŭng-gu **18** 300
paktong *see* ALLOYS → types → *baitong*
Pak Tong-jin **18** 263
Pakubuwono II, Sultan of Surakarta (*reg* 1725–49) **15** 801; **30** 9
Pakulin, Vyacheslav **7** 341
Pakulski, Józef **9** 473
Pakuriani, Apazi **3** 21
Pakuriani, Grigori **3** 21
Pak Yŏng-hyo **18** 332
Pak Yŏng-suk **18** 259
Pak Yun-mun **18** 60
Pal, Pratapaditya **30** 848
Pala **23** 805*
Pala, Dharmapala *see* DHARMAPALA, Ruler
Palaasma, Judani **13** 843
palace-boats *see under* BOATS → types
Palace of Diocletian *see under* SPLIT
Palace of Huntly **28** 224; **31** 230
Palace of Vendas Novas **32** 422
palaces **13** 238; **23** 805–26*
 historical and regional traditions
  Achaemenid **1** 116; **23** 807
  Afghanistan **1** *189*; **16** 167
  Africa **1** 242, 308–9, 314, 315; **23** 824–5*
  Anatolia, ancient **1** 824, 826; **23** 806–7*
  Ancient Near East **23** 806–7*
  Arabia **2** 250*
  Asante **1** 242
  Assyrian **23** 806
  Austria
   Baroque **11** *132*, *135*; **14** *528*, *529*; **32** *459*, *461*
   Renaissance **2** 779, *779*; **15** *867*
   18th cent. **10** *530*
  Aztec **23** 825
  Babylonian **21** *285*
  Bamum **1** 242, 309; **3** *151*, 151–2
  Bantu peoples **1** 308
  Benin, Kingdom of **1** 284
  Bhutan **3** 913
  Buddhism **30** *589*, *820*, 820
  Burma **5** 235–6, *236*
  Byzantine **9** 524, 553, 556–8*, *558*, *559*
  Cameroon **1** 309; **3** *151*
  Central Asia, Western **16** 160; **23** 815, 820*
   Islamic **6** *203*; **16** 167, *238*
   Timurid **6** *203*; **23** 820
  Chimú **23** 826
  China **6** 663, 679–84*, *680*, *683*; **23** 820*
  Crete **8** 153; **21** 651, 657, 661, 663–4*; **23** 808
  Croatia **8** 176; **9** *330*, *558*; **29** *417*
  Cyprus, ancient **8** 335–6, *336*
palaces
 historical and regional traditions—cont.
  Czech Republic **5** *79*, 702; **25** *427*
  Denmark **10** *110*
  Early Christian (*c*. AD 250–843) **9** 524, 553, 556–8*, *558*
  Egypt **16** 257
  Egypt, ancient **13** 405; **23** 807*
  England **6** 407; **10** 229, 359; **33** *247*
   Baroque **23** 812; **33** *397*
   Gothic **19** *609*; **33** *64*
   16th cent. **14** *127*; **19** 617, *618*; **23** *197*
   17th cent. **17** *635*
   see also HOUSES → types → country
  Fon **1** 309
  France
   Baroque **8** *33*
   Gothic **13** 59
   Neo-classicism **23** 812
   Renaissance **23** 810–11
   16th cent. **19** *237*
   17th cent. **4** *866*; **19** *134*; **20** *896*
   see also CHATEAUX
  Germany **12** 371; **18** *159*; **32** 682; **33** *37*
   Baroque **3** *266*; **9** *236*, *237*, *747*; **22** *309*; **23** *3*, *4*, 811–12, *812*; **25** *367*; **28** *110*, *117*
   Gothic **13** *58*
   Neo-classicism **23** *813*; **28** *101*
   Renaissance **24** *230*; **29** *739*
   Rococo **26** 495–6, *496*
   Romanesque **12** *245*
   16th cent. **29** *875*
   17th cent. **27** *196*; **33** *54*
   18th cent. **8** *530*; **17** *835*
   19th cent. **23** *814*
  Ghana **23** 824
  Gothic **13** 53
   Croatia **9** *330*
   England **19** *609*; **33** *64*
   France **13** 59
   Germany **13** *58*
   Spain **13** *283*
   Wales **27** *539*
  Greece **2** *674*
  Greece, ancient **13** 404, 405, 407; **23** 808*
  Haiti **14** *57*
  Hausa **1** 284, 315; **23** 824
  Helladic **14** 338, *339*, 340; **23** 476–7; **25** *754*; **31** *25*, 25–6
  Hittite **1** 826; **20** 540, *540*; **23** 806
  Huari culture **23** 826
  Inca **15** 162; **23** 826
  Indian subcontinent **15** 235, 248–9; **23** 816–20*
   Avadh **15** *378*
   Colonial period **15** *402*
   Islamic **15** *354*
   Madya Pradesh **23** *818*
   Malwa **15** *354*
   Mughal **15** 242, *369*, *371*
   Rajput **15** 242, 385–93, *386*, *387*, *388*, *389*, *391*, *392*; **23** *819*
   16th cent. **7** *494*
  Indonesia **15** *769*, 775
  Iran **16** 160, 234–5, 246, *265*
   Hasanwayhid **16** 160
   Islamic **16** *80*
   Safavid **23** *816*
  Iran, ancient **23** 807*
  Iraq **16** *152*, 152–3, 160, 182; **18** *483*
  Islamic **16** 130, 141, 146, 243–4, 246, 800; **23** 814–16*
   Afghanistan **16** 167
   Africa **1** 315
   Central Asia, Western **16** 160, 167, *238*
palaces
 historical and regional traditions
  Islamic—cont.
   Egypt **16** 257
   Indian subcontinent **15** *354*
   Iran **16** *80*, 160, 234–5, 246, *265*; **23** *816*
   Iraq **16** *152*, 152–3, 160, 182
   Jordan **16** *556*
   Morocco **16** 240; **23** 816
   Ottoman **16** 225, 227, 266; **23** 816
   Spain **13** *288*; **16** 187, 215, 217, *217*
   Syria **16** 148, 182, 245
   Turkey **16** 186, 204, 225, 227, 266
  Italy **22** 413; **23** 809
   Renaissance **23** 809–10
   Roman **26** *895*
   see also PALAZZI
  Japan **17** 46, *70*, *77*, *78*, *79*, *80*, 93*, *93*; **23** 821–3*, *822*
   Meiji period (1868–1912) **17** *87*
  Java **15** *769*, 775; **30** *9*
  Jordan **16** *556*
  Kassite **23** 806
  Korea **18** 260, 261, 274–6*, *275*, 281; **23** 821*
  Latvia **18** *848*
  Maya **17** *715*; **18** *578*; **20** 883; **21** *204*, *208*, 214; **23** 825, *825*, 826, 837; **28** 26, *26*
  Mesoamerica, Pre-Columbian **17** *715*; **18** *578*; **21** 204, *204*, *207*, *208*, *734*; **23** 825–6*, *825*, 837; **28** 26, *26*
  Mesopotamia **21** 272, *285*, 285–6, 291; **23** 806*
  Mexico **17** *715*; **18** *578*; **21** *734*; **23** *825*; **28** *26*
  Minoan **8** 153; **20** *203*; **21** 651, 657, 661, 663–4*; **23** 808
  Mixtec **21** *734*; **23** 825
  Morocco **16** 240; **23** 816
  Mycenaean **14** 338, *339*, 340; **23** 808; **31** *25*, 25–6
  Nepal **22** 765, *765*, 792
  Netherlands, the **14** *38*
  Nigeria **1** 314; **23** 824
  Ottoman **16** 225, 227, 266; **23** 816
  Parthian **23** 806, 807
  Peru **19** *386*; **24** *505*
  Phrygian **23** 806
  Poland **25** 97, 98, 135
   Baroque **12** *35*; **32** *870*
   Neo-classicism **32** *881*
   18th cent. **32** *875*
   20th cent. **19** *536*
  Portugal
   Baroque **28** *912*
   Neo-classicism **23** *453*
   Rococo **23** *405*
   16th cent. **28** *780*
   18th cent. **20** *402*
  Prehistoric art **1** *189*, 824; **23** 807–8*
  Romanesque **12** *245*
  Rome, ancient **3** 329*; **23** 808–9*; **26** 751, *893*, *895*; **29** *417*
  Russia **27** 373, 374
   Baroque **25** *745*
   Neo-classicism **5** *520*
   17th cent. **27** *372*
   18th cent. **22** *172*; **24** *292*, *547*; **27** *574*, *585*
  Sasanian **18** *483*; **23** 806, 807
  Scotland **9** *725*, *728*; **28** *225*
  Slovakia **4** *696*
  South America, Pre-Columbian **23** 825*, 826*
  South-east Asia **23** 823–4*
  Spain **2** *284*; **13** 285; **29** 299–300
   Baroque **8** *32*; **20** *72*; **29** *270*
   Churrigueresque **7** *289*
palaces
 historical and regional traditions
  Spain—cont.
   Gothic **12** *619*; **13** *283*
   Hispano-Flemish style **13** *731*
   Islamic **13** *288*; **16** 187, 215, 217, *217*
   Joanine **19** *776*
   Mudéjar **22** *255*
   Renaissance **8** *80*; **10** *499*, *500*; **20** *2*; **23** 811; **29** *264*; **32** *620*
   15th cent. **13** *756*
  Sri Lanka **29** 448
  Surinam **30** *14*
  Swahili **23** 824
  Sweden **29** *689*
  Syria **16** 148, 182, 245
  Syria-Palestine **23** 806*; **30** 185, 186, 187, 191, *191*
  Thailand **30** 575, 588*, *589*
  Tibet **30** 820, *820*
  Toltec **23** 826
  Turkey **9** *559*; **16** 186, 204, 225, 227, 266, *587*
  Uganda **1** 309
  Urartian **23** 807; **31** 699–700
  Wales **27** *539*
  Yoruba **1** 242, 309, 314; **23** 824; **33** 554
  Zimbabwe **1** 308
 materials
  brick **23** 807
  mosaics **17** *715*
  mud-bricks **23** 806, 807
  plaster **23** 807
 types
  block **9** 558–9*, *559*
  entre cour et jardin **25** 99
  episcopal **9** 529
  fortified **9** 557–8*; **20** *157*
  garden **23** 820
  prāsādas **23** 817
 see also BIT HILANI; CASTLES
Palace school **12** 382
Palace ware *see* POTTERY → wares → Toprakkale ware
Palacio, Augusto Pérez *see* PÉREZ PALACIO, AUGUSTO
Palacio, Gonzalo Gómez *see* GÓMEZ PALACIO, GONZALO
Palacio, Vicente Riva *see* RIVA PALACIO, VICENTE
Palácio de Congresso Nacional *see* CONGRESSO NACIONAL
Palacio Elissague, Alberto de **29** 272
Palacios, Alirio **23** 826*
 works **32** 176
Palacios, Francisco de **14** 190; **24** 392; **32** 135
Palacios, Luisa **23** 827*; **25** 824; **32** 176
Palacios, Mahoma de *see* MAHOMA DE PALACIOS
Palacios, Rafael **25** 701
Palacio San José (Entre Rios; Argentina) **2** 395
Palacios de Benaver Monastery **13** 123
Palacios y Ramilo, Antonio **23** 827*; **29** 273
Pala Colonna **25** 898
Pala del Fiore **12** 735
Pala di Collalto **12** 735
Paladini, Filippo (di Benedetto) **20** 213; **23** 827*
Paladino, Mimmo **16** 682; **23** 827–8*
 methods **10** 199
 works **9** 310; **16** 683, 709; **23** 334
Pala d'Oro *see under* VENICE → ecclesiastical buildings → S Marco
palaeography **20** 43; **23** 828*; **28** 303
Palaeolithic period *see under* PREHISTORIC ART → periods

Palaeolona **8** 339
Palaer, Jorge **23** 900
palaestrae **13** 886; **23** 828*
Greece, ancient **13** 386, 406; **23** 828
Rome, ancient **23** 828; **26** 912
see also Baths; Bath-gymnasia; Gymnasia
Paláez, Amalia **33** 316
Pala Fugger **32** 649
Palagi, (Filippo) Pelagio **10** 637; **23** 828–30*
assistants **14** 265
groups and movements **10** 644; **22** 741
patrons and collectors **16** 730; **31** 172
restorations **31** 445
works **16** 720; **23** *830*
Palagi Head **24** 593
Palagio, Carlo di Cesari del *see* Carlo di Cesari del Palagio
Palagio, del (family) **7** 333
Palaikastro **21** *651*
faience (i) (glass) **21** 683
ivory-carvings **21** 681, *681*, 682, 691
pottery **21** 667, 670, *670*
seals **21** 653
Temple of Diktaian Zeus **8** 154
towns **21** 664
wall paintings **8** 153; **21** 674
Palaiochora **18** 570, 571
Palaiokastro *see* Kastri
Palaiologan **9** 550; **23** 830–31*
Palaiologan Renaissance **9** 549, 606; **23** 831
Palaiologina, Anna **2** 509
Palaiologina, Euphrosyne *see* Euphrosyne Palaiologina
Palaiologina, Theodora **7** 228
Palaiologos, Constantine, Prince *see* Constantine Palaiologos, Prince
Palaiologos, Demetrios, Despot of Thessaloniki *see* Demetrios Palaiologos, Despot of Thessaloniki
Palaiologos, John Uroš *see* Joasaph (*1349–1423*)
Palaiologos, Manuel II, Emperor of Byzantium *see* Manuel II Palaiologos, Emperor of Byzantium
Palaiologos, Michael VIII, Emperor of Byzantium *see* Michael VIII Palaiologos, Emperor of Byzantium
Palaiologos, William VI, Margrave of Monferrat *see* William VI, Margrave of Monferrat
Palaiopyrgi **14** 351; **29** 367
palais de justice *see* Law courts
Pala Martinengo **19** 712
Palamedesz., Anthonie **23** 831–2*
attributions **25** 362
collaboration **3** 352
reproductive prints by others **19** 144
works **22** 844; **23** *831*
Palamedesz., Palamedes, I (1607–38) **22** 844; **23** 831
Palamedesz., Palamedes, II (1633–1705) **23** 832
Palampet **15** *294*, 534; **23** 832*
Ramappa Temple **15** 328, 538–9; **23** 832
Rudreshvara *see* Ramappa Temple
Palanca, Angela **31** 446
Palangana group **8** 227
Palanlı **1** 823
palanquins **2** 588*; **10** 50; **17** 302; **31** 407
Palanti, Giancarlo **1** 578; **3** 227; **21** 631; **23** 169
Palanti, M. **28** 834
Palari, Siddheshvara Temple **15** 284, 495
Pala Sforzesca **9** 263
Pala Sforzesca, Master of the **20** 741*
Palati, Temple of Apollo **22** 698–9
Palatinate Sword **9** 234; **12** 446
Palatine Bible *see under* Bibles → individual manuscripts
Palatine Chapel *see under* Aachen → Palace
Palatino, Giovanni Battista **28** 307
Palatnik, Abraham **4** 719
Palau **21** 476, 477; **23** *711*, 832–4*
architecture **23** 715, 717
body ornaments **23** 723
canoes **23** 726
erotic art **10** 474
gables **23** 833, *833*
human figures **23** *834*
lamps **23** 833
meeting-houses **23** 833, *833*
menhirs **23** 833
narratives **23** 833, *833*
pandanus **23** 735
sculpture **23** 730
shells **23** 833
wood **23** 717
wood-carvings **23** *834*
Palau, Bartolomé **30** 664
Palau, Bernard de *see* Bernard de Palau
Palau, Pere Joan **29** 333
Palaung **5** 248, 250
Palavičini, Petar **28** 453
Palawan **21** 596; **24** *607*, 625, 627
Palazuelo, Pablo **20** 75; **23** 834–5*
Palazuelos, Julio **6** 598
palazzi **16** 629, 630; **23** 806, 835–6*
Baroque **1** *622*; **13** *752*; **16** *562*, *644*, *764*; **17** *709*; **20** *45*; **27** *320*; **32** *187*
Gothic **4** *775*; **13** *64*; **24** *519*; **28** *675*, *683*; **32** *628*
Mannerism **12** *754*; **23** *864*, *865*, *868*; **26** *839*
Palladianism **3** *864*
Razionalismo **26** *15*
Renaissance **1** *562*, *607*; **2** *593*; **3** *16*; **4** *649*, 651; **5** *181*; **7** *518*, *905*; **10** *767*; **18** *861*; **21** *469*; **23** *810*, *836*; **24** *533*; **26** *819*; **27** *742*, *758*, *760*; **28** *468*; **32** *342*
Early Renaissance **16** *629*
13th cent. **11** *212*; **31** *237*
14th cent. **32** *218*
15th cent. **27** *189*; **32** *219*
16th cent. **3** *767*; **12** *752*; **13** *649*; **28** *460*
17th cent. **11** *213*; **20** *521*; **27** *194*; **28** *733*
18th cent. **5** *914*; **11** *814*; **22** *388*
19th cent. **3** *50*
20th cent. **3** *327*
Palazzi, Lazzaro **9** 75
palazzi della ragione *see* Law courts
palazzi della sapienza **31** 674, *674*
see also Universities
Palazzo, Carlo *see* Carlo di Cesari del Palagio
Palazzo Grimaldi *see under* Monaco
Palazzolo Acreide *see* Acrae
Palazzone **7** 905
Palazzo S Gervasio, Master of the **8** 139; **20** 741*
Palazzo Venezia Madonna **29** 598
Palazzo Venezia Madonna, Master of the **3** 247; **5** 164; **20** 510
Pal Barik **15** 902
Palcaro, Jacobo **23** 881
Palcr, Zdeněk **8** 388
Pale **17** 909
pale *see* Altarpieces
Palea Paphos *see* Paphos, old
Paleari, Bernardo **10** 763
Palearo, Giacomo **30** 518
Paledaen *see* Broeck, Willem van den
Palekh **23** 837*; **27** *363*
lacquer **27** 427
Museum of Palekh Art **23** 837
Museum of Palekh Crafts **27** 441
Pavel Korin House-Museum **23** 837
Palembang **6** *623*; **15** *752*, 787, 795
baskets **15** 810
coins **15** 811
Museum Budaya Sultan Mahmud Badaruddin **29** 239
sculpture **29** 231
silk **15** 794
Palencia
Cathedral **13** 68, 69, *69*; **14** 578
crypt **29** 262
furniture **29** 317
ivory-carvings **16** 524
metalwork **29** 334, 337
Oratorio de la Reina Católica **17** 674, *675*
retable **29** 289
textiles **30** 331
workshop **13** 68
Nuestra Señora de la Calle **29** 268
S Clara **26** 642
sculpture **13** 104
Palencia, Benjamín **23** 837*; **29** 286
groups and movements **5** 613; **20** 68
works **29** 286
Palencia, Pablo **29** 305, 315
Palenque **20** *882*; **21** *193*, 199, 262, *372*; **23** 826, 837–9*, *838*
caskets **21** 259
finials (architectural) **21** 207
masks **21** 254
Palace **21** 207, *208*; **29** 829
plaques **30** 786
pottery **21** 239
pyramids **31** 116
reliefs **21** 184
sculpture **21** 221–2, *222*
stairs **21** 206
stelae **29** 620
stucco **29** *828*
Tablet of the 96 Hieroglyphs **23** 838
temples **21** 214; **23** 838; **28** 640
Temple of the Cross **9** 165; **21** 214; **29** 829
Temple of the Foliated Cross **20** 883; **21** 214; **29** 829
Temple of the Inscriptions **21** 214, 215, *215*, 251, 259; **23** 837; **25** 764; **30** 449
mother-of-pearl **22** 205
sculpture **23** *839*
stucco **29** 829
tomb of Lord Pacal **23** 838; **31** 116, 118
tomb of Lord Pacal: burial mask **16** II1; **21** 243
tomb of Lord Pacal: sarcophagus **21** 188, 221, *221*; **27** 833
Temple of the Sun **20** 883; **21** 214; **29** 829
tombs **20** 883
wall paintings **21** 231
paleochrystalos **33** 628
Paleologo, Annibale **1** 529
Paleologo, Margherita **12** 561; **31** 747
Paleotti (family) **6** 361
Paleotti, Gabriele, Cardinal **7** 276; **23** 839–40*; **26** 63
works **1** 179; **4** 276; **6** 361; **8** 612; **30** 803; **31** 299
Paleotti, Gaspare Maria **14** 12
Palermo **9** *510*; **16** *103*, *621*; **23** 840–46*
Archbishop's Palace **23** 843
architecture **23** 842*
Baths of Cefalà Diana **28** 655
catacomb of S Giovanni **6** 70
catacombs **6** 70
Palermo—cont.
Cubola **16** 172
ecclesiastical buildings
Cappella Palatina **10** 833; **16** 171, 172, 253, 627; **23** 844–5*; **26** 619; **28** 655
candlesticks **26** 628
doors **9** 154
ivory-carvings **16** 524, 525
mosaics **9** 581, 645; **14** 240; **16** 655; **18** 703; **22** 162; **23** *844*, 844–5; **26** 680
muqarnas (architecture) **16** *171*; **22** 324
paintings **16** 306
wall paintings **16** 516, 530, 538; **22** 520
Cathedral of S Maria Assunta **16** 172; **23** 843*, *843*; **26** 619
retable **28** 657
sculpture **11** 899
tombs **26** 628–9; **29** 702
Il Gesù **17** 511
La Martorana *see* S Maria dell'Ammiraglio
Oratorio del Rosario **28** 657
Oratorio di S Cita **16** 704, *704*; **28** *477*; **29** 831
Oratorio di S Lorenzo **28** 657
La Pietà **1** 758
S Cataldo **7** 257; **16** 172, 627
S Domenico **22** 680
S Francesco Saverio **16** 615
S Giovanni degli Eremiti **16** 171, 627; **23** 846*
S Maria dell'Ammiraglio **9** 516, 645; **16** 171, 626; **23** 845–6*, *846*; **26** 579; **28** 655
mosaics **22** 162; **26** 680
sculpture **26** 628
S Maria dello Spasimo **28** 656
embroidery **16** 759; **26** 703
engravings **23** *842*
Fountain Pretoria **11** 342
gold **16** 742
ivory-carvings **26** 698
maiolica **16** 736
mosques **16** 171
museums
Galleria Civica d'Arte Moderna **23** 842
Galleria Regionale della Sicilia **16** 775; **23** 842; **28** 657
Museo Archeologico della Fondazione Mormino **23** 842
Museo Diocesano **23** 842
Museo Regionale di Palermo **10** 640; **13** 470; **23** 842; **27** 46
palazzi
Cuba Palace **16** 172, 627; **26** 579
Favara Palace **16** 171
Palazzo Abbatellis *see* museums → Galleria Regionale della Sicilia
Palazzo Bonagia **16** 716
Palazzo Chiaramonte **28** 656
Palazzo Gangi **16** 716
Palazzo dei Normanni **12** 71; **16** 762; **18** 71; **23** 843–4*
Palazzo Sclàfani **4** 896, 900
Palazzo Villafranca **16** 716
Royal Palace **16** 171, 172; **23** 843*
Aula Verde **16** 172
chamber of Roger II **9** 576
sculpture **5** 525
Ziza Palace **9** 558; **16** 172, 627; **22** 324; **26** 579; **28** 655
fountain **11** 340
gardens **12** 76, 78, *78*
Piazza S Francesco **28** *801*
Quattro Canti **28** 657
robes **26** 82
scripts **16** 280
Teatro Massimo **16** 646; **28** 657
textiles **16** 430, *430*, 437
throne **30** 779
urban planning **31** 717
Villa Florio all'Olivuzzo **32** 555
Palermo—cont.
Villa Igiea **28** 657
Villa la Favorita **16** 716
Villa Palagonia **32** 549
villas **32** 549
Villa Valguernera **32** 549
Palermo, Antonio Dominici **15** 881
Palermo, Antonio van **3** 23; **7** 708
Palermo, Blinky **23** 846–7*
Palermo Painter **13** 525
Palermo Stone **9** 778, 866; **10** 35
Palestine **23** 847*; **26** *852*; **30** *180*
architecture **9** 538–41*, 542–3*, 547–9*; **21** *588*; **26** 917*
baptisteries **9** 541
basalt **9** 538; **14** *273*
baths **16** *149*
bonnets **16** 459
castles **3** *691*
churches **3** *882*; **9** 538–41*, *541*, 542–3*, 547–9*, *548*; **17** *499*
dating methods **2** 300
domes **16** *147*
exhibitions **28** 548
fonts (baptismal) **11** *251*
fountains **20** *231*
glass **9** 644; **16** 517, 519
guidebooks **13** 808
icons **9** 624, 625, 627
kernoi **24** 634
lamps **27** 104, *104*
limestone **9** 538
manuscripts **9** 605, 617
martyria **17** *489*, *495*; **20** *519*
mausolea **17** 553
metalwork **9** 539
micrography **21** 475
monasteries **21** 833
mosaics **3** 882; **22** 161, 162
Byzantine **9** 567–8*, *574*
Early Christian (*c.* AD 250–843) **9** 567–8*, *574*
Jewish art **17** 557–8*
Roman **27** 63
6th cent. AD **17** *488*
mosques **22** *193*
plaques **27** *670*
pottery **16** 397
propylaia **26** *917*
refectories **18** *152*
ribāṭs **16** 155
roofs **9** 539
sculpture **14** *273*; **17** *554*
stone **9** 538
temples **17** *494*
trade
pottery **13** 486
wood **9** 539
see also Ancient Near East; Israel; Jerusalem, Latin Kingdom of; Jordan; Syria-Palestine
Palestrina *see* Praeneste
Palestrina Pietà **21** 440
Palethi, Surya Temple **15** 264
Palette, Jean **7** 466
palette knives **23** 379
Paletten **24** 451
palettes **10** 5
materials
schist **22** *509*
slate **9** 864; **14** *407*
wood **10** *4*, 5
types
ceremonial **9** 844, 868; **14** 407, *407*; **21** 554; **22** *509*; **23** 847–8*
cosmetic **1** 867; **9** 864; **10** 66; **15** 446; **24** 645
painters' **9** *898*; **10** 5; **21** 241; **23** 377, 848–9*
scribes' **10** *4*, 5
Paley, Al **16** 60
Paley, E(dward) G(raham) **9** 200
Paley, F. A. **22** 211
Pálffy (family) **28** 856

Pálffy, Ján, Count 5 771; 28 856
Palffy, Nikolaus VIII, Graf 4 663
Pálffy, Pál 15 3
Pálffy, Rudolf, Count 28 856
Palgrave, Francis 13 810; 22 352; 23 849*; 31 465
Palgrave, Mary 31 465
Pali 15 613; 29 440
  Khandoba Temple 15 493
  Shiva Temple 15 324
Pali *see* MIHINTALE
Paliachora 1 481–2
Paliani Monastery 8 156
Paliano and Castiglione, Lorenzo Onofrio Colonna, Duke of 7 621–2*
  interior decoration 7 620
  paintings 7 398, 399; 9 377; 20 375
Palikur 11 758
Palina Sape 15 818
Paling, Isaac 30 425
palisades 8 277; 9 143; 21 597; 25 522
Paliser & Paliser 25 807; 31 593
Palissy, Bernard 10 311; 23 849–50*; 24 148
  patrons and collectors 11 604; 22 31; 27 641; 31 850
  works 11 603, *603*; 12 120; 14 855; 23 540; 29 571
  writings 13 704
Palissy, Mathurin 23 850
Palissy, Nicholas 23 850
Palizzi, Filippo 22 480; 23 850, 851–3*
  groups and movements 16 678; 28 317; 32 257
  pupils 5 527; 10 512; 22 916
  teachers 4 333
  works 23 *853*
Palizzi, Francesco Paolo 23 854*
Palizzi, Giuseppe 23 850–52*
  personal collection 23 852
  works 23 *851*
Palizzi, Nicola 5 527; 8 463; 23 852–4*; 28 317
Palk, Robert 11 242
Pałka, Julian 14 155; 17 448
Palko, Anton 23 854, *854*
Palko, Franz Anton 15 13; 23 854*
  works 10 531; 23 *854*; 28 853
Palko, Franz (Xavier) Karl 2 796; 8 391; 23 854, 855*
  works 25 445; 28 853
Palla, Giovanbattista della 11 661; 16 766; 23 855–6*
Palladas, Jeremiah 24 263; 25 333
Pallade, La 24 447
palladia 19 788
Palladianism 5 538; 9 34–5; 12 129; 22 738; 23 856–62*, 871; 24 274
  art forms
    architecture 23 857, 858
      England 4 *610*, *612*, *613*, *822*; 5 *538*, *539*; 7 *174*; 17 *903*; 23 *856*, *858*; 32 *552*, *553*; 33 *224*
      Ireland 6 *64*; 9 *323*; 23 *861*
      Italy 3 *864*; 30 *424*
      Russia 17 *870*
      Scotland 28 226
      United States of America 31 590
    frames 11 426–7*, *427*
    interior decoration 31 617; 33 225, *225*
    manuals 23 860
  manuals 23 860
  pattern books 23 860
  regional traditions
    Britain 28 881
    Denmark 8 725
    England 5 537; 8 47; 10 233, 276, 361; 13 300; 23 781, 856–60; 25 266; 32 824
    France 23 856, 861
    Germany 2 94; 23 861; 33 380
Palladianism
  regional traditions—cont.
    Ireland 13 301; 16 8, 23; 23 860
    Italy 23 862
    Poland 25 99
    Scotland 23 860
    United States of America 23 860; 25 *267*
Palladio, Andrea 20 864; 23 856, 861–71*; 31 346; 32 220, 407, 648
  altarpieces 1 712
  architecture 5 617; 7 380, 382, 916; 16 635; 23 492; 24 290, 752; 27 131, 772; 32 409–10
  architectural decorations 4 776; 32 215
  cathedrals 19 673
  chapels 6 89; 20 546
  churches 4 272, 280; 7 516; 10 499; 16 635; 23 *869*; 32 187, 214, *214*
    S Francesco della Vigna (Venice) 10 744; 16 635, *636*; 22 378
    S Giorgio Maggiore (Venice) 4 774; 32 214
  palazzi
    Doge's Palace (Venice) 25 215
    Loggia (Brescia) 4 748
    Palazzo Chiericati (Vicenza) 23 836, *864*
    Palazzo della Ragione (Vicenza) 11 316; 23 *865*; 27 129; 31 238
    Palazzo Ruini-Ranuzzi (Bologna) 25 893; 30 516
    Palazzo Thiene (Vicenza) 23 858; 32 647
    Palazzo Valmarana (Vicenza) 23 492, *868*
  plans 2 *330*; 26 895; 32 411
  staircases 29 523
  temporary architecture 23 767
  theatres 1 124; 15 137; 20 412; 30 655, *655*
  triumphal arches 31 351
  villas 16 633–4; 32 547–8
    models 2 336
    Villa Badoer (Fratta Polesine) 32 *549*
    Villa Barbaro (Maser) 15 137; 20 545, *545*; 27 236, *236*
    Villa Cornaro (Piombino Dese) 20 412; 23 *866*
    Villa Foscari (Malcontenta di Mira) 11 721; 32 187
    Villa Godi-Malinverni (Lonedo di Lugo, Vicenza) 23 *863*
    Villa Poiana (Poiana Maggiore) 1 532
    Villa Rotonda (Vicenza) 14 460; 20 280; 23 857, *867*; 25 265; 28 30; 32 411
    Villa Sarego (Santa Sofia di Pedemonte) 2 *357*
  windows 3 766
  assistants 13 650; 27 347
  attributions 22 131; 25 271
  collaboration 3 202, 203; 8 706; 30 515; 32 77, 641, 647
  drawings 2 329; 26 866, 872, 900, 901, 903
  interior decoration 16 712; 27 347; 32 220, 549
  methods 14 874; 28 201
  patrons and collectors 5 690
    Barbaro (family) 3 202, 203; 32 350
    Barbaro, Daniele 3 202
    Boyle, Richard, 3rd Earl of Burlington and 4th Earl of Cork 4 609, 612; 13 301
    Contarini, Jacopo 7 775, 776
    Cornaro, Giorgio 7 861
    Grimani, Giovanni, Patriarch of Aquileia 13 659
Palladio, Andrea
  patrons and collectors—cont.
    Howard (i), Thomas, 2nd Earl of Arundel 17 633
    Jones, Inigo 2 330
    Mocenigo (family) 21 747
    Mocenigo, Leonardo 21 747
    Muttoni, Francesco 22 387, 388
    Porto, Iseppo da 25 271
    Thiene, Adriano and Marcantonio 30 731
    Thiene, Francesco di Sartorio (*d* 1593) 30 732
    Thiene, Marcantonio 30 731
    Valmarana, Giovanni Francesco 31 831
    Wotton, Henry 13 299
  reproductive prints by others 20 457
  stage design 30 656, 657
  teachers 31 346
  woodcuts 32 199
  writings 2 167–8; 14 869; 16 634; 19 160; 22 387; 23 856; 26 848; 27 236; 31 294, 296; 32 199, 410
    illustrated 9 48; 19 659
    on architectural orders 23 487
    on architecture 24 274
    on bridges 4 804
    on proportion 2 357
    on staircases 29 523
    on villas 32 550
    translated 4 203, 612, 868; 5 538; 8 496; 11 743; 12 6; 17 634; 19 144, 204, 837; 23 857; 29 269; 32 860
Palladio, Marcantonio 32 647
Palladio: Rivista di storia dell'architettura 24 448
Palladion 29 567
Palladios 9 643
palladium 10 136; 12 621, 865
Palladius, Rutilius Taurus Aemilianus 12 110; 26 884, 924
Pallady, Ferenc 29 606
Pallady, Theodor 23 872*; 26 715, 716, 723
Pallago, Carlo *see* CARLO DI CESARI DEL PALAGIO
Pallakollu 15 673
Pallandt van Klarenbeek, A. H. E., Baroness 32 377
Pallard, Jean Jacques 9 240
Pallares, Rodrigo 9 711
Pallarps, Ake 30 82
pallas 9 246
Pallás y Muig, D. Francisco 16 545
Pallava 23 872–3*
  see also:
  MAHENDRAVARMAN I, Ruler
  NANDIVARMAN II PALLAVAMALLA, Ruler
  NARASIMHAVARMAN II RAJASIMHA, Ruler
  NARASIMHAVARMAN I MAHAMALLA, Ruler
  PARAMESHVARAVARMAN I, Ruler
Pallavaram, Cave Temple 15 507
Pallavicini (family)
  architecture 1 605
  collections 2 27; 26 773
  gems 5 678
  paintings 4 638; 19 816; 20 375; 28 379; 29 388
Pallavicini, Agostino 23 873
Pallavicini, Giovanni Battista 23 873
Pallavicini, Lazzaro, Cardinal 23 873
Pallavicini, Marcello 23 873
Pallavicini, Maria Camilla, Princess of Gallicano 23 873, 874*
Pallavicini, Nicolò, Marchese (1563-1619) 23 873; 27 289
Pallavicini, Nicolò, Marchese (1650-1714) 20 *378*; 23 873, 874*; 27 346
  paintings 20 376; 24 836, 837
Pallavicini, Nicolò Maria (*d* 1759) 23 873
Pallavicini, Stefano 11 682; 23 873
Pallavicino, Cesare 15 826
Pallavicino, Cipriano 5 456
Pallavicino, Tobia 6 24
Pallavicino da Scipione, Pietro 1 748
Pallavicino Trivulzio, Giorgio, Marchese 14 265
Pallemberg 6 550
Pallenberg, Jakob 19 31
Pallesi, Alfredo 9 182
Pallettoni, Alfonso 3 211
pallia (ecclesiastical) 9 641, 642; 32 388*
  see also OMOPHORIA
pallia (secular) *see* HIMATIA
Palliardi, Ignac 25 445
Pallière, Louis-Vincent-Léon 4 106
Pallizi, Filippo 16 736
Palloni, Michelangelo 17 615; 18 440; 19 496, 497; 25 105; 32 876, 881
Pallottino, Massimo 10 638, 639; 23 874*
palls 12 331; 19 510; 26 720–21; 27 829
palm 15 720; 16 269, 487; 29 226
Palm, Gustaf Wilhelm 23 875*
Palm, Jüri 10 540
Palma, Andrea 16 640; 30 176
  works 16 *640*
Palma, Antonio 23 875, 877*
Palma, Felice 2 610; 23 880*
Palma, Nicolò 23 842
Palma, Ricardo 11 61
Palma de Mallorca 23 880–81*; 29 *259*
  Ayuntamiento 3 106
  bathhouse 3 106
  Casa de los Marqueses de Sollerich 3 106
  Casa Olesa 3 106
  Casa Palmer 3 106
  Castell del Bellver 3 106, *106*
  Cathedral of the Virgin 3 106; 13 67, *67*; 23 *881*, 881; 29 263
    buttresses 20 581
    metalwork 29 337
    Portal del Mirador 13 68
    sculpture 13 106
  Consulato del Mar *see* Museo Maritimo Balear
  Llotja 3 106; 13 68
  Market Hall *see* Llotja
  Museo de Mallorca 3 106
  Museo Maritimo Balear 23 881
  Museo de Patrimonio Nacional 3 106
  Palau Vivot 3 106
  S Eulália 3 106
  S Francesco 3 106; 13 67
  S Jaume 13 67
  S Margarita 29 263
Palma di Cesnola, Luigi 8 366; 12 266
Palma (il) Giovane(, Giacomo) (*c.* 1548-1628) 16 675; 23 875, 878–80*; 32 *191*, 194
  collaboration 11 51; 32 77, 192
  patrons and collectors 5 432; 7 776; 9 174; 14 805; 15 148; 26 284, 307; 28 5, 560; 32 6; 33 387
  pupils 4 455; 19 14
  reproductive prints by others 10 770; 12 881; 20 812; 27 503, 504
  works 1 658; 22 696; 23 381, *878*, *879*; 32 160, 191, 222, 648
Palmanova 16 *618*; 23 882*; 31 712, *713*; 32 *158*
  fortifications 32 159
Palmar Sur 29 213
Palma (il) Vecchio(, Jacopo) (*c.* 1479/80-1528) 3 771; 23 875–7*; 32 190
  assistants 20 398
  attributions 12 670
  patrons and collectors
    Augustus III, King of Poland (*reg* 1733-63) 1 633
    Benson, R(obert) H(enry) 3 740
    Butler, Charles (1822-1910) 5 311
    Contarini, Taddeo 7 775
    Crespi, Cristoforo Benigno 8 146
    Fitzwilliam, Richard, 7th Viscount Fitzwilliam 11 141
    Habsburg I., Leopold William, Archduke of Austria, Governor of the Netherlands 13 919
    Lanier, Nicholas 18 747
    Mielżyński, Seweryn Józef Stanisław 21 485
    Mond, Ludwig 26 358
    Odoni, Andrea 23 355
    Percy, Algernon, 4th Duke of Northumberland 24 390
    Poniatowski, Stanisław, Prince 25 213
    Potocki, Stanisław Kostka 25 364
    Pourtalès-Gorgier, James-Alexandre, Comte de 25 383
    Puccini, Tommaso 25 691
    Vendramin, Andrea 32 155
  pupils 24 888
  reproductive prints by others 8 495; 18 42
  works 11 36, 391; 23 *876*, *877*; 27 496; 32 191, 226
Palm Beach (FL), Royal Poinciana Hotel 14 787
Palme, Ignác, & Co.
  works 8 *410*
Palmela, Helena Maria Holstein Beck, 4th Duquesa de 29 101
Palmela, Maria Luisa de Sousa Holstein, 3rd Duquesa de 4 629; 29 101*
Palmela, Pedro de Sousa Holstein, 1st Duque de 28 431; 29 100–101*
Palmer, Alfred H. 23 886
Palmer, Bertha Honoré 5 922; 23 882*; 31 664
Palmer, Charles 30 236
Palmer, Edmund S. 23 883
Palmer, Edward 22 582
Palmer, Erastus Dow 23 882–3*; 31 610
Palmer, Frances (Flora) 8 276; 19 485; 23 883*
Palmer, F. & S. 23 883
Palmer, George 31 266
Palmer, H. S. 5 573
Palmer, James (1585-1658) 10 349; 23 883–4*; 29 800
Palmer, James le (*fl* before 1375) *see* JAMES LE PALMER
Palmer, John 3 371
Palmer, Potter 6 575
Palmer, Roger, Earl of Castlemaine 14 436
Palmer, Samuel 10 377; 23 884–7*; 29 878
  dealers 7 579
  forgeries by others 11 306, 309
  groups and movements 1 897; 10 252; 26 741
  methods 24 3
  patrons and collectors 11 331
  teachers 31 909
  works 18 714; 23 *885*, *886*; 29 *877*, *878*; 32 901, *901*
Palmer, Thomas J. 32 813
Palmer, Walter Launt 23 883
Palmer, William 7 *794*
Palmer & Hornbostel 23 41

Palmerino di Guido 2 625
Palmerston 7 790
Palmerston, Henry John Temple, 3rd Viscount *see* TEMPLE, HENRY JOHN, 3rd Viscount Palmerston
Palmerston, Henry Temple, 2nd Viscount *see* TEMPLE, HENRY, 2nd Viscount Palmerston
Palmer & Tritton Consulting Engineers 1 683
Palmer & Turner 3 177
Palmerucci, Guiduccio 22 727
palmesels *see under* SCULPTURE → types
palmettes 2 134, 135; 23 550, 556, 888–9*, *888*
see also ANTHEMIA
Palmetto ware *see under* POTTERY → wares
Palmezzano, Marco 23 889*
pupils 33 591
teachers 21 96, 97, 98
works 21 97
palm fibres *see under* FIBRES → types
Palmgren, Nils 13 864
Palmieri, Matteo 4 505
Palmieri, Pietro Giacomo 28 19
palm leaves
historical and regional traditions
Africa 1 295, *296*, 305–7; 3 331
Angola 1 *296*
Arabia 2 247
Bali (Indonesia) 15 806; 31 260
Buddhism 5 *96*; 15 570; 30 613
Burma 5 245*
Colombia 7 603
Hausa 1 305
Indian subcontinent 5 *96*; 15 544, 545, 547, 548, 561, 563–4, 570, 636, 727; 20 327
Indonesia 15 770, 809, 812
Jainism 15 545, 563–4
Java 15 772
Malaysia 20 167
Mongolia 21 876
Nepal 22 777, 778
Sudan 1 305
Thailand 30 613
Zaïre 1 *296*
uses
architecture 1 305–7
baskets 1 295, *296*; 3 331; 15 809
books 21 876
dolls 31 260
drawings 15 806
ex-votos 15 812
houses 2 247; 15 770
manuscripts 5 *96*, 245*; 15 544, 545, 547, 548, 561, 563–4, 570, 636; 20 327, *328*; 22 777, 778; 29 442; 30 613
mats 15 809
roofs 1 305; 7 603; 15 772; 20 167
thatch 1 306
trays 15 727
walls 1 306
palm nuts *see under* NUTS → types
Pal'mov, Viktor N. 2 634; 31 559
Palmqvist, Sven 12 795; 30 102
Palms Painter 10 611
Palmstedt, Erik 1 152; 23 890*
patrons and collectors 13 668
works 14 792; 29 685; 30 72, 677
Palmyra 1 *849*; 2 *246*; 13 *362*; 16 *104*; 23 *890*, 890–95*; 26 902, *915*; 28 *719*, 721; 30 178, *180*; 33 344
arches 2 297
architecture 23 891–3*; 26 918
basilica 3 329
colonnades 26 *918*
columns 26 882
forgeries 1 896
limestone 26 916
mosaics 27 65
Palmyra—cont.
mouldings 9 757
reliefs 1 882; 16 455; 23 894–5, *894*; 24 218
Sanctuary of Baalshamin 23 *892*
Sanctuary of Bel 8 64
Temple of Bel 1 887; 23 891, 894; 26 866, 916; 27 45; 30 436
sculpture 1 887; 23 894–5*; 24 217, 218; 27 102
tetrapylon 26 914
textiles 1 880, 881, 887; 7 52; 27 112
tombs 23 891, 892–3; 31 109, 110
Elahbel Tomb 1 881
Tomb of the Three Brothers 27 57
trade 30 179
urban planning 23 893
wall paintings 27 49
Palo Alto *see* STANFORD (CA)
Palo Gordo 27 780
Palo Laziale *see* ALSIUM
Palolo, Antonio 25 300
Palomar, Juan 21 382
Palomino (de Castro y Velasco), (Acisclo) Antonio 20 67; 23 895–6*; 27 276; 29 279
patrons and collectors 9 112; 14 10
personal collection 9 706
pupils 23 896
teachers 7 524
works 2 531; 7 524; 9 108; 10 191; 20 109; 26 250; 29 282, *282*, 358
illustrated 23 896
Palomino, Antonio López *see* LÓPEZ PALOMINO, ANTONIO
Palomino, Gamaniel 24 511
Palomino, Juan Bernabé 23 895, 896*
patrons and collectors 27 792
pupils 22 317
teachers 31 810
Palomino, Juan Fernando 23 895
Palomino, Matías Pérez *see* PÉREZ PALOMINO, MATÍAS
Palo Verde 27 780
Pal San *see* TAKATORI HACHIZAN
Pålsjö Faience Factory 30 97
Pálsson, Magnús 15 71; 23 896*
Paltronieri, Pietro 22 27
Paludano, Arrigo *see* BROECK, HENDRIK VAN DEN
Paludanus *see* BROECK, WILLEM VAN DEN
Paludanus, Bernardus *see* BROECKE, BERENT TEN
Palugyay, Zolo 28 853
Palumba, Giovanni Battista 20 799; 26 417; 33 356
Palumbo 31 398
Palumbo, Onofrio 3 352; 23 897*
Paluzzi degli Albertoni, Angelo *see* ALTIERI, ANGELO
Paluzzi degli Albertoni, Gasparo *see* ALTIERI, GASPARO
Paluzzi degli Albertoni, Paluzzo, Cardinal *see* ALTIERI, PADRONE, Cardinal
Palwal 15 426
Pamacallao, Basilío de Santa Cruz *see* SANTA CRUZ PAMACALLAO, BASILÍO
Pami 9 *777*
Pamiętnik sztuk pięknych 24 441
Pammukale *see* HIEROPOLIS
Pampa de las Llamas 6 521, 523
Pampa Grande 23 897–8*; 29 *156*
Huaca Fortaleza 21 750–51*; 23 897
masks 29 208
shells 29 217
Pampaloni, Luigi 16 706; 29 833
Pampas de la Llamas-Moxele 29 163
Pampatar 32 *165*
fort of S Carlos Borromeo 32 169
Pamphaios 10 612; 13 519; 23 145; 32 40, 60
Pamphili (family)
architecture 13 292; 21 805; 26 748; 31 854
collections 2 27; 16 764; 26 773
jewellery 16 752
paintings 7 902; 12 198; 13 655
Pamphili, Benedetto, Cardinal 9 175; 23 898; 31 854
Pamphili, Camillo, Prince 23 899–900*; 26 *773*
architecture 1 628; 3 198, 835; 4 434; 17 510; 23 898
collections 26 847
etchings 3 278
paintings 3 712; 4 552; 8 100; 9 175, 376; 21 807; 25 563; 33 25
sculpture 1 629; 5 376
stucco 29 830
Pamphili, Giovanni Battista, Cardinal *see* INNOCENT X, Pope
Pamphili, Olimpia *see* ALDOBRANDINI, OLIMPIA, Princess of Rossano
Pamphili, Olimpia Caffarelli, Princess *see* CAFFARELLI PAMPHILI, OLIMPIA, Princess
Pamphili, Pietro 23 898*
Pamphilos 2 523; 13 554, 561; 23 900*; 28 712
methods 10 197
pupils 2 217; 21 75; 24 283
works 13 546, 551
writings 13 549
pampilles 17 527
Pampisford, St John 26 613
Pampite *see* OLMOS, JOSÉ
Pamplona 23 900–901*; 29 *259*
armour 29 340
Cathedral of S María 13 68; 23 900–901*; 26 *521*; 29 271
ivory-carvings 16 524
metalwork 11 614; 29 335
refectory 13 *150*; 21 845
sculpture 13 105; 26 607, 642
tomb of Bishop Arnaldo de Barbazán 13 105
tomb of Blanca 13 105
tomb of Charles III and Eleanor of Castile 13 107
tomb of Miguel Sánchez de Asiaín 13 105
wall paintings 13 149; 23 409*; 29 275, *276*
gold 29 333, 337
manuscripts 17 536
metalwork 29 333
sculpture 13 105
S Domingo 4 784
S Miguel de Excelsis 26 692
Pampulha 15 886
architecture 4 714
Casa de Baile 24 291
Pamropo (NJ) 24 51
Pamukkale *see* HIERAPOLIS
Pan 29 847
Pan 2 565; 5 924; 12 394; 18 237; 21 57; 24 427, 444; 25 350; 28 342
contributors 2 565; 4 42
pan see under VESSELS → types
Pan, Barthélémy Du *see* DU PAN, BARTHÉLÉMY
Pán, Imre 10 650
Pan, Marta 23 901*
Panagal
Pachchala Someshvara Temple 15 537, 538
Shrine 3 15 538
Panagia Amasgou *see under* MONAGRI
Panagia Aphendrika 8 359
Panagia Apsinthiotissa *see under* SUKARI
Panagia Damiotissa 22 700
Panagia Kanikaria *see* LYTHRANKOMI
Panagia Phorbiotissa *see under* ASINOU
Panagiotakos, Kyriakos Fotiou 13 349; 21 735; 23 901*
Panagyurischte 4 112
Panagyurishte 13 569, 570; 30 769
Panah 'Ali, Khan (*reg c.* 1750) (Jiwanshir) 28 644
Panainos 23 901–2*; 25 177
attributions 21 513
collaboration 13 453; 18 208; 24 594
works 13 545, 550, 553; 22 514; 24 594
Panaiteanu Baldasare, Gheorghe 26 713, 714, 724, 725
Panaitios Painter 32 60
Panajacel 13 *758*
Panakton 21 556
Panama 23 *902*, 902–6*; 29 123
architecture 23 903*, 904*
bowls 29 *147*
cathedrals 23 *903*
drawings 23 904
dress 21 804, *804*
education (art) 23 904, 906
etchings 23 905
gold 29 132, *151*
haematite 21 718
lithography 23 904
metates 29 144; 32 *239*
mirrors 21 718
molas 21 804
museums 23 906
painting 23 904–5*, *905*
patronage 23 905–6*
pendants (jewellery) 29 *151*
pottery 7 *506*; 14 223–4; 29 147, 148
pyrite 21 718
roofs 23 903
sculpture 23 904–5*
monumental 29 145
Pre-Columbian 3 279; 29 143, *144*, 144–5
stone 29 *144*
spires 23 903
stone 29 *144*; 32 *239*
trade 19 385
trays 7 *506*
wood-engravings 23 904
see also COLOMBIA
Panama (City) 23 *902*, 903; 31 721
Bahā'ī temple 30 451
Caja de Ahorros 23 904
Casa de la Escultura *see* Centro de Arte y Cultura
Cathedral 23 903, *903*, 906
Central Hotel 23 903
Centro de Arte y Cultura 2 288
El Panamá Hotel 23 904
Escuela Nacional de Artes Plásticas 19 287; 23 905, 906
Grand Hotel 23 903
Hospital S Tomás 23 904
Instituto Nacional de Cultura (INAC) 23 906
Instituto Nacional de Cultura y Deportes (INCUDE) 23 906
Instituto Panameño de Arte 23 905, 906
Jesuit college 23 903, 906
La Esposición
Porras residence 23 904
La Merced 23 903
Museo Antropológico Reina Torres de Araúz 23 906
Museo de Arte Contemporáneo 23 906
Museo de Arte Religioso Colonial 23 906
Museo Nacional de Panamá 3 278; 14 224; 23 906; 29 222; 32 238
Palacio Nacional 23 904
S Ana 23 903
School of Architecture 23 904
Panama (City)—cont.
Teatro Nacional 23 904
Universidad de Panamá 1 749; 23 904, 906
Escuela de Administración y Comercio 23 904
Urraca apartment building 23 904
Panama California Exposition, 1915 *see under* SAN DIEGO (CA)
Panama Canal 23 902
Panama Canal Company 10 107
Panamalai, Talagirishvara Temple 15 513, 514, 559, *559*
Panamá la Vieja 23 *902*, 903
Casas Reales 23 903
Cathedral 23 903, 905
La Compañía 23 905
Nuestra Señora de la Concepción Treasure 23 903
Panama Pacific International Exposition, 1915 *see under* SAN FRANCISCO (CA)
Pañamarca 29 *156*
wall paintings 21 751, 754; 29 173, *173*
Panamarenko 3 574; 23 906*
Panamint Shoshone 22 660
Panammu I of Sam àl (*reg c.*800 BC) 33 684
Panaramittee 1 *37*, 40
Panari *yachi* ware *see under* POTTERY → wares
Panari Yaeyama *see* ARAGUSUKU
Panataran 14 78; 15 *753*, 765, 816; 23 906–7*
Dated Temple 15 765, *765*
Naga Temple 15 765
reliefs 15 783
Panathenaic amphorae *see under* AMPHORAE → types
Panauti 15 *261*; 22 *753*; 23 907*
Indreshvara Mahadeva temple 22 760, 792, *793*; 23 907
Panavitiya 29 *440*
rest-house 29 478
Panay 24 *607*, 616
pañcavatana 15 244*
Pancé, Le Fretay 32 279
Pancetti, José Gianini 4 718; 23 907–8*
Pančevo 28 *437*, 444
Church of the Transfiguration 28 444
National Museum 28 459
Panch *see* PENDZHIKENT
Panchal, Rajnikant 15 173
Panchen Lama 30 351, 845
Panchimalco 10 *153*
Santa Cruz 10 153, 154, *154*
Panch Mahal *see under* FATEHPUR SIKRI
panchromatic film *see under* FILM → types
panchromatic plates *see under* PHOTOGRAPHIC PLATES → types
Panciatichi, Bartolommeo 4 856; 27 849
Panciatichi, Gualtieri 32 630
Panciroli (family) 7 890
Pancorbo, Cristóbal de 29 336
Pancras (family) 4 383
Pancreac'h, Georges 32 26
Pan Cun 33 494
pandanus 1 52; 3 *330*; 15 809; 23 712, 735
pandectes 5 800, 802
Pandelis, John 30 16
Pander, H., & Zonen 14 44; 22 873, 875, 876; 23 908*; 33 387
designers 4 844
Pander, Pier 22 860; 23 908*
Panderen, Egbert van 17 599; 23 908*; 32 251
Pandit Seu 15 227, 629; 20 233; 22 438; 23 908–9*
Pandit Virji 15 614
Pando, Gédéon 5 524

Pando, Julio Mariaca see MARIACA PANDO, JULIO
Pandolfi, Giacomo 27 482
Pandolfi, Giovanni Giacomo 5 634
Pandolfini, Filippo 24 1
Pandolfini, Giannozzo, Bishop of Tróia 24 1; 27 746
Pandolfini, Giuliano 8 418
Pandolfini, Pandolfo 24 1
Pandolfini, Pier Filippo 24 1
Pandone, Porcellio 16 67
Pandrethan
 sculpture 15 482; 30 824
 Shiva Temple 15 265, *265*, 266
Pandua
 Adina Mosque 15 351–2
 Eklakhi mausoleum 15 352
 Qutb Shahi Mosque 15 353
 tomb of Sikandar Shah 15 352
Pandukeshwar Temple 15 264
Pandu Rajar Dhibi 15 718
Panduvamshi, Vasata see VASATA
Panduvasnuvara 24 1*; 29 *440*
 architecture 29 449
 council chambers 29 450
Pandya 24 2*
Pane, Gina 24 2*, 408
Pané, Ramon 14 54
Pane, Roberto 24 2–3*
Panek & Knezarek 4 460
Panelli, Terea 26 719
panelling 14 791
 Belgium 3 577
 England 10 272, *274*, 274–5, 277
 Germany 12 409, 410
 United States of America 31 *616*, 617
panel paintings 1 708; 9 13; 10 702; 14 423; 24 3–8*; 30 5
 conservation 7 IX, X; 24 6–8*, *7*, *8*
 dating methods 11 309
 historical and regional traditions
  Anglo-Saxon 2 72
  Austria 2 792*; 13 151
  Belgium 24 3
  Buddhism 6 303
  Byzantine 19 356; 24 3
  Central Asia, Eastern 6 303
  Denmark 8 730
  Early Christian (c. AD 250-843) 19 356
  Egypt, ancient 9 790
  England 13 138, 139
  Ethiopia 10 567, 570*
  Germany 12 383; 14 423; 24 3
   Gothic 13 135, 142, 151
   Romanesque 12 382
  Gothic 13 127, 129, 130–32*, 134–5, 136, 137; 24 3
   Austria 2 792*; 13 151
   England 13 138–9
   Germany 13 135, 142, 151
   Italy 13 146
   Norway 13 135, 143
   Spain 13 143, 150
  Greece 24 3
  Greece, ancient 13 543–9*, 553–5*; 24 3
   Classical 13 548–9
   Hellenistic 13 549
  Hungary 14 899
  Indian subcontinent 15 647
  Ireland 2 72
  Italy 11 379; 19 351; 24 3, 4, 5, 7, *7*, 8, *8*; 30 425
   Gothic 13 146
  Netherlands, the 14 423; 19 356; 22 834; 24 3, 4, *6*, 8
  Norway 13 135, 143
  Romanesque 12 382
  Rome, ancient 24 3; 27 50
  Russia 24 3
  Slovakia 28 851
  Spain 13 143, 150; 24 3, 6
 materials
  adhesives 24 4, 7
  aluminium 24 7
panel paintings
 materials—cont.
  balsawood 24 7
  battens 24 5, *5*, 6–7
  beech 24 3
  bone 24 4
  canvas 24 7
  casein 24 4
  chalk 13 135
  cherry-wood 24 3
  chestnut 24 3
  clay 4 254
  consolidants 7 747
  cradles (ii) (support) 8 107; 24 6–7, *7*
  fibreglass 24 7
  frames 11 379; 24 4–5
  gesso 12 501; 13 135
  glues 24 4, 5
  gold 7 627; 19 351
  gold leaf 19 356
  grasses 24 6
  grounds 13 135, 706, 708; 24 6, 798
  gypsum 13 135
  hooves 24 4
  laminates 24 4
  lime-wood 24 3
  linen 24 5
  linseed oil 13 135
  monograms 24 6, *6*
  nails 24 5
  oak 13 135; 24 3, 4, 5, *6*
  oils 13 135
  paints 24 6
  parchment 24 5
  pine 13 135; 24 3
  poplar 13 135; 24 3, 4, 5, *7*
  silver 13 135
  skins 24 4
  spruce 24 3
  tempera 13 135; 30 425, *426*
  tin leaf 24 5
  varnishes 13 544; 30 428
  walnut 24 3
  walnut oil 13 135
  wood 13 543; 24 *4*, *5*, *6*, *7*, *8*
 techniques
  brushwork 5 34
  modelling 6 569
  stamping 24 6, *6*
  transfer (conservation) 24 7; 31 281–2, 283
 see also ALTARPIECES; PREDELLAS; SPALLIERE
panels (wall) 3 575, 576; 5 159; 19 4; 28 244, 246
 see also SPALLIERE
Panel style pottery see under POTTERY → wares
Panetti, Domenico 11 4; 12 161
Panfi, Romolo 27 521
Panfilio, Prencipe 2 43
Pang, Amy Leong 31 340
Pangi 1 *401*
Panhale Kaji 15 492
Panhedel, Gielis van 33 87
Panhesy 10 53
Panhuys, Pieter 32 709
Panhuysen, Paul 29 99
Pani, Mario 21 390; 24 8–9*
 collaboration 12 920; 21 155; 22 71; 23 578
 works 21 380, 403
Panicale, Masolino da see MASOLINO (DA PANICALE)
Panico, Antonio Maria 5 867
Panico, Ugo da see CARPI, UGO DA
Paniere Farnese 5 866
Panik Church 28 445
Paniker, Jaipal 20 54
Paniker, K(olozhi) C(heerambattur) S. 15 170, 179; 20 54; 24 9*
Panilovo, St Nicholas 27 373
Panin (family) 5 332
Panin, Nikita 10 461
Panini 15 213
Panini, Giovanni Paolo 16 672; 24 9–11*; 26 774, 842
 attributions 13 347
 collaboration 12 533; 20 806
 paintings 3 708
 patrons and collectors 3 708; 4 560, 611; 5 354; 7 193; 12 594, 914; 13 301; 14 163, 190, 808; 16 563; 19 63; 20 910; 24 418; 25 150
 pupils 7 415; 17 626
 reproductive prints by others 7 495; 8 542; 19 144; 25 210; 32 689
 teachers 19 817
 works 2 164, 342; 5 686; 9 224; 11 394; 12 914; 15 862; 17 708; 23 113; 24 *10*, *11*, 834; 26 448, *775*, 840, *898*; 28 16; 31 155, 248; 32 112–13
Panipat 15 *360*
 congregational mosque 15 361, *361*
Panique group 11 552
Paniquita 7 602
Panizzi, Anthony 19 318
Panjikent see PENDZHIKENT
Panjim
 Church of the Immaculate Conception 12 827
 Palace of Yusuf ʿAdil Shah 12 826
Pankiewicz, Józef 18 428; 24 11–13*; 25 107; 32 876, 877
 groups and movements 25 108
 pupils 8 371; 17 804; 18 88; 22 423; 32 793
 works 24 *12*; 25 107; 32 877
Pankok, Bernhard 12 416; 24 13*
 groups and movements 12 427; 24 279, 591; 26 405; 28 341
 works 12 427
Pankok, Otto 24 13–14*
 groups and movements 8 825; 10 215
 pupils 13 322
 works 17 580
Pankoucke, Charles Joseph 10 207
Pankrat'yev, G. A. 6 279
Pan Ku see BAN GU
Panlongcheng 6 *615*; 7 159; 24 14*
 architecture 6 646
 bronze 4 852; 6 *838*, 841; 24 *14*
 cemeteries 6 694
 excavations 33 465
 jade 7 3
 palace 6 679
 town walls 24 14
Panmure, James Maule, 4th Earl of see MAULE, JAMES, 4th Earl of Panmure
Panmure, William Ramsay Maule, Lord see MAULE, WILLIAM RAMSAY, Lord Panmure
Pannalal 15 601
Pannartz, Arnold 4 8; 20 587; 28 306
Panneels, Herman 24 15*
Panneels, Joannes 24 15
Panneels, Willem 24 15*; 27 298
Pannemaker, André de 11 642; 19 382; 24 15
Pannemaker, de (family) 3 612; 30 317
Pannemaker, Erasmus de 24 15
Pannemaker, François de 11 642; 19 382; 24 15
Pannemaker, Pieter de 5 49; 23 525; 24 15*
Pannemaker, Stéphane 33 369
Pannemaker, Willem de 5 49; 14 5; 24 15*; 29 350; 30 317; 32 272
 workshop 5 *48*
Pannetier 24 794
Pannetier, Antoine Claude 12 731
Pannini, Francesco 24 9, 570
Pannini, Gian Paolo see PANINI, GIOVANNI PAOLO
Pannonhalma Abbey 14 884, 887, 900; 15 17
 church 14 883
 library 14 888
Pannonio, Michele 24 16*
Panofka, Théodor 4 106
Panofsky, Erwin 2 532, 536; 17 583; 24 16–17*; 26 225; 28 916; 31 672; 32 675
 collaboration 28 23
 pupils 10 447; 33 242
 works 2 138; 9 444; 13 34, 155; 15 90–91, 94–5, 880
Panopolis see AKHMIM
panorama cameras see under CAMERAS → types
Panorama-Kamera see MEGASKOP-KAMERA
Panorama Mesdag 4 203; 14 *43*; 24 19
panoramas 8 910, 911; 24 17–19*, 653–4
 historical and regional traditions
  Australia 3 427
  England 24 17–18, *18*, *19*
  France 9 370; 24 18
  Netherlands, the 14 *43*
  Poland 33 417
  Switzerland 6 66
 techniques
  photography 20 483–4; 24 659
 uses
  wallpaper 8 792; 9 370
 see also PAINTING → types → landscape
Panoram Kodak see under CAMERAS → types
Panormos Basilica (Crete) 8 155
Panormos (Naxos) 8 *304*; 22 698
 fort 8 310
Panormos (Sicily) see PALERMO
Pan Painter 13 521; 32 56, 61–2*
Pan-p'o see BANPO
Pan-presse 19 490
Panr 24 20*
Pansaers, Clement 8 438
Pansare, N. G. 15 171
Panselinos, Manuel see MANUEL PANSELINOS
Panseron, Pierre 9 420; 24 387
Pan-shan see BANSHAN
Panshanger House 2 738
pansy green see under PIGMENTS → types
Pantainos 19 312
Pantaleone of Amalfi 9 154
Pantaleone Viarecta 9 154
Pantaleon Gospels see under GOSPEL BOOKS → individual manuscripts
Pantalica 23 808; 28 653
pantaloons 5 502; 17 375; 18 771
Pantanello 21 342
Pantar 15 807
Pantazis, Périclès 24 20*; 32 679
 groups and movements 8 63; 32 591
 works 13 352
Panten, Kasper 24 21*; 27 308; 30 69
 collaboration 7 370
 patrons and collectors 31 692
 works 30 69, 70
Panteri 19 324
Panthaleon, Jehan Miquel 11 586
Pantheon 24 445
Pantheon see under ROME
Panthéon see under PARIS → ecclesiastical buildings
Pantheon Bible see under BIBLES → individual manuscripts
pantheons see under TEMPLES → types
Panther Painter 13 507
Pan Tianshou 24 21–2*; 28 553
 groups and movements 6 774
 pupils 19 375; 33 424
Pantiatichi *Madonna* 8 798
Pan T'ien-shou see PAN TIANSHOU
Pantigoso, Lorenzo de 2 386
Pantikapaion see KERCH'
pantiles see under TILES → types
Pantin, Esaïe 24 22
Pantin, Jacques 7 466
Pantin, Simon (c. 1680-1728) 24 22*
 pupils 8 62
 works 10 330; 14 856
Pantin, Simon (d 1733) 24 22
Pantocsek, Valentin Leó 15 4
 works 15 *4*
pantographic reducing machine 20 925
pantographs 10 311; 24 22*, 688; 31 496
Pantoja, Oscar 4 263
Pantoja de la Cruz, Juan 24 22–3*
 collaboration 27 706; 32 560
 patrons and collectors 13 922; 24 462; 26 307; 27 723; 32 127
 works 4 209; 9 267, 268; 24 *23*; 29 345
Pantoleon 16 589; 21 137; 24 23*
pantomimes 8 911; 30 675
Pantoni, Don Angelo 22 10
Pantović, Milorad 28 445
P'an Ts'un see PAN CUN
P'an Tsu-yin see PAN ZUYIN
Panunzi, Benito 24 24*
Panvinio, Onofrio 5 684; 10 810; 24 24*; 26 785; 33 718
 patrons and collectors 5 789
 works 26 848
Panvinius, Onuphrius 11 350
Panyam 15 299
Pan Yu 28 552
Pan Yunzheng 7 39, 141
Panza di Biumo, Giuseppe, Conte 24 24*
Panza di Biumo Collection see under VARESE
Panzani 29 547
Panzano, Master of 20 741–2*
Pan Zuyin 6 867
Pa O 5 250
Paoay Church 24 611, *613*, 613–14*
Pao-chi see BAOJI
Paola, Hypogeum of Hal Saflieni 20 210–11; 25 511
Paola, Tomie de 4 368
Paolera, Carlos Maria Della see DELLA PAOLERA, CARLOS MARIA
Paoletti (family) 12 264
Paoletti, Gaspare Maria 1 574; 24 24–5*
 pupils 5 363; 7 836; 8 597; 25 59; 27 204, 643
 works 5 363; 11 213, 214; 16 646, 772; 25 60
Paoletti, Pietro 5 378; 14 285; 17 443; 24 25*
Paoli, Paolantonio 10 414; 12 657
Paolini, Giulio 16 682; 24 25–6*
 groups and movements 2 526; 26 778
 works 16 682
Paolini, Pietro 1 104; 24 26*
 attributions 20 738
 pupils 7 553; 12 527
 works 8 139
Paolini, Pietro Antonio 28 28
Paolini, Pietro Paolo 26 766
Paolino, Fra 3 306, 307; 22 727; 24 26–7*
Paolino da Montorfano 21 533
Paolino da Venezia 32 183
Paolo, Giannicola di 3 55
Paolo, Giovanni di see GIOVANNI DI PAOLO
Paolo, Jacopo di see JACOPO DI PAOLO
Paolo, Maestro 5 656
Paolo Amadeo 12 579
Paolo d'Andrea 11 688

Paolo da San Leocadio **24** 27–8*; **29** 277
patrons and collectors **4** 409; **31** 815
Paolo da Venezia *see* PAOLO VENEZIANO
Paolo da Verona **32** 343
Paolo di Baccio **16** 845
Paolo di Bernardino d'Antonio *see* PAOLINO, Fra
Paolo di Bonaiuto **13** 96
Paolo di Giovanni Fei **13** 149; **24** 28*
collaboration **7** 329
methods **13** 139
pupils **3** 707
works **11** 381, 385
Paolo di Jacopino Avvocato **4** 274
Paolo di Mariani di Tuccio Taccone da Sezze *see* PAOLO ROMANO
Paolo di Paolo **16** 848
Paolo di Serfederigi **11** 747
Paolo Fiammingo *see* FIAMMINGO, PAOLO
Paolo Romano (*fl* 1445-70) **22** 487; **24** 28–9*; **26** 766
assistants **12** 699
attributions **16** 67; **26** 808
collaboration **16** 66
patrons and collectors **24** 731, 732
pupils **12** 582
works **11** 896; **21** 695; **26** 808, 809
Paolo Romano (*d* after 1552) **6** 147; **24** 29
Paolo Veneziano **16** 662; **24** 29–33*
attributions **20** 784
patrons and collectors **32** 213
pupils **19** 683
works **4** 275; **8** 499; **11** 382; **16** 657, 759; **24** *31*, *32*; **32** 189
Paolozzi, Eduardo **24** 34–5*; **25** 628
collaboration **10** 258; **19** 395; **20** 607
dealers **24** 213
groups and movements **10** 258; **15** 166; **17** 694; **19** 590; **25** 231
patrons and collectors **13** 629; **28** 274
pupils **5** 77
works **1** 738; **9** 2; **10** 268, 313; **21** 350; **22** 333; **24** *34*; **28** 240, 300, *300*
Paolucci, Fabrizio **21** 539
Paolucci, Francesco **3** 95
Pao Shih-Ch'en *see* BAO SHICHEN
Pap, Gyula **3** 402
Pap, Jozsef **10** 472
Pápa **14** *881*
collections **15** 17
Franciscan church **14** 900
parish church **14** 888, 895
textiles **15** 11
Papacello, Tommaso Bernabei **5** 672
Papadimitriou, J. **4** 700
Papagayo ware *see under* POTTERY → wares
Papageorge, Tod **24** 35*
Papageorgiou (family) **13** 358
Papageorgiou, A. **13** 350; **24** 803
Papago **22** 567, 662, 666, 669
Papal cross *see under* CROSSES → types
Papaleo, Pietro Francesco **24** 35*
works **20** 214, *214*
Papaloukas, Spyros **13** 353; **24** 35–6*, 803
papal roses **24** 36*, *36*
papal tiaras **26** 80
Papanasi **15** 302
paparazzi **28** 337
Paparelli, Francesco **13** 338
Papart, Max **5** 726
Papasov, George **24** 37*
Papasseit, Salvat **8** 436
Papa Westray, Knap of Howar **25** 503; **28** 223
pap-boats **24** 37*, 580
Pape, Abraham de **19** 102
Pape, H. **16** 799
Pape, Joannes de **3** 600
Pape, Lygia **4** 719; **33** 317
Papeleu-Stauthamer, E. **24** 885
Papen, Johann **20** 683
Papenbroeck, Maerten **4** 140
Papenbroek, Gerard van **26** 284; **32** 155
Papendorp *see* WOODSTOCK (SOUTH AFRICA)
Papenhoven, Alexander van **3** 570; **24** 37*
paper **1** 156; **7** 735; **24** 37–57*, *39*, *42*, *43*
conservation **15** *850*; **24** 52–5*; **25** 632–3; **32** 819
dating methods **11** 309
historical and regional traditions
Bali (Indonesia) **15** 806
Buddhism **30** 613
Cambodia **5** 501
Caribbean Islands **5** 755
Central Asia, Eastern **6** 314*
Central Asia, Western **27** 673
China **6** 725, 874, *874*; **7** 114–17*, 146–7; **22** 234; **24** 44, 46–7*, 51, 55; **25** 597; **28** 312; **31** 258
Han period (206 BC–AD 220) **6** 736; **7** 62, 63; **20** 329; **28** 310
Ming period (1368-1644) **7** *116*
Northern and Southern Dynasties (AD 310-589) **6** 740
Song period (AD 960-1279) **6** 776; **7** 64, *117*
Zhou period (*c*. 1050-256 BC) **7** 114
20th cent. **7** 113
Denmark **24** 48
Egypt **24** 48
England **10** 285; **24** 40, 48, 51, 55; **31** 258, 259
France **24** 40, 48, 51, 55; **31** 258, 259
Germany **10** 381; **24** 40, 48, 51, 55, 56; **31** 258
Indian subcontinent **15** 545, 549, 564, 706; **20** 327; **28** 310, 635
Iran **24** 55
Ireland **16** 33
Islamic **15** 549; **16** 271, 275, 351–4*, *353*; **24** 41, 45*, 48*; **25** 598; **27** 673
Italy **10** 381, 728; **24** 48, 51, 55; **31** 258
Jainism **15** 564
Japan **7** 114; **10** 776; **17** 139, 209, 210, 213–14*, 220, 305, 359*, 371, 388, 390, 392, 402–6*; **22** 234; **24** 42, 44, 47*, 51, 55, 56; **28** 312; **30** 541; **31** 259
Buddhism **17** 219
Edo period (1600-1868) **17** *403*, *405*
Heian period (AD 794-1185) **10** 776; **17** 223
Kamakura period (1185-1333) **17** 227
Korea **7** 114; **18** 264, 276, 302, 379, 380; **24** 42, 47
Malaysia **20** 180
Mesoamerica, Pre-Columbian **21** 233, 245
Mexico **24** 48
Mongolia **21** 875
Nepal **22** 779
Netherlands, the **10** 381; **24** 40, 48, 51
Ottoman **24** 55
paper
historical and regional traditions—cont.
Pakistan **23** 803
Poland **31** 259
Russia **24** 40
Sicily **20** 329
Spain **20** 329; **24** 40, 41, 48; **31** 258
Sweden **24** 40
Thailand **30** 613
Tibet **7** 114; **30** 844–5*
Turkey **24** 55, 56
United States of America **24** 40, 56
Vietnam **7** 114
materials
adhesives **1** 156; **24** 53
albumen **24** 55
alum **24** 56
aluminium **7** 115
bamboo **7** 63, 115; **24** 40; **28** 312
banana leaves **24** 40
bark **7** 114, 115; **21** 233; **28** 312; **30** 844
cane **7** 114
carnauba wax **33** 1
carragheen **24** 55
caustic soda **24** 41
chlorine **24** 42
consolidants **7** 747–8
cornflour **24** 56
cotton **24** 40
dyes **7** 115, 116; **16** 353; **17** 219; **24** 56; **30** 845
fibres **24** 40
flax **16** 352
fleaseed **24** 55
flour **7** 116; **24** 56
gelatin **24** 38
glazes **17** *405*
glues **1** 156
gold **7** 116
grasses **7** 115; **24** 40
hemp **6** 314; **7** 64, 114; **16** 352; **17** 139, 219, 403; **24** 40
inks **15** 851; **24** 55
insect repellants **7** 115
jupe **24** 40
jute **7** 114
kaolin **28** 312
lacquer **17** 359
lime **7** 114
linen **16** 352; **24** 40
linseed oil **24** 55
manila (fibre) **24** 40
mica **7** 116
mulberry **7** 64, 114–15; **17** 139, 213, 275; **24** 40
oils **24** 55
oxgall **24** 55
paper mulberry **6** 314; **7** 114; **17** 219, 227, 403
paste **24** 56*
pepper **7** 115
rags **24** 38, 40
rami (fibre) **17** 139
resins **7** 116; **24** 55
rice flour **24** 56
sandalwood **7** 115
silk **20** 328
silver **7** 116
size **16** 352; **24** 38, 44, 55; **28** 813
straw **24** 40
sugar **24** 56
textiles **7** 114
tragacanth **24** 55
turpentine **24** 55
vegetable fibres **20** 329
vinegar **24** 56
waxes **7** 114, 116; **24** 56; **33** 1
wood **24** 40
techniques
batik **24** 56
blocking **24** 55
burnishing **24** 44
paper
techniques—cont.
embossing **7** 116; **10** 177; **16** 33; **24** 55–6
gilding **24** 55–6
marbling **16** 353, *353*; **17** 404; **24** 55*, 56, I3
moulding **16** 352; **17** 403
printing **24** 55*, I2
staining **32** 815
stencilling **24** 55, 56
types
bark **21** 233, 249, *250*, 266
blotting **6** 335
brown wrapping *see* Kraft
carbon **10** 548
cardboard *see* CARDBOARD
cartonboard **24** 52
decorative **24** 55–6*, I1-3, II1-3
Dutch gilt *see* techniques → embossing; gilding
end-papers **4** 349; **24** 55
felt **24** 51
gelatin silver papers **7** 432; **24** 648
Japanese **7** 730; **25** 614; **28** 339
Kraft **24** 41
laid **30** 844
lining-papers **24** 55; **32** 814
marbled *see* techniques → marbling
paperboard *see* CARDBOARD
photographic *see* uses → photography
powdered **7** 116
rice-paper **17** 390; **24** 56; **28** 619; **32** 481
sandpaper **10** 562
tak **7** 250
tissue-paper **6** 328; **31** 282
tracing **31** 273–4, *274*
tracing-paper **2** 333
umbrella **17** 359
vellum **26** 259
wallpaper *see* WALLPAPER
waterproof **1** 121; **17** 359
waxed **10** 561
woven **30** 844
wrapping-paper **24** 55
Xuan **7** 115, *115*
uses
architecture **18** 264; **24** 51–2*
banknotes **3** 180; **7** 115
bookbindings **4** 347; **16** 353; **24** 50–51*
book covers **4** 349; **24** 55
book jackets **4** 347; **24** 50
books **4** 342; **7** 64; **15** 549
calligraphy **6** 736, 740; **17** 213–14, 219, 220, 223, 227; **24** 55
cliché-verre **7** 432
clocks **7** 448
collagraphs **7** 558
conservation **7** 730; **17** 209, 210; **28** 312, 339
décollage **8** 608
dolls **17** 371; **31** 258, 259–60*
dolls' houses **31** 263
doors **18** 276
drawings **9** 215; **15** 850; **24** 49–50*
dress **17** 359
engravings **10** 380, 381
etchings **10** 548, 561, 562
fans **10** 776; **18** 380
fibre art **11** 54
furniture **10** 285; **32** 814
hangings *see* WALLPAPER
helmets **21** 245
interior decoration **5** 755
kites **7** 113, 114, 147; **17** 388, 390; **20** 180; **31** 258
lamps **17** 359
lanterns (lights) **7** 114
lithography **25** 615
manuscripts **7** 63; **15** 545, 549, 564; **16** 275, 351–4; **20** 327, 329; **22** 779
paper
uses—cont.
masks **15** 706; **17** 390, 392
mosaics **24** 57
mounts (works on paper and scrolls) **22** 234
oil sketches **23** 380
packaging **24** 52*
painting **5** 501; **15** 806; **17** 209; **24** 49–50*
papier mâché **24** 61
partitions **17** 404; **24** 51
photography **24** 646, 647, 648, 649, 650, 651, 653, 655, 656*, 657, 658, 669, 679
plasterboard **24** 51
posters **25** 345
pottery **6** 874, *874*
printing **20** 329; **24** 50*; **25** 588
prints **17** 275; **24** 50; **25** 597–8*, 613
puppets **31** 258
sat panchee **5** 255
screens (ii) (furniture) **24** 55; **28** 619
scrolls **6** 776; **17** 139; **24** 55; **28** 310, *310*, 312
sculpture **6** 725; **17** 99
shrines (i) (cult) **28** 635
stencilling **17** 405; **28** 298
supports **6** 314; **17** 139; **18** 302; **30** 4, 6
textiles **17** 305
threads **30** 541
toys **31** 257–8
transfer (conservation) **31** 282
umbrellas **17** 359
underlays **24** 51
vestments (ecclesiastical) **6** 314
wallpaper **32** 811, 814
watercolours **24** 50, 56; **32** 899
wicker **33** 155, 158
windows **7** 114; **12** 408
writing **7** 62, 114; **15** 850; **17** 213–14
see also WATERMARKS
paperbark *see under* BARK → types
paperboard *see* CARDBOARD
paper chromatography *see under* TECHNICAL EXAMINATION → types
papercuts **24** 56–7*
Afghanistan **16** *354*
China **6** 691; **7** 114, 122, 144, 146; **24** 56, 57
Germany **24** *56*
Islamic **16** *354*, 354–5*
Japan **24** 56, 57
Jewish art **21** *743*
Mexico **24** 56
paper hangings *see* WALLPAPER
papermarks *see* WATERMARKS
paper mulberry **17** 403
historical and regional traditions
Central Asia, Eastern **6** 314
China **7** 114; **30** 560
Japan **17** 219, 403; **30** 560
uses
paper **17** 139, 213, 275; **24** 40
textiles **7** 791; **17** 312; **27** 684; **31** 143
Paperny, Vladimir **29** 89
Papero, Jacopo **11** 382
paperweights **24** 57–8*
historical and regional traditions
China **7** 91
Czech Republic **24** 57
England **24** 57
France **24** 57
Italy **32** 204
Japan **17** 386
United States of America **24** 57
materials
glass **12** 789; **17** 386; **24** 57; **32** 204
aventurine **24** 57
millefiori **24** 57
pinchbeck **24** 57
sulphides (ceramic) **24** 57

Papety, Dominique (-Louis-Féréol) **24** 58–9*
works **24** *58*
Paphos, New **8** *325*; **9** *512*; **24** 59–60*; **26** *908*
amphitheatre **8** 337
Archaeological Museum **8** 366
architecture **8** 333
basilica **8** 357, 359
Castle **8** 361
Chrysopolitissa *see* Hagia Kyriaki
glass **9** 646
Hagia Kyriaki **8** 357, 358; **9** 566
houses **8** 337
House of Aion **8** 355, *355*; **27** 64
mosaics **8** 358; **9** 566; **18** 825
House of Dionysos **8** 337, 342, 354; **27** 64
House of Orpheus **8** 337, 354
House of Theseus **8** 337, 342, 354; **9** 557; **27** 64
mosaics **8** 358; **9** 566
marble **8** 342
mosaics **8** 354; **13** 560; **18** 825; **24** *60*
odeion **8** 337
pottery **9** 632, 634
Sanctuary of Apollo Hylates **8** 336
theatre **8** 337
Tomb B **8** 356
Tombs of the Kings **8** 333, 337, *337*
urban planning **8** 336
wall paintings **8** 356
Paphos, Old **8** *325*, 332; **13** *362*; **21** 556; **24** 60–61*
copper **8** 353
helmet **13** 584
inscriptions **8** 331
ivory-carvings **8** 350, 351
mosaics **8** 354
Old Paphos Archaeological Museum **8** 366
palace **8** 336
pottery **8** 343, 346; **9** 633
Sanctuary of Aphrodite **24** 60
Temple of Aphrodite **8** 336
sculpture **8** *340*
Skales **8** 353
Papi, Antonio di **31** 517
Papi, Clemente **11** 190
Papi, Michele Agnolo di *see* MICHELE AGNOLO DI PAPI
Papian, E. **2** 428
papier collé **7** 557; **8** 242; **13** *669*; **24** 717
see also COLLAGES
papier mâché **24** 61–3*
historical and regional traditions
Britain **18** 615
China **7** 114; **24** 61
England **10** 281, 297; **24** 62, *62*
France **24** 62; **31** 262
Germany **24** 62; **28** *111*; **31** 262
India, Republic of **15** 174
Indian subcontinent **18** 609; **24** 62
Iran **16** 533; **24** 62
Islamic **16** 359, 533
Italy **12** *814*; **24** 62; **25** III
Japan **17** 373, 390; **24** 62
Ottoman **16** 359
Pakistan **23** 803
Russia **24** 62
Sweden **30** 90
Turkey **16** 359
United States of America **24** 62
uses
book covers **16** 359
buttons **24** 61
chairs **24** 62
clocks **24** 63
copies **24** 347
costumes **28** *111*
dolls **17** 373; **24** 62; **31** 262
etchings **10** 561
furniture **10** 297; **24** 62; **31** 629
papier mâché
uses—cont.
globes **12** *814*
grounds **25** 175
interior decoration **30** 90
lacquer **18** 609, 615
masks **17** 390
mirror frames **30** 90
mouldings **24** 62
relief sculpture **25** III
snuff-boxes **24** 62
trays **24** 61, *62*, 62
papiers bleus d'Angleterre see under WALLPAPER → types
papiers de tapisserie see under WALLPAPER → types
papiers peints see under WALLPAPER → types
papiers veloutés see under WALLPAPER → types
Papillon (family) **32** 812, 814
Papillon, Jean **24** 63; **32** 814
Papillon, Jean-Baptiste **33** 360
Papillon, Jean-Michel **16** 820; **24** 63; **29** 628; **32** 814; **33** 360
Papillon de La Ferté, Denis-Pierre-Jean **20** 137, 138; **24** 63*
collaboration **19** 161
writings **4** 360
Papini (family) **29** 9
Papini, Giovanni **5** 848; **12** 545; **16** 679; **24** 63–4*
collaboration **20** 427
groups and movements **4** 199; **11** 865
Papini, Guasparri di Bartolomeo **11** 194
Papisto Boy *see* SAMB, PAPE MAMADOU
Pappacoda, Luigi, Bishop of Lecce **19** 28
Pappasoff, Georges *see* PAPASOV, GEORGE
Pappenheim, Aleksander **13** 702
Pappenheim, Matthäus von **20** 793
Pappos of Alexandria **2** 312
Papraća Monastery **4** 461
Church of the Annunciation **25** 344
Papradiški, Dimitrija Andonov *see* ANDONOV PAPRADIŠKI, DIMITRIJA
Papua New Guinea **15** *751*; **23** *711*; **24** *64*, 64–86*; **25** 181
aesthetics **23** 713, *714*
anthropology **2** 137
architecture **23** 716–17; **24** 66–8*, 76–7*
arrows **24** *70*
basketwork **24** 71
beds **24** 82
body arts **23** 721–2*, *722*
body ornaments **23** 721, 735; **24** 75, *75*, 83, 84
bone **4** 314
bowls **24** 82
bows **24** *70*
canoes **23** 725–6; **24** *81*, 83
clubs (weapons) **23** 734
craftsmen and artists **24** 86
cult houses **24** 66–8, *67*, *73*
drums (musical instruments) **24** 65
hand-drums **24** 69, 74*, *75*
slit-drums **24** 68–9, *69*
education (art) **23** 736
exchange **23** 741
fans **10** 779
feathers **10** 847; **23** 721; **24** 75, *75*, *84*
headdresses **23** 721; **24** 75, *75*, 84, *84*
houseboards **24** *73*, 73–4*
houses **23** 716, *717*, *736*
ladders **24** *83*
languages **24** 65
lizard **24** 69
malangan **24** 85, *85*
Papua New Guinea—cont.
masks **24** 71–2, *72*, *77*, 77–8*, 80, 84, 85, *85*, 86
musical instruments **24** 68–9*, 79
neckrests **24** 79
painting **23** 721–2*
parinarium nuts **24** 84
pigments **23** 721, 722; **24** 73
pottery **23** 728; **24** 79
rock art
carving **23** 730, *730*
painting **23** 729
scarification **23** 721
sculpture **23** *732*, 732–3
figure **24** 70–71*, *71*, 79–80, *80*, 85–6
shells **23** 721; **24** 79, 84; **28** 581
shields **24** 69–70, *70*, 74*, 79
skull-posts **24** 79
skull racks **24** 78, *78*
skulls **24** 84
splashboards **24** *81*
tattoos **23** 722
tortoiseshell **24** 84
tourist art **24** 82
tusks **24** 79
weapons **23** 734; **24** 69–70*, *70*
wigs **23** 721; **24** 75
wood **23** 716–17, *717*, *732*; **24** *69*, *71*, *72*, *80*
wood-carvings **24** 79, *81*, 81–2, *83*, *85*
see also POLYNESIAN OUTLIERS
Papunya **1** 56, 63, 64; **25** 324; **31** 153, 767
Papworth, Alfred Wyatt **24** 86
Papworth, Collins Edgar **24** 86
Papworth, Edgar George **24** 86
Papworth, George **16** 10; **24** 86, 87*
Papworth, J(ohn) B(uonarotti) **1** 733; **10** 372; **22** 147; **24** 86–7*
collaboration **25** 711
groups and movements **10** 374
pupils **24** 87
works **7** 374; **27** 336; **32** 554, *555*
writings **8** 30
Papworth, John **24** 86
Papworth, John Thomas **24** 86
Papworth, John Woody **24** 86, 87
Papworth, Thomas **24** 86
Papworth, William **24** 86
Papworth, Wyatt (Angelicus van Sandau) **24** 86, 87*
papyri **15** 851
Egypt, ancient **9** 775, *806*, *904*, 904–6*, *905*; **10** 3, *3*, 4, 5, 6–7, 14, 20; **12** *67*; **20** 329, 336; **23** 692; **30** 701
Greece, ancient **13** 369; **20** 329
Rome, ancient **20** 329; **23** 692
papyrotype process *see under* PHOTOGRAPHY → processes
papyrus
historical and regional traditions
Africa **1** 310
Ancient Near East **1** 854
Egypt, ancient **4** *341*, *344*; **10** 7; **20** 329; **24** 87–9*; **26** 557, *557*; **31** 259
Greece, ancient **26** 556, 557
Islamic **16** 275
Rome, ancient **26** 556, 557
Uganda **1** 310
uses
bookbindings **4** 347
codices **24** 88
dolls **31** 259
drawings **9** 215
granaries **1** 310
manuscripts **16** 275
rolls **4** *341*, 342; **10** 5, 7; **20** 329; **24** 88; **26** 556–7, *557*
writing **10** 5; **20** 329; **24** 88–9
writing-tablets **4** 342
Papyrus of Tameniu **10** 473
Papzoni, Jacopino de' **32** 610
Papzoni, Pietro de' **32** 610
Paquet, Alfons **8** 825
Paquet, Pierre **2** 322
Paquet, Pierre Anne **2** 495; **3** 395
Paquier, Claudius Innocentius Du *see* DU PAQUIER, CLAUDIUS INNOCENTIUS
Paquimé *see* CASAS GRANDES
Paquin, Gladys **22** 608
Paquin, Mme **9** 291; **29** 899
Pāra **21** 299
Para (Surinam) **30** *12*, 15
parabolic arches *see* ARCHES → types → catenary
Paracas culture **24** 89–90*; **29** *156*, 160
dress **29** 182
embroidery **24** *89*
feathers **29** 207
gourds **13** 229
jars **29** 176
metalwork **29** 214
mummies **29** 218
pottery **6** 520; **24** 89; **29** 177
textiles **24** 89–90; **29** 127, 179, 180, *182*
tombs **31** 118
Paracca, Antonio **18** 849
Paracca, Giacomo **31** 899
Parachute **22** 39; **24** 430
Paraclet **13** 158
paradeisoi see under GARDENS → types
Parád Glassworks **15** 4
see also PARÁDVASAR FACTORY
Paradin, Claude **1** 584; **26** 261
Paradinas, Alfonso, Bishop of Seville **31** 188
Paradis, L. T. **31** 66
paradise **24** 90*
Paradise, Phil **19** 701
Paradise Breughel *see* BREUGHEL, JAN, I
paradise gardens *see* GARDENS → types → *paradeisoi*
Paradise Island, Paradise Grand Hotel **3** 61
Paradisi, Domenico **1** 796; **26** 778
Paradisi, Niccolò *see* NICCOLÒ DI PIETRO
Paradissi Hill
Hagios Niketas **26** 293
Haria Paraskevi *see* Hagios Niketas
Paradosso *see* TROILI, GIULIO
Parádvasar Factory **15** 4
see also PARÁD GLASSWORKS
paraffin wax *see under* WAXES → types
Paragone: Revista mensile d'arte figurativa e letteratura **19** 637; **24** 448
paragoni **14** 869; **17** 694; **19** 196; **24** 90–91*, 828; **25** 224
see also UT PICTURA POESIS
Paraguay **24** *91*, 91–102*; **29** 128
architecture **17** 513; **24** 93–7*
baskets **24** 92
beads **24** 93
body arts **24** 93
ceramics **24** 97
churches **24** *94*, 94–5, *96*
collections **24** 100–102*
cotton **24** 100
dealing **24** 100–101*
drawings **24** 99
education (art) **24** 102*
exhibitions **24** 101
feathers **24** 93
fibres **24** 92
houses **24** 94
museums **24** 101–2*
painting **14** 479; **24** 97*, 98–100*
patronage **24** 100–101*
pottery **24** 93, 97
prints **24** 98, 99
sculpture **24** *93*, 97–8*, *97*, 99*, *99*, 100*
textiles **24** 100*
weaving **24** 92
wood **24** *93*, *97*, *99*
Paraguay—cont.
wood-carvings **24** 93, 97
wood-engravings **24** 98
wool **24** 93, 100
Parakou **1** *386*
Musée de Plein-Air, d'Ethnographie et de Sciences Naturelles **3** 728
Parakramabahu I, King of Sri Lanka(*reg* 1153-86) **24** 1; **25** 169; **29** 459
Parākramapura *see* PANDUVASNUVARA
Paraloid B67 **32** 2
Paraloid B72 **7** 737; **10** 195; **12** 629; **26** 244; **28** 340; **32** 2; **33** 6
Paramaccaner **30** 13
Para-Mamluk carpets *see under* CARPETS → types
Paramara **24** 102*
see also:
BHOJA, Ruler
UDAYADITYA, Ruler
Paramaribo **24** 102–3*; **30** *12*, 15
Akademie voor Beeldende Kunste **30** 17
Bishop's House **30** 15
Cathedral of SS Peter and Paul **30** 15
Fort Zeelandia **30** 14
Governor's Residence *see* Presidential Palace
Kolonial Museum **30** 16
Ministry of Finance **30** 15
Nationale Institut voor Kunst en Kultur **30** 17
Nationale Kunstbeurs **30** 17
Ne Ve Shalom Synagogue **30** 15
Presidential Palace **30** *14*, 15
Surinaams Museum **30** 17
Parameshvaravarman I, Ruler (*reg* 669-90) (Pallava) **6** 428; **15** 303, 304, 512
Paramesvara *see* MEGAT ISKANDAR SHAH, Sultan
Páramo, Roberto **7** 609
Paramo, Santiago **23** 81
Paramonga **29** *156*
architecture **29** 162
fortifications **21** 599
temple **29** *166*, 167
Paramonov, Aleksandr **6** 279
Paramount Cinema Company **32** 257; **33** 407
Paramythia
Basilica **9** 538
statuettes **27** 89
Paraná **2** *393*
architecture **2** 396
Chamber of Deputies **2** 396
Government House **2** 396
Senate **2** 396
parana pine *see under* PINE → types
Parant, Louis-Bertin **4** 303
Parantaka I, Ruler (*reg c.* AD 907-54) (Chola) **15** 305, 515
parapets **1** 308; **8** 277; **12** 174; **21** 206, *207*, 547
Parashchuk, Michaylo **32** 78
paraskenia **13** 385, *385*, 406
Paraskos, Stass **8** 364
Parasole, Bernardino **12** 912
Parasole, Isabetta Catanea **18** 590
parasol pine *see under* PINE → types
Parasol Press **1** 24
parasols **3** 442; **11** 151, 152
Paras Pérez, Rod **24** 623
Paraspur **15** 265, 482; **30** 824
Parasuram **15** 599, 601
works **15** *601*
Parat, Pierre **2** 11
paratacamite **24** 793
Parauri Temple **15** 263

Paray-le-Monial **7** 267; **11** *505*
Abbey
church **4** 63; **11** 510; **24** *103*, 103–4*; **26** 584
cloister **7** 456
Parboni, Pietro **27** 485
Parboosingh, Karl **16** 884; **24** 104*
groups and movements **32** 910
works **16** 889
Parçay-Meslay **11** *504*; **24** 104–5*; **30** 908
barn **24** 104–5, *105*
Parçay-sur-Vienne **26** 599
parcels **20** 466
Parcent, Duquesa de **29** 308
Parcerisa i Boada, Francesco Xavier **24** 105*; **25** 786
collaboration **24** 802; **31** 750
works **29** 283
Parchim, Marienkirche **13** 161
Parchinah **1** 856; **15** 918
parchment **7** 678; **24** 106–7*, *106*; **32** 153
conservation **24** 107*
dating methods **11** 309
historical and regional traditions
China **7** 122
Egypt, ancient **4** *343*
Islamic **16** 274, 351, 356
Italy **24** 107
Netherlands, the **24** 107
Rome, ancient **20** 329; **26** 557
Spain **24** 107
Tunisia **31** *425*
uses
bookbindings **4** 347; **24** 106, 107
book covers **4** 349; **24** 106
books **4** *343*; **24** 107
codices **4** 342; **20** 329; **24** 107
doublures **16** 356
drawings **9** 215; **31** *425*
drums (musical instruments) **24** 106
lace **18** 588
lenses (spectacles) **24** 106
manuscripts **7** 513; **16** 274, 351; **20** 329; **24** 106, 107
maps **20** 363
notebooks **24** 107
painting **24** 5, 106
paintings **24** 107
pilgrim badges **24** 809
puppets **7** 122
rolls **4** 342; **26** 557
scrolls **24** 107
supports **30** 6
threads **30** 541
windows **12** 408; **24** 106
writing **15** 851; **24** 106, 107
writing-tablets **4** 342
see also VELLUM
parchment glue **1** 156
Parcieux, Château de la Grange Blanche **6** 393
parclosures *see under* SCREENS (i) (ARCHITECTURAL) → types
Parco di Racconigi **12** 118
Pardaillan de Gondrin, Louis-Antoine, Duc d'Antin *see* ANTIN(, DUC) D'
Pardee Works **13** 716
Pardiac, Bernard d'Armagnac, Comte de **11** 355
Pardies, Johann Gabriel **12** 812
Pardo, El **3** 471; **14** 104; **24** 107–8*; **29** *258*, 267; **32** 551
Casita del Príncipe **24** 108; **29** 272, 305; **32** 564
frescoes **20** 78
furniture **29** 342
paintings **12** 924; **13** 922
tapestries **4** 564; **13** 241
textiles **29** 348
Pardo, Luis **27** 501
Pardo, Manuel **24** 517
Pardo, Mercedes **24** 108*; **32** 175; **33** 317
Pardo de Lagos, Lázaro **24** 507
Pardo de Tavera, Juan, Cardinal *see* TAVERA, JUAN PARDO DE, Cardinal
Pardoe, Julia **8** 66; **25** 837
Pardoe, Thomas **32** 789
Pardo Vigarny, Gregorio **31** 89
Pardubice **8** *374*; **24** 108–9*, *109*
architecture **8** 377, 422
Castle **24** 463
crematorium **8** 373
education (art) **8** 425
houses **8** *377*
St Bartholomew **8** 384; **33** *212*
Pardubice, Pavel of *see* PAVEL OF PARDUBICE
Pardubice, Půta of *see* PŮTA OF PARDUBICE
Paré, Ambroise **21** 6
Parede, Sanatorium de Sant'Ana **25** 294
Paredes Jardiel, José **13** 725
Pareja, Juan de **24** 109–10*; **32** 131, 135
Pareja, Miguel Angel **31** 755
parekklesia **9** 544–5, 547; **24** 110*, *110*
Parement de Narbonne **13** 137, *137*, 154, 674; **18** 686; **20** 742, *742*; **31** 835
Parement de Narbonne, Master of the **3** 552; **7** 721; **17** 461; **20** 742*
patrons and collectors **31** 448, 835, 837
works **13** *137*, 154; **20** *742*
Parent, Claude **11** 527; **24** 111*, 130
Parent, Clément **19** 30
Parent, Henri-Joseph-Aubert **7** 747; **16** 851
Parent, Jean-François **2** 699
Parent, Melchior-François **28** 521
Parente, Marchese de **18** 184
Parente, Salomone de **27** 226
Parente da Silva, Domingos *see* SILVA, DOMINGOS PARENTE DA
Parenti, Marco **6** 3
Parentino *see* BERNARDINO DA PARENZO
Parentium *see* POREČ
Parentucelli, Tommaso *see* NICHOLAS V, Pope
Parenzano, Bernardino da *see* BERNARDINO DA PARENZO
Parenzo *see* POREČ
Parenzo, Bernardino da *see* BERNARDINO DA PARENZO
Parenzo, Meïr **21** 176
Parera, José Pratmarsó *see* PRATMARSÓ PARERA, JOSÉ
parerga **12** 287
Pares, John **28** 293
works **28** *293*
Paresce, Renato **16** 680
Paresi **4** 706, 724
Paret (y Alcázar), Luis **5** 750; **24** 111–12*; **25** 701
patrons and collectors **4** 564; **18** 899
sponsors **4** 564
works **4** *563*; **11** 493; **20** 70; **24** *112*; **29** 283
pargetting **24** 112*
parging *see* PARGETTING
Parhal Church **30** 306–7
Parham Church (Antigua) **2** 148
Parham House (W. Sussex; UK) **2** 450; **21** 509; **32** 244
Pariab, Ali **2** 902
Pariab, Husein **2** 902
Parial, Mario **24** 622
Parian cement **1** 516
Parian Chronicle **24** 571
Parian marble *see under* MARBLE → types
Parian porcelain *see under* PORCELAIN → types
Paricio, Ignacio **29** 861
Parienti, Marco **28** 70
parietal *see* PREHISTORIC ART → cave art
Parigi (family) **11** 181, 213
works **11** *213*
Parigi (di Santi), Alfonso (1535–90) **11** 215; **21** 23; **24** 112
Parigi, Alfonso (1606–56) **21** 26; **24** 113*; **30** 667
Parigi, Giulio **24** 112–13*; **30** 667
patrons and collectors **21** 25
pupils **3** 17; **4** 622; **5** 438; **10** 551; **12** 706; **24** 752
teachers **7** 311
works **5** 363; **11** 215; **21** 26, 27; **23** 264
Parihasapura *see* PARASAPUR
Parijs, Silvester van **3** 555
Parikia **24** 204
acropolis **24** 204
Church of Katapoliani **3** 191; **9** 538
Hekatontapyliani *see* Church of Katapoliani
Temple of Athena **7** 837
parinarium nuts *see under* NUTS → types
Parini, Giuseppe **21** 527
Pario *see* PARRI
Paris **11** *504*, 508, *524*; **24** 113–74*, *114*, *665*, *672*; **26** *905*; **31** *156*, *724*
academies and art schools
Académie Colarossi **11** 672; **14** 613
Académie d'Architecture **24** 173
Académie de l'Art Moderne **19** 80
Académie de Saint-Luc **11** 669; **24** 136
Académie des Beaux-Arts **1** 106, 107; **11** 520, 671, 672*; **14** 238; **18** 700; **24** 140, 169, 171–2*, 173*
collections **20** 454
publications **10** 210
Académie des Sciences d'Outre-Mer **1** 439
Académie Française **26** 491; **32** 864
Académie Julian **1** 106; **2** 524; **11** 672; **24** 142
Académie Ranson **25** 893
Académie Royale d'Architecture **1** 105, 106; **2** 314, 523; **4** 550; **11** 669, 670*; **20** 133; **24** 169–70*, 171
competitions **25** 637
Académie Royale de Peinture et de Sculpture **1** 101, 102, 104–5, 106, 107, 108; **2** 523; **3** 449; **4** 550; **9** 8, 762; **10** 676; **11** 536, 538, 669*; **19** 216; **20** 133, 599; **21** 759; **22** 85; **24** 135, 137, 166–8*, *169*, 171
catalogues **6** 79
collections **11** 665
competitions **7** 676; **25** 637
display **9** 16
Ecole Royale de Peinture et de Sculpture **24** 166, 167
exhibitions **7** 677; **9** 30; **10** *676*; **20** 135
groups and movements **13** 296
teachers **13** 825
Académie Royale des Inscriptions et Belles-Lettres **2** 163, 559
Académie Suisse **2** 524; **11** 672
Ecole d'Art Décoratif **25** 78
Ecole des Arts **4** 163; **11** 670
Ecole des Beaux-Arts **1** 106, 108; **2** 315, 332; **6** 80; **7** 830; **8** 593; **9** 312–13; **11** 520, 521, 522, 544, 563–4, 669, 670, 671*, 672*, 673, 675; **24** 142, 171, *173*, 173; **25** 319; **26** 190
archives **2** 370
collections **11** 673; **14** 577
Paris
academies and art schools
Ecole des Beaux-Arts—cont.
courtyard **9** *312*
Musée des Etudes **7** 831; **11** 667
paintings **8** 654
Ecole Nationale des Arts Décoratifs **1** 107; **2** 524; **3** 19; **11** 563, 669, 671
Ecole Nationale des Beaux-Arts *see* Ecole des Beaux-Arts
Ecole Nationale Supérieure des Beaux-Arts *see* Ecole des Beaux-Arts
Ecole Polytechnique **2** 315; **11** 520, 522, 671
Ecole Privée d'Architecture **11** 520
Ecole Royale des Elèves Protégés **11** 670*; **24** 168
Ecole Royale Gratuite de Dessin *see* Ecole Nationale des Arts Décoratifs
Ecole Royale de Peinture et de Sculpture *see under* Académie Royale de Peinture et de Sculpture
Ecole Spéciale de Peinture, Sculpture et Architecture **11** 671
Institut Français d'Architecture **8** 257; **14** 757
airports
Charles de Gaulle
Aérogare 1 **1** 495
Aérogare 2 **1** 495
Le Bourget **1** 494
apartment blocks **25** 52
Castel Béranger **2** 564; **11** 600; **23** 547; **24** 128
Maison Cotelle **2** 216
2 Rue de Caire **11** 519, *519*
25 Rue Franklin **2** 216; **7** 694; **16** 55; **24** *128*
7 Rue Trétaigne **7** 694; **27** 880
Arc de Triomphe de l'Etoile **4** 171; **6** 397, 463; **10** 745; **11** 523, 564, 658; **22** 47; **23** 521; **27** *310*, 311; **31** 351
reliefs **4** 618
sculpture **10** 770
Arc de Triomphe du Carrousel **10** 509; **11** 336, 564, 658; **21** 411; **22** 47, 740; **24** *124*, 124, 125, 163
Arc de Triomphe du Trône **7** 665; **24** *469*
Archives de l'Art Abstrait **3** 788
Archives Nationales **2** 365, 366
collections **11** 673
see also hôtels particuliers → Hôtel de Soubise
art forms and materials
altarpieces **9** 3; **11** 543; **31** 344
architecture **2** 510; **4** 332; **7** 693; **11** 508, 520, 523–4, 655; **26** 743
beadwork **3** 442
Bibles **4** 7, 10; **13** 130
bookbindings **4** 352; **12** 628
books **4** 372
boxes **4** *601*; **24** 147
brasses **4** 692
cabinets (ii) (furniture) **24** *150*
caricatures **5** 755
catalogues **19** 782
ceramics **24** 147–9*
chess sets **6** 558
coral **7** 835
decretals **8** 614
embroidery **11** 647, 648, *648*
enamel **10** *194*; **13** 169, *169*, *170*
engravings **10** 393
faience (ii) (ceramics) **24** 148
furniture **5** 350; **7** 167; **11** 596; **12** 414; **24** 149–51*
gems **12** 255
Paris
art forms and materials—cont.
glass **11** 611, 612
gold **10** III1; **11** 616; **24** *146*, 146–7*
guns **2** 461, 463, *463*, 466
gypsum **29** 812
hardstones **14** 170
ivory-carvings **13** 171, 172–4, 175; **16** 799
jewellery **11** 633; **17** 519, 522, 526
kaolin **24** 148
lace **11** 649
lithography **19** 491
manuscripts **4** *10*, 372; **9** 219; **11** 530; **13** 140, *140*, 141; **14** 433; **20** 332, 333, *339*, *340*, 341, *342*; **26** 660, 664; **28** *487*
Gothic **13** 138
marks
metalwork **11** 613; **20** 444
pewter **20** 445
medals **20** 924
metalwork **11** *615*, 618, 624
miniatures (manuscript illumination) **13** *140*, 140, *154*
painting **11** 532, 550; **26** 740
Gothic **13** 139, 156
panel **13** 131
portraits **13** *131*
panoramas **24** 19, 659
pattern books **24** 274
pewter **11** 628
porcelain **11** 607; **24** 148–9*, *149*; **27** 537
pottery **11** 603
printing **16** 360
railings **16** 54
rock crystal **26** 485
roofs **27** 128, 130
sculpture **11** 562; **13** 72, 77
silk **11** 644, 645, 646; **28** 716, 717, 718
silver **11** *617*, *618*, 619, 620, *620*, *622*; **24** *146*, 146–7*, *147*; **25** 313
snuff-boxes **4** *601*, 602; **11** 632
stained glass **13** 179, 180–81
steel **8** 287
tapestries **3** 606; **11** 637, 639, *640*, 640–41; **13** 195; **30** 312, 321, *321*
textiles **28** 564
wallpaper **32** 815, III, IV3
wine-fountains **23** 768
art market **2** 558, 559; **6** 79; **20** 199; **24** 136–7; **29** 375
Assemblée Nationale *see* Palais Bourbon → Salle des Séances
auction houses **2** 559
Hôtel Drouot **24** 141
banks
Banque de France *see* hôtel particuliers → Hôtel de La Vrillière
Banque Royale
paintings **24** 341
Crédit Lyonnais Head Office **4** 597
Morgan Bank **16** 876
barrières **19** 57; **22** 738
Barrière de l'Etoile **7** 360
Barrière des Bonshommes **13** 608
Bazar Bonne-Nouvelle **10** 679
Bibliothèque de France **19** 321; **24** 132
Bibliothèque de la Direction de l'Architecture **11** 674
Bibliothèque de l'Arsenal **18** 880
see also government buildings → Arsenal
Bibliothèque des Arts Décoratifs **2** 370; **11** 674; **19** 239
Bibliothèque Forney **2** 370; **11** 673

Paris—cont.
Bibliothèque Mazarine **19** 315; **20** 896
Bibliothèque Nationale **9** 86; **11** 522, 528, 573; **16** 555; **18** 583*; **19** 316, 318; **21** 823; **24** 119, 221; **25** 173; **26** 493; **27** 270; **30** 505
Cabinet des Estampes **4** 520; **8** 637, 829; **20** 455; **23** 115; **25** 631; **31** 214
Cabinet des Estampes: collections **3** 785
Cabinet des Médailles et Antiques **4** 99, 551; **27** 115
catalogues **4** 23; **18** 856
collections **4** 139, 552; **6** 322; **7** 462; **10** 422, 487, 775; **11** 673, 903; **14** 577; **15** 741, 744; **16** 854; **17** 440, 441; **19** 726; **22** 94, 425; **24** 343, 344, 712, 883; **27** 549; **30** 749
exhibitions **1** 154; **24** 683
Fonds Portugais **5** 364
Galerie Mazarine **20** 895; **26** 566
manuscripts **2** 596; **15** 741; **31** 448
photographs **29** 663
prints **9** 448
publications **10** 210
reading-room **9** 84; **16** 54
Roman collection **27** 115
Bibliothèque Ste Geneviève **2** 290; **11** 521, 522, 659; **13** 612; **16** 53; **18** 582*, *583*, 654; **19** 317; **23** 490; **25** 173; **26** 13
collections **11** 665
reading-room **18** *582*, 582*
Bourse **3** 524; **8** 65; **10** 668, 669; **14** 592; **19** 26; **20** 438; **24** 121, 123
dome **16** 53
Boutique Simultanée **13** 798
British Embassy **16** 876
building regulations **5** 135
Bureau des Marchands-Drapiers *see* hôtels particuliers → Hôtel Carnavalet
Cabinet of Natural History **12** 832
cafes and restaurants
Café Volpini **30** 174
Maxim's **2** 565; **11** 600
Le Mirliton **31** 214
carnivals **5** 788
Castel Béranger *see under* apartment blocks
cemeteries
Cimetière de Montmartre
effigy of Godefroi of Cavaignac **31** 131
Cimetière de Montparnasse
tomb of Dumont d'Urville **25** 173
Cimetière du Père-Lachaise **4** 848; **6** 166, *166*; **10** 97; **20** 868–9; **31** 130, 131
chapel of the Greffulhe family **6** 460
monument to Oscar Wilde **31** 132, *132*
Monument to the Dead **3** 291
Cimetière des Innocents **6** 165
Centre Culturel Suédois **30** 524
Chambre des Députés *see* Palais Bourbon → Salle des Séances
châteaux
Bagatelle **3** 523–4; **4** 556; **6** 509; **12** 123; **26** 449; **32** 553
collections **28** 527
metalwork **13** 234
Bastille **11** 655; **24** 115
Château de Madrid **4** 780; **6** 505; **11** 513, 656; **16** 734; **29** 833
faience (ii) (ceramics) **11** 604; **24** 148, 149
Château du Fayel **4** 887

Paris
châteaux—cont.
Château du Louvre *see* Louvre (Château du Louvre, 1200-1546)
churches *see* ecclesiastical buildings
Cirque d'Hiver **1** 798
Cirque National **13** 612
Cité de la Musique **11** 528
Cité de Refuge **11** 526; **12** 792; **19** 43
Cité des Sciences et de l'Industrie **11** 528; **14** 521; **24** 132
Cité International des Arts **3** 170
Cité Universitaire **24** 129
Pavillon Suisse **11** 526; **19** *43*, 43–4
Colisée des Champs-Elysées **19** 26
collections **17** 582
Collège Chaptal **28** 157; **31** 276
Collège de Beauvais **24** 115
Collège de Clermont **21** 39
Collège de Cluny **7** 565
Collège de Navarre **5** 666
Collège des Dix-Huit **7** 565
Collège des Quatre-Nations *see* Institut de France
colleges **7** 566
Communauté des Maîtres Peintres et Sculpteurs de Paris *see* Corporation of St Luke
Corporation of St Luke **24** 166
craftsmen and artists **13** 133; **24** 146; **25** 625
dealing **11** 664
La Défense **11** 527; **22** 49
Centre National des Industries et Technologies **7** 696; **28** *583*, 583; **33** 627–8
coloured tower blocks **24** 131
Grande Arche **11** 527, *527*, 528; **29** 526
Roussel-Hoechst Turm *see* coloured tower blocks
Tête-Défense *see* Grande Arche
Département des Estampes et de la Photographie **24** 682
Diorama **8** 449–50, 910, 911
Dôme des Invalides *see* hospitals → Hôtel des Invalides
ecclesiastical buildings
Abbaye Ste-Geneviève **5** *345*, 346; **9** 31; **23** 517; **32** 416
church **13** 37; **24** 115
see also Holy Apostles; Panthéon
Augustinian church **13** 76
Cathedral of Notre-Dame *see* Notre-Dame
Cathedral of St Etienne **24** 115
see also Notre-Dame
Chapelle Expiatoire **11** 520
Chapelle St Fernand **20** 869
Chapel of the Congrégation du St Esprit **11** 617
Chartreuse **5** 895
Church of the Jacobins **11** 406
Convent of the Celestines **11** 265; **13** 76; **24** 115
tomb of Anne of Burgundy, Duchess of Bedford **13** 79
Convent of the Petits Augustins *see* museums → Musée des Antiquités et Monuments Français
Faubourg Saint Marcel **11** 587
Holy Apostles **24** 115
see also Abbaye Ste Geneviève → church; Panthéon
La Madeleine **7** 254; **10** 745; **11** 519, 523, 544, 564, 658; **23** 521; **24** 124, 125
model **2** 337
portico **25** 268
Maison des Dames de St Chaumond **20** 298

Paris
ecclesiastical buildings—cont.
Notre-Dame **2** 347; **6** 530–31; **9** 672; **11** 510, 521, 654, 657; **13** 38, 39, 42; **24** 115, 125, 139, 151–2*, *151*, *153*; **26** 44, 45, *45*
ambulatory **1** 768
apse **2** 347
arches **23** 368
ballflower **3** 121
bosses **4** 465
buttresses **5** 319
choir-stalls **7** 192
doors **9** 156; **11** 624
gargoyles **12** 150, *150*
mouldings **22** 218, 220, 221
nave **24** *152*
paintings **20** 894
piers **24** 751
portal **11** 555
restorations **11** 306
roof **30** *900*, 901, 907
sculpture **1** 653; **7** 275; **10** 743; **11** 565; **13** 74, *75*; **24** 153–5*, *154*, *155*; **26** 39
silver **11** 622
spires **29** 413
stained glass **11** 153; **24** 156*; **26** 702; **29** 511
tie-bars **30** 853
transept **31** 281
West Portal **14** 415
see also Cathedral of St Etienne
Notre-Dame de Lorette **11** 520, *525*; **24** 125
Notre-Dame-des-Victoires **2** 724, 725; **19** *647*
Notre-Dame du Travail **2** 651
Panthéon **7** 258, 277; **11** 518, 522, 658; **22** 738; **24** 21, 121, 128, 142, 165–6*; **25** 798, *798*; **26** 12, *13*; **29** 93, *93*
dome **9** 86
doors **7** 761
model **2** 337
murals **6** 536; **8** 659; **13** 692; **22** *330*
piers **20** 576
portico **25** 267
sculpture **8** *566*; **10** 770; **11** 564; **26** 512
see also Abbaye Ste Geneviève → church; Holy Apostles
Sacré-Coeur **7** 258; **26** 704
St Ambroise **26** 704
Ste Anne-la-Royale **13** 748; **24** 118; **30** 649
St Augustin **3** 125; **11** 522; **26** 704
St Benoît **24** 115
Ste Catherine-du-Val-des-Ecoliers **24** 117
Sainte-Chapelle **6** 459; **7** 860; **11** 510, 655; **13** 42, *42*; **24** 115, *156*, 156–7*; **25** 172; **26** 45; **27** 550; **28** 631
altars **1** 697
collections **20** 251
doors **9** 152
Grand Châsse **22** 44
ivory-carvings **13** 173, *173*
manuscripts **4** 394; **11** 614
metalwork **11** 614; **13** 158
mouldings **22** 219, 221, 222
paintings **8** 856; **13** 139
reliquary of St Louis **13** 168
sculpture **7** 275; **11** 555; **13** 72, 74, 141; **24** *157*, 157–8*
stained glass **11** 530; **12** 790; **13** 135, 140, 179, 181; **19** 362; **24** *158*, 158–9*; **29** 501, 506, 511, I; **33** 246
tracery **31** 271
Treasury **13** 158
wall paintings **12** 625; **13** 132, 134; **32** 805
Ste Clotilde **11** 521

Paris
ecclesiastical buildings—cont.
Saint-Denis Abbey *see* SAINT-DENIS
St Denis-de-l'Estrée **11** 521
St Etienne-du-Mont **11** 154, 515; **13** 210
St Eugène **4** 239; **11** 522
St Eustache **11** 512, 513, 656; **13** 210; **24** 115; **29** 506
tomb of Jean-Baptiste Colbert **11** 559
wood-carvings **30** 781
Ste Geneviève *see* Abbaye Ste Geneviève → church
St Germain-des-Prés **9** 672; **11** 159; **13** 36, 37; **24** 115, 119, 159*; **32** 279
bosses **4** 465
buttresses **5** 319
capitals **24** 132
Chapel of the Virgin **26** 45
manuscripts **4** 10; **24** 132
piers **24** 751
stained glass **29** 516
wall paintings **11** *158*
St Germain-l'Auxerrois **11** 544; **24** 115, 116, 159*
altarpiece **1** 518
rood screen **13** 226
stained glass **29** 504, 506
SS Gervais et Protais **4** 865–6; **11** 154, 155, 516, *516*, 544; **24** 115, 116; **29** 504
St Jacques-la-Boucherie **24** 115
St Jacques-de-l'Hôpital **13** 76
St Jean-de-Belleville **11** 521
St Jean-de-Montmartre **7** 693; **11** 522
St Joseph des Carmes **8** 482
St Laurent **2** 320; **24** 115, 116
St Leu-St Gilles **13** 608
St Louis d'Antin **24** 120
St Louis-des-Invalides **7** 303
St Louis des Jésuites *see* St Paul-St Louis
St Louis du Louvre
tomb of André-Hercule de Fleury **7** 672–3
St Magloire **13** 36
Ste Marguerite **11** 265
Ste Marie de la Visitation **2** 725; **11** 516; **20** *289*; **24** 118
Ste Marie-Madeleine **11** 711; **13** 49
St Martin-des-Champs **1** 768; **13** 36; **22** 216, 218; **24** 115
paintings **28** *743*
roof **30** 907
see also museums → Conservatoire des Arts et Métiers
St Mathurin **31** 340
St Médard **24** 115
St Merri **11** 154, 544, 639
chapel of St Philomena **1** *759*
St Nicolas-de-Port **11** 154
St Nicolas-des-Champs **11** 558; **24** 115
St Paul-St Louis **8** 775; **11** 516; **24** 118
monument for the Heart of Henry II of Bourbon **11** 558; **27** 821, *822*
St Philippe-du-Roule **6** 396–7, *397*; **11** 520; **24** 120
St Pierre-de-Montmartre **13** 36, 37; **21** 163; **30** *900*
St Pierre de Montrouge **26** 704; **32** 84, *84*
St Pierre-du-Gros Caillou **24** 120
St Roch **24** 117
St Séverin **11** 154, 511; **13** 181; **24** 115, 116
St Sulpice **6** 397; **7** 665; **28** 485–6, *486*; **29** *636*
model **2** 337
portico **25** 267

Paris
ecclesiastical buildings
St Sulpice—cont.
stained glass **29** 506
St Sulpice-de-Favières **22** 219
St Thomas-d'Aquin **20** 894
St Victor **4** 10; **32** 415
St Vincent *see* St Germain-des-Prés
St Vincent-de-Paul **11** 159, 520; **13** 612; **14** 593, *593*; **24** 124; **25** 172
portico **25** 267
St Vincent et Sainte Croix *see* St Germain-des- Prés
Temple **7** 257; **13** 37; **14** 419
Temple de la Gloire *see* La Madeleine
Val-de-Grâce **6** 435; **9** 84; **11** 516, 536, 657; **19** 145; **20** *292*; **24** 118, 159–61*, *160*
ciborium **7** 303
portico **25** 266
Les Echelles du Baroque **2** 361
Ecole de Chirurgie *see* Faculté de Médecine
Ecole des Chartes **11** 675
Ecole des Ponts et Chaussées **11** 670; **24** 174
Ecole du Louvre **11** 675
Ecole Militaire **11** 518; **12** 595; **19** 217; **24** 121, 122
sculpture **7** 421
education (art) **16** 536
Eiffel Tower **5** 648; **10** 107, *107*, 681, 683; **11** 524; **15** 883; **16** 54; **24** 127
Esders Clothing Factory **7** *694*; **19** 365
exhibitions **10** 679; **11** 548, 550; **24** 135, 171–2
Exposition Coloniale Internationale, 1931 **10** 684; **24** 129
Musée des Arts Africains **18** 782
Exposition d'Art Musulman, 1893 **16** 559
Exposition des Arts Musulmans, 1903 **16** 559
Exposition Internationale de Peinture **8** 718; **20** 60
Exposition Internationale des Arts Décoratifs et Industriels Modernes, 1925 **2** 521–2; **7** 653; **10** 684; **11** 526, 568, 601–2; **15** 883; **20** 68; **24** 147; **27** 409, 422
architecture **25** 52
arena theatre **24** 474
Austrian Pavilion **18** 33
Catalan Pavilion **29** 308
Pavillon de l'Esprit Nouveau **19** 80; **21** 782
Pavillon de Tourisme **19** 80; **24** 129
Polish Pavilion **8** 371
Soviet Pavilion **2** 604; **21** 92, 782
Exposition Internationale des Arts et Techniques dans la Vie Moderne, 1937 **10** 684; **11** 526, 548, 569, 584; **15** 883; **19** 81; **22** 332; **27** 422; **29** 273
Japanese Pavilion **17** 88
Nouveau Palais du Trocadéro **23** 122
Pavillon de l'Air **15** *884*
Pavillon de l'Union des Artistes Modernes **24** 824
Polish Pavilion **5** 8
Spanish Pavilion **29** 286
Exposition Publique des Produits de l'Industrie Française, 1798 **15** 883
Exposition Universelle, 1855 **7** 677; **10** 682; **15** 883
Art Nouveau Bing **11** 600
Palais de l'Industrie **10** 682
Pavillon du Réalisme **10** 680

Paris—cont.
Exposition Universelle, 1867
10 94, 298, 682, *682*; **15** 883;
16 559
Exposition Universelle, 1878
10 682–3; **15** 747, 883; **16** 559;
24 127
Belgian Pavilion **3** 549
Exposition Universelle, 1889
8 123; **10** 681, 683; **14** 384;
15 883; **23** 741; **24** 127
architecture **12** 728
Galerie des Machines **9** 464;
10 683; **11** 524; **14** 384;
15 883; **16** 55, *55*
Palais des Beaux-Arts et des Arts Libéraux **22** 270
Exposition Universelle, 1900
10 683; **11** 524; **14** 384;
15 883; **24** 127; **27** 421; **28** 482
Art Nouveau Bing **2** 564;
11 582, 904
Finnish Pavilion **11** 100; **22** 331, 541
frescoes **12** 21
Grand Palais **6** 322; **10** 683;
11 524; **12** 728; **24** *127*, 127
Hall (Austria) **29** 843
Hungarian Pavilion **14** 908
monumental gateway **22** 271
Palais de l'Electricité **14** 385
Palais des Illusions **14** 385
Petit Palais **8** 715, 819; **10** 683;
11 524; **12** 728; **22** 363;
24 127, 142
Petit Palais: *see also* museums → Musée du Petit Palais
sculpture **4** 48
Faculté de Médecine **11** 518;
12 595, 898
anatomy lecture theatre **22** 738, *739*
festivals **23** 767
Fondation Dapper *see under* museums
Fondation Nationale des Arts Graphiques et Plastiques
27 225
Fontaine des Innocents **10** 744;
11 *342*, 342–3, 513, 557;
13 226, *226*; **24** 133
fountains
Fontaine des Quatre Saisons
4 509–10; **11** *560*, 561; **24** 123
Fontaine Louvois **11** 346
Galerie Aguado **18** 811
Galerie de l'Effort Moderne
27 162
Galerie Iris Clert **10** 680
Galerie Louis Carré **9** 374
Galerie Maeght **20** 75; **21** 708;
24 144
Galerie Percier **19** 66
Galeries Jouffroy **11** 524
Gaumont Film Palace **19** *368*
government buildings
Arsenal **2** 502; **11** *578*; **29** 917
see also Bibliothèque de l'Arsenal
Collège de France **24** 167
Hôtel des Monnaies **2** 172, *172*;
3 902
Ministère de la Défense
paintings **4** 124
Ministère de la Guerre *see* Ministère de la Défense
Ministère des Affaires Etrangères **13** 238
Ministère des Relations Extérieures **26** 189
Ministères des Finances **6** 534, *534*; **11** 528; **24** 132
Grande Halle de la Villette
22 748
Grand Palais *see under* Exposition Universelle, 1900
guidebooks **4** 766; **8** 846
guilds **24** 148, 579
carvers **24** 150

Paris
guilds—cont.
furniture-makers **24** 149–51
Halle au Blé *see* Bourse
Les Halles **3** *125*, 125; **4** 788;
11 524; **16** 54; **22** 333
hospitals
Hôpital Beaujon **14** 783
Hôpital de la Charité **25** 267
Hôpital des Enfants-Rouges
24 146
Hôpital-Général **24** 146
Hôpital Lariboisière **14** 783;
24 126
Hôpital St Louis **24** 118
Hôpital de la Salpêtrière **2** 657, 658; **4** 887–8
Hospice de Bicêtre **2** 657, 658
Hospice des Enfants Trouvés
22 682
Hospice des Femmes Incurables **14** 781
Hospice du Saint-Esprit **24** 146
Hôtel-Dieu **14** 782; **24** 126;
26 *448*
Hôtel des Invalides **4** 888;
7 258; **9** 86; **11** 257, 657;
14 782, 784; **24** 119, 163–5*, *164*
church **20** *294*, 294–5*;
24 164–5
Musée de l'Armée *see under* museums
paintings **11** 537; **18** 633
sculpture **5** 889; **10** 765
stained glass **29** 506
tomb of Napoleon I **11** 565;
27 831; **29** 702
hotels
Grand Hôtel **14** 786
Hôtel Continental *see* Inter-Continental Hotel
Inter-Continental Hotel **14** 786
Ritz Hotel **14** 787
hôtels particuliers
Hôtel d'Amelot **4** *225*; **14** 789
Hôtel Amelot de Bisseuil **26** 91
Hôtel des Archevêques de Sens
11 655
Hôtel d'Assy **26** 493
Hôtel d'Avaux **11** 516
Hôtel de Baudot **3** 394
Hôtel de Bautru **19** 262
Hôtel Beauharnais **25** 193
Hôtel de Beauvais **8** 65; **14** 789;
19 *211*
Hôtel de Biron **14** 789
see also museums → Musée Rodin
Hôtel Bischoffsheim **11** 584
Hôtel de la Boexière **1** 133
Hôtel Bourbon-Condé **11** 562
Hôtel de Bourgogne **30** 658, 659
Hôtel de Bourrienne **11** 411, *412*
Hôtel de Brancas **3** 523
Hôtel de Bretonvilliers **4** 574, 575, 755
Hôtel Carnavalet **4** 887; **10** 744;
11 513; **20** 292; **24** 117; **26** 91
see also museums → Musée Carnavalet
Hôtel Cernuschi *see* Musée Cernuschi
Hôtel Chalons-Luxembourg
11 516
Hôtel de Charost *see* British Embassy
Hôtel Chartraire de Montigny
18 661
Hôtel du Châtelet
Cabinet du Laque **14** 792
Hôtel de Chevry-Tubeuf **9** 22;
19 145; **20** 895–6; **29** 833
collections **9** 22
Hôtel de Choiseul
Chambre du Lit **14** 792
Premier Cabinet **14** 792
Hotel de Clisson **24** 167

Paris
hôtels particuliers—cont.
Hôtel de Cluny *see* museums → Musée de Cluny
Hôtel de St Pouange **17** 670
Hôtel Donon *see* museums → Musée Cognacq-Jay
Hôtel d'Estrées **14** 789
Hôtel d'Evreux *see* Palais de l'Elysée
Hôtel de Gallifet **14** 790
Hôtel Grimod d'Orsay
Salon Doré **14** 792; **30** 343
Hôtel Grimod de la Reynière
2 245; **7** *416*
Hôtel d'Hallwyl **14** 789
Hôtel Hesselin **11** 516
Hôtel de Jars **14** 789; **30** 530
Hôtel Lambert **5** 346; **9** 14;
11 516, 657; **14** 789; **15** 138;
18 671; **19** 263, *263*, 264, *264*
Cabinet de l'Amour **2** 904;
18 671; **19** 248, *248*; **20** 860;
24 253, 476; **30** 61
Cabinet des Bains **18** 671;
19 248
Cabinet des Muses **18** 671;
19 248; **24** 253
collections **8** 372
Galerie d'Hercule **18** 671;
19 21
interior decoration **18** 671
stucco **29** 833
Hôtel Lamoignon **3** 925; **9** 353;
11 514, 573; **23** 492
Hôtel de Langeac **17** 467
Hôtel de Lassay **22** 127
Hôtel Lauzun **5** 346; **11** 573, 575
Hôtel de La Vrillière **20** 290, 374; **26** 492–3
frescoes **24** 476
Galerie Dorée **11** 405, 578;
26 84
paintings **18** 885; **25** 390
Hôtel Le Barbier *see* Hôtel Perrault
Hôtel de Longueville **13** 825
Hôtel de Luynes **14** 791
Grand Salon **14** *791*
Hôtel de Mailly
Salon Doré **11** 577
Hôtel de Matignon **8** 63–4;
11 577; **13** 238; **14** 789
sculpture **19** 213
Hôtel Mazarin *see* Bibliothèque Nationale
Hôtel de Montmorency **14** 790;
29 523
Hôtel Morin **4** 125
Hôtel de Mortemart **3** 856
Hôtel de M Roland **29** 523
Hôtel Necker
interior decoration **11** 579–80
Hôtel de Neufville-Villeroy
24 117
Hôtel Nivernais **14** 792
Hôtel d'Ormesson **32** 338
Hôtel de la Païva **3** 278, 877;
11 599; **23** 794
Hôtel de Parabère **11** 405
Hôtel Perrault
garden **24** 467
paintings **4** 125; **24** 467
Hôtel de Pompadour *see* Palais de l' Elysée
Hôtel Pontalba **14** 790
Hôtel de Pontchartrain **26** 492
Hôtel de Rambouillet **14** 790
Chambre Bleue **11** 574;
14 790; **25** 872
interior decoration **10** 187
Hôtel de la Reine **11** 400;
24 117
Hôtel de Rohan
Cabinet des Fables *see* Green Salon
Cabinet des Singes **11** 577;
14 791; **28** 776

Paris
hôtels particuliers
Hôtel de Rohan—cont.
Green Salon **14** 791
sculpture **11** 560; **19** 118
Hôtel de Roquelaure **26** 493
Hôtel de Rouillé **26** 493
Hôtel Saint-Florentin **6** 396
Hôtel St-Julien **25** 671
Hôtel St-Pol **13** 150; **24** 115, 117; **31** 842
paintings **31** 835
Hôtel Salé *see* museums → Musée Picasso
Hôtel Séguier **28** 370; **32** 718
Hôtel de Soissons **11** 656
Hôtel de Soubise **8** 651; **11** 266
architecture **26** 494
Cabinet des Fables *see* Green Salon
Green Salon **14** 791
interior decoration **19** 723;
26 84
paintings **4** 515; **22** 682, *683*;
31 306
Salon de la Princesse **1** 133;
11 538, 578
Salon du Prince **19** *722*
Salon Ovale **11** 518, 578;
26 494, *494*
state bedrooms **14** 792
see also Archives Nationales
Hôtel de Strasbourg *see* Hôtel de Rohan
Hôtel de Sully **8** 65; **11** 514, 573, 656
Hôtel Tabary **29** 834
Hôtel Tambonneau **14** 789, *790*
Hôtel Thélusson **19** 56
Hôtel de Toulouse *see* Hôtel de La Vrillière
Hôtel des Tournelles **24** 117
Hôtel de la Trinité **24** 146
Hôtel d'Uzès **14** 789; **29** 834
Hôtel de la Vallière **18** 880
Hôtel de la Victoire **10** 186
Hôtel de Villars **11** 405; **26** 493
Hôtel Voyer d'Argenson **32** 766
Hôtel Watel-Dehaynin **21** 166
see also houses
Hôtel de Ville **11** 656; **24** 116, 125, 133, 142; **26** 190; **28** 133;
31 241
bronzes **8** 94
façade **11** *566*
Galerie des Fêtes **14** 489
Galerie des Métiers **12** 13
murals **22** 330
paintings **4** 124; **8** 654; **12** 496;
18 663; **25** 383, 750
Salon des Arts **11** 156; **12** 770
Salon Napoléon **15** 843
sculpture **9** 369; **11** 565; **12** 725
houses **11** 656, 659; **24** *121*
22 Rue de Provence **4** 332
Maison de Verre **6** 476; **11** 526, 584; **12** 792, *793*
Maison Pompéienne **4** 308;
11 580, *581*; **22** 744; **23** 209;
28 345
Tzara House **11** 526; **19** 653, *653*
see also hôtels particuliers
Institut de France **7** 567; **11** 657, 671; **19** 145, *265*; **23** 493;
24 118
collections **16** 851; **24** 389
portico **25** 266
Salle Ordinaire des Séances
9 389
tomb of Cardinal Mazarin **8** *94*;
11 559
see also academies and art schools → Académie des Beaux-Arts; Académie Française; Académie Royale des Inscriptions & Belles-Lett.

Paris—cont.
Institut de Recherche et de Coordination Acoustique et Musique (IRCAM) **1** 126
Institut des Hautes Etudes Urbaines **4** 332
Institut du Monde Arabe **11** 528;
16 556; **24** 131
Institut Néerlandais
Lugt Collection **19** 783; **28** 166
Institut Tessin *see* Centre Culturel Suédois
Louvre (Château du Louvre, 1200-1546) **6** 504; **11** 511;
24 115, 161*, *161*; **26** 43;
29 521
tapestries **31** 373
Louvre (Palais du Louvre, 1546-1793) **3** 835; **4** 547; **6** 54, 506, 507, 508; **7** 665, 916; **8** 31;
11 513, 517, 656, 658, 744;
12 259; **18** 630; **19** 140, 236–7, 265, 266–7; **20** 292–3; **23** 810, 811; **24** 116, 117, 118, 161–3*, *162*, *163*, 388, 468; **25** 81, 577;
29 92; **31** 835, 842, 848; **32** 613
Ancienne Salle du Conseil d'Etat **14** 489
Appartement des Bains **19** 248
architectural sculpture **13** 227
Ballcourt **3** 118
Cabinet de la Reine **9** 385
carpets **5** 836–7; **11** 651, 652;
27 *895*, 896
Cour Carrée **6** 506; **8** 65;
10 744; **11** 265, 516, 557, 657;
19 134, *237*
sculpture **6** 517
see also under Louvre (Musée du Louvre, 1793-)
doors **9** 158
east entrance **31** 835
exhibitions **10** 676
furniture **11** 587, 588
Galerie d'Apollon **4** 552; **5** 172;
6 508; **9** 416; **11** 575; **14** 490;
18 642; **20** 480; **23** 542;
26 91; **29** 833, *834*
frescoes **9** 329
paintings **8** 642, 643; **13** 806;
25 383
paintings (ceiling) **5** 436;
13 701; **30** 343
Grande Galerie **2** 53; **9** 31;
10 *676*; **11** 514, 536; **22** 357
carpets **4** 552
exhibitions **10** 676; **24** 168
paintings **11** 357; **25** 390–91
sculpture **14** 798; **22** 45;
23 795; **29** 733
see also under Louvre (Musée du Louvre, 1793-)
Grande Galerie du Bord de l'Eau *see* Grande Galerie
Grande Salle **30** 659
interior decoration **11** 533, 573, 722; **13** 790
King's Bedchamber **11** 572
leather **19** 3
Louis XIV Appartement **19** 248
menagerie **33** 698
metalwork **11** 626; **24** 146
paintings **18** 632
Pavillon de l'Horloge **19** *134*;
27 129, 822
sculpture **11** 558, *558*
Pavillon Henri II **10** 744
Petite Galerie *see* Galerie d'Apollon
Salle de Bal **5** 905
Salle de Diane **5** 889; **12** 158
Salle des Antiques **11** 661;
24 167
Salle des Cariatides **6** 506;
13 *227*
Salon Carré **24** 168
sculpture **5** 889; **11** 565; **13** 76, 790
staircase **31** 835

Paris
Louvre (Palais du Louvre, 1546-1793) —cont.
stucco **20** 480
studios **29** 855
Summer apartment **26** 566
Louvre (Musée du Louvre, 1793-)
9 313; **11** 258, 658, 665, 668; **14** 238; **19** 69–70; **22** 357, 362, 739; **24** 132, 163; **27** 549; **31** 593
Ancient Near East collection **1** 855
Arabian collection **2** 275
architectural sculpture **3** 314; **7** 841; **22** 465; **24** 554
Baldinucci collection **3** 97
Beisteguy collection **3** 522
Bibliothèque Centrale des Musées Nationaux **2** 370; **11** 673
Cabinet des Dessins **4** 520, 552; **5** 342, 445; **9** 230; **23** 693; **24** 712; **26** 534
Camondo collection **5** 530
catalogues **2** 165; **6** 77, 78; **10** 184; **13** 837; **21** 817
Cavaceppi collection **6** 98
ceiling paintings **14** 311
Chauchard collection **6** 516
Chinese collection **24** 343
Collection Coutan **8** 73
collections **2** 53, 559; **7** 193; **10** 487; **11** 665–6; **20** 896; **22** 296, 358; **25** 8; **30** 514
Cour Carrée **4** 301
sculpture **7** 421
see also under Louvre (Palais du Louvre, 1546- 1793)
Daru staircase **19** 154
David-Weill collection **8** 569
drawings **9** 230; **10** 432; **32** 22
16th cent. **5** 866
17th cent. **4** 128, 538; **21** 498; **26** 177
18th cent. **27** 568; **32** 584
19th cent. **24** 59
Egyptian collection **4** 308; **10** 79, 90, 93
engravings **10** 390
Etruscan collection **10** 637, 640
exhibitions **10** 676, 678; **17** 436
extension (1852-7) **28** 345, 346
extension (1985-9) **22** 368; **24** 326
see also Pyramide
Fould collection **11** 338
frames **11** 411
Galerie Campana **4** 307; **5** *536*, 537; **6** 20; **7** 876
Galerie d'Apollon **20** 873
Galerie Espagnole **10** 679; **13** 252; **30** 385
Gay collection **12** 213
Grande Galerie **24** 138, 221
lighting **9** 12
see also under Louvre (Palais du Louvre, 1546- 1793)
Greek collection **8** 366; **10** 184; **13** 469, 470, 542, 605
hardstones **11** 635
Henry II staircase **8** 829
His de la Salle collection **14** 577
Impressionist collection **10** 841; **11** 544, 887; **20** 878; **22** 94; **24** 142; **25** 150
see also museums → Musée du Jeu de Paume; Musée d'Orsay
Indian collection **15** 744
interior decoration **7** 529
Iranian collection **15** 922
Islamic collection **9** 298; **16** 555
Italian collection **4** 307; **16** 772; **31** 849
La Caze collection **18** 588; **26** 500
lighting **9** 13

Paris
Louvre (Musée du Louvre, 1793-) —cont.
Marx collection **20** 524
Melpomene Room **22** 163
Mesoamerican collection **21** 264, 265
Mesopotamian collection **21** 310
metalwork **17** 479
Musée Charles X **4** 556; **11** 258, 302, 371; **13** 692; **15** 839
ceiling paintings **14** 311
Musée Napoléon (1803-15) **2** 165; **4** 300; **11** 666
catalogues **6** 77
collections **15** 741; **16** 768
directors **8** 764; **32** 613
exhibitions **10** 678
sculpture **4** 407
Musée Napoléon III (1862-3)
catalogues **7** 412
collections **4** 307; **5** 536; **13** 542
Musée des Souverains **4** 307; **23** 126
Musée Standish **29** 535
paintings **4** 552; **27** 58
display **9** 18
16th cent. **8** 67; **10** 432; **16** 814; **32** 356
17th cent. **4** 128; **16** 814; **28** 750
18th cent. **6** 475; **8** 91; **11** 369; **31** 818
19th cent. **6** 501; **27** 263; **29** 59
paintings (ceiling) **1** 28; **24** 736; **28** 133
Pavillon de Flore **5** 824
Pavillon de Rohan **5** 824
Piot collection **24** 838
pithoi **18** 165
pottery **13** 555
Pyramide **10** 98; **11** 528, 660; **12** 794; **25** *766*, 767; **27** 131
see also extension (1985-9)
restorations **21** 429
Roman collection **27** 115
Rothschild collection **11** 664; **27** 225
Salle d'Amasis **8** 829
Salle de Diane **25** 671
Salle des Antiquités Egyptiennes **21** 411
Salle des Antonins **14** 390; **25** 671
Salle Duchâtel **21** 411
Salle Louis XVIII **20** 873
Salle Percier **21** 411
Salon Carré **22** *358*; **28** 746
sculpture **2** 559; **27** 46; **29** 564; **31** 356; **32** 237
display **9** 23
19th cent. **2** 843; **3** 357
Slovakian collection **28** 857
Soult collection **29** 96
staff **3** 314; **8** 50; **17** 464; **20** 523; **23** 778
Syria-Palestine collection **30** 198
tapestries **30** 331, 332
Thiers collection **30** 733
Lycée Louis-le-Grand **17** 670
mairie (10th arrondissement) **8** 473
mairie (19th arrondissement) **12** 496
mairie (20th arrondissement) **12** 770
Maison de l'Art Nouveau **11** 582
Maison de l'ORTF television building **24** 130
Maison des Dames de St Chaumond *see under* ecclesiastical buildings
Maison Dubois *see* Maison Municipale de Santé
Maison Municipale de Santé **11** 359

Paris—cont.
Maîtrise, the *see* Corporation of St Luke
Manufacture Nationale des Gobelins *see* GOBELINS
Marais **2** 324
markets **31** 711
Mobilier National **11** 659; **30** 331, 332
Monnaie des Médailles **8** 763
Montparnasse **2** 552
monuments and memorials
Colonne Austerlitz *see* Place Vendôme → Colonne Vendôme
Colonne de Juillet **11** 523
Colonne de la Grande Armée *see* Place Vendôme → Colonne Vendôme
Deportation Memorial **8** 224–5
monument to General Desaix *see under* Place de Victoires
monument to Henry II **10** 441
monument to Henry IV **10** 441; **11** 558
monument to Honoré de Balzac **11** 565
monument to Louis XIV *see under* Place Vendôme
monument to Louis XV *see under* Place de la Concorde
monument to Louis XVI *see under* Place de la Concorde
monument to the Triumph of the Republic **8** 472, *473*; **11** 565; **29** 566
monument to Victor Hugo **11** 566
Musée des Antiquités et Monuments Français **19** 159
Statue to the Republic **11** 565
museums **11** 665–6*
Cabinet des Dessins *see under* Louvre (Musée du Louvre, 1793-)
Caisse Nationale des Monuments Historiques et des Sites **22** 425
Centre Georges Pompidou **2** 309; **7** 670; **10** 417; **11** 528, 659, 660, 668; **14** 521; **16** 55; **19** 897; **22** 366; **24** *131*, 131, 145, 574, 697; **25** 24; **26** 540
collections **17** 517; **20** 97; **32** 659
Documentation du Musée National d'Art Moderne **2** 370; **11** 674
photographs **24** 682
staircase **29** 526
Stravinsky Fountain **11** 347, 570; **28** 315; **30** 924
see also Musée National d'Art Moderne
Conservatoire des Arts et Métiers **5** 905; **11** 159, 521, 522; **12** 487; **32** *82*, 82
collections **3** 422
see also ecclesiastical buildings → St Martin-des-Champs
Fondation Dapper **1** 437, 440; **9** 64
Galerie des Machines *see under* Exposition Universelle, 1889
Musée des Antiquités Egyptiennes **13** 692
Musée des Antiquités et Monuments Français **9** 25, 209; **11** 336, 675; **19** 159–60; **24** 171
collections **14** 876; **24** 157; **29** 515
Musée des Antiquités Orientales **2** 642
Musée de l'Armée **2** 449; **4** 307; **31** 56
Musée Arménien de France **2** 445
Musée d'Art Juif **2** 370

Paris
museums—cont.
Musée d'Art Moderne de la Ville de Paris **11** 668
collections **10** 839; **12** 724; **13** 681, 890
Musée des Arts d'Afrique et Océaniens *see* Musée National des Arts Africains et Océaniens
Musée des Arts Décoratifs **2** 563; **25** 660
collections **7** 155; **8** 569, 649, 792; **9** 158, 379; **11** 667; **16** 556; **29** 516; **30** 332; **32** 394
exhibitions **16** 559, 560; **17** 435; **23** 741; **29** 516
frames **11** 378
Musée Bourdelle **4** 569
Musée Carnavalet
collections **2** 337; **8** 510; **9** 448; **13** 879
see also hôtels particuliers → Hôtel Carnavalet
Musée Central des Arts *see* Louvre (Musée du Louvre, 1793-)
Musée Cernuschi **4** 597; **6** 345
collections **6** 868; **7** 155; **9** 448
exhibitions **15** 923
Musée Charles X *see under* Louvre (Musée du Louvre, 1793-)
Musée de Cluny **1** 765; **9** 25; **13** 208; **19** 160; **22** 359; **24** 116, 117
Abbot's Chapel **32** 92
collections **9** 458; **11** 663; **17** 580; **24** 157, 159; **26** 453; **29** 506, 515, 516; **30** 332
Roman baths *see* Palais des Thermes
Musée Cognacq-Jay **7** 528; **11** 668
Musée des Copies **7** 831; **11** 667; **26** 235
Musée Delacroix **11** 668
Musée Dupuytren **24** 552
Musée d'Ethnographie **24** 430
Musée des Etudes *see under* museums → Ecole des Beaux-Arts
Musée Français **28** 464; **32** 613
Musée Grévin **4** 568; **33** 4
Musée Guimet **13** 833
Afghan collection **1** 211, 212
Central Asian collection **6** 321, 322
Chinese collection **6** 735, 826, 925; **7** 54, 155; **8** 569
collections **24** 344
exhibitions **6** 321
Indian collection **15** 742, 744
Japanese collection **17** 434
Korean collection **18** 384
Nepalese collection **22** 795
periodicals **24** 436
South-east Asian collection **29** 240, 642
Tibetan collection **30** 834, 849
Musée Gustave Moreau **11** 668; **22** 91; **27** 239
Musée Hébert **11** 668; **14** 283
Musée de l'Homme **1** 437
collections **1** 67, 439; **21** 265, 886; **22** 376; **28** 581; **29** 221, 222, 240
exhibitions **21** 886
Musée de l'Impressionnisme *see* Musée du Jeu de Paume
Musée Instrumental du Conservatoire National Supérieur de Musique **22** 376
Musée Jacquemart-André **3** 851; **11** 668; **16** 851
collections **16** 851*
Musée Jean-Jacques Henner **11** 668; **14** 390

Paris
museums—cont.
Musée du Jeu de Paume **4** 618
see also Louvre (Musée du Louvre, 1793-) → Impressionist collection
Musée du Louvre *see* Louvre (Musée du Louvre, 1793-)
Musée du Luxembourg **5** 391; **10** 183; **11** 301
catalogues **3** 712
collections **2** 614; **3** 712; **4** 589; **6** 123; **9** 369; **11** 665, 666; **12** 568; **15** 839; **20** 118, 829; **22** 92, 384; **24** 142, 883; **27** 311
paintings **8** 718; **13** 829
sculpture **30** 743
Musée de la Marine **20** 426; **23** 693
Musée Marmottan **3** 671; **11** 668; **20** 454; **21** 868
Musée de la Mode et du Costume **12** 650
Musée des Monuments Français **9** 313; **11** 665
Musée Napoléon (1803-15) *see under* Louvre (Musée du Louvre, 1793-)
Musée Napoléon III (1862-3) *see under* Louvre (Musée du Louvre, 1793-)
Musée National *see* Louvre (Musée du Louvre, 1793-)
Musée National d'Art Moderne **11** 660, 668; **22** 360; **24** 574
collections **2** 370; **4** 661, 700; **7** 842; **13** 714; **19** 66; **20** 830
exhibitions **24** 145
see also Centre Georges Pompidou
Musée National des Arts Africains et Océaniens **1** 437; **10** 684; **17** 451
collections **1** 440; **29** 240
Musée National des Arts Asiatiques **13** 833
Musée Nissim de Camondo **5** 530; **28** 463
Musée de l'Orangerie
collections **11** 668; **21** 867
exhibitions **29** 638
Walter-Guillaume Collection **13** 826
Musée Oriental **17** 441
Musée d'Orsay **2** 727; **5** 391; **11** 660, 668; **24** 131
Camondo collection **11** 417
catalogues **6** 78
collections **4** 618; **5** 127; **6** 516; **19** 469; **24** 882; **25** 207; **26** 511
paintings **25** 150
see also Louvre (Musée du Louvre, 1793-) → Impressionist collection; stations → Gare d'Orsay
Musée du Petit Palais **11** 668
collections **5** 881; **9** 466; **26** 177
exhibitions **15** 747, 748
roof **27** 129
see also Exposition Universelle, 1900 → Petit Palais
Musée Picasso **4** 618; **12** 567; **20** 480; **24** 728; **28** 757
Musée des Plans-Reliefs **2** 337; **32** 80
Musée Renan-Scheffer **11** 668
Musée de la République *see* Louvre (Musée du Louvre, 1793-)
Musée Rodin **3** 712; **11** 668; **26** 513; **29** 858
casts **26** 514
catalogues **26** 515
collections **26** 509
see also hôtel particuliers → Hôtel de Biron

Paris
museums—cont.
Musée Royal 26 264
Musée de Sèvres 21 264
Musée des Souverains *see under* Louvre (Musée du Louvre, 1793-)
Musée des Travaux Publics 11 659; 24 474–5, *474*; 29 525
Musée de Trocadéro
collections 29 642
directors 10 401
see also Palais du Trocadéro
Musée de la Ville de Paris *see* Musée Carnavalet
Musée de la Voix 7 375
Musée Zadkine 33 590
Muséum National d'Histoire Naturelle 2 14; 7 841, 859; 9 464
Palais de Bois 24 474
Petit Palais 8 473
Observatoire 23 339, *339*
Palais Bourbon 11 564; 13 237; 24 124
Assemblée Nationale *see* Salle des Séances
Chambre des Députés *see* Salle des Séances
Deputies Library 15 88, *88*
monument to Louis XVIII 11 564
paintings 11 544; 32 584
portico 4 301
Salle de la Paix 1 661
Salle des Gardes 11 370
Salle des Séances 8 642; 11 371, 519; 13 237; 14 489; 17 629; 25 268
Salon du Roi 8 642
sculpture 8 473, 791
textiles 18 805
Palais Cardinal *see* Palais-Royal
Palais de Chaillot 8 77; 10 683, 684; 11 569
murals 11 790
Palais de la Cité 10 665; 13 59; 14 74; 24 115
gate-house 12 175
sculpture 5 666
staircase 29 521
Palais du Conseil Economique *see* museums → Musée des Travaux Publics
Palais de l'Elysée 12 496; 13 238; 21 823; 24 120
interior decoration 11 584
Palais Garnier *see* theatres → Opéra
Palais de l'Industrie *see under* Exposition Universelle, 1855
Palais de l'Institut de France *see* Institut de France
Palais de Justice 2 337; 9 *337*, 337–8; 11 521, 522; 18 888
Chambre des Requêtes 4 536
Cour de Cassation 7 831
paintings 19 153; 21 166
Salle des Pas Perdus 4 *867*
tapestries 3 639
Vestibule d'Harlay 28 345
Palais du Louvre *see* Louvre (Palais du Louvre, 1546-1739)
Palais du Luxembourg 3 853; 4 548–9, 865, *866*; 5 813, 889; 6 507; 9 363, 762; 11 515, 656; 24 118, 165*
Cabinet des Muses 4 549
Cabinet Doré 4 549
collections 10 798; 19 216
exhibitions 22 357
Galerie de Marie de' Medici 1 658; 19 161
gate-house 12 176
interior decoration 11 573, 661
Jardin du Luxembourg 8 794; 12 120; 24 180; 27 311
monument to Delacroix 11 566

Paris
Palais du Luxembourg
Jardin du Luxembourg—cont.
sculpture 8 473
paintings 4 387; 6 397, 433; 9 87; 12 770
sculpture 7 421; 8 650; 10 509; 11 562
Sénat 8 642; 11 159; 22 465
Palais Mazarin *see* hôtels particuliers → Hôtel de Chevry-Tubeuf
Palais du Quai d'Orsay 6 501; 24 125
Palais-Royal 9 12; 11 657; 13 36; 19 133; 20 860; 23 457, 517–18; 24 118, 120, 145, 167
Cabinet des Bains 13 701
collections 23 513
Galerie d'Enée 8 91; 14 584; 23 514, 515
Galerie des Fêtes 14 288
Galerie des Hommes Illustres 23 512
Galerie en Lanterne 23 516
gardens 8 794; 12 122
Grande Galerie 8 91
interior decoration 11 573; 20 467; 26 492
metalwork 11 626
oratory 6 434
paintings 14 482; 19 19
Salon d'Angle 23 *458*; 26 84
Théâtre-Français 6 377; 16 52; 23 517, 519; 30 658, *658*, 659, 669, 670, 671, 672
Palais des Thermes 26 905
Palais de Tokyo *see* museums → Musée National d'Art Moderne
Palais du Trocadéro 10 683, 770; 22 59; 28 139; 30 505
Mesoamerican collection 21 264
see also museums → Musée de Trocadéro
Palais des Tuileries 5 889; 6 437, 506; 8 *718*; 11 513; 19 693, *694*; 22 741; 24 117, 161; 32 613
Cabinet de la Reine 21 610
carpets 5 836–7; 27 896
Caryatid Rooms 10 187
Galerie des Consuls 12 862; 22 210; 29 733
gardens
sculpture 28 845
interior decoration 4 301, 303
Jardin des Tuileries 7 916; 8 94, 794; 12 106, 120, 121; 23 850
grotto 11 604; 14 855
sculpture 2 99
orders (architecture) 23 488
paintings 3 735; 5 172; 6 435; 8 89; 9 87; 14 482; 18 632
Petit Appartement Bas du Roi 21 496
Salle de Concert 4 834
Salle des Machines 30 669, 671, 672
Salle du Conseil d'Etat 12 335
sculpture 11 562
staircases 29 523, 524
tapestries 3 461
Parc des Princes stadium 29 489
Parc Zoologique de Paris *see under* VINCENNES
parks and gardens 1 686
Bois de Boulogne 24 179
Jardin de l'Archevêché 24 125
Jardin des Plantes 4 483; 7 745; 33 698
Musée d'Histoire Naturelle 26 545
Jardin des Tuileries *see under* Palais des Tuileries
Jardin d'Hiver 7 745
Jardin du Carrousel 20 121
Jardin du Luxembourg *see under* Palais du Luxembourg

Paris
parks and gardens—cont.
Parc Buttes-Chaumont 24 180
Parc de la Villette 11 528; 24 132; 31 397–8
Parc Monceau 12 105, 123; 14 798; 23 519; 24 179
Bois des Tombeaux 6 171
Parc Montsouris 24 180
Passage Choiseuil 11 524
patronage 13 128
Pavillon d'Hanovre 24 120
Pension du Roi 12 334
Petit Bourbon 30 658, 659, 669
La Petite Roquette 19 11
Petit Palais *see* Exposition Universelle, 1900 → Petit Palais; museums → Musée du Petit Palais
Piscine Molitor 19 332
Place Baudoyer 24 *121*, 121
Place Charles de Gaulle 24 *124*, 126
Place Dauphine 11 515, 656; 24 *117*, 118
Place de France 24 118
Place de la Concorde 7 666; 11 518, 658; 24 121–2, *122*, 125; 31 717
monument to Louis XV 4 510–11
monument to Louis XVI 11 564
obelisk of Ramesses II 23 331; 30 693
Place de l'Etoile *see* Place Charles de Gaulle
Place des Victoires 11 *517*, 518, 657; 23 493; 24 118, 139; 31 717
monument to General Desaix 29 565
Place des Vosges 4 785; 11 515, 656; 24 118; 31 717
sculpture 26 348
Place Louis-le-Grand *see* Place Vendôme
Place Louis XV *see* Place de la Concorde
Place Royale *see* Place des Vosges
Place Vendôme 5 167; 11 518, 657; 20 *296*, 296–7; 23 493; 24 118, *119*, 124
Colonne Vendôme 3 775; 4 301; 22 47
monument to Louis XIV 10 442; 29 565
Polish Historical-Literary Society collections 4 41
Pont Alexandre III 24 127
Pont d'Austerlitz 24 124
Pont des Arts 24 124
Pont d'Iéna 24 124
Pont Louis XVI 2 337
Pont Marie 24 118
Pont-Neuf 4 801; 7 665; 11 656; 24 117, 118
Pont Notre Dame 24 116
Porte Dorée 24 129
Porte St Denis 7 359; 12 *743*; 24 118
Porte St Martin 19 88; 24 118
Port Royal 24 118
Prison de la Nouvelle Force 12 616; 25 637
Prison Mazas *see* Prison de la Nouvelle Force
Roman amphitheatre 26 905
Roman capitolium 26 905
Roman forum 11 327
Rotonde des Panoramas 13 612
La Ruche 6 384; 8 225; 18 445, 863; 19 77; 27 307*; 29 858, *858*; 32 405; 33 590
1 Rue Danton 7 693; 14 388
Rue de Grenelle 11 657
Rue de Rivoli 11 519, 658; 24 *123*
Rue Mallet-Stevens 20 203
Rue Vavin 27 880

Paris—cont.
Salle Gaveau 7 531
Salle Louvois 8 593
Salle Pleyel 1 125; 7 687
Salon 20 135; 24 168, *169*, 171–2*
Salon de l'Art Nouveau 4 332
Salon des Tuileries 8 658
Service d'Etude et de Documentation du Département du Louvre 11 674
Service Photographique de la Réunion des Musées Nationaux 11 674
shops 24 *121*
Bercy Centre 28 623
Bon Marché, Le 2 522; 4 239, 240; 8 769–70, *769*; 10 421; 11 241, 524, 601; 16 54; 19 282; 28 900
Atelier Pomone 11 583
Classes Laborieuses 7 531
Galeries Lafayette, Les 2 522; 5 669; 8 770; 11 583, 601
Grands Magasins du Louvre 2 522; 11 601
Printemps, Au 2 522; 6 468; 8 770; 11 601; 25 79
La Samaritaine 7 528; 8 770; 11 524, 526; 17 668; 25 173; 30 506
Sorbonne 9 369; 11 676; 24 115; 25 750
Chapel 11 516, 657; 19 134, *135*; 24 118
Chapel: portico 25 266
Chapel: tomb of Cardinal Richelieu 12 *726*; 31 128
Fundacíon Cambó 5 510
library 19 313
observatory 23 342
paintings 11 156; 18 867
sculpture 6 468
see also University
stations
Gare de l'Est 11 524; 24 125; 25 *855*, 856
Gare de Lyon 24 125
Gare d'Orsay 11 524, 528; 15 849; 18 664*, *664*; 23 IV
see also museums → Musée d'Orsay
Gare du Nord 6 468; 11 524; 24 125, *126*; 25 855
Gare St-Lazare 24 125
Métro stations 2 564, 568; 13 832; 21 349; 23 547
Porte Dauphine 21 *349*
studios 29 856, 859
Atelier Benjamin Constant 11 672
Atelier Redon 32 773
Bateau-Lavoir 3 366*; 8 132; 13 668; 18 862; 20 285, 854; 21 786; 24 714; 26 75; 29 857, 858; 30 3
Maquis 29 857
Rue du Départ studios 21 852, 854, 855
synagogues 17 548
Rue de la Victoire synagogue 17 547
Rue Pavée synagogue 17 548
Temple de la Grande Armée *see* ecclesiastical buildings → La Madeleine
theatres
Ba-ta-Clan 30 679
Comédie Française *see* Théâtre de l'Odéon
Eden 30 679
Opéra 3 465; 7 666; 10 745; 11 522, *523*, 565, 659; 12 155–7, *156*, *157*; 23 546; 24 125; 26 500; 28 346; 29 525; 30 137, 677–8, 679
architectural sculpture 28 346
façade 5 824

Paris
theatres
Opéra—cont.
Foyer de la Danse 28 346
Grand Foyer 28 346
Grand Salle 32 94
Grand Staircase 29 *844*
lighting 19 366
mosaics 22 163
paintings 7 371; 11 546; 19 153; 24 817
sculpture 6 468; 10 770; 28 139
stucco 29 843
Opéra Comique
paintings 4 124; 11 156
Opéra de la Bastille 7 670; 11 528; 24 132; 30 684
Palais Garnier *see* Opéra
Théâtre des Champs-Elysées 4 568; 11 659; 23 493; 30 683
paintings 8 715
sculpture 4 *568*
Théâtre Français *see under* Palais-Royal
Théâtre de France *see* Théâtre de l'Odéon
Théâtre National de la Colline 30 684
Théâtre de l'Odéon 11 659; 24 121, 122, 581–2; 30 671; 32 768, *768*
paintings 4 536
portico 25 267
Théâtre du Vieux-Colombier 30 682, 686
Titonville 31 56
tomb of Clovis I 20 865
Tour Eiffel *see* Eiffel Tower
Tour Montparnasse 11 660
Tour Sans Fin 23 262
Tribunal de Commerce 6 468
UNESCO building 1 446; 11 527; 22 806; 24 130; 33 627
tapestries 1 142
Union Centrale des Beaux-Arts *see* museums → Musée des Arts Décoratifs
University
Bibliothèque Doucet 9 196; 11 673; 18 642
Faculté de Droit 19 296
see also Sorbonne
urban planning 1 685; 14 238, 385; 17 451; 24 117, 127–32*; 31 711, 714, 717, 723, 730
Villa Cook 11 659; 19 41–2
Villa La Roche 19 41
Villa Stein-de Monzie 2 360; 19 42, *42*; 21 783; 25 741
walls 7 360
workshops 29 852
Paris, Achille 4 842
Paris, Alexandre de *see* ALEXANDRE DE PARIS
Paris, Cardino of *see* CARDINO OF PARIS
Paris, Domenico di *see* DOMENICO DI PARIS
Paris, Ecole de *see* ECOLE DE PARIS
Paris, Harold 17 694
Paris, Jean de *see* PERRÉAL, JEAN
Paris, Joseph François 11 167
Paris, Louis-Philippe-Albert de Bourbon, Comte de 23 522
Paris, Marie Isabelle de Bourbon, Comtesse de 23 523
Paris, Matthew 12 272; 14 411, 419; 24 174–6*
works 7 241, 243; 10 244, 344; 11 *147*; 13 131, *131*, 140; 14 423; 18 687; 23 460; 24 *175*; 27 124, 528, 592; 31 153, 289
Paris, Missal of the Bishops of *see under* MISSALS → individual manuscripts
Paris, Nicholas 10 341

Pâris, Pierre-Adrien **20** 137; **24** 176–7*
assistants **24** 387
groups and movements **24** 173
personal collection **3** 873; **8** 650; **9** 229; **27** 571
works **8** 650; **9** 418; **13** 199; **22** 920; **23** 509, 510; **24** *176*; **30** 127, 672
Pâris, Pierre-François **24** 176
Paris, W. **4** 288
Parisani, Agostino **1** 605
Parisani, Napoleone **10** 641
Paris blue *see under* PIGMENTS → types
Paris Codex *see under* CODICES → individual manuscripts
Parise, Francesco *see* PERESI, FRANCESCO
Pariset, Robert-Menge **11** 723
Paris Gratian, Master of the **20** 695
Paris green *see* PIGMENTS → types → emerald green
Paris Gregory (Paris, Bib. N., MS. gr. 510) **9** 605, 614; **22** 520; **24** 177*
Parish, Capt. **30** 476
Parish, David **25** 874
Parisius *see* PARIS
Paris jet *see under* GLASS → types
Paris Master **6** 3; **20** 742–3*
Parisot, Pierre **2** 877; **10** 675
Paris Painter **10** 614
Paris photographe **22** 425
Paris Plate **27** 79
Paris Psalter *see under* PSALTERS → individual manuscripts
Paris red *see under* PIGMENTS → types
Paris Rothschild Hours *see under* BOOKS OF HOURS → individual manuscripts
Paris-van den Bruggen (family) **3** 417
Parita Church **23** 904
Parita ware *see under* POTTERY → wares
Parizeau, Marcel **5** 562, 573
Parizeau, Philippe-Louis **3** 318
Park, David **24** 182–3*
groups and movements **8** 871; **31** 608
pupils **8** 702, 870; **11** 706
Park, John **27** 562
Park, June **33** 552
Park, Patric **28** 242
parkas **22** 629–30*, *630*
park design **24** 740
Parke, Hiram Haney **24** 183
Parke-Bernet **24** 183*; **29** 88
Parker, (Richard) Barry **12** 144; **16** 891; **20** 238; **23** 194, 454; **24** 185–7
Parker, Charles (1799-1881) **3** 689; **32** 554
Parker, Charles (1895-1992) *see* PARKER, K(ARL) T(HEODORE)
Parker, George **10** 290; **18** 610, 614; **29** 530
Parker, Harley **20** 29
Parker, Harold **2** 753
Parker, Henry **29** 474
Parker, Henry Perlee **23** 21
Parker, J. **17** 897
Parker, James **7** 693
Parker, Jayne **10** 689
Parker, John (*d c.* 1765; painter) **3** 714
Parker, John (*fl* 1751-92; silversmith) **33** 158
Parker, John (*fl* 1756-85) **8** 83; **27** 356
Parker, John Henry **10** 209; **23** 690
Parker, J. P. **5** 418
Parker, K(arl) T(heodore) **24** 183*
Parker, Matthew, Archbishop of Canterbury **14** 644; **24** 184*
bookbindings **4** 352
Parker, Matthew, Archbishop of Canterbury—cont.
engravings **14** 643
manuscripts **27** 532
silver **10** 325
Parker, Obadiah **7** 693
Parker, Ray **24** 184*
Parker, Richard **1** 520; **24** 184*
Parker, Rozsika **2** 538; **33** 312
Parker, Thomas **26** 85
Parker Bros **31** 266
Parker Cut Glass factory **10** 318
Parker Knoll Ltd **10** 300; **14** 523
Parker & Thomas **27** 173
Parker & Unwin **24** 185–7*
groups and movements **10** 239
works **12** *145*; **14** 809; **24** *186*; **27** 279
Parker & Wakelin **10** 333; **12** 163; **25** 4; **29** 432
Parkes, Alexander **10** 143; **25** 25; **26** 244
Parkes, David **18** 906
Parkesine **25** 25, 26, 27; **26** 244
Parkett **24** 453
Parkham (Devon)
sculpture **15** 181, 426, *427*; **20** 817
Parkhar **6** 198
Parkin, Edmund **24** 188
Parkin, John B(urnett) **5** 562, 573; **24** 188*; **31** 243
collaboration **21** 492; **26** 261; **31** 176
works **31** *176*
Parkin, John C(resswell) **24** 188
Parkin Partnership **24** 188
Parkin Safdie Architects and Planners **23** 632
Parkinson, Donald **25** 857
Parkinson, John **19** 700; **25** 857
works **19** *700*
Parkinson, Richard **10** 580
Parkinson, Sydney **2** 743; **3** 183; **24** 188*
works **23** 57, *725*
Parkinson and Bergstrom **27** 642
Parkminster (W. Sussex) **5** 895
parks **12** 176; **24** 178–82*, *179*
historical and regional traditions
Assyrian **24** 178
China **12** 85, 86, *87*; **24** 178
England **12** 128; **22** 527; **24** 179
Germany **12** 472
Greece, ancient **24** 178
Indian subcontinent **24** 178
Iran, ancient **24** 178
Italy **12** 116–17; **24** 179
Russia **12** 134
United States of America **23** 256, *420*, *422*
types
public **12** 100; **24** 179–82*, *180*, *181*, *182*, 293
see also GARDENS → types → *jardins paysagers*; *paradeisoi*
Parks, Fanny **15** 724
Parks, Gordon (Alexander Buchanan) **24** 188*, 677
Parks, Ti **2** 754
Park Seo Bo **18** 257, 326; **24** 188–9*
Parland, Alfred **27** 578
Parlange **31** 589
Parlanti, Alessandro **12** 612
Parler (family) **13** 88, 89–90; **22** 219; **24** 189*, 192; **27** 145; **32** 453
marks **20** 441
works **12** 365, 400; **18** 539; **31** 270, 271
Parler, Heinrich, I (*fl* 1330s-1371) **24** 189–91*
attributions **12** 365
pupils **24** 191
works **11** 341, *341*; **13** 89; **28** 182
Parler, Heinrich, IV *see* HEINRICH VON GMÜND (*c.* 1354-after 1387)
Parler, Michael von Gmünd *see* MICHAEL VON FREIBURG
Parler, Johann **18** 539; **25** 440, 442
Parler, Johann von Gmünd *see* JOHANN VON GMÜND
Parler, Michael (*fl* 1330-50) **24** 190–92*
Parler, Michael von Freiburg (*d* 1387) *see* MICHAEL VON FREIBURG
Parler, Michael von Gmünd *see* MICHAEL VON FREIBURG
Parler, Peter (von Gmünd) **8** 412, 611; **24** 189–91*; **25** 430, 441
assistants **24** 191
collaboration **24** 191
patrons and collectors **19** 828, 829
works **4** 832; **8** 376, 382, 394; **13** 57, 89, 187; **18** 539, 827; **19** *829*; **20** 441; **22** 219, 221; **23** 306; **24** *190*; **25** 425, 437, 440, 441; **28** 182; **32** 92, 93
Parler, Wenzel **8** 412; **24** 191*
attributions **25** 442; **32** 452
works **25** 440
Parler von Ulm, Heinrich (i) (*fl* 1377-?1387) **24** 192*; **31** 567
Parler von Ulm, Heinrich (ii) (*fl* 1387-92) **24** 192*; **31** 567
Parler von Ulm, Michael **10** 407; **24** 192*; **31** 567
parliament buildings **31** 235
Bangladesh **3** *167*
Germany **12** *377*
Ireland **9** *316*
Pacific Islands **23** *736*
South Africa **29** *106*
see also GOVERNMENT BUILDINGS
Parlier see WARDENS
Parlington Hall (W. Yorks) **12** 639
Parma **16** *618*; **24** 192–7*; **26** *886*
Biblioteca Palatina **16** 776
Casino del Caffè dello Stradone **24** *553*
Centro Torri **16** 651
Collegio Maria Luigia **2** 128
Colonia Parmensis **24** 192
ecclesiastical buildings
Baptistery **2** 132; **3** 192, *192*; **24** 195–6*
reliefs **24** *195*
sculpture **2** *132*; **16** 687; **25** 174; **26** 621
wall paintings **16** 655; **26** 654
Cathedral of the Assumption **4** 775; **7** 889; **16** 625; **24** *193*, 194–5*; **26** 579
capitals **26** 621
crypt **8** 224
dome **9** 84
frescoes **7** *888*; **15** 137
paintings **16** 667
reliefs **24** *194*; **26** 621
sculpture **2** 132; **16** 687; **26** 595
throne **30** 778
convent of S Paolo **20** 279; **30** 886
Camera di S Paolo **1** 657; **7** 887
Oratorio di S Ilario **16** 701
S Giovanni Evangelista **5** *913*; **7** 887–9; **15** 137
S Maria della Steccata **23** 502; **24** *196*, 196–7*, 200
S Paolo **7** *886*
Galleria Nazionale **2** 132; **26** 325
INA offices **16** 650
Museo Nazionale di Antichità **24** 193
Palazzo Comunale **3** 858
Palazzo Ducale **4** 521
Palazzo del Giardino **5** 858; **7** 308
frescoes **11** 679
Parma
Palazzo del Giardino—cont.
paintings **5** 858
Sala del Bacio *see* Sala di Boiardo
Sala di Ariosto **3** 859
Sala di Boiardo **3** 859
Sala di Orfeo *see* Sala di Ariosto
Sala di Paesaggio **3** 859
Sala di Perseo **3** 859
Palazzo Lalatta *see* Collegio Maria Luigia
Palazzo della Pilotta **22** 166
Teatro Farnese **1** 601, *601*; **3** 744; **30** 666, 667, 668
Teatro Inferiore **30** 666
Roccabianca Castle **4** 196
Stradone **24** 552
Teatro Nuovo **1** 125
urban planning **27** 3
Parma, Basinio da *see* BASINIO DA PARMA
Parma, Francesco da *see* FRANCESCO DA PARMA
Parma, Giovanni Antonio da *see* GIOVANNI ANTONIO DA PARMA
Parma, Michele da *see* ROCCA, MICHELE
Parma, Scotto di *see* SCOTTO DI PARMA
Parma Gospels *see under* GOSPEL BOOKS → individual manuscripts
Parme, Julien de *see* JULIEN, JEAN-ANTOINE
Parmenon **13** 394
Parmense, Federigo *see* BONZAGNA, GIAN FEDERIGO
Parmentier **5** 193
Parmentier, André **9** 204
Parmentier, Henri **2** 56; **6** 420, 431; **24** 197*
excavations **2** 57
works **18** 769
Parmentier, Jacques **21** 907; **33** 217
Parmentier, Michel **11** 552
Parmiggiani, Claudio **16** 682; **24** 197*
Parmigianino **2** 128; **16** 766; **20** 904; **24** 197–202*, *198*; **26** 769
attributions **3** 486, 487; **28** 5
collaboration **2** 185; **7** 889
drawings **3** 487; **9** 221; **10** 130; **24** *199*
groups and movements **20** 281
paintings
ceiling **3** 487; **24** 196
mythological **23** 293; **24** *201*
portraits **2** 162
religious **16** 665, 667, *667*; **20** 278, 280; **23** 502; **24** 193, *200*
patrons and collectors
Borromeo, Federico, Cardinal **4** 426
Carraquiri, Nazario **5** 871
Coke, Thomas, 1st Earl of Leicester of the 1st creation (1697-1759) **7** 540
Doria-Pamphili (family) **9** 175
Este (i) (family) **21** 771
Faesch, Johann Jakob **10** 753
Ferdinando I, Grand Duke of Tuscany (*reg* 1587-1609) **21** 30
Francesco I, 8th Duke of Modena and Reggio (*reg* 1629–58) **10** 526
Ford, Richard **11** 304
Gondi (family) **12** 897
Jabach, Everard **16** 815
Lanier, Nicholas **18** 747
Lely, Peter **19** 124
Leoni, Leone **19** 203
Medici, Giovanni Carlo de', Cardinal (1611-63) **21** 27
Parmigianino
patrons and collectors—cont.
Medinaceli, Luís de la Cerda Fernández de Córdoba Folch de Cardona y Aragón, 9th Duque de (1660-1711) **21** 35
Morrison, James **22** 148
Ottley, William Young **23** 634
Pérez, Antonio (?1540-1611) **24** 400
Périer, Casimir **24** 418
Reynolds, Joshua **26** 280
Richelieu, Louis-François Armand-Jean Vignerod du Plessis, Duc de (1629-1715) **26** 349
Rudolf II, Holy Roman Emperor (*reg* 1576- 1612) **13** 914
Ruffo, Tommaso, Cardinal, Archbishop of Ferrara **27** 316
Seilern, Antoine, Count **28** 377
Serra, Giovan Francesco, Marqués di Cassano **28** 479
Thibaudeau, Narcisse-Adolphe, Comte de **30** 727
Udney, John **31** 525
Urban VIII, Pope (*reg* 1623-44) **3** 205
Vasari, Giorgio (1511-74) **32** 22
Vittoria, Alessandro **32** 647
Waldegrave, William, 1st Baron Radstock **32** 774
Zanetti, Anton Maria (Girolamo) (i), Conte (1680-1767) **9** 230
Zanetti, Anton Maria (Alesandro) (ii) (1706- 78) **33** 612, 613
prints **10** 550; **25** 622; **26** 229; **32** 407; **33** 365, 366
pupils **3** 486; **25** 333
reproductive prints by others **5** 844
Caraglio, Giovanni Jacopo **5** 699
Carpi, Ugo da **25** VI; **26** 229; **33** 366
Carracci, Agostino **5** 856
Fantuzzi, Antonio **10** 799
Place, Francis **25** 10
Sadeler, Aegidius, II (1570-1629) **27** 504
Sadeler, Jan, I (1550-1600) **27** 502
Tiepolo, Giambattista **30** 857
Vico, Enea **10** 477; **32** 412
Parmirbo *see* PARAMARIBO
Parnaka **1** 118
Parnass **24** 439
Parndorf Villa **26** *906*, 907
Parnell & Smith **7** 470
Pärnu **10** *536*, 537
Beach Café **10** 537
EKE (Estonian Collective Farm Administrative Building) **10** 538
Tervis sanatorium **10** 538
Paro **3** *912*
Parocel, Joseph **4** 537
Paroda, Giovanni Battista **24** 202
Parodi (family) **12** 284
Parodi, Domenico (1672-1742) **16** 702; **24** 202, 203*
Parodi, Domenico di Antomaria (1653-1703) *see* ANTOMARIA PARODI, DOMENICO DI
Parodi, Filippo **12** 284; **24** 202–3*
attributions **32** 160
collaboration **24** 835; **25** 214
groups and movements **16** 701
patrons and collectors **4** 811; **27** 878
pupils **5** 54; **10** 798; **24** 203; **25** 214; **27** 193
works **4** 311; **5** 54; **11** 9; **16** 701; **23** 756
Parodi, Giovanni Battista (*fl c.* 1630) **24** 202

Parodi, Giovanni Battista (1674-1730) 24 202
Parodi, José Laterza see LATERZA PARODI, JOSÉ
Parodia, Filippo 23 754
parodos 24 90*
Paroli 15 322, 496
Parolin, Francesco 16 738; 23 263
Paros 8 304; 9 511; 13 363; 24 204–5*
  Archilochos Capital 13 412, 413
  architecture 24 204*
  Asklepieion 24 204
  Delion 24 204, 205
  fibulae 13 601
  marble 8 314; 13 373, 387, 436; 24 204; 27 13; 29 701; 30 405
  see also under MARBLE → types
  pottery 13 497, 502
  sculpture 13 447, 450, 451, 455; 24 204–5*, 205
  korai 18 245
  stone vessels 8 317
  tholoi 30 737
Parpallo 25 491, 492, 493
parpend stones see under MASONRY → types
parquet marqueté see PARQUETRY
parquetry 20 466, 467
  historical and regional traditions
    Belgium 3 578
    England 10 275
    France 11 596; 20 467; 26 84
  materials
    king-wood 26 84
    oak 3 578
    tulip-wood 26 84
    violet-wood 11 596
  uses
    floors 3 578; 20 467
    furniture 11 596; 20 467
Parr see PARRI
Parr, Lenton 2 753; 18 64; 24 205*
Parr, Mike 2 751, 752; 24 205–6*
Parr, Nathaniel 27 465
Parr, Tom 14 511
Parr, Wolstenholme 14 131
Parra, Félix 24 206*
  works 21 385, 386
Parra, Juan de la 29 333
Parra, Vicente de la 14 714; 26 251
Parraces Monastery 29 343
Parrales, Roberto 23 85
Parralli 10 190
Parramatta
  architecture 2 737
  court-house 18 887
  Government House 2 737
  Lancer Barracks 2 737; 32 923
  Old Government House 2 737
Parras, King (reg 4th cent. BC) 24 539
Parrasio, Angelo see ANGELO (DI PIETRO) DEL MACAGNINO (DA SIENA)
Parrasio, Michele 1 690
Parreiras, Antonio (Diogo da Silva) 4 717; 13 662; 24 206*
Parreiras, Antonio, Museu see under NITERÓI
Parrhasios 7 673; 13 548, 551, 553; 16 658; 18 587; 24 206–7*; 25 44; 26 223; 32 46; 33 461
  competitions 29 665
  patrons and collectors 9 13
  works 2 682; 13 545, 553, 554, 570; 15 135; 24 593; 25 44
Parri (family) 30 68
Parri, Cristoforo 24 207
Parri, Domenico 24 207
Parri, Francesco 12 366; 24 207–8*; 32 923
Parri, Giacomo 24 207*; 25 787; 32 879
Parri, Giovanni Battista 24 207
Parris, Alexander 24 208–10*
  assistants 33 195
  groups and movements 3 730
  personal collection 8 843
Parris, Alexander—cont.
  pupils 5 64
  staff 33 195
  works 2 324; 4 472, 473; 24 209; 26 353; 31 591
Parrish, Maxfield (Frederick) 24 210*
  groups and movements 7 875
  works 4 367; 25 347; 30 869; 33 132
Parrish, Stephen 7 875; 20 604; 24 210
Parrish Painter 13 531
Parrocel, Barthélemy 24 210
Parrocel, Charles 3 388; 24 210, 211–12*
  assistants 22 725
  patrons and collectors 4 513; 19 646; 24 256
  pupils 18 804
  reproductions in tapestry 12 830
  teachers 6 122; 24 211
  works 11 539; 18 804; 24 212
Parrocel, Etienne 24 210, 212*
Parrocel, Ignace-Jacques 24 211, 212
Parrocel, Joseph 24 210–11*
  collaboration 26 386
  pupils 24 211
  works 3 388; 11 404, 407; 14 784; 20 894; 24 211
Parrocel, Joseph-François 24 211
Parrocel, Louis 24 210, 211
Parrocel, Pierre 24 210, 211*
Parrocel, Pierre-Ignace 24 211
Parrocel le Romain see PARROCEL, ETIENNE
Parrot, André 1 893; 18 797; 20 408; 30 422
Parry, Edward Warren 26 514
Parry, George Herbert 7 435
Parry, P. 4 27
Parry, William 19 157; 32 784, 790
parrying-daggers see DAGGERS → types → poignards
Pars, Henry 4 116; 25 759
Pars, William 2 164; 13 304; 24 213*
  collaboration 6 446
  sponsors 30 451
Parsch Church 2 789, 789
Parsey, Arthur 24 491
Parshandata
  seals 1 863
Parshvanatha 16 869
Parsis 15 204; 33 706
Parsons, Alfred 1 22
Parsons, Betty (Bierne) 6 80; 24 213*; 31 665
Parsons, Charles 8 276; 23 904
Parsons, David
  works 11 831
Parsons, Karl 33 132
Parsons, Lee A. 22 9; 27 780
Parsons, Samuel 32 95
Parsons, Talcott 28 927
Parsons, William E. 20 274; 24 614–15, 617
Partabgarh 15 702
Partav see BARDA
Partch, Harry 29 97
Partecipazio, Giustiniano, Doge of Venice (reg 827-9) 32 206
Parte Guelfa tondo 28 703
Partenheim, Peter Jakob von 12 808
Partenkirchen
  Jagdhaus Schachen 29 843
  St Anton 14 695
parterres (i) (gardens) 12 61, 119, 121, 128, 132, 135; 24 214*; 31 151
parterres (ii) (theatres) 24 214*
parterres de broderie 12 118, 132; 21 822
Parthaunisa see NISA
Parthenay 11 505
  Musée Municipal 11 667
Parthenay—cont.
  Notre-Dame-de-la-Coudre 24 214*; 26 600
Parthenay-le-Vieux, St Pierre 24 214*; 26 600
Parthenis, Konstantinos 24 214–15*
  pupils 8 851; 10 379; 12 546; 22 74
  works 13 353
Parthenon see under ATHENS → Acropolis
Parthian 1 852; 15 900, 901, 906, 908; 21 275; 24 215–18*
  architecture 6 198–9*; 15 912; 21 291–2*; 24 215–17*
  bone 24 218
  brick 4 772
  bronze 24 217
  clay 6 217
  coffins 24 218
  coins 1 887, 888, 888–9*; 24 215, 217
  dress 1 884, 886, 887*; 6 251
  figurines 24 218
  fortifications 2 251
  gypsum 29 814
  halls 6 198; 24 216
  iconography 24 218
  inlays 24 218
  ivory 15 915; 24 217
  iwans 15 912; 21 291–2; 24 217
  jewellery 1 876*; 24 218
  limestone 9 414
  metalwork 15 919
  mosaics 24 218
  mother-of-pearl 24 218
  nails 6 217
  palaces 23 806, 807
  plaster 29 814–15*
  pottery 21 308; 24 218
  religion 33 706
  representation 24 217–18
  rhyta 15 915; 24 217
  rock reliefs 10 171; 15 916–17; 24 217, 218
  sculpture 6 217*; 15 915; 21 302; 24 217–18*
    bronze 24 217
    relief 9 414; 24 218
  seals 1 858; 23 159; 24 218
  silk 28 715
  silver 1 888
  stucco 24 217, 218; 29 814–15*
  temples 4 772; 33 708
  textiles 1 882
  wall paintings 6 223–4
  see also INDO-PARTHIAN
Particelli, Michel, Sieur d'Emery see EMERY, MICHEL PARTICELLI, Sieur d'
particle board 24 3; 33 328
particle-induced gamma ray emission spectrometry see under TECHNICAL EXAMINATION → types
particle-induced X-ray emission spectrometry see under TECHNICAL EXAMINATION → types
Parting, J. 28 816
Partini, Giuseppe 24 218–19*, 533; 28 676
partitions 24 51
fusuma 9 163; 11 862*; 17 45, 404; 27 596; 31 676
Partizánská Ľupča 14 893; 28 851
Partoes, Alexis 24 219
Partoes, Henri Louis François 24 219*
Pártos, Gyula 5 83; 19 30; 30 212
Partoś, J. 28 838
Partridge (fl late 17th cent.) 10 342
Partridge, David 5 571
Partridge, Henry 23 59
Partridge, John Albert 14 812
Partridge, Roi 8 270
Partrishow 11 252
Partz, Felix 12 275
Paruk Clan 5 38
parures 17 524, 525, 526, 527
Parusnikov, Mikhail 3 527; 12 878
Parvez, Ahmed 23 799; 24 219*
Parviainen, Hanna 19 643
Parviainen, Johannes, Factories Ltd. 19 643
parvis 24 90
Parvis, Giuseppe 16 389
Pârvu Pârvescu see PÎRVU, MUTU
parylene 11 142
Parz Castle 2 793
Paržik, Karlo 4 460
Pas, (Hans) Henryk de see PASSE, (HANS) HENRYK VAN
Pas, Simon de 8 733
Pasadena (CA)
  architecture 2 572
  City Hall 3 83
  David B. Gamble House 31 595
  Norton Simon Museum 15 743; 19 703; 28 79, 751
Pasargadae 1 116; 15 893, 899, 901, 902, 906, 908, 911; 24 220–21*
  fire-holders 33 706
  gardens 12 66
  Gatehouse 1 116
  halls 2 213
  jewellery 1 876
  palace 15 911; 23 807
  reliefs 24 220
  sculpture 1 117
  tomb of Cyrus 31 109
  Zendan-i Sulayman 33 707
Pasca Church 7 610
Pascal, Blaise 8 786; 28 418
Pascal, François Michel 32 396
Pascal, James 11 427
Pascal, Jean-Louis 24 221*
  assistants 22 186
  collaboration 3 465
  pupils 20 877; 32 257
    Beltrami, Luca 3 687
    Burnet, J(ohn) J(ames) 5 270
    Corbett, Harvey Wiley 7 838
    Cormier, Ernest 7 858
    Cret, Paul (Philippe) 8 152
    Davis, Arthur Joseph 21 371
    Mewès, Charles Frédéric 21 371
    Monteiro, José Luís 22 13
    Nénot, Henri-Paul 22 732
    Nogueira, Miguel (José) 23 177
    Siclis, Charles 28 663
Pascali, Pino 16 709; 24 221*; 26 778
Pascall, James 10 294
Paşcani, Cantacuzino House 26 708
Pasch, Johan 24 222; 29 689; 30 88
Pasch, Lorens (1733-1805) 24 222*; 33 98
  frames 11 469
Pasch, Lorentz (1702-66) 24 222
Pasch, Ulrika Fredrika 24 222
Pascha, (Hans) Henryk van see PASSE, (HANS) HENRYK VAN
Paschal I, Pope (reg 817-24) 16 761; 24 222–3*
  architecture 5 794; 16 761; 26 754
  enamel 16 750
  mosaics 26 679, 765
Paschal II, Pope (reg 1099-1118) 26 825
paschal candlesticks see under CANDLESTICKS → types
Paschalis 7 922
Paschen, (Hans) Henryk van see PASSE, (HANS) HENRYK VAN
Paschetto, Paolo 3 193
Paschke, Ed(ward) 6 577; 24 223*; 31 609
Pascin, Jules 17 577; 24 223–4*
  dealers 33 36
  works 24 224; 32 902
Pascó, Josep 21 705; 29 308
Pascoe, Duane 8 562
Pascoe, Paul 7 210; 23 56; 24 224–5*
Pascoli, Giovanni 8 601
Pascoli, Lione 1 796; 16 781; 24 225*
Pascó y Mensa, José 25 786
Pascual, Manolo 9 117, 119
Pascual, Plácido Francés y see FRANCÉS Y PASCUAL, PLÁCIDO
Pascual de Mena, Juan see MENA, JUAN PASCUAL DE
Pascual y Colomer, Narciso 24 225*; 25 226
  pupils 8 239; 32 97
  works 4 567; 27 607
Paseas 32 62*
Pasemah 15 752, 756, 787
Paser (Governor of Thebes) 10 65
Paser II (Viceroy of Nubia) 1 96
Pasewalk Church 14 81
PAS Group 24 226*
Pasha, Ahmad Zaki 10 804
Pasha, Hüseyin Zekaî 16 537
Pasha, Osman Nuri 28 528
Pasha, Saìd Mahmet 9 398
Pashash 29 184, 185
pashm see under WOOL → types
Pashupatinatha 22 753; 24 226*
  Rajarajeshvari-ghat 22 759, 760, 761
  sculpture 22 767; 23 907
  temples 22 756, 761
Pashuprakha, King of Nepal (reg before 5th cent.) 24 226
Pasias 13 552
Pasiene 18 847
  Dominican church 18 849
Pasinati Cist 10 639
Pasinelli, Angelo 22 387
Pasinelli, Lorenzo 4 277; 12 559; 24 226–7*
  pupils 5 280; 8 158; 20 902; 21 539; 29 32, 33; 33 615
  reproductive prints by others 29 32
  teachers 5 635
Pasini, Alberto 2 106; 23 504
Pasiteles 24 227–8*; 25 45; 27 27, 29
  attributions 27 22
  pupils 29 633
  works 13 466; 25 44
  writings 13 554, 807; 25 45
Pasivenko, Vladimir 31 560
Paskali, Odhise 1 541, 546; 24 228*
Pasmore, Victor 10 375; 23 21; 24 228–9*
  groups and movements 2 553; 10 375, 652; 23 333
  patrons and collectors 7 376
  pupils 14 816
  works 10 258; 23 333; 24 229
Paso, El
  members 29 286
    Canogar, Rafael 5 622
    Chirino, Martín 7 173
    Feito, Luis 10 864
    Millares, Manolo 21 605
    Rivera, Manuel 26 429
    Saura, Antonio 20 68
    Serrano, Pablo 28 480
Pasolini, Pier Paolo 6 345; 19 637
Pasqual, Juan 13 760; 25 253
Pasqualetti, Roberto 17 622
Pasquali, Giambattista 5 55, 597; 6 91; 12 582; 24 894; 32 501, 615
Pasqualigo, Ursula 21 462
Pasqualini, Alexander (i) (1493-1559) 24 229–30*
  attributions 3 544
  works 11 876; 22 823; 24 230, 230
Pasqualini, Alexander (1567-before 1625) 24 231*; 33 279
  works 22 918

Pasqualini, Johann (i) (*c.* 1535/6-*c.* 1580/1) 24 230*
Pasqualini, Johann (ii) (1562-*c.* 1615) 24 230-31*
Pasqualini, Marc Antonio 27 *491*
Pasqualini, Maximilian, I 24 230*
Pasqualino, Alvise 2 181
Pasqualino, Antonio 2 178, 181; 16 835; 21 474
Pasqualino, il *see* ROSSI, PASQUALE
Pasqualino Veneto 7 323; 24 231*
Pasquetti (family) 3 593
Pasquier, Théodore 6 391
Pasquin, Anthony *see* WILLIAMS, JOHN
Pasquino (di Matteo) da Montepulciano 24 232*; 25 450; 31 743
 works 31 739
Pasquino Group 13 464
Passaeus, (Hans) Henryk van *see* PASSE, (HANS) HENRYK VAN
passage 6 570; 8 244
passage graves *see under* GRAVES → types
passages, wall *see* WALL PASSAGES
passage tombs *see under* TOMBS → types
Passaglia, Augusto 5 378; 9 159; 11 197
Passalacqua, Giuseppe 10 90, 92
Passalacqua, Pietro 13 626; 23 637
Passalacqua, Quintilio Lucini 22 82
Passamonti, Serafina 30 233
Passano, Pedro de Camprobín *see* CAMPROBÍN (PASSANO), PEDRO DE
Passante, Bartolomeo *see* BASSANTE, BARTOLOMEO
Passarelli, Fausto 24 278
Passarelli, Lucio 16 775; 24 278
Passarelli, Vincenzo 24 278
Passari, Bernardino *see* PASSERI, BERNARDINO
Passari, Giovanni Battista *see* PASSERI, GIOVANNI BATTISTA
Passariano, Villa Manin 32 548
Passarini, Filippo 7 746; 8 268; 24 316; 26 780
Passaro, Bernardino *see* PASSERI, BERNARDINO
Passarotti, Arcangelo 24 234
Passarotti, Aurelio 24 234
Passarotti, Bartolomeo 4 276; 16 669; 24 232-4*; 26 770
 pupils 5 856, 859; 6 113; 10 525; 31 884
 reproductive prints by others 26 229; 30 803
 works 1 *103*, 104; 2 162; 4 276; 11 701; 12 288; 24 *233*
Passarotti, Gaspare 24 234
Passarotti, Passarotto 24 234
Passarotti, Tiburzio 24 233, 234
Passarotti, Ventura 24 234
Passas Painter 13 501
Passau
 Cathedral 19 807; 29 838
 Glasmuseum und Kochbuchmuseum 19 719
 Jesuitenkirche 29 838
 Niedernburg Convent 2 824
 St Nikola 2 723
 St Salvator 32 821
 St Stephan Cathedral 12 370, *371*, *404*
  epitaph to Canon Johann Gienger von Wolfsegg 10 436
  stucco 12 404
Passau, Henry of *see* HENRY OF PASSAU
Passavant, Claude 2 877; 5 838, 839; 10 675
Passavant, Johann David 11 735; 24 234*
 pupils 28 142
 works 6 78; 9 682
  illustrated 6 78-9
  translated 9 683
Passay, Louis *see* VALLE, LOUIS DE
Passe, Crispijn (van) de, I (1564-1637) 10 389; 12 15; 24 235-7*
 collaboration 12 16; 24 237
 patrons and collectors 14 563
 printmakers 24 236
 pupils 4 150; 16 576
 reproductive prints by others 5 61
 works 2 105; 3 635; 12 242; 24 235, *235*, 236; 27 502; 29 431; 32 711
Passe, Crispijn (van) de, II (*c/0* 1593/4 - *d* after 1670) 24 236-7*
 collaboration 24 237
 pupils 19 539
 reproductive prints by others 18 812
 works 24 235; 25 461; 33 252
 writings 3 582
Passe, de (family) 25 606
Passe, (Hans) Henryk van 13 682; 24 237*
 patrons and collectors 6 127
 works 10 668; 19 568
Passe, Magdalena (van) de 10 391; 23 224; 24 235, 236*
Passe, Simon (van) de 24 236-7*
 collaboration 24 237
 patrons and collectors 29 799
 works 24 235
Passe, Willem (van) de 10 248; 24 235, 237*
Passemard, Emmanuel 16 615
Passement 11 626
passementerie 15 12*; 24 237*
Passenger, Charles 8 707
Passenger, Fred 8 707
Passepartout 7 805
Passer, Arent 10 537, 538; 11 99; 30 276, 277
Passeri, Bernardino 24 239*
Passeri, Cinzio, Cardinal 1 594
Passeri, Giovanni Battista 10 642; 24 238*
 pupils 24 238
 works 13 541; 16 781; 24 535
Passeri, Giuseppe 6 350; 24 238*; 26 246
Passerini, Margherita 27 849
Passerini, Silvio, Cardinal 5 672; 7 905; 13 827; 25 848; 32 10
Passerotti *see* PASSAROTTI
Passerotti, Archangelo 16 755
Passerotti, Bartolomeo 4 830; 20 586
Passglas *see under* GLASSES → types
Passignano, Domenico 20 242; 24 239*, 801
 assistants 11 52; 31 886
 collaboration 12 706
 patrons and collectors 1 595; 3 205; 4 549; 5 179, 735; 9 173, 174; 12 897
 pupils 5 769, 770; 8 497; 11 845; 22 190; 24 801; 26 317; 28 433; 31 886
 teachers 22 448
 works 1 596; 31 885
Passionals 27 591
 individuals manuscripts
  Hirsau Passional (Stuttgart, Württemberg. Landesbib.) 14 569
  Passional of Abbess Kunhuta (*c.* 1313-21; Prague, Libs Facs & Insts Charles U., MS. XIV A 17) 13 151; 25 431
  Stuttgart Passional (Stuttgart, Württemberg. Landesbib.) 27 592
Passionei, Domenico 12 536; 24 240*
Passion Master (*fl* after 1350; glazier) 24 158
 works 24 *158*
Passion Master (*fl* 1370s; illuminator) 17 462-3*; 31 837
Passion of Christ, Master of the 20 743*
Passmore, George *see* GILBERT AND GEORGE
Passmore, John (Richard) 18 689; 23 425; 24 241*
Passmore & Williams 31 652
Passo di Corvo 25 500
Passos, Francisco de Oliveira *see* OLIVEIRA PASSOS, FRANCISCO DE
Passos, Francisco Pereira *see* PEREIRA PASSOS, FRANCISCO
pastas houses *see under* HOUSES → types
Pastavy Church 3 527
paste 1 155, 156; 13 393; 24 56*, I1, II3; 28 312
pasteboard 6 306; 12 810; 16 356
Paštéka, Milan 28 853
pastel drawings *see under* DRAWINGS → forms
Pastellas, Pierre 27 853
pastel manner *see under* ENGRAVINGS → types
pastels 6 400; 8 127, 128, *128*; 24 241-2*, 788; 29 *234*; 33 1
 see also CRAYONS; DRAWINGS → forms → pastel
paste paper *see* PAPER → materials → paste
pasteprints 9 190; 24 245-6*, *246*
paste resist dyeing *see under* DYEING → types
Pasternak, Leonid (Osipovich) 18 215; 22 135; 24 246-7*; 33 379
Pasti, Matteo de' 24 247-8*
 collaboration 1 556
 patrons and collectors 20 160, 917
 works 1 456, *556*, 561; 13 755; 16 690; 26 398, 399, *399*, *400*
pastiches 24 248*
pastiglia 6 5-6; 13 139; 24 248-9*
 Czech Republic 13 152
 England 13 152
 Gothic 13 139, 152
 Italy 6 *6*; 11 *383*, *384*, *393*; 24 *249*
Pasto 7 *601*, 603
 Museum 7 612
Pastoe *see* UMS (Utrechtsche Machinale Stoel-en Meubelfabriek)
Pastolik
 masks 22 *573*
pastophoria 8 155
Pastor, Ludwig von 24 249*
Pastor, Valeriano 16 651
pastoral 18 700, 708, 709
 see also GEORGIC
Pastoral style pottery *see under* POTTERY → wares
Pastoret, Comte de 15 839
Pastorini, Benedetto 3 277
Pastorini, Guido 24 250
Pastorini, Pastorino (di Giovan Michele de') 16 749; 24 250*
 works 10 523; 20 919, *919*
Pastorino da Siena *see* PASTORINI, PASTORINO (DI GIOVAN MICHELE DE')
Pastoris, Federico 28 318
Pastra, Nausika 2 804
Pastrana 27 802; 29 350
 convent 29 334
Pastrana, Rodrigo de Silva, 4th Duque de *see* INFANTADO, RODRIGO DE SILVA, 4th Duque de Pastrana, Duque del
Pastura, Il 4 410
Pasture, Henri de le *see* HENRI DE LE PASTURE
Pasture, Rogelet de le *see* ROGELET DE LE PASTURE
Paśupatinātha *see* PASHUPATINATHA
Paszkowic, Jan 25 119
Pásztó 15 3
Pásztor, János 24 250-51*
Pata, Chérubino 8 57
Pataky ware *see under* POTTERY → wares
Pataliputra *see* PATNA
Patallatga 29 162
Patalung 20 179
Patamona 13 874
Patan (i) (India) 15 *276*, 347; 24 251*
 carpets 15 682
 ikat 15 671
 manuscripts 15 616
 Queen's Well *see* Rani Vav
 Rani Vav 15 314, 490; 29 635, 636
  reliefs 15 *490*
 Sindhavi Mata Vav 29 636
 temples 15 265, 266
Patan (ii) (Nepal) 22 *753*, 754-5; 24 251*
 architecture 22 759
 Bagalamukhi temple 22 759
 Bu-bahal 22 763
 Char Narayan temple 22 *761*
 Chikan-bahil 22 763, *763*
 Chyasalhiti 22 759
 Hanuman Dhoka Palace 22 770
 Haugal-bahal 22 759
 Indreshvara Mahadeva temple Uku-bahal 22 792
 Jagatnarayana temple 22 763
 Krishna temple 22 764
 Kva-bahal 22 *764*, 767, 771
  sculpture 22 *767*
 Mahabuddha-bahal 22 776
 metalwork 22 789, *790*
 Narasimha temple 22 763-4
 Nuga-Tol 22 764
 Pintu-bahil 22 763
 Red Matsyendranatha temple 22 756
 Royal Palace 22 796
 Rudravarna-mahavihara 22 760
 scrolls 22 *784*
 sculpture 22 *777*
 stupas 22 758
 Subalhiti 22 759
 Sulimha-Tol 22 774
 temples 22 755, 761
 Uku-bahal 22 763, 774, 776
 Yangvala monastery *see* YENGU-BAHAL
 Yengu-bahal 22 768
Patanazzi (family) 16 735; 24 252*
 attributions 11 268
 workshop 11 191; 31 741
Patanazzi, Alfonso 24 252
Patanazzi, Antonio 24 252; 31 742
Patanazzi, Francesco 24 252
Patanazzi, Vincenzo 24 252
Patancheru 15 537
Patanjali 15 213
Patara 19 837
 aqueducts 27 7
 bath 19 840
 Granary 19 840
 water pipes 27 7
Pa-ta Shan-jen *see* ZHU DA
Patavium *see* PADUA
Patayan 22 600
Pat Byer Studio 2 152
Patch, Thomas 19 735; 24 252*
 collaboration 13 625
 patrons and collectors 27 356
 works 13 300, 303
patchwork 2 767; 5 587; 10 354; 17 313; 24 252-3*; 25 821; 30 562, X2; 31 658
 see also APPLIQUÉ
Pate, Klytie 2 760
Patek, Philippe 7 448
 works 7 *449*
Patel, Gieve 4 291
Patel, Pierre (i) (*c.* 1605-76) 11 536; 24 253-4*
 attributions 20 860
 pupils 24 254
 reproductive prints by others 24 397
 works 4 80; 11 641; 18 710; 20 860; 24 *254*; 32 *369*
Patel, Pierre (-Antoine) (ii) (1648-1707) 24 254*
Patellani, Federico 24 255*
patens 1 697, 707; 6 398; 24 255*
 historical and regional traditions
  Byzantine 9 656, 657
  Early Christian (*c.* AD 250-843) 9 656
  England 10 322, 325
  France 21 *163*
  Germany 12 444
  Gothic 10 322
  Holy Roman Empire (before 1648) 6 *398*
  Merovingian 21 *163*
  Romanesque 6 *398*
  Romania 26 720, *720*
 materials
  enamel 21 *163*
  gold 9 657; 21 *163*
  pewter 24 580
  silver 9 656, 657
  silver-gilt 6 *398*; 26 *720*
Patent Axminster carpets *see under* CARPETS → types
Patent Graphic Telescope 31 910
patent yellow *see under* PIGMENTS → types
Pater, Antoine-Joseph 24 255; 27 659; 32 913
Pater, Jean-Baptiste 10 351; 11 539; 24 255-7*
 patrons and collectors 3 798; 12 473; 13 836; 30 523; 32 368
 reproductions in porcelain 6 I3
 reproductive prints by others 11 81; 19 216
 teachers 32 913
 works 11 34, 36, *458*; 12 292; 24 *256*
Pater, Walter (Horatio) 24 257*
 groups and movements 1 170
 works 2 530; 8 596; 12 214; 27 355
Patera Painter 13 530; 32 45
pateras 27 86
Paterna
 pottery 29 323, 324, *324*, 325
Paterni, Pietro (Pirotto) 24 850
Paternoster, Italo 27 788
paternoster beads 1 761; 7 835; 16 751; 17 520; 27 158
Paternosto, César 2 401
Paterson (Australia), C. B. Alexander Presbyterian Agricultural College 30 161
Paterson (NJ; USA), Belle-Vista Castle 18 672
Paterson, A. N. 7 530; 28 230
 works 12 *773*
Paterson, Edward, & Sons *see* PATTISON, EDWARD & SONS
Paterson, James 12 779; 28 238, 569
Paterson, John 27 656
Paterson, Oscar 27 636
Paterson Bros 2 756
pâte-sur-pâte *see under* PORCELAIN → techniques
Patey, Henri Auguste Jules 26 192; 33 163
Pathan 1 188; 23 798
Patharghata 2 139; 15 476
Pathari 3 38-9
 Shiva Temple 15 480
 see also BADOH
Pathasivarama 15 530
Pathetiker, Die 10 695; 21 55; 29 609
pathos 13 468

Pathyris *see* GEBELEIN
Paticchi, Raimondo **3** 920
Patience, J. T. **23** 247
Patin, Charles **24** 257–8*
  personal collection **29** 644
  works **5** 345; **27** 896
Patin, Charlotte Catherine **32** 356
Patin, Jacques **30** 659
patinas **24** 258–9*; **30** 393, 409
  see also TARNISHES
Patini, Teofilo **16** 678; **24** 259*
Patinir, Herry de *see* BLES, HERRI MET DE
Patinir, Joachim **1** 654; **4** 139; **24** 259–62*; **29** 374
  attributions **20** 665
  collaboration **3** 554; **21** 355
  methods **24** 493
  patrons and collectors **7** 711; **9** 185; **13** 657, 922; **28** 358, 904
  pupils **20** 665
  works **2** 194, *195*; **9** 271; **11** *454*; **18** 706, *706*; **20** 278; **24** *260*, *262*, VIII2
Patiño Ixtolinque, Pedro **21** 384; **24** 262*
patios **15** 162; **32** 169
Patirajawela **29** 445
Patkau, John **31** 864
Patkau, Patricia **31** 864
Patlan, Ray
  works **22** *336*
Patmos **8** 157; **9** *511*, *512*; **24** 262–3*
  Monastery of St John **7** *819*; **8** 155; **9** 657; **24** 263
    collections **9** 622
    icons **9** 623, 626, 628; **15** II1; **25** 333
    manuscripts **4** 4
Patna **8** 269; **15** 194, *279*, *360*, 369, 409, 592, 593; **24** 264–5*
  Audience Hall **15** 249; **23** 817
  'Azimabad **15** 370
  figurines **15** 415, 718
  gates **7** 360
  Golghar **15** 402; **24** *265*
  ivory **15** 695
  Maheshvara Temple **15** 316
  miniatures **24** 265
  mosque of Mir Ashraf **15** 370
  Murtaziganj **15** 423
  Museum **15** 181; **24** 265
  paintings **15** 653*, 724
  palace **15** 248, 737
  Patthar ki Masjid **15** 369
  sculpture **15** 423, 436; **24** 264; **30** 510
  terracotta **15** 453
  tomb of Munir al-Daula **15** 370
  trade **15** 201, 202
  University **24** 265
  woodwork **15** 720
Patnos **1** *821*, 838; **24** 265–6*
Paton, Amelia Robertson **28** 243
Paton, Claude **5** 541
Paton, J. Wallace **29** 768
Paton, (Joseph) Noel **11** 434; **19** 417; **21** 413; **24** 266*; **28** 238, 243
Paton, Richard **22** 153
Paton, Walter Hugh **24** 266
Patou, Jean **29** 899, 900
Patoun, Robert **14** 876
Patour, Jean-Augustin **14** 85
Patout, Michel **20** 450
Patout, Pierre **2** 521; **11** 602; **24** 266–7*; **27** 322
Patpator-Tolai **24** 85
Patrai **13** 419
Patras **26** *908*
  amphitheatre **26** 910
  Archaeological Museum **14** 361
  architecture **26** 908
  armour **14** 356
  mosaics **27** 63
  odeion **23** 350
  temples **26** 911
Patras, Anthony **14** 39; **30** 62
Patras, François-Joseph **19** 849
Pătraşcu, Voivode of Wallachia (*reg* 1554–9) **5** 72; **26** 707
Patrauti Church **25** 344
Patriarchal cross *see under* CROSSES → types
Patriarchate Gospels *see under* GOSPEL BOOKS → individual manuscripts
Patrick, William Rex **6** 440
Patrick, Winston **16** 884, 887
Patricolo, Giuseppe **23** 845
Patrington (N. Humberside) **29** 413
Patrington, Robert de **33** 548
Patris, Gerard **20** 604
Patrisio Church **32** 786
patrix-working **30** 770
Patrizi, Costanzo **24** 267*
Patrizi, Francesco **24** 267; **32** 639
Patrokles **17** 757
patronage **2** 557, 560; **7** 561, 562; **12** 61; **14** 868, 869; **22** 360
  historical and regional traditions **1** 105
    Achaemenid **1** 116–18
    Africa **1** 240–43*, 251*, 433–4
    Akkadian (people) **1** 508
    Antilles, Lesser **2** 152–3*
    Argentina **2** 403–5*
    Armenia (Europe) **2** 424, 444*
    Asante **1** 240, 241, 242
    Augustinian Canons **2** 724–5*
    Australia **2** 769–70*
    Austria **2** 827*
    Bahamas, the **3** 63–4*
    Bamana **1** 240
    Bamileke **3** 147
    Bamum **1** 241, 242; **3** 151
    Barbados **2** 153
    Baule **1** 243
    Beguines **3** 503–4*
    Belgium **3** 611–14*
    Belize **3** 624–5*
    Benedictine Order **3** 709–11*; **7** 218; **10** 359; **16** 762
    Benin, Kingdom of **1** 242; **3** 721–2*
    Benin Republic **3** 728–9*
    Bhutan **3** 913
    Bolivia **4** 267–8*
    Brazil **4** 718, 724–6*
    Britain **12** 30
    Buddhism
      Central Asia, Eastern **6** 294–5*
      Indian subcontinent **5** 95; **15** 737, 739
      Japan **17** 421–3; **18** 213
      Mahayana **5** 95
      South-east Asia **29** 237
      Tibet **5** 104; **30** 813–14*, 822, 828
    Bulgaria **5** 162*
    Byzantine **7** 217; **9** 519, 521–3*, 539, 623
    Camaldolese Order **5** 450–51*
    Canada **5** 588–9*
    Cappadocia **5** 674
    Carmelite Order **5** 778*
    Carolingian **12** 471
    Carthusian Order **5** 895*
    Central Asia, Eastern **6** 294–5*
    Central Asia, Western **16** 235*
    Chile **6** 600–601*
    China **6** 631, 743; **7** 143, 148, 150–52*; **33** 318
    Chokwe **1** 241, 243
    Christianity **7** 217*, 218*
    Cistercian Order **7** 350–53*; **16** 762
    Cluniac Order **7** 473*
    Colombia **7** 611*
    Costa Rica **8** 18*
    Côte d'Ivoire **8** 23
    Cuba (Caribbean) **8** 238*
    Czech Republic **8** 421–3*
    Dan (Africa) **1** 241, 243
    Denmark **8** 757–8*
    Dominican Order **9** 111–13*
patronage
  historical and regional traditions—cont.
    Dominican Republic **9** 118*
    Early Christian (*c.* AD 250–843) **7** 217; **9** 519, 521–3*, 539, 623; **16** 761–2
    Ecuador **9** 714*
    Egypt **16** 207, 382–3
    England **10** 249, 262, 359–62*; **14** 263; **19** 582
    Eritrea **10** 577–8*
    Ethiopia **10** 577–8*
    Fang **1** 241
    Finland **11** 111–12*
    Fon **1** 241
    France **2** 366; **11** 356, 652–60*; **13** 153; **20** 131
    Franciscan Order **11** 711–12*; **13** 132; **16** 762
    Fulani **1** 240, 241
    Gabon **11** 880*
    Georgia **12** 331*
    Germany **12** 446, 470–72*
    Ghana **1** 240; **12** 510*
    Gothic **13** 127–8*, 130, 132, 133, 137, 155
      France **13** 153
      Italy **13** 130
    Greece **13** 359*
    Greece, ancient **7** 561; **13** 371, 373–5*, 485–6, 487
    Grenada **2** 153
    Guatemala **13** 768–9*
    Guyana **13** 877–8*
    Haiti **14** 59–60*
    Hausa **1** 241, 242
    Hieronymites **14** 516–17*
    Hinduism **15** 206
    Honduras **14** 716–17*
    Hungary **15** 12*
    Igbo **1** 241, 243
    Inca **15** 162
    India, Republic of **15** 178–9*
    Indian subcontinent **15** 206, 207, 208, 324, 334, 651, 737*
      Buddhism **5** 95; **15** 737, 739
      Gupta **15** 738
      Hinduism **15** 206
      Islamic **15** 206, 207, 738, 739–40
      Jainism **15** 737, 739
      Rajput **15** 724
      Vijayanagara (ii) (Indian dynasty) **15** 738
    Iran **16** 126, 374
    Ireland **16** 35*
    Islam **16** 90–92*
    Islamic **16** 121–6*, 296–7
      Central Asia, Western **16** 235*
      Egypt **16** 207, 382–3
      Indian subcontinent **15** 206, 207, 738, 739–40
      Iran **16** 374
      Mamluk **16** 130
      Ottoman **16** 122, 133
      Syria **16** 146, 207, 382–3
    Israel **16** 569–70*
    Italy **13** 130; **16** 760–65*, 777; **24** 249; **32** 224
    Jainism **15** 737, 739
    Jamaica **16** 889*
    Japan **17** 46, 154, 164, 297, 345, 347, 351, 421–4*; **33** 318
      Buddhism **17** 421–3; **18** 213
    Java **15** 798–9; **29** 237
    Jesuit Order **16** 763; **17** 510–12*
    Kano (Nigeria) **1** 242
    Kenya **17** 908*
    Knights Hospitaller **18** 151–2*
    Knights Templar **18** 153–4
    Kongo **1** 241
    Korea **18** 258–9*
    Kuba (iii) (Zaïre) **1** 241, 242
    Liberia **1** 242–3; **19** 310*
    Makonde (Mozambique) **20** 149
    Malta (Republic of) **20** 219*
    Mesoamerica, Pre-Columbian **21** 191
patronage
  historical and regional traditions—cont.
    Mexico **21** 394–6*
    Mongolia **21** 884*
    Native North Americans **22** 675–8*
    Nepal **22** 769
    Netherlands, the **22** 886, 900–903*; **32** 267
    New Zealand **23** 74–5*
    Nicaragua **23** 84*
    Nigeria **23** 139*
    Norway **23** 242–3*
    Nupe **1** 241, 242
    Oratorians **23** 473–4*
    Ottoman **16** 122, 133
    Ottonian **12** 471
    Panama **23** 905–6*
    Paraguay **24** 100–101*
    Peru **24** 515–16*
    Poland **25** 93, 94, 134–7*; **27** 842
    Portugal **1** 241; **25** 317*
    Prehistoric art **25** 519, 535
    Puerto Rico **25** 703–4*
    Romanesque **26** 595
    Romania **26** 722–3*
    Rome, ancient **10** 359; **16** 760–61; **26** 855–7*, 884, 907, 911; **27** 53
    Russia **7** 217; **27** 437–8*
    Scotland **28** 267–70*
    Senegal **28** 406*
    Senufo **1** 241
    Servites **28** 489–90*
    Sierra Leone **28** 692–3*
    Slovakia **28** 856–7*
    South Africa **29** 121*
    South-east Asia **29** 236–9*, *237*
    Surinam **30** 16–17*
    Sweden **30** 117*
    Switzerland **30** 152–3*
    Syria **16** 146, 207, 382–3
    Tanzania **30** 301–2*
    Teutonic Order **30** 535–6*
    Theatine Order **30** 649*
    Tibet **5** 104; **30** 813–14*, 822, 828
    Trinidad and Tobago **31** 339*
    Ukraine **31** 564–5*
    United States of America **31** 662–3*
    Venezuela **32** 165, 178–9*
    Vietnam **32** 478
    Wales **32** 790–91*
    Yaka **1** 240
    Yoruba **1** 241
    Zambia **33** 603*
    Zimbabwe **33** 679–80
  types
    architecture **2** 362; **15** 737–8*; **16** 143*; **20** 560; **30** 649
    calligraphy **17** 217
    lacquer **17** 302
    manuscripts **26** 659–60*
    metalwork **16** 380*
    painting **15** 739–40*; **26** 656*
    sculpture **10** 265; **13** 76–7; **15** 737–8*; **27** 30
    stained glass **13** 178, 181, 183
Patrouillard Degrave, Jules-Alexandre *see* DEGRAVE, JULES-ALEXANDRE PATROUILLARD
Pattadakal **15** *276*, *294*; **24** 267*
  reliefs **15** 227
  sculpture **15** 415
  temples **6** 404; **15** 293, 297–8, *298*, 301, 526–7
    Galaganatha Temple **15** 299
    Jaina temple **15** 302, 527
    Kashivishvanatha Temple **15** 299, 300
    Mallikarjuna Temple **15** 297, 298, 526
    Papanatha Temple **15** 299, 300
    Sangameshvara Temple **15** 297, *297*, 526
Paṭṭada Kisuvolal *see* PATTADAKAL
Pattala **15** 200
Pattani *keris see under* KERIS → types
Pattaya **30** 591, 617
Patte, Pierre **24** 268*
  collaboration **11** 761; **31** 297
  works **1** *124*; **4** 163; **24** 120; **29** 92; **33** 281
  writings **1** 124; **30** 670; **31** 713
pattern *see* ORNAMENT
pattern books **4** 359; **9** 219; **21** 757; **24** 268–77*
  historical and regional traditions
    Britain **12** 333
    Byzantine **24** 269
    Czech Republic **24** 269
    England **14** 855; **24** 269, *270*, 273, 753
    France **9** 351; **24** 269, 271, *272*
    Germany **24** 271; **32** 680
    Hungary **14** 888
    Iceland **24** 269
    Islamic **16** 305
    Italy **16** 759; **24** 269, 271
    Japan **24** 276–7*
    Poland **25** 137
  types
    architecture **24** 273–6*
      Belgium **7** 480
      Britain **32** 553
      England **18** 742–3; **24** *275*; **32** 554
      Finland **6** 581
      France **9** 351; **10** 110; **22** 925; **32** 554
      Germany **9** 687; **12** 368; **17** 837; **20** 804; **28** 143, 497
      Indian subcontinent **16** 823
      Jamaica **5** 749
      Switzerland **24** *274*
      United States of America **20** 878; **24** 275; **31** 592, 593; **32** 555
      see also TREATISES → types → architecture
    calligraphy **17** 226, 227, *227*, 228, *228*, 237
    dyeing **24** 276
    furniture **6** 390
      Belgium **3** 581, 582, 585
      Britain **15** 820
      England **10** 280, 296, 299; **24** 273
      Germany **31** 680
      Portugal **25** 306
    garden **12** 105
      England **12** 130
      Netherlands, the **12** 105, *106*, 131, 133
      see also GARDEN DESIGN
    guns **2** 461, 463, 466
    houses **24** 275
    interior decoration
      Austria **2** 807
      Belgium **3** 579
      England **10** 273
      France **6** 535
      Germany **12** 409
    ironwork **14** 856
    jewellery **17** 521; **29** 345
    kimonos **24** 276–7
    lace **18** 590
    metalwork **12** 446; **24** 271; **30** 871; **33** 17
    mosaics **32** 542
    painting
      Byzantine **9** 623
      Etruscan **10** 617
      Gothic **13** 155
      Greece, ancient **13** 546
      Tibet **30** 813
    sculpture **4** *187*; **10** 261
    silver **12** 590
    textiles **27** 693
      Germany **12** 469
      Italy **16** 759
      Japan **17** 264, 354

pattern books
  types—cont.
  typography 11 359
  see also EMBLEM BOOKS; MANUALS; TREATISES
pattern cards see under CARDS → types
pattern-punching 30 770
pattern welding see under METALWORK → techniques
Patterson, Edward 1 431
Patterson, Joseph M. 14 735
Patterson, Robert Lloyd 16 42
paṭṭī 15 244*
Pattison, Edward, & Sons 31 652
Pattison, Emilia Frances see DILKE, Lady
Pattisvaram, Sri Tenupurishvara Temple 15 645
Patti Villa 9 568; 28 655
Patturelli, Giovanni 3 921
Patursson, Tróndur 10 813
Patwardhan, Sudhir 18 16
Patwin 22 549, 652
Paty (family) 10 265
Paty, Thomas 4 822; 10 265; 30 673
Paty, William 4 821; 10 265
Patzalt, Josef 29 422
Pátzay, Pál 13 638; 14 896; 29 61
Pátzcuaro 31 118
  Cathedral of S Salvador 21 375
Patzicía 13 758, 765
PAU see URBAN PLANNING WORKSHOP
paubhās 22 778, 780–83, 782
Pau de Saint-Martin, Alexandre 27 265
Paudevin, John 10 291
  works 10 291
Paudiss, Christopher 12 390; 18 467; 22 843; 24 277*
Pauelsen, Erik 8 734; 23 225
Pauer, Gyula 14 897
Päuerlin see BEIERLEIN
Pauger, Adrien de 23 31
Pauillac, Château Mouton-Rothschild
  Musée Mouton 27 225
Pau i Montaner, Pere 3 215
Paul, Master 25 111; 26 711
Paul, Patriarch 30 725
Paul, Saint 1 652
Paul I, Emperor of Russia (reg 1796-1801) 3 433; 7 193; 9 379; 26 733*; 33 579
  architecture 4 745; 5 520, 521; 12 173; 26 403; 27 198, 403; 32 697; 33 579
  drawings 29 839
  gardens 12 134
  interior decoration 22 726; 26 449
  paintings 2 690; 9 366
  sponsorship 33 522
  thrones 27 407
Paul I, Pope (reg 757-67) 26 799
Paul II, Pope (reg 1464-71) 24 277–8*
  architecture 11 685; 16 632; 19 686; 21 143; 24 731; 26 755, 804, 811
  collections 26 767, 768
  gems 12 257, 265
  medals 8 164
  plaquettes 25 19
  sculpture 3 636; 16 67; 26 791, 808
Paul III, Pope (reg 1534-50) 10 807, 808–9*; 26 769; 31 40
  architecture 5 683; 19 690; 21 79, 454, 455; 24 520, 754; 26 756, 800, 813, 822, 838; 27 742, 745; 32 503
    military 1 636; 27 744
  art policies 16 768
  coats of arms 14 416
  coins 6 140
Paul III, Pope (reg 1534-50)—cont.
  decorative works 3 645; 25 21; 26 823
  manuscripts 6 140; 26 42
  medals 4 339
  paintings 8 504; 16 665; 24 419; 28 658; 31 37, 38
    frescoes 21 439, 448; 26 816, 817, 818; 30 800
  sculpture 25 256
Paul IV, Pope (reg 1555-59) 5 698, 699*
  architecture 19 371; 26 813
  armour 13 911
  collections 7 233
  hardstones 21 725
  paintings 6 175; 8 505; 25 209; 26 769
  tapestries 26 778
Paul V, Pope (reg 1605-21) 3 296; 4 404–5*; 7 842; 17 731
  architectural history 5 767
  architecture 7 258; 11 270; 16 637; 25 227; 26 758, 796, 800, 807, 832; 30 344; 32 9
  books 10 909
  decorative works 10 908
  medals 27 767
  paintings 2 376; 5 715; 7 312; 18 730, 732; 24 239
  sculpture 3 828, 852; 7 842; 20 47, 412
Paul VI, Pope (reg 1963-78) 24 36, 278–9*
Paul, Bruno 24 279*
  collaboration 20 324
  groups and movements 2 565, 571; 10 215
  pupils 21 490
  staff 21 407
  works 11 582; 12 416, 468; 14 362; 27 871
Paul, Georges Hermann René see HERRMANN-PAUL
Paul, Jeremiah 24 279–80*
Paul, Lawrence 22 598
Paul, Raimund 14 818
Paul, Robert (1739-70) 11 338
Paul, Robert (b 1906) 33 678
Paul, Tim 22 589
Paula e Oliveira, Francisco de 26 52; 30 881
Paula Ferg, Franz de see FERG, FRANZ DE PAULA
Paula Martos, Francisco de 29 337
Paula Nebot, Francesc de 29 309
Paula Quintana, Francisco de 12 183
el Paular 5 737; 24 280*; 29 258, 292
Paulding, William 8 575; 13 208
Paule de Rigaud, Joseph-Hyacinthe-François de, Comte de Vaudreuil see VAUDREUIL, JOSEPH-HYACINTHE-FRANÇOIS DE PAULE DE RIGAUD, Comte de
Paulet, Charles, 5th Duke of Bolton 31 906
Paulette, Paulo 26 52
Paul-Frederick, Grand Duke of Mecklenburg-Schwerin (reg 1837-42) 8 706
Paulhan, Jean 2 545; 10 838; 33 305
Paulheim, Ferenc 14 523
Pauli, Adolphe 24 280*
  education (art) 3 618
  pupils 7 460; 8 765; 31 855, 888
  teachers 26 526
  works 12 519
Pauli, Fritz 30 135
Pauli, Georg 22 331; 30 81
Paulick, Richard 13 689; 22 253
Paulin, Edmond 19 809
Paulin, Pierre 32 756
Pauline Order 8 178
Paulinina glassworks 23 264
Paulinos, Bishop of Tyre (fl c. 317) 7 260, 278
Paulinus of Nola (353-431) 7 325; 16 624; 24 280*
Paulinzella Church 12 364
Paulist Fathers 24 281*
  churches 24 281
Paull, William 12 773
Paull & Bonella 31 763
Paullus, Lucius Aemilius 10 675
Paulmy, Marc-René d'Argenson, Vicomte de see VOYER, Marquis de
Paulmy, Marquis de (1722-87) 18 880
Paulo, Belchior 4 715
Paul of Caen, Abbot of St Albans 26 659, 671; 27 526
Paul of Evergetis 7 229
Paulos Silentiarios 9 656; 10 129
Paulovits, István Járdány 30 212
Paulowna, Anna, Meubelenfabriek 14 767; 22 873
paulownia 17 371, 390, 391; 18 361, 363
Paulsen (family) 25 127
Paulsen, Brian 10 398
Paulsen, Christian 25 127
Paulsen, Julius 11 475, 790; 24 281–2*
Paulson, Ronald 10 377
Paulsson, Gregor 28 917; 30 120
Paulucci, Enrico 31 446
Pauļuks, Jānis 24 282*
  works
Paulus (family) 7 921; 23 109
Paulus (fl 223 AD) 4 343
Paulus (fl 1120) 7 922
Paulus, Adolf 28 341
Paulus, Georg 10 860
Paulus, Johann 10 859
Paulyn, Horatius 25 362
Paulys, T. de 15 19
Paumgartner Altarpiece 9 433, 440, 443; 33 275
Pauni 15 450
Paur, János György 5 81
Paur, Johann Wilhelm see BAUR, JOHANN WILHELM
Paur van Ochsenfurt, Hans 27 146
Pausanias 13 421; 24 282–3*
  works 2 298, 531; 9 20; 13 369, 807; 30 286
    on acroteria 1 127
    on architectural decoration 13 604
    on architecture 2 406, 669, 670, 678; 8 446; 23 432; 27 2
    on candelabra 5 604
    on caryatids 5 904
    on cult statues 8 263
    on fountains 11 339
    on furniture 13 592
    on iconography 15 85
    on metalwork 10 625
    on monuments 22 42
    on paintings 2 684; 13 552, 553
    on sculpture 1 646; 2 133, 681; 23 441; 25 457; 26 295; 27 14; 29 814; 31 301
    on treasuries (i) 31 294
    on writing 20 328
  translated 23 79
Pausche, Paul see PREUSSE, PAUL
Pausias 24 283*; 28 712
  methods 10 197
  teachers 13 549; 23 900
  works 12 287; 13 551, 561
Pausilypos 30 718
Pauson 12 287; 13 545, 548
Pautre, Antoine Le see LE PAUTRE, ANTOINE
Pauvert de la Chapelle, J.-O. 12 266
Pauw, Maerten 14 739
Pauw, R. De see DE PAUW, R.
Pauw & Botha 25 566
Pauwels, Achiel 3 592
Pauwels, Ferdinand Wilhelm 7 346; 19 333
Pauwels, P. 3 585
Pauwels Franck see FIAMMINGO, PAOLO
Pauwelsz, Johannes 9 380
Pauwert, H. van de 2 318
Pauzié, Jérémie 27 429, 584
Pavagadh Hill 15 178
Pavao (of Dubrovnik) 8 180
Pavel (fl 1834) 5 148
Pavel of Levoča (fl early 16th cent.; sculptor) 14 893; 28 854
  works 19 281, 281
Pavel of Pardubice (fl 1514-23; master builder) 24 108, 462; 26 367
pavements
  historical and regional traditions
    Byzantine 8 155
    Cambodia 5 475
    Crete 8 154, 155
    Cyprus 8 359
    Greece, ancient 13 395, 395
    Islamic 16 145, 250
    Italy 30 886
    Rome, ancient 26 875; 27 59–60
  materials
    marble 26 875
    tiles 30 886
Paves, Pheziu see PHEZIU PAVES
Pavia 16 618; 19 549; 24 284–9*
  Castello Visconteo 4 776; 13 64; 16 722; 28 531; 32 610
    interior decoration 16 711
  ecclesiastical buildings
    Cathedral of S Stefano 4 645; 26 578
      campanile 4 775
      crypt 32 94
    Certosa 1 748; 5 894, 895; 10 743; 20 303; 21 841; 24 284–5*, 285; 32 611
      altarpiece 24 525, 526
      effigies of Ludovico Sforza and Beatrice d'Este 29 24
      ivory-carvings 13 176
      paintings 24 523
      sculpture 16 701; 24 285–7*, 286; 30 501
      woodwork 16 725
    Mezzabarba Chapel 29 832
    S Francesco 4 775; 16 725
    S Maria di Canepanova 3 249
    S Maria del Carmine 4 775; 13 64; 30 501
      tomb of Abbess Theodota 19 549, 550
    S Michele 4 141; 9 86; 16 625; 24 287–8*, 288; 26 578, 619, 620
      altar 1 696
      dome 9 84
      façade 24 287–8
      sculpture 24 288–9*; 26 620
      woodwork 16 725
    S Pietro in Ciel d'Oro 2 725; 26 620
  Ospedale di S Matteo 14 781
  Palazzo Marozzi 33 719
  Palazzo Mezzabarba see Town Hall
  Palazzo della Sapienza 31 674
  Ponte Coperto 4 801
  Regisole 10 440
  reliefs 19 549
  stools 30 776
  Torre dei Belcredi 4 776
  Torre di S Dalmazzo 4 776
  Town Hall 29 832
  University 29 833
Pavia, Belbello da see BELBELLO DA PAVIA
Pavia, Francesco da see FRANCESCO DA PAVIA
Pavia, Giacomo 4 561
Pavia, Giovanni Giorgio da see GIOVANNI GIORGIO DA PAVIA
Pavia, Leonardo da see LEONARDO DA PAVIA
Pavia, Lorenzo Gusnasco di see GUSNASCO DI PAVIA, LORENZO
Pavia, Pietro da see PIETRO DA PAVIA
Pavias, Andreas 25 332
Pavić, B. 28 452
Pavie, Antoine 24 148
Paviken 32 524
Pavilion of the Eight Paradises see ISFAHAN → Hasht Bihisht Palace
pavilion pagodas see under PAGODAS → types
pavilions (buildings) 12 61, 62, 105; 22 366; 24 289–91*
  Buddhism 18 561
  Cambodia 5 474
  Central Asia, Western 16 197
  China 6 655, 675; 24 289*; 28 552
  Egypt, ancient 12 66
  France 32 374
  Germany 8 289; 24 290
  Indian subcontinent 3 38; 10 829; 15 258, 346; 29 480
  Islamic 15 346; 16 197, 204, 225
  Italy 26 903
  Japan 18 561; 24 289*
  Korea 12 94, 94
  Netherlands, the 12 106, 131
  Ottoman 16 225; 23 638
  Rome, ancient 26 871, 903
  Russia 26 8
  South-east Asia 24 290*
  Turkey 16 204, 225; 23 638
  see also BELVEDERES; GAZEBOS; KIOSKS; TENTS
pavilions (canopy) 3 483
pavilions (crematory) 5 507*
Pavillon, Balthazar 31 175
Pavillon, Pierre 1 497
pavillons de chasse 20 131
pavimenta punica see under MOSAICS → types
paviors 20 559
Pavlenko, Oksana 2 634
Pavlov 8 374; 24 291*; 25 470, 471, 488, 492
  figurines 25 488, 489
Pavlov, A. I. 17 870
Pavlov, Georgy 27 436
Pavlov, Kapiton S. 18 38; 31 559
Pavlov, Leonid 27 381
  works 27 381
Pavlov, Yanko 5 156
Pavlova, Anna 3 87, 119
Pavlovets, Nikita Ye. 27 387, 442
Pavlović, Miloš 28 452
Pavlović, Zoran 28 451
Pavlovich, Nikolay 5 154
Pavlovich, Pavel Kamensky 27 413
Pavlovsk 5 521; 24 291–2*; 27 363, 376; 33 579
  collections 27 438
  gardens 12 134, 134; 13 5
  locks 27 425
  paintings 26 449
  Palace 4 745; 24 292; 27 403, 583
    furniture 27 583, 583
    interior decoration 27 404
    Italian Hall 27 403
    sculpture 18 416
    Upper Vestibule 4 745
  stucco 29 839
Pavlovsk Posad 27 431
Pavnar 15 464
Pavolini, Corrado 7 779
Pavón, Angel María de Barcia y see BARCIA Y PAVÓN, ANGEL MARÍA DE
Pavona, Francesco 11 241
pavonazzetto see under MARBLE → types
Pawaya
  platform 15 256
  sculpture 15 433, 451, 469, 470
Pa Wei-tsu see BA WEIZU

Paweł 32 878
Pawhuska (OK), Pawnee
  Roundhouse 22 671
Pawlak, Kazimierz 25 125
Pawlowicz, Teodor 32 878
Pawłowski, Andrzej 24 292*
Pawnee 22 551, 584
Pawtucket (RI) 25 666
  Mill 10 748
paxes 11 *86*; 17 515
Paxton (Borders)
  Paxton House 7 172; 9 727;
    28 254
  Union Bridge 4 803
Paxton, Joseph 3 245; 17 639;
  24 292–5*; 31 725; 33 449
  architecture
    conservatories 7 744; 12 137,
      791, *791*; 13 619
    country houses 2 324; 6 118
    exhibition architecture 10 235,
      319, 679, 681; 15 883; 16 53;
      19 896; 23 814; 24 *294*;
      25 173
  collaboration 5 283
  groups and movements 10 142;
    32 415
  parks 12 773; 24 179
  patrons and collectors 6 116,
    117–18, 515, 516; 27 223
Paxton, William 4 478
Pay, Johann de 12 390; 13 845;
  24 295*
Paya 14 712
Payag 3 91; 15 588, 589; 16 345;
  24 295*
Payen, Antoine A. J. 15 807;
  25 837; 33 538
Payen, Antoine Marie Joseph 5 41;
  22 33; 24 295
Payen, Auguste 24 295
Payen, Auguste Jean Joseph 3 547;
  24 295–6*; 26 192
Payer, Oskar 2 810
Payer, Peter 2 815
Payerne Abbey 7 266; 24 750;
  32 88, 89
  Notre-Dame 7 253; 26 635
Payette, Tom 23 799
Payette Associates 17 806
Paykend 6 209, 210, 264, 277
Payne, Charles 5 531
Payne, Edgar 19 701
Payne, G(eorge) D(avid) 24 296*
  works 2 740, *741*; 4 818
Payne, Henry Albert 4 87; 25 556
Payne, H. G. G. 32 27
Payne, Humphrey 24 373
Payne, Ivan 2 149
Payne, John 24 296*
  assistants 10 757
  works 28 *613*
Payne, Malcolm 29 112
Payne, Miranda 24 409
Payne, Roger 4 354
Payne, Thomas 33 377
Payne, William 12 820; 24 296–7*
Payne Knight, Richard *see*
  KNIGHT, RICHARD PAYNE
Paynter, David 29 468
Paynter, Edward William 23 75
Payogasta 29 191
Payón, José García *see* GARCÍA
  PAYÓN, JOSÉ
Paysse-Reyes, Mario 24 297*;
  31 754, 758
Paz, Alonso de la 13 764; 24 297*
Paz, Ireneo 32 571
Paz, La *see* LA PAZ
Paz, Manuel Godoy, Príncipe de la
  see GODOY (Y ALVÁREZ DE
  FARIA), MANUEL, Príncipe de la
  Paz
Paz, Manuel Marín de la *see*
  MARÍN DE LA PAZ, MANUEL
Paz, Octavio 33 575
Pažaislis 19 *494*
  Camaldolese monastery 19 496,
    497
Pazarçik (Turkey) 21 299
Pazardjik (Bulgaria), Church of
  the Councils 5 156
Pazarlı 1 833, 838; 24 691
Pazarören, Tomb of Melik Gazi
  16 186
Paz Contreras, Rey 24 620
Pázmándi, Antal 15 2
Pázmány, Petr, Archbishop of
  Esztergom 4 695; 31 353
Pazyryk 2 100; 6 *182*; 21 885;
  24 297–8*; 28 321
  Barrow 5 7 51
  belts 3 686
  carpets 2 437; 5 833; 6 186, 252;
    16 467, 469; 24 *298*
  embroidery 10 181
  felt 10 873, *873*
  harnesses 14 180, *180*
  tattoos 30 367, 769
  textiles 7 46; 25 546
  tombs 6 196
Pazzaglia, Antonio 12 263;
  24 298–9*
Pazzaglia, Stefano 24 298
Pazzi (family) 5 22
Pazzi, Andrea di Guglielmo 5 18;
  24 299*
Pazzi, Antonio 24 299
Pazzi, Girolamo de' 29 741
Pazzi, Jacopo 24 299*
Pazzi, Michel de' 2 113
Pazzi, Piero 24 299
Pazzi Chapel *see under* FLORENCE
  → ecclesiastical buildings →
  Santa Croce
Pazzini, Norberto 10 641
Pbow *see* FA'W AL-QIBLI
PC, Monogrammist 18 520;
  20 801–2*
Pčinsky, St Pročor 25 343
Pe 10 802
Peabody, George 29 221
Peabody, Robert Swain
  24 299–300*
  groups and movements 7 619;
    25 806; 28 604
  works 10 683; 25 *806*
Peabody Essex Museum *see under*
  SALEM (MA)
Peabody Museum of Natural
  History *see under* NEW HAVEN
  (CT) → Yale University
Peabody & Stearns 4 473; 5 274;
  7 485; 19 500; 23 422; 24 299;
  28 193; 33 135, 136
Peabody Trust 30 457–8
Peace, David 10 321
peace gardens *see under* GARDENS
  → types
Peach, C. Stanley 25 402; 26 111
Peach, Harry Hardy 33 157
Peacham, Henry 2 163; 13 708;
  24 300*
Peachey, James 5 564
Peach Robinson, Henry *see*
  ROBINSON, HENRY PEACH
peach stones 7 141
Peacock, James 8 495
Peacock, William 26 239
Peacock Cave 6 318
peacock feathers *see under*
  FEATHERS → types
Peacock Room *see under* LONDON
  → houses → 49 Prince's Gate
Peacock Throne 15 707; 30 784,
  785
Peake 13 22
Peake, James 28 879
Peake, Robert (1598–?1626)
  24 301*
  collaboration 19 515
  patrons and collectors 29 799
  pupils 10 757
  works 10 247; 16 823; 29 424
  writings 28 471
Peake, Robert (1602–67) 10 757;
  12 820
Peake, William 9 56; 12 820
Peak Forest Canal 2 242
Peakirk Church 26 613
Peak Sanctuary Rhyton 21 689
Peale (family) 3 129
Peale, Anna Claypoole 24 304*
Peale, Charles Willson 21 644;
  24 301–4*, *301*, 599–600;
  27 349; 31 666
  assistants 24 303
  collaboration 3 310
  patrons and collectors 12 645;
    22 678; 24 602
  pupils 24 279, 304; 25 152
  teachers 14 493; 33 92
  works 11 497; 15 140; 24 *302*;
    31 600, 601
Peale, James (1749–1831) 7 408;
  24 303*, 686
Peale, James, jr (1789–1876)
  24 303
Peale, Margaretta Angelica 24 304*
Peale, Mary Jane 24 304
Peale, Raphaelle 15 140; 24 303*;
  29 669
Peale, Rembrandt 24 303–4*, 600;
  31 666
  patrons and collectors 14 718
  pupils 24 304
  teachers 33 93
Peale, Rubens 24 304*
Peale, Sarah Miriam 24 304–5*
Peale, Titian Ramsay (1780–98)
  24 303
Peale, Titian Ramsay (1799–1885)
  10 669; 24 303
Peale Museum *see under*
  BALTIMORE (MD) → museums;
  PHILADELPHIA (PA) →
  museums
Peam Cheang 5 490
Peanut, Mr 24 409
Pearce, Edward 10 275; 11 424
Pearce, Edward Lovett 24 305–6*
  assistants 6 63
  collaboration 12 6; 16 23
  groups and movements 23 860
  works 9 316, *316*, 322; 13 237,
    301; 16 8, 23, *23*; 24 *305*;
    25 268; 32 553
Pearce, Eric 16 28
Pearce, Matthew 23 193
Pearce, Michael 33 678
Pearce, S. L.
  works 25 *403*
Pearce, Stephen 28 283
Pearce Partnership 33 678
pearling 30 839
Pearl of Brabant, Master of the
  4 594; 20 743*
pearls 17 *525*
  historical and regional traditions
    Ancient Near East 1 876
    Belgium 3 609, *609*; 10 II2
    Buddhism 6 706
    Byzantine 9 653, *653*, 657, *660*,
      662, 668
    Cambodia 5 500
    Carolingian 7 *513*
    Central Asia, Western 6 251
    China 6 706; 7 109, 110, 111,
      111, 112, *112*
      Sui period (AD 581–618) 7 *107*
    Early Christian (*c*. AD 250–843)
      9 653, *653*, 668
    Egypt 9 *653*
    Egypt, ancient 10 33
    England 10 *345*; 17 *522*
    France 11 *634*
    Germany 12 447, 462
    Gothic 13 194
    Hungary 9 *662*; 15 12
    Indian subcontinent 6 556;
      12 252
    Islamic 16 *430*
    Italy 16 751
    Korea 18 367
    Rome, ancient 27 *102*
    Russia 27 *419*, *423*
    Sicily 16 *430*
pearls
  historical and regional
    traditions—cont.
    Spain 29 349
    Switzerland 17 *520*
    United States of America
      31 *655*
  types
    pink 3 169
  uses
    beads 3 440, 442
    book covers 7 *513*
    bowls 27 *419*
    brooches 17 *520*; 31 *655*
    chess sets 6 556
    crosses 8 201
    crowns 7 110, 111, *111*, 112
    dress 6 251
    earrings 7 111; 17 523
    embroidery 3 609, *609*; 9 668;
      10 II2; 12 462; 13 194; 15 12;
      25 132; 29 349
    hair ornaments 7 *112*; 27 *102*
    headdresses 7 110
    jewellery 17 519, 522
      China 7 111, 112
      Early Christian and Byzantine
        9 653
      Egypt, ancient 10 33
      Italy 16 751
      Korea 18 367
    lace 18 590
    lockets 17 *522*
    necklaces 7 *107*, 111; 9 *653*;
      11 *634*
    papier mâché 24 61
    pendants (jewellery) 10 *345*;
      27 *423*
    rings 7 109
    robes 16 *430*
    sculpture 5 500; 6 706
Pearlstein, Philip 24 306*; 25 5
  works 19 492; 21 761; 23 297,
    297
pear mouldings *see under*
  MOULDINGS → types
Pears, A. & F., Ltd. 10 420; 21 603
  works 10 *420*
Pears, Charles 20 425
Pearsall 5 839; 18 30
Pearse, G(eoffrey) E(astcott)
  5 661; 17 602; 24 306*; 29 106
  pupils 9 686; 10 825; 29 123
Pearse, James 16 21
pear-shaped vases *see* VASES →
  types → *yuhuchun*
Pearson, Frank Loughborough
  24 307
Pearson, Gene 16 888
Pearson, James 29 506
Pearson, J. D. 16 550
Pearson, J(ohn) L(oughborough)
  5 270; 7 410; 8 48; 24 307–8*
  assistants 19 109
  collaboration 9 61
  groups and movements 10 238
  teachers 23 657
  works 4 818, 825; 10 259;
    19 615; 23 398; 24 *307*; 28 295
  writings 2 359
Pearson, John (Andrew) 8 528*;
  20 388; 23 632
Pearson, Lionel G. 6 460; 14 674
Pearson, William 24 307
Pearson Page 10 344
Pearson & Rollason 14 132
Pear Valley (VA) 32 302
  house 32 *302*
pear-wood 12 426; 18 361, 610;
  29 *318*; 33 324, III
Peascod, Alan 2 762
Pease, J. R. 14 862
peat 17 398, 399
Peate, Iorwerth C. 32 791
Peau de l'Ours, La 11 659; 19 66
pebbles
  historical and regional traditions
    Anatolia, ancient 22 159
pebbles
  historical and regional
    traditions—cont.
    Greece, ancient 22 159–60;
      23 *435*
    Prehistoric art 25 493
    Scotland 28 264
  techniques
    painting 25 493
  uses
    floors 13 556
    jewellery 28 264
    mosaics 13 556, *557*, *560*, *562*,
      562–6*, *563*, *564*; 22 154,
      159–60; 23 *435*
    tools 25 493
Peć 9 *511*; 24 308*; 28 *437*
  houses 28 444
  icons 25 339
  Monastery of the Holy Apostles
    see Patriarchate
  Patriarchate 24 308
    Church of the Hodegetria *see*
      Church of the Holy Mother
      of God
    Church of the Holy Apostles
      9 582; 24 308
      wall paintings 28 *445*, 446
    Church of the Holy Mother of
      God 28 446
      screens (i) (architectural) 9 601
    collections 28 459
  wall paintings 25 343
Pecánková, J. 25 446
Pecci (family) 28 677
Pecci altarpiece 12 *714*
Pecci-Blunt, Anna Laetitia,
  Countess 26 777
Pech 14 712
Pecháčková, Slávka 28 856
Pecham, Georg 2 794; 24 308–9*
Pecham, John 7 627; 24 486, 487;
  28 202
Pech de l'Azé 25 491
Peche, Dagobert 17 528; 24 309*;
  32 817
  collaboration 27 665
  groups and movements 33 166
  works 2 814, 821; 12 821
Peche, Ernst 24 309
Pécheux, Laurent 4 407; 8 618;
  28 19; 31 445, 447
Pech Merle 11 *505*; 24 310–11*;
  25 *470*, 476, 478, 480, 485, 487,
  650
  rock art 24 *310*
Pechstein, (Hermann) Max 4 892;
  18 79; 24 311–12*
  exhibitions 13 711
  groups and movements
    Arbeitsrat für Kunst 2 288
    Brücke, Die 4 132, 891; 10 694,
      841; 12 395; 18 77, 78
    Deutscher Werkbund 8 826
    Novembergruppe (Germany)
      3 801; 23 267
    Secession (Berlin) 3 801; 28 343
  patrons and collectors 20 880
  works 9 310; 19 491; 22 331;
    24 *311*; 25 582; 29 871; 33 363
Pecht, (August) Friedrich 24 312*
Péchy, Mihály 24 312*
Peçin
  architecture 16 202
  Karapäa Caravanserai *see*
    Menteşeid Üçgöz Caravanserai
  Menteşeid Üçgöz Caravanserai
    16 205
  palaces 16 204
  Yelli Mosque 16 202
Pécinaud 19 398
Peck, Peter 2 458; 13 905
  works 2 *458*
Peck, Robert 10 645
Peck, Sheldon 24 312–13*
Peckforton Castle (Ches) 6 61;
  27 *656*
Peckitt, William 10 675; 23 691;
  29 506; 33 545, 550

Peco, Mustafa 4 462
Pecore, Francesco delle see MOSCA, FRANCESCO DI SIMONE
Pecore, Jacopo di Simone delle 22 166
Pecori, Domenico 3 299; 18 781
Pecotic, M. 8 177
Pecovski, Dusko 19 883
Pécs 14 881; 16 103; 24 313–14*
architecture 14 891
Cathedral of St Peter 14 883, 889; 24 313–14*; 26 570, 594
altarpiece 14 894
furniture 14 906
reliefs 24 314
sculpture 14 885, 892; 26 636, 638
congregational mosque 16 222
Csontváry Museum 15 17; 24 313
Endre Nemes Museum 22 730
Ferenc Martyn Collection 15 17
Inner city parish church 14 886
Janus Pannonius Museum 15 17
mosque of Gázi Kasim Pasha Jami see Inner city parish church
mosque of Pasha Yakovali Hassan 14 886
Uitz Museum 15 17; 31 542
Uránváros estate 14 891
Vasarely Museum 15 17
Pécsi, József 3 876
pecten see under SHELLS → types
pectoral crosses see under CROSSES → types
pectoral ornaments
historical and regional traditions
Chimú 3 442
China 7 107
Egypt, ancient 10 29, 30
Greece, ancient 12 869
Huastec 14 831
Mesoamerica, Pre-Columbian 21 266
Mixtec 21 253
Native North Americans 22 616
Rhodes (island) 12 869
materials
gold 7 107; 10 30; 12 869
jade 7 107
shells 14 831
silver 22 615
Pecul (family) 29 342
Pecul, Domingo 29 343
Pecul, Felipe 29 343
Pecul, Francisco (1768-1804) 29 343
Pecul, Francisco, the younger (fl 1854) 29 343
Pecul, Luis 29 337
Pecul y Crespo, Luis 29 342
Pecz, Samu 21 118; 26 241
pedal looms see under LOOMS → types
Pedatumbulam, Ramadeva Temple 15 328
Peddie, J(ohn) Dick (1824-91; father) 24 315*
Peddie, J(ohn) M(ore) Dick (1853-1921; son) 4 884; 24 315
Peddie & Kinnear 24 315*
groups and movements 28 288, 289
staff 4 884
works 28 228, 229
Peddle Thorpe & Harvey 4 818
Peddle Thorpe & Walker 4 818
Pede, Hendrik van 3 543
works 3 544
Pedemuro, Giovanni da 23 862
Pedemuro, Girolamo da 23 862
Pedersen, Carl-Henning 24 315–16*
groups and movements 7 488; 8 736
patrons and collectors 8 758
works 24 316
Pederson, William 18 193*
Pedery-Hunt, Dora de 5 571; 20 927
pedestals 24 316–17*
Buddhism 15 448
Cambodia 5 496
England 24 316; 28 665
France 24 316
Greece, ancient 13 393
Guatemala 13 767
Indian subcontinent 15 448
Italy 9 21; 24 316
pedestal tables see under TABLES → types
Pedevilla, Giovanni Battista 20 371
Pedgaon, Lakshmi-Narayana Temple 15 316
Pedi 1 257, 289, 414, 415, 417, 418, 419
pedigrees 12 271–2
pediments 24 317–20*; 25 264
historical and regional traditions
Burma 5 230
Cambodia 5 470, 476
Ecuador 9 710
Etruscan 24 317
Greece, ancient 13 377, 378, 390, 391, 398, 414, 424–5, 431–2*, 432, 445–6; 24 317–19*, 319
Archaic 7 849
Rome, ancient 24 317, 318, 319–20*; 26 878, 923; 27 30, 32
Syria 28 351
Thailand 12 II2
materials
brick 26 878
sculpture 24 318–20*, 319
teak 12 II2
types
broken 4 843*
Pedoulas, Church of the Holy Cross 9 627
Pédoya 18 864
Pedra do Ingá 29 196
Pedrajas, Francisco Javier 1 741; 24 320*
Pedrali, Giacomo 33 608
Pedraza, Bernardo 29 336
Pedraza, Carlos 6 598
Pedraza, Cristóbal 29 336
Pedraza, Felipe 29 336
Pedraza, Herminio 4 264
Pedraza, Juan 29 336
El Pedregal 30 866
Pedrera, Esteban de 29 335
Pedretti, Giuseppe Carlo 3 466
Pedriel, Santos 27 705
Pedrini, Domenico 20 497; 24 320–21*
Pedrini, Filippo 20 497; 24 320, 321*
Pedrini, Giovanni 26 440
Pedro, Bishop of Évora 13 101
Pedro, Constable of Portugal 11 483
Pedro (of Alcobaça), Frei 24 321–2*; 25 301
works 24 322
Pedro, António 2 903; 24 321*; 25 300
Pedro, Francesco del 12 582
Pedro, Hermano 24 297
Pedro, Luis Martínez see MARTÍNEZ PEDRO, LUIS
Pedro, Master 23 414
Pedro Alexandrino see CARVALHO, PEDRO ALEXANDRINO
Pedro de Aponte 1 127
Pedro de Coma 19 518
Pedro de Montoya, Bishop of Burgo de Osma 27 727
Pedro de Pennafreita 19 518
Pedro de Rasínes 20 493
Pedro de Ribadeo 13 165; 29 333
Pedro de Toledo 20 653
Pedro Díaz de Oviedo see DÍAZ DE OVIEDO, PEDRO
Pedro el Pintor see GOSSEAL, PEDRO
Pedro Juan de Valogona see PERE JOHAN
Pedro Pintor 13 104
Pedrosa del Rey 26 642
Pedroso, João 19 879
Pedroso, Mateo 8 231
Pedro the Goldsmith 26 690
Pedroza, José Trinidad see TRINIDAD PEDROZA, JOSÉ
Pedrozzi, Giovanni Battista 3 428
works 3 429
pedyā 15 244*
Pee, Engelhard de 28 189; 30 34
Pee, Jan van 14 757
Pee, Theodor van 28 724
Peebles, Don 7 211; 33 58
Peebles Church (Borders) 28 288
Peel, Mildred 5 570
Peel, Paul 5 566; 24 322*
Peel, Robert (fl 18th cent.) 2 869, 874*; 8 36; 24 849
Peel, Robert (1788-1850) 10 266; 24 322*; 28 370
architecture 28 874
collections 4 602; 7 579
drawings 3 854
furniture 12 639
paintings 7 572; 10 365; 20 238; 33 190, 216
Peemans, Gerard 9 763
workshop 5 50
Peemuggina, Peter
works 1 62
peepshow boxes 24 322*, 489
Peers, Charles 26 380
Peet, T(homas) Eric 10 81
Peeters 19 116
Peeters, Bonaventura, I (1614-52) 24 323–4*
collaboration 22 718
works 3 560; 24 323
Peeters, Bonaventura, II (1648-1702) 24 324
Peeters, Catharina 24 323
Peeters, Clara 7 369; 24 324*; 33 308
works 3 561; 5 352; 29 666
Peeters, Gillis, I 24 323, 324
Peeters, Henk 2 422; 8 668; 23 298; 28 159
Peeters, Jan, I 24 323, 324; 32 700
Peeters, Jozef 2 197; 3 564; 24 324*; 29 872
Peev, Stoyko, Factory 5 159
Peffenhauser, Anton 2 473
Pefteuawiamun Tjaiemhorimu 2 690
PEG (polyethylene glycol) 7 748; 33 327
Pegado, Bernardo Pereira see PEREIRA PEGADO, BERNARDO
Pegasus Roman see under TYPE-FACES
peg dolls see under DOLLS → types
Pegg, William 8 776
pegged rugs see under RUGS → types
Pegia
basilica 8 357; 9 566
Hagios Giorgios 8 359
peg knitting see under KNITTING → types
Pegna, Hyacinth La see LA PEGNA, HYACINTH
Pegram, Henry 32 788
Pegrassi, Salesio Angelo 3 179
pegs 5 474
Pegu 5 221, 225; 6 623; 24 324–5*; 29 225
architecture 5 238
ceramics 5 255, 263
Kyaik-pun 5 241
palaces 5 235
sculpture 5 240
Shwe-gu-gyi 5 241
Shwe-maw-daw 5 234, 240
tiles 5 254
Peham, Barthel see BEHAM, BARTHEL
Peham, Georg see PECHAM, GEORG
Peham, Sebald see BEHAM, SEBALD
Pehem, Hans see BEHEIM, HANS (1455/60-1538)
Pehlevi script see under SCRIPTS → types
Pehowa 15 484
Pehrson, Karl-Axel Ingemar 7 699; 30 81
Pei, I(eoh) M(ing) 14 803; 22 367; 24 132, 325–6*
architecture 7 429
city halls 8 470
concert halls 1 126; 7 688; 8 470
hotels 14 788
museums 22 365, 367, 368; 24 325; 32 888
office buildings 22 36
pyramids 11 528, 660; 12 794; 24 163; 25 766, 767; 27 131
skyscrapers 8 470; 10 417; 11 347; 12 794; 14 203, 720, 721; 28 834
space-frames 29 250
urban planning 5 562; 7 429; 12 381
collaboration 1 184; 31 176
groups and movements 10 98
staff 14 325; 19 288; 31 792
teachers 4 762
Pei-ching see BEIJING
Peichl, Gustav 2 831; 24 326–7*
works 2 789; 11 735; 24 327; 32 439
Peierlin see BEIERLEIN
Peignot see under TYPE-FACES
Peignot, G., & Frères 2 733; 13 318
P'ei Hsiao-yüan see PEI XIAOYUAN
P'ei Hsiu see PEI XIU
Pei I-yüan see BEI YIYUAN
Peikon 13 484
Peile, Gen. 1 648
Peiligang-Cishan culture 7 159
Peill & Putzler 32 757
Peinado, Joaquín 29 286
Peiner, Werner 22 711
peineta chairs see under CHAIRS → types
Peintner, Johann 23 339
Peinture/Cahiers Théoriques 24 429, 442; 30 6
peinture à la colle see PAINTS → types → distemper
Peiraeus 13 363, 372, 401; 24 327–9*; 26 908
architecture 13 409; 24 327–8*
Arsenal of Philon 13 381, 394, 407; 30 903
harbour 9 58
limestone 13 387
measurements 13 411
mosaics 13 560
sculpture 13 438; 24 328, 328–9*; 32 527
bronze 13 448, 460, 460; 24 328–9
cult statues 8 262; 18 409
relief 22 733
shipwreck 26 854
town walls 21 556
urban planning 13 419, 420; 14 564
Peiraeus Athena 13 460, 460
Peiraikos 12 287; 13 547; 24 329*; 29 665
Peirce, Charles Sanders 28 396–7*; 30 163
Peirce, William, P. 24 622
watercolours 24 621
Peire, Luc 3 565; 17 518; 24 329*
Peiresc, Henri Fabri de 12 266
Peiresc, Nicolas-Claude Fabri de 11 356; 24 329–30*, 571
drawings 25 833
illustrated writings 6 396
Peiresc, Nicolas-Claude Fabri de— cont.
manuscripts 8 38; 9 603
paintings 11 115
collections 11 661, 665
sponsorship 18 76
Peisianix 25 176
Peisistratos 2 674, 683, 688; 13 373; 19 312; 24 331*
Peisley, Bartholomew 31 234
Peisser, Hans 18 575; 20 799; 23 309; 24 331–2*
works 8 384; 23 309; 25 21; 32 608
Peithner von Lichtenfels, Eduard 3 821
Pei Xiaoyuan 6 631
Pei Xiu (224-71 AD) 20 361
Pei Xiu (fl c. 855 AD) 6 748
Peixotto, E. C. 33 132
Pejë 1 543
Pejeng 15 754
drums (musical instruments) 15 816; 29 229, 229
Pek, J(an) E(rnst) van der 17 910; 24 332*
Pekalongan 15 790, 791, 792
Pekan see TAIWAN
Pekárna 8 374; 24 332–3*; 25 470, 471, 492
Pekhsukher 9 860
Peking see BEIJING
Peking Opera 7 136
costumes 7 137
stage 7 136
Peking stitch see under STITCHES
Pēkšēns, Konstantīns 18 853, 854; 24 333*; 26 383
Pektin, Bekir 31 454
PEL 3 814; 6 391; 7 483; 10 284, 299
Pela, il see LAMBERTI, NICCOLÒ DI PIERO
Pelacani, Biagio 23 753
Péladan, Joséphin 8 701; 24 333–4*; 27 639
groups and movements 3 564; 28 423; 30 169
illustrated works 27 140, 141
Peláez (del Casal), Amelia 8 233; 18 834; 24 334*
works 8 236, 236; 18 835
Peláez, Antonio 24 334*
Peláez, Diego, Bishop 27 793
Pelagi, Pelagio 4 277
Pelagius I, Pope (reg 556-61) 1 764
Pelagius II, Pope (reg 579-90) 26 799
Pelagonnesou-Alonnesou 9 633
Pelayo, Bishop 26 676
Pelayo, Marcelino Menéndez y see MENÉNDEZ Y PELAYO, MARCELINO
Pelbart, Oswald 33 354
Pełcznica altarpiece 25 110
Pelegrinus 26 622; 32 343
Pelekita 8 153
Peleliu see BELILIOU
Pelende 33 482
Pélerin, Jean 24 334–5*, 488; 25 405; 31 299
Peleş Castle 26 718, 722, 725
Peleset see PHILISTINE
Peleus Painter 13 522; 32 64
Pelham (family) 14 599; 33 444
Pelham, Charles, 4th Earl of Yarborough 4 157
Pelham, Henry, 4th Duke of Newcastle 28 873
Pelham, James 33 158
Pelham, Peter 7 809; 21 416; 24 335*; 28 870
works 4 477
Pelham-Clinton-Hope, Henry, 8th Duke of Newcastle 2 560
Pelham Gold Cup 33 158

Pelham-Holles, Thomas, Marquess of Clare and 1st Duke of Newcastle 4 805; 7 374; 31 860
Pelican History of Art 4 24; 10 377
Pelican Press 22 117
pelikai 13 475, *475*, 478, 518, *524*; 24 335*
Pelikai Painter 13 534
Pelikan, Franz Anton 8 410
Pelikan inks 28 197
Pélissier, Pierre 19 382
Pelizeus, Wilhelm 10 90, 93
Pell, F. Livingston 7 838
Pella(i) (Jordan) 17 655; 24 335–6*; 30 *180*
 Husn, Tell 24 336
 metalwork 16 369
 pottery 16 396
 stelae 29 613
 stele 24 *335*
Pella (ii) (Macedonia) 13 *362*, *363*; 19 880; 24 337–8*
 agora 24 337
 houses 13 383, 407; 23 808; 24 337–8
  House I1 13 557, 559, 560, 562, 564, *564*; 24 *337*, 337–8
   mosaics 13 564–5; 24 338
  House I5 13 557, 559, 560, 562, *563*, 564
   mosaics 13 564–5; 24 338
  House of Dionysus *see* House I1
  House of Helen *see* House I5
 mosaics 2 348; 12 826; 13 383, 545, 556, 557, 559, 561, 563, 565; 22 155, 159; 24 337, 338*
 palace 13 561
Pella (Russia) 27 376
Pellan, Alfred 22 39; 24 338*
 groups and movements 11 302, 550; 25 635; 27 639; 31 146
 works 5 568; 22 335
Pellar, Hans 11 464
Pellatt, Apsley, I (*fl c.*1790) 19 595
Pellatt, Apsley, II (1791-1863) 10 319; 19 595; 24 57
 works 10 *319*; 12 *783*
Pellatt, Henry 19 158
Pellechet, Jules 4 600
Pellegrini, Aldo 2 400, 525, 546
Pellegrini, Angelo 26 810
Pellegrini, Carlo 3 834; 19 484; 24 339*; 26 810
Pellegrini, Carlos Enrique 2 395, 399; 24 339*
Pellegrini, Giovanni Antonio 14 584; 16 676; 24 339–42*; 32 195
 groups and movements 10 372
 patrons and collectors 2 559; 4 609; 11 348; 14 807; 21 908; 33 280
 pupils 8 484; 32 615
 works 6 65; 9 223, 242; 10 249, 277; 14 *585*; 19 142; 24 *340*, *341*, 865; 31 858
Pellegrini, Giovanni Battista 15 139
Pellegrini, Girolamo 20 546
Pellegrini, Ignazio 11 213, 214
Pellegrini, Ludovica Antonia 21 533
Pellegrini Chapel, Master of the *see* MICHELE DE FIRENZE
Pellegrino, Francesco 13 700; 27 588
Pellegrino da Pontremoli 33 585
Pellegrino da San Daniele 24 342*
 patrons and collectors 5 432
 pupils 11 219
 works 9 308; 33 356
Pellegrino (di Giovanni) di Antonio 12 302
Pellegrino di Giacomo 26 399
Pellegrino di Mariano 6 4
Pelleluhu 24 82
Pellens, E. 9 196
Peller, Martin 17 711; 33 294
Pellerano, Soucy de 9 118
Pellerin (*fl* mid-18th cent.) 3 288
Pellerin (family; *fl* 1850-70) 15 142
Pellerin (*c.* 1890-1910) 31 258, 263
Pellerin, Auguste 6 375; 22 55
Pellerin, J. 1 210
Pellerin, Jean-Charles 33 360
Pellestrina 32 206
Pellet, Gustave 19 86, 489; 20 603
Pelletan, Edouard 4 365
Pelletier (family) 14 856
Pelletier, Jean 11 426; 14 856; 19 592
Pellew, Charles 31 659
Pellezuoli, Donato Buoni de *see* BUONI DE PELLEZUOLI, DONATO
Pelli, Cesar 14 803; 24 342–3*
 collaboration 1 149
 works 10 417; 12 794; 14 203; 19 578; 23 43; 24 *343*; 25 *656*; 28 834
Pelli, Domenico 14 369
Pelli, Giuseppe Bencivenni *see* BENCIVENNI PELLI, GIUSEPPE
Pelliccia, Bartolomeo 18 586
Pellicciaio, Giacomo di Mino del *see* GIACOMO DI MINO DEL PELLICCIAIO
pellicea *see* CASSOCKS
Pellicer, Alexandre Cirici *see* CIRICI PELLICER, ALEXANDRE
Pellicer, Carlos 21 396
Pellicioli, Mauro 24 343*
Pelling-Gill, Harry 25 560
Pellini, Eros 21 533
Pellini, Eugenio 16 706
Pellini, Luigi 27 788
Pelliot, Paul 6 320, 772; 7 159; 9 394; 18 494; 24 343–4*; 30 848; 31 422
 collections 6 299, 321; 7 118, 155
 personal collection 6 321
Pellipario, Nicolò 6 18; 11 268; 31 747
Pellizza da Volpedo, Giuseppe 16 678; 24 344–6*
 exhibitions 24 708
 teachers 3 857
 works 14 589; 16 679; 24 *345*, *346*; 31 446
Pellón, Gina 24 347*
Pelloquin, Jean-François 22 242
Pellworm, Alte Kirche 11 253
Pelo, Bernardo 3 224
Pelo, Ludovico 3 224
Peloro, Giovanni Battista 24 347*, 533
Pelouse, Léon 18 32
Pelplin Abbey 4 783; 13 57; 24 *347*, 347–8*; 25 *92*, 104, 119
 church 25 114
Pelrott-Csara, Vilmos 30 207
Pels, Andries 18 651
Pelsaert, Francisco 21 717
Pelseneer, Guillaume 3 585
Pelsers, Joest *see* VREDIS, JUDOCUS
Peltant, Charles 19 396
Peltenburg, E. J. 19 131
pelts 24 106
Peltzer, Zacharias 19 93; 25 435, 436
Pelucca, Paolo 13 293
Peluffo, Martha 2 401; 24 348*
Peluffo, Valero 4 315
Péluse, Gaspard Monge, Comte de *see* MONGE, GASPARD, Comte de Péluse
Pelusium 9 848
Pelz, Paul Johannes 19 346; 28 888
Pematang 15 787
Pematang Purba 21 595
Pemba 30 300
Pemba, George (Mnyaluza) 29 109
Pemba Island 1 *407*
Pemberton, Jane *see* SMALL, JANE
Pemberton, John E. 10 421
Pemberton, Samuel 10 335
Pemberton, Sophie 5 566
Pembroke 32 *780*
Pembroke, Aymer de Valence, Earl of *see* VALENCE, AYMER DE, Earl of Pembroke
Pembroke, (Marie de St Pol,) Countess of 5 511; 24 348*
Pembroke, Henry Herbert, 9th Earl of *see* HERBERT, HENRY, 9th Earl of Pembroke
Pembroke, Philip Herbert, 4th Earl of *see* HERBERT, PHILIP, 4th Earl of Pembroke
Pembroke, Philip Herbert, 5th Earl of *see* HERBERT, PHILIP, 5th Earl of Pembroke
Pembroke, Thomas Herbert, 8th Earl of *see* HERBERT, THOMAS, 8th Earl of Pembroke
Pembroke, William Herbert, 3rd Earl of *see* HERBERT, WILLIAM, 3rd Earl of Pembroke
Pembroke Castle 3 209; 6 54; 12 173
 Horseshoe Gate *see* Inner Gate
 Inner Gate 12 174
Pembroke tables *see under* TABLES → types
Pemdje *see* OXYRHYNCHUS
Pemon 13 874
Pemzashen 2 434
Pen, Semyen 2 893; 3 88; 17 872
Pen, Yury (Moiseyevich) 24 350*; 32 412
 pupils 2 903; 6 383
 works 3 529
Pen, Yury, Museum *see under* VICIEBSK
Pena, Antonio 31 755
Peña, Arnau de la *see* ARNAU DE LA PEÑA
Peña, Eduardo Cano de la *see* CANO DE LA PEÑA, EDUARDO
Peña, Eugenio 7 609
Peña, Gaspar de la 10 498; 24 350–51*
Peña, Juan Antonio de la 2 868
Peña, Juan Bautista de la 20 67; 24 351*
Peña, Manuel Francisco Alvarez de la *see* ALVAREZ DE LA PEÑA, MANUEL FRANCISCO
Peña, Pedro de la 24 350; 29 637; 31 171
Peña, Tonita (María Antonia) 22 594; 24 351*; 32 122
Peña, Umberto 8 234
Peña, Virgilio Narcisso Diaz de la *see* DIAZ DE LA PEÑA, VIRGILIO NARCISSO
Penaat, Willem 4 73; 21 362; 22 867, 875, 883; 24 351*
 groups and movements 22 868, 875; 33 323
Penacchi da Treviso, Girolamo 33 356
Peña Defillo, Fernando 9 117
Peña de Toro 29 270
Penadura, Cristoforo *see* BONADURA, CRISTOFORO
Peñafiel, Antonio 33 472
Peñaflor (family) 9 699
Peña Ganchegui, Luis 3 217
Penalba, Alicia 3 462; 24 352*; 30 329, 330
Peñalba, Rodrigo 23 81, 85; 24 352*
 patrons and collectors 23 84
 pupils 13 830; 25 455
Peñaloza, José Antonio 32 173
Peñaloza, Pedro de 4 257; 29 893
Penalva, Marquis of 8 221
Penalva, Gastão 4 725
Peña Montoya, Nicolasa 20 498
Penan 5 11; 20 182
Pen and Ink Group MSS 20 682
Penang 20 *162*, 169; 21 575; 29 *225*
 Cathedral of the Assumption 20 168
 Civil Service buildings 20 168
 St George's 20 168
 State Museum 29 240
 University of Science of Malaysia 20 184
penannular brooches *see under* BROOCHES → types
Peñaranda, Gaspar de Bracamonte y Guzmán, 3rd Conde de 4 619*; 28 479; 29 353
Peñaranda de Duero, Palacio de los Condes de Miranda 22 256; 29 299
Peñarrubia 29 364
Penarth (S. Glams), St Augustine's 32 783
Peñas, Sabino de Medina y *see* MEDINA Y PEÑAS, SABINO DE
Penataran *see* PANATARAN
penboxes *see under* BOXES → types
Pencaitland (Lothian), Winton House 32 799
Pencarrow (Cornwall), Music Room 23 790
Penchaud, Antoine-Xavier 24 353
Penchaud, Michel-Robert 8 18; 24 352–3*
Penchaud, Robert 24 352
Penchester, Stephen of *see* STEPHEN OF PENCHESTER
Pencil Points *see* PROGRESSIVE ARCHITECTURE
pencils 5 33; 8 128, 129; 24 353–4*
 see also BRUSHES; CRAYONS; DRAWINGS
Penck, A. R. 24 354–5*
 collaboration 15 147
 groups and movements 25 360
 works 12 397, 408; 29 98; 33 364
Pencz, Georg 2 716; 10 385; 20 799; 24 355–6*
 collaboration 3 69; 18 574
 groups and movements 19 501
 patrons and collectors 16 866; 33 275
 reproductive prints by others 1 592
 restorations by others 17 711
 works 12 386, 815; 19 813; 23 308; 24 *355*; 25 126; 27 256; 33 354
pendants (i) (roofs) 24 356*
pendants (ii) (pairs of works) 11 226; 24 357*, *357*
pendants (jewellery) 17 518, 519, 520, 521, 522; 21 243
 historical and regional traditions
  Aboriginal Australia 1 52
  Africa 1 367
  Ancient Near East 1 855, 877
  Anglo-Saxon 10 322
  Antilles, Lesser 5 747
  Baule 3 *409*
  Belgium 3 *605*
  Byzantine 9 645, *659*, *663*
  Canaanite 30 186
  Caribbean Islands 5 748
  Central Asia, Western 6 *274*
  China 7 2, *2*, *5*, 76, 103, *104*, *107*, 111
  Coclé culture 29 *151*
  Colombia 28 *781*; 30 *240*
  Costa Rica 29 154, *154*
  Crete 21 687, *687*
  Cyprus, ancient 8 328, 338, 352
  Early Christian (*c.* AD 250-843) 9 645, *659*
  Egypt 17 III1
  Egypt, ancient 10 29
  England 10 *345*
   Anglo-Saxon 10 322
   Gothic 13 170
   16th cent. 17 522
   19th cent. 17 *528*
pendants (jewellery)
 historical and regional traditions—cont.
  Etruscan 10 *635*
  Germany 12 *455*; 17 *521*
  Gothic 13 170
  Gran Chiriquí culture 13 *291*
  Gran Nicoya culture 13 311, *312*
  Greece, ancient 13 *600*, 601–2
  Helladic 14 *357*
  Huastec 21 260
  Hungary 15 10, *10*
  Indian subcontinent 15 736
  Islamic 17 III1
  Italy 10 *635*
  Kazakhstan 17 *868*
  Luba 1 350; 19 743–4*
  Maori 23 720
  Marquesas Islands 23 720
  Maya 21 243, 247
  Mesoamerica, Pre-Columbian 21 241
   Huastec 21 260
   Maya 21 243, 247
   Mixtec 21 243
   Olmec 21 242
   Toltec 21 243, 260
  Mesopotamia 1 855
  Minoan 21 687, *687*
  Mongolia 21 878
  Native North Americans 22 614
  Nigeria 15 *118*
  Olmec 21 242
  Pacific Islands 23 720
  Panama 29 *151*
  Pende 1 350
  Prehistoric art 25 472, 473, 489, 545, 546
  Puerto Rico 29 *199*
  Punic 25 735, *735*
  Russia 10 *721*; 27 *423*
  Saladoid culture 29 *199*
  Scotland 28 *263*
  Sinú 28 *781*
  South America, Pre-Columbian 29 154, *154*
   Colombia 28 *781*; 30 *240*
   Costa Rica 29 154
   Gran Chiriquí culture 13 *291*
   Gran Nicoya culture 13 *312*
   Panama 29 *151*
   Puerto Rico 29 *199*
   Sinú 28 *781*
   Tairona 29 155, 217; 30 *240*
  Syria-Palestine 30 186
  Tairona 29 155, 217; 30 *240*
  Toltec 21 243, 260
  Vietnam 32 487
 materials
  amethyst 17 *528*
  bone 21 247
  bronze 10 *635*; 13 *600*, 601; 15 *118*; 25 546
  cameos 10 *345*
  chrysolite 17 *528*
  clay 25 546
  diamonds 3 *605*; 10 *345*
  enamel 10 *194*; 11 *307*; 13 170; 15 10, *10*; 17 III1
  faience (i) (glass) 1 877
  figurines 25 489
  glass 9 645
  gold 11 *307*
   Baule 3 *409*
   Byzantine 9 *663*
   Central Asia, Western 6 *274*
   China 7 111
   Early Christian (*c.* AD 250-843) 9 *659*
   England 10 *345*
   Helladic 14 *357*
   Hungary 15 *10*
   Indian subcontinent 15 736
   Islamic 17 III1
   Minoan 21 *687*
   Scotland 28 *263*
   Sinú 28 *781*

pendants (jewellery)
materials
gold—cont.
South America, Pre-Columbian **13** *291*; **29** *151*
hardstones **29** 154
ivory **7** 103, *104*
jade **7** 2, *2*, *5*, 76, *107*, 111; **13** 311, *312*; **29** *154*, *199*
mother-of-pearl **27** *423*
onyx **10** *345*
pearls **10** *345*; **27** *423*
picrolite **8** 328
rock crystal **6** *274*
rubies **10** *345*
serpentine **29** *199*
shells **1** 52; **21** 260; **29** 217
silver **3** *605*; **12** *455*; **17** *868*; **22** 614; **27** *423*
silver-gilt **25** *735*
turquoise **27** *423*
techniques
filigree **27** *423*
pendant vaults *see under* VAULTS (CEILING) → types
Pende **18** 484; **24** 357–60*
architecture **1** 406
chairs **1** 366
divination instruments **1** 357
figurines **1** 273
gesture **1** 266
iconography **1** 261
ivory **24** 359–60
masks **1** 256, 290, 333, 405; **24** *358*, 358–9*
pendants (jewellery) **1** 350
raffia **24** *358*
sculpture **1** 403
staffs **24** 360
whistles **24** 359–60
wood **24** *358*
wood-carvings **24** *359*, 360
Pendennis (Cornwall) **21** 568
Castle **21** 550, 568
pendentives **9** 85; **16** 142; **24** 360*
see also SPANDRELS
pendentive vaults *see* VAULTS (CEILING) → types → sail
Pendergast, David M. **1** 735; **18** 666
Pendlebury, John D. S. **10** 81; **17** 824; **18** 165
Pendleton, William S. & John **8** 276; **18** 726
pendulum clocks *see under* CLOCKS → types
Pendzhikent **6** *182*, 199, 209, 210, *210*; **24** 360–62*; **28** *719*; **30** 251, *252*
architecture **32** 320
Blue Hall **6** *230*; **24** 362
earrings **6** 238
fortifications **21** 591
glass **6** 267, 268
houses **6** 200
jewellery **6** 273
ossuaries **23** 609
paintings **6** 230; **28** 722
wall **6** 193, 228–30, 244, 248; **11** 145; **16** 252
palace **6** 200, 230; **32** 321
pottery **6** 255
Room 28, Sector XXV **6** *200*
Roudaki Abuabdullo Republican Historical Regional Museum **6** 283
sculpture **6** 219, 220, *220*
temples **6** 200; **30** 440
Temple I **24** 360–61, *361*; **30** 441
reliefs **6** 219
Temple II **24** 360–61, *361*; **30** 440, 441
reliefs **6** 219
wall paintings **6** 228
terracottas **6** 275, 276
wood-carvings **6** 277
Pène du Bois, Guy **1** 773; **4** 93; **24** 362*, 432
Penekkale Cathedral *see* BANA CATHEDRAL
Penelope Painter **13** 523
Peñeranda, Conde de **4** 381
Peney, Antoine **13** 126
Penfield, Edward **4** 367; **25** 347
Pengcheng **6** 913
P'eng Chun-pao *see* PENG ZHUNBAO
Peng Daya **21** 885
Penghu Liedao *see* PESCADORES ISLANDS
Pengkalan Bujang **16** 519; **20** 163
Pengshan **6** 700
P'eng Ta-ya *see* PENG DAYA
Penguin Books **4** 369; **13** 811; **31** 396, 498
Pengxi, Baofan Temple **6** 779
Peng xian **6** 843
Peng Zhunbao **7** 16
Peniarth 22 manuscript **32** 788
Pénicaud (family) **10** 195; **19** 396
Pénicaud, Jean (i) (*c.* 1490-after 1543) **24** 362
Pénicaud, Jean (ii) (*c.* 1515-*c.* 1588) **24** 362*
Pénicaud, Jean (iii) (*fl c.* 1650-1570) **24** 362
Pénicaud, Nardon **10** 195; **19** 396; **24** 362*
Pénicaud, Pierre **24** 362
Peniche **25** 317
Penicuik, James Clerk, 3rd Baronet of *see* CLERK, JAMES, 3rd Baronet of Penicuik
Penicuik, John Clerk, 1st Baronet of *see* CLERK, JOHN, 1st Baronet of Penicuik
Penicuik, John Clerk, 2nd Baronet of *see* CLERK, JOHN, 2nd Baronet of Penicuik
Penicuik House (Lothian) **28** 227, 269
dovecot **9** 202
drawings **7** 418
gardens **12** 128, *129*
Hall of Ossian **7** 418
paintings **1** 488; **7** 418; **15** 148; **21** 34; **27** 333
Penicuik Jewels **28** 263
Penicuik Locket **28** 263
Penig Church **12** 461
Peninsula *keris* *see under* KERIS → types
Penkill Castle (Strathclyde) **28** 249, 276–7
Penkov, Ivan **32** 78
Penley, Aaron **18** 61; **23** 57
Penmaen Castle (W. Glam) **6** 53; **12** 173
Penman, James
works **28** *261*
Penmon Priory (Anglesey) **26** 617; **32** 781
cross **32** 786
Penn, Irving **24** 363*
Penn, John (1729-95) **1** 184; **10** 849; **14** 492
Penn, John (1760-1834) **8** 588; **10** 806
Penn, Thomas **14** 492
Penn, William (1644-1718) **11** 785; **24** 596
Penn, William (*fl* 1800) **10** 753
Penna, Agostino **25** 322
Penna, Cesare **19** 28
works **19** *28*
Pennacchi, Girolamo di Giovanni *see* GIROLAMO DI GIOVANNI PENNACCHI
Pennacchi, Pier Maria **3** 667; **5** 688; **24** 363*
Pennafreita, Pedro de *see* PEDRO DE PENNAFREITA
Pennant, George Day Hawkins **6** 61; **23** 210; **32** 784
Pennant Melangell (Powys), St Melangell **26** 612
shrine of St Monacella **26** 617; **32** 781
Penne, Olivier **29** 306
Penne de Castillo, María Luisa **25** 701
Pennefather River **1** 44
Pennell, Joseph **24** 363–4*; **29** 245
collaboration **20** 604
groups and movements **19** 492; **25** 629
works **4** 365; **9** 309; **15** 830; **19** 488
Pennelli, Enrico **10** 639
Pennelli, Pietro **10** 639
Pennethorne, James **22** 528; **24** 364–5*
patrons and collectors **4** 170; **14** 148
teachers **25** 710
works **7** 667; **8** 249; **19** 575; **22** 528
Pennethorne, John **23** 490; **24** 368
Penni, Giovan Francesco **24** 365*; **29** 853
collaboration **6** 583; **7** 560; **25** 902, 908; **26** 818
patrons and collectors **21** 17
works **3** 858; **6** 139; **21** 17; **24** *365*; **26** 818
Penni, Lorenzo **4** 616; **11** 264; **24** 366
Penni, Luca **24** 365–6*, 419
groups and movements **11** 264, 265
patrons and collectors **8** 856; **18** 579
reproductive prints by others **12** 558; **21** 499; **27** 212
pennies *see under* COINS → types
Penniman, John Ritto **11** 138; **28** 525
Pennino, Leonardo **16** 705
pennons **6** 305; **11** 148; **12** 272; **14** 408
Pennsylvania Railroad Company **19** 538
Pennut **23** 280
Penny, Edward **10** 372; **24** 366–7*
pupils **4** 46
reproductive prints by others **14** 803
works **7** 786, 787; **12** 293; **24** *366*
Penny, Thomas **33** 146
Penny Black **25** 328, *329*
Penobscot **22** 673
Peñol de Juchipila **21** *193*, *372*; **24** 367*
Peñón del Río **24** 367–8*; **29** *136*
Penone, Giuseppe **2** 527; **24** 368*
Penraat, Jaap J. **22** 869
Penrhyn *see* TONGAREVA
Penrhyn, Edward Gordon Douglas, Lord *see* DOUGLAS, EDWARD GORDON, Lord Penrhyn
Penrhyn Castle (Gwynedd) **6** 61; **23** 210, *210*; **32** 784
paintings **4** 595; **23** 876; **26** 169
wallpaper **32** 818
Penrice, Thomas **4** 330
Penrice Villa (Penrhys) **32** 782
Penrose, Elizabeth *see* MILLER, LEE
Penrose, F(rancis) C(ranmer) **7** 502; **13** 393; **24** 368*
works **23** 490; **25** 402
Penrose, George **32** 903
Penrose, Roland **5** 531; **21** 607; **24** 368–9*
collections **10** 367
groups and movements **10** 257; **19** 591; **30** 22
writings **10** 268
Penrose, William **32** 903
pens **24** 348–50*
historical and regional traditions
Central Asia, Eastern **6** 307
pens
historical and regional traditions—cont.
Egypt, ancient **10** *4*, 5; **24** 348
Islamic **16** 276; **24** 348
Rome, ancient **24** 348
materials
bone **4** *314*
feathers **24** 349
felt **24** 350
gold **24** 349
metal **24** 349–50*
nylon **24** 350
quills **4** 343; **9** 216; **24** 348, 349*; **28** 303–4
reeds **9** 216; **10** *4*; **16** 276; **24** 348–9*; **28** 303
rushes **10** 5
silver **24** 349
steel **24** 350
types
ballpoints *see* biros
biros **24** 350
felt-tip *see* fibre-tip
fibre-tip **24** 350
fountain **24** 350
mapping **24** 350
reservoir **24** 350
uses
calligraphy **24** 348, 349
drawings **9** 216; **15** 855; **24** 348, 349, 350
painting **10** 5
scripts **24** 348
sketches **24** 350
underdrawings **24** 350
writing **10** *4*, 5; **15** 850, 853; **24** 348, 349; **28** 303–4
Pensée, Charles
works **23** *509*
pensée, première *see* PENSIERO, PRIMO
Penseurs, Les *see* PRIMITIFS, LES
Penshurst Place (Kent) **8** 42; **10** 227, 275; **18** 685; **23** 398; **28** 301, *301*
furniture **10** 287
hall **14** 76
Leicester Square cottages **8** *830*
metalwork **20** 217
paintings **10** 159; **19** 121
pensiero, primo **24** 369*
see also DRAWINGS; SKETCHES
Pensionante del Saraceni **24** 369*; **27** 817
Penson, Thomas (1790-1859) **23** 211
Penson, Thomas Mainwaring (1818-64) **6** 561
pentagonal beaked towers *see under* BASTIONS → types
pentagonal forts *see under* FORTS → types
Pentagon Process **21** 390
Pentagram **25** 354
pentagraphs *see* PANTOGRAPHS
pentaptychs *see under* ALTARPIECES → types
pentastyle **24** 370*
Pentateuch Master **26** 667
Penteado, Yolanda **4** 727
Pentecost **31** 890, 891, 892
Pentecost Plaque **26** 693
Pentelic marble *see under* MARBLE → types
Pentenrieder, Johann Martin **2** 715
Penther, Johann Friedrich **30** 676; **31** 298
Penthesilea Painter **13** 523, 535, 550
Penthièvre, Louis de Bourbon, Duc de **11** 592; **25** 872
Pentik **11** 106
Pentima, Tancredi da *see* TANCREDI DA PENTIMA
pentiments **24** 370*
Pentney Hoard **2** 80; **10** 322
Penton, Henry **19** 572
Pentre Bach, Capel Bilidu **32** *783*
Penttilä, Timo **24** 370*
works **14** *372*
Pentz, Georg *see* PENCZ, GEORG
Penukonda **15** 539
Rama Temple **15** 539
Shiva Temple **15** 329, 539
Penz, Franz de Paula **2** 783; **24** 370*
Penza, Regional Museum **27** 440
People's Art Guild **17** 578
peori *see under* PIGMENTS → types
Peparelli, Francesco **10** 525; **24** 371*; **27** 194
Pepe, Mario **2** 517
Pepers, Pieter, I (1730-85) **3** 571; **24** 371*
Pepers, Pieter, II (1761-94) **24** 371
Pepersack, Daniel **26** 113
Pepijn, Marten **5** 352
Pepin I, King of Aquitaine (*reg* 817-38) **7** 718
Pepin, Claude **11** 410
Pépin, Joseph **25** 817
Pepin, M. **8** 69
Pépin de Huy, Jean *see* JEAN PÉPIN DE HUY
Pepin Reliquary **5** 806, 808; **7** 720; **11** 613
Pepin the Short, King (*reg* 751-68) **27** 549
architecture **5** 793; **6** 482; **27** 539
coins **7** 534
doors **9** 153
textiles **9** 666
Pepler, Hilary **12** 631
Peploe, S(amuel) J(ohn) **9** 725; **24** 371–2*; **28** 238, 289, 290
peploi **9** 246, 247, 248, 254
Peplos Kore **29** VIII1
Pepo, Benciviene di *see* CIMABUE
Pepo, Cenni di *see* CIMABUE
Pepoli, Alessandro, Conte **24** 372
Pepoli, Cornelio, Conte **24** 372
Pepoli, Ercole, Conte **8** 141, 159; **24** 372
Pepoli, Giacomo **24** 372
Pepoli, Giovanni **24** 372
Pepoli, Sicinio, Conte **24** 372
Pepoli, Taddeo **5** 653; **24** 372
pepper **7** 115
Pepper, Beverly **24** 372*
Pepper, Thomas **10** 348
Pepy I (*reg c.* 2289-*c.* 2256 BC) **9** *776*
architecture **9** 829, 830; **10** 80, 81; **27** 812; **30** 433
sculpture
bronze **4** 851
copper **9** 855, 870; **10** 35, *35*; **14** 514
schist **9** 869
slate **9** 860
statuettes **10** 91
Pepy II (*reg c.* 2246-*c.* 2150 BC) **9** *776*
architecture **10** 76, 80; **25** 763, *763*; **27** 812
reliefs **9** 871, 877
sculpture **9** 859, 869; **10** 91
stelae **22** 398
Pepyankh **21** 61
Pepyn, Katherine **24** 372
Pepyn, Maarten **3** 559; **24** 372–3*
Pepys, Elizabeth **4** 884
Pepys, Samuel **24** 373*; **25** *280*
personal collection **8** 495; **10** 329, 420, 657, 658; **11** 423; **15** 723; **25** 631
works **4** 373; **14** 268; **19** 5; **25** 280
Pepysian Model Book (Cambridge, Magdalene Coll., Pepys MS. 1916) **11** 421; **24** 269, *270*
Péquart, Marthe **20** 542
Péquart, Saint-Juste **20** 542
Pequeñas Monografías del Arte **26** 314

Peracca, Giovanni Antonio 4 405; 29 559
Perachora 13 *363*; 24 373–4*
cisterns 7 354
ex-votos 13 376
fibulae 10 591
Harbour Stoa 13 406
hestiatoria 13 417
ivory-carvings 13 596
models 24 *374*
Sanctuary of Hera 13 371; 24 373–4
altar 1 691, 692
bronze 13 441
seals 13 595
Pera Chorio, Church of the Holy Apostles 8 358, 359
Peradeninuvara 29 450
Peral, Andrés de 25 *286*
Peral, Torcuato Ruiz del *see* RUIZ DEL PERAL, TORCUATO
Perales, María Elena 25 702
Peralta (family) 23 841
Peralta, Ramín 24 622
Peralta, Tole 6 601
Peralta Ramos, Federico 2 397
Peramore di Bartolomeo 11 382
Peranda, Sante 10 525; 20 83; 25 227
Perast 22 *17*
Municipal Museum 22 19
Perate, Vicente 29 337
Perati 13 *363*; 14 353; 24 374–5*
Pérau, G.
works 24 *164*
Peraza, Nilda 18 833
Perazancas 26 609
Per-Bastet *see* BUBASTIS
Percaccino *see* PROCACCINI
Perce, Moses 19 75
perception 24 375–85*, *376*, *378*, *379*, *380*, *382*, *384*, 742; 26 61, 62, 223–4
Perceptismo 2 400; 24 386*
Perceval, John (*fl* 1712) 18 31
Perceval, John (de Burgh) (*b* 1923) 4 606; 24 386–7*
groups and movements 2 161, 750
works 2 749, 760–61, *761*
Percier(-Bassant), Charles 11 256, 257–8, 523; 12 731; 24 387–9*; 25 193
architecture
architectural decorations 29 834
façades 11 519; 24 123, *123*
galleries (art) 24 163
libraries 11 *257*; 25 408
palaces 11 258; 33 217
urban planning 26 743
assistants 26 268
book illustrations 4 361; 8 867
collaboration 8 593; 9 12; 19 251; 21 411; 22 47; 23 544; 28 732; 31 351
decorative works 4 42
drawings 27 545, 548, 549
furniture 3 485; 6 390; 11 261, 597; 24 *389*; 29 315, 318
groups and movements 10 97, 186; 13 201; 22 734, 740; 26 189
interior decoration 1 110; 6 390; 11 579; 13 702; 24 317; 29 305, *305*
marquetry 20 468
metalwork 11 305, 621
patrons and collectors 4 301, 302, 306, 565; 25 364; 27 536
porcelain 28 523
pupils
Abadie, Paul, the elder (1783-1868) 1 13
Bourla, Pierre (Bruno) 4 586
Debret, François 8 592
Destailleur, François-Hippolyte 8 816
Duc, (Joseph-)Louis 9 336
Gärtner, Friedrich von 12 167
Percier(-Bassant), Charles
pupils—cont.
Gisors, Alphonse (-Henry) de 12 746
Grandjean de Montigny, Auguste-Henri-Victor 13 295
Hetsch, G(ustav) F(riedrich) 14 497
Hittorff, Jacques-Ignace 14 592
Lebas, Louis-Hippolyte 19 11
Leclère, (Achille-) François-René 19 35
Lesueur, Jean-Baptiste-Cicéron 19 250
Letarouilly, Paul-Marie 19 251
Lusson, Adrien-Louis 19 812
Mazois, Charles-François 20 901
Penchaud, Michel-Robert 24 352
Pitloo, Anton Sminck (van) 24 892
Renard, Bruno 26 191
Roelandt, Louis Joseph Adrien 26 525
Suys, Tieleman-Frans 30 47
Visconti (ii), Louis-Tullius-Joachim 32 613
Zanth, Ludwig von 33 616
staff 22 25
teachers 24 582; 32 80
writings 2 332; 3 584; 11 520; 23 209; 25 193
Perčinlić, Ljubomir 4 461
Perckhamer Altarpiece 26 105
Perco, Rudolf 32 439
Percy (family) 14 419; 21 549; 33 547
Percy, Algernon, 10th Earl of Northumberland 24 389–90*
dealing 10 363
decorative works 32 402
gems 12 266
paintings 5 554; 12 243; 19 120, 121; 24 389; 29 716
Percy, Algernon, 4th Duke of Northumberland 24 390*
architecture 5 616
collections 10 90, 92
paintings 10 367
sculpture 12 598
Percy, Arthur 30 101
Percy, Henry, 9th Earl of Northumberland 24 389*
Percy, Hugh, 3rd Duke of Northumberland 12 831; 33 145
Percy, Hugh Smithson, 1st Duke of Northumberland *see* SMITHSON (PERCY), HUGH, 1st Duke of Northumberland
Percy, J. 4 683
Percy, Samuel 24 391*
Percy, Thomas 10 421; 24 391*
Percy Folio 24 391
Percy Thomas Partnership 1 126
Perdomo, Michelle 3 623
Pere 1 404; 19 74
Perean, Pura Yeh Gangga 15 767–8
Pereda, Antonio de (*d* 1622) 24 391
Pereda, Antonio de (1611-78) 20 66; 24 391–3*; 29 279, 281
patrons and collectors 4 378; 32 129
pupils 2 376; 6 343
teachers 8 254
works 9 110; 20 71; 24 *392*; 29 340, 667
Pere de Sant Joan 13 106; 23 881
Peredvizhniki *see* WANDERERS
Peregrina pearl 17 523
Peregrino da Cesena 16 750; 23 115, 116; 24 393*
Peregrino da Salerno 3 235; 13 98; 24 393*
Perehudoff, William 5 569
Pereins, Simón 21 383, 404; 24 393*
collaboration 7 689
works 21 *383*
Pereira 7 *601*, 605
Museo Arqueológico 7 612
Pereira (family) 2 829
Pereira, António (i) (1621-57) 24 394*
Pereira, António (ii) (*fl* early 18th cent.) 3 815; 24 394*; 30 881
Pereira, Dolores 31 758
Pereira, Fernandes 25 292
Pereira, João 24 395
Pereira, José Maria, jr 19 468
Pereira, Manuel 24 394–5*; 29 292
patrons and collectors 31 89
works 1 587; 14 658; 20 67
Pereira, Manuel Francisco 10 729
works 25 *311*
Pereira, Nuno Teotónio 24 395*
works 25 294
Pereira, Tomás Romero *see* ROMERO PEREIRA, TOMÁS
Pereira, William 27 731
Pereira Arouca, José 4 710; 23 669
Pereira Campanhã, Caetano 24 395
Pereira Campanhã, Francisco 24 395*; 26 254
Pereira Camponeschi, Maria *see* CAMPONESCHI, MARIA PEREIRA
Pereira Capote, Luís 10 729; 25 311
Pereira da Azevedo, Damião 24 395
Pereira da Costa, Luís 24 395–6*
collaboration 7 521; 26 253; 27 805; 28 732
Pereira da Costa Noronha, Manuel 24 396*; 28 732
Pereira da Magalhães, José Tiburcio 3 535
Pereira da Silva, Oscar 4 708
Pereira da Silva, Teodoro Marques *see* MARQUES PEREIRA DA SILVA, TEODORO
Pereira de Lemos, António Alves *see* ALVES PEREIRA DE LEMOS, ANTÓNIO
Pereira de Melo, Fontes 25 293
Pereira de Melo, Nuno Alvares, Duque de Cadaval *see* CADAVAL, NUNO ALVARES PEREIRA DE MELO, Duque de
Pereira de Sampajo, Manuel 12 762
Pereira dos Santos, João 24 395
Pereira dos Santos, Vitalino 4 722
Pereira Júnor, José Maria 30 882
Pereira Passos, Francisco 26 414
Pereira Pegado, Bernardo 5 903
Péreire (family) 21 69
Péreire, Eugène 4 597
Péreire, Isaac 11 524; 24 396*; 27 591
Péreire, Jacob-Emile 11 524; 14 188; 16 876; 18 869; 24 396*; 27 591
Pereiro de Melo, Florência Leite 22 534
Pere Johan 3 218; 11 482; 13 107; 26 249; 27 818; 29 289; 30 347
Pérelle, Adam 2 853; 6 453; 24 397*; 27 315
works 6 *454*; 12 *121*
Pérelle, Adrien 24 397
Pérelle, Gabriel 2 614; 10 657; 11 358; 14 394; 24 397*; 25 833; 28 742
Pérelle, Nicolas 7 569; 11 358; 24 397*; 27 315; 28 742
Perennius, M. 27 106
Perényi (family) 14 885
Pérényi, Peter 9 754; 14 574
Perera, J. D. A. 29 467
Peresi, Francesco 24 397*
Peresinotti, Antonio 1 598; 27 438
Peresopnitsky Gospels *see under* GOSPEL BOOKS → individual manuscripts
Peressuti, Gino 23 753
Peressutti, Enrico 3 438; 26 536
Péret, Benjamin 8 438, 439; 30 17, 19, 22
Père Tanguy, Le *see* TANGUY, JULIEN-FRANÇOIS
Perete, Pedro 24 475
Pere Terrenchs 1 684
Peretola, S Maria 30 497
Perets, David 23 16
Peretti (family) 11 662
Peretti (-Montalto), Alessandro, Cardinal 8 182; 27 160
Peretti, Camilla 24 397
Peretti, Elsa 30 867; 31 655
Peretti, Felice *see* SIXTUS V, Pope
Peretti (-Montalto), Francesco, Cardinal 18 733; 24 397, 399; 25 563
Peretti, Michele, Prince 24 397, 399
Peretti, Pietro 3 530; 19 497; 29 839
works 19 *496*
Peretti-Montalto, Alessandro, Cardinal 24 399*
architecture 3 56; 24 397; 30 649
paintings 2 493; 13 275; 18 730, 732, 733, *733*; 26 836
sculpture 3 57
Peretu 30 770, 771
Peretyatkovich, Marian (Marianovich) 24 400*; 27 378
collaboration 3 733, 734; 18 658; 26 241
works 22 173
Peretz, David 4 603
Pereyaslav 31 545, *546*, 551
architecture 31 546, 547, 548
Cathedral of St Michael 31 548
Church of the Saviour 31 548
palace 31 548
Pereyaslavl'-Zalessky 27 382
Cathedral of the Transfiguration 27 369
Pereyns, Simón *see* Pereins, Simón
Pérez, Alberto 3 123; 6 598
Pérez, Antonio (*fl* 1404) *see* PERIS, ANTONI
Pérez, Antonio (?1540-1611) 8 237; 24 400*; 29 352
Pérez, Antonio (*fl* 1634) 22 342; 23 410
Pérez, Antonio Gisbert *see* GISBERT PÉREZ, ANTONIO
Pérez, Bartolomé (*fl* 1604) 29 340
Pérez, Bartolomé (1634-93) 2 381; 24 400–401*; 29 668
Pérez, Carlos Andrés 29 89
Pérez, Francisco de Sales *see* SALES PÉREZ, FRANCISCO DE
Pérez, Gonzalo *see* PERIS, GONÇAL
Pérez, Guillo 9 117
Pérez, Irene 18 832
Pérez, Joaquín 29 270
Pérez, José Gestoso y *see* GESTOSO Y PÉREZ, JOSÉ
Pérez, José Luján *see* LUJÁN PÉREZ, JOSÉ
Pérez, José Victoriano Carmelo Carlo González *see* GRIS, JUAN
Pérez, Juan Bautista *see* PETRI, JOHANNES
Pérez, Marta María 8 229
Peréz, Mateo Santander *see* SANTANDER PERÉZ, MATEO
Pérez, Matilde 6 598
Pérez, Pedro 7 612
Pérez, Ramón Atiles y *see* ATILES Y PÉREZ, RAMÓN
Pérez, Régulo 24 401*; 32 176
Perez, Rod Paras *see* PARAS PEREZ, ROD
Pérez, Sebastián Martínez *see* MARTÍNEZ PÉREZ, SEBASTIÁN
Pérez, Silvestre 4 562; 29 272
Perez, Tommaso 22 482
Pérez, Toribio 14 714
Pérez Barradas, Antonio 3 272
Pérez Barradas, Rafael *see* BARRADAS, RAFAEL (PÉREZ)
Pérez Calvillo, Fernando 17 676
Pérez Calvillo, Pedro 17 676
Pérez Castiel, Juan 31 813, 814
Perez d'Aleccio, Matteo 20 213
Pérez de Aguilar, Antonio 21 384
Pérez de Alesio, Adrian 24 401
Pérez de Alesio, Mateo 24 401*
works 3 387; 4 261; 19 385; 24 506; 26 815, 817
Pérez de Arce, Mario 6 594
Pérez de Arroyo, Marcelino 7 605; 25 233
Pérez de Bocanegra, Juan 24 507
Pérez de Holguín, Melchor *see* HOLGUÍN, MELCHOR PÉREZ DE
Pérez de Irazábal, Juan 21 173
Pérez de la Roche, Roger 23 81, 84, 85; 25 455; 29 34
Pérez del Cuadro 2 386; 24 503
Pérez de León, Enrique 13 770
Pérez de Merida, Juan 33 571
Pérez de Montalto, Antonio 29 336; 31 89
Pérez de Moya, Juan 15 83
Perez de Villahoz, Pedro 5 202
Pérez Galdós, Benito 21 81
Pérez González, Antonio 25 354
Pérez-Mínguez, Rafael 13 6
Pérez Mink, Domingo 11 886; 30 22
Pérez Palacio, Augusto 21 380; 24 401–2*
Pérez Palomino, Matías 5 410; 24 503
Pérez Pita, Estanislao 27 784
Pérez Rayón, Reinaldo 21 380
Perez Valle, Francisco 24 402*
Pérez Villaamil, Jenaro 23 627; 24 402–3*; 26 362; 29 284
works 13 *756*; 20 59; 24 *403*; 29 283
Pérez Villalta, Guillermo 13 6
Pérez y Martínez, Silvestre 27 767
Perfetti 4 842
perforators 25 494
performance art 7 685; 8 612; 10 416, 680; 17 805; 22 279, 381; 24 403–9*, 679; 25 645, 647
collections 29 16
regional traditions
Austria 5 *31*
Bolivia 4 264
England 10 258; 24 *408*
Germany 24 *406*
Mexico 21 390
Poland 17 448
Russia 20 886
United States of America 23 397; 31 609
Performing Garage 24 409
perfume burners 9 *520*; 29 *338*
perfume containers 3 442; 7 *60*; 16 799; 24 645
China 7 58
Perg, Wenzel 28 380
Pergamene appliqué ware *see under* POTTERY → wares
Pergamene ware *see* POTTERY → wares → Eastern Sigillata A
Pergamon 9 *512*; 13 *362*, *363*; 16 477; 24 410–16*, *411*; 26 *908*; 31 456
Altar of Zeus *see* Great Altar of Zeus
Archaeological Museum 13 470
architects 13 389
architecture 9 524; 13 404; 26 911
arsenal 13 381

Pergamon—cont.
- Asklepieion **19** 312
- coins **4** *686*; **13** 588, *588*, 589; **27** *98*
- collections **13** 555
- congregational mosque **16** 202
- excavations **13** 606; **14** 655
- figurines **13** 581
- fortifications **9** 524; **21** 558
- gates **7** 358
- Great Altar of Zeus **1** 692; **3** 807; **13** 369, 380, 406, 432, 464, 468, 470, 606; **15** 85; **22** 411; **24** 411, *412*, 415–16*; **26** 135
  - Great Frieze **1** *692*; **13** 426; **22** 514, *514*; **24** 415, *415*
  - Little Frieze **24** 416
- gymnasium **13** 406, 886
- houses **9** 561
- Kızıl Avlu **3** 329
- library **13** 464; **19** 312
- marble **13** 434
- masonry **13** 388; **20** 572
- mosaics **13** 557, 558, *558*, 559, *559*, 560, 561, 567; **22** 160; **24** 411
- Museum **2** 365; **9** 20
- orders (architecture) **23** 484
- Palace IV **13** 567
- palaces **23** 808
- Palace V **13** *558*, 567
  - mosaic **13** *559*
  - tessellated floor **14** 400
- parchment **20** 329; **24** 106
- pottery **13** 540; **27** 106, 107
- Sanctuary of Asklepios **26** 881
- Sanctuary of Demeter **25** 657
- sculpture **13** 423, 430, 462, *463*, 463–4, 469, 470; **23** 291; **24** 413–14*, *414*, *415*, 415–16*; **27** 29
- stadium **29** 488
- stoas **13** 406; **29** 681
- stone **13** 387
- storehouses **13** 407
- temples **13** 405
- terracottas **27** 111
- theatre **24** *413*
- Unswept Room **29** 86

Pergamonmuseum *see under* BERLIN (GERMANY) → museums
Pergaut, Dominique **19** 801
Perge **13** *362*; **24** 416–17*; **26** *908*
- arches **2** 297
- architecture **26** 913
- Basilica A **31** 280
- churches **9** 536
- columns **26** 882
- fortifications **21** 558
- macellum **19** 889

pergolas **5** 344; **12** 62, 110, 112, 115
Pergolesi, Michelangelo **1** 111; **4** 540
Perhtold, Kustos **2** 790
Peri, Jacopo **7** 311
Peri, László **2** 553; **7** 771; **24** 417–18*; **29** 872
Peri, Menahem **26** 65
Peri, Pellegrino **12** 197
periaktoi **30** 657, 659, 662, 667
Periam, George August **24** 418*
periboli *see under* WALLS → types
peribolos tombs *see under* TOMBS → types
Peribsen **9** *776*; **29** 614
Perić, Milan **22** 18
Pericas, Josep Maria **3** 216; **23** 260
Pericles **13** 415; **24** 418*
- architecture **2** 666, 676–8; **13** 368, 374, 394; **21** 556; **23** 349
- sculpture **13** 374, 439

Pericoli, Filippo **26** 779
Pericope books
- individual manuscripts
  - Echternach Pericope Book (Bremen, Staats- & Ubib., MS. b. 21) **9** 698, *698*; **28** 308
  - Pericope Book of Custos Berthold (New York, Pierpont Morgan Lib., MS., M. 780) **23** 655
  - Pericope Book of Henry II (Munich, Bayer. Staatsbib., Clm. 4452) **22** 520; **28** 25
    - book cover **5** 810
  - *see also* GOSPEL BOOKS → individual manuscripts → Codex Aureus of St Emmeram → book cover (ivory)
  - Pericopes of Abbess Uta (Munich, Bayerische Staatsbibliothek, Cod. 1m 13601) **13** *19*
  - Uta Pericope (Munich, Bayer. Staatsbib., Clm. 13601) **7** 513

Péridiez, Louis **17** 666
peridots **12** I; **17** 524; **29** 699
Périé, Antoine-Hilaire-Henri **25** 581
Périer, Casimir **24** 418*
Périer, Gaston-Denys **33** 596
Perier, Jean **27** 250
Périer-d'Ieteren, C. **3** 619
Peries, Leela **29** 462
Perignac Church **26** 600
Périgny, Maurice de **26** 412
Périgoy, Antoine **24** 148
Périgueux
- Cathedral of St Front **7** 257; **26** 584
- Maison du Coderc **29** 522
- St Etienne **26** 584

Periklytos **2** 160
Péril, Robert **3** 555
perilla **8** 235
perilla oil *see under* OILS → types
Perilli, Achille **7** 782; **9** 168; **11** 314; **16** 681; **26** 777
Périn, Alphonse **3** 867; **23** 573
Perinetti, José Cúneo *see* CÚNEO (PERINETTI), JOSÉ
Peringsdörfer, Katharina **33** 300
- altarpieces **33** *301*

Peringsdörfer, Sebald **33** 300
- altarpieces **33** *301*

Peringskjöld, Johan **23** 255
Perini, Domenico **3** 303
Perini, Fortunato Antonio **25** 217
Perini, Gherardo **25** 558
Perino del Vaga **7** 918; **9** 172; **16** 766; **24** 419–20*; **26** 769, 770
- assistants **8** 504; **11** 268; **24** 365; **25** 255; **28** 657, 658; **32** 237
- collaboration **14** 171; **24** 199, 827; **25** 256, 909; **26** 818; **29** 737; **30** 800; **31** 524; **32** 503
  - Polidoro da Caravaggio **25** 148
- decorative works **10** 810
- furniture **16** 725
- groups and movements **20** 281
- paintings
  - frescoes **25** 71
    - Castel Sant' Angelo (Rome) **24** *420*
    - Palazzo Doria Pamphili (Genoa) **1** 657; **12** *283*; **23** 680
    - S Marcello (Rome) **8** 504
    - SS Trinità dei Monti (Rome) **33** 717
    - Vatican Palace (Rome) **26** 817, 818
  - mythological **10** 476, 477
- patrons and collectors **9** 172; **10** 809; **12** 283; **20** 587; **21** 35
- personal collection **8** 268
- pupils **31** 907
- reproductive prints by others **3** 817; **5** 699; **12** 558; **32** 412
- stucco **21** 441; **26** 818; **27** 653

Perinthos
- stelae **23** *888*, 889

Period Home, for those who Own and Enjoy Listed Buildings **24** 445
periodicals **4** 25–6; **10** 210; **22** 360; **24** 420–53*, 665, 671, 672, 677
- historical and regional traditions
  - Africa **24** 429–30*
  - Australia **24** 437–8*
  - Austria **24** 438–9*
  - Belgium **24** 439*
  - Bulgaria **22** 539
  - Burma **24** 437
  - Canada **22** 39; **24** 430–31*
  - Canary Islands **11** 886
  - China **19** 831; **24** 435–6*
  - Czech Republic **20** 254; **24** 440*
  - Denmark **24** 451*
  - Ecuador **9** 749
  - England **10** 255; **24** 422, 423–4, 445–6*
  - Finland **24** 452*
  - France **13** 663; **24** 421–2, 423, 442–3*
  - Germany **12** 416; **24** 421, 423, 443–5*
  - Hungary **24** 440–41*
  - Iceland **24** 452*
  - India, Republic of **4** 290
  - Indian subcontinent **24** 436*
  - Indonesia **24** 437
  - Ireland **16** 42
  - Islamic **16** 550
  - Italy **24** 423, 447–9*; **32** 233
  - Japan **24** 436–7*; **30** 256
  - Latin America **24** 434–5*
  - Malaysia **24** 437
  - Netherlands, the **22** 911–15*; **24** 449–50*
  - New Zealand **24** 437–8*
  - Northern Ireland **16** 42
  - Norway **24** 452*
  - Poland **24** 441–2*
  - Portugal **24** 453*
  - Russia **24** 450–51*; **27** 392, 441, 443, 444
  - Scandinavia **24** 451–2*
  - Slovakia **24** 440*
  - South-east Asia **24** 437*
  - Spain **24** 452*
  - Sweden **24** 451*
  - Switzerland **24** 453*
  - Thailand **24** 437
  - Union of Soviet Socialist Republics **24** 424, 677
  - United States of America **24** 424, 431–4*, 673, 677
- types
  - aesthetics **23** 108
  - architecture **24** 275
    - France **8** 476; **11** 359
    - Germany **12** 641
    - United States of America **24** 431–2, 433–4; **28** 844
  - archives **2** 368*
  - engraving **2** 399
  - photography **24** 432, 434, 658, 661
  - scientific **12** 208
  - urban planning **28** 801; **32** 380

periodization **24** 453–5*; **30** 382
Peri-Peri **29** 195
peripteral **24** 455*
perirrhanteria **16** 612, *612*
- *see also* BASINS

Peris, Antoni **24** 455*
Peris, Gonçal **24** 455*
- collaboration **20** 383
- teachers **23** 109
- works **24** 400

Perišić, Brankica **4** 462
Peristeria **14** 339
- Tholos Tomb I **30** 738

peristyle courtyards **9** 557, 832; **13** 382, *382*; **24** 456
peristyle houses *see under* HOUSES → types
peristyles **24** 456*
- Greece, ancient **13** 376–7, *376*, 380, 383, 397

peristyles—cont.
- Rome, ancient **26** 863, 869, *870*
- *see also* COLONNADES

periwinkle shells *see under* SHELLS → types
Periz de Estella, Juan **23** 409
Periz de Estella, Martin **23** 402
Perizinotti, A. **24** 546
Perjeconter **25** 570
Perkasa Alam Johan, Sultan **20** 171
Perkin, W(illiam) H(enry) **23** 786; **24** 789; **30** 562; **32** 816
Perkins, Charles C(allahan) **10** 210; **24** 456*; **31** 671
Perkins, Christopher **23** 60; **24** 456–7*; **33** 58
Perkins, Dwight Heald **6** 578; **13** 647; **24** 457; **25** 446
Perkins, F(rederick Francis) Mason **24** 448, 457*
Perkins, Frank E. **25** 700
Perkins, Jacob **3** 180; **28** 831
Perkins, Lawrence B(radford) **24** 457
Perkins, Wheeler & Will **24** 457; **27** 475
Perkins and Will Partnership **24** 457
Perkins & Will **24** 457*
Perkois, Jacobus **28** 165
Perlan, Henri **24** 467; **27** 821; **32** 864
Perlaska, Dominik **28** 451
Pērle, Rūdolfs
Perleberg **25** 522
Perlee **21** 885
Perli, Ipolit **19** 497
Perli, Jozeph **19** 497
Perlingeiro, Max **4** 725
Perlmuter, Pearl **22** 861
Perlmuttapeten see under WALLPAPER → types
Perlmutter, Izsák **30** 211
Perlrott Csaba, Vilmos **17** 876; **22** 434; **24** 457*
Perm' **24** 457–8*; **27** *362*, 387, 389
- Art Gallery **24** 458

permanent green *see under* PIGMENTS → types
permanent violet *see* PIGMENTS → types → manganese violet
Per-Medjed *see* OXYRHYNCHUS
Permeke, Constant **3** 564, 614; **24** 458–9*
- groups and movements **2** 516; **10** 696; **18** 626
- pupils **32** 269
- works **3** 564, *565*; **24** *459*

Permeke, Henri-Louis **24** 458
Permeniates, Ioannis **25** 332
Permeribo *see* PARAMARIBO
Permont, Thomas **10** 103
Permoser, Balthasar **12** 460; **24** 460–61*; **27** 664
- assistants **9** 752
- collaboration **8** 904; **9** 145, 235, 242
- patrons and collectors **9** 238; **28** 15; **33** 114
- pupils **9** 238; **10** 264; **19** 772; **21** 818; **24** 585; **27** 242
- works **9** *236*, 242; **12** 373, 405; **23** 812; **24** *461*; **25** 240, 241, 727; **29** 574

Perna, Artur **10** 537
Perna, Pietro **29** 673
Pernaa Church, monument to Arvid Tönnesson Wildeman and Anna Hansdotter Björnram **11** 99
Pernat, Marko *see* PERNHART, MARKO
per neser see SHRINES (i) (CULT)
Pernes-les-Fontaines, Notre-Dame **26** 603
Pernéty, Antoine Joseph **10** 207
Pernevi, Palle **30** 86
Pernhart, Marko **24** 461*
- works **28** 860, *861*

Pernicharo, Pablo **24** 461*
Pernier, L. **24** 589
Pernik, House of Culture **5** 159
Pernkopf, Eduard **1** 845
Pernon, Camille **9** 379; **11** 646
Pernot, François Alexandre **31** 373
Pernštejn (family) **8** 422; **24** 462*
- architecture **2** 213
- collections **8** 423
- paintings **8** 390
- sculpture **8** 384

Pernštejn, Jan of *see* JAN OF PERNŠTEJN
Pernštejn, Vilém of *see* VILÉM OF PERNŠTEJN
Pernštejn, Vojtéch of *see* VOJTÉCH OF PERNŠTEJN
Pernštejn, Vratislav of *see* VRATISLAV OF PERNŠTEJN
Pernštejn Castle **8** *374*, 377; **24** 462–3*, *463*
per nu see SHRINES (i) (CULT)
Peró, Agustín **20** 64
Pêro, Mestre **13** 102; **24** 463*; **25** 300
Perold, Ivor A. **29** 117
Peroli (family) **32** 620
Peroli, Francesco **29** 300
Péron, François **1** 50, 66
Peroni, Francesco **1** 630
Peroni, Giuseppe **1** 631; **25** 851
Perot, Lena **8** 832
Perotti, José **22** 114
Perouse **12** 368
Peroux, Joseph Nikolaus **23** 675
Perov, Vasily (Grigor'yevich) **24** 464–5*; **27** 390, 391
- groups and movements **22** 178; **27** 579; **32** 835
- patrons and collectors **31** 311
- pupils **2** 417; **17** 827; **18** 389; **19** 276; **22** 811; **27** 459
- teachers **33** 622
- works **22** *177*; **24** *464*

Perovsk, Pioneer Palace **27** 381
Perpendicular style *see under* GOTHIC → styles
Perpète **9** 197
Perpignan
- Bibles **17** 562
- Castillet **4** 780
- Cathedral of St Jean-le-Vieux **11** 252; **26** 609, 610
- manuscript illumination **17** 561
- Sainte-Chapelle **27** 551
- silk **11** 646

Perrache **21** 430
Perrache, Antoine-Michel **3** 785; **17** 683; **19** 846; **29** 91
Perragod, François **10** 752
Perramón, J. B. **32** 536
Perrat, Pierre **21** 362
Perraud, Jean-Joseph **24** 467*
Perraud, Laurent **22** 919
Perrault, Charles **7** 665; **23** 474; **24** 470*
- patrons and collectors **24** 467
- works **1** 897; **2** 171, 518; **4** 360; **11** 657; **13** 704, *704*; **24** 468
  - illustrated **4** 366; **31** 510

Perrault, Claude **7** 665; **11** 515, 517; **24** 467–70*; **26** 12
- attributions **24** 163
- collaboration **12** 747; **19** 267; **23** 811
- competitions **7** 665
- groups and movements **24** 170
- patrons and collectors **4** 551; **24** 467
- works **6** 508; **11** 258; **17** 670; **19** 267; **23** 339, *339*, 489; **24** 162, *163*, *469*; **29** 525
- writings **2** 358; **23** 488; **24** *468*; **31** 296, *297*
  - illustrated **19** 34
  - translated **16** 893

Perrault, Dominique **11** 528; **19** 321; **24** 132

Perrault, Henri-Maurice 24 470–71*
collaboration 23 616
works 5 561; 22 36
Perrault, Jean 24 467*
Perrault, Maurice 24 470
Perrault, Mesnard & Venne 24 471
Perrault d'Armancourt 4 360
Perréal, Jean 23 788; 24 471–2*; 29 638
assistants 3 646
collaboration 11 556; 21 72; 25 570
methods 24 242
patrons and collectors 7 595; 13 905; 31 845, 846
works 4 828, 870; 7 595; 17 485; 24 472; 27 546
Perreau 8 890
Perreau, Claude 19 630
Perreault, John 12 218
Perrecy-les-Forges 26 602
Perregaux, Alexandre 18 873
Perrenot de Granvelle, Antoine see GRANVELLE, ANTOINE PERRENOT DE
Perret, A. G., Architectes 24 473
Perret, Auguste 11 525; 16 55; 23 493; 24 128, 472–5*; 26 192
architecture 2 361
apartments 2 216; 4 48; 7 694; 19 39; 24 128
churches 13 204; 14 82; 19 365; 24 473
factories 7 694, 694; 19 365
houses 11 659
museums 24 474
skyscrapers 11 525
theatres 4 568; 30 683
towers 19 91
assistants 11 47
collaboration 17 463
competitions 7 670
groups and movements 25 747
pupils 12 871; 19 746; 20 299; 22 728; 26 37; 28 809
staff 17 808
staircases 29 525
urban planning 11 527; 19 91; 25 375
Perret, Claude 24 473
Perret, Claude-Marie 24 472
Perret, Clement 10 389
Perret, Gustave 11 525; 16 55; 24 472–5*
architecture
apartments 7 694; 19 39; 24 128
churches 14 82; 19 365; 24 473
factories 7 694, 694
museums 24 474
staircases 29 525
theatres 30 683
assistants 11 47
collaboration 17 463
groups and movements 25 747
Perret, Louis 32 308
Perret, Pedro (1555-1625) 24 475*
pupils 32 557
works 4 911; 11 486; 14 476; 24 239; 27 885; 29 377
Perret, Pedro (d 1639) see PERETE, PEDRO
Perret et Fils 24 472–3
Perret Frères 11 526, 527; 13 733; 21 780; 24 473; 26 15
Perret-Gentil, Moise 17 713
Perreux, Alexandre Millin Du see MILLIN DU PERREUX, ALEXANDRE
Perrey, Nicholas 5 694
Perri, Giacomo 25 890
Perriand, Charlotte 19 51; 24 475–6*
collaboration 17 463
groups and movements 11 526; 31 581, 582
works 19 48; 30 755
Perricci, Ignazio 22 99
Perriccioli, Giuliano 21 27
Perrichon, Camille 19 849
Perrier, Charles 26 53
Perrier, François 11 534; 24 134, 476*
collaboration 13 655
patrons and collectors 3 745; 18 885
pupils 9 371; 11 833; 19 19
teachers 18 733; 19 14
works 2 163; 4 408; 13 783; 24 476; 26 230; 32 236
Perrier, Guillaume, I (d 1656) 2 707
Perrier, Guillaume, II (1626-59) 2 707
Perrier, Maurice 11 628
Perrier, Mme 11 599
Perrière, Guillaume de La see LA PERRIÈRE, GUILLAUME DE
Perrin, Sainte-Marie 4 466
Perrin (La Veuve) 11 606; 20 474
Perrin, Claude 20 474
Perrin, Hyacinthe-Marie 26 205
Perrin, Jean-Charles-Nicaise 9 417; 24 477–8*
Perrin, Léon 19 40
Perrin, Luis 4 260
Perrin, Patricia 23 69
Perrinetto da Benevento 19 180
Perring, John Shae 10 79
Perrins, Charles William Dyson 24 478*
Perrissin, Jean 14 855; 24 478–9*; 33 357
Perritt, Thomas 29 835
Perrodin, François 11 553
Perrois, Louis 1 232
Perron, Maurice 2 839
Perron, Philipp 29 843; 33 283
Perronet, Henri 6 138; 14 469
Perronet, Jean-Rodolphe 11 670; 24 121, 479–80*
groups and movements 24 174
pupils 9 420; 19 85
works 2 337; 4 801; 20 567; 24 122; 26 347
writings 4 804
Perroni Museum 6 179
Perronneau, Jean-Baptiste 3 101; 4 391; 11 460; 22 846; 24 135, 480–81*
methods 24 242; 29 863
patrons and collectors 4 307; 7 528; 9 196
works 9 224; 24 242
perrons 24 479*
Perrot, Bernard 11 612; 21 720
Perrot, Georges 1 520; 7 171; 10 84
Perrot, L. 27 484
Perrot, Pierre Josse 2 704; 5 837
Perrottet, Jean 2 699
Perrottet and Fabre 2 700
Perroud, Laurent 30 136
Perry, Lila Cabot 21 868; 24 481*
Perry, Mary Chase 30 887; 31 639
Perry, William (fl 1960s) 17 806; 23 799
Perrycroft 21 779
PERSAGI (Union of Indonesian Painters) 15 808
Persant, Philippart 31 835
Persatuan Ahli Gambar see PERSAGI
Perscheid, Nicolas 24 674
Persephone Painter 32 28
Persepolis 1 116, 849, 895; 2 213; 15 893, 897, 899, 901, 902, 906, 907, 908, 912, 919; 24 481–4*
Achaemenid Treasury 13 550
apadana 2 213; 6 480; 15 911; 24 482–3, 483
citadel 24 482
dress 1 887
excavations 14 487
façade decoration 10 742
furniture 1 890
glass 1 868
inscriptions 1 895; 6 186
Persepolis—cont.
murals 15 922
palace 15 902; 23 807; 29 520; 33 707
polychromy 25 171
reliefs 1 117, 690, 886; 6 251, 479; 15 902, 914, 915, 916; 21 275; 26 134; 33 707
sculpture 13 438; 29 395
seals 1 117
temple 15 911
tomb of Artaxerxes III Ochus 33 707
vaults (ceiling) 28 537
Perséus, Edvard 3 776; 17 8; 18 449
Pershore Abbey (Hereford & Worcs) 26 590; 32 91
Pershore Censer Cover 10 338
Persia see IRAN; IRAN, ANCIENT
Persian 1 116–18, 851; 15 900, 902, 905–6; 21 275
dress 1 886; 16 456
Persian capitals see under CAPITALS → types
Persian period see EGYPT, ANCIENT → periods → 27th Dynasty
Persico, Edoardo 4 88; 24 484*; 31 446
collaboration 23 169
groups and movements 26 15
works 16 649, 650
Persico, Luigi 32 892
Persijn, Reinier van 8 291
persimmon 17 359, 399; 30 560
Persis 1 889
Persius, (Friedrich) Ludwig 24 484–5*
collaboration 5 905; 19 156; 28 102
groups and movements 13 202
patrons and collectors 14 655
teachers 28 102
works 2 478; 12 376, 415; 14 490; 25 173, 366, 366, 367, 368; 32 554
Persivale Serrano, Jaime 24 506
persjarnia 23 369; 25 133
Perskie, Leon 23 26
Persky, Mathias 28 859
Personico 30 145
personifications 1 651, 654; 9 519–20*
Personnaz, Antonin 24 883
Persoons, Nicolaes (Jeremiasz.) 24 485*
Perspecta: The Yale Architectural Journal 24 434
perspective 1 101, 102, 107; 14 869; 22 378; 24 375, 377–80, 485–95*; 28 202; 30 649
grids 24 828
historical and regional traditions
China 24 492
France 18 704
Greece, ancient 13 472
Italy 16 658; 20 529; 30 654, 656, 668
15th cent. 9 98, 101
Japan 17 186
Prehistoric art 18 807
Rome, ancient 27 48
theories see under THEORIES → types
types
acuity 24 492, 493, 494
aerial 24 378, 492, 494
anamorphic see ANAMORPHOSIS
atmospheric see aerial
colour 24 492, 493
curvilinear 24 491*
isometric 24 491
linear 24 377, 378, 380, 381, 486–91*, 487, 488, 489, 490
China 24 486
Greece, ancient 24 486
Italy 24 486–7
Japan 24 486
perspective
types
linear—cont.
Netherlands, the 24 486, 490
orthographic 24 491*
synthetic 24 380
see also VANISHING POINT
perspectographs 24 488; 28 203
Perspektief: Quarterly Photography Magazine 24 450
Perspex 10 267; 24 495*; 25 23, 27, 612; 26 244; 31 283
Persson, A. W. 18 580
Persson, Hjelt Per 30 116
Persson, Jerker 30 103
Persson, Nils 30 116
Persson, Sigurd 12 451; 30 109, 113
Persson-Melin, Signe 30 101
Pertevniyal Valide Sultan 16 227
Perth (Australia) 1 37; 2 736; 24 495–6*
architecture 2 738, 740, 741
Art Gallery of Western Australia 2 770; 15 748; 24 496
Cathedral 2 738
Government House 2 755
Lawrence Wilson Art Gallery 24 496
State Library
Alexander Building 19 320
Western Australian Museum 1 66; 24 495, 496
Perth (Tayside; UK)
art schools 28 274
cabinetmaking 28 254
Fergusson Gallery 28 273
museums 28 273
Museum and Art Gallery 28 273
Tower Ridge 4 789
Perthes, James Boucher de see BOUCHER DE PERTHES, JAMES
Perthes, P.-J.-E. de 31 241
Perth-Nedlands, University of Western Australia
Anthropology Research Museum 1 66
Perthshire Paperweights Ltd 28 260
Pertinchamp, La Ramée see LA RAMÉE PERTINCHAMP
Pertsch, Johann Nepomuk 2 714
Pertsch, Matteo 24 496*; 28 859; 31 329
Pertsch, Nicolò 24 496; 28 859
Pertwanger, A. 18 505
Peru 15 161; 24 497–518*, 498
adobe 29 168
aguana 24 515
albumen 19 386
alpaca hair 29 182
antependia 24 511
archaeology 2 300; 23 702
architectural decorations 6 441
architecture 24 500–506*; 32 25, 306
archives 2 369, 371*
aryballoi 29 175
baskets 3 330
bottles 28 650
boxes 24 512
brick 19 385
bridges 19 385
bronze 24 510
carpets 5 829
cathedrals 24 501, 503
cedar 24 515
centrolobian 24 515
ceramics 24 514*
chairs 24 514
chullpas 31 47
churches 2 386; 24 500–504
citadels 20 3
cloisters 24 502
clyster tubes 29 133
coats of arms 14 411
cocobola 24 515
coins 7 537
Peru—cont.
collections 24 515–17*
erotic art 10 487
photographs 24 518*
concrete 24 505
conopas 24 500
copper 28 651
cotton 30 IX
crowns 29 214
dolls 31 259, 260, 261
dolls' houses 31 264
drinking vessels 10 474
education (art) 24 517*
embroidery 24 513
emeralds 29 155
engravings 24 506
erotic art 10 474
fans 10 780
feathers 29 207
friezes 6 607
furniture 24 514–15*
gold 8 272; 28 651; 29 214
gourds 13 229; 24 500
government buildings 19 387
granite 29 167
guidebooks 13 811
hats 24 512
headdresses 28 651
heraldry 14 411
iconography 29 134
ikat 24 513
incense burners 24 512
jade 16 861
jars 6 440; 21 752
jet 21 718
kilns 3 364
knitting 18 157; 24 513
leather 31 260
libraries 24 518*
looms 30 544
mantles 24 513
marble 24 510
marquetry 33 332
masks 29 208–9, 209
masonry 14 827
metal 24 512
metalwork 24 500, 511–12*
mirrors 21 718
monstrances 24 511
mortars (building) 19 386
mother-of-pearl 33 332
mud 6 607
museums 24 516–17*
narratives 22 518
painting 24 506–11*
portraits 24 508
wall 19 385; 29 135
palaces 19 386; 24 505
parana pine 24 515
patronage 24 515–16*
photography 10 580
portraits 24 515
pottery 24 500; 27 621; 31 261
Nazca 22 707
Pre-Columbian 6 440; 8 272, 272; 21 752, 752–4*
pyramids 21 750, 750–52*
queros 24 499, 499
relief 6 607; 29 168
repoussé 29 214
retables 24 499; 26 252
rock art 22 708
rose-wood 33 332
sarcophagi 27 833
sculpture 24 506–11*, 507, 510
Pre-Columbian 29 167
shields 14 411
shrines (i) (cult) 28 641
silver 7 537; 24 500, 511–12, 512; 28 651
stone 19 385
stone-carvings 6 350, 521; 29 169, 170, 171
syringes 29 133
tabernacles (ii) (receptacle) 24 511
tapestries 29 181; 30 III1
temples 29 166

Peru—cont.
textiles **23** *564*; **24** 512–13*; **29** *182*
threads **24** 512
tortoiseshell **33** *332*
trade **32** 180
silver **4** 723
tumi **28** *651*
tunics **29** *181*, *207*; **30** IX
turquoise **28** *651*
vases **32** *418*
vaults (ceiling) **24** 501
velvet **24** *512*
wall paintings **24** 506–7
walnut **24** 515
women artists **24** 509
wood **24** *499*
wool **24** *513*; **30** III1
Péru, Jean-Baptiste, II **4** 391
Peru, Upper *see* BOLIVIA
Perugia **10** *583*, 585; **16** *620*; **24** 518–25*; **26** *886*
academy **1** 103
bronzes **10** 626, 627
churches
Cathedral of S Lorenzo **16** 724
Chapel of S Bernardino **3** *254*, 254
S Bernardino **10** 743
S Bevignate **16** 655
S Domenico **13** 193
tomb of Benedict XI **13** 96
S Manno **1** 695
S Maria dei Fossi **25** 184
S Matteo **1** 695, 696
S Pietro **16** 725; **24** 524–5
S Prospero **7** 302; **13** 96
Collegio del Cambio **3** 173; **13** 700; **24** 523
Sala dell'Udienza **14** 869; **16** 724; **24** 525
Collegio della Mercanzia **16** 711
dress **9** 259
Fontana Maggiore **11** *340*, 341; **22** 44; **24** 870–71
sculpture **13** 96
fortifications **10** 588
Galleria Nazionale dell'Umbria **24** 520
see also Palazzo dei Priori
gateways **10** 602
mirrors **10** 629
Museo dell'Opera del Duomo **16** 774
Palazzo Comunale *see* Palazzo dei Priori
Palazzo dei Priori **16** 627; **24** *519*; **31** 236
altarpieces **24** 522, 525
Cappella dei Priori **4** *317*; **24** 522
frescoes **4** 316
sculpture **13** 96
see also Galleria Nazionale dell'Umbria
Palazzo dell'Università Vecchia **11** 118
Porta Augusta **2** 295; **26** 887, *887*
Porta Marzio **7** 359; **21** 566
Rocca Paolina **21** 566
sculpture **27** 9
stools **30** 776
tapestries **16** 756
Tomb of the Volumnii **10** 598, 600; **16** 622
urn of Arnth Velimnas **10** 588
vase paintings **10** 592
Perugia, Cavaliere *see* CERRINI, GIOVANNI DOMENICO
Perugia, Rubeus da *see* RUBEUS DA PERUGIA
Perugia Painter **10** 615
Perugini, Giuseppe **3** 439; **25** 792
Perugino **3** 917; **4** 494; **11** 184; **16** 661, 662; **24** 520–27*; **28** 676; **29** 853
assistants **16** 694, 749; **19** 200; **27** 769
Perugino—cont.
attributions **3** 858; **11** 117; **19** 676; **26** 765, 815; **27** 847
collaboration **7** 676; **24** 829; **26** 186
Baccio d'Agnolo (Bartolommeo d'Agnolo di Donato Baglione) **3** 15
Bartolomeo della Gatta **3** 299
Bencivenni, Antonio (da Mercatello) **3** 701
Botticelli, Sandro **4** 494
Ghirlandaio, Domenico **12** 551
Rosselli, Cosimo **27** 175
Signorelli, Luca (d'Egidio di maestro Ventura de') **26** 815; **28** 700
drawings **9** 220
groups and movements **26** 187
methods **21** 758, 768; **23** 376
paintings
allegorical **10** 130; **15** 86, *86*
altarpieces **3** 305; **19** 183; **24** *526*
erotic art **10** 476
frescoes **3** 173; **13** 700; **24** *522*; **26** 815, 817
landscape **18** 705
mythological **24** *523*
religious **19** 675; **20** 684; **24** *524*, 776
patrons and collectors **14** 869; **16** 770
Alexander, Francis **1** 611
Amboise, Georges I d', Cardinal (1460-1510) **1** 766
Anne of Brittany, Queen of France (1477-1514) **31** 846
Baglioni (Perugian family) **3** 55
Bardini, Stefano **3** 228
Cacault, François **5** 356
Campbell, John, 1st Baron Cawdor (1755-1821) **5** 541
Carafa, Oliviero, Cardinal **5** 698
Correggio (*d* 1534) **7** 891
Eastlake, Charles Lock (1793-1865) **9** 683
Francis-Joseph, Prince of Liechtenstein (*reg* 1772-81) **19** 338
Gondi, Bartolomeo **12** 897
Isabella I, Queen of Castile-León (*reg* 1474-1504) **2** 278
Isabella d'Este, Marchesa di Mantua (1474-1539) **10** 520; **14** 870; **16** 659; **29** 860
Julius II, Pope (*reg* 1503-13) **27** 272, 273
Lorenzo the Magnificent, Lord of Florence (*reg* 1469-92) **21** 14
Mellon, Andrew W(illiam) **21** 90
Moore, Morris J. **22** 58
Pucci, Dionigi **25** 690
Richelieu, Armand-Jean Du Plessis, Cardinal de **11** 662
Ryerson, Martin A(ntoine) **27** 463
Sixtus IV, Pope (*reg* 1471-84) **7** 218; **16** 661; **27** 271
Thibaudeau, Narcisse-Adolphe, Comte de **30** 727
William II, King of the Netherlands (*reg* 1840-49) **23** 469
pupils **1** 620; **3** 13, 858; **8** 510; **10** 651; **12** 277; **15** 60; **25** 897; **27** 740
stained glass **13** 193
teachers **32** 366
Perugino, Bartolomeo di Pietro **9** 112; **24** 781, 830
Perugino, Paolo *see* GISMONDI, PAOLO
Perulli, Count **11** 395
Perushtitsa **5** *144*; **9** *511*; **24** 528–9*
Red Church **5** *145*, 146, 150; **9** 538; **24** 528–9
wall paintings **9** 572
Perusia *see* PERUGIA
Per-Usir *see* ABUSIR
Péruwelz **13** 113
Peruzzi (family) **3** 173; **11** 183
Peruzzi, Baldassare **16** 778; **24** 529–34*; **28** 676
architecture **4** 280; **8** 101
bastions **24** *532*
castles **20** 840; **24** 219
churches **26** 187
façade decoration **10** 737
façades **13** 210; **24** *530*; **30** 655
fortresses **5** 683
palazzi **6** 82; **8** 504; **23** 810; **24** *533*; **28** 675
porticos **24** 567
theatres **27** 179; **30** 656
tombs **31** 320
urban planning **31** 714
villas **8** 503; **15** 137; **32** 545
assistants **4** 749
attributions **4** 272; **11** 693; **28** 683
collaboration **6** 355; **10** 130; **26** 805; **27** 743
drawings **2** 328; **16** 712; **28** 469
fountains **16** 845
interior decoration **16** 634; **23** 680
paintings **20** 279, 840; **22** 412; **24** *531*; **26** 836
patrons and collectors **10** 808
Chigi, Agostino (i) (1466-1520) **6** 583; **16** 633; **26** 769
Leo X, Pope (*reg* 1513-22) **21** 16
Massimo, Pietro (*d* 1489) **20** 587
Paul III, Pope (*reg* 1534-50) **10** 808; **21** 79; **26** 813
Pio, Alberto III (1475-1531) **24** 833
productions **21** 16
pupils **6** 82; **8** 503; **18** 790; **22** 804; **24** 347; **28** 466
reproductive prints by others **12** 699
stage design **15** 137; **30** 656, 657
Peruzzi, Emilia **11** 190
Peruzzi, Giovanni Sallustio **5** 699
Peruzzi, Sallustio **19** 371, 372
Peruzzi Chapel Altarpiece **12** 686
Peruzzi de Medici, Edith Marion, Marchesa **29** 724
Peruzzini, Antonio Francesco **20** 95; **21** 30; **26** 320
per wer see SHRINES (i) (CULT)
Pery, William, 3rd Earl of Limerick (1840-96) **12** 840; **16** 25
Peryer, Peter **24** 534*
Peryn', Church of the Birth of the Mother of God **27** 370
Pešánek, Zdeněk **8** 387; **22** 748
Pesarese, il *see* CANTARINI, SIMONE
Pesaro (Italy) **16** *620*; **24** 534–6*, *535*
bastion **3** 359
maiolica **24** 535*
manuscripts **17** 565
Palazzo Ducale **12** 279; **27** 274
Teatro del Sole **30** 667
Villa Imperiale **3** 162; **7** 560; **12** *278*; **24** 536*; **27** 274, 323; **32** 546
Camera delle Cariatidi **18** *707*
frescoes **32** 550
paintings **18** 708
Villa Ruggieri **32** 555
Pésaro (family) **3** 660; **32** 217
Pesaro, Alessandro Sforza, Lord of **28** 529, 530*
altarpieces **5** 127
architecture **18** 861; **24** 534, 536
paintings **2** 183; **19** 788; **21** 96; **33** 126
Pesaro, Franco da *see* FRANCO DA PESARO
Pesaro, Galeazzo Sforza, Lord of **10** 521
Pesaro, Gerolamo **24** 537
Pesaro, Giovanni **19** 629
Pesaro, Giovanni Sforza, Lord of **11** 699; **24** 534
Pesaro, Jacopo, Bishop of Paphos (1466-1547) **24** 536–7*
Pesaro, Jacopo da (*fl* 1540-68) **32** 200
Pesaro, Lunardo **24** 537
Pesaro, Mariotto de *see* MARIOTTO DE PESARO
Pesaro, Paolo di **3** 643
Pesaro, Tomaso **29** 326
Pesaro *Coronation of the Virgin* **3** 662–3
Pesaro Madonna **24** 536; **32** 217
Pesatti, Sof'ya (Isaakovna) *see* DYMSHITS-TOLSTAYA, SOF'YA
Pescador, Mariano **25** 419
Pescadores Islands **6** 331
Pescadoret, el *see* JULIÁ, ASCENSÍO
Pescara, Marchesa di *see* COLONNA, VITTORIA
Pescatore, J. P., Musée *see under* LUXEMBOURG
Pescatore, Pietro *see* VISSCHER, PIETER
Peschernyy Monastery *see under* VARDZIA
Peschka, Anton **28** 88
Pesci, Gasparo Prospero **1** 633
Pesci, Girolamo **24** 537*
Pescia
Palazzo Vescovile **1** 711
S Francesco **1** 708; **3** *808*; **13** 541
Pescia, Benedetto Pagno da *see* PAGNO DA PESCIA, BENEDETTO
Pescia, Pier Maria Serbaldi da *see* SERBALDI DA PESCIA, PIER MARIA
Pescia Romana Painter **10** 614
Pescio (family) **1** 579
Pesellino **9** 98; **24** 537–9*
attributions **20** 743; **29** 786
collaboration **19** 894
methods **30** 427
patrons and collectors **12** 32; **13** 272; **14** 675; **19** 736; **21** 13
teachers **19** 444; **24** 539
works **4** 196; **6** 3; **8** 850; **11** 384; **19** 443; **24** *538*
workshop **16** 660
Pesellino, Compagno di *see* APOLLONIO DI GIOVANNI (DI TOMASO)
Pesello **24** 537, 539*
collaboration **11** 892
works **11** 893; **19** 674; **31** 513
Pesenti, Francesco **27** 483
Pesenti, Pietro Martire **27** 483
Pesenti, Vincenzo **27** 483
Pesev, Khristo **5** 156
Peshawar **15** *264*, *360*; **23** *797*; **24** 539–41*
Archaeological Museum **23** 804
Bala Hisar **24** 540
Islamia College **24** *540*
metalwork **23** 803
Museum **23** 804
pottery **23** 802
sculpture **15** 459
University **23** 801, 803
Peshitta Gospels *see under* GOSPEL BOOKS → individual manuscripts
Peshkopi Historical Museum **31** 451
Peshkov, Aleksey *see* GOR'KY, MAKSIM
Peshtera
Oryahovo Monastery
St Nikola **5** 147
St Dimiter **5** 148
Pešina, J. **8** 426
Peška, Juozapas **19** 498
Pesne, Antoine **3** 798; **24** 541–2*
attributions **13** 268
patrons and collectors **14** 651, 652; **25** 368; **31** 852
pupils **12** 391; **18** 158; **21** 147; **26** 506; **30** 713
reproductive prints by others **14** 132
works **11** 37, 458, *458*, *459*, 470; **12** 391; **15** 139; **23** 113; **24** *542*; **31** 328
Pesne, Henriette **24** 542
Pesne, Jean **9** 8
works **9** *9*
Pesne, Thomas **24** 541
Pesoa, Isaac **2** 858
Pesochenskaya Factory **27** 414
Pesqueiras, S María **26** 642
Pesquera, Diego de **24** 542*; **28** 513, 518
Pessac **7** 695
Pesser, Hans *see* BESSER, HANS
Pessina, Giovanni Battista **26** 318
Pessinous Temple **13** 405
Pessinus **24** 690
Pessoa, Alberto **1** 752
Pest *see* BUDAPEST
Pestagalli, Pietro **21** 534
Pestalozzi, Heinrich **30** 132
Pestalozzi, Johann Heinrich **7** 183
Pest Art Association **14** 896
Pestel', Vera Ye. **8** 10; **20** 151
Pestels de Lévis, Anne-Claude-Philippe de Tubières de Grimoard de, Comte de Caylus *see* CAYLUS, Comte de
Pesther Kunst-Verein *see* ARTISTS ASSOCIATION OF PEST
Pesti Műegyesület *see* ARTISTS ASSOCIATION OF PEST
Pestinien, Jean de *see* JEAN DE PESTINIEN
pestles **17** 341, 352; **25** 477; **29** 133
Pestravka **27** 415
Pestrikov, Treyak **27** 419
Peszka, Józef **12** 821; **25** 106
Petaling Jaya **20** 170
Petal ware *see under* POTTERY → wares
Petamenopet **9** 805, 841
Petăr **5** 160
pétards **24** 542*
Petau, Denis **20** 455
Petau, P.
works **27** *589*
Pete, Juan **26** 518
Petel, Clement **24** 542
Petel, Georg **2** 45; **12** 460; **24** 542–4*
attributions **12** 239
works **3** 598; **12** 404; **22** 725; **24** *543*, *544*; **29** 571
Peter (*fl* 1383-4) **27** 217
Peter, Abbot of St Calmine **26** 692
Peter, Archpriest **22** 714
Peter, Duke of Kurland (*reg* 1769-95) **17** 472
Peter, Master (*fl* 1185) **27** 604
Peter, Master (*fl* 1402) **20** 186; **21** 846
Peter, Master (1422-1528) *see* TORRIGIANI, PIETRO (DI TORRIGIANO D'ANTONIO)
Peter, Master (*fl c.* 1460) **1** 576
Peter, Metropolitan **22** 181
Peter I, Emperor of Brazil (*reg* 1822-31) **4** *631*, 711; **19** 468; **28** 431
architecture **24** 584
Peter I, King of Aragon (*reg* 1094-1104) **7** 475; **19** 520
Peter I, King of Castile-León (*reg* 1350-66; 1367-89) **22** 255; **28** 511, 514, 518; **29** 298
Peter I, Tsar and Emperor of Russia (*reg* 1682-1725) **3** 85; **13** 729; **21** 473; **26** 729-31*
amber **1** 762

Peter I, Tsar and Emperor of Russia (*reg* 1682-1725)—cont.
architecture **6** 572; **19** 17; **20** 839; **24** 546; **26** 7, *730*; **27** 373, 438, 572, 573, 575, 585, 586; **28** 117; **31** 317, 318; **33** 621
palaces **20** 839
ceramics **30** 884
coins **7** 538
collections **6** 237; **15** 745; **27** 440; **28** 321
dress **10** 356
education (art) **27** 442
enamel **27** 426
furniture **2** 812; **27** 582
gardens **11** 345; **12** 134
glass **12** 897
hardstones **27** 427
interior decoration **27** 401
lacquer **18** 614; **27** 427
metalwork **8** 904; **28** 325
paintings **4** 374; **22** 50; **27** 438; **28** 724
prints **19** 751
sculpture **24** 820; **27** 389
ships **8** 95
silver **3** 122; **30** 105
tapestries **27** 430; **30** 324
textiles **19** 418
Peter I, Voivode of Moldavia (*reg* 1375-91) **26** 707; **29** 892
Peter II, Bishop of Le Puy **12** 209
Peter II, Count of Savoy (*reg* 1263-8) **6** 602
Peter II, Duke of Bourbon (*reg* 1488-1503) **4** 542, *543*, 545*; **31** *833*
manuscripts **11** 355; **16** 854; **26** 454
paintings **4** 544; **20** 731, 732, 734
Peter II, Duke of Brittany (*reg* 1450-7) **4** 827; **24** 775
Peter II, Emperor of Brazil (*reg* 1831-89) **4** *631*, 705, 728; **26** 413
collections **4** 725, 726, 727
daguerreotypes **5** 320
sponsorship **1** 681, 774
Peter II, King of Cyprus (*reg* 1369-82) **8** 361
Peter II, King of Portugal (*reg* 1683-1706) **4** *631*, 634–5*
architecture **2** 189
metalwork **25** 313
paintings **7** 522; **25** 297
textiles **25** 315
Peter II, Vladika of Montenegro (*reg* 1830-51) **22** 18
Peter III, Bishop of Le Puy **12** 209
Peter III, Emperor of Russia (*reg* 1762) **19** 219, 563
Peter III, King of Portugal (*reg* 1777-86) **4** *631*, 632, 637*
architecture **4** 632; **25** 814; **26** 471
Peter III, Voivode of Wallachia (*reg* 1583-5) **26** 707; **29** 892
Peter IV, King of Aragon (*reg* 1336-87) **2** 276*
altarpieces **4** 423
architecture **25** 58
coats of arms **14** 413
manuscripts **3** 339; **8** 140, 817; **26** 563; **31** 88
metalwork **13** 165; **29** 332
sculpture **13** 106; **22** 70; **25** 58
wood-carvings **3** 220
Peter IV, King of Portugal *see* PETER I, Emperor of Brazil
Peter IV, Voivode of Wallachia (*reg* 1574-7; 1578-9; 1582-91) **15** 55
Peter V, King of Portugal (*reg* 1853-61) **4** *631*; **19** 468
Peter, Alexander **9** 727; **28** 252
Peter, Hans **29** 422
Peter, Marc **29** 807
Peter, Marvine Sakvan **22** 656
Peter, Thomas **30** 761
Peter, Victor **26** 514
Peter, Wenzel **4** 407; **31** 679
Peterborough (Ont.; Canada), Trent University **5** 562
Peterborough (Cambs; UK) **10** *225*; **24** 544–6*
brick **4** 768; **10** 236
Cathedral of St Peter, St Paul and St Andrew (Abbey) **1** 723; **10** 228; **12** 6; **24** 544–6*, *545*; **26** 588; **30** 729; **31** *155*
Abbot Kirkton's gate **14** 420
arches **2** 294
choir **26** *589*
choir gallery **8** 856
Hedda sarcophagus **2** 70
Lady Chapel **18** 622
manuscripts **26** 661
piers (ii) (masonry) **24** 751
pinnacles **24** 826
retrochoir **24** 465, 466
roof **27** 131
sculpture **13** 82
spires **29** 413
vaults **20** 579
wall paintings **31** 499
roofs **30** 907
St John's **13** 211
Thorpe Hall **2** 545; **27** 130; **32** 551
Peterborough Psalter *see under* PSALTERS → individual manuscripts
Peterborough ware *see under* POTTERY → wares
Petercels, Jan **4** 417
Peter Damian, Saint **5** 450
Peter de Caraman **21** 798
Peter des Roches, Bishop of Winchester **7** 350
Peterdi, Gabor **10** 397, 398; **20** 605
Petergof *see* PETERHOF
Peterhans, Walter **3** 403; **7** 818; **29** 641
Peterhof **24** 546–7*; **27** *363*, 373, 377
gardens **4** 311; **11** 345; **12** 134; **24** 546
Grand Cascade **24** *547*; **28** 643
Grand Palace **24** 546; **26** 7; **27** 213, 401
hardstones **27** 427–8
interior decoration **27** 401
Monplaisir **5** 348; **27** 438
Chinese study **27** 427
furniture **27** 407
interior decoration **27** 401
lacquer **18** 614
palace **24** *547*; **27** 374
Pavilion **23** 861
sculpture **28** 193
Peterhof lapidary factory **24** 547
Péterinck, François-Joseph **3** 590, 591; **31** 220
Péterinck-Gérard, Charles **3** 591; **31** 220
Peter Jones **10** 299
Peterlee (Tyne & Wear) **19** 747; **31** 733
Peter of Amiens **28** 428
Peter of Beaujeu *see* PETER II, Duke of Bourbon
Peter of Celle *see* PIERRE DE CELLE
Peter of Colechurch **4** 800
Peter of Eboli **7** 243; **14** 412, 423; **26** 662
illustrated works **14** *413*
Peter of Gloucester, Abbot **26** 688
candlesticks **26** *688*
Peter of Navarre **5** 895
Peter of Poitiers **7** 241
illustrated works **7** *242*
Peter of St Omer **20** 324
Peter of Spain **11** 420
Peter of Thessaloniki, Bishop of Constantinople **9** 638
Peter Orseolo, King of Hungary (*reg* 1038-41) **5** 80
Peters, Cornelis Hendrik **1** 803; **14** 45; **24** 547*
Peters, Dewitt **1** 425; **5** 751; **17** 660; **21** 894; **23** 332
Peters, Edward C. **2** 693
Peters, Luthor **33** 452
Peters, Matthew William **8** 864; **24** 547–8*; **28** 819; **29** 675
Peters, Richard **24** 596
Peters, Susie **22** 595
Peters, Wilhelm **23** 227
Peters, Wolfram **31** 576
Petersberg Church **5** 797
Petersburg Artel **20** 151
Petersburg Circle **27** 581; **28** 585
Petersburg Press **19** 492, 493; **20** 607, 609; **25** 626
Petersdorf glass factory **12** 441
Petersen, Anders **24** 548*
Petersen, Benjamin, & Co. **23** 71
Petersen, (Johan) Carl (Christian) **8** 748; **24** 548–9*
collaboration **3** 749; **18** 136
groups and movements **13** 613
pupils **18** 136
works **3** 410; **8** 727
Petersen, Carl V. **4** 104
Petersen, Frederik **23** 225
Petersen, Hans Christian **32** 512
Petersen, Harald **10** 105
Petersen, Joachim **17** 479
Petersen, Lene Adler *see* ADLER PETERSEN, LENE
Petersen, Ove **18** 237
Petersen, Richard **21** 796
Petersen, Rolf **26** 390
Petersen, Simon **8** 730, 731
works **8** *731*
Petersen, Sophus **32** 512
Petersen, Toni **1** 13
Petersen, van (*fl* 1810) **3** 233
Petersen, Waltraud **6** 600
Petersen, William Wesley **24** 548*
Petersfels **25** 489, 492, 493
Petershausen Sacramentary *see under* SACRAMENTARIES → individual manuscripts
Peter Site **22** 571
Peters & Krouwel **31** 576
Peterson, Andrew Thomas Turton **11** 242
Peterson, David **32** 789
Peterson, E. E. **10** 759
Peterson, Frederick A. **16** 54
Pētersons, Kārlis **12** 825; **18** 852
Peterssen, (Hjalmar) Eilif (Emanuel) **23** 225; **24** 549–50*
groups and movements **28** 814
pupils **10** 105; **18** 32; **29** 15
works **11** 474
Petersz., Anthonis **22** 857
Peter the Chanter **13** 39
Peter the Cruel, King of Castile-León *see* PETER I, King of Castile-León
Peter the Great, Emperor of Russia *see* PETER I, Emperor of Russia
Peter the Mason **1** 518
Peter the Venerable **7** 476
Peter von Koblenz **32** 821
Peter von Pusica **13** 902; **14** 420; **24** 550*; **33** 164
works **2** 778; **33** 164
Peterzano, Simone **21** 525; **24** 550–51*
attributions **8** 706
pupils **5** 703
works **3** 771
Petfield, Christopher **13** 634
Pether, Abraham **24** 551
Pether, William **24** 551*
pupils **8** 584; **9** 738
teachers **11** 810
works **11** 810; **21** 417; **24** 366; **26** *231*; **33** 413
Pethes, Dávid **10** 472
Peticolas, Edward F. **22** 714
Peti Juan **7** 345; **26** 249; **31** 92
Pétion, Alexandre **14** 58, 60
Petit **30** 15
Petit, Andries **3** 600
Petit, Fernand **8** 633
Petit, Francis **8** 820; **9** 423; **11** 663; **20** 497; **24** 551*; **29** 248
Petit, Georges **6** 519; **24** 551–2*
catalogues **6** 80
dealing **2** 559; **4** 589; **15** 155; **20** 603; **21** 69, 868; **24** 143, 883; **30** 647
exhibitions **15** 155; **20** 60
Petit, Henriette **6** 597; **22** 114
Petit, Jean **16** 852; **31** 842
Petit, John Louis **13** 204
Petit, Nicholas-Martin **2** 744
Petit, Nicolas **11** 410
Petit, Philippe **11** 601
Petit, Philippe-Auguste **19** 382
Petit, Pierre (1594-1677) **27** 882
Petit, Pierre (1832-1909) **5** 763; **24** 552*, 661
Petit, Roland **25** 450
petit appareil **26** 569
Petit Chasseur, Sion **25** 529
Petit Chasseur Dolmen **25** 511
Petite Académie *see* ACADÉMIE DES INSCRIPTIONS
Petite Erculanèse **14** 442, 445
Petites Heures of Anne of Brittany *see under* BOOKS OF HOURS → individual manuscripts
Petites Heures of Jean, Duc de Berry *see under* BOOKS OF HOURS → individual manuscripts
Petite Usine, La **9** 373; **25** 78
Petit-Gérard, Baptiste **29** 610
Petitgrand, Victor **22** 40
Petitjean, Hippolyte **22** 745; **24** 552*
Petit-Montrouge, St Pierre **11** 521
Petitot, Ennemond-Alexandre **24** 552–3*
collaboration **4** 470, 521
groups and movements **22** 734
pupils **5** 650; **26** 508; **28** 913
works **1** 574; **23** 544; **24** 193, *553*
Petitot, Faule **12** 275
Petitot, Jean (1607-91) **10** 195; **24** 553–4*; **30** 148
works **10** 346; **11** 630; **14** 855; **21** 641, *641*
Petitot, Jean (1653-1702) **21** 641
Petitot, Louis (-Messidor-Lebon) **24** 554*
pupils **23** 666
teachers **5** 889
works **5** 889
Petitot, Pierre **24** 554; **27** 547
Petitpierre & Cie **11** 649
petit point *see under* EMBROIDERY → types
Petit-Radel, Louise-François **24** 554*
Petits Garçons à la Bouche Entr'ouverte, Maître des *see* OPEN-MOUTHED BOYS, MASTER OF THE
Petits Maîtres *see* LITTLE MASTERS
Petit Trianon *see under* VERSAILLES → Château
Petkov, Blagovest **5** 159
Petkov, Dusko **19** 883
Petlad **15** 347
Petle, Jörg *see* PETEL, GEORG
Peto, Harold Ainsworth **12** 141, 315*
Peto, John F(rederick) **24** 554–5*; **31** 603
groups and movements **24** 686
works **14** 188; **15** 140; **24** *555*; **29** 669
Peto Brothers **12** 315
Petondi, Gregorio **12** 282; **16** 647
Petorutti, Emilio **5** 451
Petosiris **24** 555*
altar **1** 691
coffin **10** 58
reliefs **9** 811, 818, 821, 892; **14** 462
sculpture **9** 895
tomb **9** 842
Petr **18** 396; **25** 441
Petra **1** *849*; **2** *246*; **9** *513*; **17** 500, 655; **22** 418; **24** 556–8*; **26** *915*; **30** *180*
architectural decorations **22** 419
architecture **22** 419
ceramics **22** 420, *420*
al-Dayr **24** 318, 558; **26** 882; **31** 109
houses **24** 557
Khaznat al-Fir'awn **13** 392; **24** 557–8, *558*; **26** 882; **27** 31; **31** 109
mouldings **8** 324
Monastery *see* al-Dayr
museum **17** 656
orders (architecture) **23** 484
Palace of the Pharaoh's Daughter *see* Temple of Dushara
temples **26** 916; **27** 45
Qasr Bint Fir'awn *see* Temple of Dushara
Temple of Allat **22** 419; **24** 556–7
Temple of Dushara **24** 556; **26** 917
sculpture **24** *557*
Temple of Winged Lions *see* Temple of Allat
textiles **1** 880
theatre **24** 556; **26** 916
tombs **13** 407; **24** 557
trade **30** 179
Treasury of the Pharaoh *see* Khaznat al-Fir'awn
Urn tomb **24** 558
wall paintings **27** 51
water supply **22** 419; **24** 556
Petra Cacciati **7** 329
petrachrome **19** 878
Petradura, Cristoforo *see* BONADURA, CRISTOFORO
Petragrassa, Angelo **2** 394
Petraia, La *see* LA PETRAIA
Petrakos, B. **26** 287
Petrarch, Francesco **5** 871; **12** 265; **13** 131; **14** 866, 868; **16** 780; **22** 413; **24** 558–9*
groups and movements **26** 183
on architecture **16** 768
personal collection **5** 871; **20** 508; **32** 638
scripts **28** 306
works **1** 656; **12** 244, 681, 684; **13** *834*; **15** 82; **31** 881; **32** 222
illustrated **11** 685; **13** 833; **16** 847; **20** 744
translated **16** 854
Petrarch, Master of **20** 743–4*; **33** 33
works **2** *719*; **12** 385
Petrarch Triumphs, Master of the **1** 766; **20** 744*; **31** 846
patrons and collectors **4** 547; **31** 846
works **27** 247
Petraro Villa **27** 71
Petra Sancta, Sylvester **14** 406
Petraşcu, Gheorghe **3** 88; **24** 559–60*; **26** 715, 716, 723
Petraşcu, Milița **26** 716
Petravičius, Viktoras **19** 499
Petrazzi, Astolfo **21** 27; **24** 560*; **28** 688
Petre, Francis W(illiam) **23** 54; **24** 560*
Petrelë Castle **1** 538
Petrés, Domingo de **4** 233; **7** 605; **24** 560–61*
Petrescu-Dîmbovița, Mircea **8** 252
Petri, Adam **20** 793
Petri, Giovanni Nicolo **33** 276

Petri, Heinrich 20 794
Petri, Henning 30 104
Petri, Johannes 19 172
Petri, Johann Ludwig 28 194
Petri, Lajos 33 710
Petri, Martini 19 762
Petri, Olaus 30 77
Petri, Petrus see PETRUS PETRI
Petri, Pietro de 33 638
Petri, Trude 12 437
Petrić, Vladeta 28 453
Petrick, Wolfgang 3 803; 24 561*; 31 532
Petrie, Alexander 31 649
Petrie, (William Matthew) Flinders 2 296; 10 78, 91; 24 561*
excavations 1 501, 755, 892; 8 912; 9 849; 10 26, 80, 90; 14 251, 403; 18 237, 647; 20 117; 22 488; 30 296; 33 481
exhibitions 10 94
methods 2 299, 300
personal collection 10 71, 90, 92, 94
pupils 11 732
writings 14 453
Petrie, George 6 164; 16 16, 38; 24 562*
Petrie, James 24 562
Petrie Crown 6 162
Petrie Museum see LONDON → University College
petrified wood 14 168
Petrignani, Fantino 5 705
Petřík, T. 30 221
Petrini, Antonio 24 562–3*
patrons and collectors 28 146
works 3 139; 12 371; 23 2; 24 562; 33 430, 431
Petrini, Giuseppe Antonio 24 563–4*
works 19 781; 24 564; 30 132
Petrini, Marco 24 564
Petrioli, Caetano 7 906
Petrioli, G. F. 25 894
Petrits'ky, Anatoli (Galaktionovych) 24 564–5*
works 31 559, 559
Petro, Magister see TORRIGIANI, PIETRO (DI TORRIGIANO D'ANTONIO)
Petrocchi, Pietro 33 469
Petroceni see NERI RAZZANTI, PIETRO DE'
Petrodvorets see PETERHOF
petroglyphs see ROCK ART → techniques → engraving
Petrograd see ST PETERSBURG
Petrograd State Porcelain Factory see LOMONOSOV PORCELAIN FACTORY (ST PETERSBURG)
petrol 10 561; 29 53
petroleum jelly 10 548, 561
petroleum products 15 850; 33 2
petrol stations see SERVICE STATIONS
Petronell 2 776
chapel of St Johannes der Täufer 26 634
Petroni, Alessandro, Conte 11 814
Petronia 18 212
Petronius 9 13; 10 618; 13 555; 30 218
Petronius, Saint, Bishop of Bologna 4 280
Petropavlovsk 17 865
Petro Perú 24 515
Petrópolis 4 705, 711; 24 565*
Hospital Dom Pedro II 4 711
Museu Imperial 4 711, 725, 727, 728
Palácio Rio Negro see Museu Imperial
Petrosyan, Martin 2 433
Petrov 18 504
Petrov, B. 18 39
Petrov, Ilya 5 154
Petrov, Ivan (Nikolayevich) see ROPET, IVAN (PAVLOVICH)
Petrov, Kiril 23 16
Petrov, M. E. 21 810
Petrov, Mihailo 28 451
Petrov, Nikola 5 155
Petrov, Nikolay (Aleksandrovich) 24 565*, 739
Petrov, Nikolay (Philippovich) 30 299
Petrová, E. 8 426
Petrova, Tzvetana 5 161
Petrovaradin 28 437, 444
fortress 28 444, 444
Petrović, Leonard 9 331
Petrović, Nadežda 2 890; 24 566*; 28 451
Petrović, Peter 9 331
Petrović, Roman 4 461
Petrović, Zoran 20 898; 28 451, 454
Petrovich, Paul, Comte du Nord see PAUL I, Emperor of Russia
Petrovichev, Pyotr 27 392
Petrović Njegoš, Petar see PETER II, Vladika of Montenegro
Petrov-Petersberg 4 831
Petrovsk-Port see MAKHACHKALA
Petrovsky, N. P. 6 279
Petrovsky Service 27 420
Petrov-Vodkin, Kuz'ma (Sergeyevich) 24 566*; 27 392, 394
groups and movements 11 358; 27 394; 31 583; 33 380, 740
pupils 7 377; 18 527; 27 685
Petrozavodsk 27 433
Petrozzani, Tullio 32 403
Petrucci (family; Orvieto) 27 758
Petrucci (family; Siena) 28 703
Petrucci, Carlo Alberto 5 451; 12 824
Petrucci, Francesco 3 468; 21 30; 23 444
Petrucci, Ottaviano dei 22 369
works 22 370
Petrucci, Pandolfo 3 467; 8 101; 24 567*; 28 673
Petruccio 12 749
Petruccio di Benedetto 23 587
Petrus (fl 1269) 24 783
Petrus (fl before 1550) 22 165
Petrus, Bishop of Transylvania 7 471
Petrus, Anna 30 111
Petrus Andrea 4 278; 16 733
Petrus Aurifaber 11 107
Petrus Berchorius 1 654; 10 202; 22 412; 23 679
Petrus Brunus 27 561
Petrus Christus see CHRISTUS, PETRUS
Petrus de Angicuria see PIERRE D'ANGICOURT
Petrus de Maria 7 922
Petrus de Tiergevilla 26 563
Petrus di Vinea 14 646
Petrus Italus da Lugano 26 707
Petrus Lantregen 14 893; 26 711
Petrus Luitinius 25 110
Petrus Oderisii see PIETRO DI ODERISIO
Petrusov, Georgy (Grigoriyevich) 24 567*
Petrus Petri 31 91
Petrus Rogerius, Bishop of Toulouse 31 207
Petrussen, Knud 13 620
Petsas 24 337
Petschacher, Gusztáv 5 83; 24 567–8*
Petschnigg, Hubert 14 399; 24 568*
Petsophás 8 153; 21 664
Pettenkofen, August (Xaver Karl) von 2 797; 13 332; 24 568*; 30 210; 32 445
Pettenkofen, Ferdinand 24 568
Pettenkofer, Max (Joseph) von 4 438; 24 568–9*
Petter, Anton 11 161
Pettersen, Remmert see PIETTERSZ., REMMERT
Pettersen, Sverre 23 235
Petterson, Adrian 11 851; 13 30
Petterson, Hugo Birger see BIRGER (PETTERSON), HUGO
Pettersson, Lars 11 113
petticoats 25 821
Pettie, John 24 569, 569–70*
collaboration 20 34
pupils 13 868
teachers 18 856
works 28 237, 238
Pettifer, James 10 274; 29 835
works 10 275
Pettigrew, David 16 42
Pettirossi, Benardino 6 146
Pettit, Hélène-Marie 2 142
Pettit, Paul 3 232; 11 426, 427
Pettit & Sevitt 33 373
Pettitt, Joseph Paul 4 86; 14 106
Pettondi, F. I. 2 417
Pettoruti, Emilio 6 598; 24 570*
patrons and collectors 31 758
pupils 13 869
works 2 399, 400
Petty, Bruce (Leslie) 24 571*
Petty, George 1 494
Petty, William 7 416; 14 806; 24 571–2*
Petty, William (Fitzmaurice), 2nd Earl of Shelburne and 1st Marquess of Lansdowne 5 71; 10 366; 13 696; 24 570*
furniture 15 165
Petty-Fitzmaurice, Henry, 3rd Marquess of Lansdowne 24 571*
architecture 3 283
paintings 7 572; 32 922
sculpture 33 99
Petun 22 612; 31 175
petuntse see CHINA STONE
Pétursson, Valtýr 15 70; 24 572*
Petuvash, Feliks 27 433
Petworth House (W. Sussex) 8 46; 10 275, 276
carpets 5 838
Carved Room 12 591, 592; 23 542
catalogues 3 81
ceramics 9 28
collections 7 839; 10 364, 365; 33 453
frames 11 424, 426
frescoes 15 139
furniture 4 532; 7 172; 10 291
North Gallery 9 12, 18
paintings 4 573; 5 354; 7 426; 8 454; 9 12, 18, 478; 10 159; 14 586, 754; 17 915; 19 63, 98, 121, 859; 24 637; 31 467, 471–2
portraits 24 390; 32 912
prints 9 26
sculpture 5 740; 9 23; 27 197
tapestries 9 30; 10 351
Petworth Oil Pourer 25 179
Petzold, Carl Eduard Adolf 31 488
Petzold, Hans see PETZOLT, HANS
Petzoldt, Andreas 24 572*
Petzoldt, Eduard 22 382
Petzoldt, Johann Christoph see PEZOLD, JOHANN CHRISTOPH
Petzolt (family) 23 312
Petzolt, Hans 23 312; 24 573*
collaboration 1 789
groups and movements 9 447
patrons and collectors 8 413; 10 528
pupils 16 901
works 12 443, 444; 25 22
Petzval, Josef Maximilian 24 660
Peuerlin see BEIERLEIN
Peurer, Wolfgang 20 693
Peurlin, Hanns 3 515*
Peutin, Jean 5 212
Peutinger (family) 5 199
Peutinger, Conrad 2 716; 5 199; 24 573*
patrons and collectors 13 903; 33 365
works 12 386
Peutinger Prayerbook see under PRAYERBOOKS → individual manuscripts
Peux, Jean 12 468
Pevensey Castle (E. Sussex) 20 571; 33 199
Peverel, William 23 258
Pevsner, Antoine 11 569, 877; 24 440, 573–4*
assistants 20 833
collaboration 11 877; 25 25
groups and movements 1 76; 3 120; 18 62; 27 639
Abstraction-Création 1 90
Cercle et Carré 6 342
Constructivism 1 90
Salon des Réalités Nouvelles 8 838
patrons and collectors 32 568
productions 8 850; 30 686
pupils 18 141
works 1 132; 12 408; 16 57; 24 574
Pevsner, Nikolaus (Bernhard Leon) 8 610; 11 839; 14 222; 18 827; 19 229; 24 575*; 32 415
pupils 3 172
works 2 362, 573; 10 377; 14 580; 19 896; 21 779
Pevzner, Natan Borisovich see PEVZNER, ANTOINE
Pevzner, Naum Borisovich see GABO, NAUM
Pewabic Pottery 30 887; 31 639
pews 7 283–4; 24 575–8*, 576, 577; 26 718; 28 251
Pewsey (Wilts) 14 545
pewter 21 319; 24 578–81*
display 9 30
historical and regional traditions
Armenia (Europe) 2 441
Austria 2 821
Belgium 3 603
Britain 24 578
Bulgaria 5 160
China 7 16, 96*, 100–101*, 101; 24 580
Czech Republic 8 415*, 415
Denmark 8 751, 752
England 10 341*; 12 453; 21 II2; 24 579, 579, 580, 809
France 11 624, 628*, 629; 24 578, 579
Germany 12 423, 452–4*, 453; 13 161
Gothic 13 161
Hungary 15 8
Italy 16 743
Jamaica 16 888; 24 580
Japan 17 297, 318
Jewish art 24 580
Malaysia 20 173
Netherlands, the 1 810; 12 453; 22 893, 893–4*; 24 578, 580
Norway 23 237
Rome, ancient 24 578
Scotland 28 262, 262
Spain 29 342
Sweden 30 110–11
Switzerland 30 146–7
United States of America 24 580, 581; 31 651–2*
marks see under MARKS
techniques
engraving 24 578
moulding 24 578
wrigglework 21 II2; 24 578, 579
uses
alms-dishes 24 580
altar sets 7 101
beakers 24 580
bottles 24 580
bowls 24 580
boxes 7 100
pewter
uses—cont.
candlesticks 5 611; 12 453; 24 580, 581, 581
chalices 24 580
clysters 24 580
coffeepots 24 580
cupboards 12 423
cups 7 100; 24 580
dolls' furniture 31 264
flagons 15 8; 22 893; 24 580
fonts (baptismal) 8 415, 415; 11 253; 24 580
inlays 20 467; 21 329
lacquer 7 16; 17 297
lamps 24 581
liturgical objects 24 580
loving-cups 24 580
marquetry 12 423; 20 466
measures 12 453
mugs 24 580
ointment pots 24 580
pap-boats 24 580
patens 24 580
pilgrim badges 24 809
plates 24 580
printing plates 25 612
spoons 8 284
standishes 29 535
syringes 24 580
tankards 24 579, 580
tea-caddies 7 101
teapots 7 101, 101; 24 580
tea-services 7 101
see also TIN
Pey, Johann de see PAY, JOHANN DE
Peyer (family) 29 673
glass 29 673
Pey i Farriol, Josep 29 308, 320, 329
Peyn, Caspar de 8 427
peyote 25 681
Peypus, Friedrich 29 719
Peyrat 24 96
Peyre, Antoine-François 24 581, 582–3*
groups and movements 24 173
pupils 3 124; 11 257; 15 42; 24 387, 583; 28 372; 32 80
works 12 167; 27 623
Peyre, Antoine-Marie 24 581, 583*; 32 766
Peyre, Jules 28 523
Peyre, Marie-Joseph 22 93; 24 581–3*
collaboration 19 251; 24 122; 32 768
groups and movements 22 734
pupils 24 582, 583
works 20 867; 24 582; 25 267; 29 833; 30 671
writings 20 867
Peyrefitte, Ignatius 3 624
Peyrenc de Moras, Abraham 2 701
Peyrón, B. T. 30 115
Peyron, Jacques 19 38
Peyron, (Jean-François-) Pierre 11 540; 24 583–4*
patrons and collectors 3 840
pupils 21 902
reproductive prints by others 28 474
teachers 32 427
works 8 867; 24 583
Peyrony, Denis 11 285
Peyrotte, Alexis 28 297
works 28 298
Peyster, De, Limner see DE PEYSTER LIMNER
Peytel Cup 16 366
Pezaro 11 604
Pezay, Marquise de 32 495
Pez Dorado 24 401; 32 176
Pezerat, Pierre Joseph 19 466; 24 584–5*
assistants 28 730
works 4 711; 26 413
Pezet, Paul 26 385

Pezinok, Jan Kupecký House-Museum **18** 525
Pezold, Andreas *see* PETZOLDT, ANDREAS
Pezold, August Georg **10** 539
Pezold, Johann Christoph **24** 585*
Pezolt, Hans *see* PETZOLT, HANS
Pezzo, del (family) **20** 418
Pfaff, Ferenc **33** 593
Pfaff, Judy **24** 585*
Pfaff, Nicholas **8** 395; **13** 914
Pfäffikon **27** 67
Seedamm-Kulturzentrum **30** 152
Pfaffinger, Joseph Anton **11** 120
Pfahler, Karl Georg **12** 397
Pfalzel Abbey **13** 111
Pfalzen, Friedrich von *see* FRIEDRICH VON PFALZEN
Pfalzfeld **6** 156; **25** *470*
pillars **6** *156*
sculpture **6** *156*
Pfalz-Neuburg, Wolfgang William von, Count *see* WOLFGANG WILLIAM, Count Palatine of the Rhine
Pfandzelt, Lukas **26** 731; **27** 438
Pfankuch, Peter **10** 857
Pfann, Paul **17** 853
Pfann, Wilhelm **10** 444, 445
Pfannmüller, Seyfried **8** 529
Pfau (family) **30** 143
Pfau, Bernhard **12** 379; **28** 127
Pfau, Johann Ernst **8** 747; **30** 883
Pfau, Ludwig, the elder **30** 143
Pfau, Ludwig, the younger
workshop **30** *144*
Pfautz, J. G. **29** 748
Pfeffel, Johann Andreas, I **14** 695; **18** 106
Pfeffinger, Johann Friedrich **20** 109
Pfeiffer, A. H. **17** 816
Pfeiffer, Eduard **12** 237; **33** 387
Pfeiffer, Johann Joachim **30** 284
Pfeiffer, Josef Anton **8** 410
Pfeiffer, Max Adolf **21** 67
Pfeiffer, Norman Henry **14** 174*
Pfeiffer, R. H. **23** 322
Pfeiffer, Wilhelm **33** 275
Pfeiffer-Watenphul, Max **27** 665
Pfeil, Niklaus Meyer zum *see* MEYER ZUM PFEIL, NIKLAUS
Pfelghard, Otto **14** 24
Pfemfert, Franz **24** 445, 585*; **28** 89
Pfeninger, Elsa **6** 600
Pfenninger, Johann **32** 677
Pfeufer, Joachim **11** 80
Pfeyll, Johann **17** 849
Pfieffer, Johann Georg **3** 429
Pfifferer (family) **33** 358
Pfinzing (family) **1** 788
Pfinzing, Melchior **3** 70; **9** 435; **13** 903; **28** 58, *191*; **33** 353
Pfinzing von Helenfeld, I. **24** 56
Pfinzing von Henfenfeld (family) **3** 70; **16** 900
Pfister, Albrecht **3** 140; **4** 357, *357*; **10** 725; **12** 385; **21** 337
Pfister, Hans **24** 585–6*
attributions **19** 835
works **25** 113, 130; **30** 345
Pfister, Peter **18** 518
Pflanzman, Jodocus **4** 9
Pflaum, Hans **12** 443
Pflaume, Herman **7** 581
Pflaz-Zweibrücken, Christian, Herzog von **33** 675
Pfleger, Karl Nikolaus **24** 586*
Pflock Altarpiece, Master of the **8** 118
Pflug, Franz Peter **29** 750
Pflug, Robert **18** 850; **26** 383
Pflüger, Conrad **24** 586*
works **2** 117; **19** 110; **31** 166; **33** 112
Pfnorr, Vogels Wilhelm **33** 369
Pfohl, Alexander **17** 816
Pfohl, Karl **8** 410
Pforr, Franz **24** 586–8*; **26** 776; **28** 68
groups and movements **12** 392; **14** 580; **22** 703; **32** 677
teachers **32** 751
works **11** 462; **14** 586; **24** *587*
Pforr, Johann Georg **24** 586
Pforzheim
enamel **12** 457
gold **12** 450, 451
jewellery **12** 455, 456; **17** 528
metalwork **12** 448
Schmuckmuseum **12** 451
silver **12** 449
Pfrommer, Michael **28** 324
Pfronten, Burguine Falkenstein **29** 843
Pfründt, Anna Maria *see* BRAUN, ANNA MARIA
Pfründt, Georg **4** 697; **24** 588*; **28** 193
Pfullendorf Altar, Master of the **20** 744–5*
Pfundstein, Jean Martin **29** 750
Pfundt, Christian **30** 84
Pfyffer, Louis **19** 769
Phaedrus **10** 723; **11** 307
Phagdu, Thil **30** 818
Phagspa **2** 477; **6** 307; **21** 875; **27** 600
Phaidon **12** 873; **14** 767
Phaistos **8** 153, 154, 155; **13** *362*; **21** *651*; **24** 588–91*
alabaster (gypsum) **21** 662
faience (i) (glass) **21** 683, 684
First Palace **24** 589–90
houses **21** *662*, *663*
inscriptions **21** 691
ivory-carvings **21** 681, 682
palace **8** 153; **21** 651, 657, 658, 663, 691; **23** 808; **24** *589*
wall paintings **21** 674
pottery **21** *665*, 667
seals **21** 658, 685
Second Palace **14** 338; **24** 590
staircase **21** 662
towns **21** 664
water supply **21** 662
Phaistos Disc **24** 591, *591*
Phajoding **21** 848
Phakpa **5** 112; **21** 883
Phakpa script *see under* SCRIPTS → types
Phalanstère, Le **11** 358
Phalanx **17** 761; **18** 490; **22** 304; **23** 337; **24** 591–2*; **28** 821
Phalasarna **8** 154
phalerae **30** 772–3
Phami **30** 626, 627
Phaṁpī *see* PHARPHING
phāṁsanā **15** 244*
Pham-thing *see* PHARPHING
Pham Van Don **32** 482
Phanagoria **4** 110, 111
Phānapiṅga *see* PHARPHING
Phan Piet **6** 427
Phan Ri **6** 425, 426
Phantastischer Realismus **2** 797; **4** 697; **11** 812; **13** 867; **24** 592*; **32** 447
Phantom group **10** 616
Pharai **13** 418
Pharaklas Torso **2** 686
Pharoux, Pierre **14** 743
Pharphing **22** *753*, 771; **24** 592*
Phaselis **19** 837
Phases **11** 745; **14** 219; **24** 348
Phases **2** 526; **9** 201
Phasoula **8** 333
Phat Diem Church **32** 476
Phat Tich, Van Phuc Temple **32** *468*, 472, 478, *478*
Phaulkon, Constantin **4** 796; **18** 613; **30** 575
Phayao **30** 604, 609, 610
Wat Si Khom Kham **30** 604
Pha Yu, King of Lanna (*reg* 1337-55) **6** 567
Phebus, Gaston de *see* GASTON DE PHEBUS
Pheidias **13** 435, 439, 440, 450, 453, 468, 553; **24** 592–4*; **25** 45
architecture **2** 676, 680; **13** 455–6
assistants **13** 423
attributions **2** 682, 684; **10** *139*, 140, 425; **23** 291
collaboration **1** 646; **23** 901; **24** 206; **30** 707
competitions **10** 425; **15** 894
copies **13** 464, 470; **25** 576; **27** 39; **29** 567
glass **13** 594
patrons and collectors **13** 374
personal collection **32** 49
pupils **14** 301; **18** 208
sculpture **13** 374, 435, 439, 454, 573
Athena Parthenos **2** 676, 682; **8** 262; **9** 20; **13** 379, 426, 573, 596; **15** 132; **22** 42; **24** 418, *593*; **30** 435
Athena Promachos **13** 439; **22** 42
Zeus statue **6** 388; **13** 370, 371; **23** 430, 432
teachers **1** 450
works **2** 682; **7** 245; **13** 453, *453*, 454; **25** 799
Pheidon of Argos **13** 410
Phelan, Jan **5** 582
Phelippeaux, Antoine **29** 676
Phélippes, Charles-François **21** 170
phelonia **9** 643, *643*
see also CHASUBLES
Phelps Dodge Corporation **11** 835
Phelps Stokes, I. N. *see* STOKES, I. N. PHELPS
Phélypeaux de la Vrillière, Louis *see* LA VRILLIÈRE, LOUIS PHÉLYPEAUX DE
Phendin-Klang Rama II, King of Thailand (*reg* 1809-24) **30** 639
Pheneos **13** 587
Phenix & Joyau **28** 520
phenolic resin *see under* RESINS → types
phenomenology **1** 80; **10** 686; **21** 157; **24** 594–6*; **26** 62
Pherai **13** *363*, 601
fibulae **13** *600*
pins **13** *600*
Phetchaburi **30** *571*
gold **30** 635
Phra Nakhon Khiri **30** 590
royal palace **30** 608
Wat Kamphaeng Laeng **30** 581
Wat Ko Kaeo Suttharam **30** 616
Wat Sa Bua **30** 588, *588*
Wat Yai Suwannaram **30** 616
Pheziu Pavés **10** 615
phialai **1** 118, *118*; **7** 278; **13** 477, 569, 575
Phiale Painter **13** 536
patrons and collectors **13** 542
teachers **32** 34
works **13** 521, 538
Phichit **30** 631
Phien An *see under* HO CHI MINH CITY
Phikardou Rural Museum **8** 367
Philadelphia (Lydia) **19** 840, 841
St John **9** 525
Philadelphia (Palestine) *see* AMMAN
Philadelphia (PA; USA) **2** 325; **24** 596–602*, *597*, *599*; **31** *587*, 721, 725, 735
Academy **28** 156
art forms and materials
architecture **11** 849
brass **31** 653
chairs **31** *625*
clocks **31** 624
coins **24** 626
dioramas **8** 911
frames **11** 498
Philadelphia (PA; USA)
art forms and materials—cont.
furniture **24** 601–2*; **31** 623, 625, 626, *627*, 628
glass **31** 642
interior decoration **31** 617
medals **20** 924, 925
painting **29** 669
paper **24** 48
pewter **31** 651
pottery **31** 634, 635
silver **31** 646, 647, 648, 649
textiles **31** 656
wallpaper **32** 815
Athenaeum Club **26** 190
Bank of Pennsylvania **3** 175, *175*; **10** 850; **13** 610; **31** 591
portico **25** 268
Bellevue-Stratford Hotel **14** 788
Beth Sholom Synagogue **1** 736
Broad Street Station **25** 855, 856
Carl Mackley Houses **17** 838
Centennial International Exhibition, 1876 **10** 682; **15** 883
Centre Square engine house **18** *844*
Chestnut Street Theater (1793) **30** 677, 679
Christ Church **4** 786, 787
City Hall **5** 422; **19** 867; **31** 593, 662
Columbian Gallery **27** 882
Congress Hall **31** 652
Eastern State Penitentiary **25** 637; **31** 592
Exchange **10** 669
Fairmount Park **10** 682
First Bank of the United States **3** 174
Franklin Institute *see* museums → Atwater Kent Museum
Free Library **15** 745
Girard College for Orphans **32** 827–8
Founder's Hall **32** *827*
Guild House Retirement Home **15** 887; **25** 359
Historical Society of Pennsylvania **22** 714
Independence Hall **18** 886; **31** 652
Labyrinth Gardens **23** 776
Laurel Hill Cemetery **6** 166; **20** 869; **23** 256; **31** 131
Merchants' Exchange **13** 611; **29** 771
Metro stations **21** 349
Mikveh Israel synagogue **17** 547
museums
Atwater Kent Museum **14** 246
Columbianum **23** 630; **24** 279; **27** 349; **31** 662
Memorial Hall **22** 363
Museum of Art **2** 384, 560; **12** 54; **17** 619; **22** 359; **24** 600; **31** 390, 666
archives **2** 366
Arensburg Collection **9** 359
collections **2** 450; **9** 501; **12** 15; **15** 745; **16** 557; **26** 127; **29** 657; **30** 332
exhibitions **15** 748; **24** 683
Johnson collection **19** 666; **20** 660
Peale Museum **31** 666; **33** 216
Philadelphia Museum **24** 302, 304
Rodin Museum **13** 337; **24** 601
University Museum *see under* University of Pennsylvania
National Museum of American Jewish History **17** 582
Old Church **31** 652
optics **24** 742
Pennsylvania Academy of the Fine Arts **6** 79, 176; **11** 848; **24** 600; **31** 593, 666, 669
archives **2** 367
Philadelphia (PA; USA)
Pennsylvania Academy of the Fine Arts—cont.
collections **10** 103
Pennsylvania Hospital **14** 782
Pennsylvania Hospital for the Insane **2** 658
Philadelphia Exchange *see* Merchants' Exchange
Philadelphia Savings Fund Society Building **3** 177; **14** 811; **15** 886; **28** 833; **31** 597
Provident Life and Trust Company Bank **3** 175
PSFS building *see* Philadelphia Savings Fund Society building
Public Buildings *see* City Hall
Public Library **19** 319
Richards Medical Research Laboratories **10** 417
St Mark's **13** 203
Second Bank of the United States **3** 175; **13** 611; **29** 770; **31** 591
service station **28** 488
Solitude **10** 849
State House *see* Independence Hall
synagogues **31** 649
Theatre (1766) **30** 677
Union League Club **7** 470
University of Pennsylvania
collections **10** 94; **15** 922; **21** 692; **31** 694
library **11** 849, *849*
Richards Medical Research Laboratories **17** 724; **31** 597
University Museum **10** 718; **16** 557; **21** 310, 692; **27** 47; **29** 241; **31** 354; **32** 238
Upper Ferry Bridge **4** 802
Vanna Venturi House **25** 359; **31** 598
Wanamaker's **8** 770; **30** 507
Woodlands **10** 850
Philadelphia 2449, Painter of **13** 538
Philadelphia Painter **13** 495
Philadelphia Photographer **24** 432
Philadelphia School **15** 140
Philadelphia Society of Etching **25** 629
Philae **9** *774*, 892, 896; **24** 602–3*, *603*; **26** *921*
Gate of Hadrian **9** 896
Kiosk of Trajan **18** 70; **26** 920
mammisi **20** 231, 232
obelisks **10** 90
orders (architecture) **23** 484
reliefs **9** 891
stelae **9** 890
temples **10** 81; **29** 711; **30** 237
Temple of Augustus **26** 920
Temple of Isis **2** 656; **9** 834, 835, 896; **10** 83; **23** 532
reliefs **9** 894, *894*
Philae Painter **32** 28, 62–3*
Philander, Guillaume **11** 514; **24** 603–4*; **32** 641
Philanthropinos, Nikolaos **25** 331
Philaretos, Saint **9** 649
Philbrook Art Museum *see under* TULSA (OK)
Philes, Manuel **16** 602
Philetairos **24** 412
Philia culture **8** 329
Philia-Drakos **8** *325*, 343; **13** 371
Philibert, Margrave of Baden-Baden (*reg* 1536-69) **29** 674
Philibert, Saint **7** 453; **21** 835, 844
Philibert II, Duke of Savoy (*reg* 1497-1504) **28** *2*
Philidor **20** 497
Philip, Count of Flanders (*reg* 1168-91) **4** 918
Philip, Duke of Parma (*reg* 1748-65) **3** 101; **4** 521; **9** 208; **20** 270; **23** 667; **24** 552

Philip, Duke of Pomerania-Stettin (*reg* 1606-18) **13** 630–31*; **18** 225
architecture **30** 203
collections **13** 630; **25** 137
decorative works **2** 44
furniture **2** *716*; **14** 51; **21** 127; **32** 772
Philip, Elector Palatine (*reg* 1476-1508) **19** 29; **20** 694, *920*
Philip, Prince, Duke of Edinburgh (*b* 1921) **23** 67
Philip I, Count of Savoy (*reg* 1268-85) **16** 894
Philip I, King of Castile (*reg* 1504-06) **13** *900*; **14** *2*
armour **15** 866
cradles (i) (cots) **8** 107
flags **11** 149
manuscripts **8** 857; **13** 142; **14** 726; **20** 657, 659, 725
paintings **3** 844; **4** 446; **19** 350
stained glass **26** 744
tapestries **31** 219
Philip I, King of Portugal *see* PHILIP II, King of Spain
Philip I of Anjou, Prince of Taranto *see* PHILIP IV, King of France
Philip II, Duke of Burgundy *see* PHILIP THE BOLD, 1st Duke of Burgundy
Philip II, King of Macedon (*reg* 359-336 BC) **4** 102; **24** 604*
architecture **7** 852; **13** 373, 404; **23** 430; **25** 51; **27** 692; **30** 737
coins **13** 588, *596*
gold **13** 598, 599
metalwork **12** 624
sculpture **13** 435
weapons **21** 557
Philip II, King of Portugal *see* PHILIP III, King of Spain
Philip II, King of Spain (*reg* 1556-98) **3** 213; **5** 201; **13** 922*, *922*; **14** *2*, 5; **29** 267, 356
altars **30** 802
architecture **6** 24; **14** 472, 473, 476; **20** 65; **23** 745; **30** 518; **31** 93, 822; **32** 117
churches **1** 740; **32** 505
fortifications **8** 231
military **2** 176; **23** 745; **28** 499
monasteries **30** 518
palaces **2** 284; **7** 665; **10** 498, 499, 501; **20** 70; **23** 492, 683, 811; **28** 709; **29** 300; **30** 518; **32** 117
tabernacles (ii) (receptacle) **9** 339
urban planning **19** 699
art policies **20** 462
books **2** 411; **14** 659; **19** 313
catafalques **6** 71
ceramics **33** 720
coins **13** 862; **25** 75
collections **2** 558; **12** 883; **13** 341; **14** 1, 7; **20** 66; **21** 264, 396; **27** 114; **29** 277, 352
coral **31** 285
decorative works **29** 300
drawings **14** 661, 662; **33** 454
education (architectural) **25** 319
furniture **6** 390; **29** 313; **31** 682
gardens **2** 284; **12** 124
gems **12** 260
imprese **29** 740
interior decoration **29** 300
ivory-carvings **20** 90; **29** 344
leather **19** 3
manuscripts **3** 188; **6** 25; **14** 658
maps **33** 454
medals **17** 643; **20** 921; **25** 75; **31** 319
metalwork **16** 899; **29** 334, 339
Philip II, King of Spain (*reg* 1556-98)—cont.
paintings **2** 867; **3** 257; **4** 453; **5** 172; **6** 24; **7** 562; **9** 173; **22** 63, 64; **24** 261; **27** 704; **31** 31, 41; **32** 156
allegorical **13** 341
animal subjects **27** 754
frescoes **33** 719
Grotesque **6** 25
literary themes **16** 666; **22** 413; **23** 680
miniatures **2** 868
mythological **3** 471; **23** 293; **25** 71; **32** 192
portraits **22** 63, 64; **25** 419; **31** 39–41
religious **5** 457, 735, 902; **7** 468; **8** 87; **13** 307, 909; **22** 73, 392, 694, 695; **23** 671; **31** 14; **33** 118
printing **6** 595; **25** 17
reliquaries **29** 340
retables **29** 290
sculpture **6** 25, 146; **19** 200, 203; **29** 290
silver **3** 7
stained glass **8** 103
tapestries **3** 612
tiles **29** 326
Philip II Augustus, King of France (*reg* 1180-1223) **3** 456; **4** 578; **11** 603, 655
architecture **6** 55; **11** 511; **14** 74; **27** 558; **32** 581
military **5** 369; **6** 54; **24** 115, 161; **27** 245
reliquaries **26** 146
Philip III, Duke of Burgundy *see* PHILIP THE GOOD, 3rd Duke of Burgundy
Philip III, King of France (*reg* 1270-85) **5** 726; **8** 197; **13** 158
Philip III, King of Navarre (*reg* 1328-43) **23** 402, 409
Philip III, King of Portugal *see* PHILIP IV, King of Spain
Philip III, King of Spain (*reg* 1598-1621) **8** 138; **13** *900*, *901*; **14** *2*, 6*; **31** 823
architecture **5** 411; **6** *72*; **7** 488; **22** 68; **25** 455; **32** 116
art policies **29** 301
collections **29** 352
guns **2** 462
manuscripts **20** 341
paintings **5** 411, 737; **14** 1; **31** 813; **32** 755
sculpture **2** 284; **10** 903; **14** 478; **22** 423; **29** 291, 345; **30** 228
Philip III Arrhidaios, King of Macedon (*reg* 323-317 BC) **9** *778*; **27** 691, 692
Philip IV, King of France (*reg* 1285-1314) **5** 665–6*; **9** 708; **24** 774
architecture **5** 727; **9** 708; **13** 59; **32** 573
coins **7** 536
collections **14** 10
enamel **2** 112; **13** 168
gold **13** 828
interior decoration **29** 302
manuscripts **4** 764; **5** 663; **11** 531; **14** 724–5
menagerie **33** 698
metalwork **13** 158; **14** *418*
painting **3** 554; **13** 147
paintings **14** 10; **27** 449
sculpture **10** 665; **13** 76
silver **14** 418
tapestries **13** 634
Philip IV, King of Spain (*reg* 1621-65) **4** *543*; **13** *901*; **14** *2*, 7–9*, *9*
architecture **5** 725; **14** 460; **22** 68; **24** 107; **26** 501; **29** 300; **32** 128, 551
art policies **1** 105; **29** 303
carpets **29** 347
Philip IV, King of Spain (*reg* 1621-65)—cont.
catafalques **24** 836
collections **19** 779; **27** 301; **29** 352
frames **11** 490
furniture **29** 302
gardens **12** 124
guns **2** 462
paintings **4** 619; **5** 427; **6** 24; **7** 622; **9** 16; **10** 763; **14** 1; **17** 648; **20** 899; **22** 7; **26** 436; **27** 802; **28** 479; **30** 463; **32** 125, 126, 426, 560
allegorical **5** 737
animal **32** 706
history **5** 844; **22** 21
hunting scenes **28** 898, 903
landscape **7** 394
literary themes **3** 613; **22** 414; **23** 680; **27** 296
mythological **8** 1; **22** 21; **25** 274, 809; **30** 787
portraits **4** 575; **13** 879; **29** 800
religious **3** 179; **12** 306; **14** 755; **29** 543
sculpture **2** 163, 284; **14** 714; **19** 770; **29** 291
silver **29** 336
sponsorship **32** 128
stage design **3** 17
tapestries **29** 350
teachers **20** 125
Philip V, King of Macedon (*reg* 221-179 BC) **13** 589; **21** 558
Philip V, King of Spain (*reg* 1700-24) **4** *543*, 556, *557*, 557–9*, *559*; **19** *648*; **20** 63
architecture **2** 284, 379; **17** 710; **20** 67, 71; **27** 752; **29** 271
palaces **20** 72
art policies **29** 336
ceramics **6** 332
collections **4** 558
decorative works **23** 458
drawings **26** 246
engravings **23** 896
fountains **11** 345
furniture **29** 303
gardens **12** 124
gold **29** 336
guns **2** 467
paintings **4** 559; **5** 436; **7** 682; **12** 922; **16** 49; **19** 524; **21** 79; **24** 10; **25** 2, 644, 887; **26** 386; **27** 331; **29** 352
sculpture **3** 198; **4** 588; **11** 754; **23** 412; **25** 645; **26** 553; **30** 733; **32** 8
sponsorship **6** 67; **24** 351, 461; **25** 460
tapestries **29** 350; **30** 324
Philip VI, King of France (*reg* 1328-50) **7** 536; **10** 665; **12** 723; **31** 832, *833*; **32** 581
Philip, John Birnie (1824-75) **24** 604–5*
collaboration **28** 278
pupils **19** 60
works **10** 266; **27** 629
Philip, John Moore **31** 496
Philip, P. **10** 91
Philip, Rosalind **12** 777
Philip, T. Terry **13** 811
Philip Bel, King of France *see* PHILIP IV, King of France
Philip Cox Richardson Taylor & Partners **8** 86
Philip of Burgundy, Bishop of Utrecht **5** 206, 214–15*; **13** 23; **22** 901
paintings **3** 201, 554; **4** 446; **22** 836, 837, 901
portraits **13** 25–6
sculpture **21** 71
Philip of Campello **11** 712
Philip of Cleves **10** 222; **14** 618; **20** 737
Philipon, Charles **8** 545, 546; **22** 424; **24** 605*
printmakers **13** 306
works **5** 757; **9** 169; **19** 484; **27** 871
Philipp, Prince-Bishop of Freising **33** 84
Philippa, Duchess of Aquitaine (*fl* 1098) **31** 207
Philippa of Hainault, Queen of England (1314-69) **1** 517; **17** 458; **25** 808
Roger Borsa, Duke of Apulia (*reg* 1085-1111) **19** 581
Philippart, Clemens August Josef **3** 497
Philippas, Church of Pantanassa **9** 550
Philippe, David **4** 96
Philippe, J. **3** 620
Philippe, Patek **11** 635
Philippe, Petrus **4** 96
Philippe-Auguste, Salnave **24** 605*
Philippe-Auguste de Villiers de l'Isle-Adam, Comte *see* VILLIERS DE L'ISLE-ADAM, PHILIPPE-AUGUSTE, Comte de
Philippe de Foncières **31** 842
Philippe de Mazerolles **19** 727; **20** 618; **24** 605–6*
attributions **19** 350
collaboration **20** 644
patrons and collectors **3** 555; **5** 213
Philippe de Mezières **5** 208; **19** 340
Philippe de Thaon **14** 406
Philippe le paintre **13** 195
Philippe Pigouchet **1** 765
Philippi **9** *511*; **24** 606–7*; **26** *908*
Basilica A **7** 255; **9** 538, 590
Basilica B **9** 538, 590
fortifications **9** 555
macellum **26** 910
marble **29** 702, *702*
mosaics **9** 565
Octagon **9** 590
Philippi, Gerhard **14** 865
Philippine Quarterly of Culture and Society **24** 437
Philippines **24** *607*, 607–32*
architecture **24** 610*, 614–15*
Christianity **24** 611–14*
Islamic **24** 610–11*
military **21** 596
20th cent. **20** *274*
archives **2** 369, 371*
barkcloth **24** 623
basketwork **24** 628*, *628*
beads **24** 625
benches **24** 629, *630*
betel sets **24** 627–8
boat coffins **27** 823, 831
boats **24** 624*
body ornaments **24** 625–6*
*bolo*s **24** 631
brass **24** 627–8, *627*
canoes **23** 724
ceramics **24** 626*
churches **24** 611, *612*, *613*
coins **24** 626*
containers **24** 626–8*, *627*
cotton **24** *629*
dress **24** 628*, *629*
education (art) **24** 622, 632*
embroidery **24** 624
fortifications **21** 596
furniture **24** 629*
gold **24** 626, 627*
grave markers **24** 630*
houses **24** 610–11, *611*, *615*, 615–16*, *616*
iconography **24** 609–10*
iron **29** 228
jewellery **24** 625, 626
keris **24** 631
knives **24** *631*
lutuan *see* betel sets
metalwork **24** 627–8*
mosques **24** 611
Philippines—cont.
musical instruments **24** 630*
painting **24** 620–23*
religion **24** 609–10*
santos **24** 610
scabbards **24** *631*
sculpture **24** 609, 617*, 619–20*
bulul **24** 609, 617, *618*
Christianity **24** 618–19*
Islamic **24** 618*
okir **24** 618
santos **24** 619, *619*
wood **24** *619*
silver **24** 626, 627–8*
swords **24** 631
tattoos **24** 626*
textiles **24** 623–4*
trade **6** 622
ceramics **6** 331; **24** 626; **30** 609
jewellery **29** 345
urban planning **24** 616–17*
watercolours **24** *621*
weapons **24** 630–31*, *631*
weaving **24** 623–4
wood **24** *619*, 626–7*, *630*
wood-carvings **24** 610, 617, 618, 619, *619*, 625, *630*
see also SOUTH-EAST ASIA
Philipp Morris GmbH **12** 472
Philippolis **1** 318
Philippon, Adam **19** 210
Philippopolis *see* PLOVDIV
Philippos **27** 73
Philippoteaux, Félix Henri Emmanuel **7** 529; **24** 19
Philippoteaux, Paul Dominique **24** 19
Philippotis, Demetrios **4** 297; **13** 354; **24** 632*
Philipps, Erasmus **8** 474; **32** 790
Philipp Sigismund, Bishop of Verden and Osnabrück **22** 317
Philipp von Cleve *see* PHILIP OF CLEVES
Philips *see* PHILLIPE, MAÎTRE
Philips, Caspar **3** 211
Philips, Charles (1708-48) **24** 632–3*
works **9** 282, *282*; **11** 425
Philips, Jan Caspar **11** 237
Philips, Richard **24** 632
Philips, Thomas **25** 893
Philips Electric **3** 431
Philipsen, Theodor (Esbern) **8** 735; **11** 790; **14** 572; **24** 633*
Philipson, Robin **9** 725
Philip the Arab, Emperor of Rome (*reg* 244-9) **15** *918*; **27** 6, 41
Philip the Bold, 1st Duke of Burgundy (*reg* 1363-1404) **4** 841; **5** 206–9*, *207*; **11** 654, 660; **17** 456–7; **31** 832, *833*, 834
architecture **5** 895; **8** 485, 888, 891; **26** 43
collections **5** 209; **11** 660
decorative works **7** 544
embroidery **15** 11
enamel **11** 615
gems **12** 257
gold **13** 158
hardstones **11** 635
ivory **11** 637
manuscripts **3** 614; **4** 11; **7** 525; **13** 153; **19** *389*; **20** 625, 629, 631, 652; **31** 290
paintings **3** 552; **5** 895; **10** 179; **11** 531; **17** 455, 456, 461; **19** 388; **20** 207; **21** 463; **25** 71
sculpture **3** 455, 567; **7** 405; **11** 660; **13** 76, 109; **16** 854; **17** 459, 460; **19** 544, 721; **20** 207; **28** 865; **33** 28
tapestries **3** 362; **10** 270; **11** 638; **14** 75; **25** 16; **30** 312, 313
wood-carvings **11** 438
woodcuts **33** 347

Philip the Fair, Duke of Burgundy *see* PHILIP I, King of Castile-León
Philip the Fair, King of France *see* PHILIP IV, King of France
Philip the Good, 3rd Duke of Burgundy (*reg* 1419-67) **5** 206, 209–13*, *211*; **19** *252*
architecture **8** 888; **17** 10
decorative works **3** 596, 612; **8** 524; **14** 389
embroidery **10** 181
hardstones **11** 635
jewellery **3** 604
manuscripts **3** 555, 614; **5** 213; **8** 650; **12** 524; **17** 454; **19** 350; **20** 450, 680, 686; **31** 218
religious **4** 764; **17** 454, 455; **19** 251, 252, 350; **20** 451, 749; **31** 449; **32** 728
secular **10** 705; **18** 684; **19** 251, 340; **32** 729
maps **10** 707
metalwork **13** 159
orders (chivalry) **7** 178
paintings **3** 553, 639; **8** 69, 524; **10** 705, 707, 712; **33** 117
sculpture **7** 405; **8** 662; **12** 354; **13** 78; **17** 676; **32** 674; **33** 118
silver **10** 707; **31** 147
stained glass **29** 397
tapestries **3** 397; **5** 46; **13** 634; **19** 382; **30** 313, 314; **31** 218; **32** 823
textiles **10** 709
Philip the Sincere, Count Palatine of the Rhine *see* PHILIP, Elector Palatine
Philip William of Neuberg, Elector Palatine (*reg* 1685-90) **22** 918; **33** *272*
Philiskos of Rhodes **13** 552; **24** 633*
Philistine **1** *852*; **24** 633–6*; **30** 178, 189
architecture **24** 634*
bronze **24** 635
clay **24** *635*
coffins **24** 635, *635*
figurines **24** 635
iron **24** 635
kraters **30** *197*
metalwork **24** 635–6*; **30** 195
pottery **24** 634–5*
rhyta **24** 634
seals **24** 636*
writing **24** 636
Philistine coffins *see under* SARCOPHAGI → types
Phillip, Arthur **30** 158; **33** 22
Phillip, John (1817-67) **1** 30; **24** 636*
collections **33** 138
dealers **1** 453
groups and movements **7** 436; **9** 756; **10** 254
patrons and collectors **28** 273
pupils **19** 625
teachers **17** 673
Phillipe, Maître **27** 132
Phillippo, James **16** 882
Phillipps, Thomas (1792-1872) **21** 39; **23** 212; **24** 636–7*
Phillips **2** 706; **30** 153
Phillips, Ammi **12** 54; **24** 637–8*
Phillips, Bert Greer **33** 185
Phillips, Charles (*fl c.* 1939) **30** 43
Phillips, Claude **24** 638*
Phillips, Coles **14** 751
Phillips, Duncan **4** 327; **9** 202; **24** 638*; **31** 663
Phillips, H. (18th cent.) **10** 366
Phillips, Héctor Valdés (*fl* 1942) *see* VALDÉS PHILLIPS, HÉCTOR
Phillips, Helen **14** 271
Phillips, Henry Wyndham **24** 637*
Phillips, James **24** 638
Phillips, John **32** 791; **33** 94
Phillips, Marjorie **24** 638
Phillips, Matt **21** 897
Phillips, Peter **24** 639*; **25** 231
Phillips, Philip **2** 300
Phillips, Robert (1810-81) **17** 527
Phillips, Robert C. (*fl c.* 1840s) **7** 326
Phillips, Thomas (1770-1845) **24** 637*; **29** 548; **33** 453
Phillips, Thomas (1801-67) **8** 441; **33** 106
Phillips, Tom (*b* 1937) **7** 681; **24** 639*
Phillips, William **6** 118
Phillips Brothers **18** 897
Phillips Collection *see under* WASHINGTON (DC) → museums
Philocares **13** 548
Philo Judaeus **13** 555; **17** 533, 540
Philokles **13** 549; **18** 108
Philologo, Tomaso *see* RANGONE, TOMMASO
Philomelion *see* AKŞEHIR
Philomusus, P. Cornelius **27** 53
Philon of Byzantium **13** 404, 407, 412, 413; **21** 558, 562, 577
Philon of Eleusis **13** 394, 403, 407, 409; **24** 327
Philostratos (family) **2** 517
Philostratos, Flavius *see* FLAVIUS PHILOSTRATOS
Philostratos Lemnios **24** 639–40*
works **10** 129; **13** 555, 808; **26** 857; **31** 299, 768
illustrated **10** *130*
on metalwork **10** 192
on painting **15** 135
Philostratos the younger **14** 870; **24** 640*
works **10** 129; **15** 83; **24** 639
on hardstones **15** 697
on painting **15** 135
Philoteos **9** 650
Philotimos **1** 481
Philoxenos of Eretria **24** 640*
attributions **32** 250
copies **22** 160; **25** 206
patrons and collectors **13** 551
teachers **13** 548
works **13** 551
Philoxenus, Consul **10** 776
Phimai **5** 473, 474; **30** 631
National Museum **29** 240
Phimeanakas *see under* ANGKOR
Phineus Painter **13** 516
Phintias **32** 63–5*
pupils **32** 34
teachers **32** 65
works **13** 489, 518
Phipps, Charles John **6** 415; **23** 259; **24** 641*
Phipps, Henry, 1st Earl of Mulgrave **14** 262; **16** 819; **20** 875; **33** 188
Phister, Hans *see* PFISTER, HANS
Phitsanulok **30** *571*, 591
Wat Chedi Yot Thong **30** 584
Wat Phra Si Ratana Mahathat **30** 602
Phiyang **30** 819, 832, 833
Phiz *see* BROWNE, HABLOT KNIGHT
PH lamp **14** 392
Phlyax vases *see under* VASES → types
Phnom Bakheng *see under* ANGKOR
Phnom Baset **5** 486
Phnom Bok Temple **5** 467
Phnom Da **5** 484
Phnom Dei Temple **5** 467
Phnom Krom Temple **5** 467
Phnom Kulen **5** 461
Prasat Thma Dap **5** 464
Rong Chen **5** 464, 466
sculpture **29** 642
temples **5** 464
Phnom Penh **2** 61; **5** *458*, 504; **29** *225*
betel sets **5** 508
Buddhist Institute **5** 482
Cambodiana Hotel **5** 483
Cathedral **5** 482
Chakdomukh Hall **5** 482, *482*
Chamcar Mon State Palace **5** 483
Hôtel Royal **5** 482
Kompong Sam State Brewery **5** 483
market **5** 482
Municipal Theatre **5** 483
National Museum **5** 482, 502; **22** 364; **29** 240
National Sports Complex **5** 483
Phnom Stupa **5** 481
railway station **5** 482
Royal Palace **5** 481, 482, 509; **23** 823; **29** 827
sculpture **5** 501
Silver Pagoda *see* Vat Preah Keo
Vat Botum Vodei **5** 482
Vat Onalum **5** 482
Vat Preah Keo **5** 482, *501*, 508
Phnom Srok
sculpture **5** *462*
Phocian red slip ware *see* POTTERY → wares → Late Roman ware
Phoebus, Gaston **5** 208
Phoebus Segal, Uri *see* SEGAL, URI PHOEBUS
Phoenician **1** *852*; **8** 331; **24** 641–5*; **25** 732; **26** *852*; **30** 179, 189, *189*
alphabets **1** *854*, 855, *857*; **5** 331; **24** 641; **30** 187
amulets **24** 645; **25** 734
architecture **13** 398; **24** 641–2*; **31** 426
basalt **27** 825
bowls **24** 644*, *644*; **30** 187
bronze **24** *642*, 644
coins **5** *332*; **30** 187
dyeing **1** 880
earrings **24** 644
figureheads **28** 611
figurines **24** 642–3*
furniture **16** 573
glass **1** 867, 868; **24** 645*; **25** 734
glazes **4** 172
gold **24** 644, *644*
iconography **1** 830
inscriptions **1** 828
ivory-carvings **1** 871, *872*; **16** 573, 798; **24** 643–4*; **25** 734
jewellery **24** 644*
marble **27** 825
metalwork **20** 211; **24** 644*; **30** 196
niello **5** 332
palettes **24** 645
perfume containers **24** 645
pigments
cobalt blue **4** 172
Tyrian purple **24** 645
pottery **4** 172; **24** 643*
sarcophagi **8** 341; **27** 825–6*
scripts **5** 332
sculpture **24** 642*
seals **24** 644–5*; **30** 187
ship-decoration **28** 611
shrines (i) (cult) **24** 641
silver **24** 644
statuettes **24** *642*
stelae **29** 613
temples **8** 335; **18** 98
terracotta **24** 642–3*; **27** 825
thrones **24** 642
trade **10** 590–91
chariots **10** 591
copper **10** 591
faience (i) (glass) **10** 590
fans **10** 591
glass **2** 557; **10** 55
gold **1** 876
iron **10** 591
jewellery **10** 590
metalwork **25** 734
Phoenician
trade—cont.
ostrich eggs **10** 590
parasols **10** 591
pottery **10** 591
shells **10** 590
silver **10** 590
terracottas **25** 733
see also LEBANON; PUNIC
Phoenix (AZ)
David Wright House **33** *405*
Heard Museum **22** 677, 678
Phoenix Co. **13** 297; **14** 590
Phoenix Hall *see under* UJI → Byōdōin
Phoenix Islands *see* KIRIBATI
Phoenix Jewel **10** 346
Phoenix Park **16** 886
Pho Hai **6** *418*, 420
Phoinikos **19** 837
Phokaia **13** 502, 586, 587; **15** 893
Phokas (family) **5** 676; **25** 334
Phokas (*fl* 3rd cent.) **2** 259
Phokas, Emperor of Byzantium (*reg* 602-10) **9** 513, 636; **16** 582
Phokas, Ioannis **8** 156
Phokas, Manuel **8** 156
Phokis *see* HOSIOS LOUKAS
Pholane Sonam Topgye **30** 814
Phong La **6** 428
Phong Le **6** 432
Phonodikos **13** 568
phonograms **10** 2
Photios, Patriarch of Constantinople **9** 522, 577, 638; **10** 129; **16** 593; **24** 177
photoarchives **2** 364, 365, 367, 369, 560; **4** 27; **24** 649, 678, 682–3*
Africa **1** 439*
Austria **2** 833
Belgium **2** 370
Bolivia **4** 269*
Brazil **4** 729*
Canada **5** 592*
Czech Republic **8** 425
Denmark **8** 761*
Finland **11** 112
France **11** 674
Germany **2** 366, 370; **12** 481–2*
Greece **13** 361*
Hungary **15** 19*
India, Republic of **15** 184*
Ireland **16** 38*
Israel **16** 572*
Mexico **5** 910; **21** 398*
Netherlands, the **22** 909*
New Zealand **23** 76
Portugal **25** 319*
Scotland **9** 725
Spain **29** 357–8*
Sweden **30** 119
Switzerland **30** 156*
Tibet **30** 849
United States of America **2** 365, 371; **24** 682–3; **31** 671
Uruguay **31** 758–9*
Venezuela **32** 180–81*
see also COLLECTIONS → types → photographs
Photo-Club de Paris **24** 674, 738
photocollages **4** *115*; **24** 685
photocomposition *see under* PRINTING → processes
photocopies **10** 135, *880*; **24** 654*
photoelectrotyping **25** 82
Photo-Forum **24** 534
photogalvanography *see under* PRINTING → processes
photogelatin process *see* PRINTING → processes → collotype
photogenic drawing *see under* PHOTOGRAPHY → processes
photogenic etching *see* PHOTOGRAPHY → processes → *cliché-verre*
photogrammetry *see under* TECHNICAL EXAMINATION → types
photograms **8** 852; **24** 654–5*, *654*, 676; **28** 40
see also HOLOGRAMS; RAYOGRAPHS
Photograms of the Year **24** 739
Photographic Art Association, Japan **11** 826
Photographic Art Journal **24** 432
photographic cylinders **33** 1
photographic negatives **7** 575; **9** 493; **14** 481; **24** 646–50*, 653, 656, 658, 661, 669; **25** 82; **30** 268
photographic papers *see under* PHOTOGRAPHIC PRINTS → types; PHOTOGRAPHY → materials
photographic plates **9** 493; **14** 541; **24** 651, 658, 660, 669, 670
types
albumen **24** 651
ambrotypes **7** 612; **24** 649, 651, 661
Autochrome **24** 648
calotype process **1** 148
collodion positives **24** 649–50*, 651, 661
daguerreotypes **8** 450; **24** 646, 647, 649, 650*, *650*, 659
ferrotypes **7** 612; **24** 651*, 661
gelatin dry **24** 647, 651*, 653
orthochromatic **24** 647, 663
panchromatic **9** 493; **26** 235
tintypes **24** 651, 661
wet *see* PHOTOGRAPHY → processes → collodion process
see also HOLOGRAMS; PRINTING PLATES
photographic positives **3** 422; **4** 130; **9** 493; **14** 481; **24** 646, 647–51*, 656, 658, 659, 669
see also PHOTOGRAPHY → processes → direct positive
photographic prints **23** 505; **24** 646, 647–70*
types
albumen **19** *87*; **24** 647, 648*, 649, 659, 661, 662
Brazil **24** *664*
England **5** *522*; **24** *668*; **33** *309*
France **4** 130; **19** *87*; **24** *660*, *665*
Germany **24** *667*
Russia **24** *665*
United States of America **24** *666*
blueprints **7** 432; **24** 650, 654
bromide prints **24** 648*
bromoil **24** 648*, 674
calotypes **14** *539*, 539, 540; **24** 646, 649, 658; **30** 268–70
Egypt **24** *663*
England **30** *269*
Carbondir **23** 582
carbon prints **24** 647, 649*, 655, 658, 668, 674
Cibachrome **24** 649
collodion positives **24** 668
colour **7** 432; **9** 493–4; **24** 649, 650, 655, IX, IX
United States of America **24** X, XI1, XI2
combination prints **24** 650*, 668
contact prints **24** 651
daguerreotypes
Colombia **7** 608, 612
England **7** 403
Mesoamerica, Pre-Columbian **21** 263
Netherlands, the **2** 618
United States of America **22** 150; **24** *659*
double **24** 663
Ektachrome **24** 650
gelatin silver papers **2** *663*; **22** *445*

photographic prints
types—cont.
gum bichromate **7** 432; **24** 651*, *652*, 674, IX
hand-coloured **24** 660
monochrome **24** 648, 651, 655
permanent prints **24** 647, 649
platinotypes **24** 655*
platinum prints **24** 647, 655*, *655*, 674
United States of America **24** *739*
Polaroid **24** 655
salted paper prints **24** 647, 649, 656*
France **22** *724*
sepia **24** 648
Talbotypes **24** 649
see also PHOTOGRAPHY → processes; SNAPSHOTS
photographic reproductions *see* REPRODUCTIONS, PHOTOGRAPHIC
Photographic Review **24** 739
photographs **7** 685; **9** 26; **24** 658
historical and regional traditions
Colombia **7** 609
England **4** *670*; **10** *483*
Mass Observation **20** *589*
France **4** *690*; **5** *897*
Germany **27** *718*
Guyana **13** 876
Norway **22** *293*
Scotland **24** *657*
United States of America
20th cent. **11** *728*; **17** *917*; **19** *844*; **21** *794*
see also HOLOGRAMS; RAYOGRAPHS
photography **2** 534; **3** 422; **14** 481; **24** 378, 646–84*; **26** 225, 235; **28** 203; **30** 268
conservation **2** 365, 366; **24** 683–4*
education *see under* EDUCATION (ART) → types
historical and regional traditions
Africa **10** 580
Andaman Islands **10** 580
Angola **10** 580
Australia **10** 580
Brazil **10** 580
Britain **24** 646, 658, 672; **29** 426
Cameroon **10** 580
Colombia **7** 612
colonialism **7** 615
Côte d'Ivoire **10** 580
Cuba (Caribbean) **8** 234
Czech Republic **24** *678*
England **10** 252; **15** 830; **24** 650, 668, 674
19th cent. **5** *522*; **22** *389*
France **5** 896; **24** 646, 658, 662, 663, 676
20th cent. **3** 289; **24** *672*
Germany **24** 663, 673, 674, 676, 677
20th cent. **24** *675*
Guinea **10** 580
Guyana **10** 580
Indian subcontinent **10** 580
19th cent. **15** 616
Indonesia **10** 580
Japan **24** 679
Lithuania **24** 679
Mesoamerica, Pre-Columbian **21** 263
Mexico **24** *676*
Native North Americans **10** 580
Netherlands, the **22** 853
New Guinea **10** 580
New Zealand **23** 57
North America **10** 580
Peru **10** 580
Russia **24** 672; **27** 394, 396
Scotland **33** 219
Solomon Islands **10** 580
South Africa **10** 580; **24** 679
Spain **24** *677*

photography
historical and regional traditions—cont.
Sri Lanka **10** 580
Union of Soviet Socialist Republics **24** 674, 676
United States of America **15** 830; **24** 650, 659, 661, 671, 672–3, 674, 676, 679; **25** 653; **31** 602, 605, 606, 662, 663
19th cent. **24** *673*; **29** *655*
20th cent. **1** *144*; **10** *656*; **24** *676*, *679*, *680*, *681*; **29** *656*, *745*; **33** *105*
historiography *see under* HISTORIOGRAPHY → types
instruments
aletoscopio **25** 217
dioramascopio **25** 217
electric photographic guns **20** 406
grafoscopio **25** 217
megaletoscopio **25** 217
pontioscopio **25** 217
zoopraxiscope **22** 390
materials
acetate **7** 432
acetic acid **24** 649
airbrushes **1** 494
albumen **24** 647, 648
bichromates **24** 651
bitumen **24** 655
brushes **5** 34
carbon blacks **24** 647, 649, 651
cellophane **7** 432
collodion **7** 432; **24** 649
copper **24** 646, 650, 655
dyes **9** 493; **24** 647, 648, 649, 650, 669
emulsions **7** 432; **9** 490; **24** 648, 651, 653, 656, 659, 669
ether **24** 649
film *see* FILM
flash bulbs **24** 651
frames **24** 674
gallic acid **24** 649
gaslight papers **24** 651*
gelatin **9** 490, 494; **24** 646, 647, 649, 650, 651, 653, 655, 658
gelatin silver papers **7** 432; **24** 648, 651*, 656
glass **7** 432; **24** 646, 648, 649, 650, 651
gold **24** 647
gum arabic **24** 651
hypo **24** 649, 656
inks **7** 432; **24** 648, 650, 653, 655
iodine **24** 650
iron salts **24** 650, 655
lead **24** 658
leather **24** 650
lenses (camera) **24** 654, 660, 669, 674
magnesium flash powder **24** 651
magnesium wire **24** 651, 669
mercury **24** 650
mirrors **24** 660
mordants (iii) (dyeing) **24** 647
mounts **24** 674
mylar **7** 432
negatives *see* PHOTOGRAPHIC NEGATIVES
paints **7** 432; **24** 647
paper **7** 432
photographic papers **24** 646, 647, 648, 649, 650, 651, 653, 655, 656*, 657, 658, 669, 679
pigments **24** 649, 651
plastics **7** 432; **24** 650
plates *see* PHOTOGRAPHIC PLATES
platinum **24** 647, 655
platinum paper *see* PHOTOGRAPHIC PRINTS → types → platinum prints
potassium bichromate **24** 648, 649, 659
potassium bromide **24** 649, 656

photography
materials—cont.
potassium ferricyanide **24** 650
potassium iodide **24** 648, 649
potassium oxalate **24** 655
pyrogallic acid **26** 91
salt **24** 647, 648, 650, 656
screens (photographic) **24** 651, 653, 670
shellac **1** 156
silver **24** 646, 647, 650, 659, 670; **28** 738
silver bromide **24** 648, 651, 656
silver chloride **24** 651, 656
silver gelatin **24** 647, 648
silver halides **24** 646, 651, 656, 658
silver nitrate **24** 647, 648, 649, 656
starch **24** 647, 648
sulphides (mineral) **24** 647
sulphur **24** 647
textiles **24** 651
transparencies *see* TRANSPARENCIES
tripods **24** 653
watercolours **24** 647
waxes **24** 657
see also PHOTOGRAPHY → processes → waxed paper negative process
white lead **7** 432
see also PHOTOGRAPHIC NEGATIVES; PHOTOGRAPHIC PLATES; PHOTOGRAPHIC POSITIVES; PHOTOGRAPHIC PRINTS
processes
Albertype process **24** 650
Autochrome **10** 649; **24** 647, 648*, 670
bleaching **24** 649
bromochromotype **31** 566
calotype process **3** 422; **10** 252; **24** 646, 647, 648–9*, 653, 656, 657, 658, 659, 661, 662
carbon process **2** 119; **24** 658, 659; **25** 82
chronophotography **20** 406; **24** 649*, 653
France **20** 406
Cibachrome **24** 649*, X
cliché-verre **7** 432*, 433–4*; **14** 541; **24** 655, 668
France **7** *433*
United States of America **10** 99
collodion process **8** 852; **21** 263; **24** 646–7, 649*, 651, 659, 661, 662, 663, 665
colour **9** 493; **10** 649; **24** 647–8*, 649, 650, 653, 656, 668, 670, 678, 679; **25** 82
cyanotype process **7** 432; **14** 481; **24** 650*, 654
daguerreotype process **24** 646, 650*, 653, 655, 658–9, 660–61, 662, 666, 667, 672; **25** 591
developing-out **24** 647
direct positive **3** 421–2; **24** 646, 650, 659
see also PHOTOGRAPHIC POSITIVES
distortion **24** 651
Dufaycolor **24** 647
dyeing **9** 490
dye transfer **7** 432, 434; **9** 493–4*, *494*; **24** 679, XI1
Ektachrome **24** 650*
electronic **24** 679; **25** 345
electrophotography *see* PRINTING → processes → electrography
enlarging **24** 651*, 668
flash **24** 651*, 653, 677, 679; **30** 271
gum bichromate **24** 651*, *652*
heliogravure **2** 119; **22** 723; **24** 655

photography
processes—cont.
heliotype process **7** 575; **23** 443; **24** 650
high-speed **24** 653*
infra-red **24** 653*; **30** 271
instant photographs **24** 648, 655–6, 679
Kodachrome **24** 653*; **26** 236
multiple cameras **24** 649
multiple exposures **24** 649, 653*, 663
oil pigment **24** 648, 653*
oxymel process **19** 518
papyrotype process **24** 650
photo-engraving **7** *686*; **24** 670; **30** 271
photogenic drawing **8** 852; **24** 646*, 649, 656
photograms *see* PHOTOGRAMS
photolithography *see* PHOTOLITHOGRAPHY
photomechanical **24** 647, 651–3, 669, 670
photomicrographs **30** 271
photomicrography **24** 655*
Polaroid **24** 648, 655–6*, 679
printing **24** 648
printing-out **24** 647, 656*
retouching **4** 262; **24** 656*; **25** 345
Sabattier effect **24** 657
screen film **24** 647
screen plate **24** 647
shading **24** 651
solarization process **13** 217; **21** 607; **24** *656*, 656–7; **30** 20
spotting **5** 34; **24** 651
stereoscopic **7** 403; **10** 669; **24** 648, 657*, *657*, 663, 669; **33** 134
stroboscopic **9** 721; **24** 653
toning **24** 647
transfers, oil **24** 653
tripack **24** 648, 649, 650, 653
vignetting **24** 651
waxed paper negative process **24** 646, 649, 657*, 659
wet collodion process *see* collodion process
wet-plate *see* collodion process
X-rays **24** 669
see also PHOTOGRAMS; PRINTING → processes → photomechanical; RAYOGRAPHS
uses
advertisements **9** 494; **24** 671, 678
anthropology **10** 580
archaeology **2** 300, *300*; **9** 341
architectural drawings **24** 654
architecture **3** 422
art (reproduction of works of) **2** 534; **24** 649, 655, 667; **26** 232–3
astronomy **24** 669
book illustrations **4** 363; **9** 340; **24** 649, 650, 658, 661, 662, 663, 671, 672, *673*
cameraless images *see* PHOTOGRAMS
cards **24** 661
cabinet **24** 648*, 649
cartes-de-visite **24** 648
collages **24** 654, 676, 679
copies **24** 650
documentary photography **15** 830–31; **24** 665–7*, 672–4*, 675, 679
ethnography **8** 280; **10** *578*, 578–80*, *579*; **24** 666
fashion **24** 678
medical books **21** 6
montages *see* PHOTOMONTAGES

photography
uses—cont.
movement, depiction of **8** 698; **9** 721; **20** 406; **22** 389, *389*, 390; **23** 295; **24** 649, 651, 653, 669, *670*; **29** 426
panoramas **20** 483–4; **24** 653–4*, 659
photocopies **24** 654*
plans **24** 650, 654
political *see* documentary photography
portraits *see under* PORTRAITS → media
postage stamps **25** 329
posters **24** 671; **25** 345, 349, 352
printing **7** 575–6*, *576*; **20** 603; **24** 655; **25** 591
see also PHOTOLITHOGRAPHY
prints **25** 596, 617–18*
propaganda **10** 580
reproductions **24** 649, 651–3, 654, 655, 661
screenprinting **28** 299
sculpture **24** 688
social documentation *see* documentary photography
surveys **2** 300, *300*; **24** 662
technical examination **24** 653; **30** 395*
20th cent. **24** 674–7*
see also CAMERAS; FILM; FILMS; MOVING PICTURES; SNAPSHOTS; TRANSPARENCIES; VIDEOS
photography, Pictorial *see* PICTORIAL PHOTOGRAPHY
photography, rectified *see* TECHNICAL EXAMINATION → types → rectified photography
photogravure *see under* PRINTING → processes
Photo hifi Italia **24** 449
photojournalism **11** 775; **24** 656, 670, 674, 677–8*
Photo League **24** 674, 685*; **27** 164; **28** 887
photolithography **2** 619; **7** 575; **9** 303; **19** 480–81; **24** 647, 650, 653, 654, 655*, 670; **25** 82, 345, 618*; **26** 236
photometry **24** 494
photomezzotint *see* PRINTING → processes → Goupilgravure
photomicrography *see under* PHOTOGRAPHY → processes
photomontages **7** 654; **8** 436; **24** 650, 654, 676, 685–6*; **25** 352
Germany **3** 801; **13** 698; **14** 604; **24** *686*; **27** 872
Poland **30** 204
see also ASSEMBLAGES; COLLAGES
Photo Notes **24** 685
Photopane *see* PRINTING → processes → collotype
Photorealism **1** 494; **12** 296; **24** 686–8*
Bolivia **4** 264
collections **23** 7
United States of America **8** 585; **10** 532; **22** 124; **24** *687*; **31** 609
photosculpture *see under* SCULPTURE → types
Photo-Secession **7** 491; **17** 625; **23** 47; **24** 674, 688*; **29** 655; **31** 605
exhibitions **24** 739; **31** 490
members **5** 7; **10** 649; **17** 828; **29** 601; **33** 146
photo-stencilling *see under* STENCILLING → types
Phototeca **24** 449
phototype *see under* PRINTING → processes
Phourni **2** 304–5
Phournou Koriphi **8** 153; **21** *651*; **22** 403
buildings **21** 661

Phournou Koriphi—cont.
figurines 21 656
houses 21 656
Phra Bang 18 762, 768
phra bot see THAILAND → banners
Phradmon 10 425
Phraeze, Joris 18 848
Phra Kon Chai 5 485
Phra Nak 30 616
Phra Narai Ratchaniwet Lopburi 4 796
Phra Phetratcha, King of Ayutthaya (*reg* 1688-1703) 2 884
Phra Prang Yai 30 580
Phrasikleia Kore 13 447
Phraya Tak 30 592
Phrim *see* QASR IBRIM
Phrygian 1 822, 827, *852*; 24 689–91*; 26 *852*
architecture 1 831
brass 1 836; 4 *686*
bronze 1 836
coins 4 *686*
gold 1 836
iconography 1 830
inscriptions 1 830
iron 1 836
ivory-carvings 1 872
marble 9 72
megara (buildings) 13 *7*
metalwork 1 836
monuments 24 *689*
mosaics 1 890*
palaces 23 806
pottery 1 838; 24 690
religion 1 830
rock reliefs 24 *691*
screens (ii) (furniture) 13 *8*
scripts 1 830
sculpture 1 833
silver 1 836
stands 13 *8*
tombs 31 108
tumuli 24 691
wood 13 *8*
Phrygian Cap 14 456
Phrygian marble *see under* MARBLE → types
Phrygius, Dares *see* DARES PHRYGIUS
Phthiotic Thebes *see* NEA ANCHIALOS
Phuket 30 590, 617
Meridian Hotel 30 591
Phulwari Sharif Mosque 15 368
Phum Bavel 5 489
Phung Nguyen culture 29 227
Phu Ninh 6 427
Phuoc Co Tuu 30 511
Phuoc Tinh 6 430, 431
Phu Thai 18 771, 773; 30 619, 621, 623
Phya Thai palace 30 590
Phyfe, Duncan 10 851; 24 691–2*; 31 628
groups and movements 10 187
Phyfe, James 24 691
Phyfe, Michael 24 691
Phylakopi 8 *304*, 309, 310, 311, 313, 323, 324; 21 94, 95
architecture 8 309
figurines 8 310
fortifications 8 309, 310
ivory-carvings 8 323
megaron 8 309; 21 46; 23 808
Pillar Crypt 8 309, 320–21
pottery 21 95
sanctuary 8 309, 310, 322
altar 1 691
East Shrine 8 309
West Shrine 8 309
urban planning 8 310
wall paintings 8 307, 319, 320–21; 21 659
'phyongs rgyas *see* CHONGYE
Phyromachos 13 464; 24 414, 692*
Physical Cubism *see under* CUBISM → types
physiognomy 1 104; 18 880; 28 205–6*
physiognotrace 24 692*; 27 567
Physiologus 5 801; 9 686; 15 69
physionotrance 24 659
physioramas 7 924
phythiotika 8 366
Phyti 8 366
Pi, Oqwa 22 595
Pia, Peter F. 31 265
Piaay 1 96
Pia Buonanotte di Magister Fredi 7 329
Piacentini, G. B. 25 893
Piacentini, Marcello 10 820; 16 648; 24 693–5*; 26 762; 28 793
collaboration 12 718; 16 648, 650; 22 806; 24 693; 25 218
exhibitions 21 422
groups and movements 10 821; 12 718; 19 304
pupils 2 880; 20 905
staff 32 855
works 3 770, 772; 10 822; 14 581; 16 650, 731; 21 521; 24 *694*; 26 762
Piacentini, Pio 16 644; 24 692–3*; 26 776
Piacenza 16 *618*; 24 695–6*
bronzes 10 *590*, 590
churches
Cathedral of the Assumption 16 625; 20 820; 26 579
paintings 5 854
sculpture 10 476; 26 619, 620, 621
S Antonino 26 576, 690
S Eufemia 26 620
S Maria di Campagna 16 726; 31 278
S Savino 26 579, 620
S Sepolcro 31 278, *278*
S Vincenzo 30 649
Cittadella *see* Palazzo Farnese
Galleria Ricci-Oddi 16 775; 24 696
Hospital 14 781
Museo Civico 16 776; 24 695
Palazzo del Comune 4 *775*, 776; 16 627; 31 236
Palazzo Farnese 10 811; 26 320; 32 506
see also Museo Civico
Piazza Cavalli
equestrian statue of Alessandro Farnese 10 441; 21 754; 24 *696*
equestrian statue of Ranuccio Farnese I 10 441; 21 754
sculpture 16 697
urban planning 27 3
Piacenza, Alberto da *see* ALBERTO DA PIACENZA
Piacenza, Domenico da *see* DOMENICO DA PIACENZA
Piacenza, Giovanni da *see* GIOVANNI DA PIACENZA
Piacenza, Giovanni di Giuliano da *see* GIOVANNI DI GIULIANO DA PIACENZA
Piacenza, Giuseppe Battista 16 719
Piacenza, Pietro da *see* PIETRO DA PIACENZA
Piacenza, Scuola di *see* SCUOLA DI PIACENZA
Piacenza, Uberto da *see* UBERTO DA PIACENZA
Piaget, Jean 6 588; 24 696*
Piaggio, Teramo 29 831
Piamonte, Giovanni da *see* GIOVANNI DA PIAMONTE
Piamontini, Giuseppe 24 696–7*
collaboration 6 86; 11 23
patrons and collectors 21 29, 31
pupils 11 322; 22 5
reproductions in porcelain 9 58
Piamontini, Giuseppe—cont.
works 29 572
Pian, Giovanni de 6 92
Piana dei Colli 16 640
Piana di Curinga 25 501
Pianciani (family) 29 422
Pian di Meleto, Evangelista di *see* EVANGELISTA DI PIAN DI MELETO
Piane, Giovanni Maria delle 4 562
Piankoff, Alexandre 10 83
Piano, Renzo 24 697–8*; 26 540
architecture 12 282
airports 1 496; 23 593
Centre Georges Pompidou 11 528; 14 521; 19 897; 24 *131*; 25 24
museums 14 803; 21 135; 24 *697*
shopping centres 28 623
stadia 1 798; 29 489
collaboration 2 578; 10 417; 11 660; 14 521; 16 55; 22 366; 24 131; 26 333; 29 526
competitions 7 670
piano nobile 24 698*
Piano & Rogers 1 126; 2 309; 26 333, 540
pianos 20 VIII1; 22 372–3
Pianta, Francesco 16 728; 32 195
Piarco Imperial College of Tropical Architecture 31 335
Piasecki, S. 18 433
Piast (House of) 24 698; 25 94, 95
Piast, Bołeslav I, Duke of Silesia *see* BOŁESLAV I, Duke of Silesia
Piast, Bołeslav the Brave, King of Poland *see* BOŁESLAV, King of Poland
Piast, Conrad I, Duke of Mazovia *see* KONRAD I, Duke of Mazovia
Piast, Henry, Prince of Great Poland *see* HENRY III, Prince of Silesia
Piast, Kasimir I, King of Poland *see* KASIMIR I, King of Poland
Piast, Kasimir III, King of Poland *see* KASIMIR III, King of Poland
Piastrini, Giovanni Domenico 26 827
Piat, Lefebvre et Cie. 26 192
Piatra Neamt 26 710
Piatra Roșie 27 843; 30 773
Piatti, Giovanni Antonio de 1 748; 6 123; 9 75
Piatti, Ugo 27 445
Piattoli, Giuseppe 3 750, 903
Piazoll, Domenico 31 510
Piazoll, Johannes 31 510
Piazza 19 490; 33 732
Piazza, Albertino 24 699
Piazza, Callisto 24 699*
Piazza, Cesare 24 699
Piazza, Fulvio 24 699
Piazza, Martino 24 699
Piazza, Paolo 27 504
Piazza, Scipione 24 699
Piazza Armerina 9 *510*, 557; 16 *621*; 24 699–702*, *700*; 26 870, 881, *886*
mosaics 6 480; 7 834; 9 563, 568; 24 701–2*, *702*; 26 862; 27 63; 28 655; 29 423
piazzas *see* VERANDAHS
piazze *see* SQUARES (TOWN)
Piazzetta, Giacomo 24 702–3*
pupils 33 455
works 16 728; 19 630
Piazzetta, Giovanni Battista 16 676; 18 666; 21 816; 24 702, 703–8*; 28 173; 32 194
assistants 20 91
collaboration 5 594; 8 159; 24 894
patrons and collectors 1 633; 5 686; 12 355; 19 157; 22 115; 27 521, 864; 28 173; 32 196
Piazzetta, Giovanni Battista—cont.
pupils 5 908; 8 809; 18 442; 23 174; 24 894; 25 549; 31 26, 356
reproductive prints by others 3 199, 308; 4 362; 6 91; 14 49; 18 47; 24 894; 32 501, 689
works 9 110, 223; 12 292; 15 138; 20 91; 23 472; 24 *704*, *705*, *706*; 30 358; 32 194, 196, 216
Piazzola sul Brenta, Villa Simes-Contarini 19 35
Pibrac 5 346
Pic, Pere Català *see* CATALÀ PIC, PERE
Pica *see under* TYPE-FACES
Pica, Vittorio 24 448, 708*
Picabia, Francis (Marie Martínez) 2 225, 383; 19 477; 23 48; 24 428, 708–11*
dealers 26 193; 27 163
exhibitions 31 490
groups and movements 23 569, 570; 25 747; 28 347
Art informel 2 544
Cubism 8 240, 245
Dada 8 433, 435, 436, 437, 438, 439; 24 405
Dada Weststupidia 3 3 4; 8 435
Neue Leben 8 434; 22 921
Orphism 1 74; 8 245
Puteaux group 8 240
Section d'Or (ii) 2 225
Surrealism 30 19
patrons and collectors 2 383; 9 196; 21 135; 23 7
productions 3 120; 6 167; 24 405, 406
sponsorship 2 225
works 8 *435*; 11 549, *549*; 24 405, *709*, *710*; 26 51
Picard, Alexandre 5 584
Picard, Charles 9 401
Picard, Edmond 3 563; 20 862; 32 251, 591
Picard, François 24 467; 27 821
Picard, Jean (*fl* mid-16th cent.) 3 209, 210
Picard, Jean (1620-82) 30 26
Picard, Marc 18 874
Picard, Robert 32 591
Picardo, Juan 24 712*
Picart, Bernard (*fl* 1632) 24 712
Picart, Bernard (1673-1733) 24 712*
patrons and collectors 25 815
printing plates 23 612
pupils 2 851; 8 845; 11 241; 30 24
translated writings 13 324
works 4 18; 18 671; 22 684; 24 805
Picart, Etienne 24 712*; 27 270; 30 746
Picart, Guillaume 31 206
Picart, Jean 31 206
Picart, Jean-Michel 11 227; 12 801; 29 668
Picart-le-Doux, Jean 11 644; 30 328
Picasso, Musée *see under* ANTIBES; PARIS → museums
Picasso, Pablo 2 30; 3 219; 6 588; 7 385; 10 481; 11 550, 569; 18 598; 20 157, 399; 24 143, 144, 712–28*, 800; 25 584; 27 478; 29 285, 878; 31 142, 705; 32 327
assemblages 2 616; 16 57
book illustrations 4 366; 10 164; 16 823; 17 725; 20 336; 28 819; 30 488; 31 504
ceramics 11 607; 29 329
cliché-verre 7 434
collaboration 12 918; 14 486; 16 57; 20 603
Picasso, Pablo—cont.
collages 7 557, 558; 8 *242*; 15 140; 23 333; 24 *726*; 25 599, 619
dealers
Flechtheim, Alfred 11 165
Guillaume, Paul 13 826
Kahnweiler, Daniel-Henry 17 725, 726
Loeb, Pierre 19 537
René, Denise 26 193
Rosenberg, Paul 17 725; 27 162, 163
Stieglitz, Alfred 29 655; 31 605
Vollard, Ambroise 32 686
Weill, Berthe 33 36
Zwemmer, Anton 33 744
drawings 9 213, 216, 217, 226, II1; 24 243, 244
exhibitions 2 447; 10 680; 13 711; 17 436; 26 59; 31 490; 33 744
frames 11 376, 495
glass 32 204
groups and movements 25 356
Art informel 2 544
Artists International Association (AIA) 2 553
Blaue Reiter 4 132
Cubism 1 73; 8 239, 240, 241, 242, 243, 244, 245, 246; 30 19
Ecole de Paris 9 705
Elan, L' 23 694
Jack of Diamonds (Bubnovy Valet) 16 817
Junk art 17 694
Moderne Kunstkring 21 775
Post-Impressionism 25 356
School of Ceret 30 3
Surrealism 20 591; 30 18, 19, 21
livres d'artiste 32 687
methods 8 128; 24 242; 31 578
paintings 4 74; 8 596; 11 547, 548, 549, 551; 20 600; 21 761; 24 *382*, 383, *713*, *715*, *718*, *719*, *720*, *721*, *723*; 25 283
aemulatio 7 675, 831; 11 39
history 10 822; 11 550; 13 677; 14 *588*, 589; 22 523; 25 685; 29 286
landscape 18 717
murals 22 332
nude figures 23 296; 25 582, 583
portraits 29 *604*
still-lifes 29 670
papier collé 7 557
patrons and collectors 11 659; 15 883; 27 439; 30 361
Abrams, Harry N(athan) 1 71
Arensberg, Walter and Louise 2 383
Barnes, Albert C. 3 251
Beuningen, Daniel George van 3 889
Chrysler, Walter P(ercy) 7 245
Cone, Claribel and Etta 7 702
Cooper, Douglas 7 797
Dale, Chester 8 463
Dotremont, Philippe 9 189
Dutilleul, Roger 9 465
Eluard, Paul 10 164
Gallatin, A(lbert) E(ugene) 12 15
Hirsch, Robert von 14 569
Janis, Sidney 16 906
Kramář, Vincenc 8 423; 18 435
Kunstmuseum (Basle) 30 152
Lefèvre, André 19 66
Magnelli, Alberto (Giovanni Cesare) 20 97
Maitland, Ruth (Esther) 20 142
Marx, Sam and Florene 20 524
Masurel, Jean and Geneviève 19 381
Mattioli, Carlo 20 848
Morozov, Ivan (Abramovich) (1871-1921) 22 136
Museu de Arte de São Paulo 4 726

Picasso, Pablo
patrons and collectors—cont.
Museum of Art (Łódź) 2 409
Neumann, Morton G. 23 7
Noailles, Charles de, Vicomte and Marie-Laure de, Vicomtesse 23 169
Norton Simon Museum 19 703
Ōhara, Sōichirō 23 371
Open-air Museum 17 433
Penrose, Roland 24 369
Poortvliet, Marie Tak van 14 295
Quinn, John 25 823
Reber, Gottlieb Friedrich 26 59
Rilke, Rainer (Karl Wilhelm Johann Josef) Maria 12 474
Robinson, Edward G(oldenberg) and Adler, Jane Bodenheimer 26 472
Rockefeller, Abby Aldrich 26 488
Rosenberg, Léonce 27 162
Rosengart, Siegfried and Angela 30 153
Rothschild, Elie Robert de, Baron and Elie de, Baronne 27 224
Rupf, Hermann and Margrit 27 343
Sainsbury, Robert and Lisa 27 524
Schreiber, Taft and Rita Bloch 28 167
Shchukin, Sergey (Ivanovich) 28 569
Soby, James Thrall 28 914
Stein, Gertrude 11 659; 29 604–5
Stein, Leo 29 604
Stein, Michael and Sarah 29 604
Tetzen-Lund, Christian 30 532
Thompson, G(eorge) David 30 749
Vallenilla Echeverría, Pedro 32 178
Vollard, Ambroise 32 687
Walter-Guillaume Collection 13 826
Watson, Peter (Victor William) 32 912
Whitney, John Hay 33 150
personal collection 1 438; 3 127; 7 562; 23 742; 27 263; 28 757
photographed works 4 691
prints 14 271; 25 596, 599, 601, 624, 626, 628
aquatints 2 241; 20 *604*
drypoints 9 310
engravings 10 397; 24 *724*
etchings 10 557, 560; 22 416; 23 296; 25 619
linocuts 11 *495*; 19 429; 29 556
lithographs 19 491; 22 371
monotypes 21 896
posters 25 350
productions 3 119; 7 508; 8 850; 12 497; 24 405; 30 686
reproductions on postage stamps 25 329
reproductive prints by others 32 577
sculpture 6 9, 577; 7 767; 11 568; 16 57, *57*; 24 *722*; 29 295, 576
stencilling 29 628
studio 3 366; 29 858
tapestries 2 704; 11 644; 12 830; 30 328
wood-carvings 24 *716*
writings 4 691; 7 637
Picasso, Paloma 30 867; 31 655
Picasso-Sammlung *see under* LUCERNE
Picault, Jean-Michel 24 730
Picault, Robert 7 778; 24 730*; 31 281
Piccardt (family) 22 882
Piccardt, Henricus A. 22 881
Picchia, Menotti del 30 348
Picchianti, Giovanni Domenico 21 30
Picchiati, Bartolommeo 11 273; 22 472, 478; 24 731
Picchiati, Francesco Antonio 7 704; 13 801; 24 731; 28 367
Piccinato, Luigi 13 213; 16 587, 650; 21 422; 23 753; 26 364
Piccinelli, Andrea *see* BRESCIANINO
Piccinelli, Raffaello 4 749
Piccioli, Benedetto 12 706
Piccola, Niccolò La *see* LAPICCOLA, NICCOLÒ
Piccoli, Anselmo 21 32
Piccolomini (family) 19 307, 807; 20 684; 25 564; 28 677; 30 649
architecture 28 677
Piccolomini, Aeneas Silvio de', Cardinal *see* PIUS II, Pope
Piccolomini, Andrea di Nanni 24 831
Piccolomini, Caterina 10 853
Piccolomini, Francesco Todeschini *see* PIUS III, Pope
Piccolomini, Giovanni Battista 28 684
Piccolomini Altar 4 737; 22 15
Piccolomini Madonna, Master of the 20 745*
Piccolpasso, Cipriano di Michele 24 732–3*
works 4 278; 6 17
illustrated 6 *326*
translated 25 236
Pic de Leopold 24 105
Pic du Midi du Bigorre 23 342
Picelj, Ivan 8 179; 10 667; 24 733*
Piceno, Ascoli 19 560
Pichard, Pierre 29 243
Pichardo, Eligio 9 117
Pichenot workshop 24 148
Picheta 24 733*
pichets 24 580
Pichikyan, Igor R. 6 213; 30 261
Pichincha 9 710
Pichl, Luigi 2 785; 14 889
Pichler (family) 1 756
Pichler, (Johann) Anton 12 261, 262; 24 733*
Pichler, Eva 25 435
Pichler, Giacomo 24 734
Pichler, Giovanni 12 262, 263; 24 733–4*; 26 77
works 12 *263*
Pichler, Giuseppe (Johann Joseph) 24 734; 28 836
Pichler, Johann Adam 8 289, 290, 880; 11 458; 22 309; 28 110
Pichler, Johann Anton *see* PICHLER, GIOVANNI
Pichler, Johann Peter 14 508; 17 518; 21 417
Pichler, Ludvík 8 414
Pichler, Luigi (Alois) 12 264; 16 752; 24 734*
Pichler, Matthias (*fl* 1766-9) 31 510
Pichler, Matyás (1803-85) 8 414
Pichler, Walter 2 804; 32 447
Pichon Rivière, Enrique 2 525
Pichore, Jean 20 744
Picinelli, Filippo 1 658; 10 174
Pick, Frank 14 674; 15 824; 19 575; 21 349; 25 351
Pickel, Konrad *see* CELTIS, KONRAN
Pickenoy, Elias Claesz. 24 734
Pickenoy, Nicolaes Eliasz. 13 266; 14 373; 18 10; 24 734–5*
Pickering 3 209
Pickering, Evelyn, *see* DE MORGAN, EVELYN
Pickering, Gilbert 8 186
Pickering, Henry 24 735*; 33 545
Pickering, William 31 496; 33 152
Pickering Forest 16 25
Pickersgill, Henry William 24 735*
Pickery, H. 3 585
Picket & Rundell 27 336
Pickett, Byron 1 65
Pickett, Joseph 24 735*
Pickett, William 27 336
pickle 24 735*
Pico della Mirandola, Giovanni 11 838; 14 868; 16 657, 658; 22 412; 24 833; 31 428, 429
Pico della Mirandola, Lodovico, Cardinal 8 778; 11 278
Picolet, Cornelis 33 79
Pico Master 32 198
Picon, Gaëtan 20 75
Picón, Juan 32 176
Picornet, Arnoul 5 207
Picot, François-Edouard 11 544, 546; 24 736–7*
collaboration 11 159
competitions 25 638
pupils
Aman, Theodor 1 750
Belly, Léon (-Adolphe-Auguste) 3 684
Benouville, Jean-Achille 3 736
Benouville, (François) Léon 3 736
Bouguereau, William (-Adolphe) 4 527
Cabanel, Alexandre 5 341
Calderon, Philip Hermogenes 5 426
Chauvel, Théophile-Narcisse 6 519
Cibot, (François-Barthélemy-Michel-)Edouard 7 304
Clairin, (Jules-)Georges (-Victor) 7 371
Crauk, Charles-Alexandre 8 123
Giacomotti, Félix (-Henri) 12 567
Guillaumet, Gustave (-Achille) 13 828
Henner, Jean-Jacques 14 390
Israëls, Jozef 16 573
Lenepveu, Jules-Eugène 19 153
Leroux, (Louis) Hector 19 231
Lévy, Emile 19 282
Lévy, Henri Léopold 19 282
Marks, Henry Stacy 20 446
Moreau, Gustave 22 88
Mottez, Victor(-Louis) 22 207
Neuville, Alphonse (Marie-Adolphe) de 23 10
Pils, Isidore-Alexandre-Augustin 24 815
Popelin, Claudius (-Marcel) 25 236
Vedder, Elihu 32 108
works 11 159; 24 *736*
Picot, Victor Marie 29 675
Picou, Henri-Pierre 12 487; 22 745
Picqueaux, François 2 704
Picquigny, Michel-Ferdinand, Duc de 18 654
Picquot, Thomas 2 460
picric acid 9 493; 24 789
picrolite 8 328, 337, *338*; 19 131
Pictavi *see* POITIERS
Pictet, Isaak 33 638
Pictish art 24 737–8*
crosses 24 *737*, 737
iconography 24 737
manuscripts 28 233
metalwork 27 569–70
sculpture 28 233, 241
silver 27 *570*
stone-carvings 24 737–8
see also INSULAR ART
Pictographic Cave (MT) 22 592
pictographs
Ancient Near East 1 853, *854*
China 6 738
Jamaica 16 880
Mesopotamia 21 282
Native North Americans 13 332, *332*
Sumerian 31 759
United States of America 13 *332*
Picton 5 581
Pictor, Albertus *see* ALBERT THE PAINTER
Pictor, Georg 15 83
Pictor, Hugo *see* HUGO PICTOR
Pictorialism *see* PICTORIAL PHOTOGRAPHY
Pictorial Photographers of America 7 491; 24 739
Pictorial photography 24 651, 653, 668, 674, 738–40*
Australia 5 392
Britain 2 119
England 8 579; 26 472
France 8 701
Japan 23 179
United States of America 17 828; 24 *739*; 29 655
Pictorius (family) 22 315
Pictorius, Gottfried Laurenz 12 373; 24 740*; 28 106
Pictorius, Peter (i) (?1626-1685) 24 740*
Pictorius, Peter (ii) (1673-1735) 12 373; 24 740; 28 106
Pictou Academy 5 590
Pictura 3 500; 9 169, 380; 14 41, 42, 139; 19 473; 21 510; 22 907; 28 166; 29 773; 32 232
picturae compendiariae see under PAINTING → Techniques
picture-format carpets *see under* CARPETS → types
picture frames *see* FRAMES
picture galleries *see under* GALLERIES (ART) (iv) → types
picture lights *see* LIGHTING → uses →paintngs
Picture Post 14 173
picture rails 9 14
pictures, moving *see* MOVING PICTURES
pictures of collections *see* PAINTINGS → types → cabinet pictures
Picturesque 1 180; 15 828; 18 700, 713; 24 740–43*; 26 737, 740
art forms
architecture 18 394; 22 59; 26 735
engravings 24 *742*
parks 7 430
photography 24 738
regional traditions
Austria 14 216
England 10 233–5; 12 128, 130, 131, 645; 25 572–3; 33 447
France 10 464; 23 519
Hungary 18 394
Indian subcontinent 15 652
Picuris, NM 22 606
Pidluvtsi, Sanguszko Palace 31 564
Pidoplichko, I. G. 21 413
Pidsak, Sargis 2 431
piece moulding *see under* MOULDING → types
Pieck, Han 22 876
Piedad de Ulldecona, La *see* LA PIEDAD DE ULLDECONA
Piedade, Agostinho da 4 722, 723
Piedras Negras 13 *758*; 20 *882*; 21 246; 23 826; 24 743–4*
architecture 21 214; 24 *744*
bone-carvings 21 247
Building J-6 30 786
shells 21 259
stelae 21 246
Stele 14 21 221
Structure K-5 29 828
Structure P-7 3 378
temples 21 213, 214
Piehl, Karl Fredrik 10 82
Piel, Friedrich 2 834
Piel, Louis-Alexandre 4 239
Pieler 33 81
Piemans, Heinrich 3 42
Piene, Otto 18 809; 20 11; 24 744–5*
collaboration 28 829
Piene, Otto—cont.
groups and movements 12 397; 13 727; 33 636
works 1 738; 28 828, *829*; 29 99
Pieneman, Jan Willem 1 808; 21 58; 24 745*
pupils 24 745
works 22 848, *850*
Pieneman, Nicolaas 22 848; 24 745*
Pienkowski, Jan 4 368
Pien Luan *see* BIAN LUAN
Pien Shou-min *see* BIAN SHOUMIN
Pien Wen-chin *see* BIAN WENJIN
Pienza 16 *620*; 24 *746*, 746–7*; 27 182; 31 717
architecture 24 732
Cathedral of the Immaculate Virgin 16 630; 24 746, *747*
altarpiece 11 383; 20 845
font 11 254
textiles 13 195, 196; 23 461
palazzi 16 629
Palazzo Comunale 31 236
Palazzo Piccolomini 12 111–12; 16 630; 23 486; 24 746
gardens 12 *112*
Papal Palace *see* Palazzo Piccolomini
urban planning 16 629
Piepenhagen, August (Bedřich) 24 747*
Piepenhagen, Louise 24 747
Pieper, Reinhold 29 97
Piepho, Carl 24 591
Pierantoni, Giovanni 25 8
Pierantonio da Lendinara 21 904
Pierart dou Tielt 3 553
Pieratti, Domenico 5 361; 21 26; 24 752*
Pieratti, Giovanni Battista 21 26; 24 752
Pierce, Edward (i) (*fl* 1630-*d* 1658) 24 752–3*
Pierce, Edward (ii) (*c.* 1635-95) 24 752, 753–4*
assistants 8 220
collaboration 33 244
pupils 18 31
works 10 263, *275*; 24 *753*
Pierce, George 19 643
Pierce, George N., Company 17 721
Pierce, John, I (*fl* 1634-7) 24 752
Pierce, John, II (*fl* 1651-60) 24 752
Pierce, Joshua 19 643
Pierce, Margaret 24 752
Pierce, Samuel 19 643
Pierce, S. Rowland 7 668; 10 240; 16 891; 23 248; 31 243
works 10 *240*
Pierce, Thomas, I (*fl* 1632-3) 24 752
Pierce, Thomas, II (*fl* 1655) 24 752
Pierce's Park 19 643
piercing 12 866; 16 364; 21 327*
Pier Francesco da Viterbo 18 572; 24 534, 754*
Pier Francesco di Bartolomeo di Donato *see* PIER FRANCESCO FIORENTINO
Pier Francesco Fiorentino 12 713; 13 260; 20 752; 24 754–5*
works 24 *755*
Pieri, Giovan Francesco (1698-1773) 16 749
Pieri, Giovanni Francesco (*fl* 1732-8) 11 194; 22 481
Pierides, Demetrios 8 366
Pierides Gallery *see under* GLYFADA
Pieri Nerli (family) 24 218
Pierino da Vinci 19 187; 24 755–7*
attributions 12 569; 27 204
teachers 31 320
works 16 695, 696; 18 820; 19 672; 22 16; 24 *756*; 29 569

Pieris, Harry 29 468; 33 74
Pieris, Ivan 29 468
Pierleoni (family) 26 755
Pier Luigi *see* SCRIVÁ, PEDRO LUÍS
Pier Luigi, 1st Duke of Parma (*reg* 1545-7) 5 789; 10 807, 809*
- architecture 27 740; 31 278
- - military 27 744; 33 586
- medals 4 339
- paintings 28 658
Pier Maria Fiorentino *see* SERBALDI DA PESCIA, PIER MARIA
Piermarini, Giuseppe 24 757–8*
- assistants 25 154
- collaboration 1 575; 16 646; 31 268
- pupils 5 622; 24 496
- teachers 31 895
- works 1 574; 8 135; 16 646, 719, 728; 20 320; 21 520, 527; 23 263; 24 *758*; 30 667; 31 268
Piermatteo (Lauro de' Manfredi) d'Amelia 17 644; 19 445; 20 679*; 26 815
Pierneef, J(acob) H(endrik) 17 603; 24 759*; 29 110
- works 25 566; 29 108
Piero (*fl* 1506) 1 572
Piero, Albizzo di *see* ALBIZZO DI PIERO
Piero, Chimento di *see* CHIMENTO DI PIERO
Piero, Domenico di *see* DOMENICO DI PIERO
Piero, Giovanni di Domenico di *see* GIOVANNI DI DOMENICO DI PIERO
Piero d'Albino da Castiglione 24 28
Piero d'Angelo 16 839
Piero de Crescenzi
- illustrated works 24 *179*
Piero della Francesca 16 662; 24 759–67*; 26 765; 31 740
- collaboration 1 768; 3 844
- frames 11 384
- groups and movements 26 186, 187
- methods 5 898; 7 628; 18 898; 20 467; 24 487, 491, 492; 25 379; 28 200, 201, 202
- paintings
- - frescoes
- - - Residenza (Borgo San Sepolchro) 24 *764*
- - - S Francesco (Arezzo) 2 389; 5 443; 9 262; 11 709, *710*; 16 659, 837
- - - S Francesco (Rimini) 24 *762*; 26 399
- - - Vatican Palace (Rome) 26 817
- - panel
- - - allegorical 1 656
- - - altarpieces 1 711; 7 527; 12 716; 17 705; 24 *761*; 27 495
- - - portraits 18 704
- - - religious 1 818, *818*; 7 835; 9 102; 14 517; 24 520, *763*
- patrons and collectors 16 763
- - Boxall, William 4 602
- - Burton, Frederic William 3 241; 5 283
- - Clark, Robert Sterling 7 377
- - Eastlake, Charles Lock (1793-1865) 9 683
- - Este (i) (family) 11 3
- - Federigo II, 1st Duke of Urbino (*reg* 1444-82) 22 13
- - Galleria Nazionale delle Marche 31 740
- - Gardner, Isabella Stuart 12 147
- - Malatesta, Sigismondo Pandolfo 20 160
- - Poldi Pezzoli, Gian Giacomo 25 144
- pupils 4 642; 24 521; 28 700
- restorations by others 3 919
Piero della Francesca—cont.
- teachers 9 98, 103
- writings 2 345; 14 869; 16 658; 24 487; 29 636
Piero del Massaio 22 799
Piero del Pugliese 3 303
Piero de' Medici, Lord of Florence (*reg* 1464-69) 5 *300*; 11 186; 21 *8*, 12–13*
- architecture 11 204, 210
- books 32 384
- collections 18 725
- decorative works 20 552
- interior decoration 16 711
- manuscripts 11 686; 26 325
- metalwork 2 112
- paintings 3 99; 13 260; 19 443; 20 642; 24 247
- sculpture 2 39; 21 433, 466; 24 232; 26 444; 28 490
- tapestries 19 382
- tomb 32 *361*
Piero de' Medici, Lord of Florence (*reg* 1492-1503) 9 98; 25 151
Piero di Bertino 12 710
Piero di Cosimo 24 768–71*
- attributions 3 868
- patrons and collectors 3 272, 740; 13 272; 16 661; 23 523; 27 271, 737; 28 270, 271; 32 386
- pupils 3 302; 25 222; 27 846
- teachers 27 176
- works 16 660; 24 *769*, *770*; 29 362
Piero di Giovanni *see* LORENZO MONACO
Piero di Giovanni Tedesco 12 701; 13 94
- works 7 338; 11 892; 18 673; 19 673, 674; 29 405
Piero di Jacopo 24 874
Piero di Lorenzo di Pratese (di Bartolo Zuccheri) 19 894; 24 537
Piero di Niccolò (di Martino) 16 692; 19 678
Piero (di Giovanni) di Puccio 24 771*, 855
Piero Guidi, Jacopo di *see* JACOPO DI PIERO GUIDI
Pieroni, Alessandro 19 511; 21 24; 23 140
Pieroni, Francesco 24 772
Pieroni da Galiano, Giovanni 24 771–2*
- assistants 3 17
- attributions 25 446
- works 4 833; 25 426
Piero the Gouty, Lord of Florence *see* PIERO DE' MEDICI, Lord of Florence (*reg* 1464-69)
Pierotti (family) 31 262
Pierotti, Henry 31 262
- works 31 *262*
Pierpont Limner 20 745*
Pierpont Morgan Book of Hours *see under* BOOKS OF HOURS → individual manuscripts
Pierpont Morgan Situla 28 805
Pierre, André 14 58, 59; 24 772*
Pierre, Claude de la 5 367
Pierre, Fernand 14 59
Pierre, Guillaume de *see* MARCILLAT, GUILLAUME DE
Pierre, Jean-Baptiste (-Marie) 7 496; 11 670; 12 830; 24 135, 136, 137, 772–4*
- patrons and collectors 25 81, 368; 32 255
- pupils
- - Bachelier, Jean-Jacques 3 19
- - Boullée, Etienne-Louis 4 532
- - Durameau, Louis (-Jean)-Jacques 9 416
- - Jollain, Nicolas-René 17 627
- - Lavallée-Poussin, Etienne de 18 879
Pierre, Jean-Baptiste(-Marie) pupils—cont.
- - Lebarbier, Jean-Jacques-François 19 9
- - Pasch, Lorens (1733-1805) 24 222
- - Taraval, (Jean-)Hugues 30 343
- - Tierce, Jean-Baptiste 30 865
- - Vestier, Antoine 32 386
- reproductions in tapestry 22 726
- reproductive prints by others 19 144; 27 645
- works 11 261; 23 517; 24 *773*; 27 524; 29 887
Pierre, José 30 23
Pierre, Vierge 14 59
Pierre Bergé 20 470
Pierre d'Acigné 16 795
Pierre d'Angicourt 22 486; 24 774*
Pierre d'Arras 18 875
Pierre d'Aubenas *see* PIERRE DE PAIX
Pierre de Beaumetz 5 207, 208; 11 637; 30 313
Pierre de Bruxelles 3 552; 5 667
Pierre de Cajetan 14 413
Pierre de Celle 26 122, 123
Pierre de Chaule 22 486
Pierre de Chelles *see* CHELLES, PIERRE DE
Pierre de Montreuil 24 156, 774–5*
- attributions 27 558
- groups and movements 26 45
- works 24 115, 152; 27 542
Pierre de Paix 25 570
Pierre de Pons 2 112
Pierre de Thil 27 592
Pierre de Thoiry 31 840, 841
Pierre de Verone 31 837
Pierre du Billant 24 775*
Pierrefonds 6 51, 61, 510; 11 565; 13 202, 208; 21 549; 28 345
- Emperor's Bedchamber 23 546
- halls 14 74
- interior decoration 32 *597*
Pierre-Léopold of Lorraine 16 730
Pierre l'Italien 4 546
Pierre Napolitain 4 546
Pierrepont 26 598
Pierrepont, Evelyn, 1st Duke of Kingston (*fl* 1699) 10 328
Pierrepont, Evelyn, 2nd Duke of Kingston (1711-73) 21 70
Pierrepont, William, 4th Earl of Kingston 7 298
Pierre van der Meulen 3 615
Pierri, Duilio 2 401; 24 775*
Pierri, Orlando 2 400
Pierron, Jean 5 564
piers (i) (seaside) 24 747–8*, *748*
piers (ii) (masonry) 1 723; 20 576; 22 211; 24 748–52*
- historical and regional traditions
- - Early Christian (*c*. AD 250-843) 24 750
- - Egypt, ancient 24 750
- - England 24 751, *751*; 33 *547*
- - France 13 40, 43; 24 751
- - Germany 24 751
- - Gothic 13 40; 20 574; 24 751
- - - England 24 *751*
- - - France 13 43
- - - Poland 33 *259*
- - Greece, ancient 13 406; 24 750
- - Islamic 16 145, 190
- - Italy 24 752
- - North Africa 16 190
- - Ottonian 24 750
- - Poland 33 *259*
- - Romanesque 24 750–51; 26 569; 33 *547*
- - Rome, ancient 24 750; 26 863, 864
- materials
- - mouldings 22 214, 216, 217, 218, 219, 220, 221
piers (ii) (masonry)—cont.
- types
- - clustered 24 749, *749*
- - compound 22 215; 24 749, *749*, 750–51
- - crossing 20 574
- - cruciform 24 749, *750*; 27 567
- - cylindrical 24 749, *749*
- - Doric 13 406
- - drum *see* cylindrical
- - fasciculated *see* clustered
- - moulded *see* clustered
- - nave 20 575
- - *pilier cantonné* 24 749, *749*
- - quatrefoil 24 *749*, 749–50
- - rectangular *see* square
- - round *see* cylindrical
- - shaft-bundle *see* clustered
- - square 24 750
- - *trumeau* 31 392*
Pierson, Allard, Museum *see under* AMSTERDAM → museums
Pierson, Betty (Bierne) *see* PARSONS, BETTY (BIERNE)
pier tables *see under* TABLES → types
Pierzl, Wilhelm 2 832
Piesche, József 15 4
Pieskowa Skała 25 130
Piešťany 28 *848*
- Colonnade Bridge 28 850
- Napoleon Baths 28 850
Piestre, Fernand-Anne *see* CORMON, FERNAND
Pietà, Master of the 24 776
Pietà of Admont I 2 799, *799*
Pietà of Admont II 2 799
pietàs 2 3–4; 18 676; 24 775–7*, *776*; 26 183
- Austria 2 *799*
- Belgium 21 *102*
- Czech Republic 8 *383*
- France 20 *207*; 25 *796*
- Germany 9 *239*; 24 776; 28 *76*
- Gothic 2 *799*; 8 *383*; 20 *207*; 25 *796*
- Italy 24 776–7
- - Baroque 5 *860*
- - Mannerism 7 *468*; 31 *40*
- - Renaissance 3 *662*; 21 *434*; 28 *333*
- 15th cent. 5 *179*; 25 *848*
- Spain 22 *72*
Pieter de Maelre 22 835
Pieter Dircksz. 8 102
Pietermaritzburg 24 777*; 29 103, *103*
- architecture 29 105
- Natal Museum 24 777
- Tatham Art Gallery 29 121
- Town Hall 29 105
Pieters, Geertje 23 447
Pieters, Hendrik 22 201
Pieters, Simon 12 513
Pieterse, Pieter 22 891
Pietersz., Aert 1 169, 806
Pietersz., Claes 18 7
Pietersz, Doen 1 806
Pietersz., Gerrit 13 895; 18 817; 22 841; 24 777–8*
Pietersz., Hercules *see* SEGERS, HERCULES
Pietersz., Jan 1 812
Pietersz., Pieter (Claes) 1 169, 806; 7 708, 866
Pietersz., Seeger 18 817
Pietilä, Raili 11 92; 24 778; 30 284
Pietilä, (Frans) Reima (Ilmari) 24 778*; 30 284
- pupils 13 843
- works 11 92; 14 372
Pietr 32 878
Pietrabbondante *see* BOVIANUM VETUS
Pietra dell'Unzione 29 366
pietra paesina 12 461
Pietrasanta, Francesco (Cecchino) da 2 139; 9 340
Pietrasanta, Jacopo da 10 542; 16 631; 24 778–9*; 26 811
Pietrasanta, Lorenzo da 24 779
Piètre, Henri 4 847; 23 517, 518
Piètre André 13 254
pietre dure 14 168–9, I1; 16 746–8*; 24 779*
- *see also* SCAGLIOLA
Pietri, Pietro de' 26 827
Pietro (*fl* 1365) 23 94
Pietro, Cardinal (*fl* 1615-20) 12 499
Pietro, Angelo di *see* ANGELO DI PIETRO D'ASSISI
Pietro, Cecco di *see* CECCO DI PIETRO
Pietro, Gerardo di *see* GERARDO DI PIETRO
Pietro, Giovanni di (i) (*fl* 1401-23) *see* GIOVANNI (DI PIETRO) DA PISA (ii)
Pietro, Giovanni di (ii)(*b c.* 1403-*d* before 1479) *see* GIOVANNI DI PIETRO (DI GIOVANNI) (ii)
Pietro, Ippolit 18 658
Pietro, Lando di *see* LANDO DI PIETRO
Pietro, Lorenzo di *see* VECCHIETTA, IL
Pietro, Martino di 2 398
Pietro, Michelangelo di *see* MICHELANGELO DI PIETRO
Pietro, Niccolò di *see* NICCOLÒ DI PIETRO
Pietro, Sano di *see* SANO DI PIETRO
Pietro, Tommaso di *see* TOMMASO DI PIETRO
Pietro Amoroso 2 1
Pietro Andrea 30 887
- works 30 *886*
Pietroassa 9 654
Pietro Cili, Adriano di *see* FIAMMINGO, ADRIANO
Pietro d'Abano 2 650; 12 692
Pietro da Gandria 18 586
Pietro da Gorgonzola 21 532
Pietro da Messina *see* SALIBA, PIETRO DE
Pietro d'Andrea da Volterra 26 817
Pietro d'Angelo, Jacopo di *see* JACOPO DELLA QUERCIA
Pietro da Pavia 24 779*
Pietro da Piacenza 14 726
Pietro da Rimini 24 779–80*
Pietro de Benvenuti 11 3
Pietro de Bonitate 18 859
Pietro de Casolis 20 791
Pietro del Donzello *see* DONZELLO, PIETRO DEL
Pietro della Gondola, Andrea di *see* PALLADIO, ANDREA
Pietro delle Campane *see* CAMPANATO, PIETRO DI GIOVANNI BATTISTA
Pietro del Massario *see* MASSARIO, PIETRO DEL
Pietro de Petri *see* PETRI, PIETRO DE
Pietro de Saliba *see* SALIBA, PIETRO DE
Pietro di Andrea di Fiandra 10 519; 11 5
Pietro di Angicurt *see* PIERRE D'ANGICOURT
Pietro di Benedetto di Pietro *see* PIERO DELLA FRANCESCA
Pietro di Domenico da Montepulciano 20 621; 24 780*
Pietro di Domenico da Siena 24 780*
Pietro di Domenico di Norbo 11 690
Pietro di Francia 21 533
Pietro di Galeotto (di Ercolano) 24 780–81*

Pietro di Giovanni d'Ambrogio
24 781–2*
works 11 711; 24 *781*
Pietro di Giovenale 26 766
Pietro di Jacopino 20 751
Pietro di Martino da Milano
24 782*
patrons and collectors 2 276; 13 79
pupils 18 859
works 11 895; 22 487
Pietro di Migliore 7 334, 664
Pietro di Oderisio 2 481; 24 782–3*
attributions 13 97; 29 XII
works 7 919, 921; 13 97; 31 124; 32 627
Pietro di Pietro Candido *see* CANDID, PETER
Pietro di Salerno, Bishop of Anagni 1 819
Pietro di Tommaso del Minella 10 853; 16 845
Pietro Falloppi, Giovanni di *see* GIOVANNI DA MODENA
Pietro il Fiammingo *see* VERSCHAFFELT, PETER ANTON VON
Pietro Leopoldo I, Grand Duke of Tuscany *see* LEOPOLD II, Holy Roman Emperor
Pietro Sacchi da Verona 1 588
Pietroza Wodska 31 719
Pietruszka, Bogdan 12 224
Pietrzyk, Wojciech 18 429
Pietsch, Karl 8 410
Piette, Edouard 20 542
Piette, Ludovic 9 673; 24 784*
Pietersz., Remmert 8 733
Piferrer, Pablo 24 105, 802; 25 786
Pifetti, Pietro 5 192
Piffaretti, Bernard 11 553
Piffero 22 800, 801; 28 683
Piffetti, Pietro 16 716, 728; 18 618; 28 18, 19
works 16 *728*
Pigafetta, Antonio 5 11
Pigage, Anselm 24 784
Pigage, Nicolas de 14 306; 24 784–5*; 33 280
assistants 29 378
patrons and collectors 9 459
works 12 133, 413; 13 705; 16 804; 20 281, 915; 28 194
writings 6 77; 12 473
illustrated 33 292
Pigalle, Jean-Baptiste 11 561; 24 785–7*
assistants 22 210
attributions 22 210
collaboration 1 665; 26 470
groups and movements 22 740
patrons and collectors 2 724; 4 303; 8 793; 11 658; 18 660; 23 519
pupils 2 698; 14 796; 19 756; 21 800; 22 210; 25 374; 30 283; 33 226
reproductive prints by others 7 495
teachers 19 119, 142
works 4 510; 5 889; 11 *561*; 22 45; 23 295; 24 *785*, *786*; 26 113; 29 564; 30 499; 31 128
Pigalle, Jean-Pierre 24 787
Piganiol de la Force, Jean-Aimar 24 787–8*
pig bristle *see* HOG BRISTLE
Pigeon, Jean (*fl* 1448) 4 827
Pigeon, Jean (1654–1739) 12 814
pigeon houses *see under* HOUSES → types
pigeon towers *see under* TOWERS → types
Pigge, Stephanus Wijnants 22 116
piggins 16 30
Pighetti, Giacomo 23 751
Pighius, Stefanius Vinandus 2 161; 24 788*
pig iron *see under* IRON → types
Piglhein, Bruno 28 341
PIGME (particle-induced gamma-ray emission spectrometry) *see under* TECHNICAL EXAMINATION → types
pigments 20 367; 24 788–800*
historical and regional traditions
Aboriginal Australia 1 39, 50
Africa 7 635
Buddhism 30 835
Byzantine 9 623
Cappadocia 5 676
Central Asia, Eastern 6 302
China 6 775; 7 631–2
Early Christian (*c.* AD 250–843) 9 623
Egypt, ancient 9 898; 10 5
England 23 785
Etruscan 10 617
France 25 *478*, *479*
Prehistoric 23 78
Gothic 13 137
Greece, ancient 13 481, 544
Indian subcontinent 7 633; 15 548
Italy 1 588; 10 617
Japan 17 140*, *141*, 142, 277, 297, 346, 414
Mesoamerica, Pre-Columbian 21 226, 233, 241
Mesopotamia 21 308
Native North Americans 22 *545*, 561; 27 727
Ndebele 22 713
Prehistoric art 18 807; 23 78; 25 477–9*, *478*, *479*, 483; 29 227
Rhodes (island) 23 785
Rome, ancient 23 785; 25 44; 27 51
South-east Asia 29 227
Sri Lanka 29 445, 463, 476
Tibet 30 835
Vietnam 32 482
Yoruba 7 635; 33 556, 559
materials
adhesives 15 551
alizarin 9 491; 18 655, 656; 23 786; 24 796
alum 7 632; 18 655
alumina 18 655, 656
aluminium hydroxide 24 789
antimony 24 798
asphalt 24 792
azurite 6 302; 7 632; 11 763; 17 277; 23 785; 24 789, 790*
barium chromate 24 799
barium sulphate 24 797
bismuth 24 798
bismuth chromate 24 799
bistre 4 101*; 24 792
bitumen 24 792
bone black 24 789
brazil-wood 18 655; 23 786; 24 796
brochantite 24 793
buckthorn berries 18 656; 24 794, 799
burnt umber 24 792
cadmium 24 799*
calcium carbonate 18 656
calcium chromate 24 799
carbon blacks 23 376; 24 789–90*
charcoal 6 469; 24 789; 25 484
chlorophyll 24 794
chromium 24 794, 799*
chrysocolla 24 793
cinnabar 7 631–2; 11 763; 13 535, 536; 23 785; 24 795; 27 51; 29 462
clay 27 51
coal tar 24 790
cobalt 23 786
cobalt oxides 24 791
cochineal 18 655, 656; 23 786; 24 796
copper 24 793–4*
pigments
materials—cont.
copper hydroxide chloride 13 536
copper oxides 24 790*
copper resinate 24 793–4
crocoite 24 799
dayflower 17 277
dragon's-blood 24 795, 797
dyer's broom 24 799
eggs 28 338
erinite 11 763
ethiops 24 795
fixatives 11 141
flavone 9 491
flavonol 9 491
frit 24 790
fustic 24 799
gamboge 17 277; 24 800
goethite 24 792, 798; 27 51
gold 7 632, 634; 15 802
graphite 7 632
haematite 13 536; 21 241; 25 175, 477
hopanes 24 792
indigo 7 635; 17 277; 23 785; 24 791*
indigot 9 491; 24 791
indirubin 9 491
iron chromate 24 799
iron oxide 13 480; 24 790, 795
ivory 16 797
ivory black 11 763; 24 789
kermes 18 655; 24 796
lac 18 655; 24 796–7
lampblack 15 548; 23 785; 24 789–90
lapis lazuli 6 302; 15 548; 24 790
latex 28 338
lazurite 24 790
lead 7 632; 24 798–9*
lead chromate 24 799
lead monoxide 24 798–9
lichens 18 656
limonite 24 792; 27 51
litharge 24 795, 798
log-wood 18 656
luteolin 9 491; 24 799
madder 18 655, 656; 24 796
malachite 7 632; 11 763; 13 536; 23 785; 24 793
manganese dioxide 24 790; 25 175, 477
manganese oxide 24 792
massicot (lead-monoxide yellow) 24 798–9
melanin 9 491; 15 852
mercury iodide 24 796
metacinnabar 27 51
mummies 24 792
oak 18 656
ochre 7 632; 11 763; 13 536; 23 274; 24 792*, 795*, 798*
red 25 477
yellow 9 623
orpiment 7 632; 17 277; 23 785; 24 798*; 29 462
paratacamite 24 793
potassium carbonate 18 655
purpurin 9 491; 24 796
quercetin 24 799
quercitin 9 491
quercitron 18 656; 24 799
realgar 7 632; 24 798
red lead 17 277; 24 795–6*
rutile 24 798
safflower 17 277; 18 656
saffron 24 799
sepia 15 852; 24 792
shellac 24 796
shells 7 632
sienna 11 763; 24 792
silver 7 632
smalt 11 763; 23 786; 24 791*
sodium carbonate 18 655
soot 24 789
strontium chromate 24 799
titanium dioxide 24 798*
turnsole 18 656
pigments
materials—cont.
umber 11 763; 15 855; 24 792
urine 16 330; 24 799
Venice turpentine 24 793
verdigris 24 793
vine black 11 763; 24 789
viridian 6 556, *556*; 24 794
weld 24 799
white lead 24 53, 789, 795, 797*; 30 426, 427
woad 24 791*
zinc 24 797–8*
zinc oxide 23 786; 24 797
technical examination 11 309; 30 401, 409
types
anisotropic 24 789
Antwerp blue 24 791
aureolin *see* cobalt yellow
auripigmentum see ORPIMENT
azo-pigments 24 789
az(z)ur(r)o dell'Allemagna 24 790
az(z)ur(r)o della magna 24 790
azzurro oltramarino see ultramarine
Bergblau 24 790
Berggrün see MALACHITE
Berlin blue 24 791
bianco sangiovanni 11 763; 24 798
black 9 490, 491; 14 425; 15 849–52, *850*; 24 789–90*; 28 339
Ancient Near East 1 880
China 7 632
Egypt, ancient 10 5
Indian subcontinent 7 634
Indonesia 15 802, 807
Islamic 7 635
Maya 7 636
Mesoamerica, Pre-Columbian 7 636
Papua New Guinea 23 722; 24 73
Prehistoric art 25 477
Rome, ancient 27 51
Sri Lanka 29 477
Yoruba 33 559
black earth 11 763
bleu d'Allemagne 24 790
blue 4 172; 9 490, 491, 492, 493; 15 853; 24 790–92*
Ancient Near East 1 880
China 7 632
Indian subcontinent 7 634
Islamic 7 635
Japan 17 *141*
Mesoamerica, Pre-Columbian 7 636
Rome, ancient 27 51
Yoruba 33 559
see also ultramarine
blue bice 24 789, 790
blue-black 7 634; 24 789
blue-green 7 636
blue verditer 23 786; 24 790
brazilein 24 796
Bremen blue 24 790
Bresilwood 24 796
brown 9 491, 492; 14 425; 15 852; 24 792*; 25 477
brown earth 23 376, 377
Brunswick green *see* emerald green
cadmium chromate 24 799
cadmium lithopone 24 799
cadmium red 24 796
cadmium red lithopone 24 796
cadmium yellow 24 799
cadmopone *see* cadmium lithopone
caeruleum 24 791
Caledon Jade Green 9 493
caput mortuum 24 795
carmine 15 564; 24 796
Cassel earth 24 792
cenobrium 24 795
pigments
types—cont.
cerulean blue 24 791
ceruse 24 797
charcoal 25 477
Chinese blue 24 791
Chinese white *see* zinc white
chrome green 24 794
chrome orange 24 796, 799
chrome red 24 796
chrome yellow 24 794, 799
chromium oxide green opaque 24 794
chromium oxide green transparent 24 794
cinnabar green *see* chrome green
cinnabaris 24 795
cobalt blue 14 425; 24 791
Egypt, ancient 4 172
Ethiopia 4 172
Iran 4 172
Iran, ancient 4 172
Islamic 16 420, 427
North Africa 16 427
Ottoman 16 420
Phoenician 4 172
Spain 29 322, 323
Syria 4 172
cobalt green 23 786; 24 794
cobalt violet 24 797
cobalt yellow 24 799
Cologne earth 24 792
coral red 13 536
couleur 24 791
Cremnitz white 24 797
creta viridis see green earth
crimson 9 491, 492; 12 623; 23 786; 24 796
cyan 9 494
Dutch pink 10 561
Egyptian blue 6 328; 24 789, 790
Ancient Near East 1 877, 878
Egypt, ancient 32 802
Greece, ancient 13 535, 536
Iran, ancient 33 *688*
Rome, ancient 27 51
émail 24 791
emerald green 24 794
English red 24 795
eosine 18 656
Eschel 24 791
false sandarach 24 796
flake white 24 797
Frankfurt black 25 598
giallolino see lead-tin yellow
giallorino see lead-tin yellow 10 560
grain lake 24 796
green 9 491, 493; 15 852; 24 792–4*
Central Asia, Western 16 248
Iran 16 248
Islamic 7 635; 16 129, 248
Japan 17 *141*
Rome, ancient 27 51
Spain 29 322
green bice *see* green verditer
green earth 11 763; 23 376; 24 792–3*; 30 427
Cyprus 24 793
Sri Lanka 29 463
green verditer 24 793
Hooker's green 24 800
Hungarian green *see* MALACHITE
Indian lake *see* LAC
Indian red 24 795
Indian yellow 24 799–800
isotropic 24 789
kaolinite 25 477
King's yellow *see* ORPIMENT
lake 1 588; 8 128; 9 490; 12 803; 18 655–6*; 24 789, 796
England 18 656
Rome, ancient 23 785
lead-tin yellow 24 798–9
Leithner's blue 24 791
Lely green 24 794

pigments
types—cont.
light red **24** 795
lithopone **24** 797
lootwit **24** 797
magenta **9** 493, 494; **18** 656
malachite green **24** 794
manganese black **24** 790
manganese blue **24** 791
manganese brown **14** 425
manganese purple **29** 322
manganese violet **24** 797
Mars orange **24** 795
Mars red **24** 795
Mars violet **24** 795
Mars yellow **24** 795, 798
massicot *see* lead-tin yellow
masticot *see* lead-tin yellow
mauve **9** 493; **23** 786
metacinnabar **24** 795; **27** 51
mineral green *see* MALACHITE
minium **10** 560; **24** 795; **28** 338
China **7** 95, 632
molybdate orange **24** 799
molybdate red **24** 796
monastral blue *see* phthalocyanine blue
Morellensalz **24** 795
mountain blue **24** 790
mountain green *see* MALACHITE
mummy **24** 792
Munich green *see* emerald green
Naples yellow **11** 763; **24** 799
orange **9** 491, 493; **14** 425; **24** 798–800*
Japan **17** *141*
orange mineral **24** 795
pansy green **24** 794
Paris blue **24** 791
Paris green *see* emerald green
Paris red **24** 795, 796
patent yellow **24** 799
peori **16** 330; **24** 799
Perkin's mauve **24** 789
permanent green **24** 794
permanent violet *see* manganese violet
phthalocyanine blue **24** 792
pink **9** 492; **16** 249
piuri *see peori*
Pompeian blue **24** 790
porphyry **28** 778
Pozzuoli red **24** 795
Prussian blue **9** 37; **12** 623, 803; **15** 853; **24** 650, 789, 790, 791, 794; **30** 559
Germany **23** 786
Japan **17** 277, 287, 847
purple **9** 491, 492; **25** 742
Algeria **16** 448
Byzantine **9** 612
Early Christian (*c.* AD 250-843) **9** 612, 664–5
Islamic **16** 448
Morocco **16** 448
Rome, ancient **27** 51
red **9** 491, 493; **14** 425; **15** 851, 852; **24** 795–7*; **28** 778
Ancient Near East **1** 880
Byzantine **9** 623
Central Asia, Western **6** 253; **16** 485
China **7** 631, 632
Egypt, ancient **10** 5
Indian subcontinent **7** 634
Indonesia **15** 802, 807
Islamic **16** 421, 485; **30** 477
Japan **17** *141*
Maya **7** 636
Mesoamerica, Pre-Columbian **7** 636
Native North Americans **22** 561
Ottoman **16** 421
Papua New Guinea **23** 721, 722
Prehistoric art **25** 477
Rome, ancient **27** 51
Sri Lanka **29** 476
pigments
types
red—cont.
Syria-Palestine **30** 198
Yoruba **33** 559
see also HAEMATITE; OCHRE; IRON OXIDES
red antimonyoxide sulphide **24** 796
Rinmann's green *see* cobalt green
sandarack *see* REALGAR
sandyx **24** 796
sap green **24** 794
Saturn red **24** 796
Scheele's green **24** 794
schelpwit **24** 797
Schweinfurt green *see* emerald green
silver white **24** 797
sinopia **28** 778–9*
Streublau **24** 791
synthetic **24** 790
syricum **24** 796
terra di Sinope **28** 778
terra verde *see* green earth
Thénard's blue *see* cobalt blue
titanium white **13** 709; **24** 798
Titanox *see* titanium white
tomato red **16** 249
Turkey red **9** 491; **15** 795; **28** 266; **30** 559
Tyrian purple **9** 492; **24** 797; **25** 742
Ancient Near East **1** 880
Phoenician **24** 645
Syria-Palestine **30** 180
ultramarine , ; **7** 627; **11** 763; **12** 803; **24** 789, 790–91*, XII2, 3
Afghanistan **24** 790
China **24** 790
Colombia **7** 607
France **13** 833
Gothic **13** 137
Indian subcontinent **15** 551, 564; **24** 790
ultramarine red **24** 797
ultramarine violet **24** 797
Van Dyck brown **24** 792
vegetable **25** 477
Venetian colour **10** 807
Venetian red **24** 795; **28** 339
verdaccio **28** 338; **30** 427
verdetto della Magna *see* MALACHITE
vermiculus **24** 795
vermilion **7** 632, 678; **15** 851, 852; **17** 277; **18** 608; **24** 795*; **33** 5
Byzantine **9** 623
China **7** 632
Colombia **7** 607
Japan **17** 277, 297
Rome, ancient **23** 785
Veronese green *see* green earth
vert de terre *see* green verditer
vert émeraude **24** 794
Verzino **24** 796
Victoria green **24** 794
Vienna green *see* emerald green
violet **9** 491, 492; **24** 797*
white **15** 851, 856; **24** 797–8*
China **7** 632
Indian subcontinent **7** 634
Indonesia **15** 802, 807
Islamic **7** 635
Japan **17** *141*
Maya **7** 636
Mesoamerica, Pre-Columbian **7** 636
Papua New Guinea **23** 721, 722; **24** 73
Prehistoric art **25** 477
Yoruba **33** 556, 559
yellow **9** 490, 491, 492, 493, 494; **14** 425; **15** 851, 852; **24** 798–800*; **25** 477
Ancient Near East **1** 880
pigments
types
yellow—cont.
China **7** 632
Indian subcontinent **7** 634
Japan **17** *141*
Maya **7** 636
Mesoamerica, Pre-Columbian **7** 636
Papua New Guinea **23** 722
Sri Lanka **29** 477
yellow earth **11** 763
Zafferblau **24** 791
zinc green **24** 794
zinc white **10** 561; **24** 797; **32** 899; **33** 2
zinc yellow **24** 799
uses
crayons **8** 127, 128
fresco **11** 761
glazes **18** 656
icons **9** 623
inks **15** 851, 852
lacquer **17** 297; **18** 600; **32** 482
manuscript illumination **16** 330; **21** 233
painting **9** 623; **13** 137; **17** 140*, 142, 346
bark **1** 50
encaustic **10** 196
fresco **11** 763–4*; **24** 788
secco **5** 676; **28** 339
wall **21** 226
watercolours **18** 656
paints **23** 782; **24** 788
pastels **24** 788
photography **24** 649, 651
pigments **12** 803
rock art **25** 477–9*, *478*, 483
sculpture **25** 477
seals **33** 5
secco **11** 763
tattoos **17** 414; **30** 366
tiles **16** 249
waxes **33** 2
writing **10** 5
see also COLOUR
Pignatari, Decio **7** 698
Pignatelli, Princess **10** 772
Pignatelli, Antonio, Cardinal *see* INNOCENT XII , Pope
Pignatelli Cortes, Museo Diego d'Aragona *see under* NAPLES → museums
Pignatta, Giulio **11** 347
Pignatta sarcophagus *see* RAVENNA → ecclesiastical buildings → S Francesco
Pigne, Thomas **12** 257
Pignon, Edouard **11** 550; **24** 800–801*
groups and movements **11** 336; **27** 307
works **11** 551
pignon chantourné *see* GABLES → types → scrolled
pignon en cloche *see* GABLES → types → scrolled
Pignoni, Simone **24** 801*
attributions **6** 126
works **23** 294; **24** *801*
Pignoni, Zanobi **24** 801
Pignoria, Lorenzo **10** 95
Pignot, Jean **13** 231
Pigot, George **29** 809
Pigott, Gwyn Hanssen **2** 761
Pigouchet, Philippe **4** 358
Pig Painter **13** 521; **32** 56
Piguenit, William Charles **2** 746; **24** 802*
Pihaedang *see* YI YŎNG
Pihil *see* PELLA (JORDAN)
Piil, Christian Actonius Theodorus **6** 534; **25** 611
Piimänen, Antti **11** 90
Piimänen, Mikael **11** 90
Pi i Margall, Francisco **24** 105, 802*
Pijhlou, Olof **24** 811
Pijlemans (family) **3** 599
Pijnacker, Adam *see* PYNACKER, ADAM
Pijzel, Daniel **22** 891
Pike, Jimmy **1** 64; **24** 802–3*
pikes **2** 448
Pikhel'ga, Khel'ge (Krist'yanovna) **27** 423
Pikicallepata **31** 45
Pikioni-Papageorgiou, Ino **24** 803
Pikionis, Dimitris **2** 674; **13** 349, 350, 358; **24** 803*
Pikionis, Petros **24** 803
Pikirakau **23** *59*
Pila, Jacopo della *see* JACOPO DELLA PILA
Pilaer, Jan **26** 83
Pilani **15** 611
Pilapil, Imelda **24** 620
Pilar, Lever Factory **2** 397
Pilar, Martin **8** 176
Pilar, Ricardo do **4** 715; **26** 412
Pilaram, Faramarz **15** 898; **27** 810
Pilarete, André **24** 804*
pilasters **24** 804–5*
historical and regional traditions
Carolingian **5** 796
Champa **6** 421
Cyprus, ancient **8** 341
England **24** *804*
Greece, ancient **13** 376, 391
Indian subcontinent **15** 330
Italy **26** 577
Romanesque **26** 569, 577
Rome, ancient **26** 874, 878, 883
Vietnam **6** 421
materials
brick **4** 769; **26** 878
types
almohadillado *see* bolster
antae **2** 131*; **13** 376, *376*; **24** 805*
bolster **13** 761
bundled **24** 805*
lesene *see* strip
respondent **24** 805*
strip **24** 805*
see also COLUMNS
Pilát, Daniel **33** 160
Pilavaine, Jacquemart *see* JACQUEMART PILAVAINE
Pilbara **1** 41
Pilch, Anton **24** 313
Pilecki (family) **18** 693
pile dwellings *see under* HOUSES → types
Pileni **25** 181
Pileo, Gui de *see* GUI DE PILEO
Piles, Roger de **11** 662; **24** 167, 805–6*
groups and movements **27** 286, 287
personal collection **4** 568; **8** 209; **9** 230
pupils **8** 845
teachers **11** 723
works **1** 179; **2** 518, 531; **8** 612; **9** 8, 372; **11** 536, 674; **13** 301; **15** 84; **18** 700, 709; **19** 354; **22** 357; **24** 494; **31** 300, 768
illustrated **7** 864
on chiaroscuro **6** 569, *570*
on *disegno e colore* **7** 628
on painting **7** 814
translated **5** 78; **10** 376
Pilestri, Paolo di Tingo de' **19** 666
Pileta, La *see* LA PILETA
Pilet and Cougnard **11** 284
pile-weaving *see under* WEAVING → types
Pilgeram & Lefèvre **12** 31
Pilgram, Anton **24** 806–7*, *807*
works **2** 778, 800; **4** 832, *833*; **8** 383; **20** 441; **25** 725; **32** 434, 442, 452, 453
Pilgram, Franz Anton **15** 13; **16** 904; **24** 808*
patrons and collectors **10** 531
Pilgram, Franz Anton—cont.
works **4** 695; **10** 531, 871; **14** 887; **18** 443; **28** 849, *850*; **31** 786
Pilgrim II, Archbishop of Salzburg **27** 664
Pilgrim, Johann Ulrich *see* WECHTLIN, HANS
pilgrimages **13** 808
Buddhism **5** 97, *97*
Hinduism **14** 559; **31** 902
Indian subcontinent **5** 93; **14** 559; **15** 202; **31** 902
Islam **16** 87–8*, 453, 454
Japan **17** 345–6*
Sri Lanka **5** 97, *97*
pilgrim badges **8** 835; **24** 808–9*
historical and regional traditions
England **24** *809*
Spain **17** 515
materials
brass **24** 809
gold **24** 809
jet **17** 515; **24** 809
lead **18** 902; **24** 809
parchment **24** 809
pewter **24** *809*
silk **24** 809
silver leaf **24** 809
tin **24** 809
Pilgrim Flask Painter **10** 613
works **10** *614*
pilgrim flasks
historical and regional traditions
Armenia (Europe) **2** 441
China **6** 875, *875*, 887, 890
Egypt, ancient **10** 48
Greece, ancient **13** 492
Italy **16** *736*; **32** *201*
materials
faience (i) (glass) **10** 48
porcelain **16** *736*
pottery **6** 875, 887, 890
pilier cantonné piers *see under* PIERS (ii) (MASONRY) → types
Pilioko, Aloi **23** 736
Pili-Pili **33** 596, 598
Pilipko, V. N. **23** 159
P'ilippos, Catholicos **9** 732
Pilisszentkereszt Abbey **14** 883; **26** 638
sarcophagus of Queen Gertrude **14** 892
sculpture **26** 638
Pilkington, Alistair **21** 721
Pilkington, Charles Vere **29** 88
Pilkington, F(rederick) T(homas) **24** 810*; **28** 230
Pilkington, Matthew **10** 206
Pilkington, Thomas **24** 810
Pilkington, William **27** 626
Pilkington & Bell **30** 385
Pilkington's Tile and Pottery Co. **8** 122, 583
Pillaiyarpatti Cave Temple **15** 508
Pillalamarri
Erakeshvara Temple **15** 328, 538
Nameshvara Temple **15** 538
pillar clocks *see under* CLOCKS → types
Pillard, Laurent **4** 535
pillars
historical and regional traditions
Bamum **3** *151*, 152
Buddhism **15** *415*, 422–3; **17** 66; **27** 867
Cambodia **5** 474
Cameroon **3** *151*
Celtic **6** *156*; **27** *142*
Central Asia, Eastern **6** 319
France **27** *142*
Germany **6** *156*
Greece, ancient **13** 415
Indian subcontinent **15** 236–7*, 277, 302, 303, 317, 325, 424, 442, 733; **27** 844*
Buddhism **15** *415*, 422–3; **27** 867
Maurya **15** 194, 341, 413

pillars
historical and regional traditions
Indian subcontinent—cont.
2nd cent. BC **15** 430–31
5th cent. AD **15** 258, *259*
7th cent. AD **15** 303
Japan **17** 48, 53, 66
Nepal **22** 759
types
dorings **30** 816
see also CIPPI
pillar-stelae *see under* STELAE → types
pillar-stupas *see under* STUPAS → types
Pilleau, Pezé **10** 332
Pillement, Georges **31** 832
Pillement, Jean (-Baptiste) **24** 810–11*
patrons and collectors **4** 565; **25** 212
pupils **32** 425
reproductions in ceramics **20** 474
works **2** 704; **4** 361; **7** 167; **18** 614; **24** 271, *811*; **26** 303
Pillet, Edgar **8** 838; **12** 613
Pillet, M. **9** 416
Pillhofer, Josef **2** 804
Pillivuyt **14** 246
pillow lace *see* LACE → types → bobbin
pillows **6** *895*; **7** 145; **15** 795
see also HEADRESTS
Pillsbury, Alfred F. **6** 868
Pilo, Carl Gustaf **7** 805; **8** 733; **24** 811–12*; **30** 79
groups and movements **13** 864
methods **10** 199
pupils **18** 418; **24** 222
works **8** 734
Pilon, André **24** 812
Pilon, Germain (*c.* 1525-90) **20** 920; **24** 812–14*
attributions **13** 227
collaboration **3** 210; **5** 813; **30** 659
patrons and collectors **4** 303; **8** 856; **25** 383; **31** 850
works **3** 210; **11** 557; **19** 159; **20** 281; **24** 133, *133*, *813*, *814*; **27** 547, *548*; **29** 93, 571; **30** 498; **31** *124*, 125, 851
Pilon, Germain, the younger (*b* 1571) **9** 337; **24** 812
Pilon, Jacques **8** 181
Pilon, Jean **9** 405
Pilon, Raphael **24** 812
Pilon, Veno **24** 815*; **28** 860
piloncitos see under COINS → types
Piloni (family) **5** 55
pilotis **24** 815*
Piloty, Ferdinand **13** 852; **19** 482; **24** 815; **29** 776
Piloty, Karl Theodor von **22** 303; **24** 815*
pupils
Benczúr, Gyula **3** 702
Brandt, Józef **4** 671
Chase, William Merritt **6** 499
Defregger, Franz von **8** 618
Gierymski, Aleksander (Ignacy) **12** 603
Gottlieb, Maurycy (Moses) **13** 215
Iakovidis, Georgios **15** 55
Kalckreuth, Leopold (Karl Walter), Graf von **17** 736
Lenbach, Franz von **19** 150
Liezen-Mayer, Sándor **19** 351
Lytras, Nikiforos **19** 855
Makart, Hans **20** 145
Max, Gabriel (Cornelius) **20** 875
Quiquerez, Ferdo (Ferdinand) **25** 824
Schwartze, Thérèse **28** 188
Sinding, Otto Ludvig **28** 770
Székely, Bertalan **30** 205
Szinyei Merse, Pál **30** 209
Piloty, Karl Theodor von—cont.
works **12** 394; **14** 588
Pils, François **24** 815
Pils, Isidore-Alexandre-Augustin **11** 545; **24** 815–17*
groups and movements **24** 171
prizes (artists') **24** 171
pupils
Boilvin, Emile **4** 242
Brunet-Debaines, Alfred-Louis **5** 23
Buhot, Félix(-Hilaire) **5** 131
Clairin, (Jules-)Georges (-Victor) **7** 371
Duez, Ernest-Ange **9** 369
Goeneutte, Norbert **12** 842
Mednyánszky, László **21** 37
Merson, Luc Olivier **21** 166
Piette, Ludovic **24** 784
Rajon, Paul Adolphe **25** 868
Renouard, (Charles-) Paul **26** 210
works **21** 760; **24** *816*
Pilsen *see* PLZEŇ
Piłsudski, Jósef **13** 871
Pilsum **11** 253
Pilsworth, John **28** 299
Pilz, Friedrich **28** 670
Pilz, Vincenz **24** 817*
Pim, Howard **29** 110, 121
Pima **22** 550, 567, 605, 662, 666, 669
Pimenov, Georgy *see* PIMENOV, YURY (IVANOVICH)
Pimenov, Nikolay **2** 173; **27** 390
Pimenov, Stepan (Stepanovich) **24** 817–18*; **27** 390
collaboration **8** 710
works **27** 412, 579; **33** 600
Pimenov, Yury (Ivanovich) **24** 818*; **32** 661
groups and movements **27** 394; **28** 924
works **15** 830
Pimental, María Josefa de la Soledad Alonso *see* OSUNA, 9th Duquesa de
Pimental y Herrera, Juan Alfonso de, 8th Conde de Benavente *see* BENAVENTE, 8th Conde de
Pimental y Herrera, Juan Francisco Alfonso de, Conde de Benavente *see* BENAVENTE, 10th Conde de
Pimentel, Francisco **20** 109; **32** 537
Pimentel, Gaspar de Guzmán y, Conde-Duque de Olivares *see* OLIVARES, Conde-Duque de
Pimentel, Luis Serrão **4** 633
Pimentel, Serrão **25** 292
Pimentel, Vicente **9** 118
Pimm, John **7** 166
Pimonenko, Mykola (Kornylevych) **18** 38; **24** 818*
Pimpalner **15** 569
Pin, Prince *see* BIN, Prince
Pina, Alfredo **29** 575
Piña, Alonso de **14** 662
Pina, José Salomé **16** 806; **24** 818*
Pina, Juan Laureana de **24** 818–19*; **28** 516; **29** 336
Piña, Plácido **9** 117
Pina, Protásio **27** 809
Piña Chan, Román **6** 393; **18** 806; **31** 66
Pinacotheca (periodical) **19** 637
Pina da Brescia, Marco **22** 12
Pina de Brederode, António Sampaio de *see* SAMPAIO DE PINA DE BREDERODE, ANTÓNIO
pinakotheca (building) **7** 561
Pina Manique, D. I. de **1** 466; **28** 429
Pinara **19** 837, 838
Pinazo (Camarlench), Ignacio **24** 819*, 829; **31** 816
Pincas, Julius *see* PASCIN, JULES
Pincellotti, Bartolomeo **4** 621; **23** 577
Pincemin, Jean-Pierre **11** 552, 644; **30** 6
Pincevent **19** 229
Pinch, John **3** 371
pinchbeck **4** 680, 685; **7** 447; **10** 341; **17** 525; **24** 57
Pinchbeck, Christopher **10** 341
Pinches, John **27** 878
pinching *see under* POTTERY → techniques
Pinchon, Jehan **17** 10
Pinchon, Léon **14** 457
Pinciani, Alessandro **31** 800
Pincino, Lorenzo **31** 359
Pinck, Franciszek **21** 831
Pinckaert, Jeronimus **11** 871
Pinckers, Servais-André **3** 584
Pinckney, Roger **28** 281
Pinctada see under SHELLS → types
Pincum *see* VELIKO GRADIŠTE
Pincus-Witten, Robert **17** 583
Pińczów **13** 774; **25** 96, 113
Pindar **13** 568
Pindar, Paul **28** 562
Pindar, Peter *see* WOLCOT, JOHN
Pindavada Temple **15** 485
Pindaya **5** 241
Pinder, Ulrich **18** 512; **28** 57; **31** 287
illustrated works **28** *58*
Pinder, (Georg Maximilian) Wilhelm **24** 819*
Pindi *see* RAWALPINDI
Pindiga
sculpture **17** *680*
Pindu **24** 96
Pindú, Jenaro **24** 99
pine **17** 514; **33** 324
historical and regional traditions
Belgium **3** 585
Bhutan **3** 913
England **10** 277
France **11** 595
Germany **33** 326
Gothic **13** 135
Hungary **14** 903, 905
Indian subcontinent **15** 720
Japan **17** 109, 366, *366*
Korea **18** 361
Norway **6** *389*
Spain **29** *310*, *318*
types
akamatsu (red pine) **17** 46
kuromatsu (black pine) **17** 46
parana **24** 515
parasol **33** 326
screw-pine *see* PANDANUS
uses
benches **29** *310*
bonsai **17** *366*, 366
chairs **6** *389*; **29** *318*
cupboards **12** *422*
furniture **11** 595; **14** 903, 905; **18** 361
mirror frames **21** 721
panel paintings **13** 135; **24** 3
scroll rollers **28** 310
sculpture **17** 109
Pine, John **14** 519, 638; **20** 366; **24** 820; **32** 732
Pine, Matt **20** 359; **23** 63; **24** 820*
Pine, Robert Edge **3** 373; **24** 820*
pupils **22** 151
reproductive prints by others **8** 863; **29** 675
Pine, Simon **24** 820
Pineau, Dominique **7** 747; **24** 821
Pineau, Jean-Baptiste **11** 404; **24** 820
Pineau, Nicolas **6** 509; **11** 405, 577; **23** 543; **24** 820–22*; **30** 88
assistants **27** 406
collaboration **20** 298; **30** 298
groups and movements **19** 723
patrons and collectors **8** 161; **24** 546
Pineau, Nicolas—cont.
works **4** 455; **7** 168, 746; **9** 324; **11** 406, 407; **19** 231; **21** 721; **24** *821*; **26** 477, 493; **27** 401
Pineda, Antonio Hernando de **29** 340
Pineda, Bernardo Simón de **20** 234; **24** 822*
collaboration **2** 522
patrons and collectors **13** 880; **28** 515
works **20** 234; **28** 520
Pineda, Jorge **24** 622
Pinel, Philippe **2** 658
Pinelès, Charles **30** 33
Pinelli, Bartolomeo **17** 732; **24** 822–3*
Pinello, N. H. **11** 111
Pineman, Jan Willem **29** 8
pine-needles **22** 663
pinenut oil *see under* OILS → types
Pineot **2** 541
pine resin *see* ROSIN
Pines, Isle of *see* ISLE OF PINES
pine soot *see under* soot → types
Pineu-Duval, Eugène-Emmanuel *see* AMAURY-DUVAL, EUGÈNE-EMMANUEL
Pingaleshvar **15** 452
Pingchuan shanzhuang **12** 87
Pinggu **7** 21
Pingliang **7** 16
Pingo, John **24** 823
Pingo, Lewis **21** 621; **24** 823*
Pingo, Thomas **20** 924; **24** 823
Pingret, Edouard (Henri Théophile) **24** 823*
Pingsdorf ware *see under* POTTERY → wares
Pingshan **6** *615*; **7** 150; **24** 823*
architecture **6** 646
bronze **6** 832, 855, 856
gold **7** 22
plans **6** 663
plaques **6** *695*
pottery **6** *881*
tomb of Cuo, King of Zhongshan **6** 853; **24** 823
tombs **6** 648, 695, *695*
Pinguet **31** 228
Pingusson, Georges-Henri **8** 224; **24** 824*
collaboration **13** 798
groups and movements **11** 526; **31** 582
Ping Yang **25** 800
Pingyao
Dacheng dian **6** 674
hall **6** 653
Pinhas, Judah **17** 564
Pinheiro, Alfredo **4** 717
Pinheiro, Columbano Bordalo *see* BORDALO PINHEIRO, COLUMBANO
Pinheiro, Costa *see* COSTA PINHEIRO
Pinheiro, Francisco Manuel Chaves *see* CHAVES PINHEIRO, FRANCISCO MANUEL
Pinheiro, Gerson Pompeu **26** 109
Pinheiro, Manuel Gustavo Bordalo *see* BORDALO PINHEIRO, MANUEL GUSTAVO
Pinheiro, Manuel Maria Bordalo *see* BORDALO PINHEIRO, MANUEL MARIA
Pinheiro, Maria Augusta Bordalo *see* BORDALO PINHEIRO, MARIA AUGUSTA
Pinheiro, Rafael Bordalo *see* BORDALO PINHEIRO, RAFAEL
Pini, Armencio **4** 565
Pini, Biagio de' *see* PUPINI, BIAGIO
Pini, Carlo **21** 538
Pini, Ermenegildo **24** 824–5*
Pinie (family) **10** 623
Piniński, Leon **25** 138
pinjante **24** 825*
Pinjaur **15** 484
pink *see under* PIGMENTS → types
Pinkas, (Hippolyt) Soběslav **8** 392; **24** 825*
Pinker, H. R. **20** 27
Pinker, Stanley **29** 109
pinking **30** 554
Pink'un **3** 64
Pinkwas, Beniamin *see* ETTINGER, PAVEL (DAVYDOVICH)
pinnacles **2** *346*; **11** 86; **20** 564, *565*; **24** *825*, 825–6*; **27** 148; **28** 128–9, 497
ganjira **30** 842
Pinnau, Cäsar **22** 711; **24** 826–7*
Pinney, Eunice **24** 827*
Pinnis, Rūdolfs
Pino, Alfredo **2** 661–2
Pino, Don *see* BETTISI, LEONARDO
Pino, Gasper Galcerán de Gurrea Aragón y, Conde de Guimerá *see* GUIMERÁ, GASPER GALCERÁN DE GURREA ARAGÓN Y PINO, Conde de
Pino, Marco **24** 420, 827*
collaboration **8** 504; **30** 800
pupils **8** 162; **27** 779
reproductive prints by others **1** 551
Pino, Paolo **9** 142; **24** 827–8*
teachers **27** 891
works **9** 7; **16** 614, 665; **24** 90
on beauty **1** 178
on *disegno e colore* **7** 628
on *poesie* **25** 71
Pino da Messina *see* JACOBELLO D'ANTONIO
Pino di Mannaia **13** 775
Piñón, Helio **29** 274; **32** 568
Pinot, François **29** 751
pins **17** 527
historical and regional traditions
Bosnia **13** 600
China **7** 107
Cycladic **8** *322*
England **10** 340
Greece, ancient **13** 600, *600*
Prehistoric art **25** 545
Sicily **13** 600
Troadic **31** 355
materials
brass **10** 340
bronze **13** 600, *600*
ivory **7** 107
silver **6** 599; **8** *322*
turquoise **7** 107
types
cloak **6** 599
dress **2** 79; **8** 352
hairpins *see* HAIRPINS
handpins **15** 871
toggle **1** 884
Pins, Jacob **16** 570
Pinseau, Michel **22** 128
works **22** *128*
Pinsel, Master **25** 115
Pinsent, Cecil **28** 283
Pinson, Jean **24** 828
Pinson, Nicolas **24** 828*
Pinter, Klaus **14** 237*
Pinto, Caetano da Silva *see* SILVA PINTO, CAETANO DA
Pinto, de (family) **1** 802
Pinto, Edward **31** 305
Pinto, Fonseca **28** 912
Pinto, Inácio Ferreira *see* FERREIRA PINTO, INÁCIO
Pinto, Isaak de **4** 541
Pinto, Joaquín **9** 713; **24** 828–9*
Pinto, José António Jorge **19** 468; **30** 882
Pinto Alpoim, José Fernandes *see* ALPOIM, JOSÉ FERNANDES PINTO
Pinto Basto, Ferreira, (family) *see* FERREIRA PINTO BASTO (FAMILY)
Pinto de Fonseca, Manoel **10** 843; **20** 215
Pinton Frères **30** 38

Pintóo, Francesc 29 337
Pintor, Pedro *see* PEDRO PINTOR
Pintorarium 11 812
Pintori, Giovanni 7 656; 25 351
Pintos, Salustiano 31 756
Pintubi 1 52, 56
Pintura de la luz 24 829*
Pinturicchio, Bernardino (di Betto) 20 684; 24 520, 829–32*; 28 676
- assistants 2 607, 632; 10 651; 31 188
- attributions 26 765
- collaboration 3 301; 5 672; 7 676; 21 764; 24 523, 525; 25 847, 897; 28 703
- groups and movements 10 95
- patrons and collectors 3 55; 4 410; 5 537; 15 861; 16 660, 661; 24 732; 27 271, 272, 273
- restorations by others 29 892
- works 1 655; 4 650; 11 711; 12 278; 13 700; 14 416; 15 861; 18 705; 24 567, *829*, *831*; 25 184; 26 765, 817, *817*; 28 677

Pintz, Johann Georg 20 914
Pintz, Philipp Gottfried 20 915
Pinwell, G(eorge) J(ohn) 24 832*
- reproductive prints by others 19 868
- works 4 363, 868; 25 598

Pin-wewa 29 474
Pinxton porcelain factory 4 65
Pinzel' 31 561
Pinzón, José Gómez *see* GÓMEZ PINZÓN, JOSÉ
Pio, Alberto (*b* 1847) 18 694
Pio, Alberto III (1475-1531) 7 321; 24 531, 833*
Piò, Angelo Gabriello 16 704, 749; 24 834*
- patrons and collectors 1 597; 12 559
- teachers 16 699; 20 903
- works 16 749; 30 498

Pio, Beatrice da 25 18
Piò, Domenico 24 834
Pio, Giovannino del *see* BONATTI, GIOVANNI
Pio, Leonello II 24 833
Pio, Nicola 8 132; 24 537, 834*
Pio, Rodolfo, Cardinal 24 833*
Pio di Savoia, Carlo Emanuele, Cardinal 24 833
Pio di Savoia, Carlo Francesco, Cardinal 24 833–4*
Piola, Anton Maria 24 835, 836
Piola, Domenico 11 8; 16 675; 24 203, 835–7*
- collaboration 11 9; 12 283; 14 27; 24 837
- patrons and collectors 3 90; 4 811; 23 874; 27 878; 29 411
- pupils 13 816
- teachers 11 53
- works 20 371; 24 *835*, *836*; 29 75
- workshops 12 283

Piola, Giovanni Andrea 24 835, 836
Piola, Giovanni Battista 24 835
Piola, Paolo Gerolamo 4 811; 11 8; 24 837*
- collaboration 24 835, 836
- patrons and collectors 28 79
- sponsors 23 874
- works 11 10; 20 371

Piola, Pellegro 24 835
Piombi, Zamaria dei 25 216
Piombini, Giuseppe 5 853
Piombino, Ugo Boncampagni Ludovisi, Prince of 4 312; 18 184
Piombino Dese, Villa Cornaro 7 861; 20 412; 23 866, *866*; 32 548
Piombo, Sebastiano del *see* SEBASTIANO DEL PIOMBO
Pioneer Group 13 489, 490, 511; 32 53, 57
- members 13 518*; 32 41, 42, 63

Pioneers 14 221; 16 2
Piot, Eugène 13 252; 16 559; 24 837–8*
Piot, Henri 2 660; 5 609
Piot, René 12 600; 24 838*; 26 265
Piotr (*d* 1472; father) 32 873
Piotr (*d* 1459; son) 32 873
Piotr (*fl* 1694) 25 339
Piotrovsky, Boris (Borisovich) 17 822; 24 838*
Piotrowski, Maksymiljan Antoni 25 106
Piotrowski, R. 18 596
Piozzi, Hester *see* THRALE, HESTER
Pipariya 15 469, 473
pipe-bags 22 649
pipe clays *see under* CLAY → types
Piper, Adrian 7 686; 10 879, 882; 24 409
Piper, C. Wellbourne 24 648
Piper, E. M. 18 73
Piper, F(rederik) M(agnus) 12 135; 24 838–9*; 29 691; 30 89
Piper, John 24 839*
- collaboration 3 885; 20 607
- groups and movements 10 258; 22 751
- patrons and collectors 15 36
- productions 30 687
- works 4 369; 5 513, 726; 10 352, 354; 19 491, 492; 25 628; 28 808; 29 508; 32 902
- writings 22 751

Piper, Otto 19 339
Piper, Vincent 14 118
Piperno, Antonio Baboccio da *see* BABOCCIO DA PIPERNO, ANTONIO
pipes (musical) 1 891; 7 147; 8 853; 30 *637*
pipes (smoking)
- historical and regional traditions 8 672
  - Aboriginal Australia 1 53
  - Africa 1 *367*, 367–8*
  - Akan 2 590
  - Asante 1 368; 2 590*
  - Bamum 3 154
  - Bantu peoples 1 368
  - Cameroon 1 368
  - China 7 147
  - Korea 18 380
  - Native North Americans 22 584–5, *585*, 586, *586*, 651, 653, 668
  - Nigeria 1 368
  - North Africa 1 367
  - South America, Pre-Columbian 29 134
  - Sudan 1 367, *367*, 368
  - Tarascan 30 341
  - Uganda 1 368
  - Vietnam 32 481
- materials
  - bamboo 1 *367*; 18 380; 32 481
  - beads 1 *367*
  - brass 1 368
  - catlinite 22 584, *585*, *586*
  - clay 1 *367*, 368
  - feathers 22 653
  - gourds 1 367
  - pottery 30 341
  - tin 1 368
  - wood 1 368

pipestone 1 *153*
pipkins 10 301
Pippi, Giulio *see* GIULIO ROMANO
Pippin, Horace 1 443; 22 441
Pippo di Gante *see* PIPPO DI GIOVANNI DE GHANTE DA PISA
Pippo di Giovanni de Ghante da Pisa 16 66; 20 531
Piprahwa 19 790
Piquer, José 24 839; 26 308
Piqueras, Jorge 24 510
Piqueras Cotolí, Manuel 5 527
Piquereau, Guillaume 31 843
Piquer y Duart, José 1 591; 24 839–40*
- pupils 13 275
- works 20 67, *68*; 24 402; 29 294

Piquillacta 29 *156*, 220
- architecture 29 164, 166
- figurines 29 185
- sculpture 29 171

Piracurte, Antonio 18 586
Piraeus *see* PEIRAEUS
Piraeus Painter 13 506
Pir Ahmad Baghshimali 1 25; 16 318
Pir Ahmad Khwafi 16 197
Piramesse 2 850; 9 *774*, 783, 826, 851; 23 807; 24 840*
- Avaris 2 850*; 9 *774*; 24 840
- Mortuary Temple I 9 831
- pottery 8 330
- sculpture 9 863

Piramo da Monópoli, Reginaldo 1 127; 24 840*
Piran 28 *858*
- St Peter 28 859
- Tartini Square 28 860

Pirandello, Fausto 16 680; 24 840–41*; 26 777; 28 319
Piranesi, Angelo 24 841
Piranesi, Francesco 5 366; 24 845, 846; 27 484
Piranesi, Giovanni Battista 10 642, 643; 16 669, 672, 677, 744; 24 383, 384, 841–7*; 26 774; 28 646
- architecture 20 866–7; 23 489; 29 832
- assistants 30 865
- collaboration 3 645; 19 76
- dealing 4 181; 23 21; 33 19
- decorative works 26 500
- drawings 9 223; 10 637; 27 781
- forgeries 10 639
- furniture 24 *845*
- groups and movements 2 163; 10 96; 13 608; 16 717; 22 735, 738
- patrons and collectors 8 867
  - Caulfeild, James, 1st Earl of Charlemont 27 356
  - Cavaceppi, Bartolomeo 6 98
  - Clement XIII, Pope (*reg* 1758-69) 26 286
  - Gomes do Avelar, Francisco 12 889
  - Hope, John (1737-84) 14 744
  - List, Herbert 19 478
  - Meynier, Charles 21 412
  - Newdigate, Roger 23 21
  - Rezzonico (family) 26 286
  - Townley, Charles 31 244
  - Wicar, Jean-Baptiste (-Joseph) 33 154
- pattern books 24 273; 26 780
- personal collection 2 27; 4 886; 9 23
- prints 2 164; 10 83; 16 *727*; 25 599, 630; 32 113–14
  - engravings 23 21, 544; 26 *760*, *807*, 841; 33 691
  - etchings 2 331; 5 687; 9 *22*; 10 83, 554, *555*; 13 301; 24 *843*, *844*, *845*; 32 *113*
  - *vedute* 25 607, 625
- pupils 17 850
- reproductive prints by others 8 267; 20 502
- restorations 14 109
- teachers 32 70
- writings 2 164; 16 727; 26 230
  - illustrated 3 204, 645

Piranesi, Laura 24 846
Piranesi, Pietro 24 846; 27 484
Piran Round 30 653
Piraube, Bertrand 2 465, 466
Pir Budaq (Qaraqoyunlu) 2 237; 16 328, 332; 25 774
Pirckheimer (family) 30 312
Pirckheimer, Willibald 9 434, 435, 436, 440; 12 471; 24 847–8*
- collections 15 145
- drawings 14 806

Pirelli 13 782
Pires, Alvaro 2 872
Pires, António Delgado 24 848
Pires, Diogo, the elder (*fl* 1481-1515) 1 212; 24 848*
Pires, Diogo, the younger (*c.* 1470-after 1532) 6 452; 17 596; 24 848–9*
Pires, Francisco 9 40
Pires, Manuel 24 849*
- attributions 25 291; 31 179
- collaboration 1 740
- patrons and collectors 2 874; 17 511
- works 10 664; 25 291

Pireva, Evelina 5 159
Pirez, Alvaro (*fl* 1510-39) 25 295
Pirez d'Evora, Alvaro (1411-34) 24 849–50*; 25 295; 27 836
Pir Husayn 18 18
Pir Husayn Damghani 33 512
Pir Husein Stele 1 509, 884
Piribebuy 24 *91*
- Franciscan church 24 94

Pirie, John Bridgeford 1 30
Pîrîescu, Niță 13 651
piriform jars *see under* JARS → types
Pir Ilyas 1 756
Pirincay 29 155
Pirin Factory 5 158
Piri Reis 16 347
Pirita 10 *536*
- Kalev Society building 10 537
- Sailing Centre 10 538

Pirkenhammer porcelain factory 2 817
Pirmeribo *see* PARAMARIBO
Pirna 8 384, 420
- Dominikanerkirche 12 463
- St Marien 29 65

Pirna, Peter Ulrich von 2 117; 12 365
Pırnallı *see* PORTA
Pirner, Johann 30 455
Pirner, Maximilián 24 850*
- pupils 4 59; 14 840; 17 592; 18 489; 20 455; 30 52

Pirngadie, Mas 15 807, 818; 29 241
Piroli 14 445
Piroli, Tommaso 1 734; 11 163; 23 634; 26 98
Piron, Aimée 8 892
Pirosmanashvili, Niko (Aslanovich) 9 144; 12 326, 332; 24 850*
Pirot 28 454, 458
Pirot, Andreas 12 467
Pirotti (family) 16 734
Pirotti, Domenico 24 851
Pirotti, Gianfrancesco 24 850, 851
Pirotti, Gianlorenzo 24 850, 851
Pirotti, Matteo 24 850
Pirotti, Negro 24 850
Pirotti, Sebastiano 24 851
Piroux, Charles-Augustin 19 801
Pirovano, Aloisio 6 359
Pirovano, Ernesto 16 648; 24 851*
Pirovano, Ignacio 2 405, 525
Pirrone, Giuseppe 28 657
Pirvu, Mutu 5 73; 24 851*; 25 341; 26 712, 725
Pîrvu Pîrvescu *see* PÎRVU, MUTU
Pīr Yaḥyā ibn Naṣr al-Ṣūfī *see* YAHYA AL-SUFI
Piryatin *see* PYRATIN
Pisa 16 *618*, *620*; 24 852–60*, *853*
- Arch of Gaius and Lucius 27 32
- botanic garden 4 483, 484
- Cittadella Nuovo 21 566
- coins 7 535
- crucifixes 16 655; 24 *854*

Pisa—cont.
- ecclesiastical buildings 24 852, 856*
  - Baptistery 3 192; 7 256; 8 912; 10 743; 24 857, *858*, 868, 871; 28 429
    - font 11 252; 26 624
    - pulpit 7 383; 16 *687*, 688; 24 867–8; 25 724; 26 136, 182
    - sculpture 24 858–9*; 26 623
  - Campanile 5 648, 649; 10 743
  - Camposanto 2 *187*; 6 165; 10 743; 24 771; 26 233
    - frescoes 4 493; 20 *775*, 775–6; 24 *859*, 859–60
    - paintings 1 653; 13 149
    - sculpture 24 871; 26 623
  - Cathedral of S Maria 4 141; 5 291–2; 16 625; 24 *855*, 856–7*, *856*, *857*; 26 576
    - altars 29 496
    - crucifixes 13 123
    - doors 4 297; 5 360; 9 154, 158; 21 755
    - ivory-carvings 13 176
    - metalwork 26 690
    - mosaics 7 317, *318*; 22 156, 163
    - paintings 24 860
    - Porta di S Ranieri 16 688; 24 873
    - pulpit 16 688; 24 872–3; 25 723, 724, *724*; 26 136
    - sculpture 10 743; 13 93, 804; 24 858*; 25 863; 26 623
    - stained glass 13 193
    - tomb of Henry VII 31 2–3
    - transept 26 *576*
  - S Andrea 16 412
  - S Caterina 9 109; 25 463
  - S Chiara 25 462
  - S Francesco 1 709; 7 318; 23 95
  - S Giovanni a Grado 30 886
  - S Maria del Carmine 20 *531*, 531–2
  - S Maria della Spina 13 65
  - S Martino 8 212
  - S Nicola 1 696; 13 124
    - campanile 24 867
  - S Paolo a Ripa d'Arno 16 625
  - S Piero a Grado 16 625; 24 860*
  - S Sisto 16 404, 412
  - S Stefano 16 404
- glass 16 740
- Leaning Tower *see* ecclesiastical buildings → Campanile
- manuscripts 26 666
- Museo Nazionale e Civico di S Matteo 30 4
- Museo dell'Opera del Duomo 16 774
- painting 24 854, 859–60*
- Palazzo dei Cavalieri 10 *740*, 741
- Palazzo Gambacorti 10 803
- patronage 16 762
- Piazza dei Cavalieri 12 575
- pottery 27 107, 108
- sculpture 13 93; 24 854; 26 619, 622
- tower houses 16 627
- University 31 674

Pisa, Bonanus of *see* BONANUS OF PISA
Pisa, Francesco da *see* FRANCESCO DA PISA
Pisa, Giovanni (di Pietro) da *see* GIOVANNI (DI PIETRO) DA PISA (i)
Pisa, Giovanni da *see* GIOVANNI DA PISA
Pisa, Guglielmo da *see* GUGLIELMO DA PISA
Pisa, Guido 8 136
Pisa, Isaia da *see* ISAIA DA PISA
Pisa, Niccolò Braccio da *see* BRACCIO DA PISA, NICCOLÒ

Pisa, Pippo di Giovanni de Ghante da *see* PIPPO DI GIOVANNI DE GHANTE DA PISA
Pisa, Ranieri di Leonardo da *see* LEONARDO DA PISA, RANIERI DI
Pisa, Sigismondo de Pretta de *see* PRETTA DE PISA, SIGISMONDO DE
Pisac **29** 166
Pisan **18** 345
Pisan, Christine de *see* CHRISTINE DE PIZAN
Pisan, Héliodore Joseph **33** 369
Pisan-dong **18** 340
Pisanello **9** 262; **13** 155; **14** 419; **24** 860–64*; **26** 767; **32** 160
  assistants **12** 302
  attributions **4** 332; **8** 14
  collaboration **8** 180; **16** 824
  drawings **2** 102; **9** 220, *220*; **21** 758; **24** 269, *861*; **25** 557
  dress **9** 244
  groups and movements **26** 184
  medals **11** 3; **15** 149; **16** 690; **20** 917, *918*; **24** *863*
  methods **25** 279
  paintings
    frescoes **7** 620; **12** 302; **16** 659; **22** 463; **24** *862*; **26** 765; **32** 220
    landscape **18** 704
    portraits **8** 602; **24** *863*
    religious **29** 423
  patrons and collectors **2** 276; **7** 218; **10** 519; **12** 905, 906; **20** 159; **24** 247; **32** 611
  pupils **4** 332
  restorations by others **21** 825
Pisani (family)
  architecture **28** 392
  furniture **5** 54
  interior decoration **30** 860
  paintings **19** 636; **33** 714
Pisani, Villa Nazionale Già *see under* STRA
Pisani, Almorò (i) (1615-82) **24** 865
Pisani, Almorò (ii) (1660-1744) **12** 115; **24** 865; **29** 736; **30** 348
Pisani, Almorò Alvise **24** 865
Pisani, Almorò Francesco **24** 865
Pisani, Almorò Lorenzo **24** 865
Pisani, Alvise (1618-79) **24** 865
Pisani, Alvise, Doge of Venice (*reg* 1735-41) **12** 115; **29** 736
Pisani, Chiara **24** 706
Pisani, Daniele **23** 862
Pisani, Ferdinando **26** 320
Pisani, Giovanni **3** 294; **23** 862
Pisani, Giuseppe **10** 546
Pisani, Juan Ricardo **2** 397
Pisani, Lazzaro **5** 131; **20** 213; **24** 865–6*
Pisani, Luigi **20** 482
Pisani, Marco **23** 862
Pisani, Pietro **3** 294
Pisani, Pietro Vettor **5** 626; **24** 865
Pisani, Ugolino **20** 744
Pisani, Vettor **16** 682; **24** 866*
Pisani, Vittore **23** 862
Pisani-Dossi, Alberto Carlo *see* DOSSI, CARLO
Pisano (i) (family) **2** 558
Pisano (ii) (family) **2** 558
Pisano (ii), Andrea **13** 93; **24** 854, 874–6*
  methods **10** 197
  works **1** 654; **9** 154; **11** 199, *200*, 200, 201; **12** 538; **13** 93, 124; **16** 688, 743; **24** *874*, *875*; **26** 136; **30** 272
Pisano, Antonio *see* PISANELLO
Pisano, Bonanno **28** 655
Pisano (i), Giovanni **13** 52, 93, 96; **23** 292; **24** 866–74*; **28** 676
  architecture **24** 857; **28** 679
  attributions **13** 123, *124*, *176*
Pisano (i), Giovanni—cont.
  collaboration **2** 481; **16** 688; **24** 519, 868, 870, 871; **25** 724; **31** 2
  pulpits **24** *856*; **25** 724, *724*; **26** 136
  pupils **12** 709
  sculpture **9** 123, 129; **10** 743; **11** 341
    architectural **13** *93*, 93; **16** 688; **24** 858, 859; **28** *680*, 680
    pulpits **24** *872*
    relief **10** 743
    religious **13** 95; **19** 827; **24** 854, *873*; **25** 679
    statuettes **13** 171, 174, 176
    tombs **12** 282; **19** 827
  teachers **12** 759
Pisano, Giunta *see* GIUNTA PISANO
Pisano (i), Nicola **13** 98; **16** 685; **23** 292; **24** 866–71*; **28** 676
  architecture **24** 857; **28** 679
  assistants **2** 481; **13** 804; **24** 871
  attributions **4** 278; **32** 216
  collaboration **2** 483; **24** 519; **25** 724
  patrons and collectors **1** 555; **3** 228; **9** 107
  pulpits **7** 383; **16** *687*, 688; **24** 859, *869*; **25** 724; **26** 136, 182
  pupils **2** 480
  sculpture **13** 93; **24** 854
    architectural **24** 871
    fountains **11** *340*, 341; **13** 96; **22** 44
    relief **4** 279; **19** 766; **24** *870*; **28** 680
    religious **4** 275; **5** 905; **9** *106*; **10** 743
    tombs **9** 109
Pisano, Niculoso **28** 519
Pisano (ii), Nino **13** 93; **24** 854, 876*
  attributions **24** 875
  works **13** 95, 124; **24** 875–6; **32** 215
Pisano (ii), Tommaso **13** 93; **24** 854, 876*
  works **1** 709; **24** 876
Pisano tiles *see under* TILES → types
Pisanti, Giuseppe **1** 745
Pisantus, Nicola *see* PISANO (i), NICOLA
Piscator, Erwin **4** 761; **13** 687; **14** 280; **30** 683, 686
Piscator, Johannes **18** 385
Piscicelli, Antonio **29** 253
Piscina, Pietro **11** 77
piscine (i) (pool) **24** 877*
  see also ROME, ANCIENT → pools
piscine (ii) (basins) **24** 877*
Pisco **24** *498*
  La Compañía **24** 503
pisé **4** 771
pisé de terre **6** 696, 697; **7** 143; **19** 837; **32** 308
Písek **8** 376
  castle **8** 404
  St Mary **8** 388
Pi Shou *see* BI SHOU
Pishpek *see* BISHKEK
pishtāq **9** 161; **16** 160, 164, 801; **24** 877–8*
Pishwaran **16** 168
Pisidian Antioch *see* ANTIOCH (ii) (PSIDIA)
Pisis, Bona De *see* DE PISIS, BONA
Pisis, (Luigi) Filippo (Tibertelli) De *see* DE PISIS, (LUIGI) FILIPPO (TIBERTELLI)
Piso, L. Calpurnius **14** 442
Piso, Willem **2** 105
Pisones **31** 58
Pisoni, Gaetano Matteo **3** 547; **24** 878*; **30** 127
Pisoni, Paolo Antonio (1658-1711) **24** 878
Pisoni, Paolo Antonio (1738-1824) **24** 878
Pisotti, Jakob, the elder (1777-1829) **2** 816; **27** 665
Pisotti, Jakob, the younger (1792-1869) **2** 816; **27** 665
Pisquillo **6** 440
Pissarro, (Jacob Abraham) Camille **7** 674; **8** 613; **11** 416, 667; **17** 576; **19** 589; **20** 603; **24** 878–84*; **28** 797; **30** 290
  collaboration **5** 922
  dealers **3** 826, 888; **4** 589; **9** 424, 425; **15** 155; **26** 107
  drawings **5** 691; **13** 323
  exhibitions **10** 680; **15** 154, 155
  frames **11** 416, 417, 418
  groups and movements
    Impressionism **8** 621; **15** 151, 152, 153, 155
    naturalism **22** 687
    Neo-Impressionism **15** 155, 156; **22** 745, 747
    XX, Les **22** 746
  methods **5** 654; **7** 629; **9** 673
  paintings
    genre **12** 296; **15** 154, 155; **24** *879*
    landscape **11** *416*, 417; **15** 154; **24** *880*, *881*
    sporting scenes **29** 426
    topographical **31** 157; **32** 173
    townscapes **24** *882*
    watercolours **32** 902
  patrons and collectors **25** 626
    Alexandre, Arsène **1** 614
    Barnes, Albert C. **3** 251; **12** 769
    Bellio, Georges de **26** 722
    Caillebotte, Gustave **5** 391
    Clark, Robert Sterling **7** 377
    Durand-Ruel, Paul (Marie Joseph) **28** 744
    FitzGerald, Desmond **11** 141
    Havemeyer, Louisine (Waldron) **14** 244
    Khalie Museum, Cairo **5** 401
    Lambert, Catholina **18** 672
    May, Ernest (1845-1925) **20** 878
    Moreau-Nélaton, Etienne **22** 93
    Morozov, Ivan (Abramovich) (1871-1921) **22** 136
    Ōhara, Magosaburō **23** 371
    Palmer, Bertha Honoré **23** 882
    Robinson, Edward G(oldenberg) **26** 472
    Ryabushinsky, Mikhail **27** 459
    Tavernier, Adolphe-Eugène **30** 375
    Wrightsman, Charles B(ierer) **33** 416
    Zambaccian, K. H. **26** 723
  prints **19** 395; **25** 624
    aquatints **2** 240
    drypoints **9** 309
    etchings **10** 556, 559, 563
    lithographs **13** 323; **19** 488, 490; **25** 607
    monotypes **21** 896
  pupils **12** 187; **24** 884; **25** 215
  teachers **19** 93
Pissarro, Félix **24** 878
Pissarro, Georges **24** 878
Pissarro, Lucien **4** 366; **24** 878, 884–5*; **33** 369
  dealers **19** 10
  groups and movements **5** 516; **10** 255; **22** 745, 747
  patrons and collectors **3** 889
  teachers **19** 214
  works **18** 631, 716, 717; **33** 361
Pissarro, Ludovico Rodolph **24** 878
Pissarro, Orovida **24** 878
Pissarro, Paul-Emile **24** 878
Pissarskoy, Evgeniy (Gavrilovich) **18** 568
Pisses **17** 874
Pisson, Jean-Baptiste **3** 547; **12** 523; **24** 885*; **31** 864
Pistator, Meister *see* STAMPFER, PETER
Pistilli, Hugo **24** 100
Pistocchi, Giuseppe **24** 885–7*
  works **21** 520; **24** *886*
Pistoia
  Borsa Merci **16** 650
  churches
    Baptistery **3** 192
    Cathedral **7** 817
      altar **13** 163
      Cappella del Sacramento **19** *675*
      paintings **8** 212, *212*; **32** 365
      sculpture **24** 870
    Chiesa dello Spirito Santo **23** 501
    S Andrea **26** 623
      crucifix **13** 123
      pulpit **24** 872, *872*; **25** 724; **26** 136
      sculpture **13** 93
    S Bartolomeo in Pantano **25** 723; **26** 623, 624
    S Domenico **6** 466
    S Giovanni Fuorcivitas **16** 625; **25** 724; **26** 623
      sculpture **30** 497, *497*
    S Maria dell'Umiltà **32** *630*
  Falconiera, La **4** 252
  Fattoria di Celle **28** 315
  glass **16** 740
  Museo di Marino Marini **20** 429
  Parco di Collodi **13** 346
  Piazza S Francesco **27** 204
  Villa Scornio **27** 204
Pistoia, Gerino da *see* GERINO DA PISTOIA
Pistoia, Leonardo da **7** 776
Pistoia, Manfredino (d'Alberto) da *see* MANFREDINO (D'ALBERTO) DA PISTOIA
Pistoia, Matteo da *see* MATTEO DA PISTOIA
Pistoletto, Michelangelo **2** 526; **16** 682; **24** 866, 887*
Pistoli, Valentina **1** 539
pistols **2** 459, *466*
Pistoxenos **32** 40
Pistoxenos Painter **13** 484, 523, 535; **32** 41
  works **13** *535*
Pistrucci, Benedetto **16** 752; **24** 887*
  assistants **32** 682
  teachers **22** 103
  works **12** 264; **20** 924
Pistrucci, Elena **24** 887
Pistrucci, Elisa Maria **24** 887
Pistrucci, Filippo **28** 464
Pistucci Painter **13** 525
Pita, Estanislao Pérez *see* PÉREZ PITA, ESTANISLAO
Pitalkhora **5** 94; **15** *276*; **24** 887–8*
  Cave 3 **15** 434
  Cave 4 **15** 434–5
  sculpture **15** 433, 434–5*
  temple **15** 252
  wall paintings **15** 553
Pita Maha **15** 809; **29** 238
Pitareti Church **12** 320
Pitati, Bonifazio de' **16** 665; **24** 888–90*
  patrons and collectors **4** 811; **21** 348; **23** 355
  pupils **3** 343; **23** 877; **28** 81; **31** 6
  restorations by others **9** 740
  teachers **23** 877
  works **16** 726; **24** *889*
Pitati, Marco de' **24** 888
Pitau, Jacob **24** 890
Pitau, Nicolas, the elder (1632-71) **8** 525; **9** 718; **18** 879; **24** 890
Pitau, Nicolas, the younger (1670-1724) **9** 718; **24** 890
Pitcairn, Raymond **24** 890*; **29** 515
Pitcairn Island **23** *711*; **24** 890–91*
pitch **2** 239; **12** 868; **33** 2
pitch, Greek *see* GREEK PITCH
pitched-brick vaults *see under* VAULTS (CEILING) → types
pitched roofs *see under* ROOFS → types
pitchers
  historical and regional traditions
    Germany **12** 442
    Hungary **15** 3
    Italy **32** *202*
    Japan **17** *251*, 341
    Native North Americans **22** *602*
    Russia **27** 410
  materials
    gold **22** *435*
    stonewares **17** *251*
  types
    hound-handle **31** 636
  see also JUGS
Pitchford Hall (Salop) **10** 230, *231*
pitchstone **29** 702, 703
Pit culture **27** 366
pit dwellings *see under* HOUSES → types
Pite, A(rthur) Beresford **14** 743; **24** 891*
  collaboration **3** 532
  competitions **7** 668
  groups and movements **3** 269; **9** 739
  pupils **12** 314
  works **3** *533*
Pite, Alfred (Robert) **10** 185; **24** 891
Pite, William A. **20** 853
Pitento, Alberto **20** 318
Pitesti **26** 710
Pitești, Alexandru Bogdan *see* BOGDAN PITEȘTI, ALEXANDRU
Pit-grave culture **31** 545
pit-graves *see under* GRAVES → types
pith **3** 169
pīṭha **15** 244*
Pithan (family) **31** 526
Pithekoussai **10** *583*, 584, 591; **13** *362*, 372, 496; **16** *621*; **24** 891–2*
  gold **10** 631
  pottery **10** 591, 610; **13** 487, 496, 537
Pithion *see* EMPYTHION
pithoi
  Crete **8** 154; **18** *167*; **21** 671
  Cyprus, ancient **19** 131
  Etruscan **10** 613
  Greece, ancient **13** 383, 474, 538
  Helladic **14** 341, 342, *344*
  Italy **10** 613
  Minoan **18** *167*; **21** 671
  Mycenaean **14** 341, *344*
Pithom **13** 569
pithouses *see under* HOUSES → types
Pitigliano, Gianfrancesco Orsini, Conte de **21** 21; **30** 531
Pitigliano, Nicolò Orsini, Conte di **26** 726
Pitilu **24** 82
Pitiunt *see* BICHVINTA
Pitjantjatjara **1** 52, 56, 64, 68
  containers **1** *53*
Pitkänen, Pekka **24** 892*
Pitloo, Anton Sminck (van) **22** 480; **24** 892–3*
  groups and movements **16** 678; **28** 317
  pupils **12** 606; **23** 850; **32** 400
Pitman, Benn **7** 327
Pitney Brooch **2** 80; **26** 687; **32** 529
Pitocchetto, il *see* CERUTI, GIACOMO
Pitoin, Jean-Claude **24** 893
Pitoin, Quentin-Claude **11** 627; **24** 893*
Piton, Camille **3** 464

Pitons, Louis Evrard des 11 608; 21 137
Pitot, Henri 2 242
pits 12 174
Pitsa 13 370, 543, 550, 555
Pitschmann, Józef 25 106
Pitsunda see BICHVINTA
Pitt, George, 1st Baron Rivers 1 449
Pitt, Thomas, 1st Baron Camelford 13 637; 24 893*
Pitt, William (1759-1806) 26 237
Pitt, William (fl 1793) 19 11
Pitt, William (1855-1918) 2 739; 10 144; 21 75; 24 894*
Pittara, Carlo 2 10; 16 678; 28 318
Pittenhart, Wolfgang 10 739
Pittenweem Priory 21 840
Pitteri, Felice 24 895
Pitteri, Francesco 6 91
Pitteri, Marco Alvise 24 894–5*
  pupils 11 241
  works 24 707; 30 864; 32 501; 33 613
Pittermann-Longen, Emil Artur 10 107
Pitti (family) 11 893
Pitti, Luca di Bonaccorso 11 178, 213; 24 895*
Pitti, Miniato 32 11
Pitt Island see CHATHAM ISLANDS
Pitti Tondo 21 435
Pittman, W. Sidney 14 802
Pittoni, Battista 25 1*
Pittoni, Francesco 25 1
Pittoni, Giambattista 25 1–4*; 28 173
  collaboration 5 594; 8 159
  patrons and collectors 1 633; 4 560; 5 686; 27 864; 28 18, 173
  pupils 17 912
  works 17 912; 25 3
Pittoni, Giovanni Battista 18 45
pittoresco 24 741
pittoresque 24 741
Pittori, Giovanni Battista dei see BERTUCCI, GIOVANNI BATTISTA
Pitt-Rivers, Augustus Henry Lane-Fox 2 299; 10 91
Pitt-Rivers Knife-handle 9 865
Pitt Rivers Museum see under OXFORD → museums
Pitts, Gordon MacLeod 20 877
Pitts, John 6 84
Pitts, Thomas 10 332; 25 4*
Pitts, William, II (1790-1840) 10 334; 27 336
Pittsburgh (PA) 25 4–5*, 5; 31 587
  Alcoa Building 1 736; 8 278; 14 200
  Allegheny County Court House and Jail 18 888; 26 342, 342–3, 704; 31 594
  Carnegie, The 4 20; 5 781; 25 5
  Cathedral of Learning 13 204
  Center for the Arts 25 5
  exhibitions 25 5
  glass 31 642
  mills 10 748
  surveys 15 830
  Union Arcade 30 507
  Union Station 30 507
Pittsburgh Bridge Company 31 464
Pittsfield (MA)
  chairs 28 542
Pittura Metafisica 5 849; 8 602, 604, 772; 16 680; 18 717; 20 93; 21 340; 25 5–6*; 29 670; 31 852
  commentaries 27 888
  France 8 603
  Italy 8 604
Pitt & Walkley 24 894
Pitué, Pierre 4 558, 560, 588; 11 754
Pityoussa see CHIOS (ISLAND)
Pitzamanos, Angelos 25 332
Pitzamanos, Gerasimos 25 6–7*
Pitzler, Christof 5 347
piuri see PIGMENTS → types → peori
Pius II, Pope (reg 1458-64) 12 691; 24 731–2*
  altarpieces 20 845
  architecture 1 561; 10 853; 11 684, 685; 16 630, 631; 24 278, 746–7; 26 755, 811; 31 57; 32 104
  art policies 16 768
  books 12 655; 24 732; 28 677
  gardens 12 111, 112
  gold 24 36
  interior decoration 16 630
  paintings 1 621
  sculpture 10 853; 16 67; 21 693; 24 29; 26 766, 809
Pius III, Pope (reg 1503) 24 732*
  architecture 27 737; 28 677
  paintings 24 831
  sculpture 7 621; 31 189
Pius IV, Pope (reg 1559-66) 3 293; 25 7*
  architecture 4 47, 271, 272; 5 699; 9 338; 13 813; 19 372; 21 456; 22 6; 26 795, 806, 813; 28 460; 32 505
  art policies 16 768
  coats of arms 14 416
  fountains 11 342
  frescoes 5 699
  gilding 8 268
  gold 5 697
  maps 20 366
  metalwork 19 560
  paintings 27 653; 28 658; 31 524
  sculpture 19 201
  urban planning 11 272
Pius V, Pope (reg 1566-72) 25 7–8*; 26 769
  architecture 4 47; 19 631; 23 746
  clocks 7 439
  interior decoration 32 16
  paintings 22 71; 29 428; 32 16
Pius VI, Pope (reg 1775-80) 7 412; 25 8*; 32 612
  architecture 5 552; 7 493; 15 861; 16 772; 20 392, 393; 26 761; 28 755; 31 719, 800
  collections 12 474; 13 605; 27 115
  medals 32 8
  metalwork 31 799
  paintings 6 111; 11 900; 23 173; 31 679
  sculpture 6 98; 10 849; 27 46; 31 799
Pius VII, Pope (reg 1800-23) 5 555; 18 893
  architecture 22 9; 26 761; 29 639
  art policies 16 768
  carriages 1 120
  gems 24 734
  medals 12 738
  metalwork 26 389
  mosaics 5 555
  paintings 20 283; 22 338
  sculpture 5 631
Pius VIII, Pope (reg 1829-31) 5 555; 12 738
Pius IX, Pope (reg 1846-78) 4 99, 697; 12 166; 23 677; 26 761, 834; 32 385
Pius XI, Pope (reg 1922-39) 4 843; 12 738; 28 632
Pius XII, Pope (reg 1939-58) 24 278
Piva, Monastery of the Dormition of the Virgin 25 339, 340; 28 450
Pivac, Nada 4 461
Pivrncová, Vlasto 8 421
Piwarski, Jan Feliks 12 490
Piwocki, Ksawery 25 143
Piwonka, Alberto 6 594
P(article-)I(nduced) X (-ray) E(mission) see under TECHNICAL EXAMINATION → types
Pixérécourt 9 466
Piyadasa 20 172
Piye (reg c. 750-c. 719 BC) 9 777, 784; 23 281
Piyi 8 155
Pizani, Antonio 32 171
Pizano, Roberto 7 611
Pizarro, Cecilio 31 90
Pizarro, Francisco 19 385; 24 500
Pizolpasso, Francesco, Archbishop of Milan 20 783
Pizwell (Devon) 32 277
Pizzala, Andrea 25 9*
Pizzano see PISONI
Pizzicolli, Ciriaco di Filippo de' see CYRIAC OF ANCONA
Pizzigoni, Pino 16 649; 23 263
Pizzinato, Armando 11 802
Pizzino 31 534
Pizzocaro, Antonio 19 629
Pizzoli, Domenico 12 23
Pizzoli, Gioacchino 12 23
Pizzolo, Niccolò 25 9*
  assistants 20 305
  collaboration 2 130; 9 130; 12 705; 20 304, 306; 32 654
  works 12 705; 15 136; 29 665
Pizzolpasso, Francesco 32 638
Pizzoni see PISONI
Pkhotreri Church 12 322, 326
PKP group 13 525
Plá, Cecilio 2 29; 4 403; 8 2; 25 827
Pla, Francesc 29 305
Plá, Josefina 4 141; 24 98, 99
Placard, Le see LE PLACARD
Place, Francis 21 415; 25 9–11*; 33 545
  groups and movements 32 902
  pupils 28 526
  works 25 10; 32 900; 33 546
Place, L. des 3 785; 18 692
Place, Victor 1 892, 895; 21 299; 25 172
Placentia see PIACENZA
Plach, Georg 2 829; 11 33
Placidi, Francisco 18 426, 428; 19 497
Placidus, Abbot of Kremsmünster 28 380
Placzek, Adolf K. 10 212
Plá de Petracos 29 364
Plageman, Carl Gustaf 25 11*; 27 162
Plagemann, Arnold Abraham 25 11
Plaimpied 26 599
plain-line painting see under CHINA → painting
Plain of Jars 27 831
Plains (Strathclyde), St David 28 244
Plain Style (Portugal) 20 462; 25 288; 32 539
Plain style pottery see under POTTERY → wares
plain weave see under TEXTILES → types
Plain White Wheelmade ware see under POTTERY → wares
plaiting
  historical and regional traditions
    Brazil 4 706
    Marshall Islands 20 479
    Nauru 22 694
    Tonga (Pacific Islands) 31 143
  uses
    baskets 3 332; 15 809
    basketwork 22 655
    fibre art 11 54
    lace 18 589
Plá i Vila, Francesc 29 306
Pla Janini, Joaquim 25 11*
Plaka, Melos Museum 21 94
Plakes 22 396
Plakhov, Lavr (Kuzmich) 32 164
Plamadyala, Aleksandr 21 811
Plamondon, Antoine 22 597; 25 11*
  pupils 14 103
  teachers 19 75
  works 5 564
Planas, Juan Batlle see BATLLE PLANAS, JUAN
Planas Casas, José 3 380
Planat, Paul Amédée 10 209, 210
Planat, Pierre 8 476
Planché, André 8 776; 9 368; 10 308; 14 857
Planche, François de La see LA PLANCHE, FRANÇOIS DE
Planche, Gustave 25 12*; 26 53
Planché, James Robertson 30 680
Planche, Jean de 4 352
Plancher, Dom 8 894
Plancia Magna 24 417
Plancius, Petrus 12 812, 814
Planck, Max 19 355
Plancken, François van den see LA PLANCHE, FRANÇOIS DE
Plancus, L. Munatius 2 721; 19 845; 23 144; 31 57
Plandiura, Luis 29 354
Planeix, Antoine 19 41
Planella Coromina, Josep 29 306
PLANEMAK (Planejamento de Edifícios e Cidades Ltd) 20 269
planes 17 49, 49–50; 33 328
Planes, Luis 33 470
Planes, Rafael Ximeno y see XIMENO Y PLANES, RAFAEL
Planet, Louis de 8 645
Plan group 12 887
Planić, Stjepan 9 672; 15 66; 25 12*
Planicus, Petrus 32 588
Planis, Jean de see JEAN DE PLANIS
Planiscig, Leo 25 12*
plank houses see under HOUSES → types
plank masks see under MASKS → types
plank-shaped figurines see under FIGURINES → types
planning, urban see URBAN PLANNING
Plano (IL), Farnsworth House 2 360; 12 792; 21 493, 493; 24 291; 31 597
planographic printing see under PRINTING → processes
plans 20 560, 565; 24 650, 654
  Central Asia, Western 16 196
  China 6 663, 663
  Egypt, ancient 9 825; 10 63, 63–4*
  France 21 568
  Islamic 16 143, 196
  Ottoman 16 143
Plant, R. H. & S. L. 7 798
Plant, William 23 68
Plantagenet, Alphonso 14 423
Plantagenet, Anne of Bohemia, Queen of England see ANNE OF BOHEMIA, Queen of England
Plantagenet, Blanche, Princess 13 164
Plantagenet, Edward, Prince of Wales (1343-76) 33 523
Plantagenet, Edward II, King of England see EDWARD II, King of England
Plantagenet, Edward III, King of England see EDWARD III, King of England
Plantagenet, Edward IV, King of England see EDWARD IV, King of England
Plantagenet, Eleanor, Duchess of Gloucester 4 238
Plantagenet, Eleanor of Aquitaine, Queen of England see ELEANOR OF AQUITAINE, Queen of England
Plantagenet, Henry, Earl of Derby see HENRY IV, King of England
Plantagenet, Henry II, King of England see HENRY II, King of England
Plantagenet, Henry III, King of England see HENRY III, King of England
Plantagenet, Humfrey, Duke of Gloucester 5 669; 13 329, 623; 18 686–7*; 19 313
Plantagenet, Isabel, Queen of England see ISABEL, Queen of England
Plantagenet, Joan, Countess of Toulouse see JOAN, Countess of Toulouse
Plantagenet, John, King of England see JOHN, King of England
Plantagenet, John of Gaunt, Duke of Lancaster 6 50; 19 290
Plantagenet, John of Lancaster, Duke of Bedford 11 660; 18 685–6*
  architecture 3 825
  manuscripts 4 372, 764; 17 669; 18 686; 20 624, 626
Plantagenet, Margaret, Duchess of Clarence 4 372
  manuscripts 4 372
Plantagenet, Mary, Countess of Derby see MARY DE BOHUN, Queen of England
Plantagenet, Matilda see MATILDA, Duchess of Saxony and Bavaria
Plantagenet, Philippa of Hainault, Queen of England see PHILIPPA OF HAINAULT, Queen of England
Plantagenet, Richard, Earl of Cornwall, King of the Romans see RICHARD PLANTAGENET, Earl of Cornwall, King of the Romans
Plantagenet, Richard I, King of England see RICHARD I, King of England
Plantagenet, Richard II, King of England see RICHARD II, King of England
Plantagenet, Richard III, King of England see RICHARD III, King of England
Plantagenet, Thomas of Woodstock, Duke of Gloucester 4 238; 25 16*
Plantagenet-Temple-Nugent-Brydges-Chandos, Richard, 2nd Duke of Buckingham and Chandos 7 233; 10 367
plantain see under FIBRES → types
planter chairs see under CHAIRS → types
Planteri, Gian Giacomo 27 486
Planteydt, Annelies 22 897
Plantijn, Christoffel see PLANTIN, CHRISTOPH
Plantin 5 51
Plantin, Catherine 3 610
Plantin, Christoph 3 610; 25 17*, 631; 33 168, 169
  printmakers 15 42
    Borcht, Pieter van der 4 384
    Broeck, Crispin van den 4 839
    Bruyn, Abraham de 5 61
    Heere, Lucas de 14 296
    Heyden, Pieter van der 14 505
    Huys, Frans 15 43
    Huys, Pieter 15 42
    Liefrinck, Mynken 19 343
    Lorck, Melchior 19 662
    Passe, Crispijn (van) de, I (1564-1637) 24 235
    Sadeler, Jan, I (1550-1600) 27 501
    Wierix, Jan 33 168, 169
    Wierix, Jerome 33 169

Plantin, Christoph—cont.
publications **10** 389; **12** 885
illustrated **12** 17; **13** 231; **17** 599
Polyglot Bibles **2** 411; **4** 8; **15** 580; **17** 512
prints **9** 64; **14** 5
title-pages **10** 391
Plantin, Martine **3** 610
Plantin-Moretus **4** 219, 282; **6** 595; **17** 470, 471; **18** 879
workshop **25** *593*
Plantin-Moretus Museum *see under* ANTWERP → museums
Plantin Press **1** 467; **7** 120, 500; **14** 433, 616; **27** 299
plants **12** 415
Planudes, Maximus **10** 173
plaques
historical and regional traditions
Ancient Near East **1** 865, *870*, 879
Assyrian **21** *276*
Bangladesh **3** 169
Benin, Kingdom of **3** *720*, 722
Buddhism **15** *221*
Bulgaria **25** *517*
Burma **5** 230, 231, 254–5*
Byzantine **9** *514*, 590, 593, 646, 647, *650*, 650, 651, 658, 661
Carolingian **5** *811*
Central Asia, Western **27** *599*
China **6** *632*, *695*; **7** *27*, *107*, 108, 124, 140; **8** 854, *854*; **23** 496, *496*
Crete **21** *681*
Czech Republic **12** *786*
Dian culture **8** 854, *854*
Early Christian (*c.* AD 250-843) **9** *514*, 590, 647; **16** 686, *686*
Egypt, ancient **9** 890; **10** 7, 48, 58; **22** *488*
Etruscan **10** 593, 620–21, 634–5; **30** *494*
France **7** *718*; **13** 168; **24** *149*
Georgia **9** 658
Germany **7** *686*; **16** 799; **26** *696*
Gothic **13** 168
Greece, ancient **13** 370, 443, *550*, 582*, 595; **32** 67
Helladic **14** 354
India, Republic of **15** 174
Indian subcontinent **4** 794; **15** *221*, 226, 443, *459*, 695, 718
Shunga period **15** *718*
Insular art **15** *873*
Ireland **15** *873*
Islamic **16** 528
Italy **10** 593, 620–21, 634–5; **16** 686, *686*; **21** 529; **26** 486
Jainism **15** 226, 443
Japan **17** 215
Mesopotamia **1** 865; **10** *473*; **21** *276*
Minoan **21** *681*
Mongolia **23** 496, *496*
Native North Americans **29** *415*
Netherlands, the **16** 799
Ottoman **16** 528
Ottonian **23** *660*
Palestine **27** *670*
Prehistoric art **25** 491, 492, 493, 500, *517*, 540, 541
Romanesque **7** *718*; **26** *696*, *699*
Russia **2** *101*
Scandinavia **32** 523
Scythian **2** *101*
Spain **26** *699*
Sri Lanka **29** 471
Syria-Palestine **1** *870*
Tajikistan **27** *599*
Viking **32** 523
Vinča culture **25** 500
materials
amber **1** 761
baleen **28** 302
bone **2** *101*
brass **3** *720*
plaques
materials—cont.
bronze **6** *695*; **7** 108; **8** 854, *854*; **15** *873*; **21** *276*; **23** 496, *496*
clay **13** *550*
copper **29** *415*
enamel **13** 168; **23** *98*
faience (i) (glass) **1** 879; **10** 48
glass **1** 865; **9** 646; **10** 58; **12** *786*
gold **2** *101*; **6** *632*; **7** *27*, 108; **25** *517*; **27** *599*; **32** 523
hardstones **6** *632*; **7** *27*
horn **7** 124
ivory **16** 799
Byzantine **9** 647, *650*
Carolingian **5** *811*
Early Christian (*c.* AD 250-843) **16** 686, *686*
Early Christian and Byzantine **9** *514*
Egypt, ancient **22** *488*
Etruscan **10** 634–5
Greece, ancient **13** 595
Indian subcontinent **15** 695
Minoan **21** *681*
Ottonian **23** *660*
Palestine **27** *670*
Romanesque **26** *696*, *699*
jade **7** *107*; **16** 528
porcelain **24** *149*
rock crystal **21** 529; **26** 485, 486
silver **7** 108; **9** 658
slate **25** 491
terracotta **5** 230; **13** 443, 582*; **15** *221*, *459*, 718, *718*; **30** *494*
wood **7** 140
techniques
engraving **25** 491, 492
painting **25** 493
uses
architecture **4** 794
book covers **5** *811*
pulpits **23** *98*
plaquettes **25** 18–22*
historical and regional traditions
France **25** 22
Germany **12** 447; **25** 21–2, *22*
Italy **1** *35*; **16** 689; **21** 783; **25** *19*, 19–21*, *20*
Netherlands, the **25** 21
Spain **25** 20
materials
brass **25** 19
bronze **25** 19, *20*
gold **25** 19
lead **1** *35*; **18** 902; **25** 19, *22*
silver **25** 19, *19*
silver-gilt **25** *19*, *20*
see also RELIEF SCULPTURE
Plasencia **25** 22–3*; **29** *258*
Cathedral *see* S María
S María **13** 68, 70; **25** 22–3; **29** 265
choir-stalls **13** 123
retable **13** 69
Plaskin, Mikhail **8** 10
Plas Newydd **5** *687*, 688
Plasschaert, Rafaël **13** 277
plaster **29** 812–46*
conservation **29** 845–6*
France **30** *21*
historical and regional traditions
Afghanistan **29** 824–5*
Africa **1** 305; **29** 827–8*
Algeria **1** 305
Ancient Near East **29** 814–16*
Austria **29** 838–9*, 843
Aztec **29** 828
Bactria **6** 214–15
Bhutan **3** 914
Britain **29** 829
Buddhism **6** 706; **29** 823–4
Byzantine **9** 562; **29** 816–17*, *817*
Cambodia **5** 501
Canada **5** 572
plaster
historical and regional traditions—cont.
Central Asia **29** 821*
Central Asia, Eastern **29** 823–4*
Central Asia, Western **6** 214–15, *220*; **16** 200; **29** 821–3*
China **6** 706
Cyprus **29** 816, *817*
Czech Republic **8** 376, 379, *387*
Denmark **29** *541*, 840–41*
Early Christian (*c.* AD 250-843) **9** 562; **29** 816–17*, *817*
Egypt, ancient **2** 541; **6** 9; **10** *16*, 68–9*; **20** *117*; **23** 807; **29** 814*
England **9** 16; **10** 271, 274, *275*; **29** 834–5*, *836*, 843–5
Etruscan **10** 617
France **4** *568*; **5** *303*; **9** 14; **12** *564*; **24** *821*; **29** 833–4*, 843
Germany **3** *243*; **12** *406*; **29** 838*, 843
Greece **13** *354*
Greece, ancient **13** 389, 438; **29** 814*
Helladic **14** *352*
India, Republic of **15** 174
Indian subcontinent **4** 793; **15** 319; **29** 824–5*
Indonesia **15** 779
Iran **16** 165, 200
Iran, ancient **29** *815*
Ireland **16** *23*, 23–4; **29** 829
Islamic **16** 140, 142, 165, 200, 269; **29** 818–20*
Italy **9** 14, *403*; **12** *268*; **27** *18*, *19*; **29** 816–17, 829–33*, 843; **31** 523
Java **15** 779
Korea **18** 277, 300, 301, 302
Latin America **29** 841*
Maya **29** 828–9
Mesoamerica, Pre-Columbian **21** 226, 229; **29** 828–9*
Moche (culture) **29** 829
Mycenaean **14** *352*
Parthian **29** 814–15*
Poland **25** *115*; **29** 839
Portugal **29** 841–2*
Rome, ancient **2** 541; **27** 17, 18, *18*, *19*, 51
Russia **29** 839–40*
Sasanian **29** 815–16*
Scandinavia **29** 840–41*
Scotland **28** *243*, 245, 248; **29** 835, 843–5
Sogdiana **6** *220*
South America, Pre-Columbian **29** 829*
South-east Asia **29** 826–7*
Spain **29** 841–2*
Sweden **29** 840*
Syria-Palestine **30** 182, 196
Tunisia **1** 305
United States of America **29** 842*, 845; **31** 611
Uzbekistan **31** *76*
materials
alabaster (gypsum) **1** 516
alum **29** 812
barium oxide **29** 813
candelilla wax **33** 1
cement **29** 813
clay **11** 762; **15** 174; **29** 814
dextrin **29** 813
dung **15** 174
flurosilicate **29** 813
glycerin **29** 813
gum arabic **29** 813
gypsum **29** 812; **30** 196
hair **29** 813
lime **9** 562; **11** 761, 762; **21** 229; **29** 846; **30** 196
limestone **11** 762
magnesium **29** 813
marble **11** 762; **31** 523
milk **29** 813
plaster
materials—cont.
mortars (building) **29** 812
oils **29** 813
paints **29** 813
pozzolana **11** 762
sand **11** 762; **29** 812
shellac **29** 813
travertine **31** 523
waxes **29** 813
technical examination **30** 409
types
gesso spresato **28** 338
gypsum *see* GESSO
imitation **24** 61
intonaco *see* INTONACO
plaster of Paris **1** 516; **6** 7; **7** 729; **10** 306, 683; **29** 812
uses
arches **31** 351
architectural decorations **16** 142
architecture **1** 305; **4** 793; **8** 376, 379; **10** 683; **16** 165, 269
busts **5** *303*; **12** *406*; **28** *243*
casts **6** 7, 9; **10** 68; **27** 18, *18*, *19*; **28** *243*; **29** 812
ceiling decorations **28** 245, 246; **29** 812
ceramics **6** 335
chimney-pieces **16** *23*
conservation **6** 335, 336; **7** 729
death-masks **6** 9
écorchés **9** 706
etchings **10** 561
façade decoration **10** 740
floors **13** 556
frames **9** 16; **11** 377
friezes **20** *117*; **29** *817*
globes **12** 810
grounds **3** 914; **9** 623; **27** 51
houses **18** 277
icons **9** 623
interior decoration **16** 23–4; **32** *788*
masks **10** 68
mirror frames **24** *821*
models **4** *568*
mosaics **9** 562
moulds **6** 7, *8*, 327, *327*; **21** 321; **27** 17; **33** 2
ossuaries **31** *76*
overmantels **16** *23*
painting **9** 623
frescoes **11** 761, 762; **21** 226, 229
secco **28** 338
wall **5** 501; **9** 562; **32** 802
palaces **23** 807
papier mâché **24** 61
printing **10** 380
restoration **7** 729
sculpture
Bactria **6** 214–15
China **6** 706
Czech Republic **8** *387*
Denmark **29** *541*
Egypt, ancient **10** 68
England **11** *164*
France **12** *564*; **30** *21*
Germany **3** *243*
Greece **13** *354*
Greece, ancient **13** 438
Indonesia **15** 779
Italy **9** *403*; **12** *268*
Korea **18** 300, 301, 302
Mycenaean **14** *352*
Poland **25** *115*
Sogdiana **6** *220*
United States of America **31** 611
skulls **17** *484*
statuettes **10** *16*
temples **15** 319
vessels **30** 196
wall decorations **29** 812
waxes **33** 2
writing-tablets **20** 327
plasterboard **24** 51
Plasterwork *see* STUCCO AND PLASTERWORK
Plastic Fund **5** 74
Plastic Group (Australia) **29** 633
Plastic Group (Romania) *see* GRUPUL PLASTIC
Plasticiens, Les **1** 79; **5** 568; **22** 39; **25** 28*
Plasticine **29** 498; **33** 3
plastics **25** 23–8*
conservation **2** 366; **25** 27–8*
historical and regional traditions
Africa **1** 295
England **10** 285
Italy **16** *708*
Japan **17** 381; **31** *257*
Netherlands, the **22** 876, *876*
Uruguay **31** *757*
Venezuela **32** 171, *171*
techniques
electroplating **10** 136
uses
architecture **25** 24*; **32** 171, *171*
baskets **1** 295
chairs **6** 392; **22** 876
flower arrangements **17** 381
furniture **10** 285; **22** *876*; **31** 634
paint containers **23** 787
painting **25** 24–5*
paint tubes **23** 787
photography **7** 432; **24** 650
printing **4** 367
printing plates **10** 379
sculpture **16** *708*; **25** 25–6*
tapestries **31** *757*
toys **31** *257*, 259
vacuum cleaners **8** *804*
Plastique **9** 87; **24** 428, 442; **30** 235
Plastiras **8** *304*
figurines **8** 315, *315*
Plastov, Arkady (Arkad'yevich) **25** 28–9*; **27** 396
Plastyka **24** 441
Plasy Monastery **8** 378, 398; **27** 797
Plata, La *see* LA PLATA
Plataia **21** 556
paintings **13** 548
Sanctuary of Athena **13** 545, 550; **25** 177
plate **14** 418–19; **25** 29*
display **9** 29*
historical and regional traditions
Belgium **3** 596
Christianity **10** 325
England **10** 325
Russia **9** 30
Scotland **28** 261
see also GOLD; SILVER
Plate, Carl Olaf **30** 160
Platearius **14** 433
plate armour *see under* ARMOUR → types
plate-bande *see* ARCHES → types → flat
Plateelbakkerij Zuid Holland **22** 883
Plateelfabriek Rozenburg **3** 490
Plateina Monastery **25** 559
Platel, Pierre **10** 329, 330; **19** 593; **25** 29*
patrons and collectors **6** 116
pupils **18** 677
works **10** 329, 330; **14** 856; **20** 444
platemarks **25** 29*, 613
Platen, Wilhelm Friederich von **8** 726, 739; **25** 29–30*
Platen presses *see under* PRESSES → types
Plateresque style **14** 578; **25** 30–31*
Bolivia **4** 256
Dominican Republic **9** *116*
Spain **3** 32; **5** *362*; **8** *253*; **14** 662
Platerías portal, Master of the **26** 607; **29** 288
works **26** *606*

Plater-Zyberk, Elizabeth **2** 494; **18** 456
plates
historical and regional traditions
Byzantine **9** 655, *655*, 656, 657
Canada **5** *583*
China **6** *902*, *914*, *921*, II3; **23** *552*
Early Christian (*c*. AD 250-843) **9** 655, *655*
Egypt **16** *405*
England **10** *307*
France **11** *604*
Greece, ancient **13** 478, 536
Helladic **14** *342*
Iran **16** *394*
Iran, ancient **15** *920*; **27** *856*
Iraq **16** 398, *399*
Islamic **16** *394*, 398, *399*, *405*, *422*
Japan **17** *352*, 352–3
Ottoman **16** *422*
Portugal **25** *309*
Prehistoric art **25** 543
Sasanian **15** *920*; **27** *856*
Wales **32** *789*
Zulu **1** 417; **33** 724
materials
alabaster (gypsum) **9** 657
amber **1** 762
earthenwares **16** *399*, *405*
faience (ii) (ceramics) **11** *604*; **25** *309*
glass **5** *583*
gold **9** 656
pewter **24** 580
porcelain **6** *902*, *914*, *921*
pottery **6** II3; **10** *307*; **14** *342*; **16** *422*; **17** *352*; **23** *552*
silver **9** 655, *655*, 657; **15** *920*
silver-gilt **27** *856*
techniques
gilding **15** *920*
types
coupé **10** 313
photographic *see* PHOTOGRAPHIC PLATES
printing *see* PRINTING PLATES
Seder **24** 580
plate tracery *see under* TRACERY → types
platforms **3** 359
Cambodia **5** *473*
Central Asia, Eastern **6** 311
China **6** 640*, 689; **7** 33
Easter Island **9** 674; **23** 715
Greece, ancient **13** *385*, 386
Hawaii **23** 715
Marquesas Islands **23** 715
Maya **20** 881
Mesoamerica, Pre-Columbian **25** 764
Pacific Islands **23** 715
Rome, ancient **26** 864
Society Islands **23** 715; **28** 922
Spain **29** 297
Platina, Giovanni Maria *see* GIOVANNI MARIA PLATINA
Platina, il *see* SACCHI, BARTOLOMEO
plating *see under* METALWORK → techniques
Platinotype Company **24** 655
platinum
historical and regional traditions
Russia **10** *721*
South America, Pre-Columbian **29** 211
United States of America **31** *655*
marks *see under* MARKS
techniques
electroplating **10** 136
uses
brooches **10** *721*; **31** *655*
ceramics **6** 329
enamel **10** 192
gilding **12** 621, 627
jewellery **17** 529
platinum
uses—cont.
photography **24** 647, 655
watches **7** *449*
Platner, Ernst **22** 704
Platner, S. B. **2** 596
Plato **13** 419, 467, 468, 548; **14** 867; **19** 355; **22** 377; **25** 31–2*
works **26** 296
on art **1** 172, 175; **2** 518; **6** 174; **13** 553; **28** 915
on brass **4** 682
on decorum **8** 612
on painting **13** 552
on proportion **2** 345, 350; **13** 412; **14** 873
translated **18** 686
Platon, Nikolaos **2** 415; **17** 843
Platt, Charles A(dams) **7** 875, 876; **25** 32–3*
Platte Montagne, Matthieu de *see* PLATTENBERG, MATTIEU VAN
Platte Montagne, Nicolas de **6** 435, 436, 437; **25** 33
Plattenberg, Matthieu van **9** 745; **25** 33*
platters **12** *357*; **16** *737*; **31** 305
Platt Lynes, George *see* LYNES, GEORGE PLATT
Platts glasshouse **33** 13
Platzer (family) **8** 399
Platzer, Anna **25** 34
Platzer, Balthasar **23** 2
Platzer, Christoph **25** 34
Platzer, (Ignac) František (1717-87) **8** 427; **25** 33–4*
works **8** 386; **25** 438, 445; **30** 221
Platzer, František (1795-1813) **25** 34
Platzer, Ignac Karel **25** 34
Platzer, Ignác Michal **8** 386, 398, 416, 428; **11** 460; **25** 34*
works **8** *398*
Platzer, Jan Benedikt **25** 33
Platzer, Jan Nepomuk Josef **25** 34
Platzer, Johann Georg **2** 795; **7** 787; **25** 34*
Platzer, Josef Ignac **19** 500; **25** 34
Platzer, Robert **25** 34
Plauen **12** 469
synagogue **17** 548
Plautios, Novios *see* NOVIOS PLAUTIOS
Plavinsky, Dmitry **8** 10; **27** 397
Plaw, John **25** 34–5*
pupils **24** 86
works **10** 850; **25** 266; **32** 553
writings **8** 30; **32** 240
Plaxtol (Kent), Old Soar **29** 22
Playa del Carmen **9** 165
Playa de los Muertos **29** 139
Playa Grande style **19** 385
playbills **10** 419, *419*
Playfair, James **10** 96; **25** 35*; **28** 227
Playfair, William Henry **9** 727; **25** 35–6*
collaboration **25** 35
groups and movements **13** 610; **22** 741
staff **23** 256
teachers **29** 549
works **9** 723, 724; **13** 201; **16** 10; **23** 256, 340; **25** *36*, 267; **28** 156, 228, 230, 254, 272
playhouses *see* THEATRES
Playing Cards, Master of the **10** 382; **20** 628, 745–6*
attributions **20** 785
methods **10** 382
works **12** 385; **20** *746*; **24** 271
Playne, Edward **33** 382
Plaza, Exequiel **6** 597
Plaza, José Luis **32** 178
Plaza, Juan **12** 124
Plaza, Nicanor **6** 597
Plaza, Sebastián de la **27** 724
plazas *see* SQUARES (TOWN)
pleasure gardens *see under* GARDENS → types
Plečnik, Jože **25** 37*, 437, 438
pupils **31** 106
works **8** 401; **19** 516; **23** 490; **25** *37*; **28** 860
Plectrudis **7** 592
plein air **18** 715–16; **19** 355; **23** 382; **25** 38*; **26** 740, 741; **30** 17
Australia **2** 601
Finland **11** 95
France **3** *434*
Japan **18** 530
Pleistocene *see under* PREHISTORIC ART → periods
Pleite, Die **14** 280
Plekhanov, Dmitry **27** 387
Plekhanov, Georgy (Valentinovich) **20** 527; **25** 38*; **27** 444; **28** 926
plemochoai *see* KOTHONES
Plensa, Jaume **3** 220
Plepp, Joseph **3** 823; **12** 389
Plered **33** 537
Plersz, Jan Bogumił **25** 38–9*, 105; **32** 876
patrons and collectors **25** 212
works **32** 876, 881
Plersz, Jan Jerzy **25** 38*
patrons and collectors **33** 116
works **25** 115; **32** 876, 879
Pleshey (Essex) **31** 710
Castle **6** *52*; **9** 143
Plesner, Ulrik **3** 419; **8** 727; **28** 814; **29** 455, 456
Pless, Hans Heinric, Graf von **8** 816
Plessis, Alphonse-Louis du, Cardinal Archbishop of Lyon **21** 497
Plessis, Armand-Jean du, Cardinal Richelieu *see* RICHELIEU, ARMAND-JEAN DU PLESSIS, Cardinal
Plessis-Guénégaud, Henri De *see* GUÉNÉGAUD, HENRI DE
Plessis-lès-Tours Château **31** 843
Plessis-Robinson **24** 129
Plessy, Claude Le Fort du *see* LE FORT DU PLESSY, CLAUDE
Pletnyov, V. F. **25** 649
Plettenberg, Ferdinand von, Prince-Bishop **24** 562
Plettenberg, Friedrich Christian, Prince-Bishop of Münster **24** 740
Pleuer, Hermann **29** 875
pleurants see WEEPERS
Pleven
Il'ya Beshkov Art Gallery **3** 874
Mausoleum **28** 838
Museum **5** 163
Plewka-Schmidt, Urzula **30** 331
Plexiglass *see* PERSPEX
Pleydell-Bouverie, David **20** 475; **25** 39
Pleydell-Bouverie, Jacob, 2nd Earl of Radnor **25** 39*
Pleydell-Bouverie, Katherine **10** 315; **25** 39*
Pleydenwurff, Fritz **25** 39
Pleydenwurff, Hans **25** 39–40*
attributions **20** 683
house **33** 299
works **12** 385; **23** 308; **25** *40*
workshop **33** 299
Pleydenwurff, Kunz **25** 39
Pleydenwurff, Wilhelm **20** 693; **25** 39, 41*; **33** 349
collaboration **23** 310
works **3** *334*; **12** 385
Pleynet, Marcelin **11** 553
Plimack, Sylvia *see* MANGOLD, SYLVIA PLIMACK
Plimer, Andrew **21** 644
Plimer, Nathaniel **12** 228
Plint, T(homas) E(dward) **4** 879; **5** 266; **14** 849; **25** 41*
plinths **9** 23; **23** 478; **25** 41*
Pliny the elder **13** 421; **25** 42–6*
works **2** 298, 531; **10** 202, 203; **26** 223; **31** 289, 299
artists' biographies **5** 64; **8** 535; **25** 178, 456
illustrated **13** 833–4; **25** *46*
on architectural sculpture **7** 853
on architecture **10** 430, 431; **14** 69; **26** 782, 925
on art **2** 517
on artist's models **21** 757
on astronomy **2** 649
on brass **4** 681
on candelabra **5** 604
on collections **7** 561, 562
on coral **7** 834, 835
on cult statues **8** 263
on drawing **18** 108
on dyes **9** 492
on encaustic painting **10** 197, 198
on gems **12** 252; **26** 296
on genre painting **12** 287
on gilding **12** 624
on glass **27** 72
on gold **15** 706; **27** 15
on hardstones **15** 697, 698
on hypocausts **15** 51
on landscape **18** 700
on landscape painting **18** 701
on mausolea **20** 865
on mazes **18** 585
on niello **21** 329
on obelisks **23** 329
on obsidian **29** 702
on painters **9** 185; **13** 548, 551, 553
on painting **1** 619; **9** 13; **10** 616, 618, 623; **13** 375, 546, 547, 549, 551, 554, 555; **16** 658; **29** 665; **30** 425; **32** 351, 804
on pigments **13** 544; **28** 778
on portraits **13** 603
on pottery **13** 549, 570
on rolls **26** 557
on sculpture **10** 425, 625; **27** 18; **30** 496; **31** 301–2
on standards **11** 150
on stone **27** 14
on stucco **13** 602
on varnishes **13** 544
on writing **20** 328
translated **18** 699
Pliny the younger (*c*. 61-*c*. 112) **13** 462; **25** 47–8*
architecture **26** 885, 897
house **32** 544
works
artists' biographies **2** 229; **22** 402; **33** 636
on architecture **13** 408; **26** 924
on art **27** 31
on display of art **9** 20
on encaustic painting **10** 197
on furniture **33** 155
on gardens **12** 68, 69
on landscape **18** 701
on painters **27** 52
on painting **27** 52
on sculpture **13** 467, 468; **26** 292
on topiary **31** 150
on villas **12** 110, 111; **32** 541, 550
on water systems **11** 339
plique à jour enamel *see under* ENAMEL → techniques
Plischke, Anton **25** 48
Plischke, Ernst (Anton) **2** 789; **25** 48*; **33** 58
works **2** 789, 815; **23** 56, 67
Pliska **5** *144*, 146; **9** *511*; **25** 48–9*
Basilica **5** 146; **7** 261, 279; **25** 49; **26** 572
Museum **5** 163; **25** 49
palace **25** 48
reliquaries **9** 660
sculpture **5** 155
Plistik, Paraskeva (Avdyevna) *see* CLARK, PARASKEVA (AVDYEVNA)
Plitzner, Ferdinand **5** 347, 349; **9** 29; **12** 413, 423
works **5** *348*
Plíva, Oldřich **8** 411
Pljevlja, Holy Trinity **25** 340; **28** 458
Plò, Antonio **27** 481
Płock **25** *92*
Cathedral **25** 96
doors **9** 153; **25** 110, 129, 134, 137; **26** 684
metalwork **26** 687
tomb of Hieronimus Cielecki **25** 114
Jesuit college **25** 140
metalwork **26** 687
St Sigismund **25** 126
Ploeg, De **1** 647; **22** 852, 854, 861, 875; **33** 80, 162
Ploem, Guillaume Louis **22** 896
Pløen, Erik **23** 235
Plombières-les-Bains, Musée Louis Français **11** 501
Plombières-les-Dijon, Bishop's Palace **2** 699
Plomteux, Léopold **2** 510
Plongeon, Augustus Le **21** 263
Plönnies, Erich Philipp von **8** 530
Płoński, Michał **25** 106
Ploos van Amstel, Cornelis **1** 808; **22** 907; **25** 49–50*; **31** 365
assistants **18** 387
collections **22** 904
drawings **10** 864; **29** 487
methods **10** 562
personal collection **27** 271
pupils **28** 166; **33** 424
works **5** 322; **6** 89; **8** 131; **25** *50*, 622
Ploshko, I. K. **2** 893; **3** 87
Ploskovice **8** 400
Plotinus **7** 627; **19** 355; **22** 749, 750
Plotius Faustus Sertius, M. **30** 641
Plouarzel **25** 505
Plough Scythian **28** 320
ploughshare vaults *see under* VAULTS (CEILING) → types
Ploulec'h, Le Yaudet **32** *279*
Ploutarkhos *see* PLUTARCH
Plovdiv **5** *144*, 145; **9** *511*; **16** *103*; **25** 51*; **26** *906*, *915*; **27** 6; **30** 772
Djumaya Mosque **5** 148
Ethnographic Museum **5** 157
furniture **5** 158
houses **5** 148; **16** 499; **32** 319
Imaret Mosque **5** 148
interior decoration **5** *157*
metalwork **5** 160
mosaics **9** 565, 567; **27** 64, *64*
prints **5** 163
St Marina **5** 156
sculpture **5** 155
Trimoncium Hotel **5** 150
Tzanko Lavrenov Museum **18** 885
Ployardt, John **7** 812
Pluche, Noël-Antoine **11** 81
Plüddemann, Hermann Freihold **22** 329
Plüddemann, Richard **33** 417
Pluijm, Carel van der *see* PLUYM, KAREL VAN DER
Plukenet, Leonard **23** 467
Pluma, Master of the Centenar de la *see* CENTENAR DE LA PLUMA, MASTER OF THE
Plumb, Helga **25** 52*
plumbago *see* GRAPHITE
Plumbate ware *see under* POTTERY → wares
plumbers **20** 560
plumblines **13** 411
plum blossom painting *see under* PAINTING → types

plum blossom vases see VASES → types → *meiping*
Plume, La 2 562; 24 426, 442
Plumenthal, Anton 2 793
Plumet, Charles 6 489; 11 526, 600; 25 52*
Plumier, Charles 21 327
Plumier, Denis 10 372
Plumier, Pieter-Denis 3 570; 25 52–3*
assistants 28 63
patrons and collectors 8 698
pupils 8 698; 32 251
works 2 122; 5 43
Plumion, Lieven 12 523
Plumion, Pieter 12 523
Plumly, George 31 653
Plummer, James Marshall
works 16 859
Plummer, John 10 329
plums 30 560
Plumstead, Derek 1 29
Plunkett (family) 16 20
Plunkett, Bruce 12 855
PLUS 23 236, 241
Plüschow, Wilhelm von 12 817
Plutarch 14 869; 15 84; 25 53*
works
on architecture 3 329; 13 374
on painters 13 548
on painting 13 554
translated 18 686
Plutei Trajani see ANAGLYPHA HADRIANI
Plutyńska, Eleonora 25 53*, 133
Pluvinel, Antoine de 24 236
Pluym, Karel van der 22 843; 25 53–4*
Plymouth (Devon)
Bovisand Fort 21 576, 576
Charles Church 13 211
citadel 21 569
fortifications 21 569
Gogmagog 14 544
Notte Street Chapel 31 584
porcelain 4 824
Royal Hotel 14 786
Saltram House 9 17, 31; 10 278, 278
carpets 10 358
frames 11 430
paintings 12 913
wallpaper 32 818
Tinside Lido 19 332
Plymouth Porcelain Factory 7 791
Plyos, Levitan Museum 19 277
plywood 1 156; 10 300; 24 3; 31 262; 33 328
Plzeň 8 374; 25 54*
education (art) 8 425
furniture 8 402
glass 8 407
Museum of West Bohemia 8 424; 25 54
pewter 8 415
St Bartholomew 8 382, 383
sculpture 8 383
textiles 8 419
PM, Master 20 802*
PMP, Monogrammist 1 680; 3 815; 27 804; 30 881
PN, Master 28 851
pneumatic structures 30 469
Pniewski, Bohdan 5 8; 25 55*, 100, 142; 32 872
Pnotsch, Veit 22 205
Po, Andrea del 25 55, 57
Po, Giacomo del 22 479; 25 55–7*
works 3 225; 20 843; 25 56; 32 459
Pó, João Coelho see COELHO PÓ, JOÃO
Pò, Pietro del 3 521; 5 376, 413; 25 55
Po, Teresa del 25 55
Pobit Kamak 25 530
Poblano 25 57*
Poblet Abbey 7 350; 13 50; 21 838; 25 57–8*, 58; 29 259, 263
cloister 7 453
dormitory 21 843
manuscripts 4 764
tombs 13 106
Poblete, Gustavo 6 598
Poblete, Lucas 2 387; 24 504
Počaply, St Adalbert 8 875, 876
Poccetti, Bernardino 10 737; 25 58–9*
assistants 30 798
patrons and collectors 11 194; 21 28; 25 690
pupils 19 709
works 5 183; 6 126; 7 457; 8 418; 11 197, 213, 214, 216; 14 I1; 19 511; 20 586; 25 59
Poccianti, Pasquale 11 189; 25 59–61*
pupils 10 760
works 5 363; 11 213; 16 646; 19 512; 25 60
Poček, Petar 22 18
Pocetti, Bernardino 11 191
pochade see OIL SKETCHES
Pochampalli 15 672
Pochayevskaya Lavra, Trinity Cathedral 31 553
Poche, E. 8 426
Pochep Palace 31 564
Pochin, Henry Davis 4 216
Pochkhanwalla, Pilloo 15 172
Pöchlarn, Oskar Kokoschka Documentary Archive 18 200
Po Chü-i see BAI JUYI
Pochwalski, Kazimierz 4 616; 18 533
Pocitos 29 202
Pock, Johann Jacob 13 919; 32 442
Pock, Pery Juan 2 454
Pock, Tobias 2 794; 25 61*; 32 442
pocket knives see under KNIVES → types
Pocksberg, J. 20 800
Pocock, Nicholas 3 389; 20 424; 25 61*; 32 903
Pocock, William Innes 25 61
Pocock, W. W. 23 194
Pococke, Edward 16 553
Pococke, Richard 10 79, 82; 19 436; 25 61*
groups and movements 13 608
works 10 83
Po Dam 6 421
Podčasinskis, Karolis 19 497
Podeanu, Mimi 26 721
Poděbrady, George of, King of Bohemia see GEORGE OF PODĚBRADY, King of Bohemia
Podesta, Giovanni Andrea 11 53; 23 772; 25 62*
Podestá, Octavio 31 756
Podesti, Francesco 25 62*
collaboration 5 555
patrons and collectors 31 172
pupils 8 5; 27 852
reproductions on porcelain 3 49
Podgorica 22 17
Non-Aligned Countries' Art Gallery 3 170
Podhorce 25 62–3*
podia 25 63*; 26 874
Podkowiński, Władysław 25 63–4*; 32 876
works 25 64, 107; 32 877
Podlaha, A., Bishop 8 423
Podlashucq, Alexander 4 155
Podlewski, Włodzimierz 30 213
Podluzsky, Boris Petrovich 18 22
Podŏk Temple 18 311
Podolínec Church 28 853
Podoliya 31 563
Podolni-Volkmann, Artur 8 805; 18 386
Podol'sk 27 423
Podrecca, Boris 2 810; 28 155, 860
Podryabinnikov, Trifon 27 414
Podsadecki, Kazimierz 25 422
Podsekina, Mariya (Alekseyevna) 27 422
Poe, Edgar Allen 7 378; 8 528, 596; 11 697; 20 201
poeciloramas 7 924
Poel, Egbert van der 27 230
Poelaert, Joseph 25 64–5*
groups and movements 13 202
pupils 31 888
works 3 548, 548, 549, 613; 5 41; 18 889; 23 814
Poele, Jan van den 4 919, 920
works 4 920
Poelenbergh, Cornelis van see POELENBURCH, CORNELIS VAN
Poelenburch, Cornelis van 11 188; 25 65–8*; 26 772; 31 771
attributions 4 733
collaboration 3 352; 4 488; 17 880; 27 518; 30 730
groups and movements 9 462; 28 92
patrons and collectors 19 238; 21 25; 22 94, 904; 23 465; 27 133; 28 169
pupils 19 473
teachers 4 153
works 10 159, 161; 18 708; 22 843, 844; 25 66, 67
Poelenburch, Simon 32 140
Poelzig, Hans 3 795; 12 378, 480; 25 68–70*
collaboration 3 769; 29 531; 32 759
competitions 7 670
exhibitions 12 417
groups and movements 2 288; 8 825, 826; 10 697; 21 780, 782; 26 405
pupils 6 365; 10 105, 134; 12 58; 14 399; 15 66; 28 191, 353; 29 776; 32 750
works 4 788; 7 328; 10 417, 697; 14 142; 19 367; 25 69; 30 683
Poelzig, Peter 14 118; 18 114
Poensgen, Jochen 29 508
Poërson, Charles 25 70*
collaboration 14 83
patrons and collectors 31 56; 32 74
works 26 113
Poërson, Charles-François 4 536; 25 70–71*; 26 842
Poerzl 29 576
poesie 25 71–2*
see also PAINTING → types → literary themes
Poëte, Marcel 3 225; 11 526; 24 128
Poetical Stele 29 616
poetry 5 779; 25 72–3*
Byzantine 25 72
China 6 633, 636, 735, 820, 823; 25 72–3
Confucianism 25 73
Qing period (1644-1911) 25 73
Confucianism 25 73
Indian subcontinent 25 72
Islamic 25 72
Japan 1 581; 17 154–5, 212, 222, 287; 25 73
Korea 25 73
see also UT PICTURA POESIS
poetry, Concrete see CONCRETE POETRY
Poetzelberger, Robert 14 623
Pogačnik, Marjan 10 178
Poganovo Monastery
icons 5 152, 152, 154; 9 629; 28 449
St John the Theologian 5 147, 153; 25 343
icons 9 630
Pogany, Mlle 4 661
Pogány, Móric 2 416; 16 903; 25 73–4*
Pogany, Willy 7 838
Pogány & Tőry 25 73–4*
Pogatschnig, Giuseppe see PAGANO, GIUSEPPE
Poggetti, Francesco 20 70
Poggetti, Luigi 20 70
Poggi, Antonio Cesare 10 531
Poggi, Geminiano 10 526
Poggi, Giovanni (1880-1961) 25 74*; 30 731
Poggi, Giovanni, Cardinal (*fl* 1540s) 4 276; 30 800
Poggi, Giuseppe 25 74–5*
patrons and collectors 28 19
teachers 25 61
works 11 182; 16 646; 27 735
Poggibonsi Altarpiece 6 14; 12 712; 16 847; 20 748
Poggini, Domenico 6 147; 12 258; 25 75–6*
Poggini, Giampaolo 20 919; 25 75*
collaboration 6 147; 25 75
pupils 17 643
Poggini, Michele 25 75
Poggini, Michelino di Paolo 28 436
Poggio a Caiano, Villa Medici 11 704; 16 633; 21 30; 25 76–7*, 222; 27 734, 849; 32 545, 546, 549
frescoes 1 671; 12 719
paintings 15 87
portico 25 265
Sala da Pranzo 11 873, 874
Salone 21 17
tapestries 2 104; 29 741
Poggio Civitate 10 583, 638, 640; 16 620; 25 77*
friezes 10 633
gems 12 248
houses 10 598, 599
ivory-carvings 10 634
plaques 10 594
temple 10 600
Poggio della Porcareccia 25 245
Poggio del Molino see POPULONIA
Poggio Imperiale 3 359; 21 566
villa 16 646; 27 178
Poggio Montano 10 609, 610
Poggio Sommavilla Painter 10 615
Poghos 2 436; 8 198
Pögl, Ignaz 18 162
Pogliaghi, L. 9 159
Pogliaghi, Lodovico 21 533
Pogliani, Ferdinando 16 730
Pognon, Joseph 11 157
Pogolotti, Marcelo 8 233
Pohan Chae 18 259
Pohjanmaan Museo see under VAASA
Pohjola Insurance Company 14 371
Pohl, Franz (1764-1834) 4 41
Pohl, Franz (1813-84) 14 192
Pohl, Johann 14 192; 23 271
Pohle, Leon 7 346
Pohlwitz Castle 10 741
Pohnpei 21 476, 477, 477; 23 711, 723
cultural centre 23 737
Pohoří 23 264
Pohorje 28 862
Pohorylles, Gerda 5 659
Pohr see PARRI
Pohsarang
church 15 770
Institute of Technology building 15 770
Poiana, Bonifacio 23 865
Poiana Maggiore
Villa Poiana 23 865; 32 549
Poiares, Trás-os-Montes 25 315; 26 690
Pöide 10 536
church 10 536
Poidevin, Eugène (-Modeste-Edmond) see LEPOITTEVIN, EUGÈNE (-MODESTE-EDMOND)
Poieessa see PISSES
Poienari 26 706
Poignant, Etienne-Léon 3 319; 8 542; 33 44
poignards see under DAGGERS → types
Poillerat, Gilbert 11 628
Poilly, Charles de 25 77
Poilly, François de 18 46; 24 712; 25 77*
collaboration 9 718
pupils 14 53; 29 399
works 8 24; 32 95
Poilly, Jean-Baptiste de (1669-1728) 2 853; 21 498; 25 77–8; 33 44
Poilly, Nicolas de 1 787; 19 65; 20 456; 25 77*, 626; 32 242
Poincaré, Jules Henri 8 244
Poinçon, Robert 2 50; 3 362; 4 525; 30 312
works 2 50
Poinsett, Joel Roberts 21 264
Poinsot, Jean-Marc 7 895
Point, Armand 25 78*; 27 639
Point, Le 9 71
Point, Susan 22 589
Point Breeze 4 304
point d'Angleterre see LACE → types → Brussels
point de Dresde see EMBROIDERY → types → *point de Saxe*
point de France see under LACE → types
point de gaze see under LACE → types
point de Lierre see LACE → types → Limerick
point de neige see under LACE → types
point de Paris see under LACE → types
point de Saxe see under EMBROIDERY → types
point d'esprit see under LACE → types
Pointe, Arnoult de la see ARNOULT DE NIMÈGUE
Pointe Caraibe 2 152
pointed arches see under ARCHES → types
pointed bowtell mouldings see under MOULDINGS → types
pointed mouldings see under MOULDINGS → types
Pointel 11 661; 25 392, 395
Pointe-Noire 1 394
Musée Régional 'Ma-Loango' Diosso 7 709
Pointillism 7 638; 19 355; 22 745; 24 375, 880–81; 25 78*; 28 500, 501
landscape 18 716
see also DIVISIONISM; NEO-IMPRESSIONISM
pointing (i) (sculpture) 10 265; 13 438–9; 25 78*; 29 706–7*
pointing (ii) (architecture) 4 787; 25 78*
point net see under LACE → types
Point Pedro 16 864
point sizes 31 495
Poiré, Emmanuel see CARAN D'ACHE
Poiré, Pierre 5 837–8
Poirel, Nicolas 11 605; 27 248
Poiret, Paul 9 291, 373; 11 601; 25 78–9*; 32 817
collaboration 9 245, 374, 391
groups and movements 2 520, 521
works 3 462; 4 588; 9 291; 10 824; 11 582; 29 899
Poirier, Anne 11 571; 24 145; 25 79*

Poirier, Patrick 11 571; 24 145; 25 79
Poirier, Simon-Philippe 2 559; 8 448; 20 388
  furniture 3 414; 5 767; 7 658; 9 313; 11 591, 593
Poirson, Mme Paul 9 *289*
Poissant, Antoine 25 79
Poissant, Thibault 11 356, 559; 25 79–80*; 26 91
Poisson, Pierre 2 861; 11 568
Poisson, Robert 19 382
Poisson d'Etiolles, Jeanne-Antoinette, Marquise de Pompadour *see* POMPADOUR, JEANNE-ANTOINETTE, Marquise de
Poisson de Vandières, Abel-François, Marquis de Marigny *see* MARIGNY, Marquis de
Poissonnier, Arnould 31 219
Poissy 4 63
  Abbey 10 180; 13 59, 176; 24 115
    Church 31 834
  Notre-Dame 4 691; 13 76
  St Louis 13 42, 76
  Villa Savoye 11 526, 659; 12 792; 15 885; 19 42; 21 783; 24 752; 25 741; 32 556, *556*
    lighting 19 367
Poitevin, Alphonse Louis 7 575; 19 481; 24 649, 650, 651; 25 82*, 617, 618
Poitiers 9 *510*; 11 *505*; 25 82–9*, *83*, *84*; 26 *908*
  amphitheatre 29 521
  Centre d'Etudes Supérieures de Civilisation Médiévale 11 674
  Château 11 573; 21 549
  Ducal Palace 11 555; 13 59
    Tour Maubergeon 13 59
  ecclesiastical buildings
    Baptistery of St Jean 3 191; 21 163; 25 85–6*, *86*
    Cathedral of St Pierre 11 510; 13 37; 25 84*; 32 93
      metalwork 11 618
      sculpture 13 75; 25 84–5*
      stained glass 13 180, 181; 25 85*; 26 702; 29 510, 511
    Cloister of Notre-Dame 26 670
    Notre-Dame-la-Grande 1 110; 11 510, 554; 14 80; 25 86–7*, *87*; 26 585, 600
      sculpture 26 596
      spires 29 412
    Sainte-Croix 9 569
    Ste Radegonde 13 179; 26 600
    St Hilaire-le-Grand 25 87–8*; 26 600; 32 94
      capitals 25 *88*
      sculpture 26 603
      wall paintings 26 649, 655
    St Jean-de-Montierneuf 26 600
    St Nicolas 26 600
    St Porchaire 26 600
  Hôtel de Ville 25 750
  Hypogée des Dunes 21 163, 164; 25 88–9*
  Musée du Baptistère-Saint-Jean 25 86
  Musée Sainte-Croix 8 281
  Palais de Justice 14 74, *74*; 19 895
    sculpture 13 *76*, 76
    stained glass 13 179
Poitiers, Diane de, Duchesse de Valentinois *see* DIANE DE POITIERS, Duchesse de Valentinois
Poitiers, Peter of *see* PETER OF POITIERS
Poitiers 30, Master of MS. *see* ADELAIDE OF SAVOY, MASTER OF
Poitou, Joseph 11 596; 23 514
Poitou, Philippe 11 589; 12 832; 23 514
Poitras, Jane Ash 22 598
Poivrel et Fils 24 472
Poja, Francesco Alberti, Prince-Bishop of Trent 5 180
Pojan
  Archaeological Museum 1 546
  St Mary 1 538, 539
pokers 11 119
pokerwork 25 89*
Po Klaung Garai 6 424, 430, 431
Pokorný, Karel 8 387, 388
Pokorný, Zdeněk 8 251
Pokot 1 237, 254, 297, 409, 411
  headrests 1 *411*
Pokrovsky, Igor' (Aleksandrovich) 25 89*; 27 380
Pokrovsky, Vladimir (Aleksandrovich) 25 89*
  collaboration 18 99
  groups and movements 28 837
  works 19 111; 27 377; 33 601
Pokryshin, P. P. 10 889
Pol, Christiaen van 29 668
Pol, O. 31 565
Pol, Santiago 25 90*
Pola *see under* PULA
Polacca, Fannie 22 452, 609
Polacco, Leopoldo *see* POLLACK, LEOPOLDO
Polacco, Martino Teofilo *see* TEOFILOWICZ, MARCIN
Polacco, Taddeo *see* KUNTZE, TADEUSZ
Polače 9 557
  Palace 9 *558*
Połack 3 525, *525*; 25 90*
  architecture 3 526; 4 781
  Belčycki Monastery 3 527
  Cathedral of St Sophia 3 526; 27 368
  churches 27 368
  Church of the Archangel Michael 27 369
  Jesuit college 3 527
  Monastery of St Euphrosyne 31 547
    Church of the Transfiguration of the Saviour 3 527; 27 369
  monument to Francysk Staryna 3 531
  painting 27 381
Polack, Jan 22 301; 25 90–91*
  assistants 20 130
  works 12 385; 25 *91*
Pola de Lena, S Cristina de Lena 2 653; 29 261
Pola de Siero, S Martin de la Vega de Poja
  crosses 13 *165*
Polägk, Hanns *see* POLACK, JAN
Połajewo Church 25 103
Polak, Martin Teofil *see* TEOFILOWICZ, MARCIN
Polanco, Francisco 25 91*
Polanco, Miguel 25 91
Poland 25 91–143*, *92*
  alabaster (gypsum) 25 114
  altarpieces 25 110; 29 *727*
  altars 25 114
  amber 1 762
  architectural decorations 4 782
  architecture 4 783; 25 94–100*
    brick 4 783; 24 347, 698
    Cistercian Order 25 95
    Dominican Order 25 95
    Gothic 12 823; 13 56, 57; 24 347; 31 394
    Romanesque 25 94; 26 594
    vernacular 32 296
    15th cent. 23 399
  archives 2 371*
  arks 17 570
  armour 25 128, 130, *130*
  arsenals 23 *328*
  art history 25 364
  artists' biographies 25 143
  art schools 25 123
  astronomical instruments 25 139
  balustrades 25 *131*
  barrows 25 *506*, 507
Poland—cont.
  beadwork 3 442
  bells 16 867
  body ornaments 25 127
  book covers 4 352
  bowls 25 *127*
  brick 4 782, *782*, 783; 24 347, *347*, 698
  bricklaying 4 783
  bridges 24 698
  bronze 25 *131*
  cameos 25 128
  carpets 25 131, *132*
  castles 18 *431*; 20 *185*, 185–6; 25 96
  casts 25 140
  cathedrals 12 *823*; 18 430, *431*, 431
  ceramics 25 122–4*, *123*
  chairs 25 120
  chalices 13 170; 25 125
  chapels 18 *433*; 25 135
  churches 25 94–5, 96, 98, 128
    Baroque 32 895
    basilicas 25 95
    decoration 8 *590*
    Gothic 5 *28*; 6 *531*; 8 *590*
    hall 25 96, 134
    Romanesque 29 *793*
    14th cent. 4 *782*
    16th cent. 25 *96*
  clocks 25 129
  coats of arms 14 411
  coffering 25 *117*
  coffins 25 129
  coins 7 538, 539; 25 127
  collections 25 94, 136, 137–8*, 139–40*
    photographs 25 142*
  columns 29 *793*
  concrete 3 *768*
  coral 3 442
  cupboards 25 120
  damask 19 *416*
  dealing 25 137–8*
  dolls 31 259
  donjons 21 571
  drawings 23 *203*
  dress 25 132–3; 27 843
  education (art) 18 428; 25 140–42*
    architecture 25 140, 142
    design 25 140
  embroidery 25 132
  enamel 13 170; 25 *127*, 128; 26 687
  engravings 12 *223*; 25 140
  exhibitions 25 139, 141
  façade decoration 10 741
  factories 19 *536*
  faience (ii) (ceramics) 25 122, *123*
  finials (scrolls) 17 569
  flags 11 150
  fortifications 21 551
  furniture 25 119–22*
  gables 11 876
  gardens 2 414; 12 133–4*
  gates 7 *359*
  gilding 25 *120*
  glass 25 124–5*, *125*
  glasses 25 124
  goblets 25 *125*
  gold 25 125–8*, *127*, *133*, 137
  gravestones 25 115
  guilds 25 101, 119, 124, 128
  halls 3 *768*; 19 *748*
  Hannukah lamps 17 *573*
  harnesses 14 183; 25 128
  heraldry 14 405, 411*
  heritage 32 678
  hermas 25 126
  historiography 25 142–3*
  houses 25 *97*, *98*; 32 297, *297*, 298, *299*
    country 25 99
  humpen 25 124
  icons 25 341*
  insignia 14 *410*
Poland—cont.
  interior decoration 25 117–19*, *117*, *118*, 128, 131; 32 *874*, *880*, *882*
  jewellery 25 127
  kah lamps 17 573
  kaptorgas 25 125
  kilims 25 132
  Kunstkammern 25 137
  leather 4 352
  libraries 25 142*
  lime-wood 29 *727*
  lithography 25 106
  liturgical furnishings 7 *280*
  mantles 17 *570*
  manuals (architecture) 25 142
  manuscript illumination 25 137
  marble 4 *147*; 25 114, 118
  marquetry 25 *121*
  mausolea 25 135
  medals 25 127
  metalwork 25 125–8*, *127*, *128*, 129–30*
    Gothic 13 162*
    Romanesque 26 687
    17th cent. 25 *130*
  miniatures (manuscript illumination) 25 101
  monasteries 29 *792*; 32 *749*
  monstrances 13 162
  monuments 25 134, 135; 32 7
  mouldings 22 211
  museums 8 372; 25 139–40*
  napkins 19 *416*
  nephrite 16 861
  new towns 25 100, 135, 136; 31 718
  painting 9 74; 25 101–3*, 104–8*
    allegorical 4 *148*; 20 *188*; 27 *451*
    Constructivism 29 *794*
    genre 25 *64*
    Gothic 25 101, *102*
    history 20 *810*
    landscape 25 107; 29 *538*; 32 *877*
    literary themes 21 *426*
    military scenes 25 *107*
    portraits 27 843
    religious
      14th cent. 8 *430*
      16th cent. 25 *103*
      17th cent. 25 *104*
    Symbolism (movement) 21 *52*; 24 *12*
    townscapes 3 *679*
    wall 25 344*
  palaces 25 97, 98, 135
    Baroque 12 *35*; 32 *870*
    entre cour et jardin 25 99
    Neo-classicism 32 *881*
    18th cent. 32 *875*
    20th cent. 19 *536*
  panoramas 33 417
  paper 31 259
  patronage 25 93, 94, 134–7*; 27 842
  pattern books 25 137
  periodicals 24 441–2*
  photomontages 30 204
  piers (ii) (masonry) 33 *259*
  plaster 25 *115*; 29 839
  porcelain 25 123
  portals 25 95; 26 *636*
  portraits 4 *617*; 25 103, 104, 105; 31 323; 33 *456*
  posters 25 108, 354, 355
  pottery 25 122, 123
  prints 25 106
  public 2 409
  pulpits 25 115
  railings 25 130
  reconstruction 25 100
  reliquaries 25 *128*
  rugs 25 131
  sanctuaries 12 823
  sandstone 25 *109*
  sashes 25 132–3, *133*
Poland—cont.
  sculpture 25 109–16*
    architectural 25 95
    Constructivism 7 *771*
    Gothic 25 110–11, *111*
    relief 29 *793*; 31 *394*
    Rococo 25 *114*
    Romanesque 25 109–10; 26 636–7*
    stone 26 *636*, 636–7*
    tomb 32 *873*
    20th cent. 25 *115*
  seals 14 *410*
  shields 14 411
  sideboards 25 120, *121*
  silk 25 131, *133*
  silver 25 125–8*
  spice-boxes 17 572
  stained glass 13 189, *189*
  stone 26 *636*, 636–7*; 31 *394*
  stucco 29 839
  swords 25 128
  synagogues 17 543, 544–6, 548; 25 98
  szkofia 25 128
  tapestries 12 11; 25 131, 134; 30 *330*
  tas 17 569
  tefillin 17 574
  textiles 25 131–4*
  theatres 32 *871*
  theories
    painting 31 492
  threads 25 *133*
  thrones 25 *120*
  tiles 25 122
  tombs 4 *147*; 13 *774*; 22 *167*; 25 113–14; 32 *873*
  topographical views 18 *424*
  town halls 18 *424*, *425*; 25 *409*; 27 *722*; 30 *203*; 31 *196*; 33 *417*
  trappings 14 183
  treatises 29 777
    architecture 20 396, 397; 25 142
    gardens 22 202
    painting 4 837
  turbans 25 132
  tympana 25 *109*
  universities 24 699
  urban planning 22 78; 25 134; 33 605, 606
  vases 25 *123*
  vaults (ceiling)
    Gothic 13 57
    rib: jumping 13 57
    rib: star 13 57; 24 *347*, 348; 33 *259*
  vestments (ecclesiastical) 16 430
  villas 25 *100*
  wall 25 101
  weaving 25 131; 30 552
  wood 25 *96*
  woodcuts 25 106
  wool 25 131, *132*
  yew 25 *121*
Polaroid *see under* PHOTOGRAPHY → processes
Polaroid Corporation 30 391
Polášek, Josef 4 833; 25 143*
Polastron, André 31 227
Polcenigo 5 55
Polcovnicul, Nicolae 26 713
Poldi Pezzoli, Gian Giacomo 3 857; 21 825; 25 143–4*
  collections 16 769; 21 527
  decorative works 9 403
Poldi Pezzoli, Rosa Trivulzio, Marchesa 3 296, 297
Pole, Cardinal 19 547
Pole, Anne de la 27 *118*
Pole, Edward Sacheverell 22 152
Pole, Elizabeth de la, Duchess of Suffolk 10 288
Poleck, Hanns *see* POLACK, JAN
Polejowski, Maciej 19 836; 25 115, 121; 26 498
Polelonema, Otis 14 477; 22 595
Polemon 13 554, 807

Poleni, Giovanni, Marchese 25 144*
  architecture 20 579–80, _580_; 31 894
  engravings 32 615
Polenov, Dmitry (Vasil'yevich) 25 145*
Polenov, Vasily (Dmitriyevich) 25 145*; 27 391
  collaboration 27 410
  groups and movements 1 71; 20 232
  pupils 2 417; 12 877; 18 389; 19 276; 20 222; 28 596; 33 487
  works 22 178; 27 580
Polenova, Yelena (Dmitriyevna) 25 145–6*; 27 408
  collaboration 12 878; 27 410
  groups and movements 1 71; 20 232
  pupils 33 487
  workshop 27 442
Polenovo, V. D. Polenov Estate-Museum 25 145
Poleo, Héctor 25 146*; 32 175
poles 1 306, 307, 410; 22 _564_
Polesello, Rogelio 2 401; 25 146*
Polesello, Ugo 16 651
Polesini 25 491
Poleskie, Steven 20 609; 28 829
Poletti, Luigi 25 147*
  personal collection 16 776
  pupils 32 385
  teachers 29 640
  works 3 644; 26 761
Polevsko 10 773
poleyns 2 469
Pol Fruit 19 341
Polgár culture 25 513, 516, 517
Polgárdi 27 100
Polhamer, Wolfgang 15 865
Polhem, Christopher 8 189; 30 109
Polhograjski, Marko Anton 28 863
Poli, Alessandro 30 3
Poliakoff, Serge 25 147–8*
  dealers 26 193
  groups and movements 2 543, 544; 30 231
  patrons and collectors 8 10
  tapestries 12 830
  works 11 420, 551; 19 491; 25 _148_
Policansky, Max 5 668; 29 106
police stations 31 235
policies _see_ ART POLICIES
Policoro _see_ HERAKLEIA (ITALY)
Policoro Painter 13 525
Policratique of Charles V, Master of the
  works 5 _207_
Polido, Diego 28 519
Polido, Juan 28 519
Polidor(o), Jan _see_ GLAUBER, JOHANNES
Polidori, Gaetano 27 185
Polidoro da Caravaggio 25 148–9*
  collaboration 20 213; 25 909; 26 818; 27 275; 31 523
  methods 6 570; 24 493
  patrons and collectors 19 124; 26 280; 28 754
  reproductive prints by others 1 551; 3 294; 11 51; 12 4, 558; 25 570; 32 236, 407, 689
  works 9 221; 10 737; 18 707; 23 380; 24 404; 25 _149_; 27 771; 28 656; 31 448
Polidoro da Lanciano 25 149*
Polier, Antoine Louis Henri 1 583; 15 654, 741; 16 553
Polieri, Jacques 30 684
Poligino, Benedetto 21 725
Polignac, St Martin 19 223
Polignac, Melchior de, Cardinal 25 150*
  collections 12 473
  gems 8 14
Polignac, Melchior de, Cardinal—cont.
  paintings 19 646; 24 10; 26 452; 31 481; 32 113
  pupils 22 682
  sculpture 1 132, 133; 4 509; 14 652
Polignac, Winnaretta, Princesse Edmond de 25 150*
Poligny
  Church of the Poor Clares 13 78
  St Hippolyte 13 78
Poliochni 31 354, 355
  architecture 1 824
  bronze 4 850
  jewellery 1 825; 31 354
  megaron 21 46
  metalwork 1 824
Polion 13 524; 32 63–4*
Polirone, Monastery of St Benedict 26 666
Polis Basilica (Cyprus) 8 357
Polis (Ithaka) 16 782
Polis, Miervaldis 25 151*
Polis, Viktoras 16 874
Polish Applied Arts Society 8 371
Polish Art Studies 24 441; 25 143
Polish bond _see under_ BONDING
Polishchyk, L. 30 352
Polish cochineal 9 492
Polish Colourism 17 804
Polish Coronation Sword 25 126
polishes 33 1
Polish Expressionists 11 317
polishing
  historical and regional traditions
    Egypt, ancient 9 815, 818
    France 11 595
    Japan 17 276
    Vietnam 32 482
  materials
    acids 10 320
    ashes 1 761
    bamboo 16 859; 21 241
    chalk 1 761
    haematite 21 241
    silica 21 241
    waxes 24 258; 29 706
  uses
    amber 1 761
    furniture 11 595; 24 258
    gems 17 522
    glass 10 320
    hardstones 21 241
    jade 16 859
    lacquer 32 482
    metalwork 9 818
    prints 17 276
    sculpture 9 815
    stone 29 706*
polishing, French _see_ FRENCH POLISHING
Polisy, Jean de Dinteville, Seigneur de 3 209; 8 907*; 14 _669_
Politiko, Hagios Herakleidios 8 357, 358, 359
Politis, Gustavo 29 203
Polivanov Yar 25 503
Polívka, Jaroslav 14 247
Polívka, Osvald 8 379; 25 151*, 429; 33 162
Poliziano, Angelo 1 656; 13 541; 14 868, 870; 16 658; 25 151–2*
  collaboration 4 503
  groups and movements 22 412
  personal collection 32 639
Poljanski, Virgil 8 437
Polk, Brigid 10 482
Polk, Charles Peale 17 619; 25 152*
Polk, Willis J(efferson) 25 152*; 27 730; 28 604
Polke, Sigmar 25 153–4*
  works 12 397; 19 493; 22 381; 25 _153_
Polláck, Ágoston 25 154, 156; 33 514
Pollack, Giuseppe 25 154, 155
Pollack, Hanns _see_ POLACK, JAN
Pollack, Joseph 25 154
Pollack, Leopoldo 16 646; 25 154–5*
  collaboration 16 646
  works 16 719; 25 _155_
Pollack, Mihály 14 889; 25 154, 155–6*
  pupils 11 34; 33 514
  works 5 82; 14 889; 15 14, 16; 24 314; 28 850; 29 606; 30 207
Pollaiuolo, Antonio (di Jacopo d'Antonio Benci) del 11 184; 16 661, 691; 25 71, 156–63*
  assistants 3 298
  attributions 6 14; 9 103
  collaboration 2 632; 11 211
  competitions 32 362, 364
  drawings 10 441; 25 163, 557
  embroidery 10 182; 16 759, _759_; 32 343
  frames 11 382
  groups and movements 26 186
  metalwork 8 201; 11 86
  methods 21 766, 768; 28 205
  niello 16 750
  paintings 16 659, 660, 751; 18 704; 21 758; 23 292; 25 _157_, 160–61
    frescoes 13 541; 16 691; 32 549
  patrons and collectors 3 228; 9 683; 12 897, 907; 16 689; 21 14; 25 690; 27 272; 29 436
  prints 23 115; 25 605
    engravings 1 840; 10 383, _383_; 25 _160_; 26 228
  pupils 27 776
  sculpture 16 691; 25 _158_; 26 809; 27 _9_; 29 568
  textiles 13 195; 20 848
  workshop 11 185
Pollaiuolo, Piero (di Jacopo d'Antonio Benci) del 11 184; 16 661; 25 156, 160–63*
  assistants 3 298
  attributions 25 157
  collaboration 4 494; 11 211; 25 158
  competitions 32 362, 364
  patrons and collectors 12 907; 25 144, 690; 27 272; 29 46
  works 1 655; 4 493; 16 659, 660; 25 157, _161_, _162_; 27 183, 751; 29 361
  workshop 11 185
Pollaiuolo, Simone di Tomaso del _see_ CRONACA
Pöllandt, Johann 11 42
Pollard, James 2 106; 25 164*
Pollard, John 25 888
Pollard, Robert 25 164*, 619
Pollard Rowe, Ann 29 178
Pollarollo, Almeida 24 98
Pollarollo, Vicente 13 801; 24 98
Pollastra 32 22
Pollastri, Giovanni 11 194
Pollastrini, Enrico 25 164–5*; 33 515
Pöllau Church 2 783
Polleck, Hanns _see_ POLACK, JAN
Pollen, John Hungerford 23 600; 25 165*, 555
  groups and movements 5 340
  patrons and collectors 23 30
Pollias 13 518
Pollice 25 165*
Polling, Jörg von _see_ JÖRG VON HALSBACH
Pölling Church (Austria) 2 793
Polling Church (Germany) 12 369
Polling Panels, Master of the 12 385; 20 746–7*
Pollini, Gino 1 578; 10 822; 11 62–4*; 13 728; 15 885; 21 422; 26 15
Pollio, G(aius) Asinius
  library 9 20; 19 312; 27 30
  sculpture 2 416; 25 458; 26 857; 27 27, 31; 29 633
Pollio, Vedius 22 475; 27 30
Pollock, Griselda 2 538; 33 312, 313, 314
Pollock, (Paul) Jackson 10 397; 18 441; 25 165–8*, _167_, 584; 28 785; 29 877; 31 607, 665
  collaboration 20 605
  dealers 16 906; 24 213
  groups and movements 1 78, 83, 84, 85–6, 88; 2 544; 21 646; 23 48; 25 645; 29 534; 30 22, 711; 31 607
  methods 8 128
  patrons and collectors 9 189; 13 801; 21 135; 23 371; 24 213; 25 400; 26 489; 28 167; 33 45, 254
  studio 29 858
  teachers 3 748
  works 1 _86_, 129, 131, 673; 2 839; 4 75; 9 213, 310; 18 718; 25 24, _166_; 28 300; 31 142
Pollock, John 28 255
Pollock, Matthew 28 255
Pollock-Krasner Foundation 31 663
Pollockshaws Pottery 28 257
Pollok Park _see_ GLASGOW → Pollok House
Pollokshields (Strathclyde), The Knowles 28 229
Polloni factory 11 190
Polo, Agnolo di _see_ AGNOLO DI POLO
Polo, Diego (_fl_ 1617; uncle) 25 168
Polo, Diego (_c._ 1610-50/5; nephew) 25 168*; 26 436
Polo, Domenico di _see_ DOMENICO DI POLO
Polo, L. S. 31 823
Polo, Marco 6 331; 7 53, 836; 15 755; 16 443, 469
  writings 4 682; 6 320; 7 165; 10 873; 13 807; 14 137; 20 363; 30 476; 31 289
    on carpets 2 437
    on jade 7 9; 16 859, 860
    on lapis lazuli 24 790
    on mats 15 674, 681
    on observatories 23 339
    on seals 21 882
    on tents 21 885
Polo Caballero, Martín 7 604
Polo di Agnolo 1 454
Pologni, Charles 30 391
Pologova, Adelaida (Germanovna) 27 397, 411
polo grounds 16 153
Polonaise carpets _see under_ CARPETS → types
Polonceau, Antoine-Rémi 25 168*
Polonceau, Camille 25 168
Polonkoyev, Murat 27 433
Polonnaruva 25 168–70*; 29 _440_, 441
  Alahana Parivena 25 169; 29 449, 450
  architecture 29 441, 449–50
  Gal Vihara 5 98; 25 169, _170_; 29 464, _465_
    sculpture 29 442, 459
  Lankatilaka 29 449, _449_, 450
  metalwork 29 474
  monks' hospital 25 169
  moonstones 29 _443_
  royal palace 29 450
  sculpture 29 459
  shrines (i) (cult) 29 448, 450
  Thuparama 25 169
  Tivanka 25 170; 29 464–5, 476
  Uttararama _see_ Gal Vihara
Polonnoye 31 561
Polonský, Marián 28 856
Polonus, Martinus _see_ MARTINUS POLONUS
Polonus, Martinus Theophilus _see_ TEOFILOWICZ, MARCIN
Polos Painter 13 507
Polotsk _see_ POŁACK
Polotsky, Simeon 31 762
Polovtsev, A. 21 177
Polshek, James Stewart 17 549
Poltava 31 _546_
  architecture 31 551
  carpets 31 564
  ceramics 31 563
  embroidery 31 564
  Nezhinsky Lyceum 31 551
  sculpture 31 561
Polto da Bettona, Crispolto di _see_ CRISPOLTO DI POLTO DA BETTONA
Poltorack _see_ ASHKHABAD
Półtorak, Jan 25 126
Półtorak Andrzej 32 878
Poltoratsky, Yevgeny 27 381
Poltrone, Zanotta 6 392
Poltronova 2 373; 29 90
Polunin, Vladimir 30 681
Polvoir, Hames 31 842
Polvorín 29 365
Polwarth, Amabel, Lady _see_ GREY, AMABEL DE, Marchioness
Poly, Adrien 4 537
Polyaenus 10 630
Polyakov, I. 27 427
Polyakov, Leonid (Mikhaylovich) 3 685; 25 170–71*; 27 380
Polyakova, V. K. 21 812
polyalkenes _see under_ FIBRES → types
polyamides _see under_ FIBRES → types
Polyanitsa 21 551; 25 501, 503
Polyansky, Anatoly 23 426
polyautography _see_ LITHOGRAPHY
Polybius 6 68; 13 555; 21 558
Polychrome Bowls, Painter of 10 614
Polychrome group 10 614
Polychrome ware _see under_ POTTERY → wares
polychromy 7 502; 25 171–6*
  historical and regional traditions
    Afghanistan 1 198
    Africa 25 172
    Australia 4 788
    Britain 11 499
    Buddhism 1 198; 5 _100_; 6 _713_
    Catalonia 25 II2
    Central Asia, Western 6 206, _219_, 221
    China 6 _713_; 25 171, 175
    Crete 8 154
    Early Christian (_c._ AD 250-843) 25 171
    Egypt, ancient 9 _870_; 13 405; 25 171
    England 8 48; 10 238; 13 _121_; 25 I2, IV, V2; 30 _533_
    France 11 589; 13 _109_, _126_; 29 574
    Germany 10 _457_; 32 _253_
    Gothic 10 _457_; 13 _109_, _115_, _119_, _121_, _122_, _124_, _126_, 132; 25 172
    Greece, ancient 4 851; 13 377, 392–4*, 398, 405, 498; 21 341; 25 171, 799, I1; 26 134–5; 29 VIII1
    Indian subcontinent 15 354
    Islamic 7 634; 15 354; 25 171
    Italy 13 _124_; 25 III, V1; 26 _877_; 30 _498_
    Japan 17 99, 100; 25 175
    Khwarazm 6 _219_
    Mexico 25 II1
    Native North Americans 22 665
    Netherlands, the 13 _115_
    Norway 13 _119_
    Olmec 23 418
    Ottoman 23 643
    Portugal 25 171
    Romanesque 26 _647_
    Rome, ancient 26 _877_, 878; 27 16, 52
    Scandinavia 4 781
    Scotland 4 788

polychromy
historical and regional traditions—cont.
Spain **10** *903*; **13** *122*; **25** 171, 174
Tokharistan **6** 221
United States of America **4** 788
Vietnam **5** *100*
materials
beads **13** 393
gilding **13** 393
inlays **13** 393
metal **13** 393
paste **13** 393
stone **13** 393
tiles **25** 171
uses
altarpieces **13** *109*
architecture **4** 769, 781, 787–8; **13** 613; **25** 171–4*
Catalonia **25** II2
England **8** 48; **10** 238; **25** I2
Greece, ancient **25** I1
Mexico **25** II1
Rome, ancient **26** *877*, 878
bronze **4** 850, 851
cabinets (ii) (furniture) **11** 589
crucifixes **13** *122*, *124*; **26** *647*
ivory **16** 797
metal **5** 332
metalwork **21** 327–8*
pottery **23** 643
relief sculpture **25** III
sculpture **7** 740; **25** 174–6*; **29** 707; **30** 496
Afghanistan **1** 198
China **6** *713*
Egypt, ancient **9** *870*
England **13** *121*; **25** IV, V2
France **13** *126*; **20** 119
Germany **10** *457*; **32** *253*
Greece, ancient **26** 134–5; **29** VIII1
Italy **25** V1
Japan **17** 99, 100
Khwarazm **6** *219*
Netherlands, the **13** *115*
Norway **13** *119*
Rome, ancient **27** 16
Spain **10** *903*; **30** *498*
Switzerland **22** *919*
Tokharistan **6** 221
Vietnam **5** *100*
statuettes **29** 574
tiles **23** 643
see also COLOUR
Polydoros **14** 33–4*; **29** 389
attributions **13** 468
collaboration **18** 756; **25** 45
works **13** 464; **26** 292; **27** *8*
polyester *see under* FIBRES → types
polyethylene **25** 23, 28*
polyethylene glycol *see* PEG
Polyeuktos of Athens
works **13** *462*
polyeurathanes **6** 336; **7** 747; **11** 54
Polyglot Bibles *see under* BIBLES → types
Polyglott-Verlag **13** 811
Polygnotos (*fl c.* 450-425 BC) **13** 522; **25** 44; **32** 59, 64*
assistants **13** 485
methods **10** 197
pupils **32** 48
works **13** 522
Polygnotos of Thasos (*fl c.* 475-50 BC) **13** 522, 548; **25** 176–7*; **32** 60
attributions **23** 901
restorations by others **24** 283
works **8** 693; **13** 545, 550, 553
polygonal arches *see under* ARCHES → types
polygonal masonry *see* MASONRY → types → Cyclopean
polygonal termination mouldings *see under* MOULDINGS → types
polykandela **9** 656, *656*
Polykleitos (*fl c.* 450-420 BC) **2** 523; **13** 394, 395, 422, 450, 453, 454, 553, 596; **14** 870; **23** 291; **25** 177–80*; **28** 712
attributions **10** 434; **22** 690; **31** 244
competitions **10** 425, 675; **15** 894
copies **14** 443; **22** 733; **27** 39, 46
methods **21** 757
patrons and collectors **13** 605
pupils **17** 757; **22** 690
teachers **1** 450
works **2** 407; **7** 783; **13** 439, 573; **15** 101; **25** *178*, *179*
workshop **13** 459
writings **13** 412, 467; **26** 924; **28** 201; **31** 301
Polykleitos II of Argos (*fl c.* 423 BC) **2** 160; **10** 434; **22** 690; **25** 179
Polykleitos the younger (*fl c.* 380-340 BC) **30** 737
Polykles **8** 909; **25** 180–81*; **27** 27, 29; **30** 893, 915
attributions **13** 466
collaboration **8** 909
works **13** 464; **24** 227
Polykrates **25** 45; **26** 296; **27** 687
Polymedes **8** 695; **13** 445
polymer colour paints *see under* PAINTS → types
polymers **7** 747, 748; **11** 142
Polynesian outliers **25** 181–3*
barkcloth **25** 182
body ornaments **25** 182
human figures **25** 182
sculpture **25** 181–2, *182*
tattoos **25** 182
weaving **25** 182
Polyphemos Painter **32** 64*
works **13** 501, *501*
polypropylene glycolether **29** 53
polyptycha **25** 183
Polyptych of Évora Cathedral, Master of the **14** 658
polyptychs *see under* ALTARPIECES → types
polystauria **9** 643
Polystylon **9** 555
polystyrene **25** 23; **26** 244
Polytextil Gesellschaft **12** 470
polythene *see* POLYETHYLENE
polyurethane **25** 26
polyurethane foam **26** 245; **31** 687
polyurethane resin *see under* RESINS → types
polyvinyl acetate *see* PVA
polyvinyl chloride *see* PVC
Polyzalos **8** 696
Poma de Ayala, Felipe Guamán
groups and movements **8** 302
works **24** 506; **29** 130, *130*, 131, 132, 133, *183*, 209, 217, 218
Pomaire **6** 600
Pomar, Felipe Cossio del *see* COSSIO DEL POMAR, FELIPE
Pomar, Isabel **27** 304
Pomar, Júlio **19** 468; **25** 184–5*, 300, 310; **30** 882
Pomarance, Antonio Santucci dalle *see* SANTUCCI DALLE POMARANCE, ANTONIO
Pomarancio, Il *see* RONCALLI, CRISTOFORO
Pomarancio, Niccolò **25** 185*; **26** 770
collaboration **4** 840; **5** 172; **27** 122
patrons and collectors **10** 810; **13** 628; **25** 7
pupils **2** 492
works **4** 812; **26** 823, 835
Pomareda Elías, Eduardo **24** 506
Pomarede, Leon de **33** 228
Pomata **24** *498*
Church of Santiago **24** 504
Pombal
Castle **25** 311
Convento de S Francisco **13** 125
Pombal, Antônio Francisco **19** 459
Pombal, Sebastião José de Carvalho e Melo, 1st Marquês de **4** 636; **25** 185*
architecture **10** 155; **19** 464, 893; **20** 110, 403; **25** 293; **31** 717
decorative works **13** 694
gardens **7** 532; **12** 125, *125*
pottery **10** 729; **25** 310; **26** 52; **31** 865
towns **27** 804
Pombaline style **1** 753; **25** 185–6*, 288, 293; **27** 800
façades **25** *186*
Pombeiro, S Maria **26** 254
pomegranates **10** 872
Pomerance, Leo **15** 922
Pomeranian Cabinet of Art **2** *716*, 717; **14** 51
Pomerania-Stettin, Bogislav the Great, Duke of *see* BOGISLAV V, Duke of Pomerania-Stettin
Pomerania-Stettin, Franz, Duke of *see* FRANZ, Duke of Pomerania-Stettin
Pomerania-Wolgast, Philip Greifen, Duke of **13** 630
Pomerania-Wolgast, Vratislav VIII Greifen, Duke of **13** 630
Pomerantsev, Aleksandr (Nikanorovich) **25** 186–7*; **27** 580
pupils **18** 737
works **5** 149, *149*; **22** 173
Pomeroy, Frederick William **25** 187*
collaboration **22** 230; **28** 348
groups and movements **3** 269; **23** 34
patrons and collectors **14** 132
works **15** 542; **31** 241
Pomfret, Thomas Fermor, 1st Earl of *see* FERMOR, THOMAS, 1st Earl of Pomfret
Pomis, (Giovanni) Pietro (Telesphoro) de **2** 794; **25** 187–8*
patrons and collectors **13** 918
teachers **1** 35
works **2** 781, 782; **13** 329, *329*
pommels (guns) **2** 459, 462, 464, 465, *465*, 466
pommels (swords) **2** 451, 452
Pommerance collection **1** 896
Pommerscher Kunstschrank **19** 152
Pommersfelden, Schloss Weissenstein **3** 266, *266*; **8** 875; **12** *361*; **14** 529; **23** 811; **25** 188–9*; **26** 495
collections **9** 18
coral **7** 835
frames **11** 456
manuscripts **26** 673, *673*
paintings **3** 702; **4** 334; **9** 485; **17** 712; **19** 817; **26** 397; **27** 136; **28** 146
Sala Terrena **13** 705; **27** 611
Spiegelkabinett **5** 347, *348*, 349; **9** 29; **12** 413
Treppenhaus **23** *812*; **29** 525
Pommersfelden Bible *see* BIBLES → individual manuscripts → Koblenz Bible
Pommier, Hugues **5** 564
Pomo **22** 549
baskets **10** 848; **22** 641, 652, 659, *659*, 660, 668
feathers **22** 652
Pomodoro, Arnaldo **17** 530; **21** 528; **25** 189*
collaboration **17** 622; **25** 189
groups and movements **7** 782
works **1** 738
Pomodoro, Giò **17** 530; **25** 189*
collaboration **25** 189
groups and movements **7** 782, 783
works **12** 437
Pomoenia **9** 539; **20** 520
Pomona factory **10** 309; **29** 495
Pomorie **5** 145
Pomortsev, Boris **27** 434
Pompadour, Abbé de **8** 651
Pompadour, Jeanne-Antoinette Poisson, Marquise de **3** 840; **9** *283*; **11** 508; **19** 15; **20** 135; **24** ; **25** 80*
architecture **11** 658, 883; **18** 815
books **4** 360
collections **9** 467; **27** 224
decorative works **5** 379; **10** 529; **32** 815
etchings **4** 518; **11** 541
frames **11** 408
furniture **7** 658; **11** 592, 593; **23** 356; **26** 420
gems **11** 635; **13** 771
gold **11** 620
interior decoration **19** 723; **32** 338
metalwork **9** 399; **11** 619
paintings **3** 241; **4** 517; **10** 478; **11** 539; **13** 640; **14** 846; **19** 646; **23** 295; **24** 396
porcelain **11** 609; **32** 583
portraits **25** 286
sculpture **1** 133, 665; **10** 764; **24** 785; **27** 659; **28** 846; **30** 353; **32** 76
tapestries **4** 514
teachers **4** 517; **10** 119
Pompaelo *see* PAMPLONA
Pomparippu **29** 474
Pompe, Antoine **25** 190*
collaboration **4** 217; **31** 875; **32** 380
teachers **14** 604
works **3** 550, 587
Pompe, Jan-Engelbert **25** 190
Pompe, Pauwel-Martinus **25** 190
Pompe, Walter **3** 604; **6** 151; **25** 190*
works **3** 571; **30** 495
Pompei, Alessandro (Ercole), Conte **25** 191*; **32** 342
Pompeia *see* POMOENIA
Pompeian blue *see under* PIGMENTS → types
Pompeian Revival **22** 738; **25** 191–4*
Denmark **8** 740
England **4** 333; **10** 276; **25** 192, *193*
see also ARABESQUE STYLE
Pompeii **2** 164; **10** 585, 641, 644; **16** *621*; **25** 191, 192, 194–207*, *195*; **26** 230, *886*; **27** 115
aerarium **26** 867
Albergo del Gladiatore **27** 110
amphitheatre **1** 797; **25** 198; **26** 874, 889
architecture **16** 623; **25** 194–201*; **26** 856
art forms and materials
amulets **10** 487
bronzes **27** 86
cameos **27** 76
candelabra **5** 604
charcoal **6** 469
coral **7** 834
doors **9** 151
figurines **13** 581
fountains **13** 702
furniture **27** 100; **33** 332
gardens **12** 68; **26** 862; **32** 544
glass **12** 790
gold **27** 80
graffiti **13** 269
inscriptions **26** 856
ivory **15** 695
ivory-carvings **27** 100
jewellery **27** 101, 102, 103
lamps **3** 627; **27** 87
mirrors **21** *713*
mosaics **13** 551, 561; **22** 160, 161; **23** 534; **25** 205–6*; **27** 66, *66*; **31** 703
Pompeii
art forms and materials—cont.
opus sectile **32** 543
orders (architecture) **23** 484
paintings **10** 487; **27** 58
wall **5** 685; **10** 475; **12** 287; **13** 553; **16** 653; **17** 533, *534*; **22** 411, 686; **23** 291; **25** 203–5*, *204*; **26** 857, 858, 861; **27** 50, 53, 58, 74; **30** 651; **31** 265
pens **24** 349
portraits **25** 202
satires **27** 868
sculpture **10** 474; **25** 201–2*, *202*; **27** 9, 16, 22, 31, 46
copies **29** 572–3
signs (markers) **1** 164
statuettes **27** 52, 88, 89
stucco **27** 69
talismans **10** 474
terracottas **27** 109, 110, *110*
textiles **27** 112
well-heads **33** 56
Basilica **3** 328; **25** 198; **26** 867, *868*, 877, 878, 888
baths **25** 198
Central Baths **26** 871, 892
Forum Baths **3** 374; **15** 51; **26** 892; **27** 70, 71
atlantids **2** 695
stucco **27** *71*
Stabian Baths **3** 374, *374*; **15** 51; **26** 871, 888, 892; **27** 67, 70
castellum urbanum **27** 6
cisterns **27** 6
collections **13** 470
courtyards **8** 64
excavations **2** 299; **13** 605
forum **2** 294; **11** 327; **25** 196–7, *197*
fountains **27** 66, *66*
houses and villas **25** 198–201; **26** 868
House of Cicero **13** 557
House of Diomedes **32** 544
House of Dioscurides **13** *546*
House of Ephebe **5** 604
House of Fabius Rufus **12** 68
House of Iphigenia **27** 55
House of Julia Felix **27** 67, 110
House of Loreius Tibertinus **12** 69; **27** 52; **32** 544
wall paintings **27** 49, 50
House of Lucretius Fronto **29** *664*
House of Marcus Lucretius Fronto **13** 552
House of Menander **13** 547; **21** *713*; **27** 80, 81
mosaics **27** 61
wall paintings **26** 861
House of Octavius Quartio *see* House of Loreius Tibertinus
House of Octavius Quartone **13** 552
House of Pansa **26** 869, *870*
House of Paquius Proculus **27** 50
House of Pinarius Cerealis *see* House of Iphigenia
House of Polybius **12** 69
House of Sacello Iliaco **13** 552
House of Sallust **27** 53
House of the Anchor **12** 69
House of the Cithara Player **13** 552; **27** 50
House of the Coloured Capitals **26** 869
House of the Cryptoporticus **27** 54, 69
House of the Dioscuri **27** 49, 58
House of the Fated Love **27** 49
House of the Faun **13** 557, 559; **22** 155; **26** 869; **29** 665
Alexander Mosaic *see* ALEXANDER MOSAIC
mosaics **27** 61
wall paintings **27** 53

Pompeii
houses and villas—cont.
House of the Fountain with Columns **27** 66, *66*
House of the Grand Duke **27** 66
House of the Great Altar **27** 49
House of the Lararium **27** 51, *51*, 71
House of the Little Bull **12** 69
House of the Marine Venus **12** 69; **18** 703; **27** 48
paintings **12** *69*; **26** 862; **27** *48*
House of the Mosaic Atrium **26** 869
House of the Orchard **18** 702; **27** 54
House of the Priest **27** 49
House of the Priest Amandus **27** 49
House of the Prince of Naples **27** *54*
House of the Red Walls **27** 50
House of the Silver Wedding **25** *199*; **27** 54
House of the Surgeon **26** 869
House of the Tragic Poet **27** 49, 50, 58
House of the Triclinium **27** 50
House of the Vestals **15** 135
House of the Vettii **10** 475; **12** 69; **27** 49
garden **12** *68*
Ixion Room **9** 13
lararium **26** 857
paintings **13** 546; **32** 543, 803
Theban Room **26** 861
wall paintings **15** 135; **27** 49, 50, 51, 55, 58
House VIII.2.16 **27** 61, *61*
Imperial Villa **27** 54
Inn of Sotericus **27** 50
Villa of the Mysteries **10** 475; **25** 199–200; **26** 869
wall paintings **26** 858; **27** 49, 51, 53, *53*, 58; **32** 543
inns **27** 50
insulae **26** 887
macellum **19** 888, 889
markets **26** 871
masonry **26** 877
megalographia **27** 53
nymphaeum **27** 66
rediscovery **25** 206–7*
Shop of Verecundus **10** 875; **27** 50
shops **26** 871
Shrine of Our Lady **28** 632
streets **25** *196*
Temple of Isis **13** *302*; **23** 484; **27** 71
temples **25** 197–8, 201
theatres **26** 873, 888
Large Theatre **25** 198; **26** 923
Small Theatre **2** *695*, 695; **23** 349
tomb of Umbricius Scaurus **27** 71
tomb of Vestorius Priscus **27** 48
tombs **7** 642; **25** 201; **31** 109
town walls **25** 196
urban planning **25** 196–7; **27** 3
villas *see* houses and villas
walls **26** *875*
workshops **27** 28, 55
Pompeo (family) **6** 21
Pompey **12** 248, 265; **26** 764, 856, 896; **27** 96
architecture **26** 749, 856, 889
sculpture **27** 29, 30
Pompidou, Georges **7** 670; **11** 602, 660
Pompignan, Jean-Jacques Le Franc, Marquis de **13** 665
Pompon, François **2** 100, 521; **11** 568; **25** 207*
Pomponazzi, Pietro **14** 867
Pomponius Hylas **7** 642
Pomponne, Simon Arnauld, Marquis de **22** *465*
Pomposa Abbey **13** 673; **16** 625; **26** 578
frescoes **9** 260
sculpture **26** 621
Po Nagar *see under* NHA TRANG
Ponam **24** 82
Ponape *see* POHNPEI
Ponç, Joan **3** 219; **8** 538; **29** 286
Ponca **22** 551
Ponce **25** *698*, 700
Museo de Arte **5** 746; **25** 703, 704
Tibes park **25** 704
Ponce, Aguilar **23** 905
Ponce, Antonio **25** 208*; **29** 340
Ponce, Fernando García *see* GARCÍA PONCE, FERNANDO
Ponce, Jacquiot **11** 557; **25** 208*; **27** 547
Ponce, Juan García *see* GARCÍA PONCE, JUAN
Ponce, Luis Aguilar *see* AGUILAR PONCE, LUIS
Ponce, Nicolas **3** 395; **5** 440; **25** 192
Ponce de León, Fidelio **25** 208–9*
Ponce de León, Juan **25** 698
Ponce Monolith **30** 797
Poncet, François-Marie **25** 209*
Poncet, Jean **13** 79
Poncet, Pons **8** 664; **13** 79
Ponchino, Giambattista **25** 209*; **32** 348; **33** 631
Ponchon **30** 885
ponchos **2** 403, *403*; **6** *599*
Poncini, Bernardo **31** 753
Poncino, Tommaso **25** 408; **32** 895
Pončun, Matej *see* PONZONI, MATTEO
Pond, Arthur **2** 239; **9** 230; **25** 210*, *210*; **26** 229
assistants **1** 504
collaboration **18** 142
methods **10** 562
patrons and collectors **6** 117; **14** 598
personal collection **25** 631
pupils **7** 418
works **5** 756; **6** 513; **8** 130; **9** 308; **10** 178; **13** 300; **25** 619, 622; **33** 367
Pond, Edwin P.
works **22** *580*
Pond, Pond, Martin & Lloyd **28** 122
Ponda **15** *276*; **25** 210–11*
Pondicherry **15** *294*, 411, 678; **25** 211*
Government House **15** 401
Pondo **1** 368, 419
Pondomise **1** 419
ponds **12** 69, 85, 93, *94*, 95, 96, 109; **23** 417
Pondugula **15** 535
Ponętowski, Jan **25** 137
Ponfredi, Giovanni Battista **3** 712, 714
Pongdŏk Temple **18** 347
Ponge, Francis **10** 838; **17** 912
Ponggam Pogoda **23** 775
Ponghwa, Ch'ong-am-jong **12** 94
Pongnim Temple **18** 293
Pongyelok **15** 2
Po'ni *see* BRUNEI
Poniatowski (family) **25** 74
Poniatowski, Andrzej **25** 211
Poniatowski, Casimir, Duke **25** 136; **33** 722
Poniatowski, Izabella **25** 211
Poniatowski, Józef (1763-1813) **23** 530; **25** 211
Poniatowski, Józef (*fl* 1833-40) **25** 213
Poniatowski, Karol **25** 213
Poniatowski, Kazimierz **25** 211
Poniatowski, Ludwika Maria **25** 211
Poniatowski, Michał **21** 158; **25** 136, 138; **29** 839
Poniatowski, Michał Jerzy **25** 211
Poniatowski, Stanisław, Prince **25** 136, 211, 213*
architecture **31** 800; **32** 870
collections **17** 475; **25** 138
gems **12** 266
metalwork **31** 799
Poniatowski, Stanisław Augustus, King of Poland *see* STANISLAV II PONIATOWSKI, King of Poland
Poniatowski-Branicka, Izabella **4** 745
Poniky Church **14** 898
Poniński, Adam, Prince **25** 121; **32** 879
Ponirin Amin **20** 172
Ponni, Gianfrancesco **10** 810
Pons, Antoine de **23** 849
Pons, Jean **8** 149
Pons, Pierre de *see* PIERRE DE PONS
Ponsan-Debat, Edouard-Bernard *see* DEBAT-PONSAN, EDOUARD-BERNARD
Ponsang Ch'onjang *see* KWŎN TON-IN
Ponscarme, (François-Joseph-) Hubert **25** 214*
pupils **3** 474; **6** 489; **8** 41; **9** 370; **33** 285
Pons de Melgueil **7** 476
Pons de Saint-Maurice **5** 779
Ponse, Joris **28** 165; **29** 773
Pons i Ribas **29** 319
Ponso, Jacquiot *see* PONCE, JACQUIOT
Ponsonby (family) **4** 181
Ponsonby, Frederick, 10th Earl of Bessborough **14** 511
Ponsonby, Mary, Countess of Bessborough **14** 511
Ponsonby, William, 2nd Earl of Bessborough **6** 411; **12** 266; **21** 643; **28** 907
Ponsonelli, Giacomo Antonio **24** 203; **25** 214*
Ponsonelli, Giovanni **25** 214
Pont, de Carsalade du, Bishop of Perpignan *see* CARSALADE DU PONT, DE, Bishop of Perpignan
Pont, H(enry) F(rancis) Du *see* DU PONT, H(ENRY) F(RANCIS)
Pont, José Marco del **2** 405
Pont, Pierre Samuel du **19** 643
Pontadera, Andrea da *see* PISANO (ii), ANDREA
Pont-à-Lesse **3** 566
Pont-à-Mousson, St Martin **13** 79
Pontano, Giovanni **1** 127; **30** 1
Pontano, Teobaldo, Bishop of Assisi **2** 625
Pontanus, Jiři Barthold **13** 914
Pontarlier **31** 717
pontate **11** 763
Pont-aux-Choux factory **11** 606
Pont-Aven **2** 552, 732; **18** 717; **25** 214–15*; **28** 484; **30** 169
commentaries **8** 714; **28** 371
members **30** 174
Bernard, Emile **3** 813
Bevan, Robert (Polhill) **3** 893
Forbes, Elizabeth (Adela) Stanhope **11** 300
Gauguin, Paul **12** 187, 189
Hovenden, Thomas **14** 804
Loiseau, Gustave **19** 544
Peel, Paul **24** 322
Schjerfbeck, Helene (Sofia) **28** 104
Scott, William (*b* 1913) **28** 287
Sérusier, (Louis) Paul (Henri) **28** 484
Ślewiński, Władysław **28** 841
Wiik, Maria (Catharina) **33** 175
Pontbriand, Bishop of Quebec **3** 71
Pontbriant, François de **4** 155
Pontcysyllte **2** 242; **4** 802
Pont-de-Loup **3** 588
Pont du Gard *see under* NÎMES
Ponte, Antonio da **25** 215–16*
works **27** 347; **32** 186, *186*
Ponte, Baptiste de **9** 2
Ponte, dal *see* BASSANO
Ponte, Domenico de **19** 769
Ponte, Giovanni dal *see* GIOVANNI DAL PONTE
Ponte, Gottardo da **6** 357
Ponte, Hector da **24** 98, 102
Ponte, Nicolò da, Doge of Venice (*reg* 1578-85) **32** *649*
Ponte alla Badia, Villa Salviati **1** 670; **27** 448
Pontecagnano **10** 586, 631
Pontecchio Palazzo Rossi **32** 545
Ponte di Brenta, Villa Breda **4** 311
Ponte di Nona **32** 398
Pontefract (W. Yorks) **24** 808
Castle **21** 562
court-house **18** 887
Pontelli, Baccio **3** 359; **25** 216–17*; **31** 742
attributions **19** 686; **26** 836
patrons and collectors **27** 272
teachers **11** 705
works **3** *360*; **18** 862; **19** *686*; **25** *216*; **29** 665; **31** 905
Pontelli, Piero **25** 216
Ponte Lombardo, Elia di Bartolomeo da *see* ELIA DI BARTOLOMEO DA PONTE LOMBARDO
Pontevico, Comino da *see* COMINO DA PONTEVICO
Ponthier de Chamaillard, Henri-Ernest **25** 215
Ponthière, Hubert **3** 595
Ponti, Carlo **24** 664; **25** 217*
Ponti, Gio(vanni) **16** 649; **21** 363; **25** 218–19*
collaboration **11** 63; **16** 650; **22** 393, 806; **23** 263; **24** 694; **28** 834
patrons and collectors **7** 782
works **7** 696; **10** 820; **16** *93*, 93, 649, 650, 721, 731, *732*; **21** 522; **23** 263, 754, 799; **25** *218*
Pontificals **13** 130
individual manuscripts
Florence Pontificale **11** 686
Metz Pontifical (Cambridge, Fitzwilliam, MS. 298) **30** 749
Pontificale Gundecarianum (Eichstätt, Ubib.) **12** 816
Pontifical of Jean Coeur (New York, Pierpont Morgan Lib., MS. Glazier 49) **7** 596
Pontifical of Poiters (ex-Bib. Hotel de Ville, Paris; destr. 1871) **18** 685
Sens Pontifical (Brussels, Bib. Royale Albert 1er, MS. 9215) **20** 451, *452*
Sherborne Pontifical (Paris, Bib. N., MS. lat. 943) **2** 74
Thérouanne Pontifical (Haarlem, Teylers Mus., MS. 77) **20** 451
Pontigny Abbey **7** 346, 353; **9** 156; **11** *504*; **13** 38; **25** *219*, 219–20*, *220*
church **11** 510
Ponting, Herbert (George) **25** 220–21*
Pontios **22** 733
pontioscopio **25** 217
Pontis, Guillaume **19** 230; **27** 251
Pontius, Paulus **3** 561; **10** 391; **25** 221*
collaboration **9** 480; **10** 391; **22** 717; **27** 299
teachers **3** 494; **32** 700
works **26** 155
Pontius Meropius Paulinus *see* PAULINUS OF NOLA
Pont l'Abbé d'Arnoult Church **26** 600
Pont-l'Evêque, St Michel Chapel **13** 60
Pont-l'Evêque, Roger, Archbishop of York **13** 44; **33** 547, 549
Pontmain, Our Lady of Hope **28** 632
Ponton, W. V. **4** 823
Pontón de Setien, Pantaleón **27** 605
pontoons *see under* BRIDGES → types
Pontormo, Jacopo da **16** 766; **25** 221–4*; **26** 769
assistants **4** 856
attributions **19** 383
collaboration **3** 15; **4** 857; **10** 877; **12** 556, 719; **27** 848, 849
dealers **7** 234
drawings **9** 220; **21** 450
frames **11** 390
groups and movements **11** 186; **20** 280, 281
interior decoration **21** 19
methods **7** 628; **18** 898; **21** 763; **31** 578
paintings **16** 663; **25** *223*
frescoes **7** 458; **11** 204; **21** 16; **25** *222*; **31** 142; **32** 549
portraits **11** *390*; **30** 783
religious **11** 187; **20** 277, 278
spalliere **29** 362
patrons and collectors **16** 711
Baccio d'Agnolo (Bartolommeo d'Agnolo di Donato Baglione) **3** 15
Borgherini, Pierfrancesco **4** 404; **12** 897; **13** 281; **16** 766
Capponi, Ludovico (*d* 1534) **5** 16, 682
Clement VII, (Anti-) Pope (*reg* 1378-94) **25** 77
Clement VII, Pope (*reg* 1523-34) **21** 17
Cosimo I, Grand Duke of Tuscany (*reg* 1569- 74) **11** 193
Cowper, George Nassau Clavering, 3rd Earl **8** 83
Loeser, Charles Alexander **19** 538
Medici (family) **25** 76
Medici, Ottaviano de' **21** 18
Museo Nacional de Bellas Artes (Santiago) **6** 601
Palla, Giovanbattista della **23** 855
Pucci, Giovanni **25** 690
Robien, Christophe-Paul Gautron, Marquis de **26** 469
pupils **1** 730; **4** 855; **18** 781; **22** 447
restorations by others **11** 318
tapestries **27** 650; **30** 319
teachers **1** 572; **24** 771; **27** 770, 847, 851
writings **24** 90
Pontrémoli, Emmanuel **20** 450; **22** 728
Pontremoli, J. M. **10** 358
Pontremoli, Pellegrino da *see* PELLEGRINO DA PONTREMOLI
Pont-sur-Seine **5** 344; **19** 145
Pontypool (Gwent) **18** 615; **21** 331
Pontypridd (Mid Glams)
bridge **4** 801
Ynysangharad Park **32** 788
Ponz, Antonio **25** 224–5*; **29** 358; **33** 118
Ponzanelli, Giacomo **29** 292
Ponzano, Antonio **11** 819; **30** 34
Ponzano y Gascon, Ponciano **25** 225–6*; **27** 819
works **10** 501; **25** *225*; **29** 294
Ponzello, Domenico **1** 607; **25** 226*
collaboration **12** 281; **19** 806; **25** 226; **29** 523

Ponzello, Domenico—cont.
 patrons and collectors **12** 281
 works **15** 147; **19** 806
Ponzello, Giovanni
 attributions **1** 607
 collaboration **19** 806; **29** 523
 patrons and collectors **9** 173; **12** 281
 works **15** 147; **19** 806; **25** 226
Ponzio, Flaminio **12** 117; **25** 226–7*
 assistants **32** 9
 collaboration **4** 405; **25** 259
 patrons and collectors **11** 741; **32** 9
 pupils **32** 9
 works **4** 404, 405; **11** 271; **19** 632; **26** 832, 840
Ponzio, Jacquiot *see* PONCE, JACQUIOT
Ponzoni, Leonardo **3** 695; **5** 127
Ponzoni, Matteo **6** 137; **25** 227*; **33** 608
Pool, Juriaen **27** 454
Pool, Mathijs **13** 262
Poole (family) **24** 19
Poole, George Temple **2** 740; **24** 496
Poole, Paul Falconer **8** 492; **25** 228*; **32** 903
Poole Pottery Ltd **10** 313; **29** 484
Pooley, Thomas **16** 13
Pool Malebo
 sculpture **30** *419*
pools **12** 109
 Egypt, ancient **12** 66
 France **12** 120
 Indian subcontinent **20** *74*
 Islamic **16** 142
 Italy **26** *899*
 Netherlands, the **12** 132
 Rome, ancient **12** 69; **26** *899*; **27** 47
 see also PISCINE (i) (POOL)
Poompukar *see* KAVERIPATTINAM
poon **32** 488
Poon, Anthony **28** 774
Poona *see* PUNE
Poonah painting **29** 628
Poons, Larry **25** 228–9*
 groups and movements **23** 449; **25** 361
 works **1** 130; **7** 636
Poor, A. E. **23** 426
Poor, Henry Varnum **31** 640
Poor Clares, Order of *see* ORDER OF POOR CLARES
Poore, Richard, Bishop of Salisbury **27** 625, 626
Poortakker Triptych **14** 761
Poorter, Pieter Abrams **25** 230
Poorter, Willem de **22** 843; **25** 230–31*; **26** 153
 works **25** *230*
Poortvliet, Marie Tak van **14** 294
Poot, Rik **3** 574
P.O.P. *see* PHOTOGRAPHY → processes → printing-out
Pop, Misu **26** 714
Pop art **1** 79, 130; **9** 360; **10** 416; **12** 217, 296; **15** 184; **16** 906; **18** 719; **22** 279; **24** 679; **25** 231–2*; **26** 51
 art forms
  assemblages **2** 617
  collages **14** *112*
  installations **15** 868, 869
  lithography **17** *614*
  nude figures **23** 297
  painting **29** 670
   United States of America **1** *129*; **7** VII2(b), VIII1(b); **12** *217*; **17** *613*; **19** *328*, *702*; **29** *671*; **32** *862*
  photocollages **4** *115*
  screenprints **25** *232*
  sculpture **31** 615
  woodcuts **33** *364*
Pop art—cont.
 collections **6** 23; **21** 135; **23** 7; **24** 24; **28** 314; **31** 665
 commentaries **8** 609
 exhibitions **10** 680
 regional traditions
  Argentina **21** 698
  Colombia **7** 610
  England **4** 116; **6** 94; **10** 258, 268; **14** 112, 608; **17** 631; **24** 639; **30** 892
  Iceland **10** 490
  India, Republic of **18** 15
  Japan **17** 207
  United States of America **8** 522; **17** 613; **19** 328; **20** 436; **23** 397; **26** 27, 28; **27** 164, 345; **29** 670; **31** 608; **32** 862; **33** 89
Popayán **7** *601*, 603; **25** 233*
 architecture **7** 605
 Museo Arquidiocesano de Arte Religioso **25** 233
 Museo Negret **7** 609, 612; **22** 724; **25** 233
 sculpture **7** 607; **29** 146
 S Domingo **7** 605
 S Francisco **7** 605, 607, *608*
 Universidad del Cauca **7** 605
  Museo de Arte Colonial e Historia Casa Musquera **25** 233
Pŏpchu Temple **18** 266
 calligraphy **18** 329, 331
 paintings **18** 311
 P'alsang Hall **23** 775
 sculpture **18** 292
Pop de Szathmari, Carol *see* SZATHMARI, CAROL POP DE
Pope, Alexander **12** 129; **25** 233–4*
 gardens **12** 128, 129, 130
 grottoes **11** 243; **13** 704
 groups and movements **24** 741
 teachers **17** 507
 villa **32** 553
 works **27** 868
  illustrated **4** *363*, 364; **13** 646; **17** 904; **21** 59; **32** 378
 on portraits **25** 279
Pope, Alfred Atmore **25** 234*
Pope, Arthur Upham **2** 437; **15** 899; **16** 548, 560; **25** 234*
Pope, Eggers and Higgins **27** 237
Pope, Henry Martin **4** 86
Pope, John **25** 235
Pope, John Alexander **25** 234–5*
Pope, John Russell **25** 235*
 patrons and collectors **22** 400
 staff **28** 798
 works **2** 171; **21** 90; **22** 365, *365*; **23** 32; **24** 326; **26** 353; **32** 885, 887, 890
Pope, Mary Avery **25** 235
Pope, Richard **28** 259
Pope, Richard Shackleton **14** 786
Pope-Hennessy, John (Wyndham) **7** 715; **25** 236*
Popel, Zdeněk **8** 422
Popelin, Claudius (-Marcel) **25** 236*
 works **4** *307*
Popel von Lobkowitz, Christoph **33** 434
Popenko, D. I. **9** 54
Pope-Riddle, Theodate **25** 237*
Popescu, Gabriel **25** 237*; **26** 715
Popescu, Nicolae **26** 714
Popescu, Vasile **25** 237*; **26** 716
Popham, A(rthur) E(wart) **25** 237–8*
 works **25** 377
Popham, Hugh *see* POPHAM, A(RTHUR) E(WART)
Popkov, Viktor (Yefimovich) **25** 238*; **27** 397; **28** 919
poplar **24** *7*
 historical and regional traditions
  Central Asia, Eastern **6** 295
poplar
 historical and regional traditions—cont.
  France **33** 326
  Germany **12** *408*; **33** 326
  Gothic **13** 135
  Indian subcontinent **15** 311
  Islamic **16** 269
  Italy **33** 326
  Spain **33** 326
 uses
  architecture **6** 295; **16** 269
  panel paintings **13** 135; **24** 3, 4, 5
  relief sculpture **12** *408*
Poplar Forest **10** 850; **17** 468
poplin **16** 34
Popoli, Giacinto de **29** 544
Popol Vuh, Museo *see under* GUATEMALA CITY → museums
Popov, Aleksandr **22** 180; **27** 412
Popov, Gogo **19** 884
Popov, Viktor **27** 405
Popova, Lyubov' (Sergeyevna) **19** 430; **25** 238–9*; **27** 378, 392, 394; **30** 328; **32** 382, 661
 collaboration **21** 410
 exhibitions **15** 857
 groups and movements **7** 769; **8** 250, 251; **15** 856; **16** 818; **26** 504; **30** 8
 patrons and collectors **8** 10
 productions **30** 686
 teachers **21** 364; **33** 577
 works **7** 769, 770; **9** 244, 292; **25** *239*; **26** 504
Popović **8** 176
Popović, Atanasije **4** 461
Popović, Dimitrije **22** 18
Popović, Djoko **22** 18
Popović, Ljubomir-Ljuba **28** 451
Popović, Mića **28** 451, 453
Popović, P. **28** 838
Popović, V. **28** 838
Popovič-Cico, Vasilie **19** 885
Popov Porcelain Factory **22** 180; **27** 426
Popovski, Živko **19** 883
Popovski-Dada, Dragan **19** 885
Popp, Alexander **2** 813; **3** 514; **19** 434
Popp, Arnošt **8** 387, 405
Popp, Heinrich **25** 549
Popp, Sabin **26** 716
Poppehowe, Thomas **13** 84
Pöppelmann, Karl Friedrich **8** 843; **10** 109; **25** 98; **32** 870; **33** 115
Pöppelmann, Matthäus Daniel **10** 109; **25** 239–41*
 assistants **18** 162
 collaboration **4** 218; **9** 29, 235, 242; **24** 460
 groups and movements **3** 266
 patrons and collectors **9** 238; **33** 114, 115
 works **3** 527; **5** 348; **9** 235, 236, *236*, 238; **12** 373; **19** 642; **21** 64; **23** 471, 812; **25** 98, *240*; **28** 179; **29** 547
Poppelsdorf, Kreuzberg **23** 5
Poppen, Ioan **32** 589
Popper, Frank **18** 62
Poppi **11** 197; **21** 22; **25** 241*; **32** 16
Poppulin, Demetrio **25** 217
poppyheads **25** 242*
poppyseed oil *see under* OILS → types
Poprad Church **13** 162
 belfry **28** 849
Pŏpsang Buddhism *see* BUDDHISM → sects → Yogācāra
Pop Shop, The **14** 177
Pŏpsŏng Buddhism *see* BUDDHISM → sects → Dharma Nature
Popudnia **25** 502, 512
 models **25** *501*
popular art
 China **7** 142–7*, *144*, *145*, *146*
 Gabon **11** 879*
 India, Republic of **15** 177–8*, *178*
 Indian subcontinent **5** 419, *420*
 Korea **18** 376–7*
popular culture **9** 10; **20** 30
Popular Designer **32** 198
popular images *see* DEVOTIONAL IMAGES
popular prints *see under* PRINTS → types
Populer, Antonio **24** 107
Populonia **10** *583*, 586, 638; **16** *620*; **25** 245*
 bronze **10** *627*, 627
 coins **10** *632*, 632–3
 earrings **10** *631*
 iron **13** 372; **27** 93
 jewellery **10** 632
 metalwork **10** 624
 mirrors **10** 589, 628
 vases **10** 609, 612
Poquelin, Jean-Baptiste *see* MOLIÈRE
Pór, Bertalan **10** 108, 109; **25** 245–6*, *246*
Porbandar **15** 671
Porcaccino *see* PROCACCINI
Porcar, Miquel **29** 267
Porcel, E. **3** 216
porcelain **6** 330
 conservation **6** 334–6*
 display **5** 347–8*; **9** 11, 28–9*
  England **10** 276
  France **9** 30
  Germany **5** *348*; **12** 412
 historical and regional traditions
  Austria **2** 816–17*, *817*; **32** *450*
  Belgium **3** *590*, 590–91*
  Britain **19** 595
  Canada **5** *582*
  China **6** 325, 331, 868, 875, 918–21*, 923–5*; **7** 94; **9** 28; **17** 589; **25** 303, 309
   export **6** 904, 908
   Five Dynasties (AD 907-60) **7** 25
   marks **6** 903
   Ming period (1368-1644) **4** 173, *174*; **5** 12; **6** 872, *901*, 901–7*, *902*, *903*, *906*, *914*; **7** 125; **17** *589*
   Northern and Southern Dynasties (AD 310-589) **6** 885
   Qing period (1644-1911) **6** 907–11*, *908*, *909*, *910*, *911*; **7** 79, 100, 131, 132; **25** 309–10; **29** 113
   Song period (AD 960-1279) **6** 869, 895*, *895*
   Tang period (AD 618-907) **4** 172; **7** 95
   Yuan period (1279-1368) **6** 874, 897, *899*, *901*
   20th cent. **6** 912, *912*
  Czech Republic **8** 405–6*
  Denmark **7** *807*; **8** 748
  England **10** *308*, 308–10*
  Finland **11** 105, *106*
  France **5** 918; **11** 591, 607–10*; **24** *149*
   18th cent. **6** I3; **28** *521*
  Germany **4** 493; **6** 558, *558*; **9** *239*; **12** 406, 433–7*, *434*, *435*, *436*, *437*, 472; **22** 880; **31** 261, *261*
   Rococo **6** I2; **26** 498
   18th cent. **9** 234, 238; **12** *433*; **21** *64*
  Hungary **15** 2
  Iran **16** *424*, *425*
  Ireland **16** *29*, 29
  Islamic **16** 423, *424*, *425*
  Italy **7** 165; **16** 736–9*; **25** 193
porcelain
 historical and regional traditions—cont.
  Japan **17** 258, 263–4*, *265*, *341*, 351–2, 353, 399, 413; **23** 389; **31** 261
   Edo period (1600-1868) **9** 28; **17** 241, 255, *263*, *264*, 351
   Meiji period (1868-1912) **17** 353
  Korea **6** III1; **18** *255*, 337, 340*, 342–4*, *343*
  Netherlands, the **6** 333; **18** 195; **22** 882, *882*, 883
  Norway **23** 235
  Ottoman **16** 423
  Poland **25** 123
  Portugal **25** 303, 309–11*, *311*
  Russia **27** 411–14*, *412*, *414*
  Spain **29** 328–9, *330*
  Sweden **30** *99*, 99–101*, *100*
  United States of America **31** 635, 637–8, 640
   18th cent. **4** 332
   19th cent. **31** *637*
 materials
  aluminium oxides **6** 897
  bone-ash **4** 600; **10** 308
  china stone **6** 325, 869
  cobalt **6** 901; **18** 343
  copper **6** 895, 901
  copper oxides **18** 343–4, *343*
  enamel **6** 326, 872, 905, 907, 909, 910, 911; **7** 79; **14** 235; **17** *263*, 263–4*
  flint **6** 325; **29** 699
  frit **6** 326
  glazes **6** 326, 329, 894, 899
  gold **6** 895; **21** 66
  inlays **18** 344*
  inscriptions **6** 903
  iron oxide **18** 343
  kaolin **6** 325, 869, 895, 897
  silver **6** 895; **7** 25
  slip **18** 344
  soapstone **10** 309
 technical examination **30** 397, *397*, 406
 techniques
  en camaïeu **3** 590, *590*
  gilding **6** 326, 874, 905
  incising **6** 905
  lithography **30** 100
  moulding **6** 895, *895*
  overglaze decoration **6** 905, 907, 909, 911; **17** 263–4
  painting **2** 817; **10** *309*, 309–10; **14** 235
  pâte-sur-pâte **10** 312; **29** 51
  printing **10** 309, 380
  underglaze decoration **6** 326, 331, 872, 898–9, 901–5, 907; **17** *341*; **18** 343–4
 types
  blanc de chine **6** 911
   China **6** 332, 871, 907; **7** 126; **16** 425
   Iran **16** 425
   Islamic **16** 425
   see also wares → Dehua ware
  eggshell **6** 912; **22** 883, *883*
  hard-paste **6** 324, 325–6*, 329
   Austria **2** 816
   Belgium **3** 591
   England **10** 309, *309*
   France **6** 333; **11** 607, 609–10*, *610*; **28** *522*, *523*, *524*; **29** 753
   Germany **6** 333, I2; **21** 63–7, *66*
   Italy **16** *737*, *738*
   Russia **27** *414*
   Sweden **30** 100
   United States of America **31** 583
  soft-paste **6** 326*
   England **4** 600; **10** *308*, 308–9
   France **6** 923; **11** 607–9*, *607*, *608*; **28** *521*; **32** *583*

porcelain
types
soft-paste—cont.
Iran **16** *424, 425*
Islamic **16** *424, 425*
Italy **4** 176; **16** *736, 737*
Sweden **30** 99–100
United States of America **31** *635*
uses
bells **3** 627
bottles **17** *264, 265*
bowls **6** 875, 902, 903; **11** *106, 608*
brick **6** 906
brushpots **4** *175*
caskets **5** 918
centrepieces **2** *817*
chess sets **6** 558, *558*
china stone **6** 897
coffee-services **21** *65*; **32** *450*
commodes **6** I3
comports **16** *29*
crosses **8** 202
cups **7** 100; **28** *522*; **30** *99*
dolls **31** 260–61*, *261*
dolls' furniture **31** 264
ewers **6** *918*
figurines
China **6** *898*, 907, 910
England **10** *308*
France **28** *521*
Germany **6** I2; **12** *433, 437*
Italy **16** *737*
Japan **17** *263, 264, 265*
flasks **6** *910*; **16** *424*; **23** *553*
garnitures **10** *309*
ice buckets **12** *436*
incense burners **17** *265*
inkstones **7** 94, 95
jars **6** *899, 906*, III1; **17** *265*; **18** *343*
jugs **17** *264*
knife-handles **8** 285
mugs **6** *920*
netsuke **17** 399
pilgrim flasks **16** *736*
plaques **24** *149*
plates **6** *902, 914, 921*
sculpture **9** *239*
seals **17** 413
snuff bottles **7** 131, 132
snuff-boxes **11** *608*
statuettes **12** 406
sword grips **2** 456
tables **11** 591
tankards **6** 902; **12** *435*; **17** *264*
teapots **11** *607*; **16** *738*; **25** *311*
tea-services **12** *434*
tiles **6** 906
tureens **6** *921*; **12** *436*; **22** *882*; **32** *583*
vases
China **6** *898, 902*, 903, *903, 908, 909, 911*
France **11** *610*; **28** *523, 524*
Germany **21** *66*
Netherlands, the **22** *883*
Spain **29** *330*
Sweden **30** *100*
United States of America **31** *637*
wares
blue-and-white ware **4** 172
China **4** 172, 173–4*; **7** 144, 165
China: Ming period (1368-1644) **4** *174*; **6** 875, *901*, 902, *902, 903, 906*, 907, *918*; **23** *553*
China: Qing period (1644-1911) **6** 624, *908*, 909; **25** 309
China: Yuan period (1279-1368) **6** 898–9, *898, 916*
England **4** 177*
Germany **4** 176–7*
Iran **4** 172; **16** *424*
Islamic **16** *424*
porcelain
wares
blue-and-white ware—cont.
Italy **4** 176*
Japan **4** 174–5*; **17** 263
Korea **4** 174*, *175*; **18** 343
Oman **4** 173
Sri Lanka **4** 173
Vietnam **4** 173
see also kosumetsuke; *Tenkei*
Canton ware *see famille rose*
chine de commande **6** 918, 919, 921, *921*
clair de lune **6** 909
see also yuebai
Dehua wares **6** 907
see also types → *blanc de chine*
Ding ware **6** 870, 885, 895*, 913, 922; **7** 25; **23** 551
doucai **6** 905, 910
encre de Chine **6** 920
fahua **6** 332, 872, 906, *906*
famille jaune **6** 332, 910
famille noire **6** 332, 910
famille rose **6** 332, 872, *908*, 910, *910*; **10** 775*
famille verte **6** 332, 910, 919; **10** 775*
guyue xuan **6** 910; **7** 86
Imari **6** 332
China **4** 174; **6** 920
Japan **2** 414; **17** 263; **29** 114
see also ARITA → porcelain
Kakiemon ware **2** 414; **6** 332; **17** *263*, 264, 733*
see also ARITA → porcelain
kosometsuke **6** 622
see also blue-and-white ware
Kraak ware
China **4** 173; **6** 331, 904, 918, *919*; **16** 424
Iran **16** 424
Islamic **16** 424
Kubachi ware **16** 423, 424
Nabeshima **17** 263, 264, 351; **22** 421*
Old Japan ware *see* ARITA → porcelain
Parian porcelain **31** *637*
England **10** 311, *311*
Sweden **30** 100
Qingbai ware **6** 331, 894–5*, 897, 898; **23** 551
Rose mandarin *see famille rose*
Shonzui **6** 904
Swatow ware **6** 906–7
Tenkei **6** 622, 904
see also blue-and-white ware
Transitional ware **6** 331, 904, 919, *920*
whiteware **6** 326, 897–8
wucai **6** 906, 910
Xing ware **6** 870–71
Yingqing ware **6** 894
yuebai **6** 909
see also clair de lune
Zheijang greenware **6** *916*
see also CERAMICS
Porcelaine de Paris **27** 724
Porcelaines Bernardund **11** 631
Porcelaines GDA **4** 71
porcelain glass *see* GLASS → types → *lattimo*
porcelain rooms *see under* CABINETS (i) (ROOMS) → types
Porceleyne Fles **8** 667, 669; **22** 881, 882, 883, 884; **30** 506
Porceleyne Lampetkan **8** 668; **22** 879
Porceleyne Schotel **8** 668; **22** 879, 881
works **22** *878*
porcellana contrafacta see under GLASS → techniques
porcelleinglas see under GLASS → types
Porcellet (family) **2** 419
Porcellis, Jan **7** 673; **13** 894; **25** 246–8*; **27** 230
patrons and collectors **3** 615; **10** 660; **29** 799
teachers **32** 734
works **20** 424; **25** *247*
Porcellis, Julius **25** 248; **27** 230
Porcelos, Diego Rodríguez *see* RODRÍGUEZ PORCELOS, DIEGO
Porche, Pierre **33** 358
Porcher, E. A. **22** 340
Porcher, Jean **25** 248*
porches **25** 248*
Africa **1** 308
Cambodia **5** 474
France **13** *60*
Gothic **13** *60*
Greece, ancient **13** 382, 415
United States of America **32** 240
Porchier, Guillaume **20** 707
porch portals *see under* PORTALS → types
Porcinari collection **14** 114
Porco **4** 255, *255*, 265
Porcuna **15** 59
Porden, William **25** 249*; **32** 905
patrons and collectors **13** 696; **14** 145; **15** 406
teachers **7** 502
works **4** 809; **9** 17; **15** 408; **22** 59
Pordenone(, Giovanni Antonio) **16** 665; **25** 249–51*; **26** 769
attributions **1** 750; **5** 688; **19** 330
collaboration **3** 697; **4** 195; **27** 655
patrons and collectors **2** 117; **3** 55; **9** 172; **13** 658; **15** 148; **32** 155
pupils **1** 750; **3** 470
reproductive prints by others **11** 51
works **2** 102; **10** 736, 739; **13** 678; **15** 137; **24** 695; **25** *250, 251*; **31** 278, 316; **32** 191
Pordenone, Dario da *see* DARIO (DI GIOVANNI) DA TREVISO
Pordenone, Odoric of *see* ODORIC OF PORDENONE
Porębski, Mieczysław **18** 429
Poreč **8** *174*, 175; **9** *510*; **25** 251–2*
Archaeological Museum **8** 180
Basilica of Bishop Euphrasius *see* Cathedral
Bishop's Palace **9** 557
Canonika **8** 175
Cathedral **8** 175; **9** 525, 529, 573; **25** 252, *252*; **29** 816
altar **1** 694
mosaics **9** 565; **22** 161; **25** 252
Dekumanska Street 32 **8** 175
Franciscan church **8** 175
mosaics **9** 565
Sinčić Palace **8** 176
Poret, Alisa **11** 82; **12** 804
Porfyrius *see* OPTATIANUS PORFYRIUS, PUBLILIUS
Pori **11** 103
Juselius chapel **12** 21
Porimov, Victor **17** 205
Pori Puuvillatehdas Factory **11** 110
Porlezza, Paolo Sanmicheli da *see* SANMICHELI DA PORLEZZA, PAOLO
Por Loboeuk **5** 490
Pormeister, Valve **10** 538
Porne, Åke **31** 694
pornography **10** 486
Po Rome **6** *418*, 425
sculpture **6** 430, 431
wall paintings **6** 432
Poros **21** 683
poros **13** 387, 388, 389, 393
Poros (*reg c.* 326-5 BC) **15** 213
Porphyrius Publilius Optatianus **5** 779; **7** 246
Porphyrius von Neuenkirchen **29** 4, 5
Porphyrogenitos, Constantine VII, Emperor of Byzantium *see* CONSTANTINE VII PORPHYROGENITOS, Emperor of Byzantium
Porphyrousa *see* KYTHERA
porphyry **29** 702
historical and regional traditions
Aztec **21** *244*
Byzantine **27** 827
Early Christian (*c.* AD 250-843) **27** 827
Egypt, ancient **9** 813; **27** 13
Germany **20** *798*; **29** IX1
Gothic **20** *798*
Greece, ancient **27** 14
Italy **27** *43*; **30** 777
Mesoamerica, Pre-Columbian **21** *244*
Romanesque **29** IX1
Rome, ancient **26** 855, 876–7, 902; **27** 10, 13, 14, 43, *43*
Russia **27** 428
Sweden **30** 113–14*
uses
altars **29** IX1
columns **26** 902
reliefs **27** *43*
sarcophagi **27** 827
sculpture **20** *798*; **26** 855; **27** 10, 14, 43
thrones **30** 777
Porphyry (232-*c.* 305) **22** 749
Porpora, Paolo **22** 478; **25** 252–3*; **26** 61
Porporati, Carlo Antonio **13** 642
porporino see under GLASS → types
Porrata, Giacomo **8** 134
Porreras **29** 332
Porres, Diego de **2** 143; **13** 760, 761; **23** 80; **25** 253*
works **13** *761*
Porres, Diego José de **25** 253
Porres, Felipe de **13** 761; **25** 253
works **13** *761*
Porres, José de **2** 143; **13** 760, 761; **25** 253*
works **2** *143*
Porres, Joseph de
Porres, Manuel de **25** 253
Porri, Daniele de **33** 716
Porri, de *see* PARRI
porringers **9** 715; **10** 341; **31** 648
see also ECUELLES
Porro, Giovanna **4** 817
Porro, Giovan Pietro **25** 466
Porro, Girolamo **32** 199
Porro (Hidalgo), Ricardo **25** 253–4*
collaboration **13** 213
works **8** *232*, 233
porrón **8** 236, *236*; **29** *331*
Porry-Pastorel, Adolfo **28** 337
Porsche, Ferdinand **15** 825
works **15** *824*
Porsgrund Porcelain Factory **23** 235
Porta **30** 307
Porta, Antonio **5** 701; **25** 257–8*
Porta, Antonio della **25** 254–5*
assistants **32** 603
collaboration **1** 748; **3** 868; **4** 817; **11** 895, 897, 905; **23** 709
patrons and collectors **11** 556
works **8** 378; **24** 286, 287
Porta, Baccio della *see* BARTOLOMMEO, FRA
Porta, Bartolomeo della **25** 254
Porta, Carlo **12** 901
Porta, Fidias della **25** 256
Porta, Giacomo della (1532-1602) **25** 258–60*
collaboration **4** 83; **11** 78, 273; **18** 869; **31** 820
patrons and collectors **1** 595; **17** 510; **24** 398; **30** 649; **32** 547
pupils **5** 827
Porta, Giacomo della (1532-1602)—cont.
works **1** 596; **2** 336; **4** 432; **9** 82, 86; **13** 813; **20** 44, 45; **22** 5; **23** 810, 836; **25** *260*
Porta, Giacomo della (*fl* 1477-81) **25** 254
Porta, Giacomo della (1532-1602)
assistants **13** 906
collaboration **11** 271; **18** 698; **19** 638
patrons and collectors **10** 808, 810, 811; **11** 741; **13** 628; **20** 588; **26** 770; **32** 507
works **7** 692; **8** 202; **11** 343; **16** 632, 634, 635, 750; **21** 453; **25** *259*; **26** 806, 823, *823*, 838; **32** 692
Porta, Gian Giacomo della **7** 901; **25** 255*
Porta, Giovan Battista della (1535-1615) **2** 103; **5** 519
Porta, Giovanni Battista della (*d* 1597) **12** 911; **25** 257*; **26** 779; **27** 483
personal collection **4** 406
Porta, Giovanni Domenico **8** 267
Porta, Girolamo della **3** 137; **29** 25
Porta, Giuseppe *see* SALVIATI, GIUSEPPE
Porta, Guglielmo della (*fl c.* 1480) **25** 254
Porta, Guglielmo della (*fl* 1534-77) **24** 419; **25** 255–7*; **26** 769
assistants **30** 531; **31** 188
collaboration **7** 901; **9** 181; **25** 255
patrons and collectors **1** 595; **25** 7
pupils **7** 484; **31** 188
restorations **10** 812
works **3** 831; **5** 789; **10** 441; **16** 696; **25** *256*, 257; **26** 809; **29** 569
Porta, Teodoro della **25** 257*
Porta, Tomaso della **25** 257*
portable altars *see under* ALTARS → types
portable crosses *see under* CROSSES → types
Portacarrero, Cardinal **20** 375
Portaels, Jean-François **5** 44; **25** 261*
pupils **1** 453; **7** 859; **8** 628, 650, 700; **10** 735; **11** 746; **21** 86; **31** 874, 888; **32** 254, 924
teachers **22** 697
portae regiae **30** 652, 656
Portail, Jacques-André **25** 261*
Portal, Mathieu **25** 709
Portalatín, Aida Cartagena *see* CARTAGENA PORTALATÍN, AIDA
Port Alberini
painting **22** *588*
portal dolmens *see under* TOMBS → types
Portalegre **30** 328
Cathedral **25** 291; **26** 253
convent of Nossa Senhora da Conceição **25** 304
textiles **25** 315
Portalegre, João da Silva, 2nd Conde da *see* SILVA, JOÃO DA
Portalis, Roger **3** 753; **10** 210
portals **25** 261*
historical and regional traditions
Bolivia **4** *258*
Central Asia, Western **6** *203*
Denmark **8** *737*
Egypt **9** 161
England **10** 259; **23** 251
France
Gothic **2** *47*; **4** 581; **8** *892*; **9** 708; **10** *546*; **18** *759*; **27** *544*
Romanesque **2** *728*; **4** *581*; **29** *94*

portals
historical and regional traditions—cont.
Germany **11** 749; **12** *410*; **29** *6*
Gothic **31** *569*
Gothic
France **4** 581; **8** *892*; **9** 708; **10** *546*; **18** *759*; **27** *544*
France: Early Gothic **2** *47*
Germany **29** *6*; **31** *569*
Spain **13** *282*
Switzerland **18** *875*
Iran **16** 194
Ireland
Romanesque **26** *618*
Islamic **16** 142
Central Asia, Western **6** *203*
Egypt **9** 161
Iran **16** 194
Syria **8** *478*
Tunisia **16** *170, 219*
Yemen **16** 178
Italy
Romanesque **24** *858*; **26** *620*
Norway **29** 580–81
Plateresque style **8** *253*
Poland **26** *636*
Portugal **6** *451*; **23** *453*
Romanesque
Denmark **8** *737*
France **2** *728*; **4** *581*; **29** *94*
Ireland **26** *618*
Italy **24** *858*; **26** *620*
Poland **26** *636*
Spain **2** *866*; **19** *176*; **27** *795*
Spain **2** *866*; **13** *282*; **19** *176*; **27** *795*; **29** *841*
Plateresque style **5** *362*
Switzerland **18** *875*
Syria **8** *478*
Tunisia **16** *170, 219*
Uzbekistan **6** *203*
Yemen **16** 178
materials
alabaster (gypsum) **29** *841*
mouldings **22** 216, 219, 222
sandstone **29** *6*
stucco **29** *841*
types
porch **20** 820; **21** 773; **26** 621; **33** 188
see also GALILEES
stepped **25** 95
see also DOORWAYS; GATES
Portaluppi, Piero **3** 438; **16** 649; **21** 521; **23** 263
Portaña, Vicente López y *see* LÓPEZ Y PORTAÑA, VICENTE
Porta Nigra *see under* TRIER
Porta Panagia **7** 253
Port Appin **28** 241
Portas, Nuno **24** 395
portative mosaics *see* ICONS → historical and regional traditions → Byzantine; Early Christian
Port-au-Prince **14** *54*; **31** 721
Centre d'Art **14** 58, 60
education (art) **14** 60
Grand Hotel Oloffson **5** 749
Musée d'Art Haïtien **14** 60; **21** 894
Musée du Panthéon National Haïtien **14** 58
Old Cathedral **14** 57, 58
Palais National **14** 57, 58
Roman Catholic Cathedral **14** 57
St Trinité Cathedral **14** 58
Port Cergy **29** 420
Portchester (Hants; UK) **3** 209; **21** 560
fort **21** *561*
Port Chester (NY; USA), Kneset Tifereth Israel **17** 549
porte crayons **25** *261**
portcullises **12** 174
Port Dundas Pottery **28** 258
Porte, Charles Armand de La, Duc de Mazarin *see* MAZARIN, CHARLES ARMAND DE LA PORTE, Duc de
Porte, Henri Horace Roland de la *see* ROLAND DE LA PORTE, HENRI HORACE
Porte, Sébastien de la **3** 609
Porte de Schaerbeek, St Mary's **31** 887
Porte des Comtes Master **31** 209
Portela, Alfonso Sánchez *see* SÁNCHEZ PORTELA, ALFONSO
Portela Fernández-Jardón, César **25** 262*
Port Elizabeth **29** *103*
architecture **29** 105
art school **29** 123
King George VI Art Gallery **29** 121
Law Courts **29** 116
pottery **29** 116
Public Library **29** 105
St Saviour **29** 112
Portelli (da Loro), Carlo **25** 262*; **27** 732
Portengen, Lumen **31** 772
Porter, Allan **31** 660
Porter, Anna Maria **25** 264
Porter, Arthur Kingsley **25** 262–3*; **26** 589
works **31** 671
Porter, Cole **22** 350
Porter, Eliot **9** 494; **25** 263
Porter, Endymion **9** *56*; **10** 363; **19** 582; **25** 263*
Porter, Fairfield **25** 263*; **29** 670
Porter, George **30** 533
Porter, James **25** 263
Porter, Jane **25** 264
Porter, John **17** 806
Porter, Robert Ker **25** 263–4*
collaboration **22** 276
groups and movements **12** 742; **32** 903
reproductive prints by others **5** 733; **28** 86; **32** 156
Porter, Russell **23** 342
Porter, Walsh **14** 145; **25** 264*
Porter, William **20** 664
Portes **5** 894
portes cochère **25** 262*
Port Essington **1** 51, 53
Portete **29** 209
Portfolio, The **14** 106; **24** 423
Portfolio illustratori **24** 449
Port Grimaud **29** 420
Port-Harcourt **23** *129*
library **23** 135
port authority buildings **23** 135
University **23** 135
Porticello **13** 372, 373, 459
Pórtici
Museum **25** 191
Palazzo Reale **5** 671; **30** 887
collections **2** 164
furniture **16** 730
paintings **27** 58
Salottino di porcellana **5** 348; **7** 166; **9** 29; **13** 646; **16** 717, *718*; **23** 544; **32** 88
sculpture **7** 898; **14** 442
Portici, Repubblica di *see* SCUOLA DI RESINA
portico clocks *see under* CLOCKS → types
Portico group **29** 286
porticos **25** 264–8*; **29** 680–82
Argentina **2** *395*
Assyrian **18** 28
England **19** 598; **25** 265, 266, *266*, 267; **33** 10
France **25** 267
Germany **25** 267
Greece, ancient **13** 396; **25** 264; **29** *681*
Islamic **16** 145, 222
Italy **6** *18*; **25** 265
Netherlands, the **12** 748
porticos—cont.
Ottoman **16** 222
Rome, ancient **25** 265; **27** 29; **29** 681–2
Scotland **25** 267
Syria-Palestine **30** 191
Turkey **16** 222
United States of America **25** 267, *267*; **32** *894*
see also DECASTYLE; STOAS
Porticus ad Nationes **27** 32
porticus villas *see under* VILLAS → types
Portielje, Edward **25** 269
Portielje, Gérard **25** 269
Portielje, Jan (Frederik Pieter) **25** 269*
Portier **24** 883
Portier, Robbrecht **10** 704
Portigiani, Domenico **12** 576; **26** 104
Portigiani, Lapo di Pagno *see* LAPO DI PAGNO PORTIGIANI
Portigiani, Pagno di Lapo *see* PAGNO DI LAPO (PORTIGIANI)
Portigiani, Zanobi **12** 576
Portillo, Pedro de **16** 863
Portillos, Alfredo **13** 725
Portimão Church **25** 292
Portinari, Benedetto **21** 103
Portinari, Candido **4** 725; **25** 269*
works **4** 713, 718, *718*, 722; **23** 117, *118*; **28** 920
Portinari, Cândido, Casa-Museu *see under* BRODÓSQUI
Portinari, Lodovico **20** 716
Portinari, Pigello **11** 293; **21** 525
Portinari, Tommaso **25** 269–70*
paintings **3** 553, 612; **4** 920; **12** 845; **16** 659; **21** 101
Portinari Altarpiece **1** 710; **11** 224–5; **12** 845, *845*; **16** 659; **18** 704; **19** 354; **24** 769; **26** 186, 364
Portinho, Carmen **26** 109
Port Keats **1** 51
Portland (Australia) **2** *736*
Portland (Dorset; UK) **21** 568
Portland (Jamaica) **16** 879
Portland (OR; USA) **31** *587*
Art Museum **3** 682; **15** 746; **31** 596
Equitable Building **1** 736
Lovejoy Fountain **11** 346
Portland Public Services Building **7** 386; **9** 705; **25** 359; **28** 835; **31** 598, *598*
Portland (ME; USA), Museum of Art **22** 367; **24** 326
Portland, Henry Bentinck, 1st Duke of *see* BENTINCK, HENRY, 1st Duke of Portland
Portland, Margaret Bentinck, 2nd Duchess of *see* BENTINCK, MARGARET, 2nd Duchess of Portland
Portland, Richard Weston, 1st Earl of *see* WESTON, RICHARD, 1st Earl of Portland
Portland, William Cavendish-Bentinck, 4th Duke of *see* CAVENDISH-BENTINCK, WILLIAM, 4th Duke of Portland
Portland, William Henry Cavendish-Bentinck, 3rd Duke of *see* CAVENDISH-BENTINCK, WILLIAM HENRY, 3rd Duke of Portland
Portland, William John Cavendish-Bentinck, Duke of *see* CAVENDISH-BENTINCK, WILLIAM JOHN, Duke of Portland
Portland cement *see under* CEMENT → types
Portland stone *see under* LIMESTONE → types
Portland Vase **10** 58; **12** 787, *787*; **24** 330; **26** 861; **27** 74, 76
acquisition **4** 567; **5** 337; **6** 118; **14** 114
copies **10** 320; **26** 227
Port Louis **21** 573
Port Lympne **5** 688
Portman, John (Calvin) **2** 316; **25** 270–71*
works **2** 694; **5** 42; **8** 821; **12** 794; **14** 788, *788*; **25** 657
Port-Marly Hôtel de Ville **9** 175
Portmeirion (Gwynedd) **32** 784; **33** 208, *208*
Portmore, David Colyear, 1st Earl of *see* COLYEAR, DAVID, 1st Earl of Portmore
Port Moresby **24** *64*
Port Natal *see* DURBAN
Porto *see* OPORTO
Porto, A. **12** 633
Porto, Alessandro da **25** 271
Porto, António Silva *see* SILVA PORTO ANTÓNIO (CARVALHO DA)
Porto, Battista da **29** 85
Porto, Giovanni Battista del **10** 477
Porto, Giuseppe da *see* PORTO, ISEPPO DA
Porto, Iseppo da **23** 863; **25** 271
Porto, Paolo da **25** 271
Porto, Saverio **12** 586
Porto, Severiano (Mário Vieira de Magalhães) **4** 714; **25** 272*
Porto, Simone da, Canon **25** 271
Porto Alegre **4** *705*
Museu de Arte do Rio Grande do Sul **4** 727
Porto Alegre, Manuel de Araújo **4** 711, 717, 728; **13** 295
Portobello Pottery **28** 257, 258
Portobelo **23** *902*, 903
Royal Treasury **23** 903
Santiago de Gloria castle **23** 903
Santiago fortress **23** 903
S Felipe castle **23** 903
S Fernando fortress **23** 903
S Jerónimo fortress **23** 903
Portocarrero, René **8** 233, 236; **25** 272*
patrons and collectors **31** 758
works **18** 834
Porto Cheli *see* HALIEIS
Porto Ferro **27** 834
Portofino, S Fruttuoso di Capodimonte **26** 576
Port of Spain **31** *330*, 334
12 Queen's Park West **31** 335
Archbishop's House **31** 335
Cathedral of the Immaculate Conception **31** 334
free-style museum **31** 335
General Hospital **31** 334
Government House **31** 335
Hayes Court **31** 335
Holy Trinity Cathedral **31** 334
houses **31** 338
Mille Fleurs **31** 335
National Museum and Art Gallery **31** 339, 340
Queen's Park Hotel **31** 335
Queen's Royal College **31** 335
Red House *see* Government House
Rhand Credit Union Headquarters **31** 335
Roman Catholic Cathedral *see* Cathedral of the Immaculate Conception
Rosary Church **31** 335
Royal Victoria Institute *see* National Museum and Art Gallery
Union Club **31** *334*, 335
Portogallo, Luís João di *see* LUÍS JOÃO DI PORTOGALLO
Portogallo, S Andrea
catafalques **11** *276*
Portoghesi, Paolo **25** 272–3*
works **16** 650, 651; **25** *272*
writings **10** 213; **25** 359
Portois, Juliaan **3** 606
works **3** *607*
Portois & Fix **10** 722; **30** 885
Portolan charts *see under* MAPS → types
Portolli **31** 256
Portomarín, S Juan **29** 263
El Portón **27** 607
Portonaccio Group **10** 588
Porto Novo **1** *386*
Great Mosque **3** 728
Musée Ethnographique Alexandre Sènou Adande **3** 728
Musée Honmè **3** 728
Porto Rico *see* PUERTO RICO
Porto Torres, S Gavino **16** 625; **27** 836
Portoviejo **9** *709*
portrait heads *see* SCULPTURE → types → reserve heads
portraits **6** 76; **9** 244; **19** 315; **25** 273–87*
historical and regional traditions
Africa **1** 267–71*
Akan **1** 268
Bamileke **1** 269
Bangwa **1** 269
Baule **1** 269
Belgium **3** 559–60
Bembe **1** 269
Benin, Kingdom of **1** 268, 270
Benin Republic **1** 267
Buddhism **6** 811, 812; **17** 131*, 132*; **18** 308–9
Burkina Faso **1** 267
Byzantine **9** 622, 628
Cameroon **1** 269
China **6** 811, 812, 813–14, 824
Côte d'Ivoire **1** 267
Dan (Africa) **1** 267
Denmark **8** 731
Early Christian (*c.* AD 250–843) **9** 622
Edo (Africa) **1** 268
Fon **1** 267, 268, 270
Hemba **1** 269
Hungary **15** 13
Ibibio **1** 268
Ijo **1** 267
Indian subcontinent **15** 206, 231–2*
Gupta **15** 231
Kushana **15** 231
Mughal **15** 231–2
Pahari **15** 232
Rajput **15** 232
Italy **20** 509
Japan **17** 131*, 132*
Kongo **1** 269
Korea **18** 308–9
Kuba (iii) (Zaïre) **1** 268
Liberia **1** 267
Madagascar **1** 269
Nigeria **1** 267, 268
Oron **1** 267
Rome, ancient **22** 686; **26** 860–61, 862
Yoruba **1** 267, 268, 269
Zaïre **1** 268, 269
media
amber **1** 761
aquatints **16** *905*
cameos **5** 518*; **17** 522
England **10** *345*
Indian subcontinent **15** *702*
Rome, ancient **14** II2
coins **7** 537; **25** 277
Achaemenid **1** 117
Byzantine **9** *636*
Greece, ancient **13** 587, 588*, 589
Indian subcontinent **15** 231
Italy **6** 147
Rome, ancient **25** 650; **27** 96–7, *96*

portraits
media
coins—cont.
Seleucid **28** 383
drawings
Austria **8** *503*
Belgium **8** *1*; **9** *481*; **25** *284*
England: Baroque **2** *314*
England: Renaissance **9** *273*; **10** *247*; **14** *672*
England: 16th cent. **33** *720*
England: 17th cent. **10** *757*
England: 18th cent. **26** *345*
England: 20th cent. **17** *607*
France **7** 462
France: Impressionism **25** *278*
France: Renaissance **7** *463*
France: 17th cent. **9** *387*
France: 18th cent. **20** *417*
France: 19th cent. **15** *838*
France: 20th cent **14** *363*; **20** *829*
Germany **9** *428*, *429*; **18** *206*
Indian subcontinent **15** *581*
Ireland **19** *19*
Italy: Baroque **12** *202*
Italy: Renaissance **10** *521*; **21** *449*
Italy: 16th cent. **2** *373*
Italy: 17th cent. **19** *205*
Netherlands, the **12** *880*; **13** *27*; **26** *167*
Poland **33** *456*
Russia **23** *530*
drawings (pastel) **9** 224; **24** 242
France: 18th cent. **18** *842*; **19** *436*; **24** *243*, V
France: 20th cent **24** *244*
Germany: 17th cent. **24** *242*
Switzerland **30** *132*
drypoints **9** *309*
enamel **10** IV1; **17** IV1; **24** 553
engravings **4** 359; **10** 392–3; **30** 853
Belgium **10** 393
Belgium: Baroque **27** *503*
Belgium: Renaissance **33** *169*
Belgium: 17th cent. **14** *503*; **17** *598*
Czech Republic **25** *432*
Denmark **4** *67*; **8** *732*
England **10** 248, 393
France **4** *547*; **9** *9*; **10** 392; **20** *473*
Germany **1** *592*; **18** *47*; **20** *916*
Holy Roman Empire (before 1648) **25** *432*
Italy **3** *207*; **25** *411*
Mexico **10** 393
Netherlands, the **10** 392
United States of America **10** 393; **30** 853
etchings **3** *560*; **19** *349*; **25** *210*; **26** *160*
gem-engraving **12** 250, *257*, 262
glass **10** *319*
lithography **8** *764*; **12** *896*
manuscript illumination **7** 463; **8** *543*; **16** *341*
medallions **28** *242*; **33** *114*
medals **17** 524; **20** 917, 921
England **17** 522; **28** *749*
Germany **17** 522; **28** *191*
Italy **6** *140*; **16** 690; **24** *863*; **29** *408*
miniatures (manuscript illumination) **20** *724*
Belgium **3** *726*
England **5** *641*
France **4** *571*, *572*
Romanesque **5** *641*
miniatures (paintings) **17** 524; **21** 638
Austria **21** *642*
England **14** *761*; **17** 522; **21** *645*
England: Renaissance **14** *545*, *546*; **21** *639*
England: 16th cent. **23** *408*

portraits
media
miniatures (paintings)—cont.
England: 17th cent. **7** *794*
France **21** *641*
painting **5** 34; **9** 14; **26** 740
Albania **15** *103*
Argentina **2** *398*
Austria: Expressionism **28** *89*
Austria: Renaissance **14** *837*
Austria: Rococo **23** *854*
Austria: 19th cent. **1** *774*; **10** *703*
Austria: 20th cent. **18** *197*
Azerbaijan **2** 895–6, *897*
Belarus' **3** 528
Belgium: Baroque **9** *277*, *486*; **17** *653*; **25** *274*, *284*; **27** *289*, *298*
Belgium: Early Netherlandish style **3** *576*; **4** *593*, *921*, *922*; **10** *707*, *708*; **20** *670*, *676*; **21** *104*; **33** *124*
Belgium: Renaissance **18** *6*; **21** *355*; **26** *185*
Belgium: 16th cent. **18** *6*; **25** *280*
Belgium: 17th cent. **7** *833*; **13** *920*; **30** *789*; **32** *703*
Belgium: 19th cent. **3** *614*
Belgium: 20th cent. **10** *411*
Biedermeier **8** 445
Buddhism **5** 120; **17** 184, 230; **30** *830*, 830–31
Byzantine **9** 580, 609, 611, 616, 617
Canada **5** *565*
Carolingian **5** 798
Central Asia, Eastern **6** 304
Chile **6** *596*
China **6** 811–14*, *812*, *813*; **26** *216*
Christianity **25** 650
Czech Republic **8** *391*; **28** *827*
Denmark: Baroque **30** *41*
Denmark: 16th cent. **8** 732
Denmark: 17th cent. **8** 733; **33** *421*
Denmark: 18th cent. **17** *678*
Denmark: 19th cent. **1** *846*; **17** *478*
Denmark: 20th cent. **14** *119*
Early Christian (*c.* AD 250-843) **9** 609, 611, 616, 617
Ecuador **9** 713
Egypt, ancient **10** *197*; **30** V1
England **9** 245; **10** 246–7, 248–50*, 360; **14** 545, 546
England: Aesthetic Movement **33** *139*, *141*
England: Baroque **9** *278*, *281*, *483*; **19** 120–23*, *121*, *122*, *123*; **29** *802*
England: Jacobean style **8** *165*; **9** *277*; **19** *583*; **21** *509*
England: Pre-Raphaelitism **27** *351*
England: Renaissance **10** *246*, *247*, *666*; **14** *669*, *670*, *671*; **22** *64*; **25** *277*; **31** *414*
England: Rococo **8** *833*; **33** *693*
England: 14th cent. **19** *607*
England: 16th cent. **12** *515*; **13** *239*; **26** *80*; **28** *313*; **31** *889*
England: 17th cent. **9** *56*, *482*; **10** *248*; **11** *424*; **14** *806*; **15** *150*; **17** *645*; **25** *280*; **26** *393*
England: 18th cent. **3** *489*; **4** *611*; **7** *796*, *814*; **8** *20*, *26*, *454*; **9** *673*; **11** *427*, *907*, *909*; **14** *114*, *638*, *842*; **18** *143*, *146*, *891*, *892*; **21** *148*; **25** *278*, *283*; **26** *272*, *273*, *274*, *275*, *276*, *277*; **27** *118*, *119*; **29** *31*; **32** *825*

portraits
media
painting—cont.
England: 19th cent. **7** *165*; **9** *290*; **14** *147*, *754*; **18** *893*, *894*; **27** *840*; **33** *257*
England: 20th cent. **2** *712*; **3** *29*; **4** *169*; **17** *608*; **26** *78*
Etruscan **10** 620
Finland **11** 94
France: Baroque **9** *280*; **11** *537*; **18** *788*, *789*; **21** *497*, *498*; **31** *378*
France: Empire style, Second **4** *307*
France: Expressionism **29** *246*
France: Fauvism **5** *529*
France: Gothic **13** *131*; **31** 834
France: Impressionism **8** *619*; **9** *288*
France: Mannerism **7** *465*; **11** *267*; **25** *282*
France: Neo-classicism **8** *556*, *558*; **18** *660*; **19** *67*; **23** *520*; **26** *81*; **32** *585*
France: Post-Impressionism **6** *367*, *370*; **12** *858*
France: Realism **8** *55*; **11** *544*
France: Renaissance **7** *426*, *462*, *866*
France: Rococo **4** *512*; **9** *283*; **25** *275*; **27** *571*
France: Romanticism **8** *646*; **12** *335*, *353*; **13** *691*
France: 15th cent. **20** *733*
France: 16th cent. **11** *400*, *532*; **31** *849*
France: 17th cent. **4** *550*; **6** *435*, *436*, *443*; **20** *473*; **24** *134*; **25** *394*; **26** *349*, *385*
France: 18th cent. **2** *851*; **8** *507*, *866*, *890*; **9** *285*, *302*, *365*, *400*; **11** 539; **18** *576*; **22** *685*; **24** *542*; **25** *670*, *884*; **26** *248*, *387*; **31** *69*; **32** *495*, *496*
France: 19th cent. **4** *303*, *329*; **5** *813*; **10** *797*; **12** *18*; **16** *64*; **18** *866*; **23** *521*; **25** *279*
France: 20th cent **9** *2*, *292*; **14** *330*; **21** *788*; **29** *604*
Germany: Expressionism **3** *479*; **17** *452*; **21** *55*
Germany: Gothic **33** *300*
Germany: Impressionism **19** *335*
Germany: Late Gothic **12** 383; **25** *91*
Germany: Neo-classicism **31** *27*
Germany: Renaissance **1** *763*; **3** *507*; **5** *60*; **9** *431*, *439*; **10** *162*; **14** *665*; **20** *191*; **23** *306*; **25** *274*
Germany: Romanticism **27** *339*, *340*
Germany: 16th cent. **21** *484*; **22** *924*; **26** 408; **33** *85*
Germany: 17th cent. **32** *231*
Germany: 18th cent. **11** *459*; **12** *852*; **19** *111*
Germany: 19th cent. **11** *236*; **22** *101*; **32** *120*
Germany: 20th cent. **10** *869*; **13** *698*; **19** *151*, 335
Gothic: France **13** *131*
Gothic: Germany **33** *300*
Gothic: Late Gothic **12** 383; **25** *91*
Gothic: 14th cent. **13** 131–2; **31** 834
Greece **13** *353*
Holy Roman Empire (before 1648) **28** *377*
Hungary **14** *900*; **25** *246*; **26** *419*
Indian subcontinent: 19th cent. **15** *657*

portraits
media
painting—cont.
Indian subcontinent: Bilaspur **15** *624*
Indian subcontinent: Bundi school **15** *607*
Indian subcontinent: Deccan **15** *637*, 638, *639*, 639–40, *641*
Indian subcontinent: Golconda **15** *641*, 641–2
Indian subcontinent: Islamic **15** 637
Indian subcontinent: Mughal **1** *92*; **3** *92*; **4** *91*; **15** 232, 580, *580*, *586*, 586–7, *587*
Indian subcontinent: Pahari **15** 619, 621, 622, 623, *624*
Indian subcontinent: Rajput **15** 614, *614*
Iran **16** *127*, *536*
Ireland **9** *2*; **16** 13–14, *14*
Islamic **15** 637; **16** *127*, *536*
Italy: Abstraction-Création **25** *447*
Italy: Baroque **3** *382*, *383*; **4** *292*; **9** *477*, *480*; **12** *308*, *660*; **20** *378*; **23** *321*; **25** *285*; **27** *491*; **29** *42*; **30** *40*
Italy: Early Netherlandish style **17** *704*
Italy: Etruscan **10** 620
Italy: Mannerism **3** *202*; **4** *858*; **5** *843*; **11** *187*, *390*, *391*; **12** *669*; **24** *198*; **31** *14*, *42*
Italy: Pittura Metafisica **8** *604*
Italy: Renaissance **2** 180, *181*; **3** *100*, *302*, *657*, *659*, *664*; **4** *284*; **5** *128*, *743*, *820*, 822; **9** *263*; **11** *401*, *700*, *704*; **16** *659*; **19** *183*, *711*, *712*; **21** *16*; **22** *109*, *134*; **24** *863*; **25** *466*, *905*; **26** *817*, *818*; **28** *334*; **31** *741*; **32** *11*, *658*
Italy: Renaissance: Early Renaissance **16** 660
Italy: Renaissance: High Renaissance **16** 665
Italy: Rococo **25** *3*
Italy: 16th cent. **2** *93*, *374*; **5** *852*; **9** *266*; **23** *878*, *879*; **24** *233*
Italy: 17th cent. **8** *274*; **29** *33*
Italy: 18th cent. **12** *560*; **20** 805; **21** *133*; **31** *292*
Italy: 19th cent. **4** 252, *253*; **5** *555*; **21** *624*; **25** *894*
Italy: 20th cent. **11** *397*
Japan **5** 120; **11** 824; **17** 160–61*, *161*, 168, 184, 230, *335*, 750; **18** *503*; **32** *896*
Korea **18** 60, 321–3*, *322*
Maori **23** 59, *59*
Moldova **21** *812*
Netherlands, the: Baroque **1** *658, *807*; **4** *251*; **13** *895*; **14** *92*; **22** *846*; **23** I; **25** *276*; **26** *163*, *169*; **28** *50*
Netherlands, the: Early Netherlandish style **7** *239*
Netherlands, the: Mannerism **17** *924*
Netherlands, the: Post-Impressionism **12** *858*
Netherlands, the: Renaissance **22** *66*, *837*
Netherlands, the: 16th cent. **9** *275*; **16** *831*; **18** *6*; **22** *200*
Netherlands, the: 17th cent. **3** *77*; **9** *193*; **14** *41*, *139*, *289*, *374*; **18** 10, *10*; **20** *80*; **21** *486*, *510*; **22** *95*; **23** *675*; **24** *357*, *377*; **32** *263*, *376*
Netherlands, the: 18th cent. **19** *101*

portraits
media
painting—cont.
Netherlands, the: 19th cent. **22** 848*
New Zealand **23** *59*
Norway **14** *506*; **18** *464*
Peru **24** *508*, 515
Poland: 16th cent. **25** 103; **27** 843
Poland: 17th cent. **25** 104, 105; **31** 323
Poland: 20th cent. **4** *617*
Portugal: 19th cent. **4** *386*; **28** *430*
Romania **13** *652*; **26** 713, *714*
Rome, ancient **27** 50; **30** V1
Russia **27** 387, 388
Russia: Cubism **27** *581*
Russia: Neo-classicism **27** *579*
Russia: Rococo **26** *551*
Russia: Romanticism **18** *75*
Russia: 18th cent. **2** *410*; **19** *279*; **27** *388*
Russia: 19th cent. **4** *421*; **18** *438*; **30** *11*
Russia: 20th cent. **6** *384*; **28** *475*
Scotland **28** 236
Scotland: 18th cent. **25** *843*, *845*, *883*; **28** *234*, *235*, *236*
Scotland: 19th cent. **18** *856*; **24** *569*
Serbia **28** *451*
Sierra Leone **28** *692*
Spain: Baroque **7** *524*; **11** *489*; **14** *9*, *793*; **25** *645*; **32** *128*, *130*, *131*, *134*
Spain: Mannerism **13** *343*, *922*
Spain: Romanticism **10** *513*
Spain: 16th cent. **9** *267*; **24** *23*; **27** *705*
Spain: 17th cent. **5** *875*; **20** *900*; **21** *125*
Spain: 18th cent. **1** *528*; **4** *559*, *563*; **13** *244*; **19** *648*; **25** *286*; **32** *248*
Spain: 19th cent. **13** *245*, *248*; **19** *660*; **20** *59*
Sweden **18** *802*; **21** *511*; **27** *169*; **30** 77–8, *524*; **33** *705*
Sweden: 17th cent. **11** *468*
Sweden: 18th cent. **11** *470*, *471*
Switzerland **14** *667*; **21** *153*; **30** *135*; **33** *82*
Tibet **30** *830*, 830–31
Turkey **19** *436*
United States of America: Cubism **14** *204*
United States of America: 17th cent. **20** *677*; **23** *45*
United States of America: 18th cent. **7** *809*; **11** *496*, *497*; **24** *302*; **29** *805*; **31** *600*
United States of America: 19th cent. **9** *289*, *500*, *501*; **23** *765*; **24** *301*; **29** *918*
United States of America: 20th cent. **13** *11*; **25** *167*; **26** *430*
Venezuela **32** 178
Wales **32** *785*
photography **7** *294*; **24** 646, 648, 649, 650, 651, 656, 658, 659–62*, 667, 671, 672; **25** 276, 279, 281, 282, 283
Africa **1** *226*
Côte d'Ivoire **1** *226*
England **30** *270*; **33** *309*
England: 19th cent. **24** *655*
France **22** *424*; **24** *660*, *661*
Indian subcontinent **15** 232
Iran **25** 770
Japan **17** *426*; **22** *445*
Kuba (iii) (Zaïre) **10** *579*
Native North Americans **8** *537*; **10** *578*
Portugal **4** *639*

portraits
media
photography—cont.
Russia 24 675
Scotland 14 539
United States of America
2 315; 24 659, 671; 29 601
plaster 29 814
porcelain 33 377
postage stamps 25 328
pottery 21 752–3
prints 17 278, 285; 25 605–6*
relief sculpture
Egypt, ancient 9 882
Germany 24 807
Indian subcontinent 15 233
Italy 12 542; 13 911
United States of America
27 557
sculpture 14 869
Africa 1 354–5
Austria 2 799, 800
Belgium 21 499
Benin, Kingdom of 1 354
Buddhism 6 718; 17 36,
130–32*; 18 295
Buddhism: Japan 17 130
Byzantine 9 587, 587
Cambodia 5 496, 497
Celtic 6 158
China 6 718
Croatia 21 316
Cyprus, ancient 8 342, 342
Czech Republic 6 158; 9 81
Early Christian (c. AD 250-843)
9 587
Egypt, ancient 1 770, 793;
2 659; 9 875, 889; 28 492
England 4 79; 11 238; 29 564;
30 499
England: 18th cent. 33 4
Etruscan 10 608, 608–9
France 4 661; 7 450;
11 561–2*; 24 137
France: Neo-classicism 11 561
France: 19th cent. 4 458;
6 468
Germany 13 679; 18 420;
28 42
Germany: Gothic 9 257;
22 264, 692
Gothic 2 483; 5 204; 9 257;
18 420; 22 264, 692
Greece, ancient 5 298; 13 429,
451, 454, 465–6, 604; 14 70;
25 576
Indian subcontinent
15 232–4*, 540, 737–8
Indonesia 15 780
Italy: Baroque 11 189
Italy: Etruscan 10 608
Italy: Gothic 2 483
Italy: Neo-Classicism 3 295
Italy: Renaissance 16 690;
19 202
Italy: Roman 27 21
Italy: 16th cent. 16 749
Italy: 17th cent. 7 842
Japan 17 36, 130–32*
Japan: Buddhism 17 130
Java 15 780
Korea 18 295
Kuba (iii) (Zaïre) 1 354–5
Maya 25 825
Mesoamerica, Pre-Columbian
18 675; 21 222; 25 825
Mexico 18 675
Nepal 22 755
New Zealand 33 374
Norway 21 478
Olmec 23 417
Portugal 1 742; 19 893
Prehistoric art 9 81
Rome, ancient 7 642; 9 20;
10 428; 27 19, 41–2
Rome, ancient: Antonine
27 39

portraits
media
sculpture—cont.
Rome, ancient: Augustan
27 31
Rome, ancient: Constantinian
27 11, 20–21*, 44, 45
Rome, ancient: Flavian 27 34
Rome, ancient: Hadrianic
27 37
Rome, ancient: Italy 27 23
Rome, ancient: Julio-Claudian
27 33, 34
Rome, ancient: Republican
27 29
Rome, ancient: Tetrarchs
27 43
Rome, ancient: Trajanic 27 35
Seleucid 28 384
Spain 5 204; 20 68
Syria-Palestine 30 181
Turkey 9 587; 10 428; 14 70
Zapotec 18 675
seals 9 637; 25 277
silhouettes 28 713–14
silverpoints 26 156
stamps 25 277
tapestries 31 757
waxes 16 749
woodcuts
Czech Republic 13 913
Germany 13 903; 33 290
Italy 32 19
United States of America
4 476
techniques
tracing 24 659
types
artists' 10 204; 23 379; 30 499
author portraits 2 835–6*; 9 609,
610; 25 676
Byzantine 2 836; 9 605; 20 I
Carolingian 2 836; 5 801, 802;
30 166, 487
Early Christian (c. AD 250-843)
2 836
England 20 341
Germany 5 802
Insular art 4 343
Romanesque 20 341; 26 662
busts see BUSTS
cabinet 24 648
donor 15 233, 233, 234; 25 277
double 10 513, 709; 17 653;
21 484
equestrian 14 869
Evangelist portraits see author
portraits
full-length 10 709; 25 685
group 7 294
Austria 1 774
Belgium 7 833; 23 758; 27 298
Canada 5 565
Czech Republic 28 827
Denmark 14 119
England: Baroque 19 121
England: Rococo 8 833
England: 17th cent. 17 645
England: 18th cent. 11 427;
19 584; 21 148; 26 274;
28 870
England: 19th cent. 30 270
France: Baroque 9 280;
18 788
France: 18th cent. 25 670
France: 19th cent. 15 838
Germany 13 904; 27 339, 340
Italy: Early Netherlandish style
17 704
Italy: 16th cent. 5 852; 9 266
Italy: 19th cent. 25 894
Netherlands, the 14 93
Netherlands, the: Baroque
1 658, 807; 13 895; 26 169
Netherlands, the: Mannerism
17 924
Netherlands, the: Renaissance
22 837

portraits
types
group—cont.
Netherlands, the: 15th cent.
4 592
Netherlands, the: 16th cent.
1 806; 9 275; 13 26
Netherlands, the: 17th cent.
14 41
Netherlands, the: 19th cent.
26 369–70
Poland 25 104
Portugal 4 386; 28 430
Spain 4 559; 13 245; 19 648;
20 900
Switzerland 21 153
United States of America
24 302, 739
Wales 32 785
imagines maiorum 27 50
Kit-cat 18 96–7
medallion 30 487
mummy portraits 29 814; 30 V1
nisee 13 213
self-portraits 1 662, 663
African American art 1 440
Belgium 3 726; 9 486; 20 676
Czech Republic 24 190
Denmark 17 678
England 17 611
England: Gothic 33 200
England: 16th cent. 23 407
England: 18th cent. 9 673;
14 638; 25 210; 26 345
England: 20th cent. 17 607
Estonia 10 539
France: Neo-classicism 32 585
France: 17th cent. 9 9; 25 394
France: 18th cent. 9 365;
18 576, 842; 24 243; 32 496
France: 19th cent. 8 764
France: 20th cent 14 330
Germany: Expressionism
3 479; 18 206
Germany: Gothic 18 420
Germany: Impressionism
19 335
Germany: Renaissance 9 429,
429, 431; 24 807
Germany: 19th cent. 11 236;
32 120
Germany: 20th cent. 9 309;
19 151
Gothic 18 420; 33 200
Greece, ancient 13 546
Hungary 25 246
Indian subcontinent 8 543
Ireland 19 19
Italy: Baroque 12 308; 20 378;
32 191
Italy: Mannerism 24 198
Italy: Renaissance 12 542;
32 19
Italy: 16th cent. 2 93, 373
Italy: 17th cent. 27 150
Italy: 18th cent. 12 534;
21 133; 29 889
Italy: 19th cent. 21 624
Japan 28 494
Korea 18 322
Netherlands, the: Baroque
22 846; 26 160
Netherlands, the: 17th cent.
3 77; 9 193; 25 731
Norway 22 293
Pakistan 23 800
Poland 4 617; 33 456
Romania 26 714
Russia 6 384; 23 530
Scotland 24 569
Spain 13 248; 20 58; 32 248
Sweden 18 802; 33 705
Switzerland 33 82
United States of America
13 11; 24 301; 25 167
three-quarter 2 217
tronie 26 152, 154
see also CARICATURES

Portraits of Princes, Master of the
20 716, 747*; 22 535
works 4 922
Port Royal 16 878
architecture 16 882
furniture 16 885
pewter 16 888; 24 580
pottery 16 887
ports 26 864; 31 718
Port Said 9 765
Portsmouth (Dominica), Fort
Shirley Museum 2 154
Portsmouth (Hants; UK) 21 569
docks 9 58
fortifications 21 548
St Philip 28 296
Town Hall 31 241
Portsmouth (NH; USA)
Assembly House 2 618
MacPheadris-Warner House
4 786
Portsmouth, Isaac Newton
Wallop, 5th Earl of see WALLOP,
ISAAC NEWTON, 5th Earl of
Portsmouth
Portsmouth, Louise-Renée de
Kerouaile, Duchess of see
KEROUALLE, LOUISE-RENÉE
DE, Duchess of Portsmouth
Port Sunlight (Merseyside) 12 144;
19 270; 31 725
Lady Lever Art Gallery 6 605;
7 659; 10 371; 19 270
Portuense, Francisco Vieira see
VIEIRA PORTUENSE, FRANCISCO
Portugal 15 58–60; 25 287–320*,
288
agate 25 312
alabaster (gypsum) 6 452
altars 30 881
aqueducts 10 165
architecture 4 790; 19 865;
25 171, 288–94*; 29 452
Brazil 4 709
brick 4 784–5*
Byzantine 18 390
Cistercian Order 25 289
Gothic 3 362; 13 70–71*;
25 289–90
Indian subcontinent 15 401;
25 292
Manueline style 13 71;
20 325–6*; 25 290–91*
military 21 572*
Romanesque 25 289
Sri Lanka 29 452*
Uruguay 7 614–15; 31 752
art history 25 319–20*
barges 3 233
bastions 2 501
beds 3 484
bookbindings 17 566*, 567
brass 25 306
brazil-wood 25 315
brick 4 784–5*, 790
bridges 10 106; 25 293
bronze 19 893
cabinets (ii) (furniture) 25 305,
306
camphor 25 309
carpets 25 316
cartography 26 125; 32 98
castles 28 499
cathedrals 19 462; 22 533;
32 616
cedar 25 304, 305
centrepieces 25 313
ceramics 25 308–11*
chairs 25 304, 305, 306, 307, 307
chandeliers 25 303
chapels 3 362, 362; 6 43
chestnut 25 303
chests 25 303, 304, 306
choir-stalls 25 305
churches 19 866
Baroque 2 189; 13 751; 25 292;
28 911
basilicas 20 85
centrally planned 7 257

Portugal
churches—cont.
Gothic 25 289; 31 102
Mannerism 10 664
Manueline style 4 245
Neo-classicism 4 629
Romanesque 25 289
16th cent. 2 500; 30 518;
31 179
17th cent. 1 740
cloisters 25 290; 31 178
coats of arms 14 409, 410
coins 7 537, 538; 29 469
collections 25 317–19*
commodes 25 306–7
confessionals 7 703
copper 13 166
copperas 25 315
coral 25 312
cupboards 25 304, 305
dealers 25 317–18*
desks 25 304
diamonds 25 314
dining-rooms 25 304
dolls 31 261
domes 20 85
doors 18 783
drawings 14 661; 27 803;
28 432; 32 157
dyes 25 315
earrings 25 314
ebony 25 305
education (art) 25 319*
architecture 25 319
embroidery 25 316*
enamel 25 312
façades 25 186
faience (ii) (ceramics) 19 468;
25 309, 309–10*
filigree 25 314
fortifications 21 551, 572; 25 291
fortresses 29 452
forts 1 318; 21 572
furniture 25 303, 304–8*; 29 470
gardens 12 124–5*, 125
botanic 12 125
jardins à la française 26 471
glass 25 311*
glazes 25 309
gold 25 312–14*; 32 406
guilds 25 312
hardstones 25 314
headboards 25 305
heraldry 14 404, 410*
historiography 25 319–20*
hotels 25 294
houses 25 292
indigo 25 315
inlays 25 306
interior decoration 25 303,
303–4*
iron 13 166; 22 14
ivory 25 303, 305, 314
jade 16 861
japanning 25 306
jewellery 25 314
juniper 25 304
kaolin 25 311
kermes 25 315
knitting 18 157
lace 25 316, 317*
lacquer 25 314
lanterns (architecture) 10 664
lead 25 309
leather 19 4; 25 306
libraries 25 319*
limestone 13 101
liturgical objects 25 313
log-wood 25 315
mahogany 25 305, 307
manuals (architecture) 28 433
manuscript illumination 17 562*;
20 325; 25 295
marble 1 742; 28 913
marks 25 307, 312, 313
marquetry 20 468; 25 306, 307
mausolea 13 71
metal 25 305
metalwork 13 166*; 26 690*

Portugal—cont.
monasteries **1** *590*; **7** *531*; **31** *179*
monstrances **25** 312; **32** *406*
monuments **19** 893
museums **25** 318–19*
necklaces **25** *314*
nude figures **27** *615*; **28** *913*
oak **25** 303
objects of vertu **25** 314*
orders (chivalry) **7** 179
painting **25** 295–300*
allegorical **25** *298*
conversation pieces **28** 431
genre **4** *387*; **28** *736*
murals **22** 333; **25** *299*
mythological **27** *615*; **32** *425*
Prehistoric **25** 511
religious **10** *901*; **19** *655*; **25** *297*; **32** *424*
still-lifes **29** 668
15th cent. **12** *890*, *891*
17th cent. **8** 11
palaces
Baroque **28** *912*
Neo-classicism **23** *453*
Rococo **23** *405*
16th cent. **28** *780*
18th cent. **20** *402*
patronage **1** 241; **25** 317*
pattern books **25** 306
periodicals **24** 453*
photoarchives **25** 319*
plaster **29** 841–2*
plates **25** *309*
polychromy **25** 171
porcelain **25** 303, 309–11*, *311*
portals **6** *451*; **23** *453*
portraits **14** 660
group **4** *386*; **28** *430*
painting **4** *386*; **28** *430*
photography **4** *639*
sculpture **1** *742*; **19** *893*
pottery **25** 308–10*; **31** 261
blue-and-white ware **4** 175*
creamware **25** 310
tin-glazed ware **25** 309; **30** 875
promenades **27** 803
quartz **25** 314, *314*
ramps **12** 124
retables **6** *452*; **26** 252–4*; **32** 156
Rococo **26** *253*
15th cent. **25** *296*
16th cent. **7** 521
rock art **25** 475, 480
rock crystal **25** 312
rose-wood **25** *306*, 307, *307*
satin-wood **25** 307
sculpture **25** 300–302*
Gothic **13** *101*, 101–2*, 124–5*; **25** *301*
Indian subcontinent **15** 542
marble **1** *742*; **28** *913*
Neo-classicism **1** *741*
religious **6** *451*
Romanesque **26** 611*, 648*
stone **13** 101–2*; **26** 611*
wood **13** 124–5*; **26** 648*
20th cent. **25** *302*
shells **25** 306, 314
shields **14** 405, 410
shrines (i) (cult) **25** 303
sideboards **25** 304
silk **25** 315
silver **25** 303, 312–14*, *314*
silver-gilt **13** 166; **25** *313*
sissoo **25** 303, 305
squares (town) **19** *465*; **27** *800*
stained glass **13** 192*; **25** 311
stone **13** 101–2*; **26** 611*
stonewares **23** 455
stucco **29** 841–2*
synagogues **17** 545
tables **25** *303*, 307
talha **17** 595–6; **25** 303; **26** 252, 253; **30** 799
tapestries **25** 316–17*
teak **25** 303, 305
teapots **25** *311*
textiles **25** 315–17*
Portugal—cont.
theories (architectural) **26** 515
theories (art) **14** 660, 662
theosophy **28** 729
tiles **3** 222, *815*; **25** 288, 292, 303, 309; **30** 879–82*, *880*
tombs **13** *101*; **25** 511
towers **3** *534*
trade **3** 719; **6** 622; **15** 200
ceramics **6** 331; **7** 165
faience (ii) (ceramics) **25** 309, 310
furniture **15** 693; **19** 592
iron **17** 318
lacquer **18** 613
porcelain **4** 175; **6** 622, 918
quilts **15** 722
textiles **7** 53; **17** 315
tiles **30** 880
transfer (printing) **25** 310
treatises (painting) **14** 660
tulip-wood **25** 307
tureens **19** *468*
universities **7** 531
urban planning **19** *465*; **25** 186
vaults (ceiling) **9** 104; **22** 14
verandahs **32** 240
vestments (ecclesiastical) **25** 316
walnut **25** 306
woad **25** 315
women artists **25** 316
wood **13** 124–5*; **25** 303; **26** 648*
wood-carvings **32** 535, *536*
wool **25** 315
writing-boxes **25** 304
Portugal, Fadrique de, Bishop of Sigüenza *see* FADRIQUE DE PORTUGAL, Bishop of Sigüenza
Portugal, Pedro Fernández de Castro Andrade y, Conde de Lemos *see* LEMOS, Conde de
Portugal Futurista **27** 786
Portugallo, Alvaro *see* ALVARO PORTUGALLO
Portugalois, Eduart **21** 352
Português, Eduardo 'o *see* EDUARDO 'O PORTUGUÊS
Português, Simão 'o *see* SIMÃO 'O PORTUGUÊS
Portus **23** 619, 620, 621
Port-Vendres **32** 769
Portway, Douglas **29** 109
Portwood, George **29** 532
Portzamparc, Christian de **11** 528; **13** 716; **25** 320–21*
Porumbák
glass **15** 3, *3*
Porus, King *see* PARRAS, King
Porvoo **11** *87*
Cathedral **4** 781; **11** 87, 107
gold **11** 108
Jakkorila Manor **11** *102*
Porzello, Alberto **1** 588
Posada, José Guadalupe **21** 386; **25** 321*
works **25** 244, *321*; **27** 872
Posch, Leonhard **3** 804; **18** 89; **25** 322*; **32** 682
Poschinger, Benedikt von **26** 374
Poschinger, Ferdinand von **8** 885
Poschinger glass factory **12** 441
Poschmann, George **12** 452
Pose, Severino **31** 755
Poseidonia *see* PAESTUM
Posen *see* POZNAŃ
Posener, Jill **12** 219
Pošepná, Bozena **8** 420
Posey, Willi **26** 410
Posi, Paolo **25** 322–3*
pupils **24** 757; **25** 790
restorations **26** 794
works **12** 914; **25** 410
Posidonius **29** 694
Posillipo, Scuola di *see* SCUOLA DI POSILLIPO
Positano, Duca di **25** 55
positives, photographic *see* PHOTOGRAPHIC POSITIVES
Poskochin, S. **27** 410
Posnansky, Arturo **4** 260; **18** 777
Posno, J. **30** 871
Posnovis *see* UNOVIS
Posokhin, Mikhail (Vasil'yevich) **25** 323*
collaboration **25** 89
works **1** 126; **22** 174, 175, 181; **27** 380, 381
Pospíšil, Joža **28** 855
Possada, St Onufrius **25** 344
Possagno
Gipsoteca Canoviana **5** 631; **16** 775; **25** 268; **28** 35
temple **5** 630–31
Possamani, Giovanni **27** 788
Posse, Gustaf **2** 730
Possenti, Alessandro Benedetto **5** 872
Possenti, Pier Giuseppe **5** 872
Possevino, Antonio **4** 21; **25** 323*
Possibilities **24** 428, 433
Possil Pottery **28** 258
Pössneck **30** 793
Possoz, Milly **28** 781
Possum, Gabriel **25** 324
Possum, Michelle **25** 324
possum skins *see under* SKINS → types
Possum Tjapaltjarri, Clifford **1** 64; **25** 324*
collaboration **19** 258
works **1** *64*
Post, Chandler R(athfon) **25** 327*; **31** 672
Post, Frans (Jansz.) **4** 715; **13** 895; **25** 324, 325–7*
patrons and collectors **4** 725, 726
reproductions in tapestry **12** 829
reproductive prints by others **4** 868
works **2** 105; **4** 715, 724; **14** 95; **22** 536, 840; **25** *326*; **26** 65
Post, George B(rowne) **5** 274; **23** 42; **25** 327–8*; **26** 338
collaboration **12** 643; **23** 42; **28** 831
pupils **26** 468
works **10** 683; **23** 40; **28** 830; **30** 505
Post, Herbert **14** 620
Post, Jan Jansz. **25** 324
Post, J. Otis **25** 327
Post, Maurits **25** 324, 327*
works **22** 536; **23** 466; **29** 7
Post, Pieter (Jansz.) **19** 543; **22** 824, 826, 840; **25** 324–7*
collaboration **2** 385; **10** 660; **14** 635; **15** 40; **27** 509
patrons and collectors **14** 45; **20** 459
pupils **25** 327
works **4** 614, 786; **5** 543; **8** 666; **9** 179; **10** *659*; **13** 222; **14** 38, *38*, 39; **19** 100, 862; **22** 536, 825, 859; **23** 465, 492; **25** *325*; **27** 230; **32** 255, 551
Post, Theodor **31** 452
Post, William Stone **25** 327
postage stamps **10** 396; **25** 328–9*, *329*
post-and-lintel construction *see* ARCHITECTURE → techniques → trabeated construction
post-and-plank construction *see under* ARCHITECTURE → techniques
Postavy *see* PASTAVY
Post-Byzantine **25** 329–44*
churches **18** *207*
iconography **7** 222–3*
icons **8** 157, *909*; **25** 331–2*, *332*, 333–4*, *333*, 337–41*, *337*, *339*; **27** *385*, *386*
Madonneri **25** 331
manuals (painting) **25** 330, 340
painting **8** 156; **25** 330
wall **25** *330*, 334–6*, *335*, 342–4*, *342*
reliquaries **26** 149*
Post-Byzantine—cont.
see also BYZANTINE
postcards *see under* CARDS → types
Postel, Guillaume **10** 636
Postel Church **3** 541
Postel de Leopolski, Wilhelm *see* LEOPOLSKI, WILHELM
poster **25** 349
posterns **21** 547
poster paint *see under* PAINTS → types
posters **2** 372; **7** 650–56; **10** 419; **24** 662, 671; **25** 345–55*, 623, 652
conservation **2** 366
historical and regional traditions
Austria **19** 69, *485*; **25** 350; **32** *446*
Belgium **2** 510; **25** 347
Britain **7** 652, *652*, 653; **25** 347, 351, *353*, 354
Cuba (Caribbean) **25** 354
England **10** *877*
feminism **10** *877*
France **7** 652; **25** 345–7, 349–50
Art à la Rue **2** 510; **25** *346*
Art Nouveau **22** *252*
19th cent. **6** 550, *550*; **25** *347*; **31** *214*
20th cent. **25** *348*, *350*
Germany **7** *651*; **25** 348, *349*, 350, 652, *652*
Hungary **25** 348
India, Republic of **15** 177
Italy **7** *656*; **25** 348
Nazism **25** 352, 652, *652*
Netherlands, the **7** 655, *655*; **25** 347, 348
Poland **25** 108, 354, 355
Russia **7** *654*; **25** 349, 351, *351*; **26** *505*; **27** 394, 396
Suprematism **19** *475*
20th cent. **20** *887*
Spain **25** 348
Switzerland **25** 351, *354*
United States of America **7** 652; **25** 347, 352, *352*, *353*, *651*, 652
techniques
lithography **19** *475*, 488; **25** 345, *346*, *347*, *348*, *349*, *350*, *351*, *352*, *353*, *354*; **32** *446*
mass production **25** 345
photography **25** 345, 349, 352
photolithography **25** 345
photomontages **25** 352
screenprinting **25** 345
uses
décollage **8** 608
see also COMMERCIAL ART; SOUVENIRS
Posthumus, Hermann **4** 207
Posthumus Meyjes, Christian Bernardus, the elder (1859–1922) **25** 355*
Posthumus Meyjes, Christian Bernardus, the younger (*b* 1893) **25** 355
postiches **25** 355*
postici *see* OPISTHODOMOI
Postiglione, Raffaele **21** 495
Post-Impressionism **7** 630; **10** 693; **11** 315; **18** 717; **25** 355–8*
art forms
drawings **5** *922*
frames **11** 418–19
nude figures **23** 295, 296
painting
England **10** *256*; **19** *590*
France **6** *368*, *369*, *370*, *373*; **7** *675*; **25** *357*; **29** *669*; **31** *213*, *215*, *216*
Netherlands, the **7** *674*, III1; **12** *859*, *861*
portraits
France **6** *367*; **12** *858*
Netherlands, the **12** *858*
Post-Impressionism
art forms—cont.
woodcuts **25** *583*
collections **2** 561; **3** 251; **8** 62
exhibitions **5** 516; **10** 255, 680; **19** *590*; **31** 605
England **10** 547; **18** 668; **32** 753
regional traditions
Australia **8** 2
Britain **25** 358*
England **4** 168; **14** 107
France **6** 366; **25** 356–7*; **28** 340, 342
Netherlands, the **25** 358*
Poland **17** 804
Spain **21** 700
Postl, Karel **20** 252; **25** 358*
Postle, Denis **24** 34
Postma, Laurika **4** 155
Post-Minimalism **6** 23; **25** 645
Post-modernism **7** 385–6; **14** 841; **15** 880; **21** 777; **22** 743; **25** 358–60*; **26** 743
art forms
architecture **14** 581; **25** 359*
England **19** *578*
France **4** *228*; **11** *527*, 528
Italy **16** 651*; **25** *272*, 273
United States of America **17** *621*; **25** *359*
painting **25** 360*, *360*
regional traditions
France **4** 227
United States of America **30** 869
Post-Nagybánya school *see* GRESHAM GROUP
Postnik **22** 169, 184; **25** 681
works **22** *184*
Post Office (UK) **25** 353
Postojna Museum **28** 863
Postolaki, I. N. **21** 812
Post-painterly Abstraction **1** 79; **11** 706; **19** 725; **25** 360–61*
collections **21** 135
England **10** 258
United States of America **23** 184; **29** *622*; **31** 608
Postružnik, Oton **9** 672
posts **1** *47*, 47–8; **16** 45, *45*; **22** 572
see also CIPPI
postscaenia **30** 652
post seats *see under* CHAIRS → types
Post-structuralism **14** 459; **25** 361–2*
Post-Surrealism **31** 607
Postuma, Sergia *see* SERGIA POSTUMA
Postumus, Emperor of Rome (*reg* 260-69) **27** 97
posture **33** 462
posubans **1** 314
Pot, Hendrik (Gerritsz.) **13** 895; **22** 840; **25** 362–3*
pupils **23** 831
works **7** 785
Pot, Jean Le *see* LE POT, JEAN
Pot, Thomas **6** 467
Pota, Ljube **19** 883
Potain, Nicolas-Marie **25** 363*; **26** 551
works **24** 122, *122*
Potamia **8** 342
Potamies **8** 156
Potamos **18** 570
potash
enamel **10** 192
glass **10** 315; **12** 438, 439, 781; **29** 497; **30** 407
glazes **6** 329; **16** 394
potassium **7** 82; **10** 55; **24** 791
potassium-argon dating *see under* DATING METHODS → types
potassium bichromate **7** 575; **24** 648, 649, 659; **33** 1
potassium bromide **24** 649, 656
potassium carbonate **12** 781; **18** 655
potassium chloride **10** 548

potassium dichlorate 10 548
potassium ferricyanide 24 650
potassium iodide 24 648, 649
potassium oxalate 24 655
potassium oxide 6 872, 873
potassium permanganate 33 1
potassium sulphate 29 813
Potawatomi 22 552, 627
Potekhin, Pavel 23 615
Potel, M. 9 371
Potelich 31 557
  Church of the Holy Spirit 31 550, 558
Potémont, Adolphe Martial *see* MARTIAL POTÉMONT, ADOLPHE(-THÉODORE-JULES)
Poterat, Edmé 11 605; 27 248
Poterat, Louis 11 605, 607; 27 248
Poterat, Michel 11 605
Pothos Painter 13 524
Pothoven, Hendrik 14 42, 795; 22 846; 25 363*
  teachers 8 888
Potier, Antoine-Julien 8 123
Potier, Bernard 4 865
Potier, Jean 21 68
Potier & Stymus 31 621
potlatch 22 562, 565
pot-lids 18 222
Potlogi 26 722
pot-metal glass *see under* GLASS → types
Potocianum Museum 25 139
Potocka, Elżbieta 18 693
Potocki (family) 18 691; 25 138
Potocki, Aleksander, Count 17 832; 20 396
Potocki, Alfred 25 138, 364
Potocki, Anna, Countess 20 396
Potocki, Artur (1787-1832) 24 388; 25 136, 364*
Potocki, Artur (*fl c.* 1870) 5 80
Potocki, Franciszek Salezy 25 363*
Potocki, Mikołaj 25 364*
Potocki, Oskar 5 79
Potocki, Roman 18 693
Potocki, Stanisław Kostka 25 106, 136, 141, 364*; 32 881
  architecture 25 99
  books 25 142
  collections 25 138, 139
  sponsorship 1 482
  works 25 139
  writings 25 143
Potocki, Szczęsny 25 136
Potocki, Wincenty 25 138, 139, 364*
Potosí 4 255, *255*, 265, 267; 25 364–6*, *365*
  Academia Man Césped 4 269; 25 366
    see also Escuela de Artes Plásticas; Universidad Autónoma Tomás Frías
  architecture 4 258, 259
  Banco Nacional de Bolivia 4 258
  Casa del Corregidor 4 258
  Casa de Moneda 4 258
  Casa de Otavi *see* Banco Nacional de Bolivia
  Casa Vicaria 4 258
  ecclesiastical buildings 4 258
    Cathedral 4 259, 267
    convent of S Monica 4 267
    Convent of S Teresa 4 269
    El Belén 4 258
    La Compañía 4 258
    S Benito 4 258
    S Bernardo 4 258
    S Francisco 4 258
    S Lorenzo 4 *258*, 258; 21 315
    S Teresa 4 258, 261
  Escuela de Artes Plásticas 4 269; 25 366
    see also Academia Man Césped; Universidad Autónoma Tomás Frías
Potosí—cont.
  museums
    Museo del Convento de S Teresa 4 267; 25 365
    Museo del Convento S Francisco 4 267; 25 366
    Museo Nacional de la Casa de Moneda 4 268
      Archivo Histórico 4 269
      collections 13 880; 25 366
    Museo Ricardo Bohorquez 4 269
    Museo S Francisco 4 269
    Pinacoteca Colonial 4 268
    Pinacoteca Nacional *see* Museo Nacional de la Casa de Moneda
  painting 2 398; 4 261–2, 264, 268
  Sala de Dibujo Popular 4 269
  sculpture 4 264
  silver 4 255; 28 737
  textiles 4 267
  Universidad Autónoma Tomás Frías 4 258, 269; 25 366
    see also Academia Man Césped; Escuela de Artes Plásticas
Potosme, Robert 23 83
Potpeschnigg, Luise 2 832
pots 9 82
  historical and regional traditions
    Africa 1 *329*, 417–18*
    Akan 1 329
    Akye 1 328
    Anatolia, ancient 18 *513*
    Australia 2 *762*
    Bamana 1 329
    Benin, Kingdom of 1 329
    Cambodia 5 *506*
    Carib 30 13
    Central Asia, Eastern 6 *308*
    Central Asia, Western 6 *243*
    Chokwe 1 328
    England 10 *314*
    Germany 12 *443*
    Khmer 5 *506*; 30 *611*
    Korea 18 *333*
    Lwena 1 328
    Mangbetu 1 328, *329*
    Mesopotamia 21 *307*
    Prehistoric art 18 *333*
    Scythian 6 *243*
    Shona 1 418
    Tajikistan 6 *243*
    Thailand 30 *611*
    Tula (Nigeria) 1 381
    Venda 1 418
    Yoruba 1 328, 329
    Zaïre 1 *329*
    Zande 1 328
    Zulu 1 418
  materials
    bronze 15 708
    ceramics 1 *329*
    clay 1 381
    copper 6 *243*; 10 *343*
    earthenwares 18 *333*
    pewter 24 580
    pottery 18 *513*; 21 *307*
    silver 12 *443*
    stonewares 2 *762*; 5 *506*; 10 *314*; 30 *611*
    terracotta 6 *308*
  types
    coffee *see* COFFEEPOTS
    cooking
      Africa 1 369
      Asante 1 369
      Czech Republic 8 404
      England 10 301, *343*
      Germany 12 452
      Ghana 1 369
      Indian subcontinent 15 708
      Scotland 28 256–7
      Zulu 1 369
    ointment pots 10 74; 24 580
    tea *see* TEAPOTS
    water 1 369, *369*; 22 *608*
Potsdam 4 541; 12 *360*; 25 366–8*; 31 719
  Armeemuseum *see* Marmorpalais
  Astrophysical Observatory 23 340
  Charlottenhof 28 *102*
    Hofgärtnerei 12 376; 32 554
  congregational mosque 12 376
  Einsteinturm 4 788; 7 695; 10 697; 12 378; 21 119, *119*, 781
  furniture 12 *425*
  glass 4 666; 12 440
  hardstones 12 462
  interior decoration 12 410
  Marmorpalais 18 202; 27 323
  metalwork 12 452
  Mittelstrasse 4 786
  Nauener Tor 13 200
  Neuer Garten 24 181
  Neues Palais 12 424; 23 812; 25 368
    Antikentempel 14 652
    frames 11 459
    Great Grotto Hall 12 412, 462
    paintings 11 170; 14 650, 652; 18 477; 24 542; 26 564
    porcelain 3 804
  Nikolaikirche 25 *366*
  observatory 23 340
  Orangerie 28 91
  Schloss Babelsburg 13 207
    Flatow-Turm 3 689
  Schloss Cecilienhof 3 499
  Schloss Glienecke 12 376; 32 554
  Schloss Sanssouci 12 373, 410, 413, 424, 791; 13 619; 18 159; 23 812; 25 *367*, 367–8*; 26 497; 32 76
    Belvedere 3 689
    Chinesisches Haus 7 168; 12 373
    frames 11 458, 459
    gardens 12 134; 14 654; 20 1
    library 12 412, *412*
    Music Room 26 *496*
    Neptune Grotto 13 705
    Orangerie 12 416; 29 609
    paintings 4 135, 151, 536, 573; 5 711; 11 411; 14 653; 18 160; 19 646, 649; 20 415; 23 874; 24 542; 26 247; 27 288; 28 743; 30 274, 787
    Roman bath house 5 905
    Ruinenberg 27 324
    sculpture 1 133; 6 98; 9 687, 761; 12 405; 14 650; 19 141
    Voltaire Room 14 750
  silk 12 464
  Stadtschloss 12 373, 412, 414; 18 *159*, 160
    Etruscan Room 12 414
    Fortunaportal 4 218
    paintings 24 542
  Villa Keller 32 554
Pott, Anthony 2 318
Pott, Heinrich 3 804
Pott, Ignaz 12 821
Pott, Laslett J. 23 259
Pottelsberghe, Liévin van 14 760
Pottendorf, Nádasdy Castle 15 15
Pottenstein, Ulrich von *see* ULRICH VON POTTENSTEIN
Potter (firm) 25 372–3*; 32 812, 816
  staff 19 359
  works 32 *816*
Potter (family) 3 599
Potter, Albert 7 448
Potter, (Helen) Beatrix 25 372*
  reproductions in ceramics 10 314
  works 4 368; 5 422; 25 245
Potter, C., E. & J. G. 25 373
Potter, C., H. & E. 25 373
Potter, Charles 25 372
Potter, Christopher 6 454
Potter, David 2 762
Potter (ii), Edward T(uckerman) 25 371–2*; 26 468
Potter, Edwin 25 373
Potter, Graham 19 359
Potter, Harold 25 373
Potter, Isaak 11 134
Potter, John 2 163
Potter, John Gerald 25 373
Potter, Joseph 33 446
Potter (i), Paulus (Pietersz.) 22 844; 25 368, 369–71*
  collaboration 25 369
  copies 26 124
  patrons and collectors
    Arenberg, Auguste-Marie-Raymond, 6th Duke of 2 382
    Bisschop, Jan and Pieter 4 95
    Boymans, F(rans) J(acob) O(tto) 4 614
    Braamcamp, Gerrit 4 618
    Goll van Franckenstein (family) 12 876
    Josephine, Empress of the French (1763-1814) 4 303
    William IV, Stadholder of the Netherlands, Prince of Orange (*reg* 1747-51) 23 463, 468
    William V, Stadholder of the Netherlands, Prince of Orange (*reg* 1751-95) 23 469
  pupils 9 380
  reproductive prints by others 23 590
  teachers 33 110
  works 8 667; 25 *370*
Potter (i), Pieter (Symonsz.) 25 368–9*
  assistants 25 369
  reproductive prints by others 23 191
  teachers 22 841
  works 29 667; 31 882
Potter, Robert 25 728
Potter, Sally 10 689
Potter (i), Simon (Jacobsz.) 25 368
Potter (ii), William A(ppleton) 7 436; 25 371, 372*; 26 468
Potteries 10 309; 29 495
Potterne, St Mary 11 252
Potter Palmer, Mrs *see* PALMER, BERTHA HONORÉ
Potter & Robertson 25 372
Potter & Ross 25 372; 32 812
potters
  China 6 637
  Egypt, ancient 10 23
  England 10 301, 312
  Greece, ancient 13 *480*
  Inca 29 135
  Indian subcontinent 15 *729*
  Japan 17 104, 351
  Korea 17 255, 262, 351
  Netherlands, the 3 589
  South America, Pre-Columbian 29 135
Potter's Alley Glass House 9 320
Potters' Hopton Beach Camp 6 395
potter's wheels 6 326, *326*; 14 341
  historical and regional traditions
    Central Asia, Eastern 6 309
    China 6 877, 879, 880
    Crete 21 667
    Dawenkou culture 6 877
    Egypt, ancient 10 22
    Greece, ancient 13 479–80
    Indian subcontinent 15 685
    Ireland 16 28
    Islamic 16 394
    Italy 25 543
    Japan 17 241–2, 253
    Mesopotamia 21 270, 306
    Minoan 21 667
    Prehistoric art 25 542–3
    Syria-Palestine 30 185, 197
  types
    kick 10 301; 17 242
pottery
  collections *see under* COLLECTIONS → types
  conservation 6 334–6*; 7 XI1, 2
  dating methods 2 304; 16 399; 30 403–4
  display 9 28, 30
  historical and regional traditions
    Aboriginal Australia 1 64
    Achaemenid 6 255
    Afghanistan 1 207*, 210*; 16 407
    Africa 1 246, 285–6, *286*, 406, 424*, 428; 31 261
    Akye 8 22
    Algeria 16 404, 427
    Anatolia, ancient 1 644, *823*, 824, 826, 837–8*, *837*; 5 615; 14 *14*; 18 *513*
    Ancient Near East 6 333; 22 341
    Antigua (island) 2 152
    Antilles, Lesser 5 746, 747; 29 198, 200
    Arabia 2 266–9*, *267*
    Argentina 29 *191*, *202*, 203
    Assyrian 21 308
    Australia 2 760–62
    Austria 2 815–16*
    Azerbaijan 2 898*
    Aztatlán 2 904
    Aztec 2 907*; 21 240, 266
    Bactria 6 255
    Bahía (culture) 3 65; 27 609
    Bahrain 2 267, 268
    Bali (Indonesia) 15 806
    Bangladesh 3 169; 15 727
    Banshan culture 6 876, 877
    Barbados 2 152
    Belgium 3 589–90*; 21 137
    Benedictine Order 28 256
    Berber 3 755–6
    Boat-Axe culture 25 514
    Bolivia 31 *46*
    Brazil 4 706, 722*; 29 *194*
    Britain 25 513
    Buddhism 6 717; 17 252
    Bulgaria 9 633; 17 *808*
    Byzantine 9 631–4*, *633*, *634*
    Cajamarca culture 5 408–10*
    Canaanite 5 557; 30 184, 185
    Carib 13 874; 30 13
    Caribbean Islands 5 747
    Catalonia 29 323, 329
    Cedrosan Saladoid culture 29 198
    Celtic 6 156, 159, 161; 25 *543*, 544
    Central Asia, Western 6 *213*, 254–9*, *256*; 31 701
      Bactria 6 255
      Chach 6 256, 257
      Islamic 16 123, 400–402*, 407–10*, 412–14*
      Khwarazm 6 255, 257, 258, 259
      Prehistoric 6 255*
      Sogdiana 6 255, 256, 257, 258
      Tajikistan 6 259
      Timurid 16 413–14
      Turkmenistan 6 255
    Chach 6 256, 257
    Chancay 6 440
    Chavín culture 6 522*; 29 177–8
    Chican-Taíno culture 29 *199*, 200
    Chimú 6 606*; 29 177
    China 6 *686*, 868, 869, 879–89*; 7 94, 95, 107, 144
      Banshan culture 6 876, 877
      Buddhism 6 717
      Dawenkou culture 6 877–8
      Daxi culture 6 878–9
      Hemudu culture 6 877, 878
      Liao period (AD 907-1125) 6 889*, *890*, *891*
      Longshan culture 6 869, 877, *878*, 878
      Machang culture 6 876, 877

pottery
historical and regional traditions
China—cont.
Majiabang culture 6 877, 878
Majiayao culture 6 876; 20 143
Prehistoric 6 629, 772, 773, 798, 875*, 877–9*, 879; 7 128
Qijia culture 6 877
Qinlongquan culture 6 879
Qujialing culture 6 879
Shajing culture 6 877
Shang period (c. 1600-c. 1050 BC) 6 880
Song period (AD 960-1279) 6 892–4*, 894, 895*, 896*
Songze culture 6 877, 878
Tang period (AD 618-907) 6 885
Xindian culture 6 877
Yangshao culture 6 875–7*, 876, 877; 7 159
Yuan period (1279-1368) 23 552
Zhou period (c. 1050-256 BC) 6 881
Chorrera culture 7 206–7; 29 134, 151
Cistercian Order 28 256
Coclé culture 7 506–7*; 29 147
Colombia 7 603; 29 150
Condorhuasi culture 29 190
Costa Rica 9 677
Côte d'Ivoire 8 22
Crete 9 631; 13 540, 542; 21 756
Early Christian (c. AD 250-843) 9 631
Geometric (c. 900-c. 700 BC) 8 154; 13 497
Hellenistic 13 539
Minoan 8 153; 21 657, 661, 665–72*, 665, 666, 668, 669, 670, 672; 24 591
Orientalizing style 8 154; 13 498, 502
Palace style 21 671
Prehistoric 8 153
Proto-Corinthian 8 154
Protogeometric 8 154; 13 493
Special Palatial tradition 21 669
Cucuteni culture 8 252; 25 514, 514
Cupisnique 8 272, 272; 29 177
Cycladic 8 309, 311*; 13 492, 498; 14 342
Early Cycladic (c. 3500/3000-c. 2000 BC) 8 311–12*, 312
Geometric (c. 900-c. 700 BC) 13 496, 497
Late Cycladic (c. 1600-c. 1050 BC) 8 313*, 314; 30 712
Middle Cycladic period (c. 2000-c. 1600 BC) 8 312–13*, 313
Orientalizing style 13 498, 502
Sub-Protogeometric 13 492
Cyprus 9 631, 634, 634
Cyprus, ancient 8 331, 343–9*, 345, 347; 13 542
Czech Republic 8 403–5*
Dan (Africa) 8 489
Dawenkou culture 6 877–8
Daxi culture 6 878–9
Denmark 8 747
Early Christian (c. AD 250-843) 9 631–2*
Ecuador 29 150–51
Egypt 1 285; 16 402–3*, 404–5*, 405, 415–17*
Egypt, ancient 4 172; 6 333; 9 824, 864; 10 21–8*, 23, 24, 25, 28, 46; 20 593; 31 261
Naqada II (c. 3500-c. 3000 BC) 6 329; 9 827, 827
El Salvador 10 154
pottery
historical and regional traditions—cont.
England 10 300*, 303–8*
Celtic 6 161
Roman 27 108
19th cent. 10 142
Ethiopia 4 172
Etruscan 10 587, 593, 609–16*, 641; 13 540–42, 571
Etrusco-Corinthian 10 613–14*, 614
Etrusco-Geometric 10 610–11*, 611
Greece, ancient 13 514
Orientalizing style 10 611*
Fiji 11 70; 23 727, 728
Finland 11 105
France 11 603–7*; 25 543
Funnel Beaker culture 25 514
Georgia 12 330*
Germany 6 558
Gran Chiriquí culture 13 290
Gran Nicoya culture 13 310, 311; 29 147, 149
Greece, ancient 7 851; 13 370, 472–83*, 475, 480, 484–91*, 485, 490, 536*, 538*, 570–71; 16 830; 20 912
Arcadia 13 496
Archaic 13 472
Argolid 13 493, 495, 498
Attica 13 436, 493–5*, 494, 495, 571
Boeotia 13 493, 496, 498
Bronze Age 14 337–8, 359
Classical 13 472–3, 473
Corinth 13 495, 496
Corinthian 13 367
Etruscan 13 514
Euboia 13 493, 496–7, 497
Geometric (c. 900-c. 700 BC) 13 368, 471, 493–8*, 494, 495, 497; 21 95
Geometric 13 367
Geometric (c. 900-c. 700 BC) 13 472; 22 410, 513
Hellenistic 13 538–40*, 539, 540
Ionia 15 893
Italy 13 473, 525–33*, 538
Italy: Apulian 13 526–30*, 527, 528, 529
Italy: Campania 13 531, 531–2*
Italy: Lucanian 13 525–6*, 526
Italy: Paestan 13 532–3*, 533
Lakonia 13 474, 496
Late Helladic IIIC (c. 1180-c. 1050 BC) 13 367
Orientalizing style 13 471, 472, 496, 498–501*, 502–4*
Orientalizing style: Lakonia 13 498
Prehistoric 8 901
Proto-Attic 13 367, 498, 500–501*, 501
Proto-Corinthian 13 367, 498, 499–500*
Protogeometric 13 367, 368, 471, 472, 491*, 492–3*
Protogeometric: Achaia 13 492
Protogeometric: Argolid 13 492
Protogeometric: Attica 13 491–2*, 492
Protogeometric: Boiotia 13 492
Protogeometric: Corinth 13 492
Protogeometric: Dodecanese 13 492
protogeometric: Euboia 13 492–3
Protogeometric: Ionia 13 492
Protogeometric: Ithaka 13 492
Protogeometric: Lakonia 13 492
pottery
historical and regional traditions
Greece, ancient—cont.
Protogeometric: Thessaly 13 492
Protogeometric B 13 493
Rhodes (island) 26 290
Sicily 13 530, 530–31*
Sub-Mycenaean (c. 1050-c. 1000 BC) 13 367, 471
Sub-Protogeometric 13 492
Sub-protogeometric: Boiotia 13 492
Thessaly 13 496
8th cent. BC 24 892
Guadeloupe (country) 5 747; 29 199
Guangala 29 151
Guatemala 13 768*; 31 261
Gulf Coast, Mesoamerica 21 237–8
Gumelniţa culture 25 514
Guyana 13 874
Haiti 14 54
Hassuna culture 21 305
Hausa 1 246; 14 232
Helladic 8 901; 14 341–2*, 359
Argolid 14 341, 343, 346
Attica 14 341
Boeotia 14 341
Corinthian 14 341
Cyprus, ancient 8 346
Early Helladic (c. 3600/3000-c. 2050 BC) 14 335–6, 342*, 342
Euboia 14 342
Late Helladic (c. 1600-c. 1050 BC) 14 337–8, 341, 344, 344–7*, 345, 347
Middle Helladic (c. 2050-c. 1600 BC) 14 343–4*, 344
Palatial style 14 344
Thessaly 14 341
Hemudu culture 6 877, 878
Hittite 1 826, 838; 15 159–60
Hopi 22 609
Huari culture 14 828–9*
Huastec 14 831; 21 238
Igbo 1 246
Inca 15 163*
India, Republic of 15 174
Indian subcontinent 15 685–6*
Indus civilization 15 685
Iran 15 899; 16 123, 123, 124, 395, 400–402*, 407–10*, 408, 410, 412–14*, 413, 414, 423–7*, 554
Ilkhanid 16 412–13, 413
Qajar 16 425–7
Great Saljuqs 16 407
Samanid 16 401–2
Timurid 16 413–14
Zand 16 425
Iran, ancient 1 786, 851
Iraq 2 492; 16 393, 396, 397–400*
Ireland 16 28; 25 544
Islamic 6 333; 16 396*, 404*, 412*
Afghanistan 16 407
Algeria 16 404, 427
Central Asia, Western 16 123, 400–402*, 407–10*, 412–14*
Egypt 16 402–3*, 404–5*, 405, 415–17*
Iran 6 IV3; 16 123, 123, 124, 394, 395, 400–402*, 407–10*, 408, 410, 412–14*, 413, 414, 423–7*, 554
Iraq 16 396, 397–400*
Jordan 16 396, 397
Mesopotamia 16 401
Morocco 16 412, 418, 427
North Africa 16 403–4, 411–12*, 418–19*, 427–8*
Ottoman 16 419, 421, 422
Palestine 16 397
pottery
historical and regional traditions
Islamic—cont.
Sicily 16 411
Spain 16 403–4*, 411–12*, 418–19*; 29 322
Syria 16 396–7*, 397, 405, 406, 406–7*, 413, 415–17*, 416, 417
Tunisia 16 403, 404, 411, 427
Turkey 16 406, 411*, 413, 418*, 418
Italy 13 370; 25 309
Apulian 13 526–30*, 527, 528, 529
Campanian 13 531, 531–2*
Etruscan 10 587, 593, 609–16*; 13 540–42
Etrusco-Corinthian 10 613–14*, 614
Etrusco-Geometric 10 610–11*, 611
Greece, ancient 13 473, 525–33*, 538
Lucanian 13 525–6*, 526
Orientalizing style 10 611*
Paestan 13 532–3*, 533
Prehistoric 25 543; 32 563
Roman 6 333
Villanovan culture 32 562
Japan 17 104, 240*, 247–9*, 250–51*, 252*, 253–6*, 258–63*, 341, 353
Buddhism 17 252
Edo period (1600-1868) 17 234, 262, 399; 23 196
Jōmon period (c. 10,000-c. 300 BC) 17 30, 244–6*, 629
Kofun period (c. AD 300-710) 17 246–7*, 247
Prehistoric 17 242
Yayoi 17 246*, 246
Yayoi period (c. 300 BC-c. AD 300) 33 511
Jazira culture 21 269, 305
Jōmon culture 17 242, 244–6*
Jordan 16 396, 397
Karanovo culture 25 514
Kenya 1 285
Khmer 30 610–11*
Khwarazm 6 213, 255, 257, 258, 259
Kongo 1 406
Korea 18 249, 332–5*, 336–7*
Kuba (iii) (Zaïre) 1 246
La Tène culture (c. 450-.c 50 BC) 25 543, 544
Lengyel culture 25 513
Lesotho 19 241, 242
Levant 30 196
Liangzhu culture 19 302
Linear Pottery culture 25 513, 514
Longshan culture 6 869, 877, 878, 878
Lwena 7 198–9
Lydia 19 841
Machang culture 6 876, 877
Majiabang culture 6 877, 878
Majiayao culture 6 876; 20 143*, 143
Malta (Republic of) 20 209
Mangbetu 1 406
Martinique 5 747
Maya 20 883; 21 237, 239, 239, 240
Mesoamerica, Pre-Columbian 21 235, 236–40*, 249, 256, 257
Aztatlán 2 904
Aztec 21 266
Capacha-Opeño 5 660, 660
Huastec 14 831
Maya 21 239
Mexico 2 904; 7 250; 21 238, 239, 240
Mixtec 21 240
pottery
historical and regional traditions
Mesoamerica, Pre-Columbian—cont.
Olmec 23 418
tipo códice 21 737
West Mexico 21 236
Mesopotamia 6 333; 16 398; 21 269, 271, 305–8*, 306
Islamic 16 401
Samarra' 27 677
Susiana 7 186
Uruk (c. 4000-c. 2900 BC) 21 306
Mexico 21 392; 31 261
Capacha-Opeño 5 660, 660
Pre-Columbian 2 904; 7 250; 21 238, 239, 240
Midianites 2 268
Minoan 8 153; 14 338; 21 665*, 756; 24 591; 26 290
Early Minoan (c. 3500/3000-c. 2050 BC) 21 665, 666–7*, 666
Final Neolithic (c. 3800-c. 3500/3000 BC) 21 665–6*
Late Minoan (c. 1600-c. 1050 BC) 21 661, 668–72*, 669, 670, 672
Middle Minoan (c. 2050-c. 1600 BC) 21 657, 665, 667–8*, 668
Palace style 21 671
Special Palatial tradition 21 669
Mixtec 21 238, 239, 240, 737
Moche (culture) 5 761; 21 752, 752–4*, 753; 23 565; 29 134, 135, 177, 216, 221
Morocco 16 412, 418, 427
Muisca 29 150
Mycenaean 1 826; 8 346; 13 491; 14 337–8, 341, 344–7*, 344, 345, 347; 26 290
Native North Americans 20 498; 22 600–612*, 603, 607, 666, 668
Sikyatki style 22 562
Weeden Island culture 22 611, 612
20th cent. 22 451
Navajo 22 605, 677
Nazca 22 706–7*, 707; 29 133, 175
Nevis 2 152
New Caledonia 23 728
New Zealand 23 68
Nicaragua 23 82–3*
Nigeria 1 286; 15 120; 23 130
North Africa 16 403–4, 411–12*, 418–19*, 427–8*
Nuba 23 275
Nubia 17 912; 23 277, 286
Olmec 21 237; 23 418
Otomani culture 25 528
Ottoman 16 419, 420, 421, 422; 23 643
Pacific Islands 23 726–8*, 727
Palestine 16 397
Panama 7 506; 29 147, 148
Papua New Guinea 23 728; 24 79
Paracas culture 24 89; 29 177
Paraguay 24 93, 97
Parthian 21 308; 24 218
Peru 24 500; 27 621; 31 261
Nazca 22 707
Pre-Columbian 6 440; 8 272, 272; 21 752, 752–4*
Philistine 24 634–5*
Phoenician 4 172; 24 643*
Phrygian 1 838; 24 690
Phung Nguyen culture 29 227
Poland 25 122, 123
Polgár culture 25 513
Portugal 25 308–10*; 31 261

pottery
historical and regional traditions—cont.
Prehistoric art
Anatolia, ancient **1** *823*, 824, 826, *837*, 837–8*; **14** *14*
Boat-Axe culture **25** 514
Britain **25** 513
Bronze Age **6** *327*; **25** 527–9*, *528*
Bulgaria **17** *808*
Central Asia, Western **6** 255*
China **6** 798, 869, 875–9*, *876*, *877*, *878*, *879*; **7** 159; **20** *143*
Crete **8** 153
Cucuteni culture **8** 252; **25** 514, *514*
Cyprus, ancient **8** 343*
Funnel Beaker culture **25** 514
Greece **8** 901
Gumelniţa culture **25** 514
Iraq **2** *492*
Iron Age **25** 542–4*
Italy **32** *563*
Japan **17** 30, *242*, 629
Karanovo culture **25** 514
Korea **18** 332–5*
La Tène culture (*c.* 450-.*c* 50 BC) **25** *543*
Lengyel culture **25** 513
Linear Pottery culture **25** 513, 514
Neolithic **25** 513–15*, *514*
Nubia **23** 277
Polgár culture **25** 513
Romania **25** *514*
Rössen culture **25** 513
Russia **27** *366*
Sardinia **27** 834*
Serbia **29** 546
Sesklo culture **25** 514
Single-Grave culture **25** 514
South-east Asia **29** 227
Starčevo culture **25** 514
Thailand **29** 227
Tisza culture **25** 513, 514
Tripol'ye culture **25** 514; **27** *366*
Vietnam **29** 227
Vinča culture **25** 514
proto-Hassuna culture **21** 269, 305
Puerto Rico **25** 698–9, 703; **29** *199*
Punic **25** 734*
Qijia culture **6** 877
Qinlongquan culture **6** 879
Qujialing culture **6** 879
Recuay culture **26** 66
Rhodes (island) **13** 502, 503, *503*, *537*, 542; **16** 395, 420; **26** 290
Geometric (*c.* 900-*c.* 700 BC) **13** 497
Helladic **26** *290*
Romania **25** *514*
Rome, ancient **20** 593; **27** 103–5, 106–8*
England **27** *108*
Italy **6** 333
Tunisia **27** 107
Rössen culture **25** 513
Rus' **27** 410
Russia **27** *366*, 410–11*
St Lucia **2** 152
Saladoid culture **29** *199*; **31** 330
Salinar culture **27** 621
Samarran culture **21** 269, 305
Santa Cruz Islands **23** *727*, 728
Santa María culture **29** *191*
Sardinia **27** 834*
Sasanian **21** 308
Saudi Arabia **2** 267
Scotland **28** 256–7*
Serbia **25** *528*; **29** 546
Sesklo culture **25** 514
Shajing culture **6** 877
Shona **28** 621

pottery
historical and regional traditions—cont.
Sicily **13** *530*, 530–31*; **16** 411; **28** 654–5
Singapore **28** 775*
Single-Grave culture **25** 514
Sinú **29** 150
Slovakia **28** 855–6*
Sogdiana **6** 255, 256, *256*, 257, 258
Solomon Islands **23** 728
Songze culture **6** 877, 878
Sotto culture **21** 269, 305
South Africa **29** 104
South America, Pre-Columbian **9** 677, 714; **15** 67; **29** 125–7, 128, 134, *134*, 146–51*, *149*, 159, 175–8*, *187*, 187–8, 192–3*, *194*, 198, 200, 202–3*, *216*; **31** 261
Argentina **29** *191*, *202*, 203
Bahía (culture) **3** 65
Bolivia **31** *46*
Cajamarca culture **5** 408–10
Chancay **6** 440
Chavín culture **6** 522
Chorrera culture **7** 206–7; **29** 134
Coclé culture **7** 506–7*
Colombia **29** 150
Cupisnique **8** 272, *272*
Ecuador **29** 150–51
Gran Nicoya culture **13** 310, *311*
Guadeloupe (country) **29** *199*
Moche (culture) **21** *752*, 752–4*, *753*
Nazca **22** *707*
Panama **7** *506*; **29** 147, 148
Paracas culture **24** 89
Peru **6** 440; **8** 272, *272*; **14** 828–9; **21** *752*, 752–4*
Puerto Rico **29** *199*
Recuay culture **26** 66
Santa María culture **29** *191*
Valdivia culture **29** 127
Veraguas culture **32** 238
Vicús culture **32** 417–18
South-east Asia **29** 227
Spain **25** 309; **29** 322–8*; **31** 261
Almohad **16** 412
Islamic **16** 403–4*, 411–12*, 418–19*; **29** 322
Nasrid **16** 412, 418–19
Umayyad **16** 403
Starčevo culture **25** 514
Surinam **30** 13
Sweden **30** 97–9*
Syria **7** XI1
Islamic **16** 396–7*, *397*, 405, *406*, 406–7*, 413, 415–17*, *416*, *417*
Mamluk **16** 415–17
Umayyad **16** 396–7, *397*
Syria-Palestine **30** 182, 183, 184, 185, 186, 196–7*
Tairona **29** 150
Tajikistan **6** 259
Tarascan **30** 341*
Teke **1** 406
Thailand **29** 227; **30** 610–11*
Tisza culture **25** 513, 514
Toltec **21** 239
Trinidad and Tobago **31** 330–31
Tripol'ye culture **25** 514; **27** *366*
Troadic **31** 354*
Tunisia **16** 403, 404, 411, 427; **27** 107; **31** 426
Turkey **9** *633*; **16** 406, 411*, 413, 418*, *418*; **31** 455
Turkmenistan **6** 255
Ubaid culture **21** 270, 306
United States of America **22** *603*; **31** 261, 634–7, 638–40
Urartian **1** 838; **31** 701

pottery
historical and regional traditions—cont.
Uzbekistan **6** *213*
Valdivia culture **29** 127, 150; **31** 811
Vanuatu **23** 728; **31** 892
Veraguas culture **32** 238
Vicús culture **32** 417–18
Vietnam **29** 227; **32** 485
Villanovan culture **32** 562, *563*
Vinča culture **25** 514
Weeden Island culture **22** *611*, 611–12, *612*
West Mexico **21** *236*, 237
Xindian culture **6** 877
Yangshao culture **6** 875–7*, *876*, *877*; **7** 159
Yayoi culture **17** 246*, *246*
Zande **33** 610
Zapotec **21** 238, 249
materials
adhesives **13** 483
beads **25** 546
calligraphy **6** 257
cinnabar **17** 246
clay **1** 285; **6** 869; **13** 535; **16** 398, 408
cobalt **6** 258; **21** 137
copper **16** 404
enamel **6** 258; **11** 606; **16** 410*, *410*; **32** 485
flint **16** 420
frit **6** 258, IV1, 3; **16** 393, *394*, *406*, 408–9, 412, *413*, *416*, *417*, *418*, 419, 420, 421, *422*
glass **25** 546
glazes **6** 333
Central Asia **6** 257
China **6** 879, 881, 882, 886, 888, 893, 895
Early Christian and Byzantine **9** 633
Egypt, ancient **10** 46
England **10** 315
Greece, ancient **13** 504, 537
Ireland **16** 28
Islamic **16** 399, 401, 402, 408, 411, 412, 413, 415, 420, 426, 427
Japan **17** 247, 250–51, 252, 253, 255, 258
Korea **18** 336
Mesopotamia **21** 308
Syria-Palestine **30** 197
gold leaf **13** 482
graphite **25** 514
inlays **18** 338–9
inscriptions **6** 900; **10** 610; **13** 485, 487–90*, *488*, *489*, *490*, 491*; **16** 399, 414, 415; **17** 234
iron oxide **6** 885; **17** 246
Jasper ware **21** II3
kaolin **6** 876, 880
kaolinite **13** 535
lacquer **6** *881*
leaves **6** 874
manganese **16** 400
ochre **6** 874
paper **6** 874, *874*
quartz **16** 405, 408, 413, 420
resist *see* RESIST
silver **16** 404
slip **6** 255, 257, 874, 876, 882, 895; **10** 25; **16** 399, 405, 408*, 415, 420, 422; **28** 842
restoration **13** 483
technical examination **13** 480–81; **30** 393, 395, 401
techniques
appliqué **13** 540
barbotine **6** 462
burnishing **1** 207; **6** 874, 876; **16** 394; **25** 514
carving **16** 395
chattering **13** 537

pottery
techniques—cont.
coiling **6** 326, *326*; **10** 301; **16** 394; **17** 241, 245
China **6** 879
Greece, ancient **13** 479
enamel **10** 306
engraving **18** 338, 342
gilding **13** 537, 539
glazes **13** 480
hollow-building **6** 326
impressing **1** 286; **6** *327*, 874, 876, *876*, 882, *884*, *891*; **10** 612, 613; **25** 514
incising **6** 874, 882, 901; **10** 27–8, *301*, *612*, *614*; **13** 504; **16** 395, 403, 415; **25** 514
inglaze decoration **16** 395
jiggering **6** 327
luting **6** 326
marbling **18** 339; **19** 841, *841*
mass production **17** 250, 253; **21** 271
moulding **1** 285; **6** 333, 874, 883, 889; **10** 303, 306; **16** 394, *403*, 403, 415; **31** 636
overglaze decoration **16** 393, *394*, 395; **32** 485
painting **6** 887
China **6** 874, 876
Cycladic **8** 312
Egypt, ancient **10** 26
Greece, ancient **13** 535–6, *535*
Prehistoric **25** 514
South America, Pre-Columbian **29** 176–7
pinching **6** 326
polychromy **23** 643
printing **10** 307
rouletting **6** 874; **10** 301, 303; **13** 537
sgraffito **6** 895; **16** *402*, 402, 407–8*, 411, *411*, 415*; **18** 341, *341*
Six's technique **13** 482
slab-construction **6** 326; **10** 301; **16** 394
stamping **6** 881, 882; **8** 311; **10** 613; **13** *537*, 537; **16** 403
throwing **6** 326, *326*; **10** 300
transfer (printing) **11** 606
turning **6** 327
underglaze decoration **16** 393, 395, 407, 408, 412–13, 416–17*, 423, 426, *554*; **18** 339; **30** 874; **32** 485, *485*
uses
amphorae **6** *256*; **9** 632; **10** *594*; **13** *492*, *494*, *495*, *501*, *503*, *507*, *510*, *514*, *517*, *519*, *522*, *591*; **27** 106
aryballoi **13** *499*, *500*
askoi **14** *342*
basins **6** IV1; **22** *881*
beakers **6** *327*
bells **21** 256
bottles **6** 890; **10** *301*; **29** *187*
bowls
Byzantine **9** 634
China **6** *884*, *885*, III3
Cyprus, ancient **8** *347*, *348*
Egypt, ancient **9** *824*; **10** *25*
Greece, ancient **13** *540*; **14** *342*, *345*, *347*
Iran **6** IV3; **16** *123*, *554*
Iraq **23** *558*
Mexico **21** *240*
Moche (culture) **29** *134*
Nicaragua **23** *83*
Ottoman **16** *421*
Rome, ancient **27** *107*
Syria-Palestine **30** *197*
Weeden Island culture **22** *612*
boxes **6** 257
cameos **21** II3
censers **6** 883; **9** 632
chalices **21** *665*
chargers **16** *418*

pottery
uses—cont.
chess sets **6** 558
cups **13** *437*, *512*, *520*, *535*, *537*; **14** *343*; **17** *266*; **27** *108*
cup-skyphoi **13** *476*
dating methods **1** 851
dinoi **13** *507*, *509*
dolls **31** 261*
drawings **15** 806
ewers **22** *881*
figurines
China **6** 883, 887–8; **7** *55*
Costa Rica **9** 677
Cyprus, ancient **8** *329*, 338, *339*
Mesoamerica, Pre-Columbian **21** *236*, *238*, *239*
Prehistoric art **25** *528*
flasks **6** II1; **8** *343*; **21** *670*
flutes (musical instruments) **21** 257
goblets **9** *634*; **14** *343*; **21** *669*; **30** *197*
human figures **29** *194*
hydriai **10** *615*; **13** *510*, *511*, *516*, *523*
icons **9** 632, 633
incense burners **6** *882*, 900
inkstones **7** 94, 95
jardinières **22** *880*
jars
China **7** 144
Egypt, ancient **6** *329*; **10** *24*, *26*
Gran Nicoya culture **13** *311*
Helladic **14** *343*, *345*, *347*
Islamic **16** *416*
Minoan **21** *665*, *668*, *669*, *670*
Rhodes (island) **26** *290*
Syria-Palestine **30** *197*
jewellery **7** 107
jugs **8** *344*, *348*; **10** *302*; **14** *343*; **15** *822*; **21** *665*, *666*, *756*; **22** *878*
kantharoi **13** *477*; **14** *343*
kraters **10** *616*; **13** *370*, *473*, *497*, *506*, *508*, *509*, *515*, *518*, *522*, *534*, *540*; **14** *345*, *347*; **21** *672*; **30** *197*
kyathoi **13** *513*
kylikes **14** *345*
lamps **6** 257; **27** 103–5, *104*
models **6** *686*, 883–4
mugs **10** 303; **13** *537*
netsuke **17** 399
oinochoai **10** *612*; **13** *436*, *488*, *503*
ossuaries **6** *213*
pelikai **13** *524*
pilgrim flasks **6** 875, 887, 890
pipes (smoking) **30** 341
plates **6** II3; **10** *307*; **14** *342*; **16** *422*; **17** *352*; **23** *552*
pots **18** *513*; **21** *307*
pyxides (vases) **13** *505*; **14** *345*
reliquaries **15** *686*
rhyta **6** *256*; **21** *669*
sauceboats **14** *342*
sculpture **1** 285; **6** 717, 882; **16** 734; **19** *242*
stucco **29** 813
tankards **14** *342*
teabowls **6** II2; **17** *341*; **28** *410*
tea-caddies **17** *341*
teapots **15** *822*; **33** *535*
tiles **9** 632, *633*; **11** 603; **17** *262*
trays **6** 890; **7** *506*
tureens **15** *820*
urns **22** *611*; **29** *191*, *194*
vases
China **6** 890, *890*, *891*, III3
Egypt, ancient **10** *28*
Greece, ancient **13** *488*
Netherlands, the **8** *668*
Prehistoric art **25** *543*
Spain **7** XI2
Vicús culture **32** *418*
weights **30** 341

pottery
uses—cont.
wig stands **7** *166*
wares
Abraham of Kütahya ware **16** 418
Abstract style **21** 670
Abydos ware **30** 184
Agano ware **1** 448
Aghkand ware **16** 407
Aguas Buenas ware **13** 290
Alb-Salem **25** 543
alla porcellana **4** 176; **16** 733
Alligator group **13** 290
Allita Amaya **31** 46
Alternating style **21** 671
Alwa ware **23** 285
Amol ware **16** 407
a quartieri **16** 734
Argive Close style **14** 346, *347*
Aristide style **7** 506
arlecchini ware **16** 735, *735*
Arretine ware **27** 31, 106–7, *107*
Atarco style **14** 828
Atsumi **17** 260
Ayia Marina ware **14** 342
Ayios Onouphrios I ware **21** 666
Ayios Onouphrios II ware **21** 666, *666*
Aztec ware **21** 240
Baba Nakkaş ware **16** 418
Barbar ware **2** 267
Barbotine ware
Central Asia, Western **6** 257
Crete **21** 667
England **27** *108*
Islamic **16** 394
Minoan **21** 667
Rome, ancient **27** *108*
basaltes **10** 642; **33** 21, *21*
Base Ring wares **8** 330
Base Ring I ware **8** 345, *345*
Base Ring II ware **8** *345*, 346
Bencharong ware **30** 611–12
Bichrome Red ware **8** 347
Bichrome ware **8** 330, 346, 347, *348*
Bichrome Wheelmade ware **8** 345, *345*
Biscuit ware **13** 290
BI-ware **2** 268
Bizen **17** 261
Black-and-red-on-buff ware **1** 838
Black-and-red style **8** 309, *314*; **21** 95
Black-and-Red ware **15** 685
Black and White style **13** 501
Black Decorated style **14** 828
Black-figure
Etruscan **10** *594*, *614*, 614–15*, *615*; **13** 512, 516*, *516*
Greece, ancient **3** 466; **13** *367*, 368, 471, 472, 474, 475, *480*, 481–2, *482*, *483*, 486, 487, 488, 504*, 539, 549; **14** 498; **23** 145, 290; **24** 331; **32** *44*
Greece, ancient: Attica **13** 500, 501, 504, 506–11*, *507*, *508*, *509*, *510*, *511*, *591*
Greece, ancient: Boiotia **13** *513*, 513–14
Greece, ancient: Caeretan **13** 516, *516*
Greece, ancient: Chalcidian **13** *515*, 515–16
Greece, ancient: Corinth **13** 499, 504*, 505–6*, *505*, *506*
Greece, ancient: Euboia **13** 516–17*
Greece, ancient: Ionia **13** 503, *514*, 514–15*
Greece, ancient: Lakonia **13** *512*, 512–13
Italy **10** *594*, *614*, 614–15*, *615*

pottery
wares
Black-figure—cont.
Sicily **13** 512
Black-glazed
Etruscan **10** 616*
Greece, ancient **13** 471, 479, 480–83, *481*, *482*, *483*, 536–8*
Greece, ancient: Attica **13** *537*
Greece, ancient: Boiotia **13** 536
Greece, ancient: Lakonia **13** 536
Italy **10** 616*
Black Lustrous Wheelmade ware **8** 345
Black-on-red ware **8** 346, 347
Black Oribe ware **17** 255
Black Polished ware **8** 345
Black Seto ware **17** 254; **21** 651
Black-slip-and-combed ware **8** 343
Black Slip ware **8** 345
Black-topped ware **10** 25
black ware
China **6** 896*, *896*, *897*
Greece, ancient **13** 472
Korea **18** 340*
blue-and-white ware **4** 172*, 176; **9** 34
Central Asia, Western **6** 258; **16** 413
Egypt **16** 416
England **4** 177*; **7** 166
France **4** 177*; **7** 166
Germany **4** *176*, 176–7*
Iran **9** *36*; **16** 413, 414, *414*, 424
Islamic **4** *172*, 172–3*; **6** IV1, 2; **9** *36*; **16** 413, 414, *414*, 416, *417*, 418, *418*, 420, 424, 427; **30** XIII1
Mesopotamia **4** 172
Mexico **4** 175–6*
Netherlands, the **4** 176*; **7** 166; **8** *668*
North Africa **16** 427
Ottoman **4** 172, *172*; **16** 420
Portugal **4** 175*
Spain **4** 175*; **6** IV2; **30** XIII3
Syria **16** 416, *417*
Turkey **6** IV1; **16** 418, *418*; **30** XIII1
Vietnam **32** *485*, 485–6
see also Delftware
blue-on-white ware **16** 397, *398*, 400
Blue painted ware **10** 27, 28
Bontour style **31** 331
Böttgerporzellan **21** 63
Brittle ware **16** 397
Brown and red painted ware **10** 27
Brown-on-buff ware **1** *837*, 838
Bucchero **6** 353; **10** 593, 611–13*, *612*; **13** 571
Cajamarca Cursive **5** 410
Calenian Ware **13** 540
Campana C ware **13** 538
Campana group **13** 514
Candiana ware **16** 395
Cappadocian ware **1** *823*, 824, 838
Cardial-impressed ware *see* Impressed ware
Carillo Polychrome **13** 310
Cedrosan style **31** 330–31
celadon
China **6** 328, 331, 873, 892–3, *893*, 899–900, *900*, 910, *916*; **7** 95
Japan **2** 211; **17** *269*
Korea **18** 250, 317, 337–9*, *338*, *340*
Thailand **30** 609
Vietnam **32** 485
see also greenware; Longquan ware

pottery
wares—cont.
Chain-ridged ware **2** 267
Chakipampa style **14** 828
champlevé ware **9** 633; **16** 407, 411
Cheshmeh Ali ware **33** 504
Chocolate-on-White ware **24** 336
Chulmun ware **18** 333*, *333*
Cistercian ware **10** 302, 303
Cizhou ware **6** 870, 872, 874, 885, 892, 895*, *895*, 900–901*, 913, 922; **23** 551
Close style **21** *669*, 672
Codex style **21** 239
Collao **31** 46
Combed ware **8** 328, 343
compendario **16** 735
Concepción ware **13** 290
Conchopata style **14** 828
Conte Polychrome **7** *506*, 507; **28** 799
Corded ware **25** 514
Coyotlatelco ware **21** 239
creamware **6** 333; **29** 495
Czech Republic **8** *405*
England **6** 333; **10** 306–7, *307*; **22** 882
France **11** 606
Ireland **16** 28
Netherlands, the **22** 881, 882
Poland **25** 122
Portugal **25** 310
Sweden **30** 98
see also faïence fine
cuerda seca ware **16** 411, 412
Curridabat **9** 677; **13** 310
Cycladic White ceramic ware **8** 313, *313*; **21** 95
Cypro-Bucchero ware **8** 346
Damascus ware **16** 420
Dark Burnished **8** 312–13, *313*
Dark-faced Burnished ware **8** 343; **30** 196
Dark-on-light style **1** 826
Decorated ware **10** 26
Delftware **22** 879–80; **30** 875
England **6** 333; **10** 303, 305–6
Netherlands, the **4** 176; **6** 333; **7** 166, *166*; **8** *668*; **22** *878*, 879, *880*, *881*, 881–3; **29** 114
see also blue-and-white ware; FAIENCE (ii) (CERAMICS); lustreware; tin-glazed ware
Developed Stamford ware **10** 302, *302*
Diana ware **28** 653
Ding ware **6** 874, 886
Drab Polished Blue Core ware **8** 345
Eastern Sigillata A **13** 538
Echizen **17** 260
encaustic **10** 196, 199
Enmann group **13** 514
Erin Bay style **31** 331
faience *see* FAIENCE (ii) (CERAMICS)
faïence fine **3** 590, 591; **6** 333
see also creamware
faiyumi ware **16** 403, 405
Fantastic style **1** *823*, 824, 837
Fikellura style **13** 487, 503, *503*
Fine Grey ware **21** 666
Fine-line style **8** 343, *343*
Fine Orange ware **6** 580; **17** 755; **20** 884; **21** 240; **28** 373
fine paste pottery **28** 373
First Black-figure style **13** *499*, 499
Floral style **21** *669*, 670
Fortress White-on-Red Style **20** 886
Free Field style **8** 332, *348*, 348
Fustat Fatimid Sgraffito ware (FFS) **16** 405
galleyware **10** 303

pottery
wares—cont.
Galo Polychrome **13** 310
Geometric (*c.* 900–*c.* 700 BC) **21** 670
Ge ware **6** 894*
Gila Polychrome ware **22** 604
Gnathia ware **13** 539
Golden Horn ware **16** 420, 421
Grand style **13** 504
Green-and-white ware **5** 255*
green-glazed ware **17** 247–9*
Green Oribe ware **17** 255
greenware **10** 301
see also celadon
Grey bucchero ware **13** 491
Grimston-Lyles Hill **25** 513
Grooved ware **25** 514
Guan ware **6** 875, 892, 894*, *894*, 909
Haji ware **17** 241, 246–7, *247*, 249, 259, 341
Halaf pottery **2** *492*, 492; **20** 205; **21** 269–70, *305*, 305–6; **30** 183, 196; **33** 505
el Hatillo ware **14** 223–4
Hollands porceleyn **22** 879
Iga **17** 260–61, *261*
Imado **17** 262
Imitation Lustreware **9** 633
impasto ware **10** *599*, 609–10*, *610*
Impressed ware **25** 514
Insular Saladoid ware **2** 145
iron-glazed wares **18** 339*
Istoriato **16** 734, *734*, 735; **31** 741
Italo-Moresque ware **16** 733
Iznik ware **9** 633; **16** 124
Jasper ware **10** 306, 345, 642; **33** 21–2
Jaspisporzellan **6** 332; **21** 63, *64*
Jian ware **6** 873, 896, 901*, III3
Jizhou ware **6** 874, *874*, 896, 901*
Jun ware **6** 870, 895*, 900*, 909, II3
Kabeirion style **13** 513–14
Kamares ware **17** 751; **21** 657, *665*, 668, *668*
Karatsu **17** 341, *341*
Kashan style **1** 98; **16** 409–10
Kawarake **17** 259
Kaya wares **18** 335*
Kenzan ware **17** 244; **23** *366*, 367
Kerch' style **13** 524, *524*
Khabur ware **6** 386; **21** 308
Kimhae ware **18** 334–5*
Klazomenian ware **13** 487, 514, *514*, 515
Knipovitch group **13** 514
Koguryŏ wares **18** 336*
Koseto ware **17** *252*, 252–3*
Koumasa ware **21** *665*, 666
lājvardīna ware **6** IV3; **16** 412, 413
Laqabi ware **16** 406, 408
Late Roman C **16** 396
latesini ware **16** 735
lead-glazed ware **6** 333
China **6** 889
France **11** *603*, 603–4
Greece, ancient **13** 540
Ireland **16** 28
Rome, ancient **27** 106
Lebena ware **21** 666
Lefkandi I **14** 342, *342*
Lerna IV Patterned ware **14** *342*
Linru ware **6** 870, 892–3*
Longquan ware **6** 869, 893*, *893*, 899–900*, *900*, 915, 916
see also celadon
Lotus flower and crosslined ware **10** 27
Luna ware **13** 310; **23** *83*
lustreware **6** 329; **9** 37
Catalonia **29** 323

pottery
wares
lustreware—cont.
Central Asia, Western **6** 258; **16** 413
Egypt **16** 393, 404, *405*, 415–16*; **22** 515
Iran **16** 393, *394*, 401, 404, 409–10*, 412, 413, 423, 425, 427
Iraq **16** 393, 397, 399, *399*, 400, 404; **23** *558*
Islamic **6** 333, IV2; **16** 393, 394, *394*, 395, 397, 399, *399*, 400, 401, 404–5, *405*, 406, *406*, 407, 409–10*, 411, 412, 413, 415–16*, *416*, 418, 419, *419*, 423, 425, 427; **22** 515; **23** *558*
Italy **16** 734
Spain **6** 333, IV2; **7** XI2; **14** 425; **16** 404, 412, 418, 419, *419*; **20** 158; **29** 322, 323, 324–5, *325*, 326
Syria **16** 404, 406, *406*, 407, 415–16*, *416*
Turkey **16** 411
see also delftware; FAIENCE (ii) (CERAMICS) MAIOLICA; tin-glazed ware
Mabaruma style **13** 874
Macaracas Polychrome **7** 507; **28** 799
Mainland Polychrome style **14** *343*, 344
maiolica *see* MAIOLICA
majolica **20** 143*
Malacena ware **10** 616
Marine style **21** *669*, 670, *670*
Matt-painted ware **14** 337, 343, *343*, 344, 345
Mazapan ware **20** 886; **21** 239
Metope style **14** *347*
Metropolitan ware **10** 303
mezza-maiolica **6** 333
Midlands black ware **10** 303
Midlands yellow ware **10** 303
Mikarew style **24** 79
Miletus ware **16** 414, 418, 420
Minato **17** 262
Miniature style **16** 409
Mino Iga ware **17** 255
Minyan ware **14** 333, 337, 343, *344*; **23** 475
Mishima see Punch'ŏng
Modelled Alligator **13** 310
Monochrome ware **8** 345, 346
Monumental style **16** 409
Mumun ware **18** 333–4*, *334*
Namord ware **2** 267
Nanking ware **29** 114
Narumi Oribe ware **17** 255
Narushima **17** *257*
Ninevite 5 ware **21** 307
Ninsei ware **17** 244
Northampton group **13** 514
Northern Black Polished ware **15** 193, 194, 685, *686*; **22** 758
Northern Painted ware *see* Red-on-white ware
Nottingham ware **10** 306
Nuzi ware **15** 33; **21** 308; **23** 322; **30** 197, *197*
Ocros style **14** 828
Octopus style **14** *347*
Ōhi ware **25** 869
Old Hittite ware **1** 826, 838; **15** 159–60
Omuro ware **17** 244
Ongagawa ware **17** 246
Open style **21** 672
Oribe Black ware **17** 255
Oribe ware **11** 854; **17** 242, *254*, 255, 341; **21** 651
Orientalizing style **32** 30
Ornate style **13** 524, 526
Pabellón Modelled-carved ware **28** 373
Paekche ware **18** 336*

pottery
wares—cont.
Painted Grey ware **15** 193, 685
Palace style **21** *669*
Palace ware *see* Toprakkale ware
Palmetto ware **3** 59
Palo Seco style **31** 330–31
Panari *yachi* **27** 470
Panel style **8** 344
Papagayo **13** 310
Parita ware **7** 507
Pastoral style **8** 330, 346; **14** 346
Pataky **13** 310
Pataky Polychrome **29** 147
Pergamene appliqué ware **13** 540
Petal ware **9** 632
Peterborough ware **25** 513
Phocian red slip ware *see* Late Roman C ware
Pictorial style **14** *345*, *347*
Pingsdorf ware **22** 877
Plain style **13** 524, 526
Italy **13** 526
Minoan **21** 672
Plain White Wheelmade ware **8** 346
Plumbate ware **6** 580; **17** 755; **20** 886; **21** 239
Polychrome ware **9** 632–3; **10** 613
Post-Kamares ware **21** 668
pox **33** 102
Proto-Base Ring ware **8** 345
Proto-Monochrome ware **8** 345
Proto-White Painted ware **8** 346
Proto-White Slip ware **8** 345
Pseudo-Barbar ware **2** 268
Pseudo-Samian ware **16** 405
Punch'ŏng ware **18** 340–42, *341*, *342*
Pyrgos ware **21** *665*, 666
Queen ware **15** *820*
Quetta ware **25** 817
Raku ware **5** 582; **6** II2; **14** 704; **17** 256, 341, 399; **23** 367; **25** 869*; **28** *410*
Raqqa ware **16** 405, 406
Red-figure
Crete **13** 534
Etruscan **6** 333; **7** 366; **10** 615–16*, *616*; **13** 517
Greece, ancient **2** *134*; **3** 466; **6** 333; **12** 286; **13** *367*, 368, 471, 472, 475, *476*, *477*, *481*, 481–2, *482*, 488, *489*, 517*, 525–34*, *526*, *527*, *528*, *529*, *530*, *531*, *533*; **23** 290; **30** 339; **32** 31, *35*, 55, 65
Greece, ancient: Attica **13** *370*, *436*, *437*, 510, 517–25*, *517*, *518*, *519*, *520*, *522*, *523*, *524*; **29** *396*
Greece, ancient: Boiotia **13** 513–14, 533–4, *534*
Greece, ancient: Corinth **13** 534
Greece, ancient: Lakonia **13** 534
Italy **6** 333; **10** 615–16*, *616*; **13** 485, 487, 517, 525–33*, *526*, *527*, *528*, *529*, *531*, *533*; **30** 339
Sicily **13** *530*, 530–31*
Red-glazed ware **13** 538
Red Lustrous Wheelmade ware **8** 346
Red-on-black ware **8** 344, 345
Red-on-buff ware **1** 838
Red-on-white ware **8** 328, *329*, 338, 343, *343*, 345
Red Oribe ware **17** 255
Red Polished ware **8** *307*, 329, 338, 339, *339*, 344, 345
Red Polished III ware **8** *344*
Red Polished IV ware **8** 344
Red Polished V ware **8** 345
Red-ridged ware *see* Barbar ware

pottery
wares—cont.
Red Slip ware **8** 347; **16** 396; **27** 107
red spiral-burnished ware **1** 207
Red ware **10** 613*; **18** 667
relief-blue ware **16** 733, *733*
Rhenish ware **27** 108
Robles Moqo style **14** 828
Rockingham ware **31** 636
rouletted ware **29** 230
Rude style *see* Pastoral style
Rusafa ware **16** 407
Ru ware **6** 870, 892, 893–4*, *894*, 909
St Porchaire ware **6** 333
Salado Polychrome ware **22** 604
Samarra' **30** 196
Samian ware *see terra sigillata*
sancai **6** 872, 886, 888, *888*, *889*, 889, *891*, III3; **23** 389
Satsumon ware **17** 247
Scarlet ware **21** 306, *307*
Scenic ware **10** 27
Scored ware **21** 666
Second Black-figure style **13** 499, *500*
Seto **17** 341
Shigaraki **17** 260–61, *263*, 341
shiki **17** 250–51
Shino Oribe ware **17** 255
Shino ware **17** 241, 242, 254, *254*; **21** 651
Shiraiwa **17** *258*
shirashi **17** 259–61*
Siculo-Arabic ware **16** 415
Sikyatki Polychrome ware **22** *604*
Silla ware **18** *335*, 335–6*
slipwares **6** 328; **10** 303
Southern Monochrome ware *see* Combed ware
Special Palatial tradition **21** *670*, 670–71
spongewares **28** 258
Steingut see creamware
Sueki *see* Sue ware
Sue ware **17** 241, 242, 246, 249–50*, *250*, 251, 258, 259, *426*; **18** 190
Susa A **1** 894
Takatori **17** *341*
Talavera de Puebla ware **4** 175; **21** 392
Talioti ware **14** 342
terraglia see creamware
terra sigillata **6** 333; **27** 106, 107–8
terres jaspées **23** 849
Thin Orange ware **17** 755; **21** 238
three-colour glazed ware **17** 242, 247, 248*, *248*, 250, 251
tin-glazed ware **6** 333; **30** 875
Britain **30** 875
Catalonia **29** 323
England **10** 303, *304*; **30** *875*
France **30** 875
Germany **12** 430; **30** 875
Iran **16** *426*, 426
Iraq **16** 399
Ireland **16** 28
Islamic **16** 399, *426*, 426
Italy **14** 425
Mexico **21** 392, *392*
Netherlands, the **30** *876*
Portugal **25** 309; **30** 875
Scotland **28** *257*
Spain **29** 322, 323, *324*, 324–5, *326*, 326–7, *327*; **30** 875
see also Delftware; FAIENCE (ii) (CERAMICS); MAIOLIA; lustreware
Tiquisate Ware **17** 755
Tokoname **17** 260
Tonosí style **7** 506
Toprakkale ware **1** 838
Tortoiseshell Ripple ware **21** 668

pottery
wares—cont.
Tsutsumi **17** *257*
Tudor green wares **10** 302, 303
Tweeddale-type ware **28** 257
two-colour glazed ware **17** 247, 248*, 251
Ubaid pottery **30** 196
Umayyad Palace ware **16** 396, *397*
Usulután ware **17** 753; **20** 881; **21** 237
Vallejo **13** 310
Vasiliki ware **21** 666–7
Viñaque style **14** 828
Wajil ware **18** 334*, *334*
West Slope ware **13** 481, 539
Wetterau ware **27** 108
White background ware **10** 26–7
White crosslined ware **10** 26, *26*
White-ground **6** II1; **13** 471, 482, 511, *535*, 535–6*
White Mountain Redware **22** 604
White-on-dark ware **21** *665*, 667
White Painted ware **8** 338, 346, 347, *347*
White Painted I ware **8** 329, 345
White Painted II ware **8** 330, 345
White Painted IV ware **8** 345, *345*
White Painted Wheelmade ware **8** 345
White Shaved ware **8** 346
White Slip ware **8** 330
White Slip I ware **8** 345, *345*, 346
White Slip II ware **8** *345*, 346
Wild Goat style **8** 154; **13** 503, *503*; **15** 893
yamachawan **17** 250, 251, 252, 260; **33** 487–8*
Yaozhou ware **6** 870, 885, *892*, 892–3*
Yarmukian **30** 196
Yellow Seto ware **17** 254, *254*; **21** 650
Yixing ware **33** *535*, 535–6
Yue ware **6** 869, 873, 881, 884–5, *884*, 886, 892*; **7** 25
Zeuxippus ware **9** 633, 634
see also CERAMICS; EARTHENWARES; STONEWARES
Potthast, Edward Henry **25** 373*
Pottier, Jean **3** 641
Pottinger, David **16** 884; **25** 373*
potts *see under* HELMETS → types
Potts, E. **31** 241
Potuyl, H. **25** 797
Pot Viapori **11** 106
Potworowski, (Tadeusz) Piotr **17** 804; **25** 108, 373*, 409
Potyomkin, Grigory (Alexandrovich), Prince **3** 184; **12** 134; **25** 746; **27** 402, 415; **28** 599
architecture **29** 553
Potyomkin-Tavrichesky, G. A. **27** 439
Potypuszta **6** 157
Pötzsch, Eduard **25** 855
Pou **24** 82
pou see under VESSELS → types
Pou, Gabriel **11** 484
works **11** *484*
Pou Becerra, Miguel **25** 701
pouches **3** 442
historical and regional traditions
Bolivia **4** *266*
Indian subcontinent **3** 442
Native North Americans **4** I1; **22** *557*, *647*, 648, *649*, 651
United States of America **4** I1
materials
alpaca hair **4** *266*
beads **4** I1
hides **22** *557*

pouches
materials—cont.
quills **22** 651
Poucke, Karel van **3** 571; **17** 7; **25** 374*
pouffes see under STOOLS → types
Pouget **21** 907
Pouget, Jean-Henri-Prosper **17** 524; **21** 907
Pougny, Jean **25** 374–5*; **32** 412
dealers **20** 75
exhibitions **3** 802
groups and movements **1** 76; **8** 437; **16** 818; **30** 8; **31** 583
patrons and collectors **8** 10
teachers **33** 740
works **25** *375*
Pouillon, Fernand **1** 634; **25** 375–6*
Pouilloux, J. **27** 608
Pouilly, J. N. B. de **23** 31
Poulakis, Theodoros **1** 482; **7** 850; **25** 334
Poulenc, Francis **18** 863
Poulet-Malassis **4** 625; **27** 140
Poulett, John, 1st Earl Poulett (1663-1743) **12** 600
Poulett, John, 2nd Earl Poulett (*fl* 1744) **19** 531
Poulin, Julien **5** 569
Poulin, Roland **22** 39
Poullain, Antoine **3** 319
Poulleau
illustrated works **22** *739*
Poullet, Jean-Baptiste **8** 649
Poulsen, (Poul) Frederik (Sigfred) **25** 376*
Poulson, Joseph **21** 697
Poulsson, Magnus **25** 376–7*
assistants **3** 163
collaboration **2** 476; **23** 222, 232; **26** 553; **31** 243
works **23** 602, *602*
Poultier, Jean (-Baptiste) **14** 174; **25** 377*
Poulton & Woodman **23** 194
Pouncey, Philip (Michael Rivers) **6** 78; **25** 238, 377–8*
pouncing **25** 378–9*
historical and regional traditions
Buddhism **30** 845
China **25** 378
Italy **25** 378, *379*, 379
Tibet **30** 845
uses
frescoes **11** *761*, 763; **32** *806*
marquetry **20** 466
wall paintings **32** 805
Pouncy, Benjamin Thomas **24** 742
works **24** *742*
Pouncy, John **24** 651, 653
Pound, Ezra (Loomis) **24** 427; **25** 380*
groups and movements **26** 59; **32** 700, 701, 702
sculpture **12** 184
Poundbury **18** 456
Pounder, Maxwell **27** 613
pounders **25** 896, *896*
Pountney, J(ohn) D(ecimus) **33** 146
Poupart, Hiram **25** 703
poupée, à la see under PRINTING → processes
Poupelet, Jeanne **4** 391; **33** 310
Pouquette, L. F. **11** 902
Pourbus, Frans (i) (1545/6-81) **4** 839; **12** 242; **25** 381, 382*
groups and movements **26** 728
teachers **11** 222; **25** 381
works **9** 275
Pourbus, Frans (ii) (1569-1622) **11** 533; **24** 134; **25** 381, 382–3*
patrons and collectors **4** 549; **12** 903, 911; **20** 322; **28** 904
pupils **30** 40
reproductive prints by others **6** 547; **27** 503
teachers **25** 381

Pourbus, Frans (ii) (1569-1622)—cont.
works **11** *402*, 441, 533; **12** 513
Pourbus, Pieter (Jansz.) **4** 161, 921; **25** 381–2*
pupils **7** 369; **25** 382
works **3** 557; **10** 436; **17** 699; **25** *381*, 669; **31** *126*, 127
Pour l'Art **8** 701; **10** 735
Pourtalès, Jacques-Louis de **22** 920
Pourtalès-Gorgier, James-Alexandre, Comte de **3** 295; **15** 839; **25** 383–4*
Pousão, Henrique **25** 298, 384*
Pousette-Dart, Nathaniel **25** 384
Pousette-Dart, Richard **25** 384–5*
dealers **18** 162; **24** 213
groups and movements **1** 85
patrons and collectors **28** 314
Poussielgue-Rusand, Maurice **11** 622
Poussielgue-Rusand, Placide **11** 622; **13** 208
Poussin, Claude **9** 409
Poussin, Gaspard *see* DUGHET, GASPARD
Poussin, Lavallee **7** 417
Poussin, Nicolas **2** 170; **7** 383, 628; **8** 612; **9** 8, *9*, 93; **11** 356, 587, 744; **14** 583; **16** 82; **22** 378; **23** 294; **25** 385–96*, *394*; **26** 771, 772, 842
assistants **21** 497
attributions **3** 454; **6** 461; **9** 371, 376; **20** 769; **21** 89, 541; **30** 122; **32** 426
book illustrations **18** 735; **19** 197
collaboration **9** 363, 409; **13** 814; **29** 623; **31** 321; **32** 738
drawings **9** 222, 223; **21** *764*
forgeries by others **31** 871
frames **11** *403*, 404, *415*, *431*
groups and movements **3** 265; **16** 668, 670; **23** 856
methods **5** 654; **6** 570; **18** 898; **19** 354; **21** 764; **24** 493
paintings **9** 8; **16** 671–2; **21** 609; **26** 349
allegorical **1** 658; **25** *393*
altarpieces **26** 810
frescoes **7** 380
history **25** *387*
landscape **18** 709, 712; **25** *392*; **26** 772
literary themes **30** 358
mythological **10** 130, 477; **11** 535–6; **22** 414; **23** 680; **25** *390*
oil sketches **23** 381
portraits **1** 663
religious **24** VII2; **25** *391*
patrons and collectors
Altieri (family) **1** 728
Aumale, Henri-Eugène-Philippe-Louis de Bourbon, Duc d' **23** 523
Aved, Jacques (-André-Joseph) **2** 852
Barberini, Francesco, Cardinal **3** 208
Bellio, Georges de **3** 671
Bonnemaison, Ferréol de **4** 330
Bretonvilliers, Claude le Ragois de **4** 756
Brienne, Louis-Henri, Comte de **4** 807
Butler, Charles (1822-1910) **5** 311
Castel Rodrigo, Manuel de Moura y Corte Real, 2nd Marqués de **6** 30
Catherine II, Empress of Russia (*reg* 1762- 96) **26** 733
Cavendish, William, 2nd Duke of Devonshire (1671-1729) **6** 116
Charmois, Martin de **6** 488
Clement IX, Pope (*reg* 1667-70) **27** 172

Poussin, Nicolas
patrons and collectors—cont.
Clive, Robert, 1st Baron Clive **7** 437
Coke, Thomas, 1st Earl of Leicester of the 1st creation (1697-1759) **7** 540
Créquy, Charles de Blanchefort de **19** 238
Crozat, Pierre **8** 209
Desenfans, Noël Joseph **8** 792
Des Noyers, François Sublet, Baron de Dangu **29** 886
Dezallier d'Argenville, Antoine-Joseph **8** 845
Dutuit (family) **9** 466
Egerton, Francis, 3rd Duke of Bridgewater **9** 755
Einden, Jan van den **10** 114
Elizabeth Farnese, Queen of Spain (1692-1766) **4** 559
Ellis, Welbore Agar **10** 146
Esterházy, Miklós II, Prince (1765-1833) **10** 531
Fabre, François-Xavier, Baron **10** 726, 727
Felton, Alfred **10** 877
Fesch, Joseph, Cardinal **11** 32
Filomarino, Ascanio, Cardinal **11** 81; **22** 478
Fouquet, Nicolas **11** 356, 357
Francis-Joseph, Prince of Liechtenstein (*reg* 1772-81) **19** 338
Fréart (de Chantelou), Paul **11** 744
Giori, Angelo, Cardinal **12** 680
Giustiniani (i), Vincenzo, Marchese **12** 764
Hamilton, Alexander, 10th Duke of Hamilton and 7th Duke of Brandon **14** 107
Hanover, Frederick (Louis), Prince of Wales (1707-51) **14** 143
Harcourt, Simon, 1st Earl Harcourt of Stanton Harcourt and 2nd Earl Nuneham **14** 163
Henry, Bon-Thomas **14** 395
Herbert, Thomas, 8th Earl of Pembroke **14** 435
Hesselin, Louis (-Cauchon) **14** 492
His de La Salle, (Aimé-Charles-) Horace **14** 577
Hoare (i), Henry the younger (1705-85) **14** 598
Howard (ii), Frederick, 5th Earl of Carlisle **14** 808
Isham, Thomas **13** 300
Jesuit Order **17** 509
John VI, King of Portugal (*reg* 1816-26) **4** 725
Josephine, Empress of the French (1763-1814) **4** 304
Jouin, Henry(-Auguste) **17** 667
La Live de Jully, Ange-Laurent de **18** 660
Lankrink, Prosper Henry **18** 748
Las Marismas del Guadalquivir, Marqués de **18** 811
La Vrillière, Louis Phélypeaux de **18** 885
Lempereur, Jean-Denis, II **19** 144
Le Nôtre, André **19** 164
Ligne, Charles-Joseph-Emmanuel de, Prince (1759-92) **19** 369
Louis XIII, King of France (*reg* 1610-43) **4** 549
Louis XIV, King of France (*reg* 1643-1715) **4** 552; **11** 662
Lumague, Marc-Antoine (i) (*d* 1619) **19** 790
Manners, Charles, 4th Duke of Rutland **5** 357; **10** 146
Poussin, Nicolas
patrons and collectors—cont.
Marie de Medici, Queen of France (1573-1642) **4** 549
Mariette, Pierre-Jean **20** 417
Marino, Giambattista **20** 430
Massimo, Camillo (Carlo), Cardinal **20** 588; **26** 773
Mazarin, Jules, Cardinal **20** 896
Medici, Giovanni Carlo de', Cardinal (1611-63) **21** 27
Meyers, Jacques **22** 905
Morice, Humphry **22** 115
Morrison, James **22** 148
Musée Fesch **11** 32
Musée du Louvre (Paris) **11** 665
Orléans, Philippe II de Bourbon, 2nd Duc d' (1674-1723) **11** 662; **23** 516
Paignon-Dijonval **23** 777
Philip IV, King of Spain (*reg* 1621-65) **7** 394
Pointel **11** 661
Potocki, Stanisław Kostka **25** 364
Pourtalès-Gorgier, James-Alexandre, Comte de **25** 384
Pozzo, Carlo Antonio dal, II **25** 413
Pozzo (Lumbroso), Cassiano dal **25** 412, 664; **26** 773
Quentin de Lorangère **25** 815
Reynolds, Joshua **26** 280
Richards, John Inigo **26** 335
Richelieu, Armand-Jean Du Plessis, Cardinal de **11** 662; **26** 348
Richelieu, Louis-François Armand-Jean Vignerod du Plessis, Duc de (1629-1715) **11** 662
Roscioli, Giovanni Maria **27** 160
Rushout, John, 2nd Baron Northwick **27** 350
Ryabushinsky, Nikolay (Pavlovich) **27** 458
Savoy, Eugene of, Prince (1663-1736) **28** 15
Seignelay, Jean-Baptiste (-Antoine) Colbert, Marquis de **7** 546
Seymour-Conway, Richard, 4th Marquess of Hertford **28** 527
Tallard, Marie-Joseph d'Hostun, Duc de **30** 274
Temple-Nugent-Brydges-Chandos-Grenville, Richard, 1st Duke of Buckingham and Chandos **13** 637
Tessin, Carl Gustav, Count **30** 524
Thibaudeau, Narcisse-Adolphe, Comte de **30** 727
Thiers, Louis-Antoine Crozat, Baron de **8** 210
Trichet de Fresne, Raphaël **31** 321
Vassal de Saint-Hubert, Jean-Antoine-Hubert **32** 74
Vaudreuil, François, Comte de **32** 85
Walpole, Robert, 1st Earl of Orford (1676-1745) **32** 824
Watelet, Claude-Henri **32** 898
Wildenstein, Georges **33** 182
Williams-Wynn, Watkin, 4th Baronet, of Wynnstay (1749-89) **32** 790; **33** 209
pupils **3** 294; **6** 488; **8** 88; **9** 375; **10** 144; **17** 915; **25** 79; **31** 323; **33** 82
reproductions in ceramics **20** 474
reproductions in tapestry **12** 829; **23** 512
reproductions in textiles **16** 760
reproductions on porcelain **14** 323
Poussin, Nicolas—cont.
reproductive prints by others **20** 416; **21** 85; **26** 229; **30** 746
Audran, Jean **2** 709
Bergeret, Pierre-Nolasque **3** 775
Bloemaert, Cornelis, II (1603-?84) **7** 569
Chasteau, Guillaume **6** 502
Kilian, Georg **18** 47
Loir, Alexis, I (1640-1713) **19** 543
Lombart, Pierre **19** 562
Mariette, Jean **20** 416
Morghen, Raphael **10** 394
Pesne, Jean **9** 8
Picart, Bernard (1673-1733) **24** 712
Pò, Pietro del **25** 55
Poilly, François de **25** 77
Poilly, Jean-Baptiste de (1669-1728) **25** 77
Pye, John **25** 753
Rousselet, Gilles **27** 269
Simon, Pierre (*c.* 1650-1710) **28** 751
Volpato, Giovanni **32** 689
Voogd, Hendrik **32** 693
teachers **18** 662; **20** 588; **31** 908
title-pages **4** 359
writings **7** 685; **8** 613
Poussinisme **9** 8; **25** 397–8*
Poutrain, Maximilian *see* COLT, MAXIMILIAN
Pouwelsz., Claes **32** 140
Pouyat **19** 397; **24** 149
Pouyat, François **19** 397
Povedano, Tomás **8** 18
Po've'ka *see* MARTINEZ, MARIA
Poverty Point (LA) **22** *544*, 570; **25** 398*
Povey, Thomas **14** 739
Povolný, Anton **19** 281; **28** 850
Powązki **23** 202
powder **20** 465
powdered paper *see under* PAPER → types
powder flasks **16** 799
Powderham Castle (Devon) **10** 294; **26** 499
powder horns **14** 763
powder paints *see under* PAINTS → types
powder puppets *see under* PUPPETS → types
Powell, Ada Louise **33** 22
Powell, Alfred Hoare **33** 22
Powell, Barnaby **10** 321
Powell, Francis **32** 903
Powell, Geoffry **6** 409–10
Powell, Henry **9** 321
Powell, James, & Sons **10** 320; **16** 821; **19** 595; **25** 398–9*; **29** 506
designers **5** 266; **14** 677; **29** 513; **33** 132
staff **18** 882
Powell, John **26** 68
Powell, John Hardman **10** 335; **13** 207; **25** 714
Powell, Michael **25** 399
Powell, Philip **25** 399
Powell, Sebastian Pugin **25** 710
Powell and Moya **25** 399*
staff **13** 239
works **1** 736; **14** 783; **23** 689; **25** *399*; **30** 684
Powell-Cotton, Hannah **33** 610
Powell-Cotton, Percy **33** 610
Power, Alan **25** 400
Power, Albert **16** 21
Power, E(dward) J(oseph) **25** 400*
Power, John Joseph Wardell **2** 770, 772; **25** 400*
personal collection **2** 771; **30** 160
works **2** 749
Power, J. P. **2** 739; **29** 919
Power, Rupert **25** 400
Power Gallery of Contemporary Arts *see under* SYDNEY → University of Sydney
power looms *see under* LOOMS → types
Powers, Gersham **25** 637
Powers, Harriet **1** 424
works **1** *425*
Powers, Hiram **7** 327; **11** 189; **25** 400–402*; **31** 610
patrons and collectors **7** 840; **29** 651
works **25** *401*; **31** 611
Powers, Horace S. **29** 382
Powers, John **17** 431
Powers, Mrs John **17** 431
Powers, Michael **2** 318
Powers and Ball **13** 297
Powerscourt (Co. Wicklow) **12** 129; **16** *5*; **25** 402*
Powerscourt, Richard Wingfield, 3rd Viscount *see* WINGFIELD, RICHARD, 3rd Viscount Powerscourt
power stations **25** 402–3*, *403*; **28** *282*
Powhatan **30** 449
Powis Castle (Powys)
armour **14** 185
Clive Museum **15** 744
collections **7** 437; **9** 31; **15** 713, 741
gardens **32** 552
interior decoration **32** 788
paintings **4** 182; **13** 650; **15** 44
sculpture **18** 902
Powle, George **33** 380
Powles, Richard **19** 734
Pownall, William **21** 697
Powning, John **11** 361
Powolny, Michael **2** 817; **19** 719; **25** 403–4*; **32** 450
collaboration **19** 538, 539
groups and movements **33** 166
pupils **8** 406; **12** 821; **26** 365; **31** 640
works **2** 816; **12** 821
Powsner, S. **33** 507
Powys, Albert **3** 110
Powys, Marian **31** 661
pox pottery *see under* POTTERY → wares
Poyet, Bernard **25** 404*
teachers **32** 766
works **13** 237; **24** 124; **25** 268
Poyet, Jean **18** 662; **25** *405*, 405–6*; **31** 846
Poyet, Mathelin **25** 405
Poyntell, William **32** 815
Poynter, Ambrose **5** 512; **25** 406; **32** 864
Poynter, Edward John **10** 254; **14** 588; **20** 925; **23** 295; **25** 406–7*; **33** 137
groups and movements **23** 504
patrons and collectors **15** 894
personal collection **3** 184
pupils **7** 569; **21** 138; **31** 418; **33** 515
reproductive prints by others **6** 451; **9** 54
teachers **10** 373
works **5** 196; **10** 97, 254; **23** *547*; **25** *407*; **30** 503, XII
Poynter, Maude **2** 760
Poynton, Edward **28** 878
Poyntz, Francis **10** 351
Pöyry, Olli **24** 778
Poysieu (family) **7** 407
Požarevac, National Museum **28** 458
Pozdančić, Petar **31** 359
Pozen, Leonid (Volodymyrovych) **25** 407–8*
Poznań **21** 571; **25** *92*, 408–9*
architecture **25** 94, 99
art schools **25** 123, 133
bronze **25** 129
Poznań—cont.
Cathedral **25** 94, 104, 126, 134
metalwork **13** 162
painting **25** *104*
sculpture **25** 110
tomb of Adam Konarski **25** 113
tomb of Andrew and Barbara Górka **25** 113
tomb of Bishop Izbieński **25** 113
chemical factory **4** 788
collegiate church *see* St Mary
Corpus Christi **25** 126
gold **25** 127
Górka Palace *see* National Antiquities Museum
Jesuit church **25** 98; **32** 895
lithography **25** 106
metalwork **13** 162; **25** 126, 127; **26** 686
Museum of Frederick the Great **25** 139, 409
Museum of Prehistoric Archaeology **25** 139
National Antiquities Museum **25** 139, 408
National Museum **21** 485; **25** 836; **30** 332
painting **25** 101
Raczyński Library **25** 99, 408
St John **13** 162
St Mary **4** 783
St Sabina **13** 162
Stadion Lech **29** 489
State Higher School of Fine Arts **25** 141
Town Hall **25** 96, *409*, 787
Water Tower **10** 697
Wielkopolskie Museum **25** 140, 409
Poznański (family) **25** 136
Poznański, Izrael Kalmanowicz **19** 536
palaces **19** *536*
Pozo, Alberto González **22** 70
Pozo, Condesa de la Vega del *see* VEGA DEL POZO, Condesa de la
Pozo, Ismael **24** 509, 515
Pozo, José del **24** 508, 517
Pozo de Maza **29** 202
Pozo Moro **15** 59; **25** 409–10*, *470*; **30** 434
stelae **15** *60*
Pozo y Marqui, José del **22** 23; **31** 753
Pozsony *see* BRATISLAVA
Pozsonyszentgyörgy *see* JUR PRI BRATISLAVE
Pozzi (family) **12** 405
Pozzi, Andrea **11** 249; **25** 410; **31** 172
Pozzi, Andrés **29** 345
Pozzi, B. **23** 473
Pozzi, Carlo Ignazio **8** 816
Pozzi, Francesco **3** 58
Pozzi, Giovanni **25** 410
Pozzi, Giuseppe **25** 410, 411
Pozzi, Jean **15** 742; **25** 410*
Pozzi, Luigi **10** 818
Pozzi, Rocco **25** 410
Pozzi, Stefano **3** 708; **25** 410–11*
patrons and collectors **3** 707; **26** 286, 287
pupils **4** 744; **6** 111; **25** 790
reproductive prints by others **10** 770
works **29** 888
Pozzo, Amadeo dal **25** 388, 411
Pozzo, Andrea **2** 827; **16** 714; **25** 413–16*
architecture **8** 176; **9** 331; **19** 516; **28** 859; **31** 329
assistants **19** 775
collaboration **11** 754; **19** 88
methods **24** 490
pageants **26** 771

Pozzo, Andrea—cont.
  paintings 25 414
    quadratura 2 794; 13 321; 15 138; 32 443
    religious 15 121; 16 671; 25 415; 31 443
  patrons and collectors 11 32; 17 509, 510, 512; 28 14
  pupils 6 39, 350; 30 369
  sculpture 5 525; 15 121; 26 824
  stage design 30 668
  writings 6 40; 17 595; 21 762; 28 339; 31 296
    translated 16 893
Pozzo, Angelo 19 516
Pozzo, Borgino dal 1 697
Pozzo, Carlo Antonio dal, II 25 411, 412–13*
Pozzo (Lumbroso), Cassiano dal 16 671; 19 197; 25 411, 411, 412*; 30 526
  codices 24 240
  collections 2 163; 5 768; 16 764; 25 664; 26 773; 30 526
  drawings 1 533; 7 906; 9 409; 25 386
  groups and movements 6 360
  manuscripts 2 376; 20 242
  Museo Cartaceo see under ROME → museums
  paintings 12 169; 19 354; 25 388, 389, 395, 664; 32 715
  pottery 13 541
Pozzo (Lumbroso), Cosimo Antonio dal 25 411
Pozzo, Francesco da see FRANCESCO DA POZZO
Pozzo, Francesco Giuseppe 2 780
Pozzo, Gabriele dal 25 411
Pozzo, Leopoldo dal 26 322
Pozzo, Paolo 20 321
Pozzo, Ugo 1 166
Pozzo della Cisterna, Emanuele, Prince 25 412
pozzolana 7 691; 11 762; 25 748; 26 879, 889; 27 51
Pozzoserrato see TOEPUT, LODEWIJK
Pozzuoli 16 621; 24 795; 25 747–8*; 26 886
  alabastra 1 868
  amphitheatre 1 797, 797; 25 748; 26 874, 895
  glass 27 74
  inscriptions 26 885
  macellum 26 625
  markets 19 889; 20 438; 21 893; 26 871
  metalwork 27 93
  pigments 23 785
  pozzolana 7 692
  tombs 27 71
  tunnel 27 6
Pozzuoli red see under PIGMENTS → types
PPA Ltd 27 523
Prabha, B. 4 291
Prabhasa 15 695
Prabhavatigupta, Queen (reg 390–410) (Varataka) 25 885
Prabodhashiva 15 290
Praça da Ribeira 25 293
Prachatice 8 390; 10 741
Prachatitz, Peter 32 452
Prácheň
  glass 8 410
Prachinburi National Museum 29 240
Prachi Temple 15 267
Prachner, Petr 8 386; 25 417
Prachner, Richard Jiří (1705–82) 8 386, 398; 25 417, 443
Prachner, Václav 8 387, 416; 25 417*, 433
  works 8 386
Pracovní architektonická skupina see PAS GROUP
Practical Equipment Ltd see PEL
Prad, Giovanni Poulard 22 482
pradakṣiṇapatha 15 244*
Pradas, Juan García de see GARCÍA DE PRADAS, JUAN
Prader 20 119
Pradhan Gond 15 732
Pradier, Charles-Simon 4 716; 13 295
Pradier, James 11 563, 671; 15 841; 25 417–18*; 30 125
  collaboration 30 32
  groups and movements 22 742; 31 374
  patrons and collectors 8 705; 17 667; 23 521
  prizes (artists') 24 171
  pupils 6 463, 468; 10 563; 12 312; 13 826; 16 573; 19 239; 20 119
  works 11 563, 565; 20 214; 25 418; 30 137
Pradilla (Ortiz), Francisco 23 440; 25 419*
  pupils 3 12; 19 727; 27 511
  works 29 284
Pradilla, Pizano, & Caro 1 744
Prado, Blas de 19 54; 25 419*; 29 278, 280
  pupils 27 706
  works 31 89
Prado, Jerónimo del 3 45; 23 489; 31 297; 32 560
Prado, José Núñez del see NÚÑEZ DEL PRADO, JOSÉ
Prado, Marina Nuñez del see NUÑEZ DEL PRADO, MARINA
Prado, Mateo de 25 419–20*
Prado, Museo del see under MADRID → museums
Prado, Pedro de 29 344
Prado, Villa del see VILLA DEL PRADO
Prado Redemption, Master of the 20 747*; 29 691
Prado Valladares, Clarival do 4 729
Praehauser, Ludwig 2 832
Praemer, Wilhelm 2 782
Praeneste 10 583, 639, 640; 16 620; 25 420–22*; 26 886
  architecture 25 420–21*
  Barberini Tomb 10 587, 590, 626, 631
  Bernardini Tomb 1 867; 10 590, 626, 631
  bronzes 26 860; 27 85
  Castellani Tomb 10 631
  cists 10 629, 630
  Galeassi Tomb 10 631
  gardens 12 118
  mirrors 10 629
  mosaics 13 547; 22 160; 25 421*, 422; 27 60, 61
  Sanctuary of Fortuna Primigenia 16 623; 25 421; 26 865, 888; 27 1, 714; 32 86
    architecture 26 880
    Nile Mosaic see NILE MOSAIC
    sculpture 27 15
    staircase 29 520
    Temple of Fortuna Primigenia 20 571; 26 889
    well-head 33 56
  sculpture 27 29
Praenestinus, Andreas see FULVIO, ANDREA
Praesens Group 2 409; 25 100, 119, 122, 422–3*; 30 199; 32 877
  members 5 8; 7 293; 18 181, 596; 21 783; 29 582, 794; 30 199
Praesidium, Das 24 738
Praet, Jules Van see VAN PRAET, JULES
praetoria 21 559; 25 423*
Prag, Junker von see JUNKER VON PRAG
Prager, Karel 25 423*
Prager, Lorenz 28 859
Prager, Oscar 18 810
prāggrīva 15 244*
Prag-Rudniker 2 814; 15 823; 32 448
  works 33 156
Prague 8 374, 375; 14 683; 25 423–46*, 424
  academies and art schools
    Academy of Applied Art 8 414, 425; 25 435
      collections 8 424
      library 8 425
    Academy of Fine Arts 3 778; 8 425; 25 433
      library 8 425
    Academy of Performing Arts 8 425
    Bohemian Academy of Arts and Sciences 8 423
    Czechoslovakian Academy of Sciences Art History Institute 8 425
    School of Applied Art see Academy of Applied Art
    School of Arts and Crafts 8 425
    School of Decorative Arts 8 421
      lace workshop 8 421
    School of Graphic Art 8 425
  Altschul 17 547
  art forms and materials
    books 21 636
    clocks 7 442
    enamel 10 194
    furniture 8 395, 399
    gem-engraving 12 260
    glass 8 407; 25 434–5*
    gold 8 412
    Haggadot 17 565
    hardstones 14 II1; 25 435–6*
    iron 8 415, 416
    metalwork 8 414, 416; 25 436–7*; 26 686
    painting 13 131, 152; 22 414
    pewter 8 415
    porcelain 8 405
    pottery 8 404
    rock crystal 26 485, 486
    sculpture 13 85, 89
    silk 8 419
    stained glass 8 407
    textiles 8 419
  bridges
    Charles Bridge 4 698, 843, 844; 8 376, 381; 22 45; 25 424
      sculpture 8 382, 385, 387; 16 817
    Judith Bridge see Charles Bridge
    Little Quarter bridge 26 637
    Old Town bridge tower 14 420; 19 829
    Palacký Bridge 8 387
  Café Arco 8 401
  Café Corso 23 372
  Charles University 8 394
    Art History Department Library 8 425
    Carolinum 8 381
    Hrdlička Museum of Anthropology 29 241
  Clementinum 8 378; 23 339
    Italian Chapel 8 416
    library 8 425; 19 316
    St Clement 4 698–9; 32 822
  College of Technology 8 425
  colleges 7 566
  Community House 8 379
  ecclesiastical buildings 13 57
    Břevnov Monastery of St Margaret 8 397, 412, 874–5; 22 203; 25 552
    Church of Our Lady before Týn 8 394, 415; 13 161
      fonts (baptismal) 8 415
      sculpture 8 383
    Church of the Knights of the Cross with the Red Star see St Francis
    Convent of the Minorites and Poor Clares see St Agnes Convent
    Emmaus Monastery 13 151
Prague
  ecclesiastical buildings—cont.
    Holy Trinity Church 8 378
    Loreto Church 8 378; 25 443*
      monstrance 2 819
      sculpture 8 385
      Treasury 8 412, 413; 25 443
    Our Lady of the Snows 8 382, 384
    Premonstratensian monastery 8 398
    St Agnes Convent 4 782; 8 376; 25 430
    St Clement see under Clementinum
    St Francis 8 378, 379; 16 817; 25 428
      Cloister 8 400
      sculpture 8 385
    St George's Convent see under Hradčany Castle
    St James 25 766
    St John Nepomuk 32 823
    St John Nepomuk on the Rock 8 876
    St Joseph 8 396
    St Margaret 8 391
    St Mary in Týn see Church of Our Lady before Týn
    St Mary of the Snows see Our Lady of the Snows
    St Nicholas (Little Quarter) 8 378, 378, 874, 874
      paintings 8 391
    St Nicholas (Old Town Square) 8 876, 876–7; 12 372; 17 511; 32 822
    St Peter 8 394
    St Saviour 8 376, 378
    SS Simon and Jude 8 378
    St Thomas 8 396, 413; 16 908
    St Vitus' Cathedral 8 376, 379; 13 57, 58, 89; 18 827; 20 814–15; 21 757; 24 189–90, 190; 25 438*, 440, 441; 26 637
      architecture 25 438–41*
      bell 8 416
      chevets (chapels) 25 439
      choir 22 222
      choir-stalls 8 394
      crown see CROWN OF WENCESLAS
      gargoyles 12 150
      gates 8 416
      Golden Gate 8 407
      ivory-carvings 13 177
      marks 20 441
      metalwork 8 384; 26 687
      mosaics 13 134; 22 163; 25 442–3*
      oratory 8 377
      painting 13 152
      pews 8 395
      railings 8 416
      restoration 2 321
      St Vitus Madonna 8 395
      sceptres 26 81
      sculpture 8 382, 383, 384; 13 89; 25 441–2*, 442
      stained glass 8 407; 13 187
      staircases 29 522
      swords 26 82
      textiles 9 668
      tomb of Přemysl Ottakar I 13 89
      tomb of Přemysl Ottakar II 13 89
      tomb of St Wenceslas 8 412, 416
      tracery 31 271
      Treasury 8 412, 413, 414
      vaults 32 92, 93
      Vladislav II gallery 32 90
      Wenceslas Chapel 8 390, 415; 22 219
      woodwork 8 396
    St Wenceslas 8 396
Prague
  ecclesiastical buildings—cont.
    Strahov Monastery 8 376, 416; 25 444–5*
      collections 8 423
      libraries 19 316
      metalwork 8 412
      Museum of Czech Literature see under museums
      National Literary Memorial 3 91
      Philosophical Hall 8 379, 391, 399; 19 316
      Theological Hall 19 316
      woodwork 8 396
    Týn Church see Church of Our Lady before Týn
    Ursuline Convent 8 385; 25 548
  education (art) 8 425
  Equestrian Monument of St Wenceslas 25 434
  façade decoration 10 741
  fortifications 8 378
  General Pensions Institute see House of Trade Unions
  guilds 8 412; 25 431
  Hanavský Pavilion 8 416
  Hotel Juliš 8 402
  House of Trade Unions 8 380; 14 732
  houses
    By the Bell House 8 382
    Czech Cubist house 25 430
    Haus zur Minute 10 738
    House of Jiří Melantrich 8 395
    House of the Black Madonna 8 373, 380
    Müller House 8 402
  Hradčany Castle 8 376, 379; 19 828; 25 437, 437–8*; 26 366–7
    altarpieces 29 429
    Ballcourt 8 378
    Belvedere 8 377, 384, 416; 25 425; 29 624–5
      sculpture 8 384
      Singing Fountain 24 331
    collections 8 423; 9 18; 14 682
    furniture 8 395, 401, 402
    gardens 12 114, 133
    Kunstkammer 2 830; 13 914, 918; 18 522; 29 430
    Ludwig wing 8 377
    paintings 13 916, 919
    railings 8 416
    St George's Convent 8 412; 25 430
      Church 8 381; 26 594, 637
    sculpture 8 382
    towers 26 366
    Vladislav Hall 8 377; 13 58; 23 809; 26 367
  Hvězda summer house 8 384
  International Hotel 8 381
  Jesuit college 8 398
  Jewish cemetery 17 555
  Košíře cemetery
    sculpture 8 386, 387
    tomb of Bishop Lev Thun-Hohenstein 8 416
  Kotva department store 8 381
  Kunstkammern 9 14
  Legiobanka 8 373, 380, 402
  Metro stations 21 350
  Mozarteum 18 405
  museums
    Bedřich Smetana Museum 33 162
    Hrdlička Museum of Anthropology see under Charles University
    Jewish Museum 8 424; 17 581
    Museum of Czech Literature 8 424; 25 445
    Museum of Decorative Arts 8 424; 9 303; 28 176; 30 332
      library 8 425
    Museum of Ethnography 8 424

Prague
museums—cont.
Museum of the Kingdom of Bohemia see National Museum
Náprstek Museum of Asian, African and American Culture 8 424; 10 795; 15 745; 29 241
National Gallery 8 424; 18 435; 25 742; 26 1
National Museum 8 375, 379, 424; 10 795; 25 428, 429, 433; 28 133, 176
collections 8 423
Pantheon 15 49
National Technical Museum 8 425
Rudolphinum 8 379, 428
Na Můstku 8 381
New Town 8 376; 19 828
Old Town Square 8 384, 387
palaces
Archbishop's Palace 8 379, 397
Černín Palace see Czernin Palace
Clam-Gallas Palace 4 698; 23 812; 25 433
Colloredo Palace 8 396
Czernin Palace 5 701–2; 8 378, 380, 426–7; 20 572; 26 125
furniture 8 397
interior decoration 8 397
woodwork 8 396
Lobkovic Palace 8 378, 396
Michnov Palace 8 378
Morzin Palace
sculpture 8 385
Rožmberk Palace 8 378
Šternberk Palace 21 830; 29 411
Wallenstein Palace 8 378; 25 445–6*
garden 12 133; 25 445–6
interior decoration 8 397
loggia 25 427
sculpture 8 384
woodwork 8 396
patronage 13 128
Powder Tower 8 377, 383
Riunione Adriatica di Sicurta 8 373
State Institute for Conservation 8 425
State Institute for the Conservation of Historical Monuments and Nature Library 8 425
State Library see Clementinum
State Polytechnic Institute 8 425
statue of St Wenceslas 22 403
Štenc House 8 379
synagogues 17 544, 547
Klausen synagogue 17 581
Staronová Synagogue 8 376; 17 544, 544; 25 443–4*, 444
theatres
National Theatre 1 604; 8 379; 25 429
sculpture 8 387
Neues Deutsches Theater see Smetana Theatre
Nostic Theatre see Tyl Theatre
Smetana Theatre 30 678
Tyl Theatre 30 678
town halls
Jewish Town Hall 25 444
Little Quarter Town Hall 8 378
Old Town Hall
astronomical clock 7 439; 8 392
sculpture 8 382
Trade Fair Palace 8 380; 25 548; 31 492
Villa Amerika 28 163
Villa Portheim 32 554
Villa Trója 8 385; 20 814, 814
Vyšehrad 25 445*
Waterworks see museums → Bedřich Smetana Museum
Prague Art Workshops (PUD) 8 373, 401; 12 834; 16 902
Prague Gospels see under GOSPEL BOOKS → individual manuscripts
Prague Inventory 16 443
Prague Secession see SECESSION (PRAGUE)
Praha see PRAGUE
Prairie House 21 780
Prairie Printmakers 25 629
Prairie school 2 572; 6 573, 578; 25 446*; 31 595, 632
members 13 648; 25 737
Praisos 8 154; 21 681
Prakhov, Adrian 20 232; 22 338; 27 443; 32 735
Prakhov, N. A. 28 619
Prakrit 15 203
Prambanan see LORO JONGGRANG
Prämer, Wilhelm 32 435
Prämer, Wolf Wilhelm 19 336
Prampolini, Enrico 16 681; 25 446–8*; 26 776
collaboration 11 80; 20 905
exhibitions 10 821
groups and movements 1 76, 166; 8 434, 771; 11 866, 867, 868, 869; 16 648, 680
patrons and collectors 2 409
productions 4 630; 22 445
works 11 80; 16 707, 731; 25 447; 27 789; 29 97
praṇāla 15 244*
Prande, Alberts 28 715
Prandl, Petr see BRANDL, PETR
Prandocin Church 25 134
Prandtauer, Jakob 2 782; 25 448–9*; 31 510
assistants 22 296
patrons and collectors 8 378
works 2 783, 828; 5 772; 12 497; 13 279; 14 260; 18 447; 19 433; 21 83, 83–4; 25 448; 27 553
Prandtner (family) 15 8
Prandtner, János 25 449
Prandtner, József (i) (before 1783-1819) 25 449
Prandtner, József (ii) (1796-after 1839) 25 449
Prandtner, József (iii) 25 449
prang see THAILAND → tower-sanctuaries
Prang, Louis 10 421; 20 604; 25 449–50*; 30 241
works 19 485; 30 750
Prang, Louis, & Co. 4 766; 18 670; 25 449
Prangey, Joseph-Philibert Girault de see GIRAULT DE PRANGEY, JOSEPH-PHILIBERT
Prantl, Karl 2 804
Prasa 21 674, 675
Prasad, Ishwari 15 653
prāsādas see under PALACES → types
Prasaiboi 5 313
Prasat Andet
sculpture 5 484, 485
Prasat Ban Chang 30 580
Prasat Ban Phluang 30 580
Prasat Ban Thanon Hak 30 580
Prasat Beng 30 580
Prasat Damrei Krap 5 485
Prasat Khao Noi 30 579
Prasat Khna 5 470
Prasat Ku Ka Sing 30 580
Prasat Muang Sing 30 581, 599
Prasat Muang Tam 30 580
Prasat Neak Buos 5 472
Prasat Nong Hong 30 580
Prasat Phanom Rung 30 571, 580–81
lintels 30 600
sculpture 30 599
temple 30 579
Prasat Phanom Wan 30 580
Prasat Phimai 30 571, 579, 580, 581
lintels 30 600
sculpture 30 599
statue 30 599
temple 30 579
Prasat Phnom Chisor 5 472
Prasat Phra That Narai Cheung Weng 30 580
Prasat Phum Pon Temple 30 578
Prasat Prang Ku 30 580
Prasat Preah Vihear 30 580
Prasat Ra-ngaeng see PRASAT SIKHORAPHUM
Prasat Sangsilapachey 30 580
Prasat Sikhoraphum 30 581, 600
Prasat Song Phi Nong 30 580
Prasat Sra Kamphaeng Yai 30 580, 600
Prasat Srei 30 580
Prasat Ta Muen Thom 30 580
Prasat Thong, King of Ayutthaya (reg 1629-56) 2 885, 887; 30 587
Prasat Wat Prang 30 579
Prasat Yai Ngao
tower-sanctuaries 4 795
prase 21 241
Praskvica Monastery 22 17
Prassede, Ottaviano 10 654
Prassinos, Gisèle 30 21
Prassinos, Mario 3 462; 25 450*
Prat 11 483
Prat, Comtesse de 4 455
Prata Ansidónia, S Nicola 26 625
Pratapaditya, Ruler (reg c. 625-61) (Karkota) 15 265
Pratapa Malla, King (reg 1641-74) (Malla) 22 754, 775; 30 53
Pratap Singh, Maharaja of Jaipur (reg 1778-1803) (Rajput)
architecture 16 871
paintings 15 610, 610, 611
Pratello Orsini, Villa Strozzi 7 782
Prater, Christopher 10 258; 18 93; 20 606–7; 25 628; 28 300
works 28 300
Prater, Rose 25 628; 28 300
Prati, Fortunato de 5 86
Prati, Lidy 2 525, 546, 604
pratiratha 15 244*
Pratmarsó Parera, José 13 726
Prato 16 620; 25 450–51*
Cassa di Risparmio 11 679
Castello dell'Imperatore 8 138
Cathedral 25 451
Cappella del Sacro Cintolo 16 743
Chapel of the Assunta 20 747–8
frescoes 19 442–3
pulpit 25 724
stained glass 13 193
wall paintings 16 659
Centro per l'Arte Contemporaneo Luigi Pecci
library 16 777
glass 16 740
Madonna delle Carceri 26 187
Museo di Pittura Murale 25 450
Palazzo Datini 3 173; 8 535
Pieve see Cathedral
S Maria delle Carceri 7 257; 27 733–4, 734
Prato, Alessandro Negroni 3 856
Prato, Francesco (di Girolamo Ortensi) dal 25 451*
Prato, Niccolò da, Cardinal see NICCOLÒ DA PRATO, Cardinal
Pratolino 5 182–3; 11 242; 16 620; 25 452*
park 12 116
sculpture 20 279
Villa Medici 8 704–5; 21 22
fountain 16 696
Fountain of Juno 1 790
fountains 11 343; 12 570
gardens 2 837
Grotto della Galatea 13 703, 704; 27 323
grottoes 16 696
Prato Master 20 704, 747–8*; 31 517
Pratoneri, Alberto 7 890
Pratovecchio, Master of 6 14; 12 713; 16 847; 20 748*
Prats, Joan 8 538
Prats, Santiago Rusiñol i see RUSIÑOL (I PRATS), SANTIAGO
Prats-Véntos, Antonio 9 117
Pratt, Chan 3 63
Pratt, Charles Edward 28 557*; 31 864
Pratt, Christopher 5 569
Pratt, David 28 234
Pratt, Felix 29 495
Pratt, F. & R. 10 311
Pratt, George 8 46; 10 232
Pratt, George D. 29 515
Pratt, John 10 674
Pratt, José A. 24 99
Pratt, Katherine 4 480; 31 651
Pratt, Mary 5 569
Pratt, Matthew 25 452–3*
teachers 7 408; 33 92
works 25 453
Pratt, Richard Henry 22 593, 594
Pratt, Ritter & Co. 24 279
Pratt, Roger 2 314; 3 186; 13 299; 25 453–4*
assistants 24 753
patrons and collectors 3 178; 10 360
works 8 45, 46, 46; 10 231; 15 47; 19 510; 29 835
Pratt, Samuel Luke 2 450
Prault, Laurent-F. 10 823; 18 804; 22 88
Praun, Anna 2 815
Praun, Paulus 25 454*
drawings 9 446; 10 531; 14 626; 25 560
printing plates 18 474
sculpture 23 309
Pravda Porcelain Factory 27 413, 414
Praves, Diego de 25 455*
works 5 427; 7 846; 10 535; 22 67; 29 268; 31 822, 823
Praves, Francisco de 10 535; 22 68; 29 269
Prax, Valentine 33 590
Praxias 17 735
Praxias, Arnthe see ARNTHE PRAXIAS
Praxias group 10 615
Praxis 23 81, 84; 24 352; 25 455*
collections 23 84
Praxiteles 13 423, 430, 439, 460, 461, 462; 25 455–7*; 30 737
attributions 13 460, 470; 14 69; 23 432; 32 236; 33 453
collaboration 23 142
copies 11 310; 14 443; 18 148; 23 157, 291; 27 39, 46; 31 61
forgeries by others 11 307
methods 10 197
patrons and collectors 10 521; 23 326
teachers 17 910
works 2 682; 9 20; 10 474, 675; 13 423, 434, 458, 573, 606; 17 910; 18 147, 148; 21 892; 23 291; 25 45, 456
Prayaga (India) see ALLAHABAD
Prayāga (fl 1595-1655) see PAYAG
Prayerbook of Maximilian I see under PRAYERBOOKS → individual manuscripts
Prayerbooks 4 358, 369; 5 804
individual manuscripts
Magyar Benigna Prayerbook 14 899
Older Prayerbook of Maximilian (Vienna, Österreich. Nbib., Cod. 1907) 20 692, 736–7, 737
Peutinger Prayerbook (Stuttgart, Württemberg. Landesbib., MS. brev. 91) 20 512
Prayerbooks
individual manuscripts—cont.
Prayerbook of Abbot Jost Necker von Salem (Zurich, Zentbib.) 12 816
Prayerbook of Cardinal Albrecht of Brandenburg (Malibu, CA, Getty Mus., MS. Ludwig IX, 19) 3 506, 725
Prayerbook of Duke William IV of Bavaria (Vienna, Österreich. Nbib., Cod. 1880) 12 816
Prayerbook of Hans Imhoff (Nuremberg, Stadtbib., MS. Cent. V) 12 816
Prayerbook of Maximilian I (Munich, Bayer. Staatsbib.) 4 759; 8 114
Prayerbook of Otto III (Pommersfelden, Schloss Weissenstein, Cod. 347) 28 146
Royal Prayerbook (London, BL, Royal MS. 2.A.XX) 15 875
Schwarzes Gebetbuch (Österreich. Nbib., Cod. 1856) 20 618; 24 606
Prayerbooks of c. 1500, Master of the 3 555; 20 749*
attributions 20 624
groups and movements 12 525
works 19 251
prayer flags 30 845
prayer rugs see under CARPETS → types
prayer wheels 30 842
praying figures see under SCULPTURE → types
Praz, Mario 10 176; 25 458*
Prażmowo Church 25 126
Prčanj 22 17
church 22 16
Prchal, Jan Václav 17 584
Pré, Jean du see JEAN DU PRÉ
preaching-houses 23 193
Preah Khan see under ANGKOR
Preah Ko see under ROLUOS
Preah Thkol
sculpture 5 100
Preah Vihear 5 470, 472
Préault, Auguste 11 564; 20 925; 25 458–9*
groups and movements 20 498; 26 742
works 26 723; 31 131
Prebisch, Alberto (Horacio) 2 396; 21 783; 25 459*
Preca, Giorgio 20 213; 25 459–60*
precast concrete see under CONCRETE → types
Precházka, Antonin 18 492
Precht, Burchardt 25 460*
attributions 11 468
patrons and collectors 14 288
works 11 468; 30 85, 93, 93
Precht, Christian 25 460*; 29 689; 30 106
Preciado de la Vega, Francisco 5 902; 6 47; 20 283; 25 460*
Préciosité 25 461*
precious stones see GEMS
Precisionism 19 897; 25 461–2*; 28 51
United States of America 15 828; 24 686; 25 462; 28 575, 575; 29 670; 31 606
Preclík, Vladimír 8 388
Precot 7 448
Preda, Antonio 3 772
Predeau, Mathieu 24 330
predellas 1 709; 7 ; 25 183, 462–4*; 28 133
conservation 24 7
historical and regional traditions
Germany 25 464
Italy 8 443; 20 532; 25 462–4, 463; 26 456; 31 431
Netherlands, the 25 464

predellas
  historical and regional traditions—cont.
    Spain **25** 464
  see also ALTARPIECES
Predionica **25** 464*, *471*; **28** *437*
  sculpture **25** *464*
Predis, Ambrogio da *see* AMBROGIO DA PREDIS
Predis, Bernardino de **25** 464, 465, 466
Predis, Cristoforo de **25** 464, 465*
  collaboration **25** 465
  patrons and collectors **28** 531
  works **25** *465*
Predis, Evangelista de **11** 384; **19** 181; **25** 464, 466
Predis, Giovanni Ambrogio de **20** 741; **25** 464, 465–7*
  attributions **6** 102
  collaboration **19** 181; **25** 465
  patrons and collectors **20** 142
  pupils **7** 778
  teachers **25** 465
  works **11** 384; **19** 191; **25** *466*
Předklášteří u Tišnova **8** 376
Předmostí **8** *374*; **25** 467*, *470*, *471*
Přední Kopanina **8** 376
Prędota the Aged **25** 134
Predslavin **31** 547
Predynastic period *see under* EGYPT, ANCIENT → periods
Preedy, Joseph **10** 334
Preetorius, Emil **24** 826
prefabricated houses *see under* HOUSES → types
prefabrication *see under* ARCHITECTURE → techniques
Pregelj, Marij **28** 861
Prégny Château **4** 304; **7** 194
Prehistoric art **6** 152*; **25** 468–548*, *470*, *471*
  adzes **29** 227
  alabaster (gypsum) **15** 913
  alignments **25** 505*
  amber **16** 615; **25** 546
  amphorae **6** *876*
  anamorphosis **25** 479
  antlers **16** 615; **25** 472, 488, 491, 493
  architecture **25** 498–509*, 519–23*, 524
    Afghanistan **1** 189–90*
    Anatolia, ancient **1** 823, 824, 826
    Balearic Islands **3** *105*, 105–6
    Bronze Age **25** 519–24*
    Chassey culture **25** 502
    China **6** 684–5
    Cyprus, ancient **8** 333–4*
    France **25** 502–3*
    Indian subcontinent **15** 245–6*, 247*
    Iron Age **25** 535–9*
    Japan **17** 53–6*
    Korea **18** 260*, 271*
    Lengyel culture **25** 498
    Linear Pottery culture **25** 498, 500
    megalithic **5** 780, *780*; **21** 40–43*, *41*; **25** 498, 504–6*
    military **21** 551–2*
    Neolithic **25** 498–509*
    Rössen culture **25** 498
    Sardinia **25** 522
    Starčevo-Körös-Criș culture **25** 499
    stone **25** 498, 502–3
    wood **25** 499
  arm-bands **25** 542
  armour **25** 541
  arm rings **25** 545, 546
  askoi **32** *563*
  axes **25** 494, 515–16, 530
  Balangoda Points **29** 445
  bangles **25** 546
  barrows **25** 506–7, *506*, 518, 523
  basalt **14** *273*; **25** 493
  bastions **21** 551
Prehistoric art—cont.
  batons **25** 493
  beads **3** 440; **25** 473, 545, *545*, 546–7
  beakers **6** *327*; **25** 514
  belts **25** 517; **28** 806
  blades **8** 283, *283*; **25** 494, 515
  body ornaments **25** 517–18*
  bone **4** 313; **16** 615; **25** 472, 473, 488, *490*, 491, *491*, 492–3*, 518
  bone-carvings **25** *491*, *492*, 495
  bowls **25** 543
  bracelets **25** 545; **29** 228
  brick **4** 771, *771*
  brochs **21** 552; **23** 808
  bronze **1** *825*; **8** 339; **25** 518, 526–7, 547; **27** *835*; **29** *229*, 229–30
    Anatolia, ancient **1** *835*
    Bronze Age **25** 526
    China **6** 835
    Este art **10** 527
    Germany **9** 689, *690*
    Iron Age **25** 540, *540*, *541*, 541–2*, 546
    Italy **10** 527
    Japan **17** 21
  brooches **25** 540, 541, 545–6
  brushes **25** 477
  burial mounds
    Bronze Age **25** 523–4
    England **5** 292
    Germany **9** 689
    Iron Age **25** 538*, *539*
  burins (flint tools) **25** 494
  burnishing **25** 514
  cairns **25** 538
  camps (causewayed) **25** 504
  carving **25** 544–5*; **27** 365
  casting **25** 524
  castro **25** 536
  cave art **25** *476*, *477*, 487
  caves
    Borneo **29** 226
    Java **29** 226
    South-east Asia **29** 226–7
    Thailand **29** 226
    Timor **29** 226, 227
  cemeteries **6** 694; **19** 720; **25** 467, 538–9
  ceramics **6** 772; **9** 80
  charcoal **25** 477, 484
  chariots **6** 479; **25** 547–8*
  charms **25** 489
  chert **25** 493
  chevaux-de-frise **25** 536
  chronologies **2** 299; **4** 763; **16** 830; **25** 469–72*, 485, *486*
  cists **25** 506
  clay **25** *464*, *476*, 476–7, 487, 488, 502, 512, 544, 546; **32** *581*
  colour **25** 477, 480
  contours découpés **16** 615; **25** 488, 493
  copper **25** 516–17, 518
  coral **25** 546
  corbels **25** 508
  couches **9** 689
  craftsmen and artists **25** 494, 519, 524, 535, 545
  crayons **25** 477
  cups **25** 512
  daggers **25** *516*, 540
  dating methods **25** 469–72, 484–5*
  doorframes **25** 536
  drawings **25** 478, 484
  dress **25** 473
  drinking-horns **9** *690*
  drinking vessels **25** 543
  drums (musical instruments) **29** 229
  earrings **25** 545, 546
  earth **25** 506
  earthenwares **10** 527; **18** *333*, *334*; **29** *228*
  embroidery **8** 753
  enamel **25** 541, 547
Prehistoric art—cont.
  enclosures **25** 504
  engraving **25** 491–3*
  erotic art **10** 472–3
  ewers **6** *878*
  ex-votos **27** 835
  faience (ii) (ceramics) **25** 531
  feldspar **25** 477
  figurines **25** 472, 473, 488–91*, 494
    Anatolia, ancient **1** *823*, 825, *825*
    Austria **33** 197–8, *198*
    Bronze Age **25** 527, 528
    Cucuteni culture **25** 512
    Cyprus, ancient **8** *329*, 337–9*, *338*
    France **16** 615; **18** 875–6; **19** 243, *243*
    Funnel Beaker culture **25** 512
    Germany **25** *489*, *490*; **32** 679
    Gumelnița culture **25** 512
    Iron Age **25** *541*, 542
    Japan **17** 30, *97*, *102*, 102, *104*, 629
    Neolithic **25** 512
    Palaeolithic **9** 80; **16** 797
    plank figurines **8** 338, *339*
    Sardinia **25** 512; **27** 834, 835, *835*
    Serbia **25** *528*; **32** *581*
    South-east Asia **29** 228
    Thailand **29** 228
    Tisza culture **25** 512
    Tripol'ye culture **25** 512
    Vinča culture **25** 512; **32** *581*
  finger marks **25** 476, 477, 478, *478*
  flasks **8** *343*; **25** 543
  flint **8** 283; **15** 902–3; **25** 472, 493, 515, *516*
  floors **25** 487, 502
  forgeries **25** 475
  fortifications **21** 551–2*; **25** 498, 503–4*, 522, 535–6
    Bulgaria **21** 551
    Czech Republic **21** 551
    England **21** 551
    France **21** 551
    Germany **21** 551
    Ireland **21** 551
    Poland **21** 551
    Scotland **21** 551
    Spain **21** 551
  forts **9** 390–91; **21** 552
    hill-forts **21** 551; **23** 808; **25** 519, 522, 535–6, *537*
  glass **12** 789; **25** 531, *545*, 546–7*
  gold **25** 517, *517*
    Bronze Age **25** *525*, 525–6, *526*, 531
    Germany **9** *690*
    Iron Age **25** 540, 542*, 546
  granite **12** *211*; **25** 515
  graphite **25** 514
  graves **18** 119–20; **25** 506*, 507–8*, 511*, 538–9*, 540, 542
  haematite **25** 477
  hairpins **25** 546
  hammers **25** 493
  hardstones **7** 107
  harnesses **25** 541
  henges **2** *850*; **21** 40; **23** 808; **25** 498, 505–6*; **30** 434
  hides **25** 477
  hoards **25** 518
  horn-carvings **27** *365*
  houses **25** 473, 519–22
    Britain **25** 503*
    China **6** *685*
    Cucuteni culture **25** 501–2*
    Cyprus, ancient **8** *333*
    farmhouses **25** 536
    France **25** 503
    Greece **25** *499*, 500
    Gumelnița culture **25** 501
    Iron Age **25** 536
    Italy **25** 500–501
    Japan **17** *55*, 629
Prehistoric art
  houses—cont.
    Jordan **3** 514
    Korea **18** 260
    Lengyel culture **25** 500
    longhouses **25** 500, 503
    Neolithic **25** 498–503*, *499*, *501*
    pile dwellings **25** 502*
    Rössen culture **25** 500
    Scotland **28** 815, *815*
    Stroke-ornamented Pottery culture **25** 500
    Switzerland **25** 502*
    Tripol'ye culture **25** 501–2*
    Tsangli **25** 500
    Turkey **25** 499
    Ukraine **25** *501*
  human figures **1** *149*, 150; **25** 481, 490*
  iconography **17** 30*
  illite **25** 477
  impressing **6** *876*; **25** 514
  incising **25** 511, 514
  iron **9** *690*; **16** 59; **25** *540*, 540–41*, 547; **29** 228–9
  ivory **9** 81; **25** 473, 493
    mammoth **19** *243*; **25** 490; **32** 679
  ivory-carvings **25** 488, 490
    France **16** *798*
    Germany **25** *489*
    Japan **17** *102*
    Palaeolithic **16** 797; **25** 491, 493
  jade **7** *2*
  jade-carvings **7** *1*, 1–3*
  jars **18** *334*; **25** 543
  jet **25** 518
  jewellery **25** 473
    Bronze Age **25** 530–31*
    Iron Age **25** 542, 545–6*, *545*
    Linear Pottery culture **25** 517
    Palaeolithic **16** 797
    Vinča culture **25** 517
  kilns **6** 870, 875, 877; **9** 80
  knife-daggers **25** 540
  knives **8** 283
  lacquer **7** 12
  ladders **25** 479
  lamps **25** 475, 479–80, 491
  lead **25** 542
  lighting **25** 475, 479–80
  lignite **25** 488, 491, 493
  limestone **1** *194*; **25** 477, *477*, 491, 493, 494; **33** *198*
  lost-wax casting **8** 339; **25** 524
  maps **31** 152
  marls **25** 488, 493
  masonry **25** 507
  menhirs **21** 40, 134*; **25** 498, 504–5*
  metalwork **25** 518
    Afghanistan **1** 205–6*
    Anatolia, ancient **1** 824–5, 826, 834–6*, *835*
    Bronze Age **25** 524–7*
    Iron Age **25** 535, 539–42*
    Japan **17** 30
    Neolithic **25** 516–17*
  mica **25** 477
  microliths **29** 445
  mirrors **28** 806
  models **8** *307*
  monoliths **21** 40, 134
  monuments **14** 387
  see also TRILITHONS
  mortars (vessels) **25** 477
  moulds **25** 530
  mud **25** 493, 498, 499
  necklaces **25** 545, *545*
  neck rings **25** 542, 545, 546
  nude figures **33** *198*
  nuraghi
    Corsica **21** 551
    Sardinia **21** 551; **23** *304*, 304–5*, 808; **25** 522; **27** 835
  observatories **21** 42
  obsidian **25** 515
  oils **25** 477
Prehistoric art—cont.
  orthostats **12** *211*
  painting
    animal subjects **1** *835*
    China **6** 773
    Neolithic **25** 509*, 511
    Palaeolithic **25** 491, 493*
    Portugal **25** 511
    pottery **25** 514
    vase **8** *343*, 343*
    wall
      Anatolia, ancient **1** 838–9*
      France **25** 650
      Turkey **6** *74*
      Vinča culture **25** 500
  paints **23** 783*; **25** 477–9*, *478*
  palaces **1** *189*, 824; **23** 807–8*
  palisades **25** 522
  patronage **25** 519, 535
  pebbles **25** 493
  pendants (jewellery) **25** 472, 473, 489, 545, 546
  perforators **25** 494
  periods **2** 299, 300
    Aurignacian **4** 763; **25** *486*
    Azilian **20** 542
    BP **25** 472
    Bronze Age **2** 299; **25** 469, 518*, 519–31*, *520*
    Chalcolithic **2** 299; **25** 516
    Chatel-Perronian **25** *486*
    Early Bronze Age **25** 519
    Gravettian **25** *486*
    Iron Age **2** 299; **6** 152–4*; **25** 469, 533–5*, *534*, 547
    Kostyonki-Avdeyevo **18** 400
    Kostyonki-Streletskaya **18** 400
    Late Bronze Age **25** 519
    Magdalenian **4** 763; **25** 473, *486*
    Mesolithic **2** 299; **25** 469, 494–6*
    Mezin-Mezhirich **21** 413
    Middle Bronze Age **25** 519
    Mousterian **25** 472
    Neolithic **2** 299; **25** 469, 496–7*
    Palaeolithic **2** 299; **25** 468, 469, 472–3*, 488*, 491–3*
    Pavlovian **24** 291; **25** 467
    Pleistocene **25** 469, 472
    Quaternary **25** 472
    Solutrean **4** 763; **25** *486*
    Stone Age **2** 299; **25** 469
    Style I **25** 485, *486*
    Style II **25** 485, *486*
    Style III **25** 485, *486*
    Style IV **25** *486*, 487
  perspective **18** 807
  pestles **25** 477
  picrolite **8** *338*
  pigments **18** 807; **23** 78; **25** 477–9*, *478*, *479*, 483; **29** 227
  pins **25** 545
  plaques **25** 491, 492, 493, 500, *517*, 540, 541
  plates **25** 543
  portraits **9** 81
  pots **18** *333*
  potter's wheels **25** 542–3
  pottery **25** 527–8
    Alb-Salem **25** 543
    Anatolia, ancient **1** *823*, 824, 826, *837*, 837–8*; **14** *14*
    Base Ring wares **8** 330
    Bichrome ware **8** 330
    Boat-Axe culture **25** 514
    Britain **25** 513
    Bronze Age **6** *327*; **25** 527–9*, *528*
    Bulgaria **17** *808*
    Central Asia, Western **6** 255*
    China **6** 798, 869, 875–9*, *876*, *877*, *878*, *879*; **7** 159; **20** *143*
    Chulmun ware **18** *333*, 333*
    Corded ware **25** 514
    Crete **8** 153
    Cucuteni culture **8** 252; **25** 514, *514*
    Cyprus, ancient **8** 343*

Prehistoric art
pottery—cont.
Funnel Beaker culture **25** 514
Greece **8** 901
Grimston-Lyles Hill **25** 513
Grooved ware **25** 514
Gumelniţa culture **25** 514
Impressed ware **25** 514
Iraq **2** *492*
Iron Age **25** 542–4*, *543*
Italy **32** *563*
Japan **17** 30, *242*, 244–6*, 629
Karanovo culture **25** 514
Korea **18** 332–5*
Lengyel culture **25** 513
Linear Pottery culture **25** 513, 514
Mumun ware **18** 333–4*, *334*
Neolithic **17** *808*; **25** 513–15*, *514*
Nubia **23** 277
Pastoral style **8** 330
Peterborough ware **25** 513
Polgár culture **25** 513
Red-on-white ware **8** *329*
Red Polished ware **8** *307*, 329, 338, 339, *339*
Romania **25** *514*
Rössen culture **25** 513
Russia **27** *366*
Sardinia **27** 834*
Serbia **29** 546
Sesklo culture **25** 514
Single-Grave culture **25** 514
South-east Asia **29** 227
Starčevo culture **25** 514
Thailand **29** 227
Tisza culture **25** 513, 514
Tripol'ye culture **25** 514; **27** *366*
Vietnam **29** 227
Vinča culture **25** 514
White Painted ware **8** 338
White Painted I ware **8** 329
White Painted II ware **8** 330
White Slip ware **8** 330
prints **25** 478
propaganda **25** 650
quartz **25** 493; **29** 445
quartzite **25** 491, 493
rattles **22** 372
religion **21** 42
representation **25** 474
reservoirs **1** 476
rings **25** 545
ritual objects **8** 153
rock art **4** 763; **19** 229; **25** 474–7*, 480–87*, *483*, *486*
Aboriginal Australia **1** 57–8; **32** *803*
Africa **1** *220*
Algeria **1** *220*, 634
Anatolia, ancient **1** 823
Brazil **29** 195–7*
carvings **25** 509, 510, 511; **26** 133
Bronze Age **25** 531–3*
Central Asia, Western **10** 896
France **18** 806; **23** 78
Ireland **18** *169*, 169–70; **25** *509*
Malta (Republic of) **25** *510*
megalithic **25** 509–11*
Mongolia **21** 882
Neolithic **25** 509*
Russia **23** 442; **27** 365
Sweden **11** 330; **18** *103*
Central Asia, Western **6** 222–3*
drawings **15** 192
engraving **25** 476–7, 478, 480, 484–5*, *486*, 487, 494
France **12** 149; **25** *475*, 487; **31** 361
Palaeolithic **10** 381
Sicily **1** *149*, 150
South America, Pre-Columbian **29** 196–7*
Spain **1** 688–9
Sweden **25** *532*
France **2** 63; **18** 806–7, *807*; **23** 77–8; **31** 360–61, 410

Prehistoric art
rock art—cont.
hand prints **1** 688; **25** 478
Indian subcontinent **15** 551–2*
Libya **19** 323
Mesolithic **25** 494–5*
Norway **25** 495
painting **25** 473, 474–6*, 477–80*; **32** 802*
Algeria **1** *220*
Brazil **29** 195–6*, *196*
France **12** 149; **24** *310*, 310–11; **25** *475*, *478*, *479*, 487; **31** *360*
Indian subcontinent **15** 551–2*, *552*
Sardinia **27** 834
Spain **1** *689*; **29** *365*
sporting scenes **29** 422
Thailand **29** *227*
Palaeolithic **6** 46–7; **12** 149; **18** 806, *807*; **24** *310*
Russia **23** 442
Spain **1** 688–9; **25** 495; **26** 179–80; **29** 364–5*
Sri Lanka **29** 445
stencilling **29** 627
rondelles (sculpture) **25** 493
rondels (architecture) **25** 504
roofs **27** 126
sanctuaries **8** *307*; **25** 482, 538
sandstone **25** 488, 491, 493, 494
sarcophagi **25** 539
scabbards **25** 540
scaffolding **25** 479
scrapers **25** 494
sculpture **25** 491
Afghanistan **1** 193–4*, *194*
cult statues **8** *338*
Cyprus, ancient **8** 337–9*
France **25** *544*
Gumelniţa culture **25** 512
Iran, ancient **15** 913*
Iron Age **25** *544*, 544–5*
Japan **17** 102–6*
Korea **18** 297*
Malta (Republic of) **25** 512
monumental **25** 529–30*
Neolithic **10** *506*; **25** 509*, 512–13*
Nubia **23** *278*, *279*
Palestine **14** *273*
relief **8** 339; **25** *476*, 477, *477*, 487, 488, 491, 493, 494
Sardinia **27** 835
Serbia **25** *464*
statue menhirs **11** 78; **25** 529, 530; **27** 835
stone **25** 512
Syria **2** *661*
Vinča culture **25** *464*
settlements **21** 551; **25** 473, 498–503*, 504, 519–22, *521*, 535–6
shells **25** 473, 517
shields **25** 541
shrines (i) (cult) **17** *56*
signs (emblems) **25** 481, 487
siltstone **25** 488, 491, 493
silver **1** 824, *835*; **25** 542*
situlae **28** 806*, *806*, *807*
slate **25** 491, 494
soapstone **25** 493
spearheads **25** *540*
spears **25** 541
spear-throwers **25** 491, *491*, 493
spoons **8** 283
spraying **25** 478
statuettes **8** 339; **27** 834
stelae **25** 529–30
stencilling **25** 478
stone **16** 615; **25** 473, 476, 488, 491, 492–4*, 498, 512, 515–16*, 518, 524, *544*; **29** 444; **32** 679
Bronze Age **25** 530*
Neolithic **25** 502–3*
stone-carvings **12** *211*; **23** 23, *24*; **25** *512*, 513, 529–30*

Prehistoric art—cont.
stone circles **2** *850*; **25** 505*, *505*, 522; **29** *717*, 717
swords **25** 540–41*
talc **25** 477
teeth **25** 473, 518
tells **25** 498
temples **30** 433–4*
terracotta **8** 339; **29** 228; **30** 509
textiles **25** 546; **29** 228
tombs
chambered **25** 507
court **25** 507, 508*
dolmens **9** 80*; **10** 577; **21** *40*; **25** 507*; **27** *367*
France **25** 506
hypogées **25** 506, 507
Ireland **25** 508–9
Korea **18** 271*
megalithic **21** 40, *44*; **25** 507*, 509–11*
Neolithic **25** 498, 506–9*
passage **5** 780–81; **25** 507, *508*, 509–11*
rock-cut **25** 511*
Sardinia **2** 52; **25** 524; **27** 834
Scotland **20** *81*, 81–2; **25** 508
wedge **25** 508–9*
tools **16** 615; **25** 472, 473, 476, 477, 493–4, 517
Bronze Age **25** 524–5, 530
Crete **8** 153
Czech Republic **24** 332
Denmark **25** 515
Germany **32** 679
Indian subcontinent **29** 444
Iran, ancient **15** 902–3*
Iron Age **25** 541
Linear Pottery culture **25** 515
Neolithic **25** 496, 515–16*
Palaeolithic **18** 807
South-east Asia **29** 227, 228
Sri Lanka **29** 445
Thailand **29** 227, 228
Vietnam **29** 227, 228
towns **21** 551; **25** 536
trappings **25** 547–8*
tumuli **25** 538; **27** 365–6
urns **6** *877*
vases **8** 339; **25** *543*
Viereckschanzen **25** 538
wagons
ceremonial **25** 526–7, *527*
cult **25** *541*
Iron Age **25** 547–8*
wall decorations **25** 474
wheels **25** 547
woad **25** 477
wood **25** 493, 499, 547
wood-carvings **13** 5; **25** 495, *496*, 545
yokes (animal) **25** 547
Přehořovský, Count of **1** 669
Prei Khmeng **5** 464
Prei Montei **5** 462
Preindelsberger, Marianne **28** 104
Preininger, Mathias, Abbot of Admont **1** 160
Preis, Gerhard **24** 405
Preisich, Gábor **14** 890, 891
Preisler, Jan **8** 393; **20** 254; **25** 151, 548*
Preiss, František **14** 65; **25** 548*
collaboration **23** 195
teachers **18** 191
works **8** 385, 398
Preiss, Gerhard **8** 436
Preiss, P. (*fl* 1945) **8** 426
Preiss, P. Ferdinand (1882-1943) **12** 461; **29** 576
Preissig, Vojtěch **8** 393; **25** 548–9*
Preissler (i), Daniel **12** 390; **25** 549*
Preissler (ii), Daniel Josef Norbert **14** 235; **25** 549
Preissler (ii), Florian **25** 549
Preissler (i), Georg Martin **25** 549
Preissler (ii), Ignaz **8** 409; **12** 439; **14** 235; **25** 549

Preissler (i), Johann Daniel **8** 809; **12** 478; **23** 308; **25** 549*; **31** 481
Preissler (i), Johann Georg **25** 549*
Preissler (i), Johann Justin **9** 177; **13** 871; **23** 308; **25** 549*; **29** 724
Preissler (i), Johann Martin **7** 410, 805; **8** 733; **24** 222; **25** 549*
Preissler (ii), Susanna Maria *see* DORSCH, SUSANNA MARIA
Preissler (i), Valentin Daniel **25** 549
Prejevalsky, Nikolai **7** 159; **8** 411
Preleuthner, Johann **10** 907
Preljubović, Toma **28** 449, 455
Preller, Alexis **25** 550*; **29** 109
groups and movements **25** 566
works **29** 108, 110
Preller,(Ernst Christian Johann) Friedrich (1804-78) **12** 394; **14** 30; **25** 550*; **33** 37
Preller, Friedrich, the younger (1838-1901) **25** 550
Prellwitz, Arthur Henry **7** 875
Prem, Heimrad **29** 435
Premerstein, Anton von **23** 508
Premier art gothique *see* GOTHIC → styles → Early Gothic
première pensée *see* PENSIERO, PRIMO
Premierfait, Laurent de *see* LAURENT DE PREMIERFAIT
Premier Pottery **2** 760
Premonstratensian Canons **25** 551*
architecture **4** 777; **12** 471
oil sketches **20** *856*
Prémontré Church **25** 551
Premsela, Benno **22** 869
Přemysl, Margrave of Moravia (*reg* 1227-39) **31** 28
Přemysl Crucifix **8** 382
Přemyslid, Boleslav II, Duke of Bohemia *see* BOLESLAV II, Duke of Bohemia
Přemyslid, Borzhivoi I, Duke of Bohemia *see* BORZHIVOI I, Duke of Bohemia
Přemyslid, Václav I, Duke of Bohemia *see* VÁCLAV I, Duke of Bohemia
Přemyslid, Vladislav II, King of Bohemia *see* VLADISLAV II, King of Bohemia
Přemysl Ottakar I, King of Bohemia (*reg* 1197-1230) **25** 552
Přemysl Ottakar II, King of Bohemia (*reg* 1253-78) **14** 309; **18** 461; **25** 552
architecture **4** 831; **7** 350; **8** 375, 376, 421; **24** 462; **25** 425; **32** 433
metalwork **26** 687
sculpture **33** 743
silver **8** 411
Prendergast, Charles **11** 498; **25** 553; **31** 603
Prendergast, Kathy **16** 22
Prendergast, Maurice (Brazil) **25** 552–3*
groups and movements **10** 108; **23** 47; **31** 605
patrons and collectors **11** 141
works **21** 896; **25** *553*
Prene, William of *see* WILLIAM OF PRENE
Prenner, Johann Kaspar **9** 145
Přenosil, Ladislav **33** 630
Prentys, Thomas **1** 518, 519; **25** 554*
Prenzel, Robert **2** 759
Prenzlau, Marienkirche **13** 56
Preobrazhenski Monastery **5** *144*; 154
Church of the Transfiguration **5** 148, 156
Church of the Virgin **5** 148
Preosto, Gerolamo **14** 646
Prepesinthos *see* DESPOTIKON

pre-Pottery Neolithic period *see under* SYRIA-PALESTINE → periods
Pre-Raphaelite Brotherhood (PRB) **4** 878; **5** 777; **7** 226; **8** 586, 827; **10** 252–3; **14** 580; **19** 507; **20** 493; **25** 555*, 587; **26** 56, 738
dress **9** 245, 289
members **7** 572, 574; **15** 25; **21** 602; **27** 185–6, 188; **29** 633; **33** 374
periodicals **24** 426
works **1** 712
Pre-Raphaelitism **4** 604; **12** 295; **18** 100, 715; **19** 775; **21** 602, 761; **24** 50; **25** 554–6*; **32** 415; **33** 11, 251
art forms
drawings **9** 225
frames **11** 375, *375*, 432–5, *433*
painting **14** 849; **15** 165
allegorical **5** *267*; **15** *25*, *27*
genre **4** *877*, *878*; **10** *253*; **21** *601*
literary themes **5** *268*; **14** *850*; **25** *555*; **27** *187*
mythological **29** *48*
portraits **27** *351*
religious **11** *785*; **21** *602*
watercolours **27** *186*
sculpture **33** *374*
stained glass **29** *513*, VI2
tapestries **30** III2
collections **9** 757; **10** 367; **18** 906; **20** 239; **25** 41
commentaries **4** 27; **27** 351
periodicals **24** 426
regional traditions
England **10** 254
Italy **8** 509
United States of America **25** 556
Pre-Rembrandtists **25** 556–7*
members **18** 817; **21** 789; **22** 842; **25** 758; **30** 460
works **18** *818*, *819*; **25** *758*
Přerovský, J. **30** 221
Pre Rup *see under* ANGKOR
Presas, Leopoldo **2** 400; **8** 631
Presbyter, Wolframus *see* WOLFRAMUS PRESBYTER
Presbyteri, Johannes (father) **7** 922
Presbyteri, Johannes (son) **7** 922
Presbyterianism *see under* CHRISTIANITY → sects
presbyteries **25** 557*; **28** 140
Prescott (Ont), Fort Wellington **21** 575
Prescott, William H. **21** 262
Prescott Pottery **5** 582
Presencia 70 **16** 868; **24** 401; **32** 176
Presentation, Master of the **20** 767
presentation drawings *see under* DRAWINGS → types
Presenté, Georges **19** 51
preservation **22** 360; **30** 395
presidios **21** 573
Présilly **3** 209
Preslav **5** *144*, 146; **9** *511*; **25** 559*
Avradak Church 1 **5** 147
Golden Church **3** 191; **5** 146, 155; **7** 256, 261; **9** 592; **25** 559
icons **9** 633
kilns **9** 633
manuscripts **5** 152, 162
Museum **5** 163
palace **25** 559
Patleina Monastery **5** 147, 151
pottery **9** 631
Round Church *see* Golden Church
sculpture **5** 155
Selishte **5** 146
Simeon's Church *see* Golden Church
Prešov **28** *848*, 849
St Nicholas **28** 854
altarpiece **28** *854*

Prešov—cont.
Šariš Gallery **28** 857
Prespa **9** *511*; **19** *882*; **25** 559–60*
basilica **19** 882
Church of the Holy Apostles **25** 343
Hagios Achilleos **5** 146, 155
wall paintings **19** 884; **25** 343
Press, Friedrich **9** 240
works **9** *239*
Pressburg *see* BRATISLAVA
Presse, Angelot de la *see* ANGELOT DE LA PRESSE
pressed glass *see under* GLASS → techniques
presses **10** 381; **25** *593*
materials
iron **25** 592
types
Albion **25** 610
Brisset **19** 480
Columbian **25** 610
cylinder **25** 593
Platen **25** 592
rolling **25** 592
rotary **25** 593, *594*
Sigl **19** 480
Stanhope **25** 592
uses
engravings **10** 380, 381
lithography **19** 480; **24** 650; **25** 592
printing **25** 242, 588, 592–4, *593*
prints **25** 613
woodcuts **25** 609–10
pressing
amber **1** 761, 762
brick **4** 767–8
glass **7** 81; **10** 320, 321; **12** 783
press-moulding *see under* GLASS → techniques
pressure-engraving *see under* ENGRAVING → types
presswork **21** 324*
Prest, Cedar **2** 763
Prest, Godfrey **25** 16
Prest, Thomas **7** 447
Prestel, Amadeus *see* PRESTEL, JOHANN GOTTLIEB
Prestel, Ernst Gottlieb **2** 240
Prestel, Johann Gottlieb **25** 560*
Prestel, Maria Katharina **2** 240; **25** 560; **33** 14
Prestel, Theophilus *see* PRESTEL, JOHANN GOTTLIEB
Presti, Antonio **28** 657
Presti, Bonaventura **22** 485
Prestinari, Marc'Antonio **21** 533; **32** 619
Prestinari, Michele **31** 899
Presting (family) **25** 127
Preston (Lancs), Harris Library and Museum **18** 898
Preston, John **16** 24, 27
works **16** *24*
Preston, Jonathan **10** 185; **25** 560
Preston, Margaret (Rose) **1** 68; **2** 749, 760, 767; **25** 560*
works **2** *749*
Preston, Robert **12** 598
Preston, Walmsley **25** 372–3
Preston, William **2** 709
Preston, William Gibbons **25** 560–61*; **27** 884; **30** 505
Preston House (Lothian) **31** 230
Prestonpans **28** 257, 259
prestressed concrete *see under* CONCRETE → types
Prestwich, Joseph **2** 299
Prete, Juan Del *see* DEL PRETE, JUAN
Prete Genovese, Il *see* STROZZI, BERNARDO
Prete Savonese, Il *see* GUIDOBONO, BARTOLOMEO
Preti, Francesco Maria **25** 561*
works **24** 865; **29** 736; **32** 553
writings **2** 358
Preti, Gregorio **25** 562
Preti, Mattia **16** 672; **22** 479; **25** 562–5*
attributions **31** 174
collaboration **8** 100
patrons and collectors **5** 792; **10** 114; **14** 191; **21** 30; **23** 437, 898, 900; **27** 133
pupils **32** 593
works **7** 308; **15** 138; **20** 213, 214; **23** 301, 381; **25** *562*, *564*
Preti Ilario, Ugolino di *see* UGOLINO DI PRETI ILARIO
Pretoria **25** 565–6*; **29** 103, *103*
A. G. Munro House **29** 106
Anton van Wouw House **29** 122
Art Museum **25** 566; **29** 121, 122
Dutch Reformed Church **29** 105
Grupel's Court **29** 106
House Greenwood **29** 106, *107*
Kruger monument **29** 111
Meat Board building **29** 106
Melrose House **29** 116
National Cultural History and Open-air Museum **29** 114
Pierneef Museum **29** 122
Raadzaal **25** *566*; **29** 105
Radcliffe Observatory **23** 340
South African Association of Arts **25** 566
Union Buildings **3** 269; **29** 105, *106*
Pretorius, Marthinus Wessel **25** 565
Pretsch, Paul **25** 617
Pretta de Pisa, Sigismondo de **30** 914
Preu, Gerard de **21** 76
Preu, Niclas **20** 691
Preuning (family) **23** 307
Preuning, Kunz **12** 430
Preuning, Paul **12** 430
Preuss, Konrad **29** 132
Preusse, Paul **2** 480; **25** 111, 567*
Preussischer Kulturbesitz **12** 477
Preussische Staatsbibliothek *see under* BERLIN
Prevedari, Bernardo **4** 643; **26** 228
Prévert, Jacques **4** 691; **16** 808; **20** 830; **21** 709; **30** 18, 20, 291
Previati, Gaetano **16** 678, 679; **21** 527; **25** 567–8*
exhibitions **24** 708
groups and movements **9** 40
works **25** *567*
Previtali **12** 692
Previtali, Andrea **3** 771; **25** 569–70*
patrons and collectors **13** 637
pupils **23** 875
teachers **3** 667
works **3** 876; **19** 713; **25** *569*
Previtali, Giovanni **16** 782
Prevor, A. **8** 417
Prévost, Abbé **13** 653
Prévost, Benoît-Louis **7** 495; **14** 85; **33** 44
works **7** *496*
Prévost, Denis **24** 467; **27** 821
Prévost, Jacques **25** 570*
Prevost, Jan *see* PROVOOST, JAN
Prévost, Jean **25** 570*
Prévost, Louis **7** 474
Prévost, Marcel **5** 669; **6** 377
Prevost, Nicholas **7** 167; **26** 349
Prévost, Pierre (*fl* 1670-71) **11** 618
Prévost, Pierre (1764-1823) **6** 116; **8** 448; **24** 19
Prevost, Reginald **1** 846
Prévost, Zacheé **10** 559
Prevoste, Francesco **13** 344
Prevosti, Andrea **11** 280
Prey, Johann Leonhard **14** 101; **19** 815
Prey, Juan De *see* DE PREY, JUAN
Preyer, Emilie **25** 571
Preyer, Gustav **14** 216; **25** 571
Preyer, Johann Wilhelm **14** 216; **25** 571*
Prez, Jean de *see* JEAN DE PREZ
Prezel, Honoré Lacombe de *see* LACOMBE DE PREZEL, HONORÉ
Preziosi, Amadeo, Count **16** 536
Prezzolini, Giovanni **16** 679
Pr-hbyt *see* BEHBEIT EL-HAGAR
Priamo della Quercia **16** 839; **28** 682
Priam Painter **13** 473, 511; **32** 64–5*
Priam's Treasure **28** 114; **31** 355, 356, 376*, *376*
Pribčev, Stipan **8** 180
Pribiš, Rudolf **28** 855
Příbram, Church of the Holy Mount **8** 413
Pribul'sky, Anatoly I. **19** 273
Prica, Zlatko **22** 353
Price, A. G. **25** 571
Price, Bruce **25** 571*
collaboration **19** 766
groups and movements **28** 604
staff **7** 622; **25** 235
works **5** 561; **6** 513; **7** 470; **22** 36; **25** 803; **28** 831
Price, Cedric (John) **25** 571–2*
Price, Enrique **7** 609
Price, Francis **21** 765
Price, Frederick George Hilton **10** 91
Price, Frederic Newlin **32** 796
Price, Joe D. **12** 855; **17** 431
Price, Mrs Joe D. **17** 431
Price, Joshua **29** 506
Price, Kenneth **19** 492, 702; **31** 640
Price, Lucien **21** 894
Price, Robert **29** 534
Price, Tony **29** 99
Price, Uvedale **25** 572–3*
architecture **32** 783
groups and movements **12** 130, 131; **24** 741, 742, 743; **29** 890
works **8** 613; **18** 700; **26** 740
Price, William (*fl* 1696-1719) **29** 506
Price, William (*fl* 1740) **4** 472
Price, William, the younger (1703-65) **23** 691; **29** 506
Price, William G. **13** 9
Price, William L(ake) (1810-90) **24** 650, 668
Price, William L(ightfoot) (1861-1916) **11** 849; **24** 598; **25** 573*
collaboration **14** 787
groups and movements **2** 572
prices of works of art *see* ART (PRICES OF WORKS OF)
Prichard, John **5** 731; **6** 439; **25** 573*; **28** 349
pricket candlesticks *see under* CANDLESTICKS → types
Prickett, John **26** 239
pricking **24** 56
Prie, Marquise de **8** 589
Priede, Zigmunds **20** 606
Priego, Jose Alvarez y *see* ALVAREZ Y PRIEGO, JOSE
Priene **9** *512*; **13** *363*, 401; **15** 893; **25** 573–6*, *574*, 768; **26** *908*
agora **2** 297; **29** 681
architecture **15** 894; **26** 911
bouleuterion **4** 530; **24** 750
busts **13** 583
ekklesiasterion **13** 381, 407; **23** 349
figurines **13** 581
fortifications **9** 554
gymnasium **13** 886
houses **13** 382, *382*
Lower Gymnasium **13** 406; **23** 828
sculpture **13** 470; **25** 576*
stoa **13** 406; **27** 714
synagogue **17** 543
Temple of Athena **13** *377*, 379, 392, *393*, 405, 408, 410, 414, 420; **15** 894; **23** 482; **25** 575
cult statue **25** 576
entasis **10** 415
Priene
Temple of Athena—cont.
mouldings **8** 324; **9** 757
reliefs **25** 576
sculpture **25** 576*, *576*
Theatre **13** 406; **30** 651, *651*
urban planning **13** 420; **25** 573–5*
Prier, Toussaint **10** 891
Priesca, S Salvador **29** 261
Priest, John W. **7** 708
Prieter, Wolfgang Ehrenreich **31** 510
Prieto, Alejandro **5** 603
Prieto, Enrique Antonio Hernández *see* HERNÁNDEZ PRIETO, ENRIQUE ANTONIO
Prieto, Melchor **8** 50; **28** 164
Prieto, Miguel **26** 549
Prieto, Tomás Francisco **12** 57; **20** 924
Prieur, Barthélemy **9** 406; **25** 576–7*
collaboration **5** 166
patrons and collectors **28** 4
pupils **9** 405
works **2** 91; **11** 557; **27** 547; **29** 571
Prieur, Jean-Louis **11** 625, 627; **25** 212, 577–8*
collaboration **5** 380
patrons and collectors **25** 121
works **11** 627; **25** 118
Prieur, Paul **8** 752; **21** 641
Prigov, Dmitry **27** 398; **29** 89
Prijić, Aca **22** 18
Prikaz, Kamenny **22** 171
Prikhil'ny, A. **31** 552
works **31** *553*
Priknon **30** 285
Přikryl, Emil **8** 381
Prilep **19** *882*; **28** 449
museum **19** 886
PRIMA **7** 742
Primachenko, Mariya **31** 564
Primal AC33 **28** 340
Prima Porta **26** *886*; **27** 115
sculpture **25** 180; **26** 860; **27** 11, 19, 20, 46
Villa of Livia **18** 702
Garden Room **26** 862
sculpture **2** 726
wall paintings **15** 135; **27** 54, 58; **32** I2
Primario, Atanasio *see* ATANASIO PRIMARIO
Primario, Gagliardo *see* GAGLIARDO PRIMARIO
Primaticcio, Francesco **11** 262, 508, 513, 556, 656, 661; **12** 113; **24** 812, 814; **25** 578–80*
architecture **5** 166; **11** 260, 513; **20** 865; **24** 813; **27** 547, *548*, 559
assistants **1** 18; **4** 337; **5** 813; **10** 799; **22** 448; **27** 268; **30** 735
attributions **11** 260, 265, 342; **28** 468
collaboration **3** 210, 646; **9** 14; **11** 260, 557, 572; **16** 855; **24** 365; **25** 208; **32** 503
drawings **1** 18; **3** 210; **25** *580*
grottoes **13** 703; **23** 541
groups and movements **11** 260, 262, 263–4, 266; **20** 281
interior decoration **6** 506; **11** 532, 571, 572; **16** 695; **23** 540; **24** 133; **25** *579*; **29** 833
paintings **13** 700; **15** 137; **23** 293
patrons and collectors **11** 656
Catherine de' Medici, Queen of France (1519-89) **31** 850
Francis I, King of France (*reg* 1515-47) **4** 337; **14** 869; **31** 848, 849
Francis II, King of France (*reg* 1559-60) **20** 133
Guise, Charles de, Cardinal **21** 366
Primaticcio, Francesco
patrons and collectors—cont.
Lely, Peter **19** 124
Polisy, Jean de Dinteville, Seigneur de **8** 907
reproductions in tapestry **11** 262
reproductive prints by others **10** 477; **26** 229
Barbiere, Domenico del **3** 211
Chartier, Jean **6** 491
Davent, Léon **8** 549
Fantuzzi, Antonio **10** 799
Ghisi, Giorgio **12** 558
Heince, Zacharie **14** 313
Kilian, Bartholomäus, II (1630-96) **18** 46
Mignon, Jean **21** 499
Milan, Pierre **21** 538
Thulden, Theodoor van **30** 787
Vico, Enea **32** 412
restorations by others **19** 645
sculpture **3** 210; **27** 268, 547
stucco **11** *572*
tapestry **11** 639
Primato Painter **13** 526
Primavera, Jacopo **25** 581*
Primavera, L'Atelier *see* ATELIER PRIMAVERA, L'
Primavesi, Georg **29** 378
Primavesi, Otto **14** 130; **33** 166
Primavesi, Robert **14** 130
Prime, William C. **31** 671
Primera Escuela de Vallecas **1** 573; **5** 613; **20** 68
Primes, György **29** 75
priming **13** 705, 708, 709; **25** 581*
Primis *see* QASR IBRIM
Primitifs, Les **8** 558; **10** 199; **25** 581*; **26** 738
members **4** 834; **11** 738
primitive art **2** 136; **4** 185; **11** 310; **25** 582
Primitive Rajasthani **15** 602
primitivism **6** 586; **22** 440; **24** 715; **25** 582–5*
France **12** *194*
Hivaoa **12** *193*
Tahiti **12** *191*, *195*
wood-carvings **25** *584*
woodcuts **25** *582*, *583*
Primo, Luigi **4** 38; **25** 585*; **28** 92
Primoli, Giovanni Battista **25** 586*
collaboration **3** 919; **17** 514
works **5** 122; **24** 95
Primoli, Giuseppe, Conte **24** 671; **25** 586*
Primoli, Luigi **25** 586
primo pensiero *see* PENSIERO, PRIMO
primuersel **13** 708
Prince, Bart **12** 855
Prince, Engrand Le *see* LE PRINCE, ENGRAND
Prince, Gilbert **25** 15, 17
Prince, Jean-Baptiste Le *see* LE PRINCE, JEAN-BAPTISTE
Prince, Nicolas Le *see* LE PRINCE, NICOLAS
Prince Eugene Bed **2** *813*; **3** 484
Prince of Wales bastion **2** 148
Prince of Wales Island **22** *544*, 547
Prince Regent, the *see* GEORGE IV, King of Great Britain
Prince Rupert Harbour *see* SKEENA RIVER - PRINCE RUPERT HARBOUR
Princes Gate Collection *see under* LONDON → Courtauld Institute
Princes metal *see under* ALLOYS → types
Princess Charlotte Bay **1** 61
Princet, Maurice **8** 244
Princeteau, René **31** 213
Princeton Index of Christian Art **15** 96; **22** 110; **31** 671
Princeton Painter **13** 509
Princeton University (NJ) **31** 669
Art Museum **6** 826; **10** 94; **21** 265

Princeton University (NJ)—cont.
collections 9 231; 17 435; 26 358
Gordon Wu Hall 32 *235*
sculpture garden 28 315
Príncipe *see* SÃO TOMÉ AND PRÍNCIPE
principiae 21 559
Principio Furnace 31 652
Prineri (family) 4 401
Prinet, René Xavier 3 156
Pringle & Smith 2 694
Prini, Giovanni 25 586*
Prinias
fort 8 154
Temple A 8 154; 13 376, 443
Prinotto, Luigi 16 716, 728; 28 16
Prins, Nico 29 113
Prinsep, James 1 211; 15 211; 25 587*
Prinsep, Thomas 25 587
Prinsep, Val(entine Cameron) 11 434; 25 555, 587*; 27 564
Prinsep, William 25 587
Prinstet, Etienne 7 355
works 7 *355*
Print Club of Cleveland 25 629
Print Club of Philadelphia 25 629
print collections *see under* COLLECTIONS → types
Print Connoisseurs 25 629
Print Council of America 25 629
printed ephemera *see* EPHEMERAL ART
printed music *see* MUSIC (PRINTED)
printers, master *see* MASTER PRINTERS
printer's ink *see under* INKS → types
printing 15 855; 17 204; 25 588–97*
historical and regional traditions
Ancient Near East 1 855
Australia 2 768
Buddhism 5 110; 30 845
Bulgaria 5 154
Central Asia, Eastern 6 314
Central Asia, Western 6 249, *250*; 16 451
China 5 110; 7 63–5*, 117, 144; 25 588
Czech Republic 8 37
Egypt 16 361
England 8 *35*, 36, *36*; 10 307, 356*; 24 55; 30 561–2
15th cent. 6 120
France 4 130; 8 36–7; 11 649*; 19 870; 23 331; 24 55; 30 562, X1
Germany 7 625; 8 37; 13 866
Indian subcontinent 15 668–70*, 679; 16 361
Iran 16 361
Ireland 16 *34*; 30 562
Islamic 16 359–62*, *361*, 451
Italy 8 37, *37*; 14 867; 16 360; 24 55; 32 198
Japan 7 624; 17 203, 217, 220, *275*, *276*; 25 588
Korea 15 852; 25 588
Malta (Republic of) 16 361
Netherlands, the 8 36, 666; 22 899–900; 30 561
Ottoman 16 360
Romania 16 360
Russia 27 431
Scotland 8 37; 28 266
Switzerland 8 37
Tibet 30 847
Turkey 16 360
United States of America 31 657, *657*
materials
birch 30 845
cameras (ii) (photography) 25 354
cotton 15 668–70
dyes 15 852
ferric chloride 24 655
printing materials—cont.
gelatin 6 328; 7 575; 24 650
glass 7 575
gold 15 668
gum arabic 10 356; 15 668
indigo 10 356
inks 7 575; 15 849, 852–3*, 854–5*; 24 650, 653; 25 589; 27 882
iron sulphates 10 356
lasers 25 345
mica 17 220
paper 20 329; 24 50*; 25 588
plaster 10 380
plastics 4 367
potassium bichromate 7 575
presses 25 242, 588, 592–4, *593*
silk 15 670
silver 15 668
tools 17 274, 275
turmeric 15 668
type (movable) 7 624
type-faces 5 112; 15 852; 31 494
wood 25 347; 30 847
processes
à la poupée 2 239; 25 381*, 622
block *see* woodblock
chiaroscuro 16 820
collograph 7 576, *576*; 22 57; 25 618*
collotype 7 575–6*, *576*; 24 650*, *670*; 25 82, 345, 618; 26 236
colour 2 239; 4 345, 357; 7 575, 576; 15 855; 25 345, 589, 621–4*
China 7 64–5, 119–20; 15 852
England 3 421; 4 367; 25 VIII
France 12 208; 20 861
Japan 15 852; 17 272, 282–4*, *283*, 285, 286; 30 50, *51*
Scotland 25 VIII
United States of America 14 616
cross-line screen printing 26 235
diazo 24 654
electrography 10 135*; 25 589, 592
flexographic printing 32 813, 817
Goupilgravure 25 617–18*
half-tone block 7 575; 15 855; 24 647, 672; 25 617*; 26 235, 236
heliography 14 541; 23 121; 24 655; 25 617*
heliogravure *see* photogravure; PHOTOGRAPHY → processes
intaglio 25 345
Japan 20 601
line block 15 855; 25 617*
lithography *see* LITHOGRAPHY
net 17 276
offset 19 481, 493; 20 609; 25 594
photocomposition 25 589
photo-engraving 24 670
photogalvanography 25 617*
photographic 20 603; 25 591
photogravure 2 241; 10 396, 558; 24 670, 674; 25 345; 26 236; 32 813, 817
Czech Republic 18 127; 25 618*
England 28 549
France 24 647, 655*; 26 236
United Kingdom (of Great Britain and Northern Ireland) 2 119
United States of America 24 *671*, *674*
photolithography *see* PHOTOLITHOGRAPHY
photomechanical 2 241; 24 647, 669, 670; 25 345, 596, 617–18*
photomezzotint *see* Goupilgravure
printing processes—cont.
phototype 7 575; 25 617*
planographic 25 13*
process reproduction 4 363, *365*
registration 26 91*
relief 17 274
telecopy 10 135
transfer 4 177; 6 328
typesetting 25 589
woodblock 15 855; 16 359; 25 588; 26 230; 30 561; 32 *811*, 811–12, *814*, 814, 815
Bhutan 3 914
Buddhism 5 115; 7 624; 18 354–5
Central Asia, Eastern 6 307, 314
China 7 62, 63, 114, 117; 25 597
England 22 *144*
Indian subcontinent 15 668
Iran 16 450
Iraq 16 434
Islamic 16 359–60*, 434, 450
Japan 7 624; 17 185, 272, 597
Korea 5 115; 18 314, 354–6*
Tibet 30 810
Woodburytype 24 658*, 659, *661*, 670, 672; 25 617*
xerography *see* electrography
xeroradiography 10 135
states *see under* PRINTS
uses
art (reproduction of works of) 17 204; 24 649
banknotes 3 180
Bibles 4 7–9*, 17–18
books 4 342, 344; 7 63–5*, 576; 8 666; 13 866; 16 360–62, *361*; 18 354–6; 19 870
carpets 5 832
catalogues 9 16
ceramics 6 328; 10 311
colophons 7 625
cotton 6 249, *250*; 7 *52*; 8 *35*, *36*, 36–7*, *37*; 10 356*; 11 649*; 15 *669*; 23 331; 28 266; 30 561, X1; 31 *657*
decorative paper 24 12
fustian 30 561
linen 30 561
maps 20 363–5
musical notation 22 369–71*, *370*
paper 24 55*
photography 24 648
see also PHOTOGRAPHIC PRINTS
porcelain 10 309, 380
posters 25 345
reproductions, photographic 24 672
silk 24 810
textiles 30 561–2*
Ancient Near East 1 855
Australia 2 768
China 7 117, 144
Germany 12 469
Indian subcontinent 15 668–70
Iran 16 450
Iraq 16 434
Ireland 16 *34*
Islamic 16 434, 451
Netherlands, the 22 899–900
Russia 27 431
Ukraine 31 564
United States of America 31 657
tiles 30 874
wallpaper 19 429; 25 372, 373; 28 549; 32 *811*, 811–13*, *813*, *814*, 814, 815, 816, 817; 33 711
Printing Bureau (Japan) 17 203
printing-out papers (P.O.P.) *see* PHOTOGRAPHY → processes → printing-out
printing plates 10 548, 549; 17 270; 21 875; 24 650, 653
aluminium 10 548
brass 10 548
chromium steel 10 548
copper 7 814*; 10 379, 548, 549, 562; 25 612
gold 23 114, 115
iron 10 548; 25 612
Perspex 25 612
pewter 25 612
plastics 10 379
silver 10 379; 23 114, 115
steel 3 180; 5 412; 10 379, 394–6; 21 414; 25 612
zinc 10 379, 548, 562; 25 612
see also PHOTOGRAPHIC PLATES
printmakers 9 440; 10 206, 208, 210; 25 598, 625
Printmaking Workshop 20 605, 606
print publishers 25 625–6*
Belgium 7 499
Britain 25 626
France 18 745; 25 626
Italy 10 389; 25 625
Netherlands, the 25 625
United States of America 8 276; 20 609–10; 25 626
print rooms 9 26; 11 430; 16 24; 32 815
prints 15 830; 18 706; 23 505*; 24 649; 25 596–7*, 598–9*, 600–601*, 604–7*, 608*, 617–20*, 621–5*, 627–32*, 664
art (reproduction of works of)
conservation 15 856; 25 632–3*
display 1 582; 9 26*
historical and regional traditions
Algeria 1 *636*
Australia 2 751
Austria 10 *481*
Belgium 3 555–6*
Bolivia 4 261
Britain 14 638
Buddhism 5 105; 6 314; 7 117–18; 17 269, 270, *270*
Bulgaria 5 163
Cameroon 5 *524*
Canada 5 566*
Caribbean Islands 5 750
Central Asia, Eastern 6 314*
Chile 6 598
China 7 117–19*, 143, 146, *146*
Christianity 5 447; 17 271
Colombia 7 610
Costa Rica 8 18
Denmark 8 731, 733, 735, 736
Dominican Republic 9 118
England 10 *251*, 252; 27 869
France 11 540–41*; 24 883
Germany 12 391; 18 82
Guatemala 13 764
Hinduism 15 177–8, *178*
India, Republic of 15 177–8, *178*
Indian subcontinent 15 679–80*
Ireland 16 15–16, 24
Jamaica 16 884
Japan 15 855, 856; 17 269–71*, 274–96*, *281*, *282*, *283*, *284*, *294*, *296*
Buddhism 17 269, *270*
Christianity 17 271
Edo period (1600-1868) 17 *269*, *275*
Lithuania 19 498
Macedonia (ii) (former Yugoslavia) 19 885*
Mexico 21 382, 386, 388*, *390*
Montenegro 22 16–17*, 18*
Netherlands, the 2 558; 20 802; 22 854*
Nigeria 23 136
Norway 23 227
Paraguay 24 98, 99
Poland 25 106
Prehistoric art 25 478
Puerto Rico 25 702
prints historical and regional traditions—cont.
Romania 26 715
Russia 27 385, 397
Scotland 28 238
Serbia 28 450*, 451*, 452*
Slovakia 28 852, 853–4
Slovenia 28 860
South Africa 29 110–11*, 121
Spain 5 *725*
Sweden 30 80–81*
Switzerland 30 131, 133
Tanzania 30 *301*
Tibet 5 105; 6 314
ukiyoe 31 764
United States of America 20 604–7, *609*; 25 629*; 31 599, 601, 602
Uruguay 31 755
Zambia 33 602
lighting 7 732
materials
brass 17 276
casts 23 115
copper 17 276, 277
glazes 11 407
glues 11 173; 17 281
gold 15 855
gold dust 17 276
gold leaf 17 277
inks 25 598*, 612
inscriptions 20 601; 25 599–600*
lead 17 277
metal 11 173
mica 15 855; 17 276
mother-of-pearl 17 277
paper 17 275; 24 50; 25 597–8*, 613
presses 25 613
printing plates 25 612
quartz 11 173
safflower 17 282
sandbags 27 714*
scrapers 28 290
silver dust 17 277
silver leaf 17 277
tools 25 612
varnishes 11 173
wool 11 173
states 25 599*; 29 556–7*, *557*
techniques
burnishing 17 276
crachis 17 276
embossing 10 178, *178*; 17 275, 276
fukibokashi see KIRIFUKI
gaufrage 10 178; 17 275
goffering 17 275
hammering *see* repoussage
hand prints 25 478
ita bokashi 17 275
karazuri 17 275–6
kimedashi 17 275
kirifuki 17 276
manière de lavis 2 238, 239
photography 25 596, 617–18*
polishing 17 276
repoussage 26 221*
retroussage 26 257*
shading 17 275
stamping 25 600
stencilling 7 118; 17 276, 285, 288
tsuyazuri 17 276
wash manner 2 239, 241; 11 723; 32 894*
types
aquatints *see* AQUATINTS
carborundum 5 725–6*
catchpenny 6 84*; 25 244; 33 360
see also BROADSIDES
clair obscur see WOODCUTS → types → chiaroscuro
cliché-verre see under PHOTOGRAPHY → processes
collagraphs *see* COLLAGRAPHS

prints
types—cont.
devotional prints **8** 835, 837–8*, *837*, *838*; **25** 604–5
dotted *see under* ENGRAVINGS → types
drypoints *see* DRYPOINTS
empreinte veloutée see flock
engravings *see* ENGRAVINGS
etchings *see* ETCHINGS
flock **11** 173*; **25** 610
glass *see* PHOTOGRAPHY → processes → *cliché-verre*
gravure sur bois debout see WOOD ENGRAVINGS
half-tone block **24** 651–3*, 670
hand-tinted **25** 620–21*, VII2
see also PHOTOGRAPHIC PRINTS → types → gum bichromate; hand-coloured
Holzstich see WOOD-ENGRAVINGS
inbutsu **17** 270
intaglio **2** 238; **10** 547; **15** 878*; **25** 591, 608, 611–14*
kasen'e **17** 828–30*
limited editions *see under* LIMITED EDITIONS → types
lubki **3** 528; **18** 385; **19** 751*; **22** 750; **25** 243
maculatures **20** 34*
metalcuts *see* METALCUTS
mezzotints *see* MEZZOTINTS
monoprints **21** 894
monotypes **3** 495; **4** *118*, *119*; **6** 32, *34*; **21** 894–5*, *895*, 896, *896*, 897; **25** 616, VI
niello **23** 114–16*, *115*; **25** 597, 614
Otto prints **3** 96
pasteprints *see* PASTEPRINTS
photographic *see* PHOTOGRAPHIC PRINTS
photomechanical *see under* PRINTING → processes
planographic **25** 608, 614–16*
popular prints **25** 242–5*, 605
punched **25** 731–2*, *731*
see also ENGRAVINGS → types → dotted
relief **24** 670; **25** 591, 608–11*, *611*
see also GYPSOGRAPHY
Sammt-Teigdrucke see flock
shin hanga **17** 294
shunga **10** 485, *485*; **18** *92*
surimono **17** 278, 285, 286–7
tinsel **11** 173*; **25** 610
ukiyoe **4** 70; **15** 852, 855; **16** 802; **17** 23, 269, 274, 277, *280*, 280–81*, 283, 286, 290; **23** 290, 594; **30** 50
aizurie **17** 287
benie **17** 282
benizurie **17** 282
Edo period (1600-1868) **2** 7, *9*; **17** 176, *278*, 397, *397*, *415*; **18** *96*; **30** 50, *51*; **31** *766*
hashirae **17** 277, 281
hosoban **17** 277, 281, *283*
Meiji period (1868-1912) **17** 293
ōban **17** 277, *281*, 284, *289*, *291*, *292*; **31** *170*
ōkubie **17** 276, 284; **31** *765*
tane **17** *280*, 281
ukie **17** 282; **31** 169
urushie **17** 281
woodblock **15** 855; **24** 665
Australia **2** *749*
Buddhism **7** 624; **17** 270, *270*; **30** 845
Central Asia, Eastern **6** *307*, 314
China **4** 143; **7** *44*, 59, *118*, *119*, *121*; **17** 270
England **25** VII1
prints
types
woodblock—cont.
Japan **1** 582; **7** 624; **16** *561*; **17** 269, *269*, 270, *270*, 274, *275*, 279, 285–7, 293, *845*, *847*; **18** *92*, *96*, *494*; **22** *231*; **24** 276–7; **30** *51*; **31** *169*, *170*, *204*, *765*, *766*; **33** *539*
Korea **17** 270; **18** 354, *355*
Mongolia **21** 875, 884
Tibet **5** 105; **30** 836, 845*
Uruguay **31** 755
Vietnam **32** 481–2*, *482*
woodcuts *see* WOODCUTS
wood-engravings *see* WOOD-ENGRAVINGS
Yokohamae **17** 290; **33** 539, *539*
uses
book illustrations **4** 356, 357
interior decoration **16** 24
Printsellers' Association **19** 395; **25** 629
Printz, Eugène **11** 601
Prinz, Carl **33** 50
Prinz, Gershom **14** 35
Prinzhorn, Hans **25** 686
Priol, Sri Mangesh Temple **12** 827
Prior, Alfredo **2** 401; **25** 633*
Prior, E(dward) S(chroder) **25** 633–4*; **29** 507
collaboration **12** 146, 631
groups and movements **2** 575; **9** 739; **10** 239
pupils **14** 252
works **25** *634*
Prior, Matthew **4** 805; **12** 594; **25** 634–5*
Prior, Melton **3** 389; **13** 876
Prior, Thomas Abiel **25** 635*
Prior, William Matthew **12** 54
Priorato, Gualdo **28** 479
priories **25** 635*
Prior Park (Avon) **4** 801; **33** 340
Prip, John **31** 651
Prisciani, Pellegrino **10** 520
Prisma **31** 886
Prisma **24** 445
Prisme des arts **24** 442
Prisme d'Yeux **5** 568; **25** 635*
members **9** 390; **24** 338; **26** 464; **31** 146
Prism group **18** 414; **30** 338; **32** 877
Prisoner Painter **23** 285
prisons **25** 635–7*; **31** 235
England **4** 108; **8** *494*
France **19** 11
Italy **25** *636*
Rome, ancient **21** 559
United States of America **31** 592
see also COMPOUNDS
Prisse d'Avennes, (A. C. T.) Emile **10** 82, 83, 90; **16** 547
Priština **28** *437*
Ethnographic Museum **28** 454
fortress **28** 444
houses **28** 444
Imperial Mosque **28** 444
Municipal Museum **25** 464
Prisunic **11** 584
Pritam Singh, Ruler (*reg* 1767-1806) (Pahari) **15** 621
Pritchard, Jack C. **4** 762; **7** 482; **13** 688
Pritchard, Molly **7** 482
Pritchard, Thomas Farnolds **10** 265; **16** 52
works **16** *53*
Pritchard, Walter **28** 244
Pritchett, James Piggott **23** 194; **25** 268
Priteca, Marcus B. **2** 522
Prithvi Narayan, King (1768-75 (Shah) **22** 764, 775
Prithviraj III, Ruler (*reg* 1178-92) (Chahamana) **1** 502; **8** 676
Prithvi Singh, Raja of Kishangarh (*reg* 1841-80) (Rajput) **15** 613
Prithvi Singh, Ruler (*reg* 1641-64) (Pahari) **6** 405
Priuli **10** 861
Privat, Louis **31** 206
private exhibitions *see under* EXHIBITIONS → types
Private Eye **12** 152
Privat-Livemont **25** 347
Privé, Thomas **19** 544; **25** 637*; **26** 43; **31** 840
Privileges, Master of the **20** 749*
Privileges of Ghent and Flanders, Master of the **3** 555; **20** 749*
Prix, Wolf D. **7** 798–9
Prix de Rome **1** 105, 106, 107; **7** 666, 676; **8** 890; **18** 887; **19** 161; **20** 867; **22** 908; **24** 166, 167, 168, 171, 173; **25** 637–8*
Prix de Rome Architecture, Grand *see* GRAND PRIX DE ROME ARCHITECTURE
Prix Troyon **1** 107
Priymak, Boris **9** 54; **33** 518
prizes (artists') **1** 102, 104, 105; **3** 185; **19** 641; **24** 138, 140; **25** 637
Prizren **9** *511*; **25** 639*; **28** *437*
baths **28** 444
bridge **28** 444
ceramics **1** 543
Church of the Holy Archangels **28** 453
congregational mosque **28** 444
felt **1** 544
houses **28** 444
metalwork **1** 543
Monastery of the Holy Archangels **9** 561
Mother of God Ljeviška church **7** 261; **9** 552, 585; **25** 639; **28** 439, 442
wall paintings **28** 446
Pro 66 **7** 805
Proal, Jean **3** 778
Probianus **9** 649
Probota Monastery **26** 707, 712, 717
Probst, Edward **13** 271
Probst, Jakob **30** 138
Probst, Joseph **19** 827
Probst, Marvin G. **13** 271
Pröbstl, Jan Kašpar **8** 386
Probus, Emperor of Rome (*reg* 276-82) **9** 647; **27** 42
Proby, John, 1st Earl Carysfort **14** 270; **25** 639
Proby, William, 5th Earl of Carysfort **25** 639*
Procaccini (family) **32** 612
Procaccini, Andrea **20** 67; **25** 644–5*; **29** 304
collaboration **5** 854; **19** 816; **20** 377
patrons and collectors **1** 532; **4** 558, 560; **26** 778
pupils **20** 805; **25** 410
works **4** 560; **25** *645*; **26** 778; **27** 753
Procaccini, Camillo **1** 104; **25** 639, 640–42*
collaboration **21** 525
competitions **24** 551
patrons and collectors **21** 525; **28** 496; **32** 612
reproductive prints by others **27** 504
works **23** 574; **25** *641*, *642*
Procaccini, Carlantonio **25** 639, 642–4*
Procaccini, Cerano **21** 533
Procaccini, Ercole (i) (1520-95) **25** 639, 640*
Procaccini, Ercole (ii) (1605-75) **5** 289; **25** 639, 644*; **29** 722
Procaccini, Giulio Cesare **1** 104; **16** 674; **21** 533; **25** 639, 642–4*
attributions **8** 149
Procaccini, Giulio Cesare—cont.
collaboration **6** 338, 340; **22** 82
patrons and collectors **4** 425; **5** 407; **9** 174; **15** 148; **21** 526; **22** 26; **27** 878; **28** 496
works **16** 674; **25** *643*
procédé sur verre see PHOTOGRAPHY → processes → *cliché-verre*
Procellaria **8** 436
process art **1** 80; **9** 20; **15** 868, 869; **25** 645–7*; **27** 308; **28** 480; **29** 13
England **10** 258, 269
United States of America **11** 20; **25** *646*
processional crosses *see under* CROSSES → types
process reproduction *see under* PRINTING → processes
Prochaska, Eduard **19** 719
Procházka, Antonín **25** 647*
groups and movements **8** 373, 393; **10** 107, 108; **13** 711; **16** 902
works **8** 393
Procházka, K. **8** 423
Proclus **22** 749, 750
Procopé, Ulla **11** 105
Procopius of Caesarea **2** 312; **13** 808; **17** 701
Procter, Edwin **7** 326
Procter & Gamble **30** 391
Proctor, Alexander Phimister **5** 570, 593
Proctor, Dod **23** 26
Proctor, Stephen **31** 738
Proctor, Thea **2** 756, 759; **8** 2; **30** 160
proculum *see* CHALICES
Proculus **9** 595
Procureur, A. **3** 585
Prodanović, Bozidar **28** 451
Prodigal Son, Master of the **20** 750*
production, machine *see* MACHINE PRODUCTION
Production art *see* PRODUCTIVISM
Productionists **15** 857
Productivism **7** 768; **20** 887; **26** 503, 504; **27** 444
posters **26** *505*
Productivists *see* PRODUCTIONISTS
Proeleusis, Michael **30** 718
Proesch, Gilbert *see* GILBERT AND GEORGE
Profanbau **19** 327
Profil **24** 438
profiles **6** 327; **22** 211–12, 215–22
Profilm **28** 299
Progettare **24** 449
proggy rugs *see under* RUGS → types
Progonos Sgouros **9** 629
Progressive Architecture **24** 433, 434
Progressive Artists' Group **4** 290; **15** 169; **26** 48; **29** 248
Progressiven, Die **11** 768
Progressive Painting Association (Madras) **20** 54
progresso fotografico, Il **24** 447
Pro Helvetia **30** 152
Projecta **27** 84
Projecta's Casket **5** 917, *917*; **18** 825
Projectionists **26** 70
Project Method **17** 420
projectors **20** 92; **22** 390; **24** 651; **30** 685
Projekt **24** 441
Pro-Jerusalem Society **17** 492
Prokeš, Martin **28** 853
Prokhor **22** 176, 183; **27** 304, 384; **30** 707
Prokhorov, S. M. **31** 559
Prokofiev, Sergey **3** 119; **24** 565; **33** 486
Prokof'yev, Ivan (Prokof'yevich) **13** 5; **25** 647*; **27** 389, 390; **29** 778
Prokonnesos **26** *908*
marble **2** 157; **6** 555; **9** 531; **13** 387; **16** 221; **26** 854, 855, 875, 876, 885, 911; **27** 13, 826; **29** 702
see also under MARBLE → types
Prokop, August **8** 379, 426; **19** 339; **25** 648*
Prokop, Filip Jakub **14** 895; **25** 648*
Prokopios **9** 513, 519, 664; **10** 129; **15** 889; **31** 434
Prokudin-Gorsky, Sergey (Mikhaylovich) **25** 648*
Proletarian Art Movement **17** 295
Proletarian Fine Arts workshop **1** 132
Proletarskaya kul'tura **4** 231; **24** 450
Proletkul't **22** 178; **25** 649*
members **2** 578; **4** 231; **27** 283; **30** 338
Promadhattavedi, Chartvichai **30** 617
Prome **5** *221*, 259
musical instruments **5** *259*
Shwe-hsan-daw **5** 234
promenades **4** *390*; **13** 381; **27** 803
Prometei **29** 97
Prométhée **24** 442; **32** 96
Promis, Carlo **5** 425; **6** 322, 323; **19** 793; **31** 442
Promontory Partnership **22** 671
pronaoi **8** 154; **13** 376, *376*; **25** 649*
Pronaszko, Andrzej **8** 431; **11** 317; **25** 422, 649; **30** 213
Pronaszko, Zbigniew **25** 108, 649*; **32** 579
groups and movements **8** 431; **11** 317; **25** 116, 422
pupils **12** 602; **33** 416
Pronin, Boris **18** 507
Pronk, Cornelis **25** 649*
pupils **3** 900; **5** 322; **19** 347
reproductive prints by others **29** 402
works **3** 900; **6** 921
Pronnoi **17** 909
Pronomos Painter **13** 524; **32** 65*
Pronti, Domenico **25** 123
proofs **25** 650*
propaganda **1** 115; **6** 72; **14** 226; **16** 145; **24** 662; **25** 329, 650–54*, *651*, *652*; **26** 138; **27** 31, 35, *36*, 394, 413, *414*
Propertius, Sextus **11** 339
property development **25** 654–7*
Prophets, Master of the **2** 646
proportioned script *see under* SCRIPTS → types
proportions **1** 102; **12** 871; **13** 467; **14** 407; **22** 378; **28** 200–201; **30** 171
proportions (architecture) **2** 343–61*, *346*, *347*, *348*, *352*; **14** 869, 872–3; **20** 565, 576; **22** 377; **23** 484, 487; **28** 497–8
France **2** *360*
Gothic **2** 344–9*; **12** 619
Greece, ancient **2** 344, 350–51; **13** 408, 409, 410, 412–13*, *413*
5th cent. BC **15** 132
Indian subcontinent **15** 210
Japan **17** 50
Rome, ancient **13** 412; **26** 924–5
Spain **12** 619–20
see also GEOMETRY (ARCHITECTURE); MEASUREMENTS (ARCHITECTURE); MODELS → types → architectural
proportions (human) **14** 870–74*; **32** *635*
Burma **5** 224
Byzantine **14** 871

proportions (human)—cont.
Egypt, ancient 9 799–801*, 800
France 14 872
Gothic 14 872
Greece, ancient 13 422
Italy 14 871, 873
Proporzioni 19 637
Propst, Robert 23 360; 31 633
Propyläen 21 409; 24 421, 425, 443; 33 117
Propyläen Kunstgeschichte 4 24
propylaia
Greece, ancient 13 417; 25 657, 657–8*; 26 909, 909; 27 712
Palestine 26 917
Rome, ancient 26 909, 909, 917; 27 712
see also GATEWAYS
Propylaia see under ATHENS → Acropolis
Prorokov, Boris (Ivanovich) 27 396
works 27 396
Prosalentis, Aimilios 13 352
Prosalentis, Pavlos, the elder 13 353
proscenia 25 658*; 30 652
proscenium arches see under ARCHES → types
Proshian, Eatchi 2 442
Proshian, Grigor 2 436
Proskau see PROSZKÓW
Proskau, Leopold von, Prince 25 122
proskenia 13 385–6, 385, 406; 30 651
Proskouriakoff, Tatiana 20 883; 24 743; 31 507
works 24 744
Prospero da Brescia see ANTICHI, PROSPERO
Prospettiva: Rivista di storia dell'arte antica e moderna 24 449
Prosser, Richard 4 769; 30 503, 877
Prossinger, Otto 2 789
Prost, Bernard 25 658*
Prost, (Léon-) Henri 3 450; 24 130; 25 658*
collaboration 18 782; 24 128
works 16 587; 22 128; 31 729, 730
prostas houses see under HOUSES → types
Prostějov National House 8 401
prostrate figures see under SCULPTURE → types
prostyle 25 659*
prostyle temples see under TEMPLES → types
Prosymna 14 358, 359
Chamber Tomb 24 14 359
Chamber Tomb 38 14 359
Sanctuary of Hera 30 738
Prószków 12 430; 25 122
Proszowski, Jan Chryzostom 25 659*
Proszowski, Marcin 25 659
Protapopova, Lyudmila 27 414
Protarcos 2 22
proteikhisma see OUTWORKS
protein fibres see under FIBRES → types
Protestantism see under CHRISTIANITY → branches
prothesis (i) (bodies) 25 659*
prothesis (ii) (churches) 25 659*
Proti, Tommaso de' 19 683
Protić, Branko 28 451
Protić, Miodrag 28 451
Protich, Andrey 5 163
Proto-Base Ring ware see under POTTERY → wares
Proto-Canaanite see under SCRIPTS → types
Protogenes 25 659*
works 12 287; 13 546, 549, 552
writings 13 554
proto-Hassuna culture 21 269, 305
proto-Hassuna period see under MESOPOTAMIA → periods
Protokolle 24 439
Protome Painter 13 513
protomes 8 154; 13 435, 575, 575, 582–3*; 25 733
Proto-Monchrome ware see under POTTERY → wares
Proto-Sinaitic see under SCRIPTS → types
prototypes 1 107; 15 824
Proto-White Painted ware see under POTTERY → wares
Proto-White Slip ware see under POTTERY → wares
Protozanov, Yakov 10 700
Protzen, J.-P. 29 164
Proudfoot, Alexander 28 243
Proudhon, Pierre-Joseph 8 55; 25 659–60*; 28 916
groups and movements 26 55
works 28 926
Proun 19 475–6
Proussos Monastery 13 358
Proust, Antonin 25 660*
Proust, (Valentin-Louis-Georges-Eugène-) Marcel 4 127; 18 783; 25 660–61*
Prout, John Skinner 25 662*
Prout, Samuel 25 661–2*; 32 197
collaboration 20 602
patrons and collectors 23 322
pupils 14 166
works 10 236; 25 626; 31 155
Prout, Samuel Gillespie 25 662
Prouvé, Gengoult 25 662
Prouvé, Jean 25 662, 663*; 33 628
collaboration 3 450; 4 214; 5 609; 17 463; 19 535; 24 476; 28 809
groups and movements 11 526
works 8 278; 11 526, 527
Prouvé, Victor (-Emile) 12 18; 25 662–3*
groups and movements 2 564; 22 456
pupils 19 809
works 11 419; 12 18, 19
Prouveur, Jean-Marc 10 483
Provaglia, Bartolomeo 4 272
Provasoli, Eduardo 6 593
provenance 2 364, 560, 561; 4 23–4, 26; 6 76, 81; 9 26; 10 210; 11 308–9; 20 416; 22 212; 25 663–5*
Provenance Index 25 665
Provence, Comtesse de 5 767; 6 397; 15 140; 26 377
Provence, Louis, Comte de see LOUIS XVIII, King of France
Provence, Louis I, Count of see LOUIS I, Duke of Anjou, King of Naples, Sicily and Jerusalem
Provence, Louis II, Count of see LOUIS II, Duke of Anjou, King of Naples, Sicily and Jerusalem
Provence, Robert, Count of see ROBERT, King of Naples and Jerusalem
Provencher Roy 22 37
Provenzale, Ippolito 3 744; 12 707
Providence (RI) 25 666–7*; 31 587
Athenaeum 29 770
First Baptist Meeting House 25 266
Providence Arcade 20 438
Public Library 25 666
Rhode Island School of Design 13 470; 25 666
Museum of Art 25 666
Rhode Island State House 31 659
Roger Williams Park 7 430
St John's Protestant Episcopal Cathedral 13 202
Union Passenger Depot 30 412–13
Union Passenger Railroad Station 31 592
Providence Art Club 1 441
Providence Flint Glass Works production 31 643
Providence Painter 13 521; 32 34
Providential Tile Co. 4 863
Provincetown (MA), Chrysler Art Museum 7 245; 14 633
Provins 6 55; 11 504; 25 667–8*
coins 7 535
Grange aux Dîmes 25 667
Porte de Jouy 12 174
Porte St-Jean 12 174
St Ayoul 13 73
St Quiriace 13 39; 25 667
town walls 11 511; 25 667
Provis, Mary Ann 10 807
Provisore, Albert Ignaz 19 748
Provo 7 759
Provoke 22 120
Provoost, Adriaen 25 668
Provoost, Jan 3 554; 4 921; 25 668–9*
pupils 3 641
works 25 668
Provoost, Thomas 25 668
Provost 19 657
Provost, Jan see PROVOOST, JAN
Prown, Jules 31 672, 673
Prowse, (Ethel) Ruth 29 108
Prowse, Thomas 21 607
Prozorovskaya Station 12 145; 27 377; 28 403; 31 728
pṛṣṭhabhadra 15 244*
Prucha, Jindřich 8 393
Pruchert, Nikolaus see PRUGGER, NIKOLAUS
Pruckner, Josef 3 530
Prudde, John 13 184
Prudentia Cup 10 528
Prudential Assurance Co. 10 299; 14 420; 32 905
Prudentius(, Aurelius Clemens) 5 801; 14 415; 25 669*
works 1 652; 5 805; 9 603; 24 269
Prudhoe 3 209
Prudhoe lions 29 34
Prudhom, Philibert 26 745
Prud'homme, Georges (-Henri) 20 925; 25 669*
Prud'hon, Pierre-Paul 11 672; 25 660, 669–72*; 26 232
attributions 25 193
collaboration 12 158; 20 890
dealers 7 762
groups and movements 26 738
patrons and collectors
Chéramy, Paul-Arthur 6 548
Constantin, Guillaume 7 762
Coutan, Louis-Joseph-Auguste 8 73
Didot, Saint Marc 8 868
Dugléré, Adolphe 9 378
Henry, Bon-Thomas 14 396
His de La Salle, (Aimé-Charles-) Horace 14 577
Napoleon I, Emperor of the French (reg 1804-14) 4 300
Sommariva, Giovanni Battista 29 59
pupils 20 202, 891; 28 67; 32 774
reproductive prints by others 2 702; 29 676
teachers 8 834
works 8 764, 867, 868, 890; 9 286; 11 542; 20 891; 23 354; 25 670, 671; 30 747
Prudkovskaya, Nadezhda (Andreyevna) see UDAL'TSOVA, NADEZHDA (ANDREYEVNA)
Prüfening Abbey
manuscripts 26 659, 661, 663, 674, 674, 675; 31 499
wall paintings 26 652
Prugger, Maria Theresia see ASAM, MARIA THERESIA
Prugger, Nikolaus 2 579; 12 390; 25 672*
Prüm 7 265
Prunati, Santo 7 309; 31 164
Prunay 25 470
pottery 25 543
Prunet et Belpuig, La Trinité 9 156
Prunner, Hans 2 470
Prunner, Johann Michael 2 783; 25 673*; 33 286
Prunner, Matthes 24 355
Pruntrut, SS Pierre et Germain 30 146
prunts 10 317; 12 438, 438, 785*
Prusa see BURSA
Prusias I (reg 230/227-182 BC) 1 498
Prusias II, King of Bithynia (reg 182-149 BC) 1 498; 24 692
Prussia, Augustus, Prince of see HOHENZOLLERN, AUGUSTUS, Prince of Prussia
Prussian blue see under PIGMENTS → types
Pruszkowski, Tadeusz 10 793, 871, 872; 26 296; 31 106; 32 877
Pruszkowski, Witold 25 107, 673*
Pruszyński, Andrzej 32 876, 877
Prutscher, Otto 2 814; 19 719; 25 673–4*
teachers 30 755
works 32 450
Pruvot, Josef 8 400
Pr-Wadjit see FARAIN, TELL EL-
Pry, Charles 17 518
Pry, Paul see HEATH, WILLIAM
Pryanishnikov, F. I. 22 178; 27 439
Pryanishnikov, Illarion (Mikhaylovich) 25 674*; 27 390
pupils
Golovin, Aleksandr (Yakovlevich) 12 877
Ivanov, Sergey (Vasil'yevich) 16 792
Korovin, Sergey (Alekseyevich) 18 389
Malyutin, Sergey (Vasil'yevich) 20 222
Nesterov, Mikhail (Vasil'yevich) 22 811
Ryabushkin, Andrey (Petrovich) 27 459
Stepanov, Aleksey (Stepanovich) 29 631
Ul'yanov, Nikolay (Pavlovich) 31 571
Werefkin, Marianne (von) 33 77
Pryde, James (Ferrier) 8 109; 23 102; 25 347, 674*
prytaneia 8 154; 13 380; 25 674–5*
Prytz, Torolf 23 236
works 10 194; 23 237
Pryzmat group see PRISM GROUP
Przegląd artystyczny see SZTUKA
Przegląd Techniczny 20 398
Przemyśl 25 341
Franciscan church 25 115
Przesmycki, Zenon 24 441
Przeworsk
Museum of the Lubomirski Dukes 19 752
parish church 25 129
Przezdziecki, Aleksander (Narcyz Karol) 25 136, 138, 675*
Przezdziecki, Konstanty 25 136, 675
Przezdziecki, Michał 25 675
Przezdziecki, Mieczysław 25 675
Przezdziecki Library and Museum see under WARSAW → museums
Przhevalsk 18 567, 568
Przyboś, J. 2 409
Przybylski, Czesław 25 142, 675–6*; 32 872
Przybyszewski, Stanisław 18 428; 22 291; 24 441; 26 266; 33 457
Przyrembel, Georg 4 712; 28 394
Przyrembel, Hans 4 671
P.S., Master (i) (fl early 16th cent.; Germany) 20 802*
P.S., Master (ii) (fl 1535-38; Italy) 25 570
Psača, St Nicholas 28 449, 455
Psalmorum Codex see under PSALTERS → types → Mainz Psalter
Psalters 3 323; 4 3, 763; 20 332, 340; 25 676–8*; 28 487
historical and regional traditions
Anglo-Saxon 25 676; 32 517
Bulgaria 9 613
Byzantine 7 222; 9 604, 611, 613–14, 620
Carolingian 5 800, 803
Cyprus 9 613
Early Christian (c. AD 250-843) 9 604, 611, 613–14
England 25 676; 26 660
Gothic 13 129, 136
Romanesque 26 660, 662
Russia 9 613
Scotland 28 233
Serbia 9 613
individual manuscripts
Achadaeus Psalter (Cambridge, Corpus Christi Coll., MS. 271) 5 803
Alphonso Psalter (London, BL, MS. Add. 24686) 4 237; 13 141; 14 423, 424
Athelstan Psalter (London, BL, Cotton MS. Galba A. XVIII; Oxford, Bodleian Lib., MS. Rawlinson B. 484) 2 72, 74; 33 90
Barberini Psalter (Rome, Vatican, Bib. Apostolica, MS. Barb. gr. 372) 9 613
Bedford Psalter (London, BL, Add. MS. 42131) 18 685; 28 66
Besançon Psalter (Besançon, Bib. Mun., MS. 54) 13 142
Blantyre Psalter (Durham, U. Lib.) 28 233
Boswell Psalter see Kinloss Psalter
Bosworth Psalter (London, BL, Add. MS. 37517) 2 74; 5 640, 641
Bury St Edmunds Psalter (Rome, Vatican, Bib. Apostolica, MS. Reg. lat. 12) 2 77
Cathach of St Columba (Dublin, Royal Irish Acad., s. n.) 15 847, 873, 876, 892; 16 12; 29 883
Chludov Psalter (Moscow, Hist. Mus., MS. D.29) 7 180*, 181; 9 514, 604, 613
Copenhagen Psalter (Copenhagen, Kon. Bib. MS. Thott, 143.2) 26 673
Corbie Psalter (Amiens, Bib. Mun., MS. 18) 11 529; 15 848
Cormac's Psalter (London, BL. Add. MS. 36929) 16 13
Crowland Psalter (Oxford, Bodleian Lib., MS. Douce 296) 2 77
Dagulf Psalter (Vienna, Österreich. NBib., Cad. 1861) 5 801, 809, 809
Eadui Psalter (London, BL, Arundel MS. 155) 3 710; 5 641
Eadwine Psalter (Cambridge, Trinity Coll., MS. R.17.1) 5 641, 641, 646; 10 244; 21 839; 25 676; 26 671
Felbrigge Psalter 4 351
Fitzwarin Psalter (Paris, Bib. N., MS. lat. 765) 13 153; 19 818
Folchart Psalter (St Gall, Stift.-Bib., 23) 5 805; 23 653
Gewijde van Dampierre Psalter (Brussels, Bib. Royale Albert 1er, MS 10607) 3 552

Psalters
individual manuscripts—cont.
Gorleston Psalter (London, BL, Add. MS. 49622) **4** 394; **10** 245; **13** 147, *147*; **24** 478
Harley Psalter (London, BL, Harley MS. 603) **2** *76*; **5** 641; **10** 243; **20** 330, II; **25** 676
Huntingfield Psalter (New York, Pierpont Morgan Lib., MS. M. 43) **13** 140
Imola Psalter (Imola, Bib. Com., MS. 100) **25** *677*, 677
Ingeborg Psalter (Chantilly, Mus. Condé, MS. 1695) **5** 427; **11** 530; **13** 140, 179; **22** 270; **23** 523; **25** 677; **26** 677, *677*; **31** 284, *285*, 835
Iona Psalter (Edinburgh, N. Lib., MS. 1000) **28** 233
Isabella Psalter (Cambridge, Fitzwilliam, MS.300) **5** 665; **27** 565
King's Psalter (Paris, Bib. N., MS.lat. 1152) **6** 485
Kinloss Psalter (London, V&A, MS. Reid 52) **28** 234
Luttrell Psalter (London, BL, Add. MS. 42130) **4** 394; **10** 245; **12** 287; **13** 148; **18** 703, *703*; **19** 818*; **22** 686; **25** 678
Melisende Psalter (London, BL, MS. Egerton 1139) **17** 502–3, *503*; **21** 82–3*
Munich Psalter (Munich, Bayer. Staatsbib., Clm. 835) **13** 140
Ormesby Psalter (Oxford, Bodleian Lib., MS. Douce 366) **13** 147; **25** 678
Oscott Psalter (London, BL, Add. MS. 50000) **24** 478
Paris Psalter (Paris, Bib. N., MS. grec 139) **7** 220, 221; **9** 520, 613; **19** 169, 888; **22** 520; **24** 177–8*, *178*
Peterborough Psalter (Brussels, Bib. Royale Albert 1er, MSS 9961-2) **10** 245; **13** 147; **31** 499, 835
Psalterium Aureum (St Gall., Stift.-Bib., 22) **5** 805; **11** *151*
Psalter of Basil II (Venice, Bib. N. Marciana, MS. gr. 17) **9** 614; **22** 520
Psalter of Blanche of Castile (Paris, Bib. Arsenal, MS. fr. 1186) **11** 530
Psalter of Bonmont (Besançon, Bib. Mun., MS. 54) **1** 653
Psalter of Bonne of Luxembourg (New York, Cloisters, MS. 69. 88) **17** 463; **25** 694
Psalter of Charles the Bald (Paris, Bib. N., MS. lat. 1152) **5** 808, 810; **26** 81
Psalter of Duchess Mathilda (Baltimore, MD, Walters A.G., MS. W10) **26** 675
Psalter of Henry of Blois *see* Winchester Psalter
Psalter of Humphrey de Bohun (Vienna, Österreich. Nbib., Cod. 1826) **25** 676
Psalter of Jean, Duc de Berry (Paris, Bib. N., MS. fr. 13091) **4** 583; **6** 389; **16** 852; **20** 751
Psalter of Jeanne de Laval (Poitiers, Bib. Mun., MS. 41) **20** 735
Psalter of Mary Tudor *see* Queen Mary Psalter
Psalter of Robert de Lisle (London, BL, Arundel MS. 83) **13** 149
Psalter of S Egigio **4** 197
Psalters
individual manuscripts—cont.
Psalter of Yolande of Soissons (New York, Pierpont Morgan Lib., MS. M. 729) **8** 184
Purple Psalter (Oxford, Bodleian Lib., MS. Douce 59) **5** 803
Queen Mary Psalter (London, BL, Royal MS. 2.B.VII) **10** 245; **13** 147; **25** 677, *807*, 807–8*
Ramsey Psalter (London, BL, Harley MS. 2904) **2** 75; **10** 243; **25** 676; **33** 233
Ramsey Psalter (St Paul im Lavanttal, Stiftsbib., MS. 58/1) **15** 146
Rhygyfarch Psalter (Dublin, Trinity Coll. Lib) **32** 784
Riccardiana Psalter (Florence, Bib. Riccardiana, MS. 323) **17** 505
Ruodprecht Psalter (Cividale del Friuli, Mus. Archeol. N., Cod. 136) **9** 749; **23** 652, 653
Rutland Psalter (London, BL, Add. MS. 62925) **4** 394; **13** 141
St Albans Psalter (Hildesheim, St Godehardkirche) **10** 244; **20** 331; **25** 676; **26** 659, 660, 662, 671, *672*; **27** 528
St Bertin Psalter (Boulogne, Bib. Mun., MS. 20) **23** 348
St Louis Psalter (Paris, Bib. N., MS. lat. 10525) **5** 665; **11** 530; **13** 138, 141, 179; **26** 677; **27** 565*
St Omer Psalter (London, BL, Yates Thompson MS. 14) **30** 749
Southampton Psalter (Cambridge, St John's Coll.) **16** 13
Stockholm Psalter (Stockholm, Nmus., B. 2010) **33** 201
Stuttgart Psalter (Stuttgart, Württemberg. Landesbib., MS. bibl. fol. 23) **8** 200; **24** 132; **31** 774
Theodore Psalter (London, BL, Add. MS. 19352) **9** 613
Tiberius Psalter (London, BL, Cotton MS. Tib. C. VI) **10** 243; **25** 676, 677; **33** 233, *233*
Tomich Psalter (Moscow, Hist. Mus., MS. 2752) **5** 153; **32** 149
Utrecht Psalter (Utrecht, Bib. Rijksuniv., MS. 32) **2** 76; **5** 442, 802; **8** 38; **9** 219, 686; **11** 529; **13** 140; **18** 703; **25** 676; **26** 113, 671, 677; **31** *773*, 773–4*
Vespasian Psalter (London, BL, Cotton MS. Vesp. A. I) **5** 640; **10** 243; **15** 848, 875; **25** 676; **32** 385*
Westminster Psalter (London, BL, Royal MS. 2.A.XXII) **10** 244; **13** 140; **26** 677
Winchcombe Psalter (Cambridge, U. Lib., MS. Ff. 1.23) **2** 77
Winchester Psalter (London, BL, Cotton MS. Nero C. IV) **10** 244; **14** 398; **26** 660, 672; **33** 233
Winchester Psalter (London, BL, Cotton MS. Tib. C. VI) *see* Tiberius Psalter
Windmill Psalter (New York Pierpont Morgan Lib., MS. M. 102) **4** 393; **13** 136, 138
York Psalter (Glasgow, U. Lib., MS. U.3.2) **26** 673
Psalters—cont.
types
Aristocratic Psalters **9** 613
Mainz Psalter **22** 111; **25** 622
Marginal Psalters **9** 613
Psalmorum Codex **7** 625, *625*
see also BIBLES; OLD TESTAMENTS
Psammetichus (chief of doctors) **27** 813
Psammetichus I (*reg* 664-610 BC) **9** *777*, 892
Psammetichus II (*reg* 595-589 BC) **9** *777*, 892; **30** 236, 296
Psammetichus III (*reg* 526-525 BC) **9** *777*
Psammuthis (*reg* 393 BC) **9** *778*
Psamtiksaneith **9** 860
Pseira **13** *362*; **21** *651*; **25** 678*
fortifications **8** 155
paintings **21** 659, 674
pottery **21** 667, *669*, 670, *670*
towns **21** 664
Psellos, Michael **19** 888
Pseudo Antonio da Monza *see* BIRAGO, GIOVANNI PIETRO
pseudo-Apuleius **14** 432, 433
Pseudo-Barbar ware *see under* POTTERY → wares
Pseudo-Bles **2** 204; **20** 750*
works **2** *205*
Pseudo-Boccaccino *see* GIOVANNI AGOSTINO DA LODI
Pseudo-Bonaventura **7** 225; **13** 129; **25** 678–9*
Pseudo-Callisthenes **26** 563
Pseudo-Cyclax **13** 372
Pseudo-Dionysius the Areopagite **1** 176, 652; **19** 355; **22** 749; **30** 165
pseudo-dipteral **25** 679*
pseudo-dipteral temples *see under* TEMPLES → types
Pseudo-Galen **16** 456
Pseudo-Giovenone **11** 12
pseudo-isodomic masonry *see under* MASONRY → types
Pseudo-Jacopino (di Francesco Bavosi dei Papazoni) **4** 275, 276; **11** 380; **20** 751*
Pseudo-Jacquemart **20** 634, 751*
Pseudo-Mälesskircher *see* TEGERNSEE ALTAR, MASTER OF THE
Pseudo-Melioli **25** 19
Pseudo-Mostaert *see* ISENBRANDT, ADRIAEN
Pseudo-Niccolò *see* ILLUSTRATORE MASTER
Pseudo-Oppian **9** 618
Pseudo-Ortkens **2** 486; **20** 751–2*
pseudo-penannular brooches *see under* BROOCHES → types
pseudo-peripteral **25** 679*
Pseudo-Pier Francesco Fiorentino **20** 752*
Psiax **32** 31, 65–6*
attributions **23** 145
pupils **32** 65
teachers **23** 145
works **13** 511, 518
Pskov **9** *507*; **25** 679–81*; **27** *363*, 372
Cathedral of the Holy Trinity **31** 557
Church of the Epiphany **27** 370
fortifications **27** 370
icons **25** 337; **27** 382, 383, *383*
kremlin **25** *679*
painting **27** 382
St Basil on the Hill **25** *680*
Psuedo-Seneca *see* MARTIN OF BRAGA
Psusennes I (*reg c.* 1040-*c.* 997 BC) **9** *777*, 887; **10** 11, 32; **22** 284; **30** 296
Psusennes II (*reg c.* 964-*c.* 950 BC) **9** *777*
psychedelic art **25** 681*
psychoanalysis and art **1** 78; **2** 533, 538; **10** 101; **11** 765; **18** 587; **25** 681–4*; **30** 18
psychology **24** 375; **25** 684–5*; **26** 223; **28** 207–8
psychology, Gestalt *see* GESTALT PSYCHOLOGY
Psychomachia **1** 651, 652; **5** 801; **25** 669
psychophysics **7** 659; **14** 396
psychotic art **8** 441; **25** 681, 685–6*, *686*
psychrometers **7** 734
Psykhro **8** 153
psykters **13** 476, 518
Ptácek, Ondřej **8** 415
Ptahhotpe **9** 789; **27** 812; **31** 107
tomb **27** *811*
Ptahmes
dress **10** *43*
Ptahshepses **1** 97; **10** 29
Ptaszek *see* VOGEL, ZYGMUNT
Ptaszkowa Triptych **25** 101
ptera **13** 376
Ptghni **2** *423*; **9** *512*; **25** 686–7*
monastery church **2** 434; **25** 686–7
Ptoion **13** 429; **22** 700
Ptolemaic period *see under* EGYPT, ANCIENT → periods
Ptolemais **9** *507*; **13** *362*; **25** 687*; **26** *919*
amphitheatre **26** 921
fortress church **9** 535
Palace of the Columns **26** 920
tetrastyle **9** 589
Ptolemy (*c.* AD 90-168) **15** 308; **28** 721; **30** 848
manuscripts
astrology **2** 651
astronomy **2** 649, 650; **12** 812
optics **24** 492
topography **2** 695; **20** 363; **31** 151
Ptolemy I Soter I (*reg* 304-284 BC) **9** *778*
architecture **1** 614, 615; **2** 690; **13** 404; **18** 209; **22** 354; **30** 296
coins **13** 588
manuscripts **19** 312
paintings **2** 217; **23** 142
sculpture **5** 64; **9** 893
Ptolemy II Philadelphus (*reg* 285-246 BC) **9** *778*, *893*, *894*
architecture **1** 615; **18** 209; **27** 690; **30** 296, 691
paintings **23** 900
reliefs **9** 894
sculpture **9** 893; **10** 68
tents **30** 476
Ptolemy III Euergetes I (*reg* 246-221 BC) **1** 615; **2** 656; **9** 719, *778*, 894
Ptolemy IV Philopator (*reg* 221-205 BC) **9** 719, *778*, 893; **13** 407, 465; **30** 296, 701
Ptolemy V Epiphanes (*reg* 205-180 BC) **9** *778*
Ptolemy VI Philometor (*reg* 180-164 BC) **9** 719, *778*, 893, 894
Ptolemy VII Neos Philopator (*reg* 145 BC) **9** *778*
Ptolemy VIII Euergetes II (*reg* 170-163; 145-116 BC) **9** 719, *778*, 893, 894; **17** 714; **30** 693
temples **9** *720*
Ptolemy IX Soter II (*reg* 116-107; 88-81 BC) **9** 719, *778*; **17** 714
Ptolemy X Alexander I (*reg* 107-88 BC) **9** 719, *778*
Ptolemy XI Alexander II (*reg* 80 BC) **9** *778*
Ptolemy XII Neos Dionysos (*reg* 80-58; 55-51 BC) **9** 719, *778*, 894
Ptolemy XIII (*reg* 51-47 BC) **9** *778*
Ptolemy XIV (*reg* 47-44 BC) **9** *778*
Ptolemy XV Caesarion (*reg* 44-30 BC) **9** *778*
Ptolichos of Corfu **1** 481; **18** 460
PTT (Post, Telegraaf en Telefoon) **33** 743
Ptuj **28** *858*
Castle **28** 858
Minorite church **28** 859, 860
parish church **28** 858, 860
polyptychs **28** 860
Regional Museum **28** 863
Ptujska Gora, St Mary **28** 858, *858*, *859*, 861
Pu-abi, Queen (*fl c.* 2500 BC) **3** 441
Puan **18** *248*
Public Art Development Trust (Britain) **22** 333
publications, architectural *see* ARCHITECTURAL PUBLICATIONS
public buildings **10** 151
public collections *see under* COLLECTIONS → types
Public Culture **24** 436
public gardens *see under* GARDENS → types
public houses **25** 687–9*, *688*
public libraries *see under* LIBRARIES → types
public monuments *see under* MONUMENTS → types
public parks *see under* PARKS → types
public records offices *see* ARCHIVES
Public Works Administration **17** 838
Public Works of Art Project (PWAP) **9** 200; **19** 701; **22** 335
Publishers' Weekly **13** 811
publishing (photographic) **2** 690; **11** 795; **26** *235*
publishing **2** 369
Publishing on Design, Inc. **9** 121; **17** 752
Publius Ovidius Naso *see* OVID
Púbol Altarpiece **20** 514, *515*
pubs *see* PUBLIC HOUSES
Pucará **24** *498*; **29** 127, *156*; **31** 45–6
figurines **29** *185*
hardstones **29** 185
musical instruments **29** 216
pottery **29** 175, 177; **31** *46*
sculpture **29** 170–71
stone-carvings **29** *171*
Pucará de Lulumbamba *see* PUCARÁ DE RUMICUCHO
Pucará de Rumicucho **25** 689*, *689*; **29** *136*, 168
Pucci (family) **2** 854; **25** 156
Pucci, Antonio (*fl* 1380-1417) **12** 681; **25** 690
Pucci, Antonio (1418-84) **25** 690
Pucci, Antonio (*fl c.* 1515) **25** 903
Pucci, Ascanio di Pandolfo **25** 690
Pucci, Dionigi **25** 690
Pucci, Emilio **9** 294
Pucci, Francesco di Giovanni **25** 690
Pucci, Giovanni **25** 690
Pucci, Lorenzo (*fl* 1459) **9** 95
Pucci, Lorenzo (1458-1531) **25** 690
Pucci, Lorenzo di Piero (1520-92) **25** 690
Pucci, Orazio Roberto **25** 690
Pucci, Pandolfo (*fl c.* 1592; priest) **5** 704
Pucci, Pandolfo di Roberto (1509-60; patron) **25** 690
Pucci, Puccio **25** 690
Pucci, Roberto **5** 361; **25** 690
Pucci, Saracino **25** 690
Puccinelli, Antonio **8** 701
Puccini, Biagio **1** 532; **19** 524; **25** 690*
Puccini, Giuseppe **27** 204
Puccini, Niccolò **27** 479
Puccini, Tommaso **25** 690–91*

Puccini *Pietà* 21 72
Puccio, Piero (di Giovanni) di *see* PIERO (DI GIOVANNI) DI PUCCIO
Puccio di Benintendi 25 690
Puccio di Landuccio 24 857
Puccio di Simone 5 661; 23 323; 25 691*
Pucci Sardi, Andrea 13 168
Pucelle, Jean 13 142; 24 132; 25 691–4*
 attributions 11 531
 patrons and collectors 3 642, 643; 5 667; 13 153; 28 1; 31 835, 836, 837
 works 4 12, 764; 13 133, *148*, 673, *674*; 18 703; 25 *692*, *693*
 workshop 13 148, 149
Puchała, Aleksander 25 125
Puchenau 25 864
Pucherna, Antonín 25 358
Pu Ch'ien-ch'iu *see* BU QIANQIU
Puchinger, Erwin 25 673
Puchol Rubio, José 31 95
Púchov 8 419
Puchspaum, Hans 4 695; 14 884; 25 694–5*; 28 849; 32 452
Puchstein, Otto 22 731
Pu Chung-ch'ien *see* BU ZHONGQIAN
Puck 27 872
Pückler-Muskau, Hermann (Ludwig Heinrich) von 25 695–6*
 patrons and collectors 14 655
 works 12 105, 134; 22 381–2; 26 240
PUD *see* PRAGUE ART WORKSHOPS
pudding-stone 7 133
Pudsey, Bishop *see* HUGH OF LE PUISET
Puebla (Mexico) 21 *372*; 25 696–7*; 31 721
 architecture 21 376; 25 57
 Biblioteca Palafoxiana 25 697
 Casa del Alfeñique *see* Museo Regional y de Ceramica
 Casa del Canonigo Peláez 25 57
 Casa de los Muñecos 25 57
 College of Espíritu Santo 21 376
 ecclesiastical buildings 25 696
  Cathedral 21 375, 384; 25 *696*
  La Concordia 25 57
  S Catalina 25 57
  S Cristóbal 25 57
  S Domingo 25 57
   Rosario Chapel 29 841
  S Francisco 25 57
  S Inés 25 57
  S José 25 57
  S Marcos 25 57
 education (art) 21 397
 furniture 21 391
 glass 21 392
 La Victoria market 21 378
 Maternidad Tamariz hospital 21 378
 Museo Amparo 21 395
 Museo de Arte 'José Luis Bello y González' 25 697
 Museo de Arte Religioso 25 697
 Museo de las Artesanías 25 697
 Museo Industrial de Puebla 21 396
 Museo Regional y de Ceramica 25 57
 painting 21 385
 pottery 4 175–6; 21 238, 239, 392, *392*
 sculpture 21 384
 seals 21 *258*
 shields 21 255
 textiles 21 394
Puebla (Spain) 21 393
Puebla-Tlaxcala 21 737
Pueblito 29 *136*, 139; 30 240
Pueblo 1 820; 22 550, 666, 672
 altars 1 701
Pueblo—cont.
 architecture 20 571; 22 568; 31 588
 baskets 22 661
 craftsmen and artists 22 666
 dress 22 634
 historiography 22 673, 676
 houses 22 567
 jewellery 22 629
 kivas 6 *381*; 18 102–3; 22 566
 pottery 20 *498*; 22 605, 666
 religion 22 556, 557, 558, 559, 666
 ritual objects 22 562
 sculpture 22 582
 tourist art 22 668
 trade 22 562, 563
 villages 22 554
 watercolours 22 679
 weaving 22 623–4
Pueblo, Early 22 554
Pueblo Deco 22 568
Pueblo de Nuestra Señora La Reina de Los Angeles, El *see* LOS ANGELES
pueblo houses *see under* HOUSES → types
Pueblo Llano 32 177
Pueblo Nuevo 29 *136*; 32 238
Pueblo Style 22 568
Puech, Denys (-Pierre) 11 567; 25 697*
 pupils 20 839; 33 163
 teachers 10 771
Puelma, Alfredo Valenzuela 14 367
Puelma, Valenzuela 12 917
Puenta, Sancho Hurtado del *see* HURTADO DEL PUENTA, SANCHO
Puente, Alejandro 2 401; 25 697*
Puente, Diego de la 4 261; 24 506
Puente, Juan de la 7 362
Puente, P. 31 823
Puente del Arzobispo
 pottery 4 175; 29 326, 327, 329
 tiles 30 883
Puentes 24 96
Puerta de los Hispanioles *see* PORT OF SPAIN
Puerto Armuelles 23 *902*
Puerto Cabello 32 *165*
 fort 32 169
 houses 32 169
 Nuevo Templo de S José 32 169
 Real Compañía Guipuzcoana building 32 169
Puerto de la Cruz 32 *165*
Puerto de Omoa, Museo Nacional de Historia Colonial 14 717
Puerto González Viquez
 jewellery 13 *291*
Puerto Hormiga 29 *136*
 pottery 29 127, 136, 150
 shell midden 29 138
Puerto Lampira 14 *711*
Puerto Marqués 21 197
Puerto Montt 6 *590*
 Galería Manoly 6 601
Puerto Plata 9 *114*, 116
Puerto Príncipe 8 228
Puerto Rico 2 144; 5 744, *745*; 25 697–704*, *698*; 29 128
 architecture 25 700–701*; 29 200
 collections 25 703–4*
 craftsmen and artists 18 832–4*
 decorative arts 25 702–3*
 education (art) 25 704
 exhibitions 5 746
 fortifications 25 *700*
 jade 29 *199*
 masks 25 699
 museums 25 703–4*
 musical instruments 25 703
 painting 18 *833*; 25 701–2*
 patronage 25 703–4*
 pendants (jewellery) 29 *199*
Puerto Rico—cont.
 pottery 25 698–9, 703; 29 *199*
 prints 25 702
 rock art 2 145; 5 748
 sculpture 5 750, *750*; 25 702*, *702*
 serpentine 29 *199*
 stone-carvings 25 699, *699*; 29 *199*
 women artists 25 701
 wood 5 *750*
 wood-carvings 25 703
Puetro Nuevo, Monument 5 1 700
Pueyrredón, Prilidiano 2 395, 399; 25 704*
Pueyrredón, Silva de 2 405
Puga, Antonio 9 5
Pugachenkova, G. A. 2 882; 8 475; 18 16
Puget, François 25 704, 706, 707, 708, 709
Puget, Gaspard 20 472; 25 704, 705, 708
Puget, Pierre 20 *473*; 25 704–9*
 assistants 32 395
 groups and movements 16 701
 patrons and collectors 7 546; 11 356, 357; 18 660; 27 878; 28 173
 pupils 6 379; 31 174
 works 8 550; 11 559; 16 701–2; 20 472; 25 *706*, *708*; 28 612
Puget, Simon 25 704
Puget, Zbigniew 33 704
Puget de Montauron, Pierre 4 125
Puggaard, Hans 29 72
Pugh (family) 9 320
Pugh, Clifton (Ernest) 2 161; 25 710*
Pugh, Edward 32 785
Pugh, Lewis Pugh 28 349
Pugh, T. & R. 16 30
Pugin, A(ugustus) C(harles) 25 710–12*
 collaboration 27 279; 29 632
 groups and movements 13 206
 patrons and collectors 1 121
 pupils 11 22; 24 364; 25 573, 587, 712; 26 288
 works 4 *809*; 8 911; 14 128; 19 *587*; 25 *711*
 writings 4 828
  illustrated 8 *911*
  translated 4 375
Pugin, A(ugustus) W(elby) N(orthmore) 2 600; 6 605; 8 48; 25 710, 711–16*
 architecture
  cathedrals 4 85; 19 870; 23 258
  churches 7 254; 16 11; 25 *714*; 27 626; 28 230
  colleges 16 11
  country houses 1 734; 8 48; 26 361
  government buildings 10 *237*; 16 52; 19 *614*; 23 546
  restorations 5 510
  schools 28 156
  screens (i) (architectural) 28 295, 296
 candlesticks 5 612
 collaboration 3 280, 281, 282; 8 106; 9 321; 10 343; 12 635–6; 13 237; 14 167; 19 613–14
 competitions 7 667
 decorative works 25 *715*
 drawings 2 333
 fonts (baptismal) 11 256
 frames 11 432
 furniture 2 755; 10 298; 13 *207*; 30 218; 33 250
 groups and movements 3 618; 11 839; 13 203, 204, 207; 23 498; 26 743; 32 415
 interior decoration 10 281; 28 254
 jewellery 10 345
 metalwork 4 88; 8 202; 10 335; 27 336
Pugin, A(ugustus) W(elby) N(orthmore)—cont.
 patrons and collectors 3 174; 6 118; 30 267
 personal collection 3 585
 pupils 25 716
 stained glass 23 690; 29 506
 textiles 10 354
 thrones 30 783
 tiles 10 312; 30 *877*
 wallpaper 23 *546*; 32 816
 writings 1 111
  illustrated 25 573, *713*
  on architects 2 315
  on architecture 10 237, 377; 11 521; 26 14
  on decorum 8 613
  on furniture 24 273
  translated 3 585
Pugin, Cuthbert Welby 25 710
Pugin, E(dward) W(elby) 25 710, 716–17*
 collaboration 8 191; 14 46, 156
 groups and movements 13 208
 pupils 2 600
 works 1 151; 3 549, 746, 884; 16 11; 18 66
Pugin, Peter Paul 25 710, 717
Pugin & Ashlin 2 600
Puglia, Giuseppe 25 717*; 29 388
Pugliani, Cosimo 24 853
Pugliani, Domenico 6 126; 25 717–18*
Puglielli, Emilio 16 651
Puglieschi, Antonio 4 491; 25 718*
Pugliese, Piero del *see* PIERO DEL PUGLIESE
Pugliesi (family) 24 768
Pug mills 4 785; 6 325
Pugnaloni, Ottorino 32 415
Pugungraharjo 15 788
Puhar *see* KAVERIPATTINAM
Puhlmann, J. G. 3 383
P'u Hsin-yü 25 718*; 30 249
P'u I *see* PU YI
Puiforcat, Jean (Elisée) 24 147; 25 718–19*
 collaboration 27 322
 groups and movements 2 521; 31 581
 works 11 *622*, 623
Puig, Arnau 8 538
Puig, August 3 219
Puig, Vicente 10 906; 13 654; 28 729
Puig Cuyas, Ramon 29 346
Puig des Molins 3 106; 25 734, 735
Puig Gairalt, Antoni 3 216
Puig Gairalt, Ramón 23 260
Puig Garalt, Josep 23 260
Puiggari 24 105
Puig i Cadafalch, Josep 25 719*; 26 571; 29 329
 groups and movements 3 216, 219; 23 260
 works 3 216; 12 181; 29 272
Puille, Charles Pierre 22 308
Puille, Karl Ludwig 22 309
Puiset, Hugh of Le *see* HUGH OF LE PUISET
Pujili 9 709
Pujol (family) 3 218
Pujol, Alexandre Abel de *see* ABEL DE PUJOL, ALEXANDRE
Pujolle, Guillaume 2 516
 works 2 *515*
PUK 17 408
Pukapuka 7 790
Pukar *see* KAVERIPATTINAM
Pukch'ang, Ch'ŏnwang Chishin 18 272
Pukchijang Temple
 paintings 18 *310*
Pukeberg Glasbruk 30 103
Pukirev, Vasily (Vladimirovich) 25 719*; 27 390; 33 622
Pukl, Vladimír 28 491
Puksan *see* KIM SU-CH'ŎL
Pukur 3 45
Pula (Croatia) 8 *174*, 175; 9 *510*; 25 720–21*; 26 *906*; 32 *158*
 amphitheatre 1 797
 Archaeological Museum 8 180
 Cathedral of St Thomas 9 529; 25 720
 Franciscan church 8 175
 Istrian Archaeological Museum 11 312
 mosaics 9 569
 Pola 25 720*; 26 *906*
 St Marija Formosa 25 720; 29 816
 Temple of Diana 8 175
 Temple of Roma and Augustus 25 720
 temples 26 906
 Town Hall 8 175
Pula (Sardinia) 29 324
Pulai Chondong Mosque 20 166
Pulakesin II, Ruler (*reg* 609/10–642) (Chalukyas of Badami) 15 738
Pulau Carey 20 181
Puławy 25 *92*, 99, 135, 136, 138
 gardens 12 134
 Gothic House 8 372; 25 139
 Lubomirski Palace 25 98
 Temple of Sybilla 25 139
Pulburong *see* AN CHUNG-SIK
Pulcheria, Empress of Byzantium (399-453) 1 694; 7 278; 9 654; 19 787; 22 229
Pulchri Studio 4 160; 14 42
Pulguk Temple 18 354
Pulham, James 4 216
Pulham stone 2 541
Puligo, Domenico 3 15; 25 721*
Pul-i Khumri 29 824
Pulinx, Hendrik, *de jongere* (*d* 1787) 25 721
Pulinx, Hendrik, *d'oude* (1698-1781) 3 590; 12 147; 25 374, 721*
Puliti, Tito 4 842
Pulitzer, Joseph 7 648
Pulitzer and Ceas 16 731
Pulkau, Heiligblutkirche Altar 2 800
Pulkau, Master of *see* HISTORIA FRIDERICI ET MAXIMILIANI, MASTER OF THE
Pulkkinen, Mikko 24 892
Pulkovo Observatory 23 340
Pull, Georges 24 148
Pullamangai 15 *294*; 25 722*
 Brahmapurishvara Temple 15 305, *514*, 515
 reliefs 15 515
 sculpture 15 305
Pullan, Richard Popplewell 25 722*
 collaboration 5 340
 excavations 25 576
 works 14 70
Pullinen, Laila 11 101
Pullman (IL) 3 693; 25 723
Pullman, George Mortimer 25 722–3*
Pullon, Heinz 33 245
Pülmann, Jakob 29 729
Puloli 16 864
pulpita *see under* SCREENS (i) (ARCHITECTURAL) → types
pulpit altars *see under* ALTARS → types
pulpits 7 282; 25 723–8*; 28 141; 31 321
 historical and regional traditions
  Argentina 2 398
  Belgium 25 727, *727*
  Denmark 8 *740*
  England 25 724–5, 726–7
  France 23 *98*
  Germany 25 727; 29 *760*
  Gothic 24 *872*; 25 *724*, 725, *726*

pulpits
  historical and regional traditions—cont.
    Italy 16 688, 723; 20 114; 21 536, 774; 24 872; 25 723–4, 724, 725
      Romanesque 26 626, 627
    Netherlands, the 25 726
    Poland 25 115
    Romanesque 16 688; 21 774; 26 626, 627
    Scotland 28 251–2
  materials
    bronze 25 725
    marble 21 774; 24 872
    oak 25 726, 727; 28 251
    stone 26 626, 627
  types
    doophek 28 251
  see also MINBARS
Pulsano Abbey 26 628
Pulszky, Ferenc 25 728
Pulszký, František 28 857
Pulszky, Károly 25 728–9*
Pulteney, John de 8 43
Pulteney, William 30 421
Pulur 17 875
Puluwat 23 723
pulverteknikk 22 807
Pulzone, Scipione 25 729–30*; 26 770
  collaboration 31 820
  patrons and collectors 4 567; 21 24
  works 4 53; 16 665; 25 729; 30 358
Pumacahua 8 303
Pumerbo see PARAMARIBO
pumice 13 603; 24 106; 26 880; 27 51; 29 702, 706
Pumpelly, R. 6 279
Pümpin & Herzog 20 118
pumpkin domes see under DOMES → types
pump rooms 14 840
Pumpu (family) 10 620, 624; 16 652, 653
Puná, La see LA PUNÁ
Punáes 18 783–4
Pūnaka see PUNE
puncetti see under LACE → types
Punch 5 758; 9 384; 17 877; 24 605; 25 244
punch-bowls 30 105
punch-cards see under CARDS → types
punch-cutting machines 31 496
punched prints see under PRINTS → types
punches 7 532, 533; 25 730–31*
Punchestown, Long Stone 25 505
Punchinello 5 758
punching 31 147
  historical and regional traditions
    Gothic 13 139
    Islamic 16 364
  types
    ringmatting 7 109
  uses
    gold leaf 12 623; 25 730
    leather 12 623
    metalwork 16 364; 21 326
    painting 12 625; 13 139; 25 730, 730–31*
Punch'ŏng ware see under POTTERY → wares
Punct 26 716
Pundzius, Bronius 19 499
Pune 15 276; 25 732*
  National Film Archives of India 15 184
  Raja Dinkar Kelkar Museum 15 182
  St Mary 15 402
  textiles 15 664
Puni, Ivan (Al'bertovich) see POUGNY, JEAN
Punic 25 732–5*
  alabaster (gypsum) 25 733
Punic—cont.
  amulets 25 734, 735
  architecture 25 732–3*
  beads 25 734
  braziers 25 734
  bronze 25 734
  coffins 25 733
  combs (hair) 25 734
  copper 25 734
  earrings 25 734
  eggs 25 735*
  faience (i) (glass) 25 734*
  figurines 25 733–4
  fortifications 25 733
  glass 25 734*
  gold 25 735
  greenstone 25 734
  houses 25 732
  incense burners 25 733
  inscriptions 25 733
  ivory-carvings 25 734*
  jewellery 25 734–5*
  lamps 25 734
  languages 25 733
  limestone 25 733
  masks 25 733
  metalwork 25 734*
  mosaics 25 732
  moulds 25 733, 734
  necklaces 25 735
  ossuaries 25 733
  pendants (jewellery) 25 735, 735
  pottery 25 734*
  protomes 25 733
  razors 25 734
  rings 25 734
  sarcophagi 10 592
  scarabs 25 734
  sculpture 25 733–4*
  seals 25 734*
  silver 25 735
  silver-gilt 25 735
  stelae 5 892; 25 733, 733
  terracottas 25 733–4*, 735
  trade 10 592
    amulets 25 734
    metalwork 25 734
    terracottas 25 733
  tusks 25 734
  unguent vessels 25 734
  walls 25 733
Punicum 6 353; 10 583, 601
Punic wax see under WAXES → types
Punin, Nikolay (Nikolayevich) 25 735–6*; 27 444
  groups and movements 7 341, 768; 15 857; 18 536; 22 508
Punjab University see under LAHORE
Punjai Temple 15 305
Punkurí 1 701; 29 167, 170
Punnu 15 629
Puno 24 498
  Cathedral 24 504
Punt 9 780, 821; 30 693
Punt, Jan 25 736*
  pupils 32 591
  works 5 322; 31 367; 33 261
Punta Ballena
  Casa Berlingieri 31 753
  Casa Olle Perez 31 754
  La Solana del Mar Hotel 31 753
Punta del Este 8 228
  Banco de la República 31 754
  Cave 1 8 229, 229
Punta della Vipera 10 588, 592
punto in aria see under LACE → types
Punu 11 878, 879
Punuk 22 574
Punwon
  porcelain 4 174, 175
Puṇya see PUNE
Puoto see FARAIN, TELL EL-
Pupini, Biagio 3 56; 25 736*
  collaboration 5 842
  patrons and collectors 11 76
Pupluna see POPULONIA
puppets
  historical and regional traditions
    Bamana 1 385
    Cambodia 5 504–5*, 505
    China 7 122, 122–3*, 147; 31 258
    Ibibio 15 65*
    Indian subcontinent 7 122; 15 714–15*, 715
    Indonesia 15 800, 800
    Japan 17 350, 406–8*
    Java 15 801
    Laos 18 775*
    Sri Lanka 29 479
    Thailand 30 628–9*
  materials
    bamboo 17 407
    gold leaf 15 798, 798
    hair 17 407
    hides 5 505; 15 798, 798
    leather 5 505; 7 122, 147; 15 715; 16 544, 544
    paper 31 258
    parchment 7 122
    wire 7 122
    wood 7 122; 17 407, 407
  types
    bunraku 17 407, 407
    Ebisu kaki 17 406
    fire puppets 17 407
    flesh 7 122
    glove 17 408
    hand-puppets 7 123; 15 714–15; 17 406
    hotoke mawashi 17 406
    karakuri ningyō 17 408
    Kuruma ningyō 17 407
    marionettes 5 252–3*, 253; 7 122; 15 715; 17 406
    ningyō jōruri 17 406–7
    powder 7 122
    rod 15 715; 18 775
    shadow-puppets 15 799–800*
      China 7 122
      Egypt 16 545
      Indian subcontinent 15 715, 715
      Indonesia 15 797, 797, 798
      Islamic 16 543–5*, 544
      Java 15 797, 797–8, 798; 29 234
      Laos 18 775
      Malaysia 20 178, 178
      Ottoman 16 544, 544
      Thailand 30 628–9
      Turkey 16 544, 544
    string puppets see marionettes
    water puppets 32 491, 491
puppet theatre see under THEATRE → types
puppet theatres see under THEATRES → types
Puqua
  works 7 122
Pur, Kukdeshvara Temple 15 317
Pura Canggi 15 754, 784
Pura Dalem 15 754
Pura Gunung Kawi 15 754, 763–4, 784
  Queens' Tombs 15 763
Pura Kedarman 15 754, 784
Pura Kehen 15 754
  candi bentărs 15 767
Purapara
  sculpture 15 502
Pura Puseh Gaduh 15 754, 784, 785
Pura Tegeh Koripan 15 784
Pura Yeh Gangga 15 754
Purbeck 10 227; 11 253
Purbeck marble see under LIMESTONE → types
Purbuyev, Dorzhi 27 436
Purcell, Charles Henry Cuthbert 25 710
Purcell, Feick & Elmslie 25 737
Purcell, Henry 27 730
Purcell, Richard 15 28; 21 149
Purcell, William Gray 2 572; 21 649; 25 446, 737
Purcell & Elmslie 3 177; 21 650; 25 737*
Purcell & Feick 25 737
Purchase (NY)
  Neuberger Museum 22 917
  PepsiCo Headquarters 12 143, 143; 25 189
Purciems 18 846
Purdue University see under WEST LAFAYETTE (IN)
Purdy, Corydon T. 6 573; 14 658
Pure Land Buddhism see under BUDDHISM → sects
El Purgatorio 3 365; 12 71; 28 652; 29 156, 166
Pürgg 26 652, 655
  Johanneskapelle 2 790
Pürglitz Castle see KŘIVOKLÁT CASTLE
Puri 15 279, 504; 25 737–8*
  Jagannatha Temple 15 219, 319, 696, 704, 704; 25 738
    hangings 15 636
    Lakshmi Temple 15 319
    wall paintings 15 636
  pottery 15 174
  scrolls 15 730
  temples 15 309
  textiles 15 177, 672
  wall paintings 15 636
Puricelli, Giuseppe 24 344
Purija see AN CHUNG-SIK
Purini, Franco 25 738*; 30 685, 714
Puripica 29 187
Purism 1 75; 25 739–41*
  art forms
    architecture 8 247; 11 525, 840; 21 782; 25 740–41*
    painting 23 694; 24 144; 25 739, 739–40*
  exhibitions 25 740
  regional traditions
    Czech Republic 11 47; 18 445
    France 10 904; 19 40, 896; 23 694; 24 144
    Hungary 20 104
    Sardinia 27 836
Purismo 3 921–2; 16 677; 21 624; 22 383, 384; 25 741*; 26 740; 28 391
Puritans see under CHRISTIANITY → sects
Puritan spoons see under SPOONS → types
Puritan watches see under WATCHES → types
Purkersdorf Sanatorium 2 567; 33 166
Purkhu 15 629, 632–3; 25 741–2*
Purkyně, Karel 25 433, 742*
  groups and movements 2 546
  works 8 392, 392
purlin roofs see under ROOFS → types
Purmale, Liga 25 151
Purmerent, Petrus 8 104
Purnavarman, King of Taruma (reg 5th cent.) 15 756
Purnea 15 724
Purnia 15 714
Purong see AN CHUNG-SIK
purple see under PIGMENTS → types
purple codices see under CODICES → types
Purple Psalter see under PSALTERS → individual manuscripts
purporino see MOSAIC GOLD
purpurin 9 491; 24 796
Purrmann, Georg Heinrich 25 743
Purrmann, Hans 20 824; 25 743–4*; 29 604
Pursat 5 499, 500
Purser, Sarah H(enrietta) 9 318; 16 17; 25 744*; 29 507
  groups and movements 31 229
Purser, William 12 925
purses 3 442; 14 425
Purulén 6 521, 523
Purum 15 205
Purushapura see PESHAWAR
Purushavar see PESHAWAR
Purves Smith, Peter (Charles Roderick) 25 744*
Purvis, Tom 7 652, 654; 25 347, 351
  works 7 652
Purvītis, Vilhelms (Kārlis) 25 744–5*
  groups and movements 12 825
  pupils 9 296; 17 743
  works 18 850
Pury, David de 22 920
Pury, Edmond de 12 810
Puryear, Martin 1 444, 445
Purygin, Leonid 27 398
Pusa, Unto 31 886
Pusan 18 248, 250, 252, 262, 282
  Dong-A University 18 381
  Pŏmŏ Temple 18 307, 309
  University 18 381
Pusat Tenaga Rakyat see CENTRE OF PEOPLE'S POWER
Puščava Church 28 858, 859
Püschel, Konrad 33 41
Pushkar Palace 15 371
Pushkin 25 193, 745–6*; 27 363
  Aleksandriya 21 127
  Aleksandrovsky Palace 25 746; 27 403
  Aleksandrovsky Park 21 127
  apartments 27 381
  architecture 29 554
  Boblovsky Palace 25 746
  Bol'shoy Palace see Yekaterinsky Palace
  Catherine Palace see Yekaterinsky Palace
  Creaking Pavilion 24 290
  gardens 12 134; 25 746
  Mon Bijou 26 8
  Palace-Museum 23 545
  palaces 27 374
  Roman House see Palace-Museum
  St Sofia 25 746
  Yekaterinsky Palace 25 745, 745–6; 26 7–8, 731; 27 403, 407, 408, 583
    Agate Rooms 27 403
    Arabian Room 29 839
    Cameron Gallery 5 520; 13 5
    furniture 10 199; 27 583
    Green Dining-Room 29 839, 839
    interior decoration 5 520; 27 401
    Mirror Room 5 349
    Picture Hall 9 18
    Roman Baths 1 111; 5 520
    stucco 29 839
    Tabakerka study 27 415
  Yekaterinsky Park 12 134; 23 76; 26 499
    bridges 4 801
Pushkin, Aleksandr (Sergeyevich) 12 2; 18 75; 25 746*; 33 669
Pushkin Museum of Fine Arts see under MOSCOW → museums
Pushpagiri 15 540
  Chennakeshava Temple 15 540
  Satanamalleshvara Temple 15 540
Push Pin Almanack 7 292
Push Pin Graphics 7 292; 12 772
Pushpin Group Inc. 7 292
Push Pin Press 7 292
Push Pin Studios 7 292; 12 772; 25 354
Pushtun 1 209, 210
Pusica, Peter von see PETER VON PUSICA
Pusilha 21 259
Puskás, Tamás 14 891
Pusloŭsk (family) 3 529
Pussin, Jean-Baptiste 2 658

Pusteria
S Lorenzo **2** 799; **23** 707
S Sigismondo **28** 134
Pusterla, Attilio **13** 714
Pustopolje **25** 524, 529
Pustynka **25** 522
Puszcz, Joachim **32** 878
Pusztaszer Abbey **14** 892
Pûta of Pardubice **24** 108
putealia *see* WELL-HEADS
Puteanus, Erycius **12** 16
Puteaux group **8** 247; **25** 747*
members **8** 240; **23** 569; **28** 347
Duchamp-Villon, (Pierre-Maurice-)Raymond **9** 361
Gleizes, Albert **12** 806
Gris, Juan **13** 669
La Fresnaye, Roger de **18** 636
Léger, Fernand **19** 78
Marinot, Maurice **20** 431
Ribemont-Dessaignes, Georges **26** 305
Villon, Jacques **32** 576
see also CUBISM → regional traditions → France; SALON CUBISTS
Puteoli *see* POZZUOLI
PUTERA *see* CENTRE OF PEOPLE'S POWER
Puterbrot, Eduard **27** 433
Puterman-Sadłowski, Julian **32** 872
Puthois, Pierre **27** 753
Putian, Xuanmiao guan **6** 654
Sanqing Hall **6** 671
Putinati, Francesco **2** 310; **20** 924
Putini, Carlo **17** 856; **19** 497
Putini, Pietro **17** 856; **19** 497
Putinki, Church of the Birth of the Mother of God **27** 372
Putman, Andrée **11** 584
Putna **26** *705*, 712
embroidery **26** 720–21
metalwork **26** 719
Monastery **26** 707, 719, 722
Monastery Museum **26** 724
Putnam, Perley **27** 613
Pütner, Walther **28** 143
Putte, Bernard van de **19** 64
Putte, Gillis van de **5** 46
Puttemans, P. **3** 620
Putter, Pieter de **3** 900
putti **25** 748*
Putti, Giovanni **16** 705
Putti, Master of the **20** 752–3*; **32** 198
Puttinati, Alessandro **16** 706
Püttner, Walter **16** 906
Puttrich, Ludwig **18** 77
Puttur **16** 864
putty **4** 787; **6** 335; **28** 339
Putumayo **7** 603
Putún **20** 884
Putún Maya **20** 884
Putyvl' **31** 548
Putz, Leo **25** 748–9*; **28** 143
Putzel, Howard **13** 801
Puuc **17** 715; **21** 202, 205, 207; **28** 26; **31** 778; **33** 481
Puvis de Chavannes, Edouard **25** 749
Puvis de Chavannes, Pierre (-Cécile) **11** 546, 547; **18** 716; **25** 749–52*
assistants **33** 175
collaboration **6** 545
dealers **9** 424; **26** 107
groups and movements **25** 356; **30** 168; **33** 379
methods **10** 199
paintings **25** *751*
murals **25** *750*
Hôtel de Ville (Paris) **22** 330; **31** 241
Musée des Beaux-Arts (Lyon) **6** 537; **19** 848
Musée des Beaux-Arts (Rouen) **27** 248
Musée de Picardie **22** 329
Puvis de Chavannes, Pierre (-Cécile)
paintings
murals—cont.
Panthéon (Paris) **22** 330, *330*; **24** 142
Public Library (Boston, MA; USA) **4** 477; **20** 18
watercolours **32** 902
patrons and collectors **2** 881; **5** 530; **14** 244; **19** 230; **23** 882; **28** 569; **30** 375
prints **19** 489
pupils
Aman-Jean, Edmond (-François) **1** 751
Ancher, Anna (Kirstine) **1** 846
Bernadotte, Eugen (Napoleon Nicolaus), Prince of Sweden (1865-1947) **10** 648
Bussière, Gaston **5** 296
Cottet, Charles **8** 34
Morren, George **22** 136
Renan, (Cornelis) Ary **26** 191
Saleeby, Khalil **19** 7
Séon, Alexandre **28** 423
Seurat, Georges(-Pierre) **28** 500
teachers **8** 76
Puvrez, Henri **3** 573; **5** 44
Puwŏn-dong **18** 335
Pu Xinyu *see* Pu Hsin-yü
Puy, Jean **5** 530; **10** 839; **25** 752*
Puy, Le *see* LE PUY
Puyemre **9** 822
Puyenbroeck, Pierre **11** 371; **12** 230
Pu Yi **6** 826
Puymanel, Olivier de **14** 844; **32** 477
Puymaurin, Nicolas-Joseph Marcassus, Baron de **5** 366; **12** 33
Puyŏ **18** *250*, 281
architecture **18** 275
Chŏngrim Temple **18** 260, 267, 292, 328; **30** 444
pagoda **23** 775
fortress **18** 260
Kunsu Temple **18** 267, 285; **30** 444
pagodas **23** 775
lacquer **18** 369
monument to Sat'aek Chijŏk **18** 328
Muryang Temple **18** 308
Museum **18** 263, 382, 383
Sabispŏng **18** 260
temples **17** 67
tiles **18** *313*, 314
Puyo, Constant **24** 738
Puyongdong **12** 94
Puyopatamarca **29** 166
Puzur-Assur III (*reg c.* 1500 BC) **2** 637, 639
Puzurum **30** 492
Puzyr'kov, Viktor G. **31** 559
puzzles **31** 266–7*
puzzles, jigsaw *see* JIGSAW PUZZLES
PVA **1** 155, 156; **7** 737; **25** 27; **26** 244; **32** 2; **33** 6
PVC **25** 23, 26, 28*; **26** 244; **32** 817
Pwo **30** 623
PW of Cologne, Master **20** 612, 802*
Py, Bertrand **25** 752–3*
Py, Marcel **2** 660
Pyang **18** 484, 488
Pyang Ibaam **18** 484
Pyatkovskaya, Mariya *see* TENISHEVA, MARIYA (KLAVDIYEVNA)
Pyatnitsa, Paraskeva **28** 465
Pyatnitsky, Pyotr (Gavrilovich) **27** 376
Pydna **19** 880
Pye, John **4** 87; **25** 753*
pupils **4** 586; **14** 166
Pye, John—cont.
works **10** 396
writings **10** 377; **19** 586
Pye, Patrick **25** 753*
Pye, Sybil **1** 23
Pye, Thomas **24** 296
Pyell, William R. **4** 627
Pygmy Trumpeter Painter **10** 616
Pyke, George **7** 446
works **7** *445*
Pyke, John **7** 446
Pyla **8** 342
Pyle, Howard **4** 364; **24** 210
Pylipp, Hans **23** 317
pylons **9** 831, 832; **25** 753*
see also TOWERS
Pylos **13** *363*; **14** *332*; **17** 733; **25** 753–4*
fort **21** 556
furniture **14** 354
Hall 64 **14** 350, *350*
ivory-carvings **14** 354
megara (buildings) **14** 340
Museum of Pylos **17** 733
palace **14** *339*, 340; **23** 808; **25** 753–4, *754*
megaron **21** 46
Mycenaean throne-room **21** 676
wall paintings **14** 349
pottery **13** 534
wall paintings **14** 334, 348, 349, 350, *350*, 351; **29** 395
walls **14** 340
writing-tablets **14** 333, 354
Pym, Francis **3** 537; **16** 40
works **16** *39*
Pym, John **4** 599
Pynacker, Adam **25** 754–7*
groups and movements **9** 462
patrons and collectors **25** 815
works **22** 843; **25** *755*, *756*
Pynas, Jacob (Symonsz.) **25** 757–9*
attributions **25** 757
collaboration **21** 827
groups and movements **22** 842; **25** 556, 557
works **18** 708; **25** *758*; **27** 816
Pynas, Jan (Symonsz.) **25** 757
attributions **10** 158; **25** 757
groups and movements **22** 842; **25** 556, 557
pupils **31** 381
Pyne, Benjamin **14** 419; **25** 759*
works **10** 330, *330*
Pyne, Ganesh **5** 421
Pyne, George **25** 759
Pyne, James Baker **22** 274; **25** 759*
Pyne, William Henry **25** 759*
groups and movements **32** 903
patrons and collectors **1** 121
writings **22** 686
illustrated **26** 75; **29** 632; **30** 39
Pynson, Richard **19** 581
Pyochung Temple **18** 311
Py'ŏngjŏn Sarang **18** 359
P'yŏngyang **18** *248*, *250*, 261, 282
Anhak-kung **12** 94; **18** 275; **23** 821
Central Historical Museum **18** 383
exhibitions **18** 57
Fine Arts Museum of North Korea **18** 383
fortifications **21** 594
glass **18** 365
Institute of Archaeology **18** 382
Kim Il Sung University **18** 382
lacquer **18** 369
Museum **18** 383
Pubyŏng-ru Pavilion **12** 95
sculpture **18** 302
State Central Historical Museum **18** 382
temples **18** 260, 266
tombs **18** 327
Tongsu's Tomb **18** 272
wall paintings **32** 804
P'yŏngyangju Bridge **18** 280
Pyŏn Kwan-sik **7** 207; **25** 760*; **33** 534
Pyŏn Sang-byŏk **18** 317
Pyotr **23** 267; **27** 370
Pyralin *see under* IVORY → types
pyramidal roofs *see under* ROOFS → types
pyramidal stupas *see under* STUPAS → types
pyramidions **8** *456*, 456
Pyramid of Chephren *see under* GIZA → pyramids
pyramids **25** 760–67*
historical and regional traditions
Cambodia **2** 56, *56*; **5** *473*
Egypt, ancient **2** 362; **8** 456; **9** 779, 812, 813, 836, 838, 842; **10** 96; **20** 117, 863; **23** 338; **25** 760–63*; **31** 107
Early Dynastic (*c.* 2925-*c.* 2575 BC) **27** *810*
Middle Kingdom (*c.* 1966-*c.* 1630 BC) **25** 760, 763
Old Kingdom (*c.* 2575-*c.* 2130 BC) **25** 760, *761*, 762–3, *763*
Ptolemaic (304-30 BC) **9** 779
France **25** *766*
Greece, ancient **20** 863; **25** 766
Mesoamerica, Pre-Columbian **25** 760, 764–5*; **31** 116
Aztec **30** *453*
Guatemala **24** *744*
Huastec **25** 764
Maya **6** 579; **20** 881; **21** 212–16*, *214*, *215*; **24** *744*; **25** 764, 765; **30** *254*, 279–80
Mexico **7** 201, *201*; **21** *211*; **30** *254*, *453*; **31** *65*
Mixtec **25** *765*
Tarascan **25** 764; **30** 340
West Mexico **21** 197
Nubia **23** 281, 282; **25** 760
Rome, ancient **25** 766
South America, Pre-Columbian **29** 165–6*; **31** 116
Ecuador **25** *689*
Gallinazo **21** 750
Moche (culture) **21** *750*, 750–52*; **29** 160
Peru **21** *750*, 750–52*
materials
adobe **29** 160
alabaster (gypsum) **25** 762
basalt **9** 813; **25** 762
granite **25** 762
limestone **9** 812
types
step **25** 761, *761*; **27** *810*
Pyramid Texts **9** 779; **10** 80; **25** 761, 763
Pyrasos *see* NEA ANCHIALOS
Pyratin' **31** 558
Pyreikos **25** 44
Pyrenees **25** 476–7, 480, 484, 487; **29** *259*
Pyrex *see under* GLASS → types
Pyrga, Hagia Ekaterin **8** 363
Pyrgi (Greece) **9** *511*
Church of the Metamorphosis **9** 584
Hagioi Apostoloi **9** 550
Pyrgi (Italy) **6** 352; **10** *583*, 601, 638, 640; **16** *620*; **25** 767*; **26** *886*, 887
metalwork **10** 630
temenos **10** 601
Temple A **10** 596, 601
Temple B **10** 587, 603
temples **10** 588
vases **10** 613
Pyrgos **21** *651*; **22** 402–3
faience (i) (glass) **21** 683, 684
pottery **21** *665*
sarcophagi **21** 657
villa **21** 664
Pyrgos ware *see under* POTTERY → wares
Pyrgoteles (*fl* 4th century BC) **1** 613
Pyrgoteles (*fl* before 1496, *d* 1531) **12** 248; **25** 767*
Pyrikov, Abram (Yefimovich) *see* ARKHIPOV, ABRAM (YEFIMOVICH)
Pyrinos, Antonios **13** 355
pyrite **21** 241, 251, 718, 719; **29** 155
abrasives **16** 859
masks **21** 251
mirrors **21** 241, 718, 719
Pyrker, János László, Archbishop of Eger **5** 84; **8** 502; **15** 17; **20** 439
pyro-engraving *see under* ENGRAVING → types
pyrogallic acid **26** 91
pyrometers **6** 330; **33** 22
pyrometric cones **6** 330
pyrophones **29** 99
pyrophyllite **16** 857
Pyrra **19** 234, *234*, 235
Pyrrhos **2** 682
Pyrrhus Aloisius *see* SCRIVÁ, PEDRO LUÍS
Pythagoras of Rhegion (*fl c.* 475-450 BC) **13** 450; **25** 767–8*; **26** 288
works **13** 573
writings **13** 467
Pythagoras of Samos (*c.* 560-*c.* 480 BC) **12** 871; **13** 409, 412; **14** 874; **22** 377; **28** 200
Pytheas **13** 552
Pytheos **25** 768*; **32** 634
works **13** 379, 403, 405, 408, 409; **14** 69, 71; **15** 894; **18** 580; **23** 482; **25** 574, 575, 576
workshop **13** 460
Pythianice **20** 863
Pythokritos **26** 292
Python **13** 520, 532; **32** 40
python skins *see under* SKINS → types
Pyu **5** 99, 222, 223, 237; **29** 231
architecture **5** 224–5, *225*
ceramics **5** 254
coins **5** 255
sculpture **5** 238–9*, *239*
stucco **29** 826
pyxides (boxes) **1** 707; **7** 299; **14** 419
historical and regional traditions
Africa **1** 326
Byzantine **9** 648, 651; **16** 798
Early Christian (*c.* AD 250-843) **9** 648
Etruscan **10** *634*
France **13** 167
Gothic **13** 167
Greece, ancient **13** *475*, 478
Islamic **16** 525
Italy **10** *634*
Sicily **16** 525
Sierra Leone **1** 327
materials
bone **9** 651
enamel **13** 167
ivory **1** 326, 327; **9** 648; **10** *634*; **16** 525, 798
pyxides (vases) **25** 768*
historical and regional traditions
Crete **21** *656*
Cycladic **8** *312*
Greece, ancient **13** 479, 492, 493, *505*, *530*
Helladic **14** *345*
Minoan **21** *656*
Mycenaean **14** *345*
Sicily **13** *530*
materials
chlorite **21** *656*
pyxis *see* PYXIDES (BOXES)

Q

Qaa **9** *776*; **27** 810, 811
Qabr Hiram, St Cristopher **9** 539
Qabristan, Tepe **15** 904, 918
Qabus ibn Wushmgir **16** 159
Qaddafi, Col. **30** 470
Qādi Ibn ʿAdabbas **28** 511
Qadimi **16** 335
Qadisiyya **16** 151
  congregational mosque **16** 151
  Mosque of the Octagon **16** 152
al-Qahira *see under* CAIRO
Qaʾil *see* KAYALPATNAM
Qairouan *see* KAIROUAN
al-Qais **16** 431
Qaʾitbay, Sultan (*reg* 1468-96) (Mamluk) **5** 397; **14** 428; **16** 244, 382; **20** 230–31*; **21** 630
  architecture **5** 404–5; **16** 211–13, *212*; **17** 491, 497; **20** *231*, 914; **21** 32
  military **21** 587
  furniture **21** 630
  metalwork **16** 385, *385*, 386
  minbar **16** 497
Qajar **16** 119; **25** 769*
  architecture **15** 897; **17** 830; **25** 778
  paintings **21** 723
  see also:
    ʿABBAS MIRZA
    AGHA MUHAMMAD, Shah
    FATH ʿALI SHAH, Shah
    MUHAMMAD, Shah
    MUZAFFAR AL-DIN, Shah
    NASIR AL-DIN, Shah
qalʿa *see* CITADELS
Qalʿa Bani Hammad **21** 626
Qalah-i Bust *see* BUST
Qalʿa-i Dukhtar **11** 121*; **16** 801; **21** 554; **27** 855
Qalʿa-i Qahqah *see* KALA-I KAKHKAKH
Qalandar Khivaki **16** 238
Qalʿat al-Bahrain **2** 250, 251, 265
Qalʿat al-Hisn **16** 208
Qalʿat al-Mudīq *see* APAMEIA
Qalʾat ash-Sherqat *see* ASSUR
Qalʿat as Sāliḥīyah *see* DURA EUROPOS
Qalʿat Bani Hammad **16** *103*, 170–71; **25** 770–71*
  architecture **1** 634
  excavations **16** 550
  factories **16** 436
  gardens **12** 78
  Gate of the Udayas **16** 246
  gates **16** 246
  muqarnas (architecture) **22** 321
  pavements **16** 250
  pottery **16** 404
  stained glass **16** 256
Qalʿat Bani Rashid **16** 486
el-Qalʿa Temple of Min, Isis and Horus **9** 897
Qalʿat Sahyun Palace **16** 182
Qalʿat Simʿan **9** *513*, 555; **25** *771*, 771–2*; **30** 178
  Baptistery **9** 541
  St Simeon the Stylite the Elder **3** 191; **9** 540, 548, 591; **20** 520; **21** 834; **31** 280
  font **9** 591, *591*
Qalaʾun, Sultan (*reg* 1280-90) (Mamluk) **20** 56, 228*
  architecture **5** 403–4; **16** 208, *209*
  dress **16** 453
  textiles **16** 441
Qalʿa-yi Yazdagird *see* QALʿEH-I YAZDEGERD
Qalb Lozeh Church **7** 259
Qaleh **15** 921
Qalʿeh-i Yazdegerd **15** *901*, 912; **25** 773*
  architecture **24** 217
  palace **29** 816
  stucco **24** 218; **29** 814, 815
Qalinj Agha **21** 281
al-Qalqashandi **16** 277, 441, 539
Qaluq Monastery **31** 435
Qaluyu **31** 45
Qana **2** *246*, 269
qanāt **15** 901
Qandriz, Mansur **15** 898; **27** 810
al-Qandusi **16** 288
Qannas, Tell *see* HABUBA KABIRA
Qansuh al-Ghawri, Sultan (*reg* 1501-16) (Mamluk) **16** 312, 497; **17** 497; **20** 231*; **21** 587
  architecture **5** 723; **16** 213
  manuscripts **16** 310, 312
  metalwork **16** 386
  tents **30** 478
Qantīr **10** 48; **24** 840
Qar **10** 50, 51
Qarabaghlar Mausoleum **2** 892, 898
Qarajaghay Khan **16** 339
Qarakhanid **6** 203, 309; **16** 115; **27** 671
  see also:
    AHMAD I, Ruler
    ARSLAN KHAN MUHAMMAD II, Ruler
    TAMGACH KHAN, Ruler
Qaraqoyunlu **16** 117; **25** 773–4*
  see also:
    JAHANSHA, Sultan
    KHATUM JAN BEGUM
    PIR BUDAQ
Qarasunqur **16** 496
Qariet al-ʿInab *see* ABŪ-GHOSH
Qarmathian Koran **16** 280
Qart Hadasht **8** 331; **18** 98
  see also KITION; LARNACA
Qaryat al-Faw **2** *246*, 247, 249
  bronzes **2** 259
  fortress **2** 251
  glass **2** 263
  metalwork **2** 266
  palace **2** *274*
  rock art **2** 270
  vessels **2** 273
  wall paintings **2** 274–5
qaṣaba **6** 58; **21** 547
Qashqaʾi **16** 484
Qashqaʾi carpets *see under* CARPETS → types
Qasile, Tell
  architecture **24** 634
  bronze **24** 635
  rhyta **24** 634
  temple **24** 634
Qasim (Saudi Arabia) **32** 316
Qasim (*fl c.* 1597) **15** 594
Qasim ʿAli **15** 585; **16** 326; **25** 774*
  patrons and collectors **1** 645; **27** 513
al-Qasimi, Saʿid **16** 389
Qasim ibn ʿAli Chihra-gushay *see* QASIM ʿALI
al-Qasir **16** 253
qaṣr **21** 547
Qasr Abu Nasr **16** 400
Qasr al-ʿAmra *see* QUSAYR ʿAMRA
Qasr al-Banat **16** 407
Qasr al-Ghuwayda **23** 284
Qasr al-Hallabat **16** 256; **17** 656; **21** 560
Qasr al-Hayr East **16** *104*, 148; **21** 582; **25** 774*
  baths **3** 376
Qasr al-Hayr East—cont.
  excavations **16** 550
  Large Enclosure **16** 155
  Lesser Enclosure **5** 722
  pottery **16** 397
Qasr al-Hayr West **16** *104*, 148; **23** 815; **25** 774–5*
  excavations **16** 550
  floor painting **16** *251*, 251–2
  frescoes **16** 146
  palace **16** 243
  pottery **16** 397
  reliefs **16** 516
  sculpture **16** 245, 538
  stained glass **16** 256
  stucco **16** 245; **29** 818
Qasr al-Mshatta *see* MSHATTA
Qasr al-Nil Museum **10** 92
Qasr al-Tuba **17** 656
Qasr Dush **18** 20
Qasr el-Aguz *see under* THEBES (i) (EGYPT)
Qasr el Banat Monastery Church **9** 591; **21** 834
Qasr-el-Lebia **9** 570
  East Church **9** 570
Qasr el-Sagha **9** *774*; **10** 758; **25** 775*
  temple **9** 830; **10** 758; **25** 775
Qasr-e Shirin *see* QALʿEH-I YAZDEGERD
Qasr Ibn Wardan **2** 295; **9** *513*; **25** 775*
  brick **4** 773
  church **28** 537
Qasr Ibrim **9** *774*; **10** 81; **23** *276*, 286, 287; **25** 775–6*; **30** 237
  carpets **7** 827
  Cathedral **23** 287
  church **23** 288
  fortress **9** 847, 848, 849
  glass **16** 519
  Old Church **23** 287
  Temple of Amun **23** 281
  Temple of Taharqa **23** 284
Qasr Kharana **16** *104*; **17** 656; **21** 581; **25** 776*
Qasr Qarun *see* DIONYSIAS
Qasr Serij **21** 275
Qasr Zaiyan **18** 20
Qataban **2** 268
al-Qataʾiʿ *see under* CAIRO → palaces
Qatana, Tell *see* RAMAD
Qatar **15** *897*; **25** 776–7*
  architecture **25** 776*
  mosques **16** *242*
  painting **25** 776–7*
  University **25** 776
  see also ARABIA
Qatari Society for Fine Arts **25** 777
al-Qatif **27** 875; **32** 316
qatifas *see* CARPETS → types → *qtifs*
Qatna **25** 777*; **30** *180*, 185
  sculpture **30** 185
  sphinx of Ita **9** 875
  town walls **30** 190
  wall paintings **30** 198
Qattara (Abu Dhabi) **2** 248, 264
  gold **2** *264*
Qattara (Iraq) *see* RIMAH, TELL EL-
Qavām al-Dīn ibn Zayn al-Dīn Shīrāzī *see* QAVAM AL-DIN SHIRAZI
Qavam al-Din Shirazi **2** 316; **16** 196; **25** 777*
  patrons and collectors **30** 919
  works **14** 430; **16** 197; **20** 548
Qaw el-Kebir **10** 59, 77
  glass **10** 56
  tombs **9** 838, 877; **10** 60
Qawsun **20** 228; **32** 313
Qayoom Khan **24** 541
al-Qayrawan *see* KAIROUAN
Qaysariyya *see under* ISFAHAN → Bazaar
Qaytbay *see* QAʾITBAY, Sultan
Qazakh **2** *890*, 901
Qazi, Misbahuddin **23** 801
Qazi, Misbhauddin **23** 800
Qazi Ahmad **2** 519; **16** 277, 335, 343, 547; **21** 722
  writings **16** 127, 253
Qazrin Synagogue **17** 542
Qazvin **15** *897*, *901*; **16** *105*; **25** 778*
  ʿAli Qapu **16** 230
  architecture **16** 230
  carpets **16** 474
  Chihil Sutun **16** 230, 253, 334
  congregational mosque **16** 162, 234; **23** 559; **25** 778
    maqṣūra **20** 369
    sculpture **16** 245
    squinches **15** 164
  inscriptions **16** 232
  Kula-yi Farangi *see* Chihil Sutun
  manuscripts **16** 327, 331, 334–7*, 338
  Masjid-i Haydariyya **21** 506
  Mosque of the Bull *see* congregational mosque
  museums **15** 900
  rock crystal **16** 540
Qazvini **16** 373
Qedeh, Tell el- *see* HAZOR
Qenamun **9** 808, 855, 881, 902; **10** 57; **25** 778–9*
Qengo **29** 172
Qenneshre Monastery Church **9** 541
Qerétaro **21** *372*
Qermez Dere **1** 869; **2** 639
Qian Chenqun **33** 321
Qian Dian **6** 764, 765, 867
Qianfo dong *see* DUNHUANG
Qiang **6** 726
qiangjin *see under* LACQUER → types
Qian Gong **7** 119
Qian Gu **6** 819; **32** 848
Qianlong emperor (Qing; *reg* 1736-96) **6** 661, 704, 779; **7** 153, 154; **25** 779–80*
  architecture **6** 40, 41, 537, 682, 684; **25** 783
  calligraphy **6** 772
  drawings **14** 366
  enamel **7** 70
  fountains **11** 338
  glass **7** 85
  hardstones **7** 91
  jade **7** 10, 11
  jade-carvings **16** II2
  mirrors **7** 87
  paintings **2** 124; **6** 40, 811, 815; **12** 52; **13** 839; **14** 135, 823
  porcelain **4** 174
Qian Luozhi **12** 813
Qianshanyang (Wuxing) **7** 45, 74
Qian Shunju **7** 66
Qian Song **7** 130
Qian Songyan **10** 794
Qian xian **6** *615*; **25** 780*
  jade **7** 7
  Qian ling **6** 652, *698*, 698, 729, 730, *730*; **7** 7
  sarcophagus **27** 832
Qian xian—cont.
  tomb of Princess Yongtai **6** *651*, 652, 699, 808
  tomb of Prince Yide **6** 651, 652, 699, 789
  tomb of Prince Zhanghuai **6** 652, 699, 789, 808
Qian Xuan **6** 773, 790, 819; **17** 195; **25** 780–81*
  groups and movements **33** 646
  works **6** 800, 806, 810; **17** 881
qiaose **7** 8
Qi Baishi **6** 768; **25** 781–2*
  groups and movements **6** 774; **28** 555; **33** 497
  reproductions in ivory **7** 104
  works **6** *768*, 802; **25** *781*
qibla **16** 141, 144, 145; **22** 192
Qidan **5** 110; **6** 537; **7** 77
Qidfa **2** 248
Qifa Temple Stele **6** 745
Qift *see* KOPTOS
Qi Gong **7** 161
Qijia culture **6** *615*, 835, 877; **25** 782*
Qijiaping **25** 782
Qin *see* QIN SHI HUANGDI
qin *see under* ASH → types
Qingbai ware *see under* PORCELAIN → wares
Qing dynasty *see*:
  CIXI empress
  KANGXI emperor
  QIANLONG emperor
  SHUNZHI emperor
  YONGZHENG emperor
  see also CHINA → periods → Qing period
Qinglian'gang **6** *615*; **25** 784*
Qinglongshan **1** 761; **7** 83, 90, 110
Qin Gong *gui* **6** 852
Qingtian **7** 133
Qingxi *see* CHENG ZHENGKUI
Qingyang, Bei shiku Temple **6** 710
Qingyuan Kilns **6** 893
Qinlongquan culture **6** 879
Qin period (221-206 BC) *see under* CHINA → periods
Qin Shian **7** 99
Qin Shi Huangdi (Qin emperor; *reg* 221-210 BC) **6** 857; **7** 123; **25** 782; **33** 464, 466
  architecture **6** 648; **21** 593
  ceramics **6** 882
  coins **7** 72
  sculpture **6** 727; **7** 160
  stelae **6** *739*, 740; **7** 129; **29** 617
  terracottas **30** 509
  tomb **6** 648, 696; **7** *55*, 56, 97; **25** 782
Qinyang **6** 687
Qi of the North *see* QI BAISHI
Qionglai **6** 885; **7** 96
  Mt Shisun **6** 715
  pottery **6** *885*
  see also SHIFANGTANG
Qiongzhu Temple **6** 722
Qirqbize Church **1** 764
Qishan **6** 842
  see also DONGJIA CUN; FENGCHU
Qishiyi **16** 860
Qiu (?Zhu) **33** 317, 320
Qiu Ying **6** 810; **25** 784–5*; **30** 49
  groups and movements **23** 215
  works **25** *785*; **33** 436
Qivam al-Din (*fl* 1341) **16** 292
Qivam al-Din (*fl* 1420) **30** 921
Qivam al-Din (*fl* 1539-43) **16** 292
Qizil *see* KIZIL

Qočo *see* Khocho
Qom *see* Qum
Qonggyai *see* Chongye
Qos-Gabar **9** 737
Qotocalle **29** 175, 177
Qoumhané **9** 567
Qoyawayma, Al **22** 609
Qoyawayma, Polingaysi **22** 609
Qsar Skoura **32** *310*
qtifs see under Carpets → types
Quadal, Martin Ferdinand **25** 786*; **33** 545
Quadrado y Nieto, José María **24** 105; **25** 786*
Quadrante **3** 438; **16** 649; **25** 838; **26** 536
quadrant moulding *see under* Mouldings → types
quadrants **23** 339
quadrant vaults *see under* Vaults (ceiling) → types
Quadrate Painter **13** 536
quadratura see under Painting → types
quadrature **30** 430
Quadri, Bernardino **10** 763; **13** 749; **28** 11
Quadri, Martino **29** 835
Quadriga **1** 77; **25** 786*
members **2** 545; **12** 397; **13** 217, 632; **18** 449; **28** 174
quadrigas **20** 863
Quadrio, Giovanni Battista (1659-1723/7) **21** 534
Quadrio, Giuseppe **26** 319; **32** 157
Quadrio, Johannes Baptista (*d* 1590/1) *see* Quadro, Giovanni Battista
quadripartite vaults *see under* Vaults (ceiling) → types
quadriporticus **25** 787*
Quadro, Giovanni Battista **25** 787*
collaboration **24** 207
works **25** 96, 408; **32** 879
quadro riportato **25** 787*
Quaglio (family) **22** 303; **30** 669
Quaglio, Agnes **25** 787
Quaglio, Angelo, I (1784-1815) **25** 787
Quaglio, Angelo, III (1877-1917) **25** 787
Quaglio, Domenico, I (*c.* 1708-73) **25** 787
Quaglio, Domenico, II (1787-1837) **25** 787, 789*
collaboration **33** 673
groups and movements **13** 202
pupils **14** 303
restorations by others **23** 372
works **12** 415
Quaglio, Giulio, I (1601-*d* after 1658) **25** 787
Quaglio, Giulio, II (1688-1751) **19** 516; **28** 860
Quaglio, Giulio, III (1764-1801) **5** 774; **25** 787, 788–9*
Quaglio, Giuseppe **25** 787–9*; **33** 280
assistants **25** 788
pupils **25** 789
works **25** *788*
Quaglio, Lorenzo, I (1730-1805) **25** 787, 788; **33** 240
Quaglio, Lorenzo, II (1793-1869) **25** 787; **27** 319
Quaglio, Simon **25** 787
Quah Ah *see* Peña, Tonita
quahog shells *see* Shells → types → *venus mercenaria*
quaich *see under* Cups → types
Quain, Jones **21** 6
Quain, Richard **1** 844; **21** 6
Quaini (family) **4** 277
Quaini, Luigi **7** 308; **11** 679, 680, 682; **14** 27
Quaintance, George **12** 216
Quainton (Bucks), St Mary and Holy Cross **10** 265
Quakers *see* Christianity → sects → Friends, Religious Society of
Quandt, Johann Gottlob von **25** 789–90*
Quang Tri **6** 430
Quang Uyen **32** *468*, 484
Quant, Mary **9** 294
works **9** *294*
Quantel **9** 494
Quantel Paintbox **7** 681
Quanterness **25** 507, 508
Quantin, Philippe **8** 890; **25** 790*
Quantz, Johann Joachim **22** 374
Quanzhen Daoism *see under* Daoism → sects
Quanzhou **28** *719*, 721
Kaiyuan Temple
pagodas **6** 644, 645, *645*, 668
mosque *see* Qingjing Temple
Qingjing Temple **6** 658, 676–7
Quapaw **22** 551
Quaranta, Cesare **7** 704
Quaranta, Matteo da **27** 747
Quarante, Ste Marie **26** 580
Quarata Predella, Master of the **20** 704, 748
Quaratesi (family) **12** 301
Quaratesi, Andrea **21** *449*
Quaratesi, Bernardo **11** 683; **12** 302
Quare, Daniel **7** 444
works **7** *443*
Quarenghi, Giacomo **5** 366; **16** 719; **25** 790–91*
architecture
academies **25** *791*; **27** 375
churches **16** 646
gates **29** 555
halls **27** 586
houses **18** 851; **30** 73
monuments **10** 539
palaces **24** 546; **25** 746
public buildings **22** 171; **27** 575, 587
riding houses **27** 577
theatres **26** *732*; **27** 575, 585; **30** 677
assistants **27** 345
collaboration **5** 366; **24** 292; **27** 403
furniture **27** 407
groups and movements **23** 861
patrons and collectors **2** 576; **26** 731; **33** 579
Quarini, Mario Ludovico **32** 645
Quaritch, Bernard **25** 792*; **29** 88
Quarles, Francis **4** 359; **10** 175; **20** 478
Quarnström, Carl Gustaf **30** 86
Quaroni, Giuseppe **24** 693
Quaroni, Ludovico **25** 792*
collaboration **2** 880; **3** 439; **26** 364
pupils **22** 386; **25** 738
works **16** 650
Quarré, Jean **31** 834
Quarrel of the Ancients and Moderns *see* Ancients and Moderns, Quarrel of the
quarries **9** 812, 814, 815; **13** 387; **20** 560; **26** 855, 875, *876*, 876–7
Quartararo, Riccardo **28** 656, *656*
quarter-round mouldings *see under* Mouldings → types
Quarti, Eugenio **16** 721, 731; **25** 793*; **29** 59
Quarti, Mario **25** 793
Quarton, Enguerrand **25** 793–6*
attributions **2** 860; **20** 707; **32** 572
collaboration **20** 708; **32** 571
works **2** 860; **11** 531; **15** 85; **24** 776; **25** *794*, *796*; **32** 573, 574
quartz **14** 167; **26** 484
historical and regional traditions
Carolingian **5** 811
China **6** 872
Egypt **16** 405
quartz
historical and regional traditions—cont.
Egypt, ancient **10** 46
France **11** *622*
Germany **12** 450
Greece, ancient **12** 248
Iran **16** 408, 413
Islamic **16** 394, 405, 408, 413, 420
Mesoamerica, Pre-Columbian **21** 241; **22** 158
Ottoman **16** 420
Portugal **25** 314, *314*
Prehistoric art **25** 493; **29** 445
South America, Pre-Columbian **29** 153, 155
Sri Lanka **29** 445
types *see* Amethyst; Cat's-eye; Rock crystal; Rose quartz; Smoky quartz
uses
abrasives **7** 11; **16** 859
chains **12** 450
earrings **25** *314*
faience (i) (glass) **10** 46
glazes **6** 872; **16** 394
jewellery **7** 111; **25** 314
mosaics **22** 158
necklaces **25** *314*
pottery **16** 405, 408, 413, 420
prints **11** 173
seals **12** 248
tools **25** 493; **29** 445
tureens **11** *622*
vases **7** *90*
quartz crystal clocks *see under* Clocks → types
quartz crystal watches *see under* Watches → types
quartzite
historical and regional traditions
Egypt, ancient **7** XII; **9** *790*, 813*, 815; **10** 13; **27** 824; **30** *694*; **31** *482*
Prehistoric art **25** 491, 493
techniques
engraving **25** 491
uses
sarcophagi **9** 813; **10** 13; **27** 824
sculpture **7** XII; **9** 813, 815; **30** *694*; **31** *482*
stelae **9** *790*
tools **25** 493
quartz sand **21** 241
Quast, Ferdinand von **25** 797*, 804
Quast, Pieter (Jansz.) **25** 797–8*
collaboration **25** 369
reproductive prints by others **23** 191
works **25** *797*
Quaternary period *see under* Prehistoric art → periods
quatrefoil churches *see* Churches → types → tetraconch
quatrefoil piers *see under* Piers (ii) (masonry) → types
Quatremère de Quincy, Antoine (-Chrysosthôme) **11** 521, 563, 670; **12** 63, 286; **13** 392; **25** 798–9*
architecture **25** *798*; **29** 93
assistants **6** 516
collaboration **5** 888
works **3** 465; **11** 567
on display of art **9** 25
writings **10** 207, 210; **11** 674
Quatre Vents, Aux **7** 496, 499; **10** 389; **25** 625
al-Quawatir **9** 813
Quay, Pierre-Maurice **8** 558; **25** 581
Quba (i) (Azerbaijan) **2** *890*; **25** 799–800*
carpets **2** 901; **16** 479, 481
see also under Carpets → types
Quba (i) (Azerbaijan)—cont.
City Museum of Local Lore **25** 800
kilims **16** 481
rugs **2** 438
Quba (ii) (Uzbekistan) *see* Kuva
Quban **9** 845, 847
Qubilay, Khan (*reg* 1260-94) (Great Khans) **30** 476
Qué **2** 400
que *see under* Towers → types
Quebec (city) **5** *559*; **25** 801–3*, *802*
Anglican Deanery **5** 560
Assemblée Nationale **5** 561, 570; **14** 282; **30** 230
bridge **4** 803
Cathedral of Notre-Dame-de-la-Paix **5** 560
Cathedral of the Holy Trinity **5** *559*, 560
Château Frontenac Hotel **5** 561
Château of Vaudreuil **5** 558
Chevalier House **25** 802
education (art) **5** 592
Episcopal Palace **5** 558
Fargues House **25** 803
fortifications **21** 574, 575
furniture **5** 577, *577*; **25** 803*
gardens **12** 136
interior decoration **5** 572
Jesuit College and Chapel **25** 801
Mechanics Institute **5** 590
Monsignor Briand Chapel **5** 572
Musée des Beaux-Arts *see under* Université Laval
Musée de la Civilisation **5** 591; **27** 515
Musée de l'Instruction Publique **5** 590
Musée du Québec
collections **5** 590; **8** 81; **18** 659; **25** 803
directors **22** 120
Notre-Dame-des-Victoires **5** 560
Saint-Joachim Ecole des Arts et des Métiers **5** 592
Séminaire de Québec **5** 572
silver **5** 584
Université Laval
Fine Arts Division Library **5** 592
Musée de l'Amérique Française **19** 75
Musée des Beaux-Arts **5** 590
Ursuline Convent **5** 572
Queboorn, Crispijn van den **10** 720
Queborn, Christian van den **5** 441; **13** 664; **33** 28
Quebrada **29** 187
Quechan **22** 550, 605
Quechua **9** 714; **15** 162
Queckborne, Christian van den *see* Queborn, Christian van den
Quedlinburg **12** *360*
carpets **12** 468; **14** 65
Cathedral of St Wiperti **26** 572
St Servatius **23** 647; **25** 803–4*; **29** 818
carpets **5** 833
stucco **26** 632
sculpture **26** 632
tapestries **12** 465
Quedlinburg Gospels *see under* Gospel books → individual manuscripts
Quedlinburg Itala *see under* Old Testaments → individual manuscripts
Queecborn, Daniel van den **11** 443, 444
Queen Anne Revival **9** 705; **22** 809; **25** 804–7*; **26** 476; **33** 12
art forms
architecture
England **6** 439; **22** *810*; **25** *805*; **28** *157*, *562*
Queen Anne Revival
art forms
architecture—cont.
United States of America **25** *806*
furniture **31** 624–5, *625*, 626
interior decoration **23** *64*
silver **31** 648
regional traditions
Australia **10** 852
England **10** 239; **26** 190
New Zealand **28** 327
United States of America **25** 805–7
Queenborough (Kent) **6** 57
Queen Charlotte Islands **22** *544*, 547
houses **22** *564*
Queen Elizabeth *see under* Ships → named vessels
Queen Isabella's Oratory **29** 299
Queen Mary see under Ships → named vessels
Queen Mary brooches *see under* Brooches → types
Queen Mary Psalter *see under* Psalters → individual manuscripts
Queen Mlk'e Gospels *see under* Gospel books → individual manuscripts
Queen's Barrow (N. Yorks) **25** *470*, 545
jewellery **25** *545*
Queensberry, Walter Scott, 11th Duke of *see* Scott, Walter Francis John, 9th Duke of Buccleuch
Queensferry, Williams & Robinson Turbine Factory **32** 783
Queen's University *see under* Belfast
Queen's Works *see* Office of works
Queen ware *see under* Pottery → wares
Queirolo, Francesco **16** 702, 703; **25** 808*
Queirós, José Maria de Eça de *see* Eça de Queirós, José Maria de
Queiroz, Gregorio Francisco **28** 430, 431
Queiroz Duarte, Helio **4** 713
Quelepa **29** 142
Quellet & Reeves **22** 36
Quellinus (family) **3** 570
Quellinus, Arnoldus *see* Quellinus, Artus
Quellinus, Artus (i) (1609-68) **3** 559; **25** 808, 810, 811–12*
assistants **9** 760; **25** 812
collaboration **25** 727, 810; **32** 242
patrons and collectors **13** 266; **14** 650; **25** 811; **30** 85
pupils **12** 405, 591; **13** 725; **25** 812; **32** 255; **33** 197
works **1** 813; **3** 570; **10** 745; **18** 11; **22** 858–9, 895; **25** *811*; **29** 571; **30** 495; **32** 255
Quellinus, Artus (ii) (1625-1700) **3** 570; **25** 812–13*
assistants **25** 813; **29** 591
collaboration **10** 717; **22** 858; **25** 812; **33** 197
pupils **24** 37; **25** 813
teachers **25** 812
works **1** 813; **10** 717; **25** 727, *812*
Quellinus, Artus (iii) (1653-after 1686) **12** 592; **25** 812, 813*
collaboration **23** 253
works **10** 263; **19** 606
Quellinus, Cornelis **25** 812
Quellinus, Erasmus (i) (*c.* 1584-1640) **25** 808–11*
assistants **32** 242
collaboration **32** 706
pupils **25** 811

Quellinus, Erasmus (ii) (1607-78) 3 613; 4 38; 25 808, 809–11*; 32 700
  collaboration 4 222; 11 872; 17 920; 28 904; 30 730; 31 772; 32 116
  patrons and collectors 2 726
  personal collection 11 872
  pupils 25 809
  reproductive prints by others 4 283; 7 466; 17 599; 18 879
  works 3 559; 17 470, 471; 25 *809*, *810*; 27 299
Quellinus, Hubertus 25 808
Quellinus, Jan-Erasmus 25 809, 813*
  pupils 31 797
  teachers 25 811
Quellinus, Thomas 3 570; 25 812, 813*
  works 8 739; 19 746
Queluz Palace 19 524; 23 405–6; 25 *288*, 293, 304, 814*; 26 254, 471
  chamber of the Conselho de Estado 5 903
  façade 23 *405*
  gardens 12 125; 26 471
  paintings 28 430, 431
  sculpture 6 528
  tiles 30 881
Quemada, La *see* LA QUEMADA
Quemistan 29 214
Queneau, Raymond 30 18, 20
Quenington, St Swithin 26 617
Quenstedt 25 504
Quentell (*fl* 1531) 33 289
Quentell, Heinrich (*fl* 1478-1501) 2 223; 4 9
Quentin, Philippe *see* QUANTIN, PHILIPPE
Quentin, V. 11 582
  works 31 *687*
Quentin de Latour, Maurice *see* LA TOUR, MAURICE-QUENTIN DE
Quentin de Lorangère 25 815*
  collections 11 662; 12 489; 25 664
  shells 12 489
Quentin factory 11 190
Quer, Francesc 29 329
Queralt, Jaume Mercade i *see* MERCADE I QUERALT, JAUME
Querandíe 2 394; 29 203
quercetin 24 799
Quercia, Jacopo della *see* JACOPO DELLA QUERCIA
Quercia, Priamo della *see* PRIAMO DELLA QUERCIA
quercitin 9 491
quercitron 18 656; 24 799
Querelle des Anciens et des Modernes *see* ANCIENTS AND MODERNS, QUARREL OF THE
Querena, Lattanzio 14 264; 20 91
Querétaro 21 394; 25 815*
  Museo de Arte de Querétaro 25 815
  Museo Regional de Querétaro 21 396; 25 815
  retables 26 251
  S Agustín *see* Museo de Arte de Querétaro
  S Clara 21 376; 29 841
  S Rosa 21 376
Querini (family) 32 108
Querini, Angelo 6 341
Querini, Gerolamo 4 291
Querini, Polo 4 291
quérisseur statues *see under* SCULPTURE → types → healing statues
Querner, Curt 22 923
Quero Chiesa, Luis 18 832; 25 701
Querol y Subirats, Agustín 25 815–16*; 29 295; 32 125
  pupils 8 132
  sponsors 29 295
  works 29 294, 295
queros 24 *498*, 499
Querschnitt, Der 24 445
Quertenmont, A. de 19 116
Quesada, Abbot of Montecassino 22 9
Quesada, Angela Castro *see* CASTRO QUESADA, ANGELA
Quesada, Gonzalo Jiménez de *see* JIMÉNEZ DE QUESADA, GONZALO
Quesada, Jorge de 29 303
Quesada, José Francisco Salazar *see* SALAZAR QUESADA, JOSÉ FRANCISCO
Quesada, Luis Miró *see* MIRÓ QUESADA, LUIS
Quesada, Manuel 13 767
Quesada, Miguel 16 863
Quesada Garland, Luis Miró *see* MIRÓ QUESADA GARLAND, LUIS
Queseda, Museo Zabaleta 33 583
Quesnel, Abbé 8 209
Quesnel, Augustin 25 816
Quesnel, François 20 455; 25 816*
Quesnel, Jacques 25 816
Quesnel, Nicolas 25 816
Quesnel, Pierre 25 816
Quesnoi *see* DU QUESNOY
Quesnoy, Le *see* LE QUESNOY
Questel, Charles-Auguste 25 816*
  assistants 10 508
  collaboration 18 653
  pupils 4 182; 22 732; 24 221; 27 768; 31 276
  teachers 9 312
Questembert 32 278, 280
Quételet, Horace 7 408
Quetta 15 *264*; 23 *797*; 25 817*
  Serena Hotel 23 799
  University of Baluchistan 23 802, 804
Quetta ware *see under* POTTERY → wares
Quetzalcoatl crafts cooperative 23 83
quetzal feathers *see under* FEATHERS → types
Quetzaltenango 13 *758*, 762
  Banco Occidente 13 762
  Edificio Rivera 13 763
  metalwork 13 768
  Palacio Municipal 13 762
  Pasaje Henríquez 13 762
  textiles 13 766
  theatre 13 762
Quevedo, Francisco de 24 15
Quévillon, Louis (-Amable) 5 570; 25 817*
Queylar, Paul *see* DUQUEYLAR, PAUL
Quezaltepeque 10 *153*
Quft 9 850; 10 80
Qufu 6 *615*, 663; 25 817–18*
  Confucian cemetery 6 732
  Kong Family Mansion 6 661, 675
  Kong fu *see* Kong Family Mansion
  Kong lin *see* Confucian cemetery
  Kong miao *see* Temple of Confucius
  Liqi Stele 6 740
  sculpture 6 731, 733
  Shi Chen Stele 6 740, *740*
  Temple of Confucius 6 661, 674, 675, *676*; 25 818; 30 443
    altar 1 703
    Dacheng dian 6 675, 732
    Kuiwen Pavilion 6 660; 24 289
    pailou 23 780
    sculpture 6 729
  Tomb 4 7 88
  Wen miao *see* Temple of Confucius
  Zhang Menglong Stele 6 *743*, 744
Quiahuiztlán 28 640
Quiapo 24 616
Quibell, James Edward 10 80; 14 493, 513; 17 713; 27 813
  works 14 *514*
Quibor Valley 32 166
Quiccheberg, Samuel van 18 520; 25 818*
  works 18 522; 25 630; 33 271
El Quiché (Guatemala) 20 885; 27 607
Quiché culture 20 885–6; 21 183, 262
Quicherat, Jules 11 675
Quick, Kenneth 25 834
Quickborner Team 23 360
Quickeberg, Samuel 12 475
Quidor, John 10 145; 17 450; 25 818–19*
Quiduzzi, Angelo 25 438
Quiengola 21 208, 599; 33 620
Quignon, Fernand Just 19 544
Quijano, Augusto 21 382
Quijano, Jerónimo 25 819*; 29 266
Quikerberghe, Vincent van 19 382
Quileute 22 565
Quilici, Pancho 25 819*
Quillacinga 7 602
Quillaia bark *see under* BARK → types
Quillard, Pierre-Antoine 25 820*
  patrons and collectors 4 635; 5 364
  works 11 37
Quillerier, Noël 8 88; 13 878
Quilliet, Frédéric 12 839
quills
  historical and regional traditions
    Bamana 3 *135*
    Native North Americans 22 644, 648–9*, 652
  types
    bird 22 647, 648, 649
    porcupine 22 647, 648, 649, *650*, 651, 656, 663, *663*
  uses
    appliqué 22 648
    arm-bands 22 651
    baskets 22 663, *663*
    belts 22 *651*
    bracelets 22 651
    brushes 5 *32*, 33
    coats 22 651
    containers 22 651
    dress 22 648, 649, 650
    garters 22 *651*
    hair ornaments 22 649
    harnesses 22 *650*
    headbands 22 652
    headdresses 22 652
    leggings 22 649
    masks 3 *135*
    moccasins 22 648, 649, 651
    necklaces 22 651, *651*
    pens 4 343; 9 216; 24 348, 349*; 28 303–4
    pipe-bags 22 649
    pipes (smoking) 22 651
    pouches 22 651
    sashes 22 651
    shirts 22 648, 649
    weaving 22 648
quillwork
  Native North Americans 22 647–52*, *650*, 654, 655, 656
    17th cent. 22 *651*
    19th cent. 22 *649*
Quilmes 29 191
Quilon 6 *623*; 15 *294*; 25 820*
quilting 25 820–21*; 30 562
  historical and regional traditions
    Colombia 7 607
    England 10 353; 25 821, *821*
    Indian subcontinent 25 821
    Iran 25 821
    Mongolia 21 877; 25 820
    Netherlands, the 22 898
  materials
    embroidery 10 353
quilting—cont.
  uses
    dress 25 820, 821
    dresses 25 *821*
    felt 21 877
    sculpture 7 607
quilts 11 54; 25 820
  historical and regional traditions
    Africa 1 424, *425*
    Australia 2 767
    Bangladesh 3 168
    Canada 5 587
    China 7 145
    England 25 821
    India, Republic of 15 175, 176
    Indian subcontinent 15 674–5, 727
    Islamic 16 429
    North America 25 821
    United States of America 1 *425*; 30 VI3; 31 658
    Wales 25 821
  types
    Bengalla 3 168
Quimbaya 29 150, 212*
  metalwork 29 *212*
Quimper 11 *504*; 25 822*
  Bibliothèque Nationale 31 462
  Musée des Beaux-Arts 3 156
Quimper faience factory 25 822*; 30 271
Quimperlé 7 406
Quin, Henry 16 33; 30 356
Qu-i Nader 1 197
Quinal, Cruz
  works 32 *166*
Qui Nam 32 469
Quinault 22 565, 577
Quinaux, Joseph 32 254
quincha *see under* ARCHITECTURE → techniques
Quinchana 27 700
Quincy (MA)
  Crane Library 26 *341*
  Stone Temple 24 209, *209*
Quincy, de (family) 28 267
Quincy, Josiah 4 472
Quineaux, Joseph 14 25
Quinet, Mig 17 518
Quinil, Bishop of Exeter 10 672
Quinkan Galleries 1 *37*; 25 822*
Quinkhard, Jan Maurits 25 822–3*
  pupils 2 25; 3 900; 18 235; 26 97
  reproductive prints by others 14 795
  teachers 4 374
  works 22 846
Quinkhard, Julius (*fl c.* 1680-1700) 25 822
Quinkhard, Julius (1736-76) 25 823
Quinn, John 25 553, 823*; 32 702
  collections 31 663, 665
  paintings 17 607; 25 380
  sculpture 1 438; 9 359, 361
Quiñones, Alvaro de 21 701
Quiñones, Andrés García de *see* GARCÍA DE QUIÑONES, ANDRÉS
Quiñones, Jerónimo García de *see* GARCÍA DE QUIÑONES, JERÓNIMO
Quinones, Lee 3 338
Quiñones, Suero de *see* SUERO DE QUIÑONES
Quinquela Martín, Luis 31 179
Quinta de Antão de Tojal 25 292
Quintana (Simonetti), Antonio (Luis) 8 232, 233; 25 823–4*
Quintana, Ben 22 595
Quintana, Ciro 8 234
Quintana, Francisco de Paula *see* PAULA QUINTANA, FRANCISCO DE
Quintanaortuña, Chasuble of San Juan de Ortega 16 436
Quintanilla, Raúl 23 86
Quintanilla de las Viñas, S María 29 261, 287; 32 *618*, 619, *619*
Quintela, Baron *see* FARROBÓ, Conde de
Quintero, José Antonio 25 824*
Quintilian 13 468; 14 867; 25 824*; 30 487
  on decorum 8 612
  on painters 13 553
  on painting 13 554
  on sculpture 13 370; 22 402
Quintinie, Jean-Baptiste de La *see* LA QUINTINIE, JEAN-BAPTISTE DE
Quinto, Javier, Conde de 29 353
Quinto Fiorentino, Montagnola Tomb 10 634
Quintosus 27 52
Quinto Vicentino, Villa Thiene 23 492
Quintus Curtius Rufus 7 242
Quintus Pedius 27 52
Quinua 24 514
quipus 15 162; 29 130
Quiquerez, Ferdo (Ferdinand) 8 178; 22 17; 25 824–5*; 33 593
  pupils 16 795
Quiriguá 13 *758*; 20 *882*; 25 825–6*
  Altar O 1 700
  Altar P 1 700
  altars 1 700
  Monument 5 25 825; 29 620
  Monument 26 25 *825*
Quirin, Egid 11 124
Quirini, Angelo, Cardinal 14 106
Quirinus, Rochus *see* LYNAR, ROCHUS QUIRINUS
quirked roll mouldings *see under* MOULDINGS → types
Quiroa, Marco Augusto 5 356; 13 765; 25 826*; 26 549
Quiroga, Marco 4 260; 18 778
Quiroga, Vasco de, Bishop 21 249, 375, 395
Quirós, Antonio 25 826*
Quirós, Cesáreo Bernaldo de *see* BERNALDO DE QUIRÓS, CESÁREO
Quirós, Teodorico 8 18; 25 826–7*
  collaboration 1 783; 8 16; 12 919
  groups and movements 8 17; 17 586
Quiróz, Gregorio Naciaceno *see* NACIACENO QUIRÓZ, GREGORIO
Quirquincho 29 202
Quispe Tito, Diego 8 302; 24 499, 507; 25 827*
Quispez Asín, Carlos 24 510; 25 827*
Quist, Leen 22 884
Quist, W(illem) G(erhard) 25 827*
Quistorp, Johann Gottfried 11 779
Quitainer, Jan Antonín 8 386, 398; 25 445, 828*
  patrons and collectors 8 427
Quitainer, Ondřej Filip 8 385; 25 432, 443, 828*
Quito 9 *709*, 709; 25 828–9*; 31 721
  architecture 9 710, 711–12
  Banco Central de Ecuador 9 711; 24 435
    collections 29 221; 31 812
    Department de Investigaciones Históricas 9 714
  Bethlemite Hospital Chapel 9 711
  Biblioteca de Arte de la Fundación Guayasamín 9 714
  Casa de la Cultura Ecuatoriana 9 711
    Biblioteca 9 714
  Círculo Militar 9 711
  Cofradía del Rosario 9 715
  Colegio de S Andrés 9 715
  Colegio Jesuita 9 711
  collages 9 712
  ecclesiastical buildings
    Cathedral 9 710, 712, 714

Quito
ecclesiastical buildings—cont.
La Compañía **9** 710, 711
Museum **9** 714
retable **26** 252, *252*
shrine **28** 632
La Merced **9** 711
Monastery of S Agustín **2** 726; **9** 710, 712, 714
Monastery of S Domingo **9** 711
church **9** 710, 712
museum **9** 714
Monastery of S Francisco
church **9** 710, 712
museum **9** 714
Sagrario **9** 710
Santuaria de Guápulo **9** 710
S Barbara **9** 711
S Roque **9** 712
Escuela de Bellas Artes **9** 713, 715
Escuela Democrática Miguel de Santiago **9** 715
Hospital Eugenio Espejo **14** 783
Museo de Arte e Historia de la Ciudad **9** 714; **25** 829
Museo Camilo Egas **9** 749
Museo Nacional de Arte Colonial **9** 714; **18** 67; **25** 829
painting **6** 596; **7** 607; **9** 712, 714
Palacio Arzobispal **9** 711
Palacio de Gobierno **9** 711
Quito—cont.
Palacio Municipal **9** 711, 714; **25** *828*
Penal Panóptico **9** 711
retables **26** 252
sculpture **2** 398; **9** 712
Teatro Bolivar **9** 711
Universidad Central de Ecuador **9** 714, 715
wood-carvings **9** 710, 712
Quitteiner, Andreas Philipp *see* QUITANIER, ONDŘEJ FILIP
Quittner, Zsigmond **14** 889; **25** 829*; **31** 796
quivers
historical and regional traditions
Central Asia, Western **6** 261, 262
Islamic **16** 528
Japan **17** 361, 363
Mongolia **21** 875, 878
Native North Americans **22** 652
Ottoman **16** 528
materials
basketwork **3** 332
feathers **22** 652
jade **16** 528
Quivoron-Pasquiou, Marie *see* BRACQUEMOND, MARIE
Quiz, The **25** 264
Qujialing **25** 829
Qujialing culture **6** 879; **7** 159; **25** 829*
Qul Baba Kukaltash **16** 235
Qul-i-Nader **28** 625; **29** 824
Qullar-Aghasi, Husayn **15** 898
qulun *see under* LACQUER → types
Quluq Church **9** 543
Qulzum **16** 541
Qum **15** *897*; **16** *105*, 491; **25** 830*
architecture **16** 231
basilica **2** 891, 892
carpets **15** 899
cobalt **16** 394
congregational mosque **16** 162
Imamzada Ahmad Qasim **1** 98
Imamzada ʿ ibn Jaʿfar **1** 98
inscriptions **16** 232
museums **15** 900
pottery **16** 425, 426
shrine of Fatima **1** 97; **6** 172; **16** 234, 257; **25** 830; **28** 633, 634; **31** 110, 113
tiles **23** 557
tombs **16** 163
woodwork **16** 491
Qumis *see* SHAHR-I QUMIS
Qumtura *see* KUMTURA
Qunfidhah **32** 315
quoins **20** 571; **25** 830*
Quonset hut **12** 854, 855
Quost, Ernest **3** 462
Quotskuyva, Dextra **22** 609
Qur'āns *see* KORANS
Quraysh **16** 144
Qurayya **2** *246*, 268
Qurm, Oman Museum **23** 436
Qurnet Muraʿi *see under* THEBES (i) (EGYPT)
Qurra ibn Sharik **16** 146
Qurva Mosque **16** 162
Qus
ʿAmri Mosque minbar **16** 490
architecture **16** 208
glass **16** 519
tombs **31** 111
Qusayr ʿAmra **6** 564; **16** *104*, 121, 148; **17** 656; **25** 830*
Audience Hall **32** 88
baths **3** 376, 378; **16** 142
mosaics **16** 256
wall paintings **16** 251, 516, 537, 549; **22** 515
al-Qusays **2** 248, 249, 265, 273
Quseir **9** *774*; **16** *104*; **25** 830–31*
excavations **16** 550
glass **16** 519
Quṣṭantiniya *see* ISTANBUL → Constantinople
Qustul **23** *276*, 285, 286
Grave 19 **23** 277, *278*
pottery **23** 277
silver **9** 655
al-Qusur, Nestorian church **2** 252, 273, *273*
Qutb al-Din Aybak, Sultan (*reg* 1206-10) (Mamluk of Delhi) **8** 671–2, 677, 678; **20** 226
Qutb al-Din Khan Kokaltash **10** 828
Qutb al-Din Shah, Sultan (*reg* 1451-8) (Sultans of Gujarat) **27** 842
Qutb Minar *see under* DELHI → Quwwat al-Islam Mosque
Qutb Shahi **25** 831*
see also:
ʿABDULLAH QUTB SHAH, Ruler
MUHAMMAD QULI QUTB SHAH, Ruler
MUHAMMAD QUTB SHAH, Ruler
Qu xian
Shen que **6** 649; **25** 800
tomb of Feng Huang **25** 800
Quyang **6** 717
Beiyue miao **6** 657
Sanqing Hall **6** 658
Quy Nhon **6** *418*, *623*
Qu Yuan **6** 818
Qweisme **9** 543
Qwist, Christian Ludwig **2** 765

R

R, del *see* ERRI
R '33 group **6** 378
RA **25** 433
RAA (*Répertoire d'art et d'archéologie*) **4** 25–6
Raab *see* GYŐR
Raab, Georg **10** 760
Raab, Jacob **18** 848
Raab, Johann Leonhard **18** 237; **23** 529; **25** 824; **29** 578
Raab, Johann Philip
  works **5** *191*
Raab, Johann Valentin **12** 426
Raadik, Khayvi (Bernkhardovna) **27** 423
Raálo, Ervin **12** 839
Rab **8** 175
  basilica of St John **8** 175
  Benedictine church **8** 175
al-Rabadhah **16** 151
  sword guards **16** *506*
Rabaglio, Virgilio **4** 560
Rabaliatti, Franz Wilhelm **14** 306; **20** 282; **23** 339
Raban, Ze'ev **17** 566, 579; **21** 49; **29** 768
Rabanne, Paco **9** 294
Rabanus Maurus, Abbot of Fulda
  architecture **10** 109
  wall paintings **5** 797
  writings **5** 779, 803; **10** 201; **12** 255; **28** 428; **31** 289
    illustrated **5** *779*
Rabari **15** 176
Rabas, Václav **2** 546; **8** 393; **25** 832*
Rabasten, Jacques **19** 342
Rabastens **4** 780
  Notre-Dame-du-Bourg **4** 780
Rabat (Malta)
  Gesù **20** 214
  Roman Villa and Museum of Antiquities **20** 219
  St Paul's Collegiate Church Museum **20** 214, 219
Rabat (Morocco) **1** *376*; **16** *103*; **25** 832–3*
  archaeological museum **22** 129
  architecture **22** 128
  Bank of Morocco building **22** 128
  baths **16** 218
  carpets **16** 486; **22** 129
  Civic Centre **1** 319
  embroidery **16** 448
  fortifications **21** 583, 585
  French Embassy **22** 128
  Great Mosque *see* al-Sunna
  Hassan Mosque **16** 191
  Kasba of the Udaya **21** 585
  Mashwar **16** 240
  mausoleum of Muhammad V **22** 128
  Mechouar *see* Mashwar
  Musées des Antiquités **16** 558
  Oudaïa Museum **22** 129
  railway station **22** 128
  Shalom Azawi synagogue **17** 551
  al-Sunna **16** 240
  Tour Hassan **21** 626
  Udayas Gate **21** 584, *584*
Rabati, Muhammad ibn'Ali **22** 128
Rabat-Salé **22** 129
Rabbah **26** *915*
  temple **26** 917
rabbit-hair *see under* hair → types
rabbit-skin *see under* SKINS → types
Rabbula **25** 833
Rabbula Gospels *see under* GOSPEL BOOKS → individual manuscripts
Rabe, Friedrich **28** 44
Rabe, Johann Benjamin Heinrich **5** 30
Rabel, Daniel **20** 415; **25** 833*
  pupils **20** 860; **24** 397
  works **11** 401; **30** 659, *660*
Rabel, Jean **12** 203; **19** 257; **25** 833
Rabelais, François **4** 242; **14** 868, 869; **27** 868
Rabell, Arnaldo Roche *see* ROCHE RABELL, ARNALDO
Rabenden, Master of **22** 301
Räber, Hans-Ulrich **30** 136
Råberg, Per Göran **30** 120
Rabglio, Virgilio **29** 271
Rabia, Gerolamo **19** 784, 785
Rabi'a Khatun (Ayyubid) **2** 888
Rabi'a Sultan Begum (Timurid) **31** 451
Rabicano, Cola *see* RAPICANO, COLA
Rábí Castle **8** 377
Rabin, Oskar **8** 10; **18** 209; **25** 834*; **27** 397
Rabinal **13** 768
Rabindra Bhavan Art Gallery *see under* NEW DELHI
Rabine, Oscar *see* RABIN, OSKAR
Rabingan **16** 370
Rabinovich, Isaak **10** 699; **32** 601
Rabinowitch, David **5** 572; **25** 834*
Rabinowitch, Royden (Leslie) **5** 572; **25** 834*
Rabinowitz, Hym **25** 834–5*; **29** 117
Rabinowitz, Yehoshua **16** 570
Rabinowitz triptych **26** 726
Rabirius **16** 623; **25** 835*; **26** 884
  works **23** 808; **26** 784, 786, 856, 870, 895, 923
Rabl, Károly **24** 312
Rabten Kunsang **13** 884
Rabut, Charles **7** 693; **11** 770
Rabutin-Chantal, Marie, Marquise de Sévigné *see* SÉVIGNÉ, MARIE, Marquise de
Rabuzin, Ivan **22** 441
Raby, Julian **16** 550
Raby, Lord **4** 218
Raby Castle (Co. Durham) **10** 279
  Chapel **29** 515
Rabyn *see* ROBIJN
Racalcati, Antonio **10** 443
Ràcani (family) **29** 422
RACAR **24** 430
Racconigi Castello **3** 49; **10** 637; **16** 730; **17** 708
  Gabinetto Etrusco **16** 730; **23** *830*
  interior decoration **16** 720
  restorations **31** 445
raccoon-hair *see under* HAIR → types
Race, Ernest **1** 738; **6** 391; **8** 804; **10** 285, 299; **25** 835*
racecourses **10** 215; **16** 153; **29** 424
Race Furniture Ltd **25** 835
Rachchupkin, V. **30** 352
Rachette, Jean-Dominique **27** 412
Racheva-Manolova, Evgeniya **5** 159
  works **5** *159*
Rach Gia **5** 484, 485
Rachkov, N. P. **27** 439
Rachol Church **12** 827; **26** 254
Racholf **10** 109
Račić, Josip **2** 890; **8** 178, 181
Racim, Mohammed **1** 634
Racim, Omar **16** 577
Racine (WI)
  Johnson Foundation **18** 786
  Johnson Wax Administrative Building (1936-8) **12** 792; **19** 367; **23** *360*; **24** 752; **28** 834; **31** 596
    lighting **19** *367*
  Johnson Wax Tower (1950) **4** 789
Racine, François-Nicolas-Henry, Baron de Moinville *see* MOINVILLE, FRANÇOIS-NICOLAS-HENRY RACINE, Baron de
Račinskis, Karolis **19** 498
Racken group **11** 142
Ráckeve Palace **14** 886
Rackham, Arthur **4** 367; **25** 835–6*
Rackham, Richard **30** 103
Racknitz, Joseph Friedrich von **12** 413; **25** 836*; **28** 178
Rackstrow, Benjamin **33** 3
Racó Molero **29** 365
Racos Palace **14** 885
Racz, André **10** 397
Racz, Simone **6** 600
Raczyński, Atanazy, Count **25** 836*
  architecture **25** 408
  collections **25** 136, 138
  paintings **25** 409
  writings **25** 320; **28** 169
Raczyński, Edward, Count **18** 691; **25** 136, 139, 408; **33** 295
Raczyński, Kazimierz **17** 756; **25** 136
Rad, Christoph, I (1628-1710) **2** 718
Rad, Christoph, II (1676-1730) **2** 718
Rada' **32** 317
  houses **33** 519
  madrasa **16** 214
Rada, Jiménez de **22** 254
Rada, José de la Merced *see* MERCED RADA, JOSÉ DE LA
Rada, Juan de Ribero *see* RIBERO RADA, JUAN DE
Rada, Vlastimil **8** 393
Radauš, Vanja **9** 496, 672
Rădăuţi, St Nicholas **26** 707, 719
Radburn (NJ) **31** 729
Radburne Hall (Derbys) **22** 152
Radcliffe, Abraham **12** 613
Radcliffe, A. M. **5** 126
Radcliffe-Brown, A. R. **2** 137
Radclyffe, Edward **25** 837
Radclyffe, William **4** 87; **25** 836–7*
Radegund, Queen of France (*d* 987) **17** 701
Rademaker, Abraham **10** 864; **25** 837*
raden *see* INLAYS → materials → mother-of-pearl
Raden Saleh (Sarief Bustaman) **15** 807; **25** 837*
Rader, Matthäus **17** 719; **27** 503
Räderscheidt, Anton **8** 437; **22** 923; **25** 837–8*; **29** 869
Radetsky, Irina **22** 55
Radetzky, Johann Josef, Count **1** 141
Radev, Boyan **5** 163
Radev, Ivan **5** 158
Radev, Simeon **5** 163
Radewijns, Florent **4** 752; **17** 897
Radford, George K. **32** 95
Radhakrishnan, S. **15** 173
Radi, Antonio **4** 428
Radi, Lorenzo **32** 204
Radić, Zvonimir **10** 667
Radicchio, Vincenzo **21** 107
Radice, Mario **16** 681; **25** 838*; **26** 16
Radiel, Janós **14** 677
Radig, Anton **12** 2; **28** 823
Radigars (Spirit)
Radigaut, Raymond **8** 438
Radigues, Antoine *see* RADIG, ANTON
Radiguet, Raymond **32** 669
Radikale Künstler **9** 758
Radimov, Pavel **2** 633
Radimský, Viclav **5** 313
Rading, Adolf **16** 565; **25** 838–9*
  collaboration **28** 112
  groups and movements **8** 826; **26** 405
  pupils **28** 835
  works **25** *839*
Radini, Anna **17** 840
Radinoga, Masilonyane **4** 489
radiocarbon dating *see under* DATING METHODS → types
radiography, X-ray *see under* TECHNICAL EXAMINATION → types
radios **1** 762; **15** 827, *827*
Radishchev, Aleksander N., Museum *see under* SARATOV
Radivoy **5** 148; **18** 446
Radjedef (*reg c.* 2528–*c.* 2520 BC) **1** 94; **9** *776*, 779, 870
Radkan East **31** 111
Radkan West **16** 159, 161, 259
Radke, Emil **25** 128
Radke, Gustav **25** 128
Radkersburg, Johannes von *see* JOHANNES AQUILA DE RAKERSPURGA
Radloff, Wilhelm **21** 885
Radnai, Béla **13** 638
Radnicki, Zygmunt **33** 416
Radnitzky, Emmanuel *see* MAN RAY
Radnor, Jacob Pleydell-Bouverie, 2nd Earl of *see* PLEYDELL-BOUVERIE, JACOB(, 2nd Earl of Radnor)
Radnor, John Robartes, 1st Earl of *see* ROBARTES, JOHN, 1st Earl of Radnor
Radnót *see* IERNUT
Rado, Ladislav **26** 42
Radomsko **25** 122
Radončić, P. **9** 331
Radonić, Novak **28** 450
Radosav, Master **26** 712
Radoslav **22** 80; **28** 449
Radovan **2** 133; **8** 177; **25** 839–40*; **31** 359
Radović, Ivan **28** 451
Radović, Vuko **22** 18
Radovljica Church **28** 858, *858*
Radpod of Trier, Archbishop **5** 798; **26** 485
Radruzh **31** 557
Radstock, William Waldegrave, 1st Baron *see* WALDEGRAVE, WILLIAM, 1st Baron Radstock
Radtke, Emil **32** 878
Radu IV, Voivode of Wallachia (*reg* 1495-1508) **31** 23
Radu, Silvia **25** 840*
Raduga **2** 122
Radul **24** 308
Radul, Zograf **22** 17
Rådvad Værk **8** 751
Radwański, Andrzej **25** 105
Radwanski, Feliks **18** 427
Radway Grange (Warwicks) **21** 607
  Edgehill Tower **12** 176; **13** 199; **27** 323
Radwi, Abdul Halim **27** 876
Radziejowice, church **29** 839
Radziejowiski, Michał Stefan **23** 113
Radziwiłł (family)
  architecture **3** 526; **19** 496; **25** 135
  furniture **25** 121
  interior decoration **23** 113
  paintings **3** 528; **25** 137
  tapestries **25** 131
Radziwiłł, Prince (*fl* 1674-6) **29** 519
Radziwiłł, Aleksander Ludwik, Prince **25** 841
Radziwiłł, Anna, Princess **22** 449; **25** 122, 124, 132, 841*; **31** 760
Radziwiłł, Antoni **25** 136
Radziwiłł, Bogusław, Prince **25** 841*
Radziwiłł, Dominik **19** 497
Radziwill, Franz **12** 396; **25** 842*
  works **25** *841*
Radziwiłł, Helena, Princess **2** 414; **23** 203; **25** 121, 136, 138, 841; **33** 722
Radziwiłł, Hieronim Florian, Prince **25** 841
Radziwiłł, Janusz, Prince **19** 496; **25** 840*
Radziwiłł, Krzysztof, Prince **19** 496; **25** 841
Radziwiłł, Michał **25** 123
Radziwiłł, Michał Hieronim, Prince **25** 136, 138, 842
Radziwiłł, Michał Kazimierz, Prince **25** 122, 841*; **28** 863
Radziwiłł, Mikołaj Krzysztof **25** 840*
Radziwiłł Glassworks *see* NALIBOKI GLASSWORKS; URZECZE GLASSWORKS
Radziwiłł Lithuanian Brest Bible *see under* BIBLES → types
Radziwillmonty **3** 527
Radzyń **30** 535
Radzyń Podlaski **25** 99
Rae, Barbara **28** 240
Rae, George **4** 879; **8** 579; **10** 367; **27** 187
Rae, Henrietta **10** 878
Rae, Jeremias van **9** 179
Rae, Malcolm **3** 62
Rae, Ronald **28** 244
Rae, William **5** 573
Raeburn, Henry **25** 842–5*
  dealers **26** 107
  methods **9** 673
  patrons and collectors **1** 529; **28** 269
  pupils **32** 912
  reproductive prints by others **14** 288
  works **9** 725; **11** *430*, 431; **25** *843*, *845*; **28** 236–7, *236*
Raedecker, John (Anton) **3** 704; **22** 861; **25** 845*
Raedelmayer, František Michal **8** 413; **25** 443
Raedt, Anton de **3** 600
Raedt, Jean-Jacques de **14** 479
Raedt, Willem Andriesz. de **8** 103; **19** 101; **22** 897
Raeren **3** *539*; **25** 845–6*
  jugs **3** *589*
  stonewares **3** 588–9; **12** 428, 429; **22** 877

Raes (family) 30 320
Raes, Godfried-Willem 29 98
Raes, Jan 27 291, 632
works 27 294
Raes, Nicholas 30 853
Raetz, Markus 3 824; 25 846*; 30 135
works 30 135
Raeumur, René Du see Du Raeumur, René
Raevska, Yova 5 159
Raeymakers, Luis 5 53
Raf, Jan see Rav, Jan
Rafael, Joaquim 19 805; 21 348
Rafael de Marcantellis, Abbot 3 614
Rafaëlli, Jean-François 31 704
Rafajlović (family) 22 17
Rafalavičius, Karolis 19 498
Rafałowski, Aleksander 4 148
Rafaq 2 248
Rafay 1 394, 401; 33 609
Raffaele Tomás 11 482
Raffaelle de Florentia see Raffaellino del Garbo
Raffaëlli, Jean-François 11 548; 25 846–7*
collaboration 20 201
exhibitions 15 155
groups and movements 15 155; 22 687–8
methods 8 128
patrons and collectors 1 614; 23 882
works 12 296; 22 688
Raffaëlli colours 8 128
Raffaellino, il (c. 1610-62) see Romanelli, Giovanni Francesco
Raffaellino, il (1613-44) see Bottalla, Giovanni Maria
Raffaellino da Reggio see Reggio, Raffaellino da
Raffaellino del Garbo 5 698; 25 847–8*
pupils 4 855
works 19 447; 25 848
Raffaello da Brescia 14 904; 16 726; 25 849*; 27 648; 32 10
Raffaello dal Colle see Colle, Raffaello (di Michelangelo di Luca) dal
Raffaello da Montelupo 3 156, 157
Raffaello di Biagio 10 877
Raffalt, Johann Gualbert 2 797
Raffer, Josef 8 398
Raffet, (Denis-)Auguste (-Marie) 8 705; 19 486, 488; 25 849*; 27 871
Raffeueau-Delile, Alire 26 73
raffia
historical and regional traditions
Africa 1 293, 294, 294, 295, 296, 336, 382; 3 331
Bamileke 3 149, 149
Côte d'Ivoire 8 22
Kuba (iii) (Zaïre) 1 295
Madagascar 1 293; 20 40
Pende 24 358
Zaïre 1 294; 3 440
uses
baskets 1 295; 3 149, 331
fibre art 11 54
hats 1 296
headdresses 1 386
masks 1 336; 3 149; 24 358
skirts 1 295
textiles 20 40
threads 3 440; 30 537
weaving 1 293, 294
Raffles, (Thomas) Stamford 12 103; 13 812; 20 155, 163; 25 850*; 28 774
works 29 241, 866
Raffles chairs see under Chairs → types
Raffles Museum and Library see Singapore → National Museum
Rafin Kura 1 343
al-Rafiqa see Raqqa
Rafn, Aage 25 850*; 29 77
collaboration 11 139; 16 830; 17 756
teachers 17 755
works 8 728
Ràfols-Casamada, Albert 25 851*; 29 287
groups and movements 3 219
works 25 851
rafraîchissoirs 22 14
Raft, Emmanuel 2 766
rafters 15 787; 17 66
Ragama, Tewatte Basilica 29 462
Raganaldus, Abbot of Marmoutier 31 227
rag dolls see under Dolls → types
Ragghianti, Carlo Ludovico 19 637; 26 236
Raggi (family) 6 34
Raggi, (Ercole) Antonio (1624-86) 25 851–2*; 26 773
collaboration 1 631; 26 818; 29 830
patrons and collectors 10 526, 768; 23 899
pupils 11 280
works 16 699; 25 852; 26 810, 824; 28 681; 29 830
Raggi, Antonio, Marchese (fl 1640) 21 483
Raggi, Giovanni 30 862
Raggi, Pietro Paolo 3 34
Raggruppimento degli Architetti Italiano Moderni see Rami
Ragha see Rayy
Raghubir Singh 15 620
Raghugarh 15 603, 607
Raghunatha Prushti 15 636
Ragıp, Ahmet 16 537
Raglan, Lord 32 274
Raglan Castle (Gwent) 8 278; 12 174
Yellow Tower of Gwent 6 55
Ragley Hall (Warwicks) 8 46; 32 685, 825
Ragnoli (family) 3 916
Ragon, Michel 2 525, 544, 545; 24 144
Ragot, François 15 31
RA Group 8 394
rags 2 239; 24 38, 40; 27 317; 31 259, 260
Ragsdale, Christenson, Everett 22 671
ragstone 6 158
Raguenet, Nicolas 31 156
Raguier, Antoine 11 355
Ragusa (Croatia) see Dubrovnik
Ragusa (Italy) 16 640; 31 717
Ragusa, Giorgio Alegretto da see Giorgio Alegretto da Ragusa
Ragusa, Niccolò da see Niccolò dell'Arca
Ragusa, Vincenzo 17 133, 198, 420; 21 59; 33 469
Raguzzini, Filippo 25 852–4*
patrons and collectors 23 576
works 16 639, 639; 25 853; 26 760, 833; 31 713
Ragya gonpa 30 819
al-Rahal, Khalid 3 53; 16 2
Rahatgarh 15 323
Raheem, Ismeth 29 456
Rahi, Mansur 23 801
Rahim, Shaigi 29 896
Rahim Dad 15 372
Rahimi, Abdullah 15 899
Rahl, Carl 17 885; 19 718; 20 439; 25 742; 26 559; 30 205, 641
Rahman, Hamidur 3 168
Rahmanzade, M. 2 896
Rahmberg, Ulf 10 483; 30 82
Rahn, Johann Rudolf 30 156
Rahn, Rudolf 22 186
Rahner, Georg Konrad 11 731
Rahon, Alice 21 388; 30 22
Rahui, Anaha Te 32 769
Rahway (NJ) 31 634
Rai (Iran) see Rayy
Rai (people) 22 757
Raiatea 28 921, 922
Raibolini see Francia
Raichur 15 358
Raid, Ants 10 538
Raidel, Anton 12 822
Raidhu 15 568, 569
Raien 17 129
Raigern, Master of 20 753*
Raigorod 17 853
Raijō 17 98, 120, 879
Rai Kyōhei 25 866
rail chariots see under Chariots → types
railings
China 6 675; 7 136
Confucianism 6 675
Indian subcontinent 15 425, 428, 429, 437; 27 844*
Poland 25 130
Railton, William 3 79; 22 36, 47
railways 3 128; 5 41, 399; 24 597; 32 398
railway stations 25 854–7*
England 3 246; 10 236; 16 54; 19 574; 25 856
Finland 27 473
France 11 524; 18 664; 24 126; 25 855
Germany 25 856
Indian subcontinent 4 289
Italy 21 521
Malaysia 20 168
New Zealand 23 55
Russia 28 571
Switzerland 29 491
United States of America 3 693; 5 274; 17 799
see also Metro stations
Raimbach, Abraham 25 857*; 33 188, 189
Raimond de Dezest 31 844
works 31 844
Raimon de Bianya 26 610
Raimon de Via see Raimon de Bianya
Raimondi, Antonio 3 783; 24 516
Raimondi, Eliseo 8 135; 25 857*
Raimondi, Guglielmo 1 745; 22 100
Raimondi, Marcantonio 10 384, 385–6; 25 858–60*; 26 768, 818; 27 606
assistants 20 658
collaboration 3 419, 507; 10 477; 16 665; 25 904; 26 228
engravings 10 901; 20 1
forgeries by others 29 557
patrons and collectors 2 388; 8 481, 664; 10 487; 14 810; 20 416, 455
pupils 4 442; 8 765; 27 212
reproductive prints by others 5 856; 8 765; 32 412
works 2 387; 3 157; 10 386; 12 677; 13 700; 16 665, 750; 20 840; 23 292, 292; 24 812; 25 605, 618, 625, 858, 859, 904; 27 849
Raimondi, Quintiliano 31 172
Raimondi, Tommaso 20 529; 25 857
Raimondi, Vincenzo see Raymond, Vincent
Raimondi Stele see under Chavin de Huantar
Raimon Gairart see Gairard, Raymond
Raimundus Gayrardus see Gairard, Raymond
Raimundus Lombardus see Raymond the Lombard
Rainaldi, Adriano 25 860
Rainaldi, Carlo 25 860, 861–3*
assistants 13 292
attributions 3 198
Rainaldi, Carlo—cont.
collaboration 6 23; 10 782; 11 275; 25 861
competitions 7 913
patrons and collectors 6 584; 16 638; 20 240; 23 898, 899
works 2 594; 4 433, 434; 6 72; 7 276; 16 638, 638, 644; 19 632; 25 861, 862; 26 758, 759; 29 830
Rainaldi, Girolamo 12 117; 24 371; 25 860–61*; 26 842
architecture 16 638
attributions 11 741
collaboration 9 89; 13 321
patrons and collectors 1 595; 10 526, 811; 12 764; 23 898, 899
pupils 2 849; 25 861
works 1 601; 4 280, 433; 5 684; 7 276; 11 318; 16 638, 638; 25 258; 26 759; 29 250; 30 344
Rainaldi, Hieronimo see Rainaldi, Girolamo
Rainaldo 5 291; 24 856, 858; 25 863*
Rainaldo de Man Curta see Renaud de Maincourt
Rainaldo Santo da Sambuceto 24 695
Rainaldus see Rainaldo
Rainaldus, Archbishop of Bari 3 234
Rainald von Dassel, Archbishop of Cologne 7 590; 29 4
Rainaud, Bishop 2 48
rainbow beams see under Beams → types
Rainbow style see under Rome, ancient → mosaics
Raincy, Le see Le Raincy
Rainer, Arnulf 2 797, 831; 25 863–4*; 32 447
collaboration 27 215
groups and movements 28 344
patrons and collectors 9 121
works 9 310; 24 408; 25 864
Rainer, Oskar 2 832
Rainer, Roland 2 789, 810, 831; 25 864–5*
Rainer, Yvonne 10 689; 22 140; 24 407
Raineri, Giorgio 22 747
Raineri, Giuseppe 22 747
Rainerius (family) 7 921, 922; 25 865*
Rainerius, Guittone 7 922; 25 865
Rainerius, Johannes 7 922; 25 865
Rainerius, Johannes Guittonis 25 865
Rainerius, Nicolaus 25 865
Rainerius, Petrus 25 865
Rainer of Huy 25 865–6*
attributions 3 566, 566; 26 695
works 7 383; 26 681, 682
Rainov, Bogomil 5 163
Rainov, Nikolay 5 163; 25 866*
Rainwater, R. 4 24; 10 211
Raipur, Mahant Ghasi Dass Memorial Museum 15 181
Rai Rissai 17 413
Rai San'yō 17 412; 18 60; 25 866–7*; 33 322
pupils 17 198; 22 337
works 17 237, 419; 33 709
writings 17 196
raised crypts see under Crypts → types
Raiset, Frédéric 23 523
Raishō Nakajima see Nakajima Raishō
Rai Shunsui 17 237, 411, 412; 25 866
raising 4 850; 12 865; 16 363; 21 323, 324
Rai Singh, Maharaja of Bikaner (reg 1571-1611) (Rajput) 4 57
Raisio Church 11 98; 13 190
Raitenau, Wolf Dietrich von, Archbishop of Salzburg 25 867*; 27 664
architecture 2 780, 781
collections 2 829
decorative works 32 401
hardstones 27 815
paintings 17 719
pottery 27 665
silver 2 819
urban planning 27 660–61
Raiz, Abdelaziz ben 31 425
Raja, Ram see Raz, Ram
Rajab, Jehan 18 541
Rajab, Tareq al-Sayyid 18 541
Raja Budh Singh, Rao of Bundi (reg 1695-1739) (Rajput) 15 605
Raja Chandra, Ruler (reg 8th cent.) 1 15
Rajadhirajasimha, King of Kandy (reg 1782-98) 29 461
Rajagira Ghaznavid mosque 15 337
Rājagṛha see Rajgir
Rajahmundry 15 650
Rajaona 15 475
relief sculpture 15 476
Rajaraja I, Ruler (reg 985-1014) (Chola) 7 200*
architecture 15 305, 331, 332; 30 642
sculpture 15 516, 517, 518; 30 643
wall paintings 15 560
Rajaraja II (reg c. 1146-73) (Chola) 8 521; 15 518
Rajas, Pedro Albiniano de works 6 72
Rajasan 15 437
Rajasri Pattabhiramayyagaru 15 647
Rajavula 15 428
Raja Zahabuddin 20 172
Raje, Anant 15 169
Rajecka, Anna 12 203
Rajendra I, Ruler (reg 1012-44) (Chola) 7 200; 12 46; 15 333, 516, 518; 29 481
Rajendranagar 15 453
reliefs 15 452
Rajendravarman II, King of Cambodia (reg 944-68) 2 55; 5 469; 30 580
Rajewski, Czesław 14 819; 32 873
Rajgarh palace 15 371
Rajghat 15 261, 423, 424, 427; 31 902
Rajgir 15 194, 220, 279, 409; 25 867–8*
fortifications 15 248; 21 590
Maniyar Math 15 279–80, 452, 475
sculpture 15 423
Sonbhandar caves 15 475
stucco 29 824
Rajim 15 285; 25 868*
Rajivalochana Temple 15 283–4, 495
Rajk, Lászlo 14 891
Rajmahal 15 369
Sangi Dalan 15 370
Rajman, Antonin see Raymond, Antonin
Rajnapur Khinkhini 15 493
Rajniš, Martin 8 381
Rajon, Paul Adolphe 25 868*
Rajput 6 444; 12 75
Rajput (Amer) see:
Ishvari Singh, Maharaja
Jagat Singh, Maharaja
Jai Singh I, Raja
Jai Singh II, Raja
Madho Singh I, Maharaja
Man Singh, Raja
Pratap Singh, Maharaja
Ram Singh II, Maharaja
Rajput (Bikaner) see:
Anup Singh, Maharaja
Bhika, Rao

Rajput (Bikaner)—cont.
GAJ SINGH, Maharaja
GANGA SINGH, Maharaja
KARAN SINGH, Maharaja
RAI SINGH, Maharaja
SARADAR SINGH, Maharaja
SUJAN SINGH, Maharaja
ZORAWAR SINGH, Maharaja
Rajput (Bundi) *see*:
BHOJ, Rao
CHATARSAL, Rao
DEVA, Rao
RAJA BUDH SINGH, Rao
RATAN SINGH, Rao
UMAID SINGH, Rao
Rajput (Dig) *see*:
SURAJ MAL, Raja
Rajput (Ghanerao) *see*:
AJIT SINGH, Ruler
PADAM SINGH, Ruler
VIRAM DEV, Ruler
Rajput (Gwalior) *see*:
BIR SINGH DEO, Raja
KIRTTI SINGH, Raja
MAN SINGH TOMAR, Raja
Rajput (Indargarh) *see*:
INDAR SAL, Raja
Rajput (Kishangarh) *see*:
KALYAN SINGH, Raja
MOKAN SINGH, Raja
PRITHVI SINGH, Raja
RAJ SINGH, Raja
SAVANT SINGH, Raja
Rajput (Kota) *see*:
BHIM SINGH, Rao
RAM SINGH, Maharao
SHATRU SAL, Maharao
Rajput (Kachchh) *see*:
BHARMAL, Rao
DESALJI, Rao
Rajput (Marwar) *see*:
ABHAI SINGH, Maharaja
AJIT SINGH, Maharaja
BAKHAT SINGH, Maharaja
GAJ SINGH, Maharaja
JASWANT SINGH, Maharaja
JASWANT SINGH II, Maharaja
MAN SINGH, Maharaja
TAKHAT SINGH, Maharaja
Rajput (Mewar) *see*:
AMAR SINGH II, Rana
ARI SINGH, Rana
BHIM SINGH, Rana
FATEH SINGH, Rana
JAGAT SINGH I, Rana
JAGAT SINGH II, Rana
JAI SINGH, Rana
JAWAN SINGH, Rana
KUMBHA, Rana
RAJ SINGH I, Rana
RATAN SINGH, Rana
SAJJAN SINGH, Rana
SANGRAMA SINGH II, Rana
SARUP SINGH, Rana
UDAI, Rana
Rajput (Orchha) *see*:
BIR SINGH DEO, Raja
Rajput (Rawats of Deogarh) *see*:
GOKUL DAS II, Rawat
Rajput (Tomara) *see*:
ANANGAPALA, Ruler
Rajputana Museum of Archeology *see under* AJMER
(Chahamana) Rajputs *see* (CHAUHAN) RAJPUTS
(Chauhan) Rajputs **8** 676
(Sisodia) Rajputs **7** 175
(Tomara) Rajputs **8** 676; **13** 881
Rajshahi **3** *166*; **15** *279*; **25** 868*
College of Arts and Crafts **3** 169
Government College of Arts **3** 169
Raj Singh, Raja of Kishangarh (*reg* 1706-48) (Rajput) **15** 612
Raj Singh, Ruler (*reg* 1764-94) (Pahari) **6** 405
Raj Singh I, Rana of Mewar (*reg* 1652-80) (Rajput) **15** 599
Rakahanga **7** 790
Rakerspurga, Johannes Aquila de *see* JOHANNES AQUILA DE RAKERSPURGA
Rakgoathe, Dan **28** 602
Rakım, Mustafa *see* MUSTAFA RAQIM
Rakkolanjoki Ceramics Factory **11** 105, 106
Rakoathe, Dan(iel) **29** 110
Rákóczy (family) **15** 7
Rákóczy, Ferenc II, Prince of Transylvania *see* FERENC II RÁKÓCZY, Prince of Transylvania
Rákóczy, George I, Prince of Transylvania *see* GEORGE I RÁKÓCZY, Prince of Transylvania
Rakov, Mikhail (Dmitriyevich) **27** 422
Rakovszky, Géza **29** 606
Raku (family) **17** 242; **18** 552; **25** 869*
Rakuchū *see* KYOTO
Raku Dōn'yū **14** 704
Raku Ichinyū **25** 869
Raku Jōkei **14** 704
Raku ware *see under* POTTERY → wares
Rakuyō Sanjin *see* MARUYAMA ŌKYO
Ral Bhadar **15** 444
Ralegh, Walter **10** 162; **19** 143; **25** 277; **33** 146
Raleigh (NC)
Dorton Arena **23** *272*, 273; **29** 489; **30** 468
Livestock Pavilion *see* DORTON ARENA
Raleigh Ascension and Pentecost, Master of the **23** 526
Ralik **20** 479
Rallí, Aguiles **24** 511
Rällinge **32** 524
Ralph, Bishop of Bristol **18** 42
Ralston, W. C. **12** 221
Ram, Giovanni **12** 676
Ram, Gulabu **15** 621
Ram, Moti **15** 615
Ram, Udai **15** 615
Rama **15** 601
Rama I, King (*reg* 1782-1809) (Chakri) **3** 164; **28** 639; **29** 238; **30** 589, 592, 622
Rama III, King (*reg* 1824-51) (Chakri) **30** 589, 618
Rama IV *see* MONGKUT, King
Rama V *see* CHULALONGKORN, King
Rama VI, King (*reg* 1910-25) **30** 590, 601, 608
Rama IX *see* BHUMIBOL, King
Rama, Kristaq **1** 541; **14** 20; **25** 869*
Ramachandran, T. N. **15** 211
Ramacker, Henri *see* RAMAH
Ramad **25** 869–70*; **30** *180*
flax **1** 879
mud-bricks **30** 190
pottery **30** 196
skulls **30** 181
Rāmadāsa *see* RAMDAS
Ramaer, W. G. J., & Co. **22** 899; **23** 125
works **22** *900*
Ramage, John **25** 870*
Rāmagiri *see* RAMTEK
Ramagupta, Ruler (*reg c.* 376-80) (Gupta) **15** 467
Ramah (1887-1947) **5** 44
Ramah (NM), Navajo School **22** 671
Ramalho, António **25** 298, 870–71*
Ramalho Júnior, Joel **4** 715
Ramalho Ortigão, José Duarte **25** 298, 871*
Ramallah **16** 459
dresses **16** *460*
Ramana **2** 892
Ramanathapuram **15** 327
Ramalinga Vilas **15** 647
Ramannadesa **5** 225; **29** 231
Ramanujam **20** 54
Ramanzade, M. Yu. **2** 897
Ramat-Gan **17** 854
Ramathibodi I, King of Ayutthaya (*reg* 1351-69) **2** 883, 885, 887
Ramat Rahel **16** 573; **17** 552, 553
Ramavarma Kulashekhara, King (*reg* 1090-1102) (Kulashekhara) **25** 820
Ramay, Hanif **23** 800
Rambaldi, Carlo Antonio **5** 178
Rambaldoni, Vittore da *see* VITTORINO DA FELTRE
Rambeck, Aegidius **31** 574
Rambelli, Domenico **32** 405
Ramberg, Arthur von **17** 885; **29** 389
Ramberg, Johann Heinrich **9** 12; **10** 677; **25** 871–2*
works **10** *678*
Rambert Dance Company **30** 688
Rambervillers, Alphonse de **18** 836
Rambois, Achille **7** 326
Rambot, Jean-Claude **1** 497
Rambouillet **11** *504*; **25** 872*; **30** 878
Château **4** 301, 536, 537; **11** 592; **29** 834
Hôtel de Noailles **26** 449
Laiterie **8** 461; **10** 643; **11** 336; **13** 705; **17** 683; **22** 740; **26** 449; **28** 521, *522*; **30** 783
St Lubin **11** 522
Rambouillet, Marquise de **14** 790; **25** 872*
Rambouillet, Charles d'Angennes, Marquis de **25** 872
Ramboux, Johann Anton **22** 704; **25** 872–3*; **27** 346
Rambures **4** 780
Rambuteau, Comte de **24** 124, 125
Rambutyo Island **24** 82, 83
Ramdas **25** 873*
Ramdayal **15** 633
Ramdohr, Friedrich Wilhelm Basilius, Freiherr von **25** 873*
Rame, Delphine **15** 843
Rameau, Jean-Philippe **8** 533; **27** 264; **30** 672
Ramée, Daniel **10** 209; **28** 410
Ramée, Joseph **4** 302; **8** 727, 744; **25** 371, 873–4*
Ramelli, Agostino **30** 229
Ramelli, Felice **29** 887
Ramenghi, Bartolomeo *see* BAGNACAVALLO
Ramenghi, Giovanni Battista **3** 56
Ramerupt Church **13** 111
Rameses Wissa Wassef **30** 328
Rameshvara Durga Temple **15** 281
Ramesses I (*reg c.* 1292-*c.* 1290 BC) **9** *777*
Ramesses II (*reg c.* 1279-*c.* 1213 BC) **9** *777*, 859; **22** 722; **25** 874–5*
architecture **1** *95*, 95–6; **2** 155, 323; **9** 783, 835; **10** 803; **14** 462; **17** 714; **23** 279, 280, 807; **24** 840; **25** 776; **27** 813; **28** 494; **29** 386; **30** 692, 694, 695; **33** 481
military **9** 848; **21** 554
jewellery **5** 70; **10** 32
obelisks **23** 329; **30** 693
paintings **9** 805
wall **9** 903
reliefs **9** 864, 886; **30** 692
sculpture **9** 862, 863, 885; **10** 90, 97; **14** 403; **23** 280; **24** 840; **30** *297*, 433
shrines (i) (cult) **12** 227
temple **2** 657
Ramesses III (*reg c.* 1187-*c.* 1156 BC) **9** *777*; **24** 634; **25** 875*
architecture **9** 719, 825, 835, 848; **12** 174; **21** 554; **23** 807; **30** 696; **33** 246, 481
military **9** 848
dress **10** 75
furniture **10** 53
paintings **9** 805
wall **9** 807, 808, 811
reliefs **9** 886
stelae **12** 227
textiles **10** 44
Ramesses III, mortuary temple of *see under* THEBES (i) (EGYPT) → mortuary temples
Ramesses IV (*reg c.* 1156-*c.* 1150 BC) **9** *777*, 841, *885*; **10** 63, 80
paintings **9** 805
papyri **9** 805
sculpture **9** 885
tomb **10** *63*
Ramesses V (*reg c.* 1150-*c.* 1145 BC) **9** *777*; **10** 80
Ramesses VI (*reg c.* 1145-*c.* 1137 BC) **9** *777*, 805; **10** 80
Ramesses VII (*reg c.* 1137-*c.* 1126 BC) **9** *777*, 805, 860
Ramesses VIII (*reg c.* 1137-*c.* 1126 BC) **9** *777*
Ramesses IX (*reg c.* 1126-*c.* 1108 BC) **9** *777*, 805, 861, *903*; **10** 83
Ramesses X (*reg c.* 1108-*c.* 1104 BC) **9** *777*, 841
Ramesses XI (*reg c.* 1104-*c.* 1075 BC) **9** *777*, 841; **10** 32
Ramesseum *see under* THEBES (i) (EGYPT) → mortuary temples
Ramesseum Papyrus **4** *344*; **26** 557
Ramesuan, King of Ayutthaya (*reg* 1369-70; 1388-95) **2** 885
Rameswaram **15** *294*; **25** 876*
Ramalingeshvara Temple **15** 399
colonnade **15** 399, *400*
Ramey, Claude **11** 42; **17** 667; **21** 411; **25** 876*
Ramey, Etienne (-Jules) **1** 498; **8** 566; **22** 92; **24** 467; **25** 876*
Ramey, Jean **32** 114
Ramey, Jean-Etienne **12** 230
Ram factory **7** 552
Ramgarh **15** *285*; **25** 876–7*
Jogimara caves **32** 804
rock reliefs **25** 876
shrines (i) (cult) **25** 876–7
temples **15** 286
wall paintings **15** 611
Ramholz, Felix **22** 253
RAMI (Raggruppimento degli Architetti Moderni Italiani) **19** 304
rami (fibre) **17** 139, 312, 316, 354; **30** 538*
China **7** 43, 45
Japan **17** 139, 312, 316, *317*, 354
Korea **18** 358, 372, 373, 374, 375
Ramić, Afan **4** 461
Ramié, Georges **4** 700
Ram in the Thicket **21** 303
Ramírez (family) **25** 877*
Ramírez, Bernardo **13** 761; **25** 877*
Ramirez, Eduardo **4** 234
Ramirez, Francisco **18** 681
Ramírez (Benavides), José **1** 149; **25** 877*; **27** 819; **29** 293
Ramírez, José Manuel **2** 143; **13** 761; **25** 877*
Ramírez, Juan (1680-1739; sculptor) **25** 877; **27** 819
Ramírez, Juan (*fl* 1760s; painter) **25** 877
Ramírez, Juan (*d* 1782; architect) **25** 877
Ramirez, Juan Martin **20** 500
Ramírez, Jusepe **9** 5
Ramírez, Manuel **25** 877
Ramírez, Pedro **21** 383
Ramírez, Sebastián **25** 877
Ramírez, Sergio **23** 85, 86
Ramirez Amaya, Arnoldo **25** 877–8*
Ramírez Corría, Filiberto **8** 236
Ramírez de Arellano, Cristóbal **25** 878*
Ramírez de Espinosa, Gladys **23** 86
Ramirez di Montalvo (family) **1** 792; **11** 180
Ramírez Vázquez, Pedro **5** 603; **22** 314; **25** 878*
collaboration **18** 874; **22** 366
works **8** 65; **21** 380, *380*, 396, 404
Ramírez Villamizar, Eduardo **7** 609
Ramiro I, King of Asturias (*reg* 842-50) **2** 653, 654*
Ramiro II, King of León (*reg* 931-51) **19** 171; **22** 248
Ramjiawansingh, George **30** 16
Ramjidas **15** 610
Ram Jug **32** 66
Ram Jug Painter **13** 501; **32** 66*
Ramkhamhaeng, King of Sukhothai (*reg* 1279-1317) **28** 794; **29** 911
Ramkrishna **15** 633
Ramla **16** 208, 441; **17** 500
St John **17** 504, 506
Ramle **16** *565*
Ramler, Karl Wilhelm **21** 59
Ramm, Aleksandr **27** 441
Rammazijn, J. **14** 736
rammed earth *see* PISÉ DE TERRE
Rammelmayer, Adam **2** 802
Rammelsberg **4** 682, 685, 688
Ramnagar Sumari Temple **15** 405
Ramnathpur **15** 479
Ramo di Paganello **23** 585; **25** 879*
Ramón, Ricardo Bellver y *see* BELLVER Y RAMÓN, RICARDO
Ramon-Berengar IV, Count of Barcelona (*reg* 1131-62) **25** 57
Ramon de Mur **25** 879*
Ramón Ferrer, Usatges de **2** 476
Ramón y Cajal, Santiago **25** 879*
Ramos, Alfonso **19** 172
Ramos, Antonio de **20** 157
Ramos, Artur, Museu *see under* FORTALEZA
Ramos, Carlos (João Chambers) **8** 164; **25** 294, 879–80*
pupils **1** 752; **28** 812; **30** 375
Ramos, Emilio Guerrero y *see* GUERRERO Y RAMOS, EMILIO
Ramos, Federico Peralta *see* PERALTA RAMOS, FEDERICO
Ramos, Manuel de Morais de Silva *see* MORAIS DE SILVA RAMOS, MANUEL DE
Ramos, Mel **25** 232; **31** 608
Ramos, Nelson **25** 880–81*; **31** 756
Ramos, Pedro Ignacio **32** 176
Ramos, Peralta **2** 397
Ramos de Azevedo, Francisco de Paula *see* AZEVEDO, FRANCISCO DE PAULA RAMOS DE
Ramose **1** 505; **9** 839; **25** *880*, 881; **31** 107
architecture **1** 770
reliefs **9** 882, 884
wall paintings **9** 902
Ramos Martínez, Alfredo **1** 739; **6** 488; **10** 505; **25** 881*
Ramot **9** 543
Rampal *see* VIKRAMPUR
ramparts **4** 772; **21** 547, 565
Ancient Near East **4** 772
Canaanite **30** 185
Egypt **4** 772
Greece, ancient **4** 772
Rome, ancient **21** 559
Syria-Palestine **30** 185
Rampillon Church **13** 74

ramping arches *see under* ARCHES → types
Rampin Head **13** 470
Rampin Horseman **13** 430, 445
Rampin Master **13** 444
Ram Pottery **22** 884
ramps **12** 115, 124; **25** 761, 764
Rampurva
  pillar **15** 423
  sculpture **15** *413*, 415
rams **21** 556, 557
Rams, Dieter **15** 826
Ramsay, Allan (1686-1758) **28** 236, 274
Ramsay, Allan (1713-84) **1** 649; **25** 881–4*; **28** 274
  assistants **1** 504; **31** 139
  collaboration **13** 29
  methods **9** 211
  patrons and collectors **11** 362; **13** 637; **14** 144; **15** 29; **20** 910; **28** 269
  personal collection **28** 271
  pupils **20** 487; **22** 531; **26** 124
  reproductive prints by others **3** 259; **20** 487; **27** 463
  teachers **15** 54, 149; **29** 43
  works **9** 725; **10** 249; **11** *425*, 426, *427*; **22** 86; **25** *883*, *884*; **28** 235, *235*
  writings **14** 640
Ramsay, George, 4th Earl of Dalhousie (*d* 1696) **28** 252
Ramsay, George, 9th Earl of Dalhousie (*d* 1838) **5** 592
Ramsay, Hugh **25** 884*
Ramsay, James Andrew, 10th Earl of Dalhousie **28** 255
Ramsay, John **28** 271
Ramsay, M. A. **8** 501
Ramsay, Margaret **25** *883*
Ramsay, Robert **6** 455
Ramsay, Stanley C. **1** 163
Ramsay, William Mitchell **1** 520; **3** 628; **4** 67
Ramsbott, Wolfgang **18** 62, 436
Ramsbury (Wilts)
  Church of the Holy Cross **2** 71
  Manor **32** 818
Ramsden, Mel **2** 512
Ramsden, Omar **10** 336; **19** 594; **21** 324; **25** 885*
Ramsey, Agnes **25** 885
Ramsey, James **32** 903
Ramsey, John, I **23** 250
Ramsey, Ras Akyem **2** 152
Ramsey, William **19** 598, 610; **22** 220; **25** 885*
Ramsey Abbey (Cambs) **2** 66; **26** 661
  Lady **18** 622
  metalwork **13** 164, *164*
Ramsey Abbey Censer **23** 538
Ramsey Benedictional *see under* BENEDICTIONALS → individual manuscripts
Ramseyer, Walter **33** 736
Ramsey Psalter *see under* PSALTERS → individual manuscripts
Ramsgate (Kent), St Augustine **7** 254; **25** *714*, 715
Ramshaw, Wendy **10** 346
Ram Singh II, Maharaja of Jaipur (*reg* 1835-80) (Rajput) **15** 611
Ram Singh II, Maharao of Kota (*reg* 1827-66) (Rajput) **15** 606, 740
Ramsundsberget **32** 524
  memorial stones **32** *524*
Ramtek **15** 257, *285*, 317; **25** 885–6*
  Vishnu Trivikrama Temple **15** 463
Ramuicu Sarat Monastery **26** 713
Ramus, Marius **31** 382
Ramus, Pietro **10** 798
Ramusio, Giovanni Battista **23** 772
Ramuz, Charles Ferdinand **2** 700, 701; **12** 649
Ramwold, Abbot of St Emmeram **7** 513; **23** 652
Rana (family) **22** 785
Rana, Carlo Amedeo *see* RANA, CARLO ANDREA
Rana, Carlo Andrea **25** 886*
  works **25** *886*
Rana, Carlo Antonio *see* RANA, CARLO ANDREA
Rana, Juddha Shamsher **22** 776
Ranakpur **15** *276*, *279*, 314–15; **25** 886–7*
  Adinatha Temple **15** *314*, 314–15, 491
Ranaldi, Federico **24** 399
Ranasinghe, Tissa **29** 461–2
  works **29** *461*
Rana style **22** 764
Ranc, Antoine **25** 887, 895; **26** 385
Ranc, Jean **22** 35; **25** 887*; **29** 282
  collaboration **31** 229
  patrons and collectors **4** 558, 559, 635
  works **20** 67
Ranc, Luís Gil **13** 252
Rance Church **13** 113
Rancillac, Bernard **11** 552
Rand, John G. **23** 787
Rand, Paul **4** 369; **25** 353, 887–8*
Randai Nakamura *see* NAKAMURA, RANDAI
Randall, Alice *see* MARSH, ALICE
Randall-MacIver, David **13** 335
Randazzo, Filippo **27** 200
Randazzo, Ruggero de Luca di *see* RUGGERO DE LUCA DI RANDAZZO
Randel, Felix **10** 542
Randen, A. van den **30** 871
Randenbroek, Jacob van Campen, Lord of *see* CAMPEN, JACOB VAN
Randers **8** *720*
  Kunstmuseum **8** 759
Randolph, Benjamin **24** 602; **25** 888*; **31** 625
  works **17** 823; **24** 602
Random House **4** 367
Randon de Boisset, (Pierre-Louis-) Paul **13** 234; **25** 888*
  collections **3** 453; **11** 663; **20** 417
  decorative works **5** 380
  drawings **4** 517; **9** 229
  furniture **3** 414; **19** 115
Randoni, Carlo **16** 719
Ranefer **9** 855
  dress **10** *43*
Raneferef (*reg c.* 2419–*c.* 2416 BC) **1** 96; **9** *776*; **10** 47
Ranei Yamamoto *see* YAMAMOTO RANEI
Ranelagh, Richard Jones, 1st Earl of *see* JONES, RICHARD, 1st Earl of Ranelagh
Ranft, Richard **19** 490
Ranftbechern *see under* GLASSES → types
Ranftl, Johann **19** 339
Ranftl, Mathias **12** 842; **18** 419
Rang, Pierre **3** 585
Rangabé, A. **31** 25
raṅgamaṇḍapa **15** 244*
Rangamati **29** 824
Ranganatha Temple **29** 481–2
Rangdum **30** 819
Rangel, Sofí Imber de *see* IMBER DE RANGEL, SOFÍA
Ranger, Henry Ward **31** 141
Ranger, Ivan (Krstitelj) **8** 178; **25** 888*
Rangger, Johann *see* RANGER, IVAN (KRSTITELJ)
Ranghieri, Giovanni Battista **4** 286
Ranghieri, Raffaello **1** 35
Rang Mahal **15** 449, 460, 719
Rangone, Ercole, Cardinal **28** 334
Rangone, Tommaso **25** 888–9*
  architecture **27** 772
  paintings **28** 82; **31** *9*, 10
Rangone, Tommaso—cont.
  sculpture **32** 647
Rangoni, Claudio, Bishop of Piacenza **5** 854
Rangoon **5** *221*; **25** 889–90*; **29** *225*
  architecture **5** 237
  Buddhist Art Museum **29** 239
  ivory-carvings **5** 256
  National Museum **5** 241; **29** 239
  painting **5** 263
  sculpture **5** 242
  Shwe-dagon **5** 223, 234, 253, 261; **25** 889–90, *890*; **28** 639; **29** 866
    reliquaries **26** 150
  Sule Stupa **5** 224
  textiles **5** 248
  wood-carvings **5** 261
Rani Bhawani (Maratha) **31** 903
Rani Durgavati Museum *see under* JABALPUR
Ranieri, Niccolò **27** 785
Ranieri del Pace, Giovanni Battista **16** 674; **25** 890–91*
  patrons and collectors **21** 31
  teachers **27** 522
  works **27** *522*
Ranigat **15** *264*; **23** *797*; **25** 891*
Ranipur Jharial Temple **15** 505
Ranisch, Barthel **12** 224
Ranjha **15** 619, 632; **22** 439
Ranjit Singh, Maharaja (*reg* 1799-1839) (Sikh)
  architecture **1** 798; **15** 375; **18** 647; **31** 904
  throne **15** 707, *707*; **30** 785
Ranke, Hermann **10** 93
Rankei Dōryū **17** 408, 747, 748; **25** 891–2*
  works **17** *230*, 231
Ranken (family) **9** 726; **28** 259
Ranken, Frances **28** 259
Ranken, James **28** 259
Ranken, William Ford **28** 259
Rankoku *see* LANGU
Ranlett, William **15** 407
Rann, Charles **2** 395
Ranney, William Tylee **7** 840; **25** 892*; **31** 602; **33** 185
Rannie, James **7** 171
Ranong **30** 590
Ranpur **15** 635
  Jagannatha Temple **15** 395
Ransai Mori *see* MORI RANSAI
Ranseki Nakamura *see* NAKAMURA, RANSEKI
Ransen *see* TAKAHASHI YŪICHI
Ranshofen Abbey **2** 781
Ransome, Ernest L(eslie) **7** 693; **16** 55; **25** 892–3*; **26** 18
Ransome Engineering Company **7** 693
Ransome's Stone **29** 699
Ranson, France **25** 893
Ranson, Paul **11** 593; **25** 893*
  collaboration **4** 325
  groups and movements **8** 714; **22** 421, 422; **30** 169, 710
  patrons and collectors **4** 71
  productions **17** 449
  works **11** 419
Ranson, Pierre **7** 747; **26** 303
Ransonnette, Pierre-Nicolas **14** 790
Rantanen, Kirsti **11** 101
Rantei *see* SHIBA KŌKAN
Rantei Nagai *see* NAGAI RANTEI
Ranthanbor **21** 590
Räntz, Johann David **3** 428
Ranuccio *see* RAINERIUS
Ranuccio I, 4th Duke of Parma (*reg* 1592-1622) **10** 808
  architecture **1** 601; **3** 744; **22** 166; **24** 193
  paintings **28** 61; **29** 252
  sculpture **16** 697; **21** 754
Ranuccio II, 6th Duke of Parma (*reg* 1646-94) **10** 811–12*
  architecture **12** 23
  paintings **5** 850, 858; **7** 308; **21** 146; **26** 320; **31** 359, 524
Ranucius *see* RAINERIUS
Ranuzzi (family) **22** 27
Ranuzzi, Angelo Maria **25** 893
Ranuzzi, Annibale **21** 28
Ranuzzi, Giovanni Battista **25** 893
Ranuzzi, Girolamo **3** 129; **25** 893
Ranuzzi, Jacopo **32** 503
Ranuzzi, Marc Antonio **25** 893
Ranuzzi, Vincenzo, Cardinal **10** 488
Ranuzzi, Vincenzo Ferdinando **4** 46; **12** 30
Ranuzzi di Giovanni, Antonio **25** 893
Ranvoyzé, François **1** 785; **25** 894*
  works **5** 584, *585*
Ranworth (Norfolk) **10** 292
Ranzani, Rinaldo **8** 413
Ranzoni, Daniele **25** 894–5*
  dealers **13** 714
  groups and movements **16** 678; **28** 34
  teachers **3** 857
  works **25** *894*
Rao (people) **24** 80
Rao, Shikarpur Ranganath **19** 708
Rao, T. A. Gopinatha **15** 211
Rao Jie **6** 756
Rao Jodha, Maharaja of Marwar (*reg* 1458-89) (Rajput) **17** 599
Raonić, Milan **22** 18
Raos, Peter **23** 70
Raoul de Ferrières **10** 665
Raoul de Montreuil **24** 774
Raoul de Nesle **14** 418
  works **14** *418*
Raoul de Senlis **3** 460
Raoul du Mont, Abbot of Mont-Saint-Michel **22** 41
Raoulina, Theodora *see* THEODORA RAOULINA
Raoux, Jean **25** 895*
  attributions **13** 666
  patrons and collectors **4** 331; **5** 9; **22** 35
  reproductive prints by others **3** 463
  teachers **4** 536
  works **22** 34
Rao Ziran **6** 798; **19** 857
Rapa **23** *711*; **25** 896*
  adzes **25** 896
  baskets **25** 896
  fortifications **25** 896
  pounders **25** *896*, 896
  stone **25** *896*
  see also AUSTRAL ISLANDS
Rapanui **9** 674
Raper, William **9** 374
rapeseed oil *see under* OILS → types
Raphael **2** 161, 162, 319; **9** 7, 8; **11** 839; **13** 605; **14** 869; **16** 614, 661, 662, 663, 766; **21** 16; **24** 520; **25** 71, 896–910*; **26** 187–8, 769; **27** 790; **31** 740
  architecture **2** 313; **9** 181
    churches **16** 632; **20** 865; **25** 227, 766; **26** 187, 805; **27** 653
    palazzi **4** 649; **16** 634; **23** 836; **27** 740, 746
    stucco **16** 712
    theatres **30** 655
    villas **12** 752; **16** 633; **25** *907*; **32** 546
  assistants **29** 853; **31** 523
    Bagnacavallo (1484-1542) **3** 56
    Baviera **3** 419
    Colle, Raffaello (di Michelangelo di Luca) dal **7** 560
    Dossi, Battista **9** 187
Raphael
  assistants—cont.
    Evangelista di Pian di Meleto **10** 654
    Giulio Romano **12** 749
    Penni, Giovan Francesco **24** 365
    Peruzzi, Baldassare **24** 529
    Sangallo, Antonio da (ii) (1483-1546) **26** 805; **27** 742
    Sangallo, Giovan Francesco da **27** 746
    Tamagni, Vincenzo **30** 281
    Udine, Giovanni da **31** 523
  attributions **19** 25; **20** 453; **22** 21
    drawings **13** 837
    frescoes **3** 203; **24** 365
    paintings **3** 179, 305; **4** 330, 807; **10** 530; **11** 744; **12** 911; **14** 805; **19** 300; **22** 58, 314, 338; **25** 729; **28** 5; **31** 524
  cartoons **5** 47, 656, *898*, 899; **6** 470, 515; **8** 613; **10** 368; **13** 219, 646; **21** 16; **22** 153; **25** *379*, *902*; **26** 816
  catalogues **6** 78–9
  collaboration **6** 39; **12** 656, 750; **23** 492; **24** 525–7, 831; **26** 228; **27** 776
  commentaries **3** 674
  copies **12** 638
  dealers **5** 71; **10** 660; **14** 109
  drawings **6** 569; **9** 220; **25** 558, *909*
    allegorical **10** 130; **29** *883*
    architectural **2** 328, 329
    mythological **10** 130, 476
    nude figures **21** 758
    religious **21** *763*
    silverpoints **9** 216
  exhibitions **27** 171
  forgeries by others **11** 307
  frames **11** *396*, 401, 487
  gardens **12** 115
  groups and movements **10** 95; **20** 281; **26** 182, 186, 189
  house **2** 547, 550; **4** 2, 650
  methods **1** 841; **5** 898; **11** *763*; **19** 354; **21** 758, 763, 764, 765; **24** 492; **25** 379; **29** 884; **32** 805
  mosaics **22** 158, *158*, 163
  paintings **7** 380; **16** 694
    frescoes **25** 191
      bathroom of Cardinal Bibbiena (Vatican Palace, Rome) **10** 477
      Galleria Farnese (Palazzo Farnese, Rome) **15** 137
      Loggie of Leo X (Vatican Palace, Rome) **13** 700; **16** *664*, 664–5; **26** 818; **29** 747
      S Maria della Pace (Rome) **6** 583
      S Severo (Perugia) **24** 520
      Stanza d'Eliodoro (Vatican Palace, Rome) **25** 858; **26** 818, *818*
      Stanza d'Eliodoro **26** *818*
      Stanza dell'Incendio (Vatican Palace, Rome) **16** 614; **25** *901*
      Stanza della Segnatura (Vatican Palace, Rome) **1** 655, 663; **7** 383; **14** 868; **20** 278; **22** 413; **26** 817; **29** 2
      Villa Farnesina (Rome) **16** 633; **22** 413, *413*; **25** 71; **32** 549
    panel
      allegorical **1** 656, *656*; **25** *898*
      altarpieces **1** 711; **4** 276; **6** 583; **14** 582; **24** 527; **26** 842
      landscape **18** 705
      mythological **28** 332
      portraits **4** 2; **6** 39; **9** 142; **11** *401*; **14** 869; **21** *16*, 18; **25** 282, *905*; **30** 781, 783
      predellas **25** 464

Raphael
paintings
panel—cont.
religious **3** 858; **9** 188; **10** 476; **11** 186; **20** 278; **25** *897*, *900*, *903*; **27** 496; **30** 427; **31** 448
patrons and collectors **8** 83; **10** 365, 530; **11** 789; **16** 763, 769; **25** 137; **30** 274
Accademia de San Luca (Rome) **13** 275
Alba, Duques de **1** 528
Alcalá, 3rd Duque de (1583-1637) **26** 307
Aldobrandini (family) **9** 175
Alexander II, Emperor of Russia (*reg* 1855-81) **26** 734
Alfonso I, 3rd Duke of Ferrara, Modena and Reggio (*reg* 1505-34) **10** 522; **29** 860
Alfonso III, 7th Duke of Modena and Reggio (*reg* 1628-9) **10** 525
Altoviti, Bindo **1** 734
Angerstein, John Julius **2** 51
Antaldi, Antaldo, Marchese **33** 345
Arconati, Galeazzo (Maria), Conte **2** 376
Augustus III, King of Poland (*reg* 1733-63) **3** 924; **12** 473; **14** 314; **30** 859; **33** 115
Aumale, Henri-Eugène-Philippe-Louis de Bourbon, Duc d' **23** 523
Baglioni, Atalanta di Galeotto **3** 55
Baglioni, Leandra di Braccio **3** 55
Baglioni, Maddalena **3** 55
Baring, Thomas (i) (1772-1848) **3** 239
Beckford, William (1760-1844) **3** 477
Bembo, Pietro, Cardinal **3** 698
Borghese, Scipione, Cardinal **4** 406
Borromeo, Federico, Cardinal **4** 426
Bossi, Giuseppe **4** 470
Boulle, André-Charles **4** 531
Bouverie, John **4** 596
Bracciano, Livio Odescalchi, Duca di **23** 353
Butler, Charles (1822-1910) **5** 311
Canossa, Girolamo **32** 343
Carpio, Gaspar de Haro y Guzmán, 7th Marqués del **5** 845
Carpio, Luis Méndez de Haro y Guzmán, 6th Marqués del **5** 844
Charles I, King of England and Scotland (*reg* 1625-49) **2** 558; **10** 363; **23** 326; **29** 800, 801
Chigi, Agostino (i) (1466-1520) **6** 583; **24** 530; **26** 759, 769
Christina, Queen of Sweden (*reg* 1632-54) **32** 8
Churchill, John, 1st Duke of Marlborough **4** 137
Clement VII, Pope (*reg* 1523-34) **10** 675; **21** 17
Coke, Thomas, 1st Earl of Leicester of the 1st creation (1697-1759) **9** 26
Cowper, George Nassau Clavering, 3rd Earl **8** 83
Créquy, Charles de Blanchefort de **19** 238
Cromwell, Oliver **8** 186
Crozat, Pierre **8** 209
Czartoryska, Isabella, Princess (1746-1835) **8** 372
Czartoryski (family) **25** 138
Delessert, (Jules-Paul-) Benjamin (1773-1847) **8** 664

Raphael
patrons and collectors—cont.
Denon, (Dominique-) Vivant **8** 764
Díaz, Diego Valentín **8** 858
Dimsdale, Thomas **8** 901
Duarte, Diego **9** 311
Dürer, Albrecht (1471-1528) **9** 229
Egerton, Francis, 3rd Duke of Bridgewater **9** 755
Ercolani, Vincenzo, Conte **7** 890; **10** 446
Faesch, Johann Jakob **10** 753
Fesch, Joseph, Cardinal **11** 32
Feuchère, Jean-Jacques **11** 42
Flinck, Nicolaes Anthonis **11** 170
Francis I, King of France (*reg* 1515-47) **11** 661; **31** 849
Fries, Moritz, Graf von **11** 789
Galleria Nazionale delle Marche (Ubino) **31** 740
Galleria degli Uffizi, (Florence) **25** 691
Gardner, Isabella Stewart **12** 147
Gemäldegalerie Alte Meister (Dresden) **9** 239
Giustiniani (i), Vincenzo, Marchese **12** 763
Godoy (y Alvárez de Faria), Manuel, Príncipe de la Paz **12** 839
Grimani, Domenico, Cardinal, Patriarch of Aquilea **13** 657
Guidobaldo I, 2nd Duke of Urbino (*reg* 1482-1508) **22** 13
Hamilton, James, 3rd Marquess and 1st Duke of Hamilton **10** 861
Henry VII, King of England (*reg* 1485-1509) **31** 413
Herbert, Philip, 4th Earl of Pembroke and 1st Earl of Montgomery **14** 435
Hermitage Museum (St Petersburg) **7** 579
Hervey, Frederick Augustus, 4th Earl of Bristol **14** 485
Howard (i), Thomas, 2nd Earl of Arundel **14** 806, 807
Jabach, Everard **16** 815
Joachim Murat, King of Naples (*reg* 1808-15) **22** 338
John William, Elector Palatine (*reg* 1690-1716) **12** 473; **21** 31
Josephine, Empress of the French (1763-1814) **4** 304
Julius II, Pope (*reg* 1503-13) **7** 218; **16** 664, 763; **26** 769; **27** 272, 273
Lagoy, Marquis de **18** 641
Las Marismas del Guadalquivir, Alejandro María Aguado y Ramírez de Estemoz, Marqués de **18** 811
Lawrence, Thomas **18** 895
Lely, Peter **19** 124
Lempereur, Jean-Denis, II **19** 144
Leo X, Pope (*reg* 1513-22) **16** 768; **21** 16
Ligne, Charles-Joseph-Emmanuel de, Prince (1759-92) **19** 369
Louis XIV, King of France (*reg* 1643-1715) **4** 552
Ludwig I, King of Bavaria (*reg* 1825-48) **12** 476
Mariette, Pierre-Jean **20** 417
Marolles, Michel de **20** 455
Mazarin, Jules, Cardinal **11** 662; **20** 896
McLellan, Archibald **28** 271
Medici, Ferdinando de', Grand Prince of Tuscany (1663-1713) **21** 30

Raphael
patrons and collectors—cont.
Medici, Giovanni Carlo de', Cardinal (1611-63) **21** 27
Medinaceli, Luís de la Cerda Fernández de Córdoba Folch de Cardona y Aragón, 9th Duque de (1660-1711) **21** 35
Mellon, Andrew W(illiam) **2** 560; **18** 161; **21** 90
Miles, Philip John **21** 541
Mond, Ludwig **21** 849
Morgan, J(ohn) Pierpont (1837-1913) **22** 112
Musée du Louvre (Paris) **11** 665
Museo Nacional de Bellas Artes (Santiago) **6** 601
Museu Nacional de Arte Antiga (Lisbon) **4** 638
National Gallery (London) **5** 283; **8** 582
Niccolini (family) **23** 87
Orléans, Philippe II de Bourbon, 2nd Duc d' (1674-1723) **23** 515
Orsini, Fulvio **23** 577
Ottley, William Young **23** 634
Paignon-Dijonval **23** 777
Pandolfini, Giannozzo, Bishop of Tróia **24** 1
Philip IV, King of Spain (*reg* 1621-65) **14** 8; **29** 352
Poggi, Antonio Cesare **10** 531
Poniatowski, Stanisław, Prince **25** 213
Rangone, Tommaso **25** 889
Reynolds, Joshua **26** 280
Roannez, Claude Gouffier, 1st Duc de **13** 224
Robinson, John Charles **26** 473
Rogers, Samuel **26** 541
Röver, Valerius **27** 270
Ruffo, Tommaso, Cardinal, Archbishop of Ferrara **27** 316
Rushout, John, 2nd Baron Northwick **27** 350
Salamanca (y Mayol), José, Marqués de **27** 607
Solly, Edward **29** 46
Somerset, Henry, 3rd Duke of Beaufort (1707-49) **13** 301
Taddei, Taddeo **30** 231
Tallard, Marie-Joseph d'Hostun, Duc de **30** 274
Tessin, Carl Gustav, Count **30** 524
Udney, John **31** 525
Udney, Robert **31** 524
Uffelen, Lucas van **31** 526
Vatican Museums **7** 726
Villiers, George, 1st Duke of Buckingham (1592-1628) **32** 575
Vincenzo I, 4th Duke of Mantua (*reg* 1587-1612) **12** 912
Viti, Timoteo **9** 229
Waldegrave, William, 1st Baron Radstock **32** 774
Wellesley, Henry **33** 56
Wicar, Jean-Baptiste (-Joseph) **9** 229; **33** 154
Widener, Joseph E. **33** 159
William II, King of the Netherlands (*reg* 1840-49) **23** 469; **33** 345
Wright, John Michael **33** 409
personal collection **32** 641
photographed works **26** 233
pupils **12** 749; **20** 1; **24** 365, 419; **25** 148; **32** 586
reproductions in ceramics **16** 734
reproductions in tapestry **1** 671; **11** 48
reproductions on fans **10** 781
reproductions on porcelain **2** 817; **17** 445
reproductions on postage stamps **25** 329

Raphael—cont.
reproductive prints by others **10** 487; **12** 203; **20** 502; **25** 596, 625; **26** 230; **27** 502; **32** 689
Alberti, Cherubino **1** 551
Angolo del Moro, Battista dell' **2** 88
Audran, Girard **2** 708
Badalocchio, Sisto **3** 32
Bartoli, Pietro Sante **3** 294
Beatrizet, Nicolas **3** 448
Bergeret, Pierre-Nolasque **3** 775
Bernard, Jacques-Samuel **3** 813
Biard, Pierre (ii) (1592-1661) **3** 925
Bonnet, Louis-Marin **4** 330
Borgianni, Orazio **4** 413
Bos, Balthazar van den **4** 442
Bos, Jacob(us) **4** 443
Boucher-Desnoyers, Auguste-Gaspard-Louis **26** 232
Caraglio, Giovanni Jacopo **5** 699
Carpi, Ugo da **26** 229; **33** 366
Chaperon, Nicolas **6** 461
Chasteau, Guillaume **6** 502
Chéreau, François, I (1680-1729) **6** 548
Cock, Hieronymus (Wellens) **7** 499
Cort (van Hoorn), Cornelis **7** 899
Dente, Marco **8** 765
Dorigny, Nicolas **9** 176
Duchange, Gaspard **9** 362
Dupuis, Nicolas-Gabriel **9** 407
Foggo, George **11** 235
Forster, François **11** 319
Gaillard, Ferdinand **26** 233
Gautier-Dagoty, Edouard **12** 209
Ghisi, Giorgio **12** 558
Goltzius, Hendrick **12** 881
Granges, David des **13** 309
Gregori, Ferdinando **13** 625
H.F.E., Master **20** 796
Hogenberg, Franz **14** 644
Kirkall, Elisha **25** 622
Lanfranco, Giovanni **18** 730
Lélu, Pierre **19** 119
Lépicié, (François-) Bernard **19** 216
Longhi, Giuseppe **19** 636
Musi, Agostino dei **22** 369
Parmigianino **10** 550
Perrier, François **24** 476
Poilly, François de **25** 77
Raimondi, Marcantonio **10** 385; **23** 292, *292*; **25** *858*, 859–60, *904*
Rota, Martino **27** 212
Rousselet, Gilles **27** 269
Ruscheweyh, Ferdinand **27** 346
Sadeler, Aegidius, II (1570-1629) **27** 504
Selma, Fernando **28** 389
Strixner, Johann Nepomuk **29** 776
Vázquez, Bartolomé **32** 99
Vico, Enea **32** 412
Villamena, Francesco **32** 560
Volpato, Giovanni **32** 689
Vorsterman, Lucas, (i) (*c.* 1595-1675) **32** 699
Vuibert, Rémy **32** 738
restorations by others **1** 532; **21** 825; **24** 730; **25** 644
sculpture **6** 583; **16** 693
stage design **21** 16; **30** 656
tapestries **10** 275, *350*; **12** 829; **14** 416; **16** 757; **19** 834; **30** 315
teachers **24** 520, 527
workshop **11** *761*; **13** *669*; **29** 830, 853
writings **23** 486
Raphael, Antonietta **20** 82; **25** 910*
groups and movements **16** 681; **26** 777; **28** 212, 319
works **16** 708

Raphael, Flora *see* DAVID-WEILL, FLORA
Raphael, Max **2** 536–7; **19** 809; **20** 527; **28** 926
Raphael, William **22** 38
Raphelengius, Franciscus (1539-97) **16** 360
Raphina **14** *332*, 335, 338
Rapho **4** 642; **9** 71
Raphon, Hans **20** 683; **26** 1*
Rapicano, Cola **1** 127; **10** 868; **20** 144; **26** 1–2*
Rapicano, Filippo **26** 2
Rapicano, Nardo **20** 144; **26** 2
Rapid, Grip & Batten **7** 648
Rapid City (SD), Sioux Indian Museum **22** 650
rapiers **2** 453, 454, *454*, 455, 456, *456*
Rapilly, Michel **10** 823; **16** 905
Rapin, Alphonse **8** 57
Rapin, Henri **11** 602; **24** 475; **28** 525
Rapin, René **12** 122
Rapin Toyras, Paul de **32** 378
Rapisardi, Gaetano **24** 694
Rapiza, Beno de *see* BENO DE RAPIZA
Rapiza, Maria de *see* MARIA DE RAPIZA
Raponde, Dino **5** 208, 209
Raponde, Jacques **5** 208, 209; **7** 525
Rapoport, Yu. A. **31** 157
Raposo, Francisco António **25** 311
Raposo, José Aniceto **25** 307; **26** 2*
Raposo, José Maria **26** 2
Raposo, Romão José Aniceto **26** 2
Rapotec, Stanislaus **30** 160
Rapous, Michele Antonio **16** 719
Rapp, Cornelius **31** 596
Rapp, George **31** 596
Rapp, Heinrich **19** 483
Rapp, Isaac Hamilton **22** 568
Rappard, Anthon (Gerhard Alexander) van **26** 2*
Rapp Buri, Anna **30** 332
rappel à l'ordre **8** 246; **25** 739
Rappenau Staatssalinen **10** 748
Rapperswil Polenmuseum **25** 138, 139
Rappolstein, Eberhard von **4** 746
Rapson, Ralph **21** 650; **27** 475
Raqchi Temple **29** 167; **30** 447
Raqim, Mustafa *see* MUSTAFA RAQIM
Raqqa **16** *104*, 151; **23** 815; **26** 2–3*
Baghdad Gate **16** 153; **21** 583
ceramics **1** 877
congregational mosque **16** 180
glass **16** 519
houses **16** 152
mosaics **16** 256
pottery **16** 395, 396, 397, 406, 407
Raqqada **16** 156, 157, 403
Palace *see under* KAIROUAN → Musée d'Art Islamique
Ráquira **7** 603
Raritan Formation (NJ) **31** 635
Rarotonga **7** 790, 791
Ras **28** 454
fortress **28** 439, 440
St George **28** 445
St Peter **28** 445
Ra's al-Hamra **2** *246*, 248, 263, 266
Ra's al-Khayma (city) **2** *246*, 248
Ra's al-Khayma (emirate) Museum **2** 275
see also UNITED ARAB EMIRATES
Ra's al-Khayma (city) **31** 584
Museum **31** 585
Rasappa *see* RUSAFA
Rasbo **30** 83
Rasbokil **30** 76
Rasbo Master **30** 83

Rasbourgh, Antoine Van *see* VAN RASBOURGH, ANTOINE
Rascas, Pierre-Antoine de, Sieur de Bagarris *see* BAGARRIS
Rasch, Anthony **10** 851
Raschdorff, Julius (Carl) **26** 3*
assistants **33** 173
groups and movements **26** 190
patrons and collectors **14** 656
pupils **28** 192
works **3** 793, 794; **7** *582*, 582; **12** 376; **13** 717; **25** 368
Rascher, Johannes **9** 237
Rascol, V. L. **19** 847
Rasguniae *see* MATIFOU
Rashid (Egypt) **27** 593; **32** 313
Rashid (*fl c.* 1675-95) **15** 608
al-Rashid, Sultan (*reg* 1664-72) ('Alawi) **11** 49; **16** 240
Rashid al-Din **26** 3–4*
architecture **16** 92, 193, 194; **30** 223
manuscripts **16** 272, 303, 313, 314–15, *315*
works **15** 133
writings **16** 193, 443; **21** 875
Rashid Oraifi **3** 69
Rashid Swar **3** 69
Rasht **16** 450; **24** 252
Rashtrakuta **10** 147; **15** 278; **26** 4*
see also:
AMOGHAVARSHA I, Ruler
DANTIDURGA, Ruler
GOVINDA III, Ruler
KRISHNA I, Ruler
KRISHNA III, Ruler
Rašica, Božidar **8** 179; **10** 667
Rasidany **20** 36
Rasier (family) **3** 598
Rasier, Theodoor, I **3** 598
Rasiere, Laurent de **20** 81
Rasina, Pietro **26** 827
Rasinas, Juan **32** 821
Rasines, Juan de **29** 265
Rasinius
works **27** *107*
raslin *see* KAOLIN
Rasmussen, Arne Bruun **8** 759
Rasmussen, Krohn & Hartvig **3** 68; **14** 690
Rasmussen, Mads **8** 758; **24** 549
Rasmussen, Steen Eiler **8** 727, 760; **26** 4–5*; **29** 77
works **29** 77
Rasmussen, (Robert) Wilhelm **23** 230; **26** 5*
Raspal, Antoine **26** 57
Raspall (i Mayol), Manuel Joaquim **26** 5–6*
Raspantino, Francesco **9** 92
Rasparini, Giorgio **8** 158
Raspe, R. E. **30** 356
Raspopović, Ivanka **28** 445
Rass, Johann Martin **25** 673; **33** 286
al-Rassam, Abdul Qadir **16** 1
Rassam, Hormuzd
excavations
Assur **2** 636
Babylon **3** 9
Balawat **1** 892; **21** 298
Borsippa **4** 437
Nimrud **21** 298; **23** 150
Nineveh **1** 892; **21** 301; **23** 154
Sippar **28** 782, 783
Toprakkale (Armenia) **31** 158
Rassam Obelisk **21** 298
Rassegna d'arte **20** 158; **24** 448
Rassegna d'arte antica e moderna **24** 448
Rassenfosse, Armand **10** 559, 563; **25** 347; **26** 6*; **27** 140
Rastafarianism **16** 881
Rastatt **27** 196; **33** 594
Rastawiecki, Edward **7** 837; **25** 138, 143, 675
Rastell, John **22** 369
Rastic, Simun *see* SIMUN RASTIC
Rastorguyev, Mikhail **27** 586
Rāṣṭrakūṭa *see* RASHTRAKUTA
Rastrelli, Bartolomeo Carlo **8** 709; **26** 6–7*; **27** 389
assistants **12** 636
collaboration **26** 7
patrons and collectors **24** 546
pupils **26** 7
works **19** 563; **23** 26; **24** 546; **27** 406, 585; **30** 485
Rastrelli, Bartolomeo Francesco **26** 7–9*
architecture
cathedrals **26** *9*; **27** 374
churches **18** 35, *36*
hermitages **25** 746
markets **31** 827
monasteries **27** 586
palaces **5** 520; **18** 35, 36, 543, *848*, 849; **19** 17; **21** 475; **24** *547*; **25** 745, *745*; **27** 374, 585, *585*; **33** 633
pavilions (buildings) **12** 134; **26** *8*
assistants **10** 876
attributions **23** 270; **27** 401
collaboration **26** 6; **28** 41; **31** 552
furniture **27** *406*
groups and movements **26** 498; **27** 407, 575
interior decoration **24** 546; **27** 401–2; **29** 555
patrons and collectors **17** 472; **26** 729, 731; **27** 438, 585; **29** 778; **32** 697
restorations by others **27** *402*, 586
Rasul, Ghulam **23** 800, 801
Rasulid **26** 9–10*; **33** 584
Ras Welde Sellasé **10** 572
Rataba, Tell el- **9** 848; **25** 875
Ratabon, Antoine de **20** 134
Ratak **20** 479
Ratan, Tepe **29** 825
Ratanapunja *see* MANDALAY
Ratan Singh, Rana of Mewar (*reg* 1528-31) (Rajput) **7** 175
Ratan Singh, Rao of Bundi (*reg* 1607-31) (Rajput) **5** 171; **15** 604
Ratanvadi Amriteshvara Temple **15** 316
Ratchaburi Wat Phra Si Ratana Mahathat **30** 581
Ratchis altar **16** 687
Ratcliffe, William (Whitehead) **5** 516, 517; **26** 10*
Ratcliff Glasshouse **19** 595
Ratdolt, Erhard
methods **12** 386; **25** 622
printmakers **5** 198
woodcuts **4** *345*, 759; **7** 189; **21** 730; **32** 198; **33** 349, 353, 365
Rateau, Armand-Albert **11** 583, 629
works **11** *583*
Ratel *see* WEENIX, JAN BAPTIST
Ratensky, Pyotr **31** 557
Ratés, José de *see* RATÉS DALMAU, JOSÉ
Rates, S Pedro **25** 289, 300; **26** 611
Ratés Dalmau, José **7** 287; **26** 10*; **29** 292
Ratgar **26** 10–11*
Ratgeb, Jerg **26** 11*
works **11** 735; **12** 387; **26** *11*
Rath, Hans Harald **19** 522
Rath, Harald **19** 523
Rath, Marianne **19** 522
Rath, Musée *see under* GENEVA
Rath, Peter **19** 523
Rath, Stefan (i) (1876-1960) **19** 522
Rath, Stefan (ii) (1943-) **19** 523
ratha *see* BHADRA
Rathbone, Harold **26** 12
Rathbone, P(hilip) H(enry) **26** 12*
Rathbone, Richard Llewellyn **29** 484
Rathbone, William **27** 161
Rathenau, Emil **2** 566; **15** 823, 824; **26** 18; **28** 192
Rathenau, Walter **22** 291
rathikā **15** 244*
Ratia, Armi **11** 110
Ratier, Emile **2** 516
Ratingen **10** 748
ratiocinatio **13** 467
Rational Dress Society (London) **9** 290
rationales **32** 387, 388*
Rationalism (i) (architectural theory) **9** 705; **20** 846; **23** 764; **26** 12–14*
churches **26** *13*
Rationalism (ii) (style) **18** 619; **26** 14–16*
Italy *see* RAZIONALISMO
Russia **5** 333; **18** *620*
Spain **29** 273, *274*
Ukraine **31** 552
rationalized construction *see under* ARCHITECTURE → techniques
ratios *see* PROPORTIONS
Ratisbonne, Louis **11** 799
Ratlam **15** 702
Ratmann Missal *see under* SACRAMENTARIES → individual manuscripts → Ratmann Sacramentary
Ratmannsdorf, Schloss *see* SCHLOSS RATMANNSDORF
Ratnagiri **5** 96, 226; **15** *276*, 505; **26** 20*
Ratna Kanwar **16** 871
Ratnapura (Burma) *see* AVA
Ratnapura (Sri Lanka) **29** *440*
National Museum **29** 478
Ratnapura Beds **29** 444
Ratnavibhushana, Anura **29** 456
Ratna Warta **15** 809
Ratner, Eugene **26** 20*
Ratner, Yohanan *see* RATNER, EUGENE
Ratners **19** 594
Rato, Moreia **25** 302
Rato factory *see* REAL FÁBRICA DO RATO
Ratsep, Nina **18** 799
Ratshof **8** 824
rats' whiskers *see under* HAIR → types
Ratta (family) **5** 281
Ratta, Dionigio **5** 853, 854
Ratta, Marchese **32** 402
rattan *see* CANE
Rattenbury, Francis Mawson **26** 21*; **32** 414
collaboration **5** 572; **20** 30; **32** 414
works **5** 562; **6** 513; **10** 459; **31** 863
Rattenbury, James **19** 287
Ratti (company) **16** 753
Ratti, Carlo Giuseppe **26** 21*
personal collection **2** 125
works **24** 203; **29** 75
Ratti, Giovanni Agostino **26** 21
rattles
historical and regional traditions
Indonesia **15** 817
Java **15** 817
Korea **18** 346, *346*
Mesoamerica, Pre-Columbian **21** 256
Native North Americans **22** 613
Prehistoric art **22** 372
Sumatra **15** 817
materials
bamboo **15** 817
bronze **18** 346, *346*
coral **7** 835
gourds **21** 256
metal **22** 613
terracotta **21** 256
Rattlesnake *see under* SHIPS → named vessels
Rattner, Abraham **31** 660
Ratton, Charles **1** 438; **10** 91
Rat-trap bond *see under* BONDING
Rattu **15** 633
Rättvik **30** 116
Ratz, Peter **23** 311
works **23** *311*
Ratzeburg Cathedral **4** 776; **12** 403; **25** 551
Ratzel, F. (*fl* 1885-8) **1** 235
Ratzel, Friedrich (1869-1907) **17** 818
Ratzersdorfer, Herman **17** 527; **26** 191, 227
Ratzko, Peter *see* RATZ, PETER
Rau, Charles **8** 282
Rau, (Heinrich) Heinz **26** 21–2*, 286
Rau, Leopold **5** 57
Rauch, Christian Daniel **26** 22–4*; **28** 45
assistants **18** 89
collaboration **28** 98; **30** 854; **33** 154
groups and movements **3** 799
patrons and collectors **12** 406, 476
pupils **1** 119, 212; **3** 497; **4** 114; **6** 92; **9** 210; **12** 406; **26** 377; **29** 86, 609; **33** 295, 296, 391
staff **17** 739
teachers **12** 406; **28** 45
works **3** 807; **8** 531; **9** 444; **18** 123; **22** 47; **26** *23*; **28** 44, 98; **29** 566, 609; **33** 282
Rauch, E.
works **12** *167*
Rauch, Jakob **10** 858, 860; **11** 127; **26** 24*
Rauch, John **32** 234–6
Rauch, Josef **14** 632
Rauch, Leopold **22** 205
Rauchfas, Johannes **17** 480
Rauchmiller, Mathias **2** 827; **26** 24–5*
collaboration **32** 442
teachers **28** 76
works **2** 801; **4** 843; **8** 385; **12** 405; **26** *25*
Raucourt de Charleville, Antoine **14** 863
Raud, Kristjan **10** 539; **26** 25–6*; **33** 566
Raud, Paul **10** 539; **26** 26*
Raude, de *see* RHO
Raudsepp, Juhan **10** 542
Rauenstein **30** 793
Raulin **28** 136
Raulin, Gustav-Laurent **14** 458
Rauline, H.-P.-M. **1** 14
Raúl Leoni reservoir, Sun Tower **32** 176
Rauma **11** *87*
Franciscan church **11** 94
Raum und Handwerk **14** 312
Raunio, Ilpo **24** 892
Raupp, Karl **16** 874; **17** 826
Rauric, Bernat **20** 515
Rausch, Ferenc **15** 17
Rauschenberg, Robert **23** 49; **26** 26–9*; **31** 608, 614
collaboration **8** 270; **20** 605, 606, 607; **30** 924; **31** 571
dealers **6** 23; **7** 842; **24** 213
groups and movements **1** 79; **4** 110; **7** 685; **10** 416; **17** 694; **25** 231
patrons and collectors **1** 71; **6** 23; **7** 842; **9** 189; **17** 620; **20** 524; **21** 135; **24** 24; **33** 45
productions **8** 270; **24** 407
teachers **1** 549
works **2** 616, 617; **7** 557; **10** 482, 558; **12** 216; **13** 677; **19** 492; **20** *606*; **21** 892; **23** 334; **24** 407; **25** 596, 626, 628; **26** *27*, *29*, 51; **28** 52, 300; **29** 97; **31** 615
Rauscher, Johannes, II **27** 330
Rauscher, Lajos **24** 567
Rautenbach, Laura **4** 155
Rautenstrauch-Joest-Museum *see under* COLOGNE → museums
Rauwaert, Jacob **14** 292, 293
Rauws, Cornelis **26** 30*; **33** 268
Rav, Jan **20** 635; **26** 30*
Rava, Carlo Enrico **13** 728
Rava, Jacopo **4** 695
Ravanalla Cave **29** 445
Ravanica **22** 79; **28** *437*, 440
monastery church **9** 586; **28** 442, 453
Ravaschio, Francesco **31** 292
Ravat **6** 212, 242
Ravdel', Yefim **32** 661
Ravdonikas, Vladislav (Iosifovich) **26** 30*; **33** 600
Rave, Ortwin **8** 631
Rave, P. **4** 26
Raveel, Roger **3** 565; **19** 756
ravelins **21** 547, 567
Ravello
Cathedral of S Pantaleone **9** 154; **16** 626
altar **1** 695
doors **3** 240
pulpit **13** 98; **23** 107; **25** 724
S Giovanni del Toro **26** 626
Ravello, Giovan Battista **24** 837
Raven, John *see* Rav, Jan
Raven, Samuel **24** 62
Raven Castle *see* MATSUMOTO CASTLE
Ravenet, Simon Francis, the elder (1706-74) **10** 346, 392; **14** 79, 642; **26** 30–31; **27** 463
Ravenet, Simon Francis, the younger (1748-1812) **26** 31
Ravenna **7** 217; **9** *510*; **16** *618*; **26** 31–6*
Archbishop's Palace **9** 534; **18** 825
chapel of the Apostle Andrew **9** 572
ecclesiastical buildings
Arian Baptistery **3** 189; **9** 85, 533, 534; **16** 624; **26** 31–2*, *32*
icons **9** 624
mosaics **9** 571; **16** 654; **22** 161
stucco **29** 816
Basilica Ursiana *see* Cathedral
Cathedral **1** 764; **7** 301; **9** 597
ambo of Bishop Agnellus **16** 686
ambo of Bishop Marinianus **16** 686
Orthodox Baptistery **3** 189; **4** 774; **9** 524, 533; **16** 624; **26** 33*
icons **9** 624
mosaics **1** 694; **3** *190*; **9** 571
stucco **29** 816, *817*
S Apollinare in Classe **4** 774; **9** 525, 534, 573; **16** 625, 761; **18** 703; **26** 33–4*, *34*
arches **2** 297
ciborium **5** 796; **7** 301, *302*
corbels **7** 837
crypt **8** 222
mosaics **6** 173; **9** 642, 645; **12** 71; **16** 654
sarcophagus **16** 686; **27** 827
sculpture **9** 589
stained glass **29** 501; **33** 246
S Apollinare Nuovo **4** 63, 774; **7** 252; **9** 534, 572–3; **16** 625, 761; **19** 362; **22** 203; **26** 34–5*, *35*
mosaics **9** 645; **12** 790; **22** 161; **25** 742
plaques **9** 590
reliefs **9** 597
sculpture **9** 589
stucco **29** 816
Santa Croce **7** 252; **9** 533; **29** 816
S Francesco **16** 686; **27** 827
SS Giovanni e Paolo **25** 723

Ravenna
ecclesiastical buildings—cont.
S Giovanni Evangelista **9** 533; **16** 625
Santo Spirito **9** 534
S Vitale **4** 774; **7** 221, 255; **9** 85, 518, 525, 534, 576, 645, 653; **15** 882; **16** 625; **23** 485; **26** 35–6*, *36*; **27** 235
arches **2** 292
buttresses **5** 319
capitals **16** 686
ciborium **7** 302
icons **9** 624
mosaics **6** 173; **7** 828; **8** 270; **9** 251, 569, 573, *573*, 640, 642, 653, 654; **12** 790; **14** 408; **16** 654, 761; **18** 824; **19** 362; **22** 43, 161, *161*, 519; **26** 82, 138; **31** 499
plaques **9** 590
reliefs **9** 597
sculpture **9** 589
stucco **29** 816
Edicola Braccioforte
sarcophagus of Elisha **16** 686
equestrian monuments **5** 806
Mausoleum of Galla Placidia **3** 190; **4** 774; **9** 85, 534, 571; **16** 624; **18** 703, 826; **20** 865; **26** 32*, *32*
corbels **7** 837
mosaics **16** 654
Mausoleum of Theodoric **9** 534; **16** 624; **20** 865; **23** 623; **26** 32–3*, *33*; **27** 235; **31** 110, 120
mosaics **16** 761
vaults **32** 89
mosaics **9** 571, 572–3; **18** 703; **22** 158, 161, 165
Palace of Theodoric **9** 557; **16** 625
sarcophagi **9** 597; **16** 686; **27** 827
silk **9** 663
stucco **27** 72
Ravenna, Benedetto da **2** 873; **6** 43; **14** 661
Ravenna, Francesco **21** 807
Ravenna, Marco da *see* DENTE, MARCO
Ravenna, Severo (di Domenico Calzetta) da *see* SEVERO (DI DOMENICO CALZETTA) DA RAVENNA
Ravenna, Silvestro da **8** 765
Ravenna, Tommaso da *see* RANGONE, TOMMASO
Ravenscraig (Fife) **21** 564
Ravenscroft, Francis **26** 37
Ravenscroft, George **11** 612; **12** 781, 786; **26** 36–7*
works **10** 305, 316, *317*; **19** 595
Ravenstijn, Filips van **4** 161
Raventos **29** 273
Ravéreau, André (Raymond Marie) **1** 320; **20** 198; **26** 37*
works **1** 319, *320*, 634
Raverti, Matteo **21** 524; **26** 37*
collaboration **4** 736
works **10** 743; **13** 95; **21** 533
Ravesteyn **30** 879
Ravesteyn, Anthonie van **14** 139; **26** 38
Ravesteyn, Arnoldus van **26** 38
Ravesteyn, Jan (Anthonisz.) van **22** 844; **26** 37–8*
pupils **21** 509
reproductive prints by others **8** 664
works **11** *409*; **14** 41, *41*
Ravesteyn, Nicolaes van **3** 42
Ravesteyn, Sybold van **2** 318; **26** 38*; **32** 254
Ravestyn, Arnoldus van **33** 260
Ravich, Ivan A. **31** 561
Ravier, (François-)Auguste **1** 642; **26** 38–9*
Ravier, Jacques-Marie **19** 849
Ravilious, Eric (William) **10** 375; **24** 55; **26** 39*
collaboration **3** 420
patrons and collectors **28** 273
works **4** 366; **25** 628; **33** 23
Ravinder Reddy, G. **15** 173
Ravizza, Alejandro **24** 95–6
works **24** *96*
Ravnikar, Edo **19** 516; **28** 860
Ravnikar, Vojteh **28** 860
Ravrio, Antoine-André **26** 39*, 182, 375, 376
Ravy, Jean **6** 531; **24** 152, 155; **26** 39*
Rawak **6** *288*; **18** 29; **28** 720
sculpture **6** 300
stupa **6** 293, 297, *297*, 299, 302, 303; **29** 824, 867
Rawalpindi **15** *264*; **23** *797*; **26** 39–40*
metalwork **23** 803
National Council for the Arts **3** 170
Pakistan Institute of Nuclear Science and Technology **23** 799
phalerae **30** 773
Society of Contemporary Art Galleries **3** 170
al-Rawda
madrasa **16** 213
Nilometer **5** 395; **16** 155
Rawdon-Hastings, Francis, 1st Marquess of Hastings **10** 145
Rawer **9** 859, 870
Rawert, J. H. **8** 727
rawhide **22** 654
Rawi, Nouri **16** 2
Rawlins, G. E. H. **24** 653
Rawlins, Thomas **10** 265; **12** 261; **20** 923; **26** 40*
Rawlinson, Henry Creswicke **1** 892, 895; **2** 299; **4** 94, 437
Rawlinson, Robert **10** 152
Rawlinson & Barnes **29** 842
Rawnsley, David **3** 65
raw sienna *see under* PIGMENTS → types
Rawson, Jessica **7** 160
Rawsthorne, Isabel **3** *28*
raw umber *see under* UMBER → types
Raxis, Pedro (1535-1614) **26** 549
Raxis, Pedro Sardo (*d* 1581) *see* SARDO RAXIS, PEDRO
Ray, Carl **22** 597
Ray, Man *see* MAN RAY
Ray, Rezsö **14** 523
Raya, Jabatan Kerja **20** 169
Raydan **2** 263
rayḥān see under SCRIPTS → types
Rayigama **29** 450
Rayism **9** 145; **11** 867; **12** 893, 894; **18** 792, 793–4; **20** 193; **26** 40–41*; **31** 763
painting **26** *41*
Ray-Jones, (Holroyd) Tony **24** 679; **26** 41*
Raymond (*fl c.* 1700s) **26** 206
Raymond VI, Count of Toulouse (*reg* 1194-1222) **14** 408
Raymond, Antonin **17** 88; **26** 42*
collaboration **11** 47; **33** 403
pupils **20** 76
staff **33** 563
works **11** 256; **17** 89
Raymond, Eleanor **4** 475
Raymond, François *see* RÉMOND, FRANÇOIS
Raymond, Jean Arnaud **24** 173
Raymond, John **13** 299
Raymond, Marie **18** 117; **26** 193
Raymond, Pierre **19** 396
Raymond, Vincent **26** 42*
Raymond and Ebrart **20** 472
Raymond-Berengar IV, Count of Provence (*reg* 1209-54) **14** 422
Raymond du Temple **6** 494; **20** 133; **24** 132; **26** 42–3*
patrons and collectors **24** 161; **31** 832, 835, 840, 841
pupils **8** 484
works **13** 76; **24** 115; **25** 637; **29** 521; **32** 581
Raymond Gairard *see* GAIRARD, RAYMOND
Raymond the Lombard **26** 43–4*
Raynal, Guillaume-Thomas-François, Abbé **13** 663; **24** 177
Raynal, Maurice **26** 44*
collaboration **30** 488
groups and movements **8** 241, 246; **19** 92; **25** 747
writings **27** 163
Raynaud, Jean-Pierre **11** 571
Rayner, Gordon **5** 569
Raynerd, Daniel **3** 730
Rayneri y Piedra, Eugenio **8** 232
Rayneri y Sorrentino, Eugenio **8** 232
Raynham Hall (Norfolk) **8** 45
Raynolds, Dr **31** 158
Raynov, Stoyan **5** 158
Rayo, Omar **7** 610; **10** 178
rayographs **8** 438; **20** 287–8*, *288*; **24** 654; **30** 19
see also PHOTOGRAMS
Rayol, Joseph **7** 876
rayon **11** 55; **13** 766; **30** 542, *543*
Rayonism *see* RAYISM
Rayonnant style *see under* GOTHIC → styles
Rayper, Ernesto **28** 318
Raysek, Matěj *see* REJSEK, MATĚJ
Rayshev, Gennady **27** 436
Rayski, (Louis) Ferdinand von **12** 393; **26** 46*
Raysse, Martial **11** 551, 570; **26** 46–7*
collaboration **30** 924
groups and movements **10** 416; **23** 260
patrons and collectors **14** 48
works **22** 748, *748*; **23** 261
Rayts, G. S. **4** 469
Rayy **15** 899; **16** *105*; **24** 215; **26** 47*
architecture **16** 161
iconography **24** 218
metalwork **16** 370
pottery **16** 396, 397, 407, 408, 409
sculpture **16** 246
silk **16** 546
textiles **16** 435
wall paintings **16** 253
woodwork **16** 491
Raz, Ram **15** 209, 212; **26** 47–8*
Raza, Mashkoor **23** 800
Raza, Sayed Haider **4** 290, 291; **15** 169; **26** 48*
Razetti, Ricardo **32** 170
Razgrad **5** 145; **9** 557; **30** 770
Razin **2** 893
Razionalismo **10** 820; **13** 728; **23** 169; **26** 14, 15–16, 536; **28** 793
architecture **3** *438*; **11** 869; **16** 649–50*; **19** 305
factories **11** *63*
Italy **19** 421; **30** 513
office buildings **16** *649*
palazzi **26** *15*
Razlog **5** 157, 158
razors **10** 38, 67; **25** 734
Razumovsky, A. K. **27** 439
Razumovsky, Kirill, Count **3** 382; **5** 521; **18** 196, 543; **26** 403; **31** 828
Razzaguta, Gastone **28** 319
Razzanti, Pietro de' Neri *see* NERI RAZZANTI, PIETRO DE'
Razzaque, Abdur **3** 165
al-Razzaz, Mustafa **9** 766
Razzi, Girolamo Silvano **26** 48–9*
Razzo, Giachetto di Benedetto da *see* GIACHETTO DI BENEDETTO DA RAZZO
Re, Francesco **24** 865
Re, Marc'Antonio dal **12** 115, 119; **27** 321
works **12** *118*, *761*; **21** *518*
Rè, Vincenzo dal **30** 669
Rea, Alexander **1** 753
Rea, Betty **2** 553
reactive dyes *see under* DYES → types
Read, Benjamin **9** 287
works **9** *287*
Read, David Charles **9** 309
Read, Herbert (Edward) **6** 588; **9** 725; **10** 321; **13** 801; **16** 18; **19** 590; **26** 49*
groups and movements **2** 553; **19** 591; **30** 22; **31** 673
personal collection **32** 800
works **11** 315; **14** 852, 864; **28** 926; **30** 262; **33** 744
Read, James **31** 652
Read, Katherine **26** 50*; **28** 235
Read, Nicholas **27** 244
Reade, David **29** 119
Reade, J. E. **21** 299
Reade, Julian **20** 220; **30** 383
Reading (Jamaica) **16** *878*
Casa del Sol **16** 883
Ocean View **16** 883
Reading, (Berks; UK)
Abbey **3** 443; **7** 473; **13** 211; **23** 491; **26** 50*, 615
beakheads **26** 612
capitals **26** 616
cloister **7** 455
sculpture **26** 50, 611
Porsche of Great Britain **14** 521
Rowney Office Building **10** 347
St Mary's *see* Abbey
swords **32** 528
Town Hall **31** 241
University **10** 422
Reading (PA; USA), American Bank **4** 789
ready-mades **7** 685; **8** 435; **9** 356, *356*; **10** 680; **26** 50–51*
Cubism **8** 245
United States of America **13** 891; **26** *51*
Readymoney, Cowasjee Jehangir **4** 289
Reael, R. **1** 801
Real Alto **26** 51–2*; **29** *136*
Charnel House Mound **26** 52
Fiesta House Mound **26** 52
houses **26** 52
trumpets **29** 217
Real Associação dos Arquitetos e Arqueólogos Portugueses (Lisbon) **28** 732
Real Casa de Moneda (Antigua) **13** 764, 768, 770
Real Compañía Guipuzcoana **32** 169
Real de Ceniza **8** *15*, 16
Real del Sarte, Maxime **11** 568
Real Estate Corporation **3** 501
Real Fabbrica della Porcellana (Naples) **22** 482
Real Fábrica da Bica do Sapato **19** 467; **25** 310; **30** 881
Real Fábrica das Sedas (Lisbon) **4** 637; **25** 315; **26** 52
Real Fábrica de Cristales de La Granja de San Ildefonso **4** 564; **20** 67; **27** 754; **29** 330, 331–2
Real Fábrica de Custodio Ferreira Braga **19** 467
Real Fábrica de Marfiles **4** 566
Real Fábrica de Platería **20** 69; **29** 337, 338
works **29** *338*
Real Fábrica de Porcelana del Buen Retiro **12** 925; **20** 67; **27** 116; **29** 304, 329, 345
Real Fábrica de Seda (Madrid) **29** 348
Real Fábrica de Seda (Talavera de la Reina) **29** 348, 349
Real Fábrica de Tabacos **10** 748
Real Fábrica de Tapices y Alfombras de Santa Bárbara **4** 558, 564; **5** 436; **29** 350*; **30** 325
collections **4** 566; **10** 504; **29** 304
designers
Bayeu (y Subías), Ramón **3** 426
Castillo, José del **6** 47
Ginés de Aguirre, Andrés **12** 651
González Ruiz, Antonio **12** 922
González Velázquez, Antonio **12** 924
González Velázquez, Zacarías **12** 924
Goya (y Lucientes), Francisco (José) de **13** 241; **20** 67
Houasse, Michel-Ange **14** 794
Loo, Louis-Michel van **19** 648
directors **3** 424; **11** 172; **20** 77; **29** 283
production **29** 347; **30** 324, *325*
Real Fábrica do Cavaquinho **23** 454; **25** 310; **26** 479; **31** 865
Real Fábrica do Rato **19** 467; **25** 185, 310; **26** 52*; **30** 881
directors **1** 680; **5** 24
production **19** *468*
realgar **7** 632; **12** 88; **24** 798
Real Image **14** 690
realism (critical term) **12** 396; **14** 869; **15** 100; **22** 685
Bolivia **4** 261, 264
Egypt, ancient **10** 1
France **22** 687–8
Greece, ancient **2** 227
Italy **32** 256
see also MIMESIS
Realism (style) **8** 58; **12** 296; **15** 156; **21** 612; **22** 685, 686, 687; **25** 12; **26** 52–7*, 743
art forms
etchings **22** *688*
monuments **22** 47–8
nude figures **23** 295; **26** *56*
painting
Czech Republic **8** *392*
France **4** *339*, *754*; **8** *51*, *52*, *53*, *54*, *55*, *56*; **11** *544*, 544–5*; **12** *295*; **14** *587*; **19** *381*; **26** *54*, *56*
Germany **12** 393–4; **19** *97*; **21** *140*, *141*
Italy **6** *136*; **28** *705*, *706*
Russia **26** *218*, *219*
United States of America **23** *297*
sculpture **16** 706
regional traditions
Albania **1** 540
Belgium **3** 562–3; **26** 57
Britain **26** 56
Croatia **8** 178
France **6** 438–9; **8** 50, 52–4; **12** 294; **16** 850; **22** 688; **26** 53–6
Germany **21** 142–3; **26** 56
Italy **26** 56
Netherlands, the **26** 57
Norway **23** 230
Russia **26** 57, 217
United States of America **26** 57
Realism, Ugly *see* UGLY REALISM
Réalisme **9** 425; **22** 687
Realists Group **33** 689
Réalités Nouvelles, Salon des *see* SALON DES RÉALITÉS NOUVELLES
Real Laboratorio delle Pietre Dure (Naples) **4** 562, 564; **12** 262, 547; **16** 747; **22** 481–2
Reallexikon zur deutschen Kunstgeschichte **10** 212

Real Sitio de San Ildefonso *see* SAN ILDEFONSO
Real Taller de Ebanistería 29 315
Reame, Mino del *see* MINO DEL REAME
Reames, John 4 692
reamy glass *see under* GLASS → types
Reaney, James 6 410
rear-arches *see under* ARCHES → types
Reardon, Thomas 7 576
Rearte, Armando 26 57*
Reask (Co. Kerry) 15 876
Reason, Patrick 1 440
Réattu, Jacques 26 57–8*
Réau, Louis 10 211, 213; 26 58*
Réaumur, René-Antoine Ferchault de 24 40
Rebaix Church 13 113
Rebay (von Ehrenweisen), Hilla (Anna Augusta Elisabeth), Baroness 13 800; 26 58*
Rebdorf Monastery 12 373
Rebecca, Biagio 10 642, 643; 11 119
Rebel Art Centre 10 256; 19 287; 23 15; 26 59*, 466; 32 700, 753
members 2 691; 9 9; 10 547; 14 107; 23 437
Rebell, Josef 2 796; 26 59*
Rebelo, Jacinto 13 295
Rebelo, José de Avelar *see* AVELAR REBELO, JOSÉ DE
Rebelo, José Maria Jacinto 4 711; 24 565; 26 413
Rebencz, Krzysztof 25 126
Reber, Gottlieb Friedrich 13 671; 26 59*
Rebeur, Jean-Philippe 18 873
Rebeur, Pierre 18 873
Rebeyrolle, Paul 20 75; 26 59–60*; 27 307
Rebhuhn, Hans *see* RAPHON, HANS
Rebmann, Albrecht 28 171
Rebocho, Joaquim da Costa *see* COSTA REBOCHO, JOAQUIM DA
Rebouças, Diógenes 2 190; 26 60*
Reboul, Marie-Thérèse 32 427
Rebuffo, Víctor 2 399
Rebull, Santiago 16 806; 26 60*
Recalcati, Antonio 11 552
Récamier, Jacques 7 162; 10 186
Récamier, Jeanne Françoise Julie Adelaïde 7 *163*; 11 579
Recceswinth, King of the Visigoths (*reg* 649-72) 9 654; 29 345; 32 618
Recchi, Giovan Battista 16 757
Recchi, Giovanni Antonio 28 11
Recchi, Giovanni Paolo 28 11, 12
Recchi, Mario 25 447
Recco, Elena 26 61
Recco, Elena Maria 26 61
Recco, Giacomo 22 478; 26 60–61*
pupils 25 252
Recco, Giovan Battista 11 488; 22 478; 26 61*; 27 342
Recco, Giuseppe 11 32; 22 479; 26 61*
attributions 6 29
patrons and collectors 5 356
reception halls *see under* HALLS → types
reception theories *see under* THEORIES
Recerla Rudra 23 832
réchampi 26 64*
Rechany, Jorge 25 701
Rechberg Pax 22 204
Rechenberg, von 29 751
Rechenmeister (family) 20 789
Rechitsa *see* REČYCA
Rechnitz, Batthyány Castle 14 886, 893, 900
Rechte, Lieven De *see* HENDRICXZ., LIEVEN
Rechter, Yacov 16 566; 26 64, 65*
Rechter, Ze'ev 16 565; 26 64–5*, 286; 30 421
Rechter-Zarhy-Rechter 16 565; 26 64
Rechungphug 30 818
Recife 4 704, *705*; 26 65*
Assembléia Provincial 4 711
Expo Centre 4 715
Fundação Joaquim Nabuco 4 729
Guarapes Airport 4 722
Hospital Dom Pedro II 4 711
Lage 4 709
Museu de Arte Sacra 26 65
San José market 4 712
S Pedro dos Clérigos 4 710
Teatro S Isabel 4 711
urban planning 4 710
Recinos, Efraín 13 763, 770; 26 65–6*
Recke, Elisa von der 17 713
Reclam, Philipp 13 811
recliners 29 8
Reclus, Elisée 4 332
Reclus, Francisco 6 592
reconstruction 2 318–23*; 25 100; 26 226, 706
Record Art Society (Kirokugeijutsu no Kai) 14 129
Recordon, Benjamin 13 842
record reliefs *see under* RELIEF SCULPTURE → types
Recoura, Alfred-Henri 1 69; 27 270
Recques-sur-Course Château 19 233
rectangular piers *see under* PIERS (ii) (MASONRY) → types
rectified photography *see under* TECHNICAL EXAMINATION → types
rectilinear tracery *see under* TRACERY → types → bar
recto 26 66*
Rector, H. 18 887
Recuay culture 26 66*; 29 127, 130, *156*
hardstones 29 185
pottery 26 66
sculpture 26 66; 29 170
stone-carvings 29 *170*
tombs 31 118
Recuenco 29 331
Reculver (Kent)
Abbey 2 65; 10 *225*; 26 66–7*, *67*
sculpture 26 67*
Regulbium 21 560
Recum, Peter van 11 731
Rečyca Church 3 527
red *see under* PIGMENTS → types
Redam (family) 14 617
redans 21 547
red antimonyoxide sulphide *see under* PIGMENTS → types
Redback Graffix 2 751
Redcar Pier 24 748
red chalk *see under* CHALK → types
Redcliff Backs Glasshouse 4 824
Red Crow Society 30 248
Red Day Society *see* SEKIYŌKAI
Red Deer, St Mary's 5 563
Reddy, G. Ravinder *see* RAVINDER REDDY, G.
Reddy, Krishna 26 67–8*
Rede, William, Bishop of Chichester 23 686
Redecker, Gottlieb 33 245
Redel, Augustus-Casimir 15 43
Redelinghuys, Ian 29 112
Redemption of the Prado, Master of the 5 46
Il Redentore *see under* VENICE → ecclesiastical buildings
Redentore Master 20 767
Reder, Giovanni 21 831
Reder, Lorenz 26 68*; 29 787
Redfern, James Frank 5 194; 28 278
Redfern, John 9 289, 291
Redfield, Edward 2 130
Red-figure pottery *see under* POTTERY → wares
Red Fort *see* DELHI → Lal Qil'a
Red Giant Works *see* KRASNYY GIGANT WORKS
Red-glazed ware *see under* POTTERY → wares
Redgrave, John 19 734
Redgrave, Richard 7 548; 10 373; 14 148; 15 821; 26 68–9*; 28 575
collaboration 11 360; 26 68
works 10 253, *253*; 26 *69*
Redgrave, Samuel 10 210; 26 68–9*
Red Horse of Tysoe 14 544
Red House glassworks 10 320
Redi, Tommaso 11 20; 13 677; 26 69–70*
Redić, Uroš 28 450
Redijet 9 866
Redin, Ye. K. 2 880; 27 443
Redington, Thomas N. 24 87
rediscovery
Ancient Near East 1 891–5*
Aztec 21 262
Egypt, ancient 10 78–84*
see also EGYPTIAN REVIVAL
Etruscan 10 636–8*, 642–4; 13 10; 18 755
Greece, ancient 26 263; 27 45
Iran, ancient 1 894*
Italy 10 636–8*
Maya 21 262, 263
Mesoamerica, Pre-Columbian 21 262–3*
Mesopotamia 1 892
Nubia 10 81*
Rome, ancient 27 45, 115–16
South America, Pre-Columbian 29 218–20*
Sumerian 1 893
Syria-Palestine 1 892, 893
Red'ko, Klyment (Mykolayovych) 8 10; 26 70*
red lead 24 56
historical and regional traditions
Algeria 16 393
China 24 796
Gothic 24 796
Greece, ancient 13 387
Islamic 16 393
Japan 17 277
Mesopotamia 16 393
Romanesque 24 796
uses
enamel 10 192
glazes 16 393
grounds 25 174
inks 15 852
manuscript illumination 24 796
paints 24 796; 31 282
pigments 17 277; 24 795–6*
secco paintings 28 338
Redler, Jan Chrysostom 25 115
Red Lustrous Wheelmade ware *see under* POTTERY → wares
Redman, D. J. 19 483; 20 602; 25 628
Redman, Henry 23 686; 26 70–71*; 32 378; 33 306
Redman, Jane 30 330
Red Monastery *see under* SOHAG
Redmond, Granville 19 701
Red Mother *see* RØDE MOR
Redner, Ethel *see* SCULL, ETHEL
red ochre *see under* OCHRE → types
Redolfo 26 698
Redon, Gaston 4 240; 13 337; 18 782; 27 270
Redon, Odilon (Bertrand-Jean) 11 667; 22 905; 26 71–2*
collaboration 20 201, 603
dealers 9 425; 32 686
Redon, Odilon (Bertrand-Jean)—cont.
groups and movements 15 155; 22 921; 25 356, 357; 30 168; 32 591
patrons and collectors 4 142, 391; 26 534; 30 375; 33 150
productions 30 685
pupils 10 689
teachers 4 749
works 8 596; 11 230, *230*; 12 497, 830; 19 488, 489, 490; 20 602; 22 416; 24 244, *244*; 25 607, 624, 626; 26 *71*; 28 298
Red-on-black ware *see under* POTTERY → wares
Red-on-buff ware *see under* POTTERY → wares
Red-on-white ware *see under* POTTERY → wares
Red Oribe ware *see under* POTTERY → wares
redoubts 21 547
Redouté, Antoine-Ferdinand 26 72, 73
Redouté, Charles-Joseph 26 72
Redouté, Henri-Joseph 26 73
Redouté, Pierre-Joseph 26 72–3*
patrons and collectors 4 303
reproductive prints by others 4 364; 30 353
teachers 29 255
works 11 228; 13 221; 25 622; 26 *73*
workshop 7 677
Redpath, Anne 26 73–4*; 28 240
Redpath, Norma 2 753; 18 64
Redpath Museum *see under* MONTREAL → McGill University
Red Polished ware *see under* POTTERY → wares
Red-ridged ware *see* POTTERY → wares → Barbar ware
red rot 19 6
Redruth Methodist Church (Cornwall) 21 347
Redsell, Pauline 5 571
Red Slip ware *see under* POTTERY → wares
Redslob, Edwin 8 825
red spiral-burnished ware *see under* POTTERY → wares
Red Sun Society *see* RED CROW SOCIETY
Redtmer, Mårten 29 687; 30 84
reducing glasses 26 74*
reducing kilns *see under* KILNS → types
reduits 21 547
réduits modèles see under TOWERS → types
Reduktionsgotik see under GOTHIC → styles
Redura 32 6
Redusol 30 559
redware *see* EARTHENWARES
Red ware *see under* POTTERY → wares
red-wood 22 563
Redydjet 10 47
Ree, Lorentz 23 222
Reed, Alma 23 566
Reed, Barton & Co. 4 480, 481
Reed, Charles 32 867
Reed, Colin 10 321
Reed, Cynthia 2 756
Reed, Ethel 25 347
Reed, Henderson and Smart 3 368
Reed, Henry G. 4 481
Reed, John (*fl* 1819) 9 55
Reed, John (1901-81) 2 769; 23 182; 26 74*
Reed, Joseph (1823-90) 2 738; 3 368; 26 74–5*
works 2 738, 739, *739*; 21 75
Reed, Joseph H. (1857-1901) 33 409
Reed, Luman 7 550; 26 75*; 29 870
collections 23 46; 31 662, 664, 666
paintings 9 419; 14 843; 22 224
Reed, Paul 32 890, 894
Reed, Polly Jane 28 541
works 28 *541*
Reed, Smart & Tappin 26 74
Reed, Sunday 2 769; 23 182; 26 74*
Reed, Thomas 4 233; 7 605, 611; 9 711; 25 829
Reed & Barton 4 481; 5 612; 24 581; 31 650, 652
works 24 *581*
Reede, Godert van 25 327
Reede, Goort van 23 188
Reeder, John 16 888
Reed Painter 13 536; 32 46, 66*
reeds
historical and regional traditions
Aboriginal Australia 1 53
Africa 1 307, 311
Ancient Near East 20 326
Central Asia, Eastern 6 295, 306
Colombia 7 603
Egypt, ancient 5 32; 10 *4*; 24 348
India, Republic of 15 173
Indian subcontinent 15 730
Iraq 16 269; 32 *314*
Islamic 16 269, 276; 24 348; 32 *314*
Linear Pottery culture 25 500
Mesopotamia 20 326
Rome, ancient 24 348
uses
architecture 16 269; 25 500; 32 *314*
brushes 5 32
crowns 15 730
granaries 1 311
necklaces 1 53
pens 9 216; 10 *4*; 16 276; 24 348–9*; 28 303
roofs 1 307; 6 295
rugs 27 316
shields 6 306
stucco 29 813
styluses 20 326
walls 7 603
Reed & Stem 3 464; 23 40; 31 728
Reef Islands 27 778; 29 50
Reekie, David 10 321
Reekie, J. 4 627
Reeler, Ian 33 602
Re-entrant carpets *see* CARPETS → types → Bellini
Rees, St Mariä Himmelfahrt 7 300
Rees, Abraham 21 620
Rees, Jacob van 26 75
Rees, Jeremy 4 823
Rees, Lloyd (Frederic) 2 750; 26 75*; 30 160
Rees, Margaretha 22 *846*; 33 79
Rees, Otto van 8 434; 21 775; 22 852; 26 75*
Rees, T. Mardy 32 792
Rees-Dutilh, Ayda van 8 434; 26 75*
Reeve, Augustus William 26 76
Reeve, Elsie 23 71
Reeve, James 23 249
Reeve, Richard 26 75–6*
Reeve, Richard Gilson 26 75, 76
Reeves 7 639; 32 898
Reeves, Thomas (1736-99) 26 76*
Reeves, Thomas, jr (*fl* 1800) 26 76
Reeves, Oswald 19 891
Reeves, William (*fl* 1739-*d* after 1785) 26 76*
Reeves, William (*fl* 1760) 4 821
Reewijk, Hillebrant van 26 259
refectories 18 *152*; 20 *859*; 21 844–6*; 26 76*
refectory tables *see under* TABLES → types

reference books *see* DICTIONARIES; ENCYCLOPEDIAS; MANUALS; TREATISES
Reff, T. **4** 27
Re-figuración **24** 99; **26** 76*
refinements (architecture) **10** 414; **13** 413–15*, *414*; **26** 925
Refinger, Ludwig **22** 302; **26** 76*
collaboration **4** 207; **22** 302
patrons and collectors **30** 118
works **33** 271
reflectance **19** 352; **26** 76*
Reflex **17** 658
Reform **8** 824
Reformation **7** 215
Reformed Church *see under* CHRISTIANITY → sects
Reformed Cistercians *see* TRAPPISTS
Reform Village Temple **5** *755*
refractories **21** 320
Refregier, Anton **25** 653
Refus global **2** 840; **4** 402; **26** 76–7*
Rega, Filippo **12** 264; **22** 481; **26** 77*
regalia **26** 77–82*
Africa **1** 241–2, *242*, 351–5*, *352*, *353*, *355*
Akan **2** 588
Akye **1** 514–15
Asante **1** 351, 352, 353; **2** 585–8*
Bamum **1** *352*, 353
Benin, Kingdom of **1** 352, 354
Cambodia **5** 508
Cameroon **1** 242, 352
Champa **6** 432
Egypt **16** 539
Ejagham **10** 124*
England **26** *78*, *80*
France **26** *81*
Germany **26** *78*, *79*
Ghana **3** 132
Hausa **1** 242, *242*
Hemba **1** 365
Hungary **15** 11
Ife (kingdom of) **1** 352
Iran **16** 538, 539
Iraq **16** *538*
Islamic **16** 537–9*, *538*
Kuba (iii) (Zaïre) **1** 352, 354; **18** 489
Luba **1** 354, *355*
Mali **3** 132
Native North Americans **22** *549*, 653, 654
Nigeria **1** *242*, *353*
Ottoman **16** 539
Ottonian **26** *78*
Syria **16** 539
United States of America **22** *549*
Vietnam **6** 432
Yoruba **1** 352, *353*, 353
Régamey, Félix **19** 39
Régamey, Frédéric **19** 39
Régamey, Guillaume **19** 39
Regards **6** 603
Regeli **31** 787
Regello, S Giovenale di Cascia **20** 530
Regemorter, Ignatius (Joseph-Pierre) van **26** 83*
Regemorter, Petrus Johannes van **26** 83*
Régence ornament **18** 854
Régence style **23** 514; **26** 83–4*, 492–3
dress **9** 281–3*
frames **11** *403*, 404–5, *407*
furniture **26** *84*
hôtels particuliers **29** *751*
houses **22** *826*
interior decoration **19** 722; **23** *458*
sculpture **14** 651
Regency style **12** 332; **14** 145; **22** 741; **26** 84–5*
frames **11** *425*, 431, *431*
Regency style—cont.
furniture **8** 235; **29** 114, 115
interior decoration **30** XIV2
Regensburg **12** *361*; **26** 85–8*, *86*, *906*
book covers **4** IV2
churches
Alte Kapelle **16** 541
Cathedral of St Peter **12** 365; **20** 661; **23** 462; **26** 88*, 575; **27** 145–6, 147
Allerheiligenkapelle **26** 656
chapel of Bishop Hartwig **26** *575*
ciborium **7** 303
metalwork **26** 687
sculpture **13** 87
silk **16** 752
spire **29** 414
stained glass **13** 186
Dominican church *see* St Blasius
Heiligenkreuz church **13** 185
Kapelle zur Schönen Maria *see* Neupfarrkirche
Neupfarrkirche **2** 336; **12** *366*, 367; **14** 513
St Blasius **26** 74
St Emmeram **8** 223; **13** 18, 19; **26** 87–8*
altars **1** 697
ciborium **7** 300, 302
crypt **7** 265
furniture **30** 776
manuscripts **5** 808; **7** 512; **26** 660, 674
metalwork **5** 808
reliquaries **26** 144
sculpture **26** 634
transept **31** 280
wall paintings **5** 797; **23** 651
St Jakob **26** 634, 646
St Wolfgang **11** 256
cups **12** *444*
embroidery **10** 181; **12** 462
façade decoration **10** 739
fortifications **21** 565
houses **32** 281, 282
manuscripts **9** 219; **17** 534; **20** 330; **23** 652, 654; **26** 662, 674
marks **12** 442
metalwork **23** 656
painting **12** 382
Rathaus **10** 739; **31** 237
Schloss der Fürsten von Thurn und Taxis **12** 412
tapestries **12** 466
Regensburg Ordinance **4** 187; **19** 532; **20** 563, 564
Regensteiner, Else **31** 660
Regent, Master of the **20** 753*
Regent Diamond **11** 634, 635; **23** 516
Regent's Park *see under* LONDON
Reggiani, Mauro **16** 681; **22** 242; **26** 88–9*
Reggio, Baldassare da *see* BALDASSARE D'ESTE
Reggio, Carmel **8** 178
Reggio, Evangelista da *see* EVANGELISTA DA REGGIO
Reggio, Jacopino da *see* JACOPINO DA REGGIO
Reggio, Raffaellino da **3** 56; **26** 89*, 770
collaboration **33** 718
patrons and collectors **10** 810; **13** 628
reproductive prints by others **5** 856
Reggio, Sebastiano da **32** 237
Reggio di Calabria *see* RHEGION
Reggio Emilia
Casa Ghinizzini **11** 283
Casa Zanichelli **11** 283
Castello della Querciola **23** 573
Cathedral **20** 820
medals **20** 920
Museo Civico **16** 776
Reggio Emilia—cont.
S Prospero **2** *128*
Torre dell'Orologio **23** 573
Regina **5** *559*
Saskatchewan Parliament Buildings **5** 562
University **5** 590
Regina della Scala **32** 610
Regina Five **4** 169; **5** 569
Reginald of Ely **5** 511, 514; **26** 89*
Regio, Martinio **2** 285
regionalism (i) (geographic variation) **10** 76–8*; **14** 878; **26** 89–90*, 571
Regionalism (ii) (painting) **1** 772, *773*; **8** 277; **26** 90*; **33** 343
Regis, Francesco De *see* DE REGIS, FRANCESCO
registration *see under* PRINTING → processes
Registrum Gregorii, Master of the **9** 749, 750; **12** 382; **13** 18; **20** 753–4*; **23** 653; **31** 325
works **20** *754*; **23** 653, 660, *661*; **26** 695
Regisvilla **32** 744
Regius MS. (London, BL, Bibl. Reg. 17 AI) **19** 532
Regnaudin, Thomas **11** 559; **26** 91*
collaboration **12** 725; **20** 480
copies **19** 130
works **29** 571, 833
Regnauldin, Claude **22** 466
Regnauldin, Laurent *see* NALDINI, LORENZO
Regnault **19** 16
Regnault, Arthur **26** 205
Regnault, Claude *see* BAILLIF, CLAUDE
Regnault, Félix **12** 149
Regnault, Guillaume **7** 595; **27** 547
Regnault, (Alexandre-Georges-) Henri **26** 92*
dealers **4** 656; **9** 424
groups and movements **23** 503, 504
works **26** *92*
Regnault, Jean-Baptiste, Baron **10** 221; **17** 627; **26** 93–4*
assistants **19** 66
competitions **25** 638
pupils **19** 159
Aligny, Théodore Caruelle d' **1** 641
Blondel, Merry-Joseph **4** 166
Couder, (Louis-Charles-) Auguste **8** 40
Etty, William **10** 645
Foggo, George **11** 235
Guérin, Pierre (-Narcisse) **13** 791
Henry, Bon-Thomas **14** 395
Hersent, Louis **14** 481
Landon, Charles Paul **18** 699
Lecomte, Hippolyte **19** 37
Lenepveu, Jules-Eugène **19** 153
Pingret, Edouard (Henri Théophile) **24** 823
Réattu, Jacques **26** 57
Schnetz, (Jean) Victor **28** 132
Stendhal **29** 629
Vafflard, Pierre (-Antoine)-Auguste **31** 795
Wächter, (Georg Friedrich) Eberhard **32** 751
reproductive prints by others **3** 870
teachers **19** 217; **32** 427
works **26** *93*
Regnault, (Henri-) Victor **26** 91*; **28** 523
Regnault de Moulins **10** 665
Regnesson, Nicolas **22** 465
Régnier, Antoine **28** 521
Régnier, Henri de **22** 746
Regnier, Mary **31** 651
Régnier, Nicolas **9** 489; **20** 267; **26** 94–5*
dealing **10** 526; **26** 283
paintings **32** 156
patrons and collectors **12** 764; **26** 283
personal collection **26** 283
teachers **20** 267
works **26** *95*
Regnier, Pierre **23** 412; **26** 95*
Regno, Il **24** 427
Regno, Mino del *see* MINO DEL REAME
Rego, João Gaspar do **10** 729
Rego, Paula **26** 96*
methods **25** 25
works **1** 130; **22** 523, *523*; **25** 300; **29** 859
Rego Monteiro, Vicente do **4** 717, 718; **26** 96*
Regout (family) **22** 884
Regout, Petrus **19** 862; **22** 882
Regoyos (y Valdés), Darío de **26** 96–7*; **29** 284
groups and movements **24** 829; **32** 591
teachers **14** 26
works **27** 767
Regteren Altena, J(ohan) Q(uirijn) van *see* ALTENA, J(OHAN) Q(UIRIJN) VAN REGTEREN
Regters, Tibout **22** 846; **25** 823; **26** 97*
Reguengos de Monsaraz Church **25** 293
regulae (i) (architectural ornament) **11** 790; **13** 377, *378*, 393; **26** 97*
regulae (ii) (architectural element) **26** 97*
regulae (iii) (measuring tool) **26** 97*
regular script *see under* SCRIPTS → types
regulations, building *see* BUILDING REGULATIONS
Regulbium *see under* RECULVER
Régulo *see* PÉREZ, RÉGULO
Regulus **27** 15
Rehbenitz, (Markus) Theodor **26** 98*
Rehberg, Friedrich **26** 98*
Rehden *see* RADZYŃ
Rehfuss, Georg Adam **30** 147
Rehlinger, Karl **18** *44*
Rehm, Bernard **20** 190
Rehman, Habib **15** 168
Rehmann, Erwin **30** 140
Rehn, Jean Eric **26** 98–9*; **29** 689; **30** 88
groups and movements **13** 864
patrons and collectors **14** 692
pupils **11** 173; **12** 634; **28** 461, 463
works **11** 470; **14** 230; **29** *690*, 691; **30** 72, 78, 85, 89, 94, 95, 97, 106, 114, 115
Řehoř, František **8** 391
Rehotpe **9** 870; **20** 117
Rehov **17** 556
Rehovot nuclear reactor building **16** 566
Reiach, Alan **26** 99*
Reiach and Hall **26** 99
Reich, Josef **23** 358
Reich, Lilly **8** 826; **12** 470; **21** 491; **30** 755
Reich, Maria **28** 75
Reich, Philipp Erasmus **19** 111, *111*
Reich, Sigismund (Susya) *see* RICE, DAVID STORM
Reich, Steve **24** 407
Reichard, Ernst Heinrich **5** 30
Reichard, Gladys **22** 677
Reichard, Heinrich August Ottokar **13** 809
Reichardt, Charles B. **25** 268
Reichardt, Johann Friedrich **32** 751
Reichborn, Johann Joachim **23** 221
Reichel, Hans *see* REICHLE, HANS
Reichel, Oskar **28** 89
Reichel-Dolmatoff, Gerardo **29** 219
Reichenau **5** 793; **12** *361*; **26** 99–102*
manuscripts **5** 805; **12** 382; **13** *19*, 21; **20** 330; **23** 651, 652, 653, *653*, 655; **28** 25; **32** 637
metalwork **23** 656
Mittelzell Minster **3** 709; **7** 262, 265; **13** 18; **26** 100*, 572, 574
Church of SS Mary and Mark **26** 100, *100*
cloister **5** 795
manuscripts **13** 18
paintings **12** 382
piers (ii) (masonry) **24** 750
roof **27** 131; **30** *908*, 909
wall paintings **5** 797; **26** 649
Monastery of SS Mary and Mark *see* Mittelzell Minster
Niederzell
SS Peter und Paul **26** 102*, 575
wall paintings **5** 797
Oberzell **26** 101*
St Georg **26** 101*, *101*, 574, 654
wall paintings **12** 382; **23** 649, 650, *650*; **26** 101*
stucco **29** 818
Reichenau Evangeliary *see under* EVANGELIARIES → individual manuscripts
Reichenbach-Lessonitz, Gräfin **17** 853
Reichenhall Altar **20** 754
Reichenhall Altar, Master of the **20** 754*
Reichensperger, August von **3** 618; **13** 201, 205; **26** 102*
Reichenstein, Elisabeth von *see* ELISABETH VON REICHENSTEIN
Reichersberg Abbey **2** 723, 781
Reichle, Hans **26** 103–5*
collaboration **5** 360; **12** 346, 576
works **12** 403, 404; **22** 302, 725; **26** *103*, *104*; **29** 571; **33** 274
Reichle, Paul **26** 103
Reichlen, Henri **5** 408; **6** 380
Reichlen, Paule **5** 408; **6** 380
Reichlich, Marx **2** 792; **26** 105–6*
works **26** *106*
Reichlin, Bruno **25** 359; **26** 16, 106*; **30** 129
Reichlin & Reinhart **26** 106*
Reichmann, Clementina **11** 797
Reichsadlerhumpen see under GLASSES → types
Reichsamt Schönheit der Arbeit (Germany) **12** 417
Reichsgericht *see under* LEIPZIG
Reichskammer der Bildenden Künste **12** 474
Reichsstättenamt (Germany) **12** 417, 418
Reichstadt, Napoleon II Bonaparte, Herzog von, King of Rome (*reg* 1811-32) **8** 107; **30** 747
Reid, A. G. **14** 397
Reid, A. J. McNeil **19** 735
Reid, Alex(ander) **12** 776; **14** 765; **26** 107*; **28** 239
paintings **28** 272
Reid, Arthur Henry **26** 107*; **29** 105
Reid, Bill **8** 568; **22** 581, 589, 666, 674; **26** 107–8*
Reid, Edward, & Begg **3** 419
Reid, Flora Macdonald **26** 109
Reid, George A(gnew) **5** 566; **22** 335; **26** 108*; **28** 273
Reid, James W(illiam) **14** 787; **26** 108*; **27** 720
Reid, John **10** 299

Reid, John Robertson **26** 108–9*
Reid, Joseph Neel **7** 619
Reid, Lizzie **26** 109
Reid, Merritt **26** 108
Reid, Nano **16** 18
Reid, Robert (1775-1856) **28** 229; **29** 549
Reid, Robert (*b* 1924) **1** 444; **5** 570; **30** 452; **31** 716
Reid, Sylvia **10** 299
Reid, Walter **26** 107
Reid, Watson E. **26** 108
Reid, William **2** 153; **9** 727
Reid, William, & Co. **19** 508
Reid Cabral, William **9** 117
Reid-Dick, William **29** 576
Reid & East **26** 107
Reid of Auchterarder, James **12** 777
Reidy, Affonso Eduardo **26** 109–10*
collaboration **4** 712; **5** 219; **8** 7; **22** 95; **23** 117
works **4** *712*, 713, 726; **26** *110*, 414; **28** 159
Reien Mokuan *see* MOKUAN REIEN
Reifenstein **19** 661
Reifenstein, Johann Friedrich *see* REIFFENSTEIN, JOHANN FRIEDRICH
Reiff, Erik **8** 749
Reiff, Hans Franz *see* REYFF, JOHANN FRANZ
Reiffenstein, Johann Friedrich **26** 110*
Reiffstein, Johann Friedrich *see* REIFFENSTEIN, JOHANN FRIEDRICH
Reigate **10** 227
Reigen, Emperor (*reg* 1663-87) **15** 129; **17** 233
Reigl, Judit **11** 551; **30** 23
Reijers, Zeger **22** 828; **29** 8
Reijmyre Glasbruk **30** 102
Reiling, Reinhold **12** 451, 456; **17** 530
Reilly, Charles (*fl* before 1874) **26** 111
Reilly, Charles H(erbert) (1874-1948) **1** 29; **5** 876; **10** 240; **14** 676; **26** 111*
Reily, Jerry **24** 407
Reimann, Theodor **33** 157
Reimer, Georg Andreas **26** 111–12*
Reimer, Hans **12** 446; **22** 305; **33** 271, 274
Reimers (family) **23** 236
Reimers, Peter **23** 224
Reims **5** 793; **11** *504*; **26** 112–24*, *905*
art school **11** 665
bronze **11** 623
ecclesiastical buildings
Abbey of St Denis *see* Musée Saint-Denis
Cathedral of Notre-Dame **7** 383; **9** 672; **11** 509, 510; **13** 39, 40–41, 42; **14** 518, 519; **17** 461, 462; **23** 538; **26** *114*, 114–15*, *115*, *116*; **29** 413
ambulatory **7** 267
manuscripts **26** 660
metalwork **11** 616
mouldings **22** 217, 218, 220
piers **24** 751
pinnacles **24** 826
sculpture **9** 258; **11** 555; **13** 72, 73, 74–5, 99, 140; **20** 702; **22** 270; **26** 117*, *118*, *119*, 182
silver **11** 621
spire **29** 413
stained glass **13** 179; **26** 120*, *120*; **29** 508
tapestries **11** 639; **19** 382
textiles **30** 331
tombs **13** 72
Reims
ecclesiastical buildings
Cathedral of Notre-Dame—cont.
tracery **31** 270, 271
Treasury **24** *146*
vaults (ceiling) **20** 578
Vierge Dorée **10** 743
westwork **7** 265
St Denis **2** 723
St Nicaise **8** 856; **13** 42; **19** 308; **26** 44, 45, 120–21*, *121*
tracery **31** 273
St Nicolas **26** 681
St Remi **7** 266; **9** 672; **11** 509, 510; **13** 39, 180; **23** 485; **26** 121–3*, *122*, 585, 586
buttresses **5** 319
choir **13** 38, *38*
cloister *see* Musée Saint-Rémi
manuscripts **5** 803
metalwork **26** 682
mouldings **22** 217
piers **24** 751
reliquaries **26** 148
sculpture **26** 123*
stained glass **13** 179, 181; **26** 123–4*, 702; **29** 511
tapestries **11** 639
textiles **28** 715; **30** 331
St Thierry **5** 803
ivory-carvings **5** 810
lace **11** 650
manuscripts **4** 20; **5** 802, 803–4, 810; **7** 512; **9** 219, 686; **11** 653; **20** 330; **30** 486
metalwork **11** 614; **26** *682*
Musée de Reims **6** 77
Musée Saint-Denis **11** 665; **26** 113
Musée Saint-Rémi **26** 113
Porte de Mars **26** 112, 905
silk **11** 644, 645
statue of Louis XV **26** *112*
statuettes **27** 89
tapestries **11** 640; **26** 113–14*
Reims Palimpsest **13** 142
Rein, Melchior **18** 106
Rein, Toomas **10** 538; **26** 124*
Reina, Horacio **14** 716
Rein Abbey **2** 783; **24** 269
Reinagle, Charlotte **26** 124*
Reinagle, Fanny **26** 124*
Reinagle, George Philip **26** 124*
Reinagle, P. A. **26** 124*
Reinagle, Philip **26** 124*
collaboration **12** 647
pupils **14** 810; **26** 124
works **25** 883; **31** 334
Reinagle, Ramsay Richard **26** 124–5*
reproductive prints by others **31** *725*
Reinald, Bishop of Stavanger **29** 578
Reinaud, Joseph-Toussaint **4** 106; **16** 547
Reinel, Jorge **14** 698; **26** 125*
Reinel, Pedro **14** 698; **26** 125*
Reiner, Jan **26** 125
Reiner, Václav Vavřinec **26** 125–6*
patrons and collectors **8** 426
works **4** 58; **8** 391; **25** 432, 443
Reiner, Wenzel Lorenz *see* REINER, VÁCLAV VAVŘINEC
reinforced ceramic **8** 879
reinforced concrete *see under* CONCRETE → types
Reinhard & Hofmeister **7** 838
works **26** *488*
Reinhardt, Ad(olph Dietrich Friedrich) **26** 126–7*; **27** 731
dealers **24** 213
groups and movements **1** 78, 79, 84, 86, 87, 772; **31** 607
patrons and collectors **12** 15
works **7** 636, 637, VII2(d); **14** 164; **21** 892; **26** *126*
Reinhardt, Max **18** 480; **22** 293; **30** 682, 686
productions **3** 537; **7** 856; **8** 428; **29** 777; **30** 686, 687
stage design **31** 702
Reinhardt & Süssenguth **25** 857
Reinhardt Taravell, Hanns *see* TARAVELL, HANNS REINHARDT
Reinhart (family) **30** 143
Reinhart, Fabio **12** 59; **26** 16, 106*; **27** 192; **30** 129
Reinhart, Friedrich **15** 864
Reinhart, Hans (*b c.* 1500/10-1581) **12** 402; **20** 920; **26** 127*
Reinhart, Hans (*d* 1622) **26** 127
Reinhart, Heinrich **13** 315; **15** 864
Reinhart, Johann Christian **22** 703; **26** 127–9*
collaboration **1** 27
works **11** 461; **12** 392; **26** *128*
Reinhart, Oskar **30** 153; **33** 727
Reinhart, Oswald **14** 573
Reinhart, Peter **30** 146
Reinhart, Theodor **33** 727
Reinhart-Volkart, Theodor **30** 153
Reinheim **6** 155; **25** 546
Reinhold, Bernhard **3** 821
Reinhold, Friedrich Philipp **26** 129
Reinhold, Heinrich **12** 393; **26** 129*; **30** 766
Reinhold, Johann Friedrich **26** 129
Reinhold Merkelbach Co. **12** 430
Reinicke, Pancratius **13** 631
Reinicke, Peter **17** 769
Reiniger, Lotte **10** 688
Reiniger, Otto **29** 875
Reinighaus, Carl **28** 89
Reinius, Leif **1** 470; **3** 25*
Reinoso, André **19** 464; **25** 297; **26** 129*, 253
Reinoso, Antonio García *see* GARCÍA REINOSO, ANTONIO
Reinoso, Federico **24** 510
Reinoso, Jorge Vinatea *see* VINATEA REINOSO, JORGE
Reinow, Christian **9** 238
Reins **11** 526
Reins, Adriaan **21** 102
Reins, Jehan de *see* JEHAN DE REINS
Reinstorp, Henrik **4** 665
Reis, Tomb of Emir Yavtaş **16** 186
Reis, António Soares dos *see* SOARES DOS REIS, ANTÓNIO
Reis, Carlos **25** 299; **26** 130*
Reis, Gunther van der **29** 109
Reis, João Braula *see* BRAULA REIS, JOÃO
Reis, Pedro Cabrita *see* CABRITA REIS, PEDRO
Reisai **7** 183; **17** 170
Reisen, Charles Christian **12** 261
reisende und correspondirende Pallas oder Kunst-Zeitung, Die **24** 421, 443
Reiser, Joseph Ignaz **17** 657
Reiser, Matthes **12** 494
Reiser, Niklas **20** 688
Reiset, Frédéric **15** 842, 843
Reisewitz, Wolfgang **29** 608
Reismiller, Johann Benedikt **10** 215
Reisner, George Andrew **10** 71, 78, 81
excavations **10** 80
Giza **12** 767; **14** 494; **22** 398
Kerma **17** 911
Meroë **21** 160
Nag-el-Deir **22** 430
Napata **22** 467
Samaria **27** 669
writings **10** 84
Reisner, Jan **18** 440; **25** 105; **32** 875, 881
Reisner Papyri **22** 431
Reis Pereira, Júlio dos **25** 299
Reiss, Hans **5** 216
Reiss, Johanna Alexandra Jacobi *see* JACOBI, LOTTE
Reiss, Joseph Anton **3** 423
Reiss, Roland **19** 703
Reiss, Weinold **7** 326
Reiss, Wilhelm **29** 220; **31** 380
Reis-Santos, Luís **25** 320
Reissnadel, Master of the **31** 569
Reiter, Erwin **2** 804
Reiter, Jerg **32** 462
Reitharová, E. **8** 426
Reitingler **8** 716
Reitlinger, Gerald **4** 23; **16** 555; **21** 472; **26** 130*
Reitschule *see* RIDING HOUSES
Reitzmann, Heinrich **13** 722
Reizai Tamechika **17** 166
Reizei (family) **17** 225
Reizei Tamemura **33** 577
Rejchan, Alojzy **25** 106
Rejčka, Elizabeth, Queen of Bohemia **8** 421
Rejlander, O(scar) G(ustav) **24** 650, 668; **26** 131*
pupils **26** 472
works **24** *668*, 685
Rejon de Silva, Diego Antonio **10** 206
Rejsek, Matěj **8** 377, 383; **16** 866; **25** 425; **26** 131–2*
works **18** 539
Rejt, Benedikt *see* RIED, BENEDIKT
Reka, Pakatan **20** 168
Rekerdam Castle **22** 822
Rekhmire
tomb **9** 839; **26** 132*
wall paintings **9** 790, *816*, *818*, 818, *821*, 855, 861, 881, 901, 902; **10** 62, *62*; **26** 132; **31** 107
Reklama-Mechano **3** 788
relics, cult of *see* CULT OF RELICS
Relics Master **4** 582
relief beads *see under* BEADS → types
relief-blue wares *see under* POTTERY→ wares
relief etchings *see under* ETCHINGS → types
Reliefmosaik *see under* HARDSTONES → techniques
relief prints *see under* PRINTS → types
reliefs *see* RELIEF SCULPTURE; ROCK RELIEFS
relief sculpture **26** 132–7*
historical and regional traditions
Achaemenid **1** 117; **6** *479*; **15** *914*; **24** *220*
Anatolia, ancient **1** 522; **33** *685*
Hittite **14** *592*
Neo-Hittite **5** *729*
7th cent. BC **17** *810*
Ancient Near East **4** 769; **22** *511*; **25** *880*; **26** 134; **31** 530
Arabia
alabaster (gypsum) **2** *256*
stone **2** 253–6*
6th cent. BC **2** *254*
Armenia (Europe) **1** 451; **2** 433–6*
10th cent. AD **2** *434*, 435
13th cent. **2** *435*
Assyrian **1** 831, 833, 854; **2** 641, *641*; **6** *478*; **21** 296–302*, *297*, 553, 554; **22** *511*; **26** 134; **29** *701*, XI; **30** 187
Aztec **2** *907*
Bactria **6** 216–17, *217*
Bali (Indonesia) **15** *786*
Belarus' **3** *530*
Black Sea Colonies **4** *111*
bronze
Italy **24** *874*
Buddhism **5** *88*
Central Asia, Eastern **6** *299*
Central Asia, Western **6** *217*
China **6** 714
relief sculpture
historical and regional traditions
Buddhism—cont.
Indian subcontinent **5** *88*, *95*; **9** *35*; **15** *248*, *415*, 425–6, *429*, *435*, *437*, 442, 448, 453, *454*; **20** *819*
Indonesia **15** 779
Java **15** 779
Korea **18** *296*
Laos **18** 768–9
Thailand **30** *604*
Byzantine **7** *221*; **9** 594–9*, *595*, *598*; **26** 135–6*
Cambodia **5** 490–93, 495–6, *496*, 499, 500
Hinduism **5** *487*, 487–9, *488*, 490, *492*, *493*
20th cent. **5** *500*
Carolingian **5** *796*, 796–7
Central Asia, Eastern **6** *299*
Central Asia, Western **23** *608*
Bactria **6** 216–17, *217*
Buddhism **6** *217*
Islamic **6** 222
Khwarazm **6** *218*, 218–19
Sogdiana **6** 219
Uzbekistan **6** *187*, *276*; **18** *16*
Champa **6** 426; **29** IX2
Chimú **6** *607*; **29** *168*
China **6** 714, 730, *732*
Christianity **9** 596–7*; **12** 402, 405
Crete **13** 582; **21** *663*
Croatia **8** *177*
Cycladic **22** 698
Cyprus, ancient **8** 339
Czech Republic **8** *382*, *383*
Denmark **26** *305*
Dominican Order **9** *106*
Early Christian (*c.* AD 250-843) **9** 594–7*; **26** 135–6*
Egypt, ancient **9** 790, *848*, 863–4*; **10** 2; **25** 761; **26** 132, 133–4; **29** 814; **30** *696*
Amarna (1353-1333 BC) **9** 884*, *884*
Early Dynastic (*c.* 2925-*c.* 2575 BC) **1** *99*; **9** 867–8*; **14** *494*
First Intermediate Period (*c.* 2130-*c.* 1938 BC) **9** *873*, 873–4*
Graeco-Roman (332 BC-AD 395) **9** *896*, 896–7*; **10** *69*, *507*
Late Period (664-332 BC) **9** 890–92*, *891*
Middle Kingdom (*c.* 1966-*c.* 1630 BC) **2** *656*; **9** 876–8*, *878*; **21** *60*; **24** *88*
New Kingdom (*c.* 1539-*c.* 1075 BC) **1** *100*; **9** 881–2*, *882*, 885–6*; **10** *88*; **17** *714*; **22** *512*; **28** *495*
Old Kingdom (*c.* 2575-*c.* 2130 BC) **9** *820*, 871–2*, *872*; **10** 82
Predynastic (*c.* 6000-*c.* 2925 BC) **9** 865*
Ptolemaic (304-30 BC) **9** *894*, 894–5*
Second Intermediate Period (*c.* 1630-*c.* 1540 BC) **9** 879*
Third Intermediate Period (*c.* 1075-*c.* 656 BC) **9** *887*, 888*
18th Dynasty (*c.* 1539-*c.* 1292 BC) **30** *700*
Elamite **10** *133*
England
Gothic **9** *681*; **10** *674*; **27** *629*
Neo-classicism **8** *587*
New Sculpture (UK) **3** *367*
Romanesque **19** *404*, *405*; **26** *614*
Estonia **10** *538*
Etruscan **10** 593, *593*, 604
France **11** 588; **25** *476*, 477
Gothic **8** *892*; **24** *155*

relief sculpture
historical and regional traditions
France—cont.
Mannerism **24** *814*
Neo-classicism **27** *310*
Prehistoric **11** *477*
Renaissance **11** *557*; **13** *226*
Romanesque **7** *224*; **21** *798, 799*; **29** *94*; **31** *209*; **32** *397*
19th cent. **5** *825*
Georgia **12** *321*
Germany
Expressionism **12** *408*
Gothic **13** *86*; **29** *818*
Gothic: Late Gothic **22** *280*
Mannerism **33** *739*
Ottonian **7** *381*
Protestantism **12** 402, 405
Renaissance **8** *541*; **32** *606, 830*
16th cent. **19** *108*
18th cent. **28** *43*
Gothic
England **9** *681*; **10** *674*; **27** *629*
France **8** *892*; **24** *155*
Germany **13** *86*; **22** *280*; **29** *818*
Italy **7** *334*; **11** *200*; **16** *687*; **23** *587*; **24** *869, 870, 874*
Poland **31** *394*
Spain **19** *173*
Sweden **13** *103*
Greece **9** *598*
Greece, ancient **8** *690*; **10** *139*; **11** 791; **13** 370, *371*, 424, 427–8*, 430–32*, 582*; **22** *514*; **24** *415*; **26** 134–5*, *292*
Archaic **13** *582*; **30** *645*
Archaic, Late **13** *431, 447*
Classical, Early **13** *432*, 451
Classical, High **13** *455*, 455–8
Classical, Late **13** 461*
Rich style **13** *456, 458*
Turkey **10** *431*; **14** *69*
6th cent. BC **29** *368*
Helladic **14** 352–3
Hinduism
Cambodia **5** *487*, 487–9, *488*, 490, *492, 493*
Champa **6** *429*
Indian subcontinent **15** *490, 492*, 507–14, *514*; **20** *224*
Indian subcontinent: Saura **15** *536*
Indian subcontinent: Shaivism **15** 443, *489*
Indonesia **15** 780
Java **15** 780
Laos **18** *769*
Vietnam **6** *429*
Hittite **1** 522; **4** *231*; **14** *592*; **33** *513*
Honduras **7** *801*
Hungary **24** *314*
Indian subcontinent **15** *230, 233, 235, 250*, 413, 499, 719; **23** 803
Andhra Pradesh **15** *536, 537, 538, 539*
Buddhism **5** *88, 95*; **9** *35*; **15** *248, 415*, 425–6, *429, 435, 437*, 442, 448, 453, *454*; **20** *819*
Chalukyas of Badami **15** *527*
Gandhara **9** *34*; **15** *446, 447*
Gujarat **15** *490*
Gupta **8** *768*; **15** *476*
Hinduism **15** *490, 492*, 507–14, *514*; **20** *224*
Hinduism: Saura **15** *536*
Hinduism: Shaivism **15** 443, *489*
Hoysala **15** *532*
Kerala **15** *521*
Kushana **20** *818*
Kushana period **15** *452*

relief sculpture
historical and regional traditions
Indian subcontinent—cont.
Madya Pradesh **15** *497, 498*
Maharashtra **15** *451, 492*
Rajasthan **15** *489, 542*
Tamil Nadu **15** 507–14
Vijayanagara period **15** *540*
1st cent. BC **15** *235*
2nd cent. BC **15** 428, *434*
5th cent. AD **31** 520, *520*
Indonesia **15** 779, 780, 781–3, *786*
Iran, ancient **24** *220*; **33** *707*
Iraq **14** *226*; **16** 243, *247*
Islamic **6** 222; **16** *247*
Italy **16** 749; **27** *23, 26*
Baroque **1** *629*; **5** *377*; **11** *235*; **13** *815*; **19** *88*; **22** *478*; **29** *29*
Carolingian **5** *796*
Dominican Order **9** *106*
Etruscan **10** 593, *593*
Gothic **7** *334*; **11** *200*; **16** *687*; **23** *586, 587*; **24** *869, 870, 874*
Lombard art **19** *550*
Mannerism **12** *574*
Renaissance **1** *456, 748*; **3** *159, 260, 637, 860*; **8** *798*; **9** *125, 130*; **11** *184, 693*; **12** *540, 541*; **16** 689, *692, 842, 844*; **19** *208, 688*; **20** *622*; **21** *693*; **24** *756*; **25** III; **26** *327, 443, 444, 446, 766*; **30** *508*
Roman **26** *792*; **27** *38, 40, 43*; **31** *369*
Romanesque **3** *236*; **5** *550*; **11** *6*; **21** *774*; **24** *194, 195*; **26** *623, 627*; **32** *344*
13th cent. **9** *106*
15th cent. **11** *896*; **22** *476*
16th cent. **19** *556, 557*
19th cent. **32** *122*
Japan **17** *106*
Java **15** 779, 780, 781–3
Jewish art **17** 554, *554*
Khwarazm **6** *218*, 218–19
Korea **18** *296, 298*
Laos **18** 768–70, *769*
Libya **19** *223*
limestone
Romanesque **26** *614*
Lombard art **19** 549*, *550*
Lycia **19** *839*
Malaysia **20** 170
Malta (Republic of) **20** 210
Maya **5** *394*; **7** *801*; **16** 807–8; **21** 217, 266; **23** *839*; **27** 607, 780
Mesoamerica, Pre-Columbian **21** 198–9, *206*, 219*; **25** 764; **27** 780
Aztec **2** *907*
Honduras **7** *801*
Maya **6** *394*; **7** *801*; **21** 266; **23** *839*; **27** 607
Mexico **2** *907*; **8** *460*; **23** *839*; **33** *473*
Zapotec **8** *460*
Mesopotamia **21** 293, 296–302*, 308; **26** 133–4
Assyrian **2** *641*; **21** *297*; **29** XI
Early Dynastic (*c.* 2900–*c.* 2340 BC) **21** *273*
Elamite **10** *133*
2nd cent. AD **14** *226*
Mexico **2** *907*; **8** *460*; **23** *839*; **33** *473*
Minoan **21** *663*; **26** 134
Mughal **23** 803
Mycenaean **14** 352–3; **26** 134
Netherlands, the **22** *117, 855*
Norway **23** *229*
Nubia **9** 881, 896; **23** 281, *284*
Ottonian **7** *381*

relief sculpture
historical and regional traditions—cont.
Pakistan **5** *308, 309*; **23** 803
Palestine **17** *554*
Parthian **9** *414*; **24** 218
Peru **6** *607*; **29** *168*
Poland **29** *793*; **31** *394*
Prehistoric art **8** 339; **25** *476*, 477, *477*, 487, 488, 491, 493, 494
Romanesque
Croatia **8** *177*
Czech Republic **8** *382*
Denmark **26** *305*
England **19** *404, 405*; **26** *614*
France **7** *224*; **21** *798, 799*; **29** *94*; **31** *209*; **32** *397*
Hungary **24** *314*
Italy **3** *236*; **5** *550*; **11** *6*; **21** *774*; **24** *194, 195*; **26** *623, 627*; **32** *344*
Netherlands, the **22** *855*
Poland **29** *793*
Spain **2** *866, 867*; **26** *608*; **28** *728*
Sweden **26** *640*
Rome, ancient **9** *517*; **15** *92*; **22** *411*; **26** 135*, *858*, 861; **27** *23*, 23–6*, *26*, 29, 31, 33, *33*, 34, *34*, 35–6, *36*, 39, 40, 41, 42, *42, 44, 93*
Italy **26** *792*; **27** *38, 40, 43*; **31** *369*
Jewish art **17** 554
Late Antiquity **18** *824*
Libya **19** *223*
Turkey **2** *220*
1st cent. BC **9** *249*
Russia **27** *389*
Sasanian **11** *121*
Serbia **28** *453*
Sicily **13** 582
Slovenia **28** 861
Sogdiana **6** 219
South America, Pre-Columbian **6** *607*; **29** *168*
Spain
Gothic **19** *173*
Renaissance **3** *847*; **32** *493*
Romanesque **2** *866, 867*; **26** *608*; **28** *728*
Visigothic **32** *618*
Sweden **13** *103*; **26** *640*
Switzerland **2** *489*
Syria **9** *414*; **16** 243; **23** *894*
Syria-Palestine **30** 187, 190, 193, *193*
Thailand **29** *827*; **30** *604*
Toltec **31** *99*
Turkey
Byzantine **9** *595*
Greece, ancient **10** *431*; **14** *69*
Hittite **4** *231*; **33** *513*
Neo-Hittite **5** *729*
Roman **2** *220*
Ukraine **31** *560*
United States of America **31** *612*
Urartian **17** 878–9
Uzbekistan **6** *187, 276*; **18** *16*
Vietnam **6** 426, *429*; **29** IX2
Visigothic **32** *618*
Zapotec **8** *460*; **21** 219*
Zoroastrianism **23** *608*; **33** *707*
materials
adobe **29** *168*
alabaster (gypsum) **2** *641*; **21** *297*; **22** *280*; **32** *493*
amber **1** 762
basalt **33** *685*
box-wood **19** *108*
brass **32** *606*
brick **4** 769, 789–90
bronze
Assyrian **21** 296
England **3** *367*
France **24** *814*

relief sculpture
materials
bronze—cont.
Germany **7** *381*
Gothic **24** *874*
Greece, ancient **8** *690*
Italy **3** *860*; **9** *130*; **10** 604; **11** *200, 693*; **12** *540, 541*; **19** *208*; **20** *622*; **26** *327, 766*; **29** *29*; **32** *122*
United States of America **27** *557*; **31** *612*
cement **5** *500*
clay **6** *187, 218, 299*
granite **15** *233, 538*
gypsum **29** 814
inscriptions **9** 867; **13** 456–7
ivory **23** *229*
limestone **10** *674*; **15** *914*
Assyrian **22** *511*; **29** *701*
Bactria **6** *217*
Egypt, ancient **1** *100*; **9** *872, 873, 882, 884, 891*; **10** *88*; **25** *880*; **30** *696*
France **32** *397*
Germany **8** *541*
Mesopotamia **21** *273*; **29** XI
Netherlands, the **22** *117*
Romanesque **28** *728*
Syria **9** *414*; **23** *894*
marble
Black Sea Colonies **4** *111*
Byzantine **7** *221*; **9** *595, 598*
Carolingian **5** *796*
Dominican Order **9** *106*
England **8** *587*
France **11** *557*; **31** *209*
Germany **28** *43*
Gothic **23** *587*; **24** *869, 870*
Greece, ancient **13** *371, 428, 447, 455, 458*; **22** *514*; **29** *368*
Italy **5** *550*
Italy: Baroque **1** *629*; **5** *377*; **11** *235*; **13** *815*; **19** *88*
Italy: Gothic **7** *334*; **16** *687*; **23** *587*; **24** *869, 870*
Italy: Lombard art **19** *550*
Italy: Renaissance **1** *456*; **3** *159*; **8** *798*; **9** *125*; **11** *184*; **16** *842, 844*; **21** *693*; **26** *443*
Romanesque **5** *550*
Rome, ancient **9** *517*; **19** *223*; **26** *858*; **27** *23, 26, 33, 38, 40, 42*
Russia **27** *389*
Serbia **28** *453*
Spain **32** *618*
Turkey **2** *220*
papier mâché **25** III
poplar **12** *408*
porphyry **27** *43*
sandstone
Arabia **2** *254*
Cambodia **5** *492, 493, 494, 496*
Egypt, ancient **9** *887, 894, 896*; **22** *512*
Germany **13** *86*; **32** *830*
Indian subcontinent **8** *768*; **15** *230, 452, 498, 536, 537, 542*; **20** *818, 819*
Netherlands, the **22** *855*
Vietnam **29** IX2
schist **5** *308, 309*; **15** *446, 447*, 448
silver **3** *367*
slate **3** *530*; **31** *560*
soapstone **18** *298*
stone
Arabia **2** 253–6
Champa **6** *429*
Croatia **8** *177*
Czech Republic **8** *382*
Estonia **10** *538*
Gothic **13** *103*
Indian subcontinent **15** *454, 539, 540*

relief sculpture
materials
stone—cont.
Italy **16** *692*
Mexico **2** *907*; **8** *460*
Sweden **13** *103*
stucco **10** *69*; **15** 448, 499; **23** *839*; **29** 812, *818, 827*; **30** *604*
terracotta
Greece, ancient **13** 582*, *582*
Indian subcontinent **15** 499, 719
Islamic **16** *247*
Italy **3** *260*; **26** *444, 446*; **30** *501*
Uzbekistan **6** *276*
tufa **15** *786*
walnut **3** *847*
waxes **12** *574*; **16** 749; **33** 2
wood **8** *383*; **14** *494*; **18** *296, 769*; **33** *739*
techniques
gilding **12** *540, 541*; **18** *296*
moulding **6** 218
polychromy **25** III
types
record **13** 428*, *428*, 456–7
votive **8** *516, 517*; **13** 427–8*
see also PLAQUETTES; ROCK RELIEFS
relieving arches *see under* ARCHES → types
Religieuse clocks *see under* CLOCKS → types
religion and art **1** 102; **6** 510; **26** 137–41*
religious books **4** 356, 358; **10** 4
Religious Society of Friends *see under* CHRISTIANITY → sects
relining **5** 657; **7** 747; **26** 142*
reliquaries **1** 697, 707; **8** 195, 260; **17** 518, 520; **23** 401; **26** 142–51*; **28** 630–31, 632
historical and regional traditions
Afghanistan **1** *206*
Belgium **3** 593; **26** *145*
Gothic **5** *213*
Romanesque **10** IV2; **26** 683, *693*
Buddhism **26** 149–51*
Afghanistan **1** *206*
Central Asia, Eastern **6** 319
China **7** 24, 25, 82; **23** 776; **26** 150
Indian subcontinent **26** 149–50, *150, 151*
Thailand **26** 151
Tibet **30** *849*
Byzantine **5** 300; **9** *520, 647*, 657, 658, *658*, 659–60, *663*; **26** 143–4*
Carolingian **5** 806, 807–8, *808*; **10** *115*; **26** 144–5*
Central Asia, Eastern **6** 319, *321*
China **7** 24, 25, 82; **23** 776; **26** 150
Christianity **26** 142*
Early Christian (*c.* AD 250–843) **9** *647*, 659–60; **26** 143–4*; **28** 629
France **11** 616
Gothic **13** 42, 158, 168, 169, *169, 170*; **24** *146*; **26** *147*
Gothic Revival **32** *598*
Ottonian **7** 720
Romanesque **26** *692*
Germany **12** 442, 447
Carolingian **10** *115*
Gothic **13** 169; **26** *371*
Ottonian **26** *145*
Romanesque **26** *146*
Gothic **9** *3*; **26** 146–7*
Belgium **5** *213*
France **13** 42, 158, 168, 169, *169, 170*; **24** *146*; **26** *147*
Germany **13** 169; **26** *371*
Italy **13** 169

reliquaries
historical and regional traditions—cont.
Indian subcontinent **15** *686*, *698*; **26** 149–50, *150*, *151*
Insular art **15** 872; **28** *630*
Ireland **15** 872; **28** *630*
Italy **5** *808*; **9** *520*; **13** 169; **31** *535*
Korea **18** *364*, 364
Merovingian **26** 144–5*
Ottonian **7** 720; **22** *43*; **23** 656, 659; **26** *145*, 145–6*
Poland **25** *128*
Post-Byzantine **26** 149*
Romanesque **10** IV2; **26** *145*, 145–6*, *146*, 683, *692*, *693*
Spain **29** 332, 341
Thailand **26** 151
Tibet **30** *849*
materials
amethyst **26** *147*
brass **30** *849*
bronze **18** *364*; **26** *145*, *146*, *150*; **28** *630*
enamel
Belgium **5** *213*; **10** IV2; **26** *693*
Byzantine **9** *658*
France **13** 168, 169, *169*, *170*; **24** *146*; **26** *692*
Germany **13** 169; **26** *146*
Ireland **28** *630*
Italy **13** 169; **26** *144*
garnets **1** *206*
gems **5** *808*; **26** *145*
glass **3** 593; **7** 82; **18** 364
gold
Afghanistan **1** *206*
Belgium **5** *213*
Byzantine **9** *658*, *663*
France **24** *146*; **26** *147*
Germany **26** *145*
Italy **5** *808*; **26** *144*
Ottonian **22** *43*
ivory **9** *647*, 650; **16** 799; **23** 659; **26** *146*
lime-wood **26** *371*
pottery **15** *686*
rock crystal **15** *698*; **26** *147*
silver **5** *213*; **9** *3*, *520*, 657, 658; **10** *115*; **22** *43*; **26** *145*
silver-gilt **9** *520*, *658*; **13** *169*, *170*; **24** *146*
soapstone **26** *151*
wood **6** *321*
techniques
gilding **18** *364*; **26** *145*, *146*
painting **6** *321*
types
burse **26** 144
chasse **6** 500*; **28** 630
cross **26** 143, 144, *144*, 145
see also CROSSES → types → processional
staurothèques **9** 650; **26** 143
reliquary mounds *see* STUPAS
Reliquary of Elizabeth of Hungary **13** 169, *169*
Reliquary of St Cassien **11** 636
Reliquary of St Gregory Nazianzen **26** 683
Reliquary of St John the Evangelist **26** 685
Reliquary of St Lawrence **26** 683
Reliquary of St Millán **16** 436
Reliquary of St Petroc **16** 525
Reliquary of the Holy Thorn **13** 159; **24** 146, *146*; **26** *147*; **31** 837
Reliquary of the Order of the Holy Spirit **10** 323
Reliquary of the True Cross **16** 750; **24** 223
Reljić, Radomir **28** 451
Relling, Ingmar **23** 234
Relyveld, Willy **30** 15
Rem, Gaspar **1** 5
Remagen
Apollinariskirche **33** 745
Remagen—cont.
SS Peter and Paul **9** 680
remarques **25** 599, *599*; **26** 151*
Remb, Franz Carl **26** 151–2*
Remb, Johann Georg **26** 151
Rembrandt-Corpus **22** 911
Rembrandt Intaglio Printing Co. **18** 127
Rembrandt Research Project **2** 835; **7** 715; **29** 850
Rembrandt (Harmensz.) van Rijn **1** 104; **7** 226; **12** 390; **13** 895; **14** 738; **19** 348; **22** 815, 902; **26** 152–78*, *160*
assistants **10** 731
attributions **2** 835; **9** 301; **10** 146; **11** 847; **17** 666; **32** 74, 268; **33** 263, 714
drawings **18** 228
engravings **18** 228
catalogues **3** 310; **6** 78
collaboration **32** 673
commentaries **14** 740
dealers **3** 22; **9** 424
drawings **1** 585; **9** 216, 222; **24** 349; **32** 899, 900, *900*
chalk **26** *162*, 194
ink **24** *349*; **26** *167*
metalpoints **9** 217
portraits **26** *156*
frames **11** 456
groups and movements **3** 261, 264, 267; **23** 503; **30** 456
methods **5** 277; **6** 570; **9** 218, 673; **10** 191; **13** 708; **15** 147; **18** 898; **19** 353, 354, 356; **24** 741, 797; **31** 578
paintings **3** 23; **9** 149, 325; **11** 233; **25** 138
conversation pieces **7** 784
genre **26** *164*, *171*; **31** 365
history **22** 841, 842–3, *846*
landscape **18** III1; **26** *159*; **28** 359
mythological **10** 477–8; **19** 356; **23** 294; **26** *158*
portraits **1** *807*; **13** 824; **14** 584; **20** 109; **21** 759; **23** 466; **24** 377, *377*; **26** *163*, *169*
Martens, Baertge **25** *276*
Rijn, Titus (Rembrandtsz.) van **26** 391–2
Six, Jan **26** *163*
Uylenburch, Saskia van **23** I
religious **4** 881; **14** 584; **22** 521; **23** II; **26** *154*, 733
paper **17** 403; **24** 49; **25** 597
patrons and collectors **10** 365; **25** 137
Akademie der Bildenden Künste (Vienna) **2** 831
Altman, Benjamin **1** 731
André, Edouard (*b* 1827) **16** 851
Angerstein, John Julius **2** 51
Arenberg, Auguste-Marie-Raymond, 6th Duke of **2** 382
Arenberg, Engelbert-Marie, 9th Duke of **2** 382
Art Institute of Chicago **27** 463
Aved, Jacques (-André-Joseph) **2** 852
Bache, Jules Semon **3** 18
Baillie, William **3** 74
Baring, Francis (1740-1810) **3** 239
Bartsch, Adam von **3** 310
Baudouin, Silvain-Raphaël **3** 395
Beaumont, George (Howland) **3** 454
Becker, Herman (*c.* 1617-78) **3** 475
Bella, Stefano della **3** 632
Beuningen, Daniel George van **3** 889
Beurnonville, Etienne-Edmond Martin, Baron de **3** 890
Boursse, Jan **4** 587
Bouverie, John **4** 596
Rembrandt (Harmensz.) van Rijn
patrons and collectors—cont.
Braamcamp, Gerrit **4** 618
Brudenell, George, 4th Earl of Cardigan and 1st Duke of Montagu **4** 893
Bryan, Michael **5** 63
Burrell, William (1861-1958) **5** 278
Caffiéri, Philippe (ii) (1714-74) **5** 380
Cappelle, Jan van de **5** 679
Caraman, Duc de **5** 700
Carol I, King of Romania (*reg* 1866-1914) **5** 792; **26** 722
Caroline Louise, Margravine of Baden-Durlach (1723-83) **33** 594
Carr, William Holwell **5** 848
Carraquiri, Nazario **5** 871
Catherine II, Empress of Russia (*reg* 1762- 96) **26** 732, 733
Cavendish, William, 2nd Duke of Devonshire (1671-1729) **6** 116; **9** 230
Cavendish, William, 3rd Duke of Devonshire (1698-1755) **6** 117
Ceán Bermúdez, Juan Agustín **6** 124
Cheney, Edward **6** 537
Choiseul, Etienne-François, Duc de **7** 194
Clark, Robert Sterling **7** 377
Clerk, John, 1st Baron Eldin (1757-1832) **7** 419
Coats, W. A. **28** 272
Coningham, William **7** 709
Conti, Louis-François de Bourbon, Prince de (1717-76) **7** 778
Crozat, Pierre **8** 209
Czartoryska, Isabella, Princess (1746-1835) **8** 372
Denon, (Dominique-) Vivant **33** 345
Dighton, Robert (i) (1752-1814) **8** 886
Dussen, Cornelia van der **27** 271
Dutuit (family) **9** 466
Dutuit, (Etienne-Philippe-) Eugène **9** 466
Duveen, Joseph, 1st Baron Duveen of Millbank **9** 467
Ensenada, Marqués de **10** 406
Esdaile, William **10** 505; **33** 345
Esterházy, Miklós II, Prince (1765-1833) **10** 530
Everdingen, Allart van **10** 660
Faesch, Johann Jakob **10** 753
Ferdinand II, King of Portugal (1816-89) **4** 639
Fesch, Joseph, Cardinal **11** 32
Fitzwilliam, Richard, 7th Viscount Fitzwilliam **11** 141
Flinck, Nicolaes Anthonis **11** 170
Fountaine, Andrew (1676-1753) **11** 348
Frederick II, King of Prussia (*reg* 1740-86) **14** 652
Frederick Henry, Stadholder of the Netherlands, Prince of Orange (*reg* 1625-47) **23** 465
Frederick William IV, King of Prussia (*reg* 1840-61) **14** 650
Frick, Henry Clay **11** 774
Fries, Moritz, Graf von **11** 789
Gardner, Isabella Stewart **12** 147
George IV, King of Great Britain (*reg* 1820-30) **10** 365; **14** 146; **28** 527
Getty, J(ean) Paul **12** 504
Gheyn, Jacques de, III (?1596-1641) **12** 532
Rembrandt (Harmensz.) van Rijn
patrons and collectors—cont.
Goll van Franckenstein (family) **12** 876
Graham-Gilbert, John **13** 273
Guinness, Edward (Cecil), 1st Earl of Iveagh **13** 836
Gulbenkian, Calouste Sarkis **13** 841
Gustav III, King of Sweden (*reg* 1771-92) **30** 118
Haden, (Francis) Seymour **9** 309
Hall, Peter Adolf **14** 80
Havemeyer, Louisine and Henry **14** 244
Hawkins, John Heywood (1803-77) **14** 252
Heinecken, Karl Heinrich von **14** 314
Hem, Laurens van der **14** 375
Herbert, Thomas, 8th Earl of Pembroke **14** 436
Hervey, Frederick Augustus, 4th Earl of Bristol **14** 485
Hirsch, Robert von **14** 570
His de La Salle, (Aimé-Charles-) Horace **14** 577
Hoare (i), Henry the younger (1705-85) **14** 598
Holford, Robert Stayner **14** 675
Hoop, Adriaan van der **32** 708
Houbraken, Jacobus **14** 795
Hudson, Thomas (1701-99) **14** 842
Hume, Abraham, 2nd Baronet **14** 877
Hunter, William (1718-83) **15** 29
Huntington, Arabella D(uval) **15** 29
Huygens, Constantijn (i) (1596-1687) **15** 40
Jabach, Everard **16** 815
Jennens, Charles **10** 364; **17** 476
John II (Casmir), King of Poland (*reg* 1648-68) **32** 7
John V, King of Portugal (*reg* 1706-50) **4** 636
John Sobieski, King of Poland (*reg* 1674-96) **25** 138
John William, Elector Palatine (*reg* 1690-1716) **12** 473
Josephine, Empress of the French (1763-1814) **4** 303
Jullienne, Jean de **17** 684
Kann, Rodolphe **17** 777
Kneller, Godfrey **18** 145
Knight, Richard Payne **18** 150
Krasiński, Jan Dobrogost (Bonaventura) **18** 440
La Caze, Louis **18** 588
Lankrink, Prosper Henry **18** 748
La Roque, Antoine de **18** 796
Las Marismas del Guadalquivir, Alejandro María Aguado y Ramírez de Estemoz, Marqués de **18** 811
Le Brun, Jean-Baptiste-Pierre **19** 25
Lempereur, Jean-Baptiste-Denis **19** 144
Le Secq (des Tournelles), Henri (1818-82) **19** 239
Ligne, Charles-Joseph-Emmanuel de, Prince (1759-92) **19** 369
Loeser, Charles Alexander **19** 538
Louis XIV, King of France (*reg* 1643-1715) **4** 552
Loyd, Samuel Jones, 1st Baron Overstone **19** 736
Lubomirski, Henryk **19** 752
Lugt, Frits (Johannes) **19** 783
Mariette, Jean **20** 416
Mariette, Pierre-Jean **20** 417
Marolles, Michel de **20** 455
Rembrandt (Harmensz.) van Rijn
patrons and collectors—cont.
Marquand, Henry G(urdon) **20** 461
Martens, Baertge **25** 277
McLellan, Archibald **28** 271
Mead, Richard **10** 364
Medici, Leopoldo de', Cardinal **21** 28
Montagu-Douglas-Scott, Walter Francis, 5th Duke of Buccleuch, 7th Duke of Queensberry **21** 908
Morny, Charles-Auguste, Duc de **22** 127
Morrison, James **22** 148
Munro (of Novar), H(ugh) A(ndrew) J(ohnstone) **22** 314
National Gallery of Scotland **28** 272
Norton Simon Museum **19** 703
Ogiński, Michał Kazimierz, Prince **23** 369
Ottley, William Young **23** 634
Périer, Casimir **24** 418
Peter I, Tsar and Emperor of Russia (*reg* 1682-1725) **26** 729
Piles, Roger de **24** 805
Pond, Arthur **25** 210
Poniatowski, Stanisław, Prince **25** 212
Potocki, Wincenty **25** 364
Randon de Boisset, (Pierre-Louis-)Paul **25** 888
Reynolds, Joshua **26** 279, 280
Richards, John Inigo **26** 335
Richardson, Jonathan (1665-1745) **26** 346
Richter, Johann Thomas **19** 111
Ricketts, Charles (de Sousy) & Shannon, Charles **26** 360
Robert-Dumesnil, Alexandre-Pierre-François **26** 453
Rosenwald, Lessing J(ulius) **27** 166
Rothschild, James Mayer de, Baron (1792-1868) **27** 223
Röver, Valerius **14** 491; **27** 270, 271
Ruffo, Antonio **27** 316
Sachs, Paul J(oseph) **27** 493
Saint-Morys, Charles Paul Jean-Baptiste de Bourgevin Vialart de **27** 568
Saint-Non, Richard de, Abbé **27** 570
Salting, George **27** 641
Schönborn, Lothar Franz von, Bishop of Bamberg, Elector-Archbishop of Mainz **28** 146
Scriverius, Petrus **28** 309
Seilern, Antoine, Count **28** 377
Seymour-Conway, Francis Charles, 3rd Marquess of Hertford **28** 527
Seymour-Conway, Richard, 4th Marquess of Hertford **28** 527
Sheremet'yev, Pyotr (Borisovich), Count **28** 593
Simon, Norton **28** 751
Six, Jan (1618-1700) **22** 902; **28** 810
Slingelandt, Govert van, Lord of Lindt and West-IJsselmonde **28** 842
Sparre, Gustaf Adolf **29** 366; **30** 118
Steengracht van Oostkapelle, Johan **29** 592
Streeter, Robert (1621-79) **29** 767
Stuart, John, 3rd Earl of Bute (1713-92) **29** 796
Tallard, Marie-Joseph d'Hostun, Duc de **30** 274
Tarnowski, Jan Feliks, Count and Waleria **30** 345

Rembrandt (Harmensz.) van Rijn
patrons and collectors—cont.
Tarnowski, Waleria, Countess 30 345
Tessin, Carl Gustav, Count 30 524
Thibaudeau, Narcisse-Adolphe, Comte de 30 727
Thiers, Louis-Antoine Crozat, Baron de 8 209
Trip (family) 31 341
Tronchin, François 31 363
Uylenburgh, Hendrick van 31 779
Vaudreuil, François, Comte de 32 85
Verstolk van Soelen, Jan Gijsbert, Baron 32 377
Vos (ii) Jbzn, Jacob de (1803-82) 32 707, 708
Walker, (Byron) Edmund 32 794
Watelet, Claude-Henri 32 898
Wellesley, Henry 33 56
Widener, Joseph E. 33 159
Wildenstein, Georges 33 182
William I, King of the Netherlands (*reg* 1813-40) 23 469
William II, King of the Netherlands (*reg* 1840-49) 23 469
William IV, Stadholder of the Netherlands, Prince of Orange (*reg* 1747-51) 23 468
William V, Stadholder of the Netherlands, Prince of Orange (*reg* 1751-95) 23 469
William VIII, Landgrave of Hesse-Kassel (*reg* 1751-60) 12 473
Worlidge, Thomas 33 380
Yusupov, Nikolay (Borisovich), Prince (1751-1831) 33 579
Zoomer, Jan Pietersz. 25 631; 33 345, 700
personal collection 2 559; 5 351; 9 229; 22 904; 25 248; 26 313
drawings 9 150; 18 819
paintings 4 871; 15 741; 16 553; 28 359, 362
prints 5 325; 25 630; 28 361
prints 4 359; 19 395; 20 601; 25 596, 599, 600, 605, 606, 625, 631; 29 557
drypoints 9 307, 308, 308
engravings 10 478
etchings 10 553, 554; 22 906; 26 165; 28 361
landscape 25 619
mythological 23 294
religious 2 558; 5 447; 10 553; 25 618
townscapes 13 894
monotypes 21 895
pupils 1 807; 9 169
Bol, Ferdinand 4 249
Boursse, Esaias 4 587
Dijck, Abraham van 8 887
Dou, Gerrit 9 192; 19 101
Drost, Willem 9 300
Eeckhout, Gerbrand van den 9 741, 742
Fabritius, Carel 10 730, 732
Flinck, Govaert 11 169
Furnerius, Abraham 11 847; 18 228
Gelder, Arent de 12 240
Hoogstraten, Samuel van 14 737, 738
Jouderville, Isack (de) 17 666
Keil, Bernhard 17 879
Kneller, Godfrey 18 144
Koninck, Philips (de) 18 229
Leupenius, Johannes 19 258
Maes, Nicolaes 20 78
Rembrandt (Harmensz.) van Rijn
pupils—cont.
Mayr, Johann Ulrich (1630-1704) 20 894
Ovens, Jürgen 23 674
Paudiss, Christopher 24 277
Pluym, Karel van der 25 53
Poorter, Willem de 25 230
Renesse, Constantijn (Daniel) van 26 194, 194
Roghman, Roelant 26 543
Uylenburgh, Gerrit 31 779
Wet, Jacob (Willemsz.) de, I (1610-71) 33 110
Wet, Jan de 33 110
With, Pieter de 33 263
reproductions on postage stamps 25 329
reproductive prints by others
Baillie, William 3 74
Bartsch, Adam von 25 619
Burnet, John (1784-1868) 5 271
Cole, (Walter Sylvanus) Timothy 26 234
Denon, (Dominique-) Vivant 8 763
Dixon, John 9 43
Flameng, Léopold 26 234
Gaillard, Ferdinand 26 233
Gaywood, Richard 12 222
Haid (i), Johann Gottfried 14 49
Hollar, Wenceslaus 14 683
Houbraken, Jacobus 14 795
Houston, Richard 14 803
Köpping, Karl 18 237
Leeuw, Willem van der 19 64
McArdell, James 19 867
Moreau (i), Jean-Michel 22 88
Mouilleron, Adolphe 26 232, 233
Pether, William 24 551
Say, William 28 25
Suyderhoef, Jonas 30 47
Vallotton, Félix (-Emile-Jean) 31 830
restorations by others 21 429; 27 321
studio 29 855
teachers 18 817; 22 841; 25 758; 30 60
workshop 9 222; 29 850
Rembrandt van Rijn Foundation 29 121
Remède de Fortune Master 13 827; 20 631
works 13 827
Remedi, Marchese 19 793
Remee *see* LEEMPUT, REMI VAN
Remeeus, David 32 702, 705
remembrance gardens *see under* GARDENS → types
Remezov, S. U. 31 68
Remick, Christian 4 477
Remigia 25 470; 26 179–80*; 29 259
Remigio, Giovanni 19 63
Remigius, Bishop of Lincoln 19 401, 404; 26 587
Remigius of Auxerre 22 412
Remington, E., & Sons 25 589
Remington, Frederic (Sackrider) 3 390; 26 180*; 31 602, 612
dealers 18 161
works 2 106; 4 364, 365; 26 180; 29 576; 33 184
Remington, Philo 15 822
Remiremont Abbey Church 7 265
Remmelin, J. 1 841
Remmers, Johannes 14 386
Remmey, Henry, sr (1770-1865) 8 184
Remmey, Henry, jr (*fl* 1827) 8 184
Remmey, John 8 184*; 31 635
Remmi, John *see* REMMEY, JOHN
Remojadas 21 193, 197, 372; 26 181*
clay 26 181
figurines 26 181
pottery 21 237
sculpture 26 181
Rémond, François 11 625, 627; 26 39, 181–2*
collaboration 9 379; 26 376
patrons and collectors 31 480
works 11 627
Rémond, Jean-Charles-Joseph 11 800
Rémond, Joseph 27 265
Remondini (printers)
printmakers 6 91; 31 821
production 16 716; 18 614; 24 55
workshop 3 199; 10 394; 12 582
Remondini, Giambattista 32 689
Remondini, Giovanni Antonio 25 626
Removedor 31 183
Remp, Frančišek Karel *see* REMB, FRANZ CARL
Remponeau, George 14 58; 21 894
Remsey, Jenő 12 839
Remy *see* LEEMPUT, REMI VAN
Rémy, Barthélémy 11 903
Remy, Ludwig von 32 457
Remy, Perrin 5 208
Rémy, Pierre 6 81; 11 663
catalogues 2 852; 6 81; 11 662; 18 693; 30 343
dealing 11 663
Rémy, Usines 8 681
Rémy de la Fosse, Louis 14 141
Remyonov-Tyan-Shansky, P. P. 26 734
Ren (family) 7 15
Renaissance 1 105; 7 382, 383; 13 605; 14 866, 868; 24 454; 26 182–9*
academies 16 779
aesthetics 1 178–9*
architectural history 9 351
art criticism 32 18
art forms
alabaster-carvings 32 493
allegories 1 654–8*
altarpieces
Belgium 5 625; 7 424; 8 86; 11 441; 21 353; 23 525
Germany 4 759; 5 200; 8 116; 12 401; 13 721, 722
Italy 2 32, 180; 3 663, 917; 4 284; 5 307; 7 738; 8 4, 168, 170; 9 100, 101, 102; 11 28, 701; 12 162; 19 181, 441, 711, 713, 785; 20 312, 531, 787; 21 145, 904, 905; 22 477, 798, 799, 800; 24 286, 526, 761; 26 445, 457; 27 495, 766, 860, 861; 30 232; 32 104, 654, 656; 33 634
Italy: High Renaissance 3 304, 305
Portugal 6 452
Spain 11 483–4; 29 290, 290
altars 21 858
anatomical studies 1 840–41
arches 2 295
architecture (general)
Belgium 2 192; 3 544–5
commentaries 27 352
Croatia 8 175
Czech Republic 8 377; 25 425
Denmark 14 370
England 19 618
France 6 59; 11 511–14*
Germany 12 366–8*
High Renaissance 26 186–7*
Italy 4 642, 652; 5 14; 16 628–35*; 27 734
Lithuania 19 495–6
Malta (Republic of) 20 211–12
Netherlands, the 22 822–3*
Poland 24 207; 25 96
Renaissance
art forms
architecture (general)—cont.
Portugal 31 177, 178
Slovakia 28 849
Slovenia 28 859
Spain 21 126; 29 264–8*; 32 100
architecture (arsenals) 23 328
architecture (casinos) 19 371
architecture (castles) 12 367; 14 370; 18 587; 29 679
architecture (cathedrals)
Italy 11 196; 20 112; 24 747; 31 447
Spain 14 475
architecture (chapels)
France 19 691
Italy 1 562, 563; 11 186
Italy: Early Renaissance 5 18, 19, 20
Poland 18 432–3, 433
Portugal 6 43
architecture (châteaux) 2 27; 6 505, 545; 9 351, 352; 11 512, 905
architecture (churches)
Italy 1 561, 564, 566, 567, 606; 3 385, 772; 4 644, 652; 7 516; 8 188; 11 202, 207, 209, 689, 690; 21 470, 516; 24 196; 25 216; 27 734, 735, 739, 743; 31 278; 32 630
Italy: Early Renaissance 5 16, 17; 16 631; 26 183
Italy: High Renaissance 16 633
Spain 14 473; 23 625; 29 266, 268
Ukraine 31 552
architecture (clubs) 29 370
architecture (colleges) 31 823
architecture (courtyards) 16 631, 632; 21 519; 22 132; 27 741
architecture (domes) 5 15; 27 761
architecture (exchanges) 14 474
architecture (façades)
Italy 5 16; 26 398, 399; 27 772; 31 743
Spain 21 126
architecture (fortresses) 11 688
architecture (grottoes) 16 696
architecture (halls) 15 866; 23 317; 31 745
architecture (hospitals) 8 79; 31 509
architecture (houses) 1 802; 3 850; 29 750
architecture (loggias) 25 907
architecture (mausolea) 20 865*
architecture (monasteries) 10 499, 500; 21 468; 24 285
architecture (museums) 16 770–71*; 22 354–6*; 32 15
architecture (oratories) 5 18
architecture (palaces) 23 809–11*
Austria 15 867
Czech Republic 5 79
Germany 24 230; 29 739
Scotland 28 225
Spain 8 80; 10 499, 500; 20 2; 29 264; 32 620
architecture (palazzi) 1 562, 607; 2 593; 3 16; 4 649, 651; 5 181; 7 518, 905; 10 767; 18 861; 21 469; 23 810, 836; 24 533; 26 819; 27 742, 758, 760; 28 468; 32 341
Early Renaissance 16 629
architecture (squares) 2 593; 11 177
architecture (temples) 4 648
architecture (theatres) 11 3; 30 654*
Renaissance
art forms—cont.
architecture (town halls)
Belgium 2 203; 12 523
Germany 2 714; 19 110; 23 317
Poland 25 409; 27 722
architecture (villas) 32 545
Italy 12 110–12, 278, 761; 21 518; 24 530; 32 504, 546
bastions 24 532
book illustrations 9 436
books 15 50
bronze 24 258; 26 327
caricatures 21 356
cartoons (drawings) 5 898; 25 902
caryatids 13 227
coffering 8 881
concrete 7 692*
copies 11 72; 26 226
crucifixes 8 215
doors 9 156–8*, 157; 12 540
drawings 9 220–21*
Austria 2 794
France 2 27
Germany 12 386
Italy 1 841; 12 554
Netherlands, the 16 770
drawings (architectural) 2 329, 330; 5 15
drawings (chalk)
Germany 13 723
Italy 9 11; 19 186, 193; 21 758; 25 558, 909; 29 883
drawings (ink)
Belgium 4 906; 33 170
Germany 3 102; 4 760
Italy 3 157; 9 220; 14 871; 19 184, 192; 22 237; 24 861; 32 13
Switzerland 1 788; 8 822
drawings (metalpoints) 3 652
drawings (mythological) 12 214
drawings (presentation) 19 449; 25 557–8*, 558
drawings (religious) 3 651; 21 763
drawings (silverpoints) 9 217; 19 191, 192; 21 340
drawings (wash) 9 214; 32 17
effigies 29 24
engravings
Austria 2 793
Belgium 7 556
Denmark 19 662
Germany 8 114; 9 437; 10 385; 29 44, 557
Italy 5 534; 10 383; 12 698; 16 779; 23 292; 25 160, 858, 859, 904
Netherlands, the 19 758, 763
Switzerland 30 131
etchings 1 716; 4 907; 10 550; 14 574; 32 152; 33 18
exedrae 5 21
figurines 8 101
fonts (baptismal) 11 254*
fountains 11 341–3*
Czech Republic 33 435
France 11 342; 13 226
Germany 11 223; 28 138
Italy 16 690, 696; 19 372; 22 33
frames 11 375, 376
Belgium 11 440–43*, 442
France 11 399–400
Germany 11 454, 454–5*
Italy 11 381–9*, 382, 383, 384, 385, 388, 389
Netherlands, the 11 440–43*, 441, 443
Scandinavia 11 466–7*
Spain 11 483–4*
frontispieces 4 397
furniture 10 288, 289
galleries (iv) (art) 16 771*
gardens 12 110*, 114*
France 12 112–13*, 113

Renaissance
art forms
gardens—cont.
Italy **12** 110–12*, *111, 112*; **16** 633
gates **7** *360*
gateways **2** *778*; **27** *762*
intarsia **29** *860*
interior decoration **10** 270–71, 662; **11** *572*; **19** *692*
istorie **16** *613*
jewellery **10** 344
lanterns (architecture) **5** *21*
manuscript illumination **15** *91*; **20** III
manuscripts **4** *19*; **13** *834*; **20** 333–4*
France **20** *334*; **25** *405*
Italy **2** *697*; **7** *467*; **11** *686*; **20** *657*; **27** *807*; **28** *752*
medals **1** *556*; **20** 917–19*, *918*; **26** *399*; **28** 190; **29** *387*
metalwork **10** 325, *326*; **26** *329*; **33** *18*
miniatures (manuscript illumination) **29** *786*
modelli **21** 768
models **2** 336; **12** *366*
monuments **5** *128*; **22** 44*
monuments (equestrian) **6** *13*; **9** *127*; **10** 440–41*; **16** 690; **32** *363*
mosaics **22** *158*
narratives **5** *820*; **22** 521*, *522*
nude figures **23** 291–3
Belgium **33** *170*
Czech Republic **33** *435*
Germany **3** *102*; **11** *223*; **12** *402*; **29** *557*
Italy **3** *157, 665*; **4** *495, 499*; **6** *3*; **12** *656*; **14** *871*; **16** 690, *693, 694, 696*; **19** *676*; **21** *436, 758*; **24** *523*; **25** *158, 160*; **27** *773*; **28** *701*; **29** *561*; **32** *17, 809*
Netherlands, the **13** *26*; **19** *758*
orders (architecture) **1** 562; **4** 649; **6** *358*; **28** 468; **32** 638
ornament **23** 539–41*
pageants **23** 766
painting (general)
Austria **2** 793–4*
Belgium **25** 669
Croatia **8** 178
Germany **5** 198; **12** 362, 385–7*; **13** 721
High Renaissance **26** 187*
Italy **27** 494–6
Italy: Early Renaissance **16** 657–63*
Italy: High Renaissance **13** *280*; **16** 663–8*
Lithuania **19** 496
Netherlands, the **22** 836–8*
Spain **29** 276–7
Switzerland **30** 131*
painting (allegorical)
Belgium **4** *898, 899, 901, 902, 903, 906, 907*; **11** *222*
Germany **8** *117*
Italy **1** *655, 656*; **4** *494, 495*; **9** *184*; **15** *86*; **25** *898*; **27** *848*; **29** *362*; **32** *14*
painting (architectural) **2** 339–40; **14** *664*
painting (battle) **6** *2*; **12** *388*; **31** *515*
painting (ceiling) **21** *20*
painting (fresco) **4** *194*
Germany **28** *59*

Renaissance
art forms
painting (fresco)—cont.
Italy **2** *36, 37, 38, 607, 725*; **4** *317*; **5** *816*; **6** *12, 13*; **7** *457*; **8** *504*; **9** *263, 265*; **11** *13, 117, 185, 293, 710*; **12** *550*; **13** *261*; **16** *613, 664, 763*; **19** *444, 450*; **20** *305, 533, 534*; **21** *11*; **22** *413*; **24** *522, 531, 755, 762, 764, 831*; **25** *250, 901*; **26** *457*; **27** *846, 850*; **28** *80, 702, 703*; **29** *360*; **31** *513, 514*; **32** *16*
Italy: Early Renaissance **11** *7*; **16** *660*; **26** *184*
painting (genre)
Belgium **4** *904*; **7** *428*; **21** *354*
Italy **27** *890*
Netherlands, the **19** *760*
painting (glass) **32** *151*
painting (history) **9** *96*; **10** *766*; **14** *582*; **20** *10*
painting (hunting scenes) **31** *515*
painting (landscape) **4** *140, 903*; **18** *705*
painting (literary themes) **2** *228*
painting (mythological) **22** 412–14*
Italy **4** *499*; **6** *3*; **7** *322*; **9** *186*; **16** 660; **19** *676*; **24** *523, 770*; **28** *701*; **31** *429*
Netherlands, the **13** *26*
Switzerland **8** *823*
painting (*pietàs*) **3** *662*; **28** *333*
painting (predellas) **20** *532*; **26** *456*
painting (religious)
Austria **14** *836*
Belgium **2** *195*; **3** *554*; **7** *519*; **11** *221*; **19** *548*; **20** *665*; **21** *357*; **25** *668*
Germany **1** *717, 718*; **5** *59*; **8** *113*; **9** *432*; **13** *723*; **17** *601*; **26** *188*; **28** *48, 189*
Italy **1** *818*; **2** *32, 33, 179, 182, 290*; **3** *299, 650, 656, 665, 666, 751, 782*; **4** *336, 496, 497, 653*; **5** *818, 819, 820*; **6** *3, 4, 12, 356*; **7** *320, 321, 564*; **8** *167*; **9** *95*; **11** *294, 388, 702*; **12** *552, 708, 711, 753*; **16** *846*; **19** *182, 185, 442, 443, 448, 895*; **20** *123, 306, 307, 309, 313, 453, 532, 533, 771*; **21** *96, 97, 748*; **22** *108, 133, 522*; **23** *94*; **24** *365, 524, 763, 769, 829*; **25** *157, 161, 162, 251, 569, 897, 900, 903*; **26** *458*; **27** *847, 862, 891*; **28** *85, 331, 334*; **29** *2, 26*; **30** *781*; **31** *431, 432, 444*; **32** *12, 364, 365, 657*; **33** *701, 702*
Italy: Early Renaissance **3** *99*; **8** *169*; **16** *662*; **24** *538*
Netherlands, the **13** *24, 25*; **16** *834*
Spain **29** *278*
Switzerland **33** *287*
painting (*sacra conversazione*) **3** *663*; **9** *99*; **19** *447*; **24** *889*
Belgium **4** *162*
Italy **3** *917*; **5** *307*; **7** *322*; **8** *4*; **13** *259*; **19** *323, 441, 675, 711*; **20** *312*; **28** *700*; **29** *3*
Italy: High Renaissance **3** *303, 305*
painting (secco) **28** *337*
painting (townscapes) **32** *225*
painting (wall) **2** 793, *793*; **32** *805*, 805–6*
painting (watercolours) **9** *430, 433*; **32** *271*
pediments **24** 317

Renaissance
art forms—cont.
plaquettes **21** 783; **25** *19*, 19–21*, *20*
portals **6** *451*
portraits (drawings)
England **9** *273*; **10** *246*; **14** *672*
France **7** *463*
Germany **9** *428, 429*
Italy **10** *521*
Netherlands, the **13** *27*
portraits (engravings) **1** *592*; **33** *169*
portraits (frescoes) **26** *817, 818*
portraits (medals) **16** 690; **24** *863*; **28** *191*; **29** *408*
portraits (miniatures) **14** *545, 546*; **21** *639*
portraits (painting)
Austria **14** *837*
Belgium **18** *6*; **21** *355*; **26** *185*
England **10** *247, 666*; **14** *669, 670, 671*; **22** *64*; **25** *277*; **31** *414*
France **7** *426, 462, 866*
Germany **3** *507*; **5** *60*; **9** *431, 439*; **10** *162*; **14** *665*; **20** *191*; **23** *306*; **25** *274*
Holy Roman Empire **28** *377*
Italy **1** *763*; **2** *181*; **3** *100, 302, 657, 659, 664*; **4** *284*; **5** *128, 820*; **9** *263*; **11** *401, 700, 704*; **19** *183, 711, 712*; **21** *16*; **22** *109, 134*; **24** *863*; **25** *466, 905*; **28** *334*; **31** *741*; **32** *11, 658*
Italy: Early Renaissance **16** *659*
Netherlands, the **22** *66, 837*
Switzerland **14** *667*
portraits (sculpture)
Austria **2** *800*
Germany **24** *807*
Italy **12** *542*; **13** *911*; **16** 690; **19** *202*
portraits (self) **9** *429, 431*; **24** *807*; **32** *19*
portraits (woodcuts) **13** *903, 913*
prints **30** 131
proportions (architecture) **2** 352–6*; **5** 17
proportions (human) **14** *871, 873*
pulpits **20** *114*; **25** *725*
sarcophagi **27** 829–31*
screens (i) (architectural) **28** *293*, 293–4*
scripts **28** 306–7*, *307*
sculpture (general)
display **16** *770*
England **10** 360; **16** 695
France **16** 695
Germany **12** *402*
High Renaissance **26** 187*
Italy **7** 783; **16** 688–95*; **29** *561*; **30** *498, 501*
Italy: Early Renaissance **16** 689–93*
Italy: High Renaissance **16** 693–5*
Lithuania **19** 496
Netherlands, the **14** 44; **16** 695
Poland **16** 866; **18** 433
Spain **16** 695; **29** 289–91*
sculpture (allegorical)
Italy **5** *359*; **16** *766*; **21** *436, 437*; **26** *439*
sculpture (architectural) **11** *201*; **32** *226*
sculpture (busts) **5** 300–301*
Italy **5** *300*; **9** *124*, 125; **16** *691*; **21** 692, *693*, II4; **25** V1
sculpture (monumental) **12** 539; **16** *694*; **27** *773*
sculpture (mythological) **12** *402*
Czech Republic **33** *435*

Renaissance
art forms
sculpture (mythological)—cont.
Germany **11** *223*; **33** II1
Italy **2** *140, 141*; **3** *158*; **16** *693*
sculpture (*pietàs*) **21** *434*
sculpture (relief) **26** 136–7*
France **11** *557*; **13** *226*
Germany **8** *541*; **32** *606, 830*
Italy **1** *456, 748*; **3** *159, 260, 637, 860*; **8** *798*; **9** *125, 130*; **11** *184, 693*; **12** *540, 541*; **16** 689, *692, 741, 842, 844*; **19** *208, 688*; **20** *622*; **21** *693*; **24** *756*; **25** III; **26** *327, 443, 444, 446*; **27** *769*; **30** *501*
Spain **3** *847*; **32** 493, *493*
sculpture (religious)
Croatia **23** *93*
France **26** *185*
Germany **14** *450*
Italy **4** *738, 739*; **5** *361*; **9** *123, 129*; **11** *203*; **12** *539*; **16** *690, 840*; **18** *673*; **19** *560*; **20** *543, 544, 907*; **22** *32, 461*; **23** *90*; **26** *331*; **27** *448, 770, 775, 776*; **29** *561*; **32** *105, 360, 362*
Portugal **6** *451*
sculpture (statuettes)
Italy **1** *162*; **3** *861*; **25** *158*; **26** *330*; **29** 568–9*
sculpture (tomb)
Denmark **11** *219*
England **31** *190*
France **1** *766*; **7** *596*
Italy **1** *747*; **3** *138*; **4** *737*; **7** *367*; **8** *797*; **11** *27*; **21** *438*; **29** *24*
stage design **19** 195; **28** *470*
stained glass **5** *515*; **13** *909*; **14** *572*; **30** 131
staircases **4** *156*; **29** *522*
stucco **11** *572*; **29** 830
tapestries
Belgium **2** *198*; **3** *607*; **23** *527*
France **11** 571
Netherlands, the **13** *907*
terracotta **26** *331*
thrones **30** *781*
title-pages **2** *166*
tombs
Denmark **11** *219*
England **31** *190*
France **1** *766*
Italy **1** *747*; **4** *737*; **7** *367*; **8** *797*; **11** *27*; **16** 690, 840, *841*; **21** *438, 465*; **32** *361*
Spain **10** *783*
urban planning **25** 97
vaults (ceiling) **16** 630; **22** *307*
voting urns **8** *796*
woodcuts **25** VI
Germany **1** *721*; **2** *103, 223*; **5** *199*; **9** *431*; **12** 386; **23** *617*; **26** *79*; **28** *58*; **29** *434*; **33** *19, 352*
Holy Roman Empire (before 1648) **33** *355*
Italy **12** *656*
art history **32** 18
art legislation **16** 768
collections **16** 770–71
colour **7** 627–8
commentaries **21** 816
disegno **32** 19
education (art) **16** 778
gay and lesbian art **12** *214*
iconographic programmes **15** 85–7*
iconography **2** 228; **7** 225; **14** 866; **23** 680
patronage **16** 763
regional traditions
Italy **24** *863*; **26** 185–6
Netherlands, the **20** 395
see also EARLY NETHERLANDISH STYLE

Renaissance—cont.
styles
Early Renaissance **26** 182–5*
Belgium **12** *845, 846, 847*
Germany **26** 185
Italy **26** 182
Netherlands, the **26** 184, 185
High Renaissance **19** 180; **26** 186–9*
Germany **26** 188–9
Italy **19** 194, 197; **26** 186–8
Late Renaissance *see* MANNERISM
theories
architectural **1** 558–60
art **1** 555, 557
painting **1** 557–8; **19** 195–6; **27** 790
perspective **1** 557; **19** 195
proportions (human) **1** 558
sculpture **1** 558
treatises **7** 863
architecture **11** 691; **23** 869
France **32** 641
Italy **1** 555, 558–60, 568; **11** 71, 72; **28** 466, 468–71
painting **1** 555, 557–8; **16** 778; **31** 299
perspective **1** 557
sculpture **1** 555, 558
Renaissance (London) **17** 578
Renaissance (CA), Museum of Classical Chinese Furniture **7** 156
Renaissance, American *see* AMERICAN RENAISSANCE
Renaissance, Dürer *see* DÜRER RENAISSANCE
Renaissance, English *see* BAROQUE REVIVAL
Renaissance, Flower *see* FLOWER RENAISSANCE
Renaissance, Harlem *see* HARLEM RENAISSANCE
Renaissance, Justinianic *see* JUSTINIANIC RENAISSANCE
Renaissance, Kushite *see* KUSHITE RENAISSANCE
Renaissance, La (Brussels) **24** 439
Renaissance, Macedonian *see* MACEDONIAN RENAISSANCE
Renaissance, Mexican *see* MEXICAN RENAISSANCE
Renaissance, Palaiologan *see* PALAIOLOGAN RENAISSANCE
Renaissance, Saite *see* SAITE STYLE
Renaissance, Weser *see* WESER RENAISSANCE
Renaissance littéraire et artistique (Paris) **24** 426
Renaissance Revival **14** 580; **26** 189–91*
art forms
architecture **26** 189–90*
Czech Republic **25** *429*
England **3** *282*; **7** *469*
France **24** *123*
Germany **9** *459*; **12** 376, *377*; **18** *124*; **28** *398, 399*
United States of America **23** *33*; **25** *666*
furniture **26** 190; **31** 630, *631*
jewellery **17** 527, III2
regional traditions
Belgium **3** 585–6; **6** 482; **16** 906; **30** 47
Czech Republic **8** 379
France **24** 123
Germany **18** 123
Hungary **30** 210
Renaldi, Francesco **15** 654
Renan, (Cornelis) Ary **25** 751; **26** 191*
Renan, Ernest **26** 191; **28** 667; **31** 501
Renard **5** 832
Renard, Bruno **3** 547; **24** 296; **26** 191–2*

Renard, E.
works 29 *857*
Renard, Emile 30 348
Renard, Jean *see* VOLPATO, GIOVANNI
Renard, Jules 4 364; 13 232; 14 302; 21 629
Renard, L. 26 525
Renard, Léopold 26 192
Renard, Marcel 26 192*
Renard des Fonoll 19 518
Renart, Emilio 26 192*
Renascença Portuguesa 5 782
Renata of Lorraine, Duchess of Bavaria (*fl* 1568-80s) 28 189
Renatus, Flavius Vegetius *see* VEGETIUS RENATUS, FLAVIUS
Renau, Josep 26 192*; 29 286
Renaud, Madeleine 18 577
Renaud de Maincourt 11 5; 26 778
Renaud de Rome *see* REGNAULT, JEAN-BAPTISTE, Baron
Renaud de Semur, Abbot of Vézelay 32 395
Renaudie, Jean 11 528, 903; 26 192–3*
Renault (car factory) 9 71; 32 26
Renault (goldsmith) 13 171
Renault 19 382
Renault, Antoine 3 13
Ren Bonian *see* REN YI
Ren Bowen 26 211
Rendall, Joseph 18 902
Rendel, Alexander 26 316
Rendel, J. M. 33 450
Rendel, Palmer & Tritton 28 281
Render, Adam 13 334
Render, Wenzel 23 425
Rendić, Ivan 8 178
Rendón, F. Huerta *see* HUERTA RENDÓN, F.
Rendón, Gonzalo Suárez *see* SUÁREZ RENDÓN, GONZALO
Rendón, Manuel 9 713; 26 193*
Rendsborg factory 8 748
René I, Duke of Anjou (*reg* 1434-80), Duke of Lorraine, King of Naples, Sicily and Jerusalem 2 45, 49, 51, 111, 113–15*; 7 542; 11 660; 31 387
architecture 20 472
banners 6 469
embroidery 24 775
gems 12 257
gold 11 615; 13 863
hardstones 11 635
manuscripts 2 113, *114*; 12 733; 20 635, 706, *707*
medals 18 859
metalwork 11 615
miniatures (manuscript illumination) 20 *707*
paintings 1 497; 8 664; 9 4; 10 703, 716; 11 531, 799; 13 254, 264; 24 775
sculpture 11 556; 13 79; 24 782
silver 11 616
stained glass 26 471
tournaments 29 488
writings 20 706
René I, Duke of Lorraine *see* RENÉ I, Duke of Anjou, Duke of Lorraine, King of Naples, Sicily and Jerusalem
René II (of Vaudemont), Duke of Lorraine (*reg* 1473-1508) 2 111, 115*; 19 696; 31 388
manuscripts 31 388, *388*
sculpture 16 852
René II of Lorraine, Master of *see* TRUBERT, GEORGES
René, Denise 24 144; 26 193–4*
Reneb 9 *776*
Reneé de France, Duchess of Ferrara (*fl* 1570) 9 352
Renée of Lorraine, Duchess of Bavaria (*fl* 1570s) 32 612
René Master *see* KING RENÉ OF ANJOU, MASTER OF
Reneni 17 714
René of Chalon, 1st Prince of Orange (*reg* 1530-44) 28 217
Renerus *see* RAINER OF HUY
Renesse, Constantijn (Daniel) van 22 843; 26 194–5*
works 26 *194*
Renestan, El' 8 589
Renewed Church of the Brethren *see* CHRISTIANITY → sects → Moravian Brethren
Renfrew, Colin 20 81; 21 42
Renger-Patzsch, Albert 24 676; 26 195*
works 24 *675*
Rengetsu *see* ŌTAGAKI RENGETSU
Rengifo, Antonio 24 518
Rengifo, Carlos 24 518
Rengifo, Jorge 24 518
Rengyō Rokurōbei *see* ROKURŌBEI RENGYŌ
Reni, Guido 1 103, 728; 2 493; 4 277; 8 612; 12 214; 16 669, 670; 22 478; 26 195–203*
assistants 5 634–5, 870; 6 114; 18 730; 28 395, 787
attributions 4 560; 5 65; 26 283
book illustrations 18 735
catalogues 3 310; 6 78
collaboration 5 454; 6 361; 25 227; 28 529
copies 32 402
drawings 5 854; 6 470
engravings 31 347
forgeries by others 28 395
groups and movements 3 265
methods 19 354
paintings 24 467
frescoes 4 405; 9 110; 15 137; 26 *199*, 833
mythological 5 379; 26 *201*
religious 10 476; 20 213; 22 485; 23 294, 352; 25 862; 26 *197*, *198*, 840
patrons and collectors 10 365
Albarelli, Giovanni 5 432
Alcalá, 3rd Duque de (1583-1637) 26 307
Aldobrandini, Pietro (ii), Cardinal (1571-1621) 1 595
Barberini (family) (17th cent.) 5 691
Baring, Francis (1740-1810) 3 239
Barnabites 3 250
Borghese, Scipione, Cardinal 4 405, 406
Bourbon del Monte, Francesco Maria, Cardinal 4 567
Cairo, Francesco 5 407
Caraman, Duc de 5 700
Caroline Murat, Queen of Naples (1782-1839) 22 338
Carpio (family) 5 844
Carraquiri, Nazario 5 871
Charles I, King of England and Scotland (*reg* 1625-49) 29 800, 801
Clerk, John, 2nd Baronet of Penicuik (1679-1755) 7 418
Coke, Thomas, 1st Earl of Leicester of the 1st creation (1697-1759) 7 540
Colonna, Girolamo, Cardinal (1604-66) 7 620, 621
Costa (family) 8 9
Créquy, Charles de Blanchefort de 19 238
Crozat, Pierre 8 209
Dominican Order 9 111
Elizabeth Farnese, Queen of Spain (1692-1766) 4 559
Ferdinando, 6th Duke of Mantua (*reg* 1612-26) 12 912
Filomarino, Ascanio, Cardinal 11 81
Franzone, Agostino (i) (*fl* 1678) 11 739
Reni, Guido
patrons and collectors—cont.
Frederick II, King of Prussia (*reg* 1740-86) 14 652
Gregory XV, Pope (*reg* 1621-3) 19 778
Hamilton, James, 3rd Marquess and 1st Duke of Hamilton 10 861
Hanover, Frederick (Louis), Prince of Wales (1707-51) 14 143
Henrietta Maria, Queen of England and Scotland (1609-69) 29 803
Imperiale, Gian Vincenzo 15 148
Isham, Thomas 13 300
Jabach, Everard 16 814
John William, Elector Palatine (*reg* 1690-1716) 12 473
La Vrillière, Louis Phélypeaux de 18 885
Lindsay, Alexander (William Crawford), 25th Earl of Crawford and 8th Earl of Balcarres 19 412
Louis XIV, King of France (*reg* 1643-1715) 4 552
Ludovisi, Ludovico, Cardinal 19 779
Marie de Medici, Queen of France (1573-1642) 4 549
Medici, Carlo de', Cardinal 21 25
Medici, Giovanni Carlo de', Cardinal (1611-63) 21 27
Medici, Leopoldo de', Cardinal 21 27
Medinaceli, Luís de la Cerda Fernández de Córdoba Folch de Cardona y Aragón, 9th Duque de (1660-1711) 21 35
Monterrey, Manuel de Acevedo y Zúñiga, 6th Conde de 22 21
Osuna, 3rd Duque de (1574-1624) 23 626
Paignon-Dijonval 23 777
Pallavicini, Lazzaro, Cardinal 23 873
Pascoli, Lione 24 225
Polignac, Melchior de, Cardinal 25 150
Poniatowski, Stanisław, Prince 25 213
Pourtalès-Gorgier, James-Alexandre, Comte de 25 383
Reynst (family) 26 283
Richter, Johann Thomas 19 111
Ruffo, Tommaso, Cardinal, Archbishop of Ferrara 27 316
Sacchetti (family) 27 486
Salamanca (y Mayol), José, Marqués de 27 607
Sampieri (family) 27 693
Sanford, John 27 729
Sanfré, Alexandre de Sousa Holstein, Conde de 29 100
Savoy, Eugene of, Prince (1663-1736) 2 829; 28 15
Savoy, Maurice of, Cardinal 28 9
Sebregondi, Nicolo 28 337
Seignelay, Jean-Baptiste (-Antoine) Colbert, Marquis de 7 546
Serra, Giovan Francesco, Marqués di Cassano 28 479
Somerset, Henry, 3rd Duke of Beaufort (1707-49) 13 301
Spencer, John, 1st Earl Spencer 29 381
Spinola (family) 29 411
Talbot, Charles, 1st Duke of Shrewsbury (1660-1718) 30 267
Tallard, Marie-Joseph d'Hostun, Duc de 30 274
Tarnowski, Jan Feliks, Count and Waleria 30 345
Reni, Guido
patrons and collectors—cont.
Trenta, Filippo (1731-95) 31 306
Udney, John 31 525
Urban VIII, Pope (*reg* 1623-44) 3 206
Villiers, George, 1st Duke of Buckingham (1592-1628) 32 576
Vladislav IV Vasa, King of Poland (*reg* 1632-48) 32 6
Walpole, Robert, 1st Earl of Orford (1676-1745) 10 365; 32 824
Wells, William (i) (1768-1847) 33 65
pupils 5 634, 651; 7 356, 857; 11 15; 12 499; 26 317; 27 486, 893; 28 34, 395; 31 885
reproductions in hardstones 12 263
reproductions in tapestry 22 481
reproductions on fans 10 781
reproductive prints by others
Baratti, Antonio 3 199
Bervic, Charles-Clément 3 870
Chéreau, François, I (1680-1729) 6 548
Coriolano, Bartolomeo 7 857
Couvay, Jean 8 77
Cunego, Domenico 8 267
Fernández Noseret, Luis 10 906
Frey, Johannes Jakob (1813-1865) 11 770
Longhi, Giuseppe 19 636
Mattioli, Lodovico 20 848
Picart, Etienne 24 712
Poilly, François de 25 77
Rousselet, Gilles 27 269
Selma, Fernando 28 389
Strange, Robert 26 230
Traballesi, Giuliano 31 268
Valck, Gerard 31 802
Vuibert, Rémy 32 738
teachers 5 442, 851
Renialme, Johannes de 28 360, 362; 32 261
Renier, Remy-Joseph 3 600
Renier, Rodolfo 19 834
Renier collection 10 861
Renieri, Niccolò *see* RÉGNIER, NICOLAS
Renier van Tienen 8 662
Renishaw Hall (Derbys) 28 808
Renkioi Hospital 26 18
Renlies Church 13 113
Renn, Gottfried 11 813; 29 393
Rennebu, St Peter 29 580
Rennell 25 181, 182
Rennen, Peter von der 18 432; 25 127; 26 148
Rennen, von der (family) 25 127
Renner, Narcissus 26 204*
Renner, Paul 31 497
Rennes 11 *504*, 657; 26 204–6*; 31 716
Cathedral 3 609
faience (ii) (ceramics) 26 206*
gold 27 80
Hôtel Robien 26 469
Hôtel de Ville 19 141
metalwork 11 620
monument to Louis XIV 10 442
Musée des Beaux-Arts et d'Archéologie 11 665, 666; 26 205, 470
Palais de Justice 4 866; 11 515; 18 886; 26 204
paintings 8 88; 17 671
Palais du Parlement *see* Palais de Justice
Place de la Mairie 26 *205*
Place Neuve *see* Place de la Mairie
Place Royale 8 94
Seminary 18 582*
Rennie, George 26 206
Rennie, John (1761-1821) 26 206*
collaboration 2 324; 29 651
staff 2 306
works 4 801, 802; 9 58; 19 575; 23 340
Rennie, John (1794-1874) 24 747; 26 206
Rennyo 23 592
Renoir, (Pierre-)Auguste 2 12; 7 674; 11 547, 667; 26 207–10*; 30 290
ceramics 11 606
collaboration 20 201
dealers 3 826; 9 424; 32 686
drawings 9 226
exhibitions 10 680
frames 11 418
groups and movements 15 151, 152, 153, 154, 155; 23 504; 25 357; 26 432; 32 591
methods 7 629; 9 673; 13 709
paintings 15 154; 23 296
genre 9 673; 11 37; 15 152, *153*, 154; 18 715, 716; 19 355; 26 *208*, *209*
landscape 15 154
literary themes 22 379
portraits 3 434; 9 288, *289*; 15 155
still-lifes 29 669
topographical 31 157
patrons and collectors 2 707
Alexandre, Arsène 1 614; 12 769
Barnes, Albert C. 3 251
Bellio, Georges de 26 722
Bliss, Lillie P(lummer) 4 142
Caillebotte, Gustave 5 391
Chrysler, Walter P(ercy) 7 245
Clark, Robert Sterling 7 377
Cone, Claribel 7 702
Courtauld, Samuel (1876-1947) 8 62
Duret, (Jules-Emmanuel) Théodore 9 448
Fåhreu, Klas 30 118
FitzGerald, Desmond 11 141
Ford, Henry, II (*b* 1917) 24 183
Frick, Henry Clay 11 774
Hanna, Leonard C(olton) 14 139
Havemeyer, Louisine (Waldron) 14 244
Haviland, Charles 14 246
Houssaye, (François-)Arsène 14 802
Lambert, Catholina 18 672
Lane, Hugh (Percy) 18 727
Lehman, Robert 19 92
Lerolle, Henry 19 230
Lurcy, Georges 24 183
Morozov, Ivan (Abramovich) (1871-1921) 22 135, 136
National Museum (Belgrade) 28 459
National Museum of Wales (Cardiff) 5 732
Palmer, Bertha Honoré 23 882
Phillips, Duncan 24 638
Polignac, Winnaretta, Princesse Edmond de 25 150
Pope, Alfred Atmore 25 234
Robinson, Edward G(oldenberg) 26 472
Rockefeller, Abby Aldrich 26 488
Roujon, Henri 20 201
Ryabushinsky, Nikolay (Pavlovich) 27 459
Ryerson, Martin A(ntoine) 27 463
Shchukin, Sergey (Ivanovich) 28 569
Stein, Leo 29 604
Stein, Michael 29 604
Tavernier, Adolphe-Eugène 30 375
Tetzen-Lund, Christian 30 532
Tschudi, Hugo von 31 397

Renoir, (Pierre-)Auguste
patrons and collectors—cont.
Vever, Henri **32** 394
Vollard, Ambroise **32** 687
Walter-Guillaume Collection **13** 826
Whitney, John Hay **33** 150
Wildenstein, Georges **33** 182
Zambaccian, K. H. **26** 723
prints **9** 309; **19** 489; **25** 626
reproductive prints by others **32** 577
sponsorship **3** 435
teachers **12** 810
Renoir, Edmond **26** 210, 432
Renoir, Jean **5** 896
Renouard, (Charles-) Paul **26** 210–11*
Renoux, Charles **2** 614; **12** 740; **22** 243
renovatio **1** 1; **5** 792, 809; **6** 482; **7** 382–3; **26** 182
architecture **5** 793, 795; **11** 831
ivory-carvings **5** 809
manuscripts **5** 779, 800; **15** 875
sculpture **5** 796
Rénovation Esthétique **3** 813
Renqvist, (Karl) Torsten **26** 211*; **30** 81, 86
Ren Renfa **6** 631, 801; **26** 211*
works **26** *211*
Renseneb
shabtis **10** *17*
Renshichirō Kawakita *see* KAWAKITA RENSHICHIRŌ
Rensselaer (family) **18** 749
Rensselaer, Mariana Griswold Van *see* VAN RENSSELAER, MARIANA GRISWOLD
Rentis **13** 384
Renton Howard Wood Levin Partnership **1** 126
Rentz, Michal Jindřich **8** 391
Rentzel, Hinrik **14** 102
Renucci, Renuccio **28** 319
Ren Weichang *see* REN XIONG
Renwick, Aspinwall & Russell **12** 926
Renwick, James, sr (1792-1863) **26** 212
Renwick, James, jr (1818-95) **23** 39; **26** 212–15*
groups and movements **13** 203
staff **7** 436
works **7** 840; **21** 618; **26** *213*, *214*; **27** 532; **31** 592; **32** 886, *889*
Renwick and Sands **27** 137
Ren Xiong **6** 811; **26** 215–16*; **28** 553
forgeries by others **26** 215
groups and movements **28** 553
pupils **26** 216
works **6** 813, *813*
Ren Xun **26** 215; **28** 553
Ren Yi **6** 811; **26** 215–16*; **28** 553
collaboration **26** 215
groups and movements **28** 553, 554
teachers **26** 215
works **6** 802, 813; **26** *216*; **28** *554*
Ren Yu **26** 215; **28** 553
Renz, Michael Heinrich **29** 422
Renzan Aoki *see* AOKI RENZAN
Renzan Kishi *see* KISHI RENZAN
Renzhi dian **32** 840
Renzi, Juan Pablo **2** 401; **26** 216–17*
Renzi, Mario De *see* DE RENZI, MARIO
Renzio, Toni del **15** 166; **30** 22
Ren Zizhao **26** 211
Renzong, Emperor (Yuan; *reg* 1312-21) **7** 151; **19** 856; **32** 851; **33** 319
repair *see under* CONSERVATION → techniques
Reparatus, Bishop of Ravenna **26** 34
Repari, *'idgāh* **15** 340
Repentigny, Rodolphe de *see* JAURAN
Répertoire d'art et d'archéologie see RAA
Répertoire international de la littérature de l'art see RILA
Repertorium für Kunstwissenschaft **24** 423, 444, 445
Repeta, Scipione **22** 387
Repgau, Eike von *see* EIKE VON REPGAU
Repin, Il'ya (Yefimovich) **14** 588; **22** 178; **26** 217–20*; **27** 391, 442, 580; **30** 265, 464
assistants **22** 338
collaboration **12** 166
groups and movements **1** 71; **20** 232; **22** 394; **26** 57; **32** 836
patrons and collectors **12** 332; **27** 438; **31** 565
pupils **2** 108; **4** 60, 837; **6** 529; **11** 33; **13** 633; **17** 452, 812; **18** 38, 537; **20** 152, 222; **26** 26, 421; **28** 474, 570; **29** 61; **31** 75; **33** 77, 740
sponsors **30** 464
teachers **21** 811
works **3** 529; **26** *218*, *219*
Repino, Repin Museum **26** 220
replacement heads *see* SCULPTURE → types → reserve heads
replicas **2** 141; **7** 562; **11** 309; **26** 221*, 226
collections *see under* COLLECTIONS → types
see also ART (REPRODUCTION OF WORKS OF); COPIES; REPRODUCTIONS
Repnin, N. V. **27** 439
reportage **24** 670, 677–8*
Report on Archaeological Work in Burma: Archaeological Survey **24** 437
Repository of the Arts: Literature, Commerce, Manufactures, Fashions and Politics **24** 446
repoussage *see under* PRINTS → techniques
repoussé **21** 324; **26** 221*
historical and regional traditions
Buddhism **17** 320
Chavín culture **29** *214*
Denmark **13** *849*
Egypt, ancient **9** 818
Indian subcontinent **15** 713
Islamic **16** 364
Japan **17** 320
Laos **18** *776*
Native North Americans **29** *415*
Nepal **22** *755*, 775, *775*
Peru **29** *214*
South America, Pre-Columbian **29** *214*
Thracian **13** *849*; **30** 769, 770
uses
bronze **16** 364; **17** 320
copper **22** *755*; **29** *415*
gold **12** 865, 868–9; **16** 364; **21** *253*; **29** *214*
sculpture **22** *775*
silver **16** 364; **18** *776*; **24** *512*; **28** 739; **30** 770
watches **7** 446
repoussoirs **26** 221*
see also COULISSES
repp **11** 54
Reppen, Frithjof **23** 602
representatio **6** 71
representation **24** 375–85, *376*, *378*, *379*, *380*, *382*, *384*, 658; **25** 685; **26** 221–5*
Aboriginal Australia **1** 38*
Byzantine **9** 622
Christianity **13** 128–9, *129*
Early Christian (*c.* AD 250-843) **9** 622
representation—cont.
Egypt, ancient **9** 796–801*, 854; **10** 1, 3; **28** 47
Germany **12** 384
Gothic **12** 384; **13** 128–9, *129*
Greece, ancient **13** 422; **19** 853; **25** 177, 768
Italy **13** *129*
Japan **17** 284–5
Parthian **24** 217–18
Prehistoric art **25** 474
Rome, ancient **26** 855
see also MIMESIS
reproduction lace *see under* LACE → types
reproduction of works of art *see* ART (REPRODUCTION OF WORKS OF)
reproductions **24** 661; **26** 226–7*
furniture **26** 227
glass **26** 227
see also ART (REPRODUCTIONS OF WORKS OF); *see also under* COLLECTIONS → types; REPLICAS
Repton (Derbys)
Prior Overton's Tower **4** 779
St Wystan **2** 66, 70, 83; **10** 227
Repton, George Stanley **22** 526; **26** 238
Repton, Humphry **26** 237–40*; **31** 151
collaboration **7** 502; **10** 234; **20** 490; **22** 526; **33** 191
patrons and collectors **6** 118; **15** 407
works **4** 806; **8** 48; **12** 131, 136; **26** *238*, 743
writings **8** 613; **26** 14; **32** 398
Repton, John Adey **22** 526; **26** 238, 240
Repubblica di Portici *see* SCUOLA DI RESINA
Repullés **29** 272
Repullés y Vargas, Enrique **2** 866
Reqem *see* PETRA
Requa, Richard S. **27** 720, 721
Requena, Pedro **21** 383
works **21** *383*
Requeno, Vincenzo **10** 199
works **10** *196*
Requesens, Luis de **5** 411; **6** 24
Réquichot, Bernard **7** 842; **26** 240*
Requin, Henri **20** 614; **26** 240*
Requin Altarpiece **25** 795
Rerberg, Fyodor **4** 236; **26** 70
Rerberg, Ivan (Ivanovich) **26** 241*
collaboration **18** 116; **24** 400
pupils **20** 193
staff **23** 426
works **22** 173
rere-arches *see* ARCHES → types → rear-arches
reredoses **1** 707; **10** 260; **25** 183; **28** 290
Rerrich, Béla **26** 241*
works **14** 890, *890*
Resafa *see* RUSAFA
Résal, Jean **11** 770
resale royalties **2** 554
Resani, Arcangelo **26** 241–2*
Resava *see* MANASIJA
Resch, Christoph **26** 362
Resch, Josef **29** 721
Resch, Wolfgang **33** 353
Reschi, Pandolfo **26** 242–3*
Research Libraries Group **2** 368; **6** 81
Research Libraries Information Network *see* RLIN
Resen **19** *882*
Resende, José **4** 720, 728
Resende, Júlio (Martins da Silva Dias) **26** 243*
reserve heads *see under* SCULPTURE → types
reservoirs **1** 476; **7** 353, 354; **13** 381; **25** *60*
see also CISTERNS
Resettlement Administration (RA) *see* FARM SECURITY ADMINISTRATION (FSA)
Reshetilovka **31** 564
Résidence Andalous **31** 424
Resina *see* ERCOLANO
Resina, Scuola di *see* SCUOLA DI RESINA
resins **7** 116; **17** 138, 213; **26** 243–5*
materials
flour **7** 116
technical examination **30** 401, 410*
types
acrylic **7** 748; **28** 339
amber *see* AMBER
copal *see* COPAL
dammar *see* DAMMAR
epoxy **1** 156; **7** 730; **16** 797; **26** 245; **32** 2
frankincense **32** 1
kauri resin **1** 760; **26** 243; **32** 1
ketone *see* CYCLOHEXANONE
mastic *see* MASTIC
myrrh **32** 1
natural **7** 748; **26** 243–4*
Perspex *see* PERSPEX
phenolic **1** 760; **32** 2
pine **23** 792
pine *see* ROSIN
polyurethane **32** 2
rosin *see* ROSIN
sandarac *see* SANDARAC
shellac *see* SHELLAC
synthetic **5** 34; **7** 747, 748; **17** 138; **26** 142, 244–5*
see also PAINTS → types → alkyd
terebinth resin **26** 243; **32** 1
vinyl **28** 339
uses
aquatints **2** 238, 239, 240
ceramics **6** 335–6
conservation **6** 335–6; **7** 730; **10** 195; **17** 138; **28** 339
consolidants **7** 747
crayons **8** 128
encaustic paintings **10** 196
etchings **10** 560
frescoes **11** 764
glazes **12** 803; **23** 792
grounds **13** 706, 707
inks **15** 851, 853; **25** 598
jewellery **17** 530
masonry **1** 156
paints **5** 34; **23** 784, 787
paper **7** 116; **24** 55
papier mâché **24** 61
relining **26** 142
sealants **25** 174
secco paintings **28** 339
varnishes **32** 1, 2; **33** 335
waxes **33** 2
resist **26** 245*
resist-dyeing *see under* DYEING → types
resistivity surveys *see under* SURVEYS → types
Resnati **16** 563
Resobowo, Basuki **15** 807
Respaigne, Nicolaas de **27** 291
respondent pilasters *see under* PILASTERS → types
responds **22** 219, 221
response *see* THEORIES → reception
Resse, Cristoforo **19** 686, 688
Ressu, Camil **26** 245*, 715, 716, 723
pupils **7** 361; **12** 525; **20** 877; **23** 699
works **26** 715
Resta, Sebastiano **26** 245–6*
drawings **9** 26, 230; **30** 279
mounts (works on paper and scrolls) **22** 236
writings **10** 204
Resta, Vermondo **26** 246*; **28** 512; **29** 268
Restany, Pierre
exhibitions **26** 777
groups and movements **11** 551, 570; **20** 913; **23** 260; **30** 924
writings **7** 421; **19** 704
Restaurant Frognerseteren **23** 221
Restauratorenblätter **7** 743
Restenneth **28** 241
rest-houses **5** 479; **15** 202
Restif de La Bretonne, Nicolas E. **10** 823
Restle, Marcell **10** 213
restoration **7** 726–30*, 737*; **11** 306, 310; **30** 395, 853
historical and regional traditions
China **7** 729–30
Czech Republic **8** 425
Etruscan **10** 639–40
Italy **4** 247–8; **7** 738–9; **10** 639–40
Japan **7** 729–30
materials
carnauba wax **33** 1
plaster of Paris **7** 729
spermaceti wax **33** 1
uses
architecture **2** 318–25*, *321*; **7** 729; **32** 596–7
beadwork **7** 729
ceramics **7** 729
clocks **7** 729
furniture **7** 729
glass **12** 797*
paintings **7** 737–9*, *738*; **17** 209–10; **24** 569; **27** 321; **28** 340
pottery **13** 483
scrolls **7** 729–30
sculpture **2** 163; **7** 729, 739*, *739*; **9** 23; **29** *710*
Greece, ancient **9** 21
Rome, ancient **9** 21
stained glass **29** 519*
tapestries **30** 333
tomb paintings **10** 618
vases **21** 266
wall paintings **10** 618; **32** 809–10*
watches **7** 729
see also CONSERVATION; TECHNICAL EXAMINATION
Restoration style **8** 235
Restormel **6** 55
Restout, Charles **26** 246
Restout, Eustache **26** 246
Restout, Jacques **26** 246
Restout, Jean, I (1663-1702) **26** 246
Restout, Jean, II (1692-1768) **14** 83; **24** 135; **26** 246, 247–8*; **27** 248
collaboration **6** 121; **10** 842
patrons and collectors **8** 795; **25** 368
pupils **3** 204; **7** 495; **8** 794; **13** 324; **14** 84, 133; **18** 841; **26** 248, 506
reproductive prints by others **19** 261
teachers **17** 672
works **26** *247*, *248*
Restout, Jean-Bernard **11** 368; **26** 247, 248*
Restout, Marc-Antoine **26** 246
Restout, Marguérin **26** 246
Restout, Pierre **26** 246
Restout, Thomas **26** 246
Resurrección Hidalgo, Felix *see* HIDALGO, FELIX RESURRECCIÓN
Reszka, Pedro **12** 918
Reszka, Stanisław **32** 6
retables **1** 707; **26** 249–55*
Argentina **2** 398
Bolivia **4** 264
Brazil **26** *254*, 254–5

retables—cont.
Catalonia 13 106; 14 858; 20 514, 515; 26 249, 251
Colombia 26 252
Cuba (Caribbean) 8 233
Ecuador 26 252, 252
Gothic 3 218; 11 479–83, 677; 13 69, 106, 123, 169; 28 517, 518
Guatemala 26 251
Indian subcontinent 26 254
Mexico 21 383, 383
Peru 24 499; 26 252
Portugal 7 521; 25 296; 26 252–4*, 253; 32 156
Renaissance 6 452
Spain 1 710; 11 481; 13 344; 26 249–51*
Baroque 11 492; 26 251; 29 291; 31 92
Gothic 3 218; 11 479–83, 677; 13 69, 123, 169; 28 517, 518
Hispano-Flemish style 3 845
Renaissance 11 483–4; 29 290, 290
15th cent. 3 810; 4 423; 15 834
16th cent. 11 484; 26 250
17th cent. 22 3
see also ALTARPIECES; PREDELLAS
Retacco, Simone 29 371
Retalhuleu, S Antonio 13 767
Reteux, Jean 19 704
Reth, Alfred (1884-1966) 26 255*
Rethel 27 82
Rethel, Alfred (1816-59) 26 255–6*
groups and movements 12 394; 26 742
teachers 32 120
works 4 39; 11 461; 12 853; 26 256
Rethel, Otto 26 256
Rethy, Mathieu S'volders de Rethy, Abbot of Averbode *see* S'VOLDERS DE RETHY, MATHIEU, Abbot of Averbode
Rethymnon 8 156
Archaeological Museum 8 157; 21 691
fort 8 156
portal 8 156
Rimondi fountain 8 156
sculpture 21 679
Reti, Domenico 16 701
Réti, István 3 820; 22 434; 26 256*; 30 207, 212
Reti, Leonardo 26 824
reticella *see under* LACE → types
reticles 26 257*
Reticulated Background, Master of the 21 338
reticulated tracery *see under* TRACERY → types → bar
reticulated vaults *see under* VAULTS (CEILING) → types
Retimo *see* RETHYMNON
Reting 5 105; 30 818
Retiro, El *see* EL RETIRO
retouching *see under* PHOTOGRAPHY → processes
retreats *see* HERMITAGES
retrochoirs 26 257*
retroussage *see under* PRINTS → techniques
Retté, Adolphe 12 205
Retti, Leonardo 29 831
Retti, Leopoldo Mattia 26 257*
patrons and collectors 33 429
works 12 372, 373; 18 643; 29 874; 33 691
Retz, Désert de 26 257–8*, 743
Column House 11 242, 243
gardens 12 123
ruin buildings 27 324
Retz, Duchesse de 26 420
Retz, Hauptplatz 15 10 738
Retza, Franciscus de *see* FRANCISCUS DE RETZA
Retzsch, (Friedrich August) Moritz 26 258*
Reuchlen, Hans *see* REICHLE, HANS
Reuchlin, Johannes 14 868
Réunion des Musées Nationaux 11 659
Réunion Island 1 214
Reus 29 330, 343
S Pedro 29 337
Reus, Emilio 31 753
Reus, Jan de 20 81
Reusch, (Johann) Friedrich 12 405; 26 258*
reuse
altars 1 696
brick 4 772
gold 7 565
mosaics 26 691
sarcophagi 27 829
sculpture 16 245
silver 7 565
see also SPOLIA
Reusner, Nicolaus 10 174; 12 720
Reuter, Theodor 13 330
Reuter, (Christoph) Wilhelm 19 482; 20 601; 26 258*
Reuter Christiansen, Ursula 8 736
Reuterswärd, Carl Fredrik 18 809; 26 258–9*; 30 82
Reuterswärd, Patrik 30 120
Reuther, R. G. 1 66
Reutlingen, Hans von *see* HANS VON REUTLINGEN
Reutlinger, Charles 26 259*
Reutlinger, Emile 26 259
Reutlinger, Léopold-Emile 26 259*
Reuttimann, Johann Conrad 12 446
Reuvens, C(aspar) J(acob) C(hristiaan) 10 93
Reuwich, Erhard 4 358; 20 693; 26 259*; 33 349
works 13 808; 31 154
Révai, Miklós 14 888; 15 17
Reval *see* TALLINN
Revash 6 380
Revazov, U. 2 894
works 2 894
Reve, Thomas 5 514
Réveillon, Jean-Baptiste 11 579; 14 792; 25 578; 26 259–60*; 32 815
works 32 IV1
Revel, Gabriel 5 884; 26 260*
Revel, Jean 7 167; 11 646; 19 850
Revelation *see* APOCALYPSES
Reveley, Henry 8 652; 24 495
Reveley, Willey 33 385
Revell, Viljo (Gabriel) 11 92; 26 260–61*
collaboration 24 188; 31 176, 243
staff 19 798
works 2 540; 13 239; 14 372; 30 284; 31 176
Revelli, Ignazio 16 730
Revelli, Luigi 16 730
Reventlow, Claus 8 725
Révérand, Claude 23 512; 27 536
Reverdino, Cesare *see* REVERDY, GEORGES
Reverdy, Georges 20 793; 26 261*
Reverdy, Pierre 2 225, 279; 3 366; 9 196; 26 261*
groups and movements 8 244, 246
works 13 671; 20 75, 830; 30 488
writings 27 163
Rèvere, Palazzo Ducale 10 784
Revere, Joseph Warren 4 481
Revere, Paul 7 809; 26 261–2*; 31 649, 653
works 4 477, 479, 480, 481; 10 394, 851; 26 262; 31 601
Revere, Paul, Pottery 4 482
Revere Copper Co. 4 481; 26 262
Révérend, Antoine 32 386
Reverón, Armando 26 262–3*; 32 167, 175
reverse 26 263*; 32 376
Reverseaux, Guéau de 27 551
Revesby Abbey (Lincs) manuscripts 3 879, 879
revestries *see* SACRISTRIES
Révész, Imre 17 876
Révész, László 10 447
revetments 21 547
historical and regional traditions
Byzantine 9 656, 658; 16 599
Carolingian 5 794
Central Asia, Western 16 199
Early Christian (*c.* AD 250-843) 9 656
Etruscan 10 593, 603
Greece, ancient 13 424
Iran 16 199, 234, 249
Islamic 16 143, 199, 234, 243–5, 248, 249, 250, 381
Italy 10 593
Rome, ancient 26 876, 878
Turkey 16 599
materials
glazes 16 248
marble 5 794; 26 876
silver 9 656, 658
stucco 16 243
terracotta 10 603; 13 424; 26 877
tiles 16 250
Revett, Nicholas 2 164; 3 329; 7 502; 10 293; 13 303; 26 263–4*; 29 99
collaboration 2 319, 559; 6 446; 23 544
groups and movements 13 607, 608; 22 735
patrons and collectors 8 533
works 2 171, 666, 667, 672; 5 905; 13 609; 25 172
writings 2 359; 10 276; 28 242; 29 805
Review of Publications of Art 24 422
Revilla, Carlos 24 511; 26 264*
Revilla del Campo 29 333
Revillagigedo, Juan Vicente Güemes Pacheco, Conde de *see* GÜEMES PACHECO, JUAN VICENTE
Revista actual 24 435
Revista de antropofagía 24 435
Revista de ideas estéticas 5 529
Revista del Museo Nacional 24 435
revivalism 14 580–81
Revival styles *see*:
ASSYRIAN REVIVAL
BAROQUE REVIVAL
BYZANTINE REVIVAL
CELTIC REVIVAL
ENGLISH DOMESTIC REVIVAL
GOTHIC REVIVAL
GREEK REVIVAL
JACOBETHAN REVIVAL
NORMAN REVIVAL
OLD NORSE REVIVAL
OLD RUSSIAN REVIVAL
RENAISSANCE REVIVAL
ROCOCO REVIVAL
ROMANESQUE REVIVAL
SPANISH REVIVAL STYLE
Révoil, Henri-Antoine 10 508; 32 83
Révoil, Pierre(-Henri) 26 264–5*
groups and movements 9 363; 31 373, 374
patrons and collectors 4 556; 8 649
pupils 11 158; 13 806; 19 847; 21 797; 23 572
works 24 140; 26 265
Revold, Axel (Julius) 26 265–6*
collaboration 23 226
pupils 10 125, 222; 23 226; 28 828; 29 780
teachers 23 226
Revold, Axel (Julius)—cont.
works 23 226, 232, 603
Revolté, La 13 323
Revolt group (Bunt) 11 317; 25 108, 141, 409; 26 266*; 33 607
Revolution 24 427
Révolution surréaliste, La 24 144, 428, 442; 30 17, 18, 19, 20
revolving domes *see under* DOMES → types
Revue belge d'archéologie et d'histoire de l'art 24 439
Revue Blanche, La 5 669; 10 885; 22 422, 537–8; 24 426; 31 213, 830; 32 739
Revue d'art (Paris; 1858–99) 24 423
Revue d'art, La (Antwerp; 1904-29) 24 439
Revue de l'architecture en Belgique 24 439
Revue de l'art ancien et moderne 24 442
Revue des archéologues et historiens d'art de Louvain 24 439
Revue des arts décoratifs 2 564; 24 427, 442
Revue des beaux-arts de France 24 442
Revue d'esthétique 24 442
Revue Devětsilu 24 440
Revue du Lyonnais 19 848
Revue générale de l'architecture et des travaux publics 2 315, 333; 8 476; 11 359, 521; 13 204; 24 442
Revue indépendante, La 5 159; 24 426
Revue internationale de l'art et de la curiosité, La 9 424
Revueltas, Fermín 10 543; 21 387; 26 266*
Revueltas, Silvestre 10 543
Revue universelle des arts 11 675; 24 423
Rewa 15 497
palace 15 290
Rewal, Raj 15 169, 242; 26 266–7*
Rewald, John 11 676; 31 672
Rewiri, Kura Te Waru 18 529*; 20 360
Rexach, Juan 16 834; 26 267*; 31 815
Rexach, Pere 16 834; 26 267*
Rey *see* RAYY
Rey, Etienne 3 867
Rey, Guido 26 267*
Rey, Joaquín Roca *see* ROCA REY, JOAQUÍN
Rey, Mateo 29 341
Rey, Matías 29 341
Reychmuth, Johannes 26 718; 28 696
Reydams (family) 30 320
Reydams, Hendrik, II 5 50
Reyers, Willem 22 861
Reyers, Zeger 13 607; 14 42; 26 268*
Reyes, Bernabé García de los *see* GARCÍA DE LOS REYES, BERNABÉ
Reyes, Dagoberto 10 154
Reyes, Los *see* LOS REYES
Reyes, Luis Enrique 7 607
Reyes, Refugio (José) 21 379; 26 268*
Reyes Ferreira, Chucho *see* REYES FERREIRA, JESÚS
Reyes Ferreira, Jesús 26 268*
Reyff (family) 30 136
Reyff, Franz 26 268
Reyff, Franz Bartholomäus 26 268
Reyff, Johann Franz 11 773; 26 268*; 30 126, 136
Reyff, Johann Jakob 26 268
Reyff, Pankraz 26 268
Reygadas Vertiz, José 7 201; 30 452
Reykjavík 15 68; 26 268–9*
ceramics 15 72
exhibitions 15 70
Gallerí SÚM 15 71
Icelandic School of Arts and Crafts 15 68
museums
Ásmundur Sveinsson Museum 26 269; 30 54
Einar Jónsson Museum 17 646; 26 269
Living Art Museum 2 475; 15 71; 23 896
National Gallery of Iceland 15 68; 26 269
National Museum of Iceland 15 68, 70; 26 269
Sigurjón Ólafsson Museum 23 392
Myndlista og Handiðas Koli Íslands *see* Icelandic School of Arts and Crafts
Nýlistasafnið *see* museums → Living Art Museum
Thjódminjasafn Íslands *see* museums → National Museum of Iceland
urban planning 26 269
Reymerswaele, Marinus van 3 554; 10 713; 12 287; 22 836; 26 269–70*; 31 882
Reymond, Abraham-Louis 22 920
Reymond, Casimir 30 138
Reymond, Jonas-Louis 22 920
Reymond, Pierre 22 31
Reyn, de 9 485
Reyn, Toomas *see* REIN, TOOMAS
Reyna, Francisco 33 729
Reyna, Jorge González *see* GONZÁLEZ REYNA, JORGE
Reynalt van Homoet 20 758
Reyna Medina, Eduardo 21 382
Reynaud, (François-) Léonce 11 323, 522; 26 270*
collaboration 25 855
pupils 8 532
works 11 524
writings 26 13
Reynbouts (family) 30 317
Reynbouts, Maarten 5 49
Reynell, Gladys 2 760
Reyni, Ingálvur av 10 813
Reynier, Adrien 2 464
Reynière, Laurent Grimod de la *see* GRIMOD DE LA REYNIÈRE, LAURENT
Reynolds, Francis & Rohnstock 8 111
Reynolds, John Hamilton 14 736
Reynolds, Joshua 8 612; 9 212; 10 365; 19 586, 588, 620, 621; 22 480; 23 295; 26 270–82*
assistants 20 391–2; 23 213; 31 139
catalogues 6 80
commentaries 10 377
copies 5 271
exhibitions 10 677, 678; 19 507, 586
frames 11 426, 430
groups and movements 22 734, 737
house 22 122
methods 4 103; 5 519, 654; 9 673; 10 199; 23 378; 25 280, 282
paintings 4 607; 17 851
fancy pictures 10 785–6
history 14 586
portraits 9 245; 10 249
Bunbury, Sarah 25 285
Campbell, John, 1st Baron Cawdor (1755-1821) 5 541
Coussmaker, George 26 276
Delabal, Charlotte 26 277
Delmé, Elizabeth 26 274
Howard (ii), Frederick, 5th Earl of Carlisle 14 808
Keppel, Commodore 26 272

Reynolds, Joshua
paintings
portraits—cont.
Orléans, Louis-Philippe-Joseph de Bourbon, 5th Duc d' (1747-93) **23** *520*
self-portraits **20** 109
Siddons, Sarah **8** 123; **25** *278*, 279
Sterne, Lawrence **26** *273*
Worsley, Lady **9** 284
satirical **13** 300
patrons and collectors **10** 361
Alba, 17th Duque de (1878-1953) **1** 529
Angerstein, John Julius **2** 51
Arundell, Henry, 8th Baron Arundell of Wardour **2** 576
Baring, Francis (1740-1810) **3** 239
Beit, Otto (John) **3** 522
Beurnonville, Etienne-Edmond Martin, Baron de **3** 890
Boydell, John **10** 369
Brudenell, George, 4th Earl of Cardigan and 1st Duke of Montagu **4** 894
Calonne, Charles-Alexandre de **5** 439
Cavendish-Bentinck, William Henry, 3rd Duke of Portland (1738-1809) **6** 118
Curzon, Nathaniel, 1st Baron Scarsdale **8** 281
Drummond, George A(lexander) (1827-1910) **9** 305
Fox, Henry, 1st Baron Holland **11** 362
George III, King of Great Britain (*reg* 1760-1820) **14** 144
George IV, King of Great Britain (*reg* 1820-30) **14** 146
Gillott, Joseph **12** 638
Greville, Francis, 1st Earl Brooke and 1st Earl of Warwick (1719-73) **13** 644
Greville, George, 2nd Earl Brooke and 2nd Earl of Warwick **13** 644
Groult, Camille **13** 705
Guinness, Edward (Cecil), 1st Earl of Iveagh **13** 836
Hanover, William Augustus, Duke of Cumberland **14** 144
Harcourt, Simon, 1st Earl Harcourt of Stanton Harcourt and 2nd Earl Nuneham **14** 163
Howard (ii), Frederick, 5th Earl of Carlisle **14** 807
Huntington, Henry E(dwards) **15** 29
Huntington Art Gallery **19** 703
Lázaro Galdiano, José **18** 900
Leeson, Joseph Henry **19** 64
Macklin, Thomas **20** 25, 26
Mellon, Andrew W(illiam) **21** 90
Montagu-Douglas-Scott, Walter Francis, 5th Duke of Buccleuch, 7th Duke of Queensberry **21** 908
Murray, Charles Fairfax **22** 351
National Gallery of Canada (Ottawa) **1** 496
Petty, William (Fitzmaurice), 2nd Earl of Shelburne and 1st Marquess of Lansdowne **24** 570
Petty-Fitzmaurice, Henry, 3rd Marquess of Lansdowne **24** 571
Pleydell-Bouverie, Jacob, 2nd Earl of Radnor **25** 39
Proby, William, 5th Earl of Carysfoot **25** 639
Richards, John Inigo **26** 335
Rogers, Samuel **26** 541
Reynolds, Joshua
patrons and collectors—cont.
Rothschild (family) **27** 223
Rushout, John, 2nd Baron Northwick **27** 350
Sackville, John Frederick, 3rd Duke of Dorset **27** 494
Seymour-Conway, Richard, 4th Marquess of Hertford **20** 875; **28** 527
Soane, John **28** 908
Society of Dilettanti **28** 924
Spencer, John, 1st Earl Spencer **29** 380, 381
Temple-Nugent-Grenville, George, 1st Marquess of Buckingham **13** 637
Tennant, Charles **30** 464
Watson-Wentworth, Charles, 2nd Marquess of Rockingham **32** 912
Weddell, William **33** 20
Wernher, Julius **33** 84
Williams-Wynn, Watkin, 4th Baronet, of Wynnstay (1749-89) **32** 790; **33** 208
Yusupov, Nicolay (Borisovich), Prince (1751-1831) **33** 579
personal collection **2** 559; **7** 233; **10** 807; **20** 446; **22** 236
drawings **4** 330; **9** 229; **18** 895
paintings **3** 454; **12** 164; **18** 147; **19** 587; **28** 819; **29** 809
pupils **3** 280, 439; **4** 731; **9** 199; **10** 378; **12** 146; **32** 784, 910
reproductions in stained glass **23** 691
reproductive prints by others **7** 490; **16** 820; **17** 630; **21** 416; **25** 596, 619; **26** 231, 282
Bartolozzi, Francesco **3** 309
Chant, James (John) **6** 451
Cousins, Samuel **8** 69
Dickinson, William **8** 863; **24** 391
Dixon, John **9** 43
Doughty, William **9** 199
Fisher, Edward **11** 139
Green, Valentine **13** 614
Haid (i), Johann Gottfried **14** 49
Hancock, Robert **14** 132
Heath, Charles (i) (1785-1848) **14** 280
Houston, Richard **14** 803
Jones, John (*c.* 1740-*c.* 1797) **17** 630
Marcuard, Robert Samuel **20** 400
McArdell, James **19** 867
Miller, John Douglas **21** 606
Sharp, William **28** 558
Sherwin, John Keyse **28** 597
Skorodumov, Gavriil (Ivanovich) **28** 823; **29** 676, *676*
Smith, John Raphael **28** 882
Turner, Charles **31** 465
Watson, Caroline **32** 910
Watson, James **32** 910
Wilkin, Charles **33** 191
stained glass **29** 506
studio **29** 856
teachers **14** 841
writings **1** 179; **7** 675; **8** 613; **10** 402; **12** 63, 292; **13** 296–7; **14** 640; **15** 94; **22** 686; **31** 17, 300, 768; **32** 355
on contrast **7** 783
on exhibitions **10** 677
on history painting **14** 585
Reynolds, Mallica *see* KAPO
Reynolds, Samuel **7** 485, 486
Reynolds, S(amuel) W(illiam), sr (1773-1835) **26** 282*
assistants **19** 806
collaboration **21** 417
dealers **2** 614
patrons and collectors **2** 499; **28** 170
Reynolds, S(amuel) W(illiam), sr (1773-1835)—cont.
pupils **8** 69; **27** 459
works **7** 754; **24** 637
Reynolds, S(amuel) W(illiam), jr (1794-1872) **26** 282
Reynolds, William **7** 480
Reynolds-Stephens, William **26** 283*; **31** 250
assistants **9** 54
groups and movements **23** 35
works **11** *256*
Reyns, Henry of *see* HENRY OF REYNS
Reynst (family) **10** 363; **29** 804
Reynst, Gerard **9** 380; **10** 761; **19** 473; **20** 812; **22** 904; **23** 113; **26** 283–4*; **32** 155
Reynst, Jan **20** 812; **22** 904; **26** 283*; **27** 228; **32** 155
Reynst, Joan **9** 380; **26** 284
Reyntiens, Patrick **29** 508, 516; **33** 680
Reyschoot, van *see* REYSSCHOOT, VAN
Reysek, Matěj *see* REJSEK, MATĚJ
Reysher, M. I. **33** 518
Reysschoot, Anne-Marie van **26** 284, 286
Reysschoot, Emmanuel Petrus Franciscus van **26** 284, 285*
Reysschoot, Johannes Baptist Emmanuel van **26** 284, 285–6*
Reysschoot, Petrus Johannes van **26** 284*
Reysschoot, Petrus Norbertus van **26** 284, 285*
works **26** 284, *285*
Reza *see* RIZA
Reza, Jorge de la **4** 267; **23** 706
Rezanov, Aleksandr I **3** 733; **27** 578; **28** 628
Rezasco, Giovanni Battista **3** 196
Rēzekne **18** *847*
Rezeph *see* RUSAFA
Rezevic Monastery **22** *17*
Reznik, David **16** 566, 567; **26** 22, 286*
Rezza, Stefano **10** 786
Rezzonico (family) **24** 843
Rezzonico, Abbondio **5** 366, 626; **24** 298, 844
Rezzonico, Aurelio **19** 629
Rezzonico, Carlo, Cardinal *see* CLEMENT XIII, Pope
Rezzonico, Giovambattista, Cardinal **24** 844; **29** 832
furniture **24** *845*
Rezzonico, Ludovico **5** 626
Rezzuti, Piero di Neri dei **16** 746
RFR **26** 333
Rhabdios **31** 434
Rhadé **5** 503; **32** 480
Rhagae *see* RAYY
Rhakotis *see* ALEXANDRIA
Rhamnous **13** *363*; **26** 287*
sculpture **8** 262; **13** 454, 462; **24** 205
Theatre **13** 385
tombs **13** 384
Rhau, Georg **20** 791
Rhazes **21** 5
Rhäzüns, St Georg **30** 129
Rhead, Frederick Hurten **26** 287*; **27** 565; **31** 639
Rhead, George Woolliscroft **4** 879
Rhead, Louis John **19** 490; **26** 287*
Rhee, Cornelis **2** 763
Rhegion **13** *362*; **16** *621*; **26** 287–8*, *886*
coins **13** 586, 587
Museo Nazionale della Magna Grecia **26** 288
Rhein, Nicolaus **21** 417
Rheinau **30** 126
Benedictine church **26** 635
Rheinberger, Egon **19** 339
Rheindorf, Hanns **11** 256
works **23** 306, 317, *317*
Rheingold, Metzner **28** 127
Rheingruppe **1** 160
Rheinische Expressionisten **5** 543; **10** 695; **12** 395
Rheinische Sezession *see* SEZESSION (RHEINISCHE)
Rheinlande, Die *see* DEUTSCHE MONATSHEFTE
Rheinsberg, Raffael **3** 803
Rheinsberg, Schloss *see* SCHLOSS RHEINSBERG
Rheinzabern **27** 107, 108
Rhemen, Stephanus van **1** 584
Rheneia **12** 68
Rhenen, Master of **20** 754–5*
Rhenen, St Cunerakerk **2** *341*; **22** 819, 857
Rhenish ware *see under* POTTERY → wares
Rher, Juan de **24** 503
Rhesafa *see* RUSAFA
Rheu, Le *see* LE RHEU
Rheydt **12** 379
Rhijn, Titus van *see* RIJN, TITUS (REMBRANDTSZ.) VAN
Rhijs, Peter **7** 832
Rhind, Alexander Henry **10** 7, 90, 92
Rhind, David **26** 288*
groups and movements **28** 289
pupils **24** 315
works **9** 724; **28** 156, 228
Rhind, Ethel **31** 229
Rhind, John (1828-92) **28** 243
Rhind, John Massey (1858-1936) **3** 31
rhinoceros horn *see under* HORN → types
rhipidia **10** 775
Rhisnes **12** 836
Rhitsona **13** 579
Rhiwaedog Gate-house **32** 782
Rhizaion **9** 556
Rho, Adolphe **19** 59
Rho, Carlo da **4** 400
Rho, Gabriele da **26** 288–9*
Rho, Giovanni Pietro da **26** 288, 289*
Rho, Manlio **16** 681; **25** 838; **26** 289*
Rho, Paganino da **26** 288
Rhoads, Samuel **14** 782
Rhode Island School of Design **31** 669
Rhoden, Johann Martin von *see* ROHDEN, JOHANN MARTIN VON
Rhodes (island) **9** *511*, *512*; **13** *362*, *363*; **26** *289*, 289–95*
architecture **14** 420; **26** 291*, 295*
Byzantine **26** 293*
Early Christian (*c.* AD 250-843) **26** 293*
Knights Hospitaller **26** 294, *294*
basilicas **26** 293
bronze **26** 292
carpets **16** 473
ceramics **1** 877; **13** 358
coins **7** 535; **13** 587, 588; **18** 152
earrings **13** 598, *598*
electrum **13** *598*
embroidery **13** *356*
faience (i) (glass) **1** 878; **13** 589
fibulae **10** 591; **13** 601
figurines **13** 578
glass **1** 868; **13** 593
gold **12** *869*
gravestones **8** 341
Ibrahim Pasha Mosque **26** 295
icons **26** 293, 295
jewellery **13** 597–8
ketubbot **18** 3
lamps **13** *603*
linen **13** *356*
mosaics **13** 560
pectoral ornaments **12** *869*
Rhodes (island)—cont.
pigments **23** 785
pottery **13** 502, 503, *503*, *537*, 542; **16** 395, 420; **26** 290
Geometric (*c.* 900-*c.* 700 BC) **13** 497
Late Helladic (*c.* 1600-*c.* 1050 BC) **26** *290*
Redjeb Pasha Mosque **26** 295
Sanctuary of Athena Lindia **13** *404*, 405
sculpture **13** 423, 443, 462, 464; **26** 291–3*
bronze **26** 292
Knights Hospitaller **26** 295
silk **13** *356*
silver **13** 359
situlae **13** 515
statuettes **29** 567
stirrup jars **26** *290*
streets **26** *294*
trade **25** 733; **26** 292
wall paintings **21** 659; **26** 293
Rhodes (city) **13** 401; **26** *289*, *908*
altars **1** 692
Archaeological Museum **13** 470; **14** 361
architecture **26** *294*
armour **2** 449
churches **26** 293
Hagia Triada **26** 295
Hagioi Apostoloi **26** 294
Latin Cathedral *see* Orthodox Cathedral of the Panagia tou Kastrou
Orthodox Cathedral of the Panagia tou Kastrou **26** 294, 295
Panagia tis Nikis **26** 294
Panagia tou Bourgou **26** 294
Panagia tou Kastrou *see* Orthodox Cathedral of Panagia tou Kastrou
St John of the Collachium **26** 294
Hagios Phanourios **26** 293
fortifications **21** 558
funerary stelae **26** *292*
glass **13** 594
Knights Hospitaller compound **18** 152
mosaics **13** 562, 565
reliefs **26** *292*
sculpture **26** 292
Second Hospital of the Knights of St John **14** 780
stadium **29** 488
Süleymaniye Mosque **26** 295
Tongue of England **26** 295
town walls **21** 557
urban planning **13** 419, 420, 421; **14** 564; **26** 291
wall paintings **26** 294–5
Rhodes, Benjamin **14** 419
works **14** *418*
Rhodes, Cecil **3** 81; **29** 105, 114, 116; **31** 488
Rhodes, Daniel **31** 640
Rhodes, David **10** 307; **33** 20
Rhodes, Dennis Sun *see* SUN RHODES, DENNIS
Rhodes, Greville **2** 318
Rhodes, Lis **10** 689
Rhodes, Pauline **7** 211
Rhodes, Philiskos of *see* PHILISKOS OF RHODES
Rhodes, Zandra **9** 294
Rhodesia, Northern *see* ZAMBIA
Rhodesia, Southern *see* ZIMBABWE
Rhodian houses *see under* HOUSES → types
rhodium **10** 136
Rhoikos of Samos **1** 480; **13** 394, 439; **26** 295–6*; **27** 687
works **13** 380, 572; **15** 893
Rhomboidal Pyramid *see* DAHSHUR → pyramids → Bent Pyramid

Rhondda Group **32** 786
Rhondda Pottery **32** 790
Rhone and Iredale **19** 321; **31** 864
Rhoplex *see under* PAINTS → types
Rhuddlan Castle (Clwyd) **16** 894, *895, 896*; **21** 564
Rhygyfarch Psalter *see under* PSALTERS → individual manuscripts
Rhymni (Mid Glams) **32** 783
Rhyn, Rembrandt (Harmensz.) van *see* REMBRANDT (HARMENSZ.) VAN RIJN
Rhys **32** 781
Rhys, Charles du **9** 354
rhyta **26** 296*
historical and regional traditions
Central Asia, Western **6** *256*, 270–71, *271*; **23** *160*
China **7** *89*
Crete **21** 668, *669*
Cyprus, ancient **18** *98*
Greece, ancient **13** 477, 569
Helladic **14** 355
Iran, ancient **15** 905, *915*
Minoan **21** 668, *669*
Mycenaean **14** 355
Parthian **15** *915*; **24** 217
Philistine **24** 634
Sogdiana **6** *256*
Thracian **30** 770
Turkmenistan **6** *271*; **23** *160*
materials
faience (i) (glass) **18** *98*
ivory **6** 270–71, *271*; **15** *915*; **23** *160*; **24** 217
pottery **6** *256*; **21** *669*
Rhythm group (Rytm) **25** 108; **26** 296*; **32** 877
members **18** 414; **29** 791; **33** 285
rhythmos **13** 467
Riace **13** *362*
Riace Bronzes **2** 171; **4** 851; **13** 421, 434, 450, 453, *453*, 469, 606; **23** 291; **24** 593; **26** 288, 296–8*, *297*; **27** 45
Riadh *see* RIYADH
Rian, Johannes **23** 227
Riancho, Agustín **14** 26; **24** 829; **26** 298*; **27** 783; **29** 284
Riancho, González **27** 783
Riaño, Diego de **26** 298–9*; **29** 265
attributions **29** 266
groups and movements **25** 30, 31
works **28** 512, 518, 726
Riaño, Luis de **8** 302; **24** 507
Riario (family) **26** 756
Riario, Raffaele (Sansoni), Cardinal **26** 299*, 836
architecture **16** 631; **24** 530; **26** 756, 836; **32** 640
paintings **6** 355
sculpture **2** 558; **21** 433
Rib, Johan Kaspar **30** 884
RIBA *see* LONDON → Royal Institute of British Architects
Riba, Prat de la **27** 304
Ribaberikin Kiribati *see* KIRIBATI
Rib-Addi **5** 331
Ribadeo, Pedro de *see* PEDRO DE RIBADEO
Riba Fria, Gaspar Gonçalves do *see* GONÇALVES DO RIBA FRIA, GASPAR
Ribagorza, Martín Gurrea y Aragón, Conde de *see* VILLAHERMOSA, MARTÍN GURREA Y ARAGÓN, Duque de
Ribaldi, Giovanni di Francesco **19** 686
works **19** *685*
Ribalta, Francisco **26** 299–302*; **29** 280; **31** 815
assistants **26** 302
attributions **6** 30
collaboration **6** 29, 30
groups and movements **30** 456
Ribalta, Francisco—cont.
patrons and collectors **4** 565; **26** 306
pupils **26** 302, 309
works **11** 490, 710, *710*; **26** 250, *300, 301*
Ribalta, Juan **6** 29, 30; **26** 299, 301, 302*
Ribas, Felipe de **26** 302*; **29** 292
Ribas, J. M. **20** 516
Ribas, M. **20** 516
Ribas, Pons i *see* PONS I RIBAS
Ribas i Anguera, Josep **29** 321
Ribat-i Malik **5** 722; **6** *182*, 201, 206; **16** *105*; **26** 302–3*; **31** *781*
fortifications **21** 592
inscriptions **16** 258
pīshṭāq **24** 877
portals **6** *202*
Ribat-i Sharaf **5** 722; **16** *105*, 163; **26** 303*
arches **2** 295
architectural decorations **16** 165
bowls **16** 533
palaces **23** 815
pīshṭāq **16** 164; **24** 877
squinches **16** 164, 169
woodwork **16** 491
ribāṭs **16** 151, 154, 155, 156
see also CARAVANSERAIS; KHĀNAQĀHS
Ribaucourt, Comte de **18** 572
ribbed domes *see under* DOMES → types
ribbons **7** 179; **22** 654; **26** 703; **28** *310*
see also BRAIDS
ribbonwork **26** 303–4*, *304*
Ribchester (Lancs)
helmets **27** *95*
Ribe **8** *720*; **26** 304–5*
architecture **32** 533
brooches **32** 531
Cathedral of Our Lady **8** 722, 723; **24** 316; **26** 304–5*, 593
Citizens' Tower **4** 781; **8** 723
sculpture **8** 737, 738; **26** *305*, 640
tomb of Christopher I **8** 738
chests **8** 757
metalwork **32** 524
painting **8** 733
St Catherine **8** 723
sculpture **8** 737
stone **8** 721
Ribeira, António Simões *see* SIMÕES RIBEIRA, ANTÓNIO
Ribeira Grande, Mangualdqdia **25** 292
Ribeiro, Diogo **26** 125
Ribeiro, Gabriel **4** 710
Ribeiro, Mário Emilio **25** 272
Ribeiro, Paulo Antunes *see* ANTUNES RIBEIRO, PAULO
Ribeiro da Fonseca, Maria Inês Carmona *see* MENEZ
Ribeiro da Rocha, Lourenco **4** 723
Ribeiro Soares da Silva, André *see* SOARES DA SILVA, ANDRÉ RIBEIRO
Ribeisen (family) **20** 794
Ribelles, José **4** 378
Ribemont **25** 538
Ribemont-Dessaignes, Georges **8** 438, 439; **21** 709; **26** 305–6*
works **21** 176
Ribemont-sur-Ancre **26** 905
Riber, Lauritz Andersen *see* ANDERSEN RIBER, LAURITZ
Ribera, Antonio de **24** 95
Ribera (ii), Carlos Luis Ribera y Fieve *see* RIBERA Y FIEVE, CARLOS LUIS
Ribera, Catalina de **28** 513
Ribera (i), Fadrique Enríquez de, 1st Marqués de Tarifa *see* TARIFA, 1st Marqués de
Ribera, Fadrique Henríquez de *see* HENRÍQUEZ DE RIBERA, FADRIQUE
Ribera (i), Fernando Enríquez Afán de, 3rd Duque de Alcalá *see* ALCALÁ, 3rd Duque de
Ribera, José de *see* RIBERA, JUSEPE
Ribera, Juan Antonio **4** 378; **20** 58
Ribera (ii), Juan Antonio Ribera y Fernández *see* RIBERA Y FERNÁNDEZ, JUAN ANTONIO
Ribera (i), Juan de, Archbishop of Valencia **26** 306*
architecture **31** 815
paintings **22** 73; **26** 300, 301; **27** 842
Ribera, Juan Félix de **26** 313
Ribera, Juan Vicente **1** 587
Ribera, Jusepe de **22** 478; **26** 309–13*, 772; **29** 281
assistants **11** 364
attributions **9** 52; **18** 840
engravings **26** *310*
frames **11** 487
groups and movements **30** 456
paintings **16** 673
genre **12** 289
religious **22** 484; **23** 294, 625; **26** *309, 311, 312*; **32** 775
patrons and collectors **22** 486
Alcalá, 3rd Duque de (1583-1637) **26** 307
Alexander I, Emperor of Russia (*reg* 1801-25) **26** 733
Altamira, Vicente Joaquín Osorio Moscoso y Guzmán, 11th Conde de **1** 690
Arce, Pedro de **2** 291
Bourbon del Monte, Francesco Maria, Cardinal **4** 567
Coke, Thomas, 1st Earl of Leicester of the 1st creation (1697-1759) **7** 540
Doria, Marcantonio **9** 174
Esterházy, Pál, Prince (1786-1866) **10** 530
Ferdinand VII, King of Spain (*reg* 1808; 1814-33) **4** 566
Giustiniani (i), Vincenzo, Marchese **12** 764
Godoy (y Alvárez de Faria), Manuel, Príncipe de la Paz **12** 839
Harrach, Ferdinand Bonaventura, Graf von **14** 190
Iriarte, Domingo de **16** 48
Las Marismas del Guadalquivir, Alejandro María Aguado y Ramírez de Estemoz, Marqués de **18** 811
Louis-Philippe, King of the French (*reg* 1830-48) **30** 385
Mauroner, José **2** 404
Mead, Richard **20** 910
Medici, Leopoldo de', Cardinal **21** 28
Medinaceli, Luís de la Cerda Fernández de Córdoba Folch de Cardona y Aragón, 9th Duque de (1660-1711) **21** 35
Medina de las Torres, Ramiro Nuñez de Guzmán, Duque de **21** 36
Monterrey, Manuel de Acevedo y Zúñiga, 6th Conde de **22** 21; **29** 353
Museo del Prado (Madrid) **4** 566
Museo Provincial (Cádiz) **5** 368
Osuna, 3rd Duque de (1574-1624) **23** 626
Pourtalès-Gorgier, James-Alexandre, Comte de **25** 383
Roomer, Gaspar **27** 133
Rosso, Antonio del (1600-1668) **27** 205
Ribera, Jusepe de
patrons and collectors—cont.
Salamanca (y Mayol), José, Marqués de **27** 607
Serra, Giovan Francesco, Marqués di Cassano **28** 479
Tallard, Marie-Joseph d'Hostun, Duc de **30** 274
Uffelen, Lucas van **31** 526
Yusupov, Nikolay (Borisovich), Prince (1751- 1831) **33** 579
pupils **3** 352; **6** 108; **9** 52; **10** 762; **12** 660; **27** 149
reproductive prints by others **10** 658; **18** 237, 812; **21** *415*; **25** 629; **26** 517
Ribera, Marcos **8** 302
Ribera, Pedro (Domingo) de **26** 313–14*
groups and movements **7** 289
patrons and collectors **29** 270
works **2** 864; **20** 63
Ribera (i), Per Afán de, 1st Duque de Alcalá *see* ALCALÁ, 1st Duque de
Ribera y Fernández, Juan Antonio **26** 308*; **29** 283
patrons and collectors **4** 566
pupils **1** 600; **26** 308
works **1** 743
Ribera y Fernández, Manuel **26** 308
Ribera y Fieve, Carlos Luis **26** 308–9*
Ribero Rada, Juan de **7** 362; **10** 535; **23** 681; **27** 605; **29** 268; **31** 823
Ribes (i Marco), Demetri **26** 314*
Ribestein, Michel **26** 314*
Ribiṭa Church **26** 711
Ribnica **28** *858*
Ribot, Théodule (-Augustin) **11** 547; **26** 315*
groups and movements **26** 54
patrons and collectors **30** 375
works **11** 230; **12** 294
Riboud, Marc **6** 500; **20** 99
Riboulet, Pierre **26** 192
Ribouté, C.-H. **19** 161
ribs
historical and regional traditions
Central Asia, Western **16** 164
Germany **29** 392
Iran **16** 164
Islamic **16** 142, 164
Rome, ancient **26** 903, *903*
materials
brick **26** 879, 903, *903*
cast iron **3** 524
mouldings **22** 211, 212, 213, *213*, 214, 215, 216, 217, 218*, 219, 220, 221
uses
domes **16** 164
vaults (ceiling) *see under* VAULTS (CEILING) → types
Ricamatori, Giovanni dei *see* UDINE, GIOVANNI DA
Ricard, André **29** 322
Ricard, (Louis) Gustave **26** 315–16*
Ricard, Prosper **16** 554; **22** 129
Ricard de Montferrand, August *see* MONTFERRAND, AUGUST RICARD DE
Ricardo, Francisco **32** 169
Ricardo, Halsey (Ralph) **5** 419; **8** 707; **26** 316*; **30** 507
Ricardo, Master **5** 205
Ricardo di Montefuscolo **6** 16
Ricardos, Felipe **5** 691
Ricards, R. F. **23** 212
Ricardus Franciscus **20** 664
Ricaria *see* ARCHAR
Ricart, E.-C. **2** 542
Ricart, Josep Gudiol i *see* GUDIOL I RICART, JOSEP
Ricaud de Tirregaille, Pierre **25** 363; **33** 115
Ricca, Gianbattista (1691-1756) **26** 316–17*
Ricca, Giovanni (*fl* 1630s-40s) **29** 544
Riccardi (family) **11** 181, 845; **26** 242
Riccardi, Domenico **5** 872
Riccardi, Luigi **12** 608
Riccardi, Marcantonio **23** 880
Riccardi, Pio **10** 639
Riccardi, Riccardo **10** 639
Riccardi, Teodoro **10** 639
Riccardi, Virgilio **10** 639
Riccardiana Psalter *see under* PSALTERS → individual manuscripts
Riccardiana Virgil (Florence, Bib. Riccardiana, MS. 492) **2** 649
Riccardin, Francesco, Marchese **12** 661
Riccardi type-face *see under* TYPE-FACES
Riccardo da Foggia **24** 774
Riccardo da Lentini **6** 83; **28** 656
Riccardo dei Conti di Segni **15** 860
Riccati (family) **25** 561
Riccati, Giordano **25** 561; **31** 316
Ricchi, Pietro **5** 845; **26** 317*
Ricchieri, Antonio **18** 733, 734
Ricchini, Bernardo **26** 317
Ricchini, Francesco Maria **21** 532; **26** 317–19*
collaboration **3** 250; **16** 562
patrons and collectors **4** 426
works **3** 355, 773; **12** 372; **16** 641; **21** 518, 533; **26** *318, 319*
Ricchini, Giovanni Domenico **26** 319
Ricchino *see* RICCHINI, FRANCESCO MARIA
Ricci (family; Italian) **10** 249; **14** 584
Ricci (family; Spanish) *see* RIZI
Ricci, Alessandro **3** 179; **10** 91
Ricci, Alvise **28** 332
Ricci, Corrado **16** 774, 782; **24** 448; **26** 325*
Ricci (de Guevara), Francisco *see* RIZI (DE GUEVARA), FRANCISCO
Ricci, Giovan Battista **4** 404
Ricci, Giovanni (1440/50-1523) **11** 51; **20** 721
Ricci, Giovanni, Cardinal (fl c. *1550)* **4** 47; **5** 541; **11** 740; **27** 652
Ricci, Giovanni (*fl* 1680s) **8** 140
Ricci, Girolamo **26** 319
Ricci, Joaquín Toesca y *see* TOESCA Y RICCI, JOAQUÍN
Ricci, Juan Andres **9** 418
Ricci, Lanfranco **1** 512, 513
Ricci, Marco **11** 188; **26** 319–24*; **32** 194, 195
attributions **5** 594
collaboration **5** 594; **8** 159; **24** 340, 341
patrons and collectors **5** 686; **7** 780; **14** 144; **21** 908; **22** 115; **28** 173, 884; **33** 613
reproductive prints by others **3** 308; **11** 329; **12** 582; **16** 820; **25** 622; **32** 689; **33** 359, *359*, 367
works **5** 594, 686; **9** 223; **10** 277; **15** 139; **18** 711; **26** 321, *322, 324*; **32** 900
Ricci, Mario **30** 675
Ricci, Matteo **7** 120, 153; **10** 379; **12** 814; **17** 513
Ricci, Sebastiano **11** 188; **12** 559; **16** 673; **23** 637; **26** 319–24*; **31** 444; **32** 194, 195
assistants **26** 323
attributions **7** 915
collaboration **8** 159; **26** 323
copies **13** 741
dealers **2** 559
dealing **21** 30

Ricci, Sebastiano—cont.
drawings **9** 223
groups and movements **16** 674, 676
interior decoration **11** 214
paintings
frescoes **10** 277; **15** 138
Castle Howard (N. Yorks) **31** 859
Royal Hospital (London) **15** 138
S Bernardino alle Ossa (Milan) **21** 527
S Marziale (Venice) **32** 194
Villa Nazionale Già Pisani (Stra) **24** 865
oil
allegorical **26** *322*
ceiling **2** 795; **26** *321*; **32** 460
landscape **26** *324*
mythological **26** *322*
oil sketches **23** 381
religious **28** *17*; **32** 196, 215
patrons and collectors **10** 811; **24** 703
Algarotti, Francesco **1** 633
Augustus III, King of Poland (*reg* 1733-63) **1** 633
Blundell, Henry **4** 181
Boyle, Richard, 3rd Earl of Burlington and 4th Earl of Cork **4** 609
Conti, Stefano **7** 780
Ferdinando I, Grand Duke of Tuscany (*reg* 1587-1609) **21** 30
George III, King of Great Britain (*reg* 1760-1820) **14** 144
Gibbs, James **12** 594
Isham, Thomas **13** 300
Lennox, Charles, 2nd Duke of Richmond and Lennox **19** 157
McSwiny, Owen **5** 686
Mocenigo (family) **21** 747
Sasso, Giovanni Maria **27** 864
Schulenburg, Johann Matthias, Graf von der **28** 173
Smith, Joseph, Consul (*c.* 1674-1770) **28** 884
Vassal de Saint-Hubert, Jean-Antoine-Hubert **32** 75
Victor-Amadeus II, 15th Duke of Savoy (*reg* 1675-1730) and King of Sardinia (*reg* 1720-30) **28** 16
Yusupov, Nikolay (Borisovich), Prince (1751-1831) **33** 579
Zanetti, Anton Maria (Girolamo) (i), Conte (1680-1767) **33** 613
pupils **9** 47; **11** 286; **13** 277; **26** 323; **33** 612
reproductive prints by others **3** 308; **6** 91; **10** 770; **11** 286; **19** 437; **21** 831
Ricci, Seymour de **26** 325*
Ricci, Stefano **8** 19; **11** 189, 206; **16** 705
Ricciani, Antonio **5** 412
Ricciardelli, Daniele *see* DANIELE DA VOLTERRA
Ricciardelli, Gabriele **4** 154; **22** 480
Ricciardi **20** 404
Ricciardi, Gabriele **19** 28
works **19** *28*
Ricciardo di Nanni, Ser **11** 686; **26** 325–6*
Ricciarelli, Daniele *see* DANIELE DA VOLTERRA
Riccio, Agostino (*fl* before 1515) **5** 31
Riccio, Agostino del (*fl* 1597) **14** 167
Riccio, Andrea **26** 326–31*; **31** 570; **32** 192
attributions **2** 453; **11** 248; **19** 556; **28** 509
Riccio, Andrea—cont.
collaboration **9** 340
patrons and collectors **20** 400
pupils **6** 119
teachers **3** 636; **29** 568
works **3** 637; **13** 292; **25** 20; **26** *327, 329, 330, 331*; **29** 568
Riccio, Domenico *see* BRUSASORCI, DOMENICO
Riccio, Il *see* NERONI, BARTOLOMMEO (DI SEBASTIANO)
Ricciolini, Michelangelo **26** 331*; **28** 163
Ricciolini, Nicolò **6** 350; **26** 331–2*; **27** 646
Riccobaldo Ferrarese **12** 681, 683
Riccomanno, Leonardo **11** 897
rice **3** 331; **5** 755; **15** 812; **18** 601
Rice (family) **32** 784
Rice, David Storm **14** 192; **16** 549; **26** 332*
Rice, D(avid) Talbot **9** 725; **26** 332*
Rice, John Andrew **4** 109; **31** 670
Rice, Peter **13** 667; **14** 521, 522; **24** 698; **26** 332–3*
rice flour **24** 56; **30** 558, 561
rice-paper *see under* PAPER → types
rice paste
historical and regional traditions
Indonesia **15** 790
Japan **17** 309, 310, *310*, 314, 355, 414
Java **15** 790
Ryūkyū Islands **27** 470
uses
batik **3** 378
dyeing **17** 309, 310, *310*; **27** 471
dyes **17** 355
lacquer **18** 609
paints **32** 898
scrolls **28** 310
tattoos **17** 414
Ricevuto, Lapo di *see* LAPO DI RICEVUTO
Rich, Charles A. **28** 604
Rich, Claudius James **1** 891, 895; **4** 437; **16** 554; **21** 310
Rich, Fred **20** 926
Rich, Henry, 1st Earl of Holland **27** 360
Rich, John **28** 486
Rich, Obadiah **4** 480
Rich, Peter **29** 107
Rich, Richard **19** 568
Rich, Victor **4** 390
Richard, Deacon (*c.* 1259) **13** 86
Richard I, Duke of Normandy (*reg* 942-96) **6** 52, 55; **22** 41; **27** 245
Richard I, King of England (*reg* 1189-99) **6** 511; **19** 895; **29** 488
Richard I, Prince of Capua *see* CAPUA, RICHARD I, Prince of
Richard II, King of England (*reg* 1377-99) **19** *607*; **25** 16–17*
architecture **10** 163; **14** 454; **19** 609
coats of arms **14** 423
heraldry **7** 179
paintings **10** 359
tapestries **10** 348; **30** 313
Richard III, King of England (*reg* 1483-85) **5** 514
Richard, Elizabeth **22** 594
Richard, Fleury (-François) **26** 333–4*
groups and movements **9** 363; **31** 373, 374
patrons and collectors **4** 303, 305
pupils **7** 876; **11** 157; **16** 849; **19** 847
works **11** 542; **24** 140
Richard, Francis (*fl* 1986) **15** 748
Richard, François (*fl c.* 1739-40) **14** 447
Richard, Giulio **16** 739
Richard, Jean (-Baptiste)-Claude *see* SAINT-NON, RICHARD DE, Abbé
Richard, Jules **8** 819; **16** 554; **22** 340; **25** 770
Richard, Karl Friedrich Wilhelm **14** 79
Richard, Théodore **4** 678
Richard de Fournival **3** 879
Richard-Ginori **25** 218; **27** 724
Richard of Oxford **19** 581
Richard of St Vannes **7** 265
Richard of St Victor **32** 416
Richard of Verdun **13** 142; **14** 725; **26** 334*
Richard of Wallingford, Abbot of St Albans **7** 438
Richardot, Jacques **3** 590
Richard Plantagenet, Earl of Cornwall, King of the Romans (*reg* 1189-99) **10** 322; **13** 46; **26** 81
Richards, Ceri **20** 607; **26** 334–5*
collaboration **20** 607
groups and movements **23** 333
works **19** 492; **32** 786
Richards, Eugene **20** 99
Richards, Godfrey **23** 856
Richards, Ivor **20** 491
Richards, James (*fl* 1718-59) **3** 232
Richards, James (*b* 1907) **20** 475
Richards, J. M. **4** 366; **26** 39
Richards, John Inigo **18** 672; **26** 335*
Richards, M. C. **4** 109
Richards, Peter **22** 375
Richards, Vanjah **19** 310
Richards, William Trost **25** 556; **26** 335–6*
works **26** *336*
Richards, Winston **19** 310
Richardson (family) **31** 646
Richardson, Albert E(dward) **26** 336–7*; **32** 257
groups and movements **22** 743
pupils **28** 798; **29** 379
teachers **29** 695
works **32** 257
Richardson, Antonio **18** 832
Richardson, Benjamin **10** 319
Richardson, Charles Douglas **2** 752; **14** 307
Richardson, Charles James **26** 337*; **29** 748
Richardson, Edgar **31** 671
Richardson, Francis **31** 648
Richardson, George (*d c.* 1813) **1** 140; **26** 337*
Richardson, George (*fl* 1818-28) **31** 652
Richardson, H(enry) H(obson) **2** 315; **4** 474, 479; **25** 327; **26** 338–43*; **31** 622
architecture **4** *474*; **25** 4; **28** 591; **31** 593
churches **4** 474; **13** 204; **18** 627; **26** *339*; **31** 689
hospitals **5** 124
houses **14** 454
law courts **18** 888; **26** *342*
libraries **4** 477; **19** 318; **26** *341*
monuments **25** 766
office buildings **14** 203
warehouses **6** 573; **26** *343*; **32** 861
assistants **14** 317
collaboration **10** 104; **23** 422
competitions **7** 668
groups and movements **2** 572; **6** 578; **7** 619; **25** 806; **26** 704; **28** 604
staff **20** 16; **28** 591
Richardson, J. (1806-71) **8** 400
Richardson, Jonathan (1665-1745) **7** 714; **14** 842; **26** 344–6*
attributions **7** 175
collaboration **33** 377
collections **30** 727
Richardson, Jonathan (1665-1745)—cont.
drawings **18** 626; **25** 210
groups and movements **29** 889
mounts (works on paper and scrolls) **22** 236
patrons and collectors **4** 611; **20** 910; **26** 280
pupils **14** 841; **18** 142
teachers **26** 394
works **1** 632; **2** 518; **4** *611*; **26** 246, *345*; **32** 378
writings **9** 229; **10** 249, 364; **13** 300, 301
Richardson, Jonathan (1694-1771) **9** 229; **18** 626; **22** 236; **25** 634; **26** 345, 346
Richardson, Joseph (1711-84) **31** 648
works **31** *648*
Richardson, Marion **6** 588, 589
Richardson, Samuel **4** 361; **13** 324
Richardson, Thomas Miles **23** 21
Richardson, W. H., B. & J. **10** 319
Richardson, William Cummings **14** 207*
Richardson Associates **28** 328
Richardson & Gill **26** 337
Richard-Troncy, Laura **3** 630
Richard van der Capelle, Canon **3** 612
Richarius, Saint **27** 588
Richart, Eude **2** 113
Richarte, Antonio **25** 224
Richartz, Johann Heinrich **7** 584; **26** 346*
Richborough Castle (Kent) **20** 571
Richecourt, Emanuelle de **3** 812
Richelet, César-Pierre **5** 344
Richelieu **11** *504*, *505*, 657; **26** 346–9*, *347*; **31** 719
architecture **32** 278, 280
Château **6** 507; **19** 133; **26** 348–9
Galerie des Batailles **26** 348
gardens **12** 120
King's apartments **26** 349
paintings **25** 389
Queen's apartments **26** 349
church **11** 516
Richelieu, Armand, Duc de (1696-1788) **19** 725
Richelieu, Armand-Jean Du Plessis, Cardinal de **11** 657; **26** 348–9*, *349*; **31** 227
architecture **6** 507; **11** 657; **19** 133–4; **24** 118; **26** 346–7, 349; **30** 658, 735
collections **4** 550; **11** 661, 662
furniture **11** 587
gardens **12** 120; **27** 314
interior decoration **11** 573
manuscripts **17** 449
metalwork **11** 617
paintings **6** 36, 434; **8** 785; **9** 363; **11** 357, 534; **18** 648, 840; **19** 19, 238; **20** 521, 860; **23** 512; **25** 389, 390, 391; **29** 623; **32** 509, 718
personal collection **11** 535
sculpture **1** 626; **3** 853; **12** 577; **25** 383; **27** 821
Richelieu, Louis-François Armand-Jean Vignerod du Plessis, Duc de (1629-1715) **4** 389; **11** 662; **22** 899; **26** 349*
collections **7** 545; **27** 301
paintings **4** 552; **18** 633
sculpture **12** 727, 832
Richelieu, Maréchal de **24** 120
Richelot, Louis **26** 205
Richels, Jürgen **14** 103
Richemont, Arthur de **20** 723
Richental, Ulrich von *see* ULRICH VON RICHENTAL
Richenza, Empress **18** 226
Richeôme **17** 511
Richepin, Jean **29** 612
Richer, Jean **4** 546
Richer, Louis **19** 562
Richert, Franz **22** 305
Riches, Martin **29** 98
Richeterre, Michel Dessailliant de *see* DESSAILLIANT DE RICHETERRE, MICHEL
Richier (family) **7** 842
Richier, Gérard **26** 349, 350
Richier, Germaine **11** 569; **26** 351–2*; **30** 139
assistants **22** 274
collaboration **32** 423
dealers **16** 820
groups and movements **11** 302
pupils **22** 274
works **26** *351*; **29** 576
Richier, Jacob **19** 238
Richier, Jean **26** 350–51
Richier, Joseph **26** 350
Richier, Ligier **26** 349–51
works **26** *350*
Richings (Berks) *see* RISKINS (BERKS)
Richis Church **13** 189
Richland Center **32** 861
Richman, Robert **32** 889
Richmond (N. Yorks; UK)
Castle **6** 52, 53, 54, 56
High School for Girls **28** 158
Temple Lodge
Culloden Tower **11** 242
Theatre Royal **30** 674
Richmond (Surrey; UK)
Asgill House **32** 553
Doughty House **7** 788
Ham House **10** 275; **20** 141, 476
Blue Drawing Room **10** *274*
frames **11** 424
furniture **7** 166; **10** 290, 291, *291*; **11** 119; **31** 684
Green Closet **9** 12, 14, 17, *26*, 27
interior decoration **10** 276; **23** 789
leather **19** *4*, 5
manuscripts **16** 876
Miniature Room **7** 431
mouldings **11** 422
paintings **3** 245; **4** 150; **9** 14; **10** 897; **13** 309; **19** 121, 123
Queen's Closet **28** 28; **31** 682
sculpture **2** *541*; **7** 480
silver **10** 328
tapestries **10** 351
Hermitage **14** 460, *460*
Richmond Park **24** 179
Riverside Development **7** 385; **22** 743
Sheen Charterhouse **5** 895
Sheen Palace **4** 779; **12** 126, 127; **13** 782; **14** 75; **31** 413
chapel **25** 15
Theatre **19** 576; **30** 679
Richmond (VA; USA) **26** 352–3*; **31** *587*
Agecroft Hall **10** 327
Capitol Square **23** 256
Monumental Church **10** 850; **21** 616, *617*
Valentine Museum **26** 353
Virginia Museum of Fine Arts **10** 94; **14** 296; **15** 746; **19** 286; **21** 91; **26** 353
Virginia State Capitol **10** 850; **13** 237; **17** 467; **18** 887; **22** 738; **26** *352*; **31** 591, *591*
model **2** 337
Virginia State Penitentiary **31** 591
Richmond, George **10** 394; **26** 353–4*
groups and movements **1** 897; **23** 884
works **14** 680; **16** 820; **21** 606
Richmond, John **7** 236
Richmond, William Blake **3** 269; **10** 641; **14** 809; **26** 354*; **30** 506

Richmond and Derby, Margaret Beaufort, Countess of *see* BEAUFORT, MARGARET, Countess of Richmond and Derby
Richmond and Lennox, Charles Lennox, 2nd Duke of *see* LENNOX, CHARLES, 2nd Duke of Richmond & Lennox
Richmond and Lennox, Charles Lennox, 3rd Duke of *see* LENNOX, CHARLES, 3rd Duke of Richmond & Lennox
Richmond and Lennox, Frances Theresa Stuart, Duchess of *see* STUART, FRANCES THERESA, Duchess of Richmond and Lennox
Richomme, Théodore **15** 841
Richon-Brunet, Richard **6** 597
Rich style **13** 452, 455, *456*, 456–8, *457*, *458*
Richter **31** 258
Richter, Abraham **26** 354
Richter, Albrecht **26** 354
Richter, Alfred W. **5** 671
Richter, Bengt **9** 145, 147
Richter, Carl August **26** 358
Richter, Caspar **19** 110
Richter, Christian (1678-1732; Swedish) **21** 641
Richter, Christian, I (*d* 1667) **19** 110; **26** 354; **29** 547
Richter, Christian, II (1655-1722) **26** 354*; **33** 36
Richter, Christian, III (1676-1730; German) **26** 354
Richter, David **21** 641
Richter, Erich **3** 796
Richter, F. F. **22** 183, 184
works **22** *183*
Richter, Franz **13** 888
Richter, Fredrik **19** 796
Richter, Gerhard **26** 355–6*; **30** 201
groups and movements **1** 81; **25** 153
works **2** 241; **12** 397; **18** 74; **19** 493; **21** 892; **26** *355*
Richter, Gisela **33** 310
Richter, Gustav **32** 111
Richter, H. (*fl* 1628) **4** 147
Richter, Hans (Siegfried) **22** 380; **26** 356–7*
groups and movements **7** 770, 771; **8** 433, 434, 436, 437; **9** 758; **12** 396
works **9** 758; **10** 687; **26** *357*
Richter, Hans Theo **26** 357*
pupils **12** 886; **18** 1; **31** 539; **33** 30
works **9** 237
Richter, Helmuth **2** 789
Richter, Jakob **11** 89; **26** 357–8*
Richter, Jan **8** 414, 416
Richter, Jean-Louis **30** 148
Richter, Jean Paul **19** 197; **21** 849; **22** 102; **26** 358*
Richter, Jeremias **26** 354
Richter, Johann Adolf **18** 465; **26** 354–5*; **31** 371; **33** 36
Richter, Johann Georg **26** 354
Richter, Johann Moritz, I (1620-67) **26** 354; **33** 36
Richter, Johann Moritz, II (1647-1705) **26** 354
Richter, Johann Moritz, III (1679-after 1735) **26** 354
Richter, Johann Thomas **19** 111; **29** 376
Richter, (Adrian) Ludwig **21** 66; **26** 358–60*; **33** 369
collaboration **12** 393
groups and movements **26** 740
patrons and collectors **29** 376
pupils **9** 233
works **26** *359*
Richter, Vjenceslav **10** 667
Richter, Wilhelm, I (1626-1702) **26** 354
Richter, Wilhelm, II (after 1670-1712) **26** 354
Richtofen, Ferdinand von **28** 718
Rickard, Bruce **2** 742; **30** 161
Rickards, Charles **32** 922
Rickards, Edwin Alfred **5** 731; **14** 863; **18** 690*
works **5** *731*
Rickards, Maurice **10** 421
Ricke, Herbert **10** 81, 84
Ricke de Marsalaer, Jodoco *see* MARSALAER, JODOCO RICKE DE
Rickels, Horst **29** 98
Rickert, Franz **12** 451
Ricketson, Edith **31** 507
Ricketson, Oliver **31** 507
Ricketts, Charles (de Sousy) **4** 366; **24** 426; **26** 360*; **33** 369
patrons and collectors **14** 132; **33** 180
productions **4** 74
works **28** 555; **33** 180
Ricketts, William **2** 760
Rickey, George (Warren) **26** 360–61*
groups and movements **7** 772; **18** 62, 63
patrons and collectors **28** 167
works **16** 58; **21** 746
Rickham, Thomas **11** 785
Rickman, James **19** 734
Rickman, Thomas **2** 64; **8** 610; **12** 773; **24** 465; **26** 361*
architecture **13** 210
assistants **33** 639
groups and movements **9** 669; **13** 202
works **4** 85; **5** 512; **13** 34; **16** 10; **19** 506
writings **10** 377
rickshaws **3** 169, *169*; **15** 177
Rickson, Gary **1** 445
Ricla, Conde de **29** 303
Ricla, Condesa de **3** 7
Rico, Andrea *see* RITZOS, ANDREAS
Rico, Bernardino **26** 362
Ricoeur, Paul **14** 459
Ricolais, Robert Le *see* LE RICOLAIS, ROBERT
Riconucci, Domenico *see* BARBIERE, DOMENICO DEL
Ricordi record factory **4** 199; **11** 863; **25** 348
Ricourt, Achille **4** 655
Rico y Ortega, Martín **26** 362*; **29** 284
Ricx, Pauwels **4** 923
Rida' **16** 213
Riddell, Francis **30** 283
Riddell, George **28** 252
Ridder, Christopher **23** 237
Ridder, Willem de **31** 773
Riddere, Karel de **2** 198
Riddle, John **1** 445
Riddle, Theodate Pope **25** 234
Ridel, Bishop of Ely **10** 167
Rider Painter **13** 513; **32** 66–7*
Rider Relief **3** 419
Ridewall, John (fl c. *1330)* **1** 654; **22** 412
Ridewell, John (fl c. *1400s)* **15** 83
Ridgway **10** 310
Ridgway, B(runhilde) S(ismondo) **4** 24
Ridgway, George **26** 362
Ridgway, Job **14** 863; **26** 362
Ridgway, Job & George **26** 362
Ridgway, Job & Sons **26** 362
Ridgway, John **26** 362
Ridgway, John, Bates & Co. **26** 362
Ridgway, John & Co. **26** 362
Ridgway, John & William **26** 362
Ridgway, Smith & Ridgway **26** 362
Ridgway, William **26** 362
Ridgway, William & Co. **26** 362
Ridinger, Georg *see* RIEDINGER, GEORG
Ridinger, Johann Elias **2** 719; **21** 416; **26** 362–3*
reproductions in porcelain **21** 64
reproductive prints by others **23** 146
works **2** 105; **12** 391; **17** 186
Ridinger, Johann Jakob **26** 363
Ridinger, Martin Elias **26** 363
riding houses **25** 249; **26** 363*
riding-whips **28** 302
Ridivehera **29** 450
Ridler, Gabriel **22** 298
Ridley, Henry Nicholas **12** 103
Ridley, Matthew, 4th Baron Ridley **19** 720
Ridolfi, Agostino **5** 54
Ridolfi, Carlo **26** 363–4*
works **6** 78; **16** 767, 781; **31** 17; **32** 223, 355
Ridolfi, Claudio **5** 634
Ridolfi, Enrico **26** 364*
Ridolfi, Lorenzo **18** 820
Ridolfi, Mario **25** 792; **26** 364*
collaboration **2** 880; **25** 792
groups and movements **21** 422
works **16** 650
writings **16** 650
Ridolfi, Michele **26** 364
Ridolfi, Niccolò, Cardinal **1** 627; **6** 139; **21** 439; **24** 756
Ridolfi, Ottaviano **32** 411, 648
Ridolfi, Schiatta **5** 21
Ridout, Thomas **8** 264; **31** 176
Ridwan Bey **5** 398
Rie, Lucie **7** 808; **10** 314; **26** 365*
Riebeeck, Jan van **5** 667; **29** 116
Riebesehl, Heinrich **26** 365*
Ried, Benedikt **26** 365–8*
assistants **14** 268
collaboration **8** 383
patrons and collectors **16** 866
pupils **27** 168
works **8** 377; **13** 58; **18** 539, *539*; **22** 221; **23** 809; **25** 425, 438; **26** *366*, *367*; **30** 55
Riedel **29** 758
Riedel, August **30** 766
Riedel, Carl Josef **2** 819
Riedel, Eduard **5** 340; **9** 80; **12** 376; **23** 813; **29** 843; **33** 283
works **6** *62*
Riedel, Gottlieb Friedrich **11** 731; **19** 780
Riedel, Johann Gottfried **13** 746
Riedel, Josef **8** 410
Riedel Glassworks **2** 819
Riedenburg **2** 816; **27** 665
Rieden Retable, Master of the **13** 111
Rieder, Georg (*d* 1564) **26** 368*
Rieder, Georg (*d* 1575) **26** 368
Rieder, Georg (*fl* 1599) **26** 368
Rieder, Józsefi **30** 206
Rieder, Kaspar **2** 470
Riedinger, Georg **2** 592; **12** 369; **17** 689, 886; **26** 368–9*
Riedl, Fritz **2** 826
Riedl von Leuenstern, Joseph **12** 813
Riefstahl, Wilhelm Ludwig **28** 770
Riegel, Ernst **8** 531; **12** 450
Rieger, Christian **29** 637
Rieger, H. **29** 435
Rieger, Jacob **18** 523
Rieger, Johann **11** 230
Rieger, Renate *see* WAGNER-RIEGER, RENATE
Riegersburg Fortress **2** 805
Riegl, Alois **2** 244, 532, 833; **8** 595; **12** 483; **16** 549; **26** 63, 369–70*; **28** 917
pupils **2** 834
works **3** 262; **11** 315; **13** 34; **24** 454; **29** 879
Riego, Pedro **28** 368
Riehen
Colnaghi House **2** 512; **30** 128
Museum **30** 153
Schaeffer House **2** 512
Riek, Gustav **32** 679
Rielandt, Frans **3** 600
Riemchen *see under* BRICK → types
Riemedijk, W. F. H. **2** 148
Riemenschneider, Bartholomäus Dill **5** 180; **26** 727
Riemenschneider, Jorg **26** 372
Riemenschneider, Tilman **18** 827; **26** 370–73*
attributions **20** 705
patrons and collectors **12** 172; **33** 112
pupils **8** 682; **20** 711
works **1** 710; **3** 143; **8** 215; **12** 401, 420; **13** 91–2, *92*, 118; **26** *370*, *371*, *372*; **27** 159, 218; **28** 25, 134; **29** 728; **33** 430
workshop **12** 400
Riemer, Wilhelm Ferdinand August **3** 794
Riemerschmid, Richard **7** 584; **11** 582; **15** 823, 824; **26** 374*
architecture
factories **8** 824
garden cities **14** 362
garden city **12** 145
housing **8** 824; **14** 31
carpets **12** 468
ceramics **12** 430, 436; **21** 66
collaboration **9** 237; **12** 378; **30** 520
furniture **3** 485; **12** 428; **20** 593; **33** 156, 157
groups and movements
Arts and Crafts Movement **2** 571
Deutscher Werkbund **8** 825
Jugendstil **2** 565–6; **10** 215; **28** 341
Phalanx **24** 591
Secession (Munich; founded 1892) **28** 341
Vereinigte Werkstätte für Kunst und Handwerk **12** 416, 427; **24** 279
industrial design **8** 802
pupils **28** 126
silver **12** 450
staff **19** 283
Rienckes, Frans **3** 42
Rienzo, Cola di *see* COLA DI RIENZO
Riepenhausen, Christian *see* RIEPENHAUSEN, JOHANNES
Riepenhausen, Ernst Ludwig **26** 375
Riepenhausen, Franz **26** 374–5*; **30** 766
Riepenhausen, Johannes **26** 374–5*
Riera, Antonio de **20** 67; **26** 375*; **29** 292
Riesamburgh, Fabien van **7** 479
Riesenbeck, St Kalixtus
tomb of Reinheldis **26** 632
Riesener, Henri-François **8** 638; **26** 375
Riesener, Jean-Henri **8** 638; **11** 595, 627; **24** 150; **26** 375–7*; **31** 870
collaboration **9** 399; **11** 305
copies **28** 527
groups and movements **22** 738
patrons and collectors **4** 554, 555; **13** 665, 840; **14** 145; **17** 639; **27** 223; **28** 527
works **5** 192, *192*; **7** 658; **11** *591*, 595, 596; **12** 898; **20** 468, *469*; **26** 303, *376*
Riesener, Léon **26** 375
Rietberg, Museum *see under* ZURICH → museums
Rieter, Heinrich **4** 39
Rieth, Otto **1** 763; **26** 377*; **32** 801
Rieti, Fabio **1** 489
Rietmann, O.
works **29** *607*
Rietschel, Ernst (Friedrich-August) **9** 239; **26** 377–8*
collaboration **14** 48
patrons and collectors **12** 406
pupils **9** 145; **28** 94; **33** 284
teachers **12** 406; **26** 23
works **12** 406; **26** *377*; **28** 94
Rietveld, Gerrit (Thomas) **7** *294*; **19** 476; **22** 832; **24** 428; **26** 378–9*; **31** 771
collaboration **9** 62; **31** 867; **32** 439
groups and movements **2** 318; **7** 293; **10** 137; **21** 781; **22** 868; **26** 15; **29** 660
patrons and collectors **32** 623
works **2** 789; **4** 788; **6** 391; **8** 803; **9** 63; **12** 861; **19** 367; **21** 362, *781*; **22** 830, 831, *831*, 868, *868*, 875; **23** 548, 663; **26** *378*; **28** 666; **31** 771; **32** 556
Rietveld, Jan **10** 715
Rietveld, Wim **22** 876
Rieux, Louise de, Dame d'Ancenis **11** *532*
Rieux, Marie de, Vicomtesse de Thouars *see* THOUARS, MARIE DE RIEUX, Vicomtesse de
Rieux, Master of (fl c. *1344)* **22** 506
Rieux-Châteauneuf Master (fl c. *1500)* **7** 865
Rievaulx Abbey (N. Yorks) **7** 351; **10** *225*, 227; **12** 128; **21** 836; **26** *380*, 380–82*, *381*, 590
chapter house **26** 382
cloister **7** 455
piers (ii) (masonry) **24** 751
tiles **30** 877
Riezlmair, Georg **29** 659
Rifa'at Pasha **21** 33
works **21** *33*
Rifarto, António Vital **26** 382*
Rifer de Courcelles, Pauline **18** 156
Riffart, Hermann **9** 460; **28** 127
works **9** *459*
Rifka, Judy **21** 897; **26** 382–3*
Rig, Asser *see* ASSER RIG
Riga **18** *847*; **26** 383–4*
Arsenal **18** 851
art school **18** 851
Castle **18** 847
Circuit Court House **18** 851
ecclesiastical buildings
Cathedral of St Mary **18** 847, 848
Cathedral of SS Peter and Paul **18** 851
Ekk Convent **18** 848
Jesus Church **18** 849
Katlakalns church **18** 849
St George's Church **18** 847
St Jacob **18** 847
St Peter **18** 847, 848
exhibitions
Gostinyy Dvor market **18** 849
Great Guild Hall **18** 851
House of the Schwarzhäuptergesellschaft **18** 848
Imperial Gymnasium **18** 850
Kunstverein **18** 850
Latvian Academy of Art
Latvian Academy of Sciences
Literary and Theatre Museum *see* Jānis Rainis Museum of the History of Latvian Literature & Art
Livonian Nobility Assembly House **18** 850
museums
Jānis Rainis Museum of the History of Latvian Literature and Art
Latvian Museum of Art **18** 851; **26** 384
Latvian Open Air Museum of Ethnography **26** 384
Museum of Foreign Art **26** 384

Riga—cont.
Palace of Collective Farm Workers see Latvian Academy of Sciences
St John 18 848
Stock Exchange 18 850
Three Brothers' Houses 26 383
Town Hall 18 851
Riga Architects' Society (Rigaer Architekt Verein) 3 409; 24 333
Riga Artists' group 13 695; 17 871; 26 384*; 30 36
Rigacci, Giuseppe 11 698
Rigalt, Lluis 29 309
Rigalt i Blanch, Antoni 29 307
Riganelli, Agustín 2 399; 26 384–5*
rigā' script see under SCRIPTS → types
Riga Service 4 62
Rīgas Mākslinieku Grupa
Rigaud, C. 14 84
Rigaud, Gaspard 26 385
Rigaud, Hyacinthe (-François-Honoré-Mathias-Pierre-André-Jean) 24 134, 135; 26 385–8*
assistants 25 887; 31 223
collaboration 21 891; 24 211
copies 18 418; 21 128
methods 7 830; 9 211; 25 280, 281
patrons and collectors 3 394; 4 557; 7 897; 8 423; 14 190; 21 830; 25 150, 634; 31 56; 33 196
pupils 7 569; 19 89, 796
reproductive prints by others 2 709; 3 107; 5 884; 6 549; 8 544; 9 296, 362; 13 898; 18 795; 19 15, 216; 22 684; 24 480; 30 344; 33 195
works 11 403, 405, 537, 539; 25 281; 26 385, 387
Rigaud, Jacques 4 611, 806; 7 174, 175; 29 735
works 12 127; 29 735
Rigaud, Jean-François see RIGAUD, JOHN FRANCIS
Rigaud, John Francis 26 388*
methods 10 199
reproductions in beadwork 3 440
works 11 84; 25 192, 193
Rigaud, Joseph-Hyacinthe-François de Paule de, Comte de Vaudreuil see VAUDREUIL, JOSEPH-HYACINTHE-FRANÇOIS DE PAULE DE RIGAUD, Comte de
Rigaut, Jacques 8 438
Rigau y Ros, Hyacinthe see RIGAUD, HYACINTHE (-FRANÇOIS-HONORÉ-MATHIAS-PIERRE-ANDRÉ-JEAN)
Rigby, Elizabeth see EASTLAKE, LADY
Rig-'dzin Shakya-bzang-po 4 213
Rigel, Raphael 2 808
Rigen Daishi see SHŌBŌ
Riget, Karl Aage 8 736
Rigezzo da Como, Antonio de 4 736
Riggenbach, Christoph 3 335
riggers see under BRUSHES → types
Riggisberg, Abegg-Stiftung 7 742; 30 152, 564
Riggs, T. 4 26
Riggs, William Henry 23 126
Riggus, Michel 14 469
Righetti, Francesco the elder (1749-1819; grandfather) 13 303; 26 389*; 29 572
Righetti, Francesco the younger (b 1805; grandson) 26 389
Righetti, Francisco 2 396
Righetti, Luigi 26 389
Righi, Francesco 4 436
Righi, Tommaso 6 323; 25 115; 26 780; 29 833; 31 826; 32 579
Righini, Pietro 30 669
Right-bank Cubists see PUTEAUX GROUP
Rigny-Usse Château 11 511
Rigo d'Alemagna 11 5
Rigol, Ramon 29 309
Rigolet, M. 7 745
Rigotti, Annibale 26 389*
assistants 27 853
pupils 18 578
works 2 177; 16 648; 20 908; 30 590
Rigotti, Giorgio 26 389
Riguardi, Andrea 31 141–2
Rihab 9 540, 543
Rihei Takamatsu see TAKAMATSU RIHEI
Riihimäki Glassworks 11 106
Riis, Jacob A(ugust) 26 390*; 31 704
works 24 672, 673; 28 919
Riis, P. J. 29 907
Riisipere 10 536
manor house 10 537
Rij, Danckerts de see DANCKERTS DE RIJ
Rijckaert, David, II (1586-1642) 26 390
Rijckaert, David, III (1612-61) 7 832; 26 390–91*
works 3 560; 12 290; 26 391
Rijcke, Daneel de see DANEEL DE RIJCKE
Rijckhals, Frans 27 518
Rijeka 8 174, 175
Archaeological Museum 8 180
cultural centre 1 578
Museum 8 177
Rijf, Johan 11 91
Rijgersma, Hendrik van 2 149
Rijkhals, François 2 29
Rijkholt-Sint Geertruid 25 515
Rijkscommissie voor de Monumentenbeschrijving 13 810
Rijn, Rembrandt (Harmensz.) van see REMBRANDT (HARMENSZ.) VAN RIJN
Rijn, Titus (Rembrandtsz.) van 22 843; 26 155, 391–2*
Rijnenburg, Nicolaas 19 102
Rijneveld, Jan van 7 662
Rijnsburg Abbey Church 22 818; 27 256
Rijsby 11 465
Rijsdijk, Mezza 2 764
Rijssel, J. N. 30 16
Rijsselberghe, Octave Van see VAN RYSSELBERGHE, OCTAVE
Rijsselberghe, Théo(phile) Van see VAN RYSSELBERGHE, THÉO(PHILE)
Rijswijk, Huis ter Nieuburch 12 131; 22 813, 844; 26 392*
church 22 821
paintings 4 656; 14 730
Rike, Daneel de see DANEEL DE RIJCKE
Riken Yamamoto see YAMAMOTO, RIKEN
Rikon 26 139
Rikos, Konstantinos 8 156
Rikugo 29 547
Rikyū, Sen no see SEN NO RIKYŪ
Rikyū Tanaka see SEN NO RIKYŪ
RILA (Répertoire international de la littérature de l'art) 2 534; 4 25, 26
Rila Monastery 5 144, 154, 160; 9 511; 26 392*
Church of the Virgin 5 148
engravings 5 154
icons 5 152; 25 339
Khrelyu Tower 5 147, 151
manuscripts 5 152
prints 5 162
wall paintings 25 343
Rila Monastery—cont.
wood-carvings 9 601
Riley, Arthur Dewhurst 23 75
Riley, Bridget (Louise) 26 392–3*
groups and movements 1 79; 10 258; 23 448; 28 805
productions 30 688
works 23 449; 28 300
Riley, John 23 467; 26 393–4*
collaboration 7 461
methods 9 211
patrons and collectors 22 351
personal collection 26 345
pupils 22 352; 26 344
reproductive prints by others 3 476; 33 147
teachers 29 7
works 26 393
Riley, Thomas 16 14
Riley, W. E. 30 458
Riley factory 10 310
rilievo schiacciato see under CARVING → types
Rilke, Rainer (Karl Wilhelm Johann Josef) Maria 8 596; 26 394*, 512
groups and movements 33 383
personal collection 12 474
works 2 411; 3 127; 13 653; 17 873
Rilke-Westhoff, Clara 33 383
Rill, Johann Jakob 3 705
Rillaer, Jan van, the elder (d 1548) 19 260
Rillaer, Jan van, the younger (d 1592) 19 260
Rillaton Gold Cup 12 866
Rímac Valley 23 703
Rimah, Tell el- 1 849; 21 267, 285, 286; 26 395–6*
architecture 2 639; 4 772; 21 274, 284
faience (i) (glass) 1 879
glass 1 864, 865; 12 788
palace 21 286
Palace of Hammurabi 21 285
pottery 30 197
sculpture 21 299; 26 396
seals 1 862
shrines (i) (cult) 21 285
temple 21 286, 287, 288; 26 395, 395–6; 30 432
ziggurat 21 286; 33 675
Rimanóczy, Gyula 14 890, 891; 26 396*
Rimanóczy, Kálmán 26 709
Rimbaldesi, Giovanni 11 23
Rimbaud, Arthur 8 245; 30 53; 33 636
Rimbault, Stephen 33 692
Rimenschneider, Dill see RIEMENSCHNEIDER, TILMAN
Rimet Church 26 710
Riminaldi, Giovambattista 26 396
Riminaldi, Orazio 26 396–7*
works 11 188; 24 860; 26 397
Rimington, Alexander Wallace 22 380, 380
Rimini 16 618, 620; 20 159–60; 26 398–400*, 886
Arch of Augustus 4 776; 16 644; 26 868, 890, 891; 31 349
corbels 7 837
Biblioteca Malatestiana 20 160
bridge 4 800
patronage 16 763
pottery 16 732
S Francesco 1 561; 8 212; 22 378; 23 539; 24 247; 26 398, 398–9*, 399, 400; 31 351
portico 25 265
sculpture 26 399–400*
silk 9 665
S Maria delle Grazie 13 79; 20 755
Tempio Malatestiano see S Francesco
Rimini, Elisabetta da see ELISABETTA DA RIMINI
Rimini, Francesco da see FRANCESCO DA RIMINI
Rimini, Giovanni da see GIOVANNI DA RIMINI
Rimini, Giovanni Francesco da see GIOVANNI FRANCESCO DA RIMINI
Rimini, Giuliano da see GIULIANO DA RIMINI
Rimini, Master of 10 519; 13 79; 20 755*
Rimini, Neri da see NERI DA RIMINI
Rimini, Pietro da see PIETRO DA RIMINI
Rimiteri, Filippo 28 81*
Rimlyanin, Pavel 31 552
works 31 553
Rimmel, Eugène 6 549
Rimmer, William 11 755; 26 401–2*; 31 611; 33 151
works 26 401
Rîmnicu Sărat 26 708
Rimpacta, Antonio da see ANTONIO DA RIMPACTA
Rimpacta, Jacopo see RIPANDA, JACOPO
Rimpl, Herbert 12 379; 22 711; 26 402*; 31 730
Rimsa, Juan 4 262, 267; 15 144; 26 402–3*
Rimša, Petras 19 498; 26 403*
Rimschneider, Dill see RIEMENSCHNEIDER, TILMAN
Rimsky-Korsakov, Nikolay 4 60; 12 878; 18 389; 32 73
Rimsø 26 640
rimu 23 67
Rinaldi, Antonio 26 403–4*; 27 375, 402
patrons and collectors 12 173; 19 563
works 25 746; 27 376, 402, 575
Rinaldi, Pedro
works 5 750
Rinaldi, Raffaello see MENIA, IL
Rinaldi, Rinaldo 17 442; 31 172
Rinaldi, Tolomeo 3 355
Rinaldi, Vincenzo 28 35
Rinaldo II, Duke of Modena (reg 1694-1737) 22 288
Rinaldo, Francesco di see FRANCESCO DI RINALDO
Rinaldo, Luca, Bishop 2 731
Rinaldo, Muccio di see MUCCIO DI RINALDO
Rinaldo da Bretagna 31 432
Rinaldo di Gualtieri see WOUTERSZ., REINAUT
Rinaldo Mantovano 20 321; 26 404*
Rinascente (department stores) 25 218
rinceau 26 404*
Rinchen Sangpo 5 104
architecture 1 588; 15 311; 30 219, 816; 31 395
paintings 15 561; 30 831
sculpture 30 823
writings 15 311; 30 736
Rinck, Johann 20 720
Rinck, Peter 20 720, 759
Rincklake, Johann Christoff 18 189
Rincón, Francisco 10 902, 903; 26 404*
Rincón Mora, José 9 118
Rindisbacher, Peter 26 404–5*
Rindschleiden Church 19 827
Rinehart, W(illiam) H(enry) 31 611; 32 829
Ring, Der 3 795; 12 379; 18 878; 26 405*
members 3 795; 7 293; 8 826; 21 782
Bartning, Otto 3 292
Döcker, Richard 9 60
Ring, Der
members—cont.
Gropius, Walter (Adolf Georg) 13 688
Häring, Hugo 11 841; 14 175
Hilberseimer, Ludwig (Karl) 14 524
Korn, Arthur 18 386
Luckhardt, Hans and Wassili 19 773
Mendelsohn, Erich 21 119
Meyer, Adolf (1881-1929) 21 407
Pankok, Bernhard 24 13
Rading, Adolf 25 839
Scharoun, Hans (Bernhard) 28 55
Taut, Max 30 371
Tessenow, Heinrich 30 521
Wagner, Martin (1885-1956) 32 760
Ring, Grete 5 924; 26 405–6*
Ring, Hermann tom 11 454, 455; 26 407, 408*
Ring, Johann tom 26 407
Ring, Laurits Andersen 4 743; 8 735; 14 572; 26 406–7*
works 26 407
Ring, Ludger tom (i) (1496-1547) 26 407–8*
Ring, Ludger tom (ii) (1522-84) 26 407, 408*; 29 666
Ring, Nikolaus tom 26 407
Ring, tom (family) 12 387; 22 315
Ringbom, Lars-Ivar 11 113
Ringbom, Sixten 11 113
ring brooches see under BROOCHES → types
ring crypts see CRYPTS → types → annular
Ringebu Church 29 580
Ringel d'Illzach, (Jean-)Désiré 26 408*
Ringelheim Abbey Church 23 648
Ringenberg, Kerstken van see KERSTKEN VAN RINGENBERG
Ringerike style see under VIKING → styles
Ringering, Peter 10 761
ring forts see under FORTS → types
Ringgli, Gotthard 14 634
Ringgold, Faith 11 54; 26 410*; 33 314
ring-headed crosses see CROSSES → types → High
Ringhieri, Francesco 27 766
Ringhoffer, E. 21 150
Ringler, Joseph Jakob 12 433; 14 606; 19 780; 23 324; 33 737
Ringling, John 26 410*; 31 667
Ringling, Mable 26 410
Ringling Museum of Art see under SARASOTA (FL)
ringmatting see under PUNCHING → types
Ringness, Charles 19 492
Ring Neue Werbegestälter 32 695
Ring of Brodgar 25 505; 28 223
Ring of Minos 21 691
Ring of Nestor 14 360
Ringold, Faith 1 445
ring-ponds 27 496
rings 8 835; 17 519, 524; 32 390
historical and regional traditions
Africa 1 351
Ancient Near East 1 874
Anglo-Saxon 2 79
Asante 1 351
Byzantine 9 653
China 7 109, 111
Cyprus, ancient 8 352
Early Christian (c. AD 250-843) 9 653
Greece, ancient 13 601
Italy 16 751
Jewish art 17 574, 574–5*
Kenya 1 362
Korea 18 367, 368

rings
historical and regional traditions—cont.
Mongolia **21** 877
Prehistoric art **25** 545
Punic **25** 734
Rome, ancient **26** 485; **27** 102
Sudan **1** 362
Syria **9** 653
Syria-Palestine **1** 857
Uganda **1** 362
Vietnam **32** 487
materials
bronze **13** 601; **17** 574
diamonds **31** 654
enamel **8** *352*
gold **6** 158; **7** 109, 111; **8** *352*; **10** 33; **17** 574, II2; **21** *686*
jasper **21** *685*
pearls **7** 109
rock crystal **14** 418; **26** 485
rubies **17** II2
seals **1** 857
silver **1** 351; **7** 109, 111; **16** *504*
silver-gilt **17** 574, *574*
types
arm *see* ARM RINGS
finger **8** *352*; **15** 814; **17** 521
foot rings **6** 158
leg *see* LEG RINGS
seals **21** *685*, *686*
signet **1** 857; **14** 418; **21** *685*, *686*; **25** 285
Ancient Near East **1** 864, 876
Crete **21** *685*
Cyprus, ancient **8** 355
Egypt, ancient **10** 33, 70
Minoan **21** *685*
solitaire diamond **31** 654
thumb rings **16** *504*; **17** II2; **21** 875
torques *see* NECK RINGS
rings, dish *see* DISH RINGS
Ringsaker **23** *218*
church **23** 224
Ringseis (family) **9** 690
ring-stands *see under* STANDS → types
Ringsted **8** *720*
Sankt Bendts Kirke **4** 780; **8** 722, 723, 758
brasses **4** 691
choir-stalls **8** 738
tomb of Erik VI **8** 738
ring stones **15** 423–4
ring tables *see under* TABLES → types
ring-works *see under* CASTLES → types
Rinieri, Bernardo di Stoldo **29** 360
Rinieri Altarpiece **11** 683
Rin Jikkō **17** 412
Rin Kashō **17** 411
Rinke, Klaus **24** 408; **28** 344
Rinkel, Louis **3** 840
Rinmann **24** 794
Rinmann's green *see* PIGMENTS → types → cobalt green
Rinnagan (Co. Roscommon), St John's
metalwork **15** 872, *873*
Rinpa *see under* JAPAN → painting
Rinsai Ōkajima *see* ŌKAJIMA RINSAI
Rinsema, Thijs **22** 852; **26** 410*
Rinsumageest, Klaarkamp Abbey **4** 777
Rinuccini (family) **9** 78
Rinuccini, Cino **25** 159
Rinuccini, Cino di Filippo **11** 86
Rinuccini, Folco **14** 367
Rinuccini, Pier Francesco, Marchese **9** 78; **11** 697
Rinuccini Altarpiece **11** 380; **12** 709
Rinversi, Anna **3** 651
Rinyo **25** 503
Rinzai Buddhism *see under* BUDDHISM → sects
Rio, Alexis-François **2** 576; **26** 410–11*
Río, Antonio del **21** 262
Rio, Bernabé Gómez del *see* GÓMEZ DEL RIO, BERNABÉ
Rio, Hermilio Alcalde del *see* ALCALDE DEL RIO, HERMILIO
Río Azul **13** *758*; **20** *882*; **26** 411–12*
bone-carvings **21** 247
tombs **21** 247; **26** *411*, 411–12
wall paintings **21** 231
Riobamba **9** *709*
Cathedral **9** 710
La Concepción Museum **9** 714
Río Bec **20** *882*; **21** 214, *372*; **23** 826; **26** 412*; **29** 829
Río Bec style **5** 412; **26** 412*
Riocreux, Denis-Désiré **31** 386
Rio de Janeiro **4** 705, *705*; **24** *664*; **26** 412–14*
ABI building **26** 461–2
Academia Imperial das Belas Artes **4** 716, 727, 728; **8** 593; **26** 413; **30** 369
see also Botanical Gardens; Escola Nacional de Belas Artes
Academia Militar *see* Escola de Engenharia
Alfredo Schwarz House **4** 712
A Noite building **3** 66
architecture **4** 709, 711, 712–13
Benedictine church **4** 709
Biblioteca Nacional **4** 712, 728; **8** 10
Biblioteca Real *see* Biblioteca Nacional
Bolsa de Comércio *see* Casa França-Brasil
Botanical Gardens **4** 711
Brazilian Reinsurance Institute building **26** 462
carnivals **5** 787, 788
Casa França-Brasil **4** 711
Cathedral **4** 723
Cidade Universitária **4** 713; **22** 95
Coleção Gilberto Chateaubriand **26** 516; **28** 214
Confeitaria Colombo **4** 721
Customs House **4** 711
Edmundo Bettencourt elementary school **28** 159
Escola de Artes Visuais do Parque Lage **4** 728
Escola de Engenharia **4** 711
Escola Nacional de Belas Artes **4** 722, 728
see also Academia Imperial das Belas Artes; museums → Museu Nacional de Belas Artes
Escola Real das Ciências, Artes e Ofícios **4** 726
Flamingo Park **24** 181
Fundação Nacional de Arte **4** 729
Fundação Raymundo Ottoni de Castro Maya **4** 728; **8** 593
furniture **4** 721
Glória (1842) **4** 711
governor's residence **4** 711
Instituto Central do Cancer **4** 713
Instituto de Pesquisas Oswaldo Cruz **4** 712
Instituto Histórico e Geográfico Brasileiro **4** 725, 728
Macedo Soares House **4** 713
Marquês do Herval Building **4** 713
Ministry of Education and Health *see* Palácio da Cultura
Monteiro Garden **12** 143
museums
Fundação Roberto Marinho Collection **4** 726
Rio de Janeiro
museums—cont.
Museu de Arte Moderna do Rio de Janeiro **4** 713, 719, 726–7, 728, 729; **5** 219; **24** 682; **26** 109–10, 414
Museu Chácara do Céu **4** 726, 727; **26** 414
Museu Histórico Nacional **26** 414
Museu do Índio **4** 706
Museu Manchete **4** 726
Museu Nacional **4** 706, 711, 726; **24** 584; **26** 413
Museu Nacional de Belas Artes **4** 712, 725, 726; **9** 49; **13** 295; **26** 414
Museu do Pontal **4** 727
Museu da República **4** 711; **26** 414
Museu de Tijuca **4** 726, 727; **26** 414
Pontifícia Universidade Católica Museum **4** 711; **13** 296, *296*
Nossa Senhora da Glória do Outeiro (1717-39) **4** 710, *710*
Obra do Berço day nursery and maternity clinic **15** 886
Palácio do Catete *see* museums → Museu da República
Palácio da Cultura **4** *712*, 713; **7** 670, 695; **12** 793
Palácio do Itamarati **4** 711
Palacío de São Cristóvão *see* museums → Museu Nacional
Passeio Público **4** 716; **11** 249
Pedregulho **4** 713; **26** *110*
Piraquê Industry Building **4** 714
Santos Dumont Airport **26** 462
S Bento **4** 715, 728
S Francisco da Penitência **4** 709, 716
silver **4** 723
Solar do Monjope **4** 712
S Teresa **4** 728
Teatro Municipal **4** 712
Riofrío, Palacio del Riofrío **4** 560; **29** 271, 300
Rioja, Baltasar de Echave *see* ECHAVE RIOJA, BALTASAR DE
Rioja, Domingo de la **26** 414*
Rioja, La *see* LA RIOJA
Riollet, Marie-Catherine **3** 463
Riolo, Giovanni (di Andrea) da *see* GIOVANNI (DI ANDREA) DA RIOLO
Riom
Sainte-Chapelle **8** 611; **11** 511; **13** 59; **22** 221; **27** 551
St Pierre *see under* MOZAC
Rio Mau, S Cristovão **25** 289, 300; **26** 611
Riopelle, Jean-Paul **22** 39; **26** 414–15*
dealers **20** 75
groups and movements **1** 78; **2** 544, 839; **5** 568; **26** 76; **30** 23
patrons and collectors **20** 832
works **19** 491
Rio Piedras **25** *698*
Universidad de Puerto Rico **25** 701, 703, 704
Ríos, Demetrio de los **18** 682
Ríos, Gaspar Gutiérrez de los *see* GUTIÉRREZ DE LOS RÍOS, GASPAR
Ríos, José Amador de los *see* AMADOR DE LOS RÍOS, JOSÉ
Ríos, José López de los *see* LÓPEZ DE LOS RÍOS, JOSÉ
Ríos, Luis de la Cruz y *see* CRUZ Y RÍOS, LUIS DE LA
Ríos, Miguel Angel **12** 53
Rios, Pedro Alonso de los **20** 66; **32** 557
Ríos, Rodríguez de los *see* SANTIAGO, Marquéses de
Ríos Blanco, Alberto **10** 154
Ríos de Neybo Museum **9** 119
Río Seco **29** 158
Rioult, Louis-Edouard **12** 207
Řip **8** 376
Ripa, Cesare **9** 7; **26** 415–16*
works **1** 656, 658, 663; **15** 83, 87, 89; **22** 414
illustrated **9** *8*; **10** 174; **23** 124; **26** *415*
translated **24** 300
Ripa, Matteo **6** 39, 538
Ripanda, Jacopo **24** 526; **26** 416–17*
Ripe Archaic *see* GREECE, ANCIENT → sculpture → monumental → Archaic, Late
Riphahn, Wilhelm **12** 379; **20** 324; **28** 127
Ripicano, Cola *see* RAPICANO, COLA
Ripinski, Karol **19** 497
Ripley, Geo **9** 118
Ripley, Thomas **32** 824, 859, 860
Ripoll Abbey **26** *417*, 417–18*, 580, 581; **29** *259*, 262; **30** 663
capitals **26** 610
cloister **7** 455
manuscripts **26** 675
metalwork **26** 689
roof **27** 130
sculpture **26** 418*, 610
S Pere **11** 479
West Portal **26** 418
Ripoll Bible *see under* BIBLES → individual manuscripts
Ripon Minster (N. Yorks) **2** 65; **9** 669, 670; **13** 44
choir-stalls **7** 192
crypt **8** 222
metalwork **10** 329
misericords **21** 725
mouldings **22** 216, 217
Ripon, George Frederick Robinson, 2nd Marquess of *see* ROBINSON, GEORGE FREDERICK, 2nd Marquess of Ripon
Riposo, il *see* FICHERELLI, FELICE
Ripp, Abraham **11** 832
Ripp, J. C. **2** 127
Rippingham, T. F. O. **16** 40
Rippingille, Edward Villiers **4** 78; **26** 418–19*
Ripple Church (Hereford & Worcs) **21** 725
Rippl-Rónai, József **14** 901; **15** 2; **26** 419–20*; **33** 710
groups and movements **22** 421
works **15** 5, 12; **25** 348; **26** *419*
el-Riqqa **9** 849
Riquelme, William **22** 743; **24** 99
Riquer i Inglada, Alejandro de **25** 348; **29** 308, 320, 321
Riquet, Victor-Louis-Charles de *see* CARAMAN, Duc de
Riquinus, Master **25** 110; **26** 684
Rís, Francisco Laso de la Vega de los *see* LASO, FRANCISCO
Ris, Julia **30** 923
Risambourg, van (*fl* 1791; patron) **7** 162
Risamburgh, Bernard van (i) (*c.* 1660-1738) **26** 420*
Risamburgh, Bernard van (ii) (after 1696-1766) **5** 192; **7** 658; **11** 590, 593, 596, 626; **20** 897; **26** 420*; **30** 885
works **11** 591, 595, 596
Risamburgh, Bernard van (iii) (*c.* 1731-1800; cabinet maker) **26** 420*
Ri Sanpei **2** 414; **17** 263
Risapha *see* RUSAFA
Rîşca **26** 712
Rischer, Johann Jakob **14** 306; **20** 282
Rischoot, Petrus Johannes van *see* REYSSCHOOT, PETRUS JOHANNES VAN
Risco, Manuel **27** 763
Risely, Tom **2** 754
Risgit **22** 321; **31** 113
Rishikesh **20** 817
Rishon Le Zion **16** *565*
Rishtan **6** 259; **31** 784
Rishūbun *see* Yi Su-mun
Risinge **30** 76
Risino *see* MEZZARISA, FRANCESCO DI ANTONIO
Riskins (Berks) **30** 123
Risorgimento grafico, Il **24** 447
Ris-Paquot, Oscar Edmond **10** 208, 210
Rissai *see* KITAO MASANOBU
Rissa Ixa **31** 405
Rissanen, Juho (Vilho) **11** 96; **26** 421*; **28** 427; **33** 96
Rissani **33** 97
Ristaud, Marie *see* COTTIN, SOPHIE
Risteski, Aleksandar **19** 884
Risti **10** *536*
church **10** 538
Ristitch, Marco **30** 21
Ristori, Taddeo **30** 273
Ristoro di Andrea **20** 658
Risueño, José **9** 407; **26** 421*
works **13** 284; **29** 292
Risueño, Manuel (*fl* 1665) **26** 421
Risueño, Manuel (*fl c.* 1700) **26** 421
Ritchie, Alexander Handyside **26** 288; **28** 242
Ritchie, Alexander Hay **15** 30
Ritchie, Ian **14** 522; **26** 333
Ritchie, Walter **4** 789
Ritchie McKinley, A. A. **9** 426
Ritigala **26** 422*; **29** *440*, 470
Monastery **29** 446
Ritleng, Georges **2** 488
Ritlite Church **5** 151
Ritō Akizato *see* AKIZATO RITŌ
Ri Tōhaku **17** 410
Ritoque, Ciudad Abierta **6** 594
Ritschl, Wacław **15** 104
Ritson, Jonathan **33** 453
Ritsu Buddhism *see under* BUDDHISM → sects
Ritsuzan Shibano *see* SHIBANO RITSUZAN
Ritt, Augustin **21** 644
Rittenhouse (family) **24** 47
Rittenhouse, William **24** 48
Ritter (family) **12** 443; **23** 312
Ritter (*fl* 1928) **9** 86
Ritter, Christoph, III **24** 588; **28** 192, 193
Ritter, Erasmus **1** 31; **3** 822; **13** 871; **22** 920
Ritter, Guillaume **20** 118; **22** 920
Ritter, Heinrich Wilhelm **7** 870
Ritter, Jeremias **22** 204
Ritter, Johan Christian **29** 110
Ritter, Louis E. **17** 477
Ritter, Walter **2** 804
Ritter zu Groenesteyn, Anselm F(ranz) **4** 890; **23** 3; **26** 422*; **28** 146
Rittmeyer, Robert **26** 422–3*
Rittner, J. H. **2** 499; **13** 228
ritual objects
historical and regional traditions
Africa **1** 242–3, 257; **18** *220*
Buddhism **17** 320, 322, *322*
Canada **22** 575
Crete **8** 153
Cuba (Caribbean) **8** 230
Dorset culture **22** 575
India, Republic of **15** 174
Indian subcontinent **15** 726, 727, 729–30*
Japan **17** 320, 322, *322*
Jewish art **17** 567–8*, 571–4*, 575*; **24** 580
Kongo **1** 241; **18** 219–21*, *220*
Korea **18** *346*, 346–7, 377–8*
Native North Americans **14** 747; **22** 575
Nepal **22** 757

ritual objects
historical and regional traditions—cont.
Prehistoric art **8** 153
Venda **1** 257
materials
bronze **17** *322*; **18** *346*, 346–7
metal **15** 729–30
terracotta **15** 729
rituals
Africa **1** 257–9*, *260*, 338–9
Hinduism **14** *559*, 559–60
Indian subcontinent **14** *559*, 559–60
Japan **28** 609
Java **15** 798
Rome, ancient **26** *858*
Shinto **28** 609
Ritz (family) **30** 136
Ritz, César **14** 787; **21** 371
Ritz, Lorenz Justin **26** 423
Ritz, (Maria Joseph Franz Anton) Raphael **26** 423*
Ritzos, Andreas **8** 157; **20** 51; **24** 263; **25** 332
works **20** *51*
Ritzos, Nikolaos **20** 51; **24** 263; **25** 332
Ritzos da Candia, Maneas **20** 51
Riunsai Mochizuki *see* MOCHIZUKI RIUNSAI
Riurikid, Ivan III, Emperor of Russia *see* IVAN III, Grand Duke of Muscovy
Riurikid, Ivan the Terrible, Tsar of Russia *see* IVAN IV, Tsar of Russia
Riurikid, Vladimir I Svyatoslavich, Prince of Kiev *see* VLADIMIR I SVYATOSLAVICH, Prince of Kiev
Riurikid, Vladimir II Monomach, Prince of Kiev *see* VLADIMIR II MONOMACH, Prince of Kiev
Riurikid, Yaroslav I, Prince of Kiev *see* YAROSLAV I, Prince of Kiev
Riurikid, Yaroslav the Wise, Prince of Kiev *see* YAROSLAV I, Prince of Kiev
Rius, Alejo Rossell y *see* ROSSELL Y RIUS, ALEJO
Rius, Juan Antonio **31** 753
Rivadaneyra, Luis **5** 603
Rivafrecha y Campeche, Ignacio de **25** 701
Rivafrecha y Campeche, José de **5** 750; **25** 701, 704; **32** 173
Rivafrecha y Campeche, Manuel **25** 701
Rivaldi, Gaspare **11** 269; **20** 48
Rivaldi, Jacopo **26** 766
Rivalta, Augusto **16** 707; **26** 423*
Rivalz, Antoine **26** 423, 424*; **31** 207
pupils **26** 424; **29** 886
works **26** *424*
Rivalz, Barthélemy **26** 423
Rivalz, Jean-Pierre **26** 423–4*; **31** 207
Rivalz, Le Chevalier *see* RIVALZ, (JEAN-)PIERRE
Rivalz, (Jean-)Pierre **26** 423, 424*
pupils **4** 329; **12** 33; **27** 143
Riva Mertijn, Jacques de *see* MERTIJN, JACQUES DE RIVA
Riva Palacio, Vicente **10** 494; **14** 464; **16** 48
Rivara, João Caetano *see* CAETANO RIVARA, JOÃO
Rivara, Scuola di *see* SCUOLA DI RIVARA
Rivardi, John Jacob Ulrich **21** 575
Rivarola, Alfonso **30** 666
works **30** *666*
Rivas **23** *79*
museum **29** 222
parish church **23** 80
Puerta del Cementerio **23** 80
Rivas, Bárbaro **26** 425*; **32** 176
Rivas, Diego Rodríguez de *see* RODRÍGUEZ DE RIVAS, DIEGO
Rivas, Humberto **26** 425*
Rivas, Ricardo **33** 493
Riva San Vitale **9** *510*; **30** *124*
Baptistery **9** 533
Casa Bianchi **30** 129
Santa Croce **30** 126
Rivas Contreras, Wenceslao **29** 901
Rivas Mercado, Antonieta **26** 521
Rivas Mercado, Antonio **26** 425*
assistants **1** 589
works **21** 378, 379, 403; **23** 208
Rive, Jean-Joseph **18** 880
Rive, Pierre-Louis De La *see* DE LA RIVE, PIERRE-LOUIS
Rivenhall Church (Essex) **29** 515
Riveo, Casa Sartori **30** 129
Rivera (y Barrientos Acosta y Rodríguez), Diego (María Concepción Juan Nepomuceno Estanislao de la) **14** 589; **15** 99; **17** 721; **21** 380, 387, 397, 403, 405, 852; **22** 334; **23** 566; **26** 426–9*
assistants **6** 488; **13** 796; **23** 12, 371; **28** 536
collaboration **14** 715; **21** 155; **23** 370; **24** 401
groups and movements **8** 240, 246; **10** 543; **21** 387; **30** 21, 22
house **23** 369
methods **10** 199; **32** 807
mosaics **22** 158, 164
murals **21** 405; **22** 334; **25** 653
Escuela Nacional Prepartoria (Mexico City) **22** 334
Hospital de la Raza **14** 785
Hotel del Prado (Mexico City) **23** 335
Institute of Art (Detroit) **8** 821; **15** 830; **26** *427*
Palacio Nacional (Mexico City) **21** *405*; **27** 872; **28** 920
Rockefeller Center (New York) **25** 653
Secretaría de Educación Pública (Mexico City) **21** 387; **22** 334
Secretaría de Salubridad y Assistencia (Mexico City) **23** 335
Universidad Autónoma (Chapingo) **21** 387; **26** *428*
patrons and collectors **2** 384; **7** 834; **21** 395; **24** 278; **26** 488
personal collection **21** 395
pupils **23** 370; **29** 807; **33** 370
sculpture **21** 380
teachers **10** 727
woodcuts **33** 364
Rivera, Agustín **24** 509, 515
Rivera, Ana Delia **25** 702, 703
Rivera, Bob **18** 834
Rivera, Carlos Raquel **18** 832, 833; **25** 702; **26** 426*
Rivera, Dennis Mario **25** 702
Rivera, José De *see* DE RIVERA, JOSÉ
Rivera, Juan de **25** 700
Rivera, Julian **13** 762
Rivera, Karlo Afan de *see* AFAN DE RIVERA, KARLO
Rivera, Luis de **9** 712
Rivera, Manuel **26** 429–30*
Rivera, Miguela **24** 99
Rivera-Maestre, Miguel **13** 762
Rivera y Mir, Vicente **24** 622
river jade *see under* JADE → types
Rivero, Jacinto **24** 99
Rivero, Mariano Eduardo **6** 441
Rivero Uztáriz, Eduardo **24** 516
Rivers, George Pitt, 1st Baron *see* PITT, GEORGE, 1st Baron Rivers
Rivers, Godfrey **4** 819
Rivers, Larry **26** 430–31*
collaboration **20** 606, 607
groups and movements **25** 231
Rivers, Larry—cont.
teachers **14** 633
works **22** 523; **26** *430*
Riverside (CA; USA), Union Pacific Railroad Station **7** 619
Riverside (IL; USA) **23** 421, *421*
Riverside Press **26** 536; **31** 680
Riverstown **18** 634; **29** 835
Riverton (CT), John Tarrant Kenney Hitchcock Museum **14** 590
Rivet **24** 821
riveting **6** 335; **12** 866; **21** 324*
Riviera, Caterina della **26** 778
Riviera, Egidio della *see* VLIETE, GILLIS VAN DEN
Riviera, Maria della **26** 778
Rivière, Abbé de La *see* LA RIVIÈRE, Abbé de
Rivière, Briton **26** 431*
Rivière, Eduardo **6** 67
Rivière, Etienne de La *see* LA RIVIÈRE, ETIENNE DE
Rivière, Georges **26** 431–2*
Rivière, Gilles de *see* VLIETE, GILLIS VAN DEN
Rivière, Henri (Benjamin Jean Pierre) **2** 733; **26** 432*
collaboration **2** 733
groups and movements **17** 441
pupils **2** 733
works **17** *441*; **19** 490; **33** 361
Rivière, Hugh Goldwin **33** 382
Rivière, Joseph **4** 391
Rivière, Louis de La *see* LA RIVIÈRE, LOUIS DE
Rivière, Marquis de **32** 236
Rivière, Philippe Garçon **4** 711
Rivière, William **26** 431
Rivière Dufresny, Charles **12** 123
Rivières, Raymond Séré de *see* SÉRÉ DE RIVIÈRES, RAYMOND
Rivista d'arte **24** 423, 448
Rivista d'Italia **12** 824
Rivista fotografica universale **24** 447
Rivius, Gualtherus **1** 841; **12** 366; **26** 432–3*; **32** 641
Rivius, Walther Hermann *see* RIVIUS, GUALTHERUS
Rivoire, Apollos **26** 261
Rivoire family **20** 650
Rivoli
Castello **16** 776; **17** 708–9; **28** 16; **31** 446
Museo d'Arte Contemporanea *see* Castello
Rivolta d'Adda, S Sigismondo **26** 578, 620
Rixens, Jean-André **10** 507
Rixheim **25** 517
Musée du Papier Peint **33** 711
Rixner, Wolfgang **32** 462
riyāḍ gardens *see under* GARDENS → types
Riyadh **2** *246*; **16** *104*; **21** 588; **26** 433*
architecture **27** 875; **32** 316
Diplomatic Quarter **27** 875
Folklore Museum **27** 877
fortifications **21** 588
Great Mosque **16** 243
houses **32** 316
Institute of Art Education **27** 876
al-Khairia complex **27** 875
King Fahd International Stadium **27** 875
King Khalid International Airport **16** 258; **27** 875
King Khalid Memorial Mosque **29** 513
King Sa'ud University **2** 259; **27** 875
Murabba cultural complex **27** 877
Museum of Archaeology and Ethnography **27** 877
museums **2** 275
Qasr Masmak **21** 588
Television Centre **27** 875
Riyadh—cont.
United Nations building **27** 875
Riza **16** 76, *127*; **22** 262; **26** 433–4*
attributions **16** 295
patrons and collectors **27** 514
pupils **22** 266
works **5** 761; **16** 132, 338, 339
Riza, Shah (*reg* 1925-41) (Pahlavi) **16** 539
Riza, Ali **16** 537
Riza, Hasan **23** 695
Riza Ashraf **1** 638
Riza Imami **15** 143
Rizal 'Abbasi **16** 533
Riza-yi 'Abbasi *see* RIZA
Rize *see* RHIZAION
Rizi, Antonio **26** 434
Rizi, Francesco Maria **1** 631
Rizi (de Guevara), Francisco **20** 66; **26** 434, 435–8*; **29** 281; **30** 664
assistants **7** 523
collaboration **2** 174; **5** 874; **10** 495; **11** 491
patrons and collectors **14** 10
pupils **2** 497; **7** 522
works **7** 523; **10** 903; **11** 491; **25** 23; **26** 434, *436*, *437*; **31** 89
Rizi, Juan **26** 434–5*; **29** 281
works **26** 434, *435*
Rizio, Paolo **11** 852
Rizk, Abdel Kader **9** 766
Riznich, Ivan **27** 414
Rizo, Salvador **7** 608
Rizokarpasso **8** *325*
Hagia Mavra **8** 359
Hagios Philon **8** 357, 358
Hagios Synesios **8** 358
Panagia Syka **8** 358
Rizuti, Filippo *see* RUSUTI, FILIPPO
Rizuti, Giovanni **5** 666
Rizzetti, Giovanni **25** 561
Rizzi (family) **24** 55
Rizzi, Andrea *see* RITZOS, ANDREAS
Rizzi, Marco *see* RICCI, MARCO
Rizzo, Antonio **20** 767; **26** 438–40*; **32** 192
assistants **19** 554
attributions **19** 554
patrons and collectors **3** 201; **19** 663; **22** 127
works **3** 201, 655; **7** 518; **16** 693; **19** 554; **26** *439*; **32** 184, 192, 218, 219, *219*
Rizzo, Pietro **26** 440
Rizzo, Pippo **13** 871
Rizzoli, Giovanni Pietro **26** 440–41*
RKO **13** 709
RLIN (Research Libraries Information Network) **2** 367, 368; **4** 23, 24
RMG *see* RIGA ARTISTS' GROUP
RMJM *see* ROBERT MATTHEW, JOHNSON-MARSHALL & PARTNERS
R. M. Kliment & Frances Halsband Architects **26** 441*
Roach-Smith, Charles **11** 737
roads
England **23** 685
Inca **15** 162
Indian subcontinent **15** 202
Islamic **16** 151
Italy **26** 887
Maya **7** 484
Mesoamerica, Pre-Columbian **6** 96; **7** 484
Rome, ancient **26** 864, 887; **27** 6–7*; **32** 398
20th cent. **32** 398
see also AVENUES; CAUSEWAYS; STREETS
Road to Calvary, Master of the **3** 555
Roager Church **13** 190
Roajas, Felipe **24** 622
Roalkvam, Terje **23** 232
Roannez, Claude Gouffier, 1st Duc de **7** 464; **11** 265; **13** 224; **16** 877
Roannez, François de La Feuillade, Duc de *see* AUBUSSON, FRANÇOIS, Duc de Roannez, Duc d'
Roatán, Museo de Roatán **14** 717
Robartes, John, 1st Earl of Radnor **9** 718
Robarts, Geraldine **17** 907
Robat Sharaf *see* RIBAT-I SHARAF
Robaudy **20** 75–6
Robaut, A.-E. **19** 484, 789
Robays, C. Van *see* VAN ROBAYS, C.
Robba, Francesco **26** 441*
works **19** 516; **28** 862; **33** 592
Robbe, Emmanuel **20** 603; **26** 441–2*
Robbe, Louis **29** 644
Robbia, Andrea (di Marco) della **26** 442, 444–7*
attributions **11** 210
collaboration **26** 444, 447
patrons and collectors **27** 863
pupils **26** 446
works **14** 784; **26** *445*, *446*; **30** 497, *501*; **32** 628, 630
Robbia, della (family)
patrons and collectors **28** 560
works **16** 734; **30** 886
workshop **1** 454; **16** 658; **27** 775
Robbia, Filippo della **26** 447
Robbia, Francesco della **26** 442
Robbia, Giovanni (Antonio) della **26** 442, 446–7*
attributions **19** 412
collaboration **27** 447
works **30** 497; **32** 630
Robbia, Girolamo (Domenico) della **26** 442, 447*
works **11** 513, 604; **16** 734; **24** 148
Robbia, Luca (di Simone) della (1399/1400-82) **11** 185; **16** 741; **26** 442–4*; **31** 740
collaboration **9** 157; **11** 198, 202, 388; **20** 552; **22** 801
copies **3** 854
forgeries by others **3** 357
methods **11** 184
patrons and collectors **16** 711; **24** 299; **25** 383; **27** 729; **28** 560
pupils **22** 461; **26** 444
sculpture **16** 689
bronze **21** 466
marble
Campanile (Florence) **1** 654; **11** 201
Cathedral of S Maria del Fiore (Florence) **9** 126; **11** 197; **16** 690, 774; **26** *443*
terracotta **14** 784; **25** 175; **30** 496, 497; **31** 142
Cathedral of S Maria del Fiore (Florence) **11** 198
Palazzo Medici-Riccardi (Florence) **21** 12
Palazzo Vescovile (Pescia) **1** 711
Santa Croce (Florence) **26** *444*; **30** 501
S Domenico (Urbino) **5** 782; **20** 552
S Giovanni Fuorcivitas (Pistoia) **30** *497*
S Miniato al Monte Abbey Church (Florence) **3** 100; **11** 210; **16** 691; **21** 12; **27** 183
Santa Trinita (Florence) **3** 99
workshop **2** 114
Robbia, Luca della (1475-*d* before 1548) **26** 442, 447
Robbia, Lucantonio della **26** 447
Robbia, Marco della (*d* 1527) **26** 447

Robbia, Marco della (1468-1529/34) 26 442
Robbia, Simone della 26 447
Robe, William 5 560
works 5 560
Robecca, Isabella da see ISABELLA DA ROBECCA
Robelin, Charles 28 416
Robelin, Isaac 26 204; 31 717
Robelin, Jacques 4 391
Rõben 22 496
Robert (fl 1770s) 14 792; 20 474
Robert (fl c. 1900) 25 771
Robert, Abbot of Cîteaux (1027-1100) 7 346
Robert, Archbishop of Rouen (989-1037) 27 245, 249; 33 232
Robert, Count of Provence, King of Sicily see ROBERT, King of Naples and Jerusalem
Robert, King of Naples and Jerusalem (reg 1309-43) 2 109-10*, 632; 13 150; 22 470
Robert II, Duke of Normandy (reg 1087-1106) 23 19
Robert II, King of France (reg 996-1031) 10 546; 11 653; 24 159; 27 558
Robert II of Taranto, Prince of Achaia (reg 1333-64) 23 505
Robert, Carl 26 507
Robert, Elias 8 573; 25 301
Robert, Emile 25 663
Robert, Eugène 20 862
Robert, Hubert 4 554; 21 699; 26 447-50*, 774
architecture 8 461; 13 705
collaboration 11 658
copies 1 598
drawings 9 224
furniture 10 643; 30 783
garden design 12 123; 20 480; 21 150; 25 872; 32 372
groups and movements 13 200; 22 740
paintings 5 686; 11 410, 540; 18 713; 24 139; 26 448, 449, 450; 28 418; 31 156
capriccios 5 687
landscape 16 905
topographical 30 514; 31 156
patrons and collectors
Alexander I, Emperor of Russia (reg 1801-25) 26 733
Azincourt, Barthélémy-Augustin Blondel d' 2 904
Bergeret de Grancourt, (Pierre-) Jacques-Onésyme 3 776
Camondo, Moïse de, Comte 5 530
Charles X, King of France (reg 1824-30) 4 556
Choiseul, Etienne-François, Duc de 7 194
Cognacq, (Théodore-) Ernest 7 528
Geoffrin, Marie-Thérèse 12 312
Girardin, Louis-René, Marquis de 10 465
Hall, Peter Adolf 14 80
Henry, Bon-Thomas 14 396
Laborde, Jean-Joseph, Marquis de 18 579
Marie-Antoinette, Queen of France (1755-93) 4 555
Mariette, Pierre-Jean 20 417
Papillon de La Ferté, Denis-Pierre-Jean 24 63
Pâris, Pierre-Adrien 24 177
Paul I, Emperor of Russia (reg 1796-1801) 4 745; 26 733
Polignac, Winnaretta, Princesse Edmond de 25 150
Stroganov, Aleksandr (Sergeyevich), Count (1734-1811) 29 778
Véri (-Raionard), Louis-Gabriel, Marquis de 32 255
Robert, Hubert
patrons and collectors—cont.
Watelet, Claude-Henri 32 898
Yusupov, Nikolay (Borisovich), Prince (1751-1831) 2 417; 33 579
reproductive prints by others 13 220; 27 570, 571
sponsorship 7 193
teachers 22 683; 24 9; 28 847
tombs 6 171
Robert, Joseph Gaspard 7 762; 11 606, 609; 20 474
Robert, Karl 6 471
Robert, (Louis) Léopold 26 450-52*; 30 125
groups and movements 26 739
patrons and collectors 30 766
teachers 22 697
works 11 413, 542; 26 451; 30 133
Robert, Louis 32 816
Robert, Nicholas-Louis 24 43
Robert, Nicolas 11 229; 17 449; 26 452*
Robert, Paul 14 281; 22 920
Robert, Paul-Ponce-Antoine 6 122; 8 209; 25 622; 26 452-3*
Robert Adam Cross 28 244
Robert d'Arbrissel 11 290
Robert d'Artois 20 380
Robert de Bello, Abbot of Canterbury 5 642
Robert de Coucy 26 121
Robert de Lannoy 26 453*
Robert de Lisle, Psalter of see under PSALTERS → individual manuscripts
Robert de Luzarches 1 777; 26 453*
Robert de Moncheaux 3 397
Robert des Ruines see ROBERT, HUBERT
Robert de Varennes 31 840
Robert de Wykehampton 27 625
Robert-Dumesnil, Alexandre-Pierre-François 6 78; 26 453*; 32 377
Robertet, Florimond de 1 767; 5 285; 7 441; 11 512, 661; 19 183; 26 454*
Robertet, François 4 545; 11 355; 26 454*
Robertet, Jean 4 544; 26 453-4*
Robert-Fleury, Joseph Nicolas 4 139; 14 116, 587; 22 127; 26 454-5*
Robert-Fleury, Juste-Aurèle 23 522
Robert-Fleury, Tony 11 672; 26 455*
patrons and collectors 24 396
pupils 1 782; 3 325; 5 67; 6 377; 7 855; 10 892; 32 738; 33 175
works 8 654; 11 156
Robert Guiscard, Duke of Apulia (reg 1059-85) 8 73; 23 844; 26 698; 27 614
Roberti, Ercole (d'Antonio) de' 4 276; 9 263; 11 3; 13 293; 16 663; 26 455-9*
attributions 7 926; 11 7
patrons and collectors 8 146; 10 520, 523; 11 32
pupils 8 3; 20 904
works 7 303; 11 4; 16 659; 26 456, 457, 458
Roberti, Mirabella 21 537
Roberti, Polidoro de' 26 457
Robertinus, Magister 26 469
Robert Matthew, Johnson-Marshall & Partners 26 460-61*
works 4 790; 5 640; 9 724; 10 241; 12 775; 28 232; 31 243; 33 544
Roberto
works 19 462
Roberto, Marcelo 4 713; 26 461-2
Roberto, Márcio 26 462
Roberto, Maurício 4 713; 26 461-2
Roberto, Milton 4 713; 26 461-2
Roberto, M. M. M. 5 218; 11 365; 26 461-2*
Roberto da Montevarchi 24 525
Roberto d'Oderisi see ODERISI, ROBERTO D'
Robert of Beverley 19 598, 601, 602
Robert of Jumièges, Archbishop of Canterbury 2 77; 26 669; 33 232
manuscripts 2 77
Robert of Molesme, Saint 7 231, 354
Robert of Newminster 7 351
Roberts, Alfred C. 33 628
Roberts, Allen F.
works 1 346
Roberts, Antonius 3 62
works 3 62
Roberts, C. 18 896
Roberts, Cadman & Co. 28 577
Roberts, David (1796-1864) 9 766; 15 892; 26 463*; 28 236; 30 679
collaboration 29 536
dealers 12 30
groups and movements 23 504
paintings 7 879
patrons and collectors 4 35; 32 338
reproductive prints by others 12 925; 27 602
teachers 22 531
works 5 401, 513; 10 97, 236; 13 285; 16 210; 22 59; 24 603; 25 623; 30 680; 31 155
Roberts, David, jr (1845-1907) 29 435
Roberts, Douglas 2 749
Roberts, Gilbert 4 803
Roberts, (William) Goodridge 22 39; 26 464*
groups and movements 5 568; 25 635
pupils 8 41; 31 146
Roberts, Henry 19 509; 28 277; 30 457, 458
works 19 509
Roberts, Hera 2 756, 759
Roberts, Isabel 33 401
Roberts, James 6 513; 8 840
Roberts, John 4 70; 26 462
Roberts, Marshall O. 29 583
Roberts, Peter 4 790; 32 787
Roberts, Sarah Jane 32 789
works 32 789
Roberts, Sautell see ROBERTS, THOMAS SAUTELL
Roberts, Terrence 13 877
Roberts, Thomas (fl 1684-1714) 10 291; 29 804
Roberts, Thomas (1749-78) 10 278; 26 462-3*
works 11 428; 16 14
Roberts, Thomas Sautell (1760-1826) 16 14; 26 462, 463*
Roberts, Tom (William) (1856-1931) 2 747; 21 76; 26 464-5*
groups and movements 2 746; 14 306-7; 19 873; 29 767; 30 39
patrons and collectors 4 882
pupils 7 700
works 2 746; 26 465
Roberts, Will (b 1910) 32 786
Roberts, William (fl 19th cent.) 27 613
Roberts, William (d 1956) 33 678
Roberts, William (1895-1980) 10 374; 24 427; 26 466*
groups and movements 8 265; 13 712; 32 700, 701
patrons and collectors 16 42
works 29 426; 31 706
Roberts, Winifred see NICHOLSON, WINIFRED
Roberts-Austen, William Chandler 12 613
Roberts-Jones, Ivor 5 732; 32 788
Roberts-Jones, P. 3 619
Robertson 4 27
Robertson, Alexander 1 611; 26 466, 467
Robertson, Andrew 21 645; 22 531; 26 466, 467*; 27 173
Robertson, Anna Mary see MOSES, GRANDMA
Robertson, Archibald 26 466, 467*; 31 872
Robertson, Charles 16 15
Robertson, Daniel 25 402
Robertson, Douglas 5 668
Robertson, Eric 28 239
Robertson, Etienne Gaspard 20 92
Robertson, Fred H. 30 888
Robertson, George 5 750; 16 884, 889
Robertson, Howard (Morley) 9 685-6*; 10 240
Robertson, Hugh Cornwall 4 482; 26 467*; 30 887; 31 638
Robertson, James (1781-1868) 2 764; 8 862
Robertson, James (1830-81) 3 446; 26 467-8*
Robertson, J. B. 6 516
Robertson, John 24 294
Robertson, Louis Spier 2 740
Robertson, Patrick
works 28 262
Robertson, R(obert) H(enderson) 23 42; 25 372; 26 468*
Robertson, Sarah 22 39
Robertson, Suze 22 851; 26 468*
Robertson, William 1 135; 20 14; 26 466, 467
Robertson, Wybrow 23 340
Robertson & Sons 26 467
Robertson-Swann, Ron 2 754
Robertsport 1 386
Tubman Center for African Culture 19 310
Robert the Pious, King of France see ROBERT II, King of France
Robert the Wise, King of Naples and Jerusalem see ROBERT, King of Naples and Jerusalem
Robertus (fl 1150; Abruzzi) 23 106; 26 469*, 533-4
pupils 23 106
works 26 625
Robertus (fl mid-12th; Tuscany) 26 468-9*, 623
works 26 623
robes 9 255
historical and regional traditions
Africa 1 353
Algeria 16 459
Buddhism 18 374
Central Asia, Eastern 6 310
Central Asia, Western 6 251, 252
China 7 50, 75, 75, 77, 78, 78; 10 I1; 30 VI1
Coptic 16 431
Egypt 16 452
Hausa 1 349
Indian subcontinent 15 691
Iran 16 463, 464, 465
Islamic 16 459
Algeria 16 459
Egypt 16 452
Iran 16 463, 464, 465
Morocco 16 459
Ottoman 16 460
Sicily 16 430
Turkey 16 460, 462
Japan 17 316, 356, 356, 375, 376; 30 VII2
Korea 18 357, 358, 374, 375
Morocco 16 459
Native North Americans 22 618-21*, 619, 621, 648, 654, 655
Nigeria 1 353
Ottoman 16 460
Sicily 16 430
Turkey 16 460, 462
robes
historical and regional traditions—cont.
Uzbekistan 6 252
Vietnam 32 486, 487
Yoruba 1 353
materials
cotton 15 691; 17 356
embroidery 7 50; 10 I1
fibres 30 VII2
leather 22 654, 655
linen 16 431
pearls 16 430
rami (fibre) 17 316
silk 17 314; 18 375; 30 VI1
types
coronation 26 81-2*
court 7 77, 78
dragon 7 77
Robés, Rebeca 8 236
Robespierre, Maximilien de 18 576
Robetta 10 384; 26 469*
Robiano, de 20 281
Robiccia see CIONE, JACOPO DI
Robie, Fred 6 573; 33 401
Robien, Christophe-Paul Gautron, Marquis de 26 205, 469-70*
Robien, Paul-Christophe Gautron de 26 470
Robieson, James Frank 23 737-8
Robijn, Jan, I (d 1565) 26 470
Robijn, Jan, II (c. 1525-1600) 26 470*; 33 430
pupils 23 616
works 33 88
Robijn, Joris 26 470*
works 3 784; 24 563; 33 430
Robillard, Honoré 23 631
Robillon, Antoine 26 471
Robillon, Jean-Baptiste 26 470-71*
collaboration 25 293
gardens 25 814
palaces 25 814
patrons and collectors 4 637
works 12 125
Robillot, Claude 11 356
Robin see ROBIJN
Robin, André 2 46, 48; 26 471*
Robin, Arend 33 88
Robin, Georges 14 782; 23 616; 33 36
Robin, Pierre 27 253
Robina, Ricardo de 21 380
Robin de Fontaines 31 841
Robineau, Adelaide Alsop 26 471*; 27 565
works 31 639
Robineau, Samuel Edouard 26 471
Robinet, Edouard 28 410
Robinet d'Etampes 19 389; 31 448, 837
Robinot, Roseman 11 759
Robins, George Henry 7 500; 10 366
Robins, Henry 7 500
Robinson (family; fl 1663-9) 23 687
Robinson (textile maker; fl c. 1780)
works 16 34
Robinson, Alexander 11 141
Robinson, Anne 23 70
Robinson, Annie Louisa see SWYNNERTON, ANNIE LOUISA
Robinson, Antony 10 344
Robinson, Arnold 4 826
Robinson, Boardman 4 366; 27 872
Robinson, B. W. 16 549
Robinson, Charles Mulford 7 357; 19 700
Robinson, David 5 513
Robinson, D. M. 2 159; 23 433
Robinson, Edward G(oldenberg) 26 472*
Robinson, Fitzroy 29 380
Robinson, George Crosland 29 108, 122

Robinson, George Frederick, 1st Marquess of Ripon 5 195
Robinson, G. & J. 14 280
Robinson, Henry Peach 24 650, 668; 26 472*
groups and movements 19 424; 24 738
works 24 685
writings 24 668
Robinson, Increase 6 575
Robinson, James 16 27
Robinson, Jethro T. 20 809
Robinson, J. Lukin 8 264
Robinson, John (fl 1668-71) 26 473
Robinson, John (c. 1715-45) 1 504
Robinson, John (1778-1843) 28 248
Robinson, John Charles 9 231; 12 608; 26 472–3*
Robinson, John Henry 26 473*
Robinson, Keith 13 335
Robinson, Peter Frederick 8 30; 10 97; 32 554
Robinson, Ralph W. 19 424
Robinson, Richard, Archbishop of Armagh 7 791; 17 625
Robinson, Robert 21 416; 26 473–4*
Robinson, T. 2 643
Robinson, Theodore 15 156; 21 868; 26 474*; 31 603
Robinson, Thomas (fl c. 1627) 28 259
Robinson, Thomas (c. 1702-77) 14 808; 23 857; 26 474*; 31 858
Robinson, Thomas, 2nd Baron Grantham 7 171; 26 474–5*
works 2 148; 6 66
Robinson, Thomas Philip, 3rd Baron Grantham see GREY, THOMAS PHILIP DE, 2nd Earl de Grey
Robinson, William (c. 1643-1712) 9 315; 16 8; 26 475*
Robinson, William (1720-75) 26 474
Robinson, William (1838-1935) 12 105, 140
Robinson, William Heath see HEATH ROBINSON, WILLIAM
Robinson and Keefe 16 12
Robinson & Rhodes 10 307
Robió, Bartomeu 13 106; 19 518
Robirosa, Josefina 2 401; 26 475–6*
Robison, C. K. 5 418
Robit (family) 5 63; 8 653
Robles, Diego de 9 712
Robles, M. C. 30 16
Robles de Medina, Stuart 30 16
Robles Moqo style pottery see under POTTERY → wares
Robsjohn-Gibbings, Terence Harold 31 632
Robson, E(dward) R(obert) 26 476*
collaboration 29 650; 31 240
competitions 7 667
groups and movements 25 804
works 28 157, 157
Robson, Geoffrey 28 592
Robson, George Fennel 14 548; 26 476–7*
Robson, Philip Appleby 26 476
Robson, William 10 316
Robus, Hugo 26 477*
Robuski Monastery 25 343
Robusti see TINTORETTO
Robusti, Giovanni Battista 31 6
Robyn see ROBIJN
Robyn, Georg see ROBIN, GEORGES
Roca, Bernat 3 220, 221
Roca, Francesc Català see CATALÀ ROCA, FRANCESC
Roca, Juan de la 1 757
Roca, Miguel Garriga y see GARRIGA Y ROCA, MIGUEL
Rocafort, S María de Marquet 26 642
rocaille 26 477*, 491, 493–4
Roca i Simo, Francesc 23 881
Rocamadour 24 808; 26 653
Roca Rey, Joaquín 24 510; 30 214
works 24 510
Roc aux Sorciers see ANGLES-SUR-L'ANGLIN
rocca 6 57
Rocca, Alfred de la 4 391
Rocca, Michele 26 477*
Rocca al Mare see under IRAKLEION
Rocca d'Angera, Sala di Giustizia 16 710
Rocca Sinibaldi, Asdrubale Mattei, Duca di 20 839, 840–41*
interior decoration 18 730
paintings 7 906; 26 397; 28 472
Rocca Sinibaldi, Ciriaco Mattei, Duca di 20 839, 840*
paintings 5 711
sponsorship 20 840
Roccatagliata, Giovanni Stefano 25 413
Roccatagliata, Nicolò 26 478*; 32 192
groups and movements 16 697
works 29 570
Roccatagliata, Sebastiano 26 478
Roccatagliata, Simone 26 478
Rocchi, Andrea de' 16 725
Rocchi, Elia de' 16 725
Rocci, Gaspare 26 778
Rocco, Master 7 877
Rocco, Emanuele (Alfonso Giovanni) 8 275; 26 478*
Rocco, Ferdinando 26 478
Rocco da Vicenza 31 905; 32 409
Roc de Sers 11 505; 25 470, 477, 480, 487; 26 478–9*
rock art 25 477
Roch, Ferdinand Marie Nolasque de see GUILHERMY, FRANÇOIS DE
Rocha (family) 23 454; 25 310
Rocha, Antonio Baptista de 13 295
Rocha, Carlo Mendes da see MENDES DA ROCHA, CARLO
Rocha, João Bento da 23 454; 26 479
Rocha, João da 23 454; 26 479
Rocha, Joaquim Manuel da 25 297
Rocha, José Joaquim da 4 716; 27 644
Rocha, Lourenco Ribeiro da see RIBEIRO DA ROCHA, LOURENCO
Rocha, Manuel da 8 9; 11 249; 26 479*; 28 429, 732
Rocha, Paolo (Archias) Mendes da see MENDES DA ROCHA, PAOLO (ARCHIAS)
Rocha Borges, Leonor Augusta da 26 479
Rocha e Sousa, João da (fl 1845) 26 479
Rocha e Sousa Lima, João da (fl late 19th cent.) 26 479
Rocha Soares, Francisco da (1752-1829) 23 454; 26 479
Rocha Soares, Francisco da (1806-57) 23 454; 26 479
Rochat 7 294
Rochat, Frères 30 148
Rochdale building society 24 332
Roche, Alexander 12 779
Roche, F. Lloyd 31 733
Roche, François de la 26 73
Roché, Henri-Pierre 9 359; 10 581; 25 823; 33 304
Roche, Jean-Baptiste 29 93
Roche, (Eamonn) Kevin 8 770; 22 366, 368; 26 479–80*
Roche, Kevin, John Dinkeloo and Associates 23 43; 27 478
Roche, Martin 6 577; 14 657–8*; 17 476
Roche, Philip 9 320
Roche, Pierre 11 567, 568; 26 480–81*
collaboration 27 879
works 10 178; 29 575
Roche, Pierre De la see DE LA ROCHE, PIERRE
Roche, Roger Pérez de la see PÉREZ DE LA ROCHE, ROGER
Roche Abbey 13 43, 44; 21 838; 22 216; 26 590
Rochead, James 28 289
Rochead, John Thomas 12 773; 26 481*; 28 288
Rochechouart, Julien de, Comte 16 426
Rochechouart, Louis de 19 267
Rochefort 31 718
Rochefort, Garnier de, Abbot of Clairvaux see GARNIER DE ROCHEFORT, Abbot of Clairvaux
Rochefort, Pierre de 31 175
Rochefoucauld, Antoine de La, Comte see LA ROCHEFOUCAULD, ANTOINE DE, Comte
Rochefoucauld, François, Duc de La see LA ROCHEFOUCAULD, FRANÇOIS, Duc de
Rochegrosse, Georges (Antoine Marie) 2 642; 12 830; 26 481*
Roche Guyon (family) 3 460
Rochemonteix, Maxence de Chalvet, Marquis de 9 721; 10 82
Rochepine, Petr Filip Bechade de see BECHADE DE ROCHEPINE, PETR FILIP
Roche Rabell, Arnaldo 18 834
Rochereau, Julien 4 390
Rocherolles, Louis de 3 460
Roches, Peter des, Bishop of Winchester see PETER DES ROCHES, Bishop of Winchester
Rochester (Kent; UK)
bridge 4 800
Castle 6 54; 8 278; 10 227
Cathedral of Christ and the Blessed Virgin 1 723; 26 588, 589
chapter house 6 466
choir-stalls 7 191
effigy of John de Northwoode, Bishop of Sheppey 25 176
Lady Chapel 18 622
oliphants 23 400
pinnacles 24 826
sculpture 7 643; 26 612, 616
spire 29 412
tomb of Bishop Bradfield 31 273
Rochester (NY; USA)
First Unitarian Church 31 584
George Eastman House see International Museum of Photography
International Museum of Photography 2 372; 9 685; 24 434, 683; 27 164
William S. Kimball House 15 408
Rochester, John Wilmot, 2nd Earl of see WILMOT, JOHN, 2nd Earl of Rochester
Rochet, Louis 26 481–2*
Rochetel, Michel 19 398
rochets 32 388*
Rochette, (Désiré-) Raoul 25 172; 26 482*
Rochi, Alessandro Alonso see ALONSO ROCHI, ALESSANDRO
Röchlitz, Julius 5 83; 25 856
Rö Church 26 647
Rochussen, Charles 4 740; 22 848; 26 482–3*
teachers 23 322
works 1 809
Rochussen, Hendrik (1779-1852) 26 482
Rochussen, Henri (1812-89) 26 482
Rochus zu Linar see LYNAR, ROCHUS
rock see STONE
rock art 22 443–4
dating methods 2 269, 270; 27 696
historical and regional traditions
Africa 1 378, 402, 408; 27 695–8
Easter Island 23 729
Namibia 27 695–6
Native North Americans 22 549, 559–60*, 581–2, 589–90*, 592
New Zealand 23 728–9
Nigeria 23 130
Pacific Islands 23 728–30*
Prehistoric art 4 763; 19 229; 25 474–7*, 480–87*, 486
Aboriginal Australia 1 40–42*, 57–8; 10 474; 25 822
Africa 1 220, 370–75*
Algeria 1 220, 634
Anatolia, ancient 1 823
Arabia 2 269–70*
Argentina 29 204
Brazil 29 195–7*
Central Asia, Western 6 222–3*
Croatia 25 475
Cuba (Caribbean) 8 229, 229
Dominican Republic 9 114
Eritrea 1 373
Ethiopia 1 373
France 2 63; 18 806–7, 807; 19 229; 23 77–8; 24 310; 25 475, 486; 31 360–61, 410
Herzegovina 25 475
Indian subcontinent 15 551–2*
Iran, ancient 15 902
Italy 25 475
Kenya 1 374, 375
Libya 19 323
Malawi 1 374, 375
Mesolithic 25 494–5*
Norway 25 495
Oman 2 270
Palaeolithic 6 46–7; 12 149; 18 806, 807
Portugal 25 475
Romania 25 475
Russia 23 442
San 1 373, 375
Saudi Arabia 2 269
Somalia 1 373
South America, Pre-Columbian 29 187, 204
Spain 1 688–9; 6 46–7; 19 229; 25 475, 495; 26 179–80; 29 364–5*
Sri Lanka 29 445
Sweden 25 532
Tanzania 1 374
Uganda 1 374
Zambia 1 375
Zimbabwe 1 375
San 27 695–8
South Africa 27 696
West Mexico 33 103
Zimbabwe 27 695–6
materials
brushes 25 477
charcoal 25 477, 484
clay 25 487
colour 25 477
crayons 25 477
feldspar 25 477
frames 11 374
hides 25 477
illite 25 477
mica 25 477
mortars (vessels) 25 477
pads 25 477
paints 25 477
pestles 25 477
pigments 25 477–9*, 478, 483
talc 25 477
rock art
materials—cont.
woad 25 477
techniques
anamorphosis 25 479
carving
Buddhism 30 823
Canada 22 575
Chatham Islands 6 514, 514
China 6 743
Dominican Republic 5 748
Dorset culture 22 575
Easter Island 9 675
Egypt, ancient 9 865
Indian subcontinent 10 138
Karasuk culture 21 882
Mesoamerica, Pre-Columbian 22 443–4
Mongolia 21 881–2*
Native North Americans 22 575
Nazca 22 707–9, 708
New Caledonia 23 729, 730
Pacific Islands 23 729–30
Papua New Guinea 23 730, 730
Peru 22 708
Prehistoric art 10 896; 11 330; 18 169, 169–70, 806; 21 882; 23 78, 442; 25 484, 509–11*, 509, 510, 531–3*; 26 133
Prehistoric art: Britain 25 531, 532
Prehistoric art: Central Asia, Western 10 896
Prehistoric art: France 18 806; 23 77–8; 25 509, 511
Prehistoric art: Germany 25 511
Prehistoric art: Ireland 18 169, 169–70; 25 509, 510, 511, 531
Prehistoric art: Korea 18 297
Prehistoric art: Malta (Republic of) 25 509, 510, 510
Prehistoric art: Mongolia 21 882
Prehistoric art: Russia 23 442; 27 365
Prehistoric art: Scotland 25 532
Prehistoric art: Sweden 11 330; 18 103; 25 532
Puerto Rico 5 748
Scythian 28 321
Siberia 28 321
South America, Pre-Columbian 22 708; 29 132
Tarascan 30 341
Tibet 30 823
drawing
Antilles, Greater 2 145
Antilles, Lesser 2 145
Prehistoric art 15 192; 25 478
Puerto Rico 2 145
engraving
Aboriginal Australia 22 229
Hawaii 23 728
Moche (culture) 6 520
Pacific Islands 23 730
Prehistoric art: Anatolia, ancient 1 823
Prehistoric art 1 149, 688; 12 149; 25 475, 476–7, 478, 484–5*, 486, 487, 532; 29 196–7*; 31 361
Prehistoric art: Aboriginal Australia 1 40
Prehistoric art: Brazil 29 196–7*
Prehistoric art: France 12 149; 25 475, 480, 487
Prehistoric art: Portugal 25 480
Prehistoric art: Sicily 1 149, 150
Prehistoric art: South America, Pre-Columbian 29 196–7*

rock art
techniques
engraving—cont.
Prehistoric art: Spain **1** 688–9; **25** 480
Prehistoric art: Sweden **25** *532*
Tasmania **1** 40–41; **22** 229
finger marks
Prehistoric art **25** 476, 477, 478, *478*
hand prints
Prehistoric art **1** 688; **25** 478
incising
Prehistoric art **25** 511
painting **23** 728
Aboriginal Australia **1** 38, *41*, 41, *42*, 58–9, 61; **19** 368–9; **31** 133, 511, *511*
Buddhism **29** 462
Easter Island **9** 675
Eritrea **10** 568
Ethiopia **10** 568
Finland **11** 93
Irian Jaya **23** 729
Maasai **19** 861
Maya **22** 443–4, *444*
Mesoamerica, Pre-Columbian **21** 192, 226*, 230; **22** 443–4, *444*
Native North Americans **13** 332, *332*; **27** 727
Olmec **21** 226*
Papua New Guinea **23** 729
Prehistoric art **1** 688–9, *689*; **12** 149; **24** 310–11; **25** 474–6*, 477–80*, *478*, *479*, 487; **29** *196*, *227*, *365*, 422; **31** *360*; **32** 802*
Prehistoric art: Aboriginal Australia **1** *57*, 57–8; **32** 802, *803*, *807*
Prehistoric art: Africa **1** *220*, *372*, *375*, *376*
Prehistoric art: Algeria **1** *220*, *372*, *376*
Prehistoric art: Argentina **29** 203
Prehistoric art: Brazil **29** 195–6*, *196*
Prehistoric art: France **12** 149; **24** *310*; **25** *475*, *478*, *479*, 487; **29** 422; **31** *360*
Prehistoric art: Indian subcontinent **15** 551–2*, *552*
Prehistoric art: Russia **25** 475
Prehistoric art: South America, Pre-Columbian **29** 195*, *196*, 203
Prehistoric art: Spain **1** 688–9, *689*; **25** 487; **29** *365*, 422
Prehistoric art: Tanzania **1** *374*, *375*
Prehistoric art: Thailand **29** *227*
San **4** 489; **27** *696*, *697*
Sri Lanka **29** 462
United States of America **13** 332, *332*
relief sculpture
Prehistoric art **25** *476*, *477*, 487
sculpture **28** 241
spraying **25** 478
stencilling **25** 478; **29** 627
see also CAVE ART
Rockburne, Dorothea **4** 110; **26** 483*
rock churches *see under* CHURCHES → types
rock collections *see under* COLLECTIONS → types
rock crystal **14** 167; **26** 484–7*
historical and regional traditions
Ancient Near East **26** 485
Aztec **21** 243; **26** 487
Buddhism **26** 487
Byzantine **26** 485
Carolingian **5** 811–12*; **12** *256*; **26** 485
rock crystal
historical and regional traditions—cont.
Central Asia, Western **6** *274*
China **7** 89, 111; **26** 486
Qing period (1644-1911) **7** 91, 132
Tang period (AD 618-907) **7** 90, 109
Yuan period (1279-1368) **7** 130
Zhou period (*c.* 1050-256 BC) **7** 4, 107
20th cent. **26** 484
Crete **26** 484–5
Czech Republic **8** *414*; **25** *436*
Ecuador **29** 155
Egypt **16** 540–41, *541*; **26** 487
Egypt, ancient **26** 484
France **11** 633; **12** *257*; **26** *147*
Gothic **26** *147*
Greece, ancient **12** 247
Hinduism **26** 487
Indian subcontinent **15** 697–8*, *698*; **16** 542; **21** 717, *717*; **26** 487
Iran **16** 540
Islamic **6** 556; **12** 253; **16** 540–42*; **26** 487
Egypt **16** 540–41, *541*; **26** 487
Indian subcontinent **16** 542
Iran **16** 540*
Ottoman **16** 542, *542*
Turkey **16** *542*
Italy **3** *817*; **12** *259*; **16** 744–5*, *746*; **26** 486
16th cent. **26** *485*
Jainism **26** 487
Japan **17** 398; **26** 487
Macedonia (i) (Greece) **26** 485
Merovingian **26** 485
Mesoamerica, Pre-Columbian **1** 713; **21** 241, 243; **26** 487
Mexico **21** 393
Minoan **26** 484–5
Mixtec **21** 737; **26** 487
Nepal **26** 487
Ottoman **16** 542, *542*
Ottonian **26** 485
Portugal **25** 312
Rome, ancient **26** 485; **27** *103*
Sasanian **26** 485
South America, Pre-Columbian **29** 155
Syria-Palestine **26** 485
Thailand **26** 487
Turkey **16** *542*
technical examination **30** 405
techniques
cutting **26** 485
engraving **26** 485
painting **26** 484
staining **7** 91
uses
amulets **26** 485
beads **16** 744; **26** 487; **29** 155
belthooks **7** 107
boxes **11** 633
candlesticks **16** *541*
canteens **16** *542*
caskets **16** *745*
chandeliers **6** 443
chess sets **6** 556, 557
clocks **7** 439
crosses **8** *414*
ewers **10** *832*; **16** 541
flasks **16** 540
jewellery **7** 109, 111
mirrors **21** 717, *717*, 719
necklaces **7** 4; **27** *103*
netsuke **17** 398
pendants (jewellery) **6** *274*
plaques **21** 529; **26** 485, 486
pommels (swords) **2** 452
reliquaries **15** *698*; **26** *147*
rings **14** 418; **26** 485
rosaries **7** 90
sculpture **26** *486*
seals **7** 130; **12** 247; **26** 484
snuff bottles **7** 132; **26** 484
rock crystal
uses—cont.
sword grips **2** 452
sword hilts **2** 454
tazze **26** *485*
vases **21** 529; **26** 487
vessels **25** *436*; **26** 485
watches **7** 443
rock-cut architecture *see under* ARCHITECTURE → types
rock-cut stelae *see under* STELAE → types
rock-cut temples *see under* TEMPLES → types
rock-cut tombs *see under* TOMBS → types
Rocke, W. H., & Co. **2** 755, 758
Rockefeller (family) **2** 560; **14** 199; **26** 487*; **31** 663
collections **24** 183
interior decoration **8** 809
paintings **9** 467; **29** 605
Rockefeller, Abby Aldrich **2** 560; **26** 488*
Rockefeller, Abby Aldrich, garden court *see under* NEW YORK → museums → MOMA
Rockefeller, Blanchette Hooker **26** 489*
Rockefeller, Mrs John D. **19** 438
Rockefeller, John D(avison), I (1839-1937) **7** 838; **26** 487
Rockefeller, John D(avison), II (1874-1960) **26** 487–8*
architecture **2** 322; **7** 515; **8** 652; **11** 261; **33** 206
carpets **8** 899
interior decoration **22** 60
Rockefeller, John D(avison), III (1906-78) **15** 743; **16** 554; **26** 488*
Rockefeller, Nelson Aldrich **3** 174; **26** 488–9*
architecture **14** 200
collections **1** 439; **31** 665
interior decoration **12** 771
Rockefeller, William **14** 223
Rockefeller Foundation *see under* NEW YORK → foundations
Rockefeller Museum *see under* JERUSALEM → museums
rockeries **12** 85–90
rockers **10** *379*; **25** 612; **26** 489*
Rocket Press **25** 628
rockets **18** 353
rock gardens *see under* GARDENS → types
Rockhampton Customs House **3** 269
rocking chairs *see under* CHAIRS → types
Rockingham, Charles Watson-Wentworth, 2nd Marquess of *see* WATSON-WENTWORTH, CHARLES, 2nd Marquess of Rockingham
Rockingham, Thomas Watson-Wentworth, 1st Marquess of *see* WATSON-WENTWORTH, THOMAS, 1st Earl of Malton
Rockingham Castle (Northants) **6** 53
Rockingham ceramic factory **10** 310; **26** 489–90*
Rockingham ware *see under* POTTERY → wares
Rockox, Adriaen **14** 379
Rockox, Nicolaas **26** 490*
paintings **2** 196; **3** 558; **5** 353; **27** 290–91
personal collection **3** 613
sculpture **9** 22
rock reliefs
historical and regional traditions
Achaemenid **1** *116*; **15** 916
Anatolia, ancient **1** 827, *828*, *829*, 832–3*
Assyrian **3** 418; **21** *278*
Buddhism **5** 107; **15** *464*, *466*
rock reliefs
historical and regional traditions—cont.
China **5** 107
Egypt, ancient **9** 779
Elamite **15** *908*, 916, *917*
Hinduism **15** *465*, *477*, *508*, *510*
Hittite **1** 832–3
Indian subcontinent **15** *236*, *437*, *464*, *465*, *466*, 477, *477*, *508*, *510*, *677*
Iran **30** *337*
Iran, ancient **1** *116*; **4** *92*; **15** *908*, 915*, 916, 917, *917*, *918*, 920; **24** 217
Parthian **10** *171*
Japan **17** 106
Mesopotamia **20** 219; **21** 276, *278*, 296
Parthian **10** *171*; **15** 916–17; **24** 217, 218
Phrygian **24** *691*
Sasanian **4** *92*; **15** 917–18, *918*; **30** *337*
Seleucid **15** 916–17
Turkey **24** *691*
materials
basalt **1** *829*
granite **15** *508*, *514*
limestone **15** *510*
see also RELIEF SCULPTURE
rocks **2** 304; **12** 87–8, 94, 120
Rockwell, Norman (Percevel) **4** 367; **26** 490–91*
Rococo **26** 477, 491–500*; **28** 845; **29** 879
art forms
altarpieces **1** *712*; **26** *253*
altars **19** *364*
architecture
Austria **26** 496*
Belgium **3** 546–7, *547*
Brazil **19** 460
Czech Republic **26** 496
Denmark **10** *110*, *111*
France **11** *884*; **32** *373*
Germany **8** *289*, *290*; **12** *372*; **14** 652; **19** *316*; **26** 495–6*, *497*, 497–8*; **32** *467*; **33** *683*
Islamic **16** 226
Italy **16** 639, *639*
Ottoman **16** 226
Poland **26** 498
Portugal **23** *405*; **28** 911
Turkey **16** 226
book illustrations **4** 356, 360, *361*, 361
candlesticks **26** *493*, 493
capriccios **18** *654*
drawings **4** *164*; **32** *918*
dress **9** 281–3*
engravings **4** *361*
façades **22** *437*
frames
Denmark **11** *469*
England **11** 427–8*, *428*
France **11** 405–8*
Germany **11** 457–60*, *458*, *459*
Italy **11** *395*, 395–6*
Scandinavia **11** 469–71*
Spain **11** 492–3*, *493*
Sweden **11** *469*, *470*
United States of America **11** *496*, *497*
furniture **28** 252
England **10** 294
France **11** 590
Germany **12** 423–5*, *424*, *425*
Hungary **14** 906–7
Russia **27** *406*, 407
South Africa **29** 115
United States of America **31** *627*
gardens **3** 428; **12** *133*, 134; **26** 497; **32** 120
grilles **22** *455*
Rococo
art forms—cont.
interior decoration
Austria **2** *806*, 807, *807*
Denmark **10** 111
Finland **11** *102*
France **11** *578*; **26** *494*
Germany **3** 428, *429*; **26** *496*
Netherlands, the **22** 865–6
Russia **27** *402*
Sweden **29** *690*
United States of America **31** 618
metalwork **25** 460; **27** 420
mirrors **12** *424*; **26** 492
monstrances **26** 493
nude figures **4** *515*, *516*; **17** *627*; **23** 294–5; **25** *275*; **28** *845*; **29** *573*
ornament **23** 543–4*
painting (general) **12** 390–91*; **30** 132*
painting (allegorical) **11** *539*; **19** *142*
painting (conversation pieces) **3** *561*; **33** *694*
painting (*fêtes champêtres*) **18** *693*
painting (*fêtes galantes*) **11** *37*, *368*; **32** *914*, *915*, *916*
painting (fresco) **1** *785*; **3** *780*; **12** *391*; **13** 853; **14** *695*
painting (genre)
England **13** *324*
France **4** *514*; **17** *627*; **31** *380*
painting (history) **14** *585*
painting (literary themes) **14** *636*
painting (mythological)
France **3** *855*; **4** *515*, *516*; **11** *367*; **22** *683*; **23** *294*
Italy **25** *3*
painting (religious) **9** *48*; **19** *647*
painting (wall) **11** *102*
pattern books **24** 271
platters **12** *357*
porcelain **6** I2; **10** *308*; **26** 498
portraits (painting)
Austria **23** *854*
England **8** *833*; **33** *693*
France **4** *512*; **9** *283*; **27** *571*
Italy **25** *3*
Russia **26** *551*
satires **14** *639*
sculpture
busts **5** 302*
Denmark **8** 740
England **27** *244*
France **8** *71*; **28** *845*
Germany **1** *712*; **22** *303*; **26** 498
Hungary **14** 894–5
Poland **25** *114*
Rococo **27** *243*
Slovakia **28** *855*
Spain **29** 292–3
silver **10** 332–3; **21** *70*; **25** 460
staircases **33** *433*
stucco **10** *859*; **29** *838*; **33** *682*
tombs **27** *244*
tureens **12** *357*
regional traditions
Brazil **4** 705
Denmark **1** 686
England **10** 249; **13** 324; **26** 499–500*; **32** 825
France **4** *331*; **13** 701; **26** 83, 492–5*
Germany **12** 413; **14** 649; **28** 118; **33** 681, 683
Italy **26** 500*
Lithuania **19** 497
Peru **24** 502
Russia **26** 498–9
Scotland **28** 252
South Africa **28** 121
United States of America **31** *618*, 648

Rococo Revival 26 500–501*; 28 50
art forms
ceramics 10 310
chairs 31 630
frames 11 415, 472, 474
furniture 28 254; 31 629, 630
interior decoration 2 809; 11 581; 31 620, 620
nude figures 11 545
painting 11 545, 545–6*
wood-carvings 28 255
regional traditions
Austria 2 808
Poland 25 121
Rocoplan, Camille (-Joseph-Etienne) see ROQUEPLAN, CAMILLE (-JOSEPH-ETIENNE)
Rocourt, Dom, Abbot of Clairvaux 7 372
Rocourt, Johannes 28 362
Rocque, John 6 513; 13 645; 14 856
Rocque, Mariano de la 27 532
Rocroi 21 568
Rocznik historii sztuki 24 441; 25 143
Rocznik sztuki śląskiej 24 441
Roda (Indian subcontinent) 15 276; 26 501*
temples 15 271–2
Temple 3 15 486
Temple 5 15 272
Temple 6 15 486
Roda Madrasa (Syria) 20 230
Roda, Agustí 29 336
Roda, Cristóbal de 2 176; 26 501*
Roda Bible see under BIBLES → individual manuscripts
Roda de Isábena 26 642
Rodakowski, Henryk 4 670; 18 692; 25 106; 26 501–2*
Rodari, Bernardino 26 502
Rodari, Donato 26 502
Rodari, Giacomo 1 748; 26 502
Rodari, Giovanni 26 502
Rodari, Tommaso 1 748; 26 502–3*
Rodas, Antonio 10 154; 13 767
Rodas, Modesto Delgado see DELGADO RODAS, MODESTO
Rodchenko, Aleksandr (Mikhaylovich) 3 529; 7 770; 20 194; 24 450, 676; 26 503–5*; 27 394, 396, 434, 443; 29 632; 32 661; 33 486
collaboration 20 887; 33 631
exhibitions 15 857
groups and movements 1 75, 76, 79; 7 768; 10 415; 22 508, 509; 28 597
agitprop 1 453
Inkhuk 15 856, 857; 29 632; 32 382
kinetic art 18 62
Narkompros 22 508
Oktyabr group (Russia) 15 122; 28 643
Suprematism 30 8
patrons and collectors 8 10
pupils 19 746
works 7 654, 654, 768, 769, 770; 10 684; 21 745, 891, 892; 24 675, 686; 25 351; 26 504, 505; 27 409
Rodd, G. & E. 2 766
Rodden, Robert 22 715
Roddis, John 4 86
Roddis, Thomas 4 86
Rode, (Christian) Bernhard (1725-97) 26 506*
attributions 18 848
methods 10 199
pupils 7 183; 11 793; 12 641
restorations 13 802
works 12 392; 24 542
Rode, Christian Bernhard (d 1755) 26 506
Rode, Hermen 26 506–7*
works 10 538; 12 384; 26 507
Rode, Jean-Baptiste 16 822
Rode, Johann Heinrich 26 506
Rode, Martin van see MARTIN VAN RODE
Rode, Philipp 26 506
Rod el-Air 28 760
Røde Mor 8 736
Roden, William Thomas 4 86
Rodeñas, Pedro de 9 710
Rodenbach 6 155
Rodengo 26 655
Rodenwaldt, Gerhart 26 507*
Röder, Claus 19 110
Roder, Pankrac 25 444
Rodet, Marie-Thérèse see GEOFFRIN, MARIE-THÉRÈSE
Rodez
Cathedral of Notre-Dame 11 514; 13 79
St Claude 7 192
sculpture 13 79
Rodezno, Arturo López see LÓPEZ RODEZNO, ARTURO
Rödgen Fort 6 68
Rodger, George 5 659, 897; 6 603; 20 99
Rodger, Thomas 1 148
Rodgers, John 11 119
Rodgers, Joseph, & Sons 8 287; 15 821; 28 576
Rodgers, Richard 30 687
Rodhe, (Olof) Lennart 7 699; 26 508*
Rodi, Andrea 29 267
Rodi, Faustino 8 135; 26 508*
Rodia, Simon 2 516; 11 243; 23 334; 26 508*
Rodiči, Mateja 28 452
Rodier, Mathelin 22 464
Ródigo, Gianfrancesco Gonzaga, Conte di 12 904, 907–8*
medals 6 102
sculpture 2 140
Rodin, (François-)Auguste (-René) 5 879; 11 566, 567, 568, 569, 659, 667; 15 211; 17 134; 24 142; 26 508–14*
assistants 4 568; 8 811, 896; 23 114; 25 207
collaboration 4 626; 8 787; 19 395
commentaries 7 368; 26 394
drawings 19 490
drypoints 9 309
exhibitions 31 490
groups and movements 12 870; 32 591
patrons and collectors 3 617; 19 756; 28 344
Chéramy, Paul-Arthur 6 548
Grosvenor, Hugh Lupus, 1st Duke of Westminster 13 697
Gulbenkian, Calouste Sarkis 13 840
Museum of Modern Egyptian Art 9 768
National Museum of Wales (Cardiff) 5 732
Phillips, Claude 24 638
Rockefeller, Nelson Aldrich 26 489
personal collection 2 552; 27 206
pupils 1 578; 7 387; 12 322; 23 369; 26 351; 28 534, 597; 33 518
sculpture
busts 5 304, 304; 20 822
studio 29 857
teachers 3 314; 19 39
works 1 640; 5 44; 6 9, 176; 9 159–60; 10 480; 11 565, 566, 567; 22 48; 23 296; 26 509, 510, 511, 513; 28 524; 29 575; 30 47, 499
Rodin, Musée see under PARIS → museums
Rodin Museum see under PHILADELPHIA (PA) → museums
Rodney, George Brydges, 1st Baron Rodney 3 280
Rodney Stoke (Somerset), St Leonard 28 294
Rodno Izkustwo see NATIONAL ART SOCIETY OF BULGARIA
Rodón, Francisco 25 702
Rødovre Town Hall 8 729
rod puppets see under PUPPETS → types
Rodrigo, Joaquim (José) 25 300; 26 515*
Rodrigo, Miguel 19 388
Rodrigo Alfonso 24 280
Rodrigo de Badajoz see BADAJOZ, RODRIGO DE
Rodrigo de Osona 23 605; 29 277
Rodrigo Mazuré, Miguel see MAZURÉ, MIGUEL RODRIGO
Rodrigues, Abelardo 4 725, 727
Rodrigues, Albert 13 876
Rodrigues, António 2 875; 25 291; 26 515–16*
Rodrigues, Augusto 4 728
Rodrigues, Faustino José 18 579; 19 893
Rodrigues, Francisco de Assis see ASSIS RODRIGUES, FRANCISCO DE
Rodrigues, Gabriel 26 253
Rodrigues, Glauco 4 719; 26 516*
Rodrigues, José 4 629; 26 516–17*
Rodrigues, Nina 4 708
Rodrigues, Sérgio 4 722
Rodrigues, Simão 26 516*
collaboration 25 297; 26 253; 32 426
pupils 26 129
works 7 521
Rodrigues da Silva, António see SILVA, ANTÓNIO RODRIGUES DA
Rodrigues da Silva e Sousa, José 10 729
Rodrigues de Macedo, João 4 710; 23 669
Rodrigues de Sa Lima, António 26 479
Rodrigues dos Santos, Manoel 31 341
Rodrigues Falcate, Antonio 4 710
Rodrigues Ferreira, Alexandre 3 535
Rodrigues-Henriques, Jacques 12 649
Rodrigues Milagres, Joaquim 26 52
Rodríguez, Abel 8 233
Rodríguez, Alfonso 27 605; 28 518; 29 265
Rodríguez, Alirio 26 517*
Rodríguez, Alonzo 26 517*
Rodríguez, Anita 18 832
Rodríguez, Antonio (fl c. 1610) 26 517
Rodríguez, Antonio (fl c. mid-17th cent.) 17 676
Rodríguez, Antonio (c. 1653-1706) 9 710
Rodríguez, Bernardo 9 712, 714; 27 668
Rodríguez, Cayetano 26 517*
Rodríguez, Diego (fl 1539) 28 519
Rodríguez, Diego (fl 1638) 29 340
Rodríguez, Eduardo Luis 8 233
Rodríguez, Francisco 14 714
Rodríguez, Jeronimo 2 868
Rodriguez, Jorge 18 834
Rodríguez, José Francisco 32 173
Rodríguez, Juan (d 1544) 2 865; 26 249
Rodríguez, Juan (d c. 1675) 26 517–18*
Rodríguez, Juan (1619-?83) 27 792
Rodríguez, Juan Luis 8 18; 26 518*
Rodríguez, Lorenzo 26 518*
groups and movements 7 289
Rodríguez, Lorenzo—cont.
works 21 376, 377, 401
Rodriguez, Luigi 26 517
Rodríguez, Manuel Antonio 29 337
Rodríguez, Manuel Martín 4 563; 16 864; 27 606
Rodríguez, Mariano (b 1912) see MARIANO
Rodríguez, Marino (1897-1947) 7 606
Rodríguez, Melitón 7 612; 26 519*
Rodríguez, Nicolas 23 903
works 23 903
Rodríguez, Oscar Mesa see MESA RODRÍGUEZ, OSCAR
Rodriguez, P. (architect) 31 823
Rodríguez, Patricia (painter) 18 832
Rodríguez (Tizón), Ventura 26 519–21*; 27 819; 29 271
altars 29 341
architecture 29 271
cathedrals 16 864; 23 901; 26 521
chapels 8 253; 25 877
churches 2 215; 16 863; 20 157; 28 727
colleges 26 520
monasteries 31 823
town halls 5 202
universities 29 272
urban planning 20 63; 23 900
assistants 29 337
fountains 21 111
frames 11 493
furniture 29 315
patrons and collectors 1 689; 4 561, 562, 563, 564
pupils 2 864
retables 25 877; 26 251
screens (i) (architectural) 28 369
tombs 23 896
Rodríguez Arangoiti, Ramón 21 378, 403
Rodríguez Ayuso, Emilio 1 798; 26 521*
Rodríguez-Casas, Fernando 4 264
Rodríguez Castell, Esteban 8 232
Rodriguez de Espinosa, Jerónimo 9 52; 10 509
Rodriguez de Francia, José Gaspar 24 95
Rodríguez de la Cruz, José Miguel 8 236
Rodríguez de los Ríos see SANTIAGO, Marqueses de
Rodríguez de Rivas, Diego 14 714
Rodríguez de Soria, Antonio 21 377
Rodríguez Fuster, José 8 236
Rodríguez Galisteo, Martín 2 404
Rodríguez Hernández, Julio Antonio see JULIO ANTONIO (RODRÍGUEZ HERNÁNDEZ)
Rodríguez Juarez, Juan 7 883; 17 677; 21 384
Rodríguez Juárez, Nicolás 17 676; 21 383
Rodríguez Larraín, Emilio 24 510, 511
Rodríguez Lozano, Manuel 2 29; 20 413; 21 388, 406; 26 521–2*
Rodríguez Luna, Antonio 26 522*; 29 286; 31 415
Rodríguez Olazábal, Santiago 8 229
Rodríguez Ortega, Enrique 2 396
Rodríguez Padilla, Rafael 13 765; 26 522*
Rodríguez Porcelos, Diego 5 201
Rodríguez Riquelme, Isabel 6 596
Rodríguez Samanez, Juan 31 182
Rodríguez Urbaneta, Abelardo 9 117, 119
Rodriques Belo, Antônio 4 716
Rodt, Christoph (fl 1577-1627) 26 522
Rodt, Christoph, the younger (c. 1580-1634) 12 404; 26 522–3*
Rodt, Eduard von 3 823
Rodt, Franz Konrad von, Bishop of Konstanz 2 234
Rodulfus 4 70; 26 523*
Roe, Henry 9 322
Roe, Thomas 21 717; 24 571
Roebling, John Augustus 7 326; 26 523–4*
assistants 26 524
collaboration 4 803
works 16 55; 23 39; 26 523; 31 594
Roebling, Washington Augustus 4 803; 26 524*; 31 594
Roebling's, John A., Sons Co. 26 524
Roed, Jørgen 8 735; 26 524–5*
pupils 17 605; 32 270; 33 594
teachers 7 805
works 8 746; 26 525
Roeder, Günther 14 462
Roeder, Lorenz see REDER, LORENZ
Roeder, Max 11 18
Roederer, Louis 13 325
Roehampton (Surrey)
Roehampton House 19 250
Roehampton Housing Estate 10 241
Roelandt, Louis Joseph Adrien 3 547; 26 525–6*
assistants 8 191
collaboration 26 192; 31 864
education (art) 3 618
groups and movements 10 187
pupils 3 762; 21 623; 31 855, 887
teachers 24 387
works 3 547, 548, 578
Roelas, Juan de 26 307, 526–7*; 28 515; 29 280
works 29 280, 280
Roeleffs, Coenraet 26 527*
Roelins, Joos 4 924
Roelins, Pieter 4 924
Roelofs, Otto Willem Albertus 26 528
Roelofs, Roelof 32 465
Roelofs, Stas 4 591
Roelofs, Willem 22 849; 26 527–8*
groups and movements 14 47
patrons and collectors 11 233
pupils 21 175; 29 723
works 26 528
Roelofs, Willem Elisa 26 528
Roemer, Georg 3 474
Roemer, Hermann 10 90, 93
Roemer-Pelizaeus-Museum see under HILDESHEIM
roemers see under GLASSES → types
Rōen Hayashi see HAYASHI RŌEN
Roenspiess, Klaus 26 528–9*
Roentgen (family) 25 121
Roentgen, Abraham (fl 1730; father) 26 529
Roentgen, Abraham (1711-93; son) 26 529*
collaboration 6 451
pupils 26 529
works 12 424
Roentgen, Conrad Wilhelm 24 669
Roentgen, David 26 529–30*
collaboration 33 672
patrons and collectors 17 639
pupils 33 48
works 5 192; 7 659; 12 424, 425, 426; 20 468; 26 530; 27 583
Roerich, Nicholas 26 530–31*; 27 392, 408
groups and movements 3 119; 12 870; 27 392; 33 379
productions 8 850; 30 686; 33 608
pupils 6 384
sponsors 30 464
teachers 18 502
works 27 410; 30 265; 33 607

Roerich, Svyatoslav **26** 531
Roerich Museum *see under* NEW YORK → museums
Roermond **22** 857, 860
Munsterkerk **22** 817, 829, 855
Roesen, Hendrik **19** 260
Roesen, Severin **26** 531*
Roeser, Martin **4** 888
Roesner, Karl *see* RÖSNER, KARL
Roessler, Arthur **26** 531–2*; **28** 89, *89*
Roesslin, Eucharius **21** 7
Roestraten, Pieter (Gerritsz.) van **22** 840; **26** 532*
collaboration **14** 94
patrons and collectors **20** 142
teachers **14** 95
works **3** 599
Roettgen *Pietà* **13** 116; **24** 775, *776*, 776
Roettiers (family) **10** 764
Roettiers, Charles Norbert **26** 532
Roettiers, Georges **26** 532
Roettiers, Jacques (1707-84) **11** 619; **24** 147; **26** 532*
Roettiers, Jacques-Nicolas **11** 620; **26** 532*; **27** 584
works **11** *620*
Roettiers, James (1663-98) **20** 923; **26** 532*
Roettiers, Jan **20** 923; **26** 532*
Roettiers, Joseph (1635-1703) **8** 533; **20** 922; **26** 532; **29** 29
Roettiers, Joseph Charles (i) (1691/2-1779) **26** 532
Roettiers, Joseph Charles (ii) (1722-1803) **26** 532
Roettiers, Norbert **20** 923; **26** 532*
Roettiers, Philip (i) (1596-1669) **26** 532*
Roettiers, Philip (ii) (1640-1718) **26** 532
Roettiers, Philip (iii) (*d* 1732) **26** 533
Roeyermans, Theodoor **3** 559
Rofe, John, & Sons **18** 67
Rofrano, Prince of **27** 201
Rogalin **25** 136, 138
Armoury **25** 139
Rogaška Slatina Church **28** *858*, 859
Rogat, Emile **20** 925
Rogatin *see* IVANO-FRANKOVSK
Rogé, Pierre **19** 849
Rogel, Hans, I (1532-92/3) **26** 533*; **29** 719
Rogel, Hans, II (1560-1613) **26** 533
Rogelet de le Pasture **5** 548; **8** 525; **33** 117, 119
Rögels, Andreas **21** 896
Rogendorf, Susanna von **19** 92
Rogent, Elías **11** 291; **26** 418, 533*
Rogent, Ramón **8** 538; **26** 533*
Roger **19** 382
Roger, Bishop of Salisbury **3** 443; **26** 611, 616; **27** 624
Roger, Master **10** 672
Roger I, Duke of Apulia *see* ROGER BORSA, Duke of Apulia
Roger II, Abbot of Mont-Saint-Michel **22** 40
Roger II, King of Naples and Sicily (*reg* 1130-54) **14** 240*; **26** 628
architecture **6** 131; **9** 581; **16** 171, *171*; **23** 843, 844, 846
embroidery **16** 759
mosaics **26** 680
rock crystal **16** 744
silk **16** 752
textiles **16** 430, *430*, 437; **32** 458
wall paintings **16** 253
Roger, Barthelemy Joseph Fulcran **29** 676
Roger, F. **14** 83
Roger, Pierre **10** 118
Roger, Suzanne **19** 66
Roger Borsa, Duke of Apulia (*reg* 1085-1111) **3** 235; **14** 240
Rogerius **26** 469, 533–4*, 625
Roger-Marx, Claude **20** 524; **26** 534*
Roger of Hauteville, Count of Naples and Sicily (*reg* 1072-1101) **28** 655
Roger of Helmarshausen **10** 203; **23** 749; **26** 534–5*, 681; **30** 710
works **1** 697; **14** 366; **26** *535*, 651, 675, 683
Roger of Melfi **9** 154
Roger of Pont l'Evêque, Archbishop of York **26** 614, 615
Roger of Salerno **21** 5
Rogers, Bruce **4** 8, 366; **26** 536*; **31** 496
Rogers, Charles (1711-84) **9** 230
Rogers, Charles (1816-91) **16** 855; **26** 231; **27** 463
Rogers, Claude **10** 375, 652; **24** 228
Rogers, Edward **16** 557
Rogers, Ernesto Nathan **3** 438, 439; **26** 536*, 539
groups and movements **7** 296; **8** 8; **12** 59; **30** 391
pupils **27** 192
writings **2** 727; **16** 650
Rogers, Fairman **10** 669
Rogers, Henry **15** 25
Rogers, Isaiah **7** 326; **26** 536–8*
staff **22** 275
works **14** 786, *787*; **23** 38; **26** *537*; **27** 613; **33** 195
Rogers, James Gamble **26** 538*
works **12** 927; **19** 319; **23** 25
Rogers, John (i) (*fl* 1533-*d* 1558) **26** 538–9*
Rogers, John (ii) (1829-1904) **26** 539*; **31** 611, 664
Rogers, Joseph, & Sons **16** 61
Rogers, Louis P. **18** 54
Rogers, Malcolm **10** 213
Rogers, Phil **32** 790
Rogers, Randolph **26** 539*; **31** 611
Rogers, Richard **26** 539–41*
collaboration **2** 578; **10** 417; **11** 332, 660; **14** 521; **16** 55; **22** 366; **24** 131, 697; **26** 333; **29** 526
competitions **7** 670
groups and movements **2** 309; **11** 332
works **1** 737; **10** 242, 285, 749; **11** 528; **19** 367, 578, 897; **24** *131*; **26** *540*; **32** 783
Rogers, R. P. **23** 426
Rogers, Samuel **26** 541*
books **7** 413
decorative works **6** 455
groups and movements **2** 576
illustrated writings **12** 925; **13** 304; **18** 723; **25** 753; **26** 473; **29** 732; **31** 471, 472
Rogers, Su **11** 332; **26** 540
Rogers, Thomas **14** 768
Rogers, W. Gibbs **10** 142
Rogers, William (i) (*fl* *c.* 1589-1604) **10** 162, 247, 389; **26** 542*; **28** 357
Rogers, William (ii) (*c.* 1685-1739) **26** 542*; **31** 635
Rogers, William (*fl* 1760) **27** 336
Rogers, William R. (*fl* 1882-8) **27** 223
Rogers, Woodes **3** 63
Rogers Bros **31** 650
Rogers Statuary Co. **26** 539
Roger the Dyer **6** 407
Roget, Nicolas **24** 296
Rogge, Cornelius (Hendrik) **26** 542*
Roggenburg Monastery **12** 372
Roggiani, Guido **24** 102
Roghera, Luigi **8** 134
Roghetti, Mario **9** 111
Roghman, Geertruydt **26** 542–3*
Roghman, Hendrick (Lambertsz.) **26** 542
Roghman, Magdalena **26** 542
Roghman, Roelant **13** 647; **26** 542, 543–4*
works **26** *543*
Rogić, M. **28** 451
Rogier **11** 643
Rogiers, Hans **1** 810
Roglösa Master **30** 109
Rogni, Giacomo **12** 169
Rogoff, I. **33** 313
Rogozen Treasure **13** 568, 570; **25** *471*; **26** 544*; **30** 770, 772
beakers **30** 771
phalerae **30** 772
silver **13** 568
Rogslösa Church **9** 156; **26** 691; **30** 109
doors **9** *155*
Roguié, Pierre **11** 81
Roguier, Henri-Victor **24** 63
Roh, Frank **20** 93
Roh, Jacob P. **31** 652
Rohan (family) **1** 133; **8** 422, 423; **19** 118
Books of Hours **20** 755
manuscripts **20** *756*
Rohan, Prince de **4** 225; **20** 131
Rohan, Armand Gaston Maximilien de, Cardinal **2** 495; **19** 118
Rohan, Edouard de, Cardinal **6** 509; **27** 623
Rohan, Emmanuel de **10** 843
Rohan, François de **19** 118
Rohan, Louis Constantine de, Cardinal **8** 651; **29** 753
Rohan, Mériadeck de, Archbishop of Bordeaux **4** 389
Rohan, Pierre de **26** 454; **28** 928
Rohan Hours *see under* BOOKS OF HOURS → individual manuscripts
Rohan Hours, Master of the **19** 238; **20** 755–6*
patrons and collectors **2** 113; **4** 827
works **20** 635, *756*
workshop **6** 503
Rohan-Soubise, Armand-Gaston I, Duc de **22** 436; **28** 743
Rohault de Fleury, Charles **26** 544, 545*
works **7** 745; **11** 523; **26** 545
Rohault de Fleury, Georges **26** 544
Rohault de Fleury, Hubert **26** 544–5*
Rohde, Frederik **14** 118
Rohde, Georg **25** 127
Rohde, Gilbert **15** 824; **26** 545*; **31** 632, 633, 653
Rohde, Hans **25** 127
Rohde, Johan (Gudmann) **8** 753; **17** 479; **26** 545–6*
groups and movements **7** 805; **11** 790
pupils **28** 54
Rohde, Olof Rennart **30** 81
Rohde, Piotr **20** 14
Rohden, Johann Martin von **12** 392; **26** 546*
Rohe, Ludwig Mies van der *see* MIES VAN DER ROHE, LUDWIG
Rohl, Peter **25** 350
Rohlfs, Charles **31** 632
Rohlfs, Christian **26** 546–7*; **33** 38
groups and movements **10** 694; **12** 394; **22** 746
patrons and collectors **11** 729
works **10** 695; **12** 395, 396
Röhling, Karl **13** 810
Rohm, Otto **1** 129
Rohm and Haas Co. **1** 129
Rohner, Georges **11** 302, 550, 644; **28** 750
Rohonc *see* RECHNITZ
Rohr, Bernhard von, Archbishop of Salzburg *see* BERNHARD VON ROHR, Archbishop of Salzburg
Rohr Abbey Church **1** 712, *712*; **2** 581; **12** 372; **29** 838; **32** 89
Rohrau Schloss **20** 456
Graf Harrach'sche Familiensammlung **14** 190, 191, *191*
Rohrbach, Ignác **8** 386
Rohrbach-Holzhausen (family) **20** 792
Rohrer (family) **31** 653
Rohrer, Johann Michael Ludwig **4** 890; **5** 349; **26** 547*; **27** 196; **33** 594
Rohrer, Johann Peter Ernst **33** 594
Rohrer, Michael Ludwig Anton **26** 547
Röhrs **8** 401
Rohtas
congregational mosque **15** 368
fort **15** 368
palace **15** 368, *369*
Shergarh *see* fort
Roig, Carlos Mani i *see* MANI I ROIG, CARLOS
Roiles, Richard *see* ROYLEY, RICHARD
Roilos, Georgios **8** 602; **13** 352, 360; **26** 548*
Roissy, Charles de Gaulle Aérogare 1 **1** 495
Roisy, Claude de *see* DORICI, CLAUDE, I
Roiter, Fulvio **8** 123; **26** 548*
Roiz, António *see* RODRIGUES, ANTÓNIO
Rojankovsky, Feodor **4** 368
Rojas, Arístides **32** 178
Rojas (Luna y Saldaña), Bernardo de **26** 548*
Rojas, Carlos **7** 610
Rojas, Cecilio Guzmán de *see* GUZMÁN DE ROJAS, CECILIO
Rojas, Cristóbal (*b* 1858) **26** 548*; **32** 174, 178
Rojas, Cristóbal de (*fl* 1513) **8** 237
Rojas, Cristóbal de (1555-1614) **14** 476; **26** 548–9*; **29** 268
Rojas, Elmar (René) **5** 356; **13** 765; **25** 826; **26** 549*
works **13** *765*
Rojas, Eufrasio López de *see* LÓPEZ DE ROJAS, EUFRASIO
Rojas, Fernando de **20** 744
Rojas, Francisco Gómez de Sandoval y *see* LERMA, FRANCISCO GÓMEZ DE SANDOVAL Y ROJAS, Duque de
Rojas, Juan de **21** 383
Rojas, Miguel Angel **7** 610
Rojas, Pablo de **22** 1; **26** 549*
Rojas Luna, Fernando de **4** 258
Rojas Troyo, Ramon **13** 771
Rojo, Vicente **21** 389, 406; **26** 549*
Rojowski, Wojciech **25** 114
Rokeby Hall (N. Yorks) **23** 857; **24** 633
Rokeby *Venus* **1** 528; **5** 71; **12** 839; **13** 708; **32** 3
Rokh, Yury *see* LUKOMSKY, GEORGY (KRESKENT'YEVICH)
Rokhin, Vladimir **27** 434
Rokkaku, Kijō **26** 549–50*
Rokkaku Jakusai **31** 199
Rokkoyō *see* SIX OLD KILNS
Rokotov, Fyodor (Stepanovich) **26** 550–51*; **27** 388, 442, 579
patrons and collectors **27** 438; **31** 312
reproductive prints by others **28** 823
works **26** *551*
Roksandić, Simeon **28** 453
Rokubei V **26** 551
Rokubei VI **26** 551
Rokubei Kiyomizu I *see* KIYOMIZU ROKUBEI I
Rokujō-Madenokōji workshop **15** 158
Rokujuen *see* ISHIKAWA MASAMOCHI
Rokurōbei Rengyō **17** 160
Rokuwa **26** 551
Rokuzan *see* OGIWARA, MORIE
Rokyts'kyi, Mykola **2** 634
ROLACO **29** 321
rølakan tapestries *see under* TAPESTRIES → types
Roland, Jean-Marie **11** 666
Roland, M. **8** 787
Roland, Philippe-Laurent **19** 381; **26** 551–2*
assistants **7** 915
groups and movements **24** 171
pupils **8** 564; **10** 509
works **11** 627; **30** 496
Roland de la Porte, Henri Horace **26** 552*
works **11** 411; **29** 668
Roland Holst, Richard *see* HOLST, RICHARD (NIKOLAÜS) ROLAND
Roldán (family) **26** 552*
Roldán, Gutiérrez **21** 395
Roldán, Luisa **26** 552, 553*; **29** 292; **30** 495; **33** 308
Roldán, Marcelino **26** 553
Roldán, Pedro **16** 863; **26** 552–3*; **29** 292
attributions **29** 345
collaboration **16** 863; **24** 822
patrons and collectors **13** 880; **28** 515
pupils **9** 407; **26** 553
teachers **21** 109
works **9** 699; **16** 863; **20** 234; **26** 553; **28** 520; **31** 810
Roldana, la *see* ROLDÁN, LUISA
Roldán Villavicencio, Francisca **9** 407
Rolduc Abbey **22** 817, 855; **26** 574; **30** 907
Rolex **7** 448
Rolfsen, Alf **23** 226, 603; **26** 553–4*
Rolfsen, Nordahl **9** 751
Rolim, Antonio Pimenta **19** 523; **26** 554*
Rolin, Antoine **26** 554, 556*
Rolin, Guiguionne de Salins **26** 555
Rolin, Guillaume **26** 554, 555*
Rolin, Jean I (*fl* 14th cent.) **26** 554
Rolin, Jean II, Cardinal (1408-83) **26** 554, 555–6*
architecture **2** 840, 841
decorative works **29** 398
manuscripts **11** 726; **20** 700
paintings **20** 733
sculpture **13** 78; **17** 676
Rolin, Jean III, Canon (*d* 1501) **26** 556
Rolin, Jehanne **26** 556
Rolin, Nicolas **26** 554–5*
architecture **26** 555
interior decoration **26** *555*
paintings **3** 612; **10** 707; **14** 784; **33** 120
tiles **11** 603
Röling, Marte **22** 854
Rolin Master *see* JEAN ROLIN, MASTER OF
Roll, Alfred(-Philippe) **26** 558*
pupils **3** 43; **8** 34; **9** 382; **10** 648; **22** 136; **26** 480; **33** 76
Roll, Franz Viktor Augustin von **3** 7
Roll, Glenn **30** 113
Rolland, Benjamin **14** 283; **19** 254
Rolland, F. **12** 650
Rolland, Louis **20** 517
roll-and-fillet mouldings *see under* MOULDINGS → types
Roller, Alfred **17** 691, 744; **22** 187; **28** 344
Roller, The *see* ZAḶĀ VĀRNA
Rollet, Philippe **26** 261
Rollett, Hermann **14** 285

roll film *see under* FILM → types
roll film cameras *see under* CAMERAS → types
Rollin, Charles **15** 84; **22** 415
Rollin, Guillaume **5** 445
Rollin, Paul **25** 817
Rollin & Feuardent **10** 91
rolling **21** 323
rolling presses *see under* PRESSES → types
roll mouldings *see under* MOULDINGS → types
Rollos, Philip, the elder (*c.* 1660-1721) **10** 328, 329; **14** 485; **19** 593; **26** 558*
Rollos, Philip, the younger (*fl* 1705-*d* after 1720) **26** 558
rolls **4** 342; **12** 272; **26** 556–8*
 historical and regional traditions
  China **6** 736; **7** 63; **20** 326
  Egypt, ancient **4** *341*, 342; **10** 4, 5, 6, 7; **20** 329; **24** 88; **26** 557, *557*
  England **12** 273; **14** 423
  Greece, ancient **4** 342; **20** 329; **26** 556, 557
  Indian subcontinent **15** 731
  Islamic **16** 271
  Jewish art **26** 557
  Mesopotamia **20** *326*
  Rome, ancient **4** 342; **20** 329; **26** 556, 557
  Switzerland **12** 272
 individual manuscripts
  Guthlac Roll (London, BL, Harley Roll Y.6) **27** 592
  Hyghalmen Roll (London, Coll. Arms., 1st MS. 5) **14** 415
  Islip Roll (London, Lambeth Pal. Lib.) **27** 124
  Joshua Roll (Rome, Vatican, Bib. Apostolica, MS. Pal. gr. 431) **4** 5; **17** 664*; **19** 887
  Sant'Angelo in Formis Regesto (Montecassino Abbey, Archv, MS. Regesto 4) **26** 665
  Selden Roll (Oxford, Bodleian Lib.) **21** 184
  Vitalis Roll (Paris, Archvs. N., AE. II-138) **27** 887
 materials
  bamboo **20** 326
  leather **4** 342; **10** 5; **26** 557
  papyrus **4** *341*, 342; **10** 5, 7; **20** 329; **24** 88; **26** 556–7, *557*
  parchment **4** 342; **26** 557
  wood **20** 326
 types
  exultet **10** 700–701*; **26** 665; **27** 615
 see also MANUSCRIPTS; SCROLLS
Rolls, Charles **8** 549; **29** 691
roll-top desks *see under* DESKS → types
Rolong **19** 241
Rolph, Ernest Ross **29** 435*
Rolshoven, Julius **9** 468
Roluos **2** 54; **5** *458*, 464; **26** 558*; **29** *225*
 Bakong **5** *458*, 465, 466, *466*, 481, 485, 486
 Hariharālaya **5** *458*
 Loley **5** 466, 467
 Loley Baray **5** 464, 466
 Preah Ko **5** *458*, 465–6*, *465*; **29** 826
 stucco **29** 826
Roma **13** 50
Romá, José **10** 509
Romadin, Nikolay (Mikhaylovich) **27** 396
Roma futurista **11** 869; **26** 776
Romain, Jacques **14** 60
Romain-Defosses, Pierre **1** 431; **33** 596, 598
Romainmôtier Abbey
 church **5** 796; **7** 266; **26** 635; **30** 129
 gate-house **12** 174
Romains, Jules **26** 558–9*
 groups and movements **1** 21; **8** 243
 productions **31** 832
 works **2** 615
Romako, Anton **2** 797; **26** 559*; **32** 445
 works **26** *559*
roman *see under* TYPE-FACES
Román, Bartolomé **5** 873; **14** 6; **26** 560*
Román, Ernő **13** 889
Roman, Jacob (Pietersz) **26** 560*
 collaboration **8** 834; **22** 826
 patrons and collectors **20** 458
 works **14** 495; **22** *825*, 826; **23** 466
Roman, Jean **25** 704
Román, Nelson **9** 713, 714; **16** 806, 834
Roman, Pieter **26** 560; **28** 49
Román (Rojas), Samuel **6** 598; **26** 560–61*
Romana, La *see* LA ROMANA
Romañach, Leopoldo **24** 334; **25** 208
Romañach, Mario **8** 232
Roman Catholicism *see under* CHRISTIANITY → branches
romance manuscripts **14** 423; **20** 342; **26** 561–4*
 Belgium **26** 563*
 Byzantine **9** 519
 England **26** 564*
 France **14** 408; **26** 561–3*
 Germany **26** 563–4*
 Gothic **12** *107*; **13** 130
 Italy **26** 564*
 Romanesque **26** 662
 Spain **26** 563
 see also MANUSCRIPTS
Roman cement *see under* CEMENT → types
Roman Club **2** 164; **18** 142
Roman de la Rose of Valencia, Master of the **5** 208
Romandon, Abraham **14** 650; **26** 564
Romandon, Gedeon **3** 798; **14** 650; **26** 564*
Romanelli, Bartolomeo **26** 564
Romanelli, Ferdinando **16** 730
Romanelli, Gaspare **26** 564–5*
Romanelli, Giovanni Francesco **3** 834; **9** 93; **16** 673; **19** 265; **26** 565–6*, 773
 attributions **3** 96, 97
 collaboration **2** 92; **4** 491; **13** 656; **19** 248; **24** 476; **26** 837
 patrons and collectors **3** 206, 207; **6** 508; **9** 22; **20** 895; **22** 21
 teachers **7** 913
 works **2** 200; **11** 574; **15** 138; **18** 735; **26** *565*, 778, 810, 837, 838; **27** 160; **29** 833; **30** 322
Romanelli, Mariano d'Agnolo **28** 681
Romanelli, Pasquale **16** 706
Romanelli, Raffaele (*fl* late 16th cent.) **26** 564
Romanelli, Raffaello (*b* 1856) **9** 131
Romanescu, Eleonora **21** 812
Romanesque **26** 566–703*
 acanthus **1** 110
 alabaster (gypsum) **10** 227
 altarpieces **1** *708*
 altars **10** *113*; **26** *535*; **29** IX1
 alternating systems **26** 569, 571
 ambulatories **1** 767, *767*; **8** 223; **26** 571
 antependia **29** 275
 apses **5** 371
 aquamanilia **26** 685–6*
 arcades **4** 141; **26** 569
 arches **2** 292, 294, 295, 296, 298*
  relieving **2** 295
 architectural decorations **6** 564; **10** 228
Romanesque—cont.
 architecture **26** 568–94
  Belarus' **3** 526
  Belgium **31** 220
  Catalonia **5** 734
  Cistercian Order **26** 590, 592
  Croatia **8** 175; **26** 594
  Czech Republic **8** 376; **26** 594
  Denmark **26** 304, 592–3*
  England **2** 67; **19** 600; **23** 211; **26** 587–90*
  First Romanesque **26** 576, 577, 580
  France **4** 780; **11** 509–10*; **24** 104; **26** 571, 582–6*; **27** 566; **31** 224
   Normandy **23** 211
  Germany **12** 363–4*; **17** 482; **26** 571–5*
  Holy Roman Empire (before 1648) **26** 570, 571–5*
  Hungary **26** 594
  Ireland **5** 915, 916; **7** 459; **12** 807–8; **16** 7; **26** 592*
  Italy **16** 625–7*; **26** 575–80*, *579*
  Netherlands, the **22** 816–18*
  Norman *see* England; France; Sicily
  Norway **26** 593
  Ottonian **26** 571
  Poland **25** 94; **26** 594
  Portugal **25** 289
  Russia **26** 594
  Sardinia **27** 836
  Scandinavia **26** 592–3*
  Scotland **26** 591*
  Second Romanesque **26** 574
  Sicily **16** 171, 626–7; **28** 655
  Slovakia **28** 849
  Slovenia **28** 857–8
  Spain **26** 580–82*; **29** 262–3
  Sweden **26** 592–3*
  Transitional style **31** 283
  Wales **26** 587–90*
 archivolts **19** *405*
 articulation **26** 568
 astronomical manuscripts **26** 661
 baleen **23** *539*
 baptisteries **3** *192*; **11** *199*
 bays **26** 569
 beakheads **3** *443*; **26** 589, 612, 616
 bells **26** 686*
 Bestiaries **26** 661
 Bibles **4** 6–7; **26** 660, 666, 676
 billets **4** 63, *63*
 bookbindings **4** 348
 book covers **4** *350*, 351; **23** *539*; **26** 695
 bosses **4** *465*
 brass **26** 684–6*
 bronze **26** *145*, *146*, 690
  England **10** 322
  France **26** *682*
  Germany **26** *535*
  Holy Roman Empire (before 1648) **26** 684–6*, *685*
 candelabra **26** 686*
 candlesticks **26** 624, *682*, *688*
 capitals **5** *670*; **26** 569
  Britain **26** 611
  Catalonia **26** *610*; **27** *568*
  cushion **26** 573, *573*, 587
  England **26** 615–16
  France **5** *372*; **7** *232*, *477*; **17** *686*; **19** *224*; **22** *115*; **25** *88*; **26** 596, 597–9, *598*, *599*, *601*, 601–2, *610*; **27** 534, *534*, *552*; **31** *211*, 225
  Germany **26** *573*
  historiated **27** *534*
  Netherlands, the **19** *863*
  Sicily **21** *900*
  Spain **19** *177*; **26** *605*, 606–7; **28** *727*
  volute **10** 168, *169*
 carpets **14** 65
Romanesque—cont.
 castles **9** *203*; **10** 227; **26** 569–70; **32** *883*
 cathedrals **26** 570
  Austria **13** *857*
  Belgium **31** *221*
  England **9** *449*, *450*; **10** *166*; **12** *5*; **23** *250*, 250; **26** *588*, *589*; **27** *526*; **33** *235*
  France **2** *321*; **5** 388; **11** *509*; **26** *584*
  Germany **12** *364*; **20** *128*; **26** *575*; **29** *392*; **31** *326*
  Italy **12** *280*; **19** *766*; **21** *772*; **23** *585*; **24** *193*, *288*, *855*, *856*, *857*; **26** *576*; **32** *185*, *206*
  Montenegro **22** *18*
  Poland **18** 430
  Portugal **19** *462*
  Romania **26** 706
  Russia **26** *594*
  Sicily **21** *898*; **23** *843*; **27** *614*
  Spain **26** *581*
  Sweden **19** *795*
  Wales **27** *537*
 ceilings **26** 569
 censers **6** 173, *174*
 chalices **6** *398*
 chapels **26** 569
  England **33** *542*
  Germany **26** 574
  Ireland **26** *592*
  Spain **19** *177*
  two-storey **5** 371
 chapter houses **6** *464*
 chevets (chapels) **26** 572
 chevrons **6** 564, *565*
 choir-stalls **7** 190
 chronicles **26** 662
 chrysography **7** *246*
 churches **7** 265–6*
  basilicas **7** *253*
  Belgium **12** 520; **23** *164*
  Catalonia **5** *734*
  centrally planned **7** 257
  Denmark **8** *722*; **26** *593*
  England **10** 227–9, *228*; **12** 818; **19** *601*, *617*; **23** *685*; **26** *589*
  France **5** *370*, *371*; **7** *232*; **11** *529*; **17** *685*; **19** *527*; **23** *14*; **24** *103*; **25** *87*; **26** *122*; **31** *207*, *209*, *224*, 224; **32** *396*, *464*
  Germany **1** *723*; **7** *591*, *594*; **9** *688*; **14** *533*, *534*; **17** *483*; **26** *572*, *573*
  hall **26** 585
  Hungary **16** *872*
  Ireland **12** *807*
  Italy **2** *389*; **3** *235*; **4** *281*, *748*; **11** *210*; **16** *626*; **21** *535*; **26** *577*, *833*; **31** *316*
  Netherlands, the **19** 862; **22** *816*, *818*
  Palestine **17** *499*
  Poland **29** *793*
  Portugal **25** 289
  Scotland **27** *529*; **28** *223*
  sepulchre **28** *427*, *428*
  Spain **19** *175*, *520*
 cities **26** 570
 cloisters **3** 333, *716*; **7** 454–5*, *455*; **21** *899*; **26** *604*
 columns **21** *900*; **26** 569, 595; **29** *793*
 combs (liturgical) **7** *646*
 copper **10** 322; **26** 686*
 craftsmen and artists **26** 594
 crosiers **8** *194*; **26** *687*
 crosses **26** 618, *697*
 crucifixes
  England **10** 338
  Holy Roman Empire (before 1648) **26** 684–5
  Italy **8** *211*
  Spain **26** *643*, 698
  Sweden **26** *647*; **30** 83
Romanesque—cont.
 crypts **7** 265; **8** 223–4, *224*; **14** *501*; **26** 569, 572; **29** 391
 devotional images **8** 835
 diaper **8** 856
 dictionaries **10** 212
 domes **9** 84, 85; **26** 584
 donjons **10** 227
 door fittings **10** 338; **26** 691
 doors
  Austria **9** *152*
  England **10** *169*
  France **26** 641
  Holy Roman Empire (before 1648) **26** 684*
  Italy **16** 687; **32** *342*
  Sweden **9** *155*
 doorways **10** *169*; **18** *50*
 drawings **28** 497
 effigies **11** *290*; **26** *606*
 embroidery **15** 11; **26** 703
 enamel **26** *146*, 691–4*
  Belgium **26** 692–3*, *693*
  champlevé **10** 194, IV2; **26** *692*, *693*
  Denmark **26** 694*
  England **10** 322; **26** 694*
  France **7** 720; **26** 691–2*, *692*
  Germany **26** 693–4*
  Poland **26** 687
  Spain **26** 691–2*
 entasis **10** 415
 façade decoration **10** 742–3
 façades **5** 371, *371*
 flint **10** 227
 floors **26** 680
 fonts (baptismal) **10** 338; **26** 613, *640*, 684*; **30** 83
 fountain houses **21** *899*
 fountains **26** *623*
 galleries (i) (upper storey internal area) **26** 572
 galleries (ii) (corridors) **12** 364
 gems **26** *145*
 gilding **1** *708*; **26** *145*, *146*, *535*; **29** IX1
 gold **10** 322; **19** 351; **26** 683*, 703; **28** *631*
 grand appareil **26** 569
 granges **25** 668
 granite **10** 227; **26** *606*
 half-shafts **26** 571, 573
 halls **10** 227; **19** *401*
 herbals **26** 661
 hinges **9** 155
 houses **10** 227
 iconography **7** 224; **26** 605, 616, 651, 654–5*, 702
 initials (manuscript) **9** *257*; **15** 847; **26** 663–4
  Belgium **26** 666
  England **15** *847*; **20** *341*, V1; **26** 663, 664; **27** *591*; **33** *239*
  France **15** *848*
  Italy **26** 666
 iron **9** *155*; **26** 691
 ivory **26** *146*
 ivory-carvings **7** *646*; **8** *194*; **16** *798*; **23** *539*; **26** 695–9*, *696*, *697*, *699*; **29** IX1
 leather **4** *350*, 351
 limestone **7** *477*, *478*; **11** *290*, *554*; **26** *614*, *615*; **28** *727*, *728*; **31** *211*
  England **10** 227
 linen **26** 703
 manuscript illumination **19** 351; **26** 658–77*
  Austria **2** 790–91*; **26** 674–5*
  Belgium **26** 666–8*
  England **5** *428*; **10** 243–4*; **26** 670–73*, 677*; **27** *528*; **33** *233*
  France **10** *201*; **26** 668–70*, 677*; **27** *247*
  Germany **26** 673–4*, 675*; **33** *293*
  Italy **26** 664–6*
  Spain **26** 675–6*

Romanesque
manuscript illumination—cont.
Transitional style 26 677*
manuscripts 14 398; 20 330–31*
marble 2 132; 3 237; 5 550; 21 773; 26 576; 31 209
masonry 26 569, 574
masons 26 595
medical books 26 661
metalwork 26 681*, 686–7*
Belgium 26 682–3*
England 10 338; 26 687–8*, 688
France 7 720; 26 681–2*
Holy Roman Empire (before 1648) 26 683–6*
Hungary 26 687, 687
Ireland 26 688–9*
Italy 26 690*
Poland 26 687
Portugal 26 690*
Scandinavia 26 690–91*
Scotland 26 689*
Spain 26 689*
miniatures (manuscript illumination) 21 637
Austria 2 790; 26 676
Belgium 26 667
England 4 6; 5 288; 10 244; 26 670, 671, 672
France 26 668, 677
Germany 26 673, 674, 675
Italy 10 700; 22 11; 26 664, 665
Spain 26 676
monasteries 26 570
Austria 19 377
Cistercian Order 21 88
Cluniac Order 7 476
England 33 551
France 7 476; 26 583; 27 560, 566
Ireland 21 88
Poland 29 792; 32 749
mosaics 22 163; 26 679, 679–81*
France 26 681
Germany 26 681
Italy 21 898; 26 679–80, 679, 680, 828
Sicily 6 133; 23 844, 846; 26 679, 680
mouldings 22 211, 215–16*, 218, 220; 26 569
angle-fillet 22 213–15
face roll 22 214
hollow roll 22 214
narratives 22 520
oliphants 23 401; 26 698
orders (architecture) 23 485
ornament 23 538
painters 26 656–7*
painting 26 648–77*
Austria 2 790–91*
Czech Republic 8 388
France 11 529–30*
Germany 12 382
grisaille 26 702
Norway 23 223
panel 12 382
Spain 29 275; 30 368
wall 6 564; 26 648–57*; 32 805*, 808
Austria 2 790*; 3 711; 18 668; 26 650, 650, 653
Belgium 26 648
Czech Republic 8 389
Denmark 8 730; 26 648
England 26 650, 652, 652
France 11 529; 26 650, 651; 27 590
Georgia 8 567
Germany 26 649, 651, 653
Italy 1 819; 7 364; 26 650–51, 651, 652–3, 826; 27 784
Norway 23 223
Serbia 28 445
Spain 19 177; 26 653; 28 695; 30 368
Sweden 30 75
palaces 12 245
patens 6 398
Romanesque—cont.
patronage 26 595, 656*, 659–60*
petit appareil 26 569
piers (ii) (masonry) 24 749, 750, 750–51; 26 569; 27 567; 33 547
pilasters 26 569, 577
pinnacles 24 826
plaques 7 718; 26 696, 699
polychromy 26 647
porphyry 29 IX1
portals
Denmark 8 737
France 2 728; 4 581; 29 94
Ireland 26 618
Italy 24 858; 26 620
Poland 26 636
porch 20 820; 21 773; 26 621; 33 188
Spain 2 866; 19 176; 27 795
portraits 5 641; 20 341; 26 662
Psalters 26 660, 662
pulpits 16 688; 21 774; 26 626, 627
red lead 24 796
regionalism (i) (geographic variation) 26 571
reliquaries 10 IV2; 26 145, 145–6*, 146, 683, 692, 693
ribbons 26 703
rolls 26 665
romance manuscripts 26 662
roofs 26 569; 30 905, 907
ropework 27 139
saints' lives 26 661
sanctuaries 26 569
sandstone 10 227; 22 855; 25 109
screens (i) (architectural) 21 774
scripts 28 305
sculptors 26 595
sculpture 7 454–5*; 8 835; 22 520; 26 594–648*
animal subjects 26 617
architectural 10 742–3
Austria 26 634
Belgium 31 222
England 5 645–6, 646; 10 169; 18 50, 50
France 2 841, 842, 842; 4 581; 26 596, 596; 27 534
Italy 10 742; 21 773
Scotland 26 617*
Spain 27 796
Austria 2 798*; 26 634–5*
Belgium 26 630–31*, 644–5*
Britain 26 611–12*
bronze 26 685
Catalonia 26 605, 609–10*
column statues 6 403; 7 642; 26 602
Croatia 8 177
Czech Republic 26 637–8*
Denmark 8 737–8; 26 304, 640*
England 7 455; 19 405; 26 613–17*, 643–4*
First Romanesque 26 594
France 2 728; 7 454; 26 596–7*, 599, 600–601*, 641*; 31 225
Auvergne 26 601*
Burgundy (region) 26 601–2*
First Romanesque 26 609
Languedoc 26 602–3*
Loire Valley 26 598–9*
Normandy 26 597–8*
Provence 26 603–4*
Roussillon 26 604*, 609–10*
Germany 12 399; 26 632–3*, 634*
Holy Roman Empire (before 1648) 26 631–5*, 634, 645–6*, 684–5*, 685
Hungary 26 636, 638*
Ireland 7 458; 26 618–19*
Italy 2 132; 7 455; 16 687–8*; 26 595, 619*, 625–6*, 644*
Abruzzi 26 625*
Emilia-Romagna 26 621*
Lazio 26 624*
Romanesque
sculpture
Italy—cont.
Lombardy 26 620*
Tuscany 26 622–4*
Umbria 26 625*
Veneto 26 622*
Jerusalem, Latin Kingdom of 26 629*
monumental 2 798
Netherlands, the 26 630–31*, 644–5*
Norway 26 639*, 644; 29 580; 31 364
palmesels 26 641, 646
Poland 25 109–10; 26 636–7*
Portugal 26 611*, 648*
relief
Croatia 8 177
Czech Republic 8 382
Denmark 26 305
England 19 404, 405; 26 614
France 7 224; 21 798, 799; 29 94; 31 209; 32 397
Hungary 24 314
Italy 3 236; 5 550; 11 6; 21 774; 24 194, 195; 26 623, 627; 32 344
marble 5 550
Netherlands, the 22 855
Poland 29 793
Spain 2 866, 867; 26 608; 28 728
Sweden 26 640
religious
Belgium 26 645
England 26 615
France 7 478; 11 554
Germany 26 632
Holy Roman Empire (before 1648) 26 632
Spain 26 643
Scandinavia 26 639–40*, 646–7*
Sicily 26 619, 628–9*
Spain 7 455; 26 604–5*, 606–7*, 608–9*, 642–3*; 28 727–8; 29 288
stone 26 594–5*, 596–9*, 596, 600–603*, 604–5*, 606–7*, 608, 608–10*, 611–12*, 613–17*, 617, 618, 618–19*, 620*, 620, 621*, 622–4*, 625*, 626–9*, 630–38*, 632, 634, 636, 639–40*, 640
Sweden 19 796; 26 639*; 30 83
Switzerland 26 635*
Wales 26 617–18*
wood 26 640–41*, 642–7*, 643, 645, 648*
shafts (column) 26 569
shafts (wall) 26 589–90
shields 14 405
shrines (i) (cult) 2 867; 26 699; 28 631
signatures 26 595
silk 26 703
silver 6 173, 174; 26 145, 683*
silver-gilt 6 398
stained glass 19 129; 26 700, 700–702*, 701, 703
stone 8 382; 26 594–5*, 596–9*, 596, 600–605*, 606–7*, 608, 608–10*, 611–12*, 613–17*, 617, 618, 618–19*, 620*, 620, 621*, 622–4*, 625–9*, 630–38*, 632, 634, 636, 639–40*
stone-carvings 4 465; 26 594–5
stucco 12 399; 26 632
styles
First Romanesque 26 571
see also OTTONIAN
Norman style 23 211*; 26 361
Second Romanesque 26 571
symbolism (critical term) 26 662–3, 700–701
tapestries 14 65; 26 703
textiles 26 703*
thick-wall structures 5 370, 371; 10 228; 30 728–9, 729
Romanesque—cont.
thrones 3 237; 16 688; 30 777
tirtei 26 703
tombs 11 290; 26 628–9, 684*
towers 10 227
transepts 31 281
treatises 26 657
tympana
Austria 27 663
Denmark 26 305
England 10 169; 18 50
France 7 224, 719; 11 554; 26 600
Italy 11 6
Netherlands, the 26 630
Poland 25 109
Spain 19 176; 27 796
typological cycles 26 662
vaults (ceiling) 26 569
barrel 26 569, 581; 32 88
England 9 449, 450; 19 402; 26 589–90
France 26 586
Germany 26 575
groin 26 569
nave 26 586
quadrant 32 89
rib 26 569, 578, 586, 589; 32 92
wall passages 5 371; 26 569, 574
weaving 26 703
westworks 26 569, 574; 33 109
wood 9 152; 26 569, 640–41*, 642–7*, 643, 645, 647, 648*
wood-carvings 26 641
wool 26 703
Romanesque Revival 4 787; 26 704*; 27 336
Honduras 14 713
Hungary 14 890
Portugal 28 731
United States of America 3 128; 23 40; 26 212, 213; 31 592
see also NORMAN REVIVAL
Romanet, Antoine Louis 20 914
Romani, Romolo 16 680
Romania 16 103; 26 704–26*, 705
academies 5 73
altars 26 711, 718
amber 1 761; 7 90
architectural history 12 547
architecture 26 706–10*
armorial bearings 14 424
banks 26 709
beadwork 3 442
beakers 30 771
book covers 26 720
book illustrations 14 424
brick 26 706
bronze 30 769
carpets 16 466
castles 14 880
cathedrals 26 706
ceramics 26 718–19*
chairs 26 717–18
churches 5 72; 8 279; 26 706–7, 706, 708, 708, 710, 711–12
decoration 26 712
rock 26 483
coats of arms 14 424
collections 5 73; 26 722–3*, 725*
concrete 26 709
copper 26 714
coral 3 442
doors 26 718
drawings 26 715, 716
education (art) 5 73; 26 725–6*
embroidery 26 720–21*, 721
epitaphioi 26 721
etchings 26 716
exhibitions 5 74, 634
fortifications 21 551; 26 707
fortresses 26 706
forts 26 707
furniture 26 717–18*
glass 26 718–19*
grain elevators 26 709•
helmets 30 770
heraldry 14 411, 424
houses 26 707–8
Romania—cont.
icons 25 340–41*
interior decoration 26 717–18*
iron 30 769
jewellery 26 719–20*
libraries 26 725*
manuscript illumination 26 711
medallions 26 715
metalwork 26 719–20*; 30 770, 771
museums 26 724–5*
painting 26 710–11*, 712, 712–13*, 714, 715*, 716
fresco 26 710
wall 25 344*; 26 707, 710–11, 711, 712, 712–13
20th cent. 26 715
palls 26 720–21
patens 26 720, 720
patronage 26 722–3*
pews 26 718
portraits 13 652; 26 713, 714
pottery 25 514
printing 16 360
prints 26 715
reconstruction 26 706
rock art 25 475
screens (i) (architectural) 26 718
sculpture 26 710*, 711–12*, 713*, 714–15*, 716*
shields 14 424
silver 26 720; 30 770, 771
silver-gilt 26 720
stained glass 13 189
swords 30 769
tapestries 26 721–2
textiles 26 720–22*
thrones 26 717, 717–18
tracery 26 707
vaults (ceiling) 26 707
weaving 26 721–2*
wood 26 706, 717
wood-carvings 25 584; 26 712
woodcuts 26 716
Romanian Art (Arta Românǎ) 5 74; 26 716
Romanino, Alessandro 22 107
Romanino, Gerolamo 4 748; 26 726–8*
assistants 12 29
attributions 22 107; 24 699
collaboration 4 195; 9 185; 11 236; 22 107; 24 699
patrons and collectors 7 775
pupils 21 93; 27 148
works 5 180; 25 249; 26 727
Romanism 9 462; 22 836; 26 728–9*
Roman Master 2 622
Romano, il see ARENA, GIUSEPPE D'
Romano, Andrea 28 476
Romano, Antoniazzo see ANTONIAZZO ROMANO
Romano, Arturo 31 66
Romano, Bernardo see BERNARDO ROMANO
Romano, Clare 7 558
Romano, Evangelista see EVANGELISTA ROMANO
Romano, Gaspare 28 476
Romano, Gian Cristoforo see GIAN CRISTOFORO ROMANO
Romano, Giovanni 16 775
Romano, Giovanni Cristoforo see GIAN CRISTOFORO ROMANO
Romano, Girolamo di see ROMANINO, GEROLAMO
Romano, Giulio see GIULIO ROMANO
Romano, Luzio 24 419, 420
Romano, Marcantonio see MARCANTONIO ROMANO
Romano, Marco see MARCO ROMANO
Romano, Nardo see NARDO ROMANO
Romano, Paolo see PAOLO ROMANO

Romano, Pietro Paolo *see* GALEOTTI, PIETRO PAOLO
Romano, Salvator **28** 745
Romanoff, Boris **14** 776
Romano-Gothic style **22** 819, *819*
Romanos I Lekapenos, Emperor of Byzantium (*reg* 920-44) **9** 576, *637*, 638, 657; **16** 582; **28** 436
coins **9** *636*
Romanos II, Emperor of Byzantium (*reg* 959-63) **9** 661; **19** 886
Romanos III Argyros, Emperor of Byzantium (*reg* 1028-34) **9** 638; **16** 582
Romanos Melodos **24** 776
Romanov (House of) **22** 180; **26** 729*
Romanov, Aleksey Aleksandrovich, Grand Duke **21** 177
Romanov, Aleksey Mikhaylovich, Tsar of Moscow *see* ALEKSEY, Tsar of Moscow
Romanov, Alexander I, Emperor of Russia *see* ALEXANDER I, Emperor of Russia
Romanov, Alexander II, Emperor of Russia *see* ALEXANDER II, Emperor of Russia
Romanov, Alexander III, Emperor of Russia *see* ALEXANDER III, Emperor of Russia
Romanov, Alexandra Fyodorovna, Empress of Russia *see* ALEXANDRA FYODOROVNA, Empress of Russia
Romanov, Catherine II, Empress of Russia *see* CATHERINE II, Empress of Russia
Romanov, Charlotte Alexandra of Hohenzollern *see* ALEXANDRA FYODOROVNA, Empress of Russia
Romanov, Elizabeth, Empress of Russia *see* ELIZABETH, Empress of Russia
Romanov, Elizabeth Alekseyevna, Empress of Russia *see* ELIZABETH ALEKSEYEVNA, Empress of Russia
Romanov, Elizabeth Fyodorovna, Grand Duchess **28** 572
Romanov, Elizabeth of Baden, Empress of Russia *see* ELIZABETH ALEKSEYEVNA, Empress of Russia
Romanov, K. K. **10** 889
Romanov, Konstantin Pavlovich, Grand Duke **23** 530
Romanov, Maria, Princess of Hesse *see* MARIA ALEXANDROVNA, Empress of Russia
Romanov, Maria, Princess of Württemberg *see* MARIA FYODOROVNA, Empress of Russia
Romanov, Maria Alexandrovna, Empress of Russia *see* MARIA ALEXANDROVNA, Empress of Russia
Romanov, Maria Fyodorovna, Empress of Russia *see* MARIA FYODOROVNA, Empress of Russia
Romanov, Michael (Feodorovich), Tsar of Russia *see* MICHAEL (FEODOROVICH), Tsar of Russia
Romanov, Mikhail Mikhaylovich, Grand Duke (*fl* 1880-1900) **21** 177
Romanov, Mikhail Pavlovich, Grand Duke (1798-1849) **27** 198
Romanov, Natal'ya Alekseyevna **27** *388*
Romanov, Nicholas I, Emperor of Russia *see* NICHOLAS I, Emperor of Russia
Romanov, Nicholas II, Emperor of Russia *see* NICHOLAS II, Emperor of Russia
Romanov, Nikolay Konstantinovich, Grand Duke **6** 283
Romanov, Nikolay Y. **18** 899; **32** 600
Romanov, Paul I, Emperor of Russia *see* PAUL I, Emperor of Russia
Romanov, Peter I, Emperor of Russia *see* PETER I, Tsar and Emperor of Russia
Romanov, Peter III, Emperor of Russia *see* PETER III, Emperor of Russia
Romanov, Pyotr **27** 436
Romanov, Sophia of Württemberg, Empress of Russia *see* MARIA FYODOROVNA, Empress of Russia
Romanov, Vladimir Aleksandrovich, Grand Duke **21** 177; **28** 628
Romanov-Borisoglebsk **27** 387
Romanovich, Sergei M. **20** 151
Romans, St Barnard **26** 603
Romans, Aleksandrs
Romans, Jacob **7** 500
Roman school *see* SCUOLA ROMANA
Romański, Jerzy **15** 122; **32** 872
Romans-sur-Isère **5** 785; **27** 498
Romantic Classicism **7** 385; **9** 312; **26** 735*
Romanticism **1** 660; **10** 690; **18** 719; **25** 582; **26** 735–43*; **30** 168; **32** 110
aesthetics **1** 180; **29** 492
art forms
architecture **25** 172; **26** 709, 742–3; **32** 81
drawings **22** *152*; **26** 742; **32** *694*
England **23** *886*
gardens **2** 414; **26** 742
interior decoration **28** *908*
lithography **8** *640*
nude figures **23** 295
painting (general) **26** 737–42
France **8** 637, 646
Germany **12** 393
Switzerland **30** 133–4*
painting (allegorical)
France **1** *660*; **15** *88*
Germany **11** *781*; **22** *379*
United States of America **33** *93*
painting (animal subjects) **2** *107*
painting (architectural) **4** *136*
France **8** *449*
painting (genre) **8** *5*; **28** *736*; **30** *167*
Denmark **3** *705*
painting (history) **14** *266*
England **17** *576*
France **8** *643*; **12** *352*; **13** *690*
Italy **3** *903*
painting (landscape) **18** 714–15*
England **18** *714*; **26** *739*, *741*
Germany **4** *135*; **11** *779*, *780*, *782*; **12** *393*; **26** *359*
Norway **8** *452*
Slovenia **28** *861*
Spain **24** *403*
Switzerland **30** *133*
painting (literary themes) **8** *639*, 640; **14** *265*; **26** *739*; **31** *601*
painting (marine) **8** *451*
painting (military scenes) **12** *349*
painting (mythological) **8** *642*
painting (religious) **11** *462*
Romanticism
art forms—cont.
painting (sporting scenes) **12** *351*
painting (*vedute*) **30** 133
painting (wall) **5** *366*; **15** *88*
painting (watercolours) **23** *885*
England **12** *742*, *743*; **23** *885*
France **8** *641*
portraits
France **8** *646*; **12** *335*, *353*; **13** *691*
Germany **27** *339*, *340*
Russia **18** *75*
Spain **10** *513*
prints **26** 742
sculpture **3** *313*, *315*; **16** 706; **26** 742
sculpture (busts) **8** *565*
commentaries **16** 875
regional traditions
Belgium **3** 562*
Britain **26** 737
Denmark **18** 715
England **18** 714–15; **20** *490*; **23** 884; **26** 736
France **8** 654, 829; **12** 207; **17** 605; **26** 736; **27** 265; **29** 492
Germany **11** 778, 783; **12** 851; **18** 714; **26** 736
Italy **23** 829
Lithuania **27** 446
Poland **25** 99, 106
Russia **27** 389
Sardinia **27** 836
Spain **24** 403
United States of America **18** 715; **31** 601
Roman Urbanist group **23** 753
Romanus (*fl* late 12th cent.) **21** 900
Romanus (1504-57) *see* PENNI, LUCA
Roman Virgil **9** 603
Romay, Miguel de **5** 911; **6** 67; **26** 251
Rombauer, János **2** 546; **14** 901; **28** 853
Rombaux, Egide **3** 602, 604
Romberg, Frederick **2** 742; **4** 605; **13** 709; **26** 744*
Rombout, Joris **2** 199
Rombouts, Jan **19** 260
Rombouts, Nicolaas **26** 744–5*
works **13** 182; **26** *745*
Rombouts, Theodoor **26** 746–7*
collaboration **33** 182
reproductive prints by others **4** 283
works **3** 560; **26** *746*
Rombrich, Johann Christoph **11** 852
Romburch, P. **3** 500
Rome **9** *507*, *510*; **10** *583*; **13** 298, 299; **16** *616*, *620*; **26** 747–99*, *750*, *753*, *757*, 843*, *886*, *906*
academies
Academia Belgica **3** 620
Académie de France **1** 103, 105; **4** 550; **7** 831; **11** 536, 669–70, 673; **14** 283; **16** 697; **20** 133, 136; **24** 166, 167–8, 171
collections **13** 303
Accademia di Antichità Profane **2** 164
Accademia degli Antiquari Alessandrini **2** 164
Accademia dei Concili *see* Accademia di Propaganda Fide
Accademia Fiorentina **11** 23; **16** 699, 778; **21** 29; **26** 771
Accademia dei Lincei **6** 360; **25** 412
Accademia del Nudo **1** 103; **7** 682; **25** 411
Accademia dei Pensieri **14** 875
Rome
academies—cont.
Accademia di Propaganda Fide **2** 163
Accademia di S Luca **1** 102–3, 105, 108; **2** 523; **8** 563; **10** 676; **13** 823; **16** 637, 639, 779; **20** 866; **21** 759; **26** 770, 771, *841*, 841–2*; **32** 682; **33** 720
drawings **22** 5
Accademia della Virtù **2** 161; **32** 641
American Academy **2** 370; **5** 275
American School of Architecture *see* American Academy
Aeroporto Intercontinentale Leonardo da Vinci **26** 892
Amphitheatrum Castrense **1** 797; **26** 901
Anaglypha Hadriani **26** 782; **27** 35
Anaglypha Trajani *see* ANAGLYPHA HADRIANI
Antiquario **2** 162
aqueducts **2** 241; **26** 890
Acqua Alessandrina *see* Acqua Felice
Acqua Felice **4** 90; **26** 757
Acqua Paola **4** 90; **26** 758
Aqua Anio Novus **26** 892
Aqua Anio Vetus **26** 749; **27** 7
Aqua Appia **27** 6
Aqua Avio Novus **2** 242
Aqua Claudia **2** 242; **26** 749, 892, 901
Aqua Julia **2** 242
Aqua Marcia **2** 242; **26** 749; **27** 7
Aqua Tepula **2** 242
Aqua Trajana *see* Acqua Paola
Aqua Virgo **26** 755, 892
see also water supply; fountains
Ara Maxima *see under* Forum Boarium
Ara Pacis **1** 693; **2** 726; **7** 382; **16** 684, 760; **22** 43; **23** 534; **26** 750, *750*, *787*, 787–8*, 857, 860, 861, 890, *890*; **27** 23–4
reliefs **9** *249*; **24** 492; **27** 31, 45
Ara Pietatis **1** 693; **27** 27, 31, 33, *33*
Archiginnasio **26** 756, 759; **31** *674*, 674
Biblioteca Alessandrina **19** 314
S Ivo della Sapienza **3** 262; **4** 432*, *432*; **7** 258; **9** 84
Arch of Augustus *see under* Forum Romanum
Arch of Constantine **1** 693; **9** 519, 560; **16** 761; **18** 825; **23** 534; **26** 752, 797–8*, *798*, 868, 883, 903; **31** 350
conservation **2** 323
Great Trajanic Frieze **26** 791, 798; **27** 24, 35
Hadrianic Tondi **27** 11, 25
reliefs **2** 168; **9** 595; **10** 742; **16** 685; **26** 135; **27** 25, 43, *44*, 45
Arch of Marcus Aurelius **27** 25, 39
oratio **27** 43–4
roundels **27** 38
sculpture **27** 20
Arch of Janus **26** 868; **31** 350
Arch of Marcus Aurelius **27** 37
reliefs *see under* Arch of Constantine
Arch of Nero **26** 891
Arch of Septimius Severus *see under* Forum Romanum
Arch of the Argentarii **16** 685; **27** 41
Arch of Tiberius **26** 782
Arch of Titus *see under* Forum Romanum
Rome—cont.
Arch of Trajan *see under* Forum of Trajan
Arco di Portogallo *see* Arch of Marcus Aurelius
Arcus Novus **27** 43
Argiletum **26** *783*
Armilustrium **31** 369, *369*
art forms and materials
altarpieces **5** 809
architecture
Baroque **16** 637*
Mannerism **16** 634–5*
military **26** 751
Renaissance **16** 631–2*
Roman **26** 851–4, 856
13th cent. **7** 921
15th cent. **23** 97
books **14** 433
brick **26** 750
bronzes **26** 860
cameo **27** 76
candelabra **5** 604
cassoni **6** 7, *7*
coins **4** 687
concrete **26** 750
embroidery **16** 760
etchings **32** *113*
façade decoration **10** 737, 739, 740
façades **17** 510
frames **11** *385*, *393*, *394*
furniture **16** 723, 727; **26** 780*
gem-engraving **12** 248, 250, 257, 261
glass **9** 645; **27** 74, 75
gold **16** 742; **25** 313
hardstones **16** 746
icons **9** 3; **19** 787–9
intarsia **26** 779–80*
jewellery **16** 751, 752; **17** 526; **27** *103*
ketubbot **18** 3
manuscripts **9** 602, 603; **26** 666
maps **20** 362; **23** 190
marble **7** 918–22; **26** 751
medals **20** 919
mosaics **22** 158, 163; **26** 751, 861
Nativity groups **22** 679
orders (architecture) **23** 492; **26** 876
painting **16** 661; **18** 708–9, 711, 713
Baroque **16** 669, 670–72; **30** 456
Mannerism **16** 665*
quadratura **15** 137–8*
Renaissance **16** 664–5*
still-lifes **29** 668
vedute **24** 844; **32** 112–14
wall **13** 552; **26** 651, 857; **27** 58
panoramas **24** 659
parchment **24** 107
photographs **2** 367
pilgrim badges **24** 808, 809
plaquettes **25** 19
pottery **10** 610; **16** 732
printing **16** 360
rock crystal **26** 485, 486
sarcophagi **9** 594; **27** 826, *826*, 827
sculpture **2** 168–9; **13** 97, 466; **16** 691*, 694–5*, 696–9*; **26** 844, 845–7*
cult statues **8** 263
figurines **13** 581
reliefs **19** 549
Roman **27** 9, 28
statuettes **29** 569, 572
silk **9** 667
spolia **26** 843–4*
stage design **30** 656
stamps **26** 750
stone **26** 750
stucco **26** 751, 858; **29** 830–31
tapestries **16** 755; **26** 778–9*
terracottas **27** 109
textiles **1** 881; **27** 112

Rome
art forms and materials—cont.
thrones **30** 776, 777–8
topographical illustrations **18** 635
art market **2** 558, 559; **10** 675, 676
Atrium Libertatis **19** 312
Aula of Isis **12** 625; **26** 786
Aula Regia **26** *786*
Aurelian Wall *see under* walls
Balneum Surae **3** 375
Banca d'Italia **16** 644; **18** 184
Banca Nazionale *see* Banca d'Italia
Banco di Roma *see under* palazzi → Palazzi de Carolis
Banco di Santo Spirito **23** 492; **26** 756
Basilica Aemilia *see under* Forum Romanum
Basilica Hilariana **27** 61
Basilica Julia *see under* Forum Romanum
Basilica of Constantine *see* Basilica of Maxentius
Basilica of Junius Bassus **14** 170
Basilica of Martyrios **29** 521
Basilica of Maxentius **3** 327; **9** 560; **16** 623; **20** 577; **26** 752, 782, 796–7*, *797*, 868, 883, 902; **27** 44; **32** *113*
buttresses **5** 319
coffering **7** 527
sculpture **18** 824; **27** 46
vaults **32** 89
Basilica Opimia **26** 782
Basilica Porcia **3** 327; **26** 782, 888
Basilica Sempronia **3** 327; **26** 782, 888
Basilica Ulpia *see under* Forum of Trajan
baths **3** 375; **26** 751, 863
Baths of Agrippa **1** 463; **3** 375; **26** *749*, 751, 871
Baths of Caracalla **3** 375; **7** 692; **16** 623; **26** 795*, *796*, 872, 878, *878*, 901
capitals **26** 844
exedrae **19** 312
mosaics **27** 67
sculpture **13** 605
staircases **29** 521
wall paintings **27** 55
Baths of Claudius Etruscus **26** 925
Baths of Constantine **9** 560; **26** 752, 903
Baths of Diocletian **3** 375; **26** 868, 872, *872*, 879, 902
mosaics **27** 67
tepidarium *see* ecclesiastical buildings → S Maria degli Angeli
vaults **32** 89
Baths of Nero **3** 375; **26** 751, 871, 892
Baths of Septimius Severus **26** 901
Baths of Severus Alexander **26** 901
Baths of Titus **3** 375; **26** *750*, 751, 853, 856, 871, 895
vaults **32** 89
see also Baths of Trajan
Baths of Trajan **3** 375; **26** 788, 872, 884, 897
exedrae **19** 312
see also Baths of Titus
Stabian Baths **9** 84
bridges **26** 749
Pons Aelius *see* Ponte Elio
Ponte ai Fiorentini **26** 761
Ponte del Risorgimento **14** 388; **26** 762
Ponte Elio **26** 897; **27** 7
Ponte Fabricio **26** 758; **27** 7
Ponte Milvio **26** 755; **27** 7
Ponte Palatino **26** 761
Rome
bridges—cont.
Ponte Principe Amedeo di Savoia Aosta **26** 761
Ponte Rotto **26** 761
Ponte Sant'Angelo **3** 833; **4** 800
Ponte Sisto **26** 756
British Embassy **29** 379
building regulations **5** 134
Busiri Vici collection **5** 295
Caelian **26** 892
Caffè Aragno **29** 255
Caffè degli Inglesi **10** 83, 96
Campana House **5** 536
Campo Marzio **26** *750*; **33** *269*
amphitheatre **1** 797
baths **26** 891
gymnasium **26** 891
odeion **23** 349
sculpture **26** *858*
Campo Verano **31** 131
Capitoline **7** 921; **25** 7; **30** 655, 656
Carceri Nuove **13** 292
carnivals **5** 785, 786, *786*, 787
Casa Baldi **16** 650; **25** 273
Casa Bartholdy *see* palazzi → Palazzo Zuccari
Casa Correzzionale **25** 636, *636*
Casa dei Crescenzi **7** 921; **26** 843, *843*
Casa dei Filippini *see* ecclesiastical buildings → Oratory of S Filippo Neri
Casa Il Girasole **22** 106
Casa Lavoro per i Ciechi di Guerra **16** 649
Casa Nebbiosi **16** 649
Casa Professa **17** 510
Casino del Patriarca Biondo **30** 356
Casino Massimo
Ariosto Room **28** 136, *136*
frescoes **7** 870; **9** 690–91; **12** 393; **18** 183; **22** 704; **23** 676; **32** 119
see also villas → Villa Giustiniani
Casino of Cardinal Bessarion **32** 545
Casino Valadier **32** 554
Castel Sant' Angelo **20** 864, *864*; **26** *794*, 794–5*, 897, 899; **28** 658; **31** 110
interior decoration **24** 420
metalwork **19** 768
mouldings **9** 757
Sala dell'Apollo **14** 416
Sala Paolina **24** *420*
sculpture **3** 158
tomb of Hadrian **26** 795, 844; **27** 235
see also museums → Museo Nazionale di Castel Sant'Angelo
catacombs **9** 517; **17** 534, 535; **26** 798–9*; **27** 48
Catacomb of Calepodius **6** 70; **26** 799
Catacomb of Commodilla **10** 701; **26** 799, *799*
Catacomb of Domitilla **6** 69; **9** 534; **26** 798
Catacomb of Pontianus **26** 799
Catacomb of Praetextatus **26** 799
Catacomb of Priscilla **6** 70; **9** 562, *563*; **22** 411
Catacomb of S Agnese **26** 798
Catacomb of S Callisto **6** 69, 70; **9** 562; **26** 798, 799
basilica **7** 255
Chapel of the Popes **20** 518
wall paintings **1** 693; **16** 654
Catacomb of S Ermete **6** 71
Catacomb of SS Pietro e Marcellino **9** 517, 562, 563; **26** 798, *799*
wall paintings **22** 519
Rome
catacombs—cont.
Catacomb of S Sebastiano **6** 69; **26** 798
Catacomb of S Valentino **6** 69; **26** 798
Catacomb of the Giordiani **6** 381; **16** 654
Catacomb of the Via Latina **6** 69; **26** 798
Catacomb of Trebius Justus **26** 879
Catacomb of Turtura **9** 574
Catacombs of the Cimitero Maggiore **16** 654
Chamber of Deputies **16** 679
churches *see* ecclesiastical buildings
Circus Maximus **1** 796; **7** 341, 342, *342*; **23** 330
Circus of Maxentius **7** 342
Città Universitaria **16** 650; **24** 694, *694*; **26** 762
Cloaca Maxima **2** 295; **10** 602; **32** 87
collections **26** 773
colleges **7** 566
Collegio del Gesù **31** 787
Collegio di Propaganda Fide **4** 412, 434–5*, *435*; **23** 493; **26** 758
Collegio Romano **7** 567; **16** 771; **17** 510; **23** 340; **26** 757
Colombari di Vigna Codini **31** 110
Colombarium of Pomponius Hylas **27** 66
Colosseum **1** 797; **2** 320; **7** *499*; **16** 623; **22** 42; **23** 483, 534; **26** *750*, 751, 789–91*, *790*, 853, 856, 873, 874, 883, 888, 893, *894*, 895; **32** 384
arches **2** 297
orders (architecture) **23** 480, 484
piers (ii) (masonry) **24** 750
pilasters **24** 804
restoration **29** 639
stucco **27** 72
vaults **32** 86
Column of Antoninus Pius **16** 685; **27** 26, *26*, 37
Column of Marcus Aurelius **16** 761; **27** 25, 40, *40*, 45
comitium **26** 867
Curia Hostilia *see under* Forum Romanum
Curia Julia *see under* Forum Romanum
Curia Octavia **29** 560
Curia Senatus *see* Forum Romanum → Curia Julia
Democratic Party headquarters **16** 650
diaconiae **26** 753, 754
Domus Augustana **9** 85; **23** 808–9; **26** *786*, 787, 895, *895*
dome **9** 84
Domus Aurea **7** 692; **9** 11; **16** 623, 760; **23** 535, 808; **26** 782, 786, 788–9*, 869, 879, 880, 884, 891, 892, *893*, 893, 895, 897; **28** 510
domes **9** 83, 84
graffiti **13** 269
mosaics **27** 66
ribbonwork **26** 303
sculpture **9** 20; **27** 33; **33** 636
stucco **27** 70; **29** 829
vaults **32** 87, 89, 94
Volta Dorata **26** *788*
wall paintings **5** 685; **13** 699, 703; **25** 191; **27** 52, 54, 55, 58
Domus Flavia **26** *786*, 787, 895; **27** 22
Domus Publica **26** 782
Domus Severiana *see* baths → Baths of Septimius Severus
Rome—cont.
Domus Tiberiana **19** 312; **23** 808; **26** 786, *786*
Domus Transitoria **26** 786, 892; **27** 51, 59
ecclesiastical buildings **4** 774; **7** 190, 919–21; **9** 528–34*; **26** 569, 752
All Saints **13** 202
American Church *see* St Paul
Basilica Apostolorum *see* S Sebastiano
Basilica Constantiniana *see* S Giovanni in Laterano
Chiesa Nuova **11** 78; **16** 634; **23** 472
frescoes **7** *909*, 910; **16** 671, 763
sculpture **23** 472; **31** *787*
stucco **29** 830
Il Gesù **3** 264; **7** 254, 276; **13** 210; **16** 634, 635, 637, 763; **17** 509, 510; **23** 541; **25** 97, 259–60; **26** 822–4*, *823*; **32** 506–7
Altar of St Ignatius **16** 699; **25** 414
frescoes **12** 198–200*, *199*; **15** 138; **16** 671; **32** 101
furniture **16** 727
pilasters **24** 805
stage **25** *414*
stucco **29** 830, 831
Lateran Basilica *see* S Giovanni in Laterano
Madonna del Carmelo **21** 806
Monastery of S Alessio **26** 754
Oratorio del Crocifisso de S Marcello **32** 101, *102*
Oratory of S Filippo Neri **4** *431*, 431–2*; **23** 473, 492; **24** 805; **29** 251
Oratory of S Giovanni Decollato *see under* S Giovanni Decollato
Oratory of S Luca del Gonfalone **33** *719*
Oratory of S Venanzio **9** 575
S Adriano al Foro Romano **19** 633; **26** 752, *753*, 760, 843
see also Forum Romanum → Curia Julia
S Agnese fuori le Mura **9** 530; **16** 624; **20** 519, 865; **26** 752, 753, *753*; **27** 38
mosaics **9** 575
wall paintings **16** 654
S Agnese in Agone **4** 433–4; **12** 198; **16** 638, *638*; **25** *852*, 861; **26** 759
paintings **11** 23
sculpture **7** *276*; **16** 699
S Agostino **10** 542; **16** 631; **24** 778–9
altarpieces **1** 711, 712
Pamphili chapel **5** 376
reliquaries **26** 148
sculpture **16** 694; **27** *770*, 776–7
S Alessandro **1** 694
S Anastasia **26** 758
S Andrea al Quirinale **3** 835; **7** 258; **16** 637, 763; **17** 510–11; **20** *904*
altarpiece **1** 712
façade **5** *899*
stucco **29** 830
S Andrea della Valle **20** 44; **30** 649
frescoes **9** 90*, *92*; **15** 137; **16** 670; **18** *733*; **30** 648, 649
stucco **29** 830
S Andrea della Via Flaminia **16** 635; **32** 505
S Andrea delle Fratte **3** *95*; **4** 435*, 786; **16** 644
S Apollinare **16** 699; **26** 624
Rome
ecclesiastical buildings—cont.
SS Apostoli **3** 876; **9** 534; **26** 755, 760
Della Rovere monument **16** 691
reliefs **26** 844
Riario monument **16** 691
tomb of Clement XIV **5** 626; **16** 705; **22** *736*; **31** 130
wall paintings **16** 659
S Atanasio dei Greci **25** *260*
S Balbina **30** 777
S Bartolomeo **1** 696; **26** 844
S Benedetto Polirone **20** 820
S Bibiana **26** *753*, 758
S Carlino *see* S Carlo alle Quattro Fontane
S Carlo ai Catinari **3** *249*, 250; **12** 526; **27** 160; **29** 831
S Carlo al Corso **29** 831
S Carlo alle Quattro Fontane **3** 262, 264; **4** *429*, 429–31*, *430*, *431*; **7** 254; **16** 637, 638; **23** 541; **26** 758; **31** 340
stucco **29** 830
S Caterina da Siena a Monte Magnanapoli **25** 322
sculpture **5** *377*
S Cecilia in Trastevere **16** 625; **24** 222–3; **26** 754, 758, 760; **28** 529
altar **29** 700
ciborium **7** 303
frescoes **6** *103*, *104*; **13** 145
manuscripts **20** 331; **26** 665, *665*
sculpture **20** 47
S Cesareo **30** 778
S Clemente **7** 922; **26** 824*
see also temples → Temple of Mithras
S Clemente (Lower church) **9** 530, 532; **26** 752, 824–5*, *825*
ciborium **7** 301
schola cantorum **28** 140
wall paintings **26** 651, 656, 825–6*, *826*
S Clemente (Upper church) **16** 626, 761; **26** 576, *753*, 754, 760, 826*, *826*
ambo **1** 764
choir-screen **16** 686
frescoes **26** *827*
mosaics **7** 920; **16** 654; **22** 163; **26** 679, 827–8*, *828*
schola cantorum **7** 919; **26** 828*; **28** 141, *141*
throne **30** 777
wall paintings **16** 659; **26** 826–7*
SS Cosma e Damiano **9** 534; **26** 752, *753*, 758, 782, 784
mosaics **7** *271*, 272; **9** 574; **16** 654
S Costanza **7** 219; **9** 85, 525, 530; **16** 624; **20** 865; **22** 161; **23** 480, 485; **26** 752, *753*, *829*, 829–30*, 903, 923; **27** 235
mosaics **9** 570; **26** 830; **27** 67, *68*
vaults **32** 86
S Crisogono **8** 222; **9** 529; **26** *753*, 754; **28** 140; **29** 80; **31** 341
altar **1** 698
Santa Croce in Gerusalemme **9** 529; **16** 624; **26** 752, *753*, 843
façade **26** 761
icons **9** 630
obelisk **26** 757
oratory **9** 532
S Dionigi **31** 340
S Eligio degli Orefici **32** 101
S Francesca Romana **9** 624; **16** 654

Rome
ecclesiastical buildings—cont.
S Galla **1** 696
S Giacomo alla Lungara **26** 758
S Giacomo degli Incurabili **32** 692
S Giorgio in Velabro **26** 753, *753*
S Giovanni a Porta Latina **9** 534; **16** 654; **26** 655
S Giovanni Decollato
exhibitions **10** 676
frescoes **27** *649*
oratory **27** 648–9, 652
reliquaries **26** 148
S Giovanni dei Fiorenti **2** 336; **26** 756; **27** 486
SS Giovanni e Paolo **9** 529; **16** 761; **26** 752, *753*, 755
S Giovanni in Fonte Baptistery **27** 489
S Giovanni in Laterano **1** 595; **3** 329; **4** 432–3*; **7** 217, 252, 692; **9** 529, 654; **12** *8*; **14** 416; **15** 860; **16** 623, 761, 763; **23** 96, 109; **26** 752, *753*, 755, 760, *820*, 820–21*
Baptistery **3** 189; **9** 85, 154, 532, 533; **16** 624, 686; **22** 156; **26** 752, 758, 821–2*, *822*
Cappella Massimi **28** 658
ciborium **7** 301, 303; **13** 97
cloister **7** 455, 919, *920*, 922; **16** 626; **26** 754; **32** 75
Corsini Chapel **16** 699
crucifix **8** 216
façade **12** 8–9; **16** 639, 764; **26** 761
frescoes **1** 553; **7** 620; **12** 302
metalwork **9** 656; **10** 624
mosaics **31** 192
museum **13** 629
Obelisk of Constantius Chlorus **7** 342; **20** 570; **23** 330; **26** 757
portico **7** 919
roof **30** 905
schola cantorum **28** 140
sculpture **16** 699, 764; **20** *909*; **21** *890*; **27** 346
tomb of Cardinal Chiaves **16** 691
tomb of Damasus II **31** 121
tomb of Innocent III **26** 844
see also Lateran Palace
S Girolamo della Carità **14** 517
chapel of St Philip **9** 158
Spada Chapel **29** 251
S Gregorio Magno
cloister **26** 754
façade **29** 80, *80*
Oratoria di S Andrea **9** 88
Throne of St Gregory **30** 776
S Ignazio **13** 321; **16** 639, 763; **17** 510
frescoes **15** 138; **16** 671; **25** 414, *415*
furniture **16** 727
paintings **24** 490
reliefs **19** *88*
sculpture **16** 699
stucco **29** 830
S Isidoro **4** 104
S Ivo della Sapienza *see under* ROME → Archiginnasio
S Lorenzo fuori le Mura **7** 919, 922; **8** 260; **9** 530, 534; **14** 726; **16** 624; **20** 519; **26** 752, 753, *753*, 764
ambos **1** 764; **7** *919*
cloister **26** 754
crosses **8** 203
mosaics **7** 272
sculpture **26** 844
throne **30** 777
tomb of Cardinal Guglielmo Fieschi **31** 121, *127*
wall paintings **13** 145

Rome
ecclesiastical buildings—cont.
S Lorenzo in Damaso **2** 493; **23** 637
S Lorenzo in Lucina **29** 830; **30** 777; **31** 127
monument to Gabriele Fonseca **31** *127*
S Lorenzo in Miranda **26** 899
see also Forum Romanum → Temple of Antoninus and Faustina
SS Luca e Martina **7** 258, 911–12, *912*; **16** 637, 638, *638*; **26** 758; **29** 830
S Luigi dei Francesi **5** 380; **26** 756; **27** 491
altar **1** 695
altarpieces **8** 613
Chapel of St Louis **4** 766
Contarelli Chapel **5** 709–11; **16** 670; **30** 456
frescoes **16** 670
paintings **5** *709*, *710*
SS Marcellino e Pietro **20** 865
S Marcello al Corso **11** *275*; **27** 770; **28** 489
S Marco **16** 654; **28** 140
S Maria ad Martyres **16** 761; **26** 752, *753*, 792, 843
see also Pantheon
S Maria degli Angeli **9** 338; **16** 644; **21** 456*; **26** 844, 902
S Maria dell'Anima **9** 411; **12** *753*; **16** 665
S Maria Antiqua **7** 259; **9** 517, *517*, 534, 624; **22** 520; **26** 752, *753*, 799, 830–31*
sarcophagus **9** 596; **18** 826; **27** 827
schola cantorum **28** 140
wall paintings **8** 211; **9** 575; **16** 654; **26** 830–31, *831*
S Maria della Concezione **5** *690*, 691; **26** 758; **33** *716*
S Maria in Aracoeli **26** 755
chapel of S Pietro d'Alacantra **29** 831
frescoes **13** 145
icons **13** 131
monument to Luca Savelli **31** 123
reliefs **26** 844
sculpture **1** 490; **13** 97
tomb of Giovanni Crivelli **16** 691
tomb of Ludovico Grati Margani **27** *748*
S Maria in Campitelli **16** 638; **25** 861, *862*; **29** 830
S Maria in Campo Marzio **8** *13*
S Maria in Cosmedin **7** 190, 922; **16** *624*, 625, 761; **26** 753, *753*, 754, *754*, 760, 843
ambo **1** 764
throne **30** 777
wall paintings **26** 656
S Maria in Domnica **7** *223*; **26** 754
S Maria in Montesanto *see* S MARIA DI MONTESANTO
S Maria in Monticelli **7** 922
S Maria in Pallara *see* S Sebastiano al Palatino
S Maria in Traspontina **3** *97*
S Maria in Trastevere **9** 624; **16** 626, 761; **26** 576, 752, *753*, 754, 760, 795, 833–4*, *833*
Avila Chapel **12** 526, *526*; **21** 893; **29** 831
capitals **26** 844
frescoes **26** 834
icons **30** V2
mosaics **6** 104–5, *105*; **13** 145; **19** 353; **22** 163; **26** 679, 834
schola cantorum **28** 141
sculpture **20** *47*; **26** 624
throne **26** 624; **30** 777

Rome
ecclesiastical buildings
S Maria in Trastevere—cont.
tomb of Innocent II **31** 121
S Maria in Trivio **12** 525
S Maria in Vallicella *see* Chiesa Nuova
S Maria in Via Lata **7** 913, *913*; **26** 753, *753*
S Maria di Loreto **9** 339, *339*, *410*
S Maria Maggiore **4** 774; **7** 272; **9** 85, 515, 532; **11** 815, *815*; **13** 145; **16** 624, 761; **18** 621; **23** 96; **26** 752, *753*, 761, 831–3*
altarpiece **20** 535–6
Cappella Paolina **4** 404–5
ciborium **10** 542; **21** 693
crypt **8** 224
façade **26** 761
icons **19** *788*
mosaics **9** 518, 571; **13** 145; **16** 654; **22** 161, 519; **26** 832–3; **27** 450; **31** 192–3, *193*
obelisk **26** 757
paintings **7** 620
Pauline Chapel **20** 47
reliquaries **26** 148
Sistine Chapel **11** *272*; **29** 82
stucco **29** 816
tomb of Honorius III **31** 121
Triumphal Arch **26** *832*
S Maria dei Miracoli **16** 638; **23** *331*; **25** 861–2; **26** *758*, 759
stucco **29** 830
S Maria di Monserrato **27** *743*
S Maria di Montesanto **16** 638; **23** *331*; **25** 861–2; **26** *758*, 759; **29** 830
S Maria della Pace **4** 646–7; **7** 912–13; **16** 632; **26** *759*
Chigi Chapel **26** 759
frescoes **24** *531*
S Maria del Popolo **4** 650; **14** 417; **16** 631; **26** 759
Cerasi Chapel **5** 711; **16** 670
Chigi Chapel **6** 583; **20** 865; **22** 158, *158*, 163; **25** 766, 907; **29** 830
coffering **7** 527
Cybó Chapel **28** *379*
organ **22** 374
paintings **5** *710*; **20** *377*; **22** 521
sculpture **16** 691, 699
tomb of Cardinal Ascanio Sforza **27** 830; **31** 126
tomb of Cardinal Girolamo Basso della Rovere **16** 694; **27** 830; **31** 126
S Maria del Priorato **22** 738; **24** *844*; **29** 832
S Maria Rotonda **7** 922
S Maria sopra Minerva **5** 698; **9** 111; **13** 52; **16** 627
Cappella di S Domenico **25** 853
Carafa Chapel **13** 700; **19** 447–8
Casanatense **19** 315
monument to Clement VII **16** 696; **27** *749*
monument to Leo X **16** 696; **27** *749*
tomb of Benedict XIII **4** *621*
tomb of Cardinal Diego de Coca **4** *737*
tomb of Maria Raggi **31** 127
wall paintings **16** 659
S Maria della Vittoria
Cornaro Chapel **3** 262, *262*, 264, 831–2*; **5** 778; **12** 497; **15** 138; **16** 698; **29** 830
paintings **13** 301
S Marinella **7** 781, *781*

Rome
ecclesiastical buildings—cont.
S Martino ai Monti **5** 778; **29** 831
SS Nereo ed Achilleo **26** 758; **30** 778
S Nicola in Carcere **26** 656, 758, 843
S Omobono **27** 22
S Pantaleo **16** 644; **31** *800*
S Paolo alle Tre Fontane **16** 627
S Paolo fuori le Mura **5** 803, *804*; **7** 922; **9** 530, 532; **14** *664*, 726; **16** 624, 626; **26** 752, *753*; **30** 706
candlesticks **26** 624
Cappella del Sacramento **18** 733
ciborium **2** *481*, 481–2; **7** 303; **13** 97
cloister **7** 455; **26** 754
collections **4** 20
doors **9** 154
frescoes **6** 104; **27** 591
mosaics **6** 106; **22** 161; **26** 680
reconstruction **25** 147
roof **30** 903
sculpture **26** 624
transept **31** 280
wall paintings **9** 572; **13** 145
S Pasquale Baylon **27** 834
St Paul (American Church) **7** 226
St Peter's *see under* ROME (VATICAN)
SS Pietro e Marcellino **7** 217; **9** 530; **16** 624; **20** 519; **26** 752, *753*
see also catacombs → Catacomb of SS Pietro e Marcellino
SS Pietro e Paolo **26** 762
S Pietro in Montorio
Borgherini chapel **28** 333–4
Tempietto **4** 647–8, *648*, 652; **7** 257; **8** 224; **14** 416; **16** 632; **23** 486; **26** 186; **27** 236; **31** 270
S Pietro in Vincoli **26** 752, *753*
schola cantorum **28** 140
sculpture **16** 695
tomb of Julius II **14** 870; **16** 696; **20** 865; **21** 435–8*
S Prassede **5** *793*, 794; **22** 520; **24** 222; **26** *753*, 754
columns **29** 700
mosaics **16** 654, 761, *761*
Olgiati Chapel **2** 493
S Pudenziana **9** 518; **16** 624; **22** 161; **26** 752, *753*
mosaics **7** 272; **9** 570–71; **16** 654
sculpture **26** 624
wall paintings **26** 651, *651*
SS Quaranta Martiri *see* S Pasquale Baylon
SS Quattro Coronati **14** 416; **16** 626, 761; **26** 576, *753*, 754
cloister **26** 754, 755
frescoes **26** 82
SS Quirico e Giulitta **9** 534
S Saba **30** 777
S Sabina **7** 217, *252*; **9** 107, 518, 525, 532, *533*; **16** 624, 761; **26** 752, *753*
arches **2** 297
doors **8** 211; **9** 151, 599; **16** 686; **31** 498
mosaics **9** 571
paintings **9** 110
S Salvatore in Lauro **10** 676
S Sebastiano **9** 530, *530*; **16** 624; **20** 519; **26** 752, *753*
wall paintings **9** 563; **27** 55
S Sebastiano al Palatino **16** 654; **26** 651
S Silvestro al Quirinale **16** 699; **29** 830; **30** 649, 886
S Silvestro in Capite **26** 760

Rome
ecclesiastical buildings—cont.
S Sisto Vecchio **9** 112; **15** 860; **26** 760
Santo Spirito **26** 754
S Stefano Rotondo **3** 191; **7** 255, 259; **9** 532; **16** 624, 761; **17** 509; **26** 752, *753*, 835*, *835*; **27** 182, 235
mosaics **9** 575
wall paintings **16** 654
S Susanna **3** 264; **8** 224; **16** 635, 637; **20** 43–4, *44*; **24** 281
altars **1** 695
frescoes **8** *182*
S Teodoro **26** 753, *753*
S Tommaso in Formis **7** 920; **31** 340
Santa Trinità degli Spagnoli **31** 341
Santa Trinità dei Monti **16** 717; **26** *760*
frescoes **6** 364; **8** *504*
obelisk **26** 761
Orsini Chapel **5** 905
Scalinata della Santa Trinità dei Monti *see* Spanish Steps
sculpture **26** 624
S Urbana al Foro Traiano **7** 922
S Urbano alla Caffarella **26** 900
SS Vincenzo e Anastasio **16** 638; **19** 633, *634*
S Vitale **9** 532; **16** 761; **26** 752, *753*
Tempietto *see under* S Pietro in Montorio
Trinità dei Pellegrini **27** 710
Ecole Française **16** 777
education (art) **16** 778
Escuela Superior de Bellas Artes **2** 163
Esposizione Universale *see* EUR
Esquiline **26** 892
Lamian Gardens **27** 100
mosaics **27** 62
paintings **13** 547; **27** 58
sculpture **27** 30
tombs **26** 860
wall paintings **27** 49
Esquiline Treasure **27** 84
EUR (Esposizione Universale di Roma) **7** 331; **24** 694; **26** 762
Museo della Civiltà Romana *see under* museums
Palazzo delle Esposizioni **11** 844; **19** 305, *305*; **26** 762
excavations **13** 605; **22** 387
exhibitions **10** 676; **27** 115
festivals **23** 766
Flavian Amphitheatre *see* Colosseum
Flavian Palace **23** 808; **26** 785, 884, *895*, 895–6, 897, 901, 923, 924
fora **26** *750*, *783*, 783–5*
Fornix Fabianus *see under* Forum Romanum
Forum Adjectum **26** 781
Forum Augustum **11** 327; **26** 750, *783*, 783–4, 861, 865, 881, 889, 890, *890*, 924, 925; **27** 30, 31, 32; **30** 435
caryatids **5** 904
consoles **7** 746
sculpture **2** 726
Temple of Mars Ultor **23** 482; **26** 750, 783, *783*, *784*, 890; **27** 31, 32, 714; **30** 436, *436*
pediment **24** 319, 320
sculpture **27** 31
Forum Boarium **8** 263; **26** 865; **27** 29
Ara Maxima **27** 22
Temple of Hercules Victor **26** 875, 885, 887; **27** 9
Temple of Portunus **26** 887, *888*

Rome—cont.
Forum Julium 5 375; 11 327; 26 749, 783, 783, 856, 865, 889, 890; 27 30; 30 435
obelisks 23 330
Temple of Venus Genetrix 2 416; 12 265; 23 291; 26 749, 783, 783, 856, 865, 889, 893; 27 714; 30 435
consoles 7 746
paintings 30 916
Forum of Nerva 11 327; 26 783, 784–5, 883, 889, 895; 30 435
friezes 27 45
Porticus Absidata 26 783, 785
Forum of Trajan 11 327; 26 783, 785, 797, 866, 876, 876, 881, 884, 895, 896, 913; 27 35
Arch of Trajan 31 369
Basilica Ulpia 11 328; 26 783, 785, 868, 881, 896
columns 29 700
libraries 19 312
Library of Hadrian 26 785
Library of Trajan 26 785
Markets of Trajan 9 84, 85; 16 623; 20 438; 23 534; 26 750, 853, 871, 878, 881, 896–7, 896
sculpture 27 10, 14, 28
Temple of the Deified Trajan 26 783, 785, 896
Trajan's Column 7 381; 16 761; 22 43; 23 487; 26 783, 785, 791–2*, 792, 843, 896; 30 467
carving 27 18
facsimiles 27 115
polychromy 29 707
reliefs 2 168; 11 743; 16 684; 22 514; 23 534; 26 132, 135, 860; 27 24–5, 35, 36, 45; 30 773
ships 28 611
staircase 29 521
Forum Romanum 1 796; 4 320; 11 327, 327; 12 497; 26 748, 749, 750, 751, 781, 781–3*, 856, 901; 27 6, 35, 43
Arch of Augustus 26 781, 782, 868, 890; 31 349
Arch of Septimius Severus 10 742; 26 748, 782, 792, 868, 901, 901; 27 25, 41; 31 349–50
coffering 7 527
Arch of Titus 2 168, 297, 320; 10 742; 16 684; 22 43; 26 782, 860, 868, 876, 893, 895; 27 24, 34, 45; 31 349, 349
coffering 7 527
orders (architecture) 23 480
reconstruction 2 320, 323
Basilica Aemilia 3 327; 26 781, 782, 868, 888, 890, 925; 27 31, 32
Basilica Julia 3 328; 26 748, 752, 781, 782, 868, 890
piers (ii) (masonry) 24 750
Curia Hostilia 26 867
Curia Julia 26 752, 781, 781, 782, 867, 889, 902; 27 35
mosaics 27 59
sculpture 27 31
see also ecclesiastical buildings → S Adriano al Foro Romano
Curia Senatus see Curia Julia
decennalia monument 9 595
Fornix Fabianus 26 782
Lacus Juturnae 27 22, 29
Lapis Niger 4 320; 26 781, 782
macellum 19 888
maiolica 16 732
puteal Libonis 33 56
Regia 10 598, 600
sanctuary 27 713
sculpture 26 751; 27 20, 31
shrine of Venus Cloacina 26 781, 782

Rome
Forum Romanum—cont.
Tabularium 7 921; 26 782, 856, 867, 888
Temple of Antoninus and Faustina 26 751, 782, 866, 899; 27 45; 30 436
see also ecclesiastical buildings → S Lorenzo in Miranda
Temple of Castor and Pollux 23 809; 26 781, 782, 786, 865, 892
Temple of Concord 26 781, 782, 865; 27 30, 31, 32
consoles 7 746
mouldings 3 439; 8 324; 9 757
Temple of the Deified Vespasian 23 534; 26 782, 866, 893; 30 436
Temple of Divus Julius 26 781, 782, 865
Temple of Jupiter Stator 26 856, 865, 885, 887
Temple of Romulus 26 782, 902
temples 27 714
Temple of Saturn 25 53; 26 752, 781, 782, 867; 27 712
Aerarium Saturni 26 867
Temple of Venus and Rome 9 757; 26 751, 782, 866, 892, 896, 897, 902; 30 436
Temple of Vesta 2 319; 26 781, 782; 27 235
trophy 31 369
Forum Transitorium see Forum of Nerva
Forum of Vespasian see temples → Templum Pacis
fountains 11 341
drinking fountains 11 346
Fountain of the Bees 26 758
Fountain of the Naiads 11 346; 16 644
Fountain of the Tortoises 16 696
Four Rivers Fountain 3 832; 11 343; 16 638; 22 44, 45; 23 330, 899; 26 759
Moro Fountain 25 259
Neptune Fountain see Moro Fountain
Trevi Fountain 7 672; 10 744; 11 345; 16 705, 764; 22 45; 25 808; 26 760, 761; 27 646–7; 31 351
Triton Fountain 3 831; 11 343, 343; 22 44; 26 758
see also aqueducts; water supply
Galleria Borghese see villas → Villa Borghese
Galleria Doria Pamphili see palazzi → Palazzo Doria Pamphili
Galleria Farnese see under palazzi → Palazzo Farnese
Galleria Pallavicini see palazzi → Palazzo Pallavicini-Rospigliosi
Galleria Pamphili see palazzi → Palazzo Pamphili
gardens 12 70, 115; 26 845–7*
Gardens of Lucullus 12 118
Gardens of Maecenas 26 892; 27 14, 46
Gardens of Sallust 26 897; 27 45, 46
Germalus see Palatine
Graecostasis 26 867
grottoes 13 703
guidebooks 26 847–9*
medieval 13 808
7th cent. AD 26 799
12th cent. 26 755
15th cent. 4 75, 622
16th cent. 1 572; 11 838
17th cent. 20 495; 21 805; 27 726; 31 31
18th cent. 32 70, 237
19th cent. 18 692

Rome—cont.
Hadrianeum 26 866, 899; 27 39; 30 436
Horologium Augusti 26 750, 890
Horrea Galbana 26 879
House of Raphael see palazzi → Palazzo Caprini
houses 16 627; 26 901
House of Augustus 26 891, 892; 27 54
House of Livia 26 786, 786
wall paintings 18 702; 27 54
Yellow Frieze 13 553; 18 702
House of the Griffins 26 786, 879
mosaics 27 61
stucco 27 69; 29 814
wall paintings 27 53
House of Ulisse da Fano 10 737
hypogeum of the Via di Livenza 27 56
IBM factory 16 651
ICCROM Centre 7 742
iconography 26 859
Imperial Fora see fora
insulae 26 863, 868, 887
Isola dei Mattei 20 839–40
Istituto Centrale per il Catalogo e la Documentazione 16 777
Istituto Centrale per il Restauro Adolfo Venturi library 16 777
Istituto di Corrispondenza Archeologica 10 637, 639
Istituto Germanico 2 164
Istituto Nazionale d'Archeologia e Storia 4 23
Istituto Nazionale per la Grafica Calcografia Nazionale 16 777
collections 4 308; 16 777
Istituto per il Medio e Estremo Oriente 2 733; 3 170
Janiculum asylum 26 761
Janus Quadrifrons 26 752
Lacus Juturnae see under Forum Romanum
Lapis Niger see under Forum Romanum
Lateran Palace 19 167; 26 754, 819–20*, 819
Cappella Sancta Sanctorum 31 344
maps 20 365
Palace of Leo III 16 761
wall paintings 16 762; 26 655
libraries
Becchetti library 16 777
Biblioteca Alessandrina see under Archiginnasio
Biblioteca Apostolica Vaticana see under ROME, VATICAN → libraries
Biblioteca Casanatense 5 616; 19 89
Biblioteca dell'Istituto Nazionale d'Archeologia e Storia dell'Arte 16 776
see also palazzi → Palazzo Venezia
Biblioteca Vallicelliana 19 314
Bibliotheca Hertziana 2 366, 369, 370; 16 777
see also palazzi → Palazzo Zuccari
Library of Hadrian see under Forum of Trajan
Library of Trajan see under Forum of Trajan
Macellum Liviae 19 888
Macellum Magnum 19 888; 26 891
Macellum of Nero 26 871
marble plan see Severan marble plan
markets 20 438
Markets of Trajan see under Forum of Trajan

Rome—cont.
mausolea 20 866–7
Mausoleum of Augustus 20 864; 26 750, 750, 890; 27 235; 31 109
mausoleum of Constantia see ecclesiastical buildings → S Costanza
mausoleum of Hadrian see Castel Sant' Angelo → tomb of Hadrian
Mausoleum of Helena 20 865; 26 752
Mausoleum of Romulus 9 556; 20 864; 26 902; 27 235
see also tombs
Meta Sudans 11 339
Milliarium Aureum 26 781, 782; 27 6
Ministero di Grazia e Giustizia 24 692–3
Monte Testaccio 26 750; 27 106
monument to Giordano Bruno 29 566
monument to Marcus Aurelius see under Piazza del Campidoglio
monument to the Immaculate Conception 26 761
monument to Victor-Emanuel II 16 645, 707, 764; 22 42, 47; 26 762, 763; 27 492
museums 2 365; 27 45–6, 115
Antiquarium Comunale 26 783
Antiquarium Forense 26 783
Egyptian Museum see under Museo Capitolino
Fondazione Primoli 25 586
Gabinetto delle Stampe 24 834
Galleria Nazionale d'Arte Antica Palazzo Corsini 7 896, 897, 898; 19 524
Biblioteca Corsiniana 7 682; 13 802, 803; 27 749
directors 32 233
Galleria Corsini 6 111; 20 376
see also palazzi → Palazzo Corsini
Galleria Nazionale d'Arte Moderna 3 436; 16 648, 775; 25 586
collections 20 483; 23 852
Jewish museum 17 582
Musei Capitolini 27 45
see also Museo Capitolino; Museo dei Conservatori; Pinacoteca Capitolina
Museo Barracco 3 272; 16 774; 27 46
Museo Capitolino 13 469; 16 768; 24 240; 27 45
catalogues 4 492; 7 898
collections 1 533; 2 169; 3 708; 6 97; 9 23; 10 849; 13 303, 605; 16 771; 18 692; 22 356; 26 286, 775
Egyptian Museum 3 708
Greek collection 13 470
Roman collection 27 115
Sala degli Imperatori 9 23
sculpture 27 46
Museo Cartaceo 2 163; 7 906; 25 386
Museo della Civiltà Romana 16 775; 27 115
Museo dei Conservatori 23 492, 810
collections 13 542; 27 114, 115; 29 402
sculpture 27 46
see also palazzi → Palazzo dei Conservatori
Museo Kircheriano 18 76
Museo Nazionale d'Arte Orientale
collections 2 734; 18 384; 29 240; 30 849; 31 409
exhibitions 15 923

Rome
museums—cont.
Museo Nazionale delle Arti e delle Tradizioni Popolari 8 771; 25 448
Museo Nazionale di Castel Sant'Angelo 26 795
see also Castel Sant'Angelo
Museo Nazionale Preistorico ed Etnografico Luigi Pigorini
collections 18 165; 21 264, 265; 29 240
library 16 776, 777
Museo Nazionale Romano
collections 5 682; 16 774; 27 115
Greek collection 13 470
paintings 27 58
sculpture 27 46
Museo Nazionale di Villa Giulia
Barberini Collection 13 605
Castellani Collection 6 20; 13 605
collections 10 638, 640; 13 542, 555, 605; 16 774
see also villas → Villa Giulia
Museo del Palazzo Venezia see → palazzi → Palazzo Venezia
Museo Pigorini see Museo Nazionale Preistorico ed Etnografico Luigi Pigorini
Museo di Roma e Galleria Comunale d'Arte Moderna 27 172
see also palazzi → Palazzo Braschi
Museo di Scultura Antica see Museo Barracco
Museo della Società Geografica Italiana 29 240
Museum Chartaceum see Museo Cartaceo
Pinacoteca Capitolina 3 708; 11 386; 24 833; 27 486
see also palazzi → Palazzo dei Conservatori
Protomoteca Capitolina 7 726
see also ROME (VATICAN) → museums
National Institute of Archaeology and Art History 18 692
Norwegian Institute 19 660; 23 245
nymphaeum, Via degli Annibaldi 27 66
Olympic Games 23 431
Oppian 26 892
Orti Farnesiani 12 115
Ospedale di S Gallicano 25 853
Ospizio di S Michele a Ripa 26 760
Palace of Domitian 3 329; 12 70; 14 73; 26 751, 853
Palace of Maxentius 9 556
Palace of Septimius Severus 26 786, 787
Palace of Titus 18 756
Palatine 10 601; 23 805; 26 749, 751, 785–7*, 787, 877, 892, 893
huts 10 598
libraries 19 312
sculpture 13 605; 27 32
stucco 27 72
walls 10 601
Palatium see Flavian Palace
Palazzetto dello Sport 7 696; 22 806; 26 764; 28 583; 29 427, 489
dome 22 806
see also Palazzo dello Sport
palazzi 16 629, 631–2
Palazzetto Farnese 5 864; 10 811; 18 730
Palazzi dell'Esedra 16 644; 18 184

Rome
palazzi—cont.
Palazzo Aldobrandini (Piazza Colonna) *see* Palazzo Aldobrandini-Chigi
Palazzo Aldobrandini al Corso *see* Palazzo Doria Pamphili
Palazzo Aldobrandini-Chigi **6** 586
Palazzo Almagiá **24** 476
Palazzo Altieri **5** 653; **12** 583–4
frescoes **1** 728; **20** 588
paintings **10** 488; **11** 901; **20** 375; **31** 72
Sala dei Specchi **31** 679
Salone Verde **8** 100
Palazzo Altoviti **1** 734
Palazzo d'Aste *see* Palazzo Mischiatelli
Palazzo Baldassini **27** *741*, 741–2
Palazzo Barberini **3** 206–7, 208; **4** 428*; **16** 638; **20** 46; **26** 836–8*
bridge-ruin **27** 323
cartoons (drawings) **24** 339
collections **5** 337
frames **11** 394
frescoes **3** 96; **5** 453; **6** 568; **7** 908; **14** 583; **15** 138; **25** 148; **26** 565; **27** 487–8, *488*
Gran Salone **7** 907–8; **16** 671, 714; **26** *837*; **29** 830
guidebook **3** 208
interior decoration **16** 716
library **19** 314
paintings **3** 920; **5** 695; **6** 346; **7** 916; **11** 719; **20** 375, 377; **26** 332
sculpture **31** 244
tapestries **3** 207
Palazzo delle Belle Arti *see* museums → Galleria Nazionale d'Arte Moderna
Palazzo Bentivoglio *see* Palazzo Pallavicini-Rospigliosi
Palazzo Bernini **9** 376
Palazzo Borghese **4** 407; **19** 632; **20** 46
frescoes **5** 359; **9** 377
interior decoration **18** 871
paintings **2** 27; **7** 916; **12** 586
Sangiorgi gallery **18** 781
Palazzo Brancaccio *see* museums → Museo Nazionale d'Arte Orientale
Palazzo Branconio dell'Aquila **16** 634; **25** 907
Palazzo Braschi **25** 148
engravings **13** 626
paintings **13** 626; **29** 889
see also museums → Museo di Roma e Galleria Communale d'Arte Moderna
Palazzo di Brazzà *see* Palazzo Stati Maccarani
Palazzo Bufalo **11** 679; **33** 717
Palazzo Caetani **6** 111
Palazzo Caffarelli-Vidoni-Stoppani **31** 72
Palazzo della Cancelleria **1** 572; **2** 320; **4** 776; **16** 631; **20** 279; **23** 486, 810; **24** 752; **26** 299, 756, 791, 836*; **32** 13
courtyard **8** 65; **16** *631*
Gran Sala **1** 532
interior decoration **16** 712
paintings **19** 524; **32** 12
Sala dei Cento Giorni **3** 471; **10** 810; **12** 719; **25** 71
theatre **23** 637
Palazzo Capodiferro-Spada **3** 859; **9** 11, 14, 21
Palazzo Caprini **4** 650–51; **16** 633; **23** 492
Palazzo Cardelli **24** 833
Palazzo de Carolis **5** 812; **19** 816
Rome
palazzi—cont.
Palazzo Cesi **6** 360
Palazzo Chigi (Piazza SS Apostoli) *see* Palazzo Chigi-Odescalchi
Palazzo Chigi (Piazza Colonna) *see* Palazzo Aldobrandini-Chigi
Palazzo Chigi-Odescalchi **3** 835; **16** 639; **23** 352, 493, *493*; **26** 759
busts **23** 899
frescoes **3** 95
Salone d'Oro **16** 716, 717, *717*; **18** 779; **23** 544; **31** 799
Palazzo della Civiltà del Lavoro **26** 762
Palazzo Colonna **7** 553, 620; **20** 241, 431
collections **7** 621
frames **11** 394
frescoes **6** 568; **9** 377; **16** 671; **26** 320
Galleria Colonna **5** 344; **9** 11, *11*, 19, 377; **12** 460; **13** 292; **16** 714, 771; **21** 807; **31** 205; **33** 269
interior decoration **7** 621–2
paintings **3** 920; **7** 622; **9** 15; **25** 411
Palazzo dei Conservatori **1** 490; **16** 634; **23** 836; **26** 756
collections **2** 162, 168
frescoes **1** 595; **2** 493, *494*
sculpture **27** 271
statue of Innocent X **23** 899
see also museums → Museo dei Conservatori; Pinacoteca Capitolina
Palazzo della Consulta **11** 814, *814*
Palazzo Corsini **6** 346
murals **5** 908
paintings **25** 563; **28** 364
sculpture **28** 846
Palazzo Corsini *see also* museums → Galleria Nazionale d'Arte Antica Palazzo Corsini
Palazzo Costaguti **18** 733, 734; **21** 806; **24** 267; **26** 565
Palazzo Crescenzi **8** 138
Palazzo Deza *see* Palazzo Borghese
Palazzo Doria Pamphili **9** 175*; **13** 292; **26** 416; **30** 356
chapel **1** 596
collections **23** 898
coral **7** 835
frames **11** 394
frescoes **7** 916; **28** 38
Gabinetto degli Specchi **25** 411
Galleria Doria Pamphili **5** 635, 705, 857; **8** 143; **9** 19, 376; **20** 586, 597; **24** 827; **25** 905; **32** 12; **33** 269
Galleria Doria Pamphili: frescoes **4** 813, *813*
Galleria degli Specchi: frescoes **21** 539
paintings **3** 27, 211, 698; **4** 154; **5** 454; **9** 15, 172, 376; **11** 394; **14** 322; **23** 11; **28** 38; **30** 798
sculpture **16** 698
tapestries **5** 211; **13** 634
Palazzo dell'Esposizione **16** 644; **24** 692
Palazzo Falconieri **4** 434; **23** 836; **28** *339*; **29** 830
Palazzo Farnese **7** 664; **8** 504; **10** 808; **15** 137; **16** 633, 771; **21** 455, *455*; **23** 810, *810*; **26** 756, 838–9*, *839*; **27** *742*
Camerino Farnese **5** 861–2
collections **13** 303; **14** 661
frescoes **15** 137; **27** 652–3, *653*
Galleria Farnese **5** 864
Rome
palazzi
Palazzo Farnese—cont.
Galleria Farnese: frescoes (allegorical) **1** 659; **5** 862–4
Galleria Farnese: frescoes (grisaille) **7** 383; **13** 676; **15** 137
Galleria Farnese: frescoes (mythological) **5** 858; **15** 87; **16** 669, *669*, 670, 714; **22** 414; **23** 294, 680
Galleria Farnese: paintings **23** 523
Galleria Farnese: sculpture **9** 21
models **2** 336
Sala dei Fasti Farnesiani **16** 665; **25** 71
salotto **10** 811
staircases **29** 521
windows **12** 790
Palazzo Fiorenza **10** 849
Palazzo Gabrielli *see* Palazzo Taverna
Palazzo Gaddi **10** 737
Palazzo Gaetani *see* Palazzo Ruspoli
Palazzo Giustiniani **12** 763; **30** 428
Palazzo di Giustizia **5** 425; **16** 645; **18** 889; **26** 762
Palazzo Koch **8** 851
Palazzo Lancellotti **18** 689, 733; **30** 356
Palazzo Lante **4** 181; **5** 414; **26** 566
Palazzo Ludovisi *see* Palazzo Montecitorio
Palazzo Madama **3** 96; **6** 149; **9** 182; **20** 521, *521*
Palazzo Mancini **13** 303
Palazzo della Manifattura dei Tabacchi **26** 761
Palazzo Margherita **16** 644
Palazzo Massimo alle Colonne **8** 504; **16** 634, 712; **23** 810; **24** *533*, 533–4
Palazzo Massimo alle Terme *see* villas → Villa Negroni
Palazzo Mattei-Caetani **33** 717
Palazzo Mattei di Giove **4** 341; **7** 906; **20** 45, *45*, 840–41
Palazzo Medici *see* Palazzo Madama
Palazzo del Ministero del Tesoro **26** 762
Palazzo Mischiatelli **27** *194*
Palazzo di Monte Cavallo **15** 837
Palazzo Montecitorio **3** *327*, 835; **23** 492; **26** 759, 762
Aula Grande **27** 852
Palazzo Muti-Bussi **9** 375, 377
Palazzo Muti-Papazzurri **13** 656
Palazzo Naro **12** 525
Palazzo Nuovo **16** 634; **23** 492, 810; **26** 756
Palazzo Odescalchi *see* Palazzo Chigi-Odescalchi
Palazzo Orsini **5** 525; **23** 575
Palazzo Pacelli **16** 644
Palazzo Pallavicini-Rospigliosi **3** 744; **4** 405; **12** 706; **30** 428
Casino dell'Aurora **3** 265; **4** 813; **15** 137; **24** 239; **26** *199*
Casino delle Muse **30** *355*
frescoes **11** 845; **22** 487; **27** 172
Galleria Pallavicini **4** 154; **12** 54; **19** 894; **20** 586; **23** 873; **26** 198; **27** 643
paintings **3** 211; **12** *707*; **19** 714; **20** 805
Palazzo Pamphili **4** 433; **16** 638, 639; **26** 759
frescoes **9** 376; **23** 898
Rome
palazzi
Palazzo Pamphili—cont.
Galleria Pamphili **7** 910; **16** 671; **22** 414
library **8** 100; **15** 138
Palazzo Patrizi *see* Palazzo Costaguti
Palazzo dei Penitenzieri **24** 830
Palazzo Peretti *see* Palazzo Almagiá
Palazzo Piccolomini **30** 649
Palazzo Poli **16** 639
Palazzo del Quirinale **4** 405; **6** 362; **14** 5; **23** 677; **26** 758, 840*; **30** 356
Coffee House **3** 708; **20** 806
frescoes **7** 902; **20** 375; **21** *97*, 807, *807*; **24** 10
furniture **18** 853
Galleria di Alessandro VII **7** 910; **9** 376
gardens **1** 595
interior decoration **4** 302; **24** *845*
paintings **3** 95, 380; **5** 555; **20** 57
paintings (ceiling) **12** 584
reliefs **18** 698
Sala degli Ambasciatori **20** 283
Sala dei Corazzieri **4** 405
Sala delle Nozze Aldobrandini **4** 405
Sala Regia **3** 353; **18** 732; **27** 817; **29** 253
sculpture **30** 764
Stanza del Diluvio **5** 870
tapestries **3** 454; **31** 905
Palazzo Riario **9** 16; **32** 8
Palazzo Ricci *see* Palazzo Sacchetti
Palazzo Rondanini **12** 33
Palazzo Rospigliosi-Pallavicini *see* Palazzo Pallavicini-Rospigliosi
Palazzo Rucellai **16** 771
Palazzo Ruggieri **1** 551, 553
Palazzo Ruspoli **19** 524; **20** 394
Palazzo Sacchetti **7** 906; **16** 771; **25** 208; **27** 652
Palazzo Santacroce ai Catinari **13** 655
Palazzo del Sant'Uffizio **1** 666
Palazzo della Sapienza *see* Archiginnasio
Palazzo Sciarra-Colonna **25** 411
Palazzo Senatorio **7** 921; **16** 634; **23** 492, 810, 836; **26** 756; **31** 236
Palazzo Sforza-Cesarini **26** 755
Palazzo di S Giorgio *see* Palazzo della Cancelleria
Palazzo S Marco *see* Palazzo Venezia
Palazzo Sodalizio Piceni **2** 493
Palazzo Spada **4** 434; **21** 807
collections **11** 386
frames **11** 394
frescoes **28** *338*
Galleria Spada **20** 597, *598*; **29** 39; **31** 174
Palazzo Stati Maccarani **12** *752*, 753
Palazzo Taverna **26** 322
Palazzo Torlonia **30** 765
Palazzo dei Tribunali **4** 650; **26** 756
Palazzo della Valle **2** 162; **16** 770
Palazzo Venezia **2** 320; **11** 685; **16** 632; **23** 486; **24** 278; **26** 756
collections **16** 775
courtyard **8** 65; **16** *632*
manuscripts **2** 310
Sala del Mappamondo **20** 365
Rome
palazzi
Palazzo Venezia—cont.
see also libraries → Biblioteca dell'Istituto Nazionale d'Archeologia e Storia dell'Arte
Palazzo Wedekind **5** 552
Palazzo Zuccari **1** 662; **2** 547, *547*
frescoes **1** 662
interior decoration **3** 291
murals **7** 870; **12** *392*, 393; **22** 328, 704; **23** 676; **32** 119
see also libraries → Bibliotheca Hertziana
Palazzo dello Sport **22** 806; **29** 489
see also Palazzetto dello Sport
Palestra per la Scherma **16** 649
Pantheon **2** *167*, 319; **7** 692; **8** 260; **9** 11, 12; **16** 623; **20** 570, 577; **23** 534; **24** 21; **26** *750*, 750, 751, 752, 792–4*, *793*, 866, 880, 882, 890, 896, 897, *898*, 924; **27** 235; **28** *469*; **30** 436
arches **2** 295, 297
coffering **7** 527
dome **9** 83, 85; **20** 579; **26** 794
epigraphy **26** 884
frieze **11** 791
icons **9** 624
oculus **19** 362
orders (architecture) **23** 484
pediment **24** 318
portico **25** 265
roof **7** 813; **30** 903
sculpture **9** 20; **27** 30, 31, 32
tomb of Umberto I **29** 702
see also ecclesiastical buildings → S Maria ad Martyres
patronage **16** 761–2; **26** 773
Piazza del Campidoglio **21** 453–4, *454*; **26** 757; **27** 39, 46; **31** 236, 712
Marius trophies **31** 369
monument to Marcus Aurelius **2** 168; **10** 440; **22** 43; **27** *10*, 11, 12, 21; **29** 565
Piazza del Collegio Romano **26** 759
Piazza Colonna **26** 757
Piazza della Consolazione **9** 653
Piazza dell'Emporio **8** 263
Piazza dell'Esquilino **23** 330
Piazza della Maddalena **26** 758
Piazza Montecitorio **26** 761
Piazza Navona **4** 433–4*; **16** 638; **26** 751, 758, 873, 895
Four Rivers Fountain *see under* fountains
Moro Fountain *see under* fountains
Neptune Fountain *see* fountains → Moro Fountain
obelisk *see* fountains → Four Rivers Fountain
Piazza del Popolo **16** 638, 644; **26** *758*, 761; **31** 800–801
Obelisk of Augustus **7** 342; **23** 330, *331*; **26** 757, 758
Piazza di Porta Capena **1** 512
Piazza del Quirinale **2** 140; **9** 20; **26** 761
Piazza della Repubblica **16** 644, *648*; **26** 762
Piazza di S Ignazio **16** 639, *639*; **25** 853–4; **26** 760–61; **31** 713
Piazza delle Terme *see* Piazza della Repubblica
Piazza di Trevi **5** 826–7; **26** 758
Pincian **23** 330; **26** 761
plan (marble) *see* Severan marble plan
Porta Ardeatina **3** 359; **21** 566, *566*

Rome—cont.
Porta Maggiore 7 358; 23 484; 26 874, 892, 892
underground basilica 3 329; 26 867; 27 69–70; 29 814; 30 436
Porta Pia 7 359; 14 416; 16 634, 634; 21 456; 23 488
Porta del Popolo 26 759
Porta Portese 26 758
Portico of Octavian 25 180; 27 31
Portico of Pompey 29 521
Portico of Q. Caecilius Metellus 26 856
Porticus Absidata see under Forum of Nerva
Porticus Aemilia 26 879, 887
Porticus Deorum Consentium 26 752
Porticus Divorum 26 749, 893
Porticus Octaviae 19 312
Porticus Philippi 33 639
Porticus Vipsenia 20 365
Porto di Ripetta 26 760; 29 373–4
Post Office 16 650
Praetorian Camp 26 901, 902
Pyramid of Cestius see tombs → tomb of Caius Cestius
Quirinal 27 67
reconstruction 5 448
Regia 26 781, 782
Rostra 26 781, 781, 782, 867
Saepta Julia 26 749
Scalinata della Santa Trinità dei Monti see Spanish Steps
scholae 26 753
Secretarium Senatus 26 752
Septizodium 26 786, 787, 900, 901
Servian Walls see under walls
Severan marble plan 19 888; 26 748, 749, 784, 901
shops 26 750
shrine of Janus 26 781, 782
shrine of Venus Cloacina see under Forum Romanum
Silentium see Casa Corezzionale
silk 9 663
Spanish Steps 16 639; 26 760, 760; 27 710–11, 711; 29 525
Stabian Baths see under baths
Stadio Flaminio 26 764
Stadium of Domitian 26 895; 29 488
Stazione Centrale 26 761
Stazione di Termini 26 762
stone 26 875
Teatro Argentina 30 667
Teatro Tor di Nona 30 667
temples 26 751, 886
cult temples 26 751
Forum Boarium 26 865
Temple of Antoninus and Faustina see under Forum Romanum
Temple of Apollo (Palatine) 26 786, 786, 865; 27 30, 31, 32
sculpture 27 13; 29 VIII2
Temple of Apollo Sosianus (Circus Martius) 26 865; 27 10, 27, 30, 31
pediment 24 319, 319
Temple B (Largo Argentina) 8 263
Temple of Castor and Pollux see under Forum Romanum
Temple of Ceres 10 617
Temple of Claudius (AD 54) 23 480
Temple of Concord see under Forum Romanum
Temple of Cybele see Temple of Magna Mater
Temple of the Deified Claudius (after AD 70) 26 865, 891, 892, 893; 30 436

Rome
temples—cont.
Temple of the Deified Hadrian 26 866
Temple of the Deified Trajan see under Forum of Trajan
Temple of the Deified Vespasian see under Forum Romanum
Temple of the Dioscuri see Forum Romanum → Temple of Castor and Pollux
Temple of Divus Julius see under Forum Romanum
Temple of the Flavian family 27 34
Temple of Fortuna Virilis see Temple of Portunus
Temple of Hercules Victor see under Forum Boarium
Temple of Honor and Virtus 26 925
Temple of Julius Caesar 2 217
Temple of Juno Regina 24 319
Temple of Jupiter Dolichenus 26 867, 900; 30 436
Temple of Jupiter Optimus Maximus Capitolinus 8 263; 10 587, 601; 16 622; 26 749, 856, 865, 874, 886, 893; 27 1, 12
Temple of Jupitor Stator see under Forum Romanum
Temple of Magna Mater 26 786, 787, 879; 27 1, 27
pediment 24 319
Temple of Mars Ultor see under Forum Augustum
Temple of Minerva Medica 9 84; 26 783, 785, 879, 903, 903; 27 67, 235
arches 2 297
Temple of Mithras 26 751, 824*, 859; 27 67
Temple of Peace of Vespasian see Templum Pacis
Temple of the Penates 26 903
Temple of Portunus 30 435
Temple of Quirinus 24 320; 27 32
Temple of Romulus see under Forum Romanum
Temple of Saturn see under Forum Romanum
Temple of Serapis 26 866, 885, 900; 30 436
Temple of Sol Invictus 26 787, 900
Temple of the Sun 26 901
Temple of Titus 26 782
Temple of Veiovis 26 893; 27 12
Temple of Venus and Rome see under Forum Romanum
Temple of Venus Genetrix see under Forum Julium
Temple of Venus Victrix 26 856; 27 31
Temple of Vesta see under Forum Romanum
Templum Pacis 19 312; 26 783, 784, 796, 865, 889, 893, 925; 30 436
paintings 30 893
see also ecclesiastical buildings → S Clemente
Theatre of Marcellus 2 319; 20 572; 23 481; 26 856, 873, 873, 877, 888, 889, 891; 30 651, 655; 32 502
Theatre of Pompey 11 339; 20 572; 26 749, 750, 856, 865, 873, 879, 889; 27 29; 30 652
Thermae Alexandrinae see Baths of Severus Alexander
Thermae Antoninianae see Baths of Caracalla
Thermae Septimianae see Baths of Septimius Severus

Rome—cont.
tombs 7 642; 27 830; 31 109
Baker's Tomb see tomb of Marcus Vergilius Eurysaces
tomb of Annia Regilla 20 864; 26 877, 878, 883, 900
tomb of Caecilia Metella 20 863; 31 109
tomb of Caius Cestius 20 864; 25 766; 26 901; 31 109
tomb of Hadrian see under Castel Sant' Angelo
tomb of Marcus Vergilius Eurysaces 27 9, 25; 31 109
tomb of St Agnes 26 799
tomb of St Lawrence 26 799
tomb of the Aurelii 31 110
tomb of the Cornelii Scipiones 31 109
tomb of the Pancratii 27 72
tomb of the Valerii 27 72
see also mausolea
Tor de' Conti 15 860
Tor de' Schiavi 20 864; 27 235
Torre del Campanaro 27 38
Torre della Grascia see Torre del Campanaro
trade 9 596; 26 751
Trajan's Column see under Forum of Trajan
Trajan's Forum see Forum of Trajan
United States Embassy see palazzi → Palazzo Margherita
Università dei Pittori e Miniatori 26 766
urban planning 23 620; 27 271
Roman 26 750, 864; 27 2, 3
16th cent. 11 271, 272; 24 398; 31 713, 714, 717
17th cent. 6 584–5
20th cent. 12 718; 24 693; 25 738
Vatican see ROME (VATICAN)
Via Tiburtina 27 29
Vigna Codini 7 642
villas
Villa Albani see Villa Torlonia
Villa Altoviti 1 734
Villa Benedetti 3 706; 4 765–6
Villa Borghese 2 612–13, 646; 3 829–30; 4 404, 405, 407; 7 312, 782; 9 21, 692; 14 109; 16 644, 727; 26 762, 847
Casino 18 733; 20 456
collections 4 407; 6 98; 11 895; 16 774
Egyptian Propylaia 5 616
frescoes 5 359; 27 201
Galleria degli Imperatori 29 833
gardens 9 21; 12 116
paintings 1 596, 711; 2 180; 3 13; 4 404; 5 366, 635, 705, 711, 712, 715; 7 684, 916; 10 525; 11 396; 14 582; 16 665; 17 3; 18 733; 25 464; 26 197; 28 38
paintings (ceiling) 11 901
park 4 407; 5 616; 6 323; 12 117; 24 179
sculpture 4 407, 587; 7 383; 9 23, 26; 16 768, 771; 22 414; 23 294; 27 46; 29 562
Villa Celimontana 20 840
Villa Chigi 2 27; 16 716
Villa dei Centroni 27 66
Villa del Pigneto 7 912
Villa del Vascello see Villa Benedetti
Villa d'Este 26 846
Villa Doria 26 762
Villa Doria-Pamphili 12 117; 23 899; 31 854
Columbarium 7 642
paintings 3 712
stucco 29 830

Rome
villas—cont.
Villa Farnesina 3 674; 6 583*; 16 633; 18 702; 20 279; 24 530, 530; 27 46; 30 655; 32 545
drawings 7 903
frescoes 10 130; 22 413, 413; 25 71; 29 2; 32 549
Garden Loggia 28 332
Loggia of Cupid and Psyche 6 583; 25 905
paintings 13 546; 23 680
Sala del Fregio 23 680
Sala delle Prospettive 6 583; 15 137
Sala di Galatea 6 583; 7 383; 22 412; 24 530; 25 905
stucco 27 69, 70
wall paintings 27 52, 54, 58
Villa Galli 28 314
Villa Giulia 5 917; 16 633; 22 6; 32 504, 504–5, 546; 33 716
Fonte Basso 13 703
sculpture 26 846
see also museums → Museo Nazionale di Villa Giulia
Villa Giustiniani 9 21; 20 588
see also Casino Massimo
Villa Lante 12 752–3; 32 546
Villa Ludovisi 12 117; 26 758, 762, 847; 32 550
Bosco delle Statue 2 163
Casino Ludovisi 3 265; 4 567; 5 706; 13 786, 786; 15 137; 19 779
Casino Ludovisi: Camerino dei Paesi 32 593
sculpture 16 771
Villa Madama 10 130; 12 751–2; 13 700; 16 633; 23 492, 836; 25 191, 907; 31 523–4; 32 546
dome 9 84
frescoes 32 550
gardens 12 115
interior decoration 16 712
Loggia 25 907
sculpture 3 157; 16 770
stucco 29 830
theatre 30 655, 656
Villa Malta 26 129
Villa Massimo alle Terme see Villa Negroni
Villa Mattei 12 117; 26 847
Villa Medici 9 21; 16 771; 21 23, 30; 23 352; 26 846; 27 114; 32 546, 547
frescoes 33 722
sculpture 2 168; 3 231; 14 12; 31 787; 32 236
Villa Montalto see Villa Negroni
Villa Negroni 12 117; 18 732; 24 398, 399; 25 193
collections 17 475
paintings 18 730
sculpture 29 563
Villa of Herod Atticus 13 703
Villa of Maxentius 23 809; 26 925
Villa of the Quintilii 26 870
Villa Pamphili 9 21; 13 655; 26 847
Villa Peretti-Montalto see Villa Negroni
Villa Randanini 17 554
Villa Ruffo 6 98
Villa Torlonia 1 533; 16 644; 20 392, 393; 22 361, 735; 24 227; 26 840–41*, 847; 32 553
catacombs 17 554
collections 16 653; 27 46, 115
frescoes 16 677
Gran Salone 9 23
interior decoration 16 717
Loggia 16 772
paintings 2 27; 5 554; 20 377; 21 132–3; 23 295
ruin buildings 27 324

Rome
villas
Villa Torlonia—cont.
sculpture 1 533, 646; 9 23, 409; 16 771; 29 633; 31 63
stucco 29 833
Tempietti 24 290
walls 26 754, 901, 902
Aurelian Wall 26 751
Servian Walls 26 749, 874, 887
water supply 11 339
see also aqueducts; fountains
Zoo 33 699
Rome (Vatican) 26 800–818*
Accademia di Bacchio Brandin see under Palace → Cortile del Belvedere (great)
Appartamento Borgia see under Palace
Casino of Pius IV 19 371, 371; 24 290; 25 7; 26 846; 29 830; 33 718
paintings 3 254
cemetery 27 113, 113
collections 2 370, 559; 10 487; 13 470; 24 240, 834
books 19 313
sculpture 4 697
textiles 28 715
Cortile del Belvedere (great) see under Palace
Cortile del Belvedere (small) see museums → Museo Pio-Clementino → Cortile Ottagono di Belvedere
Cortile di S Damaso see under Palace
Galleria delle Statue see under museums → Museo Pio-Clementino
Giardino della Pigna 23 86
Grotte Vaticane
sarcophagus of Junius Bassus 9 518; 16 686; 27 828
sculpture 16 691; 27 271
tomb of Boniface VIII 2 482
tomb of Gregory V 31 121
tomb of Paul II 21 694
tomb of Sixtus IV 25 158
libraries
Biblioteca Ambrosiana 24 249
Biblioteca Angelica 19 314, 315; 24 240
Biblioteca Apostolica Vaticana 7 218; 8 781; 14 867; 19 313, 315
archives 2 370
Camera dei Papiri 7 412; 10 96; 21 133
catalogues 4 409; 7 306
codices 24 240
collections 1 439, 532; 2 596; 4 21; 15 744; 18 692; 23 96; 32 8
frescoes 12 549–50
manuscripts 15 862
paintings 4 840; 24 492
Salone Sistino 24 399
Biblioteca Greca 6 14
Bibliotheca Latina 27 271
Loggie of Leo X see under Palace
museums 2 365; 8 781; 13 541; 27 46, 115; 30 332
Astarita Collection 24 278
catalogues 6 77
Chiaramonti corridor 14 265
collections 21 265
Collezione d'Arte Moderna Religiosa 24 278
directors 30 459
Galleria degli Arazzi 26 800
Galleria Clementina 7 897; 9 29
Galleria Lapidaria 1 532
Musei Lateranesi 24 240
Museo Chiaramonti 5 679; 7 726; 16 774; 26 800, 814
Braccio Nuovo 3 644; 16 774; 29 640, 640
frescoes 32 119

Rome (Vatican)
museums—cont.
Museo Clementino *see* Museo Pio-Clementino
Museo Gregoriano Egizio **13** 629; **16** 774; **26** 800
collections **10** 94, 95
Museo Gregoriano Etrusco **13** 629; **16** 774; **26** 800
collections **9** 29; **10** 637, 640; **13** 542, 555
pottery **13** 541
Museo Gregoriano Profano **16** 775; **26** 287, 800
collections **13** 629
frescoes **25** 411
paintings **27** 58
sculpture **27** 46
Museo Missionario Etnologico **16** 775; **24** 278
Museo Pio-Clementino **2** 165, 169; **5** 552, 679; **7** 411–12; **9** 12, 23; **16** 772; **22** 362; **25** 8; **26** 756, 775, 800, 814; **27** 115; **28** 754; **29** 833; **32** 612, 613
catalogues **33** 385
collections **2** 168; **6** 98; **9** 23, 29; **16** 705, 768; **22** 356; **24** 240; **25** 8
Cortile Ottagono di Belvedere **2** 226; **27** 114; **28** 314, 754–5
Galleria delle Statue **9** 23; **15** 861
interior decoration **31** 679
Sala a Croce Greca **28** 755
Sala delle Muse **28** 755
Sala Rotonda **9** *12*; **22** *361*; **28** 755
sculpture **13** 605; **16** 770, *773*; **22** 355; **27** 46
Museo Pio-Cristiano **16** 775
Museo Sacro **3** 708; **22** 110; **24** 240; **25** 411
Museo Storico **24** 278
Museum of Christian Antiquities *see* Museo Sacro
Pinacoteca Vaticana **16** 774; **26** 800
sculpture **10** 849
Palace **7** 620; **15** 860; **19** 371; **23** 97; **26** 755, 810–14*, *812*, 815*, 817–18*
apartments **1** 572
Appartamento Borgia **1** 655; **4** 410; **10** 95; **13** 700; **16** 660; **26** 817
Belvedere *see* Cortile del Belvedere (great)
Belvedere Chapel **20** 311
Chapel of Nicholas V **2** 37–8*, *38*; **16** 659; **26** 184
Cortile del Belvedere (great) **1** 572; **4** 648–9, *649*; **7** 218, 383; **8** 65; **9** 23; **22** 362; **26** *813*, 846; **29** 522; **32** 546; **33** 718
Accademia di Bacchio Brandin **16** 778
Pine Cone **11** 346
sculpture **2** 162; **3** 690; **9** 20; **13** 605; **25** 7
Cortile del Belvedere (small) *see* museums → Museo Pio-Clementino → Cortile Ottagono di Belvedere
Cortile di S Damaso **23** 898
Galleria delle Carte Geografiche **4** 812; **8** 513; **20** 366; **26** 565
Loggie of Leo X **12** 750; **13** *669*, 700; **21** 16; **25** 148, 191, 902; **32** 586
frescoes **29** 747
paintings **24** 365
stucco **29** 830
Papal Audience Hall *see* Sala Regia
Pauline Chapel **21** *447*, 447–8*

Rome (Vatican)
Palace—cont.
Sala Clementina **1** 553, 595; **4** 813; **11** *762*
frescoes **1** *552*
Sala dei Chiaroscuri **26** 818
Sala dei Misteri della Fede **3** 301; **4** 410; **24** 830; **26** 817, *817*
Sala dei Paramenti **26** 817
Sala dei Santi **4** 410; **24** 830; **26** 817
Sala del Concistoro **1** 595
Sala del Credo **4** 410; **24** 830; **26** 817
Sala della Contessa Matilda **3** 206, 207; **26** 565
Sala delle Arti Liberali **24** 830; **26** 817
Sala delle Scienze e delle Arti **4** 410
Sala delle Sibille **4** 410; **24** 830; **26** 817
Sala del Pappagallo *see* Sala dei Chiaroscuri
Sala di Carlo Magno **1** 20; **25** 411
Sala di Costantino **3** 387; **15** 137; **25** 902; **26** 818
frescoes **12** 751; **24** 398; **32** 806
paintings **13** 628; **24** 365
Sala Regia **22** 806; **27** 655; **28** 658, *658*; **33** *717*, 718
frescoes **23** 265
paintings **13** 628; **32** 17
Sala Vecchia degli Svizzeri **23** 97; **26** 818
Scala di Bramante **29** 522
Scala Regia **3** 837*; **26** *814*; **29** 524
equestrian statue of Constantine **23** 899
stucco **29** 830
Sistine Chapel **4** 697; **6** 459, 460; **7** 218, 676; **20** 684; **21** 134; **26** 756, *815*, 815–17*
cleaning **7** 727
conservation **7** 747
frescoes **4** *840*; **8** 612; **15** 87; **16** 614, 659, 661, 664, 763; **20** 279; **21** 446–7; **23** 293; **24** 521–2, *522*, 830; **25** 411; **26** 186, 189, *816*; **28** 700–701; **32** 805, *806*
paintings **16** 665; **22** 521
photographed works **26** 233
restorations **32** *809*
Sistine Ceiling **12** 503; **13** 676; **15** 137; **19** 352; **21** 443–5*, *444*; **23** 292, 293; **31** 501
tapestries **14** 416; **30** 315, 322
Stanza d'Eliodoro **21** 16; **24** 493; **25** 901; **26** 818
frescoes **25** 71; **26** *818*
wall paintings **32** 806
Stanza dello Incendio **21** 16; **24** 526; **25** 901–2; **26** 818
frescoes **25** *901*
secco paintings **28** *337*
Stanza della Segnatura **3** 674; **14** 868; **16** 664; **22** 413; **25** 899–901; **26** 817
frescoes **1** 655; **7** 383; **16** 664, *664*; **24** 419; **32** 805
furniture **12** 708
Stanze **4** 653; **14** 582; **25** 899–902*; **26** 186
frescoes **3** 203; **16** 763; **24** 526; **26** 188, 189
stufetta **10** 477; **13** 700; **24** 365; **31** *523*
tapestries **32** 586
Terza Loggia **20** 366
Torre dei Venti **4** 812; **13** 628; **18** 707; **23** 339
Torre di S Giovanni *see* Torre dei Venti

Rome (Vatican)
Palace—cont.
Tribunale della Ruota Romana **33** 718
Piazza S Pietro **3** 264, 835–7*, *836*; **10** 744; **16** 763; **23** 541; **26** 759, 807
obelisk **23** 330; **26** 757
St Peter's (Old) **3** 329; **5** *793*; **7** 217, 252, 253, 260, 692; **8** 64, 260; **9** 530; **15** 860; **16** 623; **20** 519, 520; **26** 752, *753*, 755, 800–801*, *801*, 802–3*, *803*; **28** 629
altar **1** 694
altarpieces **25** 462–3
Benediction Loggia **11** 684–5; **16** 631; **24** 731; **26** 755
choir **16** 631; **26** 756
crypt **8** 222, *223*
doors **9** 157; **16** 691; **25** 19
frescoes **26** 802
gate-house **22** 163
metalwork **6** 173; **9** 656
mosaics **7** 920; **22** 163; **26** 802, 803
proportions **2** 350
roof **30** 903
shrine of St Peter **20** 518, *518*
tabernacle **16** 691
tomb of Innocent VIII **16** 691
tomb of Sixtus IV **16** 691
transept **31** 280
vaults **32** 86
wall paintings **13** 145
St Peter's **1** 594–5; **2** 319, 320; **3** 206, 293, 830–31, *836*; **4** 404, 649–50; **7** 258, 692; **10** 909; **16** 632, 637, 761; **20** 44–5; **21** 454–5; **25** 260; **26** 186, 187, 756, 758, 791, 804–8*, *804*, *806*, *807*, *809*, 809–10*, 859; **29** 888
altarpieces **1** 712
Baldacchino **1** 698; **3** 830*; **4** 428; **7** 226, 301, 303; **14** 416; **16** 712; **23** 489, 541; **28** 632
bell **3** 627
campanile **3** 835
candlesticks **12** 260
Cappella del Coro **11** 682
Cappella del Sacramento **7** 907
Cathedra Petri **1** 698; **3** *832*, 832–3*; **5** 810; **7** 226; **16** 698, 712; **30** 776, 779, 781
clock tower *see* tower of Paul V
columns **26** 624
crosses **8** 202
crucifixes **8** 216
dome **9** 82, 86; **20** 579–80, *580*
doors **9** 157, 159, *159*; **11** *71*, 71–2
façade **16** 637
liturgical furnishings **16** 761
metalwork **16** 742, 743
models **2** 336
monument to Clement XIV **27** 831
monument to Constantine the Great **10** 442
monument to Innocent XII **27** 831
monument to Pius X **9** 159
monument to Urban VIII **3** 206, 831*; **22** 44; **27** *830*, 831
mosaics **11** 23; **22** 158, 162; **31** 314–15
orders (architecture) **23** 492
paintings **13** 628
Parchment Plan **4** 649
piers (ii) (masonry) **24** 752
Pietà **1** 711; **21** *434*, 434–5; **24** 777
sacristy **20** 392–3

Rome (Vatican)
St Peter's—cont.
sculpture **7** 860; **9** 109, 410; **16** 697–8, 699, 763; **21** 755, *755*, 831; **23** 645; **26** *766*, 808–9*
tapestries **16** 755
Tomb B **9** 562
Tomb M **9** 562; **27** 67
tomb of Alexander VII **3** 833; **22** 44
tomb of Clement XIII **5** 626–7; **27** 831; **31** 130
tomb of Countess Matilda **3** 206
tomb of Fannia Redempta *see* Tomb B
tomb of Gregory XIII **27** 346–7, *347*; **31** 128
tomb of Leo XI **1** 627; **27** 831; **31** 128
tomb of Nicholas V **2** 166
tomb of Paul III **16** 696; **25** 256
tomb of Pius XII **31** 132
tomb of the Julii *see* Tomb M
tomb of Valerius Herma **27** 72
tombs **22** 156, 161; **26** 900; **31** 109
tower of Paul V **10** 908–9; **26** 756
Sala a Croce Greca *see under* museums → Museo Pio-Clementino
Sala delle Muse *see under* museums → Museo Pio-Clementino
Sala Rotonda *see under* museums → Museo Pio-Clementino
S Anna dei Palafrenieri **16** 635; **32** 505
Scala Regia *see under* Palace
silk **16** 752
Terza Loggia *see under* Palace
Villa Belvedere **2** 168; **15** 861
Rome, ancient **26** 849–925*, *886*, *904*, *905*, *906*, *908*, *915*, *919*, *921*, *922*; **27** 1–116*
acanthus **1** 109
acroliths **27** 29, 32
aeraria **26** 867
aesthetics **1** 176*; **26** 924
agate **12** 250
alabaster (gypsum) **27** 15
alae **26** 865
allegories **1** 652, *652*
alloys **21** 329–30
altars **1** 693*, 696; **26** *787*, 787–8, *890*; **27** *23*, 23–4, 712–13
funerary **27** *34*
amber **1** 761
amphitheatres **1** 796–7*; **21** 559; **26** 863, 864, 892, 904; **27** 712; **29** 521
Augustan **26** 873, 891
Flavian **26** 895
France **2** *418*; **23** 147; **26** 874
Greece **26** 910
Italy **1** *797*; **25** 198, 748; **26** 789–91*, 888, 889, *896*; **27** 781; **32** 340
Spain **30** *347*
amphorae **12** *787*; **26** 880, 903; **27** 106
amulets **1** 816, 817; **12** 251–2*, *252*; **26** 485
antefixes **2** 131; **26** 878
apses **22** 161; **26** 923
aqueducts **7** 353; **11** 339, 802–3; **26** 864, 890; **27** 6*, 7*
Greece **26** 910
North Africa **26** 919
Spain **2** *242*; **28** *368*
arcades **2** 242, *242*; **26** 888, *888*, *894*
archaeology **32** 544*
arches **2** 295, 297*; **26** 863, 877, 890, *892*, 922, 923, 924; **27** 41
flat **2** 294
Greece **26** 909
Italy **26** 887, *887*

Rome, ancient
arches—cont.
round **2** 295, 297
Syria **2** 297
triple **7** 917; **26** 868
architects **2** 312–13; **26** 864, 884–5*
architectural decorations **23** 534–5; **26** 878, 916*; **27** 9
architecture **4** *771*, 772; **7** 691–2; **12** 497; **13** 404, 412; **16** 623; **25** 171; **26** 854, 855–6, 863–925*, *872*; **27** 1–7*
brick **23** *621*; **26** *912*, *914*
Christianity **26** 907
Crete **8** 154–5
Cyprus **8** 337*
Egypt, ancient **26** 920
France **11** 509*; **26** 904
Greece **26** 908–11*
Ionia **15** 894
Italy **16** 623; **26** 886–9*; **27** *4*
Jordan **26** 918*
marble **26** 889
military **3** 329*; **21** 548, 558–61*
Nabataea **26** 917–18*
North Africa **26** 919–22*
Palestine **26** 917*
prefabrication **21** 559; **26** 911
Republican **26** 886–9*
Spain **26** 904
stone **26** 874–5*
Syria **26** 916–17*, 918*
Turkey **26** *923*
wood **26** 856
archives **2** 364
armour **2** 469; **27** 94–5*
armouries **21** 559
art (imitation of works of) **11** 306
art (reproduction of works of) **26** 230
art history **25** 824
artists' biographies **8** 535
art market **9** 20; **10** 675
atlantids **10** *426*
atria **2** 696*
attics (i) (architectural order) **26** 923
auctions **27** 29
azurite **23** 785
balneae **26** 872, 919
banners **14** 407
baptisteries **27** 60
barracks **21** 559
basalt **26** 880
basilicas (non-ecclesiastical) **3** 327–9*; **26** *748*, 867–8, *868*, 890, 902, 907; **27** 3; **31** 235
Britain **3** 328; **26** 905
Germany **31** *324*
Greece **26** 910
Italy **3** *328*; **7** 917; **26** *797*, 888
Libya **3** *328*; **19** *222*
basketwork **3** 332
bath-gymnasia **26** 912, 914; **27** 837, *837*
baths **3** 374–5*; **15** 51, *51*; **21** 559; **22** 161; **26** 863, 864, 868, 871–2*, *872*, 877, 902, 912, 924; **27** 48
Germany **26** 907; **31** 323
Greece **26** 909–10
Italy **3** *374*; **26** 888
Libya **19** *221*
Tunisia **5** 891
Turkey **26** *912*
1st cent. BC **26** 891
1st cent. AD **26** 892
2nd cent. AD **26** 897
3rd cent. AD **26** 901
4th cent. AD **26** 903
beakers **27** *79*
beds **3** 483
bekhen stone **27** 14, *14*
berms **21** 559
boats **26** 892
bone **9** 647; **27** 101
book illustrations **23** 692

Rome, ancient—cont.
books **20** 327
bowls **12** VIII2; **26** *859*
  Central Asia, Western **6** *267*
  Germany **27** *75*
  Italy **27** *107*
  Kyrgyzstan **6** *267*
  Switzerland **27** *77*
bracae **9** 251
bracelets **27** 102, *102*
brass **4** 687, 852
brick **4** 767, 769, *771*, 772; **23** *621*; **26** 864, *877*, 877–9*, *878*, 900, 903, *903*, 911, *912*, *914*
bricklaying **26** 878
bridges **4** 800; **26** 864; **27** 7*
bronze **4** 852, 855; **8** 263; **20** 328; **21** 1; **24** 258; **25** 43; **27** 10–11, 12, 17, 85–92*, 105; **28** *383*; **29** *561*, *562*, 567
  Augustan **27** 32
  Egypt **27** *89*
  Italy **2** 168
  Late Antiquity **18** *824*
  Republican **24** 258; **25** *202*; **27** 29, *30*
  Switzerland **27** *91*
  1st cent. BC **14** *443*; **21** 713
  2nd cent. BC **8** 342
  5th cent. BC **27** *9*
  1st cent. AD **11** *151*; **27** *95*
  2nd cent. AD **27** *86*
  3rd cent. AD **27** *88*
building regulations **5** 134–5; **26** 887, 891
busts **5** 298*, 299*, *299*; **7** 642; **9** 246; **26** 861; **27** *12*, *15*, *30*, 35, *37*, *41*
  Italy **27** *110*
buttresses **5** 319
caementa **26** 879
caldaria **26** 919
calendars **9** 603
callipers **26** 861
cameos **1** *652*; **12** 250; **14** II2; **21** *162*; **27** 34
camps (military) **6** 68–9*; **25** 423; **26** 905, 907; **27** 4
candelabra **5** 604, *604*
capitals **5** *670*; **26** 875, 877
  Composite **1** 109
  Corinthian **26** *876*
  Doric **32** *502*
capitolia **26** 905; **27** 3
capriccios **5** 685
carpets **26** 855
carving **21** 326
caryatids **5** 904*; **27** 29, 30, 31, 39
caskets **5** *917*
castella urbana **27** 6
casting **27** 17–18*, *18*
casts **6** 9; **7** 562; **27** 18, *18*, *19*, 30
catacombs **9** 562; **26** 798–9; **31** 110
cathedrals **26** 908
caveae (i) (seating) **26** 873; **30** 651–2
ceilings **27** 47, 51, 55
cement **26** 879
cemeteries **14** 515
cenotaphs **6** 170
censers **6** 173
censorship **6** 174
chairs **6** 388; **13** 591
chariots **6** 480*
chasubles **9** 251
chests **27** 100
chisels **27** 16
chlamydes **9** 251
churches **12** 362; **26** 752, 859; **27** 60
cinnabar **23** 785; **27** 51
cippi **27** 6, 33
circuses **5** 891; **7** *342*; **26** 864, 873; **27** 712
cisterns **7** 353, 354; **26** 864
cities **23** 300; **26** 853, 854
  Classicism **7** 382

Rome, ancient—cont.
clay **26** 877, 879; **27** 17, 51, *104*
cloaks **9** 251
codices **4** 342; **20** 327, 329
coffering **7** 526–7*
coins **4** 687; **7** 533; **11** *151*; **21** 1, 162; **25** 650; **26** 860; **27** 29, 31, 32, 39, 95–8*, *96*, *98*
  Etruscan **10** 586
  Indian subcontinent **15** 200
  Phoenician **5** *332*
collections **2** 558; **10** 675; **13** 469, 555; **14** 867; **16** 765; **26** 782, 861; **27** 29, 31, 114–16*
  erotic art **10** 487
  paintings **7** 562; **13** 555; **27** 58*
  public **25** 43
  royal **26** 784
  sculpture **7** 561–2, 564; **9** 23; **26** 856; **27** 34, 45–7*
colonnades **26** 858, 863, *918*, 922
columns **4** 769, 772; **26** 135, 863, 874, 875, 876, 877, 878, 882–3, *892*, 905, 922, 923, 924, 925; **27** 39, 40
  Belgium **26** 905
  Britain **26** 905
  Doric **11** 231
  engaged **26** 874, 878
  Germany **26** 905
  Greece **26** *909*
  historiated **26** 791
  Italy **27** *40*
  Turkey **26** *923*
comitia **28** 867
concrete **2** 297; **6** 9; **7** 691–2; **20** 572; **25** 748; **26** 864, 871, 874, 877, 879–80*, 881, 889, 893, 904
  Crete **8** 155
  Italy **26** 887
construction machinery **26** 864
contrapposto **7** 783
copies **2** 557; **13** 423; **26** 861; **27** *104*, 105
  busts **28** *383*
  sculpture **2** *156*; **7** 561, 830; **10** 311; **11** 72; **13** *450*, *462*, 464, 469; **15** *92*; **19** *853*; **23** *291*; **26** 226, 854; **27** 10, 30, 39, 40
copper **8** 354
coral **7** 834; **16** 750
corbels **7** 837
cornelian **12** *250*, 251
couches **3** 483; **27** 99–100; **29** 8
courtyards **8** 64
craftsmen and artists **9** 647; **13** 468; **27** 52–3*, *93*
crucifixes **9** 518
cups **23** *535*; **27** *76*, 80
  cage-cups **27** 73*, 76*, 78*
  hunt cups **27** *108*
curiae **26** 867; **27** 3
cutting **27** 75–6*
dalmatics **9** 251
decadence and decline **8** 595–6*
derricks **7** 764
diptychs **18** *826*; **26** 862
display of art **9** 13, 20
ditches **21** 559
dolls **31** 259
domes **9** 11, 84, 85; **26** *793*, 879, 880, 903, *903*, 923
doors **9** 150–51*
dress **9** 245–6*, 249–50*, 251*; **27** 112, *113*, 113–14
drills **27** 16, *17*
dromoi **29** 487
dyes **27** 112
earrings **27** 102
education (art) **26** 864, 884–5*
emblems **27** 61, *61*, 62
enamel **27** *76*, 78*
encyclopedias of art **25** 42
engineering (civil) **30** 26
engraving **27** 17, 76*
entablatures **26** 875, 876, 878; **32** *502*

Rome, ancient—cont.
entasis **10** 414, 415
epigraphy **26** 883–4*
erotic art **10** 474–5; **27** 48, 50
exedrae **10** 670
exhibitions **10** 675; **27** 31, 47, 115–16
ex-votos **26** 858, 859; **27** 52, 109–12*, 712
façade decoration **10** 742*
façades **2** 541; **26** 863, 873, 923
fans **10** 775
felt **10** 875
figureheads **28** 611
figurines **27** 109–12*
filigree **21** 327; **27** 101, 102, *102*
flags **11** 146*
flint **26** 874
floors **26** 877; **27** 59–65*
flutes (columns) **11** 231; **26** 878
fora **11** 327–8*; **12** 497; **26** 781–5, 863, 867, 890, 905; **27** 3
  Britain **26** 905
  Greece **7** *852*
  Italy **11** *327*; **26** *748*, 889
forgeries **2** 558; **7** 561; **27** 105
fornices **26** 888, *888*
fortifications **21** 548, 558–61*, *560*, *561*; **26** 905, 907, 909
forts **6** 68–9*; **21** 558–61; **23** 300; **25** 423
  Britain **26** 907
  England **14** 23, *23*
  France **26** 907
  Serbia **28** 439
  shore forts **21** 560, *561*
fountains **11** 339; **12** 69; **22** 161; **26** 863
  Greece **26** 910
  Italy **12** *68*; **27** *66*
frames **11** 379
friezes **11** 791; **26** 792, *792*, *890*; **27** 24–5, *26*, 33, 35, 38, 39, 40, 41, 44, *44*
funeral pyres **6** 72
furniture **26** 875; **27** 94, 99–100*; **33** 155
galleries (iv) (art) **9** 13, 20
games **26** 872
garden design **12** 68–70
gardens **12** 65, *68*, 68–70*, *70*, 287; **26** 862, *862*, *899*; **27** 29, 48; **32** 543–4
gargoyles **12** 150
garnets **27** *103*
gates **7** 358, *358*; **23** *147*; **32** *342*
gateways **26** 864, *891*, 909, *909*
gay and lesbian art **12** 213
gem-engraving **12** *250*, 250–52*, *252*
gems **25** 45
geometry **26** 924
Gesamtkunstwerk **12** 497
gilding **12** 624, 625, 626, 627; **27** *10*, 15, 29
glass **12** 783, 785, 786, 787, 788, 789, 790; **21** 713; **26** 855, 871; **27** 66, 72*, 74–7*, *78*, *79*
  cameo **12** 787, *787*; **27** 73–4*, 76–7*, *77*, 78*; **30** *407*
  casting **27** 74*
  Central Asia, Western **6** *267*
  Egypt **27** 78
  Germany **7** 586; **27** *75*
  glassblowing **12** 784; **27** 72–3*, 74–5*, 77–8*
  Italy **12** VIII2; **27** *76*
  Kyrgyzstan **6** *267*
  moulding **27** 73, 74
  Netherlands, the **22** 884
  Spain **29** 330
  Switzerland **30** 144
gold **8** 263; **21** 1; **25** 43; **27** *15*, 15–16, 79*, 80*, *103*
gold leaf **27** 15, 51
Graecostasis **26** 867
granite **26** 874, 876–7; **27** 14; **29** 700
greenhouses **13** 619

Rome, ancient—cont.
grottoes **22** 161; **27** 29
guidebooks **13** 807–8*
guilds **26** 855
guilloche **13** 830
gymnasia **8** *368*; **26** 872
gypsum **27** 13
haematite **12** 251, 252, *252*
hair ornaments **27** *102*
hairstyles **9** 249–50
halls **14** 73*
hangings **27** *114*
hardstones **14** 169–70
harnesses **14** 181*
heating systems **15** 51, *51*; **26** 879
helmets **27** *95*
himatia **9** 246, 251
historicism **14** 581
hortus see gardens
hospitaliae **30** 652
hospitals **21** 559
houses **26** 856, 868–70, 877, 891
  atria **26** 869, 904
  Corinthian **26** 869
  displuviate **26** 869
  England **10** 226
  farmhouses **26** 869
  Germany **26** 906
  Italy **14** *441*; **25** *199*; **26** 888
  peristyle **26** 869, *870*, 888, 904, 920
  testudinate **26** 869
  tetrastyle **26** 869
  town **32** 72
  Tuscan **26** 869
human figures **27** 29
hydraulic works **26** 864
hypocausts **3** 374; **13** 404; **15** 51*, *51*; **26** 871, 879, 888
hypogea **31** 110
iconography **5** 801; **9** 517; **10** 211; **22** 411; **26** 857, *858*, *859*, 859–63*, *862*; **27** 11–12*, 31, 47–50*; **32** 86; **33** 241
  Late Antiquity **26** 862–3, *863*
illusionism **15** 135
indigo **23** 785
industrial scenes **15** 827
inks **15** 851
inns **27** 50
inscriptions **26** 861, 864; **27** 2, 32, 61
insignia **32** 394
insulae **10** 426–7; **15** 869–70*, *870*; **23** *621*; **26** 863, 868, 869, 887, 891, 901; **27** 4, 55
interior decoration **25** 191–4; **29** 665
interlace **15** 881
iron **27** 93–4*
ivory **16** 798; **18** *826*
ivory-carvings **27** 100–101*, *101*
jars **20** *471*
jasper **12** 251
jet **1** 816; **17** 516
jewellery **10** 34; **12** 456; **27** 101–2*, 103*
jugs **27** *78*, 86, *86*
kiosks **26** 919
kitchens **26** 869
knife-handles **27** 87
knives **8** 283, *283*
lampblack **23** 785
lamps **9** 11; **19** 364; **27** 87*, 103–4*, *104*
lanterns (lights) **27** *111*
lead **27** 10
leather **19** 2; **27** *105*, 105–6*
libraries **9** 20; **19** 311–12*; **26** *909*, *914*; **27** 30
lighting **9** 11
lime **11** 762; **26** 879; **29** 812
limestone **26** 874, 875, 879; **27** 9–10, 13, 14
  Numidian **27** 14
  travertine **26** 874; **27** 13
linen **20** 327; **27** 112
lost-wax casting **27** 17
lunettes **9** 11

Rome, ancient—cont.
macella **19** 888*, *889*; **26** 867, 871
  Greece **26** 910
  North Africa **26** 919
malachite **23** 785
mantles **9** 251
manuals **12** 68; **26** 884
manuscript illumination **26** 862, *863*
manuscripts **20** 329
maps **20** 362; **31** 153
marble **5** 298, 604; **25** 44–5; **26** 854–5, *858*, 864, 865, 875–7*, *876*, 878, 885, 911–12, 925; **27** 826; **29** 702; **30** 436
  Antonine **5** *299*; **8** 342; **27** *17*, *40*
  Augustan **26** 889; **27** 10, 13–14, *32*, *41*, *42*
  bardiglio **26** 875
  Black Sea Colonies **4** *113*
  Carrara **27** 13, 826, *826*
  cipollino **26** 876
  Constantine **27** 45
  Crete **8** 155
  Docimian **27** 13
  England **19** *579*
  giallo antico **26** 876
  Greece, ancient **5** *604*
  Hadrianic **27** *37*, *38*
  Italy **9** *517*; **27** *21*, *22*, *23*, *26*
  Julio-Claudian **27** *33*; **29** *389*
  Libya **19** *223*
  marmor lunensium **26** 875, 876
  Parian **27** 13
  pavonazzetto **26** 875, 876; **29** VIII2
  Pentelic **23** *536*; **26** 876; **27** 13
  Phrygian **27** 13
  Prokonnesian **26** 876
  Republican **2** *169*; **13** *462*; **19** *853*; **23** *291*; **25** *178*; **26** 887, 889; **27** *8*, 12–13, 15, 29
  Thasian **26** 877; **27** 13
  Turkey **2** *220*; **10** *428*
  verde antico **26** 877
markets **19** 888; **20** 438; **26** 867, 871
marks **6** 333; **20** 441, 443; **27** 80, 106
masonry **20** 570; **26** 877–8
  ashlar **26** 874, 904, 911, *912*
  Cyclopean **20** 571; **26** 874; **27** 7
  opus Africanum **20** 572
  opus incertum **20** 572; **26** 874, 879, *879*
  opus mixtum **26** 877
  opus quadratum **26** 874
  opus quasi-reticulatum **26** 879
  opus reticulatum **4** 772; **8** 856; **20** 572; **26** 874, *875*, 877, 879, *879*, 889
  opus testaceum **20** 572; **26** 877, 879, *879*
  rubble **20** 572; **26** 877, 879, 911, *912*
  rustication **26** 874, 892, *892*
masons **26** 884–5*
mausolea **20** 863–5*, *864*; **26** *794*
mazes **18** 585
meander **20** 912, *912*
measurements **26** 867, 924–5
measuring instruments **30** 26
medallions **21** 1–2*, *2*, *3*; **27** *96*
metalwork **27** 79–84*, 93–4*
milestones **27** 6
mirror frames **21** 713
mirrors **4** 855; **21** 713*, *713*
Mithraea **26** 859, 867; **30** 436
models **27** 18–19*, *19*
modillions **26** 865
moles **26** 864
monopteroi **21** 892–3*
monuments **26** 860, 864, 867, 911; **27** 39, 41, 43
  equestrian **10** 440*; **27** *10*, 12, 29, 30, 35, 39
  funerary **27** 25–6*, 31

Rome, ancient
monuments—cont.
public **22** 43*; **27** *23*, 23–5*, *26*
Italy **26** *900*
triumphal arches **2** 297; **10** 742; **22** 43; **26** 135, 863, 864, 868; **27** 24, 25; **31** 349–50*
Augustan **26** 890; **27** 32
Constantine **26** 797–8*, 903; **27** 43–4, *44*
Flavian **26** 895
France **2** 286–7, *287*; **27** 31
Italy **3** 715; **26** *748*, *798*, *891*, *901*; **31** *349*
North Africa **26** 920, *920*
Republican **27** 29
Tetrarchs **27** 43
Trajanic **26** 897
mortars (building) **26** 879, 911, *912*
mosaics **13** 559; **22** 160–61; **23** 622; **26** 691, 861; **27** 58–68*; **30** 408; **31** 254; **32** 542
Africa **1** 377–8
Algeria **27** *63*
Ancient Near East **27** 64
Black and White style **23** *623*; **27** 59, 60, 61
Britain **27** 62; **32** 542
Crete **8** 155
Cyprus, ancient **8** 333, 354–5, *355*; **24** *60*; **27** 63
Egypt **1** *617*
emblemata **22** *155*, 160; **27** 59, 60
First Style **29** 665
Floral style **27** 61
France **27** 62; **32** 542
Germany **21** III1; **27** 62
Greece, ancient **27** 63
Italy **22** *159*; **23** *623*; **25** *206*, 421, *422*; **27** 60, 61–2*, *61*, *62*, 65–7*, *66*, *68*; **31** *62*
Late Antiquity **26** 862; **27** 64
Monochrome style *see* Black and White Style
Muiltiple Décor style **27** 62
North Africa **27** 63; **32** 542
opus musivum **27** 58–9, 65
opus signinum **27** 59, 61
opus tessellatum **27** 58–9, 61
opus vermiculatum **27** 59, 61
Palestine **27** 63
Rainbow style **27** 64
Sicily **24** 700, 701–2, *702*; **27** 63
Silhouette style **27** 61, *62*
Spain **27** 63
Syria **2** *157*; **27** *64*, 64, *65*
Tunisia **1** *377*; **32** *543*
moulding **12** 783; **27** 17–18*
mouldings **9** 757; **22** 211, 215
moulds **27** 17, 18
mud-bricks **26** 877
museums **26** 782; **27** 45–7*, 114–16*
nails **9** 151
narratives **22** 514*; **26** 792, 861
naturalism **22** 686
necklaces **27** 102, *103*
niches **22** 161; **26** 923, *923*
niello **10** 381; **27** 102
nude figures **23** 291; **29** *562*
Egypt **27** *89*
Greece, ancient **25** *178*
Italy **14** *443*; **25** *202*; **27** *8*, *14*; **31** *60*
Republican **2** *169*; **19** *853*; **23** *291*; **29** *561*
nymphaea **11** 339; **12** 69; **13** 703; **26** 910; **27** 29, 65–6
obelisks **23** 330*
ochre **27** 51
oculi **9** 11; **26** 880
odeia **23** 349–50; **26** 910; **27** 712
odeion **26** 874
onyx **12** 251; **14** II2
opus sectile **14** 170; **26** 875; **27** 47, 59, 60; **32** 543
Rome, ancient—cont.
orchestras **26** *920*; **30** 651, 652
orders (architecture) **23** 477; **26** 863, 865, 924
Composite **23** 477, 480
Corinthian **23** 480, 482–3, *483*; **26** 875, 889; **30** 436
Doric **23** 478, *479*, 481
giant **23** 491*
Ionic **23** 478, 482
Tuscan **23** 477
ornament **23** 533–5*
orpiment **23** 785
painting **25** 43–4; **26** 860; **27** 16, 47–58*, 78*
ceiling **27** *55*
display **9** 13
encaustic **24** 3
floor **27** 47
flower **27** 49
fresco **8** 462; **18** *702*; **27** 51
genre **12** 287*
glass **12** 798
history **27** 39
Italy **16** 653
landscape **18** 700, 701–3, *702*; **26** 862; **27** 48, 50, 53
lime secco **27** 51
mythological **26** 860, 861
panel **24** 3; **27** 50
secco **27** 51
still-lifes **26** 861–2, *862*; **27** 50; **29** *664*, 665
see also xenia
tomb **27** 48–9, 57
wall **8** *462*; **13** 699; **22** 686; **26** 857, 861, *862*; **27** 47–50*, 51–7*; **32** 543, 803–4*
Ancient Near East **27** 57
Britain **27** 56–7
Constantinian **27** 56
Egypt **1** *618*
Egypt, ancient **27** 57
First Style **15** 135; **27** 53, 69
Fourth Style **14** 444; **26** *788*, 789; **27** *48*, *54*, 54–5; **29** 665
France **27** 56, *56*
Germany **27** 56
Greece, ancient **13** *546*, *547*
Italy **9** *563*; **12** *69*; **14** *444*; **25** *204*; **27** *48*, *49*, *51*, *53*, 53–6, *54*; **32** I2
Jewish art **17** 554, 557
North Africa **27** 57
Ostian **27** 55–6
Pompeian Style **27** *53*, 53–5, *54*
Post-Pompeian **27** 55
Second Style **15** 135; **27** *53*, 53–4; **29** 665
Spain **27** 57
Third Style **27** 54; **29** *664*, 665
3rd cent. AD **26** *799*
palaces **3** 329*; **23** 808–9*; **26** 751, *893*
Croatia **29** *417*
Italy **26** *895*
palaestrae **23** 828; **26** 912
pallas **9** 246
palmettes **23** 889
papyri **20** 329; **23** 692
papyrus **26** 556, 557
parchment **20** 329; **26** 557
pateras **27** 86
patronage **10** 359; **16** 760–61; **26** 855–7*, 884, 907, 911; **27** 53
sculpture **27** 30
pattern books **32** 542
pavements **26** 875; **27** 59–60
pavilions (buildings) **26** 871, *903*
pearls **27** *102*
pediments **24** 317, 318, 319–20*; **26** 878, 923; **27** 30, 32
pens **24** 348
peristyles **26** 863, 869, *870*
perspective **27** 48
pewter **24** 578
piers (ii) (masonry) **24** 750; **26** 863, 864
Rome, ancient—cont.
pigments **23** 785; **25** 44; **27** 51
black **27** 51
blue **27** 51
Egyptian blue **27** 51
green **27** 51
lake **23** 785
metacinnabar **27** 51
purple **27** 51
red **27** 51
sinopia **28** 778
vermilion **23** 785
pilasters **26** 878, 883
piscine (i) (pool) **24** 877*
plaster **2** 541; **27** 17, 18, *18*, *19*, 51
platforms **26** 864
podia **26** 874
polychromy **26** *877*, 878; **27** 16, 52
ponds **12** 69
pools **12** 69; **26** *899*; **27** 47
see also PISCINE (i) (POOL)
porphyry **26** 855, 876–7, 902; **27** 10, 13, 14, 43, *43*
portae regiae **30** 652
porticos **25** 265; **27** 29; **29** 681–2
portraits **22** 686; **26** 860–61
amber **1** 761
cameos **14** II2
coins **25** 650; **27** *96*, 96–7
gem-engraving **12** 250
imagines maiorum **27** 50
Late Antiquity **26** 862
painting **27** 50; **30** V1
sculpture **7** 642; **9** 20; **10** *428*; **27** 11, 19, *23*, 29, 31, 33, 34, 35, 37, 39, 41–2, 43, 44, 45
ports **26** 864
postscaenia **30** 652
pottery **20** 593; **27** 103–5, 106–8*
Arretine ware **27** 31, 106–7, *107*
Barbotine ware **27** *108*
England **27** *108*
Italy **6** 333
lead-glazed ware **27** 106
Red Slip ware **27** 107
Rhenish ware **27** 108
terra sigillata **6** 333; **27** 106, 107–8
Tunisia **27** 107
Wetterau ware **27** 108
pozzolana **7** 691; **25** 748; **26** 879, 889; **27** 51
praetoria **21** 559; **25** 423*
principiae **21** 559
prisons **21** 559
propaganda **25** 650; **27** 31, 35, *36*
proportions (architecture) **13** 412; **26** 924–5
propylaia **26** 909, *909*, *917*; **27** 712
proscenia **30** 652
pumice **26** 880; **27** 51
pyramids **25** 766
quarries **26** 855, 875, *876*, 876–7
rags **31** 259
ramparts **21** 559
rediscovery **27** 45, 115–16
reeds **24** 348
refinements (architecture) **10** 414; **26** 925
religion **26** 857–9*, 867
replicas **7** 562
representation **26** 855
reservoirs **7** 353, 354
revetments **26** 876, 878
ribs **26** 903, *903*
rings **26** 485; **27** 102
rituals **26** *858*
roads **26** 864, 887; **27** 6–7*; **32** 398
rock crystal **26** 485; **27** *103*
rolls **4** 342; **20** 329; **26** 556, 557
roofs **26** 869, 877, 878, 880; **27** 127; **30** 903*
Greece **2** 408
rotundas **26** 903; **27** 235
Rome, ancient—cont.
sanctuaries **25** *421*; **26** 858, 865, 905, *905*; **27** 1–2*, *2*, 711–14*, *713*; **31** *58*
sandstone **26** 874
sapphires **27** *102*, *103*
sarcophagi **9** *250*; **22** 411, *411*; **23** *536*; **26** 135, 854–5; **27** 11, 28, 39, 40, 41, 42, *42*, 44–5, 60, 823, *826*, 826–7*
Christianity **27** 827
Italy **9** *517*
Netherlands, the **27** *99*
sard **12** 250
sardonyx **1** *652*; **15** 698
scabbards **7** *727*; **30** *394*
scaenae **26** 910, *920*; **30** 651
scaenae frontes **26** 873, 923, 924; **30** 652
scaffolding **26** 877, 880
scagliola **28** 28
scissors **8** 285
scripts **28** 305
sculptors **27** 8, 27–9*
sculpture **7** 783; **9** 34; **12** 69, 286, 625, 626, 627; **13** 466, 468; **16** 684–5; **23** 291; **24** 258, 319–20*; **25** 44–5; **26** 854, 855, 856–7, 861; **27** 8–47*; **29** 559–60
allegorical **2** *156*
Antonine **27** 39–40*
architectural **10** 742*; **27** 26–7*, 29
Turkey **10** *426*
Augustan **27** 30–32*
Black Sea Colonies **4** *113*
bronze **8** 342; **25** 43; **27** 10–11, 12
Italy **14** *443*
bronze: 5th cent. BC **27** *9*
bronze: Augustan **27** 32
bronze: Italy **2** 168
bronze: Late Antiquity **18** *824*
bronze: Republican **8** 263; **24** 258; **27** 12, 29, 85; **29** *561*, *562*
chryselephantine statues **8** 263
colossal statues **26** 855; **27** 12, 29
Constantine **27** 43–5*
Crete **8** 155
cult statues **8** 155, 262–3; **26** 858; **27** 29, 31, 88*, 711
Cyprus, ancient **8** 342*
display **9** 20; **26** *899*
England **19** *579*
Flavian **27** 34–5*
France **12** *70*; **27** 31
Greece, ancient **25** *178*
group **27** 29, 31–2, 43, *43*
Hadrianic **27** 37–9*
herms **14** 456; **27** 29
Italy **27** *9*, *10*, *14*, *18*, *19*, *21*, *32*; **29** VIII2
Julio-Claudian **27** 32–4*
Late Antiquity **18** *824*
marble **2** *169*; **8** 342; **13** *462*; **19** *853*; **23** *291*; **25** *178*; **27** *8*, 10, 12–13, *17*, 29, *32*, 45
Black Sea Colonies **4** *113*
Italy **27** *23*; **29** VIII2
Republican **19** *579*
Turkey **10** *428*
monumental **27** 33, *33*
mythological **2** *169*; **14** *443*; **27** 22, *22*
Italy **29** *389*
portraits **27** 20–21*
relief **9** *517*; **15** *92*; **22** *411*; **26** 135*, *858*, 861; **27** *23*, 23–6*, *26*, 29, 31, 33, *33*, 34, *34*, 35–6, *36*, 39, 40, 41, 42, *42*, *44*, *93*
Italy **26** *792*; **27** *38*, *40*, *43*; **31** *369*
Jewish art **17** 554
Late Antiquity **18** *824*
Libya **19** *223*
Rome, ancient
sculpture
relief—cont.
Turkey **2** *220*
1st cent. BC **9** *249*
Republican **27** 29–30*
reserve heads **10** *428*
restoration **9** 21
terminal figures **14** 456
Tetrarchs **27** 43*
Trajanic **27** 35–6*
Turkey **10** *428*
wood **27** 12
seating **26** 873; **30** 652
serpentine **27** 15
shears **7** 764
shields **3** 332
ship-decoration **28** 611
ships **26** 854
shoes **27** 105
shopping centres **26** 871
shops **23** *621*; **26** 871, 887; **27** 50
shrines (i) (cult) **18** 786*; **26** 857; **27** *2*, 50, 88–91
shuttering **4** 767
signatures **6** 333; **27** 27
signs (markers) **27** 50
silk **9** 251; **27** *113*; **28** 715
silver **23** *535*; **25** 43; **26** *859*; **27** 15, 79–84*
Augustan **27** 31
Early Christian (*c.* AD 250-843) **5** *917*
England **21** I2
Gallo-Roman **27** 82–3
1st cent. BC **27** *81*
1st cent. AD **8** 263; **21** 713, *713*
2nd cent. AD **26** *859*
3rd cent. AD **27** *82*
4th cent. AD **27** *84*
silver-gilt **21** 713
soldering **21** 325; **27** 17
solia see thrones
spikes **21** 559
spoons **8** 284, *284*; **27** 83
sporting scenes **29** 423
stables **21** 559
stadia **26** 895; **27** 712; **29** 487–8*
stage buildings **26** 863, 912
stage design **30** 651–2*
stages **30** 652
see also scaenae
staircases **29** 520–21
stamping **4** *771*, 772
stamps **26** 879
standards (vexilloid) **11** 150–51, *151*
statuettes **12** *68*; **25** *202*; **26** 923; **27** 29, 30, 87–91*, *88*, *89*, *91*; **29** 567*
steel **27** 93
stelae **8** 155; **18** 209, *209*; **29** 616–17*
stoas **27** 712, 714; **29** 681–2
stolas **9** 246
stone **2** 297; **26** 874–5*, *875*, 879
stools **6** 388
storehouses **21** 559
streets **25** *196*; **26** 863; **27** 3
stucco **2** 541; **26** 864, 878; **27** 68–9*; **29** 812, 813, 814*
albarium **27** 69
Italy **27** 53, 69–72*, *70*, *71*
opus tectorium **27** 69
studios **27** 52
sundials **32** *634*
surveyors **30** 26
surveys **27** 2–3
swords **2** 451, 452; **27** 93
symbolism (critical term) **26** 922–4*
symmetry **26** 924
synagogues **27** 60
tables **27** 99; **30** 217
tablinia **16** 801
tabularia **26** 867
tanning **27** 105
tapestries **27** 113, *114*
tattoos **30** 367

Rome, ancient—cont.
temples 26 858, 863, 864, 865–7*, 874, 878, 890, 897, 900, 907, 915–16, 924; 27 1, 3, 31, 32, 712; 30 435–6*
Britain 26 858
Celtic 26 905
cult 26 867
England 3 369
France 23 148; 26 858; 30 436
Greece 26 910–11
Italy 2 167; 26 793, 887–8, 888, 898; 30 436
Jordan 12 337
Lebanon 26 881
North Africa 26 866, 919
peripteral 12 154
podium 23 622; 26 866, 888
temple-theatres 26 865, 873, 888, 888, 889
1st cent. BC 26 784
tents 25 423; 30 467
terracotta 15 51; 26 877, 878; 27 9, 29, 51, 109–12*; 30 494
Egypt, ancient 27 111, 111
France 27 110–11
Greece, ancient 27 111
Italy 27 109–10*, 110
Spain 27 111
textiles 1 881; 9 251; 26 855; 27 112–14*, 113, 114
theatre 27 50
theatres 26 749, 863, 864, 865, 873–4, 904, 912, 916, 923, 924; 27 29, 30; 29 488; 30 651–2*
Algeria 14 564
Crete 8 155
France 30 652
Greece 26 910
Italy 26 873, 873, 888–9, 891
Libya 27 485
North Africa 26 919, 920, 921
Sicily 26 873
Syria 2 214; 4 463; 26 918
Turkey 2 605, 605; 21 543
theatre-temples see under TEMPLES → types
theories
architectural 26 922–5*
art 13 467; 25 824
sculpture 13 468
thermae 1 463; 3 375; 13 404; 26 795*, 796, 871–2, 919
thrones 6 388; 30 775*
tiles 15 51; 25 171; 26 877; 30 494
box 26 879
tegulae mammatae 26 871
timber structures 26 864
title-pages 31 48
togas 9 246, 250; 10 636
tombs 26 856, 861, 877; 27 60; 31 109–10*
columbaria 7 642*; 9 29; 31 110
tower 12 770
tools 27 16*
towers 21 559, 560
towns 26 924
fortified 2 212
new 26 864, 904, 905; 27 2–6, 4, 5
toys 31 254
trade 6 622; 15 200; 26 853, 854–5*
art 2 557
carpets 26 855
glass 3 592; 6 267; 7 83; 26 855
marble 26 854–5, 911; 27 11
porphyry 26 855
sculpture 26 854
silk 6 621; 28 715
textiles 26 855
trappings 14 181*; 27 105
treasuries 27 712
see also aeraria
treatises
agriculture 26 884
architecture 23 480, 484; 26 884, 924; 32 632
Rome, ancient
treatises—cont.
oratory 25 824
painting 31 299
tripods 27 100
trompe l'oeil 22 159; 27 48, 48, 50, 53, 53; 29 665
trophies 9 31; 31 369, 369
trousers 9 251
tubuli 26 871
tufa 26 874; 27 9
tunics 9 246, 251
tunnels 26 864; 27 7*
urban planning 11 327; 12 497; 23 618; 26 864, 904, 905; 27 1, 2–6*
Italy 27 4
Libya 27 5
North Africa 26 921
urns 7 642; 9 29; 24 845; 27 9, 33, 34
vases 26 873
vaults (ceiling) 26 864, 873, 874, 878, 880, 911, 923; 27 47, 51, 55; 32 86
annular 32 86
barrel 32 87
groin 32 89
Italy 26 796, 878
pitched-brick 32 89
rib 32 90
segmental 32 94
veneers 26 875
versurae 30 652
vessels 26 485; 27 85–7*
villas 12 110; 26 864, 869–70, 877, 891, 892, 896, 904, 907; 32 540–44*
Britain 26 906, 907; 32 542, 544
double courtyard 32 543
France 26 906; 32 543
Germany 26 906
Italy 28 496–7; 32 541, 541
porticus 26 869
Sicily 24 699–701
Spain 32 543
villa rustica 26 869
wall decorations 26 863
walls 26 875, 877–8*, 879–80
Greece 26 909
town 21 549; 26 874, 887, 901, 902, 907
warehouses 23 621; 32 860
water pipes 27 7*
water supply 2 241–2, 242
waxes 5 298; 20 327; 27 17
weapons 27 94–5*
weathervanes 33 8
weaving 27 112–13
weights 26 867
welding 27 17
well-heads 33 56–7
wheel fittings 27 91–2*
wicker 33 155
winches 7 764
windlasses 7 764
windows 26 871
wings (theatre) see alae
wire 30 394
wood 6 388; 9 151; 12 362; 20 327; 21 713; 26 856; 27 12, 12
wood-carvings 27 29
wool 27 112, 114
workshops 26 861; 27 55
writing 20 329
writing-tablets 4 342; 20 327, 328
wrought iron 27 93
xenia 29 665, 669
Rome, Jan van see ROOME, JAN VAN
Romea, Vicente Lampérez y see LAMPÉREZ Y ROMEA, VICENTE
Romeijn, Willem 3 759; 22 840; 27 116*
Romein, Jacob 27 116
Romein, Thomas Adrianus 22 828; 27 116*
Romenesil 11 612
Romeo, José 6 47
Romeos, Constantinos 2 26
Rømer (family) 23 236
Romer, A. 27 348
Rømer, Jørgen 8 736
Romero, Carlos Orozco see OROZCO ROMERO, CARLOS
Romero, Francisco 28 810
Romero, Frank 19 703
Romero, Juan Bautista 27 116*
Romero, Julião 27 117*
Romero, Marie 22 608
Romero, Raúl González see GONZÁLEZ ROMERO, RAÚL
Romero, Solón 4 263; 22 335
Romero, Susana 24 99, 100; 27 117*
Romero, Walter Solón see SOLÓN ROMERO, WALTER
Romero Brest, Jorge 2 405; 11 281
Romero de Torres, Julio 4 262; 13 880; 20 68
Romero Pereira, Tomás 24 96
Rome Secession see SECESSION, ROME
Romeu, F. 3 216
Romeyn, John le see JOHN LE ROMEYN
Romeyn, Willem see ROMEIJN, WILLEM
Römhild Church 13 160
Romieu, Paul 9 727
Romilly, Amélie 20 592
Romilly, Dessaux de 23 510
Romilly, Jean 11 630
Romiti, Gino 28 319
Rommenken 3 193
Romney, David 16 31
Romney, Frederick see ROMBERG, FREDERICK
Romney, George 22 122; 27 117–20*
groups and movements 13 297
patrons and collectors 1 496, 529; 3 179; 13 705, 836; 14 146; 19 158; 30 464
pupils 12 146
reproductive prints by others 2 234; 3 309; 4 807; 6 528; 28 283, 882
teachers 8 123; 19 157; 29 584
works 7 785, 786, 787; 10 249; 11 430; 27 118, 119
Romney, Hervin 2 494
Romney, John 13 327
Romny, St Nicholas 31 553
Romoaldus 27 120*
works 26 626, 627; 30 777, 777
Romont 30 126
Musée du Vitrail 29 516
Romsey Abbey (Hants) 1 724; 7 837; 22 220; 23 491; 26 588
rood 2 72; 27 124
sculpture 26 616
Romuald, Saint 5 449
Romualdo see ROMOALDUS
Romualdo di Candeli 22 800, 802
Romuliana see under GAMZIGRAD
Romulo Cincinnato, Diego de 10 502, 503; 13 731, 922; 14 516
Romulus 10 723, 724; 26 851
Ron 15 324, 325
Ron, Juan Alonso Villabrille y see VILLABRILLE Y RON, JUAN ALONSO
Roná, József 5 85; 14 896
Rónai, Peter 28 853
Ronald, William 5 568; 23 791; 27 120–21*; 31 177
Ronayne, Edward 7 857
Roncade
Villa Ciani-Bassetti 19 558; 32 545
Villa Giustiniani see Villa Ciani-Bassetti
Roncaioli, Pietro 24 203
Roncalli, Cesare 26 809
Roncalli, Cristoforo 26 770; 27 121–2*
collaboration 1 551
patrons and collectors 1 595; 12 912; 13 628; 17 509
pupils 6 112; 8 138; 16 835; 20 265; 33 587
works 2 492; 8 138; 19 687; 20 840, 841; 26 809; 27 121; 31 885
Ronceray Abbey Church 26 586
Roncesvalles 13 165
Ronchamp, Notre-Dame-du-Haut 2 361; 6 459; 7 277, 695; 11 527, 659; 19 46, 46, 365, 368
Rondani, Francesco Maria 2 128; 24 193; 27 122*
Rondanini, Alessandro 9 409
Rondanini Pietà 16 775; 21 439, 440, 457
rondavel huts see under HUTS → types
Ronde, Laurent 23 516
Rondel, Frédéric 14 699
Rondel, Stephane 23 73
Rondelet, Guillaume 2 103
Rondelet, Jean-Baptiste 27 123*
collaboration 29 94
patrons and collectors 28 371
pupils 13 775; 14 497
works 11 522; 24 166
writings 26 13
rondelles (sculpture) 25 493
rondels (architecture) 25 504
Rondinelli (family) 11 206
Rondinelli, Francesco 7 908
Rondinelli, Niccolò 3 667; 27 123*
works 11 489, 489
Rondinini (family) 2 27
Rondocubism see under CUBISM → types
Rondot, Natalis 7 87
rond-points 12 119
Rone Church 13 190; 14 81; 30 66
Rōnen Koji 25 892
Rongolise, S Maria in Grotta 26 653
Rongwrong 8 435; 24 428
Ronig, Ludwig Egidius 14 48
Ronis, Willy 27 123*
Rønne 8 748
Ronner, Alfred 18 157
Ronner, Alice 18 157
Ronner, Henriëtte see (RONNER-) KNIP, HENRIËTTE
Ronsard, Pierre de 9 328
Ronse, St Hermes 3 541
Ronse, Adriaan van 10 717
Ronsin 8 655
Roo, Gerard de 13 912
Rood, Mary 10 329
Rood, Ogden (Nicholas) 19 355; 27 126*
groups and movements 9 40
works 1 74; 7 629; 22 745
Rood and Hunt Binder
works 4 351
Roode, Henn 10 540
Roodish, Betty see GOODWIN, BETTY
roods 8 738; 27 123–5*, 125; 33 17
see also CRUCIFIXES
rood screens see under SCREENS (i) (ARCHITECTURAL) → types
roof bosses see BOSSES
roof-combs see FINIALS
roof decorations 7 143; 30 842
roof gardens see under GARDENS → types
roofs 27 126–31*; 30 895, 899–902*, 900, 903–11*, 908, 910
historical and regional traditions
Africa 1 305, 306, 307, 308, 320
Aztec 27 128
Bali (Indonesia) 15 773
Belgium 12 522, 522
Bhutan 3 913
roofs
historical and regional traditions—cont.
Buddhism 17 66, 72–3; 30 842
Burma 5 261
Byzantine 9 539
Cambodia 5 475
Central Asia, Eastern 6 295–6
China 5 649; 6 641–3*, 658, 691; 27 127; 30 912–14*
Colombia 7 603
Early Christian (c. AD 250–843) 9 539
Egypt, ancient 27 127
England 16 54; 30 894, 905, 906, 909, 910
Gothic 19 609; 30 904
14th cent. 27 126
19th cent. 10 236
Etruscan 1 127
France 14 592; 30 671, 907, 909, 910
Germany 27 127; 30 909
Gothic 27 128, 130; 30 907
England 19 609; 30 904
Italy 13 64
Greece, ancient 2 668; 13 390, 397; 27 127; 30 493, 902, 902–3*
Hellenistic 2 667
Roman 2 408
Inca 27 128
Indian subcontinent 15 336
Indonesia 15 773, 774
Islamic 16 141, 269; 27 127
Italy 1 127; 13 64
Japan 17 46, 47*, 48, 51, 54, 66, 259, 337–8; 23 598, 822; 30 912–14*
Buddhism 17 72–3
Java 15 764, 772
Korea 18 265, 266, 278; 30 912–14*
Malaysia 20 167
Maya 21 205; 27 128
Mesoamerica, Pre-Columbian 21 205, 206–7*, 207
Mesopotamia 9 539; 21 283, 287
Nepal 22 792–3
Nigeria 1 320
Palestine 9 539
Prehistoric art 27 126
Romanesque 30 905, 907
Rome, ancient 26 869, 877, 878, 880; 27 127; 30 903*
Greece 2 408
Russia 7 813
Ryūkyū Islands 27 470
Spain 29 311
Sudan 1 305, 306
Syria 9 539
Tibet 30 842
United States of America 27 128; 29 490
Vietnam 32 477, 487
materials
bamboo 1 307; 3 913; 15 772; 17 46
bark 17 47; 18 278
brackets 4 623
bronze 32 487
cables 29 489, 490; 30 468
canvas 13 619
cast iron 10 236; 30 671
concrete 26 880; 27 128
copper 7 813; 15 336; 17 47
cypress 23 598
glass 13 619; 16 54
grasses 1 306, 307
iron 14 592
lead 18 902; 27 131
palm leaves 1 305; 7 603; 15 772; 20 167
reeds 1 307; 6 295
shingles 17 47; 27 131
silver 32 487
slate 27 131
steel 2 512
stone 27 131

roofs
materials—cont.
straw **1** 307; **13** 619
tamarisk **6** 295
terracotta **1** 127; **13** 397; **15** 772; **32** 472, *472*
thatch **6** 692; **17** 47; **27** 131
tiles **6** 643; **17** 47, 259; **18** 278; **23** 822; **26** 877, 878; **27** 131; **30** 874
wood **9** 539; **12** *522*; **15** 772; **16** 141; **26** 569; **30** 894
wrought iron **10** 236; **16** *54*
types
collar and rafter **30** 905–7*, *906*
common-tie-beam **30** 905*
conical **27** 129, *130*
cruck **30** *901*, 908; **32** *788*
flat **2** 512; **27** 129
gambrel **27** 129
half-hipped **6** 668; **27** 129, *130*
hammer-beam **30** *900*
helm **27** 129–30, *130*
hip-and-gable **6** 668
hipped **6** 668; **27** 130, *130*
lantern **6** *295*, 296
lean-to **27** 130, *130*
mansard **27** 128, 130, *130*
Mudéjar **10** 153; **23** 903
pitched **27** *130*, 130–31
purlin **30** 907–8
pyramidal **27** *130*, 131
saddleback **27** *130*, 131
trussed **30** 899, 904–5*
China **30** *913*
Egypt, ancient **13** 404
Greece, ancient **13** 381, 390, 407
Japan **30** *913*
Korea **30** *913*
wagon **27** 131
Rooke, Noel **33** 369
Rooke, Thomas Matthews **5** 269; **25** 555
Rooker, Edward **27** 132
Rooker, Michael (Angelo) **18** 713; **23** 690; **27** 132*
rooks **11** 119
Rookwood Pottery **2** 572; **17** 441; **27** 132*; **30** 887; **31** 638, 639
works **31** *638*
Rooman, Joos **3** 545; **12** 523
Roome, Jan van **27** 132*
collaboration **21** 72
patrons and collectors **13** 905; **31** 844
reproductions in tapestry **5** 46
works **3** 606; **4** 417, 870; **13** 195
Roomer, Gaspar **4** 218; **22** 478; **27** 132–3*
paintings **10** 114, 762; **12** 664; **25** 563; **32** 826
Room Nine Society *see* KYUSHITSUKAI
Rooms, R. **3** 585
Rooney, Robert **2** 751; **27** 133*
Roopalekha **24** 436
Roore, Jacques (Ignace) de **2** 204; **27** 133–4*
Roos, Adrianus de **3** 599
Roos, Cajetan **27** 134, 136
Roos, C. S. **1** 808
Roos, Franz **27** 134
Roos, Jakob **27** 134
Roos, Johann **9** 485
Roos, Johann Heinrich **27** 134–5*
collaboration **10** 464
pupils **27** 135
reproductive prints by others **18** 47
teachers **13** 262
works **12** 390
Roos, Johann Melchior **27** 134, 135–6*
Roos, Joseph (1726-1805) **27** 134, 136*; **32** 460
Roos, Joseph, II (1760-1822) **27** 134
Roos, Peter **27** 134
Roos, Philipp Peter **4** 609; **20** 394; **27** 134, 135*; **33** 20
Roos, Theodor **27** 134, 135*
Roos, William **32** 785
Roose, Louis **12** 147
Roose, Nicolas *see* LIEMAECKER, NICOLAAS
Roosen, Jan **12** 134; **25** 745
Roosenboom, Margaretha **22** 848
Roosenburg, Dirk **27** 136*
Rooses, Max **3** 619; **6** 79; **27** 136–7*, 301
Roosevelt, Franklin D. **14** 252; **31** 606, 663
Roosevelt, Theodore **4** 364; **14** 252; **20** 19; **26** 180
works **4** *365*
Rooskens, (Joseph) Anton **7** 489; **27** 137*
Rooster, Jacques de **9** 378
Roosval, Johnny **30** 120
Roosvelt, J. F. A. Cateau van *see* CATEAU VAN ROOSVELT, J. F. A.
Root, Edward **25** 553
Root, John Wellborn **5** 272, 273; **27** 137–8*
collaboration **6** 573; **28** 830, 833; **30** 505
groups and movements **6** 577, 578; **28** 604
works **5** 274; **8** 278; **27** *138*, 463; **31** 594; **33** 174
roots **1** 295; **3** 331; **7** 142; **22** 656, 657
Roper **1** 518
ropes **7** 764, 765, 767; **10** 561; **11** 54; **16** 262; **31** 167; **33** 1
Ropet, Ivan (Pavlovich) **1** 72; **27** 138–9*, 580
groups and movements **28** 837
works **27** 377
Ropetism **22** 173
ropework **27** 139*, *139*
Röpfel, Ondřej **8** 398
Roppa, Pietro **11** 394
Rops, Félicien (Joseph Victor) **27** 139–41*
collaboration **20** 603
groups and movements **5** 44; **7** 245; **19** 321; **28** 921; **32** 591
methods **10** 563
patrons and collectors **10** 487; **26** 6
pupils **19** 85; **29** 723
works **3** 563; **8** 596; **9** 309; **10** 480; **25** 626; **27** *141*
Ropstein, Hans Gitschmann von *see* GITSCHMANN VON ROPSTEIN, HANS
Roque, Antoine de La *see* LA ROQUE, ANTOINE DE
Roque, Jean de La *see* LA ROQUE, JEAN DE
Roque, Mitre de la **11** 799
Roquefavour **2** 243
Roque-Gameiro, Alfredo **19** 879; **27** 141*; **28** 781
Roquelaure, Maréchal de **19** 231
Roquepertuse **11** *505*; **25** *470*, 536, 538; **27** 142*; **30** 434
painting **11** 528
pillars **27** *142*
sculpture **6** 158; **25** 545; **27** 142
Roqueplan, Camille (-Joseph-Etienne) **27** 142–3*
dealers **9** 423; **22** 243
groups and movements **26** 500
patrons and collectors **12** 186; **23** 522
pupils **20** 419; **29** 645
teachers **1** 28; **3** 855
works **12** 187; **27** *143*
Roques, Anne-Charlotte **27** 144
Roques, Georges **15** 669
Roques, Guillaume **27** 144
Roques, (Guillaume-) Joseph **15** 836; **27** 143–4*
Rørbye, Martinus (Christian Wedelstoft) **8** 735; **27** 144–5*
groups and movements **28** 814
pupils **11** 798
works **8** *734*; **27** *144*
Rordorff, Johann H. **22** 341
Roriczer (family) **20** 441; **26** 88; **27** 145*
Roriczer, Conrad **22** 306; **27** 145, 146*
works **23** 204, 316; **27** 146
Roriczer, Mathes **27** 145, 146, *147*, 147–8*
works **20** 564; **22** 306
writings **2** 344, 346, *346*, 347, *347*; **10** 747; **20** 564, *565*; **28** 497
Roriczer, Wenzel **27** 145–6*
Roriczer, Wolfgang **14** 308; **27** 145, 147, 148*
Rorke, Patrick **19** 242
Rorke's Drift **29** *103*
Evangelical Lutheran Church Art and Craft Centre **29** 110, 123
Rorke's Drift Pottery **29** 117
Rørlykke
horns **25** *526*
Røros **23** *218*, 220, 237
Rörstrand Ceramics Factory **11** 105, 106; **30** 97, 98, 99, 100, 101, 106, 884
marks **20** 441
works **30** *100*
Rörstrand-Gustavsberg AB
Rörstrand **30** 99, 101
Rosa, Annella de *see* ROSA, DIANA DE
Rosa, Antonio Gonçalves de *see* GONÇALVES DE ROSA, ANTONIO
Rosa, Artur **25** 300, 302
Rosa, Carlo **1** 731; **27** 149*
Rosa, Cristóbal Sánchez de la *see* SÁNCHEZ DE LA ROSA, CRISTÓBAL
Rosa (i), Cristoforo **27** 148–9*; **29** 84; **32** 223
Rosa, Diana de **3** 688; **23** 699
Rosa, Ercole **11** 15; **16** 707
Rosa, Fabián de la **20** 274; **24** 622
Rosa, Fabio **26** 842
Rosa, Fernando **22** 245
Rosa, Francesco **18** 901; **28** 109
Rosa, Gaetano *see* ROOS, CAJETAN
Rosa, Giovan Francesco de *see* PACECCO
Rosa, José **14** 697
Rosa, Joseph *see* ROOS, JOSEPH
Rosa, Manuel de la **5** 603
Rosa, Massenzio **27** 149
Rosa, Pacecco de *see* PACECCO
Rosa (i), Pietro **26** 785; **27** 149
Rosa, Salvator **3** 388; **8** 612; **11** 188; **16** 673; **22** 478; **26** 771; **27** 149–55*, *150*
attributions **21** 27
copies **5** 920; **21** 170
exhibitions **27** 171
groups and movements **29** 890
paintings **6** 586
allegorical **1** 659
patrons and collectors
Angiviller, Charles-Claude de Flahaut de la Billarderie, Comte d' **2** 53
Bourbon II., Luis Antonio, Infante of Spain **4** 565
Bracciano, Livio Odescalchi, Duca di **23** 353
Bracciano, Paolo Giordano II Orsini, Duca di **23** 576
Cairo, Francesco **5** 407
Chigi, Flavio, Cardinal **6** 585
Clement IX, Pope (*reg* 1667-70) **27** 172
Coke, Thomas, 1st Earl of Leicester of the 1st creation (1697-1759) **7** 540
Dalton, Richard **8** 474
Rosa, Salvator
patrons and collectors—cont.
Einden, van den (family) **10** 115
Francesco I, 8th Duke of Modena and Reggio (*reg* 1629-58) **10** 526
Gerini, Carlo, Marchese **12** 355
Horne, Herbert (Percy) **14** 764
Isham, Thomas **16** 82
Jennens, Charles **17** 476
Medici, Giovanni Carlo de', Cardinal (1611-63) **21** 27
Medinaceli, Luís de la Cerda Fernández de Córdoba Folch de Cardona y Aragón, 9th Duque de (1660-1711) **21** 35
Methuen, Paul (1672-1757) **21** 348
Morice, Humphry **22** 115
Paliano and Castiglione, Lorenzo Onofrio Colonna, Duke of **7** 620, 622
Poniatowski, Stanisław, Prince **25** 213
Rosso, Antonio del (1600-1668) **27** 205
Sanford, John **27** 729
Sanfré, Alexandre de Sousa-Holstein, Conde de **29** 100
Skippe, John **28** 819
Somerset, Henry, 3rd Duke of Beaufort **13** 301
Spencer, John, 1st Earl Spencer **29** 381
Streeter, Robert (1621-79) **29** 767
Talbot, Charles, 1st Duke of Shrewsbury (1660-1718) **30** 267
Tarnowski, Jan Feliks, Count and Waleria **30** 345
Temple-Nugent-Brydges-Chandos-Grenville, Richard, 1st Duke of Buckingham and Chandos **13** 637
Udney, John **31** 525
pupils **12** 560; **26** 242
reproductive prints by others **4** 607, 886; **12** 209; **25** 77; **28** 751
teachers **10** 762
works **3** 388; **11** 214, *396*; **16** 671, *671*, 672, 776; **18** 709–10; **21** 527; **27** *151*, *152*, *153*
writings **12** 289
Rosa, Salvator, frames *see under* FRAMES → types
Rosa, Scipione della, Marchese **7** 322
Rosa (i), Stefano **27** 148–9*; **29** 84; **32** 223
Rosa, Tommaso de **23** 699
Rosa da Napoli *see* ROOS, JAKOB
Rosa da Tivoli *see* ROOS, PHILIPP PETER
Rosado, Juan **25** 701; **26** 426; **31** 415
Rosado, Lucy **31** 262
Rosado del Valle, Julio **18** 832; **25** 701; **27** 155*
Rosafa *see* RUSAFA
Rosai, Ottone **16** 680; **27** 155–6*
groups and movements **7** 779; **11** 866; **16** 680
patrons and collectors **7** 782; **20** 848
works **21** 471
Rosales, Eduardo **29** 285
Rosales, Juan José **10** 773
Rosales Gallina, Eduardo *see* ROSALES MARTÍNEZ, EDUARDO
Rosales Martínez, Eduardo **27** 156–7*; **29** 284
groups and movements **24** 829
reproductive prints by others **12** 28
works **14** 587; **20** 67; **27** *156*, *157*
Rosandić, Toma **28** 453
Rosanjin Kitaōji *see* KITAŌJI, ROSANJIN
Rosapina, Francesco **23** 829
Rosaria **27** 159
rosaries **9** 108; **17** 520, 524, 525; **27** 158–60*
historical and regional traditions
Buddhism **7** 90; **17** 386
China **7** 90
England **13** 164; **27** *159*
Germany **12** 455
Gothic **13** 164
Japan **17** 386
Spain **17** 515
materials
enamel **27** *159*
glass **17** 386
gold **27** *159*
jet **17** 515
rock crystal **7** 90
Rosario (group) **7** 686
Rosario, El **20** *882*; **21** *193*, *372*; **27** 158*
Rosario, Maria do **22** 245
Rosart, N.-F. **22** 452
Rosas, Alfredo Ruiz *see* RUIZ ROSAS, ALFREDO
Rosas, Juan Manuel de **2** 395
Rosati, Rosato **3** 250; **19** 133; **20** 898; **27** 160*
Rosbach, Elias **4** 666
Rosca, Luigi **14** 222; **29** 554
Rösch, Franz Joseph **9** 177
Rosch, Georg Sigmund **11** 458
Roscher, Georg Michael **11** 458
Roscher, Wilhelm Heinrich **10** 211, 213
Roscigno **13** 570
Roscioli, Dionisio **27** 160
Roscioli, Giovanni Maria **25** 388; **27** 160*
Roscoe, Thomas **8** 84, 218; **25** 837
Roscoe, William **19** 507; **27** 161*
paintings **10** 366; **15** 57; **19** 507
sculpture **12** 597
sponsorship **19** 507
Roscommon (Co. Roscommon) **26** 688
Castle **16** 8
Rose + Croix, Salon de la *see* SALON DE LA ROSE + CROIX
Rose, Barbara **31** 672
Rose, Brian **31** 375
Rose, Edgar **4** 155; **29** 105
Rose, Franz **33** 183
Rose, Guy **19** 701
Rose, John **6** 93; **7** 480
Rose, Joseph, sr (*c.* 1723-80) **1** 140; **26** 499; **29** 835
Rose, Joseph, jr (1746-99) **1** 140; **11** 431; **16** 24; **29** 835
Rose, Joseph, & Co. **29** 835
Rosé, Manuel **31** 755
Rose, Peter **5** 563, 574
Rose, Thomas (1780-1843) **7** 480
Rose, Thomas (*fl* 1851-7) **22** 539
Rose, Willem Nicolaas **14** 45; **27** 161*
Rose, William **30** 160
Rose and Crown Club **10** 371; **19** 584
Roseau Victoria Memorial Museum **2** 153
Rosebery, Earl of **21** 732
Rosebery, William Bingham, Lord *see* BINGHAM, WILLIAM, LORD ROSEBERY
Rosebery House (Lothian) **9** 202
Rosecrans, Dirck Jacobsz. **17** *924*
Rose Hill **31** 592
Rosei, Franz **2** 804
Roselius, Ludwig **14** 622
Roselle *see* RUSELLAE
Roselli *see* ROSSELLI
Rosellini, Ippolito **10** 78, 82, 83
Rösel von Rosenhof, Franz **24** 277
rosemaling **23** 231, *232*, 242*

Rose mandarin porcelain *see* PORCELAIN → wares → *famille rose*
Rosemond, Mme Carreaud de *see* CARREAUD DE ROSEMOND, Mme
Rosemont, Franklin 30 23
Rosen, Adolf van 6 581
Rosen, Anton (Sophus) 8 727; 27 161–2*
Rosen, (Johan) Georg (Otto) von 16 67; 27 162*
Rosen, Gerd 3 802; 31 361
Rosen, Kunz von der 14 *747*
Rosen, Manuel 25 878
Rosen, Paul Gerhard, Baron von
Rosenau, Johannes of *see* JOHANNES OF ROSENAU
Rosenbach, A. S. W. 13 325
Rosenbach, Ulrike 10 879; 24 409
Rosenbaum 17 691
Rosenbaum, Fritz 30 683
Rosenbaum, Hieronymus 19 843
Rosenberg, Alexandre, the elder (*fl* 1870) 24 143; 27 162
Rosenberg, Alexandre, the younger (*fl* 1950) 27 162, 163
Rosenberg, Alfred 22 710; 28 126
Rosenberg, Eugene 33 552
Rosenberg, Harold 17 583; 24 433; 27 163*
collaboration 29 606
groups and movements 1 78, 86
works 1 131; 8 613; 13 811
Rosenberg, Johann Gottfried 3 841
Rosenberg, Léonce 4 98; 11 550; 13 670; 19 438; 21 364, 851; 24 144, 717; 27 162–3*; 28 508; 31 832
decorative works 28 508
groups and movements 8 246; 25 740; 29 661
paintings 8 606; 9 63; 14 437; 19 79
publications 22 749
sculpture 12 148
works 26 44
Rosenberg, Lev (Samoylovich) *see* BAKST, LÉON
Rosenberg, Paul 17 725; 24 144, 720; 27 162, 163*
paintings 4 676; 29 494
Rosenberg, Thomas Elliott 3 373
Rosenberg, Walle 11 108
Rosenblum, Robert 31 671, 672
Rosenblum, Walter 27 164*
Rosenburg, Alfred 12 843
Rosendael Castle 12 132; 22 *813*, 822; 27 164*
Rosendal 23 *218*
Rosendal Barony 12 135, *135*; 23 220
Rosendo, Saint 6 135; 22 247
Rosenegger, Lorenz 13 704; 14 361
Rosenfeld, Andrée 1 68
Rosenfelt, Hans 30 104
Rosengart, Angela 30 153
Rosengart, Siegfried 30 153
Rosengarten, Albrecht 17 547
Rosenholm 8 725
Rosenkrantz (family) 8 732
Rosenkrantz, Erik 23 220
Rosenquist, James 27 164–5*
collaboration 20 608
dealers 6 23
groups and movements 23 49, 261; 25 232
patrons and collectors 24 24; 28 314
works 18 719; 19 492, 493; 25 626; 31 608
Rosenrod, Johannes 20 159; 27 165*
works 30 76, *76*
Rosenthal, Constantin David 26 713; 27 165–6*
Rosenthal, Jane 3 278
Rosenthal, Léon 11 676; 24 129
Rosenthal, Philip 12 437
Rosenthal Factory 15 5
Rosenthal Gores Globe 12 813
Rosenthal-Porzellan AG 12 437; 29 117; 32 757
Rosenwald, Lessing J(ulius) 2 382; 27 166*
Rosenwald Master 20 789, 790
rose quartz 7 91, 111
Roserberg 30 89
Rose Rouge, La 6 167
Rosersberg Castle 30 *65*
architecture 30 69
furniture 30 95
Green Cabinet 9 26
Rune Hill 11 242
Rosés, Lluis Masriera i *see* MASRIERA I ROSÉS, LLUIS
Rosetsu Nagasawa *see* NAGASAWA ROSETSU
Rosetta *see* RASHID
Rosetta Stone 2 299; 10 79, 97
rosettes 13 392, 393
Rosetti, Biagio 26 459
Rosetto, il *see* TERILLI, FRANCESCO
Rose Valley (PA) 2 572; 24 598; 25 573
Roseville Pottery 26 287; 31 638
rose-wood 33 325
historical and regional traditions
Belgium 3 585
Czech Republic 8 399
England 5 192; 10 279, 297
France 11 596
Indian subcontinent 15 720
Japan 17 399
Peru 33 *332*
Portugal 25 *306*, 307, *307*
United States of America 31 *630*, *631*
uses
bureaux 5 192
cabinets (ii) (furniture) 25 *306*; 31 *631*
chairs 25 *307*
dolls' furniture 31 264
furniture 3 585; 8 399; 10 297
marquetry 25 307; 33 *332*
mirror frames 21 721
netsuke 17 399
sofas 31 *630*
veneers 11 596
Roshan Shakya 22 785
Rosheim 12 364
SS Pierre et Paul 26 633
Roshibagh Mosque 15 379
Rosi, Alessandro 8 497; 12 527; 31 187
Rosi, Zanobi 1 672, 673
Rosich, Miguel 8 232
Rosicrucians *see* SALON DE LA ROSE + CROIX
Rosier, Marc 4 545
rosin 1 155; 18 609, 610, 611; 26 243
pietre dure 14 168
varnishes 32 1
waxes 33 2
Rosincová, Š. 28 850
Rosini, Giovanni 18 811; 24 855; 27 166*; 31 516
Roskilde 8 *720*; 27 166–8*
Cathedral of the Trinity and St Lucius 4 781; 8 722, 723, 739, 758; 13 50; 26 592, 593; 27 *167*, 167–8*
choir-stalls 8 738
sculpture 8 738; 13 118
stained glass 13 190
tomb of Christian III 7 303; 11 *219*
tomb of Margaret I 8 738
wall paintings 8 730
Harald I's church 8 721
St Jørgensbjerg 27 166
Viking Ship Museum 27 167
Vor Frue Kirke 8 721
Roskó, Gábor 14 902
Roskopf, George-Frédéric 7 448
Roskopf, Wendel, I (*c.* 1480–1549) 18 539; 27 168*; 30 221
Roskopf, Wendel, II (*d* 1582) 27 168
Roškot, Kamil 8 380; 18 405; 27 168–9*
Roslagsbro 13 119
Roslin, Alexander 3 428; 12 634; 13 301; 24 137; 27 169–70*, 388; 30 78, 79
collaboration 4 517
methods 10 198
patrons and collectors 8 161; 10 531; 19 338; 30 524
pupils 11 173; 18 418; 24 222
reproductive prints by others 3 463; 19 144; 27 645
sponsorship 20 485
works 11 408, 410, 471; 27 *169*
Roslin, Marie-Suzanne 27 *169*, 170*
Roslin Chapel (Lothian) 13 56; 27 170–71*, *171*; 28 *222*, 224, 268, 497, *497*
Roslyn Woollen Mill 23 73
Rosmini, Antonio 15 54; 22 70
Rosnay, Gédéon Berbier Du Metz, 1st Comte de 20 138
Rosnay, Jean Berbier Du Metz, 2nd Comte de 20 138
Rösner, Karl 27 171*
collaboration 2 786
pupils 3 312; 11 29; 33 687
teachers
works 2 785, 808; 25 428
Rosny, Maximilien de Béthune, Baron de *see* SULLY, Duc de
Rosny-sur-Seine Château 4 556; 20 868; 29 *917*
Rosoni cycle 10 614
Rosoni Kraters, Painter of the 10 614
Rospigliosi (family) 6 568; 20 270, 375; 26 748, 773
Rospigliosi, Camillo (*d* 1670) 21 831; 27 171
Rospigliosi, Camillo, Duca di Zagarlo (1714–69) *see* ZAGARLO, CAMILLO ROSPIGLIOSI, Duca di
Rospigliosi, Clemente Domenico 23 873; 27 172
Rospigliosi, Domenico Clemente 20 805
Rospigliosi, Giovanni Battista, Duca di Zagarolo *see* ZAGAROLO, GIOVANNI BATTISTA ROSPIGLIOSI, Duca di
Rospigliosi, Giulio *see* CLEMENT IX, Pope
Rospigliosi, Giuseppe, Prince 20 805
Rospigliosi, Jacopo, Cardinal 12 285; 27 171
Rospigliosi *Athena* 30 916
Rospigliosi Cup 4 53
Rospigliosi-Pallavicini, Giovanni Battista 23 873
Rospigliosi-Pallavicini, Giuseppe 23 873
Rospigliosi Triptych 3 301
Ross (Co. Westmeath) 12 869
Ross (*fl* 1835) 14 149
Ross, Alan 21 697
Ross, Alexander 28 230
Ross, Betsy 7 408
Ross, Charles 19 355
Ross, Denman Waldo 4 168; 15 742, 745; 17 431; 26 467
Ross, Doran H.
works 1 *332*
Ross, George (Allen) 23 631; 27 173*; 31 239
Ross, Gloria F. 31 660
Ross, James 14 132
Ross, Margaret 30 469
Ross, Maria 27 173
Ross, Patrick 20 52; 21 574
Ross, Thomas (*fl* 1730–46) 20 33
Ross, Thomas (1839–92) 28 289
Ross, Thomas, & Son 2 365
Ross, William 27 173
Ross, William Charles 14 148; 26 467; 27 173*
works 21 645, *645*
Rossano, Federico 6 130; 8 716; 16 678; 22 480; 28 317, 318
Rossano Gospels *see under* GOSPEL BOOKS → individual manuscripts
Rossbach, Ed 11 54; 30 329
Ross Collection *see under* BOSTON (MA; USA) → museums → Museum of Fine Arts
Rossdhu 29 843
Rosse, Susan Penelope 12 600; 21 641
Rosseels, Jacob 3 562; 8 62; 14 507; 31 875
Rosselet, Jacob 22 920
Rosselet, Jean-Jacques 22 920
Rossell, Guillermo 5 603; 33 584
Rosselli (family) 12 814
Rosselli, Alberto 25 218
works 16 *93*
Rosselli, Alessandro 27 176
Rosselli, Bernardo (1450–1526) 27 174; 29 782
Rosselli, Bernardo di Stefano (*fl* 1460) 22 800
Rosselli, Cosimo 27 174–6*
attributions 24 25
collaboration 3 916; 7 676; 11 686; 12 551; 21 694; 26 815
patrons and collectors 4 494; 16 661; 27 271
pupils 1 569; 3 302; 10 877; 24 768
restorations by others 11 318
teachers 22 799, 800, 802
works 9 263, *263*; 11 487; 20 111; 24 521; 26 815; 27 *175*
Rosselli, Domenico (di Giovanni) 6 603; 27 177*; 31 744
Rosselli, Francesco 10 383; 27 174, 176*
attributions 6 14; 11 *178*, 687
collaboration 11 296; 20 689
works 11 687
Rosselli, Giuliano 27 174
Rosselli, Jacopo (*b* 1389) 27 174
Rosselli, Jacopo (*fl* mid-15th cent.) 8 187
Rosselli, Lorenzo 11 692; 27 174
Rosselli, Matteo 16 673; 27 177–9*
assistants 6 126
collaboration 11 845; 21 26; 25 718
patrons and collectors 5 179; 21 25
pupils 11 678; 12 706; 19 452; 25 717; 32 499
works 6 126; 27 *178*
Rosselli, Pietro di Giacomo 27 179*
Rossellino (family) 11 206
Rossellino, Antonio 24 232; 27 179–80, 183–5*; 31 717
assistants 7 366; 32 360
attributions 8 798; 21 694
collaboration 3 253; 5 129; 8 799; 27 181
methods 21 768
pupils 27 177
sculpture 27 181
altarpieces 1 711; 22 476, *477*
busts 9 127; 16 690, 691
religious 4 505
tombs 11 206, 210; 16 690; 27 *184*
Rossellino, Bernardo 12 110, 111, 112; 14 870; 16 631; 27 179–83*
architecture
architectural decorations 28 687
cathedrals 5 21; 11 196; 24 746, *747*
Rossellino, Bernardo
architecture—cont.
churches 1 560; 4 650; 26 755, 804, 835
palazzi 1 556, 562; 2 389; 10 853; 16 629; 23 486; 24 746
assistants 8 797; 32 360
attributions 24 278
collaboration 1 555–68; 11 388; 27 183
methods 24 492
patrons and collectors 5 682; 16 631; 23 97; 24 732
pupils 27 177, 183
sculpture 12 542; 16 690
tombs 5 26; 8 797, 799; 11 206; 27 *180*, 830
workshop 5 18
Rossellino, Giovanni 11 254; 23 772
Rosselló *see* ROUSSILLON, MASTER OF
Rossello di Jacopo Franchi *see* FRANCHI, ROSSELLO DI JACOPO
Rossell y Rius, Alejo 31 758
Rössen culture 25 498, 500, 513
Rosserk Abbey (Co. Mayo) 13 56
Rosset, Joseph 13 663
Rosset & Schmid 30 885
Rossetti, Biagio 27 188–91*
attributions 3 896
patrons and collectors 10 520
works 11 3; 13 293; 27 *189*, *191*
Rossetti, Carlo
works 28 *424*
Rossetti, Christina 14 850; 22 351; 27 188
Rossetti, Dante Gabriel 5 173; 27 185–8*; 28 664; 29 368
assistants 22 351
collaboration 4 879; 5 266; 10 254; 11 433; 15 26; 22 142, 143, 314; 28 349
dealers 12 30
dress 9 245, 289
frames 11 376, 432, 433, *433*, 434
groups and movements
Aesthetic Movement 1 170; 2 530; 19 588
In Arte Libertas 8 6
Japonisme 17 440
Pre-Raphaelite Brotherhood (PRB) 10 253; 14 580; 21 602; 25 554, 555
house 28 349
paintings 1 712; 5 731; 10 253, 254, 480; 31 344
literary themes 1 640; 27 *187*
watercolours 27 *186*
patrons and collectors
Boyce, George Price 4 604
City Art Gallery (Manchester) 20 239
Combe, Thomas and Martha 7 647
Graham, William 13 273
Handley-Read, Charles and Lavinia 14 132
Ionides, Aleco 15 895
Ionides, Constantine Alexander 15 895
Leathart, James 18 907
Leyland, F(rederick) R(ichard) 19 290
Murray, Charles Fairfax 22 351
Plint, T(homas) E(dward) 25 41
Stephens, F(rederic) G(eorge) 29 633
Windus, B(enjamin) G(odfrey) 33 251
personal collection 10 312; 15 895
photographed works 14 688
pupils 5 266; 22 142
reproductive prints by others 25 596
stained glass 22 143
studio 29 857

Rossetti, Dante Gabriel—cont.
teachers **4** 878
writings **4** 868; **25** 72
Rossetti, Domenico **19** 732; **33** 721
Rossetti, Gabriel Charles Dante *see* ROSSETTI, DANTE GABRIEL
Rossetti, Giorgio Giacinto **16** 737
Rossetti, Giovanni Paolo **8** 504
Rossetti, Lucy Madox **4** 879; **10** 878; **27** 188
Rossetti, William Michael **17** 440; **25** 554; **27** 188*; **28** 601
Rossi, A. de **32** 236
Rossi, Adriano **2** 404
Rossi, Aldo **6** 167; **11** 528; **16** 650; **23** 549; **27** 191–3*; **31** 735
collaboration **2** 880; **5** 123; **12** 59
groups and movements **22** 747; **25** 359; **26** 14, 16; **30** 391, 455
pupils **26** 16
works **12** 380; **14** 581; **16** 651; **18** 114, 456; **19** 862; **27** *192*; **30** 684
writings **16** 650
Rossi, Alessandro De *see* DE ROSSI, ALESSANDRO
Rossi, Angelo de **19** 274; **23** 637; **26** 810; **27** 193*
Rossi, Aniello **12** 664
Rossi, Annibale de' **16** 746; **22** 373
Rossi, Antonio **17** 706
Rossi, Attilio **10** 560
Rossi, Baldo De *see* DE ROSSI, BALDO
Rossi, Bartolomeo de' **22** 5
Rossi, Bernardino de (*c.* 1465-1514; architect) **24** 285; **27** 193–4*
Rossi, Bernardino de', Bishop of Treviso (*fl* 1505) **19** 710, *711*
Rossi, Bonaventura **13** 746
Rossi, Carlo **24** 292; **29** 842
Rossi, Carmen **33** 142
Rossi, Claudio **2** 903
Rossi, de (publishing house) **7** 897, 898; **9** 176; **26** 229
Rossi, Domenico (1657-87) **7** 861; **19** 516; **31** 186
Rossi, Domenico de (1659-1703) **27** 194
Rossi, Domenico de (*fl* 1704) **2** 164, 169; **20** 84; **31** 854
Rossi, Domenico de' (*fl* 1684-1721) **29** 251, 373
Rossi, Domenico Egidio **2** 782; **16** 641; **27** 195–6*
patrons and collectors **8** 426; **17** 512; **33** 594
works **20** 494; **27** *196*
Rossi, Domiziano **2** 903
Rossi, Eleonora Romeo **20** 607
Rossi, Evangelistra di Francesco de' **5** 672
Rossi, Federico II, Marchese di San Secondo *see* SAN SECONDO, FEDERICO II ROSSI, Marchese di
Rossi, Francesco **6** 22
Rossi, Francesco de' (1510-63) *see* SALVIATI, FRANCESCO (CECCHINO)
Rossi, Francesco de' (*fl* 1640-77) **1** 630
Rossi, Francesco dei **32** 875
Rossi, Franco dei *see* FRANCO DEI RUSSI
Rossi, Frederick **27** 197
Rossi, G. G. de (*fl* 1794) **1** 466
Rossi, Gian Alberto de' **4** 340
Rossi, Gino **16** 679; **27** 196–7*
Rossi, Giovan Battista (*fl* 1758-77) **22** 481
Rossi, Giovanni Antonio de (1616-95) **27** 194–5*
patrons and collectors **1** 728
teachers **24** 371
works **5** 377; **16** 746, *746*; **18** 689; **27** *194*
Rossi, Giovanni Antonio de' (1517-75) **20** 919; **27** 197*
patrons and collectors **12** 258
Rossi, Giovanni Battista (*fl c.* 1654) **32** 578
Rossi, Giovanni Battista de' **23** 577
Rossi, Giovanni Battista De (1822-94) *see* DE ROSSI, GIOVANNI BATTISTA
Rossi, Giovanni Domenico de **6** 34
Rossi, Giovanni Francesco **5** 376; **18** 431; **25** 114; **32** 7
Rossi, Giovanni Giacomo de' (*fl* 1640s-1699) **6** 34; **7** 466, 569; **29** 373
works **12** *526*; **29** *373*
Rossi, Girolamo **5** 635; **23** 454
Rossi, Giulio **24** 218
Rossi, Giuseppe Ignazio **28** 485
Rossi, Gregorio de **9** 340
Rossi, Henry **27** 197
Rossi, Horacio García **13** 709
Rossi, J.-J. **30** 746
Rossi, Joana **23** 454
Rossi, João **4** 141; **24** 98, 102
Rossi, John Charles Felix **27** 197*
patrons and collectors **5** 541; **33** 453
pupils **33** 449
works **19** 599, 600; **30** 503
Rossi, Josip **18** 196
Rossi, Józef **32** 876
Rossi, Karl **8** 710; **27** 198–200*, 408, 579
assistants **17** 859
collaboration **4** 598; **16** 53
teachers **4** 745
works **21** 512; **22** 25; **24** 817; **27** *199*, 345, 375, 403, 404, 576, *576*, 577, 583; **30** 486; **31** 486
Rossi, Laura Mattioli **20** 848
Rossi, Lorenzo **17** 912
Rossi, Luigi (1597-1653) **8** 88; **10** 489; **20** 895; **31** 165
Rossi, Luigi de' (*fl* 1517-19) **21** *16*
Rossi, Marcantonio de **27** 194, 195
Rossi, Mariano **2** 612; **4** 407; **27** 200–201*
Rossi, Mattia de **3** 838; **27** 194, 195*
patrons and collectors **1** 728; **6** 585; **15** 862
works **12** 649; **15** 861; **23** 352
Rossi, Michelangelo de' **27** 648
Rossi, Mino **11** 80
Rossi, Nicola Maria **14** 191; **22** 479; **27** 201*
pupils **12** 586
teachers **12** 664
Rossi, Nunzio **20** 617; **27** 202*
Rossi, Pasquale **27** 202*
Rossi, Pier Maria **3** 697
Rossi, Properzia de' **4** 280; **27** 202*; **33** 308
Rossi, Valter **20** 607
Rossi, Vincenzo (di Raffaello) de' **27** 203–4*
collaboration **19** 672
pupils **31** 787
teachers **3** 160
works **3** 159; **16** 696; **27** *203*
Rossi da Lugagnano, Raffaello **31** 291
Rossigneux, Charles **4** 308; **11** 622
Rossi Melocchi, Cosimo **27** 204*
Rössing, Mette **13** 620
works **13** *620*
Rossini, Luigi **32** 114
Rossi Osir, Paulo *see* OSIR, PAULO ROSSI
Rossiter, Mary P. *see* HARRISON, MARY P.
Rosskopf, Wendel, I *see* ROSKOPF, WENDEL, I
Rössler, Jaroslav **27** 205*
Rössler, Johann Joseph **10** 529; **11** 31; **14** 894
Rosslyn Chapel *see* ROSLIN CHAPEL
Rosslyn Pottery **28** 258
Ross & Macdonald **5** 562; **27** 173; **31** 176
Ross & MacFarlane **6** 513
Rosso, Il *see* NANNI DI BARTOLO
Rosso, Andrea del (1570-1644) **27** 205*
Rosso, Andrea del (1640-1715) **12** 661; **27** 133, 205*; **31** 886
Rosso, Antonio del (1600-1668) **27** 205*
Rosso, Antonio del (1674-1729) **27** 205*
Rosso, Domenico del **11** 194; **22** 481
Rosso, Giovanni Battista (*fl* 1639-55) **10** 528; **31** 353
Rosso, Giovanni Battista di Jacopo (1494-1540) *see* ROSSO FIORENTINO
Rosso, Giuseppe del **7** 836; **11** 181
Rosso, Lorenzo del **12** 661; **27** 133
Rosso, Lorenzo Ottavio del **27** 205
Rosso, Marco del **27** 205
Rosso, Medardo **21** 527; **27** 206–7*
groups and movements **28** 34
works **16** 706, *706*, 707; **27** *207*; **32** 257; **33** 3
Rosso, Mino **16** 708
Rosso, Ottavio del **12** 661
Rosso, Pietro **14** 469
Rosso, Zanobi del **11** 215; **16** 646; **27** 320
Rosso antico see under MARBLE → types
Rosso da Valenza, Francesco **22** 466
Rosso Fiorentino **11** 508, 513, 556, 656; **14** 869; **16** 766; **26** 769; **27** 207–10*
assistants **9** 176, 387; **30** 735
attributions **19** 18; **28** 5; **30** 735
collaboration **24** 365; **27** 848; **31** 848
drawings **10** 799; **27** *209*; **32** 10
frames **11** 391, 400
groups and movements **11** 186, 260, 262, 263, 264; **16** 663; **20** 281
interior decoration **6** 506; **9** 14; **11** 260, 513, 532, 571; **13** 700; **16** 695; **20** 278; **23** 540
methods **24** 493
paintings
allegorical **1** 657
frescoes **11** 205
nude figures **21** 759; **23** 293
religious **9** 707; **20** 280, *280*; **27** *208*
patrons and collectors **4** 379; **22** 31; **24** 133, 199; **25** 690; **31** 848; **32** 22
reproductions in ceramics **31** *742*
reproductions in tapestry **11** 262
reproductive prints by others **1** 551; **5** 699; **11** *264*, 616; **18** 46; **21** 538; **22** 369; **32** 412
stucco **29** 747, 833
teachers **27** 847, 851
Rossone, Pietro Giorgio **26** 319
Ross-on-Wye (Hereford & Worcs), St Mary's
tomb of William Rudhall **1** 519
Rosstsy *see* EFROS, ABRAM MARKOVICH
Rossum, Gerard van **6** 88
Rost, Giovanni (1535-64) *see* ROST, JAN
Rost, Giovanni (*fl* late 16th cent.) **27** 210
Rost, Jan **16** 757; **17** 812; **27** 210*
patrons and collectors **10** 523; **11** 5, 192–3
works **4** 857; **16** *757*; **26** 778; **30** 319
Rost, Karl Christian Heinrich **14** 625
Rostaing, Tristan de **20** 133
Rostand, Edmond **18** 836
Rostang, Raphaël **19** 341
Rostel, Jan *see* ROST, JAN
Rostislavov, Aleksander (Aleksandrovich) **27** 210–11*
Rosto, Jan del *see* ROST, JAN
Rostock
Marienkirche **4** 777; **13** 56; **25** 726
Neues Museum **8** 706
Rathaus **17** 699
St Nikolaus **14** 81
Rostopchin, F. V. **27** 439
Rostov **27** 211–12*, 361, *363*, 376
Church of the Resurrection **27** 387
icons **27** 212, 382
kremlin **27** 211, *211*
metropolitan's house **27** 372
Museum of Church Antiquities *see* Rostov-Yaroslavl' Architecture and Art Museum
painting **27** 382, 387
Rostov-Yaroslavl' Architecture and Art Museum **27** 211
sculpture **27** 382
wall paintings **25** 342
Rostov-on-Don **2** 425; **28** 325
theatre **27** 379, *379*
Rostovtsev, Mikhail (Ivanovich) **27** 443
Rostovtseva, Nina (Nikolayevna) **27** 417, 423
Rostov Yaroslavsky *see* ROSTOV
Rostrevor **16** 28
Rostrup, Haavard **8** 762
Rostrup Bøyesen, Peter **8** 761; **18** 543; **19** 799; **26** 508, 553; **30** 53
Rosůlek, Jan **8** 402
Rosulková, Dagmar **28** 856
Rósza, Miklós **13** 638
Roszak, Theodore **20** 832; **27** 212*; **31** 614
Rot, Diter *see* ROTH, DIETER
Rota, Bernardino **2** 731
Rota, Martino **2** 793; **10** 386; **27** 212*
patrons and collectors **13** 912
works **2** 794; **14** 899; **31** 43
Rota, Santi **28** 173
Rota Church **30** 883
Rot an der Rot Abbey Church **32** 823
Rotari, Pietro (Antonio) **26** 731; **27** 213*, 388
pupils **2** 188; **26** 550
reproductive prints by others **31** 821
teachers **3** 109
works **3** 109; **4** 407; **27** 402
Rotaru, Yelena **21** 812
rotary presses *see under* PRESSES → types
Rotati, Pietro **26** 780
Rotbertus **27** 793
Rot-Blau **3** 336; **18** 81; **27** 213*; **30** 135
members **28** 77, 172
Rotch & Tilden **8** 110
Rote Gruppe **9** 42; **28** 113
Rotella, Mimmo **11** 551; **27** 213–14*
groups and movements **8** 609; **20** 913; **23** 260; **26** 778
patrons and collectors **14** 48
works **7** 557; **16** 682
Rotellini, José Ramón **9** 118
Rotenhan, Hans Georg von **28** 146
Roth (family) **29** 684
Roth, Alfred **27** 214–15*
groups and movements **7** 296; **15** 886; **30** 391
staff **12** 744
works **27** 214
Roth, Cecil **17** 582
Roth, Dieter **15** 71; **27** 215–16*; **30** 135
collaboration **14** 112; **25** 864; **30** 748
groups and movements **13** 779
patrons and collectors **14** 48; **29** 16
works **19** 493; **27** *215*; **29** 98
Roth, Emery **3** 682; **27** 216*
Roth, Emery, & Sons **28** 834; **29** 807
Roth, Emil **27** 214*; **28** 122; **29** 531
collaboration **22** 187; **27** 214
groups and movements **7** 293; **15** 886
works **30** *128*
Roth, Franz Joseph **27** 216–17*
Roth, Harald **27** 315
Roth, Julian **27** 216
Roth, Karl-Dietrich *see* ROTH, DIETER
Róth, Miksa **15** 4
Röth, Philipp **28** 104
Roth, Richard (1905-88) **27** 216
Roth, Richard, II (*fl* 1950s) **27** 216
Roth, W. E. **1** 66, 67
Rothacher, Christian **30** 135
Rothapfel, Samuel L. **7** 327; **8** 809
Rothbletz, Johann Georg **13** 258; **18** 442
Rothbort, Samuel **23** 403
Rothbury (Northumb.), Cragside **8** 49; **9** 13; **10** 238, *238*; **25** 804
interior decoration **29** 748
Rothbury Cross **2** 70; **8** 196
Rothe, Max **21** 365
Rothenberg, Susan **2** 107; **27** 217*; **33** 364
Rothenburg, Erika **27** 872
Rothenburg, Konrad von **6** 472
Rothenburg-ob-der-Tauber **12** *361*, 385; **27** 217–18*; **33** 34
houses **32** *281*
Jakobskirche **13** 187; **27** 217–18*, *218*
Altar of the Holy Blood **12** 401; **13** 118; **14** 455; **26** *371*; **28** 134
altarpiece **14** *455*
Rathaus **12** 367; **31** 236
Sports Hall **29** 427
Rothenstein, Michael **17** 580; **27** 219; **33** 364
Rothenstein, William **10** 375; **15** 747; **17** 578; **27** 218–19*
groups and movements **23** 22
patrons and collectors **33** 181
personal collection **2** 306; **15** 742
teachers **10** 255
works **19** 488
Rother, Leopold **4** 233; **7** 606
Rothermel, Peter **23** 630
Rothfuss, Rhod **2** 400, 525; **31** 755
Rothger Micheelszoon van Colen *see* SAVOYE, RUTGER
Rothko, Mark **9** 20; **23** 48; **27** 219–22*, 731; **31** 608
dealers **16** 906; **24** 213
groups and movements **1** 78, 84, 85, 86, 87; **13** 214; **27** 563; **29** 534; **31** 607
Abstract art **1** 78
Abstract Expressionism **1** 84; **13** 214; **23** 48; **31** 138
Minimalism **21** 646
methods **7** 631; **25** 24
patrons and collectors **13** 801; **14** 575; **18** 170; **21** 135; **24** 24; **25** 400; **26** 489; **28** 314; **33** 45
works **1** 129; **6** 460; **7** 636; **18** 718; **21** 135; **27** *220*, *221*
Rothman, Gerd **12** 451, 865
Rothmann, Gerhard *see* ROTHMAN GERD
Rothmayer, Otto **8** 402; **25** 438
Rothmüller, Karl **22** 306

Rothschild (family) 16 851; 19 389; 27 223–6*
architecture 8 49; 11 735; 19 574
collections 2 829; 10 367; 11 369, 735; 12 474, 843; 13 841; 17 580
interior decoration 27 *224*
manuscripts 20 735; 25 248; 27 226
paintings 4 519; 8 599; 21 69
pattern books 24 270
Rothschild, Baronne de (*fl* 1871) 13 822
Rothschild, Adolphe Carl de, Baron (1823-1900) 27 223, 224, 225
Rothschild, Adolphe Carl de, Baronne (1830-1907) 27 225
Rothschild, Albert de, Baron 8 816
Rothschild, Alfred Charles de 27 223, 224
Rothschild, Alphonse de, Baron 31 448
Rothschild, Alphonse Mayer de, Baronne 27 225
Rothschild, Anselm Salomon de, Baron 27 224
Rothschild, Anthony Gustav de 27 224, 225
Rothschild, Anthony Nathan de 27 223
Rothschild, Edmond Adolph Maurice Jules Jacques de, Baron 11 664; 27 225
Rothschild, Edmond James de, Baron 16 552, 555; 27 223, 224, 225; 33 182
Rothschild, Elie de, Baronne (*b* 1916) 27 224
Rothschild, Elie Robert de, Baron (*b* 1917) 27 224
Rothschild, Ferdinand Anselm de, Baron 3 174; 8 817; 27 223, 224, 225
interior decoration 27 *224*
Rothschild, Guy Edouard Alphonse Paul de, Baron 27 225
Rothschild, James Armand Edmond de (1878-1957) 27 224, 225
Rothschild, James Mayer de, Baron (1792-1868) 13 778; 18 679; 24 295; 27 223, 226
Rothschild, Maurice Edmond Charles de, Baron 15 742; 16 555; 20 642; 27 224
Rothschild, Mayer Amschel, Baron (1743-1812) 27 223
Rothschild, Mayer Amschel, Baron (1818-74) 10 142; 24 295; 27 223
Rothschild, Mayer Carl de, Baron 27 224
Rothschild, Nathaniel Charles Jacob, 4th Baron 27 225*
Rothschild, Nathaniel Mayer Victor, 3rd Baron 19 519; 27 225
Rothschild, Nathan Mayer 8 37
Rothschild, Philippe de, Baron (1902-88) 27 225; 28 663
Rothschild, Philippe de, Baronne (1908-76) 27 225
Rothschild, Robert Philippe Gustave de, Baron 27 224
Rothschild, Salomon Albert Anselm de, Baron 27 223
Rothschild, Salomon James de, Baronne 27 225
Rothschild, Wilhelm Carl de, Baron 27 224, 225
Rothschild Bank 3 173
Rothschild Foundation 24 128
Rothschild Hours, Paris *see* BOOKS OF HOURS → individual manuscripts → Paris Rothschild Hours
Rothschild Hours, Vienna *see under* BOOKS OF HOURS → individual manuscripts → Vienna Rothschild Hours
Rothschild Miscellany (Jerusalem, Israel Museum, MS. 180/51) 27 226*, *226*; 32 198
Rothschild Model Book (Paris, Louvre) 24 270
Rothstein, Arthur 24 673
Rothwell, John 4 789
Rothwell, Richard 16 16; 18 895; 27 226–7*
Roti 15 *751*, 795, 813
sarongs 15 *796*
Rotival, Maurice 5 692; 32 170
Rotlinger, Hans 5 62
Rotllan, Blas Ametller *see* AMETLLER ROTLLAN, BLAS
Rotomagus *see* ROUEN
rotondas 8 155
Rotondo, Jacopo 32 5, 879
Rotondo, Paolo 21 472
Rotorua 23 *52*
New Zealand Maori Arts and Crafts Institute 20 359; 23 75
Rotse 1 273
Rotselaar, St Pieter 13 110
Rott, Hans 5 674; 9 527
Rottaler, Stephan 12 366
Rottenbuch, Augustinian church 2 723; 28 118
Rotteneck, Heinrich von, Bishop, *see* HEINRICH VON ROTTENECK, Bishop
Rottenhammer, Domenikus 27 229
Rottenhammer, Hans, I (156/5-1625) 5 76; 19 152; 27 227–9*; 32 194
attributions 23 880
collaboration 12 389; 32 772
patrons and collectors 13 631; 19 124; 28 60
reproductive prints by others 18 42; 27 504
teachers 9 133
works 12 387; 27 *227*, *228*; 30 5; 32 772
Rottenhammer, Hans, II (*d* 1668) 27 229
Rotter, Joseph Thadeus 18 417
Rotterdam 22 *813*; 27 229–31*
academy 22 907
Ahoy Centre 29 428
art forms and materials
architecture 22 831
brass 22 894, 895
bronze 22 894
ceramics 22 878
furniture 22 872
glass 22 884
ketubbot 18 3
murals 22 333
pewter 22 893
silver 22 887
tiles 22 881; 30 878, 879, *879*, 883
Bijenkorf, De 8 770; 32 696
Blijdorp 23 663
Bouwcentrum 4 790
Café De Unie 22 830
Central Library 19 320
Lijnbaan shopping centre 22 832; 28 623
museums
Boymans-van Beuningen Museum 4 217, 614; 28 891
collections 2 560; 3 889; 9 231; 11 310; 22 905, 906; 27 230; 32 269; 33 47
directors 11 233
library 22 909
Historisch Museum 17 434; 19 543; 22 906
see also Schielandshuis
Kunsthal gallery 27 231
Maritiem Museum Prins Hendrik 25 827
Rotterdam museums—cont.
Museum Hendrik Chabot 6 379
Nederlands Architectuurinstituut 18 213; 22 906, 909
Schielandshuis 4 614
Noorse Kerk 23 222
Peperklip, De 22 832
Schielandshuis 19 543; 27 230
see also Historisch Museum
Spangen 23 663
Stadhuis 30 760
Stadion Feyenoord 29 489
synagogue 17 549
urban planning 19 861
Van der Leeuw house 22 868
Van Nelle Factory 4 815, *815*; 7 695; 10 749; 12 792; 21 783; 22 830
Vreewijk 13 312–13
war memorials 22 861
Rotterdam St John on Patmos, Master of the 4 594, 595
Röttger, Jürgen 5 30
Rotthier, Philippe (Henri François) 8 257; 27 231*
Rottier *see* ROETTIERS
Rottière, Jean-Simeon Rousseau de La *see* ROUSSEAU DE LA ROTTIÈRE, JEAN-SIMEON
Rottiers, Gaspar 28 63
Rottiers, Jacobus 28 63
Rottiers, Peter 28 63
Rottland, Mario 8 232
Rottman, Franz 19 516
Rottmann, Alexander & Co. 32 817
Rottmann, Carl (Anton Joseph) 27 231–3*
attributions 8 898
exhibitions 2 546
patrons and collectors 11 787; 22 303
works 12 393; 27 *232*
Rottmann, Friedrich 11 236, 786; 27 231
Rottmann, Leopold 20 372
Rottmayr, Johann Michael 5 338; 11 130; 27 233–4*; 32 443
collaboration 30 793
patrons and collectors 5 9
teachers 19 707
works 2 794, 795, 828; 8 391; 12 390; 13 799; 14 309; 15 139; 21 84; 23 381; 25 188, 448; 27 *234*, 665; 32 454
Rottweil
Kapellenkirche Unserer Lieben Frau 12 400; 13 *88*, 88
Lorenzkapelle 13 88
Rotuma 23 *711*; 27 234–5*
see also FIJI
rotundas 2 617; 27 235–7*
Early Christian (*c.* AD 250-843) 27 235
England 27 237; 29 *735*
Italy 27 *236*, 236–7
Rome, ancient 26 903; 27 235
Spain 28 *726*
United States of America 17 *468*
see also CHURCHES → types → centrally planned
Roty, (Louis-)Oscar 4 746; 20 925; 25 214; 27 237*
Rouan, François 11 553, 644; 27 238*
tapestries 12 830
Rouart, Henri (-Stanislas) 20 351; 26 207; 27 206, 238*
Rouault, Georges (Henri) 22 91; 24 142, 144; 27 238–41*; 30 328
book illustrations 4 366
ceramics 11 606
collaboration 11 659; 14 486; 20 603; 29 508
dealers 20 75; 32 686
Rouault, Georges (Henri)—cont.
groups and movements 3 120; 10 696, 839, 840, 841; 27 639
livres d'artiste 32 687
methods 10 199
paintings 1 71; 27 *239*
patrons and collectors 3 251; 7 834; 12 724; 23 7; 24 278; 26 472; 28 272; 33 150
prints 25 624, 626, 628
aquatints 2 241; 25 599
engravings 27 *241*
etchings 10 558
lithographs 19 491
monotypes 21 896
Roubalík 25 832
Roubíček, René 8 411
Roubíčková, Miluše 23 271
Roubiliac, Louis-François 27 242–4*; 29 *31*
assistants 11 162
copies 3 79
exhibitions 10 677
groups and movements 19 585
methods 18 898, *898*; 21 770
patrons and collectors 7 540; 11 348; 14 436, 842; 17 476; 20 910
teachers 6 528; 8 71
works 5 302; 10 264; 14 856; 19 606, 619; 22 45; 27 *243*, *244*; 29 564, *564*; 31 128, 129; 32 787
Roubo, André 7 746; 11 409, 596
works 7 *746*; 33 *336*
Roubo, J(acques)-A(ndré) *see* ROUBO, ANDRÉ
Roucel, Louis 7 193
Rouché, Jacques 9 371; 24 838
Roudnice altarpiece 25 431
Roudnice nad Labem 8 423
Palace 25 258
Rouen 11 *504*; 19 27; 27 *245*, 245–55*
art forms and materials
carpets 11 652
chess sets 6 558
cotton 8 36; 11 649; 30 562
enamel 13 169
faience (ii) (ceramics) 11 604, 605, *605*; 24 316; 27 248–9*
glass 11 612
leather 19 5
manuscripts 4 372; 20 *332*, 333; 27 *247*
porcelain 6 923; 11 607
pottery 4 177; 7 166
silk 11 644, 645
tiles 30 885
Bibliothèque Municipale 9 466
Château 6 54
churches
Cathedral of Notre-Dame (1201) 11 510, 511, 654; 13 38, 42, 61, 75; 19 230; 26 570; 27 249–51*, *249*; 33 *369*
capitals 26 598
choir-stalls 7 192; 13 126
grilles 11 624
ivory-carvings 13 173
library 19 313
metalwork 13 158
misericords 21 725
nave 27 *250*
Porte des Libraires 27 252
sculpture 27 251–2*; 31 *493*
spire 29 413
stained glass 13 179, 181; 22 270; 26 701; 27 252*; 29 501
tomb of Charles V 13 76
tomb of Georges I d'Amboise and Georges II d' Amboise 1 *766*; 11 727
Notre-Dame de Bonsecours (1840-44) 13 *202*, 203
Ste Jeanne-d'Arc 27 253*
St Godard 13 181
Rouen churches—cont.
St Jean 33 64
St Maclou 11 154, 511; 13 60; 22 221; 27 253*, *253*
model 2 336
spire 29 414
tracery 31 271
St Ouen 11 155, 510; 13 59, 60, 61; 26 597; 27 254–5*
choir 27 *254*
manuscripts 26 669; 27 *247*
pinnacles 24 826
spire 29 414
stained glass 13 149, 181; 29 503, 512, VI1
St Patrice 13 181
St Vincent 13 60, 181; 27 253
Ecole de Dessin 11 671
great tower 6 52
guilds 24 579
museums 11 668
Musée des Antiquités 27 248
Musée des Beaux-Arts 8 61; 11 665, 666; 22 357; 25 750
catalogues 12 153
collections 4 127; 8 788; 27 248
directors 3 634
Musée de la Céramique 27 248
Musée Le Secq des Tournelles 9 156; 19 239; 27 248
palace 14 75
Palais de Justice 2 292; 13 236; 18 886; 27 *246*
roof 27 131
Parlement 9 416; 17 671
Rue du Gros Horloge 7 438, *438*
Rouen, Jean de (*fl* 1495-1500) *see* JEAN DE ROUEN
Rouen, Jean de (*c.* 1500-80) *see* RUÃO, JOÃO DE
Rouen, Jérôme de *see* JÉRONIMO DE RUÃO
Rouen, Robert of *see* ROBERT OF ROUEN
Rouen Echevinage, Master of the 20 757*
Rouette, Gabriel 29 668
Rouffaer, G. P. 29 241
rouge 1 761
Rougé, Marquise de 32 *495*
Rougé, Emmanuel de 10 82
Rouge, George-Louis Le *see* LE ROUGE, GEORGE-LOUIS
Rougé, Jacques de (1842-1923) 10 82
Rouge, Jacques Le (*fl* 1473) *see* JACQUES LE ROUGE
Rouge, Nicolaus le *see* LA FOSSE, LOUIS RÉMY DE
Rougement, Guy de 11 602
Rouget, Georges 8 561; 12 830
Rougeux, Pierre 11 596
Rougham 23 213
Rouille, Guillaume 8 549; 26 261
Rouille, M. 4 163
Roujon, Henri 20 201
Roulé, A. F. 3 585
Roulet de Mézerac, François de 26 451
roulettes *see under* ENGRAVINGS → materials
rouletting *see under* CERAMICS → techniques; POTTERY → techniques
Roulin, Felix 3 574
Roulland, L. 14 84
Roullet, Jean-Louis 19 154
Roumier, François 7 746; 11 405–6
round arches *see under* ARCHES → types
round barrows *see under* BARROWS → types
Round City 3 51
roundels 9 *645*; 27 255–8*, *255*, *257*
see also STAINED GLASS

Round Glass House (Dublin) **9** 320; **16** 29
round piers *see under* PIERS (ii) (MASONRY) → types
round-topped stelae *see under* STELAE → types
Roupert, Louis **17** 523
Rouppy, Jean de *see* JEAN DE CAMBRAI
Rouquet (Jean-) André **21** 641; **27** 258–9*
Rous, Thomas (*fl* 1617) **10** 304
Rousalka **5** 150
Rouse, James, Co. **28** 623
Rouse, John Owen **1** 772
Rouse, William **31** 647
Rouse & Goldstone **33** 407
Rousel, Theodore *see* RUSSELL, THEODORE
Rousham Park (Oxon) **10** *225*, 295; **12** 128; **27** *259*, 259–60*
Cuttle Mill **13** 199
furniture **10** 294
gardens **10** 233; **12** 128, 129
interior decoration **11** 428
paintings **9** 57; **17** 640
Praeneste **26** 735
sculpture **8** 644
Rous Lench (Hereford & Worcs), St Peter **26** 614
Rousse **5** 149, 156
Rousse, Georges **11** 553
Rousseau, André **7** 596, 597
Rousseau, Claude-Bernard **27** 881
Rousseau, Eugène **4** 625
Rousseau, François-Eugène **11** 613
Rousseau, Henri (-Julien-Félix) **17** 579; **27** 260–63*; **32** 327
dealers **27** 163; **32** 686
exhibitions **24** 142; **31** 490, 538; **33** 15
groups and movements **4** 132; **22** 440
patrons and collectors **2** 383; **3** 251; **5** 401; **9** 196; **13** 800, 826; **16** 906; **18** 435; **20** 848; **25** 823; **27** 162; **28** 569; **33** 150
works **2** 107; **11** 415; **13** 232; **24** *143*; **27** *261*, *262*
Rousseau, Henri, group **10** 214
Rousseau, Hester **16** 887
Rousseau, Jacques (1630-93) **27** 263–4*
collaboration **18** 633; **21** 907
patrons and collectors **16** 814; **18** 671
teachers **30** 61
works **20** 449, 450; **27** *264*
Rousseau, Jacques des (*c*. 1600-38) **26** 153
Rousseau, Jean-Hugues **4** 555
Rousseau, Jean-Jacques **10** 401, 465; **18** 714; **25** *884*; **27** 264–5*; **28** 418; **30** 132
groups and movements **26** 740
works **10** 402; **12** 292
illustrated **9** 365; **13** 324; **17** 605; **19** 136; **20** 497; **28** 754
Rousseau, Jean-Simon **4** 555
Rousseau, Jules-Hughes **13** 701
Rousseau, Marie-Anne **5** 379
Rousseau, Philippe **10** 781; **11** 230; **27** 265*
Rousseau, Pierre **32** *585*
works **19** *723*
Rousseau, Ted **19** 92
Rousseau, (Pierre-Etienne-) Théodore **11** 543; **24** 141; **27** 265–8*
cliché-verre **7** 433, 434
dealers **4** 655; **8** 820; **9** 424; **29** 248
groups and movements **3** 212, 213; **26** 54, 741; **28** 921
Rousseau, (Pierre-Etienne-) Théodore—cont.
patrons and collectors **2** 559; **5** 57; **6** 516; **11** 301; **15** 895; **18** 869; **19** 755; **23** 522
personal collection **17** 440
reproductive prints by others **6** 519
works **18** 715; **25** 607; **27** *266*, *267*
Rousseau, Victor **3** 573; **27** 268*
Rousseau, Vitor François Chartier **10** 729; **25** 311
Rousseau de La Rottière, Jean-Simeon **2** 245; **13** 701
Rousseau-Vermette, Mariette **5** 573; **30** 330
Roussel **13** 665
Roussel, Frémin **27** 268*
Roussel, Hiérome **20** 922
Roussel, Jean, Abbot **27** 254
Roussel, Ker-Xavier **27** 268–9*
collaboration **20** 603
dealers **19** 10
groups and movements **22** 421, 422
works **19** 489; **25** 626
Roussel, Nicasius **10** 326; **27** 360
Roussel, Nicolas **24** 146
Roussel, Pierre **11** 590, 595
Roussel, Theodore (1614-89) *see* RUSSELL, THEODORE
Roussel, Theodore (Casimir) (1847-1926) **27** 269*
groups and movements **19** 589; **23** 22
works **9** 309
Rousselet, Gilles **12** 832; **15** 31; **27** 269–70*; **32** 510
Rousselet, Jean **27** 270
Rousselli, Andreas *see* ROUSSEAU, ANDRÉ
Rousset, Robert **7** 155
Roussière, Etienne **6** 454
Roussillon, Master of (*fl* before 1450) **20** 757*
Roussillon, Master of the Girart de (*fl c*. 1450-70) *see* GIRART DE ROUSSILLON, Master of the
Roussillon vaults *see* VAULTS (CEILING) → types → flat-topped
Route libre **17** 518
Routhwaite and Fairfield **30** 684
Routing Linn (Northumb.) **18** 584
Routledge Publishers **10** 654
Routsi **14** 353, 354, 355
Rouvres-en-Plaine Church **13** 78
Rouvroy, Claude-Henri de, Comte de Saint-Simon *see* SAINT-SIMON, CLAUDE-HENRI DE ROUVROY, Comte de
Roux **17** 834
Roux, Alexander **22** 744; **31** 629, 630
works **31** *631*
Roux, André **2** 660
Roux, Antony **19** 395; **22** 89
Roux, Charles Le *see* LE ROUX, CHARLES
Roux, C. T. Le *see* LE ROUX, C. T.
Roux, Edouard **29** 328
Roux, Gaston-Louis **17** 726
Roux, Guillermo de **23** 904
Roux, Jacob Wilhelm Christian **10** 199
Roux, Jacques Le *see* LE ROUX, JACQUES
Roux, Louis-François **9** 338
Roux, Roulland Le *see* LE ROUX, ROULLAND
Roux-Champion, Victor **18** 477
Roux-Spitz, François-Michel Augustin **27** 270
Roux-Spitz, Michel **11** 526; **27** 270*
Rovalo, Fernando **21** 382
Rovani, Giuseppe **9** 187
Rovaniemi **11** *87*, 97
Airport **11** 93
Rovehead, Alexander **14** 783
Rovelli, Galeazzo **22** 108
Röver, Valerius **5** 326; **27** 270–71*
collections **12** 473
drawings **12** 876
paintings **14** 491
Rovere (i), della (family) **3** 254; **5** 819; **7** 899; **24** 523
Rovere, della, Missals, Master of the **20** 657–8*
works **20** *657*
Rovere, Domenico della, Cardinal **20** 657; **21** 143; **24** 830; **31** 439
Missals **20** 453
Rovere (i), Francesco della *see* SIXTUS IV, Pope
Rovere (i), Francesco-Maria I della, Duke of Urbino *see* FRANCESCO-MARIA I, Duke of Urbino
Rovere (i), Francesco-Maria II della, Duke of Urbino *see* FRANCESCO-MARIA II, Duke of Urbino
Rovere, Galeotto della, Cardinal **1** 572
Rovere (ii), Giovan Mauro della **27** 275*; **31** 899
Rovere (i), Giovanna della **25** 897
Rovere (ii), Giovanni Battista della **27** 275*; **31** 899
Rovere (i), Giovanni della *see* SENIGALLIA, GIOVANNI DELLA ROVERE, Lord of
Rovere (i), Giuliano della *see* JULIUS II, Pope
Rovere, Giulio della, Cardinal **4** 664; **21** 97
Rovere (i), Guidobaldo II della, Duke of Urbino *see* GUIDOBALDO II, Duke of Urbino
Rovere (i), Lucrezia della, Duchess of Urbino *see* LUCREZIA D'ESTE, Duchess of Urbino
Rovere (i), Vittoria della, Grand Duchess of Tuscany *see* VITTORIA DELLA ROVERE, Grand Duchess of Tuscany
Roverella altarpiece **31** 431, *431*
Roverella *Decretals* of Gratian **2** 186
Rovereto
Casa d'Arte Depero **8** 771
Casa d'Arte Futurista *see* Casa d'Arte Depero
Galleria Museo Depero **8** 771
Rovezzano Villa **11** 503
Rovezzano, Benedetto da *see* BENEDETTO DA ROVEZZANO
Roviale, Francesco **3** 471; **27** 275*
Roviana **29** 49
Rovigno, Sebastiano da **12** 708
Rovigo Synagogue **17** 544
Rovinj **8** *174*
city hall **8** 175
Rovinsky, Dmitry (Aleksandrovich) **27** 276*, 443
Rovio **30** 129
Rovira, Josep **20** 501; **29** 337
Rovira Tríes, Antonio **3** 216; **27** 276*
Rovira y Brocandel, Hipólito **27** 276*
works **29** 76, 841, *841*
Rowallen Castle (Strathclyde) **9** 727; **29** 843
Rowan, Robert A. **27** 276–7*
Rowan, Vivian **27** 277
Rowand Anderson, Paul & Partners *see* ANDERSON, ROWAND, PAUL & PARTNERS
Rowat, Jessie *see* NEWBERY, JESSIE
row carpets *see under* CARPETS → types
Rowe, Alan **3** 883; **10** 81
Rowe, Ann Pollard *see* POLLARD ROWE, ANN
Rowe, Cliff **2** 553; **22** 332
Rowe, Francis **7** 857
Rowe, Guy **4** 9
Rowe, John H. **29** 158, 219
Rowe, Nicholas **30** 675
Rowe, R. R. **5** 513
row-housing *see under* HOUSING → types
Rowland, Benjamin **27** 277*
Rowland, John **32** 785
Rowland, J. R. **20** 437
Rowlandson, Thomas **5** 756; **27** 277–9*; **33** 545
aquatints **2** 240; **4** 362; **9** 673
caricatures **5** 756; **7** 648; **9** 225; **10** 252; **19** 619; **25** 651; **27** 869
collaboration **1** 121; **17** 630; **25** 710
engravings **3** *373*; **19** *587*
erotic art **10** 479
etchings **10** 555, 562
methods **4** 184
painting **2** 105
patrons and collectors **1** 121; **10** 487; **15** 29; **21** 91
prints **8** 42; **31** 704
reproductive prints by others **1** 647; **14** 536; **25** 619; **29** 491
watercolours **27** *278*; **29** 424
Rowley, Doreen *see* GOODCHILD, DOREEN
Rowley, Richard **22** 727
Rowney **31** 300
Rowntree (family) **11** 785; **12** 144
Rowntree, Benjamin Seebohm **24** 185; **27** 279
Rowntree, Henry Isaac **27** 279
Rowntree, Joseph **27** 279
Rowntree, Kenneth **4** 369; **22** 332; **33** 552
Rowse, Herbert J. **19** 506; **26** 111
Roxbury clocks *see under* CLOCKS → types
Roxelane *see* HÜRREM SULTAN
Roxolani **28** 324
Roy, Arendt de **27** 279*
Roy, Christopher D.
works **4** *193*; **5** *329*, *330*
Roy, Claude **29** 746
Roy, Edme **11** 626
Roy, Enric Casanovas i *see* CASANOVAS I ROY, ENRIC
Roy, Jamini (Ranjan) **5** 420; **15** 180, 748; **27** 280*
Roy, Jean-Baptiste de **2** 613
Roy, Le *see* LE ROY
Roy, Matthias de **33** 279
Roy, Namba **16** 884; **27** 280*
Roy, Nicolas **28** 225; **29** 679
Roy, Peter van (*c*. 1706-45) **19** 337; **20** 855
Roy, Pierre (1880-1950) **8** 603; **25** 6; **27** 280–81*; **30** 19, 20
Roy, Shyamal Dutta **5** 421
Royal Antiquarian Society (Amsterdam) *see* KONINKLIJK OUDHEIDKUNDIG GEZELSCHAP
Royal Asiatic Society (London) **22** 795
Royal Australian Institute of Architects **2** 741, 772
Royal Axminster carpets *see under* CARPETS → types
Royal Ballet (UK) **30** 687, 688
Royal Bavarian Glass Painting Studio **29** 506
Royal Bible *see under* BIBLES → individual manuscripts
royal collections *see under* COLLECTIONS → types
Royal Commission on Historical Monuments (UK) **2** 322; **32** 274
Royal Commission on Monuments (Belgium) **3** 547
Royal Copenhagen **7** 807; **8** 749
Royal Court Terracotta Factory **8** 748
Royal Crown Derby Porcelain Co. **8** 776; **10** 313; **16** 425; **20** 441; **28** 168
Royal Doulton **9** 201
Royal Doulton Tableware Group **21** 697
Royal Dublin Society *see* DUBLIN SOCIETY
Royal Glasgow Institute of the Fine Arts **12** 776, *776*
Royal Glass Factory (Coina) **25** 311
Royal Gold Cup **10** 194, 905, III1; **11** 614, 629, 738; **12** 866; **13** 158, 169; **18** 686; **31** 837
Royal Holyrood Glass Works **28** 259
Royal Institute of British Architects (RIBA) *see under* LONDON
Royal Irish School of Art Needlework **16** 34
Royal Leerdam Glassworks **3** 431; **12** 795; **19** 12; **22** 885
Royal Lesotho Tapestry Weavers **19** 241
Royal Library Painter **13** 505
works **13** *505*
Royal Maidan *see under* ISFAHAN
Royal Manufactories *see* AUBUSSON; BEAUVAIS; GOBELINS; SAVONNERIE; SÈVRES FACTORIES
Royal Mint (Britain) **29** 469
Royal Neapolitan Porcelain factory **10** 643
Royal Photographic Society **7** 576; **24** 682
Royal Porcelain Factory (Naples) **16** 737; **29** 573
Royal Porcelain Factory (Pórtici) **16** 737
Royal Prayerbook *see under* PRAYERBOOKS → individual manuscripts
Royal Saltworks *see under* ARC ET SENANS
Royal School of Needlework **10** 354
Royal Scottish Water-Colour Society **32** 903
Royal Scythian **28** 320
Royal Shakespeare Company **30** 687
Royal Society, London **3** 329; **10** 658
Royal Society of Arts (London) **2** 371; **10** 296
see also SOCIETY OF ARTS, MANUFACTURES AND COMMERCE
Royal Society of Fine Arts (Jordan) **1** 638; **17** 655
Royal Society of Painter-Etchers and Engravers **10** 255, 397; **14** 20; **22** 351; **25** 629
Royal Standard of Ur **1** 869, 880, 881, 889, 891; **6** 478; **11** 150; **14** 169; **22** 511; **30** 774; **31** *696*
Royal State Factory **20** 441
Royal Stoa *see* ATHENS → Agora → Stoa Basileios
royalties, resale *see* RESALE ROYALTIES
Royal Windsor Tapestry Factory **10** 351; **30** 326; **31** 659
Royal Worcester **10** 312, 313; **33** 378
Royal Zoological Society **3** 533
Royas, Bernardo de Sandoval y *see* SANDOVAL Y ROYAS, BERNARDO DE, Cardinal Archbishop of Toledo
Royat, St Léger **19** 895
Roy-Audy, Jean-Baptiste **27** 281*
Royaume, Jean **24** 553
Royaumont Cistercian church **11** 654; **13** 168; **26** 44
Roybal, Alfonso **22** 594

Roybal, Juan Cruz 22 606
Roybal, Margaret Tafoya 22 606
Roybet, Ferdinand 4 655; 27 281*
Roychand, Premchand 4 288
Roy Chowdhary, Devi Prasad 15 171; 20 54
Roy Chowdhury, Hiranmoy 15 171
Roychowdhury, Sarbari 5 421
Roycrofters 14 832
Roycroft Press 14 832
Roycroft Workshops 2 572; 31 631, 653
Royen, Peter 13 727
Royen, Willem Frederik van 14 650, 706
Royer, Lodewijk 27 282*
pupils 1 650; 2 575
teachers 5 342; 12 230
works 22 860, 860
Royer, Louis *see* ROYER, LODEWIJK
Royère, Jean 11 584
Royesteyn, Jan van 22 887
Royley, Gabriel 10 261; 27 282
Royley, Richard 1 520; 10 261; 27 282*
Royne, Martin van 2 471, 472
Royo, Josep 21 709
Roza, Gustavo da 5 563
Rozanov, Nikolay Vasiliyvich 30 299
Rozanov, Vasily (Vasil'yevich) 27 283*
Rozanova, Ol'ga (Vladimirovna) 27 283*, 392, 394
collaboration 18 474, 507
groups and movements 8 251; 16 818; 22 508, 509; 30 7, 8; 31 583
patrons and collectors 8 10
teachers 33 740
works 19 491
Rōzan Yasuda *see* YASUDA RŌZAN
Roze, Jānis 18 850
Rozehnal, Bedřich 8 380; 27 283*
Rozenberg, A. V. 15 132; 18 114
Rozenbergs, Valdis *see* KALNROZE, VALDIS
Rozenburg factory 7 552; 18 195; 22 883; 28 867; 30 506; 33 743
works 22 883
Rozendaal, Willem 14 43
Rozendaal Castle *see* ROSENDAEL CASTLE
Rozendorf, Yelizaveta 27 413
Rozenshtein, Konstantin 3 684
Rozentāls, Jānis 12 825; 18 850, 852; 27 284*
Rozet, Jacques 31 881
Rozhdestvensky, Konstantin (Ivanovich) 27 284*
Rozhdestvensky, Robert 18 439
Rozhen Monastery, Church of the Virgin 5 144, 148, 156; 25 339, 343
Rozhin, Igor' (Yevgen'yevich) 12 243; 25 89; 27 284–5*; 32 670
Rožmberk Church 8 377
Rožmberk (family) 2 213; 6 363; 8 377, 395, 422, 423
Rożmberk, Peter I (*d* 1347) 20 784
Rožmberk, Petr Vok (1539-1611) 8 422; 27 285*
Rožmberk, Vilém 20 89; 27 285*; 29 738
Rožmitál (family) 8 422
Rožmitál, Leo of *see* LEO OF ROŽMITÁL
Rožmitál, Zdeněk Lev of *see* ZDENĚK LEV OF ROŽMITÁL
Rožňava Cathedral 28 851
Rožnov pod Radhoštěm Skansen 8 424
Rozpravy aventina 24 440
Rozprawy i sprawozdania muzeum narodowego w krakowie 24 441
Rozsda, Endre 30 23
Rozumovsky (family) 31 564
Rozwi 32 154
Różycki, Jan 25 127
Rrota, Simon 1 540; 27 285–6*
RS 24 452
rtsa pa brang *see* TSAPARANG
Ruaben 20 596
Ruabon, St Mary 11 255; 32 784, 787
Ruaidri Ua Conchobar, King of Connaught (*reg* 1516-56) 20 77
Ruan An 6 681
Ruanda-Urundi *see* BURUNDI; RWANDA
Ruan Yuan 6 765, 867; 27 286*
Ruão, Jerónimo de *see* JERÓNIMO DE RUÃO
Ruão, João de *see* JOÃO DE RUÃO
Ruão, Simão de 17 486
Ruatahuna Meeting House 23 54
Ruaud, Paul 11 583
Ruaud Factory 19 398
Rub'a, Tall al- *see* MENDES
Rubati, Pasquale 21 529
Rubatto, Giuseppe 16 739
rubber 1 155; 26 243
conservation 6 334
dolls 31 260
moulds 21 321
upholstery 31 687
Rubbiani, A. 3 896
rubbings 2 461; 29 617
collections *see under* COLLECTIONS → types
see also FROTTAGE
rubble masonry *see under* MASONRY → types
Rubbo, (Anthony) Dattilo 2 771; 8 2; 11 784; 20 139
Rubčić, Stanislav 14 411
Rubeis, Angelo de *see* ROSSI, ANGELO DE
Rubel, Ira W. 19 481; 25 594
Rubelles 11 606
rubellite 12 I
Rubellius Blandus 8 368
Ruben, Christian 6 344; 14 235; 19 208; 20 252; 25 742
Rubénisme 9 8; 27 286–7*
Rubens, Peter Paul 2 196; 3 613; 9 15; 12 283; 16 668, 674; 19 381; 26 772; 27 287–302*; 32 194
architecture 15 45
assistants 9 476; 32 703; 33 279
Boeckhorst, Jan (van) 4 218
Cossiers, Jan 8 1
Douffet, Gérard 9 197
Egmont, Justus van 9 762
Jegher, Christoffel 17 470; 33 367
Jordaens, Jacob (1593-1678) 17 648
Lasne, Michel 18 811
Luyckx, Frans 19 831
Neeffs, Jacob 22 717
Quellinus, Erasmus (ii) (1607-78) 25 809
Rombouts, Theodoor 26 747
Schut, Cornelis, I (1597-1655) 28 180
Snyders, Frans 28 903
Soutman, Pieter (Claesz.) 29 246
Thomas (van Yperen), Jan 30 744
Uden, Lucas van 31 522
Vos, Simon de 32 712
attributions 4 559; 8 90; 9 412; 18 816; 33 216, 298
book illustrations 1 467
catalogues 5 187; 6 79; 28 132
collaboration 3 545, 613; 13 896; 32 702
Beert, Osias, I (*c.* 1580-1624) 3 494; 11 227
Breughel, Jan, I (1568-1625) 4 913, 914, 915; 5 353
Rubens, Peter Paul collaboration—cont.
Breughel, Jan, II (1601-78) 4 916, 917
Diepenbeeck, Abraham (Jansz.) van 8 878
Fouquier, Jacques 11 357
Galle, Cornelis (i) (1576-1650) 12 17
Galle, Theodor 12 16
Jegher, Christoffel 17 470, 471
Jones, Inigo 17 634
Rockox, Nicolaas 26 490
Snayers, Pieter 28 898
Snyders, Frans 28 901, 902, 904
Thulden, Theodoor van 30 787
Vos, Cornelis de 32 703
Vos, Paul de 32 705
Wildens, Jan 33 181
Witdoeck, Hans 33 262
Costume Book 9 245; 29 892
dealers 13 337; 23 76
dealing 2 558; 5 764; 9 476
decorative works 10 717
drawings 9 245; 25 17, 284, 284, 286; 27 299
forgeries 11 307
forgeries by others 25 664
frames 11 402, 405, 443, 445, 448, 487
groups and movements 3 261, 262, 263, 264, 267
house 2 193, 196, 549, 550; 3 546
see also under ANTWERP → museums → Rubenshuis
metalwork 3 598
methods 24 4, 6; 29 53; 30 4
colour 7 628; 9 216; 24 493
drawings 8 128; 9 218; 21 765
grounds 13 708; 23 378; 24 797
modelli 21 765
paintings 9 8; 24 50
underdrawings 31 578
musical instruments 22 373
pageants 10 176; 15 84; 23 767, 769
paintings 11 666; 14 869; 17 648; 18 891; 29 281
allegorical 1 657, 658; 10 249; 19 618
altarpieces 3 263; 23 472; 26 772; 27 290; 31 344
animal subjects 2 104
battle 3 388
ceiling 33 261
conversation pieces 7 784
fêtes champêtres 11 36
genre 11 36; 12 290
history 3 559, 873
hunting scenes 3 561; 29 424
landscape 3 560; 18 711; 22 686; 27 297
Life of Marie de' Medici 1 658; 6 397; 9 762; 11 533, 666; 14 583, 583; 19 161
mythological 10 130; 22 414, 521; 25 273, 274, 275; 27 292, 293
nude figures 9 244; 23 294
oil sketches 13 676; 22 415; 23 381, 381
portraits 3 560; 9 277; 19 227
Brant, Isabella 9 277
Doria, Brigida Spinola 9 173; 27 289
Fourment, Hélène 3 560; 17 524; 21 759; 25 274; 27 298
Fourment, Susanna 25 284, 285, 286
Lipsius, Justus 19 458
religious 2 192, 203; 3 558–9; 5 514; 15 121; 17 3, 915; 22 842; 27 288, 295, 296; 33 421
patrons and collectors 25 137
Akademie der Bildenden Künste (Vienna) 2 831
Rubens, Peter Paul patrons and collectors—cont.
Alba, 17th Duque de (1878-1953) 1 529
Albert, Archduke of Austria, Regent of the Netherlands (*reg* 1599-1621) 13 917
Alcalá, 3rd Duque de (1583-1637) 26 307
Altamira, Vicente Joaquín Osorio Moscoso y Guzmán, 11th Conde de 1 690
Angerstein, John Julius 2 51
Angiviller, Charles-Claude de Flahaut de la Billarderie, Comte d' 2 53
Arenberg, Prosper-Louis, 7th Duke of, Duke of Arschot 2 382
Art Institute of Chicago 27 463
Augustinian hermits 2 725
Augustus II, King of Poland (*reg* 1697-1706; 1709-33) 33 115
Balbi, Costantino, the elder (1676-1740) 3 90
Bankes, William John 3 179
Barberini, Francesco, Cardinal 3 207
Baudouin, Silvain-Raphaël 3 395
Beaumont, Lady 5 71
Beaumont, George (Howland) 3 454
Becker, Herman (*c.* 1617-78) 3 475
Beisteguy y Benítez, Carlos de 3 522
Benavente, 10th Conde de (1584-1653) 3 700
Beuningen, Daniel George van 3 889
Beurnonville, Etienne-Edmond Martin, Baron de 3 890
Bonnemaison, Ferréol de 4 330
Borghese, Scipione, Cardinal 26 773
Boulle, André-Charles 4 531
Bourbon I., Louis de, le Grand Dauphin (1661-1711) 4 553
Breughel, Ambrosius 4 917
Brignole-Sale (family) 4 811
Brudenell, George, 4th Earl of Cardigan and 1st Duke of Montagu 4 893
Brydges, James, 1st Duke of Chandos 5 65
Buchanan, William 33 216
Butler, Charles (1822-1910) 5 311
Cairo, Francesco 5 407
Calderón, Rodrigo 5 427
Cambó y Batlle, Francisco de Asís 5 510
Cappelle, Jan van de 5 679
Carleton, Dudley, 1st Viscount Dorchester 5 764
Carol I, King of Romania (*reg* 1866-1914) 5 792; 26 722
Carpio, Luis Méndez de Haro y Guzmán, 6th Marqués del 5 844
Carr, Robert, 1st Earl of Somerset 23 326
Carr, William Holwell 5 848
Catherine II, Empress of Russia (*reg* 1762- 96) 26 732
Cavendish, William, 2nd Duke of Devonshire (1671-1729) 6 116
Champernowne, Arthur 6 438
Charles I, King of England and Scotland (*reg* 1625-49) 10 360; 19 582; 29 797, 798, 800
Christina, Queen of Sweden (*reg* 1632-54) 32 8
Churchill, John, 1st Duke of Marlborough 4 137; 10 364
Clark, Robert Sterling 7 377
Rubens, Peter Paul patrons and collectors—cont.
Clerk, John, 2nd Baronet of Penicuik (1679-1755) 7 418
Conti, Louis-François de Bourbon, Prince de (1717-76) 7 778
Crozat, Pierre 8 209
Danvers, Henry, Earl of Danby 5 764
Day, Alexander 25 665
De la Gardie, Magnus Gabriel 30 118
Desenfans, Noël Joseph 8 792
Dezallier d'Argenville, Antoine-Joseph 8 845
Doria, Gian Carlo, Prince 9 174
Duarte, Diego 9 311
Du Quesnoy, Jérôme (ii) (1602-54) 9 411
Einden, Ferdinand van den 10 114; 25 563
Einden, Jan van den 10 115
Elizabeth, Electress Palatine and Queen of Bohemia (1596-1662) 29 799
Faesch, Johann Jakob 10 753
Ferdinand III, Holy Roman Emperor (*reg* 1637-58) 13 919
Ferdinand VII, King of Spain (*reg* 1808; 1814-33) 4 566
Ferré (family) 25 704
Fountaine, Andrew (1676-1753) 11 348
Fourment, Hélène 25 274
Francesco I, 8th Duke of Modena and Reggio (*reg* 1629-58) 10 526
Frederick II, King of Prussia (*reg* 1740-86) 14 652
Frederick Henry, Stadholder of the Netherlands, Prince of Orange (*reg* 1625-47) 22 904; 23 463, 465
Gardner, Isabella Stewart 12 147
Geest, Cornelis van der 12 233
George IV, King of Great Britain (*reg* 1820-30) 14 146
Gideon, Sampson 12 601
Gildemeester, Jan (Jansz.) (1744-99) 12 620
Gillott, Joseph 12 638
Gonzaga (family) 20 318
Graham-Gilbert, John 13 273
Gran, Daniel 13 278
Grosvenor (family) 29 88
Grosvenor, Robert, 2nd Earl of Grosvenor and 1st Marquess of Westminster 13 696
Gulbenkian, Calouste Sarkis 13 841
Habsburg I., Leopold William, Archduke of Austria, Governor of the Netherlands 13 920
Habsburg II., Ferdinand, Cardinal-Infante of Spain 14 10
Hall, Peter Adolf 14 80
Hamilton, Alexander, 10th Duke of Hamilton and 7th Duke of Brandon 14 107
Hanover, Frederick (Louis), Prince of Wales (1707-51) 14 143
Hawkins, John Heywood (1803-77) 14 252
Henrietta Maria, Queen of England and Scotland (1609-69) 29 803
Hermitage Museum (St Petersburg) 7 579
His de La Salle, (Aimé-Charles-) Horace 14 577
Hohenzollern, Henry, Prince of Prussia 14 653
Holford, Robert Stayner 14 675

Rubens, Peter Paul
patrons and collectors—cont.
Howard (i), Thomas, 2nd Earl of Arundel **14** 807
Hudson, Thomas (1701-99) **14** 842
Hume, Abraham, 2nd Baronet **14** 877
Imperiale, Gian Vincenzo **15** 148
Isabella Clara Eugenia, Archduchess of Austria, Regent of the Netherlands (*reg* 1599-1633) **3** 613
Jabach, Everard **12** 243; **16** 814, 815
Jennens, Charles **17** 476
Jesuit Order **17** 509, 511
John II (Casmir), King of Poland (*reg* 1648-68) **32** 7
John V, King of Portugal (*reg* 1706-50) **4** 636
John-Adam-Andreas, Prince of Liechtenstein (*reg* 1684-1712) **19** 337
Johnson, John G(raver) (1841-1917) **17** 619
John William, Elector Palatine (*reg* 1690-1716) **9** 460; **12** 473; **33** 280
Joseph Bonaparte, King of Naples and Spain (*reg* 1806-8) **4** 304
Josephine, Empress of the French (1763-1814) **4** 303
Kneller, Godfrey **18** 146
Knight, Richard Payne **18** 150
Koninklijk Museum voor Schone Kunsten (Brussels) **3** 616
Krasiński, Jan Dobrogost (Bonaventura) **18** 440
La Live de Jully, Ange-Laurent de **18** 660
Lankrink, Prosper Henry **18** 748
La Roque, Antoine de **18** 796
Leganés, 1st Marqués de **13** 879; **29** 353
Lely, Peter **19** 124
Leopold II, King of Belgium (*reg* 1865-1909) **7** 490
Lerma, Francisco Gómez de Sandoval y Rojas, Duque de **27** 723
Leveson-Gower, George Granville, 1st Duke of Sutherland **19** 271
Liechtenstein-Castelkorn, Karel von, Bishop of Olmutz **18** 467
Long, Charles, 1st Baron Farnborough **19** 624
Louis XIII, King of France (*reg* 1610-43) **4** 549
Louis XIV, King of France (*reg* 1643-1715) **4** 552
Lowther, William, 3rd Baronet of Marske **19** 735
Marie de Medici, Queen of France (1573-1642) **4** 548; **11** 661; **24** 165
Mariette, Jean **20** 416
Mariette, Pierre-Jean **20** 417
Marolles, Michel de **20** 455
Marquand, Henry G(urdon) **20** 461
Maugis, Claude, Abbé **20** 854
Mauroner, José **2** 404
Mead, Richard **10** 364; **20** 910
Medici, Giovanni Carlo de', Cardinal (1611-63) **21** 27
Miles, Philip John **21** 541
Moltke, Adam Gottlob, Count **21** 825
Mond, Ludwig **21** 849
Montagu-Douglas-Scott, Walter Francis, 5th Duke of Buccleuch, 7th Duke of Queensberry **21** 908
Munro (of Novar), H(ugh) A(ndrew) J(ohnstone) **22** 314
Musée des Beaux Arts (Le Havre) **19** 92
Musée du Louvre (Paris) **9** 18
Neuburg, Wolfgang William, Count Palatine of **33** 279
Omazur, Nicolas **23** 437
Oratorians **23** 473
Orléans, Philippe II de Bourbon, 2nd Duc d' (1674-1723) **23** 514, 516
Pallavicini, Giovanni Battista **23** 873
Pallavicini, Nicolò, Marchese (1563-1619) **23** 873
Peel, Robert (1788-1850) **24** 322
Peiresc, Nicolas-Claude Fabri de **24** 330
Périer, Casimir **24** 418
Philip IV, King of Spain (*reg* 1621-65) **14** 1, 8; **23** 680; **24** 107; **29** 303, 352
Piles, Roger de **24** 805
Poniatowski, Stanisław, Prince **25** 213
Quellinus, Erasmus (ii) (1607-78) **25** 811
Resta, Sebastiano **26** 245
Reynolds, Joshua **26** 279
Richards, John Inigo **26** 335
Richardson, Jonathan (1665-1745) **26** 346
Richelieu, Armand-Jean Du Plessis, Cardinal de **26** 348
Richelieu, Louis-François Armand-Jean Vignerod du Plessis, Duc de (1629-1715) **11** 662; **26** 349
Richter, Johann Thomas **19** 111
Robien, Christophe-Paul Gautron, Marquis de **26** 470
Rockox, Nicolaas **3** 613; **26** 490
Rogers, Samuel **26** 541
Roomer, Gaspar **25** 563; **27** 133
Rothschild, James Mayer de, Baron (1792-1868) **27** 223
Röver, Valerius **27** 270
Ruffo, Tommaso, Cardinal, Archbishop of Ferrara **27** 316
Saint-Morys, Charles Paul Jean-Baptiste de Bourgevin Vialart de **27** 568
Salamanca (y Mayol), José, Marqués de **27** 607
Schönborn, Lothar Franz von, Bishop of Bamberg, Elector-Archbishop of Mainz **28** 146
Seilern, Antoine, Count **28** 377
Seymour-Conway, Richard, 4th Marquess of Hertford **28** 527
Sheremet'yev, Pyotr (Borisovich), Count **28** 593
Slingelandt, Govert van, Lord of Lindt and West-IJsselmonde **28** 842
Snyders, Frans **28** 904
Spencer, Robert, 2nd Earl of Sunderland (1641-1702) **29** 381
Spinola (family) **29** 411
Städelsches Kunstinstitut und Städtische Galerie (Frankfurt) **29** 487
Stanislav II Poniatowski, King of Poland (*reg* 1764-95) **25** 212
Statens Museum for Kunst (Copenhagen) **8** 758
Suttermans, Giusto **30** 41
Tallard, Marie-Joseph d'Hostun, Duc de **30** 274
Temple-Nugent-Grenville, George, 1st Marquess of Buckingham **13** 637
Thibaudeau, Narcisse-Adolphe, Comte de **30** 727, 728
Turquet de Mayerne, Théodore **31** 480
Valenti Gonzaga, Silvio, Cardinal **12** 914
Verstolk van Soelen, Jan Gijsbert, Baron **32** 377
Villiers, George, 1st Duke of Buckingham (1592-1628) **32** 575
Vincenzo I, 4th Duke of Mantua (*reg* 1587- 1612) **12** 903, 912, 913; **20** 322
Vladislav IV Vasa, King of Poland (*reg* 1632-48) **32** 7
Vos (ii) Jbzn, Jacob de (1803-82) **32** 708
Waldegrave, William, 1st Baron Radstock **32** 774
Wellesley, Henry **33** 56
(Joseph-)Wenceslas (-Lorenz), Prince of Liechtenstein (*reg* 1748-72) **19** 338
William II, King of the Netherlands (*reg* 1840-49) **23** 469
William V, Stadholder of the Netherlands, Prince of Orange (*reg* 1751-95) **23** 469
William VIII, Landgrave of Hesse-Kassel (*reg* 1751-60) **12** 473
Wit, Jacob de **33** 261
Wolfgang von Kaas, Wilhelm Friedrich **7** 584
personal collection **3** 615
drawings **9** 229, 230; **25** 664
gems **12** 266; **24** 330
ivory-carvings **3** 604; **24** 543
paintings **4** 871, 912; **5** *351*, 353; **8** 87, 464; **9** 476; **10** 158, 160, 494; **11** 807; **14** 287; **26** 313; **29** 352; **32** 705, 713; **33** 537
sculpture **5** 764; **9** 15, 23; **10** 363; **27** 114
silver **3** 598
prints **3** 206
engravings **3** 561; **10** 391; **19** 190; **26** 229
pupils **10** 248; **24** 15
Faydherbe, Lucas **10** 844
Ferdinand III, Holy Roman Emperor (*reg* 1637-58) **13** 919
Franchoys, Lucas, II (1616-81) **11** 699
Goes, Marinus Robyn van der **12** 851
Hoecke, Jan van den **14** 616
Hofmann, Samuel **14** 634
Mol, Pieter van **21** 803
Monte, Deodaat del **22** 7
Panneels, Willem **24** 15
Thulden, Theodoor van **30** 787
Vorsterman, Lucas, (i) (*c.* 1595-1675) **32** 699
Wouters, Frans **33** 388
reproductions in ivory **29** 571
reproductions in tapestry **11** 48; **12** 830
reproductive prints by others **25** 596
Baron, Bernard **3** 259
Bergeret, Pierre-Nolasque **19** 483
Boilvin, Emile **4** 242
Bolswert (family) **4** 282
Bolswert, Boetius (Adamsz.) (à) **4** 282
Bolswert, Schelte (Adamsz.) (à) **4** 282–3
Browne, John **4** 886
Clouwet, Albert **7** 466
Clouwet, Pieter **7** 466
Collaert, Jan Baptist, II (*c.* 1590-1627) **7** 557
Daullé, Jean **8** 544
Rubens, Peter Paul
reproductive prints by others—cont.
Duchange, Gaspard **9** 362
Elsheimer, Adam **10** 157
Follin, Bartolomeo **11** 241
Galle, Cornelis (i) (1576-1650) **12** 16, *17*
Galle, Cornelis (ii) (1615-78) **12** 17
Galle, Joannes **12** 17
Goes, Marinus Robyn van der **12** 851
Gregori, Carlo **13** 625
Gribelin, Simon, II **13** 646
Huret, Grégoire **15** 31
Jode, Pieter de (i) (1570-1634) **17** 599
Jode, Pieter de (ii) (1606-74) **17** 599
Lasne, Michel **18** 811
Lauwers, Conrad **18** 879
Lauwers, Nicolaes **18** 879
Leeuw, Willem van der **19** 64
Lempereur, Louis-Simon **19** 144
Louys, Jacob **19** 731
Masson, Antoine **20** 592
McArdell, James **19** 867
Moitte, Pierre-Etienne **21** 800
Muller, Jan (Harmensz.) **22** 272
Nattier, Marc **22** 684
Panderen, Egbert van **23** 908
Passe, Magdalena (van) de **24** 236
Pontius, Paulus **25** 221
Punt, Jan **25** 736
Rodríguez, Cayetano **26** 517
Snyers, Hendrick **28** 904
Sompel, Pieter van **29** 62
Soutman, Pieter (Claesz.) **8** 644; **29** 246–7, *247*
Suyderhoef, Jonas **30** 47
Swanenburg, Willem (Isaacsz.) van (1581-1612) **30** 60
Thurneysen, Johann Jakob, I (1636-1711) **30** 793
Vorsterman, Lucas, (i) (*c.* 1595-1675) **2** 196, *196*; **32** 699, *699*
Vorsterman, Lucas, (ii) (1624-66) **32** 700
Wit, Jacob de **33** 261
restorations by others **7** 339
sculpture **30** *499*
studio **9** 12; **29** 855
tapestries **1** 658; **5** 49; **7** 908; **11** 641, 643; **24** 15; **26** 778, 838; **27** *294*; **30** 320, 321, *321*, 331; **31** 501
teachers **23** 201; **32** 114, 115, 250
title-pages **4** 359, *360*
woodcuts **17** 470, 471
workshop **3** 559
writings **2** 162, 170; **4** 568; **5** 351; **32** 551
Rubens, Philip **27** 300
Rubens-Francken *see* FRANKCEN, FRANS, III
Rubenshuis *see under* ANTWERP → museums
Ruberti (della Grana), Giovanni Francesco **12** 908; **20** 800
Rubeus da Perugia **23** 586
Rubiales, Pedro de **27** 275
Rubicano, Cola *see* RAPICANO, COLA
Rubieri, Jacopo de' **25** 630; **33** 347
rubies **12** 268, 270, I
historical and regional traditions
China **7** 91, 111, 112
England **10** *345*
Indian subcontinent **6** 556; **12** 252; **17** II2; **21** *717*
Islamic **12** 253; **16** *507*, *542*
Laos **7** 91
Ottoman **16** *506*, *542*
Turkey **16** *542*
techniques
cutting **12** 269
rubies—cont.
uses
amulets **1** 817
canteens **16** *542*
chess sets **6** 556
crowns **7** 112
helmets **16** *507*
jewellery **7** 111; **17** 519
mirror frames **21** *717*
pendants (jewellery) **10** *345*
rings **17** II2
Rubik Saviours Monastery **1** 542
Rubin (family) *see* ROBIJN
Rubin (*fl* 1930s) **30** 421
Rubin, Arnold **1** 233; **17** 679
works **17** *680*
Rubin, Deann Joy **31** 661
Rubin, Lawrence **18** 161
Rubin, Reuven **16** 567, 571; **17** 579; **27** 303*
Rubín de la Borbolla, Daniel **21** 396
Rubinetto di Francia **11** 5; **31** 431
Rubini, Agostino **20** 412; **32** 411, 646, 648
Rubini, Lorenzo **20** 412; **32** 646
Rubini, Vigilio **32** 646, 650
Rubini, Vincenzo **32** 411
Rubino, Edoardo **5** 413; **27** 303*
Rubino, Giovanni **21** 632; **23** 754; **27** 304*
Rubinstein, Héléna **1** 439; **11** 583; **12** 871; **20** 399; **22** 425; **29** 900
interior decoration **11** *582*
Rubinstein, Ida **3** 87; **12** 878; **28** *475*
Rubio, Felipe **31** 814
Rubio, José Puchol *see* PUCHOL RUBIO, JOSÉ
Rubio, Martin **18** 833
Rubio, Pablo **25** 702
works **25** *702*
Rubió i Bellver, Joan **12** 182; **27** 304*
Rubiò i Tudurí, Nicolau Maria **3** 216; **9** 373; **23** 260
Rubira, Andrés **20** 499
Rubislaw Den **28** 229
Rublyov, Andrey **15** 77; **22** 176; **27** 304–5*, 384
collaboration **8** 506; **9** 601; **30** 707
icons **15** *76*, 77; **27** *305*
Moscow **22** 183
Sergiyev Posad **27** 384; **28** 464
Vladimir (Russia) **7** 279; **28** 291; **32** 665
Zvenigorod **33** 741
patrons and collectors **8** 506
Rubo, F. A. Frants **13** 633; **24** 19
rubrics **16** 291
Rubruck, Willem van **10** 874; **21** 874, 885; **30** 476
Rubuntja, Wenten **1** 64
Rucabado (Gómez), Leonardo **27** 306*, 783; **29** 273
Rucellai (family) **9** 492
architectural decorations **12** 710
architecture **1** 792; **11** 178
paintings **22** 801; **30** 649
sculpture **23** 855
Rucellai, Bernardo (di Giovanni) **26** 848; **27** 306, 307*
Rucellai, Giovanni (di Paolo di Messer Paolo) **18** 662; **27** 306–7*
architecture **1** 556, 561–4; **11** 186, 209; **12** 710
spalliere **29** 360
Rucellai, Orazio **33** 722
Rucellai, Palla **27** 307
Rucellai Chapel *see under* FLORENCE → ecclesiastical buildings → S Pancrazio
Rucellai *Madonna* **1** 708; **8** 857; **9** *342*, 342–3, 349; **11** 183; **12** 625
Ruch, Earnest **19** 242
Ruchat, Flora **4** 491; **12** 5

Ruche, La *see under* PARIS
Ruchet, Berthe **23** 336
Ruchti, Frederico **27** 307
Ruchti, Jacob (Mauricio) **27** 307–8*
Ruck, Arthur **14** 120
Rucker, Thomas **16** 60
Ruckers, Hans **2** 195; **22** 373
 works **22** *372*
Rückert, Fyodor, I **22** 180; **27** 426
Rückriem, Ulrich **27** 308*
Ruckstall, Frederic **31** 612
Rucqueville **26** 598
Rud' **21** *810*
 monastery church **21** 810
Rudavská, Mária **28** 856
Rudavský, Andrej **28** 855
Rudbeck, Olof (1630-1702) **21** *511*; **27** 308–9*; **30** 78
 works **24** 21; **30** 70; **31** 692, 693
Rudbeck, Olof, jr (*fl* 1670) **27** 308; **30** 78
Rudd, Jean-Baptiste **5** 320; **8** 637
Rudder, Hélène De *see* DE RUDDER, HÉLÈNE
Rudder, Isidore De *see* DE RUDDER, ISIDORE
Rudder, Louis Henri de **25** 849
Rude, François **11** 563, 564, 659, 671; **27** 309–12*
 collaboration **30** 32
 groups and movements **26** 742; **28** 345
 patrons and collectors **6** 397; **11** 659
 pupils **5** 392, 824; **6** 514; **7** 238, 841; **11** 753
 teachers **5** 889; **8** 834, 891
 works **7** 915; **8** 648; **10** 745; **11** *564*, 565; **22** 47; **26** 137; **27** *310*, *311*; **29** 574; **31** 131
Rude, Olaf **8** 736
Rudenica **22** 79
 monastery church **28** 442
Rudenko, Sergey (Ivanovich) **21** 885; **24** 297; **27** 312*
Rude style pottery *see* POTTERY → wares → Pastoral style
Rudge, William E. **26** 536
Rudhardsche Schriftgiesserei **9** 703
Rudier **11** 629
Rudier, Alexis **19** 395; **26** 514
Rudier, Eugène **26** 514
Rudier, Georges **26** 514
Rudnay, Gyula **13** 333; **14** 553
Rudnay, Sándor, Archbishop **10** 546
Rudnev, Lev (Vladimirovich) **27** 313*, 378
 collaboration **11** 245
 groups and movements **29** 530
 pupils **19** 12; **29** 388
 works **2** 894; **22** 174, *175*; **27** 378, 380, 578
Rudnyánszky, József **23** 462
Rudofsky, Bernard **4** 109
Rudolf, Archduke of Austria *see* RUDOLF II, Holy Roman Emperor
Rudolf, Count Palatine of the Rhine (*reg* 1294-1317) **33** *272*
Rudolf I, Holy Roman Emperor (*reg* 1273-91) **24** *587*; **33** 736
Rudolf II, Holy Roman Emperor (*reg* 1576-1612) **2** *374*, 775, 827; **5** *301*; **8** 422; **13** *900*, *901*, 912–15*, *913*; **21** 264; **25** *432*; **27** 885; **29** 737
 animal subjects **2** 104; **14** 626
 architecture **2** 213, 778, 779; **8** 378; **11** 77; **12** 149; **19** 433; **25** 54, 437, 438
  hunting-lodges **10** 889
 art policies **1** 663
 clocks **7** 439
 coins **20** 190
 collections **2** 830; **8** 390, 423; **9** 443; **10** 487; **15** 145; **18** 522; **22** 355; **29** 738; **30** 118
Rudolf II, Holy Roman Emperor (*reg* 1576-1612)—cont.
 decorative works **24** 573; **32** 401, 402
 drawings **2** 374; **9** 229, *446*; **12** 530, 881, 883; **14** 626; **29** 648
 engravings **27** 501, 504
 fountains **13** 910; **16** 900
 furniture **8** 395; **16** 746
 gardens **12** 133
 gems **8** 416; **12** 259, 260, 266
 glass **8** 407; **12** 439; **19** 93; **25** 435
 gold **14** 766
 hardstones **8** 417, 418; **14** 171; **21** 726; **25** 435
 imprese **29** 740
 ivory **33** 669
 ivory-carvings **12** 460
 manuscripts **14** 619, 620; **16** 553; **29** 740
 medals **1** 35
 metalwork **2** 732; **8** 411, 412–13; **16** 899; **19** 152; **25** 39
 paintings **1** 5; **2** 828; **3** 257, 613; **4** 453, 897, 913; **8** 390; **9** 16, 446; **11** 732; **12** 387; **13** 847, 899; **14** 319, 381, 626; **23** 516; **25** 432; **27** 885; **28** 189; **29** 648; **31** 13
  allegorical **2** 374
  genre **2** 340
  miniatures **11** 65, 803; **21** 640
  mythological **3** 257; **14** 319; **29** 428–31
  portraits **25** 382
  religious **22** 272; **27** 228; **29** 428
 plaquettes **25** 22
 printing plates **12** 882
 regalia **32** 458
 rock crystal **26** 486
 sculpture **1** 36; **8** 384; **11** 62; **12** 348, 576; **32** 730, 731
 silver **16** 901
 sponsorship **19** 662
 thrones **16** 60
Rudolf IV, Duke of Austria (*reg* 1358-65) **2** 827; **13** 899–901*, *900*; **14** 418
 architecture **2** 777; **21** 424; **32** 431, 452
 sculpture **2** 799
Rudolf, Konrad **31** 816
Rudolf, Paul **16** 101
Rudolf von Ems **7** 241; **31** 326
Rudolph, 4th Prior of Camaldoli **5** 449
Rudolph, Paul (Marvin) **27** 313–14*
 pupils **23** 385
 staff **7** 895; **16** 819; **30** 869
 teachers **4** 762
 works **4** 475; **7** 695; **23** 25; **27** *314*
Rudolph, Wilhelm **13** 322
Rudolphi, Andreas **29** 578
Rudolphi, Frédéric-Jules **5** 392; **11** 621
Rudradeva, Ruler (*reg c.* 1158-95) (Kakatiya) **14** 130
Rudston **32** 542
Rudva Glava **25** 516
Rudyerd, John **19** 360
Rudzka-Cybisowa, Hanna **17** 804; **33** 416
Rue, Jean-Baptiste de La *see* LA RUE, JEAN-BAPTISTE DE
Rue, Lizynka *see* MIRBEL, Mme de
Rue, Philibert-Benoît de La *see* LA RUE, PHILIBERT-BENOÎT DE
Rued, Benedikt *see* RIED, BENEDIKT
Rueda, Esteban de **9** 354; **27** 314*; **29** 291
Rueda, Jorge **4** 234; **7** 607
Rueda, Lope de **30** 664
Rueda, Teodosio Sánchez de *see* SÁNCHEZ DE RUEDA, TEODOSIO
Rüegg, Arthur **33** 736
Rueil
 château **12** 832
 garden **12** 120, *121*; **27** 314–15*
Rueil-Malmaison *see* MALMAISON
Ruel **4** 666
Ruel, Marie-Fernande **9** 423
Ruelas, Julio **21** 386, 397; **23** 565; **27** 315*
Ruelens, Charles **27** 137
Ruelle, Claude de La *see* LA RUELLE, CLAUDE DE
Ruelles, Jan Frans de **7** 466
Ruellet, G. **8** 892
Ruental *see* RUNDĀLE
Ruesch, Nikolaus **33** 286
Ruesga, Juan de **14** 578
Ruez **12** 405
Ruf, Franz **12** 379; **27** 315
Ruf, Sep **10** 105; **12** 379; **27** 315*
Rufail **16** 350
al-Rufaya
 statue **2** 256, *257*
Ruff, Franz **27** 316
Ruff, Ludwig **27** 316*
Ruffinelli **17** 565
Ruffino **24** 228
Ruffins, Reynold **7** 292; **12** 772
Ruffo, Antonio **27** 316*
 paintings **12** 308; **26** 164, 168, 177, 311; **27** 202; **29** 697
Ruffo, Marco **22** 169; **27** 371, 400
Ruffo, Tommaso, Cardinal, Archbishop of Ferrara **27** 316*
 paintings **7** 682; **8** 159; **13** 330; **28** 755
Rufford Old Hall (Lancs) **10** 270
ruffs **9** 266–7, 286
Rufini, Alessandro, Bishop of Melfi **11** 740
Rufinus, L. Cuspius Pactumeius *see* PACTUMEIUS RUFINUS, L. CUSPIUS
Rufus, L. Annius Mammianus **14** 440
Rufus, L. Mammius Maximus **14** 441
Rufus, M. Spurius **14** 441
Rugar, John **32** 815
Rugård **14** 781
Rugby School (Warwicks) **25** 173, I2; **28** 156
Rugendas, Christian **27** 319
Rugendas, Georg Philipp, I (1666-1742) **2** 719; **27** 319*
 pupils **14** 49; **26** 363
 reproductive prints by others **23** 146
 works **12** 391; **21** 416
Rugendas, Georg Philipp, II (1701-74) **27** 319
Rugendas, Jeremias Gottlob **27** 319
Rugendas, Johann Lorenz **27** 319
Rugendas, Johann Moritz **6** 596; **26** 414; **27** 319*; **31** 754
 works **2** 399; **4** 706, 708, 717; **24** 508
Rugenn, Jürg **12** 272
Rüger **8** 904
Ruger, Master **20** 564
Ruger, Albert **4** 81
Rugerus *see* THEOPHILUS (PRESBYTER)
Rugerus of Helmarhausen *see* ROGER OF HELMARHAUSEN
Ruggero, Marco di *see* ZOPPO, MARCO
Ruggero, Pablo **24** 96
Ruggero de Luca di Randazzo **2** 181
Ruggieri, Cosme **30** 659
Ruggieri, Federico **21** 31
Ruggieri, Ferdinando **16** 646; **24** 24; **27** 319–20*
Ruggieri, Genaro **23** 904
Ruggieri, Giovanni **13** 655; **27** 320–21*
 works **21** 519; **27** *320*; **32** 548
Ruggieri, Giovanni Battista **9** 92
Ruggieri, Giuseppe **24** 24
Ruggieri, Maria **22** 727
Ruggieri, Ruggiero de **9** 328; **11** 266; **20** 673; **31** 850
Ruggiero **20** 323
Ruginoasa Palace **26** 718
rugs **27** 316–18*
 historical and regional traditions
  Armenia (Europe) **2** 437–9*, *438*
  Britain **27** 317*
  Canada **5** 588; **27** 317–18*
  Central Asia **10** 873
  Central Asia, Western **10** *874*
  Germany **12** 409, 413
  Israel **16** 569
  Native North Americans **22** 669; **30** VIII2
  Navajo **5** 829; **22** 626; **27** 317; **30** VIII2
  Norway **5** 829
  Ottoman **23** 643
  Pakistan **23** 802
  Poland **25** 131
  Spain **29** 297
  Sweden **5** 829, 830
  Tibet **30** *837*
  Turkey **2** 438
  United States of America **27** 317*; **30** VIII2
  Venezuela **32** 177, *177*
 materials
  appliqué **27** 316
  bark **27** 316
  burlap **27** 317
  embroidery **27** 316
  felt **10** 873, *874*; **27** 316
  jute **27** 317
  linen **27** 317
  rags **27** 317
  reeds **27** 316
  sacking **27** 317
  wool **30** VIII2
 techniques
  crochet **27** 318
  knitting **27** 318
  weaving **27** 316
 types
  bed **27** 318
  braided **27** *317*, 318
  button *see* dollar
  chenille *see* shirred
  clippy *see* proggy
  cloutie *see* proggy
  dollar **27** 318
  hooked **27** *317*, 317–18*
  jergas **27** 316
  Kazak **2** 438, 439
  Kuba **2** 438
  Kumkapu **2** 439
  list **27** 318
  long-pile **5** 831
  pegged *see* proggy
  proggy **27** 318
   Britain **27** *318*
  shirred **27** 318
  Shirvan **2** 438
  short-pile **5** 831
  tongue **27** 318
  yarn-sewn **27** 318
 see also MATS
al-Ruhā *see* URFA
Ruhe, Ed **1** 66; **21** 733
Ruhe, Ed, Collection *see under* LAWRENCE (KS)
Ruhemann, Helmuth **14** 385; **27** 321*
Ruhental *see* RUNDĀLE
Ruhl **9** 691
Ruhl, Christian **26** 22
Ruhl, Johann Christian **27** 322
Ruhl, Ludwig Sigismund **27** 322*
Rühle, Christoph **9** 241
Ruhlmann, Jacques-Emile **11** 583, 601; **27** 322*
 collaboration **9** 391
 groups and movements **2** *520*, 521
Ruhlmann, Jacques-Emile—cont.
 works **1** 112; **11** 601, 602; **20** 469; **24** 266; **28** 525; **31** 224
Ruhlmann & Laurent, Etablissement **27** 322
Ruhnau, Werner **8** 631; **18** 118, 119
Ruhuna University *see under* MATARA
Ruian **7** 83
 Huiguang Pagoda **7** 15, 25
Ruichang, Tomb of Li Yanghu **7** 82
Ruicheng Yongle gong **6** 657, 672
 Chongyang Hall **6** *672*
 Sanqing Hall **6** 657, *657*, 672; **14** 78
 wall paintings **6** 779, 786, *787*
Ruijsdael, Salomon (Jacobsz.) van *see* RUYSDAEL, SALOMON (JACOBSZ.) VAN
Ruijsscher, Johannes *see* RUISSCHER, JOHANNES
Ruijven, Pieter Claesz. van **32** 267
ruin buildings **12** 130, *130*; **13** 703; **24** 741; **27** *323*, 323–4*
Ruini, Carlo **2** 105
ruin mounds **1** 851; **21** 268
 see also TELLS
Ruis, Juan Antonio **22** 24
Ruischer, Johannes *see* RUISSCHER, JOHANNES
Ruisdael, Isaack van **27** 324, 455
Ruisdael, Jacob (Isaacksz.) van **22** 843; **27** 324–9*, 455
 attributions **17** 920
 collaboration **3** 757; **22** 843; **23** 611; **32** 145
 copies **26** 124
 patrons and collectors
  Altman, Benjamin **1** 731
  Aumale, Henri-Eugène-Philippe-Louis de Bourbon, Duc d' **23** 523
  Beit, Otto (John) **3** 522
  Boyle, Richard, 3rd Earl of Burlington and 4th Earl of Cork **10** 364
  Boymans, F(rans) J(acob) O(tto) **4** 614
  Catherine II, Empress of Russia (*reg* 1762- 96) **26** 732, 733
  Cavendish, William, 2nd Duke of Devonshire (1671-1729) **10** 365
  Choiseul, Etienne-François, Duc de **7** 194
  Feitama, Sybrand (1620-1701) **10** 864
  Goll van Franckenstein (family) **12** 876
  Hall, Peter Adolf **14** 80
  Harvey, Thomas **8** 184
  Johnson, John G(raver) (1841-1917) **17** 619
  Livois, Marquis de **19** 510
  Marigny, Marquis de **25** 81
  McLellan, Archibald **28** 271
  Napoleon III, Emperor of France (*reg* 1852-70) **4** 306
  Peel, Robert (1788-1850) **24** 322
  Ryerson, Martin A(ntoine) **27** 463
  Seymour-Conway, Richard, 4th Marquess of Hertford **28** 527
  Stuart, John, 3rd Earl of Bute (1713-92) **29** 796
  Verstolk van Soelen, Jan Gijsbert, Baron **32** 377
  Waldegrave, William, 1st Baron Radstock **32** 774
 pupils **14** 600; **17** 920
 reproductive prints by others **4** 169; **8** 539; **21** 800; **23** 590
 restorations by others **21** 429
 works **10** 553; **13** 894; **18** 710, *711*; **22** 840; **25** 606; **27** *325*, *326*, *327*, *328*

Ruisel, Juan du *see* JUAN DU RUISEL
Ruisell, Hermann 31 840
Ruislip Lido 19 332
Ruisscher, Johannes 27 330*; 32 907
Ruissel, Herman 5 207
Ruiz (*fl* 18th cent.) 22 480
Ruiz (Costa Rica) 29 214
Ruiz (family) 7 846
Ruiz, Alonso 7 488
Ruiz, Andrés 29 268
Ruiz, Antonio (*fl* 1536) 31 865
Ruiz, Antonio (*d* 1800) 29 337
Ruiz, Antonio (1785-1829) 29 337
Ruiz, Antonio (1897-1964) 21 388; 23 370; 27 331*
Ruiz, Antonio González (1711-88) *see* GONZÁLEZ RUIZ, ANTONIO
Ruiz, Bartolomé 29 152
Ruíz, Cristóbal 25 701; 27 155
Ruiz, David 3 625
Ruiz, Fernando 29 334
Ruíz, Florencio 13 768
Ruiz, Gilberto 18 835
Ruíz, Guillermo 21 389, 397; 33 728
Ruiz, Hernán, I (*d* 1558) 7 844; 27 330*
Ruiz, Hernán, II (*c.* 1500-69) 14 464; 23 343; 27 330-31*; 29 338
works 4 784, *784*; 28 513, 518; 29 266
writings 29 637
Ruiz, Hernán, III (*c.* 1559-1606) 27 331; 29 268
Ruiz, Jose Tence *see* TENCE RUIZ, JOSE
Ruiz, Juan 3 471; 21 156; 29 298, 334
Ruiz, Miguel Angel 14 715
Ruíz, Noemí 25 702
Ruiz Blasco, José 24 713
Ruiz de Florindo, Alonso 23 626
Ruiz de la Iglesia, Francisco Ignacio 5 874, 875; 27 331*
works 6 *71*
Ruiz del Peral, Torcuato 26 421
Ruiz de Luna 29 329
Ruiz de Salces, Antonio 17 447; 20 64; 29 355
Ruiz Gijón, Francisco 8 216
Ruíz González, Pedro 5 875; 27 331*
Ruiz Picasso, Pablo *see* PICASSO, PABLO
Ruiz Rosas, Alfredo 24 510; 27 332*
Ruiz Ullán, Antonio 32 167
Rujiazhuang (Baoji) 3 187; 6 848; 7 80
Rukani Basilica 8 155
Rukhin, Yevgeny 27 397, 581
Rukhlyadev, Aleksey Mikhaylovich 18 458; 29 529
Rūķis *see* GNOME, THE
Rukn al-Dawla, Amir (*reg* 947-77) (Buyid) 16 373
Rukn al-Dīn Baybars al-Jāshankīr *see* BAYBARS II
Ruknuddin 15 608
Rukupo, Raharuhi 20 355; 23 53; 27 332*
Rul, Manuel González *see* GONZÁLEZ RUL, MANUEL
Ruldu 15 631, 633
rulers 22 182
rules 11 763; 13 411
Rulier, Jean 29 348
Rümann, Wilhelm von 27 332*
pupils 14 47; 19 661; 22 917; 29 721
works 32 758; 33 283
Rumayla 2 264, 267, 272
Rumbold, Thomas 10 643
Rumfa, Muhammadu 1 242; 17 778
Rumford, Benjamin Thompson, Count *see* THOMPSON, BENJAMIN, Count Rumford
al-Rumi 16 285
Rumicolca 29 164
Rumicucho, Pucará de *see* PUCARÁ DE RUMICUCHO
Rummer, Johann Michael 32 879
Rummindei *see* LUMBINI
Rumohr, Carl Friedrich Ludwig Felix von 2 532; 8 761; 12 482; 14 766; 29 46, 879
rumorarmonio 27 446
Rump, (Christian) Godtfred 27 332-3*
Rump, Johannes 8 759; 12 423; 27 333*; 30 533
Rumphius 29 229
Rumpler, Franz 7 368; 16 874; 17 517; 22 187; 24 568
Rumprecht von Graben 11 752
Rumsey, Mrs Charles 9 359
Rumsey, Edward 2 705; 23 54
Rumyantsev, Nikolay 27 439, 440
Rumyantsev, Sergey 27 440
Rumyantsev Museum *see under* MOSCOW → museums
Runa, Asilo de Invalidos 25 293
Runciman, Alexander 9 724; 23 208; 27 333-4*; 28 235, 236, 274
patrons and collectors 7 418, 419; 28 269, 273
teachers 28 236
works 28 235, 236
Runciman, John 9 724; 27 333, 334*; 28 235, 236
Runcorn (Ches) 31 733
Rundāle 18 *847*
Palace 18 *848*, 849
Rundbogenstil 6 565; 9 704; 14 839; 26 743; 27 334-6*
Belgium 31 887
Germany 12 *167*, 376; 14 *840*; 27 334-6*, *335*
United States of America 27 334; 31 690, *691*
Rundell, Bridge & Co. 27 337
Rundell, Bridge & Rundell 15 820; 19 593; 22 889; 27 336-7*
designers 10 264; 11 164; 25 712
groups and movements 26 85
patrons and collectors 14 145
staff 3 78; 29 723
works 10 334, 345; 24 887
Rundell, Edmond Waller 27 336
Rundell, Philip 22 719; 27 336
Rundell & Bridge 27 336
Runeberg, Johan Ludvig 9 717; 18 800
Runeberg, Walter Magnus 11 99, 105; 27 337*; 30 258
runes 10 592; 32 517, 518
rune-stones 23 227; 31 748
Runge (family) 27 *340*
Runge, Daniel 27 337
Runge, Philipp Otto 12 394; 14 102; 22 378; 27 337-41*
groups and movements 22 540; 26 736, 738, 741
patrons and collectors 12 853; 29 376
teachers 18 395
works 12 393, *393*; 19 355; 22 *379*; 27 *339*, *340*; 28 714
writings 7 629; 26 737
Rüngeling, John *see* RINGLING, JOHN
Rungštelė, Antanas 19 499
Rungu 20 175, 176
Runhau, Werner 11 778
Runk, Ferdinand 19 338
running script *see under* SCRIPTS → types
running stitch *see under* STITCHES
running tracks 13 381, 386, 403, 406
Runwaso 15 323
Ruo, Gennaro 4 333
Ruodprecht 23 652
Ruodprecht Psalter *see under* PSALTERS → individual manuscripts
Ruofen *see* YUJIAN
Ruokokoski, Jalmari 23 266; 27 633
Ruoppolo, Carlo 27 342
Ruoppolo, Francesco 27 342
Ruoppolo, Giovanni Battista 11 32; 22 479; 26 61; 27 342*
Ruoppolo, Giuseppe 27 342
Ruotte, Louis Charles 3 309; 29 676
Ruovesi Studio 12 20; 22 541
Rupam 5 420; 24 436
Rupar 15 423
Rupbas 15 *261*; 27 342*
Rupe, Alano de *see* ALANO DE RUPE
Rupert, Holy Roman Emperor (*reg* 1400-10) 12 492; 14 305; 33 *272*
Rupert, Saint *see* HRODBERT, Bishop of Worms
Rupert III, Elector Palatine *see* RUPERT, Holy Roman Emperor
Rupert IV, Abbot of Kremsmünster 18 447
Ruperti, C. A. 31 371
Rupertsberg Antependium 12 462
Rupert's metal *see under* ALLOYS → types
Rupf, Hermann 17 725; 27 343*
Rupf, Margrit 27 343*
Rupio, Fermín Vivaceta *see* VIVACETA RUPIO, FERMÍN
Ruppert, Karl 5 411
Rüppurr 17 817
Ruprecht-Karls-Universität *see under* HEIDELBERG
Ruprich-Robert, Victor-Marie-Charles 5 370, 875; 7 761; 12 312; 27 343*
Ruptura (Mexico) 10 866
Rupture (Belgium) 5 286
Rupy, Jean de *see* JEAN DE CAMBRAI
Rural Industries Bureau 25 821
Rus' 27 361
architecture 27 368; 31 546-7*
pottery 27 410
urban planning 31 547
workshops 27 441
see also UKRAINE
Rusafa 9 *513*, 523, 554; 16 *104*, 150; 27 343-4*
architecture 9 538
Basilica A 27 344; 29 816
Basilica B 1 722; 27 344
church 9 539, 541
martyrium of St Sergius *see* Basilica B
north gate 4 63; 27 *344*
pottery 16 407
SS Sergius and Bacchus 3 191; 7 279; 9 540, 654
Rusahinili *see* TOPRAKKALE
Rusa II, King of Urartu (*reg c.* 680-640 BC) 3 356; 9 731; 17 822; 31 158, 699
Rusai.URU.TUR *see* BASTAM
Rusakov, Aleksandr 7 341
Rusca, Bartolomeo 4 310
Rusca, Carlo Francesco 24 894
Rusca, Grazioso 21 533
Rusca, Luigi 24 458; 27 345*, 408; 30 277
Rusca, Michele 3 90
Rusce, Bartolomeo 29 304
Ruscelli, Girolamo 21 579
Ruscha, Edward (Joseph) 27 345*
collaboration 20 606, 607
groups and movements 19 702; 25 232
patrons and collectors 33 45
works 19 492, 493; 25 620; 31 608
Ruscheweyh, Ferdinand 7 870; 27 345-6*
Ruschi, Francesco 16 676
Rüschlikon 30 144
Rusconi, Benedetto *see* DIANA, BENEDETTO
Rusconi, Camillo 27 346-7*
assistants 20 125; 24 837; 31 826
collaboration 24 35
patrons and collectors 1 532, 597; 23 874
pupils 3 198; 12 680; 13 782; 16 699; 24 834; 28 79
teachers 11 18
works 9 158; 16 699; 20 379; 27 *347*; 31 128
Rusconi, Giovanni Antonio 27 347-8*
patrons and collectors 13 659
works 3 766; 5 531; 25 215, 889
writings 31 295
Rusconi, Giuseppe 6 67; 7 897; 16 699; 25 808; 27 347
Rusconi Sassi, Ludovico 23 637; 27 348*
Ruščyć, Ferdinand 3 529
Rüse, Hendrik 8 725
Ruseckas, B. 27 348
Ruseckas, Kanutas 3 529; 19 497; 27 348*
Rusellae 10 *583*, 585, 586; 16 *620*; 26 *886*; 27 348*
coins 10 592
town walls 10 601
vases 10 612, 616
Rush, Benjamin 33 195
Rush, Endacott & Goff 12 854
Rush, Endacott & Rush 12 854
Rush, William 24 600; 27 348-9*
works 28 613, *614*; 31 610
Rushbury, Henry 4 87
rushes 3 331; 5 *577*, 610; 6 388, *391*; 10 5; 22 662
Rusheva, Nadya (Nikolayevna) 27 349*
Rushforth, Peter 2 761
rushlights 19 364
Rushout, John, 2nd Baron Northwick 20 875; 26 463; 27 350*
Rushton Maverick, Peter *see* MAVERICK, PETER RUSHTON
Rusiñol (i Prats), Santiago 3 219; 5 509; 27 350*; 29 285
Ruska, Aloizy I. 31 551
Ruskin (family) 27 351
Ruskin, John 8 586, 802; 10 254, 479; 13 304; 15 210; 22 379; 23 546; 24 *655*; 26 63; 27 350-55*, *351*; 28 206, 276, 916
drawings 9 225; 27 *353*
education (art) 23 690
groups and movements 2 576; 13 205; 23 498; 24 743; 32 415
paintings 13 2; 27 186; 28 664; 31 472
personal collection 5 266; 11 433; 20 34; 22 351; 30 749
pupils 15 142
teachers 11 60; 14 166
writings 2 576; 5 777; 10 253, 370; 26 743
illustrated 8 66
on architecture 2 359; 5 340; 10 266; 25 173; 26 743; 32 188
on art 1 181; 10 252
on artists 31 17; 32 356
on chiaroscuro 6 570
on landscape 18 701
on painting 31 300, 768
on perspective 24 491
on photography 28 204
on polychromy 4 787; 10 238; 25 172
on restoration 2 321
translated 25 661; 29 876
Ruskin Galleries *see under* BEMBRIDGE
Ruskin Madonna 32 365
Ruskin School of Drawing and Fine Art *see under* OXFORD → colleges
Rusko Church 11 98
Rusli 15 808
Rusnati, Giuseppe 5 182; 21 533; 27 346
Rusovce Palace 14 889
Ruspagiari, Alfonso (di Tommaso) 20 920; 27 356*
Rusper 26 694
Ruspoli (family) 6 350; 20 394
Ruspoli, Alessandro Bichi 9 405
Ruspoli, Girolama Bichi, Marchesa 20 805
Russ, Jakob 7 251; 30 136
Russ, Marie Constantin *see* BASHKIRTSEVA, MARIYA (KONSTANINOVNA)
Russborough House (Co. Wicklow) 3 276; 16 8, 23; 19 63; 23 611, 860, *861*; 32 332
Russel, James 15 149; 27 356*
Rüsselbecher *see* GLASSES → types → claw-beakers
Russell 23 51, *52*
Christ Church 23 53
Pompallier House 23 53; 32 308
Russell, Andrew J. 15 830; 24 665, 667
Russell, Anthony 26 394
Russell, Bertrand 30 704
Russell, Caroline 19 591
Russell, Charles M(arion) 2 106; 27 358*; 31 612; 33 184
Russell, Christopher 2 152
Russell, Dick *see* RUSSELL, R(ICHARD) D.
Russell, Don 3 61, 64
Russell, Elias 10 345
Russell, Francis, 2nd Baron Russell of Thornhaugh *see* RUSSELL, FRANCIS, 4th Earl of Bedford
Russell, Francis, 4th Earl of Bedford 6 96; 17 635; 27 357*
Russell, Francis, 5th Duke of Bedford 27 357*
architecture 10 671; 14 681
furniture 10 295; 15 165
interior decoration 26 85
paintings 11 908
Russell, Francis, 7th Duke of Bedford 30 534
Russell, Gertrude, Dowager Duchess of Bedford 19 571
Russell, (Sydney) Gordon 8 804; 15 824; 27 358*
groups and movements 10 299
works 8 *804*; 10 284, 285
Russell, Gordon, Ltd 27 358
Russell, James *see* RUSSEL, JAMES
Russell, John 27 359*; 29 675
patrons and collectors 14 146; 25 283
reproductive prints by others 18 149
teachers 8 26
works 12 813; 25 *283*
Russell, John, 4th Duke of Bedford
architecture 19 571
furniture 10 295; 15 165; 18 746
paintings 5 597; 13 301; 32 111
sculpture 8 699
Russell, John, 6th Duke of Bedford 27 357-8*
architecture 27 357; 33 447
engravings 19 284
gardens 26 239
paintings 4 322; 14 270
sculpture 5 629; 6 456; 10 365
silver 10 334
Russell, John Fuller 27 359*
Russell, John Peter 20 822; 27 359*
Russell, John Scott 10 682
Russell, Ken 30 687
Russell, Leon B. 21 121

Russell, Lillian **14** 482
Russell, Lucy, Countess of Bedford **12** 127, 515; **27** 356–7*
Russell, Luther **22** 240
Russell, Morgan **19** 878; **27** 360*; **30** 173; **31** 607
groups and movements **1** 74; **23** 570
works **30** *173*
Russell, R(ichard) D. **25** 400; **27** 358
Russell, Robert **2** 738
Russell, Robert Tor **8** 676; **19** 822; **27** 360*
Russell, Samuel **15** 49, 402
Russell, S. B. **7** 797; **27** 360; **31** 242
Russell, Theodore **27** 360*
Russell, Thomas Cloutt **27** 359
Russell, William, 5th Earl of Bedford (1613-1700) **29** 717
Russell, William, Lord (1780-1870) **27** 357
Russell, William Hamilton **7** 436*
Russell-Cotes Art Gallery and Museum *see under* BOURNEMOUTH (HANTS)
Russell & Sons **27** 358
Russell-Taafe Chalice **9** 320
Russev, Svetlin **5** 163
Russi, Franco dei *see* FRANCO DEI RUSSI
Russia **27** 361–444*, *362*, *363*; **32** 513
academies **25** *791*; **27** 442
aesthetics **25** 38
agalmatolite **27** *437*
agate **10** *721*
aluminium **27** *397*
apartments **27** *380*
applied art **27** 394
aquamarines **10** *721*
arches **27** 368, 369–70
architecture **27** 368–81*
Baroque **27** 373–4
brick **4** 783
Empire style **29** 554
landscape **27** 376–7
military **21** 561; **27** *371*
Romanesque **26** 594
stone **27** 368
vernacular **32** 295
wood **18** 104; **27** 368
19th cent. **16** 53
20th cent. **27** *578*
archives **2** 369, 371*
art criticism **31** 416
art history **18** 215; **27** 443–4*
art legislation **2** 557
art market **2** 560
art schools **22** 177; **28** 596; **33** 740
axes **32** *527*
banknotes **3** 182
barracks **29** *555*
bastions **27** *371*
belts **32** 528
birch **33** I1
bone **2** *101*
book illustrations **11** *82*
bowenite **10** *721*
bowls **27** *419*
boxes **10** *721*, IV3
brick **4** 783*
bridges **14** 222; **27** *376*
brooches **10** *721*; **27** *429*
bureaux **27** *583*
candlesticks **10** *721*; **27** *424*
caricatures **5** 759*
carving **27** 365
cast iron **14** 222
cathedrals
Baroque **22** *182*; **26** *9*
Byzantine **29** *54*
Neo-classicism **27** *577*; **29** *552*; **32** *698*
Post-Byzantine **22** *184*
Romanesque **26** *594*
11th cent. **23** *270*
12th cent. **23** *268*; **32** *664*
Russia
cathedrals—cont.
13th cent. **27** *369*
14th cent. **33** *741*
15th cent. **11** *116*; **22** *183*
celluloid **25** *25*
ceramics **27** 410*
chairs **7** 769; **27** *408*, *409*
chess sets **6** 557
churches **27** 368–73, 374
Baroque **27** *374*; **31** *318*
Byzantine **7** 261; **25** *680*
centrally planned **7** 256
decoration **7** 273, 274
eight-on-four **22** 170
Post-Byzantine **18** *207*
Slav Revival **28** *837*
tetraconch **22** 170
12th cent. **32** *663*
14th cent. **23** *269*; **27** *370*
16th cent. **22** *170*
17th cent. **33** *507*
ciboria (i) (vessels) **7** 301
clubs (meeting places) **12** *877*; **21** *93*
coins **7** 538, 539
collections **2** 560; **6** 284–5; **27** 438–41*, 580; **31** 312
icons **18** 385
compasses **22** 182
copper **7** 813
costumes **30** *686*
cotton **27** *431*
cufflinks **10** *721*
damask **19** 418
dealing **2** 560; **27** 438–40*
decanters **27** *416*
diadems **28** *325*
diamonds **10** IV3; **12** 269; **27** 429, *429*
diplomatic gifts **16** 445
display of art **9** 18
dolls **20** 222; **31** 259
drawings **27** 389, 390
earth **19** 837
education (art) **24** 464; **26** 730–31; **27** 441–3*
architecture **27** 441–3*; **31** 543
crafts **27** 442, 443
embroidery **27** 430–31
enamel **10** 193, *721*; **27** 212, *415*, *419*, *421*, 426–7*
guilloche **10** IV3
engravings **27** 389; **29** *676*
epitaphs **27** *389*
exchanges **27** *375*
exhibitions **10** 680; **16** 808; **32** 724
façades **22** 184
factories **27** *377*
faience (ii) (ceramics) **27** 410
figurines **25** 489
filigree **27** 418, *423*, *425*, 426
fireplaces **27** *407*
fireproofing **19** 837
fortifications **21** 561; **27** 370
fortresses **25** *679*; **27** 370, 371
16th cent. **17** *872*
17th cent. **27** *211*
19th cent. **22** *181*
fountains **24** *547*
frames **9** 18; **10** *721*
furniture **9** 30; **27** 406–10*
galleries (iv) (art)
picture **9** 18
gardens **12** 122, 134*, *134*
gateways **32** 663, *663*
gems **27** *419*
glass **27** 414–18*, *415*, *416*, *418*
goblets **27** *415*
gold **10** *721*; **27** 418–23*, *419*, *421*, *429*; **28** *320*, *322*, *325*
gold leaf **32** *527*
government buildings **22** *174*; **26** *730*; **33** *600*
green belt **27** 380
guilds **27** 419
hardstones **27** 427–8*
heraldry **14** 411*
Russia—cont.
historiography **27** 443–4*
horn-carvings **27** *365*
hospitals **17** *870*; **31** *544*
houses **32** 298
country **1** *71*; **27** 377
town **27** 377
18th cent. **3** *433*
housing **12** *654*, 877; **18** *620*; **21** 622
icon covers **15** 78
icons **24** 3; **27** 305, 382–6; **31** 555
Byzantine **9** 629; **15** *76*, II2; **27** *305*, *383*, *384*; **30** V3
Post-Byzantine **8** *909*; **25** *337*, 337–8*; **27** *385*, *386*
interior decoration **27** 399–404*, 405*
Neo-classicism **27** *403*; **29** *839*
Rococo **27** *402*
17th cent. **27** *399*
iron **16** 53; **32** *527*
ivory-carvings **13** 596
jade **10** *721*; **16** 860
jasper **27** 428
jewellery **27** 428–9*; **32** 527
kaftans **9** *641*
kerchiefs **27** 430–31
knitting **18** 158
kovshy **27** *421*
lace **27** 430
lacquer **18** 614, 615; **23** 837; **27** 427*
linen **27** 430
lithography **25** *351*
mahogany **27** *583*
malachite **14** *172*; **27** 428
mansions **28** *579*, 580
manuals **29** 778
manuscript illumination **27** 385
marble **27** *389*
marks **20** 444; **22** 179; **27** 419, 420, 422
masonry **4** 783; **27** 368
mausolea **20** *870*
metalwork **27** 418*, 424*, 425–6*; **28** *320*, *322*
display **9** 30
monasteries **28** *465*; **32** *149*
fortified **27** 371, *371*
15th cent. **10** *889*
17th cent. **32** *667*
monuments **4** *598*; **22** *179*; **32** *685*
equestrian **10** *442*
mother-of-pearl **27** *423*
museums **6** 284–5; **27** 439–41*
19th cent. **22** *173*
20th cent. **20** 194; **22** 508; **27** *381*
niello **27** 419, 420, 421, 422
nude figures **28** *475*
objects of vertu **10** *721*; **27** 426*
oil sketches **25** 145
orders (architecture) **22** 182
orders (chivalry) **7** 178
ormolu **27** *424*
painting **23** 837; **27** 381–7*, 388–92*, 394–8*
Abstract art **12** *895*
allegorical **18** *792*; **32** *246*
Cubo-Futurism **20** *193*
display **9** 18
Expressionism **27** *396*
Futurism **12** *893*
genre **24** *464*
Neo-primitivism **27** *393*
19th cent. **10** *856*; **20** *154*; **32** *163*
gouache **33** *379*
hanging **9** 18
history
19th cent. **5** *25*, *68*; **16** *793*; **27** *390*; **32** *73*
20th cent. **27** *435*
Jewish art **17** 576–7*
landscape **25** 145; **27** *391*
panel **24** 3
Post-Byzantine **25** 330
Russia
painting—cont.
Rayism **26** *41*
Realism (style) **26** *218*, *219*
religious **16** *791*; **22** *176*, *177*; **27** *580*
Socialist Realism **28** *918*
Suprematism **19** *476*; **20** *194*; **25** *239*; **26** *504*; **30** *7*
townscapes **1** *599*
urban life **18** *791*
wall **25** 342*, *342*; **27** 381–2, 383, 386, 387; **30** *708*
watercolours **27** 390
19th cent. **19** *277*; **32** *736*
20th cent. **6** *385*; **10** *699*; **20** *851*; **27** *433*
palaces **27** 373, 374
Baroque **25** *745*
Neo-classicism **5** *520*
17th cent. **27** *372*
18th cent. **22** *172*; **24** *292*, *547*; **27** *574*, *585*
paper **24** 40
papier mâché **24** 62
parks **12** 134
patronage **7** 217; **27** 437–8*
pavilions (buildings) **26** *8*
pearls **27** *419*, *423*
pendants (jewellery) **10** *721*; **27** *423*
periodicals **24** 450–51*; **27** 392, 441, 443, 444
photographic prints **24** *665*
photography **24** 672; **27** 394, 396
pitchers **27** 410
plaques **2** *101*
plaster **29** 839–40*
plate **9** 30
platinum **10** *721*
porcelain **27** 411–14*, *414*
hard-paste **27** *414*
18th cent. **27** *412*
porphyry **27** 428
portraits
drawings **23** *530*
painting **27** 387, 388
Cubism **27** *581*
Neo-classicism **27** *579*
Rococo **26** *551*
Romanticism **18** *75*
18th cent. **2** *410*; **19** *279*; **27** *388*
19th cent. **4** *421*; **18** *438*; **30** *11*
20th cent. **6** *384*; **28** *475*
photography **24** *675*
self-portraits **6** *384*; **23** *530*
posters **7** *654*; **25** 349, 351, *351*; **26** *505*; **27** 394, 396
Suprematism **19** *475*
20th cent. **20** *887*
pottery **27** *366*, 410–11*
printing **27** 431
prints **27** 385, 397
lubki **18** 385; **19** 751*; **22** 750; **25** 243
propaganda **25** 652–3; **27** 394, 413, *414*
Psalters **9** 613
railway stations **28** *571*
rock art **23** 442; **25** 475; **27** 365
roofs **7** 813
rulers **22** 182
sarcophagi **13** 596
screens (i) (architectural) **7** 279, *279*; **15** 78; **25** 183
sculpture **27** 382*, 387*, 389*, 390–93*, 394, 396*, 397*, 398*
architectural **7** 274
bronze **10** *442*
Constructivism **7** *768*; **25** *25*
monumental **27** 397
mythological **27** *437*
relief **27** *389*
Socialist Realism **27** *395*
wood **30** *363*
20th cent. **27** *397*; **30** *363*
secrétaires à abattant **33** I1
Russia—cont.
shawls **27** 431
shutters (window) **13** *14*
silk **9** *641*
silver **27** 418–23*, *420*, *423*, 584; **28** 737; **32** *527*
snuff-boxes **27** *420*
sofas **27** *406*
squares (town) **27** *576*
stage design **3** *119*; **27** 392, 394, 396, 397; **30** 686
stainless steel **27** *395*
staircases **27** *402*, *404*
steel **27** *407*, *424*
stone **27** 368
stoves **27** *400*
stucco **29** *839*, 839–40*
synagogues **17** 547
tapestries **27** 430
textiles **19** 418; **27** 430–31*
theatres **26** *732*; **27** *199*, *379*; **30** 677, 683, 684
theories
art **9** 188; **11** 870; **20** 195
music **3** 692
tiles **27** *400*; **30** 884*
title-pages **17** *577*
tombs **27** *367*
towers **22** *169*; **27** 374
towns **31** 722
garden cities **12** 145; **27** 377, 378; **28** 403; **31** 728
new **5** 520; **21** 622; **27** 374, 375; **31** 719
trade
ceramics **6** 333
cotton **16** 449
glass **16** 522
metal **22** 613
metalwork **22** 180
pottery **6** 333; **16** 417, 425
trade fairs **23** 168
treatises
aesthetics **31** 97
painting **4** 237; **27** 387
urban planning **31** 486
tumuli **27** 365–6
turquoise **27** *423*
universities **22** *175*
urban planning **27** 374, 375, 376, 379; **31** 486
urns **14** *172*
vases **27** *418*
vernacular art **20** 232
vessels **27** 418, *425*
vestments (ecclesiastical) **16** 430
window displays **6** 549
wood **18** 104; **27** 368; **30** *363*
wood-carvings **13** 5, *14*
Russia leather *see under* LEATHER → types
Russian, Old *see* OLD RUSSIAN
Russian Constructivism *see* CONSTRUCTIVISM → Russia
Russian Futurism *see* FUTURISM → Russia
Russian gems trust *see* RUSSKIYE SAMOTSVETY (RUSSIAN GEMS) TRUST
Russian Orthodox cross *see under* CROSSES → types
Russian Revival *see* OLD RUSSIAN REVIVAL
Russkiye samotsvety (Russian gems) trust **27** 422, 428
Russolo, Luigi **11** 866; **22** 381; **27** 444–6*
groups and movements **4** 199; **5** 848; **6** 342; **11** 863–4, 865; **16** 679; **20** 426; **21** 527
works **27** *446*, 789; **29** 96
Russu-Cheban, V. G. **21** 811
works **21** *812*
Russwurm, Heinrich Ludwig von Gleichen *see* GLEICHEN RUSSWURM, HEINRICH LUDWIG VON
Rust, Yvonne **23** 69
Rustafjaell, Robert de **10** 91

Rustam, Tepe 3 113
Rustam 'Ali 4 49; 16 335; 22 390
Rustaq Fort 23 436
Rustavi 12 320, 330
Rustelli, Gianni 28 176
Rustem, Jan 17 832; 25 106; 32 851
Rustemas, Jonas 27 348, 446–7*
patrons and collectors 19 498
pupils 19 497
Rüstem Pasha 9 730; 16 224; 17 807; 23 641
Rustenberg 12 142
rustication *see under* MASONRY → types
Rusticelli, Faustina 20 587; 25 259
Rustichino, il *see* RUSTICI, FRANCESCO
Rustici, Cristoforo 27 447
Rustici, Francesco 27 447; 31 174
Rustici, Gabriele 3 307
Rustici, Giovanni Francesco 27 447–9*; 29 569; 30 497
assistants 19 184
attributions 20 779
collaboration 3 156; 16 694; 19 193; 26 447
patrons and collectors 11 893; 20 482
pupils 22 448
teachers 32 366
works 10 441; 19 194; 27 *448*; 32 362
Rustici, Lorenzo 27 447
Rustici, Vincenzo 27 447; 28 688
Rusticone, il *see* RUSTICI, CRISTOFORO
Rusticucci, Girolamo, Cardinal 8 182
Rusticus, Bishop of Marseille 1 694
Rusticus Helpidius 31 498
Rustwijk, George 30 16
Rusu, D. 21 *812*
Rusu, Ivan 26 725
Rusuti (family) 13 147
Rusuti, Filippo 16 655; 27 449–50*
patrons and collectors 5 666
works 13 145; 27 *449*; 31 192
Ruszczyc, Ferdynand 25 107; 27 450–51*; 32 579, 877
works 27 *451*
Ruta, Clemente 4 562; 25 191
Rutan, Charles Hercules 26 343; 28 591
Rutault, Claude 21 892
Rutelli, Mario 11 346
Rutenzwig, Hans 30 146
Rutgaart van der Wall, Willem 18 177
Rutgenssoen, Lambrecht 23 671
Rutger 22 820
Rutgers, Abraham 10 514
Rutgers, Gerrit Jan 13 632
Rutgers Group 29 73
Ruth, Theo 32 756
Ruthart, Carl Borromäus Andreas 14 709; 19 338; 27 451–2*
Ruthenbeck, Reiner 27 452*
Ruthenzweig, Bartholomäus 20 641
Rutherford, Lewis M. 10 669
Rutherglen (Strathclyde) 26 617
Town Hall 28 288
Ruthin, St Peter's 32 787
Ruth Master 33 71
Ruths, Valentin 28 104
Ruths-Speicher 9 86
Ruthwell Cross 2 68; 8 196; 23 537; 27 452–3*, *453*; 28 *222*, 241
rutile 24 798
Rutkovich, U. 31 558
Rutland, Charles Manners, 4th Duke of *see* MANNERS, CHARLES, 4th Duke of Rutland
Rutland, John Manners, 8th Earl of *see* MANNERS, JOHN, 8th Earl of Rutland
Rutland, Roger Manners, 5th Earl of *see* MANNERS, ROGER, 5th Earl of Rutland
Rutland, Violet Manners, Duchess of *see* MANNERS, VIOLET, Duchess of Rutland
Rutland Psalter *see under* PSALTERS → individual manuscripts
Rutman, Robert 29 97
Rutschmann, Antal 14 894, 907
Rutté, Paul de 2 391
Rutter, Charles 2 151
Rutter, Frank (1876-1937) 1 666; 16 42
Rutter, Frank Mowbray (1911-89) 13 876
Ruttman, Walter 10 687
Ruusuvuori, Aarno 11 92; 27 453–4*
Ruvo 13 526, 581
Ru ware *see under* POTTERY → wares
Ruweise 1 857
Ruwi National Museum 23 436
Ruxthiel, Henri-Joseph 11 563
Ruyesdaell, Salomon (Jacobsz.) de *see* RUYSDAEL, SALOMON (JACOBSZ.) VAN
Ruys, Raymond 3 602
Ruysbroeck, Jan van *see* JAN VAN RUYSBROECK
Ruysch, Anna 27 454
Ruysch, Frederik 1 842; 27 454
Ruysch, Rachel 27 454*; 33 308
patrons and collectors 5 792; 11 789; 22 846; 33 280
teachers 1 166; 28 169
works 11 228; 22 843, *847*; 27 *454*; 29 668, *668*
Ruysdael, Jacob (Salomonsz.) van 17 920; 27 329, 455
Ruysdael, Salomon van 13 894, 895; 27 455–8*
patrons and collectors 3 890; 4 304; 19 735; 24 63
pupils 23 612; 27 324
reproductive prints by others 11 760; 19 10
works 18 710; 22 840; 27 *455*, *457*
Ruyselinck, Jan 32 242
Ruyter, Michiel Adriaansz. de, Admiral 3 389
Ruyven, Pieter Claesz. van 22 902
Ruz, Alberto 31 65
Ružany, Church of the Holy Trinity 3 530
Ruzbihan Muhammad al-Tab'i al-Shirazi 16 290
Ruzhani *see* RUŽANY
Ruzhen 5 112; 6 751; 7 77
Ružička, Kamilo 9 672
Růžík, František. 25 438
Ružomberok, Ludovít Fulla Gallery 28 857
Ruzzini, Domenico 12 913
Ruzzolone, Pietro 28 656
Rwanda 1 *214*; 11 880; 27 458*
aesthetics 1 237
basketwork 1 296
earplugs 1 296
tourist art 1 252
Ry, Mathurin Du *see* DU RY, MATHURIN
Ry, Paul Du *see* DU RY, PAUL
Ryabichev, Ya. B. 9 458
Ryabinik, Nikolay L. 31 561
Ryabuchinsky, Stepan 28 580
Ryabushinsky, Mikhail 27 459*
Ryabushinsky, Nikolay (Pavlovich) 4 178; 12 870; 18 792; 27 458–9*
Ryabushinsky, Pavel 27 459*
Ryabushinsky, Stepan 27 459*
Ryabushinsky, Vladimir 27 459*
Ryabushkin, Andrey (Petrovich) 24 465; 27 459*
Ryall, Henry Thomas 27 459–60*
Ryan, Aeneas 16 32
Ryan, Ann 7 557, 558
Ryan, Thomas 16 18
Ryan, Tony 16 36
Ryangina, Serafima (Vasil'yevna) 27 395, 460*
Ryazan' 27 *363*, 460*
Cathedral of the Dormition 27 372
City Museum of Local Lore 27 460
enamel 27 426
jewellery 27 428
metalwork 27 418
Regional Art Museum 27 460
tiles 30 884
Ryazhsky, Georgy (Georgiyevich) 27 395; 31 64
Ryback, Issachar 17 576, 577
Rybák, Jaromír 8 411
Rybak, Taty 27 460*
Ryberg, Simson 30 106
Rycault, Paul 30 479
Rychner, Claude 2 447
Rychner, Hans 33 297
Rychnov nad Kněznou 8 423
Ryckaert, David, III *see* RIJCKAERT, DAVID, III
Rycke, Daneel de *see* DANEEL DE RIJCKE
Ryckhals, François 27 230
Ryckmans, Nicolaes 17 598
Ryckwaert, Cornelis 8 816
Rycote (Oxon), Chapel of St Michael 7 283, *283*
Rycroft Painter 13 511; 32 65, 67*
Ryd, Carl Magnus 33 566
Rydam (family) 30 324
Rydams, Hendrik 17 649
Rydberg, Gustaf (Fredrik) 27 460–61*
Rydberg, Victor 30 120
Rydboholm 30 89
Rydén, S. 29 202
Ryder, A. F. C. 3 723
Ryder, Albert Pinkham 27 461–2*; 31 603
patrons and collectors 7 379; 24 638
works 2 107; 18 161; 27 *462*
Ryder & Yates & Partners 23 20
Rydzyna Palace 29 912
Rye (E. Sussex) 10 302
Ryebeke, Katelijne van 21 102
Ryed, Benedikt *see* RIED, BENEDIKT
Rye House (Herts) 4 779
Ryer, Pierre Du *see* DU RYER, PIERRE
ryers see under CARPETS → types
Ryerson, Egerton 5 570
Ryerson, Martin A(ntoine) 6 575; 27 463*, 778
Ryerson Library *see under* CHICAGO (IL) → museums → Art Institute
Ryes 26 598
Ryff, Walther Hermann *see* RIVIUS, GUALTHERUS
rygal mtshan see GYELTSEN
rygal rtse *see* GYANTSE
Rygård Castle 4 781
Rygg, Kittil 23 242
Rygge Church 26 646
Ryggen, Hannah 23 239
Rygh, Aase Texmon 23 231
Rygier, Teodor 25 115, 130
Rygnestad 30 116
ryijys see under CARPETS → types
Ryj, Dankers de *see* DANCKERTS DE RIJ
Rykantai 19 *494*
church 19 496
Rykr, Zdeněk 8 393
Ryland, Edward 27 463
Ryland, William Wynne 5 216; 9 43; 27 463*
works 5 216; 8 131; 13 220; 26 231; 27 716; 29 675; 32 426
Rylands, John, Library *see under* MANCHESTER (UK)
Rylands Haggadah *see under* HAGGADOT → individual manuscripts
Rylestone (N. Yorks), Burton Farm
roof 30 *908*
Ryley, John *see* RILEY, JOHN
Rylov, Arkady (Aleksandrovich) 27 463–4*
groups and movements 27 395; 31 582
pupils 6 499
teachers 18 502
Rym, Daniel 20 687
Rymaker, Hans 33 182
Ryman, James 23 690
Ryman, Robert 27 464*; 31 609
groups and movements 1 81
patrons and collectors 24 24; 27 478
prints 2 241
works 21 892
Rymschnyder, Dill *see* RIEMENSCHNEIDER, TILMAN
Rymsdyck, Jacob van 28 206
Rymsdyk, Jan van 1 844; 21 7
Ryn, Titus van *see* RIJN, TITUS (REMBRANDTSZ.) VAN
Ryn, W. Am 32 757
Rynck, de (family) 3 610
Ryndin, Vadim (Fyodorovich) 27 396, 464*
Rynkeby Cauldron 6 159
Ryōchū 17 747
Ryōkan 27 464–5*
works 17 216; 27 *465*
Ryōko Maki *see* MAKI RYŌKO
Ryorikh, Nikolay (Konstantinovich) *see* ROERICH, NICHOLAS
Ryōsai
works 17 *399*
Ryosai *see* URAGAMI GYOKUDŌ
Ryōsa Kohitsu *see* KOHITSU RYŌSA
Ryōsei 17 131
Ryōshū Maruyama *see* MARUYAMA, RYŌSHŪ
Ryōtai Tatebe *see* TATEBE RYŌTAI
Ryōyū 17 219
Ryozan Kuroda *see* KURODA RYOZAN
Ryōzen 17 170; 27 465*
Ryōzen Nishimura *see* NISHIMURA RYŌZEN
Rysbrack, Gerard 27 465
Rysbrack, Jacob 27 465
Rysbrack, Ludovicus 27 465
Rysbrack, (John) Michael 3 570; 10 372; 12 594; 27 465, 466–9*
collaboration 10 264; 12 595; 14 785; 17 768; 19 606
metalwork 7 446
methods 30 496
patrons and collectors 4 611; 7 286, 540; 12 594; 14 598, 842; 20 33; 25 635; 29 734; 30 890; 32 824
sculpture 10 264; 30 451, 499
equestrian monuments 4 821; 27 *467*
portraits 28 64, 844; 30 *499*
tombs 22 45, *46*; 27 *467*; 31 *128*, 129
Rysbrack, Pieter 27 465
Rysbrack, Pieter Andreas 4 611; 7 175; 27 465–6*
Rysbraeck *see* RYSBRACK
Ryssel, Paul Van *see* GACHET, PAUL(-FERDINAND) (1828-1909)
Rysselberghe, Octave Van *see* VAN RYSSELBERGHE, OCTAVE
Rysselberghe, Théo(phile) Van *see* VAN RYSSELBERGHE, THÉO(PHILE)
Ryssen, Warnard van 14 621
Rysum 23 501
Ryswyck, Dirk van 22 205
Ryszkiewicz, Andrzej 25 143
Ryt (Association of Polish Graphic Artists) 32 877
Ryt, Herman de 31 772
Rytkönen, Kerttu 2 317
Rytm *see* RHYTHM GROUP
Rytwiany Church 25 104
Ryuami 17 380
Ryuboku Chiba *see* CHIBA RYUBOKU
Ryūchikai (Dragon Pond Society) 17 200
see also NIHON BIJUTSU KYŌKAI
Ryūhei Murayama *see* MURAYAMA, RYŪHEI
Ryūho Hinaya *see* HINAYA RYŪHO
Ryuho Nonoguchi *see* NONOGUCHI RYUHO
Ryūichi Kuki *see* KUKI, RYŪCHI
Ryujo Hori *see* YAMADA, MATSUE
Ryū-jo Yamazaki *see* YAMAZAKI RYŪ-JO
Ryū Kobi *see* RYŪ SŌRO
Ryūkōkaku *see* IKENAGA DŌUN
Ryūkōsai 17 288
Ryūku Ingen *see* INGEN RYŪKU
Ryūkyū Islands 27 469–71*
architecture 27 470
blood 27 471
carving 18 601
castles 27 470
dyeing 27 470
earthenwares 27 470
gold leaf 27 471
ikat 27 471
lacquer 18 601, 602; 27 471, *471*
limestone 27 470, 471
manuals 27 471
mother-of-pearl 27 471, *471*
painting 27 470*
pottery 27 470
rice paste 27 470
roofs 27 470
sculpture 27 470*
silver leaf 27 471
stonewares 27 470
tattoos 17 414
temples 27 470
textiles 27 470–71*
tombs 27 470
trade 27 471
trays 27 471, *471*
Ryūmin *see* ONO MATAEMON
Ryumin, A. V. 17 805
Ryūmonji kiln 27 873
Ryurikovo Gorodishche 32 527
Ryūryūkyo Shinsai 17 287
Ryūsa 17 401
Ryūsai *see* ANDŌ HIROSHIGE
Ryūsei Kishida *see* KISHIDA, RYŪSEI
Ryūsendō Mayuyama *see* MAYUYAMA, RYŪSENDŌ
Ryushi *see* KOMADA, ISAMU
Ryūshi Kawabata *see* KAWABATA, RYŪSHI
Ryū Sōro 17 236, 411
Ryūzaburō Shikiba *see* SHIKIBA, RYŪZABURŌ
Ryūzaburō Umehara *see* UMEHARA, RYŪZABURŌ
Ryūzō Torii *see* TORII, RYŪZŌ
Rýžmberk (family) 8 422; 26 367
Rzaguliyev, A. A. 2 897
Rząsa, Antoni 18 429
Rzeszów Church 25 114

S

S, Master (*fl c.* 1520) 3 556; 20 802–3*
S, Painter (*fl c.* 520-480 BC) 13 511
S(udarsono), Srihadi 15 808
Sá, Estácio de 26 412
Saabye, August Vilhelm 8 741; 17 481
Sa'adan Toraja 15 789
Sa'adat 'Ali Khan 19 775
Sa'ad-Awwam 2 255
Saadi 10 486
Sääksmäki, Master of 11 98
Saal, Georg 28 104
Saalburg 27 105
Sā al-Hagar *see* SAIS
Saalhausen, Anton von 28 194
Saalkirchen see under CHURCHES → types
Saami art 11 110; 23 217; 27 472*; 32 288
Saarbrücken
  Ludwigskirche 19 815; 29 630
  Schloss 2 234; 5 348
Saarburck, Bartolomé *see* SARBURGH, BARTHOLOMÄUS
Saarela, Heikki 24 370
Saarinen, Eero 9 502, 503; 27 474–8*
  architecture
    airports
      John F. Kennedy Airport, Transworld Airlines Terminal (New York) 1 495; 7 696; 23 43; 27 *128*, 129; 30 853
      Washington Dulles International Airport (Chantilly, VA: USA) 27 *477*; 30 468
    chapels 4 790; 27 212
    commercial buildings 3 858
    government buildings 8 278
    museums 22 365
    public monuments 19 305; 22 48; 27 565; 31 352
    stadia 23 25; 29 *490*
    theatres 14 200; 30 684
    university buildings 4 475
  collaboration 7 259; 23 273; 24 457; 29 489; 31 597, 633
  competitions 7 669
  furniture 1 738; 31 633
  groups and movements 10 698
  sculpture 24 574
  staff 24 342; 26 479; 32 234
  tables 30 218, *218*
Saarinen, Eero, and Associates 27 476
Saarinen, (Gottlieb) Eliel 11 92, 110; 12 498; 27 473–5*
  collaboration 19 407; 24 457; 27 475; 31 597
  groups and movements 23 498
  pupils 33 29
  works 10 683; 11 92, 100, 104, 105; 12 145; 14 371; 20 460; 22 365; 27 *473*; 30 349; 31 595, 728
Saarinen, Loja 11 54; 31 660
Saarinen, Swanson and Saarinen 27 476
Saarinen and Swanson 27 476; 33 254
Saarnio, Bertel 19 114
Saatchi, Charles 2 561; 10 367; 19 590; 27 478*
Saatchi, Doris 2 561; 27 478
Saavedra, Gustavo 23 369
Saavedra, Hernandarias de 24 93
Saavedra, Juan de 31 852
Saa y Faría, José Custodio de 31 753
Saba (Netherlands Antilles) 2 144; 5 *745*
  see also ANTILLES, LESSER; ANTILLES, NETHERLANDS
Saba (*fl* early 9th cent.) 30 305
Saba' (Yemen) 2 268
Saba'a (Iraq) 21 299
Sabadini, Lorenzo *see* SABATINI, LORENZO
al-Sabah (Kuwait) *see*:
  ABDULLAH AL-JABER AL-SABAH, Shaykh
  HUSSA SABAH AL-SALEM AL-SABAH, Shaykha
  NASSER SABAH AL-AHMAD AL-SABAH, Shaykh
Sabah (Malaysia) 5 *10*; 15 *751*; 20 162, 164
  architecture 21 45
  brass 20 173, 180
  headcloths 20 176
  jewellery 20 180
  keris 20 174
  Sabah State Museum 29 240
  sarcophagi 27 831
  see also MALAYSIA
Sabará 4 *705*
  Nossa Senhora do Ó 4 710
Sabartés y Gual, Jaime 13 765; 24 722; 26 522; 27 478*
Sabatelli, Luigi 5 918; 11 189; 16 677; 21 527; 27 478–9*
  patrons and collectors 4 471
  pupils 3 856, 903; 15 819
Sabatier, François 24 59
Sabatier, R. G. B. 10 91
Sabatier effect *see under* PHOTOGRAPHY → processes
Sabatini, Andrea 27 479*
Sabatini, Lorenzo 27 480*
  assistants 26 89
  collaboration 5 441; 8 181; 32 17
  patrons and collectors 13 628
  pupils 4 308, 812
  reproductive prints by others 5 856
  works 26 818
Sabatini, Rodolfo 5 19
Sabatios *see* SAVVATY
Sabatke, Manfred 3 510
sabatons 2 469
Sabattini, Lino 24 147
Sabattini, Lorenzo *see* SABATINI, LORENZO
Sabaudia 16 650; 31 730
Sabaudian Residences, Master of the 28 12
Sabavala, Jehangir 4 291
Sabbas of Palestine, Saint 26 483
Sabbatini, Francesco 27 480–82*; 31 88
  assistants 29 341; 31 72
  collaboration 31 72
  patrons and collectors 4 561, 562, 563, 565; 27 487; 29 271
  teachers 31 895
  works 2 284; 20 73; 24 108; 27 *481*, 753; 28 369; 29 271, 293, 315, 341; 31 823
Sabbatini, Innocenzo 10 820
Sabbatini, Lorenzo *see* SABATINI, LORENZO
Sabbatini, Niccolò 24 534; 27 274, 482*; 30 667, 668
Sabbioneta 12 910; 16 *618*; 27 482–4*, *483*; 31 712
  Palazzo Ducale 27 483
    Galleria degli Antichi 1 551; 12 910; 16 771
Sabbioneta—cont.
  Teatro Ducale 27 483–4; 28 32, *32*; 30 656
Sabbioneta, Vespasiano Gonzaga, Duca da 12 *904*, 910–11*
  architecture 20 278; 27 482–3; 28 32; 31 712
  paintings 1 551; 5 547
  sculpture 16 771; 19 203
Sabereebi 12 323
Sabi *see* PUYŌ
Sabi Abyad, Tell 30 196
Sabina, Empress of Rome (*fl* 117-138) 27 37
Sabina von Steinbach 33 308
Sabine, Wallace Clement 1 122; 4 474; 13 757
Sabine Shawl 7 828
Sabinov 7 301; 14 899; 28 854
Sabinus, G. 23 680
Sabioneda, Gianlorenzo Gonzaga, Duke of, Prince of Bezzolo *see* RÓDIGO, GIANFRANCESCO GONZAGA, Conte di
Säbisch, Albrecht von 19 815
Sabit Khan 1 639
sable *see under* HAIR → types
Sablet, (Jean-)François 27 484*
Sablet, Jacob (1720-98) 27 484
Sablet, Jacques (-Henri) (1749-1803) 27 484–5*
sablé work *see under* BEADWORK → types
Sablier, Editions du 20 547
Sablière, Charles-Michel Trudaine de la *see* TRUDAINE DE LA SABLIÈRE, CHARLES-MICHEL
Sabloff, Jeremy A. 28 26
Sablonière, H. de Lussanet de la *see* LUSSANET DE LA SABLONIÈRE, H. DE
Sablons, Moly-Sabata *see* MOLY-SABATA
Sabni 2 656
Sabni and Mekhu 2 656; 9 838
Sabogal (Diéguez), José 27 485*
  pupils 5 527; 13 322; 14 875; 29 434
  works 24 509
Sabogen *see* SAVOYE
Sabon *see under* TYPE-FACES
Sabongida-Ora 9 734
Sabouret, V. 20 584
Sabouroff Painter 13 523, 536; 32 28
Sabra al-Mansuriyya *see* AL-MANSURIYYA
Sabratha 9 *510*; 13 *362*; 27 485*
  baptisteries 3 191
  basilica 9 570
  Mausoleum B 13 407
  pottery 13 536
  sculpture 27 18, 19
  theatre 11 231; 26 873, 883, 919, *920*; 30 651
sabres 2 456; 6 261; 16 503, *506*, 508
Sabri, 'Ata 16 2
Sabri, Mahmoud 16 2
Sabry, Ahmed 9 766
Sabsay, Pinkhos 2 895; 15 133
Sabsovich, Leonid 27 379
Šabuneiūski, S. 3 527
Saburō Asō *see* ASŌ, SABURŌ
Saburō Hasegawa *see* HASEGAWA, SABURŌ
Saburō Murakami *see* MURAKAMI, SABURŌ
Saburōsuke Okada *see* OKADA, SABURŌSUKE
Sabya 32 315
Sa Canova 3 105
Sacastene *see* SISTAN
Sacavém factory 30 881, 882
Sacca, Paolo 31 278
Sacchetti (family) 27 485–6*
  architecture 7 911, 912
  collections 16 768
  paintings 3 708; 4 491; 7 902, 906; 26 198
Sacchetti, Alessandro 7 910; 27 485–6
Sacchetti, Franco 15 85
Sacchetti, Giovanni Battista 17 710; 27 485, 486–7*; 29 304
  assistants 26 519; 32 563
  patrons and collectors 4 558, 560; 5 902
  works 2 379; 20 72, *72*; 27 753; 29 271
Sacchetti, Giovanni Francesco 27 485–6
Sacchetti, Giulio, Cardinal 4 491; 27 485–6
Sacchetti, Marcello 25 386; 27 485–6
Sacchetti, Urbano, Cardinal 27 486
Sacchetto, Bartolomeo 5 180
Sacchi, Andrea 27 487–91*
  assistants 5 454; 12 648; 20 374
  book illustrations 18 735
  collaboration 5 453, 454; 7 907; 21 483; 27 643, 893
  groups and movements 3 266
  mosaics 26 810
  paintings
    altarpieces 26 810
    frescoes 1 659; 12 679; 16 671; 26 822, 837; 27 *488*
    history 17 *511*; 32 101
    oil sketches 23 381
    portraits 4 560; 27 *491*
    religious 5 450; 27 *489*, *490*
  patrons and collectors 10 406; 32 75
    Barberini, Antonio, Cardinal 3 208
    Barberini, Taddeo 3 208
    Bourbon del Monte, Francesco Maria, Cardinal 4 567
    Castel Rodrigo, Manuel de Moura y Corte Real, 2nd Marqés de 6 30
    Einden, Jan van 10 114
    Ensenada, Marqués de 10 406
    Giori, Angelo, Cardinal 12 680
    Jesuit Order 17 511
    Medinaceli, 9th Duque de 21 35
    Pascoli, Lione 24 225
    Spencer, John, 1st Earl Spencer 29 381
    Urban VIII, Pope (*reg* 1623-44) 3 206
    Vassal de Saint-Hubert, Jean-Antione-Hubert 32 75
  pupils 3 96; 12 169; 20 374; 33 82
  reproductive prints by others 3 208
  teachers 1 534, 535
Sacchi, Bartolomeo 12 907; 27 806
Sacchi, Benedetto 27 487
Sacchis(, Giovanni Antonio) de *see* PORDENONE
Sacco Altarpiece 6 113
Saccomanno, Stefano 31 131
Sacconi, Carlo 21 30
Sacconi, Giuseppe 27 492*
  works 16 645, 764; 19 687; 22 42, 47; 26 762, *763*
Sacerdos, Nicolaus 31 279
Sachar, Edith 27 220
Sachelarie-Vladimirescu, Wanda 27 493*
Sacher, Maja 3 336
Sáchez-Felipe, Alejandro 25 701
Sachio Ōtani *see* ŌTANI, SACHIO
Sachs, Conrad 18 450; 20 747
Sachs, Curt 22 376
Sachs, Hans 19 661; 28 143, 144; 29 719; 33 354
  works 12 *621*; 24 *106*
Sachs, Paul J(oseph) 9 231; 27 493*; 31 671
Sachse, E. and Company
  works 2 *121*
Sachse, Edward 4 81
Sachse, Louis Friedrich 3 800
Sachse, Melchior 20 791
Sachsen, Clemens Wenzeslaus von, Elector and Archbishop of Trier 24 582; 27 623
Sacilotto, Luís 4 719
Sackenheim, Rolf 13 727
Sackett, Augustine 24 51
sacking 27 317
Sackler, Arthur M. 6 868; 7 156; 27 493*
Sackler, Arthur M., Museum *see under* CAMBRIDGE (MA; USA) → Harvard University
Sackler, Arthur M. Gallery *see under* WASHINGTON (DC) → museums
Säcklingen, Fridolinsmünster
  Fridolin Shrine 12 447
Sackville, Anne, Countess of Dorset 18 795
Sackville, Charles, 2nd Duke of Dorset (1711-69) 13 301
Sackville, Charles, 6th Earl of Dorset (1638-1706) 30 783
Sackville, Edward, 4th Earl of Dorset 9 *277*
Sackville, John Frederick, 3rd Duke of Dorset 26 276; 27 494*
Sackville, Lionel Cranfield, 1st Duke of Dorset 18 146; 19 418; 27 493–4*
Sackville, Richard, 3rd Earl of Dorset 18 795
Sackville, Thomas, 1st Earl of Dorset 23 689
Sackville, Victoria 28 384, 528
Sackville-West, Vita 12 142; 27 494
Saco, Carmen 24 509
Sacoccia, Cola 26 766
Sacquesepée, Adrien 27 494*
Sacquesepée, Pierre 27 494
sacra conversazione see under PAINTING → types
Sacra di San Michele Abbey 16 625
Sacramenia 29 263
Sacramentaries 1 697; 5 800; 21 729
  individual manuscripts
    Drogo Sacramentary (Paris, Bib. N., MS. lat. 9428) 5 803, 810; 20 330; 21 *729*, 729; 31 499
    Figeac Sacramentary (Paris, Bib. N., MS. lat. 2293) 26 670
    Gellone Sacramentary (Paris, Bib. N., MS. lat. 2048) 21 164, 729
    Hildoard Sacramentary (Cambrai, Bib. Mun., MS. 164) 25 743
    Hornbach Sacramentary (Solothurn, Ursuskirche) 23 653

Sacramentaries
individual manuscripts—cont.
Marmoutier Sacramentary (Autun, Bib. Mun., MS. 19bis) 31 227
Mont-St-Michel Sacramentary (New York, Pierpont Morgan Lib., MS. M. 641) 26 669
Petershausen Sacramentary (Heidelberg, Ubib., Cod. Sal. IXb) 23 653
Ratmann Sacramentary (Hildesheim, Diözmus. & Domschatzkam., Cod. 37) 14 532; 26 662, 675
Sacramentary of Gelasianum (Rome, Vatican, Bib. Apostolica, MS. Reg. lat. 316) 6 174; 11 529; 21 164
Sacramentary of Henry II (Munich, Bayer. Staatsbib., Clm. 4456) 7 513; 23 652, 654; 28 25
Sacramentary of Limoges Cathedral (Paris, Bib. N., MS. lat. 9438) 8 857; 11 530
Sacramentary of Robert Jumièges see MISSALS → individual manuscripts → Missal of Robert of Jumièges
Sacramentary of St Alban (Malibu, CA, Getty Mus., MS. Ludwig V.2) 23 655
Saint-Amand Sacramentary (Valenciennes, Bib. Mun., MS. 108) 26 668
St Gereon Sacramentary (Paris, Bib. N., MS. lat. 817) 23 654
Šibenik Sacramentary (Šibenik, Franciscan Monastery) 8 177
Utrecht Sacramentary (Berlin, Staatsbib. Preuss. Kultbes., MS. 691) 22 833
see also MISSALS
sacrament houses 9 680, 681
Sacramento, Antonio 29 296
Sacrati (family) 12 162
Sacrati, Bartolomeo 31 430
Sacrati, Francesco 31 165
Sacrati, Pietro 31 430
Sacrati, Uberto 31 430
sacred groves 12 68; 13 *418*, 418–19
sacred lakes 9 832; 27 496–7*; 30 432
sacred monuments see under MONUMENTS → types
sacrimonti 27 497–500*, *498*; 31 *898*
see also MONASTERIES
Sacripanti, Maurizio 25 738
Sacriste, Eduardo 2 397
sacristries 27 497*
sacristy cupboards see under CUPBOARDS → types
Sacristy of Siena Cathedral, Masters of the see SIENA CATHEDRAL, MASTERS OF THE SACRISTY OF
Sacrobosco, Joannes de see JOANNES DE SACROBOSCO
Sacro Speco see SUBIACO → San Beneddetto Abbey
Sacrow, Heilandskirche 25 173
Sacs, Joan 29 308
Sacsahuaman 23 826; 27 501*; 29 *156*; 30 447
fortifications 21 599
masonry 29 164
temple 29 167
Săcueni 26 712
Saʿd 16 127
SAD see SOCIÉTÉ DES ARTISTES-DÉCORATEURS
Saʿda
congregational mosque 16 214, 500
domes 16 215
houses 33 519, *519*
Saʿda—cont.
silver 33 520
Sada, Carlo 31 442
Sada, D. 21 396
Sadahide Utagawa see UTAGAWA SADAHIDE
Sadaie no Fujiwara see FUJIWARA NO TEIKA
Sadajirō Yamanaka see YAMANAKA, SADAJIRŌ
Saʿd al-Din al-Isʿirdi 16 379
Sadali, Achmad 15 808
Sadamasa Katagiri see KATAGIRI SEKISHŪ
Sadamasa Motonaga see MOTONAGA, SADAMASA
Sadamitsu Sugimoto see SUGIMOTO, SADAMITSU
Sadang 18 338, 339, 340
Sadanobu, Fujiwara no see FUJIWARA NO SADANOBU
Sadanobu Hasegawa (i) see HASEGAWA SADANOBU (i)
Sadanobu Kano see KANŌ KŌI
Sadanobu Matsudaira see MATSUDAIRA SADANOBU
Saʾdan Toraja 15 789, 807; 23 555
houses 15 *807*
Sadao, Shoji 11 835
works 12 *311*
Sadarbs (Co-operation) 28 715; 33 601
Sada Shrine 17 160
Sadatoki Hōjō see HŌJŌ SADATOKI, Shogunal Regent
Sadatsugu Tsutsui see TSUTSUI SADATSUGU
Sadayori, Fujiwara no see FUJIWARA NO SADAYORI
Saddam Hussein 3 10, 53; 10 833; 20 149
saddleback roofs see under ROOFS → types
saddle-bags 3 *755*; 31 *406*
Saddlers' Company 11 810
saddlery 1 762; 10 873
saddles 14 182, 186; 17 300, 301, 302, 362, 364; 21 878; 31 407
Sadée, Jacob Frederik 16 575
Sadée, Philip 14 47
Sadeleer, Raphael, I 17 918
Sadeler (family) 25 432
patrons and collectors 23 113; 25 815
works 5 605; 12 390; 17 183; 29 431
Sadeler, Aegidius, I (1560-1609) 27 501, 502–4*
collaboration 32 711
works 1 5, 663; 27 502, 503, *503*; 29 377; 32 711
Sadeler, Aegidius, II (1570-1629) 10 389; 29 648, 649
groups and movements 9 446
patrons and collectors 13 914; 27 501; 32 6
pupils 27 725; 28 826
teachers 27 501
works 1 6; 2 105; 5 606; 8 390; 9 *446*; 11 754; 12 909; 14 321, 682; 25 *432*; 27 885; 28 189; 29 431, 649
Sadeler, Daniel 2 455, 462
Sadeler, Emanuel 2 455, 462
Sadeler, Filips 5 605; 27 501, 504–5*
Sadeler, Jan, I (1550-1600) 27 501–4*
assistants 27 504
copies 25 827
methods 21 765
patrons and collectors 33 274
printmakers 33 169
pupils 4 221; 27 502, 503
works 3 230; 11 222; 22 370; 26 301; 27 *502*; 28 189; 30 35; 32 711; 33 252
Sadeler, Jan, II (1588-1665) 2 105; 27 501, 504*
Sadeler, Justus (Josse) 2 105; 25 626; 27 501, 504*
Sadeler, Philipp see SADELER, FILIPS
Sadeler, Raphael, I (1560/61-*d c.* 1628/32) 10 389; 27 501, 502–4*
collaboration 27 502, 504
patrons and collectors 27 502; 33 274
works 27 228, 501; 29 431; 32 711; 33 252, 253
Sadeler, Raphael, II (1584-after 1632) 27 504*
Sadeler, Tobias 27 501
Sadequain 23 *800*; 27 505*
patrons and collectors 23 804
works 16 288; 23 799, 800
Sadequain Museum see under ISLAMABAD
Sad Hazard 1 205
Saʿdi (dynasty) 16 119, 240; 27 505–6*
see also:
ʿABDALLAH, Sultan
AHMAD II AL-MANSUR, Sultan
Saʿdi (*d* 1292) 27 513; 28 616
Saʿd ibn Abi Wakkas 18 498
Saʿd ibn Zangi 28 616
Sadikov, Sergey 8 437
Sadiq (*fl c.* 1750-1800) see MUHAMMAD SADIQ
Sadiq, Mahmoud (*b* 1945) 17 655
Sadiq ʿAli Khan 15 380
Sadiqi 27 506*, 514
patrons and collectors 27 513
teachers 22 391
works 16 337, 338, *338*
writings 16 127
Sadis, Dionigi 5 872
Sadler (family) 16 16
Sadler, John 19 508; 29 495; 30 877
Sadler, Michael 10 367; 22 55; 23 690
Sadler, Walter Dendy 9 54
Sadler, William 23 345
Sadler & Green 10 306, 307, 346; 19 508; 33 20
works 30 *875*
Sadley, Wojciech 25 133
Sado 17 318
Bunya theatre 17 350
Fumonin 17 349
Shōbō temple 17 395
Sadolin, Ebbe 7 807
Sadoul, Georges 30 20
Sadovy 28 325
al-Sadr, Said 9 767
Sadruddin Aga Khan, Prince (*fl* 1980s) 15 743, 748; 16 295, 555
Sadsbury Township (PA)
John Truman House 32 *300*, 301
Sadun, Prince of Vaspurakan (*fl* 1273) 14 36
Sadurni, Antonio 29 349
Sadus 32 316
Sadykov, Marat (Faiziyevich) 31 783
Sadykov, Turgunbaj 18 568
Sadzeguri 1 505
Saeben Cathedral 2 776
Saebisch, Valentin von 33 417
Saedeleer, K. De see DE SAEDELEER, K.
Saedeleer, Valerius De see DE SAEDELEER, VALERIUS
Saeed, Anwar 23 799
Saeki, Yūzō 27 506–7*
Saeki Hanroku 14 37
Saeki no Emishi 22 427
Sá e Meneses, Rodrigo Aires de, Marquês de Fontes see FONTES E ABRANTES, Marquês de
Sæmundsson, Nína 15 70
Saen, Gillis de 14 709
Saenredam, Jan (Pietersz.) 10 387; 12 812; 25 625; 27 507*
collaboration 12 879
Saenredam, Jan (Pietersz.)—cont.
methods 31 578
patrons and collectors 15 40
teachers 12 532
works 4 152; 11 *456*; 12 881; 13 896; 22 839; 25 *612*; 27 *510*; 31 881
Saenredam, Pieter (Jansz.) 13 895; 27 507–11*
collaboration 4 488; 23 611
groups and movements 8 669
patrons and collectors 3 889
reproductive prints by others 1 121; 13 *893*; 32 140
works 1 *585*; 2 341; 22 686, 818, 840; 24 490; 27 *509*; 28 309; 31 769
Sáenz, Adolfo 1 783
Sáenz, Cesar 33 472
Sáenz, Leoncio 23 84, 86; 25 455
Sáenz Comacho, Alvaro 21 4
Sáenz de Oíza, Francisco Javier 21 861; 27 511*; 29 274
Saenz de Santa María, José Marcos see VALDE-IÑIGO, Marqués de
Saenz de Tejada, Carlos 10 822
Saepinum Macellum 19 889
Saether, Emil
works 10 *194*
Sætrang, Bente 23 241
Sáez, Agustín 24 622
Sáez, Carlos Federico 27 511*; 31 754, 757, 758
Sáez y López, José 28 513
S.A.F. 30 704
Safad 16 208; 18 153
Safadi 1 869; 30 183
Safar, Fuad 1 894; 10 460, 461
Safara Monastery Church 12 323
Safavid 16 119, 121, 122; 27 512–13*
architecture 17 830; 22 438; 25 778
art policies 16 100
palaces 23 816
trade
textiles 27 512
turbans 16 454
see also:
ʿABBAS I, Shah
BAHRAM MIRZA, Prince
HAMZA MIRZA
HUSAYN I, Shah
HUSSAIN, Shah
IBRAHIM MIRZA
ISMAʿIL I, Shah
ISMAʿIL II, Shah
SAFI, Shah
SAM MIRZA
SULAYMAN I, Shah
TAHMASP I, Shah
Safdar Khan 27 858
Safdie, Moshe 27 514–15*
collaboration 31 864
works 5 562, *563*, 573, 591; 10 685; 16 566–7; 22 36; 26 17
Safed 17 500
synagogues 17 552
Safed, Shalom von 27 515–16*
safes 17 358
Saff, Donald 19 493
Saffarid, ʿAmr ibn Layths see ʿAMR IBN LAYTH, Amir
ṣaff carpets see under CARPETS → types
Saffi see SAFI
safflower
historical and regional traditions
China 7 45
Iran 16 449
Islamic 16 449
Japan 17 277, 282, 308
uses
dyes 7 45; 9 492; 16 449; 17 308
lacquer 18 600
pigments 17 277; 18 656
prints 17 282
safflower oil see under OILS → types
Saffoi see SAVOYE
saffron
uses
dyes 9 492
glazes 12 623
pigments 24 799
Saffron Master 7 235
Saffron Walden (Essex) 18 585
saff-tombs see under TOMBS → types
Safi (Morocco) 16 427, 470; 22 129
Safi, Shah (*reg* 1629-42) (Safavid) 16 78
Safi, Tell es- (Jordan) 24 634
Safid Buland 16 258
Safita 6 58; 17 501; 21 564
Safiya 5 398
Safiye Sultan 8 579; 16 223
Safont, Jordi 27 516
Safont, Marc 27 516*
works 3 215, *215*; 13 69
Safronov Factory 27 413
Saftleven, Abraham 27 516
Saftleven, Cornelis 27 230, 516–18*
collaboration 27 518
patrons and collectors 7 418; 28 309
pupils 14 709
reproductive prints by others 12 851
works 27 *517*
Saftleven, Herman, I (*c.* 1580-1627) 27 516; 28 358
Saftleven, Herman, II (1609-85) 27 230, 516, 517–19*; 32 700
collaboration 27 516
methods 8 128
patrons and collectors 10 864; 27 271
personal collection 28 358
reproductive prints by others 1 681
works 27 *518*
Saftleven, Sara 27 516
Saga, Emperor (*reg* 809-23) 27 519*
calligraphy 17 214, 219, 221; 18 503
groups and movements 18 502
masks 17 391
poetry 17 154
sagabon see under BOOKS → forms
Saga dolls see under DOLLS → types
Sagaholm 25 530
Sagaing 5 *221*, 241; 27 519*; 29 *225*
Htupa-yon 5 234, *234*
Kaung-hmu-daw 5 234
Tilawka-guru 5 244
Sagalassos 13 *362*; 26 *908*; 27 519*
architecture 26 913
churches 9 536
odeion 23 349
Sagar 15 494
sculpture 15 *495*
Sagara 17 373
Sagar Tal Tomb 13 882
Sagarviñaga, Juan de 7 362, 363
Sage, Esther 3 701
Sage, Kay 27 520*; 28 914; 30 291
groups and movements 30 22
patrons and collectors 20 832
works 18 718
Sage, Le see LE SAGE
Sage, Louis 4 526
Sage, Russell, Foundation 2 698; 31 729
Sagebiel, Ernst 3 796
Sagen, Trygve 30 533
Sageot, Nicolas 11 596
Sagert, Hermann 14 304
saggars 6 329; 27 520*
China 6 869, 895
Japan 17 253

Saggi e Memorie di Storia dell'Arte 7 331
Saghen, Nicolas van 21 596
Sagla-Bazha II
bone 2 *101*
Saglio 10 211
Sagnier i Villavechia, Enrique 29 321
Sagonne, Jacques Hardouin Mansart de *see* MANSART DE SAGONNE, JACQUES HARDOUIN
Sagós 11 479
Sagot, Clovis 29 604
Sagot, Edmond 19 215, 488; 20 603
Sagra di San Michele Abbey 21 840; 26 578, 620
Sagramoro, Giacomo da *see* GIACOMO DA SANCINO
Sagredo (family) 11 871
Sagredo, Cecilia Grimani 27 521
Sagredo, Diego de 27 520*
groups and movements 25 31
patrons and collectors 11 250
works 2 356; 23 487; 24 274; 29 265, 356; 31 297; 32 641
Sagredo, Gherardo 27 521; 31 524
Sagredo, Niccolò 7 902; 20 374
Sagredo, Zaccaria 5 594; 6 36; 24 703; 27 521*
Sagrera, Antonio 27 521
Sagrera, Guillem 27 521*; 29 289
patrons and collectors 2 276
works 3 106; 13 68, 106; 23 881
Sagrestani, Giovanni Camillo 16 674; 27 521–2*
attributions 25 891
collaboration 25 890
patrons and collectors 21 31
pupils 4 315; 25 890
teachers 7 309
works 11 194; 27 *522*
Sagri *see* SANKRI
Saguia al-Hamra 33 97
Sagunto, S María 13 106
Saguntum 21 558
Sa'gya *see* SAKYA
Sahaba 23 286
Sahagún
Royal Abbey 7 473
S Benito 26 607; 29 333
S Juan 29 336
S Lorenzo 22 255; 29 263
S Tirso 22 255; 29 263
Sahagún, Bernardino de 16 859; 21 183, 191, 255, 262, 264; 31 65, 505; 33 472
Sahagún, García de 29 335
Sahaptian 22 645
Sahar, Lian 33 538
Sahara, Spanish *see* WESTERN SAHARA
Sahara, Western *see* WESTERN SAHARA
Sahara' al-Gharbiyah *see* WESTERN SAHARA
sahari see under ALLOYS → types
Sahda 9 621
al-Saheli 30 914
Saher, Eduard A. von 22 867
Saheth-Maheth *see* SRAVASTI
Sahib Ata Fakhr al-Din 'Ali 17 864; 18 234; 28 809
Sahibdin (*fl* 1628-55) 15 228, 547, 598
attributions 15 *227*
works 7 VI2; 15 *599*
Sahibdin (*fl c.* 1770) 15 615
Sahibram 15 610
Şahinefendi Monastery 5 674
Sahinyan, A. 17 827
Sahione Fadel, Sérgio 4 725
Şahkulu *see* SHAHQULI
Sahl Church 8 738
Sahle Sellasé, Emperor of Ethiopia (*reg* 1813-47) 10 573
Sahlström, Anna 33 187
Sahni, Rai Bahadur Daya Ram 14 162; 15 418
Sahri Bahlol 5 94; 15 *264*; 23 *797*; 27 522*
Mound C 15 *447*
sculpture 15 448
Sahsarām *see* SASARAM
Sahuaraura, Manuel de 24 502
Sahure (*reg c.* 2458-*c.* 2446 BC) 1 96; 9 *776*, 779, 870, 871; 30 433
Šahy Monastery 28 849
Sahyun *see* SIGON
Sai 23 *276*, 278
Saia, Jorge *see* ZONTAL, JORGE
Saichi 17 101
Saichō 5 116; 10 404; 14 302; 18 503, 549, 552
architecture 10 404
calligraphy 10 404; 17 214, 219
carvings 10 404
Sa Icu 27 835
Said, Edward 2 533
el-Said, Issam (Sabah) 16 2; 27 523*
Said, Mahmud 5 401; 9 766; 22 431; 27 523*
al-Said, Shaker Hassan 16 2; 27 523*
Saida *see* SIDON
Said Qala 1 185
Saidu Master 27 524
Saidu Sharif 27 523–4*
Swat Museum 23 804
Saigon *see* HO CHI MINH CITY
Saigyō 11 823
Saijirō Gotō *see* GOTŌ SAIJIRŌ
sai-kai see under LACQUER → types
Saikaku Ihara *see* IHARA SIKAKU
Saïkali, Nadia 3 366
Saikō Ema *see* EMA SAIKŌ
Saikyō *see* KYOTO
Saillant, Charles-Philibert Lasteyerie du, Comte de *see* LASTEYERIE DU SAILLANT, CHARLES-PHILIBERT, Comte de
Saillant, Jean 24 330
Sailly 10 782
Sailmaker, Isaac 20 424
Sailo, Alpo 22 540
sail vaults *see under* VAULTS (CEILING) → types
Saimaly Tash 10 896
Sa-im-dang *see* SIN SA-IM-DANG
Saimyōji 17 74
hondō 17 *73*
Šain, Petar 4 461
Sainsaulieu, Max 26 113
Sainsbury (family) 23 248; 27 524
Sainsbury, David 23 249; 27 524
Sainsbury, Lisa 23 249, 742; 27 524
Sainsbury, Robert 10 367, 371; 23 249, 742; 27 524*
Sainsbury Centre for the Visual Arts *see under* NORWICH → University of East Anglia
Saint, C. A. 19 274
Saint, Daniel 4 303
Saint, Jean 22 897
Saint, Thomas 3 897
St Agnes Cup *see* ROYAL GOLD CUP
St Agnes Lighthouse 19 361
Saint-Aignan, Paul-Hippolyte de Beauvillier, Duc de 27 524*
paintings 4 128; 24 772; 29 887; 31 306; 32 331
St Albans (Herts) 10 *225*; 26 *905*; 27 525–8*, *526*
Cathedral (Abbey) 10 266; 12 592; 20 571; 26 588, 589; 27 *526*, 526–7
altarpieces 11 420
Chantry Chapel of Humphrey, Duke of Gloucester 13 84
chronicles 7 243
door fittings 10 339
doors 9 155
furniture 10 287
St Albans (Herts)
Cathedral (Abbey)—cont.
gate-house 12 175
Great Screen 13 84
ivory-carvings 26 697
jewellery 10 344
Lady Chapel 3 121; 18 621, *621*
manuscripts 10 244; 26 659, *671*, 671–2; 27 *528*
rood 27 124
sculpture 13 121; 26 616
shrine 13 82; 28 630
shrine of St Alban 31 273
transept 26 *588*
Eleanor cross 27 527
fortifications 21 560
forum 26 905
hill-fort 25 536
ivory-carvings 26 696, 697
manuscripts 13 *131*; 18 674; 20 331, *341*; 26 662; 27 527–8*, *528*; 30 486
mosaics 27 63
Newhouse Park 22 *60*
Roman forum 27 525
Roman theatre 27 526
theatre 26 905
urban planning 27 3
Verulamium 27 *525*, 525–6*
St Albans, Charles Beauclerk, 1st Duke of *see* BEAUCLERK, CHARLES, 1st Duke of St Albans
St Albans, Francis Bacon, Viscount *see* BACON, FRANCIS, 1st Baron Verulam & Viscount St Albans
St Albans, Henry Jermyn, 1st Earl of *see* JERMYN, HENRY, 1st Earl of St Albans
St Albans, Hugh of *see* HUGH OF ST ALBANS
St Albans, John of *see* JOHN OF ST ALBANS
St Albans, William Beauclerk, 10th Duke of *see* BEAUCLERK, WILLIAM, 10th Duke of St Albans
St Albans Psalter *see under* PSALTERS → individual manuscripts
Saint-Amand-les-Eaux 13 19
ceramics 3 590; 31 220
manuscripts 5 804; 26 668, *668*
tiles 30 885
Saint-Amand Sacramentary *see under* SACRAMENTARIES → individual mansucripts
St Anastasio, Master of 3 818
St Anathasios 9 546
Saint-André, Jacques d'Albon, Maréchal de 19 18, 237
Saint-André, Simon Renard de 31 883
Saint-André-de-Cubzac, Château de Bouilh 6 509
Saint André-de-Sorède Church 26 609
Saint-André-la-Cateau 27 592
St Andrew, Bellevue 5 749; 16 882
St Andrew, Master of *see* LEONARD, MASTER
St Andrews (Fife) 27 528–30*; 28 *222*
Castle 27 530*
Cathedral of St Andrew 22 216; 26 591; 27 529*, *529*; 28 267
pilgrim badges 24 808
Royal and Ancient Golf Club 29 426
St Rule's Church 26 591; 27 *529*
University 7 566
library 28 275
St Salvators College chapel 28 251, 268
St Andrew's cross *see under* CROSSES → types
St Andrews Cupboard 28 250, *251*
St Anne Altarpiece, Master of the 20 797
St Ann Parish (Jamaica) 16 880
St Anns Bay (town; Jamaica), Garvey statue 16 889
St Anthony's cross *see* CROSSES → types → *tau*
St Antoine-en-Barbefosse chapel 13 100
St Antönien 30 144
Saint-Antonin-Noble-Val 11 655; 32 280
Saint-Arnoul 26 598
Saint-Aubin, Augustin de 19 641; 27 530, 531*
pupils 9 364; 28 464
reproductive prints by others 9 365
teachers 5 884
works 3 395; 4 166; 10 823; 23 520
Saint-Aubin, Charles-Germain de 9 378; 27 530*
Saint-Aubin, Gabriel (-Jacques) de 11 541; 24 135; 27 524, 530–31*
groups and movements 24 136
pupils 27 531
works 5 354; 10 677; 11 631; 19 26; 24 135; 27 *531*; 31 704
writings 8 210
Saint-Aubin, Gabriel-Germain de 27 530
St Aubin, J. P. 29 695
Saint-Aubin, Louis-Michel de 27 530
St Augustine (FL) 27 531–2*; 31 *587*
Castillo de San Marcos *see* Fort Marion
Fort Marion 5 124; 14 814; 21 573; 22 593, 594; 27 532, *532*; 28 741; 31 588
Ponce de Leon Hotel 14 787
St Augustine, Master of 20 757–8*
St Augustine Gospels *see under* GOSPEL BOOKS → individual manuscripts
St Auta, Master of 20 758*
Saint-Avit-Sénieur Church 26 584
St Barbara, Master of the Legend of *see* LEGEND OF ST BARBARA, MASTER OF THE
St Barlaam 9 548; 12 331
St Barthélémy (French Antilles) 2 144; 5 *745*
St Bartholomew Altar, Master of the 7 583; 20 758–9*
works 12 384, *409*; 20 *758*
Saint Béat 27 13
St Beatus, Master of 20 641
St Bees Priory (Cumbria) 26 614
St Beňadik on the Hron 28 851
Saint-Benoît-sur-Loire Abbey 3 708; 7 266; 11 *504*; 26 599; 27 533–5*
capitals 26 596
church 7 *253*; 26 585, 586; 27 *533*, 533–4*
capitals 27 *534*
choir-stalls 13 126
sculpture 26 595; 27 534–5*
manuscript illumination 2 76; 5 803; 30 487
metalwork 11 613
sculpture 11 553
St Bento, Master of 19 655
St Bertin, Goscelin of *see* GOSCELIN OF ST BERTIN
St Bertin, Odbert of *see* ODBERT OF ST BERTIN
St Bertin Altar 20 *451*, 451, 452
St Bertin Altar, Master of the *see* MARMION, SIMON
St Bertin Psalter *see under* PSALTERS → individual manuscripts
Saint-Bertrand-de-Comminges 3 328, 375; 11 327; 27 31
Cathedral 7 454; 23 461
Saint-Beury, Hugues de Thil, Lord of 27 592
St Blasien 12 413
Monastery 12 374, 462
St Blasius 16 *804*
St Boniface, Eglise du Précieux Sang 5 563
Saint-Bonnet, Jean de, Marquis de Toiras *see* TOIRAS, JEAN DE SAINT-BONNET, Marquis de
St Bruno Album *see under* ALBUMS → individual manuscripts
Saint-Calais 9 668
St Calais, William of, Bishop of Durham *see* WILLIAM OF ST CALAIS, Bishop of Durham
St Catherine
Arawak Indian Museum 2 147; 16 890
Colbeck Castle 5 749; 16 882
pictographs 16 880
St Catherine, Master of 21 338
St Cecilia Master (*fl* 1290-1320) 2 624; 5 124; 11 183; 20 713, 759–60*; 23 743; 29 599
attributions 12 692
works 2 624; 12 693; 13 145; 20 *760*
St Cecilia Master (*fl* 17th cent.) 7 689
St Chéron Master 6 498
Saint-Christol 26 604
St Clair, Staunton 13 876
St Clare, Master of
works 25 *229*
Saint-Cloud 27 535–7*
ceramics 23 512; 24 148; 27 536–7*
Château 4 301; 19 211; 22 740; 23 511–12; 27 535–6*
carpets 27 896
cascade 19 *212*
furniture 5 192; 11 595, 627
gardens 12 122, *122*; 27 536*
interior decoration 4 303; 11 305; 27 263
paintings 4 556; 13 793; 23 173, 517
sculpture 1 132
tapestries 3 461
porcelain 6 923; 11 607, *607*; 27 536–7
St Contest 7 837
St Croix (Lesser Antilles) 2 144
Estate Whim Plantation Museum 5 749
see also ANTILLES, LESSER; VIRGIN ISLANDS
St Croix Abbey (France) 21 164
St Cuthbert Gospel of St John *see under* GOSPEL BOOKS → individual manuscripts
Saint-Cyprien, Musée Fondation François-et-Souza-Desnoyer 8 810
Saint-Cyr, Augustinian College 2 *724*, 725
St David's (Dyfed) 27 537–9*; 32 *780*
Bishop's Palace 27 538*, *539*; 32 781
Cathedral of SS Andrew and David 10 228; 13 82; 27 *537*, 537–8*
Saint-Denis
Abbey 3 710; 5 *793*, 793–4; 6 482; 7 218, 267; 8 257, 260, 261; 9 671, 672; 11 *504*, 509, 510, 530, 653; 13 36–7, 42; 20 762; 26 44; 27 539–42*, *540*, *541*, *542*, 543*; 29 902–3*
altars 1 697; 5 808; 7 263
ambulatory 1 768; 27 *541*
apse 2 347
arches 2 295, 298
Baptistery 3 191
bosses 4 465
Bourbon Chapel 11 516; 20 866

Saint-Denis
Abbey—cont.
brasses 4 691
buttresses 5 318
capitals 27 545*
choir 11 510; 13 34, 36, 36–7
chronicles 7 243
cloister 7 455; 27 545*
collections 7 564
crypt 8 222; 23 485
doors 9 153
effigy of Mahaut, Comtesse d'Artois 13 99
enamel 13 168, 169
flags 11 147
gold 11 613
hardstones 14 170
ivory-carvings 5 810; 13 173, 175; 26 697
manuscripts 7 512; 9 603
metalwork 5 808; 11 614; 26 681; 29 334
misericords 21 725
Monument for the Heart of Francis I 11 265
mosaics 7 275; 13 134; 22 163; 26 679, 681
mouldings 22 216, 217
outer crypt 5 795
paintings 13 691–2
piers (ii) (masonry) 24 751
portals 11 554
Porte des Valois 27 545*
reliquaries 26 146
reliquary of St Denis 13 168
restorations 8 593
sculpture 7 642; 13 72, 73, 99; 27 543–5*, 543, 544
shrines (i) (cult) 5 807
south transept portal 27 545*
stained glass 12 790; 19 356; 26 701, 702; 27 548–9*, 549; 29 501, 506, 509, 510, 510, 511, 516, 851
stone-carvings 21 163
Throne of Dagobert see THRONE OF DAGOBERT
tiles 11 603
tombs 3 455; 13 72; 22 44; 24 139; 27 546–8*
Arnegunde, Queen 10 181; 21 162
Charles V, King of France (reg 1364-80) 13 76, 77; 31 120
Charles VIII, King of France (reg 1483-98) 11 556
Dagobert, King of Austrasia and Neustria (reg 623-39) 20 762
Francis I and Claude de France 11 513, 557; 31 125
Henry II and Catherine de' Medici 11 557; 24 813; 27 547, 548; 31 125
Isabella of Aragon, Queen of France (1234-71) 31 122
Louis IX, King of France (reg 1226-70) 31 129
Louis, Crown Prince 27 829
Louis XII and Anne of Brittany 11 513, 556, 727; 27 546–7, 547; 31 125
Orléans (Bourbon House of) 11 556
Pepin the Short, King (reg 751-68) 7 267
Philip III, King of France (reg 1270-85) 13 77
Philippe Dagobert 33 28
transept 31 280
Treasury 13 158; 24 132; 27 549–50*
Valois Chapel 11 513; 20 865
wall paintings 5 797
west portals 27 543–5*
westwork 5 795
Factory 7 693
Saint-Denis Missal see under MISSALS → individual manuscripts
St-Didier 27 682
St Dié, Jean de see JEAN DE ST DIÉ
Saint-Dizier 31 717
Musée d'Archéologie 11 667
Saint-Domingue see HISPANIOLA
St Dominic's Press 12 631; 17 632
St Donat's (S. Glams), Castle Church 32 784
Sainte Chapelle Evangeliary see under EVANGELIARIES → individual manuscripts
Sainte-Chapelle Gospels see under GOSPEL BOOKS → individual manuscripts
Sainte-Claude Cathedral 13 126
Sainte-Colombe 25 542
bronze 13 575
Sainte-Colombe-les-Sens 11 603
St Edmundsbury see BURY ST EDMUNDS
St Elias limestone see under LIMESTONE → types
St Elisabeth Panels, Master of the 20 755
St Elizabeth 16 879
Sainte Magnance 26 602
Sainte-Marie, Hugh de see HUGH DE SAINTE-MARIE
Sainte Marie (Quebec), Ste Marie de la Beauce 3 73
Ste Marie du Parc 26 666
Ste Marie du Parc Bible see under BIBLES → individual manuscripts
Sainte-Maure, Benoît de see BENOÎT DE SAINTE-MAURE
Sainte-Maure, Charles Montausier, Duc de 17 449; 18 880; 19 267; 26 452
Saintenoy, Gustave 27 551
Saintenoy, Paul (Pierre Jean) 3 550, 619; 27 551*; 28 41
St Epiphanius, Master of 20 711
St Erasmus, Master of 20 628
Saintes 11 505; 26 905; 27 551–3*
Abbaye-aux-Dames 26 600; 27 552–3*
St Eutrope 26 585, 600; 27 551–2*
altars 7 263
capitals 27 552
crypt 8 224
sculpture 27 552*
Saintes-Chapelles see under CHAPELS → types
Saintes Islands 2 144; 5 745
see also ANTILLES, LESSER; LEEWARD ISLANDS
Saintes-Maries-de-la-Mer, Musée Camarguais 14 457
Sainte-Suzanne Champaione, Catherine of see CATHERINE OF SAINTE-SUZANNE CHAMPAIONE
Saint-Etienne Préfecture 18 865
St Eustatius 2 144; 5 745
see also ANTILLES, LESSER; ANTILLES, NETHERLANDS
Saint-Evroult-de-Montfort 11 253, 623
St Evroult-Notre-Dame-du-Bois 26 669
St Fagans (S. Glams) 32 780
Castle 32 782
Welsh Folk Museum 32 781, 783, 791
Saint-Far, Eustache de 4 302; 19 641
St Fleury, Jean de 29 336
Saint-Florentin, Comte de 6 396
Saint Florentin Church 13 181
St Florian Abbey 2 776, 781, 783; 5 772, 772; 27 553–4*
candelabrum 26 686
frescoes 1 659; 29 602
furniture 2 811, 812; 17 470
St Florian Abbey—cont.
interior decoration 2 806
library 15 87
manuscripts 2 792; 13 151; 26 675; 27 554*
metalwork 2 822
paintings 1 659, 717, 733; 2 792
sculpture 27 873
stucco 29 838
Saint-Foix, Claude-Pierre-Maximilien Radix, Comte de 4 848
Saint-Foix, Poullain de 4 518
Saint-Fond, Barthélemy Faujas de see FAUJAS DE SAINT-FOND, BARTHÉLEMY
St Francis, Master of 20 760–61*
attributions 2 632
works 2 621–2, 622; 8 212; 11 709; 12 III1; 20 761
St Francis, Master of the Bardi see BARDI ST FRANCIS, MASTER OF THE
St Francis, Master of the Legend of see LEGEND OF ST FRANCIS, MASTER OF THE
St Francis's Obsequies, Master of 12 692
Saint-Gabriel 26 603, 604
St Gall 30 124
Abbey 7 263; 13 18; 26 588; 27 554*; 30 126, 137
book covers 5 808
church 27 554–5*; 32 822
cloister 5 795
gardens 12 107
glass 30 144
ivory-carvings 5 810
library 19 316
manuscripts 5 805; 11 653; 12 382; 15 875; 32 637, 638
Monastery plan 2 313, 325, 349; 5 794–5; 7 190, 231, 264, 265, 453; 12 107, 108, 363; 14 780; 19 312; 21 835, 843, 844; 27 555, 555–6*; 28 308
refectories 21 844
paintings 5 797; 12 382
Cathedral see Abbey
ceramics 30 144
curtains 30 141
embroidery 30 151
lace 30 152
manuscripts 9 219, 668; 20 330; 23 652
Museum für Völkerkunde 30 155
Wirtschaftshochschule 30 129
St Gall Gospels see under GOSPEL BOOKS → individual manuscripts
Saint-Gaudens, Augustus 16 21; 20 16, 925; 25 5; 27 556–8*
assistants 33 42
collaboration 3 30; 33 42
groups and movements 7 875; 23 46; 30 868
pupils 20 30
teachers 17 667
works 4 477; 7 357, 875, 876; 18 627; 20 18; 22 48; 27 557; 29 575–6; 31 611, 612; 33 8, 28
Saint-Gaudens, Homer 5 530
Saint-Gaudens, Louis 20 18; 27 556, 557
St Gelais, Octavien de, Bishop of Angoulême 30 529
Saint-Généroux Church 26 585, 586
Saint-Genis-des-Fontaines 11 505, 554; 26 609; 27 558*
Saint-Genis-Laval, Château de l'Haye 19 790
Saint-Genou Church 26 586, 599
St George (Barbados), Drax Hall 2 148, 150; 5 749
St George, Master of see MARTORELL, BERNAT
St George Codex, Master of the 20 649–50*
works 2 860; 20 650
St George on the Řip 26 594
St George's (Grenada)
architecture 2 148
Fort St George 2 148
Grenada National Museum 2 153
St George 2 148
St Georges (French Guiana) 11 756
Saint-Georges see JOURDAIN, JULES (LOUIS)
Saint-Georges, Guillet de see GUILLET DE SAINT-GEORGES
St George's Art Society 2 575
St George's Caye 3 622
St Gereon Sacramentary see under SACRAMENTARIES → individual manuscripts
Saint-Germain, Jean-Joseph de 11 625, 626, 627; 25 577; 27 558*
St Germain, Mademoiselle 19 56
Saint-Germain, Pierre-Marie Gault de see GAULT DE SAINT-GERMAIN, PIERRE-MARIE
Saint-Germain-de-Livet Château 6 504
Saint-Germain-en-Laye 11 504
Château Neuf (destr. 1777) 6 506; 11 513; 19 693; 24 117; 27 559, 559
fountains 11 343
gardens 12 120, 121
grotto 13 704
interior decoration 11 533
paintings 4 549; 9 328, 385; 25 391; 32 717
Château Vieux 4 780; 6 415; 11 513, 656; 26 45; 27 558–60*
glass 11 611
Musée des Antiquités Nationales de France 11 667; 23 126; 27 560
Musée Départemental du Prieuré 8 715
Sainte-Chapelle 13 42; 26 45; 27 558
Saint Germain-lès-Corbeil 13 179
St Germans (Cornwall) 10 303
Saint-Germer-de-Fly 13 37, 38
Lady Chapel 6 458; 13 42; 26 45; 27 550; 31 273
stained glass 26 702
St Giles, Master of 20 761–3*
works 20 762
Saint-Gilles-du-Gard Abbey 11 505, 554; 23 485; 26 182; 27 560–61*; 31 351
façade 27 560
pilgrim badges 24 808
sculpture 26 596, 603
Saint Gobain factory 10 748; 11 575; 21 720; 29 332
St Gorgonius Abbey 3 709; 7 231, 262; 8 222; 13 18
crypt 7 265
wall paintings 5 797
Saint-Guilhem-le-Désert Abbey 26 582, 603
St Helena 21 574
Longwood 5 169
St Hilarion Castle 8 357, 358, 361
Saint-Hubert
Château 6 509; 10 764
St Hubert 3 552; 13 211; 26 666, 667
Saint-Hubert, Jean-Antoine-Hubert Vassal de see VASSAL DE SAINT-HUBERT, JEAN-ANTOINE-HUBERT
Saint-Idesbald, Musée Paul Delvaux 8 700
Saint-Igny, Jean de 27 248, 561–2*
reproductive prints by others 4 468
teachers 25 833
works 29 424
St Ildefonso, Master of 20 763*
St Ives (Cornwall) 1 77, 78; 3 628; 18 754; 23 104; 27 562–3*; 32 800
Barbara Hepworth Museum 14 402; 28 314
Tate Gallery 10 371; 27 563
St Ives group 10 258, 267; 11 362, 363, 804; 20 368; 33 175
members 14 401, 465; 28 104
painting 27 562
Saint-James, Baudart de 13 234
Saint-James, Claude Baudard de 3 524
St James Parish (Barbados)
Cockade House 2 151
Maddox 2 151
Mango Bay 2 151
St James Parish (Jamaica), Rose Hall 5 749; 16 882, 886
Saint-Jean (French Guiana) 11 756, 758
St Jean (Que; Canada) 5 581
Saint-Jean, Simon 27 563*
Saint Jean-aux-Bois, St Jean 13 181
St Jean d'Acre see 'AKKO
Saint-Jean-de-Côle Church 26 584
Saint-Jean-de-Losne Church 13 78
Saint Jean-du-Doigt, St Jean-Baptiste 11 616
St Jerome, Master of 19 393
St Johannes, Master of 20 711
Saint John (NB; Canada)
furniture 5 578
Market Hall 5 561
monument to Samuel de Champlain 5 570
St John (US Territory; Caribbean) 2 144
see also ANTILLES, LESSER; VIRGIN ISLANDS
St John, Barr & Co. 8 34
St John, Oliver 2 545; 21 615
St John, Order of see KNIGHTS HOSPITALLER
St John Altarpiece, Master of the 16 832; 20 763*
St John Hope, W. M. 33 250
St John Lampadistis see KALOPANAGIOTIS
St John-Mildmay, Humphrey 3 239
St John's (Antigua)
Barclays Bank 2 153
Museum of Antigua and Barbuda 2 154
St John's (Nfld; Canada) 5 559
Mechanics Institute 5 590
St Johns (Que; Canada) see ST JEAN (QUE; CANADA)
St Johns Stone Chinaware Co. 5 581; 10 814
St John's Wood Clique 10 254; 27 563–4*
members 5 426; 20 446; 25 587; 33 515
St John's Wood School of Art see under LONDON → academies and art schools
St John the Baptist, Master of 20 763*
St Joseph 25 340
St-Josst-ten-Node, Musée de l'Hôtel Charlier 6 487
Saint-Jouin-des-Marnes 26 599, 600
Saint-Julien, Baron de 11 368
Saint-Julien-de-Jonzy 26 602
Saint-Julien-du-Sault Church 24 159
Saint Junien 26 601
St Jura, Fritz 11 759
Saint-Just (Narbonnais) 26 603
Saint-Just (Valcabrère) 26 603
St Kitts 2 144; 5 745
architecture 2 148
Brimstone Hill Museum 2 153, 154
carnivals 5 788

St Kitts—cont.
costumes **2** *146*
Government Administration Building **2** 149
libraries **2** 153
masks **2** 146
museums **2** 153, 154
Olovaze Plantation **2** 151
Rawlins **2** 148
Romney Manor **2** 148
textiles **2** 151
see also ANTILLES, LESSER; LEEWARD ISLANDS
St Lachtin's Arm **32** 530
St Lambrecht Abbey **2** 781; **12** 370
St Lambrecht Votive Altarpiece, Master of the **2** 792; **14** 159; **20** 764*; **32** 441
St Laurence, Master of **33** 186
Saint Laurent, Yves **5** 921; **9** 294; **20** 470
Saint-Laurent-du-Maroni **11** *756*, 758, 759
St Lawrence Glass Co. **5** 583
Saint-Léger-en-Yvelines Château **19** 691; **24** 117
Saint-Léon, Arthur Dufresne de *see* DUFRESNE DE SAINT-LÉON, ARTHUR
Saint-Leonard de Noblat **9** 156
St Leonards (E. Sussex)
New Palace Pier **24** 748
parish church **25** 728
Saint Leu-d'Esserent **4** 465; **22** 217
St Nicolas **13** 39
Saint Lizier Cathedral **4** 780; **11** 616
Saint-Lô **26** 598
Hôpital-mémorial France-Etats-Unis **14** 785
Musée d'Archéologie **11** 667
Saint-Louis (Guadeloupe) **31** 721
St Louis (Haiti) **14** 57
St Louis (MO; USA) **27** 564–5*; **31** *587*
artificial stone **30** 505
Art Museum **14** 174; **22** 363; **27** 565
collections **4** 73; **6** 826; **9** 231; **10** 640; **16** 554, 555; **20** 880; **30** 332
Bellefontaine Cemetery
Wainwright Tomb **20** 869
court-house **18** 887
Eads Bridge **16** 54
Festival Hall **10** 683
Jefferson National Expansion Memorial **22** 48; **31** 352, 597
Loew's State Cinema **7** 327
Louisiana Purchase International Exposition, 1904 **10** 683; **15** 883; **22** 679; **27** 565
Hungarian Manor House pavilion **14** 909
Mississippi Bridge **9** 499
Reliance Building **6** 578
terracotta **30** 505
Trova Studio **31** 375
Wainwright Building **4** 788; **6** 578; **23** 493; **29** 913–15; **30** 505; **31** 594, *594*
lighting **19** 365
St Louis (Senegal) **1** *381*; **28** 405
Musée de Saint-Louis du Sénégal **28** 406
Saint-Louis, Compagnie des Verreries & Cristalleries de *see* COMPAGNIE DES VERRERIES &CRISTALLERIES DE SAINT-LOUIS
St Louis, Joan **31** 335
St Louis Psalter *see under* PSALTERS → individual manuscripts
Saint-Loup-de-Naud Church **13** 73
St Lucia **2** 144; **5** *745*
architecture **2** 148
houses **2** 147
libraries **2** 153
St Lucia—cont.
museums **2** 153
pottery **2** 152
sculpture **2** 149
textiles **2** 151
see also ANTILLES, LESSER; WINDWARD ISLANDS
St Lucy, Master of the Legend of *see* LEGEND OF ST LUCY, MASTER OF THE
St Lucy altarpiece **7** 628; **16** 661, *662*; **27** 495
St Lukas **2** 829
St Luke's Society (Amsterdam) **1** 808, 809; **21** 851
St Maarten *see* ST MARTIN **2** 144
St MacDara's Church (Co. Galway) **16** 7
Saint-Maixent Abbey **13** 210, 211; **26** 600
Saint-Mandé **2** 92
Saint-Marceaux, Charles-René de Paul de **25** 207; **27** 566*
Saint-Marcel **26** 641
altar **1** 694
St Margarethan **2** 804
St Martens-Lennik **9** 681
St Martha, Master of *see* CHAOURCE, MASTER OF
St Martin **2** 144, 148; **5** *745*
see also ANTILLES, LESSER; ANTILLES, NETHERLANDS
Saint-Martin, François Goret de *see* GORET DE SAINT-MARTIN, FRANÇOIS
Saint-Martin-aux-Bois **31** 273
Saint-Martin-de-Boscherville
St Georges **6** 467; **13** 72; **30** 729
Saint-Martin-des-Aires **2** 725
St Martin des Sées **26** 669
Saint-Martin-du-Canigou Abbey **1** 723; **11** *505*; **27** *566*, 566–7*
capitals **26** 609
church **11** 509; **26** 580, 585
cloister **7** 454; **26** 610
piers (ii) (masonry) **24** 750
sculpture **27** 567
St Mary (Jamaica) **16** 879
St Mary Magdalene, Master of the Legend of *see* LEGEND OF ST MARY MAGDALENE, MASTER OF THE
St Mary's City (VA), Roman Catholic chapel **4** 786
St Mary's Platt (Kent), Hop Field **7** 712
Saint-Mathurin, Suzanne de **2** 63
St Maurice, Saint-Maurice d'Agaune (destr.; Switz) **3** 191; **5** 794, 796
chancels **12** 363
ciborium **10** 322; **26** 688
Treasury **5** 806; **26** 683
Saint-Maur-les-Fossés **11** 645; **27** 592
Château **11** 513; **19** 690
St Mawes Castle (Cornwall) **21** 550, 568, *569*
St-Maximin **31** 121
Saint-Médard-des-Prés **10** 197
St Médard Gospels *see under* GOSPEL BOOKS → individual manuscripts → Soissons Gospels
Saint-Mémin, Charles B(althasar) J(ulien) F(évret) **27** 567*; **28** 714
Saint-M'Hervé, Moulin d'Haroult **32** 279
St Michael
Barbados Community College **2** 154
Barbados Museum and Historical Society **2** 153, 154; **5** 746
St Michael Cup **3** 597
Saint-Michel-de-Cuxa **11** *505*, 509; **22** 247; **27** 567–8*, *568*
church **7** 454; **26** 581, 610
sculpture **26** 603, 610
Saint-Michel-de-Touch **25** 502
St Michel Gaillac Gradual *see under* GRADUALS → individual manuscripts
St Monans (Fife) **28** 251, 267
St Moore, R. **4** 810; **24** 748, *748*
Saint-Morien, M. de **24** 494
Saint-Morys, Charles Paul Jean-Baptiste de Bourgevin Vialart de **8** 845; **27** 568*
Saint-Morys, Etienne Bourgevin Vialart, Comte de **5** 445; **19** 11
St Mungo **29** 743
Saint-Nectaire-le-Haut
priory church of St Nectaire **26** 681
capitals **26** 601
metalwork **11** 614
reliquaries **26** 145
sculpture **26** 601
sculpture **11** 554
St Neophytos Monastery **7** 229; **8** *325*; **9** *512*; **26** 483; **27** 569*
Enkleistra **8** 359; **9** 580, 626
Katholikon **8** 362
wall paintings **7** *229*; **9** 523
Saint-Nicholas-de-Port **13** 59, 60
St Ninian's Cave **28** 241
St Ninian's Isle Treasure **24** 738; **27** 569–70*, *570*
Saint-Non, Richard de, Abbé **2** 239; **9** 416; **27** 570–71*, *571*
collaboration **8** 763
illustrated writings **2** 84; **4** 360; **8** 772, 815; **11** 541; **13** 871; **24** 176; **28** 657; **30** 865; **32** 685
personal collection **9** 230
pupils **2** 240
Saint-Omer
Abbey of St Bertin
crypt **7** 265
ivory-carvings **26** 696
manuscripts **5** 803; **26** 666, 668; **27** 617
Cathedral of Notre-Dame **11** 614, 623
ivory-carvings **11** 636
tapestries **11** 639
tiles **30** 885
St Omer, Peter of *see* PETER OF ST OMER
St Omer Psalter *see under* PSALTERS → individual manuscripts
St Oswald, Rowland Winn, 1st Baron *see* WINN, ROWLAND, 1st Baron St Oswald
Saint-Ouen Museum **4** 555
Saint-Ours, Jacques **27** 571
Saint-Ours, Jean-Pierre **12** 276; **27** 571–2*; **30** 125, 133; **31** 363
St Patrick's Bell-shrine **32** 530, *530*
Saint-Paul (France) **30** 885
St Paul (MN; USA)
Minnesota Museum of Art **21** 650
Minnesota State Capitol **7** 357; **12** 614
warehouses **32** 861
Saint-Paul, Claude **11** 723
Saint Paul, Paul **5** 584
Saint-Paul-de-Mausole **26** 603
Saint-Paul-de-Varax **26** 602
Saint-Paul-de-Vence, Fondation Maeght **2** 542; **8** 65; **12** 567; **20** 75–6; **28** 315, 483, *483*
collections **21** 709
lighting **19** 365
St Paul Master **4** 20
St Paul's Walden (Herts), All Saints **28** *294*, 295
Saint-Paul-Trois-Châteaux, Cathedral of St Paul **26** 603
Saint-Périer, René de **16** 615; **19** 243
Saint-Périer, Suzanne de **16** 615
St Peter (Barbados), St Nicholas's Abbey **2** 148, 150
St Petersburg **2** 425; **27** *362*, *363*, 373, 572–87*, *573*
academies and art schools
Academy of Sciences **25** *791*; **27** 375, 438
see also museums → Peter the Great Museum of Anthropology and Ethnography
All-Russian Academy of Arts **27** 443
Dzerzhinsky Higher Naval Engineering Academy *see* Admiralty Building
Imperial Academy of Arts **1** 105, 106; **18** 196–7; **22** 177; **25** 141; **27** 388, 402, 438, 439, 442, 575, 579, 580; **28** 646
archives **2** 371
directors **19** 118
Petrograd Institute of Painting, Sculpture and Architecture **27** 443
I. Ye. Repin Institute of Painting, Sculpture and Architecture **27** 443
Russian School **27** 442
Admiralty Building **13** 238; **22** 741; **27** 373, 375; **30** 885; **33** 599–600, *600*
Aleksandrinsky Theatre *see* Pushkin Theatre
apartments **27** 381
art forms and materials
architecture **27** 375–6, 377, 378
ceramics **27** 582*
enamel **27** 426
furniture **11** 104; **27** 409, 582–4*
glass **27** 415, 582*
gold **27** 584*
lace **27** 430
marks **27** 584
medals **20** 924
metalwork **27** 419, 420–21, 422, 424
polychromy **25** 171
porcelain **27** 412
silver **27** 584*
tapestries **30** 326
textiles **27** 430, 431
tiles **30** 884
Bronze Horseman *see* monument to Peter the Great
Buddhist Temple **30** 821
ecclesiastical buildings
Aleksandr Nevsky Monastery **27** 586*
Cathedral of the Trinity **29** *552*, 552–3
Church of the Annunciation *see* Museum of Town Sculpture
Museum of Town Sculpture **27** 586
Cathedral of St Nicholas **6** 562; **27** 374; **28** 837
Cathedral of SS Peter and Paul **14** 82; **27** 373; **31** 317, *318*
Kazan' Cathedral **27** 375; **32** 697, *698*
St Isaac's Cathedral **16** 53; **27** 428, 577, *577*
Smol'ny Convent **26** 8–9; **27** 586–7*
Cathedral **26** *9*; **27** 374
Voskresensky Novodevichy Monastyr *see* Smol'ny Convent
education (art) **27** 442
Engineers' Castle **4** 745
Exchange *see* museums → Central Naval Museum
gardens **22** 25
German Embassy **23** 493
government and state buildings
Arsenal **2** 502
A.M. Gorky Palace of Culture **27** *578*
House of Soviets **27** 380
St Petersburg
government and state buildings—cont.
Marine Regiment Courtyard **27** 373
Pavlovsky Barracks **27** 375; **29** *555*
Senate **27** 376
State Bank **27** 375
Synod Building **27** 376
Imperial Library and Museum *see* museums → Peter the Great Museum of Anthropology and Ethnography
institutes
Alexander Institute **27** 402
Institute of Oriental Studies of the Russian Academy of Sciences **6** 284
Institute of the History of Material Culture of the Russian Academy of Sciences **6** 284
Mining Institute **27** 375
Smol'ny Institute **27** 402
Inzhenernyy Zamok *see* Engineers' Castle
Metro stations **21** 350
Mikhaylovsky Castle *see* Engineers' Castle
monument to Peter the Great **10** 442, *442*, 765; **22** 45; **29** 565
monument to the Victims of the Revolution **27** 378
Moscow Gates **29** 555
museums
Agricultural Museum **18** 99
Aleksandr Blok Museum **27** 581
Brodsky Apartment Museum **4** 838
Central Naval Museum **10** 669; **22** 741; **25** 268; **27** 375, *375*, 575; **30** 748
City Museum *see* Museum of the History of St Petersburg
Dostoyevsky Museum **27** 581
Hermitage Museum **3** 735; **18** 125, 161; **22** 362; **27** 440, 444, 575, 578, 585; **30** 486
Arabian collection **2** 275
archives **2** 371
atlantids **2** 695
Campana Collection **5** 536
catalogues **26** 734
Central Asian collection **6** 284, 321
Chinese collection **7** 54, 156
collections **2** 559; **6** 284; **7** 579; **14** 569; **26** 729, 732, 733, 734; **27** 438, 439, 441, 579, 581, 586; **28** 321, 646; **29** 778
Crozat collection **8** 210; **11** 663
directors **5** 26; **26** 734
display **9** 24, 25, 30
drawings **7** 416; **21** 85
Egyptian collection **10** 90, 94
Etruscan collection **10** 637
exhibitions **6** 285, 286; **16** 560
gems **4** 874; **12** 266
Greek collection **13** 470, 542, 605
Indian collection **15** 710, 745
Iranian collection **15** 923
Islamic collection **16** 556
Kozlov collection **30** 849
Mongolian collection **21** 886
Morozov collection **22** 136
paintings **21** 90; **27** 439, 440
Pallavicini collection **23** 874
portraits **27** 439
Roman collection **27** 46
Russian collection **27** 428
sculpture **4** 304; **11** 371; **30** 766
South-east Asian collection **29** 241
tapestries **30** 332
Theatre **26** *732*; **30** 677

St Petersburg
museums
Hermitage Museum—cont.
see also palaces → Winter Palace
Jewish Ethnographic Museum **17** 581
Kunstkamera see Peter the Great Museum of Anthropology and Ethnography
Kushelyov Gallery **27** 439
Museum of Anthropology and Ethnography *see* Peter the Great Museum of Anthropology and Ethnography
Museum of Artistic Culture **15** 857; **20** 194, 301; **30** 362
Museum of Ethnography **6** 284; **16** 485; **21** 886
Museum of Political History **12** 856
Museum of the History of Religion **6** 284; **21** 886
Museum of the History of St Petersburg **15** 133; **33** 522
Museum of the Revolution *see* Museum of Political History
Museum of Town Sculpture *see under* ecclesiastical buildings → Aleksander Nevsky Monastery
Peter the Great Museum of Anthropology and Ethnography **6** 572; **20** 839; **27** 373, 574
collections **26** 729; **27** 440
observatory **23** 339
see also academies → Academy of Sciences
A. S. Pushkin Apartment Museum **27** 581
Russian Military History Museum **25** 89
Russian Museum **1** 148; **26** 734; **27** 198–9, 376, 404, 577; **29** 556
Benois Wing **3** 733
catalogues **32** 724
collections **6** 284; **27** 439, 440, 441, 580
directors **27** 312
paintings **31** 537
Stieglitz Museum **3** 889; **21** 177
Suvorov Museum **12** 856
Neva Porcelain Factory *see* LOMONOSOV PORCELAIN FACTORY (ST PETERSBURG)
observatory *see under* museums → Peter the Great Museum of Anthropology and Ethnography
palaces **27** 374
Anichkov Palace **18** 661; **27** 401, 408, 583
Chesme Palace **28** 643
Marble Palace **26** 403; **27** 402; **28** 643
Menshikov Palace **9** 760; **27** 401, *574*, 581
Mikhail Palace *see* museums → Russian Museum
Mikhaylovsky Palace *see* museums → Russian Museum
Summer Palace of Peter I **27** *400*, 401, 581
Tauride Palace **23** 813; **27** 375; **29** 551–2
gardens **12** 134
interior decoration **27** 402
Winter Palace **9** 209; **11** 287; **13** 740; **16** 53; **26** 9, 499; **27** 374, 408, 583, *585*, 585–6*
1812 Gallery **27** 200, 440
collections **8** 580; **27** 438, 440
furniture **27** 407, 408, 583, 584
interior decoration **27** 401, 403

St Petersburg
palaces
Winter Palace—cont.
Jordan Staircase **27** *402*; **30** 486
see also museums → Hermitage Museum
Yelagin Palace **27** 404, 581
Palace Square **27** 199, 375, *576*
Peter and Paul Fortress **28** 585
Peter's Palace *see* PETERHOF
Petrograd **27** 378
Police Bridge **14** 222
Post Office **27** 375
Pushkin Theatre **16** 53; **27** *199*, 376, 404
Saltykov-Shchedrin State Public Library **2** 371; **6** 284
Singer Company building **1** 148
Society for the Encouragement of the Arts **27** 438, 442, 580
Society of Architects **27** 580
Summer Garden **4** 311; **12** 134
Hall of Glorious Ceremonials **27** 401
synagogue **17** 547
Twelve Colleges **26** *730*; **27** 373
Senate Hall **27** 401
see also A. A. Zhdanov State University
University *see* A. A. Zhdanov State University
urban planning **15** 133; **18** 543; **21** 512; **31** 718
Ust-Rudista workshop **27** 415, 582
Vasil'yevsky Island **31** 317–18
Yeliseyev trading house **1** 148
A. A. Zhdanov State University **6** 284; **31** 317–18
Zimny Dvorets *see* palaces → Winter Palace
St Petersburg Album *see under* ALBUMS → individual manuscripts
St Petersburg Electroforming, Casting and Mechanical Plant **10** 136
St Petersburg Glass Factory *see* IMPERIAL GLASS FACTORY (ST PETERSBURG); IMPERIAL CHINA AND GLASSWORKS (ST PETERSBURG)
St Petersburg Porcelain Factory *see* IMPERIAL PORCELAIN FACTORY, ST PETERSBURG
Saint-Phalle, Niki de **11** 551, 570; **27** 587*
collaboration **11** 570; **19** 782; **28** 315; **30** 924; **31** 571
groups and movements **10** 416; **23** 261
patrons and collectors **14** 48; **21** 135; **29** 420
works **11** 347; **15** 869; **30** 924
Saint Philibert **17** 684
Saint-Philibert-de-Grand-Lieu Abbey Church
crypt **5** 795; **7** 265; **8** 222
St Philip, Master of *see* CIAMPANTI, ANSANO DI MICHELE
St Philip (Barbados), Sam Lord's Castle **2** 149, 151
Saint-Pierre, Jacques-Henri Bernardin de **4** 364; **8** 868; **11** 500
Saint-Pierre, Joseph **3** 428; **14** 652; **27** 587–8*, 777, 778
Saint-Pierre de Plesguen **11** 724
St Pierre de Préaux **26** 669
Saint-Pierre-le-Moûtier **26** 601
Saint-Pierre-sur-Dives **32** 278, 280
Abbey **11** 603; **30** 885
St Pius X Basilica **7** 258
Saint-Pol, Count of **3** 646
Saint-Pol, Anne de Caumont, Comtesse de **4** 572

Saint-Pol, Enguerrand, Count of **14** 408
Saint-Pol, Hugues Candavène, Count of **14** 408
seal **14** *408*
Saint-Pol, Louis de Luxembourg, Count of **10** 222
Saint-Pol, Marie de *see* PEMBROKE, Countess of
St Pölten **2** 777, 783
Saint-Porchaire **11** *505*, 603; **27** 588*
St Porchaire ware *see under* POTTERY → wares
St Prex **30** 145
Saint-Quénin **1** 693
Saint-Quentin
collegiate church **13** 40, 179, 180
Labyrinth **18** 584
tracery **13** 41
Musée Antoine Lécuyer **18** 842
Saint-Quentin, Jacques-Philippe-Joseph **3** 463; **16** 905
Saint-Quentin-en-Yvelines **4** 227; **12** 185; **24** 131
Arcades du Lac **11** 528
Saint-Rémy de Provence *see* GLANUM
Saint-Rémy-en-Rollat **11** 603; **27** 110
Saint-Restitut **26** 603
Saint-Riquier Abbey **3** 708; **5** 794; **7** 263, 264, 265; **11** *504*, *505*, 509, 511, 653; **13** 19; **27** 588–90*, *589*, *590*
altar **7** 263
church **12** 5
ciboria (ii) (structure) **7** 302
crypt **7** 265
spire **29** 412
westwork **5** 795; **7** 264; **33** 106
St Rollox Glassworks **28** 259
Saint-Romain, Jean de *see* JEAN DE SAINT-ROMAIN
Saint-Romain-en-Gal **27** 60
St Rupert Cross **10** 322; **27** 663
Saint-Saëns, Marc **11** 644; **30** 328
Saint-Savin-sur-Gartempe **11** *505*; **22** 520; **27** 590–91*
Abbey Church **11** 510; **14** 80; **26** 585, 600
wall paintings **11** *529*, 530; **26** 649, 650
piers (ii) (masonry) **24** 751
wall paintings **26** 654, 655
St Sebastian, Master of (i) (*fl c.* 1470-90) **20** 764*
St Sebastian, Master of (ii) (*fl* 1493-1505) *see* LIEFERINXE, JOSSE
Saint-Servan, Tour Solidor **8** 902
Saint-Sever Abbey **11** 619; **13** 36; **26** 670
St Severin, Master of **20** 764–5*
attributions **20** 717
patrons and collectors **27** 159
teachers **20** 692
works **7** 590; **12** 384
Saint-Séverin Church **3** 541
St Simeon **17** 500
Saint-Simon, Charlotte de, Princesse de Chimay *see* CHIMAY, CHARLOTTE DE SAINT-SIMON, Princesse de
Saint-Simon, Claude-Henri de Rouvroy, Comte de **11** 522; **12** 144; **27** 591
Saint-Simonism **27** 591*
saints' lives **27** 591–2*
Byzantine **9** 616; **21** 138
Early Christian (*c.* AD 250-843) **9** 616
England **13** 136
Gothic **13** 128, 130, 136
Italy **16** 837
Romanesque **26** 661
Saint-Sorlin, Jean Desmarets de *see* DESMARETS DE SAINT-SORLIN, JEAN

SS Paul and Barnabas, Master of **20** 250
St Stephen reliquary **5** 807
Saint-Sulpice-du-Tarn **13** 174
Saint-Thibault-en-Auxois **11** *504*
priory church **13** 125; **27** 592–3*
side chapel **22** 221
St Thomas (Jamaica), Stokes Hall **5** 749; **16** 882
St Thomas (Virgin Islands) **2** 144, 148
Synagogue **17** 545
see also ANTILLES, LESSER; VIRGIN ISLANDS
St Thomas-in-the-East (Jamaica) **16** 888
Saint-Trond *see* SINT-TRUIDEN
St Tropez, Musée de l'Annonciade **9** 396
Saint-Urbain **30** 126
Saint-Urbain, Ferdinand de **14** 287; **20** 922; **23** 515; **27** 593*
Saint-Urbain, Marie-Anne de **27** 593
St Urban **30** *124*
Abbey **4** 777; **30** 136, 142, 143, 884
St Urban, Master of **20** 711
Saint-Ursanne **30** 136
Collegiate Church **26** 635
St Ursula Silk **9** 667
Saint-Vaast Abbey **3** 552; **5** 804
St Vaast Bible *see under* BIBLES → individual manuscripts
St Vannes, Richard of *see* RICHARD OF ST VANNES
St Veronica, Master of **7** 583; **20** 765–6*; **33** 186
teachers **7** 724
works **7** 590; **11** 438; **12** 383; **20** *765*
St Victor, Adam of *see* ADAM OF ST VICTOR
St Victor, Hugh of *see* HUGH OF ST VICTOR
Saint-Victor, Jacques Benjamin **24** 418
St Vincent **2** 144, 149; **5** *745*
Archaeological Museum **2** 154
Calliaqua Estate Villa **2** 151
carnivals **2** 146
libraries **2** 153
museums **2** 154
painting **2** 149
see also ANTILLES, LESSER; WINDWARD ISLANDS
St Vrain Schwankowsky, Frederick John de *see* SCHWANKOWSKY, FREDERIC JOHN DE ST VRAIN
Saint-Wandrille **3** 708
Fontanella Abbey **6** 464; **7** 453; **21** 835, 836; **29** 412
St Willibrord Gospels *see under* GOSPEL BOOKS → individual manuscripts → Echternach Gospels
St Wolfgang im Salzkammergut Church **2** 800; **28** 134, *184*
altarpiece **1** 710; **11** 452; **12** 401; **13** 117; **23** *707*, *708*, 708–9, *709*; **26** 186
Saint-Yrieix **11** 607, 609; **28** 521
Saint-Yrieux-la-Perche **13** 125
S Zeno Master, First **20** 767*
S Zeno Master, Second **20** 767*
Saínz, Casimiro **27** 783
Sáinz de la Lastra, Severiano **1** 149
Saiō *see* NISHIKAWA SUKENOBU
Saiōin, Yodominoseki **17** 340
Saionji (family) **17** 150, 160
Saionji Kintsune **18** 561
Sais **9** 773, *774*, 891; **27** 593*
sacred lake **27** 497
Saisunaga **27** 593–4*
see also:
AJATASHATRU, King
UDAYI, King
Saitama **17** 433
Honeiji **17** 122

Saiter, Daniel *see* SEITER, DANIEL
Saite Renaissance *see* SAITE STYLE
Saites **9** 784
Saite style **9** 888, 889, 891–2
Saito, Katsutoshi **17** 402
Saitō, Sogan **17** 135
Saito, Takako **11** 232
Saitō, Yori **17** 205
Saitō, Yoshishige **17** 207; **27** 594*
works **17** *136*
Saitō Jūrōbei **31** 203, 204
Saitō Setsudo **33** 709
Saitō Yoemon **31** 204
Sajet, Philip **22** 897
Saji, Keizō **17** 430
Sajimachi **17** 355
Sajjad, Shahid **27** 594*
works **23** 801, *802*
Sajjan Singh, Rana of Mewar (*reg* 1871-84) (Rajput) **15** 601
Sajnu **15** 634
Sajsawaman *see* SACSAHUAMAN
Saka (family) **14** 37
Saka-Acquaye **12** 509
Sakaguti, Adolfo **4** 715
Sakai (Japan) **17** 19, 358
tea ceremonies **17** 335
textiles **17** 311
tomb of Emperor Nintoku **17** 57, *57*, 58; **18** 190; **23** 157*
sarcophagus **27** 832
weapons **17** 363
Sakai (people) **20** 167
Sakai (family) **14** 551; **17** 430; **23** 364; **27** 596; **30** 52
Sakai, Kazuya **27** 595*
Sakaida (family) **17** 267
Sakaida Kakiemon (1596-1666) **17** 733
Sakaida Kakiemon XIV (*b* 1934) *see* KAKIEMON, SAKAIDA, XIV
Sakai Dōitsu **17** 180
Sakai Hōitsu **17** 165, 180; **23** 365, 367; **27** 595–6*; **30** 378
attributions **31** 204
collaboration **30** 52
pupils **30** 52
works **14** 551; **17** 166; **27** *596*
Sakakibara, Kōshū **15** 129
Sakakibara, Seiyō **11** 811
Sakakibara, Shihō **17** 201
Sakakibara Kōshū **17** 409, 413
Sakaki Hyakusen **17** 188, 189; **27** 596*
Sakakura, Junzō **11** 526; **17** 88; **27** 597*
collaboration **33** 563
staff **2** 598, 909; **15** 128
works **17** 88, 89, *89*, 90
Sakalava **1** 294; **20** 35, 36–7, 38, 40
textiles **20** *40*
Sakamoto, Hanjirō **27** 597*
exhibitions **17** 436
groups and movements **17** 205; **31** 82
works **17** 205
Sakamoto, Issei *see* SAKAMOTO, KAZUNARI
Sakamoto, Kazunari **27** 598*
Sakamoto Sukehachi *see* YI KYOUNG
Sakanoue no Tamuramaro **17** 746; **18** 549
Sakarra **15** 323
Sakata (Africa) **1** 363, 403
Sakata (Japan), Domon Ken Memorial Museum **9** 122
Sakça Gözü **1** *821*, 893; **27** 598*; **30** *180*; **31** 456
architecture **1** 831
Coba Höyük **27** 598
pottery **21** 306
reliefs **30** 190
sculpture **1** 833
Sakellarakis, E. **2** 304
Sakellarakis, John **15** 98
Sakellarakis, Y. **2** 304
Sakevem
sculpture **16** *43*

śākhā **15** 244*
Sakharna **21** *810*
  Monastery **21** 810
Sakharov, Aleksandr **22** 921
Sakhibov, Safar **30** 253
Sakhnovs'ke **31** 562
Sakiestewa, Ramona **27** 599*
Sakitama tomb group **15** 160
Sakje-Geuzi *see* SAKÇA GÖZÜ
Sakkas, Hagios Giorgios **8** 358
Sakkizabad **15** 921
sakkoi **9** 643
Sakonides **13** 510
Sakor Shiva Temple **15** 255
Saksanokhur **6** *182*, 197; **27** 599*; **30** *252*
  metalwork **6** 238; **27** *599*
Saku **10** *536*
  manor house **10** 537
Saku Beer Factory **10** 541
Sakubei *see* TAKAMATSU RIHEI
Sakuma, Tōtarō **21** 634
Sakuma Shōzan **17** 793
Sakunojō **14** 36
Sakura, National Museum of Japanese History **2** 598
  Nomura Collection **17** 311, *311*, *316*
Sakuragaoka **17** *11*; **27** 599–600*
Sakurai
  Chausuyama burial mound **17** 58
  Hashihaka **17** 58
  West Monjuin Tomb **17** 59
Sakurai, Hideo **17** 402
Sakuraidani
  coffins **17** *426*
Sakvan Peter, Marvine *see* PETER, MARVINE SAKVAN
Sakya **5** 105; **27** 600*; **30** *806*, 818
  Northern Monastery **27** 600
  sculpture **22** 775
  Southern Monastery **27** 600; **30** 818
  stupas **2** 477
Sakyapa Buddhism *see under* BUDDHISM → sects
Sakyol Pulur **1** 824
sal **22** 793
Sal, Isaac **32** 771
Sala (Java) *see* SURAKARTA
Sala Forum (Mauritania) **11** 328
Sala (Sweden)
  Aguéli Museum **1** 466
  mines **30** 104
Sala, Emilio **4** 127
Sala, Francesco **8** 386
Sala, George Augustus (Henry Fairfield) **27** 601*
Sala, Ignacio de **23** 903
Sala, Joan **29** 309
Sala, Miguel **3** 218
Sala, Pierre **24** *472*
Sala, Sebastian **25** 114; **32** 874
Salaboss, Melchior **27** 601*
Sălacea **25** *471*, 523; **30** 434
  temple **25** *523*
Sala Colonia **25** 832
Saladin *see* SALAH AL-DIN, Sultan
Saladin, Henri **9** 527; **16** 548
Saladin, P. A. **11** 80
Salado **22** 600, 622
Saladoid culture **5** 746–7; **25** 698–9
  pendants (jewellery) **29** *199*
  pottery **29** *199*; **31** 330–31
Salado Polychrome ware *see under* POTTERY → wares
Salagon **26** 604
Salah *see* BARIŞ TEPE
Salah al-Din, Sultan (*reg* Egypt 1169-93; Diyarbakir 1185-95) (Ayyubid) **16** 490; **20** 55, 56; **21** 630; **33** 614
  architecture **5** 403; **16** 175
  dress **16** 452
  fortifications **2** 888; **5** 396, 402
Salah al-Din Yusuf, Sultan (*reg* Aleppo 1237-60) (Ayyubid) **2** 889
Salahi, Ibrahim el- **27** 601*
  works **1** 245, 433; **29** 896
Salahuddin, Asad **23** 800
Salaì *see* CAPROTTI, GIAN GIACOMO
Salakhov, Tahir (Teymur-Ogly) **2** 896; **27** 601–2*
  works **2** *897*
Salala **23** 436
Salamah, Darwish **27** 876
Salama ibn Jandal **16** 545
Salamanca **26** *904*; **27** *602*, 602–6*; **29** *258*
  art forms and materials
    embroidery **29** 350
    furniture **29** 314, 315
    gold **27** 606*; **29** 337
    metalwork **29** 337
    painting **13** 150
    sculpture **29** 290
    silver **27** 606*
    tapestries **29** 350
  bridge **4** 800
  Casa de las Conchas **29** 299
  Casa de las Muertas **29** 296
  La Clerecía *see* Colegio Real de la Compañía de Jesús
  Colegio Real de la Compañía de Jesús **12** 56; **22** 68; **29** 269, *269*
    Claustro de los Estudios **7** 288
  colleges **7** 566
  Corredera **31** 718
  ecclesiastical buildings
    convent of Las Agustinas Descalzas **29** 353
    convent of the Carmelitas del Carmen de Abujo **11** 492
    New Cathedral **13** 69, 211; **22** 221; **25** 30; **27** 605–6*, *606*; **29** 265, 270
      sculpture **26** 642
      stained glass **13** 192; **29** 504
    Old Cathedral **13** 70; **27** 604–5*; **29** 263
      altarpiece **1** 710
      corbels **7** 837
      gold **29** 334
      organ shutters **23** 500
      paintings **29** 276
      pinnacles **24** 826
      retable **11** 482
      sculpture **26** 609
      spire **29** 414
      Torre del Gallo **27** *605*
    S Cristóbal
      sculpture **26** 642
    S Esteban **26** 250; **29** 265, 292
      retables **11** *492*; **26** *251*
    S Maria de la Vega
      cloister **7** 455
  Palacio de Monterrey **12** *619*, 619; **29** 299; **30** 501
  Plaza Mayor **29** 270
  Universidad de Salamanca **25** 31; **27** 603; **29** 265; **31** 674
    gate-house **12** 175
    library **12** 19
    Palacio Anaya **17** 674
    sculpture **3** 847; **29** 289
Salamanca, Antonio (Martínez de) **10** 389; **25** 625; **27** 606*
  copies **18** 635
  personal collection **3** 448
  printmakers **4** 443; **5** 906
  works **2** 162; **27** 650; **30** 746
  workshop **12** 760
Salamanca, Francisco de **13** 732; **14** 474; **31** 718, 822
Salamanca, Gabriel of *see* GABRIEL OF SALAMANCA
Salamanca (y Mayol), José, Marqués de **20** 64; **27** 606–7*
  architecture **24** 225
  collections **29** 352, 353
  paintings **4** 565
Salamanca, Juan de **14** 474; **28** 294
Salamá Valley **13** *758*; **20** *882*; **27** 607*
Salamis **8** *325*, 331; **9** *512*; **13** *362*; **26** *908*; **27** 607–9*
  amphitheatre **8** 337
  aqueduct **8** 356
  cenotaph **6** 170
  chariot **6** 480
  coins **8** 349
  glass **1** 867
  gymnasium **8** 332, 337
  Hagios Epiphanios **8** 357, 358; **9** 566
    Baptistery **3** 191
  Hagios Varnavas **8** 358
  harnesses **14** 179
  House of the Oil Press **29** 816, *817*
  ivory-carvings **8** 351; **24** 643; **27** *608*
  Kampanopetra **8** 357
  marble **8** 342
  monastery of Apostolos Banrabas **8** 367
  mosaics **8** 354; **27** 67
  Phaneromeni Monastery **25** 336
  pottery **8** 346
  Royal Tombs Museum **8** 366
  sculpture **8** 332, 341, 342; **27** *609*
  shrine of Nikodemos **8** 359
  Temple of Zeus Olympios **8** 332, 336
  theatre **8** 337
  tombs **8** 332, 335, 347; **31** 108
    Tomb 79 **8** 353, *354*
    Tomb 80 **8** 356
  wall paintings **8** 356
Salampasu **1** 403
  masks **1** *405*
Salamzade, S. **2** 896
Salamzade, V. **28** 644
Salango **27** 609–10*; **29** *136*
Salangome *see* AGUA BLANCA
Salão de Maio **4** 718
Salar **16** 209, 210, 384
Salardú **26** 642
Salar Jung III, Nawab **15** 182, 742
Salar Jung Museum *see under* HYDERABAD
Salas, Antonio **5** 365; **9** 713, 714; **27** 610
Salas, Carlos **29** 293, 294
Salas, Cristóbal Martínez de, Bishop of Panama
Salas, José Antonio (*fl* 1864) **31** 229
Salas, José de (*fl* late 18th cent.) **2** 398
Salas, Juan **32** 170
Salas, Rafael **27** 610*
Salas, Tito **32** 174, 178, 180
Salas, Tovar y *see* TOVAR Y SALAS
Salas (y Bosch), (Francisco) Xavier de **27** 610*
Salas retable **29** 332
Salathé, Friedrich **30** 133
Salavin-Fournier triptych **28** 753
Salayev, F. E. **2** 895
Sala y Sarda, José **23** 606
Salazar, Hernando da **27** 606
Salazar, Juan de **13** 767
Salazar, Nazario **8** 236
Salazar, Pedro de Liendo y *see* LIENDO Y SALAZAR, PEDRO DE
Salazar, Ponciano **7** 645; **21** 228
Salazar de Mendoza, Pedro **2** 28; **27** 611–12*
Salazar Herrera, Carlos **1** 783
Salazaro, Demetrio **8** 588
Salazar Quesada, José Francisco **8** 16
Salazar y Espinosa, Juan **24** 93
Salazar y Mendoza, José **23** 32
Salcedo, Bartolomé Zumbigo y *see* ZUMBIGO Y SALCEDO, BARTOLOMÉ
Salcedo, Bernardo **7** 610; **27** 612*
Salcedo, Francisco Antonio de, 1st Marqués de Vadillo *see* VADILLO, FRANCISCO ANTONIO DE SALCEDO, 1st Marqués de
Salcedo, Gregorio de Tapia y *see* TAPIA Y SALCEDO, GREGORIO DE
Salcedo y Azcona, Luis de **20** 499
Salces, Antonio Ruiz de *see* RUIZ DE SALCES, ANTONIO
Salcman, Martin **30** 162
Säld, Jörg *see* SELD, JÖRG
Šalda, František Xaver **8** 393
Saldae, Mons Aeflanus tunnel **27** 7
Saldaña, Bernardo de Rojas Luna y *see* ROJAS (LUNA Y SALDAÑA), BERNARDO DE
Saldanha, Eduardo de Almeida *see* ALMEIDA SALDANHA, EDUARDO DE
Saldanha, Flaminio **4** 714
Saldanha, Iona **33** 317
Saldanha, Manuel Cardoso de *see* CARDOSO DE SALDANHA, MANUEL
Saldern, Caspar van **10** 461
Saldini, Cesare **21** 521; **29** 486
Salé (Burma) **5** *221*, 242
Salé (Morocco) **1** *376*
  Abu'l-Hasan Madrasa **16** 218; **20** 57
  Bu 'Inaniyya Madrasa **16** 250
  embroidery **16** 448
  fortifications **21** 584
  houses **1** 315
  Rabbi Yaakov Ashraf synagogue **17** 551
  Rabbi Yaakov Bibas synagogue **17** 551
  Zawiyat al-Nussak **16** 218
Sale (Ches; UK), Methodist Church **21** 347
Sale, della (family) **9** 185
Saleeby, Khalil **7** 858; **19** 7
al-Saleem, Muhammad Mossa **27** 876
Saleh, Raden *see* RADEN SALEH (SARIEF BUSTAMAN)
Salelles, Lluís Brui i *see* BRUI I SALELLES, LLUÍS
Salem (Germany)
  Abbey Church **12** 372, 404, 405; **13** 57; **32** 821; **33** 163
  Kaisersaal **11** 43
Salem (South Africa) **29** 116
Salem (MA; USA) **27** 612–13*; **31** *587*
  Assembly House *see* Hamilton Hall
  brick **4** 786
  Chestnut Street **27** *613*
  furniture **2** 150; **31** 628
  Gardner-Pingree House **31** 591
  Hamilton Hall **2** 618
  Peabody Essex Museum
    collections **3** 916; **7** 30, 156; **17** 435; **18** 384; **21** 886; **27** 613
    directors **22** 148
  silver **31** 649
Salem (NC; USA) **22** 80; **31** 634, 635
Salem, Ali ben **31** 425
Saleman, Georg **21** 641
Salempur **15** 423
Salerno **9** *510*; **10** 638; **16** *621*; **27** 613–15*
  Cathedral of S Matteo **9** 645; **16** 626; **26** 619, 625, 626; **27** 614–15*
    ivory-carvings **26** 698
    mosaics **7** 275; **26** 679, 680; **27** 614
    oliphants **23** 401
    Porta dei Leoni **27** *614*
    pulpit **26** *626*
    throne **30** 777
    Treasury **27** 615*
  Chiesa della Sacra Famiglia **25** *272*
  ivory-carvings **26** 698
  manuscripts **14** *432*; **21** 5
Salerno—cont.
  Museo Diocesano Provinciale **27** 615
  Teatro Verdi **22** 99
Salerno, Andrea da **22** 477
Salerno, Fratte di **10** 585
Salerno, Girolamo da *see* GIROLAMO DA SALERNO
Salerno, Muriolus of *see* MURIOLUS OF SALERNO
Salerno, Osvaldo **24** 99, 101; **26** 76
Salerno, Peregrino da *see* PEREGRINO DA SALERNO
Salerno, Roger of *see* ROGER OF SALERNO
Salerno di Coppo di Marcovaldo **7** 817
salerooms *see* AUCTION HOUSES; AUCTIONS
sales *see* ART MARKET; AUCTION HOUSES; AUCTIONS; COLLECTING; DEALING; TRADE
Sales Catalog Index Project Input Online *see* SCIPIO
sales catalogues *see* CATALOGUES → types → auction
Sales Pérez, Francisco de **21** 462
Salet, Francis **30** 332
sale terrene see under HALLS → types
Salette, La *see* LA SALETTE
Salford (Greater Manchester)
  Museum and Art Gallery **1** 453; **20** 239
  Philips and Lee Mill **19** 366; **28** 831
  Royal Peel Park Museum *see* Museum and Art Gallery
Salgado, José Veloso **27** 615–16*
  works **25** 299; **27** *615*
Salgado, Samuel **14** 715, 716
Salgado, Sebastião **20** 99; **24** 679; **27** 616*
Salghetti-Drioli, Francesco **27** 616*
Salginatobel Bridge **4** 803
Salgótarján **14** 890
Sali, Piero di Bartolomeo **11** 86
Saliagos **2** 160; **8** 314
Salian (House of) **12** 471; **27** 616*
Salian, Conrad II, Holy Roman Emperor *see* CONRAD II, Holy Roman Emperor
Salian, Henry III, Holy Roman Emperor *see* HENRY III, Holy Roman Emperor
Salian, Henry IV, Holy Roman Emperor *see* HENRY IV, Holy Roman Emperor
Salian, Judith of Flanders *see* JUDITH OF FLANDERS
Saliba, Antonio de **2** 178; **16** 824; **20** 213; **23** 751; **27** 617–18*; **28** 656
Saliba, Pietro de **2** 178; **20** 213; **27** 618*
Salicka, Judyta Maria **32** 749
Salicrup, Fernando **18** 833
salient angle **21** 547
Salietti, Alberto **23** 264
Saliger, Ivo **22** 711
Salignac de La Mothe-Fénelon, François de *see* FÉNELON, FRANÇOIS DE SALIGNAC DE LA MOTHE-
Saligny, Anghel **26** 709
al-Salih, Muhammad *see* MUHAMMAD AL-SALIH
Salih, Sultan (*reg* 1351-4) (Mamluk) **17** 497
Salih, Zeid **16** 2
Salih al-Ustadh **31** 585
al-Salih Najm al-Din, Sultan (*reg* Damascus 1239, 1245-9; Egypt 1240-9) (Ayyubid) **2** 888; **5** 396; **16** 176, 381
al-Salih-Tala'i' **5** 396; **16** 175, 490
salilāntara **15** 244*

Salim 15 808
Salim, Hajj Muhammad 16 2
Salim, Hajj Suad 16 2
Salim, Jawad 16 2; 27 523, 618*
Salim, Naziha 27 618
Salim, Nizar 27 618
Sa Lima, António Rodrigues de *see* RODRIGUES DE SA LIMA, ANTÓNIO
Salim al-Mosuli, Hajj Muhammad 27 618
Salimbeni (family) 3 16
Salimbeni, Arcangelo 27 620; 31 884
Salimbeni, Francesco 6 139
Salimbeni, Iacopo 27 618, 619; 31 740
  works 27 *619*
Salimbeni, Lorenzo 27 618–20*
  works 27 *619*; 31 740
Salimbeni, Luigi 4 407
Salimbeni, Ventura 16 674; 27 620–21*
  collaboration 19 383
  pupils 20 264; 22 81; 29 740
  works 24 860; 26 823; 27 *620*; 28 687, 688; 30 355
Salim Chisti, Shaykh 10 827
Salimgarh Fort 15 409
Salim Shah *see* JAHANGIR
Salin, Bernhard 21 502; 32 514, 534
Salin, Nikolaus 12 426
Salina 25 522
Salinar 31 118
Salinar culture 27 621*
Salinas (González-Mendive), Fernando 8 232, 233; 27 621*
Salinas Calado, Rafael 19 468
Salinas Moro, Raúl 24 401
Salincorno, Mirabello di *see* CAVALORI, MIRABELLO (D'ANTONIO DI PACINO)
Saline de Chaux 10 748
Salini, Tommaso 27 621–3*
  attributions 31 5
  pupils 20 431
  works 27 *622*; 29 667
Salins, Hugues I, Archbishop 3 872
Salins Church 4 923
Salins de Montfort, Nicolas-Alexandre 6 509; 12 414; 27 623*; 29 378
Salis, Rodolphe 13 317
Salisbury, Rhodesia *see* HARARE
Salisbury (Wilts) 10 *225*; 27 624–30*, *625*; 31 708, 709
  bookbindings 4 351
  Castle 6 407
  Cathedral of the Blessed Virgin Mary 1 724; 7 267; 9 670; 10 228; 13 44, 45–6, 55, 81; 18 621; 27 626–8*, *627*, *628*
    arches 2 295
    ballflower 3 121
    chantry chapels 7 267
    chapter house 6 466; 13 80
    choir-screen 13 81
    clock 7 438
    cloister 7 456
    Lady Chapel 13 45–6
    mouldings 11 420; 22 217, 218, 222
    pinnacles 24 826
    restorations 33 446
    retrochoir 14 82
    roof 30 908
    sculpture 27 628–9*, *629*; 29 96
    spire 27 628; 29 412, 413
    stained glass 13 183; 14 422; 27 629–30*
    tomb of Bishop Roger 31 122
    transept 9 *669*; 31 281
  houses 2 324
  King's House *see* Salisbury and South Wiltshire Museum
  manuscripts 13 140
  market 31 711
Salisbury (Wilts)—cont.
  Salisbury and South Wiltshire Museum 27 626
Salisbury, James Cecil, 5th Earl of *see* CECIL, JAMES, 5th Earl of Salisbury
Salisbury, John of *see* JOHN OF SALISBURY
Salisbury, Robert Cecil, 1st Earl of *see* CECIL, ROBERT, 1st Earl of Salisbury
Salisbury Breviary *see under* BREVIARIES → individual manuscripts
Salisbury Breviary St Stephen, Master of the 20 626
Salish 22 548; 29 743
  architecture 22 565
  basketwork 22 645, 656, 657, 659
  beadwork 22 640
  dress 22 632
  metalwork 22 613
  religion 22 559, 666
  sculpture 22 577, *577*
  tourist art 22 668
saliva 10 549
Salivahana *see* SATAVAHANA
Salivahana, Ustad 15 596
  works 15 *596*
Saliyev, A. 18 569
Saljuqs 27 630*
Great Saljuqs 5 722; 16 113, 115; 27 630–31*
  ceramics 26 221
  see also:
  ALP ARSAN, Sultan
  MALIKSHAH, Sultan
  SANJAR, Sultan
Saljuqs of Anatolia 5 722; 16 141; 18 233; 27 631–2*
  see also:
  'ALA AL-DIN KAYQUBADH I, Sultan
  GHIYATH AL-DIN KAY KHUSRAW I, Sultan
  GHIYATH AL-DIN KAY KHUSRAW II, Sultan
  'IZZ AL-DIN KAYKA'US I, Sultan
  JAWHAR NASIBA
  KILIC ARSLAN II, Sultan
  MAHPERI KHWAND KHATUN
  MAS'UD I, Sultan
Saljuqs of Rum *see* SALJUQS OF ANATOLIA
Salkhad 9 543
Salkind 28 294
Salkojidari Bridge 18 280
Sallaert, Anthonis 3 559; 27 632–3*
  works 17 471; 21 895; 33 358
Sallaert, Jan Baptist 27 633
Sallando, Pierantonio 20 453
Sallandrouze de la Mornaix 11 643
Sallarts, Anthoni *see* SALLAERT, ANTHONIS
Salle, David 27 478, 633*; 31 609
Salle, Gigaud de la 21 425
Salle, (Aimé-Charles-) Horace His de La *see* HIS DE LA SALLE, (AIMÉ-CHARLES-) HORACE
Salles, Georges 4 677
sallets *see under* HELMETS → types
Sallieth, Mattheus de 18 176, 739
Sallinen, Tyko Konstantin 11 96; 23 266; 27 633–4*
Sallinger, Michael 22 306
Sallo, António 2 87
Sallust 4 362
Sally Lunn 3 370
sallyports *see* POSTERNS
Salm (family) 19 807
Salm, Abraham 3 397; 27 634
Salm, Adriaen van der 27 230
Salm, Den 2 201; 3 588
Salm, Gerlof Bartholomeus 1 803; 2 416; 3 397; 27 634*
Salm, Nikolaus II, Count of 14 836, 837
Salman ibn Ma'ali 16 490
Salmansweiser, Hans Saphoy von *see* SAVOYE, JOHANN
Salmantica *see* SALAMANCA
Salm-Dyck, Prince de 32 81
Salmeggia, Chiara 27 634
Salmeggia, Enea 6 343; 27 634*
Salmeggia, Francesco 27 634
Salm foundry 8 416; 10 907
Salmi, Mario 24 449; 27 635*, 657
Salm-Kryburg, Friedrich 2 173
Salmon, Mrs 33 3
Salmon, André 3 366; 27 635*
  groups and movements 24 405; 25 747
  works 8 774; 11 568
Salmon, François 2 142
Salmon, Gabriel 22 455; 33 357
Salmon, James 12 774, 775; 27 636*; 33 565
Salmon, Robert 20 425; 27 635–6*
Salmon, Son & Richie 4 884
Salmon, Thomas 32 378
Salmon, William (1644-1713) 8 128; 29 437
  works 29 *437*
Salmon, William (*c*. 1703-79) 10 205; 23 860; 24 275
Salmon, William (*fl* 1850-1870) 28 881
Salmon, William Forrest 12 773; 27 636
Salmona, Rogelio 4 234; 5 887; 7 606, 607
  works 7 *606*
Salmond, J. L. 14 743
Salmon & Gillespie 7 694; 12 775; 27 636*; 28 228
Salmons, Jill
  works 15 *62*, *64*
Salm-Reifferscheid, Franz Xaver Altgraf zu, Bishop of Klagenfurt 28 68
Salm-Salm, Franz, Prince zu 22 426
Salm-Salm, Konstantin, Prince zu 22 426
Salmson, Hugo (Fredrik) 27 636*
Salmson, Jean-Jules-Bernard 27 636–7*
Salnecke Palace 30 69
Salò, Antonio Scaino da 3 118
Salò, Domenico di Pietro da 27 637*
Salò, Francesco di Tommaso da 27 637
Salò, Gasparo da 27 637
Salo, Giannantonio da 20 546
Salo, Markku 11 107
Salò, Pietro di Lorenzo da 6 89; 27 637*
Salomě 10 483
Salomon 22 246
Salomon, Andrea 4 401
Salomon, Bernard 11 533; 27 637*
  works 22 414; 23 680
Salomon, Erich 24 677; 27 637*
Salomon, Geskel 17 576
Salomon, N. 33 313
Salomone (family) 1 579
Salomoni, Ruggiero 32 6
Salomons, Edward 10 679
Salomons, Vera Bryce 16 558, 571
Salomonson, Hein 21 362; 22 869
Salon *see under* PARIS
Salona 8 *174*; 9 *510*; 27 637–8*, *638*
  Anastasius Mausoleum 20 519
  architecture 26 906
  Basilica 9 538
  mosaics 9 565, 566
Salon Cubists 8 240, 244
  see also PUTEAUX GROUP
Salon d'Art Idéaliste 8 701; 30 169
Salon d'Automne 3 642; 14 120; 19 77; 24 142, 143, 172; 27 239
Salon de la Nouvelle Génération 11 302
Salón de la Plástica Mexicana 6 520
Salon de la Rose + Croix 27 639*
  members 30 169
    Bernard, Emile 3 813
    Bussière, Gaston 5 296
    Chabas, Maurice 6 377
    Delville, Jean 8 701
    Desboutin, Marcellin (-Gilbert) 8 787
    Fabry, Emile 10 735
    Gausson, Léo 12 205
    Hodler, Ferdinand 14 614
    Khnopff, Fernand 3 564
    Marcel-Lenoir 20 385
    Martin, Henri (-Jean-Guillaume) (1860-1943) 20 488
    Minne, George 21 648
    Péladan, Joséphin 24 333
    Point, Armand 25 78
    Schwabe, Carlos 28 181
    Séon, Alexandre 28 423
    Vallotton, Félix (-Emile-Jean) 31 830
Salon de Mai 1 142; 8 77
Salon de Nu 17 207
Salon des Artistes Français 24 172
Salon des Iconomaques 19 827
Salon des Indépendants 2 90; 10 680; 24 142, 143, 172; 26 191; 28 171
Salon des Réalités Nouvelles 1 79; 2 544; 11 569; 27 639*
  members
    Delaunay (ii), Sonia 8 659
    Dewasne, Jean 8 838
    Domela (-Nieuwenhuis), César 9 87
    Freundlich, Otto 11 769
    Gorin, (Albert) Jean 13 10
    Herbin, Auguste 14 437
    Klein, Yves 18 118
    Pellan, Alfred 24 338
    Pevsner, Antoine 24 574
    Poliakoff, Serge 25 147
    Rouan, François 27 238
    Zeid, Fahrelnissa 33 628
Salon des Refusés 10 680; 24 140, 172
Salon des Surindépendants 14 205, 776
Salon des Tuileries 8 811; 9 371
Salon du Palais des Arts Libéraux 2 124
Salone 26 *906*
Salonen, Johan 11 91
Salonen, Matti 11 91
salon exhibitions *see* EXHIBITIONS → types → fine arts
Saloniki *see* THESSALONIKI
Salón Independiente 5 881
Salon of Romanian Artist Sculptors 16 877
salons 19 264
Salopian China Manufactory 6 93; 14 132
Salor 6 253; 16 485
  works 6 *253*; 16 *484*
Šaloun, Ladislav 27 640*; 28 836
  collaboration 25 151
  pupils 28 855
  works 8 387; 25 433
Salsedo, Stefano Carrillo y *see* CARRILLO Y SALSEDO, STEFANO
Salses Fortress 3 359; 21 550
Salsta 30 93
salt
  bidri 4 687
  brick 4 797
  dyeing 27 471
  gilding 12 623
  glazes 3 *589*; 4 769; 5 581; 6 329; 10 *312*, 315; 12 429; 16 394, 427; 28 258; 30 875
  photography 24 647, 648, 650, 656
  stucco 29 813
Salt (Jordan) 17 654
Salt, Henry 10 82, 90, 92, 93
Salt, John 19 493; 24 686
Salt, Titus 3 893; 27 641*; 31 725
Salta 2 392, *393*, 394
  architecture 2 394
  Cathedral 2 396
  chapels 2 394
  ponchos 2 403
Saltaire 27 641; 31 725
Saltash (Cornwall), Royal Albert Bridge 4 802, *802*
Salters, Edward 10 316
Saltillo 21 394
  Cathedral 21 393
Salting, George 1 454; 27 641–2*
  collections 7 155; 10 367; 29 416
Salting diptych 13 176
Salting Leaf 13 172
salt jars *see under* JARS → types
Salt Lake City (UT) 22 126; 27 *642*, 642–3*; 31 *587*
  Museum of Church History 22 126; 27 642
  Museum of Fine Arts 22 126; 27 642
  Salt Lake Art Center 27 642
  Salt Lake Temple 22 126; 30 450
  Utah State Historical Society 22 126
Saltman, Carlyn
  works 1 *287*
Salt Mine (Saudi Arabia) 2 270
Salto, Axel (Johannes) 27 643*; 28 22; 29 72
  groups and movements 19 799
  works 8 748
Salto, Naja 8 755
Salton, N. C. 30 95
saltpetre 6 872
salts 10 419; 27 640–41*
  historical and regional traditions
    Africa 1 326, *326*, *327*
    Benin, Kingdom of 1 327, *327*
    England 10 325; 27 *640*
    France 6 *143*
    Sierra Leone 1 *326*, 327
    Spain 29 *335*
    Sweden 30 *106*
  materials
    coral 7 835
    enamel 6 *143*
    gold 6 *143*
    ivory 1 326, *326*, 327, *327*; 16 799
    silver-gilt 27 *640*; 29 *335*; 30 *106*
    verre églomisé 27 *640*
  see also CASTERS; CRUETS
Saltsjö-Duvnäs 19 798
Saltwood, Lord Clark of *see* CLARK, KENNETH
Saltykov, Ivan 27 426
Saltykov-Shchedrin, Mikhail 18 504; 22 50
Saltykov-Shchedrin State Public Library *see under* ST PETERSBURG
Salucci, Alessandro 21 483; 27 643*
Salucci, Giovanni 27 643–4*; 33 616
  patrons and collectors 33 429
  works 20 868; 29 874
Saluces, Georges de *see* GEORGES DE SALUCES
Saluces Altarpiece 4 417; 23 524
Saluces Hours, Master of the 28 1
Saludianus, Paulus Galarius 8 11
Salud Madrid Alcalá-Zamora, María de la 1 741
Salurt, Claudio 19 387; 24 505
Salutati, Coluccio 14 867, 870; 16 658
Saluzzi, Alessandro *see* SALUCCI, ALESSANDRO
Saluzziano Codex *see under* CODICES → individual manuscripts

Salvador 4 *705*, 709; 13 781; 27 644*
Casa de Câmara 4 710
Central Administration of Bahia (CAB) Chapel 4 *714*, 714
churches
Cathedral 4 709, 715
Chapel of the Blessed Sacrament 4 723
Church of the Third Order of S Francisco da Penitência 4 709
Golden Chapel 4 710
Misericórdia 4 709, 716
Nossa Senhora da Conceição da Praia 4 710, 716
S Bento 4 709, 722, 723, 728
S Francisco 4 710
S Marcelo 4 709
S Teresa 4 709
Jesuit college 4 715
church *see* churches → Cathedral
museums
Museu de Arte da Bahia 4 725, 726
Museu de Arte Moderna de Bahia 4 727
Museu de Arte Popular do Unhão 3 227; 4 721
Museu de Arte Sacra da Bahia 4 727
Museu da Coleção Abelardo Rodrigues 4 727
Museu da Fundação Carlos Costa Pinto 4 708, 727
Pálacio da Vitória 4 726
silver 4 723
Solar do Ferrão 4 725
Salvador, El *see* EL SALVADOR
Salvador Carmona, José 27 644
Salvador Carmona, Juan Antonio 27 644, 645
Salvador Carmona, Luis 27 644–5*; 29 292
collaboration 32 557
teachers 32 557
works 15 889
Salvador Carmona, Manuel 27 644, 645*
pupils 1 776; 10 906; 28 389
Salvador da Bahia 1 422, 423
Salvador Goméz, Vicente 27 645*
Salvage, Jean-Galbert 1 845; 9 706
Salvart, Jenson 3 825; 27 250
Salvati, Cintio de *see* CINTIO DE SALVATI
Salvatierra, José Francisco Sarmiento, Conde de 11 872; 32 706
Salvatierra de los Barros Church 21 393
Salvatierra y Barriales, Valeriano 27 646*
collaboration 3 199
pupils 21 36
works 3 199
Salvatierra y Serrano, Mariano 27 646; 31 89
Salvation Army 19 43
Salver, J.
works 33 *431*
salvers 16 31; 27 646*; 28 *738*; 32 *161*
see also TAZZE
Salvestrini, Cosimo 21 26
Salvetat, Alphonse-Louis 6 924; 28 523
Salvi, Gaspare 7 421
Salvi, Giovanni Battista *see* SASSOFERRATO
Salvi, Nicola 27 646–7*
assistants 13 661
collaboration 11 345; 22 45; 25 292, 808; 31 894
competitions 7 672
patrons and collectors 3 708; 4 635; 7 897; 19 777
pupils 2 612
Salvi, Nicola—cont.
works 3 835; 10 744; 12 762; 16 639; 23 352; 27 *647*
Salvi, Tarquinio 27 864
Salviani, Ippolito 2 103
Salviati (family)
architecture 4 47; 27 748
frescoes 1 671
paintings 1 670; 24 239
sculpture 12 576
Salviati (company) 5 340
Salviati, Alamanno, Cardinal 1 670; 4 857; 22 5; 27 648
Salviati, Antonio (1816-90) 3 270; 32 204
glass 26 227
mosaics 18 897; 22 158, 163; 28 278; 29 871
stained glass 27 538
Salviati, Antonio (Maria), Cardinal (*fl* 1590s) 32 692
Salviati, Averardo 3 305
Salviati, Bernardo, Cardinal 27 648
Salviati, Francesco (Cecchino) 4 276; 16 665, 766; 26 769, 770; 27 648–55*
assistants 29 740
attributions 9 176; 11 265
collaboration 4 857; 25 262; 32 10
drawings 25 558
frames 11 389, 488, 489
groups and movements 6 360; 20 281
methods 28 339
paintings 15 137; 26 836; 27 *649, 652, 653*; 31 524
altarpieces 5 450; 28 335
frescoes 11 211; 16 665; 20 278; 25 71; 27 *651*, 655; 33 717
portraits 1 734; 5 789
patrons and collectors
Accolti, Benedetto, Cardinal 11 193
Chigi, Agostino (i) (1466-1520) 6 583
Cosimo I, Grand Duke of Tuscany (*reg* 1569- 74) 11 193; 16 664; 21 20
Farnese, Alessandro, Cardinal (1520-89) 5 789; 10 810
Farnese, Ranuccio, Cardinal 10 811; 26 838
Grimani, Marino, Cardinal, Patriarch of Aquileia 13 658
Grimani, Vettor 13 658
Medici (family) 24 853
Orsini, Fulvio 23 577
Pier Luigi, 1st Duke of Parma (*reg* 1545-7) 10 809
Pius IV, Pope (*reg* 1559-66) 25 7
Salviati, Giovanni, Cardinal 27 648
pupils 5 182; 27 275, 654
reproductive prints by others 4 96; 20 796; 27 275; 32 412
stage design 30 657
tapestries 11 *193*; 16 757, *757*; 17 812; 30 319
teachers 27 851; 32 10
Salviati, Giovanni, Cardinal 3 817; 6 139; 27 648
Salviati, Giuseppe 27 654–5*
attributions 28 5
collaboration 19 330; 28 658
methods 21 766
paintings 32 223
teachers 27 654
works 26 818; 27 653, *655*; 32 212; 33 356
Salviati, Jacopo 1 670; 12 576; 19 672; 27 648
Salviati, Lorenzo 27 748
Salviati and Son 31 163
Salviatis, Bernardinus de 8 551
Salvi d'Andrea 27 655–6*
Salvi di Michieli 9 330
works 9 *330*
Salvin, Anthony (1799-1881) 27 656–7*
assistants 22 809; 28 561
collaboration 22 808
groups and movements 10 142; 13 202
patrons and collectors 25 39
restorations 5 510; 19 617
staff 24 307
works 5 264; 6 61; 23 250, 689; 24 390; 27 *656*; 29 835; 33 250
Salvin, Anthony (1827-81) 27 657
Salvini, Roberto 27 657*
Salvioni, Giovanni Maria 17 706
Salvisberg, Otto Rudolf 27 657–8*; 30 128
collaboration 3 796
pupils 23 440; 26 744
Salvisburg & Brechbühl 3 823
Salvo 16 683; 27 658*
Salvo d'Antonio 2 178; 8 14; 20 213; 27 658*; 28 656
Salvotti (family) 25 3
Salvucci (family) 27 750
Salway, William 2 122
Saly, Jacques-François-Joseph 1 105; 7 805; 8 760; 11 561; 27 659*
patrons and collectors 5 380; 8 758
pupils 24 222
reproductions in ceramics 8 748
works 3 841; 7 802; 8 740; 10 *110*
Salza, Jakob von, Bishop of Breslau 24 207
Salzburg 2 774, 775, *776*; 25 867; 26 *906*; 27 659–65*, *660*
art forms and materials
ceramics 27 665*
embroidery 2 824
faience (ii) (ceramics) 2 815, *815*
furniture 2 811
gold 2 819
manuscripts 2 790, 792; 5 803; 15 875; 20 330; 23 655; 26 674–5
metalwork 26 683
painting 2 792; 12 382
pewter 2 821
pottery 2 815–16
Cemetery of St Sebastian 6 165
ecclesiastical buildings
Cathedral of SS Rupert and Virgil 2 776, 777, 780, *781*, 790, 824; 29 27
reliquaries 2 819
sculpture 2 801; 26 634
tympanum 27 *663*
Cemetery of St Sebastian Gabrielskapelle 2 800
mausoleum of Wolf Dietrich von Raitenau 2 781
Church of Maria Plain 8 526
Dreifaltigkeitskirche 2 782; 11 132, *133*
Erhardskirche 2 781
Franciscan church 2 799; 4 777; 26 635; 32 88, 93, 821
altar 27 *661*
Kajetanerkirche 2 794
Kollegienkirche 2 782; 11 132
Michaelbeuern Monastery
sculpture 13 *799*
Nonnberg Abbey
chairs 12 419
furniture 30 776
manuscripts 2 790; 26 675, *676*
sculpture 2 801; 26 635
stained glass 13 188, *188*; 29 504, IV
wall paintings 2 790; 26 652
St Peter - Stift 2 781, 819, 822, 824; 6 165; 22 204; 26 635, 675
mother-of-pearl 22 *204*
Theatine church 2 781
Salzburg—cont.
Festspielhaus 30 683
frescoes 27 *664*
Hohensalzburg
Goldene Stube 2 805
Internationale Sommerakademie für Bildende Kunst 2 831
Mozarteum 2 831; 27 662
Residenz 2 781
paintings 11 720; 27 233
Residenzgalerie 4 574; 8 427, 428
Residenzplatz 27 *662*
Salzburger Museum Carolino Augusteum 27 665
Schloss Altenau *see* Schloss Mirabell
Schloss Anif 2 786, 802
Schloss Mirabell 2 782, 801; 26 498; 27 *661*
theological college of St Joseph 2 789
University 2 789
Salzburger Cristallglas 2 818
Salzburger Gewerbeblatt 28 800
Salzburger Museumsblätter 24 438
Salzedas Abbey 25 289
Salzedo, Lourenço de 2 874
Salzenberg, Wilhelm 27 665–6*
Salzillo, Nicolás 27 666; 29 293
Salzillo y Alcaraz, Francisco 27 666*; 29 293
Salzillo y Alcaraz, Inéz 27 666
Salzillo y Alcaraz, Juan Antonio 27 666
Salzillo y Alcaraz, Patricio 27 666
Salzmann, Alexander von 24 591
Salzmann, Auguste 16 395; 24 663; 27 667*
Salzmann, Friedrich Zacharias 25 367
Samacchini, Orazio 27 667*
patrons and collectors 25 7
reproductive prints by others 5 856; 30 803
Samada 30 *806*, 812, 818, 825
Samad al-Shan 2 265
Samain (family) 11 628
Samal 24 630
Sam'al *see* ZINCIRLI
Samandağı, Monastery of St Simeon the Stylite 2 159; 3 191; 9 540, 548, 591
Saman Deme *see* DEME SAMAN
Samanez, Juan Rodríguez *see* RODRÍGUEZ SAMANEZ, JUAN
Sam'ani 1 203
Samanid 27 667–8*
see also ISMA'IL I BIN AHMAD, Amir
Samaniego, Lorenzo 6 348
Samaniego y Jaramillo, Manuel 9 712, 714; 27 668*
Samar 24 *607*, 627
Samara 27 425
Samaraka 11 759
Samaras, Lucas 1 71; 13 355; 18 170; 27 668*
Samari, Hwasŏldang 12 94
Samaria 1 *849*; 14 465; 16 *565*, 573; 26 *915*; 27 668–71*; 30 *180*
churches 9 549
glass 1 866, 867
ivory-carvings 1 870; 24 643
palace 16 573; 17 552
plaques 27 *670*
St John 17 504, 506
Temple of Rome and Augustus 26 917
Samarina, Zoodochos Pigi 9 545
Samarkand 1 *849*; 6 *182*, 186, 197, 201, 203, 209, 210, *623*; 16 *105*; 27 671–7*, *672*; 28 *719*, 721; 30 253; 31 *781*, 781
art forms and materials
architecture 6 210; 16 196; 30 252; 31 782
coins 6 265, 266
Samarkand
art forms and materials—cont.
domes 9 84
embroidery 6 250; 31 783
glass 6 268, 269
inscriptions 6 379
ivory-carvings 6 271
jewellery 6 241, 274
manuscripts 6 234, 236; 16 321, 323, 342
metalwork 6 245, 246; 16 370
ossuaries 23 607
paintings 28 722
wall 1 882; 6 193, 228, 248; 16 252
paper 16 351; 24 48; 27 673
pottery 6 257, 258; 16 400, 413; 23 558; 28 723
reliefs 6 *276*
rock crystal 16 540
stucco 29 821–2
tents 23 820; 30 476
terracottas 6 275
textiles 6 249, 250; 16 443, 451; 31 783
tiles 6 207; 16 413
wood-carvings 6 277
woodwork 16 502
Baghcha Pavilion 6 208
Bagh-i Dilkusha 16 253
bazaars 6 211
Chini-khana 6 208
citadel 6 210
fortifications 21 589, 591, 592
gardens 16 197
Gulyamov Institute of Archaeology 6 283
Gur-i Mir 6 203; 16 *140*, 197, 199; 27 675–6*; 31 112
dome 9 84
doors 16 501, 526
mosaics 6 208
tomb of Timur 6 272; 16 527
wood-carvings 6 277
houses 16 154
Ishrat-Khana 6 208
Islamic religious buildings
madrasa of Abu Sa'id ibn Kuchkunji 16 235
madrasa of Shaybani Khan 16 235
madrasas of Yalangtush Bi Alchin 16 235
minarets 16 237
Mosque of Bibi Khanum 6 203; 16 91, 196, 199; 22 194; 24 877; 27 675*, *676*; 30 *918*
textiles 6 249
Shir Dar Madrasa 6 205, 208; 16 236, 239
Tamgach Bogra Khan Madrasa 6 201
Tilla Kar Madrasa 6 205; 16 236
Ulughbeg Madrasa 6 203, 205; 16 197; 20 57; 24 878
mausoleum of Ibrahim ibn Hasan 6 207
musalla 22 354
museums 6 282
Afrasiab Museum 6 283; 27 674
Ikramov Museum of the History of the Culture and Art of Uzbekistan 6 283; 27 674
Museum of History 6 283
Ulughbeg Memorial Museum 27 674, 677
Observatory 6 203; 16 198; 23 338; 27 677*
wall paintings 16 253
palaces
Blue Palace *see* Gok Saray
Bustan Saray 23 820
Garden Palace *see* Bustan Saray
Gok Saray 23 820
Ilkhanid palace 6 230–31
Samanid palace 6 206, 233
ramparts 6 211

Samarkand—cont.
Registan 6 205; 16 235–6, *236*; 27 676–7*
Shah-i Zinda 6 203; 16 197, 200; 27 *674*, 674–5*, *675*; 28 634, 636; 30 917; 31 113
mausoleum of Amir-Zada 6 208
mausoleum of Shrinibeg Aga 6 208
mausoleum of Tuman-Aga 6 208
doors 16 501
shrine of Qutham ibn ʿAbbas
cenotaph 6 172, 203, 277; 16 250; 28 634, 636
doors 16 501
tiles 6 207, 208; 16 250
tomb of Khwaja Ahmad 6 203
tomb of Qutluq Aqa 16 249
tomb of Shad-i Mulk 6 203, 208; 16 249
tomb of Ulugh Sultan Begum 6 203
State University 6 283
tomb of Khwaja Ahrar 16 237
town walls 6 199, 209, 211
Ulughbeg Madrasa 6 203
urban planning 6 209, 211
Samarkand Ewer 16 369
Samarlakota 15 534, 537
Bhimeshvara Temple 15 537
Mandava Narayana Temple 15 537
Samarra' 16 2, *104*, 112, 151; 21 *267*; 23 557, 560; 27 677–81*, *681*
art forms and materials
architecture 3 894; 4 791
ceramics 6 330, 915
glass 16 517, 518
iron 21 269
pottery 16 135, 396, 397, 398, 399, 400; 21 305; 23 557, *558*; 27 *677*, 677–8*; 30 196
rock crystal 16 540
stucco 29 819
wall paintings 16 252
woodwork 16 488, *489*
cantonments 16 151, 153
excavations 14 487; 16 550; 27 846
gardens 12 77–8
Great Mosque of al-Mutawakkil 16 151, *151*, 152; 27 680
minaret 16 152; 21 *626*, 626
mosaics 16 256
Pharaoh's Tray 11 339
houses 16 153
kiosks 18 70
mosque of Abu Dulaf 16 152; 22 194
minaret 16 152
mosques 22 193
musallas 16 152
ornament 16 133
palaces 16 142, 153, 243, 517; 23 814, 815
Balkuwara Palace 16 244; 27 *680*
gardens 12 77
Dar al-Khilafa 16 151, *152*, 153, 256; 23 815; 27 678
gardens 12 77
Jawsaq al-Khaqani 16 248, 252, 400, 452, 530; 23 815
Qasr al-ʿAshiq 16 153; 27 681
polo grounds 16 153
Qubbat al-Sulaibiyya 27 681; 31 110
racecourses 16 153
shrine of Imam al-Dawr 16 181; 29 820
Samarran culture 21 269*, 305
Samarra period *see under* MESOPOTAMIA; ANCIENT NEAR EAST → periods
Samassa, Albert 28 863
Samassa bell-foundry 28 863
Samate 22 245
Samatya Baths 16 224
Samb, Pape Mamadou 28 405
Samba, Cheri 33 597
works 33 *597*
Sambach, Kaspar Franz 2 795; 14 900; 30 206
works 30 *206*
Samba Pediados 21 656
Sambaquí culture 29 128, 197–8*
sculpture 29 *197*, 197–8*
Sambhal 15 *360*
congregational mosque 15 361
Sambhar 15 449
Sambiliturai 16 864
Sambin, Claude 27 681
Sambin, David 27 682
Sambin, Guillaume 27 681
Sambin, Hugues 27 681–2*
works 8 890, 891; 11 400, 514; 13 700; 27 *681*, *682*
writings 11 586; 23 489
Sambin, Mammès 27 681
Sambolín, Nelson 25 702
Sambor Prei Kuk 5 *458*, 464*; 29 826
lintels 5 464
sculpture 5 484
Sambourne, Linley 4 363; 21 312
interior decoration 10 *283*
Sambourne, Linley, House *see under* LONDON → museums
Sambucus, Johannes 10 174; 14 296
Samburu 1 254, 297, 350; 17 906
jewellery 1 *350*
Samch'ŏk, Chuksŏ-ru Pavilion 12 95
Samch'ŏk tonghae pi 14 702
Same 30 301
Sameba Church 12 320
Sameh 9 543
Samgijae *see* CH'OE PUK
Samgori 12 318
Samhan 18 382
Samhuram 23 436
Sami (1838-1912) 27 683*
Sami (Kephallinia) 17 909
Sami, Ali 24 220
Samian ware *see* POTTERY → wares → *terra sigillata*
Samico, Gilvan 4 719; 23 400
Samida Takarazuka mirror 17 54
Samloti 15 632
Sammacchini, Orazio *see* SAMACCHINI, ORAZIO
Sammartino, Giuseppe *see* SANMARTINO, GIUSEPPE
Sammartino, Marco 27 683*
Sammicheli, Matteo 31 447
Sammicheli (da Verona), Michele *see* SANMICHELI, MICHELE
Sam Mirza (Safavid) 2 235; 16 301, 343; 21 704
Sammlins, Benjamin 3 24
Sammlung nützlicher Aufsätze und Nachrichten die Baukunst betreffend 12 641; 24 443
Sammlung vermischter Schriften zur Beförderung der schönen Wissenschaften und der freyen Künste 24 443
Sammt-Teigdrucke prints *see* PRINTS → types → flock
Sammyo, Great Tomb of Kangso 18 313
Samnon Buddhism *see* BUDDHISM → sects → Madhyamika
Samnyŏn 21 594
Samo *see* BASQUIAT, JEAN-MICHEL
Samoa 27 683–5*
architecture 23 715, 717, 718
bark 27 684
body arts 27 *684*
canoes 27 683
craftsmen and artists 23 718
hair 23 720
headdresses 23 720
houses 27 683
languages 27 683
Samoa—cont.
mats 23 735
paper mulberry 27 684
stone 23 715
tattoos 23 718, 719; 27 683–4, *684*
wood 23 717, 718
Samoa, Western *see* WESTERN SAMOA
Samobor 8 *174*
kindergarten 8 177
Samohelová, Helena 8 406
Samokhvalov, Aleksandr (Nikolayevich) 7 341; 27 394, 395, 685*
Samokish, Nikolay (Semyonovich) 27 685*
Samokov 5 *144*
Bayraklı Mosque 5 148
Church of the Dormition 5 148
furniture 5 157
glass 5 159
Municipal Historical Museum 33 695
printing 5 154
prints 5 162
Sarafska House 5 156
sculpture 5 156
synagogue 17 545
Samokov school 5 154, 156; 27 685–6*; 33 695
Samonà, Alberto 27 686
Samonà, Giuseppe 27 686*
groups and movements 26 16
works 16 650; 28 657
writings 16 650
Šamorín Church 4 782; 14 898
Sa Morokot Reservoir 30 581
Samos 13 *363*; 15 893; 26 *908*; 27 687–90*
aqueducts 13 381
architecture 13 374
art forms and materials
bronzes 13 571, 572, 573
cauldrons 13 575
ceramics 13 358
fibulae 10 591
figurines 13 578
helmets 10 585
ivory-carvings 13 596
lamps 13 *603*
marble 13 434; 27 688, *689*
metalwork 10 591
pottery 13 497, 512, 515
sculpture 13 371, 445, 447, 592; 15 893; 18 409; 27 688–90*, *689*
korai 18 245
kouroi 13 445
South Stoa 27 687
stelae 13 427
Cheramyes Kore *see* CHERAMYES KORE
First Dipteros *see* Temple of Hera
fortifications 21 556, 558
Geneleos Group *see* GENELEOS GROUP
Heraion *see* Sanctuary of Hera
measurements 13 411
Sanctuary of Hera 13 371, 380, 416, 433, 592; 26 911; 27 687–8
bronze 13 372, 373, 435, 572
ivory-carvings 13 596, *596*
propylon 25 657
reliefs 13 427
sculpture 18 409; 26 857
Temple of Hera 13 555
1st Temple 13 376, 396, 442; 15 893; 24 456; 27 687
2nd Temple 13 374, 397; 24 456
3rd Temple 13 380, 394, 398, 399, 408; 15 893; 23 481, 484; 27 *687*, 687–8
4th Temple 13 373; 27 *688*
Temple of Rhoikos *see* Temple of Hera → 3rd Temple
Samos
Sanctuary of Hera—cont.
wood-carvings 13 604
tombs 13 384
tools 33 328
town walls 21 556
trade 13 486
tunnel 13 373, 411
water pipes 13 419
water supply 30 26
Samos, Rhoikos of *see* RHOIKOS OF SAMOS
Samos, Theodorus of *see* THEODORUS OF SAMOS
Samosata 17 499
Samostrzelnik, Stanisław 16 867; 25 103
Samothrace 13 *363*; 27 690–92*, *691*
fortifications 9 555
Nike *see* NIKE OF SAMOTHRACE
Sanctuary of the Great Gods 13 417, 425; 27 690–92*, *691*
Anaktoron 27 690
Arsinoeion 13 390, 391; 27 691–2; 30 737, *737*
Hall of Votive Gifts 14 73
Hieron 13 380, 389, 405; 24 319; 27 690; 30 435
Propylon of Philip II of Macedon 27 692
Propylon of Ptolemy II 13 392; 25 657; 27 690–91
tholoi 30 737
Sanctuary of Hera 1 128
sculpture 26 292; 27 692*, *692*
Samoyed 27 433
Sampaio, João Coelho *see* COELHO SAMPAIO, JOÃO
Sampaio, Joaquim da Costa Lima *see* COSTA LIMA SAMPAIO, JOAQUIM DA
Sampaio, José Coelho *see* COELHO SAMPAIO, JOSÉ
Sampaio de Pina de Brederode, António 29 101
Sampajo, Manuel Pereira de *see* PEREIRA DE SAMPAJO, MANUEL
Samper Ganneco, Germán 21 4
Sampieri (family) 27 693*
Sampilov, Tsyrenzhap 27 436
Sample, Paul 19 701
samplers 27 693–4*
Belgium 27 694
England 9 493; 27 693, 694
Germany 27 693, 694
Italy 27 *693*
Netherlands, the 27 694
Scandinavia 27 694
Spain 27 694
Switzerland 30 150–51
United States of America 27 694; 31 658
see also EMBROIDERY
Samprangan 15 785
Sampson, George 3 174; 28 905
Sampson, Joseph 21 896
Sampson the Painter *see* STRONG, SAMPSON
Sampung culture 29 226
Samra, Faisal 27 876
Samrong Sen 5 *458*, 459
Sam Saen Thai, King of Lan Xang (*reg* 1373-1416) 18 762
Samsam al-Dawla, Amir (*reg* 983-98) (Buyid) 16 372
Samsat *see* SAMOSATA
Samshvilde, Church of Sioni 12 319
Samson (family) 11 621
Samson, Edmé 27 694
Samson, Edmé, & Cie 24 149; 27 694*
Samson, Emile 11 631; 26 227; 27 694
Samson Master 12 399; 20 766*; 26 633; 33 71
Samsonov Brothers' Faience Factory 27 410
Samtavisi Church 12 *319*, 320; 27 129
Samtsevrisi Church 12 319
Sam Tung Uk 14 720
Samuda, Joseph 24 560
Samudio, Juan A. 24 98, 101, 102
Samudragupta, Ruler (*reg c.* 335-76) (Gupta) 1 647; 10 444; 15 461, 688
coins 15 *688*
inscription 15 475
Samudra-Pase 15 811
Samuel, King of Bulgaria (*reg* 976-1014) 5 146
Samuel, Gabriel 17 683
Samuel, George 12 742; 25 264
Samuel, Godfrey 20 475; 30 411
Samuel, H. (company) 19 594, 596
Samuel, Hava (*fl* 1932) 16 568
Samuel, Lewis 31 334
Samuel, Rafael 31 335
Samuel, Sigmund 5 589; 27 694–5*
Samuel, Sigmund, Canadian Museum *see under* TORONTO → museums and galleries
Samuel, Sigmund Gallery *see under* TORONTO → museums and galleries → Royal Ontario Museum
Samuel, Vera Evelyn 13 615
Samuel Alcock & Co. 10 310
works 10 *311*
Samuel ben Jacob 21 475
Samuels, Emerson 13 876
Samuels, Jeffrey 1 65
Samuels, Sarah *see* STEIN, SARAH
Samuely, F. J. 10 173; 14 613
Samun Dukiya 23 *129*, 130
Samuolis, Antanas 19 499
Samuru Iwase *see* KITAO MASANOBU
Samus (*fl* 1st cent. AD) 26 885
Samus' (Russia) 27 365
Samwell (family) 21 148
Samwell, William 13 696; 20 141
Samye 5 104; 21 848; 27 695*; 30 *806*
sculpture 30 822
Utse Temple 27 695; 30 815, *815*
wall paintings 30 829
Samyŏng 18 330
San 1 *381*, 417; 4 489; 19 241; 27 695–8*; 29 102; 33 678
beads 1 297; 4 489
beds 1 366
eggs 1 297
lamps 1 385
rock art 1 373, 375; 4 489; 27 695–8, *696*, *697*
shells 28 581
shelters 1 306
Saña (Peru) 24 *498*
S Agustín 24 502
S Francisco 24 502
Sanʿa (Yemen) 2 *246*; 16 *104*, 144; 27 698–9*, *699*
Abhar Mosque 16 500, *500*
Abraha Church 16 255
architecture 16 213; 32 317; 33 519
Bakiriyya Mosque 16 229
Dar al-Saʿada *see* National Museum
education (art) 33 520
fortifications 21 588
Gallery Number One 33 520
Great Mosque 16 177, 178; 27 698
ceiling 16 500
coffering 7 527
grilles 16 500
minaret 16 178
sculpture 16 245
jewellery 16 532
manuscripts 16 289
Masjid al-Abhar 16 215
minaret 16 215
metalwork 33 520
museums 2 275

San'a (Yemen)—cont.
National Museum **33** 520
Nizamiyya **16** 215
printing **16** 361
silver **33** 520
temple of Huqqa **2** 253
textiles **16** 438; **31** 21, 22
tomb of Salah al-Din **16** 215
tower houses **33** 519
windows **16** 257
Sanabria, Gregorio F. **14** 716
Sanabria, Juan **21** 378
Sanabria, Tomás José **32** 171
Sanadze, K. **12** 327
Sanage **17** *11*, *241*
ceramics **27** 699–700*
kilns **17** 250
pottery **17** 242, 248–9, 251, *251*, 260, 351; **33** 487
San Agustín (Colombia) **7** *601*; **29** *136*
metalwork **29** 212
mounds **29** 139
pottery **29** 150
stelae **29** 620
stone-carvings **29** 134
tombs **31** 118
San Agustín Convent (Mexico) **21** 383
San Agustín, Marcelo de **24** 621
San Agustín culture **27** 700–701*; **29** 132
crypts **27** 700
religion **29** 130
sarcophagi **27** 833
sculpture **27** 700, *700*, 701; **29** 127, 145–6
stone **27** *700*
Sanahin
Monastery **2** *423*; **27** 701*
Church of the Holy Mother of God **2** 434; **27** 701
Church of the Saviour **2** 434, 444; **27** 701
khatchk'ars **2** 436
library **2** 427, 444
Treasury **2** 444
Tuteordi *khatchk'ar* **2** 436
pottery **2** 439
Sanahuja, Manuel de **27** 702*
works **4** 259; **5** 551; **18** 777, *778*; **25** 365
Sanakht (*reg c.* 2650–*c.* 2630 BC) **9** *776*, 868; **29** 615
Ṣān al-Ḥagar *see* TANIS
Sanam **23** *276*, 281, 282; **30** 237
Temple of Amun **23** 281
San'ami **1** 776
Sanandaj *see* SENNA
San Antimo Abbey **26** 576
San Antolín de Tóques **26** 642
San Antonio (Belize) **3** 623
San Antonio (Costa Rica), Escuela 'Country Day' **8** 17
San Antonio (Ecuador) **9** 710
San Antonio (TX; USA)
Alamo church **31** 589
S Antonio de Valero *see* Alamo church
S José y S Miguel de Aguayo **31** 589
San Antonio, Bartolomé de **24** 111
San Antonio del Oriente **14** *711*, 713
sanatoria **14** *628*; **15** *886*; **23** 221
Sanatruq I (*fl* AD 177–8) **14** 224
Sanatruq II (*fl* AD 240–1) **14** 224
Sanavio, Natale **17** 442
San Bartolo Atepehuacán **21** 192
San Bartolomé de Xala, Conde de **21** 377, 395, 401; **26** 518
Sanba Shikitei *see* SHIKITEI SANBA
San Beat **29** 702
Sanbei Kingae *see* RI SANPEI
San Benedetto Abbey *see under* SUBIACO
San Benedetto Po Abbey (Emilia-Romagna) **26** 621
San Benet de Bages **7** 455
San Bernardino Master **13** 820
San Biagio **21** 342
San Blas Hospital **22** 255
Sanbontōge kiln **30** 287
Sanborn, John **32** 421
Sanburov, P. A. **26** 734
Sanbutsuji **17** 129
Nageiredō **17** 68, *68*
sancai pottery *see under* POTTERY → wares
San Candido, SS Candido e Corbiniano **26** 635, 646
San Carlos, Duque de **29** 342
S Carlos Castle (Nicaragua) **23** 80
San Carlos Church (Panama) **23** 904
San Carlos Church (Uruguay) **31** 753
San Casciano, S Maria del Prato **13** 94
S Cassiano Altarpiece **2** *180*; **27** 495
San Cebrián de Mazote **2** 294; **22** 246, 247; **29** 288
S Cecilia Bible *see under* BIBLES → individual manuscripts
Sancha, Queen of Aragon (*d* 1208) **26** 656; **28** 695
Sancha, Queen of Castile and León (*d* 1067) **2** 222; **8** 213; **19** 178; **29** 288
Sancha of Majorca, Queen of Naples (1286–1345) **2** 110; **13** 163; **22** 470, 476
Sanches, Rui **25** 302
Sánchez **9** *114*
church **9** 116
Sánchez, Adán **4** 260; **18** 777
Sánchez, Alberto *see* ALBERTO
Sánchez, Bartolomé **8** 231
Sánchez, Benito **7** 362
Sánchez, Cristobal **28** 519
Sánchez, Diego **27** 702*
Sánchez, Edgar **27** 702*
Sánchez, Emilio **18** 834; **27** 703*
Sánchez, Fabián **24** 511
Sánchez, Félix **21** 382
Sánchez, Humberto Jaimes *see* JAIMES SÁNCHEZ, HUMBERTO
Sánchez, Jerónimo **27** 706
Sanchez, José Luis **29** 296, 309
Sánchez, Juan (*fl* 1980s) **18** 834
works **18** *833*
Sánchez, Juan, II (*fl* 1590–1600) **27** 702*
Sánchez, Juan Félix **27** 703*; **32** 167
Sánchez, Luis **21** 382
Sanchez, Manuel **27** 666
Sánchez, Mariano (Ramón) *see* SANCHIS, MARIANO (RAMON)
Sánchez, Martín **13** 123
Sanchez, Maurice **19** 492
Sánchez, Nufro **21** 604
Sánchez, Pedro (*fl* 1560s) **24** 514
Sánchez, Pedro (1568–1633) **3** 418; **22** 68; **29** 269
Sánchez, Pedro, I (*fl c.* 1500) **27** 702*
Sánchez, Pedro, II (*fl* after 1500) **27** 702*
Sánchez, Ramona **12** 915
Sánchez, Roberto M. **14** 716
Sánchez, Samuel **25** 701
Sánchez Barba, Juan **20** 67; **27** 703*
Sánchez Bonifacio, Martín **13** 757; **21** 125; **27** 703*
Sánchez Bort **29** 271
Sánchez Canton, Francisco Javier **27** 704*; **31** 172
Sánchez Cerro, Luis **24** 516
Sánchez Coello, Alonso **27** 704–6*
collaboration **29** 278
patrons and collectors **1** 529; **2** 409, 874; **13** 922; **14** 5, 517; **24** 462; **26** 307; **32** 127
pupils **19** 303; **24** 22
Sánchez Coello, Alonso—cont.
works **9** 267, 268; **10** 502; **15** 121; **20** 66; **22** 695; **27** *705*; **29** 345
Sánchez Cotán, Juan **27** 706–7*; **29** 280
groups and movements **30** 456
teachers **25** 419
works **15** 140; **27** *707*; **29** 667; **31** 89
Sánchez de Castro, Juan **27** 702*
Sánchez de Guadalupe, Antón **27** 702*
Sánchez de la Rosa, Cristóbal **24** 818
Sánchez de Rueda, Teodosio **15** 33; **27** 708*
Sánchez Eliá, Santiago **2** 397
Sanchez Falconete, Pedro **28** 520
Sánchez Felipe, Alejandro **31** 415
Sánchez Galque, Adrian **9** 712; **18** 835
Sánchez García, Alfonso **1** 624
Sánchez Gomez, Jávier **2** 397
Sanchez-Heredero, José Francés y *see* FRANCÉS Y SANCHEZ-HEREDERO, JOSÉ
Sánchez Portela, Alfonso **1** 624
Sánchez Solís, Felipe **13** 868
Sánchez Soto, Cristóbal **29** 337
Sanchi **8** 269; **15** 194, 245, *285*; **21** 847; **27** 708–10*
Archaeological Museum **15** 181
art forms and materials
architecture **14** 77; **15** 248, 737
ivory **15** 695
reliefs **2** 297; **6** 481; **13** 3; **15** 248, *248*, 249, 416, 442, 677; **21** 590; **23** 817; **30** 438
sculpture **5** 94, 95; **15** 220, 229, 412, 431–3*, 451, 468, 469, 470, *470*, 494, 677, 744, 750
gateways **15** 248
Great Stupa **12** 72; **15** 249, 412; **27** *709*; **29** 442, 526, 864, *864*
reliefs **15** *235*
sculpture **15** *431*, 431–3
iconography **15** 213
pillar **15** 423, 430, 431
stupas **15** 303; **19** 717; **22** 516
Stupa 2 **15** 428–9*, *429*, 433
Stupa 3 **15** 433, 451
temples **15** 237
Temple 17 **14** 77; **15** 253–4
Temple 18 **15** 252, 494
Temple 40 **15** 251
toraṇa **31** 160
toraṇas **15** 431
Sanchis, Mariano (Ramón) **4** 565; **27** 710*
Sancho, King of Aragon (*reg* 1063–94) **19** 520
Sancho I, King of Portugal (*reg* 1185–1211) **7** 531
Sancho IV, King of Castile and León (*reg* 1284–95) **2** 452; **16** 439
Sancho V, King of Aragon (*reg* 1076–94) **31** 209
Sancho, Antonio **29** 335
Sancho de Zamora **31** 88
Sancho of Aragon, Archbishop of Toledo **16** 440
Sanchor Mosque **15** 349
Sanchotene, J. **12** 43
Sancino, Giacomo da *see* GIACOMO DA SANCINO
San Clemente a Casáuria Abbey **26** 625
San Clemente al Vomano **16** 626
church **26** 533, 625
S Climente, Master of **29** 275; **30** 368
San Coamo **25** 700
church **25** 700
San Cosmé **24** *91*
Mission Church **24** 94
Museum **24** 101
San Cristobal (Solomon Islands) **29** 50, 51
bowls **29** *50*
San Cristóbal (Venezuela) **32** *165*
Palacio de Gobierno **32** 170
San Cristobal de las Casas, Casa de Andrés de Tobilla **21** 376
San Cristóbal Totonicapán **13** 768
San Cristoforo factory **16** 739
Sanctis, Francesco de' **27** 710–11*
catalogues **16** 769
works **15** 862; **16** 639; **26** *760*; **27** *711*; **29** 374
Sanctis, Giovanni de *see* VASANZIO, GIOVANNI
Sanctis, Guglielmo de *see* DE SANCTIS, GUGLIELMO
Sanctis, Orazio de **27** 711*
Sancti Spíritus **8** 228, *228*
sanctuaries **27** 711–14*
Bali (Indonesia) **15** 758, 767–8
Bolivia **4** *257*
Britain **27** *2*
Buddhism **6** 296–7, *422*; **15** 759–62, *761*
Cambodia **5** 467, 468–9*, *473*, 475, 477, 496
Celtic **27** 142
Central Asia, Eastern **6** 296–7
Champa **6** 420, *421*
Christianity **27** 714*
Crete **8** 153; **18** 164
Cyprus, ancient **8** *307*, 334, 341
Early Christian (*c.* AD 250–843) **27** 714
Egypt, ancient **9** *828*, *833*; **12** *227*; **29** 386
Etruscan **10** 608
Germany **26** *905*
Greece, ancient **8** 692, *692*, 868; **13** 369, 371, 376, 380, 381, 386, 396, *404*, 416–17*, *416*, *418*, 418–19*, 420, 568; **18** *393*; **27** 711–14*, *712*; **29** 680
Hinduism **15** 762
Indonesia **4** 419, *419*; **15** 758–68*
Buddhism **15** 759–62, *761*
Hinduism **15** 762
8th cent. AD **15** *759*
14th cent. **15** *765*
15th cent. **15** *766*
Iran, ancient **15** 913
Italy **25** *421*; **31** *58*
Japan **16** 74
Java **15** 758–62, *759*, *761*, 764–6, *765*, *766*
Khmer **5** 477
Maya **23** 838
Mesoamerica, Pre-Columbian **23** 838
Minoan **8** 153; **18** 164
Poland **12** 823
Prehistoric art **8** *307*; **25** 482, 538
Romanesque **26** 569
Rome, ancient **25** *421*; **26** 858, 865, 905; **27** 1–2*, 711–14*, *713*
Britain **27** *2*
Germany **26** *905*
Italy **31** *58*
Shinto **16** 74
Sumatra **15** 766–7
Syria-Palestine **30** *190*
Vietnam **6** 420, *421*
Zoroastrianism **15** 913
see also HEROA
Sanctuary of Apollo Ptoios (Boeotia) **18** 409
sanctuary-temples *see under* TEMPLES → types
Sancy Diamond **11** 634, 635
sand **6** 324
historical and regional traditions
Aboriginal Australia **1** 44–5*, *45*
Africa **29** 827
Central Asia, Eastern **6** 301
Central Asia, Western **6** 224
Greece, ancient **29** 706
Turkmenistan **6** 224
sand—cont.
uses
abrasives **1** 761; **29** 706
arriccio **10** 740
brick **4** 767
casting **28** 739
ceramics **6** 328, 330
enamel **10** 192
etchings **10** 562
glass **29** 497
grounds **6** 224, 301; **25** 174
moulds **21** 320
plaster **11** 762; **29** 812
sculpture **1** 44–5*, *45*
stucco **29** 812, 827
Sand, Georges **17** 605; **26** 54
Sanda
church **14** 81
memorial stone **32** 522
Sandal (W. Yorks) **6** 55; **9** 144
Sandal (*fl* 1304–6) **20** 229
sandalwood **7** 115; **15** 720, 721, 724; **17** 399; **28** 310; **32** 488; **33** 325
sandalwood bark *see under* BARK → types
San Daniele, Pellegrino da *see* PELLEGRINO DA SAN DANIELE
Sandanski, Hotel **5** 159
sandarac **6** *71*; **12** 803; **16** 729; **20** 58; **26** 243; **29** 305
glazes **23** 792
japanning **18** 610
lacquer **18** 609, 611
varnishes **32** 1
sandarack *see* REALGAR
San Davino, Master of **13** 733
Sandawizaya, King (*reg* 1710–31) (Myohaung) **2** 281
shrines (i) (cult) **2** *281*
Sandbach, Henry **12** 598
Sandbach, Margaret **12** 598
sandbags **27** 714*
Sandbeck Park (N. Yorks) **19** 793; **21** 368; **23** *781*
Sandberg, Johann Gustav **10** 127; **22** 329; **30** 79, 80
Sandberg, Ragnar **10** 805; **13** 31; **30** 81
Sandberg, Willem (Jacob Henri Berend) **1** 810; **22** 852; **27** 714–15*
Sandblad, Nils Gösta **30** 120
sand-blasting **4** 789; **12** 787*
Sandburg, Carl **29** 602
Sandby, Paul **14** 166; **23** 258; **27** 715–17*
methods **10** 559
patrons and collectors **14** 163; **33** 209
pupils **7** 501; **14** 163, 451; **19** 98; **27** 132
reproductive prints by others **13** 693
works **1** 649; **2** 239, 240; **10** 251, *559*, 562; **14** 641; **15** 828; **20** 109, 569; **27** *716*; **32** 785, 900
writings **14** 640
Sandby, Thomas **10** 372; **23** 258; **27** 715*
patrons and collectors **14** 144
pupils **27** 715
works **27** *715*
sand casting *see under* CASTING → types
sand drawings *see under* DRAWINGS → forms
Sande, Diego de **6** 67
Sande, Jan van de **33** 169
Sande Bakhuyzen, Hendrik van de **22** 908; **26** 527
Sandels, (Adrian) Gösta (Fabian) **27** 717*; **30** 81; **33** 566
Sandeman, George **28** 252
Sander, August **13** 727; **24** 673; **27** 717–18*
works **27** *718*
Sander, Gunther **27** 718

Sander, Wilhelm 22 450; 33 245
Sanders, Herbert 31 640
Sanders, Jan 12 288
Sanders, Theodorus 3 787
Sanders, William T. 17 753; 30 483
Sanders, W. J. 2 765
Sanderson, Arthur 27 719
Sanderson, Arthur, & Sons Ltd 10 285; 14 53; 17 470; 27 719*; 32 721, 812; 33 372
Sanderson, Arthur Bengough 27 719
Sanderson, Elijah 10 852
Sanderson, Harold William 27 719
Sanderson, Ivan Couper 27 719
Sanderson, Jacob 10 852
Sanderson, John 17 877; 23 21, 859; 29 540
Sanderson, John Ward 27 719
Sanderson, Robert 4 479; 31 647
Sanderson, William 23 208; 27 719*
Sanders van Hemessen, Jan *see* HEMESSEN, JAN SANDERS VAN
Sanderus, A.
 works 4 *920*
Sandford Reliquary 10 338
sāndhāra see under TEMPLES → types
Sandi, Antonio 3 199; 21 831; 27 719–20*
Sandía (NM) 22 606
San Diego (CA) 27 720–21*; 31 *587*
 Hotel Coronado 14 787
 Museum of Art 15 743; 16 555, 557; 22 795; 27 720
  Binney Collection 2 236
 Panama California Exposition, 1915 10 683
 Woman's Club 27 *720*
Sandier, Alexandre 28 524
Sandilands 3 61
Sandilands, Robert Douglas 12 775
Sandl 12 798
Sandle, Michael 10 269; 27 721*
San Domenico di Fiesole, Badia Fiesolana 23 485; 26 576; 32 88, 384
Sandomierz 25 *92*; 27 721–3*
 Cathedral 25 115, 121, 126, 127, 129
 Diocesan Museum 27 722
 Długosz's House 25 134
 fortifications 4 783
 Museum 25 140
 St James 4 782; 25 95
 Town Hall 27 *722*
Sandon Park (Staffs) 3 690; 26 345
Sandoval, Gregorio Mariá de Silva Mendoza y, Duque del Infantado y Pastrana
Sandoval, Santiago Cristóbal 21 384
Sandoval y Rojas, Bernardo de, Cardinal Archbishop of Toledo 27 724*
 furniture 29 314
 illustrated writings 2 645
 paintings 31 89
Sandoval y Rojas, Francisco Gómez de, Duque de Lerma *see* LERMA, FRANCISCO GÓMEZ DE SANDOVAL Y ROJAS, Duque de
Sandoway 5 247
Sandoz (company) 19 808
Sandoz, Adolf Karol 25 751
Sandoz, Edouard-Marcel 19 398; 27 724*
Sandoz, Gérard 2 521; 17 529
sand painting *see under* PAINTING → forms
sandpaper *see under* PAPER → types
Sandrart, Gerrit van 5 1
Sandrart, Jakob von 11 457
Sandrart, Joachim von (1606-88) 2 717, 794; 11 674, 735; 12 390, 478; 14 869; 19 501; 22 302; 23 308; 26 772; 27 724–6*; 30 526; 33 276
 collaboration 29 400
 dealing 9 410; 13 919; 31 526
 groups and movements 24 741; 28 92
 patrons and collectors 19 238
 personal collection 9 229
 pupils 21 152
 reproductive prints by others 14 25; 18 46; 30 47
 teachers 14 730; 16 576; 27 504
 works 2 163; 6 78; 7 400; 12 389, 390; 17 656; 18 668; 27 *725*; 28 380
 writings 2 531; 7 389; 9 443; 10 204; 12 764; 15 82; 20 267
  illustrated 18 46
Sandrart, Joachim von (1668-91) 27 724
S Andres Semetabaj 13 760
Sandrié, Charles 7 778
Sandrik 28 856
Sandrino di Giovanni 31 447
Sandro, Iacopo di 26 816
Sandrock, Brian 25 566
Sands, Anthony 27 726
Sands, Joseph 26 214
Sands, Robert 14 736
sandstone 29 703*
 conservation 7 747
 historical and regional traditions
  Africa 1 305
  Arabia 2 *254*
  Belgium 29 *660*
  Buddhism 5 *100*, *462*, *498*; 15 *440*, *441*, *455*, *456*, *457*; 20 *819*; 27 *844*; 30 *600*, 606; 33 *574*
   China 6 706, *714*, *716*
  Cambodia 5 *100*, 459, *462*, 474, *485*, *488*, *489*, *492*, *493*, *494*, *496*, *497*, *498*
  Champa 29 IX2
  China 6 706, *714*, *716*, *718*; 33 *574*
  Czech Republic 8 376
  Denmark 8 *741*
  Egypt, ancient 9 773, 813*, 814, 815, *883*, *887*, *894*, *896*; 10 5; 29 703
   Egypt, ancient 22 *512*
  England 10 224, 227
  Etruscan 10 602
  Germany 3 *142*; 11 *751*; 12 *343*, *344*; 13 *86*, *91*, *92*, *684*; 29 *6*; 32 *830*
   Gothic 26 *370*, *372*
  Gothic 11 *751*; 12 *343*, *344*; 13 *86*, *91*, *92*, 102; 26 *370*, *372*; 29 *6*
  Hinduism 5 *485*, *488*, *489*, *492*, *493*, *494*; 15 *214*, *218*, *495*, *496*, *497*
  Huastec 14 *830*, 830
  Iberia (peninsula) 15 59, *60*
  Indian subcontinent 8 *768*; 15 *427*, *440*, *441*, *442*, *444*, *452*, *536*, *537*; 20 *819*
   Gupta 15 *253*
   Indian subcontinent 20 *818*
   Islamic 15 340; 16 239
   2nd cent. BC 15 *430*
   3rd cent. BC 15 *423*; 27 *844*
   5th cent. AD 15 *455*, *456*
   6th cent. AD 15 *457*, *460*
   7th cent. AD 15 *229*, *495*
   8th cent. AD 15 *214*, *495*
   9th cent. AD 15 *536*
   10th cent. AD 15 *218*, *230*, *496*
   11th cent. 15 324, *497*
   15th cent. 15 *498*
   17th cent. 27 *867*
   19th cent. 15 *413*, *542*
  Islamic 15 340; 16 239
sandstone
 historical and regional traditions—cont.
  Israel 17 *579*
  Jainism 15 *442*
  Jewish art 17 *579*
  Khmer 30 *600*
  Mauretania 1 305
  Mesoamerica, Pre-Columbian 14 *830*; 21 719; 27 *832*
   Huastec 14 830
  Mexico 14 *830*; 27 *832*
  Netherlands, the 22 *855*; 23 *188*
  Olmec 27 *832*
  Ottonian 23 646, *647*
  Poland 25 *109*
  Prehistoric art 25 488, 491, 493, 494
  Romanesque 10 227; 22 *855*; 25 *109*
  Rome, ancient 26 874
  Sweden 13 102
  Thailand 30 *600*, 606
  Vietnam 29 IX2
 techniques
  engraving 25 491
 types
  Baumberg 13 *683*
  Millstone Grits 29 703
  Old Red 10 227
  Yorkstone 29 703
 uses
  abrasion 1 761
  abrasives 16 859
  altarpieces 26 *372*
  architecture 1 305; 8 376; 9 773; 15 340; 16 239; 26 874; 29 703
  capitals 15 *413*; 22 *705*; 27 *844*
  chimney-pieces 23 *188*
  crucifixes 12 *343*
  erasers 10 5
  figurines 25 488
  friezes 15 *230*
  mirrors 21 719
  monuments 27 *867*
  portals 29 *6*
  relief sculpture 22 *512*
   Arabia 2 *254*
   Cambodia 5 *492*, *493*, *494*
   Egypt, ancient 9 *887*, *894*, *896*
   Germany 13 *86*; 32 *830*
   Indian subcontinent 8 *768*; 15 *452*, *498*, *536*, *537*, *542*; 20 *818*, *819*
   Netherlands, the 22 *855*
   Vietnam 29 IX2
  sarcophagi 27 *832*
  sculpture 5 *100*; 9 815; 15 *218*, *495*
   Belgium 29 *660*
   Buddhism 5 *462*; 6 *716*, *718*
   Cambodia 5 *462*, *485*, *488*, *489*, *497*, *498*
   China 6 706, *714*, *716*, *718*; 33 *574*
   Denmark 8 *741*
   Egypt, ancient 9 *883*
   Germany 3 *142*; 11 *751*; 12 *344*; 13 *91*, *92*, *683*, *684*; 26 *370*
   Gothic 13 *91*, *92*, 102; 29 *6*
   Hinduism 15 *478*, *479*, *480*, *481*
   Iberia (peninsula) 15 59, *60*
   Indian subcontinent 15 *214*, *229*, *230*, *423*, *427*, *430*, *440*, *441*, *442*, *444*, *455*, *456*, *457*, *460*, *478*, *479*, *480*, *481*, *495*, *496*, *497*
   Jewish art 17 *579*
   Mesoamerica, Pre-Columbian 14 830, *830*
   Ottonian 23 646, *647*
   Poland 25 *109*
   Romanesque 25 *109*
   Thailand 30 *600*, 606
   Vietnam 32 *478*
  temples 15 *253*, 324
sandstone
 uses—cont.
  writing 10 5
sandstone (silicified) *see* QUARTZITE
Sandström, Margareta 30 113
Sandström, Sven 30 120
Sandtner, Jakob 15 835; 22 299
Sandur 15 526
 Parvati Temple 15 295, 298, 300
Sandwich (Kent), Old House 10 272
Sandwich glass *see under* GLASS → types
Sandy Lane Hotel 2 148
Sandys, Edwin 16 15
Sandys, Emma 27 727
Sandys, Francis 2 337; 5 287; 14 485
Sandys, (Anthony) Frederick (Augustus) 23 249; 27 726–7*
 groups and movements 10 253; 25 555
 reproductive prints by others 25 868
 works 11 433, 434, 435; 25 266
Sandys, George 7 431; 10 78; 13 298; 23 680
sandyx see under PIGMENTS → types
Sandzhiyev, Nikita 27 433
San Emigdiano Range 22 *544*; 27 727*
Sanen, Simon van 28 217
San Esteban de Gormaz, S María del Rivero 16 436
San Esteban y Gormaz, García de 27 727*
Sanetaka Sanjōnishi *see* SANJŌNISHI SANETAKA
Sanetomo *see* MINAMOTO NO SANETOMO, Shogun
Sanfelice, Ferdinando 13 802; 27 727–9*
 works 16 640; 22 473; 27 *729*; 29 525
San Felipe (Chile) 6 *590*
 Museo San Francisco de Curimón 6 601
San Felipe School (NM; USA) 22 671
San Felipe de Arecibo 25 700
San Felipe y Santiago de Montevideo *see* MONTEVIDEO
San Feliú de Guixols, Puerta Ferrada 29 262
San Fernando de Omoa 14 713
Sanfilippo, Antonio 1 112; 9 168; 11 314; 26 777
Sanford, Claire 4 481
Sanford, F. 6 174
Sanford, John 21 348; 27 729*
San Francisco (CA) 27 729–31*; 31 *587*
 Alamo Square 27 *730*
 Art Institute 26 427
 building regulations 5 136
 Citizens' Federal Savings and Loan Association building 31 598
 City Hall 31 242
 coins 24 626
 Coit Tower 25 653
 Fox Cinema 7 327
 Golden Gate Bridge 4 803; 25 892
 Golden Gate International Exposition 22 674
 Haas-Lilienthal House 9 685
 International Airport 1 495
 Metro stations 21 350
 museums
  Asian Art Museum 15 743; 18 384; 22 795; 25 234; 27 731
   collections 3 916; 6 735, 826; 7 156; 15 746
  California Palace of the Legion of Honor 27 731
San Francisco (CA)
 museums—cont.
  M. H. de Young Memorial Museum 22 276; 27 731; 31 667
  Museum of Modern Art 27 731; 28 167
 Old St Mary's 24 281
 Old Vedanta Temple 15 408
 painting 25 681
 Palace Hotel 14 787
 Palace of Fine Arts 10 683
 Panama Pacific International Exposition, 1915 10 683; 15 883; 27 730, 731; 31 605
 Sacred Circles gallery 22 678
 Sea Ranch development 22 *53*
 Tanho Temple
  Conservatory of Flowers 7 745
 urban planning 7 357; 31 735, 738
San Francisco de Quito *see* QUITO
San Francisco de Veraguas 23 *902*
 church 23 904
San Francisco Tapestry Workshop 1 145; 31 660
Sanfré, Alexandre de Sousa Holstein, Conde de 29 100*; 32 425
San Friano, Maso da 25 262; 27 732*
 pupils 10 188; 23 764
 works 10 858; 27 *732*
Sanfront, Ercole Negro di *see* NEGRO DI SANFRONT, ERCOLE
Sang, Jacob 22 885
Sanga 1 305
San Gaggio, Master of 2 514
San Galgano Abbey 16 627
Sangallo (family) 25 906
Sangallo, Antonio da (i) (*c.* 1460-1534) 21 566; 27 733, 739–40*
 architecture 3 299; 16 633; 19 511; 27 736, *739*
 assistants 22 15
 attributions 26 836; 32 692
 collaboration 3 15, 16; 7 541; 8 187; 11 705; 16 633; 23 492; 27 733, 734, 735
 drawings 27 736
 patrons and collectors 2 390; 7 366
 works 2 390; 11 179
Sangallo, Antonio da (ii) (1483-1546) 7 542; 20 865; 21 566; 26 769; 27 741–8*; 31 714
 architecture
  banks 23 492; 26 756
  bastions 21 *566*
  chapels 22 12
  churches 5 552; 7 692; 9 182, 339; 16 635; 18 573; 19 686; 24 196; 25 260; 26 187, 805; 27 *743*, 770; 33 586
  fortifications 19 686
  fortresses 1 605; 2 1; 5 683; 7 359; 21 19; 24 520, 754; 31 581
  military 2 593; 3 359; 21 566
  mints 27 *744*
  monasteries 22 10
  palazzi 4 650; 12 790; 16 633; 19 159, 688; 23 810, *810*; 26 838; 27 486, *741*, *742*; 29 521
  wells 23 584
 assistants 4 47; 7 331; 27 740
 attributions 1 605; 24 754
 collaboration 18 572, 573; 20 271; 21 17; 25 906; 26 805; 27 733, 747, 748, 771
 drawings 2 329; 22 10; 30 657
 methods 21 765
 models 2 336
 patrons and collectors 3 158; 4 410; 10 808, 809; 20 587; 21 16, 79; 26 813; 31 825
 pupils 24 237
 writings 32 640–41

Sangallo, Aristotile da *see* SANGALLO, BASTIANO DA
Sangallo, Bastiano da **7** 542; **27** 733, 740–41*
collaboration **27** 746
patrons and collectors **24** 1
works **21** 442; **26** 816
Sangallo, (Giovanni) Battista da **22** 10; **27** 733, 747–9*; **32** 640
collaboration **27** 743
patrons and collectors **27** 648
works **27** *748, 749*
Sangallo, Francesco da **27** 733, 746–7*
collaboration **1** 490; **19** 688
patrons and collectors **3** 228
works **19** 688, *688*; **21** 16; **29** 569
Sangallo, Giovan Francesco da **22** 15; **24** 1; **27** 733, 746*
Sangallo, Giuliano da **2** 161; **3** 359; **11** 384; **21** 566; **24** 852; **27** 656, 733–41*
architecture **21** 16
churches
St Peter's (Vatican, Rome) **16** 632
S Lorenzo (Florence) **23** 486
S Maria delle Carceri (Prato) **20** 112; **25** 451; **26** 187; **27** *734*
S Maria di Loreto **19** 686
S Maria Maddalena dei Pazzi (Florence) **27** *735*
Santo Spirito (Florence) **11** 705; **27** 656
models **8** 187; **16** 629
palazzi **11** 178; **16** *629*; **23** 809
sarcophagi **27** 830
theatres **27** 179
university buildings **31** 674
villas **11** 705; **16** 633; **25** 265; **27** 775; **32** *546*
assistants **21** 143
attributions **5** 22
collaboration **3** 15; **8** 187; **11** 705; **12** 656; **25** 906; **26** 804, 805; **27** 739; **32** 629
drawings **2** 328, *330*; **16** 632; **27** 781
frames **11** 382, 384
patrons and collectors
Alfonso II, King of Naples (*reg* 1494-95) **2** 277
Cosimo I, Grand Duke of Tuscany (*reg* 1569- 74) **2** 390
Ferdinand I, King of Naples (*reg* 1458-94) **21** 14
Gondi, Bartolomeo **12** 897
Julius II, Pope (*reg* 1503-13) **27** 272
Leo X, Pope (*reg* 1513-22) **21** 16
Lorenzo the Magnificent, Lord of Florence (*reg* 1469-92) **21** 14; **25** 76; **32** 545
Sassetti, Francesco (di Tommaso) **27** 863
Strozzi, Filippo, the elder (1428-91) **29** 782
personal collection **24** 273, 274
pupils **9** 94; **27** 741, 746, 769
Sanganer **15** 670
Sangaste **10** *536*
Castle **10** 537
Sang Bast **16** 198
tomb **16** 164, 165, 259
San Geminiano, Master of **33** 188
Sänger, Johann Jacob **12** 412
San Germán **25** 698, *698*, 700
church **25** 700
hermitage of Porta Coeli **25** 700
painting **25** 701
San Gerolamo *see* BIELLA
San Gervasio **20** 884
Sanggodang *see* KIM KWANG-SU
Sanggye Gyatso **30** 836
Sanghadasa **15** 226
Sanghamitta **5** 97
Sanghol **15** 229, *264*, 442; **20** 819; **27** 750*
Sangi 'Ali Badakhshi **16** 354
Sang-i chīnī *see* CHINA STONE
San Gil, Francisco de *see* FRANCISCO DE SAN GIL
San Gimignano **6** 57; **16** *620*; **27** 750–51*, *751*
Cathedral of S Maria Assunta *see* Collegiata Pieve
Collegiata Pieve **12** 109; **27** 751
chapel of St Fina **12** *550*, 550–51
frescoes **3** 246–7; **13** 149
sculpture **16** 842
S Fina Monument **20** 114
wall paintings **16** *656*, 657
Palazzo del Popolo **16** 710; **19** 454; **21** *107*; **27** 750
S Agostino **2** 725; **27** 751
altarpiece **25** *162*
frescoes **2** 725, *725*; **13** 260, *261*; **16** 659
tower houses **16** 627
Town Hall **19** 449
Sangines, Ponce **29** 219
Sangiorgio, Abbondio **16** 705; **20** 99; **30** 215
San Giorgio, Adamino da *see* ADAMINO DA SAN GIORGIO
San Giorgio, Eusebio da *see* EUSEBIO (DI JACOPO DI CRISTOFORO) DA SAN GIORGIO
San Giorgi seals **21** 691
San Giovanni **31** 711
San Giovanni, Achille **17** 203
Sangiovanni, Carlos **9** 118
San Giovanni, Giovanni da *see* GIOVANNI DA SAN GIOVANNI
San Giovanni Lipioni **10** 609
San Giovenale **10** *583*; **16** *620*; **27** 752*
huts **10** *598*, 599
vases **10** 613
Villa Sambuco **26** 869
Sangistan, mausoleum of Muhammad 'Ali **6** 277
San Giuliano **10** 617, 620, 640
San Giusto, Giuliano di Colino degli Scarsi da *see* GIULIANO DI COLINO DEGLI SCARSI DA SAN GIUSTO
Sanglada, Pedro *see* ÇA ANGLADA, PERE
Sanglier, Henri, Archbishop **28** 414
Sango (peoples) **11** 878; **18** 401, 403
Sang'o (Korea) **23** 775
Sangram Singh II, Rana of Mewar (*reg* 1710-34) (Rajput) **15** 599, 600
Sangro, Raimondo di, Prince of Sansevero **7** 882; **16** 703; **25** 808
Sangüesa **29** *259*
metalwork **29** 333
S María la Real **7** 643; **27** 752*
monstrance **29** 333, 335
sculpture **26** 605, 607, 608
tomb of Blanche of Navarre **26** 642
Sangui **11** 878
Sanguigni, Battista di Biagio **29** 785
Sanguin, Cardinal **21** 366
sanguine *see* CHALK → types → red
Sanguinetti, Garth **16** 889
Sanguszko (family) **25** 138
Sanguszko, Roman, Prince **16** 475
Sanguszko carpets *see under* CARPETS → types
Sangyong **18** 353
San-hsing-tui *see* GUANGHAN
Sani, Atsidi **22** 614
Sani, Domenico Maria **4** 558; **25** 645; **29** 304
Sani, Paolo **9** 403; **16** 729
Sani, Tommaso **2** 752
Sani' al-Mulk *see* GHAFFARI, ABU'L-HASAN
San Ignacio **24** *91*
Mission Church **24** 94
Museum **24** 101
San Ignacio Miní **2** 392, 394
San Ildefonso (Spain) **27** 752–4*; **29** *258*
Centro Nacional del Vidrio **29** 332
Palace **2** 379; **4** 557–8, 560; **27** 753
collections **25** 645; **29** 352
Fountain of Perseus and Andromeda **11** 345
furniture **29** 315
gardens **12** 124; **27** *753*, 753–4; **30** 733
sculpture **4** 588; **11** 754
interior decoration **29** 304, 306
paintings **4** 559; **5** 907; **8** 12; **15** 149; **19** 524; **24** 10; **25** 2; **29** 41
palace **27** 752–3; **29** 270
San Ildefonso (NM; USA) **20** 498–9; **22** 606, 668
San Ildefonso Watercolor Movement **22** 594
Sanis, Lorenzo de *see* SENES, LORENZO
sanitary wallpaper *see under* WALLPAPER → types
San Jacinto **29** 150
Sanjar, Sultan (*reg* 1118-57) (Saljuq) **16** 161; **21** 169
Sanjar al-Jawli **16** 209, 210
Sanjaya **29** 237
San Jerónimo **24** *498*
church **24** 500
San Jerónimo, Juan de **27** 754*
Sanjō (family) **18** 561
San Joan de les Abadesses, Collegiate Church **13** 106, 122
Sanjōnishi (family) **17** 781
Sanjōnishi Sanetaka **17** 167; **30** 259; **31** 197
S Jorge, Master of *see* MARTORELL, BERNAT
San José (Costa Rica) **8** *15*
Almacén Borbón **8** 16
architecture **8** 16
barracks **8** 16
Casa del Artista **8** 18
Central Bank of Costa Rica **29** 222
Club Unión **8** 16
Comandancia **8** 16
Edificio Correos y Telegráficos **8** 16
Edificio Metálico **8** 16
Escuela de Arte y Decoración Esempi **8** 18
Escuela Nacional de Bellas Artes **8** 18
Hospital S Juan de Dios **8** 16
Jane Davidson de Salazar house **8** 17
La Merced **8** 16
La Sabema national airport *see* Museo de Arte Costarricense
Museo de Arte Costarricense **8** 16, 18
Museo Nacional de Costa Rica **29** 222
National Insurance Institute **29** 222
Nuestra Señora de Desamparados **8** 16
Palacio Nacional **8** 16
Puci Poli **8** 17
Schyfter building **8** 17
Secretaría de Salubridad Pública **8** 16
S Isidro de Coronado **8** 16
Teatro Nacional **8** 16
Trejos Gonzaléz building **8** 16
Universidad de S Tomás **8** 16
San José (Uruguay) **31** *751*
San José culture **29** 190
San José de Oruna **31** *330*, 334
San José Mogote **21** 195, 196, 199, 219, 718
San Juan (Argentina) **2** 392, 394
San Juan (Puerto Rico) **25** *698*
architecture **25** 700
Arsenal de La Puntilla **25** 704
Cabildo **25** 700
Capitolio **25** 700
Caribe Hilton **25** 701
Castillo de S Cristobál **25** 700, 704
Castillo de S Felipe de El Morro **25** 700, *700*, 704
Cathedral **25** 700
Convent of S Tomas Aquino **25** 700
Corte Suprema de Justicia **25** 701
Escuela de Artes Plásticas **25** 704
fortifications **21** 573
Instituto de Arte Puertorriqueña **25** 703
Museo de Arte e Historia de San Juan **25** 704
Museo del Grabado Latinoamericano **25** 704
Museo de Las Américas **25** 704
painting **25** 701
Real Intendencia **25** 700
San Jerónimo **25** 704
San Juan (NM; USA) **22** 606
San Juan (Venezuela) **32** 177
San Juan, Andrés de *see* ANDRÉS DE NÁJERA
San Juan, Juan de **28** 516
San Juan Bautista *see* PUERTO RICO
San Juan de Boada **22** 247
San Juan de la Peña **22** 247; **26** 656; **27** 754–5*; **29** *259*, 263
Monastery **7** 455; **26** 607, 609; **29** 262
San Juan de la Peña Master **27** 752, 754
San Juan de Limay **23** 86
San Juan del Oriente **23** 82, 83; **29** 224
San Juan de Siguas **2** 386
San Juan Ostuncalco **13** 768
Sanka **17** 759; **22** 339; **30** 240
Sankai Zōkei Bijutsu Kyōkai (Three Division Plastic Arts Society) **17** 206; **20** 873
San Kamphaeng **30** 609, 610
Sankar Sompura, Prabha **15** 212
Sankasha **33** 560
Sankasya **8** 269; **15** 220, *261*; **27** 755*
pillar **15** 423
ring stones **15** 423
Sankei Hara *see* HARA, SANKEI
Sankei Shimbun Press **30** 286
Sankey, Ira David **7** 216
San Khan **5** 248
Sankhare *see* MENTUHOTPE
Sankhavaram **15** 686
Sankhu **22** *753*; **27** 755*
Gum Vihara **27** 755
Sankisa *see* SANKASYA
Sankofa **12** 510
Sankoh, Osman **28** 692
works **28** *691*
Sanko Kohei **17** 401
Sankri
Hagios Artemios **9** 575; **22** 700
Hagios Ioannis Theologos **9** 575
Hagios Nikolaos **22** 700
Sankt Sigmund Church **27** 755–6*
San Lázaro **8** 232
San Leocadio, Felipe Pablo de *see* FELIPE PABLO DE SAN LEOCADIO
San Leocadio, Miguel Juan de *see* MIGUEL JUAN DE SAN LEOCADIO
San Leocadio, Paolo da *see* PAOLO DA SAN LEOCADIO
San Leonardo al Lago **19** 457
San Leonardo di Siponto **26** 628
San Leucio **31** 713
casino **11** 136
S Liberatore alla Maiella **16** 626
San Lorenzo (Italy), Museo del Tesoro **16** 775
San Lorenzo (Paraguay) **24** *91*
Museo Etnográfico Guido Roggiani **24** 102
S Lorenzo del Escorial *see* ESCORIAL
S Lorenzo della Costa, Master of **20** 766–7*
San Lorenzo Nuovo **31** 719
San Lorenzo S.p.A. **32** 501
San Lorenzo Tenochtitlán **21** *193*, 195, 237, *372*; **23** 416–17, 418; **27** 756*
architecture **7** 636; **21** 209
colossal heads **21** 219
jade **21** 242
mirrors **21** 718
Monument 1 **23** *417*
Monument 34 **5** 408
pendants (jewellery) **21** 241
sculpture **21** 218
water supply **21** 208
San Lorenzo Vecchio **10** 602
San Lúcar, Duque de *see* OLIVARES, Conde-duque de
San Lúcar de Barrameda **29** 343
Sanlucar la Mayor, S María **13** *122*
San Luis **2** 392, *393*, 394, 403
San Luis Jilotepeque **13** 768
San Luis Potosí
Caja de Agua **21** 378
Cathedral **21** 377
Teatro de la Paz **21** 378; **23** 208
tools **21** 192
Sanlun Buddhism *see under* BUDDHISM → sects
Sanluri, Master of **27** 836
San Mamés, Marqués de **30** 418
Sanmaniego, Félix María de **17** 587
San Marco, Master of **3** 340; **13** 150; **20** 767*
S Marco Altarpiece **21** 10
San Marco Argentano **6** 57
San Marco d'Alunzio **6** 57
S Marcos *see* PERU → retables
San Marino (CA)
Huntington Art Gallery **15** 30; **19** 703
Huntington Library **9** 231; **14** 510; **15** 30; **19** 319, 703
San Martín **10** 190
San Martín, Cosme **13** 9
San Martín, José de **24** 518
San Martín, José Luis Zorrilla de *see* ZORRILLA DE SAN MARTÍN, JOSÉ LUIS
San Martín, Juan de **29** 336
Sanmartín, Vicente **28** 513
San Martin de Unx **26** 607
San Martino, Carlo Arrigo di **26** 810
Sanmartino, Giuseppe **22** 479; **27** 756–7*
pupils **32** 651
works **12** 748; **16** 704; **22** 485, *681*; **26** 500; **29** 573
San Martino, Marco *see* SAMMARTINO, MARCO
San Martino, Master of **24** 854
San Mateo **29** 332
San Mateo de Valparaiso, Condesa **21** 377
San Mateo de Valparaiso, Marqués de **13** 797; **21** 395, 401
San-men-hsia *see* SHANGCUN LING
Sanmenxia *see* SHANGCUN LING
S Mercuriale at Forlí, Master of **23** 101
Sanmi, Lady **33** 318
Sanmichele (da Verona), Michele *see* SANMICHELI, MICHELE
S Michele a Castello, Master of **23** 743
San Michele Extra, Madonna di Campagna **16** 635; **27** 761

S Michele tapestry factory (Rome) 16 758
Sanmicheli, Bartolomeo 27 757
Sanmicheli, Giovanni Girolamo 5 6; 27 757; 32 159
Sanmicheli, Michele 3 359; 5 617; 23 864; 27 757–63*; 32 340
 architecture 5 6; 16 635; 32 341
  churches 27 761
  fortifications 8 156; 23 752; 27 762; 32 159
  gates 7 359, 360
  monuments 3 698
  palazzi 2 295; 13 650; 23 492; 27 347, 758, 760; 32 187, 342, 342
 attributions 13 658; 22 131
 collaboration 5 6; 18 572; 23 756; 27 743, 747
 groups and movements 20 281
 paintings 32 12
 patrons and collectors 3 896; 7 861; 13 659; 27 273; 28 533
Sanmicheli da Porlezza, Paolo 33 586
San Michiel, (da Verona), Michele Da see SANMICHELI, MICHELE
San Miguel (Argentina), Casa Caveri 2 397
San Miguel (El Salvador) 10 153, 154
San Miguel (Philippines) 24 617
San Miguel, Andrés de 27 763*
San Miguel de Allende, Escuela de Bellas Artes 28 785
San Miguel de Escalada 22 246, 247; 27 763, 763–4*; 29 258, 262, 288
 Abbey Church 26 580
 manuscript illumination 29 275
 sculpture 26 642
San Miguel de Foces 13 144
San Miguel de Lillo 29 261
San Miguel Totonicapán 13 768
San Millán de la Cogolla 7 527; 22 247; 29 262, 288
 ivory-carvings 22 248; 26 699
 manuscript illumination 29 275; 26 676
 Monastery 26 642
 S Millán de Suso 22 246
Sanminiatelli, Bino 25 447
Sanminiati (family) 12 661
Sanmizuka Tomb 17 320
Sanmon see ŌTSU → Enryakuji
Sanmyakuin see KONOE NOBUTADA
Sannazaro, Jacopo 12 656; 14 870; 18 708; 30 1
San Nazzaro Sésia Abbey Church 26 578
Sannesio, Clemente see COLLELUNGO, CLEMENTE SANNESIO, Marchese di
Sannesio, Giacomo, Cardinal 18 730; 27 764*
San Niccolò di Lido, Jewish Cemetery 17 555
S Nicola Chapel, Master of the 2 625
San Nicolás, Lorenzo de 10 206; 27 765*
 works 29 637; 31 297
 writings 29 269, 357
Sannini, Santillo 29 544
San' o see KIM (i) CHE
Sano, Emmanuel 22 296
Sano, Turino di see TURINO DI SANO
Sano di Matteo 27 765*
Sano di Pietro 1 622; 7 328; 16 662; 20 738; 27 765–6*; 28 684
 attributions 4 30
 collaboration 12 715; 32 103
 forgeries by others 17 644
 paintings 11 383; 16 470
  altarpieces 27 766
  cassoni 6 4
Sano di Pietro
 paintings—cont.
  frescoes 9 95; 11 711; 27 862; 28 686, 687
 pupils 3 750
Sá Nogueira(, Rolando de) 27 766–7*; 30 882
Sanot, Girolamo del see TESSARI, GIROLAMO
S Pablo de Yuririapundaro 21 375
S Paolo Eremita, Master of 21 533
San Pedro 3 623
San Pedro, Pedro González de see GONZÁLEZ DE SAN PEDRO, PEDRO
San Pedro Carchá Museum 13 769
San Pedro culture
 bottles 29 187
 containers 29 189
 tablets 29 188
San Pedro de Alcántara 9 510
 church 9 533; 29 261
San Pedro de Arlanza 16 436
San Pedro de Atacama 6 592
 Museo de Arqueología 'R. P. Gustave Le Paige, S. J.' 29 187
San Pedro de la Mata Church 29 261
San Pedro de Montes 16 436
San Pedro de Moxos 4 269
San Pedro de Nora 29 261
San Pedro de Roda see SANT PERE DE RODES
San Pedro Marcoris 9 114
 Casa Salene 9 117
San Pedro Sula 14 711, 711, 713
 Casa Castro 14 714
 Casa Cordova 14 714
 Club Social del Banco Sogerín 14 714
 masonic temple 22 256
 Museo de San Pedro 14 716
Sanpei Ri see RI SANPEI
San Pieri, Abate di 27 693
San Pier Maggiore Altarpiece 24 8
San Pietro
 shipwreck 26 855
 Villa Il Boschetto 5 533
San Pietro ad Montes 16 626; 26 625
S Pietro ad Oratorio 16 626
San Pietro di Castello 32 182
 Campanile 7 516
 church 19 629, 629–30
Sanpitsu 17 221; 18 502; 27 519; 30 231
San Polo in Chianti, Master of 8 443
San Quirce 26 607
Sanquirico, Alessandro 24 758
Sanquirico, Paolo 27 486, 767*
Sanquirico, Pio 24 344
San Quirico d'Orcia 16 724
Sanraku Kanō see KANŌ SANRAKU
Sanredam see SAENREDAM
Sanron Buddhism see under BUDDHISM → sects
Sansai see KIMURA KENKADŌ
San Salvador 3 59; 10 153, 153
 Candelaria church 10 154
 Casa Reales 10 153
 Cathedral 10 154
 Church of Santiago 10 153
 Escuela Nacional de Artes Gráficas 10 154
 marks 13 768
 Museo Nacional David J. Guzmán 10 155
 S Sebastián 10 153
 textiles 13 766
S Salvador de Fuentes 26 689
San Salvador de Penedos 26 642
San Salvatore Maggiore Abbey 23 649
Sansar Chand, Maharaja (reg 1775-1823) (Pahari) 15 632, 740
San Sebastián (Spain) 27 767–8*; 29 259
 Club Nautico 29 273
San Sebastián (Spain)—cont.
 Escuela de Armería 27 768
San Sebastián Church (Peru) 24 502
San Sebastián de Urabá 7 600, 603
San Secondo, Bertrando de' Rossi, Conte di 20 709
San Secondo, Federico II Rossi, Marchese di 26 320
San Secondo Parmense, La Rocca 3 859
Sansedoni (family) 28 677
Sansegundo, Carlos 13 725
Sansei Suzuki see SUZUKI, SANSEI
Sanseki 11 822; 17 221–2, 227; 23 445
 works 17 222
Sansetsu Kanō see KANŌ SANSETSU
Sanseverino, Aurora, Duchessa di Laurenzano see LAURENZANO, AURORA SANSEVERINO, Duchessa di
Sanseverino, Federigo, Cardinal 12 908
Sanseverino, Galeazzo da see GALEAZZO DA SANSEVERINO
Sanseverino, Giulio see LETO, POMPONIO
Sanshō Wada see WADA, SANSHŌ
Sans i Cabot, Francesc 29 306
San Sigismondo see SANKT SIGMUND
San Simeon (CA), Hearst Castle 6 63; 14 452; 27 47
San Simone, Francesco see FRANCESCO DA SAN SIMONE
Sanskrit 6 420; 15 193, 203; 29 440
Sansom, Gareth 27 768*
Sanson, Paul-Ernest 3 77; 27 768*; 28 463
Sanson, S.
 works 10 355
Sansoni, Barbara 29 456
Sansoni, Guglielmo see TATO
Sansott, Odette 6 600
Sansovino, Andrea 11 217; 26 769; 27 775–7*
 architecture 2 500; 4 650; 11 691; 19 688
 assistants 19 710; 22 166
 attributions 25 76
 collaboration 27 656, 769; 29 403
 methods 21 765
 patrons and collectors 20 482; 21 16; 23 326; 27 273; 32 22, 386
 pupils 1 490; 7 331; 16 694; 27 769
 sculpture 11 186; 16 695
  reliefs 11 254; 19 688, 688; 22 15; 23 756; 26 137; 31 320
  religious 1 711; 4 650; 8 512; 27 775, 776
 sugar 30 219
 tombs 27 830; 31 126
Sansovino, Francesco 27 769, 774*
 works 13 808; 16 781; 32 193, 196, 214
Sansovino, Jacopo (d'Antonio) 13 909; 16 665, 688, 689; 23 754; 26 769; 27 769–74*; 32 192, 220, 349
 architecture 13 658, 678; 16 635, 693; 32 185
  architectural decorations 31 237; 32 223
  churches 3 202; 21 16; 22 378; 25 215; 26 756; 28 37
  façades 10 744; 25 889; 27 772
  government buildings 6 89; 23 864; 31 717; 32 187
  libraries 5 532; 16 770; 19 313, 560; 28 82; 31 717; 32 222
  palazzi 3 766; 16 712; 32 187
  scuole 32 228
 assistants 18 691; 19 562; 21 647; 32 222, 646
Sansovino, Jacopo (d'Antonio)—cont.
 attributions 13 658; 25 176; 30 498
 collaboration 1 789; 4 748; 6 89; 27 743, 847; 28 37; 31 581; 32 647
 dealing 10 521
 methods 21 768
 patrons and collectors
  Altoviti, Bindo 1 735
  Campagna, Girolamo 5 531
  Contarini, Federico 7 776
  Cornaro (family) 7 861
  Cosimo I, Grand Duke of Tuscany (reg 1569- 74) 3 293
  Ercole II, 4th Duke of Ferrara, Modena and Reggio (reg 1534-59) 10 523
  Gaddi (ii), Giovanni de' 11 893
  Grimani (family) 13 659
  Grimani, Marino, Cardinal, Patriarch of Aquileia 13 658
  Rangone, Tommaso 25 889
 pupils 6 89; 10 798; 18 691; 19 560, 562; 27 637; 31 320; 32 646
 sculpture 3 16; 16 694; 32 192–3
  doors 4 739; 9 157, 157; 32 220
  modelli 16 749; 30 496; 33 2
  mythological 27 773; 29 561; 32 220
  reliefs 11 711; 21 632; 25 175, III
  religious 27 769, 770
  statuettes 29 569
  terracottas 30 495, 497
 studio 29 853
 teachers 16 694; 27 777
Sansovino frames see under FRAMES → types
Sanspareil 12 134, 361; 27 777–8*
San Sperate
 nuraghi 23 304
Sanssouci see POTSDAM → Schloss Sanssouci
San Stefano 31 717
Sant, George 27 778
Sant, James 27 778*
 reproductive prints by others 4 807; 31 138
Sant, Lorenzo de Muretto de see SENES, LORENZO
Sant, Tom Van see VAN SANT, TOM
Santa 6 520
Santa Ana (Philippines) 24 617
Santa Ana (Solomon Islands) 29 50, 51
Santa Ana (NM; USA) 22 607
Santa Ana Chautempan 21 394
Santa Ana do Riacho 29 196
Santa Anita Ixtapalapa 10 505
Santa Apolonia 13 758, 768
Santa Bárbara (Chile) 29 187
Santa Barbara (CA; USA)
 Museum of Art 13 470; 27 47
 University of California 4 27
 University Art Museum 19 802
Santa Cándida 2 396
Santa Catalina 29 50, 51
Santa Catalina mission 2 394
Santa Catarina
 sculpture 29 197
S Caterina Polyptych 1 709; 13 138; 24 854
Santa Cecilia Acatitlán 25 765
Santacilia, Carlos Obregón 12 920
Santa Clara (NM) 22 606, 609
Santa Clara, António de see ANTÓNIO DE SANTA CLARA
Santa Clara-a-Velha Convent 13 166
Santa Coloma de Cervello, Colonia Güell Chapel 4 789; 12 182; 29 508
Santa Coloma de Farnés 29 330
Santa Cristina-Palilatino 30 434
Santacroce (family) (fl 15th cent.) 3 667
Santacroce (family) (fl 17th cent.) 13 655; 24 371
Santacroce, Filippo 16 725
Santacroce, Francesco da 27 778; 31 13
Santacroce, G. (fl c. late 18th cent.) 31 818
Santacroce, Girolamo da (1480/5-1556) 9 21; 20 418; 27 778*
 works 11 383
Santacroce, Marcello, Cardinal 13 656
Santa Croce Altarpiece 31 533, 534
Santa Cruz (Bolivia) 4 255, 255
 Cathedral 4 259, 267
 Escuela de Bellas Artes see Taller de Artes Visuales
 Museo de Arte Contemporáneo 4 269
 Museo de Arte Sacro S Lorenzo Martir 4 269
 painting 4 262
 Taller de Artes Visuales 4 270
Santa Cruz (Philippines) 24 616
Santa Cruz, Álvaro de Bazán, Marqués de 4 566
Santa Cruz, Alvaro de Bazán y Guzmán, 1st Marqués de 6 24; 7 901; 29 299; 32 620
Santa Cruz, Antonio de 29 337
Santa Cruz, Basilio 6 596
Santacruz, Francisco 3 218
Santa Cruz, Leocadia 5 355
Santacruz, S. 22 314
Santa Cruz Islands 23 711; 27 778–9*; 29 48, 50
 body ornaments 27 778, 779, 779
 canoes 27 779
 headdresses 27 779
 masks 27 779
 pottery 23 727, 728
 sculpture 23 732
 weapons 23 734
 wood-carvings 27 779
Santa Cruz Pachacuti Yamqui, Juan de see YAMQUI, JUAN DE SANTA CRUZ PACHACUTI
Santa Cruz Pamacallao, Basilío de 8 302
Santaella, Rodrigo de 28 512
Santa Eufemia 31 717
Santa Fe (Argentina) 2 393
 architecture 2 395
 La Compañía 2 398
 Museo Provincial de Bellas Artes 'Rosa Galisteo de Rodríguez' 2 404–5
  library 2 406
 painting 2 398
 S Francisco 2 394
Santa Fe (NM; USA) 31 587
 Governor's Palace 31 588
 Indian Day School 22 594
 Institute of American Indian Art (IAIA) 22 592, 596, 597, 666, 677
 Santa Fe Indian Market 22 677
 Santa Fe Indian School see Institute of American Indian Arts
 The Studio 22 591, 595
Santafede, Fabrizio 22 478; 23 626; 27 779–80*; 29 543
Santa Fe de Antioquia see ANTIOQUIA
Santa Fe de Bogotá see BOGOTÁ, SANTA FE DE
Santa Fosca, Piovano di 27 228
Sant'Agata, Francesco (di Giovanni) da 27 780*; 29 569
Sant'Agata dei Goti
 Cathedral 26 625
 S Menna 26 625
Santa Gertrudis, Juan de 27 700
Santa Inés 27 158; 32 170

Santa Isabel 29 49
shields 28 II2
Santa Isabel de Siguas 2 386
Santa Isabel Iztapán 21 192
Santal 3 165; 15 634, 732
Santalinea (family) 29 332
Santalinea, Bernat 29 332
Santa Lucía Cotzumalhuapa 13 *758*; 20 *882*; 27 780*
Santamarca, Bartolomé Eladio, Conde de 27 781*; 29 354
Santamarca y Donato, Carlota, Duquesa de Nájera *see* NÁJERA, CARLOTA DE SANTAMARCA Y DONATO, Duquesa de
Santa María, Master of 30 369
Santamaría, Alfredo 29 344
Santa María, Andrés de 7 609, 611; 27 781*
Santamaría, Arturo 29 344
Santa María, José Marcos Saenz de *see* VALDE-IÑIGO, Marqués de
Santa María, Juan de 7 458
Santamaría, Mariano 7 605
S Maria ad Martyres Bible *see* BIBLES → individual manuscipts → Pantheon Bible
S María de Bamba 22 246, 247; 29 275
S María del Campo Church 29 266
paintings 29 *277*
Santa Maria Capua Vetere 9 *510*; 16 *621*; 27 781–3*
Cathedral of S Maria 9 533
Conocchia 20 865
S Prisco 27 *782*, 782–3*
Santa María culture 29 190
pottery 29 *191*
Santa María de Bendones 29 261
Santa María de Guadianilla 25 698
Santa María de las Misiones Museum 24 101
Santa Maria de l'Estavy 16 436
Santa Maria della Torre 5 893
Santa María del Puerto Príncipe 8 236
Santa María del Río 21 394
Santa María de Mur 26 649
Santa María de Tarrasa 26 657
Santa Maria di Falerii *see* FALERII NOVI
Santa Maria di Portonovo Church 26 577, *577*
Santa Maria di Sala, Villa Farsetti 10 819
S María de Eunate 29 263
S Maria di Foroclaudio 16 626
Santa Maria in Valle Porclaneta Church 26 625
Santa María la Antigua del Darién 7 600, 603
S María de Lebeña 22 247
S María de Marquet 22 247
S Maria di Monte d'Oro 16 635
S María de Peñalba 22 247
S Maria di Portonovo 16 625
Santa Maria dei Servi, Master of 3 918
Santa María y Sedano, Marceliano 27 511
Santamarina, Antonio 2 404, 406
Santamarina, Mercedes 2 404
Santa Marinella *see* PUNICUM
Santa Marta 7 600, *601*, 603
Museum 7 612
Santa Monica (Menorca) 3 105
Santa Monica (CA; USA)
Frank O. Gehry's house 1 737; 2 *552*; 12 236
Getty Center for the History of Art 19 703; 24 683; 31 671; 33 405
graffiti 13 *270*
Museum of Art 19 703
Santana do Riacho
rock art 29 *196*
Sant'Anastasia 30 434
Santander 27 783–4*; 29 *258*
furniture 29 315
Santander—cont.
Museo Municipal de Bellas Artes 27 783
Palacio de la Magdalena 29 321
Santander, Francisco de Paula 7 611
Santander, Sancho de 3 738
Santander Peréz, Mateo 8 236
Sant'Andrea Priu-Bonorva 2 52
Sant Andreu, Casa Bloc 29 273
Sant'Angelo di Pianella
S Maria Maggiore 26 625
S Paolo di Peltuino 26 625
Sant'Angelo in Formis 16 *621*, 626; 26 625; 27 784*
church 26 580
frescoes 16 654; 26 650, 653, 654, 655, 656; 27 *784*
Sant'Angelo in Formis Regesto *see under* ROLLS → individual manuscripts
Sant'Angelo in Lauro 26 650
Santans, Terrier de, Marquis 3 866
Sant'Antimo, Ruffo di, Prince 14 267
Sant'Antine 25 522
Santarelli, Emilio 16 705
Santarelli, Giovanni Antonio 12 264; 20 924
collaboration 5 363
patrons and collectors 4 305; 12 264
Santarém (Brazil) 4 *705*, 722; 27 785*
pottery 4 706; 27 785; 29 177, 192–3*
roads 29 192
sculpture 29 193
Santarém (Portugal) 25 *288*
Church of Marvila 30 880, *880*, 881
Graça church 25 289
metalwork 25 313
Piedade church 25 292
S Clara
tomb of Doña Leonor 13 102
S João de Alporão 25 289
textiles 25 315
Santarém, Visconde de 28 *430*
Santa-Rita(, Guilherme Augusto Cau da Costa) 25 299; 27 786*
Santa Rita Corozal 3 *622*; 20 *882*; 27 786*
brick 4 796
wall paintings 21 232, 256
Santa-Rita-Pintor(, Guilherme Augusto Cau da Costa) *see* SANTA-RITA(, GUILHERME AUGUSTO CAU DA COSTA)
Santa Rosa (Argentina) 2 *393*
Government House 2 397
Santa Rosa (Paraguay), Our Lady of Loreto Chapel 24 98
Santa Rosa de Copán 14 *711*
Santa Rosa Xtampak 21 206, 231
Palace 21 207
Santa Severa *see* PYRGI
Santa Sofia di Pedemonte, Villa Sarego 2 357, *357*; 23 866
Santa Tirso 25 291
Santa Trinità di Saccargia 27 836
Santayana, George 1 181; 10 691; 27 786–7*
Santayana, Jorge (Augustín Nicolás Ruiz de) *see* SANTAYANA, GEORGE
Sant Cugat del Vallès Abbey 29 263
cloister 7 455; 26 610
manuscripts 4 764
retables 11 481
sculpture 26 642
Sante Alari, Conte 3 903
Sante di Apollonio del Celandro 11 118
Sante Druden, Godert von *see* GODERT VON SANTE DRUDEN
Sant'Elia 24 448
Sant'Elia, Antonio 27 787–9*; 31 728
groups and movements 8 247; 11 843, 865, 867, 868; 21 781; 26 15
works 11 *868*; 16 648, 721; 25 173; 27 *788*; 28 833; 31 706
Santelices, Juan de 4 265
Santelli, Serge 31 424
Santen, Giovanni van *see* VASANZIO, GIOVANNI
Santerelli, Emilio 27 785
Santerelli, Giovanni Antonio 27 785*
Santerre, Jean-Baptiste 27 789*
attributions 13 666
patrons and collectors 18 693
reproductive prints by others 6 549
teachers 4 536
works 11 537
Santes Creus Abbey 7 350, 353; 13 50, 68, 69, 191; 21 838; 29 263
cloister 7 453
dormitory 21 843
tomb of Blanche of Anjou 13 105
tomb of James II of Aragon 13 105
tomb of Peter III of Aragon 13 105; 29 288
tomb of Peter II of Aragon 7 303
Santhanaraj 20 54
Santi, Andriolo de' 27 789–90*
works 1 725; 5 871; 11 708; 13 95, 747; 31 316
Santi, Carolina 27 791
Santi, Ciro di Natale 27 790
Santi, Dionisio 27 791
Santi, Domenico 5 651
Santi, Giosuè di *see* GIOSUÈ DI SANTI
Santi, Giovan Gioseffo 5 653
Santi, Giovanni (1435/40-94) 16 662; 21 98; 25 897; 27 790*; 31 740
attributions 10 654; 17 705; 31 744
patrons and collectors 8 763; 22 13
pupils 10 653
teachers 21 97
works 16 781
Santi, Giovanni de' (*d* 1392) 27 790
Santi, Lorenzo 27 790–91*; 32 188
Santi, Raffaello *see* RAPHAEL
Santiago (de Chile) 6 589, *590*; 27 791–2*
Academia de Pintura *see* Escuela Nacional de Bellas Artes
Academia de San Luis 6 602
architecture 6 591–4
Arcis 6 602
Avenida Pocura 6 594
Biblioteca Nacional 6 591, 601
Brazilian Embassy 6 593
Casa Colorado 6 592
Casa Edwards 6 595
Casa Fuenzalinda 6 595
Casa Marta de Duhart 6 594
Casa Peña 6 594
Centro de Estudios de la Arquitectura (CEDLA) 5 129; 6 594
Centro Nacional de Conservación y Restauración 6 601
Colegio de Arquitectos de Chile 6 600
library 6 601
Colegio del Verbo Divino 6 594
Congreso Nacional 6 592, 593
Conjunto Plaza Lyon 6 594
ecclesiastical buildings
Basilica del Salvador 6 593
Cathedral 6 591, 592, 599
Divina Providencia 6 593
Santiago (de Chile)
ecclesiastical buildings—cont.
Iglesia de la Recoleta Domínica 6 593
Iglesia de la Veracruz 6 592
La Cañadilla 6 592
La Compañía 6 591–2
La Merced 6 592
Preciosa Sangre 6 593
S Agustín 6 596
S Augustín 6 593
S Domingo 6 592, 599
S Francisco 6 591, 592, 599
S Ignacio 6 593
Edificio Commercial Edwards 6 594
Edificio Fundación 6 594
Edificio Oberpaur 6 594; 18 797
Edificio S Lucia 6 594
education (art) 6 594
Escuela de Escultura Ornamental y Dibujo en Relieve 6 601
Escuela Militar 6 593
Escuela Nacional de Bellas Artes 6 591, 601, 602
Exposición Internacional, 1910 6 597
Fundación Mi Casa 6 594
Hospital de S Juan de Dios 6 592
houses 6 594
Instituto de Arte Contemporáneo 6 602
Instituto Nacional 6 591
Luis Cousiño Park 24 181
museums
Museo Abierto 6 601
Museo del Alba Arturo Pacheco Altamirano 6 601
Museo de Arte Colonial de San Francisco 6 601; 27 792
Museo de Arte Contemporáneo 6 601; 27 792
Museo de Arte Popular Americano 27 792
Museo de Artes Decorativas 6 601
Museo Chileno de Arte Precolombino 7 207; 18 797; 31 812
Museo de la Escuela Militar 6 601
Museo de Historia Natural 6 593
Museo Histórico Nacional 6 601
Museo Nacional 24 516
Museo Nacional de Bellas Artes 2 190; 6 597, 600, 601; 27 792
library 6 601
Museo de Pinturas *see* Museo Nacional de Bellas Artes
Palacio de Bellas Artes 6 594
Palacio de la Alhambra 6 593, 601
Palacio Arrieta 6 593
Palacio Cousiño 6 593
Palacio Díaz Gana 6 593
Palacio Edwards 6 593
Palacio Errázuriz *see* Brazilian Embassy
Palacio para la Exposición Internacional *see* Museo de Historia Natural
Palacio Pereira 6 593
Palacio Presidencial *see* Real Casa de Moneda
Palacio Rivas 6 593
Partenón *see* → museums → Museo Nacional de Bellas Artes
Portal de Sierrabella 6 592
Posada del Corregidor 6 592
Real Aduana 6 592
Real Audiencia 6 592
Real Canal de San Carlos de Maypu 6 592
Real Casa de Moneda 6 592, *593*
silver 6 599
Teatro Municipal 6 592
Teatro Nacional 6 593
Santiago (de Chile)—cont.
tiles 6 591
Torre S Ramón 6 594
Tribunales de Justicia 6 594
United Nations building 7 695
Universidad Católica de Chile 6 594, 598, 601, 602
library 6 601
Universidad de Chile 6 591, 593, 602; 27 *792*
Escuela de Bellas Artes 6 598
Escuela de Medicina 6 594
Facultad de Derecho 6 594
library 6 601
Universidad de S Felipe 6 590
Universidad Metropolitana de Ciencias de la Educación 6 602
urban planning 6 592
Santiago (Costa Rica) 9 679
Santiago (Dominican Republic) 9 *114*, 116; 31 721
Museum 9 119
Santiago (Panama) 23 *902*
Santiago (Paraguay) 24 *91*, 98
Edificio El Partenón 19 458
Museum 24 101
Santiago, Cayetano Rodríguez de los Rís, 3rd Marqués de 27 793
Santiago, Fernando Augustín Rodríguez de los Rís, 2nd Marqués de 27 793
Santiago, Francisco Esteban Rodríguez de los Ríos, 1st Marqués de 27 792–3
Santiago, María de la Soledad, Marquésa de 27 793
Santiago, Martín de *see* MARTÍN DE SANTIAGO
Santiago, Matías de 4 233
Santiago, Miguel de 2 726; 9 712, 714
Santiago Atitlán 13 *758*, 765
Santiago de Calimaya, Condes de 13 797
Santiago de Compostela 26 570; 27 793–6*; 29 *258*
art forms and materials
jet 17 515
metalwork 29 341
pilgrim badges 24 808, 809
sculpture 29 292
Cathedral of Santiago 1 723, 767; 5 911; 6 458; 8 260, 261; 13 50, 51; 20 811; 26 570, 581; 27 793–4*, *794*; 28 629; 29 262, 270, 271
altarpieces 1 518; 9 262
Baldacchino 26 251
Basilica 2 653
capitals 26 606
choir-stalls 26 605
collections 2 654
crypt 29 262
iconography 26 605
metalwork 6 174; 29 336
nave 26 *581*
Pórtico de la Gloria 10 743; 13 103; 27 795–6, *796*; 29 288
Puerta de las Platerías 7 642; 26 *606*, 607; 27 795, *795*; 29 288
retable 26 249
sculpture 26 605, 607, 608, 609; 27 795–6*
transept 31 281
collections 17 582
colleges 7 566
guidebooks 13 808
Hospital de los Reyes Católicos 14 781; 29 265
Instituto de Estudios Gallegos Padre Sarmiento 29 358
Palacio del Gelmírez 29 263
S Martín Pinario 26 251
S Pelayo de Antealtares 7 642
University 31 674
Santiago de Cuba 8 228, *228*
Cathedral 8 231, 237
collections 8 238

Santiago de Cuba—cont.
education (art) 8 238
El Morro 8 231
Galería Oriente 8 238
Santiago Hotel 8 233
Santiago de Guatemala *see* ANTIGUA
Santiago de las Vegas *see under* HAVANA
Santiago de Leon de los Caracas *see* CARACAS
Santiago del Estero 2 392, *393*, 394, 403
Santiago de los Caballeros *see* LEÓN (NICARAGUA)
Santiago de Peñalba 22 246, 247, *247*, 248; 29 275
Santiago de Pupuja 24 *498*, 500
church 24 504
Santiago de Villa Rica *see* VILLARRICA
Santiago Gate 20 168
SS Apostoli (island) 32 182
Santifaller, Franz 15 865
Santillana, Diego de 19 174
Santillana, Iñigo López de Mendoza, Marqués de 9 264; 13 731; 15 834–5
Santillana del Mar Church 26 609
Santini (-Aichel), Giovanni 27 796–8*
collaboration 17 776
groups and movements 13 200
works 2 785; 8 378, 398; 13 199; 18 539; 25 427, 438; 27 *797*, *798*
Santini, Paolo 30 230
Santiniketan 5 420
Santiponce
amphitheatre 26 874
houses 26 870, 904
Italica 16 616*; 26 *904*; 28 510; 29 *258*
mosaics 27 63
S Isidoro del Campo 22 3, *3*; 29 264; 30 882
S Marina 30 882
Santipore 15 723
Santisteban, Conde de 21 35
Sant Joan, Pere de *see* PERE DE SANT JOAN
Sant Joan les Fonts 26 642
Sant Just Desvern, Walden 7 4 227
Sant Miquel de Fluviá Church 26 609
Il Santo *see under* PADUA → ecclesiastical buildings
Santo, Augusto 25 302
Santo, Cesare da *see* CESARE DA SANTO
Santo, Dionísio del 4 719
Santo Antão da Faniqueira Chapel 13 111
Santo Bona Nuova, Villa Zenobio 16 719
Santo Chocano, José 13 668
Santo d'Apollonio 5 672
Santo Domingo (Chile), Casa García Huidobro 6 595
Santo Domingo (Dominican Republic) 8 231; 9 *114*, 116
Academia de Dibujo, Pintura y Escultura 9 119
Alcázar 5 749; 9 116
apartments 9 116
APEC Escuela de Arte 9 119
architecture 5 749
art market 9 118
Asociación de Ahorros y Prestamos 9 116
Banco Central 9 116
Banco Hipotecaria Domenicano 9 117
Casa de Engombe 9 116
Cathedral of S María de la Encarnación 9 116, *116*
Colegio Dominicano de Artistas Plasticas 9 119
Escuela de Artes Plásticas 9 119
Santo Domingo (Dominican Republic)—cont.
Escuela Nacional 9 119
Escuela Nacional de Bellas Artes 9 119
Galería de Arte Moderno *see* Museo de Arte Moderno
Galería de Bellas Artes 9 119
Galería Nacional de Bellas Artes 9 119
Galerias Comerciales 9 117
Hospital of Nicolas de Ovando 9 116
La Compañia Church 9 116
Museo de Arte Moderno 5 746; 9 118
Museo de las Casas Reales 9 118
Museo del Hombre Dominicano 9 116, *117*
Museo Nacional 9 119
Palacio de Bellas Artes 9 116, 119
Palacio Nacional 9 116
S Barbara 9 116
S Francisco 9 116
Torre del Hominaje 9 116
Universidad Autónoma de Santo Domingo 9 118
see also HISPANIOLA (ISLAND)
Santo Domingo (Honduras) 29 139
Santo Domingo (NM; USA) 22 607, 614, 668
Santo Domingo de la Calzada 27 799*; 29 *258*, *259*
Cathedral 26 249, 605, 608; 27 799
metalwork 29 333
Santo Domingo de la Española Cathedral 29 334
Santo Domingo de Oaxaca 33 481
Santō Kyōden *see* KITAO MASANOBU
Santomaso, Giuseppe 27 799*; 32 197
groups and movements 11 802; 13 727; 16 681
works 19 491
San Tomé de Guayana 32 *165*
Fort of S Francesco *see under* ANGOSTURA
Santon Downham (Suffolk), St Mary 26 613
Santoni, Emile Gérard 8 22
Santori, Giulio, Cardinal 2 492
Santorini *see* THERA (ISLAND)
Santorio, Giulio Antonio, Cardinal 26 834
Santoro, Francesco 14 479
Santoro, Suzanne 10 879
santos see under SCULPTURE → types
Santos, Marquesa de 4 711; 24 584
Santos, Agnaldo Manoel dos 1 425; 4 709, 719
works 4 *708*
Santos, Antonio dos 2 87
Santos, Bartolomé (*fl* 1661) 8 858
Santos, Bartolomeu (Cid) dos (*b* 1931) 27 799*
Santos, Deoscóredes Maximiliano dos 4 709
Santos (da Carvalho), Eugénio dos 27 799–804*
assistants 20 402; 27 803
attributions 19 468
collaboration 20 110; 25 186
pupils 27 803
works 19 464, *465*; 20 110; 25 185, *186*, 293; 27 *800*, 804; 31 717
Santos, Francisco de los 10 502; 27 802*; 32 557
Santos, João Pereira dos *see* PEREIRA DOS SANTOS, JOÃO
Santos, Joaquim Marques dos *see* MARQUES DOS SANTOS, JOAQUIM
Santos, Josefina 2 397
Santos, Manoel Rodrigues dos *see* RODRIGUES DOS SANTOS, MANOEL
Santos, Manuel dos 27 802*; 30 881
Santos, Mauro Malang *see* MALANG SANTOS, MAURO
Santos, Reinaldo dos 25 320; 27 802*
Santos, Reinaldo Manuel dos 27 803–4*
patrons and collectors 4 637
works 19 893; 20 403; 23 406; 27 *803*
Santos, Teotónio dos 3 815; 27 804*; 30 881
Santos, Vitalino Pereira dos *see* PEREIRA DOS SANTOS, VITALINO
Santos e Carvalho, Eugenio dos 1 675
Santos Leal, José do Couto dos *see* COUTO DOS SANTOS LEAL, JOSÉ DO
Santos Pacheco 18 783; 24 396; 26 253; 27 804–5*; 28 732
groups and movements 17 595, 596
works 11 19
Santo Spirito Conversazione, Master of the 19 677
Santos Simões, J. M. 25 320
Santos Vasconcellos, Juan de los 6 592
Santos y Ávila, Diego de los 21 376
Santos Zelaya, Juan 23 84
Sant Pere de Burgal 3 710
Sant Pere de Cassèrres 24 750
piers 24 *750*
Sant Pere de Rodes 27 805*; 29 *259*, 262; 32 89
manuscripts 26 675
metalwork 26 689
sculpture 20 *639*; 26 609, 610
S Trovaso, Master of 20 767*
Santry, Denis 28 772; 29 120
Santucci, Geronimo, Bishop of Fossombrone 27 177
Santucci dalle Pomarance, Antonio 12 813
Santuccio, Villa Strozzi 32 545
Santu Pedru-Alghero 2 52
Santurce
Eduardo Georgetti House 25 701
Museum of Contemporary Puerto Rican Art 25 703, 704
Teodoro Moscoso House 25 701
Santurini, Francesco 22 299; 30 676; 33 276
Santvoort, Abraham 5 39
Santvoort, Anthonie 28 388
Santvoort, Dirck (Dircksz.) 27 805–6*
Santvoort, Jan van 9 729
Santvoort, Pieter Dircksz. 27 805
Santvoort, Willem van 7 498
Santwijk, Philippus van 22 872
Sanudo, Marco 19 208
Sanŭng *see* KIM (iii) HONG-DO
San'unsuigetsu Shūjin *see* IKENAGA DŌUN
Sanur 15 806
ceramics 15 811
drawings 15 807, 808
Hyatt Hotel 12 104
Sanuti, Nicolò, Conte di La Poretta *see* LA PORETTA, NICOLÒ SANUTI, Conte di
Sanuti, Nicolosa, Contessa di La Poretta *see* LA PORETTA, NICOLOSA SANUTI, Contessa di
Sanuto (family) 5 819
San Valentino di Marsciano 10 626
San Valero 16 436, 439, 440
S Venanzio 16 654
San Vicente 10 *153*
Pilar church 10 153
Teatro Nacional 10 154
San Vicente dels Horts 29 330
San Vicentejo de Trevino 26 609
S Vincenzo al Volturno 16 *621*, 654; 27 806*
Sanvitale (family) 4 456
Sanvitale, Galeazzo 24 198
Sanvito, Bartolomeo 27 806–7*
attributions 12 171
collaboration 12 656
manuscripts 18 872
works 2 166; 20 III; 27 *807*; 32 198
Sanvittale, Marchese 31 164
San Vittore del Lazio, S Maria la Rosa 13 97
San Vivaldo, Sacromonte 27 498, *498*, 499, 500
Sanxay 27 2
Sanxingdui *see* GUANGHAN
Sanyal, Bhabesh Chandra 8 677
San'yō Rai *see* RAI SAN'YŌ
Sanyuan, Tomb of Li Shou 6 699
Sanyuangong 8 582
San Yuste *see* YUSTE MONASTERY
Sanz, Juan Pablo 9 711
works 9 *711*
S Zaccaria (island) 32 182
Sanz de Sautuola, Marcelino 1 688; 25 474
Sanzeno 6 157
metalwork 6 *153*
Sanzio, Raffaello *see* RAPHAEL
Sao 1 329, 330, *394*; 30 509
figurines 1 *330*
São Bento, Bernardo de 4 709
São João, Macário de 4 709
São João da Tarouca Abbey, Tomb of Pedro, Count of Barcelos 13 102
São João del Rei, S Francisco de Assis 26 *254*, 255
São Joaquim, Barão de 4 725
São José 4 722
São José, Francisco de *see* FRANCISCO DE SÃO JOSÉ
Saonara Park 17 442
Saône Castle 17 502; 21 563; 32 89
Saong *see* KIM KWAN-P'IL
São Paulo 4 *705*, 722; 27 807–8*
architecture 4 712, 714
Casa Modernista 4 721, 724
Centro de Documentação e Informação Sobre Arte Brasileira Contemporânea 2 370
Citibank building 4 715
Companhia Siderúrgica Exhibition Building 4 713
Documentação Social e Estatística, Divisão 4 729
Estúdio Gravura 1 70
furniture 4 721
libraries 4 729
Louveira residential building 4 713
Luz 4 728
Mairinque Railway Station 4 712
museums
Museu de Arqueologia e Etnologia *see under* Universidade de São Paulo
Museu de Arte 3 227; 4 721, 726; 22 366; 27 808, *808*
directors 3 227
Museu de Arte Moderna 4 726, 727; 27 808
Museu de Arte Sacra 4 727; 27 808
Museu de Arte Técnica Popular e Folclore 4 727
Museu da Discoteca 4 708
Museu da Imagem e do Som 4 728
Museu Lasar Segall 4 727
Museu Paulista *see under* Universidade de São Paulo
Pinacoteca do Estado 4 726; 27 808
São Paulo—cont.
Pacaembú Modernistic House 4 712
Palacio Bandeirantes 25 269
Parque de Ibirapuera 4 731; 31 756
patronage 4 717
Rex Gallery 19 61
São Paulo International Biennale 4 726
S Teresa 4 723
UFA Palace 19 271
Universidade de São Paulo
Faculty of Architecture and Urbanism 2 *543*; 4 714
Instituto de Estudos Brasileiros 4 725, 727, 728
Museu de Arqueologia e Etnologia 4 708; 27 808
Museu de Arte Contemporânea 4 714, 727, 728; 6 99; 21 123; 27 808; 33 185
Museu Paulista da Universidade de São Paulo 4 706, 726, 728
Villa Penteado 4 712, 721
Warchavchik's house 4 712
São Pedro de Sintra Casa do Cipreste 25 294
Saora 15 174, 205, 734
São Salvador 1 *401*; 2 85; 18 218
Cathedral of São Salvador 2 85
São Tomé 27 809
Fort of São Sebastião *see* Museu Nacional de São Tomé e Príncipe
Museu Nacional de São Tomé e Príncipe 27 809
Portuguese Cultural Centre 27 809
Reading-Room Francisco Tenreiro 27 809
Saotome 17 364
São Tomé and Príncipe 1 *214*; 11 880; 27 809*
masks 27 809
wood-carvings 27 809
Sapaca, Marcos *see* ZAPATA, MARCOS
Sapalli Tepe 6 196; 7 51
Sapara 12 *317*
St Saba 12 320, 321, 322
Sapareva Banya, St Nikola 5 146
Saparua Duurstede Fort 21 596
Sape, Palina *see* PALINA SAPE
sap green *see under* PIGMENTS → types
Saphoy, Hans *see* SAVOYE, JONATHAN
Saphoy von Salmansweiser, Hans *see* SAVOYE, JOHAN
Sapi culture 1 263, 387
sculpture 1 *388*
Sapieha (family) 19 496; 25 135
Sapieha, Jan Fryderyk 8 843
Sapieha, Leon 25 138
Sapovius, Christoph 28 115
Sapp, Allen 22 597
sappan-wood 7 45
sapphires 12 268, 270, I; 29 699
historical and regional traditions
Australia 12 269
Belgium 3 *609*
Burma 7 91
Byzantine 12 254
China 7 91, *107*
England 17 *522*
France 11 *634*; 17 *525*, II3
Indian subcontinent 12 252
Islamic 12 253
Rome, ancient 27 *102*, *103*
Sri Lanka 12 268
techniques
cutting 12 269
uses
amulets 1 816, 818
bodice ornaments 17 *525*
earrings 17 *525*
embroidery 3 *609*
hair ornaments 17 *525*; 27 *102*

sapphires
uses—cont.
jewellery **17** 519, II3
lockets **17** *522*
necklaces **7** *107*, *109*; **11** *634*; **27** *103*
Sappho Painter **13** 511
Sapporo **17** 18, 97
Historical Museum of Hokkaidō **17** 433
Hokkaidō Museum of Modern Art **17** 433
Saprid, Solomon **24** 620
Saptarshi calendar *see under* INDIAN SUBCONTINENT → calendars
Sapunov, Nikolay (Nikolayevich) **27** 809–10*
groups and movements **4** 178; **22** 178; **27** 392; **33** 379
patrons and collectors **4** 178; **22** 135
teachers **19** 277
Saqqakhana **15** 898; **27** 810*; **30** 286; **33** 634
Saqqara **7** *819*; **9** *507*, 773, *774*, 866; **10** 81; **26** *921*; **27** 810–14*
art forms and materials
columns **23** 532
furniture **10** 50, 51
inscriptions **10** 82
mummies **22** 284, 286
paintings **13** 516, 543, 555
rolls **26** 556
sanctuary **9** 807
sarcophagi **27** 825
saws **9** 821
sculpture **9** 858, 873
architectural **27** 814
relief **9** 871, 873, 885; **10** 64
reserve heads **9** 863
statuettes **10** 16
stelae **9** 890; **29** 615
Deir Apa Jeremiah *see* Monastery of St Jeremias
funerary complex of Djoser **10** 50, 72, 84; **27** *810*, 811–12
funerary complex of Pepy I **10** 81
funerary complex of Sekhemkhet **9** 779; **27** 812
funerary temple of Pepy II **9** 877
Great Enclosure **25** 761
heb-sed court of Djoser **9** 825, 833
South Building **2** 296
houses **9** 852
Monastery of St Jeremias **7** 820, 821, 822; **9** 574; **27** 813–14; **30** 776
wall paintings **27** 814
monuments **7** 820
mortuary temple of Sahure **9** 871
mortuary temple of Userkaf **25** 762
necropoleis **9** 843, 899; **22** 286
pyramids **25** 763
Buried Pyramid **25** 761
Ibi **27** 812
Isesi **27** 812
Khendjer **25** 763; **27** 812
Merenre **27** 812
Pepy I **10** 80; **27** 812
Pepy II **10** 76, 80; **25** 763, *763*; **27** 812
Sekhemkhet **10** 81
Step Pyramid **9** 779, 790, 819, 844, 891; **10** 72, 81, 84; **11** 231; **15** 146; **20** 571, 863; **23** 807; **25** 761, *761*; **27** *810*, 810, 811, 813; **31** 107
furniture **10** 50
reliefs **9** 868
sculpture **9** 867
tiles **10** 47, *47*
Teti **10** 80; **27** 812
Unas **10** 83; **25** 763; **27** 812
Userkaf **25** 762; **27** 812
Wenis **9** 804; **10** 29, 80
Pyramid Texts *see* PYRAMID TEXTS
Saqqara—cont.
Serapeum **9** 843, *843*; **10** 80, 93; **27** 813
sarcophagi **27** 825
stelae **29** 616
Temple T **9** 850
tomb chapels **9** 838
tombs **9** 778, *839*
mastabas **20** 596; **27** 810–11
private **9** 838, 850
Akhhotpe **27** *811*, 812; **31** 107
Akhpet **27** 812
Ameneminet **27** 812
Amuntefnakht **9** 842
Ankhmahor **9** 872
Aperia **27** 812
Bekenrenef **9** 841, 891; **27** *811*, 813
Djanenjebu **27** 813
Hemaka **9** 822
Hesyre **9** 822, 899; **10** 50; **14** 493–4*, *494*; **20** 596; **27** *811*, 812; **29** 615
Idut **9** *872*; **27** *811*, 812
Ihy **9** 877
Ipuia **27** 812
Kagemni **27** *811*, 812
Karenen **9** 820
Khentika **9** 790
Khnumhotpe **10** 50; **27** *811*, 812
Maya (*fl c.* 1320 BC) **27** 812
Mehu **9** 899
Mereruka **9** 673, 790, 808, 817, *817*, 822, 904; **10** 51, 65, 83; **20** 596; **21** 149–50; **27** *811*, 812
Mes **27** 812
Nebet **27** *811*, 812
Nefer and Kahay **9** 820, 821, 822, 838; **10** 51; **27** *811*, 812
Neferenpet **9** 904; **27** 812
Niankhkhnum **10** 50; **27** *811*, 812
Niankhpepi **9** 838
Padyenaset **10** 68
Psammetichus (chief of doctors) **27** 813
Ptahhotpe **9** 789; **27** *811*, 812; **31** 107
Ruaben *see* Tomb 2302
Sheikh el-Beled **28** 577
Tomb 2302 **20** 596
Tomb 3070 **20** 596
Tomb C8 *see* Sheikh el-Beled
Ty **9** 802, 808, 819, 820, *820*, 822; **27** *811*, 812; **31** 491*
royal **9** 779; **10** 68, 72, 81
Adjib **27** 810
Aha **27** 810
Djer **27** 810
Hetepsekhemwy **27** 811
Horemheb (*reg c.* 1319–*c.* 1292 BC) **9** 839, 885; **14** 758; **27** *811*, 812
Khaemwese **9** 843
Mastabat Faraun **9** 779; **10** 81; **27** 812
Merneith **27** 810
Ninetjer **27** 811
Qaa **27** 810, 811
Tia **27** 812; **31** 107
Wadimu **27** 810, 811
Wadj **27** 810
tools **9** 821
Saqsaywaman *see* SACSAHUAMAN
Saqueti, Giovanni Battista *see* SACCHETTI, GIOVANNI BATTISTA
Saqundi, El **5** 833
SAR *see* STICHTING ARCHITECTEN RESEARCH
Sara **1** 363
Sarab, Tepe **15** 913; **21** 269, 305
Sarabhai, Gautam **15** 742
Sarabīṭ al Khādim *see* SERABIT EL-KHADIM
Sarabiyye, Ibrahim **19** 7
Saraburi **30** 595
Saracchi (family) **14** 171; **16** 745; **27** 814–15*
works **8** 407; **26** *485*, 486
Saracco, Bartolomeo **27** 814
Saracco, Costanzo **27** 815
Saracco, Gabrielo **27** 815
Saracco, Gasparo **27** 815
Saracco, Giovanni Ambrogio **11** 279; **21** 529; **27** 814, 815; **33** 274
Saracco, Michele **11** 279; **21** 529; **27** 814
Saracco, Pietro Antonio **27** 815
Saracco, Raffaello **11** 279; **21** 529; **27** 814
Saracco, Simone **11** 279; **21** 529; **27** 814; **33** 274
Saracco, Stefano **11** 279; **21** 529; **27** 814; **33** 274
Saracen Foundry **28** 263
Saraceni, Carlo **16** 670; **27** 815–17*
assistants **3** 353
attributions **11** 723; **19** 35, 205; **29** 253
collaboration **4** 405; **18** 732; **26** 840; **29** 253; **30** 356; **31** 436
groups and movements **30** 456
patrons and collectors **4** 567; **5** 451; **12** 912; **27** 133, 724
pupils **20** 737; **24** 369; **32** 102
reproductive prints by others **19** 35
works **3** 354; **19** 35; **27** 724, *816*, *817*
Saraceni, Pensionante del *see* PENSIONANTE DEL SARACENI
Saracenic ivory-carvings *see under* IVORY-CARVINGS → types
Saracen Pottery **28** 258
Saracini (family) **28** 677
Saracini **11** 384
Saradar Singh, Maharaja of Bikaner (*reg* 1851-72) (Rajput) **15** 609
Saragossa **16** *103*; **26** *908*; **27** 817–19*, *818*; **29** *259*
academy **29** 293
La Alfería **29** 323
Aljafería Palace **12** 79; **16** 133, 187, 189–90, 244; **21** 505; **29** 262, 263
ceiling **16** 493
Throne Room **2** 529
art forms and materials
architecture **6** *72*
astrolabes **16** 369
Bibles **17** 562
gold **13** 165; **29** 335, 337
metalwork **29** 332
painting **29** 280
pottery **16** 411; **29** 323
sculpture **26** 609; **29** 294
Casa Miguel Donlope **29** 267
Casa Zaporta **29** 267
churches
Cathedral of La Seo **13** 69, 70, 211; **29** 263, 265; **30** 313, 331
altarpieces **25** 184
monstrance **29** 335
retable **13** 107
retables **26** 249
textiles **13** 197
tomb of Archbishop Lope Fernández de Luna **13** 106
Cathedral of Nuestra Señora del Pilar **29** 269, 334, 337, 341
paintings **29** 283
retables **26** 249; **29** 290
sculpture **29** 293
sepulchre of *General Ena* **25** *225*
towers **4** 784
wood-carvings **29** 312
La Magdalena **22** 255
parish church of Belchite **11** 482
S Engrácia **29** 265
S Pablo **29** 337
Coso Theatre **30** 663
education (art) **29** 357
Saragossa—cont.
Exchange **29** 267
Fundación-Museo Pablo Serrano de Zaragoza **29** 355
Instituto y Museo Camón Aznar **5** 529
Museo Pablo Gargallo **12** 148
palace of the Conde de Morata **29** 267
Palacio de Argillo *see* Museo Pablo Gargallo
Palacio de los Condes de Sástago **29** 301
Rincón de Goya **29** 273
Torre Nueva **13** 68; **22** 255
Saragozza, Llorenz *see* LORENZO ZARAGOZA
Saraguru **9** 710
Saragwala *see* LOTHAL
Sarah Fuller Arawak Pottery **2** 152
Sara Hildén Art Museum *see under* TAMPERE
Sara Hildén Foundation **11** 112
Sarai Amanat Khan **15** 366, 680
Saraimiran **17** 778
Saraina, Torello *see* SARAYNA, TORELLO
Saraiva, Cardinal **25** 319
Saraj al-Din Badr **17** 864
Sarajas-Korte, Salme **11** 113
Sarajevo **4** *459*; **16** *103*; **27** 819–20*
Academy of Arts **4** 462
Ali Pasjia Mosque **4** *460*
architecture **4** 460
Art Gallery **4** 463
basilica **4** 459
dress **16** 463
Ferizbey Baths **4** 460
Gazi Husrefbey Mosque **4** 460
Holiday Inn **4** 460
Institute of Physics and Chemistry **4** 460
Jewish Museum **27** *820*
Kal Grandi synagogue **17** 547
Marindvor Centre **4** 460
Museum of the City of Sarajevo **4** 463
National Museum **4** 460, 463
National Theatre **4** 460
Officers' Pavilions **4** 460
Palace of Justice **4** 460
Parliament Building **4** 460
Philosophy Faculty **4** 460
Railway Council Building **4** 460
Slavija apartment building **4** 460
State School of Painting **4** 461
Svrzo House **4** 460
Technical Faculty **4** 460
Town Hall **4** 460
water supply **27** 819
Sarakhs **16** 164
Saralegui y López-Castro, Leandro de **27** 820*
Saramaccaner **30** 13
Saramaka
cloaks **1** *424*
sarangi **22** 376
Saransk Sychov Mordovian Picture Gallery **10** 494
Sarao, Gennaro **16** 748
Sarapalli **15** 537
sarapes **21** 394; **22** *625*
Sarapuu, Lembit **10** 540
Sarapyan, E. A. **13** 653
Sarasota (FL), Ringling Museum of Art **14** 675; **26** 410; **31** 667
Saratov **27** *363*, 442
Aleksander N. Radishchev Museum **4** 232; **27** 440
Saravia, Fernando **23** 81, 82, 85
Sarawak **5** *10*; **15** *751*; **20** 162, *162*, 164; **29** *225*
architecture **20** 165; **21** 45, 596
baskets **3** 332; **4** I2
beadwork **3** 442; **4** I2
brass **20** 173, 180
cane **4** I2
fortifications **21** 596
Sarawak—cont.
jewellery **20** 180
Sarawak Museum **29** 240
shells **4** I2
tattoos **15** 809
see also MALAYSIA
Sarawak Museum Journal **24** 437
Saray **16** 412
Sarayacu **9** 709
Sarayama **17** 260
Saray Berke **6** 258
Sarayna, Torello **5** 816; **27** 820*
Sarazin, Benigne **27** 822
Sarazin, Charles **27** 879–80
Sarazin, Jacques **24** 134, 167; **26** 772; **27** 821–2*
assistants **13** 790
collaboration **5** 323; **19** 225; **20** 291; **23** 460; **24** 467
patrons and collectors **5** 168; **14** 492; **28** 370; **29** 886
pupils **19** 88, 95; **20** 480; **25** 79
restorations by others **32** 580
teachers **13** 825
works **7** 422; **9** 90; **11** *558*, 558–9; **19** 134, 642; **27** 548, *822*
Sarazin, Jean-Philippe **4** 888
Sarazin, Pierre **27** 822
Sarazm **6** 236, 255; **30** 440
Sarbiewo Church **25** 126
Sarburgh, Bartholomäus **27** 822–3*
Sarça, Diogo de **25** 304; **27** 823*
Sarcham **16** 193
sarcophagi **27** 823–33*; **31** 121
historical and regional traditions
Ancient Near East **27** 825*
Bali (Indonesia) **27** 831
Borneo **27** 831
Byzantine **9** 596–7; **27** 827–8*
Chachapoyas **27** 833
China **27** 832*
Christianity **9** 596–7; **27** 827
Colombia **27** 833
Crete **2** *879*; **8** 155; **21** 657; **26** 855; **27** 825
Cyprus, ancient **27** 825
Early Christian (*c.* AD 250-843) **9** 594, 596–7; **16** 686; **27** 827*, *828*
Egypt, ancient **1** 516, *516*; **9** 813, *843*; **10** 12–13*; **27** 823–5*, *824*
Etruscan **10** 588, 592, 594, *607*, 607–8; **27** 823, 826*
France **27** *829*
Greece, ancient **13** 383, 515, 596; **26** 855; **27** 825–6*
Indian subcontinent **15** 686
Indonesia **15** 788; **27** 831, *831*
Insular art **5** 916
Ireland **5** 916
Italy **27** 829–31
Baroque **27** *830*
Early Christian (*c.* AD 250-843) **16** 686
Etruscan **10** 588, 594, *607*
Punic **10** 592
Roman **9** *517*
Japan **17** 58, 59*, 106, *106*; **27** 832*
Java **27** 831
Jewish art **17** 554
Korea **27** 832*
Laos **27** 831
Lycia **19** *839*
Maya **27** 823, 832
Merovingian **21** 163–4*
Mesoamerica, Pre-Columbian **27** *832*, 832–3*
Mesopotamia **27** 825
Mexico **27** *832*
Minoan **2** *879*; **21** 657; **27** 825
Mycenaean **27** 825
Netherlands, the **27** *99*
Olmec **27** 832, *832*
Peru **27** 833
Phoenician **8** 341; **27** 825–6*
Prehistoric art **25** 539

sarcophagi
historical and regional traditions—cont.
Punic **10** 592
Rome, ancient **9** *250*; **22** 411, *411*; **23** *536*; **26** 135, 854–5; **27** 11, 28, 39, 40, 41, 42, *42*, 44–5, 60, 823, *826*, 826–7*
Christianity **27** 827
Italy **9** *517*
Netherlands, the **27** *99*
Russia **13** 596
Sabah (Malaysia) **27** 831
San Agustín culture **27** 833
South America, Pre-Columbian **6** 380; **27** 833*
South-east Asia **27** 831*
Sumatra **15** 788; **27** 831, *831*; **31** 115
Syria **26** 855
Syria-Palestine **27** 825; **28** *668*
Ukraine **31** 561
materials
alabaster (gypsum) **27** 824
alabaster (limestone) **1** 516, *516*
basalt **27** 824, 825
bronze **27** *830*
clay **13** 515; **27** 825
granite **10** 13; **27** 824, 825
limestone **2** *879*; **10** *607*; **27** 823, 824, 825
marble **9** *517*; **23** *536*; **26** 854–5; **27** *42*, 825, 826, *826*, 827, *828*; **28** *668*; **31** 561
molasse **27** 831
porphyry **27** 827
quartzite **9** 813; **10** 13; **27** 824
sandstone **27** *832*
schist **27** 824, *824*
stone **10** 607–8; **17** 59; **27** 824, 825, 826, 827, 828, *831*
terracotta **15** 686; **27** 825, 826
tufa **27** 831
wood **27** 825
reuse **27** 829
types
boat coffins **27** 823, 831
Philistine coffins **27** 825
see also COFFINS; MUMMY CASES
sarcophagus altars *see under* ALTARS → types
Sarcophagus of Doña Sancha, Master of the **16** 816
Sarcophagus of the Mourning Women **13** 461; **27** 825
sard **12** 250, *263*; **14** *170*
Sarda, José Sala y *see* SALA Y SARDA, JOSÉ
Sardar, Arbab Mohammad **23** 801
Sardar, Tepe **1** *186*, *849*; **27** 833*
Room 52 **1** 203
sculpture **1** 196, 197, 198; **27** 833
stucco **1** 196; **29** 824, *825*
stupas **1** 192; **27** 833
wall paintings **1** 201, 202, 203
Sardarapat, Museum of the Ethnography of Armenia **2** 445
Sardë **1** 538
Sardegna *see* SARDINIA
Sardi, Andrea Pucci *see* PUCCI SARDI, ANDREA
Sardi, Gaetano **3** 920; **28** 379
Sardi, Giuseppe (*fl* 1621-99) **3** 202; **7** 900; **32** 188, 195, 229
works **32** *229*
Sardi, Giuseppe (1680-1753) **1** 532; **2** 26; **5** 293; **27** 833–4*
Sardinia **16** *616*, *620*; **25** 732; **26** *886*; **27** 834–6*
altars **27** 836
architecture **27** 836
Cistercian Order **27** 836
Franciscan Order **27** 836
Gothic **27** 836
megalithic **21** 43
Prehistoric **25** 522
Romanesque **27** 836
vernacular **32** 290, 291
Sardinia—cont.
askoi **10** 610
bronze **25** 734; **27** 835, *835*
churches **27** 836
copper **16** 743; **25** 734
coral **7** 834, 835
ex-votos **27** 835
figurines **25** 512; **27** 834, 835, *835*
fortifications **21** 551
gold **6** 158
ivory-carvings **25** 734
jewellery **25** 735
moulds **25** 734
nuraghi **3** 311; **21** 551; **23** 304–5*, *304*, 808; **25** 522; **27** 835
ostrich eggs **25** 735
painting **27** 834, 836
periods
Prehistoric **27** 834–5*
pottery **27** 834*
razors **25** 734
sculpture **25** 734; **27** 835, 836
statuettes **27** 834
stone-carvings **25** 530
temples **30** 434
tin **10** 624
tombs **2** 52; **25** 524; **27** 834
trade
paintings **27** 836
tin **13** 372; **14** 333
Sardis **1** *849*; **9** *512*; **13** *363*; **19** 840, 841; **26** *908*; **27** 837–8*
acropolis **19** 841
arcades **9** 524
architecture **9** 524; **15** 894; **26** 913
Basilica **9** 536
bath-gymnasium **3** 375; **23** 483; **26** 912, 914; **27** 837, *837*
Church E **9** 550
coins **1** *888*
mosaics **9** 564, 565
sculpture **27** 838*
silver **19** 841
stadium **29** 488
synagogue **9** 564; **15** 894; **17** 543
Temple of Artemis **13** 405; **19** 841
tombs **19** 841
urban planning **26** 913
sardonyx **14** 167
historical and regional traditions
Byzantine **9** 661; **12** 254
Etruscan **12** 249
France **11** *636*; **12** *264*
Greece, ancient **12** 248
Indian subcontinent **15** 698, *702*
Rome, ancient **1** *652*; **15** 698
uses
cameos **1** *652*; **12** 248, *264*; **15** *702*
chalices **9** 661
ewers **11** *636*
scarabs **12** 249
Sardo Raxis, Pedro **26** 549
Sarduri II, King of Urartu (*reg c.* 764-734 BC) **31** 700
Sarenput I (*fl* 1971-1926 BC) **2** 657
Sarenput II (*fl* 1929-1892 BC) **2** 657; **9** 838
Sarepta **24** 643; **30** 187
Saret, Alan **3** 291
Sarfaraz Khan, Nawab of Bengal (*reg* 1740-66) **15** 378
Sarfati, Alain **27** 838*
Sarfatti, Margherita **27** 838–9*; **28** 792
groups and movements **10** 820; **16** 680; **23** 263
Sargadelos **18** 598; **29** 329
Sargathon **31** 434
Sargent, Charles Sprague **10** 814
Sargent, Henry **27** 839*
Sargent, John Singer **27** 839–41*; **31** 603; **32** 197
dealers **18** 161
Sargent, John Singer—cont.
groups and movements **1** 22; **26** 57; **32** 591
methods **6** 471
patrons and collectors **3** 740; **7** 377; **11** 141; **28** 808; **33** 151
pupils **3** 631
works **3** 390; **4** 477; **9** 225, 288, *289*; **20** 18; **27** *840*, *841*
Sargh, Hendrik **31** 704
Sargin **31** 453
Sargon (*reg* 2334-2279 BC) **1** 508–9*; **21** 272
vases **1** *867*
Sargon II (*reg* 721-705 BC) **21** 274; **25** 650
architecture **1** 891; **2** 297, 638, 640; **18** 27; **21** 288–90; **23** 150, 151, 153, 806
reliefs **28** 611
sculpture **21** 299–300*
Sargon's palace *see under* KHORSABAD
Sargon Vase **1** 867, *867*, 868; **23** 150
Sargsyan, Ara **2** 436
Sarha Mosque **16** 177
Sari (Iran) **16** 408
Sari (Java) **29** 865
Sari, Fujiwara no *see* FUJIWARA NO SARI
Sarian, Martiros (Sergeyevich) *see* SARYAN, MARTIROS (SERGEYEVICH)
Sarianidi, V. I. **6** 285
Sarif, Abdurāhmān M. **10** 574
Sarıgöl Church **5** 675
Sarigüzel **9** 597
Sari Kubur **31** 701
Sariñena, Juan **26** 306; **27** 842*; **29** 267; **31** 815
Saripolos **13** 359
Sar-i Pul **16** *105*
architecture **16** 161
Imam-i Khurd *see* Imamzada Yahya
Imamzada Yahya **16** 163, *163*, 165, 168
inscriptions **16** 169
mausoleum of Imam-i Kalan **16** 166
Sar-i Pul-i Zuhab **15** 916
sārīs **15** *670*, 692
Šariš **28** 856
Šarišské Museum *see under* BARDEJOV
Sariyev, Shaimardan **17** 867
Sark **30** 770, 772, 773
Sarkhej **15** *279*, 347, 348; **27** 842*
tomb of Shaykh Ahmad Khatu **15** 349
Sarkis **11** 553
Şarkışla **1** 835
Sarkissof, Denise **3** 76
Sarlandie, Jules **19** 396
Sarlis, Maligawage **29** 461, 467
works **29** *467*
Sarmaj Palace **16** 160
Sarmatia **27** 842
Sarmatian **25** 533; **27** 842; **28** 320, 324–6*
diadems **28** *325*
gold **28** *325*
metalwork **28** 321, 324
standards (vexilloid) **11** 151
see also SCYTHIAN
Sarmatism **25** 105, 118, 131, 132–3; **27** 842–3*
Sarmiento, José Francisco, Conde de Salvatierra *see* SALVATIERRA, JOSÉ FRANCISCO SARMIENTO,Conde de
Sarmiento, Martín de **23** 413
Sarmiento, Pedro, Cardinal, Archbishop of Santiago de Compostella **13** 862
Sarmin **16** 441
mosque **16** 179
Sarmizegethusa **25** *471*; **26** *705*, 906, *906*; **30** 434, 773
Sārnate **18** 846, *847*
Sarnath **5** 94; **8** 269; **15** 220, *261*, *279*; **27** 844*
apsidal temple **15** 251, 256
Archaeological Museum **15** 181
architecture **15** 263
capitals **27** *844*
Dhamekh Stupa **15** 262, *262*, 281; **29** 869
park **24** 178
pillar **15** 423; **27** 844
platform **15** 256
sculpture **15** 413, 415, 416, 423, 424, 426, 427–8, 440, 454, 455, *455*, 456, *456*, 457, 480, 499; **20** 819
Sarnelli, Antonio **27** 845*
Sarnelli, Gennaro **27** 845
Sarnelli, Giovanni **27** 845*
Sarnelli, Pompeo **23** 577
Sarnen **30** *124*, 145
Kollegiumkirche **30** 128
Sarno **26** 888
Sarnowo **25** *471*
barrow **25** *506*
Sa'robi **1** 189
Saroldi (family) **11** 611
sarongs **15** 791, 793, 795, *796*, 813; **20** 180; **30** XI
Saronno, S Maria dei Miracoli **15** 137
Sárospatak **14** *881*
Castle **14** 885
Lorántffy wing **14** 885
chests **14** 905
collections **15** 17
Cultural Centre **14** 891
Rákóczi Museum **15** 17
Sarotrataniman, Phra **30** 590
Sarouk **16** 483
Sarpaneva, Timo **11** 100, 106, 110
Sâr Peladan *see* PELADAN, JOSÉPHIN
Sarphati, Samuel **1** 803; **23** 670
Sarpsborg Stadion **14** 229
Sarrabat, Charles **27** 845
Sarrabat, Daniel **7** 640; **24** 810; **27** 845*
Sarrabat, Isaac **12** 637; **21** 416; **27** 845*
Sarrabat, Pierre **18** 804
Sarrabezolles, Charles **10** 689; **11** 568, 569; **31** 224
Sarrasin, Clemens **31** 219
Sarrazin, Jacques *see* SARAZIN, JACQUES
Sarre, Friedrich **16** 327, 548, 550, 554, 556, 559; **27** 845–6*
assistants **18** 501
collaboration **14** 487; **16** 548
personal collection **16** 559
Sarrett, John **31** 653
Sarria, Pedro Fernández de Castro Andrade y Portugal, Marqués de *see* LEMOS, Conde de
Sarria de Masaya, Antonio **23** 81
Sarrocchi, Tito **24** 218, 219
Sarsi **22** 551
Sart *see* SARDIS
Sart, Cornelis du *see* DUSART, CORNELIS
Sart, Johann Gregor van der *see* SCHARDT, JOHANN GREGOR VAN DER
Sartain, John S. **4** 73; **14** 166; **21** 418; **23** 634
Sartain, William **3** 464
Sarte, Maxime Real del *see* REAL DEL SARTE, MAXIME
Sar Temple **2** 251
Sarteneja **21** 248
SAR theory *see* SUPPORTS THEORY
Sarti, Antonio **26** 761, 824, 842; **31** 172
Sarto, Andrea del **11** 532, 703; **16** 694, 766; **27** 846–51*
assistants **25** 222
Sarto, Andrea del—cont.
collaboration **3** 15; **12** 719; **25** 222; **27** 740, 770
drawings **9** 220
forgeries by others **11** 307
frames **11** 387
methods **21** 768
paintings **16** 663; **22** 727; **24** 860
allegorical **27** *848*
altarpieces **11** 186; **26** 321; **27** 496
frescoes **9** 264; **11** 204, 703; **13** 676; **21** 16; **25** 76; **27** *846*, *850*
portraits **16** 663
religious **27** *847*; **29** 14
patrons and collectors
Alcalá, 3rd Duque de (1583-1637) **26** 307
Anna Maria Luisa de' Medici, Electress Palatine **21** 31
Arconati, Galeazzo (Maria), Conte **2** 376
Baudot (family) **3** 394
Benintendi, Giovan Maria **3** 15
Benson, R(obert) H(enry) **3** 740
Borgherini (family) **4** 404; **16** 711
Borgherini, Pierfrancesco **3** 15; **4** 404; **13** 281; **28** 334
Bourbon II., Luis Antonio, Infante of Spain **4** 565
Butler, Charles (1822-1910) **5** 311
Carr, William Holwell **5** 848
Charles IV, King of Spain (*reg* 1788-1808) **4** 565
Confraternity of St John the Baptist **7** 457
Corte, Valerio **5** 456
Créquy, Charles de Blanchefort de **19** 238
Dezallier d'Argenville, A(ntoine)-N(icolas) **8** 845
Faesch, Johann Jakob **10** 752
Francesco I, 8th Duke of Modena and Reggio (*reg* 1629-58) **10** 526
Francis I, King of France (*reg* 1515-47) **11** 264; **31** 849
Fries, Moritz, Graf von **11** 789
Gaddi (ii), Giovanni de' **11** 893
Hesselin, Louis (-Cauchon) **14** 492
Leemput, Remi van **19** 63
Medici, Carlo de', Cardinal **21** 25
Medici, Ferdinando de', Grand Prince of Tuscany (1663-1713) **21** 30
Medici, Ottaviano de' **21** 18
Musée du Louvre (Paris) **11** 665
Museo Nacional de Bellas Artes (Santiago) **6** 601
Palla, Giovanbattista della **23** 855
Philip II, King of Spain (*reg* 1556-98) **9** 173
Philip IV, King of Spain (*reg* 1621-65) **5** 844; **14** 8
Poniatowski, Stanisław, Prince **25** 213
Richelieu, Armand-Jean Du Plessis, Cardinal de **26** 348
Roscoe, William **27** 161
Salviati (family) **27** 648
Serra, Giovan Francesco, Marqués di Cassano **28** 479
Servites **28** 489
Tallard, Marie-Joseph d'Hostun, Duc de **30** 274
Urban VIII, Pope (*reg* 1623-44) **3** 205
Villiers, George, 1st Duke of Buckingham (1592-1628) **32** 575
William II, King of the Netherlands (*reg* 1840-49) **23** 469

Sarto, Andrea del—cont.
pupils **3** 13; **7** 776; **18** 781; **25** 721; **27** 207, 648; **32** 10
reproductions in tapestry **11** 48
reproductions in textiles **16** 759
reproductive prints by others
Alberti, Cherubino **1** 551
Cock, Hieronymus (Wellens) **7** 499
Cort (van Hoorn), Cornelis **7** 899
Danckerts, Hendrick **8** 495
Forster, François **11** 319
Heyden, Pieter van der **14** 505
Krüger, Dietrich **18** 476
Mignon, Jean **21** 499
Musi, Agostino dei **22** 369
Zuccarelli, Francesco **33** 714
restorations by others **24** 730
sculpture **21** 72
teachers **24** 771; **25** 848
Sartori, Angioletta **16** 780
Sartori, Giambattista **5** 631
Sartori, Joseph Anton **24** 313
Sartorio, Giulio Aristide **25** 793; **26** 776; **27** 852*
groups and movements **8** 509
works **16** 678, 679
Sartoris, Alberto **7** *294*; **16** 681; **27** 853*
collaboration **5** 919; **30** 513
groups and movements **15** 886; **21** 422; **26** 15, 16
works **11** 80; **16** 649
Sartorius (family) **21** 91; **29** 424
Sartorius, C. J. **27** 853*
Sartorius, Francis (i) (1734-1804) **27** 853*
Sartorius, Francis (ii) (*fl* 1799-1808) **27** 853*
Sartorius, G. W. **27** 853*
Sartorius, Jan Adam Dominik **8** 413
Sartorius, J(ohn) F(rancis) (1775-1831) **27** 853*
Sartorius, J(ohn) N(ost) (1759-1828) **10** 250; **27** 853*
Sartorius, John (1700-80) **27** 853*
Sartorius, M. **27** 853*
Sartorius, Tomáš, Abbot of Broumov **8** 396
Sartre, Jean-Paul (Charles Aymard) **1** 182; **2** 508; **10** 685, 686; **27** 853–4*
groups and movements **24** 144
productions **1** 142; **13** 322; **18** 577
works **12** 565
illustrated **33** 305
Sarug, Jacob of *see* JACOB OF SARUG
Saruhanid **16** 202
Sarup Singh, Rana of Mewar (*reg* 1842-61) (Rajput) **15** 601, *601*
Sárvár, Nádasdy Castle **14** *881*, 885, 899, 905; **15** 15
Festsaal **29** 839
Sarvasaddhi Acharya **24** 267
Sarvastivada Buddhism *see under* BUDDHISM → sects
Sarvavarman, Ruler (*reg c.* 576-80) (Maukhari) **15** 458
Sarvistan **15** *901*, 912; **16** *105*; **27** 854*
palace **24** 877
Saryan, Martiros (Sergeyevich) **2** 431; **27** 854–5*
groups and movements **4** 178; **11** 358; **12** 871; **27** 392
house **13** 653
patrons and collectors **4** 178
teachers **28** 475
works **2** 431, 432; **28** 918
Saryg **23** 607
Saryk **6** 254; **16** 485
rugs **10** *874*
Sarzana
Cathedral of S Maria Assunta **8** 211
Sarzana—cont.
S Francesco
tomb of Guarniero degli Antelminelli **13** 94
Sarzana, il *see* FIASELLA, DOMENICO
Sarzec, Edmond de **1** 892
Sarzec, Ernest de **30** 422
Sasa, Pedro Antonio **29** 338
Sasaki, Shōdō **17** 324
Sasaki Shizuma **17** 236, 238
Sasamón S María la Real **13** 104
Sasanian **1** *852*; **6** 187; **15** 900, 906–7; **21** 275*; **27** 855–7*
architecture **11** 121; **15** 912–13; **21** 292–3*, 554
carpets **16** 469
chalcedony **1** *858*
coins **1** 204, *888*, 889*; **6** 264; **7** 82; **27** *855*
crowns **1** 888
diadems **1** 888
dress **1** *884*, 887–8*
earrings **1** 876
façades **18** *483*
fortifications **21** 554
gilding **15** *920*
glass **7** 83; **9** 645
iwans **27** 855
jewellery **1** 876*
metalwork **6** 238; **15** 920
palaces **18** *483*; **23** 806, 807
plaster **29** 815–16*
plates **15** *920*; **27** *856*
pottery **21** 308
religion **33** 706
rock crystal **26** 485
rock reliefs **4** *92*; **15** 917–18, *918*; **30** *337*
sculpture **11** *121*; **15** 915; **21** 302
seals **1** 858, *858*; **27** 857
silk **16** 429; **28** 715
silver **15** *920*; **27** *855*, 856
silver-gilt **27** *856*
standards (vexilloid) **11** 151
stucco **27** 856; **29** 815–16*
textiles **1** 882–3
trade
silk **28** 721
vaults (ceiling) **27** 857
wall paintings **18** *499*
Sasaniya **22** 758
Sasaram **15** *279*, *360*; **27** 857–9*
tombs **15** 368; **27** *858*, 858
Sasave **26** 607
Sasayama, Old Tanba Pottery Museum **17** 433
SASDLR *see* SURRÉALISME AU SERVICE DE LA RÉVOLUTION
Sasebo Shinwa Bank **17** 90
Saseki *see* FUJIWARA NO SARI
Sash, Cecily **29** 109
sashes **7** 179
historical and regional traditions
Canada **5** 588
China **7** 75
Hawaii **14** 249
Indian subcontinent **3** 442
Indonesia **15** 792
Iran **16** 465
Islamic **16** 429, 461, 462, 465
Japan **17** 315–16, 377, 386
Java **15** 792
Madagascar **20** *39*
Micronesia, Federated States of **21** *477*
Morocco **16** 429
Native North Americans **22** 627, 651
Ottoman **16** 461, 462
Poland **25** 132–3, *133*
Turkey **16** 461, 462; **25** 132
materials
beads **17** 386; **21** *477*
beadwork **3** 442
cotton **15** 792
feathers **14** 249
fibres **21** *477*
quills **22** 651
sashes
materials—cont.
shells **21** *477*
silk **15** 792; **20** *39*; **25** *133*
wool **21** *477*
Sashizudō **17** 125
sash windows *see under* WINDOWS → types
Saskatoon **5** *559*
Mendel Art Gallery **5** 590
sa skya *see* SAKYA
Sasliha **5** 411
Sass, Else Kai *see* KAI SASS, ELSE
Sass, Henry **7** 839; **8** 827; **10** 373
pupils **7** 801; **9** 756; **11** 795, 804; **14** 768; **21** 601; **27** 185; **30** 384, 569
Sassari Palazzo Provinciale **28** 213
Sassetta **12** 717; **27** 859–63*
attributions **1** 621, 622; **20** 738
patrons and collectors **6** 393; **7** 782; **15** 39; **28** 676, 677
pupils **24** 781; **27** 765; **32** 103
restorations by others **24** 343
works **11** 709; **16** 662, 845; **18** 705; **27** 765, *860*, *861*, *862*
Sassetti, Baro **31** 534
Sassetti, Francesco (di Tommaso) **11** 186; **16** *763*; **27** 863*
frescoes **12** 551; **31** 124
manuscripts **20** 413
paintings **16** 763
sculpture **26** 444
Sasseville, François **5** 585, 586
Sasseville, Joseph **5** 585
Sassi, Ludovico Rusconi *see* RUSCONI SASSI, LUDOVICO
Sassi, Riccardo **26** 809
Sassia, Hospital of S Spirito **27** 271
Sasso, Antonio **13** 321
Sasso, Francesco **4** 564
Sasso, Giovanni Maria **27** 863–4*; **29** 746; **33** 385
paintings **14** 877
Sassocorvaro Fortress **3** 359; **11** *688*
Sassoferrato (1609-85) **27** 864–5*
attributions **21** 497
patrons and collectors **5** 537; **12** 638; **24** 225
reproductive prints by others **26** 517
works **8** 99; **9** 110; **27** *864*; **32** *4*
Sasso Ferrato, Bartolo di *see* BARTOLO DI SASSO FERRATO
Sassoferrato, Palazzo Communale **2** 185
Sassoon (family) **4** 289
Sassoon, Philip **5** 688; **22** 60
Sassú, Aligi **13** 872; **16** 681; **21** 528; **27** 865*
Sassuolo, Palazzo degli Estense **2** 849; **7** 356; **15** 138
Sastri, M. S. Kuppuswami **28** 808
Sasuk Chae **18** 259
Sasvár **15** 11
Sas-Zaloziecky, Wladimir **2** 833, 834
Sas-Zubrzyski, Jan **25** 99
Satakarni, King (*reg c.* 1st cent. BC) (Satavahana) **15** 431
Satake (scrolls) **11** 826; **17** 829
Satake Shozan **14** 565; **17** 417; **23** 347; **27** 865–6*
Satake Sōshichi **17** 401
Satariano, Saverio **20** 217
Satavahana **27** 866*
see also:
GAUTAMIPUTRA YAJNA SATAKARNI, King
NAGANIKA, Queen
SATAKARNI, King
SHIVAMANKA SADA, King
VASISHTHIPUTRA PULUMAVI, King
Satawan *see* MORTLOCK ISLANDS
satellites **2** 301
Satgaon **15** 674, 722; **25** 821
Vishnu Temple **15** 316
Satha, King of Cambodia (*reg* 1576-1594) **2** 56
Sathing Phra **30** 596, 608
sculpture **30** *597*
Satie, Erik
films **8** 439; **10** 687; **24** 710
groups and movements **8** 438, 439
productions **3** 119, 120
Le Fils des étoiles **27** 639
Mercure **24** 718
Parade **3** 119; **7** 508; **8** 246; **24** 405, 718; **30** 18
Relâche **6** 167; **24** 405, 710
Socrate **5** 423
Saties, Vel *see* VEL SATIES
satin **30** 551*
historical and regional traditions
Austria **2** *824*
China **7** 49, *51*
England **10** 353
Indian subcontinent **30** *564*
Iran **16** 449, *450*
Islamic **16** 449, *450*
Japan **17** 311, *311*, 313, 315, *327*
Spain **29** *348*
uses
chasubles **2** *824*
embroidery **10** 353
engravings **10** 380
helmets **30** *564*
kimonos **17** *327*
tents **30** 470
satinet **31** 656
satin stitch *see under* STITCHES
satin-wood **11** 595
historical and regional traditions
Britain **7** 445
England **5** 192; **10** 293, *293*
France **11** *592*
Netherlands, the **5** 192
Portugal **25** 307
South Africa **29** 115, *115*
Sri Lanka **29** 470
uses
bookcases **31** *628*
bureaux **5** 192; **31** *628*
cabinets (ii) (furniture) **29** *115*
clocks **7** 445
commodes **11** *592*
desks **5** 192
furniture **10** 293; **29** 115
marquetry **25** 307
mirror frames **21** 721
tables **10** *293*
satires **5** 755; **7** 648; **25** 283; **27** 868–72*
Colombia **27** 872
Egypt, ancient **9** 805*, *806*; **27** 868
England **7** 648; **25** 651; **27** 869–70*
Rococo **14** *639*
18th cent. **27** *869*
19th cent. **5** *272*
France **25** 651; **27** *870*, 870–71*
Germany **27** 869, *871*, 871–2*
Greece, ancient **27** 868
Japan **7** 649; **17** 348
Mexico **27** 872
Nazism **27** 872
Spain **27** 870
United States of America **27** 872*
see also CARICATURES
Satirical Papyrus **10** 65
satī stones *see under* MONUMENTS → types
Satō, Chōzan **14** 218; **17** 135
Satō, Chūryō **27** 872–3*
Satō, Shotaro **17** 295
Satomi, Katsuzō **17** 206; **27** 506
Satomi Takejiro
works **17** *265*
Satoru Hoshino *see* HOSHINO, SATORU
Sato Take
works **17** *265*
Satour, Jacques **18** 541
sat panchee **5** 255–6*
Satrap Sarcophagus **13** 458; **28** 667–8
Satricum **27** 9
Satrunjaya **15** 314
Satsuma **17** *11*, *241*
ceramics **6** 332; **27** 873*
lacquer **17** 356
porcelain **17** 352
textiles **17** 354
Satsumon ware *see under* POTTERY → wares
Satsunan islands **27** 469
Sattagydian **1** 887
Sattamini, João Leão **4** 725; **26** 414
Satterthwaite, Linton **5** 696
Sattler (company) **24** 794
Sattler, Christoph **12** 381
Sattler, Hubert **7** 924
Sattler, Johann Michael **7** 924
Sattler, Leonhard **27** 873–4*
works **2** 806, 811, 812; **17** 470; **27** 553
Satu Mare
castle **14** 885
Concert Hall **14** 890
Pannonia Hotel **14** 890
Saturiq *see* TAKHT-I SULAYMAN
Saturn red *see under* PIGMENTS → types
Satus **15** 777
Satyavolu **15** 535
Ramalingeshvara Temple **15** 535
sculpture **15** 535
temples **15** 295, 299
Satyros **13** 460; **14** 69
sauceboats **8** 311; **10** 330, *333*; **14** 342, *342*
saucer domes *see under* DOMES → types
saucers **14** *342*
Sauchy-Lestrée, St Aubert
relief sculpture **18** *659*
Saucière Duplessis **9** 398
Saudé, Jean **29** 628
Saudek, Jan **27** 874*
Saudi **27** 874*
see also:
'ABD AL-'AZIZ II, King
FAHD, King
TURK'I, Imam
Saudi, Muna **17** 655
Saudi Arabia **16** *104*; **27** 874–7*
airports **1** *495*
architecture **27** 875–6*; **32** 315–16*
coins **16** 514
collections **1** 896
education (art) **27** 876
jewellery **27** 877
mihrabs **21** 32
mosques **21** 32, *33*; **27** *876*
museums **2** 275
pottery **2** 267
rock art **2** *269*
tombs **2** *250*
wall paintings **2** *274*
see also ARABIA
Saudi Arabian Society for Culture and Arts **27** 876
Sauen **28** 41
Sauer, Carl **2** 904
Sauermann, Heinrich **23** 185
Sauern, Gottfried Albrecht von **18** 741
Sauerweid, Gottlob **18** 849; **30** 915
Saufkie, Gracilda **22** 616
Saufkie, Lawrence **22** 616
Saugal **22** 770–71
Saugrain, Elise **22** 88
Saugus (MA) **31** 652
Sauk **22** 552, 627
Šauka, Šarūnos **19** 500
Saúl, Benjamín **10** 154
Saul, Peter **27** 872; **31** 609
Saul (Co. Down), St Patrick's Memorial Church **16** 39
Saulcy, Félicien Caignart de **27** 667
Sauli (family) **1** 605, 608; **25** 226

Sauli, Bendinelli, Cardinal **27** 877
Sauli, Domenico **27** 878
Sauli, Filippo, Bishop of Brugnato **27** 877
Sauli, Francesco Maria **27** 878
Sauli, Gerolamo, Archbishop of Genoa **1** 605; **27** 878
Sauli, Giulio, Doge of Genoa (1578-1668) **27** 878
Sauli, Ottavio **27** 878
Sauli, Stefano **27** 877
Saulieu **7** 456
Saulini, Luigi **12** 265; **27** 878*
Saulini, Tommaso **12** 265; **27** 878*
Saulles, George William de **4** 599; **27** 878–9*
Saulnier, Etienne **4** 544, 546
Saulnier, Jules **27** 879*
  works **10** 748; **16** 54; **22** 270; **30** 504
Saulnier, Sébastien Louis **10** 90, 93
Saulteaux **22** 546
Saulterre, Georges **3** 595
Saumon, Michelet **31** 839
Saumur **11** 616
  château **6** 504; **29** 522
Saunders, David **10** 852
Saunders, Gail **3** 64
Saunders, George **1** 124; **30** 674
  works **1** *124*
Saunders, Helen **32** 701
Saunders, Joseph **19** 497; **27** 348
Saunders, Paul **7** 171; **10** 351; **30** 324; **33** 715
Saunders, Winston **3** 64
Saundersas, Juozapas *see* SAUNDERS, JOSEPH
Saunderson, Richard, 4th Earl of Scarborough **24** 741
Saundford, Fulk de, Archbishop of Dublin *see* FULK DE SAUNDFORD, Archbishop of Dublin
Sauneron, Serge **10** 82
Saunier, Charles **22** 538
Saunier, Claude-Charles **7** 658; **11** 595
Saupique, Georges **4** 520; **11** 568
Saur, Corbinian **11** 467; **12** 446
Saur, K. G. **2** 369; **10** 212
Saura *see under* HINDUISM → sects
Saura, Antonio **27** 879*
  groups and movements **2** 545; **8** 538; **20** 68; **29** 286
  works **19** 491; **29** 286
Sauras **31** 434
Saurashtra
  beadwork **3** 442
  figurines **15** 174
  shawls **15** 671
  textiles **15** *176*
Saurios of Samos **13** 549; **18** 108
Sauroens, Jean Vion di *see* VION DI SAUROENS, JEAN
Sauromatian **28** 320, 324
Sauser, Frédéric Louis *see* CENDRARS, BLAISE
Saushtatar, King of Mitanni (*reg c.* 1450-1400) **4** 641
Saushtatar letter **23** 322
Sausmarez, Maurice de **26** 392
Saussard, Auguste **29** 750
Saussey, Bourdon du **23** 510
Saussure, Ferdinand de **1** 182; **25** 362; **28** 396*; **29** 787; **30** 163
Saussure, Horace-Bénédict de **31** 149
Sauter, Samuel Friedrich **4** 39
Sauter, Ulrich **30** 147
sautoirs **17** 526
Sautuola, Marcelino Sanz de *see* SANZ DE SAUTUOLA, MARCELINO
Sauvage, Barthélemy Thomas
  works **3** *600*
Sauvage, (Frédéric) Henri **27** 879–81*
  groups and movements **2** 564; **11** 869; **21** 782
Sauvage, (Frédéric) Henri—cont.
  patrons and collectors **8** 257
  staff **19** 235
  works **4** 48; **7** 694; **8** 770; **11** 526; **24** 129; **27** *880*; **29** 843; **32** 555
Sauvage, Piat Joseph **7** 677; **11** 261; **14** 791; **15** 140; **24** 148
Sauvage, Tristan *see* SCHWARZ, ARTURO
Sauvageot, Louis **27** 248
Sauvaget, Jean **16** 262, 548, 549; **27** 881*
Sauval, Henri **11** 574; **27** 881–2*
Sauvan, Philippe **3** 107; **32** 331
Sauvan, Pierre **29** 348
Sauwa-Erma
  shields **16** *47*
Sava (Iran) **16** 162, 230, 409
Sava, Archbishop of Thessaloniki (*fl* 1219-35) **28** 436, 438, 455; **30** 718
Sava, Patriarch (1354-75) **28** 449
Savadi **15** 326
Savage, Augusta **1** 442, 443; **23** 48; **27** 882*; **33** 314
Savage, Edward **17** 450; **18** 64; **27** 882*
Savage, James **10** 235
Savage, Robert **18** 117
Savage, Samuel **18** *143*
Savage, William **25** 590, 622; **27** 882*
Savageot
  works **27** *550*
Savage Studio of Art and Crafts **27** 882
Sava Gospel Book *see under* GOSPEL BOOKS → individual manuscripts
Savai'i **27** 683
Savain, Petion **14** 58
Savall, P. B. **32** 536
Savalo **26** 659
Savang Vatthana, King of Laos (*reg* 1959-75) **18** 770
Savannah (GA) **22** 80; **27** *883*, 883–4*; **31** *587*, 721
  Chatham County Court House **18** 887
  Cotton Exchange **30** 505
Savant Singh, Raja of Kishangarh (*reg* 1748-64) (Rajput) **15** 612–13, 740
Savar **8** 846
  National Monument **3** 167
Savaria *see* SZOMBATHELY
Savaria, Jean **6** 417
Savary de Brèves, Francois (*fl* 1592-1604) **16** 360
Savasse, Feliciano de **20** 218
Sāvatthī *see* SRAVASTI
Savayan, Efrem **2** 432
Savelli (family) **9** 340; **16** 762; **32** 216
Savelli, Prince **11** 662
Savelli, Cencio *see* HONORIUS III, Pope
Savelli, Paolo, Cardinal **20** 376
Savelli, Sperandio **20** 918
Savel'yev, Dmitrij **23** 531
Savel'yev, L. **27** 409
Savel'yev, Yury (Petrovich) **27** 423
  works **27** *423*
Savel'yeva, Lyubov' **27** 418
  works **27** *418*
Saveri, Jan Baptist *see* XAVERY, JAN BAPTIST
Savernake Horn **10** 322
Saverne Château **6** 509; **19** 118
Savery, Hans, I (*fl* 1564-1622) **27** 884
Savery, Hans, II (1589-1654) **27** 884, 886
Savery, Jacob, I (1565-1603) **22** 841; **26** 542; **27** 884–5*
  attributions **4** 894
  pupils **23** 124; **27** 884, 885
  teachers **4** 251
Savery, Jacob, I (1565-1603)—cont.
  works **4** 905
Savery, Jacob, II (1592-after 1651) **27** 884
Savery, Jacob, III (1617-66) **27** 884
Savery, Jan Baptist *see* XAVERY, JAN BAPTIST
Savery, Roelandt **3** 613; **22** 841, 843; **25** 432; **26** 543; **27** 884, 885–7*; **31** 771
  attributions **4** 894, 905; **12** 884; **20** 769
  copies **4** 657
  patrons and collectors **9** 150; **10** 660; **13** 914, 916; **14** 375, 682; **22** 94; **29** 799
  pupils **10** 660
  reproductive prints by others **24** 236; **27** 504
  teachers **27** 884
  works **2** 104, 696; **4** 905; **8** 390; **11** 225, 226; **18** 707; **27** *886*
Savery, Salomon **25** 369; **27** 884; **32** 588
  works **14** 96; **32** 671
Savery, William **24** 602; **27** 887*; **31** 626
Saverys, Jan **2** 510
Savescu, Constantin **26** 710
Savickas, Augustinas **19** 499
Savicki, Michail **3** 530
Savignac, Raymond **25** 353
Savignies **11** 603
Savigny **26** 602; **27** 887
Savigny, Order of **3** 709; **7** 347; **27** 887*
Savile, John, 1st Earl of Mexborough (1719-78) **33** 217
Savile, John, 2nd Earl of Mexborough (*d* 1830) **25** 279
Saville, Marshall **29** 145
Saville, Samuel **4** 611
Savin, Fyodor **29** 54
Savin, Istoma **27** 386; **29** 779
Savin, Nazary **27** 386; **29** 779
Savin, Nikifor (Istomin) **25** 338; **27** 386; **29** 779
Savin, Paolo di Matteo **20** 623; **27** 888*
  collaboration **5** 537; **32** 192; **33** 633
  works **19** 559
Savin, Sila **27** 387
Savin, Thomas **28** 349
Savina, Jo(seph) **19** 49; **27** 888*
Savinien, Saint **28** 413
Savinio, Alberto **8** 602; **24** 448; **26** 776; **27** 888–9*; **28** 793
  groups and movements **16** 680; **25** 5–6; **31** 852
  writings **25** 447; **27** 163
Savin Monastery **25** 343
Savino, Gennaro **16** 748
Savino da Montepulciano, Domenico **12** 117
Savino Guido di *see* ANDRIES, GUIDO (*d* 1541)
Savinov, Aleksandr **12** 804
Savins Church **13** 125
Savinšek, Jakob **28** 862
Savio, Francesco, Lo *see* LO SAVIO, FRANCESCO
Savio, John Andreas **27** 472
Savitsky, Igor (Vital'yevich) **31** 783
Savitsky, Konstantin (Apollonovich) **3** 529; **22** 394; **27** 391, 889*
Savitsky, Mikhail (Andreyevich) **27** 889*
Savoia (family) **23** 175
Savoia, Carlo Emanuele Pio di, Cardinal *see* PIO DI SAVOIA, CARLO EMANUELE, Cardinal
Savoia, Carlo Francesco Pio di, Cardinal *see* PIO DI SAVOIA, CARLO FRANCESCO, Cardinal
Savoie, Jaques de **9** 352
Savoie, Louise de, Comtesse d'Angoulême *see* ANGOULÊME, LOUISE OF SAVOY, Comtesse d'
Savoie-Carignan, Marie Thérèse Louise de, Princesse de Lamballe *see* LAMBALLE, Marie Thérèse Louise de Savoie-Carignan, Princesse de
Savoieye *see* SAVOYE
Savoldo, Giovanni Girolamo **4** 748; **27** 889–92*; **32** 190
  patrons and collectors **7** 775; **21** 27, 525; **23** 355; **28** 433, 533; **31** 849
  pupils **24** 827
  works **12** 288; **27** *890, 891*
Sávoly, Pál **14** 891
Savona **16** *618*; **27** 893*
  Cathedral of S Maria Assunta **16** 725
  Palazzo Gavotti **13** 816; **14** 27
  Palazzo Rovere **27** 737
  pottery **16** 735
Savonanzi, Emilio **27** 893*
Savonarola, Girolamo **11** 186; **12** *257*; **27** 894*
  works **6** 175; **9** 14; **15** 80; **16** 658
Savonarola, Michele **12** 683; **16** 780
Savonese, il Prete *see* GUIDOBONO, BARTOLOMEO
Savonetti (family) **3** 593
Savonetti workshop
  works **3** *594*
Savonnerie **4** 302, 550, 552; **5** 836–7, 839; **11** 576, 652; **12** 828; **20** 133; **27** 894–6*; **29** 92
  carpets **2** 559; **5** *837*, I; **9** 30; **27** *895*
  designers **5** 841; **9** 379; **11** 575
  exhibitions **10** 678
Savorelli, Gaetano
  works **13** *669*
Savoretti, Giovanni di *see* GIOVANNI DA ORIOLO
Savorgnan, Germanico **23** 746
Savorgnan, Giulio **23** 882; **31** 70, 712; **32** 159
  works **31** *713*
Savory, Ronald **13** 877
Savot, Louis **5** 344; **11** 515, 573; **27** 896*
Savoy (House of) **12** 276; **28** 1–3*, *2*, 20*
  gardens **12** 115, 118, 119
  manuscripts **31** 449
  tapestries **31** 446–7
Savoy, Adelaide Henrietta of *see* ADELAIDE HENRIETTA OF SAVOY, Electress of Bavaria
Savoy, Amadeus I, 1st Duke of *see* AMADEUS VIII, Count of Savoy
Savoy, Amadeus of, King of Spain *see* AMADEUS OF SAVOY, King of Spain
Savoy, Amadeus VI, Count of *see* AMADEUS VI, Count of Savoy
Savoy, Amadeus VII, Count of *see* AMADEUS VII, Count of Savoy
Savoy, Amadeus VIII, Count of *see* Amadeus VIII, Count of Savoy
Savoy, Anna Victoria of, Princess **28** 15
Savoy, Blanche of Burgundy, Countess of *see* BLANCHE OF BURGUNDY, Countess of Savoy
Savoy, Charles-Albert, King of Sardinia *see* CHARLES-ALBERT, Duke of Savoy and King of Sardinia
Savoy, Charles-Emanuel I, 11th Duke of Savoy *see* CHARLES-EMANUEL I, 11th Duke of Savoy
Savoy, Charles-Emanuel II, 14th Duke of *see* CHARLES-EMANUEL II, 14th Duke of Savoy
Savoy, Charles-Emanuel IV, Duke of *see* CHARLES-EMANUEL IV, Duke of Savoy and King of Sardinia
Savoy, Charles-Felix, King of Sardinia *see* CHARLES-FELIX, Duke of Savoy and King of Sardinia
Savoy, Charles I, 5th Duke of *see* CHARLES I, 5th Duke of Savoy
Savoy, Charles III, Duke of *see* CHARLES III, Duke of Savoy
Savoy, Charlotte of, Queen of France *see* CHARLOTTE OF SAVOY, Queen of France
Savoy, Christina, Duchess of *see* CHRISTINA, Duchess and Regent of Savoy
Savoy, Emanuel-Philibert, 10th Duke of *see* EMANUEL-PHILIBERT, 10th Duke of Savoy
Savoy, Eugene-Maurice of, Prince (1633-73) **28** *2*
Savoy, Eugene of, Prince (1663-1736) **28** *2*, 15*
  architecture **14** 528
    cabinets (i) (rooms) **5** 344, 348
    military **14** 527; **32** 435
    palaces **2** 782; **11** 131
      Belvedere (Vienna) **2** 782, 828, 830; **3** 689; **14** 529, 530; **32** 458
      Ráckeve **14** 886
    stables **29** 485
    town houses **8** 21
  atlases **2** 696
  books **14** 375
  collections **16** 48; **32** 444
  drawings **9** 230; **18** 120
  furniture **2** 812, *813*; **32** 448
  gardens **12** 723
  interior decoration **9** 176; **19** 69
  paintings **1** 533; **2** 829; **4** 320; **8** 141; **12** 559; **25** 56; **28** 18; **29** 32; **32** 443
    battle **28** 18
    frescoes **5** 774
  prints **20** 416; **25** 631
  sculpture **12** 748; **14** 445, 894
  silver **3** 122
  textiles **7** 167; **24** 253
Savoy, Isabel of, Queen of Portugal *see* MARIA FRANCISCA (ISABEL), Queen of Portugal
Savoy, Louise of, Comtesse d'Angoulême *see* ANGOULÊME, LOUISE OF SAVOY, Comtesse d'
Savoy, Madeleine of *see* MONTMORENCY, MADELEINE OF SAVOY, Duchesse de
Savoy, Marguerite de Valois, Duchess of *see* MARGUERITE DE VALOIS, Duchess of Savoy
Savoy, Maria Luisa Gabriela, Queen of Spain *see* MARIA LUISA GABRIELA OF SAVOY, Queen of Spain
Savoy, Maria of, Duchess of Milan *see* MARIA OF SAVOY, Duchess of Milan
Savoy, Maria Teresa Felicia of Liechtenstein, Comtesse de Soissons *see* SOISSONS, MARIA TERESA FELICIA OF LIECHTENSTEIN, Comtesse de
Savoy, Marie-Adelaïde of, Duchesse de Bourgogne *see* BOURGOGNE, MARIE-ADELAÏDE OF SAVOY, Duchesse de
Savoy, Mary Christina of Naples, Duchess of Savoy and Queen of Sardinia *see* MARY CHRISTINA, Duchess of Savoy and Queen of Sardinia
Savoy, Mary Joanna, Duchess of *see* MARY JOANNA OF SAVOY-NEMOURS, Duchess and Regent of Savoy

Savoy, Maurice of, Cardinal 1 535; 28 2, 8–9*, 395
Savoy, Peter II, Count of see PETER II, Count of Savoy
Savoy, Philibert II, Duke of see PHILIBERT II, Duke of Savoy
Savoy, The 2 562; 3 446
Savoy, Thomas I, Count of see THOMAS I, Count of Savoy
Savoy, Thomas of, Prince of Carignano see CARIGNANO, THOMAS OF SAVOY, Prince of
Savoy, Victor-Amadeus, King of Sicily see VICTOR-AMADEUS II, 15th Duke of Savoy and King of Sardinia
Savoy, Victor-Amadeus I, 12th Duke of Savoy see VICTOR-AMADEUS I, 12th Duke of Savoy
Savoy, Victor-Emanuel II, King of Sardinia and Italy see VICTOR-EMANUEL II, Duke of Savoy and King of Sardinia, King of Italy
Savoy, Victor-Emanuel III, King of Italy see VICTOR-EMANUEL III, King of Italy
Savoye, Michael (fl after 1350) 22 820; 28 20
Savoye, Michael (fl c. 1373-81) 28 20
Savoye, Michael (fl c. 1415-35) 28 20
Savoye, Johann (fl 1552-93) 2 779, 780; 28 20
Savoye, Johannes (fl c. 1373-4) 28 20
Savoye, Rutger 28 20*
Savoye, Villa see under POISSY
Savoy glasshouse
  production 10 317
Savoy Hours see under BOOKS OF HOURS → individual manuscripts
Savoy-Nemours, Charles-Amédée of, Duc de Nemours see NEMOURS, CHARLES-AMÉDÉE OF SAVOY, Duc de
Savoy-Nemours, Maria Francisca (Isabel) of, Queen of Portugal see MARIA FRANCISCA (ISABEL), Queen of Portugal
Savoy-Nemours, Mary Joanna of, Duchess of Savoy see MARY JOANNA OF SAVOY-NEMOURS, Duchess and Regent of Savoy
Savoy-Nemours, Philip of, Duc de Nemours see NEMOURS, PHILIP OF SAVOY, Duc de
Savrasov, Aleksey (Kondrat'yevich) 27 391; 28 21*
  groups and movements 22 178; 27 579
  pupils 2 417; 18 389; 19 276
Savromats 2 100
Sävstaholm 31 362
Savu 15 775, 795, 813
Savva, Christoforos 8 364; 28 21*
Savvateyev, Yuriij A. 33 600
Savvaty 29 51
Savvides, Andreas 8 364
Savvidis, Symeon 13 352; 28 21*
Savy, Honoré 20 474
Sawa 22 287
  masks 22 287
Sawada Tōkō 17 235
Sawade, Jürgen 30 685
Sawaemon Tsukatani see TSUKATANI SAWAEMON
Sawai Jaipur see JAIPUR
Sawai Jai Singh II, Maharaja of Jaipur see JAI SINGH II, Maharaja of Amer
Sawakin see SUAKIN
Sawalo 26 669
Sawan see ASWAN
Sawankhalok 5 12; 30 582, 609
sawari see under ALLOYS → types
sawdust 18 601; 25 174; 31 258, 260, 261
sawing 16 859
sawmills 12 419
Sawos 24 68
saws 9 815, 821; 17 48–9, 49; 21 241
Sawston 14 76
Sawu see SAVU
Sawwan, Tell es- 1 894; 21 267; 28 21–2*
  alabaster (gypsum) 1 516
  figurines 21 293; 28 22
  flax 1 879
  fortifications 21 552
  houses 21 280, 280
  stone 21 269
Sawyer, Alan 29 223
Sawyer, Philip 20 19
Saxbo 8 720, 749; 28 22*
Saxe, Adrian 31 640
Saxe, Charles Jewett 2 308
Saxe, C. S. 7 859
Saxe, Henry 5 571; 28 23*
Saxe-Coburg, Augusta of, Princess of Wales see HANOVER, AUGUSTA, Princess of Wales
Saxe-Coburg, Ernest II, Duke of see ERNEST II, Duke of Saxe-Coburg and Gotha
Saxe-Coburg and Gotha, Albert, Prince of see ALBERT, Prince of Saxe-Coburg-Gotha
Saxe-Coburg and Gotha, Ernest I Wettin, Duke of see ERNEST I, Duke of Saxe-Coburg and Gotha
Saxe-Coburg-Gotha, Ferdinand, Prince of see FERDINAND II, King of Portugal
Saxe-Coburg-Saalfeld, Ferdinand, Prince of 33 110
Saxe-Coburg-Saalfeld, Francis Wettin, Duke of see FRANCIS, Duke of Saxe-Coburg-Saalfeld
Saxe-Coburg-Saalfeld, Leopold, Prince see LEOPOLD I, King of Belgium
Saxe-Coburg-Saalfeld, Victoria of, Duchess of Kent 14 480
Saxe-Gotha (family) 33 81
Saxe-Gotha, Augusta, Princess of see HANOVER, AUGUSTA, Princess of Wales
Saxe-Gotha, Emile-Leopold-August, Prince 13 320
Saxe-Gotha, Ernest Ludwig II, Herzog von 14 797
Saxe-Gotha, Frederick I, Duke of (1646-91) 21 640
Saxe-Gotha, Frederick II, Duke of (fl 1712-30) 5 345
Saxe-Gotha, Luise-Dorothee, Duchess 18 465
Saxe-Gotha-Altenburg, Ernest, Duke of see ERNEST, Duke of Saxe-Gotha-Altenburg
Saxe-Lauenburg, Julius Franz, Herzog von 8 408
Saxe-Meiningen, Adelaide, Duchess of see ADELAIDE, Duchess of Saxe-Meiningen
Saxe-Meiningen, George II, Duke of see GEORGE II, Duke of Saxe-Meiningen
Saxe-Teschen, Albert (Casimir) Wettin, Herzog von, Governor General of the Netherlands (1780-92) 3 613; 9 426; 33 110, 110, 116*
  architecture 22 33; 32 767
  collections 2 829; 14 11; 32 444
  drawings 3 310; 8 448; 9 229, 230
  paintings 18 418
  prints 2 830; 25 631
  sculpture 5 628
  sponsorship 28 69
Saxe-Teschen, Marie Christine Wettin, Herzogin von 3 613; 5 767; 8 448; 22 33
Saxe-Weimar, Anna Amalia, Duchess of see ANNA AMALIA, Duchess of Saxe-Weimar
Saxe-Weimar, Bernhard, Duke of 24 588
Saxe-Weimar, Caroline, Princess of 28 376
Saxe-Weimar, Charles Augustus, Grand Duke of see CHARLES AUGUSTUS, Grand Duke of Saxe-Weimar
Saxe-Weimar, Charles Frederick, Grand Duke of see CHARLES FREDERICK, Grand Duke of Saxe-Weimar
Saxe-Weimar, Ernest Augustus Wettin, Duke of see ERNEST AUGUSTUS, Duke of Saxe-Weimar
Saxe-Weimar, John Wettin, Duke of see JOHN, Duke of Saxe-Weimar
Saxe-Weimar, Louise, Princess of 28 376
Saxe-Weimar, William Ernest, Duke of 26 354; 33 116
Saxe-Weimar, William Wettin, Duke of see WILLIAM, Duke of Saxe-Weimar
Saxe-Weimar-Eisenach, Charles Alexander, Grand Duke of see CHARLES ALEXANDER, Grand Duke of Saxe-Weimar-Eisenach
Saxl, Friedrich see SAXL, FRITZ
Saxl, Fritz 1 154; 2 536; 28 23*, 916; 32 854
  collaboration 24 16
  works 15 91, 93
Saxons 8 527; 14 408; 21 500
Saxony (House of) 11 760; 28 24*
Saxony, Christian I, Elector of see CHRISTIAN I, Elector of Saxony
Saxony, George, Duke of 2 117; 9 235; 19 131
Saxony, Henry I, Holy Roman Emperor see HENRY THE FOWLER, Holy Roman Emperor
Saxony, Henry II, Holy Roman Emperor see HENRY II, Holy Roman Emperor
Saxony, Ludolphus of see LUDOPHUS OF SAXONY
Saxony, Mathilda, Duchess of see MATHILDA, Duchess of Saxony
Saxony, Otto II, Holy Roman Emperor see OTTO II, Holy Roman Emperor
Saxony, Otto III, Holy Roman Emperor see OTTO III, Holy Roman Emperor
Saxony, Otto the Great, Holy Roman Emperor see OTTO I, Holy Roman Emperor
Saxton, Christopher 14 643; 18 73; 20 366
Say, Constance 16 876
Say, Frederick Richard 28 25
Say, William 21 417; 28 25*
Saya Aye 5 246
Sayaji Rao III, Maharaja (reg 1875-1936) (Gaekwad) 7 173; 15 182; 22 364; 31 793
Saya Khin 5 262
Saybrook (CT) 31 623
Sayce, Archibald Henry 1 893
Sayën, H. Lyman 24 600
Sayer, James see SAYERS, JAMES
Sayer, Robert 29 675
  printmakers 5 216; 9 506; 11 139; 14 803; 26 30; 32 910
  works 4 361; 24 366
Sayer, Roger 8 529; 19 531
Sayer and Bennett 26 278
Sayers, James 28 25*
Sayf al-Dawla, Ruler (reg 945-67) (Hamdanid) 16 539
Sayf al-Din Qaymari 16 181
Sayf al-Din Tankiz al-Husami 17 491; 20 228
Sayf al-Din Turumtay 1 756
Sayf Khan 15 369
Say Fong 18 762
Sayi 14 377
al-Sayid, Tawfik 17 655
Sayil 20 882, 884; 21 262, 372; 23 826; 28 26*
  Great Palace 20 884; 28 26, 26
  sculpture 9 165
  stucco 29 829
Säynätsalo 11 92
  Civic Centre 31 243
  Town Hall 1 10
Sayn bei Neuwied, Royal Prussian Ironworks 12 374
Sayod 16 253
Sayramsu 6 241, 274
Saytour, Patrick 11 552, 570; 30 6
Say'un, Sultan's Palace 33 520
Saywite 29 172
Sayyed 6 182, 222; 28 26–7*; 29 822; 30 252
Sayyid 8 673–4; 28 27*
Sayyid, Mu'izz al-Din Mubarak Shah see MU'IZZ AL-DIN MUBARAK SHAH, Sultan
al-Sayyida al-Hurra Arwa bint Ahmad, Ruler (reg 1099-1138) (Sulayhid) 29 912
Sayyid Abdallah 21 50
Sayyid Ahmad (fl 15th cent.) 30 921
Sayyid Ahmad Khan (fl 1870) 1 639
Sayyid Aqā Jalāl al-Dīn Mīak al-Ḥasanī see AQA MIRAK
Sayyid Ibrahim 14 217
Sayyid Mirza 3 193; 16 534, 535; 22 260; 28 27*
Sayyid Yusuf 16 501
saz 16 133, 349, 388; 28 27*
Sazangwiyo 2 86
  works 2 86
Sazhin, M. M. 31 559
Sazhina, N. N. 21 812
Sazikov 22 180; 27 421, 584
Sazō Idemitsu see IDEMITSU, SAZŌ
SB, Monogrammist 25 103
Sbaraglia, Marco 8 159
Sbarra, Francesco 5 264; 18 535
Sbarri, Manno di Bastiano 3 817; 8 202; 10 810; 14 171; 16 745
Sbeïtla see SUFETULA
Sbobel, Conrad see PFLÜGER, CONRAD
Sbraga di Gabriele see URBINO, NICOLA DA
Sbraghe, Nicola di Gabriele 31 741
Sbrolius, Richardus 29 433
SBUAM see SOCIÉTÉ BELGE DES URBANISTES ET ARCHITECTES MODERNES (SBUAM)
SC, Master 20 803*
scabbards 14 426
  conservation 7 727
  historical and regional traditions
    Austria 14 88
    Celtic 6 157, 160; 14 88; 18 828
    Central Asia 6 270, 305
    England 6 160–61; 30 394
    Indian subcontinent 15 678
    Indonesia 15 817
    Iran 16 516
    Islamic 16 508, 516
    Italy 19 3
    Japan 17 300
    La Tène culture (c. 450-.c 50 BC) 2 451; 18 828
    Ottoman 16 508
    Philippines 24 631
    Prehistoric art 25 540
    Rome, ancient 7 727; 30 394
    Tajikistan 6 270
    Turkey 16 508
  materials
    bronze 6 157; 14 88
    enamel 16 516
    gold 15 678, 817; 16 508, 516
    iron 6 157; 15 817
scabbards
  materials—cont.
    ivory 6 270
    lacquer 17 300
    leather 19 3
    steel 16 508, 516
    velvet 15 678
  techniques
    damascening 16 516
Scacciati, Andrea 2 239
scaenae 13 385–6, 385, 406; 26 910, 920; 28 27*; 30 650, 651
scaenae fissa 30 656
scaenae frontes 26 873, 923, 924; 28 28; 30 652, 655
Scafati 27 90
scaffolding 7 764; 25 479; 26 877, 880
scaffolds 30 653
Scaglia, Cesare Alessandro, Abbé 9 482
Scaglia, Desiderio, Cardinal 4 656
Scaglia, Girolamo 24 26
scagliola 2 541; 28 28*; 29 813
  see also PIETRA DURE
Scaglion, Robert 13 311
Scaino da Salò, Antonio see SALÒ, ANTONIO SCAINO DA
Scala 16 777
Scala, Alberto I della, Captain-General of Verona see ALBERTO I, Captain-General of Verona
Scala, Bartolomeo 3 861; 27 733, 736
Scala, Basilio della 18 152
Scala, Cangrande I della, Lord of Verona see CANGRANDE I, Lord of Verona
Scala, Cangrande II della, Lord of Verona see CANGRANDE II, Lord of Verona
Scala, Cansignorio della, Lord of Verona see CANSIGNORIO, Lord of Verona
Scala, della (family) 32 340
  architecture 13 64; 32 341
  coats of arms 14 421
  collections 32 343
  paintings 16 710
  sculpture 20 865; 31 120
  tombs 32 345, 346
Scala, Giorgio 27 878
Scala, Giovanni Battista 29 251
Scala, Mastino II della, Lord of Verona see MASTINO II, Lord of Verona
Scala, Regina della see REGINA DELLA SCALA
Scalé, Bernard
  works 9 316
scale armour see under ARMOUR → types
Scaletti, Sebastiano 3 868
Scalfurotto, Giovanni Antonio 16 641; 24 841; 25 266; 30 423
Scaligeri see SCALA, DELLA
scalps 22 652
Scalza, Ippolito 23 584
Scalzi, Alessandro see PADUANO, ALEXANDER
Scamozzi, Bertotti 23 861
Scamozzi, Giandomenico 28 29, 30*
Scamozzi, Ottavio Bertotti 2 358
Scamozzi, Vincenzo 23 870; 28 29, 30–33*
  architecture 2 162; 16 640; 19 313, 628; 21 579; 23 869, 882; 31 712; 32 186, 410
    churches 2 780; 23 754; 25 867; 27 352, 661
    fireplaces 32 220
    libraries 32 222, 223
    palazzi 3 770; 5 328; 20 278
    theatres 27 483; 28 32; 30 655, 656
    urban planning 31 713
    villas 23 867, 867; 27 237; 28 31; 32 411, 548

Scamozzi, Vincenzo—cont.
attributions **11** 77
collaboration **5** 532; **19** 627; **28** 30; **29** 85
patrons and collectors **4** 612; **7** 776; **12** 910; **17** 633; **25** 271; **30** 732
pupils **19** 627
reproductive prints by others **20** 457
stage design **15** 137; **30** 656
writings **21** 579; **24** 274; **28** 30; **30** 852; **31** 296
illustrated **25** 1
on architectural orders **23** 487
on lighting **9** 12
on models **2** 338
on proportion **2** 357
on stage design **30** 656
on villas **32** 550–51
translated **2** 868; **8** 496
Scamp, William **20** 212
Scandellari, Filippo **20** 903; **24** 834
Scandiano Castle **1** 17
Scandinavia **8** 719; **32** 512–25*
acanthus **1** 110
alphabets **10** 592
architects **14** 151
architecture **23** 222
brick **4** 780–81*
Cistercian Order **13** 50
Gothic **13** 50*, 56–8*
megalithic **21** 43
military **21** 570*
Romanesque **26** 592–3*
stone **31** 363
Viking **32** 532–4*, *533*
wood **31** 363
baskets **3** 332
beds **3** 485
benches **32** *519*
bonding **4** 781
brick **4** 780–81*
bronze **32** *513*, *515*, *516*
brooches **32** *514*, 515, *516*, 520, 524, 531
chess sets **6** 557
churches **4** 780–81; **32** 517, 532
coins **7** 538
cups **32** *516*
cutlery **8** 284
design **8** 803*
desks **5** 192
door fittings **26** 691
dress **9** 254*
ex-votos **32** 523
felt **10** 875
figureheads **28** 611
filigree **32** 524, 531
fortifications **21** 570*
frames **11** 465–78*
gardens **12** 135*, *135*
gold **32** *516*, 523, 524
granite **11** 100
halls **32** 532
harness-mounts **32** *513*, *515*
helmets **14** 412
heraldry **14** 410*
historiography **32** 534*
houses **32** 532, 533
human figures **32** 520–21*
iconography **32** 519–24*
insignia **7** 178
iron **26** 691
jewellery **32** 516, 528
knitting **18** 158
looms **30** 546
masks **32** 520–21*
mass production **32** 524
memorial stones **32** 517, *517*, 518, *518*, 521–2*, *522*, *523*, *524*, 525
metalwork **13** 166–7*; **32** 513, 515, 516, 524*
Romanesque **26** 690–91*
monuments **32** 521–2*
narratives **32** 521–3*, *522*, *523*
niello **32** *516*
ornament **32** 519–21*, 523–4*
Scandinavia—cont.
painting **13** 143*
parterres (i) (gardens) **12** *135*
periodicals **24** 451–2*
plaques **32** 523
plaster **29** 840–41*
polychromy **4** 781
roods **27** 124
runes **10** 592; **32** 517, 518
samplers **27** 694
sculpture **11** 100
Gothic **13** 102–3*, 118–20*
Romanesque **26** 639–40*, 646–7*
stone **13** 102–3*; **26** 639–40*; **32** 513
Viking **32** 513
wood **13** 118–20*; **26** 646–7*
ship-decoration **28** 611
silver **32** *514*, *516*, 524, 531
stained glass **13** 190–91*
statuettes **32** 524
stone **13** 102–3*; **26** 639–40*; **31** 363; **32** 513
stone-carvings **25** 513
Viking **32** 516, *517*, *518*, *522*, 523, *523*, *524*, 525*
stucco **29** 840–41*
swords **2** 452
tapestries **23** 238
textiles **32** 523
thrones **30** 778
tiles **30** 883–4*
tombs **21** 41
tracery **31** 273
trade **3** 588, 592, 602
women **32** 521
wood **13** 118–20*; **26** 646–7*; **30** 778; **31** 363
wood-carvings **13** 143; **32** *519*, 524, 525*
workshops **32** 524
writing **23** 227
see also DENMARK; FINLAND; NORWAY; SWEDEN; VIKING
Scandinavian Bank **3** 784
Scandrett, Thomas
works **10** *282*
Scanga, Italo **22** 690
Scaniglia, Stefano **12** 282
Scannabecchi, Dalmasio (di Jacopo) *see* DALMASIO (DI JACOPO) SCANNABECCHI
Scannell (family) **16** 21
Scannelli, Francesco **28** 33–4*
Scanzi, Giovanni **31** 131
Scapigliati, Gli **16** 678; **21** 527; **25** 567; **28** 34*
members **16** 706
Boito, Camillo **4** 246
Casnedi, Raffaele **5** 918
Cremona, Tranquillo **8** 136
Dossi, Carlo **9** 187
Grandi, Giuseppe **13** 294
Grubicy (De Dragon), Vittore **13** 714
Ranzoni, Daniele **25** 894
works **16** *706*
Scapitta, Giacomo Bernadini **30** 102
Scappi, Giovanni Battista **11** 700
scapulars **9** 644, *644*
scarabs
historical and regional traditions
Ancient Near East **1** 857*, *857*
Egypt, ancient **1** 857; **9** 879; **10** 20, 30, 70–71*, *71*; **22** 285; **28** 34*, *34*
Etruscan **12** 248–50, *249*
Greece, ancient **12** 247, *247*, *248*
Judah **1** 857
Palestine **1** 857
Syria-Palestine **1** 857, *857*
materials
agate **12** *247*, 249
amber **1** 761
basalt **28** 34
cornelian **12** 249, *249*
scarabs
materials—cont.
faience (i) (glass) **28** 34
greenstone **25** 734
jasper **12** *248*
limestone **28** *34*
sardonyx **12** 249
serpentine **28** 34
soapstone **1** *857*; **10** *71*; **28** 34
see also SEALS→ types → stamp
Scaramuccia, Giovanni Antonio **6** 347; **12** 746; **28** 34
Scaramuccia, Luigi Pellegrino **28** 34–5*
patrons and collectors **28** 479
pupils **18** 755
works **4** 21
Scaravelloto **29** 306
Scarbantia *see* SOPRON
Scarborough (Tobago) **31** *330*
Court House **31** 334
Scarborough (N. Yorks; UK) **10** 302
Grand Hotel **30** 503
St Martin **25** 728
Scarborough, Richard Lumley, 1st Earl of *see* LUMLEY, RICHARD, 1st Earl of Scarborough
Scarborough, Richard Saunderson, 4th Earl of *see* SAUNDERSON, RICHARD, 4th Earl of Scarborough
Scarborough Civic Centre (Ont; Canada) **5** 563
Scardeone, Bernardino **28** 35*
works **23** 754
Scarfe, Gerald **5** 758
scarification **1** 254, *255*, 344–6, *345*, 409; **10** 474; **11** 830; **23** 721
see also CICATRICES
Scarisbrick, Charles **8** 48; **25** 712
Scarisbrick Hall (Lancs) **8** 48
Scarlatti, Alessandro **5** 593; **23** 637; **24** 340
Scarlet ware *see under* POTTERY → wares
scarp **21** 547
Scarpa **25** 729
Scarpa, Carlo **8** 803; **16** 721; **28** 35–6*
pupils **4** 490; **13** 213
works **16** 650, 775; **28** *36*, 657; **32** 196, 204, 342
Scarpagnino, Antonio **28** 36–8*
attributions **13** 649
collaboration **29** 369
patrons and collectors **13** 912; **19** 663
works **5** 178; **13** 678; **19** 560; **28** *37*; **29** 522; **32** 186, 187, 220, 227
Scarpatia, Vittore *see* CARPACCIO, VITTORE
Scarperia, Palazzo del Vicariato **6** 14
Scarpettini, Giovanni **22** 481
Scarron, Paul **11** 593; **30** 24
Scarsdale, 1st Baron *see* CURZON, NATHANIEL, 1st Baron Scarsdale
Scarsella, Ippolito *see* SCARSELLINO
Scarsella, Sigismondo **28** 38
Scarsellino **28** 38–9*
patrons and collectors **10** 525
pupils **18** 685
works **11** 4, 487; **28** *39*
Scarsi da San Giusto, Giuliano di Colino degli **20** 531
scarves **9** 643; **28** 718
see also HEADSCARVES
Scassa, Ugo **16** 758
Scasso, Juan Antonio **31** 753
Scattergood & Telfer **22** 74
Scattola, Luciano **22** 27
Scaurus, Marcus Aemilius **12** 265; **24** 283; **26** 856
Scavezzi, Prospero *see* ANTICHI, PROSPERO
Sceaux **11** 606
Château **12** 122; **25** 377, 705
Musée de l'Ile-de-France **10** 839
Parc de Sceaux **2** *663*; **24** 120
Scelleur, Jehan le *see* JEHAN LE SCELLEUR
scena per angolo **30** 665, 668, *668*, 672
Scena Robotnicza **14** 541
scenery **24** 741, 742; **30** 685
scenery, stage *see* STAGE SCENERY
Scenic ware *see under* POTTERY → wares
scent bottles *see under* BOTTLES → types
sceptres **26** 80–81*
historical and regional traditions
Asante **1** 388
Byzantine **26** 80
China **7** 141
England **26** 81
France **26** 81
Germany **12** 442
Japan **17** 386
materials
glass **17** 386
wood **7** 141
types
zhang **7** 3
Scerpswert, Elias **13** 159
Scerrier, Michiel **4** 161
Scève, de **30** 660
Scève, Maurice **10** 175
Scevola, Lucien-Victor Guirand de *see* GUIRAND DE SCEVOLA, LUCIEN-VICTOR
Scey-Montbéliard, Winaretta Singer, Princesse de **5** 881
Schaaffhausen, Maria Theresa von **7** 591
Schaak, Jean **19** 827
Schaár, Erzsébet **14** 896; **15** 5; **28** 39*; **32** 579
Schaarbeek **3** 618
Schabaelje, Jan Philips **25** 605
Schabbelt **4** 667
Schabert, Ernst David **18** 849
Schacherl, Franz **28** 179
Schacht, Lienhard **18** 575; **23** 395
Schachtel, Ferdinand **8** 413
Schack, Adolf Friedrich von, Graf **28** 39–40*
collections **22** 303
paintings **4** 205; **12** 274; **19** 151; **20** 404
Schack-Galerie *see under* MUNICH → museums
Schad, Christian **24** 654; **28** 40–41*
groups and movements **3** 802; **8** 433, 434, 436; **12** 396; **20** 93; **22** 304, 923
Schadaeus, O. **29** 756
Schadde, Joseph Henri Martin **3** 549; **28** 41*
collaboration **3** 585
pupils **27** 551
teachers **3** 763
works **2** 194
Schädel, Gottfried (Johann) **19** 563; **28** 41*
works **18** 35, 39, 40; **27** 573, *574*; **31** 551, 552
Schader, Jacques **28** 41–2*; **33** 736
Schadographs **24** 654
Schadow, Albert **15** 407
Schadow, Cornelius Wilhelm **22** 703
Schadow, Friedrich Gottlieb **12** 413, 414
Schadow, Friedrich Wilhelm **28** 42
Schadow, Johann Gottfried **28** 42–5*
collaboration **12** 273
groups and movements **3** 799; **32** 243
patrons and collectors **12** 406; **14** 653
Schadow, Johann Gottfried—cont.
pupils
Begas, Reinhold **3** 497
Gilly, Friedrich **12** 641
Hübner, (Rudolph) Julius (Benno) **14** 838
Lucae, Richard **19** 754
Olivier, Friedrich (Woldemar) **23** 412
Rauch, Christian Daniel **26** 22
Schadow, Ridolfo **28** 45
Tieck, (Christian) Friedrich **30** 854
Wichmann, Ludwig (Wilhelm) **33** 154
Wolff, Emil **33** 296
Wredow, August (Julius) **33** 391
teachers **30** 353
works **3** 799, 805; **5** 758; **12** 406; **28** *42*, *43*, 672; **33** 282
writings **14** 872
Schadow, Ridolfo **28** 42, 45–6*
groups and movements **22** 704
patrons and collectors **6** 117
pupils **33** 296
teachers **28** 45
Schadow, (Friedrich) Wilhelm (von) **9** 460; **14** 587; **28** 46*
collaboration **7** 870; **14** 838; **23** 676
groups and movements **12** 393, 394; **22** 704
patrons and collectors **3** 291; **30** 766
pupils **3** 703; **9** 460; **11** 45; **14** 838; **19** 243; **28** 104, 169; **29** 16, 66
works **22** 328
Schaefer, Carl **5** 567
Schaefer, Herwin **19** 896
Schaefer, John **1** 157
Schaefer Beer Company **30** 391
Schaeffer, Claude F. A. **1** 893; **31** 529
Schaeffer, Rudolph **8** 455
Schaer, Ernst **12** 744
Schaerbeek *see* BRUSSELS
Schaeuffelein *see* SCHÄUFELEIN
Schaezler **2** 714
Schäfer, Carl (Wilhelm Ernst) **28** 46–7*
pupils **3** 769; **23** 617; **25** 68
restorations **14** 305
works **21** 63
Schäfer, Friedrich **7** 211
Schäfer, Fritz **30** 684
Schäfer, Heinrich **10** 84, 93; **28** 47*
Schaffer, Jacob **24** 40
Schäffer, Nicholas *see* MORELLI, GIOVANNI (LORENZO)
Schaffgotsch, Christoph Leopold, Graf von **8** 409
Schaffhausen **30** *124*
Allerheiligenkirche **26** 635
bridge **4** 802
glass **9** 646
Haus zum Ritter **10** 737; **29** 673
stucco **30** 136
town walls **30** 126
Schaffhausen glass *see under* GLASS → types
Schaffhausen Onyx **17** *520*
Schaffner, Marcel **30** 135
Schaffner, Martin **28** 47–8*
attributions **21** 157
teachers **29** 684
works **12** 387; **28** *48*; **29** 684; **31** 570
Schaffrath, Ludwig **29** 508; **33** 680
Schäftlarn Monastery Church **12** 406; **32** 822
Schaick, G. T. Dentz van *see* DENTZ VAN SCHAICK, G. T.
Schaidhauf, Thomas **22** 796; **28** 49*
Schairt, Gisbert **22** 821
Schalch, Johann **33** 3

Schalcken, Godfried 22 846; 28 49–50*
  patrons and collectors 23 468, 469
  pupils 4 374; 22 50
  reproductive prints by others 8 481; 33 196
  teachers 9 194; 14 739; 22 845
  works 28 *50*
Schalek, František Karel 8 400, 401
  works 8 *400*
Schall, Jean-Frédéric 8 791; 28 50*
Schallaburg, Schloss *see* SCHLOSS SCHALLABURG
Schallautzer, Hermes 2 780; 32 434
Schaller, Johann Nepomuk 2 802; 22 704
Schaller, Ludwig 22 28; 28 186
Schall von Bell, Adam 6 678; 7 120
Schamberg, Morton Livingston 23 48; 24 600; 28 51*
  groups and movements 8 435
  patrons and collectors 2 384
  works 26 51; 31 613
Schammade, Die 3 4; 8 438; 24 428
Schanaert, Antoine 19 238
Schänis, St Sebastian 5 796; 26 635
Schantz, Karl (*b* 1944) 1 738
Schantz, (Karl) Philip (Gunnar) von (*b* 1928) 28 51*; 30 82
Schaper, (Hugo Wilhelm) Fritz 28 51–2*
  pupils 4 762; 5 57; 18 128, 480; 28 164; 31 688; 33 72
Schaper, Johann 12 439; 14 235; 23 313
  works 12 *439*
Schapiro, Meyer 2 532, 834; 21 134; 28 52–3*
  pupils 22 206; 26 126; 27 668
  works 20 528; 25 683; 29 880, 881; 31 672
Schapiro, Miriam 1 81; 6 577; 28 53*
Schapiro, Rosa 4 892
Schardt, Johann Gregor van der 22 857; 23 395; 28 53*; 29 571
  attributions 4 640
  collaboration 12 402; 18 575
  patrons and collectors 13 910; 15 145; 25 454
  works 8 739; 12 *402*; 23 309, *309*
Scharf, George (1788-1860) 9 27; 28 53; 33 515
Scharf, George (1820-95) 28 53–4*
  assistants 6 100
  exhibitions 10 679
  works 18 633; 21 907
Scharf, Kenny 3 338
Scharfeneck, Conrad de *see* CONRAD DE SCHARFENECK, Bishop of Metz
Scharff, Anton 4 220; 20 925
Scharff, Edwin 4 181; 28 54*
Scharff, Johann Gottlieb 27 584
Scharff, (Niels) William 8 736; 28 54–5*
Scharff, William 8 755
Scharmburg, Ernst von, Count 27 229
Scharoun, Hans (Bernhard) 3 795; 12 378, 380; 25 839; 28 55–6*
  collaboration 3 293, 795; 11 299; 14 118; 28 112
  groups and movements 8 826; 11 842; 15 885; 21 781, 782; 23 498, 500; 26 405
  pupils 28 835
  staff 28 835
  works 1 126; 3 796–7; 7 688; 12 379, 380; 14 176; 21 *783*; 28 *56*; 30 684; 31 731
Scharpaza, Vittore *see* CARPACCIO, VITTORE
Scharvogel, Jacob Julius 2 565; 8 531
Schasler, Max (Alexander Friedrich) 28 56*
Schat, Anneke 22 896
Schatz, Boris 3 901; 16 567, 568, 571; 17 579, 582; 28 56–7*
  pupils 29 768
  works 5 156
Schatz, David 18 465
Schauberg, Katherina 23 13
Schauberger, Johann Georg 17 585
Schaubert, Edouard 2 673; 13 358; 14 149; 18 124
Schaudt, Emil 14 102; 19 54; 29 566
Schauenburg, Adolf II, Count of (*fl* 1143) 19 745
Schauenburg, Adolf III, Count of (*d* 1225) 14 100
Schauensee, Franz Josef Meyer von *see* MEYER VON SCHAUENSEE, FRANZ JOSEF
Schauer, Bertold 22 204
Schäufelein, Hans, I (*c.* 1484-1539/40) 2 718; 9 433, 440; 13 903; 23 308; 28 57–60*; 32 680
  collaboration 3 474
  methods 31 578
  pupils 12 494
  reproductive prints by others 28 57
  works 9 433; 12 386; 17 700; 27 256; 28 57, *58*, *59*; 29 787; 31 287; 33 353, 354
Schäufelein, Hans, II (after 1515-*c.* 1582) 14 572; 23 310, 312
  teachers 28 57
Schauff, Johann Nepomuk 5 84; 14 888; 15 18
Schaum, Johann Valentin 11 832
Schauman, Sigrid 31 886
Schaumberger, Johann Martin 6 363
Schaumberg Lippe-Bückeburg, William, Graf von 10 165
Schaumburg, Adolf VI, Graf von 5 76
Schaumburg, Bruno von, Bishop 18 467
Schaumburg, Ernst von, Graf 28 60–61*
  architecture 5 76; 23 252
  fountains 33 426
  sculpture 23 252; 32 731; 33 425
Schaumburg-Lippe, Christian, Graf 6 568
Schaumburg-Lippe, Wilhelm, Graf von 10 155
Schaupp, Wilhelm 27 315
Schaur, Eda 11 778
Schaur, Johann Caspar 2 717
Schaus, William 29 382
Schauss, Ferdinand 17 736; 26 546
Schawinsky, Xanti 4 109; 24 406, 407
Schayck, Jan van 22 855
Schayes, Antoine Guillaume Bernard 3 547, 619; 28 61*
Scheben, Gerhard 24 231
Schedel, Hartmann 12 385; 23 310; 25 41; 33 301
  works 3 *334*
Schedoni, Bartolomeo 28 61–2*
  patrons and collectors 7 778; 10 525
  reproductive prints by others 3 33
  works 28 *62*
Schedoni, Giulio 28 61
Scheel, Heinrich 18 851
Scheel, Sebastian *see* SCHEL, SEBASTIAN
Scheele, Carl Wilhelm 23 786; 24 794, 799
Scheele's green *see under* PIGMENTS → types
Scheemaeckers, Peter (1652-1714) 3 570; 28 63*
  assistants 10 372
  pupils 3 417; 28 63; 32 694
  teachers 32 242
  works 24 37
Scheemakers, Henry 6 528; 23 253; 28 64*
Scheemakers, Peter (1691-1781) 3 570; 10 372; 28 63–4*
  assistants 11 162; 28 64; 29 540
  collaboration 8 698; 19 606; 25 53
  patrons and collectors 4 611; 7 540; 20 910
  pupils 3 183; 14 599; 23 189; 31 389
  works 10 264; 14 862; 27 260; 28 *64*; 29 806; 30 451, 452
Scheemakers, Thomas 28 64*; 29 806
Scheemda 23 501
Scheen, Pieter, jr 28 65
Scheen, Pieter A(rie), snr 28 65*
Scheerbart, Paul 28 65*; 29 872
  groups and movements 10 696
  works 12 792; 25 173
Scheermaecker, J. 3 601
Scheerre, Herman (*fl c.* 1405-25) 28 66*
  works 20 624; 28 *66*
Scheerre, Hermann *see* SCHERER, HERMAN
Schéfer, Charles 16 554, 559
Schefer, Jean-Louis 29 787–8
Schefer Hariri 16 137, 300, 309, *309*
Scheffau, St Ulrich 2 801
Scheffauer, Philipp Jakob 8 508; 19 781
Scheffel, Johan Henrik 18 418
Scheffel, Victor von 33 82
Scheffer, Anton 3 386
Scheffer, Ary 11 663; 26 191; 27 266; 28 67–8*
  assistants 24 456
  dealers 26 233
  patrons and collectors 27 223
    Demidov, Anatoly, Prince 8 705
    Fodor, Carel Joseph 11 233
    Gaugain, (Armand-Pierre-) Henri 12 186
    Louis-Philippe, King of the French (*reg* 1830-48) 23 521
    Orléans, Ferdinand-Philippe (-Louis-Charles- Henri) de Bourbon, 7th Duc d' (1810-42) 23 522
    Péreire (family) 24 396
    Plint, T(homas) E(dward) 25 41
    Pourtalès-Gorgier, James-Alexandre, Comte de 25 383
  pupils 22 848
    Armstrong, Thomas 2 475
    Bartholdi, Frédéric-Auguste 3 289
    Colin, Gustave 7 554
    Coutan, Louis-Joseph-Auguste 8 72
    Gallait, Louis(-Joseph) 12 12
    Orléans, Ferdinand-Philippe (-Louis-Charles- Henri) de Bourbon, 7th Duc d' (1810-42) 23 522
    Orléans, Marie (-Christine-Caroline-Adélaïde-Françoise-Léopoldine) de Bourbon, Princesse d' 23 522
    Popelin, Claudius (-Marcel) 25 236
    Verlat, Charles 32 259
  teachers 13 794
  works 22 849; 23 522; 28 *67*; 31 346
Scheffer, Cornelia 28 67
Scheffer, Henri 9 169; 25 749; 26 191; 28 67
Scheffer, Joannes *see* SCHEFFERUS, JOHANNES (GERHARD)
Scheffer, Johann-Bernhard 28 67
Schefferus, Johannes (Gerhard) 28 68*
Scheffer von Leonhardshoff, Johann (Evangelist) 2 796; 22 703, 704; 28 68–9*
Scheffler, Felix Antonín 19 748; 25 443
Scheffler, Karl 28 342
Scheffler, Thomas Christian 2 580; 3 779
Schega, Franz Andreas 28 69*
Scheggia 11 683; 20 532; 28 69–70*
  attributions 29 360
  collaboration 4 32
  patrons and collectors 29 360
  works 6 4; 9 102; 11 388; 28 *70*
  workshop 16 660
Scheibe, Richard 14 310; 20 395; 22 712; 28 70–71*
Scheibenkreuz see under CROSSES → types
Scheiber, Hugo 14 901; 28 71–2*
Scheibler (family) 25 136
Scheid, Karl 12 437
Scheid, Ursula 12 437
Scheidler, Anton 33 240
Scheiffelin *see* SCHÄUFELEIN
Scheil, Vincent 28 782
Scheinberg, Simón 2 404
Scheithauerová, Linka 10 107; 25 647
Scheits, Andreas 14 141; 20 350
Scheits, Matthias 28 72*; 32 757
Schel, Sebastian 15 865
Schelfhout, Andreas 28 72*
  collaboration 23 590
  patrons and collectors 11 233; 33 46
  pupils 14 42; 15 807; 19 99; 23 321; 25 837; 33 46
  works 11 448; 22 847
Schelfhout, Lodewijk 21 775, 852; 28 72
Schelkens, Abraham 31 526
Schellenburg, Johann Rudolf 4 39; 28 72–3*
Schellenburg, Johann Ulrich 13 268; 28 72
Scheller 3 594
Scheller brothers 28 48
Schellincks, Willem 2 696
Schelling, Friedrich (Wilhelm Joseph von) 1 660; 28 73*
  works 1 180; 22 102
Schelling, H. J. G. 25 857
Schelling, S. van der 8 209
Schellink, Sam 22 883
  works 22 *883*
Schellinks, Daniel 28 73
Schellinks, Willem 28 73–4*
  collaboration 3 757; 22 443
  patrons and collectors 14 375
  reproductive prints by others 23 191
  works 22 208; 28 *74*
schelpwit see under PIGMENTS → types
Schembera, Victor K. 28 800
Schembri, Benedict 13 875
Schemerl von Leytenbach, Joseph 2 785; 32 437
Schenau, Johann Eleazar *see* ZEISSIG, JOHANN ELIAS
Schenck (family) 26 24; 30 136
Schenck, Christoph 12 404; 28 74, 75*
Schenck, Christoph Daniel 12 405, 460; 28 74, 75–6*
  works 12 404; 28 *76*
Schenck, Frederick 10 267
Schenck, Hans 28 74–5*; 30 703
Schenck, Johann Caspar 12 405; 28 76*
Schenck, Johann (Hans) Christoph 28 75*
Schenck, Petrus (*fl* 1713) 21 368; 28 77
  works 33 *54*
Schenck, Pieter (1660-1713) 21 415; 28 76–7*; 31 802
  methods 30 568
Schendel, Maria 4 719
Schendel, Petrus van 22 848; 28 77*
Schendler, Johannes 29 5
Schenherr, Simón 25 233
Schenk, Christoph 12 405
Schenk, Daniel 9 689; 25 188; 27 611
Schenker, Nicolas 20 592
Scheper, Hinnerk 3 402
Schepers, Gaetano 5 671; 20 69
Schepers, Livio 5 671
Scheppers, Paul 13 862
Scherber, Christian Theodor 25 124; 31 760
Scherer, Hans Ulrich der 12 343
Scherer, Hermann (1893-1927) 28 77*
  collaboration 18 81
  groups and movements 3 336; 18 81; 27 213; 30 135
  works 30 138
Scherhauff, Marx 20 779
Schermerhorn, Edmund H. 19 346
Schermerhorn, William 19 346
Schernier, Jan *see* CONINXLOO, JAN VAN, I
Scherpenheuvel, Onze Lieve Vrouw 3 545, 613
Scherrebek tapestry workshops 9 703; 12 468; 30 326
  production 30 *327*
Schers, Leonhard 18 61
Scherzer, George 6 924
Scherzhauser, Martha 2 815; 23 332; 27 665
Schesslitzer, Hans 23 311
  works 23 *311*
Schetky, J(ohn) C(hristian) 28 78*
Scheu, Ludwig 31 568
Scheubel, Johann Joseph 12 467
Scheuer, Ruth 31 661
Scheuer Tapestry Studio *see* CENTER FOR TAPESTRY ARTS
Scheult, François-Lénard *see* SEHEULT, FRANÇOIS-LÉNARD
Scheult, Saint-Félix *see* SEHEULT, SAINT-FÉLIX
Scheuren, Caspar 28 104
Scheurich, Paul 12 437; 21 66; 25 348
Scheurl, Christoph 9 440, 442; 28 78*; 33 112
Scheurl von Defersdorf (family) 3 70
Scheurmann, Samuel 32 677
Scheutz, Matthias *see* SCHEITS, MATTHIAS
Scheveningen
  Pavilion 22 828
  Pier 24 747
Scheving, Gunnlaugur 15 70; 28 78*
Scheyer, Emmy *see* SCHEYER, GALKA
Scheyer, Galka 17 453; 28 78–9*
  groups and movements 4 177; 17 766
  paintings 18 111
Scheyern Abbey 26 674
Scheyndel, Aegidius van 5 324; 14 97; 28 79*
Scheyndel, Gillis van *see* SCHEYNDEL, AEGIDIUS VAN
Scheyrer, Daniel
  works 12 *811*
Schiaffino, Bernardo 28 79*
  collaboration 24 835
  patrons and collectors 27 878
  pupils 16 702; 25 808; 28 79
  works 8 550; 16 702; 27 878
Schiaffino, Eduardo 2 404, 405

Schiaffino, Francesco Maria 1 680; 28 79–80*
collaboration 24 835
pupils 23 412; 31 292
works 5 773; 16 702
Schiaminossi, Rafaello 5 437; 28 80*
Schiaparelli, Elsa 8 466; 9 245, 293; 11 727
Schiaparelli, Ernesto 16 774
Schiassia *see* SCIASSIA
Schiavi, Prospero 5 432
Schiavo, Marco 28 81
Schiavo, Paolo 28 80–81*
attributions 6 *3*, 14
collaboration 20 558
pupils 6 11
works 28 *80*
Schiavon (family) 5 376; 22 14
Schiavon, Alessandro 28 81
Schiavon, Domenico 28 81
Schiavon, Francesco (di Stefano) 5 376
Schiavon, Giovanni 28 81
Schiavon, Jacopo (di Stefano) 5 376; 28 81
Schiavon, Matteo 28 81
Schiavon, Michele (di Stefano) 5 376; 28 81
Schiavon, Piero 5 376; 28 81
Schiavon, Stefano 5 376; 28 81
Schiavone, Andrea 16 665; 28 81–3*
attributions 27 210
collaboration 19 330; 31 6
methods 9 308
patrons and collectors 5 847; 11 304; 26 284; 32 155
pupils 31 6
reproductive prints by others 2 88
works 8 178; 16 726; 28 *83*; 32 223; 33 356
Schiavone, Giorgio (di Tommaso) 28 84–5*
patrons and collectors 8 763
teachers 23 754; 29 436
works 28 *85*
Schiavonetti, Luigi 3 309; 4 120; 5 733; 8 186; 28 85–6*; 29 676
Schiavonetti, Niccolo 5 733; 28 86; 29 676
Schiavoni, Natale 20 91
Schiavonni, Giovanni 26 725
Schiche, Martin 4 286
Schick, (Christian) Gottlieb 12 392; 14 586; 28 86*
Schick, Jan Melchiar 8 413
Schick, Karl Friedrich 31 389
Schick, Maria Seraphia Susanna Magdalena 19 734
Schickedanz, Albert 14 908; 28 87*
collaboration 14 889; 30 762
pupils 30 762
works 5 83
Schickhardt, Hans 33 711
Schickhardt, Heinrich, I (1464-1540) 28 87
Schickhardt, Heinrich, II (1558-1635) 11 766; 12 368, 369, 370; 19 815; 28 87–8*
collaboration 3 492
works 12 369; 28 *88*; 29 875; 31 720
Schickhardt, Lukas, I 28 87
Schickler, Aaron 18 797
Schider, Fritz 5 215
Schidone, Bartolomeo *see* SCHEDONI, BARTOLOMEO
Schiebling, Christian 8 895; 25 549
Schiedam
church 22 820
Gemeentemuseum 22 906
St James's Hospital Church 12 748
Schiedhelm, Manfred 5 609; 30 391
Schiedmayer & Söhne 7 346
Schiefler, Gustav 4 892
Schiele, Egon 14 630; 28 88–91*; 29 763
commentaries 26 531
groups and movements 2 776; 10 695, 696; 14 33; 23 1, 2; 24 585; 33 166
patrons and collectors 2 370, 829; 3 715; 25 282
works 2 797; 10 481; 23 297; 25 285; 28 *89*, *90*; 32 446
Schiele, Egon, Gesellschaft *see under* TULLN
Schiele, Moik 30 330
Schiertz, Franz Wilhelm 22 320; 23 221
Schiess, Hans 18 81
Schiess, Traugott 29 600
Schievelbein, Hermann (Friedrich Anton) 12 505; 28 91*; 33 392
Schifano, Mario 16 682; 26 778
Schiff, Hart M. 19 346
Schiff, Mortimer L. 12 504; 26 325
Schifferstadt 25 525
Schikaneder, Jakub 28 92*
Schikel, William 23 40
Schikowski, John 29 872
Schilardhi, D. U. 24 204
Schilbach, I. D. 5 345
Schilbach, Walter 26 405
Schilder, Roelof de 14 293
schilderachtig 24 741
Schildersbent 9 462; 26 772; 28 92–3*
members 12 233; 22 843
Asselijn, Jan 2 614
Bijlert, Jan (Hermansz.) van 4 52
Bloemen, Norbert van 4 153
Bloemen, Pieter and Jan Frans van 4 153
Bor, Paulus 4 377
Bossuit, Frans van 4 471
Boulogne, Valentin de (1591-1632) 4 538
Bramer, Leonard 4 656
Breenbergh, Bartholomeus 4 733
Cabel, Adriaen van der 5 343
Crabeth, Wouter (Pietersz.) (ii) (1594-1644) 8 104
Fyt, Jan 11 871
Geest, Wybrand (Symonsz.) de, I (1592-*c.* 1662) 12 233
Genoels, Abraham, II (1640-1723) 12 285
Glauber, Johannes 12 801
Hoogstraten, Samuel van 14 738
Laer, Pieter (Boddingh) van 18 622
Liss, Johann (*c.* 1595-1631) 19 471
Miel, Jan 21 482
Moucheron, Isaac de 22 208
Poelenburch, Cornelis van 25 65
Primo, Luigi 25 585
Roos, Philipp Peter 27 135
Schellinks, Willem 28 74
Schrieck, Otto Marseus van 28 169
Schut, Cornelis, I (1597-1655) 28 179
Terwesten, Augustinus 30 517
Weenix, Jan Baptist 33 25
Withoos, Matthias 33 264
Wittel, Gaspar (Adriaansz.) van 33 269
paintings 2 *615*; 8 *104*; 28 *93*
Schildknecht, Georg 4 598
Schildknecht, Nikolaus 30 126, 127
Schildt, Mona Morales *see* MORALES SCHILDT, MONA
Schildwächter 14 404
Schilkin, Michael 11 106
Schillemans 30 879
Schiller, Carl 27 601
Schiller, (Johann Christoph) Friedrich (von) 12 *406*; 28 93–4*; 33 37
collaboration 12 851, 852
productions 20 282; 25 787, 788
works 1 180; 11 315; 26 736
illustrated 26 258
Schiller Painter 13 526
Schilling, Diebold 7 244; 30 130
works 20 *560*
Schilling, Erna 25 600
Schilling, Jakob 19 542
Schilling, Johannes 9 239; 28 94–5*
assistants 19 54
patrons and collectors 28 95
teachers 26 378
works 12 406
Schilling, Rudolf 28 95
Schilling & Gräbner 18 140; 28 95*
Schillmark, Nils 11 94; 28 95–6*
Schilperoort, Coenraat Arentsz. van 13 255
Schimkowitz, Othmar 2 803
Schimmel, Fred 29 111
Schimmel, Norbert 1 839, 896; 10 95; 15 922
Schimmelman, J. 4 23
Schimmelpfenning, Adolf 20 397
Schimpf, Edouard 29 751
Schindler, Andreas *see* SCHINDLER, ONDŘEJ
Schindler, Emil Jakob 2 797; 21 819; 24 568; 32 445
Schindler, Joseph 5 584, 585
Schindler, Ondřej 25 54
Schindler, Philipp Ernst (1695-1765) 32 449
Schindler, Philipp Ernst, II (1723-93) 2 823
Schindler, Phillip Emmanuel 14 767
Schindler, Rudolph (Michael) 2 788; 28 96*; 31 596, 632
collaboration 1 490; 23 10
groups and movements 21 782
house 23 9
works 2 815; 19 701; 28 *96*
Schinkel, Karl Friedrich 1 106; 7 205; 28 97–103*
architecture 12 374, 375–6; 14 460; 25 136, 367
brick 4 787
bridges 4 114; 33 296, 391
cathedrals 4 541
churches 11 782; 12 642; 14 490; 25 366, *366*; 29 863
concert halls 3 791; 7 687
galleries (art) 25 408
government buildings 23 490; 31 241
guardhouses 3 *793*; 7 360; 30 521
houses 14 876; 18 456; 25 99
mausolea 3 792, 807; 14 82; 20 867, 868
monuments 18 124; 20 1; 22 47; 28 44
museums 2 359; 3 799, 807; 4 324; 9 18, 25; 12 *375*, 476; 14 575; 18 89; 22 358, 362; 25 172; 29 46
observatories 23 340
palaces 2 673; 3 807; 18 124; 23 813, *813*; 25 368; 28 *101*
pilasters 24 805
porticos 25 267
restorations 20 186; 33 458
schools 28 *100*
theatres 3 797; 12 642; 28 45, *99*; 30 677
universities 19 111; 23 602
urban planning 3 794
villas 18 208; 24 *290*; 28 *102*; 32 554
assistants 14 878; 24 484; 29 45, 658; 33 155, 745
attributions 8 133
Schinkel, Karl Friedrich—cont.
collaboration
Gentz, (Johann) Heinrich 12 311
Grosch, Christian Henrich 13 693
Kolbe, Carl Wilhelm (i) (1759-1835) 18 202
Lassaulx, Johann Claudius von 18 813
Lenné, Peter Joseph (1789-1866) 19 156
Persius, (Friedrich) Ludwig 24 484
Rauch, Christian Daniel 26 22
Strack, Johann Heinrich 29 736
Stüler, Friedrich August 29 863
Tieck, (Christian) Friedrich 30 854
drawings 2 332
frames 11 461
furniture 3 485; 6 391; 12 426, 427, *427*; 26 303
groups and movements 23 545
Gothic Revival 13 201, 202, 207
Greek Revival 13 610
Neo-classicism 22 741
Pompeian Revival 25 193
Renaissance Revival 23 546
Romantic Classicism 26 735
Romanticism 26 743
Vereins der Kunstfreunde im Preussisches Staat 3 799
interior decoration 3 807; 9 17; 12 414; 28 46; 31 *686*
jewellery 3 804; 12 454
lithographs 19 482
metalwork 12 448
painting 7 872; 8 911; 12 393
patrons and collectors 14 649, 653, 654, 655; 25 364
pattern books 24 273
polychromy 25 172, 173
productions 10 97
pupils 3 807; 14 593; 19 243; 24 484; 25 797; 29 736, 863
sculpture 5 905; 31 131
teachers 14 575; 26 13
writings 3 890; 4 243
Schinnagel, Marx 22 299
Schinnagl, Maximilian Josef 2 795
Schinnerer, Adolf 33 161
Schinz, Johann Kaspar 8 790
Schiöler, Inge 10 805; 13 31; 30 81
Schiotling, Johannes 1 811; 22 889
Schippers, Wim T(heodor) 11 232; 28 103–4*
Schira, Albert *see* Skira, Albert
Schira, Cynthia 11 55; 30 330
Schirmer, Heinrich Ernst 14 140; 23 221
Schirmer, Johann Wilhelm 12 394; 17 818; 19 244; 28 104*
groups and movements 9 460; 12 394
pupils
Achenbach, Oswald 1 119
Böcklin, Arnold 4 204
Eckersberg, J(ohan) F(redrik) 9 702
Fries, (Jacob Daniel Georg Gottlieb) Bernhard 11 787
Gude, Hans Fredrik 13 776
Hart, James McDougal 14 202
Hilgers, Carl 14 535
Thoma, Hans 30 739
Werner, Anton (Alexander) von 33 82
works 9 460
Schirnagel, Marx 33 276
Schirren, Ferdinand 28 104*
groups and movements 4 618, 619; 5 44; 23 399
works 2 197; 3 564
schist
historical and regional traditions
Afghanistan 1 193, 195, *196*
Buddhism 1 *196*; 15 *222*, 448
schist
historical and regional traditions—cont.
Egypt, ancient 22 *509*; 27 824, *824*
Hinduism 28 *544*
Indian subcontinent 15 *222*, *446*, *447*, 448, *461*, 499; 28 *544*
Nubia 21 *160*
Pakistan 5 *308*, *309*
Scotland 15 *892*
uses
crosses 15 *892*
palettes 22 *509*
relief sculpture 5 *308*, *309*; 15 *446*, *447*, 448
sarcophagi 27 824, *824*
sculpture 1 193, 195, *196*; 15 *222*, *461*, 499; 28 *544*
tablets 21 *160*
Schit, Nicolaus 20 693
Schjerfbeck, Helene (Sofia) 11 95, 96, 112; 28 104–5*
dealers 11 111
Schjetnan Garduño, Mario 21 382
Schläger 1 93
Schlaggenwald *see* SLAVKOV U BRNA
Schlaggenwald porcelain factory 2 817
Schlagmetall see under ALLOYS → types
Schlater, Georg Friedrich 10 539
Schlaubitz, Jan Gotfryd 25 128; 28 105*
Schlaubitz, Nataniel 25 127; 28 105*
Schlaun, Johann Conrad 28 105–7*; 33 277
works 5 7; 8 288; 12 373; 19 269; 22 315; 24 740; 28 *106*
Schlegel, August Wilhelm (von) 1 660; 9 239; 28 107*
pupils 20 526; 23 410
works 2 518; 26 737
Schlegel, Caroline 9 239; 28 107
Schlegel, (Carl Wilhelm) Friedrich (von) 1 660; 28 107–8*; 31 283
collaboration 28 107
groups and movements 26 736
works 26 736
Schlegel, Frits 8 728; 30 750; 33 699
Schleich, August 21 896
Schleich, Eduard 28 108–9*
patrons and collectors 28 40
pupils 17 885; 20 372
works 8 432
Schleich, Hans 22 302; 33 274
Schleichach 23 6
Schleiermacher, Friedrich (Daniel Ernst) 3 799; 14 458; 28 109*
Schleiss 25 404; 33 723
Schleiss, Emilie 12 821
Schleiss, Franz, the elder (*d* 1887) 12 821
Schleiss, Franz, the younger (*fl* 1913) 12 821
Schleiss, Leopold 12 821
Schleissheim, Schloss *see under* OBERSCHLEISSHEIM
Schleissner, J. D., & Söhne 12 449
Schlemmer, Carl 28 111
Schlemmer, Oskar 3 411; 5 531; 28 110–12*; 29 875
collaboration 3 411; 25 839
groups and movements 3 400, 401, 402, 403; 12 396; 24 406; 25 6
productions 10 863; 12 497; 24 406
pupils 3 93; 4 104; 33 254
teachers 14 694
works 12 407, 497; 19 491; 21 896; 22 331; 24 *406*; 28 *111*; 30 686
Schlenkier (family) 25 136
Schlepkau, Jacob 32 757

Schlepper, Berthold Christian 27 584
Schlesier, Niklas see SCHLESITZER, NIKLAS
Schlesinger, Joseph 25 444
works 25 444
Schlesinger, Niklas see SCHLESITZER, NIKLAS
Schlesinger, Walter 4 290
Schlesitzer, Niklas 22 302; 28 112–13*
Schleswig 8 737
amber 1 761
Cathedral 12 403; 26 640
ceramics 8 748; 30 884
St Michael 8 723
Schleswigfahrer 29 4
Schleswig-Holsteinische Strom Company 14 644
Schleswig lace see under LACE → types
Schletter, Adolf Heinrich 19 112
Schletterer, Jakob Christoph 9 147; 11 123; 18 225; 21 313; 32 453; 33 623
Schlettstadt, St Fides 30 884
Schleynig, Gregor 7 471
Schlichten, Johann Franz van der 33 280
Schlichter, Rudolf 28 113*
groups and movements 3 802; 22 923; 25 6
works 3 802
Schlick (family) 8 422; 19 807
Schlick, Gräfin 14 316
Schliemann, (Johann Ludwig) Heinrich (Julius) 23 475, 476; 28 113–14*; 29 61; 31 25
excavations 1 892; 2 299; 11 854; 16 782; 22 395; 31 355, 375
groups and movements 13 613
house 29 885; 33 677
personal collection 2 560; 31 356
translated works 22 352
Schlierbach Abbey 2 781; 29 838
Schlobach, Willy 10 517; 32 591
Schlör, Sem 33 429
Schloss, Arleen P. 24 409
Schloss Ambras see under INNSBRUCK
Schloss Arenenberg 4 305; 31 374
Schloss Bauschlott 18 523
Schloss Bellevue see BRÜDER GRIMM MUSEUM
Schloss Brunnsee 11 230
Schloss Churburg 2 449, 470
Schloss Dyck 12 134
Schlossel, András 22 310
schlösser see GERMANY → castles; palaces
Schlosser, Julius von 2 833; 4 25; 22 102; 28 114–15*
pupils 12 887; 18 458; 25 12; 28 350; 30 157
teachers 33 159
Schloss Eurasburg 19 706
Schloss Frain an der Thaya see VRANOV NAD DYJÍ → Castle
Schloss Friedau 13 279
Festsaal 2 795
Schloss Frondsberg 2 805
Schloss Goldegg 2 793
Schloss Göppingen 12 369
Schloss Güstrow 12 366
Schloss Haidenburg 11 32
Schlosshalde 6 157
metalwork 6 153
Schloss Herrenchiemsee see under HERRENINSEL
Schloss Hochosterwitz 2 779
Schlosshof im Marchfeld 2 783
Schloss Horben 33 291
Schloss Horst 12 367
Schloss Kirchberg 29 60
Schloss Kirchheim 12 403
Schloss Lichtenstein, Master of 20 768*
Schloss Liebenburg Chapel 33 241
Schloss Linderhof see under GRASWANGTAL
Schloss Marienburg 12 415; 13 202
Schloss Maurach
sculpture 11 43, 44
Schloss Moritzburg 17 888
Monströsensaal 28 743
Schloss Moyland 18 230
Schloss Neuburg an der Donau 11 33
Schloss Neuhaus 33 88
Schloss Neuschwanstein see under SCHWANGAU
Schloss Oranienburg 5 347, 349; 14 650
Heinkel works 26 402
porcelain 9 29
Schloss Porcia see under SPITTAL AN DER DRAU
Schloss Rastatt 27 196
Schloss Ratmannsdorf 2 805
Schloss Rheinsberg 24 541
Schloss Salamanca see SPITTAL AN DER DRAU → Schloss Porcia
Schloss Schallaburg 2 776, 779; 28 50–51*
Schloss Scharffeneck 12 369
Schloss Schleissheim see under OBERSCHLEISSHEIM
Schloss Schlosshof 2 808, 813; 14 530
Schloss Sierndorf 2 800
Schloss Tirol see TIROLO → Castel Tirolo
Schloss Tratzberg 2 805; 20 191
Schlöth, Ferdinand 18 91; 28 115*; 30 137
Schlotthauer, Joseph 29 380
Schlottheim, Hans 7 439; 8 413
works 7 440
Schlumberger, Daniel 16 550; 30 17
Schlumberger, Jean 30 867; 31 655
Schlüsselfelder St Christopher, Master of the 23 308
Schlüter, Andreas 3 798; 12 404; 27 389; 28 115–18*
architecture 3 798; 12 373
architectural decorations 12 34; 17 615; 18 440; 25 98; 32 875, 875, 881
arsenals 2 502; 3 790
castles 30 703
palaces 3 790, 805; 20 839; 23 811; 28 117
villas 3 790–91
collaboration 24 460; 25 366; 27 401
furniture 12 424
interior decoration 26 8
patrons and collectors 12 479; 14 647, 650, 651; 26 730
sculpture 3 798; 12 405; 25 114, 727; 28 116
equestrian monuments 3 798
Schlütter, Jozef Franciszek Teodor 25 122
Schmädl, Franz Xaver 9 6; 12 405; 28 49, 118*
Schmahl, Henrik 28 118*
Schmalenbach, Werner 28 119*
Schmalhofer, Karl 32 439
Schmalix, Hubert 32 447
Schmalkalden, Schloss Wilhelmsburg 12 368
chapel 19 815
Schmalz, Otto 28 119*
Schmalzigaug, Jules 3 564; 28 119*
Schmarsow, August 3 262; 13 34; 24 819; 28 119–20*
Schmauss, Friedrich Ritter von 12 483
Schmeck, C. H. 17 878
Schmela, Alfred 28 120*
Schmelcher, Leonhard 22 918
Schmid, Caspar 3 20
Schmid, David Aloïs 28 120*
Schmid, Franz 28 120
Schmid, Hans 14 893
Schmid, Heinrich Alfred 30 157
Schmid, Jan Pavel 8 396
Schmid, Johann Georg 9 241
Schmid, Johann Karl 3 794
Schmid, M. (d 1720/30) 23 313
Schmid, Martin (1694-1772) 4 259; 28 120*
Schmid, Martin (1786-1842) 28 120
Schmid, Thomas 14 665; 30 131
Schmidhammer, Jörg 6 171
Schmidt 14 910
Schmidt, A. K. 28 163
Schmidt, Anton 28 853
Schmidt, Balthasar 10 893
Schmidt, Claus 12 446
Schmidt, Daniel Heinrich 28 121*
works 29 115, 115, 119
Schmidt, Erich F. 16 550; 19 812; 24 481
Schmidt, Ernst (c. 1875-1930) 2 450; 29 415
Schmidt, Ernst (b 1938) 22 256
Schmidt, Ferdinand von 23 372
Schmidt, Ferenc 14 894; 33 593
Schmidt, Florent 24 838
Schmidt, Friedrich Otto 2 814; 32 448
Schmidt, Friedrich von 28 121*
assistants 33 173
groups and movements 13 203
patrons and collectors 19 339
pupils 3 878; 4 270; 13 273, 677; 14 227; 21 129, 757; 28 172; 29 606
works 2 787; 8 176; 13 204; 19 522; 24 314; 28 859; 31 241; 32 437; 33 593
Schmidt, Fritz 24 565
Schmidt, Garden & Erickson 21 492; 28 122
Schmidt, Garden & Martin 28 121–2*; 31 464; 33 408
Schmidt, Georg Friedrich 1 633; 6 563; 10 393; 11 57; 12 391
Schmidt, H. (fl 1891) 32 421
Schmidt, Hans (1893-1972) 7 294; 28 122–3*; 29 531; 30 127
collaboration 2 512, 513; 22 187; 33 41
groups and movements 21 783; 25 842
works 3 335; 30 128, 128
writings 27 214
Schmidt, Hans Wolfgang (1676-1710) 23 313
Schmidt, Heinrich, Freiherr von (1850-1928) 17 853
Schmidt, Heinrich von (fl c. 1470-1541) 19 111
Schmidt, Hubert 8 252
Schmidt, Izaak 2 25
Schmidt, J. (fl late 20th cent.) 31 759
Schmidt, Joerg (d 1596) 29 750
Schmidt, Johann (fl 19th cent.) 9 468
Schmidt, Johann Georg (1685-1748) 23 425; 28 123*
patrons and collectors 31 510
teachers 29 789
Schmidt, Joost 3 402, 403; 25 350
Schmidt, Jörg (1568-1628) 26 368
Schmidt, Jürgen (fl late 20th cent.) 16 549
Schmidt, Karl (Karlovich) (b 1866) 27 377
Schmidt, Karl (1873-1954) 2 571; 8 824; 12 145; 14 362; 26 374
Schmidt, Käthe see KOLLWITZ, KÄTHE
Schmidt, Kremser see SCHMIDT, MARTIN JOHANN
Schmidt, Kurt 24 406
Schmidt, Leonhard 12 430
Schmidt, Lorenz 3 823
Schmidt, M. 24 309
Schmidt, Martin Johann 18 446; 28 123–4*
patrons and collectors 31 510
works 2 795, 796; 8 392; 19 516; 27 665; 28 860
Schmidt, Nikolaus 8 413; 12 445; 23 312; 25 22
Schmidt, Peter 10 403
Schmidt, Richard E(rnst) 6 578; 28 121–2
Schmidt, Samuel Gotthelf 32 878
Schmidt, Thomas Lanigan 12 218
Schmidt, Wiener see SCHMIDT, JOHANN GEORG
Schmidt, Wilhelm 12 265
Schmidt, Willem Hendrik 30 373
Schmidthammer (fl 1919; architect) 3 422
Schmidthammer, Heinrich (fl 1589) 8 416
Schmidt-Kugel, Maria 12 450
Schmidt-Pecht 12 432
Schmidt-Reutter, Ludwig 8 658; 18 490
Schmidt-Rottluff, Karl 4 143, 892; 18 717; 25 582; 28 124–6*
groups and movements 2 288; 4 891; 10 694, 841; 12 395; 14 284; 18 77; 24 585
personal collection 4 893
works 9 310; 11 464, 465; 12 407, 408, 450; 19 491; 25 582, 582; 28 125; 29 871; 33 363
Schmidt von der Launitz, Eduard see LAUNITZ, EDUARD VON DER SCHMIDT
Schmiedecker 31 358
Schmiedel, Jan Antonín 8 419
Schmieden, Heino 13 685; 28 672
Schmit, Tomas 11 232
Schmithals, Hans 28 126*
Schmitt, F. G. 12 454
Schmitt, Max 9 500
Schmitt, Peter 9 685
Schmitthenner, Paul 28 126–7*
groups and movements 2 288; 4 143, 309
works 12 379; 22 711; 29 874, 875
Schmittner, Johann Georg Melchior 28 127*
Schmitz, Bruno 28 127*
collaboration 21 365
teachers 32 801
works 3 795; 12 406; 19 111, 434; 20 282; 22 47
Schmitz, Hans 13 727
Schmitz, Max 9 121
Schmoll von Eisenwerth, Fritz see EISENWERTH, FRITZ SCHMOLL VON
Schmölz+Huth 28 127
Schmölz, Hugo 28 127
Schmölz, Karl Hugo 15 38; 28 127–8*
Schmoranz, František (the elder) (1814-1902) 28 128*
Schmoranz, František (the younger) (1845-92) 25 435; 28 128; 33 162
Schmoranz, Gustav 28 128*
Schmoranz, Jan 28 128*
Schmoranz, Josef 28 128*
Schmuklerski, Israel see LERSKI, HELMAR
Schmuttermayer, Hanns 28 128*
works 20 564
writings 2 344; 20 564, 565; 28 497
Schmutzer see SCHMUZER
Schmutzer, Andreas 21 512; 28 525
Schmutzer, Ferdinand 28 344
Schmutzer, Jakob Matthias 1 27; 9 426; 11 766; 17 857; 25 358; 28 450; 31 358
Schmutzer, Johann (fl early 18th cent.) 21 512
Schmutzer, Josef (fl 1728; engraver) 28 525
Schmuz-Baudiss, Theodor 12 436
Schmuzer (family) 29 838
Schmuzer, Franz (Xaver), I (1676-1741) 28 129–31*
collaboration 28 129, 130, 131
works 29 838
Schmuzer, Franz Xaver, II (1713-1775) 28 130–32*
collaboration 28 130; 31 512
works 28 131; 33 41
Schmuzer, Jacob 3 310
Schmuzer, Johann (1642-1781) 28 129–30*; 29 838
collaboration 28 129, 130
pupils 28 130
works 28 130
Schmuzer, Joseph (1683-1752; architect and stuccoist) 23 636; 28 130*; 29 838
collaboration 3 491; 28 129
pupils 28 130
works 28 130
workshop 28 129
Schmuzer, Matthias 28 129
Schnaase, Carl 12 482
Schnabel, Heinrich 22 921
Schnabel, Julian 28 132*; 31 609
groups and movements 10 696; 25 360
methods 10 199
patrons and collectors 2 561; 17 620; 27 478
works 23 334
Schnatterpeck, Hans 28 58
Schneck, Adolf G. 8 826; 30 755
Schneckendorf, Josef Emil 8 531
Schneckendorf, Kurt 23 317
Schneeberg, St Wolfgang 12 365
Schneegas, Gebrüder 31 264
Schneemann, Carolee 10 879; 17 694; 24 407
Schneevogt, C(arl) G(ottfried) Voorhelm 28 132*
Schneeweiss, Urban 9 240
Schnegg, Lucien 4 391
Schneider, A. M. (fl 1920s-30s) 9 527
Schneider, Andreas (1861-1931) 23 235
Schneider, Christian Gottfried 8 409
Schneider, Elizabeth Ann
works 22 713
Schneider, Gérard 26 193
Schneider, Herbert 9 237
Schneider, Josef 11 125
Schneider, Juste 19 40
Schneider, Karl 26 405
Schneider, Leonhard 13 268
Schneider, Martin 11 125
Schneider, Roman 25 122
Schneider-Esleben, Paul 1 495; 12 379, 380; 33 490
Schneider-Manzell, Toni 20 808; 27 665
Schneiders, Toni 29 608
Schneider von Lindau, Hans 33 417
Schneidler, Ernst 28 307
Schnell, Martin 9 238; 12 423; 18 614, 615; 28 297
Schnelle, Eberhard 23 360
Schnelle, Wolfgang 23 360
schnellen see under TANKARDS → types
Schnellenbühel, Gertraud von 22 306
Schneller, Ludwig 17 491
Schnell & Steiner 13 811
Schnepf, Bob 25 353
Schnetz, (Jean) Victor 4 527; 8 40; 28 132–3*
Schnetzler, Johann Ulrich 14 133
Schniep, Hans 7 443
works 7 443
Schnirch, Bedrich 30 467

Schnirch, Bohuslav 25 433; 27 640; 28 133*
Schnitgen , Johann 7 425
Schnitzaltar see under ALTARPIECES → types
Schnitzler, Arthur 19 539
Schnitzler, Hermann 31 328
Schnorr von Carolsfeld, Johann Veit 5 901; 28 134, 135
Schnorr von Carolsfeld, Julius (Veit Hans) 18 123; 26 98; 28 135–7*; 31 397; 33 282
  assistants 23 412
  collaboration 22 308
  groups and movements 2 796; 12 393; 22 703, 704
  methods 10 199
  patrons and collectors 22 303, 328
  pupils 8 790; 24 815; 26 98
  works 11 *460*, 462; 22 328, *328*; 23 412; 28 *135*, *136*; 33 282
Schnorr von Carolsfeld, Ludwig Ferdinand 28 134–5*
Schnütgen, Wilhelm Alexander 7 584
Schnyder, Jean-Frédéric 28 137*
Schobbens, Alexander 31 807
Schobinger, Bernhard 9 759
Schoch, Johann 28 137–8*
  pupils 13 776
  works 12 369; 14 305; 28 *138*; 29 750
Schocken, Deganit 16 569
Schocken, Salman 16 570; 21 119, 120
Schödlberger, Wilhelm Johann Nepomuk 32 775
Schoeffer, Peter 4 357, 358; 14 433; 22 369; 33 349
Schoefft, Jozsef Ágost 4 438
Schoelcher 24 149
Schoellkopf, Jean-Louis 11 553
Schoemaker, R. L. A. 15 770
Schoeman, Amy 33 245
Schoen, Arnold 13 638
Schoen, Eugene 31 654
Schoenberg, Arnold (Franz Walter) 28 138–9*
  groups and movements 4 132; 8 434; 23 2
  house 19 653
  productions 28 112
  pupils 5 381; 21 762
  works 29 97
Schoenberg Castle 19 166
Schoenberger, Guido 17 583
Schoenborn, Mrs Wolfgang *see* MARX, FLORENE
Schoenewerk, Pierre-Alexandre 28 139*
Schoenfeldt, Johann Heinrich 22 478
Schoenhut, Albert 31 259, 263
Schoenmaekers, M. H. J. 1 74
Schoevaerdts, Mattijs 4 522
Schöffer, Johann 19 825
Schöffer, Nicolas 28 139–40*
  dealers 26 193
  groups and movements 18 62, 63
  works 29 97
Schöffer, Peter 4 344; 7 189, 625; 13 808; 25 622
Schofield, John 3 476; 28 140*
Schofield, Levi T. 7 428
Schofield, Robert 28 140
Schokotnigg, Joseph 18 225
schola cantorum 28 140–41*, *141*
Scholander, Fredrik Wilhelm 29 689; 30 73; 31 693; 33 638
scholars' tables 28 141*
Scholastikia 10 427
Scholder, Fritz (William IV) 22 598, 666, 667; 28 142*
Scholderer, Otto 12 394; 28 142*
Scholds, K. 17 874
Scholer, Friedrich Eugen 4 309; 25 856
Scholes, Michael 29 107
Scholl, Inge 4 61
Scholl, Johan Baptist, the elder (1784-1854) 28 142
Scholl, Johann Baptist, the younger (1818-81) 28 142–3*
Scholl, Joseph Franz 4 114
Scholle, Die 12 394; 16 906; 25 748; 28 143*
Schöllhammer, Johann Melchior 2 127
Scholte, Rob 22 853
Scholten, Désirée 30 331
Scholten, Herman 11 54; 30 330, 331
Scholten, Jobst 14 369
Scholtz, Alina 13 871
Scholtz, Benjamin von 32 449
Scholtz, Hans 19 835
Scholtz, Johannes *see* SCHOUTEN, JOHANNES
Scholz, Bernhard 10 176
Scholz, Georg 22 923
Scholz, Werner 12 396
Schomberg, Duke of 9 718
Schomburgk, Julius 2 765; 33 73
Schomburgk, Robert Hermann 13 876
Schommer, François 11 581
Schön, Erhard 20 794; 23 310; 28 143–4*
  attributions 29 719
  works 12 386, 815; 19 813; 25 605, 621; 28 *144*; 29 433, 719
Schon, Gerardo 2 397
Schön, Heinrich, the elder (1600-1640) 28 144–5*
  patrons and collectors 33 275
  works 12 369; 22 299, 307; 28 109
Schön, Heinrich, the younger (*d* 1645) 28 145
Schön, Marx, III 28 143
Schonaeus, Cornelis 12 879
Schönau, Jan, Knight of 8 405
Schönau, Johann Eleazar *see* ZEISSIG, JOHANN ELIAS
Schönauer, Alexander 12 449; 13 209; 14 103
Schönauer, Heinrich 2 786
Schonau von Schwenstatt, Franz Anton von 20 216
Schönberg, Meinhard von 33 295
Schönberger, Armand 14 901
Schönberger, Lorenz 32 677
Schönborn (family) 1 724; 12 467; 28 *145*
  architecture 12 471; 23 2; 26 422, 495; 28 381; 33 432
  collections 32 447
  decorative works 23 2
  paintings 12 664
  sculpture 2 844
Schönborn, Damian Hugo von, Cardinal, Prince-Bishop of Speyer and Konstanz 4 890; 23 3; 26 422, 547; 28 146*; 29 577
Schönborn, Franz Georg von, Elector-Archbishop of Mainz 23 4; 30 866; 33 672
Schönborn, Friedrich Karl von, Prince-Bishop of Würzburg 28 146*
  architecture 3 140; 14 528, 529, 530; 18 495; 23 2, 3; 32 466; 33 432
  drawings 18 120
  paintings 3 702; 5 339; 29 789
  sculpture 2 843
Schönborn, Johann Philipp Franz von, Prince-Bishop of Würzburg (1673-1724) 4 225; 23 2; 28 146*; 33 65, 431
Schönborn, Johann Philipp von, Prince-Bishop of Würzburg, Elector-Archbishop of Mainz (1605-73) 9 194; 10 451; 28 145–6*
Schönborn, Lothar Franz von, Bishop of Bamberg, Elector-Archbishop of Mainz 28 146*
  architecture 3 140; 8 875; 25 188; 26 422; 32 456
  drawings 18 120
  glass 12 897
  interior decoration 13 705; 27 611
  paintings 3 109, 702; 5 338; 7 308; 9 18; 12 473; 19 817; 25 188; 27 135; 29 789; 31 314
  porcelain 5 347; 9 29
Schönbornslust 23 4
  faience factory 19 734
Schönborn-Wiesentheid, Franz Erwein von, Graf 28 45
Schönbrunn (family) 10 455
Schonburg 6 57
Schöndorff, Max 19 848
Schöne, Albrecht 10 176
Schöne, Johann Daniel 21 65
Schöne, Ludwig 30 212
Schönebeck, Eugen 3 323, 803; 12 397; 28 146–7*
Schöne Künste 24 439
Schönenberg Church 12 371; 32 821
Schonenfahrer Altarpiece 23 *254*, 255
Schöner, Johannes 12 813
schöner Stil see under GOTHIC → styles
Schönfeld, Johann Heinrich 2 719; 22 302; 28 147–9*; 33 276
  collaboration 29 400
  patrons and collectors 18 467
  pupils 14 324; 28 127
  works 12 389, 390, *390*; 28 *147*, *148*
Schönfeld, Josef 14 364
Schönfeldt, Joachim 29 113
Schongau 12 403
Schongauer, Barthel 20 792
Schongauer, Caspard 28 149
Schongauer, Erhard 20 794
Schongauer, Georg 12 341; 28 149; 30 146
Schongauer, Ludwig 28 149, 152, 154*
Schongauer, Martin 10 382; 12 341, 385; 25 607, 624; 28 149–54*
  attributions 20 770; 33 19
  drawings 12 *385*
  engravings 6 173; 10 *382*, 713; 12 420; 26 228; 28 *153*
  methods 10 382–3
  paintings 7 579; 28 *150*, *151*
  patrons and collectors 8 481; 14 810
  prints 8 838; 25 604
  pupils 5 198; 9 442
  reproductive prints by others 20 792, 799
Schongauer, Paul 28 149
Schöngrabern 2 *776*
  Church of Mariae Geburt *see* St Mariä Himmelfahrt
  St Mariä Himmelfahrt 2 798; 26 575, 635; 28 154–5*
Schönheit, Johann Carl 21 65
Schönherr, Matyáš 8 386; 25 33, 443
Schöninger 12 813
Schönkind (family) 30 311
Schönleber, Gustav 17 818
Schönpflug, Fritz 17 897
Schönsperger, Johann 2 716; 13 903; 20 737, 744
Schönthal, Otto 14 749; 28 155*; 29 843
Schönthaler, Franz 2 809, 814; 28 155*; 32 448
Schönthal Monastery Church 26 635
Schönwald 12 437
Schoock, Hendrick 14 621
Schoolcraft, Henry R. 9 685
School cup 13 490
Schoolmaster Printer 25 622
School of Art Needlework *see* ROYAL SCHOOL OF NEEDLEWORK
School of Ceret 30 3
School of London 10 258
  works 10 *258*
School of Paris *see* ECOLE DE PARIS
School of Rome 14 901
schools 28 155–9*
  Austria 2 *784*; 13 *204*
  Britain 26 19
  China 6 676
  Confucianism 6 676; 18 269–71, *270*, *271*
  Egypt 5 *399*; 16 229
  England 10 241; 23 194; 26 461, 476; 28 156–9
    Gothic Revival 25 I2
    Queen Anne Revival 25 804; 28 *157*
    20th cent. 26 *19*
  Finland 11 *90*
  France 28 156, 157
  Germany 4 *61*; 27 *335*; 28 156, 158
  Greece, ancient 13 381
  Islamic 5 *399*; 16 141, 229, 241, 265
  Korea 18 269–71, *270*, *271*
  Netherlands, the 11 *840*
  Ottoman 16 229, 265
  Scotland 28 156
  Turkey 16 265
  United States of America 26 19; 28 157, 159; 32 *827*
  see also COLLEGES; UNIVERSITIES
schools of painting 9 18*; 15 *597*, *619*, *637*; 22 *356*, 357
  see also COLLECTIONS → types → classified
Schoon, Theo 28 159*
Schoonbeke, Gilbert van 31 714
Schoonebeeck, Adriaan 26 729; 33 712, 713
Schoonejans 33 567
Schoonhoven
  church 22 820
  Nederlands Goud-, Zilver- en Klokkenmuseum 22 906
  Stadhuis 22 822
  tapestries 22 897; 30 318
Schoonhoven, Jan 28 159*
  groups and movements 2 422; 8 668; 22 852; 23 298
Schoonjans, Anthoni 13 729; 18 46
Schoor, Lodewijk van 30 320
Schoor, Lucas 27 133
Schooten, Floris (Gerritsz.) van 13 895; 22 840; 28 159–60*
Schooten, Joris van 3 77; 19 101, 348; 22 841
Schopen, J. 32 682
Schopenhauer, Arthur 1 181; 28 160–61*
Schopenhauer, Johanna 33 309
Schöpf, Johann Adam 2 580; 4 58
Schopf, Johann N. 30 914
Schöpf, Josef 21 818; 25 443; 26 713; 28 161*
Schöpf, Peter 14 135
Schöpfer, Abraham 33 271
Schöpfer, Hans, I (*c.* 1505-69) 28 161*
  patrons and collectors 30 118; 33 271
  pupils 21 485
Schöpfer, Hans, II (*fl* 1569-1610) 28 161; 33 271
Schopfer, Jean 22 538; 32 740
Schöpp, Herthe 33 84
Schoppe, Julius 4 39
Schoppenzaun, Ulrich IV, Abbot of Kremsmünster 18 447
Schopper, Hartman 29 44
Schöppingen, Master of 20 768*
Schor (family) 15 139; 28 162
Schor, Bonaventura 28 162
Schor, Christoph 19 632; 28 162
Schor, Egid 2 795; 28 162–3*
  collaboration 28 162
  pupils 13 845; 15 865; 28 163; 32 775
  works 2 794
Schor, Hans 28 162*
Schor, Johann 28 162
Schor, Johann Ferdinand 28 162, 163*
Schor, Johann Paul 16 727; 28 162*
  collaboration 10 782
  patrons and collectors 6 586
  pupils 32 775
  teachers 7 913
  works 7 621; 16 714; 26 771, 780, 810
Schor, Philipp 11 130; 28 162
Schorchuck 28 720
Schorkens, Jan 28 163–4*; 32 427
Schorn, Karl 24 815
Schorquens, João *see* SCHORKENS, JAN
Schossel, András 14 896
Schotel, Johannes Christiaan 9 169; 22 847; 28 164*
Schotel, Petrus Johannes 28 164*
Schoten, Floris van 29 666
Schott 1 841; 20 794; 33 18, 33
Schott, Andrée 24 788
Schott, Franz 7 916; 13 808
Schott, John 23 37
Schott, Margarethe 12 437
Schott, van der (botanist) 19 55
Schott, Walter 28 164*
Schottenstift, Master of the Vienna *see* VIENNA SCHOTTENSTIFT, MASTER OF THE
Schott & Gen. Glassworks 12 441; 32 757
Schöttl, Heinrich 8 432
Schottmüller, Frida 28 165*
Schou, Olaf 23 243
Schou, Philip 18 462
Schoubroeck, Pieter 11 731; 28 165*
Schoukhaieff, Basil *see* SHUKHAYEV, VASILY (IVANOVICH)
Schouman, Aert 22 885; 28 165–6*; 33 262
  pupils 23 588
  reproductive prints by others 14 795
  works 2 105; 9 169; 14 707; 28 *166*
Schouman, Martinus 9 169; 13 607; 22 847; 28 164, 165
Schout, Jacob Maertensz. 10 216
Schouten, Gerrit 30 15
Schouten, H. M. 6 89
Schouten, H(ermanus) P(etrus) 28 166*
Schouten, J. L. 18 481; 20 275
Schouten, Johannes 28 166
Schouten, Lydia 22 853
Schoutte, R. Van *see* VAN SCHOUTTE, R.
Schoy, Auguste 3 620
Schoy, Johann Jakob 29 533, 761
Schrader, H. 25 576
Schrägeschnitt see BEVELLED STYLE
Schram, Alois Hans 22 330
Schramm, Alexander 28 167*
Schramm, Friedrich 28 167*
Schrammel, Imre 15 2
Schrank *Madonna* 25 110
Schrattenbach, Siegmund Christoph, Archbishop of Salzburg 27 662
Schraudolph, Johann von 29 392
Schreck, Andreas 33 41
Schreck, Johann Veit 3 429

Schreckengost, Viktor **8** 82; **31** 639
Schreib, Werner **28** 394
Schreiber, Charlotte (Elizabeth) (1813-95) **10** 782; **28** 168*
Schreiber, Charlotte (1834-1922) **5** 566
Schreiber, E. **7** 576
Schreiber, Georg **1** 762; **17** 740; **28** 168*
Schreiber, J. **15** 4
Schreiber, Rita Bloch **28** 167
Schreiber, Taft **28** 167
Schreiber, Wilhelm Ludwig **4** 144; **28** 168*
Schreiber Glassworks **28** 856
Schreibtisch *see* DESKS → types → writing-desks
Schreier, Ulrich **2** 792; **28** 168*
Schreiner, Károly **14** 132
Schreiter, Johannes **29** 508
Schreitmüller, Johan Jakob **2** 127
Schrenck von Notzing, Jacob **13** 912; **15** 867
Schrenkeisen, M. & H. **22** 744
Schretter, I. **3** 528
Schreyer, Adolf **2** 106; **23** 503, 504
Schreyer, Lily **5** 582
Schreyer, Lothar **3** 400, 401; **24** 406; **29** 872
Schreyer, Sebald **32** 608
Schrezheim **12** 430, 431
chapel of St Anthony **12** 431
Schriber, James **31** 634
Schrick, Andreas **15** 8
Schrieck, Otto Marseus van **11** 228; **22** 843; **28** 168–9*; **29** 374; **30** 274; **33** 264
Schriften **17** 578
Schrijver, Pieter *see* SCRIVERIUS, PETRUS
Schrimpf, Georg **12** 396; **22** 304, 922, 923; **28** 169*
Schritsen **22** 879, 881
Schro, Dietrich **14** 627, 649
Schro, Peter **12** 401
Schröckh, Johann Matthias **26** 506
Schroda **1** 418
Schrödel (family) **9** 240
Schrödel, Carl David **12** 447
Schröden, Caspar **30** 85
Schröder **10** 453
Schroder, Abel **11** 468
works **11** *467*
Schröder, Christian Fredrik (1722-89) **11** 91; **31** 461
Schröder, Erich **19** 783
Schröder, Georg Engelhardt **11** 469; **27** 169
Schröder, Kristián **4** 668; **27** 797
Schröder, Rudolf Alexander **4** 42; **33** 383
Schröder-Schräder, Truus (G. A.) **26** 379
Schröder-Sonnerstern, Friedrich **7** 842
Schrödter, Adolf **12** 394; **28** 169*
groups and movements **12** 394
patrons and collectors **26** 111
pupils **33** 82
Schrödter, Karl Friedrich Heinrich **28** 169
Schroeder, Hans **2** 395
Schroeder, Ulrich von **30** 848
Schroedter, Gerta **12** 450
Schröger, Efraim *see* SZREGER, EFRAIM
Schrotblatt *see* ENGRAVINGS → types → dotted prints
Schröter, Victor *see* SCHRETER, VIKTOR (ALEKSANDROVICH)
Schroth, Claude **2** 499; **7** 754; **8** 867; **11** 663; **14** 861; **28** 170*; **29** 248
Schteyngel', Baron **4** 312
Schubert, Christian Gottlieb **11** 852
Schubert, Ernő **10** 650; **14** 901
Schubert, Franciszek **32** 878
Schubert, Gotthilf Heinrich von **23** 412
Schubert, Marie-Thérèse **8** 73
Schübler, Andreas Georg **29** 422
Schübler, Johann Jakob **24** 271
Schuch, Adolf Franciszek **28** 171
Schuch, August **28** 408
Schuch, Carl **2** 797; **14** 30; **28** 170*; **31** 397
Schuch, Jan Chrystian **28** 170–71*
Schuchbauer, Anton **7** 471; **26** 713, 718
Schüchlin, Hans (*fl* 1430-68) **28** 171
Schüchlin, Hans (*c.* 1430-1505) **28** 171*
works **28** *171*
Schucht, Franz **33** 592
Schuer, Theodorus van der **30** 517
Schuffenecker, (Claude-) Emile **12** 191; **28** 171–2*; **30** 174
Schuh, Gotthard **28** 172*
Schuhknecht, Friedrich **8** 530
Schuhmacher, G. **21** 47
Schuhmacher, Ivan **27** 374
Schuhmacher, Wim **22** 852; **28** 172*
Schuitema, Paul **7** 655; **23** 450
works **7** *655*
Schukale, Robert **29** 877
Schulc, Daniel **32** 7
Schüle, Johann Heinrich **2** 714, 717; **12** 469
Schulek, Frigyes **5** 85; **28** 172*
works **5** 83; **14** 889; **16** 872; **26** 241; **32** 615
Schulenberg, Johann Matthias, Graf von der **25** 3; **27** 494; **28** 173*; **32** 196
collections **24** 703
paintings **3** 109; **5** 598; **6** 352; **12** 559; **13** 741; **20** 415; **23** 174; **24** 705; **25** 4; **28** 755
Schulenburg Schloss **33** 88
Schüler, Johann Valentin **17** 571
works **17** *571*
Schüler, Karl Ludwig **33** 256
Schule von Beuron *see* BEURON SCHOOL
Schulin, J. S. **8** 742
Schüller, J. C. **20** 275
Schulte-Frohline, Julius **12** 379
Schulthess Painter, De *see* DE SCHULTHESS PAINTER
Schultz **3** 527
Schultz, Daniel, II **19** 496; **28** 173*; **32** 875
works **12** 390; **25** 104
Schultz, Friedrich **20** 484
Schultz, Johann **10** 537; **30** 276
Schultz, Lili **12** 451
Schultz, Lotte **24** 99
Schultz, Peter **11** 99
works **11** *99*
Schultz, Robert Weir **2** 5; **9** 527; **28** 173–4*; **29** 797; **33** 342
Schultz, Sigurd **8** 762
Schultz-Codex *see under* SKETCHBOOKS → individual manuscripts
Schultze, Bernard **28** 174*
groups and movements **12** 397; **13** 727; **21** 341; **25** 786
Schultze-Fielitz, Eckard **11** 778
Schultze-Naumburg, Paul **28** 175*
groups and movements **4** 143
works **12** 379, 416, 418; **22** 711; **25** 367
writings **4** 143
Schulz, Christoph **10** 339
Schulz, Heinrich Wilhelm **28** 175*
Schulz, Josef **25** 429; **28** 175–6*
assistants **10** 795
collaboration **10** 795; **25** 429; **28** 133; **33** 687
pupils **16** 902; **18** 434; **29** 553
works **8** 379; **25** *429*
Schulz, P. (*fl* 1940s) **28** 483
Schulz, P. W. (*fl* 1900) **16** 554, 559
Schulze, Alfred Otto Wolfgang *see* WOLS
Schulze, E. **18** 193
Schulze, H. J. **9** 693
Schulze-Rose, Wilhelm **19** 112
Schulz Solari, Oscar Agustín Alejandro *see* XUL SOLAR
Schum, Gerry **32** 420
Schumacher, Emil **28** 176–7*
groups and movements **2** 545; **12** 397; **13** 727
works **28** *177*
Schumacher, F., & Co. **31** 659
Schumacher, Fritz (Wilhelm) **12** 378; **28** 177–8*
groups and movements **8** 824, 826
pupils **14** 284; **32** 759
teachers **28** 374
works **31** 728
Schumacher, G. **12** 337; **27** 669
Schumann, T. **9** 303
Schumer, Johann **23** 195
Schünnemann, Johannes **33** 435
Schuppen, Jacob van **1** 105; **2** 795; **18** 790; **23** 358; **32** 443
Schuppen, Pierre-Louis van **19** 65; **21** 497; **24** 805; **28** 178*
Schürch, Robert **30** 135
Schürer (family) **8** 407
Schürer, Hans Christoph **1** 6
Schürer, Paul **10** 772
Schuricht, Christian Friedrich **2** 305; **8** 40, 379; **9** 236; **28** 178–9*
Schurman, Anna Maria van **22** 885, 898
Schürstab, Anton **13** 187
Schurterre, John *see* JOHN SCHURTERRE
Schuss, Hendrik Adolph **22** 891
Schussele, Christian **1** 22; **2** 130; **24** 600
Schussenried Monastery **12** 369
Schust, Florence **31** 633
Schuster, Franz **2** 815; **28** 179*
Schuster, Jean **30** 23
Schuster-Woldan, Raffael **22** 711
Schut, Cornelis (*fl* 1600) **17** 598
Schut, Cornelis, I (1597-1655) **28** 179–80*, 898; **30** 320
collaboration **28** 364; **30** 730; **33** 182, 262
patrons and collectors **27** 133
reproductive prints by others **32** 700; **33** 262
teachers **5** 49
works **3** 559; **4** 923; **11** 194; **14** 617; **23** 11; **28** *180*
Schut, Cornelis, III (*c.* 1629-85) **28** 180
Schut, Pieter **30** 878
Schutte, Hans Olufsen *see* OLUFSEN SCHUTTE, HANS
Schutte, Herman **5** 662, 667
Schütte-Lihotzky, Grete **20** 879; **33** 41
Schütter, Franciszek Jozef Teodor, Baron **32** 879
Schütz (family) **28** 862
works **28** *863*
Schütz, Carl **2** 512
Schütz, Johannes **31** 512
Schütz, Johann Georg **33** 116
Schütz, Sebastian **12** 494
Schutz factory **22** 895
Schuur, Theodoor van der **22** 846
Schuylenburch, Cornelis van **8** 887; **14** 39; **20** 459
Schuyler, Mrs *see* VAN RENSSELAER, MARIANA GRISWOLD
Schuyler, Montgomery **28** 180–81*
Schwab, Kaspar **3** 20
Schwabach **12** 468; **30** 324
SS Johann und Martin **12** 626
Schwabe, Alexander **18** 851
Schwabe, Carlos **27** 639; **28** 181*; **30** 169
Schwabe, Conrad *see* PFLÜGER, CONRAD
Schwabe, Kaspar **12** 369
Schwäbisch Gmünd **12** *361*
Cathedral of the Holy Cross **12** 364, 365; **14** 81; **18** 827; **22** 220, 221; **24** 189; **28** 181–2*, *182*; **32** 821
choir **22** 221
sculpture **12** 400; **13** 89; **28** 182–3*
vaults **32** 90
gold **12** 450, 451
jewellery **12** 455–6
metalwork **12** 448
Schwäbisch-Hall
Rathaus **17** 699
St Katharina **13** 111
St Michael **13** 112
Schwager, Carl **28** 670
Schwager, János **25** 449
Schwaiger, Antal **14** 677
Schwaiger, Hanuš **25** 832; **28** 183*
Schwaiger, Imre **15** 742, 745
Schwaigern Church **32** 821
Schwalbe, Ole **8** 755; **28** 183–4*
Schwanardt, Georg **14** 171
Schwanenburg, Hans von **22** 305
Schwanfeld **25** 500
Schwanfelder, Charles Henry **14** 146
Schwangau
Schloss Hohenschwangau **12** 415; **13** 202
Schloss Neuschwanstein **6** 62, *62*; **12** 376, 416; **13** 209; **23** 546, 813; **33** 283
stucco **29** 843
Throne Room **5** 340
Schwanhardt, Georg, the elder (1601-67) **12** 439; **19** 93; **23** 313; **25** 435; **26** 486
Schwanhardt, Georg (*d* 1676) **12** 439; **23** 313
Schwanhardt, Heinrich **12** 439; **23** 313
Schwankowsky, Frederick John de St Vrain **25** 165
Schwanthaler (family) **12** 404
Schwanthaler, Franz Jakob **28** 184, 186*
Schwanthaler, Franz Xaver **28** 186
Schwanthaler, Hans **28** 184
Schwanthaler, Johann Franz **28** 185
Schwanthaler, Johann Georg **28** 186
Schwanthaler, Johann Peter, I **28** 184, 185–6*
Schwanthaler, Ludwig (Michael) von **19** 525; **28** 184, 186–7*
groups and movements **26** 742
patrons and collectors **6** 117; **12** 406, 476; **22** 303
pupils **14** 304, 631; **30** 137; **33** 160
works **2** 802; **12** 406; **14** 48; **18** 124; **22** 300, 308; **27** 665; **33** 160, 282
Schwanthaler, Thomas **2** 801; **28** 184–5*
works **28** *184*
Schwanz, Christoph **4** 832
Schwanzer, Karl **2** 810; **22** 363; **28** 187*
Schwartau, Wilhelm Friedrich Meyer **30** 204
Schwartz, Buky **28** 187*
Schwartz, F. C. **30** 642
Schwartz, Feliks Jan **25** 128
Schwartz, Frans **11** 84
Schwartz, Jan Maciej **20** 186; **25** 128; **32** 878
Schwartz, Jerzy *see* SZWARC, JERZY
Schwartz, John **25** 130
Schwartz, Mikołaj **28** 187*
Schwartz, Shmuel **16** 566
Schwartz, Stanisław **25** 127; **28** 187*
Schwartz, Stefan **28** 188*; **30** 888
Schwartz, Wojciech **5** 121; **25** 127; **28** 187*
Schwartze, Georg **1** 808
Schwartze, J. G. **28** 188
Schwartze, Thérèse **28** 188*
Schwarz (family) **14** 664
Schwarz, Arturo **28** 188*
Schwarz, Christoph **22** 302; **28** 188–90*
patrons and collectors **11** 819; **12** 387; **30** 35; **33** 271
reproductive prints by others **18** 44; **27** 503
teachers **4** 208
works **28** *189*; **33** 274
Schwarz, Conrad **28** 188
Schwarz, Damascen **33** 255
Schwarz, Fritz **28** 190*
Schwarz, Hans **2** 718; **28** 190–91*
attributions **18** 475
groups and movements **9** 447
works **12** 402; **20** 920; **23** 311; **28** *191*
Schwarz, Martin **33** 274
Schwarz, Matthäus **1** 764; **26** 204
Schwarz, Peter **22** 796
Schwarz, Rudolf **11** 734; **12** 380; **28** 127, 191*
collaboration **12** 379
groups and movements **8** 826
staff **4** 235
works **2** 789; **7** 582; **11** 256; **19** 434; **31** 730
Schwarz, Stephan **28** 190
Schwarz, Willi **14** 632
Schwarzberg, Albrecht von, Graf **26** 470
Schwarzberg, Günther von, Graf **26** 470
Schwarzburg (family) **33** 81
Schwarzburg, Anton Günther von, Prince **5** 345
Schwarzburg-Rudolstadt, Prince of (*fl c.* 1740) **18** 465
Schwarzburg-Rudolstadt, Princess of **18** 465
Schwarzburg Werkstätten **12** 437
works **12** *437*
Schwarze, Peter *see* PALERMO, BLINKY
Schwarzenacker **27** 89
sculpture **27** *88*
Schwarzenbach **6** 155
Schwarzenberg (family) **8** 404, 422; **13** 278; **26** 496
Schwarzenberg, Adam, Graf von **6** 364
Schwarzenberg, Adam Franz, Graf von **11** 134; **13** 277; **20** 494
Schwarzenberg, Johann, Freiherr zu **20** 744
Schwarzenberg, Otto Heinrich, Graf zu **1** 6
Schwarzes Gebetbuch *see under* PRAYERBOOKS → individual manuscripts
Schwarzes Gebetbuch, Master of the *see* ANTOINE OF BURGUNDY, MASTER OF
Schwarzkogler, Rudolf **28** 192*
groups and movements **1** 513; **5** 30; **22** 256; **32** 447
works **10** 483; **24** 408
Schwarzlot enamel *see under* ENAMEL → types
Schwarzmann, Herman J. **10** 682
Schwarzrheindorf, St Klemens **12** 364; **26** 654
Schwatlo, Carl **3** 794
Schwechenmacher, Hans **22** 305
Schwechten, Franz **3** 795; **8** 816; **25** 408; **28** 192*
Schwedler, Johann Wilhelm **25** 856
Schwedtfeger, Theodore **27** 586
Schwegler, Daniel **20** 793–4*

Schwegler, Jakob 33 727
Schwegler, Johannes 14 865
Schweickardt, Heinrich Wilhelm 14 42
Schweickard von Kronberg, Johann, Elector-Archbishop of Mainz 17 689; 26 368
Schweidnitz see ŚWIDNICA
Schweigel, Ondřej 8 386, 426
Schweiger, Antal 10 531
Schweiger, Anton Ferdinand 26 125
Schweigger, Georg 28 192–3*
  attributions 10 444
  collaboration 24 588
  pupils 29 683
  works 23 309
Schweigger, Immanuel 28 192
Schweikard von Kronberg, Johann, Prince-Bishop of Mainz 2 592; 3 598; 13 720
Schweikart, Johann Adam 2 239
Schweinberger, Anton 8 413; 13 914; 25 436
Schweinfurt, Jacob von see HAYLMANN, JACOB
Schweinfurt green see PIGMENTS → types → emerald green
Schweinfurth, A(lbert) C(icero) 28 193
Schweinfurth, Charles F(rederick) 7 428; 28 193
Schweinfurth, Charles Julius 28 193
Schweinfurth, Georg A. 20 267; 25 775; 33 610
  works 20 268
Schweinfurth, Henry Green Bronson 28 193
Schweinfurth, Julius A(dolph) 28 193
Schweinitz, Rudolf 4 115
Schweitzer, Adolf 3 288
Schweitzer, Erich Otto 32 439
Schweitzer-Alessina, Francesco 24 784
Schweitzer-Cumpana, Rudolf 13 653
Schweizer (group) 18 205; 29 600
Schweizer, Herman 14 279
Schweizer, Ludwig 11 766
Schweizer, Otto-Ernst 31 730
Schweizer Bau und Ingenieur Kalender 29 491
Schweizerische Gesellschaft für Erhaltung historischer Kunstdenkmäler 13 810
Schweizerischer Werkbund 19 541; 27 214
Schweizerische Vereinigung für Landesplanung 29 603
Schweizer Museumsführer 30 155
Schweizersbild 25 492
Schwendi, Lazarus 13 329; 15 867; 29 375
Schwenke, David 28 194*
Schwenke, Hans 28 194
Schwenke, Michael 28 194*
Schwenter 32 607
Schwerdfeger, Jean-Ferdinand-Joseph 28 194*
  patrons and collectors 4 555; 11 627
  works 11 627
Schwerdtfeger, Kurt 18 62
Schwerin
  Cathedral 13 56
  faience (ii) (ceramics) 12 430
  painting 12 394
  Schloss 6 62; 23 813; 26 190
  Staatliches Museum 8 706; 20 848; 33 296
Schwertfeger, Otto 12 447
Schwetzingen 12 361, 413; 28 194*
  Baroque Garden 12 133; 28 213
  bathhouse 18 173
  Temple of Apollo 13 705
Schwetz-Lehmann, Ida 12 821
Schwimmer, Max 12 886; 14 323; 18 1; 19 112; 31 539; 33 30
Schwind, Moritz (Ludwig) von 11 735; 28 194–6*; 32 882
  groups and movements 26 740
  patrons and collectors 28 40
  pupils 29 848
  teachers 28 134
  works 11 462; 12 393, 394, 415; 22 328; 25 789; 28 196
Schwinger, Hermann 23 313
Schwink, Konrad 5 72; 26 709
Schwippert, Hans 8 826; 12 379; 28 191
Schwiter, Louis-Auguste 28 196*
Schwitters, Kurt (Herman Edward Karl Julius) 19 476; 23 603; 24 428; 25 108; 28 196–8*
  assemblages 2 616
  collaboration 19 476; 26 410
  exhibitions 32 775
  groups and movements
    Abstract art 1 73
    Abstraction-Création 1 90
    Abstrakten Hannover, Die 5 75; 7 771; 32 695
    correspondence art 7 895
    Dada 1 75; 8 437; 12 396; 17 694
    environmental art 10 416
    Ring Neue Werbegestälter 32 695
    Stijl, De 29 661
  house 2 552
  methods 21 171
  patrons and collectors 2 409; 30 749
  productions 26 357
  pupils 14 393
  works 7 557, 558, 558; 9 25; 11 465; 12 407; 14 605; 19 491; 23 333–4; 28 197; 29 872; 30 704
Schwob, Marcel 18 577
Sciacca 16 736; 30 887
  S Giorgio 30 887
  Stereopinto 28 657
Sciamerone, Pippo see FURINI, FILIPPO
Sciarra (family) 16 769
Sciasca (family) 12 370
Sciasca, Domenico see SCIASSIA, DOMENICO
Sciasca, Lorenzo 12 370, 372; 28 199*; 32 822
Sciassia, Domenico 2 781; 12 370; 19 378; 28 198–9*
Scibec de Carpi, Francisco 2 28; 11 260, 532, 571
science and art 28 199–208*, 200, 201, 204, 207
Sciences, Techniques, Urbanisme, Confort, Art see S.T.U.C.A
scientific books 4 356, 358, 358
  Caribbean Islands 5 750
  Iraq 16 309–10
  Islamic 16 132, 297–9*, 298, 309–10
scientific instruments 7 444; 16 799; 28 208–12*
Sciortino, Antonio 20 214; 28 212*
SCIPIO (Sales Catalog Index Project Input Online) 4 24; 6 81
Scipio Africanus 16 616; 26 871; 27 30; 31 349
Scipion de Corvisart, Charles Louis, Baron 27 563
Scipione 28 212–13*
  groups and movements 16 681; 20 82; 25 910; 26 777; 28 319
  patrons and collectors 20 848
Scipione, Giulio di see GIULIO DI SCIPIONE
Sciri, Sciro 31 742
scissors 8 285–7*, 286
Sciuti, Giuseppe 22 99; 28 213*, 657
Sckell, Friedrich Ludwig von 27 231; 28 213*; 33 280
  collaboration 11 128
  works 2 591; 12 134; 22 300, 309; 24 180; 28 194; 32 375
Sckell, Wilhelm 28 213
S Claudio al Chienti 16 625
Sclavonus see SCHIAVONE, GIORGIO (DI TOMMASO)
Scliar, Carlos 4 718, 719; 28 213–14*
Scliefen 17 834
Sclua 27 566
Scodra see SHKODËR
Scofield, John see SCHOFEILD, JOHN
Scolari (family) 5 19
Scolari, Filippo see SPANO, PIPPO
Scolari, Giovanni Baptista di 33 274
Scolari, Giuseppe 28 214–15*
  works 28 214; 33 356
Scolari, Massimo 30 455
Scoles, Ignatius 13 875
Scoles, J. J. 23 473
Scollay, Mrs John 11 496
sconces (earthworks) 21 547
sconces (lighting) 9 13; 28 215*
Sconditi, Bastiano 11 193
Scone, David, Lord 7 641
Sconenberghe, Hendrik 19 260
Scone Palace (Tayside) 20 487; 28 248; 33 188
Sconzani, Ippolito 21 84
scorched leather see under LEATHER → types
scorching 20 466
Scorder, Joseph 10 729
Scored ware see under POTTERY → wares
Scorel, Jan van 7 424; 28 215–19*
  assistants 14 291; 25 381
  attributions 17 657
  collaboration 4 161; 7 869; 22 857; 23 188
  groups and movements 9 462; 26 728
  patrons and collectors 4 614; 11 140; 12 676; 22 535, 906
  pupils 22 63, 837; 23 200
  teachers 13 28; 14 291; 20 615
  works 1 806; 8 666; 22 837; 23 188; 28 216, 217; 33 355
  workshop 31 771
Scorel, Pieter van 28 219
scores, musical see MUSICAL SCORES
scoria 26 916
Scorretti marble 1 199
Scorţaru 30 769
Scorticone, Domenico 11 53
Scorza, Sinibaldo 16 675; 28 219–21*
  patrons and collectors 3 90; 15 148
  pupils 6 32
  teachers 23 772
  works 28 220
Scorzelli, Lello 24 278
Scot, Michael 2 650
Scotch carpets see under CARPETS → types
Scotch tape 24 53
scotiae 13 393; 23 478; 28 221*
Scotin, François-Gérard 28 221
Scotin, Gérard, I (b 1643) 28 221
Scotin, Gérard (-Jean-Baptiste), II (1698-after 1755) 10 392; 28 221*, 751
Scotin, Gérard-Jean-Baptiste (1671-1716) 28 221
Scotin, Jean-Baptiste 28 221
Scotin, Louis-François 28 221
Scotin, Louis-Gérard 14 642; 28 221
Scotin, Pierre 21 368
Scotland 28 221–77*, 222; 31 585, 585
  academies 20 22; 28 235
Scotland—cont.
  amulets 17 516
  architecture 2 5; 4 788; 12 773; 27 171; 28 223–32*
    Gothic 13 56
    military 21 549
    Neo-classicism 25 36
    Romanesque 26 591*
    vernacular 28 229
    19th cent. 28 288–9*
  art history 9 725
  art market 28 239
  assembly rooms 2 617
  banks 28 228
  bannock racks 28 261, 262
  basins 28 261
  bastions 21 550
  beds 28 245, 252
  bird's-eye views 9 723
  bookbindings 4 349
  bottles 28 257, 259
  boxes 28 264
  brackets 28 245
  brass 2 462
  bridge design 30 421–2
  bridges 29 651; 30 422
  brooches 28 263–4
  busts 28 243
  cabinetmaking 28 252, 253–5
  calico 28 266
  cameos 28 263
  cane 28 252
  carpets 5 830, 839; 28 248, 252, 266
  cast iron 28 255, 263
  castles 6 60; 28 224, 230; 29 679
  cathedrals 12 778; 28 224
  ceilings 28 245, 246, 247
  ceramics 28 256*, 257–8*
  chairs 6 391; 11 850; 28 251, 252, 253, 253, 256
  chests 28 255
  chimney-pieces 28 246, 247
  churches 27 171, 529; 28 223, 223–4, 227, 230–31; 30 751
  cinemas 28 250
  closets 28 252
  coal 28 255
  coats of arms 14 409, IV
  collections 28 267–74*, 275
  colleges 25 36
  cooking pots 28 256–7
  cotton 8 37; 28 266
  courtyards 28 225
  craftsmen and artists 28 235, 250, 252
  crosses 15 892; 24 737; 27 453
  cupboards 28 245, 251
  cups 28 261
    quaich 25 789; 28 261, 261
  damask 28 265–6
  dealing 28 272*
  decorative arts 32 530*
  dovecots 9 202
  drypoints 9 309
  dyeing 28 266
  dyes 28 266
  earthenwares 28 257
  ebony 28 246
  education (art) 28 271, 274–5*
    applied art 28 274, 275
  embroidery 28 264–5*, 265
  enamel 28 263
  engraving 12 776; 28 236, 259
  etchings 28 236, 238
  exhibitions 11 338
  fibreglass 11 55
  fireplace furnishings 28 263
  fortifications 21 549, 551, 569; 28 223
  forts 21 551, 569
  foundries 28 242
  furniture 11 850; 28 244–5, 248, 250–55*, 254, 256*
  gardens 12 126, 128, 129, 129
  genealogies 12 271
  gesso 19 876
  glass 28 231, 259–60*, 259
  glass paste 28 242
Scotland—cont.
  glazes 28 258
  goblets 28 259
  gold 28 260–62*, 263
  Gospel books 28 233
  guilds 28 262
  guns 2 462, 464, 467
  gun stocks 2 462
  hangings 28 265
  henges 25 498
  heraldry 14 409, 412, IV
  houses
    country 28 226, 230, 289
    laird's 28 225–6
    Prehistoric 28 815, 815
    taighean tugha 28 229
    tower 6 59; 28 224, 288; 31 229–31, 231
    20th cent. 20 23, 24
  inlays 28 246
  interior decoration 28 244–5*, 245, 247, 247, 248–50*, 249, 252, 286
  iron 2 462; 28 228
  ivory 28 246
  jack of plates 2 472
  jet 17 516–17*
  jewellery 17 516; 28 263, 263–4
  knitting 28 266
  laburnum 28 252
  lace 28 266
  laminates 28 256
  leather 27 105; 28 252
  lecterns 28 251
  libraries 28 275*
  linen 19 417, 419; 28 264, 265, 265–6
  liturgical furnishings 7 283
  maces 28 260
  madder 28 266
  mahogany 28 252, 253
  manuscript illumination 15 875; 28 233–4
  manuscripts 28 233–4
  marks 20 444; 28 260, 262
  mass production 28 255
  Mauchline ware 28 264
  mazers 28 261
  measures 28 262, 262
  metalwork 13 164, 165; 26 689*; 28 260–63*, 262
  mills (industrial) 28 228
  misericords 28 250
  monasteries 8 550
  monuments 32 530
  mouldings 22 216
  mulls 28 264
  museums 28 231, 272–4*
  napkins 19 419; 28 265–6
  narratives 23 476
  National Art Survey 2 5
  oak 6 391; 11 850; 28 251, 251
  objects of vertu 28 263–4*
  office buildings 12 775
  painting 28 233–40*
    ceiling 28 234, 244, 245
    genre 9 725; 33 189
    history 33 190
    landscape 28 235–6
    townscapes 9 726
    wall 28 233
    19th cent. 28 237, 277
    20th cent. 28 239
  palaces 9 725, 728; 28 225
  panels (wall) 28 244, 246
  patronage 28 267–70*
  pebbles 28 264
  pendants (jewellery) 28 263
  pews 24 576; 28 251
  pewter 28 262, 262
  photoarchives 9 725
  photographic prints 1 148
  photography 33 219
    19th cent. 24 657
  piers (ii) (masonry) 24 749
  plaster 28 243, 245, 248; 29 835, 843–5
  plate 28 261
  polychromy 4 788

Scotland—cont.
  pommels (guns) **2** 462
  porticos **25** 267
  portraits
    medallions **28** *242*
    painting **25** *843*, *845*; **28** *234*, *235*, 236, *236*
      18th cent. **25** *883*
      19th cent. **18** *856*; **24** *569*
    photography **14** *539*
    self-portraits **24** *569*
  pottery **28** 256–7*, *257*
    spongewares **28** 258
  printing **8** 37; **28** 266
    colour **25** VIII
  prints **28** 238
    monotypes **25** VIII
  Psalters **28** 233
  pulpits **28** 251–2
  rock art **25** 532; **28** 241
  rushes **6** *391*
  schist **15** *892*
  schools **28** 156
  screens (i) (architectural) **28** 233
  sculpture **11** *55*; **26** 617*; **28** 241–4*
  shawls **28** 266
  shields **14** 409
  sideboards **28** 253
  signatures **28** 241
  silk **28** 264, *265*
  silver **27** *570*; **28** 260–62*, *261*, *262*, 273
  smelting **28** 263
  snuff-boxes **28** 264
  stained glass **29** 508
  steel **28** 228
  stone **24** *737*, 737–8; **26** 617
  stone-carvings **25** *512*
  stonewares **28** 258
  stucco **28** 246, *247*; **29** 835
  tables **28** 245, 253
  tapestries **28** 244, 266–7, *267*
  tartans **28** 266
  textiles **20** *25*; **28** 248, 250, 264–7*, *265*
  tiles **28** 246
  tombs **20** *81*, 81–2; **25** 508
  topographical views **12** 128
  tortoiseshell **28** 246
  towers **21** 552; **22** 241–2; **23** 808; **28** 223
  town halls **28** *229*; **31** 239
  towns **12** 635; **31** 710
  trade **28** 248
    textiles **28** 250
  transfer (printing) **28** 257–8
  trappings **27** *105*
  treatises
    architecture **28** 252
  turrets **21** *550*
  tweeds **28** 266
  urban planning **28** 227–8, 229
  veneers **9** 727
  villages **28** 228
  villas **28** 230
  walnut **28** 246
  women artists **28** 235
  wood-carvings **28** 250, *251*, 255
  wool **28** 265, 266, *267*
  wrought iron **28** 263; **30** 422
  see also BRITAIN
Scotland, Abbot **26** 587
Scotland and Runge **4** 743
Scotney Castle (Kent) **10** 142
Scott, A. D. **16** 890
Scott, A. D., Collection *see under* KINGSTON (JAMAICA) → National Gallery of Jamaica
Scott (ii), Adrian Gilbert **22** 59; **28** 277, 282–3*
Scott, Alex T. **3** 82
Scott, Anne Douglas, Countess of Buccleuch **21** 907
Scott, Bob **5** 569
Scott, C. A. **16** 889
Scott, Caudill Rowlett **14** 803
Scott, Charlotte Sophia **18** *856*
Scott, David (*fl* 1787) **25** 35
Scott (i), David (1806-49) **28** 238, 275–6*
Scott, Digby **10** 334
Scott, Edmund Evan **4** 810; **7** 415
Scott (ii), Elizabeth Whitworth **7** 670; **10** 240; **28** 277, 283*
Scott, F. J. **9** 205
Scott, Francis, 2nd Duke of Monmouth and Buccleuch **10** 292; **13** 744; **25** 882
Scott, Francis Seyton **19** 424
Scott, Geoffrey **28** 283*
Scott (ii), George Gilbert, I (1811-78) **4** 787; **10** 170; **16** 820; **23** 54; **24** 604; **25** 173; **28** 277–80*
  architecture
    churches
      All Souls (Halifax) **28** *278*
      Anglican Cathedral (Christchurch) **7** 210; **22** 230; **23** 54
      Cathedral of St John the Baptist (Norwich) **23** 247
      Cathedral of the Holy Trinity (Shanghai) **6** 678
      St John's Chapel (Cambridge) **5** 513
      St Mary in Castro (Dover) **9** 203
      St Mary's (Bury St Edmunds) **5** 287
      St Nikolai (Hamburg) **14** 102
      St Osmund (Salisbury) **27** 626
      St Peter (Edensor) **6** 516
    government buildings **7** *668*; **13** 238; **19** 573; **33** 450
    hotels **3** 246, 885; **10** 237; **14** 786; **19** 575; **25** 856
    monuments **6** 171; **10** 266; **18** 903, *903*; **22** 47; **23** 689
    restorations
      Cathedral of Christ and the Blessed Virgin (Chester) **6** 561
      Cathedral of St Peter (Exeter) **10** 673
      Cathedral of SS Andrew and David (St David's) **27** 538
      Cathedral of the Blessed Virgin Mary (Salisbury) **27** 628
      Cathedral of the Holy Trinity (Ely) **10** 165, 167, 168; **18** 585
      Christ Church Cathedral (Oxford) **2** 320
      New College Chapel (Oxford) **23** 691
      Tewkesbury Abbey **22** 144
      Westminster Abbey (London) **19** 604
    screens (i) (architectural) **28** 296; **33** 237
    town halls **31** 241
    university buildings **4** 288; **12** 773; **15** 403; **28** 229
  assistants **3** 81; **7** 410; **14** 259
  collaboration **2** 474
  competitions **7** 667, 668
  crockets **8** 184
  groups and movements **9** 705; **13** 201, 204, 209; **26** 190; **27** 336
  pupils **4** 214; **28** 280; **33** 148
  staff **2** 5; **14** 301; **26** 476; **29** 650, 764
  stained glass **7** 410
Scott (ii), George Gilbert, II (1839-97) **4** 214; **28** 277, 280*
  assistants **24** 315
  pupils **3** 110; **22** 58
  teachers **28** 279
  works **5** 510; **22** 58
Scott (ii), Giles Gilbert **28** 277, 280–83*
  collaboration **4** 215; **28** 283
  competitions **7** 670
  restorations **19** 566
  teachers **22** 59
Scott (ii), Giles Gilbert—cont.
  works **5** 513; **6** 459, *459*; **10** 240, 335; **18** 73; **19** 319, 506, 576, 615; **23** 689; **25** 403, *403*; **28** *282*
Scott, Henry, 3rd Duke of Buccleuch **3** 276
Scott, Henry Young Darracott **11** 360; **14** 149; **16** 54; **22** 363; **30** 503
  works **30** *504*
Scott, Ian **23** 61
Scott, James (1809-89) **3** 366; **28** 283*
Scott, James, 1st Duke of Monmouth and Buccleuch (*d* 1685) **18** 144; **33** 177
Scott, Johan **30** 82
Scott, John (*fl* 1639) **28** 245
Scott, John (1774-1828; engraver) **8** 65; **20** 477
Scott, John (*fl* 1803; architect) **22** 539
Scott, John (Colin) (*b* 1924) **23** 56; **28** 283–4*; **33** 58
  works **23** *56*
Scott, John Murray **28** 528
Scott (ii), John Oldrid **28** 277, 279, 280*
  attributions **4** 597
  collaboration **28** 279
  groups and movements **5** 340
  restorations **27** 538
  staff **33** 219
  teachers **28** 279
  works **23** 247
Scott, Jonathan **16** 553
Scott, Marian **21** 816; **22** 39, 335
Scott, Mary **5** 569
Scott, M(ackay) H(ugh) Baillie *see* BAILLIE SCOTT, M(ACKAY) H(UGH)
Scott, Michael **9** 318; **16** 12; **26** 479; **28** 284*
Scott, Niall **28** 284
Scott, Patrick **16** 18; **28** 284*
Scott, Philipe **31** 524
Scott, Richard Falcon **25** 221
Scott (ii), Richard Gilbert **28** 282
Scott (i), Robert **5** 271; **28** 275, 276
Scott, Samuel **28** 284–5*
  collaboration **18** 672
  patrons and collectors **14** 436
  personal collection **32** 144
  pupils **12** 645; **20** 449
  works **20** 424; **28** *285*; **32** 111
Scott, Thomas Seaton **5** 67; **22** 36; **33** 213
Scott, Tim **1** 80; **10** 268; **16** 58; **28** 285–6*
Scott, Walter (1771-1832) **28** 286–8*
  groups and movements **24** 743; **26** 85
  house **2** 692; **4** 170; **10** 298; **28** 248, *286*; **29** 549
  personal collection **4** 806; **5** 169; **9** 31
  works **9** 286; **28** 288
    illustrated **1** 649; **5** 271; **8** 218; **11** 362; **13** 327; **14** 267; **17** 605; **18** 723; **19** 515; **22** 532; **30** 752; **31** 374, 471, 777
Scott, Walter (*c*. 1811-75) **31** 249
Scott, Walter Francis John Montagu-Douglas-, 9th Duke of Buccleuch *see* MONTAGU-DOUGLAS-SCOTT, WALTER FRANCIS JOHN, 9th Duke of Buccleuch **28** 215
Scott, Walter Francis Montagu-Douglas-, 5th Duke of Buccleuch *see* MONTAGU-DOUGLAS-SCOTT, WALTER FRANCIS, 5th Duke of Buccleuch
Scott, William (1685-1704) **9** 727; **28** 252
Scott, William (*b* 1913) **3** 373; **16** 40; **28** 287–8*
  dealers **16** 820
  groups and movements **2** 545
  works **19** 492
Scott, William, & Sons **5** 589
Scott (i), William Bell **18** 906; **23** 21; **28** 276–7*
  groups and movements **7** 436; **25** 554; **32** 415
  pupils **1** 678
  works **15** 829, *830*; **28** 249, *277*; **29** 748
Scott, William E. **1** 442
Scott Brown, Denise **31** 735; **32** 234–6
Scott Brownrigg & Turner **1** 495
Scotti, Annibale, Marchese **4** 310
Scotti, B. **19** 807
Scotti, Desiderio **13** 764
Scotti, Ernesto **20** 513
Scotti, Giosuè **5** 775
Scotti, Giovanni **4** 745; **27** 402
Scotti, K. **12** 633
Scotti, Mikhail (Ivanovich) **20** 151; **23** 16
Scotti, Orazio **18** 731
Scotti, Pietro **19** 780
Scottis, Gottardo de *see* GOTTARDO DE SCOTTIS
Scottish Arts Council **28** 240, 270
Scottish Baronial **6** 62; **9** 724; **28** 224, *286*, 287, 288–9*, *289*
Scottish Colourists **10** 899; **28** 238, 270, 273, 289–90*
  collections **26** 107
  members **24** 372
Scottish Cooperative Wholesale Society **28** 249, 256
Scottish Society of Watercolour Painters **12** 776
Scott Mitchell, David *see* MITCHELL, DAVID SCOTT
Scott Morton & Co. *see* MORTON, SCOTT & CO.
Scotto, Gian Stefano **11** 13; **19** 783
Scotto di Parma **3** 526
Scottsdale (AZ)
  Frank Lloyd Wright Foundation **2** 364, 372
  Ralph Jester House **2** 360
Scotus, Duns *see* DUNS SCOTUS
Scotus, Michael *see* MICHAEL SCOTUS
Scougall, David **9** 724
Scougall, Stuart **20** 419; **21** 733; **33** 573
Scoullar & Chisholm **23** 66
scraperboards **28** 290*
scrapers **25** 494; **27** 234; **28** 290*
Scrattenbach, Sigismund, Graf von **14** 32
Scratton, Michael **22** 795
screen film processes *see under* PHOTOGRAPHY → processes
screen plate processes *see under* PHOTOGRAPHY → processes
screenprinting **24** 679; **25** 592, 608; **28** 298–301*
  historical and regional traditions
    African American art **1** *444*
    Australia **2** 767, *768*
    Denmark **8** 736
    England **10** 258; **28** *300*
    Finland **11** 97; **23** 207
    Native North Americans **22** 589
    South Africa **29** 110
    United States of America **1** *444*; **20** 609; **25** *232*
  materials
    inks **15** 853, 855
    paints **15** 855
    squeegees **29** 438
  uses
    posters **25** 345
    textiles **28** 299; **30** 562
    wallpaper **19** 415; **32** 813
screenprinting—cont.
  see also SERIGRAPHY
screens (i) (architectural) **28** 290–96*
  historical and regional traditions
    Africa **1** 313
    Bulgaria **5** 159
    Byzantine **9** 600–601*; **28** 291*
    Early Christian (*c*. AD 250-843) **28** 291*
    Egypt **16** *496*
    England **10** *270*; **28** 293–5, *294*, *295*, 296
      Renaissance **28** *293*
    France **28** 292
    Germany **28** 292
    Gothic **13** 127
    Indian subcontinent **23** 803
    Islamic **16** 257, 269, *496*, 500
    Italy **28** 293; **32** 217
    Mughal **23** 803
    Pakistan **23** 803
    Spain **30** 664
    Yemen **16** 500
  materials
    marble **21** *774*
    stucco **16** 257
    wood **16** 269, 500
  types
    arcade **30** 655, 656
    cancelli **28** 290
    choir-screens **7** 281–2; **12** 399
    iconostases **15** 98*; **28** 290
      Bulgaria **5** 155
      Byzantine **7** 279, *279*; **9** 622–3, 625, 627; **28** 291
      Macedonia (ii) (former Yugoslavia) **19** *884*
      Romania **26** 718
      Russia **7** 279, *279*; **15** 78; **25** 183
    parclosures **28** 290
    pulpita **28** 292
    rood **1** 695; **27** 123; **28** 290, 292; **33** *17*
      England **28** 292
      France **28** *292*
      Gothic **13** 127
      Italy **21** *774*; **28** 292
      Romanesque **21** *774*
      Scotland **28** 233
    templa **28** 291, *291*
screens (ii) (furniture) **28** 296–8*
  historical and regional traditions
    Africa **1** 291
    China **6** 773; **7** 33, 140; **28** 296–7
    Egypt **16** 496
    England **19** 5
    France **28** 298, *298*
    Ijo **1** 257; **15** 125, *125*
    Islamic **16** 487, 496, 500
    Japan **17** 215, *236*, 359; **28** 296, 297
      Momoyama period (1568-1600) **17** *376*
    Korea **18** 315, 362; **28** 297
    Phrygian **13** *8*
    Turkey **13** *8*
    Yemen **16** 500
  materials
    decorative paper **24** 55
    ivory **7** 102
    lacquer **7** 166; **18** *601*
    leather **19** 5; **28** 297
    mother-of-pearl **18** *601*
    soapstone **18** *601*
    tracery **31** 271
    walnut **28** *298*
    wood **7** 140; **13** *8*; **15** *125*; **16** 487, 496, 500
  techniques
    painting *see under* PAINTING → forms
  types
    rood **28** *292*
    shōji **17** 45, 359, 384; **28** 619*, *619*
    table-screens **7** 102; **18** *601*

screens (fire) *see* FIRE-SCREENS
screens (photographic) **14** 271; **24** 651, 653, 670
screens passages **28** *301*, 301–2*
Screta, Carlo *see* ŠKRÉTA, KAREL (ŠOTNOVSKÝ ZE ZÁVOŘIC)
screw-pine *see* PANDANUS
screws **2** 449
scribal education *see under* EDUCATION (ART) → types
scribes
- Egypt, ancient **9** 897; **10** 3, 4, 5–6*, 7
- Japan **17** 28, 214

scribes' palettes *see under* PALETTES → types
scribe statues *see under* SCULPTURE → types
scribing **21** 326, *326*
Scribner, Charles, & Sons **31** 680
Scrigni, Giorgio Contarini dagli *see* CONTARINI DAGLI SCRIGNI, GIORGIO
scrimshaw **27** 139; **28** 302–3*, *303*
scriptoria **5** 800; **9** 604, 698, *698*; **17** 211, 214, 218–19; **28** 308*; **29** 851
scriptors *see under* CABINETS (ii) (FURNITURE) → types
scripts **28** 303–7*
- historical and regional traditions
  - Afghanistan **16** 166
  - Akkadian (people) **1** 508
  - Ancient Near East **1** 850, 854–5*
  - Aztec **21** 233
  - Britain **28** 307
  - Byzantine **9** 606
  - Carolingian **28** *303*
  - Central Asia **6** 308; **16** 166
  - China **2** *208*; **4** 344; **6** 737–9, *738*, *740*, 741
  - Coptic **10** 1
  - Cyprus, ancient **1** 855
  - Egypt, ancient **9** 896
  - Elamite **1** 854
  - England **28** 305
  - France **28** 305
  - Germany **3** 512; **28** 307
  - Gothic **28** 305–6*, *306*
  - Greece, ancient **13** 490–91*
  - Hittite **1** 855; **14** 591
  - Indian subcontinent **15** 192, 193, 198–9*
  - Indus civilization **15** 192, 193; **25** 468
  - Insular art **28** *304*
  - Iran **16** 273
  - Ireland **28** 305
  - Islamic **15** 198; **16** 166, 216, 217, 273, 285–7*, 367–8
  - Italy **14** 867; **28** 305
  - Japan **17** 210–14*, *213*, 217, 226, 234, 238–40*, *239*, *240*
    - Muromachi period (1333-1568) **7** 624
  - Manichaeism **6** 308
  - Maya **21** 233
  - Mesoamerica, Pre-Columbian **21** 233*; **25** 468
  - Mesopotamia **25** 467
  - Minoan **1** 855
  - Mongolia **6** 308; **21** 882–3*
  - Ottonian **28** 305
  - Pakistan **16** 166
  - Phoenician **5** 332
  - Semitic **15** 198
  - Sogdiana **6** 308; **21** 882
  - Soyombo **5** 106; **21** 883
  - Spain **16** 216, 217
  - Tibet **30** 836
  - United States of America **28** 307
  - Uruk **1** 854
  - Visigothic **28** 305
- materials
  - inks **15** 855
  - pens **24** 348

scripts—cont.
- types
  - alphabetic
    - Anatolia, ancient **1** 830
    - Ancient Near East **1** 851, 893
    - Mesopotamia **3** 12; **21** 274
    - Phrygian **1** 830
  - *andalusī* **16** 282
  - antique **14** 867; **23** 86
  - Arabic **4** 344; **6** 202; **16** 258, 277–8, 359; **29** 619
  - Aramaic **6** 308; **15** 198
  - *bafen* **6** 741–2
    - *see also* clerical
  - *bihārī* **16** 286
  - bird seal *see* seal, bird
  - book script **6** 307
  - Brahmi **6** 307
  - broken kufic *see* New Abbasid style
  - calligraphic **13** 491
  - *cancelleresca corsiva* *see* chancery cursive
  - chancery cursive **28** 306
  - clear **21** 882
  - clerical
    - China **6** 739, 740, *740*, 742, 743, 755, 758, 763, *763*, 764–5, 767, 770; **7** 63; **29** 617
    - Japan **17** 214, 234
    - *see also bafen*
  - clerical, cursive **6** 764
  - copperplate **28** 307
  - Coptic **10** 1
  - correct *see* regular
  - cuneiform
    - Anatolia, ancient **1** 830
    - Ancient Near East **1** 850, 851, 853–4*, *854*, 893, 895; **24** 481
    - Assyrian **1** 854
    - Hittite **1** 893
    - Iran, ancient **24** 481
    - Mesopotamia **1** 850, 853–4; **2** 299; **31** 827
    - Neo-Assyrian (*c.* 883-*c.* 612 BC) **1** *854*
    - Urartian **1** 830
  - cursive **28** 304, 306
    - Afghanistan **16** 169
    - Central Asia, Eastern **6** 307, 308
    - Central Asia, Western **16** 169
    - China **6** 735, 737, 741, 742–3, 745, *747*, 749, 754, *754*, 756, 757, *757*, 758, 759, 760, 761, 763, 765, 767, 769, 770; **14** 820
    - China: 20th cent. **33** 581
    - Egypt **16** 432
    - Egypt, ancient **10** 3
    - Gothic **28** 305
    - Islamic **12** 513; **16** 169, 258, 259–60, 368, 432
    - Japan **17** 211, 214, 221, 226, 237
    - Maya **23** 838
    - Mesoamerica, Pre-Columbian **23** 838
    - Rome, ancient **28** 305
    - Tibet **6** 307
  - cursive, draft **6** 739, 741, 743, 754–5, 756, 757, 760, 767, 769
  - cursive, large **6** 762
  - cursive, modern **6** 739, 741, 742, 743, 754
  - cursive, running **6** *750*, 755, 758, 759, 761, *762*
    - *see also* running
  - cursive, small **6** 755
  - cursive, wild **6** *747*, 747–8, 749, *749*, 756, 758, *758*, 760, 771
  - cursive clerical *see* clerical, cursive
  - demotic **1** 854; **10** 1, 4*, 79
  - *dīvānī* **16** 287
  - draft **6** 735
    - *see also* cursive

scripts
- types—cont.
  - draft cursive *see* cursive, draft
  - early Abbasid **16** 278–9, *279*, 280
  - eastern kufic *see* New Abbasid style
  - *fāsī* **16** 282
  - figural **16** 375–6
  - fingernail **16** 276
  - *gayrawānī* **16** 282
  - grass *see* cursive
  - *haesŏ* *see* regular
  - half-uncial **28** 305
  - Hephthalite **6** 307
  - hieratic
    - Ancient Near East **1** 854
    - Egypt, ancient **10** 1, 2, 3–4*, *3*, 5–6
  - hieratic, abnormal **10** 4
  - hieroglyphic
    - Anatolia, ancient **1** 827, 855; **17** 810
    - Ancient Near East **1** 855
    - Egypt, ancient **1** 854, 855; **2** 299; **10** 1–4*, 79, 83
    - Hittite **1** 827, 829, *854*
    - Hurrian **1** 827
    - Maya **17** 753; **20** 883; **22** 443; **26** *411*
    - Mesoamerica, Pre-Columbian **17** 753; **22** 443; **26** *411*
  - *hihaku* **17** 213, 219
  - *hihakutai* **17** 214
  - *ḥijāzī* **16** 278; **18** *240*
  - *hiragana* **17** 211, 212, *212*
  - ideographs **15** 192, 193
  - Indus Valley **1** 854; **15** 198
  - italic **14** 867; **32** 199
  - *jawi* **15** 757; **20** 171
  - *jiudie wen* **7** 129, 130
  - *kana* **17** 157, 211–12*, *223*; **18** 231
  - *katakana* **17** 211
  - Kufesque **16** 135
  - kufic **16** 169, *176*, 258–9, 273, *275*, 278, 367, 510–12, 542–3, *543*; **29** *618*, 619
    - Afghanistan **16** 169
    - Central Asia, Western **16** 169
    - Egypt **16** *176*, 258, *259*
    - Indian subcontinent **15** 338
    - Spain **16** 215, 216
  - kufic-*naskh* *see* New Abbasid style
  - large regular *see* regular, large
  - large running *see* running, large
  - large seal *see* seal, large
  - literati **17** 234–8, *235*, *236*, *237*
  - *littera antiqua* *see* antique
  - *maghribī* **16** 280, *281*, 281–2*
  - majuscule **28** 304
  - *man'yōgana* **17** 211
  - minuscule **28** 304
    - Anglo-Saxon **28** 305
    - Byzantine **9** 514, 604, 606
    - Carolingian **6** 483; **28** 305
    - Early Christian (*c.* AD 250-843) **9** 604, 606
    - England **28** 305
    - Italy **28** 305, 306, *307*
    - Romanesque **28** 305
  - modern cursive *see* cursive, modern
  - *muḥaqqaq* **16** *275*, 282; **18** *241*
  - *naskh* **15** 338; **16** 278, 282, *283*, 386, 513
    - Iraq **16** *283*
    - Ottoman **16** 285
    - Spain **16** 386
    - Syria **16** *275*
    - Turkey **16** 285
  - *nasta'līq* **16** 285–6, *286*, 368
    - Central Asia, Western **16** 378
    - Indian subcontinent **16** 514
    - Iran **16** *286*, 378, 390, 391, 514
  - Nestorian **6** 308
  - New Abbasid style **16** 280–81*, *280*

scripts
- types—cont.
  - New Style I *see* New Abbasid style
  - oracle bone **6** 737–8, *740*, 767
  - Pahlavesque **16** 510
  - palace style *see kungch'e*
  - Pehlevi **1** 858
  - Persian **16** 258, 285, 329
  - Phakpa **21** 883
  - Phakpa, horizontal **21** 883
  - proportioned **15** 67; **33** 503
  - Proto-Canaanite **1** 855
  - Proto-Sinaitic **1** 855
  - *rayḥān* **16** *275*
  - regular
    - China **6** 737, 739, 741, 742, 743–4, *744*, 745, 749, 751, 753, 755, 757, 758, 760, 763, 765, 766, 767, 768, 770, 771; **23** 166; **29** 617
    - China: Tang period (AD 618-907) **6** 745, 746, *746*, 748
    - China: Yuan period (1279-1368) **6** *753*
    - Japan **17** 211, 218, 220, 226
    - Korea **18** 327–8
  - regular, large **6** 754, 761
  - regular, running **6** 758
  - regular, small **6** 756, 757, 758, 759, 764
  - *rigā'* **16** 282
  - running
    - China **6** 736, 737, 739, 741, 742–3, *742*, 748, 749, *751*, *752*, 759, *759*, 760, 761, 763, 764, 766, 767, 768
    - China: Tang period (AD 618-907) **6** 745, 747
    - Japan **17** 211, 226
  - running, large **6** 763, 766
  - running, small **6** 757, 759
  - running cursive *see* cursive, running
  - running regular *see* regular, running
  - seal
    - China **5** 36; **6** 758, 760, 764, 765, *765*, 766, 768, *768*, 770; **7** 130; **29** 617
    - Mongolia **21** 883
  - seal, bird **6** 739
  - seal, large **6** 737, 738–9, *738*, 741, 766, 767
  - seal, small **6** 738, 739, *739*, 740, 741, 767, 769; **7** 63, 129
  - semi-cursive **6** 736, 745, 747, 759, 760
    - *see also* running
  - Semitic **8** 153
  - *shakyōtai* **17** 211
  - *shikasta nasta'līq* **16** 287
  - Six Pens **16** 280, 282–4*
  - small regular *see* regular, small
  - small running *see* running, small
  - small seal *see* seal, small
  - *sōgana* **17** 239
  - standard *see* regular
  - *sūdānī* **16** 282
  - *ta'līq* **16** 286
  - *tawqī'* **16** 282
  - *thuluth* **16** 169, 282, 368, 513
    - Afghanistan **16** 169
    - Central Asia, Western **16** 169
    - Egypt **16** *275*, 368, 386
    - Indian subcontinent **16** 514
    - Iran **16** 514
    - Ottoman **16** 285
    - Syria **16** 368
    - Turkey **16** 285
  - true *see* regular
  - Turkish **16** 258
  - *uchen* **30** 832
  - Ugarit **1** 855
  - uncial **9** 610, 612; **19** 733; **28** 305
  - Uygur **6** *307*, 308; **21** 882, 883
  - Vagindra **21** 882

scripts
- types—cont.
  - western kufic *see* New Abbasid style
  - wild cursive *see* cursive, wild
- *see also* ALPHABETS; WRITING

Scriva, Luis **28** 308
Scrivá, Pedro Luís **11** 691; **13** 906; **18** 785; **28** 308–9*
Scriven, Edward **28** 693
Scriverius, Petrus **1** 585; **22** 841; **28** 309*
scroll cases **28** 312; **29** *475*
scrolled gables *see under* GABLES → types
scroll mouldings *see under* MOULDINGS → types
scroll paintings *see under* PAINTING → forms
scroll rollers **17** 386; **28** 310, *310*
scrolls **28** 309–12*
- conservation **7** 729–30; **28** 312*
- historical and regional traditions
  - Buddhism **6** 779–81*; **22** 784, *784*; **28** 311; **30** 823
  - Central Asia, Eastern **6** 306
  - China **6** 761, 776; **7** 63; **17** 158; **22** 233; **28** 309, 310–11, 312
    - Buddhism **6** 779–81*
  - Hinduism **22** 784
  - Indonesia **15** *801*, 801–2
  - Japan **17** 149–50, 157, 219–20, 343; **22** 234; **28** 309, 312
    - Buddhism **28** 311
    - Edo period (1600-1868) **17** *272*; **29** *925*; **30** *376*
  - Jewish art **20** 327
  - Korea **18** *315*; **28** 309, 311
  - Nepal **22** *784*, 784–5*
  - Sogdiana **6** 306
  - Syria-Palestine **1** 881
  - Tibet **22** 234; **30** 823, 835
- materials
  - bamboo **28** 310
  - brocades **28** 310, 312
  - leather **20** 327
  - mounts **22** 233, *233*, 234
  - paper **6** 776; **17** 139; **28** 310, *310*, 312
    - decorative **24** 55
  - parchment **24** 107
  - ribbons **28** *310*
  - rice paste **28** 310
  - silk **6** 776; **7** 63; **17** 139; **28** 310, *310*, 312
  - size **28** 310
  - supports **28** 312
  - textiles **28** 309, 310
  - wood **28** 310, *310*
- restoration **7** 729–30
- techniques
  - inscriptions **28** 310
  - painting *see under* PAINTING → forms
- types
  - *emakimono* **17** 21, 22, 149–50, 153, 750; **25** 72; **28** 610
  - handscrolls **28** 309, 310, *310*
    - Buddhism **17** 145, 149–50
    - China **6** 740, 773, *809*, *810*, *812*, *823*; **7** *34*, *35*; **28** 311; **32** *839*; **33** *463*
    - China: Tang period (AD 618-907) **19** *299*
    - Japan **17** 139, 145, 149–50, 161, *168*, 214, 217, 234, 342–4, *829*; **28** 311; **29** *925*
  - hanging **28** 309, 310, *310*
    - Buddhism **6** 779, *784*; **7** *49*; **17** 145, *230*
    - China **6** 779; **7** 729–30
    - Japan **2** *210*; **17** 139, 145, 159, 161, *230*, 341, 343, *343*, *797*; **28** 311, *610*; **32** *896*
    - Japan: Kamakura period (1185-1333) **17** *230*
    - Shinto **28** *610*
  - horizontal *see* handscrolls

scrolls
types—cont.
tangkas **28** 310, 311
Bhutan **28** 309
Buddhism **28** 309; **30** 827, 828, 830, 832–5, 845, 846
Mongolia **21** *880*
Nepal **28** 309
Sikkim **28** 309
Tibet **28** 309; **30** 809, 810, 827, 828, 830, 832–5, *838*, 845, 846
vertical *see* hanging
see also ROLLS
Scrope (family) **24** 576
Scrope, Richard le, 1st Baron Scrope of Bolton **19** 290
Scrope, Stephen **7** 236
Scrope, William **18** 721
Scrots, Guillim **20** 753; **28** 313*
works **10** 246; **28** *313*
Scrovegni, Enrico **3** 173; **23** 756
Scrovegni Chapel *see* PADUA → churches → Arena Chapel
Sčučyna, St Teresa **3** 527
Scudéry, Georges de **25** 461
Scudéry, Madeleine de **25** 461; **32** 97
Scüldt, Fritiof **19** 428
Scull, Ethel **28** 314
Scull, Robert C. **28** 314*
Scully, Sean **21** 897; **28** 314*; **32** 902
Scully, Vincent J. **28** 604; **29** 653
sculptors
Buddhism **31** 676
China **6** 705
Egypt, ancient **9** 853, 855
England **10** 265
Greece, ancient **13** 395; **25** 455
Inca **29** 135
Indian subcontinent **15** 207, *414*, 414–15*, 543
Japan **17** 28*; **31** 676
Netherlands, the **10** 261
Romanesque **26** 595
Rome, ancient **27** 8, 27–9*
South America, Pre-Columbian **29** 135
Sculptor's Cave **28** 241
sculptors' guilds *see under* GUILDS → types
Sculptors' Society of Canada **5** 570; **33** 343
sculpture **12** 62, 105; **14** 869; **27** 10; **29** 559–67*
conservation **7** 729, *739*, 739–40*, XII
copies *see under* COPIES → types
display **9** 11–13, 20–26*; **22** 355, 356; **28** 314
Africa **22** 360
Belgium **9** 15–16, 22
England **9** 22, 23–5
France **9** 22, 23, 25
Germany **22** 362
Greece, ancient **7** 561; **9** 20
Italy **9** *15*, 20–22, 23, *26*; **11** *190*; **16** *770*, *773*; **22** *361*; **26** *899*
Netherlands, the **9** 15, 22
Rome, ancient **9** 20; **26** *899*
Sweden **9** 23, *26*
education *see under* EDUCATION (ART) → types
forms
architectural **10** 741–5*
Africa **1** 314
Anatolia, ancient **1** 832–3*; **17** *810*
Armenia (Europe) **2** 433–5*; **7** 274
Assyrian **10** 742
Austria **32** *441*
Babylonian **10** 742
Belgium **10** 745, *745*; **31** *222*
Bulgaria **5** 155
Byzantine **7** 273–4*; **9** 588, 589*, 599*
Champa **6** 428
Early Christian (*c*. AD 250-843) **9** 588, 589–92*, 599*
Egypt **9** 591; **16** 244
Egypt, ancient **10** 741–2*
England **5** 645–6; **10** 266, 476, 744; **18** 50
England: Gothic **33** *62*
England: Romanesque **5** *646*; **10** *169*; **18** *50*
England: 12th cent. **10** *475*
Etruscan **10** 588, 593, 595, 596, 603–4, *604*
France **10** 744–5
France: Baroque **11** *558*
France: Gothic **2** *47*; **6** *497*; **26** *118*, *119*; **27** *544*; **28** *416*
France: Neo-classicism **8** *566*
France: Romanesque **2** *841*, 842, *842*; **4** *581*; **26** 596, *596*; **27** 534
France: 20th cent **4** *568*
Georgia **7** 274
Germany **10** 745
Germany: Baroque **28** *116*
Germany: Gothic **20** *89*; **22** *315*; **29** *6*
Gothic **10** 741, 743
Gothic: Austria **32** *441*
Gothic: England **33** *62*
Gothic: France **2** *47*; **26** *118*, *119*; **27** *544*; **28** *416*
Gothic: Germany **20** *89*; **22** *315*; **29** *6*
Gothic: Italy **5** *430*; **13** *93*; **26** *400*; **32** *227*
Gothic: Spain **10** 743–4
Gothic: Switzerland **14** *318*
Greece, ancient **10** 742*; **13** 391, 392, 393, 424–7*, 431–2*, 445–7, 470
Greece, ancient: Archaic **2** 679, *679*; **7** *849*
Greece, ancient: Classical, Early **2** 679–81, *680*; **10** *434*; **13** *432*, 451–2
Greece, ancient: Classical, High **13** *425*, *426*
Greece, ancient: Classical, Late **13** 460*
Greece, ancient: Hellenistic **2** *667*
Greece, ancient: Sicily **28** *387*
Hinduism **15** *496*; **17** *761*
Indian subcontinent **15** 206, 326, 397–8, *398*, *400*, 412–13*; **30** *642*
Indian subcontinent: Hinduism **15** *496*; **17** *761*
Indian subcontinent: Islamic **15** 413
Indian subcontinent: Madya Pradesh **15** *496*
Indian subcontinent: Maha-Gurjara **15** 274
Indian subcontinent: Maharashtra **15** 275
Indian subcontinent: Nolamba **15** *531*
Indian subcontinent: Orissa **15** 505
Indian subcontinent: Vijayanagara period **15** 335, *335*
Iran **16** 246
Iran, ancient **10** 742
Ireland **10** 476; **31** *402*
Islamic **16** 243–7*
Islamic: Egypt **16** 244
Islamic: Indian subcontinent **15** 413
Islamic: Iran **16** 246
Islamic: Great Saljuqs **16** 246
Islamic: Spain **16** 246
Italy **9** 21; **10** 743, 744
Italy: Etruscan **10** 588, 593, 595, 596, *604*
Italy: Gothic **5** *430*; **13** *93*; **26** *400*; **32** *227*
Italy: Renaissance **11** *201*; **32** *226*
Italy: Romanesque **10** 742; **21** *773*
Italy: 13th cent. **14** 647; **32** *208*
Italy: 14th cent. **10** *744*
Japan **17** 98
Mesopotamia **10** 742*; **21** 296
Netherlands, the **10** 745
Nubia **23** 288
Poland **25** 95
Romanesque **10** 742–3
Romanesque: Austria **26** *634*
Romanesque: Belgium **31** *222*
Romanesque: England **5** 645–6, *646*; **10** *169*; **18** 50, *50*
Romanesque: France **2** *841*, 842, *842*; **4** *581*; **26** 596, *596*; **27** 534
Romanesque: Italy **10** 742; **21** *773*
Romanesque: Scotland **26** 617*
Romanesque: Spain **27** *796*
Rome, ancient **10** *426*, 742*; **27** 26–7*, 29
Russia **7** 274
Scotland **26** 617*; **28** 241
Sicily **28** *387*
Spain: Gothic **10** 743–4
Spain: Islamic **16** 246
Spain: Neo-classicism **29** *294*
Spain: Romanesque **27** *796*
Sri Lanka **29** 865
Switzerland **14** *318*
Syria **16** 245
Syria-Palestine **30** 190
Turkey **10** *426*
Ukraine **7** 274
Vietnam **6** 428; **32** 480–81
monumental
Achaemenid **1** 116
Albania **1** *541*
Anatolia, ancient **1** 832–3*, *833*
Armenia (Europe) **2** 436
Austria **2** 798; **5** *264*
Bolivia **30** *796*
Buddhism **6** 298; **22** *497*
Central Asia, Eastern **6** 298
Central Asia, Western **6** *219*
China **6** 725, 727, 730
Colombia **29** 145–6
Costa Rica **29** 145
Cyprus, ancient **8** 332
Easter Island **9** 674–5, *675*
England **10** 265–6
Etruscan **10** 588, 593
France **13** 140, 141
Germany **3** 498, *498*; **26** *377*
Gothic **13** 140, 141
Gran Nicoya culture **29** 142
Greece, ancient **13** 368, 421*, 428–32*, 470; **23** 290–91
Greece, ancient: Archaic **27** 689
Greece, ancient: Archaic, Late **13** *431*
Greece, ancient: Classical, Early **13** *432*
Greece, ancient: Classical, Late **13** 458–61*
Hittite **1** 832–3, *833*
Huastec **21** 217, 222*
Indian subcontinent **15** 194 .
Iraq **16** *3*
Italy **10** 588, 593; **12** 539
Italy: Mannerism **1** *790*
Italy: Renaissance **16** *694*; **27** *773*
Japan **22** *497*
Khwarazm **6** *219*
Korea **18** 302
Manteño culture **29** 127, 145
Maya **1** 14–15; **16** 806–8; **20** 885; **22** 8–9; **25** *825*, 825–6; **28** *373*
Mesoamerica, Pre-Columbian **21** 196, 217–18*, 219, 222, 236
Mesoamerica, Pre-Columbian: Classic period **21** 220–22*
Mesoamerica, Pre-Columbian: Maya **1** 14–15; **22** 8–9; **25** *825*, 825–6; **28** *373*
Mesoamerica, Pre-Columbian: Olmec **18** *645*; **21** 195; **23** 416–18
Mesoamerica, Pre-Columbian: Post-Classic period **21** 222–5*
Mesoamerica, Pre-Columbian: Pre-Classic period **21** 218–20*
Mesoamerica, Pre-Columbian: Zapotec **21** 195
Mexico **18** *645*; **21** 386
Mongolia **21** 883
Nicaragua **29** 145
Olmec **18** *645*; **23** 416–18
Panama **29** 145
Prehistoric art **25** 529–30*
Romanesque **2** 798
Rome, ancient **27** 33, *33*
Russia **27** 397
San Agustín culture **29** 127, 145–6
Seleucid **28** 383
South Africa **29** 111
South America, Pre-Columbian **29** 127, 145–6*; **30** *796*
Toltec **21** 217, 222–3*
United States of America **31** *611*
Zapotec **21** 219*, 221*
relief *see* RELIEF SCULPTURE
social **3** 893
tomb **13** 424
Austria **5** *628*
Belgium **3** *417*, *571*; **9** *413*
Czech Republic **8** *386*
Denmark **11** *219*
England: New Sculpture **12** *611*
England: Renaissance **31** *190*
England: Rococo **27** *244*
England: 15th cent. **10** *260*
England: 16th cent. **10** *262*
Finland **11** *99*
France: Baroque **2** *91*; **12** *726*; **24** *786*; **28** *846*
France: Gothic **13** *78*
France: Mannerism **16** *856*
France: Renaissance **1** *766*; **7** *596*
France: 16th cent. **3** *210*; **27** *547*, *548*
France: 17th cent. **8** *94*; **27** *822*
Germany **18** *479*; **32** *833*
Gothic: France **13** *78*
Gothic: Italy **13** *96*, *97*
Gothic: Portugal **13** *101*
Gothic: Spain **13** *107*, *108*; **28** *724*
Gothic: Switzerland **22** *919*
Ireland **14** *500*
Italy: Baroque **1** *627*; **16** *704*; **27** *347*
Italy: Gothic **13** *96*, *97*
Italy: Neo-Classicism **22** *736*
Italy: Renaissance **1** *747*; **3** *138*; **4** *737*; **7** *367*; **8** *797*; **11** *27*; **16** *841*; **21** *438*; **29** *24*
Italy: 13th cent. **2** *480*
Italy: 14th cent. **22** *475*
Poland **32** *873*
Portugal **13** *101*
Spain: Baroque **9** *407*
Spain: Gothic **13** *107*, *108*; **28** *724*
Sweden **30** *84*
Switzerland **22** *919*
see also BRASSES (MONUMENTAL); EFFIGIES; MONUMENTS → types → funerary; TOMBS
galleries *see under* GALLERIES (iv) (ART) → types
historical and regional traditions
Aboriginal Australia **1** 42–5*, *45*
Achaemenid **15** 914–15; **21** 302
Afghanistan **1** 193*, 194–9*, 208*, *487*; **29** 824
Buddhism **1** *197*, 197–8*, *198*, *199*, 207
Hellenistic **1** *197*
Hinduism **1** 199
Prehistoric **1** 193–4*, *194*
Africa **1** *219*, 257–8*, 278, 285, 300–301*, 321–8*, *322*, 330–32*, *332*, 378, 385–6, 402, *404*, 418, 422–3*, 427–8
Kalabari Ijo **1** *247*
United States of America **1** *422*
Yoruba **4** I3
19th cent. **1** *323*, *324*, *325*, *404*
20th cent. **1** 251
African American art **1** 440, *441*; **19** 286
Akan **1** 257, 274, 278, 330, 503
Akkadian (people) **1** 509; **2** 639; **21** 294*
Alamito culture **29** 190, *190*
Albania **1** 541*
Algeria **1** 634–6
Anatolia, ancient **1** 823, 827, 832*
Anglo-Saxon **2** 68–72*; **10** 259
Angola **1** 359; **2** 86*
Antilles, Lesser **2** 152
Arabia **2** 253*, 256–9*, *257*, 260*
Argentina **2** 398–9*, 401; **33** *569*
Constructivism **2** *400*
Pre-Columbian **29** *190*
Armenia (Europe) **2** 433*
Asante **1** 322; **2** 589*
Assyrian **2** 639; **14** *64*; **21** 296*; **25** 650
Australia **2** 752–4*, *754*
Austria **2** 798*, 799–800*, 802–3*
Baroque **2** 801–2*
Gothic **2** 798–9*
Neo-classicism **2** 802
Romanesque **2** 798–9*; **26** *634*, 634–5*
18th cent. **27** *661*
20th cent. **2** 803–4*, *804*
Azerbaijan **2** 894–5*
Aztec **2** 905–7*; **21** 217, 222, *400*; **29** 901
Post-Classic (*c*. AD 900-1521) **21** 223–5*
Babylonian **21** 302*
Bactria **6** *214*, 214–17*, *215*, *216*; **9** 34; **15** 914
Baga **1** 322; **3** *46*; **13** 834
Bahamas, the **3** 62–3*
Bali (Indonesia) **15** 776, 783*, *786*
Bamana **1** 278, 385; **3** 132–3
wood **3** *133*
19th cent. **1** *323*
Bamileke **1** 322
Bangladesh **15** *502*
Bantu peoples **29** 111
Baule **1** 322, *324*
Belarus' **3** 530–31*

sculpture
historical and regional traditions—cont.
Belgium **3** 566–7*, 568–71*, 572*, 573–4*
Abstract art **3** *574*
Gothic **13** 98–101*, 109–15*, *112*
Gothic: Late Gothic **8** 662
Romanesque **26** 630–31*, 644–5*
Surrealism **20** *102*
19th cent. **3** *573*
20th cent. **4** *861*; **29** *660*
Belize **3** 624*, *624*
Bembe **1** 418; **3** 694, *694*
Benedictine Order **28** 861
Benin, Kingdom of **1** *219*, 278, 322, 329; **3** *723*, *724*
Benin Republic **11** *246*
Bhutan **3** 913*, 914, *914*
Bijogo **4** 56*
Black Sea Colonies **4** 111, *113*
Bolivia **4** 264–5*, *265*
Bon (religion) **30** 822
Bosnia **4** 460–62*
Brazil **4** 715*, 717–20*, *720*
Pre-Columbian **29** *197*, 197–8*
wood **4** *708*
20th cent. **4** *720*
Britain **2** 541; **15** 542; **26** 611–12*
Buddhism **9** 34; **17** 138; **18** 606
Afghanistan **1** *196*, 197–8*, *198*, *199*, 207
Burma **5** 239–42*, *240*, *241*; **18** *607*
Cambodia **5** *100*, *462*, 484, 485, 490, *494*, 494, 495–500*, *498*
Central Asia, Eastern **6** 294, 297–301*, *300*; **29** *823*
Central Asia, Western **6** *194*, 215–17, *216*, *221*, 221–2*
Champa **6** 427–8*; **9** 133
Champa: Mahayana **6** *428*
China **6** 706–23*, 835; **7** 68, 98, 99, 161; **19** *639*
China: Han period (206 BC-AD 220) **12** 626
China: Lamaism **6** 722; **30** 443
China: Liao period (907-1125) **5** *111*
China: Ming period (1368-1644) **6** *719*, *720*
China: Northern and Southern Dynasties (AD 310- 589) **6** *708*, *710*; **12** 901; **19** *638*; **33** *574*
China: Northern Zhou period (AD 557-81) **23** 216
China: Qing period (1644-1911) **6** *722*
China: Song period (AD 960-1279) **6** *718*
China: Sui period (AD 581-618) **6** *713*
China: Tang period (AD 618-907) **6** *714*, *716*; **7** 14
China: Tantric **6** 719–20
Gelugpa **30** 822
Indian subcontinent **10** 484; **15** *222*, *223*, 415–16, *425*, *431*, 439–42*, *440*, *441*, 446–9, 451, 453–4*, *455*, *456*, *457*, *462*, *470*, 476, 499–502, *500*, *501*, 505, *505*, 521, *530*; **17** 857; **20** 818–19; **30** *220*
Indonesia **15** 776, *778*, 778–9, *782*
Japan **5** 120; **12** 626; **17** 97–8, 100, 106*, *114*, 126–7*, 130–32*, 320; **31** 167
Japan: Asuka-Hakuhō period (*c.* 552-710) **17** *375*
Japan: Asuka period (AD *C.* 552-645) **17** *34*, 106–9*, *107*, *109*

sculpture
historical and regional traditions
Buddhism—cont.
Japan: Edo period (1600-1868) **17** *126*
Japan: Esoteric **17** 118
Japan: Hakuhō period (AD 645-710) **17** *99*, *110*, 110–12*, *111*, *112*
Japan: Heian period (AD 794-1185) **17** *116*, 116–21*, *117*, *118*, *120*
Japan: Kamakura period (1185-1333) **17** 121–6*, *123*, *125*
Japan: Nara period (AD 710-94) **17** 113–16*, *113*, *299*
Java **15** 778, *778*, 779, *782*
Khmer **5** 100; **6** 430; **30** *600*
Korea **12** 626; **18** 282–96*
Korea: 6th cent. **18** *284*
Korea: 7th cent. **5** *114*; **18** *283*, *285*
Korea: 8th cent. **18** *287*, *288*
Korea: 9th cent. **18** *290*
Korea: 10th cent. **18** *288*, *291*, *292*
Korea: 14th cent. **18** *294*
Korea: 16th cent. **18** *295*
Laos **18** 763, 767, *768*
Mahayana **6** 427
Maitreya **5** *114*
Malaysia **20** 170*
Nara period (AD 710-94) **17** *130*
Nepal **22** *758*, 758–9, 768–9, *769*, 770, *771*, 771, 773, *777*
South-east Asia **5** 100*; **29** 231
Sri Lanka **29** *457*, *460*, 461, *479*
Thailand **5** 100; **29** *911*; **30** 573–4, 593–5*, *594*, *595*, 596–7*, *597*, *598*, 599*, *600*, *601*, 601–4*, *602*, *605*, 605–6*, 607, *607*
Tibet **30** 351, 809, 821–7, *823*, *824*, *825*, *826*, *827*
Vietnam **5** *100*; **6** 427–8*; **9** 133; **32** 478, *478*, *479*, 479–80
Vietnam: Mahayana **6** *428*
Bulgaria **5** 155–6*
Burma **5** 238–42*, *239*
Buddhism **5** 239–42*, *240*, *241*; **18** *607*
Hinduism **5** 240*
Byzantine **9** 587–8*, 589*, 594–602*
Cambodia **5** 483*, 484–5*, 490–95*, *497*, 498*
Buddhism **5** *100*, *462*, 484, 485, 490, *494*, 494, 495–500*, *498*
early Angkor period **5** 486–90*
Hinduism **5** 484–5, *485*, 486–90, *489*
Khmer **5** 499
Cameroon **1** 278; **5** 523–4*
Canada **5** 570–72*, *571*; **14** 282; **22** 574–5
Caribbean Islands **5** 750–52*, *753*
Carolingian **5** 796*; **12** 398
Carthusian Order **28** 861
Catalonia **26** 609–10*
Celtic **6** 152, 156, 158–9
Czech Republic **6** *158*
Scotland **28** 241
Central Asia **9** 34
Central Asia, Eastern **6** 294, 297–301*, *300*; **29** *823*
Central Asia, Western **6** 211*, 212–14*, 219*, 222, 275–6
Bactria **6** *214*, 214–17*, *215*, *216*
Buddhism **6** *194*, 215–17, *216*, *221*, 221–2*

sculpture
historical and regional traditions
Central Asia, Western—cont.
Islamic **16** 239
Kazakhstan **6** 220
Khwarazm **6** 218*
Kyrgyzstan **6** 220
Parthian **6** 217*
Sogdiana **6** 219–21*, *220*
stone **6** 220
Tajikistan **6** *214*
Tokharistan **6** *221*, 221–2*
Champa **6** 426–7*, 429–31*
Buddhism **6** 427–8*, *428*; **9** 133
Hinduism **6** 427, 428–9*, 430
Chavín culture **6** 521–2*; **29** 167, *167*, 169–70
Chile **6** 595–9*, *598*
China **6** 705*, 725–33*, 882; **7** 98, 99, 135, 143, 160
Buddhism **6** 706–23*, 835; **7** 68, 98, 99, 161
Buddhism: Han period (206 BC-AD 220) **12** 626
Buddhism: Lamaism **6** 722; **30** 443
Buddhism: Liao period (907-1125) **5** *111*
Buddhism: Ming period (1368-1644) **6** *719*, *720*
Buddhism: Northern and Southern Dynasties (AD 310-589) **6** *708*, *710*; **12** 901; **19** *638*; **33** *574*
Buddhism: Northern Zhou period (AD 557-81) **23** 216
Buddhism: Qing period (1644-1911) **6** *722*
Buddhism: Song period (AD 960-1279) **6** *718*
Buddhism: Sui period (AD 581-618) **6** *713*
Buddhism: Tang period (AD 618-907) **6** *714*, *716*; **7** 14; **19** *639*
Buddhism: Tantric **6** 719–20
Daoism **6** *628*, 723*, *724*
Five Dynasties (AD 907-60) **7** *99*
Han period (206 BC-AD 220) **6** *727*, *728*; **8** *853*
Liao period (AD 907-1125) **6** *891*
Ming period (1368-1644) **6** 701; **7** *57*; **30** *398*
Northern and Southern Dynasties (AD 310-589) **6** *729*
Qing period (1644-1911) **6** *733*; **7** *134*
Qin period (221-206 BC) **19** *432*; **30** *509*
Shang period (*c.* 1600-*c.* 1050 BC) **13** *736*
Song period (AD 960-1279) **6** *731*; **7** *100*
Tang period (AD 618-907) **6** *730*; **25** 175
Zhou period (*c.* 1050-256 BC) **12** 625
20th cent. **6** *734*
Chokwe **1** 359, *404*
Christianity
Germany **12** 403
Lutheranism **12** 403
Protestantism **12** 402, 403
Roman Catholicism **12** 402–3
Cistercian Order **13** 97–8
Cluniac Order **26** 596
Colombia **7** 607–8*, *608*, 609
Pre-Columbian **27** 700, *700*, 701
colonialism **7** 615, *616*
Cook Islands **7** 790–91*
Coptic **7** 821–2*
Corsica **11** 78

sculpture
historical and regional traditions—cont.
Costa Rica **8** 17–18*; **9** 677–9, *678*, *679*; **29** 143
Côte d'Ivoire **8** 22–3, *23*
Crete **8** 154
Daidalic **13** 443
Minoan **8** 153; **21** 656, 657–8, 659, 678–80*, *679*
Roman **8** 155
Croatia **8** 177–9*
Cuba (Caribbean) **8** 229, 230, *230*, 233–4*
Cyprus **8** 363, 364–5*
Cyprus, ancient **8** 333, 337*, 339–41*; **27** *609*
Archaic **24** 61
Hellenistic **8** 342*
Prehistoric **8** 337–9*
Roman **8** 342*
6th cent. BC **8** *340*
Czech Republic **8** 381*; **22** 403
Celtic **6** *158*
Cubo-Expressionism **8** *249*
Romanesque **26** 637–8*
20th cent. **8** *388*; **22** *404*
Daoism **6** *628*, 723*
Denmark **8** 737*, 738*, 739–40*, 741–2*
Gothic **13** 118; **26** 304
Romanesque **8** 737–8; **26** 304, 640*
Dian culture **8** *853*
Dogon **1** *322*
Dominican Republic **9** 117–18*
Early Christian (*c.* AD 250-843) **9** 587–8*, 589*, 594–7*, 599–602*
Italy **16** 686*
Spain **29** 287
Easter Island **23** 731
Ecuador **9** 712*, 713*, 714*
Edo (Africa) **9** 736–7
Egypt **7** 821–2*; **9** 765–6*, *766*
Egypt, ancient **9** 779, 813, 815, *815*, *816*, 853–5*, 864*; **10** 3, 55, 57, 68, 84, *472*; **12** 625; **13** *465*
Amarna (1353-1333 BC) **9** 883–4*, *883*
Early Dynastic (*c.* 2925-*c.* 2575 BC) **9** 866–7*, *867*
First Intermediate Period (*c.* 2130-*c.* 1938 BC) **9** 872–3*
Graeco-Roman (332 BC-AD 395) **9** 895–6*, *895*; **13** 465
Late Period (664-332 BC) **5** *71*; **9** 888–90*, *889*
Middle Kingdom (*c.* 1966-*c.* 1630 BC) **2** *659*; **9** 874–6*, *876*; **10** *77*
New Kingdom (*c.* 1539-*c.* 1075 BC) **9** 880–81*, *881*, 884–5*, *885*; **10** *58*; **28** 407
Old Kingdom (*c.* 2575-*c.* 2130 BC) **9** 869–71*, *869*, *870*; **10** *35*, *37*; **29** X1
Predynastic (*c.* 6000-*c.* 2925 BC) **9** 864–5*
Ptolemaic (304-30 BC) **9** 892*, *893*, 893–5*
Second Intermediate Period (*c.* 1630-*c.* 1540 BC) **9** 878*, 879*
Third Intermediate Period (*c.* 1075-*c.* 656 BC) **9** 886–7*
5th Dynasty (*c.* 2465-*c.* 2325 BC) **1** 96
18th Dynasty (*c.* 1539-*c.* 1292 BC) **28** *433*
Ejagham **10** 123*, *123*, 124*
Elamite **15** 914, *919*; **30** *28*
El Salvador **10** 154–5
England **10** 259*, 261–7*; **12** 129; **19** 605; **30** 499*; **33** 3
Abstract art **5** *790*
Anglo-Saxon **2** 68–72*; **10** 259

sculpture
historical and regional traditions
England—cont.
Gothic **7** 456; **10** 266; **13** 80–83*, *81*, *84*, 84–5*, *121*, 121–2*; **33** 550
Gothic: Decorated style **10** 673
Gothic: Early Gothic **33** 61
Modernism **22** *57*
New Sculpture **23** *34*; **30** *762*
Renaissance **16** 695
Roman **19** *579*
Romanesque **7** 455; **19** 405; **26** 613–17*, 643–4*
Viking **2** 71*; **32** 529
15th cent. **33** 238
18th cent. **27** *468*
20th cent. **10** *268*, *438*; **11** *157*; **14** *401*; **24** *34*
Eritrea **10** 576–7*
Estonia **10** 538–40*
Ethiopia **10** 576–7*
Etruscan **10** 587, 589, 602–9, *603*, *604*, *605*, *606*, *608*, 639; **16** 683, *684*; **27** 9
bronze **10** 602, 604–6, 608
stone **10** 602; **32** 744
Wiry Geometric style **10** 604
Fang **1** 282, 322, 359; **10** *788*, 788–92*, *789*, *790*
Finland **11** 97–9*, 100–101*, 106
19th cent. **28** 814
Fon **1** 278; **11** *246*, 246–7*
France **11** 553–71*; **30** 498–500*; **33** 3
biomorphism **2** *491*
Constructivism **24** *574*
Cubism **2** *311*; **9** *362*; **18** *863*; **24** *716*; **33** *590*
Gothic **7** 455–6; **13** 72–9*, *76*, 125–6*, 169; **24** 159
Jewish art **17** 577*
Neo-classicism **25** *418*
Nouveau Réalisme **6** *354*
Prehistoric **25** *544*
primitivism **12** *194*
Renaissance **16** 695
Roman **12** *70*; **27** 31
Romanesque **2** 728; **7** 454; **26** 596–7*, 600–601*, 641*; **31** 225
Romanesque: Auvergne **26** 601*
Romanesque: Burgundy **26** 601–2*
Romanesque: First Romanesque **26** 609
Romanesque: Languedoc **26** 602–3*
Romanesque: Loire Valley **26** 598–9*
Romanesque: Normandy **26** 597–8*
Romanesque: Provence **26** 603–4*
Romanesque: Roussillon **26** 604*, 609–10*
Romanticism **26** 742
Surrealism **12** *564*; **30** *21*
18th cent. **2** 53
19th cent. **11** *564*
20th cent. **4** *660*, *661*, *662*; **7** *697*; **8** *773*; **9** *356*; **11** *569*, *570*; **12** *184*, *566*; **20** *120*, *825*, *828*; **21** *787*; **22** *748*; **24** *722*; **26** *351*; **30** *924*
Franciscan Order **24** 98
Fremont culture **22** 582
French Guiana **11** 759
Gabon **1** 282, 359; **11** *879*, 879*
Gambier Islands **31** 403–4
Gandhara **15** 416
Georgia **12** 321–2*, *322*
Germany **12** 398–405*, 406–8*, 472
Baroque Revival **12** 406

sculpture
historical and regional traditions
Germany—cont.
Carolingian **12** 398
Expressionism **18** *78*
Gothic **12** *344*; **13** 86–7, *160*; **20** *129*
Gothic: Early Gothic **12** 399–400; **22** 692
Gothic: Late Gothic **13** *316*; **32** *605*
Holy Roman Empire (before 1648) **26** 634*
Jugendstil **12** 407
Lutheranism **12** 403
Nazism **12** 408; **22** 711–12
Neo-classicism **12** 406
Ottonian **7** 590; **12** 399
Protestantism **12** 402, 403
Rococo **26** 498
Roman Catholicism **12** 402–3
Romanesque **12** 399; **26** 632–3*, 634*
Surrealism **3** *672*
16th cent. **26** *103*; **28** 492
19th cent. **9** *692*; **14** *526*
20th cent. **3** *243*, *891*; **19** *95*; **20** *396*, *808*
Ghana **1** 331; **12** 509*, *509*
Gothic **7** 455*; **13** 71–2*, 109*, 139; **28** 402
Austria **2** 798–9
Belgium **13** 98–101*, 109–15*, *112*
Belgium: Late Gothic **8** 662
Cistercian Order **13** 97–8
Denmark **13** 118; **26** 304
England **7** 456; **10** 266; **13** 80–83*, *81*, *84*, 84–5*, *121*, 121–2*; **33** 550
England: Decorated style **10** 673
England: Early Gothic **33** 61
France **7** 455–6; **13** 72–9*, *76*, 125–6*, 169; **24** 159
Germany **12** *344*; **13** 86–7, *160*; **20** *129*
Germany: Early Gothic **12** 399–400; **22** 692
Germany: Late Gothic **13** *316*; **32** *605*
Holy Roman Empire (before 1648) **13** 85*, 86–7*, 115–18*, *160*
Hungary **14** 893
Italy **13** 87–92*, 93*, 123–4*; **16** 688*
Italy: Campania **13** 98*
Italy: Emilia-Romagna **13** 95–6*
Italy: Lazio **13** 97–8*
Italy: Lombardy **13** 94–5*
Italy: Tuscany **13** 93–4*
Italy: Umbria **13** 96–7*
Italy: Veneto **13** 95*
Netherlands, the **13** 98–101*, 109–15*
Norway **13** 102, 119
Poland **25** 110–11
Portugal **13** 101–2*, 124–5*; **25** *301*
Scandinavia **13** 102–3*, 118–20*
Spain **13** 103–8*, 122–3*; **29** 288–9
Sweden **13** 102–3, 119, 120; **30** 83
Switzerland **30** 136
Gran Nicoya culture **13** 310–11
Greece **13** 353–5*, *354*

sculpture
historical and regional traditions—cont.
Greece, ancient **2** 678–82; **13** 374*, 392, 421–8*, *422*, *423*, 433–8*, 439*, 440*, 441*, 450*, 467–71*; **22** 733; **23** 290, *291*; **24** 318–19*, *319*, *414*; **25** 177, *179*, *576*; **26** *297*; **29** 559, *710*
Archaic **8** 457, 458; **12** 625; **13** *367*, 438, 439*, 441*, 444*; **22** 699; **27** *689*
Archaic, Early **13** 442–5*
Archaic, Late **13** 447–9*, *448*
Archaic, Middle **13** 445–7*, *447*
Attica **13** 447
Boeotia **18** 409
Classical **7** 783; **9** 34; **13** *367*, 438–9*; **24** 258; **25** *178*
Classical, Early **2** 681–2; **8** *695*, *696*, *697*; **13** 450–52*
Classical, High **2** 682; **13** 452–8*, *453*, *454*; **24** *593*
Classical, Late **2** 682; **13** *459*; **25** *456*
Daidalic **13** 442–4*
Dark Age (*c*. 1050–*c*. 750 BC) **13** 441*
Early Christian (*c*. AD 250–843) **6** 9
Geometric (*c*. 900–*c*. 700 BC) **2** 681; **13** *367*, *441*, 441–2*
Hellenistic **2** 682; **9** *248*; **12** 286–7; **13** *367*, 461–2*; **25** *179*
Hellenistic, Early **13** *462*, 462–4*, *463*
Hellenistic, High **13** 464–5*, *465*
Hellenistic, Late **13** 465–7*, *466*
Ionia **15** 893
Italy **30** 339
marble **14** *69*, *70*; **27** *692*
Orientalizing style **13** 442
Proto-Daidalic **13** 442*
Rich style **13** 452, 455, 456–8
Roman **13** *367*
Severe style (i) (Greece, ancient) **13** *450*, 450–52, *452*, 468
Turkey **8** *870*; **14** *70*
5th cent. BC **23** *433*
Guatemala **10** 154; **13** 763–6*, *767*
Gulf Coast, Mesoamerica
Classic (*c*. AD 250–*c*. 900) **21** 220*
Pre-Classic (*c*. 2000 BC–*c*. AD 250) **21** 218–19*
Gumelniţa culture **25** 512
Guyana **13** *877*, 877
Haida **22** 580–81*
Haiti **14** 58
Hawaii **10** *848*; **14** 250; **23** 731
Helladic **14** 351*
Early Helladic (*c*. 3600/3000–*c*. 2050 BC) **14** 351*
Late Helladic (*c*. 1600–*c*. 1050 BC) **14** 351–2*
Middle Helladic (*c*. 2050–*c*. 1600 BC) **14** 351*
Herzegovina **4** 460–62*
Hinduism
Afghanistan **1** 199
Bangladesh **15** *502*
Burma **5** 240*
Cambodia **5** 484–5, *485*, 486–90, *489*
Champa **6** 427, 428–9*, 430
India, Republic of **15** *79*

sculpture
historical and regional traditions
Hinduism—cont.
Indian subcontinent **1** *484*; **5** 95; **15** *219*, *416*, *417*, 443–4*, *468*, *469*, *471*, 502, *503*, 503–5, *504*, 514–20, *515*, *516*, *517*, *518*, *519*, 523, *524*, *525*; **23** 832; **28** *544*
Indian subcontinent: Saura **15** *216*, 444, *482*, *504*
Indian subcontinent: Shaivism **15** *214*, *438*, *463*, *479*, *480*, *481*, *482*, *488*, *496*, *497*, *502*, *530*, 535, *728*
Indian subcontinent: Shakta **15** *218*
Indian subcontinent: Vaishnavism **15** *472*, *484*, *495*, *502*
Indonesia **15** 778–9
Java **15** 778
Malaysia **20** 170*
Nepal **5** *121*; **6** *449*; **22** *767*, 767–8, *768*, 770, *770*, 771, *772*, 772–3
Shaivism **14** *561*
South-east Asia **29** 231
Thailand **30** 574, 598
Vietnam **6** 427, 428–9*, 430
see also SCULPTURE → types → *liṅga*
Hittite **1** 827
Holy Roman Empire (before 1648) **13** *160*; **26** 684–5*
Germany **26** 634*
Gothic **13** 85*, 86–7*, 115–18*, *160*
Romanesque **26** 631–5*, *634*, 645–6*, 684–5*, *685*
Honduras **14** 714–16*
Hong Kong **6** 562
Huari culture **14** 829*; **29** 171
Huastec **14** *830*, 830–31; **21** 188, 222
Hungary **14** 891*, 893–7*
Gothic **14** 893
Romanesque **26** 636, 638*
15th cent. **5** *86*
19th cent. **14** *895*
20th cent. **14** *897*
Iberia (peninsula) **15** 59
Ibibio **1** 332
Iceland **15** 69–71*
Idoma **15** 102–3
Ife (kingdom of) **15** *105*, 106*, *106*, *107*; **23** 131; **33** 555, 559
Igbo **1** 274, 330, 331; **5** 761
Inca **15** 163*; **29** 171–2
India, Republic of **15** *79*, 171–3*, *172*, *173*, 174, 175, 177
Indian subcontinent **14** *557*; **15** 206, *229*, 232, 411–12*, 414–17*, *421*, 422–38*, 439–45*, 449*, 451–2*, 454*, 458–9*, 476–84*, 498–506*, 541–2*, 548, 708, 719, 727, 730, 733; **23** 290, 832; **29** 438, 824; **30** 510
Andhra Pradesh **15** 438–9*, 533–41*, *534*
Bengal **15** 498–503*, 541
Bhil **15** *735*, 735
Bihar **15** 498–503*
Buddhism **10** 484; **15** *222*, *223*, 415–16, *431*, 439–42*, *440*, *441*, 451, 453–4*, *457*, *462*, 476, 499–502, *501*, 505, *505*, 521, *530*; **17** 857; **20** 818–19
Buddhism: 1st cent. **15** 449
Buddhism: 2nd cent. BC **15** *425*
Buddhism: 2nd cent. **15** 446

sculpture
historical and regional traditions
Indian subcontinent—cont.
Buddhism: 5th cent. **15** *455*, *456*, *470*
Buddhism: 7th cent. **15** *500*
Buddhism: 10th cent. **15** *500*
Buddhism: 11th cent. **30** *220*
Buddhism: 12th cent. **15** *501*
Chalukyas of Kalyana **15** 531–2
Chandella **15** 481
Chola **15** 514–18*
colonialism **7** *616*
Colonial period **15** 542–3*
Gandhara **15** *222*, 416, 445–9*, 452, 458
Gujarat **15** 449–50*, 461–3*, *462*, 484–91*, 541
Gupta **8** 768; **15** 194, 454–8*, 475–6*
Gurjara-Pratihara **15** 480–81, 486
Haryana **15** 484*, *484*
Himachal Pradesh **15** 483*
Hinduism **5** 95; **15** 443–4*, 502, *503*, 503–5, *504*, 514–20, *519*, 523, *524*; **23** 832; **28** *544*
Hinduism: 5th cent. **15** *416*, *468*, *469*, *471*
Hinduism: 8th cent. **15** *417*
Hinduism: 10th cent. **15** *515*
Hinduism: 11th cent. **15** *219*, *516*, *517*
Hinduism: 16th cent. **15** *518*
Hinduism: Saura **15** *216*, 444, *478*, *504*
Hinduism: Shaivism **1** *485*; **15** *214*, *438*, *463*, *480*, *481*, *482*, *488*, *496*, *497*, *502*, *530*, 535, *728*
Hinduism: Shakta **15** *218*
Hinduism: Vaishnavism **15** *472*, *484*, *495*, *502*
Hoysala **15** 532–3
Indus civilization **15** 417–22*
Islamic **15** 497
Jainism **5** 95; **15** *442*, 442–3*, 453, 467, 497–8, 508, 522, 523, 531; **20** 817
Jammu **15** *482*, 482–3*
Karnataka **15** 525–33*, 541
Kashmir **15** 458–9, 482–3*
Kerala **15** 521–5*, *523*, 541
Kushana **6** 215; **15** 439–41*, *444*, 444
Kushana period **15** 416, *440*, *442*, 451, 452–3*
Madya Pradesh **15** 467–75*, 494–8*, *496*
Madya Pradesh: 5th cent. **15** *468*, *469*, *470*, *471*, *472*
Madya Pradesh: 7th cent. **15** *495*
Madya Pradesh: 8th cent. **15** *495*
Maharashtra **15** 450–51*, 463–6*, 491–3*
Malwa **15** 460, *460*, *461*
Maratha period **15** 493
Mathura **7** 793
Maurya period **15** 422–4, *423*
Naga (people) **15** *733*
Nayaka period **15** 519–20*
Nolamba **15** 529–30
Orissa **15** 503–6*
Pala-Sena period **15** 498–503*
Pallava **15** 509–14
Punjab **15** 483–4*
Rajasthan **15** 449–50*, 459–60*, 484–91*, *487*, *488*, 541
Rashtrakuta **15** 492–3
Shunga period **15** 425
Tamil Nadu **15** 506–20*

sculpture
historical and regional traditions
Indian subcontinent—cont.
Uttar Pradesh **15** *480*, *481*, *482*
Vidarbha **15** 463–4*
Vijayanagara period **15** 329, 518–19*, 533, 539
Western Ganga **15** *528*
wood **15** 721, *733*
7th cent. AD **15** 478–9*
8th cent. AD **15** 479–80*
19th cent. **15** *725*
Indonesia **4** *420*; **15** 776*, 777–89*, *781*, *786*
Buddhism **15** 776, *778*, 778–9, *782*
Hinduism **15** 778–9
Indus civilization **15** 417–22*
Insular art **15** 876–8*
Iran, ancient **15** 913–15*, *914*
Elamite **15** *919*
Prehistoric **15** 913*
Ireland **16** 18–22*
Dark Age (ii) (*c*. 5th-8th cent. AD; Western Europe) **15** 876–8*
Romanesque **7** 458; **26** 618–19
20th cent. **16** *21*
Irian Jaya **16** *43*; **23** 733
Islamic **16** *135*
Central Asia, Western **16** 239
Indian subcontinent **15** 497
Malaysia **20** 170–71*
Philippines **24** 618*
Israel **16** 567*; **17** *579*, 579–80*
Italy **1** 711; **11** 192; **12** 110, 111, 116; **16** 683–8*, 734; **30** 496–8*; **33** 2, *3*
Arte Povera **2** *527*; **16** *708*
Baroque **7** *276*; **16** 697–704*; **20** *47*; **27** *830*
Cistercian Order **13** 97–8
Early Christian (*c*. AD 250–843) **16** 686*
Etruscan **10** 587, 589, *603*, *604*, *605*, *606*, *608*, 639; **16** *684*; **32** 744
Futurism **4** *201*; **11** *868*
Gothic **13** 87–92*, 93*, 123–4*; **16** 688*
Gothic: Campania **13** 98*
Gothic: Emilia-Romagna **13** 95–6*
Gothic: Lazio **13** 97–8*
Gothic: Lombardy **13** 94–5*
Gothic: Tuscany **13** 93–4*
Gothic: Umbria **13** 96–7*
Gothic: Veneto **13** 95*
Greece, ancient **30** 339
Lombard art **16** 686
Mannerism **12** *571*; **16** 695–7*
Neo-classicism **16** 704–7*
Néo-Grec **9** *404*
Renaissance **7** 783; **16** 688–95*; **30** *498*, *501*
Renaissance: Early Renaissance **16** 689–93*
Renaissance: High Renaissance **16** 693–5*
Roman **27** *14*, *18*, *19*, *21*, *23*, *32*; **29** VIII2
Romanesque **7** 455; **16** 687–8*; **26** 595, 619*, 625–8*, 644*
Romanesque: Abruzzi **26** 625*
Romanesque: Emilia-Romagna **26** 621*
Romanesque: Lazio **26** 624*
Romanesque: Lombardy **26** 620*
Romanesque: Tuscany **26** 622–4*
Romanesque: Umbria **26** 625*
Romanesque: Veneto **26** 622*
Verismo **9** *178*, *403*
15th cent. **20** *303*

sculpture
historical and regional traditions
Italy—cont.
17th cent. **30** 228
19th cent. **12** _268_; **27** _207_
20th cent. **4** _101_; **5** _279_; **16** _707_, 707–9*; **20** _353_, _429_
Jainism **5** 95; **15** _442_, 442–3*, 453, 467, 497–8, 508, 522, 523, 531; **20** 817
Jamaica **16** 883–5*, _884_
Japan **12** 626; **17** 97–106*, 133–9*, 267, 299, 341, 348*; **25** 175, 176; **31** 676
Asuka period (AD _c._ 552-645) **17** 106–9*, _107_, _109_
Buddhism **5** 120; **12** 626; **17** 97, 100, 106*, 126–7*, 130–32*, 320; **31** 167
Buddhism: Asuka-Hakuhō period (AD _c._ 552- 710) **17** _375_
Buddhism: Asuka period (AD _c._ 552-645) **17** _34_, 106–9*, _107_, _109_
Buddhism: Edo period (1600-1868) **17** _126_
Buddhism: Esoteric **17** 118
Buddhism: Hakuhō period (AD 654-710) **17** _99_, _110_, 110–12*, _111_, _112_
Buddhism: Heian period (AD 794-1185) **17** _116_, 116–21*, _117_, _118_, _120_
Buddhism: Kamakura period (1185-1333) **17** 121–6*, _123_, _125_
Buddhism: Nara period (AD 710-94) **17** 113–16*, _113_, _114_, _130_, _299_; **22** 504
Hakuhō period (AD 645-710) **17** _110_
Hakuhō style **17** 97, 107, 110–12*, _111_, _112_
Meiji period (1868-1912) **17** _134_, 134
Shinto **17** 31–2, 98, 127–9*; **28** 610–11*
Shōwa period (1926-89) **17** _136_, _137_
20th cent. **1** _738_; **17** 135–8
Java **15** 776, 777–83*, _781_; **29** 234
Buddhism **15** 778, _778_, 779, _782_
Hinduism **15** 778
Jerusalem, Latin Kingdom of **26** 629*
Jewish art **17** 575–80*, _579_
Jōmon culture **17** 97
Jordan **17** _655_
Karasuk culture **21** 883
Kassite **17** _837_; **21** 295
Kazakhstan **6** 220; **17** 867*
Kenya **17** 907–8*, _908_
Khmer **5** 486–90; **30** 599–600*
Buddhism **5** 100; **6** 430; **30** _600_
Cambodia **5** 499
Vietnam **6** 430
Khwarazm **6** 212, 218*
Knights Hospitaller **26** 295
Kongo **1** 263, 274, 322; **2** 86
Korea **18** 282*, 297–302*
Buddhism **18** 282–96*
Buddhism: 4th cent. **12** 626
Buddhism: 6th cent. **18** _284_
Buddhism: 7th cent. **5** _114_; **18** _283_, _285_
Buddhism: 8th cent. **18** _287_, _288_
Buddhism: 9th cent. **18** _290_
Buddhism: 10th cent. **18** _287_, _291_, _292_
Buddhism: 14th cent. **18** _294_
Buddhism: 16th cent. **18** _295_
Prehistoric **18** 297*
20th cent. **18** _302_

sculpture
historical and regional traditions—cont.
Kota (ii) (Gabon peoples) **18** 402*, _402_
Kuba (iii) (Zaïre) **1** 242, 322; **18** _486_
Kyrgyzstan **6** 220
Laos **5** 484; **18** 767–9*
Buddhism **18** 763, 767, _768_
Latvia
Lebanon **19** 8
Lega **19** 73–4
Lesotho **19** 242, _242_
Liberia **19** 310*
Lithuania **19** 496, _499_
Lombard art **16** 686
Luba **19** 742–3*
Lycia **33** _459_
Macedonia (ii) (former Yugoslavia) **19** _884_, 885*
Madagascar **20** 36–8*, _38_
Makonde (Mozambique) **30** 301
Malawi **20** _161_
Malaysia **20** 170*
Buddhism **20** 170*
Hinduism **20** 170*
Islamic **20** 170–71*
Mali **1** 274; **20** 199*
Malta (Republic of) **20** 209–10, _210_, 213–14*; **25** 512
Mande **1** 386
Mangbetu **1** _404_
Manteño culture **20** 316–17; **29** 193
Maori **20** _360_; **23** 62, 63, 731
Marquesas Islands **23** 731
Maya **1** 735; **4** 296–7; **17** 753; **21** 218, 254; **24** 743; **25** 825; **33** 511
Chacula style **27** 158
Merovingian **21** 163–4*
Mesoamerica, Pre-Columbian **1** 735; **17** 753; **21** _185_, _188_; **24** 743; **33** 617, 618
Aztec **21** _400_
Chacula style **27** 158
Huastec **14** _830_, 830–31
Maya **4** 296–7; **21** 254; **33** 511
Maya region **21** 219–20*, 221–2*, _222_, 225*
Mexico **5** _409_; **14** _830_; **30** _341_; **33** _618_
Remojadas **26** _181_
Tarascan **30** 340–41, _341_
Toltec **5** _409_; **31** 99
West Mexico **33** _103_
Mesopotamia **4** 641; **21** 271, 293–6*, 302*
Elamite **30** _28_
Kassite **17** _837_
Sumerian **18** _798_; **29** X2; **30** _423_; **31** _760_
Uruk (_c._ 4000-_c._ 2900 BC) **4** _641_
Mexico **21** 383, 385–7*, 390*; **29** 901, _901_
Pre-Columbian **5** _409_; **14** _830_; **21** _400_; **26** _181_; **30** _341_; **33** _618_
Minoan **8** 153; **21** 678*
Early Minoan (_c._ 3500/3000-_c._ 2050 BC) **21** 656, 678–9*
Late Minoan (_c._ 1600-_c._ 1050 BC) **21** 659, _679_, 679–80*
Middle Minoan (_c._ 2050-_c._ 1600 BC) **21** 657–8, 679–80*
Neolithic **21** 678–9*
Moche (culture) **29** 171
Moldova **21** 811–12*
Mongolia **21** 883*
Morocco **22** 129
Mossi **1** 383
Mozambique **22** 244*
Muisca **29** 146
Mycenaean **14** 351–2*

sculpture
historical and regional traditions—cont.
Nabataea **22** 419*, _419_
Native North Americans **22** 573–86*
Nazism **12** 408; **22** 711–12
Nepal **22** 758, 766–73*, 774–7*, 793–4
Buddhism **22** _758_, 758–9, 768–9, _769_, 770, _771_, 771, 773, _777_
Hinduism **5** _121_; **6** _449_; **22** _767_, 767–8, _768_, _770_, 770, 771, _772_, 772–3
Malla period **22** 773–6*, _774_, _775_, _776_
Netherlands, the **12** 132; **22** 854–6*, 857–9*, 860*, 861–2*
Gothic **13** 98–101*, 109–15*
Renaissance **16** 695
Romanesque **26** 630–31*, 644–5*
20th cent. **22** _861_
New Caledonia **23** 17–18, 731
New Zealand **23** 62–3*, _63_
Nicaragua **23** 81
Niger **1** 330
Nigeria **1** _247_, 281, 331; **4** I3; **23** 137–8*
Yoruba **15** 105*, _105_, _106_, 106–7*, _107_
20th cent. **23** _138_
Nok **1** 258, 274, 329, 330
Northern Ireland **16** 40–41*
Norway **3** 783; **14** 229; **21** 478; **23** 227–31*
Gothic **13** 102, 119
Romanesque **26** 639*, 644; **29** 580; **31** _364_
20th cent. **32** _497_
Nubia **23** _278_, _279_
Nupe **1** 281
Old Bering Sea culture **22** 574
Olmec **5** 408; **21** _185_, 217
Pre-Classic (_c._ 2000 BC-_c._ AD 250) **21** 218–19*
Ottonian **7** 590; **12** 399; **23** 646*, _647_, 647–9*, _648_
Pacific Islands **23** 730–33*, _732_
Pakistan **23** 801–2*, _802_
Palau **23** 730
Palestine **14** _273_
Panama **3** 279; **23** 904–5*; **29** 143, _144_, 144–5
Papua New Guinea **23** _732_, 732–3
Paraguay **24** _93_, _97_, 97–8*, 99*, _99_, 100*
Parthian **6** 217*; **15** 915; **21** 302; **24** _217_, 217–18*
Peru **24** 506–11*, _507_, _510_; **29** _167_
Philippines **24** 609, 617*, _619_, 619–20*
bulul **24** 609
Christianity **24** 618–19*
Islamic **24** 618*
Phoenician **24** 642*
Phrygian **1** 833
Pictish art **28** 233, 241
Poland **25** 109–16*
Constructivism **7** _771_
Gothic **25** 110–11
Romanesque **25** 109–10; **26** 636–7*
20th cent. **25** _115_
Portugal **25** 300–302*
Gothic **13** 102*, 124–5*; **25** _301_
Indian subcontinent **15** 542
Romanesque **26** 611*, 648*
19th cent. **28** _913_
20th cent. **25** _302_

sculpture
historical and regional traditions—cont.
Prehistoric art **25** 491
Afghanistan **1** 193–4*, _194_
Cyprus, ancient **8** 337–8*, 339*
France **25** _544_
Gumelniţa culture **25** 512
Iran, ancient **15** 913*
Iron Age **25** _544_, 544–5*
Japan **17** 102–6*
Korea **18** 297*
Malta (Republic of) **25** 512
Neolithic **10** _506_; **25** 509*, 512–13*
Nubia **23** _278_, _279_
Palestine **14** _273_
Sardinia **27** 835
Serbia **25** _464_
Syria **2** _661_
Vinča culture **25** _464_
Puerto Rico **25** 702*, _702_
Punic **25** 733–4*
Recuay culture **26** 66; **29** 170
Remojadas **26** _181_
Rhodes (island) **13** 423; **26** 291–3*
bronze **26** 292
Daidalic **13** 443
Knights Hospitaller **26** 295
Romanesque **7** 454–5*; **8** 835; **22** 520; **26** 594–5*, 635–6*, 640–41*
Austria **2** 798–9*; **26** 634–5*
Belgium **26** 630–31*, 644–5*
Britain **26** 611–12*
Catalonia **26** 609–10*
Croatia **8** 177
Czech Republic **26** 637–8*
Denmark **8** 737–8; **26** 304, 640*
England **7** 455; **19** 405; **26** 613–16*, 643–4*
France **2** 728; **7** 454; **26** 596–7*, 600–601*, 641*; **31** 225
France: Auvergne **26** 601*
France: Burgundy **26** 601–2*
France: First Romanesque **26** 609
France: Languedoc **26** 602–3*
France: Loire Valley **26** 598–9*
France: Normandy **26** 597–8*
France: Provence **26** 603–4*
France: Roussillon **26** 604*, 609–10*
Germany **12** 399; **26** 632–3*, 634*
Holy Roman Empire (before 1648) **26** 631–5*, _634_, 645–6*, 684–5*, _685_
Hungary **26** 636, 638*
Ireland **7** 458; **26** 618–19
Italy **7** 455; **16** 687–8*; **26** 595, 619*, 625–8*, 644*
Italy: Abruzzi **26** 625*
Italy: Emilia-Romagna **26** 621*
Italy: Lazio **26** 624*
Italy: Lombardy **26** 620*
Italy: Tuscany **26** 622–4*
Italy: Umbria **26** 625*
Italy: Veneto **26** 622*
Jerusalem, Latin Kingdom of **26** 629*
Netherlands, the **26** 630–31*, 644–5*
Norway **26** 639*, 644; **29** 580; **31** _364_
Poland **25** 109–10; **26** 636–7*
Portugal **26** 611*, 648*
Scandinavia **26** 639–40*, 646–7*
Sicily **26** 619, 628–9*
Spain **7** 455; **26** 604–5*, 606–7*, 608–9*, 642–3*; **28** _727_, 727–8; **29** 288

sculpture
historical and regional traditions
Romanesque—cont.
Sweden **19** _796_; **26** 639*; **30** 83
Switzerland **26** 635*
Wales **26** 617–18*
Romania **26** 710*, 711–12*, 713*, 714*, 715*, 716*
Rome, ancient **12** 69, 286, 625, 626, 627; **23** 291; **25** 43, _178_; **26** 854, 856–7, 861; **27** 8*, 9–19*, 20–29*, 32, 43, 85
Antonine **27** 39–40*
Augustan **27** 29*, 30–32*, 41–2*
Black Sea Colonies **4** _113_
Classical **7** 783; **9** 34; **27** 8–9*
Classical, Late **23** _291_
Constantine **27** 43–5*
Crete **8** 155
Cyprus, ancient **8** 342*
Denmark **27** _17_
Early Christian (_c._ AD 250-843) **27** _19_
Egypt **26** 855
England **19** _579_
Etruscan **24** 319–20*
Flavian **27** 34–5*
France **12** _70_; **27** 31
Greece **13** _462_; **25** 44–5, _178_; **27** 85
Hadrianic **27** 37–9*
Hellenistic **13** 466
Italy **2** 168; **16** 684–5; **27** _8_, _14_, _18_, _21_, _23_, _32_; **29** _562_, VIII2
Julio-Claudian **27** 32–4*
Late Antiquity **18** _824_
Republican **13** 468; **24** 258; **27** 29–30*; **29** 559–60, _561_
Tetrarchs **27** 43*
Trajanic **27** 35–6*
Turkey **10** _428_
Russia **27** 382*, 387*, 389*, 390–93*, 396*, 397*, 398*
Constructivism **7** _768_; **25** _25_
20th cent. **27** _397_; **30** _363_
Ryūkyū Islands **27** 470*
Sambaquí culture **29** _197_, 197–8*
San Agustín culture **27** 700, _700_, 701
Santa Cruz Islands **23** 732
Sardinia **25** 734; **27** 835, 836
Sasanian **15** 915; **21** 302
Scandinavia **11** 100
Gothic **13** 102–3*, 118–20*
Romanesque **26** 639–40*, 646–7*
Scotland **11** _55_; **28** 241–4*
Seleucid **21** 302; **28** 383
Senegal **28** 406*
Senufo **1** 278, 279, 322
Serbia **25** _464_; **28** 452–4*
Shinto **17** 31–2, 98, 127–9*, _128_; **28** 610–11*
Sicily **16** 688; **28** 654
Romanesque **26** 619, 628–9*
6th cent. BC **28** _654_
Singapore **28** 774–5*
Slovakia **28** 854–5*
Slovenia **28** 861–2*
Society Islands **28** 922
Sogdiana **6** 219–21*, _220_
Solomon Islands **23** 732
South Africa **29** 104, 111–13*, _112_
South America, Pre-Columbian **29** 141–5*, 166*, 167–72*, 193–4*
Alamito culture **29** _190_
Argentina **29** _190_
Chavín culture **6** 521–2*; **29** 167, _167_
Colombia **27** 700, _700_, 701

sculpture
historical and regional traditions
South America, Pre-Columbian—cont.
Costa Rica **9** *678*, *679*; **29** 143
Gran Nicoya culture **13** 310–11
Panama **29** 143, *144*, 144–5
Peru **29** *167*
Recuay culture **26** 66
Sambaquí culture **29** *197*, 197–8*
San Agustín culture **27** 700, *700*, 701
stone **9** 677–9
Tiahuanaco **29** 168
Veraguas culture **32** 238–9
South-east Asia **30** 510
Buddhism **5** 100*; **29** 231
Hinduism **29** 231
Shaivism **14** *561*
Spain **25** 174; **29** 287–9*, 293–5*
Abstract art **23** *629*
Baroque **29** 291–3*
Churrigueresque **29** 292
Cubism **12** *919*; **16** *57*
Early Christian (*c.* AD 250-843) **29** 287
Gothic **13** 103–8*, 122–3*; **29** 288–9
Neo-classicism **29** *20*
Philippines **24** 618–19
Renaissance **16** 695; **29** 289–91*
Rococo **29** 292–3
Romanesque **7** 455; **26** 604–5*, 606–7*, 608–9*, 642–3*; **28** 727–8; **29** 288
Visigothic **29** 287
5th cent. BC **15** *60*
16th cent. **3** 844
20th cent. **10** *910*; **12** *148*; **16** *57*; **21** *709*; **29** 295–7*, *296*
Sri Lanka **29** 456–9*, 460–62*, 478
Buddhism **5** 98; **29** *457*, 461, *479*
20th cent. **29** *461*
Sudan **29** 897*, *897*
Sumatra **15** 776, 787–8*; **29** 231
Sumerian **18** *798*; **21** 294; **29** X2; **30** *423*; **31** *760*
Surinam **30** 16*
Swaziland **30** 63
Sweden **30** 83–7*
Gothic **13** 102–3, 119, 120; **30** 83
Neo-classicism **30** *86*
Romanesque **19** *796*; **26** 639*; **30** 83
20th cent. **30** *87*
Switzerland **30** 136–40*
Concrete art **30** *138*
Gothic **30** 136
Romanesque **26** 635*
20th cent. **30** *139*
Syria **2** *661*; **13** 465
Syria-Palestine **1** 491–2, *492*; **14** *64*; **20** *410*; **30** 185, 186, 187, 192–4*, *193*
Hurrian **15** *33*
Tabwa **1** 282
Tahiti **12** *191*
Tairona **29** 146, 193
Tajikistan **6** *214*; **30** 252–3*
Tanzania **30** 301*
Tarascan **21** 217; **30** 340–41, *341*
Mesoamerica, Pre-Columbian **30** 340–41
Post-Classic (*c.* AD 900-1521) **21** 225*
Teutonic Order **28** 861

sculpture
historical and regional traditions—cont.
Thailand **5** 484; **29** 231; **30** 593*, 597–8*, 599–601*, 603–4*, 605–6*, 607–8*
Buddhism **5** 100; **28** *640*; **29** *911*; **30** 573–4, 593–5*, *594*, *595*, 596–7*, *597*, *598*, 599*, *600*, *601*, 601–4*, *602*, *605*, 605–6*, 607, *607*
Hinduism **30** 574, 598
Thracian **5** 155
Tiahuanaco **29** 168, 171
Tibet **30** 821–7*
Bon (religion) **30** 822
Buddhism **30** 351, 809, 821–7, *823*, *824*, *825*, *826*, *827*
Togo **31** *74*
Tokharistan **6** *221*, 221–2*
Toltec **5** *409*; **31** 99
Tonga (Pacific Islands) **31** 144
Torres Strait Islands **23** 733
Trinidad and Tobago **31** 335–6*
Tunisia **31** 424–6*
Turkey **31** 454–5*
Greece, ancient **8** *870*; **14** *70*
marble **14** *69*, *70*
Roman **10** *428*
Urartian **31** *700*
Turkmenistan **31** 459*
Uganda **31** 528*
Ukraine **31** 560–61*
United Arab Emirates **2** *260*
United States of America **1** *422*; **3** 114; **31** 610*, 612–15*; **33** 4
Abstract art **1** *80*; **23** *29*
African American art **1** *441*
Cubism **19** *437*
Jewish art **17** 578*
Minimalism **2** *12*; **19** *289*; **21** *646*
Neo-classicism **25** *401*
Surrealism **31** *613*
19th cent. **15** 23; **26** *401*
20th cent. **9** *357*, *359*; **12** *795*, VII2; **16** *58*; **18** *594*; **22** *426*; **23** *12*, *397*; **28** *877*; **31** *614*, *615*; **33** *97*
Urartian **31** *700*, 700
Uruguay **31** 754–6*
Uzbekistan **31** 782–3*
Valdivia culture **29** 169
Vanuatu **23** 732
Venda **1** 415, 418
Venetian Empire **32** 160
Venezuela **32** 172–6*
Veraguas culture **32** 238–9
Vietnam **5** 484; **32** 478–81*
Buddhism **5** *100*; **6** 427–8*; **9** 133; **32** 478, *478*, *479*, 479–80
Buddhism: Mahayana **6** *428*
Champa **6** 426–7*, 429–31*
Hinduism **6** 427, 428–9*, 430
Khmer **6** 430
Socialist Realism **32** *480*
Viking **2** 71*; **32** 529
Vinča culture **25** *464*
Visigothic **29** 287
Wales **26** 617–18*; **32** 786–8*
West Mexico **33** 103, *103*
Yayoi culture **17** 97
Yemen **2** *258*, *259*
Yoruba **1** 274, 278, 322, 331, 332, 427; **4** I3; **15** *105*, *106*, 106–7*, *107*; **33** 555–7*
Nigeria **15** 105*
Zaïre **18** *486*
Zambia **1** 261; **33** 603*
Zapotec **21** 217, 218; **33** 619
Zimbabwe **33** 679, *679*
Zulu **1** 323; **29** 104
historiography *see under* HISTORIOGRAPHY → types

sculpture—cont.
materials **14** 787
agalmatolite **27** *437*
alabaster (gypsum)
Arabia **2** *256*
Denmark **11** *219*
England **10** 260
France **1** *766*
Germany **21** *72*
Iran, ancient **15** 913
Netherlands, the **3** *456*; **22** *858*
Poland **25** 114
Rome, ancient **27** 15
alabaster (limestone) **25** 733; **29** X1
aluminium **1** 737–8*, *738*; **12** *610*, 613; **24** *34*; **27** *397*
artificial stone **2** 541, *541*; **19** *95*
basalt **4** *265*; **5** *121*; **14** *64*, *273*; **21** *188*; **22** *419*; **23** 417; **30** *341*
beads **1** *325*; **4** I3; **7** *197*; **29** 104
beeswax **33** 1
bekhen stone **9** *881*; **22** *399*; **27** 14, *14*
box-wood **29** *728*
brass
Benin, Kingdom of **3** *723*, *724*
China **6** 706; **30** *398*
England **10** *268*
Germany **32** *605*
Ife (kingdom of) **15** *106*
India, Republic of **15** *173*
Indian subcontinent **15** 733, 735, *735*
Kota (ii) (Gabon peoples) **18** *402*
Tibet **30** 822, *823*, *824*, *825*, *826*, *827*
brick **4** 789; **5** *487*; **15** 413
bronze **4** 851, 855; **7** 564, 670–72; **10** 702; **29** 559
Aegean **8** 262
Afghanistan **1** 207
Albania **1** *541*
Arabia **2** 258–9
Argentina **33** *569*
Australia **2** 752, *753*
Austria **2** *800*, 802, *803*; **10** *894*
Baroque **27** *830*
Belgium **3** *571*; **21** *499*
Buddhism **6** 298, 706; **17** 120
Buddhism: Afghanistan **1** 207
Buddhism: Burma **5** *240*, 241
Buddhism: Cambodia **5** 485
Buddhism: China **6** 706, 707, *708*, *710*, 712, 718, *719*, *720*, 720–22, 835; **7** 68
Buddhism: Indian subcontinent **15** *223*, 476, *530*, 530–31
Buddhism: Japan **17** *34*, *107*, *110*, 110–12, *111*, *112*, *113*, 320, *375*
Buddhism: Korea **5** *114*; **18** *284*, *285*, *287*, *294*
Buddhism: Laos **18** 768, *768*
Buddhism: Sri Lanka **29** *460*, *479*
Buddhism: Thailand **30** 593–5*, 596–7, *597*, *598*, *601*, 601–2*, *602*, *605*, *607*
Buddhism: Tibet **30** 351
Burma **5** 239, *240*, 241
Cambodia **5** 485, 497–8*
Central Asia, Eastern **6** 298
Chile **6** *598*
China **6** 718, 726–7, 733, 835, 855–6; **7** 68; **24** 258
China: Buddhism **6** *719*, *720*
China: Daoism **6** *628*
China: Han period (206 BC-AD 220) **8** *853*
China: Ming period (1368-1644) **6** 720–22

sculpture
materials
bronze—cont.
China: Northern and Southern Dynasties (AD 310- 589) **6** 707, *708*, *710*, 712
China: Qing period (1644-1911) **6** *733*
China: Shang period (*c.* 1600-*c.* 1050 BC) **7** 160; **13** *736*
China: Tang period (AD 618-907) **6** 730
China: Zhou period (*c.* 1050-256 BC) **29** *906*
Crete **8** 154; **21** *679*, 679–80
Croatia **21** *316*
Cyprus, ancient **8** 342
Czech Republic **8** *249*; **32** *731*; **33** *435*
Daoism **6** *628*
Dian culture **8** *853*
Early Christian (*c.* AD 250-843) **18** *824*
Edo (Africa) **9** 736
Egypt, ancient **5** *71*; **9** 855, *856*, 860, *861*, 886
Ejagham **10** 124*
Elamite **15** *919*
England **10** *438*
England: New Sculpture **23** *34*; **30** *762*
England: 19th cent. **11** *238*
England: 20th cent. **11** *157*
Etruscan **10** 587, 602, 604–6, *605*, *608*, 608; **16** *684*
France: Baroque **7** *423*; **24** *786*
France: Mannerism **11** *558*
France: Neo-classicism **14** *798*; **27** *311*
France: Romanticism **3** *313*, *315*
France: 16th cent. **27** *548*
France: 17th cent. **8** *94*; **27** *822*
France: 19th cent. **26** *509*, *510*
France: 20th cent **4** *661*; **9** *362*; **12** *566*; **20** *825*, *828*; **26** *351*
Georgia **12** *322*
Germany **28** 492
Germany: Baroque **3** *798*
Germany: Gothic **13** *160*
Germany: Mannerism **12** *346*, *347*; **18** *478*, *479*; **26** *104*
Germany: Renaissance **11** *223*; **12** *402*
Germany: 20th cent. **20** *396*
Gothic **13** *160*
Greece, ancient **13** 434–5*
Greece, ancient: Archaic **8** 262, 458; **13** 422; **24** *328*
Greece, ancient: Archaic, Late **13** 448
Greece, ancient: Classical, Early **1** 481; **6** 9; **8** *696*; **13** 433, 438; **23** 290; **24** 258; **25** 177, *178*, *179*
Greece, ancient: Classical, High **8** 262; **13** *429*, *453*; **26** *297*
Greece, ancient: Classical, Late **13** *460*; **25** *456*
Greece, ancient: Geometric **8** *262*; **13** 441–2, *442*
Greece, ancient: Hellenistic **30** 339
Greece, ancient: Proto-Daidalic **13** *443*
Hinduism **15** *219*, *516*, *517*, 523, *728*
Holy Roman Empire (before 1648) **13** *160*; **26** 684–5*, *685*
Hungary **14** *897*
Hurrian **15** *33*
India, Republic of **15** 175

sculpture
materials
bronze—cont.
Indian subcontinent **14** *557*; **15** *223*, 453, 476, *516*, 516, *517*, 521, 522, 523, *523*, 524, *525*, *530*, 530–31, 708, *725*, *728*, 730
Indonesia **15** 776, 777
Iran, ancient **15** *919*
Ireland **16** *21*
Islamic **16** *135*
Italy **12** 539; **30** 339
Italy: Baroque **2** *609*; **5** *533*; **27** *830*
Italy: Etruscan **10** 587, *605*, *608*; **16** *684*
Italy: Futurism **4** *201*; **11** *866*
Italy: Mannerism **1** *791*; **3** *162*, *469*; **6** *142*, *145*; **12** *572*
Italy: Renaissance **2** *140*, *141*; **3** *637*; **9** *127*; **12** *539*; **16** *690*; **19** *202*; **27** *448*; **29** *561*; **32** *105*, *360*, *362*
Italy: Roman **14** *443*; **27** *9*, *10*
Italy: 17th cent. **7** *842*
Italy: 20th cent. **16** *707*; **20** *353*, *429*
Jainism **15** 453, 531
Japan **17** 100–101*, 110–12, 120, 320
Japan: Asuka-Hakuhō period (*c.* 552-710) **17** *34*, *375*
Japan: Asuka period (AD *C.* 552-645) **17** *107*
Japan: Hakuhō period (AD 645-710) **17** *110*, *111*, *112*
Japan: Nara period (AD 710-94) **17** *113*; **22** *497*
Java **15** 777
Korea **5** *114*; **18** *284*, *285*, *287*, *294*, 297, 300, 301, 302
Laos **18** 768, *768*
Latvia
Mesopotamia **30** *28*
Mexico **21** *384*
Minoan **21** *679*, 679–80
New Zealand **23** 63, *63*; **33** *374*
Norway **3** 783; **23** *230*; **32** *497*
Pakistan **23** *802*
Parthian **24** *217*
Peru **24** *510*
Portugal **19** *893*
Prehistoric art **25** *527*
Punic **25** 734
Rhodes (island) **26** 292
Romanesque **26** 684–5*, *685*
Rome, ancient **8** 342; **25** 43; **27** 10
Rome, ancient: Augustan **27** 32
Rome, ancient: Italy **2** 168; **14** *443*
Rome, ancient: Republican **8** 263; **24** 258; **27** *9*, 10–11, 12, 29, 85; **29** *561*, *562*
Russia **10** *442*
Sardinia **25** 734
Seleucid **28** 384
Slovakia **28** *855*
South Africa **29** *112*
Spain **21** *709*
Sri Lanka **29** *460*, *461*, 478, *479*
Switzerland **30** *138*
Syria-Palestine **15** *33*; **30** 193
Thailand **30** 573, 593–5*, 596–7, *597*, *598*, *601*, 601–2*, *602*, *605*, *607*
Tibet **30** 351
Turkey **31** *700*
United States of America **18** *594*; **31** 611, *613*
Urartian **31** 700, *700*
Vietnam **32** 480
Yemen **2** *258*, *259*
20th cent. **22** *426*
camphor-wood **17** *99*, *109*

sculpture
materials—cont.
cast iron **7** 98, 99–100, *99*, *100*; **8** *386*
celluloid **25** 25, *25*
cement **1** 331–2, *332*; **5** 500; **10** 124; **15** 64, 65; **18** 769; **23** 137–8; **31** *74*
ceramics **1** 44, 328*; **11** 106; **17** 267–8
chlorite **15** *504*, 913, 914
clay **6** *219*; **7** 607; **10** 702
Afghanistan **1** 193, 196, 197, *197*, 198, *199*
Africa **1** 418
Bhutan **3** 914
Central Asia, Eastern **6** 298, 299, *300*
Central Asia, Western **6** *194*, *214*, *215*, 216, *216*, 217, 218, 219–20, *221*, 221–2
China **6** 706, 708, 717, *734*
Greece, ancient **13** 436–7*
India, Republic of **15** 174
Indian subcontinent **30** *220*
Japan **17** *31*, 98–9
Korea **18** *292*, 295
Mesoamerica, Pre-Columbian **21** 236; **26** *181*; **33** 617
Nubia **23** *278*
Serbia **25** *464*
concrete **5** *753*; **7** 691*, 696–7*, *697*; **23** *138*
copper **2** 639; **15** *223*; **22** *772*
Bhutan **3** 914, *914*
Egypt, ancient **10** 35, *35*
Ife (kingdom of) **15** *105*
India, Republic of **15** *173*
Kota (ii) (Gabon peoples) **18** *402*
Nepal **22** *755*, *769*, *776*, *777*
Tibet **30** 822
coral **6** 706
cypress **17** 100
diorite **2** *661*; **9** *869*; **21** 294; **29** X2; **30** *423*
drills **27** *17*
earthenwares **6** *891*; **17** *105*
electricity **29** 97
enamel **7** 68; **13** 169; **30** *497*
feathers **10** *848*
felt **3** *891*
fibreglass **11** 55, *55*; **18** *831*; **25** 26
gesso **6** 717, 725; **12** 501, 626
gilding **6** *300*; **15** *501*; **22** *497*
glass **1** *233*; **2** *588*; **6** 717; **10** 55, 57, *58*; **12** *795*, 795–6*, VII2; **17** 100; **25** 176
glazes **25** 175
gold **8** 261, 263; **10** *37*; **13** 435, 596; **23** 647; **27** 15–16; **30** 823
Baule **3** 407
gold leaf **5** 747; **17** 100, *116*; **27** 15
granite
Egypt **9** *766*
Egypt, ancient **9** 815, *857*, *862*, *876*, *879*, *885*, *889*, *893*; **10** *77*; **14** *758*; **28** *492*; **30** *297*
Finland **11** 100
Indian subcontinent **15** *515*, *518*, *519*, *534*; **17** *761*
Japan **17** 102
Korea **18** *283*, *288*, 298, 302
Malawi **20** *161*
Nubia **23** *279*
Rome, ancient **27** 14
South America, Pre-Columbian **29** *167*
grasses **15** 727
greenstone **21** *185*
grounds **25** 174–5*
Guaiacum wood **16** *879*
gypsum **10** 606, *606*; **26** *401*; **27** 13; **29** *923*
hair **1** *404*; **3** *672*; **6** 299; **7** *197*
hemp **17** 101

sculpture
materials—cont.
Hornton stone **22** *57*
inlays **3** 914; **15** 414
inscriptions **15** 440, 443; **17** 107, 126
iron **10** 702; **16** 56–8*
Africa **1** *233*, 385
Bamana **3** 133–4
Benin Republic **11** *246*
China **6** 706, 721, *724*, 730, 731
Côte d'Ivoire **8** *23*
Czech Republic **8** *388*
France **24** *722*; **30** *21*
Italy **16** *708*
Japan **17** 102*
Korea **18** 289, *290*, *291*
Spain **12** *148*; **16** *57*
Switzerland **30** 139
ivory **1** *219*, 325–8*; **13** 435, 596, 597; **16** 798, 799
jackfruit-wood **15** 730
lacquer **17** 100
Buddhism **18** 606
Burma **18** *607*
Cambodia **5** 500
China **6** 706, 725; **7** 14, 138
Japan **17** 99, 101–2*, *114*, 115–16, *116*, 117, 118, *130*, *136*, 299, *299*
Laos **18** 768
Vietnam **32** 479, *479*
lead **1** *133*; **10** 264; **18** 902–3; **27** 10
leather **1** *322*; **15** *172*; **23** 254
light **29** 97
limestone **9** 590–91; **29** 701
Aegean **8** 262
Afghanistan **1** 193, *194*
Anatolia, ancient **1** *833*
Arabia **2** *257*
Austria **2** *804*
China **19** *638*
Cyprus, ancient **8** 340, *340*, *342*
Czech Republic **13** *90*
Egypt, ancient **1** *793*; **9** *815*, 815, *858*, *859*, *863*, *867*; **30** *297*
England **10** *262*
France **4** *546*; **7** *478*; **11** *554*
Germany **14** *450*
Gothic **2** *799*; **4** *583*; **13** *90*
Greece, ancient **13** 434*, 443
Hungary **5** *86*
Indonesia **15** *781*
Iran, ancient **15** 914
Jordan **17** *655*
Ottonian **23** 646
Portugal **13** *101*
Romanesque **26** *615*
Rome, ancient **27** 9–10, 13, 14
Scandinavia **13** 103
Sicily **28** 654, *654*
Sri Lanka **29** *457*
Thailand **30** *595*
United States of America **19** *437*
Zambia **33** 603
lime-wood **10** *455*, *457*; **13** *316*; **22** *281*; **23** *648*, *887*; **29** *729*, *761*
magnesite **15** *914*
mahogany **3** *574*; **13** *767*; **16** *884*
marble **29** 559
Afghanistan **1** 198–9
African American art **1** *441*
Austria **5** *628*
Belgium **3** *417*, *571*; **9** *413*
Black Sea Colonies **4** *113*
Brazil **4** *720*
Byzantine **9** 587, *587*
China **6** 706; **7** *57*
Croatia **23** *93*
Cyprus, ancient **8** 340, 342; **27** *609*
Denmark **11** *219*; **30** *764*, *765*

sculpture
materials
marble—cont.
Early Christian (*c.* AD 250–843) **9** 587, 588
Egypt, ancient **9** *895*; **13** *465*
England: Baroque **10** *264*
England: Baroque Revival **22** *28*
England: Neo-classicism **5** *629*; **10** *265*; **11** *163*
England: Rococo **27** *244*
England: Roman **19** *579*
England: 16th cent. **10** *262*
England: 18th cent. **3** *184*; **4** *79*; **27** *468*; **28** *64*; **29** *564*
England: 19th cent. **6** *456*; **12** *598*
England: 20th cent. **3** *78*
Etruscan **10** 589, *589*
Finland **11** *99*
France: Baroque **2** *91*; **12** *725*, *726*; **24** *785*, *786*; **25** *706*; **28** *846*; **29** *563*
France: Baroque Revival **5** *879*
France: Cubism **33** *590*
France: Mannerism **24** *813*
France: Neo-classicism **4** *301*; **6** *517*; **8** *566*; **10** *764*; **11** *561*; **25** *418*
France: Renaissance **1** *766*; **7** *596*
France: Rococo **8** *71*; **28** *845*
France: 16th cent. **11** *503*; **24** *133*; **27** *547*
France: 17th cent. **8** *94*
France: 18th cent. **4** *510*; **7** *450*; **23** *795*
France: 19th cent. **6** *468*; **11** *564*
France: 20th cent **2** *491*; **4** *660*; **20** *120*
Germany: Gothic **12** *400*
Germany: Neo-classicism **9** *691*
Germany: Rococo **1** *712*
Germany: 18th cent. **28** *42*
Germany: 19th cent. **9** *692*; **14** *526*
Gothic **13** *94*, *96*, *97*, *108*; **20** *728*; **26** *400*
Gothic: Italy **2** *482*, *483*; **24** *873*, *875*
Greece, ancient **13** *422*, *423*, 433, 436
Greece, ancient: Archaic **2** 679; **8** 457, *688*, *695*, *697*, *870*; **13** 434*, 445, *446*; **18** *244*, *409*, *410*; **22** 699, *699*; **27** 688, *689*
Greece, ancient: Archaic, Late **10** *449*; **13** *448*, *449*; **18** *244*
Greece, ancient: Classical, Early **1** *480*; **13** *425*, *452*; **24** *205*; **25** *179*
Greece, ancient: Classical, High **8** 262, *689*; **13** 438, *454*, *456*; **23** *433*; **25** *576*
Greece, ancient: Classical, Late **10** *434*; **13** *459*; **14** *69*, *70*; **19** *853*; **23** *291*
Greece, ancient: Hellenistic **13** *463*, *466*; **24** *414*; **27** *692*
Greece, ancient: Roman **13** 438
Hungary **14** *895*
Ireland **14** *500*
Italy: Baroque **1** *627*, *711*; **3** *262*, *828*, *829*; **11** *18*, *189*, *280*; **16** *698*; **20** *47*, *909*; **27** *347*, *830*; **29** *563*; **31** *790*
Italy: Etruscan **10** *589*, 589
Italy: Gothic **2** *482*, *483*; **13** *94*, *96*, *97*; **20** *728*; **24** *873*, *875*; **26** *400*; **28** *680*; **32** *227*
Italy: Mannerism **1** *790*, *791*; **8** *511*; **12** *571*; **16** *696*; **27** *203*; **29** *558*, *562*

sculpture
materials
marble—cont.
Italy: Neo-Classicism **3** *295*, *296*; **5** *627*; **16** *705*; **22** *736*
Italy: Néo-Grec **9** *404*
Italy: Renaissance **1** *747*; **3** *138*, *158*; **4** *738*; **5** *359*, *361*; **7** *367*; **9** *123*; **11** *27*, *203*; **16** *691*, *693*, *694*, *766*, *840*; **18** *673*; **19** *560*; **21** *434*, *436*, *437*, *438*; **22** *32*, *461*; **26** *439*; **27** *769*, *770*, *773*; **29** *24*
Italy: Roman **27** *21*, *22*, *32*; **29** *389*, VIII2
Italy: Romanesque **2** *132*; **21** *773*
Italy: 15th cent. **10** *854*; **20** *303*
Italy: 16th cent. **6** *90*; **19** *557*; **25** *256*
Italy: 17th cent. **21** *755*
Italy: 18th cent. **21** *890*
Japan **17** *137*
Lithuania **19** *499*
Mesopotamia **31** *760*
Nigeria **23** *138*
Peru **24** *510*
Poland **25** 114
Portugal **1** *742*; **28** *913*
Romanesque **21** *773*
Rome, ancient **25** 44–5; **26** 854
Rome, ancient: Antonine **8** 342; **27** *17*
Rome, ancient: Augustan **27** 10, 13–14, *32*
Rome, ancient: Black Sea colonies **4** *113*
Rome, ancient: Constantinian **27** 45
Rome, ancient: Italy **27** *21*, *23*; **29** VIII2
Rome, ancient: Julio-Claudian **27** *33*
Rome, ancient: Republican **2** *169*; **13** *462*; **19** *579*, *853*; **23** *291*; **25** *178*; **27** *8*, 12–13, 15, 29
Rome, ancient: Turkey **10** *428*
Spain **13** *108*; **20** *68*; **23** *629*; **29** *20*, 291, *294*, *296*
Sumerian **31** *760*
Sweden **28** *462*
Turkey **8** *870*; **9** *587*; **10** *428*; **14** *69*, *70*
United States of America **1** *441*; **25** *401*
16th cent. **32** *649*
metal **10** 702
Africa **1** *322*
China **6** 726
Egypt, ancient **10** 35–7*
Haiti **14** 58
Indian subcontinent **15** 499, *500*, *501*, 505
Korea **18** 301
Nepal **22** 768–9*, 771–3*, 774–6*
mica **17** 99
mirrors **1** *219*
mixed-media **1** 300–301*
mosaics **11** 192; **21** 254
mud **1** 330–31*
nails **6** 217
neon **2** *400*; **16** *708*; **22** 747, *748*
oak **13** *114*, *119*, *121*; **22** *856*; **24** *776*
oil-drums **14** 58
paints **25** 477
paper **6** 725; **17** 99
pastiglia **13** 139
pearls **5** 500; **6** 706
pear-wood **33** II1
Perspex **10** 267
picrolite **8** *338*
pigments **25** 477
pine **17** 109

sculpture
materials—cont.
pith **3** 169
plaster
Bactria **6** 214–15
China **6** 706
Czech Republic **8** *387*
Denmark **29** *541*
Egypt, ancient **10** 68
England **11** *164*
France **12** *564*; **30** *21*
Germany **3** *243*
Greece **13** *354*
Greece, ancient **13** 438
Indonesia **15** 779
Italy **9** *403*; **12** *268*
Korea **18** 300, 301, 302
Mycenaean **14** *352*
Poland **25** *115*
Sogdiana **6** *220*
United States of America **31** 611
plastic **25** 25–6*
plastics **16** *708*
porcelain **9** *239*
porphyry **20** *798*; **26** 855; **27** 10, 13, 14, 43
pottery **1** 285; **6** 717, 882; **16** 734; **19** *242*
quartzite **7** XII; **9** 813, 815; **30** *694*; **31** *482*
ragstone **6** *158*
rock crystal **26** *486*
sand **1** 44–5*, *45*
sandstone
Belgium **29** *660*
Buddhism **5** *100*, *462*; **6** *716*, *718*
Cambodia **5** *462*, *485*, *488*, *489*, *497*, *498*
China **6** 706, *714*, *716*, *718*; **33** *574*
Denmark **8** *741*
Egypt, ancient **9** 815, *883*
Germany **3** *142*; **11** *751*; **12** *344*; **13** *91*, *92*, *683*, *684*; **26** *370*
Gothic **13** *91*, *92*, 102; **29** *6*
Hinduism **15** *479*, *480*, *481*, *482*
Iberia (peninsula) **15** 59, *60*
Indian subcontinent **15** *214*, *218*, *229*, *423*, *427*, *430*, *440*, *441*, *442*, *444*, *455*, *456*, *457*, *460*, *478*, *479*, *480*, *481*, *495*, *496*, *497*
Jewish art **17** *579*
Mesoamerica, Pre-Columbian **14** 830, *830*
Ottonian **23** 646, *647*
Poland **25** *109*
Romanesque **25** *109*
Thailand **30** *600*, 606
Vietnam **32** *478*
schist **1** 193, 195, *196*; **15** *222*, *461*, 499; **28** *544*
sealants **25** 174*
serpentine **27** 15; **33** *679*
shells **1** *283*; **5** 747; **7** 138
silver **8** 261, 263
France **4** *458*
Germany **13** *679*
Guatemala **13** *767*
Indian subcontinent **15** *223*, *500*, *502*
Nepal **22** *777*
Ottonian **23** 647
Rome, ancient **27** 15
Tibet **30** 823
silverplate **15** *173*
slate **3** 914; **15** *216*
soapstone
Africa **1** *388*
China **7** *134*, 135
Egypt, ancient
Gabon **11** *879*
Gothic **13** 102
Kenya **17** *908*
Nigeria **23** *133*

sculpture
materials
soapstone—cont.
Norway **31** *364*
Swaziland **30** 63
sound **22** 375
stainless steel **10** *268*; **27** *395*
statuettes **12** 406
stearine **33** 2
steel **1** *247*; **2** *754*; **16** 56–8*, *57*, *58*; **28** *877*; **29** *897*; **31** *614*
stone **10** 702
Africa **18** *217*, *219*
Arabia **2** 253, 256–8
Argentina **29** *190*
Austria **26** *634*, 634–5*
Aztec **2** 906–7
Bactria **6** 216–17
Bangladesh **15** *502*
Belgium **13** 98–101*, *99*, *100*; **26** 630–31*
Britain **26** 611–12*
Buddhism **6** 221, *428*, 706, *713*, 718; **15** *500*, *501*, *505*, *778*, *782*; **18** 295; **22** *758*, 758–9, 770, *771*; **30** 593–5*, *594*, 823
Burma **5** *239*
Byzantine **9** 589*, 594–9*
Catalonia **26** 609–10*
Central Asia, Western **6** 216–17, 220, 221
Champa **6** *428*
China **6** 706, 718–19, 725, 726, *727*, 727–30, *728*, *729*, *730*, *731*
China: Sui period (AD 581-618) **6** *713*
Colombia **27** *700*
Costa Rica **9** 677–9, *678*, *679*
Czech Republic **4** *698*, *844*; **26** 637–8*
Denmark **8** 737; **26** 640
Early Christian (*c.* AD 250-843) **9** 589*, 594–7*
Easter Island **9** 674–5, *675*
Egypt, ancient **9** 815*, 855, 886
Ejagham **10** 123*, *123*
England **13** 80–83*, *81*, *84*, 84–5*; **26** 613–17*, *617*; **32** 529; **33** *62*
Etruscan **10** 602, 606–8; **32** 744
France **13** 72–9*; **26** 596–7*, 598–9*, 600–601*, 603–4*, 609–10*
France: Baroque **11** *558*
France: Gothic **13** *74*, *75*, *76*, *78*; **24** *157*
France: Late Gothic **19** *138*
France: Prehistoric **25** *544*
France: primitivism **12** *194*
France: Romanesque **26** *596*, 597–8*, 601–3*
France: 20th cent **21** *787*
Germany **13** 86–7, *88*; **22** *264*; **26** *632*, 632–3*, 634*
Gothic **5** *430*; **13** 72–9*, *74*, *75*, *76*, *78*, 80–83*, *81*, *84*, 84–5*, 86–92*, *88*, 93–108*, *93*, *99*, *100*, *104*, *105*, *107*; **22** *264*, *692*; **33** *62*
Greece, ancient **8** 262; **13** 435–6*, 439; **29** *710*
Hinduism **6** *449*; **15** *463*, *482*, *484*, *488*, *502*, *503*, *504*; **22** *767*, 767–8, *768*, 770, *770*, 771
Holy Roman Empire (before 1648) **13** 85*, 86–7*; **26** 631–5*, *632*, *634*
Hungary **26** 638*
Indian subcontinent **15** 412, 414, *414*, 452, *463*, *482*, *484*, *487*, *488*, *500*, *501*, *502*, *503*, *504*, *505*; **23** 832
Indonesia **4** *420*; **15** 777, *778*, *782*
Ireland **26** *618*, 618–19
Islamic **16** 243
sculpture
materials
stone—cont.
Italy **13** 87–92*, 93–8*, *93*; **26** 619*, 620*, *620*, 621*, 622–4*, 625–8*; **32** 744
Japan **17** 102
Java **15** 777, *778*, *782*
Jerusalem, Latin Kingdom of **26** 629*
Kongo **18** *217*, *219*
Korea **18** 295, 298–9, *299*, 301
Malta (Republic of) **20** *210*
Mesoamerica, Pre-Columbian **30** 340–41; **33** *103*
Mexico **21** *400*
Nepal **6** *449*; **22** *758*, 758–9, 766–8*, *767*, *768*, *770*, 770–71*, *771*, 773–4*
Netherlands, the **13** 98–101*; **26** 630–31*
Norway **26** 639*
Ottonian **23** 646–7
Panama **29** *144*
Poland **26** *636*, 636–7*; **31** *394*
Portugal **13** 101–2*; **26** 611*
Prehistoric art **25** 512, *544*
Romanesque **26** 594–5*, 596–9*, *596*, 600–604*, 606–7*, *608*, 608–10*, 611–12*, 613–17*, *617*, *618*, 618–19*, 620*, *620*, 621*, 622–4*, 625–9*, 630–38*, *632*, *634*, *636*, 639–40*, *640*
San Agustín culture **27** *700*
Scandinavia **13** 102–3*; **26** 639–40*; **32** 513
Sicily **26** 628–9*
Sogdiana **6** 220
South America, Pre-Columbian **9** 677–9, *678*, *679*; **27** *700*; **29** *144*, *190*
Spain **13** 103–8*, *104*, *105*, *107*; **26** 604–5*, 606–7*, *608*, 608–9*
Sweden **26** 639, *640*
Switzerland **26** 635*
Syria-Palestine **20** *410*
Tarascan **30** 340–41
Thailand **30** 593–5*, *594*
Tibet **30** 823
Vietnam **6** *428*; **32** 478
Viking **32** 513, 529
West Mexico **33** *103*
Zimbabwe **33** 679
straw **6** 706; **17** 99
string **8** *23*
stucco
Afghanistan **1** 193, 196, 197–8
Buddhism **29** *823*
Central Asia, Eastern **6** 298
Germany **12** 399
Indian subcontinent **15** 413, 414, 475; **29** 824
Islamic **16** 243
Italy **26** *400*
Mesoamerica, Pre-Columbian **18** *675*; **21** *222*
Ottonian **23** 646, *647*
Romanesque **26** 632
Sweden **30** 85
Thailand **30** 595*, 602–3*
sugar **21** 383; **29** *901*, 901–2*; **30** 219
teak **20** *808*
terracotta **8** 262; **30** 495–500*
Africa **1** 257, 258
Arabia **2** 260
Central Asia, Western **6** 275–6
China **19** *432*; **30** *509*
Cyprus, ancient **8** 338, 340, 342
Edo (Africa) **9** 736
England **30** *499*
Etruscan **10** 593, *604*, 608
France **30** *500*
Germany **4** *376*; **26** *104*
Greece, ancient **7** *854*; **13** 433*, 436–7*, 441, *441*, 450; **23** *433*
sculpture
materials
terracotta—cont.
Ife (kingdom of) **15** *107*
Indian subcontinent **15** 449, 453, *462*, 719; **30** 510
Italy **3** *496*; **12** *570*; **20** *778*, *907*; **23** *90*; **26** *331*; **30** *497*, *498*
Kassite **17** *837*
Korea **18** *302*
Mesoamerica, Pre-Columbian **33** *618*
Nepal **22** 758
Nigeria **23** *132*
Rome, ancient **27** 9, 29
Sicily **28** 654
South-east Asia **30** 510
Spain **31** *191*
Sweden **30** *86*
Thailand **30** 595*
United Arab Emirates **2** *260*
Vietnam **6** 426
textiles **6** 214, 706
tin **5** *571*
tools **27** 16*
tree trunks **3** *891*
tufa **15** 787; **27** 9
turquoise **6** 706
waxes **10** 197, 702; **29** 712; **33** 1, 2–4*
England **33** *4*
Germany **10** *702*
Italy **16** *706*; **27** *207*; **33** *3*, 725, *726*
Rome, ancient **27** 17
see also WAXWORKS
wire **7** *197*; **17** 99
wood **3** *405*; **8** 261; **9** *67*; **12** *191*; **15** *172*, 721; **17** *693*; **20** *150*; **30** *363*; **33** 325–6*
Africa **1** *232*, *233*, 251, 321–5*, *322*, *323*, *324*, *325*, *359*, *397*, *398*, 402, *404*, *415*, *422*; **18** *220*
Angola **7** *197*, *198*
Asante **2** 588, *588*
Austral Islands **2** *773*
Austria **13** *799*
Aztec **2** 907
Baga **3** *46*
Bali (Indonesia) **15** 784, 785–7*, *786*
Bamana **1** *323*; **3** 132–3, *133*
Baule **1** *233*, *324*
Belgium **13** 109–15*, *111*, *112*; **26** 644–5*, *645*
Bembe **3** *694*
Brazil **4** *708*
Buddhism: Central Asia, Eastern **6** 298, 300
Buddhism: China **6** 706, 717, 718, 721, *722*, 722
Buddhism: Japan **17** *116*, 116–26*, *117*, *118*, *120*, *123*, *125*, *126*
Buddhism: Korea **18** *292*, *295*, 295
Buddhism: Laos **18** 768
Buddhism: Vietnam **5** *100*; **30** 823; **32** 479, *479*
Burkina Faso **22** *197*
Byzantine **9** 599–602*
Cambodia **5** 499
Caribbean Islands **5** *748*
Central Asia, Eastern **6** 298, 300
Central Asia, Western **6** 220
China **6** 706, 717, 718, 721, 722, *722*; **7** 138, 140, 141
Chokwe **1** *404*; **7** *197*
Czech Republic **8** 383, *388*
Denmark **8** 738
Dogon **1** *262*, *322*; **9** *66*
Dominican Order **9** *110*
Early Christian (*c.* AD 250-843) **9** 599–602*
Egypt, ancient **2** *659*; **9** 886
England **13** 121–2*; **26** 643–4*
sculpture
materials
wood—cont.
Fang **1** *232*; **10** *788*, *789*, *790*
Fiji **11** 68
France **4** *661*; **13** 125–6*, *126*; **24** *716*; **26** 641*
Germany **3** *672*; **9** *752*; **22** *303*; **24** *461*; **32** *253*
Ghana **12** *509*
Gothic **13** 109–20*, *111*, *112*, *115*, 121–3*, 124–6*, *126*; **14** *892*
Greece, ancient **8** 262; **13** 433–4*, 442
Guinea **1** *359*
Guyana **13** *877*
Hemba **14** *377*
Hinduism **15** *524*
Holy Roman Empire (before 1648) **13** 115–18*; **26** 645–6*
Hungary **14** *892*
Igbo **15** *113*, *115*
Indian subcontinent **7** *616*; **15** 412, 414, 523–4, *524*, *733*
Indonesia **15** 784, 785–7*, *786*, 789
Irian Jaya **16** *43*
Italy **9** *129*; **13** 123–4*; **26** 644*
Jamaica **5** *748*
Japan **17** 99–100*, *116*, 116–26*, *117*, *118*, *120*, *123*, *125*, *126*, *128*, *134*, *137*, 348, 729
Khmer **5** 499
Kissi **1** *359*
Kongo **1** *233*; **18** *220*
Korea **18** *292*, 295, *295*, 300, 301
Kuba (iii) (Zaïre) **18** *486*
Laos **18** 768
Luba **1** *325*; **19** *742*, *743*
Madagascar **20** *38*
Mali **1** *262*
Malta (Republic of) **20** *214*
Mangbetu **1** *404*
Mossi **22** *197*
Native North Americans **22** 668
Nepal **22** 774*
Netherlands, the **13** 109–15*, *115*; **26** 644–5*
Nigeria **15** *113*, *115*
Ottonian **23** 647–9*
Ovimbundu **7** *199*
Papua New Guinea **23** *732*; **24** *71*, *80*
Paraguay **24** *93*, *97*, *99*
Philippines **24** *618*, *619*
Portugal **13** 124–5*; **26** 648*
Puerto Rico **5** *750*
Romanesque **26** 640–41*, 642–7*, *643*, *645*, 648*
Rome, ancient **27** 12
Scandinavia **13** 118–20*; **26** 646–7*
Senufo **28** *419*, *420*
Shinto **17** *128*
Slovenia **28** 862, *862*
Sogdiana **6** 220; **18** *500*
Songo **7** *198*
Spain **3** *846*; **9** *110*; **10** *903*; **13** 122–3*; **21** *173*; **22** *4*; **26** 642–3*, *643*; **29** 291, *292*, *296*
Spain: 20th cent. **10** *910*
Tajikistan **18** *500*
Teke **30** *419*, *420*
Tibet **30** 823
United States of America **1** *422*
Vietnam **5** *100*; **32** 479, *479*
Yoruba **1** *283*, 283–4
Zaïre **1** *359*; **14** *377*; **18** *486*
Zambia **33** 603
Zande **1** *359*
wrought iron **12** *919*
ziricote **3** *624*
sculpture—cont.
restoration **2** 163; **7** 729, 739*, *739*; **9** 21, 23; **29** *710*
technical examination **25** 175*; **30** 396
techniques
casting **27** 17–18*, *18*
engraving **27** 17
gilding **8** 262; **12** 625–6*, 627; **25** 175
Buddhism **18** *607*
China **6** 706, 707, *708*, *710*, *719*, *720*, *722*
Greece, ancient **13** 435
Indian subcontinent **15** 414
Japan **17** *34*, *107*, 110–12, *111*, *112*, *113*
Korea **18** *285*, *287*, *294*, *295*
Nepal **22** *755*, *772*, 774, *774*, *775*, *776*
Rome, ancient **27** *10*, 15, 29
Slovenia **28** *862*
Sri Lanka **29** *460*
joinery **5** 408
lost-wax casting **22** *774*, 774–5, *775*
mass production **3** 114; **15** 448; **17** 320
moulding **1** 198; **6** 298; **27** 17–18*
oiling **24** 258
painting **6** 216, 725; **7** *616*; **8** 262; **14** *352*; **15** *79*, 548; **17** 99; **27** 16
photography **24** 688
polishing **9** 815
polychromy **7** 740; **25** 174–6*; **29** 707; **30** 496
Afghanistan **1** 198
China **6** *713*
Egypt, ancient **9** *870*
England **13** *121*; **25** IV, V2
France **13** *126*
Germany **10** *457*; **32** *253*
Greece, ancient **26** 134–5; **29** VIII1
Italy **25** V1
Japan **17** 99, 100
Khwarazm **6** *219*
Netherlands, the **13** *115*
Norway **13** *119*
Rome, ancient **27** 16
Spain **10** *903*; **30** *498*
Switzerland **22** *919*
Tokharistan **6** 221
Vietnam **5** *100*
quilting **7** 607
repoussé **22** 775, *775*
sgraffito **7** 607
soldering **27** 17
stamping **6** 214
stone-carvings **26** 595
varnishing **24** 258
welding **27** 17
treatises *see under* TREATISES → types
types
acro-elephantine **13** 597
acrolithic **1** 127*; **8** 262; **13** 434
allegorical
Austria **9** *146*
Champa **6** *429*
Czech Republic **8** *387*
Denmark **29** *541*
England **22** *28*
France: Baroque **24** *785*; **25** *706*
France: Neo-classicism **4** *301*; **27** *311*
France: Rococo **8** *71*
France: 19th cent. **26** *510*
Germany **18** *478*
Gothic **5** *176*
Italy: Baroque **4** *621*; **16** *698*; **33** *726*
Italy: Gothic **5** *176*
Italy: Mannerism **8** *511*; **12** *570*; **20** *279*

sculpture
types
allegorical—cont.
Italy: Renaissance **5** *359*; **16** *770*; **21** *436*, *437*; **26** *439*
Italy: Romanesque **2** *132*
Italy: 16th cent. **20** *778*
Norway **23** *230*
Portugal **1** *741*
Romanesque **2** *132*
Rome, ancient **2** *156*
animalier **2** 99–100*
ba statues **23** 283
block statues **9** 856–7*, *857*, 874
bulul **24** 617, *618*
cat statues **5** 70, *71*
chacmools **21** 223, *223*
chrysaliform figures **9** 866
chryselephantine statues **7** 245*
Germany **29** 576
Greece, ancient **8** 262, 458; **13** 387, 435*, 596; **16** 798; **24** 593, 594
Rome, ancient **8** 263
colossal heads **21** 219; **22** 8–9; **23** 417, *417*
colossal statues
Afghanistan **3** 149
Buddhism **3** 149; **25** *170*; **29** 442, *458*
Commagene **22** *731*
Egypt, ancient **1** 770; **9** 815, *816*, *862*, 862–3*; **30** *297*, 694, *694*, 695; **31** *482*
Germany **3** 155; **28** 186
Greece, ancient **8** 262; **24** 593, 594; **27** 689
Indian subcontinent **15** 528, *528*; **29** 438
Italy **7** *842*
Mesoamerica, Pre-Columbian **21** 218
Olmec **21** 209
Rome, ancient **26** 855; **27** 12, 29
Sri Lanka **5** 98; **25** *170*; **29** 442, 458, *458*
Turkey **22** *731*
column statues **7** 275, 642–3*
France **1** *781*; **6** *403*, *495*; **7** 642, *642*; **9** *257*; **13** 73, *74*; **26** 602; **29** 902
Gothic **1** *781*; **6** *495*; **7** 642; **9** *257*; **13** 73, *74*
Romanesque **6** *403*; **7** *642*; **26** 602
composite statues **9** 884
cult statues **8** 261–3*; **17** 524
Aegean **8** 262
Anatolia, ancient **8** 261
Ancient Near East **8** 261
Canaanite **8** 261
Crete **8** 154, 155
Cyprus, ancient **8** *338*
Egypt, ancient **8** 261; **9** 795*; **30** 433
Greece, ancient **2** *686*; **8** 262, *262*; **10** 423; **13** 370, 424; **27** 711; **29** 567
Hittite **8** 261
Indian subcontinent **15** 727–9*, 730
Mesopotamia **8** 261
Prehistoric art **8** *338*
Rome, ancient **8** 155, 262–3; **26** 858; **27** 29, 31, 88*, 711
dvārapāla **15** 507, *534*, *542*
dyads **9** 858–9*, *858*, 869–70; **22** 398, *399*
equestrian **1** 280
Africa **1** 280–81*
Bamana **1** 280
Benin, Kingdom of **1** 280
Dogon **1** 280
Indian subcontinent **15** *735*
Nigeria **1** 280
Senufo **1** 280
Sudan **1** 280
Yoruba **1** 280

sculpture
types—cont.
equestrian monuments *see under* MONUMENTS → types
figure
Aboriginal Australia **1** *62*
Africa **1** 230–34, *232*, *233*, 321–5*, *322*, *323*, *324*, *325*, 382, *388*, 396–8, *397*, *398*, 402–5, *404*, 410, *415*, 415–16; **18** *217*, *219*, *220*
Akan **1** 392, 514; **2** 588
Akye **1** *515*
Angola **7** *197*, *198*
Arabia **2** 256–8, *257*
Asante **2** 588*, *588*, 590
Aztec **2** 906–7; **21** *244*
Bamana **1** *323*, 323; **3** 132–4*, *133*
Bamileke **3** *146*, 147
Bangwa **1** 323, 324; **3** 170–71*, *171*
Baule **1** 231, *233*, 323, *324*, 392; **3** 404–5, *405*
Bembe **1** 403, 404; **3** 693–4, *694*
Bijogo **1** 391
Buddhism **6** 318–19
Burkina Faso **22** *197*
Bwa **5** 330*
Cameroon **1** 396; **3** *171*
Caribbean Islands **5** 747–8, *748*
Caroline Islands **25** *182*
Central Asia, Eastern **6** 318–19
Chamba (ii) (Africa) **1** 382; **6** 406; **22** 287
Chokwe **1** 322, 403, *404*; **7** 196–7*, *197*
Côte d'Ivoire **1** 514, *515*
Cuba (Caribbean) **8** 229, 231
Dan (Africa) **8** 488–9*
Dogon **1** 231, *322*, 322; **9** *66*, 66–7*, *67*
Egypt **16** 245
Fang **1** 231, 232, *232*, 322, 323, 324
Fiji **11** 68
Gran Chiriquí culture **13** 290–91
Gurunsi **5** 330*
Hemba **1** 403; **14** 376–8*, *377*
Ibibio **15** *63*, 63–4*, *64*
Igbo **15** 109, *112*, *113*, 113, 114, 115*, *115*
Ijo **15** 124, *125*
Indian subcontinent **15** 415, 424, 539–40, 734
Iraq **16** 245
Jamaica **5** *748*; **16** *879*, 880
Jukun **1** 382; **17** 679*, *680*
Kongo **1** *233*, 403; **8** 230; **18** *217*, 217–21*, *219*, *220*
Kota (ii) (Gabon peoples) **1** 323
Kuba (iii) (Zaïre) **1** 403; **18** 485–7*, *486*
Lega **1** 404
Lobi **19** 521–2*
Luba **1** 323, 324, *325*, 403
Lwena **1** 403
Makonde (Mozambique) **1** 410; **20** 149, 150, *150*
Mangbetu **1** 404, *404*
Maya **4** 296–7; **5** *394*; **16** 807–8; **27** 780
Mende (Sierra Leone) **21** 117*
Mesoamerica, Pre-Columbian **4** 296–7; **5** *394*; **21** *244*; **27** 780
Mossi **22** *197*, 197–8*
Mumuye **1** 382; **22** 287*
Nigeria **15** *63*, *64*, *112*, *113*, *115*; **23** *132*, *133*
Ovimbundu **1** 403; **7** *199*, 199–200
Papua New Guinea **24** 70–71*, *71*, 79–80, *80*, 85–6
Pende **1** 403

sculpture
types
figure—cont.
Polynesian outliers **25** 181–2, *182*
Senufo **1** 234, 323; **28** *419*, 419–20*, *420*
Songo **1** 403; **7** *199*
Songola **1** 404
Songye **1** 403; **29** *69*, 69–70*
Syria **16** 245
Tabwa **1** 403; **30** 225, *225*
Teke **1** 403; **3** 694; **30** 418–19, *419*
Togo **31** 73
Turkey **16** 245
Venda **1** 415, 416; **32** 155
Yaka **1** 403; **33** 485, *485*
Yoruba **1** 231
Zaïre **14** *377*; **18** *486*; **29** *69*; **30** *225*
Zande **1** 404; **33** 609–10*
group
Germany **16** 799
Greece, ancient **13** 424, 458; **27** 689
Netherlands, the **16** 799
Rome, ancient **27** 29, 31–2, 43, *43*
guérisseur statues *see* HEALING STATUES
haniwa **17** 30–31, *31*, 104–6, *105*, 425; **18** 190; **23** 157
heads, colossal *see* colossal heads
healing statues **9** 888
heraldic **14** 420–21*, *421*
herms **14** 455–6*
Greece, ancient **5** 298–9; **13** 429; **14** 455–6
Rome, ancient **14** 456; **27** 29
Spain **8** 80
kneeling figures **9** 859–60*, 866, 871
korai **29** 559
Etruscan **10** 593
Greece, ancient **8** 688; **13** 371, 422, 429, 444–5, 451; **18** 243–5*, *244*; **29** VIII1
Italy **10** 593
kouroi **18** *409*, 409–10*, *410*; **24** *328*; **27** *689*; **29** 559
Etruscan **10** 593
Greece, ancient **13** 371, 422, 429, 444–5, *446*, *449*, 451; **22** 699, *699*; **23** 290; **27** 689
Italy **10** 593
limited editions *see under* LIMITED EDITIONS → types
liṅga **14** 561; **15** 332, 412, *438*, 443–4, 729
mummiform figures *see* chrysaliform figures
mythological **22** 410–11*
Australia **2** *753*
Austria **10** *894*
Czech Republic **32** *731*; **33** *435*
Denmark **8** *741*; **30** *764*, *765*
England **12** 613
England: Neo-classicism **5** *629*
England: New Sculpture **12** *610*
England: 18th cent. **2** *541*; **3** *184*
England: 19th cent. **12** *598*
Etruscan **10** *589*
France: Baroque **1** *133*; **7** *423*; **12** *725*; **29** *563*
France: Baroque Revival **5** *879*
France: Neo-classicism **6** *517*; **10** *764*; **14** *798*
France: Rococo **28** *845*
France: 16th cent. **11** *503*
France: 18th cent. **4** *510*; **23** *795*
France: 19th cent. **30** *500*
Germany: Neo-classicism **4** *376*; **8** *509*; **9** *691*

sculpture
types
mythological—cont.
Germany: Renaissance **11** *223*; **12** *402*; **33** II1
Germany: Rococo **22** *303*
Greece, ancient **8** *688*, *689*; **10** *449*
Greece, ancient: 5th cent. BC **24** *205*
Greece, ancient: Classical, Early **1** *480*
Greece, ancient: Classical, High **13** *429*
Greece, ancient: Classical, Late **7** *854*; **13** *460*
Greece, ancient: Geometric (*c.* 900–*c.*700 BC) **13** *442*
Greece, ancient: Proto-Daidalic **13** *443*
Italy: Baroque **3** *829*; **29** *563*
Italy: Etruscan **10** *589*
Italy: Mannerism **3** *162*; **6** *142*, *145*; **12** *572*; **27** *203*; **29** *558*, *562*
Italy: Neo-Classicism **5** *629*; **16** *705*
Italy: Renaissance **2** *140*, *141*; **3** *158*; **16** *693*
Italy: Roman **14** *443*; **27** *9*, *22*; **29** *389*
Late Helladic (*c.* 1600–*c.* 1050 BC) **14** *352*
Mycenaean **14** *352*
Netherlands, the: 16th cent. **22** *858*
Rome, ancient **2** *169*; **14** *443*; **27** *9*, *22*, *23*; **29** *389*
Russia: 20th cent. **27** *437*
Sweden **28** *462*
nāga **15** 444
naophorous statues **9** 855, 860–61*
okir **24** 618
Osirid statues **9** 862
palmesels **23** 887*, *887*; **26** 641, 646
photosculpture **24** 688*
portraits *see under* PORTRAITS → media
praying figures **9** 866
prostrate figures **9** 861–2*
religious
Austria **13** *799*
Baga **3** *46*
Belgium: Baroque **9** *411*; **25** *811*, *812*
Belgium: Gothic **13** *99*, *100*, *111*
Belgium: Romanesque **26** *645*
Brazil **19** *461*
Catalonia **20** *639*
Croatia **23** *93*
Czech Republic **4** *698*, *844*; **13** *90*; **25** *442*
Dominican Order **9** *110*
England: Gothic **10** *259*; **19** *603*
England: Neo-classicism **11** *164*
England: Romanesque **26** *615*
England: 19th cent. **3** *78*
France **33** 3
France: Gothic **4** *583*; **13** *126*; **19** *138*; **24** *157*; **28** *866*; **31** *382*
France: Mannerism **24** *813*
France: Renaissance **26** *185*
France: Romanesque **7** *478*; **11** *554*
France: 14th cent. **11** *555*
France: 16th cent. **4** *546*; **24** *133*
Germany: Baroque **9** *752*; **13** *684*, *777*
Germany: Gothic **7** *589*; **11** *751*; **12** *400*; **13** *91*, *92*; **22** *281*; **26** *370*; **29** *728*, *729*

sculpture
types
religious—cont.
Germany: Late Gothic **10** *455*, *457*
Germany: Mannerism **12** *346*; **26** *104*
Germany: Renaissance **14** *450*
Germany: Rococo **1** *712*
Germany: Romanesque **26** *632*
Germany: 16th cent. **21** *72*
Germany: 18th cent. **13** *851*; **24** *461*; **29** *761*; **32** *253*
Gothic: Belgium **13** *99*, *100*, *111*
Gothic: Czech Republic **13** *90*
Gothic: England **10** *259*; **19** *603*
Gothic: France **4** *583*; **13** *126*; **19** *138*; **24** *157*; **28** *866*; **31** *382*
Gothic: Germany **7** *589*; **10** *455*, *457*; **11** *751*; **12** *400*; **13** *91*, *92*; **22** *281*; **26** *370*; **29** *728*, *729*
Gothic: Hungary **14** *892*
Gothic: Italy **2** *482*; **13** *94*; **20** *728*; **24** *873*, *875*; **28** *680*
Gothic: Netherlands, the **3** *456*; **13** *114*, *115*
Gothic: Norway **13** *119*
Gothic: Poland **25** *111*
Gothic: Spain **13** *109*
Guinea: Baga **3** *46*
Holy Roman Empire (before 1648) **26** *632*
Hungary **14** *892*
Italy: Baroque **1** *711*; **2** *609*; **3** *262*, *828*, *832*; **9** *410*; **11** *18*, *280*; **16** *698*; **20** *909*; **31** *790*
Italy: Gothic **2** *482*; **13** *94*; **20** *728*; **24** *873*, *875*; **28** *680*
Italy: Mannerism **3** *469*; **16** *696*
Italy: Renaissance **4** *738*, *739*; **5** *361*; **9** *123*, *129*; **11** *203*; **12** *539*; **16** *690*, *840*; **18** *673*; **19** *560*; **20** *543*, *544*, *907*; **22** *32*, *461*; **23** *90*; **26** *331*; **27** *448*, *769*, *770*, *775*, *776*; **29** *567*; **32** *105*, *360*, *362*
Italy: 15th cent. **10** *854*; **18** *859*
Italy: 16th cent. **3** *496*; **6** *90*; **25** *256*; **31** *787*; **32** *649*
Italy: 17th cent. **10** *800*; **21** *755*
Italy: 18th cent. **21** *890*
Malta (Republic of) **20** *214*
Netherlands, the **3** *456*; **13** *114*, *115*; **22** *856*
Norway **13** *119*
Poland **25** *111*, *114*
Portugal **6** *451*
Romanesque: Belgium **26** *645*
Romanesque: England **26** *615*
Romanesque: France **7** *478*; **11** *554*
Romanesque: Germany **26** *632*
Romanesque: Holy Roman Empire **26** *632*
Romanesque: Spain **26** *643*
Slovakia **28** *855*
Slovenia **28** *862*
Spain: Baroque **29** *292*
Spain: Dominican Order **9** *110*
Spain: Gothic **13** *105*
Spain: Mannerism **3** *846*
Spain: Romanesque **26** *643*
Spain: 16th cent. **17** *693*
Spain: 17th cent. **9** *110*; **10** *903*; **21** *173*; **22** *4*

sculpture
types—cont.
reserve heads
Egypt, ancient **9** 863*, *863*, 870
Rome, ancient **10** *428*
Turkey **10** *428*
santos **5** 750, *750*; **24** 610, 619, *619*
scribe statues **9** 857–8*, 870, *870*; **14** *758*, 759
seated figures **9** 855–6*, *856*, 866, *867*, 869, *869*, 870, *876*, *879*; **20** 117
servant statues **9** 854, 871; **10** *16*, 16–17*
soft *see* SOFT ART
squatting statues **9** 859*, *859*
standard-bearers **9** 881
standing figures **9** 855*, 866, 873, *881*, *883*, 888
statue menhirs **11** 78; **21** 134; **25** 529, 530; **27** 835
stelophorous statues **9** 860–61*
tatemono see haniwa
terminal figures **14** 456; **30** 491*
terms *see* terminal figures
theophorous statues **9** 860–61*, *861*
triads **9** 858–9*
vishap **2** 435
votive statues **10** 702, *702*; **13** 424; **24** 97; **29** *923*
see also EX-VOTOS
yakṣa **15** 413, 426–7, *427*, 429–30, *430*
yakṣī **15** 413, *425*, 429–30
uses
altarpieces **1** 711
architectural decorations **16** 239
churches *see under* CHURCHES → decoration
cloisters **7** 453–6*
crucifixes **8** 213–16*
façade decoration **10** 741–5*, *744*, *745*
fountains **16** 696; **29** 563–4
gardens **28** 314; **29** 563–4
grottoes **16** 696
pediments **24** 318–20*, *319*
tea ceremonies **17** 341
sculpture gardens *see under* GARDENS → types
Sculpture International **24** 429
Sculpture In The Environment *see* SITE
sculpture porcelain *see* PORCELAIN → wares → Parian
Scultetus, Joannes **21** 6
Sculthorpe (Norfolk), All Saints **26** 613
Scultori, Adamo **10** 386; **28** 316
Scultori, Diana **10** 386; **28** 316–17
Scultori, Giovanni Battista **10** 386; **12** 557; **28** 316*
scumble **12** 803; **28** 317*
Scuola di Pergentina **28** 705
Scuola di Piacenza **26** 621
Scuola di Piazza del Popolo **26** 778
Scuola di Posillipo **12** 606; **16** 678; **22** 480; **28** 317*; **32** 400
members **24** 893; **32** 256, 379
Scuola di Resina **8** 716; **16** 678; **22** 480; **28** 317–18*
members **6** 130; **21** 472
Scuola di Rivara **2** 10; **16** 678; **28** 318*
Scuola di Staggia **1** 152; **16** 678; **19** 870; **28** 318–19*
Scuola di Via Cavour **16** 680; **20** 82; **24** 841
Scuola etrusca *see* ETRUSCAN SCHOOL
Scuola Labronica **19** 512; **28** 319*
Scuola Romana **10** 822; **20** 82, 93; **21** 87; **26** 776; **28** 319*
members **2** 183; **5** 382, 671; **11** 18; **16** 680; **25** 910; **28** 212
works **26** *777*
scuole **28** *37*; **32** *226*
see also HALLS; VENICE → guilds
Scupi *see* SKOPJE
Scuri, Enrico **30** 358
Scutari (Turkey) *see* ISTANBUL
Scutari (Albania) *see under* SHKODËR
Scutenaire, Louis **20** 101; **30** 20
SČVU *see* UNION OF CZECHOSLOVAK ARTISTS
Scylax of Caryanda **13** 807
scyphuses *see* CHALICES
Scythian **2** 100; **5** 94; **6** 186, 187; **12** 316; **25** 533; **28** 319–26*
amphorae **28** *324*
bronze **6** 242; **28** 322
calligraphy **6** 307
carving **6** 212
copper **6** *243*
dress **1** 886; **6** 251
gold **2** *101*; **28** *320*, 321, 322, *322*
graves **6** 212
harnesses **14** *180*
metalwork **6** 237; **15** 919; **28** *320*, 321, *322*, 322–4
plaques **2** *101*
pots **6** *243*
rock art **28** 321
silver-gilt **28** *324*
stone-carvings **28** 321
swords **6** 260
tattoos **30** 367, 769
trade **28** 323; **30** 772
weapons **6** 261
see also SARMATIAN
Scythopolis *see* BETH SHAN
Seabrook, Norman H(ugh) **2** 742; **28** 326*
sea charts *see under* MAPS → types
Seacliffe, Borders **28** 288
Sea Dayak *see* IBAN
Seager, Richard B. **21** 756; **25** 678; **32** 70
Seager, Samuel Hurst **7** 210; **23** 54; **28** 326–7*; **33** 342
Sea Islands (SC) **1** *426*
seal amulets *see under* SEALS → types
sealants **25** 174*
seal bags *see under* BAGS → types
sealing wax *see under* WAXES → types
Seal of Michelangelo **3** 48
seals **1** 855; **7** 532; **11** 309; **14** 408, 416, 417–18; **15** 149; **28** 327*
collections *see under* COLLECTIONS → types
historical and regional traditions
Achaemenid **1** 116, 117–18
Afghanistan **16** *552*
Anatolia, ancient **1** 826; **2** 504
Ancient Near East **1** 855*, 868, 877–8, 883, 886; **2** 504
Sumerian **10** *802*
Arabia **2** 270–71*
Aztec **21** 258
Byzantine **9** 635–8*, *637*; **33** 5
Central Asia **6** 314–15*, *315*; **23** 159
China **7** 102, 128–31*, *129*, *130*, *131*, 134, 135; **15** 851; **17** 408
Han period (206 BC–AD 220) **7** 117
Qing period (1644–1911) **7** 65; **8** 713; **17** *411*
Crete
Minoan **8** 153; **21** 656–7, 658, 682, 684–6*
Orientalizing style **8** 154
Popular group **21** 686
Talismanic group **21** 686
Cyprus, ancient **8** 355–6*; **19** 131; **24** 645
Early Christian (*c.* AD 250–843) **9** 635–7*
Egypt **10** 69–70*
Egypt, ancient **10** 69*, 70–71*
seals
historical and regional traditions—cont.
England **12** 273; **14** 413, 416; **19** *580*; **33** *5*, 6
France **14** *408*, 413
Germany **14** 413
Greece **7** 532
Greece, ancient **12** 246–8*; **13** 595
Bronze Age **14** 338, 359*, *359*
Popular group **14** 360
Helladic **14** 359*, *359*
Early Helladic (*c.* 3600/3000–*c.* 2050 BC) **14** 336
Late Helladic (*c.* 1600–*c.* 1050 BC) **14** 338
Popular group **14** 360
Hurrian **15** 33
Indian subcontinent **15** 192, 213, 476
Indus civilization **15** 213
Iran, ancient **1** 868; **15** 904
Islamic **16** 542–3*, *543*, *552*; **33** 5
Israelite **16** 573
Japan **7** 624; **9** 73; **17** 399, 408–14*; **31** 77
Edo period (1600–1868) **15** 129; **17** *410*, *412*; **33** *709*
Judah **16** 573
Kassite **17** 836–7
Korea **18** 371–2*
Maya **21** 258
Mesoamerica, Pre-Columbian **21** 258*
Huastec **21** *258*
Mexico **21** *258*
Toltec **21** *258*
Mesopotamia **12** 212; **21** 269, 272, 274, 275, 278; **28** 783
Mexico **21** *258*
Minoan **8** 153; **21** 682, 684–6*
Early Minoan (*c.* 3500/3000–*c.* 2050 BC) **21** 656–7
Middle Minoan (*c.* 2050–*c.* 1600 BC) **21** 658
Popular group **21** 686
Talismanic group **21** 686
Mitannian **1** 877; **15** 33
Mongolia **21** 882*
Mycenaean **14** 338
Olmec **21** 258
Parthian **23** 159
Philistine **24** 636*
Phoenician **24** 644–5*; **30** 187
Poland **14** *410*
Punic **25** 734*
Sasanian **27** 857
Sumerian **1** 880; **10** *802*
Syria **2** 660–61
Syria-Palestine **30** 187
Toltec **21** 258
materials
agate **12** 247
beeswax **33** 5
beige stone **1** *857*
blackstone **1** *856*
bone **12** 247
brass **16** *543*; **21** 882
bronze **6** 315, *315*; **7** 128, 129, *129*, 130, *130*; **17** 409; **21** 882
chalcedony **1** *858*; **12** 247, 248
clay **1** 856; **15** 192
copper **6** 315; **15** 420
cornelian **12** 247; **16** 543, *543*
cream stone **1** *856*
faience (i) (glass) **1** 877–8; **21** 684
garnets **12** 248
glass paste **12** 247, 248
gold **7** 128; **21** *686*, 882
greenstone **1** *858*
haematite **16** *543*
horn **7** 130
huaru **7** 130
inks **15** 851
inscriptions **7** 128; **16** 542, *543*
iron **21** 882
seals
materials—cont.
ivory **7** 102, 128, 130; **12** 247; **13** 595; **16** 798
jade **7** 128, 129, 130; **21** 882
jasper **1** *857*; **12** 247; **16** *543*; **21** *685*
lapis lazuli **16** *543*
lead **9** *637*
limestone **10** 70; **12** 246
marble **12** 246
onyx **16** *543*
pigments **33** 5
porcelain **17** 413
quartz **12** 248
rock crystal **7** 130; **12** 247; **26** 484
serpentine **12** 246, 247
shellac **33** 5
silver **7** 128; **21** 882
soapstone **1** 856; **7** 134, 135; **10** 70; **15** 192, 420
stone **6** 315; **7** 128, 130
terracotta **15** 420
Venice turpentine **33** 5
waxes **19** *580*; **33** *5*, 5–6*
wood **6** 315; **7** 128; **10** 70
types
artists' **7** 129
collectors' **7** 129
conoid **1** 857
cylinder
Achaemenid **1** *863*, 864
Afghanistan **1** 850
Akkadian (people) **1** 510, 860–61; **21** *277*
Anatolia, ancient **1** 828, 850, *859*, 863; **2** 504
Ancient Near East **1** 853, 856, 858–64*, *859*, 874; **2** 504; **22** 510
Arabia **2** 270–71
Assyrian **1** 850, *861*, 861–2
Babylonian **1** 861, 862
Canaanite **30** 184, 186
Cyprus, ancient **8** 355
Egypt, ancient **10** 69*
Helladic **14** 358
Indian subcontinent **1** 850; **15** 421
Indus civilization **15** 421
Iran, ancient **1** 850, 856, 858, *863*, 863–4
Iraq **1** 858
Kassite **1** *861*, 861
Mesoamerica, Pre-Columbian **21** 258
Mesopotamia **1** 850, 856, 858, *859*, *860*, 860–62, *861*; **4** 641; **21** 271, *271*, 276, *277*, 310
Mitannian **1** 862, *862*; **21** 730, *731*; **23** 322
Mycenaean **14** 358
Sumerian **29** 924*
Syria-Palestine **1** 858, *859*, *862*, 862–3; **30** 184, 185, 186
Urartian **17** 879
fob **14** 418
ring
Ancient Near East **1** 857
Crete **21** *685*, *686*
Minoan **21** *685*, *686*
Parthian **24** 218
Syria-Palestine **1** 857
seal amulets **1** *856*; **10** 69–70
stamp
Achaemenid **1** 118, 858
Anatolia, ancient **1** 827, 855, 856–7, *857*
Ancient Near East **1** 855–8*, *856*, *857*, *858*, 864
Arabia **2** 271
Assyrian **1** 856
Babylonian **1** 856, 858, *858*
Bahrain **2** 271
Crete **21** 684
Cyprus, ancient **8** 355
seals
types
stamp—cont.
Egypt, ancient **10** 69–70*; **28** 34
Hittite **1** 827, 857*, *857*
Huastec **21** *258*
Indian subcontinent **15** 420–21
Indus civilization **15** 420–21
Iran, ancient **1** *856*, 858
Mesoamerica, Pre-Columbian **21** 258, *258*
Mesopotamia **1** 855, *856*, 858; **4** 641
Minoan **21** 684
Parthian **1** 858
Sasanian **1** 858, *858*
Syria-Palestine **1** 855, *857*
Toltec **21** *258*
see also SCARABS
stamp-cylinder **1** 863; **31** 701
thread **17** 409
votive **1** 859
uses
body arts **21** 258
colophons **7** 624
netsuke **17** 399
rings **1** 857; **21** *685*, *686*
tombs **10** 70
Sealy, John **2** 541; **7** 480
Sealy, William **30** 502
Sea Peoples **24** 633–4; **30** 197, 695
Sea Ranch (CA) **31** 598
Searchers (Keresők) **10** 108
Searle, John **25** 233
Searle, Ronald **5** 758
Searles, Charles **1** 445
Sears, David **8** 843
Sears, Mrs Montgomery J. **5** 922
Sears, Willard T. **4** 477; **8** 265
Sears Roebuck Co. **15** 825; **19** 538; **20** 594
seascapes *see* PAINTING → types → marine
Seaside (FL) **18** 456
seated figures *see under* SCULPTURE → types
seating **13** 380, 385, *385*, 386; **26** 873; **30** 652
seating, garden *see* GARDEN SEATING
Seaton Delaval (Northumb.) **8** 47; **10** 232; **31** *861*, 861–2
Seattle (WA) **28** 327–8*; **31** *587*
Art Museum **28** *328*
collections **7** 156; **15** 746; **17** 434; **22** 795; **28** 327
exhibitions **18** 301
Katherine White Collection of African Art **28** 328
Century 21 Exposition, 1962 **15** 883
Seattle Center **14** 90
Henry Art Gallery *see under* University of Washington
Northgate Shopping Center **28** 622, *623*
St Alphonsus
Fritts-Richard organ **22** 375
Sound Garden **28** 315
Tacoma Narrows Bridge **4** 803
University of Washington
Henry Art Gallery **28** 328
Washington State Museum **28** 328
Seattle Engraving Company **30** 753
Séaux, Jean **2** 510; **29** 369
Seaver, Henry **16** 39
Seaview Farm **2** 152
Seaweed, Joe **28** 330
Seaweed, Willie **22** 581, 589, 674; **28** 329–30*
works **22** *579*, 588; **28** *329*
seaweeds **7** 747; **9** 492; **17** 138
Seawright, James **18** 63; **29** 98
Sébah, Pascal **16** 591
Sebaste (Israel) *see* SAMARIA

Sebaste (Turkey) **9** 588, 590, 593; **26** 913
Sebastea *see* SIVAS
Sebastian, King of Portugal (*reg* 1557-78) **2** 869, 875*; **26** 515; **30** 517
Sebastián, Enrique Carbajal **3** 624; **12** 844; **22** 21; **28** 330*
Sebastian, Georges **31** 424
Sebastián de Almonacid **28** 331; **31** 92
Sebastián de Toledo **28** 330–31*; **29** 289
collaboration **7** 345; **13** 757; **26** 249
works **13** *108*, 108; **28** 369; **31** 88, 92
Sebastiani, Sebastiano **9** 158
Sebastiano del Piombo **16** 766; **21** 457; **28** 331–6*
attributions **4** 304; **12** 670, *671*, 673, 674; **25** 860
collaboration **16** 664
frames **11** 387
methods **28** 339
paintings **6** 583; **10** 476; **12** 670; **21** 450
altarpieces **27** 653
frescoes **25** 71
portraits **9** 172; **21** 19; **27** 877; **28** *334*
religious **26** 424; **28** *331*, *333*, *334*; **32** 628
patrons and collectors
Angerstein, John Julius **2** 51, 559; **5** 63
Aretino, Pietro **2** 388
Bankes, William John **3** 179
Baring, Thomas (ii) (1799-1873) **3** 239
Beit, Otto (John) **3** 522
Borgherini, Pierfrancesco **4** 404
Carr, William Holwell **5** 848
Chigi, Agostino (i) (1466-1520) **6** 583; **26** 769
Clement VII, Pope (*reg* 1523-34) **10** 675; **21** 17
Cobos, Francisco de los **7** 488
Coningham, William **7** 709
Contarini, Caterina **7** 775
Demidov, Anatoly, Prince **8** 705
Doria-Pamphili (family) **9** 175
Francis I, King of France (*reg* 1515-47) **31** 849
Grimani, Marino, Cardinal, Patriarch of Aquileia **13** 658
Guastalla, Ferrante Gonzaga, Duca da **12** 910
Howard (i), Thomas, 2nd Earl of Arundel **14** 805
Imstenraedt, Franz Gerhard von **15** 158
Lanier, Nicholas **18** 747
Medici, Ottaviano de' **21** 18
Medinaceli, Luís de la Cerda Fernández de Córdoba Folch de Cardona y Aragón, 9th Duque de (1660-1711) **21** 35
Orléans, Philippe II de Bourbon, 2nd Duc d' (1674-1723) **23** 516
Orsini, Fulvio **23** 577
Percy, Algernon, 4th Duke of Northumberland **24** 390
Philip IV, King of Spain (*reg* 1621-65) **29** 352
Pourtalès-Gorgier, James-Alexandre, Comte de **25** 383
Pulszky, Károly **25** 729
Soult (Jean de Dieu), Maréchal **29** 96
Thyssen-Bornemisza, Heinrich, Baron von **30** 795
Valori, Baccio **31** 851
Vich, Jéronimo de **31** 815
William II, King of the Netherlands (*reg* 1840-49) **23** 469
pupils **18** 869
Sebastiano del Piombo—cont.
reproductive prints by others **26** 233
teachers **3** 667
Sebastiano di Giacomo di Bologna da Conegliano *see* FLORIGERIO, SEBASTIANO
Sebastiano di Marforio **6** 18
Sebastiyah *see* SAMARIA
Sebèce, Alain **31** 841
Sebekaa **21** 744
Sebekemsaf I **9** 879, *879*
Sebekhotpe (12th Dynasty) **2** 657; **21** 744
tomb **2** *656*
Sebekhotpe I (13th Dynasty) **9** 878
Sebekneferu (*reg c.* 1760-*c.* 1756 BC) **9** *776*; **10** 43
Sebellin, Baldassar **16** 739
Sebenico, Giorgio da *see* GIORGIO DA SEBENICO
Sebennytos **9** 892
Seberth, Wilhelm Jakob **2** 825
Sebeş Church **14** 892; **26** 707, 712
Sebidi, Helen (Mmakgoba) **29** 109
Sebiumeker **23** 283
Sebregondi, Nicolo **12** 912, 913; **28** 336–7*
Sebring (OH) **31** 639
Sebring Pottery Co. **31** 639
Sebrogondi, Nicolo **24** 772
Sébron, Hippolyte-Victor-Valentin **8** 450, 911
Seccadenari, Ercole **4** 280
Secchiaroli, Tazio **28** 337*
Secco, Niccolò **12** 761
secco paintings **11** 763; **28** 337–40*; **32** 802, 808
conservation **28** *339*, 339–40*
historical and regional traditions
Buddhism **6** 301
Byzantine **9** 562
Cappadocia **5** 676
Central Asia, Eastern **6** 301
China **6** 776
Denmark **8** 730
Early Christian (*c.* AD 250-843) **9** 562
Gothic **13** 132, 133–4*, 135
Indian subcontinent **15** 548
Italy **13** 132, 135; **28** *337*, *338*, *339*
Mesopotamia **21** 308
Rome, ancient **27** 51
Slovenia **28** 860
types
lime secco **19** 394–5*; **27** 51; **28** 337; **32** 802
see also FRESCOES; MURALS; WALL PAINTINGS
Secco-Suardo, Giovanni **22** 102; **28** 340*
Seçen, Islam **23** 391
Šećerinski, Risto **19** 883
Secession (Berlin) **3** 801; **14** 175; **22** 257; **23** 186; **28** 340, 341–3*
exhibitions **3** 477; **11** 768; **22** 689; **28** 840; **29** 609
galleries (art) **14** *176*
members **12** 394; **24** 591
Beckmann, Max **3** 478
Bruguière, Francis **5** 7
Cassirer, Paul **5** 924
Corinth, Lovis **7** 856
Dettmann, Ludwig **8** 821
Feininger, Lyonel **10** 862
Friedrich, Nikolaus **11** 784
Gaul, August **12** 196
Kolbe, Georg **18** 203
Kollwitz, Käthe **18** 205
Kruse, (Carl) Max **18** 480
Kubin, Alfred (Leopold Isidor) **18** 490
Lehmbruck, Wilhelm **19** 94
Leistikow, Walter **19** 112
Liebermann, Max **19** 335
Minne, George **21** 648
Secession (Berlin) members—cont.
Neumann, J. B(er) (1887-1961; dealer) **23** 7
Pechstein, (Hermann) Max **24** 311
Purrmann, Hans **25** 743
Putz, Leo **25** 748
Tuaillon, Louis **31** 401
Uphues, Joseph (Johann Ludwig) **31** 688
Vallgren, Ville **31** 828
Walser, Karl **32** 827
Wenck, Ernst (Gustav Alexander) **33** 72
paintings **28** *342*
Secession (Budapest) **28** 340
Secession (Cologne) **20** 12
Secession (Croatia) **8** 178
Secession (Dresden) **4** 208; **9** 41; **10** 870; **28** 340
Secession (Düsseldorf) **28** 340
Secession (Graz) **21** 316; **30** 755
Secession (Japan) **14** 761; **17** 88; **33** 488
Secession (Karlsruhe) **28** 340
Secession (Kraków) **28** 340
Secession (Leipzig) **19** 112; **28** 340
Secession (London) **24** 739
Secession (Munich; founded 1892) **17** 736; **19** 277; **22** 304, 338; **28** 340–41*, 839; **30** 739; **31** 828
exhibitions **24** 739
members **12** 394
Behrens, Peter **3** 511
Bouzianis, Giorgos **4** 598
Carrière, Eugène **5** 881
Corinth, Lovis **7** 855
Diez, Julius **8** 885
Hirth, Georg **14** 576
Jank, Angelo **16** 906
Khnopff, Fernand **18** 24
Marussig, Piero **20** 521
Putz, Leo **25** 748
Riemerschmid, Richard **26** 374
Stuck, Franz von **29** 847
Trübner, (Heinrich) Wilhelm **31** 389
Uhde, (Friedrich Hermann Karl) Fritz von **31** 537
Secession (Photo-) *see* PHOTO-SECESSION
Secession (Poland) **25** 107, 123
Secession (Prague) **18** 405; **28** 340
see also MÁNES UNION OF ARTISTS
Secession (Rome) **5** 740, 919; **21** 87; **25** 586; **28** 340
Secession (Vienna) **2** 566–7, 776, 788; **3** 68; **12** 497; **14** 762; **28** 340, 343–4*, 670
art forms
architecture **19** 749; **21** 779; **22** 365
ceramics **30** 885
furniture **15** 823; **33** 156, *156*
metalwork **2** 822
posters **32** *446*
sculpture **2** 803
exhibitions **1** 783; **2** 571, 809; **6** 79; **14** 628; **18** 625; **19** 875; **20** 22; **21** 369; **28** 90; **33** 165
members **2** 571, 797; **12** 780; **14** 33; **32** 446, 762
Bacher, Rudolf **3** 21
Bauer, Leopold **3** 398
Bernatzik, Wilhelm **3** 821
Cézanne, Paul **6** 371
Czeschka, Carl Otto **8** 428
Egger-Lienz, Albin **9** 760
Fałat, Julian **10** 760
Forstner, Leopold **11** 320
Frampton, George (James) **11** 499
Hanak, Anton **14** 130
Hoffmann, Josef (Franz Maria) **14** 628
Hrdlicka, Alfred **14** 818
Secession (Vienna) members—cont.
Jettmar, Rudolf **17** 517
Kempf-Hartenkampf, Gottlieb Theodor von **17** 897
Klimt, Gustav **18** 129
Klinger, Max **18** 136
Knüpfer, Benedikt **18** 171
Kubin, Alfred (Leopold Isidor) **18** 490
Kurzweil, Max(imilian) **18** 534
MacNair, (James) Herbert **20** 31
Makovskaya-Luksh, Yelena (Konstantinovna) **20** 152
Malczewski, Jacek **20** 188
Mayreder, Julius **20** 895
Metzner, Franz **21** 365
Meyer, Adolf (Gayne) de, Baron (1868-1949) **21** 407
Minne, George **21** 648
Moll, Carl **21** 819
Moser, Kolo(man) **22** 187
Olbrich, Joseph Maria **23** 393
Orlik, Emil **23** 529
Powolny, Michael **25** 404
Putz, Leo **25** 748
Thorn Prikker, Johan **30** 760
Vallgren, Ville **31** 828
Wagner, Otto **32** 762
Weiss, Wojciech **33** 45
Zülow, Franz von **33** 723
periodicals **24** 438
sponsors **2** 829; **33** 284
writings **18** 131
Secession (Weimar) **28** 340
Secessione, La *see* SECESSION (ROME)
Secessione Artistica Italiana, Nuova *see* FRONTE NUOVO DELLE ARTI
Secession ((Münchner) Neue; founded 1913) *see* SEZESSION (NEUE)
secessions **21** 776; **28** 340*
see also SEZESSION
Séchan **24** 396; **28** 399
Séchas, Alain **11** 553
Sechelt Image **29** 743
Sechín *see* CERRO SECHÍN
Sechín Alto **29** *156*
architecture **29** *165*
temple **29** 165
Seckau Abbey
Engelskapelle **2** *798*
mausoleum of Charles II **2** 793, *793*, 800, 822
sculpture **2** 798; **26** 646
Seckel, Kryštof **25** 438
secondary ion mass spectroscopy *see under* TECHNICAL EXAMINATION → types
Secondat, Charles-Louis, Baron de Montesquieu *see* MONTESQUIEU (, Baron de)
Second Division Society *see* NIKAKAI
Second Empire style **9** 705; **28** 345–6*
architecture **10** 238; **23** *671*; **26** 190; **31** 593
frames **11** 414–15, *415*
interior decoration **11** *581*
portraits **4** *307*
Second Intermediate Period *see under* EGYPT, ANCIENT → periods
Second Mesa (AZ), Hopi Cultural Center **22** 568, 670
Second Mutual Credit Society **19** 332
Second Nuremberg Haggadah *see under* HAGGADOT → individual manuscripts
Second Order of St Francis *see* POOR CLARES, ORDER OF
Second Romanesque *see under* ROMANESQUE → styles
Second Star of Africa **12** 269
Second Style painting *see under* ROME, ANCIENT → painting → wall
Secoton **22** *552*
Secq (des Tournelles), Henri Le *see* LE SECQ (DES TOURNELLES), HENRI
Secqueville-en-Bessin **26** 598
secretaire-bookcases **5** 192
secretaires **5** 350; **9** 29; **11** 591; **12** 421, 423, 425, 426; **23** *66*; **26** *376*; **31** 631
see also BUREAUX; DAVENPORTS; DESKS
secrétaires à abattant *see under* DESKS → types
secrétaires à cylindre *see under* DESKS → types
secrétaires en pente *see under* DESKS → types
Secretan, Francine **5** 872
Secretaria do Patrimônio Histórico e Artístico Nacional (SPHAN) (Rio de Janeiro) **4** 728, 729
secretary drawers *see* ESCRITOIRES
secret gardens *see* GARDENS → types → *hortus conclusus*
Secret Room Painting *see* MISSHITSUGA
Section d'Or (i) *see* GOLDEN SECTION
Section d'Or (ii) **8** 246; **23** 569; **25** 747; **28** 347*
members
Apollinaire, Guillaume **2** 225
Csáky, Joseph **8** 225
Duchamp, (Henri-Robert-) Marcel **9** 355
Duchamp-Villon, (Pierre-Maurice-)Raymond **9** 361
Dunoyer de Segonzac, André (Albert Maris) **9** 396
Exter, Alexandra (Alexandrovna) **10** 699
Gleizes, Albert **12** 806
Gris, Juan **13** 669, 671
La Fresnaye, Roger de **18** 636
Léger, Fernand **19** 78
Lhote, André **19** 297
Marchand, Jean (Hippolyte) **20** 387
Marcoussis, Louis **20** 399
Metzinger, Jean **21** 363
Picabia, Francis (Marie Martínez) **24** 709
Survage, Léopold **30** 25
Villon, Jacques **32** 576
Secundus, Janus **13** 906
Securo, Francesco **18** 778
Sédaine, Michel-Jean **30** 672, 675
Sedan **11** 650
Sedang **32** 489
Sedano, Alonso de *see* ALONSO DE SEDANO
Sedano, Jan de **8** 551
Sedano Triptych **8** 551
Sedat, David W. **27** 607
Sedd al-Bahr **21** 586
Seddin **25** 524
Sedding, Edmund **28** 347; **29** 765
Sedding, J(ohn) D(ando) **28** 347–8*; **31** 151
collaboration **3** 368; **25** 187; **33** 132, 219
groups and movements **2** 575
pupils **12** 649
staff **33** 219
teachers **29** 765
Seddon, George (*c.* 1727-1801) **7** 659; **19** 592; **28** 348*
Seddon, George (1765-1815) **28** 348
Seddon, George (1796-1857) **28** 348
Seddon, George, & Co. **10** 297
Seddon, J(ohn) P(ollard) **5** 731; **10** 298; **28** 348, 349*
collaboration **25** 573
pupils **3** 893; **32** 720

Seddon, J(ohn) P(ollard)—cont.
works 10 281
Seddon, Thomas (1761-1804) 28 348
Seddon, Thomas (1792-1864) 28 348
Seddon, Thomas (1821-1856) 28 348*
groups and movements 10 253; 25 554
teachers 19 775
works 4 878
Seddon & Sons 28 348
Sedefkar see MEHMED AĞA
Sedeinga 23 279; 27 78
Tomb W T1 30 237
Sedelgem Church 11 253
Sedelmayr, Jeremias Jacob 13 278
Sedelmeyer, Charles 2 829; 6 548; 18 237; 22 311
Sedeño, Tomas Alberto 25 700
Seder sets 17 573*
Sedes 13 384
Sedgefield, St Edmund 28 295
sedges 3 331
Sedgley, Richard 4 353
Sedgwick, William 1 612; 9 374
Sedgwick Manciewicz, Alice see WERNHER, ALICE SEDGWICK
Sedia di S Marco 30 776
sedilia 28 349*
Sédille, Charles-Jules 28 349
Sédille, Paul 4 331; 8 770; 28 349–50*
Sedlaček, Vojtěch 8 393
Sedlec
Abbey Church (1703) 8 379
Cathedral 8 376
Cistercian church (c. 1280) 13 57
Sedlec monstrance 8 412
Sedlmayr, Hans 2 833, 834; 11 315; 28 350*
teachers 28 115
works 13 34; 26 63
Sedlmayr, János 14 891
Sedlyar, F. 4 605
Sedlyar, Vasyl' 2 634
Sedment 14 403
Tomb 254 10 53, 53
Sednev see SYNDIV
Sédrata 29 820
palace 16 244
Sedulius 5 801
Seebass, Alfred Richard 3 804
Seeberg Observatory 23 340
Seebüll, Stiftung Ada-und Emil Nolde 23 186
seed hairs see under FIBRES → types
seed pods 3 440
seeds 1 53, 296; 13 874
Seefried, Georg Christian 11 886
Seeger, Ernst 21 473
Seege von Laurenberg, Sigismund see LAURENBERG, SIGISMUND SEEGE VON
Seehof Schloss 2 234
Seeia 26 915; 28 350–51*
sculpture 22 419
Temple of Baalshamin 28 350–51
Temple of Dushara 26 918; 28 351
Seekatz, Johann Conrad 11 735; 12 853; 28 351*
Seekatz, Johann Ludwig 28 351
Seel, Eberhard 14 328
Seele, Johann Baptist 28 351*
pupils 14 307, 322; 18 456
works 12 392
Seelig, Warren 11 54
Seeliger, J. C. E. 19 731
Seeling, B. 18 506
Seelos, Hans 15 865
Seelos, Ludwig 15 865
Seely, Charles 11 331
Seeman, Enoch, the elder (b c. 1661) 28 352
Seeman, Enoch (c. 1694-1744) 28 352*
Seemann, E. A., (company) 10 212; 28 344
Seemann, Ernst Arthur 19 112
Seenat 11 106
Seenu Stupa 20 188
Seeon, Master of 20 768–9*
Seeon Abbey 13 90; 23 654; 28 25
Seeon Pietà 24 776
Sées, Cathedral of Notre-Dame 8 183; 13 42, 179; 29 413
Seesselberg, Friedrich 30 371
Seethaler, Johann Alois 12 447
Seetzen, Ulrich 12 337; 33 520
Seeu, Marinus de 26 269
Seeurosaari, Kekkonen Museum 29 769
Seewagen, Heini 20 797
Seewald, Richard 10 825
Sefar
rock art 1 376
Şefik Bey see MEHMED ŞEFIK
Sefton, Charles-William Molyneux, 3rd Earl of see MOLYNEUX, CHARLES-WILLIAM, 3rd Earl of Sefton
Sefton (Lancs), St Helen 24 576
pews 24 576
Šega, Franc Andrej 28 862
Segal, Arthur 3 802; 28 352*
groups and movements 8 434
pupils 20 877; 23 120
works 3 801; 11 465
Segal, George 28 353*; 31 615
dealers 16 906
groups and movements 10 416; 25 232
patrons and collectors 24 24; 28 315
works 29 671
Segal, Hanna 25 683
Segal, Uri Phoebus 17 564
Segal, Walter 28 352–3*
Segal, Zelig 16 568
Segala, Francesco 23 754; 28 354*
groups and movements 16 697
patrons and collectors 20 400
works 29 570
Ségalen, Victor 7 161
Segalino, Francesco see SEGALA, FRANCESCO
Segall, Lasar 4 717, 718; 28 354*
works 32 855
Segall, Lasar, Museu see under SÃO PAULO → museums
Segalla, Francesco see SEGALA, FRANCESCO
Segantini, Giovanni 5 126; 16 678, 679; 21 527; 28 354–7*
dealers 13 714–15
groups and movements 9 40
patrons and collectors 23 371; 28 344
works 22 330; 28 355, 356; 30 134
Segar, Francis 28 357
Segar, William 28 357*
works 8 828; 10 246; 15 150
illustrated 26 542
Segarra, Juan de 29 268
Segawa, Kokichi 10 580
Segenschmied, Franz Xaver 32 461
Seger, Hermann 12 436
Segers, Hercules (Pietersz.) 28 357–62*
attributions 27 330
copies 4 657
methods 9 308; 10 548, 559
patrons and collectors 5 679; 14 563; 26 160
teachers 22 840
works 10 553–4; 25 606, 614, 621; 28 359, 360, 361
Segerstrale, Lennart 11 97
Segersz., Pieter 18 817
Segesser, Placid 19 769
Segesta 13 362; 16 621; 26 886; 28 363*
metalwork 13 568
Segesta—cont.
temple 10 415; 13 414; 16 622, 622; 24 317; 28 363
theatre 26 873, 888
Segesvár see SIGHIŞOARA
Segewold see SIGULDA
seggars see SAGGARS
Seghers, Antheunis 21 102
Seghers, Daniel 17 512; 28 363–4*
collaboration 4 915; 25 811
patrons and collectors 1 690; 12 473; 23 463, 465
pupils 10 144; 30 730
works 3 561; 11 225, 227, 443; 28 364; 29 666
Seghers, Gerard 20 267; 28 364–5*
collaboration 32 705; 33 182
pupils 11 698
reproductive prints by others 4 283; 18 879; 22 717; 25 221; 32 700
works 28 365
Seghers, Hercules (Pietersz.) see SEGERS, HERCULES (PIETERSZ.)
Seghers, Jan Baptist 28 364
Seghizzi, Andrea 3 90; 6 28; 11 9; 15 138; 24 227
Segiriya see MIHINTALE
segmental arches see under ARCHES → types
segmental domes see under DOMES → types
segmental vaults see under VAULTS (CEILING) → types
Segna, Niccolò di see NICCOLÒ DI SEGNA
Segna di Bonaventura 28 365–6*
attributions 9 347
collaboration 9 346
patrons and collectors 9 306
teachers 9 349
works 13 146; 28 366, 684, 686
Segni (family) 11 888
Segni, Antonio 25 558
Segni, Bruno of see BRUNO OF SEGNI
Segni, Lotario dei Conti de see INNOCENT III, Pope
Segodnya see TODAY
Segoffin, Victor 28 366–7*
Segola, Philip 4 489
Segonzac, André (Albert Maris) Dunoyer de see DUNOYER DE SEGONZAC, ANDRÉ (ALBERT MARIS)
Segorbe y Cardona, Duque de 28 367*
Ségou 1 381; 20 199
Colonial Government Offices 20 198
fort 20 198
Segovia 26 904; 28 367–9*, 368; 29 258
Alcázar 19 896; 27 129
Arca del Tesoro 13 166
aqueduct 2 242, 242, 297; 4 800; 6 178; 27 7; 28 368
ecclesiastical buildings
Cathedral 13 70, 211; 25 30; 28 368–9*, 369; 29 265
metalwork 29 336
screen 28 294
stained glass 13 192; 29 504, 505
Corpus Christi 29 263
El Parral 13 70; 26 249
Jesuit church 26 250
La Vera Cruz 7 257; 9 112; 13 70; 18 154; 29 263, 275
S Antonio el Real 13 112
S Juan de los Caballeros see Museo Zuloaga
S Millán 2 528; 7 527; 28 368*
embroidery 29 350
Museo Zuloaga 28 368; 33 723
sculpture 26 607
Seminary 29 268
stage machinery 30 664
synagogue 22 254
Segovia, Master of see BENSON, AMBROSIUS
Segovia, Juan de see JUAN DE SEGOVIA
Segromigno, Villa Mansi 31 72
Seguí, Antonio 2 401; 28 369–70*
Séguier, Dominique, Bishop of Meaux 17 449; 19 162
Seguier, John 28 370
Séguier, Pierre 11 537; 24 167, 258; 28 370*
paintings 19 19, 20; 32 718
sculpture 27 821
sponsorship 12 725; 19 20
Seguier, William 13 696; 14 146; 19 588; 28 370*
Seguin, Abbot of La Chaise Dieu 5 893
Séguin, Armand 10 559; 19 10; 25 215; 28 371*
Seguin, Olivier 12 921
Segundo de Lema, José 10 501; 25 226
Segura, Antonio de 33 578
Segura, Jorge 24 511
Segura, Juan 21 379; 28 371*
Segura de la Ancuña, Andrés de see SAN MIGUEL, ANDRÉS DE
Segurado, Jorge 25 880
Seguros Carabobo 32 179
Segusini, Giuseppe 15 865; 28 371–2*
Segvić, N. 8 177
Şehabeddin Pasha 9 730
Sehetepneteru see FARAS
Seheult, François-Lénard 28 372*
Seheult, Saint-Félix 28 372*
Seh Gabi 12 838
Seh Hammad, Tell see SHEIKH HAMMAD, TELL
Sehring & Lachmann 8 770
Sehwan, Shrine of Shaykh 'Uthman Marvandi La'l Shahbaz 15 337
Şehzade Mehmed
paper 16 353
Şehzade Mustafa (Ottoman) 16 350
Seia see SEEIA
Sei a Torino 5 919; 31 446
Seibal 13 758; 20 882, 884; 21 246; 23 826; 28 372–3*, 373
architecture 20 885
Structure A-3 21 213; 28 372
Seibei 18 553
Seibu Department Stores 30 286
Seichō 17 122, 746
Seidan, Tomáš 22 403; 27 640
Seidenstücker, Friedrich 28 373*
Seidl, Alfred 32 450
Seidl, Andreas 10 860
Seidl, Emanuel von 9 382; 28 341, 374
Seidl, Gabriel von 28 373–4*
collaboration 19 152
pupils 3 878
staff 11 129
works 7 694; 22 363; 29 390
Seidler, Harry 5 602; 28 374–5*
collaboration 22 806; 28 834
groups and movements 2 756
staff 4 415
works 2 742; 4 818; 7 696; 28 375; 30 159
Seidler, Louise (Caroline Sophie) 14 655; 28 375–6*; 33 37
Seidl-Heck, Annie 25 404
Seidlin von Pettau 2 823
Seido Fujii see FUJII, SEIDŌ
Seiemon Nonomura see NONOMURA NINSEI
Seifert, Richard 19 577, 578; 28 376*
Seifert, Richard, Co. Partnership 12 775
Seiffert, Carl 14 657
Seifū Tsuda see TSUDA, SEIFŪ
Seigai, Kinoshita 30 246
Seignelay, Jean-Baptiste (-Antoine) Colbert, Marquis de 3 752; 6 518; 7 544, 546*; 21 498
bronze 11 626
fountains 11 344
interior decoration 3 752
paintings 23 515
sculpture 6 518
Seigneur, Jehan du 26 742
Seihakusai see Kanō Tsunenobu
Seihō Takeuchi see TAKEUCHI, SEIHŌ
Seiichi Izumi see IZUMI, SEIICHI
Seiichi Mizuno see MIZUNO, SEIICHI
Seiichi Shirai see SHIRAI, SEIICHI
Seijas Cook, Rafael 32 170
Seiji 17 399
Seijiro Tsukamoto see TSUKAMOTO, SEIJIRO
Seiji Tōgō see TŌGŌ, SEIJI
Seijurō Nakamura see NAKAMURA, SEIJURŌ
Seikaji 17 119
Seika Takiwaki see TAKIWAKI SEIKA
Seike, Kiyoshi 28 376*
Seikei 17 122
Seiki Kuroda see KURODA, SEIKI
Seiki, Yuzō 17 205
Seiki Yokoyama see YOKOYAMA SEIKI
Seiko 7 449
Seikō Kanō see KANŌ SEIKŌ
Seiko Kawachi see KAWACHI, SEIKO
Seiko Okuhara see OKUHARA SEIKO
Seiler-Baldinger, Annemarie 29 178
Seilern, Antoine, Count 7 579; 28 377*
Seilern Triptych 20 669, 672
Seiller, Johann Georg 27 136
Seima 28 321
Seimei Tsuji see TSUJI, SEIMEI
Seimu, Emperor 17 312
Seinai Dominican Church 19 497
Seine, de see DESEINE
Seinsheim, Adam Friedrich von 30 866; 32 120, 758
Seinsheim, Joseph Franz, Graf von 13 851
Seinsheim, von (family) 8 290
Seiran Watanabe see WATANABE SEIRAN
Seirullo (family) 1 579
Seiryūji
sculpture 17 126
Seisai see KITAO MASANOBU
Seisenegger, Jakob 2 716; 28 377–8*
collaboration 4 207
patrons and collectors 13 908
works 2 793; 8 390; 28 377
Sei Shōnagon 17 371
Seishūken see IKENAGA DŌUN
Seismic Baroque 14 713
seismic surveys see under SURVEYS → types
Seisnegger, Jakob 27 285
Seison Maeda see MAEDA, SEISON
Seissel, Joseph 8 437
Seisui Okuhara see OKUHARA SEISUI
Seitaro Miyazaki see MIYAZAKI, SEITARO
Seitenstetten Abbey 2 783, 825, 829
Seiter, Daniel 26 771; 28 378–9*
dealing 31 443
groups and movements 28 92
patrons and collectors 28 15
works 28 379
Seitone (family) 1 579
Seitz, Alexander Maximilian 28 380, 381
Seitz, Anton 20 549

Seitz, František Josef **8** 413
Seitz, Franz von **33** 283
Seitz, Gustav **12** 408; **19** 54; **28** 380*; **29** 733
Seitz, Heribert **2** 450
Seitz, Jiří **8** 413
Seitz, Johann **28** 380*
Seitz, Ludovico **26** 817; **28** 380–81*
Seitz, Otto **4** 598; **14** 840
Seitz, Rudolf von **8** 885; **28** 374
Seitz, William C. **23** 448
Seiwert, Franz **8** 437, 438; **13** 727; **22** 923; **25** 837, 838; **29** 869
Seixas, (Artur Manuel Rodrigues do) Cruzeiro *see* CRUZEIRO SEIXAS (ARTUR MANUEL RODRIGUES DO)
Seixas, José de Figueiredo *see* FIGUEIREDO SEIXAS, JOSÉ DE
Seiyōdo *see* SHIMIZU TOMIHARU
Seiz, Georg **28** 381
Seiz, Johannes **28** 381*; **31** 325
Seizan Matsuura *see* MATSUURA SEIZAN
Seizō Katō *see* KATŌ, SEIZŌ
Seizō Ōta *see* ŌTA, SEIZŌ
Seizo Sugawara *see* SUGAWARA, SEIZO
Sejdini, Bukurosh **1** 540
Šejka, Leonid **28** 451
Sejo, King of Korea (*reg* 1455-68) **7** 208; **18** 330; **28** 426
Sejong, King of Korea (*reg* 1418-50) **4** 174; **18** 356; **28** 381–2*
Séjourné, Paul **4** 802; **11** 770
Sejruk, M. **3** 529
Sekal, Zbyněk **8** 388
Sekani **22** 546, 645
Şeker Ahmet Pasha *see* AHMED, ALI
Sekhar **30** 818
śekharī **15** 244*
Sekhemka **10** 50
Sekhemkhet (*reg c.* 2611–*c.* 2604 BC) **9** *776*, 779
 architecture **10** 81; **15** 146; **25** 761; **27** 812
 stelae **29** 615
Sekhemre-Upmaat Inyotef **9** 879; **10** 10
Seki **17** 97, 358
sekibo *see under* FIGURINES → types
Sekien Toriyama *see* TORIYAMA SEKIEN
Sekijinyama Tomb **17** 143
Sekine, Shōji **17** 205; **23** 179
Sekino, Tadashi **7** 161; **18** 259; **22** 239
Seki Shikyō **17** 235
Sekishū Katagiri *see* KATAGIRI SEKISHŪ
Sekisui Itō *see* ITŌ, SEKISUI
Sekitei Kiuchi *see* KIUCHI SEKITEI
Sekitoleko, Francis **31** 528
Sekiyō *see* HYOBU SAIYO
Sekiyōkai **14** 260
Sekka Kamizaka *see* KAMIZAKA, SEKKA
Sekkyakushi **7** 183; **17** 170
Sekondi Teachers Training College **1** 319
Sekoto, Gerard **28** 382*; **29** 109
Selaʿ *see* PETRA
Selaković, Kemal **4** 462
Selam, Alle Felege *see* FELEGE SELAM, ALLE
Selangor **20** 163
 House of T. Y. Chiew **20** 169
 Roof-Roof House **20** 169
Selangor Pewter Company **20** 173
Sélavy, Rose *see* DUCHAMP, MARCEL
Selborne Priory (Hants) **29** 659
Selby Abbey **3** 709; **8** 611; **10** 228; **26** 614
Selchau, Jørgen **4** 417; **18** 799
Selçikler Köyü *see* SEBASTE (TURKEY)
Selçuk **9** 554; **10** 430*
 carpets **16** 470
 Ephesos Archaeological Museum **13** 470; **27** 115
 Isa Bey Mosque **16** 202, *203*; **22** 193
Selçuk (dynasty) *see* SALJUQ
Selcuks of Rum *see* SALJUQS OF ANATOLIA
Seld, Jörg **2** 718; **10** 220; **28** 382*
Selden, John **10** 420; **11** 424; **14** 806; **33** 453
Selden Roll *see under* ROLLS → individual manuscripts
Selectasine **28** 299
Select Committee on Arts and their Connections with Manufacture **10** 372
Sélection (gallery) **3** 564; **8** 809; **17** 508; **31** 502
Sélection (magazine) **5** 44
Select Society for the Encouragement of Arts, Sciences and Manufactures **28** 269
Selenica, David **1** 540
selenite **28** 28
selenium **12** 782
Seler, Eduard **21** 265, 734; **31** 310; **33** 472
Sélestat, Ste Foy **26** 633, 634
Seleucia **27** 63
Seleucia-on-the-Tigris **15** 912; **21** 268, 275; **28** 383
 architecture **24** 216; **28** 383
 iconography **24** 218
 iwans **16** 801; **21** 291
 jewellery **24** 218
 tower **24** 216
Seleucia Pieria **9** 539, 541
Seleucid **1** *852*; **15** 908; **21** 275; **28** 382–4*
 architecture **13** 405; **28** 383
 bronze **28** 384
 busts **28** *383*
 coins **13** 588, 589; **28** 383, 384
 glass **28** 384
 orders (architecture) **28** 384
 portraits **28** 383, 384
 rock reliefs **15** 916–17
 sculpture **21** 302; **28** 383, 384
 statuettes **28** 383
 stoas **13** 406
 temples **13** 405; **28** 383, 384
 see also:
 ANTIOCHOS III, King of Syria
 ANTIOCHOS IV EPIPHANES, King of Syria
 ANTIOCHOS VI EPIPHANES, King of Syria
 SELEUKOS I NIKATOR, King of Syria
Seleukia of Eulaios *see* SUSA (MESOPOTAMIA)
Seleukos (*fl* 25 BC) **27** 52
Seleukos I Nikator, King of Syria (*reg* 305-281 BC) **28** *383*
 architecture **28** 383
 temples **8** 869; **23** 392; **31** 747
 towns **1** 602; **2** 155, 213; **15** 912
 coins **13** 588
Selevac **25** 499, 516
Seley, Jason **17** 660
Self, Colin **10** 268; **25** 231
self-patterned tabby *see under* WEAVING → types
self-portraits *see under* PORTRAITS → types
self-weathering steel *see under* STEEL → types
Selge **26** 912, 913
Selham (W. Sussex), St James **26** 616
Seligenstadt-am-Main, SS Peter und Marcellinus **5** *793*, 794; **7** 265; **8** 222; **12** 363, 471
 piers (ii) (masonry) **24** 750
Seligmann, Jacques **27** 224; **28** 384*, 528
Seligmann, Jacques, & Co. Inc. **2** 559; **14** 139
Seligmann, Kurt **28** 384–5*; **30** 135, 139
 groups and movements **1** 666; **30** 22, 135
 works **19** 491
 writings **1** 666
Selim I, Sultan (*reg* 1512-20) (Ottoman) **8** 478; **16** 542, 545; **28** 811
Selim II, Sultan (*reg* 1566-74) (Ottoman) **16** 333, 347, 595, 610; **20** 914; **21** 33; **23** 639, 641; **28** 768
Selim III, Sultan (*reg* 1789-1807) (Ottoman) **16** 291, 611
Şelimbăr **26** 719
Selime Monastery **5** 674
Selimiye Mosque *see under* EDIRNE
Selinos, Church of the Holy Fathers **8** 156; **25** 334
Selinunte *see* SELINUS
Selinus **13** *362*, 587; **16** *621*; **28** 385–7*
 coins **13** 586
 figurines **13** 579
 fortifications **21** 556; **28** 654
 houses **13** 401
 North Gate **21** 558
 orders (architecture) **23** 484
 pottery **13** 499
 sculpture **28** 386, 654
 temples **13** 374; **28** *385*, 385–6
 Temple B **13** 612
 Temple C **13** 398, 432, 447, 612; **28** 386
 Gorgoneion **13** 390
 sculpture **28** *387*
 Temple D **13** 398
 Temple E **10** 415; **13** 432, 434, 451, 470
 Temple G **13** 378, 398; **16** 622; **23** 481
 Temple of Hera *see* Temple E
Selje, St Alban **26** 593
Seljuk *see* SALJUQ
Selkirk (Man.; Canada) **22** 645
Selkirk (Borders; UK)
 law courts **28** 288
Selk'nam **29** 204
Sella, Quintino **26** 762
Sella, Vittorio **28** 387*
sella curulis *see under* CHAIRS → types
Sellaer, Vincent **3** 554; **28** 388*
Sellaio **7** 334
Sellaio, Arcangelo del *see* ARCANGELO DEL SELLAIO
Sellaio, Francesco **13** 94
Sellaio, Jacopo del *see* JACOPO DEL SELLAIO
Sellán, Juan **29** 338
Sellari, Girolamo *see* CARPI, GIROLAMO DA
Sellari, Tommaso **10** 523
Sellars, James **28** 228
Selle, de **12** 185
Seller, Abraham **2** 163
Sellers, Coleman **10** 669, 670
Sellers, J(ames) Henry **33** 343
Selles-sur-Cher, St Eusice **21** 163; **26** 586, 599
Sellier, Charles-François **15** 841; **28** 388*
Sellier, Henri **24** 129, 130
Sellier, Jacques **11** 596
Sellier, Louis **29** 93
Sellin, Ernst **17** 483; **28** 573
Selling (Kent), St Mary **13** 183; **14** 422
 stained glass **14** *422*
Sellitto, Carlo **22** 478; **28** 388–9*
Sellitto, Sebastiano **28** 388
Sellius, Gottfried **11** 171
Sellner, Gustav Rudolf **33** 386
Sello **24** 485
Sellotape **24** 53
Selma, Fernando **28** 389*
Selman, Eduardo **9** 117
Selmanović, Behaudin **4** 461
Selmecbánya *see* BANSKA ŠTIAVNICA
Selmer, Harald **4** 69
Selmersheim, Tony **11** 600; **25** 52
Selmesheim, Pierre **11** 602
Selous, Henry Courtney **28** 389*
 works **15** *884*
Sels'kyi, Roman **23** 262
Seltendorff, Friedrich **19** 110
Selva, Domenico **5** 519
Selva, Giovanni Antonio **28** 389–90*
 collaboration **7** 306
 groups and movements **22** 741
 teachers **30** 424
 theatres **28** *390*
 works **16** 646; **24** 496; **25** 268; **32** 188
Selva, Roberto de la **23** 81
Selva de Montirac, Pierre, Cardinal of Pamplona **32** 574
Selvatico (family) **8** 483
Selvatico (Estense), Pietro, Marchese **28** 391–3*
 patrons and collectors **28** 371
 works **28** *392*, *393*
 writings **25** 741; **27** 166
Selve, George de, Bishop **14** *669*
Selvi, Antonio Francesco **11** 347; **20** 922; **28** 393*
Selwyn, George Augustus **23** 53; **30** 646
Selymbria **9** 555
Selyuk Island **27** 367
Selz, Peter **17** 694; **31** 673
Selzaete **31** 875
Semaine des Constructeurs, La **8** 476
Seman, Clause **33** 353
Semana de Arte Moderna **4** 712, 717, 725; **28** 393–4*
 members **4** 731; **6** 99; **26** 96
Sema Naga **15** 205, 733
Semanario pintoresco español, El **24** 452
Semang **20** 163
Semantic art **28** 394*
Semarang
 Borsumij Company building **15** 770
 Cultuurmaaatschappij der Voorstenlanden building **15** 769
 Sisters Railway Company building **15** 770
 Sobokartti Folk Theatre **15** 770
Semashkevich, Roman (Matveyevich) **28** 394–5*
Semashko, Iosif **7** 244
Sembatsu Shūsaku Bijutsu Ten (Exhibtion of Selected Outstanding Art) **17** 135
Sembiyan Mahadevi *see* SHEMBIYAN MAHADEVI
Semedo **8** 11
Semeghini, Pio **16** 679; **28** 395*
Semenov, A. A. **16** 549
Semenov, P. P. **6** 280
Sementi, Giovan Giacomo **4** 666; **26** 197, 200; **28** 9, 395*
Semenza, Marco **21** 521
Semerkhet **9** *776*
Šemešys, Adomas **19** 498
Semian, Ervín **28** 853
Semibratny **13** 570
 silver **13** 372, 373, 568, *570*
semicircular mouldings *see under* MOULDINGS → types
semi-cursive script *see under* SCRIPTS → types
semi-domes *see under* DOMES → types
Seminario, Manuel Rendón *see* RENDÓN SEMINARIO, MANUEL
Semino, Alessandro **9** 173; **28** 395
Semino, Andrea **28** 395–6*
 collaboration **28** 395, 396
 patrons and collectors **9** 173; **29** 411
 pupils **6** 25
 teachers **28** 395
Semino, Antonio **28** 395
Semino, Giulio Cesare **9** 173; **28** 395
Semino, Ottavio **13** 307; **28** 395–6*
Semino, Paggi **9** 173
Seminole **22** 553, 663, 670; **24** 253
 beadwork **4** I1
semiotics **2** 533, 537; **3** 289; **7** 661; **15** 100; **24** 377; **26** 222–3; **28** 396–7*; **31** 769
Semipalatinsk **17** *865*; **27** 375
Semipalatka **17** 866
semi-precious stones *see* HARDSTONES
Semirani, Luciano **16** 651
Semirechye
 altars **6** *243*
 gold **6** 241
 metalwork **6** 242
 sculpture **6** 212
 silver **6** 240; **28** *723*
Semitecolo, Nicoletto **13** 747; **23** 753; **25** 442; **28** 397*
Semiz Ali Pasha **9** 730
Semmel, Joan **10** 483
Semna **9** *774*; **23** *276*; **30** 237
 fort **9** 844, 845–6, *845*; **10** 81; **21** 554
 stelae **29** 615
 Temple of Amun **23** 281
 temples **23** 279
Semnan *see* SIMNAN
Semna South **9** 845; **21** 554
Semolei, Il *see* FRANCO, (GIOVANNI) BATTISTA
Semon, John **14** 203
Šemov, Simon **19** 885
Semp, Johan **8** 725
Sempé, Jean-Jacques **5** 759
Semper, Gottfried **2** 826; **9** 236–7; **10** 298, 740; **15** 211; **25** 172; **28** 397–401*; **29** 879
 architecture **12** 376
 government buildings **22** 300, *300*
 houses **25** 172; **32** 554
 museums **2** *786*, 787, 830; **9** 12; **22** 363, 364; **25** 240; **29** 525
 observatories **23** 340
 palaces **23** 813; **32** 760, 762
 railway stations **33** 735
 schools **13** 842; **30** 127; **33** 735
 synagogues **17** 547, *548*; **22** 60
 theatres **2** 808; **9** 239, 242; **28** *398*, *399*; **30** 506, 677, 678, *678*
 assistants **14** 216
 collaboration **28** 95; **32** 437, 457; **33** 131
 groups and movements **26** 190; **27** 336
 pupils **2** 478, 711; **4** 182; **22** 60; **29** 791
 teachers **12** 178
 writings **26** 491
Semper, Hans **2** 834
Sempere, Eusebio **1** 620; **28** 401*; **29** 296, 309
Semple, George **9** 317
Semple, John **28** 401*
 works **16** 10, *10*
Semplice da Verona, Fra **12** 913
Sempoliński, Jacek **2** 502; **25** 108; **28** 402*
Sempringham (Lincs), St Andrew **10** 339; **21** 840
Sempukuji cave **17** 244
Semsales **30** 145
Semur-en-Auxois **11** *504*; **28** 402–3*
 Notre-Dame **13** 41; **28** 402–3*
Semur-en-Brionnais **26** 602

Semyonov, A. A. **28** 596
Semyonov, Vasily **27** 421
Semyonov, Vladimir (Nikolayevich) **27** 379; **28** 403*
works **3** 88; **12** 145; **22** 174; **27** 377, 379; **31** 730
Semyonova, Mariya **27** 426
Semyonov-Tyan-Shansky, P. P. **27** 439
Šen, Edo **8** 766; **28** 403*
Sen, Paritosh **5** 420
Sena **23** 805*
Sena, António **25** 300
Senaca, Antonio **16** 724
Senanayake, Laki **29** 456
Senanayake, Senaka **29** 468
Senanque Abbey **7** 453; **21** 837, 843, *843*
Senarclens, Claude de **1** 584
Senart, Emile **11** 335
Senate Park Commission *see* McMillan Commission
Senatne un Māksla **28** 715
Senault, Guillaume **3** 924; **11** 904
Senbel, Mustafa **27** 876
Šenberga, Dace **33** 378
Šēnbergs, Georgs
Senbergs, Jan **1** 147; **28** 403–4*
Senbi **9** 877; **21** 61
Sendai **17** 84, 95, 358
Osaki Hachiman Shrine **17** 63
Sendak, Maurice **4** 368
works **4** *368*
Sendangduwur **15** 783
cemetery **15** 768
gateways **15** *769*
Seneb **9** 858, *858*, 872
Senebtisi **10** 66; **19** 470
Seneca (people) **16** 61; **22** 552, 612
Seneca(, Lucius Annaeus) (4 BC–AD 65) **12** 68; **15** 51; **26** 871
Senefelder, Georg **19** 482
Senefelder, J(ohann) N(epomuk) F(ranz) Alois **15** 855; **19** 479, 481, 482; **25** 345, 615; **28** 404*; **33** 685
methods **20** 601; **25** 591
works **12** 392; **19** 481, *482*; **22** 370; **25** 623
Senefelder, Theobald **19** 482
Senefelder Club **19** 492
Seneffe, Comte de **32** 767
Seneffe Château **3** 547
Senegal **1** *214*, 380; **28** 404–6*
architecture **21** 43; **28** 405*
collections **28** 406
compounds **1** 311
dyeing **3** 379
education (art) **28** 406*
gold **1** 288
houses **1** 313
museums **1** 440; **28** 406*
painting **28** 405–6*, *406*
patronage **28** 406*
sculpture **28** 406*
tapestries **28** *405*
trade
oils **1** 250
Sen'ei Ikenobō *see* IKENOBŌ SEN'EI
Sen'emon Kawai *see* KAWAI SEN'EMON
Senenfelder, Alois **8** 128
Senenmut **9** 790, 826, 859, 860, 880; **28** 407*
paintings **9** 805, 902
sculpture **9** 795, 857
Sénèque, Clement **9** 427; **29** 108
Senes, Lorenzo **25** 97, 118; **28** 407*
Senex, John **12** 815
Senff, Karl August **10** 539; **28** 408*
Senftenberg **21** 551; **25** 536
Sengai Gibon **5** 120; **17** 165, 194, 231; **28** 408–9*
Sengele **19** 74
Senge Namgyel, Ruler of Basgo (*reg c.* 1570 1642) **14** 383; **15** 397; **19** 90; **21** 593
Sengetsohip **21** 881
Sengge, Princess **7** 151, 153
Senghim **18** 26
Senghimaghiz **6** 296
Seng-ke, Princess *see* SENGGE, Princess
Senglea **20** 215
Sengoku *see under* HACHIŌJI → Miyata
Sengoku period *see under* JAPAN → periods
Śeṅgu *see* SVAYAMBHUNATHA
Sengyō Ikenobō *see* IKENOBŌ SENGYŌ
Senhora, Feliciano de Nossa, Bishop of Lamego *see* NOSSA SENHORA, FELICIANO DE, Bishop of Lamego
Senhouse, George **8** 832
Senigallia, Giovanni della Rovere, Lord of **11** 690; **25** 217
Senigallia *Madonna* **1** 818, *818*; **7** 835; **24** 764
Senillosa, Felipe **2** 395
Senior, David **2** 148
Senis, Mey de *see* MEO (DI GUIDO) DA SIENA
Senj **8** *174*, 175
Senkadagala *see* KANDY
Senkaku **27** 469
Senkamanisken (*reg* 643-623 BC) **23** 282
Senke **17** 336
Senkei Ikenobō *see* IKENOBŌ SENGYŌ
Senkin, Sergey **24** 686
Senkō Ikenobō II *see* IKENOBŌ SENKŌ II
Senkschmelz enamel *see under* ENAMEL → techniques
Senkyūhyaku Sanjū Kyōkai (1930 Society) **17** 206; **27** 506
Senlis **11** *504*; **26** *905*; **28** 409–10*
Cathedral of Notre-Dame **1** 723; **9** 48–9, 672; **11** 155, 510; **13** 37, 61; **28** *409*, 409–10*
piers (ii) (masonry) **24** 751
sculpture **7** 643; **11** 555; **13** 73; **28** 410
spire **29** 412
St Vincent **2** 723, 725
town walls **21** 560
Victorine church **32** 416
Senlis, Alice de, Countess of Northampton **14** 418
coats of arms **14** *417*
Senlis, Raoul de *see* RAOUL DE SENLIS
Senlis, Séraphine de *see* SÉRAPHINE
Senn, Otto **30** 128
Senn, Paul **28** 410*
Senna (Iran) **15** *897*, 899; **16** 483; **18** 48
kilims **18** *48*
Sennacherib (*reg* 704-681 BC) **1** *854*; **21** 274, 304, 553
aqueducts **2** 241
architecture **1** 892; **2** 638, 640–41; **3** 418, 419; **9** 85; **18** 896; **21** 287, 290; **23** 153–4; **30** 25
cotton **1** 880
dams **12** 66
gardens **12** 66; **21** 291
reliefs **20** 220; **21** *278*, 300–301*
rock reliefs **12** 66
sculpture **30** 774
Senna knots *see* KNOTS → asymmetrical
Sennar (Sudan) **16** *104*, 519; **23** 289, 290
Senneby, Anette **30** 87
Sennedjem **2** 296; **9** 840, 903; **10** 53
tomb **30** *700*
Sennefer **9** 840, 857, *857*; **11** 374
Sennett, Mack **1** 21
Senneval, Marquis de **13** 308
Senneville, Leroy de **11** 595
Sennhauser, H. R. **27** 554
sennit **23** 712, *712*
Senno Ikenobō *see* IKENOBŌ SENNO
Sen no Rikyū **12** 98; **17** *335*, 343, 365, 381; **21** 828; **23** 594; **28** 410–13*; **30** 376
collaboration **18** 553
personal collection **17** 343; **18** 559
pupils **11** 854; **23** 347
teachers **30** 259
works **15** 108; **17** 215, 323, 335–6, 337, 339, 343, 423, 424; **25** 869
Sennosuke Takeda *see* TAKEDA, SENNOSUKE
Sennuwy **2** 659; **17** 911
Senō Kanayama *see* KANAYAMA SENŌ
Senones **28** 413
Senorbí **27** 834
Senpan Maekawa *see* MAEKAWA, SENPAN
Senro Kawai *see* KAWAI, SENRO
Senryūsai *see* UTAGAWA TOYOHARU
Sens **11** *504*, 653; **26** *905*; **28** 413–18*
Cathedral of St Etienne **1** 723; **6** 413; **8** 288; **9** 672; **11** 154, 510; **13** 37, 39, 42, 61; **22** 218; **28** 413–15*, *414*, *415*
apse **2** 347
buttresses **5** 319
nave **13** *37*
piers (ii) (masonry) **24** 751
sculpture **11** 554; **13** 73, 75
architectural **28** 416*, *416*
stained glass **13** 179, *179*; **26** 702; **28** 416–17*, *417*; **29** 501, 506, 510
textiles **4** 544; **9** *666*, 667; **18** 157; **23** 461; **26** 703; **30** 314
tracery **31** 273
transept **31** 281
Treasury **28** 417–18*
roofs **30** 907
St-Pierre-le-Vif **1** 767; **7** 266; **8** 224
Salle Synodale **32** *595*
silk **9** 663
Sens, William of *see* WILLIAM OF SENS
Senseki Takami *see* TAKAMI SENSEKI
Sensen *see* QIAN XUAN
Sensenruth Church **13** 182
Sensheim, Adam Friedrich von, Prince-Bishop of Würzburg **12** 134
sensibilité **12** 292, 293; **28** 418*
Sensier, Alfred **9** 424; **21** 430
Sen Sōtan **17** 215, 336, 343
Sens Pontifical *see under* PONTIFICALS → individual manuscripts
Sens propre **5** 44
Sensuke Naitō *see* NAITŌ SENSUKE
Senta Museum **28** 459
Sentaro Iwaki *see* IWAKI, SENTARO
Sentenach, Narciso **19** 303
Šentevski, Nikola **19** 885
Sentigny, Jacques **12** 467
Sentout, Pierre **19** 510
Šentrupert Church **28** 858
Šentvid **28** 860
Senufo **1** 310, 385; **8** 21; **28** 418–23*
bracelets **1** 357
burial practices **1** 258–9*
divination instruments **1** 357–8
doors **1** 280, 314; **9** 164
fibres **28** *422*
Senufo—cont.
figurines **1** 273, *281*
iconography **1** 275, 280
jewellery **1** 279
masks **1** 241, 279, 301, 338, 341; **28** 420–21*, *421*, *422*
meeting-houses **1** 310
mixed-media **1** 301
musical instruments **1** 360
painting **8** 22
patronage **1** 241
sculpture **1** 234, 278, 279, 280, 322, 323; **8** 22; **28** *419*, 419–20*, *420*
staffs **1** 263; **28** 421–3*
textiles **1** 258, 290
tools **1** 370
wood **1** *281*; **9** 164; **28** *419*, *420*, *421*, *422*
Senusertankh **19** 471
Senusert-Senebefny **9** 857, 860
Senusret III *see* SESOSTRIS III
Senwosre
seals **10** *71*
Senza Graffito Painter **10** 614
Senzoku Tomb **17** 143
Seoane, Luis **2** 400; **28** 423*; **29** 286
Seo de Urgel, Cathedral of S María **26** 43; **29** 337
Seoka, Phuthuma **29** 113
Séon, Alexandre **27** 639; **28** 423*
Seoul **18** *248*, *250*, 261, 262, 282; **28** 423–6*, *424*
Academy of Painting and Calligraphy **18** 381
architecture **18** 264; **28** 426
Bank of Korea **18** 264
British Ambassador's residence **18** 262
Capitol Building **18** 262
Chŏngdong **18** 262
Chŏngdong Church **18** 262
Chongmyo **23** 821
Chongmyo Royal Ancestral Shrine **18** 269
Daehan Life building **18** 264
Daewoo Centre **18** 264
fortifications **21** 594
fortress **18** 260
French Embassy **18** 263
gates **18** 279
Great East Gate **18** 261, *262*
South Gate **18** 265
glass **18** 365
Hilton Hotel **18** 264
Hwashin department store **18** 263
Ihwa school for girls **18** 262
Korean Traditional Performing Arts Centre **18** 264
Kyŏngsŏng Electric Corporation building **18** 262
Kyŏngsŏng government office **18** 262
Kyŏngsŏng Institute for Commercial and Industrial Support **18** 263
Lucky Goldstar Corporation **18** 264
Mt Pukhan **18** 291
Munhwajae Kwalliguk Research Institute of Cultural Properties Preservation **18** 381
museums
Art Museum of the Korean People **33** 491
Central National Museum **6** 321; **18** 383, 384
Ho-am Art Museum **18** 383
Horim Art Museum **18** 383
Kansŏng Art Museum **18** 383
Museum of the Government-general of Korea **18** 382
National Ethnographical Museum *see* National Folklore Museum
National Folklore Museum **18** 383; **28** 425
Seoul
museums—cont.
National Museum **5** 175; **7** 154
National Museum of Korea *see* Central National Museum
National Museum of Modern Art **18** 383
Sunggyun'gwan University Museum **18** 330
Tongguk University Museum **18** 308, 329
Whanki Museum **18** 56
Myŏngdong Cathedral **18** 262
National Assembly Building **18** 264
National Theatre **18** 264
Olympic Sculpture Park **18** 302
Olympic Stadium **18** *263*
Paejae school for boys **18** 262
palaces **28** 425–6
Ch'angdŏk Palace **12** 94; **18** 276; **23** 821
garden **18** 276
paintings **7** 208
Piwŏn **12** 94, *94*; **18** 72
throne **30** 785
Yŏn'gyongdang house **18** *278*, 278–9
Ch'anggyŏng Palace **12** 94; **18** 276; **23** 821
Kyŏngbok Palace **12** 94; **18** 276; **23** 821; **28** 425
Hwangwŏnjong **18** 72
Kalhang Temple **23** 775
Kŭnjŏng Hall **18** *275*
stupa **29** 869
throne **30** 785
Yŏngje Bridge **18** *280*
Tŏksu Palace **18** 276; **28** 425–6
Art Gallery **18** 263, 383
Savings Bank **18** 263
sculpture **18** 301
Sejong Cultural Centre **18** 264
Sŏnggyun'gwan Academy
Munmyo Shrine **18** 269; **30** 445
Sŏngmo Hospital **18** 263
stele **18** 328
Sup'yo Bridge **18** 280
Tongbang Life Office **18** 264
universities
Dankook University **18** 381
Ehwa Women's University Library **18** 264
Hanyang University **18** 381
Hong'ik University **18** 301
Koryŏ University **18** 381
National University **18** 301, 381
Sŏgang University **18** 263
Sunggyun'wan University Museum *see under* → museums
Tongguk University Museum *see under* → museums
Yonsei University **18** 381
Sep **3** 848
Sepa **9** 866
Sepahan *see* ISFAHAN
Sepharvaim *see* SIPPAR
sepia **15** 852, 855; **24** 648, 792
see also PHOTOGRAPHIC PRINTS → types
Sepino, Tomb of C. Ennius Marsus **20** 864
Sepins, S João Baptista **26** 611
Sepmann, Henno **10** 538; **30** 276
SEPRA **2** 397; **30** 525
Sepsibükszád Glassworks **29** 249
Sepsiszentgyörgy *see* SFÎNTU GHEORGHE
Sept Arts *see* 7 ARTS
Septemberhópurinn *see* SEPTEMBRISTS
Septembrists **2** 412; **24** 572; **28** 828
Septem group **11** 96; **23** 266; **28** 427*
members **10** 200; **11** 83; **26** 421; **27** 633

Septimius Severus, Emperor of Rome (*reg* 193-211) **8** 477; **9** 895, *895*; **26** 900–901; **27** 41, 45, *98*, 670; **28** 509–10*
architecture **16** 578; **19** 222; **26** 784, 853, 867, 875, 885, *900*, 901*; **27** 4, 41; **30** 694; **31** 349–50
coins **27** 97
monuments **26** *901*
propylaea **26** 920
sculpture **27** 41
sepulchral monuments *see* MONUMENTS → types → funerary
sepulchre churches *see under* CHURCHES → types
Sepúlveda, Fernando de *see* FERNANDO DE SEPÚLVEDA
Sepúlveda, João de Deus **4** 716; **26** 65
Seqenenre Tao, II (*reg c.* 1560 BC) **9** 879; **10** 87
Sequana **27** 2
Sequani **18** 828
Sequeira, Domingos António de **14** 586; **28** 429–32*
patrons and collectors **29** 100
personal collection **5** 367
pupils **4** 637
works **24** 243; **25** 298, *298*, 307, *313*, 314; **28** *430*, *432*
Sequeira, José da Costa **28** 433*
Sequeiros, David Alfaro *see* ALFARO SEQUEIROS, DAVID
sequence dating *see under* DATING METHODS → types
Sequens, František **18** 525
sequins **4** II; **15** 795
Sera **30** *806*, 819, 820, 846
Sera, Cosimo del **22** 423
Sera, Paolo del **4** 455; **21** 27, 28; **28** 433*
Serabaglio, Giovanni Battista **2** 455
Serabi carpets *see under* CARPETS → types
Serabit el-Khadim **9** *774*; **28** 433–4*
inscriptions **1** 855
reliefs **29** 394
sculpture **28** *433*, 760
statuettes **1** 770
stelae **29** 616
Temple of Hathor **9** 831; **28** 434
Serafi, D. **29** 638
Serafimovski, Aleksandar **19** 883
Serafimovski, Tome **19** 885
Serafini, Paolo **28** 434*
Serafini, Serafino **28** 434–5*
works **28** *435*; **31** 104
Serahuli **12** 32
Serai Doraha **15** 364
Serai Nur Mahal **15** 364
Šerák, Václav **8** 406
Serambos **1** 481
Sérangeli, Gioacchino Giuseppe **8** 867; **12** 830; **13** 793
Serantoni, Antonio **1** 844
Seraph, Master of the *see* OTTO VAN MOERDRECHT, MASTER OF
Séraphim, Juliana **19** 8
Séraphine **22** 440, 441; **28** 435–6*
Serapion (*fl* 1st cent. AD) **27** 52
Serapion (the younger) **14** 432
Serbaldi, Antonio **28** 436
Serbaldi da Pescia, Pier Maria **28** 436*
patrons and collectors **3** 48; **21** 16
pupils **32** 393
works **12** 258; **14** 170; **16** 746
Serbelloni (family) **5** 650
Serbia **28** 436–59*, *437*; **33** 571
architecture **28** 439–42*, 444–5*
Byzantine **9** 552–3
vernacular **32** 293, 294
19th cent. **3** *620*
beds **28** 454
Serbia—cont.
book covers **28** 456
bowls **28** *455*
ceramics **28** 454*
churches **9** 552–3; **13** *264*; **28** 440–42, *441*, *442*
clay **25** *464*; **32** *581*
coins **14** 411; **28** 454–5
collections **28** 458–9*
dress **28** 456–7, 458
education (art) **28** 451
embroidery **28** 457–8*
epitaphioi **28** *457*
figurines **25** *528*; **32** *581*
fortresses **28** 440, *444*
forts **28** 439
furniture **28** 454*
heraldry **14** 411
icons **25** *339*, 339–40*; **28** *447*, 447–9*, *448*
interior decoration **28** 454*
jewellery **28** 456
kilims **28** 458
linen **28** 456
manuals **25** 340
manuscript illumination **28** 449–50*
marble **28** *453*
masonry **4** 773
metalwork **28** 454–6*
miniatures (manuscript illumination) **28** *449*
monasteries **28** 440
museums **28** 458–9*
painting **22** 80; **28** 445*, 450–52*
wall **22** *79*; **28** 445–7*
Byzantine **28** *445*, *446*
Post-Byzantine **25** 343–4*
Romanesque **28** 445
portraits **28** *451*
pottery **25** *528*; **29** 546
prints **28** 450*, 451*, 452*
Psalters **9** 613
sculpture **28** 452–4*
Prehistoric **25** *464*
relief **28** *453*
silk **28** 456, *457*
silver **28** *455*, 456
textiles **28** 456–7*, 458*
trade **9** 515; **28** 456
tympana **28** *453*
vestments (ecclesiastical) **28** 457–8
wool **28** 456
Serçe Limanı **16** 406
shipwreck **16** 517, 518
Ser Cenni, Cenni di Francesco di *see* CENNI DI FRANCESCO DI SER CENNI
Serdika *see* SOFIA (BULGARIA)
Serebriakoff, Alexander
works **10** *285*
Serebryakova, Zinaida (Yevgen'yevna) **3** 732; **18** 749; **27** 392; **28** 459*
teachers **30** 464
Séré de Rivières, Raymond **21** 568
Serednikovo **27** 376
Şeref, Abdurrahman **16** 611
Seregni (di Bonardo), Vincenzo **28** 460–61*
collaboration **1** 608; **12** 761; **19** 561
pupils **3** 354
works **1** 462; **21** 532; **28** *460*
Seregni, Vitruvio **28** 461
Seremban **20** *162*, 169
Istana Hinggap **23** 823
Negeri Sembilan State Mosque **20** 166
Serena, Francesco Leone **12** 595; **29** 835
Serena, La *see* LA SERENA
Serenghi, Counts **1** 726
Serenyi, László **2** 546
Serer **28** 404
Serfederigi, Paolo di *see* PAOLO DI SERFEDERIGI
Serfka **9** 822
Serfolio, Giacomo (di Bartolomeo) **4** 620; **20** 901; **28** 461*
Ser Francesco, Antonio da Giovanni di *see* ANTONIO DA GIOVANNI DI SER FRANCESCO
Sergardi, Filippo **27** 648; **28** 335
serge **16** 445; **30** 845
Sergeant, Peter **4** 472
Sergel, Johan Tobias **24** 137; **28** 461–3*; **29** 689
collaboration **10** 100
groups and movements **13** 864
patrons and collectors **8** 161; **30** 268
personal collection **5** 366
pupils **5** 339; **11** 99; **13** 31
works **5** 302, *303*; **26** 99; **28** *462*; **30** 85, *86*, 109
Sergent, Francés Tené **2** 405
Sergent, René **5** 530; **18** 782; **28** 463–4*
Sergent, Tené **5** 123
Sergent-Marceau, Antoine Louis François **28** 464*
Serghini, Mohamed **22** 129
Sergi, Sergio **2** 399
Sergia Postuma **25** 720
Sergioupolis *see* RUSAFA
Ser Giovanni (da Firenze), Leonardo di *see* LEONARDO DI SER GIOVANNI (DA FIRENZE)
Sergius I, Pope (*reg* 687-701) **6** 173; **26** 803
Sergius II, Pope (*reg* 844-47) **26** 821
Sergius III, Pope (*reg* 904-11) **26** 821
Sergius Orata **15** 51; **26** 871
Sergius Radonezhsky, Saint **28** 464
Sergiyev Posad **27** *363*; **28** 464–5*
Monastery of the Trinity and St Sergius **27** 370, 371, 373, 387; **28** 464–5, *465*
bell-tower **27** 374
Cathedral of the Dormition **27** 371
collections **27** 440
manuscripts **27** 385
St John the Baptist **29** 779
Trinity Cathedral **27** 384
Serguidi, Antonio *see* GUIDI, ANTONIO
Séri, Robert de *see* ROBERT, PAUL-PONCE-ANTOINE
seriation **2** 300; **30** 382
Serigiers, G. **2** 516; **3** 614
serigraphy **25** 616; **28** 298, 299, 465*
see also SCREENPRINTING
Sérilly, Mme de **26** 551
Seri Menanti, Istana Lama **23** 823
Seringapatam **15** 678
Seripando, Girolamo **32** 12
Seripando, Gualtiero **22** 486
Seriphos **8** *304*
Serizawa, Keisuke **21** 635; **28** 466*
groups and movements **17** 295; **21** 634
patrons and collectors **17** 433; **23** 371
pupils **22** 114
works **17** 310
serjeant painters **28** 466*
Serjilla **3** 376
Serlachius, Gösta **11** 111, 112
Serlachius, Gustaf Adolf **11** 111
Serlachius Art Foundation **11** 111, 112
Serlachius Art Museum *see under* MÄNTTÄ
Serlio, Sebastiano **11** 513, 656; **12** 113; **14** 869; **16** 635, 665; **20** 133, 488, 864; **25** 580; **26** 432; **28** 466–71*
altars **10** 799
architecture **31** 34
cathedrals **9** 86
Serlio, Sebastiano
architecture—cont.
châteaux **11** 259, 260, 513, 572, 656; **28** *467*; **32** 551
hôtels particuliers **14** 789
palaces **28** *468*
town halls **23** 864
attributions **11** 260
ceilings **13** 678
chimney-pieces **6** 604; **28** *469*, *470*
groups and movements **11** 263
patrons and collectors **25** 271; **29** 738
writings **14** 789; **23** 486; **29** 739
on architectural orders **14** 660; **23** *486*; **31** 294
on architecture **16** 632; **24** 274; **32** 187
on caryatids **5** 905
on coffering **7** 527
on Donato Bramante **4** 652
on façade decoration **10** 738, 739
on gates **7** 359
on lighting **9** 12
on military architecture **29** 739
on proportion **2** 356
on Roman architecture **2** 167; **26** 848; **27** 236; **31** 295
on stage design **30** 657, *657*, 659
on villas **20** 112; **32** 550
translated **7** 519; **10** 534; **20** 488; **22** 823; **27** 331; **29** 267
Sermei, Cesare **2** 626
Sermezy, Mme de **31** 374
Sermoneta, Girolamo da *see* SICIOLANTE, GIROLAMO
Sermoneta, Michelangelo Caetani, Duca di **6** 20
Serna, Ceferino Enríquez de la **2** 865
Serna, Miguel Fisac *see* FISAC SERNA, MIGUEL
Sernada, Fernand **32** 669
Serner, Walter **8** 433, 434, 436
Sernesi, Raffaello **16** 678; **19** 870; **20** 482, 483
Serodine, Giovanni **28** 472–3*
patrons and collectors **20** 841; **28** 271
works **13** 275; **28** *473*; **30** 131
Serodine, Giovanni Battista **28** 472
Ser-Odjav **21** 885
Serós, Santa Cruz **26** 607
Serour, Habib **9** 195
Séroux d'Agincourt, Jean-Baptiste (-Louis -Georges) **28** 473–4*
personal collection **18** 641; **31** 532
works **11** 674; **29** 550; **31** 516
Serov, Valentin (Aleksandrovich) **27** 391, 408, 581; **28** 474–5*; **30** 265; **33** 740
collaboration **27** 410
groups and movements **1** 71; **12** 870; **20** 232; **22** 178; **31** 582; **33** 379
patrons and collectors **12** 332; **22** 135; **27** 438
productions **20** 232
pupils
Fal'k, Robert (Rafailovich) **10** 771
Kravchenko, Aleksey (Il'ich) **18** 444
Kuznetsov, Pavel (Varfolomeyevich) **18** 542
Larionov, Mikhail (Fyodorovich) **18** 792
Mashkov, Il'ya (Ivanovich) **20** 548
Petrov-Vodkin, Kuz'ma (Sergeyevich) **24** 566
Sapunov, Nikolay (Nikolayevich) **27** 809
Saryan, Martiros (Sergeyevich) **27** 854
Serov, Valentin (Aleksandrovich)
pupils—cont.
Sudeykin, Sergey (Yur'yevich) **29** 899
Tatlin, Vladimir (Yevgrafovich) **30** 361
Ul'yanov, Nikolay (Pavlovich) **31** 571
Yuon, Konstantin (Fyodorovich) **33** 577
works **28** *475*
Serowe **4** 490
Serpa, Ivan (Ferreira) **4** 727, 728; **28** 476*
groups and movements **4** 719
pupils **23** 382
works **4** 719
serpentine **16** 857, 858
historical and regional traditions
China **7** 1, 3
Costa Rica **29** 153
Crete **21** *690*
Egypt, ancient **10** 29; **28** 34
Gabon **11** 879
Greece, ancient **12** 246, 247
Mesoamerica, Pre-Columbian **18** *881*; **21** 241
Mexico **18** *881*
Minoan **21** *690*
Olmec **18** *881*
Puerto Rico **29** *199*
Rome, ancient **27** 15
South America, Pre-Columbian **29** 155, *199*
Zimbabwe **33** 679, *679*
types
bowenite **21** 241
williamsite **21** 241
uses
jewellery **10** 29; **29** *199*
scarabs **28** 34
sculpture **27** 15; **33** *679*
seals **12** 246, 247
vases **21** *690*
serpents **22** 375
serpent-stones **15** 728, *728*
Serpin, Jean **1** 766
Serpotta, Gaspare **28** 476*
Serpotta, Giacomo **28** 476–7*
attributions **28** 477
collaboration **28** 476
works **16** 703, 704, *704*, 716; **28** *477*, 657; **29** 831
Serpotta, Giovan Maria **28** 476
Serpotta, Giuseppe **28** 476–7*
Serpotta, Procopio **20** 370; **28** 476, 477*; **29** 831
Serpuchovo **27** 431
Serpukhov Art Museum **27** 440
Serpukhovsky, Vladimir Andreyevich, Prince **9** 521; **30** 707
Serra (Egypt) **23** 289
Serra (family) **28** 478*
Serra, Agostino **14** 885
Serra, Antoni **29** 329
Serra, Enric **29** 329
Serra, Eudald **29** 286
Serra, Francisco **28** 478
Serra, Giacomo **13** 785; **28** 478*
Serra, Giovan Francesco, Marqués di Cassano **4** 619; **28** 479*
Serra, Jaime **11** 481; **20** 767; **27** 818; **28** 478*, 656; **29** 276
Serra, Josep **29** 319
Serra, Juan **28** 478
Serra, Junípero **27** 720
Serra, Luigi **28** 479*
Serra, Paolo **3** 922
Serra, Pedro **11** 481; **20** 811; **26** 249; **28** 478*; **29** 276
Serra, Richard **28** 479–80*
dealers **6** 23
groups and movements **10** 416; **24** 743; **25** 645–6
patrons and collectors **24** 24
works **15** 869; **18** 903; **25** *646*; **29** 13; **31** 615

Serrabone, Ste Marie 26 603, 610
capitals 26 610
Serra de la Arrabida 27 498
Serraglio, Tambo di see TAMBO DI SERRAGLIO
Serrahina 29 309
Serra i Abella, Josep 29 329
Serra i Fiter, Antoni 29 329
works 29 330
Serralongue, Assomption de la Vierge 9 156
Serrano, Andres 6 176
Serrano, Francisco J. 12 921; 21 379, 381; 28 480*
Serrano, Jaime Persivale see PERSIVALE SERRANO, JAIME
Serrano, Luis G. 2 692
Serrano, Mariano y Salvatierra y see SALVATIERRA Y SERRANO, MARIANO
Serrano, Pablo 28 480*; 29 309, 355
patrons and collectors 9 113
works 29 296, 336
Serrano Camargo, Gabriel 4 234; 7 606
Serrão, Domingos Vieira see VIEIRA SERRÃO, Domingos
Serre, Michel 20 472; 23 666
Serre, Puget de La see LA SERRE, PUGET DE
Serres (Germany) 12 368
Serres (i) (Greece) 9 511, 555, 556; 28 480–81*
Monastery of Hagios Ioannis Prodromos 9 629
Old Metropolis 9 579, 598, 598
Serres, August de 5 83
Serres (ii), Dominic(k) (1722-93) 3 389; 20 424; 28 481–2*
collaboration 28 482
patrons and collectors 21 91
Serres (ii), Dominic M. (c. 1761-1804) 28 481
Serres (ii), John Thomas 28 481–2*
Serres, Oliver de 12 120
Serreta de Alcoy, La see LA SERRETA DE ALCOY
Ser Ricciardo di Nanni 31 165
Serristori, Bernardo 2 19
Serro, Antonio 33 279
Serro, Giovanni 12 371
Serro, Johann 1 550; 22 918
Serrurier, Louis 28 482
Serrurier-Bovy, Gustave 3 550; 28 482*
collaboration 14 604
groups and movements 2 571
works 3 579, 586–7; 14 138
Serstevens, Marcus 't, I 3 599
Sert, Jackson & Associates 20 147
Sert (y Badia), José María 1 529; 5 509; 10 822; 11 904; 22 332; 25 150
Sert (i López), Josep Lluís 7 294, 606; 11 526; 19 51; 28 483*; 29 273, 321
collaboration 3 217; 31 184
groups and movements 3 219; 7 293, 296; 12 177; 31 184
pupils 14 596
staff 4 315; 30 260
works 3 217; 20 76; 21 710; 28 483; 29 273, 274, 355
Sertzen, Pieter 3 90
Sérusier, (Louis) Paul (Henri) 25 893; 28 484–5*
collaboration 4 325
groups and movements 7 451; 8 714; 22 421, 422; 25 215, 356; 30 169, 710
productions 17 449; 32 258
pupils 3 88; 18 636
teachers 12 189
works 11 418; 12 497; 28 484; 30 174
Servaes, Albert 28 485*
groups and movements 2 516; 3 564; 10 696; 18 626; 21 648
works 3 564
Servaes, Herman 9 476
Servandoni, Giovanni Niccolò 28 485–6*
assistants 5 907; 16 803; 27 587; 32 766
attributions 19 468
competitions 7 665
pupils 5 613; 6 396; 18 660; 20 5; 30 672
works 2 337; 9 238; 12 747; 25 267; 28 486; 30 672
Servandoni, Jean-Adrien-Claude 28 486
Servandus, Bishop 22 246
Servatius Cross 9 749; 26 144
Serveau, Clement 25 450
Servi, Costantino de' 6 95; 17 633; 29 799
Service books 21 729; 28 486–7*
Service des Antiquités 20 418
service stations 28 488*
Servien, Abel 19 264; 21 366
Servières, Eugénie 31 373
Servites 28 488–90*; 32 402
painting 28 489; 32 402
Servius 15 83; 22 412
Servolini, Benedetto 19 70
Servranckx, Victor 5 44; 28 490–91*
Serwouters, Pieter 32 588
Šerých, Jaroslav 28 491*
sesame oil see under OILS → types
Sese 30 418
Sesebi 9 831, 832; 23 276, 279–80
town walls 9 848
Seshadhari, Premalata Hanumantha 20 54
seshime see under LACQUER → types
Seshseshet 10 65
Sesklo 13 363; 21 46, 551; 28 491*
Sesklo culture 25 514
Sesklo period see under GREECE, ANCIENT → periods
Sesonji see under JAPAN → calligraphy
Sesonji Tsunetada 11 856; 17 224, 225, 227
Sesonji Yukifusa 17 224, 226
Sesonji Yukisue 17 224
Sesonji Yukitada 17 224, 225
Sesonji Yukitaka 17 224
Sesonji Yukiyoshi 17 224
Sesostris I (reg c. 1918-c. 1875 BC) 9 776; 14 331
architecture 9 830, 831, 831; 10 758; 18 70, 238; 19 470; 25 763; 30 433
military 9 844, 845, 846; 23 278
obelisks 23 329
reliefs 2 659; 9 877
sculpture 9 874–5; 17 713
Sesostris II (reg c. 1844-c. 1837 BC) 9 776
architecture 9 844, 850; 10 758; 25 763
jewellery 10 30
reliefs 9 877
sculpture 25 874
Sesostris III (reg c. 1837-c. 1818 BC) 9 776, 819; 28 491–2*, 492
architecture 6 170; 8 456; 9 830; 10 80; 18 647
military 9 780, 844, 845, 846; 23 278
reliefs 9 877, 878
sculpture 9 855, 856, 875
stelae 29 615
Ses Paisses 3 105
sesquipedales see under BRICK → types
Sessa Aurunca, Cathedral of S Pietro 16 626; 26 626
Sessarego, Rómulo 24 518
Sesselschreiber, Gilg 28 492*
patrons and collectors 13 904
works 2 800, 800; 6 171
Sesshin see KANŌ YUKINOBU
Sesshū, Toso see TOSO SESSHŪ
Sesshū Tōyō see TŌYŌ SESSHŪ
Sesson Shūkei 28 493–4*
works 17 40, 174; 28 494
Sesson Uno see UNO, SESSON
Sesto, Cesare da see CESARE DA SESTO
Sesto, Giovanni Battista da 24 286, 287
Sesto, Giovanni Stefano da 24 286, 287
Sesto Fiorentino 10 592
Sesto San Giovanni, Villa Pelucca 19 784
Sestri, il see TRAVI, ANTONIO
Seta, Lombardo della see LOMBARDO DELLA SETA
Setagaya Museum see under TOKYO → museums
Setalia see ANTALYA
Setau 17 714
setback buttresses see under BUTTRESSES
Sethe, Kurt 10 82
Sethnakht (reg c. 1190-c. 1187 BC) 9 777; 10 80
Sethos I (reg c. 1290-c. 1279 BC) 9 777, 841; 12 227; 28 494–5*, 495
architecture 1 101; 2 850; 6 170; 9 835; 10 79; 23 279; 24 840; 28 434; 30 433, 695
drawings 9 904
Exhibition 10 94
inscriptions 10 83
obelisks 23 331
paintings 9 805
wall 9 897, 903
reliefs 9 791, 807, 848, 864, 886; 23 280
sarcophagus 1 516, 516; 10 13, 90, 97; 27 824; 28 908
sculpture 9 848, 861, 885; 30 692
shrines (i) (cult) 12 227
stone vessels 10 74
tomb 9 841; 31 107
Sethos II (reg c. 1204-c. 1198 BC) 9 777; 10 80; 14 462
Seti I see SETHOS I
Seti (scribe) 9 880
Setien, Pantaleón Pontón de see PONTÓN DE SETIEN, PANTALEÓN
Sétif 1 634; 9 570; 13 547
Museum 1 636
Seto 17 11, 241, 352
Aichi Prefectural Ceramic Museum 17 433
ceramics 17 256; 28 495–6*
Hora kilns 17 352–3
Kita Shintani kiln 28 496
porcelain 17 264
pottery 17 242, 251, 252, 252, 253–5*, 351, 352, 353; 33 487
Seto, Black, ware see under POTTERY → wares
Seto, Hiroshi 17 268
Seto, Yellow ware see under POTTERY → wares
Seton (E. Lothian)
Castle 22 740
Collegiate Church 28 251
Seton, Alexander, 1st Earl of Dunfermline 32 799
Seton, Ernest Thompson 4 364
Seton, George, 3rd Earl of Winton 7 614; 32 799
Seton, George, 5th Lord Seton 31 889, 889
Seton, Grace 4 364
Seton, John Thomas 28 235
Seto Ohashi Bridge 4 803
Şetran, Ioana 26 719
sets 15 137; 30 667, 668, 672, 681
Setshogo, Thamae 4 489
works 4 490
set squares 11 763; 13 411
Setsudo Saitō see SAITŌ SETSUDO
Setsujō Nakazawa see NAKAZAWA SETSUJŌ
Setsu Watanabe see WATANABE, SETSU
Setsuyō Kubota see KUBOTA SETSUYŌ
Setsuzan Kitajima see KITAJIMA SETSUZAN
Settala, Manfredo 2 104; 28 496*
collections 4 484; 16 771
furniture 16 747
Sette Bassi Villa 26 870
Settecamini 23 584
Settecamini Painter 10 615
settees 15 813; 29 8, 8
Settefinestre 12 70; 16 620; 26 886; 27 116; 28 496–7*
Settei Tsukioka see TSUKIOKA SETTEI
Sette Pittori del Novecento see NOVECENTO ITALIANO
setters 20 559, 561, 562
Settevechi, Ludovico 10 524
Setthathirath, King of Vientiane (reg 1548-71) 18 764; 32 465
Setti, Godfrey 33 602
Setti Camini 27 67
Settignano see FLORENCE → villas → Villa I Tatti
Settignano, Antonio di Piergiovanni di Lorenzo da see ANTONIO DI PIERGIOVANNI DI LORENZO DA SETTIGNANO
Settignano, Antonio Marchesi da see MARCHESI DA SETTIGNANO, ANTONIO
Settignano, Desiderio da see DESIDERIO DA SETTIGNANO
Settignano, Pagno di Antonio di Berti da see PAGNO DI ANTONIO DI BERTI DA SETTIGNANO
Settignano, Simone da see CIOLI, SIMONE (DI MICHELE)
Settimo, Ruggero 23 842
setting out 28 497, 497–8*, 498
Settle, Elkanah 26 474; 30 674
settlement 20 575–6*
settlements 14 336, 338, 340; 15 192; 21 551; 25 473, 498–504*, 519–22, 521, 535–6
see also COMPOUNDS; VILLAGES
settles 29 8
Setúbal 25 288; 28 498–500*
Castelo de S Filipe 28 499
metalwork 25 313
Monastery of Jesus 13 71, 192
church 4 245; 20 325; 25 290
paintings 25 295
Museu de Setúbal 25 318
tiles 30 880
urban planning 25 294
Setúbal, Francisco de 28 429
Setubal, Morgado de see BARROS, JOSÉ ANTÓNIO BENEDITO DE
Seu d'Urgell, La see LA SEU D'URGELL
Seu d'Urgell, Master of see CANAPOST, MASTER OF
Seuffert, Anton 23 66
works 23 66
Seuna see YADAVA
Seunties, Nicolaas 22 896
Seupel, J. A. 12 342
Seuphor, Michel 3 564; 6 342; 11 550; 12 894; 18 793; 21 854; 22 749; 24 144, 324
Seurat, Georges (-Pierre) 11 547; 28 500–505*, 697
collaboration 18 866
dealers 9 425; 19 10; 26 107
drawings 9 217; 28 503
exhibitions 3 826; 10 680
frames 11 417, 418
Seurat, Georges(-Pierre)—cont.
groups and movements
Impressionism 15 155, 156
Neo-Impressionism 15 828; 22 745–6
Post-Impressionism 25 355, 356, 358
Salon des Indépendants 24 142
XX, Les 2 562; 5 44; 32 591
methods 7 629, 638; 8 128; 19 355; 24 3; 25 78; 28 201, 203
paintings 21 761; 22 746; 23 296
genre 8 596; 28 502
landscape 18 716, 716
marine 20 426
still-lifes 29 669
urban life 28 501
patrons and collectors
Alexandre, Arsène 1 614
Art Institute of Chicago 6 575
Barnes, Albert C. 3 251; 12 769
Courtauld, Samuel (1876-1947) 8 62
Doucet, Jacques (-Antoine) 9 196
Lehman, Robert 19 92
Lévy, Pierre and Denise 19 282
Maitland, Alexander 28 272
Quinn, John 25 823
Whitney, John Hay 33 150
periodicals 4 42
pupils 24 552
teachers 19 93
Seurre, Bernard-Gabriel 28 506*
Seurre, Charles-Emile 28 506*
Seurre, Emile 23 521
Seusenhofer, Hans (d 1555) 2 472
Seusenhofer, Hans (d 1580) 2 472
Seusenhofer, Jörg 2 821
Seusenhofer, Konrad 2 472
Seuter, Abraham 14 235
Seuter, Bartolomäus 14 235
Seuthopolis 5 145; 23 808; 30 772
Seutter 20 364
Seutter, Albrecht Carl 2 719
Seutter, Daniel see SEITER, DANIEL
Seutter, Matthäus 2 719; 3 620; 12 815
Seutter, Tobias Conrad Lotter 2 719
Sevan Monastery 2 436
Sevastopol' 31 551
Sevast'yanov Cross 9 663
Sève, Gilbert de 11 641; 12 832; 28 506*
assistants 12 285
collaboration 12 828; 19 21
reproductive prints by others 20 592
Sève, Pierre de 7 600; 12 832; 19 21; 28 506
Sève, Robert 6 179
works 6 179
Seven (Hetek) 13 840; 31 541
Seven Brothers 28 323
Seven & Five Society see 7 & 5 SOCIETY
Seven in October 8 394; 25 433
Seven Masters of Anatolia 16 285
Seven Stars Painting Forum see RED CROW SOCIETY
Seven Wonders of the World see:
ALEXANDRIA (EGYPT) → Pharos lighthouse
BABYLON (MESOPOTAMIA) → Hanging Gardens
COLOSSUS OF RHODES
EPHESOS → Temple of Artemis
GIZA → pyramids
HALIKARNASSOS → Mausoleum
OLYMPIA → Zeus statue
Severance, H. Craig 31 855
Severan marble plan see under ROME
Severano, Giovanni 4 457
Severence, John L. 33 407

Severe style (i) (Greece, ancient) **13** 468
sculpture **13** *450*, 450–52, *452*
thrones **13** *452*
Severe style (ii) (Russia) **27** 396; **28** 919; **33** 658
Severi, Giovanni Battista **8** 497
Severin, Mark **4** 366
Séverin, Nicolas-Pierre **11** 596
Severini, Gino **24** 448; **26** 776; **28** 506–8*, 808; **29** 878
dealers **27** 162
exhibitions **10** 255, 822; **31** 490
groups and movements **11** 865; **31** 852
Cubism **8** 240, 246, 247
Divisionism **9** 41
Futurism **1** 74; **4** 199; **11** 863, 866; **16** 679; **20** 426; **25** 358; **27** 445
Italiani di Parigi **16** 680
Neo-Impressionism **22** 747
Novecento Italiano **10** 821
patrons and collectors **20** 848; **33** 254
pupils **24** 572
works **7** 557, 905; **11** 398, 844; **16** 681; **20** 427; **23** 754; **28** *507*
writings **27** 163
Severino, Jorge **9** 118
works **9** *115*
Severinus, Pope (*reg* 640) **26** 802
Severn, Arthur **28** 509
Severn, Joseph **23** 36; **28** 509*
Severn, Mary **28** 509
Severn, Walter **28** 509
Severnaya chern' (northern niello) craft collective **27** 422, 423
Severn Bridge **4** 803
Severo, Ricardo **2** 903; **4** 712
Severo (di Domenico Calzetta) da Ravenna **16** 691; **26** 327; **28** 509*; **29** 568
Severs, Ann **19** 865
Severud, Fred **29** 489
Severus (i) (*fl c.* 59 AD; mason) **26** 885
Severus (ii) (*fl* mid-1st cent. AD; architect) **2** 312; **16** 623; **26** 884, 892; **28** 510*
patrons and collectors **22** 804
works **26** 788
Severus, Bishop of Naples (362-408) **9** 571
Severus Alexander, Emperor of Rome (*reg* 222-35) **2** 312; **8** 477; **16** 777; **22** 804; **23** 808; **26** 901; **29** 488
Sevesi, Fabrizio **16** 720
Sévigné, Marie de Rabutin-Chantal, Marquise de **17** 526
Sevilla, Ferran García *see* GARCÍA SEVILLA, FERRAN
Sevilla, Gonzalo Lobo *see* LOBO SEVILLA, GONZALO
Sevilla, Juan de **5** 618; **26** 421
Sevilla La Nueva *see* NEW SEVILLE
Seville **16** *103*; **26** *904*; **28** 510–20*, *511*, *512*; **29** *258*, 307
Alcázar **4** 784; **22** 255; **23** 683; **28** 518–19*; **29** 264, 277
chapel of the Visitation **30** 883
gardens **12** 79, *80*, 114
Hall of the Ambassadors **16** 495
Montería **16** 495
al-Mubarak palace **12** 80
muqarnas (architecture) **22** 324
Oratory chapel **16** 734; **29** 325
Patio de las Doncellas **29** 323; **30** 882
Salón de Embajadores **22** *255*
tiles **29** 326
Aljama Mosque **16** 494
see also ecclesiastical buildings → Cathedral of S María de la Asunción
Archbishop's Palace *see* Palacio Arzobispal
Seville—cont.
art forms and materials
architecture **16** 190
armour **29** 340
catafalques **6** 71
coins **16** *513*
embroidery **29** 349
gold **29** 333
iron **29** 340
leather **19** 3
manuscripts **16** 307
metalwork **16** 369, 386; **28** 516*; **29** 334, 340, 343
painting **29** 279, *280*, 281, 282, 284
pottery **25** 309; **29** 323, 325–6, 327
reliquaries **29** 341
sculpture **13** 108; **14** 714; **29** 291–2, 294
silk **29** 348
silver **28** 516
stage machinery **30** 664
tiles **29** 327; **30** 879, 882
woodwork **16** 492
Ayuntamiento **29** 266
Casa de Pilatos **22** 256; **28** 519–20*; **29** 299, 325; **30** 882
gardens **12** 114
paintings **29** 278
churches *see* ecclesiastical buildings
Colegio de S Buenaventura **14** 469; **33** 730
Colegio de S Telmo *see* Palacio de S Telmo
Doña Elvira Theatre **30** 663
ecclesiastical buildings
Augustinian church **2** 726
Cathedral of S María de la Asunción **13** 68; **26** 299; **28** 516–18*, *517*; **29** 263, 266, 268
books **13** 880
bosses **4** 465
Chapel of S Francisco **14** *471*
Chapel of S José **11** 492
chapter house **6** 364, 467; **25** 30
choir-stalls **13** 123
crucifix **8** 216
furniture **29** 317
Giralda Tower **4** 784, *784*; **10** 513; **16** 191; **21** 626; **22** 255
gold **29** 334
metalwork **11** 614; **28** 516; **29** 333, 338
misericords **21** 725
monstrance **29** 337
paintings **17** *896*; **22** *344*; **29** 278
pax of S Ana de Triana **29** 333
Puerta del Nacimiento **13** 108
retable **13** 69, 123; **26** 249; **28** 518; **29** 290
Sacristía de los Cálices **22** 2, *2*
Sacristía Mayor **29** 266
screen **28** 294
sculpture **21** 146–7; **29** 292
stained glass **13** 191, *191*; **29** 504, 505
tiles **30** 882
tomb of Cardinal Juan de Cervantes **13** 108; **21** 146; **29** 289
vaults **32** 91
weathervane **33** 8
Charterhouse *see* University Church
Convento de la Madre de Dios **30** 883
Convento de la Merced Calzada **11** 66; **30** 883
see also Museo de Bellas Artes
Convento de Porta Coeli **9** 110
Convento de S Clara **30** 883
Convento de S Clemente **22** 344
Seville
ecclesiastical buildings—cont.
Convento de S Paula **29** 325; **30** 882
church **5** 618–19; **13** 108
Hospital de la Sangre Church **27** 331; **29** 266
Omnium Sanctorum **22** 255; **29** 264
El Salvador **29** 271
S Ana **30** 883
S Catalina **29** 264
S Isidoro del Campo **29** 345
S Luis **11** 66; **29** 271
S Marcos **22** 255; **29** 264
S María de las Flores **30** 883
S María la Blanca **17** 544; **22** 345
S María Magdalena **11** 65–6; **31** 182
Capilla de la Quinta Angustia **22** 255; **29** 264
S Marina **22** 255; **29** 264
S Pablo *see* S María Magdalena
S Tomás **9** 110
University Church **29** 290
tomb of Doña Catalina Ribera **11** 898
education (art) **29** 357
Exchange *see* Lonja
exhibitions
Expo '92 **28** 516
Pabellon del Futuro **24** 291
Exposición Iberoamericana, 1929 **28** 516; **29** 273
Fábrica de Tabacos **28** *514*
see also Universidad de Sevilla
factories **16** 436
fountains **11** 340
Giralda Tower *see under* ecclesiastical buildings → Cathedral of S María de la Asunción
Great Mosque *see* Aljama Mosque
guilds **29** 312
Hospicio de los Venerables Sacerdotes **23** 11
Hospital de la Caridad **14** 784; **28** 520*
church **20** 234; **22** 346
paintings **31** 883
sculpture **31** 810
Hospital de las Cinco Llagas **14** 781
Hotel Madrid **30** 883
Lonja **10** 668; **14** *474*; **29** 268
Maritime Museum *see* Museo Nautico
Museo Arqueológico Provincial **12** 502
Museo de Bellas Artes **19** 658; **29** 355, 357
see also ecclesiastical buildings → Convento de la Merced Calzado
Museo Nautico **28** 511
Palacio Arzobispal **4** 209; **29** 353
Palacio de S Telmo **7** *289*; **23** 523; **29** *270*, 271
Parque María Luisa **24** 181, *181*; **29** 273
Plaza de España **29** 273
Real Academia de Bellas Artes de S Isabel de Hungría **22** 345; **29** 357
synagogues **22** 254
Torre del Oro *see* Museo Nautico
Universidad de Sevilla **31** 674
Laboratorio de Arte Francisco Murillo Herrera **29** 357
see also Fábrica de Tabacos
Sévin, Louis Constant **11** 622; **28** 520*
Sevin, Pierre Paul **30** 219
Şevki Efendi *see* MEHMED ŞEVKI
Sevlievo **5** 156; **30** 769
Church of the Prophet Elijah **31** 393
Sèvres **11** 649
Ecole Royale de Dessin **11** 669
Musée National de Céramique **6** 535; **8** 814; **29** 638
Sèvres Porcelain Factory **5** 825; **6** 333; **8** 448, 763; **9** 29; **11** 609, 610, 658; **13** 206; **19** 723; **20** 133, 388; **22** 882; **25** 193; **28** 520–27*
collections **4** 302, 554; **5** 530; **6** 439; **7** 194, 528, 561; **9** 29; **10** 97; **20** 897; **25** 80, 82, 138; **28** 527; **33** 55
designers
Aubé, Jean-Paul **2** 700
Beaudin, André **3** 450
Bergeret, Pierre-Nolasque **3** 775
Boucher, François **4** 515, 517
Brongniart, Alexandre-Théodore (1739-1813) **4** 848
Chaplain, Jules-Clément **6** 461
Chenavard, (Claude-)Aimé **6** 535
Chéret, Jules **6** 550
Coutan, Jules-Félix **8** 72
Defernex, Jean-Baptiste **8** 617
Denon, (Dominique-)Vivant **8** 764
Desportes, (Alexandre-)François **2** 105
Devéria, Achille (-Jacques-Jean-Marie) **8** 829
Drolling, Martin **9** 299
Dubois, Paul (i) (1829-1905) **9** 326
Dumont, Edme **9** 388
Duplessis, Jean-Claude-Thomas (Chambellan) (*c.* 1730-83) **9** 398; **11** 627
Falconet, Etienne-Maurice **10** 763, 764; **23** 295; **29** 573; **30** 219
Fontana, Lucio **11** 281
Fragonard, Alexandre-Evariste **11** 366, 371
Fragonard, Théophile **11** 366
Froment (-Delormel), (Jacques-Victor-) Eugène (1820-1900) **11** 798
Galanis, Demetrios **12** 2
Garneray, (Ambroise-)Louis **12** 153
Gendron, (Etienne-)Auguste **12** 271
Guardiola, Josep **29** 329
Hamon, Jean-Louis **14** 120
Hutin, Pierre-Jules **15** 39
Hynais, Vojtěch **15** 49
Isabey, Jean-Baptiste **16** 64
Jalabert, Charles (-François) **16** 876
Lebas, Louis-Hippolyte **19** 11
Martinet, François-Nicolas **20** 497
Mercié, (Marius-Jean-)Antonin **21** 147
Os, Georgius (Jacobus Johannes) van **23** 590
Penalba, Alicia **24** 352
Percier (-Bassant), Charles **24** 387, 388
Puech, Denys(-Pierre) **25** 697
Rodin, (François-)Auguste (-René) **26** 511
Saint-Aubin, Louis-Michel de **27** 530
Sandoz, Edouard-Marcel **27** 724
Solon, Marc-Louis-Emanuel **29** 51
Spaendonck, Gerard van **11** 229; **29** 255
Thomire, Pierre-Philippe **30** 747
Viollet-le-Duc, Eugène-Emmanuel **13** 208
directors **3** 19; **4** 248; **5** 879; **8** 608; **11** 561; **18** 643; **26** 91
exhibitions **10** 678
marks **20** 441
Sèvres Porcelain Factory—cont.
painters **17** 445; **30** 63, 369
potters **5** 880; **6** 462
production **1** 110; **5** 767; **6** 924; **7** 166, 658; **8** 448; **19** 115, 723; **20** 388; **23** 605; **24** 149; **25** 193; **26** 303; **27** 139; **28** *521*, *522*, *523*, *524*
panels **6** 13
pupils **10** 728
reproductions **26** 227
stained-glass workshop **29** 506; **32** 597
teachers **4** 319
tiles **30** 885
Sevrugin, Antoine **25** 770; **30** 415
Sevso Treasure **9** 655; **18** 825; **27** 83, 84
Sewak Ram **15** 653
Sewa Mende **21** 116
Sewell, Brooke **6** 868
Sewell, Robert **1** 753
sewing **24** 107; **30** 562–3*
historical and regional traditions
Ancient Near East **1** 879
Byzantine **9** 640
Early Christian (*c.* AD 250-843) **9** 640
Islamic **16** 356
Korea **18** 379
uses
bookbindings **4** 346–7*; **16** 356
see also NEEDLEWORK
sewing-machines **9** 287; **15** *821*; **20** 593; **30** 563
sewing-tables *see under* TABLES → types
sexpartite vaults *see under* VAULTS (CEILING) → types
sextants **23** 338, 339
Sextilius Pollio, C. **26** 911
Seybert, Elise Felice Amélie *see* MODEL, LISETTE
Seybold, Christian **2** 795; **28** 525*
Seydelmann, Apollonie **21** 131
Seydelmann, Jacob C. **15** 852; **24** 792
Seydl, Zdeněk **8** 394
Seydou, Chris **20** 199
Seydov, I. **2** 897
Seyfer, Hanns *see* SYFER, HANS
Şeyh Hamdullah *see* HAMDULLAH, ŞEYH
Şeyh Kuşteri **16** 544
Seyitgazı Church **9** 590
Seyma **27** 367
Seymour (family) **28** 525
Seymour, Charles, 6th Duke of Somerset
collections **10** 364
frames **11** 426
furniture **10** 291
interior decoration **12** 591
metalwork **8** 149
paintings **8** 454; **18** 97; **24** 633
Seymour, David *see* CHIM
Seymour, Dermot **16** 41
Seymour, Edward, 1st Duke of Somerset **8** 273; **10** 231; **28** 526*
Seymour, Henry (*fl* 1882-1901) **18** 68
Seymour, Henry, Lord (1805-59) **8** 599
Seymour, James (*d* 1739) **28** 526
Seymour, James (1702-52) **28** 526*
patrons and collectors **21** 91
reproductive prints by others **20** 144
works **2** 105, 106; **29** 424
Seymour, John **4** 479; **10** 852; **17** 823; **28** 525*; **31** 627
works **33** 112
Seymour, Robert **28** 526*
Seymour, Thomas **3** 38; **4** 479; **10** 852; **17** 823; **28** 525–6*; **31** 627
Seymour-Conway, Francis Charles, 3rd Marquess of Hertford **14** 145; **28** 527*

Seymour-Conway, Hugh Edward, 8th Marquess of Hertford **32** 685
Seymour-Conway, Richard, 4th Marquess of Hertford **9** 451; **28** 527–8*
collections **11** 663; **28** 384
paintings **4** 519; **8** 599; **14** 95, 603; **20** 497, 498, 875; **21** 69; **27** 143, 563; **28** 527; **33** 345
tapestries **28** 528
Seymour Haden *see* HADEN, (FRANCIS) SEYMOUR
Seymour Harris Partnership **5** 732
Seymour & Son **28** 525
Seyon, Fré **10** 570
Seyrig, Théophile **23** 454
Seyssel, Claude de *see* CLAUDE DE SEYSSEL
Seyter, Daniel *see* SEITER, DANIEL
Seytres, Joseph de, Marquis de Caumont *see* CAUMONT, JOSEPH DE SEYTRES, Marquis de
Seyyid Naskhbendi Mustafa **25** 51
Seyyit, Süleyman **16** 536, 537, 591; **28** 528*; **31** 453
Sežana **28** *858*, 860
Sezemice **4** 782
Sezenius, Valentin **10** 195; **12** 457
works **10** *194*
Sezession (Freie) **5** 924; **12** 196; **17** 857; **18** 128; **25** 842; **28** 343, 354, 779
Sezession (Neue) **3** 801; **22** 304; **28** 343
members
Hofmann, Hans (Georg Albert) (1880-1966) **14** 632
Klein, César **18** 115
Kubišta, Bohumil **18** 492
Morgner, Wilhelm **22** 114
Mueller, Otto **22** 257
Nolde, Emil **23** 186
Pechstein, (Hermann) Max **24** 311
Scharff, Edwin **28** 54
Segal, Arthur **28** 352
Thöny, Wilhelm **30** 755
Weisgerber, Albert **33** 44
Wiedemann, Guillermo **33** 161
Sezession (Rheinische) **1** 160; **10** 825; **12** 874
Sezessionstil *see* ART NOUVEAU
Sezincote (Glos) **7** 502; **8** 505; **15** 406, *407*; **26** 85
dairy **8** 461
Seznec, Jean Joseph **28** 528–9*
Sezon group **30** 286
Sezze, Paolo di Mariani di Tuccio Taccone da *see* PAOLO ROMANO (*fl* 1445-70)
Sfax
Archaeological Museum **31** 427
architecture **16** 219
bowls **31** 426
congregational mosque **16** 156
Dar Jalluli *see* Museum of Popular Arts and Tradition
fortifications **16** 156
houses **32** 312
jewellery **16** 532
medina **31** 424
Museum of Popular Arts and Traditions **31** 427
Sfîntu Gheorghe, District Museum of Covasna **18** 394
Sfondrato, Niccolo, Cardinal *see* GREGORY XIV, Pope
Sfondrato, Paolo Emilio, Cardinal **20** 47; **26** 196, 758; **28** 529*; **31** 884
Sforni, Gustavo **12** 546
Sforza (family) **8** 134; **28** 529
architecture **21** 456
coats of arms **32** *201*
coins **7** 537
glass **32** 201, *201*
maiolica **24** 535
manuscripts **20** 334; **26** 564
Sforza (family)—cont.
paintings **3** 695; **18** 704
Sforza, Cardinal (*fl* 1646) **16** 768
Sforza, Alessandro, Lord of Pesaro *see* PESARO, ALESSANDRO SFORZA, Lord of
Sforza, Anna Maria, Duchess of Ferrara, Modena and Reggio *see* ANNA MARIA SFORZA, Duchess of Ferrara, Modena and Reggio
Sforza, Antonio Maria *see* ANTONIO MARIA DA VILLAFORA
Sforza, Ascanio Maria, Cardinal **4** 646; **28** 529, 532–3*
Sforza, Beatrice, Duchess of Milan *see* BEATRICE D'ESTE, Duchess of Milan
Sforza, Bianca Maria, Duchess of Milan *see* BIANCA MARIA VISCONTI, Duchess of Milan
Sforza, Bianca Maria, Holy Roman Empress *see* BIANCA MARIA SFORZA, Holy Roman Empress
Sforza, Bona, Duchess of Milan *see* BONA SFORZA, Duchess of Milan
Sforza, Caterina, of Forlì **21** 97
Sforza, Francesco, Marchese di Caravaggio *see* CARAVAGGIO, FRANCESCO SFORZA, Marchese di
Sforza, Francesco I, 4th Duke of Milan *see* FRANCESCO I, 4th Duke of Milan
Sforza, Francesco Maria, Duke of Milan *see* FRANCESCO II, Duke of Milan
Sforza, Galeazzo, Lord of Pesaro *see* PESARO, GALEAZZO SFORZA, Lord of
Sforza, Galeazzo Maria, Duke of Milan *see* GALEAZZO MARIA, 5th Duke of Milan
Sforza, Ginevra **11** 699
Sforza, Giovanni, Lord of Pesaro *see* PESARO, GIOVANNI SFORZA, Lord of
Sforza, Guido Ascanio, Cardinal **21** 79; **25** 258
Sforza, Ippolita **19** 784; **20** 697
Sforza, Isabella of Aragon, Duchess of Milan *see* ISABELLA OF ARAGON, Duchess of Milan
Sforza, Ludovico il Moro, Duke of Milan *see* LUDOVICO (MARIA), 7th Duke of Milan
Sforza, Maria Cesarini **5** 911
Sforza, (Ercole) Massimiliano, Duke of Milan *see* (ERCOLE) MASSIMILIANO, 8th Duke of Milan
Sforza Book of Hours, Master of the *see* BIRAGO, GIOVANNI PIETRO
Sforza da Caravaggio, Giovanni Paolo **19** 784
Sforza da Caravaggio, Violante **19** 784
Sforza Hours *see under* BOOKS OF HOURS → individual manuscripts
Sforza Pallavicini (family) **8** 156
Sforza Triptych **5** 127; **28** 530; **33** 126
Sforzesca, Master of the Pala *see* PALA SFORZESCA, MASTER OF THE
sfregazzi **28** 533*
sfumato **5** 34; **6** 570; **24** 379
sgabello chairs *see under* CHAIRS → types
Sgarlatta, Filippo T. **28** 533–4*
Sgaw **30** 623
Sgibnev, Akim Alexeyevich **18** 568
S Giorgi, Nannocio della Costa a *see* COSTA A S GIORGI, NANNOCIO DELLA
S Giorgio in Velabro, Cardinal *see* PASSERI, CINZIO, CARDINAL
S Giorgio Maggiore, island of *see* ISOLA S GIORGIO
Sgouros, Progonos **23** 374
sgraffito **28** 534*
historical and regional traditions
Central Asia, Western **16** 407–8*
China **6** 895
Colombia **7** 607
Egypt **16** 415*
Gothic **13** 139
Iran **16** *402*, 402, 407–8*
Islamic **16** 248, 250, *402*, 402, 411, *411*, 415*
Italy **23** 754
Spain **16** *411*
Syria **16** 415*
Turkey **16** 248, 411
uses
ceramics **6** 328; **28** 534
façade decoration **10** *740*, 740–41*
frescoes **28** 534
gold **12** 623, 625, 626
paintings **13** 139
pottery **6** 895; **16** *402*, 402, 407–8*, 411, *411*, 415*; **18** 341, *341*
sculpture **7** 607
tempera **30** 427
tiles **16** 248, 250; **30** 874
's Gravenhage *see* HAGUE, THE
's Gravesande, Arent Arentsz. van *see* ARENTSZ. VAN 'S GRAVESANDE, ARENT
's Gravesande, W. J. **20** 92
Sguazzella, Andrea **27** 851
al-Sha'aba **2** 261
Shaar-ha-Golan **30** 182, 196
Shaba
stools **14** *378*
Shabaka (*reg c.* 719-*c.* 703 BC) **9** *777*; **23** 281
Sha'ban I, Sultan (*reg* 1345-6) (Mamluk) **17** 497
Sha'ban II, Sultan (*reg* 1363-76) (Mamluk) **16** 284, 385; **20** 229*
Shaba Virasena **15** 467
shabracks **21** 878
Shabran **2** 898
shabti containers **10** *19*, 19–20*
shabtis **10** *17*, 17–19*, 48, 57
Shabwa **2** *246*, 247, 252, 259, 275
Shackleford (Surrey), Norney Grange
South Lodge **12** 177
Shackleton, Ernest **15** 32
Shackleton, John **25** 883
Shackleton, Thomas **28** 348
Shadad **1** 863
Shadbolt, Jack (Leonard) **5** 569; **28** 534*; **31** 864
Shadbolt, Maurice **4** 642
Shaddadid, Abu'l-Asvar Shavur I *see* ABU'L-ASVAR SHAVUR I, Ruler
shading **17** 275; **24** 651
Shadjabad *see* MANDU
Shadow Painter *see* APOLLODOROS
shadow-puppets *see under* PUPPETS → types
shadow theatre *see under* THEATRE → types
Shadr, Ivan (Dmitriyevich) **27** 396; **28** 534*; **33** 601
Shaduppum *see* HARMAL, TELL
Shadwell (VA), Monticello **4** 787; **10** 850; **22** 30*; **31** *587*, 591; **32** 553
portico **25** 266, *267*
Shadwell, Thomas **28** 210; **30** 674
Shafa **16** 460
Shaffner, Ruth **17** 908
shaffrons **2** 448
Shafi' **16** 339
al-Shaf'i, Imam **2** 889; **16** 91
Shafi'a, Tell Abu el- **24** 840
Shafi' 'Abbasi *see* MUHAMMAD SHAFI'
Shafi'i, Farid
works **16** *173*
Shafirov, Pyotr **26** 7
shaft-bundle piers *see under* PIERS (ii) (MASONRY) → types
Shaftesbury, Anthony Ashley Cooper, Earl of *see* COOPER, ANTHONY ASHLEY, 3rd Earl of Shaftesbury
Shaftesbury Abbey (Dorset) **26** 672
shaft graves **13** 383; **28** 652
shaft looms *see under* LOOMS → types
shaft-rings **22** 218
shafts (column) **22** 217, 218, 219, 222; **23** 477, 478, 484; **26** 569
shafts (wall) **26** 589–90
shaft tombs *see under* TOMBS → types
Shagal, Mark (Zakharovich) *see* CHAGALL, MARC
shagreen *see under* LEATHER → types
Shah, Jamil **23** 802
Shah, Prithvi Narayan *see* PRITHVI NARAYAN, King
Shah Alam, Institute of Technology, MARA **20** 184
Shah 'Alam II, Emperor (*reg* 1760-1788; 1788-1806) (Mughal) **15** 592
Shahamat Jang (Nawabs of Bengal) **15** 379
Shahaziz, Ervand **2** 445
Shahba' *see* PLOVDIV
Shah Bahadur II **8** 680
Shahbazgarhi **15** *264*; **23** *797*, 798; **28** 535*
Shahdad **15** 904, 907, 919
Shaheinab **10** 81
Shaḥḥāt *see* CYRENE
Shah-i Mashhad **16** 166, 169
Shahinshah ibn Sulayman ibn Amir Ishak **9** 41
Shah Jahan, Emperor (*reg* 1628-58) (Mughal) **15** 196, 364, 371–2; **26** *167*
albums **15** 547; **22** 258
architecture **8** 676; **15** 371; **16** 239
military **8** 680; **15** 370
mosques **8** 680; **16** 239
palaces **3** 238; **15** 373; **23** 818
pavilions **29** *480*
tombs **1** 459, 460
towns **1** 473, 502; **15** 372; **17** 717; **18** 646; **20** 251; **27** 342; **29** 481; **30** 647
urban planning **1** 458; **15** 364–7, 410
cameos **15** 698, 701, *702*, 723
gardens **11** 340; **12** 74; **18** *646*
gold **15** 707
jade **6** 272, 285; **15** 699, *699*
manuscripts **16** 345
miniatures (manuscript illumination) **15** 588, 589; **21** 703
mirrors **21** 717
paintings **1** 31; **3** 92; **15** 547; **18** 186; **24** 295; **25** 873
sculpture **6** 405
throne **30** 785
urban planning **8** 675
weapons **15** 713
Shahjahanabad *see under* DELHI
Shah Jahan Diamond **12** 270
Shah Jehan, Begum of Bhopal (*reg* 1868-1901) **3** 908
Shah-ji-ki-Dheri **5** 94; **15** *264*; **23** *797*; **28** 535*
reliquaries **15** 446; **26** 149, *150*
Shahkund **15** 475
Shah Mahmud Nishapuri **16** 286, 292, 333, 335, 337; **27** 513
Shah Mansur Tabrizi **16** 346
Shah Miri *see* ZAIN AL-ABIDIN, Sultan
Shah Mosque *see under* ISFAHAN → mosques
Shah Muhammad, Ustad **15** 361
Shah-Muzaffar **1** 645; **15** 578; **28** 811
Shahn, Ben **10** 656; **17** 578, 580; **23** 48; **28** 535–6*; **31** 606
collaboration **20** 603
groups and movements **1** 86, 773; **4** 110
patrons and collectors **26** 488
works **14** 35; **15** 830; **17** *578*; **25** 653; **28** 919; **31** *606*, 705
Shahpur **15** 678
Shahquli **28** 536*
patrons and collectors **23** 641
pupils **17** 807
works **16** 346; **28** 27
Shah Quli Khan **15** 363
Shahr-e Suxteh *see* SHAHR-I SOKHTA
Shahr-i Nav **8** 672
Shahr-i Qumis **15** *901*, 906, 912; **24** 215, 216; **28** 536–7*, *537*
carpets **16** 469
seals **24** 218
Shahr-i Sabz **6** *182*; **16** *105*; **28** 537–8*; **31** *781*
Aq Saray **6** 203, *203*; **16** 196, 197, 248; **23** 815, 820
mosaics **6** 208
embroidery **31** 783
Gumbad-i Sayyidan **6** 277
jewellery **6** 241, 274
pottery **6** 259
textiles **6** 250
tiles **6** 208
urban planning **16** 264
White Palace *see* Aq Saray
Shahr-i Sokhta **1** 185, 850, 894; **10** 132; **15** *901*, 904, 921; **28** 538*
lapis lazuli **15** 902
metalwork **15** 919
pottery **28** 538
seals **1** 863
shahristān **21** 547
Shahr Rey *see* RAYY
Shahrukh, Sultan (*reg* 1405-47) (Timurid) **30** 917, 918–19*
architecture **4** 100; **14** 430; **25** 777
bookbindings **16** 358
manuscripts **16** 303, 322–3*, 325, 551; **18** 30
Shahsavur al-Katib **16** 331
Shahsawar **15** 573
Shah Shuja', Amir (*reg* 1364-84) (Muzaffarid) **15** 370
Shah Sri Chandrapala **15** 739
Shah Tepe **15** 919
Shahzada, Laila **23** 801
Shah Zaman **26** 40
Shaikhan Dheri **15** 446
Shaikh Hassan, Tell **21** 285
Shaikhupura **15** 363
Shailendra **29** 231, 237
Shaivism *see under* HINDUISM
Shajarat al-Durr (Ayyubid) **2** 888
Shajing culture **6** 877
Shaka *see* SCYTHIAN
Shaka, Maues *see* MAUES, King
Shaka calendar *see under* INDIAN SUBCONTINENT → calendars
Shakadō **17** 103
Shakar Dara **1** 199
Shakar Tangai *see* SIKRI (PAKISTAN)
Shake **18** 401
Shake Hands **18** 212
Shaker Heights *see under* CLEVELAND (OH)
Shakers **28** 538–42*
architecture **28** 539*
barns **28** *540*
chairs **28** *542*
decorative arts **28** 542*

Shakers—cont.
drawings **28** 540–41, *541*
furniture **28** 542
maple **28** *542*
painting **28** 540–41*
Shakespeare, William **30** 661, 662
Shakhorazar **2** 439
Shakhovsky, Dmitry **27** 397
Shakhrinau **6** *182*, 209, 217; **28** 543*
citadel **6** 198
fortifications **28** 543
Shakhristan **6** 231
Shakhrisyabz *see* SHAHR-I SABZ
Shakhsuvarova, S. Yu. **2** 898
Shakhtakhtinskaya, E. G. **2** 896, 897
Shakhty Cave **6** 222
Shaki **2** *890*, 900, 901
summer palace of the khans **2** 893, 896
Shakua *see* FUJIWARA NO SHUNZEI
shakudō see under ALLOYS → types
Shakuzuru Yoshinari **17** 393
Shakya, Ananda Muni *see* ANANDA MUNI SHAKYA
Shakya, Kesh Raja *see* KESH RAJA SHAKYA
Shakya, Kubera Simha *see* KUBERA SIMHA SHAKYA
Shakya, Man Jyoti *see* MAN JYOTI SHAKYA
Shakya, Roshan *see* ROSHAN SHAKYA
Shakya, Siddhi Muni *see* SIDDHI MUNI SHAKYA
Shakya, Yog Man *see* YOG MAN SHAKYA
Shakyamuni *see* SIDDHARTA GAUTAMA
shakyōtai see under SCRIPTS → types
shale **7** 95; **17** 514
Shalfak **21** 554
fortress **9** 844, 846; **21** *555*
Shalimar Gardens *see* SRINAGAR → Shalimar Bagh
Shalivahana **15** 617
Shallalat **23** 153
Shalmaneser I (*reg* 1273-1244 BC) **2** 637, 639; **23** 149, 153; **28** 578
Shalmaneser III (*reg* 858-824 BC) **2** 640; **21** 274
architecture **2** 637, 638; **21** 288; **23** 150–51, *150*, 153
reliefs **1** 892; **18** 896; **21** 298; **30** 187
Shalmaneser V (*reg* 726-722 BC) **21** 288
Shalom of Safed *see* SAFED, SHALOM VON
Shalu **28** 543*; **30** *806*, 813
collections **5** 105
roofs **30** 842
sculpture **22** 775; **30** 825
temple **30** 818
wall paintings **30** 830, 831
al-Sham *see* DAMASCUS
Shamakhy **2** *890*
carpets **16** 479, 481
Djuma mosque **2** 891
embroidery **2** 901
jewellery **2** 900
kilims **18** 49
pottery **2** 898
textiles **2** 900
Shamalaji **15** *276*; **28** 544*
sculpture **15** 450, 461, 462–3; **28** *544*
shamanism **25** 482; **28** 545–7*
art forms
altars **1** 704, 705
architecture **18** 268; **28** 638
historical and regional traditions
China **6** 625; **7** 136
Indian subcontinent **15** 205
Korea **18** 252, 377
Mongolia **21** 879, 884
shamanism
historical and regional traditions—cont.
Native North Americans **22** 557–8, 563; **28** 546
Nepal **22** 757
Siberia **28** *546*
South America, Pre-Columbian **29** 133–4*
Taiwan **28** 546, *547*
Venezuela **28** 547
iconography **18** 253–4
Shamay **18** 401, 403
Shambar **15** 488
Shami **10** 170; **24** 216
inlays **24** 218
sculpture **1** 887; **10** 170; **15** 919; **24** *217*
bronze **24** 217; **28** 384
Shammout, Ismail **28** 548*
Shamon Gyōmyō **17** 392
Sham Qala **1** 196
shamsa **16** 291
Shams al-Din (Nizami) (*fl* 1328) **33** 512
Shams al-Din (*fl* 14th cent.) **1** 24, 474; **16** 314, 318; **17** 687
Shams al-Din (*fl* 17th cent.) **16** 232
Shams al-Din ʿAdil Shah, Sultan of Maʿbar (*reg c.* 1368-72/3) **15** 359
Shams al-Din al-Hasani
works **16** *394*
Shams al-Din Baysunghuri **16** 285
Shams al-Din Muhammad (Juvanyni) **28** 809
Shams al-Din Qattabi **16** 864
Shams al-Din Yusuf Shah, Sultan (*reg* 1474-81) (Line of Ilyas Shah) **12** 204
Shams al-Mulk Nasr **16** 258; **26** 303
Shamshernagar, tomb of Shamsher Khan **15** 370
Shamshi **6** 238
Shamshi-Adad I (*reg* 1813-1781 BC)
architecture **2** 637, 639; **19** 105; **21** 285, 286; **23** 153
seals **1** 115
Shamshi-Adad V (*reg* 823-811 BC) **2** 638; **21** 298; **23** 153
stele **29** *614*
Shamshi-ilu **2** 640; **30** 873
Shams Khan Dandani, Khan (*reg* 1405/6-1418/9) (Dandani) **15** 349
Shan **5** 247, 248, 249, 253, 257, 262
dress **5** 250
silver **5** 259
Shanahan, Michael **14** 485
Shanballyedmond **25** 508
Shanchengzi **18** 281
Shand, Philip Morton **20** 475; **28** 548*
Shandi *see* SHENDI
Shand Kydd, William **28** 548*
works **32** V2
Shand Kydd Ltd **19** 415; **28** 548–9*; **32** 812, 817
Shangcun ling **6** *615*; **28** 549*
belthooks **3** 685
bronze **6** 850, 854
Burial 1727 **28** *549*
lacquer **7** 12
Shangdu **6** 665; **21** 874
Violet Tower of Kublai Khan **4** 794
Shang dynasty *see* FU HAO; *see also* CHINA → periods → Shang period
Shangguan Zhou **14** 824
Shanghai **6** *615*; **28** 550–53*, *551*
Academy of Fine Art **7** 149; **28** 553
art forms and materials
carpets **7** 51, 68
dolls **31** 259
Shanghai
art forms and materials—cont.
enamel **7** 71
gardens **12** 89, 93
ivory-carvings **7** 104
painting **6** 807
pottery **6** 878
prints **7** 120
silver **7** 29, 30
textiles **7** 51, *52*
Cathedral of St Ignatius **6** 678
Cathedral of the Holy Trinity **6** 678
Hongkong & Shanghai Bank **3** 177
Hongkou Park
statue of Lu Xun **6** 733
Museum of Art **6** 734, 772, 868, 925; **24** 436; **28** 553
Painting Academy *see* Academy of Fine Art
tomb of Lu Shen **7** 10
tomb of Pan Yunzheng **7** 39
trade **6** 624
Yu yuan **6** 692; **7** 99; **12** *88*, 89; **28** 552
Huxin ting Pavilion **28** *552*
Zhenru Temple **6** 658
see also SONGJIANG
Shanghai Art Publishing Agency **6** 540
Shanghai school **6** 774, 802; **28** 553–5*; **33** 497
members **6** 540; **33** 420
works **28** *554*
Shang Hsi *see* SHANG XI
Shanglinhu **6** 885
Shanglin yuan **12** 86
Shang period *see under* CHINA → periods
Shangsunjia (Datong, Qinghai) **20** 143
Shang-ts'un ling *see* SHANGCUN LING
Shangu Laoren *see* HUANG TINGJIAN
Shang Xi **6** 817; **21** 633
Shangyu **6** 885
Shanidar **21** 269
Shankadi **1** 323
Shankaragana, Ruler (*reg c.* 750-75) (Haihaya) **15** 495
Shankarapattana *see* PATAN (i) (INDIA)
Shankaravarman of Kashmir (*reg* AD 883-902) (Utpala) **15** 266
Shankargadh **15** 470, 473
Shankland, Edward **5** 274
Shankland & Cox **18** 541
Shanks, Duncan **28** 240
Shanks Leighton Kennedy & Fitzgerald **16** 40
Shannon, Charles (Hazelwood) **28** 555*; **33** 369
personal collection **26** 360
works **19** 488; **33** 180
Shannon Airport (Co. Clare) **1** 494
Shanshan **6** 308
Dongfengchang Cemetery **6** *308*
Shan-Tai **5** 220
Shantao **5** 109
Shantarakshita **5** 104; **27** 695
Shantiniketan **15** 657
art school **30** 235
Hindi Bhavan **22** 267
library **15** 657
Vishva-Bharati University **15** 173
Shantou **6** 332, 906; **28** *719*, 721
Shao'ang, Zhao **10** 794
Shaohao, Emperor (*reg*? mid-3rd millenium BC) **25** 818
Shao Mi **28** 555–6*
Shaoxing **6** *615*; **7** 151; **28** 556*
bronze **6** 856
house of Xu Wei **6** 687
kilns **6** 885
mirrors **6** 863; **21** 715, 716
Shen yuan **6** 687
Tomb 306 **7** 21
shape *see* FORM
Shapira, Ileana *see* SONNABEND, ILEANA
Shapiro, Joel **1** 81
Shapiro, Jory **6** 576
Shapiro, Joseph **6** 576
Shapiro, Konstantin **33** 667
Shapo cun (Xi'an) **7** 23
Shaposhnikov **17** 547
Shaposhnikov, K. N. **27** 422
Shapur I (*reg* 241-72)
architecture **16** 801; **21** 292
cities **15** 906, 912; **23** 160; **25** 778; **27** 856
coins **1** *888*
dress **1** 887
mosaics **27** 65
sculpture **15** 915, *918*
Shapur II (*reg* 309-79) **25** 778; **27** 856
Shaqra **32** 316
Sharaf al-Abawani **16** 415
Sharaf al-Dawla Muslim, Ruler (*reg* 1061-85) (ʿUqaylid) **22** 322
Sharaf al-Din ʿAli Yazdi **12** 82; **16** 196, 321; **30** 921
works **16** *325*
Sharaf al-Din Muhammad ibn Sharaf ibn Yusuf **16** 284; **20** 229
Sharaf al-Din Qummi **16** 163; **26** 303
Sharaf Khan **15** 355
Sharakusai **31** 204
Sharaku Tōshūsai *see* TŌSHŪSAI SHARAKU
Sharav, Balduugin *see* BALDUUGIN SHARAV
Shardeloes **25** 266
Sharer, Robert J. **6** 394; **27** 607
Shargh **16** 370
Shargorod Synagogue **31** 550
Sharif, Mohammad Haji **22** 489
Sharifah Fatimeh Zubir **20** 172
Sharif Amidi **20** 231
Sharifs of Morocco *see* ʿALAWI; SAʿDI
Sharifzade, S. **2** 896
Sharipov, Savzali Negmatovich **30** 253
Sharits, Paul **10** 688
Sharjah
exhibitions **31** 585
King Faisal Mosque **31** 584
Museum of Archaeology **31** 585
museums **2** 275
New Souk **31** 584
see also UNITED ARAB EMIRATES
Shar-Kali-sharri (*reg* 2217-2193 BC) **1** 508
Sharleman, Iosif **12** 327; **31** 398; **32** 601
Sharon, Arieh **16** 565; **26** 21; **28** 556–7*
collaboration **16** 565
groups and movements **15** 886; **30** 421
staff **33** 507
works **16** 566; **17** 492
Sharon, Eldar **16** 566; **28** 557
Sharp, Alfred *see* SHARPE, ALFRED
Sharp, George Lister Thornton **28** 557*
Sharp, Joseph Henry **33** 185
Sharp, Robert **3** 476
Sharp, Thomas **9** 465
Sharp, Thompson, Berwick, Pratt & Partners **5** 562; **28** 557*; **31** 863, 864
Sharp, William **10** 393; **21** 414; **28** 557–8*
Sharp and Thompson **31** 863
Sharpe, Alfred **23** 58; **28** 558*
Sharpe, C. W. **20** 28
Sharpe, Edmund **22** 211; **30** 503
works **30** *502*
Sharpe, John **11** 84; **30** 752; **33** 152
Sharpe, Joseph H. **2** 121
sharp fillet mouldings *see under* MOULDINGS → types
Sharples, Felix Thomas **28** 558
Sharples, Guy **13** 876
Sharples, James (1751/2-1811) **28** 558*
Sharples, James (*c.* 1788-1839) **13** 875; **28** 558
Sharples, Rolinda **28** 558*
Sharpness **32** 861
Sharqi, Husayn Shah *see* HUSAYN SHAH, Sultan of Jaunpur
Sharuḥen *see* AJJUL, TELL EL-
Sharukh **21** 169
shaseiha see MARUYAMA-SHIJŌ SCHOOL
Shash *see* CHACH
Shashanka, Ruler (*reg c.* early 7th cent.) (Gauda) **15** 503
Shashin shūho15 **18** 194
Shatin **14** 720
Shatrunjaya, Motishah Tuk **15** 405
Shatru Sal, Maharao of Kota (*reg* 1866-89) (Rajput) **15** 606
Shattuck, Aaron Draper **28** 559*
Shatz, Boris *see* SCHATZ, BORIS
Shaub, V. **27** 578
Shaubak *see* KRAK DE MONREAL
Shaugh Moor **25** *521*, 522
Shaukat Rai **17** 803
Shavdia, G. **12** 320
Shavei Zion **9** *513*, 567
Shavgar *see* TURKESTAN (TOWN)
Shaw, (John) Byam (Liston) **25** 556; **28** 559*
Shaw, George Bernard **3** 446; **4** 367; **9** 290; **26** 360
Shaw, Henry **23** 546; **24** 273; **26** 234; **28** 307
works **10** *286*
Shaw, Howard Van Doren **25** 446
Shaw, (John) James Byam **6** 78; **7** 579; **28** 559, 560*
Shaw, John (i) (1776-1832) **10** 373; **28** 559*
Shaw, John (ii) (1803-70) **28** 559*
Shaw, Joshua **14** 536; **28** 560*
Shaw, Martin **8** 109
Shaw, Quincy Adams **28** 560*
Shaw, Richard (*b* 1941) **31** 640
Shaw, Richard Norman (1831-1912) **1** 146; **2** 333; **7** 668; **10** 235, 239, 298, 374; **17** 440; **18** 66; **22** 809; **28** 560–64*
architecture
brick **4** 788
country houses **7** 789; **8** 49; **10** *238*, 239; **11** 75; **18** 903; **19** 625; **23** 398
hotels **10** 239
houses **19** 574; **23** 547; **25** *805*; **28** *562*; **30** 504
office buildings **19** 506; **23** 359; **28** *563*
public houses **25** 688
tiles **30** 879
urban planning **4** 157
assistants **2** 575; **5** 65; **18** 655; **19** 252
collaboration **10** 239; **16** 821; **19** 506; **22** 809; **25** 633
fountains **15** 542
furniture **10** 298
groups and movements
Baroque Revival **3** 269
Gothic Revival **13** 209
Neo-Georgian **22** 743
Old English style **10** 238; **13** 204; **22** 752; **23** 398; **32** 277
Queen Anne Revival **9** 29; **25** 804, 805
patrons and collectors **13** 615; **14** 680, 768; **29** 716
staff **23** 36; **28** 173
teachers **27** 657; **29** 765
Shaw, Thurstan **15** 116; **23** 130
Shawa, Leila (Rashad) **28** 564*

al-Shawbak *see* KRAK DE MONREAL
shawls **28** 564–5*
historical and regional traditions
Austria **2** 825
England **8** 36; **28** 564
France **28** 564
India, Republic of **15** 175, 176
Indian subcontinent **28** 564
Kashmir **15** 665*, *666*, 676, 723
Mughal **15** 665
Italy **8** *37*
Russia **27** 431
Scotland **28** 266
materials
cotton **8** 36, 37, *37*
embroidery **15** 676
lace **18** 593
silk **28** 564
wool **28** 564
Shawnee **22** 552
Shaybanid **28** 565–6*
architecture **6** 211
manuscript illumination **6** 234
see also:
ʿABD AL-ʿAZIZ, Khan
ʿABDALLAH II, Khan
ʿABD AL-MUʾMIN, Khan
MUHAMMAD SHAYBANI, Khan
ʿUBAYDALLAH, Khan
Shaybani Khan *see* MUHAMMAD SHAYBANI, Khan
Shaydullin, Shamil' **27** 435
Shayer, William **4** 808; **28** 566*
Shayer, William Joseph **28** 566
Shayista Khan **8** 847
Shayk ʿAbdallah **16** 354
Shaykh ʿAbbasi **16** 339; **28** 566*
Shaykh ʿAbdullah ibn Qasim al-Thani **25** 777
Shaykhet, Arkady (Samoylovich) **1** 685; **28** 567*
Shaykh Hamad ibn ʿAbdullah al-Khalifa **3** 68
Shaykh Ḥamdullah ibn Mustafa Dede *see* HAMDULLAH, ŞEYH
Shaykhi **28** 567*
attributions **16** 328
collaboration **8** 533
patrons and collectors **16** 328
works **28** 811
Shaykh Lutfallah Mosque *see under* ISFAHAN → mosques
Shaykh Mahmud Haravi **16** 285
Shaykh Mahmud Zarin-qalam **16** 864
Shaykh Muhammad **28** 567–8*
works **16** 335, *336*, 337
Shaykh Muhammad Amir **15** 653
Shaykh Murshid **16** 329
Shaykh Salim Chisti, tomb of *see under* FATEHPUR SIKRI
Shaykhzada (*fl* 1302-28) *see* AHMAD AL-SUHRAWARDI
Shaykhzada (*fl* 1520-40) **14** 431; **16** 332, 333, 343; **28** 568*
Shaykh Zain al-Din **15** 593
Shayzar **21** 583
Shazhong (Jiangling) **7** 33
Shazhou *see* DUNHUANG
Shazitang (Changsha) **7** 133
Shchavinsky, V. **31** 565
Shchedrin, Feodosy (Fyodorovich) **27** 389, 390, 579; **28** 568*
pupils **3** 530
works **24** 546; **31** 561; **33** 600
Shchedrin, Semyon (Fyodorovich) **12** 2; **20** 850
Shchedrin, Sil'vestr (Feodosiyevich) **27** 389; **28** 568–9*
Shchekotikhina-Pototskaya, Aleksandra **27** 413
Shchelinsky, V. **17** 805
Shcherbatova, Maria Grigorievna, Princess **29** 652
Shcherbinina, S. **30** 352
Shchuchino *see* ŠČUČYNA
Shchuchynka **31** 562
Shchukin, Ivan (Ivanovich) (1869-1908) **22** 178
Shchukin, Ivan (Sergeyevich) (1885-1975) *see* STCHOUKINE, IVAN (SERGEEVICH)
Shchukin, Piotr **15** 742, 745
Shchukin, Sergey (Ivanovich) **4** 489; **11** 664; **20** 272; **28** 569*
collections **11** 659; **27** 439; **30** 361
murals **22** 331
paintings **17** 725; **20** 193, 824, 826; **24** 716; **27** 441; **31** 416
Shchukin, Stepan **19** 279; **27** 579; **31** 369
Shchuko, Vladimir (Alekseyevich) **27** 378; **28** 570–71*; **33** 486
assistants **3** 685; **12** 243; **25** 170
collaboration **15** 890; **27** 379
groups and movements **11** 358; **22** 508; **29** 529
pupils **11** 245; **19** 273; **27** 284
teachers **3** 734
works **19** 319; **22** 174; **27** 379, *379*
Shchusev, Aleksey (Viktorovich) **17** 867; **28** 571–2*
architecture **3** 88; **7** 174; **27** 377
churches **18** 40; **22** 173; **28** *837*; **31** 553
hotels **27** 409
mausolea **20** 870, *870*; **27** 379; **31** 132
railway stations **22** 173, 349; **28** *571*
theatres **29** 823; **31** 782
urban planning **22** 174
assistants **9** 73; **12** 876; **23** 426; **25** 323
collaboration **22** 173
groups and movements **11** 358; **28** 837; **29** 529
pupils **6** 526
staff **21** 92
teachers **3** 734
Shchusev, Aleksey (Viktorovich), State Research and Scientific Museum of Russian Architecture *see under* MOSCOW → museums
Sheard, Joseph **31** 176
Shearer, Thomas **14** 400
shears **7** 764, 765, 766; **8** 285, *286*
Sheba **16** 438
Shebitku (*reg c.* 703–*c.* 690 BC) **9** *777*; **23** 281
Shebuyev, Vasily (Kuz'mich) **5** 25; **28** 573*; **31** 537; **32** 851
Shechem **16** *565*; **28** 573*; **30** *180*
gateways **30** *190*, 191
martyrium **20** 520
Migdol Temple **21** 553; **30** 191, *191*
temples **30** 185
Shechori, Ran **16** 571
Shedel', Gotfried Iogann *see* SCHÄDEL, GOTTFRIED (JOHANN)
Shedov, Ivan (Stepanovich) **27** 423
sheds **21** 600
Shedu **9** 822
Shee, Martin Archer **16** 16; **19** 271; **28** 573–4*, 924
Sheeler, Charles (Rettew) **2** 383; **23** 48; **24** 676; **28** 574–5*; **31** 606, 662; **32** 328
collaboration **29** 745
groups and movements **8** 435; **23** 48; **24** 686; **25** 461, 462
patrons and collectors **2** 384; **3** 251; **26** 488
teachers **2** 130; **6** 500
works **15** 828; **25** *462*; **28** *575*
Sheene, Alice **10** 329
Sheepshanks, John **10** 361; **28** 575–6*
architecture **11** 360
collections **10** 366, 370
engravings **25** 753
paintings **7** 801; **33** 16
prints **28** 362
sheepskin *see under* SKINS → types
Sheerness Boat Store (Kent) **16** 55
sheets **11** 54; **18** *591*
Sheets, Millard **14** 538; **19** 701
Sheets, Payson **3** 278
Sheffield (S. Yorks) **10** *225*; **28** 576*
Britannia metal **10** 343; **24** 579
Carver Street Chapel **21** 347; **23** 193
Cathedral of St Peter and St Paul **10** 261
Graves Art Gallery **10** 371
Guild of St George **27** 354
knives **8** 285
marks **20** 444; **28** 576
scissors **8** *286*, 287
sculpture **4** 789, 790
silver **10** 331, 333; **28** 739
silverplate **28** 576
steel **16** 61
Town Hall **7** 667; **31** 240, 241
University **10** 375
urban planning **31** 738
Sheffield, John, 2nd Duke of Buckingham **5** 78
Sheffield plate *see under* SILVERPLATE → types
Sheikan **29** 898
Sheikh, Gulam (Mohammed) **18** 16; **28** 577*
Sheikh, Tell esh- **30** 196
Sheikh Abd el-Qurna *see under* THEBES (i) (EGYPT)
Sheikh el-Beled **9** 855, 871; **28** 577–8*
Sheikh Hammad, Tell **1** *849*; **21** 299; **28** 578*; **30** *180*, 198
el-Sheikh Ibada *see* ANTINOÖPOLIS
Sheikhley, Ismail **14** 221; **16** 2
el-Sheikh Said **3** 848
tomb of Serfka **9** 822
Shekhr-Islam **6** 274
Shekhtel', Fyodor (Osipovich) **28** 578–80*
assistants **11** 244
groups and movements **28** 837
works **22** 173; **27** 377, *377*, 378, 404, *404*, 459; **28** *579*
Sheki *see* SHAKI
Sheki Silk Combine **2** 901
Shekwan *see* SHIWAN
Shelarvadi **17** 695
Shelburne, William (Fitzmaurice) Petty, 2nd Earl of *see* PETTY, WILLIAM (FITZMAURICE), 2nd Earl of Shelburne and 1st Marquess of Lansdowne
Shelburne Museum (VT) **14** 244
Sheldon (family) **10** 349; **20** 366
Sheldon, George **25** 807
Sheldon, Gilbert, Archbishop **23** 687; **33** 393
Sheldon, Rufus **21** 896
Sheldon, William **10** 349; **30** 318
works **30** *318*
Sheldon Memorial Art Gallery *see under* LINCOLN (NE; USA) → University of Nebraska
shelf-clocks *see under* CLOCKS → types
shelf dolls *see under* DOLLS → types
shellac **1** 155; **9** 492; **18** 608, 655; **25** 23, 26; **26** 243
consolidants **7** 747
fixatives **11** 142
gilding **12** 621
lacquer **18** 599, 607, 609, 611
photography **1** 156
pigments **24** 796
shellac—cont.
plaster **29** 813
seals **33** 5
stencilling **28** 298
varnishes **32** 2, 3
Shellal **2** 656; **9** 567
Shell Bahamas Ltd **3** 64
Shelley, Percy Bysshe **13** 304
Shelley, Samuel **21** 644; **32** 910
Shelley Pottery **10** 314
works **10** *314*
shellfish **9** 492
shell gold *see under* GOLD → types
shell keeps *see under* DONJONS → types
shell middens **18** 7; **29** 138
Shell Polishing Office *see* KAIZURI BUGYŌSHO
shells **22** 204–5; **28** 580–82*
dating methods **2** 304
Mesoamerica, Pre-Columbian **21** 251
historical and regional traditions
Aboriginal Australia **1** 52
Africa **1** 296; **28** 581
Ancient Near East **1** 869
Austral Islands **2** 773
Aztec **21** 260
Bamum **3** *152*
Cameroon **3** *152*
Caribbean Islands **5** 747
Chimú **29** 218
China **7** 14, 106, 107, 138; **21** 715
Colombia **29** 217
Ecuador **29** 217
Egypt, ancient **10** 29
England **28** *581*
Fiji **11** *69*
Hawaii **28** 581
Huari culture **29** 218
Huastec **21** 260
Inca **15** 163
Iroquois **28** 582
Japan **17** 400; **18** 601
Lengyel culture **25** 517
Linear Pottery culture **25** 517
Malaysia **4** I2
Maori **28** 581
Maya **21** 251, 259–60
Mesoamerica, Pre-Columbian **21** 246, 251, 257, 259–60*, 719; **22** 158
Mesopotamia **1** 869
Moche (culture) **23** 897; **29** 218
Native North Americans **22** 637–40*, 641–2*, *641*, 644*; **28** 582
Olmec **21** 260
Pacific Islands **23** 721*; **28** 581
Palau **23** 833
Papua New Guinea **23** 721; **24** 79, 84
Portugal **25** 306, 314
Prehistoric art **25** 473, 517
San **28** 581
Sarawak **4** I2
Society Islands **28** 922, *922*
Solomon Islands **28** 581; **29** 49, *50*
South America, Pre-Columbian **28** 581; **29** 217–18*
Sumerian **22** 159; **31** *696*
Tiahuanaco **29** 218
Toltec **21** 260
Torres Strait Islands **31** 186
Vanuatu **31** 892
Vinča culture **25** 517
West Mexico **33** 103
Yoruba **28** 581
techniques
carving **28** 581
types
abalone **20** 466; **28** 580, II1
busycon **21** 259
Cassis *see* helmet
clam **7** 632; **21** 259; **28** 580
conch **3** 441; **29** 217; **30** 843–4
Buddhism **28** 582, *582*
shells
types
conch—cont.
Huastec **14** 831
Indian subcontinent **15** 729
Maya **21** 260
Mesoamerica, Pre-Columbian **14** 831; **21** 260
Tibet **28** *582*
Conus **28** 580, 581; **29** 217
cowrie **3** *441*, 441; **28** 580
Africa **1** 295, 362; **28** 581
Igbo **1** 284
Indian subcontinent **15** 734
Kuba (iii) (Zaïre) **18** *488*
Nigeria **3** 331
Yoruba **1** *283*
Zaïre **18** *488*
Cypraea *see* cowrie
Dentalium **28** 580
eggshells *see* EGGSHELLS
Haliotis *see* abalone
helmet **28** 580
malea **29** 217
Melo **28** 580
mussel **28** 580
Mytilidae *see* mussel
Nassa **28** 580
nautilus **7** 14; **11** *616*; **17** 524; **22** 694; **28** 580, I1
Nerita **28** 580
oliva **21** 259; **29** 217
ostrea *see* oyster
oyster **29** 217
oyster (pearl) *see* *Pinctada*
oyster (thorny) **3** 442; **21** 259; **28** 580; **29** 217, 218
pecten **29** 217
periwinkle **17** 524
Pinctada **21** 259; **28** 580; **29** 217
quahog *see* *venus mercenaria*
Spondylus *see* oyster (thorny)
strombus **21** 259; **29** 217
tortoise-shell *see* TORTOISE-SHELL
Tridacna *see* clam
Triton **28** 580
turtle-shell *see* TORTOISESHELL
venus mercenaria **3** 441
uses
architectural decorations **21** 259
baskets **1** 295; **3** 331; **4** I2
beads **1** 296; **3** 440, 441, 442; **21** 259, 260
belts **25** 517
body ornaments **23** 721; **29** 217–18
bowls **29** *50*
breastplates **11** *69*
cameos **12** 264
canoes **28** 611
caskets **21** 259
chairs **25** 306
collars **29** 217
costumes **3** 441
cups **22** 694
discs **29** 218
dress **28** 922, *922*
earrings **14** 831
ear-spools **21** 260
ewers **28** I1
figurines **29** 218
furniture **3** *152*
grottoes **28** 581
grounds **25** 174
headdresses **28** II1; **31** 186
houses **1** 284
inlays **7** 14; **29** 218; **31** *696*
interior decoration **28** *581*
jewellery **2** 773; **7** 106, 107; **10** 29; **17** 524; **21** 260; **22** 642; **25** 517; **31** 186
lacquer **18** 600, 601, 609
lintels **20** *355*
marquetry **20** 466
masks **18** *488*; **21** 251
mirrors **7** 14; **21** 715, 719
mosaics **22** 154, 158, 159; **29** 217, 218

shells
uses—cont.
necklaces **21** 259, 260; **29** 217
nefs **11** *616*
netsuke **17** 400
paint containers **23** 787
pectoral ornaments **14** 831
pendants (jewellery) **1** 52; **21** 260; **29** 217
pigments **7** 632
sashes **21** *477*
scrimshaw **28** 302
sculpture **1** *283*; **5** 747; **7** 138
shields **29** 49
talismans **15** 734
textiles **21** 259
trumpets **21** 257, 260; **28** *582*; **29** 217
see also MOTHER-OF-PEARL
shell structures **7** *695*; **22** *806*; **28** 582–4*, *583*, *584*
Shell UK Ltd **7** 652, 653; **13** 811; **17** 850; **19** 485, 538; **28** 273; **29** 641
Shelomi **9** 543
shelters **1** 49, *49*, 306, 307; **30** 191; **33** 571
Shelton collection *see under* NEWARK (NJ; USA) → Newark Museum
shelves **6** 330; **9** 11, 15, 21, 28, 29, 30; **17** 76, *81*, *385*; **19** 313, 314, 316
see also BATS
Shema **16** 573
Shemakha carpets *see under* CARPETS → types
Shembe **33** 725
Shembiyan Mahadevi, Queen (*fl c.* 950) (Chola) **15** 234, 305
Shemi, Yehiel **28** 584–5*
Shemokmedi **12** 330
Shemshara **21** 269
Shem tov ben Abraham ibn Gaon **17** 661
Shemyakin, Mikhail (Mikhaylovich) **27** 397, 581; **28** 585*
Shemza, Anwar Jalal **16** 288; **23** 800; **28** 585*
Shen **25** 800
Shenango Pottery Co. **31** 639
Shen Can **6** 756–7
Shen Cheng **28** 589
Shen Chou *see* SHEN ZHOU
Shen Dasheng **7** 60
Shendi **23** 290
Shen Du **6** 756–7
Shen Fucan **33** 652
Shen Fu-ts'an *see* SHEN FUCAN
Shengavit **2** 439, 440
Shenge **33** 598
Sheng Hong **28** 586
Shengle **6** 664
Sheng Mao **28** 586*
Sheng Maoye **28** 586–7*
works **28** *587*
Sheng Mao-yeh *see* SHENG MAOYE
Sheng Mou *see* SHENG MAO
Shen Hengji **28** 589
Shen Hsin-yu *see* SHEN XINYOU
Shen Hsi-yüan *see* SHEN XIYUAN
Shenkhorov, Chingiz **27** 436
Shen Mo **7** 104
Shenmu **7** 3
Shen Nanpin **9** 737; **28** 587–8*
works **17** 183, 184*, 189, 195; **22** 429
Shen Nanpin school **17** 184–6*
Shen Shichong **28** 588*
Shen Shih-ch'ung *see* SHENG SHICHONG
Shenstone, William **12** 130; **18** 906; **24** 391; **29** 890
Shen Ta-sheng *see* SHEN DASHENG
Shen Ts'an *see* SHEN CAN
Shen-tsung, Emperor *see* SHENZONG, EMPEROR
Shen Tsung-ch'ien *see* SHEN ZONGQIAN
Shen Tu *see* SHEN DU
Shen Tzu-an *see* SHEN ZIAN
Shen Xi **33** 535
Shen Xinyou **7** 120
Shen Xiyuan **6** 817
Shenyang
Chongzheng dian (Hall of Esteem for Government) **6** 684
Dazheng dian (Hall of Great State Affairs) **6** 684
Dragon Throne **30** 785
Fenghuang lou (Phoenix Tower) **6** 684
Fu ling **6** 704
Imperial Palace **6** 684, 732
Liaoning Provincial Museum **6** 772
Northern Tombs **6** 662, 732
pailou **23** 779
Qingning gong (Palace of Pure Peace) **6** 684
Wensu ge (Pavilion of Remembering Literature) **6** 684
Zhao ling **6** 704
Shen Yao-ch'u **30** 249
Shen Yinmo **6** 767
Shen Yu **6** 538
Shen Zhenji **28** 589
Shen Zhou **6** 757, 774, 820; **7** 148; **11** 307; **21** 633; **28** 588–90*; **30** 49
groups and movements **29** 244; **30** 49
personal collection **6** 757
pupils **19** 833; **33** 67, 436
teachers **6** 547
works **1** 581; **6** 760, 785, 791, *791*, 806; **7** 675; **14** 823, 825; **25** 73; **28** *590*; **30** 48, *48*; **33** 435–6, *436*
Shen Zifan **7** 49
Shenzong, Emperor (Song; *reg* 1068-85) **8** 255; **13** 854
Shen Zongqian **6** 798, 814
she-oak **2** 757, *758*
Shepard, Jesse **27** 720
Shepenwepet **9** 887
Shepherd, Charles **4** 587; **26** 468
Shepherd, (Richard) David **17** 907; **28** 591*
Shepherd, Edward **3** 370; **10** 233; **30** 673; **33** 340
Shepherd, J. C. **17** 473; **28** 283
Shepherd, Rupert **29** 110
Shepherd, W. L. **19** 395
Shepherd Islands **31** 893
Shepley, Bulfinch, Richardson & Abbott **28** 591
Shepley, George Foster **26** 343; **28** 591
Shepley, Henry R. **29** 716
Shepley, Rutan & Coolidge **13** 617; **26** 343; **28** 591*
staff **20** 877; **22** 275; **29** 382
works **4** 474
Sheppard, Oliver **16** 37; **28** 592*
works **9** 322; **16** 21, *21*
Sheppard, Richard (Herbert) **28** 592*
Sheppard, Richard, Robson & Partners **5** 513; **28** 592
works **5** *513*
Sheppard, T. **2** 153
Sheppard, William **3** 244; **18** 484
Sheppard Hardware Co. **31** 257
Sheppard Robson Architects **28** 592
Shepseskaf (*reg c.* 2472–*c.* 2467 BC) **9** *776*, 779; **22** 398; **27** 812
Shepseskare (*reg c.* 2426–*c.* 2419 BC) **1** 97; **9** *776*
Sheraton, Thomas **10** 293; **26** 303; **28** 592–3*
works **5** 192; **6** 390; **8** 107; **10** 297; **12** 333; **18** 614; **24** 273
Sheraton, Thomas—cont.
writings **10** 296; **25** 307; **26** 85; **28** 253
Sherbakov, Valentin **27** 413
Sherborn, Charles William **4** 373; **10** 396
Sherborne (Dorset)
Abbey **10** 227; **13** 55
monument to Sir John Dutton **31** *128*, 129
Old Castle **3** 443; **22** 352; **26** 616
Sherborne, William **13** 634
Sherborne Missal *see under* MISSALS → individual manuscripts
Sherborne Pontifical *see under* PONTIFICALS → individual manuscripts
Sherbro-Bullom **1** 241, 247, 391; **21** 115
Sherbro islands **18** 90
Sherbrooke (Que), Plymouth Trinity Church **5** 560
Sherburne, Annie **10** 875
Sher-e-Bangla Nagar *see under* DHAKA
Sheremet'yev (family) **2** 409; **18** 536; **22** 177; **27** 441
Sheremet'yev, Nikolay (Petrovich), Count **23** 615; **27** 439; **28** 593
Sheremet'yev, Pyotr (Borisovich), Count **12** 134; **28** 593*
Sherf, Walter **12** 453
Sher-Gil, Amrita **15** 180, 657, 748; **28** 593*
Sheridan, Richard Brinsley **19** 728
Sheridan School of Crafts and Design **5** 583
Sheriff, Charles **12** 237
Sheriff, W. C. **19** 515
Sherlock, Cornelius **19** 318, 505
Sherlock, Philip **16** 890
Sherman, Cindy **10** 882; **25** 360; **28** 594*; **31** 610
Sherman, Claire Richter **33** 309
Sherman, Hoyt L. **19** 328
Sherman, John B. **5** 273; **27** 137
Sherman, Stuart **24** 409
Sherman, Welby **1** 897; **23** 884
Sherman, William Watts **20** 16; **25** 806
Sherman & Smith **15** 858
Shernborne (Norfolk), SS Peter and Paul **26** 613
Sherpa **22** 757, 787, 794
Sherpur Mosque **15** 369
Sherrin, George **1** 163; **18** 690; **23** 473
Sherring, J.
works **25** *244*
Sherringham, John **33** 372
Sher Shah, Sultan (*reg* 1538-45) (Sur) **15** 362, 410; **22** 258; **24** 264; **27** 858; **30** 9
architecture **8** 675, 679; **15** 362, 368; **27** 858, *858*
's Hertogenbosch **22** *813*; **28** 594–5*
brick **4** 778
Cathedral of St Jean *see* St Janskerk
collections **22** 905
glass **22** 884
masons' lodges **22** 820
Noordbrabants Museum **28** 594
Onze Lieve Vrouwekerk organ loft **22** 858
Provincehuis **30** 329
retables **22** 856
St Janskerk **1** 526; **3** 542; **6** 458; **13** 61, 62, 160; **22** 820; **28** 595*, *595*
choir-stalls **13** 114; **22** 856
sculpture **13** 100, 114, *114*; **22** 855
silver **22** 886
Stadhuis **8** 778; **30** 787
Shervashidze, Aleksandr (Konstantinovich) **28** 596*
Shervud, Leonid (Vladimirovich) **19** 13; **28** 596–7*; **33** 522
Shervud, Vladimir (Osipovich) **28** 596*
pupils **18** 116; **28** 596
works **22** 173, *173*
Sherwin, James **2** 759
Sherwin, John Keyse **28** 597*
Sherwin, William **21** 415; **25** 630
Sherwin & Cotton **30** 877
works **30** *877*
Sherwood Pottery *see* ORZEL POTTERY
Shestakov, F. M. **22** 172
Shestakov, Sergey **22** 173; **27** 378
Shestkovitsky **31** 562
Shestovitsa **32** 527
Shetelig, Haakon **31** 748; **32** 534
Shetland Islands **28** *222*
architecture **25** 503
baskets **3** 332
heraldry **14** 409
jumpers **18** 158
knitting **18** 157
lace **18** 158
Shetland wool *see under* WOOL → types
Shevardnadze, D. **12** 326
Shevchenko, Aleksandr (Vasil'yevich) **28** 597*
groups and movements **9** 144; **20** 151; **22** 750; **26** 504
Shevchenko, Taras (Hryhorovych) **17** 867; **18** 38; **28** 598*
patrons and collectors **31** 565
works **31** 559
Shevtsov, Yevgeniya **28** 841
She-wolf **2** 162, 168; **10** 587; **27** *9*, 10, 114
She xian **7** 93, 94, 119, 120
Shey **15** 311, 397
castle **21** 592
Shi *see* CHACH
Shiba Kōkan **17** 165; **28** 598–9*
attributions **31** 204
teachers **14** 565; **17** 185
works **17** 283
writings **17** 417
Shibam **16** 177, 271; **33** 519
Shibanid *see* SHAYBANID
Shibani Khan *see* SHAYBANI KHAN
Shibano Ritsuzan **17** 236; **29** 926
Shibanov, Mikhail **28** 599*
Shiba Shun *see* SHIBA KŌKAN
Shibata Junzo I **28** 599
Shibata Zeshin **17** 399; **28** 599–601*
methods **17** 140
teachers **17** 197; **23** 386
works **17** 200, 305; **18** 605; **28** *600*
Shiber, Saba George **18** 541
shibori *see under* DYEING → types
Shibrain, Ahmed Mohammed **29** 896
works **29** *896*
shibuichi *see under* ALLOYS → types
Shibusawa, Keizō **17** 345
Shicheng **17** 804
Shichiemon Hayahiya *see* HAYAHIYA SHICHIEMON
Shichiemon Iizumiya *see* IIZUMIYA SHICHIEMON
Shichijō-Ōmiya workshop **15** 158
Shi Chong **12** 86; **25** 785
Shi Dabin **33** 535
Shidon Kenpō *see* KENPŌ SHIDON
Shield bowls *see under* BOWLS → types
Shieldhall Cabinet Works **28** 256
Shield of Achilles **10** 334
Shield of Scipio **27** 83
shields **2** 468, 469; **14** 404–13*, *413*, 417–26
historical and regional traditions
Aboriginal Australia **1** 54, *55*, 56
shields
historical and regional traditions—cont.
Africa **1** 299, 362*, 411, *412*; **3** 332
Aztec **14** 411; **21** *250*; **22** 164
Belgium **2** *473*
Britain **14** 409
Byzantine **14** 408
Celtic **6** *161*
Central Asia **6** 261, 262, 306
China **7** 12–13
Dacian **30** 773
Egypt, ancient **10** 41
England **6** *161*; **14** 405, 407, 412, 413, 419, 420, 425; **15** 150
Ethiopia **1** 362
France **14** 409, 413
Germany **14** 409–10, 421
Gothic **14** 405
Greece, ancient **13** 583; **14** 407; **15** 149
Hungary **14** 411
Inca **14** 411
Irian Jaya **16** 47, *47*
Islamic **14** 428; **16** 503, 505, 507
Italy **14** 405, 410–11, 412, 413
Kenya **1** *412*
Maasai **1** 362, 411
Mesoamerica, Pre-Columbian **14** 411; **21** 245, 246, 249, *250*, 255; **22** 164
Mixtec **21** 255, 737
Morocco **16** 505
Native North Americans **22** *562*, 653, 654, *654*
Norway **23** 223
Ottoman **16** 507
Pacific Islands **23** 734; **28** II2
Papua New Guinea **24** 69–70, *70*, 74*, 79
Peru **14** 411
Poland **14** 411
Portugal **14** 405, 410
Prehistoric art **25** 541
Romanesque **14** 405
Romania **14** 424
Rome, ancient **3** 332
Scotland **14** 409
Solomon Islands **28** II2; **29** 49
Somalia **1** 362
Spain **14** 405, 410, 411, 412, 428; **16** 505
Sudan **1** 362
Tanzania **1** 299
Tarascan **30** 342
Turkey **31** *159*
Urartian **31** *159*
Yoruba **33** 556
Zaïre **1** 296
Zande **33** 610
Zulu **1** 362
materials
basketwork **1** 296; **3** 332
bronze **6** *161*; **31** *159*
coral **6** *161*
feathers **10** 848; **21** 245, 249, *250*; **22** 653; **30** 342
gold **21** 250
hides **22** *562*
iron **30** 773
lacquer **7** 12–13
leather **1** 299; **6** 262; **19** 2; **21** 245; **22** *654*
mosaics **21** 255
mother-of-pearl **28** II2
reeds **6** 306
shells **29** 49
silk **16** 508
turquoise **21** 737
wicker **6** 261, 262; **16** 507
wood **1** *55*, *412*; **16** *47*, 503
techniques
painting **23** 223
types
hoplon **13** 584
Shields, Frederic(k James) **14** 764; **20** 239; **28** 601*

Shields, F. W. 25 293
Shifangtang (Qionglai) 6 885
Shifrin, Nisson 28 924; 32 601
Shiga, Shigeo 2 761
Shigai Kitamura *see* KITAMURA, SHIGAI
Shigan Sō *see* SONG ZIYAN
Shigaraki 17 *11*, *241*
  Kōyama kiln 17 353
  Nakaide 28 601
  pottery 15 108; 17 255, *255*, 256, 260–61, 262, 267, 351; 28 601*
Shigaraki ware *see under* POTTERY → wares
Shigatse 21 593; 30 820, 831
Shigemasa 17 401
Shigemasa Ishikawa *see* ISHIKAWA TATSUEMON SHIGEMASA
Shigemasa Kitao *see* KITAO SHIGEMASA
Shigemori, Mirei 12 100; 17 381; 18 560
Shigemura, Tsutomu 30 392
Shigenaga Nishimura *see* NISHIMURA SHIGENAGA
Shigenobu Yanagawa *see* YANAGAWA SHIGENOBU
Shigeru Aoki *see* AOKI SHIGERU
Shigetaka Katō *see* KATŌ, SHIGETAKA
Shigetaka Mōri *see* MŌRI SHIGETAKA
Shigir' peat-bog 13 5; 27 365
Shihab al-Din Abu Hafs 'Umar al-Suhrawardi 1 473
Shihab al-Din Ahmad, Ruler *see* AHMAD I WALI, Ruler
Shihab al-Din Mahmud, Ruler (*reg* 1482-1518) (Bahmani) 15 681
Shihab al-Din Pasha 25 51
Shihab al-Din Tughril 16 380
Shihan 9 737
  stele 29 613; 30 194
Shih-ch'eng *see* SHICHENG
Shih Ch'ung *see* SHI CHONG
Shih-hsi *see* KUNCAN
Shih-hu *see* SHIHU
Shih I *see* SHI YI
Shih Jui *see* SHI RUI
Shih K'o *see* SHI KE
Shih Lu *see* SHI LU
Shihō Sakakibara *see* SAKAKIBARA, SHIHŌ
Shih-sou *see* SHISOU
Shih-t'ao *see* DAOJI
Shih T'ien-chang *see* SHI TIANZHANG
Shihu 7 66
Shih Wan-ts'ai *see* SHI WANCAI
Shiin *see* IKENAGA DŌUN
Shiinomine 17 351
Shii Sō *see* SŌ SHII
Shi'ite *see under* ISLAM → branches
Shijaku, Sali 1 540; 28 602*
Shijiahe culture 7 159
Shijiazhuang 7 113
  military cemetery 7 99
  statue of Norman Bethune 6 733
Shijō school 20 836
  works 20 *836*
  see also MARUYAMA-SHIJŌ SCHOOL
Shikai Irie *see* IRIE, SHIKAI
Shikanosuke Oka *see* OKA, SHIKANOSUKE
shikasta nasta'liq script *see under* SCRIPTS → types
Shikata Annosuke 17 323
Shi Ke 28 602*
Shikhaliyev, O. Yu. 2 898
Shikhly, S. M. 2 901
Shikiba, Ryūzaburō 21 634
Shikibu Murasaki *see* MURASAKI SHIKIBU
Shikida, Koichiro 9 765
Shikin Katsu *see* KATSU SHIKIN
Shikitei Sanba 17 845
shiki ware *see under* POTTERY → wares
Shikō 10 121
Shikohabad 15 409
Shikō Imamura *see* IMAMURA, SHIKŌ
Shikoku 17 10, *11*, 18, *241*
Shikō Munakata *see* MUNAKATA, SHIKŌ
Shikō Sō *see* SŌ SHIKŌ
Shikō Watanabe *see* WATANABE SHIKŌ
Shikshin 28 720
Shilakoe, Cyprian 1 433; 28 602*; 29 110
Shilakoe, Mpho *see* SHILAKOE, CYPRIAN
Shilhak-Inshushinak (*reg* 12th cent. BC) 30 28
Shilipu 7 15
Shilluk 1 295, 368, 409
  pipes (smoking) 1 *367*
Shil'nikovsky, Yevstafy (Pavlovich) 27 422
Shilo, M. K. 33 518
Shilou 6 *615*; 28 603*
Shi Lu 6 807
Shimada, Izumi 3 363, 365
Shimada Shujiro *see* SHUJIRO, SHIMADA
Shimadate (family) 20 835
Shimal 2 *246*
  jewellery 2 264
  pottery 2 266
  stone vessels 2 272
Shimamoto, Shōzō 13 866
Shimaoka, Tatsuzō 17 266; 21 634
Shimazu (family) 17 262, 386, 430, 793
Shimazu Yoshihiro 27 873
Shimbar 1 *849*; 10 172
Shimizu (company) 17 53
Shimizu, Uichi 17 267
Shimizu Gan'ō 17 410
Shimizu Onoe 17 401
Shimizu Ryūkei 17 98, 127
Shimizu Tomiharu 17 401
Shimjŏn *see* AN CHUNG-SIK
Shimogari 17 56
  shrine 17 *56*
Shimomura, Kanzan 14 219; 17 180, 200, 201; 28 603–4*
Shimonoseki Municipal Museum of Art 17 433
Shimotsusa 17 328
Shim Sa-chŏng 18 317
Shimshi, Siona 16 568, 569
Shin Bunten (New Bunten; New Japanese Art Exhibition) 17 206
Shinch'ŏn, Tomb 9 18 273, 350
Shindae 18 343
Shindaibutsuji 17 131
shinden *see under* HOUSES → types
Shindo Tsuji *see* TSUJI, SHINDO
Shine, Archie, Ltd 10 299
Shin'etsu Tōkō *see* TŌKŌ SHIN'ETSU
Shingei Geiami 1 776*; 7 716; 17 423; 28 493
  patrons and collectors 17 898
  pupils 17 898
  works 17 173, 437
Shingen Takeda *see* TAKEDA SHINGEN
Shingi Buddhism *see under* BUDDHISM → sects
Shing-kun *see* SVAYAMBHUNATHA
shingles 17 47; 27 131
Shingle style 10 185; 20 16, *17*; 23 498; 25 372, 806; 26 341; 28 604*; 31 593
Shingo Honda 21 892
Shingon Buddhism *see under* BUDDHISM → sects
Shingu, Susumu 26 550
Shingwi 18 272
shin hanga *see under* JAPAN → prints
Shin Harai *see* HARAI, SHIN
Shin Hongō *see* HONGŌ, SHIN
Shin'ichi Okada *see* OKADA, SHIN'ICHI
Shinji 2 86
Shinjidai Yōga Ten (New Era Western Painting Exhibition) 17 206
Shinji Hiraki *see* HIRAKI, SHINJI
Shinjin Gakai (Painting Society of New Talent) 17 207; 20 834
Shinjirō Okamoto *see* OKAMOTO, SHINJIRŌ
Shinjukai 17 137
Shinkai, Taketarō 17 134, 135; 22 444
Shin Kenchiku Kōgei Kenkyūjo 17 421
Shinki Huamán, Venancio 28 604–5*
Shinkō Chūan *see* CHŪAN SHINKŌ
Shinkurō Kunisawa *see* KUNISAWA, SHINKURŌ
Shinn, Everett 14 393; 28 605*; 31 605
  groups and movements 2 596, 597; 10 108; 12 769; 23 47
  works 21 897
Shin Naitō *see* NAITŌ, SHIN
Shinna Mitsui *see* MITSUI SHINNA
Shin Nanpin *see* SHEN NANPIN
Shinnie, P. L. 21 160
Shin'nin, Prince 17 196, 197
Shinnō Nōami 1 776*; 7 716; 17 380, 423; 22 338
  works 17 170, 173, 437; 18 563
  writings 17 428, 437
Shinnō Shūken 1 776
Shinnō Son'en *see* SON'EN, Prince
Shinobu Kawase *see* KAWASE, SHINOBU
Shinoda, Morio 1 738
  works 1 *738*
Shinoda, Tōkō 17 240; 28 605*, 627
Shinoda Kaishin 17 413, 861
Shinohara, Kazuo 17 92; 28 605–6*
  pupils 14 212; 27 598
  works 17 92; 28 *606*
Shinohara, Ushio 22 742
Shino Oribe ware *see under* POTTERY → wares
Shino ware *see under* POTTERY → wares
Shinoyama, Kishin 28 606–7*
Shinozaki Shōchiku 17 237, 412
Shinozaki Yōchiku 33 709
Shinran 5 119; 17 22
Shinsai Ryūryūkyo *see* RYŪRYŪKYO SHINSAI
Shin Sang-ho 18 344
Shin Sawbu, Queen of Pegu (*reg* 1453-72) 25 889
Shin Seisaku Kyōkai (New Art Work Society) 17 135, 137, 206; 27 872
Shinsen'en 17 69
Shinsen Tokuoka *see* TOKUOKA, SHINSEN
Shinsŏng on Namsan Stele 18 328
Shinsō Sōami 1 776–7*; 7 716; 17 380, 423; 18 550
  works 1 776, *776*; 17 172, 173, 437; 18 560, 561, 563
  writings 2 598; 17 428, 437
Shinsui Itō *see* ITŌ, SHINSUI
Shin Takamatsu *see* TAKAMATSU, SHIN
Shintarō Yamashita *see* YAMASHITA, SHINTARŌ
Shinten'ō Amanaka *see* AMANAKA SHINTEN'Ō
Shinto 5 117; 12 62, 95; 17 21; 28 *607*, 607–11*
  altars 1 703, *704*
  architecture 17 74
  collections 17 432
  dress 17 374
  iconography 10 485; 17 31–3*
Shinto—cont.
  mandalas 17 32, *32*, 151–3*, *152*, *153*; 28 *610*, 610
  masks 17 390, 394, 395
  musical instruments 17 396
  paintings 17 32–3, 151–3*, *153*; 28 610–11*
  rituals 28 609
  sanctuaries 16 74
  scrolls 28 610, *610*
  sculpture 17 31–2, 98, 127–9*, *128*; 28 610–11*
  shrines (i) (cult) 16 72, 74, 812, *812*; 17 46, 60–64*, *61*, *62*, *63*, *64*; 20 833; 22 231, *491*; 28 609–10*, 638–9
  wood 17 *128*
Shinuiju, State Historical Museum 18 382
Shinyōkai (Spring Sun Society) 33 552
Shinyōken Yada *see* YADA SHINYŌKEN
Shinzen 18 222
Shinzō Fukuhara *see* FUKUHARA, SHINZŌ
Shiokawa Bunrin 17 197, 200; 18 231; 23 386
Shiomgvime 12 *317*, 319
  monastery church 12 321
Shiomi (family) 17 304
Shiomi Masanari 17 304
Ship Clock 11 627
ship-clocks *see under* CLOCKS → types
ship-decoration 15 810–11; 28 611–14*, *612*, *613*, *614*
Shipibo 24 513, 514
Shipka Peak 5 156
Shiplake (Oxon), White House 22 744
Shipley, William 10 372; 15 820; 19 585; 28 614–15*
  groups and movements 8 802
  pupils 13 693; 14 879; 17 640; 22 152; 33 133
Shipman, Ellen 7 876
Shippen (family) 24 599; 33 91
Shippen, William 28 885
ships 10 197; 28 611–14
  historical and regional traditions
    Indonesia 15 810
    Japan 17 347
    Rome, ancient 26 854
  named vessels
    Andrea Doria 25 218
    Cutty Sark 28 614
    Giulio Cesare 25 218
    HMS Colossus 13 541
    Leonardo da Vinci 16 758
    Mary Rose 7 748
    Pocahontas 28 613, *614*
    Queen Elizabeth 33 382
    Queen Mary 3 631
    Rattlesnake 28 613
    Sovereign of the Seas 28 612, *613*
    USS Lancaster 28 613
    Victory 28 612, 613
    Wasa 7 748; 28 612
  types
    state *see* BARGES → types → ceremonial
    steam 28 614
ships' castles 28 611
ship's chests *see under* CHESTS → types
Ship's Master 23 600; 32 515
Shi Qiang *pan* 6 842
Shiraga, Kazuo 13 866; 17 207
Shirai, Seiichi 17 90; 28 615*
Shirai, Uzan 17 133
Shirai Kayō 17 417
Shiraiwa kiln 17 258
Shiraiwa pottery *see under* POTTERY → wares
Shirakaba *see* WHITE BIRCH SOCIETY
Shirakavan 2 426
Shirakawa Shizan 32 896
Shirakoya Ichibei 31 170
Shiraoi, Ainu Museum 17 433
Shira-Punu 1 393, 396, *399*
Shirashi ware *see under* POTTERY → wares
Shirayama Shōsai 17 305
Shiraz 15 *897*, 898; 16 *105*; 28 615–17*
  Arg 16 233
  art forms and materials
    architecture 16 229, 233–4
    carpets 16 482, *482*, 484
    dress 16 465
    glass 16 522
    lacquer 16 534, *534*
    manuscripts 16 124, 294, 296, 303, 317, *317*, 318, 321, 322, 324, 327, 328, 329, 331, 337–8*; 28 616–17
      15th cent. 16 328
    metalwork 16 *376*, 392
    woodwork 15 899
  Divankhana 16 233
  fortifications 21 589
  Friday Mosque 1 25
  gardens 12 82, 83
  library 19 316
  maidan 16 233
  Masjid-i Vakil 16 233, *234*
  mosque of Nasir al-Mulk 16 234
  musalla 22 354
  Naranjistan 28 *615*
  palace 16 233
  Pars Museum 15 900
  royal palace 16 160
  tombs 16 230
Shiraz, Ara 2 437
Shirburn Castle (Oxon) 21 549; 23 210
shire halls 18 886
Shirin *see* KURKAT
Shirinov, M. 2 902
Shirin Painter *see* MUHAMMAD (*fl* c. 1825-50)
Shirkov Church 27 373
Shirlaw, Walter 9 233; 23 46; 28 617*
Shirley, Anthony 16 475
Shirley, E. P. 25 573
Shirley, Frederick Stacey 22 240
Shirley, Thomas 9 374
Shirley, William 14 197
Shirley-Smith, Hubert 5 419
Shirner, Robert 10 669
shiro *see* JAPAN → castles
Shirohatayama *see under* IIZUKA CITY
Shirō Kasamatsu *see* KASAMATSU, SHIRŌ
Shiroko 17 355; 29 627
Shirone 17 389, 390
  Giant Kite History Museum (Odako Rekishi no Yakata) 17 390
Shiro Nomura *see* NOMURA, SHIRO
Shirō Otani *see* ŌTANI, SHIRŌ
shirred rugs *see under* RUGS → types
shirts 11 54
  historical and regional traditions
    Africa 1 348, *349*
    Akan 1 348
    Asante 1 *349*
    Byzantine 9 252
    Central Asia, Eastern 6 309
    England 9 274, 275
    Iran 16 463, 464
    Islamic 16 *137*, 459, 460, 463, 464
    Laos 18 771
    Native North Americans 22 636, 648, 649, 654
    Ottoman 16 *137*, 460
    South America, Pre-Columbian 29 182
    Turkey 16 *137*, 460
  materials
    inscriptions 16 *137*

shirts
materials—cont.
leather 1 *349*; 22 654
linen 16 *137*
quills 22 648, 649
Shi Rui 21 633
Shirvan 2 438, 901, 902
Shirvandjough Basilica 2 425
Shirvanzade, Aleksandr 2 432
Shiryayev, V. 28 598
Shiryū Morita *see* MORITA, SHIRYŪ
Shisan ling *see* CHANGPING → Ming Tombs
Shiseki Sō *see* SŌ SHISEKI
shisham 23 803
Shishkin, Ivan (Ivanovich) 27 391, 442; 28 617–18*
groups and movements 27 579
pupils 27 436, 450
Shishkin, V. A. 29 821; 31 896
Shishmanovich, John Alexander, King of Bulgaria *see* JOHN ALEXANDER, King of Bulgaria
Shisou 6 866
Shitao *see* DAOJI
shitenno *see* FOUR GREAT PUPILS OF KANŌ TAN'YŪ
Shi Tianzhang 7 61
works 7 *61*
Shivagupta, ruler of South Kosala (*reg c.* 7th cent. AD) 15 494
Shivaji 12 652
Shivalal 15 599, 601
Shivamaka Sada 27 866
Shivamitra 29 439
shivviti 21 743
Shiwan 28 618*
figurines 28 *618*
Shi Wancai 7 71
Shixi *see* KUNCAN
Shiyamangalam 15 509, 516
cave temple 15 507
Shi Yi 6 733
Shiz *see* TAKHT-I SULAYMAN
Shizan Shirakawa *see* SHIRAKAWA SHIZAN
Shizan Sō *see* SŌ SHIZAN
Shizhaishan 6 *614*; 8 853; 28 618–19*; 29 230
bronzes 8 852, 853
spearheads 8 854
Tomb 1 8 *853*
Tomb 13 7 89; 8 *854*
Shizhuang (Jingxing) 6 700
Shizuoka 17 84
Ganjōjuin 17 122
Kuwabara 17 122
Municipal Serizawa Keisuke Art Museum 28 466
Shūzenji 17 122
Shkodër 1 *537*, 538, 546
art schools 1 547
ceramics 1 543
guns 1 544
metalwork 1 543
Migjeni Theatre 1 539
National Exhibition of Folk Culture 1 546
Scutari 32 *158*
seraglio 1 539
silk 1 544
silver 1 543
textiles 1 545
Shkol'nik, Iosif 18 507; 22 508; 31 583
Shmarinov, Dementy (Alekseyevich) 27 396; 28 619*
Shobdon (Herts)
St John the Evangelist 25 726; 26 616
Shobdon Court 26 616
Shōbō 18 557
Shobwa *see* SHOOWA
Shodai kiln 17 258
shoden *see* JAPAN → sanctuaries
Shōdenji 12 99
Shōdoshima 17 331, 332
Shoebridge & Rising 25 688
shoe horns 14 763
Shōei Kanō *see* KANŌ SHŌEI
Shōeki Dokuryū *see* DOKURYŪ SHŌEKI
Shōen Uemura *see* UEMURA, SHŌEN
shoes 9 256; 20 594; 32 390
historical and regional traditions
China 7 145, *145*
Egypt, ancient 10 61
Islamic 16 452, 461
Japan 17 386
Ottoman 16 452, 461
Pakistan 23 803
Rome, ancient 27 105
Turkey 16 461
materials
beads 17 386
cotton 7 *145*
leather 10 61
shofarot 17 572
Shōga Takuma *see* TAKUMA SHŌGA
Shōgorō Tsuboi *see* TSUBOI, SHŌGORŌ
Shōhachi Kimura *see* KIMURA, SHŌHACHI
Shoha Hidai *se* HIDAI, SHOHA
Shōhaku Soga *see* SOGA SHŌHAKU
Shōhei Tanaka *see* TANAKA SHŌHEI
shōhekiga *see under* JAPAN → painting → wall; door panel
Shōhin Noguchi *see* NOGUCHI SHŌHIN
Shōichi Ida *see* IDA, SHŌICHI
shoin *see under* HOUSES → types
Shōitsu Kokushi *see* ENNI
shōji *see under* SCREENS (ii) (FURNITURE) → types
Shoji, Mitsuo 2 762
Shōji Hamada *see* HAMADA, SHŌJI
Shōji Kamoda *see* KAMODA, SHŌJI
Shōjin Gekkōtei *see* GEKKŌTEI SHŌJIN
Shōji Sekine *see* SEKINE, SHŌJI
Shōjō Shōkadō *see* SHŌKADŌ SHŌJŌ
Shojo Tenmin 17 400
Shōkadō Shōjō 14 703; 28 619–20*
groups and movements 17 215, 232, 343
works 17 228, 232–3, 236
Shōkaji 17 116
Shōkaku 18 557
Shōkaku *see* SOGA SHŌHAKU
Shōkei Kenkō *see* KENKŌ SHŌKEI
Shōkei Tenyū *see* TENYŪ SHŌKEI
Shokhin, N. A. 22 173
Shokin Hidai *see* HIDAI, SHOKIN
Shōko *see* NISHINO, SHOTARO
Shōkōsai Hanbei *see* HANBEI SHŌKŌSAI
Shoman, Suha 17 655
Shōmei Tomatsu *see* TOMATSU, SHŌMEI
Shomeron *see* SAMARIA
Shōmin Unno *see* UNNO, SHŌMIN
Shōmu, Emperor (*reg* 724-49) 17 23; 18 213; 28 620*
architecture 17 422, *422*; 22 491, 496; 23 592
calligraphy 17 218
collections 17 21, 428; 22 494, 504
sculpture 17 97, 113, 114
textiles 17 312
Shona 1 428; 13 334; 28 620–21*; 32 154; 33 678
architecture 1 414
axes 1 361; 28 621
barkcloth 28 621
beadwork 1 419
dice 28 621
headrests 1 *416*, 416–17*; 28 621, *621*
houses 1 313
iron 28 621
knives 28 621
Shona—cont.
metalwork 28 621
pots 1 418
pottery 28 621
snuff bottles 28 621
snuff-boxes 1 367
staffs 1 417
stone-carvings 1 429
wood 1 *416*; 28 *621*
wood-carvings 1 416, 417
Shōnagon Sei *see* SEI SHŌNAGON
Shō Nei 27 470
Shōnen Suzuki *see* SUZUKI, SHŌNEN
Shonzui porcelain *see under* PORCELAIN → wares
Shook, Edwin 17 753; 22 9; 31 507
Shoolbred, James, & Co. 8 576
Shoosmith, Arthur (Gordon) 28 622*
Shoowa 1 406; 18 484
shop-houses *see under* HOUSES → types
shopping centres 13 716; 28 622–3*
Austria 32 439
Rome, ancient 26 871
United States of America 28 622–3, *623*, *799*; 31 735
see also DEPARTMENT STORES
shops
Egypt 16 175
France 24 *123*
Germany 2 *566*; 31 *876*
Greece, ancient 13 381
Islamic 16 141, 175, 266
Italy 23 *621*; 26 887
Japan 17 357, 358–9; 18 *551*
Ottoman 16 266
Rome, ancient 23 *621*; 26 871, 887; 27 50
Turkey 16 266
United States of America 3 35; 23 *31*
see also DEPARTMENT STORES
Shorapur 15 642
Shorchuk 6 *288*, *614*; 28 624*; 30 441
sculpture 6 298, 300
Temple XXV 6 300
wall paintings 6 304
Shore, Arnold 2 772; 3 628
Shore, Henrietta 33 105
Shore, Stephen 23 37; 28 624*
works 24 XI2
shore-forts *see under* FORTS → types
Shoreham (Australia) 2 *736*
Shoreham (Kent; UK) 26 353
Shoreham-by-Sea (W. Sussex) 5 173
Shōren'in *see under* JAPAN → calligraphy
Shōren'in no Miya, Prince 2 211
Shōri no Uonari 17 391
Short, Frank 9 309; 14 165; 21 418
Short, Gladys 29 116
Short, Richard 5 564
Short, William 32 234
short coats *see under* COATS → types
Shorter, Colley 7 434
Short Hills (NJ), B'nai Jeshurun 17 549
short-pile rugs *see under* RUGS → types
Shōsen'in Tadanobu Kanō *see* KANŌ SHŌSEN'IN TADANOBU
Shōsen Soga *see* SOGA SHŌSEN
Shoshenq I (*reg c.* 950-*c.* 929 BC) 2 690; 9 *777*, *887*
Shoshenq II 9 *777*; 10 11, 32
Shoshenq III 9 *777*, 861, 887; 30 296
Shoshenq V 9 *777*
Shoshenq kings 5 70
Shōshi no Fujiwara *see* FUJIWARA NO SHŌSHI
Shōshō Hōrin *see* HŌRIN SHŌSHŌ
Shoshone 22 633
Shoshone (Northern) 22 549
Shoshone (Western) 22 549, 633, 641
Shoshoni 22 551
tepees 22 *569*
Shōshō Soga *see* SOGA SHŌSHŌ
Shōsōin *see under* NARA
Shōson *see* OHARA, KOSON
Shostakovich, Dmitri 26 505
Shōtarō Koyama *see* KOYAMA, SHŌTARŌ
Shotaro Nishino *see* NISHINO, SHOTARO
Shotaro Satō *see* SATŌ, SHOTARO
Shōtei Hokuju 17 286, 287, 848
Shōtei Takahashi *see* TAKAHASHI, SHŌTEI
Shōtetsu 17 228
Shōtō Bokusai 15 129; 28 624*
Shōtoku, Empress (*reg* 764-70) 17 270; 22 495; 33 318
Shōtoku, Prince 17 21, 97, 142; 28 624–5*
architecture 2 655; 5 115; 14 773, *774*; 18 555, 556; 22 500; 23 596
attributions 17 214
dress 17 374
manuscripts 17 217, 402
sculpture 23 595
textiles 17 313
Shotor, Tepe 1 211; 14 19
Museum 1 212
sculpture 1 193, 196, 197
stucco 1 196, 197; 29 824, 825
stupas 1 192
Tyche of Niche V2 1 196, *197*
wall paintings 1 201, *201*
Shotorak 1 *186*; 28 625–6*
reliefs 1 188
sculpture 1 196; 28 625–6
Shotover (Oxon), Gothic Temple 13 199
Shotridge, Louis 10 580
Shotters, Joos 12 523
Shotts Iron Co. 28 263
Shoturgay 6 185
Shou hsien *see* SHOU XIAN
shouldered arches *see under* ARCHES → types
shoulder-handled amphorae *see* AMPHORAE → types
Shoumen 5 156, 162
Shōun Maeda *see* MAEDA SHŌUN
Shōunsai Shōno 17 365
Shoura, Nasir 30 177
Shou xian 6 *615*; 7 150, 247; 28 626–7*
tomb of Marquis Zhao of Cai 7 247; 28 *626*
bronzes 6 851; 28 626–7
gold 7 21
Zhujiaji
tomb of Prince You of Chu 28 627
Shovell, Cloudesley 8 *454*
shovels 11 119
Shō Village 17 116
Shovkoplias, I. G. 21 413
Shovkunenko, Aleksey A. 31 560
Shōwa period *see under* JAPAN → periods
showcases 9 30, 31
Shōya Yoshida *see* YOSHIDA, SHŌYA
Shōyū Itsunen *see* ITSUNEN SHŌYŪ
Shōzaburō Watanabe *see* WATANABE, SHŌZABURŌ
Shozan Satake *see* SATAKE SHOZAN
Shōzō Shimamoto *see* SHIMAMOTO, SHŌZŌ
Shōzō Uchii *see* UCHII, SHŌZŌ
Shpat *see* VALËSH
Shpataraku, Kostandin 1 540
Shpirag 1 542
Shqipëri *see* ALBANIA
Shrapnell, James, Parker & Wakelin 19 596
Shravana Belgola *see* SHAVANA BELGOLA
Shreter, Viktor (Aleksandrovich) 4 335; 17 859; 18 99; 28 627–8*; 31 551
Shreve, Lamb & Harmon 7 766; 28 628–9*
works 23 43, 359; 28 *629*; 31 596
Shreve, Richmond Harold 28 628–9
Shreve, Stanwood & Co. 4 480
Shreve & Lamb 28 629
Shrewsbury (Salop)
Assembly Rooms 2 617
houses 10 230
mills (industrial) 21 600
St Mary 6 *565*; 22 217
school 28 156
sculptors 10 265
shire hall 18 887
Shrewsbury, Charles Talbot, 1st Duke of *see* TALBOT, CHARLES, 1st Duke of Shrewsbury
Shrewsbury, Edward James 33 219
Shrewsbury, Elizabeth Talbot, Countess of *see* TALBOT, ELIZABETH, Countess of Shrewsbury
Shrewsbury, George Talbot, 6th Earl of *see* TALBOT, GEORGE, 6th Earl of Shrewsbury
Shrewsbury, John Talbot, 16th Earl of *see* TALBOT, JOHN, 16th Earl of Shrewsbury
Shrewsbury, John Talbot, 1st Earl of *see* TALBOT, JOHN, 1st Earl of Shrewsbury
Shrewsbury Book (London, BL, Royal MS. 15. E. VI) 20 772
Shridarani, Sundari 8 677
Shriharsha 15 228
Shrimpton, Henry 4 481
shrines (i) (cult) 28 629–41*
historical and regional traditions
Africa 1 289, 309–10, 313, 331, *332*
Asante 1 309; 2 589*
Aztec 28 640
Bamana 1 261
Belgium 28 630
Benin, Kingdom of 1 289
Bijogo 4 55
Britain 27 *2*
Buddhism
Central Asia, Eastern 28 *636*, 637
Indian subcontinent 28 635
Japan 28 639
Korea 28 638
Sri Lanka 17 769; 25 169
Thailand 28 *640*
Burkina Faso 1 289; 19 *522*
Burma 2 280–81, *281*; 28 639, 640
Byzantine 9 656
Cambodia 2 57; 5 474
Carolingian 5 807
Central Asia 28 635*
Central Asia, Eastern 28 *636*, 637*
Central Asia, Western 28 635–6*
Champa 28 639
China 28 *637*, 637–8*
Christianity 28 629
Confucianism 18 269; 28 638
Crete 21 *663*, 663–4*
Early Christian (*c.* AD 250-843) 9 656; 28 629–30*
Ecuador 28 632
Edo (Africa) 9 *736*, 736–7
Egypt, ancient 9 *827*, 827–35; 30 432
England 28 630
France 23 *99*; 28 632
Germany 12 442; 23 99, *311*; 28 630, *631*, 632, IV2

- shrines (i) (cult)
  - historical and regional traditions—cont.
    - Ghana 1 289, 309, *332*
    - Gothic 13 *94*; 23 *311*; 28 IV2
    - Greece, ancient 13 418–19
    - Hinduism 14 559; 15 *331*; 19 *695*; 25 169; 28 635
    - Holy Roman Empire (before 1648) 28 IV2
    - Ibibio 1 310
    - Igbo 1 289; 15 113*
    - Inca 28 *641*
    - Indian subcontinent 15 249–51*, 309, 310–11, 324, 325–8, *326*, *327*, 727–9*; 25 303; 28 635*, III2
      - Buddhism 28 635
      - Hinduism 14 559; 15 *331*; 28 635
      - Islamic 15 *308*
      - Kerala 15 336
      - Vijayanagara period 15 330, *331*
    - Insular art 28 *630*
    - Iran 25 830; 28 IV1
    - Iraq 28 *633*
    - Ireland 28 *630*; 32 *530*
    - Islamic 28 632–5*
      - Central Asia 28 636, 637
      - Indian subcontinent 15 *308*
      - Iran 28 IV1
      - Iraq 28 *633*
      - Kazakhstan 16 *198*
    - Italy 13 *94*; 28 632
    - Japan 17 56, *56*, 301, 345–7; 28 638–9*
      - Buddhism 28 639
      - Shinto 16 72, 74, 812; 17 46, 60–64*, *62*; 22 *491*; 28 609–10*, 638–9
      - Shinto: Edo period (1600-1868) 16 *812*; 17 *61*, *63*
      - Shinto: Kamakura period (1185-1333) 20 833
    - Java 19 *695*; 28 639
    - Jewish art 17 538–9
    - Kazakhstan 16 *198*
    - Korea 18 269; 28 638*
    - Laos 18 776
    - Lobi 19 *522*
    - Mali 1 261
    - Maya 28 640
    - Mesoamerica, Pre-Columbian 28 640–41*
    - Mesopotamia 33 675, 676
    - Minoan 21 *663*, 663–4*
    - Mongolia 28 637
    - Native North Americans 28 641*
    - Nepal 22 759, *760*, 793
    - Nigeria 1 289; 9 *736*
    - Pakistan 30 *380*
    - Peru 28 *641*
    - Phoenician 24 641
    - Portugal 25 303
    - Prehistoric art 17 *56*
    - Romanesque 2 *867*; 26 699; 28 *631*
    - Rome, ancient 27 *2*
    - shamanism 28 638
    - Shinto 16 72, 74, 812, *812*; 17 46, 60–64*, *61*, *62*, *63*; 20 833; 22 231, *491*; 28 609–10*, 638–9
    - South America, Pre-Columbian 28 640–41*, *641*
    - South-east Asia 28 639–40*
    - Spain 2 *867*; 26 699; 28 632
    - Sri Lanka 17 769; 25 169, 303; 29 448
    - Thailand 28 639, 640, *640*
    - United States of America 28 632
    - Vietnam 32 471
    - Viking 32 *530*
    - Yoruba 1 289
    - Zambia 1 289, 310
  - materials
    - bronze 28 *630*, IV2; 32 *530*
- shrines (i) (cult)
  - materials—cont.
    - cement 1 331
    - domes 28 634
    - enamel 28 *630*
    - filigree 32 *530*
    - glass 32 *530*
    - gold 23 *99*; 28 *631*; 32 *530*
    - hardstones 32 *530*
    - ivory 26 699
    - lacquer 17 301
    - marble 13 *94*
    - paints 1 289
    - paper 28 635
    - silver 9 656; 23 *311*; 32 *530*
    - tiles 28 634
    - wood 18 776; 28 *636*
  - types
    - bark *see* TEMPLES → types → peripteral
    - *bodhighara see* tree-shrines
    - circular 15 249–50, *251*
    - elliptical 15 251
    - lararia 18 786*; 26 857; 27 50, 88–91
    - spirit-houses 28 III1; 30 638
    - square 15 249
    - tree-shrines 15 249, 728; 29 442
  - *see also* CHAPELS; CULT HOUSES; MAUSOLEA; MARTYRIA; RELIQUARIES; SANCTUARIES; TEMPLES; TOMBS → types → confessio
  - *see also* TOMBS → types → confessio
- shrines (ii) (altarpieces) 23 656; 28 133, 641*
  - *see also* ALTARPIECES; PREDELLAS
- Shrinivasanallur Temple 15 305
- Shri Singh, Ruler (*reg* 1844-70) (Pahari) 6 405
- Shroud of St Columba 16 436
- Shroud of St Froilan 16 436
- Shroud of St Josse 16 100, 430, 435, *435*
- Shroud of Turin 20 251; 28 5; 30 403
- shrouds 3 442; 9 *666*; 10 14; 20 38
- Shrubland Park (Suffolk) 12 139, *139*
- Shryock, Gideon 13 611; 28 641*
- SHS 4 461
- Shtakenshneyder, Andrey (Ivanovich) 28 641–2*
  - assistants 18 99
  - works 18 543; 24 546; 27 377, 578
- Shteller, Pavel P. 19 12, 732; 25 323
- Shterenberg, Abram 28 642–3*
- Shterenberg, David (Petrovich) 17 577; 27 441; 28 642*; 32 661
  - assistants 19 746
  - groups and movements 10 843; 22 508; 27 394; 28 924
- Shterenberg, Vasily I. 18 38; 30 915; 31 559
- Shteynberg, Eduard 27 397
- Shtiglits, A. L., Baron *see* STIEGLITZ, A. L., Baron
- Shtil'man, Ilya M. 31 560
- Shtorm, Ivan V. 31 553
- Shu (people) 6 726
- Shu (family) 17 595
- Shubat Enlil *see* LEILAN, TELL
- Shubhakarasimha 5 109
- Shubin, A. V. 21 813
- Shubin, Fedot (Ivanovich) 27 389, 442, 579; 28 643*
  - patrons and collectors 27 438
  - works 24 546; 26 403; 27 402, 403; 29 551, 552
- Shūbun school 17 172
- Shūbun Tenshō *see* TENSHŌ SHŪBUN
- Shūchō Tamagawa *see* TAMAGAWA SHŪCHŌ
- Shūdan Gendai Chōkoku (Modern Sculptue Group) 17 137
- *shuden* 17 *76*, 77
- Shufflebotham, Jean 28 592
- Shugborough (Staffs) 13 608; 25 267; 29 806
  - Tower of the Winds 8 461
- Shugendō 5 118
  - dress 17 *43*
  - iconography 17 42–4*
  - *maṇḍalas* 17 43–4
- Shūgetsu Higuchi *see* HIGUCHI SHŪGETSU
- Shūgetsu Tōkan 31 251, 252
- Shugyō Oguchi *see* OGUCHI, SHUGYŌ
- Shuhda 16 276
- Shūhei Ogata *see* OGATA SHŪHEI
- Shūhō Mori *see* MORI SHŪHŌ
- Shūhō Myōchō *see* DAITŌ KOKUSHI
- Shuichi Gotō *see* GOTŌ, SHUICHI
- Shuihudi *see* YUNMENG
- Shuitema, Paul 24 686
- Shuitianban 14 136
- Shujaʿ al-Daula, Nawab of Avadh (*reg* 1754-75) 15 376, 654, 712
- Shujaʿ ibn Manʿa al-Mawsili 16 381
  - works 16 *381*
- Shūji Hosoda *see* HOSODA SHŪJI
- Shujiro, Shimada 7 161
- Shūkei 17 132
- Shūkei Sesson *see* SESSON SHŪKEI
- Shūken Shinnō *see* SHINNŌ SHŪKEN
- Shukhayev, Vasily (Ivanovich) 27 392; 28 643*
  - collaboration 33 486
  - pupils 1 507; 8 277; 31 398
- Shukhov, V. G. 22 173
- Shukhuti 12 *317*, 323
- Shukō Murata *see* MURATA SHUKŌ
- Shukri, Akram 16 2
- Shuksu *see* SUKAS, TELL
- Shulgi (*reg* 2094-2047 BC) 30 28
- Shul'gin, V. 2 894
- Shultz, Robert Weir 12 316
- Shuman *see under* DUSHANBE
- Shume *see* KANŌ NAONOBU
- Shumemaru 17 401
- Shu Min 6 637
- Shumi yuan 6 897
- Shumsher, Chandra 22 765
- Shumun *see* HERMOPOLIS MAGNA
- Shūnan 17 411
- Shunboku Ōoka *see* ŌOKA SHUNBOKU
- Shun-chih emperor (Ch'ing) *see* SHUNZHI EMPEROR (QING)
- Shunchō Katsukawa *see* KATSUKAWA SHUNCHŌ
- Shun'ei Katsukawa *see* KATSUKAWA SHUN'EI
- *shunga see* JAPAN → prints → types
- Shunga (Indian subcontinent) 28 644*
- Shungyoku Katsukawa *see* KATSUKAWA SHUNGYOKU
- Shunjōbō Chōgen *see* CHŌGEN
- Shunjuike Ichiyo 17 381
- Shunkei lacquer *see under* LACQUER → types
- Shunkin Uragami *see* URAGAMI SHUNKIN
- Shunkō Katsukawa (1743-1812) *see* KATSUKAWA SHUNKŌ
- Shunkō Katsukawa (*fl* 1806-21) *see* KATSUKAWA SHUNSEN
- Shunkōsai Hokuei 17 289
  - works 17 *289*
- Shunkōsai Hokushū 17 288
- Shunkyō Yamamoto *see* YAMAMOTO, SHUNKYŌ
- Shunman Kubo *see* KUBO SHUNMAN
- Shun'oku Sōen 17 343
- Shunsen Katsukawa *see* KATSUKAWA SHUNSEN
- Shunsen Natori *see* NATORI, SHUNSEN
- Shunshō Katsukawa (1726-92) *see* KATSUKAWA SHUNSHŌ (1726-92)
- Shunshō Katsukawa (1743-1812) *see* KATSUKAWA SHUNKŌ (1743-1812)
- Shunsō Hishida *see* HISHIDA, SHUNSŌ
- Shunsui Katsukawa *see* KATSUKAWA SHUNSUI
- Shunsui Rai *see* RAI SHUNSUI
- Shunsuke Matsumoto *see* MATSUMOTO, SHUNSUKE
- Shuntei Katsukawa *see* KATSUKAWA SHUNTEI
- Shunwa Katsukawa *see* KATSUKAWA SHUNWA
- Shunyōkai (Spring Season Society) 17 205; 23 383; 31 82, 575
- Shunzan Katsukawa *see* KATSUKAWA SHUNZAN
- Shunzei, Fujiwara no *see* FUJIWARA NO SHUNZEI
- Shunzhi emperor (Qing; *reg* 1644-61)) 6 704
- Shuo xian, Chongfu Temple 6 778
- Shuqafa, Kom el- *see under* ALEXANDRIA (EGYPT)
- Shuri *see* NAHA
- Shurmak culture 28 325
- Shuruppak *see* FARA, TELL
- Shusaku Arakawa *see* ARAKAWA, SHUSAKU
- Shūsei 30 466
- Shūseki Watanabe *see* WATANABE SHŪSEKI
- Shūsh *see* SUSA (MESOPOTAMIA)
- Shusha 2 *890*, 894; 16 *105*; 28 644*
  - carpets 2 438, 901; 16 479, 481
  - embroidery 2 901
  - jewellery 2 900
  - Museum of the History of Shusha 28 644
  - textiles 2 900
- Shūshin Gidō *see* GIDŌ SHŪSHIN
- Shushtar 15 897, *897*
- Shu-Sin, King of Ur (*reg* 2037-2029 BC) 21 552
- Shustar 8 861
- Shūsū Daigaku *see* DAIGAKU SHŪSŪ
- Shute, John 2 314; 9 367; 13 298; 28 645*
  - works 2 312, 356, 362; 31 297
- Shūtoku 31 252
- Shutov, Sergey 27 398
- Shutruk-Nahhunte I (*reg* 12th cent. BC) 15 910; 30 28
- Shutruk-Nahhunte II (*reg* 7th cent. BC) 1 879; 30 29
- shuttering 4 767; 7 690, *690*; 28 645*
- shutters (camera) 22 390; 24 653, 669
- shutters (window) 9 12
  - historical and regional traditions
    - Belgium 3 575
    - Dogon 9 *69*
    - France 9 12
    - Islamic 16 500
    - Netherlands, the 9 12
    - Russia 13 *14*
    - Yemen 16 500
  - materials
    - iron 9 *69*
    - wood 9 *69*
- shuttlecocks 7 147
- Shutze, Philip Trammell 2 694; 28 645–6*
- Shutze and Armistead 28 645
- Shuvalov (family) 27 441
- Shuvalov, Ivan (Ivanovich), Count 19 563; 27 438; 28 646*
  - collections 27 439
- Shuvalov, Ivan (Ivanovich), Count—cont.
  - education (art) 27 442
  - paintings 27 438
- Shuvalov, Yevgraf (Sergeyevich) 27 417
- Shuvalov Painter 13 523, 524
- Shuvayeva, S. 30 352
- Shuvelyany 2 893
- Shuweimiyeh 14 21
- Shuzaku, Emperor (*reg* 930-46) 23 445
- Shuzan Nagamachi 17 400
- Shūzan Yoshimura *see* YOSHIMURA, SHŪZAN
- Shuzenji 17 405
- Shūzo Ōura *see* ŌURA, SHŪZO
- Shūzui Keisho *see* KEISHO SHŪZUI
- Shvarts, Vyacheslav (Grigor'yevich) 28 646–7*
- Shvartsman, Mikhail M. 8 10; 27 397
- Shvetambara *see under* JAINISM → sects
- Shvidkovsky, Aleksandr 12 878
- Shwartz, Stefan 20 925
- Shwebo 5 238
- Shwedaung 5 *221*, 247
- Shwegu 5 263
- Shwe-hsan-daw, Shin bin 29 826
- Shweibou Tin Maung 5 252
- Shyama Sundara 15 594
- Shyrock, Gideon 18 887
- Si 8 490
  - works 1 *291*
- Siʿ *see* SEEIA
- SIA *see* SOCIETY OF INDEPENDENT ARTISTS
- Siagu 9 535
- Siak 15 811
- Sialk, Tepe 1 894; 10 132; 15 *901*, 902, 903, 904, 905, 920, 921; 28 647*
  - ceramics 15 *921*
  - jewellery 1 874
  - metalwork 15 918
  - pottery 15 920; 28 647
- Sialkot 15 678, 713
- Siam *see* THAILAND
- Siamun (*reg c.* 973-*c.* 964 BC) 9 *777*, 879, 887; 30 296
- Siana 13 508
- Siana cups *see under* CUPS → types
- Siano, Antonio Capecelatro, Duca di 25 665
- Siarhiejevič, P. 3 529
- Siba 15 629
- Sibbald, Robert 28 242
- Sibelius, Jean 22 540
- Sibellino, Antonio 2 400; 28 647*
- Šibenik 8 *174*
  - Cathedral 8 175
  - Franciscan Monastery 8 177
  - St James's Cathedral 8 178; 12 666–7, *667*
- Šibenik Sacramentary *see under* SACRAMENTARIES → individual manuscripts
- Siberechts, Jan (*fl* 1620) 28 647
- Siberechts, Jan (1627-1703) 2 196; 28 647–8*
  - works 3 560; 4 80; 18 711; 28 *648*
- Siberia 27 *363*, 435–7
  - carpets 16 467
  - citadels 31 68
  - dolls 31 260
  - dress 28 *546*
  - felt 10 873, *873*
  - figurines 25 489
  - hardstones 14 172
  - ivory 7 102; 16 796, 799
  - leather 31 260
  - metalwork 28 321, 322, 324–6
  - nephrite 7 11; 16 860
  - rock art 25 488; 28 321
  - trade
    - iron 22 613
    - textiles 1 118

Siberia—cont.
  see also RUSSIA
Siberian Collection 6 212, 237
Siberian red lead *see* CROCOITE
Sibermann, Gustav 25 623
Sibi, Narasimhasvami Temple 15 649
Sibilla, Angelo 27 192
Sibilla, Gaspare 4 622; 25 8
Sibiu 26 *705*; 28 648–9*
  architecture 14 884
  Astra Library 26 724
  Brukenthal Museum 26 708, 718, 722, 724; 28 649
    collections 5 8–9*; 26 717
  Chapel of the Cross 26 711
  church 26 707
  City Library 26 724
  Evangelical parish church *see* St Mary
  font 26 719
  fortifications 26 707
  furniture 14 903
  German Evangelical College 26 724
  houses 26 707, 712
  Jesuit church 26 713
  Jesuit college 26 708
  metalwork 15 7; 26 719
  Museum of History 28 649
  pews 26 718
  St Mary 14 883; 26 711; 28 649
  sculpture 14 893
Sibley, Joseph 5 578; 28 649*
Sibley, Michael 28 649
Sibmacher, Hans Melchior 28 649
Sibmacher, Johann 28 649*
  works 14 406, *412*
Sibri 15 421
Sibrium *see* CASTELSEPRIO
Sibsagar 15 396
  Vishadol Temple 15 396
Sibt ibn al-Jawzi 16 379
Sibundoy 7 602
Sibutu 24 *607*, 628
Sic 24 442
Sican 19 822
Sicán Archaeological Project 3 363, 365
Sicán culture 28 650–52*
  alloys 28 651
  architecture 28 652
  bottles 28 *650*
  bronze 28 651
  copper 28 *651*
  emeralds 29 155
  gold 28 651, *651*, *652*
  headdresses 28 *651*
  iconography 28 651
  knives 28 651, *652*
  masks 28 651
  metalwork 28 651–2; 29 210
  shaft graves 28 652
  silver 28 *651*, *652*
  turquoise 28 *651*
Sicard, Bishop of Cremona 31 295
Sicard, Claude 10 79
Sicard, François 2 769
Sicardi, Louis-Marie 21 643
Sicasica Church 4 258
Siccama, Hora 13 875
Siccardi (family) 1 579
Siccardsburg, August Siccard von 31 872–3*
  collaboration 2 786
  pupils 3 312; 11 29; 14 216; 21 757; 25 648; 28 175; 29 722; 32 760; 33 687
  teachers
  works 2 808
siccatives 28 653*
Sicciolante, Girolamo 13 628
Sicevo, St Nicholas 25 343
Sichartus, Abbot of Farfa 10 804
Sichelbein (family) 28 147
Sichelbein, Johann Friedrich 14 324
Sichem, Christoffel van, I (1546-1624) 33 358
Sichem, Christoffel van, II (1581-1658) 33 358
Sichem, Christoffel van, III (1618-59) 33 358
Sichem, Christoffel van, IV (1642-*c.* 1692/8) 33 358
Sichmüller, Johannes 8 398
Sichuan wenwu 24 435
Sichulski, Kazimierz 25 108
Siciliano, Antonio 10 713; 13 24, 659
Siciliano, Lorenzo 5 704
Sicily 16 *103*, *616*, *621*; 25 732; 28 653–7*
  amber 1 761
  architecture
    Baroque 16 640–41
    Islamic 16 171–2*
    military 21 556, *557*
    Romanesque 16 171, 626–7; 28 655
    vernacular 32 292
  bone-carvings 28 653
  bronzes 13 572
  capitals 21 *900*
  carnivals 5 787
  caskets 16 525
  cathedrals 21 *898*; 23 *843*; 27 *614*
  churches 16 *640*; 23 *846*
  circuits 21 556
  clay 26 877
  cloisters 21 *899*
  coins 7 536; 13 586, 587, *587*; 28 654
  columns 21 *900*
  coral 7 834; 16 750; 31 285
  eggs 25 735
  embroidery 16 *430*
  figurines 13 580, 581
  finials (scrolls) 17 569
  fortifications 16 172; 21 556, *557*
  forts 21 *557*
  fountain houses 21 *899*
  fountains 12 *78*
  gardens 11 340; 12 *78*
  gold 16 *430*, 742
  heraldry 14 412
  historiography 16 547
  ivory-carvings 16 525–6*, 799; 26 698
  lamps 13 *603*
  limestone 28 654, *654*
  maiolica 16 735, 736
  marble 21 *900*
  mosaics 22 162, 163
    Byzantine 9 581
    Roman 24 700, 701–2, *702*; 27 63
    Romanesque 6 *133*; 23 *844*, *846*; 26 *679*, 680
  moulds 25 734
  muqarnas (architecture) 22 324
  oliphants 26 698
  painting 16 253, 525–6; 28 *656*
  paper 20 329
  pearls 16 *430*
  periods
    Prehistoric 28 653*
  pins 13 600
  pottery 28 654–5
    Black-figure 13 512
    Diana ware 28 653
    Greece, ancient 13 *530*, 530–31*
    Islamic 16 411
    Red-figure 13 *530*, 530–31*
    Siculo-Arabic ware 16 415
  protomes 13 583
  pyxides (boxes) 16 525
  pyxides (vases) 13 *530*
  robes 16 *430*
  rock art 1 *149*; 25 475
  sculpture 13 582; 16 688; 28 *387*, 654
    Romanesque 26 619, 628–9*
    stone 26 628–9*
    6th cent. BC 28 *654*
  silk 13 197; 16 *430*, 436, 437, 752
  silver 13 *587*; 16 742
Sicily—cont.
  stelae 29 619
  stone 26 628–9*
  stone-carvings 6 30
  stucco 28 *477*
  Tellaro Villa 27 63
  temples 13 392, 398; 28 654
    dipteral 13 398
    Doric 1 511, *511*
    Greece, ancient 13 378
    Ionic 13 398
  terracotta 13 582; 28 654
  textiles 16 437
  theatres 26 873
  threads 16 *430*
  thrones 30 777
  tiles 30 887
  tombs 26 628–9
  tortoiseshell 16 748
  trade 9 515
    pottery 13 487; 16 415; 28 654
  urban planning 28 654
  vaults (ceiling) 16 *171*
  villas 24 699–701
  well-heads 33 56
Sicinio-Bibiena, Giovanni Carlo 25 292
Siciński, Karol 17 874
Siciolante (da Sermoneta), Girolamo 24 420; 26 770; 28 657–8*
  collaboration 7 777; 11 721
  patrons and collectors 10 809; 25 7
  works 26 818; 28 *658*
sick building syndrome 10 417
Sickelpart, Ignatius 6 41, 539
Sickert, Bernard 19 589
Sickert, Oswald Adalbert 28 659
Sickert, Walter Richard 3 373; 4 810; 19 621; 28 659–62*; 32 197
  groups and movements 1 666; 5 516, 517; 10 254, 255; 15 156; 19 589, 591, 623; 23 22, 23
  patrons and collectors 16 42; 20 476
  pupils 4 293; 5 516; 13 29; 14 718; 17 472, 631
  teachers 33 141, 144
  works 9 309; 10 256; 12 296; 21 761; 28 *659*, *660*; 29 426
Sickinger, Anselm 19 150
sickles 30 *181*
Sickman, Laurence Chalfant Stevens 28 663*
Siclis, Charles 28 663–4*
Sicre, Juan José 5 730
Siculi 31 57
Siculo-Arabic ivory-carvings *see under* IVORY-CARVINGS → types
Siculo-Arabic ware *see under* POTTERY → wares
Šid
  Petar Dobrović Gallery 28 459
  Savo Šumanović Gallery 28 459
Sidama 10 567, 577
Sidamon-Eristavi, V. 12 326
Sidaogou 6 315
Siddal, Elizabeth (Eleanor) 10 253; 28 664*; 33 314
Siddalingasvami, Silpi 22 404
Siddhanakola 1 485
Siddha Pal Singh, Ruler (*reg c.* 1500) (Pahari) 15 705
Siddharta Gautama 5 87
Siddhi Muni Shakya 22 785
Siddhinarasimha, King (*reg c.* 1620) (Malla) 22 764
Siddington Barn (Glos) 30 908
Siddiqi, I. R. 23 804
Siddons, Sarah 25 *278*; 30 675
siddurim 28 664*
Side 13 *362*; 26 *908*; 28 664–5*
  Basilica CC 9 536
  baths 26 913
  Building M 26 923, *923*
Side—cont.
  cutting 27 7
  fortifications 21 558
sideboards 28 665–6*
  historical and regional traditions
    Belgium 3 585
    England 28 *665*
    Poland 25 *121*
    Portugal 25 304
    Spain 29 302, 314
    Switzerland 30 142
    United States of America 31 628, 631
  materials
    oak 3 585
    silver 29 302
    yew 25 *121*
  techniques
    gilding 28 *665*
    marquetry 25 *121*
  types
    służba 25 120
    stage-top 28 253
sidelighting *see under* LIGHTING → types
Sidés, Fredo 27 639
side tables *see under* TABLES → types
sidewalks 28 728
Sidh Sen, Ruler (*reg* 1684-1727) (Pahari) 15 633
Sidi Bou Said 31 424, 426, 427
Sidih *see* ISFAHAN
Sidi-Kacem 16 418
Sidi Qasim al-Jalizi 16 220, 427
Sidiqqi, Shakeel 23 800
Sidló, Ferenc 12 839
Sidney, Frances, Countess of Sussex 5 511
Sidney, Margaret 14 219
Sidney, Philip 8 50; 13 298; 28 666*
Sidney, Robert, 2nd Earl of Leicester 19 120; 24 390
Sidon 1 850; 17 505; 19 8; 24 641; 26 *915*, 917; 28 666–8*, *719*, 721; 30 179, *180*
  architecture 19 7; 24 642
  coffins 24 642
  coins 1 888
  dyes 1 880; 9 664
  figurines 24 643
  glass 26 855; 27 72
  halls 30 191
  harbour 24 642
  houses 16 269
  ivory-carvings 24 644
  mummy cases 28 *667*
  sarcophagi 13 458, 461, 470; 27 825; 28 666–8, *668*
  sculpture 24 642
Sidonius Apollinaris 19 846; 28 669*
Sidorkin, Eugene 17 867
Sidorov, Aleksey (Alekseyevich) 27 444; 28 669*
Sidorov, Valentin 27 398
Sidra Synagogue 17 544, 545
Sidun 7 2; 19 302; 33 425
Sidur, Vadim (Abramovich) 27 397; 28 669*
  works 27 *397*
Sidzhak 6 274
Siebe, Johan 8 752
Siebelist, Arthur 1 470
Siebenerklub 3 398; 22 187; 28 670*
Sieber, Roy 1 231
Siebers, Alphonsus 23 450
Siebmacher, Hans *see* SIBMACHER, JOHANN
Siebner, Herbert 32 414
Siebold, Alexander 28 670
Siebold, Heinrich 28 670
Siebold, Philipp Franz von 17 429, 434; 22 429; 28 670*
  collaboration 17 187
Sieciech 25 134
Siècle des lumières *see* ENLIGHTENMENT, THE
Sieczkowski, Tadeusz 14 819; 17 824
Siedler, Wolf Jobst 18 114
Sieff, Jeanloup 28 670*
Siegburg 12 *361*
  metalwork 26 683
  St Michael's Abbey 26 673
    St Anno shrine 23 100
  stonewares 7 586; 12 428, 429; 22 877; 28 671*
  textiles 16 434
Siegburg Lectionary Cover 28 806
Siegburg Lion Silk 9 665, 666
Siegburg *Madonna* 26 *632*, 633
siege engines 13 413; 21 556–7
Siegel, Christian Heinrich 13 354, 360; 24 632
Siegel, Gustav 2 809, 814; 18 192
Siegel, Karl August Benjamin 14 25; 28 178
Siegel, Margot 28 671*
Siegel, Robert 13 884
Siegelaub, Seth 7 685
Siegel Diamond Architects 28 671*
Siegen, Ludwig von 2 239; 21 414; 28 671–2*
Siegersdorf, Hensel of *see* HANS SIGERSDORFER
sièges courants *see under* CHAIRS → types
siege-sheds 21 556, 557
sièges meublants *see under* CHAIRS → types
siege-towers *see* TOWERS → types → siege
Siegfried of Lorraine 19 825
Siegwart (family) 30 145
Siegwart, Hugo 33 736
Siegwitz, Johann Albrecht 25 115; 33 417
Sielski, Margit 2 528
Sielski, Roman 2 528
Siematycze, Natural History Museum 25 139
Siembab, Carl 7 917
Siemens 12 472; 14 694; 21 782
Siemens, Hans 21 721
Siemering, (Leopold) Rudolf 14 879; 28 672*
Siemering, Wolfgang 28 672
Siemigmowski, J. E.
  works 25 *128*
Siemiradzki, Henryk 25 107; 28 672–3*
Siem Reap 5 *458*
  houses 5 *483*
  sculpture 5 499
  Vat Preah Eynkosei 5 500
Siemsicki, Kryzsztof 28 187
Siena 16 *620*; 28 673–89*, *674*; 31 709
  Archivio di Stato 2 371
  art forms and materials
    agate 14 167
    altarpieces 25 183
    biccherne 4 29–30, 351
    cassoni 6 1, *4*, 4–5*, 6
    coats of arms 14 410
    coins 7 535
    crucifixes 16 655
    enamel 13 163, 169
    flags 11 150
    frames 11 382, 387
    furniture 16 723, 724, 730
    gold 16 741; 24 36
    maiolica 16 732, 734
    manuscript illumination 14 424
    painting 7 815; 13 146; 16 661, 662; 24 776; 27 859; 28 *677*
    sculpture 13 93; 16 688, 691–2*
    silk 13 197
    tapestries 13 196
    vases 10 616
    wrought iron 16 743
  building regulations 5 135

Siena—cont.
Campo **24** 567; **28** *675*
Fonte Gaia **11** 341; **16** 692, 840–41
Casa dei Borghesi **10** 739
collections **10** 637
ecclesiastical buildings
Baptistery
font **11** 254; **12** 539–40, *540*; **16** 692, 842, 843; **24** 487; **26** 136
Cathedral of the Assumption **4** 774; **7** 664; **9** 86; **13** 52, 65; **16** 627, 762; **24** 567, 867, 871; **28** 677–80*, *678*, *679*
altar **16** 692
altarpieces **1** 709; **9** 343–5; **13** 146; **25** 183, 463; **27** 859–61
Chapel of S Giovanni **16** 724
doors **9** 159
font **11** 254
gargoyles **12** 150
Libreria Piccolomini **14** 416; **24** 829, 831–2
metalwork **13** 163; **28** 455
mosaics **6** 569; **22** 163
Museo dell'Opera del Duomo *see under* museums
paintings **13** *129*, 130
pavement **16** 662
polychromy **25** 171
pulpit **16** 688; **24** 868–70, *869*, *870*; **25** 724; **26** 136
S Crescenzio Altarpiece **19** 671
sculpture **13** *93*, 93; **16** 688; **28** *680*, 680–81*
spire **29** 414
S Savino Altarpiece **19** 666–7
stained glass **13** 192, *193*
tomb of Bishop Giovanni Pecci **16** 690; **31** 122
tomb of Cardinal Riccardo Petroni **14** 416; **31** 3, *123*, 124
chapel of the Nove *see under* Palazzo Pubblico
Convent of S Caterina di Siena **11** 875
Madonna della Grotta oratory **13** 192
Osservanza **8** *101*; **13** 124
S Agostino **3** 246
Azzoni Chapel **24** 781, *781*
S Francesco **6** 466
S Maria della Scala **28** 681–3*; **32** 105
frescoes **28** *682*
sculpture **32** *105*
see also Ospedale di S Maria della Scala
S Maria dei Servi **7** 815–16
altarpiece **1** 708
paintings **11** 379; **19** *454*
S Martino **27** 861
S Niccolò **19** 666
Fonte Gaia *see under* Campo
fortifications **24** 532
see also town walls
guilds **28** 676
kilns **4** 774
Loggia di Mercanzia **10** 853
sculpture **10** *854*
Museo dell'Opera del Duomo **16** 774; **24** 219
Ospedale di S Maria della Scala **10** 738; **14** 784
frescoes **9** 95
Pellegrinaio **16** 659, 662
see also ecclesiastical buildings → S Maria della Scala
Palazzo Bindi-Sergardi **3** 468; **27** 121
Palazzo Chigi-Saracini **29** 2
Palazzo del Magnifico **12** 278; **24** 567, 832; **28** 703; **29** 2
Palazzo Petrucci *see* Palazzo del Magnifico
Palazzo Piccolomini **19** 831
Siena—cont.
Palazzo Pubblico **4** 776; **14** 421, 868; **16** 627; **19** 869; **20** 504, 510; **23** 806, 809; **28** *675*, 676, *683*, 683–4*; **29** *406*; **31** 236
altarpieces **20** 506, 510
Antecappella **28** *687*
Chapel of the Nove **25** 462
collections **10** 640
frescoes **2** 339; **11** 711; **13** 128, 135, 146; **19** 670; **20** 509; **26** 182; **29** 3, 406; **30** 232; **31** 154; **32** 805
paintings **12** 625; **19** 671; **28** 684–9*
railings **16** 743
Sala del Concistoro **15** 86; **28** *688*
Sala della Giunta **9** 95
Sala della Pace **1** 654; **19** 669–70, *670*; **31** 703
frescoes **16** 762; **28** *686*
Sala del Mappamondo **19** 671; **28** *685*
frescoes **16** 762; **20** 506; **28** *685*; **32** 112
paintings **20** 505
Sala del Risorgimento **16** 764
Sala di Balía **27** 765
Torre del Mangia **4** 776; **7** 837
Palazzo Sansedoni **20** 909
Palazzo della Sapienza **31** 674
Palazzo Venturi *see* Palazzo Bindi-Sergardi
Pinacoteca Nazionale di Siena **28** 683
town walls **31** 710
Porta Romana **7** 359
Porta S Viene **24** *532*
see also fortifications
urban planning **31** 711
Villa Cetinale **32** 549
Villa le Volte **24** 529
water supply **31** 711
Siena, Gano da *see* GANO DI FAZIO
Siena, Giovan Battista da (*fl* 1527–8) **7** 331
Siena, Giovanni da *see* GIOVANNI DI STEFANO
Siena, Giovanni di Stefano da *see* GIOVANNI DI STEFANO DA SIENA
Siena, Guido da *see* GUIDO DA SIENA
Siena, Luca di Giovanni da *see* LUCA DI GIOVANNI DA SIENA
Siena, Matteo da **13** 628; **26** 818, 835
Siena, Meo (di Guido) da *see* MEO (DI GUIDO) DA SIENA
Siena, Mino Parcis da *see* MINO PARCIS DA SIENA
Siena, Minuccio Jacobi da *see* MINUCCIO JACOBI DA SIENA
Siena, Pietro di Domenico da *see* PIETRO DI DOMENICO DA SIENA
Siena, Ugolino da *see* UGOLINO DI NERIO
Siena, Vigoroso da *see* VIGOROSO DA SIENA
Siena Cathedral, Masters of the Sacristy of **3** 707; **13** 733; **23** 93
Siena Codex *see under* CODICES → individual manuscripts
Sieniawska, Elżbieta **3** 431; **8** 843; **25** 38, 135; **32** 876, 881
Sieniawski, Adam Mikołaj **25** 124
Sienicki, Jacek **2** 502
sienna **11** 763; **24** 792
Sieradz, Franciszek of *see* FRANCISZEK OF SIERADZ
Sieraków Church **25** 120
Sierakowski, Charles **24** 496
Sierakowski, Sebastian **25** 142
Sierakowski, Wacław Hieronim **25** 142
Sierck, Jacob von **12** 342
Sierndorf, Schloss *see* SCHLOSS SIERNDORF
Sierpes Cross **29** 340
Sierra, Andrés **25** 702
Sierra, Francisco de **28** 690*
collaboration **28** 689; **29** 293
works **28** *689*
Sierra, Jacinto de **28** 690*
Sierra, José de **28** 690*
Sierra, Miguel Aguado de la *see* AGUADO DE LA SIERRA, MIGUEL
Sierra, Pablo Zelaya *see* ZELAYA SIERRA, PABLO
Sierra, Paul **18** 835; **25** 209; **28** 690*
Sierra, Pedro de **28** 689–90*
collaboration **29** 293
works **28** *689*
Sierra, Tomás de **28** 689–90*; **29** 293
Sierra de Filabres **29** 289
Sierra Leone **1** *214*, 386; **28** 690–93*
architecture **28** 691*
bowls **1** 241
collections **28** 692–3*
currency **1** 363
dress **1** 347
dyeing **3** 379
education (art) **28** 693
forks **1** 327
horns **1** 327
iconography **1** 261
ivory **1** 241, 293, 326–7, *326*
knife-handles **1** 327
masks **1** *237*, 256, 282, *282*, 340
megaphones **1** 360
paintings **28** *691*, 691–2*, *692*
lorry **28** *691*, 692
wall **1** *261*
patronage **28** 692–3*
portraits **28** *692*
pyxides (boxes) **1** 327
salts **1** *326*, 327
spoons **1** 327
stone **1** 292
stone-carvings **1** 263
trade
oils **1** 250
women **1** 247, 340
wood **1** *282*
Siese **9** 877, *878*
Siete Iglesias, Marqués de *see* CALDERÓN, RODRIGO
Siete Pintores Abstractos **2** 400; **6** 376; **24** 348
Sievänen, Jaako (Olavi) **11** 97; **28** 693*
Sieveking, Karl **12** 414
Sieveking, Syndikus **29** 376
Siever **24** 96
Sieverding, Katarina **24** 408
Sievert, Mary Ann
works **31** *660*
Sievier, Richard **32** 911
Sievier, Robert William **28** 693–4*; **33** 101
Siewers, Wolter **30** 104
Siewierz, Chapel of St John the Baptist **30** 906
Sifer, Conrat **27** 125; **28** 694*; **29** 758
Sifer, Hans **31** 286
Siferwas, John de *see* JOHN DE SIFERWAS
Sifnos **29** 701
Sifr, Tell **21** 304
Sigacik *see* TEOS
Sigala, José **28** 694*
Sigalin, Józef **29** 634
Sigalon, (Alexandre-François-) Xavier **11** 543; **13** 794; **28** 694–5*
Siga Tomb **23** 299
Sigeion **13** 568
Sigena Monastery **28** 695–6*; **29** *259*
chapter house **6** 466
ceiling **2** 528
wall paintings **10** 244; **13** 143; **26** 653, *653*, 656; **28** *695*, 695–6*
coffering **7** 527
S María **26** 643
Sigersdorfer, Hans *see* HANS SIGERSDORFER
Sigeru Miwa *see* MIWA, SIGERU
Sighişoara **26** *705*; **28** 696*
Deal church **26** 711, 719
fortifications **26** 707
houses **26** 707
metalwork **26** 719
monastery church **26** 718
Municipal Museum **28** 696
St Nicholas **13** 189; **14** 884
sculpture **26** 712
tabernacle **26** 718
Sighizzi, Andrea *see* SEGHIZZI, ANDREA
Sigifridus **12** 442
Sīgiri *see* SIGIRIYA
Sigiriya **28** 696–7*; **29** *440*
architecture **29** 446
caves **28** 697
furniture **29** 470
gardens **29** 448
jewellery **29** *473*, 478
metalwork **29** 474
palace **29** 448
wall paintings **15** 543; **29** 462–4, *463*, 470, 472, 476, 478
Sigismondi, Sigismondo de' **7** 246
Sigismund, Count of Tyrol (*reg* 1439–96) **2** 470; **15** 863
armour **2** *470*
Sigismund, Duke of Bavaria-Munich (*reg* 1460–67) **25** 90
Sigismund, Holy Roman Emperor (*reg* 1410–37), King of Hungary (*reg* 1387–1437) and King of Bohemia (*reg* 1420–37) **19** 830–31*; **23** *306*
architecture **4** 694, 695; **5** 80, 86; **14** 884, 893; **18** 396; **32** 614
collections **8** 423
gold **24** 36
sculpture **5** 87
Sigismund, King of Sweden *see* SIGISMUND III, King of Poland
Sigismund, Master **18** 724; **20** 678
Sigismund I, King of Poland (*reg* 1506–48) **16** 866–7*; **18** 427–8; **25** 134; **32** 874
architecture **3** 711; **11** 713; **18** 430, 432, *433*; **25** 96; **27** 722
clocks **7** 439
embroidery **25** 132
gold **25** 137
medals **5** 699
metalwork **18** 574; **20** 395; **25** 126
painting **4** 400; **9** 445; **19** 496; **24** 356
silver **3** 69–70; **23** 307
tapestries **1** 165
Sigismund II Augustus, King of Poland (*reg* 1548–72) **16** 867–8*; **25** 134
architecture **13** 774; **32** 879
collections **16** 866
guns **3** 98
painting **4** 400; **19** 496
sculpture **22** 167
tapestries **18** 431; **25** 117, 137; **30** 316
Sigismund III, King of Poland (*reg* 1587–1632) **32** 5–6*
architecture **4** 147; **6** 22; **12** 745; **18** 431; **25** 135; **31** 312
carpets **16** 475
gold **25** 127
paintings **4** 913; **9** 74; **25** 104, 137; **29** 246
Sigismund III, King of Poland (*reg* 1587–1632)—cont.
sculpture **4** 146
teachers **31** 767
textiles **16** 553
Sigismund-Francis, Count of Tyrol (*reg* 1662–5) **13** 845, 921
Sigl, Georg **25** 593
siglos *see under* COINS → types
Sigl press *see under* PRESSES → types
Sigmaringen **14** 497
Schloss **12** 410
Rhäzmas Hall **12** 415
Sigmaringen, Master of *see* STRÜB, HANS
Sigmond, Géza **15** 5
Sigmond, Peter **28** 889
Sigmundr, Master **30** 75
Sigmund relief **3** 426
Signac, Paul **7** 630; **28** 697–8*
collaboration **20** 603
dealers **9** 425
exhibitions **10** 680
groups and movements **9** 40; **15** 155, 156; **22** 745, 746, 747; **24** 142, 592; **25** 358; **32** 591
methods **19** 355
patrons and collectors **10** 885
personal collection **6** 375; **19** 767; **20** 823
works **4** 42; **8** 596; **11** 417, 418; **13** 323; **15** 828, *829*; **19** 488, 489; **20** 473; **25** 624; **28** *698*
writings **25** 78
Signac, Pierre **8** 649; **21** 641
Signakhi **12** 320
Signals **24** 428
signal-towers *see under* TOWERS → types
signatures **10** 205, 210, 380; **11** 308; **20** 442; **24** 6, *6*, 674
Ancient Near East **1** 859
Aztec **21** 249
China **7** 15, 64, 129; **17** 229
Egypt **16** 415, 496
Egypt, ancient **10** 6, 7
Etruscan **10** 629
Greece, ancient **7** 830; **13** 439, 440, 484, 488, 489*, *489*, 490, 587; **20** 441; **24** 892; **32** 27
Indian subcontinent **15** 208, 415, 532
Iran **16** 232, 331, 410
Iraq **16** 399
Islamic **16** 126, 127, 232, 325, 331, 399, 410, 415, 496, 508
Italy **10** 629; **16** 685; **20** 441
Japan **17** 347, 391, 399, 400, 422
Mesoamerica, Pre-Columbian **21** 249
Netherlands, the **22** 894
Ottoman **16** 508
Romanesque **26** 595
Rome, ancient **6** 333; **27** 27
Scotland **28** 241
South-east Asia **29** 236
Syria **16** 415, 496
Tibet **30** 811
see also MONOGRAMS
signet rings *see under* RINGS → types
Signia **27** 9
Signo **3** 123
Signol, Emile **11** 544; **28** 699*
collaboration **8** 40
pupils **19** 38
Signoraccio, Bernardino del *see* BERNADINO DEL SIGNORACCIO
Signorelli, Francesco **28** 703
Signorelli, Luca (d'Egidio di maestro Ventura de') **28** 676, 699–704*; **29** 853; **31** 740
attributions **20** 684
collaboration **3** 299; **11** 690; **20** 684; **24** 521, 522; **26** 186
drawings **21** 758, *758*; **25** 557
groups and movements **26** 187

- Signorelli, Luca (d'Egidio di maestro Ventura de')—cont.
  - paintings
    - altarpieces **28** *700*
    - frescoes
      - Cathedral of the Assumption (Orvieto) **1** 840; **9** 263; **13** 700; **16** *613*; **23** 586; **28** *703*
      - Monte Oliveto Maggiore **7** 457; **28** *702*; **29** 1
      - Palazzo del Magnifico (Siena) **12** 278; **24** 567; **28** 677
      - Palazzone **7** 905
      - Sistine Chapel (Rome, Vatican) **26** 815
      - S Maria di Loreto **19** 687
    - literary themes **1** 640
    - mythological **28** *701*
  - patrons and collectors **3** 55, 241, 740; **7** 218; **16** 661; **19** 412; **24** 526; **27** 271
  - pupils **12** 277
  - restorations by others **29** 892
- Signoretti, Gian Antonio **20** 920
- Signorini, Edoardo **28** 705
- Signorini, Egisto **28** 705
- Signorini, Giovanni **28** 705
- Signorini, Telemaco **16** 678; **24** 448; **28** 318, 704–7*
  - groups and movements **19** 870, 871; **20** 482; **32** 108
  - pupils **4** 252
  - works **28** *705*, *706*
- Signot, Jacques **13** 808
- signs (emblems) **8** 782; **10** 1–2; **25** 481, 487
- signs (markers)
  - Belgium **2** 510
  - England **32** *324*, *325*, 326, *327*
  - France **2** 510
  - Japan **17** 358*
  - Mali **20** *200*
  - Rome, ancient **27** 50
- Sigoli, Simone **16** 384
- Sigolsheim, SS Pierre et Paul **26** 633
- Sigon **9** 555
- Sigraf **26** 639
  - works **26** *640*
- Sigresten (family) **30** 136
- Sigrist, Franz **2** 795; **28** 707–8*
  - collaboration **21** 512
  - patrons and collectors **10** 531
  - teachers **31** 358
  - works **9** 754
- Sigrist, Kurt **30** 140
- Sigsig **28** 651
- Sigtuna
  - altarpiece **13** 120
  - metalwork **32** 524
  - St Mary **4** 781; **30** 66
  - St Olof **26** 593; **30** 66
  - St Per **26** 593; **30** 66
- Sigüenza **28** 708–9*; **29** *259*
  - Cathedral of the Asunción de Nuestra Señora **28** *708*, 708–9; **29** 263, 334
  - paintings **29** 278
  - tomb of Bishop Alonso Carillo de Albornoz **13** 106, *107*
- Sigüenza, José de **10** 498, 502, 503; **13** 922; **23** 811; **28** 709–10*
  - teachers **2** 411
  - works **15** 85; **29** 300; **30** 803
  - writings **27** 802
- Sigüenza y Góngora, Carlos de **21** 264
- Sigüenza y Góngora, José Cayetano **21** 377
- Sigulda **18** *847*
- Sigulda Castle **18** 847
- Sigurdson, Sveinn Franklin John **11** 880
- Sigurðsson, Helgi **15** 70
- Sigurjón Ólafsson Museum *see under* REYKJAVÍK → museums
- Sigward, Bishop of Minden **26** 651
- Sīhagiri *see* SIGIRIYA
- Sihanaka **1** 269; **20** 36, 40
- Sihigiri *see* SIGIRIYA
- Sihlali, Durant **29** 113
- Sihoniya Kakanmath **15** 292, 497
- Siimes, Aune **11** 105
- Siinmaa, Olev **10** 537
- Siintămăria-Orlea Church **14** 898
- Siirt **16** 379
  - minbar **16** 497
- Siitonen, Tuomo **14** 328*
- Sijelmassi, Abdelhaq **22** 129
- Sijelmassi, Abdelrahim **22** 128
- Siji Dosekun Partnership **9** 179
- Sijilmasa **16** *103*; **33** 97
- Sijmons, K. L. **1** 804; **33** 616
- Sika, Jutta **2** 817
- Sikaiana **25** 181, 182
- Sikandara *see* SIKANDRA
- Sikandar 'Adil Shah, Ruler (*reg* 1672-86) ('Adil Shahi) **15** 640
- Sikandar Shah I, Sultan (*reg* 1358-90) (Line of Ilyas Shah) **15** 351
- Sikandar Shah II, Sultan (*reg* 1489-1517) (Lodi) **8** 674; **15** 345, 409; **19** 533
- Sikander, Begum of Bhopal (*reg* 1845-68) **3** 908
- Sikandra (Agra) **1** 458; **15** *261*, *360*; **28** 710–11*
  - tomb of Akbar **15** 363; **17** 512; **28** 710–11, *711*; **31** 114
    - gardens **12** 74
  - tomb of Maryam Zamani **28** 711
- Sikandra (Bayana) **15** 345, 346
  - congregational mosque **15** 345, 346
  - La'l Darvaza **15** 346
- Sikar **15** 671
  - Harasnath Temple **15** 270, 488
- Sikasingo **1** 403
- Sikelianos, Eva **23** 566
- Sikendeng **15** 776
- Sikh, Ranjit Singh *see* RANJIT SINGH, Maharaja
- śikhara temples *see under* TEMPLES → types
- Sikhism **15** 190, 202, 204; **28** 711–12*
  - architecture **15** 375, *375*
  - iconoclasm **15** 79
- Sikiana **29** 50, 51
- Sikimić, Gojko **4** 462
- Sikinos **8** *304*
- Sikka **15** 810
- Sikkim **22** *753*; **28** 309
- Siklós
  - congregational mosque **14** 886
  - Siklós Centre **15** 2
- Sikora, Rudolf **28** 853
- Sikoutinos, Leo **30** 718
- Sikri (Pakistan) **15** *264*; **23** *797*; **28** 712*
- Sikri (Rajasthan), Delhi Darwaza Mosque **15** 346
- Sikri (Uttar Pradesh) *see* FATEHPUR SIKRI
- SIKSI **24** 452
- Sikyatki (AZ) **22** 609
- Sikyatki Polychrome ware *see under* POTTERY → wares
- Sikyon **9** 565; **13** *363*; **28** 712–13*
  - bouleuterion **4** 530; **14** 73
  - bronzes **13** 572
  - galleries (iv) (art) **10** 675
  - gymnasium **13** 406
  - mosaics **13** 556, 559, 561, 562, *562*, 563
  - painting **13** 549, 551, 554, 561
  - pottery **13** 534
  - sculpture **13** 440, 462–3, 596; **19** 852; **25** 179
  - theatre **13** 391
- Sikytala **22** 614
- Sil, S Esteban de Ribas **29** 263
- Siladeva **29** 439
- silane **7** 747
- Silanion **13** 458, 459; **24** 329; **28** 713*
- Silanus, Governor of Bithynia **23** 142
- Šilar, Lubomir **8** 406
- Silber, Jonas **23** 312; **25** 22, 731; **28** 713*
- Silberberg **21** 571
- Silberburg, C.W. **14** 747
- Silbermann, A. **28** 917
- Silbermann, Gottfried **9** 241; **11** 749
- Silbermann, Jean-Claude **30** 23
- Silchester *see* CALLEVA ATREBATUM
- Sile Fortress **9** 848, *848*
- Šileika, Jonas **19** 498
- Silenos **13** 408
- Silen Painter **10** 614
- Silesian glasses *see under* GLASSES → types
- silhouettes **24** 57, 659; **28** 713–14*
  - Greece, ancient **13** 481, 492, 493, 498, 504, 535
  - Switzerland **28** *714*
  - Turkey **24** 56
- silica **6** 324; **7** 747
  - historical and regional traditions
    - China **6** 873; **7** 80
    - Egypt **16** 404
    - Egypt, ancient **10** 55
    - Islamic **16** 404
    - Mesoamerica, Pre-Columbian **21** 241
  - uses
    - conservation **6** 336
    - glass **7** 80; **10** 55; **12** 781; **32** 200
    - glazes **6** 329, 873; **16** 404
    - polishing **21** 241
- silica gel **7** 736; **23** 793
- silicate painting *see under* PAINTING → forms
- Sililo, Ranford **33** 602
- Silin **27** 63
- Siliņš, Jānis **28** 714–15*
- Silis, Nicholay Andreyovich **31** 459
- Silistra **5** 150; **9** 640; **27** 49
- Silivanovič, Mikalaj **3** 529
- Silivri, Büyük Çekmece Bridge **16** 225
- silk **7** 731, 735; **9** 37; **28** 715–18*; **30** 552
  - historical and regional traditions
    - Abbasid **28** 716
    - Africa **1** 293
    - Albania **1** 544
    - Ancient Near East **1** 880, *882*; **30** 551, 552
    - Anglo-Saxon **2** *84*
    - Armenia (Europe) **2** *443*
    - Austria **2** 824, 825; **32** *389*, *391*
    - Bali (Indonesia) **15** 793
    - Belgium **3** *607*, 609, *609*, 610; **4** *923*; **10** II2; **30** I2, II1; **31** *218*
    - Bhutan **3** 915, *915*
    - Buddhism **18** *254*, 305, *374*
    - Burma **5** 247, 248*
    - Byzantine **9** 520, *640*, *641*, 663–4, *664*, *665*, 665–9, *666*, *668*; **16** 429; **28** 715; **30** 552
    - Cambodia **5** 501, 502, *502*
    - Central Asia, Eastern **6** 304, 309, 316
    - Central Asia, Western **6** 248–9*, *248*, 250, 251, *252*, 253; **28** 715
      - Islamic **16** 435
      - Sogdiana **6** 285; **28** *722*
      - Timurid **16** 430
    - China **6** 773, 776; **7** 43, 45, *49*, 74, 140; **10** 776; **16** 428; **30** 551, VI1
      - Han period (206 BC-AD 220) **6** 736; **7** *46*, 63; **28** 310; **31** *153*
      - Ming period (1368-1644) **7** 50, *50*, 64
- silk
  - historical and regional traditions
    - China—cont.
      - Northern and Southern Dynasties (AD 310-589) **20** 327
      - Prehistoric **7** 45–8; **28** 715
      - Qing period (1644-1911) **7** 19, 51, *51*, *67*, 68, *78*; **10** I1; **28** 312
      - Shang period (*c.* 1600-*c.* 1050 BC) **7** 44
      - Song period (AD 960-1279) **7** 49, 76; **19** *857*, *858*
      - Tang period (AD 618-907) **7** *45*, *49*, 77
      - Yuan period (1279-1368) **7** 50
      - Zhou period (*c.* 1050-256 BC) **7** 51–2, 62
      - 20th cent. **7** 51, 113; **22** 233; **28** 718
    - Cyprus **8** 356
    - Czech Republic **8** 419
    - Denmark **8** *754*, 755*
    - Early Christian (*c.* AD 250-843) **9** *640*, *641*, 663–4, *664*, *665*, 665–9
    - Egypt
      - Byzantine **9** *640*, *665*, 668
      - Islamic **16** 431, *433*, 441–2, *442*; **28** 715; **31** 21
      - Mamluk **16** 430; **28** 716
    - Egypt, ancient **30** 552
    - England **2** *84*; **10** *182*, 278, *290*, *350*, *352*, 353, 356–7*, *357*; **21** 600; **23** *461*; **28** 716, 717, *717*; **30** *541*, III2, X3
    - Fatimid **28** 716
    - France **9** 279; **11** 589, *638*, *640*, 644–7*, *645*, *646*, *648*; **16** 850; **24** 810; **28** 716, 717; **30** I1, II2
      - chinoiserie **7** 167
      - 8th cent. AD **9** *252*
    - Germany **10** *181*; **12** 462, 463–4*, *463*, *464*, 467, 469; **23** *337*
    - Ghana **1** 293
    - Gothic **11** *638*; **13** 194, 197*; **30** *541*, 552; **32** *389*
      - Germany **10** *181*
      - Italy **13** *197*, 197
      - Sicily **13** 197
      - Spain **13** 197
    - Greece **9** *668*; **13** 355
    - Guatemala **13** 766
    - Hungary **15** 11, 12
    - Indian subcontinent **15** 661–5*, *664*, 667, 668, 670, *670*, *675*; **28** 717, 718
      - Bengal **15** 662, *663*
      - Kashmir **15** 661, 662
      - Punjab **15** 661
    - Indonesia **15** 790, 792, 793, 794
    - Iran **5** 829; **16** 428, 430, 435, *435*, 443, *444*, 449, *450*, 465, 474, *475*; **18** 48, 49; **25** 131; **28** 715, 716
    - Iran, ancient **1** 882, *882*
    - Iraq **16** 434–5; **28** 715
    - Ireland **16** 33–4
    - Islamic **16** 124, 428–9, 430, *430*, 431, *433*, 434–5, *435*, 436–7, *437*, *438*, *439*, 440, 441–2, *442*, 443, *444*, 445, 446, *446*, 447–8, *448*, 449, *450*, 462, 465, 466, 473, 474, *475*, 508; **28** 715–16; **30** VIII; **31** 21
    - Italy **11** *193*; **16** 445, 752–4*, *753*, 760; **21** 600; **27** *693*; **28** 716, 717
      - chinoiserie **7** 167
      - Gothic **13** *197*, 197
    - Japan **17** 139, 161, 209, 305, 306, *307*, 311, *311*, 312, 313, *314*, 315–16, *316*, 317, *362*, 371; **18** 601; **22** 234; **28** 312, 718; **30** 560
- silk
  - historical and regional traditions—cont.
    - Java **15** 790, 792
    - Khmer **5** *502*
    - Korea **18** *254*, 302, 305, *315*, 357, 358, 372, 373, *374*, *375*, *380*; **30** X2
    - Laos **18** 771
    - Madagascar **1** 293; **20** 38, *39*
    - Malaysia **20** 175
    - Mongolia **21** *876*, 877
    - Morocco **16** 429, *448*
    - Native North Americans **22** *645*
    - Netherlands, the **22** 899
    - New Zealand **23** 74*
    - Nigeria **1** 293
    - North Africa **16** 447–8; **28** 715
    - Ottoman **16** 430, 445, 446, *446*, 462, 508; **23** *639*; **28** 716
    - Parthian **28** 715
    - Poland **25** 131, *133*
    - Portugal **25** 315
    - Rhodes (island) **13** *356*
    - Romanesque **26** 703
    - Rome, ancient **9** 251; **27** *113*; **28** 715
    - Russia **9** *641*
    - Sasanian **16** 429; **28** 715
    - Scotland **28** 264, *265*
    - Serbia **28** 456, *457*
    - Sicily **13** 197; **16** *430*, 436, 437, 752
    - Sogdiana **6** *248*, 248–9, 285; **28** 721, *722*
    - South-east Asia **29** 231
    - Spain **13** 197; **16** 428, 436–7, *437*, *438*, *439*, 440; **28** 715, 716, 717; **29** *348*, 348–9*; **30** VII1
    - Sumatra **15** 794
    - Sweden **28** 717; **30** 90, 115*
    - Switzerland **30** 151
    - Syria **16** 428, 429, 430, 431, 441–2, *442*; **28** 715, 716
    - Thailand **5** 503
    - Tibet **30** 846
    - Transoxiana **16** 428, 435
    - Turkey **16** 430, 445, *446*, 446, 462; **23** *639*; **25** 131
    - United States of America **31** 657
    - Uzbekistan **6** *252*; **31** *783*
    - Venetian Empire **28** 716
    - Vietnam **32** 489, 491
  - techniques
    - dyeing **9** 490, 492; **15** 667, 668, *670*, 790, 792
    - printing **15** 670; **24** 810
    - weaving **9** 665–9; **16** 849; **17** 306; **30** 547
  - types
    - bizarre **4** 103*; **11** 646
    - half-silk **16** 433; **31** 21
    - *point rentré* **19** 850
    - *Van* **32** 489, *489*
  - uses
    - armour **17** *362*
    - banners **6** 304
    - batik **3** 378
    - bookbindings **7** 63, 64
    - brocades **30** 553
    - calligraphy **6** 736
    - carpets **5** 829, 831; **6** 253; **7** *67*, 68; **16** 466, 473, 474, *475*; **28** 716
    - chairs **11** 589
    - chasubles **12** *464*; **13** *197*; **32** *389*, *391*
    - costumes **32** 491
    - dalmatics **16** *444*
    - damask **30** 551
    - dolls **17** 371
    - dolls' furniture **31** 264
    - drawings **15** 850
    - dress **3** *915*; **5** *248*; **6** 251, *252*, 309; **7** 76, 77, *78*; **9** 251; **16** 462, 465; **18** 357, 358; **27** *113*; **28** 715, 717; **31** *783*
    - dresses **10** *357*

silk
uses—cont.
embroidery 10 181
Armenia (Europe) 2 443
Austria 2 824
Belgium 3 609, 609, 610; 10 II2
Canada 22 645
China 7 44, 45, 49, 50, 50, 51
Early Christian and Byzantine 9 668
England 10 182, 353; 30 541
France 11 648
Germany 10 181; 12 462, 463, 463; 23 337
Gothic 13 194
Greece 13 356
Hungary 15 12
Italy 16 760; 27 693
Morocco 16 448
Scotland 28 264, 265
Spain 29 349, 349
Switzerland 30 151
Uzbekistan 6 250
engravings 10 380
epitaphioi 9 668; 28 457
etchings 10 561
fans 10 776
figurines 7 140
flags 11 145
gauze 28 715; 30 551
grounds 18 315
hangings 15 675
interior decoration 28 717; 30 90
jewellery 17 530
kaftans 9 641; 16 446
kilims 18 48, 49
kites 7 113
knitting 18 158
lace 12 469; 18 588, 590
lacquer 7 19; 18 601
manuscripts 7 63
maps 31 153
mounts (works on paper and scrolls) 22 233, 234
norigae 18 380
paintings 5 501, 656; 6 773; 17 139, 161, 209; 18 305; 19 857, 858
paper 20 328
passementerie 24 237
patchwork 24 252, 253; 30 X2
pilgrim badges 24 809
robes 17 314; 18 375; 30 VI1
sashes 15 792; 20 39; 25 133
satin 30 551
scarves 28 718
scrolls 6 776; 7 63; 17 139; 28 310, 310, 312
shawls 28 564
shields 16 508
shrouds 9 666; 20 38
stencilling 30 560
stoles (ecclesiastical) 2 84
supports 17 139; 18 302
tapestries 30 308
Belgium 3 607; 4 923; 5 47, 48, 50; 30 I2, II1; 31 218
Denmark 8 754
Egypt 16 433
England 10 350, 352; 30 III2
France 11 638, 640; 30 I1, II2
Germany 12 467
Italy 11 193
threads 7 50, 51, 51; 12 463, 467, 469; 15 11; 21 877; 23 461; 30 537, 538, 539*, 541, 541
ties (dress) 28 718
tiraz 31 21
tunics 9 640; 21 876
upholstery 10 290; 28 715
velvet 28 715; 30 553
vestments (ecclesiastical) 32 391
waistcoats 30 X3
wall coverings 10 278
wallpaper 32 813
silk
uses—cont.
weaving 1 293; 12 463; 16 447–8; 17 311, 313, 317
writing 7 62; 15 850; 20 328
Silk and Textile Printers 2 767
Silkeborg Kunstmuseum 8 759, 760; 17 658, 659
silk moiré 32 812
Silko 23 286
Silk Route 6 186, 290–91, 616, 618, 621; 16 107; 21 592; 28 718–23*, 719; 31 781
Buddhism 6 618; 15 200
ceramics 6 330
Islam 6 619
jade 7 6
silk 7 52; 16 428; 28 715
textiles 6 248
silk screen printing see SCREENPRINTING; SERIGRAPHY
silkworkers guilds see under GUILDS → types
Silla, Giacomo see LONGHI, SILLA
Silla da Viggiù see LONGHI, SILLA
sillas de cadera see under CHAIRS → types
Silla ware see under POTTERY → wares
Sillett, James 18 618; 23 248; 30 735
sillimanite 16 857
Sillon, Le 14 137
Silluk Temple 4 795; 18 295; 23 775
Sillustani 29 162
chullpas 31 47, 47
Sillyon 13 404; 21 558
Silo, Adam 28 723–4*
Silo, Pascual Herráiz y see HERRÁIZ Y SILO, PASCUAL
Siloé, de (family) 29 311
Siloé, Diego de 28 725–6*; 29 289, 313
choir-stalls 29 289
collaboration 8 79; 23 494; 26 250; 27 603; 31 92; 32 493
groups and movements 25 30, 31
patrons and collectors 7 488; 11 250
works 2 23; 5 201, 203, 204, 205, 621; 10 534; 13 283; 20 157; 25 23; 26 250; 28 518, 726; 29 265, 266, 637; 31 510, 865; 32 124
Siloé, Gil de 28 724–5*
collaboration 5 204; 8 872; 26 249
patrons and collectors 2 278
works 5 201; 13 108; 28 724; 29 289; 31 822, 823; 32 124
Silos 29 258
manuscripts 29 275
S Domingo 22 247; 26 582, 607; 28 727–8*; 30 663
capitals 28 727
cloisters 7 454, 455; 26 607, 609
manuscripts 22 248; 26 676
metalwork 22 248; 26 689
monstrance 29 333
reliefs 26 605
sculpture 26 608; 28 728
silos see GRAIN ELEVATORS
Silsbee, Joseph Lyman 20 106; 28 728*; 31 595
assistants 33 400
groups and movements 28 604
pupils 12 632
staff 25 737
Silsbee, Ralph 28 728
siltstone 25 488, 491, 493
Silva, (José) Marques da 23 454; 25 294, 319; 28 731*
Silva, Aires Gomes da see GOMES DA SILVA, AIRES
Silva, André Ribeiro Soares da 28 731
Silva, Antonio 4 832
Silva, Antonio José Dias da see DIAS DA SILVA, ANTONIO JOSÉ
Silva, António Rodrigues da, the elder (1836-c. 1900) 28 729
Silva, António Rodrigues da, the younger (1868-1937) 28 729*
Silva, A. S. H. de 3 419
Silva, Boaventura José da 28 731
Silva, Carlo (fl 1706) 8 142
Silva, Carlos (1930-87) 2 401; 28 729*
Silva, Carlos Miguel Fitz-James Stuart y, 14th Duque de Alba see ALBA, 14th Duque de
Silva, Conceição (Francisco) 25 294; 28 729*
Silva, Cristino da 4 638
Silva, Diego Antonio Rejon de see REJON DE SILVA, DIEGO ANTONIO
Silva, Domingos Parente da 25 293; 28 730*
Silva, Ena de 3 419; 29 455
Silva, Federico 12 844; 28 330, 730–31*
Silva, Ferdinando da, Count of Cifuentes see CIFUENTES, FERDINANDO DA SILVA, Count of
Silva, Filipe da 12 888; 26 253
Silva, Francis Augustus (1835-86; painter) 19 791
Silva, Francisco Augusto Nogueira da (1830-68; engraver) see NOGUEIRA DA SILVA, FRANCISCO AUGUSTO
Silva, Gerardo Aguilera see AGUILERA SILVA, GERARDO
Silva, Jacinto da 28 731*
Silva, J. A. Pinto da 28 429
Silva, J. H. Pais da see PAIS DA SILVA, J. H.
Silva, João Carlos da 27 809
Silva, João Charters de Almeida e see CHARTERS DE ALMEIDA E SILVA, JOÃO
Silva, João Cristino da see CRISTINO DA SILVA, JOÃO
Silva, João da 28 730*
Silva, João Paulo da 18 578
Silva, Joaquín Bethencourt da see BETHENCOURT DA SILVA, JOAQUÍN
Silva, José Antônio da 4 719
Silva, José Claudio da 23 400
Silva, José da Costa e see COSTA E SILVA, JOSÉ DA
Silva, Júlio César da 30 882
Silva, Luís Manuel da 28 731
Silva, Manuel da 25 306
Silva, Manuel Duarte da see DUARTE DA SILVA, MANUEL
Silva, Manuel Fernandes da see FERNANDES DA SILVA, MANUEL
Silva, Manuel Francisco da 24 396
Silva, Maria Elena Vieira da see VIEIRA DA SILVA, MARIA ELENA
Silva, Maria Luiza da 2 87
Silva, Miguel da, Cardinal 28 730*; 32 616
Silva, Miguel Francisco da 28 731–2*
collaboration 26 253; 27 805
works 8 9; 24 396; 28 731
Silva, Minette de 29 455
Silva, Monica 22 607
Silva, Niccolo da 2 472
Silva, Oscar Pereira da see PEREIRA DA SILVA, OSCAR
Silva, (Joaquím) Possidónio (Narciso) da 19 468; 28 732*
Silva, Rufino 18 832
Silva, Severino José da 1 680; 23 454; 26 52
Silva, Teodoro Marques Pereira da see MARQUES PEREIRA DA SILVA, TEODORO
Silva, Valentim da Fonseca e see FONSECA E SILVA, VALENTIM DA
Silva, Viriato 19 468
Silva Castro e Vasconcelos, Félix Machado da see MACHADO DA SILVA CASTRO E VASCONCELOS, FÉLIX
Silva e Silva, António José 23 455
Silva e Sousa, José Rodrigues da see RODRIGUES DA SILVA E SOUSA, JOSÉ
Silva Figueroa, Garcia 24 481
Silvagni, Giovanni 30 364
Silva Lemos, Francisco da 2 402
Silva Lisboa, Inácio Augusto da 19 467
Silva Mendoza y Sandoval, Gregorio Mariá de, Duque del Infantado y Pastrana see INFANTADO Y PASTRANA, GREGORIO MARIÁ DE SILVA MENDOZA Y SANDOVAL, Duque del
Silvan
Castle 16 247
el-Hadra church 9 543
fortifications 31 434
Jacobite church 9 543
Martyropolis 9 512, 513
minaret of Abu'l Muzaffar 16 247
mosque 16 179
Silvani, Francesco 28 733*
Silvani, Gherardo 28 733–4*
assistants 28 734
patrons and collectors 27 205
pupils 23 264
works 5 360, 361; 16 641; 27 736; 28 733
Silvani, Pierfrancesco 28 733, 734–5*
patrons and collectors 7 897
works 5 361; 7 912; 11 23; 21 28; 27 319; 28 735
Silvani, Salvatore 28 733
Silvani, Silvano 28 733
Silvanus, C. 27 52
Silva Pinto, Caetano da 24 395
Silva Pires Keil do Amaral, Maria da see KEIL DO AMARAL, MARIA DA SILVA
Silva Porto, António (Carvalho da) 28 735–6*
groups and movements 4 386
pupils 26 130; 32 98
works 19 466; 25 298; 28 736
Silva Porto Society 26 130
Silva Ramos, Manuel de Morais de see MORAIS DE SILVA RAMOS, MANUEL DE
Silvashi, Tibery 31 560
Silveira, Bento Coelho da see COELHO DA SILVEIRA, BENTO
Silveira, Luís de 31 178
silver 14 419; 28 737–41*
alloys
cadmium 10 136
copper 9 657; 17 318; 21 319; 29 211
gold 9 657; 12 864, 865; 17 318; 29 211
lead 17 318
cleaning 7 727
conservation 7 727
historical and regional traditions
Achaemenid 1 118, 888
Afghanistan 1 204, 204, 210; 16 366, 375, 378
Africa 1 350, 351
Albania 1 543
Anatolia, ancient 1 824, 834, 835, 836
Ancient Near East 1 873, 888
Anglo-Saxon 2 79, 80; 10 322; 31 316–17
Argentina 2 401–2*
Armenia (Europe) 2 441–2
Australia 2 764–6, 765; 28 737
Austria 2 819–21*, 821, 824
Bangladesh 3 169; 15 502
silver
historical and regional traditions—cont.
Belgium 3 596–601*, 602, 604, 605, 606, 607; 5 213; 13 159; 22 885; 26 145
17th cent. 3 599
18th cent. 3 600
Berber 3 756
Bhutan 3 914, 916
Bolivia 4 255, 256, 265–6*
Bosnia 4 462
Brazil 4 723, 723–4*
Britain 7 442, 445
Brunei 5 11–12
Buddhism 15 223, 500; 18 348; 22 777; 30 823
China 7 21, 23, 24, 25
Korea 18 351–2
Bulgaria 5 152, 160, 160
Burma 5 259
Byzantine 8 199; 9 520, 612, 623, 652, 654–6*, 655, 656, 657–8*
Cambodia 5 507, 508, 508
Canada 5 584–6*; 28 737
Carolingian 5 806; 7 534; 10 115
Celtic 6 159; 22 371
Central Asia, Eastern 6 305, 306, 309
Central Asia, Western 6 188, 193, 236–42*, 239, 241, 250, 262, 263, 274; 16 378; 28 723
Chile 6 599*
China 7 21–7*, 26, 72, 79, 106, 108, 109, 116, 128, 632; 21 715
Buddhism 7 21, 23, 24, 25
export 7 28, 28–30*, 29
Liao period (AD 907-1125) 7 25
Ming period (1368-1644) 7 111
Qing period (1644-1911) 7 27, 111, 112
Shang period (c. 1600-c. 1050 BC) 7 106, 107
Song period (AD 960-1279) 6 895; 7 110
Tang period (AD 618-907) 7 14, 14, 23, 24, 82, 109; 23 551, 551
Yuan period (1279-1368) 7 124
Zhou period (c. 1050-256 BC) 6 853, 855; 7 98, 107; 21 714
Colombia 7 600, 610–11*
Crete 21 658, 686–7, 688
Cuba (Caribbean) 8 237, 237
Cycladic 8 322*, 322
Cyprus 8 360*, 365
Cyprus, ancient 8 349, 353; 21 334
Czech Republic 7 535; 8 411–14*
Dacian 30 773
Denmark 8 750–51*, 751, 752, 753; 13 849; 32 516
Celtic 22 371
Early Christian (c. AD 250-843) 5 917; 8 360*; 9 612, 652, 654–6*, 655, 656
Ecuador 9 714
Egypt 16 384, 385, 389, 404, 504; 21 718
Egypt, ancient 9 817; 10 29, 29, 36, 51; 21 711
England 6 443; 10 291, 322*, 323–30*, 327, 331, 331–7*, 332, 333, 355
Anglo-Saxon 2 80; 10 322–3*
chinoiserie 7 167
Gothic 7 535; 23 461; 30 541, 542
Modern Movement 10 337
New Sculpture 3 367
Roman 21 I2
7th cent. AD 10 350
16th cent. 7 537; 14 418, 419

silver
historical and regional traditions
England—cont.
17th cent. **2** *456*, *466*; **14** 856; **28** *740*
18th cent. **3** *627*; **19** *594*; **28** *737*
19th cent. **10** 142, *335*
Etruscan **10** 624, 625, 630–32*, *632*
Finland **11** 107, *108*
France **11** 613–23*
Rococo **21** *70*
Roman **27** *82*, 82–3
16th cent. **6** 443; **11** *616*
17th cent. **2** *463*; **9** 30; **11** 576, *618*; **14** *418*
18th cent. **8** 68; **11** *620*, *621*; **12** *357*; **24** *147*
19th cent. **4** *458*; **5** 836; **11** *622*
20th cent. **11** *622*
Georgia **9** 658; **12** *328*, 328–9*, *329*
Germany **6** 173, 557; **12** 442–50*, *449*, 463; **18** *522*
Baroque **12** 423
Gothic **23** *311*
Roman **27** *81*
Romanesque **6** 173, *174*
9th cent. AD **10** *115*
12th cent. **7** *535*
15th cent. **12** *443*
16th cent. **2** *718*; **7** *440*; **12** *444*; **16** *900*
17th cent. **7** *538*; **9** 234
18th cent. **12** *435*, *445*; **13** *679*
19th cent. **12** *450*
20th cent. **12** 450–51*, *451*
Gothic **9** *3*; **13** 135, 159, 168, 194; **23** *311*; **30** *541*
Greece **13** 358–9
Greece, ancient **3** 483; **13** 390, 391, 568–71*, *569*, *570*, 573, 585, *585*, *587*, *588*, 588, 589
Guatemala **13** *767*, 767–8*
Helladic **14** 354–5*
Herzegovina **4** 462
Hinduism **15** *502*
Hittite **8** 261
Holy Roman Empire (before 1648) **26** 683*
Hong Kong **7** 29, 30
Hungary **15** 5–8*, *11*
Iceland **15** 73*
Inca **15** 164
Indian subcontinent **4** 687; **6** 556; **15** 200, *223*, *500*, 664, 668, *688*, 707–8*, 712*; **21** 717
4th cent. BC **15** 687
12th cent. **15** *502*
17th cent. **15** *708*, *714*
18th cent. **15** *711*
Indonesia **15** 813*
Insular art **2** *378*; **8** *782*; **15** *872*, 873
Iran **16** *371*, 375, *376*, 450, *511*, *513*
Iran, ancient **1** *118*; **7** *187*; **15** 905, *920*; **27** *855*; **30** 770
Iraq **16** *380*, *512*
Ireland **2** *378*; **8** *782*; **15** *872*, 873; **16** 30–32*, *31*, *32*, 34; **32** *530*
Islamic **4** 688; **6** 556; **16** 363, 364, 371–3*, *381*, *383*, *504*, 532; **21** *718*
Afghanistan **16** *366*, *375*, *378*
Algeria **16** 532
Central Asia, Western **16** *378*
Egypt **16** *384*, *385*, *389*, 404
Iran **16** *371*, 375, *376*, 450, *511*, *513*; **21** 11
Iraq **16** *380*, *512*
Syria **16** *99*, *384*, 389, 510, *511*
Tunisia **16** *512*
Umayyad **21** *505*

silver
historical and regional traditions
Islamic—cont.
Yemen **16** *533*
Italy **5** *917*; **9** 30, *520*; **11** *86*; **12** 868; **16** 690, *741*, 741–3*; **20** *922*; **25** *19*; **32** 212
Etruscan **10** 624, 630–32*, *632*
Jamaica **16** *889*
Japan **17** 219, 220, 297, 298, *305*, 313, 318, 321, 370, 401
Edo period (1600-1868) **10** *777*; **17** *370*
Momoyama period (1568-1600) **17** 370
Muromachi period (1333-1568) **17** *228*, *301*
Nara period (AD 710-94) **17** 369
Jewish art **5** 612
Kazakhstan **17** *868*; **28** *723*
Khwarazm **6** *193*, 238
Knights Hospitaller **20** 216
Korea **18** *348*, 349–52*, *356*, 357, 366, 370
Laos **18** 775, 776, *776*
Madagascar **20** 38
Malaysia **20** 173, 174, 175, 180
Malta (Republic of) **20** 216–17*, *217*
Mesoamerica, Pre-Columbian **21** 253
Mesopotamia **21** 303, *303*, 304
Mexico **7** 537; **21** 392–3*; **28** 737
Minoan **21** *658*, 686–7*, 688*
Mongolia **7** *836*; **21** 876, 877, 878, 882, 884
Mycenaean **14** 355*
Native North Americans **22** 614, *615*, 668–9
Navajo **22** 614, *615*
Nepal **22** *777*
Netherlands, the **3** 598; **13** 159; **22** 885–92*, *886*, *888*, *890*, *891*, *892*; **28** *739*
Indonesia **15** 813*
New Zealand **23** 70–72, *71*
Nicaragua **23** 83*
North Africa **16** 532
Norway **23** 236*, *237*, 238; **32** *514*
Nubia **23** 286, *286*
Ottonian **22** *43*; **23** 647, 656–7*
Pakistan **23** 803
Parthian **1** *888*
Peru **7** 537; **24** 500, 511–12, *512*; **28** *651*
Philippines **24** 626, 627–8*
Phoenician **24** 644
Phrygian **1** 836
Pictish art **27** *570*
Poland **25** 125–8*
Portugal **25** 303, 312–14*, *314*
Prehistoric art **1** 824, *835*; **25** 542*
Punic **25** 735
Rhodes (island) **13** 359
Romanesque **6** 173, *174*; **26** *145*, 683*
Romania **26** 720; **30** *770*, *771*
Rome, ancient **23** *535*; **25** 43; **27** 15, 79–84*
Augustan **27** 31
Early Christian (*c.* AD 250-843) **5** *917*
England **21** 12
Gallo-Roman **27** 82–3
1st cent. BC **27** *81*
1st cent. AD **8** 263; **21** 713, *713*
2nd cent. AD **26** *859*
3rd cent. AD **27** *82*
4th cent. AD **27** *84*
Russia **27** 418–23*, *420*, *423*, 584; **28** 737; **32** *527*
Sasanian **15** *920*; **27** *855*, 856

silver
historical and regional traditions—cont.
Scandinavia **32** *514*, *516*, 524, 531
Scotland **27** *570*; **28** 260–62*, *261*, *262*, 273
Serbia **28** *455*, 456
Sicán culture **28** *651*, *652*
Sicily **13** *587*; **16** 742
Sogdiana **6** *239*, *241*
South Africa **19** 709; **28** 121; **29** *115*, *119*, 119–21
South America, Pre-Columbian **28** *651*, *652*; **29** 211
Spain **27** 15; **29** 301, 302, 332–8*, *334*, 349
Sri Lanka **29** 474, *475*
Sumatra **15** 812
Sweden **29** 689; **30** 104–9*, *107*, *108*
Switzerland **30** 146, 147, 151
Syria **9** 655; **16** *99*, *384*, 389, 510, *511*; **21** *718*
Syria-Palestine **30** 179, 194, 195
Thailand **30** *626*, 631, 635–6*
Thracian **13** 848–9, *849*; **30** 769, 770, *770*, *771*
Tibet **30** 823, 839, 840, *840*, 841
Troadic **31** 355*, *355*
Tunisia **16** *512*
Ukraine **31** 562
United States of America **10** 851, *851*; **26** 262, *262*; **28** 737; **31** 646–51*, *648*
Baroque **31** *647*
17th cent. **31** *646*
20th cent. **31** *651*
Urartian **1** 836
Uruguay **31** 756*
Uzbekistan **6** *188*
Venezuela **32** 176–7*
Vietnam **32** 487, 488
Viking **32** *514*, *516*, 524, *527*, *530*, 531
Yemen **16** 532, *533*
marks *see under* MARKS
patinas **21** 329*
reuse **7** 565
technical examination **30** 400, 408
techniques
casting **28** 739
chasing **15** *708*; **28** 740
embossing **22** 888; **30** *840*
engraving **15** *708*; **28** 740
filigree **7** 112
gilding **12** *328*, 445, 624
lost-wax casting **28** 739
repoussé **16** 364; **18** *776*; **24** *512*; **28** 739; **30** 770
rolling **3** 367
soldering **28** 739
stamping **12** 448
undercutting **21** 878
uses
alabastra **13** *569*
altars **9** 656; **16** *741*
antependia **24** 511
axes **7** *187*; **32** *527*
badges **14** *419*
basins **22** 890
baskets **22** 890
beads **3** 440, 442
beakers **10** *337*; **15** *708*; **22** 886, 890; **30** 105, *771*; **31** *646*
beds **3** 483
bells **3** 627, *627*
belthooks **7** *98*, 107
belts **7** 108, 109, 111; **18** *776*
betel sets **5** 254, *508*, 508; **18** 776; **20** 175; **30** 631
bookbindings **2** 442
book covers **9** 656, 658; **26** 720
books **21** 876
bowls **6** *188*, *241*; **7** 23, *24*, *26*; **9** 657; **16** 31; **18** 351; **24** 644; **26** *262*, *859*; **28** *455*; **29** *119*

silver
uses—cont.
boxes **11** *108*; **16** 32, *32*, *889*, *900*; **24** 512; **30** *840*; **32** 488
bracelets **7** 109; **10** *29*; **18** 366; **22** 614
braids **30** 542
braziers **29** 301, 302
brooches **2** *80*; **15** *872*; **32** *514*
brushes **5** 33
busts **3** *604*
cabinets (ii) (furniture) **29** *115*
calligraphy **17** 219, 220, *228*
candlesticks **5** 611, 612; **10** *332*; **16** *31*, 31, 32
canopies (ii) (textile coverings) **10** 51
carpets **5** 836
caskets **5** *917*; **22** *890*
cauldrons **13** *849*
censers **6** 173, *174*; **9** 656
ceramics **6** 329
chairs **29** 301
chalices **2** *378*; **6** 398; **8** *782*; **9** 656, 657
chandeliers **6** 443; **9** 13
châtelaines **7** 109
chess sets **6** 556, 557, 558
ciboria (i) (vessels) **9** 656
clocks **7** 439, *440*, 442, 445
coffeepots **2** *821*; **12** *451*; **20** 217; **22** *891*; **24** *147*; **30** 106
coffee-urns **3** *600*
coffrets **11** *622*
coins **7** 534–7
Afghanistan **1** 204, *204*
Arabia **2** *262*
Carolingian **7** *534*
Celtic **6** 159
Central Asia, Eastern **6** 309
Central Asia, Western **6** *263*
China **7** *72*
Cyprus, ancient **8** 349
England **7** 535, 536, *537*; **14** 419
Etruscan **10** 632, *632*
Germany **7** *535*, *538*
Greece, ancient **13** 585, *585*, *587*, *588*, 588, 589
Indian subcontinent **15** 687, *688*
Islamic **16** 510, *511*, *512*, *513*; **21** *505*
Japan **17** 318, 369, 370, *370*
Korea **18** *356*, 357
Malaysia **20** 180
Parthian **1** *888*
Sasanian **27** *855*
Sumatra **15** 812
combs (hair) **7** 110
containers **3** 916
cradles (i) (cots) **10** 326
crosses **8** 199, 201, 203, 204; **9** 656, 658; **29** *334*
crowns **7** 25, *25*; **23** *286*
cult statues **8** 261, 263
cups
Australia **2** *765*
China **7** *23*, 82; **23** *551*
Cyprus, ancient **21** *334*
Denmark **32** *516*
England **28** *740*
Germany **12** *444*
Greece, ancient **13** *570*
Hungary **15** 6
Ireland **16** 31
Laos **18** 776
Netherlands, the **22** 886, *886*, 889
New Zealand **23** *71*
Rome, ancient **23** *535*; **27** 80
Troadic **31** *355*
diadems **8** *322*
dish rings **16** 32
dolls' furniture **31** 264
doors **13** 390, 391
earrings **22** 614; **25** *314*
ecuelles **11** *621*; **20** 217

silver
uses—cont.
electroplating **10** 135
embroidery **2** *824*; **12** 463; **13** 194; **15** *11*; **30** *541*
emulsions **24** 669
enamel **7** 79; **10** 192; **13** 168; **15** 707, *711*, 712*
ewers **6** *239*, 599; **7** 23; **16** *371*; **22** 890; **32** *401*
exchange **5** 255
fans **9** 656; **10** *777*
fibulae **30** 773
filigree **7** 111; **12** 868; **20** 216; **32** 531
flagons **10** *327*
frames **9** 658
fringes **3** 483
furniture **9** 30, 234; **10** 291, 328; **11** 576, 617–18; **12** 423, 445, 448
gates **20** *217*
gilding **12** 627; **17** 321
glass **12** 782
glass holders **22** 887, 889
grounds **13** 135
gun stocks **2** *463*, *466*
hairpins **7** 109
hats **24** *512*
headdresses **7** 109, *836*; **28** *651*
helmets **30** *770*
hookas **15** *711*
icon covers **15** 77, *77*
icons **5** 152; **9** 623, 658; **12** *328*, *329*
incense boats **4** *723*
incense burners **7** 110; **24** 512
inks **15** 851, 852
inkwells **9** 657
inlays **21** 329
Afghanistan **16** *375*
Bhutan **3** 914
China **6** 853, 855; **7** 14, 22, 107
Egypt **16** *385*, *389*
Germany **4** 688
Greece **13** 573
Indian subcontinent **15** 707, 712, *714*
Iran **16** *376*
Iraq **16** *380*
Islamic **16** *99*, 364, *366*, 375, *378*, *381*, *383*, *384*
Korea **18** *348*
Rajasthan **4** 687
Syria **16** 389
Turkey **4** 688
jewellery **17** 522
Afghanistan **1** 210
Africa **1** 350
Belgium **3** *605*
Berber **3** 756
Central Asia, Western **6** 274
China **7** 106, 107, 112
Early Christian and Byzantine **9** 652, 657
Egypt, ancient **10** 29
Islamic **16** 532
Laos **18** 775
Madagascar **20** 38
Minoan **21** 686
Mongolia **21** 877
Native North Americans **22** 614, *615*
Philippines **24** 626
Phoenician **24** 644
Portugal **25** 314
Ukraine **31** 562
Vietnam **32** 487
jugs **10** *335*; **16** 31, 372
kantharoi **21** *658*
keris **20** 174
kettles **6** 599
knife-handles **8** 285
knives **28** *651*
lace **10** 355; **16** 34; **30** 151, 542
lacquer **7** *14*, 25, 107; **17** 297, 298, *301*, *305*; **18** 370, 604
laminates **12** 621
lamps **9** *520*, 656, 657

silver
uses—cont.
liturgical objects **9** 656
maces **8** *237*
manuscripts **9** 612
medals **16** 690; **20** 917, *922*
mirror frames **21** 717, 719, 721
mirrors **21** 711, 713, *713*, 714, 715, *718*; **28** 738
monstrances **3** *599*
monteiths **31** *647*
mosaics **22** 155
mounts (porcelain) **9** 28
mugs **7** 29, *29*
necklaces **8** *753*; **16** *533*; **25** *314*
nefs **11** *616*
netsuke **17** 401
oinochoai **13** *569*
paintings **13** 135; **17** 319
paper **7** 116
patens **9** 656, 657
paxes **11** *86*
pectoral ornaments **22** *616*
penboxes **21** I1
pendants (jewellery) **3** *605*; **12** *455*; **17** *868*; **22** 614; **27** *423*
pens **24** 349
perfume burners **9** *520*
phialai **1** *118*
photographic plates **24** 658, 660
photography **24** 646, 647, 650, 659, 670; **28** 738
pigments **7** 632
pins **6** 599; **8** *322*
plaques **7** 108; **9** 658
plaquettes **25** 19, *19*
plates **9** 655, *655*, 657; **15** *920*
platters **12** *357*
polykandela **9** 656, *656*
porcelain **6** 895; **7** 25
pots **12** *443*
pottery **16** 404
printing **15** 668
printing plates **10** 379; **23** 114, 115
relief sculpture **3** *367*
reliquaries **5** *213*; **9** *3*, *520*, 657, 658; **10** *115*; **22** *43*; **26** *145*; **31** *535*
revetments **9** 656, 658
rings **1** 351; **7** 109, 111; **16** *504*
roofs **32** 487
salvers **16** 31
sauceboats **10** *333*
scissors **8** 287
scroll cases **29** *475*
sculpture
France **4** *458*
Germany **13** *679*
Guatemala **13** *767*
Indian subcontinent **15** *223*, *500*, *502*
Nepal **22** *777*
Ottonian **23** 647
Rome, ancient **27** 15
Tibet **30** 823
seals **7** 128; **21** 882
shrines (i) (cult) **9** 656; **23** *311*; **32** *530*
sideboards **29** 302
silverplate **28** 576
snuff-boxes **27** *420*
soldering **21** 325
spoons **8** 284; **9** 654, 656; **27** 83; **28** *739*
spurs **6** 599
stained glass **13** 178
standishes **29** 535
statuettes **10** *36*
sword hilts **2** *456*
swords **6** 262, 305, 306
tabernacles (ii) (receptacle) **24** 511
tables **9** 30
tankards **12** *435*; **30** 104–5
tapestries **3** 606, *607*; **5** *48*
tazze **22** 886
tea-caddies **28** *737*
silver
uses—cont.
tea-grinders **7** *24*
teapots **5** 584; **16** 31; **20** 217; **22** *891*; **30** 106
tea-services **3** *602*; **7** *28*; **22** *892*
tea-urns **10** *851*
textiles **17** 313; **28** 716
threads **30** 308, 540, 541–2
Belgium **10** II2; **14** III2; **30** II1, 2
Central Asia, Western **6** 250
England **10** *350*; **23** *461*; **30** *541*
France ,
Germany **12** 463
Gothic **13** 194
Hungary **15** *11*
Indian subcontinent **15** 664
Islamic **16** 450
Spain **29** 301, 349
toilet services **11** *618*
toys **31** 255
trappings **31** 756
trays **20** 217
tunics **30** *626*
tureens **11** *620*, *622*; **12** *357*; **21** *70*; **22** *888*
varnishes **8** 447
vases **7** *27*; **21** *303*
vessels **7** *27*
wallpaper **32** 812
watches **7** 444
wine-coolers **10** *331*
wire **21** 324; **28** 738
writing *see* CHRYSOGRAPHY
writing sets **18** *522*
see also PLATE; SILVER GELATIN
Silver, Arthur **10** 283; **28** 742
silver, German *see under* ALLOYS → types
Silver, Harry **2** 137; **28** 742
Silver, James **28** 742
Silver, L. **15** 91
Silver, Rex (Reginald) **6** 164; **28** 742
silver, Sterling *see under* ALLOYS → types
Silvera, Eudoro **23** 905; **28** 741*
Silver Birch Master **9** 375; **20** 769*
silver bromide **9** 493; **24** 648, 651, 656
silver chloride **12** 788; **24** 651, 656
Silvercroon, Johan-Philips **17** 648
silver dust **17** 277; **25** *620*; **30** 540
boullework **20** 466
chromolithography **25** *620*
lacquer **18** 604, 605, 606
marquetry **20** 466
prints **17** 277
silver foil *see* SILVER LEAF
silver gelatin **24** 647, 648
silver-gilt
historical and regional traditions
Austria **2** *820*
Bactria **6** *237*
Belgium **3** *597*
Byzantine **8** *199*; **9** *520*, 623, 657, *658*, *660*
Carolingian **5** *807*
Central Asia, Western **6** *237*, *240*
China **7** 108, 109, 110, 112
Czech Republic **8** *412*, *414*
England **10** *326*, *330*; **13** *164*; **23** *461*; **27** *640*; **28** *738*; **30** *541*
Gothic **10** *323*
19th cent. **10** *334*
France **11** *615*, *617*; **13** *158*, *168*, *169*, *170*; **24** *146*
Germany **2** *453*; **8** *200*, *201*; **12** 424, *444*, *445*, *449*; **16** *899*, *901*; **17** *888*; **28** I1
Gothic **7** *300*; **13** *158*, 166; **30** *541*
England **10** *323*
France **11** *615*; **13** *168*, *169*, *170*
silver-gilt
historical and regional traditions
Gothic—cont.
Italy **13** *163*
Spain **29** *333*
Holy Roman Empire (before 1648) **6** *398*
Hungary **15** *3*, *6*, *11*
Iran **16** *372*
Iran, ancient **27** *856*
Islamic **16** *372*
Italy **5** *807*; **6** *140*; **9** *520*; **16** *541*, *742*, *746*; **25** *19*, *20*
Gothic **13** *163*
Jewish art **17** 574, *574*
Mexico **21** *393*
Netherlands, the **1** *811*; **32** *400*
Ottoman **23** *639*
Portugal **13** 166; **25** *313*
Punic **25** *735*
Romanesque **6** *398*
Romania **26** *720*
Rome, ancient **21** 713
Sasanian **27** *856*
Scythian **28** *324*
Sogdiana **6** *240*
Spain **29** *333*, *335*, *336*
Sweden **30** *104*, *105*, *106*, *108*
Switzerland **30** *146*, *147*
Tajikistan **30** *253*
Turkey **23** *639*
Turkmenistan **31** *459*
Ukraine **28** *324*
United States of America **4** *480*
uses
altars **5** *807*
amphorae **28** *324*
basins **11** *617*; **15** *6*; **17** *888*
bosses **6** *237*
bowls **6** *240*; **8** *412*
boxes **30** *105*
breast-ornaments **30** *253*; **31** *459*
candlesticks **16** *541*, *742*
caskets **16** *745*; **30** *108*
casters (vessels) **29** *335*
censers **13** *164*
centrepieces **16** *899*; **25** *313*
chalices **6** *398*; **13** *163*; **21** *393*
ciboria (i) (vessels) **7** *300*
combs (hair) **7** 109
crosses **8** *199*, *200*, *201*, 201, *414*
crowns **7** 110
cups **4** *480*; **10** *323*, *326*, *334*; **12** *449*; **16** *901*
custodia **29** *333*
diadems **7** 110
embroidery **15** *11*; **30** *541*
ewers **3** *597*; **11** *615*; **15** *6*; **28** I1; **29** *336*; **32** *400*
figurines **30** *147*
flasks **15** *3*
furniture **12** 424
glass holders **1** *811*
goblets **2** *820*
hair ornaments **7** 108
icon covers **15** 77
icons **9** 623
jewellery **7** 112
medals **6** *140*
mirror frames **21** 713
patens **6** *398*; **26** *720*
pendants (jewellery) **25** *735*
perfume burners **9** *520*
plaquettes **25** *19*, *20*
plates **27** *856*
reliquaries **9** *520*, *658*; **13** *169*, *170*; **24** *146*
rings **17** 574, *574*
salts **27** *640*; **29** *335*; **30** *106*
salvers **28** *738*
standishes **29** 535
statuettes **13** *158*
swords **2** *453*
tabernacles (ii) (receptacle) **13** *168*
tankards **30** *104*
silver-gilt
uses—cont.
threads **15** *11*, 12; **23** *461*, *639*; **30** 308, *541*
trays **16** *372*
vessels **30** *146*
waiters **10** *330*
wire **7** 110
silver halides *see under* PHOTOGRAPHY → materials
Silverhorn **22** 63; **28** 741–2*
silvering **10** 135–6
Silver Lake, Van der Leeuw Research House **23** 10
silver leaf **21** 330, 331
historical and regional traditions
Bali (Indonesia) **15** 806
Belgium **3** 575
China **7** 13
Egypt, ancient **3** 482
Japan **17** 140, 277, 298, 314
Ryūkyū Islands **27** 471
Syria-Palestine **21** *331*
uses
beds **3** 482
drawings **15** 806
dress **17** 314
figurines **21** *331*
gilding **12** 621; **19** 2
lacquer **7** 13; **17** 298; **27** 471
manuscript illumination **20** 347
mosaics **12** 622
painting **17** 140
panels (wall) **3** 575
pilgrim badges **24** 809
prints **17** 277
textiles **17** 314
threads **30** 540
wallpaper **32** 812
Silverman, Burt **18** 797
Silverman, Helaine **5** 388
silver nitrate **13** 136; **21** 721; **24** 647, 648, 649, 656; **29** 498
silver oxides **16** 394, 518
silverplate **31** 650
types
Sheffield plate **5** 612; **10** 135–6, 331–2; **21** 325, 331; **28** 576–7*
United States of America **31** 649
uses
candlesticks **5** 612
sculpture **15** *173*
silverpoints *see under* DRAWINGS → forms
silversmiths
Barbados **2** 152
Bhutan **3** 916
England **10** 331
Indian subcontinent **15** 723
United States of America **31** 647
silversmiths guilds *see under* GUILDS → types
Silver & Sons **6** 484
silver-stain **13** 136, 178, 183, 186, 193; **29** 498, 499; **33** 549
Silver Studio **28** 742*; **32** 817; **33** 372
collaboration **19** 415
designers **18** 170
patrons and collectors **19** 311
works **19** 359
Silverstyne, Isaac **28** 242
Silver Towers **6** 420, 423, 430, 432
silver white *see under* PIGMENTS → types
silver wire **30** 839
Silves **25** 289
Silvestre (i), Alexandre **28** 742
Silvestre (i), Israël **19** 16; **20** 415; **25** 626; **28** 742–3*
assistants **20** 457
collaboration **30** 61
pupils **28** 743
reproductive prints by others **12** *121*
works **4** 756; **14** 394; **19** *162*, 300; **23** 512; **27** 315; **30** 659; **31** 156; **32** *97*
Silvestre (i), Louis de (1669-1740) **28** 742
Silvestre (ii), (Paul-)Armand **15** 153, 157; **28** 744*
Silvestre (i), Louis de (1675-1760) **25** 105; **28** 742, 743–4*
collaboration **12** 27
patrons and collectors **33** 115
pupils **5** 908
works **3** 528; **9** 242; **28** *743*
Silvestre (ii), Théophile **11** 674; **28** 744*
Silvestre (i), Charles-François **28** 742
Silvestre, Jacques-Augustin **2** 702
Silvestre, J. B. **26** 234
Silvestre (i), Suzanne **28** 742
Silvestri, Bartolommeo **25** 74
Silvestro dell'Aquila (*fl* 1439-40; goldsmith) **28** 745
Silvestro (di Giacomo da Sulmona) dell'Aquila (*fl* 1471-1504; sculptor) **18** 785; **28** 744–5*
Silvestro della Torre *see* SILVESTRO (DI GIACOMO DA SULMONA) DELL' AQUILA
Silvestro di Paolo di Stefano **32** 366
Silvio, Enea **27** 195
Silvio, Giampietro **3** 470; **32** 229
Silvy, Camille **24** 661, 663; **28** 745*
Silwood Ceramics **29** 117
Šima, Josef **25** 433; **28** 745–6*
groups and movements **2** 546; **7** 772; **30** 20, 22
works **8** 393, *393*, 394
Šima, Ladislav **13** 711
simae **8** 154
Sima Guang **12** 87; **25** 785
Simaika, Morcos **5** 401
Sima Jinlong **7** 34
Simalungun Batak **15** 788
Simanonis, Kazimeras (Vintsovich) **27** 423
Simão, Julio **12** 826; **25** 291
Simão 'o Português **25** 295
Sima Qian **6** 320; **8** 852; **18** 281; **19** 431; **21** 884
Simart, Pierre-Charles **11** 565, 567; **12** 461; **28** 746*
Simavik **23** 218
Simbale, Vina **20** 162
Simberg, Hugo (Gerhard) **28** 746–7*
works **10** 200; **11** 96; **29** 63; **30** 284
Simberg-Ehrström, Uhra **11** 110
Śimbhu *see* SVAYAMBHUNATHA
Simbirsk Museum **27** 440
Simbirtsev, Vasily (Nikolayevich) **28** 747*
groups and movements **32** 695
works **22** 174; **27** 380, 409; **32** 685
Simbo **29** 49
Sim Chŏng-ju **28** 758
Simeon, Abbot of Ely **10** 165, 166
Simeon, Emperor of Bulgaria (*reg* 925-27) **5** 162; **25** 559
Simeon Movilă, Voivode of Wallachia (*reg* 1600-02) **26** 721
Simetite *see* AMBER
Simetria **9** 70
Simferopol Treasure **16** 531
Simhachalam **15** 537
Narasimha temple **15** 328, 539
siṁhakarṇa **15** 244*
siṁhamukha **15** 244*
Simhavishnu (*reg c.* 550-70) (Pallava) **15** 234, 507
Siṁhinera *see* SINNAR (INDIA)
Simiane **26** 604
Simiane, Marquise de **32** 331
Simias **4** 345
Simicioglu, Michael **13** 358
Simiolus **24** 449, 450
Simiruni painters **15** 899

Simitthus 26 *876*
  marble 23 300; 26 876; 27 14; 29 702
  temple 23 300
Simla 15 *264*; 28 748*
  architecture 15 411
  Himachal State Museum 15 180; 28 748
  Town Hall 31 241
  Viceregal Lodge 12 75
Simmel, Georg 28 917; 31 728
Simmler, Andreas 25 121; 32 879
Simmler, Hans Jakub 32 879
Simmler, Jakub Karol 32 879
Simmler, Johann 5 168
Simmler, Józef 25 106
Simmonds, T. C. 24 185
Simmons, Anthony 10 851
Simmons, Edward 12 614; 30 452
Simmons, James 5 640
Simmons, Paula 31 660
Simmons, Philip 1 422
Simmons, William Henry 12 30; 28 748*
Simms, Jane 16 41
Sim Mun-sŏp 18 301
Simnan 16 *105*, 160, 161; 28 748*
  congregational mosque 16 234
Simo, Franceso Roca y *see* ROCA Y SIMO, FRANCESCO
Simoēs, J. M. Santos *see* SANTOS SIMÕES, J. M.
Simões, M. 20 371
Simões de Almeida, José 28 748–9*
  pupils 8 11; 26 130; 27 141, 615
  works 25 302
Simões Ribeiro, António 19 523
Simon (family) 26 113
Simon (*fl* early 13th cent.; Poland) 32 749
Simon (*fl* late 13th cent.; England) 33 547
Simon (*fl* 1470-1508) 32 586
Simon (the glassmaker; *fl* 1509) 26 269
Simon, Abbot of St Albans 26 659, 677
Simon, Abraham 20 923; 28 749*
Simon, André 17 725
Simon, Bernhard 33 297
Simon, Brigitte 26 113
Simon, Caspar 3 711
Simon, Constant 26 509
Simon, Eduard 12 474; 21 311
Simon, Elizabeth 8 95
Simon, Felix 21 311
Simon, Friedrich Rudolf 28 750*
Simon, George 13 877
Simon, James 10 93; 12 474
Simon, Jean (1675-1751) 19 384; 24 335
Simon, Jean-Henri 26 486
Simon, Jean-Pierre 29 676
Simon, John *see* SIMON, JEAN
Simon, Joseph 3 595; 24 820
Simón, Juan (*fl* 1571) 29 339
Simon, Louis 24 267
Simon, Lucien 14 486; 28 750*
  groups and movements 3 156
  pupils 5 920; 24 338; 28 593; 29 638; 32 174
Simon, Luke 22 598
Simon, Marcia *see* WEISMAN, MARCIA
Simon, Melvin, & Associates 28 623
Simon, Norton 28 750–51*; 33 45
  collections 15 743; 19 703; 31 665
  sculpture 22 795
Simon, Norton, Museum *see under* PASADENA (CA)
Simon, Oliver 22 117
Simon, Pierre (*c*. 1650-1710) 28 751*
Simon, Pierre (before 1750-1810) 11 912
Simon, Samuel 28 299
Simon, Thomas 8 186; 10 657; 12 261; 20 923; 26 532; 28 749–50*; 33 6
  works 28 *749*
Simon, Yochanan 16 567; 23 25
Simonau, François 28 751*
Simonau, Gustave Adolphe 28 751*
Simonau, Pierre 28 751
Simoncini, Giorgio 5 912
Simon de Châlons *see* MAILLY, SIMON DE
Simon de Courcy 20 719
Simondi, Bernardino 19 341, 342
Simonds, Charles 28 751–2*; 31 615
Simonds, Ossian C. 14 657
Simone (*fl* 1366-8) 7 338
Simone (*fl* 1469) 20 323
Simone, Maestro (*fl* 1550s-60s) 6 18
Simone, Alfredo De *see* DE SIMONE, ALFREDO
Simone, Antonio De *see* DE SIMONE, ANTONIO
Simone, Francesco De *see* DE SIMONE, FRANCESCO
Simone, Puccio di *see* PUCCIO DI SIMONE
Simone Ardizone da Reggio *see* ARDIZZONI DA REGGIO, SIMONE
Simoneau, P. 14 84
Simone Camaldolese 5 451; 28 752–3*
  works 28 *752*
Simone da Bologna, Archbishop of Palermo 23 843
Simone da Orsenigo 21 530
Simone da San Pellegrino 33 633
Simone da Settignano *see* CIOLI, SIMONE (DI MICHELE)
Simone da Sirtori 21 532
Simone dei Crocefissi 4 275; 28 753–4*
  collaboration 20 751
  pupils 16 848; 19 453; 28 434
  works 4 276; 8 212; 28 *753*
Simone de Orsenigo 21 534
Simone di Filippo Benvenuti da Bologna *see* SIMONE DEI CROCEFISSI
Simone di Tomaso del Pollaiuolo *see* CRONACA
Simonelli, Giuseppe 12 663, 664
Simonelli, Niccolò 28 754*
Simone Martini *see* MARTINI, SIMONE
Simonet, Adrien-Jacques 28 754
Simonet, Jean 26 778
Simonet, Jean-Baptiste (-Blaise) (1742-1813) 28 754*
Simonetta, Carlo 5 182; 16 563; 21 533
Simonetta, Giacomo, Cardinal of Perugia 20 271
Simonetta, Giovanni 4 76
Simonetti, Ivan 28 754*
Simonetti, Michelangelo 28 754–5*
  collaboration 5 552; 9 12
  patrons and collectors 7 411; 16 772; 25 8
  works 9 *12*; 16 *773*; 22 *361*, 362; 26 814; 29 833
Simonetti carpet 16 472
Simon Fraser University *see under* BURNABY
Simon Gibbon Salt 10 326
Simon & Halbig 31 261
Simoni, Gustavo 23 504
Simoni, Michelangelo di Lodovico Buonarroti *see* MICHELANGELO (BUONARROTI)
Simonides 13 553; 31 768
Simonides, Constantine 10 92
Simonin, Claude 2 465
  works 2 *465*
Simonin, Francine 30 135
Simonin, Jacques 2 465
Simonini, Francesco 5 908; 28 755*
Simonis, (Louis-)Eugène 3 613; 28 756*
  assistants 6 487
  pupils 9 326; 31 874; 32 590
  teachers 17 921
  works 3 572; 5 43
Šimonis, Kazys 19 498
Simonneau, Charles 6 502; 12 833; 25 70; 28 756*
Simonneau, Louis 28 756*
Simonneau, Philippe 3 639; 28 756
Simon of Aigina 1 481
Simonos Petra 9 546
Simonot, Francesco 12 534
Simonov, Grigory A. 11 244; 12 234; 23 144
Simons, Anna 3 512; 4 369; 28 307
Simons, Aurelius Augustinus 3 599
Simons, François Marcus 22 891
Simons, Frans 2 197; 32 591
Simons, P. 33 313
Simons, Ralph 5 511
Simonsen, Niels 33 594
Simonson, Lee 30 687
Simonson, Otto 22 60
Simonsson, Birger Jörgen 28 821; 33 566
Simonsuuri, Lauri 32 599
Simonton, Dean Keith 25 685
Simon van Harlem 20 731
Simonyan, Ripsime 2 437
Simor, János, Archbishop of Esztergom 10 545; 15 17
Simorre Church 4 780
Simos 13 552
Šimotová, Adriena 8 388; 28 756–7*
Simounet, Roland 19 381; 28 757*
Simov, Viktor (Andreyevich) 27 396; 28 757*
Simpasa, Akwila 33 603
Simpelveld sarcophagus 27 99, *99*
Simplicius, Pope (*reg* 468-83) 16 761; 26 752
Simplizissimus 2 565; 14 313–14; 26 715
Simpol, Claude *see* SAINT-PAUL, CLAUDE
Simpson, Archibald 1 30; 20 14; 28 228, 230, 757–8*
Simpson, A. W. 28 326
Simpson, C. W. 1 496
Simpson, John W. 28 273; 29 489; 33 204
Simpson, Jonathan 14 673
Simpson, Lawson & Rayne 23 20
Simpson, Lorna 10 882
Simpson, Mel 23 70
Simpson, Norah 2 748
Simpson, Ralph 10 303; 29 495
Simpson, Wallis Warfield *see* WINDSOR, WALLIS, Duchess of Windsor
Simpson, W. B. 19 109
Simpson, W. B., & Co. 5 194; 8 583; 28 881
Simpson, William (1823-99; draughtsman) 1 211; 7 579; 23 503
Simpson, William (*fl* 1878-9; archaeologist) 14 19
Simpson, William E. (1818-72) 1 440
Simpson Mackennal, John *see* MACKENNAL, JOHN SIMPSON
Simpson & Wilson 4 803
Sims (family) 27 613
S(econdary) I(on) M(ass) S(pectroscopy) *see under* TECHNICAL EXAMINATION → types
Sims, Charles 33 145
Sims, Henry 26 468
Sims, James Peacock 10 718
Sims, Karl 28 204
Sims, Paddy Japaljarri 28 758*
  works 1 *63*
Sim Sa-jŏng 7 203; 28 758–9*
  works 28 *759*
Simsbury (CT) 31 653
Simthoka Dzong 21 848
Simu, Anastase 26 723, 724
Simukanga, Shadreck 33 602
simultaneity 8 244
Simun Rastic 24 32
Sin
  caravanserai 16 193
  minaret 16 165, 248
Sinaba, S. 20 199
Sinagua 22 600, 622
Sinai 7 *819*; 9 *507*, *774*; 28 760–65*, *760*, *761*
  copper 9 817
  gold 9 817
  icons 28 *762*, *763*
  inscriptions 1 855
  manuscript illumination 28 *764*
  manuscripts 28 764–5*
  metalwork 9 818
  rock reliefs 9 779
  trade
    turquoise 9 786; 10 28
  see also MT SINAI
Sinai Gregory (MS) 9 *614*, 615
Sinaitic, Proto- *see under* SCRIPTS → types
Sinan (i) (shipwreck) 28 765*
  bronzes 6 864
  ceramics 4 173; 6 331; 28 765*
  stonewares 6 899
Sinan (ii) (*c*. 1500-88) 2 316; 16 143, 220, 221, 223; 28 766–9*
  architecture
    aqueducts 2 242; 16 585
    baths 3 376, *377*
    bridges 16 225
    caravanserais 5 *723*
    cisterns 16 608
    commercial buildings 9 730
    imarets 16 224
    mausolea 16 595
    mosque complexes 1 603; 9 730; 18 509; 21 50
    mosques 8 579; 9 86, *730*; 10 493; 14 886; 16 221, 222, *223*, *224*, 604; 22 196; 28 *766*, *767*, *768*
    palace buildings 16 610
    pavilions 16 499
  patrons and collectors 23 639, 641; 29 18
  pupils 1 474; 8 579; 21 50
Sinan, Koca *see* SINAN (ii)
Sinan Beg 16 348
Sinan Pasha 5 81, 398; 10 546; 16 291; 28 444
Sinas *see* FAFI
Sinas, Simon 13 359
Sinatra, Vincenzo 11 899; 16 640; 23 258; 28 769–70*
Sincency 11 605
Sin Cham 28 770*
Sinck, Lucas 1 801
Sinclair (Ballesteros), Alfredo 23 905; 28 770*
Sinclair, William, 3rd Earl of Orkney and 1st Earl of Caithness 27 170; 28 224, 268
Sinclairtown Pottery 28 258
Sincrai 26 719
Sind 1 887; 16 *105*
  mausoleum of Mirza ʿIsa Khan 15 372
Sindelfingen
  Galerie der Stadt Sindelfingen 18 114
  Lütze-Museum *see* Galerie der Stadt Sindlfingen
  St Martin 26 686
Sindicato de Arquitectos de Cataluna 31 184
Sindicato de Obreros Técnicos, Pintores y Escultores 21 405; 22 334; 26 426
Sindicato Fascista degli Artisti 10 821
sindicatul Artelor Frumoase *see* Fine Arts Union
Sindinera *see* SINNAR (INDIA)
Sinding, Otto Ludvig 28 770*
Sinding, Sigmund 28 770
Sinding, Stephan (Abel) 17 646; 23 230; 28 770–71*
Sinding-Larsen, Holger 22 319
Sinding-Larsen, Ståle 23 245
Sindos 13 598; 19 880
Sindt, Christian 2 825
Sind University *see under* JAMSHORO
Sinebrychoff, Paul 11 111
Sine-Ngayene 21 43
sinew 1 295; 3 440
Sinforiano Bogarín, Juan 24 101
Sing, Johann Kaspar 22 302; 29 398
Singapore 20 163, 164, 169; 28 771–5*, *771*; 29 *225*
  art forms and materials
    architecture 21 575; 28 771–4*
    calligraphy 6 772
    painting 28 774*
    pottery 28 775*
    sculpture 28 774–5*
    stained glass 28 772
  Assembly House *see* Parliament House
  Botanical Gardens 4 484; 12 103, 104
    Burkhill Hall 28 773
  Bukit Laranggam citadel 28 771
  churches
    Armenian Church of St Gregory 28 772
    Cathedral of St Andrew 28 772
    Cathedral of the Good Shepherd 28 772
    Chapel of St Joseph's Institution 28 772
    Chinese Presbyterian Church 28 772
    Church of Our Saviour 28 772
    St Andrew's 28 772
    St Bernadette 28 772
    St Ignatius 28 772
    Wesley Church 28 772
  Clock-Tower 28 772
  collections 7 154
    calligraphy 6 772
  Court House 28 772
  fortifications 21 575
  General Post Office 28 772
  Golden Bell 28 773
  Government House 28 772, 773
  houses 28 773–4, *773*
  Indoor Stadium 28 772
  Jurong Town Hall 28 772
  law courts 18 890
  mosques 28 772
    Abdul Gaffoor Mosque 28 772
    al-Abrar Mosque 28 772
    Darul Aman Mosque 28 772
    Jamae Mosque 28 772
    Sultan Mosque 28 772
  Municipal Building 28 772
  Nanyang Academy of Fine Arts 28 774
  National Museum 28 772; 29 240
  National Stadium 28 772
  National Trade Union Congress Conference Hall 28 772
  Parliament House 28 771
  People's Park 28 772
  Police Court 28 772
  Police Station 28 771
  Post Office 28 771, 772
  Raffles Institution *see* Singapore Institution
  Raffles Museum and Library *see* National Museum
  Singapore Institution 25 850
  Supreme Court 28 772
  temples 28 772–3
    Chee Tong Temple 28 772

Singapore
temples—cont.
Chettiar Temple **28** 773
Hong San See Temple **28** 772
Kong Meng San Phor Kark See Temple **28** 772
Siong Lim Temple **28** 772
Sri Mariamman Temple **28** 773
Sri Perumal Temple **28** 773
Sri Ruthra Kaliamman Temple **28** 773
Thian Hock Keng Temple **28** 772
Teo Hoo Lye **28** 773
Town Hall **28** 772
urban planning **28** 774*
Victoria Concert and Memorial Hall **28** 772
villas **28** 773
see also SOUTH-EAST ASIA
Singapore Arts **24** 425
Singaraja **15** 806, 807
Singburi **30** 609
Singer **30** 503
Singer, Cassian *see* SINGER, KASSIAN
Singer, Franz **2** 783; **28** 775*
Singer, Hans Wolfgang **10** 213
Singer, I. M., & Co. **15** 822; **30** 202
sewing-machines **15** *821*
Singer, Isaac **15** 822
Singer, Jakob (*fl* 1728-56; Austrian architect) **28** 775
Singer, Jakob (1718-88; Swiss architect) **28** 775*
Singer, Johann Anton **28** 775
Singer, Josef **28** 775*
Singer, Kassian **28** 775–6*
Singer, Paul **7** 108
Singer, Susi **31** 640
Singer, Winaretta, Princesse *see* SCEY-MONTBÉLIARD, WINARETTA SINGER, Princesse de
singeries **7** 168; **28** 776*, *776*
Singh, Arpita **8** 677; **15** 171; **28** 777*
Singh, Babbu **15** 711
Singh, Bhai Ram **14** 148
Singh, Bhupindra **5** 320
Singh, Kuldip **15** 169
Singh, Paramjeet **28** 777
Singh, Sardar Bhai Ram **15** 407; **22** 364
Singh, Shiv **15** 173
Singh, Sri Pratap, Museum *see under* SRINAGAR
Singh, Tara **15** 627
Singh, Zalim **24** 251
Singhasari **14** 560; **15** 781
Singher, Hans *see* DUYTSCHER, HANS DE
Singhpur **15** 496
Singidunum **3** 620; **28** 439
Singier, Gustave **3** 462; **19** 491; **28** 777*
Single-Grave culture **25** 514
Singleton, Henry **5** 216; **18** 887; **27** 565; **28** 777–8*
Singleton, William **28** 777
Singleton Copley, John *see* COPLEY, JOHN SINGLETON
Singleton Hall (W. Sussex) **14** 76
single-warp knots *see under* KNOTS → types
Singora **20** 179
Singüenza, Francisco Jiménez de *see* JIMÉNEZ DE SINGÜENZA, FRANCISCO
Sin Hak-ch'ŏl **18** 327
Sinhala **29** 449, 450
Sinhalese **29** 440, 441, 470
Sin Hŏn **18** 331
Sinhŭng Temple **18** 321
Sinibaldi, Bartolomeo *see* MONTELUPO, BACCIO DA
Sinibaldi, Raffaello da *see* MONTELUPO, RAFFAELLO DA
Sin Ik-sŏng **18** 329
Sinjar **16** 256; **21** 275
al-Sinkara, Tell *see* LARSA
sinking **12** 865; **16** 363; **21** 323
Sinkoti Church **12** 319
Sînmiclăuş **26** 707
Sinmun, King (*reg* 681-92) **18** 298
Sin Myŏng-yŏn **18** 317; **28** 759, 760*
Sinnar (India) **15** *276*, 316; **28** 778*
Ayeshvara Temple **15** 317
Gondeshvara Temple **15** 315, *315*, 316
Sinnar (Sudan) *see* SENNAR
Sinnicoară Crucifix **26** 719
Sinnicq, Gilbert van *see* ZINNICK, GILBERT VAN
Sino-Central Asia *see* CENTRAL ASIA, EASTERN
Sinolfo di Castellotteri **1** 621
Sinop **28** 778
Saray Mosque **16** 202
Süleyman Pervane Madrasa **16** 184
Sinope **4** 110, 112, 113
Sinope Gospels *see under* GOSPEL BOOKS → individual manuscripts
sinopia see under PIGMENTS → types
sinopie **9** 214; **11** 763; **13** 556; **22** 156; **28** 778–9*, *778*; **32** 802, 805
see also UNDERDRAWINGS
Sinsabaugh, Art(hur Reeder) **28** 779*
Sinsacate, Jesuit mission **2** 394
Sin Sa-im-dang **18** 317, 329; **33** 523–4*
works **33** *524*
Sin-Shar-Ishkun (*reg* ?-612 BC) **2** 638, 641; **21** 290, 302; **23** 151
Sinskul'ptarkh *see* ZHIVSKUL'PTARKH
Sinssheim, Conrat von *see* SIFER, CONRAT
Sin Suk-chu **18** 259
Sîntămărie Church **26** 710
Sintana de Mureş **26** 710
Sintenis, Renée **28** 779*
Sint-Kruis, Monastery of St Truiden **13** 113
Sint-Martens-Latem *see* LAETHEM-SAINT-MARTIN
Sint Niklaas, Onze Lieve Vrouwekerk **3** 548
Sint Odilienberg **26** 631
Sintra **25** *288*, 318; **28** 779–81*
Monserrate Palace **25** 293
Palácio Nacional **25** 308; **28** 780, *780*; **30** 879, 880
Palácio da Pena **10** 496–7; **25** 293, 304
Palácio de Seteais **12** 125; **24** 810
Palácio da Vila *see* Palácio Nacional
Quinta de São Sebastião **24** 811
Quinta do Relôgio **25** 293
stained glass **13** 192
Sint-Truiden **3** *539*
Abbey **3** 552; **8** 257; **12** 469; **26** 666
Begijnhof **3** 504
marks **3** 601
Onze Lieve Vrouwekerk **13** 110
silver **3** 598
tapestries **3** 606
Sintzenich, Heinrich **3** 309; **29** 676
Sintzig, Johann Wilhelm von **13** 683
Sinú **28** 781–2*
gold **28** *781*
lost-wax casting **28** *781*
metalwork **29** 211, 213
musical instruments **29** 217
pendants (jewellery) **28** *781*
pottery **29** 150
Sinu Carib **29** 132
Sinulfo di Castel Ottieri **20** 521
Sinurin **5** 741
Sin Wi **18** 325, 331; **28** 759–60*
Sinyavsky, M. I. **3** 287; **22** 174
Sin Yun-bok **28** 782*
works **18** 257, 320, *320*
Sinzendorf (family) **3** 488
Sinzendorf, Count **5** 772
Sinzig Church **12** 364
Sio **24** 84
Sion
Cathedral of Notre-Dame
metalwork **5** 806
organ shutters **23** 500, *500*
textiles **9** 668; **18** 157
silk **9** 664
Sion Gospels *see under* GOSPEL BOOKS → individual manuscripts
Sioni Cathedral *see under* ATENI
Sion Treasure **9** 656, *656*
Siopis, Penelope **29** 109
Siot-Decauville **11** 629
Sioux **22** 552, 584, 592, 629, 642, 649, 650, 655, 669, 673
dolls **31** 260
Sioux (Santee) **22** 585, 649
Sioux (Yankton) **22** 649
Sioux Indian Museum *see under* RAPID CITY (SD)
Sipahi **15** 629
Sipán **31** 116
Siphnos **8** *304*
ceramics **13** 358
copper **8** 323
sculpture **14** 455
silver **13** 568
Sipinen, Arto **11** 92
Siponto, Cathedral of S Maria Maggiore di Siponto **26** 626; **30** 777
Sippar **1** 508, *849*; **3** 11; **20** 361; **21** *267*, 268, 274; **28** 782–3*
architecture **21** 291
fortifications **21** 552
religion **21** 277
seals **1** *860*, 861; **28** 783
stelae **1** 509
temple **19** 311
Siptah (*reg c.* 1198-*c.* 1193 BC) **9** *777*; **10** 80
Siqueira, Nuno José de **19** 468
Siqueiros, David Alfaro **10** 505; **14** 589; **21** 387, 388, 397, 403, 405; **23** 566, 578; **25** 653; **28** 783–6*; **29** 670
assistants **3** 625; **6** 10; **13** 837; **25** 166; **28** 730
collaboration **13** 796; **15** 172; **26** 522
groups and movements **21** 387; **26** 426
methods **1** 129; **22** 335; **28** 339
patrons and collectors **21** 395; **31** 757
pupils **12** 55; **19** 725; **24** 104
works **14** 785; **15** 830; **21** 380; **22** 334; **25** 24, 653; **28** *784*, *785*, 920; **33** 364
Siracusa *see* SYRACUSE (SICILY)
Siraf **13** 328; **16** *105*; **28** 786*
architecture **16** 142
ceramics **6** 915, 917
congregational mosque **16** 153, 400
excavations **16** 550
glass **16** 517
houses **16** 154
kilns **16** 398
mosques **16** 154
pottery **16** 397, 398, 399, 400, 401
stelae **29** 618
Sir Ahmed, Tag el **29** 896
śirahpaṭṭī **15** 244*
Siranes **23** 202
Sirani, Anna Maria **28** 787
Sirani, Barbara **28** 787
Sirani, Elisabetta **16** 780; **28** 787–8*; **33** 308
patrons and collectors **12** 559; **31** 307
pupils **7** 857
works **10** 476; **28** *787*
Sirani, Giovanni Andrea **5** 651; **24** 226; **26** 200; **27** 486; **28** 787
Şirato, Francisc **26** 715; **28** 788*
Sirbegović, Kemal **4** 461
Sircello, Guy **10** 692
Sirel, Nejat **31** 454
Sirén, Hannu **11** 101
Sirén, Heikki **11** 92; **14** 372; **19** 434; **28** 788–9*
Sirén, J(ohan) S(igfrid) **11** 92; **14** 371; **24** 778; **28** 788*
Sirén, Kaija **11** 92; **14** 372; **19** 434; **28** 788–9*
Sirén, Osvald **27** 720; **28** 789*; **30** 120; **33** 89
works **2** 539; **7** 161
Siren Painter **13** 485
Siret (family) **19** 704
Siret, Holy Trinity Church **26** 707
Sireuil **25** 488
Sireul, Jean-Claude Gaspard de **4** 517; **28** 789–90*
Sirhandi, Khalid **23** 804
Sirhandi, Marcella **23** 804
Siri *see under* DELHI
Siriès, Carlo **28** 790
Siriès, Cosimo **28** 790
Siriès, Louis (1743-1811) **28** 790
Siriès, Louis (*c.* 1686-after 1766) **11** 636; **12** 262; **28** 790*; **33** 691
Siriès, Violante Beatrice **11** 743; **28** 790
Sirigatti, Lorenzo **32** 860
Sirigatti, Ridolfo **3** 827; **4** 408; **21** 768
Sirignano, Giuseppe Caravita, Prince of **8** 463; **16** 721
Sirikit, Queen (*b* 1932) **30** 622
Sirikye **1** 229
el-Siririya **29** 386
Sirissea, Marino di **26** 269
Sirius **8** 433
Sirjan **16** 397, 400, 401
Sirkap *see under* TAXILA
Sirks, Jan **29** 397
Sirleto *see* SIRLETTI
Sirletti, Carlo (i) (*b* 1753) **28** 790
Sirletti, Carlo (ii) (*b* 1818) **28** 791
Sirletti, Filippo **28** 790*
Sirletti, Flavio **12** 261, 262; **28** 790*
Sirletti, Francesco **28** 790*
Sirletti, Gioacchino **28** 790
Sirletti, Giovanni (i) (*b* 1723) **28** 790*
Sirletti, Giovanni (ii) (*b c.* 1788) **28** 790
Sirletti, Pietro **28** 790
Sirletti, Raimondo **28** 790*
Sirletto *see* SIRLETTI
Sirmione **16** *618*; **26** 897; **28** 791*
Sirmium *see under* SREMSKA MITROVICA
Siro, Lorenzo **10** 804
Sirocco Screenprints **20** 609
Sirois, Pierre **12** 489; **24** 255; **32** 914
Sirolli, Renato **21** 528
Sironi, Mario **11** 843; **16** 680; **28** 792–3*
collaboration **19** 421; **20** 905; **22** 393; **23** 263
exhibitions **10** 821, 822
groups and movements **5** 849; **10** 821; **11** 866; **16** 680; **20** 522; **21** 528; **23** 263; **25** 6
patrons and collectors **7** 782; **20** 848
works **11** 843; **16** 681, 708; **22** 332; **25** 652; **28** *792*
writings **27** 889
Siroto, Leon **1** 231
Sirpur **15** *223*, *279*, *285*, *294*; **28** 793*
Archaeological Museum **15** 181
Lakshmana Temple **15** 284, *284*, 494
Rama Temple **15** 284
Sirsa **15** 484
Sirsukh *see under* TAXILA
Sirval **15** 300, 527
Sirwah **2** *246*
Temple of Almaqah **2** 252, 253
Siryaqus **16** 208
Sis *see* KOZAN
sisal **1** 296; **11** 54
Sisala **5** 328
Sisal de Valladolid Monastery **33** 571
Sisapu **24** 795
Si Satchanalai **28** 793–4*; **29** *225*; **30** *571*
architecture **30** 582
ceramics **30** 608, 611–12
pottery **29** 236
stucco **30** 603
Wat Chang Lom **28** 794; **29** 866; **30** *583*, 584, 612
Wat Chang Rop **30** 584
Wat Chedi Chet Thaeo **30** 583
Wat Sorasak **30** 584
Wat Suan Kaeo Uthayan Noi **30** 584, *584*
Síscara, Juan **27** 532; **31** 588
works **27** *532*
Sise, Hazen **23** 632
Sisian **2** 434
St Hovhannes **2** 434
Sisibek
sarcophagus **27** *824*
Siskind, Aaron **6** 577; **28** 794*
groups and movements **1** 83, 85, 86; **4** 110; **24** 685
pupils **16** 84
Sisley, Alfred **28** 794–7*
dealers **4** 589; **9** 424; **26** 107
exhibitions **10** 680
groups and movements **8** 621; **15** 151, 152, 153, 154, 155
methods **7** 629
paintings **22** 687
landscape **18** 716; **28** *795*
marine **20** 426
townscapes **15** VII; **28** *796*
patrons and collectors
Barnes, Albert C. **3** 251; **12** 769
Bellio, Georges de **26** 722
Burrell, William (1861-1958) **5** 278
Caillebotte, Gustave **5** 391
Camondo, Isaac de, Comte **5** 530
Coquelin, Ernest **7** 832
Duret, (Jules-Emmanuel) Théodore **9** 448
Faure, Jean-Baptiste **10** 837
FitzGerald, Desmond **11** 141
Havemeyer, Louisine (Waldron) **14** 244
Lambert, Catholina **18** 672
Lurcy, Georges **24** 183
Moreau-Nélaton, Etienne **22** 93
Morozov, Ivan (Abramovich) (1871-1921) **22** 136
Palmer, Bertha Honoré **23** 882
Phillips, Duncan **24** 638
Shchukin, Sergey (Ivanovich) **28** 569
Silvestre (ii), (Paul-) Armand **28** 744
Tavernier, Adolphe-Eugène **30** 375
Van Horne, William (Cornelius) **31** 880
Vever, Henri **32** 394
Zambaccian, K. H. **26** 723
prints **19** 489
teachers **12** 810
Sisojevac **22** 79
Sisopo *see* SISAPU

Sisovath, King of Cambodia (*reg* 1904-27) 5 482
Sissinghurst Castle (Kent) 12 142
Sisson, Marshall (Arnott) 28 798*
sissoo 25 303, 305
Sistan 15 901, 902, 905; 16 370, 414
Siste 27 244
Sisti, Nicolo 11 191; 16 736
Sistine Chapel *see under* ROME (VATICAN) → Palace
Sistine Madonna 3 924; 9 188; 14 314; 16 664; 25 903; 27 496
Sisto di Firenze 9 111
Siston, St Anne 26 688
sistra 10 48, 64; 22 372
Śiśunāga *see* SAISUNAGA
Sisupalgarh 3 909; 15 248, *279*; 28 798*
Sisuro, Wirot 30 446
Sisyphus Painter 13 526
works 13 *527*
Sit, Ventura 4 560; 27 754; 29 331
Sitagroi 25 517
Sitamun 10 52; 30 775
Sitaram 15 612
sitars 22 376
Sitavaka 29 450
SITE 25 359; 28 798–9*
works 4 790; 19 286; 27 323; 28 *799*
Síteia
Folklore Museum 8 157
Síteia Museum 8 157
Sitemu 3 45
Sitges 27 350
Sithathoriunet 10 30, 52, 66, 90; 22 284
pectoral ornaments 10 *30*
Si Thep 30 *571*, 576, 577, 580, 592
Sithole, Lucas 29 112
Sitifis *see* SÉTIF
Sitio Conte 28 799–800*; 29 *136*
bowls 29 *147*
gold 7 507
metalwork 29 213
mirrors 21 718
pendants (jewellery) 29 *151*
pottery 7 507
trays 7 *506*
Sitka 1 95
Sitnikov, Aleksandr 27 397
Sitorai-Makhi-khossa 29 822
Sittannavasal Jaina Temple 15 543, 559; 32 804
Sittard 3 580; 22 856; 25 500
church 22 821
Sitte, Camillo 28 800–802*
pupils 23 393
works 23 424; 28 *801*, *802*
writings 31 727
Sitte, Franz 22 273; 28 800
Sitte, Willi 28 802–3*
Sittingbourne (Kent), Borden Hall 10 272
Sittow, Michel 3 554; 9 274; 28 803–4*
attributions 10 538
patrons and collectors 8 758; 13 905; 23 395
works 8 731; 11 466; 17 674; 28 *804*
Sittwe 2 282; 5 241, 247
Situation 7 529; 10 258; 14 816; 19 591; 22 279; 28 804–5*
situlae 28 805–7*
historical and regional traditions
Este art 10 528
Germany 28 *805*
Hallstatt culture (*c*. 750-*c*. 450 BC) 28 806
Italy 28 806, *807*
Ottonian 23 659–60; 28 *805*
Prehistoric art 28 806*, *806*, *807*
Rhodes (island) 13 515
Slovenia 28 806, *806*
materials
bronze 28 *806*
situlae
materials—cont.
ivory 23 659–60; 28 *805*
see also BUCKETS
Situlpavuva 29 458
Sitwell (family) 3 447; 28 508; 33 627
Sitwell, Edith (Louisa) 28 808*
Sitwell, George 28 808*
Sitwell, (Francis) Osbert (Sacheverell) 14 120; 28 808*
Sitwell, Sacheverell 28 808*
Siunik' 2 426
Siuntio Church 11 94
Siūt *see* ASYUT
Sivaramamurti, Calambur 15 211; 28 808*
Sivas 16 *104*; 28 808–9*
architecture 16 202
Buruciye Madrasa 16 184
carpets 2 439; 16 479
Çifte Minareli Madrasa 22 323, *323*
Gök Madrasa *see* Museum
Great Mosque 16 183
Güdük Minare Türbesi 16 204
hospital of ʿIzz al-Din Kayka'us 16 184, 247
Museum 16 184, 247; 28 809
Sive, André 12 871; 25 663; 28 809*
Sivers, Angelica von 11 106
Sivert, Denis 29 332
Siviero, Carlo 2 214
Sivisa Church 5 675
Sívori, Eduardo 2 399, 405; 28 809–10*
pupils 32 415
Sivrihisar
church 5 675
congregational mosque 16 202, 497
Siwa Oasis 9 *774*, 834; 28 810*
Six, Collectie *see under* AMSTERDAM → museums
Six, Jan (1618-1700) 9 179; 22 902; 26 *163*; 28 810*
collections 22 904
drawings 26 164, 166, 176; 27 270
etchings 14 795; 27 271
paintings 18 820; 26 284
sculpture 11 170; 26 284; 32 155
Six, Jan (*fl* 1692-1707) 29 116
Six, Les 3 119, 120; 7 508
Six, Willem 25 631
Six and Four Art Club 11 59
Six Associates 22 671
Sixdeniers, Alexandre Vincent 19 115
Sixdeniers, Christiaan 3 545
Six Kiowas 22 63
Six Masters 16 283
Six Old Kilns 9 697; 17 259
Six Orthodox Masters 23 579–81
Six Pens *see under* SCRIPTS → types
Six's technique 23 145
Sixtus III, Pope (*reg* 432-40) 3 189; 28 810*
architecture 16 624, 761; 26 752, 831, 832
frescoes 24 521–2
silver 6 173
Sixtus IV, Pope (*reg* 1471-84) 21 *96*; 26 800, 844; 27 271–2*
architecture 7 218; 16 631, 632; 25 216; 26 756, 811, 815
art policies 16 768
collections 26 767, 768
frescoes 21 96; 28 700, 701
manuscripts 2 186; 12 655
museums 27 45
painting 4 494; 16 661; 26 765, 766
sculpture 2 162, 168; 27 114; 29 402
textiles 2 632; 16 836
urban planning 24 398
Sixtus V, Pope (*reg* 1585-90) 12 912; 24 397–9*; 26 841
architecture 8 513; 11 270, 271–3; 18 699; 19 313; 24 397; 26 747, 757–8, 769, 811, 814, 818, 819, 832, 840; 29 82
urban planning 11 *271*
art policies 1 102
education (art) 16 779
frescoes 8 182
medals 4 323; 25 76
models 32 660
obelisks 23 330
paintings 1 552; 4 840; 13 795; 19 383; 22 715; 32 658
sculpture 2 139; 26 791
tombs 29 82
Siyah Qalam 16 328; 28 811*
works 16 131, *132*, 137, 328
Siyavush 16 337; 22 391; 28 811–12*; 32 148
Siyavuş Pasha 12 84; 16 348
Siysk Gospel *see under* GOSPEL BOOKS → individual manuscripts
Siyu 30 57
Siza, Alvaro 25 880; 30 375
Siza Vieira, Alvaro 25 294; 28 812*
size 28 812–13*
historical and regional traditions
Egypt, ancient 9 898
Islamic 16 352
Japan 17 140
materials
alum 28 813
chalk 28 310
formalin 28 813
glycerin 28 813
honey 28 813
kaolin 28 310
lime 28 310
skins 28 310
vinegar 28 813
uses
canvas 5 654; 13 706
consolidants 7 747
gesso 12 501
gilding 6 328; 12 628, 629; 24 55; 28 813
grounds 13 706; 28 812
painting 17 140
paints 32 898
paper 15 850; 16 352; 24 38, 44, 55; 28 813
scrolls 28 310
sealants 25 174
silk 15 850
wall paintings 9 898
wallpaper 32 812
see also GLUES
Sizergh Castle (Cumbria) 10 272
SJA 3D Co. Ltd 17 686
Sjlev, Mihailo 19 884
Sjöberg, Petter Adolf 30 107
Sjonhem Church 13 190
Sjoo, Monica 10 483; 28 813*
groups and movements 10 878, 879
works 12 217
Sjöstrand, Carl Eneas 28 813–14*
pupils 27 337; 30 258; 31 828
works 11 99
Sjöström, Cyril *see* MARDALL, CYRIL
Sjöström, Frans Anatolius 14 371; 19 411; 23 326
Skagen 1 845; 4 105, 807; 8 *720*, 735; 12 296; 14 572; 18 463, 469, 470, 717; 23 162; 24 550; 28 814*; 30 647; 31 485
Hotel Brøndum 28 814
painting 17 605
Skagens Museum 1 845; 8 760; 28 814
Skagerfors, Olle 30 81
Skaill 32 517, 530
Skal, Hubertus von 12 451
Skala 17 909
Skala: Nordisk magasin for arkitektur og kunst 24 451
Skalica Church 28 849
Skalk 24 451
Skallerup 25 526–7
Skälvum 26 639
Skånberg, Carl (Emmerick) 28 814–15*
Skandagupta, Ruler (*reg c*. 455-67) (Gupta) 15 738
Skandar, Tepe 1 *186*, 199, 211
skandhavedī 15 245*
Skanes Tourist Centre 1 320
Skånska Glasbruk 30 102
Skąpska, Barbara 29 743
Skara 30 106, 111
Cathedral 13 102; 26 639
Skara Brae (Orkney) 25 *470*; 28 *222*, 815*
architecture 25 503; 28 223, 815
House 1 28 *815*
rock art 25 511
Skarah Dheri 15 446, 448
skaramangia 9 252, 641
Skarbek, Ignacy 19 752
Skarbina, Franz 12 394; 32 244
Skarðsbók (Reykjavík, Arnamagnean Inst., AM 350 folio) 15 69, *69*
Skare, Giovanni Gregori de *see* SCHARDT, JOHANN GREGOR VAN DER
Skarnos, Jurij 28 862
Skaryna, Francysk 3 528; 28 815–16*
Skarzhynska, K. 31 565
Skatins Robe 22 *621*
Skattunge Altarpiece 13 120
Skaun Church 11 465
Skavronsky, Y. 24 458
Skawina majolica factory 18 822
Skeaping, John Rattenbury 14 400–401; 19 623; 29 426; 33 23
Skeen, William Louis Henry 10 580; 28 816*
Skeena River - Prince Rupert Harbour 22 *544*; 28 816*
Skeibrok, Mathias 10 105; 23 230; 32 497
skeleton clocks *see under* CLOCKS → types
Skellefteå Church 11 99; 26 647
Skellern, Victor 33 23
Skellig Michael 16 *5*, 6; 28 816–17*
Skelmorlie 28 241
Aisle mausoleum 28 245
Skelton, Jonathan 13 302; 18 672; 28 817*; 32 900
Skelton, Joseph 9 31
Skelton, Robert 15 212
skene
skene see scaenae
Skepidis, Michael 5 678
Skerin Langberg, Harald 8 761
Skerne 23 536
Skerryvore Lighthouse 19 361
sketchbooks
individual manuscripts
Antwerp Sketchbook (Chatsworth, Derbys) 9 476
Bergamo Sketchbook (Bergamo, Bib. Civ. A. Mai, MS. D. vii. 14) 13 149; 24 270
Coner Sketchbook (London, Soane Mus.) 2 596
Dresden Sketchbook (Vienna, Österreich. Nbib., Cod. vind. min. 3) 9 243*
Errera Sketchbook (Brussels, Mus. A. Anc.) 7 499; 21 360
Fairfax Murray Sketchbook (New York, Pierpont Morgan Lib., MS. M. 86) 24 269
Italian Sketchbook (London, BM) 9 478, 480, 484, 485
Madrid Codex (Madrid, Bib. N. MS. 8936) 10 441
sketchbooks
individual manuscripts—cont.
Roman Sketchbook (Basle, Bib. Öffentlicher Kstsamml., MS. U.iv.6-U.iv.29) 11 220
Schultz-Codex (Leipzig, Mus. Ksthandwks) 14 766
Travelling Sketchbook 31 807
Venetian Sketchbook (London, BM, L. B. 13) 26 271
Vienna Sketchbook (Vienna, Albertina, Cim Kasten, Fach 6 no. 55) 32 462–3*
Zoubaloff Sketchbook (Paris, Louvre) 12 350
Sketch Club 2 130; 15 834
see also CENTURY CLUB
sketch clubs 32 902–3*
sketches 1 582; 19 *585*; 24 350; 28 817*
see also DOODLES; DRAWINGS; MODELLI; PENSIERO PRIMO; OIL SKETCHES; SUR LE MOTIF
sketches, oil *see* OIL SKETCHES
Sketching Society (England) 12 742
Sketching Society (Japan) *see* FYŪZANKAI (SKETCHING SOCIETY)
Skevra 2 442, 444
Monastery 2 430
skew arches *see under* ARCHES → types
skiagraphia see under DRAWINGS → techniques
skias 30 736
Skibet Church 8 730
Skidmore, Francis, the elder 10 335; 13 209; 28 278, 279
Skidmore, Francis, the younger 10 335
Skidmore, Francis Alexander 30 533
Skidmore, Louis 28 817*
Skidmore, M. & G. 11 119
Skidmore, Owings & Merrill (SOM) 2 315; 3 682; 14 803; 28 817–18*; 31 738
architecture 2 742; 12 874; 14 203; 25 5; 26 353; 29 456; 31 597, 598
airports 1 *495*; 30 469
banks 3 177; 13 *762*, 763; 27 731
galleries (iv) (art) 5 124
hotels 7 326; 14 788
office buildings 12 792; 15 *887*; 19 578; 23 43, 258, 359
skyscrapers 17 603; 28 834, *834*; 29 106; 31 242
collaboration 2 216, 217; 3 682; 6 574; 16 587; 24 826; 31 452
groups and movements 15 887
staff
Ardalan, Nader 2 378
Bunshaft, Gordon 5 175
Goldsmith, Myron 12 873
Jackson, Daryl 16 819
Johansen, John M(aclane) 17 605
Maki, Fumihiko 20 147
Meier, Richard (Alan) 21 56
Okada, Shin'ichi 23 385
Smith, Adrian D. 4 476
Tigerman, Stanley 30 869
Vignelli, Lella 32 500
Weese, Harry (Mohr) 33 29
Skidmore's Art Manufactures 30 266
Skien, Fylkesmuseet for Telemark og Grenland 23 231
Skikda Museum 1 636
Skilleman, Adriaen 20 731
Skillin (family) 28 613
Skillin, John (Simeon) 3 38; 4 479; 28 818–19*; 31 610
Skillin, Samuel 28 818–19*
Skillin, Simeon, sr (1716-78) 28 818; 31 610

Skillin, Simeon, jr (1756-1806) **3** 38; **28** 818–19*; **31** 610
Skillitzi, Stephen **2** 763
Šķilters, Gustavs **12** 825
Skinner, Bailey & Lubetkin **30** 411
Skinner, E. **29** 454
 works **29** *454*
Skinner, Francis **20** 475; **30** 411
Skinner, Halcyon **5** 832
Skinner, James **15** 208, 655
Skinner, John **31** 651
Skinner, Peter **25** 399
Skinner, Samuel **2** 759
Skinner, William **28** 227
Skinner & Dyke **10** 366; **19** 587
skins **19** 1
 historical and regional traditions
  Aboriginal Australia **1** 56*
  Africa **1** 295, 418
  Aztec **21** 252
  Ejagham **10** 122, *122*
  Japan **17** 305
  Mesoamerica, Pre-Columbian **21** 234, 245, 252, 257, 261
  Mesopotamia **1** 883
  Native North Americans **22** 654–5*
 techniques
  dyeing **9** 490
 types
  bird **22** 653
  calfskin **1** 299
  deerskin **21** 233; **22** 654, *654*; **31** 260
  goatskin **19** 1; **24** 106
   Africa **1** 299, 307, *307*
   Egypt **16** *357*
   Fulani **1** *307*
   Islamic **16** *357*
   Libya **19** 3
   Niger **1** *307*
   Syria **16** *357*
  kangaroo **2** *758*
  kid-skin **31** 260, 262
  leopard **3** 145; **6** 305
  lizard **24** 69
  possum **1** 56*
  python **3** 145
  rabbit **31** 282
  sheepskin **24** 106
   Africa **1** 299
   Central Asia, Western **6** 251
   Native North Americans **22** 654
  tiger **6** 305
  uterine **24** 106
  yaks **28** 310
 uses
  armour **6** 305; **21** 246
  baskets **1** 295
  cloaks **1** 56*; **20** *358*
  costumes **1** 418
  dolls **31** 260, 262
  dress **6** 251
  drums (musical instruments) **24** 69
  glues **15** 850; **31** 282
  helmets **21** 245
  inks **15** 850
  manuscripts **21** 234
  masks **10** 122, *122*; **21** 252
  musical instruments **21** 257
  panel paintings **24** 4
  parchment **24** 106
  size **28** 310
  tents **1** 307
  textiles **17** 305; **21** 261
  upholstery **2** *758*
 see also HIDES; LEATHER
Skiold, Birgit **10** 178; **20** 609
Skippe, John **28** 819*; **33** 367
Skipper, G. (1856-1948) **23** 248
Skipper, G., jr (*fl* 1960s) **23** 248
Skipper, Matcham **2** 766
Skipper, Peter **28** 819*
Skira, Albert **20** 208, 829; **24** 453; **28** 819–20*; **32** 234
 printmakers **3** 450; **24** 726; **26** 236
Skira, Albert—cont.
 staff **26** 44; **30** 488
 works **4** 366; **8** 775; **24** 721
Skirbeck (Lincs), Rochford Tower **4** 779
skirts
 historical and regional traditions
  Africa **1** *410*
  China **7** 76, 77, 78
  England **9** 276
  France **9** 276
  Iran **16** 466
  Islamic **16** 466
  Japan **17** 375
  Kuba (iii) (Zaïre) **1** 295, 348
  Laos **18** 772, 773, 774
  Native North Americans **22** 652
  Tanzania **1** *410*
  Thailand **30** *626*
  Zulu **33** 724
 materials
  appliqué **30** *626*
  beadwork **1** *410*; **3** 442
  cotton **30** *626*
  embroidery **30** *626*
  feathers **22** 652
  leather **1** *410*; **33** 724
  raffia **1** 295
 types
  hooped **9** 264, 278
Skirving, Archibald **28** 237
Skislewicz, Anton **21** 421
 works **21** *421*
Skitnik, Syrak **5** 155, 163; **28** 820*
Skjaak, Ola Rasmussen **23** 242
Skjeberg **26** 639
 Centre for the Blind *see* Storedal Kultursenter
 Storedal Kultursenter **14** 229
Skjöldebrand, Anders Fredrik **30** 80
Sklarzska Poreba **8** 409
Sklaverokhori, Hagios Georgios **8** 156
Sklavos, Yerasimos **13** 355; **28** 820–21*
Sklenář, Zdeněk **20** 254
Sklenoteplice Glassworks **15** 3
Sklėrius, Kajetonas **19** 498
Skoczylas, Władysław **11** 317; **18** 507; **26** 296; **32** 877
Skoda, R. **19** 111
Skoda Works **8** 428
Škofja Loka **28** *858*
 ceramics **28** 862
 church **28** 858
 convent of the Ursulines **28** 863
 sculpture **28** 862
Skokloster **30** *65*, 109
 Castle **30** 69; **33** 622
  interior decoration **10** 458; **11** 468
  paintings **2** 730; **33** 421
  stucco **2** 95
 parish church **1** 898; **13** 118; **29** 840
  chapel of General Herman Wrangel **30** 85
Sköld, Otte **28** 51, 821*; **30** 52, 81
Skookum Glass **5** 583
Skopas **13** 394, 459; **27** 29, 31, 692; **28** 821–2*
 attributions **22** 729
 collaboration **5** 64; **19** 170
 copies **23** 157
 works **10** 431; **12** 250; **13** 423, 425, 426; **14** 69; **18** 148; **24** 205; **30** 413
 workshop **13** 460
Skopelos **13** 358
Skopin **27** 411
Skopje **9** *511*; **16** *103*; **19** *882*; **28** 440, 822–3*
 Archaeological Museum of Macedonia **19** 886; **28** 823
 Art Gallery **19** 882, 886; **28** 823
 Chamber of Commerce **19** 883
 Daut-Pasha Amam baths *see* Art Gallery
Skopje—cont.
 District Labour Insurance Building **19** 883
 Ethnographical Museum **19** 886
 Girls' Lyceum **19** 883
 Governor's Palace **19** 883
 Historical Museum **28** 823
 Ibni Pajko Building **19** 883
 Main Post Office **19** 883
 Market Centre **19** 883
 Museum of Contemporary Art **28** 823
 National Bank **19** 883
 Radio Skopje Building **19** 883
 St Andrew **19** 882, 884; **28** 447
 St Niketas **28** 446
 St Saviour **19** *884*
 School for Applied Arts **19** 885
 Suli Han caravanserai **19** 882
 Sultan Murat Mosque **19** 882
 wall paintings **19** 884
Skopljak, Mustafa **4** 462
Skordilis, Emmanouil (*fl* 1651-80) **1** 482
Skordylis, Antonios **25** 334
Skordylis, Emmanuel (*fl* late 18th cent.) **25** 334
Skordylis, Ioannis (*fl* 1729-40) **25** 334
Skórewicz, Kazimierz **23** 113
Skorina, Frantsisk *see* SKARYNA, FRANCYSK
Skorodumov, Gavriil (Ivanovich) **27** 389; **28** 823*; **29** 676
 works **29** *676*
Skorodumov, Ivan **28** 823
Škorpil, Hermingild **5** 163
Škorpil, Josef **25** 54
Škorpil, Karel Václav **5** 163
Skosana, Christina
 works **1** *313*
Skotarek, Władysław **26** 266
Skoteino **8** 153
Skoteinos, George **8** 364
Skotnes, Cecil **1** 433; **17** 603; **28** 823–4*
 pupils **18** 514; **20** 368; **29** 112
 works **29** 108, 110
Skotnes, Pippa **29** 110
Skotnicki, Jarosław Bogoria, Archbishop of Gniezno **12** 823
Skottorp Manor **30** 96
Skouphos, Philotheos **25** 334
Skovgaard, Joakim (Frederik) **8** 735, 755; **11** 790; **14** 572; **28** 824*
Skovgaard, Niels (Kristian) **8** 735; **11** 790; **28** 824–5*
Skovgaard, P(eter) C(hristian Thamsen) **8** 735; **14** 543, 572; **28** 824*
 pupils **28** 824
 works **28** *824*
Skovkloster *see under* NÆSTVED
Skovorodko, Church of Michael the Archangel **27** 383
Skramlík, J. **8** 401
Skredsvig, Christian **28** 825–6*
 groups and movements **23** 225; **28** 814
 works **28** *825*
Škréta, Karel (Šotnovský ze Závořic) **25** 432; **28** 826–7*
 reproductive prints by others **18** 45
 works **8** 390, *391*; **25** 436; **28** *827*
Škréta group **1** 604
Skriblyak (family) **31** 564
Skrīde, Ārijs **25** 745
Skripou *see under* ORCHOMENOS
Skrwilno **25** 127
Skryabin, Aleksandr **22** 380; **29** 97; **30** 684
Skrzyński (family) **18** 691
sku 'bum *see* KUMBUM
Skudrian **1** 886
Skúlason, Thorvaldur **15** 70; **18** 543; **28** 828*
Skull, Edwin **14** 522
Skull, Walter **14** 522
skullcaps **32** 390*
skull-posts **24** 79
skull racks
 Mesoamerica, Pre-Columbian **1** 701; **21** 188; **31** 505–6*, *506*; **33** 101
 Mexico **31** *506*
 Papua New Guinea **24** 78, *78*
 Toltec **1** 701; **31** 99
skulls
 historical and regional traditions
  Maya **21** 248
  Mesoamerica, Pre-Columbian **21** 248; **31** 505–6
  Papua New Guinea **24** 84
  Syria-Palestine **30** 181, 192
   Pre-pottery Neolithic B (*c.* 7000–*c.* 6000 BC) **17** *484*
  Vanuatu **31** *891*
 uses
  headdresses **31** *891*
  masks **24** 84
skull troughs **15** 754
Skulme, Oto **26** 384
Skulme, Uga **26** 384
Skultuna **30** 110, 111
Skum, Nils Nilsson **27** 472
Skunder *see* BOGHOSSIAN, ALEXANDER
Skupi *see* SKOPJE
Skupina 42 *see* GROUP 42
Skurjeni, Matija **22** 441
Skursky, George **31** 787
Skutecký, Dominik **28** 853
Skuttunge Church **30** 865
Sky, Alison **28** 798
sky art **24** 744; **28** 828–9*, *829*
sky-domes *see under* DOMES → types
Skye **29** 702
Skylitzes, John *see* JOHN SKYLITZES
Skylitzes Chronicle *see under* CHRONICLES → individual manuscripts
Skyllis **8** 457; **13** 439, 596; **25** 44
Skymnos **18** 460
skyphoi **13** 476, 492; **19** *841*; **28** 830*
 Attic **13** *475*, 476
 Corinthian **13** *475*, 476
 cup *see* CUP-SKYPHOI
 Kabeiric **13** 533
Skyros **13** 357, 358
skyscrapers **7** 764, 765, 766; **28** 830–35*
 historical and regional traditions
  Australia **2** 742; **28** *375*, 834
  Brazil **14** 295; **21** 631
  England **24** *343*
  Germany **28** 834, 835
  Hong Kong **14** *720*
  Japan **17** 90
  South Africa **29** 106
  United States of America **5** 175; **7** 326; **11** 144; **12** 643; **17** 477; **18** 54; **23** 41; **25** 327; **28** 831–3*; **31** 594, 595, 596, 597, 662
   Art Deco **28** *629*, *833*
   International Style **5** *136*
   Post-modernism **25** *359*
   19th cent. **5** 126; **28** *832*; **29** *914*; **30** *506*; **31** *594*
   20th cent. **6** *574*; **11** 25; **12** *614*; **14** 200, *735*, *803*; **23** *44*; **26** *488*; **28** *834*; **30** *507*
 materials
  concrete **7** 326
  steel **31** 594, *594*
Skythes **10** 474; **13** 519
Slaatto, Nils **19** 798*
Slabbinck, Rik **17** 518
slab-construction *see under* POTTERY → techniques
slab stelae *see under* STELAE → types
slab tombs *see under* TOMBS → types
Slade, Felix **11** 738
Slade School of Fine Art *see under* LONDON → art schools
Sladka Gora Church **28** 859
Slager, Petrus Marinus **17** 664; **28** 595
Sláma, Bohumil **11** 47
Slane Castle **6** 61
Slangerup Church **4** 781
Slaoui, Hassan **22** 129
Šlapeta, Čestmír **28** 835
Šlapeta, Lubomír **8** 402; **28** 835*
slashing **30** 554
slate
 historical and regional traditions
  Belarus' **3** *530*
  Bhutan **3** 914
  China **7** 94
  Czech Republic **8** 376
  Egypt, ancient **9** 864; **14** *407*, *415*
  England **10** 236, 297
  Hinduism **15** *216*
  Indian subcontinent **15** *216*
  Mesoamerica, Pre-Columbian **21** 718, 719
  Prehistoric art **25** 491, 494
  South America, Pre-Columbian **29** 155
  Ukraine **31** *560*
  Wales **10** 236
  West Mexico **21** 718
 uses
  abrasives **16** 859
  architecture **8** 376; **10** 236
  furniture **10** 297
  inkstones **7** 94
  mirrors **21** 718, 719
  palettes **9** 864; **14** *407*
  plaques **25** 491
  roofs **27** 131
  sculpture **3** *530*, 914; **15** *216*; **31** *560*
Slater, John **9** 201
Slater, Samuel **31** 656
Slater, William **5** 828
Slatina Monastery **26** 721
Slătineanu, Alexandru **26** 723
Slatkin, Charles E. **31** 660
Slaughter, Stephen **16** 13; **28** 835–6*
Slavata, Vilém **8** 422
slaves
 Africa **3** 60; **4** 707–8; **5** 753; **7** 603; **9** 115; **16** 880; **30** 13
 Bahamas, the **3** 60
 Brazil **4** 707–8
 Caribbean Islands **5** 753
 Colombia **7** 603
 Dominican Republic **9** 115
 Jamaica **16** 880
 Surinam **30** 13
Slavey **22** 546, 648, 656
Slavíček, Antonín **8** 392; **25** 433; **28** 836*
Slavin **4** 24
Slavin, L. M. **23** 427
Slavkovski, Krsto **19** 885
Slavkov u Brna **8** *374*; **28** 836–7*
 architecture **8** 377
 Castle **28** 836*
 pewter **8** 415
 porcelain **8** 405
 sculpture **8** 386
Slavonice Castle **8** 378, 390; **10** 741
Slav Revival **28** 837–9*
 churches **28** *837*
Slavs **21** 500, 501; **25** 94; **28** 857
Sławski, Roger **25** 408
Sleaford (Lincs) **31** 709
 dress **9** *253*
 St Denys **8** *836*
Sleator, James **16** 17
sledges **1** 296; **17** 59
Sledmere House (Humberside) **30** 507

sleeping-chairs *see under* CHAIRS → types
Sleeping Satyr 3 830; 12 474; 13 470; 23 701
sleeves 9 256–7, 260
Sleigh, Alison 28 283
Sleigh, Sylvia 10 483, 879; 28 839*
Slendzinski, Aleksander 19 497
Ślendziński, Ludomir 25 108, 141; 28 839*; 32 579
Slepče Monastery 19 882
Slesier, Niklas *see* SCHLESITZER, NIKLAS
Slesin, Susan 14 521
Slesinger, Niklas *see* SCHLESITZER, NIKLAS
Slesińska, Alicja 25 116
Sleter, Francesco 5 65; 10 278; 30 451
Slevogt, Max 28 839–41*
  dealers 5 924
  groups and movements 3 511; 12 394; 23 505; 28 341, 342
  patrons and collectors 11 777; 18 186
  works 4 366; 19 490; 28 *840*
Slevogthof *see under* LEINSWEILER
Ślewiński, Władysław 25 108; 28 841–2*; 32 877
  groups and movements 25 215
  pupils 33 264
Ślęża 25 109
  Church of the Canons Regular 26 636
Slezer, John 12 128; 28 235; 33 147
slides
  collections *see under* COLLECTIONS → types
  types
    glass 26 236
    lantern 20 92; 24 651, 672; 26 236
  see also TRANSPARENCIES
sliding doors *see* PARTITIONS → types → *fusuma*
Sliedrecht, Dirk van 22 876
Sliegh, J.
  works 19 *484*
Sligo (Co. Sligo) 16 37
  Abbey 16 20; 31 273
  Museum and Art Gallery 16 36
Sligo, Howe (Peter) Browne, 2nd Marquis of *see* BROWNE, HOWE (PETER), 2nd Marquis of Sligo
Slijper, Salomon Bernard 19 537
Šlik, Count 20 813
Slimbridge (Glos), St John's 29 659
Slingeland, Pieter (Cornelisz.) van 28 842*
  groups and movements 19 102; 22 841
  teachers 9 194
Slingelandt, Govert van, Lord of Lindt and West-IJsselmonde 28 842*
  collections 22 905; 23 463
  paintings 14 42; 22 905; 23 469
Slingeneyer, Ernest 11 746
Slingherlandt, Pieter (Cornelisz.) van *see* SLINGELAND, PIETER (CORNELISZ.) VAN
slings 2 448; 10 40
slip 6 326, 327; 28 842*
  historical and regional traditions
    Central Asia, Western 6 255, 257, *257*; 16 408*
    China 6 874, 876, 882, 886, 895
    Egypt 16 405, 415*
    Egypt, ancient 10 25
    England 6 325
    Etruscan 13 571
    Iran 16 408*
    Iraq 16 399
    Islamic 16 395, 399, 405, 408*, 415*, 420, 422
    Korea 18 339, 342, 344
    Ottoman 16 420, 422
slip
  historical and regional traditions—cont.
    Syria 16 415*
  materials
    tin 16 420
  uses
    ceramics 6 327, 328
    earthenwares 6 *257*, 874, 886; 16 427
    glazes 6 329
    porcelain 18 344
    pottery 6 255, 257, 874, 876, 882, 895; 10 25; 16 399, 405, 408*, 415, 420, 422
    stonewares 18 339, 342
slip casting clay *see under* CLAY → types
slipper-coffins *see under* COFFINS → types
slipwares *see under* POTTERY → wares
Slisselburg 27 431
slit-drums *see under* DRUMS → types
slit-tapestry *see under* TEXTILES → types
Sliven 5 161
  Museum 5 163
Slivenc Church 8 407
Slivenec 13 187
Šlizys, Rimantas 19 500
Sloan, C. G., & Co., Inc. 32 890
Sloan, David 22 671
Sloan, John (1871-1951) 14 393; 22 674, 679; 24 600; 28 842–3*; 31 605
  collaboration 20 604
  exhibitions 2 447
  groups and movements 2 596, 597; 10 108; 12 769; 23 47; 28 925
  pupils 3 31; 5 422; 13 214, 272; 19 60; 26 464
  teachers 2 130
  works 2 *596*; 12 296, 769; 15 828; 21 897; 24 *601*; 28 919; 31 705
Sloan, John (1890-1970) 5 571
Sloan, Samuel 11 361; 22 398, 539; 28 843–4*
Sloane, Eric 5 531
Sloane, Hans 28 844*
  collections 1 437; 10 368; 13 605; 22 739
  gems 12 266
  medical books 21 6
  plaquettes 25 18
  prints 7 120
  writings 16 882
Sloane, Joseph C. 2 530; 22 688
Sloane Collection *see under* LONDON → museums → British Museum
Sloan & Stewart 28 843
Slodki, Marcel 8 434
Slodtz (family) 20 137, 497; 26 420
Slodtz, Dominique-François 28 845
Slodtz, Jean-Baptiste 28 845
Slodtz, Michel-Ange *see* SLODTZ, RENÉ-MICHEL
Slodtz, Paul-Ambroise 28 845*
  collaboration 28 845
  patrons and collectors 11 626
  works 7 657; 28 *845*; 32 511
Slodtz, René-Michel 11 559, 560; 20 137; 24 137; 28 845–7*
  patrons and collectors 3 708
  pupils 3 843; 4 248; 12 862; 14 796; 24 371; 26 448; 30 353
  reproductive prints by others 11 171
  works 7 195; 8 72; 11 410; 28 *846*
Slodtz, Sébastien (?1655-1726) 3 570; 11 625; 15 38; 28 845*
  collaboration 11 626
  teachers 12 727
Slodtz, Sébastien (?1655-1726)—cont.
  works 11 626; 24 165
Slodtz, Sébastien-Antoine (1695-1754) 28 845*
  collaboration 28 845
  patrons and collectors 11 626
  works 7 657
Slomcynski, André 8 57
Slonim, Cistercian Church 3 *525*, 526
Słonski, Gabriel 18 425
Sloper, Ernest Willmott 3 82
Slot, Gerardo 11 5
Slott-Møller, Agnes 11 790; 28 847*
Slott-Møller, Harald 28 847–8*
  groups and movements 11 790
  works 8 748; 11 478, *478*
Slough (Berks)
  St Mary's 29 508
  Wexton Park Hospital 14 783
Slous, George 28 389
Slous, Henry Courtney *see* SELOUS, HENRY COURTNEY
Slovakia 28 *848*, 848–57*
  altarpieces 19 *281*, 281; 28 *854*
  architecture 28 849–50*
  bronze 28 *855*
  castles 4 *695*
  churches 3 *224*; 28 848, 849, *850*; 31 *353*
  collections 28 856–7*
  decorative arts 28 855–6*
  dyeing 30 558
  embroidery 28 856*
  felt 10 875
  fortifications 21 551
  glass 28 856*
  lace 18 593; 28 856
  manuscript illumination 28 851
  metalwork 28 856*
  museums 28 857
  painting 28 850–54*
    panel 28 851
    urban life 28 *853*
    wall 28 850–51, *851*, *852*, 852
  palaces 4 *696*
  patronage 28 856–7*
  periodicals 24 440*
  pottery 28 855–6*
  prints 28 852, 853–4
  sculpture 28 854–5*, *855*
  spice-boxes 17 572
  synagogues 17 548
  town halls 3 *224*
  universities 4 694
Slovenes 28 857
Slovenia 28 857–63*, *858*; 33 571
  architecture 28 857–60*; 32 293
  bronze 28 *806*
  cast iron 28 863
  ceramics 28 862
  churches 28 *859*
  collections 28 863*
  decorative arts 28 862–3*
  education (art) 28 863
  gilding 28 *862*
  glass 28 862
  glassworks 28 862
  helmets 28 807
  metalwork 28 862–3
  monuments 28 862
  museums 28 863*
  painting 28 860–61*, *861*
  prints 28 860
  sculpture 28 861–2*
    Baroque 28 *862*
    Gothic 28 861
    relief 28 861
    wood 28 *862*, 862
  situlae 28 806, *806*
  textiles 28 863
  vases 28 *863*
  wood 28 862, *862*
Slovenská Ľupča Castle 28 852
Slovenske Gorice Church 28 859
Słucak 3 525, *525*; 25 133; 28 863–4*
  St Michael 3 526
Sluijters, Georges Joseph van *see* FEURE, GEORGES DE
Sluijters, Gijsbertus Antonius 28 864
Sluijters, Jan (Carolus Bernardus) 21 851; 22 851; 28 864–5*
Sluijters, J. M. Janssen Eijken *see* JANSSEN EIJKEN SLUIJTERS, J. M.
Sluis, Jacob van der 19 102
Sluis Stadhuis 22 822
Sluntchev Bryag 5 150
Sluperius 19 64
Sluter, Claus 3 568; 5 43; 11 555; 13 156; 17 460; 20 207; 22 855; 28 865–7*
  assistants 7 405
  collaboration 20 207
  groups and movements 26 184
  patrons and collectors 3 567; 5 206, 207, 208, 209, 895; 11 655, 660; 33 28
  teachers 17 460
  works 7 405; 8 890, 892, *892*, 893; 10 743; 11 *555*; 13 77; 17 460; 20 207, 614; 26 *185*; 28 *866*; 31 122; 33 *28*, 28
Slutsk *see* SŁUCAK
Slutzky, Naum 12 450, 456
Sluys, Cornelis van der 22 868, 876
Sluyterman, Th(eodorus) K(arel) L(odewijk) 28 867*
Sluyters, Jan 21 775
służba see under SIDEBOARDS → types
Smaele, De 8 633
Smakauskas, Vincentas 19 498
Small, Jane 21 *639*
Small, John W. 28 255
Small, William (*fl* 1871) 28 919
Small, William F. (1798-1832) 18 845
small-format cameras *see* CAMERAS → types → miniature
Small Landscapes, Master of the 20 769*; 32 621
small regular script *see under* SCRIPTS → types
small running script *see under* SCRIPTS → types
small seal script *see under* SCRIPTS → types
Small *Shāhnāmas* 16 296
small-swords *see under* SWORDS → types
Small Trades, Master of the 18 622
smalt 6 869; 11 763; 12 803; 16 394; 23 786; 24 791*
Smara 33 98
  mosque of Shaykh Ma al-'Aynayn 33 98
Smărăndescu, Paul 3 124
Smargiassi, Gabriele 5 527; 8 716; 22 480; 23 850, 852; 28 317
Smarje, St Rochus 29 839
Šmarna Gora Church 28 859
Smart, Borlase 18 754; 27 562
Smart, Charles P. 3 368*
Smart, Francis Joseph 26 74
Smart, Jeffrey 28 867–8*
Smart, John 4 601; 21 644
Smart, William 5 288
Smbat II, King of Armenia (*reg* 890-914) 2 97, 444; 14 36
Smeaton, James 5 640
Smeaton, John 7 693; 9 58; 18 843; 19 360; 28 868*
Smeatonian Society 28 868
Smederevac, Petar 28 456
Smederevo 28 *437*, 440
  fortress 28 440, 444
  jewellery 28 455
  manuscript illumination 28 449
  palace 28 440
Smee, William, & Son 2 755, 758
Smeers, Frans 23 398
Smeesters, Theodoor 3 599
Smeeton, Burn 19 214
smegmatothekeai *see* KOTHONES
Šmejkal, F. 8 426
Smellie, William 1 844; 21 7; 32 910
smelting 21 319–20*
  historical and regional traditions
    China 7 98
    Egypt, ancient 9 817–18
    Indian subcontinent 21 *320*
    Japan 17 318–19*
    Scotland 28 263
  materials
    charcoal 21 319
    coke 21 319, 320
    iron 7 98
  uses
    bronze 17 318
    iron 16 50; 17 318; 28 263
    steel 17 319
Smeltzing, Jan 20 923; 28 868*
Smeltzing, Martin 28 868
Smendes (*reg c.* 1075-*c.* 1045 BC) 9 *777*, 887
Smenkhkare (*reg c.* 1335-*c.* 1332 BC) 9 *777*; 10 80
Smeraldi, Francesco 32 648
  works 32 *649*
Smeraldo di Giovanni 6 2; 12 700
Smet, Cornelis de (*fl c.* 1580) 7 487
Smet, Cornelis de (1742-1815) 3 571; 28 868–9*
Smet, Gustave De *see* DE SMET, GUSTAVE
Smet, Hendrik de 19 260
Smet, Jules De *see* DE SMET, JULES
Smet, Léon de (*fl* 1490-1513) 3 606; 5 46; 27 132
Smet, Léon De (1881-1966) *see* DE SMET, LÉON
Smet, Lucie De *see* DE SMET, LUCIE
Smet, Martin de 22 116
Smetana, Bedřich, Museum *see under* PRAGUE → museums
Smetana, Pavel 28 850
Smetham, James 28 869*
Smetius, Martinus 19 458
Smeyers, Nicolas 11 698
Smibert, John 4 477; 9 724; 23 32, 46; 28 235, 869–70*; 31 665
  patrons and collectors 4 599; 8 463
  reproductive prints by others 24 335
  works 4 472; 28 *870*; 31 599
Smibert, Nathaniel 28 870
Smidt, Andrès de 28 871*
Smidt, Firmin de 12 520
Smidth, Hans Ludvig 14 572; 28 871*
Smidt vom Gelder, Pieter 2 196
Smies, Jacob 10 126
Smijtere, Jan de 14 296
Smikros 13 484, 518, 573; 32 42
Smilis of Aigina 1 480; 13 439
Smillie, James 9 309; 25 629
Smillie, Thomas William 17 625
Smiřice Chapel 8 391, 874; 26 498
Smiřický, Zikmund 25 426
Smiriglio, Mariano 28 657
Smirke, Mary 28 871
Smirke, Richard 19 612; 28 871
Smirke, Robert (i) (1753-1845) 28 871–2*
  reproductive prints by others 10 378; 25 164
  works 4 601
Smirke, Robert (ii) (1780-1867) 2 332, 560; 28 871, 872–5*
  architecture 4 822
    castles 5 194
    clubs (meeting places) 7 469
    law courts 18 887
    libraries 19 318, *318*; 28 *874*
    museums 9 25; 10 *234*, 235, 369, 745; 19 573; 22 362; 25 267

Smirke, Robert (ii) (1780-1867)
architecture—cont.
parliament buildings **19** 613
post offices **25** 268
prisons **14** 172
theatres **27** 197; **28** *873*
groups and movements **13** 610
methods **7** 693
patrons and collectors **19** 735; **24** 322
pupils **7** 502
staff **5** 263; **32** 864
watercolours **10** *186*
Smirke, Sydney **3** 325; **7** 470; **9** 1, 55; **11** 360; **16** 54; **28** 871–2*
Smirnoff, George **19** 866
Smirnov, Boris (Ivanovich) (1792-1837) *see* ORLOVSKY, BORIS (IVANOVICH)
Smirnov, Boris (1903-87) **27** 417
Smirnov, Veniamin (*b* 1937) **27** 434
Smirnov, V. I. (*fl* 1930) **33** 518
Smirnov, Yakov (Ivanovich) **28** 875*
Smíšek, Jan **18** 539
Smíšek, Michal **18** 540
Smísek, Mirek **23** 69
Smissaert, Frans A. E. L. **26** 528
Smit, A. (*fl* 1767-92) **3** 211
Smit, Arie (*b* 1916) **15** 809
Smit, Daneel, and Partners **29** 121
Smit, E. **8** 177
Smit, Frans de **17** 649
Smit, Hans **2** 152
Smit, Robert **22** 896
Smith (family) **8** 47; **12** 595
Smith, Abraham **10** 271; **29** 834
Smith, Adam **13** 300
Smith, Adrian D. **4** 476
Smith, A. L. (*fl* 1873/4) **18** 888
Smith, A. Ledyard (*fl* 1920-30) **28** 372; **31** 507
Smith, Andrew Lawrenson (1620-92) **23** 224
Smith, Arnold Dunbar **28** 888*
Smith, Barr (family) *see* BARR SMITH (FAMILY)
Smith, Benjamin (1764-1823) **27** 336
patrons and collectors **10** 334; **27** 139
teachers **4** 541; **29** 723
works **3** 79; **10** 334
Smith, Benjamin (*d* 1833) **31** 777
Smith, Bernard (*fl* 1694) **19** 599
Smith, Bernard (*b* 1916) **2** 161, 750, 769; **10** 852; **25** 710
Smith, B. F.
works **21** *618*
Smith, Brian Arthur **14** 850
Smith, Charles **15** 164*
Smith, Charles Hamilton **21** 412
Smith, Charles R. **22** 809
Smith, Chris **29** 426
Smith, Colvin **16** 62; **28** 237
Smith, Daniel **3** 476
Smith, David (Roland) **28** 875–7*
dealers **18** 162
groups and movements **1** 83, 84, 85, 87, 772
patrons and collectors **14** 575
works **1** 738; **15** 829; **16** 58, *58*; **28** *877*; **29** 628, *628*; **31** 613–14, *614*
Smith, Dennis A. **25** 874
Smith, Derek **2** 762
Smith, E. Baldwin **9** 528; **31** 672
Smith, Eben **31** 652
Smith, Edward **23** 336
Smith, Edwin **10** 92; **28** 877–8*
Smith, E. H. Dean **14** 603
Smith, Elizabeth **1** 153
Smith, Emma **28** 883
Smith, Eric **30** 160
Smith, Ernest **12** 650
Smith, Eustace **2** 475
Smith, Evan **24** 296
Smith, E. Willard **1** 157
Smith, Francis **28** 878*; **29** 835
Smith, Frank Eugene *see* EUGENE, FRANK
Smith, Franklin Webster **26** 214
Smith, Frithjof **3** 481; **29** 15
Smith, George (1714-76) **10** 280; **28** 879*
Smith, George (*fl c.* 1786-1828) **28** 879*
groups and movements **26** 85
works **10** 296, *296*
writings **10** 297; **28** 253
Smith, George (1783-1869; English architect) **27** 527
Smith, George (1793-1877; Scottish architect) **26** 288
Smith, George (*fl* 1850s) **2** 636
Smith, George (1849-1924) **7** 428
Smith, George W. (*fl* 1857) **11** 361
Smith, George Washington (1876-1930) **7** 619; **28** 879–80*
Smith, Gordon **5** 569; **10** 459
Smith, Grace Cossington *see* COSSINGTON SMITH, GRACE
Smith, Hamilton (P.) **7** 429; **22** 366
Smith, Harry **21** 108
Smith, Henry Holmes **7** 434; **20** 912; **24** 679; **31** 525
Smith, Hinchman & Grylls **8** 821
Smith, Hugh **21** 616
Smith, Isaac (*fl* 1769) **11** *497*
Smith, Isaac (1795-1871) **5** 560
Smith, J. **10** 377
Smith, Jabez **27** 613
Smith, Jack **28** 880*
groups and movements **10** 258; **18** 97
works **10** 688; **18** *97*
Smith, James (*fl* 1659) **28** 880
Smith, James (1645-1731) **22** 400; **28** 880–81*
collaboration **28** 226
groups and movements **23** 857, 860
house **28** 226
patrons and collectors **20** 866
works **5** 538; **28** 225, *226*, 226, 227, 246
Smith, James (*fl* 1719) **10** 330
Smith, James (*fl* 1792-1809; silversmith) **10** 334; **27** 139
Smith, James (*fl* 1802; potter) **14** 863
Smith, James (1808-63) **14** 108
Smith, James (*b* 1925) **6** 598
Smith, Jaune Quick-to-see **22** 599; **28** 881*
Smith, Jeremiah **14** 863
Smith, J. Forbes **24** 315
Smith, J(ohn) Moyr **9** 295; **28** 881*
Smith, John (1580-1631) **14** 675
Smith, John (i) (*c.* 1654-*c.* 1742) **10** 758; **18** 147; **28** 881*; **31** 786
teachers **3** 476
works **7** 461; **17** 915; **18** 748; **21** 416; **23** 468; **26** 231; **33** 260
Smith, John (*fl* 1673-80) **23** 789
Smith, John (*c.* 1717-64) **28** 879
Smith, John (1781-1852) **20** 14; **28** 229
works **1** 30
Smith, John (ii) (1781-1855) **10** 366; **24** 322; **28** 882*
dealing **14** 146
works **14** 635
Smith, John Orrin **19** 431
Smith, John Raphael **1** 153; **6** *457*; **21** 416; **22** 123; **28** 882*
printmakers **5** 216
pupils **8** 842; **14** 550; **26** 282; **32** 856
works **21** 417; **22** 122; **26** 231; **29** 676; **33** 413
Smith, John Rubens **12** 605; **19** 259; **28** 883
Smith, John Shaw **28** 883*
Smith, John Thomas **10** 560; **23** 190
Smith, John 'Warwick' **13** 304; **26** 774; **28** 883*
patrons and collectors **14** 598
works **18** 713
Smith, Jolyon **3** 62
Smith, Joseph, Consul (*c.* 1674-1770) **5** 595–7; **28** 883–4*; **32** 196
architecture **32** 615
catalogues **5** 55
collections **19** 437; **29** 796
dealing **2** 559
drawings **3** 308; **5** 600; **6** 36; **9** 230; **24** 707; **26** 323; **27** 521
engravings **6** 91; **32** 195, 615
etchings **5** 598
gems **3** 817; **9** 28
groups and movements **23** 861
paintings **5** 593, 595, 598, 878; **8** 474; **10** 366; **14** 144; **23** 175; **26** 319, 322, 323; **32** 111, 615; **33** 598, 714, 715
printmakers **5** 597
prints **25** 631
sculpture **11** 902
Smith, Joseph (1805-44) **22** 125; **27** 642
Smith, Kiki **3** 338; **10** 882
Smith, Leon Polk **22** 667
Smith, Louis Laybourne **2** 772
Smith (e Ibarra), Manuel María de **28** 884*
Smith, Mara **4** 789
Smith, Marshall **19** 583
Smith, Marshall J., jr **23** 32
Smith, Martin **10** 315
Smith, Mathinus Lourens **29** 119
works **29** *119*
Smith, Matthew (Arnold Bracy) **10** 257; **19** 623; **28** 884–5*
Smith, May **23** 74
Smith, Michael **24** 409
Smith, Myron Bement **16** 548
Smith, Nathaniel **27** 244; **33** 227
Smith, Oliver **30** 687
Smith, Percy **28** 307
Smith, Peter **33** 678
Smith, Philip E. L. **12** 46
Smith, Rata Lovell *see* LOVELL-SMITH, RATA
Smith, R. H. **24** 336
Smith, Richard **28** 885*
assistants **5** 77
groups and movements **25** 231; **28** 804
pupils **5** 77
Smith, Robert (i) (1722-77) **8** 505; **24** 596; **28** 885*; **31** 590
Smith, Robert (*fl* 1926-37; archaeologist) **31** 507
Smith, Robert (Chester) (ii) (1912-75; art historian) **17** 595; **25** 320; **28** 886*
Smith, Roger, & Gale **17** 897
Smith, Roger Thomas **7** 701
Smith, Roland Ingleby **16** 39
Smith, Sidney R. J. **10** 370; **30** 359; **32** 801
Smith, Stephen Catterson (1806-72) **28** 886*
Smith, Stephen Catterson, jr (1849-1912) **28** 886
Smith, Sydney Ure *see* URE SMITH, SYDNEY
Smith, Thomas (i) (1513-77) **28** 526, 886*
Smith, Thomas (ii) (*d* 1691; American painter) **28** 887*; **31** 599
Smith, Thomas (*fl* 1685; English painter) **29** 58
Smith, Thomas (*d* 1767; painter) **28** 882; **32** 652
Smith, Thomas (*d* 1769; engraver) **5** 295
Smith, Thomas C(arl) **31** 583, 637
Smith, Tony (Peter) **23** 49; **28** 887*
groups and movements **21** 645
works **16** 58; **31** 615
Smith, T. Roger **28** 158
Smith, Vincent (*fl* 1880-1908) **15** 211
Smith, Vincent (*b* 1929) **1** 445
Smith, Vivian **24** 342
Smith, W. A. **11** 433
Smith, Walter **31** 669
Smith, W(illiam) Eugene **24** 677; **28** 887–8*
works **24** *677*
Smith, William (1661-1724) **28** 878
Smith, William (1705-47; builder) **28** 878
Smith, William (1707-64; painter) **28** 879
Smith, William (1817-91) **6** 62; **14** 149; **28** 248, 288; **30** 385
Smith, William & Andrew **28** 264
Smith, William Ronald *see* RONALD, WILLIAM
Smith, William Stevenson **9** 798; **10** 84
Smithard, G. S. **29** 110
Smith-Barry, John **16** 25
Smith & Brewer **5** 732; **28** 888*; **32** 784, 791
Smith Brothers **14** 536
Smith College Museum of Art *see under* NORTHAMPTON (MA; USA)
Smither, James **31** 649
Smither, Michael **28** 888*
Smithers, James G. **7** 613; **18** 896; **29** 453, 454, 478
Smithers, Leonard **3** 446
Smith & Julius **2** 769; **32** 770
Smithmeyer, John L. **28** 888–9
Smithmeyer, John L., & Co. **28** 889
Smithmeyer & Pelz **19** 318; **28** 888–9*; **32** 886
Smith of Chichester, George *see* SMITH, GEORGE (1714-76)
Smithson, Alison **28** 889–90*
collaboration **24** 34
exhibitions **33** 218
groups and movements **5** 56; **7** 295; **11** 527; **15** 166; **20** 475; **23** 17; **30** 391
works **2** 361; **10** 241–2; **28** 158, *890*
Smithson (Percy), Hugh, 1st Duke and 2nd Earl of Northumberland **24** 390*
architecture **10** 361
furniture **15** 165; **19** 531
paintings **1** 533; **5** 598; **21** 132
sculpture **31** 826
silver **10** 333
Smithson, Huntingdon *see* SMYTHSON, HUNTINGDON
Smithson, James **24** 390; **31** 666; **32** 889
Smithson, Peter **28** 889–90*
collaboration **24** 34
exhibitions **33** 218
groups and movements **5** 56; **7** 295; **10** 241–2; **11** 527; **15** 166; **20** 475; **23** 17; **30** 391
pupils **7** 788
works **2** 361; **7** 295; **28** 158, *890*; **30** 391
Smithson, Robert **23** 49; **28** 890–91*
groups and movements **1** 80; **24** 741, 743; **25** 646
methods **28** 206
works **9** 26; **18** 694, *694*, 695; **31** 615
Smithsonian Institution *see under* WASHINGTON (DC) → museums
Smithsonian Studies in American Art see AMERICAN ART
smithsonite *see* CALAMINE
Smits, Eugène **22** 697; **28** 891*
Smits, George **29** 99
Smits, Hendrik **22** 891
Smits, Jakob **2** 516; **3** 614; **9** 189; **28** 891–2*
Smitz, Gaspar **16** 13; **28** 881
smoking **22** 654; **24** 258
smoking pipes *see* PIPES (SMOKING)
Smoky, Lois **22** 595
smoky quartz **7** *90*
Smolderen, Joseph **2** 194
Smolensk **27** *363*, 374; **28** 892*
architecture **4** 781; **31** 548
fortress **27** 371
painting **27** 381
Regional Museum **28** 892
SS Peter and Paul **27** 369
S. T. Konyonkov Museum of Art **28** 892
Tinisheva collections **30** 265
Smoliansky, Gunnar **28** 892*
Smollett, Tobias **8** 218; **11** 858; **13** 301
Smolyan **5** 150
Smout, Willem **12** 884
Smrečany **28** 851
Smrekar, Hinko **28** 860
Smrěková, Ludvika **8** 411
Smuglewicz, Franciszek **3** 528; **19** 497; **25** 106, 141; **28** 892*; **32** 579
assistants **27** 446
collaboration **4** 744
patrons and collectors **19** 498
pupils **19** 497
teachers **8** 374
works **25** 105
Smuglewicz, Łukasz **21** 757; **28** 892
Smurfit, Michael **16** 36
Smyrna (Old) **13** 396; **15** 893; **21** 556; **28** 892–3*, *893*
architecture **15** 893
fortifications **13** 396; **15** 893
pottery **13** 502, 514
Temple of Athena **13** 418; **28** 893
Tomb of Tantalus **31** 108
town walls **21** 555
Smyrna **13** *363*
Smyrna (New) *see under* IZMIR
Smyrna, Theon of *see* THEON OF SMYRNA
Smyrna carpets *see under* CARPETS → types
Smyrna-Teppich-Fabrik **9** 703
Smyth, Bishop of Lincoln **23** 686
Smyth, Edward **9** 322; **14** 500; **16** 21, 37; **28** 894*
Smyth, Hervey **5** 564
Smyth, James Carmichael **3** 63
Smyth, John (*fl* 1429-*c.* 1460) **7** 419
Smyth, John (*fl* 1758-69) **9** 323
Smyth, John (*fl c.* 1773-1840) **9** 322; **16** 21; **28** 894
Smyth, Robert Brough **1** 55, 67
Smyth, Thomas *see* SMITH, THOMAS (i) (1513-77)
Smythier, Robert **10** 329, 330
Smythson (family) **3** 186
Smythson, Huntingdon **28** 897
Smythson, John **28** 896–7*
works **2** 330; **6** 59, *60*; **28** 894; **32** 551
Smythson, Robert **20** 893; **28** 894–6*
assistants **28** 896
groups and movements **9** 739; **10** 143
patrons and collectors **10** 360
works **2** 330; **10** 230; **12** 790; **23** 258; **24** 274; **28** *895*, *896*; **30** 266, 267, 794; **32** 551
Snagov Monastery **26** 718
Snailwell (Cambs) **25** 541
Snaiter, Lorenzo **16** 748
Snake Bay **1** *47*
snake kilns *see* KILNS → types → climbing

Snakenburg, Theodoor **31** 366
Snaketown (AZ) **22** *544*, 566; **28** *897*, 897–8*
mirrors **21** 718
pottery **22** *601*, 602
Snape, Michael **2** 754
Snaphaen, Abraham **19** 102
snapshots **14** 481; **24** 647, 656*, 662, 679
snarling **12** 868
Snarskis, Michael **9** 677; **18** 586
Snayers, Pieter **28** 898*
patrons and collectors **14** 8, 10
pupils **21** 367
teachers **32** 723
Snedker, Mogens **31** 138
Sneferu (*reg c.* 2575–*c.* 2551 BC) **9** *776*
cities **9** 850
pyramid **20** 863
pyramids **2** 296; **8** 456; **10** 81; **20** 117; **25** *761*, 762; **31** 107
reliefs **9** 871
sculpture **9** 869, 870
Sneferu-Seneb **9** 863
Snel, Willibrord **30** 26
Snell, H. Saxon **32** 720
Snell, Johan **29** 687; **30** 77
Snellinck, Abraham **28** 899
Snellinck, Andries **28** 899
Snellinck, Daniel (*fl* 1531-44) **28** 898
Snellinck, Daniel, III (1576-1627) **28** 899
Snellinck, Geraerd **28** 899
Snellinck, Jan, I (1544/9-1638) **17** 3; **28** 898–9*; **32** 706
Snellinck, Jan, II (1579-1627/38) **28** 899
Snelling, Douglas **2** 756, 759
Snell-Walker, Teresa **2** 752
Snelson, Kenneth **1** 738; **4** 110; **28** 899*
Snetogorsk Monastery, Cathedral of the Birth of the Virgin **27** 383
Snettisham (Norfolk) **6** 161
Snettisham Torc **6** *153*, 160; **12** 864
Sneyd, John **12** 640
Sneyd, Walter **5** 623
Sneyers, Léon **28** 899–900*
Snichkov, Yu. **18** 568
Snijers, Hendrick *see* SNYERS, HENDRICK
Snischek, Max **2** 826
Snitker, Johan *see* GRONINGEN, JOHAN VAN
Snoek-van Utrecht (family) **32** 703
Snofru *see* SNEFERU
Snook, John Butler **28** 900*
collaboration **2** 699
patrons and collectors **31** 870
pupils **14** 223
staff **27** 137
Snotingeham *see* NOTTINGHAM
Snoů, Rdultovsky Palace **3** 527
Snow, Carmel **2** 852; **4** 691
Snow, George Washington **30** 899
Snow, Michael **28** 900*; **31** 177; **33** 163
works **5** 569, 571, 574; **10** 688; **29** 98
Snow, W. A., & Co. **31** 653
Snowdon(, Anthony Armstrong-Jones, 1st Earl of) **25** 571; **28** 900–901*; **30** 784; **33** 700
Snozzi, Luigi **4** 491
snuff bottles
historical and regional traditions
China **7** 86, 91, 103, 131–3*, *132*, *133*; **16** IV; **26** 484
Mongolia **21** 884
Shona **28** 621
materials
amber **1** 761
chalcedony **7** 132, *132*
copper **7** 132
enamel **7** 132, *133*
glass **7** 86, 132, *133*
snuff bottles
materials—cont.
hardstones **7** 91
ivory **7** 103, 132
jade **7** 132; **16** IV
jadeite **7** 132
porcelain **7** 131, 132
rock crystal **7** 132; **26** 484
snuff-boxes
historical and regional traditions
Afghanistan **1** 210
Africa **1** 351, 367*
Austria **2** 823
Bantu peoples **1** 367
England **10** 342, 346, 347, *347*
France **4** *601*; **7** 167, *194*; **11** *608*, *631*, 632, *632*, 633, *633*; **24** 62
Germany **12** 457–9*, *458*, *459*
Malawi **1** 367
Netherlands, the **22** 897
Russia **27** *420*
Scotland **28** 264
Shona **1** 367
Sweden **30** 111, *112*
materials
agate **10** *347*; **12** *459*
diamonds **12** *459*
enamel **2** 823; **4** *601*; **10** 346; **11** *631*, 632, *633*; **30** *112*
gold **2** 823; **4** 601, *601*; **10** 347, *347*; **11** *631*, *632*, *633*; **12** *459*; **30** *112*
hardstones **11** 632; **12** 457–9, *458*
horn **1** 367
lacquer **11** 632
mother-of-pearl **11** 632
papier mâché **24** 62
porcelain **11** *608*
silver **27** *420*
wood **1** 367
types
boîtes à portrait **24** 62
snuffers **28** 901*
see also CANDLE HOLDERS
snuff trays **29** 133
snuff tubes **29** 133
Snyder, Joan **20** 609
Snyders, Frans **16** 674; **28** 901–4*
assistants **32** 705
collaboration **3** 108; **4** 218, 913, 915; **5** 764; **17** 6; **27** 298; **32** 705, 713; **33** 181
patrons and collectors
Altamira, Vicente Joaquín Osorio Moscoso y Guzmán, 11th Conde de **1** 690
Carleton, Dudley, 1st Viscount Dorchester **5** 764
Francis-Joseph, Prince of Liechtenstein (*reg* 1772-81) **19** 338
Guinness, Edward (Cecil), 1st Earl of Iveagh **13** 836
Habsburg II., Ferdinand, Cardinal-Infante of Spain **14** 10
Hondecoeter, Melchior d' **14** 706
Jabach, Everard **16** 815
Philip IV, King of Spain (*reg* 1621-65) **14** 8; **32** 129
Rockox, Nicolaas **26** 490
Röver, Valerius **27** 270
pupils **4** 221, 521; **8** 811; **11** 871; **16** 832
teachers **4** 910; **13** 234
works **2** 104, *104*; **3** 561; **28** 902, *902*, *903*; **29** 424, 666
Snyers, Hans **32** 709
Snyers, Hendrick **18** 879; **28** 904*
Snyers, Pieter **3** 562
Snyers-Ring **3** 585
So, Guillem de, Vescomte d'Evol *see* EVOL, GUILLEM DE SO, Vescomte d'
Soada *see* SUWAYDA
Soady, Rose **19** 413
Sŏam *see* KIM YU-SŎNG
Sōami Shinsō *see* SHINSŌ SŌAMI
sōan *see under* HOUSES → types
Soane, John **9** 25; **23** 544; **28** 904–10*
architecture **10** 234; **16** 10
arches **2** 307
banks **3** 174; **19** 571; **25** 268; **26** 13; **28** *906*; **30** 386
chimney-pieces **6** 605
country houses **28** *907*
dairies **8** 461
galleries (iv) (art) **9** 12; **10** 369; **19** 588; **22** 362
government buildings **19** 612, 613; **28** *909*
mausolea **20** 867, 868, *868*
opera houses **30** 677
pilasters **24** 805
staircases **19** *613*
assistants **5** 688
caryatids **5** 905; **30** 503
collaboration **8** 105; **29** 835; **31** 466
competitions **7** 666
drawings **2** 333
groups and movements **13** 608; **22** 741; **26** 85, 735, 743
house **2** *550*, 552; **9** 12, 13; **10** 234, 279; **14** 810; **28** *908*
methods **7** 693
patrons and collectors **2** 577; **4** 576; **13** 637; **14** 485; **24** 893
pattern books **24** 275; **32** 553
personal collection **8** 495; **9** 24; **10** 90, 97; **14** 550; **19** 588
pupils **3** 324; **26** 337; **28** 872
staff **12** 45
teachers **8** 494
writings **2** 314, 358
Soane Hours *see under* BOOKS OF HOURS → individual manuscripts
Soans, Anton **10** 537; **30** 277
works **10** *537*
Soans, Jaak **10** 540; **30** 277
soap **10** 560
aquatints **2** 240
crayons **8** 127, 128
etchings **10** 559
inks **15** 853; **25** 598
lithography **19** 480
soapstone **6** 400; **16** 857
historical and regional traditions
Africa **1** 292, *388*
Ancient Near East **1** 856, *857*
Buddhism **26** *151*
Byzantine **9** 647, 651
China **7** 133–5*, *134*; **18** *601*
Crete **18** *168*
Egypt, ancient **10** 29, 46, 47, 70, *71*; **12** 246; **28** 34, *433*
Gabon **11** *879*
Gothic **13** 102
Indian subcontinent **15** 192, 324, 327, *419*, 420; **26** *151*
Indus civilization **15** *419*, 420
Iran, ancient **15** *903*
Kenya **17** *908*
Korea **18** *298*
Mesopotamia **21** *295*
Minoan **18** *168*
Native North Americans **22** 668
Nigeria **23** *133*
Norway **13** 102; **31** *364*
Prehistoric art **25** 493
Swaziland **30** 63
Syria-Palestine **1** *857*; **30** *195*
uses
beads **10** 47
boxes **7** 133, 134
brushpots **7** 134, *134*
brush-rests **7** 134
figurines **15** *419*, *903*
inkstones **7** 134–5
jewellery **10** 29
moulds **30** *195*
porcelain **10** 309
relief sculpture **18** *298*
soapstone
uses—cont.
reliquaries **26** *151*
scarabs **1** *857*; **10** *71*; **28** 34
screens (ii) (furniture) **18** *601*
sculpture
Africa **1** *388*
China **7** *134*, 135
Egypt, ancient **28** *433*
Gabon **11** *879*
Gothic **13** 102
Kenya **17** *908*
Nigeria **23** *133*
Norway **31** *364*
Swaziland **30** 63
seals **1** 856; **7** 134, 135; **10** 70; **15** 192, 420
statuettes **21** *295*
temples **15** 324, 327
vases **18** *168*
see also TALC
Soares, Ernesto **25** 320
Soares, Francisco da Rocha *see* ROCHA SOARES, FRANCISCO DA
Soares, João **27** 141
Soares, Manuel José **23** 454, 455; **25** 310
Soares da Silva, André Ribeiro **28** 910–12*
works **2** 285–6; **4** 629; **13** 831; **25** 293; **26** 254; **28** *911*, *912*; **30** 799; **32** 535
Soares dos Reis, António **20** 464; **28** 912–13*
pupils **5** 781; **30** 417
teachers **17** 667
works **25** 302; **28** *913*
Soares Rego, Margarida Emília **23** 455
Soave, Carlo Felice **28** 913–14*
Soay wool *see under* WOOL → types
Soba **23** *276*, 287
Sobachko-Shostak, Anna **31** 564
Sobaïc, Milos **3** 366
Šobajić, Ilija **22** 18
Sobalvarro, Orlando **23** 84, 86; **25** 455
Sobata **9** 543
Soběchleby **8** 419
Sōbei Kinkozan *see* KINKOZAN SŌBEI
Sobek **32** 878
Soberano, Domingo **11** 324
Soběslav Church **8** 376
Sobey (family) **5** 590
Sobieski, John III, King of Poland *see* JOHN SOBIESKI, King of Poland
Sobieski Hours *see under* BOOKS OF HOURS → individual manuscripts
Sobieszczański, Franciszek Maksymilian **25** 143
Sobkemsaf **9** 876
Sobko, Nikolai (Petrovich) **27** 443
Sobocki, Leszek **29** 743
Sobolev, D. M. **28** 403
Sobolewski, R. **21** 288
Søborg Castle **8** 723
Sobótka **25** 109, 515
Sobrado, Master of **17** 693
Sobrinho, Francisco Matarazzo *see* MATARAZZO SOBRINHO, FRANCISCO
Sobrinho, Simões Almeida
Sobrino, Francisco **13** 709; **19** 209; **28** 914*; **29** 297
Soby, James Thrall **28** 914*
socarrats *see under* TILES → types
Socchi, Giovanni **16** 719, 729; **30** 783
Sochaczew **25** 131
Soche, Karl **18** 446
Sōchin **30** 259
Sōchin Kokei *see* KOKEI SŌCHIN
Sochos, Antonēs **13** 354; **28** 915*
Sochos, Lazaros **13** 354
social history **7** 565
social history of art **26** 63; **28** 915–17*
see also ART HISTORY
socialism **15** 830; **29** 529; **30** 170
Socialistická scená **18** 462
Socialist Realism **15** 99; **28** 917–20*
art forms
painting **1** *540*; **12** 397; **28** *918*
sculpture **6** 733; **25** 116; **27** *395*; **32** *480*
historical and regional traditions
Albania **1** 540, 541, 547
Bulgaria **5** 155, 162
China **7** 150; **28** 919
Croatia **8** 179
Czech Republic **8** 394; **18** 463
Germany **3** 803; **12** 472
Korea **18** 247, 302; **28** 919
Poland **18** 182; **25** 108, 136; **33** 416
Russia **15** 891; **22** 268; **27** 395; **32** 836
Union of Soviet Socialist Republics **6** 176; **25** 351, 653; **28** 917–19
Vietnam **28** 919; **32** 480
social realism **15** 830; **22** 333; **25** 653; **26** 53; **28** 919–20*
Britain **22** 332
England **11** *74*
India, Republic of **20** 159
Italy **21** *473*
South Africa **29** 109
United States of America **1** 84, 772; **29** 249; **31** 606
social sculpture *see under* SCULPTURE → forms
Sociedad de Arquitectos (Peru) **24** 505
Sociedad de Arquitectos Mexicanos **20** 436; **21** 379
Sociedad de Artistas Ibéricos **24** 452
Sociedad de Artistas Plásticas (Cochabamba) **7** 493
Sociedad Bach **24** 515
Sociedad de Bellas Artes (Lima) **24** 516, 517
Sociedad Damas de Caridad (Buenos Aires) **2** 404
Sociedad Económica de Amigos del País **24** 70; **32** 180
Sociedade Martins Sarmento **25** 294; **28** 731
Sociedade Nacional de Belas-Artes (Lisbon) **25** 317
Sociedade Pró-Arte Moderna (São Paolo) **4** 718
Sociedad Española de Amigos del Arte **29** 308
Sociedad Española de Diseño Industrial **29** 322
Sociedad Filarmónica **24** 515
Sociedad de Foment de les Arts Decoratives *see* FAD
Sociedad Nacional de Bellas Artes (Santiago) **6** 601; **12** 918
Società degli Acquarellisti **26** 776
Società Aemilia Ars **16** 755
Società di Amatori delle Belle Arti **21** 538
Società Columbaria **2** 164
Società Fotografica Italiana **1** 643
Società Leonardo da Vinci di Scienze, Lettere ed Arti **11** 190
Società per l'Arte di Gaetano Previati **25** 568
Società Promotrice Fiorentina **11** 190
Società Salviati e Compagni **18** 897
Società S Giorgio **12** 506
Société des Amateurs d'art et des Collectionneurs **31** 503
Société Anonyme **9** 233, 358; **17** 766; **18** 111; **21** 854; **23** 48; **24** 574; **28** 920–21*; **31** 605
members **20** 287

Société des Antiquaires de Normandie **11** 521
Société des Aquafortistes **5** 284; **10** 562; **20** 256; **25** 629
Société des Aquarellistes Français **16** 851; **18** 679; **32** 902
Société Archéologique (Bruges) **33** 8
Société de l'Art Contemporain **7** 405; **14** 507
Société d'Art Décoratif Français **13** 318
Société des Artistes-Décorateurs (SAD) **11** 241, 582, 600, 601, 602; **13** 318
Société des Artistes Indépendants **9** 324
Société des Artistes Lithographes Français **19** 488
Société des Arts de Genève **12** 277; **30** 156
Société de Banque Suisse **18** 91
Société des Beaux-Arts (Algeria) **1** 634
Société des Beaux-Arts, La (Glasgow) **26** 107
Société Belge des Urbanistes et Architectes Modernes (SBUAM) **3** 550, 551; **4** 217; **31** 874
Société Centrale d'Architecture (Belgium) **3** 44
Société Centrale des Architectes *see* ACADÉMIE D'ARCHITECTURE
Société Céramique **22** 882, 884
Société des Edifices Religieux **11** 521
Société de l'Estampe Originale **19** 488
Société Française d'Archéologie **6** 95
Société Française de Photographie **19** 86
Société Française des Architectes Urbanistes **1** 447; **14** 385; **17** 451
Société Française des Habitations à Bon Marché **5** 363
Société des Gens des Lettres **11** 565
Société des Graveurs au Burin **26** 233
Société Héliographique **19** 86, 239; **24** 682; **31** 831
Société de l'Histoire de l'Art Français **11** 675
Société Internationale de l'Art Populaire **22** 252
Société Internationale des Ecoles Berlitz **13** 807
Société du Jing-lar **17** 441
Société Libre des Beaux-Arts **3** 562; **10** 517; **28** 891, 921*
members **2** 511; **5** 44; **9** 325; **14** 507, 838; **21** 369; **27** 140; **29** 645; **32** 380
Société Nationale des Beaux-Arts **5** 813; **6** 79; **12** 496; **18** 177; **19** 94, 296; **20** 498; **21** 69; **24** 172; **26** 191
Société Normande de Peinture Moderne **25** 747
Société des Peintres Algériens et Orientalistes **1** 634
Société des Peintres-Graveurs Indépendants **4** 588
Société des Peintres-Graveurs Français **4** 626; **31** 214
Société des Peintres Orientalistes Français **1** 634; **15** 747
Société Primitive, La *see* PIONEERS
Société de la Propriété Artistique et des Dessins et Modèles (SPADEM) **2** 554
Société Républicaine des Arts **24** 138
Société des Trois **19** 90; **33** 137, 139
Société des Urbanistes Belges *see* SOCIÉTÉ BELGE DES URBANISTES ET ARCHITECTES
Société des Voyageurs et des Artistes **7** 923
societies, exhibiting *see* EXHIBITING SOCIETIES
Society for Canadian Artists of Native Ancestry (SCANA) **22** 598
Society for the Advancement of Truth in Art **14** 536; **26** 335
Society for the Mineral and Battery Works **10** 339
Society for the Promotion of Fine Arts (Towarszystwo Zachęty Sztuk Pięknych) **25** 139
Society for the Promotion of Hellenistic Studies **23** 36
Society for the Protection of Ancient Buildings (SPAB) **2** 321; **22** 144; **33** 13
Society for the Protection of Historical Monuments (Warsaw) **20** 397
Society for the Study of Poetical Language *see* OPOYAZ
Society Islands **23** *711*; **28** 921–3*
adzes **23** *712*
architecture **28** 922*
barkcloth **28** 922, *922*
basalt **23** *712*
breastplates **28** 922
canoes **28** 923, *923*
coconuts **28** *922*
dress **28** *922*, 922–3
feathers **28** *922*
forgeries **23** 737
headdresses **28** 922, *922*
platforms **23** 715; **28** 922
sculpture **28** 922
sennit **23** *712*
shells **28** 922, *922*
tattoos **28** 923
textiles **28** 922–3
wood **23** *712*
Society of American Artists **6** 516; **7** 577; **23** 46; **26** 474; **27** 462, 557; **28** 617; **30** 868; **33** 43
Society of American Etchers *see* SOCIETY OF AMERICAN GRAPHIC ARTISTS
Society of American Graphic Artists **25** 629
Society of American Wood Engravers **25** 629
Society of Antiquaries **2** 163, 559; **10** 376; **19** 585; **24** 46; **25** 192
directors **13** 225
drawings **5** 890; **7** 385, 839
members **8** 38; **14** 598; **28** 869; **30** 279
staff **3** 329; **8** 852; **32** 378
Society of Architectural Historians **2** 533
Society of Artists (Lithuania) **19** 498
Society of Artists (Australia; Melbourne) **2** 747
Society of Artists (Australia; Sydney) **2** 747
Society of Artists Book **24** 438
Society of Artists of Bulgaria *see* NATIONAL ART SOCIETY OF BULGARIA
Society of Artists of Great Britain **19** 586; **23** 781; **26** 272
see also INCORPORATED SOCIETY OF ARTISTS
Society of Artists of Revolutionary Russia **2** 633
Society of Arts (London) **3** 287; **8** 802; **10** 677; **19** 586; **24** 46
Society of Arts, Manufactures and Commerce **15** 820–21, 883; **19** 585, 588; **28** 614
see also ROYAL SOCIETY OF ARTS (LONDON)
Society of Arts and Crafts (Boston, MA) **4** 480
Society of Beaux-Arts Architects **11** 143
Society of Canadian Artists **5** 565; **22** 38
Society of Cypriot Studies **8** 366
Society of Decorative Arts of New York City **33** 134
Society of Dilettanti **2** 164, 559; **7** 385, 713; **10** 376; **19** 585; **28** 924*
architecture **29** 806
drawings **7** 839; **10** 79
excavations **25** 576; **29** 99
groups and movements **13** 608
members **10** 364
Brudenell, John, Marquess Monthermer and Baron Montagu **4** 894
Coke, Thomas, 1st Earl of Leicester of the 1st creation (1697-1759) **7** 540
Dashwood, Francis, 15th Baron Le Despenser **8** 533
Dawkins, James **8** 581
Gell, William **12** 243
Greville, Charles Francis **13** 644
Harcourt, Simon, 1st Earl Harcourt of Stanton Harcourt and 2nd Earl Nuneham **14** 163
Knapton, George **18** 142
Reynolds, Joshua **26** 273
Robinson, Thomas, 2nd Baron Grantham **26** 475
Temple, Henry, 2nd Viscount Palmerston **30** 451
Weddell, William **33** 20
Wood, Robert (*c.* 1717-71) **33** 345
Zuccarelli, Francesco **33** 715
publications **6** 446; **22** 736; **26** 230, 263; **29** 805
staff **26** 273; **33** 192
surveys **13** 304; **24** 213, 368
Society of Easel Painters (OST) **18** 574; **22** 178; **25** 653; **27** 394; **28** 924*; **32** 579
members **2** 123; **8** 844; **18** 527; **24** 818; **28** 642; **31** 502
Society of Eight **28** 290
Society of Eleven (Jūichikai) **2** 578
Society of Female Artists *see* LADY ARTISTS
Society of Fine Arts (Egypt) **9** 766
Society of Formative Artists **18** 541
Society of Friends *see* CHRISTIANITY → sects → Quakers
Society of Icelandic Printmakers (Íslensk grafík) **10** 222
Society of Independent Artists (Lithuania) **19** 499
Society of Independent Artists (USA) **9** 233, 357; **23** 701; **28** 925*
Society of Jesus *see* JESUIT ORDER
Society of Korean Archaeological Studies *see* HANGUK KOGOHAK YŎN'GUHOE
Society of Lake District Artists **7** 570
Society of Medallists **18** 751
Society of Moscow Artists (OMKh) **9** 296; **22** 178
Society of Painters in Pastel **4** 179; **33** 43
Society of Painters in Water-Colours, The **8** 163; **19** 586; **32** 901, 903
Society of Patriotic Friends of Art **8** 422, 423, 425
Society of Polish Applied Art (Towarzystwo Polska Sztuka Stosowana) **18** 429; **25** 119, 133; **30** 328
works **25** *118*
Society of Romanian Architects **21** 631
Society of Russian Sculptors (ORS) **22** 178
Society of St Peter Martyr **32** 902
Society of Scottish Artists **28** 238
Society of the Friends of Art **9** 766
Society of the Sons of St George **29** 918
Society of Transylvanian Museums **26** 724
Society of Trinidad Independents **31** 335, 339, 340
Society of Twelve **8** 109
Society of Virtuosi of St Luke (London) **10** 371; **19** 584, *584*
Society of Wood-Engravings **8** 109
Society of Young Artists (Obmokhu) **21** 38; **22** 178; **29** 626
Sociological art **25** 108
sociology of art *see* ART (SOCIOLOGY OF)
Söckler, Johann Michael **29** 760
socles **28** 928*
Socnopaiou Nesos **9** 852
Socolescu, Ion N. **26** 709
Socrate, Carlo **9** 135; **26** 776
Socrate, Virgilio *see* FUNI, ACHILLE
Socrates **13** 394, 548, 568; **25** 31; **33** 461
Socrates Master **32** 34
soda
enamel **10** 192
glass **10** 317; **12** 438, 781; **29** 497; **30** 407; **32** 200
glazes **6** 329; **16** 394
soda-lime **7** 82; **10** 315; **12** 438; **17** 385
Sodang *see* YI CHAE-GWAN
Sōdeisha **33** 480
Soderberg, Elizabeth **2** 766
Soderigo da Tito **5** 180
Soderini (family) **22** 801
Soderini, Francesco, Cardinal **3** 697
Soderini, Mauro **11** 20
Soderini, Niccoló, Conte **3** 714
Soderini, Piero (di Tommaso) **28** 928*
interior decoration **3** 15
paintings **3** 304, 305
pupils **27** 737
Soderini, Tommaso di Lorenzo **22** 799, 800, 801
Söderköping **30** 64, *65*
Södermanland, Charles Philip, Duke of **24** 21
Södermark, Olaf Johan **29** 1*
Sodersten, Emil **2** 741, 771; **5** 601
sodium **10** 55
sodium carbonate **18** 655
sodium hydroxide **30** 538
sodium sulphides **24** 106; **30** 559
sodium thiosulphite *see* HYPO
Sōdōji **17** 196
Sodoma **12** 214; **25** 900; **28** 676, 684; **29** 1–3*
attributions **27** 634
patrons and collectors **6** 583; **24** 526; **27** 273
pupils **22** 804; **27** 447; **30** 281
teachers **29** 366
works **10** 130, 476; **24** 860; **25** 275; **26** 817; **28** 687–8; **29** *2*, *3*
Sødorp Church **23** 229
Sōdosha *see* GRASS AND EARTH SOCIETY
Södra Råda Church **30** *65*, 67, 75, 76
Sodré, Niomar Muniz *see* MUNIZ SODRÉ, NIOMAR
Sodwalls **32** 308
Soeder, Hans **26** 405
Soeffrens, Nicolas (*d* 1694) **18** 848
Soeffrens, Nicolas, the younger (1662-1710) **18** 848
Soelen, Jan Gijsbert Verstolk van, Baron *see* VERSTOLK VAN SOELEN, JAN GIJSBERT, Baron
Soemmerring, Samuel Thomas **1** 844
Sōen Josui *see* JOSUI SŌEN
Soen Kian *see* KIAN SOEN
Sōen Shun'oku *see* SHUN'OKU SŌEN
Soerensen **1** 690
Soesmans, Leib **4** 18
Soest **12** *360*; **29** 4–7*
Cathedral of St Patrokli **13** 18; **29** 4, 510; **33** 109
painting **12** 382; **13** 151
St Maria zur Höhne **26** 646
crosses **28** 71
St Maria zur Wiese **12** 365; **13** 56; **22** 220, 221; **29** 5*, *5*
sculpture **29** *6*, 6–7*
St Pauli **22** 220
sculpture **13** 114
Soest, Conrad von *see* CONRAD VON SOEST
Soest, Cord van *see* CORD VAN SOEST
Soest, Gerard **10** 273; **19** 125; **29** 7*
patrons and collectors **22** 351
pupils **26** 393
works **10** 249
Soest Antependium **13** 142
Soestdijk **22** *813*; **23** 466; **29** 7–8*
architecture **22** 828
gardens **12** 132
paintings **14** 381; **18** 652; **22** 846; **24** 745
Soeterbeeck, Master of **13** 114
Soetsu Yanagi *see* YANAGI, MUNEYOSHI
sofas **29** 8*; **31** 684
Austria **2** *814*
France **2** *564*; **11** 594
Germany **12** 426
Russia **27** *406*
United States of America **31** 628, 630, *630*, 633
Soffici, Ardengo **4** 199; **5** 848; **11** 190; **16** 680; **24** 448; **27** 207; **29** 9–10*
collaboration **20** 427; **24** 63
exhibitions **13** 711
groups and movements **11** 863, 865; **16** 679; **27** 307
works **7** 557; **29** *10*
soffit roll mouldings *see under* MOULDINGS → types
soffits **2** 292, *292*; **22** 213, 215, 217, 218, 220; **29** 10*
see also INTRADOS
Sofia (Bulgaria) **5** *144*, 145, 149; **9** *511*; **16** *103*; **26** *906*; **29** 10–11*
Army Club **5** 149
Art Academy **5** 163
art forms and materials
architecture **5** 150
metalwork **5** 160
sculpture **5** 156, 162
Bulgaria Hotel and Concert Hall **5** 149
Bulgarian National Bank **5** 149; **32** 78
Central Department Store **5** 150
Central State Photo Archive **5** 163
Communist Party Building **5** 150
congregational mosque **16** 222
Cyril and Methodius National Library **5** 149, 162
Daskalov house **5** 157
ecclesiastical buildings
Alexander Nevski Cathedral **5** 149, *149*, 162, 163; **28** 448
Holy Synod building **5** 149
St George **5** 150, 151; **29** 11
St Petka Samardjiiska **5** 148, 160; **25** 343
St Sophia **5** 146; **9** 538, 565

Sofia (Bulgaria)—cont.
Gallery for International Art **5** 150
Genshov house **5** 157
House of Teachers **5** 159
Institute of Architecture **5** 163
Ivan Lazarov Museum **18** 900
Kuyumdzhioglu house **5** 157
Mineral Baths **5** 149
Museum of Sofia's History **5** 163
National Art Gallery **5** 163, 326
National History Museum **5** 163
National Palace of Culture **5** 150; **31** 785, 905
National Swimming Complex **5** 159
National Theatre **5** 149
Old Royal Palace *see* National Art Gallery
Raikov house **5** 157
School of Drawing *see* Art Academy
Sheraton Hotel **5** 150, 163
Surmdiyev House **5** 149
tombs **5** 150
University Library **32** 78
urban planning **32** 78
Vitosha-New Othany Hotel **5** 159
Yablanski House **5** 149
Zaimov housing project **5** 150
Sofia (Russia) **5** 520
Sofronie, Master
works **26** *712*
Sofronievo **30** 769
Sofronova, Antonina **8** 10
soft art **11** 156; **23** 397; **25** 646; **29** 11–13*, *12*
United States of America **23** *397*
softeners *see under* BRUSHES → types
soft-ground etchings *see under* ETCHINGS → types
Soft Machine **4** 608
softness *see* MORBIDEZZA
soft-paste porcelain *see under* PORCELAIN → types
Soft Style *see* GOTHIC → styles → *weicher Stil*
Sōfū Ōkabe *see* OKABE, SŌFŪ
Sōfu Teshigahara *see* TESHIGAHARA, SŌFU
soga (dye) **30** 558
Soga (family) **17** 107
Soga Chokuan **17** 163; **23** 594; **29** 13*
Soga Dasoku *see* SOGA JASOKU
Sogai Tani *see* TANI SOGAI
Soga Jasoku **18** 560; **29** 13
Soga Kurayamada Ishikawamaro **17** 65
Sŏgam, Tomb 9 **18** 366
sŏgana script *see under* SCRIPTS → types
Soga Nichokuan **17** 164; **23** 594
Soğanlı
Karabaş Kilise **5** 676, 678
St Barbara **5** 674, 676, 677, 678; **9** 580
Soga no Umako **12** 95; **16** 82; **17** 65
Sogan Saitō *see* SAITŌ, SOGAN
Sogari *see* SPANI, PROSPERO
Soga school **29** 13*; **30** 466; **33** 535
Soga Shōhaku **17** 165, 194; **18** 552; **29** 13–14*
Soga Shōsen **29** 13
Soga Shōshō **29** 13
Soga Sōjō **29** 13
Soga Sōyo **29** 13
Sogdiana
amphorae **6** *256*
architecture **6** 197, 200, 201
bowls **6** *240*, *241*
castles **6** 200
clay **6** 219–20
dress **1** 886; **6** 251
ewers **6** *239*
Sogdiana—cont.
fortifications **6** 199
friezes **6** *230*, *231*
houses **6** 200, *200*, 229–30
manuscripts **6** *189*; **7** 114
metalwork **6** 238–41*
mud-bricks **6** 199
nude figures **18** *500*
ossuaries **6** 193; **23** 607
paintings **6** 228–32*; **28** 722
plaster **6** *220*
pottery **6** 255, 256, *256*, 257, 258
rhyta **6** *256*
scripts **6** 308
scrolls **6** 306
sculpture **6** 219–21*, *220*; **18** *500*
silk **6** *248*, 248–9, 285; **28** 721, *722*
silver **6** *239*, *241*
silver-gilt **6** *240*
stone **6** 220
swords **6** 261
temples **30** 440–41
terracotta **6** 275, 276
textiles **16** 435
vambraces **6** 262
weapons **16** 505
wood **6** 220; **18** *500*
Sōgenshodōkai **17** 239
Soggi, Niccolò **11** 217; **12** 760
Sogliani, Giovanni Antonio **19** 677; **29** 14*
patrons and collectors **12** 897
works **24** 860; **31** 54
Sognot, Louis **11** 601
Sogn-Valdres style **29** 580
Sōgo **8** 461
Sōgō Jūshiya *see* JŪSHIYA SŌGŌ
Sogō Setsudō **17** 413
Sogoyan, F. M. **18** 38
Söğüt Mosque **16** 205
Sŏgyang-jŏng *see* YI CHŎNG (i)
Sōgyū Tsuda *see* TSUDA SŌGYŪ
Sohag **7** *819*; **9** *507*; **29** 14–15*
Red Monastery (Deir el-Ahmar) **7** *819*, 820; **29** 14–15
White Monastery (Deir el-Abyad) **7** *819*, 820, 823; **23** 289; **29** 14
Sohagpur **15** *285*; **29** 15*
sculpture **15** 496, *496*
Virateshvara Temple **15** 291, 323
Sohar **21** 588
Museum **23** 436
Sōhei Takahashi *see* TAKAHASHI SŌHEI
Sohier, Hector **11** 512
Sohlberg, Harald Oskar **18** 717; **22** 540; **23** 225; **29** 15*
Sohm, Hanns **29** 16*
Sohn, Carl Ferdinand **29** 16*
collaboration **14** 838; **18** 204
groups and movements **9** 460; **12** 394
pupils **5** 290; **10** 99; **18** 143, 204; **31** 288; **32** 95; **33** 371
teachers **14** 838
Sohn, Wilhelm **16** 63
Söhnlein Rheingold **21** 431
Sohnu **15** 627
Søholm **8** 729
Sōhō Takuan *see* TAKUAN SŌHŌ
Soho Tapestry Works **10** 277; **30** 324
Sŏhwa hyŏphoe **33** 534
Sŏhwa misulhoe **18** 57
Sŏhwa yŏn'guhoe **18** 57
Soi, Ancent **17** 907
Soiaro, il *see* GATTI, BERNARDINO
Sōichirō Ōhara *see* ŌHARA, SŌICHIRŌ
Soignies, St Vincent **3** 568; **22** 216; **26** 574
sculpture **13** *100*, 100, 113
Soil de Moriamé, E. **3** 619
soils *see* MUD
Soirées de Paris, Les **24** 427, 442
Soissons **11** *504*; **29** 16–18*
Cathedral of SS Gervais and Protais **9** 672; **11** 510; **13** 38, 39–40; **14** 518; **26** 44; **29** *17*, 17–18*; **30** 729
mouldings **22** 217
stained glass **13** 179, 180, 181; **24** 890; **29** 511
tie-bars **30** 853
tracing floor **31** 275
transept **31** 281
manuscripts **7** 512
St-Jean-des-Vignes **13** 172
St Médard **7** 246, 265
Soissons, Comte de **20** 293
Soissons, Louis (Emmanuel Jean Guy de Savoie-Carignan) De *see* DE SOISSONS, LOUIS (E. J. G. DE SAVOIE-CARIGNAN), Vicomte d'Ostel, Baron Longroy
Soissons, Maria Teresa Felicia of Liechtenstein, Comtesse de (1694–1772) **21** 313
Soissons, Yolande de *see* YOLANDE DE SOISSONS
Soissons Gospels *see under* GOSPEL BOOKS → indivdual manscripts
Soitoux, Jean-François **3** 289
Sōi Yōsō *see* YŌSŌ SŌI
Sojae *see* YI SONG-MIN
Sōji Yamanoue *see* YAMANOUE SŌJI
Šojlev, Mihailo **19** 884
Sōjō **17** 173
Sojo, Felipe **29** 18*
Sojŏng *see* PYŎN KWAN-SIK
Sōjō Soga *see* SOGA SŌJŌ
SOK (Suomen Osuuskauppojen Keskuskunta) **15** 39
Sōka Gakkai Buddhism *see under* BUDDHISM → sects
Sokchang **18** 382
Sŏkchŏng **18** 312
Sŏkch'on Tomb **18** 369
Sokei **17** 122
Sōkei Nanbō *see* NANBŌ SŌKEI
Sōkei Nanpō *see* NANPŌ SŌKEI
Sōkei Oguri *see* OGURI SŌKEI
Sōkei Tanaka *see* TANAKA SŌKEI
Soken Yamaguchi *see* YAMAGUCHI SOKEN
Sokhumi **12** 320
Sokić, Ljubica **1** 820; **28** 451
Sŏkkuram **18** 250, 261, 265; **30** 444
sculpture **18** 286, *288*, 289
shrine **5** 115
Sŏk Kyŏng **29** 18*
Soknopaiou Nesos **9** 895; **10** 6
temple **10** 759
Sōko *see* MORITA, KISABURO
Sōkō Kogaku *see* KOGAKU SŌKŌ
Sokol, Koloman **28** 853
Sokollu Mehmed Pasha **29** 18–19*
architecture **9** 730; **16** 222, 223, 224, 225; **28** 768, *768*
manuscripts **16** 348
Sokol'niki, Rusakov House of Culture **27** 379
Sokolnikoff, Ruby *see* SCULL, ROBERT C.
Sokolov, B. Ye. **21** 813
Sokolov, Ivan I. **31** 559
Sokolov, N. (*fl* late 18th cent.) **17** 744
Sokolov, Nikolai (Aleksandrovich) (*fl* 1940s) **18** 504; **25** 352
Sokolov, Pyotr (Ivanovich) (1753–91) **27** 579
Sokolov, Pyotr (Fyodorovich) (1791–1848) **27** 390, 579; **29** 19*
pupils **31** 536
reproductive prints by others **28** 823
Sokolov, Pyotr (Petrovich) (1821–99) **29** 19*
Sokolov, V. D. **33** 518
Sokolova, Lydia **3** 119
Sokolova, Nina (Aleksandrovna) **27** 423
Sokolova Mogila **28** 324
Sokolov-Skalya, Pavel (Petrovich) **27** 395; **29** 19*
Sokołów **25** 121
Sokołowska, Barbara *see* BRUKALSKI, BARBARA
Sokołowski, Jan Seweryn **4** 234; **28** 402
Sokołowski, Marian **25** 143
Sokoryntsi, Galagan Palace **31** 564
Sokoto **1** *381*; **23** *129*
Shehu Mosque **1** 316
university **23** 135
Sokoto Caliphate **23** 302
Sokov, Leonid **29** 89
Sokpong *see* HAN HO
Sokra group **10** 616
Sokrates of Thebes **2** 682
Sŏktam *see* YI (i) I
Sŏktu **18** 312
Sŏ Kubang **18** 306
Sokuhi Nyoitsu **17** 231, 234, 235, 409; **20** 286; **29** 19–20*
Sōkyū Imai *see* IMAI SŌKYŪ
Sōkyū Negoro *see* NEGORO SŌKYŪ
Sōkyū Ueda *see* UEDA, SŌKYŪ
sol *see under* LACE → types
Sola **1** *401*
Sola, Antonio **1** 742; **3** 219; **29** 20–21*, 294; **32** 538
works **29** *20*
Solana, José (Gutiérrez) **10** 822; **20** 68; **29** 21*, 286
Solanki **29** 21*
see also:
BHIMA I, Ruler
JAYASIMHA SIDDHARAJA, Ruler
KARNADEVA, Ruler
UDAYAMATI, Queen
Solano, Mesa Gabriel **7** 606
Solano, Susana **29** 21*
Solano, Valentín Carderera y *see* CARDERERA Y SOLANO, VALENTÍN
Solano López, Francisco **24** 92, 95, 100
Solar, Antonio **13** 330
Solar, Xul *see* XUL SOLAR
Solari (i) (family) **9** 75
Solari, Agostino **25** 254
Solari (i), Alberto **29** 22
Solari, Amadeo **24** 286
Solari, Antonio (1700-73) **6** 572; **32** 879; **33** 116
Solari (i), Betolo **29** 22
Solari, Cristoforo (*c.* 1468/70–1524) **1** 748, 767; **21** 533; **29** 23–5*
patrons and collectors **10** 522
works **6** 357; **8** 135; **10** 744; **24** 286; **26** 503; **29** *24*
Solari, Cristoforo (*fl c.* 1570-85) **29** 27
Solari (i), Francesco **24** 286; **29** 22, 23*
Solari, G. A. **5** 867
Solari, Giorgio **21** 533
Solari (i), Giovanni **9** 75; **29** 22–3*
Solari (i), Guiniforte **9** 75; **11** 72; **21** 532; **29** 22–3*
collaboration **29** 23
patrons and collectors **9** 112
works **4** 645; **21** 534; **24** 284; **26** 289; **29** 22
Solari, Ignazio **29** 27
Solari, Luis **10** 509; **29** 26*; **31** 756, 758
Solari, Museo *see under* FRAY BENTOS
Solari (i), Pietro **29** 22
Solari (i), Pietro Antonio **27** 400; **29** 22, 23*
pupils **29** 23
works **22** 169; **27** 371
Solari, Santino **29** 26–7*
patrons and collectors **2** 828; **12** 133; **14** 361
works **2** 780, *781*, 782; **8** 526; **13** 703; **14** 645; **27** 323, 661
Solari, Tommaso **4** 562
Solario, Andrea **1** 767; **21** 525; **29** 22, 25–6*
copies **22** 190
patrons and collectors **1** 766, 767; **22** 26; **25** 144
works **1** 767; **3** 50; **19** 191; **22** 477; **29** *26*
Solario, Antonio (*fl* 1502-14) **1** 767; **29** 27–8*
works **8** 171; **29** *28*
solarization process *see under* PHOTOGRAPHY → processes
Solaro, Carlo **27** 878
solars **6** 407; **29** 21–2*, *22*
see also CHAMBERS
solar temples *see under* TEMPLES → types
Solbes, Rafael **10** 443; **29** 286
Sŏlcham *see* KIM SI-SŬP
Soldaïa *see* SUDAK
Soldán, Felipe Paz **19** 386
Soldani (Benzi), Massimiliano **11** 188; **29** 28–30*
assistants **28** 393
patrons and collectors **7** 286; **10** 140; **11** 234; **13** 301; **19** 337; **21** 29, 31; **27** 878
pupils **3** 198; **28** 393; **33** 15
reproductions in porcelain **9** 58
works **16** 700; **20** 214, 922; **26** 148; **29** *29*, 572
Soldata, Giuseppe **2** 212
Soldatenkov, K. G. **27** 439
Soldati, (Anton) Atanasio **16** 681; **22** 242; **29** 30–31*
Soldati, Giacomo **32** 631
Soldati, Giovanni Battista **29** 833
Soldati, Tommaso **8** 426
Soldatović, Jovan **28** 453
Soldé, M. **10** 781
Soldenhoff, Max **33** 737
soldering **20** 367
historical and regional traditions
Afghanistan **21** *325*
China **7** 100
Egypt, ancient **9** 818
Rome, ancient **21** 325; **27** 17
materials
borax **12** 866; **21** 325
chrysocolla **24** 793
copper **21** 325
lead **7** 100; **21** 325
mercury **21** 325
silver **21** 325
tin **7** 100; **21** 325
uses
bronze **4** 850; **10** 625
conservation **7** 730
gold **12** 866–7; **24** 793
metalwork **9** 818; **21** 324–5*
sculpture **27** 17
silver **28** 739
stained glass **29** 499
soldering, colloidal *see* METALWORK → techniques → granulation
soldering, eutectic *see* METALWORK → techniques → granulation
Soldi, Andrea **29** 31–2*
works **29** *31*
Soldi, Antenore **28** 318
Soldiero, Domenico *see* MORELLI, DOMENICO
Soldner, Paul **31** 640
Soldo, Giacomo **31** 901
Sole, Giovanni Antonio Maria dal **29** 32
Sole, Giovanni Gioseffo dal **4** 277; **29** 32–3*
collaboration **8** 141
patrons and collectors **4** 611; **5** 178; **7** 779; **12** 559; **27** 316

Sole, Giovanni Gioseffo dal—cont.
pupils **3** 488; **12** 3; **19** 117; **22** 26; **26** 320; **33** 690
teachers **24** 227
works **24** 227; **29** *33*
Sole, Giuseppe dal **12** 25
Soleb **9** *774*; **23** *276*, 279; **29** 33–4*
temple of Amenophis III **9** 831; **23** 279, *279*, 280; **29** 33–4
sole bends *see under* LEATHER → types
Soledad, María de la, Marquésa de Santiago *see* SANTIAGO, MARÍA DE LA SOLEDAD, Marquésa de
Soledad Alonso Pimental, María Josefa de la *see* OSUNA, 9th Duquesa de
Solentiname **23** *79*
Solentiname primitivist painting **23** 81, 84, 85; **29** 34*
Soler, Luis Blanco, *see* BLANCO SOLER, LUIS
Soler, Ramón López *see* LÓPEZ SOLER, RAMÓN
Soleri, Paolo **29** 34–5*
collaboration **8** 257
methods **28** 645
pupils **33** 223
works **29** *35*
Solerio, Carlo Guasco, Marqués de **11** 872
Soler y Faneca, Juan de **29** 271
Solesmes Abbey **11** 555
Solf & Wichards **13** 686
Solger Hours *see under* BOOKS OF HOURS → individual manuscripts
Solgŏ **29** 36*
Sŏlgok *see* Ŏ MONG-NYONG
Soli **8** *325*
basilica **8** 357, *357*, 359; **29** 816
marble **8** 342
mosaics **8** 354
nymphaeum **8** 337
sculpture **8** 342, 354
temple **8** 336
Soli, Aratus of *see* ARATUS OF SOLI
Soli, Giuseppe Maria **2** 175; **27** 790
solia see ROME, ANCIENT → thrones
Soliani **33** 358
solidi *see under* COINS → types
Solier, René de **26** 352; **33** 305
Solier, W. du **14** 831
Solihull (Warwicks) **29** 413
Solikowski, Jan Dymitr, Archbishop **3** 918
Solimani, Nicolò **19** 305, 307
Solimani, Zeno **19** 305
Solimena, Angelo **29** 36–7*
Solimena, Francesco **22** 479; **29** 36–43*; **31** 444
assistants **27** 201
attributions **25** 891
collaboration **13** 347; **25** 2; **29** 36
patrons and collectors
Auldjo, John **2** 727
Bourbon II., Luis Antonio, Infante of Spain **4** 565
Buonaccorsi, Raimondo **5** 178
Cacault, François **5** 356
Charles VI, Holy Roman Emperor (*reg* 1711- 40) **32** 444
Coke, Thomas, 1st Earl of Leicester of the 1st creation (1697-1759) **13** 301
Elizabeth Farnese, Queen of Spain (1692-1766) **4** 560
Filangieri, Gaetano **11** 70
Harrach, Aloys Thomas, Graf von **14** 191
Maria Amalia, Queen of Spain (1724-60) **4** 562
Solimena, Francesco
patrons and collectors—cont.
Medinaceli, Luís de la Cerda Fernández de Córdoba Folch de Cardona y Aragón, 9th Duque de (1660-1711) **21** 35
Ramsay, Allan (1713-84) **28** 271
Ruffo, Tommaso, Cardinal, Archbishop of Ferrara **27** 316
Savoy, Eugene of, Prince (1663-1736) **28** 15
Tallard, Marie-Joseph d'Hostun, Duc de **30** 274
Theatine Order **30** 648
Victor-Amadeus II, 15th Duke of Savoy (*reg* 1675- 1730) and King of Sardinia (*reg* 1720-30) **28** 16
pupils
Altomonte, Bartolomeo **1** 733
Bonito, Giuseppe **4** 323
Caro, Lorenzo de **5** 790
Conca, Sebastiano **7** 681
Gioffredo, Mario Gaetano **12** 657
Gran, Daniel **13** 277
Mura, Francesco de **22** 326
Narice, Francesco **22** 507
Ramsay, Allan (1713-84) **25** 882
Rossi, Nicola Maria **27** 201
Rotari, Pietro (Antonio) **27** 213
Sanfelice, Ferdinando **27** 727
Traversi, Gaspare **31** 291
Vaccaro, Domenico Antonio **31** 789
Zeiller, Johann Jakob **33** 629
Zoffany, Johan (Joseph) **33** 692
reproductive prints by others **3** 204; **8** 267
works **2** 828; **14** 900; **15** 139; **16** *672*, 673; **22** 479; **29** *37*, *38*, *40*, *42*; **31** 883; **32** 443, 459
Solimena, Giulio **1** 796
Solimena, Orazio **29** 36
Solin *see* SALONA
Solingen **7** 586
Deutsches Klingenmuseum **18** 114
metalwork **12** 454
scissors **8** 286, *286*, 287
Solinus **31** 289
Solís, Felipe Sánchez *see* SÁNCHEZ SOLÍS, FELIPE
Solís, Francisco de **22** 103; **29** 45*; **32** 557
Solís, Juan de **2** 381; **29** 45*
Solís, Mario **9** 713
Solis, Nikolaus **29** 43, 44*
Solis, Virgil **2** 455; **11** 48; **23** 310; **28** 671; **29** 43–4*
collaboration **1** 788
pupils **29** 44
works **12** 386, 446, 455; **14** 424; **16** 901; **23** 680; **24** 271; **25** 607; **29** *44*, 747; **33** 354
Solivella, Guillermo **19** 518
Solkhat Krym *see* STARYY KRYM
Sollentuna **30** 83
Soller, August **19** 754; **29** 45*
works **3** 794; **25** 173; **29** 5
Soller, Louis **10** 689
Sollers **11** 553
Søllested Grave **32** 525
Sollier, Louis **17** 451
Sollis, Hans **29** 43
Sollogub, N. M. **27** 439
Solly, Edward **29** 46*
paintings **2** 560; **10** 366; **14** 653; **21** 824
Solly, Sarah **29** 46
Solly *Madonna* **29** 46
Solms, Friedrich Magnus, Graf von **32** 676
Solms-Braunfels, Amalia, Countess von *see* AMALIA VON SOLMS, Princess of Orange
Solna Church **30** 66
Solnhofen Basilica **26** 634
Solntsev, Fedor **27** 579
Solo *see* SURAKARTA
Solodkin, Judith **19** 492
Soloeis **28** 654
Soloi Basilica **9** 566
Solokha **4** 111
Solomatkin, Leonid (Ivanovich) **27** 390; **29** 46–7*
Solomerto **15** 778
Solomon **30** 727
Solomon, Abraham **29** 47*
Solomon, Gladstone **15** 657
Solomon, J. M. **5** 668; **29** 105; **32** 792
Solomon, King of Israel (*reg c.* 961-922 BC)
architecture **16** 572; **17** 487, 493, 494, 532; **21** 553; **30** 431
thrones **30** 775
Solomon, Rebecca **29** 47*
Solomon, Simeon **12** 216; **29** 47–8*
groups and movements **23** 504; **25** 555
patrons and collectors **15** 895; **25** 41; **33** 180
works **11** 434; **23** *547*; **29** *48*; **30** 123
Solomon, Solomon J. **9** 54; **17** 578
Solomon ben Isaac **17** 563
Solomon-Godeau, Abigail **33** 312
Solomon ha-Kohen **14** 35
Solomonic order *see under* ORDERS (ARCHITECTURAL) → types
Solomon Islands **23** *711*; **24** 64, *64*; **25** 181; **27** 778; **29** 48–51*
beads **29** *49*
body ornaments **27** *779*; **29** 49, 51
bowls **29** 50, *50*
canoes **23** 724, 725, *726*; **29** 49
clubs (weapons) **29** 49
figureheads **29** 49, *49*
forgeries **23** 738
headdresses **27** *779*
houses **23** *726*; **29** 50–51
mother-of-pearl **28** II2
photography **10** 580
pottery **23** 728
sculpture **23** 732
shells **28** 581; **29** 49, *50*
shields **28** II2; **29** 49
tattoos **23** 722
weapons **23** 734
wood **29** *49*, *50*
wood-carvings **29** *49*, 49–51
see also POLYNESIAN OUTLIERS
Solomon Master **33** 71
Solomons, Israel **17** 582
Solon, Albert **30** 888
Solon, Léon-Victor **17** 722; **29** 51
Solon, Marc-Louis-Emanuel **21** 697; **29** 51*
groups and movements **17** 441
works **10** 312; **12** 261; **24** 149
Solongo **1** 403
Solón Romero, Walter **29** 51*
Solo Press **19** 492
Solórzano, Bartolomé de *see* BARTOLOMÉ DE SOLÓRZANO
Solorzano, Juan Javier Mijares de *see* MIJARES DE SOLORZANO, JUAN JAVIER
Solórzano, Martín de *see* MARTÍN DE SOLÓRZANO
Solosmeo, Antonio **27** 851
Solothurn **30** *124*
Cathedral of St Ursus **12** 372; **30** 127
faience (ii) (ceramics) **30** 144
fountains **30** 136
Jesuit church **32** 821
Kunstmuseum **5** 75
sculpture **30** 136
town walls **30** 126
Solothurn school **14** 86
Solovetsky Monastery **27** *363*, 371; **29** 51–2*
Cathedral of the Transfiguration **27** 371
Solov'yev, Sergey **27** 440, 441
Solovyov, Vladimir **3** 692
Solsona, Cathedral of S María **26** 610, 642
Solsona, Justo **2** 397
Solt'an *see* HAN SI-GAK
Sołtan, Jerzy **15** 122; **29** 52*; **30** 391
Soltaniye *see* SULTANIYYA
Soltau, Pauline **29** 905
Soltynski, Roman **17** 824
Solutrean period *see under* PREHISTORIC ART → periods
Solvay, Armand **14** 770
Solvay, Louis **3** 619
Solvay Company **14** 770
solvents **1** 155; **7** 92; **8** 899*; **23** 791; **29** 53*
types *see*: BUTANOL; DIACETONE ALCOHOL; GENKLENE; ISO PROPANOL; OILS → types → lavender; PETROL; POLYPROPYLENE GLYCOETHER: TOLUENE; TURPENTINE; WHITE SPIRIT; XYLENE
uses
cleaning **29** 53
glazes **23** 792
paints **23** 792; **29** 53
varnishes **33** 335
Sölvesborg Factory **30** 97
Sol'vychegodsk **27** *363*, 426; **29** 53–5*
Cathedral of the Annunciation **29** 53–4, 779
Cathedral of the Presentation of the Virgin **27** 373; **29** 54, *54*, 779
embroidery **27** 430
lace **27** 430
Solvyns, F(rançois) Baltazard **29** 55*
SOM *see* SKIDMORE, OWINGS AND MERRILL
Sōma **17** 353
Somada (family) **17** 399
Somaini, Francesco **29** 55*
Somali **1** 229, 295, 306, 366; **9** 50; **29** 55
Somalia **1** *214*, 378; **29** 55–7*; **30** 693
architecture **29** 56–7
basketwork **1** 296
jewellery **29** 56
mats **1** 296
metalwork **29** 56
rock art **1** 373
shields **1** 362
windows **29** *56*
wood-carvings **29** 56, *56*
Somaliland, French *see* DJIBOUTI
Somanatha **15** 79, 533; **29** 61
Somapalem Chennakeshava Temple **15** 540, 645, 647
Somapura Vihāra *see* PAHARPUR
Somaré, Enrico **29** 57*
Somazzi, Giovanni **29** 251, 290
Sombor **28** *437*
Cathedral of the Holy Trinity **28** 444
Municipal Museum **28** 458
Somenzi, Mino **1** 166; **8** 771; **11** 867, 869
Somer, Bernaert van **7** 510; **29** 57
Somer, Jan van **21** 415
Somer, Paul van **10** 248; **21** 416; **29** 57–8*
works **10** 247; **16** 823
Somera, Francisco **21** 403
Someren, Barent van **9** 470
Someren, Pauwels van *see* SOMER, PAUL VAN
Somerford, Tommy **7** 327
Somerhill, Ulick de Burgh, Baron *see* BURGH, ULICK JOHN DE, 14th Earl of Clanricarde
Somerley House (Hants) **9** 13
Somers (family) **3** 598
Somers, Charles, 3rd Earl of Somers **29** 58*; **32** 922
Somers, John, 1st Lord Somers
drawings **6** 116; **8** 209; **9** 230; **26** 246; **30** 279
paintings **9** 327; **29** 58
Somers, John, Baron **26** 345
Somers, Wierick, III **3** 598
Somerset, Charles Noel, 4th Duke of Beaufort **5** 598; **27** 468; **28** 790
Somerset, Charles Seymour, 6th Duke of *see* SEYMOUR, CHARLES, 6th Duke of Somerset
Somerset, Edward Seymour, 1st Duke of *see* SEYMOUR, EDWARD, 1st Duke of Somerset
Somerset, Henrietta *see* WILLIAMS-WYNN, HENRIETTA SOMERSET, Lady, of Wynnstay
Somerset, Henry, 1st Duke of Beaufort(, 3rd Marquess of Worcester) (1629-1700) **29** 58*
Somerset, Henry, 3rd Duke of Beaufort (1707-49) **5** 350; **13** 301; **17** 902; **29** 31
Somerset, Henry, 10th Duke of Beaufort (1900-84) **2** 560
Somerset, Richard Gay **20** 239
Somerset, Robert Carr, 1st Earl of *see* CARR, ROBERT, 1st Earl of Somerset
Somersham Church (Cambs) **10** 286
Somerton (Oxon), St James **10** 261
Somerville, Henry B. T. **10** 580
Somerville, William **4** 362
Somerville Stone **28** 241
Someshvara III (*reg c.* 1126-63) (Chalukyas of Kalyana) **15** 550
Something Else Press **29** 16
Somezée *Warrior* **23** 441
Sōmi Tanaka *see* TANAKA SŌMI
Somkovsky, Sebastian **31** 510
Somm, Henry **20** 602; **26** 432; **29** 58*
Sommariva, Giovanni Battista **29** 59*
collections **11** 663
gems **3** 687; **24** 734
paintings **2** 232; **8** 560; **13** 793; **19** 786; **25** 383, 671
sculpture **30** 764
Sommariva, Luigi **29** 59
Sommaruca **27** 852
Sommaruga, Giuseppe **29** 59*
collaboration **25** 793
groups and movements **2** 567
teachers **4** 247, 842
works **16** 648, 721; **20** 908
Sommavilla, Godofredo **11** 62
Somme, Charles de **29** 668
Somme-Bionne **6** 481
Sommelsdijk, Cornelis van Aerssen van *see* AERSSEN VAN SOMMELSDIJK, CORNELIS VAN
Sommer (family) **33** 36
Sommer, Carlos (late 19th century) **29** 60
Sommer, Caspar **29** 59–60
Sommer, Charles (late 17th century) **12** 832
Sommer, Eberhardt **29** 59
Sommer, Ferdinand **14** 614
Sommer, Frederick **7** 434; **29** 60*
Sommer, Georg Christoph **29** 60
Sommer, Giorgio **29** 60–61*
Sommer, Jacques **11** 589
Sommer, Johann Andreas **29** 60
Sommer, Johann Daniel **29** 59–60*
Sommer, Johann Eberhardt **29** 59
Sommer, Johann Friederich **29** 60

Sommer, Johann Jakob **29** 60
Sommer, Oskar **10** 451, 669; **11** 735; **31** 241
Sommer, Philipp Christoph **29** 60
Sommer, Philipp Jakob **29** 60
Sommerard, (Simon-Nicolas-) Alexandre du *see* DU SOMMERARD, (SIMON-NICOLAS-) ALEXANDRE
Sommerau, Ludwig **20** 915
Sommerfeld, Adolf **13** 687
Sommerhuber **25** 403, 404
Sommer & Son **29** 573
Sommerville, Maxwell **12** 266
Sommier, François-Clément *see* SOMM, HENRY
Sommier, M. Alfred **32** 97
Somnath **15** 308; **16** 245
 Maipuri Dargah **15** 349
Somnathpur **15** *294*, 532; **29** 61*
 Keshava Temple **15** 327, 533
Somodevilla y Bengoechea, Zenón *see* ENSENADA, Marqués de
Somodor **27** 92
Somogyi, Árpád **29** 61*
Somogyi, József **14** 896
Somogyvár **14** *881*
 Abbey of St Giles **14** 883; **26** 638
  St Adalbert **14** 892
  sculpture **14** 892
Somolo **1** 311
Somorja *see* ŠAMORÍN
Somov, A. S. **27** 443
Somov, Konstantin (Andreyevich) **27** 580; **29** 61–2*
 collaboration **8** 506
 groups and movements **8** 849; **12** 870; **27** 580; **31** 582; **33** 379
 patrons and collectors **22** 135
Sompel, Pieter van **29** 62*
Sompting (W. Sussex), St Mary **26** 616; **27** 130; **29** 659
Sompura (family) **15** 179
Somville, Roger **5** 45; **17** 518
Son **8** 490
Son, Adrian van *see* VANSON, ADRIAN
Soná **32** 238
Sŏnam-sa Temple **18** 281
Sonargaon Folk Art and Craft Museum **3** 170
Sŏn Buddhism *see under* BUDDHISM → sects
Son Carla **3** 105
Sonchin **17** 228
Sonchō **14** 703; **17** 228
Soncini, Eugenio **16** 650; **25** 218
Soncino **17** 565; **28** 664
Soncino, Andrea **9** 340
Soncino, Eliezer **29** 62
Soncino, Gershom (*d* 1534; grandfather) **4** 18; **17** 565; **21** 176; **29** 62
Soncino, Gershom (*d* 1562; grandson) **29** 62
Soncino, Joshua **4** 18; **29** 62
Soncino, Moses (grandfather) **29** 62
Soncino, Moses (grandson) **29** 62
Soncino, Solomon **29** 62
Soncinus, Hieronymus *see* SONCINO, GERSHOM
Sonck, Lars (Eliel) **29** 63–4*
 collaboration **3** 177
 groups and movements **22** 541; **23** 498
 works **11** 92; **14** 371; **29** *64*; **30** 284; **32** 861
Sondani **15** *279*, *285*; **29** 64*
 pillars **15** 286
 sculpture **15** 457, 460, *460*, 474
Sonde **29** 97
Sonden **17** 228
Sonder *see* MOLLER
Sonderborg, K(urt) R(udolf) H(offmann) **29** 64–5*
Sonderbund **17** 764; **21** 775; **31** 538
Søndergaard, Jens (Andersen) **8** 736; **29** 65*
Sondergotik see under GOTHIC → styles
Sønder Jernløse Church **8** *730*
Sonderland, Fritz **29** 66
Sonderland, Johann Baptist **29** 66*
Sondersø **9** 156
Sondes, George **2** 545
Sondō **17** 228
 works **17** *228*
Sŏndŏk, Queen of Silla (*reg* 632-47) **18** 546
Sŏndong **18** 342, 343
Sondre Tveito
 farmhouses **32** *287*
Sone, Tatsuzo **17** 87
Son'en, Prince **11** 856; **29** 66*
 works **17** 215, 225–6, 227, *227*, 228
 writings **17** 226–8, 229; **29** 902
Son'en school *see* SHŌREN'IN
Son'en Shinnō *see* SON'EN, PRINCE
Sone Sunsai **17** 413
Song, King (*reg* 523-54) **18** 275
Songak *see* KAESONG
Songayla, Mikolas (Aleksandro) **17** 856; **19** 499; **29** 66*
Song Bai **19** 326
Song Boren **7** 118
Song Chun-gil **18** 330
Song Di **6** 784
Song dynasty
 see:
  GAOZONG, Emperor
  HUIZONG, Emperor
  TAIZONG, Emperor
 see also CHINA → periods → Song period
Songe *see* SONGYE
Song Guang **6** 756
Songguk **18** 271
 pottery **18** *334*
Songgung **18** 345
Songgwang Temple (North Cholla) **18** 296
Songgwang Temple (South Cholla) **12** 94; **18** 281; **28** 638
 metalwork **18** 348
 paintings **18** 307, 308, 309
 sculpture **18** 295
Songhai **1** 246, 310, 315; **11** 829; **23** 127
Songhe (Jingshan) **6** 850
Sŏng Im **18** 329
Song In **18** 329
Songjae *see* CH'OE PUK
Songjiang **6** 756, 760–61; **7** 151
 see also SHANGHAI
Sŏngjong, King (*reg* 1469-94) **18** 317, 324, 329
Sŏngju **18** 341
Sŏngjung *see* KIM KWANG-SU
Song Ke **6** 756, 757
 works **6** *757*
Songkhla **30** 590
 sculpture **30** 597, *598*
 Wat Matchimawat **30** 616
Song Luy **6** 426
Songnim Temple **18** 331
Songo **2** 86; **7** 195–6, 199*
 body arts **1** 342
 clubs (weapons) **7** *198*
 sculpture **1** 403; **7** *198*
 wood **7** *198*
Songola **1** 404; **19** 72, 74
Songor A **21** 280
Songor B **21** 281
Songor C **21** 281
Song period *see under* CHINA → periods
Sŏng Sam-mun **18** 329
Songsan **18** 260
 Tomb 6 **18** 272
Sŏng Se-ch'ang **18** 329; **29** 68*
Song Si-yŏl **18** 330
Sŏng Su-ch'im **18** 331
Song Sui **6** 756
Song Su-nam **18** 326
Songtsen Gampo, King of Tibet (*reg* 620-49) **19** 293; **30** 815
Songwŏl **18** 312
Song Xu **28** 588; **29** 68*; **33** 652, 657
Songye **29** 68–71*
 baskets **1** 251
 divination instruments **1** 356, 357
 masks **1** 405, 406; **29** 69, *70*, 70–71*
 metalwork **29** 69
 sculpture **1** 403; **29** *69*, 69–70*
 textiles **29** 69
 wood-carvings **14** 378
Song Yingxing **4** 684; **7** 83, 115
 works **4** *683*
Song Yŏng-su **18** 301
Song Yun **6** 311, 320; **28** 637
Songze culture **6** 877, 878
Song Ziyan **17** 185; **29** 86
Sonia, Anwar Khamis **23** 436
Soninke **3** 132, 379; **20** 198, 861
Sŏnjo, King (*reg* 1567-1608) **14** 137; **18** 300, 314, 330; **29** 72*
Sonjun **17** 229
Sonkai *see* CHON'GYE
Sonkamsari, Temple 1 **15** 267
Sonkh **15** 252; **20** 817
 sculpture **20** 817, *818*
 temple **20** 818
Sonnabend, Ileana **6** 23
Sonne, Jørgen (1771-1823) **29** 72
Sonne, Jørgen (Valentin) (1801-90) **4** 68; **27** 643; **29** 72*
Sonne, Edvard **29** 72
Sonne, Edvard Christian **14** 595
Sonneberg **31** 255, 262
Sonnenschein, (Johann) Valentin **29** 73*; **30** 137; **33** 737
 pupils **31** 764
 works **3** 823; **19** 781
Sonnetti, Bartolomeo da li **27** 176
Sonnier, Keith **6** 23; **22** 748; **25** 645; **29** 73*
Sonnin, Ernst Georg **14** 101; **19** 815
Sonning (Berks), Deanery **9** 739; **12** 141; **19** *820*
Sonnini de Manoncour, Charles **10** 79
Sonnō *see* SON'Ō
Sonntag, William Louis **29** 73–4*
Sonntagberg **2** 799
 Pilgrimage Church **25** *448*
Son'ō **17** 228
Sono, Toshihiki **29** 219
Sonoda, Kojō **17** 413, 414
Sonoma (CA), El Novilfero **12** 143
Sono Noguchi *see* NOGUCHI, SONO
Sonora Desert Museum **33** 700
Son Real **3** 105
Sons, Jan **23** 502; **28** 61
Sons of Liberty **26** 262
Sons of Liberty Punch Bowl **26** 262, *262*
Sonsonate **10** *153*, 154
Sonsorol **23** 832
Sontag, William Louis *see* SONNTAG, WILLIAM LOUIS
Söntgen, Johann Joseph **13** 805; **22** 456
Sonuga, Gbenga **15** 57
Sŏn'un Temple **18** 294, 295, 311
Sony Corp. **15** 827
 radios **15** *827*
Sŏnyŏng *see* YU SUK
Sonzino, Il *see* CAPORALE, FRANCESCO
Soon, Tay Kheng **19** 384; **28** 772
Soonde **1** 403, 405
soot
 historical and regional traditions
  China **6** 736; **7** 91
  Islamic **16** 276
  Japan **17** 387, 388
 types
  pine **6** 736; **7** 91, 92, *93*; **17** 213
soot—cont.
 uses
  bistre **4** 101
  calligraphy **6** 736; **17** 213
  inks **6** 736; **7** 91, 92, *93*; **15** 849, 851, 852; **16** 276; **17** 213
  inksticks **7** 91, 92, *93*; **17** 387, 388
  pigments **24** 789
  tattoos **30** 366
  writing **17** 213
Sōotarō Yasui *see* YASUI, SŌOTARŌ
Sopara **15** 200, 492
 Chakreshvara Temple **15** 493
Soper, Alexander **7** 161
Sopers, Antoine **3** 572
sophia **13** 467
Sophia, Electress of Hanover (*fl c.* 1696) **3** 806; **14** 469; **23** 513
Sophia, Empress of Byzantium (before 530-after 600) **9** *637*; **17** 701; **26** 143
Sophia, Princess of Armenia (*fl c.* 931) **2** 429
Sophia Charlotte, Queen of Prussia (1668-1705) **5** 347
Sophia-Dorothea, Queen of Prussia (1687-1757) **11** *459*; **14** 647; **18** 475; **24** 541
Sophia Magdalena, Queen of Sweden (*fl c.* 1770s) **26** 99; **29** 689
Sophianus, Nikolaus **32** 681
Sophia van Bylant **20** 758
Sophie, Electress of Saxony (*fl c.* 1585) **17** 887
Sophie, Margravine of Ansbach (*fl* 1486-1503) **31** 286
Sophie, Queen of Poland (?1405-61) **25** 675
Sophie Amalie, Queen of Denmark (*fl c.* 1665) **8** 725
Sophie Magdalen, Queen of Denmark and Norway (1746-1813) **10** 111
Sophienholm **8** 727
Sophilos (*fl c.* 600-570 BC) **32** 67*
 works **13** 507, *507*
Sophilos (*fl c.* 200 BC) **1** 617; **13** 557; **29** 74*
 works **1** *617*; **13** 557, 558, 566, 567; **21** 122; **22** 160
Sophocles **1** 450; **9** 618; **30** 650
Sopianae **24** 313
Sopik, St Mary **1** 542
Sopoćani, Holy Trinity Monastery **9** *511*, 552; **28** 440; **29** 74–5*
 church **28** 441
 icons **9** 628
 sculpture **28** 452
 wall paintings **9** 582, 583; **28** 446, *446*
Sopolis **13** 549
Sopot **25** 123, 133
Sopotskin Synagogue **17** 544
Soprani, Raffaele **24** 836, 837; **28** 219; **29** 75*
Sopranzi, Agostino **17** 444
sopraporte *see* OVERDOORS
Sopron **14** *881*; **26** *906*; **29** 75–6*
 All Souls **14** 900
 architecture **14** 889
 Church of the Holy Ghost **29** *75*
 Franciscan church **14** 883
 pottery **25** 543
 St George **29** 76
 St Michael **14** 883, 884; **29** 75
 sculpture **14** 894
 synagogue **17** 544
Sopron-Bécsidomb **6** 157
Sopronhorpács Church **26** 638
Soradir, St Ēdjmiadzin **2** 426
Soragni, Bonifacio Lupi di *see* BONIFACIO LUPI DI SORAGNI
Sorai Ogyū *see* OGYŪ SORAI
Soranus of Ephesos **9** 618
Soranzo, Alvise **27** 760
Soranzo, Jacopo **5** 623
Sorbi, Raffaello **7** 344
Sorbonne *see under* PARIS
Sorch, Hendrick de *see* SORGH, HENDRICK (MAERTENSZ.)
Sorčuq *see* SHORCHUK
Sordini, Ettore **20** 352
Sordino, Il *see* CALVI, JACOPO ALESSANDRO
Sordo, il *see* VIVIANI, ANTONIO
Sordo, Javier **21** 382
Sordo Madaleno, Juan **19** 84; **21** 380, 397; **29** 76*
Soreau, Daniel **29** 725
Soreau, David **12** 389
Soreau, Isaak **11** 227; **12** 389
Soreda, Juan de **29** 278
Sorel, Edward **7** 292; **12** 772
Sorella, Simone **32** 229
Sorello, Miguel **29** 76*
Sørensen, Carl Theodor (Marius) **8** 728; **21** 820; **29** 76–7*, 601
Sørensen, C. F. **30** 647
Sorensen, Christen **5** 573
Sørensen, Erik Christian **29** 77*
Sørensen, Henrik (Ingvar) **23** 603; **29** 77–9*
 collaboration **23** 226
 groups and movements **10** 696
 teachers **23** 226
 works **23** 603; **29** *78*
Sørensen, Jørgen Haugen *see* HAUGEN SØRENSEN, JØRGEN
Sørensen, Jorn Ole **8** 729
Sørensen, Margrethe **8** 742
Soresina Vidoni, Bartolomeo **3** 687
Soresini, Giuseppe Maria **13** 169
Sorge, Peter **3** 803; **31** 532
Sörgel von Sorgenthal, Conrad **2** 816; **32** 449
Sorgh, Hendrick (Maertensz.) **29** 79*
 attributions **27** 518
 reproductive prints by others **12** 851
 teachers **32** 673
 works **27** 230; **31** 246
sorghum **30** 557
Sŏ-ri (Korea) **18** 340
Sori (Papua New Guinea) **24** 82
Soria
 Bibles **17** 561
 Cathedral **2** 294
 manuscripts **4** *16*
 sculpture **26** 605, 609
 S Pedro **32** 821
Soria, Antonio Rodríguez de *see* RODRÍGUEZ DE SORIA, ANTONIO DE
Soria, Giovanni Battista **29** 79–80*
 collaboration **13** 292, 321
 patrons and collectors **3** 250; **4** 406; **32** 9
 teachers **22** 5
 works **22** 5; **27** 160; **29** *80*
Soria, Martín de *see* MARTÍN DE SORIA
Soriano, Esteban **18** 832
Soriano, Federico Aparici y *see* APARICI Y SORIANO, FEDERICO
Soriano, Juan **21** 406; **29** 81*
Soriano, Rafael **18** 834; **29** 81*
Soriano, Raphael S(imon) **18** 189; **19** 701; **29** 81*
Soria y Mata, Arturo **12** 144; **31** 728
Sorim *see* CHO SŎK-CHIN
Sōritsu Oguri *see* OGURI SŌRITSU
Sōri Yanagi *see* YANAGI, MUNEMICHI
Sorko **1** 317
Sorleir **20** 603
Sormani, Leonardo **29** 82*
 collaboration **2** 139; **25** 257; **31** 787
 works **26** 833
Sormeau, Pérot **4** 544

Sorø 8 *720*; 13 50
Abbey Church 4 780; 8 722, 723, 738
altarpiece 8 733
crosses 28 71
funerary monument of Archbishop Absalon 8 738
funerary monument of Christopher II 8 738
tomb of Valdemar III 8 738
Art Museum 8 760
Soroka, Grigory (Vasil'yevich) 27 389; 29 82–3*; 32 164
Soroki 21 *810*
castle 21 810
Sorokin, Yevgraf (Semyonovich) 24 247; 29 631
Sorolla y Bastida, Joaquín 29 83–4*; 31 816
groups and movements 24 829
patrons and collectors 1 529; 3 869; 12 504; 31 757
works 27 767; 29 *84*, 285
Soros, George 10 541
Sōrosha 17 239
Sorri, Pietro 5 769; 29 783; 31 886
Sorrisi, Giovanni Maria 29 830
Sorte, Cristoforo 16 712; 21 765; 29 84–5*; 31 17
Sorunda 30 77
Sörup Font 11 253
Sosa, Antonieta 29 85*
Sosa, Joaquín 32 180
Sosabravo, Alfredo 8 236
Sosaburō Eiraku *see* EIRAKU SOSABURŌ
Sosa Dede 11 247
Sōsai 29 241
Sōsaku hanga see CREATIVE PRINT MOVEMENT
Sŏ Sang-wu 18 331
Sŏsan Taesa *see* HYUJŎNG
Sos del Rey Católico 27 752
S Esteban 29 263
Sōsei Iten *see* Iten Sōsei
Sōseki Daishitsu *see* DAISHITSU SŌSEKI
Sōseki Musō *see* MUSŌ SŌSEKI
Sōseki Natsume *see* NATSUME, SŌSEKI
Sosen Mori *see* MORI SOSEN
Sŏ Se-ok *see* SUH SE OK
Soshenko, Ivan M. 31 559
Sō Shigan *see* SONG ZIYAN
Sō Shii 17 412, 414; 18 190, 191; 29 85–6*
Sō Shikō 29 86
Soshinskaya, Lyudmila (Anatol'yevna) 27 411
Sōshirō Nishimura *see* NISHIMURA SŌSHIRŌ
Sō Shiseki 29 86*
pupils 27 595; 28 598
works 14 565; 17 185; 23 347; 28 588
Sō Shizan 28 588; 29 86
Sōshū Kanō *see* KANŌ SŌSHŪ
Sosianus Hierocles 23 893
Sosias Painter 13 518
Sosibios 22 733
Sosikles 13 454
Sosnowski, Kajetan 4 234
Sosnowski, Tomasz Oskar 25 100, 115, 142; 28 839; 29 86*; 32 872, 877
Sosonghoe 18 57
Sosos 22 160; 24 411; 29 86–7*
copies 22 *159*
works 13 557; 15 135
Sos, S Esteban 26 607
Sosten, Dietrich von 30 284
Sostratos 10 650; 25 767
Sostres Maluquer, Josep Ma 3 217; 13 726; 29 87*
groups and movements 20 516; 29 274
Sōsui *see* OUCHI, JIRO
Sota, Alejandro de la 29 274
Sotades 13 523; 32 68
Sotades Painter 32 67–8*
Sōtan Genpaku *see* GENPAKU SŌTAN
Sōtan Oguri *see* OGURI SŌTAN
Sōtan Sen *see* SEN SŌTAN
Sōtarō Kubo *see* KUBO, SŌTARŌ
Sōtatsu Tawaraya *see* TAWARAYA SŌTATSU
Sōtatsu Tsuda *see* TSUDA SŌTATSU
Soter, Bishop of Naples 3 191
Soteriou, George Angelos 9 527, 528; 29 87*
Soteriou, Maria 29 87
Sōtern, Philip Christoph von, Prince-Bishop of Speyer, Elector of Trier 28 138
Sōtern, von (family) 29 578
Sotes 32 53
Sotheby, John 29 88
Sotheby, Samuel 29 88
Sotheby, Samuel Leigh 29 88
Sotheby, Wilkinson & Hodge 29 88
Sotheby, William 13 304
Sotheby & Co. 4 403; 29 88
Sotheby-Parke-Bernet 24 183
Sotheby's 2 559, 560–61, 706; 6 81; 9 725; 10 366; 15 888; 19 586; 24 183; 29 88*
catalogues 4 23
Denmark 8 759
Israel 16 570
Spain 29 354
Switzerland 30 153
Times-Sotheby Index 15 888
United States of America 32 890
Sotho 19 241; 22 712; 32 154
aprons 1 419
architecture 1 414
dolls 1 419
knives 1 417
sculpture 1 415
wall decorations 1 414
wall paintings 1 313
Sotillo, Alvaro 19 257; 29 88*
Sotira 8 *325*, 329, 334
Sotiriou, M. G. 28 828
Sotnikov, Aleksei (Georgevich) 27 411, 414; 32 661
Soto, Armando 18 833
Soto, Cristóbal Sánchez *see* SÁNCHEZ SOTO, CRISTÓBAL
Soto, D. Manuel 30 883
Soto, Elaine 18 833, 834
Soto, Emilio de 8 232
Soto, Hernando do 9 165; 30 449
Soto, Jesús (Rafael) 29 88–9*; 32 180
dealers 26 193
groups and movements 1 79; 10 416; 11 570; 23 298, 448, 449
patrons and collectors 23 85
works 32 176, 568
Soto, Jesús, Fundación Museo de Arte Moderno *see under* CARACAS → museums
Soto, Jesús, Museo *see under* CIUDAD BOLÍVAR
Soto, Jorge 18 833
Soto, Luis Gutiérrez *see* GUTIÉRREZ SOTO, LUIS
Sōtō Buddhism *see under* BUDDHISM → sects
Šotola, Vratislav 7 210; 23 271
Sotomayor, Enrique de 25 700
Sotomayor, Fernando Alvarez de *see* ALVAREZ DE SOTOMAYOR, FERNANDO
Sotomayor, Juan de Herrera y *see* HERRERA Y SOTOMAYOR, JUAN DE
Šotra, Branko 4 461; 28 451
Sots art 5 142; 18 209; 27 397, 398; 28 919; 29 89*
members 17 716
works 27 *398*
Sotta, Joachim 8 659
Sotte Cleef *see* CLEVE (i), CORNELIUS VAN
Sotto, Tell es- 21 269, 305
Sottocornola, Giovanni 5 918
Sotto culture 21 269, 305
Sottsas, Enrico 30 887
Sottsass, Ettore, sr (1892-1953) 16 649; 21 422; 29 89
Sottsass, Ettore, jr (*b* 1917) 8 803; 15 826; 16 651, 732; 29 89–90*
groups and movements 22 242
works 8 803; 15 *826*; 25 27
Sottsass Associati 29 90
Sotz art *see* SOTS ART
Souar, Henchir 31 426
Soubourou, Jeanne 19 396
Souburg 13 25; 22 837
Souch, John 10 248; 29 90*
Souchal, François 10 212
Souchal, Geneviève 30 332
Souchon, François 5 812; 8 859; 12 206
Soucy, Elzéar 5 570
Soudain, Jean 31 382
Soudan, Henry 31 384
Soudavar, Abolala 16 555
Soufflot, François 27 123; 29 94
Soufflot, Jacques-Germain 11 518; 12 829; 24 121; 29 90–94*
altars 28 486
architecture
churches 11 518, 522; 20 135; 24 122, 166; 25 267, 798; 26 12, *13*; 29 *93*
exchanges 10 668; 29 *92*
grottoes 13 705
hospitals 29 *91*
models 2 337
palaces 24 163, *163*
theatres 3 124; 30 670
assistants 19 225; 27 123
collaboration 9 390; 28 847
groups and movements 22 738
illustrated writings 9 390
patrons and collectors 11 658; 25 81
pupils 13 775; 24 552
reproductive prints by others 30 343
Soufflot le Romain 24 166
Souffron, Pierre 4 801
Soufi, Hassan 31 426
Soufli 13 358
Soufli Magoula 14 353
Sougez, (Louis-Victor-) Emmanuel 29 94*
Souillac Abbey 11 *505*; 13 158; 26 584; 29 *94*, 94–5*
sculpture 26 602
Soukens, Jan 32 700
souks *see* ISLAMIC → markets
Soulages, Jules 10 755; 11 663
Soulages, Pierre 11 551; 29 95*
groups and movements 2 543; 30 231; 33 635
Soulas, Louis-Joseph 8 63
Souldenbalch, Evert van *see* EVERT VAN SOULDENBALCH
Soule, Isaac Newton 10 814
Soulés, Felix 10 771
soul-houses 9 850; 10 17
Soulier, Charles 8 644
Soulier, Edouard 11 60
Soulignac, Antoine 29 506
Soulouque, Faustin, Emperor of Haiti *see* FAUSTIN SOULOUQUE, Emperor of Haiti
Soult (Jean de Dieu), Maréchal 11 663; 28 520; 29 95–6*
collections 4 811
Soult, Nicolas-Jean 16 904
Soul to Art 3 623
Soumaine, Simeon 31 648
sound and art 29 96–9*
sound sculpture *see under* SCULPTURE → materials
Sounier, Léon 2 565
Sounion 13 *363*; 29 99*
fort 21 556
Sounion—cont.
Sanctuary of Poseidon
propylon 25 *657*, 657
sculpture 18 409
Temple of Poseidon 1 128; 13 470; 24 319
Temple of Athena 13 379
SOUP '69 18 780
Soupault, Philippe 2 279; 4 753; 8 438; 11 549; 30 17, 18; 31 503
Soûr *see* TYRE
Source see ZDOŘJ
Source-de-la-Roche 6 159
Sources-de-la-Seine 6 159
Source Yubu 33 610
Sourdéac, Marquis de 30 660
Sourdeau, Jacques 4 155
Sourdel-Thomine, Janine 13 812; 16 549
Sourdis, François de, Archbishop of Bordeaux 4 391
Souris, André 30 20
Sousa, Alberto de 27 141
Sousa, Ângelo (César Cardoso) de *see* ÂNGELO (CÉSAR CARDOSO) DE SOUSA
Sousa, Antonio de 24 395
Sousa, Aurélia de 25 299; 29 100*
Sousa, Caetano Tomás de 5 375; 19 468; 25 293
Sousa, Cipriano da Cruz *see* CIPRIANO DA CRUZ
Sousa, Diogo de, Archbishop of Braga 4 628
Sousa, Ernesto de 25 302
Sousa, Francisco António de 5 376
Sousa, Francisco de 2 189
Sousa, João 25 313
Sousa, João da Rocha e *see* ROCHA E SOUSA, JOÃO DA
Sousa, José Rodrigues da Silva e *see* RODRIGUES DA SILVA E SOUSA, JOSÉ
Sousa, Manuel Caetano de *see* CAETANO DE SOUSA, MANUEL
Sousa, Manuel de *see* CIPRIANO DA CRUZ
Sousa, Victor 22 245
Sousa Coutinho, Rodrigo de, 1st Conde de Linhares *see* LINHARES, RODRIGO DE SOUSA COUTINHO, 1st Conde de
Sousa Coutinho, Vitorio Maria de, 2nd Conde de Linhares *see* LINHARES, VITORIO MARIA DE SOUSA COUTINHO, 2nd Conde de
Sousa Holstein (family) 4 630; 25 318
Sousa Holstein, Alexandre de, Conde de Sanfré *see* SANFRÉ, ALEXANDRE DE SOUSA HOLSTEIN, Conde de
Sousa Holstein, Catarina Juliana de 29 100
Sousa Holstein, Francisco de Borja Sousa Holstein, 1st Marquês de 29 101*
Sousa Holstein, Maria Luisa de, 3rd Duquesa de Palmela *see* PALMELA, MARIA LUISA DE SOUSA HOLSTEIN, 3rd Duquesa de
Sousa Holstein, Pedro de, 1st Duque de *see* PALMELA, PEDRO DE SOUSA HOLSTEIN, 1st Duque de
Sousa Lima, João da Rocha e *see* ROCHA E SOUSA LIMA, JOÃO DA
Sousa Loureiro, Artur José de *see* LOUREIRO, ARTUR JOSÉ DE SOUSA
Sousa-Pinto, José Júlio de 29 101*
Sousa Viterbo, Francisco, Marques de 25 320; 29 101–2*
Sousee 1 315
Souskiou 8 337, 338
Sousse 16 *103*; 29 102*; 31 427
Archaeological Museum 31 427
Sousse—cont.
architecture 1 377; 16 219
factories 16 436
Great Mosque 16 157
Hadrumetum 29 102
Khalaf al-Fata 16 156
lighthouse 19 360
medina 31 424
mosaics 27 60, 63, 67
mosque of Bu Fatata 16 157
ribāṭ 16 157; 21 582
*ribāṭ*s 16 156
stelae 25 733
Souter, Camille 16 18
South, Robert 2 462
South Africa 1 *214*; 29 102–23*, *103*
aquatints 29 110
architectural decorations 1 313, *313*
architecture 26 18; 29 102, 104–7*; 30 728
art market 29 121
Australian black-wood 29 116
beads 22 *713*; 29 104
beadwork 1 262; 3 442
book illustrations 29 121
bowls 29 *119*
bronze 29 *112*
cabinets (ii) (furniture) 29 *115*, 115
candle stands 29 115
candlesticks 28 121
ceramics 29 116–17*
chairs 29 115–16
cloaks 10 848
coins 29 120
collections 29 121–2*
coromandel 29 115
corrugated steel 29 105
cupboards 29 115
dealing 29 121*
desks 29 115
diamonds 12 269; 29 103
drawings 1 *431*; 29 108, 109, *109*
dress 22 *713*; 29 104
eastern beef-wood 29 115
ebony 29 114, 115
education (art) 1 433; 29 122–3*
applied art 29 123
architecture 29 123; 30 728
design 29 123
engravings 29 110
etchings 29 110
ethnographic art 29 121
exhibitions 29 121, 122*
feathers 10 848
figurines 1 273
furniture 29 114–16*
gables 11 876
galleries (iv) (art) 29 121
gardens 12 142
glass 29 *118*, 118–19*
gold 12 864; 29 103, 105
hangings 29 104
houses 1 *313*, 318; 5 662, *662*; 29 104, 105, *107*
huts 1 *311*
imbuia 29 116
interior decoration 29 113–14*
jars 29 *118*
lacquer 29 114
law courts 18 887
libraries 29 121
linocuts 29 110, *111*
lithography 29 110, 121
maps 29 121
marks 29 120–21*
metalwork 29 119–21*
mosques 9 427; 29 105
museums 29 121–2*
new towns 29 105
painting 29 107–10*, 121
parliament buildings 29 *106*
patronage 29 121*
photography 10 580; 24 679
pottery 29 104, 114
prints 29 110–11*, 121
rock art 27 696

South Africa—cont.
satin-wood **29** *115*, 115
screenprints **29** 110
sculpture **29** 104, 111–13*, *112*
silver **19** 709; **28** 121; **29** *115*, *119*, 119–21
skyscrapers **29** 106
sponsorship **29** 121
squares (town) **25** *566*
stink-wood **29** 114, *115*, 115, 116
stonewares **29** *117*
tables **29** 115–16
teak **29** 114
temples **29** 105
terracottas **1** *222*
textiles **29** 104
topographical illustrations **29** 110, 121
toys **29** 104
trade **1** 250; **29** 114
vases **29** *117*
veneers **29** 115
verandahs **29** 105; **32** 240
women artists **29** 104
wood-carvings **29** 104
woodcuts **29** 110
South African Artistic Potteries **29** 117
South African Fine Arts Association *see* CAPE TOWN → South African Association of Arts
South African Glass Co. Ltd **29** 118
South African Library **29** 122
South African Society of Artists **5** 668
Southall, Joseph Edward **4** 87; **11** 436, 786; **25** 556; **30** 427
works **11** *437*, *785*
South America *see* LATIN AMERICA
South America, Pre-Columbian **29** 123–224*, *125*, *130*, *136*, *156*
adobe **4** 796; **29** 160, 162, *168*
agate **29** 155
alloys **21** 332; **28** 651; **29** 211, *212*; **32** 238
altars **1** 701*
amber **1** 761
architects **29** 135
architectural decorations **6** *441*
architecture **29** 138–40*, 159–60, 161–7*, *163*, 192
Chavín culture **6** 522–3*
military **21** 599*
Puerto Rico **29** 200
Sicán culture **28** 652
stone **30** 240
Tairona **30** 240
argyllite **29** 155
armour **29** 204*, 205–6*
art history **2** 533
aryballoi **29** *175*
basketwork **29** 188, 194
beads **29** 155
body arts **29** 204
body ornaments **29** 155, 217–18
bone-carvings **29** 206–7*
book illustrations **29** *130*
bottles **28** *650*; **29** *187*
bowls **29** *134*, *147*, *150*, *186*, *193*, *194*
brass **4** 681
brick **4** 796*
bronze **28** 651
cairns **28** 640
caricatures **5** 761*
casting **29** 211–12
ceramics **29** *221*; **30** 282
chairs **20** *317*; **29** 145
chert **29** 155
chronologies **6** 520–21; **29** *126*
chullpas **31** 47, *47*
citadels **20** *3*
clay **29** 175, *193*
clubs (weapons) **29** 205
clyster tubes **29** 133

South America, Pre-Columbian—cont.
collars **29** 217
collections **7** 609; **29** 218–21*, 222*; **30** 282
gold **7** 612
pottery **7** 612
Uruguay **31** 758
colour **7** 635–6*
compounds **29** 166
containers **29** *189*
copper **28** *651*; **29** 211; **30** 240, *240*
coral **7** 836
cotton **29** 178; **30** IX
craftsmen and artists **29** 134–5*, *134*
crowns **29** *214*
crypts **27** 700
discs **29** 218
dolls **31** 261
doors **9** 166*
dress **29** 151–2*, 181, 182, *183*, 183–4, 188–9, 194*
embroidery **24** *89*
emeralds **29** 155
exhibitions **7** 609; **29** 220*, 221*, *221*
fans **10** 779–80*
feathers **29** 155, *207*, 207–8*
figurines **18** 835; **22** 266; **29** 134, *185*, 218; **30** 511–12
Chorrera culture **30** *512*
Costa Rica **9** 677; **29** *143*
Inca **29** 218
flasks **29** *212*, 212–13
forgeries **29** 222*, 223–4*
fortifications **21** 599*
fortresses **15** *162*
friezes **6** *607*
gardens **12** 71*
gilding **29** 212
gold **12** 866; **13** *291*; **28** 651, *651*, *652*, *781*, 800; **29** 132, *151*, 152, 211
Chavín culture **29** *214*
Coclé culture **7** 507
Colombia **29** 135, *211*; **30** 240, *240*
Cupisnique **8** 272
Gran Chiriquí culture **13** *291*
Muisca **29** *211*
Panama **29** 132
Peru **8** 272; **29** *214*
Tairona **30** 240, *240*
Veraguas culture **32** 238
gourds **13** 229*; **29** 159, *159*, 188
granite **29** *131*, *167*
gravestones **9** *679*
greenstone **29** 155
haematite **21** 718
hair **29** *182*
hammering **29** 211
hammers **29** 211
hammocks **29** 194*
hardstones **9** 679–80; **29** 152–4*, 155*, 184–6*, 198–9
hats **29** 151
headdresses **28** *651*
houses **29** *139*
human figures **29** *176*, *194*
iconography **6** 521–2*; **28** 651; **29** 129–34*, 190
inlays **29** 218
jade **13** 311–12, *312*; **29** 152–3, *154*, 155, *199*
jars **6** *440*; **13** *312*; **21** *752*; **29** 176, *176*, *177*, *221*
jet **21** 718
joinery **5** 408
kilns **3** 364
knitting **18** 157
knives **28** 651, *652*
labyrinths **18** 586*
lead **29** 211
limestone **29** 155; **30** *796*
looms **29** 135
lost-wax casting **29** 211–12
maces **29** 205

South America, Pre-Columbian—cont.
mantles **29** 152
marble **29** *153*
masks **28** 651; **29** 208–10*, *209*
masonry **14** *827*; **23** 415; **29** 162*, *162*, 163–4*, *164*
masons (master) **29** 135
mass production **29** 135
mazes **18** 586*
metal **21** 718
metalwork **29** 127, 135, 210–15*
Chavín culture **29** 214–15
Costa Rica **9** 679–80
Inca **29** 133
Sicán culture **28** 651–2
Veraguas culture **32** 238
metates **9** 678–9; **13** 310–11; **29** 141*, *141*, 142*, *142*, 144, *144*; **32** 238–9, *239*
mirrors **21** 718*; **29** 134
models **29** *139*
mortars (vessels) **29** 133
mosaics **29** 217, 218
mounds **29** 139
mud **6** *607*
mummies **29** 132
museums **29** 220–21*, 222*
musical instruments **29** 215–17*
narratives **22** 517–19*
necklaces **29** 217
obelisks **29** *131*
observatories **23** 338
obsidian **29** 155
ornament **23** 564–5*
painters **29** 135
painting
wall **29** 135, 172–4*, *173*, *174*; **32** 803*
paints **29** 176–7
palaces **23** 825*, 826*
pendants (jewellery) **29** 154, *154*
Colombia **28** *781*; **30** *240*
Costa Rica **29** 154
Gran Chiriquí culture **13** *291*
Gran Nicoya culture **13** *312*
Panama **29** *151*
Puerto Rico **29** *199*
Sinú **28** *781*
Tairona **29** 155, 217; **30** *240*
periods **29** 125*
Early Ceramic **29** *126*
Early Horizon **29** *126*, 160*, 169–70
Early Intermediate **29** *126*, 160–61, 170–71
Early Regional Development **29** *126*
Initial **29** *126*, 159–60*
Integration **29** *126*
Late Horizon **29** *126*, 161
Late Intermediate **29** *126*, 161
Late Regional Development **29** *126*
Middle Horizon **29** *126*, 161, 171
Pre-Ceramic **29** *126*, 158–9*, 168–9
Prehistoric **25** 468
Regional Development **29** *126*
pestles **29** 133
pipes (smoking) **29** 134
plaster **29** 829*
platinum **29** 211
poporos *see* flasks
portraits **21** 752–3
potters **29** 135
pottery **15** 67; **29** 125–7, 128, 134, *134*, 146–51*, *149*, 159, 175–8*, *187*, 187–8, 192–3*, 198, 200, 202–3*, *216*; **31** 261
Aguas Buenas ware **13** 290
Alligator group **13** 290
Allita Amaya **31** 46
Argentina **29** *191*, *202*, 203
Aristide style **7** 506
Atarco style **14** 828
Bahía (culture) **3** 65
Biscuit ware **13** 290

South America, Pre-Columbian pottery—cont.
Black Decorated style **14** 828
Bolivia **31** *46*
Brazil **29** *194*
Cajamarca culture **5** 408–10
Cajamarca Cursive **5** 410
Chakipampa style **14** 828
Chancay **6** 440
Chavín culture **6** 522
Chorrera culture **7** 206–7; **29** 134
Coclé culture **7** 506–7*
Collao **31** 46
Colombia **29** 150
Concepción ware **13** 290
Conchopata style **14** 828
Conte Polychrome **7** *506*, 507; **28** 799
Costa Rica **9** 677
Cupisnique **8** 272, *272*
Curridabat **9** 677
Ecuador **9** 714; **29** 150–51
Gran Nicoya culture **13** 310, *311*
Guadeloupe (country) **29** *199*
Macaracas Polychrome **7** 507; **28** 799
Moche (culture) **21** *752*, 752–4*, *753*
Nazca **22** *707*
Ocros style **14** 828
Panama **7** *506*; **29** 147, 148
Papagayo **13** 310
Paracas culture **24** 89
Parita ware **7** 507
Pataky Polychrome **29** 147
Peru **6** 440; **8** 272, *272*; **14** 828; **21** *752*, 752–4*
Puerto Rico **29** *199*
Recuay culture **26** 66
Robles Moqo style **14** 828
Santa María culture **29** *191*
Tonosí style **7** 506
Valdivia culture **29** 127
Veraguas culture **32** 238
Vicús culture **32** 417–18
Viñaque style **14** 828
pyramids **21** *750*, 750–52*; **25** *689*; **29** 160, 165–6*; **31** 116
pyrite **21** 718; **29** 155
quartz **29** 153, 155
quipus **29** 130
rediscovery **29** 218–20*
religion **29** 129–34*
repoussé **29** *214*
rock art **29** 187, 204
carvings **22** *708*; **29** 132
engraving **29** 196–7*
painting **29** 195*, *196*, 203
rock crystal **29** 155
sarcophagi **6** 380; **27** 833*
sculptors **29** 135
sculpture **29** 141–5*, 167–72*, 193–4*; **30** 282
Alamito culture **29** *190*
Argentina **29** *190*
Chavín culture **6** 521–2*; **29** 167, *167*
Colombia **27** 700, *700*, 701
Costa Rica **9** 677–9; **29** 143
Gran Nicoya culture **13** 310–11
monumental **29** 127, 145–6*; **30** *796*
Panama **29** 143, *144*, 144–5
Peru **29** *167*
Recuay culture **26** 66
relief **6** *607*; **29** *168*
Sambaquí culture **29** *197*, 197–8*
San Agustín culture **27** 700, *700*, 701
stone **9** *678*, *679*; **27** *700*; **29** *144*, *190*
Tiahuanaco **29** 168
Veraguas culture **32** 238–9
serpentine **29** 155, *199*
shaft graves **28** 652

South America, Pre-Columbian—cont.
shell middens **29** 138
shells **28** 581; **29** 217–18*
shirts **29** 182
shrines (i) (cult) **28** 640–41*, *641*
silver **28** *651*, *652*; **29** 211
slate **29** 155
snuff trays **29** 133
snuff tubes **29** 133
spear-throwers **29** 204–5
staircases **29** 527–8*
statuettes **29** *143*, *144*
stelae **29** 145, 619–20*
stone **9** 677–9, *678*, *679*; **20** *317*; **27** *700*; **29** *143*, *144*, 145–6*, *185*, *186*, *190*; **30** 240; **32** 238–9, *239*
stone-carvings **6** *350*, *521*; **29** 155, *169*, *170*, *171*, *199*, 200
stools **9** 679; **29** 134
stucco **29** 829*
sundials **23** 338
syringes **29** 133
tablets **29** *188*, 189
tangas **20** *372*; **29** 193
tapestries **29** 180, *181*
temples **29** *165*, 165–6*, *166*; **30** 447–8*
terracotta **20** *372*; **30** 511–12*, *512*
textiles **23** *564*; **24** 89–90; **29** 134–5, 151–2*, 155, 178–84*, *182*, 194*, 207–8
thrones **30** 786*
tin **29** 211
tombs **31** 118–19*, *119*
tools **29** 184
trade
emeralds **29** 155
hardstones **29** 155
metalwork **21** 252
shells **29** 217
trays **7** *506*
trumpets **29** 217
tubes **29** 189
tunics **29** *181*, 188, *207*; **30** IX
turquoise **28** *651*; **29** 155, 217
urns **29** *191*, 193, *194*
vases **29** *153*; **32** *418*
weapons **29** 204–6*
weaving **29** 159, 194*
wood **29** *188*, *189*
wood-carvings **29** 135, 189, 200
Southampton (Hants)
City Art Gallery **4** 798
Civic Centre **31** 242
docks **9** 59
ivory-carvings **2** 81
Marchwood power station **25** 403
town walls **31** 710
Southampton, Nicolás de *see* NICOLÁS DE ANTONA
Southampton, Thomas Wriothesley, 4th Earl of *see* WRIOTHESLEY, THOMAS, 4th Earl of Southampton
Southampton Psalter *see under* PSALTERS → individual manuscripts
South Cerney (Glos) **10** 261
All Hallows **8** 213; **26** 616, 643
South-east Asia **29** 224–43*, *225*
adzes **29** 227
altars **1** 705–6*
architecture **21** 595–6*; **29** 226
art history **29** 241–3*
bamboo **29** 226
bracelets **29** 228
brick **4** 795–6*
bronze **29** 228, *229*, 229–30
caves **29** 226–7
ceramics **29** 231–2
chronologies **29** 231, 241
collections **7** 154; **29** 239–41*
cotton **29** 232
craftsmen and artists **29** 235–6*
dating methods **29** 241

South-east Asia—cont.
doors **9** 163–4*
dowries **29** 236
drums (musical instruments) **29** 229, *229*
earthenwares **29** *228*
fans **10** 778*
figurines **29** 228
fortifications **21** 595–6*
gongs **4** 855
guilds **29** 236
halls **14** 77–8*
hardstones **29** 227
historiography **29** 241–3*
houses **29** 226
iconography **5** 91
inks **15** 850, 851
inscriptions **29** 231
iron **29** 228–9
jars **29** 232, *232*
languages **29** 224–6*
mother-of-pearl **22** 205
museums **29** 239–41*
ornament **23** 554–6*
palaces **23** 823–4*
palm **29** 226
patronage **29** 236–9*, *237*
pavilions (buildings) **24** 290*
periodicals **24** 437*
periods
Prehistoric **29** 226–30*
pigments **29** 227
plaster **29** 826–7*
pottery **29** 227, 230
sarcophagi **27** 831*
sculpture **5** 100*; **14** *561*; **29** 231; **30** 510
shrines (i) (cult) **28** 639–40*
signatures **29** 236
silk **29** 231
staircases **29** 528*
stone **29** 227–8
stucco **29** 826–7*
stupas **5** 99; **28** 639; **29** 865–7*
temples **14** 560; **29** 236–7; **30** 446–7*
terracotta **29** 228; **30** 510–11*
textiles **29** 228, 232–3, *233*, 235–6
thrones **30** 785–6*
tombs **31** 115*
tools **29** 227, 228
tourist art **29** 236, 238–9*
tower-sanctuaries **28** 639
trade **29** 230–33*
ceramics **6** 904, 908, 916–17*; **29** 231–2
ikat **15** 671
iron **29** 228
textiles **29** 231, 232–3
wood **29** 226
see also BURMA; BRUNEI; CAMBODIA; INDONESIA; LAOS; MALAYSIA; PHILIPPINES; SINGAPORE; THAILAND; VIETNAM
Southend Pier (Essex) **24** 747, 748
Southern, Clara **14** 307; **29** 243*
Southern Artistic Association **30** 248
Southern Methodist University *see under* DALLAS (TX)
Southern Monochrome ware *see* POTTERY → wares → Combed wares
Southern Netherlands *see* BELGIUM
Southern Printmakers **25** 629
Southern school (China) **6** 820, 824; **7** 147, 148; **17** 188; **23** 579; **29** 243–4*
members **6** 760; **9** 142; **17** 696; **18** 59; **21** 420; **32** 850
works **6** 789; **7** 632; **9** *141*; **21** *419*; **32** *849*
Southern school (Japan) **33** 577
Southern school (Korea) **33** 577
Southern Song period *see under* CHINA → periods
Southern Suku *see* SUKU (SOUTHERN)
Southey, Robert **8** 218; **32** 240
South Foreland Lighthouse **19** 366
Southill Park (Beds) **10** 279; **12** 646; **21** 832; **26** 85
South Kensington Art Pottery Studio **10** 312; **21** 697
South Kyme (Lincs), St Mary and All Saints **2** 70
South Littleton (Worcs), Hathaways **8** 46
South Mexican International Style **21** 254
South Mimms (Herts) **6** 53, 55; **9** 143; **21** 562
Southoe Church (Cambs) **26** 613
South Pacific Commission **23** 735
Southport Pier (Merseyside) **24** 748
Southrop (Glos), St Peter **11** 252; **26** 613, 617
South Shields **27** 93
South Stoa I *see under* ATHENS → Agora
Southwark pottery **4** 177; **7** 166
Southwark school **7** 641; **10** 261–2; **19** 605
Southwell, George **32** 414
Southwell Minster (Notts) **9** 670; **13** 54; **23** 538; **26** 588
crockets **8** 183
pulpitum **2** 295; **32** 89
sculpture **13** 82
South West Africa *see* NAMIBIA
South-Western Townships *see* SOWETO
Southwest Indian Art Project *see under* TUCSON (AZ) → University of Arizona
Southwold (Suffolk), St Edmund **11** 421; **13** 139
South Wootton (Norfolk), St Mary **11** 252; **26** 613
Southworth, Albert Sands **29** 245
Southworth, Nancy *see* HAWES, NANCY
Southworth & Hawes **24** 661; **29** 245*
works **24** *659*, 666
Soutine, Chaïm **17** 577; **21** *788*; **29** 245–6*
dealers **33** 627
groups and movements **9** 705; **10** 696; **11** 550; **18** 445; **27** 307
patrons and collectors **3** 251; **9** 465; **13** 826; **19** 282; **27** 524
studio **29** 858
works **29** *246*
Soutman, Pieter (Claesz.) **22** 839; **25** 104; **29** 246–7*
attributions **25** 362
collaboration **10** 391; **14** 46; **19** 731; **32** 622
patrons and collectors **8** 644; **32** 6
pupils **19** 64, 731; **29** 62; **32** 622
reproductive prints by others **30** 47
works **29** 62, *247*
Souto, Antonio **26** 549
Souto, Arturo **9** 696
Soutter, Louis **29** 247–8*
Souttoukeny **15** 701
Souty, P. **11** 413; **29** 248*
Soutzos, Alexandros **13** 359
souvenirs **17** 526; **24** 664, 672
Greece, ancient **13** 478
Iran **16** 414
Islamic **16** 414
Native North Americans **22** 668
see also TOURIST ART
Souverbie, Jean **33** 424
Souvigny **7** 535
St Pierre
tomb of Charles I, Duke of Bourbon, and Agnes of Burgundy **13** 79
Souvigny
St Pierre—cont.
tomb of Louis II of Bourbon and Anne of Auvergne **13** 79
Souvigny Bible *see under* BIBLES → individual manuscripts
Souvré, Anne de, Marquise de Louvois *see* LOUVOIS, ANNE DE SOUVRÉ, Marquise de
Souvré de Courtenvaux, Jacques **19** 95
Souyia **8** 155
Souza, Madame de **22** 126
Souza, Francis Newton **4** 290, 291; **15** 169; **29** 248*
Souza, Jorge **2** 604
Souza, Luiz de Vasconcelos e *see* VASCONCELOS E SOUZA, LUIZ DE
Souza, Manuel Joaquim de **29** 101
Souza, Tomé de **4** 709
Souza, Wladimir Alves de *see* ALVES DE SOUZA, WLADIMIR
Souza Aguiar, Francisco Marcelino de *see* MARCELINO DE SOUZA AGUIAR, FRANCISCO
Souza-Cardoso, Amadeo de *see* AMADEO (DE SOUZA-CARDOSO)
Souza Leão, Joaquim de **4** 725
Sovana, S Maria **7** 302, *303*
Ssovánka, István **15** 4; **28** 856; **29** 249*
Sövenbürger, Jakob, I *see* LUCIUS, JAKOB, I
Sovereign of the Seas *see under* SHIPS → named vessels
Sovetskiy Muzey **27** 441
Sovetskoye Dekorativnoye iskusstvo **27** 444
Sovetskoye iskusstvoznaniye **27** 444
Soviet Central Asia *see* CENTRAL ASIA, WESTERN
Soviet Culture Fund **19** 376
Soviet Union *see* UNION OF SOVIET SOCIALIST REPUBLICS
Sovremennaya Arkhitektura **7** 770; **12** 36; **23** 590; **24** 428; **32** 382
Sowa, Jan **32** 878
Sōwa Kanamori *see* KANAMORI SŌWA
Sowerby Ellison Glassworks **10** 320, 321
Sowers, Thomas **21** 573
Soweto **29** *103*, 106
African Institute of Art **29** 123
Anglican Church **29** 107
Jubilee Art Centre **1** 433
Soyama, Yukihiko **11** 821; **17** 203, 420
soy-beans **17** 310
Soyer, Isaac **29** 249
Soyer, Moses **1** 772, 773; **12** 771; **17** 578; **29** 249*
Soyer, Paul **5** 921
Soyer, Raphael **1** 71, 773; **12** 771; **17** 578; **19** 492; **29** 249*; **31** 606
Soyer, Robert **23** 509
Soyfertis, Leonid **27** 396
Soyhier, Daniel **32** 588
house **32** *589*
Soyinka, Wole **15** 56; **23** 139
Soyllot, Clays **23** 524
Soyo **1** *401*
Soyombo script *see under* SCRIPTS → types
Sōyo Soga *see* SOGA SŌYO
Sŏ Yu-gu **18** 259
Soyuz Deyatelei Iskusstv *see* UNION OF ART WORKERS
Soyuzfoto **11** 775; **15** 122
Soyuz khudozhnikov *see* UNION OF ARTISTS
Soyuz kudozhnikov i poetov 'Iskusstvo - zhizn'' *see* MAKOVETS
Soyuz Molodyozhi *see* UNION OF YOUTH
Sozan Kaneshige *see* KANESHIGE, SOZAN
Sozansky, V. A. **9** 54
Sozi-Carafa, Bishop of Lecce **32** 651
Sozio, Alberto di *see* ALBERTO DI SOZIO
Sozo Ozaki *see* OZAKI, SOZO
Sozopol **4** 110; **5** *144*, 145; **26** *906*
Church of the Virgin **5** 156
coins **4** 112
icons **25** 338
pottery **4** 112
sculpture **4** 112
Temple of St Joan **5** 154
Temple of the Virgin **5** 154
Sozzi, Olivio **20** 513; **23** 845
Sozzo, Niccolò di ser *see* NICCOLÒ DI SER SOZZO
Sozzo di Stefano **23** 95
Spa **7** 166; **18** 614
SPAB *see* SOCIETY FOR THE PROTECTION OF ANCIENT BUILDINGS
Spaccarelli, Attilio **24** 693
SPACE **19** 591
space-frames **16** *56*; **29** 249–50*, *250*
Spackman, Charles **3** 241, 373; **18** 891
Spada (family) **1** 627; **20** 375; **28** 379
Spada, Bernardino, Cardinal **29** 250–51*
architecture **20** 521; **29** 251
collections **26** 773
paintings **7** 509, 553
Spada, Leonello **9** 111; **29** 251–2*
collaboration **4** 830
patrons and collectors **10** 525; **19** 238
works **29** *252*
Spada, lo *see* MARASCALCHI, PIETRO DE'
Spada, Orazio, Marchese **20** 375
Spada, Paolo Orazio **29** 250
Spada, (P.) Virgilio **23** 899; **29** 250–51*
architecture **4** 431; **13** 292; **23** 473
collaboration **20** 520
Spadafora, Adriano **26** 306
Spada Reliefs **27** 38
Spadarino, lo **21** 25; **26** 840; **29** 252–3*
Spadaro, Micco **22** 478; **29** 253–5*
collaboration **7** 509
patrons and collectors **10** 115; **22** 486
teachers **10** 762
works **7** *509*; **18** 709; **29** *254*
Spada Varalli, Fabrizio, Cardinal **6** 568; **26** 773; **29** 39
SPADEM *see* SOCIÉTÉ DE LA PROPRIÉTÉ ARTISTIQUE ET DES DESSINS ET MODÈLES
Spaendonck, Cornelis van **22** 848; **29** 255, 256*
patrons and collectors **4** 303
pupils **19** 116
works **11** 228; **29** 668
Spaendonck, Gerard van **22** 848; **29** 255–6*
patrons and collectors **19** 847
pupils **11** 229; **18** 156
works **11** 228; **29** *256*, 668
Spaers, Joachim **3** 738
Spägl, Andreas **1** 532
Spagna (family) **31** 799
Spagna, Carlo **12** 309; **16** 742
Spagna, Giovanni **24** 525
Spagna, Paolo **26** 838
Spagnoli, Battista **12** 908
Spagnolo, Giuseppe **21** 528
Spagnolo, Roviale *see* ROVIALE, FRANCESCO
Spagnuolo, Fernando *see* FERNANDO SPAGNUOLO
Spagnuolo, lo *see* CRESPI (ii), GIUSEPPE MARIA
Spain **15** 58–60; **16** *103*; **26** *904*; **29** 256–359*, *258*, *259*
aesthetics **21** 128; **23** 578–9, 628
alabaster (gypsum) **1** 516; **29** *841*
alabaster-carvings **32** *493*
alicatados **30** 882
alphabets **12** 889
altarpieces **11** *481*; **25** 184
altars **11** *479*
amber **29** 302
ambulatories **2** *864*
amphitheatres **30** *347*
amulets **17** 514, *515*, 515
antependia **11** 479; **29** 275, *349*
appliqué **29** 349
aquatints **13** *243*; **20** *604*
aqueducts **2** 242, *242*; **28** *368*
arabesques **2** *245*
arcades **1** 743; **2** *242*
arches **2** 294; **16** 158, 188, *188*
architectural decorations **16** *189*; **32** *619*
architecture **4** 790; **25** 171; **29** 261–74*
Almohad **16** 187
Almoravid **16** 187, 190
Baroque **29** 268–71*
brick **4** 784–5*
Cistercian Order **13** 50; **29** 263
criticism **32** 563
Gothic **13** 35, 50–51*, 66–70*; **19** 171; **29** 263, 265
Islamic **16** 157–8*, 187–91*, 215–17*; **29** 287–8
military **21** 573*, 584–5
Mozarabic **22** *247*
Nasrid **16** 215–17
Philippines **24** 611–14
Renaissance **29** 264–8*
Roman **26** 904
Romanesque **26** 580–82*; **29** 262–3
Umayyad **16** 149, 157–8, 187, 189*
vernacular **32** 290–91*
wood **16** 494–5
20th cent. **20** *516*; **29** 273–4*
archives **2** 369, 371*
armorial bearings **14** 428
armour **29** 343
art criticism **21** 128
art history **29** 358–9*
artists' biographies **6** 124; **10** 208; **23** 896
astrolabes **16** 369, 386
badges **29** *346*
basins **29** *325*
baskets **3** 331
bastions **21** 551
beds **3** 483, 484; **29** 310, 315*, 316, 319
benches **29** *310*, 310
Bibles **4** 5, 14; **26** 676
bodice ornaments **17** *523*
bone **6** 558; **29** 313
bookbindings **4** 347, 349; **12** 628; **17** 566*, 567
book covers **4** 350, 351, 352, 353; **12** 628; **16** 357
book illustrations **4** 365; **31** 750
bowls **16** 404, 419
braziers **25** 734; **29** 301, 302
brick **4** 784–5*, 790; **13** 68
bridges **16** 217
brocades **29** *348*
bronze **16** *368*, 386, *387*, *506*; **20** 51; **29** 339, 341, *343*
busts **29** *328*
cabinets (ii) (furniture) **5** 191, 350
calligraphy **16** 215
camarín **21** 859
candle holders **29** 338
capitals **16** 188; **19** *177*; **26** *605*, 606–7; **28** *727*
caps **18** 157
caricatures **5** 757
carnivals **5** 786
carpenters **29** 312

Spain—cont.
carpets **5** 833–5*, *834*, *835*; **8** 252; **29** 297, 298, 347–8*
  Islamic **16** 430, 466, 468, 471
  15th cent. **29** *347*
cartouches **16** 215, 216
carving **29** *317*
caskets **16** 524, *525*; **17** 516; **29** 302
casters (vessels) **29** *335*
castles **6** 58*, *58*
  Mudéjar **7** *491*
  14th cent. **23** *403*
  15th cent. **18** *681*; **31** *181*
catafalques **6** 72
catalogues **25** 224
cathedrals
  Baroque **5** *368*
  Churrigueresque **27** *794*
  Gothic **2** *864*; **5** *203*; **13** *67*, 68, *69*; **19** *172*; **23** *881*; **27** *605*, *606*; **31** *91*, *814*; **33** *604*
    Early Gothic **28** *708*
  Plateresque style **8** *253*
  Renaissance **14** *475*
  Romanesque **26** *581*
  16th cent. **16** *863*; **28** *369*
  18th cent. **26** *521*
caves **1** 688–9, *689*
ceilings **16** 216, 494–5, *495*; **19** 658
  artesonado **2** 528–9, *529*
ceramics **29** 322*, 327–30*
chairs **19** 5; **29** 297, 301, 309–10, 314*, 315–16, *316*, 318, 319
  folding **29** 310
  Gothic Revival **29** *318*
  Nasrid **29** 314, *314*
  peinetas **29** 316
  sillas de cadera **29** 311
chalices **13** 169
chandeliers **16** *387*
chapels **6** *135*; **17** 693; **19** *177*
charters **14** 423
chess sets **6** 557, 558
chests **29** 310, 312*
choir-stalls **7** *192*; **13** 123; **28** *689*, 689–90; **29** 311
churches **29** 261, 311
  Gothic **3** *215*; **12** 619–20; **13** *70*
  pilgrimage **27** 794
  Plateresque style **14** 662
  Renaissance **14** *473*; **23** *625*; **29** *266*, *268*
  Romanesque **19** *175*, *520*
  United States of America **31** *589*
  Visigothic **29** 261
  9th cent. AD **2** *652*, *653*; **29** *264*
  10th cent. AD **27** *763*
  16th cent. **10** *502*; **31** *93*, *865*
  18th cent. **7** *288*
cinnabar **23** 785
circuses **7** 342
cisterns **16** 217
citadels **16** 215–16
clocks **7** 438
cloisters **7** 455; **31** *87*
coats of arms **12** 272; **14** 410, 411, 412, 423, 425, 428, IV
coffers **29** 310
cofre de Valencia **5** 350
coins **7** 532, 534, 536, 537, 538; **16** 513, *513*
collections **5** 509; **9** 18; **21** 35; **29** 351–5*
colleges **29** *269*; **31** *823*
columns **16** 188
  see also Estípites
combs (hair) **25** 734
consoles **29** 315
copper **16** 394; **29** 339, 340, 342
costumes **30** 664*
cotton **8** 35
courtyards **8** *65*; **13** *288*, *731*
craftsmen and artists **29** 315; **32** 180
crosses **13** 165, *165*; **17** 515; **29** 332, *334*

Spain—cont.
crowns **29** 345; **32** *617*
crucifixes **8** 213, 216
  Gothic **13** 122, *122*
  Romanesque **26** *643*, 698
  11th cent. **29** *288*
  17th cent. **22** *2*
cupboards **29** 312*
cupolas **10** 500
curtains **29** 298; **30** VII1
cushions **18** *157*; **29** 297
custodia **29** *333*
dados **16** 216
daggers **2** 452; **16** *506*
dealing **29** 354*
desks **5** 350; **29** 312–14*, *313*
diamonds **17** *523*
dictionaries of art **10** 206, 208
diptychs **9** 4
display of art **9** 15, 18
dolls **31** 261
domes **33** *604*
donjons **6** 50; **9** 144
doors **16** 495
drawings **6** *46*; **9** II1
dress **9** 259–60, 261–2*, 264*, 267–8*, 277; **16** 457, 458
dyes **5** 834; **19** 3
earthenwares **16** *411*, *419*; **29** *324*, *325*, *326*, *327*, 327–8, *328*
education (art) **29** 356–7*; **31** 93
effigies **26** *606*
eggs **25** 735
embroidery **13** 195; **29** 349–50*, *349*
emeralds **17** *523*
enamel **2** *454*; **14** 419; **29** 334, *336*, *346*
  basse taille **13** 169
  cloisonné **16** 515
  Gothic **13** 169
  Islamic **16** *504*
  Nasrid **16** 515
  Romanesque **26** 691–2*
engravings **20** *66*; **27** *602*; **29** *302*
epigraphy **16** 216, 217
etchings **2** *241*; **28** *515*
ewers **29** *336*
exchanges **14** *474*; **31** *815*
exhibitions **29** 294
ex-votos **27** 111
façade decoration **10** 743–4
façades **14** *579*; **21** *126*
factories **16** 436
fans **10** 782
festivals **23** 766
figurines **27** 111
films **10** *687*
fortifications **21** 551, 573*, 584–5; **25** 733
fortresses **16** 217; **20** *157*; **31** 588
forts **21** 551
fountains **11** 340; **16** *368*
frames **11** 373, 375, 376, *479*, 479–96*, *484*, *486*, *488*, *489*, *492*, *493*, *495*, *496*
furniture **29** 309–17*, 318–22*
galleries (iv) (art) **9** 15, 18
gardens **2** 284; **12** 124–5*
  Baroque **27** *753*
  botanic **12** 125
  Islamic **12** 78–81*, *80*, *81*
  landscape **32** 564
gates **5** *202*; **16** 216
gateways **27** *481*
gems **29** 349
gilding **11** *488*, *489*; **12** 628; **19** 3; **29** *343*
glass **29** 330–32*, *331*
gold **2** *454*; **17** *523*; **29** 301, 332–8*, *333*, *346*, 349
  Islamic **7** 534; **16** *513*
gowns **9** 275
granadilla **29** 315
granite **26** *606*; **29** 700
grasses **3** 331
grilles **29** *339*
guidebooks **11** 304; **13** 809, 810

Spain—cont.
guilds **17** 515
  carpenters **29** 312
  furniture-makers **29** 315
  goldsmiths' **29** 332, 336
  painters' **14** 8
guns **2** 462, 464, 466, 467
hangings **19** 3; **29** 298
harnesses **14** 419
headdresses **9** 260, 264
helmets **16** *504*
heraldry **12** 272; **14** 404, 410*, 411, 412, 428, IV
hieroglyphs **6** 72
historiography **11** 304; **16** 547; **29** 358–9*
hose **9** 267
hospitals **8** *79*; **14** *781*; **31** *509*
houses **29** *274*; **32** *291*
humanism **14** 868
iconography **26** 605
inlays **29** 311, 313, *313*
inscriptions **14** 410; **16** *387*, 513, 524
insignia **29** *346*
interior decoration **29** 297–309*, *298*, *299*, *300*, *302*, *304*, *305*, *307*; **31** *90*
iron **12** *148*; **16** *57*, *504*; **29** 338–9*, *339*, 340, 341
  Gothic **13** 166
ivory **6** 558; **16** *506*; **29** *288*, *313*
ivory-carvings **16** 799; **29** 344–5*
  Islamic **16** 524–5*, *525*, 799
  Punic **25** 734
  Romanesque **26** 698–9, *699*
jacaranda **29** 315, 319
jade **16** 861
jars **29** 322, 323, *324*
jet **17** 514–16*, *515*
jewellery **16** 515; **17** 516, 521; **29** 345–6*
kermes **19** 3
kiosks **18** 71
knitting **18** 157, *157*; **29** 350
knots **5** 835
lace **18** 588; **29** 351
lamps **29** *343*
lanterns (architecture) **16** 216
lattice work **29** 311
leather **4** 351, 352, 353; **17** 566; **19** *2*, 3*, 5; **29** 312, *314*
  guadameci **19** 3; **29** 297, 301
libraries **29** *272*, 357–8*
lignum vitae **29** 315
limestone **28** *727*, *728*
linocuts **11** *495*
lithography **21** *708*; **29** 283
locks **29** 340, *340*
macramé **29** 350
mahogany **29** *313*, 314
maiolica **16** 418
mansions **30** 663
manuals
  aesthetics **21** 127
  painting **10** 651
manuscript illumination **14** 423; **23** 683; **29** 275, 297
  Gothic **13** 144; **29** 275, *852*
  Islamic **16** *302*, 306–7*
  Jewish art **17** 560–62*, *561*, *562*
  Romanesque **26** 675–6*
  10th cent. AD **27** 763
  13th cent. **9** *259*
manuscripts
  Byzantine **9** 603
  Early Christian (*c.* AD 250–843) **9** 603
  10th cent. AD **20** 330
maps **20** 363; **33** 454
maqṣūras **16** *188*, 188; **20** 368
marble **10** *783*; **13** *108*; **20** *68*; **23** *629*; **29** *20*, 291, *294*, *296*; **32** *618*
marks **13** 165; **20** 444; **29** 332, 333, 335, 336, 337
marquetry **20** VIII3
masonry **25** 410
metal **1** 743; **29** *349*

Spain—cont.
metalwork **25** 734; **29** 332–44*, *338*
  Gothic **13** *165*, 165–6*
  Islamic **16** 368–9*, 386–7*; **20** 51
  Romanesque **26** 689*
mihrabs **16** 188, *188*
minarets **21** 626
minbars **16** *493*
miniatures (manuscript illumination) **4** *16*; **17** *536*; **26** *676*
mirrors **29** 302
models **14** *475*
monasteries **10** *499*, *500*
monstrances **2** 390; **11** 713; **29** *333*
monuments **10** *502*; **25** *225*
mosaics **6** 177; **16** 216; **27** 63; **30** 882
mosques **7** *845*; **16** 157–8, 188
mouldings **22** 216, 217, 218, 219, 221
moulds **19** *2*; **25** 734
muqarnas (architecture) **16** 216, 494; **22** 324
museums **29** *272*, 332, 354–6*; **32** *565*
nude figures **27** *157*; **29** *294*; **32** 131, *132*
objects of vertu **29** 344–6*
observatories **32** *566*
oil sketches **12** *588*
orders (architecture) **8** 79; **23** 492
painting **29** 274–87*
  allegorical **12** *924*; **24** *392*
  Art informel **30** *336*
  Baroque **29** 278–82*
  battle **5** *737*
  bodegones **4** 209–12*, *210*, *211*; **12** 289; **32** *126*
    see also genre; still-lifes
  display **9** 15, 18
  Ecuador **9** 712
  flower **29** 668
  fresco **29** 275
    Gothic **13** 135, 150; **29** *276*
    Romanesque **30** *368*
    16th cent. **5** *456*; **10** *504*
    17th cent. **10** *504*; **21** 732
    18th cent. **3** *425*; **12** *924*
  genre **12** 289–90*
    17th cent. **22** *343*, *347*
    18th cent. **24** *112*
    19th cent. **11** *325*; **27** *157*; **29** *84*, 284, *284*
    see also bodegones
  Gothic **13** 143–4*, 149–50*; **29** 275–6
  hanging **9** 15, 18
  history **27** 157
    Baroque **19** *179*; **26** *437*
    Cubism **14** *588*
    Mannerism **13** *342*
    17th cent. **5** *874*; **14** *516*; **20** *126*
    19th cent. **11** *324*; **13** *246*; **27** *156*; **29** 284
  landscape
    Baroque **32** *131*
    Romanticism **24** *403*
    17th cent. **7** 559
    19th cent. **29** 284–5, *285*
  military scenes **32** *129*
  mythological **32** *132*, *133*
  Noucentisme **3** *219*
  panel **13** 143, 150; **24** 3, 6
  pietàs **22** *72*
  religious
    Baroque **5** *526*, *618*, *619*; **7** *522*; **11** *710*; **12** *58*; **20** *617*; **22** *695*; **26** *435*, *436*; **29** *280*, *281*, *282*; **31** *809*; **32** *127*; **33** *729*, *731*
    Franciscan Order **11** *710*
    Gothic **29** *277*
    Hispano-Flemish style **8** *872*

Spain
painting
  religious—cont.
    Mannerism **7** *225*; **13** *340*, *343*; **23** *705*; **31** *347*
    Renaissance **20** *10*; **29** *278*
    14th cent. **9** *261*
    15th cent. **9** *264*; **20** *384*; **29** *298*
    16th cent. **5** *736*
    17th cent. **2** *878*; **5** *738*; **6** *365*; **7** *559*; **10** *510*; **14** *470*, *471*; **20** *500*; **22** *344*; **23** *571*; **26** *300*, *301*
  Romanesque **29** 275; **30** 368
  still-lifes **29** 664, 667–8
    Baroque **33** *730*
    16th cent. **25** 419; **27** 706
    17th cent. **14** *104*; **27** *707*
    18th cent. **21** *80*
    see also bodegones
  Surrealism **8** *466*, *467*; **9** *293*
  topographical **13** *344*; **20** *63*, *71*
  townscapes **27** *818*
  vanitas **31** *810*, 883
  wall **13** 144, *150*; **19** *177*; **26** *653*; **27** 57; **28** *695*; **29** 274–5
    19th cent. **13** *248*
  16th cent. **3** 844
  19th cent. **19** *763*
  20th cent. **13** *6*; **25** *851*; **29** 285–7*, *287*
paints **29** 349
palaces **29** 299–300
  Baroque **8** *32*; **20** *72*; **29** *270*
  Churrigueresque **7** *289*
  fortified **20** *157*
  Gothic **12** *619*; **13** *283*
  Hispano-Flemish style **13** *731*
  Islamic **13** *288*; **16** 187, 215, 217, *217*
  Joanine **19** *776*
  Mudéjar **22** *255*
  Nasrid **13** 285
  Renaissance **8** *80*; **10** *499*, *500*; **20** *2*; **23** 811; **29** *264*; **32** *620*
  15th cent. **13** *756*
  16th cent. **2** *284*
paper **20** 329; **24** 40, 41, 48; **31** 258
parchment **24** 107
parks
  public **24** *181*
patchwork **24** 252
pattern books **29** 345
paxes **17** 515
pearls **29** 349
pear-wood **29** *318*
perfume burners **29** *338*
periodicals **24** 452*
pewter **29** 342
photoarchives **29** 357–8*
photography **24** *677*
piers (ii) (masonry) **24** *750*
pigments **29** 322, 323
pilgrim badges **17** 515
pine **29** *310*, *318*; **33** 326
plaques **26** *699*
plaquettes **25** 20
plaster **29** 841–2*
platforms **29** 297
polychromy **10** *903*; **13** *122*; **25** 171, 174
poplar **33** 326
porcelain **29** 328–9, *330*
porrón **29** *331*
portals **29** *841*
  Gothic **13** *282*
  Plateresque style **5** *362*
  Romanesque **2** *866*; **19** *176*; **27** *795*
portraits
  double **10** *513*
  group **4** *559*; **19** *648*; **20** *900*
    19th cent. **13** *245*

Spain
portraits—cont.
painting 13 922
Baroque 7 524; 11 489; 14 9, 793; 25 645; 32 128, 130, 131, 134
Mannerism 13 343
16th cent. 9 267; 24 23; 27 705
17th cent. 5 875; 20 900; 21 125
18th cent. 1 528; 4 559, 563; 13 244; 19 648; 25 286; 32 248
19th cent. 13 245, 248; 19 660; 20 59
Romanticism 10 513
sculpture 5 204; 20 68
self-portraits 13 248; 20 58; 32 248
posters 25 348
pottery 25 309; 29 322–8*, 329; 31 261
Almohad 16 412
blue-and-white ware 4 175*; 6 IV2; 30 XIII3
cuerda seca ware 16 411
Islamic 16 403–4*, 411–12*, 418–19*; 29 322
lustreware 6 333, IV2; 7 XI2; 14 425; 16 404, 412, 418, 419, 419; 20 158; 29 322, 323, 324–5, 325, 326
Nasrid 16 412, 418–19
terra sigillata 27 107
tin-glazed ware 29 322, 323, 324, 324–5, 326, 326–7, 327; 30 875
Umayyad 16 403
predellas 25 464
prints 5 725
propaganda 25 652
proportions (architecture) 12 619–20
ramps 12 124
rapiers 2 454, 456
red lead 16 393
reliquaries 29 332, 341
retables 1 710; 13 344; 26 249–51*
Baroque 11 492; 26 251; 29 291; 31 92
Gothic 3 218; 11 479–83, 677; 13 69, 123, 169; 28 517, 518
Hispano-Flemish style 3 845
Renaissance 11 483–4; 29 290, 290
15th cent. 3 810; 4 423; 15 834
16th cent. 11 484; 26 250
17th cent. 22 3
rock art 19 229; 25 475
engraving 1 688–9; 25 480
hand prints 1 688
painting 1 688–9, 689; 25 487; 29 365, 422
Prehistoric 1 688–9; 6 46–7; 25 495; 26 179–80; 29 364–5*
romance manuscripts 26 563*
roods 27 124
roofs 29 311
rosaries 17 515
rotundas 28 726
ruffs 9 267
rugs 29 297
salts 29 335
samplers 27 694
sandstone 15 60
satin 29 348
satires 27 870
scissors 8 286
screens (i) (architectural) 30 664
scripts 16 215, 216, 217, 386
sculpture 25 174; 29 287–97*
Abstract art 23 629
architectural
Gothic 10 743–4
Islamic 16 246
Neo-classicism 29 294
Romanesque 27 796
Spain
sculpture—cont.
Baroque 29 291–3*
Churrigueresque 29 292
Cubism 12 919; 16 57
Early Christian (c. AD 250-843) 29 287
Gothic 13 103–8*, 122–3*; 29 288–9
herms 8 80
Mannerism 3 846
marble 13 108; 23 629; 29 20, 291, 296
Neo-classicism 29 20
Philippines 24 618–19
relief 19 173
Renaissance 3 847; 32 493
Romanesque 2 866, 867; 26 608; 28 728
Visigothic 32 618
religious 9 110
Baroque 29 292
Gothic 13 105
Mannerism 3 846
Romanesque 26 643
16th cent. 17 693
17th cent. 10 903; 21 173; 22 4
Renaissance 16 695; 29 289–91*
Rococo 29 292–3
Romanesque 7 455; 26 604–5*, 606–7*, 608–9*, 642–3*; 28 727–8; 29 288
stone 13 103–8*, 104, 105, 109; 26 604–5*, 606–7*, 608, 608–9*
tomb
Baroque 9 407
Gothic 13 107, 108; 28 724
Visigothic 29 287
wood 9 110; 10 903; 13 122–3*; 22 4; 26 642–3*, 643; 29 291, 292, 296
5th cent. BC 15 60
16th cent. 3 844
20th cent. 10 910; 12 148; 16 57; 21 709; 29 295–7*, 296
settlements 25 473
sgraffito 16 411
shields 14 405, 410, 411, 412, 428; 16 505
shrines (i) (cult) 2 867; 26 699; 28 632
sideboards 29 302, 314
silk 13 197; 16 428, 436–7, 438, 439, 440; 28 715, 716, 717; 29 348, 348–9*; 30 VII1
silver 27 15; 29 301, 302, 332–3*, 334, 335–8*, 349
silver-gilt 29 333, 335, 336
skirts 9 278
spires 29 414*
squares (town) 20 61, 62; 31 717
stage design 30 663–4*
stage machinery 30 664
stage scenery 29 306; 30 663, 664
stained glass 31 92
Gothic 12 740; 13 191, 191–2*; 19 174
Islamic 16 257
Romanesque 26 702
16th cent. 29 V
staircases 8 79; 10 504; 29 521
steel 16 57; 29 340
stelae 15 60; 29 617, 619
stone 13 103–8*, 104, 107, 109; 26 604–5*, 606–7*, 608, 608–9*
stone-carvings 2 245
strapwork 16 411
stucco 16 189, 217; 29 841, 841–2*
sword hilts 2 454
swords 2 452; 16 506
synagogues 17 544; 31 86
tables 29 314–15*, 316, 317
tanks 16 246
Spain—cont.
tapestries 29 297, 301, 350*; 30 324, 325
temples 30 434
terracotta 27 111; 31 191
textiles 29 301, 346–51*
Baghdad Group 16 436
Islamic 16 436–7*, 439–40*
theatres 30 663*
theories
architectural 5 700–701; 32 563
art
16th cent. 32 558
17th cent. 5 736, 739; 23 705–6
18th cent. 13 251
20th cent. 23 578–9
threads 29 301, 349, 349
thrones 30 778
tiles 16 216, 217; 29 297, 322, 323, 325, 326, 327; 30 875, 875, 882–3*, 883, XIII3
tin 10 624; 16 393
tiraz 16 436
tombs
Gothic 9 748; 13 107, 108; 28 724
Renaissance 10 783
tortoiseshell 29 314
towers 4 784; 13 68; 16 143, 215, 216
towns
garden cities 12 181
new 31 718
toys 31 258
trade 6 624; 10 592; 19 385
art (works of) 32 180
carpets 5 833, 834, 835
ceramics 6 331, 333; 16 395, 409, 412; 25 309; 31 338
chairs 3 582
coral 16 750
furniture 19 592
glass 16 522
icons 31 815
jet 27 793
jewellery 29 345
metal 22 613
metalwork 3 602; 16 368; 25 734
paintings 27 836
pottery 16 395
tapestries 3 607; 29 350
textiles 7 53; 17 315
tiles 3 575; 30 880
travel books 4 443
treatises 12 619–20
architecture 23 487; 31 297*
Baroque 29 269
military 28 367
16th cent. 25 31; 27 520
17th cent. 5 411, 700–701, 700; 24 350; 27 763, 765; 31 171
fortifications 14 476
16th cent. 12 921; 26 548
17th cent. 2 542; 26 548
painting 5 313; 13 870
urban planning 2 379
vaults 31 171
trompe l'oeil 29 668
tubular steel 29 321
tympana 13 104, 109; 19 176; 27 796
universities 26 520; 27 603
upholstery 29 314
urban planning 22 67; 31 724, 822
vases 7 XI2; 16 419, 419; 29 327, 330
vaults (ceiling) 8 79; 13 69; 16 217; 26 581
vellum 24 107
velvet 29 349
verandahs 32 240
vestments (ecclesiastical) 32 391
villas 32 543
walls 13 285
walnut 3 847; 29 311, 314, 317; 33 326
Spain—cont.
water supply 2 242
weathervanes 33 8
weaving 16 436, 439–40; 30 VII1
windows 13 191; 20 157; 29 301
wood 10 903; 26 642–3*; 29 291
Baroque 29 292
Gothic 13 122, 122–3*
Islamic 16 216, 493, 494–5, 506
Mudéjar 19 658
Renaissance 3 846
Romanesque 26 643
15th cent. 2 529
17th cent. 9 110; 21 173; 22 2, 3, 4
20th cent. 29 296
woodcuts 33 350, 358
woodwork 16 492–5*
wool 29 347
workshops 29 852
writing-boxes 20 VIII3
wrought iron 12 919
see also CATALONIA
Spain, Cosh & Dods 9 61
Spain, Peter of see PETER OF SPAIN
Špála, Václav 29 359*
groups and movements 8 373, 393; 13 711; 16 902; 33 710
works 8 393
Spalato see SPLIT
Spalatum see under SPLIT
Spalek, J. 4 27
spalliere 9 30; 16 711; 29 359–62*, 361, 362
see also CASSONI; PANEL PAINTINGS; PANELS (WALL)
spalling 7 747; 20 574, 576
Spalt, Johannes 2 287–8, 789, 815; 14 693
Spampani, Carlo 3 527
spandex 30 543
Spandikov, Eduard 18 507; 31 583
Spandini, Armando 29 255*
spandrels 2 292, 292; 29 363*
see also PENDENTIVES
Spangenhelm see under HELMETS → types
Spängler, Johann Jakob (Wilhelm) 8 776
spangles 18 590, 591
Spango Valley (Strathclyde), IBM Building 28 232
Spanheim, Bernhard 19 516
Spanheim, Engelbert, Count von 15 146
Spani, Andrea 29 363
Spani, Bartolomeo 29 363*
Spani, Girolamo 29 363
Spani, Prospero 10 523, 524; 29 363*
Španiel, Otakar 8 387; 28 855
Spanish chairs see under CHAIRS → types
Spanish Colonial Revival 7 619
Spanish Forger 11 306, 308
Spanish Levantine rock art 29 364–5*, 365
Spanish Revival style 28 879
Spanish Sahara see WESTERN SAHARA
Spanish style 8 235
Spanish Town 16 878, 882
architecture 16 882
Cathedral of St James 16 882
House of Assembly 16 882
monument to Admiral Rodney 16 884, 889
Old King's House 16 882, 886, 887
pottery 16 887
Spanjaard, Frits 22 868, 876
Spannocchi (family) 28 677
Spannocchi, Ambrogio 20 112
Spannochi, Tiburzio 26 501; 30 518
Spannring, Luise 27 665
Spano, Antonio 29 344
Spano, Francisco 29 345
Spano, Pippo 20 555, 556
Spanocchi (family) 20 684
Spanocchi, Tiburzio 11 772; 25 291
Spanzotti (da Casale), Giovanni Martino 29 365–6*
attributions 11 11
pupils 11 11; 29 1
works 31 443, 444
Spanzotti, Pietro 29 365
Sparāns, Aigars 33 378
Sparkes, John 23 34
Sparling, Marcus 10 887
Sparlösa 32 521
Sparmann, Carel 14 33
Sparre, Gabriel, Baron 30 97; 31 362
Sparre, Gustaf Adolf 29 366*; 30 118
Sparre, Louis, Count 11 83, 104, 105, 108, 110, 476; 12 21
Sparre, Ulrika 30 523
Sparro, Pavel I. 18 39; 31 553
Sparta 13 362, 363; 14 332; 26 908; 29 367–8*
Archaeological Museum 14 361
art forms and materials
architecture 26 909; 29 367–8*
bronzes 13 571, 572, 572
cenotaphs 6 170
combs (hair) 13 595
ivory-carvings 14 354
metalwork 32 660
mosaics 13 560; 27 63
pottery 13 496, 512, 534
reliefs 29 368
sculpture 13 443; 29 368*
seals 13 595
statuettes 13 596
Menelaion 21 46; 29 367
Sanctuary of Artemis Orthia 13 595
bronze 13 441
figurines 13 373
jewellery 13 600
masks 13 582
workshop 13 371
Temple of Athena Chalkioikos 13 391
theatre 26 910
Spartali, Marie 4 879; 11 434; 29 368–9*, 671
Spárti see SPARTA
sparto grass see under GRASSES → types
Sparton Corporation 30 391
Sparzo, Marcello 9 173
Spasimo di Sicilia 14 582; 25 903
Spät, Casper 2 455, 462
Spata 14 354
Spătaru, Mircea 29 369*
Spätgotik see under GOTHIC → styles
Spatialisme 2 510; 29 369*
Spatio see SPAZIO
spatter painting see under PAINTING → techniques
spatulas 10 197
Spatz see SPAZIO
Spaulding, John T. 17 431
Spaulding, Sumner 19 700
Spaulding, William S. 17 431
Spaulding collection see under BOSTON (MA; USA) → museums → Museum of Fine Arts
Spaun, Friedrich Franz von 19 719
Spaun, Maximilian Robert Johann von 19 719
Spaun, Max Ritter von 19 719
Spavento, Giorgio 19 558; 29 369–70*
patrons and collectors 19 663
works 5 177; 13 678; 29 370; 32 187
Spaveto, Giorgio 28 36
Spaxton Church (Somerset) 24 577
Spaz see SPAZIO

Spazialismo **5** 671; **8** 162; **9** 132; **11** 281, 282, *282*; **16** 709; **29** 370–71*
Spazio **22** 106
Spazio, Bernardo **1** 607; **29** 372*
Spazio, Giovanni (before 1644-after 1698) **14** 885; **29** 372
 assistants **2** 212
 works **8** 377
Spazio, Johann Jakob **4** 1; **29** 371
Spazio, Johann Peter, II **29** 371, 372*
Spazio, Lucius **29** 371
Spazio, Markus **29** 371, 372*
Spazio, Martin *see* SPAZIO, MARKUS
Spazio, Martino de **30** 914
Spazio, Marx *see* SPAZIO, MARKUS
Spazio, Pietro (*fl* 1623-44) **29** 371
Spazio, Pietro (*fl* 1629- *d* after 1643) **29** 371
Spazio e società **24** 449
Spazzapan, Luigi (di Giusto) **28** 861; **29** 372–3*; **31** 446
Spazzio, Giovanni **32** 870, 881
 works **32** *870*
Spazzio, Johann Baptist II **29** 371
Spazzo, Giovanni Pietro **10** 528
Spazzo, Pietro **14** 885
Spear, Francis **24** 839
Spear, Laurinda Hope **2** 494
Spearhafoc **29** 851
spearheads
 historical and regional traditions
  China **7** 58
  England **25** *540*
  Helladic **14** 356
  Japan **17** 364
  Mesoamerica, Pre-Columbian **21** 192, 245
  Mycenaean **14** 356
  Prehistoric art **25** *540*
 materials
  bamboo **7** 58
  bronze **14** 356; **25** *540*
  chalcedony **21** 192
  chert **21** 192
  iron **25** *540*
  obsidian **21** 192, 245
spears **2** 448
 Aboriginal Australia **1** 53–4
 Africa **1** 362
 Egypt, ancient **10** 40
 Indonesia **15** 818
 Java **15** 818
 Luba **19** 740*
 Maasai **1** 362
 Malaysia **20** 174
 Mesoamerica, Pre-Columbian **21** 245
 Prehistoric art **25** 541
 Sumatra **15** 818
Spear Thrower **10** 587
spear-throwers
 historical and regional traditions
  France **25** *491*
  Maya **21** 246
  Mesoamerica, Pre-Columbian **21** 245, 246
  Mixtec **21** 737
  Moche (culture) **29** 204–5
  Prehistoric art **25** 491, *491*, 493
  South America, Pre-Columbian **29** 204–5
 materials
  antlers **25** 493
  bone **25** *491*
  ivory **25** 493
Specchi, Alessandro **29** 373–4*
 patrons and collectors **1** 532; **5** 812
 works **11** 814; **29** 251, *373*; **32** 111, 112
Special Commission for Cultural Affairs **3** 916
Speciale, Pietro **11** 896
specialization **7** 830; **13** 133; **29** 374–5*
specifications (*syngraphe*) **13** 409
specimens (*paradeigma*) **13** 409
Speck, Henry **22** 589
Speckaert, Jan *see* SPEECKAERT, JAN
Speckle, Daniel **9** 750; **21** 579; **29** 375–6*, 750
speckle interferometry *see* TECHNICAL EXAMINATION → types → interferometry (speckle)
Specklin, Veit **33** 354
Speckner (family) **8** 160
Speckner, Lorenz **8** 161; **12** 430
Speckter, Erwin **12** 394; **29** 376*
Speckter, Hans **29** 376*
Speckter, Johann Michael **29** 376*
Speckter, Otto **29** 376*
Speckter & Co. **29** 376
Speck von Sternburg, Maximilian **19** 111; **29** 376–7*
Spectator **18** 507
spectrometry **11** 309
Spectrum, 't **22** 876; **32** 623
Speculatie *see* TEYLER, JOHANNES
speculation **2** 557, 558; **7** 562
speculative building *see* PROPERTY DEVELOPMENT
speculum metal *see under* ALLOYS → types
Spedaletto **22** 519
 Villa Medici **12** 551
Spedos **8** 315, *316*
Speeckaert, Jan **26** 728; **29** 377*
Speed, J.B., Art museum *see under* LOUISVILLE (KY)
Speed, John **20** 364; **29** 377*
 works **9** *314*; **23** *197*, 198; **29** 532; **33** *231*, 231, *544*
 writings **2** 163; **8** 38
Speed Graphic *see under* CAMERAS → types
Speer, Albert **11** 526; **22** 711; **29** 377–8*, 752
 assistants **2** 216
 staff **10** 755; **24** 826; **26** 402
 teachers **30** 521
 works **3** 796; **4** 741; **10** 684; **12** 379, 417, 477; **13** 238; **18** 444; **22** 711; **23** 814; **25** 268, 652; **31** 730, *731*
Speer, Martin **33** 692
Speeth, Peter **12** 375; **29** 378*; **33** 431
Speier, Johann Emerich of *see* JOHANN EMERICH OF SPEIER
Speier, Wendelin of *see* WENDELIN OF SPEIER
Speight, George **26** 489
Speight, Sadie **20** 491; **28** 158
Speinshart Abbey Church **29** 838
Speiser, Ephraim A. **1** 894; **12** 211
Spejo, Hernando de **29** 341
Speke Hall (Merseyside) **5** 169
Spelies
 Church of the Hodegetria **9** 584
 Hagia Thekla **9** 584
Spello
 S Lorenzo **16** 725
 S Maria Maggiore
  Baglioni Chapel **24** 830–31, *831*
spelter *see* ZINC
speltering **4** 683–5*
Speluzzi, Giuseppe **16** 731
Spence, Basil (Urwin) **5** 531; **29** 379–80*
 collaboration **2** 578; **28** 231
 competitions **7** 670
 works **2** *322*, 323; **4** 808; **6** 459; **7** 192; **10** 242; **28** 231, 232, 256, 488; **29** *379*; **30** 38, 782; **33** 58
Spence, Benjamin Edward **12** 598
Spence, Glover & Ferguson **9** 724; **12** 775
Spence, Jo (*fl* 1970s) **10** 879
Spence, Joseph (*fl* early 18th cent.) **13** 300; **25** 233
Spence, T. R. **23** 20
Spence, William **28** 228
Spence, William Blundell **11** 189; **28** 270; **29** 380*
 collections **14** 675
 dealing **12** 32; **19** 412
Spencer (family) **1** 520; **13** 789
Spencer, August **15** 823
Spencer, Charles (*fl* 1982) **31** 505
Spencer, Charles, 3rd Duke of Marlborough (1706-58) **8** 149; **10** 332
Spencer, Charles, 3rd Earl of Sunderland (1674-1722) **9** 718; **29** 380
Spencer, Dowager Countess **11** 163
Spencer, George, 4th Duke of Marlborough **10** 365; **12** 263, 266; **14** 833; **15** 165; **20** 389
Spencer, George John, 2nd Earl Spencer **10** 334; **12** 263; **14** 110, 681; **25** 843; **29** 380
Spencer, Gervase **21** 643
Spencer, John, 1st Earl Spencer **10** 366; **29** 380, 381*
 collections **17** 475; **18** 143
 interior decoration **29** 806
Spencer (Jungarrayi), Larry
 works **1** *63*
Spencer, Lavinia Bingham, Countess *see* BINGHAM LAVINIA, Countess Spencer
Spencer, Lilly Martin **29** 381–2*
Spencer, Niles (Maurice) **1** 772; **25** 461; **29** 382*; **31** 606
Spencer, Robert, 2nd Earl of Sunderland (1641-1702) **29** 380–81*
 frames **11** 423
 paintings **10** 364; **19** 122
Spencer, Robert, Lord Teviot (*fl* 1679) **16** 82
Spencer, Robert C(lossen) **6** 578; **25** 446; **29** 382*
Spencer, Stanley **19** 621; **29** 382–5*
 groups and movements **23** 23; **25** 356, 556
 patrons and collectors **9** 467; **16** 42; **20** 476; **28** 273
 teachers **31** 146
 works **6** 460; **9** 2; **10** 257, 482; **22** 332; **29** *383*, *384*
Spencer, Thomas **28** 526
Spencer, W. (*fl* 1860) **12** 163
Spencer, W. Baldwin (1860-1920) **1** 51, 66, 67; **2** 769
Spencer, William, 6th Duke of Devonshire **22** 28
Spencer and Powers **19** 453
Spencer Bower, Olivia **29** 385*
Spencer Cameron Gallery **2** 151
Spencer-Churchill, Edward George **10** 91
Spencer-Stanhope, Charles **14** 480
Spender, Humphrey **20** 590; **26** 540; **29** 385–6*
 works **20** *589*
Spender, M. **18** 890
Spender, Michael **29** 385
Spender, Stephen **24** 839
Spengler, Adam **33** 737
Spengler, Lazarus **12** 816
Spengler, Lorenz **29** 386*
 works **8** 753; **31** 481, *481*
Spengler, Oswald **8** 595
Spenyng, Laurenz **14** 884; **25** 695
speoi *see* EGYPT, ANCIENT → temples → rock-cut
Speos Artemidos *see under* BENI HASAN
Spera, Clemente **20** 95
Sperandio (Savelli) **10** 519; **29** 386–7*
 patrons and collectors **3** 743; **12** 907; **20** 322; **27** 272
 works **29** *387*; **30** 498
Sperandio, Giovanni Battista **13** 845; **29** 388
Sperandio, Giovanni Colleto **29** 387–8*
Sperandio Savelli, Bartolomeo **29** 386
Speransky, Sergey (Borisovich) **2** 99; **17** 753; **29** 388*
Speranza, Giovanni Battista **25** 717; **29** 388*
Speranza, Stefano **29** 388
Sperber, Dan **30** 163
Sperges, Norbert, Baron von **18** 683
Sperl, Johann **29** 388–9*
Sperling, Hieronymus **23** 146
Sperling, Johann Christian **33** 80
Sperlonga **13** *362*; **16** *620*, *621*; **26** *886*; **29** 389–90*
 Grotto of Tiberius **13** 555; **14** 33; **27** 46, 66
 Museo Archeologico Nazionale **27** 46
 sculpture **13** 464; **26** 292; **27** 11, 30; **29** *389*, 389–90*
 Tiberius' villa **25** 45; **27** 33
spermaceti wax *see under* WAXES → types
Spero, Nancy **10** 883; **12** 886; **29** 390*; **31** 609
Spescha, Matias **30** 135
Spes Nostra, Master of **20** 656
Spetchley Roman Catholic School (Hereford & Worcs) **28** 156
Speth, Balthasar **11** 33
Speyer **12** *361*; **29** 390–93*
 Cathedral of SS Maria and Stephan **9** 86; **12** 363, 364; **23** 645; **26** 570, 573–4, 575, 620; **27** 617; **29** 390–93*, *391*; **30** 729; **31** 821–2
  architecture **29** 391–3*, *392*
  Building I **29** 391*, *392*
  Building II **29** 391–3*, *392*
  buttresses **5** 319
  Chapel of St Emmeram **14** 81
  ciborium **7** 303
  crypt **8** 224, *224*
  manuscripts **23** 655
  oliphants **23** 400
  roof **27** 130
  sculpture **29** 393*
  vaults **32** 89
  vessels **26** 685
 Dreifaltigkeitskirche **19** 815
 Emmeramskapelle **7** 257
 Historical Museum **29** 390
 Purrmann House **25** 744
 silk **12** 463
 synagogue **17** 547
 watches **7** *443*
Speyer, von *see* TRAUT (VON SPEYER)
Spezia, La *see* LA SPEZIA
Spezza *see* SPAZIO
Spezza, Andrea **25** 97; **29** 371*; **33** 259
 attributions **25** 446
 collaboration **24** 772
 patrons and collectors **19** 751
 works **18** 426; **25** 445; **29** 371
Spezza, Antonio **28** 849; **31** 353
 works **31** *353*
Spezza, Carlo **29** 371
Spezza, Giovanni Antonio **29** 371
Spezza, Giovanni Battista **29** 371
Spezza, Giovanni Pietro **29** 371
Spezza, Pietro **14** 886; **28** 849; **31** 353
 works **31** *353*
Spezza, Rocco **29** 371
Sphakia, Hagios Paolos **8** 155, 156
sphalerite **4** 684
SPHAN *see* SECRETARIA DO PATRIMÔNIO HISTÓRICO E ARTÍSTICO NACIONAL
spheres, armillary *see* ARMILLARY SPHERES
spherical domes **28** 584
Sphinx, De **9** 62; **29** 397*
Sphinx, Great *see under* GIZA
sphinxes **29** 393–7*
 Ancient Near East **29** 394–5*, *395*
 Egypt, ancient **2** 362; **9** 862, 870, 875; **21** *109*; **29** 393–4*, *394*
 Greece, ancient **8** *695*; **13** 429; **29** 395–7*
Sphinx Factory **22** 882, 884
Sphoungaras **21** 657, 684
S. P. H. Stoffe **29** 696
sphyrelaton technique *see under* BRONZE → techniques
Sphys, Friedrich **22** 306
Spicart, Jan *see* SPEECKAERT, JAN
Spicchio, Simone da **4** 30
spice-boxes **10** 419; **17** 572*, *572*
Spicer, William **30** 794
Spicer-Simson, Theodore **29** 397*
Spicre, Guillaume **29** 397
Spicre, Pierre **11** 639; **26** 556; **29** 397–8*
Spicymir **30** 345
Spiegel, Christinus **32** 681
Spiegel, Frigyes **14** 909; **20** 447; **29** 398*
Spiegel, Jacobus van der **31** 647, 648
Spiegelhalter, Ilona **31** 396
Spiegelman, Art(hur) **5** 759; **7** 649
Spiegler, Franz Joseph **29** 398–9*; **30** 132
 collaboration **3** 58
 pupils **2** 876
 works **7** 211; **10** 859; **11** 125; **15** 139
Spieker, Paul **23** 340
Spieler, Mathias *see* SPIHLER, MATHIAS
Spiennes **25** 515
Spierinck, Claes **5** 213; **20** 724, 725
Spierinck, Jan **22** 835
Spierinck, Nicolaas **20** 333
Spierinck, Pieter **23** 665
Spierincx, Frans **2** 199; **22** 844
Spiering (family) **30** 320
Spiering, Aert **22** 897
Spiering, Frans **8** 667; **10** 349; **20** 366; **22** 897; **30** 318; **32** 732
Spiering, Pieter **9** 194; **22** 897
Spierre, Claude **29** 399
Spierre, François **7** 569; **11** 23; **29** 399*
Spiers **28** 256
Spiers, Albert van **33** 261
Spiers, Richard Phené **2** 333; **4** 157; **28** 349; **32** 257
Spies, Walter **15** 807, 809; **29** 234, 238
Spieskappel, St Johannes **7** 303
Spiess, Hans **8** 377, 383; **25** 438; **26** 365, 367; **27** 168
Spifami, Catherine **11** 799
Spihler, Mathias **29** 399–400*; **30** 70
spike *see* OILS → types → lavender
spiked hollow mouldings *see under* MOULDINGS → types
spikes **21** 559
Spilberg, Adriana **22** 721; **33** 280
Spilberg, Johann, II **33** 279
Spilem *see* SPOILUM
Spilia, Church of the Dormition **8** 156
Spilimbergo **22** 158
Spilimbergo, Irene di **29** 400*; **33** 308
Spilimbergo, Lino Eneas **2** 400, 707; **6** 10; **29** 400*
Spillem *see* SPOILUM
Spillenberger, Johann, I (*fl* 1619-50) **28** 852; **29** 400, 612
Spillenberger, Johann, II (1628-1679) **2** 794, 795; **18** *45*; **29** 400–401*
 collaboration **27** 452
 works **12** 390; **29** *401*
spiller **1** 762
Spiller, Gottfried **4** 666; **12** 440

Spilliaert, Léon(tius-Petrus-Ludovicus) **2** 516; **3** 564; **29** 401–2*
spillikins **31** 266
Spillman, Samuel **28** 713
Spilman, Hendrik **3** 900; **25** 649; **29** 402*
Spilsbury, John **31** 266
Spilsbury, Samuel **12** 163
Spilzer, Andreas
 works **12** *813*
Spina **10** *583*, 585, 592, 638
 bronze **10** 627
 gems **12** 249
 jewellery **10** 632
 pottery **13** 533
Spinacci, Giovanni **13** 773
Spinario **2** 162, 168; **21** 23; **27** 87, 114; **29** 402*, 561, *561*
Spinazzi, Innocenzo **8** 83; **22** 5; **23** 157; **29** 402–3*
Spindler, Hans **8** 626; **12** 404
Spindler, Heinrich Wilhelm **12** 424; **29** 403
 works **12** *425*
Spindler, Jakob **29** 403
Spindler, Johann **29** 403
Spindler, Johann Dietrich **33** 429
Spindler, Johann Friedrich **12** 411, 424; **29** 403
 works **12** *425*
spindles **21** 236; **30** 540
Spinelli, Andrea **29** 409–10*
 works **29** *409*
Spinelli, Antonio **3** 229
Spinelli, Domenico di Niccolò *see* DOMENICO DI NICCOLÒ
Spinelli, Ferrante, Prince of Tarsia *see* TARSIA, FERRANTE SPINELLI, Prince of
Spinelli, Giacomo **29** 409
Spinelli, Giovanni Battista **29** 410–11*, 544
 works **29** *410*
Spinelli, Luca di **29** 403, 404
Spinelli, Marcantonio **29** 409
Spinelli, Niccolò (*fl c.* 1360-1402) **29** 407
Spinelli, Niccolò di Forzore (1430-1514) **2** 19; **18** 673; **29** 403, 408–9*
 works **20** 919; **29** *408*
Spinelli, Parri **2** 389; **20** 621; **29** 403, 407–8*
 collaboration **29** 406
 works **13** 676; **29** *407*
Spinelli, Sergio **28** 337
Spinellini, Giovanni **22** 800
Spinellino di Luca *see* SPINELLO ARETINO
Spinello *see* SPINELLI
Spinello Aretino **2** 389; **13** 149; **29** 403–7*
 assistants **29** 407
 collaboration **19** 673, 678; **23** 95
 patrons and collectors **13** 644; **26** 541
 pupils **12** 700
 teachers **2** 19
 works **11** 210, 380; **24** 855, 860; **27** 765; **28** 687; **29** *405*, *406*
spinels **12** I; **29** 699
Spineta, Giovanni Battista **1** 669
Spineta, Pietro, II **6** 363
spinets **22** 372–3
Spingola, François *see* LESPINGOLA, FRANÇOIS
Spini (family) **22** 801
Spini, Gherardo **6** 148; **11** 216
Spini, Giovanni (*fl* 1452) **22** 799
Spini, Giovanni, Conte (*fl* 1820s) **5** 783
Spini, Salvestro **22** 799
Spink, Walter **1** 500
Spink & Son Ltd **7** 233; **10** 91
spinning (metalwork) **12** 865; **16** 363; **21** 323
spinning (textile) **30** 539–40*
 historical and regional traditions
  Africa **1** 294
  Ancient Near East **1** 880
  Anglo-Saxon **2** 83
  Egypt, ancient **9** 824; **30** 540
  Indian subcontinent **15** 660
  Korea **18** 372
  Native North Americans **22** 619
  New Zealand **23** 74
 types
  S-spinning **16** 468
  Z-spinning **16** 432, 468
Spinning Jenny **30** 540
spinning-wheels **7** 43; **13** 766; **30** 540
Spinny, Guillaume Jean Joseph de **14** 42
Spinola (family) **12** 280; **30** 232
 architecture **12** 283; **24** 836
 paintings **6** 34
 sculpture **25** 707
 silk **12** 284
Spinola, Agustín de, Cardinal **29** 353
Spinola, Ambrogio **2** 126; **27** 295
Spinola, Andrea **29** 411
Spinola, Angelo Giovanni **29** 411
Spinola, Battista **29** 411
Spinola, Cattaneo **29** 411
Spinola, Cristoforo **29** 411
Spinola, Eliano **29** 411
Spinola, Ernestina Stahrenberg, Marchesa **5** 626
Spinola, Francesco **11** 897
Spinola, Giacomo **29** 411
Spinola, Giambattista (*fl* 1563-6) **29** 411
Spinola, Giambattista, Cardinal (*fl* 18th cent.) **29** 411
Spinola, Giovanni Domenico **3** 922; **10** 786
Spinola, Guilio **29** 411
Spinola, Lazzaro **29** 411
Spinola, Luca (*fl* 1562) **29** 411
Spinola, Lucano (*fl* 1328-30) **31** 277
Spinola, Nicola, Cardinal **3** 920
Spinola, Oberto **29** 411
Spinola, Paolo **25** 226
Spinola, Taddeo **29** 411
Spinola Hours *see under* BOOKS OF HOURS → individual manuscripts
Spínola y Guzmán, Ambrosio Ignacio *see* GUZMÁN, AMBROSIO IGNACIO SPÍNOLA Y
Spinowski, Teofil **25** 841
Spintharos **8** 694; **13** 395
Spira, Johannes Emericus de *see* JOHANN EMERICH OF SPEIER
Spira, Vindelinus de *see* WENDELIN OF SPEIER
spirae **23** 478
spiral coats *see under* COATS → types
Spirale **24** 428
Spiral group **1** 444
Spire, Charles **11** 619
spires **20** 581; **29** 412–14*
 Austria **32** 450
 Belgium **13** 62–3; **29** 414
 Czech Republic **25** 54
 England **13** 55–6; **19** 597; **29** *412*, *413*, 413–14*
 France **29** 412–13, 414*
 Germany **13** 56, 58; **29** 414
 Gothic **13** 55, 56, 58, 62–3; **27** 628; **29** *412*, 412–13, *413*
 Holy Roman Empire (before 1648) **29** 414*
 Indian subcontinent **15** 318, *318*, 319
 Italy **2** *177*; **29** 414
 Netherlands, the **13** 62–3
 Panama **23** 903
 Spain **29** 414*
Spiridon, Joseph **5** 509; **11** 32
Spiridonov, Nikita **29** 415
Spiridonov, Seymon **29** 414–15*; **33** 507
Spiridonov, Vasily **29** 415
Spiridony of Kiev **31** 557
 works **31** *558*
spirit, white *see* WHITE SPIRIT
Spirit Cave *see* XIANREN DONG
spirit fresco *see under* FRESCOES → techniques
spirit-houses *see under* SHRINES (i) (CULT) → types
Spirit of Denmark Clock **11** 627
spirit poles **16** 46; **18** 300
Spirituals **11** 707
spirit varnishes *see under* VARNISHES → types
Spiro, Elizabeth **3** 127; **18** 138
Spiro Mounds **22** *544*, 560; **29** 415*; **30** 449
 metalwork **29** *415*
 textiles **22** 628
Spirovska, Mira **19** 885
Spiš **28** 856
Spiskin, Jean **3** 543
 works **3** *543*
Spišská Kapitula Cathedral **14** 898, 899; **28** 849, 851
Spišská Nová Ves **28** *848*
 theatre **28** 850
Spišska Sobota Church **13** 162
Spišske Podhradie Altarpiece **14** 893
Spišský Štvrtok **21** 551
 St Ladislas, Zápolya Chapel **14** 884; **28** 849
Spitakavor Church of the Mother of God **2** 434, 435
Spital am Pyhrn, Abbey Church **2** 783, 822
Spiti **15** 311
Spits, Arnoult van der *see* ARNOULT DE NIMÈGUE
Spittal an der Drau, Schloss Porcia **2** *776*, 779; **25** 248–9*
Spitting Image Workshop **30** 389
spittoons **29** 470
Spituk **15** 311; **30** 819
Spitzer, Frédéric **21** 413; **27** 641; **29** 415–16*
 armour **28** 528
 collections **6** 393; **28** 384
 stained glass **29** 515
Spitzly, Caspar **20** 803
Spitzweg, Carl **22** 304; **29** 416–17*
 groups and movements **26** 740
 works **12** 394; **29** *416*
Splanchnopt Painter **13** 523
splashboards **24** *81*
Splenger, Jakob **9** 108
Splinter, Gerrit **4** 150
Split **8** *174*, 175; **9** *510*; **26** *906*; **29** 417–19*; **32** *158*
 Archaeological Museum **8** 180
 Benedictine nunnery **12** 667
 Cathedral of the Blessed Virgin Mary **8** 177, 178, 180; **26** 907; **29** 419
  Baptistery **8** 177, *177*
  doors **8** 180
  mausoleum of Diocletian **8** 175; **20** 864; **29** 418; **31** 110
 Cindro Palace **8** 176
 fortifications **32** 159, *159*
 Galerija Meštrović **8** 181; **21** 316; **29** 419
 Gallery of Fine Arts **8** 181
 Palace of Diocletian **8** 175; **9** 554, 556, 557; **21** 560; **23** 809; **26** 854, 870, 882, 902, 907; **29** *417*, 417–18
  arches **2** 297
  basilica **3** 329
 Spalatum **29** 417–18*
 stadium **8** 177; **29** 489
 wood-carvings **9** 601
split ply twining *see under* TWINING
split stitch *see under* STITCHES
splitting **29** 703–4*
Spode, Josiah, I (1733-97) **10** 309; **29** 419*; **33** 136
Spode, Josiah, II (1755-1827) **4** 177; **29** 419*, 495
Spode, Josiah, III (*d* 1829) **29** 419
Spode Ceramic Works **4** 177; **10** 307, 310; **26** 85; **29** 419*, 495
Spoede, Bernhard **24** 740
Spoede, Jean-Jacques **18** 841
Spoerri, Daniel **11** 551; **29** 419–20*; **30** 135, 140
 collaboration **30** 923
 groups and movements **23** 260; **33** 636
 patrons and collectors **14** 48; **29** 16
 works **2** 617; **23** 261; **26** 51; **30** *139*
Spoerry, Bernard **29** 420
Spoerry, François (Henry) **11** 528; **29** 420*
Spohr, von **17** 834
Spoilum **6** 624; **13** 733, 734*; **14** 721
Spoldy, Anibal **16** 877
Spolek výtvarných umělců *see* MÁNES UNION OF ARTISTS
Spoleto **16** *620*; **26** *886*; **29** 420–22*
 aqueduct **2** 242
 Cathedral of the Assumption **8** 211; **16** 625, 725
  frescoes **19** *444*
 Museo Civico **29** 422
 S Pietro **16** 625; **26** 625
 S Salvatore **16** 624; **26** 625; **29** *421*
Spoleto, Tizio da **33** 718
spolia **2** 319; **9** 531; **15** 207, 338; **26** *843*
spolia masonry *see under* MASONRY → types
spolveri **29** 422*
Spolverini, Pier Ilario **10** 812; **28** 755
Spon, Jacob **2** 162; **11** 661; **13** 608; **33** 136
Spondylus shells *see under* SHELLS → types
spongewares *see under* POTTERY → wares
spongotypes **21** 896
Spon Lane glassworks **10** 319
Sponlee, John de *see* JOHN DE SPONLEE
sponsorship **29** 121; **31** 669
Spool Gripper Axminster carpets *see under* CARPETS → types
spoons **8** 283–5*
 historical and regional traditions
  Africa **1** *291*, 326, *368*, 368–9*
  Asante **1** 369
  Benin, Kingdom of **1** 328
  Byzantine **9** 654, 656
  Dan (Africa) **1** *291*, 368, *368*; **8** 489*, *489*
  Early Christian (*c.* AD 250-843) **9** 654, 656
  Egypt, ancient **10** *66*
  England **8** *284*; **10** 324; **14** *763*
  Ghana **1** 369
  Guro **13** 861
  Hausa **1** 247
  Kota (ii) (Gabon peoples) **18** 404
  Liberia **1** *291*, 368; **8** *489*
  Madagascar **20** 39
  Netherlands, the **28** *739*
  Prehistoric art **8** 283
  Rome, ancient **8** 284, *284*; **27** 83
  Sierra Leone **1** 327
  Sri Lanka **29** 471
  Zulu **1** 369
 materials
  aluminium **1** 247
  bone **8** 283, 284
  brass **8** 284
  clay **8** 283
  enamel **28** *739*
spoons
 materials—cont.
  horn **8** 284; **14** *763*
  ivory **1** 326, 327, 328; **29** 471
  pewter **8** 284
  silver **8** 284; **9** 654, 656; **27** 83; **28** *739*
  wood **1** *291*, *368*; **8** 283, 284, *489*; **10** *66*; **31** 305
 types
  Puritan **8** *284*, 285
  trefid **8** *284*, 285
Spoor, Cornelis **21** 851
Spoor, Matthias **10** 732
Spoorwater, Evert **13** 62, 896; **22** 820–21
Sporck, Franz Anton, Graf von **8** 391; **29** 422*
 architecture **1** 669; **8** 422; **18** 504, 506
 sculpture **4** 698; **8** 385; **18** 192, 506
Sporing, Herman **3** 183
Spornberg, Jacob **3** 373
Sporring, Ole **8** 736
Sportes, Ronald Cécil **11** 584
sporting scenes **29** 422–7*
 Britain **29** 422, 426, *427*
 Denmark **12** *602*
 Egypt, ancient **9** 811*
 England **3** 245; **10** 250; **29** 422, 425; **33** *376*
 Etruscan **10** 594, *594*
 France **8** *620*; **12** *351*; **19** *297*; **20** *260*; **29** 426
 Greece, ancient **29** 422, 423
 Indian subcontinent **29** 422
 Italy **10** 594, *594*
 Rome, ancient **29** 423
 United States of America **3** *680*; **29** 425, 426
 see also HUNTING SCENES
sports centres **22** *806*; **23** *272*; **29** 427–8*
spotlights **3** 537; **9** 13
Spotswood, Alexander **31** 590; **33** 207
Spott, J. V. **8** 401
spotting *see under* PHOTOGRAPHY → processes
Spottiswoode, Hugh **18** 882
Spøttrup Castle **4** 781; **8** 724
spout gables *see under* GABLES → types
Spovieri, Giuseppe **11** 865
sprang **8** 753; **10** 76; **30** 550, 563
Spranger, Bartholomäus **8** 390; **16** 674; **25** 432; **27** *503*; **29** 428–31*
 collaboration **12** 881
 copies **11** 803
 groups and movements **26** 728
 methods **10** 387
 patrons and collectors **5** 792; **12** 387; **13** 910, 912, 914, 915; **14** 868; **25** 8
 reproductive prints by others **1** 662; **9** 79; **10** *388*; **12** 881; **13** 847; **17** 598; **18** 42; **22** 272; **27** 502, 503, 504
 teachers **20** 249
 works **8** *390*; **10** 436; **12** 881; **22** 839; **23** 294; **29** *429*, *430*
Sprangher, Barthollomeus *see* SPRANGER, BARTHOLOMÄUS
Spratling, William **21** 393
Spratt **24** 589
Sprawozdania komisji do badania historii sztuki w polsce **24** 441
spraying **25** 478
Spreafico, José **29** 431*
Sprechman, Thomas **31** 754
Sprechsaal für Keramik, Glas, Email, silikate **24** 444
Spreckels, Adolph B. **27** 731
Spreckels, Alma **27** 731
Spreckelsen, Otto von **11** 527, 528; **24** 132; **26** 333; **29** 526
 works **11** *527*

Spreeuwen, Jacob van **19** 102
Sprenger, (Wilhelm) Paul Eduard **2** 785, 786, 787; **3** 779; **29** 431*; **32** 437
Spriet, Joan van der **32** 258
sprigging *see under* CERAMICS → techniques
Sprimont, Nicholas (*c.* 1678-1744) **29** 432
Sprimont, Nicholas (1716-71) **6** 533; **19** 593, 595; **29** 432*
  collaboration **6** 451; **8** 149
  patrons and collectors **14** 143; **27** 641
  works **10** 308, 332; **14** 857
Spring (family) **24** 576
Spring *see* VESNA
Spring, Jakob **30** 136
Spring, Peter **30** 136
Springer, Anton **8** 426; **14** 635; **15** 89; **24** 825; **28** 916
Springer, Cornelis **29** 432–3*
  collaboration **32** 375
  patrons and collectors **11** 233
  pupils **13** 633
  teachers **17** 825
  works **22** 848
Springer, Ferdinand **21** 311
Springer, Hendrik **29** 432
Springer, J. B. **1** 803; **29** 433
Springer, J. L. **1** 803; **29** 433
Springer, Willem **29** 433*; **33** 48
springewölbe vaults *see* VAULTS (CEILING) → types → rib: jumping
Springfield (MA), South Congregational Church **25** 372
springing lines **2** 292
Springinklee, Hans **23** 310; **29** 433–4*
  collaboration **9** 436, 440; **17** 700; **28** 58, 143
  patrons and collectors **13** 902, 903; **33** 353
  pupils **29** 719
  restorations by others **17** 711
  teachers **23** 308
  works **12** 386; **29** *434*, 719; **33** 353
Springmeyer, Frederic **3** 685
Springmeyer, John H. **3** 685
Springmeyer, William **3** 685
Springmeyer Bros **3** 685
Spring of Khusraw **12** 77; **16** 469
springs **3** 585; **7** 439, 441; **31** 685, 686
Spring Season Society *see* SHINYŌKAI
Spring Slumber Studio **12** 50
Springsteen & Goldhammer **32** 851
Spring Sun Society *see* SHINYŌKAI
Springuett, Sabino **29** 434*
  groups and movements **24** 510
  patrons and collectors **24** 515
  pupils **28** 604
  works **24** 510
Springwood, Norman Lindsay Gallery and Museum **2** 771
Sprinkle, Annie **10** 882
sprinkled lacquer *see under* LACQUER → types
sprinklers **32** *203*
sprinkles **6** 32
Sproatt, Henry **29** 435*
Sproatt & Rolph **29** 435*; **31** 176
Sprotborough (S. Yorks), St Mary's **30** 778
Spruance, Benton **19** 492
spruce **15** 720; **22** 563; **24** 3; **33** 324
Sprüngli, Niklaus **3** 822
Spur **29** 435*
Spurey, Kurt **32** 450
Spurgeon, Charles Haddon **23** 194
Spurinas group **10** 615
Spurinna (family) **10** 622
spurs **6** 599
Spy *see* WARD, LESLIE
Spybuck, Ernest **22** 594
Spychalski, Jan **25** 409
spyglasses **17** 399
Spynie, Archbishop's Palace **31** 230
Spyropoulos, T. G. **23** 476; **30** 285
Spyropoulos, Yannis **2** 545; **29** 435*
Spytihněv II, Duke of Bohemia **25** 439
Squarcione, Francesco **16** 778; **29** 435–6*
  assistants **8** 526; **28** 84, 85
  attributions **28** 85
  personal collection **25** 163
  pupils **20** 304; **23** 754; **25** 9; **28** 84; **33** 700, 702
square piers *see under* PIERS (ii) (MASONRY) → types
squares (town) **11** 342; **31** 714, 717–18
  Austria **27** *662*
  France **31** 717
    Louis XIV style **11** *517*
    17th cent. **11** 518; **24** *117*, *119*
    18th cent. **8** *889*; **22** *454*, *455*; **24** *122*; **26** *205*
  Germany **14** 492; **28** *802*
  Hungary **14** *890*
  Inca **15** 162
  Iran **27** 512
  Italy
    Baroque **3** *836*
    Mannerism **21** *454*
    Neo-classicism **16** *648*; **31** *442*
    Renaissance **2** *593*; **11** *177*
    Rococo **16** *639*
    12th cent. **28** *675*
    13th cent. **11** *212*
    16th cent. **27** *483*
    17th cent. **6** *18*; **31** *439*
    18th cent. **19** *685*
    19th cent. **28** *801*
  Mesoamerica, Pre-Columbian **21** 195
  Olmec **23** 417
  Portugal **19** *465*; **27** *800*
  Russia **27** *576*
  South Africa **25** *566*
  Spain **20** *61*, *62*; **31** 718
squaring up **11** *762*, 763; **29** *437*, 437–8*
squatting statues *see under* SCULPTURE → types
squeegees **29** 438*
squeezes **7** 65, 117
Squerryes Court (Kent) **10** 277
Squier, Ephraim George **6** 441; **13** 311, 811; **23** 703; **29** 218, 219, 222
Squier, Robert **18** 881
Squillace **6** 57
Squillace, Giovanni Battista Borgia, Prince of **4** 409
Squilli, Benedetto di Michele **11** 193
squinches **9** 85; **29** 438*
  Afghanistan **16** 168–9
  Central Asia, Western **6** 199; **16** 161, 168–9
  Egypt **16** 176
  Indian subcontinent **15** 340
  Iran **16** 161, 164
  Iran, ancient **15** 912
  Islamic **15** 340; **16** 142, 161, 164, 168–9, 176
Squinzano, Santa Maria delle Cerrate **26** 628
Squire, Raglan **22** 719
squirrel-hair *see under* HAIR → types
Squirru, Carlos **2** 401
Sra **8** 490
  works **8** *489*
Šrámek, Jan **8** 381; **29** 438*
Šrámková, Alena **8** 381; **29** 438
Sras Srang *see under* ANGKOR
Sravana Belgola **15** 204, *294*, 301, 528; **29** 438–9*
  Chamundaraya Basti **15** 528
  Chandragupta Basti **15** 528
  Gommateshvara **15** 528, *528*
  Jaina *maṭha* **15** 531, 649
  sculpture **15** 226, 529
Sravasti **15** 220, *261*, *264*, 409; **29** 439*
  plaques **15** 227
  sculpture **15** 440, 441, *441*
Srbinović, Mladen **28** 451
Srebrenica **4** *459*
  church **4** 460
Sredets **5** 147
Sredi kollektsionerov **27** 439
Sregier, Efraim *see* SZREGER, EFRAIM
Srei Santhor **2** 61
  architecture **5** 481
  stupas **5** 481
  Vat Srei Sar Chhor Monastery **5** 498, 499
  sculpture **5** *498*
  Vat Vihear Suor Monastery **5** 498
Sremska Mitrovica **9** *510*, *511*; **26** *906*; **28** *437*, 439
  architecture **9** 560
  Roman circus **7** 342
  Sirmium **28** 791*
  Sremska Museum **28** 458
Sremski Karlovci **28** *437*, 444
Śrihaṭṭa *see* SYLHET
Sri Indraditya, King of Sukhotai (*reg* 1238-75) **30** 582
Srikshetra **5** *221*, 222, 223; **29** 231
  architecture **5** 225, 227, 237
  Bawbaw-gyi **5** 225, *225*; **29** 866
  Bebe **5** 225, 238
  coins **5** 255
  Le-myet-hna **5** 225, 238
  Paya-gyi **5** 225
  Paya-ma **5** 225
  stelae **5** 239
  tablets **5** 242
  Ze-gu, East **5** 225
Srikurmam **15** 636
Sri Lanka **29** 439–79*, *440*
  architectural decorations **29** 475, 477–8*
  architecture **29** 441, 446–51*, 452–6*
    Buddhism **29** 446–8*, 449
    Hinduism **29** 448
    megalithic **29** 445
    military **21** 572, 575
    prefabrication **29** 453
  armour **29** 468–9*
  Balangoda Points **29** 445
  blacksmiths **29** 474
  boxes **29** 470
  bronze **29** *460*, *461*, 474, 478, *479*
  burial mounds **29** 442
  cabinets (ii) (furniture) **29** 470, 471
  calamander **29** 470
  cane **29** 470, 471
  caskets **29** 471, *472*, 479
  cave art **29** 462
  chairs **25** 305; **29** 470, *471*
  chests **29** 470
  cinnabar **29** 462
  clay **29** 475
  clubs (weapons) **29** 469
  coins **29** 469*
  collections **29** 473, 478–9*
  combs (hair) **29** 471
  copper **29** 474
  dāgabas **5** 98; **29** 446, 447, *447*, 864–5*
  department stores **29** *454*
  diamonds **20** 302
  domes **9** 86
  doors **29** 471
  dress **29** 470*
  dyes **29** 476
  ebony **29** 470
  ethnography **29** 473
Sri Lanka—cont.
  exhibitions **29** 478
  figurines **29** 471, 475, *476*
  flags **29** 477, *477*
  foils (iii) (swords) **29** 469
  fortifications **21** 572, 575
  fortresses **29** 452
  forts **21** *572*
  furniture **29** 470–71*
  gammalu **29** 477, *478*
  gardens **29** 448
  gems **29** 471
  gilding **29** *460*
  gold **20** 329; **29** 472, *473*, 474–5
  government buildings **29** *455*
  graffiti **29** 464
  grounds **29** 462
  guns **29** 469
  hospitals **25** 169
  houses **29** 453
  iconography **29** 442–4, *443*, 458, 459
  image-houses **25** 169; **29** 443, 448–9*, *449*, 451
  iron **16** 59; **29** 468, 474
  ivory **29** 469, 470
  ivory-carvings **29** 471*, *472*, 479
  jak **29** 470
  jewellery **29** 470, 471–3*, *473*
  kaolin **29** 462
  knaaps *see* spittoons
  kumbuk **29** *471*
  lacquer **18** 608
  laterite **29** 452
  limestone **29** *457*
  looms **29** 476
  manuals
    architecture **29** 446
    jewellery **29** 473
    pottery **29** 475
    weapons **29** 468
  manuscript covers **20** *328*
  manuscript illumination **29** 462, 465
  manuscripts **20** *328*; **29** 442, 478
  maps **32** 99
  masks **29** 473–4*
  mats **29** 470
  metalwork **29** 474–5*
  microliths **29** 445
  monasteries **29** 446–8*
  moonstones **29** 443, *443*
  museums **29** 478–9*
  nadun **29** 470
  ochre **29** 463
  orpiment **29** 462
  painting **29** 466–8*, 479
    Buddhism **29** 466
    murals **29** *468*
    wall **29** 462–5*, *463*, *465*, 466, *466*
      Buddhism **5** *97*; **25** 170; **29** 443, 462*
    20th cent. **29** *467*
  palaces **29** 448
  periods
    Prehistoric **29** 444–5*
  photography **10** 580
  pigments **29** 445, 463, 476
    green earth **29** 463
    yellow **29** 477
  pilgrimages **5** 97, *97*
  plaques **29** 471
  porcelain **4** 173
  puppets **29** 479
  quartz **29** 445
  religion **29** 440, 441–4*, *443*
  rock art **29** 445
  sapphires **12** 268
  satin-wood **29** 470
  scroll cases **29** *475*
  sculpture **29** 456–9*, 460–62*
    architectural **29** 865
    bronze **29** *460*, *461*, 478, *479*
    Buddhism **5** 98; **29** *457*, *460*, 461, *479*
    colossal statues **5** 98; **25** *170*; **29** 442, *458*, 458
Sri Lanka—cont.
  shrines (i) (cult) **17** 769; **25** 169, 303; **29** 448
    tree-shrines **29** 442
  silver **29** 474, *475*
  spittoons **29** 470
  spoons **29** 471
  staircases **29** 526; **33** *503*
  steel **16** 51; **29** 468
  stupas *see dāgabas*
  swords **29** 469
  tamarind **29** 470
  teak **29** 470
  tempera **29** 462
  temples **29** *451*
  terracottas **29** 475–6*, *476*
  textiles **29** 476–7*
  tools **29** 445
  trade **20** 302
    chairs **25** 305
    iron **16** 59
    porcelain **4** 175; **6** 622
    shrines (i) (cult) **25** 303
  varnishes **29** 462
  weapons **29** 468–9*, 471, 474
  weaving **29** 476
  wood **20** *328*; **29** 477–8*
  wood-carvings **29** 450, 477–8*, *478*
  writing **20** 329
Sri Menanti Royal Palace **20** 167
Srimushnam, Bhu Varaha Temple **15** 399
Srinagar **15** *264*, *360*, *619*; **28** *719*, 721; **29** 480–81*
  carpets **16** 485
  fountains **11** 340
  Garden of Joy *see* NISHAT BAGH
  Hari Parbat Fort **15** 362, 364
  maps **15** 705
  mosque of Mulla Shah Badkhshani **15** 367
  Nishat Bagh **12** 74; **15** 364
  painting **15** 628
  Pari Mahal **15** 367
  Shalimar Bagh **11** 340; **12** 74, *75*; **15** 364, 366
    Black Pavilion **29** *480*
  Sri Pratap Singh Museum **15** 180
  tomb of Madin Sahib **15** 687
  Vernag **15** 364
Śrīnagara *see* SINNAR (INDIA)
Sri Nathji **30** 559
Sringa Verapura **15** *261*; **29** 481*
Sringeri, Vidya Shankara Temple **15** 331, 533
Sri Nivasa, King (*reg c.* 1661-*c.* 1684) (Malla) **22** 754
Srinivasan, K. R. **15** 212
Srinivasan, P. **20** 54
Srinivasulu **20** 54
Sripura *see* SIRPUR
Srirangam **15** *294*; **26** 48; **29** 481–2*
  gateways **15** 405
  ivory **15** 696
  Ranganatha Temple **15** 334, 335, 399, 518, 519, 647; **29** *481*
    Sheshagiri Mandapa **15** 518, *518*
  Tiruvannaikovil
    Jambukeshvara Temple **14** 77; **15** 399
Srirangapattana **15** 648
Srisailam **15** *294*; **29** 482*
  Mallikarjuna Temple **15** 329, 540
  sculpture **15** 540
  Shiva temples **15** 539
Srī Sajjanālaya *see* SI SATCHANALAI
Srivijaya **29** 231
Sri Vikrama Rajasimha, King of Kandy (*reg* 1798-1815) **17** 769; **29** 451, 472, 478
Srivilliputtur, Sri Andal Temple **15** 647
Srnec, Aleksandar **8** 179; **10** 667
Srnec, Jiří **2** 4
Sroda, Gostomski Chapel **25** 129
Srour, Habib **7** 858; **19** 7
Srubnaya culture **28** 321

Santa Rufina factory 25 310
Ssangbong Temple
pagoda 23 775
stupa 29 869
Ssanggye Temple (South Cholla) 18 308
Ssanggye Temple (South Kyŏngsang) 18 307, 308, 310, 311, 328
SS Marinus and Anianus (Rott am Inn) 11 125, 127; 12 372, 372, 406; 13 851; 26 498
Ssu-ma Ch'ien see SIMA QIAN
Ssu-ma Chin-lung see SIMA JINLONG
Ssu-ma Kuang see SIMA GUANG
Sta, Herbrand 23 242
Staal, Arthur 22 832; 29 482, 484*
collaboration 29 483
groups and movements 4 221; 22 831
Staal, J. F. (fl late 19th cent.; father) 29 482
Staal, J(an) F(rederik) (1879-1940; son) 29 482–4*
collaboration 18 436, 469; 21 122; 29 484; 33 676
groups and movements 1 815
pupils 29 483
staff 14 693
works 1 804
Staal-Kropholler, Margaret 18 469; 29 482, 483*
Staates, Forbes J. 23 697
Staatliche Porzellanmanufaktur, Berlin see KÖNIGLICHE PORZELLANMANUFAKTUR (BERLIN)
Staatliches Bauhaus see BAUHAUS → Weimar
Staats (family) 22 111
Staats Forbes, James see FORBES, JAMES STAATS
Staber, Johann 32 440
Stabiae 10 585; 26 886
Villa of Carmiano 27 48
Villa S Marco 27 51, 71
wall paintings 13 547; 16 653; 27 50, 51, 53, 58
workshops 27 55
Stabile, Luigi 6 136
stabiles 29 484*
Stabili, Giovanni Battista 22 453
Stabilimento Stefano Johnson 6 42
stabilization see under CONSERVATION → techniques
Stabius, Johannes 9 435; 13 902, 903
Stabler, Harold 19 594; 29 484*
pupils 19 431
works 10 337
Stabler, Phoebe 29 484
stables 3 273; 21 559; 29 484–6*, 485, 486
Stabrowski, Kazimierz 25 141
Stacchini, Ulisse 29 486*
works 16 648; 21 521, 521; 25 857
stacco method 22 165
Stache, Friedrich 11 29
Stachowicz, Michał 18 428; 25 105
Stack bond see under BONDING
Stackelberg, Otto von 13 612
stacking dolls see DOLLS → types → Matryoshka
Stacpoole, Frederick 26 431; 29 486*
Stacquet, Henry 8 63
Stade, Hartwig von see HARTWIG VON STADE
Städel, Johann Friedrich 11 735; 29 487*
Städel-Jahrbuch 24 445
Staden, Hans 4 706
Stadholder Maria, Master of the see REGENT, MASTER OF THE
stadia 1 798; 29 427, 487–90*
Britain 29 489
stadia—cont.
Greece, ancient 13 386, 403, 418; 16 612; 27 712; 29 487–8*, 488
Italy 29 489
Korea 18 263
Rome, ancient 26 895; 27 712; 29 487–8*
Sweden 14 227
United States of America 1 798; 29 489, 490
see also AMPHITHEATRES; CIRCUSES (ROMAN)
Stadil Church 8 738
Stadion, Johann Caspar von 24 588
Stadler, Anselm 30 135; 33 30
Stadler, Anton 29 490
Stadler, August Conrad 29 490
Stadler, Bernhard, workshops 7 346
Stadler, Ferdinand (Caspar) 3 335, 824; 29 490, 491*
Stadler, Hans Caspar 29 490, 491
Stadler, Hans Conrad (1712-74) 29 490
Stadler, Hans Conrad (1752-1819) 29 490
Stadler, Hans Conrad (1788-1846) 10 496; 29 490–91*
Stadler, Hans Ludwig, I 21 407
Stadler, Hermann Augustus 29 490, 491*
Stadler, Joseph Constantine 29 491*
pupils 19 284
works 2 238; 10 806; 18 906
Stadler, Julius Jakob 13 842
Stadler, Toni (1888-1982) 19 707; 22 267; 29 491–2*
Stadler, Toni von (1850-1917) 29 491
Stadler, Voit 14 893; 31 353
Stadl-Paura, Dreifaltigkeitskirche 2 783
Städtebau, Der 14 300; 28 801; 31 728
Stadthagen Schloss 33 88
Staebler, Stephen De 24 281; 31 640
Staeck, Edition see EDITION STAECK
Staeck, Klaus 29 492*
Staedtler, J. S. 8 128
Staehr-Nielsen, Eva 8 749; 28 22
Staël (-Holstein), (Anne-Louise-Germaine,) Mme de 29 492*
personal collection 30 854
works 2 530; 26 736
illustrated 13 779
Staël, Nicolas de 29 492–5*
dealers 27 163
groups and movements 2 543; 26 414
patrons and collectors 7 797; 19 282; 30 749
works 11 551; 29 493, 670
Staets, Hendrick (Jacobsz.) 1 801; 18 8; 32 673
staff 10 683
staffage 29 495*
Staffel, Rudolf 31 640
Staffelkirche see CHURCHES → types → hall
Stafford, Edward, 3rd Duke of Buckingham 1 746; 6 59
Stafford, George Leveson-Gower, 2nd Marquess of see LEVESON-GOWER, GEORGE, 1st Duke of Sutherland
Stafford, Henry Valentine Fitzherbert, 9th Baron see FITZHERBERT, HENRY VALENTINE, 9th Baron Stafford
Stafford, Spencer 31 652
Stafford, William Howard (i), Viscount see HOWARD (i), WILLIAM, Viscount Stafford
Stafford Pottery (St Cunegonde) 5 581
Staffordshire 29 495–6*
designers 10 312
enamel 17 525
figurines 10 308
pottery 10 303, 306
see also POTTERIES
staffs
historical and regional traditions
Africa 1 265, 278, 355, 402, 417, 417
Akye 1 514
Asante 1 354; 2 587*
Baule 3 407
Cook Islands 7 790
Côte d'Ivoire 1 263
Easter Island 9 675
Edo (Africa) 9 735
Ghana 1 278
Luba 1 354, 355; 19 740*
Madagascar 20 40
Ndebele 1 417
Pende 24 360
Senufo 1 263; 28 421–3*
Shona 1 417
Thailand 30 639
Tonga (Pacific Islands) 31 144, 144
Venda 1 417
Yoruba 1 265; 33 556, 557
Zaïre 1 402
Zulu 1 417, 417; 33 724
materials
barkcloth 7 790
brass 1 265
fibres 1 355
leather 1 355
wood 1 355, 402; 7 790; 30 639; 31 144
Stafhell, Anders 30 107
Stafhell, Gustaf 25 460; 30 106
Stag Cabinet Co. 10 299
stage buildings 13 385–6, 385, 391; 26 863, 912
stage design 5 686; 19 728; 30 653, 679–82*, 685–8*
Armenia (Europe) 2 432
Azerbaijan 2 897
Belgium 30 665
Britain 30 687–8, 688
England 17 638; 30 653, 662, 662–3*, 674–5*, 681
France 30 653, 659–60*, 671–2*, 686
Germany 30 685, 686, 687
Greece, ancient 1 450; 30 650–51*
Italy 30 655, 656–7*, 657, 667–9*, 668
Baroque 25 414
Renaissance 19 195; 28 470
16th cent. 5 184; 27 740
18th cent. 12 25
Japan 17 325–6*
Rome, ancient 30 651–2*
Russia 3 119; 27 392, 394, 396, 397; 30 686
Spain 30 663–4*
United States of America 15 824; 30 687, 688
stage machinery 30 653, 654, 657, 658, 663, 664, 668, 674; 31 166
stage-painting see STAGE SCENERY
stages 30 650
historical and regional traditions
China 7 135–6
France 30 653
Germany 30 685
Greece, ancient 13 385, 386, 406; 30 651
Japan 17 326, 329–32*
Olmec 23 417
Rome, ancient 30 652
materials
stucco 30 656
stage scenery 30 650, 665, 679, 680
historical and regional traditions
Britain 30 680–82
stage scenery
historical and regional traditions—cont.
China 7 138
England 30 653, 662, 673, 674, 681
France 30 681
Greece, ancient 1 450; 30 650
Italy 30 654, 657
Spain 29 306; 30 663, 664
types
cycloramic 30 682
Fortuny cupola 11 326
Stage Society 30 685
stage-top sideboards see under SIDEBOARDS → types
Staggemeier, L. 4 354
Staggi, Gioacchino 25 121, 212
Staggia, Scuola di see SCUOLA DI STAGGIA
Stagi, Bernardino 29 496
Stagi, Giuseppe 29 496
Stagi, Lorenzo 3 742; 7 367; 29 496
Stagi, Stagio 24 855; 29 496*
collaboration 1 789; 7 918
works 3 742; 24 858
Staglieno, David da see DAVID DA STAGLIENO
Stagno, Bruno 8 17
stag-stones see under STELAE → types
Stahi, Constantin 26 714
Stahija 25 344
Ståhl, Efraim 30 95
Stahl, Johann Georg 4 890
Stahl, Leonhard 29 392
Stahl, P. J. 11 798
Stahlavsky, Zdenek 19 523
Stahly, François 29 496–7*
collaboration 11 569
groups and movements 2 544; 10 581
patrons and collectors 19 848; 27 224
works 11 569
Stahrenberg, Graf von 20 494
Staiger, Otto 13 726; 27 213; 30 134
Staikov, Vesselin 5 155
Stain, Jörg 22 305
Stainbank, Mary 9 427; 29 111
Stainborough House see WENTWORTH → Castle
Staindle, Matthias see STEINL, MATTHIAS
stained glass 12 790; 14 422; 29 497–519*, 499; 33 246
cleaning 29 518*
collections see under COLLECTIONS → types
conservation 29 517, 517–19*
exhibitions see under EXHIBITIONS → types
historical and regional traditions
Anglo-Saxon 2 83*
Australia 2 763; 11 756
Austria 13 151, 186, 188; 29 IV
Belgium 13 181–3*, 182, 909; 26 745
Cistercian Order 7 353; 13 136; 26 702; 29 502
Czech Republic 8 407; 13 187, 189
Denmark 13 190
England 29 505, 506, 507, 508; 30 654; 33 549
Anglo-Saxon 2 83*
Gothic 5 647, 647–8, 648; 13 135, 136, 140, 142, 152, 178, 183–5*, 184; 14 422; 19 406; 29 501, 503, II; 33 64, 549
Pre-Raphaelitism 29 513, VI2
Renaissance 5 515
Romanesque 26 702
16th cent. 5 514
19th cent. 22 143, 143; 29 507
Finland 13 190
stained glass
historical and regional traditions—cont.
France 29 504, 505–6, 508
Gothic 3 459; 4 582; 6 494, 498; 13 135, 136, 136, 140–41*, 142, 143, 149, 178–81*, 179, 180; 16 837; 24 158; 26 120, 123; 27 549; 29 501, 503, 510, 511, 759, I, VI1
Gothic: Channel style 13 143
Gothic: Early Gothic 28 417
Romanesque 19 129; 26 700, 702, 703
20th cent. 29 509
Franciscan Order 11 712
Germany 23 315; 29 503–4, 506, 508
Gothic 2 720; 7 590; 10 452; 13 135, 142, 185, 185–8*, 186; 29 502, III
Gothic: Early Gothic 12 382; 22 693
Renaissance 14 572
Romanesque 26 701, 702
16th cent. 27 255; 29 512
Gothic 13 127, 132*, 134, 135–6, 178*, 189*; 19 356; 29 501–3
Austria 13 151, 186, 188; 29 IV
Belgium 13 181–3*, 182
Cistercian Order 13 136
Czech Republic 13 187, 189
Denmark 13 190
England 5 647, 647–8, 648; 13 135, 136, 140, 142, 152, 178, 183–5*, 184; 14 422; 19 406; 29 501, 503, II; 33 64, 549
Finland 13 190
France 3 459; 4 582; 6 498; 13 135, 136, 136, 140–41*, 142, 143, 149, 178–81*, 179, 180; 16 837; 26 120, 123; 27 549; 29 501, 503, 510, 511, 759, I, VI1
France: Channel style 13 143
France: Early Gothic 28 417
Germany 2 720; 7 590; 10 452; 12 382; 13 135, 142, 185, 185–8*, 186; 29 502, III
Germany: Early Gothic 22 693
Holy Roman Empire (before 1648) 13 185–8*; 29 502, 503
Italy 13 192–3*, 193
Norway 13 190
Poland 13 189, 189
Portugal 13 192*
Romania 13 189
Scandinavia 13 190–91*
Spain 12 740; 13 191, 191–2*; 19 174
Sweden 13 190–91, 190
Switzerland 13 186; 30 130*
Wales 13 183, 184
Holy Roman Empire (before 1648) 13 185–8*; 29 502, 503
Hungary 12 839
Iran 16 257
Ireland 29 507, VII
Islamic 16 256*, 257
Italy 29 504
Gothic 13 192–3*, 193
Romanesque 26 702
13th cent. 2 631
16th cent. 13 827; 29 504
Morocco 16 257
Netherlands, the 2 485; 8 102, 103; 14 737; 27 257
Northern Ireland 16 41
Norway 13 190
Ottoman 16 257
Poland 13 189, 189
Portugal 13 192*; 25 311

stained glass
historical and regional traditions—cont.
Romanesque **19** 129; **26** *700*, 700–702*, *701*, *703*
Romania **13** 189
Scandinavia **13** 190–91*
Scotland **29** 508
Singapore **28** 772
Spain **31** 92
Gothic **12** *740*; **13** *191*, 191–2*; **19** *174*
Islamic **16** 257
Romanesque **26** 702
16th cent. **29** V
Sweden **13** 190–91, *190*
Switzerland **11** 773; **13** 186; **30** 130*, 131, 134
Turkey **16** 257
United States of America **18** 627; **29** 508; **30** 868–9; **31** 689
20th cent. **18** *101*
Wales **13** 183, 184
historiography *see under* HISTORIOGRAPHY → types
materials
armatures **29** 501
borax **29** 498
enamel **2** 485; **29** 498
iron oxide **29** 498
lead **29** 499
Plasticine **29** 498
silver **13** 178
silver nitrate **13** 136; **29** 498
waxes **29** 498
restoration **29** 519*
technical examination **29** 518*
techniques
cartoons (drawings) **23** *315*; **29** 498
cutting **29** 498*
firing **29** 499*, *499*
grisaille paintings **13** 136, 178, 181, 183, 672–3*; **19** 406; **26** 702; **29** 502–3, VII
France **13** *136*
Gothic **13** *136*
painting **29** 498–9*
silver-stain **13** 136, 178, 183, 186, 193; **29** 498, 499; **33** 549
soldering **29** 499
yellow-stain *see* SILVER-STAIN
treatises *see under* TREATISES → types
uses
architectural decorations **16** 256*
churches *see under* CHURCHES → decoration
see also ROUNDELS
Stainer, Ferdinand **11** 801
Stainer, Thomas *see* STAYNER, THOMAS
Stainhart, Dominicus **22** 302; **29** 519–20*
collaboration **29** 519
works **12** 460
Stainhart, Franz, I (1651-95) **29** 519*
collaboration **29** 519
works **12** 460
Stainhart, Franz II (*fl* 1683-1724) **29** 519
Stainhart, Johann Franz **29** 519
Stainhart, Joseph **29** 519
Stainhart, Matthias **29** 519*
staining
chalcedony **12** 270
glass **12** 788*
see also STAINED GLASS
ivory **16** 797
marble **5** 336
paper **32** 815
rock crystal **7** 91
wood **33** 335, 338
stainless steel **16** 51
historical and regional traditions
Denmark **8** 752
stainless steel
historical and regional traditions—cont.
England **10** *268*
Russia **27** *395*
uses
coins **7** 539
knives **8** 285
sculpture **10** *268*; **27** *395*
Stainmüller, Christian *see* STEINMÜLLER, CHRISTIAN
Stains Drancy **11** 526
Stainton, Lavinia *see* HANDLEY-READ, LAVINIA
Stainville, Etienne-François, Comte de *see* CHOISEUL, ETIENNE-FRANÇOIS, Duc de
Stainz, Matthias **31** 510
staircases **29** 520–28*
Austria **27** *661*
Aztec **29** 527, *527*
Belgium **14** *770*
Crete **29** *521*
England **10** 279; **19** 567; **29** 524
Neo-classicism **6** *412*; **19** *613*
17th cent. **10** *275*
France **29** 521, 523–4
Renaissance **4** *156*
16th cent. **13** 224
17th cent. **19** 264; **29** *523*, 524, *524*
20th cent. **24** *474*
Germany **25** 188; **29** *522*; **33** *433*
Greece, ancient **13** 385, *385*
Indian subcontinent **29** *526*, 526–7*
Italy **12** 115, 116; **29** 521
Baroque **26** *760*, *814*; **27** *711*, *729*
Renaissance **32** 225
17th cent. **32** *229*
18th cent. **29** 525; **31** *895*
Maya **29** 527
Mesoamerica, Pre-Columbian **29** 527*, *527*
Mexico **29** *527*
Minoan **29** *521*
Rome, ancient **29** 520–21
Russia **27** *402*, *404*
South America, Pre-Columbian **29** 527–8*
South-east Asia **29** 528*
Spain **8** 79; **10** *504*; **29** 521
Sri Lanka **29** 526; **33** *503*
Sweden **29** *525*
see also PERRONS
stairs **13** 387; **18** 280; **21** 206*; **25** 764, 765
stairs, holy **23** 5
stairwells **29** 526
Stais, V. **1** 478
Staithes **18** 149
Stajić Tošković, Jovan *see* TOŠKOVIĆ, JOVAN STAJIĆ
Stajuda, Jerzy **29** 528*
stakes **14** 378
staking *see* LEATHER → techniques → stretching
Stakna Monastery **15** 397
Stalać **28** 440
stalactite vaults *see under* VAULTS (CEILING) → types
Stalbemt, Adriaen van **29** 528*
attributions **11** 732
collaboration **4** 916; **22** 718
works **1** 663; **10** 250
Stalder, Anselm **29** 529*
Stalen, Antoine van **17** 643
Stålhane, Carl-Harry **30** 101
Stalinabad *see* DUSHANBE
Stalingrad *see* VOLGOGRAD
Stalinist architecture **15** 890; **22** *175*; **26** 709; **29** 529–30*
Stalker, John **10** 290; **18** 610, 614; **29** 530
Stalker, J. S. **28** 245
Stalker and Parker **7** 166; **24** 273; **29** 530*
Stallaert, Joseph **8** 700; **22** 697; **28** 891
Stalnaker, Budd **30** 330
Stalpaert, Daniël **22** 902; **29** 530*
works **1** 801, 802, 813; **31** 715
Stalpaert, Jeronimus **23** 665
Stalybridge (Ches), Methodist Church **21** 347
Stam, Johan *see* WENDELSTAM, JOHAN
Stam, Mart(inus Adrianus) **7** *294*; **12** 480; **19** 476; **21** 362; **22** 908; **28** 122; **29** 530–31*; **30** 128
assistants **27** 214
collaboration **4** 815; **10** 163; **21** 156; **22** 187; **28** 122
groups and movements **7** 293; **8** 826; **15** 885; **21** 407, 781, 782; **22** 868; **23** 450
pupils **18** 435; **31** 867
staff **21** 156
works **1** 804; **4** 761, *815*; **22** *875*, 876
writings **27** 214
Stamati, Iacov **1** 728
Stam-Beese, L. **1** 804
Stambruges Church **13** 110
Stambul *see* ISTANBUL
Stamford (Lincs) **10** *225*; **29** 531–3*, *532*; **31** 710
ceramics **29** 533*
pottery **10** 300
Stamford, George Harry Grey, 5th Earl of *see* GREY, GEORGE HARRY, 5th Earl of Stamford
Stamman, Hugo **14** 87
Stammel, Johann Georg **29** 533
Stammel, Josef **1** 161; **2** 801; **19** 316; **29** 533*
Stammler (family) **12** 648
stamnoi **13** *475*, 476, *485*; **29** 533*
Stamo, Ye. N. **25** 323
Stamos, Theodoros **1** 85; **24** 213; **29** 533–4*
Stampa, Massimiliano **19** 561
Stampe, Baron **30** 766
Stamperia Valdonga **20** 404
Stampfer, Hans Jakob **2** 606; **29** 534*; **33** 736
Stampfer, Hans Ulrich, I **2** 606
Stampfer, Peter **2** 811
Stämpfli, Peter **29** 534*
stamping
historical and regional traditions
Central Asia, Western **6** 274, 275
China **6** 881, 882
Egypt **16** 403
Islamic **16** 403
Italy **20** 509
Jewish art **17** 566
Mongolia **21** 878
Rome, ancient **4** *771*, 772
uses
baskets **22** 662, 663
bookbindings **17** 566
brick **3** 588; **4** *771*, 772; **26** 750, 879
glass **16** 517
jewellery **6** 274
leather **21** 878
metalwork **21** 327*
painting **20** 509; **24** 6, *6*
pottery **6** 881, 882; **8** 311; **10** 613; **13** 537, *537*; **16** 403
prints **25** 600
sculpture **6** 214
silver **12** 448
stonewares **18** 341, *341*
terracottas **6** 275
textiles **1** 856; **6** 249; **17** 309; **30** 553
stamps **14** 424
Bactria **6** 214
Belgium **3** 588
Byzantine **9** 655
Central Asia, Western **6** 214, 249
Early Christian (*c.* AD 250-843) **9** 655
stamps—cont.
Egypt **16** 517
Greece, ancient **13** 537, *537*
Islamic **16** 517
Japan **17** 309
Korea **18** 341, *341*
Mesoamerica, Pre-Columbian **21** 236
Native North Americans **22** 662, 663
Netherlands, the **22** 887
Rome, ancient **26** 879
Tajikistan **33** *509*
see also MARKS
stamps, postage *see* POSTAGE STAMPS
Stams Abbey Church **28** 163
Stana, Varjuvár **18** 394
Stanchi, Giovanni **20** 432
stanchions **28** 874
Stančić, Miljenko **8** 179
Standard Aircraft Factory **33** 407
Standard Bank **29** 121
standard-bearers *see under* SCULPTURE → types
Standard Inscription **21** 297
standardization **14** 564; **15** 821, 823, 824; **20** 593–4
Standard-Möbel **4** 761; **30** 755
Standard Oil **28** 488
standards (flags) **11** 144, 150
Anatolia, ancient **1** *521*
Egypt, ancient **14** 407
England **11** *145*, 148; **12** 272
Syria-Palestine **30** 183, *183*
standards (vexilloid) **11** 144, 150–53*, *150*, *151*, *152*; **23** 496, *496*; **30** 342
standards, building *see* BUILDING REGULATIONS
standard script *see* SCRIPTS → types → regular
Standchev, Khristo **5** 154
Standen (W. Sussex) **10** 239; **33** *12*
standing figures *see under* SCULPTURE → types
standing stones *see* MENHIRS; MONOLITHS
Standish, Frank Hall **23** 521, 523; **29** 535*; **30** 385
Standish, Musée *see under* PARIS → Louvre (Musée du Louvre, 1793-)
standishes **29** 535*
see also INKSTANDS
Standlake (Oxon) **2** *300*; **6** 160
stand mirrors *see under* MIRRORS → types
stand oil *see under* OILS → types
stands
historical and regional traditions
China **6** 827; **7** 139
Cyprus, ancient **8** 353, *354*
Egypt **16** *389*
England **9** 29, 30
Islamic **16** *389*, 517
Phrygian **13** *8*
Turkey **13** *8*
materials
brass **16** *389*
bronze **6** 827, *855*; **7** 139
horn **7** 125
iron **8** *354*
lacquer **18** *603*
wood **7** 139; **13** *8*; **16** 487, 497, *501*
types
bows **19** 740–41
cult **15** 729; **24** 634–5
cup **6** 875, *875*
drum **6** *855*
Koran stands **16** 487, 497, *501*
lamp *see* LAMPSTANDS
mirror **18** *603*
ring-stands **7** 125
Stanecki, Szymon **32** 878
Staneika, Adalbertas **19** 498
Staňek, Master **30** 221
Ştaneşti Bilkea Church **25** 344
Stăneşti Monastery **26** 721
Stanetti, Giovanni *see* STANETTI, JOHANN
Stanetti, Johann **2** 801; **32** 453
Stanfield, Clarkson (Frederick) **29** 535–6*; **30** 679; **32** 197
assistants **7** 789
collaboration **26** 463
patrons and collectors **4** 35; **19** 875; **24** 322, 571
reproductive prints by others **8** 66
teachers **22** 531
works **7** 924; **8** 911; **20** 424; **29** *535*; **30** 680; **31** 156
illustrated **29** 634
Stanfield, George **33** 227
Stanfield, George Clarkson **29** 536
Stanfield, William Clarkson *see* STANFIELD, CLARKSON (FREDERICK)
Stanford, Jane **29** 536
Stanford, Leland (1824-93) **22** 390; **29** 426, 536*
Stanford, Leland, jr (1869-84) **23** 422; **29** 536
Stanford Bishop (Hereford & Worcs), St James **6** 389; **10** 287
Stanford Hall (Leics) **22** 744
Stanford University (CA), Art Gallery and Museum **25** 892; **26** 511; **29** 536
Cassirer collection **5** 924
Memorial Arch **31** 351
Stang, Rudolf **28** 188; **33** 266
Stanga, Cristoforo **26** 289
Stanga, Marchesino **26** 289
Stânga Church **13** 103
Stange, Alfred **8** 514; **29** 536–7*
Stangenglas *see under* GLASSES → types
Stangl, J. Martin **31** 639
Stanhope, Anne Hussey Delaval, Lady **8** *26*
Stanhope, Arthur Philip, 6th Earl of Stanhope **33** 565
Stanhope, Charles, 3rd Earl of Stanhope **25** 592
Stanhope, James, 1st Earl of Stanhope **7** 461; **8** 813
Stanhope, Philip, 2nd Earl of Stanhope **25** 882
Stanhope, Philip Dormer, 4th Earl of Chesterfield **7** 171; **10** 276; **13** 809; **18** 677; **23** 860
Stanhope, (John) Roddam Spencer **29** 537*
groups and movements **25** 555
patrons and collectors **25** 41
pupils **8** 707
works **11** 397, 434
Stanhope Forbes, Elizabeth (Adela) *see* FORBES, ELIZABETH (ADELA) STANHOPE
Stanhope Press **33** 152
Stanhope presses *see under* PRESSES → types
Staniątki Nunnery **25** 104
Stanić, Vojo **22** 18
Stanier, Ymbert **7** 525
Stanigar, Marguerite **16** 888
Stanimaka **5** *144*
Asen church **9** 552
Church of the Archangels Michael and Gabriel **5** 147
Petrichka Virgin **5** 147, 151
St George **5** 148
Stanislav, Duke of Lorraine *see* STANISLAV I LESZCZYŃSKI, King of Poland
Stanislav I Leszczyński, King of Poland (*reg* 1704-09) **13** 805; **19** 800; **22** 454; **29** 537–8*
architecture **14** 447; **19** 697; **21** 699; **22** *455*
Stanislav II Augustus, King of Poland *see* STANISLAV II PONIATOWSKI, King of Poland

Stanislav II Poniatowski, King of Poland (*reg* 1764-95) **8** 792; **10** 366; **25** 136, 140, 211-13*; **32** 876
architecture **11** 17; **17** 756; **19** 725; **21** 158; **25** 99; **32** 870, 880
collections **22** 202; **25** 138, 139; **30** 345
decorative works **5** 380; **24** 810
faience (ii) (ceramics) **25** 122; **32** 879
furniture **20** 90; **25** 121
gardens **28** 170
interior decoration **25** 118; **32** 879
paintings **3** 15, 678; **4** 517; **12** 203; **13** 803; **14** 84; **18** 418, 495, 683; **23** 203, 369; **25** 38, 105; **32** 112, 678
sculpture **32** 579
sponsorship **18** 490
Stanislavsky, Konstantin **9** 747; **12** 878; **26** 530; **28** 757; **29** 899; **30** 685; **31** 572
Stanisławów **25** 133
Stanisławski, Jan (Grzegorz) **18** 428; **24** 441; **25** 107; **29** 538-9*
pupils **20** 153
works **29** *538*
Staniuta, M. **3** 529
Stankēvic, Aleksandrs
Stankiewicz, Richard **29** 539*; **31** 614
groups and movements **17** 694
teachers **19** 83
works **2** *616*, 617; **16** 58; **17** *694*; **31** 614
Stankiewicz, Zofia **32** 877
Stańko, Tomasz **32** 865
Stankowski, Anton **29** 540*
Stanley (family) **8** 123
Stanley, Carl Frederik (i) (*c.* 1738-1813) **8** 740; **29** 540-41*
assistants **31** 342
works **27** 168; **29** *541*
Stanley, Carl Frederik (Ferdinand) (ii) (1769-1805) **29** 541*
Stanley, Charles **11** 427; **29** 835
Stanley, Edward, 11th Earl of Derby **29** 807
Stanley, Edward Geoffrey, 14th Earl of Derby **18** 904
Stanley, Elizabeth, Countess of Derby **10** 642
Stanley, F. D. G. **2** 739
Stanley, George **10** 366
Stanley, John **29** 88
Stanley, John Mix **7** 840; **29** 541-2*; **31** 602; **33** 185
Stanley, Max **1** 439
Stanley, Simon Carl **29** 540*
Stanley Engineering Company **18** 200
Stanley Pool *see* POOL MALEBO
Stanleyville *see* KISANGANI
Stanmore (Middx)
Bentley Priory **13** 608
Stanmore Hall **5** 268; **10** 352
Stannard, Alfred **4** 808; **29** 542
Stannard, Alfred George **29** 542
Stannard, Eloise Harriet **29** 542
Stannard, Joseph **29** 542*
Stannard, William John **25** 591
Stannus, Hugh **29** 646
Stano **1** 539
Stanojev, M. **28** 452
Stanojević, Veljko **28** 451
Stansfield, H. S. **5** 573
Stansted Airport (Essex) **1** 495; **10** *241*, 242
Stanton (family) **10** 263, 372; **29** 542*
Stanton, Edward **29** 542-3*
Stanton, Elizabeth **9** 289
Stanton, Hervey de *see* HERVEY DE STANTON
Stanton, J.E.
works **1** *46*
Stanton, Thomas (1610-74) **29** 542*
Stanton, Thomas (*fl c.* 1720) **29** 543
Stanton, William (1639-1705) **10** 263; **19** 606; **29** 542*, 581
Stanton, William (*d* 1753) **29** 543
Stanton, William (*fl* 1763) **29** 543
Stanton Harcourt (Oxon) **9** 646; **14** 163
Parsonage **8** 46
Stanwell (Surrey), St Mary's
tomb of Lord Knyvett and his wife **1** 520
Stanyl' **31** 557
Stanzione, Massimo **22** 478, 479; **29** 543-5*
collaboration **7** 509; **26** 311
patrons and collectors **11** 70; **21** 73; **22** 486; **27** 133
pupils **3** 671; **6** 108; **13** 753; **23** 699; **27** 149; **29** 410
works **22** 484; **29** *544*, *545*
workshop **16** 673
Stapfer, Albert **8** 640
Staphorst, Abraham **7** 785
Staphorst, Nicolaus **11** 714
Staplehurst (Kent) **32** 277
All Saints **9** 155; **10** 339
Stapleton, Michael **9** 317, 323
Stąporków **25** 130
Stappen, Charles Van der *see* VAN DER STAPPEN, CHARLES
Stapran, O. **27** 409
Stará Boleslav **8** 378, 385, 395
Starace, Gaetano **20** 843
Starace, Nicola **16** 748
Stará Role **8** 405, 406
Staraya Ladoga **27** *363*; **29** 545-6*; **32** 527
St George **27** 382
Stara Zagora **5** *144*, 145, 158; **30** 769, 772-3
Starčevo **25** *471*; **28** *437*; **29** 546*
Starčevo culture **25** 499, 514
Starčevo-Körös-Criș culture **25** 499
starch **16** 433; **17** 209; **24** 647, 648; **32** 898
Starchev, Valentin **5** 156, 162
Starchikov, Nikolai **27** 408
starch paste *see* PASTE
Starck, Constantin Karl **29** 546*
Starck, Johann Heinrich **14** 655; **20** 386; **29** 863
Starck, Philippe **8** 805; **11** 584, 602; **29** 546-7*
Starcke, Johann Georg **9** 235; **12** 373; **19** 110; **29** 547*
Starck-Lilienborg, Hilda **30** 115
Starck Product **29** 546
Starczewski, Antoni **29** 547-8*
Staré Hradisko **6** 159; **21** 551; **25** 544
Staren, Dirk van *see* VELLERT, DIRK (JACOBSZ.)
Starey, Benjamin **5** 315
star forts *see under* FORTS → types
Star Fresco **30** 198
Stargard Szczecinski
St Mary's **4** 783; **5** 27-8, *28*; **32** 91
Town Hall **31** 238
Starhemberg **2** 782
Stari Bar *see* BAR
Stari Church **28** 858
Starigrad **8** *174*, 175
Staring, Adolph **29** 548*
Stari Slankamen **28** 439
Staritsa, Cathedral of SS Boris and Gleb **27** 371; **30** 884
Stark, Adele von **17** 744
Stark, Arthur James **29** 548
Stark, James **23** 248; **29** 548*
illustrated writings **11** 362
pupils **7** 789
teachers **8** 185
Stark, William **12** 773; **29** 548-9*
groups and movements **13** 610
pupils **25** 35
works **12** *773*; **18** 887; **25** 268
Starke **3** 461
Starke, Johann Georg **18** 121
Starke, Mariana **13** 303, 304, 810
Starke, Sampson *see* STRONG, SAMPSON
Starkey, J. L. **10** 759; **18** 596
Starkey, Sampson *see* STRONG, SAMPSON
Starkie, Edyth **25** 835
Starkopf, Anton **10** 540; **29** 549*; **32** 511
Starkopf Atelier Museum *see under* TARTU
Starmayr, Johann Gottlieb **28** 123
Starnina, Gherardo (di Jacopo) **20** 621-2; **29** 549-50*; **31** 815
pupils **20** 553
works **29** *550*
Star of Africa **12** 269
Starogród **25** 103
Staro Nagoričano **9** *511*; **19** *882*; **29** 551*
St George **9** 552, 585; **19** 882; **28** 442; **29** 551
icons **28** 448
screen **28** 291
wall paintings **28** 446
Staronosov, Piotr Nicholaevich **30** 253
Starov, Ivan (Yegorovich) **27** 442, 579; **29** 551-3*
collaboration **27** 403
patrons and collectors **27** 438
pupils **33** 599
teachers **31** 828
works **3** 526; **23** 813; **25** 681; **27** 375, 376, 402, 586; **29** *552*; **31** 551
Starowiejski, Franciszek **25** 354; **32** 878
Starožitnosti **8** 424
Starr, R. F. S. **23** 322
Starr, Sidney **19** 589
Starr Carr (S. Yorks) **2** 300; **4** 313
Starre, Abraham **6** 88
Starrett and Eken **28** 629
star vaults *see under* VAULTS (CEILING) → types
Starý, Oldřich **29** 553*
Stary, Stanisław **25** 102
Stary Orkhey Castle **21** 810
Stary Otwock **25** 98
country houses **25** *98*
Staryye gody **20** 152; **27** 439, 441, 580; **32** 724
Staryy Krym **29** 553*; **31** *546*
Starzyński, Juliusz **25** 143
Stasack, Edward **7** 558
Stasiewicz, Mikołaj **22** 449
Stasio, Stefano Di *see* DI STASIO, STEFANO
Stasov, Vasily (Petrovich) **27** 198, 404, 408, 577, 579; **29** 554-5*
collaboration **8** 710; **27** 345
groups and movements **28** 837
works **3** 527; **22** 172; **25** 746; **27** 345, 375, *402*, 408, 576, 583, 585, 586, 587; **29** *555*; **32** 579
Stasov, Vladimir (Vasil'yevich) **17** 576; **27** 443; **29** 554, 556*
Stastny-Burke **22** 671
State Academy of Artistic Sciences *see* GAKHN
State Art Committee **11** 112
state boats *see* BARGES → ceremonial
state collections *see under* COLLECTIONS → types
State Free Art Studios *see* SVOMAS
State Institute of Artistic Culture *see* GINKHUK
State Jewish Theatre *see* GOSET
Staten Island (NY)
New Dorp, Moravian Cemetery **20** 869
quilts **30** VI3
Statens Kunstfond **8** 758; **22** 332
State Public Works Department (India) **15** 168
states *see under* PRINTS
state ships *see* BARGES → ceremonial
State University of New York *see under* PURCHASE (NY)
Stathmi **4** 598; **13** 228; **32** 78
Stati, Cristoforo **12** 753; **29** 558-9*
works **29** *558*
Stati, Francesco **29** 559
Stationers' Company **3** 233
barges **3** *234*
stationery **24** 55
stations, railway *see* RAILWAY STATIONS
stations, underground *see* METRO STATIONS
Statius, Achilles **15** 89
Statius, Publius Papinius **26** 924, 925; **29** 560
Stattler, Wojciech Kornel **13** 702; **19** 208; **25** 106
statue menhirs *see under* SCULPTURE → types
Statue of Liberty *see under* NEW YORK
statues *see* SCULPTURE
Statues of Coudewater, Master of the **22** 856
statuettes **29** 567-76*
historical and regional traditions
Austria **2** *801*
Bactria **6** 275
Bamum **3** 154
Belgium **29** 575
Bhutan **3** 914
Buddhism **6** 298
Canaanite **30** 186
Carolingian **5** *806*
Celtic **6** 159
Central Asia, Eastern **6** 298
Central Asia, Western **6** 275
Champa **6** 427
Colombia **29** *143*
Cyprus, ancient **8** 339, 353; **10** *400*
Egypt, ancient **9** 860; **10** 35-7, 47
Late Period (664-332 BC) **22** *690*
Middle Kingdom (*c.* 1966-*c.* 1630 BC) **10** *47*
New Kingdom (*c.* 1539-*c.* 1075 BC) **10** *36*
Roman **27** *89*
Third Intermediate Period (*c.* 1075-*c.* 656 BC) **10** *36*; **14** *403*
England **29** 575*
New Sculpture **10** *266*; **11** *303*; **25** IV; **29** *575*
Etruscan **10** 587, 627
France **29** 571-2*, 573-5*
Baroque **29** *572*
Carolingian **5** *806*
Gothic **13** *158*, 172-4, *173*
Rococo **29** *573*
Roman **27** 89, 90
13th cent. **16** 799
18th cent. **5** *381*
19th cent. **2** *100*
Germany **12** 406; **29** 574*
Baroque **23** *309*
Roman **27** *88*
17th cent. **24** *543*
18th cent. **12** *445*
Gothic **13** *158*, 172-4, *173*
Greece, ancient **13** 436, 571-4*, *572*, *574*, 578-82*, 595-6, *596*; **29** 567*, *567*
Classical, Early **13** *573*
Italy **30** *339*
statuettes
historical and regional traditions—cont.
Holy Roman Empire (before 1648) **29** 570-71*
Indian subcontinent **4** 687
Italy **9** 21; **16** 689; **29** 568-70*, 572-3*
Baroque **2** *610*; **16** *700*
Etruscan **10** 587
Greece, ancient **30** *339*
Mannerism **29** *569*
Renaissance **1** *162*; **3** *861*; **25** *158*; **26** 327, *330*
Roman **12** *68*; **25** *202*
15th cent. **3** 636
16th cent. **9** *340*
Khwarazm **6** 275
Kissi **18** 89-91, *90*
Mali **21** 478-81
Mende (Sierra Leone) **18** 90
Mesopotamia **21** *295*
Middle Niger cultures **21** 478-81*
Nepal **22** *774*
Netherlands, the **29** 571*
Ottonian **23** *661*
Phoenician **24** *642*
Prehistoric art **8** 339; **27** 834
Rome, ancient **12** *68*; **25** *202*; **26** 923; **27** 29, 30, 87-91*, *88*, *89*, *91*; **29** 567*
Sardinia **27** 834
Scandinavia **32** 524
Seleucid **28** 383
South America, Pre-Columbian **29** *143*
Switzerland **27** *91*
Syria-Palestine **30** 186
Tokharistan **6** 275
United States of America **29** 575-6*
Vietnam **6** 427
Viking **32** 524
Yaka **33** 482
materials
alabaster (gypsum) **22** *690*; **29** 571
biscuit **29** 573
brass **4** 687
bronze **8** 339; **10** 35-7, *36*; **13** 571-2*; **15** 459; **29** *572*
Carolingian **5** *806*
Celtic **6** 159
Cyprus, ancient **10** *400*
Egypt, ancient **9** 860
England **10** *267*; **11** *303*; **29** *575*
France **2** *100*; **5** *381*, *806*
Germany **23** *309*
Greece, ancient **13** 571, *573*, 573*; **29** 567, *567*; **30** *339*
Italy **1** *162*; **2** *610*; **3** 636, *861*; **9** *340*; **16** 689; **25** *202*; **26** 327, *330*; **29** *569*; **30** *339*
Phoenician **24** *642*
Roman **27** *91*
Rome, ancient **27** 87-91, *88*, *89*
Vietnam **6** 427
clay **6** 298
copper **22** *774*; **29** 572
enamel **13** *158*
faience (i) (glass) **10** 47, *47*
gold **14** *403*
iron **17** 323
ivory **16** 799
Austria **2** *801*
Belgium **29** 575
England **10** *267*
France **29** 571, 574
Germany **24** *543*; **29** 574
Gothic **13** 172-4, *173*
Greece, ancient **13** 595-6, *596*
Netherlands, the **29** 571
Ottonian **23** *661*
kaolin **29** 574
marble **29** 567
mother-of-pearl **10** *267*

statuettes
materials—cont.
ormolu **29** 572
plaster **10** *16*
silver **10** *36*
silver-gilt **13** *158*
soapstone **21** *295*
stone **18** 89–91, *90*; **29** *143*
terracotta **6** 275; **13** 578–82*; **29** 567, 573, *573*
wood **29** 570, 571
types
funerary *see* SCULPTURE → types → servant statues; SHABTI
okimono **17** 323
see also FIGURINES
Statz, Vincenz **29** 576–7*
assistants **11** 813
groups and movements **13** 204
pupils **30** 485; **33** 173
works **2** 787; **19** 434
Staub, Hans Jacob **33** 737
Staub, Johann Baptist **32** 453
Staub, John F. **14** 803
Staubles, Coast Guard Marine Museum **31** 339
Stauch, Hellmut (Wilhelm Ernst) **25** 566; **29** 106, 577*; **33** 245
Stauder, Franz Karl **29** 577
Stauder, Jakob Karl **22** 811; **29** 577*; **30** 132; **33** 671
Staudigel, Master **27** 217
Staudt, Matthias **29** 577–8*
Stauerbout, Martin **27** 430
Stauffenberg Altar **28** 149
Stauffenberg Altar, Master of the **14** 87; **20** 770*
Stauffer-Bern, Karl **10** 396; **18** 205; **29** 578*
Stauff zur Ehrenfels (family) **11** 852
Staunton, Howard **6** 558
Staunton Harold **13** 211; **19** 622
Staupitz, Johann von **9** 442; **20** 754
Stauris, Rinaldo de' **8** 135; **20** 302
staurothèques *see under* RELINQUARIES → types
Stavanger **23** *218*, 219; **29** 578–9*
Cathedral of the Holy Trinity **13** 102; **23** 219; **26** 593; **29** 578–9*
Christ Church *see* Cathedral of the Holy Trinity
Stavanger Faste Galleri **23** 243
Swithin's Church *see* Cathedral of the Holy Trinity
Stavba **7** 293; **24** 440; **29** 553
stave churches *see under* CHURCHES → types
Staveley Coal and Iron Company **24** 185
Stavelot Abbey **1** 697; **13** 18, 19
crypt **7** 265
manuscripts **3** 552; **20** 331; **26** 666
reliquaries **26** 146
sculpture **26** 645
Stavelot Bible *see under* BIBLES → individual manuscripts
Stavelot Triptych **11** 438; **22** 111; **26** 693, *693*; **31** 343, 499
Staveren, Johan Adriaensz. van **19** 102
Staverton Builders Ltd **8** 810
Stavitel **24** 440
Stavoprojekt **11** 365
Stavrinides, (Christakis) Panayiotis **8** 364; **29** 581*
Stavros Mill **8** 361
Stawiński, B. **18** 433
Stayner, Anthony **29** 581
Stayner, Thomas (*c.* 1668-1731; father) **10** 263; **29** 581*
Stayner, Thomas (*fl* 1702; son) **29** 581
Staythorpe Power Station (Notts) **25** 403
Stażewski, Henryk **29** 582*
groups and movements **1** 76, 90; **2** 409; **4** 148; **7** 772; **25** 108, 422, 423
Stazio, Abbondio **29** 831
works **29** *832*
Stazio, Andrea **30** 855
Stazio, Giovanni **25** 54; **29** 582–3*
Stchoukine, Ivan (Sergeevich) **15** 211; **16** 101, 549; **28** 569–70*
works **16** 295
Steadman, Benjamin **16** 799
Steadman, Ralph **4** 368; **5** 759
steam engines *see* ENGINES (STEAM)
steam looms *see under* LOOMS → types
steam ships *see under* SHIPS → types
stearic acid **8** 128
stearine *see under* WAXES → types
Stearns, John Goddard **10** 683; **24** 299
Stearns, Junius Brutus **29** 583*
Stearns Collection *see under* ANN ARBOR (MI) → University of Michigan
steatite *see* SOAPSTONE
Stebbing, Henry **8** 66
Stebbins, Emma **19** 286; **29** 583*; **31** 611; **33** 309
Steblin, Fyodor Petrovich **18** 568
stećaks see BOSNIA → gravestones
Stecchi, Domenico **20** 70
Stech, Andreas **12** 390; **25** 104; **29** 583*
Štech, Václav Vilém **8** 426; **13** 711
Stechlin, Gillis (Egidius) **20** 794
Stechone, Bartolomeo **29** 315
Stechow, (Ferdinand Ernst Günther) Wolfgang **14** 635; **29** 583–4*
Steckborn **30** *124*, 143, 151
Steckhoven, Adriaen van **32** 461
Stecki (family) **25** 138
Stedman, E. C. **33** 136
Stedman, John Gabriel **30** 15
Stedum **22** *813*
church **22** 819
steel **16** 49–51*, 59*, 60–61*; **21** 319
historical and regional traditions
Africa **1** *247*, 287
Argentina **1** 743
Australia **2** 740, *754*
Belgium **3** 576
Canada **5** 562
Central Asia, Western **6** 261
China **7** 57, 96–7*, 98, 100
Egypt **21** *718*
England **2** *471*; **10** 341–2, 345
17th cent. **10** *342*
18th cent. **21** II3
19th cent. **16** *61*
20th cent. **10** 284
France **11** *625*; **16** *55*
Germany **10** 697; **12** 454*; **16** *59*; **30** 734
India, Republic of **15** 169
Indian subcontinent **15** *678*; **16** 51
Iran **16** 391, *508*, *516*
Islamic **16** 143, 363, *508*, *516*; **21** *718*
Iran **16** 391
Ottoman **16** 507, 508
Italy **2** *470*, *472*
Japan **17** 50, 86, 319, 361
Korea **18** 266
Malaysia **20** 174
Mesopotamia **21** 304
Mongolia **21** 878
Nigeria **1** *247*
Ottoman **16** 507, *508*, 508
Rome, ancient **27** 93
Russia **27** *407*, *424*
Scotland **28** 228
Spain **16** *57*; **29** *340*
Sri Lanka **16** 51; **29** 468
steel
historical and regional traditions—cont.
Sweden **30** 109–10*, *110*
Switzerland **2** 512
Syria **21** *718*
Syria-Palestine **30** 194
Turkey **16** *508*
United States of America **4** *761*; **16** *56*, *58*; **22** 336; **27** 565; **28** 488, *877*; **31** 594, *594*, *596*, *614*
patinas **21** 330*
technical examination **30** 397, 409
techniques
electroplating **10** 135, 136, 137
etching **30** 110, *110*
smelting **17** 319
types
chromium *see* CHROMIUM STEEL
corrugated *see* CORRUGATED STEEL
Cor-Ten steel **16** 51, 56
self-weathering **16** 51
stainless *see* STAINLESS STEEL
tubular *see* TUBULAR STEEL
watered **16** 60
uses
architecture **1** 743; **5** 562; **15** 169; **16** 51*, 54–6*, *55*, 143; **17** 86; **18** 266; **20** 570; **21** 631; **28** 228; **30** 27; **31** 596, *596*
armour **2** 448, *471*; **7** 57
boxes **30** *110*
bridges **4** 802–3*; **27** 565; **31** 594
buckles **21** II3
candlesticks **27** *424*
carving **21** 878
caskets **10** *342*
chairs **4** *761*
châtelaines **16** *61*
clocks **7** 439
coins **7** 539
daggers **16** *516*
domes **30** 734
drinking-horns **30** *110*
engravings **26** 742
factories **10** 697
fireplaces **27** *407*
furniture **10** 284; **16** 61
game-boards **31** 265
guns **16** 508
halberds **17** 361
helmets **2** *470*, *472*; **6** 261; **16** 507
jewellery **10** 345; **17** 525, 530
keris **20** 174
keys **11** *625*
knives **8** 284, 285
locks **16** *59*; **29** *340*
mezzotints **28** 25
mirrors **3** 576; **21** *718*
murals **22** 336
pens **24** 350
piers (i) (seaside) **24** 748
postage stamps **25** 329
printing plates **3** 180; **5** 412; **10** 379, 394–6; **21** 414; **25** 612
roofs **2** 512
scabbards **16** *508*, *516*
scissors **8** 286, 287
sculpture **1** *247*; **2** *754*; **16** 56–8*, *57*, *58*; **28** *877*; **29** *897*; **31** *614*
service stations **28** 488
skyscrapers **31** 594, *594*
space-frames **16** *56*
swords **15** *678*; **16** 60, *506*, *508*; **17** 361
theatres **30** 677
tie-bars **30** 853
tools **17** 50
weapons **7** 97
Steel, Andrew **2** 151
Steel, Robert **4** 353
Steel, Thomas **26** 489
Steelandt, Livinia van **14** 760
Steelchrome **10** 299
Steele, Christopher **27** 117; **29** 584*
Steele, Florence **10** 373
Steele, Joshua **2** 151
Steele, Louis John **2** 706; **23** 59
Steele, Richard **1** 150
Steele, William L. **25** 737
Steell, John (*fl* 1804-24; carver and gilder) **29** 584
Steell, John (1804-91; sculptor) **5** 751; **21** 908; **29** 584–5*
works **9** 724; **28** 242
steel-pan drums *see under* DRUMS → types
Steen (family) **23** 236
Steen, Franciscus van der **27** 725
Steen, Jan (Havicksz.) (1626-79) **13** 255, 894, 895; **29** 585–92*
patrons and collectors **4** 618
Arenberg, Prosper-Louis, 7th Duke of, Duke of Arschot **2** 382
Art Institute of Chicago **27** 463
Bonnemaison, Ferréol de **4** 330
Boymans, F(rans) J(acob) O(tto) **4** 614
Fagel (family) **10** 754
George IV, King of Great Britain (*reg* 1820-30) **14** 146
Gildemeester, Jan (Jansz.) (1744-99) **12** 620
John II, Prince of Liechtenstein (*reg* 1858-1929) **19** 339
Johnson, John G(raver) (1841-1917) **17** 619
Papillon de La Ferté, Denis-Pierre-Jean **24** 63
Peel, Robert (1788-1850) **24** 322
Seymour-Conway, Richard, 4th Marquess of Hertford **20** 875; **28** 527
Sparre, Gustaf Adolf **29** 366
Steengracht van Oostkapelle, Johan **29** 592
Tronchin, François **31** 362
Turner, Dawson **31** 465
Wellesley, Arthur, 1st Duke of Wellington **33** 55
reproductive prints by others **12** 515
teachers **13** 257; **19** 101; **23** 609
works **1** 659; **9** 457, 755; **11** 444, 446; **12** 290; **22** 841; **29** *586*, *587*, *588*, *589*; **31** 246
Steen, Jan van der (1633-1725) **3** 570; **14** 488; **18** 742; **29** 591*
Steen, Jasper van der **29** 591
Steen, Knud **23** 231
Steen, Ole J. **23** 236
Steenberg, Jan **8** 761
Steenbergen **24** 808
Steengracht van Duivenvoorde, Hendrick Adolf **19** 782; **29** 592
Steengracht van Oosterland, Hendrick **29** 592
Steengracht van Oostkapelle, Johan **29** 591–2*
Steenvoorde, van **8** 495
Steenwijk Church **22** 820
Steenwijk, Hendrick van (i) (*c.* 1550-1603) **29** 592*; **31** 803
patrons and collectors **11** 718
pupils **3** 23; **22** 718; **29** 592
works **2** 340; **3** 560
Steenwijk, Hendrick van (ii) (1580-1649) **29** 592*
copies **8** 663
patrons and collectors **20** 142
pupils **22** 718
works **2** 341
Steenwijk, Susanna van **29** 593*
Steenwinckel, Hans van (i) (1550-1601) **29** 593*
attributions **14** 542
works **4** 640, 781; **8** 725; **31** 138
Steenwinckel, Hans van (ii) (1587-1639) **29** 594*
patrons and collectors **14** 369; **23** 396
works **4** 786; **7** 802; **14** 542; **19** 815; **23** 339; **27** 168; **29** 593
Steenwinckel, Hans van (iii) (1639-1700) **29** 594*
Steenwinckel, Lourens van, I (*fl* 1567) **29** 593
Steenwinckel, Lourens van, II (1585-1619) **29** 593–4*
collaboration **29** 594
patrons and collectors **23** 396
works **4** 786; **7** 802; **10** 668; **27** 168
Steenwinckel, Maarten (Morten) van **8** 733; **14** 369; **17** 879
Steenwinkel, Anton van **8** 758
Steenwinkel, Hans van **12** 47
Steenwyck, Harmen van **3** 78; **22** 841; **29** 667; **31** 882
Steenwyck, Pieter van **3** 78; **22** 841; **29** 667; **31** 882
Steeple, John **4** 86
Steer, Philip **29** 594
Steer, Philip Wilson **4** 880; **10** 374; **19** 589; **29** 594–6*
groups and movements **10** 254; **15** 156; **19** 589; **23** 22
patrons and collectors **16** 42
pupils **9** 53; **12** 493
works **18** 716; **21** 761; **29** *595*
Steers, William **10** 308
Steevens, George **4** 607
Stefan (*fl* 1445; painter) **26** 711
Stefan (*fl* before 1464; *d* before 1499; architect) **3** 224; **14** 884; **18** 397; **28** 854; **29** 596*
Stefan, Bedřich **8** 387, 414, 416
Stefan, Christoph **21** 129
Stefaneschi (family) **16** 762; **26** 765
Stefaneschi, Bertoldo **6** 104; **26** 765; **29** 597
Stefaneschi, Giacomo Gaetani, Cardinal **2** 860; **6** 104; **29** 596–7*
architecture **2** 861
paintings and mosaics **12** 683; **20** 508; **26** 765
Stefaneschi Altarpiece **25** 462, *463*; **26** 765
Stefani, De *see* DE STEFANI
Stefanini, Bruno **30** 152
Stefan Krumenauer *see* KRUMENAUER, STEFAN
Stefano, Francesco di *see* PESELLINO
Stefano, Giovanni di *see* GIOVANNI DI STEFANO
Stefano, Silvestro di Paolo di *see* SILVESTRO DI PAOLO DI STEFANO
Stefano, Tommaso di **11** 389
Stefano a Libris **19** 322
Stefano (di Giovanni) da Verona **17** 455; **29** 597–8*
pupils **22** 130
teachers **21** 463
works **20** 321; **24** 269; **29** *598*
Stefano de Donabona **11** 4
Stefano degli Azzi **23** 91
Stefano di Franceso **24** 537
Stefano di Giovanni di Consolo *see* SASSETTA
Stefan of Cologne **19** 527
Stefano Fiorentino **2** 626; **5** 661; **12** 694; **29** 598–9*
Stefano Godefroy **2** 109
Stefanov, Dyanko, Glass and Porcelain Factory **5** 159
Stefanov, Gligor **19** 885; **29** 599*
Stefano Veneziano **9** 261
Stefánsson, Jón **15** 70; **29** 599*
Steffan, Johann Gottfried **11** 798; **29** 600*
Steffani, Agostino **14** 141

Steffeck, Carl (Constantin Heinrich) **18** 116; **19** 333; **20** 404; **29** 600*
Steffelaar, Cornelis **32** 375
Steffeswert, Jan van *see* JAN VAN STEFFESWERT
Steg, Jim **7** 558
Stege, Erwin von **20** 794
Stegel, Hans **20** 797
Steger, Adolf **33** 735
Steger, Hans **11** 320; **31** 166
Stegh, Andrzej *see* STECH, ANDREAS
Stegmann, Karl Martin von **12** 506; **29** 600*; **33** 37, 687
Stegmann, Povl **8** 728; **11** 139; **21** 820; **29** 600–601*
Stegner, Matthias **25** 443
Stehli, Bea **29** 119
Stehlík, M. **8** 426
Steib, Katharina **30** 129
Steib, Wilfrid **30** 129
Steichen, Edward J(ean) **24** 648, 676, 678, *739*; **29** 601–2*; **31** 141
collaboration **29** 655
groups and movements **8** 435; **24** 688, 739; **29** 655; **31** 490
pupils **7** 491
translated writings **5** 169
works **24** 675; **29** *601*; **31** 141
writings **29** 655
Steidl, Melchior **13** 845; **18** 447, 668; **27** 553; **29** 602*
Steiermark, Karl von, Archduke **18** 877
Steiff (company)
teddy bears **31** *260*
Steiff, Margarete **31** 260
Steig, Robert M. **2** 815
Steig, William **5** 759
Steiger, Karl **29** 602
Steiger, Peter **17** 886
Steiger, Rudolf **7** *294*; **29** 602–3*; **30** 128
collaboration **14** 24; **22** 187
groups and movements **21** 783
works **29** *603*; **30** *128*; **33** 735
Steigerwald firm **25** 435
Stein (Austria)
Göttweiger Hof Chapel **2** 791
Minorite church **2** 791
Stein (family) **31** 664
Stein, Allan **9** 181
Stein, (Marc) Aurel **7** 159; **10** 873; **29** 605*; **30** 848
excavations **6** 311
Astana **2** 645
Bampur **3** 150
Dandan-oilik **8** 496
Dunhuang **6** 740, 767, 772, 826; **9** 394
Kalibangan **17** 738
Karakhoto **17** 807
Khadalik **6** 318
Khotan **18** 29
Loulan **6** 316, 776; **7** 53; **19** 727
Luristan **19** 812
Miran **6** 313; **21** 703
Niya **23** 165
Shami **10** 170
Shorchuk **28** 624
Turfan **31** 438
Yarkhoto **33** 505
Yotkan **33** 563
personal collection **6** 321; **7** 118, 155; **15** 180; **30** 849
writings **6** 320
Stein, Clarence **17** 547; **20** 890; **23** 273; **31** 729
Stein, Gertrude **11** 360; **29** 603, 604–5*, *604*; **32** 327
collections **2** 693; **11** 659; **24** 714; **29** 604
groups and movements **8** 240
paintings **7** 702; **17** 725; **20** 824; **24** 716; **30** 532
portraits **25** 283
Stein, Gertrude—cont.
writings **29** 655
illustrated **13** 671
Stein, Henri **10** 209
Stein, Joël **13** 709, 710; **18** 809; **21** 746
Stein, Johann Andreas **13** 897
Stein, Joseph Allen **15** 169
Stein, Karl, Reichsfreiherr vom und zum *see* VOM UND ZUM STEIN, KARL, Reichsfreiherr
Stein, Leo **29** 603, 604*
collections **24** 714; **30** 532
drawings **22** 425
paintings **20** 824
Stein, Meir **8** 762
Stein, Michael **19** 41; **29** 604*; **30** 532
Stein, Peter **30** 688
Stein, Sarah **4** 888; **7** 702; **19** 41; **20** 824; **29** 604
Stein, Theobald **17** 479
Stein, Theodor **25** 856
Steinach Church **8** 215
Steinacher, G. **28** 513
Steinamanger *see* SZOMBATHELY
Stein am Rhein **27** 76
glass **27** *77*
Haus zum weissen Adler **10** 737, 738
Monastery of St Georg **12** 409; **30** 131
Steinbach, Erwin von *see* ERWIN
Steinbach, Sabina von *see* SABINA VON STEINBACH
Steinbach Abbey Church **4** 776; **5** 794, 797; **7** 265; **12** 471; **31** 280
Steinbauer, Raimund **25** 648
Steinbeck, John **3** 748
Steinberg, Edward **8** 10
Steinberg, Leo **2** 532; **21** 134
Steinberg, Saul **5** 759; **28** 52; **29** 605–6*
works **5** *759*
Steinbrecht **20** 186
Steinbüchel-Rheinwall, Rambald von **13** 330
Stein Collection *see under* LONDON → museums → British Museum
Steindl, Ferenc **29** 606*
works **14** 908, *908*
Steindl, Imre **5** 85; **29** 606–7*
collaboration **3** 412
groups and movements **13** 203
pupils **18** 655; **30** 762
restorations **3** 224
works **5** 83; **13** 237; **14** 580, *888*, 889; **23** 814; **27** 129
Steindl, Janos **29** 606
Steindl, Matthias *see* STEINL, MATTHIAS
Steindorff, Georg **10** 81, 93
Steinebach, Michel **2** 699
Steinegg, Bernhard von Stein von *see* STEIN VON STEINEGG, BERNHARD VON
Steinen, Karl von den
works **4** *707*; **23** *719*
Steiner, Fridolin **3** 890; **22** 329
Steiner, Gotlieb A. **8** 537
Steiner, Hans (*fl c.* 1593) **33** 711
Steiner, Heinrich (*fl* 1522-48) **1** 589
Steiner, Henry (*fl* 1862-78) **2** 765
Steiner, Johann **29** 607*
Steiner, Johann Nepomuk (1725-93) **17** 585
Steiner, Ralph **21** 762; **33** 146
Steiner, Rudolf **15** 143; **29** 607–8*
groups and movements **2** 138; **10** 698; **30** 710
works **2** 337; **29** *607*
Steiner Master **8** 315
Steinert, Otto **12** 246; **17** 878; **26** 365; **29** 608*
Steinfeld, Franz **2** 796; **4** 838; **12** 821
Steinfeld Abbey **29** 503, 512
stained glass **29** *512*
Steingaden Abbey **28** *131*
Steingruber, Johann David **33** 691
Steingut *see* POTTERY → wares → creamware
Steinhard *see* STAINHART
Steinhardt, Antal **24** 313
Steinhardt, Jacob **16** 567; **29** 609*
groups and movements **10** 695; **21** 55
works **14** 35; **17** 566
Steinhaus **2** 552
Steinhausen Church **12** 372; **26** 497; **29** 838; **32** 823; **33** 683, *683*
Steinhäuser, Adolph **29** 609
Steinhäuser, Carl (Johann) **19** 244; **29** 609*
Steinhäuser, Georg Andreas **29** 609
Steinhäuser, Wilhelm **29** 609
Steinheil, Adolphe-Charles-Edouard **29** 610
Steinheil, Louis-Charles-Auguste **2** 846; **6** 497; **24** 158; **29** 609–10*
Steinhof, Eugen Gustav **33** 386
Steinhöwel, Heinrich **10** 724, 725
works **10** *725*
Steinicken & Lohr **30** 350
Steinkopf, Johann Friedrich **19** 780
Steinl, Matthias **2** 827; **22** 297; **29** 610–11*
collaboration **2** 819; **28** 123; **29** 789
patrons and collectors **31** 510
works **2** 783, 801, *801*; **18** 140; **19** 748; **25** 728
Steinle, Bartholomäus **8** 627; **24** 543
Steinle, Eduard Jakob von **29** 611*
assistants **11** 813
collaboration **31** 428
pupils **19** 103
teachers **32** 120
works **12** 393, 394
Steinlen, Théophile-Alexandre **2** 733; **29** 611–12*
collaboration **20** 602, 603
groups and movements **2** 510
productions **3** 120
pupils **29** 609; **31** 416
works **4** 365; **5** 758; **12** 296; **13** 323; **19** 490; **25** 346
Steinmann, Johann **4** 717
Steinmeyer, Vincentius **20** 743
Steinmüller, Christian **29** 612*
Steinmüller, Johann (Hans) **11** 819; **26** 105; **29** 612
Stein Quadriptych **3** 726
Steinsel **19** 826
Stein von Steinegg, Bernhard von **22** 188
Steinweg, Klara **23** 362; **29** 613*
Steir, Pat **29** 613*
Stejskal, K. **8** 426
Stel, Simon der **29** 105
stelae **29** 613–20*
historical and regional traditions
Akkadian (people) **1** 508–9, *509*
Anatolia, ancient **29** 614
Ancient Near East **24** *335*; **29** 613–14*, *614*
Arabia **2** 255
Assyrian **29** 614
Aztec **29** 620
Babylonian **3** *12*
Black Sea Colonies **4** 111
Buddhism **6** *711*; **15** 448
Central Asia, Western **29** 618, 619
Champa **6** 420
China **6** 740, 741, *743*, 744, *744*, 745, 764; **8** 713; **29** 617*; **33** 464
Buddhism **6** *711*
Nestorianism **22** *812*
stelae
historical and regional traditions—cont.
Christianity **22** *812*
Coptic **7** *822*
Dan (Africa) **8** 489
Egypt **7** *822*
Egypt, ancient **9** 890; **10** 1, 2, 48; **29** 614–16*
Early Dynastic (*c.* 2925-*c.* 2575 BC) **1** *99*
New Kingdom (*c.* 1539-*c.* 1075 BC) **9** *790*
Roman **18** 209, *209*
Elamite **10** *133*
Eritrea **10** 565
Ethiopia **10** 565
Etruscan **10** 587
Greece, ancient **6** *388*; **13** *457*, *544*; **29** 616–17*
Guatemala **29** *620*
Helladic **14** 338
Honduras **7** *801*
Huastec **29** 620
Indian subcontinent **15** 231, 413
Buddhism **15** 448
Islamic **29** 619
Pala-Sena period **15** 499
Iran **29** 618, 619
Iran, ancient **29** 614
Islamic **29** 617, 618, 619
Italy **10** 587
Jordan **24** *335*
Korea **29** 869
Manteño culture **29** 145, 620
Maya **5** 412; **7** *801*; **16** *807*, 807–8; **20** 883; **21** 266; **24** 743; **25** 825; **27** 780; **28** *373*; **29** 620, *620*
Mesoamerica, Pre-Columbian **24** 743; **25** 825; **27** 780; **29** 619–20*
Classic (*c.* AD 250-*c.* 900) **21** *220*
Honduras **7** *801*
Maya **5** 412; **7** *801*; **16** *807*; **21** 266; **28** *373*; **29** *620*
Mexico **16** *807*
Pre-Classic (*c.* 2000 BC-*c.* AD 250) **21** 219
Mesopotamia **21** 271, *296*, 296; **29** 613–14
Babylonian **3** *12*
Elamite **10** *133*
Mexico **16** *807*
Morocco **29** 618
Mycenaean **14** 338
North Africa **29** 613
Nubia **29** 615
Olmec **21** 219; **23** 417; **29** 619
Ottoman **29** 618
Phoenician **29** 613
Punic **5** *892*; **25** 733, *733*
Rome, ancient **18** 209, *209*; **29** 616–17*
Sicily **29** 619
South America, Pre-Columbian **29** 145, 619–20*
Spain **29** 617, 619
Syria **29** 617, 618
Syria-Palestine **9** *694*; **29** 613, 614; **30** 193
Toltec **29** 620
Turkey **29** 618, 619
Vietnam **6** 420; **32** 476
materials
basalt **9** *694*; **21** *296*
brick **29** 618
ceramics **29** 618
faience (i) (glass) **10** 48
inscriptions **29** 617, *618*, 619
limestone **1** *99*, *509*; **7** *822*; **25** *733*; **29** 614, *614*, *615*, *620*; **30** *189*
marble **3** *12*; **13** 427, *457*; **29** *616*, *618*
quartzite **9** *790*
wood **29** 614, 618
stelae—cont.
techniques
painting **13** *544*
types
commemorative **29** 613
China **29** 617*
Egypt, ancient **9** 868; **29** *615*, 615–16*
Mesopotamia **21** 276
false door **9** 825; **29** 615
funerary **29** 613
Champa **6** 420, 431
China **29** 617
Crete **8** 155
Cyprus, ancient **8** 342
Egypt **29** *618*
Egypt, ancient **9** 868, 877; **29** 614–15*
Eritrea **10** 577
Ethiopia **10** 577
Etruscan **10** 594
Greece, ancient **13** 427*, 430–31, *431*, 456, *457*; **26** *292*; **29** *616*
Islamic **29** 617–19*, *618*
Italy **10** 594
Prehistoric **25** 529–30
Rome, ancient **8** 155
Vietnam **6** 420
see also GRAVESTONES
pillar-stelae **15** 59, *60*
rock-cut **29** 614, 616*
round-topped **29** 615, 616
slab **29** 615
stag-stones **21** 882, 883
votive **29** 617
wanfo bei **29** 617
Stelea Monastery **26** 708, *708*
Stele of Hegeso **13** 427
Stele of Naram-Sin **1** 892; **21** 273
Stele of Prime Minister Yi Wŏn-ik **14** 702
Stele of the Vultures **1** 508; **6** 478; **21** 272, *273*, 294; **29** 614, 923; **30** 422
Stelian, Toma **26** 724
Stella, Franco (*b* 1944) **16** 651
Stella, François (1563-1605) **20** 482
Stella, Frank (*b* 1936) **10** 398; **20** *607*; **29** 621–2*; **31** 609, 660
collaboration **20** 608
dealers **6** 23; **18** 162
groups and movements **1** 79; **23** 449; **25** 361
patrons and collectors **6** 23; **17** 620
productions **8** 270
works **1** 130, 738; **7** 636; **13** 677; **19** 492, 493; **21** 892; **28** 52; **29** *622*; **33** 364
Stella, Giacomo (*c.* 1545-1630) **26** 818
Stella, Jacques (1596-1657) **11** 536; **24** 134; **29** 622–4*
dealing **11** 662
patrons and collectors **18** 671; **19** 238; **23** 513; **29** 803, 886
pupils **6** 488
reproductive prints by others **21** 85; **25** 77; **27** 269
works **26** 113, 349; **29** *623*
Stella, Joseph **29** 624*
exhibitions **2** 447
groups and movements **8** 435; **25** 461; **28** 925
patrons and collectors **15** 830
teachers **6** 500
works **15** 828; **31** 705
Stella, Paolo **29** 624–5*
patrons and collectors **8** 384; **13** 908
works **8** 377; **22** 167; **25** 425, 438; **33** 303
Stellaert, François **29** 622
Stella Milanese, Paolo **29** 625
stellar vaults *see* VAULTS (CEILING) → types → rib: star

Stella St John's Studio Gallery **2** 151
Stellenbosch **18** 887; **29** *103*, 105
 architecture **29** 114
 Dutch Reformed Church **14** 33
 furniture **29** 114
 Museum **29** 122
Stelletsky, Dmitry (Semyonovich) **27** 392; **29** 625*; **30** 464
Stellingwerf, Jacobus **14** 794
Stelliola, Niccolò Antonio **5** 888
Stello **7** 708
stelophorous statues *see under* SCULPTURE → types
Steltman (company) **26** 379
Steltman, Johannes **22** 892
Stelush Castle **1** 538
Stelzmann, Volker **29** 625*
Stelzner, Anna Carolina **29** 626
Stelzner, Carl Ferdinand **4** 75; **24** 660; **29** 625–6*
Stelzner, Carl Gottlob **29** 625
Stem, Allen **32** 867
Stematsky, Avigdor **16** 571; **17** 577; **29** 626*
 groups and movements **23** 25
 pupils **18** 525
Stemnitsa **13** 358
stem stitch *see under* STITCHES
Sten, Henrik **30** 98, 100
Sten, John **30** 81
Stenberg, Georgy (Avgustovich) **29** 626*
 collaboration **21** 38
 groups and movements **7** 768; **15** 857
 works **7** 768; **25** 351, *351*; **27** 394; **30** 686
Stenberg, Lidiya (Avgustovna) **29** 626
Stenberg, Sten **29** 626
Stenberg, Vladimir (Avgustovich) **29** 626*
 collaboration **21** 38
 groups and movements **7** 768; **15** 857
 works **7** 768, *768*; **25** 351, *351*; **27** 394; **30** 686
Stenbock (family) **20** 391
Stenbock, Gustaf Otto **5** 817
Stenč, Jan **8** 401
stencil-dyeing *see under* DYEING → types
stencilling **25** 597, 615; **29** 626–8*, *627*
 historical and regional traditions
  Buddhism **30** 835
  Central Asia, Eastern **6** 302
  China **7** 49, 118; **29** 627; **30** 560, 561
  Fiji **11** 69; **29** 627
  Germany **24** 56
  Indian subcontinent **30** 561
  Japan **17** 276, 285, 288, 293, *309*, 309–10*, 313, 314, *314*, 315, 348, 355, 405; **29** 627; **30** 560, 561
  Korea **18** 303
  Nigeria **30** 561
  Prehistoric art **25** 478
  Tibet **30** 835
  Tonga (Pacific Islands) **31** 143
  United States of America **29** 628, *628*
 materials
  inks **15** 855
  lacquer **28** 298
  leather **24** 56
  paper **17** 405; **28** 298
  paper mulberry **30** 560
  persimmon **30** 560
  shellac **28** 298
  silk **30** 560
  velvet **29** 628
 types
  hand **25** 478
  photo-stencilling **28** 299
 uses
  dolls **31** 259
stencilling
 uses—cont.
  leather **17** 313, 355
  paintings **18** 303
   wall **6** 302; **25** 478
  paper **24** 55, 56
  prints **7** 118; **17** 276, 285, 288
  rock art *see under* ROCK ART → techniques
  screenprinting **28** 299
  textiles **7** 49; **11** 69; **17** *309*, 309–10, 313, 314, *314*, 315, 355; **29** 627; **30** 560–61*
  wallpaper **32** 812*
Štenclová, Jitka **8** 421
Stendal
 Cathedral of St Nikolaus **13** 187; **14** 81
 St Marien **14** 81
Stendhal **24** 140, 741; **26** 739; **29** 629–30*
Steneberg, Karl Erik **30** 120
Stenersen, Rolf E. **11** 142; **22** 807; **23** 243
Stengel, Friedrich Joachim M(ichael) **19** 815; **29** 630*
Stengel, Wilhelm **14** 772
Stengel Co. **26** 236
Stengg, Andreas **2** 783; **13** 330
Stengg, Johann Georg **2** 783; **13** 330
Stenglein, Johann Eberhard **2** 127
Stenhouse **28** 257
Steninge **30** 93
Stenius, Per **11** 478
Sten Knudsen, Nina **8** 736
Stenman, Gösta **7** 251; **11** 112; **28** 104
Steno, Nicolaus **4** 360
Stenrat, Johannes **13** 120; **29** 630–31*
Stenstadvold, Håkon **23** 239
Stenström, Nils Petter **30** 95
Stent, Peter **6** 80; **14** 684; **21** 721; **25** 626
Stent, Sydney **17** 897
Stent, Thomas **13** 203; **23** 632
Stentas, Spyridon **25** 334
Stepanakert *see* XANKÄNDI
Stepanavičius, J. **19** 499
Štěpánek, Josef **11** 812
Stepanov, Aleksey (Stepanovich) **29** 631*
Stepanov, Nikolay (Aleksandrovich) **29** 631*
Stepanov, Yevgeny **27** 440
Stepanova, Varvara (Fyodorovna) **7** 770; **24** 450; **25** 239; **27** 394; **29** 632*; **32** 661
 collaboration **21** 410; **33** 631
 exhibitions **15** 857
 groups and movements **7** 768; **15** 857; **22** 508; **32** 382
 patrons and collectors **8** 10
 teachers **33** 577
 works **7** 769, 770; **9** 244, 292; **26** 504
Štěpánský, Karel **29** 438
Step'anyan, Suren **2** 436
step gables *see under* GABLES → types
Stephan, Christoph **4** 114; **10** 155
Stephan, Pierre **4** 824
Stephanoff, Fileter **29** 632
Stephanoff, Francis Philip **10** 378; **29** 632*
Stephanoff, Gertrude **29** 632
Stephanoff, James **29** 632
Stephanoni, P. Giovanni Francesco **2** 908
Stephanos **24** 227; **27** 27; **29** 633*
Stephanos of Aila (*fl* mid-6th cent. AD) **28** 761
Stephanos of Alexandria (*fl* 7th cent. AD) **4** 688
Stephanus (*fl* 1430) **18** 685
Stephanus Magius (*fl* 13th cent; marble-worker) **7** 922
Stephanus Oderisii (*fl* 1250; wood-carver) **24** 783
Stephen (*fl c.* 1100) **26** 657
Stephen, King of England (*reg* 1135-54) **3** 369; **7** 473; **26** 615
Stephen, Prince of Serbia (*reg* 1389-1427) **22** 79; **28** 440, 442, 447
Stephen, Saint, King of Hungary (*reg* 997-1038) **1** 530; **13** 887; **15** 11; **26** 82, 638; **31** 786
Stephen I, King of Hungary *see* STEPHEN, SAINT, King of Hungary
Stephen II, Duke of Bavaria-Landshut (*reg* 1347-75) **33** *272*
Stephen II, Pope (*reg* 752-57) **26** 801
Stephen III, Count of Blois and Champagne (*reg* 1089-1102) **25** 667
Stephen III, Voivode of Moldavia (*reg* 1457-1504) **15** 55; **26** 712, 719, 722; **29** 892; **32** 696
Stephen, Clive (Travers) **29** 633*
Stephen, Dorothy **29** 633
Stephen, George **11** 743
Stephen, William **25** 311
Stephen Bathory, King of Poland (*reg* 1533-86) **3** 526; **4** 146; **13** 774; **14** 756; **25** 96
Stephen Bathory, Voivode of Transylvania (*fl* 1479-94) **14** 884; **23** 324
Stephen Nemanja, Grand Župan of Serbia (*reg* 1168-96) **28** 436, 440, 441, 445, 447, 455; **29** 849
Stephen Nemanjić, King of Serbia (*reg* 1196-1227) **25** 639; **28** 455
Stephen of Holland *see* HERWIJCK, STEVEN VAN
Stephen of Penchester **8** 138
Stephen Radoslav, King of Serbia (*reg* 1227-34) **29** 849
Stephens, C. J. **28** 772
Stephens, Edward Bowring **10** 674; **12** 270
Stephens, F(rederic) G(eorge) **10** 367; **25** 554; **29** 633*
Stephens, John Lloyd **18** 577
 collaboration **6** 87
 photographs **21** 263
 writings **7** 800; **13** 811; **16** 803; **21** 262; **31** 420
Stephens, Oswold **23** 68, 69
Stephenson, Arthur (George) **2** 742; **29** 634*
Stephenson, David **9** 55; **23** 20
Stephenson, George **25** 854
Stephenson, Ian **10** 375
Stephenson, James **13** 327; **29** 634*
Stephenson, J. J. **30** 504
Stephenson, John **31** 640
Stephenson, Jonathan **25** 628
Stephenson, Mathilda Coxe **22** 676
Stephenson, Robert **4** 802; **16** 53; **23** 20; **25** 854; **29** 651
Stephenson, Sam **16** 12
Stephenson, Suzanne **31** 640
Stephenson & Royston **3** 245
Stephenson & Turner **2** 742; **26** 744; **29** 634
Stephens *Shāhnāma* **16** 316
Stephen the Great, Voivode of Moldavia *see* STEPHEN III, Voivode of Moldavia
Stephen Tvrtko I, King of Bosnia (*reg* 1376-91) **22** 16
Stephen Uroš I, King of Serbia (*reg* 1243 -76) **9** 583; **28** 446; **29** 74
Stephen Uroš II Miliutin, King of Serbia (*reg* 1282-1321)
 architecture **9** 552–3; **13** 264; **25** 639; **28** 440; **29** 551
 metalwork **28** 455
 paintings **2** 646; **9** 585; **23** 373; **28** 446
Stephen Uroš II Miliutin, King of Serbia (*reg* 1282-1321)—cont.
 textiles **28** 457, *457*
Stephen Uroš III Dečanski, King of Serbia (*reg* 1321-31) **8** 599; **28** 446, 448, 455
Stephen Uroš IV Dušan, Emperor of Serbia (*reg* 1331-55)
 architecture **8** 599; **9** 553; **25** 639; **28** 442
 heraldry **14** 411
 paintings **28** 446, 448; **29** 75
Stephen Uroš V, King of Serbia (*reg* 1355-71) **9** 553
Stephen Vladislav, King of Serbia (*reg* 1234-43) **9** 582
Stępinski, Zygmunt **29** 634–5*
stepped portals *see under* PORTALS → types
Step Pyramid *see under* SAQQARA → pyramids
step pyramids *see under* PYRAMIDS → types
steps **13** 380
stepwells **15** 192, 341, 343, 349; **29** *635*, 635–6*
 see also WELLS
Stequi, Domingo *see* STECCHI, DOMENICO
Sterbak, Jana **5** 572; **10** 879
Sterckshof Castle
 Provinciaal Museum voor Kunstambachten Sterckshof **3** 616
stereobatai **29** 636*
stereoscopes **24** 651, 657, 663; **33** 134
stereoscopic photography *see under* PHOTOGRAPHY → processes
stereotomy **19** *691*; **29** *636*, 636–7*
stereotyping **25** 610
Steriadi, Jean Al(ex) **23** 699; **26** 716, 723; **29** 638*
Steriadi, Nora **26** 719, 721; **29** 638*
Sterk, Isaac Elink **20** 434
Sterk, Izidor **5** 83
Sterligov, Vladimir (Vasil'yevich) **12** 804; **27** 581
Sterling, Charles (Jacques) **29** 638*, 665
Sterling Furnace **31** 652
Sterling silver *see under* ALLOYS → types
Stern, A. Biró de *see* BIRÓ DE STERN, A.
Stern, E. (*fl* mid-15th cent.) **20** 794
Stern, Ernst (1876-1954) **24** 591
Stern, Friedrich Siegmund **9** 364; **10** 539
Stern, Georg **33** 274
Stern, Giovanni **18** 779; **26** 780; **29** 639
Stern, Grete **2** 525; **7** 818; **29** 641*
Stern, Henry **19** 489
Stern, Ignaz **29** 639*
Stern, Irma **29** 108, 641*
Stern, Irma, Museum *see under* CAPE TOWN
Stern, Johann *see* STERN, GIOVANNI
Stern, Jonasz **18** 429, 433; **29** 641–2*
Stern, Josef **8** 392; **18** 467
Stern, Leonard **8** 324
Stern, Ludovico (i) (1709-77) **29** 639
Stern, Ludovico (ii) (1780-1861) **29** 639
Stern, Philippe **5** 483; **6** 420; **15** 211; **29** 642*
 pupils **9** 401
 works **29** 241–2
Stern, Raffaele **29** 639–40*
 collaboration **7** 726
 pupils **25** 147
 restorations **7** 726; **26** 791
Stern, Raffaele—cont.
 works **3** 644; **7** 726; **9** 25; **26** 814; **29** *640*
Stern, Robert A(rthur) M(orton) **7** 385; **17** 549; **23** 490; **29** 642*; **31** 598
 groups and movements **25** 359
Stern, Veronica **29** 639
Sternberg, Harry **1** 772
Sternberg, Josef von **23** 10; **29** 642–3*
Šternberk, F., Count **8** 422
Šternberk, Václav Vojtěch, Count **8** 422; **20** 814
Sternburg, Maximilian Speck von *see* SPECK VON STERNBURG, MAXIMILIAN
Sterne, Hedda **24** 213
Sterne, Lawrence **8** 218; **19** 891; **26** *273*
Sterne, Maurice **29** 643*
Sternefeld, Anna Sibilla *see* BIERMANN, AENNE
Sternen, Matej **2** 890; **16** 874; **28** 860
Sterner, Albert Edward **19** 492; **20** 604; **21** 897
Sterner, F. J. **14** 787
Sterns, John G. **28** 604
Sternschuss, Moshe **17** 717
Sterre, Chrysostomus van, Abbot of Antwerp **8** 877
Stertinius, L. **31** 349
Sterzing *see* VIPITENO
Sterzing Altarpiece, Master of the **20** 770*
Stethaimer, Hanns von *see* HANS VON BURGHAUSEN
Štetić, Rizah **4** 461
Stetten, Paul von, II **29** 643*
Stetten, von (family) **29** 786
Stetter, Wilhelm **29** 643*
Stettin *see* SZCZECIN
Stettin, Nicholaus von *see* NICHOLAUS VON STETTIN
Stettler, Wilhelm **29** 644*
Steuart, George **10** 145; **14** 539
Steuben, Charles de **8** 51; **12** 336; **17** 453
Steuben Glass Works **7** 875; **14** 252; **24** 58; **29** 644*; **31** 644
 designers **13** 326; **30** 390
 directors **5** 730
Steubenville Pottery **31** 639; **33** 410
Steudlin, J. M.
 works **17** *817*
Steur, A. van der **4** 614; **27** 231
Steurbout, Hubrecht **4** 590
Steurbout, Maarten **2** 199
Steurs, Victor de **10** 731
Stevanović, Andra **28** 444
Stevanović, Borivoj **28** 451
Steven, Jan *see* CALCAR, JAN STEVEN VAN
Stevenage (Herts) **19** 577; **31** 733
Stevenage New Town Corporation **13** 239
Stevens (family) **31** 652
Stevens, Alfred (George) (1817-75) **29** 645–7*
 competitions **7** 673
 groups and movements **13** 297; **26** 500
 methods **23** 788
 patrons and collectors **14** 675
 pupils **11** 360; **14** 849
 works **10** 343; **16** 60; **19** *600*; **22** 163; **27** 831; **29** *646*, *647*; **31** 488
Stevens, Alfred (Emile-Léopold) (1823-1906) **3** 615; **10** 298; **11** 545; **20** 60; **29** 644, 645*
 assistants **30** 162
 collaboration **12** 496
 exhibitions **2** 516
 groups and movements **8** 718
 patrons and collectors **7** 377
 personal collection **17** 440

Stevens, Alfred (Emile-Léopold) (1823-1906)—cont.
 pupils 24 481
 teachers 22 697; 33 197
 works 1 69; 3 563; 19 600
Stevens, Alice Barber
 works 33 *311*
Stevens, Anton 29 649
Stevens, Arthur 29 644
Stevens, Charles Frederick 29 647
Stevens, Francis 6 402
Stevens, Frederick William 29 647*
 works 4 289, *289*; 15 403; 31 241
Stevens, James 10 212
Stevens, J. & E. 31 257, 264
Stevens, Johann Jakob 29 649
Stevens, John 4 80
Stevens, John Calvin 28 604; 29 647–8*
Stevens, John Hargrave 21 349
Stevens, John Howard 29 648; 33 192
Stevens, Joseph 5 44; 29 644–5*
Stevens, Léopold 29 644
Stevens, May 27 872
Stevens, Paul Anton 29 649
Stevens, Pieter 3 613; 10 709; 29 648–9*
 groups and movements 11 732
 patrons and collectors 13 914
 personal collection 10 710; 21 354
 reproductive prints by others 14 709; 27 504
 works 8 390; 29 *649*
Stevens, Richard 10 143, 662; 29 650*
Stevens, Suzanne 29 693
Stevens, Thomas 2 760
Stevens, Wallace 8 435
Stevens, Will Henry 23 32
Stevens, Zachariah 31 652
Stevens & Gregson & Co. 29 454
Stevens & Hunt 8 770; 30 507
Stevenson, Alan 19 361
Stevenson, C. R. 19 506
Stevenson, J(ohn) J(ames) 26 476; 29 650*
 assistants 4 884; 5 65
 groups and movements 25 804, 805
 staff 31 375
 teachers 28 279
Stevenson, J. J., and Douglas, Campbell 20 27
Stevenson, Laura 28 232
Stevenson, Robert 19 361; 29 651*
Stevenson, Robert Macaulay 28 569
Stevenson, T.
 works 19 *360*
Stevenson & Higgins 28 255
Stevens & Williams 5 730; 10 320; 15 824
Steven the Almayne *see* HASCHENPERG, STEFAN VON
Stevers *see* PALAMEDESZ., ANTHONIE
Stevin, Simon 28 202
Stevini, Barbara 18 830
Stevns, Gjorslev Castle 8 724, *724*
Stevns, Niels Larsen *see* LARSEN STEVNS, NILS
Stevyns, Thomas 4 692
Steward, Donn 20 606
Steward, Joseph 4 764; 9 504; 32 777
Steward, Toby 10 304
Stewardson, Emlyn Lamar 7 808
Stewardson, John 7 808; 10 718; 11 849
Stewardson & Page 7 808
Stewart, Alexander Turney 29 651*
 architecture 17 891
 paintings 9 332; 20 60; 21 69; 33 581
Stewart, Ann Linsell 33 678
Stewart, A. T., & Co. 29 651
Stewart, David 5 71
Stewart, Donald 5 570
Stewart, Dugald 2 136
Stewart, Gilbert *see* STUART, GILBERT
Stewart, James 18 690
Stewart, James, & Co. 22 275
Stewart, John (*fl* 1867) 17 798
Stewart, John S. (*fl* 1852-7) 28 843
Stewart, Margaret, Countess of Lennox 32 679
Stewart, Matthew, 4th Earl of Lennox 32 679
Stewart, McClure & Mullgardt 22 275
Stewart, Patrick, 2nd Earl of Orkney 28 268
Stewart, Robert, 1st Duke of Albany (*fl* 1415) 32 823
Stewart, Robert, 2nd Marquess of Londonderry (1769-1822) 5 631; 22 338
Stewart, Theodore 14 188
Stewart, Thomas S. 26 353
Stewart, William, 1st Earl of Blessington 16 26
Stewart, William Drummond 21 605
Steynberg, Coert 4 155; 29 111
Steynemeulen, Siger van 2 201
Steynemolen, van (family) 20 915
Steyner 33 33
Steyner, Heinrich 20 743, 744
Steynrot, Johannes *see* STENRAT, JOHANNES
Steyr
 Dominikanerkirche 2 781
 globes 12 *811*
 metalwork 2 822
 Michaelerkirche 2 781
 SS Agid und Koloman 32 93
Sthapati, V(aidyanatha) Ganapati 15 171; 29 651–2*
Sthapit 22 792
Sthaviravada Buddhism *see under* BUDDHISM → sects
Sthennis 4 112; 19 170; 29 652*
STI *see* SOCIETY OF TRINIDAD INDEPENDENTS
Štiavnica Church 28 849
Stibar 20 801
Stibbert, Frederick 11 189
Stibbington Hall (Cambs) 10 230
Stibor, Master of the 5 87
Stibral, Jiří 29 652*
sticharia 9 642, *643*
Stichele, Gillis de 4 923
Stichting Architecten Research 13 898; 29 652*
 see also SUPPORTS THEORY
Stichting Goed Wonen 22 868, 876
Stichting voor Culturele Samenwerking met Suriname en de Nederlandse Antillen (STICUSA) 30 17
stick-back chairs *see under* CHAIRS → types
Stickelberg, Ernst *see* STÜCKELBERG, ERNST
Stickells, Robert 32 551
stick lac 24 796
Stickley, Gustav 10 147; 24 432; 29 653*; 31 653
 groups and movements 2 572; 31 595
 works 6 391; 30 218; 31 621, 631
Stickley, J. George 31 631, 653
Stickley, Leopold 31 631, 653
Stickley Bros Co. 13 297
sticks, vomiting *see* VOMITING STICKS
Stick style 29 653*; 31 593
Stična Monastery 28 857, *858*, 860
STICUSA *see* STICHTING VOOR CULTURELE SAMENWERKING MET SURINAME EN DE NEDERLANDSE ANTILLEN
Stiebel, George 16 886
Stiefel, Eduard 22 113
Stiegel, Henry William 29 654*; 31 641, 652
 works 26 227; 31 *641*
Stieglitz, A. L., Baron 3 733; 5 26; 20 404; 24 566; 27 442; 29 515
Stieglitz, Alfred 1 438; 11 360; 23 387; 24 432, 675, *739*; 29 654–7*; 31 605, 663; 33 15
 collaboration 10 649; 24 710; 33 146
 groups and movements 7 491; 8 435; 23 47; 24 688, 739; 31 490
 personal collection 24 683; 29 601
 works 9 357; 10 655; 24 688; 29 *655*, *656*; 31 157
Stieglitz, Christian Ludwig 29 657–8*
Stieglitz, Joseph 16 570
Stiehl, Christian Gottlieb 12 458
Stiehle, Juan 9 711
Stieler, Johann Friedrich 19 654
Stieler, Joseph Karl 29 658*
 groups and movements 25 789
 pupils 33 256
 works 12 393; 22 308; 33 282
Stiemer, Felix 10 869
Stieng 32 487
Stienne (family) 3 599
Stienne, Louis 29 758
Stier, Gustav 29 658
Stier, Hubert 14 142; 25 854, 856; 29 658
Stier, Wilhelm 4 335; 29 658*
Stierlein, Georg 12 816
Stierlin, Henri 27 756
Stiernsund 30 90
stiff-leaf 29 659*, *659*
Stiffneck group 33 710
Stifter, Adalbert 20 705; 29 659*
Stift-Melk 25 176
Stiftung Ada-und Emil Nolde *see under* SEEBÜLL
Stiftung für Kunst, Kultur und Geschichte 30 152
Stigell, Robert 11 100
Stigliano, Mele da *see* MELE DA STIGLIANO
Stiglmaier 12 406
Stijl, De 1 74, 75, 90, 810, 815; 10 137; 11 360; 19 897; 23 548
 architecture 8 247; 21 781, *781*, 782; 31 771
 collections 18 466; 27 162
 exhibitions 9 63; 26 379; 28 920
 furniture 22 875
 interior decoration 22 868
 members 1 76; 7 293, 630; 23 124; 25 173
  Arp, Hans (Peter Wilhelm) 2 490
  Baljeu, Joost 3 111
  Doesburg, Theo van 9 63
  Domela (-Nieuwenhuis), César 9 86
  Eesteren, Cornelis van 9 745
  Hoff, Robert van 't 14 625
  Leck, Bart (Anthonij) van der 19 32
  Mondrian, Piet(er Cornelis) 22 852
  Oud, J(acobus) J(ohannes) P(ieter) 23 663
  Rietveld, Gerrit (Thomas) 8 803
  Vantongerloo, Georges 31 890
  Vordemberge-Gildewart, Friedrich 32 695
  Wils, Jan 33 215
 painting 9 *63*; 19 *32*; 22 851
 sculpture 29 *660*
Stijl: Maandblad voor de moderne beeldende vakken, De 9 62; 15 36; 19 32; 21 851, 853; 22 749, 830, 868, 875; 24 428, 449; 26 379; 29 660–61*
Stijović, Risto 22 18
Stile, Lo 25 218
stile floreale *see* STILE LIBERTY
Stile Futurista 25 447
stile liberty 2 567; 4 100; 8 532; 21 779
 architecture 16 648*
 fountains 16 *648*
 frames 11 397, *397*
 furniture 25 793
Stilicho 9 649
 works 9 *251*
Stilkunst 28 343
Still, Clyfford 23 48; 27 731; 29 661–3*
 dealers 24 213
 groups and movements 1 78, 83, 84, 85, 86, 87; 21 646; 23 48; 29 534; 31 607
 patrons and collectors 9 189; 13 801; 25 400; 33 45
 works 7 636; 18 718; 29 *662*
Still, Nanny 11 106
Stillberg, Jakob Axel 12 634
Stillfried & Anderson 29 663
Stillfried & Co. 29 663
Stillfried-Rathenitz, Raimund, Baron von 3 447; 18 534; 24 666; 29 663*
Stilling, Harald Conrad 14 497
Stillingfleet (N. Yorks), St Helen 9 155; 10 339
still-lifes *see under* PAINTING → types
Stillman, Clark 1 439
Stillman, James 5 922
Stillman, Mrs William *see* SPARTALI, MARIE
Stillman, William James 24 431; 29 671–2*
 groups and movements 25 556
 illustrated writings 7 551
Stillorgan (Co. Dublin) 12 128
Stil' modern *see* ART NOUVEAU
Stilo 9 *510*; 16 *621*; 29 672*
 architecture 9 523
 Cattolica church 16 626; 29 672
stilted arches *see under* ARCHES → types
stilts (kiln furniture) 6 330
stilts (walking) 20 *463*
Stimm, Thomas 2 804
Stimmer, Abel 29 672, 674*
Stimmer, Christoph (*c.* 1490-1562) 29 672*
Stimmer, Christoph (*c.* 1520/25-1562) 29 672*
Stimmer, Gideon 29 672*
Stimmer, Hans Christoffel 29 672
Stimmer, Josias 29 672–3*
Stimmer, Tobias 29 672–4*; 30 131
 collaboration 22 341
 works 10 736, 737; 12 720; 29 *673*, *674*, 674; 30 131; 33 354, 357, 366
Stinchcombe (Glos), Stancombe Park 11 243
Stinche, della, tabernacle 12 706
Stind Factory 5 159
Stingl, Vince 14 449; 15 2
stink-wood 29 114, 115, *115*, 116; 33 325
Štip 19 *882*, 884
 museum 19 886
Štipl, Karel 8 414; 25 435
stippling *see under* ENGRAVING → types; PAINTING → techniques
Stirewalt, James 8 574
Stirling (Central)
 carpets 28 266
 Castle 28 *222*, 225, 234, 250; 29 678–80*, *679*
  Chapel Royal 28 225, 234
  interior decoration 28 244
  Presence Chamber 28 244
 Holy Rude Church 28 224, 251
 Mar's Wark 28 268
 tolbooth 28 269
Stirling (Central)—cont.
 University 28 232
  Principal's House 28 231
Stirling, David 5 561; 14 193, 259
Stirling, James (Frazer) 29 677–8*
 collaboration 12 793; 13 239
 groups and movements 15 166; 30 391
 staff 18 456
 works 5 513; 7 386, *386*; 9 19; 10 242, 285, 371; 12 477; 14 803; 19 591; 22 367; 29 *678*, 874; 31 735, *736*
Stirling, Marion 3 65
Stirling, Matthew W. 3 65, 278; 14 223; 18 881; 27 756; 31 310
Stirling, T. G. 14 108
Stirling, William *see* STIRLING-MAXWELL, WILLIAM
Stirling, William & Sons 28 266
Stirling and Wilford 18 114
Stirling & Gowan 5 56
Stirling Heads 28 225, 242, 244, 250
Stirling-Maxwell, William 12 777; 26 232; 29 358, 680*
Stirn & Lyon 31 263
Stirn Secret *see under* CAMERAS → types
stirrup jars *see under* JARS → types
stirrups 17 300, 302, 362, 364
Stitchbury, Peter 23 69
stitched-bound books *see under* BOOKS → forms
stitches 30 563
 back 31 21
 blanket 31 21
 Bokhara 21 877
 chain 6 250; 7 44, *47*; 17 313; 21 877; 31 21
 cross 6 250
 float 17 314
 long-and-short 17 315
 Peking 21 877
 running 17 317
 satin 3 *609*; 6 250; 7 44, 50; 17 313, 315
 split 3 *609*, 610; 16 *759*
 stem 17 313, 315
 weave 17 317
stitching *see under* DYEING → types
stitch-resist dyeing *see under* DYEING → types
Štítnik Church 28 851
Stitzen *see* FLAGONS → types
Stiven, Charles 28 264
Stix, Alexander 10 718
Stjärnorps Church 30 112
Stjärnsund (factory) 30 109
Stjernsund (manor) 30 73
Stoa Basileios *see under* ATHENS → Agora
Stoakes, William 5 169
Stoa of Attalos *see under* ATHENS → Agora
Stoa of the Herms *see under* ATHENS → Agora
Stoa of Zeus *see under* ATHENS → Agora
Stoa Poikile *see* ATHENS → Agora → Painted Stoa
stoas 13 236; 29 680–82*
 Crete 8 154
 Greece, ancient 8 *686*; 13 381, *381*, 386, 389, 402–3, 406, 416, 417, 418; 27 712, 714; 29 680–81, *681*; 31 294
  6th cent. BC 13 *402*
  7th cent. BC 27 687
 Rome, ancient 27 712, 714; 29 681–2
 Seleucid 13 406
 see also PORTICOS
stoat-hair *see under* HAIR → types
Stobbaerts, Jan 29 682*
Stobi 9 *511*; 19 *882*; 26 *906*; 29 682–3*
 architecture 9 560

Stobi—cont.
Baptistery **7** 302; **9** 574
basilicas **19** 882, 884; **29** 682
Bishop's Palace **9** 557
church **9** 565
houses **9** 560
mosaics **9** 565, 566
Museum **29** 683
synagogue **9** 565
Stobwasser, Georg Siegmund **18** 615; **24** 62; **33** 54
Stocade, Nicolaas de Helt *see* HELT STOCADE, NICOLAAS DE
Stock, Andries (Jacobsz.) **10** 387; **14** 709; **33** 181
Stock, Hans **10** 81
Stock, Ignatius van der **4** 521; **11** 358; **31** 793
Stock, Joseph Whiting **29** 683*
Stockade Building System **11** 834
Stockamer, Balthasar **12** 405; **21** 27; **29** 683*
Stockar, Rudolf **8** 414, 416
Stockbridge (Hants; UK) **31** 709
Stockbridge (MA; USA), Chesterwood (Daniel Chester French Studio and Museum) **3** 30; **11** 756
stock catalogues *see under* CATALOGUES → types
Stöckel (family) **18** 511
Stöckel, Joseph **29** 683*
Stockelsdorff factory **8** 748
Stocker, Anton **29** 684
Stocker, Felix **29** 684
Stocker, Hans **30** 134
Stocker, Jörg **28** 47; **29** 683–4*
stock exchanges *see* EXCHANGES
Stockham, Alfred **4** 823
Stockhamer, Sebastian **10** 174
Stockhausen, Karlheinz **7** 688; **22** 381; **23** 777
Stockholm **29** 684–91*, *685*; **30** 64, *65*
academies **21** 759
academy **1** 105, 107
art forms and materials
architecture **30** 69
copper **30** 111
damask **19** 418; **30** 115
dioramas **8** 911
embroidery **30** 115
furniture **30** 92
glass **30** 102
jewellery **30** 112
lacquer **18** 614
metalwork **29** 688–9*; **30** 106
painting **22** 333; **30** 79
pewter **30** 110
sculpture **30** 83
silk **30** 115
silver **30** 104, *105*, *107*
snuff-boxes **30** *112*
tapestries **30** 332
Bolinder House **30** 73
cemetery **31** 131
Central Post Office **30** 74
Central Railway Station **30** 73, 110
churches
Adolf Fredrikskyrka **30** 72
Engelbrekt Church **32** 765
Franciscan church **30** 76, 77
Hedvig Eleonora church **30** 70
Karl Johans Church **30** 73
Katarinakyrka **8** 661; **19** 815; **30** 70, 71
Riddarholmskyrka **20** 866; **30** 109
Caroline Mausoleum **20** 866
sarcophagus of Karl XIV **30** 113
St Jakob **30** 70, 84
textiles **16** *753*
St Klara **30** 69
St Mary **6** 165
Stockholm
churches—cont.
Storkyrka **4** 781; **23** 255; **30** 67, 72, 93
altarpieces **13** 120; **23** *255*; **30** 83
monument to Jesper Kruus **30** 84
sculpture **13** 118
wall paintings **30** 76, 77
Ulrika Eleanora church **30** 70
City Library **2** 612; **19** 319; **30** 74, *74*
Concert Hall **30** 75
craftsmen and artists **11** 111
Customs House **30** 72
Dramatiska Teater **18** 802; **30** 74
Exchange **30** 72
exhibitions **29** *688*
Garrison Hospital **30** 73
Globe **14** 227
Gustav I statue **30** 85
Gustav II Adolf statue **30** 85
Gustav III statue **30** 86
Hall of Justice **30** 74
Home Exhibition of the Swedish Society of Arts, 1917 **8** 803
House of the Nobility *see* Riddarhus
Konsthögskolans Arkitektskola Library **30** 119
Kungliga Akademi för de Fria Konsterna **1** 105
library **30** 119
Kungliga Bibliotek **8** 455; **30** 119
Kungsträdgård **12** 114; **21** 815
Kunstbibliotek **30** 119
Lifeguards' Barracks *see* museums → Statens Historiska Museum
Metro stations **21** 350
museums
Dansmuseum **3** 120
Ekolsund Museum **7** 156
Etnografiska Museum
collections **7** 54; **14** 287; **17** 440; **21** 886; **29** 241
periodicals **24** 430
Gustav IIIs Antikmuseum *see under* palaces → Kungliga Slott
Hallwylska Museum **14** 88
Liljevalchs Konsthall **3** 784; **23** 207; **30** 74
Moderna Museum **1** 466; **9** 758; **21** 861; **29** 688; **30** 119
Museum of Far Eastern Antiquities *see* Östasiatiska Museum
Musikmuseum **22** 376
National Maritime Museum **23** 616
Nationalmuseets Arkiv **8** 455
Nationalmuseum **18** 802; **22** 362; **29** 863; **30** 73, 523
collections **4** 128; **8** 161, 455; **11** 234; **14** 80, 537, 692; **18** 635; **21** 85; **24** 834; **28** 462, 463; **30** 118, 119, 524
directors **3** 777
drawings **2** 708
frescoes **18** 801
paintings **18** 803
prints **25** 631
Nordiska Museum **2** 371; **7** 379; **23** 615; **30** 73, 91
library **2** 371
Östasiatiska Museum
collections **6** 321, 735, 826, 868, 925; **7** 156; **13** 864; **14** 287; **17** 815; **30** 119
directors **17** 816
exhibitions **33** 89
Prins Eugens Waldemarsudde **1** 466; **10** 648; **30** 91
RÖHSSKA Konstslöjdsmuseum **30** 119
Skansen **22** 540; **30** 91, 119; **32** 274
Stockholm
museums—cont.
Statens Historiska Museum **8** 649; **9** 156; **30** 73, 86
Thielska Galleri **30** 119, 730
Olympic Stadium **29** 489
Operakällare **4** 105
palaces
Bååth Palace **30** 70
Drottningholm Slott **29** *690*, 690–91*; **30** 70, 117, 467
beds **30** *93*
Chapel **11** 469
Court Theatre **29** 691; **30** 72, 90, *676*, 677
frames **11** 470, 472
furniture **30** 93, 94
gardens **11** 345; **12** 135
Gothic Tower **11** 242
interior decoration **11** 473; **13** 864
Kina Slott **1** 152; **29** 691; **30** 72
leather **19** 5
paintings **10** 100; **19** *136*, 137; **30** 78, *78*, 163
sculpture **30** 85; **32** *731*
stucco **29** 840
tapestries **3** 752
Kungliga Slott **29** *689*, 689–90*; **30** 66, 67, 68, 70, 117, 522–3
frames **11** 471
furniture **30** 92, 93, 95
gardens **12** 135
Gustav IIIs Antikmuseum **2** 165; **9** 23
interior decoration **4** 511; **11** 469, 470; **13** 864; **30** 88–9
paintings **11** 336
sculpture **30** 85
Slottskyrka **30** 93
stucco **29** 840
tapestries **30** 114
theatre **30** 675
Makalös Palace **18** 459–60; **30** 69
Rosendals Slott **30** 73, 90, *90*, 113
furniture **30** 95
paintings **33** 98
Wrangel Palace **30** 94
Parliament Building **30** 73
Petersenska House **9** 188; **30** 69, 84
Riddarhus **10** 100; **24** 222; **30** 70, 78
Royal Opera House **13** 864; **18** 802; **30** 72, 117, 677
Royal Palace *see* palaces → Kungliga Slott
Scharp House **30** 70
Skandia Cinema **2** 611; **7** 328
Skogskyrkogården *see* Woodland Cemetery
Stadhus **7** 668; **13** 204; **23** 615–16; **30** 74, 96, *96*; **31** 242, *242*
State Bank Building **30** 75
Stockholm Exhibition, 1930 **2** 612
synagogue **30** 73
Technological Institute **30** 73
Tullpackhus *see* Customs House
University **30** 118
Library **30** 75, 119
urban planning **31** 718
Van der Noot House **30** 70
Vitterhetsakademi Library **30** 119
Wasa *see under* SHIPS → named vessels
Wasavarv **30** 84
Woodland Cemetery **19** 283–4, *284*
chapel of the Resurrection **30** 75
World Trade Centre **29** *525*, 526
Stockholm Codex Aureus *see under* GOSPEL BOOKS → individual manuscripts
Stockhpaur, Hans **27** 665
Stocking, Thomas **10** 278
Stocking, William **4** 821
stockings **18** 157; **32** 390
Stöckl, Anselm **30** 34
Stockley, Henry **20** 590
Stockomer, Balthasar *see* STOCKAMER, BALTHASAR
Stockport (Ches)
Hazel Grove Church **21** 347
Town Hall **31** 241
stocks *see* GUN STOCKS
Stocks, Lumb **29** 691*
Stockt, Bernaert van der **20** 716, 747; **29** 691
Stockt, Jan van der **29** 691
Stockt, Michiel van der **29** 691
Stockt, Vrancke van der **3** 553; **8** 524; **20** 747; **29** 691–3*
collaboration **8** 501
teachers **5** 43
works **29** *692*
Stockton **23** 67
Stoclet, Adolphe **29** 693*
architecture **2** 567; **14** 628; **20** 203; **33** 166
Stoclet *Madonna* **9** 348
Stoczek Church **25** 130
Stodart & Currier **8** 276
Stoddard-Karmay, Heather **30** 848
Stoddart, Alexander
works **28** *243*
Stoddart, Sandy **28** 244
Stoecklin, Niklaus **22** 921; **25** 351; **30** 135
Stoeger Passion, Master of the **21** 337
Stoenescu, Eustaţiu **3** 88
Stoep, Reyner **4** 591
Stoer, Lorenz *see* STÖR, LORENZ
Stoer, Niklas *see* STÖR, NICLAS
Stoevere, Gheeraert de *see* GHEERAERT DE STOEVERE
Stoevere, Liévin de *see* LIÉVIN DE STOEVERE
Stoevig, Bernhard **12** 416
Stoffels & Co.
tea-services **22** *892*
Stöffler, Johann **12** 812
Stogursey (Somerset), St Andrew **26** 616
Stöhr, Martin **5** 792
Stöhrer, Walter **29** 693*
works **3** 803, *803*
Stoica, Master **26** 708
Stoichiţă, Graziella **26** 721
Stoicism **1** 176; **29** 693–4*
Stojanović, Sreten **13** 263; **28** 451, 453
Stojanović-Sip, D. **28** 451
Stojić, Vojin **28** 453
Stojko **22** 797
Stok, Jacobus van der **29** 432
Stoke (Staffs) **29** 495
Stoke-on-Trent (Staffs) *see* BURSLEM; FENTON; HANLEY; LONGTON; STOKE; TUNSTALL
Stoke Prior Bell Salt **27** 640
Stoke Prior Double Salt **10** 326
Stokes, Adrian **29** 694–5*
groups and movements **19** 591; **27** 563
paintings **32** 800
works **7** 631; **25** 683
Stokes, George Henry **2** 324; **10** 142; **24** 294; **27** 223
Stokes, I. N. Phelps **14** 812
Stokes, Leonard (Aloysius Scott Nasmyth) **29** 695*
groups and movements **9** 739
patrons and collectors **23** 473
staff **26** 336; **33** 342
teachers **29** 765
works **13** 875, *876*
Stokes, Marianne *see* PREINDELSBERGER, MARIANNE
Stokesay (Salop)
Castle **8** 277; **10** 269; **14** 76; **29** 22
St John the Baptist **24** 577
Stokoe, John **23** 20
Stokomer, Balthasar *see* STOCKAMER, BALTHASAR
Stokowski, Leopold **26** 531
Stolac **4** *459*
gravestones **4** *461*
stolas **9** 246
Stolba, Leopold **28** 344
Stolberg **4** 688
brass **4** 688, *689*
Stolberg, Louisa Maria von, Countess of Albany *see* STUART, LOUISA MARIA VON STOLBERG, Countess of Albany
Stoldo Rinieri, Bernardo di *see* RINIERI, BERNARDO DI STOLDO
stoles (ecclesiastical) **2** *84*; **9** 642–3; **32** 389*
stoles (secular) **21** 394
Stolf, Francisco **31** 816
Stolichny bank **27** 440
Stolitsa i Usad'ba **27** 580
Stoll, Beverly *see* PEPPER, BEVERLY
Stolle, Juliusz **25** 124
Stolle, Rudi **21** 67
Stolling, Reinecke **12** 410
works **12** *410*
Stollmeyer, Hugh **31** 335
Stołpie Castle **4** 782
Stoltenberg, Matthias **29** 696*
Stoltikov, Count **27** 583
Stöltzel, Samuel **4** 493; **14** 766; **32** 449
Stolz, Michael **8** 618
Stolz, Rudolf **15** 866
Stolzenfels Schloss **13** 202
Stolzer, Eugen **17** 855
Stölzl, Gunta **12** 468; **16** 789; **28** 556; **29** 696*; **30** 327
groups and movements **3** 402; **12** 470
works **11** 54; **12** 468; **30** *328*
Stölzle **2** 818
Stom, Matthias **29** 696–7*
attributions **20** 640
groups and movements **30** 456
works **11** 393; **29** *697*
stomachers **17** 524
Stombuco, Andrea Giovanni **2** 738; **29** 698*
Stomer, Matthias *see* STOM, MATTHIAS
Stomfa **15** 2
Stomme, Hans Verhagen der *see* VERHAGEN DER STOMME, HANS
Stomme van Kampen, de *see* AVERCAMP, HENDRICK (BARENTSZ.)
Ston
Church of the Archangel Michael **22** 16; **28** 445
St Blaise **25** 332
stone **25** 484; **29** 698*, 703*, 706–7*
cleaning **29** *710*, 712–13
conservation **7** 747; **29** 707–13*, *708*
historical and regional traditions
Africa **1** 292*, 296, 305, 350, 377; **18** *217*, *219*
Algeria **1** 305
Anatolia, ancient **1** 823
Ancient Near East **9** 150
Antilles, Greater **2** *145*
Arabia **2** 253–8, 271–3
Argentina **29** *190*
Austria **26** *634*, 634–5*
Aztec **2** 906–7, *907*; **21** 218
Bactria **6** 216–17
Bangladesh **15** *502*
Belgium **3** *568*, 575, 578; **13** 98–101*, *99*, *100*; **26** 630–31*
Berber **1** 305
Bhutan **3** 913
Britain **26** 611–12*; **32** 276

stone
historical and regional traditions—cont.
Buddhism 6 221, 428; 15 454, 500, 501, 505, 778, 782; 18 295; 22 758, 758–9, 770, 771; 30 593–5*, 594, 823
China 6 706, 713, 718–19
Burma 5 226, 239
Byzantine 1 694; 9 538, 562, 589*, 594–9*; 27 827
Caribbean Islands 5 748
Catalonia 26 609–10*
Celtic 6 156
Central Asia, Eastern 6 315
Central Asia, Western 6 216–17, 220, 221, 224, 260; 16 199
Champa 6 428, 429
China 6 644–5*, 706, 725, 726; 7 94, 128, 130
Han period (206 BC-AD 220) 6 697, 697, 727, 727–30, 728
Ming period (1368-1644) 7 18
Northern and Southern Dynasties (AD 310-589) 6 729
Qing period (1644-1911) 6 704; 7 19
Shang period (c. 1600-c. 1050 BC) 6 726
Song period (AD 960-1279) 6 718–19, 731
Sui period (AD 581-618) 6 713
Tang period (AD 618-907) 6 730
Yuan period (1279-1368) 7 130
Colombia 27 700; 29 143
Costa Rica 9 677–9, 678, 679; 29 143
Crete 21 656, 659, 689–90
Archaic 8 154
Croatia 8 177
Cyprus, ancient 27 825
Czech Republic 4 698, 844; 8 379, 382; 24 190; 26 637–8*
Denmark 8 721, 737; 26 640*; 27 167
Early Christian (c. AD 250-843) 1 693, 693; 9 538, 562, 589–92*, 594–7*; 27 827; 30 776
Easter Island 9 674–5, 675; 23 715
Ecuador 20 317; 29 145
Egypt 16 176
Egypt, ancient 2 296; 9 779, 812–16*, 825, 855, 864, 865, 886; 10 71–4*, 73; 22 159; 25 761; 27 811, 824, 825; 30 433
Ejagham 10 123*, 123
England 1 707; 10 224, 236; 11 254; 13 80–83*, 81, 83, 84, 84–5*; 26 613–17*, 617; 32 529
Estonia 10 538
Ethiopia 1 305
Etruscan 6 388; 10 588, 602, 606–8; 27 826; 32 744
France 1 693, 707; 9 191; 11 558; 13 72–9*, 74, 75, 76; 25 544; 26 596–9*, 596, 600–604*, 609–10*; 32 278
Gothic 13 78
Prehistoric 25 502–3*
Georgia 12 318
Germany 1 709; 4 776; 6 156; 13 86–7, 88; 22 264, 692, 693; 26 632, 632–3*, 634*; 32 281, 679
Gothic 1 709; 5 430; 8 382; 9 191; 13 72–9*, 74, 75, 76, 78, 80–83*, 81, 84, 84–5*, 86–92*, 88, 93–108*, 93, 99, 100, 103, 104, 107, 109; 22 264, 692, 693

stone
historical and regional traditions—cont.
Greece, ancient 1 692; 8 262; 13 376, 386–9*, 388, 389, 393, 435–6*, 439, 445, 543; 22 160; 29 710
Guinea 1 292
Hinduism 6 429, 449; 15 463, 482, 484, 488, 502, 503, 504; 22 767, 767–8, 768, 770, 770, 771
Holy Roman Empire (before 1648) 13 85*, 86–7*; 26 631–5*, 632, 634
Hungary 26 638*
Inca 29 186
Indian subcontinent 4 794; 15 253–6*, 412, 414, 417–20*, 452, 502, 505; 27 844*; 29 444
Islamic 16 239
2nd cent. AD 15 454
5th cent. AD 15 463
7th cent. AD 15 500, 503
9th cent. AD 15 482, 484, 487
10th cent. AD 15 488
11th cent. 15 414, 501, 504, 540
13th cent. 15 539
Indonesia 4 420; 15 777, 778, 782; 27 831
Indus civilization 15 417–20*
Insular art 7 460
Iran 16 199
Iraq 16 150
Ireland 1 468; 7 460; 12 6; 26 618, 618–19
Islamic 6 557; 16 141, 142, 243, 255, 256, 269; 20 166; 21 630
Central Asia, Western 16 199
Egypt 16 176
Indian subcontinent 16 239
Iran 16 199
Iraq 16 150
Ottoman 16 266
Syria 16 182
Turkey 16 186, 266
Italy 5 430; 7 516, 517; 13 87–92*, 93–8*, 93; 16 692; 26 619*, 620*, 620, 621*, 622–4*, 625–8*; 32 744
Jamaica 16 885
Japan 17 59, 102*, 398, 400
Java 15 777, 778, 782
Jerusalem, Latin Kingdom of 26 629*
Kissi 1 292; 18 89–91, 90
Kongo 1 292; 18 217, 219
Korea 18 264, 265, 266, 271, 281, 298–9, 299
16th cent. 18 295
20th cent. 18 301
Malaysia 20 166
Malta (Republic of) 20 210
Manteño culture 20 317; 29 145
Maori 23 715
Mariana Islands 23 715
Mesoamerica, Pre-Columbian 2 907; 8 460; 21 206; 30 340–41; 33 103
Mesopotamia 9 538
Mexico 2 907; 8 460; 21 400
Micronesia, Federated States of 23 716
Minoan 21 656, 659, 689–90
Morocco 1 305
Nabataea 24 557
Native North Americans 21 718
Nepal 6 449; 22 758, 758–9, 766–8*, 767, 768, 770, 770–71*, 771, 773–4*
Netherlands, the 13 98–101*; 26 630–31*
Nigeria 1 292
Norway 26 639*
Olmec 21 218
Ottoman 16 266

stone
historical and regional traditions—cont.
Ottonian 23 646–7
Pacific Islands 23 715*, 716
Pakistan 23 803
Palestine 9 538
Panama 29 144; 32 239
Peru 19 385
Poland 26 636, 636–7*; 31 394
Portugal 13 101–2*; 26 611*
Prehistoric art 16 615; 25 473, 476, 488, 491, 492–4*, 498, 512, 515–16*, 518, 524, 544; 29 444; 32 679
Bronze Age 25 518, 530*
Neolithic 25 502–3*
Romanesque 8 382; 26 594–5*, 596–9*, 596, 600–605*, 606*, 608, 608–10*, 611–12*, 613–17*, 617, 618, 618–19*, 620*, 620, 621*, 622–4*, 625–9*, 630–38*, 632, 634, 636, 639–40*
Rome, ancient 2 297; 26 874–5*, 875, 879
Russia 27 368
Samoa 23 715
San Agustín culture 27 700
Scandinavia 13 102–3*; 26 639–40*; 31 363; 32 513
Scotland 24 737, 737–8; 26 617
Sicily 26 628–9*
Sierra Leone 1 292
Sogdiana 6 220
South America, Pre-Columbian 9 677–9, 678, 679; 20 317; 27 700; 29 143, 144, 185, 186, 190; 30 240
Panama 32 239
Veraguas culture 32 238–9, 239
South-east Asia 29 227–8
Spain 13 103–8*, 107, 109; 26 604–5*, 606–7*, 608, 608–9*
Sumatra 27 831
Sweden 13 103; 26 639*; 30 66
Switzerland 26 635*
Syria 9 538; 16 182
Syria-Palestine 20 410; 30 179, 181, 183, 190
Tairona 30 240
Tajikistan 33 510
Tarascan 30 340–41
Thailand 29 227–8; 30 593–5*, 594, 633
Tibet 30 823
Tokharistan 6 221
Tonga (Pacific Islands) 23 715
Tuareg 1 305
Turkey 16 186, 266
Turkmenistan 6 224
Ukraine 31 546, 547
Veraguas culture 32 238–9, 239
Vietnam 6 428, 429; 29 227–8; 32 472, 478, 489
Viking 32 513, 529
Wales 32 787
West Mexico 33 103
Zapotec 8 460
Zimbabwe 1 292, 305; 33 679
patinas 24 258
technical examination 29 711; 30 393, 397, 399, 404–6*, 406, 409
techniques
abrasion 29 706*
carving *see* STONE-CARVINGS
drilling 29 705–6*
engraving 25 492–3*
flaking 25 530
painting 25 493
polishing 29 706*
sawing 29 155
splitting 29 703–4*
uses
altarpieces 1 707, 709, 709

stone
uses—cont.
altars 1 692, 693, 693, 694; 6 704
arches 2 296, 297
architectural decorations 16 142
architecture 1 305; 2 362; 16 150
Africa 1 377
Bhutan 3 913
Britain 32 276
Burma 5 226
Byzantine 9 538
Central Asia, Western 16 199
China 6 644–5*
Czech Republic 8 379
Denmark 8 721
Early Christian (c. AD 250-843) 9 538
Egypt 16 176
Egypt, ancient 9 779, 825; 25 761; 27 811
France 32 278
Georgia 12 318–19
Germany 32 281
Greece, ancient 13 386–9*
Indian subcontinent 4 794; 16 239
Iran 16 199
Islamic 16 141, 176, 182, 186, 199, 239, 266, 269
Korea 18 264, 265, 266
Malta (Republic of) 20 210–11
Micronesia, Federated States of 23 716
Ottoman 16 266
Pacific Islands 23 715, 716
Prehistoric art 25 498, 502–3*
Rome, ancient 26 874–5*
Russia 27 368
Scandinavia 31 363
South America, Pre-Columbian 30 240
Sweden 30 66
Syria 16 182
Syria-Palestine 30 190
Tairona 30 240
Turkey 16 186, 266
Ukraine 31 546
beads 1 296, 297; 3 441; 9 815; 30 633
beakers 10 72
bosses 13 83; 22 693
bowls 29 186
bracelets 1 350
bridges 4 802*; 18 281; 19 385; 26 749
busts 6 429; 24 190, 557
caryatids 11 558
chairs 6 388; 20 317
chess sets 6 557
churches 4 776; 9 538; 27 167; 31 547
concrete 26 874
crosses 1 468; 7 460; 24 737; 32 787
doors 9 150
figurines 2 145; 9 677, 865; 15 417–20*; 25 488; 29 143, 185
floors 3 575, 577, 578
fonts (baptismal) 9 191; 11 252*, 254
fortifications 21 559, 561–2
furniture 26 875
game-pieces 31 266
grounds 6 224
houses 3 575
inkstones 7 94
jars 10 74
lacquer 7 18, 19
lithography 25 600
mansions 12 6
masks 5 748
masonry 20 559, 560, 573, 574
metates 32 238–9, 239
minbars 21 630
mirrors 21 718

stone
uses—cont.
mosaics 9 562; 13 556; 16 255, 256; 22 154, 155, 159
mosques 20 166
moulds 25 530
musical instruments 32 489
netsuke 17 398, 400
pagodas 6 668; 18 261
pillars 6 156
plinths 13 389
polychromy 13 393
pounders 25 896
pulpits 26 626, 627
railings 27 844*
relief sculpture 2 253–6
Champa 6 429
Croatia 8 177
Czech Republic 8 382
Estonia 10 538
Gothic 13 103
Indian subcontinent 15 454, 539, 540
Italy 16 692
Mexico 2 907; 8 460
Sweden 13 103
rondelles (sculpture) 25 493
roofs 27 131
sarcophagi 10 607–8; 17 59; 27 824, 825, 826, 827, 828, 831
sculpture 4 420; 10 702; 15 452; 16 243; 20 210; 21 400; 33 679
Africa 18 217, 219
Arabia 2 253, 256–8
Argentina 29 190
Austria 26 634, 634–5*
Aztec 2 906–7
Bactria 6 217
Bangladesh 15 502
Belgium 13 98–101*, 99, 100; 26 630–31*
Britain 26 611–12*
Buddhism 6 221, 428, 706, 713, 718; 15 500, 501, 505, 778, 782; 18 295; 22 758, 758–9, 770, 771; 30 593–5*, 594, 823
Burma 5 239
Byzantine 9 589*, 594–9*
Catalonia 26 609–10*
Central Asia, Western 6 216–17, 220, 221
Champa 6 428
China 6 706, 718–19, 725, 726, 727, 727–30, 728, 729, 730, 731
China: Sui period (AD 581-618) 6 713
Colombia 27 700
Costa Rica 9 677–9, 678, 679
Czech Republic 4 698, 844; 26 637–8*
Denmark 8 737; 26 640*
Early Christian (c. AD 250-843) 9 589*, 594–7*
Easter Island 9 674–5, 675
Egypt, ancient 9 815*, 855, 886
Ejagham 10 123*, 123
England 13 80–83*, 81, 84, 84–5*; 26 613–17*, 617; 32 529; 33 62
Etruscan 10 602, 606–8; 32 744
France 13 72–9*; 26 596–9*, 600–601*, 603–4*, 609–10*
France: Baroque 11 558
France: Gothic 13 74, 75, 76, 78; 24 157
France: Late Gothic 19 138
France: Prehistoric 25 544
France: primitivism 12 194
France: Romanesque 26 596, 601–3*
France: 20th cent 21 787
Germany 13 86–7, 88; 22 264, 692; 26 632, 632–3*, 634*

stone
uses
sculpture—cont.
Gothic **5** *430*; **13** 72–9*, *74*, *75*, *76*, *78*, 80–83*, *81*, *84*, 84–5*, 86–92*, *88*, 93–108*, *93*, *99*, *100*, *107*, *109*; **22** *264*, *692*; **33** *62*
Greece, ancient **8** 262; **13** 435–6*, 439; **29** *710*
Hinduism **6** *449*; **15** *463*, *482*, *484*, *488*, *502*, *503*, *504*; **22** *767*, 767–8, *768*, 770, *770*, 771
Holy Roman Empire (before 1648) **13** 85*, 86–7*; **26** 631–5*, *632*, *634*
Hungary **26** 638*
Indian subcontinent **15** 412, 414, *414*, *463*, *482*, *484*, *487*, *488*, *500*, *501*, *502*, *503*, *504*, *505*; **23** 832
Indonesia **15** 777, *778*, *782*
Ireland **26** *618*, 618–19
Italy **13** 87–92*, 93–8*, *93*; **26** 619*, 620*, *620*, 621*, 622–4*, 625*, 626–8*; **32** 744
Japan **17** 102
Java **15** 777, *781*, *783*
Jerusalem, Latin Kingdom of **26** 629*
Kongo **18** *217*, *219*
Korea **18** 295, 298–9, *299*, 301
Mesoamerica, Pre-Columbian **30** 340–41; **33** *103*
Nepal **6** *449*; **22** *758*, 758–9, 766–8*, *767*, *768*, *770*, 770–71*, *771*, 773–4*
Netherlands, the **13** 98–101*; **26** 630–31*
Norway **26** 639*
Ottonian **23** 646–7
Panama **29** *144*
Poland **26** *636*, 636–7*; **31** *394*
Portugal **13** 101–2*; **26** 611*
Prehistoric art **25** 512, *544*
Romanesque **26** 594–5*, *596*, 596–9*, 600–605*, 606–7*, *608*, 608–10*, 611–12*, 613–14*, 615–17*, *617*, *618*, 618–19*, 620*, *620*, 621*, 622–4*, 625–9*, 630–38*, *632*, *634*, *636*, 639–40*, *640*
San Agustín culture **27** *700*
Scandinavia **13** 102–3*; **26** 639–40*; **32** 513
Sicily **26** 628–9*
Sogdiana **6** 220
South America, Pre-Columbian **9** 677–9, *678*, *679*; **27** *700*; **29** *144*, *190*
Spain **13** 103–8*, *107*, *109*; **26** 604–5*, 606–7*, *608*, 608–9*
Sweden **26** 639*, *640*
Switzerland **26** 635*
Syria-Palestine **20** *410*
Tarascan **30** 340–41
Thailand **30** 593–5*, *594*
Tibet **30** 823
Vietnam **6** *428*; **32** 478
Viking **32** 513, 529
West Mexico **33** *103*
seals **6** 315; **7** 128, 130
stairs **21** 206
statuettes **18** 89–91, *90*; **29** *143*
stools **5** 748; **9** 679
stripwork **29** 775
temples **13** 376, 445; **15** 253–6*; **30** 433; **32** 472
theatres **26** 749
thrones **30** 776
tombs **6** 697, *697*; **18** 271; **25** 524
tools **16** 615; **25** 473, 476, 493–4*, 515–16*; **29** 227–8, 444; **32** 679
toys **31** 254, 258

stone
uses—cont.
tracery **31** 270
trays **33** *510*
tympana **26** *600*
urns **10** 588, 607, 608
vaults (ceiling) **26** 874
vessels
Arabia **2** 271–3*
Bahrain **2** 272
Crete **21** 656, 689–90*
Cycladic **8** 308, 317*, *317*
Egypt, ancient **9** *814*, 814–15*, 864; **10** 71–4*, *73*
Minoan **21** 656, 659, 689–90*
wall paintings **13** 543
walls **26** *875*, 879
weapons **6** 260
see also LITHICS
Stone (iii) (family) **29** 715*
Stone, Alfred E. **25** 666
Stone, Arthur J. **4** 480; **31** 651
works **4** *480*
stone, artificial *see* ARTIFICIAL STONE
Stone, Benjamin
works **19** *614*
Stone, Carpenter & Willson **25** 666
works **25** *666*
stone, china *see* CHINA STONE
Stone, Doris **14** 716
Stone, Edward A. **7** 327; **22** 60
Stone, Edward Durrell **29** 716*
works **16** 94; **22** 365; **23** 799, 904; **30** 468; **32** 888
Stone (ii), Frank **20** 239; **29** 715–16*
Stone (i), Henry **29** 714–16*
stone, imitation *see* IMITATION STONE
Stone (i), John **29** 715–16*
assistants **5** 263; **7** 297
collaboration **29** 715
Stone (ii), Marcus **3** 646; **8** 863; **22** 744; **29** 716*
Stone, Michelle **28** 798
Stone (i), Nicholas, I (1586/7-1647) **18** 11; **19** 582; **29** 713–16*
attributions **8** 38
collaboration **17** 616
pupils **18** 8, 11
teachers **16** 892
works **1** 520; **2** 545; **5** 764; **10** 262, 263; **19** 509, 568, 599, 605; **22** 858; **23** 686; **27** 357; **29** *714*; **31** 122
Stone (i), Nicholas, II (1618-1647) **29** 715*
personal collection **30** 495
Stone, Reynolds **4** 367, 373; **19** 606
Stone, Symon **29** 716–17*
Stone Age *see under* PREHISTORIC ART → periods
stone-carvings **29** 704–5*
historical and regional traditions
Africa **1** 292
Ancient Near East **24** *335*
Anglo-Saxon **2** 68–72*, *69*, *70*, *71*
Antilles, Lesser **29** 200
Aztec **2** *906*; **21** *223*, *224*
Belarus' **3** 530
Bosnia **4** *461*
Britain **25** 513
Caribbean Islands **5** 748
Catalonia **26** 595
Celtic **6** *156*, 161
Chavín culture **6** *521*
Chican-Taíno culture **29** *199*, 200
Colombia **29** 155
Corsica **11** 78
Crete **8** 153
Denmark **17** *474*; **32** *517*
Dominican Republic **29** *199*
Ecuador **29** 155
Egypt, ancient **9** 815; **29** 704

stone-carvings
historical and regional traditions—cont.
England
Anglo-Saxon **2** 68–72*, *69*, *70*, *71*
Romanesque **4** *465*
Viking **2** 71*; **26** *409*; **32** 516, 523, *529*
France **12** *211*; **26** 595
Germany
Celtic **6** *156*
Merovingian **21** *164*
Migration period **21** *502*
Romanesque **26** 595
Ife (kingdom of) **1** 292
Inca **15** 163; **29** 145
Indian subcontinent **15** 338
Insular art **15** *876*
Ireland **15** *876*; **23** 23, *24*
Islamic **2** *245*; **15** 338
Isle of Man **32** 523, 530*
Jamaica **16** *885*
Japan **17** 348–9
Jordan **24** *335*
Korea **18** *299*
La Tène culture (*c.* 450-.*c* 50 BC) **6** *156*
Maldives, Republic of **20** 189
Merovingian **21** *164*
Mesoamerica, Pre-Columbian
Aztec **2** *906*; **21** *223*, *224*
Classic (*c.* AD 250-*c.* 900) **21** *221*
Maya region **21** *221*
Olmec **6** *394*; **18** 645; **23** 418
Zapotec **22** *8*
Mexico **2** *906*; **6** *394*; **18** 645; **21** *374*
Migration period **21** *502*
Minoan **8** 153
Native North Americans **22** 573
Nigeria **15** 107
Norway **32** *518*
Nubia **21** *160*
Olmec **5** 761; **6** *393*; **18** 645; **23** 418
Peru **6** *350*, *521*; **29** *169*, *170*, *171*
Pictish art **24** 737–8
Prehistoric art **12** *211*; **23** 23, *24*; **25** *512*, 513, 529–30*
Puerto Rico **25** 699, *699*; **29** *199*
Romanesque **4** *465*; **26** 594–5
Sardinia **25** 530
Scandinavia **25** 513
Viking **32** 516, *517*, *518*, *522*, 523, *523*, *524*, 525*
Scotland **25** *512*
Scythian **28** 321
Shona **1** 429
Sicily **6** 30
Sierra Leone **1** 263
South America, Pre-Columbian **6** *350*, *521*; **29** 155, *169*, *170*, *171*, *199*, 200
Spain **2** *245*
Sweden **32** *518*, *522*, *523*, *524*
Tairona **29** 155
Valdivia culture **29** 155
Viking **32** 525*
Borre style **32** 516
Denmark **32** *517*
England **2** 71*; **32** 516, 523, *529*
Isle of Man **32** 523, 530*
Mammen style **17** *474*; **32** *517*
Norway **32** *518*
Ringerike style **26** *409*; **32** *518*
Sweden **32** *518*, *522*, *523*, *524*
Urnes style **32** *518*
Yoruba **15** 107
Zapotec **22** *8*
materials
andesite (volcanic) **21** *223*
chisels **29** 704
tools **29** *704*, 704–5

stone-carvings—cont.
processes
pointing *see* POINTING (i) (SCULPTURE)
stone circles **2** *850*; **21** 41; **25** 505*, *505*, 522; **29** *717*, 717
Stone City Colony **33** 344
Stone Drum Inscriptions **6** 739, 766
Stone Head of the Virgin, Master of the **22** 856
Stonehenge (Wilts) **10** *225*, 226; **14** 387; **21** 40; **25** *470*, 505; **29** *717*, 717–18*; **30** 434
archaeology **2** 299, 323; **30** 405
construction **21** 41, *41*, 42; **23** 338; **24** 750; **25** 505–6, 522
Stonehouse (Devon), Royal Naval Hospital **14** 783
stone ink *see under* INKS → types
Stoneleigh Abbey (Warks) **17** 915; **26** 613
Stone of the Five Suns **2** 907
stones **17** 366
stones, standing *see* MENHIRS; MONOLITHS
Stones of Steness **25** 505
stone-throwers **21** 557
stonewares **6** 325*, 330
historical and regional traditions
Australia **2** *762*
Belgium **3** 588, 589*, *592*
Cambodia **5** 506*, *506*
Canada **5** 581
China **6** 868, 869, 870, 871, 872, 873, 875, 879, 880, 881, 884, 885, 886, *886*, 892, *892*, *893*, 895, *895*, *900*, *917*; **7** *94*; **17** *595*; **28** *618*
Denmark **8** 748
England **10** *304*, 304–5, 306, 308, *312*, *314*
France **11** 604
Germany **12** 428–30*, *429*
Hungary **15** 2
Islamic **16** 406
Japan **17** 249–50, *250*, *252*, *255*, *256*, *261*, 262–3*, *263*, *268*, 350, 352, 353; **18** *554*; **27** 699; **31** *77*
Edo period (1600-1868) **17** *254*, *257*, *258*; **18** *555*; **23** *196*, *365*, *366*
Heian period (AD 794-1185) **17** *251*, 252
Khmer **5** *506*; **30** 610–11, *611*
Korea **18** 332–3, 335, *335*, 336, *336*, 337–9*, *338*, *339*, 340–42*, *340*, *341*, *342*
Netherlands, the **22** 877
Norway **23** 235
Portugal **23** 455
Ryūkyū Islands **27** 470
Scotland **28** 258
South Africa **29** *117*
Sweden **30** 99
Syria **16** 406
Thailand **30** *610*, 610–11, *611*
United States of America **31** 635–7, *640*
Vietnam **32** 484
materials
clay **23** *365*
copper oxides **18** 339, *340*
enamel **6** 872; **18** *554*, *555*; **23** *196*
glazes **5** 506; **6** 328, 329, 872, 873, 893; **17** 350, 352; **18** *335*, 337, 338; **27** 699; **32** 484
gold **18** 339
inlays **18** *339*, 341
iron oxide **18** 339, 342, *342*
slip **18** 339, 342
techniques
impressing **6** 892
incising **6** 892
moulding **6** 893, 899
stamping **18** 341, *341*

stonewares—cont.
uses
bottles **6** *896*; **10** *304*; **12** *429*; **17** *256*, *258*
bowls **6** *897*; **18** *336*, *555*; **30** *611*
ewers **17** *254*
figurines **28** *618*
flasks **17** *252*, *257*
jars **6** *886*; **17** *255*, *257*, *260*; **21** *64*; **23** *196*; **31** *77*
jugs **3** *589*
mugs **10** *304*
pillows **6** *895*
pitchers **17** *251*
pots **2** *762*; **5** *506*; **10** *314*; **30** *611*
teabowls **17** *255*, *256*, *595*
tea-caddies **17** *255*
tea ceremonies **17** 262–3
vases **10** *312*; **17** *254*, *261*, *268*; **18** *554*; **30** *610*
Stöng **32** 533
Stonorov, Oskar **14** 811; **29** 718*
collaboration **17** 723, 838
staff **32** 234
Stonor Park (Oxon) **4** 770, *770*
Holy Trinity chapel tower **4** 779
Stonyhurst (Lancs) **30** 872
Stonyhurst Gospels *see* GOSPEL BOOKS → individual mss → St Cuthbert Gospel of St John
stools
historical and regional traditions
Africa **1** 353, 365–6, *366*
Ancient Near East **30** 774
Asante **1** 353; **2** *585*, 585–6*
Bahamas, the **3** 59
Bamileke **3** *147*, 147–8
Bamum **3** 152
Baule **3** 407
Belgium **3** 581
Cameroon **1** 365
Caribbean Islands **5** 748
China **7** 34, 39, 145
Colombia **7** *603*
Costa Rica **9** 679
Egypt, ancient **10** 51, 52–3; **23** *533*
England **10** *290*
Etruscan **10** *633*, 634
Finland **8** *803*
France **11** 587
Hemba **1** 365
Italy **10** *633*
Java **30** 785
Kota (ii) (Gabon peoples) **18** 404
Liberia **1** 365
Luba **19** 740*, *740*
South America, Pre-Columbian **9** 679; **29** 134
Tabwa **1** *366*
Valdivia culture **29** 134
Zaïre **1** *366*
Zambia **1** 365
materials
beadwork **3** *147*, 148
birch **8** *803*
brass **2** *585*; **3** 148
bronze **6** 388
glass **2** *585*
gold **1** 353; **2** *585*
iron **6** 388
ivory **10** 52
leather **10** 52
stone **5** 748; **9** 679
wood **1** 365, *366*; **3** *147*; **5** 748; **14** *55*, *378*; **19** *740*
types
caryatid **14** 378, *378*
dujos **14** 54, *55*
folding **6** 388; **16** 516; **30** 775, 776
footstools **6** 388; **30** 774, 779
Early Christian (*c.* AD 250-843) **30** 776
Egypt, ancient **30** 775
Helladic **14** 354

stools
types
footstools—cont.
Hemba **1** 365
pouffes **6** 391
Stoop, Dirck (Willemsz.) **29** 718–19*
Stoop, Maerten (Willemsz.) **29** 718; **33** 26
Stoop, Petrus Paulus **3** 763
Stoop, Willem Jansz. **29** 718
Stopany, D. **29** 691
Stopendael, Bastiaen **18** 73; **29** 7
Stopforth, Paul **29** 109, 113
stoppers **14** 763
stopping-out *see under* ETCHINGS → techniques; WATERCOLOURS → techniques
Stoppino, Giotto **13** 629
Stör, Lorenz **2** 716; **12** 421; **26** 533; **29** 719–20*
Stör, Niclas **25** 621; **29** 719–20*
Storace, Claudio **3** 195
Stora Väsby **30** 89
Storch, F. L. **14** 607
Storck (i), Abraham **29** 720–21*
works **20** 424; **29** *720*
Storck, Carol **26** 715; **29** 721
Storck (ii), Friederic **29** 721*
Storck, H. B. **8** 727; **14** 572
Storck, Henri **18** 577
Storck (i), Jacobus **29** 720*
Storck, Josef von **2** 814; **29** 721–2*
works **2** 808; **18** 101; **19** 522
Storck (ii), Karl **5** 73; **26** 725; **29** 721*
pupils **12** 316; **31** 802
works **23** 472; **26** 714
Storehouse **7** 725
storehouses **15** 162; **17** 55; **21** 559; **22** *494*; **23** *219*
Store Kongensgade Faience Factory **8** 747–8; **30** 97, 883
production **8** *747*
Storer, Bartholomäus **29** 722
Storer, Johann Christophorus **12** 390; **18** 46; **29** 722*
Storer, John **33** 403
Storer, Maria Longworth *see* NICHOLS, MARIA LONGWORTH
stores, department *see* DEPARTMENT STORES
Storey, Ellsworth Prime, II **29** 722*
Storey, G. A. **27** 564
Storey Brothers **18** 127
storeyed pavilion pagodas *see under* PAGODAS → types
Storez, Maurice **3** 675
Storff, Paul **22** 418
Storia della città **24** 449
Storia dell'arte **24** 449
Störklin, Johann Joseph **20** 915
Storm, Graeme **23** 69
Storm, Per Palle **1** 12; **14** 229
Storm, William George **5** 572; **8** 264; **11** 836; **23** 632; **31** 176
Stormont (Co. Down)
Parliament Buildings **16** 39
St Molua's **16** 42
Storm van 's Gravesande, Carel Nicolaas **29** 722–3*
Storm van 's-Gravesande, Laurens **13** 875; **30** 14
Stornaloco, Gabriele **1** 748; **2** 347; **20** 566; **21** 531
works **21** *531*
Storne, Ferenc **29** 75
Storr, Paul **29** 723*
collaboration **10** 334
groups and movements **26** 85
patrons and collectors **3** 476
works **3** 79; **10** 334, *334*, 335; **27** 336
Storr & Co. **27** 336; **29** 723
Storrer, Johann Christophorus *see* STORER, JOHANN CHRISTOPHORUS
Storr & Mortimer **27** 336; **29** 723
Storrs, John **20** 604; **31** 613
Storrs, Ronald **3** 883; **17** 492
Storrs Hall **5** 169
Störtenbecker, Nikolaus **33** 627
Stortenbeker, Pieter **2** 224; **20** 435
Story, Edith Marion *see* PERUZZI DE MEDICI, EDITH MARION, Marchesa
Story, Julian Russell **29** 724
Story, Waldo **29** 724
Story, William Wetmore **29** 723–4*; **31** 611
Story-Maskelyne, Nevil **19** 519
Stosch, Philipp, Baron von **1** 533; **2** 559; **29** 724*
collections **12** 473
gems **12** 262; **31** 481
manuscripts **24** 240
paintings **12** 534, 536
sculpture **14** 652
writings **12** 262, 266
illustrated **25** 549
Stoskopff, Sebastien **11** 535; **27** 724; **29** 725–6*
teachers **4** 747; **12** 389
works **29** 668, *725*; **31** 882
Stoss, Andreas **29** 729
Stoss, Florian **29** 726
Stoss, Johannes **28** 696; **29** 726
Stoss, Martin **25** 126; **29** 726
Stoss, Matthias **25** 126; **29** 726
Stoss, Stanislas **18** 427, 430; **29** 726
Stoss, Veit, the elder (*c*. 1445/50–*c*. 1533) **12** 401; **13** 91; **23** 307; **25** 126; **26** 712; **28** 193; **29** 726–31*
assistants **14** 835; **24** 331
attributions **18** 452; **20** 705
groups and movements **26** 186
metalwork **23** 311
paintings **18** 427; **23** 316–17
altarpieces **1** 710; **11** 455; **13** 117–18; **25** 117, 134, 140
icons **27** 159
patrons and collectors **13** 822; **28** 492
sculpture
altarpieces **3** 143; **12** 401; **25** 111; **29** *727, 730*
crucifixes **8** 214, 215
monuments **2** 800; **23** 314; **25** 129
religious **23** 309; **29** *728, 729*
statuettes **29** 570
tomb **13** 92; **18** 432
Stoss, Veit, the younger (*d* before 1531) **29** 726
Stoss, Willibald **29** 726
Stössel **20** 803
Stothard, Charles Alfred **29** 732–3*
works **19** 611, *611*
Stothard, Thomas **5** 272; **29** 731–2*
book illustrations **26** 541
collaboration **14** 810
patrons and collectors **22** 314; **26** 541; **33** 251
reproductive prints by others **10** 378; **14** 280; **18** 149; **26** 473; **28** 86, 597; **29** 675
works **3** 79; **7** 413; **8** 186; **10** 334; **19** 483; **27** 336; **28** 558; **29** *732*
Stotz, Paul **19** 661
Stötzer, Werner **29** 733*
Stoudena, Church of the Archangel Michael **5** 156
Studios **16** 580, 600
Stoudios, Theodore of *see* THEODORE OF STOUDIOS
Stoudt, John Jacob **31** 634
Stouf, Jean-Baptiste **4** 618; **6** 516; **11** 561; **29** 733*
Stoughton, William **7** 702
stoups **7** 282, 835; **31** *567*
Stourbridge (Wilts) **10** 320
Stourhead (Wilts) **3** 173; **5** *539*; **10** *225*, 233; **14** 597–8; **23** 856; **29** 733–5*, *734*; **32** 553
collections **2** 27; **9** 28
Stourhead (Wilts)—cont.
frames **11** 426
furniture **7** 172; **10** 294; **13** 634; **16** 746; **26** 85
gardens **10** 361; **12** 61, 129, 130; **22** 740
sculpture **6** 528
Market Cross **29** 707
paintings **8** 455; **9** 18; **11** 411; **14** 598; **15** 148; **18** 642; **20** 378; **23** 874; **26** 335
Pantheon **2** 541
portico **25** 266
sculpture **19** 250; **27** 468
watercolours **9** 366
Stout, Renée **1** 438
stoves **11** 119
historical and regional traditions
Austria **2** 815
Belgium **3** 575, 588
Finland **11** 105
Germany **12** 410, 411
Hungary **14** 904
Norway **23** 237
Russia **27** *400*
Sweden **8** 190; **30** 89, 97
Switzerland **30** 143, *144*
United States of America **31** 652
materials
cast iron **3** 575
ceramics **3** 575, 588; **11** 105
faience (ii) (ceramics) **30** *144*
tiles **2** 815; **3** 575; **27** *400*; **30** 89, 97, 874, 876
types
Bath stoves **11** 119
Venetian stoves **11** 119
Stow (Lincs), St Mary **2** 67
Stow, John **10** 339; **19** 567, 597
Stowarzyszenie Artystów Plastyków Rytm *see* RHYTHM GROUP
Stowarzyszenie Plastyków Szkoła Warszawska *see* WARSAW SCHOOL ASSOCIATION OF PLASTIC ARTISTS
Stowasser, Friedrich *see* HUNDERTWASSER, FRIEDENSREICH
Stowe (Bucks) **10** *225*; **29** 735–6*; **30** 451–2
collections **2** 560; **29** 88
Dido Grotto **13** 704
garden bridge **4** 801
gardens **4** *806*, 874–5; **10** 233, 361; **12** 61, 63, 105, 128, 129, 130; **24** 741; **29** *735*
Gothick Library **26** 85
interior decoration **13** 637
Pantheon **27** 237
pyramid **25** 766
sculpture **27** 466
Temple of Ancient Vertue **27** 237
Temple of British Worthies **6** 171
Temple of the Sun **27** 237
Temple to the Liberty of our Ancestors **13** 199
wall paintings **10** 199
Stowe, Harriet Beecher **3** 489
Stowell, John **13** 85
Stowe Missal *see under* MISSALS → individual manuscripts
Stowe-Nine-Churches (Northants), St Michael **10** 262
Stow Longa Church (Cambs) **26** 613
Stoyanova, Milka **5** 159
Stozharov, V. F. **27** 397
Stra **16** *618*
Villa Nazionale Già Pisani **12** 119; **24** 865; **29** 736*; **30** 348; **32** 553
gardens **12** 115
interior decoration **16** 719
paintings **16** 719; **30** 860
sculpture **20** 423
Straat, Jan van der (1523-1605) *see* STRADANUS, Joannes
Straaten, J. van **33** 177
Strabo **13** 555; **16** 454; **30** 285
on Alexandria **1** 614
on architecture **3** 327; **8** 869
on brass **4** 682
on marble **26** 855
on paintings **12** 287
on Scythians **28** 324
on weapons **15** 677
Strabo, Walafrid *see* WALAFRID STRABO
Strachan, Alexander James **10** 348
Strachan, David **30** 160
Strachan, John, Bishop of Toronto **3** 854
Strache, Hugo **20** 801
Strache Altar, Master of the **20** 801
Strachey, Lytton **4** 168
Strachey, Richard **1** 648
Strachovský, Josef **30** 221
Strachulfus **30** 144
Strack, Heinrich **29** 737
Strack, Johann Heinrich **29** 736–7*
assistants **18** 208; **32** 801
pupils **9** 761; **14** 227, 631; **21** 311
works **3** 807; **4** 375; **20** 1; **25** 268
Strada, Famiano **3** 415; **7** 902; **21** 483
Strada, Giovanni della *see* STRADANUS, JOANNES
Strada, Jacopo **2** 161; **29** 737–40*; **32** 442
assistants **29** 740
attributions **32** 456
collaboration **29** 740
dealing **11** 818; **18** 521; **27** 285
patrons and collectors **5** 79; **13** 908, 910, 911, 912, 914
works **2** 20, 778; **8** 268; **9** 181, 750; **10** 889; **22** 307; **29** *739*; **33** 271
writings **28** 470, 471
Strada (a Rosberg), Ottavio **8** 413; **13** 914; **29** 737, 738, 740*
Strada, Vespasiano **29** 740*
Stradanus, Joannes **29** 740–42*
collaboration **32** 14; **33** 722
patrons and collectors **21** 21
pupils **30** 428
reproductive prints by others **1** 840; **3** 558; **7** 556, 901; **10** 389; **12** 16; **27** 502, 504; **29** *854*
teachers **1** 168
works **2** 104; **4** 923; **10** 130; **11** 193; **12** 881; **16** 757; **18** 590; **21** 22; **29** *741, 742*; **32** 14, 16
Stradanus, Scipione **29** 741
Stradella, S Marcello in Montalino **26** 578
Stradioto **4** 620
Stradivari, Antonio **8** 135
Stradonice **21** 551; **25** 536, 541, 547
Straehuber, Alexander **19** 97
Straet, Jan van der (*d* 1535) **29** 740
Straet, Jan van der (1523-1605) *see* STRADANUS, JOANNES
Straeten, Charles Van der *see* VAN DER STRAETEN, CHARLES
Strafford, Thomas Wentworth, 1st Earl of *see* WENTWORTH, THOMAS, 1st Earl of Strafford
Strahan, John **3** 370
Strahl, Edvard **28** 863
Strahl, Karl **28** 863
Strähuber, Alexander **6** 532; **7** 181; **10** 760; **12** 603; **18** 398
Strähuber, Sigmund **1** 141
Straide, Dominican friary **16** 20
Straight Ahead (Wprost) **29** 742–3*
straight-edges **13** 411
strainer arches *see under* ARCHES → types
Strait of Georgia **29** 743*
Straits Chinese **20** 166
Straits *keris* *see under* KERIS → types
Straka von Nedabylice, Petr **5** 338
Strakonice
Castle **24** 462
Commandery of St John **8** 382; **13** 151
Stralsund **12** *360*; **29** 744*
Kulturhistorisches Museum **29** 744
Meeresmuseum **29** 744
St Nikolai **4** 777; **13** 56
Ünglinger Tor **4** 777
Stralsund Faience Factory **30** 97
Strambi, Domenico **13** 260; **20** 124
Strambino, SS Michele e Solutore del Rosario **25** 886, *886*
Stramm, August **29** 872
Strand, Paul **24** 676; **29** 744–6*
collaboration **28** 574
patrons and collectors **29** 657
pupils **5** 896; **27** 164
works **29** *745*
Strand, Rune **30** 103
Strang, David **25** 627; **29** 746
Strang, Ian **29** 746
Strang, Peter **21** 67
Strang, William **21** 418; **29** 746*
methods **10** 396; **21** 340
works **28** 238
Strange, John **27** 864; **29** 746*; **33** 697
Strange, Robert **13** 301; **29** 746–7*
methods **10** 393
sponsors **1** 533
teachers **28** 236
works **1** 844; **26** 230
writings **19** 586
Strängnäs **13** 167; **30** *65*
Cathedral **1** 898–9; **4** 781; **13** 50; **29** 840; **30** 66, 67, 109
monument to Duke Karl **30** 84
wall paintings **30** 76
Strängnäs Altarpiece **8** 25; **13** 120
Stranigar, Patrick **16** 883
strap backs *see* LEATHER → types → harness leather
strapwork **11** 875; **23** 540; **29** 747–8*
Belgium **29** *748*
Central Asia, Western **31** 784
Egypt **16** 487
France **13** 700
Islamic **6** 557; **16** 487; **23** 560; **31** 784
Italy **32** 647
North Africa **16** 487
Spain **16** 487
Syria **16** 487
Strasbourg **11** *504*; **29** 749–59*
art forms and materials
engravings **10** 381
faience (ii) (ceramics) **11** 606, *606*; **19** 723; **29** 753*
marks **12** 442
metalwork **11** 624
pewter **11** 628
porcelain **11** 607, 609; **12** 433
prints **25** 625
sculpture **12** 399; **13** 85, 88
silver **11** 620, 621
stained glass **13** 180
tapestries **12** 466; **29** 752–3*
watermarks **32** *908*
woodcuts **33** 360
Aubette entertainment complex **10** 137, 415
Bibliothèque Nationale et Universitaire **19** 318
Café de l' Aubette **1** 75; **29** 661; **30** 234
Cathedral of Notre-Dame **9** 192, 680; **10** 492; **12** 356, 362; **13** 48, 49, 56, 58, 142; **14** 117; **23** 485; **29** 753–5*, *754, 756, 757*, 758–9*
baptismal font **9** *192*
clock **2** 837; **7** 438, 439
epitaph to Conrad von Busang **31** 127

Strasbourg
Cathedral of Notre-Dame—cont.
font **11** 253
mouldings **22** 216, 219, 220, 221
nave **29** *753*
plans **2** 326, *326*, 327
pulpits **25** 725
St Catherine chapel **13** 88; **32** 92
St John's Chapel **12** 343
St Laurent chapel **22** 221
screen **28** 292
sculpture **9** 259; **12** 400; **13** 86, 87, 88; **22** 270; **29** 711, 755–8*; **33** 308
spire **14** 866; **29** 412
stained glass **13** 142, *143*, 186, 187; **29** 502, *503*, *759*
tapestries **25** 70
Tomb of Christ **9** 680
tracing house **31** 274
westwork **33** 109
Château **4** 303
Cité Rotterdam **3** 450
Dominican church **22** 219, 221
garden city **8** 824
garrison church **14** 82
guilds **12** 442; **20** 599; **24** 579
Hospices Civils **14** 781
Maison Kamerzell **29** *750*
masons' lodges **13** 823; **19** 532
Musée d'Art Moderne **29** 516
Musée des Beaux-Arts **11** 666
Musée de l'Oeuvre Notre-Dame **29** 516
New Chancellery **12** 342–3, *344*; **13** 91
observatory **23** 341
Palais du Conseil de L'Europe **1** 13
Palais Rohan **6** 509; **8** *33*; **29** *751*
St Blaise **12** 442
St-Pierre-le-Jeune **32** 821
St Thomas **32** 821
Karman **31** 128
tomb of Maurice, Maréchal de Saxe **11** 561; **24** 786, *786*
synagogue **17** 548
Strasbourg, Jacob of *see* JACOB OF STRASBOURG
Strasbourg, Nicholas Wurmser of *see* WURMSER OF STRASBOURG, NICHOLAS
Strasbourg, Ulrich of *see* ULRICH OF STRASBOURG
Strasbourg Bible *see under* BIBLES → types
Strasbourg Cock **2** 837, *838*
Strasbourg turpentine **26** 243
Strasfogel, Ian **24** 745; **28** 829
Strassburg, Gottfried von *see* GOTTFRIED VON STRASSBURG
Strassburger, August **33** 37
Strasser, Arthur **2** 803; **12** 872; **25** 403
Strata Florida **7** 350; **32** 781
Straten, Henri Van *see* VAN STRATEN, HENRI
Stratensis, Giovanni *see* STRADANUS, JOANNES
Stratfield Saye (Hants) **3** 241; **4** 330; **11** 430; **24** 811; **33** 55
Stratford (Ont.; Canada), Shakespeare Festival Theater **1** 125; **30** 684
Stratford Hall (VA; USA) **4** 787; **31** 590
Stratford-upon-Avon (Warwicks) **31** 709
Grammar School (Guildhall) **13** 822
guilds **13** 822
Holy Trinity Church **13** 822
Shakespeare Hotel **30** *896*
Shakespeare Memorial Theatre **7** 670; **10** 240
Strathearn Glass Ltd **28** 260
Strathmann, Carl **24** 591
Stratico, Simone **25** 144
stratigraphy **2** 299, 301, *302*, *303*; **4** 763
Stratios **29** 617
Stratonice Master **20** 770–71*
attributions **7** 296
works **20** *771*
Stratonikeia **5** 742
Stratonikos **16** 85*; **24** 414
Stratos **13** *363*; **29** 759*
Temple of Zeus **13** 391, 418; **29** 759
town walls **21** 557
Stratter, Erasmus **28** 168
Strattman **2** 782
Stratton (Cornwall), St Andrew **28** 293
Stratton, Mary Chase **8** 821
Stratton Park (Hants) **25** 267
Straub (family; 16th cent.) **23** 312
Straub (family; 18th cent.) **21** 313
Straub, Franz Anton **29** 760
Straub, Georg **30** 151
Straub, Hans **23** 312
Straub, Johann Baptist **22** 302; **29** 759, 760–61*
attributions **12** 447
collaboration **8** 290
groups and movements **26** 498
patrons and collectors **33** 278
pupils **4** 375; **13** 850, 852; **17** 657; **21** 313
works **11** 124, 125; **12** 406; **22** *303*; **25** 728; **29** *760*, *761*
workshop **12** 405
Straub, Johann Georg, the elder (*d* 1730) **29** 759, 760, 761, 762
Straub, Johann Georg, the younger (1721-73) **29** 760
Straub, Josef **29** 760, 762*
works **28** 862, *862*
Straub, Philipp Jakob **14** 894; **21** 313; **29** 760, 761*
Straube, William **11** 807
Straubing
St Peter **26** 634
Ursuline church **2** 584
Straubing, Heinrich von **22** 306
Strauch, Adolph **7** 326
Strauch, Georg **17** 656; **29** 762*; **31** 371
Strauch, Hans **29** 762
Strauch, Lorenz **12** 389; **29** 762*; **31** 370
Strauch, Ludwig Karl **29** 763*
Štraus, Ivan **28** 445
Straus, Percy Selden **29** 763*
Straus Madonna, Master of the **3** 247; **20** 510, 771*; **29** 763
Strauss, Bernhard **10** 529; **22** 205
Strauss, George **7** 483
Strauss, Isaac **17** 580
Strauss, Joseph Baermann **4** 803; **27** 730
Strauss, Louise **10** 467
Strauss, V. F. **28** 628
Stravinsky, Igor
groups and movements **3** 119; **8** 434
productions **22** 150; **28** 112
Apollon musagète **3** 391
Feu d'artifice **3** 116
Histoire du soldat **2** 701
Le Rossignol **8** 771; **20** 828
L'Oiseau de feu **12** 878
Mavra **30** 25
Rite of Spring **23** 183
straw **29** 763*
historical and regional traditions
Africa **1** 307
Ancient Near East **4** 771
Britain **29** 763
Buddhism **6** 706
Central Asia, Eastern **6** 301
China **6** 706
Indian subcontinent **15** 548
Japan **17** 99, 371, 373
Linear Pottery culture **25** 500
Switzerland **30** 151
straw—cont.
types
rice **17** 358
uses
adobe **4** 767
architecture **25** 500
arriccio **10** 740
baskets **17** 358
brick **4** 771
chairs **29** 763
dolls **17** 371, 373
furniture **29** 763
grounds **6** 301
lace **30** 151
paper **24** 40
roofs **1** 307; **13** 619
sculpture **6** 706; **17** 99
secco paintings **15** 548
Strawberry Hill *see under* TWICKENHAM (MIDDX)
Strawberry Hill Press **32** 825
Strawson, P. F. **7** 661
Strazdiņš, Jēkabs
Strážky Church **28** 852, 857
Strazza, Giovanni **16** 706
Strazzarolo da Aviano, Girolamo *see* GIROLAMO DI BARTOLOMEO STRAZZAROLO DA AVIANO
Strazzo, Giovanni **30** 215
streaky glass *see under* GLASS → types
streamlining **15** 824
streams **12** 85, 109
Streatfield, Henry **20** 866
Strebelle, Claude **3** 551; **29** 764*
Strebelle, Olivier **5** 45; **16** 849
Strecius, Johann **14** 894; **29** 764*
Strecius, Johann Georg **14** 894; **29** 764
Strecken, Geraert van der **9** 763
Strecken, van der (family) **14** 617; **30** 320
Středa, Jan of *see* JAN OF STŘEDA
Streek, Hendrick van **2** 342; **33** 267
Street, Arthur Edmund **29** 766
Street, G(eorge) E(dmund) **25** 173; **29** 764–6*
architecture **4** 787; **9** 322
cathedrals **4** 825; **10** 266; **18** 42
churches **5** 268; **7** 663; **14** 863; **18** 874; **26** 776; **27** 626; **29** *765*
law courts **10** 237; **18** *888*; **27** 131; **29** *766*
schools **28** 156
assistants **28** 561; **29** 695
competitions **2** 337; **7** 667, 668; **18** 889
groups and movements **9** 705; **10** 237; **13** 202, 203, 207, 209
metalwork **10** 335
pupils **7** 559; **8** 528; **22** 142; **28** 347
restorations by others **12** 926
staff **33** 11
stained glass **7** 410
teachers **28** 279
Streeter, Robert (1621-79) **29** 766–7*; **33** 393
patrons and collectors **5** 900
reproductive prints by others **33** 147
works **10** 249; **15** 47; **23** 687
Streeter, Robert (*d* 1711) **29** 767
Streeter, Tal **28** 829
Streeter, Thomas **29** 767
street lighting *see under* LIGHTING → types
Streeton, Arthur (Ernest) **2** 747, 769; **21** 76; **29** 767–8*
groups and movements **2** 746; **14** 306–7; **19** 873; **30** 39
works **2** 746, *746*, 747, 748; **29** *767*
streets
Belgium **2** 510
Etruscan **10** 602
France **2** 510; **20** *474*
streets—cont.
Islamic **16** 206, 261–2, *266*
Italy **10** 602; **25** *196*
Knights Hospitaller **26** *294*
Ottoman **16** 206, *266*
Rhodes (island) **26** *294*
Rome, ancient **25** *196*; **26** 863; **27** 3
Turkey **16** 206, *266*
see also AVENUES; CAUSEWAYS; ROADS
Street-Wilson, William **9** 426; **24** 777; **29** 105, 768*
Strehlow, Karl **1** 66
Streicher, Franz Nikolaus **18** 683
Streichman, Yehezkel **16** 571; **17** 577; **29** 768–9*
groups and movements **17** 579; **23** 25
pupils **9** 747
Strei Church **26** 710
Streisingeorgu Church **26** 710, 711
Strel'bitsky, M. **21** 811
Strelcha **5** 155
Strelitzas Bathas, Markos *see* BATHAS, MARKOS STRELITZAS
Strelkov, A. S. **30** 490
Strel'na **12** 134; **27** 373
Streng, Henryk *see* WŁODARSKI, MAREK
Strengell, Gustaf **11** 805; **29** 769*
Strengell, Marianne **11** 54
stress **20** 573–4
stressed-skin construction **21** 407
Stretcher bond *see under* BONDING
stretchers **29** 769*
stretching **5** 654; **19** 1, *1*; **24** 106; **28** 559
Stretes, Gwillm *see* SCROTS, GUILLIM
Stretton Sugwas (Hereford & Worcs), St Mary Magdalene **26** 616
Strettweg **25** *470*, 542
models **25** *541*
Streublau see under PIGMENTS → types
Streuvels, Stijn **3** 579
striation **29** 769*
Strichen **14** 544, 545
Strick, Peter **3** 873
Strickland, Francis William **29** 771
Strickland, Walter **16** 38
Strickland, William **14** 246; **29** 769–71*
collaboration **25** 4
groups and movements **13** 611
pupils **28** 641
teachers **18** 845
works **3** 175; **10** 669; **17** 547; **23** 776; **24** 597; **29** *770*, *771*; **31** 591; **32** 827
Strickland Brooch **10** 322
Strickner, Johann Michael **15** 865
Strick van Linschoten (family) **4** 53
Strict Style *see under* CELTIC → periods
Strider, Marjorie **7** 685
Striening, J. **20** 437
Strigel, Bernhard **20** 745; **29** 772, 773*
collaboration **33** 629
patrons and collectors **13** 903–4, 908
teachers **33** 629
works **11** 453; **12** 384; **16** 866
Strigel, Hans, I (*fl* 1430-62) **29** 772
Strigel, Hans, II (*fl* 1450-80) **29** 772, 773*
pupils **29** 773
works **29** *772*
Strigel, Ivo **29** 772, 773; **30** 136
Strigelli, Vincenzo **7** 915
strigillation **11** 231
Strij, Abraham van, I (1752-1826) **22** 848; **29** 773–4*; **33** 262
works **9** 169
Strij, Abraham van, II (1790-1840) **29** 773
Strij, Jacob van **22** 847; **29** 773, 774*
works **2** 105; **9** 169
Strij, Leendert van **29** 773
Strijcker, Willem **22** 843
Striker, L. **16** 599
striking **20** 917, 921; **29** 774*
Strindberg, (Johan) August **8** 596; **29** 774–5*
groups and movements **22** 291
productions **30** 682
writings **12** 192
Strindberg, Frida **19** 591
Strindberg, Sven **11** 112
string **1** 52; **8** *23*; **10** 561; **29** 813
Stringa, Francesco **10** 527; **29** 775*; **33** 690
Stringa, Giovanni **27** 774; **32** 196
string courses **22** 215, 218, 222; **29** 775*
string puppets *see* PUPPETS → types → marionettes
Strioński, Stanisław **25** 105
striped masonry *see* MASONRY → types → *ablaq*
stripwork **20** 571; **29** 775–6*, *776*
Strixner, August **23** 9
Strixner, Johann Nepomuk **9** 443; **19** 482; **28** 404; **29** 776*
Strizhakov, Vasily **2** 417
Strizhkov, Filip (Vasil'yevich) **27** 428
Strižić, Zdenko **8** 177; **29** 776–7*
Strnad, Oskar **2** 789, 815; **29** 777*; **32** 448
assistants **13** 798
pupils **10** 495; **14** 25; **25** 48
works **2** 788, 789, 810; **30** 684
Strnad and Vaníček **8** 401
Strnadel, Antonín **8** 393
Strobel, Bartholomäus, II **19** 496; **25** 104; **29** 777*; **32** 875
Strobel, Johann **22** 305
Strobel, Mathias **25** 731
Strobl (family) **27** 665
Strobl *see* STRUDEL
Stróbl, Alajos **5** 85; **14** 896; **15** 14; **18** 86
Strobl, Zsigmond Kisfaludi *see* KISFALUDI STROBL, ZSIGMOND
stroboscopic photography *see under* PHOTOGRAPHY → processes
Ströch, Gerhard *see* ALTENBOURG, GERHARD
Strochevyshivka workshop **2** 901
Stroe **25** 340
Stroebel, Johannes **20** 433
Stroe from Tîrgovişte **26** 712
Stroganov (family) **29** 778–9*; **32** 697
architecture **29** 53
collections **27** 441
embroidery **27** 430
icons **25** 338; **27** 385, 438
lace **27** 430
manuscripts **29** 53
paintings **7** 172; **29** 53
Stroganov, Aleksandr (Sergeyevich), Count (1734-1811) **27** 438; **29** 778*
collections **27** 439; **29** 778
hardstones **27** 428
paintings **12** 2; **27** 439
Stroganov, Aleksandr (Sergeyevich), Count (1818-64) **29** 778, 779*; **32** 697
Stroganov, Anika (Fyodorovich) **29** 53, 778
Stroganov, Grigory S., Count **26** 734; **29** 54, 778, 779
Stroganov, Maksim **29** 779
Stroganov, Nikita **29** 54, 779
Stroganov, Pavel S., Count **26** 734; **29** 778

Stroganov, Sergey (Grigor'yevich), Count **27** 442; **29** 778–9*
Stroganov school **22** 176; **25** 338; **27** 385–6; **29** 54, 778, 779*
  works **22** *176*
Ströhber, Karl **11** 735
Ströhling, Eduard **19** 338
Stroiński, Stanisław **25** 363
Stroitel'stvo i Arkhitektura Moskvy **19** 732
Stroj, Mihael **8** 178; **28** 860; **29** 779*
Strojnowska, Waleria *see* TARNOWSKI, WALERIA, Countess
Strojnowski, Hieronim **30** 345
Stroke-ornamented Pottery culture **25** 500
Strömberg **13** 811
Strömberg, Edvard **30** 103
Strömberg, Erik **30** 103
Strömberg, Gerda **30** 103
Stromberg, Klosterkirche **7** 703
Strömbergshyttan Studioglas AB **30** 103
strombus shells *see under* SHELLS → types
Strömdahl, Åke **30** 113
Stromer, Ulman **23** 310
Stromer, Wolf Jakob **17** 711; **18** 575
Stromer von Auerbach, Heinrich **19** 110
Strömholm, (Ture) Christer **24** 548; **29** 780*
Strømme, Olav **29** 780*
Stromness (Orkney), Pier Art Centre **28** 274
Strömsholm Castle **30** 93; **32** 814
Stronach, Alexander **31** 239
Stronach, David **23** 318; **24** 220; **28** 537; **33** 504
Stronczynski, Kazimierz **25** 143
Strong, Edward **31** 234
Strong, Emilia Frances *see* DILKE, Lady
Strong, Sampson **23** 690; **29** 781*
Strong, William D(uncan) **5** 388; **14** 820; **23** 703
Strongylion **13** 453; **29** 781*
  collaboration **17** 910
  works **2** 682; **13** 454
Stronsvick, Gustav **14** 716
strontium chromate **24** 799
Stroobant, François **29** 781*
Strossmayer, Josip Juraj, Bishop of Zagreb **8** 178, 180; **18** 473; **27** 616; **28** 754
Stroud (Glos.), Stanley Mill **21** 601
Strouts, Frederick **33** 342
Stroy, Mihael *see* STROJ, Mihael
Strozzi (family) **24** 770; **25** 59
  architecture **3** 896; **11** 178; **27** 748; **28** *733*
  collections **4** 209
  gems **8** 14
  manuscripts **2** 186; **11** 296
  metalwork **6** 140
  paintings **6** *2*; **11** 697, 888; **19** 446; **24** 768; **30** 649
  sculpture **23** 855
  wrought iron **16** 743
Strozzi, Alessandro **21** 53
Strozzi, Alfonso **29** 782
Strozzi, Bernardo **12** 283; **16** 675; **29** 783–5*; **32** 194
  attributions **6** 126
  patrons and collectors **1** 633; **3** 90; **9** 174; **13** 920; **15** 148; **26** 283; **29** 411
  pupils **3** 34; **11** 14; **31** 293
  works **11** 392; **29** *784*, *785*
Strozzi, Filippo, the elder (1428-91) **29** 782*
  architecture **8** 187; **27** 735; **32** 545
  manuscripts **11** 295
  paintings **3** 917; **19** 447
  sculpture **20** 113
Strozzi, Filippo, the elder (1428-91)—cont.
  sponsorship **19** 445
Strozzi, Filippo, the younger (1489-1538) **29** 782
Strozzi, Giovanni Battista **28** 733
Strozzi, Leo **12** 266
Strozzi, Lorenzo **29** 782
Strozzi, Luigi **11** 662
Strozzi, Niccolò **21** *692*
Strozzi, Nofri **29** 781
Strozzi, Palla (di Nofri) **14** 867; **29** 781–2*
  paintings **2** 34; **11** 184; **12** 300, 303; **19** 681
Strozzi, Roberto **21** 440
Strozzi, Tommaso di Rosello **7** 333
Strozzi, Zanobi (di Benedetto di Caroccio degli) **11** 686; **29** 785–6*
  collaboration **20** 689; **31** 165
  works **29** *786*
Strozzi Altarpiece **7** *333*, 333–4; **11** 184, 209, 380; **12** *300*, 300–301*; **13** 149
Strozzi key **16** 59
Strüb, Hans **29** 786*
Strüb, Jakob **29** 786*
Strüb, Peter (*fl* 1475-1504) **29** 786
Strüb, Peter (*d* ?1540) **29** 786–7*; **33** 674
Strubicz, Maciej **25** 840
Struck, Hermann **3** 43; **29** 609
Structon Group Architects **2** 689
Structural Information Theory **24** 384
Structuralism **2** 537, 538; **3** 289; **15** 100; **19** 275; **25** 361; **29** 787–8*; **31** 769
Structure **1** 79; **3** 111
structures, pneumatic *see* PNEUMATIC STRUCTURES
structures, tension *see* TENSION STRUCTURES
structures, timber *see* TIMBER STRUCTURES
Structurism **4** 38
Structurist **24** 428
Strudel (family) **13** 921
Strudel, Dominik **29** 788
Strudel, Paul **29** 788–9*
  collaboration **32** 442
  patrons and collectors **32** 457
  works **2** 801; **26** 25; **29** *789*; **32** *442*, 443
Strudel, Peter **2** 831; **29** 788–90*; **32** 443
  collaboration **28** 123
  patrons and collectors **32** 457
  works **2** 795; **29** *790*; **32** 456
Strudwick, John Melhuish **5** 269; **11** 397, 436; **25** 555
Struga, St George **9** 628
Strumica **19** *882*
  Virgin Eleousa **9** 579; **19** 882
Struna, Palace of Florian Hrabnicki **3** 526
Strunke, Niklāvs **26** 384
Strunmica Museum **19** 886
Struss, Karl F. **7** 491; **24** 739; **33** 146
Strutt, Alfred William **29** 791
Strutt, Joseph **10** 206; **24** 820; **29** 790
Strutt, Rosa **29** 791
Strutt, William (1756-1830) **16** 52; **28** 831
Strutt, William (1825-1915) **2** 771; **23** 58; **29** 790–91*
Strutt, William Thomas **29** 790
Struycken, Peter **22** 852, 854, 861; **29** 791*
Struys, Alexander **17** 736; **26** 546
Strydom, Willem **29** 112
Strydonck, Guillaume van **11** 448
Stryjeńska, Zofia **25** 108; **26** 296; **29** 791*
Stryjeński, Karol **25** 122; **29** 791
Stryjeński, Tadeusz **8** 371; **29** 791*
Stryker, Roy **10** 493, 656; **19** 60; **24** 673
Stryme **13** 537, 538
Strynkiewicz, Franciszek **17** 448; **25** 116
Strzałecki, Antoni **20** 397
Strzegom, SS Peter and Paul **13** 57
Strzelno Abbey **25** *92*; **29** 792–4*
  Church of the Holy Trinity **25** 95, 109; **29** *792*, 792–3*, *793*
    sculpture **29** 792–3*
  Premonstratensian convent **4** 782
  St Procopius Rotunda **29** *792*, 793–4*
  sculpture **25** 95
Strzemiński, Władysław **3** 529; **18** 181; **25** 142; **29** 794–5*
  groups and movements
    Abstract art **1** 76
    a.r. group **2** 409; **19** 537; **25** 108
    Block group **4** 148; **7** 772; **25** 423; **30** 8
    Kraków group **18** 434
    Praesens Group **25** 422
  pupils **11** 66; **29** 547
  works **29** *794*
  writings **18** 181
Strzygowski, Josef **2** 832, 833; **29** 795*
  excavations **9** 528
  pupils **8** 708, 885, 899; **18** 437
  works **2** 428
    translated **8** 474
Stuart (House of) **29** 797*
Stuart, Col. **22** 123
Stuart, Anne of Denmark, Queen of England and Scotland *see* ANNE OF DENMARK, Queen of England and Scotland
Stuart, Athenian *see* STUART, JAMES
Stuart, Bernard (*fl* 1736) **11** 120
Stuart, Bernard, Lord (1623-1645) **9** *278*
Stuart, Charles (1753-1801) **29** 796
Stuart, Charles, Duke of Lennox and Richmond **21** 615
Stuart, Charles Edward, Prince **28** 261
Stuart, Charles 'Hindoo' (1757/8-1828) **15** 741, 744
Stuart, Charles I, King of England and Scotland *see* CHARLES I, King of England and Scotland
Stuart, Charles II, King of England and Scotland *see* CHARLES II, King of England and Scotland
Stuart, Elizabeth, Queen of Bohemia *see* ELIZABETH, Queen of Bohemia
Stuart, Enrico Bencoletto, Bishop of Frascati **18** 524
Stuart, Frances Theresa, Duchess of Richmond and Lennox **9** *281*
Stuart, Francis, 10th Earl of Moray **9** 723; **12** 635
Stuart, Gilbert **4** 477; **16** 15; **23** 32; **24** 599; **29** 804–5*
  assistants **4** 882
  collaboration **24** 279; **31** 872
  copies **31** 872
  patrons and collectors **4** 599; **7** 379; **11** 774; **12** 645; **27** 694; **33** 151
  pupils **4** 882; **17** 666; **23** 37
  teachers **33** 92
  works **29** *805*; **31** 600
Stuart, Henrietta Anne, Duchesse d'Orleans *see* ORLÉANS (ii), HENRIETTA ANNE, Duchesse d'
Stuart, Henrietta Maria, Queen of England *see* HENRIETTA MARIA, Queen of England
Stuart, Henry, Duke of Gloucester **14** *139*
Stuart, Henry (Frederick), Prince of Wales **29** 797, 798–9*
  architecture **6** 95; **10** 368; **11** 242; **17** 633
  books **19** 792
  collections **9** 167; **19** 582
  gardens **12** 126
  gems **12** 266
  paintings **10** 363; **19** 617; **23** 326; **24** 301
  sculpture **12** 577; **30** 228
  stage design **17** 637
Stuart, Henry Benedict, Cardinal **14** 106
Stuart, Ian **16** 22
Stuart, James **2** 164; **7** 502; **10** 293, 642; **12** 43; **13** 303; **26** 263; **29** 805–6*
  architecture **13** 623; **25** 267
  bookbindings **4** 353
  collaboration **2** 559; **3** 285; **23** 544; **28** 64
  drawings **2** 666
  furniture **10** 293
  groups and movements **2** 163; **12** 332; **13** 607, 608; **22** 734, 735, 738
  interior decoration **14** 163; **22** *737*; **23** 544; **25** 192
  metalwork **4** 540; **9** 30; **10** 333
  patrons and collectors **12** 601; **29** 381
  sculpture **10** 265
  writings **2** 171, 359, 667; **5** 905; **10** 276; **25** 172; **28** 242
    collaboration **2** 319
    illustrated **2** *672*; **3** 329; **13** *609*; **24** 213
Stuart, James Francis, Old Pretender **6** 568; **14** 106
Stuart, James I, King of England *see* JAMES I, King of England and Scotland
Stuart, James II, King of England and Scotland see JAMES II, King of England and Scotland
Stuart, James IV, King of Scotland *see* JAMES IV, King of Scotland
Stuart, John, 3rd Earl of Bute (1713-92) **29** 796*
  architecture **5** 731; **24** 570; **33** 84
  collections **8** 474
  gardens **18** 4
  paintings **8** 474; **13** 624; **25** 883; **33** 693
  sculpture **17** 7
Stuart (ii), John, 4th Earl and 1st Marquess of Bute (*d* 1814) **29** 796
Stuart, John, Lord (*fl* 1639) **9** *278*
Stuart, John Patrick Crichton, 3rd Marquess of Bute *see* CRICHTON-STUART, JOHN PATRICK, 3rd Marquess of Bute
Stuart, Louisa Anne, Marchioness of Waterford *see* DE LA POER, ANNE, Marchioness of Waterford
Stuart, Louisa Maria von Stolberg, Countess of Albany **7** 541; **10** 726, 727; **20** 389
Stuart, Maria Clementina, Princess **20** *922*
Stuart, Martinus **5** 322
Stuart, Mary, Princess *see* ORANGE NASSAU, MARY STUART, Princess
Stuart, Mary, Queen of Scotland *see* MARY, Queen of Scotland
Stuart, Mary II, Queen of England and Scotland *see* MARY II, Queen of England and Scotland
Stuart, Mary of Modena, Queen of England *see* MARY OF MODENA, Queen of England
Stuart, Michelle **29** 807*
Stuart Crystal **26** 39
Stuart de Rothesay Hours *see under* BOOKS OF HOURS → individual manuscripts
Stuart enamel *see under* ENAMEL → techniques
Stuart-Fitz-James y de Silva, Cayetana, Duquesa de Alba **29** 355
Stuart & Sons **10** 321
Stuart y Falcó, Jacobo Fitz-Stuart, 17th Duque de Alba *see* ALBA, 17th Duque de
Stuart y Silva, Carlos Miguel Fitz-James, 14th Duque de Alba *see* ALBA, 14th Duque de
Stuba, Dionizy **18** 431
Stübben, Joseph **7** 581; **9** 460; **25** 408; **32** 380
Stubbins, Hugh A(sher) **6** 460; **29** 807*; **30** 684
Stubbs, Dorman **3** 62, 64
Stubbs, George **29** 807–10*; **33** 22, 545
  groups and movements **22** 740; **26** 740
  methods **10** 199; **23** 378; **24** 4
  patrons and collectors
    Blundell, Henry **4** 181
    George IV, King of Great Britain (*reg* 1820-30) **14** 146
    Grosvenor, Richard, 1st Earl Grosvenor (1731-1802) **13** 696
    Hunter, William (1718-83) **15** 29
    Mellon, Paul **21** 91
    Spencer, John, 1st Earl Spencer **29** 381
    Watson-Wentworth, Charles, 2nd Marquess of Rockingham **32** 912
    Whitney, John Hay **33** 150
    Wrightsman, Charles B(ierer) **33** 416
  reproductive prints by others **5** 216; **9** 43, 506; **33** 372
  works **1** 844; **2** 106; **4** 361; **7** 814; **10** *198*, 250; **11** 430, *430*; **21** 7; **22** 686; **25** 619; **28** 206; **29** 424, *425*, 676, *809*, *810*
Stubbs, George Townly **29** 676, 810
Stübel, Alfons **29** 220; **31** 380
Stubenberg, Georg Augustin von **29** 811*
Stubenberg, Otto Gall von **29** 811*
Stubenberg, Rudolf Wilhelm von **29** 811*
Stuber, Kaspar Gottfried **29** 811
Stuber, Nikolaus Gottfried **22** 302; **28** 110; **29** 811–12*; **33** 277
S.T.U.C.A. **13** 10
stucco **29** 812–46*
  conservation **29** 845–6*, *846*
  historical and regional traditions
    Afghanistan **1** 193, 196, 197–8; **16** *163*; **29** 824–5*, *825*
    Africa **29** 827–8*
    Algeria **16** 190
    Ancient Near East **29** 813, 814–16*
    Arabia **2** 273*
    Austria **29** 838–9*, 843
    Aztec **29** 828
    Belgium **3** 577, 578
    Buddhism **1** 197–8; **30** 595*, 602–3*, *604*, 823
      Central Asia, Eastern **6** 298; **29** *823*, 823–4
      Indian subcontinent **15** 448; **29** 824
      Thailand **29** 826
    Burma **5** 230, 231; **29** 826
    Byzantine **29** 816–17*, *817*
    Cambodia **29** 826
    Carolingian **5** 796
    Central Asia **29** 821*
    Central Asia, Eastern **6** 298; **29** *823*, 823–4*
    Central Asia, Western **16** 160; **29** 821–3*, *822*

stucco
historical and regional traditions—cont.
Crete **13** 603; **29** 814
Cyprus **29** 816
Denmark **29** *840*, 840–41*
Early Christian (*c.* AD 250-843) **29** 816–17*, *817*
Egypt **29** 819
Egypt, ancient **10** 68*, *69*; **29** 813–14*
England **10** 278; **29** 813, 835–7*, *837*
Etruscan **29** 814*
France **11** *572*; **25** *579*; **26** 123; **29** 833–4*, *834*, 843, *844*
Germany **11** *44*; **12** 372; **26** 632; **29** 838*, 843
Baroque **12** *404*; **28** *130*
Gothic **29** 818, *818*
Rococo **10** *859*; **29** *838*; **33** *682*
Romanesque **12** 399
18th cent. **28** *131*
Gothic **29** 818, *818*
Greece, ancient **13** 383, 389, 602–4*; **29** 813, 814*
Holy Roman Empire (before 1648) **26** 632
Indian subcontinent **15** 338, 413, 414, 448, 475, 499; **29** 824–5*
Gandhara **29** 824
Indus civilization **29** 824
Indus civilization **29** 824
Iran **16** 158, 160, 165, *200*, *233*, *244*; **21** 506; **29** 818, *820*
Iran, ancient **29** *815*
Iraq **16** 153, 243; **27** *681*; **29** 819
Ireland **29** 835
Islamic **16** 133, 140, 243–5, 250, 257; **21** 506; **29** 818–20*
Afghanistan **16** *163*; **29** 825
Algeria **16** 190
Central Asia, Western **16** 160
Egypt **29** 819
Indian subcontinent **15** 338; **29** 825
Iran **16** 158, 160, 165, *200*, *233*, *244*; **29** 818, *820*
Iraq **16** 153, 243; **27** *680*; **29** 819
Jordan **29** *819*
Morocco **16** 190, 257
Ottoman **16** 257
Spain **16** *189*, 217
Syria **31** *573*
Turkey **16** 248, 257
Yemen **16** 214, 215
Italy **2** 541; **4** 776; **16** 712, *712*, *713*, *722*; **25** 578; **26** *400*; **29** 812, 813, 816, 829–33*, 843; **30** 656; **32** *193*, 550
Baroque **1** *626*; **16** *704*; **29** 830, *832*
Byzantine **29** 816–17, *817*
Early Christian (*c.* AD 250-843) **29** 816–17, *817*
Etruscan **29** 814*
Lombard art **16** 687*
Mannerism **30** *800*
Renaissance **29** 830
Roman **27** 53, 69–72*, *70*, *71*
Jordan **29** *819*
Khmer **29** 826
Korea **18** 277
Kuwait **2** *273*
Laos **29** 827
Latin America **29** 841*
Lithuania **19** *496*
Lombard art **16** 687*
Maya **20** 881; **21** 266; **23** *839*; **29** *828*, 828–9
Mesoamerica, Pre-Columbian **18** *675*; **21** *222*, 266; **23** *839*; **29** *828*, 828–9*
Mexico **18** *675*; **23** *839*
Minoan **29** 814
Moche (culture) **29** 829

stucco
historical and regional traditions—cont.
Morocco **16** 190, 257
Netherlands, the **22** 866; **29** 837*
Ottoman **16** 257
Ottonian **23** 646, *647*
Parthian **24** 217, 218; **29** 814–15*
Poland **29** 839
Portugal **29** 841–2*
Romanesque **12** 399; **26** 632
Rome, ancient **2** 541; **26** 864, 878; **27** 68–9*; **29** 812, 813, 814*
albarium **27** 69
Italy **27** 53, 69–72*, *70*, *71*
opus tectorium **27** 69
Russia **29** *839*, 839–40*
Sasanian **27** 856; **29** 815–16*
Scandinavia **29** 840–41*
Scotland **28** 246, *247*; **29** 835
Sicily **28** *477*
South America, Pre-Columbian **29** 829*
South-east Asia **29** 826–7*
Spain **16** *189*, 217; **29** *841*, 841–2*
Sumatra **29** 826
Sweden **29** 840*; **30** 85, 88; **32** 923
Switzerland **30** 136
Syria **31** *573*
Tajikistan **29** *822*
Thailand **29** 826–7, *827*; **30** 595*, 602–3*, *604*
Buddhism **29** 826
Tibet **30** 823
Turkey **16** 248, 257
United States of America **29** 842*, *842*, 845
Yemen **16** 214, 215
Zapotec **18** *675*
techniques
gilding **29** 818, 825; **32** *193*
moulding **29** 813, 825
types
Fibrous Plaster **29** 813
imitation **24** 61
stucco bianco **29** 812
stucco duro **29** 813
uses
altarpieces **1** 707
architectural decorations **16** 165, *189*, 190, 215, *244*, 250
architecture **12** 372; **15** 338; **16** 133, 158, 160, 214, 217
busts **29** 814
capitals **29** *822*
cassoni **16** *722*
catafalques **6** 71
ceilings **3** 577; **28** 246, *247*; **29** 812
façades **2** 541; **4** 776
friezes **31** *573*
grilles **16** 257
houses **18** 277
interior decoration **29** *839*
masks **20** 881
mihrabs **16** *163*, *244*, 245; **21** 506; **29** *820*
portals **29** *841*
relief sculpture **10** *69*; **15** 448, 499; **23** *839*; **29** 812, *818*, *827*; **30** *604*
revetments **16** 243
screens (i) (architectural) **16** 257
sculpture
Afghanistan **1** 193, 196, 197–8
Central Asia, Eastern **6** 298
China **29** *823*
Germany **12** 399; **23** 646, *647*; **26** 632
Indian subcontinent **15** 413, 414, 475; **29** 824
Islamic **16** 243
Italy **26** *400*

stucco
uses
sculpture—cont.
Mexico **18** *675*; **21** *222*
Sweden **30** 85
Thailand **30** 595*, 602–3*
stages **30** 656
vaults (ceiling) **16** *200*, *233*; **19** *496*
wall decorations **29** 812
walls **13** 389
Stuchs, Georg **28** 128
Stuck, Franz von **29** 846–8*
collaboration **23** 192
groups and movements **12** 394; **28** 341
house **2** 365, *550*, 552
pupils **1** 120; **12** 237; **17** 761; **18** 108; **25** 743; **33** 44
works **4** 42; **11** 456, 464, *464*; **12** 427; **22** 330; **25** 348; **29** *847*
Stucke, William Henry **4** 155; **29** 105, 848*
Stückelberg, Ernst **22** 329; **29** 848–9*; **30** 134
Stucki, Jakob **30** 144
Stucky-Schürer, Monika **30** 332
Studebaker **19** 538
Studenica Monastery **9** *511*, 561; **28** *437*, 440; **29** 849*
Church of the Mother of God **9** 646; **25** 343; **28** 441, *441*; **29** 849
icons **28** 447
sculpture **28** 452, *453*
wall paintings **9** 582; **28** 445
collections **28** 459
Hermitage of St Savva **25** 343
icons **25** 339
Katholikon *see* Church of the Mother of God
King's Church **28** 446, 455
metalwork **28** 454
SS Joachim and Anne **9** 585
textiles **16** 444; **28** 457
vestments (ecclesiastical) **28** 458
Studer, E. **30** 128
Studer, Friedrich **2** 711
Studer, G. **30** 128
Studholme, Joe **20** 607
studies **9** 213–15*, 220; **11** *64*
Studies in Conservation **7** 743
Studi Etruschi **10** 638
Studii și cercetări de istoria artei **24** 425
Studio, The **2** 562; **12** 780; **24** 424, 426, 446; **29** 858
contributors **3** 445; **18** 24; **20** 22
on wicker **33** *156*, 157
Studio Artemide **3** 439
Studio August Sander für Kunstphotographie und Malerei **27** 717
Studio AYDE **2** 880
Studio Blumberg & Hermann **27** 717
Studio Cinco **22** 24
Studio Club, The **24** 739
Studio d'Arte Palma **3** 227; **4** 721
studio di musica **22** 376
Studio Dongo **20** 101
Studio International **24** 424, 429, 446
studioli **5** 344; **9** 11, 14, 21; **16** 770; **29** 859–61*, *860*, *861*
Studio Nervi **22** 805
Studio Per **29** 861*
studios **1** 103; **2** 552; **9** 12; **29** 850–59*
Belgium **11** 220; **29** *854*
England **10** 248; **29** 856, 858
France **11** 544*, 671*; **23** *788*; **29** 855, *857*, *858*
India, Republic of **9** *180*
Ireland **9** *319*
Islamic **16** 122
Italy **2** *170*; **6** *98*; **10** *196*; **29** 853, *889*; **30** *121*

studios—cont.
Netherlands, the **26** *171*; **29** 854, *855*
Rome, ancient **27** 52
United States of America **15** 21
see also ARTISTS' HOUSES; ATELIERS; WORKSHOPS
Studio Sander & Stukenberg **27** 717
Studites, Theodore *see* THEODORE OF STOUDIOS
Studius *see* LUDIUS
Studland Art Industries **19** 6
Studley Bowl **10** 323
Studley Royal (N. Yorks) **10** *225*; **11** 348; **12** 128; **22** 716; **29** 861–2*
Chinese kiosk **18** 72
stucco **29** 835
Studnička, Alois **18** 525
studs **30** 896, *896*; **32** 276
study collections *see under* COLLECTIONS → types
Study Group for Calligraphy and Painting *see* SŎHWA YŎN'GUHOE
Stuers, Victor (Eugène Louis) de **19** 862; **22** 903; **29** 862*
Stufa, della (family) **11** 206
Stufenhalle see CHURCHES → types → hall
stuffing *see under* LEATHER → techniques
Stuhlweissenburg *see* SZÉKESFEHÉRVÁR
Stukeley, William **2** 299; **29** 515, 862*; **30** 123
Stukenberg, Franz **27** 717
Stukenbrock, Johachim Andreas **23** 221
Stüler, Friedrich August **18** 161; **29** 863*
architecture
academies **5** 82; **30** 210
cathedrals **3** 792–3; **7** 872
chapels **3** 805, *806*
exchanges **10** 669
museums **3** 807; **12** 376; **22** 362; **25** 268; **26** 3; **29** 686; **30** 73, 119
palaces **6** 62; **12** 416; **14** 490; **23** 813
collaboration **28** 102
groups and movements **3** 799; **18** 160; **26** 190
interior decoration **12** 415
patrons and collectors **14** 654
pupils **30** 210
teachers **28** 99
Stulhof, Sebestyén **14** 907
Stumme, Absalom **4** 418; **12** 384
Stumpf, Johann **14** 424
Stumpf, William **31** 633
Stumpff, Johanna **3** 398
stumping **29** 863*
stumps **29** 863
Stunder, Jan **14** 901; **19** 281; **28** 853
Stuoka Gucevicius, Laurynas *see* GUCEWICZ, WAWRZYNIEC
Stuosz, Veit *see* STOSS, VEIT
stupas **22** 376; **29** 863–9*
historical and regional traditions
Afghanistan **1** 191–2, *192*, 198; **3** 113
Bali (Indonesia) **15** 763
Buddhism **5** 88; **9** 86; **29** 863
see also DĀGABAS
Burma **5** 223, 224, *225*, 227, *231*, 231–2*, 234*, *234*; **25** *890*; **29** 866, *866*
Cambodia **5** 481
Central Asia **5** 102; **29** 867*
Central Asia, Eastern **6** 297, *297*
China **29** 868*

stupas
historical and regional traditions—cont.
Indian subcontinent **1** *500*, *754*; **4** 794; **5** 94, *95*; **15** 194, 220, 237*, 249*, *262*, 431; **23** 772; **27** *709*; **29** 863–4*, *864*
Jainism **15** 226; **29** 864
Indonesia **29** 865, *866*
Jainism **15** 226; **29** 863, 864
Japan **29** 869*
Korea **18** 266; **29** 868–9*
Laos **18** 764, 765*
Nepal **5** *103*; **22** 760; **29** 867–8*
South-east Asia **5** 99; **28** 639; **29** 865–7*
Sri Lanka **29** 446, 447, *447*
Thailand **29** 866–7; **30** 576, *576*, *583*, 583–4, *584*, *586*, 586, *587*
Tibet **13** *885*; **29** 867–8*; **30** 815–16, 817, 818, 819, 842
Vietnam **32** 473, 476
materials
brick **4** 794; **32** 476
granite **29** 869
types
bkra-shis sgo-mang mchod-rten **29** 868
kumbum **13** 884–5, *885*; **29** 868
pagoda-stupas **22** *459*; **23** 773, *774*; **29** 868
pillar-stupas **29** 868
pyramidal **29** 867
terrace-stupas **29** 867
votive **29** 867
see also CAITYAS; CHORTENS
Stupica, Gabrijel **28** 861; **29** 869*
Stupid group **8** 438; **25** 837; **29** 869–70*
Stupin, A. V. **27** 442
Stupinigi, Palazzina Mauriziana di Caccia **3** 266; **7** 571; **17** *709*, 709–10; **26** 500; **32** 549
frescoes **8** 193; **15** 139; **19** 646; **31** 445
gardens **12** 119; **18** 618
interior decoration **11** 396; **16** 716, 719
paintings **11** 396
Sala degli Scuderi **28** 19
stables **29** 486
Stur, Karl *see* DUBOIS, LOUIS (JEAN-BAPTISTE)
Sturbridge (MA) **31** 652
Sturck, Jan Jansz. **29** 720
Sturckenburch, Johannes **29** 720
Šturdík, Jozef **28** 853
Sture, Birgitta Gustafsdotter **16** 790
Sture, Sten **23** 255
Sturefors **30** 89
Sturehof **13** 864
Sturel-Paignée, Marie-Octavie **4** 306
Sturges, Jonathan **9** 419; **22** 224; **29** 870*
Sturgis, John Hubbard **25** 806; **29** 870–71*; **30** 505
Sturgis, Julian **25** 805
Sturgis, Russell, jr (*fl* 1834) **29** 870
Sturgis, Russell (1836-1909) **29** 871*; **33** 174
assistants **3** 6; **20** 16
writings **10** 213
Sturgis & Brigham **4** 474; **32** 793
Sturkelov, Konstantin **5** 155
Stürler, Albrecht **3** 822; **30** 127
Stürler, Franz Adolph von **15** 839; **22** 383; **25** 741
Stürler, Ludwig Samuel **22** 920
Sturm, Abbot of Fulda **11** 831; **26** 10
Sturm, Anton **4** 375; **12** 405
Sturm, Ferdinand *see* ESTURMIO, HERNANDO DE
Sturm, György **15** 6
Sturm, Helmut **29** 435

Sturm, Leonhard Christoph 10 739; 29 872–3*
works 7 258; 23 489; 31 298
writings 12 368, 475
Sturm, Meyer J. 14 783
Sturm: Wochenzeitschrift für Kultur und die Künste, Der 10 695; 12 395; 20 849; 24 406, 427, 445; 25 626; 29 871–2*; 32 774
contributors
Arp, Hans (Peter Wilhelm) 2 488
Campendonk, Heinrich 5 543
Cendrars, Blaise 6 167
Felixmüller, Conrad 10 869
Klee, Paul 18 109
Kokoschka, Oskar 10 696; 18 198
Morgner, Wilhelm 22 114
Schwitters, Kurt (Herman Edward Karl Julius) 28 196
Segal, Arthur 28 352
exhibitions 23 570; 25 375
Sturmberg, Johann Adam 28 63; 29 540
Sturmberger, Johan Christopher 8 739
Sturmbühne 32 775
Sturmer, Johann 33 255
Sturmer, Matthew von 23 72, 73
Sturm-Galerie *see under* BERLIN
Sturmio, Hernando de 23 626
Sturmkunsthochschule 29 872; 32 775
Sturmschule see STURMKUNSTHOCHSCHULE
Sturm und Drang 12 851; 14 316; 26 737
Sturovo 25 500
Štursa, Jan 29 873*
collaboration 18 405
pupils 18 472; 22 393; 28 855
works 8 387, 402
Štursa, Jiří 8 402; 24 226*
Štursová, Vlasta 8 402
Sturt, John 4 34; 19 165, 583
Sturtevant, Benjamin Franklin 28 831
Sturt Pottery 2 761
Sturt's Meadow 1 41; 22 62
Sturt Workshops 2 767
Stürtzel, Konrad 33 32
Stury, Richard 25 16
Sturzig 32 879
Sturzwage, Léopold *see* SURVAGE, LÉOPOLD
Stutterheim, Willem Frederik 15 809; 29 873*
Stuttgart 12 *361*, 413; 29 873–5*
Altes Schloss 12 366, 369; 29 875*, *875*; 31 311
Neuer Bau 28 87
Neues Lusthaus 3 491–2; 12 368; 33 711
paintings 33 711
collections 12 481
Danneckerei 8 508
exhibitions 10 678
Grabkapelle 20 868
Grosses Lusthaus 29 607
Inselbad Untertürkheim 19 332
Landesbibliothek 1 23
museums
Design Center Stuttgart 29 875
Galerie der Stadt Stuttgart 29 875
Linden-Museum 1 67; 7 155; 24 430
Museum der Bildenden Künste *see* Staatsgalerie
Natural History Museum 27 644
Staatliches Museum für Völkerkunde *see* Linden-Museum
Staatsgalerie 7 386, *386*; 10 242; 12 477; 22 367; 29 677; 31 735, *736*
archives 2 370
Archiv Sohm 29 16
Stuttgart
museums
Staatsgalerie—cont.
collections 9 121; 29 875
Koenig-Fachsenfeld Collection 13 788
Württembergisches Landesmuseum 21 250, 265; 29 875
Neues Schloss 12 371, 373; 26 257
Aeneas Gallery 13 853
painting 12 391, 392
railway station 12 379; 25 856
Schloss Rosenstein *see* museums → Natural History Museum
Schloss Solitude 26 497
Schocken Store 8 770; 21 782
Städtische Bibliothek 27 644
tapestries 30 324
tiles 30 884
urban planning 31 715
Villa Wilhelma 22 59
Weissenhofsiedlung 7 293, 695, 698; 8 *826*; 12 379, 416; 21 490, 782; 23 663; 25 741; 26 15; 28 126; 30 458
Wilhelmspalais *see* Städtische Bibliothek
Württembergische Landesbibliothek 12 482
Stuttgart Global Strip 12 814
Stuttgart Gospels *see under* GOSPEL BOOKS → individual manuscripts
Stuttgart Passional *see under* PASSIONALS → individual manuscripts
Stuttgart Psalter *see under* PSALTERS → individual manuscripts
Stuttgart school 4 309
Stuven, Ernst 21 508
Stuyck (family) 29 347
Stuyck, Juan Bautista 29 347
Stuyck, Livinio 29 350
Stuyt, Jan 29 875–6*
collaboration 8 300
pupils 23 662
staff 27 136
works 28 594
Stuyvenburg, P. A. 2 148
Stuyvesant (family) 18 749
Stuyvesant, Peter 12 136; 23 38, *45*
Stwosz, Wit *see* STOSS, VEIT
Stýblo, Zbyšek 8 381
Styka, Jan 18 398; 29 539; 33 417
style 29 876–82*
see also ART HISTORY
Style, The *see* STIJL, DE
Style 1900 see ART NOUVEAU
style coup de fouet see ART NOUVEAU
Style François Ier *see* FRANÇOIS IER STYLE
Style I *see under* MIGRATION PERIOD → styles; ANGLO-SAXON → styles; PREHISTORIC ART → periods
Style II *see under* MIGRATION PERIOD → styles; ANGLO-SAXON → styles; PREHISTORIC ART → periods
Style III:E *see under* VIKING → styles
Style III:F *see under* VIKING → styles
Style Jules Verne see ART NOUVEAU
Style Métro *see* ART NOUVEAU
Style moderne see ART DECO
Style nouille see ART NOUVEAU
Style of 1200 *see* GOTHIC → painting → Transitional style
style ogival, le 13 34
styles 25 362; 30 382–3*
styling 15 823, 824; 20 593
stylobatai 13 *376*, 414; 29 883*
Stylos Basilica 8 155
styluses 6 736; 10 197; 20 326; 29 883–4*
Stymphalos 13 587
Sanctuary of Artemis 13 604
water-clock 13 382
Styria Studios 20 609
Štyrský, Jindřich 29 884*
collaboration 31 250
groups and movements 8 393, 829; 25 433; 30 22
Suakin 1 317, *379*; 16 *104*, 269; 23 290; 29 884*
Suardi (family) 3 770, 771
Suardi, Bartolomeo *see* BRAMANTINO
Suarès, André 9 196; 27 240, 241; 28 750
Suárez, Alfredo Gálvez *see* GÁLVEZ SUÁREZ, ALFREDO
Suárez, David Muñoz *see* MUÑOZ SUÁREZ, DAVID
Suarez, Diego 12 143
Suárez, Francisco 24 621
Suárez, González 24 828
Suárez, Jaime 25 702, 703
Suárez, José 29 884*
Suárez, Lorenzo 23 571
Suárez de Figueroa, Lorenzo 2 284
Suárez Rendón, Gonzalo 7 604, 607, 611
Suavius, Lambert 19 547; 29 885*
Suazey 2 144
Subandhu, King (*reg* late 5th cent.) 15 470
Subashi 6 *288*; 18 495; 28 720; 30 441
figurines 6 300
reliquaries 6 292, 303, 319, *321*, 321
South-western Stupa 29 867
Stupa H 6 297
wall paintings 6 312, *312*
Subbotovo, Church of the Prophet Elijah 31 552
Subbuteo 31 266
subcinctoria 32 388*
Subes, Raymond Henri 2 521; 11 601, 628
Subh 7 844; 16 524
Subhanquli Khan 3 113; 16 236
Subha-pabbata *see* YAPAHUVA
Subiaco
Church of Sacro Speco 11 708
Nero's villa 26 892
S Benedetto Abbey 21 144; 26 665
S Scolastica 1 696; 16 646
Subic, Georg
works 14 *438*
Šubic, Janez 28 860; 29 885*
Šubic, Jurij 28 860; 29 885*
Šubic, Štefan 29 885
Šubič, Vladimir 28 860; 29 885*
Subirachs (i Sitjar), Josep Maria 29 886*
groups and movements 3 220; 8 538
patrons and collectors 9 113
works 29 296
Subirana, Joan Baptista i *see* BAPTISTA I SUBIRANA, JOAN
Subirats, Agustín Querol y *see* QUEROL Y SUBIRATS, AGUSTÍN
Subisati, Sempronio 4 560; 29 304
Subject-matter *see* ICONOGRAPHY
Subjektive Fotografie 17 878; 29 608
Sublet de Noyers, Pierre 11 722
Sublet Des Noyers, François, Baron de Dangu *see* DES NOYERS, FRANÇOIS SUBLET, Baron de Dangu
Subleyras, Matthieu 29 886
Subleyras, Pierre 26 774; 29 886–9*, *889*
collaboration 9 399; 19 525
patrons and collectors 27 524; 31 306
Subleyras, Pierre—cont.
pupils 14 133; 18 420
reproductive prints by others 3 204
teachers 26 424; 32 670
works 11 *409*; 29 *887*
Sublime, The 8 94; 14 697; 15 828; 18 700, 713; 24 741; 26 736–7; 29 889–91*
works 29 *890*
Sub-Minoan periods *see under* MINOAN → periods
Subotica 28 *437*, 444
Bačka Gallery 28 459
Cathedral of St Theresa 28 444
Municipal Museum 28 458
Subramanyan, K(alpathi) G(anapathi) 15 170, 748; 28 577; 29 891*
Subramanya Raju, Y. 22 404
Subsidiary Queen Mary Artist 4 237
Subterranean Imitation Realists 2 120
Subtiaba
Museum 29 222
S Juan Bautista 23 80
suburbs 25 655
suburbs, garden *see* TOWNS → types → garden cities
subway art *see* GRAFFITI
Succa, Antoine de 29 892*
Succi, Domenico 29 892
Succi, Giacomo 29 892
Succi, Pellegrino 29 892
Suceava 26 *705*, 710; 29 892–3*
altar curtains 2 442
architecture 2 427
fort 26 707
guilds 26 725
metalwork 26 719
St Elias 25 344
St George 26 149
Suceava, Toma de la *see* TOMA DE LA SUCEAVA
Sucevița 26 *705*
church 26 *712*
textiles 26 721
wall paintings 25 344; 26 712
Sucgang, Telesforo 24 622
Suchadoûski, January 3 528
Suchard 10 421
Sucharda, Stanislav 29 893*
collaboration 8 401; 25 151
groups and movements 20 254
pupils 17 718
works 8 387; 20 926; 25 433
Suchindram
Shiva Temple 15 398
Sthanunathasvami Temple 15 524
Suchodolski, January 25 106; 32 876
Suchomel, J. (fl. 1920) 30 221
Suchomel, Jiří 8 381
Suchumi, Abkhazian Museum 12 332
Suckow, L. J. D. 31 298
Sucre 4 255, *255*; 29 893–4*; 31 721
architecture 4 256–7, 259–60
art school *see* Universidad Mayor Real y Pontificia de S Francisco Xavier
Banco Argandoña 4 260
Banco Nacional 4 259; 5 551
Biblioteca Nacional de Bolivia 4 270
Biblioteca y Archivo Nacional 4 269
Capilla Redonda 4 259
Casa Consistorial 4 257
Casa de la Libertad 4 268; 29 894
Casa del Gran Poder 4 257
Casa de Moneda 4 257
ecclesiastical buildings
Cathedral 4 256, 266, 267
Convent of S Clara 4 257, 267, 269
Sucre
ecclesiastical buildings—cont.
Convent of S Teresa 4 257, 267
Hospital de S Bárbara Church 4 257
La Recoleta 4 267, 269
S Augustín 4 257
S Domingo 4 257
S Felipe Neri 4 259
S Francisco 4 257
S Lázaro 4 257
Las Monicas 4 258
Museo Catedralicio 4 269; 29 894
Museo Charcas *see under* Universidad Mayor Real y Pontificia de S Francisco Xavier de Chuquisaca
painting 4 261, 262, 264
Palacio Arzobispal 4 257
Palacio de la Glorieta 4 260
Palacio de Gobierno 4 260
Palacio Torre Tagle 4 257
sculpture 4 264
Teatro Gran Mariscal 4 260
textiles 4 267
Universidad Mayor Real y Pontificia de S Francisco Xavier de Chuquisaca 4 257, 263, 269
Museo Charcas 4 268; 29 894
Sud, Anupam 8 677
Suda, Issei 29 894*
Suda, Kunitarō 29 894*
Sudak 29 894–5*; 31 *546*
Sudan 1 *214*, 378; 29 895–8*
animal subjects 1 237, *238*
architecture 29 895–6*
bamboo 1 *367*
baskets 1 295
beads 1 *367*
beds 1 285
body arts 1 288, *344*
bracelets 1 362
brick 1 305
calligraphy 29 *896*
clay 1 *367*
compounds 1 311, 312
cotton 8 34
drawings 29 *896*
education (art) 1 433
gold 9 817
grasses 1 *306*, 307
guidebooks 13 811
houses 1 306, 307, 311, 319
huts 1 *306*
kilns 1 305
knives 1 *361*
leather 1 299
megaphones 1 360
mihrabs 21 505
mosques 1 284, 316
mud 1 285
mud-bricks 1 284
museums 29 898
oils 1 305
painting 1 289; 29 896–7*
palm leaves 1 305
pipes (smoking) 1 367, *367*, 368
religion 1 229, 230
rings 1 362
roofs 1 305, *306*
sculpture 1 280; 29 897*, *897*
shields 1 362
tents 1 307
Sudan, French *see* MALI
Sudanese Antiquities Service 10 81
sūdānī script *see under* SCRIPTS → types
sudaria 32 390*
Sudarshana 15 227
Sudbury, Adam de *see* ADAM DE SUDBURY
Sudbury Hall (Derbys) 10 274, 275; 26 394; 29 835
Great Staircase 10 *275*
Sudek, Josef 25 433; 29 898–9*
works 24 678, *678*
Sudeley (family) 29 515

Sudeley Castle (Glos) **7** 435; **31** 469
Sūden Ishin *see* ISHIN SŪDEN
Sudervė **19** *494*
  Rotunda church **19** 497
Sudety Glassworks **25** 125
Sudeykin, Sergey (Yur'yevich) **29** 899*
  collaboration **13** 654; **33** 486
  groups and movements **4** 178; **27** 392
  patrons and collectors **4** 178; **27** 458
  pupils **18** 750
  writings **32** 724
Sudhammavati *see* THATON
Sudi, Mallikarjuna Temple **15** 325, 327
Sudjojono **15** 807, 808, 818
  works **15** *808*
Sudler, James **25** 218
Sudo **18** 342
Sudoeste **1** 676
Su Dongpo *see* SU SHI
Sudre, Pierre **15** 841
Sudus **21** 588
Sue **17** *241*
Sue, Eugène **13** 779
Süe, (Marie-)Louis **11** 582, 601; **29** 899–900*
  groups and movements **2** 520, 521, 522
  works **5** 841; **11** *582*, 601, 602; **20** 399
  writings **32** 578
Süe, Olivier **29** 900
Sueda Art Gallery *see under* ŌITA
Sueda no Jimaro **22** 497
Süe et Mare **9** 371
Sueharu Fukami *see* FUKAMI, SUEHARU
Sueji Umehara *see* UMEHARA, SUEJI
sueki *see under* POTTERY → wares
Suemura **17** *241*, 249
Suenaga Takezaki *see* TAKEZAKI SUENAGA
Suensen, Palle **29** 77
Suermondt, Edwin **22** 689
Suero de Quiñones **11** 677
Suescun, Luis **29** 335
Suessula **10** 585
Suessula Painter **13** 484, 534
Suess von Kulmbach, Hans *see* KULMBACH, HANS SÜSS VON
Suetin, Nikolay **27** 284, 413; **30** 8; **31** 677
Suetonius **7** 246
Sueur, Le *see* LE SUEUR
Sue ware *see under* POTTERY → wares
Suez **9** 765
Sufenas Proculus, M. **8** 368
Sufetula **9** *510*; **29** 900*
  architecture **31** 427
  Arch of Diocletian **26** 920; **31** 350
  Basilica **9** 535, 570
  Roman capitolium **26** 919
  temple **2** 297
Suffolk, Charles Brandon, Duke of *see* BRANDON, CHARLES, Duke of Suffolk
Suffolk, Elizabeth de la Pole, Duchess of *see* POLE, ELIZABETH DE LA, Duchess of Suffolk
Suffolk, Henry Howard, 12th Earl of *see* HOWARD, HENRY, 12th Earl of Suffolk
Suffolk, Thomas Howard, 1st Earl of *see* HOWARD (i), THOMAS, 1st Earl of Suffolk
Suffolk, William *see* WILLIAM OF SUFFOLK
al-Sufi **2** 650
  works **2** *650*
Sufism *see under* ISLAM → branches
Sugai, Kumi **19** 491; **29** 900*; **30** 172
Sugai Baikan **30** 295
Sugao Yamanouchi *see* YAMANOUCHI, SUGAO
sugar **10** 559; **24** 56
  historical and regional traditions
    Egypt **31** 260
    Mexico **29** 901, *901*
  uses
    aquatints **2** 239, 240
    consolidants **7** 748
    dolls **31** 260
    sculpture **21** 383; **29** *901*, 901–2*; **30** 219
    stucco **29** 813
sugarbite aquatints *see* ETCHINGS → types → lift-ground
sugar bowls *see under* BOWLS → types
sugar-lift etchings *see* ETCHINGS → types → lift-ground
sugarloaf vaults *see* VAULTS (CEILING) → types → *muqarnas*
Sugarman, George **29** 900–901*
Sugawara **13** 328
Sugawara, Seizo **9** 391; **11** 583; **18** 615
Sugawara no Michizane **17** 227, 228, 322; **18** 395; **29** 902*
Sugdaea *see* SUDAK
Suger, Abbot of Saint-Denis **11** 653; **24** 132; **29** 902–3*; **30** 779
  architecture **3** 710; **7** 218; **8** 261; **11** 510; **13** 36; **24** 751; **26** 656; **27** 539, 540
  bronze **9** 153
  collections **7** 564
  enamel **26** 691, 693
  gold **31** 499
  hardstones **26** 681
  metalwork **5** 806; **11** 614; **26** 681, 682; **27** 550
  mosaics **13** 134; **26** 679; **27** 543
  reliquaries **8** 260
  rock crystal **16** 744
  sculpture **27** 544
  stained glass **19** 356; **26** 701; **27** 548, 549; **29** 500, 501, 509, 511, 851
  writings **8** 612; **19** 356; **31** 295
sugi (Japanese cedar) *see under* CEDAR → types
Sugimoto, Sadamitsu **17** 267
Sugimura Jihei **14** 577; **17** 280
Sugita, Hideo *see* EI, KYŪ
Sugita Genpaku **23** 347
Sugiura, Kohei **29** 904*
Sugiyama, Yasushi **17** 202; **29** 904*
Sugrañes, Claudio Lorenzale y *see* LORENZALE Y SUGRAÑES, CLAUDIO
Sugrañes i Gras, Domenech **12** 183
Sugu (Africa) **6** 406
Sugu (Japan) **17** 246
Sūhāg *see* SOHAG
Šuhájek, Jiří **8** 411; **17** 816
Su Hanchen **6** 817; **7** 36; **14** 137; **29** 904–5*
  works **7** *36*
Suhis I (*reg* early 10th–early 9th cent. BC) **5** 729
Suhis II (*reg* early 10th–early 9th cent. BC) **5** 729
Suhr, Christoph **21** 540
al-Suhrawardi **23** 561
Suhrlandt, Carl **29** 905
Suhrlandt, Johann Heinrich **29** 905
Suhrlandt, Pauline *see* SOLTAU, PAULINE
Suhrlandt, Rudolph (Friedrich Carl) **29** 905*
Suhrlandt, Wilhelmine **29** 905
Suh Se Ok **18** 326; **29** 905*
Suhut **9** *512*
  St Trophimos **9** *592*, 593
Suida, Wilhelm **2** 833; **12** 873
Suigetsu Ōnishi *see* ŌNISHI SUIGETSU
Sui hsien *see* SUIZHOU
Suiko **23** 595
Suindinum *see* LE MANS
Suinin, Emperor (*reg* ?29 BC–AD 70) **17** 104
suint *see under* WAXES → types
Suiō Genro **14** 63; **17** 194
Sui period *see under* CHINA → periods
Suiseki Hirata *see* HIRATA SUISEKI
Suisse, Charles Alexandre **8** 51; **25** 849
Suisse, Charles Louis **8** 890
Suita National Ethnological Museum **17** 92
suites *see under* FURNITURE → types
Suits, Gustav **33** 565
suits, three-piece **9** 279, 287
Suiun, Komuro **14** 744
Sui xian *see* SUIZHOU
Suizan, Miki **17** 295
Suizhou **6** *614*, *615*, 727; **7** 13, 150; **29** 906–7*
  bronze **6** 855, *855*
  jade **7** 5
  lacquer **7** 13
  tomb of Marquis Yi of Zeng **3** 626; **6** 648, 695, *696*; **7** 80, 247; **23** 550; **29** 906–7
    armour **7** 56
    bells **6** 829
    bronzes **6** 828, 830, 834, 852, 855; **33** 660
    gold **7** 22
    sculpture **29** *906*
Šujanová, Katarína **28** 856
Sujanpur Tira **22** 785
Sujan Singh, Maharaja of Bikaner (*reg* 1700–36) (Rajput) **15** 609
Sujas Mosque **16** 162
Su Jian **29** 905
Sujigou **23** 496
Su Jingqing **29** 905
Sujong Temple **18** 295
sukanāsā **15** 245*
Sukari, Panagia Apsinthiotissa **8** 358, 359
Sukarnapura
  wood-carvings **16** *45*
Sukarno **15** 808; **29** 907*
Sukas, Tell **29** 907*; **30** *180*, 196
Sukchong, King (*reg* 1674–1720) **18** 331
Sukehachi Sakamoto *see* YI KYOUNG
Sukemasa, Fujiwara no *see* FUJIWARA NO SARI
Sukenik, E. L. **3** 880
Sukenobu Nishikawa *see* NISHIKAWA SUKENOBU
Sukeyoshi Karasumaru *see* KARASUMARU SUKEYOSHI
Sukezaēmon Ichimonjiya *see* ICHIMONJIYA SUKEZAĒMON
Sukhadeva **15** 602
Sukhanov, Prince Volkonsky's church **29** 554
Sukharam **15** 609
Sukhodillya, Church of the Mother of God **31** 550
Sukhothai **29** 224, *225*, 907–12*, *908*, *909*; **30** 571, *571*, 574
  architecture **30** 582, 591
  betel sets **30** 631
  ceramics **6** 331; **30** 609
  enamel **30** 632
  Ram Khamhaeng National Museum **29** 240
  sculpture **14** 562
  stucco **30** 603
  urban planning **30** 592
  Wat Chang Lom **30** 582–3
  Wat Chetupon **29** 911*
  Wat Mahathat **29** 867, 908–9*, *909*; **30** 575, 582, 584
Sukhothai—cont.
  Wat Phra Phai Luang **29** 911*; **30** 581, 582, 602–3
  Wat Saphan Hin **29** 911, *911*; **30** 603
  Wat Sa Si **29** *909*
  Wat Si Chum **29** 911*; **30** 582, 638
  Wat Si Sawai **29** 909–11*, *910*; **30** 578, 581
  Wat Trakuan **30** 602
  Wat Trapang Thong Lang **29** 826, 912; **30** 603
  Wat Traphang Ngoen **30** 584
Sukhovo-Kobylin **7** 769; **21** 410
sukiya *see* HOUSES → types → teahouses
Suku **33** 482, 483
  drums (architecture) **1** 357
  masks **1** 256, 405
  sculpture **1** 301, 403; **33** 485
Suku (Southern) **1** 405, 406
Sukuma **1** 411
Sukuro, Etale **17** 907
Suky, Benedek **15** 10
Sulá **21** 231
Sulaiman, Caliph (*reg* 715–717) (Umayyad) **16** 146, 255, 455
Sulawesi **15** *751*; **29** 226; **30** 558
  architecture **15** 774*; **21** 45
  baskets **15** 810
  batik **3** 379; **15** 796
  beadwork **15** 814
  caves **29** 226
  ceramics **15** 811
  hats **15** 810
  houses **15** 774*, *774*, 789
  ikat **15** 795; **24** 624
  iron **15** 817
  jewellery **15** 814
  Leang Burung 2 **29** 227
  painting **15** 806, *807*
  roofs **15** 774
  sculpture **15** 789
  spears **15** 818
  textiles **15** 796; **29** 232
Sulayhid **29** 912*
Sulayhid, al-Sayyida al-Hurra Arwa Bint Ahmad *see* AL-SAYYIDA AL-HURRA ARWA BINT AHMAD, Ruler
Sulayman I, Shah (*reg* 1666–94) (Safavid) **16** 80, 231, 232, 509, 539; **28** 633
Sulayman II, Sultan (*reg* 1520–66) (Ottoman) *see* SÜLEYMAN THE MAGNIFICENT, Sultan
Sulaymanya **16** 2
Sule *see* KASHGAR
Suleiman, Khalid ben **31** 426
Suleiman, Ziauddin **17** 654
Suleiman Haji Esa **20** 172
Suleimeh, Tell **14** 128
Suleyman, Caliph (*reg* 715–717) (Umayyad) *see* SULAIMAN, Caliph
Süleyman Kanuni *see* SÜLEYMAN THE MAGNIFICENT, Sultan
Süleyman Pasha **5** 398
Süleyman Seyyit *see* SEYYIT, SÜLEYMAN
Süleyman the Magnificent, Sultan (*reg* 1520–66) (Ottoman) **16** *118*, 347; **23** 638, 641–2*; **28** 767
  architecture **16** 266; **17** 491, 496; **18** 509; **23** 639
    bridges **9** 730
    madrasas **16** 224; **20** 914
    military **21** 587
    mosques **3** 2; **16** 604; **21** 33; **28** *766*
    pavilions **16** 254
  crowns **16** 539
  dress **16** 446, 452
  ivory-carvings **16** 526
  miniatures (manuscript illumination) **16** *348*
  mirrors **21** 718
Süleyman the Magnificent, Sultan (*reg* 1520–66) (Ottoman)—cont.
  painting **17** 807; **28** 536
  poetry **16** 349
  sabres **16** 508
  stained glass **16** 257
  teachers **13** 358
Sulgrave **2** 67; **10** 226
Sulhamstead (Berks), Folly Farm **8** 49
al-Suli **16** 277
Sulibhavi **1** 485
Sulimovka *see* SULYMIV KA
Suli Pasha **17** 864
Sulka **24** 83, 84
Sułkowski, Aleksander Józef **11** 739; **29** 912; **33** 115
Sułkowski, August **25** 138; **29** 912*
Sulla (Felix, Lucius Cornelius) **13** 469; **26** 749, 764, 782, 856; **29** 420; **33** 639
Sullivan, Edmund Joseph **4** 367
Sullivan, Françoise **2** 840; **5** 572; **26** 77
Sullivan, Kay **16** 889
Sullivan, Louis (Henri) **17** 476; **23** 548; **28** 180; **29** 913–16*; **31** 622
  architecture
    banks **3** 176; **29** *916*
    commercial buildings **4** 788; **23** 493; **27** 642; **30** *506*; **31** *594*
    department stores **6** 573; **8** 770; **29** *915*; **33** 246
    exhibition architecture **5** 274; **15** 883
    mausolea **20** 869; **25** 766
    skyscrapers **29** *914*; **30** 505
    theatres **1** 111; **29** 845; **30** 678
    warehouses **32** 861
  collaboration **1** 158; **5** 124; **6** 573; **10** 683; **14** 787; **19** 365; **25** 737; **28** 833; **31** 594
  groups and movements **2** 568; **6** 577, 578; **11** 840; **21** 780, 781; **23** 498
  patrons and collectors **27** 565
  pupils **21** 780
  staff **9** 305; **11** 840
  teachers **11** 848; **32** 84
  writings **31** 594
Sullivan, Luke **14** 640; **21** 643; **23** 105
Sullivan, Michael **7** 161
Sully, James **6** 586
Sully, Lawrence **29** 918
Sully, Maurice de, Bishop **14** 74; **24** 151
Sully, Maximilien de Béthune, 1st Duc de **20** 133; **21** 567; **29** 917–18*
  architecture **2** 502; **4** 865; **6** 503; **9** 353; **11** 656
Sully, Maximilien-François de Béthune, 2nd Duc de **19** 267
Sully, Thomas **22** 714; **24** 600; **29** 918–19*
  patrons and collectors **7** 840; **12** 645; **32** 753
  pupils **15** 858; **21** 605
  reproductions in hardstones **12** 265
  teachers **3** 701; **33** 93
  works **29** *918*
Sulman, John **2** 739, 740, 741; **29** 919*
Sulman Rhodes **29** 919
Sulmona
  Palazzo Sanità **8** 682
  Sanctuary of Hercules Curinus **27** 88
Sulmona, Camillo Borghese, Cardinal and Prince of *see* PAUL V, Pope
Sulmona, Giacomo di Paolo *see* GIACOMO DI PAOLO SULMONA

Sulmona, Marcantonio Borghese, Prince of 1 626
sulphides (ceramic) 10 319; 12 789*; 24 57
sulphides (mineral) 24 647
sulphur 1 156; 23 115; 24 647; 25 619
sulphuric acid 10 192, 548; 30 559
Sulpitius van Vorst 3 542; 19 260; 20 812, 813
Sultan, Donald K. 18 161; 23 50
Sultanabad see ARAK
Sultanabad carpets see under CARPETS → types
Sultan ʿAli 15 594
Sultan ʿAli Mashhadi 15 586; 29 919*
collaboration 4 49
patrons and collectors 1 645; 16 286, 553; 30 922, 922
works 6 235; 16 277, 292, 342, 345; 30 922
Sultan Ali Saifuddin mosque 5 11
Sultan Al-Nisa Begum, princess (Mughal) 15 364
Sultan Alsiliety 25 777
Sultanatabad 16 235
sultanes 29 8
Sultanganj 4 853; 15 475, 499, 500, 706
Sultan Han 5 722; 16 186; 24 878
Sultaniyya 16 105; 29 919–20*
architecture 16 193
cenotaphs 16 501
coins 16 513
khānaqāh 18 18
mausoleum of Uljaytu 2 295; 16 194, 194, 366; 29 920; 31 112
inscriptions 16 259
manuscripts 16 282, 283
minarets 21 628
mosque 21 628
textiles 16 444
Sultan-Muhammad 16 390; 22 260; 29 920*
patrons and collectors 16 332; 27 514
pupils 27 513; 33 626
works 16 333, 333
Sultan Muhammad Khandan 29 919
Sultan Muhammad Nur 1 645; 16 332; 29 919
Sultanov, N(ikolay) V(ladimirovich) 23 615; 27 443; 29 920–21*
Sultans of Gujarat see: AHMAD SHAH I, Sultan MAHMUD BIGARA, Sultan MUHAMMAD SHAH, Sultan QUTB AL-DIN SHAH, Sultan
Sulter, Maud 10 882; 29 921*
Sulu Islands
boats 24 625
dress 24 628
grave markers 24 630
weapons 24 631
weaving 24 623
Sulu keris see under KERIS → types
Sulymiv Ka, Church of the Protecting Veil of the Mother of God 31 552
Sulzbachner, Max 13 726
Sulzberger, Mayer 17 581
Sulzer, D. 10 176
Sulzer, J(ohann) G(eorg) 29 921–2*; 30 125, 132
works 6 570; 10 207, 208
illustrated 21 59
Sulzer, Johannes (1652-1717) 32 883
Sulzer, Johannes (1748-94) 10 781
SÚM 2 475; 11 774; 13 779, 780; 15 71
sumac 3 331; 7 45; 19 1
Suma group 21 390
Sumaka Mosque 16 152
sumak weaving see under WEAVING → types
Suman, Nusret 31 454
Sumana 30 604
Šumanović, Sava 28 451; 29 922*
Sumatra 15 751, 752; 29 225
appliqué 15 795
architecture 15 771–2*
bamboo 20 327
bark 20 327
baskets 3 331; 15 810
blouses 15 795
cane 15 810
ceramics 15 811
chess sets 6 557
cobalt oxides 4 173
coins 15 811, 812
copper 15 812
cotton 15 794, 794
dance 15 802
drawings 15 806–7*
dress 15 794, 813*
drums (musical instruments) 15 787
embroidery 15 795
gold 15 794, 810, 811
houses 15 771–2*, 807
ikat 15 794; 30 554
jewellery 15 814, 815
lacquer 15 810
looms 15 794
lutes 15 817
manuscripts 20 327, 327
masks 15 804
meeting-houses 15 771
metal 15 795
painting 15 804, 806–7*
pillows 15 795
rattles 15 817
sanctuaries 15 766–7
sarcophagi 15 788; 27 831, 831; 31 115
boat coffins 27 823
sarongs 15 795, 813
sculpture 15 776, 787–8*; 29 231
sequins 15 795
silk 15 794
silver 15 812
spears 15 818
stone 27 831
stucco 29 826
textiles 15 794–5*
tin 15 811
trade 6 557; 29 230
ceramics 15 811
wall hangings 15 794
yarn 15 795
Sumatran keris see under KERIS → types
Sumba 15 751; 30 554
architecture 15 756; 21 45
baskets 15 810
beadwork 15 814
dress 15 813; 29 235
jewellery 15 814, 815, 816
mantles 15 795
sarcophagi 27 831
sculpture 15 776, 789
textiles 9 III1; 15 795; 29 232
Sumbawa 15 818; 29 235
Sümeg 14 881; 29 922*
Episcopal Palace 14 906
Franciscan Monastery 14 900
parish church 14 900
Sumegne, Joseph-Francis 5 524
works 5 524
Sumenu Sacred Lake 27 496
Sumer 3 11; 21 267, 268, 272
alabaster (gypsum) 1 516
seals 21 271
trade
beads 3 440
Sumer 16 550
Sumerian 1 508, 851, 852; 21 267; 29 922–4*; 33 373
alabaster (gypsum) 9 45
architecture 29 924*
beads 1 873
bitumen 22 159
Sumerian—cont.
casts 6 9
copper 22 159
diorite 29 X2
dress 1 881
figurines 9 45
gold 1 874
gypsum 9 45; 29 923
harps 22 372
inlays 1 869; 31 696
ivory-carvings 1 869
languages 1 853–4
lapis lazuli 31 696
limestone 9 45; 22 159; 31 696
lyres 22 372
marble 31 760
mosaics 22 158
pictographs 31 759
rediscovery 1 893
religion 21 277
sculpture 18 798; 21 294; 29 923, X2; 30 423; 31 760
seals 1 880; 10 802; 29 924*
shell 22 159
shells 31 696
terracotta 22 158
writing 1 853; 20 361; 29 924*
writing-tablets 2 364
ziggurats 33 675
Sumerian King List 21 272
Sumgait 2 890, 894
Sumin, Avenir (Ivanovich) 27 422, 428
Sumin, Ivan 27 428
suminagashi see PAPER → techniques → marbling
Suminokura Sōan 14 703, 704; 17 271; 30 376
Sumitomo (family) 23 595
Sumitomo Kichizaemon, Baron 6 868
Sumiyoshi Gukei 29 925–6*
works 29 925
Sumiyoshi Hiromori 29 926
Sumiyoshi Hironao 29 926
Sumiyoshi Hirotsura 29 926
Sumiyoshi Hiroyasu 29 926
Sumiyoshi Hiroyoshi 29 926
Sumiyoshi Hiroyuki 29 926
Sumiyoshi Jokei 17 165; 29 924–6*
Sumiyoshi Keion 29 924
Sumiyoshi school 17 166, 419, 424, 438; 18 552; 29 924, 925–6*; 31 81, 200
works 29 925
Summer, Charles 33 364
Summerhayes, Geoffrey 2 770
Summerhill 16 8
summerhouses see under HOUSES → types
Summerly, Felix see COLE, HENRY
Summerly's, Felix, Art Manufactures 10 311; 15 821; 26 69
Summers, Charles 2 752; 29 926*
Summers, Charles Francis 29 926
Summers, George 29 926
Summers, Gerald 10 284
Summers, Roger 13 335
Summerson, John (Newenham) 29 926–7*; 32 800
Summersperger, Hans 2 453
Summit (NJ), Unitarian Meeting House 7 619
Summonte, Pietro 30 1*
Sumner, Alan 2 763; 28 300
Sumner, (George) Heywood (Maunoir) 14 770; 17 469; 30 1*; 31 250
Sumner, Maud 29 108
Sumner, Polly 1 65
Sumner, William 20 222
Sumsion, Calvin 5 382
Sumu 14 712
Sumukhwa (Indian ink) movement 18 326
Sumun see YI SU-MUN
Sumy 31 551
Sunar Furniture 13 326
Sunar Hauserman 31 633
furniture 31 633
Sunbeam Glassworks 23 70
Sunch'ŏn 18 343
Sun Chün-tse see SUN JUNZE
Sunda 15 801
Sunda, Lesser, Islands 15 751
baskets 15 810
bronze 29 229
palm leaves 15 810
sarcophagi 31 115
Sundahl, Eskil 1 470; 30 2*
Sunda Kelapa see JAKARTA
Sundanese 15 753; 29 235
Sundara-pabbata see YAPAHUVA
Sunday Jack Akpan 15 65
Sundborn, Carl Larsson-Gården 18 802; 30 91, 91, 119
Sundby Memorial Stone 32 518, 518
Sund Church 11 88, 94
Sunder see MOLLER
Sunderland (Tyne & Wear)
Grange Congregational Chapel 23 194
St John's, Ashbrooke 21 347
Sunderland, Charles, 3rd Earl of see SPENCER, CHARLES, 3rd Earl of Sunderland
Sunderland, Robert Spencer, 2nd Earl of see SPENCER, ROBERT, 2nd Earl of Sunderland
Sunderland, Thomas 8 96
Sunderland frames see under FRAMES → types
Sundermann, F. A. 11 852
Sundi 1 403
sundials 7 437; 17 399; 23 338; 28 209, 211; 32 634
Sundqvist, Carl Petter 11 104
Sundström, Heljä Lukko 30 884
Sundt-Hansen, Carl Frederik 23 225; 30 2*
Sundvall, Carl Fredrik 30 73, 90, 95; 31 693
Suneson, Palle 8 728
Śuṅga see SHUNGA
Sungai Kedayan 5 11
Sungailangsat 15 788
Sungai Lumut 5 12
Sunghir 4 313; 25 473
Sung Hsü see SONG XU
Sungir' 25 488; 27 364, 365
Sŭngju, Sŏnam-sa Temple 12 94
Sung K'o see SONG KE
Sung Kuang see SONG GUANG
Sung period see under CHINA → periods
Sung Sui see SONG SUI
Sung Ti see SONG DI
Sung Tzu-yen see SONG ZIYAN
Sun Guoting 6 760, 770; 30 2*
Sung Ying-hsing see SONG YINGXING
Sung Yün see SONG YUN
Sun I see SUN YI
Sun I-jang see SUN YIRANG
Sunjong, Emperor (reg 1907-10) 18 60, 300
Sun Junze 33 463
sunk chamfer mouldings see under MOULDINGS → types
Sun King see LOUIS XIV, King of France
Sunko, Dinko 33 593
Sun Kuo-t'ing see SUN GUOTING
Sünnesheim, Conrat von see SIFER, CONRAT
Sunni see under ISLAM → branches
Sun of Taiwan 30 248
Suñol, Jerónimo 21 81; 29 294; 30 3*
Sunpangkat, Jim 15 808
Sunqua 14 721
Sun Rhodes, Dennis 22 671
Sünshen, Conrat von see SIFER, CONRAT
Sunshing 7 30
Sun Stone 28 241
Suntai 6 405, 406
Suntory Ltd 17 433
Su Nuraxi 3 311–12*; 21 551
Sunyer, (i de Miró), Joaquim 23 260; 30 3*
groups and movements 3 219
works 3 219; 18 717
Sun Yi 2 95
Sun Yirang 6 867
Suō 17 318
Suomenlinna Fortress 11 87, 90; 30 3*
Suomen Taideyhdistys see FINNISH ART ASSOCIATION
Suotniemi Faience and Porcelain Factory 11 105
La Superga see under TURIN → churches
Superior (WI), Great Northern Railway grain elevator 13 274
Super Realism 22 124; 23 297
see also PHOTOREALISM
superstructures 4 794; 15 286, 397
Superstudio 2 373; 16 651; 30 3–4*
Supervielle, Jules 27 281
Superville, David Pierre Humbert de see HUMBERT DE SUPERVILLE, DAVID PIERRE
Supino, Igino Benvenuto 24 448; 30 4*
Suppiluliuma I (reg 1380-1335 BC) 20 541, 549
Suppiluliuma II (reg c. 1200 BC) 33 514
supporters 14 404, 416
supports 30 4–6*
conservation 24 6–8
historical and regional traditions
Central Asia, Eastern 6 303, 314
China 28 312
Greece, ancient 13 543
Japan 17 139–40*; 28 312
Korea 18 302
materials
aluminium 31 283
blockboard 24 3
boards 30 5
canvas 24 3; 30 5
chipboard 31 283
copper 30 5
fibreboard 31 283
grounds 13 705, 708
hardboard 24 3
ivory 16 799
mahogany 24 3
marine ply 31 283
millboard 24 3
oak 30 5
panel see wood
paper 6 314; 17 139; 18 302; 30 4, 6
parchment 30 6
particle board 24 3
Perspex 31 283
plywood 24 3
silk 17 139; 18 302
vellum 30 6
veneers 24 3
wood 6 303; 13 543; 24 3–8, 4, 5, 6, 7, 8
see also under PANEL PAINTINGS → materials
technical examination 30 395
uses
prints 9 26
scrolls 28 312
transfer (conservation) 31 283
supports, ceramics see CONES
Supports-Surfaces 1 80; 11 570; 24 145; 30 6*
members 5 612; 11 552; 14 160; 32 399
supports theory 13 898–9
see also STICHTING ARCHITECTEN RESEARCH
Supraśl Monastery 3 527; 25 344

Suprematism 1 75; 8 251; 11 360; 15 99; 18 141; 19 474–6; 20 194; 21 776, 892; 24 405; 25 239, 374; 26 503; 27 379, 392; 30 6–8*; 31 519, 763
collections 8 10
drawings 25 *375*
exhibitions 16 818
painting 19 *476*; 20 *194*; 25 *239*; 26 *504*; 30 *7*
posters 19 *475*
Supremus 30 8
Supremus 30 8
Sur (Afghan dynasty) 30 9*
see also:
HASAN SUR
ISLAM SUR, Sultan
SHER SHAH SUR, Sultan
Sur (Lebanon) *see* TYRE
Sura, Najmi 23 800
Surabaya 15 769, 780, 819
Suraj al-Daula, Nawab of Bengal (*reg* 1756-7) 15 379, 634
Suraj Mal, Raja of Dig (*reg* 1755-63) (Rajput) 15 390
Surakarta 15 *753*, 775; 30 9–10*
art schools 15 819
batik 15 790
dance 15 802
figurehead 15 810
Kashunanan Palace 15 775
Mangkunagaran Palace 15 772, 775; 30 10
Pendopo Agung 30 *9*
patronage 29 238
Prince Mangkunegaran Palace Museum 29 239
puppets 15 797, 798, 801
Radya Pustaka Museum 29 239
Surakarta Museum 30 10
Susuhunan's palace 30 10
Surakhana fire temple complex 2 893
Surakhany 2 893
Surakhare 3 376
Sura Mosque 15 352, 353
Suranadi 12 103
Śūrasenaka 15 245
Surat 15 201
factories 15 401
maps 15 705
metalwork 15 714
textiles 15 664, 723
surbased arches *see under* arches → types
Surcea 30 773
surcoats 2 469; 14 404, 421
Sureda, Bartolomé 20 69, 70
Sureda, Guillermo 25 701
Surenyants, Vardyes 2 431
Suresnes 24 129
Mont-Valérian 27 498, 500
surface analysis *see under* TECHNICAL EXAMINATON → types
Surgis, Louis de *see* SURUGUE, LOUIS
Surikov, Vasily (Ivanovich) 14 588; 27 391, 580; 30 10–12*
groups and movements 32 836
works 22 178; 27 *390*; 30 *11*
surimono see under PRINTS → types
Surinaamse Akademie voor Beeldende Kunsten 30 17
Surinaamse Kunstkring 30 16
Surinam 30 *12*, 12–17*
architecture 30 14–15*
calabashes 30 13
cedar 30 16
cloaks 1 *424*
collections 30 17
combs (hair) 1 *423*
cotton 1 *424*
decorative arts 30 16*
drawings 30 15, *15*
dress 30 13
education (art) 30 16–17
engravings 21 154, *154*
Surinam—cont.
exhibitions 30 16
feathers 30 16
furniture 30 16*
houses 30 15
huts 30 13
jewellery 30 16
lithography 30 15
mahogany 30 16
museums 30 17
painting 30 15–16*
palaces 30 *14*
patronage 30 16–17*
pottery 30 13
sculpture 30 16*
slaves 30 13
synagogues 17 545
textiles 1 424; 30 13–14
tourist art 30 13
wood 1 *423*
wood-carvings 30 13
Surio Subroto, Abdullah 15 807, 818
Suriqui 31 47
Sur Jur'eh 14 21
Surkhat, Church of the Holy Cross 2 427
Surkh Dum 19 811, 812
Surkh Kotal 1 *186*, 188, *191*, 211, *849*; 6 *182*; 30 17*, 440
architecture 1 191
capitals 6 217
inscriptions 1 187
sculpture 1 196; 15 737
stucco 29 824
temple 30 17
sur le motif 30 17*
see also DRAWINGS → types → life-drawings
Surlet, Jean-Ernest de 14 727
Surlet, Jean-Ignace de 14 727
Sürlin *see* SYRLIN
Suro, Darío 9 117
Surovyy stil' *see* SEVERE STYLE
Surozh *see* SUDAK
Surpatele Monastery 26 720
Surpele, Govaert van 17 *653*
surplices 32 388*
Surraco, Carlos 31 753
Surrealism 2 279, 488; 4 74; 8 439, 465–6; 9 104; 10 466, 468, 470–71, 481–2; 11 360; 15 99; 20 100, 590; 21 340, 776; 23 698; 25 582, 683, 686; 26 743; 30 17–23*, 168, 389; 31 52, 508
art forms
assemblages 2 617
collages 10 *468*
decalcomania (ii) (printing) 9 *105*
décollage 8 608
films 10 687, *687*
fumage 23 697
furniture 16 *721*
installations 15 868
magazines 33 183
mobiles 21 745
nude figures 3 *672*; 8 *700*
objets trouvés 23 334
painting 8 438; 18 717; 19 537; 25 6; 29 670; 32 5
Australia 12 804
Belgium 8 *700*; 20 *101*, *102*; 31 *51*
Czech Republic 8 *393*
England 1 449; 5 277, *277*
France 4 *700*; 10 *467*, *469*; 11 549–50; 30 *20*, *292*
Greece 10 379
mythological 22 416
Portugal 8 433
Slovenia 28 861
Spain 8 *466*, *467*; 9 *293*
Sweden 14 865
United States of America 1 84; 20 *838*; 31 607
wall 5 *45*
sculpture 17 694; 20 34; 29 12
Belgium 20 *102*
Surrealism
art forms
sculpture—cont.
France 12 *564*; 30 *21*
Germany 3 *672*
United States of America 31 613, *613*
collections 2 384; 6 23; 7 812; 20 832; 21 135; 23 7; 28 273
France 10 164
exhibitions 9 132; 10 416, 680; 11 886; 20 75; 23 385; 26 51; 28 920; 30 22; 33 183
Belgium 30 22
France 26 414; 30 19
Mexico 21 388
periodicals 24 428
regional traditions
Argentina 2 400
Belgium 5 44; 7 489; 8 699; 9 188; 20 100, 414; 21 176; 30 20, 23; 31 866
Brazil 4 718
Britain 20 34; 24 369; 33 744
Canary Islands 9 104; 11 886
Chile 30 22
Czech Republic 8 393; 16 908; 20 153; 22 393; 29 884; 30 22, 416
Denmark 4 105; 8 736; 11 744
Egypt 2 511; 30 22
England 10 257, 268, 655; 23 23; 30 22
France 1 75; 2 225, 490, *514*; 3 672–3; 4 699; 5 449; 7 562; 8 246; 10 164; 12 564; 14 160, 271, 852; 20 100, *591*, 837; 21 706; 23 358; 24 143, 404, 405–6, 720; 26 261, 306; 27 280; 28 820; 30 17–20, 53, 291; 31 504
Honduras 14 716
Japan 11 827; 17 206; 30 22
Mexico 17 721; 18 900; 30 22
Netherlands, the 19 259
Peru 30 22
Poland 25 108; 30 23
Portugal 8 221; 24 321
Spain 29 286
Switzerland 23 456
United States of America 7 655; 13 12; 14 175; 18 441; 20 287, 837; 22 674, 679; 27 280; 28 385; 30 22, 23
Venezuela 32 175
writings 2 513; 4 753
see also BIOMORPHISM; DECALCOMANIA; METALOMORPHISM
Surréalisme au service de la révolution, Le (*SASDLR*) 24 428, 442; 30 20
Surréalisme même 30 23
Surréalisme Révolutionnaire, Le 2 693
Surréalisme Révolutionnaire, Le 24 428
Surrealismus 24 440
Surrealist Group 25 433
Surrealists, The (Lisbon) 2 902; 6 359; 8 221
Surrey, Gundrada, Countess of *see* GUNDRADA, Countess of Surrey
Surrey, Philip H. 5 568
Surrey, Richard *see* BROOKER, BERTRAM (RICHARD)
Surrey, Thomas Holland, Duke of *see* HOLLAND, THOMAS, Duke of Surrey
Surrey, William of Warenne, Earl of *see* WILLIAM OF WARENNE, Earl of Surrey
Surrey enamel *see under* ENAMELS → techniques
Surry County (VA) Bacon's Castle 4 786; 12 62
Surso, Baldino di *see* BALDINO DI SURSO
Sursock, Nicholas Ibrahim, Museum *see under* BEIRUT
Sursock, Nicolas Ibrahim 19 8
Sursum 31 792; 33 710
Surtees, Robert Smith 4 363
Sur Telbis 14 21
Surugue, Denise-Charlotte 30 24
Surugue, Louis 4 513; 6 473; 12 489; 24 256; 30 24*
Surugue, Marie 30 24
Surugue, Pierre 30 24, 499
Surugue, Pierre-Etienne 30 24
Surugue, Pierre-Louis de 30 24*
Survage, Léopold 8 240; 22 380; 28 347; 30 24–5*
Survey, The 15 830, 831
surveyors 7 420; 30 25–7*
Surveyors' Club 2 314
surveys 2 301; 13 411–12; 24 662; 27 2–3
surveys, photographic 22 27
Surwaya 15 289, 413
monasteries 15 292
sculpture 15 497
Shiva Temple 15 292
stepwell 29 635
temples 15 292
Surya (*fl* 1039) 15 788
Suryavarman, Prince (*fl c.* 554) (Maukhari) 15 260
Suryavarman I, King of Cambodia (*reg* 1002-50) 2 55; 5 472
Suryavarman II, King of Cambodia (*reg* 1113-50) 2 55, 57; 5 460, 462
Susa (Italy)
Cathedral of S Giusto 16 722; 26 690
S Maria Maggiore 16 722
Susa (Mesopotamia) 1 116, 508, *849*, 850, 892, 894; 2 *246*; 10 132–3; 15 *897*, 899, *901*, 902, 904, 905, 906, 907, 908, 909, 912, 913, 920, 921, 922; 21 *267*, 287; 30 27–9*
apadanas 1 879; 2 213; 15 *911*
Arch of Augustus 2 297; 31 349
art forms and materials
architecture 4 771; 15 909
ceramics 6 330; 15 *921*
coins 2 261
façade decoration 10 742
faience (i) (glass) 1 878, 879
figurines 1 885
glass 1 868
gold 1 876
ivory-carvings 1 872
jewellery 1 874, 877
metalwork 15 918, 919, *919*
murals 15 922
pottery 1 894; 16 397, 398, 399, 400, 401
reliefs 26 134
rock crystal 16 540
sculpture 1 117, 886; 15 913, 914; 21 294, 295; 24 217; 29 395; 30 *28*
seals 1 856, 863–4, 877, 883; 21 553
stamp 2 271
statuettes 1 885
stelae 1 509, *509*, 510
stone vessels 2 272
toys 31 254
writing-tablets 1 854
Ayadana 15 *911*
congregational mosque 16 153
kudurrus 21 276
palace 15 902; 21 275; 23 807; 30 29; 33 707
shrine of Daniel 28 634
statue of Darius I 9 888
temples 15 910; 30 432
ziggurat 33 675, 676
Sūsa (Tunisia) *see* SOUSSE
Sūsa, A. 12 77
Susa A pottery *see under* POTTERY → wares
Susanne, Jean 31 834
Suscipi, Lorenzo 24 659
Susenyos, Emperor of Ethiopia (*reg* 1607-32) 10 566
Su Shi 6 748–9, 750, 752, 783, 789, 804, 818; 7 147; 10 692; 17 231; 19 298; 25 785; 30 29–31*, 49
groups and movements 6 630, 819; 14 825; 29 244
patrons and collectors 6 772
works 1 581; 6 823; 18 323; 25 72, 73; 30 *30*
writings 6 771, 773
illustrated 33 647
sushi 17 382
Su Shih *see* SU SHI
Susiana period *see under* MESOPOTAMIA → periods
Sušienka, Jozef 28 856
Susillo (Fernández), Antonio 29 295; 30 31*
Susini, Antonio 29 570; 30 31–2*
collaboration 12 571, 576
patrons and collectors 3 158; 13 906
pupils 30 32
works 12 576
workshop 4 551
Susini, Clemente 16 749
Susini, Francesco 30 31, 32*
patrons and collectors 21 26
works 11 215; 29 570
workshop 4 551
Susini, Giovan *see* SUSINI, FRANCESCO
Susisaari *see* SUOMENLINNA FORTRESS
Suslov, Vladimir (Vasilevich) 27 443
susŏk see KOREA → rocks
Su Song 7 438
suspension bridges *see under* BRIDGES → types
Susquehannock 22 612
Susse, Albert 30 32
Susse, Amédée 30 32
Susse, André 30 33
Susse, Eugène 30 32
Susse, (Emile-Jean-)Jacques 30 33
Susse, Jean 30 32
Susse, Léon 30 32
Susse, Michel-Victor 30 32
Susse, Nicolas 30 32
Susse, Victor 30 32
Susse Frères 8 510; 11 629; 25 418; 30 32
Sussex, Augustus Frederick, Duke of *see* HANOVER, AUGUSTUS FREDERICK, Duke of Sussex
Sussex, Eleanor Lee, Countess of *see* LEE, ELEANOR, Countess of Sussex
Sussex, Frances Sidney, Countess of *see* SIDNEY, FRANCES, Countess of Sussex
Sussex bond *see under* BONDING
Sussex chairs *see under* CHAIRS → types
Sussex stretcher bond *see under* BONDING
Sussex University *see under* FALMER (E. SUSSEX)
Sussman, Eliezer 17 546, 559
works 17 *558*
Süssmann-Hellborn, Louis 3 499
Süssner (family) 8 385
Süssner, Jeremias 8 385; 16 817
Süssner, Konrad Max 8 385
Süss von Kulmbach, Hans *see* KULMBACH, HANS SÜSS VON
Susteren, J. A. van 3 546
Susteren Church 22 816
Sustermans, Justus *see* SUTTERMANS, GIUSTO
Sustjepan, St Stephen 25 340
Sustris, Friedrich 30 34–6*
assistants 5 605; 32 403
collaboration 5 768; 23 757; 33 274

Sustris, Friedrich—cont.
patrons and collectors **11** 819; **12** 387, 897; **17** 511; **30** 33
reproductive prints by others **27** 504
works **9** 750; **11** 193; **12** 346, 368, 389; **13** 701, 703; **15** 137; **22** 302, 305, 307; **26** 103; **30** *35*; **33** 274
Sustris, Lambert **2** 716; **30** 33–4*
pupils **30** 34
works **30** *33*; **33** 355
Sustris, Ottheinrich **25** 672
Susu **1** 393; **3** 47; **13** 834
Susugama
marks **17** *244*
Susumu Ikuta *see* IKUTA, SUSUMU
Susumu Koshimizu **21** 892
Susumu Tange *see* TANGE, SUSUMU
Suta, Romans **26** 384; **30** 36*
Sutchava *see* SUCEAVA
Sutcliffe, Frank Meadow **24** 669; **30** 36–7*
Sutcliffe, Thomas **30** 36
Šutej, Miroslav **30** 37*
Sutemi Horiguchi *see* HORIGUCHI, SUTEMI
Suter, Johann **33** 455
Sutermann, Lambert *see* SUAVIUS, LAMBERT
Sutherland **28** 241
Sutherland, George **30** 39
Sutherland, George Leveson-Gower, 1st Duke of *see* LEVESON-GOWER, GEORGE, 1st Duke of Sutherland
Sutherland, George Leveson-Gower, 2nd Duke of *see* LEVESON-GOWER, GEORGE, 2nd Duke of Sutherland
Sutherland, Graham (Vivian) **2** 560; **30** 37–9*
collaboration **29** 379
groups and movements **18** 718; **22** 751
patrons and collectors **1** 496; **7** 376, 797; **10** 362; **13** 629; **15** 36
tapestries **28** *267*
teachers **13** 649
works **4** 369; **7** 434; **9** 293; **19** 491; **25** 283, 628; **30** *38*, 329, 332, IV1
Sutherland, Helen **32** 800
Sutherland, Jane **14** 307; **30** 39*
Sutherland, John Sutherland Egerton, 6th Duke of *see* EGERTON, JOHN SUTHERLAND, 6th Duke of Sutherland
Sutherland, Thomas **30** 39*
Sutherland-Leveson-Gower, Ronald (Charles) *see* GOWER, RONALD (CHARLES)
Su Ting **21** 885
Sutjeska Franciscan Monastery **4** 462
Sutkovtsy, Church of the Protecting Veil of the Mother of God **31** 550
Sutkus, Antanas **18** 542; **20** 7
Sutnar, Ladislav **8** 402, 406, 411; **11** 845
sutra mounds **17** 321
Sutrapada **15** 267
sutras
Buddhism **5** 90; **7** *118*, 624; **17** 211, 214, 270, 423
China **6** 781–2*; **7** *118*
Japan **7** 624; **17** 148, 211, 214, 217–21, 270, 321, 423
Sutri, Domenico da **2** 453
Su-tsung, Emperor (T'ang; *reg* AD 756-62) *see* SUZONG, EMPEROR
Sutter, Joseph **22** 703, 704; **23** 675; **24** 587; **26** 98
Sutter, Pieter de **14** 326; **32** 374
Suttermans, Cornelis **30** 42
Suttermans, Frans **30** 41
Suttermans, Giusto **3** 560; **16** 673; **21** 25; **30** 39–42*
collaboration **25** 383
patrons and collectors **10** 526; **12** 913
pupils **11** 873
reproductive prints by others **7** 466; **29** 399
works **30** *40*, *41*
Suttermans, Jan **30** 40
Suttermans, Matthias **30** 42
Sutton, Ann **11** 54
Sutton, Denys (Miller) **30** 42*
Sutton, John (*fl* 1662-72) **29** 532
Sutton, John (*fl* 1847) **23** 502
Sutton, Richard **23** 686
Sutton, Robert **1** 518; **25** 554
Sutton, W(illiam) A(lexander) **30** 43*
works **7** *210*, 211
Sutton Bonnington (Notts), St Michael **11** 252
Sutton Courtenay (Oxon), Rectory House **30** 909
roof **30** *908*
Sutton Hoo (Suffolk) **2** *303*; **10** *225*; **23** 537; **30** 43–5*
cauldron **16** 59
enamel **10** 346; **30** *44*
helmet **14** 412
ivory-carvings **2** 80
jewellery **2** 79; **10** 322, 344
metalwork **15** 872; **16** 369
musical instruments **22** 372
silver **9** 655
sword **2** 452; **26** 82
whetstone **30** *45*
Sutton Place (Surrey) **8** 44; **14** 76
architectural decorations **4** 779; **30** 502
gardens **12** 143
Sutton St Mary (Cambs) **29** 413
Sutton Scarsdale (Derbys) **29** 835
Sutton's Panoramic *see under* CAMERAS → types
Sutton Walls **2** *303*
Su Tung-p'o *see* SU SHI
Su Tzu-mei *see* SU ZIMEI
Suun *see* YU TOK-CHANG
Suure-Jaani **10** *536*
church **10** 536
Suvée, Joseph-Benoît **11** 672; **30** 45–6*
competitions **25** 638
groups and movements **24** 171
patrons and collectors **13** 665
pupils **6** 151; **20** 890; **23** 354; **31** 149
reproductions in tapestry **12** 830
teachers **32** 427
works **3** 562; **11** 448; **30** *46*; **31** 390
Suvero, Mark Di *see* DI SUVERO, MARK
Suveş, Church of the Forty Martyrs **5** 676
Suwarrow **7** 790
Suwa Shrine **17** 98
Takehara Tomb **10** 776; **17** *11*, 143; **30** 259*
Suwayda **30** 178
Museum **30** 178
Tomb of Hamrath **13** 407; **20** 863
Suwŏn **18** 282
fortifications **18** 266; **21** 594
gates **18** 279
Hwahong Gate **18** 279
Yŏnju Temple **18** 348
Suxena Altarpiece **12** 162, *162*
Suyapa **14** 714
Suycker, Elizabeth Cornelisdr. **22** 879
Suyderhoef, Jonas **30** 47*; **32** 6, 377
Suyetin, Nikolay **8** 10
Su Yijian **17** 696
Suys, Léon-Pierre **3** 548, 549, 613; **5** 41; **30** 47*
Suys, Tieleman-Frans **3** 547; **30** 47*
attributions **3** 547
collaboration **26** 192, 525
pupils **17** 8; **30** 47
staff **7** 479
works **3** 547; **5** 54; **22** 828
Suytburg *see* SOUBURG
Suzdal' **32** 665–7*
Cathedral of the Birth of the Virgin **27** *369*, 382
Convent of the Protective Veil **32** 666, *667*
Episcopal Palace **27** *369*
kremlin **32** 666
monasteries **32** 666–7*
Monastery of the Saviour and St Euthymius **32** 666–7
sculpture **27** 382
wall paintings **27** 382
see also VLADIMIR-SUZDAL
Suzhou **6** *615*; **7** 151; **30** 47–50*; **33** 435, 642
Academy of Art **7** 149
Baoen Temple
pagoda **6** 655
calligraphy **6** 756, 757–60
coverlets **7** *144*
Duanguang Temple **6** 780, *781*
Embroidery Research Institute **7** 51, 142
enamel **7** 79
gardens **12** 89; **30** 49
houses **6** 687, 692
Huqiu ta **6** 655
Hu yuan **12** 88
jade **7** 9, 10
lacquer **7** 18
Liu yuan **12** 90, 92, *92*
Yuanyang Hall **6** 643
painting **6** 790; **17** 189
paper **7** 116
prints **7** 119, 120
Ruiguang si **7** 114
pagoda **7** 15
silver **7** 110
tomb of Wang Xijue **7** 39
tomb of Zhang Shicheng **7** 77
trade **6** 620
urban planning **6** 662
Wangshi yuan **12** 90, 91, 93
Xuanmiao guan **6** 654
Yi yuan **12** 91, *91*
Zhuozheng yuan **6** 687; **12** 90, 91, *91*, 92
kiosks **18** 72
see also TAOHUAWU
Su Zhuo **29** 905
Su Zimei **30** 49
Suzong, Emperor (Tang; *reg* AD 756-62) **6** 730
Suzor-Coté, Marc-Aurèle de Foy **5** 566, 570; **30** 50*
Suzu **17** 259, 351
Suzuki, Akio **29** 99
Suzuki, Chokichi **17** 324
Suzuki, Kei **7** 161
Suzuki, Makoto **2** 363; **17** 91; **30** 50*, 260
Suzuki, Osamu **14** 452; **17** 267, 268; **33** 480
Suzuki, Sansei **17** 266
Suzuki, Shōnen **31** 525
Suzuki Harunobu **17** 281, 282, 284, 792; **30** 50–52*
collaboration **15** 896; **17** 844
patrons and collectors **10** 487
pupils **16** 561; **28** 598
works **10** 485; **17** 273, 276, 277, 280, 282, 283, 284, *284*, 288, *397*; **23** 391; **30** *51*
Suzuki Harushige *see* SHIBA KŌKAN
Suzuki Hiroshige II (1826-69) **17** 177
Suzuki Hiroshige III (1842-94) **17** 177
Suzuki Kiitsu **17** 180; **30** 52*
teachers **27** 596
Suzuki Kiitsu—cont.
works **17** *180*
Suzuki Reitan **27** 596; **30** 52
Suzuki Shuitsu **17** 180; **30** 52
Suzuki Tetsugoro **17** 401
Švabinský, Max **18** 467; **30** 52*
pupils **25** 832
works **8** 393; **25** 435
Svanberg, Max Walter **30** 52–3*
groups and movements **14** 865; **15** 142, 143; **21** 696; **30** 23
works **10** 483; **21** 696; **30** 81
writings **15** 142–3
Svankmajer, Jan **30** 23
Svankmajerova, Eva **30** 23
Svärdsjö **30** 116
Svarichevsky, Georgiy (Mikhailovich) **31** 782
Svartorp Church **26** 639
Svartsjö Castle **11** 469; **30** 68–9, 71
Svatý Kopeček **8** 398
clocks **8** *397*
St Mary **8** 391
Svayambhunatha **5** 102; **22** *753*; **30** 53*
Harati temple **22** 775
Museum **22** 796
sculpture **22** 774
stupa **22** 756
Svayambhu Stupa **5** *103*
Svaz Českého Díla **8** 423
Sveaborg *see* SUOMENLINNA FORTRESS
Svear **30** 64
Švec, Jindřich **8** 420
Svedberg, Lena **30** 82
Šveics, Erasts **26** 384
Sveinsdóttir, Júlíana **15** 70, 74; **30** 53–4*
Sveinsson, Ásmundur **4** 807; **15** 70; **30** 54*
Sveinsson, Ásmundur, Museum *see under* Reykjavik → museums
Sven **26** 639
Svenskt Tenn **29** 689; **30** 110
Svenneby **27** 124
Svenska Kristallbruken **30** 102
Svenska Slöjdförening **8** 803; **30** 90, 91, 99
Svensk Form *see* SVENSKA SLÖJDFÖRENING
Svenskt Tenn **2** 815; **11** 728
Svensson, Carl O. **21** 696
Svensson, Holger S. **4** 804
works **4** *804*
Sverchkov, D. **22** 170; **26** 149
Sverdlovsk *see* YEKATERINBURG
Sverre, Ole **2** 476; **22** 319
Sverstorp **30** 92
Sveshnikov, Boris **8** 10
Sveshtari **4** 112; **5** 150, 155; **30** 769, 772
Svetieva, Aneta **19** 885
Svetoslavsky, Sergey (Ivanovich) **18** 38; **31** 559, 782
Svidník, Museum of Ukrainian Culture **28** 857
Švihov, Jindřich **30** 55
Švihov, Půta **30** 54
Švihov, Václav **30** 55
Švihov Castle **8** *374*, 377; **30** 54–5*, *55*
Svin'in, Pavel (Petrovich) **12** 2; **27** 439, 440
Svishchov-Paola, Nikolay (Ivanovich) **30** 55*
Svishtov **5** *144*
Church of the Holy Trinity **5** 148
Museum **5** 162
Svistoonoff, Nicolás **9** 714; **30** 56*
Svitnitsky, S. Z. **21** 696
Sviyazev, Ivan **24** 458
Sviyazh Monastery, Cathedral of the Dormition **25** 342
Svoboda, Jan **30** 56*
Svoboda, Jiri **9** 80
Svoboda, Petr **8** 406
Svoboda, Rudolf **8** 388
Svobodniye (gosudarstvenniye) khudozhestvenniye masterskiye *see* SVOMAS
Svobodova, Miloslava **3** 596
Svojanov Castle **24** 462
s'Volders de Rethy, Mathieu, Abbot of Averbode **3** 609
Svolinský, Karel **8** 393
Svomas **3** 684; **4** 811; **9** 296, 747; **13** 654; **17** 764; **18** 181; **19** 13; **20** 301; **22** 178; **27** 442, 580, 685; **28** 597; **30** 56*
teachers
Baranoff-Rossiné, Vladimir (Davidovich) **3** 196
Benois, Leonty (Nikolayevich) **3** 734
Dokuchayev, Nikolay (Vasil'yevich) **9** 73
Fal'k, Robert (Rafailovich) **10** 772
Klyun, Ivan (Vasil'yevich) **18** 141
Konchalovsky, Pyotr (Petrovich) **18** 215
Korolyov, Boris (Danilovich) **18** 388
Kuprin, Aleksandr (Vasil'yevich) **18** 528
Lentulov, Aristarkh (Vasil'yevich) **19** 166
Mashkov, Il'ya (Ivanovich) **20** 549
Petrov-Vodkin, Kuz'ma (Sergeyevich) **24** 566
Pevsner, Antoine **24** 574
Popova, Lyubov' (Sergeyevna) **25** 239
Tatlin, Vladimir (Yevgrafovich) **30** 362
Udal'tsova, Nadezhda (Andreyevna) **31** 520
SVU Mánes *see* MÁNES UNION OF ARTISTS
Swaanswijk, L(ubertus) J(acobus) *see* LUCEBERT
Swabe, Conrad *see* PFLÜGER, CONRAD
Swabian Master
works **11** *453*
Swaelmen, Louis Van der *see* VAN DER SWAELMEN, LOUIS
Swaenken, Michiel int **13** 22
swags **11** 33
Swahili **1** 229, 251, 411; **17** 906; **30** 56–8*
architectural decorations **1** 317
architecture **1** 315, 410; **30** 56–7*
body arts **1** 409
chairs **30** 57
doors **9** 165; **30** *57*
furniture **30** 57*
mats **30** 57
metalwork **30** 57
palaces **23** 824
tombs **30** 57
towns **1** 251
trade **1** 249
wood **9** 165; **30** *57*
woodwork **30** 57
Swain, John Barak **33** 369
Swain, Joseph **1** 666; **32** 794
Swaine, Francis **30** 58*
Swaine, Monamy **30** 58
Swainson, Harold **5** 340; **9** 527
Swakeleys (Middx) **8** 45; **11** 876
Swakopmund **22** 450
Woermann House **22** 450
Swalberg, H. **30** 277
Swales, Francis S. **31** 729
Swali, H. K. **22** 795
Swallow Painter **10** 613
Swami Malai **15** 179
Swamimalli
bronze **4** 853, *853*
Swaminathan, Jagdish **15** 170; **30** 58*
Swan, Abraham **23** 860; **24** 275; **30** 59*

Swan, John 3 280
Swan, Joseph 19 366; 28 831
Swan, Joseph Wilson 24 649
Swan chairs *see under* CHAIRS → types
Swane, Christine 30 59
Swane, Lars 30 59
Swane, Leo 8 762
Swane, Sigurd 30 59*
Swanenburg, Claes van 30 59
Swanenburg, Isaac Claesz. van 22 901; 30 59–60*
 pupils 13 255; 19 101; 30 60; 32 114
 works 19 101; 22 841
Swanenburg, Jacob (Isaacsz.) van 30 59, 60*
 collaboration 23 191
 pupils 19 101; 26 152, 153
 works 22 841
Swanenburg, Willem (Isaacsz.) van (1581-1612) 10 387, 391; 28 309; 30 59, 60*; 33 419
Swanevelt, Herman van 28 754; 30 60–61*
 attributions 24 253
 collaboration 19 248
 groups and movements 9 462
 patrons and collectors 3 745; 6 30; 18 671; 19 238
 personal collection 18 624
 pupils 27 263
 reproductive prints by others 32 693
 works 20 860; 30 *60*
Swank, Luke 25 5
Swan Mazer 10 323
Swann, Joseph 30 542
Swanpool Garden Suburb *see under* LINCOLN
Swansea (W. Glams) 32 *780*
 art school 32 792
 chalets 6 395
 Glyn Vivian Art Gallery and Museum 32 791
 Guildhall 4 672
 potteries 32 789
 Royal Institution of South Wales 32 791
 School of Art 32 790, 792
 Town Hall 31 242
 Weaver Flour Mill 7 693
Swansea porcelain factory 5 732; 7 481
Swansea Triptych 1 518, *519*; 11 421
Swanson, Gloria 29 *601*
Swanson, Harold F. 2 760
Swanson, J. Robert F. 27 475
Swanson Associates 27 476
Swanton, R. John 9 719; 22 676
Swanzy, Mary 16 17; 30 61*
Swart (van Groningen), Jan (*c.* 1500-60) 3 555; 8 102; 14 381; 30 61–2*; 33 355
 works 1 658; 27 256; 30 *62*
Swart, Jan (1754-94) 1 808
Swart, Pieter de 14 39; 22 865; 30 62*
 works 22 827; 28 594
Swartwout, Egerton 30 62–3*
Swartz, Johann David 30 78
Swartzmann, Henry J. 22 363
Swarzędz 25 122
Swasey, Albert E. 14 207
swastikas 8 195; 23 562
Swatch 28 798
Swatow *see* SHANTOU
Swatow ware *see under* PORCELAIN → wares
Sway (Hants), Peterson's Tower 11 242
Swazi 1 289, 297, 416, 417, 418, 419
Swaziland 1 *214*; 30 63*
Swazo Hinds, Patrick 22 596
sweating 24 106
Sweatman, Estelle Mary *see* SWEATMAN, JO
Sweatman, Jo 29 243
Swebach, François-Louis 30 63
Swebach, Jacques-François (-Joseph) 4 300, 888; 21 429; 30 63–4*
Swebach-Desfontaines, Jean-François 11 610
Swedberg, Rolf 30 111
Sweden 30 64–120*, *65*; 32 512
 altarpieces 13 120; 23 *255*; 30 77, 83
 aquatints 11 173
 architecture 30 66–7*, 68–75*
  brick 30 66
  Gothic 13 50, 56
  military 21 570
  Romanesque 26 592–3*
  stone 30 66
  vernacular 32 286–9*
  wood 32 286–7
 archives 2 371*
 art history 30 119–20*
 banknotes 3 180
 bark 31 260
 basins 30 *111*
 beakers 30 105
 beds 30 *93*
 benches 32 *519*
 bonader see friezes
 bone china 30 100–101
 books 30 77
 boxes 30 *105*, *110*, 111, 112*
 brass 30 111
 brick 30 66
 bronze 30 111; 32 *513*, *516*
 brooches 32 *516*
 bureaux 5 191
 busts 5 *303*
 cabinets (ii) (furniture) 30 *95*
 caskets 30 *108*
 cast iron 30 109, 110
 castles 14 *368*; 30 67, *67*, *68*
 cathedrals 19 *795*; 31 *693*
 ceramics 30 97*
 chairs 30 *96*
 chandeliers 30 111
 chapels 19 *284*
 chests-of-drawers 30 94, 95
 churches 30 66–7, *71*, 75–7; 31 *794*
 coffeepots 30 106
 coins 7 538, 539
 collections 11 851; 30 118–19*
  erotic art 10 487
  paintings 29 366
 commodes 7 659; 30 *94*
 copper 30 111, *111*
 crucifixes 26 *647*; 30 83
 cups 30 *99*
 damask 19 418; 30 115*
 dealing 30 118*
 design 8 803
 diplomatic gifts 16 445
 display of art 9 23, 26, *26*
 dolls 31 260
 doors 9 *155*, 156
 drawings 9 *758*
 drinking-horns 30 *110*
 earthenwares 30 *98*
 embroidery 30 115*
 enamel 28 68; 30 112, *112*
 engravings 11 174; 12 634; 29 *685*; 30 78
 erotic art 10 473, 483; 21 *644*
 etching 30 *110*
 ewers 30 *111*
 exhibitions 29 *688*
 faience (ii) (ceramics) 30 97
 felt 10 875
 figureheads 28 612
 follies 11 242
 fonts (baptismal) 26 *640*; 30 83
 fortifications 21 570
 frames 11 *468*, *469*, *470*, *471*, 471–2, *472*, *474*, *475*, *476*
 friezes 30 116*
 funerary monuments 30 84, *84*
 furniture 20 468; 30 92–6*, *93*, *96*
Sweden—cont.
 gables 11 876
 galleries (iv) (art) 9 23, *24*
 gardens 12 135
 gilding 30 *94*
 glass 30 *101*, 101–3*, *103*
 goblets 30 *101*, 102
 gold 30 104–9*, 112*, *112*, *113*
 granitelle 30 113
 harness-mounts 32 *512*, *513*
 heraldry 14 404
 historiography 30 119–20*
 houses 32 286, 287–8, 532
 industrial scenes 30 79
 interior decoration 13 864; 29 *690*; 30 87–92*, *88*, *89*, *90*, *91*
 iron 9 *155*, 156; 30 109–10*
 jewellery 30 112–13*; 32 528
 lace 30 115*
 leather 19 5*
 libraries 30 *74*, 119*
 limestone 13 103
 linen 30 115
 lithography 30 100
 mahogany 30 *95*
 manuscript illumination 30 77
 maps 20 299
 marble 5 *303*; 28 *462*
 marks 30 104, 108, 110
 marquetry 20 468
 memorial stones 32 518, *518*, 521, *522*, *523*, *524*, 525
 metalwork 13 167; 30 104–11*
 mirror frames 30 90
 mirrors 30 95
 monasteries 7 703
 moss 32 286
 museums 30 118–19*
 narratives 32 *522*, *523*
 necklaces 30 *113*
 nude figures 17 *662*; 28 *462*
 objects of vertu 30 112–14*
 painting 30 75–80*, 81–2*
  allegorical 30 *78*
  animal subjects 19 *379*
  battle 19 *136*
  genre 10 100
  landscape 22 *541*; 23 *206*; 30 79; 31 707
   19th cent. 30 *80*
  miniatures 21 641, *644*; 28 68
  mythological 17 *662*
  still-lifes 30 78
  wall 30 75–7, *76*, *77*
   19th cent. 17 *8*
   20th cent. 30 *82*
 palaces 29 *689*
 paper 24 40
 papier mâché 30 90
 patchwork 24 252
 patronage 30 117*
 periodicals 24 451*
 pewter 30 110–11
 photoarchives 30 119
 plaster 29 840*
 porcelain 30 *99*, 99–101*, *100*
 porphyry 30 113–14*
 portraits
  painting 21 *511*; 30 77–8
   17th cent. 11 *468*
   18th cent. 11 *470*, *471*; 27 *169*; 30 *524*
   19th cent. 33 *705*
   20th cent. 18 *802*
  self-portraits 18 *802*; 33 *705*
 pottery 30 97–9*
 print rooms 9 26
 prints 9 26; 30 80–81*
 punch-bowls 30 105
 rock art 11 330; 18 *103*; 25 532, *532*
 roods 27 124
 rugs 5 829, 830
 runes 32 518
 rune-stones 31 748
 salts 30 *106*
 sandstone 13 102
Sweden—cont.
 sculpture 30 83–7*
  display 9 23, *24*
  Gothic 13 102–3, 119, 120; 30 83
  marble 28 *462*
  Neo-classicism 28 *462*; 30 *86*
  relief 13 *103*; 26 *640*
  Romanesque 19 *796*; 26 639*; 30 83
  stone 26 639*, *640*
  tomb 30 *84*
  20th cent. 30 *87*
 ship-decoration 28 612
 silk 28 717; 30 90, 115*
 silver 29 689; 30 104–9*, *107*
 silver-gilt 30 *104*, *105*, *106*, *108*
 snuff-boxes 30 111, *112*
 stadia 14 227
 stained glass 13 190–91, *190*
 staircases 29 *525*
 steel 30 109–10*, *110*
 stone 13 *103*; 26 639*; 30 66
 stone-carvings 32 *518*, *522*, *523*, *524*
 stonewares 30 99
 stoves 8 190; 30 89, 97
 stucco 29 840*; 30 85, 88; 32 923
 tankards 30 *104*, 104–5
 tapestries 30 114–15*, *114*, 320
 teapots 30 106
 terracotta 30 *86*
 textiles 19 418; 30 114–15*
 theatres 30 675, *676*, 677
 tiles 30 89, 97, 884*
 timber structures 32 287
 town halls 31 *242*
 towns 31 718
 trade 6 624
  ceramics 6 332
  sculpture 11 98
  silk 28 717
 trays 30 97
 treatises (painting) 28 68
 trompe l'oeil 30 89
 universities 30 *72*
 vases 30 *98*, *100*, *103*
 vernacular art 30 116–17*
 villas 2 *611*
 wallpaper 30 89, 90
 walls 32 *601*
 wood 23 *255*; 26 *647*; 32 286–7
 wood-carvings 30 84; 32 *519*
 see also SCANDINAVIA; VIKING
Swedish Craft Union *see* SVENSKA SLÖJDFÖRENING
Swedish East India Company 17 895; 30 97
Swedish Friends of Textile Art 30 329
Sweelinck, Gerrit Pietersz. *see* PIETERSZ., GERRIT
Sweeney, James Johnson 21 855; 23 121; 30 120–21*; 31 613
Sweersz., Hendrik 4 148
Sweert, Emmanuel 11 225
Sweerts, Michiel 5 43; 11 226; 30 121–2*
 groups and movements 3 143
 patrons and collectors 21 541
 works 9 706; 11 445; 12 289; 30 *121*
Sweet, William 29 118
sweeteners *see under* BRUSHES → types
Sweetheart Abbey (Dumfries & Galloway) 28 224
sweetmeat dishes 31 *635*
sweetness 6 570
Sweet Style 16 690–91*
Sweezy, Carl 22 594
 works 22 *594*
Swegher, Jan Gerritsz. 20 666
Swell (Glos), Manor House 6 604
Swellendam 29 *103*, 114
Swenet *see* ASWAN
Sweringen, Mantis J. van 7 429
Sweringen, Oris P. van 7 429
Swerts, Jan 1 604; 17 474; 22 329; 33 635
Sweynheim, Konrad 4 8; 20 587; 28 306
Swiczinsky, Helmut 7 798–9
Swidde, Willem 8 455
 works 29 *685*
Świdnica 21 571
 SS Stanislas and Wenceslas 13 57; 25 111
Swid Powell 30 870
Świerczyński, Rudolf 25 100, 142; 30 122*
Świerzań 25 124
Swierzy, Waldemar 25 354
Święta Lipka Church 25 130
Swieten, Johannes Cornelisz. van 19 102
Swieten, Johan van 20 458
Swieten, van (family) 14 495; 22 836
Świetopełk II, Duke of Gdańsk (*d* 1266) 12 223
Swift, Henry 13 710
Swift, Jonathan 4 366; 16 25; 21 776; 24 252; 27 868
Swift Robe 22 *619*
swimming pools 32 439
 see also BATHS; LIDOS
Swinburn, Jorge 6 594
Swinburne, Algernon Charles 1 170; 2 530; 19 588; 30 122–3*
Swinburne, Henry 8 763; 13 303
Swinburne Pyx 10 322
Swinden, Albert 1 772
Swindon (Wilts)
 Reliance Controls Factory 14 521
 Renault Distribution Centre 10 749; 14 521, *522*; 16 55; 30 468
swing bridges *see under* BRIDGES → types
Swing Painter 13 509; 32 68*
Swinomish (WA) 22 671
Swint, Cornelio 2 103
Swinton Pottery 26 489
Swiny, Stuart 33 688
swish *see under* ARCHITECTURE → techniques
Swiss Archaeological Institute 10 81
Swiss Provinces Exhibitions, 1939 *see under* ZURICH
Swiss Stores 16 889
Swithun, Bishop of Winchester 33 229
Switzer, Stephen 4 806; 12 128, 129; 30 123*
Switzerland 30 123–57*, *124*
 altarpieces 11 *452*
 architecture 4 777, 789; 30 125–9*
  Carolingian 27 554
  Gothic 30 125–6
  Modernism 29 *603*
 archives 2 371*
 arm rings 6 155
 art history 30 156–7*
 artists' biographies 30 156
 art legislation 2 561
 art market 30 153–4
 auction houses 30 153
 book illustrations 4 *358*
 bowls 27 *77*
 brick 4 777, 788, 789
 bridges 14 388; 20 118, *119*
 bronze 25 547; 27 *91*; 30 *138*, *146*
 brooches 6 157; 17 *520*
 busts 27 *15*
 cameos 17 *520*
 cane 33 157
 caricatures 30 133
 carnivals 5 786
 castles 6 *602*
 cathedrals 12 *276*; 14 *518*
 cemeteries 6 157
 ceramics 30 143–4*
 chalets 6 395, *395*

Switzerland—cont.
chess sets **6** 557
churches **3** 886; **22** 186, *186*; **30** *126*
clocks **10** 135
cloisters **3** 333
coats of arms **12** 272; **14** 420
coins **7** 537, 538, 539
collections **15** 888; **17** 886; **30** 152–5*
public **3** 336; **30** 154
collections, public **1** 771
commercial art **7** 655, 656
concrete **20** 118; **22** 186; **31** 465
cotton **8** 37
crypts **27** 554
cupboards **30** *142*
daggers **30** 146
dealing **30** 153–4*
dictionaries of art **30** 156
drawings
allegorical **19** *414*
ink **19** *257*
landscape **19** *257*
Renaissance **1** *788*; **8** *822*
16th cent. **13** *268*; **29** *673*
18th cent. **30** *132*
20th cent. **25** *686*
education (art) **30** 155–6*
applied art **30** 155, 156
crafts **30** 155
embroidery **30** *150*, 150–51*
enamel **25** 547; **30** *145*, 148
engravings **30** *131*
etchings **13** 267; **21** *152*; **25** VII2
façade decoration **10** 737, *739*, 741
faience (ii) (ceramics) **30** 143, *144*
fans **10** *781*
figurines **30** *147*
flagons **30** 146
fountains **11** *346*; **30** 136
frames **11** *452*
furniture **30** 142–3*; **33** 157
genealogies **12** 272
glass **9** 646; **27** *77*; **30** 144–5*, *145*
gold **6** 155; **17** *520*; **27** 15, *15*; **30** 145–6, 147, 151
government buildings **11** *841*
guidebooks **13** 810
guilds **30** 154
heraldry **12** 272; **14** 416
historiography **30** 156–7*
horsehair **30** 151
houses **25** 502*
Arts and Crafts Movement **3** *75*
farmhouses **30** 126–7, *127*
Gothic **11** 773
pile dwellings **25** 502*
town **30** 127
housing **3** 841; **30** *128*
iconography **30** 136
interior decoration **30** 140–41*, *141*
iron **30** 139
jade **16** 861
jewellery **17** 526; **25** 547; **30** 148
knitting **18** 157
lace **18** 590; **30** 151–2*
libraries **30** 156*
linen **13** 194
lithography **25** *354*
manuals (mining) **8** 823
manuscript illumination **12** 272; **13** 151; **30** 130*
manuscripts **5** 805
marcasite **17** 525; **30** 148
marks **30** 146, 147
mass production **7** 448
metalwork **6** 157; **30** 145–7*
miniatures (manuscript illumination) **3** *188*; **20** *560*
models
architectural **29** *607*
modules **14** 86
monasteries **10** *116*; **22** *61*
monstrances **30** 145

Switzerland—cont.
monuments **5** *446*
museums **30** 154–5*
neck rings **6** 155
nude figures **12** *798*; **19** *414*
objects of vertu **30** 148*
onyx **17** *520*
painting **30** 129–35*
Abstract art **1** *77*; **18** *112*
allegorical **14** *615*; **24** *564*
Baroque **30** 132*
fresco **22** 385
glass **12** *798*; **22** *341*
landscape **30** 133; **33** 287, *291*
Romanticism **30** *133*
miniatures **21** 641
mythological **8** *823*; **17** *682*
Neo-classicism **30** 132–3*
religious **21** *136*; **30** *130*; **33** *287*
Renaissance **30** 131*
Rococo **30** 132*
Romanticism **30** 133*
Symbolism (movement) **30** 134*
vedute **30** 133
wall **30** 129–30*
watercolours **12** *500*; **29** *673*; **32** VIII2
16th cent. **11** *788*; **14** *438*
20th cent. **16** *788*; **19** *541*; **30** 134–5*
panoramas **6** 66
patronage **30** 152–3*
pattern books **24** *274*
pearls **17** *520*
periodicals **24** 453*
pewter **30** 146–7
photoarchives **30** 156*
portals **18** *875*
portraits
group **21** *153*
Renaissance **14** *667*
17th cent. **21** *153*; **33** *82*
18th cent. **30** *132*
20th cent. **30** *134*
posters **25** 351, *354*
printing **8** 37
prints **25** VII2; **30** 131, 133
railway stations **29** 491
rolls **12** 272
roofs **2** 512
samplers **30** 150–51
sculpture **30** 136–40*
bronze **30** *138*
Concrete art **30** *138*
Gothic **14** *318*; **22** *919*; **30** 136
relief **2** *489*
Romanesque **26** 635*
stone **26** 635*
20th cent. **30** *139*
sideboards **30** 142
silhouettes **28** *714*
silk **30** 151
silver **30** 146, 147, 151
silver-gilt **30** *146*, *147*
stained glass **11** 773; **13** 186; **30** 130*, 131, 134
statuettes **27** *91*
steel **2** 512
stone **26** 635*
stoves **30** 143, *144*
straw **30** 151
stucco **30** 136
synagogues **17** 544
tapestries **30** 148–9*, 311*
Gothic **13** 194, 196
Heidnischwerk **30** 148
15th cent. **30** *149*
tempera **8** *823*
textiles **30** 148*, *150*, 150–52*
theatres **30** 665
theories
architectural **33** 297
art **33** 297–8
tiles **30** 143, 884–5*
tombs **22** *919*; **30** 136
towns **30** 127

Switzerland—cont.
trade
dress **1** 347
paper **24** 48
tureens **30** *146*
veneers **30** *142*
vessels **30** *146*
villas **19** *40*
watches **7** 448; **30** 148
wicker **33** 157
willow **33** 157
wood-carvings **30** 136
woodcuts **4** *358*; **25** *610*; **29** *674*
Swoboda, Karl Maria **2** 833
Swoll, Hendrick van **32** 268
Swopp, Conrat *see* CONRAT SWOPP
sword fittings **7** 81
sword grips **2** 451, 452, 456; **6** *260*
sword guards **2** 451, 453; **14** 429; **16** *506*
sword hilts **2** 451, 452, 454, *454*, *456*; **7** *835*; **15** 696; **16** 527, 528
see also POMMELS; SWORD GRIPS; SWORD GUARDS
Sword of Aurangzeb **16** 60
sword ornaments **2** *587*, 587; **17** 98
swords **2** 448, 451–7*; **14** 404; **26** 82
historical and regional traditions
Aboriginal Australia **1** 54
Africa **1** 361
Anglo-Saxon **2** 452
Asante **1** 242, 354, 361; **2** *586*, 586–7*
Azerbaijan **2** 900; **16** *506*
Benin, Kingdom of **1** 354, 361
Britain **2** 452
Burma **5** 259–60
Celtic **6** 157, 159; **18** 828; **25** 540
Central Asia, Eastern **6** 305
Central Asia, Western **6** 260, 261, 262
China **7** 7, *22*, 56, 97
Egypt **16** *506*
Germany **2** *452*, 453, *453*
Greece, ancient **2** 451
Hallstatt culture (*c.* 750–*c.* 450 BC) **2** 451
Helladic **14** 356
Indian subcontinent **15** 677, 678, *678*
Indonesia **15** 818
Indus civilization **15** 677
Iran **16** *508*
Iraq **16** *506*
Islamic **2** 452; **16** 503–4, 505, *506*, 508, *508*, 509
Italy **2** 453
Japan **17** 28, 302, 361, 362, 363, 364, 386; **22** 433
Korea **18** 345
La Tène culture (*c.* 450–.*c* 50 BC) **2** 451; **18** 828
Mesoamerica, Pre-Columbian **21** 245
Minoan **2** 451
Mongolia **21** 878
Mycenaean **2** 451; **14** 356
Nigeria **33** *555*
Ottoman **16** 508, *508*, 509
Ottonian **23** 658
Philippines **24** 631
Prehistoric art **25** 540–41*
Romania **30** 769
Rome, ancient **2** 451, 452; **27** 93
Scandinavia **2** 452
Scythian **6** 260
Sogdiana **6** 261
Spain **2** 452; **16** *506*
Sri Lanka **29** 469
Syria **16** *506*
Thracian **30** 769
Turkey **16** *506*, *508*
Viking **2** 452
Yoruba **33** *555*

swords—cont.
materials
bronze **2** 451; **7** 56; **14** 356; **16** *506*; **18** 345
chalcedony **6** 261
enamel **2** 452
glass **17** 386
gold **2** *452*; **6** 261; **7** *22*; **15** *678*; **16** *506*, *508*
iron **2** 451; **7** 56, 97; **23** 658; **27** 93
ivory **16** *506*; **33** *555*
jade **7** 7, 56
lacquer **17** 302
obsidian **21** 245
silver **6** 262, 305, 306
silver-gilt **2** *453*
steel **15** *678*; **16** 60, *508*; **17** 361
turquoise **6** 261, 262
techniques
casting **2** 452
chasing **2** 452
chiselling **2** 454, 455, 456
cut-steel work **2** 456
damascening **2** 454–5
etching **2** 449, 452, 453
Goldschmelz **2** 453
pattern welding **2** 451
types
karabela **25** 128
small-swords **2** 456, *457*
Swymmer, Anthony Langley **27** 356
Swynnerton, Annie Louisa **10** 878; **19** 620; **30** 157*
Swynnerton, Joseph **30** 157
Sy, Jean de *see* JEAN DE SY
Sybaris **13** 386, 586
Syberg, Anna **30** 158
Syberg, Fritz (Christian Friedrich Wilhelm Heinrich), Baron von **8** 735; **30** 157–8*; **33** 595
sycamore **6** 559; **11** *591*; **14** 903, 907; **20** 466; **33** 324
Sychem, Pieter van **3** 598
Sychen, van (family) **3** 599
Sychev, N. **33** 516
Sychra, Vladimír **8** 393, 394
Sychrov Castle **8** 379
Syder, Daniel *see* SEITER, DANIEL
Sydney **1** *37*; **2** *736*; **30** 158–61*, *159*
7 Cranbrook Avenue, Cremorne **2** 741
Académie Julian **2** 771
Ancher's House **30** 160
Anzac House **2** 742
Anzac War Memorial **2** 741, 753
Archibald Fountain **2** 769
architecture **2** 736, 738, 739, 742, 743; **4** 790; **32** 307
Art Gallery of New South Wales **2** 739, 770; **32** 339
collections **2** 769; **7** 155; **19** 626; **24** 802; **29** 241
paintings **15** 746
Australia Council library **2** 773
Australian Museum **3** 252; **19** 287
collections **1** 66; **17** 434; **23** 739; **29** 241
Australia Square **28** 375
Bahā'ī temple **30** 451
Barncleuth house **2** 740
Carthona **2** 738
Cohen House **30** 161
College of the Arts **2** 601, 771, 772
Darling Harbour **9** 59
Darlingshurst Court House **2** 738
East Sydney Technical College **2** 753, 772
Eryldene **2** 741; **7** 620
Exhibition Centre **2** 743
exhibitions **2** 762
Forbes Street Housing, Woolloomooloo **2** 743
furniture **2** 757, 759
General Post Office **2** 739, 752
Gladesville Bridge **4** 803

Sydney—cont.
glass **2** 763
Government House **2** 737, 738, 758; **4** 787
Government Stables *see* NSW Conservatorium of Music
Greenway **7** 620
Highlands **2** 740
Hyde Park Barracks **2** 737; **13** *622*
IBM Building **2** 742
Kuring-gai College of Advanced Education **30** 161
lithography **2** *744*
Lucas's House **30** 160
Macquarie Street church **26** 18
Mechanics School of Art **2** 772
metalwork **2** 764, 765
Mint **2** 737
Mitchell Library **2** 772
MLC Centre **2** 742; **7** 696; **28** *375*, 834
Modern Art Centre **4** 107
Muller's House **30** 161
Museum of Applied Arts and Sciences **30** 160
Museum of Contemporary Art **2** 771; **30** 160
library **2** 773
Power collection **25** 400
Nelson House **2** 740
New South Wales Club **7** 470
New South Wales Parliament **2** 737
New South Wales University of Technology **2** 772
NSW Conservatorium of Music **2** 738
Opera House **2** 742; **7** 670, 696; **23** 426; **27** 129; **30** 684; **31** 776, *777*
lighting **19** 367
painting **2** 744, 745, 746
Power Gallery of Contemporary Arts *see* University of Sydney → Power Gallery of Contemporary Arts
Queen Victoria Markets Building **2** 740
St Andrew's Cathedral **2** 738
St James **2** 737
St Mary's Roman Catholic Cathedral **2** 738
Seidler House **2** 742
State Library of New South Wales
collections **2** 771
Supreme Court **18** 887
Sydney Harbour Bridge **4** 803
Sydney International Exhibition, 1879–80 **15** 883
Town Hall **2** 739
Union Club **7** 470
University of Sydney **2** 741
Great Hall **2** 738
library **2** 772
Power Bequest **25** 400
Power Gallery of Contemporary Arts **2** 771; **25** 400
Power Institute of Fine Arts **2** 749, 770
Tin Sheds Art Workshop **2** 772
Victoria Memorial **16** 21
Water Board headquarters **2** 742
Woolley house **33** 373
Sydney 9 **30** 160*
Sydney Group **11** 784; **23** 336; **30** 160*
Sydney school **30** 160–61*; **33** 373
Sydney Subscription Cup **2** 764
Sydykhanov, Abdrahshid **17** 867
Syed Ahmad Jamal **20** 171, 172
Syed Thajudeen **20** 172
Syene *see* ASWAN
syenite **29** 700
Syfer, Conrat *see* SIFER, CONRAT
Syfer, Hans **14** 159; **19** 29; **29** 393; **30** 161*
Syfer, Lenhart **30** 161

Syfrewast, John de *see* JOHN DE SIFERWAS
Sygma **27** 616
Syjalon, Antoine **11** 604
Sykes, Godfrey **11** 360; **30** 162*
Sykes, Mark **30** 507; **33** 345
Sykes, Tatton **29** 765
Sýkora, Zdeněk **8** 394; **30** 162*
Sylhet **3** *166*; **15** 727; **30** 162*
syllabaries **17** 211
syllabograms **1** 853
Syllas, Leo de **2** 318
Sylva, Carmen **20** 380
Sylva-Tarroucca, Arnošt Emanuel, Count **29** 652
Sylvester (family) **33** 4
Sylvester II, Pope (*reg* 999-1003) **2** 349
Sylvester, David **18** 97; **28** 880
Sylvester, L. **12** 468
Sylvester Petrus Sancta *see* PETRUS SANCTA, SYLVESTER
Sylvestine Order **3** 709
Sylvestre, François **24** 211
Sylvestre, Israël **7** 194
Sylvestre, Louis **4** 536
Sylvestris, Bernard **19** 356
Sylvius, Balthazar **3** 598
Sylvius, François de la Boë *see* BOË SYLVIUS, FRANÇOIS DE LA
Sylvius, Johan **29** 690; **30** 163*
symbolism (critical term) **1** 651, 660; **15** 89, 94–6, *95, 96*; **18** 739; **19** 355–7; **22** 686
Africa **1** 260–64*
architecture **5** 476, 479
Buddhism **6** 632
Byzantine **9** 519–20*
China **6** 630–33*, 726
Daoism **6** 632
Early Christian (*c.* AD 250-843) **9** 519–20*
Greece, ancient **13** 415–16*
Indian subcontinent **15** 424*
Indonesia **15** 758
Islamic **16** 136, 468
Netherlands, the **15** 94
Prehistoric art **25** 474
Romanesque **26** 662–3, 700–701
Rome, ancient **26** 922–4*
Symbolism (movement) **1** 661; **5** 880; **7** 451; **12** 194; **15** 44, 156; **18** 716; **19** 36; **21** 340; **22** 422; **23** 504; **24** 743; **26** 743; **30** 168–70*
art forms
drawings **3** *564*; **24** 243; **31** *148*
frames **11** *450, 477*
painting **22** 416
Belgium **11** *450*; **18** *24*
Denmark **23** 116; **33** *214*
Estonia **10** *540*
France **5** *880*; **12** *190*; **22** *90, 91*; **30** *170*
Netherlands, the **8** 778
Norway **22** *292*
Poland **21** *52*; **24** *12*
Russia **27** 392
Switzerland **14** *615*; **30** 134*
sculpture **3** 291
theatre **30** 685
collections **18** 466
commentaries **7** 388; **13** 232; **17** 723; **20** 853
exhibitions **8** 715
periodicals **24** 426
regional traditions
Austria **17** 517
Belgium **3** 563–4; **14** 137; **18** 23, 626; **32** 251, 591
Czechoslovakia **4** 60
Denmark **8** 741
Finland **11** 95, 96
France **2** 732; **3** 813; **8** 245; **10** 884; **12** 189; **14** 396; **22** 91, 421; **23** 569; **24** 334; **25** 356; **26** 72, 191; **27** 639; **28** 181, 502; **32** 739; **33** 142
Iceland **18** 106
Symbolism (movement)
regional traditions—cont.
Poland **25** 107
Russia **3** 692; **4** 156, 178; **12** 870; **30** 389
symbols **1** 660; **10** 1; **15** 412; **30** 163–7*, 811
see also HIEROGLYPHS; SIGNS
Syme, David **2** 601
Syme, John **28** 237
Symeon **25** 335
Symeon, Archbishop of Thessaloniki **9** 641
Symeon d-Zayte, Bishop of Harran (700-34) **31** 435
Symeon Metaphrastes (*fl* mid-10th cent.) **9** 616
Symeon the New Theologian **7** 229
Symi **9** 566
Symmachi **9** 3
Symmachus, Pope (*reg* 498-514) **26** 801
Symmachus, Q. Aurelius **27** 53
symmetria **13** 467; **26** 924–5
symmetrical knots *see under* KNOTS
symmetry **13** 412; **26** 924; **30** 171*
Symondes, Simon **5** 515
Symonds, John Addington **12** 214; **30** 171–2*
Symonds, Richard **30** 172*; **33** 409
works **13** 708; **23** 788; **29** 437
Symons (family) **12** 429
Symons, Arthur **3** 446; **8** 596
Syn **30** 172*
synaesthesia **30** 169
synagogues **17** 538, 540–52*, 568*; **30** 173*
Afghanistan **17** 551
Algeria **17** 551
Ashkenazi **17** 544–5
Australia **17** 547
Belarus' **17** *546*
Bosnia **17** 547; **27** *820*
Bulgaria **17** 545
China **17** 551
Czech Republic **17** 544, *544*, 547; **25** *444*
Denmark **17** 547
Egypt **17** *550*, 551
England **17** 544, 548
France **17** 545, 547, 548
Germany **17** 543, 544, 546, 547, 548, *548*, 549
Neo-classicism **33** *40*
Gothic **25** *444*
Greece **17** 540, 543
Hungary **17** 544, 547
Iraq **17** 550
Israel **17** *540, 541*
Italy **17** 543, 544, 545, 546, 547, 548
Jordan **17** 543
Kurdistan **17** 550
Lydia **19** 841
Morocco **17** 551
Netherlands, the **17** 544, 545, 548, 549
Northern Ireland **17** 548
Poland **17** 543, 544–6, 548; **25** 98
Portugal **17** 545
Rome, ancient **27** 60
Russia **17** 547
Sephardi **17** 545
Slovakia **17** 548
Spain **17** 544; **31** *86*
Surinam **17** 545
Switzerland **17** 544
Syria **17** 543, 550
Tunisia **17** 543, 551
Turkey **17** 543, 545, *545*, 551
Ukraine **17** 545, 546; **31** 550
United States of America **14** 198; **17** 545, 547, 548, 549, *549*
Yemen **17** 551
Synchromism **1** 74; **4** 888; **19** 878; **27** 360; **29** 670; **30** 173*; **31** 607
works **30** *173*
Syndiv, Lizogub house **31** 551
Synergetics Incorporated **11** 835
Syng, Philip, sr (1676-1739) **31** 648
Syng, Philip, jr (1703-89) **31** 648, 653
Synge, John Millington **33** 516
Synkovičy Church **3** 526
Synnada *see* SUHUT
Synod of Carthage **9** 642
Synpunkt **24** 451
Synthetic Cubism *see under* CUBISM → types
synthetic dyes *see under* DYES → types
synthetic fibres *see under* FIBRES → types
Synthetism **7** 451; **22** 421; **30** 169, 173–4*; **32** 738
France **3** 813; **25** 215; **28** *484*, 484
Norway **22** 291
syntroni *see under* BENCHES → types
Syon Abbey (Middx) **21** 840
Syon Cope **10** 353; **14** 425; **23** 461; **30** *541*, 542
Syon House (Middx) **1** 136, *137*; **8** 48; **9** 27; **10** 233, 361; **22** 738; **24** 390; **25** 192
Ante Room **28** 28
carpets **5** 839; **10** 358
furniture **10** 296
gate lodges **12** 176
interior decoration **5** 907; **10** 279; **23** 544
paintings **3** 286; **9** 482; **13** 303; **19** 121, 123; **26** 393; **31** 413
sculpture **6** 98
Sype, Laurenz van de **12** 369
Syracuse (Sicily) **13** *362*, 401; **16** *103, 621*; **26** *886*; **30** 174–6*, *175*
Altar of Hieron II **13** 406
Altar of Zeus Eleutherios **13** 380
amphitheatre **1** 797; **28** 655
art forms and materials
architecture **16** 640
catapults **21** 557
coins **13** 586, 587, *587*; **28** 654
copies **13** 587
figurines **13** 579, 580, 581
pottery **13** 496, 502; **28** 654
sculpture **13** 462; **27** 29
Augusta **16** 172; **28** 656
Castello Maniace **16** 172; **28** 656
Catacombs of S Giovanni **28** 655
Catacombs of Vigna Cassia hypogeum A **28** 655
Cathedral **16** 640, *640*
see also Temple of Athena
Euryalus fort **21** *557*, 558
fortifications **21** 556, 558; **28** 654
Ionic temple **13** 398; **30** 434
Museo Regionale Archeologico **28** 653, 657
Neapolis **28** 654
Olympieion *see* Temple of Olympian Zeus
Piazza del Duomo **28** *801*
Piazza Minerva **28** *801*
Temple of Apollo **13** 398, 399; **16** 622
Temple of Athena **13** 390; **28** 655
Temple of Olympian Zeus **2** 351; **13** 398
Theatre **13** 385
town walls **21** 556
Syracuse (NY; USA), Everson Museum of Art **24** 326
Syracuse Printmakers **25** 629
Syrewicz, Bolesław **9** 394
Syria **13** *362*; **16** *104*; **21** *267*; **30** 176–81*, *180*
ambos **1** 764
arches **2** 295, 297
architectural decorations **16** 146, 245, *255*
architecture **13** 405
brick **4** 791
Syria
architecture—cont.
Byzantine **9** 538–41*, 542–3*, 547–9*
Early Christian (*c.* AD 250-843) **9** 538–41*, 542–3*
Islamic **4** 791; **16** 145–9*, 155–6*, 182*, 207–13*
Mamluk **16** 207–13
military **21** 582–3, *583*, 587–8
Ottoman **16** 228, *228*
Roman **26** 916–17*, 918*
stone **16** 182
Umayyad **16** 146–9*, 243
vernacular **30** *177*; **32** 314–15*
baptisteries **9** 541
basalt **26** 916
basins **16** *384*, 397; **20** *228*
baths **3** 376, 377; **16** 148
beakers **16** *521*
belts **9** 653; **16** 530
book covers **16** 357, *357*
boxes **16** 497
brass **16** *99*, 379, *384*
brick **4** 791
bronze **16** *511*
calligraphy **16** *275*
canteens **16** *99*
caravanserais **16** 148, 228
carpets **16** 466; **28** 716
castles **6** *52*; **18** 421, 422, *422*
cenotaphs **6** 171
censers **6** 174
churches **7** 259, 260, 261; **9** 538–41*, *539, 540*, 542–3*, 547–9*
basilicas **3** 329
centrally planned **7** 255
domus ecclesiae **9** 416
cities **14** 12
clay **16** 393
cloisters **7** 453
coins **13** 588, 589; **16** 510, *511*, 512, 538
colonnades **23** *892*; **26** *918*
cotton **16** 428
courtyards **16** *148*
craftsmen and artists **16** 146
domes **16** 182, 270
doublures **16** 356
dress **9** 644; **16** 452, 454, 455, 457
earthenwares **4** 172; **16** 406
enamel **16** 515, 520, *520, 521*
Islamic **12** IV1
façades **16** *148*, 179
flax **16** 428
fonts (baptismal) **9** *591*
forgeries **16** 545
fortifications **18** 422; **21** 582–3, *583*, 587–8
fountains **11** 340
friezes **31** *573*
frit **16** *406, 416, 417*
gardens **12** 77
gates **27** *344*
gilding **16** *357, 520, 521*
glass **9** 644; **12** IV1; **16** 515, 517, 519, 520, *520, 521*, 521
glazes **4** 172; **16** 415
gold **16** 311, *384, 511*; **21** *718*
guidebooks **13** 811
headdresses **16** 454, 459
helmets **16** *504*
heraldry **14** *427*
hospitals **8** *478*; **16** 181
houses **9** 560; **16** 152, 269; **32** 315
icons **9** 627
ikat **30** 554
incising **16** 415
inlays **16** *99*, 381–2, *384*, 389, 497
inscriptions **16** 258, 381, 383, 415, 441–2, 510, 512
Islamic **16** 147, 277
iron **16** *504*
ivory **16** 497
ivory-carvings **16** 523–4*
jars **16** 397, *416*
jewellery **16** 529–30*
Syria—cont.
kiosks **18** 70
lamps **16** 397, *520*; **27** 104
mosque **12** IV1
lead **16** 415
limestone **9** 538, 591, *591*; **23** *894*
liturgical furnishings **7** 279*
madrasas **4** 464; **16** 180, *181*; **20** 56
manuscript illumination **9** 619; **16** 307–12*, *311*
marble **21** *505*
marquetry **16** 490
masonry **2** 888; **16** 180, 182; **33** 614
mausolea **16** 181, 207
medallions **16** 538
metalwork
Byzantine **9** 539
Early Christian (*c.* AD 250-843) **9** 539
Islamic **14** *427*; **16** 367, 369*, 379*, 380*, 381–6*, 389–90*
Mamluk **16** 382
Ottoman **16** 386
mihrabs **1** *603*; **21** 505, *505*
minarets **16** 180; **21** 627
minbars **16** 496–7; **21** 629
mirrors **21** 717, *718*
monasteries **21** 834; **25** *771*
mosaics **16** 147, *255*, 256; **22** 162
Abbasid **16** 256
Byzantine **9** *567*, 567–8*
Early Christian (*c.* AD 250-843) **9** *567*, 567–8*
Islamic **16** 146, 148
Roman **2** *157*; **27** 64, *64, 65*
Umayyad **16** 255
mosques **8** 479–80, *480*; **16** *148*, 179–80
hypostyle **16** 146–8
moulding **16** 415
mouldings **16** 182
mud-bricks **30** *177*
muqarnas (architecture) **22** 322–3
orders (architecture) **23** 491
painting
floor **16** *251*
glass **12** 798
wall
Early Christian (*c.* AD 250-843) **9** 416
Islamic **16** 148
Jewish art **9** *415*; **17** 556–7*, *557*
20th cent. **30** *178*
palaces **16** 148, 182, 245
patronage **16** 146, 207, 380*, 382–3
pigments **4** 172
portals **8** *478*
pottery **7** XI1
blue-and-white ware **16** 416, *417*
Brittle ware **16** 397
Islamic **16** 396–7*, *397*, 405, 406–7*, 413, 415–17*, *416*, *417*
Laqabi ware **16** 406
Late Roman C **16** 396
lustreware **16** 404, 406, *406*, 407, 415–16*, *416*
Mamluk **16** 415–17
Raqqa ware **16** 405, 406
Red Slip ware **16** 396
Rusafa ware **16** 407
Umayyad **16** 396–7, *397*
Umayyad Palace ware **16** 396, *397*
regalia **16** 539
rings **9** 653
roofs **9** 539
sarcophagi **26** 855
scoria **26** 916
scripts **16** *275*, 368
sculpture
figure **16** 245
Hellenistic **13** 465

Syria
sculpture—cont.
relief **9** *414*; **23** *894*
Umayyad **16** 243, 245
sgraffito **16** 415*
signatures **16** 415, 496
silk **16** 428, 429, 430, 431, 441–2, *442*; **28** 715, 716
silver **9** 655; **16** *99*, *384*, 389, 510, *511*; **21** *718*
skins **16** *357*
slip **16** 415*
stands **16** 497
steel **21** *718*
stelae **29** 617, 618
stone **9** 538; **16** 182
stonewares **16** 406
strapwork **16** 487
stucco **31** *573*
swords **16** *506*
synagogues **17** 543
temples **13** 405; **23** *892*
textiles **16** 441–2*
theatres **2** 214; **4** *463*; **26** 918
thrones **30** 776
tiles **16** 422
tombs **16** 207
towers **21** 583
town walls **21** 583
trade **9** 786; **30** 179
antiquities **1** 896
craftsmen and artists **16** 146
glass **7** 83; **10** 591
metalwork **16** 383, 390
pottery **6** 333; **16** 396, 397, 405, 415, 416, 417
silk **16** 430
textiles **16** 441
tunics **9** *252*
urban planning **16** *261*
vaults (ceiling) **33** 614
weaving **16** 441
wood **9** 539
woodwork **16** 488–91*, 496–7*
see also ANCIENT NEAR EAST; MESOPOTAMIA; SYRIA-PALESTINES
Syriac Bible *see under* BIBLES → individual manuscripts
Syrian arches *see under* ARCHES → types
Syrian knot masonry *see* MASONRY → types → interlinked
Syrians **7** 818; **16** 573
Syria-Palestine **2** 660; **9** 786; **16** 572; **21** 266; **30** 178–99*, *180*
alabaster (gypsum) **5** *186*
alphabets **30** 187
animal subjects **15** *33*
arches **30** 190
architectural models **10** *173*
architecture **30** 182, 184, 185, 187, 190–92*, *190*, *191*
military **21** 553; **30** 185
stone **30** 190
basalt **9** *694*; **14** *64*
bit hilani **30** 185, 186, 187, *190*, 191, *191*, 194
body ornaments **30** 182
bone **30** 181, *181*, 184, 192
bowls **30** 187, *197*
carinated **30** 185, *197*
brick **4** 771
bronze **15** *33*; **21** *331*; **30** 180, 193, 194, 195
catalogues **30** 199
cedar **30** 179
chariots **6** 478
chronologies **1** *852*, 853
clay **27** 825; **30** 182
coins **30** 187, 196
collections **30** 198–9*
columns **30** 191
copper **30** 179, *183*, 194–5
arsenical **30** 195
craftsmen and artists **30** 180
crowns **30** 183
diorite **2** *661*
dress **1** *884*, 885; **30** 181

Syria-Palestine—cont.
exhibitions **30** 199
faience (i) (glass) **1** *878*
figurines **5** *186*; **21** *331*; **30** 182, 185, 195, *195*
forgeries **1** 896
fortifications **21** 553, *553*; **30** 185, 186, 190–91, *190*
furniture **30** 187
gates **30** 185
gateways **30** 190, *190*
glass **1** 865*, 867, 868
glazes **30** 197
goblets **1** *878*; **30** *197*
gold **30** 195
gypsum **30** 196
halls **30** 187, 191
headdresses **1** 885
houses **10** *173*; **30** 182, 185, 186
human figures **1** 491–2, *492*; **30** 181
iconography **30** 188–9*
inlays **1** *869*
iron **30** 194
ivory-carvings **1** *869*, *870*, 871; **5** *557*; **30** 180, 183, 186, 194
jars **30** 185, *197*
jasper **1** *857*
jewellery **30** 187
kraters **30** *197*
lead **21** *331*
lime **30** 196
limestone **30** *189*, *193*
looms **30** 546
lost-wax casting **30** 183
masks **30** 182
masonry **30** 180, 182, 190, 192
metalwork **30** 180, 183, *183*, 186, 187, 194–6*, *195*
moulds **30** *195*
mud-bricks **30** 182, 190
mummy cases **28** *667*
museums **30** 198–9*
niello **30** 195
oils **30** 180
orthostats **30** 185, 190
ossuaries **30** 183
painting **30** 197–8*, *198*
palaces **23** 806*; **30** 185, 186, 187, 191, *191*
pediments **28** 351
pendants (jewellery) **30** 186
periods
Amuk **30** 182
Bronze Age **30** 184*
Byzantine **1** *852*
Ceramic Neolithic (*c*. 6000–*c*. 5000 BC) **1** *852*
Chalcolithic (*c*. 5000–*c*. 3500 BC) **1** *852*
Chalcolithic **30** 182–4*
Early Bronze Age (*c*. 3500–*c*. 2000 BC) **1** *852*
Early Bronze Age **30** 184–5*
Graeco-Roman (332 BC–AD 395) **1** *852*
Iron Age **30** 186–8*
Islamic **1** *852*
Late Bronze Age (*c*. 1700–*c*. 1200 BC) **1** *852*
Late Bronze Age **30** 186*
Mesolithic (*c*. 14000–*c*. 8000 BC) **1** *852*
Mesolithic **30** 181*
Middle Bronze Age (*c*. 2000–*c*. 1700 BC) **1** *852*
Middle Bronze Age **30** 185–6*
Neolithic **30** 181–2*
Pre-pottery Neolithic A (*c*. 8000–*c*. 7000 BC) **1** *852*; **30** 181
Pre-pottery Neolithic B (*c*. 7000–*c*. 6000 BC) **1** *852*; **30** 181
pigments
red **30** 198
Tyrian purple **30** 180
pisé **4** 771
plaques **1** *870*

Syria-Palestine—cont.
plaster **30** 182, 196
porticos **30** 191
potter's wheels **30** 185, 197
pottery **30** 182, 183, 184, 185, 186, 196–7*
Abydos ware **30** 184
Dark-faced Burnished ware **30** 196
Halaf pottery **30** 183, 196
Khabur ware **6** 386
Nuzi ware **30** 197, *197*
Samarra' **30** 196
Ubaid pottery **30** 196
Yarmukian **30** 196
ramparts **30** 185
rediscovery **1** 892, 893
religion **30** 188–9*
reservoirs **1** 476
rings **1** 857
rock crystal **26** 485
sanctuaries **30** *190*
sarcophagi **27** 825; **28** *668*
scarabs **1** 857, *857*
scrolls **1** 881
sculpture **1** 491–2, *492*; **14** *64*; **30** 181, 182, 185, 186, 187, 192–4*, *193*
architectural **30** 190
bronze **15** *33*; **30** 193
Hurrian **15** *33*
portraits **30** 181
Prehistoric **2** *661*
relief **30** 187, 190, 193, *193*
stone **20** *410*
seals **1** 855, 857, *857*, 858, *859*, *862*, 862–3; **2** 660–61; **30** 184, 185, 186, 187
shelters **30** 191
sickles **30** *181*
silver **30** 179, 194, 195
silver leaf **21** *331*
skulls **17** *484*; **30** 181, 192
soapstone **1** *857*; **30** *195*
standards (flags) **30** 183, *183*
statuettes **30** 186
steel **30** 194
stelae **9** *694*; **29** 613, 614; **30** *189*, 193
stone **20** *410*; **30** 179, 181, 183, 190
synagogues **17** 550
tapestries **1** 881
tells **30** 190
temples **30** 184, 185, 186, 188, 191, *191*, 432
terracottas **10** *173*
textiles **1** 881; **30** 180, 182
timber structures **30** 190
tombs **30** 190
tools **30** 182, 192, 194
towers **30** 190
watch **21** 553
trade **8** 345; **21** 652; **30** 179–81
bowls **15** 902
ivory-carvings **10** 591
urban planning **30** 190, 191
vaults (ceiling) **30** 190
vessels **30** 196
wall decorations **30** 182
walls **30** 182, 190–91
weapons **30** 194
weaving **30** 182
wood **30** 179
wrought iron **30** 194
see also ISRAEL; JORDAN; LEBANON; NABATAEA; PALESTINE; SYRIA
syricum see under PIGMENTS → types
syringes **23** 787, *787*; **24** 580; **29** 133
Syriskos **13** 484
Syriskos Painter **13** 520
Syrkov, Dmitry **23** 269
Syrkus, Helena **7** 293; **25** 100; **30** 199–200; **32** 872

Syrkus, Szymon **25** 100, 142; **30** 199–200*
groups and movements **7** 293; **25** 422
works **25** 119; **32** 872
Syrlin, Hans **28** 171
Syrlin, Jörg (*c*.1420-91) **10** 454; **12** 401; **21** 725; **30** 136, 200*; **31** 566
pupils **18** 451
works **12** 420; **13** 117; **28** 171; **31** 570
Syrlin, Jörg (1455-1523) **30** 200–201*; **31** 569; **33** 19
Syron, Gordon **1** 65
Syros **8** *304*, 305, 308; **13** *363*; **30** 201*
bastions **21** 551
collections **8** 323; **13** 359
silver **8** 322, *322*
Syrrako **13** 358
Systems art **21** 645; **30** 201*
systems building *see under* ARCHITECTURE → techniques
Sytin, Ivan **31** 566
Syunnerberg, Konstantin (Aleksandrovich) *see* ERBERG, KONSTANTIN (ALEKSANDROVICH)
Syuzor, Pavel (Yul'yevich), Count **1** 148; **30** 202*
Sy & Wagner **12** 449
Syzk, Arthur **17** 566
Syzmanowski, Wacław **18** 430
Syzmonowicz-Siemiginowski, Jerzy Eleuter **6** 366
Szablowski, Jerzy **25** 143
Szablya-Frischauf, Ferenc **12** 10; **18** 141
Szabo **25** 663
Szabó, Ákos **14** 902
Szabo, Albert **29** 52
Szabó, Julius **28** 854
Szafran, Tadeusz **25** 123
Szalay, Ferenc **13** 333
Szalay, László **2** 546
Szamossy, Elek **22** 310
Szamosújvár *see* GHERLA
Szamotuły **25** 103
Szanajca, Józef **5** 8; **18** 596; **21** 783; **25** 100, 119, 422; **32** 872
Szandház **18** 116
Szaniawski, Konstanty Felicjan **25** 135
Szańkowski, Maciej **17** 448
Szapocznikow, Alina **25** 116; **30** 202*; **32** 878
Szárhegy *see* LAZAREA
Szarmizegethusa **27** 843*
Szarogród **33** 606
Szászsebes *see* SEBEŞ
Szathmari, Carol Pop de **5** 73, 791; **26** 713; **30** 202*
Szathmári, György, Bishop of Pécs **14** 885
Szatmár *see* SATU MARE
Szczecin **21** 571; **25** *92*; **30** 203–4*
Bismarck Monument **20** 870
Museum of the City of Szczecin **30** 204
National Museum **30** 203, 204
St James's **5** 28
Town Hall **30** *203*
Szczepkowski, Jan **25** 116, 123; **30** 204*
Szczerbinski, K. **32** 879
Szczuka, Mieczysław **30** 204*
collaboration **30** 199
groups and movements **4** 148; **7** 772; **25** 108, 422
Sze, Arthur **27** 599
Szecesszió *see* SECESSION (BUDAPEST)
Széchenyi, Ferenc, Count **14** 900; **15** 16
Széchenyi, György, Bishop of Veszprém **29** 922
Széchenyi, István, Count **14** 888; **15** 18

Szécsény **14** *881*
Franciscan Monastery **14** 884
Szécsi, Denes, Archbishop **10** 544, 546
Szécsisziget Church **14** 894
Szécy, Mária **14** 905
Szeged **13** 333; **14** *881*
Dom Square **14** 890, *890*
Votive Church **14** *890*
Szegedi, Márton **15** 7
Székely, Bertalan **5** 85; **14** 901; **30** 204–6*
collaboration **8** 585
pupils **2** 415; **10** 888; **13** 886; **18** 388, 822; **22** 433
works **24** 567; **30** *205*
Székesfehérvár **14** 881, *881*; **30** 206–7*
Cathedral of St Stephen **14** 883, 884; **15** 11; **24** 314; **30** 206
chapel of Louis I, King of Hungary and Poland **14** 892
sculpture **14** 892, 907; **26** 636, 638
Church of Our Lady **26** 638
Coronation Church *see* Cathedral of St Stephen
Garden of Ruins **14** 890
parish church **14** 888
St Anne Chapel **14** 884
St John Nepomuk **14** 894, 900
sarcophagus **14** 891
Székessy, Karin **33** 427
Szekrényessy, Dániel **2** 547
Szekszárd
Abbey Church **14** 883
Old County Hall **14** 889; **15** 14
sculpture **26** 638
Szelepchényi-Pohronec, Juraj **28** 852
Szelepcsényi, György, Archbishop of Esztergom **14** 899
szellem, A **24** 440
Szemere, Madeleine **17** 894
Szendrő **13** 162
Szènes, Arpad **4** 719; **7** 376; **32** 423
Szentendre **3** 111; **14** *881*
Barcsay Museum **15** 17
Collection of Serbian Orthodox Ecclesiastical Art **15** 17
Ferenczy Museum **10** 892; **15** 17
Imre Ámos-Margit Anna Collection **15** 17
Lajos Vajda Museum **15** 17; **31** 798
Margit Kovács Ceramics Collection **15** 17; **18** 412
Szentendre colony **8** 431; **14** 901; **18** 386; **30** 207*; **31** 174, 798
members **1** 796; **3** 223; **23** 794
Szentes **15** 1
Szentgotthard **14** 900
Szentgyörgyi, Jozsef **10** 472
Szentjóby, Tamás **14** 897
Szentkirály **26** 638
Szentpéteri, József **15** 8, 9; **30** 207*
Szentsimon **14** 899
Szepeshely *see* SPIŠSKÁ KAPITULA
Szepeskortvélyesi **13** 162
Szepesség **14** 884
Szepesszombat *see* SPIŠSKA SOBOTA
Szepesváralja *see* SPIŠSKE PODHRADIE
Szeptycki, Atanaze, Bishop of L'viv **19** 836
Szerda **24** 440
Szermentowski, Józef **25** 107; **30** 207–8*
Szewczyk, Andrzej **30** 208*
Szigetvar Congregational Mosque **14** 886
Szilágyi, Sándor **13** 638
Szilassy, Johannes **15** 7, 10; **28** 856; **30** 208–9*
Szily, János, Bishop of Szombathely **14** 298; **15** 15; **30** 212

Szinyei Merse, Pál **14** 901; **30** 209–10*
works **30** *209*
Szinyei Merse Society **15** 14; **22** 434; **30** 210
Szirtes, János **14** 902
Szivessy, Tibor **17** 876
Szkalnitzky, Antal **5** 83; **14** 889; **19** 30; **28** 87; **30** 210*
Szkalnitzky & Koch **30** 210*
szkofia **25** 128
Szkoła Warszawska **32** 877
Szlányi, Lajos **30** 211
Szlapka, P. L. **4** 803
Szlekys, Olgierd **25** 122
Szmaj, Stefan **26** 266
Szobotist **15** 2
Szobotka, Imre **13** 638
Szoldatits, Ferenc **22** 704; **30** 210*
Szolnok **14** *881*
Szolnok colony **1** 16; **2** 797; **8** 585; **10** 888; **13** 332; **14** 901; **17** 876; **30** 210–11*
Szombathely **14** *881*; **26** *906*; **30** *211*, 211–12*
Bishop's Palace **14** 888; **15** 15
Cathedral **14** 888, 895
Gyula Derkovits and Dési Huber Memorial Museum **8** 780
Picture Gallery **15** 17
Savaria Museum **15** 17; **30** 212
Szongtágh, Pál **19** 31
Szontagh, Aranka **15** 12
Szontagh, Erzsébet **15** 12
Szőnyi, István **13** 638; **14** 901; **23** 577; **30** 212*
Szöri, József **13** 333
Szpilowski, Hilary **25** 141; **32** 871
Szreger, Efraim **30** 212–13*; **32** 871
collaboration **29** 839
patrons and collectors **25** 212
works **12** 824; **25** 38, 99; **31** 196
Sztálinváros *see* DUNAÚJVÁROS
Sztehl, Otto **3** 224
Sztehlo, Lili **2** 416
Szternfeld, Paul **30** 213*
Sztuka **24** 441
Sztuka Polish Artists Society **4** 617; **10** 760; **20** 188; **21** 52; **27** 450; **29** 539; **33** 45, 457
see also SECESSION (KRAKÓW)
Sztuka stosowana **24** 441
Sztuki piękni **24** 441
Szulc, Daniel, II *see* SCHULTZ, DANIEL, II
Szulc, M. **4** 148
Szwaner, Stefan **32** 875, 881
Szwankowski, Jan **33** 606
Szwarc, Jerzy **25** 119
Szweiser, Dominik **25** 127
Szydłowiecki, Krzysztof **25** 135
Szyller, Stefan **3** 527; **25** 99; **28** 838; **32** 872
Szymanowski, Wacław **25** 115, 130; **32** 877
Szymanski, Rolf **3** 803
Szymin, David *see* CHIM
Szymon **25** 119
Szymonowicz, Georg **3** 95
Szymonowicz-Siemiginowski, Jerzy Eleuter **17** 615; **25** 105; **32** 875, 881
Szynalewski, Feliks **20** 187
Szyszko-Bohusz, Adolf **8** 429; **24** 441; **30** 213*; **33** 259
Szyszkowitz, Michael **23** 500; **30** 214
Szyszkowitz-Kowalski **30** 214*
Szyszkowski, Marcin, Bishop of Kraków **31** 312
Szyszlo (Valdelomar), Fernando de **24** 510, 511; **30** 214*
works **24** *510*

T

Taafe, Philip 1 81
Tabacchi, Odoardo 30 215*
pupils 4 100; 5 413, 623; 13 294; 27 303
works 16 706; 21 533
Tabachetti see WESPIN(, DE)
Tabaguet see WESPIN(, DE)
Tabajares 29 194
Tabaka, Maija 30 215*
Tabaković, Ivan 9 672; 28 451
Tabanan 15 806
Ṭabaqat Faḥl see PELLA (JORDAN)
Tabar (island) 24 85
Tabar (people) 24 85
Tábara 29 275
Tábara, Enrique 9 713; 30 216*
Tabarant, Adolphe 30 216*
Tabard, François 2 704; 19 808
Tabard, Maurice 30 216*
al-Tabari 6 239; 16 146, 304
Tabarka 12 71
Chapel of Martyrs 9 570
mosaics 32 543
Tabary, James 16 20, 22, 25
Tabary, John 16 22, 25
Tabary, Louis 16 22, 25
Tabary, Pierre-René de 19 56
Tabasqueño 26 412
Tabatabai, Jazeh 15 898
Tabbaa, Samer 17 655
works 17 655
Tabbat al-Hammam 24 642
tabby weave see under WEAVING → types
Tabennesis 7 227
tabernacle cabinets see under CABINETS (ii) (FURNITURE) → types
tabernacle clocks see under CLOCKS → types
tabernacle frames see FRAMES → types → aedicular
tabernacles (i) (place of worship) 30 217*
tabernacles (ii) (receptacle) 1 697, 707; 25 183; 30 217*
historical and regional traditions
Austria 22 204
Belgium 3 568
Canada 19 261
France 13 167, 168; 25 183
Gothic 3 568; 13 167, 168
Italy 32 215
Peru 24 511
materials
enamel 13 167, 168
ivory 16 799
mother-of-pearl 22 204
silver 24 511
silver-gilt 13 168
Taberth, Hans 33 353
Taberyová, Marta 8 406
Tabet, Antoine 19 7
Tabio, Emma Alvarez see ALVAREZ TABIO, EMMA
Tabiyev, Bakhtiyar 17 867
Tablada de Lurín 19 385
table altars see under ALTARS → types
table amphorae see under AMPHORAE → types
tableaux en découpures see SILHOUETTES
tableaux vivants 23 769
Table Bay see CAPE TOWN
table carpets see under CARPETS → types
table clocks see under CLOCKS → types
tablecloths 19 415, 416
Table of the Marshalls 24 388
table ornaments 10 419; 22 722; 30 218–19*
tables 30 217–18*
historical and regional traditions
Africa 1 366
Austria 2 811–12
Bamum 3 153
Belgium 3 581, 582, 584
Byzantine 9 656
Cameroon 3 153
Canada 5 578
China 7 34–5, 37, 40, 40–41, 41; 30 217
Czech Republic 8 398
Egypt, ancient 10 51, 53; 30 217
England 10 288, 292, 293
Arts and Crafts Movement 2 572
Greek Revival 30 218
Neo-classicism 10 293
Renaissance 10 288
Ethiopia 1 366
Etruscan 10 633
France 11 587, 589, 590–91*, 599, 602
Germany 12 419–20, 423, 424, 426; 14 426
Greece, ancient 13 592*; 30 217
Ireland 16 27
Italy 10 633; 14 426; 16 726
Korea 18 361, 363
Malta (Republic of) 20 215
Netherlands, the 22 868, 870
New Zealand 23 67
Portugal 25 303, 307
Rome, ancient 27 99; 30 217
South Africa 29 115–16
Spain 29 314–15*, 316, 317
United States of America 31 619, 623, 626, 628, 631, 633
materials
beech 11 589
bronze 23 67
fibreglass 30 218
gesso 10 292
gingko 18 363
gold 9 656
huang huali 7 40
intarsia 12 423
kauri 23 67
mahogany 5 578; 16 26, 27
marble 10 293, 293; 11 589
oak 11 589; 12 423; 23 67
porcelain 11 591
satin-wood 10 293
silver 9 30
tubular steel 30 218
veneers 11 602
walnut 10 288; 12 423; 29 317
wood 2 572
wrought iron 7 747
zitan 7 41
techniques
carving 29 317
painting 33 331
types
card-tables 30 218
console tables 7 746, 746–7*; 30 217
Austria 2 811
France 11 575, 589, 595
Germany 12 423, 424, 424
counters 28 245
crib 14 903
draw 30 217
dressing-tables 31 623, 626
en cabaret 11 591
étagères 31 631
gate-leg 10 290; 30 217; 31 623
globus 14 907
tables
types—cont.
guéridon see pedestal
heraldic 14 426
lobby 28 253
lowboys 31 623
offering tables see OFFERING TABLES
pedestal 10 294; 11 590
Pembroke 30 218
pier 33 331
refectory 29 314; 30 217
ring 23 233
sewing-tables 12 426
side 9 30; 16 26; 30 217
sideboards see SIDEBOARDS
Tatar table 15 826
toilet 31 623
trestle 30 217
tric-trac 11 590
whatnots 10 297; 31 631
writing-tables see BUREAUX
table-salts see SALTS
table-screens see under SCREENS (ii) (FURNITURE) → types
table services 30 218–19*
see also COFFEE-SERVICES; TEA-SERVICES
tablets
historical and regional traditions
Anatolia, ancient 1 859
Ancient Near East 1 859, 859
Buddhism 17 230; 30 596, 606, 638*
Burma 5 240
China 7 4, 102
Denmark 8 732
Egypt, ancient 9 828
Japan 17 230
Maya 21 243
Mesoamerica, Pre-Columbian 21 243
Nubia 21 160
San Pedro culture 29 188
South America, Pre-Columbian 29 188, 189
Thailand 30 596, 606, 638*
materials
bronze 20 328
clay 30 596
ebony 9 828
ivory 7 102
jade 7 4
schist 21 160
wood 29 188
see also LABELS
tablet weaving see under WEAVING → types
Tabley, John Fleming Leicester, Baron de see LEICESTER, JOHN FLEMING, Baron de Tabley
Tabley Hall (Cheshire) 10 365
tablinia 16 801; 30 219*
Tablos, Juan de Candamo de los see CANDAMO DE LOS TABLOS, JUAN DE
Tabnit 28 667
Tabo 5 104; 15 264; 30 219–20*, 237, 806
Golden Temple see Serkang
paintings 15 561
sculpture 23 282, 283; 30 220, 810, 823
Serkang 30 833, 846
statue of Arensnuphis 23 283
statue of Sebiumeker 23 283
temples 23 281
wall paintings 30 831
Tabois, Gaston 16 884
Tábor 8 374; 30 220–21*, 221
Church of the Transfiguration 8 377
façade decoration 10 741
furniture 8 398
Tabor, Phil 8 256
Tabora 1 249, 407
Taborda, J. C. 25 319
Tabota, Anton 11 123
tabourets see STOOLS
Tabourin, Y. 25 494
Tabqa 1 895
Tabriz 15 897; 16 105; 30 221–4*
Arg 30 222
art forms and materials
architecture 16 193
bookbindings 18 609
carpets 15 899; 16 474, 483; 30 223
coins 6 266; 16 513
lithography 16 342
manuscripts 2 895; 16 286, 292, 293, 295, 315, 315, 316, 318, 320, 326, 327, 331–4*; 30 222–3
metalwork 16 373, 378, 390
miniatures (manuscript illumination) 16 319, 328, 333
painting 16 122, 125
pottery 16 414, 423
printing 16 360, 361
rock crystal 16 542
textiles 16 443, 444, 449, 450
tiles 16 249
Blue Mosque 16 198, 248; 24 877; 30 223*, 224
tiles 16 199
congregational mosque 16 193
fortifications 21 589
funerary complex of Ghazan Khan 16 194, 247
funerary complex of Rashid al-Din 16 194
gardens 12 83
Hasht Bihisht Palace 16 198, 253; 18 71
houses 16 269
mosque of ʿAlishah 4 792
Muzaffariyya 16 198
Nasriyya 16 198
painting 7 V
Rabʿ-i Rashidi 16 194, 313; 30 222, 223*
Tabrizi, Sadeq 15 898; 27 810
Tabu (group) 8 438; 9 354
Tabu (periodical) 24 428
Tabuchi, Yasukazu 30 224*
Tabuena, Romeo 24 622
Tabula Bembi see MENSA ISIACA
Tabula Cebetis 15 84
Tabulae Cybelicae 10 638
Tabula Peutingeriana 19 99; 20 362; 24 573; 31 153
tabularia 26 867
Tabwa 19 739; 30 224–6*
body arts 1 344
cicatrices 1 346, 346
divination instruments 1 357
scarification 1 409
sculpture 1 282, 403; 30 225, 225
stools 1 366
wood-carvings 1 366; 30 225
TAC (The Architects Collaborative) 3 797; 4 475; 10 120; 13 689; 14 596; 30 226–7*
Tác see GORSIUM
Taca, Antonio (fl 1532-6) 13 192
Taca, Antonio (fl 1569-96) 13 192
Tacca, Ferdinando 30 227, 229*
attributions 11 234
works 21 26, 27; 29 570; 30 228
workshop 4 551
Tacca, Giovan Pietro della 6 139
Tacca, Pietro 30 227–9*
collaboration 5 360
patrons and collectors 4 548; 21 25, 26
pupils 4 254; 12 902
teachers 12 575; 16 699
works 4 402, 524; 10 441, 504; 11 215; 12 576; 16 700; 19 512; 21 24; 22 3; 26 250; 29 291, 341, 570; 30 228, 229; 31 305
workshop 4 551
Tacca, Simone 18 900
Taccino, Giovanni 12 656
Taccola, Mariano (di Jacopo) 21 578; 30 229–30*
Taccone, Mariani di Tuccio 24 28
Taccone da Sezze, Paolo di Mariani di Tuccio see PAOLO ROMANO (fl 1445-70)
Tacconi (family) 5 852
Tacconi, Francesco 3 667
Tacconi, Innocenzo 5 867; 30 230*
Tâché, Eugène-Etienne 5 561, 570; 25 803; 30 230*
Tâcheron, Pierre 9 706
T'a-chi see TAJI
Tachibana 17 69
Tachibana, Zuichō 23 628
Tachibana Minkō 17 282
Tachibana Morikuni 17 273; 23 594
Tachibana no Hayanari 17 221; 18 502; 27 519; 30 231*
Tachibana no Konakichi 14 774
Tachibana no Michiyo 14 775; 17 110
Tachibana no Toshitsuna 12 96; 17 417
Tachihara, Norigoshi 17 402
Tachihara Kyōsho 17 412
Tachikui 30 287
Tachism 1 77, 78; 2 515, 543; 24 144; 30 231*
members 2 545; 18 750; 33 305, 588
works 2 839; 20 815, 816
writings 20 815
Tachtigers 4 740; 16 576; 33 266
Tacitus, Emperor of Rome (reg 275-76) 5 785; 9 252; 19 565, 579; 26 750
Tacitus, Aeneas see AENEAS TACITUS
tack bond see under BONDING
tackets 24 107
Tacoma Dome (WA) 22 748
Tacubaya
Barragán House 8 65; 21 381
observatory 23 341
Tacuinium sanitatis 18 704
Tada 4 854
Tadaharu Katsura see KATSURA TADAHARU
Tadamasa Hayashi see HAYASHI, TADAMASA
Tadamasa Honda see HONDA TADAMASA
Tadamichi, Fujiwara no see FUJIWARA NO TADAMICHI
Tadanobu Okubo see OKUBO TADANOBU
Tadanori Yokoo see YOKOO, TADANORI
Tadao Andō see ANDŌ, TADAO

Tadaoki, Hosokawa *see* HOSOKAWA TADAOKI
Tadashige Ono *see* ONO, TADASHIGE
Tadashige Takahashi *see* TAKAHASHI TADASHIGE
Tada Shin'ai **17** 238
Tadashi Sekino *see* SEKINO, TADASHI
Tadayoshi Honda *see* HONDA TADAYOSHI
Tadcaster **10** 227
Tadda, Francesco (Ferrucci) del *see* FERRUCCI DEL TADDA, FRANCESCO
Tadda, Francesco del *see* FERRUCCI, FRANCESCO (DI GIOVANNI)
Taddei, Francesco Antonio **29** 841
Taddei, Jacopo **29** 404
Taddei, Michel Angelo **29** 841
Taddei, Taddeo **18** 895; **30** 231*
Taddei Tondo **21** 435, 457; **30** 231
Taddel, Heinrich **12** 458
Taddeo, Francesco di *see* FERRUCCI, FRANCESCO (DI GIOVANNI)
Taddeo da Ferrara *see* CRIVELLI, TADDEO
Taddeo di Bartolo **13** 149; **28** 676, 677, 684; **30** 231–3*
  patrons and collectors **14** 868; **29** 411
  pupils **9** 94; **13** 626
  works **11** 380, *380*; **16** 657; **25** 183, *184*; **27** 751, 862; **28** 684, 687, *687*; **29** 406; **30** *232*
Taddi, Agnolo **11** 206
Taden, La Grand' Cour **32** 279
Tadevossian **7** *294*
T'adevosyan, Egishe **2** 431, 432
Tadić, Radoslav **4** 462
Tadini, Emilio **21** 528
Tadjoura **9** 50
Tadla **21** 585
Tadmor *see* PALMYRA
Tadmor, H. **21** 299
Tadolini, Adamo **16** 705; **19** 386; **24** 509; **30** 233*
Tadolini, Enrico **30** 233
Tadolini, Francesco **17** 442; **31** 180
Tadolini, Giulio **30** 233
Tadolini, Petronio **30** 233
Tadolini, Scipione **30** 233
Tadolini, Tito **30** 233
Tadpatri **15** *294*, 540; **30** 234*
  Parvati Temple **15** 540
  Ramalingeshvara Temple **15** 331, 540; **30** 234
  reliefs **15** 539
  sculpture **15** 540
  Venkataramana Temple **15** 331, 645, 647
Tadrart Acacus **1** 370, *371*
Tadubaste **2** 690
T'aech'ŏn **18** 368
Taegam, National Master *see* T'ANYON
Taegok **18** 334
Taegu **18** *248*
  bronze **18** 347
  Tonghwa Temple **18** 289
  Yongnam University **18** 381
T'aejo, King of Korea (*reg* 918-43) **18** 268
T'aejo, King of Korea (*reg* 1392-8) **7** 208*; **18** 321
Taejŏn **18** 297
  Ch'ungnam University **18** 381
Taejo Temple **18** 292
Taemon **14** 704
taeniae **11** 790; **13** 377, *378*, 393; **23** 478; **30** 234*
Taenk **14** 392
Taensa **30** 449, 450
Taer si *see* KUMBUM
Taeryong *see* HŎ MOK
T'aesang **18** 273
Taesŏng Temple, Myŏji Hermitage **18** 292
T'aesu *see* YI PUL-HAE
Taesung Temple **18** 296
Taewŏn'gun **7** 208
Taeye, Lodewijk Jan De *see* DE TAEYE, LODEWIJK JAN
taffeta **30** 553
Tafi, Andrea **11** 199, 887
Tafí culture **29** 190
Taft Mosque **16** 199
Tafur, Pero **7** 178
TAGA *see* TALLER DE ARTES GRÁFICAS
Taganrog **27** 375, 409; **28** 325
Tagao **1** 198, 199
Tagar (Siberia) **2** 100
Tağar Church (Turkey) **5** 674, 678
Tagara *see* TER
Tagar culture **27** 367; **28** 322
Taga Shinkō *see* HANABUSA ITCHŌ
Taggart, R. T. **16** 39
Taggart, W. D. R. **16** 39
Tagi, Kōji **22** 120
tagidashi see under LACQUER → types
Tagiolini, Filippo **29** 573
Tagish **22** 546
Tagisken **6** 196, 273
Tagiyev, Ta. **2** 896
Tagizade, Rza **2** 901
Tagliacarne, Giacomo **28** 436
Tagliacarne, Il *see* SERBALDI DA PESCIA, PIER MARIA
Tagliaferri, Elena **24** 200
Tagliafichi, Andrea **3** 922
Tagliente, Giovanni Antonio **11** 386; **28** 307
Tagliolini, Filippo **22** 480, 482
Tago **1** 329
Tagore (family) **15** 183
Tagore, Abanindranath **5** 420; **15** 656–7; **30** 235, 236*
  patrons and collectors **15** 180
  personal collection **15** 742
  pupils **4** 455; **15** 171
  works **15** 747
Tagore, Gaganendranath **15** 657, 742; **30** 235, 236*
Tagore, Pradyot Kumar **24** 739
Tagore, Rabindranath **5** 420; **6** 814; **15** 656, 657, 725; **30** 235*
  collaboration **15** 657
  works **15** 748
Taguemont **16** 532
Taha **16** 431
Taha, Mahmoud **17** 655
Tahaa **28** 921
Tahala Synagogue **17** 551
Taharqa (*reg c.* 690-*c.* 664 BC) **9** *777*; **23** 154; **30** 236–7*
  architecture **23** 281, 284; **30** 691
  sculpture **9** 891; **23** 282
  shabtis **10** 18
  stelae **17** 859–60
Tahart Mosque **16** 493
Tahbo, Mark **22** 609
Tahdauli Temple **4** *793*; **15** 262, 413
Tāherī *see* SIRAF
Taherit **3** 523
Tahir, Mehmed **16** 604
Tahirid **33** 584
Tahirid, ʿAmir II *see* ʿAMIR II, Ruler
Tahiti **28** 921
  adzes **23** *712*
  canoes **23** 725; **28** *923*
  dress **28** 922
  fans **10** 779
  feathers **23** 720
  forgeries **23** 737
  platforms **23** 715; **28** 922
  sculpture **12** *191*
  shells **28** 922
  tattoos **23** 737; **28** 923; **30** 367
  weapons **23** 734
  wood **23** 712
Tahiti—cont.
  woodcuts **12** *195*
Tahiwi, Aromea **20** 360; **30** 237*
Tahltan **22** 546, 639
Tahmasp I, Shah (*reg* 1524-76) (Safavid) **16** 123; **22** 260, 263; **25** 778; **27** 513–14*; **30** 223
  architecture **16** 230, 253; **20** 548; **21** 589
  manuscripts **7** 717; **9** 461; **16** *301*, 319, 332, 334; **21** 705, 722, 723; **27** 512
    Fālnāma **16** 334
    Garshāspnāma **27** 506
    Haft awrang (Jami) **16** 335; **22** 391
    Kalila and Dimna **1** 474
    Khamsa (Nizami) **16** 292, *293*, 295, 334
    Koran **16** 334
    Shāhnāma **2** 235; **4** 50; **9** 461; **16** 272, *302*, 303, 332, 333, 353, 552; **22** 390; **28** 567
  paintings **2** 235; **4** 49; **16** 122, 127; **29** 920
Taho **18** 251, 369
  lacquer **18** *369*, 379
Tahoma, Quincy **22** 595, 596; **30** 238*
Tahoua **31** 406
Ta-hsi *see* DAXI CULTURE
Tahta **9** 896, 897
Tahuata *see* MARQUESAS ISLANDS
Tahull *see* TAÜLL
Tai **18** 772–3; **30** 619–22
Tai, Marchioness of *see* DAI, Marchioness of
Taiapa, Pine **13** 272; **20** 359; **30** 238*
Tai Chin *see* DAI JIN
Tai Daeng **18** 771, 772
Tai Dam **18** 771, 772; **30** 619, 621
  textiles **18** *773*
Taide **24** 452
Taidehalli **24** 452
Ta'if **16** 271; **27** 875; **32** 315
Taiga Ike *see* IKE TAIGA
taighean tugha see under HOUSES → types
Taiheiji **17** 749
Taiheiyō Bijutsukai *see* PACIFIC FINE ART SOCIETY
Taiheiyō Gakai (Pacific Painting Society) **17** 204, 435; **22** 444
  see also MEIJI FINE ARTS SOCIETY (MEIJI BIJUTSUKAI)
Taihō **17** 184
Taihō Yamazaki *see* YAMAZAKI, TAIHŌ
T'ai-hsü *see* TAIXU
Taiji Kawajiri *see* KAWAJIRI, TAIJI
Taijishan **8** 852
Taikai Shiomi *see* ZŌROKU IV
Tai Kanbara *see* KANBARA, TAI
Taikan Yokoyama *see* YOKOYAMA, TAIKAN
Tai Khao **18** 771, 772–3
Taikō Gyōū **17** 746
Tai K'uei *see* DAI KUI
Taikyōan *see* HON'AMI KŌETSU
Tai Lao **18** 770; **30** 619
Tailfeathers, Gerald **22** 597
Tailhade, Laurent **14** 457
Taillasson, Jean-Joseph **19** 217; **30** 238–9*
Taillebert, Urbain **30** 239*
Taillebourg, Cave *see under* ANGLES-SUR-L'ANGLIN
Taillepied de Bondy **4** 847; **12** 725
Taillibert, Roger **29** 489
Tailly, Martin de **5** 39
tailpieces **30** 239*
Tai Lue **18** 771, 773; **30** 619, 620, 623
Taiman **7** 25
Tai Muai **18** 771
Taimuran **15** 921
Taimu Tatehata *see* TATEHATA, TAIMU
Tain, tolbooth **31** 239
T'ai-nan
  architecture **6** 674
  Da Tian hou gong *see* Ta T'ien hou kung
  K'ai-yuan ssu **30** 245
  Ta T'ien hou kung **30** 244
  workshop **6** 787
Tainaron **29** 702
Taine, Hippolyte (-Adolphe) **11** 675; **28** 916; **30** 239–40*
  groups and movements **22** 540
  pupils **21** 428
  works **28** 926
Tai Neua **18** 771, 772
Taíno **5** 746, 747–9; **8** 228, 229; **9** 114; **14** 54; **16** 878, 879; **25** 698, 699; **29** 207
  dujos **14** *55*
  sculpture **5** *748*
  stone-carvings **25** *699*
  trigonolites **9** *114*
taipa de pilão see under ARCHITECTURE → techniques
Taipei **6** *614*; **30** 244
  Chang Foundation Museum **7** 154
  Chiang Kai-shek Memorial Hall **30** *245*, *246*
  Gugong Bowuguan *see* National Palace Museum
  Longshan si *see* Lung-shan ssu
  Lung-shan ssu **30** 244–5
  National Museum of History **7** 154
  National Palace Museum **7** 161; **14** 859; **17** 697; **19** 326; **30** *245*
    collections **3** 518; **6** 772, 826, 868, 925; **7** 11, 26, 27, 62, 154; **30** 245
    exhibitions **7** 157
  National Taiwan Art Gallery **19** 504
  National Theatre and Concert Hall **1** 126
Tai Pen-hsiao *see* DAI BENXIAO
Tai Phuan **18** 771, 773; **30** 619, 620
Taiping **7** 115
  Perak Museum **29** 240
Taira (family) **14** 705; **17** 148, 423; **30** 376
Taira **29** 187
Taira no Kiyomori **16** 786; **17** 148, 219, 404, 423
Tairoku Yanagida *see* YANAGIDA, TAIROKU
Tairona **30** 240–41*
  architecture **30** 240
  beads **29** 155
  copper **30** 240, *240*
  gold **30** 240, *240*
  masks **29** 193
  metalwork **29** 213
  musical instruments **29** 217
  pendants (jewellery) **29** 155, 217; **30** *240*
  pottery **29** 150
  sculpture **29** 146, 193
  stone **30** 240
  stone-carvings **29** 155
Taïrov, Alexander **10** 699; **12** 893; **21** 38; **22** 268; **29** 899; **30** 686; **32** 382; **33** 486
Tairyūkyo *see* SHIBATA ZESHIN
Taisei **17** 53
Taisei Meigaten (Exhibitions of Famous Works of the Occident) **17** 207
Taishin Ikeda *see* IKEDA TAISHIN
Taishō period *see under* JAPAN → periods
Taiso Yoshitoshi *see* TSUKIOKA YOSHITOSHI
Tait, Arthur Fitzwiliam **30** 241*; **31** 602
  patrons and collectors **31** 870
Tait, Arthur Fitzwiliam—cont.
  reproductive prints by others **8** 276
  works **33** 185
Tait, Gordon **20** 238
Tait, Norman **22** 581
Tait, Thomas (Smith) **30** 241–2*
  collaboration **10** 173
  groups and movements **3** 465; **9** 740; **21** 783
  works **5** 271; **9** 724; **28** 231
Tait, W. D. **30** 266
Tait, William Nairne **33** 565
Taiteilija **24** 452
Taiten **33** 709
Taito **17** 288
T'ai-tsu, Emperor (Sung; *reg* 960-76) *see* TAIZU, Emperor
T'ai-Tsung, Emperor *see* TAIZONG, Emperor
Taiun Yanagida *see* YANAGIDA TAIUN
Taiwan **6** *614*; **10** 580; **30** 242–50*
  architecture **21** 44
  calligraphy **6** 772; **30** 246
  coins **7** 73
  collections **6** 772; **7** 154
  education (art) **7** 150
  exhibitions **30** 248–9
  fans **10** 777
  gateways **30** *246*
  halls **30** *245*
  inks **15** 850
  jewellery **7** 112
  museums **30** *245*
  nephrite **16** 861
  painting **30** 246–50*, *247*, *248*, *249*
  temples **30** 244
  trade **6** 624; **17** 47
  see also CHINA
Taixi (Gaocheng) **7** 159
  cemeteries **6** 694
  lacquer **7** 12
  metalwork **7** 97
  see also GAOCHENG
Taixu **5** 113
Tai Yai **30** 623
Taiyang Fine Arts Association **30** 247
Tai Yong **6** 776
Taiyuan (China) **6** *615*; **30** 250–51*
  Cave 7 **29** 905
  Chongshan Temple **6** 660; **30** 250*
  Dabei Temple *see* Chongshan Temple
  Jin ci **6** *653*, 654, 724; **7** 99, *100*; **28** 638
  Jin Family Shrines *see* JIN CI
  Yongzhao Temple **23** 773, *774*
Tai Yuan (people) **30** 571, 619, 620, 621
T'ai-yung *see* TAIYONG
Taizan Hine *see* HINE TAIZAN
Taizhou *see* TIANSHUI
Taizong, Emperor (Tang; *reg* AD 626-649) **6** 651, 698, 745, 746, 751; **7** 76, 152; **30** 251*
  calligraphy **6** 745, 746; **30** 288
  painting **6** 808
  paintings **13** 739; **33** 498, 499
  tomb **6** *700*
Taizong, Emperor (Song; *reg* 976-97) **6** 751; **7** 118, 152; **29** 67; **32** 836, 837; **33** 500
Taizu, Emperor (Song; *reg* 960-76) **6** 635
Ta'izz **16** *104*
  architecture **16** 213; **33** 519
  Asadiyya Madrasa **16** 214
  Ashrafiyya Madrasa **16** 214, 215, 500
  Husayniyya **16** 229
  Imam Ahmad Palace Museum **33** 520

Ta'izz—cont.
minarets 16 215
Mu'tabiyya Madrasa 16 214
Muzaffariyya Mosque 16 213, *214*
palace 16 213
Salah Palace Museum 33 520
Taj al-Din 'Ali Shah 14 260
Taj al-Din Firuz, Sultan (*reg* 1397-1422) (Bahmani) 3 66
Taj al-Din Salmani 16 286
Taji 7 110
Tajik 1 188; 6 252, 274; 16 451
Tajikistan 6 181; 16 *105*; 30 251–4*, *252*
architecture 16 166; 30 252*
breast-ornaments 30 *253*
capitals 29 *822*
carpets 16 466
collections 6 283*
copper 6 *243*
decorative arts 30 253–4*
gold 27 *599*
historiography 6 279–80*
ivory 6 *270*
ivory-carvings 6 *270*; 30 *262*
jewellery 30 253
manuscripts 6 *189*
mihrabs 16 *492*
museums 6 283*
nude figures 18 *500*
painting 30 252–3*
wall 5 *172*; 17 *734*
plaques 27 *599*
pots 6 *243*
pottery 6 259
scabbards 6 *270*
sculpture 6 *214*; 18 *500*; 30 252–3*
silver-gilt 30 *253*
stamps 33 *509*
stone 33 *510*
stucco 29 *822*
tents 30 473
textiles 30 253
toys 6 277
trays 33 *510*
wood 18 *500*
woodwork 16 *492*
Tajimi, Eihōji 17 73
Tajín 21 190, *193*, 197, 200, 262, *372*; 23 565; 30 254*
ballcourts 3 118; 21 187
hardstones 21 243
mirrors 21 719
Museum 12 921
Pyramid of the Niches 30 *254*, 254
pyramids 25 764
reliefs 21 249; 22 518
religion 21 186
sculpture 21 185, 220
stele 29 620
talud-tablero 21 206; 30 280
Tajin Chico 7 692
Tajiri, Shinkichi 7 489; 22 861; 30 255*
Taj Mahal *see under* AGRA → tombs
Taju, Sheikh 15 606
Tak 30 584
Takada, Chikuzan 17 414, 861
Takada, Hiroatsu 17 135
Takada, Kenzo 9 294
Takada Keiho 29 13
Takaezu, Toshiko 31 640
Takagamine 14 703; 17 232
Takahari, Bhavani Temple 15 316, 317
Takahashi, Genkichi 30 256
Takahashi, Shōtei 17 293
Takahashi Dōhachi (*fl* 1751-64) 30 255
Takahashi Dōhachi (1783-1855) 17 258, 399; 30 255*
Takahashi Kumakichi 17 400
Takahashi Mitsuoki *see* TAKAHASHI DŌHACHI (1783-1855)
Takahashi Sōhei 17 192; 30 299
Takahashi Tadashige 17 372
Takahashi Yūichi 17 198; 30 255–6*
exhibitions 17 435
teachers 17 198, 420
works 28 599
Takahisa Furukawa *see* FURUKAWA, TAKAHISA
Takaichi, Prince 30 257
Takai Kitō 20 836
Takaishvili, E. 12 331
Takakane Takashima *see* TAKASHIMA TAKAKANE
Takako Araki *see* ARAKI, TAKAKO
Takako Saito *see* SAITO, TAKAKO
Takāku Aigai 30 295
takamakie see under LACQUER → types
Takamasa Yoshizaka *see* YOSHIZAKA, TAKAMASA
Takamatsu 17 18
Kagawa Prefectural Government Office 17 90; 30 289
Rural Residence Museum 17 434; 21 648
Shikoku Minka Hakubutsukan *see* Rural Residence Museum
Takamatsu, Jirō 14 568; 17 207; 30 256*
Takamatsu, Shin 17 92; 30 256–7*
Takamatsu-chō, Tsukuriyama 17 57
Takamatsu Rihei 18 553
Takami Senseki 23 390
Takamitsu Azuma *see* AZUMA, TAKAMITSU
Takamura, Kōtarō 17 134; 21 59; 30 241, 257–8*
groups and movements 17 135
works 17 135
writings 17 440
Takamura, Kōun 17 133, 134, 135; 30 257
works 17 *134*
Takamura, Toyochika 17 324
täkänäs 11 109
Takanashi, Yutaka 22 120
Takanen, Johannes 27 337; 30 258*
Takanobu, Fujiwara no *see* FUJIWARA NO TAKANOBU
Takanobu Kanō *see* KANŌ TAKANOBU
Takaoka 17 358, 407
Takasabu Ryūtatsu 30 376
Takasaki 17 105
Gunma Prefectural Museum of Modern Art 1 737; 16 563; 17 92
Takashi Kimizu *see* KIMIZU, TAKASHI
Takashi Masuda *see* MASUDA, TAKASHI
Takashima Takakane 17 154, 160, 367
Takasima 2 564
Takatora Tōdō *see* TŌDŌ TAKATORA
Takatori (Japan) 17 *11*, *241*; 30 258–9*
Takatori (family) 30 259
Takatori Hachirō 30 258
Takatori Hachizan 30 258
Takatsugu Tōdō *see* TŌDŌ TAKATSUGU
Takauji Ashikaga *see* ASHIKAGA TAKAUJI, SHOGUN
Takawira, Bernard 1 429
Takawira, John 1 429
Takayama, Hida Folklore Museum 17 434
Takayama, Tatsuo 30 259*
Takayama Hida *see* HIDA TAKAYAMA
Takayuki Masaki *see* MASAKI, TAKAYUKI
Takechi no Ōkuni 22 497
Takeda, Goichi 3 176
Takeda, Hideo 17 296
Takeda, Kinosuke 17 408
Takeda, Sennosuke 17 408
Takeda Kizaemon 17 342
Takeda Shingen 17 363
Takefu 17 358
Takefumi Aida *see* AIDA, TAKEFUMI
Takehara Tomb *see under* SUWA SHRINE
Takehisa, Yumeji 17 202, 295
Takehisa Kosugi *see* KOSUGI, TAKEHISA
Takei, Katsuo 17 421
Takeji Fujishima *see* FUJISHIMA, TAKEJI
Takejiro Satomi *see* SATOMI TAKEJIRO
Takekoshi, K. 10 563
Takelot 9 887
Takelot I 9 *777*
Takelot II 9 *777*
Takelot III 9 887
Takemoto Gidayū 17 406
Takenaka 17 53
Takenaka Komuten Co. Ltd 14 259; 16 811
Takenobu Kanō *see* KANŌ TAKENOBU
Takeno Jōō 17 323, 342; 23 594; 28 411; 30 259–60*
Takenuchi, Kyūichi 17 133
Ta Keo *see under* ANGKOR
Takeo kiln 17 351, 811
Takeo Yamaguchi *see* YAMAGUCHI, TAKEO
Take Sato *see* SATO TAKE
Takeshirō Kanokogi *see* KANOKOGI, TAKESHIRŌ
Taketarō Shinkei *see* SHINKEI, TAKETARŌ
Taketomi 27 471
Takeuchi, Kimiaki 17 267
Takeuchi, Seihō 17 198, 200; 18 231; 30 260*; 31 399
Takeyama, Minoru 2 363; 3 52; 17 91; 30 260*
Takeyama, Minoru, and the United Actions 30 260
Takezaki Suenaga 17 362
Takhat Singh, Maharaja of Marwar (*reg* 1843-73) (Rajput) 15 616
Takht-i-Bahi 5 94; 15 *264*; 23 *797*; 30 261*
halls 14 77
stucco 29 824
stupa 15 249
Takht-i Jamshid *see* PERSEPOLIS
Takht-i Kubad 1 *186*, *849*; 6 *182*, 237; 15 *901*; 30 *252*
coins 23 691
see also OXUS TREASURE
Takht-i Malyan *see* MALYAN, TALL'I
Takht-i Marmar 30 784
Takht-i Nadiri 30 784
Takht-i Sangin 1 *186*; 6 *182*; 30 *252*, 261–2*
ivory-carvings 6 270; 30 *262*
metalwork 1 206
sculpture 1 188; 6 214
Temple of Oxus 6 196, *197*, 197–8; 30 261–2, 440
ivory-carvings 6 270, *270*
jewellery 6 273
metalwork 6 237, 242–3
sculpture 6 213, *214*
Takht-i Sulayman 15 899, *901*; 16 *105*, 193; 30 262*
fortifications 21 554
muqarnas (architecture) 16 133; 22 322
palace 16 250; 18 71; 23 815
pottery 16 407
temple 15 *911*, 913; 33 708
Takhut, Queen (*fl* 595-89 BC) 2 690
Takiguchi, Shūzō 30 22, 262*; 33 488
Taking of Christ, Master of the 22 835
Takinomotobō 17 232
Takis 11 570; 30 262–3*
groups and movements 10 416; 18 63
works 1 738; 13 355; 29 97, 98
Takita, Kōichi 17 266; 21 634
Takiwaki Seika 23 390
Taki Yūden 17 417
Takizawa Bakin 17 288, 846
Taklē, Afawarq 1 433; 10 573, 577
Takonda' 10 565
tak paper *see under* PAPER → types
Takrit 16 488
Takrouna 1 305; 3 755
Takṣaśilā *see* TAXILA
Taksin *see* PHRAYA TAK
Takuan Sōhō 5 120; 17 193, 232; 23 594; 30 263*
Takua Pa 29 231; 30 598
Taku kiln 17 811
Takum 6 405; 17 680; 23 *129*
Takuma (school) 17 29; 30 264*
Takuma Chōga 30 264
Takuma Eiga 30 264*
Takuma kiln *see under* NOGATA
Takuma Ryōga 30 264
Takuma Shōga 30 264*
Takuma Shunga 30 264
Takuma Tamehisa 30 264
Takuma Tamemari 30 264
Takuma Tametoki 30 264
Takumi Asakawa *see* ASAKAWA, TAKUMI
Takushit 9 887; 10 36
Takutea 7 790
takyas 16 234
tal see TELLS
Tala 15 *279*; 30 264–5*
architectural decorations 30 265
Deorani Temple 15 474; 30 264–5
Devarani Temple *see* Deorani Temple
Jethani Temple 15 474
sculpture 15 474
Shiva temples 15 283
talacchanda 15 245*
Talachkino 2 568
Taladuro, Athanasios 26 392
Talamanca de Tibás jewellery 29 *154*
Talamantes, Baltasar 33 358
Talamone 10 588, 601
al-Talamsani, Kamil 2 511
Talani, Teresa 12 264
Talarn, Domingo 25 816
talars 16 234, 238, *238*
Talas *see* ZHAMBYL
Talasea 24 84
Talashkino 20 223; 27 *363*, 408, 438; 30 265*
members 26 530
pottery 27 410
Russkaya Starina 30 464
Talaswaima, Terrance 22 598
talatat-blocks 1 505; 9 832, 883
Talava Temple 5 *97*
Talavera, Cristobal de 25 697
Talavera (y Heredia), Juan 28 513; 30 265–6*
Talavera, Juan de *see* JUAN DE TALAVERA
Talavera de la Reina
antependia 30 881
Ermita del Prado 30 883
furniture 29 321
potters 4 175
pottery 4 175; 25 309; 29 322, 325, 326, *326*, *327*, 327, 329
tiles 29 300, 327; 30 883, *883*
Talavera de Puebla ware *see under* POTTERY → wares
Talavera y de la Vega, Juan 30 265
talavitāna 15 245*
talayots 25 522
Talbert, Bruce J(ames) 30 266*
groups and movements 1 171; 13 209
works 6 391; 28 255
writings 10 281, 298
Talbot (family) 14 423
Talbot, Aletheia *see* HOWARD (i), ALETHEIA, Countess of Arundel
Talbot, Charles, 1st Duke of Shrewsbury (1660-1718) 2 307; 30 267*
Talbot, Charles, 15th Earl of Shrewsbury (*d* 1827) 1 733
Talbot, Christopher 30 268
Talbot, Constance 30 *270*
Talbot, Elizabeth, Countess of Shrewsbury 30 266–7*
architecture 6 115, 116, 515; 10 360; 28 894
furniture 10 288; 20 467
interior decoration 29 834
paintings 19 531
tapestries 14 422
Talbot, George, 6th Earl of Shrewsbury 28 894; 30 266
Talbot, John, 1st Earl of Shrewsbury (*c.* 1388-1453) 20 772
Talbot, John, 16th Earl of Shrewsbury (1791-1853) 30 267*
architecture 25 712, 713, 716
gardens 1 734
paintings 4 106
Talbot, John, Master of *see* TALBOT MASTER
Talbot, Luke 10 305
Talbot, Reginald 1 146
Talbot, Suzanne 11 583; 13 328
Talbot, Thomas Mansel 30 268*; 32 782, 791
Talbot, William Henry Fox 8 652; 11 363; 19 519; 24 646, 647, 648, 651, 653, 654, 655, 656, 658, 659; 28 203; 30 268–71*
methods 25 591
works 10 252; 24 646; 26 232; 30 *269*, *270*; 33 134
Talbot Hours *see under* BOOKS OF HOURS → individual manuscripts
Talbot Master 20 772*
Talbotypes *see under* PHOTOGRAPHIC PRINTS → types
talc 1 292; 6 336; 7 133; 14 167; 25 477, 530
see also SOAPSTONE
Talca 6 *590*
Museo de Bellas Artes O'Higgins 6 601
Tal-Coat, Pierre 11 302, 550; 30 271–2*
Taleides 13 510
Talenti, Francesco 13 94; 30 272–3*
attributions 11 203
collaboration 30 273
competitions 7 664
works 11 176, 195, 200; 13 65, *66*; 16 627; 24 875
Talenti, Jacopo 11 208, 209; 30 272–3*
Talenti, Lodovico 2 117
Talenti, Piero 30 272
Talenti, Simone 13 94; 30 272, 273*
collaboration 7 334
works 11 203; 13 65
talha 17 595–6; 25 303; 26 252, 253; 30 799
Talhatan Baba Mosque 16 162
Talheim 25 504
Taliaris 32 782
Taliesin (Spring Green, WI) 31 596
Taliesin Associated Architects 24 548

T'alin 2 *423*, 435; 9 *512*; 30 274*
Cathedral 2 426, *426*, 429; 30 274
ta'līq script *see under* SCRIPTS → types
T'alish *see* ARUCH
Talisman of Charlemagne 1 4; 5 807; 26 145
talismans 7 834; 8 835; 17 518
Indian subcontinent 15 726, 734
Islamic 16 136–7, *137*, 245, 453
Japan 17 399
Ottoman 16 *137*
Turkey 16 *137*
Tall, Papa Ibra 1 432; 28 405
works 28 *405*
Tallageda College (AL) 1 442
Tallard, Marie-Joseph d'Hostun, Duc de 6 81; 9 467; 30 274*
Tallberg, Axel 10 563; 30 81, 275*
Tallberg, Julius 27 474
tallboys *see under* CHESTS OF DRAWERS → types
Tallensi 1 312; 10 778
El Taller 16 868
Taller 99 2 190; 6 598; 9 204
Taller Alacrán 20 513
Taller Boricua 18 833
Taller de Arquitectura 4 226–8
Taller de Artes Gráficas (TAGA) 10 511; 23 827; 32 176, 180
Taller de Fundición Artística Mexicana 7 784
Taller de Gráfica Panarte 23 905
Taller de Gráfica Popular 21 388; 23 371; 30 275*
members 1 739; 2 90; 3 688; 6 520; 21 123; 33 600
Taller de Integración Plástica 6 520
Talleres de Maestranza 31 758
Talleres Reales 29 304, 305, 315, 318
Taller Kyron 8 254
Taller Libre de Arte 1 72; 5 873; 16 868; 24 401; 32 176, 494
Taller Montevideano 31 757
Taller Torres García 11 249; 30 275*; 31 183, 755, 758
Talleyrand, Princesse de 2 869
Talleyrand-Périgord, Charles-Maurice, Duc de 4 330; 5 71; 7 194; 11 609; 29 88
Tallgren, A. M. 22 50
Tallherr, József 24 312
Tall Hum *see* CAPERNAUM
Talliard, Jean-Baptiste 6 401
Tallinn 10 *536*; 27 474; 30 275–7*
Academy of Sciences 10 541
Art Hall 10 537, *537*, 541; 30 277
churches
Cathedral of St Mary *see* Toomkirik
Charles Church 10 537
Church of the Holy Spirit 10 538
Kaarli *see* Charles Church
Metsakalmistu Cemetery chapel 10 537
Pühavaimu *see* Church of the Holy Spirit
St Nicholas 10 536; 30 *276*
altarpiece 10 538
chapel of St Anthony 10 538
Clodt Chapel 10 537
Museum of Medieval Art 10 541; 30 276
St Olav 10 536
Toomkirik 10 536
monument to Admiral S. Greigh 10 539
monument to Pontus de la Gardie 10 538
wood-carvings 10 539
Cottage of Peter the Great 30 277
Estonian National Library 10 541
Estonia Theatre 10 537
Flower Pavilion 10 538
fortifications 10 537
Tallinn—cont.
Governor's Palace 10 537
House of the Schwarzhäupter Brotherhood 10 537, 538
Kadriorg Palace 10 537, 538
Main Guildhall 10 537
museums
Adamson-Eric Museum 10 541
Art Museum of Estonia 10 541; 30 277
City Museum 22 365; 30 277
Eesti Kunstimuuseum *see* Art Museum of Estonia
Estonian Museum of Architecture 10 541
Estonian Open-Air Museum 30 277
Estonian Park Museum 10 541
Kristjan Raud Museum 10 541
Museum of Applied Art 10 541; 30 277
Museum of Medieval Art *see under* churches → St Nicholas
Parliament Building 10 537
Railway Hospital 10 537
Raua Street schoolhouse 10 537
St Olav's Guildhall 10 537
Song Festival Amphitheatre 10 537
Soros Centre 10 541
Suurgildi hoone *see* Main Guildhall
Town Hall 10 537, 538
villas 10 537
Tallino di Jacopo d'Ognabene 2 19
tallit 17 574
Tallmadge, Thomas E. 6 577, 578; 29 915
Tallman, William 5 78
Tallman & Bucklin 5 78; 30 412; 32 866
Talloment, Gédéon 18 649
Tallon, Ronald 28 284
Tallone, Cesare 21 527; 30 277*
pupils 5 842, 848; 11 843
works 16 562; 24 344
Tallone, Filippo 21 533
tallow 5 610; 8 128; 10 548, 561; 13 706; 23 378
Tally, Thomas L. 7 327
Talma, François-Joseph 8 638; 30 675
Talmage, Algernon 3 628
Talman, John 7 860; 10 292; 22 236; 30 277, 279*
Talman, William 6 65; 14 127; 30 277–9*
attributions 6 515; 8 834
groups and movements 23 857
patrons and collectors 4 131; 6 115, 116, 128, 515; 14 126, 127
personal collection 10 292
works 5 65; 8 47; 11 39; 30 *278*; 33 244
Talmanca de Jarama 29 334
Talon, Denis 5 167
Talor, William 10 303; 29 495
Talos Painter 13 524; 32 68*
Talowski, Teodor Marian 28 838; 30 279*; 31 553
Talpa, Bartolo 12 907
Talpino, il *see* SALMEGGIA, ENEA
Talpush-atili 4 641
Talsŏng, Dodong *sŏwŏn* 18 *270*
Talucchi, Giuseppe 5 615; 17 707; 31 442
talud-tablero 21 198, 200, 205–6*, *206*; 25 764; 30 279–80*, *280*
talus 8 277; 21 547
Talwin 10 356
Tamagawa Shūchō 15 896
Tamagni, Vincenzo 27 751; 30 281*; 31 448
Tamagnini, Paolo 20 585
Tamagnino, Antonio *see* PORTA, ANTONIO DELLA
Tamamizu 25 869
Taman 30 737
Tamana, Eijani West Tomb 17 59
Taman Bali 15 783
Tamang 22 757
Tamanrasset 1 636
Taman Siswa 15 808, 818
T'amanyan, Alek'sandr 30 281*
collaboration 13 653
groups and movements 29 529
works 2 428, 436; 10 449, 450, *450*
Tamar, Queen of Georgia (*reg* 1179-1212) 12 331
Tamara, Empress of Byzantium (*fl* 13th cent.) 9 3
tamarind 29 470
Tamarind Lithography Workshop 1 145; 19 492, 702; 20 606, 607, 608; 33 7
Tamarind Papers, The 1 145
tamarind seed mucilage *see under* GUMS → types
tamarisk 6 295, 296; 16 500
Tamarit de Litera, S Miguel 9 109
Tamaro, Bruna Forlati *see* FORLATI, BRUNA
Tamasch, Andreas 12 404
Tamassos 8 *325*
architecture 8 336
pottery 32 53
Sanctuary of Astarte 8 353, 356
sculpture 8 341, 342
tombs 8 332, 335
Tamaulipas 14 829
Tamayo, Camilo Cuéllar *see* CUÉLLAR TAMAYO, CAMILO
Tamayo, Rufino 21 388, 390, 406; 30 281–3*
patrons and collectors 21 395
personal collection 23 327
pupils 11 729; 16 811; 18 832
works 19 492; 22 21, 334; 30 *282*
Tamba 33 596, 598
Tambach glass factory 12 439
Tamba-kanda 29 474
Tambapanni 29 474
Tambapittigama 29 474
Tambarattha 29 474
Tambdi Surla 12 826
Tamberma 1 383
Tambo Colorado 29 *156*, 161, 162, *163*, 166
Tambo di Serraglio 23 742
Tambonneau, Jean 19 262
Tambo Quirquincho, Museo *see under* LA PAZ → museums
tambour (i) (embroidery) 30 283*
tambour (ii) (furniture) 30 283*
tambourwork *see under* BEADWORK → types
Tambo Viejo 29 *156*; 30 283*
Tambura 1 *379*, *401*; 33 609
Tamburini, Francisco 2 396; 9 335
works 2 *396*
Tamburlaine *see* TIMUR
Tam Chi 17 388; 24 47
Tame 8 490
works 8 *487*, *488*
Tamechika Reizai *see* REIZAI TAMECHIKA
Tamehisa, Fujiwara no *see* FUJIWARA NO TAMEHISA
Tameie, Fujiwara no *see* FUJIWARA NO TAMEIE
Tamemura Reizei *see* REIZEI TAMEMURA
Tamenari 17 156
Tamerlane *see* TIMUR
Tametaka *see* KITA KIUEMON
Tameuji, Fujiwara no *see* FUJIWARA NO TAMEUJI
Tamgach Khan, Ruler (*reg* 1052-68) (Qarakhanid) 27 674
Tamgrout 33 97
Tami 23 735; 24 79, 80
Tamietti, Carlo 16 739
Tamikichi Katō *see* KATŌ TAMIKICHI
Tamil 15 193; 29 440, 441, 442
Tamine, Laurent-Joseph 30 283*
Taminne, Laurent-Joseph *see* TAMINE, LAURENT-JOSEPH
Tamit Basilica 23 287
T'amjin *see* CH'OE KYŎNG
Tamjing 18 304; 30 284*
Tamjol *see* KANG HŬI-ŎN
Tam Ky 6 427
Tamluk 15 200
figurines 15 415, 700
plaques 15 717, 718, *718*
terracotta 15 453
Tamm, Franz Werner von 2 827; 30 284*
collaboration 29 789
patrons and collectors 23 874
works 2 795; 12 390
Tamm, Vaino 30 349
Tammisaari 11 103
Tamms, Friedrich 12 379; 32 439
Tamoni 27 238
Tampa (FL), University of South Florida-Tampa 19 493; 20 609
Tampaksiring *see* PURA GUNUNG KAWI
Tampang 15 787
Tampella Factory 11 110
Tampere 11 *87*; 30 284*
Cathedral 11 92, 96; 22 541; 28 747; 29 63
Kaleva Church 11 92
Metalworkers' Union Training Centre 14 328
Public Library 11 92
Pyynikinlinna 11 827
St John *see* Cathedral
Sara Hildén Art Museum 11 112; 30 284
State Granary *see* Sara Hildén Art Museum
UKK Institute 14 329
Tampinco, Isabelo 24 619
Tamposoque 14 829
Tamralipti *see* TAMLUK
Tamstone Press 20 608
Tamsweg 2 811
St Leonhard 2 819
Tam-tam 24 440
Tamtok 14 829
Tamub 20 886
Tamuín 14 829; 21 222, 226, 227
Tamura, Kōichi 17 267
Tamura Gozaemon 18 537
Tamworth (Staffs) 6 55; 9 144
Tamyang, Sosoewon 12 94
Tan, Joseph 20 172
Tanabe, Takao 5 569
Tanabe Gengen 17 413
Tanagra 13 *363*; 14 *332*; 26 *908*; 30 285–6*
figurines 12 286; 13 433, 579, *579*, 581; 15 895
pottery 13 513
sarcophagi 27 825; 30 285
sculpture 13 445
T'anahat
Church of the Holy Sign 2 434
St Step'anos 2 435
Tanaina 22 546, 639
Tanais 4 110, 111
reliefs 4 *111*
Tanaka, Atsuko 13 866; 17 207
Tanaka, Hideho 11 55
Tanaka, Ikko 17 752; 30 286*
Tanaka, Ikko, Design Studio 30 286
Tanaka, Kyōkichi 23 441
Tanaka, Shintarō 22 742
Tanaka, Toyotarō 21 634
Tanaka Chōjirō 17 342, 424; 18 553*; 25 869; 28 412
works 28 *410*
Tanaka Design Atelier *see* TANAKA, IKKO, DESIGN STUDIO
Tanaka Dōnyū 25 869
works 6 II2
Tanaka Jōkei 25 869
Tanaka Kakudō 23 594
Tanaka Masanobu 17 283
Tanaka Minko 17 400
Tanaka Nikka 17 197
Tanaka Nonkō *see* TANAKA DŌNYŪ
Tanaka Rikyū *see* SEN NO RIKYŪ
Tanaka Shōhei 25 869
Tanaka Sōkei 25 869
Tanaka Sōmi 25 869
Tanaka Totsugen 17 166; 31 545
Tan An 1 706
Tanana 22 546
Tanana, Upper 22 546
Tananarive 1 *413*
Tănăsescu, Radu 26 719
Tanavoli, Parviz 15 898; 16 288; 27 810; 30 286*
Tanazević, Branko 28 444, 838
Tanba 17 *241*
pottery 17 255, *255*, 256, 260, 261, 351, 352; 30 287*
Tanba Tachikui 17 353
Tanba ware *see under* POTTERY → wares
Tañcai *see* THANJAVUR
Tancanhuitz 14 829
Tañcavūr *see* THANJAVUR
T'an Chih-jui *see* TAN ZHIRUI
tanchras see under CARPETS → types
Tan Cikai 6 767
Tancol 21 200
Tancred, Prince of Antioch (*reg* 1111-12) 14 239; 17 502; 22 705
Tancredi, Parmeggiani 13 801
Tancredi da Pentima 18 785
Tancrémont Church 26 645
Tandarini, Carlantonio 31 901
Tanderagee 6 162
Tandyryul 6 212
tane see under PRINTS → types → *ukiyoe*
Tanejiro Kanae *see* KANAE TANEJIRO
Taneji Yamazaki *see* YAMAZAKI, TANEJI
Tanenbaum, Ruth *see* SCHEUER, RUTH
Tanesara-Mahadeva 15 460, *461*
Tanetsugu, Fujiwara no *see see* FUJIWARA NO TANETSUGU
Tanev, Nikola 5 155
Tang, José 24 510
Tanga (Tanzania) 1 *407*
Museum 30 302
Tanga (*d* 1954) 11 879
Tanganyika *see* TANZANIA
tangas 20 *372*; 29 193
Tängbro 32 524
T'ang Cheng-chung *see* TANG ZHENGZHONG
Tangdai 3 517; 6 818
Tang Da Wu 28 774
Tang Di 30 287*
Tange, Kenzō 17 53, 89, 93; 18 532, 541; 20 76; 23 386, 427; 25 878; 30 288–90*
architecture 7 695; 17 90
city halls 31 243, *243*
exhibition architecture 10 685
government buildings 17 90, *92*; 23 135
museums 14 568; 17 53, 89; 21 650
public buildings 22 474
stadia 1 798; 17 90; 29 489; 30 *289*; 31 79
university buildings 3 68
urban planning 17 90, 96; 19 883; 27 875; 31 80, 733, *734*
competitions 28 823
groups and movements 15 887; 21 318; 25 359
pupils 14 161; 16 563; 18 532; 20 147; 21 318; 33 509
staff 18 40; 23 628
Tange, Kenzō, & Urtec 16 563; 30 288
Tange, Susumu 17 408

Tangei Tsuruzawa *see* TSURUZAWA TANGEI
Tangente, Edition *see* EDITION TANGENTE
Tangermünde Church **14** 81
Tangga **24** 85
Tang He **7** 27
T'ang Ho *see* TANG HE
Tang Hou **6** 751, 824; **19** 299
Tang-i Botan *see* SHIMBAR
Tang-i Chogan **4** *92*, 92
Tangier
fortifications **21** 585
jewellery **16** 532
Musée d'Art Contemporain **21** 79; **22** 129
Museum of Military Miniatures **11** 301
synagogues **17** 551
Tang-i Sarvak **1** *849*, 887; **10** 172; **24** 218
tangkas see under SCROLLS → types
Tangmere (W. Sussex), St Andrew **11** 252
Tang Mun Kit **28** 774
Tang period *see under* CHINA → periods
Tangshan **6** *615*, 912, 913; **30** 290*
Tang Shisheng **19** 378
Tang Souyu **33** 319, 322
T'ang-tai *see* TANGDAI
T'ang Ti *see* TANG DI
Tan'gu *see* KIM (iii) HONG-DO
Tanguma, Leo **18** 831
Tangut **5** 110; **6** 308, 314; **30** 475
Tanguy, Julien-François **6** 375; **11** 449; **12** *858*; **30** 290*
Tanguy, Yves **27** 520; **30** 291–2*; **31** 607
groups and movements **30** 18, 19, 20, 21, 22
patrons and collectors **7** 812; **16** 892; **20** 832; **28** 914
teachers **14** 271
works **11** 549; **18** 718; **30** *20*, *292*
Tan'gwang **18** 369
Tang Yin (1470-1524) **6** 758, 810; **30** 49, 292–4*; **33** 659
patrons and collectors **28** 555
works **6** 781, 785; **17** 189; **30** *294*; **33** 436
Tangyin (Henan) **7** 99
Tang Ying (*fl* 1736-56) **6** 908; **17** 589
Tangyue **23** 780
Tang Zhengzhong **6** 804
Tanh Ho **6** 426
Tanh Loi **6** 426
Tani, Angelo di Jacopo **3** 612; **30** 294*
Tani, Jacopo **30** 294
Tani Bunchō **17** 188, 412; **30** 294–5*
groups and movements **17** 797
pupils **32** 896
works **3** *144*; **17** 191, 848; **18** 60; **30** *295*
writings **17** 419
Tanida Chubei **18** 606
tanida-makie see under LACQUER → types
Taniguchi, Kōkyō **17** 201
Taniguchi, Yoshirō **17** 88; **30** 296*
Tani Kankan **17** 191
Tanimbar islands **1** 706; **15** *751*, 789, 810
Tanis **9** 773, *774*, 783; **10** 77, 80; **24** 840; **30** 296–7*
colossal statue **30** *297*
colossi of Mermesha **9** 879
glass **10** 59
jewellery **10** 33
metalwork **10** 37
mummy cases **10** 14
mummy masks **10** 13
obelisk of Ramesses II **23** 329
reliefs **9** 887
sacred lake **27** 496
Tanis—cont.
sculpture **9** 863; **30** 296
shabtis **10** 18
sphinxes
sphinx of Ammenemes II **9** 875
sphinx of Ammenemes III **1** 793; **9** 879
statue of Ammenemes I **9** 874
statue of Ammenemes III **9** 875
statue of Osorkon III **9** 886
Temple of Amun **30** 296
tombs **9** 841; **10** 74; **30** 296
Amenemope (*reg c.* 998–*c.* 989 BC) **22** 285
Psusennes I (*reg c.* 1040–*c.* 997 BC) **9** 887; **10** 11, 32; **22** 284
Shoshenq II **10** 11, 32
Tani Sogai **31** 204
Tanjavur *see* THANJAVUR
Tanjé, Pieter **14** 795; **26** 477; **30** 297*; **31** 367
Tanjore *see* THANJAVUR
tankards
historical and regional traditions
China **6** 902
Cycladic **8** *312*
England **19** 4; **24** *579*
Germany **12** *431*, *435*, 444, 447
Helladic **14** *342*
Japan **17** *264*
Netherlands, the **22** 893
Norway **23** 236
Ottoman **16** *860*
Sweden **30** *104*, 104–5
Turkey **16** *860*
materials
amber **1** 762
coins **12** 444, 447
earthenwares **12** *431*
gold **16** *860*
ivory **16** 799
leather **19** 4
nephrite **16** *860*
pewter **24** *579*, 580
porcelain **6** 902; **12** *435*; **17** *264*
pottery **14** *342*
silver **12** *435*; **30** 104–5
silver-gilt **30** *104*
types
cimarres **7** 324–5*
schnellen **3** 588
Tankardstown **16** 28
Tankei **17** 122, 124, 729, 879; **31** 676
works **17** *123*
Tanken, Johannes **11** 99
Tankerville, Forde Grey, Earl of *see* GREY, FORDE, 1st Earl of Tankerville
Tankō **17** 126
tanks **16** 246
Tanlay **19** 145
Petit Château **6** 506
Tanmok **18** 58
Tanna **31** 890, 892
Tannauer, Gottfried *see* DANHAUER, GOTTFRIED
Tanneguy du Chastel, 1st Vicomte de La Bellière and Baron de Derval **6** 502–3*; **16** 854
Tanner, Benjamin **30** 853
Tanner, Henry Ossawa **1** 441; **25** 5; **30** 297*; **31** 603; **33** 370
tanneries **16** 262
Tannevot, Michel **24** 170, 821; **30** 298*
tanning **19** 1; **21** 878; **22** 654; **27** 105
alum **19** 6
brain tannage **22** 654
chamoising *see* oil tannage
mineral tannage *see* tawing
oil tannage **19** 1, 6; **22** 654
tawing **19** 1, 2; **22** 654; **27** 105
vegetable tannage **19** 1, 6
Tanning, Dorothea **10** 469; **29** 12; **30** 22, 298*
tannins **9** 490; **15** 851; **17** 359; **24** 106
Tannir, Hassan **19** 7
Tanno *see* CHO HŬI-RYONG
Tano, Nicolas **10** 92
Tanomura Chikuden **17** 198; **18** 60; **30** 298–9*
pupils **17** 192
works **17** 190
writings **17** 417
Tanomura Chokonyū **17** 198
Tanqasi culture **23** 285
Tanqueray, Anne **10** 329; **30** 299
Tanqueray, David **14** 856; **19** 593; **30** 299*; **33** 195
Tansey, Mark **25** 360
works **25** *360*
tansu see JAPAN → chests of drawers
Tansykbayev, Ural (Tansykbayevich) **30** 299–300*; **31** 783
Tanta **16** 90
Tantamani (*reg c.* 664-*c.* 657 BC) **9** *777*; **23** 281
Tantardini, Antonio **16** 706; **30** 215
Tantardini, Carlo Antonio **28** 13
Tan Teng Kee **28** 774
Tantisuket, Sawasdi **30** 617
Tantra **5** 93, 96*, 103
tantras **5** 90, 103
Tantric Buddhism *see under* BUDDHISM → branches
Tantric Hinduism *see under* HINDUISM → sects
T'an Tz'u-k'ai *see* TAN CIKAI
Tanucci, Marchese **14** 445
Tanum **25** 532
T'anŭn *see* YI CHŎNG (i)
Tanwŏn *see* KIM (iii) HONG-DO
Tan Yankai **6** 767
Tanyao **6** 709; **33** 574
Tanyao Caves *see under* YUNGANG
T'an Yen-k'ai *see* TAN YANKAI
T'anyon **18** 329
Tan'yū Kanō *see* KANŌ TAN'YŪ
Tanzania **1** *214*; **30** 300–302*
beadwork **1** *410*; **3** 442
caves **1** 304
collections **30** 302*
doors **9** 165; **30** *57*, 300
earrings **1** 351
education (art) **30** 302*
exhibitions **30** 302
figurines **1** 273
houses **1** 311; **30** 300, 302
leather **1** 299, *410*
metal **1** 287
museums **30** 302*
musical instruments **1** 358
painting **30** 301*
palisades **21** 597
patronage **30** 301–2*
prints **30** *301*
rock art **1** 374, *374*, *375*
sculpture **30** 301*
shelters **1** 306
shields **1** 299
skirts **1** *410*
tembes **1** 311
trade **30** 300
wood **9** 165; **30** *57*
Tanzanian Handicrafts Marketing Corporation (HANDICO) **30** 302
Tanzen *see* SHIBATA ZESHIN
Tan Zhirui **6** 783
Tanzio, il *see* TANZIO DA VARALLO
Tanzio da Varallo **27** 499; **30** 302–4*
collaboration **31** 899
works **16** 674; **30** *303*, *304*
Tao-chi *see* DAOJI
T'ao Ch'ien *see* TAO YUANMING
Tao Hongjing **6** 744; **7** 716; **16** 860
Tao-hsüan *see* DAOXUAN
Taohuawu **7** 120
see also SUZHOU
T'ao Hung-ching *see* TAO HONGJING
Tao-Klarjeti **9** *512*; **30** 305–7*
architecture **30** *305*, *306*
manuscript illumination **12** 324
wall paintings **12** 323
Tao-kuang emperor (Ch'ing) *see* DAOGUANG EMPEROR (QING)
Taolean culture **29** 226
Tao Qian *see* TAO YUANMING
Taosi (Xiangfen) **7** 138
Taos Pueblo (NM) **22** 606, 634; **31** *587*
Taos Ten **33** 185
T'ao Tsung-i *see* TAO ZONGYI
Tao Yuanming **6** 795; **12** 86
Tao Zongyi **7** 89, 90; **9** 141
tapa see BARKCLOTH
Tapa-é-Top-é-Kalan *see* TEPE KALAN
Tapajó **4** 706; **27** 785; **29** 193
Tapar **15** 265
Vishnu Temple **15** 265
Taparelli, Massimo, Marchese D'Azeglio *see* D'AZEGLIO, MASSIMO (TAPARELLI), Marchese
Taparelli, Roberto, Marchese D'Azeglio *see* D'AZEGLIO, ROBERTO TAPARELLI, Marchese
Tapa Sardar *see* SARDAR TEPE
tape lace *see under* LACE → types
tapestries **3** 388–9; **5** 829–30; **6** 388; **11** 54; **14** 422; **30** 307–35*, *308*, 553*
collections *see under* COLLECTIONS → types
conservation **30** 332–5*, *333*, *334*
display **9** 30*
historical and regional traditions
Ancient Near East **1** 880
Australia **2** 767
Austria **2** 823, 826
Belgium **2** *200*; **3** 576, 605–8*; **4** *923*, 923; **5** *47*, *48*, *50*; **30** 312–17*, 320, 324; **31** *218*, 219
Baroque **17** *649*; **27** *294*
Renaissance **2** *198*; **3** *607*; **23** *527*
15th cent. **5** 43; **30** I2
16th cent. **30** *316*, II1
17th cent. **3** *608*
Brazil **4** 724
Burma **5** 248*
Byzantine **9** 666
China **7** 48, *48*, 49, 51, *51*, *67*
Coptic **7** 826, *827*, 828; **16** 431; **30** IV2
Czech Republic **8** *420*
Denmark **8** *754*, 754–5*; **30** 320
Early Christian (*c.* AD 250-843) **9** 666
Egypt **7** *827*; **9** *767*; **16** 431, 432, *433*; **30** IV2; **31** 21
Egypt, ancient **10** 44, 75, *75*
England **10** 270, 275, 277, 348–52*; **30** 318, 322, *326*
chinoiserie **7** 167
Pre-Raphaelitism **30** III2
16th cent. **30** *318*
17th cent. **10** *350*
18th cent. **10** *352*
20th cent. **30** IV1
France **11** 589, 637–44*; **12** 829; **30** 312–14*, 318, 321–4
Baroque **30** *321*
chinoiserie **7** 167, *168*
Gothic **2** 49–51, *50*, 111; **11** *638*; **13** *195*, 196
Mannerism **8** *67*
Renaissance **11** 571
14th cent. **30** *313*
15th cent. **20** *777*; **29** *423*; **30** I1
17th cent. **11** *640*; **12** *829*; **21** *366*, *367*; **30** II2
18th cent. **2** *703*; **3** *462*; **11** *642*; **30** *323*
tapestries
historical and regional traditions
France—cont.
20th cent. **11** *644*; **13** 681; **19** *808*
Germany **12** 464–5*, 467–8*; **14** 422; **30** 310–12*, 319, 324, *327*
chinoiserie **7** 167
Gothic **13** 194, 196
Romanesque **14** 65; **26** 703
12th cent. **12** *465*
15th cent. **12** *466*; **30** *312*
17th cent. **5** 606, *606*
20th cent. **30** *328*
Gothic **13** 194–7*
France **2** 49–51, *50*, 111; **11** *638*; **13** *195*, 196
Germany **13** 194, 196
Netherlands, the **13** 196
Switzerland **13** 194, 196
Greenland **13** *620*
Huari culture **29** *181*
Hungary **15** 12*
Inca **15** 163
Iraq **16** 434
Islamic **16** 431, 432, *433*, 434; **31** 21
Italy **20** 318, 323; **30** 314, 319; **32** 205
Mannerism **30** *319*
14th cent. **16** 755–8*, *756*
15th cent. **16** 711
16th cent. **11** *193*; **16** *757*
17th cent. **30** 322
18th cent. **30** 324
Lesotho **19** 241
Netherlands, the **22** 862, 897*; **30** 317, 320
Gothic **13** 196
Renaissance **13** *907*
New Zealand **23** *74*
Norway **23** 238–9*, *239*, *240*, 241
Peru **29** *181*; **30** III1
Poland **12** 11; **25** 131, 134; **30** *330*
Portugal **25** 316–17*
Romanesque **14** 65; **26** 703
Romania **26** 721–2
Rome, ancient **27** 113, *114*
Russia **27** 430
Scandinavia **23** 238
Scotland **28** 244, 266–7, *267*
Senegal **28** *405*
South America, Pre-Columbian **29** 180, *181*
Spain **29** 297, 301, 350*; **30** 324, *325*
Sweden **30** 114–15*, 320
Switzerland **13** 194, 196; **30** 148–9*, *149*, 311*
Syria-Palestine **1** 881
United States of America **1** *146*; **31** 659*, *660*, 660–61*
Uruguay **31** 755, 757, *757*
materials
cartoons (drawings) **30** 310
cotton **30** 308
gold **3** 606, *607*; **5** *48*
hemp **11** 637
linen **12** 465; **13** 194; **16** *433*; **30** 308, IV2
plastics **31** *757*
silk **30** 308
Belgium **3** *607*; **4** *923*; **5** *47*, *48*, *50*; **30** I2, II1; **31** *218*
Denmark **8** *754*
Egypt **16** *433*
England **10** *350*, *352*; **30** III2
France **11** *638*, *640*; **30** I1, II2
Germany **12** 467
Italy **11** *193*
silver **3** 606, *607*; **5** *48*
threads **10** *350*; **11** *193*; **30** 308, II1, 2

tapestries
materials—cont.
wool **9** 490; **30** 308
Belgium **3** *607*; **4** *923*; **5** *47*, *48*, *50*; **30** I2, II1; **31** *218*
Coptic **30** IV2
Denmark **8** *754*
Egypt **9** *767*
England **10** *350*, *352*; **13** 196; **30** III2, IV1
France **2** *703*; **11** *638*, *640*; **30** *313*, I1, II2
Germany **12** 465, 467
Gothic **13** 194
Italy **11** *193*
New Zealand **23** *74*
Norway **23** *239*
Peru **30** III1
Scotland **28** *267*
United States of America **31** *660*
restoration **30** 333
types
à alentours **11** 643; **12** 829
flamsk **30** 114, *114*
Heidnischwerk **30** 148
millefleurs **14** 422, III2
rølakan **30** 114
uses
blankets **3** 606
canopies (ii) (textile coverings) **8** *754*
chairs **9** 30; **11** 589
cushion covers **3** 606; **12** 467
maps **20** 366*
tiraz **31** 21
tunics **29** *181*
tapestry carpets *see under* CARPETS → types
tapestry-weavers' guilds *see under* GUILDS → types
Tapetenmuster style **27** 56
tapete tiles *see under* TILES → types
Tapia, Amalia **23** 905
Tapía, Andres de **21** 252; **31** 505
Tapia, Cristobal de **9** 116
Tapia, Francisco de **5** 410; **24** 503
Tapia, José Manuel de **5** 410; **24** 503
Tapia, Luis **18** 832
Tapia y Alarcón, Rodrigo de **30** 335*
Tapia y Salcedo, Gregorio de **24** 15
Tapié, Michel **2** 514–15, 543, 544, 545; **11** 551; **26** 777; **33** 305
Tàpies, Antoni **30** 335–6*
dealers **16** 820; **20** 75
groups and movements **1** 78; **2** 543, 545; **3** 219; **8** 538; **20** 846; **29** 286
house **7** 512
patrons and collectors **24** 24; **25** 400
works **3** 219; **5** 726; **19** 491; **30** *336*
Tapiola **10** 492; **11** 92
Cultural Centre **11** 92
Tapioszentmarton **28** 323
Tapiró Baró, José **29** 284
tapis à languette **5** 588
Tapley, John **27** 337
Taplow **2** 79
Tappa **11** 78
Tapper, Kain **11** 100; **30** 336–7*
Tappert, Georg **3** 801; **22** 114
Tappin, N. B. **26** 75
tappit hens *see under* MEASURES
Taprell, Holland & Son **14** 682
Taprell, Stephen **14** 682
Taprell & Holland **14** 682
Ta Prohm *see under* ANGKOR
Tapureli **9** 590
Tapuskyansky, B. **28** 642
Taq-i Bustan **1** *849*; **15** *901*, 918; **27** 856; **30** 337*
metalwork **15** 920
reliefs **1** 882; **16** 530
Taq-i Bustan—cont.
rock reliefs **1** 887; **11** 151; **15** 907, 915, 917; **30** 337, *337*
sculpture **30** 337
Tar, András **15** 6
Tar, Illés **15** 7
Tara **15** 601; **30** 338*
Tara Brooch **6** 164; **15** 872, *872*; **16** 36
Tarabukin, Nikolay (Mikhailovich) **7** 341; **15** 857; **30** 338*
Tara Chandi Hill **27** 857
Tarade, Jacques **29** 750
Taragarh, Shrine of Sayyid Husayn Khing Sawar **15** 371
Taragros, Ter-Vardanyan **2** 436
Tara Kalan *see* TARA
Taramelli, Antonio **2** 52; **17** 751
Taramgambadi *see* TRANQUEBAR
Taranatha **26** 20
Taranchi **30** 473
Taranczewski, Wacław **25** 108, 409; **30** 338–9*
Taranga **15** 314
Taranto
Cathedral of S Cataldo **1** 698; **26** 627; **30** 777
chamber **13** 383, 384
coins **13** 587
couches **13** 592
figurines **13** 579, 580, 581
limestone **13** 434
metalwork **13** 568; **32** 660
Museo Nazionale **13** 555
pottery **13** 512, 526, 528, 530, 540
sculpture **13** 582; **27** 29, 31; **30** *339*
Taras **13** *362*; **16** *621*; **30** 339–40*
temples **30** 339
terracottas **13** 582
trade **14** 337
Taras *see under* TARANTO
Tarascan **21** 177, 204; **30** 340–42*; **33** 102
architecture **30** 340*
basalt **30** *341*
cloaks **30** 342
dress **30** 342
feathers **21** 249; **30** 342
gourds **30** 341
hardstones **30** 341
headdresses **30** 342
humming-bird feathers **21** 249
metalwork **21** 254; **30** 341
mitres **21** 249
pipes (smoking) **30** 341
pottery **30** 341*
pyramids **25** 764; **30** 340
rock art **30** 341
sculpture **21** 217, 225*; **30** 340–41, *341*
shields **30** 342
standards (vexilloid) **30** 342
stone **30** 340–41
textiles **30** 342
tombs **31** 118
weapons **21** 245
weights **30** 341, 342
wood **30** 342
yácatas **31** *504*
Tarascon **19** 895
Bergière **29** 488
Ste Marthe **26** 603
Tarasewicz, Aleksander **19** 496
Tarasewicz, Leon **19** 496
Tarasin, Jan **2** 502; **30** 342–3*
Tarasov **33** 658
Taras Painter **32** 37
Taravai *see* GAMBIER ISLANDS
Taraval, Guillaume-Thomas (-Raphael) **8** 161; **9** 455; **29** 689; **30** 78, 343, 524
Taraval, (Jean-)Hugues **30** 343*
patrons and collectors **13** 665
pupils **12** 186; **30** 343
works **14** 792; **17** 627
Taraval, Jean-Gustave **30** 343
Taraval, Louis-Gustave **30** 343
Taravell, Hanns Reinhardt
works **25** *436*
Taraz *see* ZHAMBYL
Tarazona Cathedral **29** 263, 337
Tarbell, Edmund C(harles) **4** 478; **11** 141; **30** 343–4*
groups and movements **23** 47; **30** 452; **31** 603
pupils **11** 322
Tarbişu
Nergal Temple **21** 290
palace **21** 290
Tarbolton, Harold Ogle **18** 68
Tarburg **12** 431
Tarchaneiotes, Michael Glavas *see* MICHAEL GLAVAS TARCHANEIOTES
Tarchetta, Alesso **1** 747
Tarchiani, Filippo **12** 706
Tarchon *see* TARRAGONA
Tarchuna *see* TARQUINIA
Tard, Antoine **10** 771
Tardessire, Guillaume **11** 604; **19** 849
Tardieu, Jacques-Nicolas **30** 344
Tardieu, Nicolas-Henry **30** 344*
pupils **3** 259; **5** 884; **11** 171; **19** 10; **27** 531
works **10** 391; **14** 85
Tardieu, Pierre-Alexandre **8** 557
Tardieu, Pierre-François **30** 344
Tardieu, Victor **32** 492
Tarentum *see* TARAS
Tarfaya **33** 98
'Tarffa, Tebaba **10** 574
Target *see* DONKEY'S TAIL
Targmantchats Gospels *see under* GOSPEL BOOKS → individual manuscripts
Targone, Pompeo **4** 405; **26** 779; **30** 344–5*
Targowica Synagogue **17** 559
Taricco, Sebastiano **29** 831
el-Tarif *see under* THEBES (i) (EGYPT)
Tarifa, 1st Marqués de **12** 114; **26** 306*; **28** 519
Tarifa, Marquesa de **29** 299
Tarifa, Per Afán de Ribera, 2nd Marqués de *see* ALCALÁ, 1st Duque de
Tarija **4** 255, *255*, 270
Museo de la Casa Dorada **4** 269
Museo S Francisco **4** 269
Tarim **33** 520
al-Afqa Library **33** 520
Tariq, Tawfiq **30** 177
Tarishlak **6** 294
Tarissel, Pierre **1** 777; **6** 414
Tarjanne, Onni **11** 92
Tarkhan **10** 59
coffins **33** 330
dress **10** 45
furniture **30** 775
Grave 415 **10** 50
Tomb 1845 **20** 596
Tomb 852 **20** 596
tombs **9** 837
Tarkhan-Mouravi, R. **12** 327
Tarkowski, Andrei **26** 106
Tarkunia *see* TARQUINIA
Tarlati, Guido **19** 665
Tarlé **8** 776
Tarlo, Relly **29** 99
Tarmita **6** *182*, 198; **30** 489
Tarnapowicz, Jan **22** 449; **25** 124
Tarner (family) **22** 891
tarnishes **9** 30
see also PATINAS
Tărnovo *see* VELIKO TURNOVO
Tarnovsky, Veniamin **31** 565
Tarnów **25** *92*; **30** 345*
Cathedral **25** 126; **30** 345
tomb of Barbara Tęczyńska Tarnowska **25** 113
tomb of Jan Tarnowski and his Son Jan Christopher Tarnowski **22** *167*; **25** 113
Tarnów
Cathedral—cont.
tomb of the Ostrogski Family **25** 113
District Museum **30** 345
Museum **25** 140
Tarnowski (company) **32** 879
Tarnowski (family) **18** 691; **25** 138
Tarnowski, Jan Feliks, Count **25** 136, 138; **30** 345*
Tarnowski, Waleria, Countess **25** 138; **30** 345*
Tarocchi, Mattia **24** 853; **30** 430
Tarocchi Baglioni (tarot) *see* TAROCCHI COLLEONI
Tarocchi Brambilla (tarot) **33** 626
Tarocchi Colleoni (tarot) **33** 626
Tarocchi Visconti di Modrone (tarot) **33** 626
Taroi, Wero **32** 769
Tarone, Josef **8** 419
Tarō Okamoto *see* OKAMOTO, TARŌ
Tarouca
S João de Tarouca **25** 289
S Pedro Velho **26** 611
Taroudant Synagogue **17** 551
Tarpoley Painter **13** 525, 526
Tarquinia **10** *583*, 585, 601, 637, 638, 642; **16** *620*; **26** *886*; **30** 346*
bronze **10** 604, 624, 627
coins **10** 633
excavations **30** 346
glass **9** 646
gold **10** 631
metalwork **10** 630
mirrors **10** 628
Monterozzi necropolis **10** 587; **30** 346
Museo Nazionale Tarquinese **10** 640
pottery **10** 610, 613; **13** 542
sarcophagi **10** 588, 607, 608
sculpture **10** 591
S Maria di Castello **7** 919, 922; **25** 865
temple **23** 480
tombs **10** 591, 592, 617, 621–4, 637
Aninas Tomb **10** 620, 623
Bartoccini Tomb **10** 621
Bocchoris Tomb **10** 587
Bruschi Tomb **10** 618, 623
Giglioli Tomb **10** 623, 633
Querciola I Tomb **10** 619, 622
Tomb 1560 **10** 622
Tomb 3697 **10** 622
Tomb 4813 **10** 622
Tomb 5187 **10** 622
Tomb 5517 **10** 622
Tomb 6071 **10** 622
Tomb of Hunting and Fishing **10** 594, 618, 619, *619*, 621; **18** 701; **31** 109
Tomb of Orcus I **10** 622
Tomb of Orcus II **10** 596, 617, 620, *620*, 622, 632
Tomb of the Augurs **10** 594, 618, 619, 621, 634
Tomb of the Baron **10** 595, 621
Tomb of the Biclinium **10** 637
Tomb of the Black Sow **10** 618, 619, 622
Tomb of the Blue Demons **10** 622
Tomb of the Bulls **10** 595, 596, 621, *621*; **18** 701; **31** 109
Tomb of the Cardinal **10** 623, 637
Tomb of the Ceisinie (Family) **10** 637
Tomb of the Chariots **10** 617, 618, 619, 621; **16** 653
Tomb of the Charuns **10** 617, 623, *623*
Tomb of the Cock **10** 622
Tomb of the Congress **10** 624
Tarquinia
tombs—cont.
Tomb of the Funeral Couch **10** 618, 619, 622
Tomb of the Garlands **10** 617, 623
Tomb of the Hunter **10** 618, 621, 636
Tomb of the Hut **10** 621
Tomb of the Jade Lions **10** 621
Tomb of the Jugglers **10** 619, 621
Tomb of the Leopards **10** 618, *618*, 621
Tomb of the Lionesses **10** 618, 621
Tomb of the Lotus Flower **10** 621
Tomb of the Maiden **10** 622
Tomb of the Monkey **10** 619
Tomb of the Olympic Games **10** 618, 619, 621
Tomb of the Panthers **10** 621
Tomb of the Red Lions **10** 621
Tomb of the Shields **10** 623, 632
Tomb of the Ship **10** 618, 622; **13** 540
Tomb of the Stag Hunt **10** 622
Tomb of the Tapestry **10** 637
Tomb of the Triclinium **10** 618, 621, 622; **16** 653
Tomb of the Tritons **10** 621
Tomb of the Typhon **1** 692; **10** 588, 594, 620, 624; **16** *652*, 653
Tomb of the Warrior **10** 622
trade **10** 584, 591
vase paintings **10** 614, 615
vases **10** 609, 610, 611, 612, 613, 616
wall paintings **10** 617, 618–20*; **16** 652
Tarquinia *Madonna* **15** 135
Tarquinius Priscus **8** 263; **10** 601; **27** 22
Tarquinius Superbus **10** 601
Tarraco *see* TARRAGONA
Tarragona **26** *908*; **29** *259*; **30** 346–7*
amphitheatre **30** *347*
Cathedral **3** 309; **13** 69; **29** 263; **30** 347*
metalwork **13** 166
retable **9** 262; **11** 482; **13** 107; **29** 289
retables **26** 249
sarcophagus **9** 596
sculpture **26** 610
textiles **30** 331
tomb of Archbishop Juan de Aragón **13** 105
cemetery **29** 261
Civil Government building **29** 274
glass **27** 74
gold **13** 165
Roman circus **7** 342
sarcophagi **9** 597
sculpture **29** 287
S María del Milagro **29** 261; **30** *347*
Tomb of the Scipios **31** 109
Tarragona, Juan de *see* JUAN DE TARRAGONA
Tarrant, Margaret **21** 32
Tarrasa **9** *510*
Fábrica Aymerich *see* Museo de la Ciència i de la Tècnica de Catalunya
Museo de la Ciència i de la Tècnica de Catalunya **21** 849
S Pere **9** 533
Tarraths, Joan Josep **29** 286
Tarrytown (NY)
Knoll *see* Lyndhurst
Lyndhurst **7** 745; **8** *575*, 575; **13** 208; **14** 482
Tarsia, Antonio **7** 900; **30** 347–8*

Tarsia, Bartolomeo 24 546
Tarsia, Ferrante Spinelli, Prince of (*c.* 1651) 10 762; 11 321
Tarsila 4 717, 718; 30 348*; 33 316
  works 4 708; 28 394; 30 *348*; 32 855; 33 317
T'arsus (Armenia) 2 427
Tarsus (Turkey) 1 *821*; 17 500; 27 *102*
  coins 13 587
  figurines 1 833
  jewellery 27 103
  mosaics 13 565
  pottery 1 826; 8 343; 27 107
  stamps 9 655
  temple 1 826
  tents 30 478
  terracottas 27 111
Tartaglia, Niccolo 27 347
Tartalı 24 691
tartans 9 492; 28 266
tartaric acid 30 559
Tartas, David de Castro *see* CASTRO TARTAS, DAVID DE
Tartessos 10 592; 25 410
Tartölten 22 375
Tartous *see* ANTARADUS
Tartu 10 *536*; 30 349*
  Estonian National Museum *see* Museum of Ethnography
  Folk Museum of Estonia *see* Museum of Ethnography
  fortifications 10 537
  monument to Barclay de Tolly 10 539
  Museum of Art 10 541; 30 349
  Museum of Ethnography 10 541; 30 349; 33 566
  Pallas art school 10 539
  Raadi manor 10 540
  St John 10 536, 538
  Starkopf Atelier Museum 29 549
  Students' Society building 10 537
  Town Hall 10 537
  Town Hall Square 10 537
  University 10 537, 539, 541; 19 497
  University Museum of Classical Archaeology 30 349
  Vanemuine Theatre 10 537
Tartuffi, Emilio 12 559
Tartus 12 248; 18 153; 30 179
  museum 30 178
Taruffi, Emilio 7 308; 30 349*
Taruga 1 *381*; 23 *129*, 130, 179, 181
Tarut Island 2 *246*, 267, 271, 272
Tarvas, Peeter 30 349
Tarvaspää, Gallen-Kallela Museum 12 21
Tarvisium *see* TREVISO
Tarxien 25 *470*, 512
  carvings 25 510, *510*
Tarxna *see* TARQUINIA
Tarzona Cathedral 29 335
tas 17 569, *570*
Tasaki Museum of Art *see under* KARUIZAWA
Taschner, Ignatius 14 632; 30 349–50*
Tasco 10 505
tas-de-charge 30 350*, *350*
Ta-senet *see* ESNA
Tash-Air 30 350*; 31 *546*
Tashichoiling Monastery 21 875
Tashi-khatun 33 482
Tashilhunpo 30 351–2*, *351*, *806*, 819, 820
  Maitreya Chapel 30 351, 821
  paintings 22 785, 786
  prints 30 845
  woodwork 30 846
Tashi Namgyel, Ruler of Basgo (*reg* 16th cent.) 15 311, 397; 19 90
Tashkent 6 *182*, 379; 16 *105*; 30 352*; 31 781, *781*
  Alisher Navoi metro station 31 782
Tashkent—cont.
  architecture 31 782
  coins 6 266
  fortifications 21 589, 592
  jewellery 6 274
  Khamza Institute for Knowledge of the Arts 6 283
  manuscripts 16 342
  museums 6 282
    Museum of Applied Art 6 283
    Museum of the Arts of Uzbekistan 6 283; 31 783
    T. Aybek Museum of the History of the Peoples of Uzbekistan 6 283
  Navoi Opera and Ballet Theatre 29 823
  ossuaries 23 607
  Palace of Friendship of the People 31 782
  ramparts 6 211
  Soviet Theatre 29 823
  State University 6 283
  textiles 6 250; 31 783
  Theatre of Opera and Ballet 31 782
  woodwork 16 502
Tashtimur 32 313
Tashtyk culture 27 367; 28 325
Tasker, James R. 4 802
Tasker, Rita 29 117
Taslitzki, Boris 11 337
Tasman, Abel 23 51, 57
Tasmania 1 *37*
  baskets 1 52
  necklaces 1 53
  painting 1 51
  rock art 1 40–41; 22 229
  textiles 2 767
  see also ABORIGINAL AUSTRALIA; AUSTRALIA
Tasmola 2 100
Tasneem, Mohammad 23 801
Tasnière, Georges 3 35; 24 836, 837; 28 12
Tasri, Agostino 6 586
TASS 29 19
Tassa, Aleksander 33 566
Tassaert, Félix 30 352
Tassaert, Henriette Felicité 30 352, 353*
Tassaert, Jean-Joseph-François 14 192; 30 352, 353*
Tassaert, Jean-Pierre-Antoine 3 571; 30 352, 353*
  assistants 28 42
  patrons and collectors 4 303
  pupils 12 835; 30 353
  teachers 28 845
Tassaert, Marie-Edmée *see* MOREAU, MARIE-EDMÉE
Tassaert, (Nicolas-François-) Octave 5 57; 23 788; 30 352, 353–4*
Tassaert, Paul 30 353
Tassaert, Philippe-Joseph 28 370
Tassel 14 770
Tassel, Jean 30 354–5*
  works 8 890; 30 *354*
Tassel, Pierre 30 354
Tassel, Richard 8 893; 30 354*
Tasselli, Domenico 26 800
tassels 24 237
Tasset, Paulin 32 338
Tassi, Agostino 3 862; 12 307; 30 355–6*
  assistants 8 783
  attributions 3 38
  collaboration 4 405; 9 90; 12 305; 18 732, 733; 27 817; 32 826
  patrons and collectors 21 25; 24 267
  pupils 7 389; 12 307
  works 2 493; 3 *57*; 4 405; 12 305; 15 137; 18 689, 708; 26 840; 30 *355*
  workshop 3 56
Tassi, Francesco Maria 5 872; 6 148
Tassie, James 2 11; 12 263; 16 33; 30 356*
  assistants 3 25
  personal collection 3 812; 12 547; 24 734
  teachers 11 338
  works 17 525; 28 242, *242*, 264, 790
Tassie, William 28 242; 30 356
Tassili N' Ajjer 1 *376*
  painting 1 274, 343, 370, 373
  rock art 1 *220*, 333, 370, 377
Tassili National Park 1 634
Tassilo III, Duke of Bavaria (*reg* 748-88) 5 806; 18 446, 447
Tassilo Chalice 5 806; 6 398; 27 663
Tassis, Antoon de 3 615
Tassis, Iñigo Vélez de Guevara y *see* OÑATE Y DE VILLAMEDIANA, Conde de
Tasso, Chimenti del 16 724; 24 768
Tasso, Clemente del *see* TASSO, CHIMENTI DEL
Tasso, del (family) 9 142; 11 388, 389; 16 724; 20 111
Tasso, Domenico del 6 7; 16 712, 724
Tasso, Filippo 30 357
Tasso, Francesco 20 414, 415
Tasso, Giovan Battista di Marco del 30 357*
  works 16 724; 30 *357*
Tasso, Giuliano del 16 712
Tasso, Leonardo del 16 724
Tasso, Marco del 16 712
Tasso, Torquato 30 358*
  productions 3 744
  sponsorship 12 911
  works 29 400; 31 881
    illustrated 4 362; 5 857; 6 25; 30 428
Tasso, Zanobi del 16 724
Tasso y Nadal, Torcuato 28 647
taste 2 557, 561; 6 76; 7 561; 14 868; 15 888; 17 800–802; 22 355; 24 667, 742
  France 1 898
  Italy 20 242
Taster, The *see* 'ALI IBN ILYAS AL-TABRIZI AL-BAVARJI
Tastil 29 191
Tata (Hungary) 15 2
  English Garden 14 888
  Piarist school 15 17
Tata (family) 15 742; 17 428
Tata, J. N. 4 289; 15 411
Tata faience factory 10 531
Tatam, Henry 29 532
tatami see under MATS → types
Tatar 14 183; 27 434
Tatarescu, Aretia 26 723
Tatarkiewicz, Józef Jakub 25 115; 30 359*; 32 876
Tatarkiewicz, Władysław 25 143; 33 704
Tatarnas Monastery 9 630
Tatar tables *see under* TABLES → types
Tatarup 27 432
Tata Trusts 4 290
Tatatungo 21 882
Tate, Henry 10 370; 23 26; 30 359*; 32 907
Tatebayashi Kagei 17 179; 23 367
Tatebe Ryōtai 17 273; 18 494
Tate Gallery *see under* LONDON → museums; LIVERPOOL; ST IVES (CORNWALL)
Tatehata, Taimu 17 134
Tateishi, Kōichi 17 207
tatemono see under SCULPTURE → types
Tateno kiln 27 873
Tat'ev Monastery 2 *423*; 30 360*, *360*
  chapel of St Grigor the Illuminator 30 360
Tat'ev Monastery—cont.
  Church of the Mother of God 30 360
  SS Paul and Peter 2 429, 434; 30 360
  Treasury 2 444
Tatevosyan, Egish 18 404
Tatevosyan, Oganes (Karapetovich) 31 783
Tatham, Arthur 1 897; 23 884
Tatham, C(harles) H(eathcote) 10 644; 28 908; 30 361*
  groups and movements 10 97
  teachers 7 502
  works 6 66; 10 296; 14 808; 20 868; 24 273
  writings 10 279, 296, 334; 26 85
Tatham, Frederick 1 897; 23 884
Tatham, Thomas 9 31; 10 279
Tatham & Bailey 30 783
Tati, Pier Antonio di Benvenuto 25 7
Tatís, José Gabriel 7 608
Tatishchev, Vasily 24 458; 33 517
Tatishvili, G. 12 326
Tatius, Achilles 15 85
Tatlef 27 434
Tatler, Elijah 19 165
Tatlin, Vladimir (Yevgrafovich) 7 770; 17 764; 27 284, 393, 443, 580; 30 361–4*; 32 661; 33 486
  collaboration 26 504; 31 519
  groups and movements 1 76
    Abstraction-Création 1 90
    agitprop 1 453
    Association of Revolutionary Art of Ukraine (ARMU) 2 634
    Constructivism 7 767
    Dada 8 437
    Donkey's Tail 9 144; 22 750
    environmental art 10 415
    Inkhuk 15 856, 857
    kinetic art 18 62
    Narkompros 22 508
    Union of Youth 31 583
    World of Art (Mir Iskusstva) 33 380
  patrons and collectors 8 10
  productions 30 686
  pupils 19 746; 20 301; 25 238
  staff 32 381
  works 1 737; 7 769; 20 888; 22 42, 173; 23 333; 26 504; 27 378, 409; 30 *363*
Tato 1 166; 8 771; 11 867
Tatoi, Loverdos House 13 349
Tatoti, Antonio *see* GHERARDI, ANTONIO
Tatsuaki Kuroda *see* KURODA, TATSUAKI
Tatsuno, Kingo 3 176; 17 87; 30 364*; 31 79
Tatsuoki Nanbata *see* NANBATA, TATSUOKI
Tatsuo Takayama *see* TAKAYAMA, TATSUO
Tatsusuke Kuriki *see* KURIKI, TATSUSUKE
Tatsuyuki Nakanishi *see* NAKANISHI, TATSUYUKI
Tatsuzō Shimaoka *see* SHIMAOKA, TATSUZŌ
Tatta *see* THATTHA
Tattarescu, Gheorghe 5 73; 15 56; 26 713, 725; 30 364–5*
Tattegrain, Francis 22 329, 330
Tattershall (Lincs) 10 *225*
  Castle 4 779; 6 54; 9 144; 10 227; 19 896; 30 *365*, 365–6*
  chimney-piece 6 603
  Holy Trinity Church 24 576; 30 366*
Tatti, Jacopo *see* SANSOVINO, JACOPO (D'ANTONIO)
tatting 18 593; 30 549
Tatto Group 1 636
Tatton, Henry, & Son 28 262
Tatton-Brown, William 20 475
tattoos 30 366–7*
  Africa 1 344–5, 346–7
  Ainu 17 414
  Berber 1 346
  Britain 30 367
  Burma 5 250–51*, *251*; 30 366
  Coptic 7 829*; 10 68; 30 367
  Cyprus, ancient 8 338
  Egypt 7 829*
  Egypt, ancient 10 66, 67, 68; 30 366
  Fiji 11 70; 27 234
  Fulani 1 346
  Greece, ancient 30 367
  Greenland 30 366
  Hausa 1 346, 347
  Hawaii 14 249–50; 23 719
  Indian subcontinent 15 733, 735
  Indonesia 15 809
  Japan 17 414–15*, *415*
  Maori 20 358; 23 713, 719; 30 366, *367*
  Marquesas Islands 20 462; 23 719, *719*
  Marshall Islands 23 723
  Micronesia, Federated States of 21 477
  Native North Americans 22 630, 631; 30 366
  Nigeria 1 346
  Nubia 1 346
  Pacific Islands 23 713, 718–19*, *719*, 722*, 723
  Papua New Guinea 23 722
  Philippines 24 626*
  Polynesian outliers 25 182
  Rome, ancient 30 367
  Ryūkyū Islands 17 414
  Samoa 23 718, 719; 27 683–4, *684*
  Sarawak 15 809
  Scythian 30 367, 769
  Society Islands 28 923
  Solomon Islands 23 722
  Thracian 30 769
  Tonga (Pacific Islands) 23 719
  Tunisia 30 366
  Tuvalu 31 484
  United States of America 30 366
  Vietnam 32 487
  Yoruba 1 346
Ta-t'ung *see* DATONG
Ta Ty 32 483
Tatz, Eduardo Bross *see* BROSS TATZ, EDUARDO
Tau 1 417
Taube, Evert, Baron 11 901
Täuber-Arp, Sophie 2 490; 11 569; 24 428; 30 139, 234–5*, 328
  collaboration 2 488, 490; 9 63; 10 137
  groups and movements 30 135
    Abstract art 1 75
    Abstraction-Création 20 97
    Cabaret Voltaire (group) 8 434
    Concrete art 1 75, 76
    Dada 8 434
    environmental art 10 415
    Neue Leben 8 434; 22 921
    Salon des Réalités Nouvelles 9 87
    Stijl, De 29 661
  pupils 30 330
  works 1 *77*; 24 405; 30 138
Taubes, Frederick 14 538
Taubman, A. Alfred 29 88
Tauchen, Jost 25 111
Taucher, (Jarl) Gunnar 4 160; 30 367–8*
tau cross *see under* CROSSES → types
Taudin (family) 10 341
tau du Mans 26 696
Tauerbach, Sebastian 16 867; 18 431; 25 111, 119
tauf 21 280
Taugelchee, Daisy 30 368*
Taugelchee, Priscilla 30 368
Taujėnai Church 19 497

Taulier, Jean 9 196
Taüll 29 *259*
  benches 29 310, *310*
  S Climente 11 479; 30 368–9*
  frescoes 29 275; 30 *368*
  S Maria 26 642, 655; 30 368–9*
  S María 26 *643*
Taunay, Auguste-Marie 4 716; 8 593; 13 295; 30 369
Taunay, Félix Emile 4 727
Taunay, Nicolas-Antoine 4 716; 13 295; 26 414; 30 369*
  groups and movements 31 373
  reproductive prints by others 8 791
  works 8 867; 26 *413*
Taunay, Pierre-Henri 30 369
Taung 19 241
Taung-gyi 5 241
Taungthaman 5 223
Taunton Britannia Manufacturing Co. 31 652
Taupin 11 405
Taupin, Pierre 2 701
Taurel, André Benoît Barreau *see* BARREAU TAUREL, ANDRÉ BENOÎT
Taurellus, Nicolaus 10 175
Taurini (family) 16 726
Taurisano, Duque de 5 427
Taurisci 6 159
Tauriskos 2 229*; 10 812; 25 45; 26 292
Taurnhauser, Hans 13 315
Tauromenion 23 349
Taurus 16 526
Taurus, T. Statilius 1 797
Tausch, Christoph 14 900; 28 852; 30 369–70*; 33 417
Tausert (*reg c.* 1193–*c.* 1190 BC) 5 70; 9 *777*, 805
Tausug 24 618, 628
Taut, Bruno 3 795; 8 824; 11 129; 12 378; 16 591; 17 88; 30 370–71*, 521
  collaboration 3 795; 21 495; 27 657
  competitions 7 669
  groups and movements 2 288; 3 801; 8 825, 826; 10 697; 21 490, 781; 26 405
  staff 19 746
  works 3 795, *796*, 841; 7 582; 8 824; 10 683; 12 792; 14 581; 19 332; 25 172, 173; 26 19; 30 *370*; 32 759
Taut, Max 3 795; 12 378; 30 371–2*
  collaboration 29 531; 30 370
  groups and movements 2 288; 8 826; 10 697, 698; 21 490, 781; 26 405
  works 3 797; 12 380
Tautenhayn, Josef 33 285
Tăutu, Ion 26 711
Tauu 25 181, 182
Tauzin, Henri 4 240
Tauzin, Mario 10 483
Tavakarashvili, Mamuka 12 325
Tavant 11 530; 26 599
Tavárez, Rosa 9 118
Tavarone, Lazzaro 30 372–3*
  collaboration 5 457; 6 25; 13 307
  patrons and collectors 9 173
  works 10 503; 22 484; 30 *372*
Tavast, Magnus II, Bishop of Turku 11 98, 714
Taveira, Tomás 25 294
Tavella, Carlo Antonio 4 811
Tavenraat, Johannes 30 373*
Taver, Nicolás 5 544
Tavera, Juan Pardo de, Cardinal 3 847; 5 305; 8 78; 30 373–4*; 31 88; 32 559
Taverna, Ferdinando 11 741
Taverna, Gaudenz 11 798
tavern clocks *see under* CLOCKS → types
Taverner, Jeremiah 30 374
Taverner, William (*d* 1731) 30 374
Taverner, William (1703–72) 18 672; 30 374*; 32 900
Tavernier 11 524
Tavernier, Adolphe-Eugène 30 375*
Tavernier, Jean-Baptiste 11 634; 15 698; 16 542
Tavernier, Jean Le *see* LE TAVERNIER, JEAN
Tavernier, Melchior 4 467; 5 294; 18 745; 19 257; 20 415
Tavern Society *see* SOCIETY OF ANTIQUARIES
Taverny Church 13 41
Tavetsch 30 144
Tavira 25 317
  Misericórdia 24 804
Tavola Strozzi 22 470, *470*
Tavoliere Plain 25 500, 503
Távora, Fernando 25 294, 880; 28 812; 30 375*
Távora e Noronha Leme Cernache, Jerónimo de 22 533, 534
Tavoy 5 *221*, 247, 255
Tawahka 14 712
Tawaraya 17 314
Tawaraya Sōri 17 179
Tawaraya Sōsetsu 17 178–9; 30 378
Tawaraya Sōtatsu 9 738; 14 702; 17 165, 177, 409; 18 552; 30 375–8*
  assistants 14 703
  attributions 14 704
  works 10 777; 14 703, 705; 17 166, *178*, 232, 334; 18 557; 30 *376*, *377*
Ta-wen-k'ou *see* DAWENKOU
Taweo 31 891
Tawer, Bartholeme *see* DAUHER, BARTHOLOMÄUS
Tawfiq, Khedive (*reg* 1879–92) (Muhammad ʿAli's Line) 16 557
tawing *see under* TANNING
Tawi-Tawi 24 *607*, 625
Tawney, Lenore 11 54; 30 329
tawqīʿ script *see under* SCRIPTS → types
TAX 21 382
Taxco, SS Prisca y Sebastián 9 418; 21 377, 383, 395
taxes 7 561
Taxila 5 94; 8 269; 15 *264*, 409; 21 847; 23 *797*; 30 378–81*, *379*
  apsidal shrines 15 252
  Archaeological Museum 23 804; 30 380, 381
  arrowheads 15 677
  Bhir Mound 30 378–9*
  brass 4 687
  Dharmarajika 15 445, 446; 30 381*
  figurines 15 446, 719
  glass 15 694
  halls 14 77
  hardstones 15 *698*
  Hathial Mound 30 378
  ivory 15 695
  Jandial 30 380–81*
  Jaulian 15 458; 30 381*
  jewellery 15 700
  Kachcha Kot 30 379
  mirrors 21 716
  Mohra Moradu 15 446; 30 381
  monasteries 30 381*
  reliquaries 15 698; 26 149
  ring stones 15 423
  sculpture 15 453, 458
  seals 15 698
  Sirkap 15 249; 30 379–80*
    apsidal temple 15 252
    figurines 15 719
    palettes 15 446
    sculpture 15 446
    Shrine of the Double-headed Eagle 30 380, *380*
Taxila—cont.
  Sirsukh 30 379–80*
  stucco 29 824, 825
  swords 15 677
  trade 15 202
  urban planning 23 817
Taxkorgan 7 89
Taxner, Karel 8 413
taxonomy 22 354; 30 381–3*
Taya, Tell 2 639; 21 *267*, 307; 30 383*
  temple 21 283
Tayac 6 160
Tayali, Henry 33 602
  works 33 *603*
Tayasal 13 *758*; 20 *882*; 30 383*
Taybad 16 197, 200
Tay Bridge 4 799, 802
Tayinat, Tell 1 *821*; 30 *180*, 384*
  reliefs 30 187
  sculpture 1 816, 833; 30 187
  temple 30 187
Tayk' 2 426
Tay Kheng Soon *see* SOON, TAY KHENG
Tayler, A(lexander) Chevallier 23 26
Tayler, (John) Frederick 30 384*
Tayler, Lloyd 2 739; 33 409
Tayloe, John, III 30 761
Taylor, Andrew T(homas) 30 385*
  works 5 562
Taylor, Basil 21 91
Taylor, Bayard 23 904
Taylor, Brook 24 490; 28 202
  works 24 *490*
Taylor, Charles 24 446; 30 384
Taylor, E. A. 28 256
Taylor, Edward 2 395; 24 95; 33 545
Taylor, Edward Richard 4 87
Taylor, Ernest Archibald 18 65
Taylor, George Watson 19 115; 28 370
Taylor, H. A. C. 20 16
Taylor, Harold (*fl* 1965–78) 2 64
Taylor, Harry (1871–1956) 7 798
Taylor, Henry W. 22 276
Taylor, Howard 5 573
Taylor, I. & J. 30 384
Taylor, Isaac (1730–1807) 3 897; 30 384
Taylor, Isaac (1759–1829) 30 384
Taylor, Isidore-Justin-Séverin, Baron 23 521; 30 385*
  collaboration 5 392; 8 867; 11 521
  dealing 20 59; 24 402
  drawings 21 425
  illustrated writings 4 321; 11 60, 371; 19 484; 25 626; 31 156
    Ciceri, Eugène 7 304
    Dauzats, Adrien 8 548
    Huet, Paul 14 848
    Isabey, (Louis-)Eugène (-Gabriel) 16 65
    Viollet-le-Duc, Eugène-Emmanuel 32 594
  paintings 4 523; 20 59
Taylor, James (1745–99; England) 30 384
Taylor, James (*fl* 1790s; USA) 18 66
Taylor, James (1785–1829; Australia) 2 744
Taylor, James Knox 7 619; 12 614
Taylor, Janet 30 330; 31 660
Taylor, Jennifer 30 160
Taylor, Jeremy 10 757
Taylor, J. G. 10 460; 31 694
Taylor, John (*fl* 1688; Jamaica) 16 885
Taylor, John (*fl* 1695; England) 23 690
Taylor, John, & Sons 2 755; 28 255
Taylor, John N. (1842–1914) 18 169
Taylor, Joseph 24 275
Taylor, Joshua 31 673
Taylor, Josiah 28 593; 30 384
Taylor, J. W. Chapman 23 55
Taylor, Lloyd 1 151
Taylor, Luke 1 68
Taylor, Max(well) 3 62, 64
Taylor, Obed 27 642
Taylor, Paul Schuster 18 738
Taylor, Robert (1690–1742) 30 385, 386
Taylor, Robert (1714–88) 10 374; 30 385–7*
  collaboration 8 492; 27 626
  groups and movements 10 643
  patrons and collectors 7 552
  pupils 7 501
  staff 22 526
  teachers 6 528
  works 3 174; 4 876; 8 47; 18 754; 27 626; 28 905; 30 *386*; 32 553; 33 445
Taylor, Robert Minton 30 458
  works 30 *877*
Taylor, Sandra 2 762
Taylor, Soilleux & Overend 23 679
Taylor, Thomas 6 100; 33 9
Taylor, Warrington 22 143
Taylor, W. B. Sarsfield 10 199
Taylor, W. Howson 2 570
Taylor, William Watts 27 132
Taylor-Bushay, Jean 16 888
Taylor & Gilles 31 335
Taylor & Gordon 30 385
Taylorian Institution *see under* OXFORD
Taylor & Johnson 7 328
Taylor & Jones 4 78
Taylor of Ongar *see* TAYLOR, ISAAC (1759–1829)
Taylor & Soilleux 23 679
Taylor Woodrow 7 788
Tayma' 2 *246*, 247, 249
  museum 2 275
  pottery 2 268
  relief sculpture 2 254–5, *254*
  stelae 2 255
  town walls 2 250
Tayma' Stone 2 254; 27 877
Taymouth Castle (Tayside) 28 230, 248, 254; 29 835
Tay Ninh 32 *468*
  Great Temple of Caodai 32 471
Taynton (Oxon) 23 684
Tayob, (Abdool) Aziz (Ahmed) 29 107; 30 387*
Tay Phuong Temple 32 *473*, 474, 480
Tay Son 32 486
Taza
  Bastiun 21 585
  congregational mosque 16 218, 495
  Great Mosque 16 386–7
  minbars 21 629
Tazlău Monastery 26 718
Tazoli, Gaspare dei 16 746
Tazoult Lambèse *see* LAMBAESIS
Tazumal 21 252
Tazza Farnese *see* FARNESE CUP
tazze 11 617; 12 444; 19 *397*; 22 886; 26 *485*; 30 387*
Tazzini, Giacomo 31 878
Tbeti 12 *317*; 30 305
  Cathedral 12 323; 30 306
Tbeti Gospels *see under* GOSPEL BOOKS → individual manuscripts
Tbilisi 2 425; 9 *512*; 12 *317*, 320; 16 *104*; 30 387–9*
  Academy of Arts 12 317
  Armenian Cultural Society 2 444
  art forms
    architecture 2 428
    coins 6 266
    curtains 2 442
    pottery 12 330
    sculpture 2 436
  Church of Anchiskati 12 318
  citadel 12 319
Tbilisi—cont.
  Ethnographic Society 2 444
  Georgian Bank of the Nobility *see* National Library of Georgia
  Georgian Picture Gallery 12 326; 30 389
  Hotel Tbilisi 12 320
  House of the Georgian Artists 12 332; 30 389
  Institute of Manuscripts 12 317
  K. S. Kekelidze Institute of Manuscripts 12 332
  Kvashveti Church 12 320
  Metekhi Church 30 *388*
  monument of Mother Georgia 12 322
  monument to Three Hundred Aragvian Heroes 12 322
  museums
    G. Chubinashvili Institute of the History of Georgian Art 12 332
    Georgia State Museum of Art *see* Museum of Art of Georgia
    Jewish museum 17 581
    Museum of Art of Georgia 12 320, 332; 30 389
      collections 12 317, 331; 24 850
      directors 1 786
    Museum of Georgia 12 332
    Museum of Georgian Folk Architecture and Local Lore 12 332
    Museum of the History of Georgia 30 389
  Narikala Fortress 30 *388*
  National Library of Georgia 12 320
  Opera House 12 320
  Philharmonic Concert Hall 12 320
  Post Office 12 320
  railway station 12 320
  Rustaveli Theatre 12 320
  Sports Palace 12 320
  statue of Aleksandr Pushkin 12 322
  M. I. Toidze people's art studio 12 317
  tomb of I. Chavchavadze 12 322
't Binnenhuis *see* BINNENHUIS, 'T
T'boli 24 625, 626
Tchalenko, G. 9 560
Tchalenko, Janice 10 315; 30 389*
Tchapkonov, Georgi 5 156
Tchébétchou, René 5 524
Tchelitchew, Pavel 28 808; 30 389–90*
  groups and movements 3 120, 753; 22 752
  productions 16 892; 30 686
  teachers 10 699
  works 16 892; 28 914
Tchernykhov, Yakov (Georgievich) *see* CHERNIKOV, YAKOV (GEORGIEVICH)
Tchirnhaus, Ehrefgried Walther von 6 924
Tchiyanagi, Toshi 24 407
Tchlenov 30 421
Tchokossi 31 73
Tchórzewski, Jerzy 25 108; 32 878
T. D. Tekhnicheskaya estetika 24 451
teabowls 6 896, II2; 17 *255*, *256*, 341, 342, *595*; 28 *410*; 30 847
teabush-wood 17 399
tea-caddies 7 101, 167; 17 *255*, 301, *341*; 28 *737*
tea ceremonies 7 53; 17 215, 231, 258, 262–3, 301, 322, 323, 334–44*, 351, 358, 383, 424, 428, 438; 28 410
  Buddhism 17 336
  Christianity 17 341
  Edo period (1600–1868) 20 287
  Kamakura period (1185–1333) 17 382

tea ceremonies—cont.
Momoyama period (1568-1600) **17** 365
Muromachi period (1333-1568) **12** 98; **17** 254, 259; **30** 259
20th cent. **5** 120
tea gardens *see under* GARDENS → types
tea-grinders **7** *24*
Teague, John **5** 561; **32** 414
Teague, Walter Dorwin **8** 802; **15** 824, 825; **30** 390–91*
works **10** 684; **19** 897
teahouses *see under* HOUSES → types
tea jars *see under* JARS → types
teak
historical and regional traditions
Bangladesh **3** 169
Egypt **16** *490*
Germany **20** *808*
Indian subcontinent **6** 555; **15** 720, 721; **25** 303
Indonesia **15** 813
Iraq **16** 488, *489*
Islamic **16** 269, 488, *489*, *490*
Portugal **25** 303, 305
South Africa **29** 114
Sri Lanka **29** 470
Thailand **12** 112; **30** 631, 639
Vietnam **32** 488
uses
architecture **16** 269
betel sets **30** 631
chess sets **6** 555
doors **16** *489*, *490*
furniture **15** 813; **29** 114
inlays **32** 488
pediments **12** 112
sculpture **20** *808*
Team 4 Architects **11** 332; **14** 521; **26** 540
Team Ten **5** 609; **7** 296; **10** 242; **15** 887; **22** 832; **27** 313; **28** 889; **29** 52; **30** 391–2*
members **7** 511; **10** 490, 715; **11** 527; **14** 155; **20** 475; **29** 52; **31** 867
Team Zoo **17** 92; **30** 392*; **33** 563
Te ana a Nunuku **6** *514*
Cave **6** 514
teapots **20** 595
historical and regional traditions
Australia **2** *761*
Austria **21** 13
Canada **5** 584
Central Asia, Eastern **6** 313
China **7** 101, *101*; **24** 580; **33** *535*
England **10** *314*; **15** *820*
France **11** *607*
Germany **12** 447
Ireland **16** 31
Italy **16** *738*
Korea **18** *338*
Malta (Republic of) **20** 217
Netherlands, the **22** *891*
Portugal **25** *311*
Sweden **30** 106
materials
basketwork **7** 101
clay **7** 101
coconuts **7** 101
copper **21** 13
earthenwares **2** *761*; **7** 101, *101*; **10** *314*
ebony **22** *891*
enamel **25** *311*
jade **7** 101, *101*
niello **21** 13
pewter **7** 101, *101*; **24** 580
porcelain **11** *607*; **16** *738*; **25** *311*
pottery **15** *822*; **33** *535*
silver **5** 584; **16** 31; **20** 217; **22** *891*; **30** 106
Teare, Wallace S. **7** 429
tea-rooms **17** *337*, 337–40*, *338*
tea-services
historical and regional traditions
Austria **2** *820*
Belgium **3** *602*
China **7** *28*, 101
England **10** *314*
Germany **12** *434*
Netherlands, the **22** *892*
materials
earthenwares **10** *314*
ebony **22** *892*
gold **2** *820*
ivory **3** *602*
pewter **7** 101
porcelain **12** *434*
silver **3** *602*; **7** *28*; **22** *892*
Teatro Guiñol **1** 739
Teatro Scientifico **30** 685
tea-urns **10** 341, *851*
tea utensil collections *see under* COLLECTIONS → types
tea utensils **17** *341*
tebako *see under* BOXES → types
Tebaldi (family) **24** 768
Tebar, Jesús Múñoz *see* MÚÑOZ TEBAR, JESÚS
Tebar, Luis Múñoz *see* MÚÑOZ TEBAR, LUIS
Tebessa *see* THEVESTIS
Tebtunis **10** 6, 759
techne **13** 467
Techni **13** 353
technical examination **7** 726, 730*; **30** 392–402*, 403–4*, 410*
types
atomic absorption spectrometry (AAS) **30** 398
autoradiography **30** 400*
bulk elemental analysis **30** 398–9
chromatography **30** 401–2*
column chromatography **30** 401
contouring (holographic) **30** 396
differential thermal analysis **30** 401
electron-probe microanalysis (EPM) **30** 400*
gas-liquid chromatography **30** 401–2
high-performance liquid chromatography (HPLC) **30** 401
holography **30** 395–6*
inductively coupled plasma spectrometry (ICPS) **30** 398
infra-red spectrometry **30** 401, 402*
interferometry (holographic) **30** 395
interferometry (speckle) **30** 396
isotope analysis **30** 400*, 405, *406*
microscopy (electron) **28** 206; **30** *397*, 397–8, *407*
microscopy (low power) **30** 393
microscopy (optical) **30** *396*, 396–7*
microscopy (video) **30** 393
Mössbauer spectroscopy **30** 401
neutron activation analysis (NAA) **30** 399
nuclear magnetic resonance spectrometry (NMR) **30** 402*
optical emission spectrometry (OES) **30** 398
organic analysis **30** 401*
paper chromatography **30** 401
particle-induced gamma-ray emission spectrometry (PIGME) **30** 399, *399*
particle-induced X-ray emission spectrometry (PIXE) **30** 399
photogrammetry **30** 395*
photography **24** 653; **30** 395*
rectified photography **30** 395
secondary ion mass spectroscopy (SIMS) **30** 400
surface analysis **30** 399–400*
thermal analysis **30** 401
technical examination
types—cont.
thermogravimetric analysis **30** 401
xeroradiography **30** 395
X-ray fluorescence spectrometry (XRF) **30** *398*, 398–9
X-ray photoelectron spectroscopy (XPS) **30** 400
X-ray powder diffraction analysis **30** 401, 405
X-ray radiography **11** 309; **30** 394–5, *399*
uses
alloys **30** *396*, 397, 408
architecture **30** 395, 409*
bone **30** 397, 410
brass **30** *398*, 408
brick **30** 409
bronze **30** 408
cement **30** 409
ceramics **6** 334*; **30** 393, 395, 397, *397*, 400, 406–7*
concrete **30** 409
copper **30** 400, 408
craquelure **30** 393
enamel **30** 407–8*
forgeries **11** 309–10*
gems **30** 401
glass **12** 796–7*; **30** 393, 400, 401, *407*, 407–8*
glazes **30** 401
glues **30** 410*
gold **30** 408
grounds **30** 401
inks **15** *850*
iron **30** 397, 409
ivory **30** 410
lead **30** 400, 408
leather **30** 410
maps **30** 395
marble **30** 400, 405, *406*
metal **21** *319*; **30** 395, 397, *408*, 408–9*
mortars (building) **30** 409
mosaics **30** 409
niello **30** 409
paintings **2** 835; **30** 393, 395, 397, 400, 409–10*
paints **30** 396, 402
patinas **30** 393, 409
pigments **11** 309; **30** 401, 409
plaster **30** 409
porcelain **30** 397, *397*, 406
pottery **30** 393, 395, 401
preservation **30** 395
resins **30** 401, 410*
restoration **30** 395
rock crystal **30** 405
sculpture **30** 396
silver **30** 400, 408
stained glass **29** 518*
steel **30** 397, 409
stone **29** 711; **30** 393, 397, *399*, 404–6*, *406*, 409
supports **30** 395
textiles **30** 410–11*, 565–6*
tiles **30** 409
wall paintings **30** 409
wallpaper **30** 395
waxes **30** 410*
wood **30** 409, 410; **33** 337
wood-carvings **30** 396
see also DATING METHODS
technology and art **1** 107
Teck, Mary of, Queen of Great Britain *see* MARY OF TECK, Queen of Great Britain
Tecpán, Iximché Archaeological Museum **16** 803
Técső colony **12** 10; **14** 687; **15** 36
Tecton **18** 807; **19** 747; **24** 224; **30** 411*
collaboration **7** 695
groups and movements **15** 886; **20** 475
staff **2** 577; **8** 256
Tecton—cont.
works **5** 905, *905*; **7** 698; **10** 241; **19** 747; **33** 699
Tęczyński (family) **25** 135
teddy bears **31** 260, *260*
see also DOLLS
Tederigho Memmi **3** 247; **19** 454, 455; **20** 510; **21** 108
Tedesco, Carlo **20** 391
Tedesco, Giovanni Paolo *see* SCHOR, JOHANN PAUL
Tedesco, Gulielmo *see* TETRODE, WILLEM DANIELS
Tedesco, Jacopo *see* LAPO
Tedesco, Michele **28** 317
Tedesco, Piero di Giovanni *see* PIERO DI GIOVANNI TEDESCO
Tedhi Singh, Ruler (*reg* 1742-67) (Pahari) **15** 397
Tedice, Enrico di *see* ENRICO DI TEDICE
Tedice, Ugolino di *see* UGOLINO DI TEDICE
Tedros, Michael **10** 567
Teec-nos-pos (AZ) **22** 626
Teels, Pierre **13** 909
teepees *see* TEPEES
Teerlinc, Levina **3** 725; **21** 639; **30** 411–12*; **33** 308
works **30** *412*
Teerlink, Abraham (Alexander) **24** 892; **30** 412*
teeth **16** 796
historical and regional traditions
Africa **1** 296
China **7** 106
Prehistoric art **25** 473, 518
types
bear **17** 399
dogs **12** 622
elephant **16** 796
fox **25** 473
hippopotamus **1** 868; **16** 796; **17** 399
leopard **3** 145
tiger **17** 399
whale **16** 796, 797; **17** 399; **23** 720; **28** 302, *302*
China **7** 102
wolf **17** 399
uses
beads **1** 296
body ornaments **23** 720; **25** 518
burnishing **12** 622
jewellery **7** 106
netsuke **17** 399
scrimshaw **28** 302
Tefft, Thomas (Alexander) **5** 78; **25** 666; **30** 412–13*; **31** 592
tefillin **17** 574
Tegallingga **15** 764
Tegdaoust **1** 305, *376*
Tégé **30** 418, 419
Tegea **13** *363*; **30** 413*
bronzes **13** 571
pottery **13** 534
Temple of Athena Alea **13** 379, 387, 401, 460; **24** 205; **28** 821, 822; **30** 413
acroteria **1** 128
altar **1** 692
ex-votos **27** 712
metopes **13** 426
pediments **13** 425; **24** 319
Tegeda, Carlos **12** 921
Tegelen, Hans von, I **32** 771
Tegelstein, Carl Johann **27** 584
Tegeo, Rafael *see* TEJEO, RAFAEL
Tegernsee
Klosterkirche **2** 579; **20** *192*, 772; **23** 659
sculpture **29** *761*
manuscripts **23** 655
metalwork **26** 684
Tegernsee Altar **20** 192
Tegernsee Altar, Master of the **12** 385; **13** 675; **20** 192, 747, 772*
Tegg, Thomas **27** 279
Teggiano Cathedral **13** 98
Tegucigalpa **14** *711*, 712, 713; **30** 414*
architecture **14** 714
Archivo Nacional **14** 716
Banco Central de Honduras **14** 714, 715
Biblioteca Nacional **14** 716
Casa Presidencial **14** 713
Casa Vieja **14** 713
Cathedral of S Miguel **14** 713, *713*, 714; **26** 252
Escuela Nacional de Bellas Artes **14** 715, 716
Financiera **14** 713
Galería Nacional de Arte **14** 716; **30** 414
Instituto Hondureño de Antropología e Historia (IHAH) **14** 716
Los Dolores **14** 713
Ministerio de Hacienda **14** 714
Museo del Banco Atlántida **14** 717
Museo Historico de la República **14** 716
Museo Nacional **14** 716
Palacio del Distrito Central **14** 713
Palacio Legislativo **14** 714, 716
tegulae mammatae *see under* TILES → types
Tegurwangi **15** 787
Te Hau Ki Turanga **20** 355; **23** 53
Tehneh **29** 386
Těhník, Libor **8** 406
Tehran **15** *897*; **16** *105*; **30** 414–16*
architecture **16** 229
Ardebil Shrine **6** 331
College of Decorative Arts **15** 898
fortifications **21** 589
galleries (iv) (art) **15** 898
glass **16** 522
Gulistan Palace **15** 743; **16** 234, 425; **21** 506; **30** 414–15
Iran Centre for Management Studies **15** 897
lacquer **16** 534
lithography **16** 342
manuscripts **16** *341*
mausoleum of Ayatollah Khomeini **15** 898, *898*
museums
Archaeological Museum **12** 834; **15** 899; **16** 557; **20** 448; **30** 415
collections **6** 898, 925; **7** 155; **12** 507; **15** 922, 923; **20** 222; **33** 688
Carpet Museum **15** 900; **16** 557; **30** 415
Crown Jewels Museum **15** 899; **30** 415
Decorative Arts Museum **15** 899
Gulistan Palace Museum **15** 899; **30** 415
Iran Bastan Museum *see* Archaeological Museum
Museum of Contemporary Art **8** 862; **15** 897, 900; **30** 415
Museum of Ethnography **15** 899; **16** 557; **30** 415
Museum of Glass and Ceramics **15** 900; **16** 557; **30** 415
Nigaristan Museum **15** 899; **16** 555, 557; **30** 415
Riza 'Abbasi Museum **15** 899; **16** 557; **30** 415
Nigaristan Palace **1** 25; **16** 535
Nizamiyya Palace **12** 507
palaces **30** 415
Parliament Building **15** 899
pottery **16** 426
printing **16** 361
Qasr-i Qajar **16** 234
Shams al-'Imarat **16** 234

Tehran—cont.
Sipahsalar Mosque 16 234
textiles 16 450
University, College of Fine Arts 15 898
urban planning 16 241
Tehri 15 628
Tehuacán Valley 21 192, 194, 239
Tehubaryan, Ghukas 2 437
Tehuelche 2 394; 29 204
Teibi Insha 17 861
Teichert, Minerva 22 126
Teigdrucke see Pasteprints
Teige, Karel 8 380, 393, 402; 30 416*
groups and movements 7 182, 293, 772; 8 829, 830; 11 47, 365; 14 732; 30 22
works 31 250
writings 33 710
Teiichi Hijikata see Hijikata, Teiichi
Teijiro Nakahara see Nakahara, Teijiro
Teika, Fujiwara no see Fujiwara no Teika
Teikan Tō see Tō Teikan
Teiko Ishii see Ishii, Teiko
Teikoku Bijutsuin Tenrankai see Teiten (Imperial Art Academy Exhibition)
Teinfrith 2 64
Teinitzerová, Marie 8 419
works 8 *420*
Teirich, Valentin 2 814
Teisai Hokuba 31 253
Teishebaini see Karmir Blur
Tei Shin see Fenollosa, Ernest Francisco
Teisias 13 484
Teisikrates 33 461
Teiten (Imperial Art Academy Exhibition) 17 135, 205, 305
Imperial Art Academy (Teishitsu Gigeiin) 17 29, 435
see also Bunten
Teiwes, Helga 10 580
Teixeira, Diogo 19 464; 30 416*
collaboration 25 296; 26 253; 32 157
works 25 296; 32 156
Teixeira, Luís 30 416–17*
Teixeira, Manuel 25 313
Teixeira, Vitor Manuel see Viteix
Teixeira Lopes, António 25 302; 28 913; 30 417*
Teixeira Lopes, José Joaquim 30 417
Teixidor, Andrés Aleu y see Aleu y Teixidor, Andrés
Teixidor, Felipe 21 398
Teixidor, Jordi 31 816
Teixidor, Pere 20 515
Teja, Casimiro 28 318
Tejada, S Pedro 26 607
Tejada, Carlos Saenz de see Saenz de Tejada, Carlos
Tejada, Francisco de 30 417*
Tejada, Hernando 7 610
Tejada, Juan de 25 700
works 25 *700*
Tejada, Rafael 29 343
Tejapala 8 848; 22 225
Tejeda, Antonio
works 4 *296*
Tejeda Fonseca, Antonio 12 53
Tejeo, Rafael 4 378; 30 417–18*
Tejerrina, Juan 17 674
Tejima, Yūkei 17 240
Tejima Toan 17 348
Teka grona konserwatorów galicji zachodniej 24 441
Teka konserwatorska 24 441
Te Kanawa, Diggeress (Rangituatahi) 14 495; 20 360; 30 418*
Teke 1 393; 8 154; 21 679; 30 418–20*
figurines 1 273
Teke—cont.
gesture 1 265, 266
masks 1 290; 30 419–20, *420*
painting 30 420*
pottery 1 406
sculpture 1 403; 3 694; 7 708; 30 418–19, *419*, *420*
wood 30 *419*, *420*
Tekelü, Ahmed 23 641
Tekena, Melchor Huki see Huki Tekena, Melchor
Tekes 6 309
Tekhné 4 217; 24 439; 32 380
Tekin see Magnesia on the Maeander
Tekirova see Phaselis
Tekke (Central Asia) 6 253, 254; 16 485
breast-ornaments 31 *459*
Tekke (Crete) 13 597
tekkes see Khānaqāhs
Tekor Church 2 426, 434
Tektaios 8 458, 688; 17 742
Tekta Society 31 491
Te Kuiti, Meeting House 23 54
Tela 14 *711*, 714
Telade 9 543
Teladur, Atanas 5 156; 27 686
telamons see Atlantids
Tel Anafa 13 594
Telanissos see Deir Sim'an
Telavi 12 320
museum 12 332
Tel Aviv 16 *565*; 30 421*
apartments 16 565
Art Teachers Training College 16 571
Avni Art Institute 16 571
collections 17 582
El Al Headquarters 16 565
F. R. Mann Auditorium 16 565
Gordon Gallery 16 570
Ha'aretz Museum 17 582
Museum of Art 10 719; 16 566; 30 421
collections 16 570, 571
library 16 572
Sam and Ayala Zacks Hall 16 570
Museum of Ethnography and Folklore 2 370
Nahum Goldmann Museum of the Jewish Diaspora 17 582
Rubin House 16 571
Sick Fund Administrative Centre 16 565
University 10 719; 16 566
Yehoshua Rabinowitz Tel Aviv Foundation for the Arts 16 570
Telbin, William Lewis 30 681
works 30 *681*
Telbis Island 14 21
Telč 8 378, 390, 422; 10 741
houses 8 *377*
Telcs, Ede 14 896; 18 86
Tele, Catherine 6 469
Telechany 23 369
Telecomunicações de Moçambique 22 245
telecopy see under Printing → processes
Telefolmin 24 73, 74
Telegdi, Csanád, Archbishop 10 544
Telegdy, Barbara 13 162
Teleglobe Canada 26 108
Teleilat el-Ghassul see Ghassul, Teleilat el-
Teleki (family) 14 904
Teleki, Mihály 14 904
Teleki, Samuel, Count 15 15
Telekles 26 296
Telemann, Georg Philipp 22 380
Télémaque, Hervé 11 552
Telephanes 13 549
Telephos frieze see Great Frieze
Telephos Painter 13 523; 32 55
Teles, Rodrigo de Moura see Moura Teles, Rodrigo de
telescopes 23 338, 339; 28 210, 211; 30 26
Telesmora 30 99
televisions 8 911; 15 827, 885; 24 678; 26 236
Telford (Salop), Ironbridge Gorge Museum 7 481
Telford, Thomas 23 105; 30 421–2*
collaboration 4 802; 9 58; 19 573
works 2 242; 4 803; 7 693; 24 747
writings 4 802
Teliagarhi fort 15 370
Telje, Are 23 602
Telje-Torp-Aasen 23 222
Telkibánya 15 2
Telkupi 15 320, 321
Temple 6 15 321
tell 21 268
Tell, et- see Ai
Tella, di (family) 2 404
Tellaeche, Julian de 27 768
Tellem 9 64, 65, 66
Teller, Andreas 17 816
Tellez, Germán 5 887
Téllez de Meseses (family) 13 105
Tellez Girón, Juan, Count of Ureña see Ureña, Juan Tellez Girón, Count of
Téllez Girón y Guzmán, Pedro, 3rd Duque de Osuna see Osuna, 3rd Duque de
Téllez Girón y Pacheco, Pedro de Alcántara see Osuna, 9th Duque de
Tellier, François Michel Le, Marquis de Louvois see Louvois, Marquis de
Tellier, Michel Le see Le Tellier, Michel
Tellier, Pierre Le see Le Tellier, Pierre
Tellippalai 16 864
Tello, Julio C. 6 520; 24 516; 29 131
excavations
Cerro Sechín 6 348
Chavín de Huántar 6 523; 29 219
Huaca Las Ventanas 3 363
Pachacamac 23 703
Paracas peninsula 24 89
personal collection 24 518
Tello, Luis Felipe 24 515
Telloh 1 508, 509, *849*; 21 *267*; 30 422–3*
sculpture 21 273, 294; 29 X2; 30 *423*
silver 21 303, *303*
statues 1 892
stone vessels 2 272
writing-tablets 1 853, 895
tells 1 851*; 25 498; 30 190
see also Ruin mounds
Telmessos 19 838; 31 109
Amyntas Tomb 19 839
Tel-neshin see Deir Sim'an
Telorac, Alexander 2 127
Telovani 12 323
Telvatta 29 466
Tel'zhanov, Kanify 17 867
Temanza, Antonio 30 423
Temanza, Tommaso 30 423–4*
assistants 24 842
groups and movements 23 861
pupils 28 389
works 30 *424*; 32 196
writings 2 358
temazcals see Mesoamerica, Pre-Columbian → baths
Tembe, Ernesto see Neto
tembes 1 311
Tembladera 6 521; 29 134
Tembo 1 405; 19 72
Tembo, Friday 33 603
Temboury, Jean 20 156
Tembu 1 351, 418, 419; 33 725
temenoi 21 283; 30 424*
Temesa heroön 14 466
Temesvár see Timişoara
Temir-Khan-Shur see Buynaksk
Temizer, Racı 15 159
Temne 1 261, 262, 263, 387, 391–2*; 21 115; 28 690
headdresses 3 47
masks 1 247, 256, 392
painting 1 *261*
shrines (i) (cult) 1 263, 387
Témoignage group 10 581; 19 848; 29 496
Tempel, Abraham (Lambertsz.) van den 22 841; 30 425*
groups and movements 22 841
pupils 21 487; 22 50, 383; 32 683
teachers 16 833
works 1 659
Tempel, Lambert Jacobsz. van den 30 425
Tempelaere, Ferdinand 30 425
Tempelaere, Gustave 10 798; 30 425*
Tempelaere, Julien 30 425
Tempelman, Olof 13 864; 30 72; 31 693
works 30 *72*
Tempelman, Theo 22 876
tempera 5 33; 10 191; 23 783; 24 789; 30 425–8*
conservation 30 427–8*
historical regional traditions
Afghanistan 1 200, 202
Buddhism 1 202; 29 462
Egypt, ancient 9 898
Germany 12 383
Gothic 13 134, 135
Greece, ancient 13 393, 544
Italy 20 *557*; 30 425
Mesoamerica, Pre-Columbian 21 226*
Sri Lanka 29 462
Switzerland 8 *823*
materials
albumen 30 425
brushes 30 426
eggs 30 425
egg yolks 23 783; 30 425
grounds 30 426
oils 30 427
techniques
gilding 30 427
sgraffito 30 427
uses
altarpieces 12 383
icons 30 425
painting 8 *823*
ceiling 28 245
encaustic 10 196
panel 13 135; 30 425, *426*
secco 28 338–40*
wall 1 200, 202; 21 226
wallpaper 32 811, 818
Temperello, il see Caselli (da Parma), Cristoforo
Tempest see under Type-faces
Tempest, Pierce 25 10
Tempesta, Antonio 30 428–9*; 31 55
assistants 8 783
collaboration 3 827; 4 812; 5 437; 10 551
copies 22 242
patrons and collectors
Alcalá, 3rd Duque de (1583-1637) 26 307
Berchem, Nicolaes (Pietersz.) (*c.* 1620-83) 3 758
Borromeo, Vitaliano VI, Conte (1620-90) 4 427
Créquy, Charles de Blanchefort de 19 238
Gregory XIII, Pope (*reg* 1572-85) 13 628
Hinloopen, Michiel (Thijmensz.) 14 563
Tempesta, Antonio
patrons and collectors—cont.
Peretti (-Montalto), Alessandro, Cardinal 24 399
Savoy, Maurice of, Cardinal 28 9
pupils 14 394, 834
reproductive prints by others 23 908; 29 59; 30 746
works 2 105; 3 56; 4 457; 5 684; 10 551; 15 *93*; 23 680; 26 818, 835; 30 358, *429*
Tempesta, Pietro 7 621
Tempesti, Domenico 11 348, 743; 22 465
Tempesti, Giovanni Battista 8 12; 30 429–30*
Tempietto see under Rome → ecclesiastical buildings → S Pietro in Montorio
templa see under Screens (i) (Architectural)
Templar, Knights see Knights Templar
template formers 22 212
templates 13 409, 556; 20 560; 22 211; 30 430–31*, *431*
carpentry 28 498
mouldings 28 497
vaults (ceiling) 28 498
Temple, Henry, 2nd Viscount Palmerston 10 366; 24 213; 30 451*
Temple, Henry John, 3rd Viscount Palmerston 7 667
Temple, Isaac M. Wise 22 60
Temple, Jean du 26 43
Temple, Raymond du see Raymond du Temple
Temple, Richard 29 735
Temple, Richard, 1st Viscount Cobham 30 451–2*
architecture 10 361; 13 199; 29 735
gardens 4 805, 874; 12 105; 13 636; 29 736
paintings 23 189
sculpture 27 466
Temple, Richard Grenville, 1st Earl see Grenville, Richard, 1st Earl Temple
Temple, William 12 127
works 2 *758*
Temple area workshop 26 629
Temple of Artemis Alpheiosa 18 108
Temple Combe (Berks) 11 243
temple-mountains
Cambodia 2 56, *56*; 5 461, 467–72*, 473, *473*, 474
Hinduism 5 464, 466, *466*, *469*, *471*
Khmer 5 479
Temple-Nugent-Brydges-Chandos-Grenville, Richard, 1st Duke of Buckingham and Chandos 2 595; 13 637*; 23 777
Temple-Nugent-Grenville, George, 1st Marquess of Buckingham 13 637*
temple offerings 18 776*
temple-ponds 27 496
temples
historical and regional traditions 2 362; 6 76; 30 431*, 442*, 447*, 450–51*
Africa 1 309–10
Anatolia, ancient 1 826; 24 265; 30 432
Ancient Near East 30 431–2*
Arabia 2 251–3*, *252*
Assyrian 30 432
Aztec 7 481; 30 449, *453*
Bactria 6 197–8
Bahā'ī 30 450
Bali (Indonesia) 3 *872*; 15 785; 30 447
Bangladesh 15 279–81*
Bhutan 3 913, *913*

temples
historical and regional traditions—cont.
Britain **26** 858; **30** 434
Buddhism **30** 431; **32** *473*
Bhutan **3** *913*
Burma **5** 233*; **23** *763*
Cambodia **5** 463*, *479*
Central Asia, Eastern **3** 902*; **6** 294, 319; **30** 441–2, *442*
Central Asia, Western **6** 200; **30** 440
China **5** 107; **6** 667–71, *670*; **9** 393–4; **30** 442–3*
China: Lamaism **30** 443
Ferghana **6** 200
Indian subcontinent **3** *905*; **15** *280*; **30** 437
Japan **10** 404; **12** 97; **17** 46, 65–8*, *67*, *68*, *72*, 432; **30** *445*, 445–6*
Japan: Edo period (1600-1868) **17** *74*; **20** *286*
Japan: Esoteric **18** 222
Japan: Heian period (AD 794-1185) **5** *335*; **10** *405*; **17** *71*
Japan: Kamakura period (1185-1333) **17** *73*, *748*
Japan: Nara period (AD 710-94) **22** *490*, *503*
Japan: Pure Land **30** 445
Japan: Shingon **30** 445
Japan: Shōtoku **14** *774*
Japan: Tendai **30** 445
Japan: Zen **30** 446
Java **30** 446
Khmer **30** *579*, 581
Korea **18** 260, 266–8*, *268*; **30** 444–5
Laos **18** 764–5*
Mongolia **30** *442*
Ryūkyū Islands **27** 470
Sri Lanka **29** *451*
Tendai **10** 404, *405*
Thailand **3** 164, *164*; **30** 446, *579*, 581, 589–90
Tibet **19** *294*; **30** *815*, 818–19, 842
Tokharistan **6** 200
Vietnam **30** 446; **32** 471–4*, *472*, *473*
Burma **5** 222, 227–30*, *227*, *228*, *229*, 233*; **23** *763*
Cambodia **2** 55; **5** 461, 467–72*, *473*, 473–80, *475*; **30** 446
Buddhism **5** *479*
Hinduism **5** 463–7*, *465*, *469*, *470*, *471*, 473
Khmer **2** *58*; **5** *477*, *478*
Canaanite **5** 557; **30** 184, 185
Caribbean Islands **5** 755
Celtic **26** 905
Central Asia **30** 440*
Central Asia, Eastern **30** 441–2*
Buddhism **3** 902*; **6** 294, 319; **30** 441–2, *442*
Manichaeism **30** 442
Central Asia, Western **30** 440–41*
Bactria **6** 197–8
Buddhism **6** 200; **30** 440
Sogdiana **30** 440–41
Champa **6** 420, 421, *421*, *424*
China **6** *538*, *652*, *654*, 662; **30** 442*, 443–4*
Buddhism **5** 107; **6** 667–71, *670*; **9** 393–4; **30** 442–3*
Confucianism **6** 674–5, *676*; **30** 443
Daoism **6** 671; **30** 443, *444*
Christianity **22** *126*; **30** 450
Confucianism
China **6** 674–5*, *676*; **30** 443
Korea **30** 445
Vietnam **32** *474*, 474–5*
Crete
Archaic **8** 154
Greece, ancient **18** *210*, 210–11

temples
historical and regional traditions
Crete—cont.
Hellenistic **8** 154
7th cent. BC **8** 154
Cyprus, ancient **8** 335, 336
Daoism **6** 671; **30** 443, *444*
Egypt, ancient **1** 770; **9** 719, *720*, 795, 824, 827*, *831*, *834*, 844; **10** 1, 2, 6; **21** 554; **30** 432–3*
Early Dynastic (*c.* 2925-*c.* 2575 BC) **9** 828–9*
Graeco-Roman (332 BC-AD 395) **8** *711*; **9** 834–5*; **24** *603*
Late Period (664-332 BC) **9** 834*; **14** *461*
New Kingdom (*c.* 1539-*c.* 1075 BC) **9** 831–4*; **30** *433*
Old Kingdom (*c.* 2575-*c.* 2130 BC) **9** 829–30*
Predynastic (*c.* 6000-*c.* 2925 BC) **9** 827–8*
Ptolemaic (304-30 BC) **2** *422*
England **3** 369; **10** 226; **12** 129
Etruscan **2** *355*, *356*; **10** 588, 593, 596, *600*, 600–601*, *601*, 603–4; **26** 865, 886; **27** 712; **30** 435
Ferghana **6** 200
France **30** 434
Roman **23** *148*; **26** 858; **30** 436
Greece, ancient **2** 362, *664*, *672*, *688*; **8** *370*, *685*; **13** 375, *375*, *376*, 376–80, *377*, 387, 390, 391, 392, 393, 394, *395*, 396, 397–401*, *400*, *404*, 405–6, *406*, 408, 409, 412, 414, *414*, 415, *416*, 424, 431–2*, 443, 445, 556; **21** 46; **22** 354; **23** 429, 477; **27** 712; **30** 434–5*, 902–3
Archaic **7** 849
Crete **18** *210*, 210–11
Doric **23** *759*
Hellenistic **13** 410
Ionia **15** *894*
Italy **16** *622*; **30** 339
Libya **8** *367*
Lydia **19** 841
Naxos (Greece) **22** *698*
Roman **26** 910–11
Sicily **13** 378
Turkey **5** *742*; **8** *869*
5th cent. BC **13** *401*
6th cent. BC **7** *852*
7th cent. BC **28** 893
Guatemala **24** *744*
Hinduism **30** 431
Bali (Indonesia) **3** *872*
Cambodia **5** 463–7*, *465*, *469*, *470*, *471*, 473
Champa **6** 420
Indian subcontinent **1** *484*; **3** *911*; **13** *882*; **14** 77, 559; **15** 257, *282*, *312*, 312, *315*, *316*, *318*, *320*, *321*, *330*, *332*, *334*; **17** *760*; **18** *13*, *14*; **20** *224*; **29** *481*; **30** 437–9*, *439*; **31** *542*
Indian subcontinent: Shaivism **15** *263*, *286*, *287*, *289*, *291*, *310*, *323*
Malaysia **20** 156
rock-cut **30** 431
Shaivism **1** *485*; **3** *911*
Singapore **28** 773
South Africa **29** 105
South-east Asia **14** 560
Trinidad and Tobago **5** *755*
Vaishnavism **15** 394
Vietnam **6** 420
Hittite **1** 826; **15** 159
Igbo **1** 309
Inca **29** *166*; **30** 447–8

temples
historical and regional traditions—cont.
Indian subcontinent **4** *793*, 794; **9** 161–2; **13** 885; **15** 195, 206, 207, 234, 237–41*, 250, 253*, 260, 266–75*, 279–83, 304–5, 309, 317–22, 385, 393, *397*, 405–6; **26** 48; **30** 436–7*
Andhra Pradesh **15** 293–302*, 328, 534
Assam **15** 396*
Bengal **15** 279–81*, 395–6*, *396*
Bihar **15** 279–81*, 321–2*
Buddhism **3** *905*; **15** *280*; **30** 437
Chalukyas of Badami **15** *297*, *298*, *299*, 526–7
Chalukyas of Kalyana **15** *326*
Chalukyas of Vengi **15** *301*, 301
Chandella **15** *289*
Chola **7** 200; **15** 305, 331–4, *332*, *334*
Deccan **15** 240
drāviḍa **15** 239–41, *240*, 258, 259–60, 278–9, 293–8, *296*, 300, 302–3, 317, 324–7, 328, 333; **30** 437–9*
Gujarat **15** 266–7, *267*, *268*, *272*, *274*
Gupta **15** 194, 237, 252–7*, *253*, *254*, *255*, *256*
hāveli **15** 394–5
Himachal Pradesh **15** *310*, 396–7*, *397*
Hinduism **1** *484*; **3** *911*; **13** *881*; **14** 77, 559; **15** 257, *282*, 312, *312*, *315*, *316*, *318*, *320*, *321*, *330*, *332*; **17** *760*, *761*; **18** *13*, *14*; **20** *224*; **29** *481*; **30** 437–9*, *439*; **31** *542*
Hinduism: Shaivism **1** *485*; **15** *286*, *287*, *289*, *291*, *310*, *323*
Hoysala **15** *327*, 327–8
Jainism **15** 301, 312, *313*, 313, *314*, 314, 528
Kalinga **15** 317
Karnataka **15** 293–302*, 324–8*
Kashmir **15** 264–6, *265*
Kerala **15** 336*
Kosala **15** 283–4, *284*
Kulu **15** *310*
kūṭina **15** 239, *240*
Ladakh **15** 397
latina **15** *238*, 239, 284, 298
Madya Pradesh **15** 285–93, *286*, *287*, 322–4, *323*
Maha-Gurjara **15** 268, 270, 271–5, *272*, *273*, *274*
Maha-Maru **15** 267–71, *269*, *270*, *271*, 275
Maharashtra **15** 315–17, 493
Maru-Gurjara **15** 271, 275, 311–15, *312*, *314*
nāgara **15** *238*, 239, 258, 260, 266–75, 277–8, 298–300, 309–11, 316, 318, 326, 327, 328, 405; **30** 437–9*
Nayaka **15** 397–400*, *398*, *400*
Orissa **15** 281–3*, 317–20*, *318*, *320*, 395*; **18** 213, *214*
Pallava **15** *304*, *305*
Paramara **15** *291*
Rajasthan **15** 267–75, *269*, *270*, *271*, *273*
Rashtrakuta **15** 527–8
Shaivism **15** *263*
Sikhism **15** *375*
Surashtra style **15** 266–7, *267*, *268*
Tamil Nadu **15** 240
Tripura **15** 396*
Uttar Pradesh **15** 260–63; **31** *904*

temples
historical and regional traditions
Indian subcontinent—cont.
Vaishnavism **15** 394
Vanga **15** 320–21*
Vijayanagara period **15** 328–31, *330*, *335*, 335–6, 644
vimāna **15** *297*, *298*, 301–2, 325–6, 333
Western Ganga **15** 528–9
Yadava **15** *315*, *316*
8th cent. AD **15** 262
9th cent. AD **15** 306
11th cent. **30** 642
17th cent. **20** *74*
20th cent. **15** *405*
Indonesia **15** 758–68*, 785
Iran, ancient **30** 432
Italy **9** 21
Etruscan **2** *355*, *356*; **10** 588, 593, 596, *600*, 600–601*, *601*; **26** 886; **30** 435
Greece, ancient **16** *622*; **30** 339
Renaissance **4** *648*
Roman **2** *167*; **26** *793*, 887–8, *888*, *898*; **30** *436*
Jainism
Indian subcontinent **15** 301, 312, 313, *313*, 314, *314*, 528
Japan **14** 429; **17** 94; **23** 596–7
Buddhism **17** 46, 65–8*, *67*, *68*, 432; **30** *445*, 445–6*
Buddhism: Edo period (1600-1868) **17** *72*, *74*; **20** *286*
Buddhism: Esoteric **18** 222
Buddhism: Heian period (AD 794-1185) **5** *335*; **10** *405*; **17** *71*
Buddhism: Kamakura period (1185-1333) **17** *73*, *748*
Buddhism: Nara period (AD 710-94) **22** *490*, *503*
Buddhism: Pure Land **30** 445
Buddhism: Shingon **30** 445
Buddhism: Shōtoku **14** *774*
Buddhism: Tendai **10** 404; **30** 445
Buddhism: Zen **17** 748–9; **30** 446
Java **30** 446
Jewish art **17** *538*, 538–9; **30** 431
Jordan **12** *337*
Khmer **2** *58*, 59; **5** *477*, *478*; **30** 446
Buddhism **30** *579*, 581
Cambodia **5** *477*
Laos **18** 764*
Thailand **30** 578–81
Korea **18** *265*; **30** 444–5*
Buddhism **18** 260, 266–8*, *268*; **30** 444–5
Confucianism **30** 445
Laos **18** 764–5*, 767
Lebanon **3** *3*; **26** *881*
Libya **8** *367*
Lydia **19** 841
Malaysia **20** 156
Malta (Republic of) **20** 210; **30** 433–4
Manichaeism **30** 442
Maya **6** *580*; **20** 884, 885; **21** 212–16*, *214*, *215*; **24** *744*; **30** *448*, 448–9, *449*, *872*; **31** *420*; **33** *510*
Mesoamerica, Pre-Columbian **6** *580*; **21** *211*, *214*, *215*; **25** 764; **30** 448–9*
Aztec **30** *453*
Guatemala **24** *744*
Maya **30** *448*, *449*, *872*; **31** *420*; **33** *510*
Mexico **30** *448*, *449*, *453*, *872*; **31** *420*; **33** *510*
Mesopotamia **4** *772*; **19** *105*; **21** 281, 282, 283, 285, 286, 287; **30** 431, *432*
Neo-Babylonian (*c.* 627-539 BC) **21** 291

temples
historical and regional traditions—cont.
Mexico **30** *448*, *449*, *453*, *872*; **33** *510*
Pre-Columbian **31** *420*
Minoan **2** 305
Mongolia **30** *442*
Native North Americans **22** 572; **30** 449–50*, *450*
Nepal **22** 760, 761–4, *762*, 792
16th cent. **22** *761*
17th cent. **22** *762*
Nigeria **1** 309
North Africa **26** 919
Nubia **23** 279
Olmec **30** 448
Palestine **17** *494*
Parthian **4** *772*; **33** 708
Peru **29** *166*
Phoenician **8** 335; **18** 98
Prehistoric art **30** 433–4*
Rome, ancient **26** 858, 863, 864, 865–7*, 874, 878, 890, 897, 900, 907, 915–16, 924; **27** 1, 3, 31, 32, 712; **30** 339, 435–6*
Britain **26** 858
Celtic **26** 905
England **3** 369
France **23** *148*; **26** 858; **30** 436
Greece **26** 910–11
Italy **2** *167*; **26** *793*, 887–8, *888*, *898*; **30** *436*
Jordan **12** *337*
Lebanon **26** *881*
North Africa **26** 919
1st cent. BC **26** *784*
Ryūkyū Islands **27** 470
Sardinia **30** 434
Seleucid **13** 405; **28** 383, 384
Sicily **13** 378, 392, 398; **28** 654
Sikhism **15** *375*
Singapore **28** 772–3
Sogdiana **30** 440–41
South Africa **29** 105
South America, Pre-Columbian **29** *165*, 165–6*, *166*; **30** 447–8*
South-east Asia **14** 560; **29** 236–7; **30** 446–7*
Spain **30** 434
Sri Lanka **29** *451*
Syria **13** 405; **23** *892*
Syria-Palestine **30** 184, 185, 186, 188, 191, *191*, 432
Taiwan **30** 244
Thailand
Buddhism **3** 164, *164*; **30** 446, *579*, 581, 589–90
Khmer **30** 578–81
Tibet **19** *294*; **30** 815, *815*, 816, 818–19, 842
Tokharistan **6** 200
Toltec **6** *580*
Trinidad and Tobago **5** *755*
Turkey **5** *742*; **8** *869*
United States of America **22** *126*, 572; **30** 450
Urartian **1** 729, 831; **24** 265; **31** 700
Vietnam **6** 420, 421, *421*, *424*; **32** 471–5*
Buddhism **30** 446; **32** 471–4*, *472*, *473*, *474*
Confucianism **32** *474*, 474–5*
Yoruba **1** 309
materials
basalt **15** 328
brick **4** *772*, *793*, 794; **15** 256–7*, 280, 328
concrete **5** 755
granite **15** 329
marble **26** 865, 887; **30** 436
mats **30** 433
mud **5** 755
mud-bricks **9** 844; **13** 376; **30** 433
plaster **15** 319
sandstone **15** *253*, 324

temples
materials—cont.
soapstone **15** 324, 327
stone **13** 376, 445; **15** 253–6*; **30** 433; **32** 472
terracotta **26** 878
wood **5** 755; **13** 376; **18** 266; **30** 433; **32** 471
types
amphiprostyle **1** 796*; **13** 376
apsidal **15** *251*, 251–2*, 259
ātishgāh **15** 913
chahār ṭāq **15** *911*, 912, 913
colossal **13** 399
Corinthian **13** 405
cult
Egypt, ancient **9** 827–35*, *827*, *829*; **18** *19*
Greece, ancient **13** 396, 417
Rome, ancient **26** 867
degas **22** *761*, 761–3, *762*
dipteral **9** 3*; **13** 376, 398
distyle **13** *376*
Doric
Greece, ancient **1** *479*, 511, *511*; **2** *677*, 684; **13** 377–9, *378*, 387, 401, 405, *414*, 415; **17** *745*; **23** *759*; **30** *435*; **31** *269*
Sicily **1** 511, *511*
Turkey **2** 635
elliptical **15** 251
funerary **12** 497; **20** 863; **30** 433
hall **15** 300
hekatompeda **13** 397, 415
hexastyle **13** 398
hundred-footers *see hekatompeda*
Ionic **13** *379*, 379–80, 398–400, 415
kutai Amidadō **17** 660
mammisi **9** 835; **20** 231–2*
mortuary
Egypt, ancient **9** 827, 835*; **25** 760, 762; **27** 811; **30** 695
Japan **17** 58
pantheons **24** 21*
peripteral
Armenia **12** *154*
Egypt, ancient **9** 833
Greece, ancient **10** 423; **13** 376, 397, *397*, 398, 415
Roman **12** *154*
peristyle **13** 397; **24** 456*
podium **23** *622*; **26** *866*, *888*
prostyle **13** 376
pseudo-dipteral **13** 378, 405
rock-cut
Bali (Indonesia) **15** 763–4
Buddhism **6** 626; **15** 252–3, 464, 492; **22** 239; **30** 431, 437, 442–3*
Cambodia **2** 57
China **6** 626, 650; **22** 239; **30** 442–3*
Egypt, ancient **1** *95*, 95–6; **9** 830, 831, 833; **12** *227*; **29** 386*
Hinduism **15** 465–6, 477, 521–2
Indian subcontinent **1** *485*; **10** *149*; **15** *250*, *251*, 252–3, 275–9, *277*, *278*, 293, 302–4, 306, 464–6, 477, 492, 507, 521–2, 534, 535; **30** 437*
Indonesia **15** 763–4
Nubia **23** 279
Tibet **30** 817, 818
sanctuary-temples **30** 434–5
sāndhāra **22** 423
śikhara **5** 229–30; **22** 763–4
śikhara **15** 244*
solar **30** 433
sun temples **1** *91*
temple-theatres
Italy **26** 888, *888*, 889
Rome, ancient **26** 865, 873, 888, *888*, 889
treasury-temples **30** 434, 435
tripteral **13** 376

temples
types—cont.
valley **25** 760, 762
see also SHRINES (i) (CULT)
Temple Site *see* CAÑO, EL
Temple Street Glasshouse **4** 824
temple-theatres *see under* TEMPLES → types
Templeton, James, & Co. **4** 788; **5** 840; **17** 640; **28** 250
Templetown, Elizabeth **33** 22
works **21** 113
Templier, Raymond **2** 521; **17** 529
temporary architecture *see under* ARCHITECTURE → types
Temporiti, Joseph-François **12** 832
Temps Nouveaux, Les **13** 323
Temuka Pottery **23** 68, 69
Temür Güregen *see* TIMUR
TEN **21** 382
Ten, The (1898-1918) *see* Ten American Painters
Ten, The (1935-40) **13** 214; **27** 219
Tenafly (NJ), African Art Museum **1** 228
tenailles **21** 547, 567, 571, 580
Ten American Painters **23** 47; **30** 452*; **33** 43
members **3** 740; **8** 598, 841; **14** 220; **21** 342; **30** 344; **31** 487
Tenampua fortress **29** 140
Tenam Rosario **27** 158
Tenancingo **21** 394
Tenango del Valle **21** 265
Tenasserim *see* MERGUI
Tenayuca **21** *193*, *372*; **30** 452–3*
coatepantli **7** 481; **30** 452
double pyramid **25** 765; **30** 452–3, *453*
skull racks **31** 506
wall paintings **21** 230
Ten Bamboo Studio **7** *116*, 117
Tenby **32** 787
Tenca, Francesco **8** 16
Tencala, Giovanni Giacomo **30** 454
Tencalla (family) **32** 435
Tencalla, Carpoforo **2** 794; **8** 391
collaboration **30** 454*
patrons and collectors **10** 529
works **14** 899; **18** 467; **28** 852
Tencalla, Constante **30** 453–4*
patrons and collectors **32** 5, 7
works **19** 496; **25** 114; **32** 578, 874
Tencalla, Giovanni Giacomo **4** 1; **19** 55, 336
Tencalla, Giovanni Pietro **30** 454–5*
works **2** 782; **4** 832; **8** 386; **18** 467; **23** 424; **32** 456
Tencalla, Pietro **19** 55
Tence Ruiz, Jose **24** 620
Tenda **1** 392
Tendai, Morris **33** 679
Tendai Buddhism *see under* BUDDHISM → sects
Tendenza **11** 528; **26** 14; **30** 455*
tenderness **6** 570
Tendilla, Iñigo López de Mendoza, Conde de **10** 783; **32** 100
Tendilla Retablo **11** 485
Tendring Hall **4** 779
Tène, La *see* LA TÈNE
Tenea Kouros **13** 470
tenebrism **4** 261; **19** 353; **30** 456*
Tenedos **19** 235
tenements **10** 98; **17** 83; **30** *457*, 457–9*
see also HOUSES
Tenerani, Carlo **30** 459
Tenerani, Giambattista **30** 459
Tenerani, Giuseppe **21** 36; **30** 459
Tenerani, Pietro **20** 214; **26** 776; **30** 459*
groups and movements **3** 921; **25** 741

Tenerani, Pietro—cont.
patrons and collectors **4** 106; **31** 172
pupils **29** 86; **32** 538
teachers **30** 766
works **16** 705; **26** 810
tenerezza *see* TENDERNESS
Tenerife **18** 588
Ténès Treasure **9** 653
Ten Eyck (family) **31** 647
Tenganan Pegeringsingan **15** 793
Tengbom, Anders **30** 460
Tengbom, Ivar (Justus) **3** 784; **30** 459–60*
groups and movements **13** 613
pupils **2** 611; **19** 283
staff **1** 470, 475; **6** 151; **11** 363
teachers **18** 663
works **29** 686; **30** 75
Teng Ch'un *see* DENG CHUN
Tengenenge Sculpture Community **33** 679, 680
Tenggara, Arkitek **28** 772
Tengnagel, Jan **25** 757; **30** 460*
groups and movements **22** 842; **25** 556, 557
Ten Great Disciples **17** 196; **22** 118, 429
Teng Shih-ju *see* DENG SHIRU
Tengström, F.
works **14** *371*
Teng Wen-Yüan *see* DENG WENYUAN
Tenhola church **11** 94
Tenicheff, Mariya (Klavdiyevna) *see* TENISHEVA, MARIYA (KLAVDIYEVNA)
Teniers (family) **5** 65; **32** 368
Teniers, Abraham **30** 460
Teniers, David, I (1582-1649) **2** 196; **4** *895*; **5** 43; **9** 16; **30** 460–61*
attributions **19** 25
collaboration **4** 916, 917
copies **3** 873
patrons and collectors
Aumale, Henri-Eugène-Philippe-Louis de Bourbon, Duc d' **23** 523
Balbi, Giovanni Agostino **3** 90
Caffiéri, Philippe (ii) (1714-74) **5** 380
Du Bois, Simon **9** 327
Elizabeth Farnese, Queen of Spain (1692-1766) **4** 559
George IV, King of Great Britain (*reg* 1820-30) **14** 146
Gideon, Sampson **12** 601
La Caze, Louis **18** 588
Meynier, Charles **21** 412
Quentin de Lorangère **25** 815
Salamanca (y Mayol), José, Marqués de **27** 607
personal collection **4** 917
pupils **29** 79; **30** 461
reproductions on porcelain **28** 521
reproductive prints by others **3** 463; **14** 288; **19** 10, 136; **23** 908; **25** 10
tapestries **29** 350; **30** 333
works **1** 663; **5** 50; **9** 412; **12** 290, 292, 670
Teniers, David, II (1610-90) **1** 104; **2** 181; **3** 615, 617; **4** *895*; **10** 351; **17** 919; **25** 811, 813; **29** 375; **30** 460, 461–4*
collaboration **2** 540; **22** 718; **31** 521; **32** 700, 705
dealing **32** 728
paintings
portraits **13** *920*
patrons and collectors
Blathwayt, William **4** 131
Bourbon II., Luis Antonio, Infante of Spain **4** 565
Brukenthal, Samuel, Baron von **5** 9

Teniers, David, II (1610-90)
patrons and collectors—cont.
Catherine II, Empress of Russia (*reg* 1762- 96) **26** 732, 733
Dundas, Lawrence **9** 392
Faesch, Johann Jakob **10** 753
Fould, Louis **11** 338
Gildemeester, Jan (Jansz.) (1744-99) **12** 620
Gillott, Joseph **12** 638
Habsburg I., Leopold William, Archduke of Austria, Governor of the Netherlands **3** 354; **6** 77; **13** 919, 920
Johnson, John G(raver) (1841-1917) **17** 619
Orléans, Philippe II de Bourbon, 2nd Duc de (1674-1723) **32** 919
Papillon de la Ferté, Denis-Pierre-Jean, **24** 63
Peel, Robert (1788-1850) **24** 322
Ryerson, Martin A(ntoine) **27** 463
Sparre, Gustaf Adolf **29** 366
Temple-Nugent-Grenville, George, 1st Marquess of Buckingham **13** 637
Vilas Boas, Manuel (do) Cenáculo **32** 539
pupils **2** 40; **30** 874
reproductions in porcelain **12** 434
reproductions in tapestry **4** 924
reproductive prints by others **6** 527, 547; **8** 544; **21** 147; **25** 221
works **3** 560; **5** 50; **7** 784; **9** 18; **16** 767; **30** *461*, *462*, *463*
Teniers, David, III (1638-85) **3** 613; **4** 894; **29** 350; **30** 460
Teniers, Juliaan (1572-1615) **23** 76; **30** 460
Teniers, Juliaan (1616-79) **30** 460
Teniers, Theodoor **30** 460
Tenies **4** 460
Tenisheva, Mariya (Klavdiyevna) **27** 438; **30** 464*
architecture **20** 223
collections **27** 439
paintings **3** 734
pottery **27** 410
sponsorship **30** 265
Tenjikujō *see* DAIBUTSU
Tenju Kan *see* KAN TENJU
Tenjukoku mandara shūchō **17** 374
Tenkai Togarō **31** 251
Tenkei *see under* PORCELAIN → wares
Tenmon **4** 803
Tenmu, Emperor (*reg* 672-86) **17** 217; **22** 499; **23** 597
Tenmyō **17** 322
Tennant, Charles **1** 454; **30** 464*
Tennent, H. M. **19** 868
Tennessee Valley Authority (TVA) **31** 596; **32** 851
Tenniel, John **30** 464–5*; **33** 369
works **4** 363, 868; **5** 758; **6** 605; **19** 614; **31** 266
tennis-courts *see* BALLCOURTS
Tennyson, Alfred **15** 26
architecture **18** 169
groups and movements **24** 743
illustrated works **10** 254; **32** 502
Doré, Gustave(-Paul) **4** 364
Ehninger, John W(hetten) **10** 99
Homer, Winslow **14** 699
Hughes, Arthur **14** 850
Millais, John Everett **4** 363; **21** 602
Rossetti, Dante Gabriel **27** 186
Victoria, Empress of Germany (1840-1901) **14** 656
Tenochtitlán **21** *193*, 201, 398–400*, *399*
architecture **21** 211–12
causeways **6** 97
excavations **21** 399–400

Tenochtitlán—cont.
fortifications **21** 598
gardens **12** 71
Great Pyramid **21** 212, 224
Great Temple *see* Templo Mayor
hanging gardens **12** 65, 71
hardstones **21** 243
masks **21** 252
mosaics **21** 255
platform **25** 764
pottery **2** 907
religion **21** 182
sculpture **21** 218, 223, 400, *400*
relief **21** 224
skull racks **31** 506
stone-carvings **21** *223*, *224*
stucco **29** 829
talud-tablero **30** 280
Temple of Huitzilopochtli
reliefs **2** *907*
Templo Mayor **21** 252, 255, 260, 398, *399*, 399–400, 719; **23** 825; **25** 765; **30** 449
chacmools **28** 640
coatepantli **7** 481
painting **2** 907
reliefs **21** 224
sculpture **2** 905–6; **21** 240, 400
skull racks **21** 188; **31** 505, *506*
urban planning **21** 398–9
wall paintings **21** 230
water supply **21** 208
see also MEXICO CITY
Tenorio, Pedro **31** 91
Tenorio, Robert **22** 607
Tenos **8** *304*; **13** 383, 497
ten Raa, E. **1** 374
Tenrai Hidai *see* HIDAI, TENRAI
Tenreiro, Jesús **32** 171
Tenreiro, Joaquim **4** 721
Tenri
Chōgakuji **17** 121
Sankōkan Museum **6** 735; **15** 746; **17** 433
Tenrikyō **17** 430, 433; **28** 609
tensegrity **11** 835; **12** 311
Tenshin Okakura *see* OKAKURA, TENSHIN
Tenshō Shūbun **17** 29, 409; **18** 552; **30** 465–6*
attributions **17** *172*
pupils **23** 371; **29** 13; **31** 251
works **2** 598; **17** 172–3; **30** *466*
tenshu *see* JAPAN → donjons
tension structures **23** *272*, 273; **30** 467–9*
Tenskwatawa **22** 559
Tensta Church **27** 165; **30** *65*, 66, 76
wall paintings **30** *76*
Tenta *see* KALAVASOS
Ten Thousand Buddha Stelae *see* STELAE → types → *wanfo bei*
tents **30** 467, 469–80*
historical and regional traditions
Afghanistan **30** 473
Africa **1** 307, *307*
Algeria **30** 473
Arabia **30** 471
Azerbaijan **16** 193; **30** 473
Berber **1** 307; **3** 755; **30** 473
Central Asia **10** 873; **30** 473–6*
Central Asia, Western **16** 197, 485; **23** 820
China **30** *475*
Egypt **30** 477
Egypt, ancient **10** 61
England **2** *339*
Fulani **1** *307*, 307
Indian subcontinent **15** *716*, 716–17*; **30** *472*
Iran **16** 193; **30** *472*, 473, 480*
Iran, ancient **30** 476
Islamic **15** 716–17*; **16** 124, 193, 197, 429, 485; **30** *472*, 476–80*
Israelite **30** 471
Jordan **30** 473

tents
historical and regional traditions—cont.
Mongolia **21** 873, 883, 884–5; **30** 473–6*
Morocco **30** 473
Niger **1** *307*
Ottoman **30** 478–80*
Rome, ancient **25** 423; **30** 467
Sudan **1** 307
Tajikistan **30** 473
Tuareg **1** 307
Turkestan (region) **30** 473
Turkey **30** 473–6*, *474*
Turkmenistan **30** 473
20th cent. **23** 635
materials
brocades **15** 716; **30** 470, 476
calico **30** 470
canvas **30** 470, 474
chintz **15** 717
embroidery **15** 717
felt **10** 873, 874; **16** 485; **30** 470, 473, *474*, *475*
goat-hair **1** 307; **30** 470, 471, *472*
leather **1** 307; **10** 61
satin **30** 470
skins **1** 307
velvet **15** 716; **30** 470
wood **21** 883
see also KIOSKS; TEPEES; YURTS
Tentyris *see* DENDARA
Ten'yū Kamiya *see* KAMIYA TEN'YŪ
Tenyū Shōkei **17** 172; **30** 466
Tenzin Gyatso *see* DALAI LAMA, 14th
TEO *see under* NARKOMPROS
Teocalli de la Guerra Sagrada **2** 907
Teodoli (family) **20** 394
Teodoli, Girolamo, Marchese **4** 333; **30** 481*, 667
Teodorescu, Nicolae **30** 364
Teodorico da Orvieto, Cardinal **13** 775
Teodorico de Alemania **13** 98
Teodoro d'Errico *see* HENDRICKSZ. (CENTEN), DIRCK
Teodorović, Djurdje **28** 451
Teodoru, Horia **30** 481*
T'eodosia St Sargis **2** 427
Teo Eng Seng **28** 774, 775
Teofil (*fl c.* 1313-50) **26** 710
Teofil (*fl c.* 1505-11) **3** 224
Teofilo, Martino *see* TEOFILOWICZ, MARCIN
Teofilo di Jacopo Cesena **31** 432
Teofilowicz, Marcin **18** 177; **30** 482*
Teopantecuanitlán **21** 208, 219
Teopanzolco **25** 765
staircase **29** *527*
Teophorous statues *see under* SCULPTURE → types
Teopilos **13** 549
Teos (Turkey) **13** *363*; **15** 893; **29** 702; **30** 482*
Temple of Dionysos **23** 482
Teos (*reg* 365-360 BC) **9** *778*
Teotenago **21** 599
Teotihuacán **20** 882; **21** 177, 181, 192, *193*, 197, 198, 200, 263, 264, *372*; **23** 826; **30** 482–5*, *483*; **33** 101
architecture **21** 205, 207, 209–10, *210*; **25** 764; **30** 483–4
Avenue of the Dead **6** 96–7; **30** *483*
causeway **6** 96–7
Ciudadela **21** 598
figurines **21** 185, 242, 243, 249
hardstones **1** 713; **21** 242
houses **21** 208
joinery **5** 408
masks **16** *861*; **21** 242, *243*, 251, 254
mines **1** 713
Teotihuacán—cont.
mirrors **21** 718
mosaics **21** 254
Museo Arqueológico de Teotihuacán **21** 396
narratives **22** 518
Palace of Atetelco **21** 227–8
Palace of Quetzalpapálotl **5** 408; **9** 166; **21** 206, *207*
Palace of Tepantitla **21** 227, *228*
Palace of Tetitla **21** 228
plaques **30** 786
pottery **21** 238; **30** 484–5*
Pyramid of Quetzalcóatl **21** 205, 207, 210; **25** 764
Pyramid of the Moon **21** 207, 210; **25** 764; **30** *483*
Pyramid of the Sun **21** 210; **25** 764; **30** *483*
religion **21** 186, 189
roofs **21** 206
sculpture **21** 217, 220*; **30** 484*
seals **21** 258
shells **21** 257, 259, 260
shields **21** 246
stele **21** *220*; **29** 620
Stele of La Ventilla **5** 408
stucco **29** 829
talud-tablero **21** 205; **30** 279
Temple of Quetzalcóatl **21** *206*, 220, 260; **29** 829; **30** 448
temples **30** 448
Temple of the Sun **30** 448, *448*
Tepalcayo 1 **25** 764
urns **21** 242
wall paintings **7** 636; **21** 226, 227–8, 246, 249, 261; **30** 484*, *484*
water supply **21** 208
Teotim **28** 458
Teozacoalco
manuscript illumination **21** *738*
Tepantitla **21** 246
tepe **1** 851; **21** 268
Tepe, Alfred **30** 485*
Tepeaca Franciscan Monastery **21** 375
tepees **2** 362; **9** 165; **22** 568–9, *569*, 570, 653, 655; **30** 470
see also TENTS
Tepelena, Ali Pasha **18** 243
Tepexi el Viejo **21** 599
tepidaria **13** 386
Teplá monastery **8** 376
Teplice **15** 3
Ceramics School **8** 406
House of Culture **8** 381
Teplov, A. G. **27** 439
Tepotzotlán
College of S Martín *see* Museo Nacional del Virreinato
Museo de Arte Colonial **21** 396
Museo Nacional del Virreinato **17** 513; **21** 376, 396
Tepper (family) **25** 136
Tepper, Piotr **30** 213
Tep Pranam **5** 480
Tepti-Ahar **15** 909; **29** 814
Tequixquiac **21** 192, 250
Ter **15** 257, 259–60, *276*, *294*; **30** 485*
ivory **15** 695
sculpture **30** 510
temples **15** 295
yakṣī **15** 450
Terahi **15** 292
Mohajamata **15** 292
monasteries **15** 292
Shiva Temple **15** 288
Terai Yōsetsu **17** 236
Teramo **27** 61
Téran, F. Collantes de *see* COLLANTES DE TÉRAN, F.
Terasawa (family) **17** 811
Terasawa Hirotaka **17** 811
Te Rauparaha **33** 57
Ter-Avetisyan, Smbat **9** 471
Terayama, Shūji **33** 540
Terborch *see* BORCH, TER
Terbruggen, H. **14** 643
Terbrugghen, Hendrick *see* BRUGGHEN, HENDRICK (JANSZ.) TER
Tercan, tomb of Mama Hatun **16** 185
Terciis, Francesco de *see* TERZIO, (GIOVANNI) FRANCESCO
Ter Doest Abbey **3** 552
Terebenyov, Aleksandr (Ivanovich) **30** 486*; **33** 516
Terebenyov, Ivan (Ivanovich) **30** 485–6*; **33** 600
terebinth resin *see under* RESINS → types
Teredon *see* BASRA
Terence **30** 486–7*
works **10** 534
illustrated **4** 358; **5** 801; **9** 603; **26** 662, *671*; **30** *487*, 655, 656; **31** *49*
Térence des Ducs (Paris, Bib. Arsenal, MS. 664) **20** 625; **30** 487
Terence of Martin Gouge (Paris, Bib. N., MS. lat. 7907 A) **30** 487
Terengganu Royal Palace **20** 167
Terenozhkin, A. **1** 504
Terenuthis *see* KOM ABU BILLO
Terenzano, Master of *see* CAPPELLA MEDICI POLYPTYCH, MASTER OF THE
Tér és forma **4** 378
Tereshchenko, M. **31** 565
Tergeste *see* TRIESTE
Tergnier **11** 526
Terhai **15** 496
Tériade **3** 450; **4** 691; **6** 384; **20** 830; **28** 820; **30** 488*; **33** 362
collaboration **18** 864; **26** 44
paintings **13** 359
sponsorship **30** 709
works **4** 366
Terilli, Francesco **30** 488*
Terk, Sonia *see* DELAUNAY (II), SONIA
T'erlemezyan, P'anos **2** 431, 432
Ter-Maruk'yan, Andreas **2** 436
Termehüyük **15** 159
Termeno S Giacomo **26** 654
Termessos **26** *908*, 913; **30** 488–9*
bouleuteria **13** 407
temple **26** 913
theatre **23** 349; **26** 912
Termez **6** *182*, 201; **16** *105*; **30** 489–91*; **31** *781*
architecture **16** 161
capitals **6** 217
congregational mosque **16** 159
Fayaz Tepe **6** 198; **28** 635; **30** 491*
sculpture **6** 216, 217
wall paintings **6** 224, 225, 226, 228
houses **16** 154
ivory-carvings **6** 270
Kara Tepe **6** *182*, 198; **30** *490*, 490–91*
capitals **6** 217
Complex B **6** 225–6, *226*
Complex D **6** 226
Complex G **6** 194
pottery **6** 255
sculpture **6** *194*, 214, 216, 217, 221; **29** 821
statuettes **6** 275
wall paintings **6** 194, 224, 225–6, 228
mausoleum of Sultan Sa'dat **6** 207
minaret **16** 160
Museum **6** 283
ramparts **6** 211
Regent's Palace **6** 207; **16** 160, 165, 244; **23** 820
glass **6** 269
plaster **29** 822
sculpture **6** 222; **16** 246
stucco **29** 820
Termez—cont.
stupas **29** 867
tomb of al-Hakim al-Tirmidhi **16** 259; **28** 636
Termikelov, G. M. **2** 893; **3** 87, 88
terminal figures *see under* SCULPTURE → types
Termine, Guilio Cesare **4** 635
Termini, Giovan Battista **11** 194
Termini, Stefano **11** 194
terminology of architecture *see* ARCHITECTURE → terminology
terminology of art *see* ART (TERMINOLOGY OF)
Termoli, Alfanus of *see* ALFANUS OF TERMOLI
terms *see* SCULPTURE → types → terminal figures
Ternate Benteng Toloko **21** 596
Terneuzen Town Hall **31** *868*
Terningen **13** 848
Terni Palazzo Spade **20** 244
Ternovets, Boris (Nikolayevich) **30** 491*
Térouanne, Pierre **22** 701
Terqa **1** *849*, 850; **30** 179, *180*, 492*
Terra, Daniel J. **24** 481
Terra, (Miguel) Ventura **30** 492–3*
assistants **8** 74
pupils **22** 14; **25** 879
works **19** 466; **25** 294
terra alba **1** 516
terraced gardens *see under* GARDENS → types
Terrace Glass Works **7** 857; **16** 30
terrace houses *see under* HOUSES → types
terraces **12** 61
Cambodia **5** 474
England **9** 367; **12** 127
France **12** 120
Inca **15** 162
Italy **12** 115, 116
terrace-stupas *see under* STUPAS → types
Terracina **26** *886*
Cathedral of S Cesario **7** 919
insulae **26** 871, 887
terracotta **30** 493–512*
conservation **30** 512*
historical and regional traditions
Aegean **8** 262
Afghanistan **16** 166, 169
Africa **1** *221*, *222*, 285; **18** *218*; **30** *508*, 508–9*
Akan **1** 257, 503; **2** 589; **30** 509
Ancient Near East **9** 150
Arabia **2** 260
Asante **2** 589
Bangladesh **3** 169
Belgium **3** 588
Brazil **20** *372*
Buddhism **6** *298*; **15** *221*, *462*; **30** 595*
Burma **5** 255; **30** 511
Central Asia **30** 510*
Central Asia, Eastern **6** *298*, *308*, 315–16*, *316*
Central Asia, Western **6** 206–7, 274*, 275–7*
Islamic **16** 166, 169, 245
Sogdiana **6** 275, 276
Tokharistan **6** 275
Uzbekistan **6** *276*
Champa **6** 426
China **6** 9; **7** *55*, 80; **30** 509*, *509*
Chorrera culture **30** *512*
Crete **8** 154; **13** *443*, 582; **21** *680*; **27** 825
Cycladic **8** 309
Cyprus, ancient **8** 338–9, 340, 342
Edo (Africa) **9** 736
Egypt, ancient **9** 864, 865, *865*; **27** 111, *111*, 825
terracotta
historical and regional traditions—cont.
England **10** 266; **27** *243*; **30** 499*, *499*, 501–4*, *502*, 506–7*; **32** *905*
Etruscan **1** 127; **10** 587, 588, 593, 602–4, *603*, *604*, 608, *633*; **27** 9, 826; **30** 494, *494*; **32** *119*
France **14** *797*; **29** *573*; **30** 498–500*, *500*, *501*
Roman **27** 110–11
Germany **4** *376*; **26** *104*
Ghana **1** 285
Greece, ancient **7** *854*; **10** 742; **13** 376, 390–91, 393, 424, 433*, 436–7*, 441, *441*, *443*, 450, 577–83*, *603*; **21** *342*; **22** 160; **23** 427, *433*; **24** *374*; **27** 825; **29** 567; **30** *493*, 493–4; **31** 259
Archaic **13** 578–9*, *579*, *582*
Attica **13** *580*
Boeotia **13** *579*, *580*
Classical **13** 579–81*, *580*
Daidalic **13** 443
Hellenistic **13** *581*, 581–2*
Roman **27** 111
Helladic **14** *352*
Huastec **14** 830–31
Ife (kingdom of) **1** 329; **15** *107*; **30** 509
Igbo **30** 509
Indian subcontinent **15** 395, 414, *421*, 453, 717–20*, 727, 728; **30** 510*, *510*
Baluchistan **15** 213
Bangladesh **15** *726*
Gond **15** *734*
Gupta **15** 719
Indus civilization **15** 213, 420, 421–2*
Kushana period **15** 719
Maurya period **15** 718
Pala period **15** 719
Pala-Sena period **15** 499
Prehistoric **15** 686
Rajasthan & Gujarat **15** 449
Satavahana period **15** 719
Shunga period **15** *718*, 718
Tamil Nadu **15** *729*
4th cent. AD **15** *459*, *462*
9th cent. AD **15** *221*
20th cent. **15** 719, 729, 730
Indus civilization **15** 213, 420, 421–2*, 717–18
Iran **16** 165
Iraq **16** *247*
Islamic **16** 140, 143
Afghanistan **16** 166, 169
Central Asia, Western **16** 166, 169, 245
Iran **16** 165
Iraq **16** *247*
Pakistan **16** 166
Italy **1** 127, 707; **10** 587; **21** *770*; **30** 496–8*, 501*
Baroque **11** *279*
Etruscan **10** 587, 588, 593, *603*, *604*, *633*; **32** *119*
Greece, ancient **21** *342*
Mannerism **12** *570*
Renaissance **3** *260*; **8** *101*; **9** *124*; **20** *907*; **23** *90*; **25** V1; **26** *331*, 443, *444*, *445*, *446*; **30** *497*, *498*, *508*
Roman **27** 109–10*, *110*
16th cent. **3** *496*; **20** *778*; **32** *649*
18th cent. **22** *681*
Japan **17** 47; **30** 509–10*
Java **15** 772
Kassite **17** *837*
Kongo **18** *218*
Korea **18** *302*; **30** 509–10*
Lwena **30** 509
Mali **1** 285; **21** 478–81, *479*

terracotta
historical and regional traditions—cont.
Mesoamerica, Pre-Columbian 14 830–31; 21 256; 30 511–12*; 33 *618*
Mesopotamia 17 *837*; 21 295, 302
Mexico 33 *618*
Middle Niger cultures 21 478–81*, *479*; 30 509
Minoan 21 *680*; 27 825
Mycenaean 14 *352*; 27 825
Nepal 22 758, 790*
Nigeria 1 *221*; 15 *107*; 23 *132*, 179–81, *180*, *181*; 30 *508*
Nok 1 221, *221*, 258, 342; 21 481; 30 508
Pakistan 16 166
Parthian 24 218
Phoenician 24 642–3*; 27 825
Prehistoric art 8 339; 29 228; 30 509
Punic 25 733–4*, 735
Rome, ancient 15 51; 26 877, 878; 27 9, 29, 51, 109–12*; 30 494
Egypt, ancient 27 111, *111*
France 27 110–11
Greece, ancient 27 111
Italy 27 109–10*, *110*
Spain 27 111
Sicily 13 582*; 28 654
Sogdiana 6 275, 276
South Africa 1 *222*
South America, Pre-Columbian 20 *372*; 30 511–12*, *512*
South-east Asia 29 228; 30 510–11*
Spain 27 111; 31 *191*
Sri Lanka 29 475–6*, *476*
Sumerian 22 158
Sweden 30 *86*
Syria-Palestine 10 *173*
Thailand 29 228; 30 511, *511*, 595*
Tokharistan 6 275
United Arab Emirates 2 *260*
United States of America 30 505*, 507*, *507*
Uzbekistan 6 *276*
Vietnam 6 426; 32 472, *472*
Yoruba 15 *107*; 30 509
Zande 30 509
materials
glazes 26 443; 30 505
techniques
appliqué 29 475
dating methods 21 479–80
impressing 6 275
moulding 6 275
stamping 6 275
uses
acroteria 1 127–8
altarpieces 1 707; 26 *445*
antefixes 10 603
architectural decorations 10 266; 15 719; 16 143, 166, 169, 245, *247*; 27 9; 30 *504*, *507*; 32 *119*
architecture 16 165, 169; 30 501–7*; 32 *905*
beads 7 80
brick 4 768–9*
busts 6 *316*; 13 *443*, 583*; 14 *797*; 27 *110*; 30 495
England 27 *243*
Italy 9 *124*; 32 *649*
casts 6 9
churches 30 *502*
coffins 24 218
cult statues 8 262
dolls 31 259
doors 9 150
écorchés 9 706
ex-votos 13 376; 27 109–12
façade decoration 10 742
figurines 13 *580*; 15 728
Central Asia, Eastern 6 315–16

terracotta
uses
figurines—cont.
Central Asia, Western 6 276
Crete 8 154
Cyprus, ancient 8 339
Egypt, ancient 9 865, *865*
Greece, ancient 13 578–82*, *579*, *581*; 23 427
Huastec 14 830–31
Indian subcontinent 15 213, 414, *421*, 421–2*, 718, 719, *729*; 30 *510*
Italy 8 *101*; 22 *681*
Mesopotamia 7 *186*; 21 295
Minoan 21 *680*
Mycenaean 14 *352*
Nepal 22 790
Phoenician 24 642–3*
Rome, ancient 27 109–12
South America, Pre-Columbian 30 511–12, *512*
South-east Asia 29 228
Thailand 30 *511*
friezes 10 *633*; 21 *342*
lamps 13 *603*
lanterns (lights) 27 *111*
masks 13 582*; 15 *734*
modelli 11 *279*; 21 768, *770*; 30 495
models 24 *374*
mosaics 13 556, 565; 22 154, 155, 158, 160
moulds 6 *298*; 25 734
murals 22 333
ossuaries 6 276
plaques 5 230; 13 443, 582*; 15 *221*, *459*, 718, *718*; 30 *494*
pots 6 *308*
protomes 13 582–3*
rattles 21 256
relief sculpture
Greece, ancient 13 582*, *582*
Indian subcontinent 15 499, 719
Islamic 16 *247*
Italy 3 *260*; 26 *444*, *446*; 30 *501*
Uzbekistan 6 *276*
revetments 10 603; 13 424; 26 877
ritual objects 15 729
roofs 1 127; 13 397; 15 772; 32 472, *472*
sarcophagi 15 686; 27 825, 826
sculpture 30 495–500*
Africa 1 257, 258
Arabia 2 260
Central Asia, Western 6 275–6
China 19 *432*; 30 *509*
Cyprus, ancient 8 338, 340, 342
Edo (Africa) 9 736
England 30 *499*
Etruscan 10 593, *604*, 608
France 30 *500*
Germany 4 *376*; 26 *104*
Greece, ancient 7 *854*; 13 433*, 436–7*, 441, *441*, 450; 23 *433*
Ife (kingdom of) 15 *107*
Indian subcontinent 15 449, 453, *462*, 719; 30 510
Italy 3 *496*; 12 *570*; 20 *778*, *907*; 23 *90*; 26 *331*; 30 *497*, *498*
Kassite 17 *837*
Korea 18 *302*
Mesoamerica, Pre-Columbian 33 *618*
Nepal 22 758
Nigeria 23 *132*
Rome, ancient 27 9, 29
Sicily 28 654
South-east Asia 30 510
Spain 31 *191*
Sweden 30 *86*
Thailand 30 595*
United Arab Emirates 2 *260*

terracotta
uses
sculpture—cont.
Vietnam 6 426
seals 15 420
statuettes 6 275; 13 578–82*; 29 567, 573, *573*
tangas 20 *372*
temples 26 878
tiles 1 *126*; 3 588; 13 390–91; 15 51; 17 47; 30 *493*, 493–4
toys 6 276; 15 *726*, 730
urns 10 588, 602–3, *603*; 18 *218*; 27 9
vases 30 *501*
wall paintings 27 51
Terra de Barros 32 618
terra di Sinope *see under* PIGMENTS → types
Terra d'Otranto, Giacomo Bellanti di *see* GIACOMO BELLANTI DI TERRA D'OTRANTO
terraglia *see* POTTERY → wares → creamware
Terragni, Attilio 27 789; 30 512
Terragni, Giuseppe 16 681; 28 793; 30 512–14*
collaboration 11 63; 19 421; 24 694; 27 789
exhibitions 10 821
groups and movements 13 728; 15 886; 21 422; 25 838; 26 15, 289
works 7 695; 16 649, *649*, 650, 721
Terranova, Charles of Aragon, Duke of 12 242
Terranova, Guglielmo *see* NIEULANDT, WILLEM VAN, I
Terranova, Matteo da 30 514*
terra portugesa 7 894
terra sigillata *see under* POTTERY → wares
Terrassa
S María 6 564; 29 262, 275
S Miquel 29 262, 275
S Pedro 4 *423*; 29 262
Terrasse, Henri 16 548; 30 514*
Terrasson, Pierre *see* BERCHOD, PIERRE
terra verde *see* PIGMENTS → types → green earth
Terray, Antoine-Jean, Vicomte de Rosières 30 515
Terray, Joseph-Marie 5 380; 11 663; 20 135; 22 210; 24 787; 30 514–15*
Terraza, Eduardo 22 21
terrazzi *see under* FLOORS → types
Terregles Church 13 211
Terreni, Giuseppe Maria 16 719
terres jaspées *see under* POTTERY → wares
terrets *see* CHARIOT FITTINGS
Terribilia, Antonio 4 272; 30 515*
Terribilia, Francesco 4 272, 280; 30 515–16*
Terriesi, Francesco 21 29
Terro, Francesco *see* TERZIO, (GIOVANNI) FRANCESCO
Terry, Carden 7 858; 30 516*
works 16 32, *32*; 33 204
Terry, Eli 7 446; 31 629
Terry, Emilio 11 727
Terry, Fernando Belaúnde *see* BELAÚNDE TERRY, FERNANDO
Terry, Jane *see* WILLIAMS, JANE
Terry, Leonard 23 327; 30 516*
works 2 705, 738; 7 470; 23 54
Terry, (John) Quinlan 23 490; 30 516–17*
collaboration 10 462
groups and movements 22 743
works 2 361; 7 385; 10 242; 23 359; 32 556
Terskel/Threshold 24 452
Tersteeg, Jan 13 295
Ter Step'annos 9 733
Tertiaries 11 707

Tertio, Francesco *see* TERZIO, (GIOVANNI) FRANCESCO
Tertullian 6 173; 22 42, 411; 25 46
Teruel
Cathedral 13 68; 29 263, 290, 323
ceiling 2 529
metalwork 29 337
paintings 29 275
metalwork 29 335
pottery 29 323, 326, 327, 328
S Martín 29 263, 323
S Pedro 22 255
S Salvador 22 255; 29 263, 323
Terumasa Ikeda *see* IKEDA TERUMASA
Terumoto Mōri *see* MŌRI TERUMOTO
Tervarent, Guy de 10 213; 15 91
Tērvete 18 847
Tervuren
hunting-lodge 19 650; 27 309
Koninklijk Museum voor Midden Afrika 3 616; 29 69
collections 1 437, 439
library 3 618
musical instruments 22 376
Tervuren colony 4 529; 5 44; 11 359; 14 838
Terwesten, Augustinus 3 798; 14 651; 22 846; 30 517*
Terwesten, Matthäus 3 798; 14 42, 651; 30 517
Terwesten, Pieter 14 622; 22 910
Terylene 30 543
Terzaga, Isotta de *see* ISOTTA DE TERZAGA
Terzi, Aleardo 31 268
Terzi, Filippo 30 517–19*
attributions 1 740
collaboration 32 156
patrons and collectors 14 662; 27 274
pupils 20 462
works 1 741; 14 474, 475; 23 453; 25 291; 26 516; 27 274, 482; 28 499, *499*; 30 *518*; 31 1, 102, *178*, 745
Terzi, Girolamo 19 713
Terzi, Margherita 16 780
Terzio, (Giovanni) Francesco 8 384; 13 912; 24 331; 30 519*
Tesauro, Emanuele 1 658; 10 176; 23 770; 24 837; 28 11; 33 276
Tesch, Nils 2 603
Teschendorff, John 2 762
Teseo 8 806
Těšetice-Kyjovice 25 504
Teshigahara, Hiroshi 17 381
Teshigahara, Sōfu 17 381
Teshikago, Akan Wagoto Museum 22 249
Teshima, Ted 22 120
Tesi, Mauro Antonio 1 633; 4 280; 30 519–20*
Tessai Hokuba 17 177
Tessai Tomioka *see* TOMIOKA TESSAI
Tessari, Battista 30 520
Tessari, Girolamo 30 520*
Tesseki Fujimoto *see* FUJIMOTO TESSEKI
Tessel, Christoffer 5 817
tessellae *see* MOSAICS
tessellarii 22 154
tessellated floors *see* MOSAICS → types → *opus tessellatum*
Tesselschade, Maria 22 885, 898
Tessenow, Heinrich 30 520–21*
collaboration 9 237
groups and movements 2 288; 8 824, 826; 26 405
pupils 28 179; 29 377; 32 750
works 8 824; 12 378, 416; 14 362, 363; 30 *521*, 682
tesserae *see* MOSAICS → materials
Tesshi Nagamo *see* NAGAMO, TESSHI
Tesshū Tokusai 17 170; 30 521–2*
Tessié du Motay, C. M. 7 575

Tessier, Germaine 22 441
Tessin, Carl Gustav, Count 12 634; 29 689; 30 523–4*, *524*
collections 23 669; 30 119, 727
drawings 8 209; 9 176, 229; 14 692; 18 626; 21 85; 24 834; 30 522, 523
engravings 11 173
interior decoration 30 88
paintings 4 516; 14 692; 19 117; 23 174; 30 118, 856
prints 25 631
Tessin, Nicodemus (1615-81) 12 135; 30 522*
assistants 29 399
house 2 550
patrons and collectors 14 288; 29 690
works 5 817; 11 31, 344; 20 866; 29 685, 687; 30 69, 70, *71*, 93, *93*, 522*
Tessin, Nicodemus (1654-1728) 3 752; 12 135; 30 522–3*
assistants 6 519
collaboration 14 177; 25 460; 30 522
patrons and collectors 8 650; 13 668; 14 288; 29 690; 30 117
personal collection 4 128; 30 163
pupils 1 152; 14 177
teachers 11 274
works 8 660, 725, 739; 11 344, *468*, 470; 20 391; 29 685, 689, *689*, 690, 840; 30 70, 85, 93, 522; 31 *684*, 694
Tessitori, L. P. 17 738
Tessmann, Günter 10 788, 789
Testa, Baron 17 444
Testa, Clorindo 30 524–5*; 31 757
collaboration 3 485, 712
groups and movements 2 401; 13 725
works 2 397; 30 *525*
Testa, Giovanni Cesare 30 528
Testa, Pasquale 16 726
Testa, Pietro 7 569; 9 93; 26 771; 30 525–9*
commentaries 27 726
methods 19 354; 21 763
patrons and collectors 1 728; 12 764; 25 412; 26 773
works 1 113, 659, 663; 2 163; 6 570; 9 222; 10 551; 16 672; 30 *526*, *528*
Testard, Alphonse 4 80
Testard, Robinet 30 529–30*
works 20 613; 30 *529*
Testelin, Gilles 30 530
Testelin, Henri 30 530*
reproductive prints by others 18 46
works 4 *550*
writings 6 570; 8 612; 24 494
Testelin, Louis 30 530*
testers 3 483
Testolini, Gaetano 28 86
Testone, Gaspare 27 200
testoni *see under* COINS → types
testoons *see under* COINS → types
Testore, Caterina del 31 5
Test Roll *see under* LONDON → Palace of Westminster → House of Lords
testudinate houses *see under* HOUSES → types
Tesuque (NM) 22 606
Tétard, Jean 11 623
Tetbury Market Hall (Glos) 31 239
Tête du Lion 25 *470*, 479, 484
rock art 25 *479*
Te Teko Meeting House 23 54
Teteven 5 160
Teti (*reg c.* 2325–*c.* 2291 BC) 9 *776*; 10 64, 80; 27 812
Teti, Girolamo 3 207, 208; 5 454
works 3 *207*
Tetiaroa 28 921
Tetitla 21 207

Tetla **21** 205
Tetlamixteca **21** 736
Teton **22** 551
Tétouan
ceramics **22** 129
embroidery **16** 448
Escuela Preparatoria de Bellas Artes **22** 129
scrolls **21** 49
synagogues **17** 551
Tetova, Ali **1** 544
Tetova, Hasan **1** 544
Tetovo **19** *882*
Dervish School *see* Municipal Museum
Municipal Museum **19** 882
tetraconch churches *see under* CHURCHES → types
Tetrahelix Inc. **11** 835
tetrapyrgia see under FORTS → types
tetrastyle **30** 530*
tetrastyle houses *see under* HOUSES → types
Tetrawan
sculpture **15** *501*
Tetri Tskharo Church **12** 321
Tetrode, Willem Danielsz. van **30** 530–31*; **33** 29
works **22** 857, *858*; **29** 571
Tetsugoro Suzuki *see* SUZUKI TETSUGORO
Tetsugorō Yorozu *see* YOROZU, TETSUGORŌ
Tetsuharu *see* TŌGŌ, SEJI
Tetsujo Kuwana *see* KUWANA, TETSUJO
Tetsumi Kudō *see* KUDŌ, TETSUMI
Te-tsung, Emperor (T'ang; *reg* 780–805) *see* DEZONG, Emperor
Tetsuō Hidaka *see* HIDAKA TETSUŌ
Tetsuo Kanō *see* KANŌ, TETSUO
Tetsuo Okada *see* OKADA, TETSUO
Tetsurō Komai *see* KOMAI, TETSURŌ
Tetsurō Yoshida *see* YOSHIDA, TETSURŌ
Tetsuya Noda *see* NODA, TETSUYA
Tetsuzan Mōri *see* MŌRI TETSUZAN
Tett, A **1** 131; **17** 833; **24** 440
Tetteh, E. K. **12** 509
Tettelbach, Gottfried Benjamin **12** 263
Tetter, Mikołaj **25** 130
Tettnang Palace **12** 369
Tetum **9** 164
Tetzcotzingo **21** *193*, 208, 211; **23** 825; **30** 531–2*
Tetzel (family) **24** 573
Tetzen-Lund, Christian **8** 759; **19** 799; **30** 532–3*
Teubel, Jan Zygmunt *see* DEYBEL, JAN ZYGMUNT
Teuber, Johannes Martin **29** 386
Teucher **31** 70
Teuchitlán
architecture **21** 216–17; **33** 102
crypts **21** 217
platforms **21** 217
pyramids **21** 197
tombs **21** 216
wall paintings **21** 217
Teuchitlán-El Refugio **21** 217
Teufel, Nicolaus **33** 295
Teuffel, Georg **10** 537
Teuffenbach, Christophe von **1** 584
Teugels, Jean **18** 577
Teugels-Schippers **3** 585
Teulon, Samuel **30** 533
Teulon, S(amuel) S(anders) **8** 48; **30** 533–4*
works **30** *533*
Teulon, W. Milford **30** 533
Teuné, François-Gaspard **11** 591
Teunissen, Cornelis *see* ANTHONISZ., CORNELIS
Teunisz., Barent **26** 153
Teurnia, Friedhofskirche **2** 776
Teutenberg, Anton **23** 62, 71
Teutones **6** 159
Teutonic Order **6** 531; **24** 698; **25** 93, 126; **30** 534–6*
amber **1** 762
architecture **3** 57, 58; **6** 57; **17** 505; **21** 564; **26** 706
castles **20** *185*, 185–6; **30** 535
coats of arms **14** 411
gonfanons **11** *147*
paintings **14** 87
patronage **30** 535–6*
sculpture **28** 861
tombs **30** *535*
Teutsch, János Máttis *see* MÁTTIS TEUTSCH, JÁNOS
Teutsche, Der see NEUE TEUTSCHE, DER
Teutsche Mercur **33** 116
Tevan, Margit **15** 8
Tevdore **12** 323
Teversall (Notts), St Catherine's **24** 577
Tevet, Nahum **30** 536*
Teviot, Robert Spencer, Lord *see* SPENCER, ROBERT, Lord Teviot
Tewa **22** 606
Tewar **15** 290
Tewin Water **3** 522
Tewkesbury Abbey (Glos) **22** 144; **23** 491; **26** 590, *590*; **30** 729
ballflower **3** *121*
bosses **13** *83*
chantry chapels **7** 267
piers (ii) (masonry) **24** 751
pinnacles **24** 826
stained glass **14** 422
tomb of Hugh, Lord Despenser **31** 271
Trinity Chapel **31** 271
vaults **32** 88, 92
Tewkesbury Baptist meeting house **7** 283
Tew Park **5** 169
Texaco **30** 390
Texas Homecare **10** 285
Texcoco
Franciscan Monastery **21** 373
gardens **12** 71
textiles **21** *261*, 394
Texcotzingo *see* TETZCOTZINGO
Texedor, Rafael *see* TEJEO, RAFAEL
Texier, Charles (-Félix Marie) **9** 72; **16** 548; **30** 536–7*; **31** 456
collaboration **5** 340; **25** 722
works **9** 527
Texier Lavigne, Paul **22** 35
textiles **7** 731; **14** 425; **30** 537–67*, *549*
cleaning **30** 566*
conservation **30** *563*, 563–7*, *564*, *567*
dating methods **9** 492; **11** 309
display **30** 565*
historical and regional traditions
Aboriginal Australia **1** 64; **2** 768
Achaemenid **1** 118
Afghanistan **1** 209–10*; **16** 451
Africa **1** 348–9, 378, 406, 423–4*, 428; **23** 131; **30** 562
Akan **1** 295
Albania **1** 544–5*
Algeria **1** 636; **16** 448*
Anatolia, ancient **1** 881
Ancient Near East **1** 855, 856, 879–83*, *882*; **30** 774
Anglo-Saxon **2** 83–4*
Antilles, Lesser **2** 151–2*
Argentina **2** 402–3*
Armenia (Europe) **2** 442–3*
Asante **1** 290, 294, 424
Australia **2** 766–9*
Austria **2** 823–6*
textiles
historical and regional traditions—cont.
Azerbaijan **2** 900–901*
Bactria **6** 214
Bali (Indonesia) **15** 793*, 806
Bamana **1** 285, 294; **3** 136–7
Bamum **3** 153
Bangladesh **3** 168*
Barbados **2** 151
Baule **1** 294; **3** 408; **8** 22
Belgium **3** 578, 605*; **26** 703
Benin Republic **1** 349
Bhutan **3** 914, 915–16*
Bolivia **4** 266–7*
Bosnia **4** 462
Brazil **4** 724*
Britain **19** 418; **21** 600
Buddhism **5** *104*; **6** 706; **18** 374
Bulgaria **5** 161*
Burma **5** 247–9*
Byzantine **9** 663–9*
Cambodia **5** 502–3*; **6** 432
Cameroon **1** 400
Canada **5** 586–8*
Cape Verde Islands **1** 424
Carib **29** 194
Central Asia, Eastern **6** 303, 316–18*, *317*
Central Asia, Western **6** 247–8*
Bactria **6** 214
Islamic **16** 435, 443, 451*
Champa **6** 432–3*
Chancay **6** 440; **29** 181
Chavín culture **29** 180
Chile **6** 599–600*
Chimú **6** 606*; **29** 181, 207
China **1** 881; **6** 706; **7** 43–53*, 144–5; **29** 627; **30** 559, 560, 561
Han period (206 BC–AD 220) **7** 114, 117
Qing period (1644–1911) **7** *51*
Colombia **7** 602; **29** 152
Coptic **7** 826–8*; **9** 492, 664; **16** 431
Côte d'Ivoire **1** 290; **8** 22
Cyprus **8** 363, 366*
Czech Republic **8** 418*, 420–21*
Dan (Africa) **8** 490
Denmark **8** 753–6*
Early Christian (*c*. AD 250–843) **9** 663–9*
Ecuador **9** 709–10
Edo (Africa) **9** 736
Egypt **7** 826–7*; **16** 431–2*, 441–2*
Egypt, ancient **9** 823–4*; **10** 74–6*; **30** *563*
England **10** 271, 348*; **21** 600–601; **28** *565*; **30** 561–2
Anglo-Saxon **2** 83–4*
Romanesque **26** 703
18th cent. **9** 284
19th cent. **22** *144*; **32** *722*
Etruscan **10** *635*, 635–6*
Fiji **11** 69
Finland **11** 109–10*
Fon **1** 295, 424
France **11** 574, 576, 637*; **30** 562
Romanesque **26** 703
18th cent. **9** 284
French Guiana **1** 424
Fulani **11** 829–30*; **23** 128
Georgia **12** 330–31*
Germany **12** 462*, *463*, 469–70*; **26** 703
Gothic **13** 194–7*
Greece **13** 355–7*
Greece, ancient **13** 604*
Guatemala **13** *766*, 766–7*
Guinea-Bissau **13** 835
Hausa **1** 251; **14** 231–2*
Herzegovina **4** 462
Hinduism **15** 176, 548, 599, 669, 673
Huari culture **14** 829*
Hungary **14** 904; **15** 11–12*
textiles
historical and regional traditions—cont.
Ibibio **15** 64, *64*
Iceland **15** 73–4*
Igbo **1** 349
Ijo **1** 349
Inca **15** 163–4*; **29** 135, 181, 207
India, Republic of **15** 175–7*
Indian subcontinent **15** 200, 201, 548, 549, 562, 658–9*, 660–72*, 673*, 674*, 722–3; **30** 559–60, 561
Assam **15** 662
Bengal **15** 201, 723
Deccan **15** 664
Gujarat **15** 202, 671*, 672, 723
Hinduism **15** 599, 669, 673
Islamic **15** 664*; **16** 452*
Jainism **15** 565, *566*
kalamkārī **15** 673–4*
Orissa **15** 636
Punjab **15** 669
Rajasthan **15** 669, 671*
8th cent. AD **28** 309
18th cent. **15** 548; **29** *233*
Indonesia **15** 758, 789*, 790–92*, 793*, 794–6*, 807*, 810; **29** 239
Iran **16** 435*, 443, 449, 451*, 546
Iran, ancient **1** *882*, 882–3
Iraq **16** 433–5*
Ireland **16** 33–5*, *34*; **30** 562
Iroquois **22** 628
Islamic **6** 557; **14** 428; **16** 124, 428–30*, 431*, 439*, 443–7*, 503; **31** 20–22
Afghanistan **16** 451
Algeria **16** 448*
Central Asia, Western **16** 435, 443, 451*
Egypt **16** 431–2*, 441–2*
India, Republic of **15** 176
Indian subcontinent **15** 664*; **16** 452*
Indonesia **15** 758
Iran **16** 435*, 443, 451*
Iraq **16** 433–5*
Java **15** 758
Morocco **16** 447–8
North Africa **16** 436–7*, 439–40*, 447–8*
Ottoman **16** 121, 444, 447
Sicily **16** 437
Spain **16** 436–7*, 439–40*
Syria **16** 441–2*
Transoxiana **16** 435, 443
Tunisia **16** 448
Turkestan (region) **16** 451
Turkey **16** 444
Uzbekistan **16** 451
Yemen **16** 438–9*
Israel **16** 569*
Italy **10** *635*, 635–6*; **16** 714, 752–4*
Jainism **15** 565, *566*
Japan **17** 235, 297, 305–18*, 326–7, 353–7*, 390, 392; **29** 627; **30** 559, 560, 561; **31** 260
Edo period (1600–1868) **17** *354*
Momoyama period (1568–1600) **12** 621
Nara period (AD 710–94) **17** *309*, 386
Yayoi period (*c*. 300 BC–*c*. AD 300) **33** 511
Java **15** 758, 790–92*; **29** 239
Jewish art **1** 881; **16** 451
Jukun **17** 680
Kazakhstan **17** 867–8*
Kenya **17** 906
Khmer **5** 502–3*
Khwarazm **31** 21
Kongo **18** 484
Korea **18** 372–6*
textiles
historical and regional traditions—cont.
Kuba (iii) (Zaïre) **1** 295
Kyrgyzstan **18** 569*
Laos **18** 770–74*, *773*
Libya **19** 324
Macedonia (ii) (former Yugoslavia) **19** 885*
Madagascar **20** 36, 38*, 40, *40*
Malaysia **20** 175–6*, 182
Maldives, Republic of **20** 189
Mali **20** 198–9*, *199*
Malta (Republic of) **20** 218–19*
Maori **20** 357–8
Maya **13** 766, *766*; **21** 259
Mende (Sierra Leone) **21** 117
Mesoamerica, Pre-Columbian **21** 181–2, 259, 260–62*, *261*
Mesopotamia **1** 881
Mexico **21** 394*, *394*
Milagro-Quevedo **29** 152
Moche (culture) **29** 135
Mongolia **21** 876
Montenegro **22** 19
Morocco **16** 447–8
Mossi **22** 199*
Mughal **3** 168
Muisca **29** 152
Native North Americans **22** 562, 618–28*, *625*, 663
Navajo **22** *625*
Nazca **29** 180
Ndebele **29** 104
Nepal **22** *791*, 791–2*
Netherlands, the **22** 864, 897–900*, *898*; **30** 561
Romanesque **26** 703
New Zealand **23** 73–4*
Niger **23** 128
Nigeria **1** 349; **15** *64*; **23** 131; **30** 561
North Africa **16** 436–7*, 439–40*, 447–8*
Norway **23** 238–41*; **32** 523
Nupe **23** 302
Ottoman **16** 121, 444–7*; **23** *639*
Pacific Islands **23** 723
Pakistan **23** 802*
Paracas culture **24** 89–90
Paraguay **24** 100*
Parthian **1** 882
Peru **23** *564*; **24** 512–13*; **29** *182*
Philippines **24** 623–4*
Poland **25** 131–4*
Portugal **25** 315–17*
Prehistoric art **25** 546; **29** 228
Romanesque **26** 703*
Romania **26** 720–22*
Rome, ancient **1** 881; **9** 251; **26** 855; **27** 112–14*, *113*, *114*
Russia **19** 418; **27** 430–31*
Ryūkyū Islands **27** 470–71*
St Kitts **2** 151
St Lucia **2** 151
Sasanian **1** 882–3
Scandinavia **32** 523
Scotland **20** *25*; **28** 248, 250, 264–7*, *265*
Senufo **1** 258, 290
Serbia **28** 456–7*, 458*
Sicily **16** 437
Slovenia **28** 863
Society Islands **28** 922–3
Sogdiana **16** 435
Songye **29** 69
South Africa **29** 104
South America, Pre-Columbian **23** *564*; **24** 89–90; **29** 134–5, 151–2*, 155, 181, *182*, 184*, 194*, 207–8
South-east Asia **29** 228, 232–3, *233*, 235–6
Spain **29** 301, 346–51*
Islamic **16** 436–7*, 439–40*
Sri Lanka **29** 476–7*
Sumatra **15** 794–5*

textiles
historical and regional traditions—cont.
Surinam **1** 424; **30** 13
Swaziland **30** 63
Sweden **19** 418; **30** 114–15*
Switzerland **30** 148*, *150*, 150–52*
Syria **16** 441–2*
Syria-Palestine **1** 881; **30** 180, 182
Tajikistan **30** 253
Tarascan **30** 342
Thailand **5** 503; **6** 432; **30** 619–22*, 623–8*
Tibet **5** *104*; **30** 845–6*
Togo **1** 349; **31** 73
Transoxiana **16** 443
Tunisia **16** 436, 448
Turkestan (region) **16** 451
Turkey **16** 444; **23** *639*
Ukraine **31** 563–4
United States of America **10** 852; **21** 601; **31** 616–17, 655–7*, *657*, 659*, 660–62*
Bangladesh **3** 168
18th cent. **25** 666
Uruguay **31** 756–7*
Uzbekistan **16** 451
Valdivia culture **29** 152
Venezuela **32** 166, 177–8*
Vietnam **6** 432–3*; **32** 489–90*, *490*
Viking **32** 523
Wales **32** 790*
Yemen **16** 438–9*
Yoruba **1** 242; **33** 559*
Zaïre **1** 349
legislation **8** 35, 36; **25** 315–16
lighting **7** 732
materials
airbrushes **1** 494
alpaca hair **27** 641; **29** *182*
bark **1** 493; **7** 43; **31** 143
beads **17** 386; **25** 546
dyes **6** 249; **7** 826; **13** 194
feathers **21** 261; **29** 207–8
flax **16** 431
fur **21** 261
glass **25** 546
glazes **16** 433; **31** 21
glues **1** 156
gold **15** 793, 794; **16** *753*; **17** 313; **20** 175; **28** 716; **29** 152
gold leaf **20** 176
grounds **13** 708
gum arabic **20** 176
hair **3** 915; **16** 449; **22** 791
hemp **7** 43, 45
inscriptions **16** 430, 431, 432, 433, 434, *438*, 439, 441–2, 450; **31** 20–22, *21*
mud **1** 285
nettles **1** 493; **3** 915; **22** 791
paper **17** 305
raffia **20** *40*
resist *see* RESIST
sequins **15** 795
shells **21** 259
silver **17** 313; **28** 716
silver leaf **17** 314
skins **17** 305; **21** 261
threads **30** 537–43*, *540*, *543*
waxes **20** 176; **33** 1
yarn **15** 795
technical examination **30** 410–11*, 565–6*
techniques
braiding **22** 626; **30** 550
calligraphy **17** 235
dyeing **9** 490, 491; **10** 74–5*; **20** 367; **30** 554–6*, *555*, *557*, 557–8*, 559*
Indian subcontinent **15** 667*, 670*, 672*
Islamic **16** 457
Japan **17** 308, 314
Mali **20** 198
textiles
techniques
dyeing—cont.
Scotland **28** 266
embroidery *see* EMBROIDERY
gilding **12** 621
knotting **30** 550
linking **30** 549
looping **10** 75; **29** 179; **30** 549
looping, crossed **30** 549
looping, inter-connected **30** 549
mass production **17** 317; **21** 600; **31** 656
netting *see* LACE → types → lacis
netting, knotless *see* looping, crossed
painting **5** *104*; **6** 303; **15** 548, 565, *566*, 636, 673–4*, 806, 807; **16** 434; **17** 313, 314; **30** 559–60*
pinking **30** 554
printing **30** 561–2*
Ancient Near East **1** 855
Australia **2** 768
China **7** 117, 144
Germany **12** 469
Indian subcontinent **15** 668–70*
Iran **16** 450
Iraq **16** 434
Ireland **16** *34*
Islamic **16** 434, 451
Netherlands, the **22** 899–900
Russia **27** 431
Ukraine **31** 564
United States of America **31** 657
screenprinting **28** 299; **30** 562
sewing **30** 562–3*
slashing **30** 554
spinning (textile) **30** 539–40*
sprang **29** 179; **30** 550
stamping **1** 856; **6** 249; **17** 309; **30** 553
stencilling **7** 49; **11** 69; **17** *309*, 309–10, 313, 314, *314*, 315, 355; **29** 627; **30** 560–61*
twining **22** 627
split-ply **30** 550
twining, weft **22** 626; **29** 179; **30** 550
watered **30** 553
weaving **15** 660*; **16** 429, 434–5; **29** 179; **30** 543–9*, *544*, *545*, *546*, *547*, 550–54*
types
aya **17** 306, 312, 313
Baghdad Group **16** 436
batik *see* BATIK
brocades *see* BROCADES
cambric *see* CAMBRIC
Chinese weave **17** 314
compound warp-faced **7** 46
corduroy *see* CORDUROY
cotton *see* COTTON
crochet *see* CROCHET
damask *see* DAMASK
dhaka cloth **22** 791, *791*
fustian *see* FUSTIAN
gauze *see* GAUZE
ikat *see* IKAT
kain songket **20** 175–6
knitting *see* KNITTING
lace *see* LACE
linen *see* LINEN
lùn taya **5** 248, *248*
macramé *see* MACRAMÉ
maśrū **15** 664*
metal-ground **16** 450
moiré *see* MOIRÉ
Nhieu **32** 489
nishiki **17** 306–7, 311, 313
open-weave **17** 313
plain weave **17** 306, 312, 313; **21** 261
pleated **10** 76
rølakan **23** 240
satin *see* SATIN
textiles
types—cont.
silk *see* SILK
slit-tapestry **21** 261
tapestries *see* TAPESTRIES
tatting *see* TATTING
The **32** 490
velvet *see* VELVET
velveteen *see* VELVETEEN
warp float **21** 261
warp-pile **7** 46
weft pile **21** 261
weft-warp openwork **21** 261
wool *see* WOOL
yuzen **17** 315, *316*
zandanījī **16** 435
uses
armour **16** 503
book covers **4** 349, 350
ceiling paintings **15** 562
chess sets **6** 557
collagraphs **7** 558
dolls **31** 260*
etchings **10** 562
fibre art **11** 54–5
grounds **3** 914
hangings **15** 636
interior decoration **3** 578; **11** 574, 576; **22** 864
lacquer **17** 297; **18** 606
manuscript covers **15** 548, 549
manuscripts **15** 549; **20** 327
masks **17** 390, 392
mirror-cases **10** 636
painting **15** 599
paper **7** 114
photography **24** 651
scrolls **28** 309, 310
sculpture **6** 214, 706
stucco **29** 813
tea ceremonies **7** 53
upholstery **31** 680
waxes **33** 2
windows **29** 301
textiles guilds *see under* GUILDS → types
Textron Corporation **13** 9
texture screens *see* PHOTOGRAPHY → materials → screens
Teyateyaneng Handicrafts Centre *see* TY HANDICRAFTS CENTRE
Teybell, Jan Zygmunt *see* DEYBEL, JAN ZYGMUNT
Teyfel, Jan **25** 426
Teyjat **25** 487, 492
Teyler, Johannes **25** 622; **30** 568*
Teyler (van der Hulst), Pieter **13** 894; **22** 905; **30** 568*; **32** 466
Teylers Museum *see under* HAARLEM
Teylingen Castle **22** 822
Teymurova, R. **2** 902
Teynard, Félix **30** 568–9*
Teyssedre, B. **2** 537
TF, Monogrammist **25** 103
TG, Monogrammist **11** 221
al-Tha'alabi **16** 456; **23** 561
Thaaning, Niels **23** 225
Thaasetimu
dress **10** *43*
Thabaud, Hyacinthe-Joseph-Alexandre *see* LATOUCHE, HENRI DE
Thabit ibn Qurra **2** 650
Thabong Cooperative **19** 241
Thacker, Christopher **12** 65
Thackeray, William Makepeace **9** 209; **22** 743; **30** 569*; **32** 794
Thaddeus, Henry Jones **16** 17
Thadominbya **5** 237
Thadou Kuki **15** 205
Thaenae **3** 375
Thaeter, Julius **7** 872
Thai **30** 571
Thailand **29** *225*; **30** 569–640*, *571*
amber **3** 441
appliqué **30** *626*
Thailand—cont.
architecture **2** 884; **30** 574–5*, 576–81*, 582–4*, 585–8*, 589–92*
brick **2** 884; **4** *795*
Buddhism **30** 576–7
military **21** 595
wood **30** 585–6*, *586*
art history **2** 530; **29** 241
bags **30** *626*
bai sema *see* boundary stones
bamboo **30** *637*
banners **30** 612–13, *613*
barges **30** 639
basketwork **30** 630*
beads **30** 633
beadwork **3** 441
betel sets **30** 631*
blankets **30** *621*
boats **30** 631*
book covers **20** 327
books **30** 613, *614*
boundary stones **30** 575
bowls **30** *611*
brick **2** 884; **4** *795*, 796
bronze **4** 855; **29** 228, 229; **30** 593–5*, 596–7, *597*, *598*, *601*, 601–2*, *602*, *605*, *607*, 633
caves **29** 226
ceramics **5** 12; **29** 232; **30** 608–9*, 611–12*
chariots **30** 639
chests **30** 618
clay **30** 596
coffins **30** 639
coins **30** 631–2*
coral **3** 441
costumes **30** 629
cotton **30** *621*, *626*
cupboards **30** 618
doors **9** 163, *163*
dress **30** 619*, 622–8*, *625*
drums (musical instruments) **22** 376; **30** *637*, 637
dyeing **30** 558
earthenwares **29** *228*
education (art) **30** 640*
embroidery **30** 625, *625*, *626*
enamel **30** 611, 632*
ephemeral art **30** 632–3*
figurines **29** 228; **30** *511*
flower arrangements **30** 632–3
flutes (musical instruments) **30** *637*
fortifications **21** 595
garden design **12** 102
gardens **12** 102–4*, *103*
gates **30** 639
gems **12** 268
gilding **12** 625, II2
glass **18** 604; **30** 633*
glazes **30** 610
gold **30** *619*, 631, 635–6*
gold leaf **30** 618
gongs **30** 637
granaries **30** 639
halls **30** 575
headdresses **3** 441
houses **30** 591–2, 639
iconography **29** 826; **30** 573–4*, 594, 635
ikat **5** 502, 503; **30** 554
inks **15** 850
inlays **30** 636*, *636*
iron **29** 228
jade **7** 112
jewellery **30** 633–4*
lacquer **30** 617–19*, *619*, 631, *636*
urushi **18** 604
limestone **30** *595*
lintels **30** 599–600
manuscript illumination **30** 613–14*, *614*
masks **30** 629, *629*
metalwork **30** 635–6*
Thailand—cont.
monasteries **2** *886*; **29** *910*; **30** 574–5, 582, 585–6, *586*, 587–8, *588*
mother-of-pearl **30** 636*, *636*
musical instruments **30** 636–7*
new towns **17** 686
niello **30** 635–6
ornament **23** 555
painting **30** 612*, 613–14*, 616–17*
Buddhism **30** 612–14*, *613*, *617*
wall **12** 625; **30** 615–16*; **32** 804
Buddhism **30** *615*, 615–16*
palaces **30** 575, 588*, *589*
palm leaves **30** 613
paper **30** 613
pediments **12** II2
periodicals **24** 437
phra bot *see* banners
pipes (musical) **30** *637*
pots **30** *611*
pottery **29** 227; **30** 609, 610–12*
prang *see* tower-sanctuaries
puppets **30** 628–9*
religion **30** 573–4*
reliquaries **26** 151
repoussé **30** 635
rock art **29** *227*
rock crystal **26** 487
sandstone **30** *600*, 606
sculpture **5** 484; **29** 231; **30** 593*, 597–8*, 599–601*, 603–4*, 605–6*, 607–8*
bronze **30** 573, 593–5*, 596–7, *597*, *598*, *601*, 601–2*, *602*, *605*, *607*
Buddhism **5** 100; **28** *640*; **29** *911*; **30** 573–4, 593–5*, *594*, *595*, 596–7*, *597*, *598*, 599*, *600*, *601*, 601–4*, *602*, *605*, 605–6*, 607, *607*
Hinduism **30** 574, 598
relief **29** *827*; **30** *604*
stone **30** 593–5*, *594*
shrines (i) (cult) **28** 639, 640, *640*, III1; **30** 638*
silk **5** 503
silver **30** *626*, 631, 635–6*
skirts **30** *626*
staffs **30** 639
stone **29** 227–8; **30** 593–5*, *594*, 633
stonewares **30** *610*, 610–11, *611*
stucco **29** 826–7, *827*; **30** 595*, 602–3*, *604*
Buddhism **29** 826
stupas **29** 866–7; **30** 576, *576*, *583*, 583–4, *584*, *586*, 586, *587*
tablets **30** 596, 606, 638*
teak **12** II2; **30** 631, 639
temples
Buddhism **3** 164, *164*; **30** 446, *579*, 581, 589–90
Khmer **30** 578–81
terracotta **29** 228; **30** 511, *511*, 595*
textiles **5** 503; **6** 432; **30** 619–22*, 623–8*
theatre **30** 628–30*
thrones **30** 785
tools **29** 227–8
tower-sanctuaries **4** *795*; **30** 575, 587
trade **18** 252; **29** 230
ceramics **30** 609, 611–12
porcelain **4** 175
treatises **30** 614
tunics **30** *626*
turbans **30** *626*
turquoise **3** 441
urban planning **30** 592–3*
vases **30** *610*
vessels **29** *228*
weapons **30** 638*
wood **20** 327; **30** 585–6, *586*, *637*, 639
wood-carvings **12** II2; **30** 639*
xylophones **30** 636

Thailand—cont.
see also SOUTH-EAST ASIA
Thair *see* TER
Thaj **2** *246*, 249, 252; **27** 877
coins **2** 261
figurines **2** 260
fortifications **2** 250
incense burners **2** 269
pottery **2** 268
seals **2** 270
vessels **2** 273
Thakali **22** 794
Thaler, Franz Christian **14** 834
Thaler, Raphael **15** 865
Thalhofer, Johann Baptist **5** 339
Thallherr, Johann Josef **5** 81
Thallmayr, Nikolaus **22** 306
Thal Shrine **15** 265
Thame Park (Oxon), Abbot's Lodgings **10** 272
Thames Bank workshops **19** 614; **25** 805
Thame School **28** 156
Thames & Hudson **23** 8
Thamsen, Peter Christian **11** 473
Thamugadi **1** 634; **9** *510*; **23** 300; **28** 757; **30** 640–41*
Arch of Trajan **23** 491; **26** 868, 920, *920*; **31** 350
basilica **3** 328
markets **11** 328; **19** 889; **26** 871, 919
mosaics **27** 63
Rogatinus Library **19** 312
Roman capitolium **26** 867, 919, 921; **30** 436
South Baths **26** 872
urban planning **26** 853, 921; **27** 3, 4
Thamyris **33** 307
Than, Mór **14** 315, 901; **30** 641*
Tha Na **18** 771
Thanatos Painter **13** 536; **32** 48
Thancoupie **1** 44, 64
Thandwei **5** 247
Thanet (Kent), Prospect Inn **25** 689
Thanet, Sackville Tufton, 8th Earl of *see* TUFTON, SACKVILLE, 8th Earl of Thanet
Thango, François **33** 596
Thang Tran Phanh **32** 482
Thanh Ho **6** 426
Thanh Hoa, Trach Lan Temple **32** 476
Thanh Lu **6** 426
Thanjavur **15** *294*, 305; **30** 641–3*
Art Gallery **15** 182; **30** 641
Brihadeshvara Temple *see* Rajarajeshvara Temple
bronze **15** 708
Darbar Hall **15** 647
metalwork **15** 709, 713; **21** 328
paintings **15** 652, 672
Rajarajeshvara Temple **7** 200; **15** 230, 309, 331–3, *332*, 516, 518, 560, *560*; **30** 642–3*
frescoes **30** 642–3, *643*
gopuras **13** 4
reliefs **30** 642
sculpture **15** *516*; **30** *642*, 643
Subrahmanya shrine **15** 399
wall paintings **15** 543
Sarasvati Mahal Library **15** 647
temples **15** 738
textiles **15** 177, 664, 672
wall paintings **15** 646, 647
Thann (Austria) **2** 799
Thann (France), St Thiébaut **10** 751–2; **11** *504*; **30** 643–4*
Thannhauser, Justin K. **12** 474
Thantia **9** 540
Thaon, Philippe de *see* PHILIPPE DE THAON
Thao Sin Kaeo **18** 770
Thaothong, Preecha **30** 617
Thapa, Bhimsen **22** 764
Thapahiti **22** 770–71
Thapar, Bal Krishen **17** 738
Thap Mam **6** 423, 430
Thapong International Artists' Workshop **4** 490
Thapsos **16** *621*; **23** 808; **25** *470*; **30** 644*
pottery **28** 653
Thap Thap **6** 432
Tharaud Factory **19** 398
Thari, Hagios Michailis **26** 293
Tharpaling **21** 848
Tharrats (i Vidal), Joan-Josep **3** 219; **8** 538; **30** 644*
Tharros **25** 732
architecture **25** 733
faience (i) (glass) **24** 645
fortifications **25** 733
ivory-carvings **25** 734
jewellery **25** 734, 735
seals **24** 645; **25** 734
Tharwas **9** 805
Thasian marble *see under* MARBLE → types
Thasos (island) **9** *511*; **13** *363*; **19** 880; **30** 645*
cenotaph **14** 466
coins **13** *585*, 586
figurines **13** 579
marble **26** 854; **27** 13, 826; **29** 702
metalwork **13** 568
plaques **9** 590
pottery **13** 504
reliefs **30** *645*
sculpture **13** 445, 451
Thasos (town) **26** *876*, *908*; **30** 645*
Basilica **9** 538
bronzes **13** 571
friezes **13** 390
marble **26** 875, 877
mosaics **13** 559
reliefs **30** *645*
stoa **13** 414
town walls **13** 394; **21** 556
Thasos, Polygnotos of *see* POLYGNOTOS OF THASOS
thatch **1** 306, 307, 308; **6** 692; **17** 47; **18** 266, 278; **27** 131
grasses **1** 307, 308
palm leaves **1** 306
Thatcher, Frederick **2** 705; **23** 53; **30** 646*; **33** 57
works **23** 53
Thatcher, John P. **20** 382
Thaton **5** *221*, 222, 225; **29** *225*, 231
ceramics **5** 254
inscriptions **5** 257
sculpture **5** 238
Thattha **15** *264*, 687; **23** *797*; **30** 646–7*
congregational mosque **15** 372; **22** 195; **30** 647
Makli Hill necropolis **30** 646
tomb-mosque of Nizam al-Din II **30** 646
tomb of Jam Nizam al-Din **15** 338
tomb of Mirza Jani Beg **30** 646
Thaulow, Frits (Johan Fredrik) **23** 225, 602, 603; **30** 647*
groups and movements **15** 156; **23** 225; **28** 814
pupils **22** 289; **33** 76
teachers **13** 776
works **28** 569
Thaur, Maria Himmelfartskirche **13** 188
Thausing, G. **10** 83
Thausing, Moritz **2** 833; **33** 159
Thax *see* DIONYSIOS
Thayer, Abbott Handerson **30** 647–8*
patrons and collectors **11** 748
works **11** 498
writings **5** 530
Thayngen-Weier **25** 502
Thay (Master) Temple **32** 472
Theaetetus **2** 350
Theatine Order **30** 648–9*
iconography **30** 648–9*
patronage **30** 649*
theatra **13** *385*, 385–6; **30** 650, 688*
theatre
historical and regional traditions
Bali (Indonesia) **15** 797, 802–4*
Burma **5** 251*
China **7** 122, 136–8*
Indonesia **15** 797*, 802–4*
Japan **17** 324*
Java **15** 797, *801*, 801–2*
Laos **18** 774–5*
Malaysia **20** 177*
Rome, ancient **27** 50
Thailand **30** 628–30*
Vietnam **32** 490–92*
types
bugaku **17** 333–4*, *334*
bunraku **17** 350
gagaku **17** 325
kabuki **17** 328–9*, 332–3*
kyōgen **17** 325, 328
nō **17** 324–5*, *326*, 326–8*; **28** 609
puppet **15** 800, *800*, 801*; **17** 350, 406
shadow
Bali (Indonesia) **15** 799–800*
Cambodia **5** 503, 504–5*, *505*
China **7** 122
France **26** 432
Indonesia **15** 797–800*, *797*, *798*, 804
Islamic **16** 544–5
Java **15** *797*, 797–9*, *798*
Malaysia **20** 177–8*, *178*
Ottoman **16** 544–5
Thailand **30** 628
Turkey **16** 544–5
water puppet **32** 491–2*, *491*
wayang beber **15** *801*, 801–2*
Théâtre-Antoine **15** 58; **30** 682, 685
Théâtre d'Art (Fort) **28** 484; **32** 739
Théâtre de l'Art (Lugné-Poe) *see* THÉÂTRE DE L'OEUVRE
theatre boxes **1** 124; **30** 666, 667, 670
Théâtre-Libre *see* THÉÂTRE-ANTOINE
Théâtre du Marais **30** 658, 659, 660, 669
Théâtre de l'Oeuvre **28** 484; **30** 682, 685; **32** 739
theatres **7** 688; **12** 105, 106; **16** 143; **27** 499; **30** 649–79*, 682–5*
acoustics **1** 122, 123–5*, *124*; **30** 662, 667
historical and regional traditions
Algeria **14** 564
Armenia (Europe) **10** *450*
Austria **10** 871; **30** 676
Belgium **30** 665*
Britain **30** 677
Bulgaria **5** 150
Byzantine **9** 553, 560
Cambodia **5** 503–4*
China **7** 135–6*, *136*
Crete **8** 155
Czech Republic **25** *429*; **30** 677
Early Christian (*c.* AD 250–843) **9** 553, 560
England **30** 660–62*, *662*, 673–4*, *685*
Greek Revival **28** *873*
Renaissance **30** 654
17th cent. **30** *661*, *673*
19th cent. **24** 641
20th cent. **25** *399*
Finland **14** *372*
France **30** *653*, 658–9*, 669–71*
Neo-classicism **19** *726*; **32** *768*
Post-modernism **4** *228*
Renaissance **30** 654
Roman **30** *652*
theatres
historical and regional traditions
France—cont.
17th cent. **30** *658*
18th cent. **29** 91; **30** *670*
Germany **14** 491; **30** 676*, *678*, *683*, 684; **32** 339
Baroque **14** 469
Expressionism **10** *697*
Neo-classicism **28** *99*
Renaissance Revival **28** *398*, *399*
Rococo **8** *290*
19th cent. **7** *582*
20th cent. **31** *877*
Greece, ancient **1** 123; **13** 380, 385–6*, *385*, 391, 403, 406, 418; **19** 234; **21** 341; **29** 488; **30** 650–51*, *651*
Hellenistic **24** *413*
Roman **26** 910
4th cent. BC **13** *402*
Helladic **19** 234
Holy Roman Empire (before 1648) **30** 665*
Italy **1** 125; **12** 114, 115, 119; **30** 650, 655–6*, *657*, 666–7*
Baroque **1** *601*
Mannerism **30** *655*
Neo-classicism **3** *196*; **23** *88*; **24** *758*; **28** *390*
Renaissance **30** 654
Roman **26** 873, *873*, 888–9, 891
16th cent. **27** 483–4; **28** *32*
17th cent. **1** 601; **30** *666*
Japan **33** 539
Libya **27** 485
Mexico **13** *730*; **21** *379*; **23** 208
Netherlands, the **30** 665*, 676
North Africa **26** 919, *920*, 921; **30** 652
Poland **32** *871*
Renaissance **11** 3
Rome, ancient **26** 749, 863, 864, 865, 873–4, 904, 912, 916, 923, 924; **27** 29, 30; **29** 488; **30** 651–2*
Algeria **14** 564
Crete **8** 155
France **30** *652*
Greece **26** 910
Italy **26** *873*, 873, 888–9, 891
Libya **27** 485
North Africa **26** 919, *920*, 921
Sicily **26** 873
Syria **2** 214; **4** *463*; **26** 918
Turkey **2** 605, *605*; **21** *543*
Russia **26** *732*; **27** *199*, *379*; **30** 677, 683, 684
Sicily **26** 873
Spain **30** 663*
Sweden **30** 675, *676*, 677
Switzerland **30** 665
Syria **2** 214; **4** *463*; **26** 918
Turkey **2** 605, *605*; **21** *543*
Ukraine **23** *354*
United States of America **1** *158*; **30** 677*
Venezuela **32** *171*
lighting **30** 657, 666, 669, 685
materials
brick **30** 667
cast iron **30** 650
concrete **30** 677
masonry **30** 667
steel **30** 677
stone **26** 749
wood **30** 667
types
anatomy **22** *739*
kabuki **17** 329–32*, *330*, *331*
nō **17** 325–6*
puppet **17** 406
see also CONCERT HALLS; OPERA HOUSES
theatre-temples *see under* TEMPLES → types
Theau, Louis **5** 838
Thebaldi, Francesco **2** 780
Thebes (i) (Egypt) **1** 756; **9** 773, *774*, 780; **10** 62, 76, 77, 93; **26** *921*; **30** 688–702*, *689*
art forms and materials
baskets **10** *41*
coffins **10** 12
colossal statues **9** 863; **28** 491
faience (i) (glass) **10** 48
furniture **10** 53; **27** 99
glass **10** 55, 58
harps **10** *65*
inscriptions **10** 83
jewellery **10** 31, 32
looms **10** 75
mummies **10** 66, 80, 91
mummy cases **10** 14
ostraca **9** 810, *810*, 811, *903*, 904
papyri **9** *905*
pottery **10** 27
reliefs **9** 799, 805, 868, 876, 881; **10** 37, 86; **22** 722
sculpture **9** 854, 873, 885; **10** 90
shabtis **10** 18, 19
silver **9** 655
statues **1** 793; **9** 855, 875, 879, *879*, 880, 886; **28** 491; **30** 236
statuettes **1** 770
stelae **29** 615
tomb paintings **9** 804
tools **9** 816
wall paintings **9** 805, 806, 807, 808, *809*, 809, 810, 898, 900–903; **10** 37, 65, 82–3; **29** 437
writing **10** 4
Asasif **9** 841; **30** 699, 700
bark of Amun **30** 693, 694, 695
Colossi of Memnon *see under* temples (mortuary) → Amenophis III
craftsmen and artists **9** 789
dealers **10** 92
Deir el-Bahri **9** 784, 839; **10** 51, 52, 65, 81; **30** 690, *693*, 693–4*
Deir el-Medina **9** 839, 851, *852*; **10** 5, 23, 53, 81; **30** 689, 698, 700–701*; **31** 107
Deir el-Shelwit **30** 702
Dra Abu el-Naga **9** 841; **30** 697, 699
fortress **9** 824
Gebel Tarif *see* el-Tarif
Gem Pa-Aten *see* temples (cult) → Temple of the Aten
Ipet-resyt *see* temples (cult) → Temple of Amun, Luxor
Karnak **1** *376*, 377; **9** *774*, 892; **10** 81; **23** 281; **30** 690–91*, *690*
bark-stations **9** 892
reliefs **9** 891
sacred lakes **27** 497
el-Khokha **30** 699
Luxor **7** *819*; **10** 79; **30** 692–3*
avenue of sphinxes **30** 692, *692*
Luxor Museum **10** 92
quay and nilometer **30** *692*
Malqata **9** 851; **30** 701–2*
Medinet Habu **9** *774*; **23** 281; **30** 237, 689, 695–6*
east gate **9** 826; **30** 695
reliefs **9** 891
sacred lake **27** 496
tomb chapels of the Divine Adoratrices of Amun **2** 295, 296; **9** 841; **30** 696
vaults **32** 87
Window of Appearances **30** 695
New Gourna **1** 319; **10** 830, *831*; **16** 241
Northern Monastery *see* Deir el-Bahri
palaces
palace of Amenophis III **23** 807; **30** 689, 701, *701*
wall paintings **9** 898
palace of Ramesses II **23** 807

Thebes (i) (Egypt)
palaces—cont.
palace of Ramesses III 9 825; 23 807; 33 246
Qurnet Mura'i 30 699
Royal Cache *see under* tombs (royal) → Inhapy (TT 320)
Sanctuary of Isis and Montu 9 896; 30 697
Sheikh Abd el-Qurna 30 699
Shelwit, Deir el- *see* Deir el Shelwit
el-Tarif 9 839; 30 697
temples 29 386; 30 696–7*
temples (cult) 9 833
Great Temple of Amun, Karnak 9 821, 825, 826, 861, 886, 887; 10 65; 15 53; 25 874, 875; 27 496; 30 433, *433*, 688, 689, 691
altar 1 691
Botanical Room 10 54
Cachette Court 9 *889*; 30 691*
chapel of Amenophis I 9 882
Festival Hall 9 831, 833
gardens 10 54
gold 10 35
Great Hypostyle Hall 9 783, 826; 25 874; 28 494; 30 433, 694
kiosk of Sesotris I 9 830
obelisk of Hatshepsut 23 329, *330*
obelisk of Tuthmosis I 23 329
obelisk of Tuthmosis III 23 330
Pylon III 9 830, 831, *831*
Pylon X 29 616
reliefs 9 848, *848*, 886, 887, *887*; 10 35
sculpture 9 *883*
seals 10 70
statue of Tuthmosis III 9 880, *881*
statues 9 880, 885
Table of Kings 10 90
Taharqa's Column 30 237
Temple of Khons 9 783; 10 83; 30 694
White Chapel 9 831, *831*; 18 70; 30 433
precinct of Amun, Karnak 9 883
Temple of Amun *see* temples (cult) → Great Temple of Amun, Karnak
precinct of Mut, Karnak 25 875; 27 496, 497; 30 237
Temple of Amun, Luxor 9 807; 10 64; 20 231; 24 750; 30 689, 692, *692*
colonnade of Tutankhamun 30 692–3, *692*
colossal statues 31 *482*
court of Amenophis III 30 692, *692*, 693
court of Ramesses II 25 874; 30 692, *692*, 694
obelisk of Ramesses II 23 329, 330; 30 693
pylon of Ramesses II 25 874; 30 692, *692*, 694
reliefs 9 882, 886; 30 692
sanctuary 30 692
Temple of Serapis 26 920
triple bark shrine of Ramesses II 30 692, *692*
vestibule 30 692
wall paintings 7 822
Temple of Amun and Hathor 30 693, *693*
Temple of the Aten 1 505; 9 832, 883; 10 82; 11 231
colossal statues 9 883–4
reliefs 9 884
Temple of Hathor and Ma'at 9 833; 29 *615*; 30 697, 701
Temple of Mentuhotpe III 9 831
Thebes (i) (Egypt)
temples (cult)—cont.
Temple of Montu, Karnak 1 770
Temple of Thoth, Qasr el-Aguz 30 697
temples (mortuary) 9 790, 832; 12 174
Amenhotpe, son of Hapu 9 835; 30 697
Amenophis II (*reg c.* 1426–*c.* 1400 BC) 30 697
Amenophis III (*reg c.* 1390–*c.* 1353 BC) 30 689, 697
Colossi of Memnon 1 770; 9 782, 813, 862, 863; 30 689, 694*, *694*, 697
sculpture 9 781, 881
Hatshepsut (*reg c.* 1479–*c.* 1485 BC) 9 807, 821, 825, 826, 835; 10 80, 81; 12 497; 14 226; 20 231; 24 750; 30 689, 693, *693*
altar 1 691
gardens 10 54
reliefs 23 329
sculpture 9 880
shrine of Anubis 11 231
wall paintings 9 810, 903
Horemheb (*reg c.* 1319–*c.* 1292 BC) 30 697
Mentuhotpe II (*reg c.* 1957–*c.* 1945 BC) 9 779, 811; 10 80; 12 67; 30 693, *693*
Bab al-Husan *see* cenotaph of Mentuhotpe
cenotaph of Mentuhotpe 30 693
reliefs 9 874, 876
statues 9 874
wall paintings 9 900
Mentuhotpe III (*reg c.* 1945–*c.* 1938 BC 30 696
Merneptah (*reg c.* 1213–*c.* 1204 BC) 30 697
Ramesses III (*reg c.* 1187–*c.* 1156 BC) 9 783, 835, 848; 21 554; 24 634; 25 875; 30 695–6
reliefs 9 886; 30 *696*
wall paintings 9 805, 807, 808, 811
Ramesses IV (*reg c.* 1156–*c.* 1150 BC) 30 697
Ramesses II *see* Ramesseum
Ramesseum 9 825, 835; 25 874; 30 689, 694–5*, *695*
arches 2 292, 296
colossal statue 9 863; 30 695
court 30 695
hypostyle 30 695
inscriptions 10 83
King's audience hall 30 695
paintings 9 805
palace 30 695
papyri 9 844
pylon 30 695
reliefs 9 886
Temple of Touy 30 695
vaults 32 87, 89
Sethos I (*reg c.* 1290–*c.* 1279 BC) 9 886; 30 694, 697
reliefs 9 886
Siptah (*reg c.* 1198–*c.* 1193 BC) 30 697
Small Temple of Hatshepsut and Tuthmosis III 30 696
Tausert (*reg c.* 1193–*c.* 1190 BC) 30 697
Tuthmosis II (*reg c.* 1482–*c.* 1479 BC) 9 811
Tuthmosis III (*reg c.* 1479–*c.* 1426 BC) 30 697
Tuthmosis IV (*reg c.* 1400–*c.* 1390 BC) 30 697
tombs 9 823, 824, 840; 10 53
tombs (private) 9 840; 10 65; 25 763; 30 689, 698–700*
Amenemhab (TT 85) 9 840
Amenemhet (TT 48) 9 840
Thebes (i) (Egypt)
tombs (private)—cont.
Amenhotpe (TT 40) 1 885
Amenirdis 9 *839*
Ankhorkawy (TT 359) 9 840
Benia (TT 343) 29 615
Daga (TT 103) 9 824
Djar (TT 366) 9 900
Djehutinefer (TT 104) 9 808
Djeserkareseneb (TT 38) 10 65
Harwa (TT 37) 9 892
Ibi (TT 36) 9 891; 30 700
Ineni (TT 81) 9 901; 10 54
Inyotefoqer (TT 60) 30 699
Ipy (TT 217) 9 790, 840, 903; 10 46; 25 875
Kha (TT 8) 10 46, 57, 61, 74, 75
Khaemhet (TT 57) 1 770; 9 902; 30 699
Kharuef (TT 192) 1 770; 9 882; 10 83
Maiherpri (KV 36) 10 80; 20 118*
Meketre (TT 280) 9 820, *823*, 824; 10 46, 81
models 9 850, *851*
reliefs 9 877
statuettes 10 16, *16*
Menkheperraseneb (TT 86) 9 822, 902
Menna (TT 69) 9 839; 10 87; 21 136; 30 699
wall paintings 9 902; 29 664
Mentuemhet (TT 34) 9 805, 841, 891, *891*, 892; 21 139; 30 700
Min (TT 109) 9 811
Mose (TT 254) 9 825
Nakht (TT 52) 9 902; 22 446*; 30 699
Nebamun (TT 90) 9 810, 825
wall paintings 9 *807*, 902; 32 I1
Nebamun (unknown tomb) 9 *901*, 902
Nebamun and Ipuky (TT 181) 9 789, 820, 821, 822, 840; 10 52
Neferrenpet (TT 43) 9 840
Paser (TT106) 10 65; 30 699
Petamenopet (TT 33) 9 805, 841
Puyemre (TT 39) 9 822
Qenamun (TT 93) 9 808; 25 778–9
shabtis 10 57
wall paintings 9 855, 881, 902
Ramose (TT 55) 1 505, 770; 9 839; 25 *880*, 881*; 30 699, *700*; 31 107
reliefs 9 882, 884
wall paintings 9 902
Rekhmire (TT 100) 9 787, 788, 790, 821, 839, 861; 26 132*; 30 699; 31 107
wall paintings 9 *816*, 818, *818*, *821*, 855, 881, 901–2; 10 62, *62*
Senenmut (TT 71) 28 407
Senenmut (TT 353) 9 787, 805, 902; 28 407; 30 693
Sennedjem (TT 1) 2 296; 9 *839*, 840; 30 *700*
furniture 10 53
wall paintings 9 903
Sennefer (TT 96) 9 839; 11 374; 30 699
Tharwas (TT 232) 9 805
User (TT 260) 10 75
Userhet (TT 56) 9 808, 811, 902; 10 10
Wah (TT 1102) 10 29, 46; 22 284
tombs (royal) 9 825, 841; 10 68; 22 716; 25 763; 30 697–8*
Ahhotpe (*d c.* 1550–30 BC) 1 469; 10 94
axes 10 41
coffin 10 10
daggers 9 818
Thebes (i) (Egypt)
tombs (royal)
Ahhotpe (*d c.* 1550–30 BC)—cont.
jewellery 10 31, *31*
sarcophagus 10 90
Akhenaten (*reg c.* 1353–*c.* 1336 BC) *see* Unknown royal personage (KV 55)
Amanishakheto, queen (early 1st cent.) 10 93
Amenhirkhopshef (QV 55) 30 698
Amenophis II (KV 35) 10 7, 80; 30 698
drawings 9 904
glass 10 57
wall paintings 9 903
Amenophis III (KV 22) 30 698
Ashayt 10 12, 43
Hatshepsut (KV 20) 10 80, 94; 14 226
Horemheb (KV 57) 9 791, 903; 10 80; 14 758
Inhapy (TT 320) 9 841
Royal Cache 30 694, 698
Inyotef I (*reg c.* 2081–*c.* 2065 BC) 9 839
Inyotef II (*reg c.* 2065–*c.* 2016 BC) 9 839
Inyotef III (*reg c.* 2016–*c.* 2008 BC) 9 839, 873
Inyotef kings 9 876; 30 697
Kauit 10 12
Mentuhotpe II (*reg c.* 1957–*c.* 1945 BC) 9 779; 10 94; 30 688
Merneptah (KV 8) 9 805
Nefertari (QV 66) 10 83; 22 722; 25 875; 30 698, *698*; 31 107
wall paintings 9 903
Nefertiti *see* Unknown royal personage (KV 55)
Neferu 9 876
Ramesses III 10 44, 53, 75
Ramesses IV (KV 2) 9 805, 841; 10 63, *63*
Ramesses VI (KV 9) 9 805; 30 698
Ramesses VII (KV 1) 9 805
Ramesses IX (KV 6) 9 805, 861; 10 83
Ramesses X (KV 18) 9 841
Ramesses XI (KV 4) 9 783, 841
Sethos I (KV 17) 9 791, 841, *841*; 10 87, *88*, 94; 28 *495*; 30 698; 31 107
drawings 9 904
paintings 9 805, 897, 903
sarcophagus 1 516, *516*; 10 13, 90
Siptah (KV 47) 10 80
Tausert (KV 14) 9 805
Tiye, Queen (*c.* 1550–1307 BC) *see* Unknown royal personage (KV 55)
Tutankhamun (KV 62) 2 300; 5 890; 9 150, 782; 10 53, 54, 60, 65, 81, 94, 95, 98; 19 716; 31 107
alabaster (limestone) 1 516
beadwork 3 441
chariot 6 *477*
chests 6 559; 10 15
coffin 10 10
collars 17 IV2
daggers 9 817
dress 10 44, 61, 75
fans 10 775, *775*
furniture 9 808, 811, 822, 823; 10 52, *52*, 53, 57, 61; 20 466; 23 *533*; 30 775; 33 III1
glass 10 57, 58
ivory 16 797
jewellery 10 32
metalwork 10 37
models 28 611
mummy 22 284
mummy mask 10 13
Thebes (i) (Egypt)
tombs (royal)
Tutankhamun (KV 62)—cont.
musical instruments 10 35; 22 372
paintings 14 *179*
palettes 23 788
reliefs 9 886
sarcophagus 9 813
shabtis 10 18, 20
textiles 10 74, 75, 76
Tuthmosis I (KV 38) 10 56, 80
Tuthmosis III (KV 34) 9 841; 10 80; 27 824; 30 698
glass 10 56
wall paintings 9 903
Tuthmosis IV (KV 43) 10 43–4, 75, 80
textiles 10 *75*
Unknown royal personage (KV 55) 10 80
Yuya and Tuya (KV 46) 1 770; 9 822; 10 52, 80; 33 580*, *580*
furniture 10 53; 30 775
glass 10 54
al-Ufsur *see* Luxor
Valley of the Kings 9 783, 784, 903; 10 80, 81; 30 689, 694, 697; 31 107
Valley of the Queens 30 689, 697
Thebes (ii) (Greece) 13 *362*, *363*; 14 *332*; 30 702–3*
Archaeological Museum 14 361
art forms and materials
armour 14 356
bracelets 13 *600*
faience (i) (glass) 14 358, 359
figurines 13 579
furniture 14 354
ivory-carvings 14 354
jewellery 14 356, 357
lapis lazuli 1 850
mosaics 9 566
pottery 13 496, 533
sculpture 13 442, *443*; 14 353
seals 17 836
wall paintings 14 334, 348, 350
Hagios Georgios 9 592
houses 9 561; 14 338
palace 14 349
tombs 30 702
tomb of Teiresias 6 170
Thebes, Nikomachos of *see* NIKOMACHOS OF THEBES
Thedy, Max 10 888; 26 546
Theed, William, I (*fl* 1757–62) 27 336
Theed, William, II (1764–1817) 27 336; 29 723; 30 703
Theed, William, III (1804–91) 14 148; 19 614; 30 703*
Theiss, Caspar 3 805; 14 650; 30 703*
Theiss, Siegfried 14 749; 32 439
Thék, Endré 14 908, 910
Thelot, Johann Andreas *see* THELOTT, JOHANN ANDREAS
Thelott, Israel 30 703
Thelott, Johann Andreas 2 718; 30 703–4*
Thélusson, Marie-Jeanne 13 234; 19 9, 56
Thembu 1 297
Themerson, Stefan 30 704*
Themistokles 21 556; 24 327
Thenae Baths 26 872, 919
Thénard 24 791
Thénard's blue *see* PIGMENTS → types → cobalt blue
Thenaud, Jean 20 334
Thendu 15 733
Thenkoh Konyak 15 733
Thény, Řehoř 8 386; 18 505
Theo(dotos) 10 434; 13 460
Theobald I, Count of Blois (*reg* 975) 6 50
Theobald II, Count of Champagne (*reg* 1102–52) 7 371; 25 219

Theobald III, Count of Blois (*reg* 1037-89) **25** 667
Theobald IV, Count of Champagne (*reg* 1201-53) **25** 667
Theobald VI, Count of Blois and Chartres (*reg* 1205-18) **4** 155
Theobald, Lewis **31** 871
Theobald de Lyxheim **21** 362
Theobalds Park (Herts) **12** 126
Theochares, D. **15** 891
Theocritus **9** 618; **18** 701
Theocritus Cup **10** 334; **29** 723
Theoda *see* TIODA
Théodard, Archbishop of Narbonne **22** 504
Theodegrimus **31** 227
Theodoli, Girolamo, Marchese *see* TEODOLI, GIROLAMO, Marchese
Theodolinda, Queen (*d* 625) **8** 203; **26** 79, 143
Théodon, Jean (-Baptiste) **13** 814; **26** 771; **30** 704–5*
  assistants **19** 118
  collaboration **15** 121, 862; **23** 644; **26** 810
  patrons and collectors **17** 510
  works **19** 213; **26** 824
Theodor, Bishop of Aquileia **2** 243
Theodora (*fl* 3rd cent. AD) **30** 722
Theodora, Empress of Byzantium (*reg c.* 527-36) **9** 654; **28** 761
  architecture **9** 537
Theodora, Empress of Byzantium (*reg* 810-after 858) **30** 705*
Theodora, Empress of Byzantium (*reg c.* 1042-50) **9** 638
Theodora Palaeologos, Empress of Byzantium (*reg* 1261-82) **9** 550; **23** 830
Theodora Petraleipha **2** 509
Theodora Raoulina **23** 831
Theodore (*fl* 1066) **9** 613
Theodore (*fl* end 14th cent.) **1** 588
Théodore (*fl* 17th cent.) **21** 609
Theodore I, Pope (*reg* 642-49) **26** 835
Theodore I Laskaris, Emperor of Byzantium (*reg* 1204-22) **9** 555
Theodore II Laskaris, Emperor of Byzantium (*reg* 1254-8) **9** 549; **16** 810
Theodore Apseudes **9** 580; **27** 569
Theodore Metochites **9** 522, 550; **23** 830
  architecture **9** 559, 584; **16** 584, 597
  paintings and mosaics **9** 523; **16** 597; **22** 163
  sculpture **9** 592
Theodore of Ser **9** 601
Theodore of Stoudios **7** 229; **9** 613; **30** 705*
  architecture **16** 601
  manuscripts **9** 604
Theodore Psalter *see under* PSALTERS → individual manuscripts
Theodorescu-Sion, Ion **26** 716
Theodore Studites *see* THEODORE OF STOUDIOS
Theodore Tourkeles **9** 657
Theodoric, Master **25** 431; **30** 705–6*
  works **8** 389; **11** 451; **13** 152, *152*; **17** 820, 821; **30** *706*
Theodoric the Great, King of the Ostrogoths (*reg* 489-526) **23** 623*
  architecture **2** 319; **9** 534; **16** 761; **26** 31, 33, 795
  banners **11** 146
  mosaics **22** 161
  sculpture **22** 43
Theodoros **18** 571
Theodoros of Phokaia **8** 694; **30** 737
  tholoi **8** *694*
Theodoros of Samos **1** 480; **2** 312; **13** 394, 408, 411, 439; **26** 295–6*; **27** 687
  works **10** 430; **13** 399, 408, 572; **15** 893
Theodorus of Phocis *see* THEODOROS OF PHOKAIA
Theodosia *see* KAFFA
Theodosiopolis *see* ERZURUM
Theodosios I, Emperor of Rome (*reg* 379-95) **21** *3*; **30** 706*
  architecture **9** 509, 540; **26** 752; **30** 719
Theodosios II, Emperor of Byzantium (*reg* 408-50) **9** 647, 654; **21** 562
Theodosios the Great, Emperor of Rome *see* THEODOSIOS I, Emperor of Rome
Theodotos **13** 395
Theodotos Kassiteras, Patriarch of Constantinople **9** 638
Theodotus (*fl* 740) **26** 831
Theodulf, Bishop of Orléans **5** 779; **30** 706–7*
  architecture **5** 794; **12** 484
  manuscripts **5** 803; **6** 483
  mosaics **12** 485
  writings **7** 224
Theokles **8** 458
Theokosmos **13** 438, 596; **24** 594; **30** 707*
Theolinde, Queen (*d* 625) **19** 549
Theologos *see* SELÇUK
Theon (*fl c.* 160-150 BC) **18** 148
Theon of Samos (*fl* late 4th cent. BC) **13** 547, 551, 553
Theon of Smyrna (*fl c.* 115-40 AD) **2** 349
Theophanes Continuatus **12** 71
Theophanes the Cretan **8** 157; **21** 344; **30** 707*
  attributions **22** 228
  works **10** 437; **22** 228; **25** 333, 334–5, *335*
Theophanes the Greek **7** 217; **27** 384; **30** 707–9*
  collaboration **9** 601; **27** 304
  works **7** 261; **9** 521, 586, 629; **22** 176, 183; **23** 269; **25** *342*; **27** 383; **30** *708*
Theophano, Empress (*d* 991) **7** 594; **9** 650; **26** 572
Theophanu, Abbess **12** 363; **26** 574, 695
Theophilos (*fl c.* 1332-3) **2** 602
Theophilos (*c.* 1868-1934) **13** 353, 359; **30** 709*
Theophilos, Bishop of Thessaloniki **30** 723
Theophilos, Emperor of Byzantium (*reg* 829-42) **9** 522; **30** 709*
  architecture **16** 607
  furniture **30** 779
  palaces **9** 558
Theophilus (Presbyter) **8** 910; **9** 646; **26** 535; **30** 709–10*
  works **10** 203; **13** 135; **20** 324; **29** 851; **31** 299, 302
    on art **2** 518
    on brass **4** 682, 688
    on censers **6** 174
    on chrysography **7** 245
    on enamel **13** 134; **26** 691
    on engraving **21** 337
    on gilding **12** 624
    on glazes **12** 803
    on glues **5** 912
    on inks **15** 851
    on metalwork **26** 681
    on mosaics **22** 156
    on niello **21** 329
    on oil painting **23** 375
    on painting **5** 656; **13** 138
Theophilus (Presbyter) works—cont.
    on stained glass **26** 700, 701; **29** 497, 498
    on varnishes **32** 1; **33** 335
    on wall painting **26** 657
Theophrastus **12** 108; **14** 432; **22** 354
Theopompos **4** 682
Theopropos **1** 481
Theorem painting *see* POONAH PAINTING
Theorianos, John **23** 373, 374
theories
  architectural **10** 205; **26** 12
    England **22** 139; **23** 213; **33** 341, 386, 387
    France **4** 533; **24** 469
    Germany **4** 179, 504; **11** 853; **12** 368–9; **27** 334; **28** 119, 400
    Gothic **13** 34
    Greece, ancient **13** 403, 408–9*; **25** 768
    India, Republic of **15** 169
    Italy **1** 558–60; **22** 106; **32** 638
    Japan **17** 26
    Portugal **26** 515
    Rome, ancient **26** 922–5*
    Spain **5** 700–701; **32** 563
    Switzerland **33** 297
    United States of America **1** 610–11
  art **1** 102, 172, 173–4; **2** 505–6, 538–9; **14** 869; **15** 99; **25** 684
    Britain **5** 215; **20** 527–8
    Buddhism **29** 462
    Byzantine **15** 75
    China **2** 531; **6** 631, 634, 637, 769; **21** 418
      Daoism **6** 634
    Confucianism **6** 631, 634, 637; **7** 704*
    Daoism **6** 634
    Egypt, ancient **28** 47
    England **5** 777; **7** 570–71, 796; **14** 642; **30** 171–2
      19th cent. **27** 352
    France **1** 524; **13** 232; **31** 820–21
      17th cent. **1** 897–8; **25** 392
      19th cent. **8** 661; **10** 183–4; **18** 631; **25** 659–60; **30** 174, 239
      20th cent. **3** 784; **4** 200; **10** 164; **20** 436–7; **27** 854
    Germany
      17th cent. **27** 726
      18th cent. **12** 852; **14** 99, 446; **17** 801–2; **18** 880; **26** 278–9; **27** 264
      19th cent. **14** 298–300, 526; **23** 123; **26** 369; **28** 107–8, 109, 160–61
      20th cent. **1** 73; **3** 400, 731, 891; **18** 110; **20** 527; **24** 16–17; **33** 383
    Greece, ancient **13** 467–9*, 545, 548; **25** 177
      4th cent. BC **25** 31–2
    Indian subcontinent **15** 205
    Islamic **15** 206
    Italy **25** 71–2
      Mannerism **19** 546–7
      Renaissance **1** 557; **32** 18–21
      15th cent. **6** 169; **8** 601–2; **16** 658
      16th cent. **2** 388, 531; **4** 198; **6** 39; **7** 646; **9** 74; **12** 244; **31** 906
      17th cent. **33** 720
      18th cent. **21** 600
      20th cent. **8** 182–3
    Japan **17** 419
    Marxism **2** 533, 536, 538; **6** 768; **14** 234; **20** 526–8
    Netherlands, the **18** 226
    Norway **13** 726
    Portugal **14** 660, 662
    Rome, ancient **13** 467, 468; **25** 824
theories art—cont.
    Russia **9** 188; **11** 870; **20** 195
    Spain **5** 736, 739; **13** 251; **23** 578–9, 705–6; **32** 558
    Stoicism **29** 694
    Switzerland **33** 297–8
    Union of Soviet Socialist Republics **20** 527
    United States of America
      20th cent. **8** 839; **20** 527, 528; **27** 787; **33** 16
      19th cent. **2** 562; **11** 57–8; **19** 61; **22** 102; **27** 354
      20th cent. **2** 573; **10** 101; **14** 303–4; **18** 459; **20** 208; **21** 157–8; **33** 284
    see also AESTHETICS
  calligraphy **6** 769–71; **8** 519; **17** 226
  colour **7** 627, 628–31; **10** 203; **12** 853; **24** 375–7; **26** 737
    France **14** 396; **22** 745; **28** 504
      19th cent. **6** 564
    Germany **1** 74; **18** 449; **27** 341
    Italy **7** 627–8
      19th cent. **1** 74; **27** 126
  culture **20** 208
  form **11** 312–14; **13** 468; **22** 102; **24** 383; **25** 31
  fortifications **32** 79
  garden **8** 845; **12** 124, 130
  hanging chain **20** 567
  intuition **13** 468
  landscape **8** 519*, 771; **18** 700; **22** 540
  masonry **20** 575*, 580, 581
  music **3** 692
  painting
    China **6** 795–8, 814, 818, 821–5*; **7** 147; **25** 72
      Qing period (1644-1911) **8** 519–20*
      11th cent. **6** 789
    England **9** 8; **19** 412; **26** 345; **27** 353
    France **1** 73; **8** 782; **9** 8–9; **18** 630; **30** 170
    Germany **14** 446; **19** 245; **22** 385
    Greece, ancient **13** 553–4*
    Italy **18** 708
      Mannerism **19** 546–7
      Renaissance **1** 557–8; **19** 195–6; **27** 790
      16th cent. **9** 6–7; **24** 827–8
      17th cent. **9** 7–8; **20** 221
    Japan **17** 439
    Netherlands, the **14** 740–41
    Poland **31** 492
    Portugal **8** 11
    Renaissance **19** 195–6
  perception **2** 476–7; **6** 586; **21** 157; **24** 375, 696; **26** 223–4
  perspective **24** 375, 377–80, 492, 493
    Greece, ancient **13** 553
    Italy **1** 113, 557; **19** 195, 546
  poetry **17** 26; **25** 72
  proportions **1** 558; **18** 898; **19** 546; **24** 469
  reception **26** 61–4*
  representation **10** 690; **11** 334; **19** 327; **26** 222–4
  restoration **32** 596–7
  sculpture **1** 558; **13** 467–9*
    Germany **12** 407; **14** 446
    Rome, ancient **13** 468
  urban planning **5** 170; **7** 293
theosophy **1** 75; **21** 851; **30** 168, 710–11*
  Germany **29** 607
  Portugal **28** 729
Theotocopoulos, Jorge Manuel **30** 711*
  collaboration **21** 159; **31** 89
  works **13** 344; **27** 612; **31** 348
Theotokopoulos, Dominikos *see* GRECO, EL
Theotokopoulos, Menegos *see* GRECO, EL
Thera (island) **8** *304*, 305; **13** *363*; **14** 337; **30** 711–13*
  Akrotiri *see* AKROTIRI
  architecture **32** 294
  faience (i) (glass) **21** 684
  houses **32** *294*
  jewellery **13** 597
  neck rings **13** 601
  pottery **8** 309; **13** 497, 512; **30** *712*
  pumice **13** 603
  Sanctuary of Dionysos **30** 713
  stone vessels **8** 317
  vase paintings **8** 309
  wall paintings **8** 309, 318–20*, *318*, *320*; **21** 673, 674, 675, 677; **30** *713*
Thera (town) **30** 713
Theranda *see* PRIZREN
Theravada Buddhism *see under* BUDDHISM → branches
Therbusch, Anna Dorothea **3** 799; **30** 713–14*; **33** 308
Thérémin, François Claude **27** 584
thericleians **13** 537
thermae **26** 871
  Italy **1** 463; **26** 795*, *796*
  North Africa **26** 919
  Rome, ancient **1** 463; **3** 375; **13** 404; **26** 795*, *796*, 871–2, 919
  see also BATHS; BALNEAE
thermal analysis *see under* TECHNICAL EXAMINATION → types
Thermes, Laura **25** 738; **30** 714*
Thermi **19** 234, *234*, 235
thermocouples **6** 330
thermogravimetric analysis *see under* TECHNICAL EXAMINATION → types
thermohygrographs **7** 734
thermoluminescence dating *see under* DATING METHODS → types
thermometers **7** 734
Thermon **13** *363*; **30** 714–15*
  Megaron B **13** 376, *377*, 397
  metopes **13** 543; **30** 714–15
  Temple of Apollo **13** 377, *377*, 390
    gargoyles **12** 150
    metopes **13** 398, 425; **30** *714*
Thermopylae **9** 554
Thern, Richard **22** 671
Thernberg **2** 799
Thero, Manjusri **29** 468
Theron **1** 511; **13** 373
Theron, Daniel **29** 106
Thérouanne Cathedral **1** 767; **8** 224; **9** 70; **13** 37
Thérouanne Pontifical *see under* PONTIFICALS → individual manuscripts
Therouyn, Regnault **1** 766
thesaurus of art *see* ART (THESAURUS OF)
Theselius, Mats **30** 110
Thesenblätter **18** 45
Theseus Painter **13** 511; **23** 146
Thesleff, Ellen **11** 96, 97; **28** 427; **30** 715*
Thesmar, Fernand **11** 623, 631
Thespiai **6** 170
  Polyandrion **13** 533
Thespis **30** 650
Thessaloniki **9** *511*, 513, 515; **13** *363*; **19** 881; **26** *908*; **30** 716–26*, *717*
  Archaeological Museum **13** 360, 470; **17** 808; **30** 719; **32** 249
  Arch of Galerius **9** 519; **26** 909; **27** 43, 45; **30** 719*; **31** 350
  Aristoteleion University Department of Applied Arts **13** 360

Thessaloniki
Aristoteleion University—cont.
Department of Architecture 13 360
Experimental School 13 349
art forms and materials
architecture 4 774; 9 551, 560; 26 909
coins 9 638–9
embroidery 30 718
icons 9 622, 626, 629, 630
jewellery 19 *881*
ketubbot 18 3
metalwork 13 359
mosaics 9 571–2; 13 561
pottery 9 631, 634
silk 9 *668*
textiles 9 669; 28 458
wall paintings 9 520
ecclesiastical buildings 9 523, 526, 576
Acheiropoietos 7 278; 9 571, 589
Church of the Acheiropoietos 7 252; 9 582
Hagia Aikaterini 9 551, 585; 28 446
Hagia Sophia 7 221; 9 542, *542*; 30 723*
ambo 9 590
mosaics 9 575, 577; 30 *723*, 723–4*
plaques 9 590
wall paintings 9 578; 30 724*
Hagioi Apostoloi 9 551, 585, 599; 30 724*, *725*
mosaics 9 *585*; 30 725*
Hagios Demetrios 1 722; 3 329; 7 252; 9 538; 13 349; 20 520; 26 572; 30 720–21*; 31 280
altar 7 278
ambo 9 590
chapel of Hagios Euthymios 9 585
chapel of St Euthymius 24 110
ciborium 7 301
ex-votos 10 701
marble revetments 30 721–2*
mosaics 7 272, *278*; 9 573, 575; 22 162; 30 *721*, 721–2*
plaques 9 590
sculpture 30 722*
Hagios Georgios 30 719–20*
ambo 9 590
collections 30 719
mosaics 9 571; 22 162; 30 720
wall paintings 9 577
Hagios Giorgios 7 255, 272; 9 556
ambo 7 278
Hagios Menas 9 590
Hagios Nikolaos Orphanos 9 585
Hagios Panteleimon 9 551
Hosios David 9 579; 30 722*
mosaics 9 571–2, *572*; 30 722–3*
wall paintings 30 723*
Panagia Chalkeon 9 545, *546*; 30 724*
capitals 9 592
wall paintings 9 577; 30 724
Profitis Elias 9 551; 30 725–6*
Rotunda *see* Hagios Georgios
Vlatadon Monastery 9 629
fortifications 9 524, 553, 555; 26 909
House of Leo Sikountenos 9 520
hypogea 15 52
Mausoleum of Galerius 26 903
Museum of Popular Art 30 719
odeion 23 350
palace 9 565; 23 809; 26 910
patronage 9 523
Roman circus 7 342
Serayli Mosque *see* ecclesiastical buildings → Profitis Elias
Thessaly 14 *332*, 335; 26 *876*, 877
Thesson, Johan *see* TIJSEN, JOHAN
The textiles *see under* TEXTILES → types
Thetford (Norfolk) 2 83; 10 300, 301
Abbey 18 622
Castle 9 143
Thetford Treasure 26 859; 27 83, 102, 103
Theti, Carlo 21 579
Thetis Painter 13 533
Theudelinda 9 654
Theunis, Pierre 20 925
Theunissen, Cornelis *see* ANTHONISZ., CORNELIS
Theuriet, André 19 296
Theus, Jeremiah 30 726*; 31 600
Thévenet, Louis 3 564; 4 618; 23 399; 28 104; 30 726–7*
Thévenin, Jacques-Jean 4 555; 8 461; 22 740; 25 872
Thévenin l'imagier 4 544
Thévenot, Jean de 10 78
Thevestis 1 634; 9 *510*; 30 727*
Arch of Caracalla 26 920; 31 350
Baptistery 7 302
Basilica 7 255; 9 535, 569; 20 520; 21 834; 30 727
Thevet, André 4 706; 10 78
Thewasathan Prang Khaek Temple 30 579
Theyer, Leopold 8 532
Thibaud, J. 27 575
Thibaudeau, Narcisse-Adolphe, Comte de 30 727–8*
Thibault, Gérard 4 282; 8 665; 23 908
Thibault, Jean-Thomas 1 527; 4 302; 11 257; 22 828; 24 387; 33 674
Thibault, L(ouis) M(ichel) 30 728*
collaboration 5 662; 9 420
works 5 667; 18 887; 29 105
Thibault, Marie-Elisabeth 9 370
Thibault de Maisières, M. 3 620
Thibaut, Willem 7 799
Thibaw, King of Burma (*reg* 1879-85) 5 236, 246
Thibron 20 98
Thickness, P. C. 19 506
works 19 *506*
Thicknesse, Philip 11 908
thick-wall passages *see* THICK-WALL STRUCTURES
thick-wall structures 5 370, 371; 10 228; 30 728–9*, *729*
Thiébaud, Jonas 2 718
Thiebaud, Wayne 27 731; 30 729–30*
groups and movements 25 232
patrons and collectors 1 71
pupils 28 142
works 31 608
Thiebaut de Luxembourg 1 782
Thiébaut Frères 7 783; 10 771
Thiel, Ernest 17 9; 30 117, 118, 730*
paintings 17 8
sponsorship 19 379
Thiele, Elert 10 538
Thiele, Johann Alexander 1 463; 8 880; 33 115
Thiele, O'Brien
works 22 *336*
Thielen, Anna-Maria van 30 730
Thielen, Francisca-Catherina van 30 730
Thielen, Jan Philips van 3 561; 25 811; 29 666; 30 730*
Thielen, Maria-Theresia van 30 730
Thielens, Emile 31 856
Thieler, Fred 3 803; 14 613; 30 730–31*
Thiem, Daniel 25 130
Thieme, Ulrich 10 212; 12 483; 14 635; 28 165; 30 731*
Thieme-Becker 4 26; 10 212; 30 731*; 33 308
Thiene 30 731*
Villa Porto-Colleoni 29 85; 32 545
Thiene, Adriano 30 731
Thiene, Enea 30 732
Thiene, Francesco (*d* 1556) 30 732
Thiene, Francesco di Sartorio (*d* 1593) 30 732
Thiene, Gaetano *see* CAJETAN, Saint
Thiene, Giulio 1 601; 31 745
Thiene, Jan van 10 494
Thiene, Marcantonio 30 731
Thiene, Marco 30 732
Thiene, Odoardo 30 732
Thiene, Orazio di Francesco 30 732
Thiene, Paul 33 407
Thiene, Teodoro 30 732
Thienen, Jacob van *see* JACOB VAN THIENEN
Thienen, Jan van 4 415; 30 732
Thienen, Peter van 30 732
Thienen, Renier van (i) (*fl c.* 1465–98) 4 415; 30 732*
Thienen, Renier van (ii) (*fl c.* 1484–*c.* 1530) 4 415, 417; 13 160; 30 732*
Thienpondt, Carl Friedrich 12 457
Thienpont 3 578
Thienpont, Joseph 33 167
Thiepval, Memorial to the Missing of the Somme 2 360, 362; 19 *823*
Thierrat, Augustin 3 785
Thierriat, Augustin-Alexandre 2 232; 27 563
Thierry (*fl* 1327) 13 672
Thierry, Abbot of Jumièges (*d* 1027) 17 684
Thierry, Abbot of Reims (*fl* 1035-46) 26 122
Thierry, Archbishop of Nicosia (*fl* 1206) 3 638
Thierry, Augustin 16 904; 18 865
Thierry, Jacques-Nicolas-Augustin 27 591
Thierry, Jean (*fl* mid 14th cent.) 31 384
Thierry, Jean (1609-79) 30 733
Thierry, Jean (1669-1739) 30 733*
collaboration 11 754; 14 174
patrons and collectors 4 558, 588
works 3 258; 12 125; 27 753, *753*, 754
Thierry de Masmines 18 572
Thierry de Ville d'Avray, Arnaud 20 138
Thierry de Ville d'Avray, Marc-Antoine 20 138
Thierry-Lagrange, François 28 463
Thiers 8 287
Thiers, A. 9 527
Thiers, (Louis-) Adolphe 4 *329*; 11 667; 30 733*
sculpture 6 463; 27 311
writings 25 849
Thiers, Louis-Antoine Crozat, Baron de 8 208, 209–10*; 30 274
Thiersch, August 30 734
Thiersch, Friedrich von 30 733–4*
assistants 14 606
competitions 7 668
groups and movements 28 341
pupils 3 840, 878; 9 382; 17 853; 28 177; 30 520; 32 421; 33 66
works 18 890; 22 301
Thiersch, Ludwig 13 360
Thiéry, A. 19 260
Thiès 28 405
Manufactures Sénégalaises des Arts Décoratifs 28 406
Thieulloye Abbey, La *see* LA THIEULLOYE ABBEY
Thieu Tri, Ruler of Hue (*reg* 1841-7) 14 845; 32 476
Thievaert, Daniel 33 110
Thijm, Josephus Albertus Alberdingk *see* ALBERDINGK THIJM, JOSEPHUS ALBERTUS
Thijs, Pieter 30 734*
collaboration 4 222; 11 872; 14 617
works 3 559
Thil, Hugues de, Lord of Saint-Beury *see* SAINT-BEURY, HUGUES DE THIL, Lord of
Thil, Pierre de *see* PIERRE DE THIL
Thilenius, Georg 23 740
Thilo von Lorich 9 3
works 9 *3*
Thim, Reinholt 8 733; 11 467; 30 734*
thimbles 10 340
Thimphu 3 *912*
textiles 3 *915*
Thina 27 57
Things Jamaican 16 887
Thinis 9 778
Thinissut 25 734
Thinissut, Baal of *see* BAAL OF THINISSUT
Thinite period *see under* EGYPT, ANCIENT → periods
Thin Orange ware *see under* POTTERY → wares
Thins, Maria 3 8; 32 262
Thira *see* THERA (ISLAND)
Third Artel 27 426
Third Eye 12 546
Third Intermediate Period *see under* EGYPT, ANCIENT → periods
Third Style painting *see under* ROME, ANCIENT → painting → wall
Third Text: Third World Perspectives on Contemporary Art and Culture 24 425, 429, 436, 446
Thiret, Nicolas 16 853
Thirion, André 30 20
Thiriot, Jean 21 346; 26 346; 30 734–5*
Thirkleby Flagon 10 327, *327*
Thirlestane Castle (Borders) 28 226
Thirslund, Jens 17 720
Thirteen 28 394
Thirtle, John 18 618; 23 248; 30 735*
Thirugokarna, Thirugokarneshvara Temple 15 647
Thiry, Georges 33 596
Thiry, Léonard 30 735*
attributions 8 549
groups and movements 11 264, 265
reproductive prints by others 4 616; 24 271
works 13 700; 25 607
writings 13 701
Thisbe Treasure 14 360
Thisong Detsen 5 104
thistle brooches *see under* BROOCHES → types
thistle-cups *see under* CUPS → types
Thistle-Hamilton *see* HAMILTON, KARL WILHELM DE
Thívai *see* THEBES (ii) (GREECE)
Thjomsonn, James 4 107
Thmuis *see* MENDES
Thoiry, Jean de *see* JEAN DE THOIRY
Thoiry, Pierre de *see* PIERRE DE THOIRY
Thoison, Charles 19 266
thokchak 26 141; 30 840–42
Thola, Benedikt da 10 741
Thola, Gabriel da 10 741
Tholen, Willem Bastiaan 11 885; 14 43, 47; 30 735–6*
Tholen Church 22 820
Tholens, K. P. 14 693
Tholing 5 104; 30 736*, *806*, *817*
Golden Temple *see* Serkang
manuscript illumination 30 835
paintings 15 561
sculpture 30 824
Serkang 30 816
stupas 30 817
wall paintings 30 831, 833
Yeshe Ö Temple 30 816, 819
tholoi 8 692, *694*; 13 380, 390, 401; 14 73; 27 235, 691; 29 367; 30 736–7*, *737*
Tholos of Lathuresa 30 736
tholos tombs *see under* TOMBS → types
Thom, Alexander 21 41
Thom, Ivor 13 877
Thom, Ron(ald James) 5 562; 28 557; 30 739*; 31 176, 864
Thoma, Hans 17 818; 30 739–40*
groups and movements 26 56
patrons and collectors 31 397
pupils 14 623
teachers 28 104
works 4 42; 11 *463*, 463–4; 12 394; 30 *740*
Thoma, Hans, Museum *see under* KARLSRUHE → museums
Thoma, Ludwig 14 313; 30 350
Thomae, Benjamin 9 238; 17 768; 21 64
Thoman, Johann Valentin (Anton) 30 740–41*
Thomann, Heinrich 33 737
Thomann, Johann Valentin (Anton) *see* THOMAN, JOHANN VALENTIN (ANTON)
Thomar Abbey *see* TOMAR ABBEY
Thomas, Master 31 384
Thomas, Saint (1st half of 1st cent. AD) 15 819
Thomas I, Count of Savoy (*reg* 1189-1233) 6 602
Thomas, Albert-Théophile-Félix 12 728
Thomas, Alexis-François 30 743
Thomas, Alfred Brumwell 30 742–3*
groups and movements 3 269; 9 739
works 3 537; 6 171; 16 11; 31 241
Thomas, Alma 33 314
Thomas, Antoni 12 740
Thomas, Brodrick 25 402
Thomas, Bruno 2 450
Thomas, Cecil 6 129*; 30 743*
Thomas (ii), Cyrus Pole 30 741, 742
Thomas, David 17 530
Thomas, Dewi Prys 32 784, 792
Thomas, D. J. 25 293
Thomas, Dylan 32 912
Thomas, Emile 8 789, 818
Thomas, Félix 25 172
Thomas, F. G. 28 281
Thomas, F(rancis) Inigo 4 157; 9 305; 30 743*
Thomas, Gabriel-Jules 4 568; 8 41; 28 345; 30 743–4*
Thomas, Gary 13 877
Thomas, George 30 744
Thomas, George H. 14 148
Thomas (i), Griffith 30 741*
Thomas, Isaiah 10 421
Thomas, J. 28 259
Thomas, James Havard 30 744*
Thomas (van Yperen), Jan 21 414; 28 904; 30 744*
Thomas, John (1810/11-89; potter) 5 580
Thomas (ii), John (1813-62; sculptor) 30 741, 742*
patrons and collectors 14 148, 149; 22 809
works 19 613; 26 288
Thomas, John Evan 32 787
Thomas, Joseph 4 120
Thomas, Julian 21 42

Thomas, Koso 28 692
Thomas, Lloyd Goodrich 31 672
Thomas, Percy, Partnership 4 823
Thomas, Percy E. 5 731, 732; 31 242
Thomas, R. G. 1 151
Thomas, Rodney 22 719
Thomas, Rover 1 64; 30 744*
Thomas (i), Thomas 30 741*
Thomas, Walter Aubrey 19 506
works 19 *506*
Thomas (ii), William 30 741–2*; 31 176
Thomas, William Brodrick 30 743
Thomas, William Cave 1 678
Thomas, William Meredydd 32 787
Thomas (ii), William Tutin 30 741, 742
Thomas à Kempis *see* KEMPIS, THOMAS À
Thomas Altar, Master of the *see* ST BARTHOLOMEW ALTAR, MASTER OF THE
Thomas Aquinas 1 176, 177, 653; 7 627; 13 138; 30 744–5*
Thomas Aquinas, Master of the Glorification of *see* GLORIFICATION OF THOMAS AQUINAS, MASTER OF THE
Thomas Becket, Saint (1120-70) 18 621; 30 745*
house 28 416
textiles 10 181; 26 703; 29 349
Thomas de Burgo 16 30
Thomas de Cantimpré 3 879; 10 202; 21 5
Thomas de Guerard 25 667
Thomas de Leghtune 9 155; 10 339; 13 164
Thomas de Leightone *see* THOMAS DE LEGHTUNE
Thomas de Maubeuge 31 834
Thomas James, Bishop of Dol 2 697
Thomas of Bayeux, Archbishop of York 26 588, 614; 33 542, 546
Thomas of Brantingham 7 420
Thomas of Canterbury 12 819; 30 745*
Thomas of Cantimpré *see* THOMAS DE CANTIMPRÉ
Thomas of Cluj 28 851
Thomas of Hatfield 19 290
Thomas of Kent 26 564
Thomas of Oxford 13 183, 184; 23 689, 691; 33 238, 550
Thomas of Witney 30 745–6*
assistants 17 673
works 10 672, 673; 33 61, 236
Thomason, Edward 4 88, 541; 8 534; 10 335; 20 925
Thomason, Yeoville 4 85; 31 240
works 4 *86*
Thomas Reservoir 1 *37*; 30 746*
Thomassen, Otto 13 620
Thomassin 14 725
Thomassin, Henri-Simon 30 746; 32 914
Thomassin, Philippe 10 389; 30 746*
assistants 8 783
pupils 5 437
works 3 448; 8 783; 11 754; 24 239; 28 506
Thomassin, Simon 12 833; 14 84; 19 225; 30 733, 746*; 31 379
Thomas & Son 30 741
Thomastown Chapel (Co. Kilkenny) 6 *443*
Thomas von Villach *see* ARTULA VON VILLACH, THOMAS
Thomé, Valter 14 371
Thomé, Verner 11 96; 28 427
Thomerle 15 866
Thomery, Musée-Atelier Rosa-Bonheur 4 318
Thomese, Albert de 14 42
Thomessen, Erik 7 488
Thomire, Duterme & Cie 30 747
Thomire, Luc-Philippe 30 747
Thomire, Pierre-Philippe 11 625, 627, 629; 30 747*
collaboration 8 107; 11 305; 24 893; 26 376; 28 194; 32 458; 33 48
groups and movements 10 186
patrons and collectors 23 354
works 8 523; 11 119, 627, *627*; 20 445; 24 388; 29 318, 342, 573
Thomisen, Daniel *see* TOMMISEN, DANIEL
Thomkins, André 30 135, 140, 747–8*
Thommesen, Erik 8 741
Thomon, Thomas-Jean de 27 404; 30 748*
groups and movements 13 611; 22 741
patrons and collectors 4 302
works 10 669; 23 353; 25 268, 790; 27 375, *375*, 575; 31 551
Thomopoulos, Thomas 2 218
Thompson, Art 22 581, 589
Thompson, Benjamin (*b* 1918) 2 324; 30 226, 227; 31 735
Thompson, Benjamin, Count Rumford (1753-1814) 8 897
Thompson, Berwick, Pratt & Partners 5 563; 10 458; 28 557; 30 739; 31 864
Thompson, Cephas 30 749
Thompson, Cephas Giovanni 30 749
Thompson, Charles 33 369
Thompson, Charles Joseph 28 557*
Thompson, Charles Thurston 26 233
Thompson, Christopher 5 582
Thompson, D'Arcy (Wentworth) 28 206; 30 748–9*
Thompson, Edward H. 21 263
Thompson, Elizabeth Southerden *see* BUTLER, Lady
Thompson, Eric 1 14
Thompson, F. F. 10 669
Thompson, Francis 16 53; 25 855
Thompson, Gary 29 118
works 29 *118*
Thompson, G(eorge) David 30 749*
Thompson, George K. 18 54
Thompson, Hamilton 30 365
Thompson, Henry (1733-1843) 28 25
Thompson, Henry (1820-94) 13 709; 33 142
Thompson, Henry Yates 30 749*
Thompson, Jerome 30 749–50*
Thompson, John (*fl* 1779) 33 95
Thompson, John P. (*fl* 1804) 32 156
Thompson, Jon (*fl* 1990s) 19 591
Thompson, J. Walter 3 423; 7 652; 29 602
Thompson, Launt 31 611
Thompson, Marguerite *see* ZORACH, MARGUERITE
Thompson, Mark 2 762
Thompson, Martin E. 2 502; 19 626; 31 232
Thompson, R. Campbell 20 205; 23 153
Thompson, Richard 21 416; 31 786
Thompson, Robert 1 444; 2 151
Thompson, Samuel 25 267
Thoms, Frederik, Count von 23 468
Thoms, Patrick 28 231
Thomsen, C. J. 2 299
Thomsen, Edvard (Johan) 8 728; 17 755; 30 750*
Thomson, Adam Bruce 9 725
Thomson, Alexander 30 750–51*
groups and movements 22 742
Thomson, Alexander—cont.
works 12 773, 774; 25 267; 28 228, 229, 230, 243, 248, *249*, 254; 30 *751*; 32 554
Thomson, Charles 10 851
Thomson, David Croal 4 589
Thomson, Donald 1 66
Thomson, E. 4 27
Thomson, George 19 589; 30 750
Thomson, Henry 30 751–2*
Thomson, Hugh 4 363
Thomson, James (1700-1748) 17 904; 18 712; 24 741; 29 675; 30 752*
Thomson, James (1789-1850) 14 268
Thomson, James (1800-83) 22 719
Thomson, James (1835-1905) 12 773, 775
Thomson, John (1778-1840) 18 855; 30 752*
teachers 22 531
works 28 236
Thomson, John (1837-1921; photographer) 30 752–3*
works 14 721; 24 664, 666, 672
Thomson, John (1859-1933; architect) 12 775
Thomson, J. T. 28 773, 774
Thomson, Kenneth 5 590
Thomson, Leslie Grahame 28 231
Thomson, Tom (John) 30 753–4*
groups and movements 5 566
patrons and collectors 5 589
works 30 *754*
Thomson, William George 30 327
Thomson Gallery *see under* TORONTO
Thomson of Duddingston *see* THOMSON, JOHN (1778-1840)
Thomy-Thiéry, George 6 516
Thonauer, Hans, I *see* DONAUER, HANS, I
Thonburi 3 165; 30 *571*, 593
urban planning 30 592
Wat Arun 30 589, 607
Wat Daowadungsaram 30 616
Wat Dusidaram 30 616
Wat Kalayanamit 30 589
Wat Ratcha Orot 30 589, 607, 616
Wat Ratchasittharam 30 616
Wat Suwannaram 30 616
Thonet, August 30 754
Thonet, Franz 30 754
Thonet, Gebrüder 2 814; 4 761; 8 802; 15 823; 18 192; 25 674; 32 448
works 15 *822*
Thonet, Jakob 30 754
Thonet, Josef 30 754
Thonet, Michael (1796-1871) 20 593; 30 753–5*; 32 448
collaboration 19 113
groups and movements 24 475
works 2 808, *809*, 813; 6 391; 19 896; 30 *755*
Thonet, Michael (1824-1902) 30 754
Thonet & Co. 10 299; 14 908
Thonet-Mundus 30 755
Thonisz., Cornelis *see* ANTHONISZ., CORNELIS
Thons, Jean Du Châtelet III, Baron des 12 309
Thöny, Eduard 27 871
Thöny, Wilhelm 2 797; 30 755–6*
Thooft, Joost 8 667; 22 882
Thoolne, Jan van der *see* TOOLNE, JAN VAN DER
Thopas, Johan 30 47
Thor, Le *see* LE THOR
Thor, Walter 4 598
Thorak, Josef 12 408; 14 130; 22 711, 712
Thorbecke, J. R. 22 903
Thorbecke, Marie-Pauline
works 1 *339*, *352*
Thoré, (Etienne-Joseph-) Théophile 11 675; 24 140; 30 756*
groups and movements 26 54
works 24 837; 32 268
Thoreau, Henry 11 840
Thorén, Theodor Esaias 14 89
Thorer, Bartholeme *see* DAUHER, BARTHOLOMÄUS
Thoresby (Notts) 6 407; 7 298
Thoresby, John, Archbishop of York 33 548
Thoreuil, Le *see* LE THOREUIL
Thorfinnr munnr 32 523
Thorgrimsson, Gestur 15 72
Thoricourt Castle 4 785
Thorigny, Jacques III de Goyen-Matignon, Comte de 8 64
Thorigny, Jean-Baptiste Lambert, Sieur de *see* LAMBERT, JEAN-BAPTISTE
Thorikos 14 335, 354
Theatre 13 385
tombs 30 738
Thörl 2 792
Thorláksson, Thórarinn B(enedikt) 15 70; 30 757–8*
works 30 *757*
Thorma, János 22 434
Thormeyer, Gottlob Friedrich 9 236; 30 758*
Thorn (Netherlands)
church 22 821
tower 22 816
Thorn (Poland) *see* TORUŃ
Thornbury Castle (Glos) 6 59; 10 228
Thornely, Arnold 3 269, 537; 16 39; 19 506
works 19 *506*
Thorney (Cambs) 30 534
Abbey 26 588, 613
Thorneycroft, Mary 30 761
Thorneycroft, Thomas 30 761
Thornham Parva (Suffolk), St Mary 11 421
Thornhill, Cuthbert Bensey 1 648
Thornhill, James 10 249; 12 594; 19 584; 28 466; 30 758–9*
drawings 19 584
groups and movements 10 372
paintings
frescoes 30 *759*
patrons and collectors 14 127
Brydges, James, 1st Duke of Chandos 5 65
Cavendish, William, 1st Duke of Devonshire (1640-1707) 6 116, 515
Churchill, John, 1st Duke of Marlborough 4 137; 7 286
Clarke, George 7 379
Harley, Edward, 2nd Earl of Oxford 14 178
Howard, Hugh 14 810
Hudson, Thomas (1701-99) 14 842
personal collection 27 263
prints 25 630
pupils 14 637, 641
reproductive prints by others 31 871
restorations by others 33 515
works 10 249, 274, 277; 13 623; 14 784; 15 139, V; 23 381, 678, 690; 30 675
Thornhill, John 21 765
Thornir, Peter 31 510
Thornley, Geoffrey 23 61
Thorn Prikker, Johan 22 850, 900; 30 760*
groups and movements 22 875; 23 120; 25 358
house 14 31
pupils 5 543
works 1 734; 2 568; 14 31; 20 808; 22 851; 29 508
Thornton, Bonnell 32 327
Thornton, John 13 184; 33 549
works 33 *549*
Thornton, Robert John 4 362; 9 506; 10 394; 18 714; 26 124
Thornton, Thomas 12 646
Thornton, Wallace 30 160
Thornton, William 30 760–61*
assistants 11 426
competitions 7 666
works 10 850; 13 237; 14 20; 29 842; 30 503; 31 591, 662; 32 891
Thornton Abbey (Humberside) 4 779; 10 227; 12 175
Thornycroft, (William) Hamo 20 925; 25 238; 30 761–2*
assistants 31 488
groups and movements 3 269; 23 33, 34
works 3 532, 533; 29 575; 30 *762*
Thornycroft, Thomas 29 575
Thoroczkai Wigand, Ede 12 839; 14 890; 30 762*
Thoronet Abbey 7 *232*
Thoroton, John 33 447
Thorp, Alfred H. 25 371
Thorp, Peddle 2 770
Thorp, Richard 21 732
Thorpe, John (*c*. 1565-?1655) 30 762–3*
patrons and collectors 28 908
works 3 186; 10 163; 24 274
Thorpe, John (*d* 1792) 2 576, 577; 4 181
Thorpe, Robert de 19 641
Thorpe, Thomas (*fl* 1570) 30 762, 763
Thorpe, Thomas (*fl* 1620) 30 762
Thorsager 7 257
Thorsburg 9 640
Thorsen, Kura (Te Waru) Rewiri *see* REWIRI, KURA TE WARU
Thorsteinsson, Sigurður 15 73
Thorsteinsson, Sivert 8 751
Thorvaldsen, Bertel 3 645; 8 719, 740, 741; 10 907; 15 144; 16 705; 17 921; 22 363; 26 776; 30 763–6*; 33 282
assistants 4 41; 10 895; 11 767, 768; 29 645; 30 459
collaboration 4 68; 33 296
copies 4 41; 15 144
groups and movements 13 612; 22 734; 26 742
methods 21 770
patrons and collectors 4 302; 6 117; 14 744, 876; 25 836; 27 357; 31 172
personal collection 5 366; 7 805; 8 758, 759; 26 129; 27 145
pupils 28 242
Bissen, Hermann Wilhelm 4 97
Clésinger, (Jean-Baptiste-) Auguste 7 421
Crawford, Thomas 8 124
Gibson, John (i) (1790-1866) 12 597; 27 878
Greenough, Horatio 13 621
Jerichau, J(ens) A(dolf) (1816-83) 17 481
Kessels, Mathieu 17 920
Michelsen, Hans 21 471; 23 229
Orlovsky, Boris (Ivanovich) 23 531
Salvatierra y Barriales, Valeriano 27 646
Schievelbein, Hermann (Friedrich Anton) 28 91
Tatarkiewicz, Józef Jakub 30 359
Theed, William, III (1804-91) 30 703
Vilar, Manuel 32 538
Widnmann, Max von 33 160
Wyatt, Richard James 33 449
reproductions in hardstones 12 265
reproductions in porcelain 7 807
restorations 7 739; 29 *710*

Thorvaldsen, Bertel—cont.
sculpture 15 837; 23 295; 30 459
monuments 22 47; 25 115; 32 876
mythological 22 415; 29 562; 30 764, 765
reliefs 10 479; 16 719; 26 137
restorations 32 759
tombs 18 431; 24 855; 26 810; 31 130
Thorvaldsen, Gotskálk 30 763
Thorvaldsens Museum see under COPENHAGEN → museums
Thory, Claude-Antoine 26 73
Thoryson, Peter see TORRIGIANI, PIETRO (DI TORRIGIANO D'ANTONIO)
Thott, Otto, Count 8 758; 18 418
Thou (family) 11 716
Thouars, Marie de Rieux, Vicomtesse de 20 723
Thougga see DOUGGA
Thouin, Gabriel 12 64, 124
Thouret, Nikolaus Friedrich von 30 767*
groups and movements 13 200
patrons and collectors 19 780; 33 429
pupils 14 307
works 13 200; 29 874; 33 37
Thourion 14 564
Thourneysser, Johann Jakob, I see THURNEYSEN, JOHANN JAKOB, I
Thouron, Jacques 21 643
Thovez, Enrico 4 100; 30 767*
Thoyars, Laquin de
works 12 518
Thoynard de Vougy, Barthélémy 8 589
Thrabaca see TABARKA
Thracian 2 100; 5 143; 6 159; 25 533; 26 852; 30 767–72*
beakers 30 771, 771
bowls 30 769
bronze 30 769, 770
cauldrons 13 849
craftsmen and artists 30 770
cups 30 769
cymbals 30 769
gilding 30 769
glass 30 769
gold 30 769, 770
greaves 30 771
helmets 30 770, 770–71
iconography 30 771
iron 30 769
jugs 30 770
metalwork 26 544; 30 767, 768–72*, 770, 771
repoussé 13 849; 30 769, 770
rhyta 30 770
sculpture 5 155
silver 13 848–9, 849; 30 769, 770, 770, 771
swords 30 769
tattoos 30 769
tombs 5 155
trade 30 772
wall paintings 30 768
see also SKUDRIANS
Thrale, Hester 4 167; 13 303
Thran, Christian
works 17 817
Thrän, Ferdinand 31 568
Thrane, Henrik 19 812
Thrasybulus 1 646
Thrasyllos 2 666, 667
Thrasymedes 10 434; 13 440, 596; 30 774*
Thrax 13 484
threads 30 537–43*, 540, 543
historical and regional traditions
Africa 1 343
Belgium 3 610; 10 II2; 14 III2
Byzantine 9 668
Central Asia, Western 6 250
China 7 45, 50, 50, 51, 51, 53
Early Christian (c. AD 250-843) 9 668
threads
historical and regional traditions—cont.
Egypt, ancient 30 540
England 10 350; 23 461; 30 541, 542
France 30 542
Germany 10 181; 12 463, 464; 30 542
Gothic 10 181; 13 194
Hungary 15 11, 11, 12
Indian subcontinent 15 663, 675
Iran 16 450; 18 48, 49
Islamic 16 430, 443, 450
Italy 11 193
Japan 17 308; 30 541
Malaysia 20 176
Mongolia 21 877
Peru 24 512
Poland 25 133
Sicily 16 430
Spain 29 301, 349, 349
United States of America 30 542
materials
alpaca hair 30 538, 539*
camel hair 30 538, 539*
cashmere 30 539*
copper 30 540, 542
cotton 3 440; 30 538*, 541
goat-hair 30 538, 539*
gold 10 181; 30 308, 540, 541–2
Anglo-Saxon 2 83, 84
Belgium 10 II2; 14 III2; 30 II1, 2
Central Asia, Western 6 250
China 7 45, 50, 50, 51, 51, 53
Early Christian and Byzantine 9 668
England 10 350
France 30 II1
Germany 12 463, 464
Gothic 10 181; 13 194
Indian subcontinent 15 663, 675
Iran 16 450
Islamic 16 430, 450
Malaysia 20 176
Poland 25 133
Romanesque 26 703
Spain 29 301, 349
gold dust 30 540
gold leaf 30 540
grasses 30 538
hemp 30 537–8*
jute 30 538
kapok 30 538*
leather 3 440
linen 12 463, 464, 469; 30 537*, 541
llama-hair 30 538, 539*
metal 18 48, 588, 590; 30 540–42*
Belgium 3 610
Byzantine 9 668
Germany 12 462, 463, 467, 469
Hungary 15 11, 12
Iran 18 49
Islamic 16 443
Italy 11 193
Peru 24 512
Spain 29 349
mohair 30 539*
nettles 30 538
paper 30 541
parchment 30 541
raffia 3 440; 30 537
rami (fibre) 30 538*
silk 7 50, 51, 51; 12 463, 467, 469; 15 11; 21 877; 23 461; 30 537, 538, 539*, 541, 541
silver 30 308, 540, 541–2
Belgium 10 II2; 14 III2; 30 II1, 2
Central Asia, Western 6 250
England 10 350; 23 461; 30 541
France 30 II1
Germany 12 463
Gothic 13 194
threads
materials
silver—cont.
Hungary 15 11
Indian subcontinent 15 664
Iran 16 450
Islamic 16 450
Spain 29 301, 349
silver dust 30 540
silver-gilt 15 11, 12; 23 461, 639; 30 308, 541
silver leaf 30 540
sinew 3 440
vicuña-hair 30 539*
wool 30 538–9*
techniques
gilding 30 541
uses
bookbindings 4 346
braids 30 540, 542
embroidery 10 181, 181; 17 308; 30 540
hairstyles 1 343
lace 18 588, 590; 30 540, 542
stoles (ecclesiastical) 2 84
tapestries , ; 10 350; 11 193; 30 308, II1, 2
tattoos 30 366
Threave 31 230
Three Brushes of Ōbaku see ŌBAKU SANPITSU
Three Brushes of the Kan'ei see KAN'EI NO SANPITSU
Three Brushes of the Late Edo period see BAKUMATSU NO SANPITSU
Three Candles Press 16 18
three-cell tombs see under TOMBS → types
three-colour glazed ware see under POTTERY → wares
three-colour scheme 18 706
Three Division Plastic Arts Society see SANKAI ZŌKEI BIJUTSU KYŌKAI
Three Graces Clock 11 627
Three Kingdoms see under CHINA → periods
Three Kings Mazer 10 325
Three Kings' Shrine 26 683
Three Nagasaki bunjin 17 189, 199
three-quarter hollow mouldings see under MOULDINGS → types
Three Tower Reliquary 13 169
Throckmorton, Arthur 17 616
Throndhjem see TRONDHEIM
Throne Images, Master of the 4 20
Throne of Dagobert 5 806; 11 623; 30 776, 779
Throne of Maximian 6 389; 30 776, 776
thrones 6 387, 389; 30 774–86*
historical and regional traditions
Achaemenid 30 774
Africa 1 352, 353
Ancient Near East 1 890; 30 774*
Assyrian 30 774
Bamum 1 352, 353; 3 152, 152
Buddhism 30 785
Burma 5 261; 30 785
Byzantine 9 656
Cambodia 30 785
Cameroon 3 152
Carolingian 30 776
Central Asia, Eastern 6 311
China 7 40; 30 785*
Denmark 8 745; 30 782
Early Christian (c. AD 250-843) 30 776*
Ecuador 30 786
Egypt 30 776
Egypt, ancient 29 393; 30 774–5*
England 30 778, 778, 780
Etruscan 10 633, 633
France 30 781–2
Greece, ancient 13 452; 30 775*
thrones
historical and regional traditions—cont.
Indian subcontinent 15 693, 707, 707; 30 784–5*
Indonesia 30 785
Islamic 16 516; 30 784*
Italy 30 776, 777, 777–8
Baroque 3 832
Etruscan 10 633
Renaissance 30 781
Romanesque 3 237; 16 688
Japan 17 36–7; 30 785*
Korea 30 785*
Laos 30 785
Malaysia 30 785
Manabi 30 786
Mesoamerica, Pre-Columbian 30 786*
Phoenician 24 642
Poland 25 120
Romanesque 3 237; 16 688; 30 777
Romania 26 717, 717–18
Rome, ancient 6 388; 30 775*
Scandinavia 30 778
Sicily 30 777
South America, Pre-Columbian 30 786*
South-east Asia 30 785–6*
Spain 30 778
Syria 30 776
Thailand 30 785
materials
amber 1 762
bronze 30 774
canopies (ii) (textile coverings) 30 778, 778
gold 9 656; 15 707, 707
ivory 30 774, 775, 776
leather 30 775
linen 30 776
marble 3 237; 13 452; 30 777, 777
metal 30 775
porphyry 30 777
stone 30 776
veneers 30 775
wicker 30 775
wood 1 353; 25 120; 26 717; 30 775, 776, 776, 778, 778
techniques
gilding 25 120
types
block-thrones 30 775
see also CHAIRS
thronos see under CHAIRS → types
Throop, Louisa 24 691
Throp, Bernard 25 399
throwing see under CERAMICS; POTTERY → techniques
throwing knives see under KNIVES → types
throwsticks 10 40
thrymsas see under COINS → types
Thuan Dong 6 425
thūbhas see STUPAS
Thubon (India) 15 285; 30 786*
Thu Bon (Vietnam) 6 430
Thubron, Harry 10 375; 14 816
Thuburbo Maius 31 427
gardens 12 70
markets 19 888, 889
mosaics 27 63
Temple of Ceres 26 919
Temple of Mercury 26 867; 30 436
Thucydides 2 666; 13 415; 21 556; 22 42
Thugga see DOUGGA
Thuilius, Johannes 10 174
Thuison 5 895
Thula 32 317
Thulden, Theodoor van 30 787–9*
collaboration 14 46; 28 904
reproductive prints by others 12 851; 22 717
teachers 4 182; 5 49
Thulden, Theodoor van—cont.
works 1 18, 658, 659; 3 559, 560; 23 769; 25 579; 27 296; 30 788, 789
Thule 13 620; 22 546, 574, 575, 655
Thulié, Jean-Baptiste-Henri 9 425
Thulin, Waldred 11 498
thuluth script see under SCRIPTS → types
Thum, Christian 30 78
Thumann, Paul 19 333
Thumb, Christian 23 636; 30 790*
collaboration 12 371
pupils 22 61
works 30 790; 32 822
Thumb, Johann Baptist 30 790
Thumb, Johann Christian see THUMB, CHRISTIAN
Thumb, Kaspar 30 790
Thumb, Michael 30 790*
assistants 30 790
collaboration 12 371
pupils 3 490; 30 790
works 32 821, 822
Thumb, Peter, I (fl c. 1635-40) 30 790
Thumb, Peter, II (1681-1766) 30 790–92*
works 12 372; 27 554; 30 126, 791; 32 822
thumb rings see under RINGS → types
Thun (Switzerland) 17 526; 25 525; 30 124
Thun (family) 19 807; 21 757
Thun, Count 20 813
Thun, Mateo 2 815
Thung Setthi 21 595
Thun-Hohenstein, F. A. von, Graf 11 780
Thun-Hohenstein, Guidobald von, Cardinal, Archbishop of Salzburg 27 661; 30 792–3*
Thun-Hohenstein, Johann Ernst von, Archbishop of Salzburg 11 132; 30 793
Thun-Hohenstein, Michael Oswald 20 814
Thuot, Carl Ludwig 12 798
works 12 798
thūpas see STUPAS
Thupelo workshops 29 113
Thür, Georg 23 340
Thurah, Laurids (Lauridsen) de see DE THURAH, LAURIDS (LAURIDSEN)
Thuraine and Le Hollandois 2 464
Thurber, Gorham 13 9
Thurber, James 5 759
Thureau-Dangin, François 1 889; 2 503; 30 873
Thurgau 30 142
Thurgau Crucifix 13 142
Thürheim, Graf 25 673; 29 372
thuribles see CENSERS
Thurii 13 401, 587
Thüringen, Kyffhäuser monument to Emperor William I 12 406
Thüringen Frick, von 10 413
Thuringia 12 361; 30 793*
metalwork 26 683
Thuringia, Hermann I, Landgraf von 33 588
Thuringians 21 500, 501
Thüring von Ringoltingen 30 149
Thurloe, John 21 615; 28 749
Thurmann, Peder C. 14 506
Thurmayr, Johannes 33 271
Thürmer, Joseph 14 25; 23 108
Thurn, Everard im 10 580
Thurn, Franz 23 340
Thurn, H. P. 28 917
Thurn, Jakob Maximilian, Graf, Prince-Bishop of Gurk 31 357
Thurnauer, Gérard 26 192
Thurneysen, Johann Jakob, I (1636-1711) 4 128; 10 392; 30 793*

Thurneysen, Johann Jakob, II (1668-1730) 30 793
Thurneysser, Leonhard 22 340
Thurn und Taxis, Alexander Ferdinand, Prince of 33 692
Thurn und Taxis, Anselm, Prince of 8 33
Thurn und Taxis, Leonard von 8 87
Thurn und Taxis, Princes of 26 87
Thurstan, Archbishop of York 7 351; 26 380
Thurston, Stephen 31 660
Thurtle, John *see* THIRTLE, JOHN
Thury, Jacques Cassini de *see* CASSINI DE THURY, JACQUES
Thury, Levente 15 3
Thury, Pierre de 18 685
Thurzo, Stanislav 18 467; 30 793–4*
Thutmose 9 791; 10 68; 30 794*
 house 22 723
 works 9 884
 workshop 1 756; 22 *723*
thuya 3 585
Thwaites, John Anthony 33 635
Thwaites & Son 2 758
Thyateira 19 840, 841
Thybault, Willem 13 893
Thynne, John 30 794*
 architecture 8 44; 20 893; 28 526, 894
 interior decoration 9 367; 29 834
 tapestries 10 349
Thynne, John Alexander, 4th Marquess of Bath 8 106
Thynne, Thomas, 2nd Marquis of Bath 33 447
Thyreatis Treasure 14 356, *357*
Thys, Gaston 18 866
Thys, Pieter *see* THIJS, PIETER
Thysdrus
 amphitheatre 1 797; 26 919; 31 426
 mosaics 27 63
 sculpture 27 19
Thyssen, Fritz, Foundation 2 369
Thyssen-Bornemisza (family) 19 782
Thyssen-Bornemisza, Hans Heinrich, Baron von 5 354; 30 795*
Thyssen-Bornemisza, Heinrich, Baron von 30 794–5*
Tia 27 812; 31 107
Tiahuanaco 4 255, *255*; 23 565; 29 127, 132, *156*, 161, 219; 30 795–7*, *796*
 Akapana 30 447
 architecture 4 256; 29 135, 161, 164; 30 796; 31 47
 church 4 256
 doors 9 166
 Gateway of the Sun 9 166; 29 168; 30 *796*, 797
 graves 29 133
 hardstones 29 185
 joinery 5 408
 Kalasasaya 29 167; 30 447
 masonry 29 162
 musical instruments 29 216
 pottery 30 797; 31 *46*
 religion 29 130
 sculpture 29 168, 171; 30 *796*, 796–7
 shells 29 218
 spear-throwers 29 205
 stelae 29 620
 stirrup jars 29 176
 temple 29 165
 textiles 29 180
 tombs 31 118
Tianjin 6 *615*; 30 797–8*
 carpets 7 51, 68
 congregational mosque 6 677
 French Church 6 678
 kites 7 113
 Laoxikai *see* French Church
 Museum of Art 6 772; 30 798
Tianjin—cont.
 Museum of Tianjin Opera 30 798
 Notre-Dame-des-Victoires 6 678
 Qingzhen si *see* congregational mosque
 Wanghai lou *see* Notre-Dame-des-Victoires
 see also YANGLIUQING
Tianlongshan *see* MT TIANLONG
tianqi *see* LACQUER → types → filled-in *urushi*
Tianshui 28 718, *719*
Tian So Po, Thierry 11 759
Tiantai Buddhism *see under* BUDDHISM → sects
Tianwai yi xianren *see* DOKURYŪ SHŌEKI
Tianxingguan (Jiangling), Tomb 1 7 139, *139*, 140
Tiao Kuan *see* DIAO GUAN
tiaras 17 527; 32 390
tiaras, papal *see* PAPAL TIARAS
Tiaret 1 634
Tiarini, Alessandro 4 277, 334; 30 798–9*
 assistants 11 15
 attributions 8 149
 patrons and collectors 9 111; 10 525
 reproductive prints by others 7 857; 33 358
 works 30 *798*
Tiarini, Antonio 30 799
Tiarini, Francesco 30 799
Tibães Abbey 25 *288*, 291; 26 254; 30 799*
 carvings 32 *536*
 sculpture 25 301
Tibaldi, Domenico 30 803–4*
 pupils 5 856
 works 1 637; 4 280; 20 898; 30 799
Tibaldi, Maria Felice 26 841; 29 887
Tibaldi, Pellegrino 4 426; 21 525; 24 420; 26 769; 30 799–803*
 altars 21 525
 architectural decorations 26 317
 architecture 5 327; 8 224; 10 499; 21 518, *519*, 532; 28 4; 30 *800*
 assistants 5 327
 attributions 30 803
 collaboration 7 777; 8 504; 10 503
 interior decoration 19 687; 30 *800*
 metalwork 19 371
 paintings 2 1; 10 503; 30 799
  altarpieces 10 502
  frescoes 4 276; 10 502, 503; 15 137; 28 709; 29 *300*, 301
 patrons and collectors 4 425, 655; 5 792; 13 922; 14 516; 28 5
 pupils 27 667; 30 803
 reproductive prints by others 1 551
 sculpture 21 534
Tibaldi, Tebaldo 30 799
Tibas 9 678
Tibau, Manuel 26 479; 30 804*
Tibau, Samuel 25 305; 30 804*
Tibble, Geoffrey 10 652; 23 333
Tiberghien, Pierre Joseph Jacques 3 600
Tiberiapolis *see* KONYA (TURKEY)
Tiberino, Il 24 447
Tiberio (Raineri di Diotallevi) d'Assisi *see* ASSISI, TIBERIO (RAINERI DI DIOTALLEVI) D'
Tiberios I, Emperor of Byzantium (*reg* 578-82) 16 581, 607
Tiberios II, Emperor of Byzantium (*reg* 698-705) 9 636, *637*
Tiber Island
 Sanctuary of Asklepios 27 1
 Temple of Asklepios 27 2
Tiberius, Emperor of Rome (*reg* 14-37) 29 389; 30 804*
 architecture 2 156; 5 684; 19 312; 26 782, 784, 786, 869, 875, 891, 892; 27 66, 837; 31 349
 coins 27 96
 paintings 9 13; 24 207; 25 44
 sculpture 27 31, 32, 33, *33*, 34
Tiberius Bede (London, BL, Cotton MS. Tib. C.II.) 15 875
Tiberius Claudius Italicus 2 606
Tiberius Psalter *see under* PSALTERS → individual manuscripts
Tibertelli, Ernesta 8 772
Tibes 29 200
Tibesti 1 370, *371*
Tibet 6 *614*, 616; 30 804–50*, *806*
 aesthetics 30 809
 agate 30 839
 altars 1 704–5*
 amulets 30 839, 840, 845
 appliqué 30 846
 aprons 3 442
 archaeology 30 847*
 architectural decorations 30 842, 846
 architecture 21 44, 592–3*; 30 812, 814–21*
 art criticism 30 848
 art history 30 848*
 banners 30 828
 bark 30 844
 beads 30 839
 beadwork 3 442
 bells 30 843
 birch 30 845
 bone 4 314
 bookbindings 30 836
 book covers 30 836, 846, *846*
 book illustrations 30 835, 836
 books 30 835–6*
 boxes 30 840, *840*, 847
 brass 4 687; 30 822, *823*, *824*, *825*, *826*, *827*, 839, 841, *849*
 brocades 30 846
 bronze 30 351, 839, 840–41, *841*
 calligraphy 30 845
 carpets 30 836–7*
 casting 30 842
 caves 30 817, 818
 cemeteries 30 815
 chortens 29 868; 30 815–16, 817, 818, 819
 clay 30 823
 coins 30 837*
 collections 30 813–14*, 848, 849*, 850
 colophons 30 *836*
 copper 30 822, 841, *844*
 coral 7 836; 30 839
 craftsmen and artists 13 885; 30 809, 811–13*
 doorframes 30 846
 dress 30 807, 837–9*, *838*
 drums (musical instruments) 30 844
 dyes 30 845
 education (art) 30 812–13*
 embossing 30 *840*
 embroidery 30 846
 ethnography 30 848
 exhibitions 30 850*
 felt 10 875; 30 846
 fibulae 30 841, *841*
 fortifications 21 592–3*
 gilding 12 624; 28 *582*; 30 *844*
 gold 30 823, *836*, 836, 839, 840, 841, *841*
 guidebooks 13 812
 guilds 30 843
 gyeltsen 30 842
 hair 30 845
 hardstones 7 91; 28 *582*
 harnesses 14 184*
 headdresses 30 840
 historiography 30 848*
 iconography 5 91; 30 809–11*, 813, 822, 825–6, 845
Tibet—cont.
 inks 15 850
 inlays 30 *841*
 inscriptions 13 885; 30 809, 813
 iron 30 841
 jewellery 7 836; 30 839–40*, *840*
 languages 30 804
 looms 30 837, 845
 lost-wax casting 30 823
 lutes 30 844
 maṇḍalas 5 *104*, 104; 22 *234*
 manuals
  painting 28 543
  sculpture 28 543
 manuscript illumination 30 827, 828, 830, 832, 835, *836*, 836
  Buddhism 30 *836*
 manuscripts 6 306; 30 835–6*, 845
 masks 30 839
 metalwork 30 808, 812, 840–43*, *849*
 miniatures (manuscript illumination) 30 835
 mirrors 30 840–41, *841*
 monasteries 30 813–14, 819, 820
  Buddhism 5 105; 21 847–8*; 27 695; 30 *351*, 808, *817*, 818, 828
 monoliths 30 816
 mounts (works on paper and scrolls) 22 234*, *234*
 museums 30 849*, 850
 musical instruments 30 843–4*
  Buddhism 30 843
 painting 22 *234*, 785
  Buddhism 5 *104*; 21 880–81; 30 *810*, 827–35*
  ceiling 15 562
  portraits 30 *830*, 830–31
  scroll 30 *829*, *830*, *831*, *833*, *834*
  wall 30 827, 828, 829–30, 831–2, *832*, 833–5
 palaces 30 820, *820*
 paper 7 114; 30 844–5*
 patronage 5 104; 30 813–14*, 822, 828
 pattern books 30 813
 photoarchives 30 849
 pigments 30 835
 pillars 30 816
 pinnacles 30 842
 pouncing 30 845
 prayer flags 30 845
 prayer wheels 30 842
 printing 30 810, 847
 prints 6 314
  Buddhism 5 105
  woodblock 5 105; 30 836, 845*
 religion 30 808*, 822
 reliquaries 30 *849*
 rock art 30 823
 roof decorations 30 842
 roofs 30 842
 rugs 30 *837*
 scripts 6 307; 30 832, 836
 scrolls 22 234; 30 823, 835
  tangkas 28 309; 30 827, 828, 830, 832–5, *838*, 845
 sculpture 30 821–7*
  Bon (religion) 30 822
  bronze 30 351
  Buddhism 21 880–81; 30 351, 809, 821–7, *823*, *824*, *825*, *826*, *827*
  stone 30 823
  wood 30 823
 serge 30 845
 shells 28 *582*; 30 843–4
 signatures 30 811
 silk 30 846
 silver 30 823, 839, 840, *840*, 841
 stencilling 30 835
 stone 30 823
 stucco 30 823
 stupas 13 884–5, *885*; 29 867–8*; 30 815–16, 817, 818, 819, 842
 symbols 30 811
Tibet—cont.
 tangkas 30 809, 810
 tantras 5 103
 teabowls 30 847
 temples 30 815, 816, 819
  Buddhism 19 *294*; 30 *815*, 818–19, 842
 rock-cut 30 817, 818
 textiles 5 *104*; 30 845–6*
 thokchak 26 141; 30 840
 timber structures 30 816
 tombs 30 805, 847
 tools 30 842
 trade 30 807–8*
  brocades 30 807
  cotton 30 807
  gold 30 807
  pigments 30 807
  silk 30 807
 trappings 14 184*
 treatises 30 813
  aesthetics 30 848
  painting 30 848
  sculpture 30 848
 trumpets 28 *582*; 30 844, *844*
 turquoise 30 839
 window-frames 30 846
 wood 30 823, 835, 836, *846*, 846–7
 wood-carvers 30 847
 wood-carvings 30 836, 846–7*, *846*
 wool 30 845
 writing 30 836
Tibidabo, Casa Arnus 29 321
Tibur *see* TIVOLI
Tiburgueta 3 339
tiburio 30 851*
Tiburnus 31 57
Tiburtine Sybil, Master of the 20 772–3*; 22 835; 23 671
 attributions 20 795
 teachers 4 594
 works 20 *773*
Ticciati, Girolamo 11 188; 30 851*; 31 129
Tichborne, William 16 22
Tichborne Dole 9 *279*, 279
Tichelaar factory 22 883; 30 879, 883
Tichitt 1 305, *376*; 20 861
Ticho, Albert Abraham 16 571
Ticho, Anna 16 567, 571; 30 851*
Tichter, Michel 18 452
Tichý, František 8 393
Tichy, Karol 18 429; 25 122
Ticinese school 4 491
Ticino, Banca del Gottardo 30 153
Tickencote, St Peter's 26 589
Tickhill Barbican 6 54
Tickner, Lisa 33 312
Ticonderoga *see* FORT VAUDREUIL
Ticozzi, Stefano 10 208; 16 781; 30 852*
Tidemand, Adolph 23 232; 30 852*
 collaboration 13 776
 groups and movements 9 461
 pupils 16 63; 23 204; 33 697
 reproductive prints by others 29 66
 works 23 225
Tidemanis, Jānis
Tidemann, Philipp 30 853*
 reproductive prints by others 31 802
 works 22 *373*; 23 502
Tidjikdja 20 861
 library 20 862
Tidö Castle 30 *65*, 70, 92
Tiéard, Guillaume 19 341
tie-bars 9 599; 20 576; 30 853*
Tiebout, Cornelius 30 853*; 31 601
Tieck, (Christian) Friedrich 30 854*; 33 155
 assistants 18 89
 collaboration 26 22; 28 98

Tieck, (Christian) Friedrich—cont.
groups and movements **3** 799; **26** 738
patrons and collectors **12** 406
pupils **1** 119
teachers **28** 45
works **22** 47; **33** 282
Tieck, Ludwig **9** 443; **11** 820; **26** 375; **27** 338; **32** 751
tied arch bridges *see under* BRIDGES → types
Tiede, August **3** 794
Tiedemann, Friedrich **1** 844
Tiedra, Diego de **8** 253
tie-dyeing *see under* DYEING → types
Tiefenbronn an der Enz, St Mary Magdalene **12** 384; **22** 188, *188*; **26** 184; **28** 171, *171*
Tieffenbrücker, Gaspar **22** 374
attributions **22** *374*
Tieffental, Hans **14** 86
Tiegem, Maarten van **2** 198
Tiegen, Jan van **5** 47, 49; **16** 867; **30** 317, 319
Tiel Church **22** 820
tieli **7** 31
Tielke, Joachim **22** 374
Tiellandt, Willem Hendrik Jacob Westreenen van, Baron van *see* WESTREENEN VAN TIELLANDT, WILLEM HENDRIK JACOB, Baron van
T'ien-chin *see* TIANJIN
Tienen, Hendrik van *see* HENDRIK VAN TIENEN
Tienen, Jacob van *see* JACOB VAN TIENEN
Tienen, Onze Lieve Vrouwe ten Poel **13** 62, 100
Tienen, Renier van *see* RENIER VAN TIENEN
T'ien-lung-shan *see* MT TIANLONG
Tiepolo (family) **3** 228; **14** 584; **32** 195, 201
Tiepolo, Giambattista **4** 46; **13** 740; **16** 669, 677; **20** 67; **22** 415; **23** 294; **30** 854–64*; **32** 194, 195, 196
assistants **30** 854, 863–4
attributions **7** 894; **25** 1
caricatures **5** 756
collaboration **12** 582; **20** 585
drawings **9** 223
etchings **5** 685; **10** 554
groups and movements **3** 261; **26** 495, 500
methods **19** 354; **23** 378
paintings **5** 884
frescoes **15** 138–9; **16** 676; **32** 194, 410
Chinese Palace (Lomonosov) **27** 402
Colleoni Chapel (Bergamo) **3** 772
Doge's Palace (Venice) **32** 220
Palacio Real (Madrid) **20** 72; **29** 283, 304
Palazzo Canossa (Verona) **32** 342
Palazzo Clerici (Milan) **16** 674, *674*, 716; **21** 527
Residenz (Würzburg) **23** 3; **30** *858*; **33** *433*, 434
S Maria del Rosario (Venice) **9** *109*
S Maria degli Scalzi (Venice) **5** 778
Villa Nazionale Già Pisani (Stra) **16** 719; **24** 865; **25** 561; **29** 736; **32** 553
Villa Valmarana (Vicenza) **16** 719; **30** *859*; **32** 553
oil
allegorical **1** 659; **30** *860*
altarpieces **23** 756
literary themes **30** 358
mythological **30** *857*
Tiepolo, Giambattista
paintings
oil—cont.
oil sketches **23** 381
religious **3** 773; **30** *863*
patrons and collectors **32** 196
Algarotti, Francesco **1** 633
André, Edouard (-François) (1833-94) **16** 851
Angiviller, Charles-Claude de Flahaut de la Billarderie, Comte d' **2** 53
Archinto (family) **2** 310
Augustus III, King of Poland (*reg* 1733-63) **1** 633
Barbaro (family) **3** 202
Beurnonville, Etienne-Edmond Martin, Baron de **3** 890
Bonaparte, Mathilde, Princess **4** 308
Borromeo (family) **16** 562
Buckner, Richard **5** 78
Butler, Charles (1822-1910) **5** 311
Capuchins **5** 690
Carmelite Order **5** 778
Charles III, King of Spain (*reg* 1759-88) **4** 562
Cheney, Edward **6** 537
Cognacq, (Théodore-) Ernest **7** 528
Crespi, Cristoforo Benigno **8** 146
Dominican Order **9** 110
Felton, Alfred **10** 877
Francis-Joseph, Prince of Liechtenstein (*reg* 1772-81) **19** 338
Gerini, Andrea, Marchese **12** 355
Greiffenklau, Karl Philipp von, Prince-Bishop of Würzburg **13** 631–2
Horne, Herbert (Percy) **14** 764
Kuen, Franz Martin **18** 497
List, Herbert **19** 478
Louisa Ulrica, Queen of Sweden (1720-82) **30** 118
Mocenigo, Alvise I, Doge of Venice (*reg* 1570-77) **21** 747
Munro (of Novar), H(ugh) A(ndrew) J(ohnstone) **22** 314
Museu Nacional de Belas Artes (Rio de Janeiro) **4** 726
Poldi Pezzoli, Gian Giacomo **25** 144
Poniatowski, Stanisław, Prince **25** 213
Rezzonico (family) **26** 286
Ryerson, Martin A(ntoine) **27** 463
Sasso, Giovanni Maria **27** 864
Schwiter, Louis-Auguste **28** 196
Seilern, Antoine, Count **28** 377
Strange, John **29** 746
Tessin, Carl Gustav, Count **30** 523
Van Horne, William (Cornelius) **31** 880
Wrightsman, Charles B(ierer) **33** 416
Yusupov, Nikolay (Borisovich), Prince (1751- 1831) **2** 417; **33** 579
prints **25** 607
pupils **5** 168; **18** 410, 683; **23** 497; **30** 132, 863
reproductive prints by others **32** 501
Bartolozzi, Francesco **3** 308
Cattini, Giovanni **6** 91
Giampiccoli, Giuliano **12** 582
Monaco, Pietro **21** 831
Saint-Non, Richard de, Abbé **27** 571
Tiepolo, Lorenzo (Baldissera) **30** 864
Volpato, Giovanni **32** 689
Zucchi, Francesco **33** 721
Tiepolo, Giambattista—cont.
teachers **18** 901
Tiepolo, Giandomenico **16** 669, 677; **30** 854, 863–4*; **32** 194
attributions **30** 864
collaboration **13** 632
patrons and collectors **4** 308; **27** 864
pupils **14** 834
reproductive prints by others **27** 571
teachers **30** 862
works **5** 756; **9** 223, 224, *224*; **10** 554; **11** 37; **12** 292; **16** 719; **30** *863*; **32** 194, 553
Tiepolo, Jacopo, Doge of Venice (*reg* 1229-49) **32** 184, 216
Tiepolo, Lorenzo (Baldissera) **24** 894; **30** 854, 862, 864–5*; **32** 194
Tierce, Jean-Baptiste **3** 840; **30** 865*
Tiercelet **19** 145
tierceron vaults *see under* VAULTS (CEILING) → types
Tiergevilla, Petrus de *see* PETRUS DE TIERGEVILLA
Tieri, Francesco da *see* FRANCESCO DA TIERI
Tiermes **27** 76
Tierp Church **30** 76, 865
Tierp school **16** 790; **30** 76, 865*
Tierra de Campas **26** 607
Tierradentro **7** *601*; **29** 132, *136*; **30** 866*
pottery **29** 150
sculpture **29** 146
tombs **30** 866; **31** 118
Tiers, Daniel **5** 579
Tiersch, Friedrich **31** 25
ties (architecture) *see* TIE-BARS
ties (dress) **9** 287; **28** 718
Tieshenggou (Gong xian) **7** 98
Tietgen, C. F. **21** 77
Tietharth, Joseph **29** 922
Tietz, (Adam) Ferdinand **30** 866–7*
groups and movements **26** 498
works **12** 405; **28** 381; **32** 120
Tietz, Johann Adam **30** 866
Tietze, Hans **30** 867*; **33** 159
Tietze-Conrat, Erica **30** 867; **33** 310
Tieze, Franz **9** 320
Tifalmin **24** 73, 74
houses **24** *73*
Tiffany, Charles Louis **30** 867*; **31** 654
Tiffany, Louis C., & Associated Artists **7** 577, 622; **14** 244; **15** 408; **30** 868; **31** 621; **33** 134
Tiffany, Louis Comfort **12** 788; **18** 627; **24** 671; **26** 353; **29** 498; **30** 867–9*; **31** 639
collaboration **4** 325; **33** 134
groups and movements **1** 171; **2** 564, 568; **31** 621
patrons and collectors **4** 71; **29** 516
works **13** 715; **23** 547; **29** 508, 516; **30** *868*; **31** 644, 654; **32** 109
Tiffany & Co. **9** 295; **28** 739, 741; **30** 867*; **31** 650, 653, 654, 655
designers **2** 208; **31** 650, 655
jewellery **31** *655*
metalwork **31** *650*
rock crystal **26** 486
stained glass **33** 246
Tiffany Glass and Decorating Co. **30** 868
Tiffany Glass Co. **24** 57; **30** 868
Tiffany Pottery **31** 639
Tiffany Studios **27** 557; **30** 868; **31** 654
Tiffany style *see* ART NOUVEAU
Tiffany & Young **30** 867; **31** 654
Tiffin, Charles **4** 818
Tiflis *see* TBILISI
Tiflis Ewer **16** 369, *370*
Tigak **24** 85
Tiger, Jerome **22** 597
Tigerman, Fugman, McCurry **30** 870
Tigerman, Stanley **30** 869–70*
works **30** *870*
Tiger's Eye: On Arts and Letters **24** 428, 433
tiger teeth *see under* TEETH → types
Tiglath-Pileser I (*reg* 1114-1076 BC) **2** 637, 639; **23** 153; **24** 178
Tiglath-Pileser III (*reg* 744-727 BC) **2** 503, 640
architecture **2** 638; **21** 288
reliefs **21** 299*
wall paintings **23** 151
Tigowa **15** *285*; **30** 870–71*
Kankali Devi Temple **15** *253*, 253–4, 469
Narsing Temple *see* KANKALI DEVI TEMPLE
sculpture **15** 470, 495
Tigrane Pasha **10** 91
Tigran Honents **2** 98, 429
Tigran II, King of Armenia (*reg* 95-56 BC) **2** 441; **9** 731
Tigre (people) **1** 305, 311; **10** 564
El Tigre **29** 142
Tigua **9** 710
Tihany Abbey **26** 638
Church of St Anianus **14** 883, 907
Tihanyi, Lajos **30** 871*
groups and movements **1** 131; **10** 108; **14** 901
works **10** 109
Tihrani, Hasan **15** 899
Tijdschrift voor Indische taal-, land- en volkenkunde **24** 437
Tijdschrift voor Photographie **2** 619
Tijen, Willem van **19** 861; **22** 832; **27** 230; **30** 871*
assistants **31** 867
collaboration **4** 815; **13** 685; **29** 531
groups and movements **23** 450
staff **19** 861
works **1** 804
Tijou, Jean **30** 871–2*
patrons and collectors **6** 116, 515; **14** 127
works **10** 275, 342; **14** 856; **16** 59; **19** 595, 599; **23** 467
writings **14** 856
Tijsen, Johan **29** 687; **30** 84
Tikal **13** *758*; **20** 881, 882, *882*, 883; **21** *193*, 196, 199, 246, 264, 266; **23** 826; **30** 872–3*
architecture **20** 883; **21** 214
bone-carvings **21** 247
Burial 116 **21** 247
caskets **21** 259
causeway **6** 97
fortifications **21** 599
graffiti **13** 269
lintels **9** 165
masks **21** 251
mouldings **21** 206
North Acropolis **30** 448
plaques **30** 786
pottery **21** 239
pyramids **25** 765; **31** 116
Pyramid Str 5D-33 **21** 213
Pyramid Structure 33-3 **29** 828
shells **21** 259
stairs **21** 206
stelae **20** 883; **21** 221, 246; **29** 620
Stele 4 **21** 259
Stele 16 **29** *620*
Stele 31 **20** 883; **21** 259
talud-tablero **30** 280
temples **21** 213; **30** 448, 449
Temple I **21** 213, 215; **25** 765; **30** 449, *872*
Temple II **21** 207, 213; **25** 765
Temple III **21** 213
Tikal
temples—cont.
Temple IV **21** 213, 215
Temple 5D-22, 1st **21** 213
Temple V **21** 213
Temple of the Giant Jaguar *see* Temple I
tombs **31** 118
Painted Tomb **27** 832
wall paintings **20** 881; **21** 231
Tikal, Václav **8** 394; **20** 254
Tikal Park, Museo Arqueológico-Sylvanus G. Morley **13** 769
Tikar **1** 289, 309
Tikhanov, Ivan **27** 401, 407, 427
Tikhanov, Mikhail **22** 619
Tikhonov, G. **27** 425
tikim **17** 568*, *568*
Tikkanen, Johan Jakob **11** 113
Tikopia **25** 181, 182; **29** 50, 51
Tikotin, Felix **17** 432
Tiktse **30** 819
Tikveša, Halid **4** 462
Tila
shields **24** *70*
Tilaganga **22** 767, 770
Tilantongo **21** 202, 235; **31** 118
Tilaurakot **19** 790; **22** 758
Til Barsip **1** 889; **2** 640; **21** *267*; **30** *180*, 873–4*
architecture **2** 640
necropolis **30** 873
palace **21** 288; **30** 873–4
sculpture **2** 640; **21** 301
wall paintings **2** 640; **21** 309, *309*; **30** 873–4
Tilbergs, Jānis Roberts
Tilborgh, Gillis van **30** 874*
works **9** 279, *279*
Tilburg, Onze Lieve Vrouw Abbey **3** 564
Tilcara **29** 191
Tilden, George **14** 207
Tilden, Philip **22** 60
Tilden, Samuel J. **32** 95
Tile Club **27** 557; **33** 43
tile graves **13** 383
tile pattern carpets *see under* CARPETS → types
tiles **14** 424–5; **30** 874–88*
historical and regional traditions
Afghanistan **16** 169
Austria **2** 815; **30** 884–5*, *885*
Belgium **3** 575, 576, 577, 588; **30** 878
Britain **30** 876–7*
Bulgaria **5** 159
Burma **5** *254*
Byzantine **9** 632, 633, *633*
Catalonia **29** 328, 329
Central Asia, Western **6** 202, 204, 206, 207–8*, *207*; **16** *140*, 169, 199, *236*, 239, 248
Champa **6** 432
China **6** 643, 685, 686, 691, 772, *788*, 882, 906; **7** 94, 143, 144
Cistercian Order **7** 353
Czech Republic **8** 403–4
Denmark **8** 747; **30** 883–4*
Egypt, ancient **10** 47, 48; **22** 159
England **4** 787; **10** 311–12; **30** *875*, 876–7*, *877*, XII
Etruscan **1** *126*; **30** 494
Finland **30** 884*
France **11** 603; **30** 885–6*
Germany **12** 409, 430; **30** 506, 884–5*
Greece, ancient **13** 387, 390, 411, *411*; **30** *493*, 493–4
Hungary **5** 85; **16** 422
Indian subcontinent **15** 336, *374*, 374–5, 686–7*
Bengal **15** 686
Islamic **15** 337, 338, 342, 354, 686
Mughal **15** 686–7
Rajput **15** *687*

tiles
historical and regional traditions—cont.
Iran 1 98; 6 172; 16 165, 193, 195, 199, 199, 234, 248, 249, 425; 28 615
Iraq 16 400, 404
Ireland 30 877
Islamic 16 140, 143, 158, 248–50*, 259, 269, 395; 21 506; 22 154
Afghanistan 16 169
Central Asia, Western 6 202, 204, 207; 16 140, 169, 199, 236, 239, 248
Indian subcontinent 15 337, 338, 342, 354, 686
Iran 6 172; 16 195, 248, 249
Iran: 9th cent 16 248
Iran: 12th cent. 16 165
Iran: 13th cent. 1 98; 16 193
Iran: 15th cent 16 199, 199–200
Iran: 18th cent. 16 234, 425
Iraq 16 400, 404
Morocco 16 250
North Africa 16 427
Ottoman 16 206, 221, 419, 420, 421, 422, 423
Spain 16 216, 217
Syria 16 422
Tunisia 16 250, 427
Turkey 16 206, 221, 248, 418; 30 XIII1
Yemen 16 215
Italy 1 126; 16 422, 735; 30 886, 886–7*
Japan 17 47, 259, 262; 23 822
Khwarazm 6 207
Korea 18 264, 278, 299, 313, 378
Mexico 25 II1
Morocco 16 250
Netherlands, the 22 878, 880–81; 25 303; 30 876, 878–9*, 879, XIII2
North Africa 16 427
Norway 30 884*
Ottoman 16 206, 221, 260, 419, 420, 421, 422, 423, 604; 23 643
Poland 25 122
Portugal 30 879–82*, 880
Rome, ancient 15 51; 25 171; 26 877; 30 494
Russia 27 400; 30 884*
Scandinavia 30 883–4*
Scotland 28 246
Sicily 30 887
Spain 16 216, 217; 29 297, 323, 325, 326; 30 882–3*, 883, XIII3
Sweden 30 89, 97, 884*
Switzerland 30 143, 884–5*
Syria 16 422
Transoxiana 6 207
Tunisia 16 250, 427
Turkey 5 282; 9 633; 16 206, 221, 248, 418, 604
Islamic 30 XIII1
United States of America 30 887–8*; 31 637
Vietnam 6 432; 32 485
Yemen 16 215
materials
clay 23 822; 30 874
earthenwares 30 874, 877
enamel 9 633; 30 874
faience (i) (glass) 10 47, 47, 48
faience (ii) (ceramics) 30 875
glazes 16 165, 239, 248; 30 874–5*, 876*
inlays 30 874
inscriptions 6 208
maiolica 30 875, 886, 886
manganese dioxide 16 248
marble 13 387, 390
masonry 13 757
ochre 16 248

tiles
materials—cont.
pigments 16 249
porcelain 6 906
pottery 9 632, 633; 11 603; 17 262
terracotta 1 126; 3 588; 13 390–91; 15 51; 17 47; 30 493, 493–4
technical examination 30 409
techniques
carving 16 248
mass production 30 877, 882, 887
moulding 6 772
painting 30 874
polychromy 23 643
printing 30 874
sgraffito 16 248, 250; 30 874
transfer (printing) 30 877
types
Akoustolith 13 757
alfardón 30 883
alfardón mig 30 883
arista 30 879, 882
aves e ramagens 30 881
azulejos 4 722
Portugal 3 222, 815; 25 288, 292, 303, 309; 30 879, 882
Spain 29 327; 30 882
azulejos de xadrez 30 879
box 26 879
caixilho 30 880, 880
chimneys 13 390
cuenca 30 875*, 879, 882
cuerda seca 30 875*
Central Asia, Western 16 239
Islamic 16 199, 239, 249, 250
Ottoman 16 199
Portugal 30 879
Spain 29 322; 30 875, 875, 882
Turkey 16 199
encaustic 4 769; 30 876*, 876, 877, 885, 886
enxaquetado 30 880, 880
enxaquetado rico 30 880, 880
grinaldas 30 881
laçarias e rosas 30 881
laggioni 27 893
lājvardīna 16 249, 412
lustre 16 216, 248, 249; 28 634
mīnā'ī 16 249
olambrillas 30 882
painted 16 248–9
pantiles 13 390
Pisano 30 883
socarrats 29 325; 30 883
tapete 30 880, 880
tegulae mammatae 26 871
vitreous 30 874
uses
architectural decorations 15 338, 342, 374–5; 16 143, 169, 206, 215, 221, 234, 239, 248–50*, 249; 25 292, II1
architecture 16 217, 236, 269; 18 264
cenotaphs 6 172
chimney-pieces 30 874
churches *see under* CHURCHES → decoration
dairies 30 876
façades 28 615; 30 875, 876, 885
fireplaces 3 576; 30 876
floors 3 575, 577; 16 250; 26 877; 29 75; 30 874, 876
hypocausts 15 51; 26 879
inkstones 7 94
inscriptions 16 165, 248
interior decoration 28 246; 30 875, 876
mausolea 16 140
mihrabs 5 282; 16 249; 21 506
mosaics 6 208; 16 195, 199, 216, 248, 249, 250, 259; 22 159; 30 506, 882
pavements 30 886
polychromy 25 171

tiles
uses—cont.
revetments 16 250
roofs 6 643; 17 47, 259; 18 278; 23 822; 26 877, 878; 27 131; 30 874
shrines (i) (cult) 28 634
stoves 2 815; 3 575; 27 400; 30 89, 97, 874, 876
tombs 15 686
vaults (ceiling) 26 878
walls 4 787; 26 877; 30 874, 876
Tilghman, Benjamin 12 787; 24 41
Tilgner, Victor (Oscar) 30 888–90*; 32 445
assistants 10 750
teachers 4 220
works 2 802; 30 889
Tilia, Giuseppe 24 481
Tilich 31 557
Tilimsān *see* TLEMCEN
Tiljak, Duro 9 672
Tillander 27 584
Tillander, Aleksandr 27 422, 426
Tilla Tepe *see* TILLYA TEPE
Tillberg, Peter 30 82
Tillbergs, Olegs
Tille, Christoph 4 666
Tille Höyük 1 889
Tillemans, James 30 890
Tillemans, Peter 29 424; 30 890*
assistants 8 832
patrons and collectors 20 33; 21 91
pupils 23 189
works 7 785; 10 250
Tiller, Lars 13 726
Tillers, Imants 2 751; 30 890–91*
Tillet, Titon du *see* TITON DU TILLET
Tilliard, Jacques-Jean-Baptiste
attributions 11 594
Tillia Tepe *see* TILLYA TEPE
Tillin 17 551
Tilling, Larissa 27 426
Tilliot Hours *see under* BOOKS OF HOURS → individual manuscripts
Tillot, Guillaume Du *see* DU TILLOT, GUILLAUME
Tilly, Lorenz von, Graf 2 580
Tillya Tepe 1 186, 211; 6 182, 196; 28 719; 30 440, 891–2*
clasps 30 891
gold 1 205; 6 187
jewellery 6 273
medallions 1 188
metalwork 1 206; 6 237; 28 722
sculpture 6 212, 214
Tilmanis, Osvald 26 384
Tilmann van der Burch 7 593
Tilmen 1 826
Tilmun *see* BAHRAIN
Tilney, Richard Child, 1st Earl of *see* CHILD, RICHARD, 1st Earl of Tilney
Tiloka, King of Chiang Mai (*reg* 1442-87) 6 567; 30 604
Tilori 15 322
Vishnu Temple 15 293
Tilson, Henry 30 892*
Tilson, Joe 30 892–3*
groups and movements 25 231; 27 563
pupils 5 77
works 5 726; 28 300
Tilt 12 210
tilting buttons 28 542
tilting chests *see under* CHESTS → types
Tiltman, R. Stavers 4 810
Tim, Arab-Ata mausoleum 6 201, 206, 206; 16 159; 22 321; 31 112
pīshṭāq 16 160; 24 877
squinches 16 161
stucco 29 821
Timagoras 30 476
Timai, Tell 29 74

Timanthes 13 551; 30 893*
works 13 545, 552, 553; 16 613
Timarchides (the elder) 8 909; 27 27; 30 893*, 915
Timarchides (the younger) 8 909; 30 893*
Timarchos 18 394; 25 455, 457–8*
Timarete 33 307
Timay, Tall *see* MENDES
Timba Colorado 9 166
Timbal, Charles 9 298
timber *see* WOOD
timber graves *see under* GRAVES → types
timber structures 30 894–9*
historical and regional traditions
Africa 1 306
Anglo-Saxon 2 64, 66
Britain 32 276
China 6 640; 22 240
Denmark 32 285
England 19 609; 30 894, 895, 896, 897
Finland 32 287
France 30 895; 32 278–9
Germany 30 895; 32 282–3
Guyana 13 875
Islamic 16 269
Japan 17 45, 46–7*
New Zealand 23 54
Norway 32 287
Rome, ancient 26 864
Sweden 32 287
Syria-Palestine 30 190
Tibet 30 816
United States of America 32 302
types
balloon frames 5 562; 30 898–9*, 898; 31 593
box frames *see* wall frames
Chicago construction *see* balloon frames
cross frames 30 894–6*, 895
floor frames 30 895, 896, 897*
roof frames *see* ROOFS
wall frames 30 895, 896–7*
Timbira 4 706, 707
Timbrell, Benjamin 12 594
Timbuktu 1 386; 30 914*
architecture 20 198
fortifications 21 597
Great Mosque 4 793
Sankoré Mosque 1 316
textiles 20 198
Time Buddhism *see* BUDDHISM → sects → Ji
Times, The 22 118; 31 498
Times Furnishing Ltd 14 523
Times-Sotheby Index 2 561; 15 888
Times Square Show, The 3 338
Timgad *see* THAMUGADI
Timişoara 26 705, 708; 30 914–15*
Banat County Museum 26 724
Castle *see* District Museum
Cathedral 14 887
District Museum 30 914
fortifications 26 708
interior decoration 26 718
Jesuit college 26 708
metalwork 15 9
Museum of Art 30 914
Presidential House *see* Museum of Art
Timm, Georg Wilhelm 18 851; 27 390; 30 915*
Timm, Johan 8 733
Timm, Reinold *see* THIM, REINHOLT
Timm, Vasily (Fyodorovich) *see* TIMM, GEORG WILHELM
Timmaji 15 648
Timmons, Edward J. Finley 11 322
Timna' 2 246, 247, 249; 33 520
bronzes 2 259
sculpture 2 257, 258
textiles 1 881
vessels 2 273

Timofey 8 908
Timofeyev, Ivan 4 599
Timokles 8 909; 30 893, 915*
Timomachos 13 547; 25 44; 30 915–16*
Timonidas 13 504
Timor 15 751
baskets 15 810
caves 29 226, 227
drawings 15 807
dress 15 813
headdresses 15 814
houses 15 775
jewellery 15 814, 815
masks 15 804
weaving 15 795
Timoriyev, Vasily 27 413
Timoshenko, S. P. 28 838
Timotesubani Church 12 323
Timotheo, Fabio 5 448
Timotheus (411-354 BC) 19 169
Timotheos (*fl c.* 380-*c.* 350 BC) 13 440, 453; 19 170; 27 29, 31; 30 916*
collaboration 5 64
works 10 434, 434; 13 454, 460; 14 69
workshop 13 460
Timoto-Cuicas 32 166
timpani 22 375
Tims, Michael *see* BRONSON, A. A.
Timuca 22 552
Timucua Indians 19 143
Timur, Sultan (*reg* 1370-1405) (Timurid) 16 501; 30 917–18*
architecture 5 137; 6 203, 203, 210, 211; 8 673; 16 196, 197, 198; 23 815, 820; 27 673, 675; 28 537, 538; 30 918; 31 451
basins 6 285
gardens 12 82; 16 197
manuscripts 16 272, 284, 320
metalwork 14 431; 16 366, 377
paintings 1 25; 6 233; 16 200, 253
porcelain 16 413
pottery 6 258; 27 673
tents 23 820; 30 478
Timurid 16 116; 30 916–22*
architecture 6 202, 211; 27 675
books 30 920
glass 6 269
manuscripts 14 431; 30 922
mosques 30 918
palaces 6 203; 23 816
trade 16 860
women 30 917
see also:
ABU'L-QASIM BABUR, Sultan
ABU SA'ID MIRZA, Sultan
BABUR, Emperor
BADI' AL-ZAMAN, Sultan
BAYSUNGHUR
GAWHARSHAD
HUSAYN BAYQARA, Sultan
IBRAHIM SULTAN
ISKANDAR SULTAN
KHALIL, Sultan
MIRANSHAH, Sultan
MUHAMMAD JUKI, Prince
MUHAMMAD SULTAN
RABI'A SULTAN BEGUM
SHAHRUKH, Sultan
TIMUR, Sultan
ULUGHBEG, Sultan
Tīmūr-i Lang *see* TIMUR, Sultan
Timurov, Rashid (Mukhamedovich) 31 783
Timur Shah, King (*reg* 1773-93) (Durrani) 17 717
tin 4 688; 24 578
alloys 24 578
antimony 21 319; 24 578
bismuth 24 578
copper 4 848, 849, 855; 12 621; 17 318; 21 319; 24 578; 29 211
see also BRONZE
lead 17 318; 21 319; 24 578, 809
see also PEWTER

tin—cont.
historical and regional traditions
Afghanistan **1** 850; **4** 849
Anatolia, ancient **1** 850
Austria **21** *314*
Bantu peoples **1** 368
Belgium **3** 602, 603
Bolivia **4** 256
Britain **16** 393
Canada **5** *571*
Central Asia, Western **6** 257
China **7** 97, 100; **8** 852; **15** 812
Cyprus, ancient **8** 353
Czech Republic **8** 415
Dian culture **8** 852
Egypt **16** 404
Egypt, ancient **4** 688
England **4** 688; **18** 615
Etruscan **10** 624
France **10** 624
Germany **31** *256*, *263*
Gothic **13** 139
Iran **16** 402, 413
Iran, ancient **15** 902
Iraq **16** 399
Islamic **16** 363, 393, 395, 399, 402, 404, 413, 420
Japan **17** 318; **21** 716
Java **15** 811
Malaysia **16** 393; **20** 179, 180
Mesopotamia **21** 304
Nigeria **4** 854; **15** 118
Ottoman **16** 420
Sardinia **10** 624
South America, Pre-Columbian **29** 211
Spain **10** 624; **16** 393
Sumatra **15** 811
Turkey **4** 849
United States of America **18** 615; **31** 652–3*
uses
brushes **5** 33
busts **21** *314*
coins **15** 811, 812; **20** 179, 180
dolls **31** 262*
dolls' houses **31** *263*
dyes **9** 490
gilding **24** 55
glass **30** 408
glazes **6** 257, 329; **16** 393, 395, 399, 402, 404, 413
see also FAIENCE (ii) (CERAMICS); POTTERY → wares → delftware; lustrewares; tin-glazed wares
inks **15** 852
lacquer **18** 605, 615
mirrors **21** 716, 720
mosaics **22** 155
paintings **13** 139
paint tubes **23** 787
pilgrim badges **24** 809
pipes (smoking) **1** 368
sculpture **5** *571*
slip **16** 420
soldering **21** 325
solders **7** 100
toys **31** 255–6*, *256*
weapons **7** 97
tinajas see under JARS → types
tinajón see under JARS → types
tinctures **14** 405, 406*, 409, 425
Tindale, Norman **1** 66
Tindle, David **12** 501
Tinduli *see* TAHDAULI TEMPLE
Tinelli, Luigi **16** 739
Tinelli, Tiberio **6** 91; **10** 861; **28** 433; **30** 923*
Tinerimea Artisticä *see* ARTISTIC YOUTH
tin foil *see* TIN LEAF
Ting, Walasse **19** 491
Tingatinga, Edward Saidi **1** 430; **30** 301, 302
Ting Chieh-yin *see* DING JIEYIN
Ting Ching *see* DING JING
Tingelstad
antependia **13** 135, *144*; **23** 223
Tingelstad—cont.
painting **13** 143, *144*
Tinggården **8** 729
Tingham, Edmond **4** 609; **9** 322
Ting Kao *see* DING GAO
tin-glazed ware *see under* POTTERY → wares
Tingmei *see* LIU JUE
Tingmogang **15** 311
Tingqua **6** 624; **13** 733, 734–5*; **24** 621
Tingry, Christian-Louis de Montmorency-Luxembourg, Prince of **8** 63
Tingstäde Church **13** 119; **30** 66
Ting Tao-hu *see* DING DAOHU
Tinguely, Jean **11** 551, 570; **22** 375; **30** 125, 923–5*
collaboration **11** 570; **18** 118; **19** 782; **27** 587; **28** 315; **29** 420; **31** 571
dealers **7** 421; **26** 193
groups and movements **10** 416; **17** 694; **18** 62, 63; **23** 260
methods **19** 395
patrons and collectors **14** 48; **21** 135
works **2** 837, 838; **11** *346*, 347, 773; **15** 869; **16** 58; **21** 746; **22** 381; **23** 261, 334; **29** 97; **30** 140, *924*
Tinguian **24** 624, 625, 626, 627, 628
Ting Yün-p'eng *see* DING YUNPENG
Tinian, House of Taga **20** 412, *412*
Ti-n-Lalan **10** 473
tin leaf **11** 764; **12** 621, 625; **19** 2; **21** 331; **24** 5, 245
Tinmal **16** *103*
congregational mosque **16** 191, *191*; **29** 820
mihrab **21** 505
Tinne, Alexandrine **30** 925*
Tinney, John **4** 886; **32** 793; **33** 372
Tinney, J. P. **7** 753
Tinnis **16** 431, 432; **31** 21, 22
Tinoco, João Nunes **25** 292; **31** 1–2*
patrons and collectors **4** 634
works **25** 292, *292*
Tinoco, José Martins **31** 2*
Tinoco, Pedro Nunes **25** 292; **31** 1*
Tinoco da Silva, Francisco **2** 188
Tino di Camaino **13** 93, 98; **28** 676; **31** 2–5*
collaboration **2** 109; **24** 873
works **2** 110; **11** 197; **13** 93; **14** 416; **19** 827; **22** *475*, 476, 484; **24** 854; **31** *3*, *4*, *123*, 124
T-in-O maps *see under* MAPS → types
Tinos **13** 387; **29** 701
tin-plate **31** 256–7*, 265
Tinqua *see* TINGQUA
tinsel **15** 812
tinsel prints *see under* PRINTS → types
Tintagel Monastery (Cornwall) **21** 834
Tintal **29** 619
Tinted Venus **12** *598*
Tintern Abbey **8** 610; **32** *780*, 781
Tinti, Camillo **8** 267
Tintoi **15** 463
Tintore, Francesco del **24** 26
Tintore, Simone del **24** 26; **31** 5*
Tintoretto, Domenico **31** 5, 15, 19*
cartoons **32** 205
collaboration **30** 358; **32** 77, 222
friezes **32** 222
patrons and collectors
Federico I, 3rd Marchese of Mantua (*reg* 1478-84) **12** 907
Gillott, Joseph **12** 638
Tintoretto, Domenico
patrons and collectors—cont.
Herbert, Philip, 4th Earl of Pembroke and 1st Earl of Montgomery **14** 435
Medinaceli, Luís de la Cerda Fernández de Córdoba Folch de Cardona y Aragón, 9th Duque de (1660-1711) **21** 35
Museu de Arte de São Paulo **4** 726
Soult (Jean de Dieu), Maréchal **29** 96
Zamoyski, Jan **33** 606
personal collection **14** 806
works **31** 5
Tintoretto, Jacopo **9** 7; **16** 665; **26** 478; **31** 5–19*; **32** 190, 194
assistants **11** 52; **31** 19, 70
attributions **5** 847; **19** 790; **26** 363
collaboration **31** 19; **32** 77, 406
commentaries **26** 363
drawings **6** 470; **9** 221
frames **11** 387, 401, 487
methods **5** 654, 657; **6** 570; **8** 128; **9** 216; **13** 708; **18** 898; **19** 354; **21** 766; **23** 376; **24** 493; **30** 456
mosaics **22** 163; **32** 212
paintings **32** 191, 223, 352
allegorical **1** 658
altarpieces **13** 678; **32** 215
architectural **2** 340
ceiling **9** 14; **32** 220, 222
genre **16** 666
history **32** 160, 222
literary themes **30** 358
mythological **10** 476; **20** 277
oil sketches **23** 381
organ shutters **22** 374; **23** 502
portraits **2** 162; **31** *14*; **32** 223
religious **10** 476, 503; **16** 667; **20** 278, 280; **21** 525; **31** *6*, *8*, *9*, *11*, *12*; **32** 215, 222, 226, 227, *227*
wall **32** 220
patrons and collectors
Alcalá, 3rd Duque de (1583-1637) **26** 307
Aretino, Pietro **2** 388
Aved, Jacques (-André-Joseph) **2** 852
Bellori, Giovanni Pietro **3** 673
Bonnemaison, Ferréol de **4** 330
Borromeo, Vitaliano VI, Conte (1620-90) **4** 427
Bracciano, Paolo Giordano II Orsini, Duca di **23** 576
Butler, Charles (1822-1910) **5** 311
Carleton, Dudley, 1st Viscount Dorchester **5** 764
Carpio, Gaspar de Haro y Guzmán, 7th Marqués del **5** 845
Carpio, Luis Méndez de Haro y Guzmán, 6th Marqués del **5** 844
Carr, William Howell **5** 848
Cavendish, William, 2nd Duke of Devonshire (1671-1729) **6** 116
Choiseul, Etienne-François, Duc de **7** 193
Christina, Queen of Sweden (*reg* 1632-54) **30** 118
Contarini (family) **7** 775
Contarini, Jacopo **7** 775, 776
Contini Bonacossi, Alessandro, Conte **7** 782
Cornaro, Alvise (1484-1566) **7** 863
Crozat, Pierre **8** 209
Doria, Agostino **9** 173
Duarte, Diego **9** 311
Egerton, Francis, 3rd Duke of Bridgewater **9** 755
Ensenada, Marqués de **10** 406
Este (i) (family) **21** 771
Tintoretto, Jacopo
patrons and collectors—cont.
Francis-Joseph, Prince of Liechtenstein (*reg* 1772-81) **19** 338
Gerbier, Balthazar **12** 340
Godoy, Juan Silvano **24** 101
Goering, Hermann (Wilhelm) **12** 843
Gonzaga (family) **19** 834
Habsburg I., Leopold William, Archduke of Austria, Governor of the Netherlands **13** 919
Hamilton, Alexander, 10th Duke of Hamilton and 7th Duke of Brandon **14** 107
Hanover (House of) **14** 128
Henry III, King of France (*reg* 1574-89) **31** 851
Herbert, Thomas, 8th Earl of Pembroke **14** 436
Hervey, Frederick Augustus, 4th Earl of Bristol **14** 485
Hesselin, Louis (-Cauchon) **14** 492
Howard (i), Aletheia, Countess of Arundel **14** 807
Imperiale, Gian Vincenzo **15** 148
John William, Elector Palatine (*reg* 1690-1716) **12** 473
Kerr, Robert **28** 270
Leoni, Leone **19** 203
Louis XIV, King of France (*reg* 1643-1715) **4** 552
Mauroner, José **2** 404
Mocenigo, Alvise I, Doge of Venice (*reg* 1570-77) **21** 747
Orléans, Philippe II de Bourbon, 2nd Duc d' (1674-1723) **23** 515
Philip II, King of Spain (*reg* 1556-98) **13** 922; **14** 1
Potocki, Stanisław Kostka **25** 364
Rangone, Tommaso **25** 889
Régnier, Nicolas **26** 95
Reynolds, Joshua **26** 280
Ricketts, Charles (de Sousy) **26** 360
Santiago, Francisco Esteban Rodríguez de los Ríos, 1st Marqués de **27** 792
Scuola Grande di S Marco (Venice) **13** 824
Seignelay, Jean-Baptiste (-Antoine) Colbert, Marquis de **7** 546
Serra, Giovan Francesco, Marqués di Cassano **28** 479
Strada (a Rosberg), Ottavio **29** 740
Strange, John **29** 746
Tallard, Marie-Joseph d'Hostun, Duc de **30** 274
Velázquez, Diego (de Silva y) (1599-1660) **32** 130
Vendramin, Andrea **32** 155
Villiers, George, 1st Duke of Buckingham (1592-1628) **32** 575
pupils **11** 51; **25** 187; **31** 18, 41; **32** 708
reproductions in textiles **16** 760
reproductive prints by others **5** 856, 857; **6** 114; **11** 51; **18** 42, 44; **20** 812; **25** 622; **27** 504
Kilian, Philipp Andreas (1628-93) **18** 45
Mellan, Claude **19** 790
Picart, Etienne **24** 712
Sadeler, Raphael, I (1560/61-*d c.* 1628/32) **27** 503
restorations by others **9** 740; **14** 265; **24** 343
studio **29** 853
workshop **22** 111
Tintoretto, Marco **31** 5, 15
Tintoretto, Marietta **16** 668; **31** 5, 15, 18–19*
tintypes *see under* PHOTOGRAPHIC PLATES → types
Tinworth, George **9** 201; **10** 312
Tio **1** 395
Tioda **31** 19*
Tio Fotografer **17** 623
Tipai **22** 550
Tipaza **9** *510*
Basilica **9** 535
houses **26** 920
sarcophagi **9** 562
tomb of the Christian woman **23** 299
tipo códice **21** 737
Tippur **29** 438
Tipra **3** 165
Tiptoft Master **32** 198
Tipungwuti, Giovanni **1** 64
Tipu Sultan, Khan of Mysore (*reg* 1782-99) **3** 163; **15** 648, 713, 724, 744; **16** 554; **17** 639
throne **15** 707
Tique, João **22** 245
Tiraboschi, G. **12** 719
Tirali, Andrea **16** 641; **25** 144, 266; **28** 32; **32** 188, 216
Tiranë **1** *537*, 538; **31** 20*
art schools **1** 546, 547
ceramics **1** 543
Ethem Bey mosque **1** 539, 540, *542*
furniture **1** 542; **31** 20
Jordan Misja Arts Lyceum **23** 747
metalwork **1** 543, 544
monuments **1** 541
museums **1** 546; **18** 459
Archaeological-Ethnographic Museum *see* National Museum of Archaeology
Art Gallery **1** 543, 546
Enver Hoxha Museum *see* International Centre of Culture
Gallery of Figurative Art **1** 546
International Centre of Culture **1** 539
Museum of the National Liberation War **1** 546
Museum of the People's Army **1** 546
National Historical Museum **1** 546
National Museum of Archaeology **1** 546
Pinakoteka *see* Gallery of Figurative Art
Palace of Congresses **1** 539
Palace of Culture **1** 539
Partizani Sports Palace **1** 543
textiles **1** 545
Youth Park restaurant **1** 543
Tiranë Factory of Furniture for Institutions **31** 20
Tiranë Glassworks **1** 543; **31** 20
Tiranë Porcelain Factory **12** 862; **18** 458; **31** 20, 451
Tiranë Textile Combine **1** 545
Tiraspol' **21** *810*
Higher Agricultural School **21** 810
Pedagogical Institute **21** 810
Theatre Square **21** 810
tiraz **16** 121, 432, *433*, 433, 436, 438, 455, 457; **28** 716; **31** 20–22*, *21*
Tire **16** 205
Kazırzade Mosque **16** 202
Tiree **28** 229; **29** 702
Tirenum *see* TRANI
Tiretta, Edward **15** 402; **24** 264
Tîrgovişte **26** *705*, 708
Archaeological Museum **31** 23
architecture **31** 23*
books **14** 424
Museum of Printing and Early Printed Books **31** 23
palace **26** 707

Tîrgovişte, Constantinos of *see* CONSTANTINOS OF TÎRGOVIŞTE
Tîrgovişte, Dobromir of *see* DOBROMIR OF TÎRGOVIŞTE
Tîrgovişte, Stroe from *see* STROE FROM TÎRGOVIŞTE
Tîrgu-Jiu **4** 662; **26** 716, 723; **28** 314
  sculpture **4** *662*
Tîrgu-Mureş **15** 15
  metalwork **15** 9
  Museum of Art **26** 724
  Palace of Culture **14** 890; **15** 4; **26** 718
  Roman Catholic College **26** 724
  Town Hall **14** 890
Tirhakah *see* TAHARQA
Tirilye *see* ZEYTINBAGI
Tirion, Isaac **3** 900; **29** 402
Tiriyo **4** 707
Tirmidh *see* TERMEZ
Tirol, Hans **4** 58; **25** 426; **31** 23*
Tirolo, Castel Tirolo **2** 792; **26** 634
Tiron, Jean-Marie **11** 633
Tiron, Napoleon **31** 23–4*
Tironensian Order **8** 550
Tironi, Francesco **27** 719
Tirregaille, Pierre Ricaud de *see* RICAUD DE TIRREGAILLE, PIERRE
Tirtagangga **12** 103
  palace **15** 776
  water garden **12** *102*
tirtei **26** 703
Tiruchcharanattumalai **15** 522
  temple **15** 306
Tiruchirapalli **15** *294*; **31** 24*
  cave temple **15** 507
  ikat **15** 672
  inscription **15** 508
  paintings **15** 652
  reliefs **15** 508–9, 510, 511
  rock reliefs **15** *508*
  sculpture **15** 506, 507
  textiles **15** 664, 665
Tirukkulashekharapuram *see under* MAKOTAI
Tirumala *see* TIRUPATI
Tirumalai **15** 331
  Kundavi Jinalayam **15** 560, 645
Tirumalai, Ruler (*reg* 1623-59) (Nayaka) **15** 233, 398, 506; **20** 73, 74; **22** 702
  sculpture **15** 519
Tirumalaipuram **15** 559
Tirumangai Alvar **15** 304
Tirunandikkara **15** 306, 559
Tiruparangundram **15** 358
Tirupati (Andhra Pradesh) **15** *294*; **31** 24*
  Govindaraja Temple **15** 399, 540
  sculpture **15** 540
  temples **15** 331
  Venkateshvara Temple **15** 541
Tirupatti (Tamil Nadu) **15** 713
Tirupparuttikunram, Vardhamana Temple **15** 646
Tiruppudaimarudur
  Narumbunatha Temple **15** 646
  Virabhadra Temple
    paintings **15** *645*
Tirurangadi **15** 358
Tiruvaduturai, Gomukteshvara Temple **15** 233
  sculpture **15** *233*
Tiruvalanjuli, Kapardishvar Temple **15** 645
Tiruvanandapuram *see* TRIVANDRUM
Tiruvanchikulam *see* MAHODAYAPURAM
Tiruvankadu
  sculpture **15** *219*
Tiruvannaikovil *see under* SRIRANGAM
Tiruvannamalai **15** *294*; **31** 24–5*
  Arunachaleshvara Temple **13** *4*, 5; **15** 334, *334*, 335
  thousand-columned hall **15** 335
Tiruvanur **5** 432
Tiruvarur, Thyagaraja Temple **15** 647
Tiruvattar, Adikeshava Temple **15** 524
Tiruvelangadu **15** 516
Tiruvellarai, Pundarikaswami Temple **15** 645
Tiruvengadu **15** 517, *517*
  Svetaranyasvami Temple **15** 517
Tiruvippirambedu *see* GUDIMALLAM
Tiruvitāṅkoṭu *see* TRAVANCORE
Tiryns **13** *363*; **14** *332*, 360; **31** 25–6*, *25*
  floors **13** 560
  fortifications **14** 340
  granaries **14** 339
  ivory-carvings **14** 353
  megara (buildings) **14** 340; **21** 46
  megaron **21** 46
  palace **14** 340, 349; **21** 46; **23** 808
  pottery **4** 172; **14** 342
  sculpture **14** 351, 353
  Treasure **14** 360
  wall paintings **14** 334, 340, 348, 350–51
Tisac (family) **12** 440
Tisavar **21** 560
Tischbein, Anton Wilhelm **5** 286
Tischbein, August Anton **31** 26, 28*
Tischbein, Christian Wilhelm **27** 323; **31** 26, 28*
Tischbein, (Johann) Friedrich (August) **31** 26, 27*
  works **12** 392; **31** *27*
Tischbein, Jacob **31** 27
Tischbein, Johann Heinrich (1682-1764) **31** 26
Tischbein, Johann Heinrich, I (1722-89) **14** 492; **31** 26–7*
  patrons and collectors **14** 492
  pupils **26** 110; **31** 27
  reproductive prints by others **26** 375
  works **11** 459; **12** 392
Tischbein, Johann Heinrich, II (1742-1808) **10** 562; **21** 850; **22** 320; **24** 586; **31** 26, 579
Tischbein, Johann Valentin **14** 42; **31** 26, 27
Tischbein, (Johann Heinrich) Wilhelm **22** 480; **31** 26, 27–8*, 579
  collaboration **14** 114
  groups and movements **10** 644; **22** 740
  patrons and collectors **33** 116
  pupils **12** 853
  works **2** 164; **12** *852*; **13** 303, 541
Tischer, (Carl) Marcus *see* TUSCHER, (CARL) MARCUS
Tischler, Ludwig **14** 724
Tischler, Severin **8** 386
Tisdall, Hans **4** 369
Tishinin (family) **20** 147
Tisi, Benvenuto *see* GAROFALO
Tismana **25** 344; **26** 712, 719, 721
Tismice Basilica **8** 376
Tišnov Abbey **8** *374*; **31** 28–9*
  Church of the Assumption **26** 638
  sculpture **8** 381
  west portal **31** 29
Tišov, Ivan **31** 29*
Tissamaharama **29** 474
Tissendier, Jean, Bishop of Toulouse **13** 76
Tissot, James **14** 363; **31** 29–31*
  groups and movements **23** 504; **26** 55
  patrons and collectors **4** 308
  personal collection **17** 440
  works **4** 9; **9** 309; **10** 254; **11** 417; **12** 296; **21** 418; **25** 600; **31** *30*, 704
tissue-paper *see under* PAPER → types
Tisza culture **25** 512, 513, 514, 516, 517
Tita **6** 294, 302
Titaedius Labeo **27** 52
titanium **17** 530
titanium dioxide **24** 789, 798*
titanium oxide **6** 328, 873
titanium white *see under* PIGMENTS → types
Titanox *see* PIGMENTS → types → titanium white
Titchfield (Hants)
  Abbey **7** 456
  St Peter **2** 65
Tite, William **7** 667; **10** 668; **25** 268; **31** 31*
Titel, Friedrich Wilhelm **12** 902
Titelberg **19** 826
Titge, Gebhard Jürgen **12** 405
Titi, Filippo **31** 31*
Titian **2** 716; **6** 569; **9** 7, 8, 9; **15** 93; **16** 665, 666, 766; **26** 769; **31** 14, 16, 31–44*; **32** 106, 190, 349
  assistants **6** 99; **8** 765; **9** 187; **30** 33; **32** 107, 243
  attributions **19** 25
    drawings **6** 114; **10** 525
    paintings **8** 765; **10** 146; **12** 670, *670*, *672*, 674, 677, 678; **25** 149, 168; **29** 400; **33** 387
    woodcuts **5** 415; **10** 823; **32** 381
  collaboration **5** 535; **10** 389; **12** 676, 756; **32** 106, 107, 199, 220
  commentaries **3** 265
  copies **5** 920; **26** 170; **27** 704
  drawings **2** 412; **6** 470; **9** 221
    cartoons **8** 766; **32** 205
    landscape **9** *218*
  exhibitions **27** 171
  forgeries by others **5** 535; **11** 307
  frames **11** 384, *386*, 387, 389, 401, 487, 494
  methods **5** 657; **6** 570; **13** 708; **15** 147; **19** 354; **23** 376; **24** 370, 493; **30** 5
  mosaics **22** 163; **32** 212
  paintings **12** 560; **27** 149; **32** 220
    allegorical **1** 656, *656*, 657; **27** 149; **29** 84, 423; **31** *32*, *33*; **32** 223
    architectural **2** 340
    battle **3** 387; **14** 583
    fêtes champêtres **11** 34, 35, *35*, 36; **16** 665
    frescoes **9** 264; **10** 737, 738; **19** 663; **23** 754; **32** 191
    landscape **18** 708
    mythological **3** 665; **10** 130, 443, 476, 477; **13** 922; **16** 665, *666*; **18** 708; **22** 413; **23** *377*, 680; **25** 71; **26** 221; **31** *34*, *35*, *36*, *39*; **32** 191
    nude figures **23** 292, *293*
    portraits **2** 102, 162, 458; **7** 784; **9** 265; **13** *922*; **25** *282*; **31** *42*; **32** 191
    religious **1** *710*, 711; **4** 748; **10** 476, 503; **13** 678; **16** 665; **18** 677; **19** 356; **23** 878; **24** 777; **27** 496; **28** 709; **31** *37*, *38*, *40*, 316, 740; **32** 191, 216, 217
    wall paintings **24** 231, 523; **32** 229
  patrons and collectors **2** 561; **10** 365; **16** 763
    Akademie der Bildenden Künste (Vienna) **2** 831
    Alba, 17th Duque de (1878-1953) **1** 529
    Alba, Fernando Alvárez de Toledo, Gran-Duque de, Governor of the Netherlands **1** 528
    Albarelli, Giovanni **5** 432
    Alcalá, 3rd Duque de (1583-1637) **26** 307
Titian
  patrons and collectors—cont.
    Aldobrandini, Pietro (ii), Cardinal (1571-1621) **1** 595
    Alfonso I, 3rd Duke of Ferrara, Modena and Reggio (*reg* 1505-34) **3** 306; **10** 522; **11** 4; **14** 870; **16** 665; **19** 559; **29** 860; **32** 192
    Altman, Benjamin **1** 731
    Angerstein, John Julius **2** 51
    Archinto, Filippo, Archbishop of Milan **2** 310
    Aretino, Pietro **2** 388; **25** 281
    Augustus II, King of Poland (*reg* 1697-1706; 1709-33) **33** 115
    Augustus III, King of Poland (*reg* 1733-63) **33** 115
    Avalos, Alfonso d' **21** 525
    Bankes, William John **3** 179
    Bellori, Giovanni Pietro **3** 673
    Bembo, Pietro, Cardinal **3** 698
    Benson, R(obert) H(enry) **3** 740
    Borghese, Scipione, Cardinal **4** 404, 406
    Borromeo, Federico, Cardinal **4** 426; **16** 771
    Borromeo, Vitaliano VI, Conte (1620-90) **4** 427
    Bourbon I., Louis de, le Dauphin (1729-65) **4** 553
    Bracciano, Livio Odescalchi, Duca di **23** 353
    Butler, Charles (1822-1910) **5** 311
    Cambó y Batlle, Francisco de Asís **5** 510
    Canino, Lucien Bonaparte, Prince of (1775-1840) **4** 304
    Carlo Borromeo, Saint **4** 424
    Carpio, Gaspar de Haro y Guzmán, 7th Marqués del **5** 845
    Carpio, Luis Méndez de Haro y Guzmán, 6th Marqués del **5** 844
    Carr, Robert, 1st Earl of Somerset **5** 847
    Carr, William Holwell **5** 848
    Carraquiri, Nazario **5** 871
    Cesare, 6th Duke of Modena and Reggio (*reg* 1597-1628) **10** 525
    Champernowne, Arthur **6** 438
    Charles I, King of England and Scotland (*reg* 1625-49) **2** 558; **8** 166; **10** 363; **13** 309; **19** 582; **23** 883; **29** 797, 800, 801
    Charles II, King of England and Scotland (*reg* 1660-85) **26** 283; **29** 804
    Charles V, Holy Roman Emperor (*reg* 1519-58) **8** 87; **13** 906, 907; **16** 665; **21** 19; **29** 352; **33** 578
    Christina, Queen of Sweden (*reg* 1632-54) **30** 118; **32** 8
    Churchill, John, 1st Duke of Marlborough **4** 137
    Clovio, Giulio **7** 469
    Colebrooke, George **7** 552
    Coningham, William **7** 709
    Contarini, Alessandro **7** 775
    Contarini, Jacopo **7** 775, 776
    Corte, Valerio **5** 456
    Cosimo I, Grand Duke of Tuscany (*reg* 1569- 74) **3** 293
    Créquy, Charles de Blanchefort de **19** 238
    Crozat, Pierre **8** 209
    Czernin, Jan Rudolf, Count **8** 428
    De la Gardie, Magnus Gabriel **30** 118
    Demidov, Anatoly, Prince **8** 705
    Dennistoun, James **8** 763
    Doria (family) **9** 173
Titian
  patrons and collectors—cont.
    Doria, Gian Carlo, Prince **9** 174
    Duarte, Diego **9** 311
    Dyck, Anthony van **9** 480
    Egerton, Francis, 3rd Duke of Bridgewater **9** 755
    Emanuel-Philibert, 10th Duke of Savoy (*reg* 1553-80) **28** 4
    Faesch, Johann Jakob **10** 753
    Federico II, 5th Marchese and 1st Duke of Mantua (*reg* 1519-40) **12** 909; **16** 667
    Ferdinand III, Holy Roman Emperor (*reg* 1637-58) **13** 919
    Ferdinand VII, King of Spain (*reg* 1808; 1814-33) **4** 566
    Ferdinando I, Grand Duke of Tuscany (*reg* 1587-1609) **21** 30
    Fitzwilliam, Richard, 7th Viscount Fitzwilliam **11** 141
    Francesco II, 10th Duke of Milan (*reg* 1521- 35) **28** 533
    Francesco-Maria I, Duke of Urbino **27** 273
    Francis I, King of France (*reg* 1515-47) **31** 849
    Frick, Henry Clay **11** 774
    Ganay, Hubert de, Marquis **11** 664
    Gardner, Isabella Stewart **7** 579; **12** 147
    Giulia Varano, Duchess of Urbino (*fl* 1547) **25** 280
    Giustiniani (i), Vincenzo, Marchese **12** 763
    Godoy (y Alvárez de Faria), Manuel, Príncipe de la Paz **12** 839
    Gonzaga, Ercole, Cardinal **12** 910
    Gozzi, Alvisio **20** 278
    Grimani, Antonio **13** 657
    Grimani, Domenico, Cardinal, Patriarch of Aquilea **13** 657
    Gritti, Andrea, Doge of Venice (*reg* 1523-39) **13** 678
    Guidobaldo II, 4th Duke of Urbino (*reg* 1538-74) **27** 274
    Guzmán, Ambrosio Ignacio Spínola y, Archbishop of Seville **13** 880
    Habsburg I., Leopold William, Archduke of Austria, Governor of the Netherlands **13** 919
    Herbert, Philip, 4th Earl of Pembroke and 1st Earl of Montgomery **14** 435
    Hervey, Frederick Augustus, 4th Earl of Bristol **14** 485
    Hesselin, Louis (-Cauchon) **14** 492
    Hopton, Arthur **14** 755
    Howard (i), Aletheia, Countess of Arundel **14** 807
    Howard (i), Thomas, 2nd Earl of Arundel **14** 806
    Hume, Abraham, 2nd Baronet **14** 877
    Imperiale, Gian Vincenzo **15** 148
    Isabella d'Este, Marchesa di Mantua (1474-1539) **10** 521
    Jabach, Everard **11** 662; **16** 814
    John William, Elector Palatine (*reg* 1690-1716) **12** 473
    Joseph Bonaparte, King of Naples and Spain (*reg* 1806-8) **4** 304
    Josephine, Empress of the French (1763-1814) **4** 304
    Jullienne, Jean de **17** 684
    Lane, Hugh (Percy) **18** 727
    Las Marismas del Guadalquivir, Alejandro María Aguado y Ramírez de Estemoz, Marqués de **18** 811

Titian
patrons and collectors—cont.
Lastanosa, Vicencio Juán de **18** 816
La Vrillière, Louis Phélypeaux de **18** 885
Leemput, Remi van **19** 63
Leganés, 1st Marqués de **13** 879
Leoni, Leone **19** 203
Lerma, Francisco Gómez de Sandoval y Rojas, Duque de **27** 723
Liechtenstein-Castelkorn, Karel von, Bishop of Olmutz **8** 423
Louis XIV, King of France (*reg* 1643-1715) **4** 552
Ludovisi, Ludovico, Cardinal **19** 779
Mary of Hungary, Regent of the Netherlands (1505-58) **13** 909; **22** 64
Mauroner, José **2** 404
Mazarin, Jules, Cardinal **20** 896
McLellan, Archibald **28** 271
Medici (family) **21** 27
Medici, Ottaviano de' **21** 18
Medinaceli, Luís de la Cerda Fernández de Córdoba Folch de Cardona y Aragón, 9th Duque de (1660-1711) **21** 35
Mond, Ludwig **21** 849
Munro (of Novar), H(ugh) A(ndrew) J(ohnstone) **22** 314
Murray, Charles Fairfax **22** 351
Musée du Louvre (Paris) **11** 665
National Gallery (London) **8** 571
Nave, Bartolomeo della **22** 696
Nicholas I, Emperor of Russia (*reg* 1825-55) **26** 734
Nys, Daniel **23** 326
Odoni, Andrea **23** 355
Orléans, Louis-Philippe-Joseph de Bourbon, 5th Duc d' (1747-93) **8** 87
Orléans, Philippe II de Bourbon, 2nd Duc d' (1674-1723) **23** 515
Ottley, William Young **23** 634
Percy, Algernon, 10th Earl of Northumberland **10** 363, 367; **24** 390
Percy, Algernon, 4th Duke of Northumberland **24** 390
Pérez, Antonio (?1540-1611) **24** 400
Pésaro (family) **32** 217
Pesaro, Gerolamo **24** 537
Pesaro, Jacopo, Bishop of Paphos (1466-1547) **24** 536
Petty, William **24** 572
Philip II, King of Spain (*reg* 1556-98) **9** 173; **10** 503; **13** 922; **14** 1; **23** 292; **29** 352
Philip III, King of Spain (*reg* 1598-1621) **5** 737
Philip IV, King of Spain (*reg* 1621-65) **22** 21; **29** 302, 352; **32** 127
Philip V, King of Spain (*reg* 1700-24) **29** 303
Pinacoteca Comunale (Ancona) **2** 2
Poniatowski, Stanisław, Prince **25** 213
Porter, Endymion **25** 263
Pourtalès-Gorgier, James-Alexandre, Comte de **25** 383
Puccini, Tommaso **25** 691
Pulzone, Scipione **25** 729
Radziwiłł (family) **25** 137
Ram, Giovanni **12** 676
Richelieu, Louis-François Armand-Jean Vignerod du Plessis, Duc de (1629-1715) **26** 349
Richter, Johann Thomas **19** 111
Ricketts, Charles (de Sousy) **26** 360

Titian
patrons and collectors—cont.
Rogers, Samuel **26** 541
Rudolf II, Holy Roman Emperor (*reg* 1576- 1612) **18** 522
Ruffo, Tommaso, Cardinal, Archbishop of Ferrara **27** 316
Rushout, John, 2nd Baron Northwick **27** 350
Saint-Morys, Charles Paul Jean-Baptiste de Bourgevin Vialart de **27** 568
Savoy, Eugene of, Prince (1663-1736) **2** 829; **28** 15
Seignelay, Jean-Baptiste (-Antoine) Colbert, Marquis de **7** 546
Seisenegger, Jakob **28** 378
Sera, Paolo del **28** 433
Serra, Giovan Francesco, Marqués di Cassano **28** 479
Seymour-Conway, Francis Charles, 3rd Marquess of Hertford **28** 527
Sigismund II Augustus, King of Poland (*reg* 1548-72) **16** 867
Soult (Jean de Dieu), Maréchal **29** 96
Souza, Madame de **22** 126
Spencer, Robert, 2nd Earl of Sunderland (1641-1702) **29** 381
Stone, Symon **29** 716
Strange, John **29** 746
Suttermans, Giusto **30** 41
Tallard, Marie-Joseph d'Hostun, Duc de **30** 274
Tejada, Francisco de **30** 417
Temple, Richard, 1st Viscount Cobham **30** 451
Tessin, Carl Gustav, Count **30** 524
Thibaudeau, Narcisse-Adolphe, Comte de **30** 728
Tintoretto, Jacopo **31** 15
Torlonia (family) **31** 172
Trolle-Bonde, Gustaf, Count **31** 362
Vendramin, Gabriele **32** 156
Villahermosa, Martín Gurrea y Aragón, Duque de **13** 862
Villiers, George, 1st Duke of Buckingham (1592-1628) **10** 363; **12** 340; **32** 575
Wellesley, Henry **33** 56
Wernher, Julius **33** 84
Wilson, Andrew **33** 216
Wotton, Henry **33** 387
Wright, John Michael **33** 409
Yusupov, Nikolay (Borisovich), Prince (1751- 1831) **33** 579
prints **1** 656; **7** 899; **13** 338; **25** 606; **32** 199; **33** 356, *356*
pupils
Barendsz., Dirck **3** 230
Bordone, Paris **4** 398
Calcar, Jan Steven van **5** 415
Greco, El **13** 339; **32** 190
Micheli, Parrasio **21** 462
Moretto (da Brescia) **22** 107
Peterzano, Simone **24** 550
Rosa (i), Pietro **27** 149
Spilimbergo, Irene di **29** 400
Tintoretto, Jacopo **31** 6
Vecellio, Cesare **32** 107
Vecellio, Orazio **32** 107
reproductive prints by others
Angolo del Moro, Battista dell' **2** 88
Baron, Bernard **3** 259
Boldrini, Nicolò **4** 254
Britto, Giovanni **4** 828
Bry, Theodor de **5** 63
Campagnola, Giulio **26** 229
Caraglio, Giovanni Jacopo **5** 699
Cartaro, Mario **5** 888
Cort (van Hoorn), Cornelis **7** 899, *899*; **26** 229

Titian
reproductive prints by others—cont.
Cunego, Domenico **8** 267
Danckerts, Hendrick **8** 495
Fontana (ii), Giovanni Battista **11** 270
Fontana (ii), Giulio **11** 270; **15** *92*
Gautier-Dagoty, Edouard **12** 209
Gaywood, Richard **12** 221
Greche, Domenico dalle **13** 338
Gregori, Carlo **13** 625
Jackson, John Baptist **25** 622
Jode, Arnold de **17** 599
Jode, Gerard de **17** 598
Jode, Pieter de (i) (1570-1634) **17** 599
Jode, Pieter de (ii) (1606-74) **17** 599
Kilian, Lucas **18** 42
Köpping, Karl **18** 237
Lasne, Michel **18** 812
Macbeth, Robert Walker **19** 868
Mariette, Pierre (i) (1596-1657) **20** 415
Masson, Antoine **20** 592
Pontius, Paulus **25** 221
Raimondi, Marcantonio **14** 810
Rodríguez, Cayetano **26** 517
Sadeler, Aegidius, II (1570-1629) **27** 504
Sadeler, Jan, I (1550-1600) **27** 502
Sadeler, Raphael, I (1560/61-*d* *c.* 1628/32) **27** 503
Selma, Fernando **28** 389
Snyers, Hendrick **28** 904
Strange, Robert **26** 230
Thurneysen, Johann Jakob, I (1636-1711) **30** 793
Tibaldi, Domenico **30** 803
Uberti, Lucantonio degli **31** 511
Vico, Enea **32** 412
restorations by others **1** 763; **5** 737; **9** 481, 740; **27** 321
studio **29** 853
teachers **3** 667
workshop **8** 582
writings **25** 71
Titicaca Basin **4** *255*; **31** 45–7*
title-pages **4** 345, *345*, 358, 359; **22** 370; **31** 48–9*; **32** 501
Anglo-Saxon **31** 48
Belgium **4** *360*
Carolingian **31** 48
Greece, ancient **31** 48
Italy **2** *166*; **9** *224*; **10** 389; **31** *49*; **32** *642*
Jewish art **17** *537*, *577*
Merovingian **31** 48, *48*
Netherlands, the **17** *537*; **20** *245*
Ottonian **31** 48
Rome, ancient **31** 48
Russia **17** *577*
titles of works of art **6** 76; **31** 49–53*
title-vignettes *see* TITLE-PAGES
Tito, Diego Quispe *see* QUISPE TITO, DIEGO
Tito, Ettore **24** 708; **32** 197
Tito, Santi di **16** 673; **31** 53–5*
collaboration **8** 268
methods **25** 280
patrons and collectors **9** 174; **25** 7; **27** 648; **32** 106
pupils **7** 297, 311; **21** 754; **23** 764; **25** 185; **30** 428
teachers **4** 859
works **7** 457; **16** 664; **31** *54*, *55*
Tito, Sodegerio da *see* SODEGERIO DA TITO
Tito, Tiberio di **31** 55
Tito Bustillo **25** 477, 479, 484, 487
Titograd *see* PODGORICA
Titon, Jean-Baptiste **31** 56
Titon, Maximilien **31** 56*

Titon du Tillet, Evrard **12** 159; **31** 56
Titov Veles **19** *882*
museum **19** 886
St Panteleimon **19** 883
tituli see under CHURCHES → types
Titus, Bishop of Crete **8** 155
Titus (Flavius Vespasianus), Emperor of Rome (*reg* 79-81) **31** 56–7*
architecture **2** 156; **26** 751, 789, 866, 893; **31** 349; **32** 384
sculpture **9** 20; **18** 756; **25** 45; **27** 34
triumphal arches **31** *349*
Titus-Carmel, Gérard **31** 57*
Titus Livius *see* LIVY
Titus (Rembrandtsz.) van Rijn *see* RIJN, TITUS (REMBRANDTSZ.) VAN
Tityos Painter **10** 614
Titzenthaler, Waldemar **24** 673
Tiv **1** 236, 245, 281, 303, 346, 382; **17** 680; **23** 134
Tivali, Andrea **27** 352
Tivar **1** 546
Tiverton Town Hall (Devon) **31** 241
Tivey, Hap **19** 702
Tivissa **15** 60
Tivoli **16** *620*; **26** *886*; **31** 57–64*
architecture **7** 921
Cathedral of S Lorenzo **26** 644
Hadrian's Villa **1** 734; **9** 85; **10** 95, 849; **11** 339; **14** 34; **16** 623; **23** 809; **24** 290; **26** 853, 870, 879, 881, 896, 897–9; **27** 39, 67; **28** 314; **31** 58–9*, *59*, 61–3*
Academy **31** 61, *62*
basilica **3** 329
candelabra **5** 604
Canopus Canal **5** 904; **11** 339; **26** 882, *899*; **31** 60
excavations **13** 605
gardens **12** 70, 79
graffiti **13** 269
Island Villa **14** 460; **27** 235; **31** 61
monopteros **21** 892
mosaics **22** 160; **27** 59, 61, 62; **31** 61*, *62*
nymphaeum **13** 703; **27** 66
Piazza d'Oro **9** 84; **26** 882, *882*, 924; **31** 61
sculpture **1** 533, 646; **2** 169; **9** 20; **24** 570; **26** 861; **27** 11, 15, 22, 45, 46, 357; **31** *60*, 60–61*, 244
Serapeum **11** 339; **26** *899*
Small Baths **3** 375
Stadium Garden **12** 70
stucco **27** 72; **29** 814
Vale of Tempe **31** 61
wall paintings **27** 55
Rocca Pia **19** 896
Sanctuary of Hercules Victor **26** 888, *888*; **31** 58, *58*
Temple of Vesta **23** *483*; **26** 882, 887, 889; **27** 235
Villa d'Este **7** *572*; **19** 372–3; **23** *886*; **31** 63–4*, *64*; **32** 547, 549
Ballcourt **3** 118
Fountain of Rometta **19** *372*
Fountain of the Dragon **12** 116
gardens **11** 343; **12** 61, 63, 110, 115, 116; **16** 633; **31** 63–4
grotto **13** 703
Oval Fountain **12** 116
paintings **4** 154
Water Organ **12** 116; **29** 96
Villa of Horace **27** 66
wall paintings **27** 58
Tivoli, Rosa da *see* ROOS, PHILIPP PETER
Tivoli, Serafino De *see* DE TIVOLI, SERAFINO

Tiwa **22** 606
Tiwanaku *see* TIAHUANACO
Tiwi **1** 39, 43, 44, 47–8, 51, 52, 53, 63, 64, 66; **2** 768
posts **1** *47*
Tiwi Designs Cooperative **1** 64
tixi see LACQUER → types → *guri*
Tiya **10** 577
Tiye (*c.* 1070-945 BC) **10** 33
Tiye, Queen (*fl* 14th cent. BC) **9** 781; **10** 80, 93; **23** 279; **28** 34, *433*, 434
Tizatlán **4** 796; **21** 226, 229, 738
Tizio, Sigismondo **19** 669, 671
Tiznit **16** 532
Rabbi Simeon ben Yohai synagogue **17** 551
Tizoc and Ahuizotl Stone **1** 701; **20** 201
Tizón, Ventura Rodríguez *see* RODRÍGUEZ (TIZÓN), VENTURA
Tizoni, Fermo **20** 98
Tjakamarra Nelson, Michael *see* NELSON (TJAKAMARRA), MICHAEL
Tjallingii **30** 879
Tjamerery **22** 431
Tjaminji, Paddy **30** 744
Tjanefer **9** 857
Tjanehebu
shabtis **10** *17*
Tjangala, Wuta Wuta *see* UTA UTA (JANGALA)
Tjapaltjarra Leura, Tim *see* LEURA (TJAPALTJARRI), TIM
Tjapaltjarri, Clifford Possum *see* POSSUM TJAPALTJARRI, CLIFFORD
Tjayasetimu **11** 306
Tjele manor house **8** 724
Tjety
dress **10** *43*
Tjupurrula, Jack **22** 729
Tkabha-Erdy Church **27** 432
Tkachenko', I **2** 894
Tkachov, Aleksey (Petrovich) **27** 397; **31** 64*
Tkachov, Sergey (Petrovich) **27** 397; **31** 64*
Tkadlík, František **8** 392; **20** 252; **25** 433; **31** 64*
Tlacochahuaya **8** 460
Tlacolula **33** 481
Dominican Monastery **21** 375
Tlalancaleca **21** 205; **25** 764
Tlalmanalco **30** 786
Tlalnextipantli **21** 260
Tlalpan, Capillo de las Capuchinas **8** 65
Tlapacoya **21** 250
architecture **25** 764
figurines **21** *193*, 194
tools **21** 192
Tlapán **10** 505
Heroico Colegio Militar **21** 381
Tlatelolco **21** *193*, 266, 399; **31** 65*
architecture **25** 765
ceramics **10** 780
pyramid **31** *65*
Santiago de Tlatelolco **31** *65*
skull racks **31** 505, 506
trade **31** 65
wall paintings **21** 230
Tlatilco **21** *193*, 196, 237, *372*; **31** 66*
figurines **31** 66
masks **21** 188, 250
pottery **31** 66
seals **21** 258
tombs **31** 117
Tlaxcala
drums (musical instruments) **21** 256
Franciscan Monastery **21** 373
Sanctuario de Ocotlán **21** 377; **25** 57
S José Tlaxcala **21** 393
Tlaxcaltec **11** 152

Tlemcen **16** *103*; **31** 66–7*
- Abu Maydan Mosque **16** 217, 250
- Archaeological Museum **16** 494; **31** 66
- architecture **1** 634; **16** 217
- carpets **16** 485, 486
- congregational mosque *see* Great Mosque
- Great Mosque **16** 190, 493; **21** 505; **22** 193, 324; **29** 820; **30** 905; **31** 273
- madrasas **20** 57
- mosque of al-'Ubbad *see* Abu Maydan Mosque
- mosque of Idris I **16** 493
- mosque of Sidi Bel Hassan *see* Archaeological Museum
- mosque of Sidi Brahim **16** 217
- Museum of Antiquities **1** 636
- tomb of Sidi al-Halwi **16** 217
- tomb of Sidi Bu Madyan **16** 217

Tleson **13** 484, 510; **32** 58, 69*
Tli **28** 321
Tlingit **22** 547, 674
- basketwork **22** 657
- beadwork **22** 639, 640, *640*
- copper **22** 612, 613
- daggers **22** 613
- dress **22** 632
- embroidery **22** 645
- headdresses **28** III1
- houses **22** 564
- shells **22** 640
- textiles **22** *547*, 620, *621*
- wood-carvings **22** *580*, 581, 668

Tlingit (Inland) **22** 546
Tlos **19** 837; **24** 691
- Bellerophon Tomb **19** 839

TLV mirrors *see under* MIRRORS → types
Tmutarakan **9** 631
T. N. T. **8** 435
Toaldo, Giuseppe **6** 340
Toam *see* YI CHAE
Toan, Vo **22** 128
Toan Tejima *see* TEJIMA TOAN
toastmasters' glasses *see under* GLASSES → types
Toba, Emperor (*reg* 1107-23) **17** 219
Toba Batak **3** 144; **15** 788, 807, 814, 817; **23** 555
tobacco-boxes *see under* BOXES → types
tobacco jars *see under* JARS → types
tobacco juice **7** 102
tobacco pipes *see* PIPES (SMOKING)
tobaccoseed oil *see under* OILS → types
tobacco spit *see under* GLAZES → types
Tobago *see* TRINIDAD AND TOBAGO
Toba Kisō **17** 387
Tobari, Kōgan **17** 134
Toba Sōjō **17** 154, 166; **23** 444
Tobe **17** 264, 352, 353
Tobeen **4** 391
Tobei Kamei *see* KAMEI, TOBEI
Toberentz, Robert **19** 54
Tobey, Mark **25** 584; **31** 67–8*
- groups and movements **1** 83, 86
- patrons and collectors **9** 189; **28** 328
- works **12** 216; **21** 897; **31** *68*, 607

Tobin, Maurice **11** 119
Tobin, Michael **4** 801
tobine *see under* WEAVING → types
Tobol'sk **27** *362*; **31** 68–9*
- churches **27** 374
- Historical Museum **31** 68
- kremlin **31** 68
- metalwork **27** 420
- Picture Gallery **31** 68

Tobón Mejía, Marco **7** 609; **31** 69*
Toby jugs *see under* JUGS → types
Toca da Boa Vista I **29** 195
Toccagni, Callisto de *see* PIAZZA, CALLISTO
Tō Chō **17** 411, 414
Tocqué, Louis **22** 685; **27** 388; **31** 69–70*
- attributions **19** 543
- patrons and collectors **30** 524
- pupils **31** 799
- reproductive prints by others **9** 407; **33** 195, 196
- works **3** 841; **8** 743; **10** 531; **11** 405, 458; **31** *69*

El Tocuyano *see* RODRIGUEZ, JOSÉ FRANCISCO
El Tocuyo **32** *165*
- linen **32** 178
- painting **32** 173
- rugs **32** 177
- S Francisco **32** 168
- textiles **32** 178

el-Tod **1** 850
- sacred lake **27** 496
- temple **10** 68
- Temple of Montu **9** 830
- vases **21** 658

Tod, Joanne **5** 569
Toda **15** 205, 732, 735–6
- cloaks **15** *736*

Toda, Masatoshi **7** 656
Tōdaiji *see under* NARA
Toda Rai Singh **15** 603, 607
Today (Segodnya) **33** 522
Todd, Michael **19** 703; **29** 581
Todeschini, Giulio **31** 70*
Todeschini Piccolomini, Francesco *see* PIUS III, Pope
Todeschino, Giovanni *see* GIOVANNI TODESCHINO
Todi **10** *583*
- Cathedral of SS Annunziata **13** 96
- forgeries **10** 638
- pottery **16** 732
- sculpture **10** 605, *605*
- S Fortunato **13** 52
  - choir **13** *52*
- S Maria della Consolazione **7** 258, 541; **16** 633, *633*; **26** 187
- tapestries **16** 756

Todi, Jacopone da *see* JACOPONE DA TODI
Todi, Pietro Paolo da **26** 809
Todini, Michele **22** 373
Todleben, Franz Edouard Ivanovich **21** 581
Todmorden Town Hall (W. Yorks) **31** 241
Tōdo **23** 383
Todorov, Tseno **4** 603; **5** 154
Todorović, Mica **4** 461
Todorović, Stevan **28** 450
Todorovski, Dimo **13** 263; **19** 885
Tōdō Takatora **15** 108
Tōdō Takatsugu **15** 108
Todros, Boulos **10** 92
T'oech'on *see* KIM (i) SIK
Tō Eifu **17** 410
Tōeki Unkoku *see* UNKOKU TŌEKI
Toen Morikawa *see* MORIKAWA TOEN
Toeput, Lodewijk **21** 828; **31** 15, 70–71*
- works **31** *71*

Toesca, Pietro **19** 637; **31** 71–2*
Toesca y Ricci, Joaquin **6** 592, 602; **31** 72*
- works **6** *593*; **27** 791

Tōetsu **31** 252
Tofanelli, Agostino **31** 72
Tofanelli, Stefano **31** 72–3*
Toffetti, Gaspare San Giovanni **5** 694
Tofinou **1** 311
Toft, Albert **5** 732; **23** 34
Toft, Thomas **10** 142, 303; **29** 495
Toftrees (Norfolk), All Saints **26** 613
Tōgai Kawakami *see* KAWAKAMI, TŌGAI
Togaku Mori *see* MORI, TOGAKU
Togansai *see* HASHIMOTO GAHŌ
Tōgan Unkoku *see* UNKOKU TŌGAN
Togarō Tenkai *see* TENKAI TOGARŌ
togas **9** 246, 250, 639–40; **10** 636
Tōgen Nagahashi *see* NAGAHASHI TŌGEN
Toggenburg, Frederick of *see* FREDERICK OF TOGGENBURG
toggles **14** 763; **17** 398
- *see also* NETSUKE

Togguere Doupwil **21** 480
togidashi makie *see under* LACQUER → types
Togliacozzi, Gaspare **21** 6
Togo **1** *214*, 386; **31** 73–4*
- basketwork **31** 73
- calabashes **31** 73
- cement **31** *74*
- clay **1** 305
- compounds **1** 312
- dance-crests **31** 73
- earthenwares **31** 73
- furnaces **1** *287*
- houses **1** 305, 311, 312
- iconography **1** 282
- metal **1** 287
- sculpture **31** 73, *74*
- textiles **1** 349; **31** 73
- wood-carvings **31** 73

Tōgō, Seiji **17** 205; **31** 74*
Togolese Republic *see* TOGO
Togolok 1 **2** 251; **30** 440
Togolok 21 **2** 251; **6** 196; **30** 440
Tōgo Murano *see* MURANO, TŌGO
togu na *see* DOGON → meeting-houses
Togyū Okumura *see* OKUMURA, TOGYŪ
Tōhaku Hasegawa *see* HASEGAWA TŌHAKU
Tōhan Unkoku *see* UNKOKU TŌHAN
Tō Hittan **17** 412
Tohn, Aleksandr A. **29** 555
Toho, Shiozuki **30** 246
Tohono O'Odham **3** 331; **22** 550
Tohwasö **18** 57
toichobatai **13** 388, 389
Toidze, Mose (Ivanovich) **12** 326; **31** 75*
Toikka, Inkeri **11** 107
Toikka, Oiva **11** 107
toilé *see under* LACE → types
toile de jouy **32** 815
toilet-boxes *see under* BOXES → types
toilet services **5** 611; **10** 328; **11** *618*
toilet tables *see under* TABLES → types
Toiras, Jean de Saint-Bonnet, Marquis de **20** *922*
Toit, Paul Du *see* DU TOIT, PAUL
Tojbel', A. **3** 527
Tōjinmachi kiln *see under* KARATSU
Tōjirō Kitade *see* KITADE, TŌJIRŌ
Tojirō Oshita *see* OSHITA, TOJIRŌ
Tōkan Shūgetsu *see* SHŪGETSU TŌKAN
Tokara **27** 469
Tokat **16** *104*
- architecture **16** 183, 202
- Çukur Madrasa **16** 184
- curtains **2** 442
- Gök Madrasa **16** 184
- Halifet Gazi cloister **16** 204
- metalwork **2** 441
- mosque of Ali Pasha **16** 222
- street **16** *266*
- Sumbul Baba cloister **16** 204
- tomb of Ebu'l-Kasim **16** 185
- urban planning **16** *266*

Toke, Brian *see* TUKE, BRIAN
Tokelau **23** *711*; **31** 75*
- canoes **31** 75, *75*
- craftsmen and artists **31** *75*
- mats **31** 75

tokens **1** 853, 855; **4** *509*; **21** 271
Tokeshi, Eduardo **24** 511
Tokharians **6** 187, 307
Tokharistan
- castles **6** 199, 200
- clay **6** *221*, 221–2
- fortifications **6** 199
- houses **6** 200
- mud-bricks **6** 199
- polychromy **6** 221
- sculpture **6** *221*, 221–2*
- statuettes **6** 275
- stone **6** 221
- temples **6** 200
- terracotta **6** 275
- wall paintings **6** *232*, 232–3*

Tŏkhu *see* YI SONG-MIN
Tokimasa Hōjō *see* HŌJŌ TOKIMASA, Shogunal Regent
Tokimune Hōjō *see* HŌJŌ TOKIMUNE, Shogunal Regent
Tokiwa, Daijo **7** 161
Tokiyama **17** 243
Tokiyori Hōjō *see* HŌJŌ TOKIYORI, Shogunal Regent
Tok-kala **6** *182*; **31** 75–6*, *781*
- ossuaries **6** 233; **23** 607; **31** *76*

Tokkuz-tepa *see* KALA-I KAFIRNIGAN
Toklas, Alice B. **29** 605
Tokmadjan, Levon **2** 437
Tokmak **18** *567*, 568
- textiles **18** *569*

Tokoi, Oskari **32** 600
Tōkoku *see* SUZUKI TETSUGORO
Tokoname **17** *11*, *241*
- pottery **17** 241, 243, 255, 256, 260, 267, 350, 351; **31** 76*, *77*; **33** 487

Tokoname ware *see under* POTTERY → wares
tokonoma **17** 47, 77, 80, 343, 367, 435; **28** 311; **31** 77*
Tōkō Shin'etsu **17** 409; **31** 77*
Tōkō Shinoda *see* SHINODA, TŌKŌ
Tokoudagba, Cyprien **3** 728
- works **3** *729*

Tŏksan *see* HWANG KI-NO
Toksun **6** 308
Toktaliyev, E. **18** 569
Tokuan Ōtani *see* ŌTANI, TOKUAN
Tokudaiji Sahei **31** 84
Tokugawa (family) **17** 344
- architecture **17** 63, 749; **18** 238
- art policies **6** 175
- calligraphy **17** 215
- collections **17** 433
- emblems **23** 554
- lacquer **17** 301, 302; **28** 599
- paintings **17** 175, 184, 423, 788, 789, 793, 794, 796
- pottery **17** 262
- silk **17** 311
- weapons **17** 424

Tokugawa Hidetada, Shogun (*reg* 1605-23) **17** 383
- architecture **18** 564
- paintings **17** 786, 787, 789; **30** 376
- pottery **25** 869

Tokugawa Iemitsu, Shogun (*reg* 1623-51) **17** 304, 370; **31** 202
- architecture **17** 748; **18** 224, 564; **30** 263; **33** 540
- cities **18** 551
- dress **17** 315
- interior decoration **17** 788
- paintings **17** 789, 791

Tokugawa Ieyasu, Shogun (*reg* 1603-5) **17** 195, 370, 378; **31** 78
- architecture **17** 63; **18** 180, 181
- armour **17** 363
- castles **17** 84; **18** 564; **22** 432; **31** 83
- cities **17** 19, 96

Tokugawa Ieyasu, Shogun (*reg* 1603-5)—cont.
- coins **17** *370*
- dress **17** 377
- fans **11** 152
- paintings **14** 214
- screens (ii) (furniture) **17** 42

Tokugawa Mitsukuni **17** 730; **31** 77, 84
Tokugawa Nariaki **17** 730
Tokugawa period *see under* JAPAN → periods
Tokugawa Tsunayoshi, Shogun **18** 558
Tokugawa Yorifusa **31** 84
Tokugawa Yoshimune, Shogun (*reg* 1716-45) **17** 371
Tokugawa Yoshinao **22** 432
Tōkuma Katayama *see* KATAYAMA, TŌKUMA
Tokuoka, Shinsen **31** 78*
Tokuriki, Tomikichirō **17** 295
Tokuro Katō *see* KATŌ, TOKURO
Tokusai Tesshū *see* TESSHŪ TOKUSAI
Tokyo **17** *11*, 18, 19, 84, 95, 96; **31** 78–84*, *79*, *82*, *734*
- academies and art schools
  - Kōbu Bijutsu Gakkō (Technical Art School) **17** 133, 198, 203, 420, 435; **21** 59
  - School of Fine Arts *see* University of Fine Arts and Music
  - Tenkai Gakusha (Tenkai Rō; Tenkaisha) **30** 256
  - Tōkyō Bijutsu Gakkō (Tokyo Art School) **17** 133, 204, 420, 421, 798
  - Tōkyō Geijutsu Daigaku *see* University of Fine Arts and Music
- Angelo Tarlazzi Building **17** 92
- art forms and materials
  - enamel **17** 378
  - furniture **17** 358
  - kites **17** 389
  - lacquer **17** 302, 303
  - painting **17** 189
  - printing **7** 624; **17** 272
  - prints **17** 278, 280, 290
  - puppets **17** 408
  - seals **17** 409–10, 412
  - textiles **17** 315
- art market **2** 561
- auction houses **2** 561
- Bansho Shirabesho (Office for the Study of Western Documents) **17** 198; **30** 256
- calligraphers **17** 237
- Cathedral of St Mary **17** 90
- Central Post Office **17** 88, *88*
- Central Telegraph Office **17** 88
- City Hall **25** 359
- commercial buildings
  - Asahi Brewery **29** 546
  - Bank of Japan, Nihonbashi **3** 176; **17** 87
  - Kasumigaseki Building **17** 90
  - Matsuzakaya Department Store **21** 634
  - Nihon Life Insurance Building **17** 90
  - Nihon Sogo Bank **17** 89
  - Nippon Kangyō Bank **3** 176
  - Reader's Digest Building **17** 89; **26** 42
  - Yamato International Office Building **1** 737; **17** 92
- Communications Ministry Hospital **15** 886
- Daigaku Seminary Housing **17** 91
- Daikanyama Hillside Terrace Flats **17** 91
- Deer Cry Pavilion *see* Rokumeikan
- Diet **17** 87; **19** 320
- Edo **17** 96*; **31** 78*, 80–81*

Tokyo—cont.
Edo Castle 17 45, 52, 84, *96*, 796; 23 823; 31 78, 83–4*
exhibitions 31 81
French Embassy 8 77
gates 7 361
Hotel Okura 12 101
houses 17 83
Iwasaki Villa 17 *86*, 87
Mirror House 15 408
Silver Hut 16 783–4, *784*; 17 92
Imperial Hotel 14 788; 17 88
institutes
Japan Art Institute *see* Nihon Bijutsuin
National Art Research Institute 18 532
National Research Institute of Cultural Properties 7 744; 17 138
New Japan Art Institute *see* Saikō Nihon Bijutsuin
Nihon Bijutsuin (Japan Art Institute) 17 134, 200, 201, 420, 435; 28 603; 33 541
Saikō Nihon Bijutsuin (New Japanese Art Institute) 17 201
Tōkyō Kōgyō Daigaku (Tokyo Institute of Technology)
Alumni Memorial Hall 17 92; 28 *606*
Centennial Hall *see* Alumni Memorial Hall
Hydraulics Laboratory 30 296
Kabukiza 17 329
Law Courts 17 87
Meiji Shrine 12 100
Metropolitan Festival Hall *see* Municipal Festival Hall
Metropolitan Government Office 17 *92*, 93
Ministry of Justice 17 87
Municipal Festival Hall 17 90; 20 *76*
museums
Bridgestone Art Museum 17 433, 436
Eisei Bunko 6 826; 7 154
Gotō Museum 7 154; 33 562
Gyokudō Art Museum 33 562
Hatakeyama Collection 17 429
Idemitsu Museum of Art 7 154; 28 409
Imperial Museum 7 701; 17 87, 204; 22 365
see also National Museum
Japan Calligraphy Museum (Nihon Shōdo Hakubutsukan) 17 433
Japanese Sword Museum 17 364, 433
Japan Folk Art Museum *see* Nihon Mingeikan
Matsuoka Art Museum 15 746
Museum of Art and History *see under* University of Fine Arts and Music
Museum of Calligraphy (Shōdo Hakubutsukan) 6 772; 17 433
National Museum 17 89, 426; 20 76; 22 358; 32 896
collections 6 321, 735, 772, 826, 925; 7 54, 154; 15 75; 17 432
exhibitions 17 436
Hōryūji Treasure House 14 773
Matsukata collection 20 834
Ogura Collection 18 383
see also Imperial Museum
National Museum of Modern Art 17 136, 433, 436
archives 2 371
collections 24 682
exhibitions 17 137, 436
National Museum of Western Art 20 834; 22 365; 27 597; 33 563
Tokyo
museums—cont.
Nezu Art Museum 6 735, 826; 7 154; 18 383
Nihon Mingeikan (Japan Folk Art Museum) 17 265, 344, 429; 21 634; 31 82
collections 17 433; 18 383; 33 491
Nihon Shōdo Hakubutsukan *see* Japan Calligraphy Museum
Ōkura Shūkokan Museum 15 746; 16 783
Seikadō Bunko (Seikadō Art Museum and Library) 7 154; 17 429, *430*
Setagaya Museum 31 518
Shōdo Hakubutsukan *see* Museum of Calligraphy
Suntory Museum of Art 17 433
Taimaiken Japan Kite Museum 17 390
Tōgō Seiji Museum 17 433
Ueno Royal Museum *see* Imperial Museum
Nagasakin Capsule Tower 17 90; 21 *317*; 28 834
National Gymnasia 1 798; 16 55; 17 90; 28 627; 29 489; 30 *289*, 468
National Theatre 17 329
Nihon Dental College Hospital 17 88
Office for the Study of Western Documents *see* Bansho Shirabesho
palaces
Akasaka Detached Palace 17 *87*, 88; 21 59
Imperial Palace *see* Edo Castle
Katō Palace 18 239
Onarigoten 17 378
parks and gardens 12 99
Hibiya Park 12 100
Kōrakuen 12 99; 31 84*
Rikugien 12 99
Shinjuku Imperial Garden 12 100
Tenrikyōkan roof garden 12 101
Ueno Park 12 100; 24 181
pattern books 24 276
Rise Cinema 1 737
Rokumeikan (Deer Cry Pavilion) 17 87
roofs 17 47
St Anselm's 11 256
Shizuoka Press and Broadcasting Center 17 90
Supreme Court 18 890; 23 385
sushi 17 382
temples
Gokokuji 17 315
Jindaiji 17 112, *112*
Manganji 17 410
Shōfukuji 17 73, 419
Zōjōji 17 47
Zuishōji 21 802
theatres 17 329, 330
Tokyo Station 21 59
University of Fine Arts and Music 17 29, 200, 295, 304, *420*; 21 59
Museum of Art and History 29 241
urban planning 17 90
Wacoal Art Centre 1 737, *737*; 17 92; 20 147
Yushima Seidō shrine 17 435
Tokyo Art School *see* TOKYO → academies and art schools → Tōkyō Bijutsu Gakkō
Tokyo School of Fine Arts *see* TOKYO → University of Fine Arts and Music
Tokyo Society for Photographic Research 23 179
Tokyūsai *see* HON'AMI KŌETSU
Tol, Dominicus van 9 194; 19 102
Tola, Benedikt de 32 830
Tola, José 24 511
Tolai 24 83, 84
Tolaitola *see* TOLEDO
Tolchkov
Church of the Prophet Elijah 27 387
St John the Baptist 27 387
Tolchkovo, John the Prophet 25 342
Toledano, Eliézer *see* ELIÉZER TOLEDANO
Toledo (Spain) 16 *103*; 26 *904*; 29 *258*; 31 84–92*, *85*
Alcázar 8 79, *80*; 14 473–4; 29 267, 523
art forms and materials
armour 29 343
astrolabes 16 369
ceramics 29 322
clocks 7 438
embroidery 29 349, *349*, 350
furniture 29 310, 311
manuscript illumination 17 560–61; 30 778
manuscripts 26 563
marble 29 315
marks 31 90
metalwork 13 166; 16 369; 21 330; 29 333, 335, 336, 342; 31 90*
painting 13 144, 150; 29 278
pottery 16 411
scissors 8 286
sculpture 13 108
silk 29 348
swords 2 454
textiles 16 436
tiles 29 326; 30 883
weapons 29 340
Casa del Greco 4 785
Casa de Mesa 22 255; 29 263
Casa-Museo Victorio Macho 19 897; 31 90
Corral de Don Diego 22 255
ecclesiastical buildings
Cathedral 7 345; 13 51, 69; 29 263, 333; 30 374; 31 88, 90–92*, *91*
alabaster-carvings 32 *493*
altarpiece 1 710
Capilla Mayor 29 339, *339*
chapel of Santiago 13 106; 19 793
chapter house 2 529; 11 484
crowns 26 79
effigy of Juana Manuel 9 262
furniture 29 311
Great Retable 11 483
ivory-carvings 13 173
Lions' Gate *see* Puerta de los Leones
metalwork 11 615; 13 159; 29 333, 334, 337, 339, 341
monstrance 29 333, *333*
paintings 29 277
Puerta de Los Leones 1 599–600; 29 339
Puerta del Reloj 13 105
reliquaries 29 333
retables 13 123; 26 249
sacristy 31 *90*
sculpture 3 847, *847*; 10 476; 13 103; 29 293; 31 92*
silver 3 598
spire 29 414
stained glass 13 191, 192; 29 502, 504; 31 92*
swords 2 452
textiles 13 197; 16 437, 439; 23 461; 29 348; 30 331
tomb of Álvaro de Luna and Doña Juana de Pimentel 13 69, 106, *108*, 108; 28 330
tomb of Archbishop Alonso Carrillo de Alborñoz 29 290
tomb of Archbishop Pedro Tenorio 13 105
tomb of Cardinal Francisco Jiménez de Cisneros 29 289
Toledo (Spain)
ecclesiastical buildings
Cathedral—cont.
tomb of Cardinal Gil De Albornoz 13 105
tomb of Cardinal Mendoza 29 290
Transparente 11 492; 23 543; 26 251; 29 270, 292; 31 133–4
Treasury 26 689
workshop 13 68
convent of S Clara 29 290
convent of S Juan de la Penitencia 30 883
Cristo de la Vega 29 263
El Cristo de la Luz 2 294; 4 792; 16 189; 22 254; 31 86
monastery of Santa Cruz 30 883
Nuestra Señora del Tránsito 4 784; 17 544, 570; 22 254, 255; 29 263
Santiago del Arrabal 2 529; 4 784; 22 254; 29 263
Santo Domingo el Antiguo 6 44
S Bartolomé 22 254
S Juan Bautista 23 489
S Juan de los Reyes 2 278; 13 69, 70, *70*, 108, 757; 14 578; 29 263; 32 92
arches 2 295
cloister 31 *87*
staircases 29 521
S Leocadia 29 263
S María la Blanca 4 784; 17 544; 22 254; 29 263; 31 *86*
ceiling 2 529
S Miguel 29 263
S Pedro Mártir 20 125
S Román 22 254; 29 263
S Tomé 4 784; 22 254; 29 263
El Tránsito synagogue *see under* ecclesiastical buildings → Nuestra Señora del Tránsito
guilds 29 312
Hospital de Afuera *see* Hospital de S Juan Bautista
Hospital de Santa Cruz 14 781, *781*; 25 31; 29 265
Hospital de Santa Cruz *see also* Museo Arqueológico y de Bellas Artes; Museo de Santa Cruz
Hospital de S Juan Bautista 8 79, *79*; 29 267; 30 374
Hospital de Tavera *see* Hospital de S Juan Bautista
Ibn Shoshan synagogue *see* ecclesiastical buildings → S María la Blanca
Instituto de Estudios Visigoto-Mozárabes de S Eugenio 29 358
Jewish museum 17 582
mausoleum of Las Vegas de Pueblanueva 29 261
Mosque of Bab al-Mardum *see* ecclesiastical buildings → El Cristo de la Luz
Museo Arqueológico y de Bellas Artes 31 87
Museo de los Concilios y de la Cultura Visigoda 31 85; 32 618
Museo de la Fundación Duque de Lerma 31 87
Museo de Santa Cruz 29 355
Nuncio 2 658
palace of Cárdenas de Ocaña 22 256
Palacios de Galiana 29 297
Plaza de Zocodover 14 476
Puerta del Sol 29 263
railway station 22 256
Roman circus 7 342
Santiago del Arrabal 29 336
Sinagoga del Tránsito *see under* ecclesiastical buildings → Nuestra Señora del Tránsito
S Servando Castle 8 138
Toledo (Spain)—cont.
stelae 29 618
Taller del Moro 22 255; 29 263
Town Hall 14 474
urban planning 31 711
Toledo Museum of Art (OH; USA) 17 385; 19 304; 27 47; 31 645, 667
Toledo, Aldary Henriques *see* HENRIQUES TOLEDO, ALDARY
Toledo, Antonio 24 615
Toledo, Archbishop 29 130
Toledo, Eleonora of *see* ELEONORA OF TOLEDO, Duchess of Florence
Toledo, Fernando Alvárez de, Governor of the Netherlands *see* ALBA, FERNANDO ALVÁREZ DE TOLEDO, Gran-Duque de
Toledo, Fernando de 4 453
Toledo, Francisco (*b* 1940) 31 92–3*
patrons and collectors 21 395
personal collection 21 397
works 21 390, *390*
Toledo, Francisco de, Viceroy of Peru (1515-82) 8 302; 21 264, 396; 25 365
Toledo, Juan Antonio 10 443
Toledo, Juan Bautista de 10 535; 20 70; 31 93–4*
assistants 14 473
attributions 14 474
collaboration 8 65; 23 492; 29 522
patrons and collectors 2 284; 13 922; 14 5, 517
works 2 284; 10 498, 499, *499*, *500*, 501; 14 473; 19 226, 227; 20 72; 23 811; 24 107; 29 267, 300; 31 *93*, 822
Toledo, Luigi da 1 551
Toledo, Pedro Alvarez de, Marqués de Villafranca *see* VILLAFRANCA, PEDRO ALVAREZ DE TOLEDO, Marqués de
Toledo, Pedro de *see* PEDRO DE TOLEDO
Toledo, Pietro di 5 525
Toledo, Sebastián de *see* SEBASTIÁN DE TOLEDO
Toledo y Gonzaga, José Alvárez de *see* ALBA, JOSÉ ALVÁREZ DE TOLEDO Y GONZAGA, 17th Duque de
Toledo y Gutiérrez, Cipriano 8 303; 33 617
Tolentino, S Nicola da Tolentino 6 466, *467*
Tolentino, Guillermo 20 274; 24 619
Tolerazzi, Fortunato 16 737
Toletum *see* TOLEDO (SPAIN)
Tolibowski, Wojciech, Bishop of Poznán 28 187
Tolima 29 210
Tolita *see* LA TOLITA
Toljić, Mirko 22 18
Tölk 14 749
Tolla, Bartolomeo 29 841
Tollan *see* TULA
Toller, Melchiorre 16 836
Tollet, Johann Septimius von *see* JÖRGER VON TOLLET, JOHANN SEPTIMIUS
Tollet, Tony 25 752
Tolley, William 25 836
Tolli, Vive 10 540
Tollman, J., & Co. 14 53
Tollu, Cemal 31 94*, 454
Tollus, Adrianus 22 828
Tolmeita *see* PTOLEMAIS
Tolmer 4 368
Tolmezzo, Gianfrancesco da *see* GIANFRANCESCO DA TOLMEZZO
Tolnai, Vagujhelyi Károly *see* TOLNAY, CHARLES ERICH DE

Tolnay, Charles Erich de **14** 901; **21** 460; **28** 115; **31** 94–5*
Tolomei (family) **28** 677
Tolomei, Cardinal **8** 12
Tolomei, Claudio **2** 161; **25** 278; **31** 95*; **32** 641
Tolosa, Pedro de **2** 864; **29** 267
Tolowa **22** 549
Tolozan (family) **8** 653
Tolpan **14** 711, 712
Tölpus, Uno **30** 349
Tolsá, Manuel **29** 294; **31** 95–6*
pupils **24** 262
works **13** 730; **20** 351; **21** 378, 384, *384*, *401*, 402; **25** 697; **31** 307
Tolson, Edgar **22** 441
Tolson, Michael **28** 204
Tolstaya Mogila Pectoral **4** 111; **28** 323–4
Tolstov, Sergey (Pavlovich) **18** 414; **31** 96*, 157
Tolstoy, Aleksey (Nikolayevich), Count **28** 619
Tolstoy, Fyodor (Petrovich) **20** 924; **27** 390; **31** 96*
Tolstoy, Ivan (Ivanovich) **31** 96*
Tolstoy, Leo *see* TOLSTOY, LEV (NIKOLAYEVICH)
Tolstoy, Lev (Nikolayevich) **24** 247; **31** 96–7*
works **1** 181; **4** 366
illustrated **25** 28
on art **1** 172
on expression **10** 690
Tolstoy, M. P., Count **19** 333
Tolstoy, Paul **31** 66
Toltec **6** 579; **20** 884; **21** 177, 200–201, 202–3; **31** 97–100*
altars **1** 701
architecture **31** 98–9
armour **21** 246
ballcourts **3** 118, *118*; **31** 99, 505
beads **21** 243
ceramics **31** 99
chacmools **21** 223
coatepantlis **7** 481–2, *481*
colour **21** 183
figurines **31** 100
friezes **31** 99, *99*
jade **21** 243
joinery **5** 408
limestone **21** *223*; **31** 99
manuscripts **21** 233
obsidian **31** 98
palaces **23** 826
pendants (jewellery) **21** 243, 260
pottery **21** 239
sculpture **5** *409*; **21** 222–3*, *223*; **31** 99
monumental **21** 217
relief **31** *99*
seals **21** 258, *258*
shells **21** 260
skull racks **1** 701; **31** 99
stelae **29** 620
temples **6** *580*
weapons **21** 246
Tolteca-Chichimeca **31** 97
Toltecat **20** 886
toluene **12** 629; **29** 53
Toluvila **29** 459
Tołwiński, Tadeusz **25** 142; **31** 100*; **32** 872
Toma (people) **1** 279, 363
Toma (*fl* late 14th cent.) **4** 679
Toma (*fl* 1428) **26** 711
Toma, Gioacchino **22** 480; **32** 257
works **16** 678, *679*
Tomacelli, Lucrezia **25** 257
Toma de la Suceava **31** 101*
Tomadjan **1** 786
Tomáharo **24** 93
Tomajuoli, Giuseppe **25** 56
Tomalin, H. F. **29** 454
Tomanović, Luka **22** 18
Tomar **25** *288*
Abbey **6** 43–4; **20** 325–6; **25** *288*; **31** 101–2*, 178
Charola **23** 414; **31** 101*
choir **25** 291
Church of the Order of Christ **2** *500*; **7** 257, *257*; **13** 71; **25** 296; **27** 139; **31** *102*
gargoyles **12** 150
sculpture **13** 125
cloister **25** 291; **31** *178*
stained glass **13** 192
Templars' Rotunda *see* Charola
wall paintings **25** 295
architecture **25** 291
Chapel of Nossa Senhora da Conceição **6** *43*; **25** 291
synagogue **17** 545
Tomara *see* (TOMARA) RAJPUTS
Tomara, Anangapala *see* ANANGAPALA TOMARA
Tomás, José **13** 275
Tomás, Leão de *see* LEÃO DE TOMÁS
Tomás, Raffaele *see* RAFFAELE TOMÁS
Tomás de Sousa, Caetano *see* SOUSA, CAETANO TOMÁS DE
Tomasello **26** 193
Tomasini, G. F.
works **4** *483*
Tomasino da Vimercate **20** 783; **31** 102–3*
works **20** 710; **31** *103*
Tomaso da Modena **13** 152; **31** 103–5*
patrons and collectors **8** 423
teachers **32** 626
works **9** 261; **13** 149; **17** 819; **28** 434; **30** 705; **31** *104*, *105*, 316
Tomaso de Vigilia **28** 656
Tomaso di Calisto **25** 19
Tomaso di Maurienne, Saint **10** 804
Tomaszewski, Henryk Albin **25** 125; **31** 106*
Tomaszewski, Lech **15** 122; **29** 52
Tomaszów **25** 123
tomato red *see under* PIGMENTS → types
Tomatsu, Shōmei **14** 779; **24** 679; **31** 106*
Tomaz, Victor **22** 245
Tomažič, France **28** 860; **31** 106*
tombak **16** 388
Tombazis, Alexandros N. **13** 351
tomb chapels *see under* CHAPELS → types
tomb-chests *see under* TOMBS → types
tomb of Emperor Kimmei **17** 58
tomb of Emperor Ōjin **17** 58
tomb of Emperor Richū **17** 58
tomb of Khai Dinh **32** 480
tomb of King Muryŏng **18** 297
tomb of Tran Hien Tong **32** 478
tomb of Tran Thu Do **32** 478
Tombos Stele **9** 781
Tombouctou *see* TIMBUKTU
tomb painting *see under* PAINTING → forms
Tomb period *see* JAPAN → periods → Kofun
Tombros, Mikhaēl **2** 218; **13** 354; **31** 133*
tombs **2** 362; **5** 301; **6** 165; **8** 222; **14** 420–21; **31** 106–32*
historical and regional traditions
Afghanistan **16** *163*
Anatolia, ancient **1** 521–2
Austria **5** *628*; **7** *554*
Aztec **31** 118
Bali (Indonesia) **15** *763*
Belgium **3** *417*; **14** *421*
Bulgaria **5** 150, 155
Central Asia, Western **6** 196
Islamic **16** 159–60, 163–4, 197, 237, 492
tombs
historical and regional traditions
Central Asia, Western—cont.
Samanid **16** 159
Chancay **31** 118
Chimú **31** 118
China **4** *794*; **6** 631, 693–9*, 700–705*; **7** 73, 133; **31** 115
Han period (206 BC-AD 220) **6** 648, *697*; **33** 532–3
Ming period (1368-1644) **6** *701*, *702*, *703*
Qing period (1644-1911) **6** *704*
Shang period (*c.* 1600-*c.* 1050 BC) **6** *694*
Song period (AD 960-1279) **6** *699*, *700*
Tang period (AD 618-907) **6** *651*, *698*
Zhou period (*c.* 1050-256 BC) **6** *695*, *696*
Crete **18** 164; **21** 656, 657, 659, 664–5*; **31** 107
Cycladic **8** 310
Cyprus, ancient **8** 333, 335, *337*
Denmark **11** *219*
Egypt **5** *403*; **16** 175, 207, 208–9; **31** *113*
Egypt, ancient **9** 836–8*; **10** 1, 2, 3; **20** 863; **31** 107*
Graeco-Roman (332 BC-AD 395) **9** 842*
Late Period (664-332 BC) **9** 841–2*
Middle Kingdom (*c.* 1966-*c.* 1630 BC) **9** 838*
New Kingdom (*c.* 1539-*c.* 1075 BC) **9** 839–41*, *840*, *841*
Predynastic (*c.* 6000-*c.* 2925 BC) **9** 837*
England **1** 520; **10** 259, 261, 262, 359
Gothic **1** *517*; **13** 84; **19** *605*
Gothic Revival **31** *345*
Neo-classicism **22** *46*
New Sculpture **12** *611*
Renaissance **31** *190*
Rococo **27** *244*
15th cent. **10** *260*
16th cent. **10** *262*
19th cent. **31** *131*
Ethiopia **10** 577
Etruscan **10** 587, 588, 597–9*, 603, 617–24*; **13** 486, 506; **20** 863; **30** 346; **31** 109
France
Baroque **2** *91*; **12** *726*; **24** *786*
Gothic: 15th cent. **13** *78*
Mannerism **16** *856*
Prehistoric **25** 506
Renaissance **1** *766*
Romanesque **11** *290*
14th cent. **17** 459
16th cent. **11** 556; **26** *350*; **27** *547*
17th cent. **8** *94*
Germany **14** 421
Baroque **26** *25*; **32** *833*
Gothic **13** 160; **30** *535*
Gothic: Late Gothic **32** *607*
Ghirza **31** 109
Gothic
England **1** *517*; **13** 84; **19** *605*
France **13** *78*
Germany **13** 160; **30** *535*; **32** *607*
Italy **13** 95–6, *96*, *97*
Portugal **13** *101*
Spain **13** *107*, *108*; **28** *724*
Switzerland **30** 136
Greece, ancient **13** 383, *384*, 391, 396, 404, 407, *407*, 568; **31** 107*, *108*
Guatemala **17** *754*
Helladic **14** 340–41
Holy Roman Empire (before 1648) **26** 684*
tombs
historical and regional traditions—cont.
Inca **31** 119
Indian subcontinent **6** 165; **15** 686, 734; **31** 114–15*
Bahmani **15** 356, 358
Deccan **15** *384*
Ghurid **20** *251*
Islamic **15** *337*, 342, 343, 349; **31** 111, 113, 114, *115*
Mughal **1** *459*; **8** *679*; **15** *364*; **28** *711*
Prehistoric **21** *44*
Punjab **15** *374*
15th cent. **8** *674*
16th cent. **8** *674*
17th cent. **15** *373*
Indonesia **15** *763*
Iran **16** 159–60, 163–4, 197, 492; **31** *112*
Iran, ancient **15** 904
Iraq **16** 159
Ireland **16** 19–20; **25** 508–9
Islamic **16** 90, 128, 141, 142; **28** 633–5; **31** 110–13*
Afghanistan **16** *163*
Central Asia, Western **16** 159–60, 164, 197, 237, 492
Egypt **5** *403*; **16** 175, 207, 208–9; **31** *113*
Indian subcontinent **15** *337*, 342, 343, 349; **31** 111, 113, 114, *115*
Iran **16** 159–60, 163–4, 197, 492; **31** *112*
Morocco **16** 240, *240*
Ottoman **16** 206
Syria **16** 207
Tunisia **16** 220
Turkey **16** 185–6, 206; **31** *114*
Uzbekistan **27** *675*
Yemen **16** 177, 214–15
Italy **9** 125; **16** 688; **27** *180*, 181, *184*
Baroque **1** *627*; **4** *621*; **16** *703*; **27** *347*
Etruscan **10** 587, 588, 597–9*, 617–24*; **20** 863; **30** 346
Gothic **13** 95–6, *96*, *97*; **31** *3*, *4*
Renaissance **1** *747*; **4** *737*; **7** *367*; **8** *797*; **11** *27*; **16** 690, 840, *841*; **21** *438*, *465*; **32** *361*
Roman **26** *877*
13th cent. **2** *480*, 481
14th cent. **12** 303; **22** *475*; **28** *29*
15th cent. **4** *736*; **19** *555*
16th cent. **27** *748*, *749*
20th cent. **4** *101*
Japan **17** 57–9*; **27** 832; **28** 608; **31** 115
Kofun period (*c.* AD 300-710) **17** *58*, *59*, 142–4*
Yayoi period (*c.* 300 BC-*c.* AD 300) **33** 511
Korea **18** 260, 271–4*, 289, 298–300, 316
Prehistoric **18** 271*
6th cent. AD **18** *272*
7th cent. AD **18** *274*
Lycia **19** 838–40, *839*
Lydia **19** 841; **31** 108
Macedonia (i) (Greece) **15** 53; **31** 109
Madagascar **20** 36
Maya **17** *754*; **20** 885; **21** 213; **26** *411*, 411–12; **31** 117, 118
Mesoamerica, Pre-Columbian **25** 764; **31** *117*, 117–18*
Guatemala **17** *754*
Maya **17** *754*; **26** *411*, 411–12
Zapotec **18** 675–6
Mesopotamia **31** 107*
Milagro-Quevedo **31** 118
tombs
historical and regional traditions—cont.
Minoan **18** 164; **21** 664–5*; **31** 107
Early Minoan (*c.* 3500/3000-*c.* 2050 BC) **21** 656
Late Minoan (*c.* 1600-*c.* 1050 BC) **21** 659
Middle Minoan (*c.* 2050-*c.* 1600 BC) **21** 657
Mixtec **31** 118
Moche (culture) **31** 118, *119*
Morocco **16** 240, *240*
Mughal **1** *459*
Mycenaean **14** 340–41
Nabataea **2** 249–50, *250*
Native North Americans **22** 571
Nubia **23** 279, 282
Numidia **23** 299
Olmec **31** 117
Ottoman **16** 206
Pakistan **23** 803
Phrygian **31** 108
Poland **4** *147*; **13** *774*; **22** *167*; **25** 113–14; **32** *873*
Portugal **13** *101*
Prehistoric art
Bronze Age **25** 524
France **25** 506
Ireland **25** 508–9
Korea **18** 271*
Neolithic **25** 498, 506–9*
Sardinia **2** 52; **27** 834
Scotland **20** *81*, 81–2; **25** 508
Recuay culture **31** 118
Romanesque **11** *290*; **26** 628–9, 684*
Rome, ancient **26** 856, 861, *877*; **27** 60; **31** 109–10*
Ryūkyū Islands **27** 470
Sardinia **2** 52; **25** 524
Saudi Arabia **2** *250*
Scotland **20** *81*, 81–2; **25** 508
Sicily **26** 628–9
South America, Pre-Columbian **31** 118–19*, *119*
South-east Asia **31** 115*
Spain
Gothic **9** *748*; **13** *107*, *108*; **28** *724*
Renaissance **10** *783*
Swahili **30** 57
Switzerland **22** *919*; **30** 136
Syria **16** 207
Tarascan **31** 118
Teutonic Order **30** *535*
Thracian **5** 155
Tibet **30** 805, 847
Tunisia **16** 220
Turkey **16** 185–6, 204, 206; **31** *114*
Urartian **31** 700
Uzbekistan **27** *675*
Veraguas culture **31** 118
Vicús **31** 118
Vietnam **31** 115; **32** *475*, 475–6, *476*
Yemen **16** 177, 214–15
Zapotec **18** 675–6; **31** 118
materials
alabaster (gypsum) **1** *517*, 520; **10** 261; **13** 84
brick **4** *793*; **6** 648, 696, 697, 698; **18** 271; **26** *877*
bronze **8** *94*; **26** 684*
domes **16** 214–15
limestone **10** *262*; **11** *290*; **13** *101*
marble
England **10** *260*, 262, *262*; **31** *122*
Finland **11** *99*
France **8** *94*; **12** *726*; **16** *856*
Gothic **13** *96*, *97*, *108*
Italy **1** *627*, *747*; **2** *480*; **4** *101*, *621*; **5** *628*; **7** *367*; **8** *797*; **16** *841*; **19** *555*; **21** *465*; **27** *347*; **28** *29*; **31** *3*, *4*

tombs
  materials
    marble—cont.
      Poland 4 147
      Spain 10 783
    masonry 25 507
    stone 6 697, 697; 18 271; 25 524
    tiles 15 686
    tracery 31 271
    vaults (ceiling) 15 53
    wood 6 696; 18 271
  types
    arch door 10 597*
    beehive see tholos
    caditoia 10 598*
    chamber
      Crete 13 383, 396; 21 659
      Etruscan 10 593, 597, 597–9
      Greece, ancient 13 383, 384, 396
      Italy 10 593, 597, 597–9
      Japan 16 82
      Korea 18 271
      Minoan 21 659
      Sardinia 27 834
      see also passage
    chambered 25 507
    chapel 9 836, 837, 838, 839–42
    ciborium 7 303
    cist
      Egypt, ancient 9 842
      Greece, ancient 13 383, 396
      Korea 18 271
    columbaria 7 642*; 9 29; 31 110
    confessio 7 703*
    corbel 10 597*
    court 25 507, 508*
    dolmens 9 80*; 25 507*
      England 21 40
      Eritrea 10 577
      Ethiopia 10 577
      France 9 80
      Germany 9 80
      Korea 18 271
      Prehistoric art 21 40; 25 507; 27 367
      Russia 27 367
      Syria-Palestine 30 190
    dolmens (à couloir) 9 80
    dolmens (portal) 9 80
    heroa see Heroa
    hypogées 25 506, 507
    iwan 16 186
    keyhole 17 57, 57, 58–9; 23 157
    lunette 10 597*
    Macedonian 13 384, 391, 404, 407
    mastabas 9 779, 836, 837, 839, 899; 20 596*, 863; 25 760; 31 107
    megalithic 9 80
      France 21 42
      Germany 21 41
      Indian subcontinent 21 44
      Prehistoric art 21 40, 44; 25 507*, 509–11*
      Scandinavia 21 41
    passage 5 780–81; 25 507, 508, 509–11*
      see also chamber tombs
    peribolos 13 384
    private 9 836, 840; 30 700
    pyramids see Pyramids
    rock-cut
      Egypt, ancient 9 837; 31 107
      Etruscan 10 597
      Greece, ancient 31 108
      Italy 10 597
      Japan 17 58
      Jewish art 17 553
      Nabataea 24 558
      Prehistoric art 25 511*
    royal 9 791, 836, 836, 840–41; 10 7, 63; 17 57–8*; 25 760
    saff-tombs 9 839; 30 697
    shaft 2 209; 21 197, 216*; 33 101, 102
    slab 31 122, 122–3*
tombs
  types—cont.
    tholos 30 737–8*
      Crete 21 656; 30 738
      Greece, ancient 13 383; 31 108
      Helladic 14 338, 339, 340, 340–41; 23 476
      Minoan 21 656; 30 738
      Mycenaean 14 338, 340, 340–41; 23 476; 30 738, 738; 31 107
    three-cell 10 598*
    tomb-chests 31 121*, 121, 122
    tower
      Central Asia, Western 16 159–60
      France 12 770
      Iran 16 158, 159–60, 160, 194; 23 559
      Islamic 16 158, 159–60, 160, 185–6, 194, 204; 23 559; 31 113
      Rome, ancient 12 770
      Turkey 16 185–6, 204; 31 113
    tunnel 17 106
    two-cell 10 598*
    wall 31 123–7*
      England 31 124, 127
      France 31 124, 125
      Gothic 31 124
      Italy 31 123, 124, 125, 126–7
    wedge 25 508–9*
    zenpōkōen see keyhole
  see also Brasses (monumental); Burial mounds; Catacombs; Cemeteries; Effigies; Graves; Hypogea; Mausolea; Monuments → types → funerary; Necropoleis; Pyramids
Tombs, The 1 37; 31 133*
Tombs of Christ 9 680–81*, 681
tomb statues see under Sculpture → types
tombstone headdresses see under Headdresses → types
tombstones see Gravestones
tomb towers see Tombs → types → tower
Tomé (family) 28 368; 29 291
Tomé, Andrés 31 133
Tomé, Antonio 31 133
Tomé, Diego 31 133, 823
Tomé, Giovanni de see Giovanni de Tomé
Tomé, Narciso 31 133–4*, 674
  groups and movements 7 289
  works 11 492; 23 543; 26 251; 29 270, 292; 31 89, 92, 823
Tomé, Simón Gavilán 28 690
Tomečko, Pavel 28 856
Tomeo, Leonico 3 649
Tomić, Mihailo 28 453
Tomice Church 25 129
Tomich Psalter see under Psalters → individual manuscripts
Tomicki, Piotr 25 135
Tomiharu Shimizu see Shimizu Tomiharu
Tomikichirō Tokuriki see Tokuriki, Tomikichirō
Tomiko Hino see Hino Tomiko
Tomilov, Aleksey Romanovich 18 74; 27 438, 439
Tomimoto, Kenkichi 17 266, 267, 268, 433; 18 555, 901; 21 635; 31 134*
  groups and movements 21 634
  works 23 179, 371
Tominaga, Yuzuru 17 92; 31 134–5*
Tominc, Jožef 28 860; 31 135*
Tominz, Giuseppe see Tominc, Jožef
Tomioka Tessai 17 188; 31 135–7*; 33 322
  patrons and collectors 17 433
  works 17 199; 31 137
Tomio Miki see Miki, Tomio
Tomis see Constanța
Tomishko, Antony 12 856
Tomita, Keisen 17 201
Tomita, Reiko 30 392
Tomitarō Aoki see Hara, Sankei
Tomitarō Hara see Hara, Tomitarō
Tomiyama Keijun 17 412
Tomkin, S(amuel) N(orton) 14 157*
Tomkins, Charles 24 18; 31 137
Tomkins, Charles Algernon 31 137
Tomkins, Charles John 31 137–8*
Tomkins, Peltro William 3 309; 29 675; 31 137
Tomkins, William 31 137
Tomkinson & Adam 5 832, 840
Tomkinsons Ltd 18 30
Tomlin, Bradley Walker 1 83; 24 213; 26 489; 31 138*
Tomlinson, William 29 419
Tommasi, Angiolo 19 71
Tommasi, Giuseppe 19 525
Tommasi, Lodovico 19 71
Tommasi, Tommaso 30 429
Tommasi foundry 19 438
Tommaso, Bartolomeo di see Bartolomeo di Tommaso (da Foligno)
Tommaso da Barisini see Tomaso da Modena
Tommaso da Maroggia see Rodari, Tommaso
Tommaso da Milano 32 409
Tommaso da Ravenna see Rangone, Tommaso
Tommaso de Celano 11 708
Tommaso di Bartolommeo see Maso di Bartolommeo
Tommaso di Cristofano Fini see Masolino
Tommaso di Pietro 11 28
Tommaso di Ser Giovanni di Mone Cassai see Masaccio
Tommè, Luca di see Luca di Tommè
Tommen, Gabriël van der 5 49
Tømmerby 8 720
  Church 8 722, 722
Tommisen, Daniel 31 138–9*
Tomoe Yabe see Yabe, Tomoe
Tom of Finland 12 216
Tomon, Toma de see Thomon, Thomas-Jean de
Tomonobu Kanō see Kanō Tomonobu
Tomorowicz, Kazimierz 20 153
Tomotada see Iizumiya Shichiemon
Tomoto Kobori see Kobori, Tomoto
Tomov, Evtim 17 868
Tomovski, Dragan 19 883
Tomovski, K. 19 883
Tomovski, Sotir 19 883
Tomoyoshi Murayama see Murayama, Tomoyoshi
Tompal, Kamilo 9 672
Tompieme 8 490
Tompion, Thomas 7 442; 32 368
  works 7 443
Tomruk, Mehmet Mahir 31 454
Toms, Carl 21 312; 31 139*
Toms, Peter 8 26; 9 212; 31 139*
Toms, William Henry 4 607; 6 513
Tomsk 27 362, 374, 378
Tomsky, Nikolay (Vasil'yevich) 31 139*
Ton, Konstantin (Andreyevich) 27 377; 31 140*
  assistants 3 733
  groups and movements 28 837
  pupils 28 628
  works 16 794; 22 173, 181, 181; 27 377
Tonalá 20 882; 21 193, 372; 31 140–41*
Tonalamatl Aubin see under Codices → individual manuscripts
Tonal Impressionism 31 393
Tonalism 22 350; 31 141*; 33 442
Tonalismo 21 87
Tonauer, Hans, I see Donauer, Hans, I
Tonbridge (Kent) 6 56; 31 423
  Castle 12 173
Tonconogy, Alberto 2 397
Tønder 8 720, 756, 757
  Sønderjyllands Kunstmuseum 8 760
Tønder lace see under Lace → types
tondi 4 496; 9 14; 31 142*
Tondino di Guerrino 13 775; 31 141–2*
Tondo 24 616
tondo frames see under Frames → types
Tone, Mariya (Aleksandrovna) 27 423
Tone, Sister 15 103
Tone, Voldemārs 26 384
Tonelli, Carlos 31 756
Tonelli, Giuseppe 26 321
toners 24 647
Tonga (Africa) 1 310, 368, 414, 416, 417, 418, 419; 20 161
Tonga (Pacific Islands) 23 711; 31 142–5*, 145
  architecture 23 715
  bark 31 143
  barkcloth 23 735
  basketwork 31 143
  bone 4 314
  canoes 23 725
  craftsmen and artists 23 718
  fans 10 779
  feathers 31 143
  headdresses 31 143
  ivory-carvings 31 144, 145
  mats 23 735; 31 143
  paper mulberry 31 143
  plaiting 31 143
  postage stamps 25 329
  sculpture 31 144
  staffs 31 144, 144
  stencilling 31 143
  stone 23 715
  tattoos 23 719
  wood 31 144
  wood-carvings 31 143–4
Tongareva 7 790
Tongatapu Island 23 715
Tongbong see Kim Si-sŭp
Tongchuan 6 885, 892, 913
Tongdao 7 27
T'ŏngdo Temple 18 331
  metalwork 18 348
  paintings 18 309
  sculpture 18 295
  wall paintings 18 307
Tongeren 3 539
  architecture 3 540
  Begijnhof 13 114
  glass 3 592
  marks 3 601
  Onze Lieve Vrouwebasiliek 10 703; 13 62, 159
    ivory-carvings 23 660
    jewellery 3 604
    objects of vertu 3 603
    sculpture 13 110; 26 644, 645
  Provincial Gallo-Romeins Museum 3 592
  sculpture 3 566
  silver 3 598
Tongeren, P. van 12 885
Tongeren, Willem van 10 707
Tongerlo Abbey 3 546, 570; 13 100
Tongerloo, Georges van see Vantongerloo, Georges
Tong'gou 18 250
  palace 18 275
Tong'gou—cont.
  tombs 18 272, 318
    Kakcho Tomb 18 272
    Muyong Tomb 18 272, 313, 318, 319, 373
    Tomb of the Dancers see Muyong Tomb
Tongguan 6 885, 915, 917
  pottery 6 917
Tonglü shan 6 830
Tongoa 31 893
To Ngoc Van 32 482
tongs 11 118, 119
Tongsamdong 18 365, 372
Tongsŏng, King (reg 479-501) 18 275
Tongsu 18 272, 373
tongue rugs see under Rugs → types
Tong' yŏnsa (Society for Joint Research) 18 60; 25 760; 33 534
Tongzhi emperor (Qing; reg 1862-74) 7 153
Toni, Angelo Michele 8 140
Toniná 20 882; 21 372; 29 620; 31 145*
toning see under Photography → processes
Tonio di Baccio 16 845
Tonitza, Nicolae (N.) 3 4; 26 716, 723; 31 145–6*
Tonjae see Sŏng Se-ch'ang
Tonkawa 22 551
Tonkin 18 613; 32 486
Tonks, Henry 4 880; 10 374; 19 589; 31 146*
  groups and movements 23 23
  pupils 19 591
    Biller, Olive Allen 4 63
    Dobell, William 9 53
    Fox, Ethel Carrick 11 363
    Gertler, Mark 12 493
    John, Augustus (Edwin) 10 255; 17 608
    Leach, Bernard (Howell) 18 901
    Perkins, Christopher 24 456
    Roberts, William (1895-1980) 26 466
    Spencer Bower, Olivia 29 385
  teachers 4 880
Tonnancour, Jacques (Godefroy) de 8 41; 25 635; 31 146*, 228
Tonnay-Charante, Prince de 18 654
Tonne, Jehan de la see Toolne, Jan van der
Tonnelier, Georges 19 75; 26 486
  works 26 486
Tonnelier, Louis-Auguste Le, Baron de Breteuil see Breteuil, Louis-Auguste Le Tonnelier, Baron de
Tonnerre, Charles-Henry de Clermont- see Clermont-Tonnerre, Charles-Henry de
Tonnerre, Hôpital Notre-Dame des Fontenilles 11 511; 14 780, 780; 30 909
Tönnis, Cord 33 87
Tōnomine, Suhara House 27 596
Tonomura, Kichinosuke 21 634
Tonomura Otai 17 411
Tonosí style pottery see under Pottery → wares
Tonson, Jacob 11 426; 18 97, 145; 30 759; 31 871
Tonti, Michelangelo, Cardinal 5 870
Tontine Heads 28 242
Tonwerke Kandern 12 432
Töoffer, Wolfgang Adam 20 592
Tooke, Brian see Tuke, Brian
Tooker, George 20 93; 21 606
Tookey, J. 15 57
tooling 31 147*
Toolne, Jan van der 31 147*

tools
 historical and regional traditions
  Africa **1** 291, *364*, 364–5*
  Baule **1** *364*
  Burkina Faso **1** *364*
  China **6** 841; **7** 97
  Côte d'Ivoire **1** *364*, 370
  Crete **8** 153, 154
  Czech Republic **24** 332
  Denmark **25** 515
  Germany **32** 679
  Greece, ancient **13** 371
  Guinea **1** *364*
  Indian subcontinent **15** 192, 193; **29** 444
  Iran, ancient **15** 902–3*
  Japan **17** 47–50*, *49*, 274, 275, *275*, *276*
  Kissi **1** *364*, 365
  Kuba (iii) (Zaïre) **1** *364*
  Linear Pottery culture **25** 515
  Luba **1** *364*
  Mesoamerica, Pre-Columbian **21** 190, 195, 247
  Mesopotamia **21** 304
  Minoan **8** 153
  Mossi **1** *364*
  Prehistoric art **16** 615; **25** 472, 473, 476, 477, 493–4*, 517
   Bronze Age **25** 524–5, 530
   Crete **8** 153
   Czech Republic **24** 332
   Denmark **25** 515
   Germany **32** 679
   Indian subcontinent **29** 444
   Iran, ancient **15** 902–3*
   Iron Age **25** 541
   Linear Pottery culture **25** 515
   Neolithic **25** 496, 515–16*
   Palaeolithic **18** 807
   South-east Asia **29** 227, 228
   Sri Lanka **29** 445
   Thailand **29** 227, 228
   Vietnam **29** 227, 228
  Rome, ancient **27** 16*
  Sampung culture **29** 226
  Senufo **1** 370
  South America, Pre-Columbian **29** 184
  South-east Asia **29** 227, 228
  Sri Lanka **29** 445
  Syria-Palestine **30** 182, 192, 194
  Taolean culture **29** 226
  Thailand **29** 227–8
  Tibet **30** 842
  Tura (people) **1** *364*
  Urartian **31** 700
  Vietnam **29** 227, 228
  Zaïre **1** *364*
  Zande **1** *364*
 materials
  antlers **16** 615; **25** 472, 493
  basalt **25** 493
  bone **8** 153; **16** 615; **21** 247; **25** 472
  bronze **6** 841; **29** 228
  chert **25** 493
  copper **25** 517
  diamonds **20** 302
  flint **15** 192; **25** 472, 493, 515
  granite **25** 515
  iron **7** 97; **8** 154; **15** 193; **17** 47; **29** 228; **31** 700
  ivory **25** 493
  limestone **25** 493
  obsidian **21** 195; **25** 515
  pebbles **25** 493
  quartz **25** 493; **29** 445
  quartzite **25** 493
  steel **17** 50
  stone **16** 615; **25** 473, 476, 493–4*, 515–16*; **29** 227–8, 444; **32** 679
  wood **25** 493
tools—cont.
 types *see*:
  ADZES; BOUCHARDES; DRILLS; HAMMERS; MALLETS; PORTS CRAYON; ROCKERS; ROULETTES; SAWS; SCRAPERS
 uses
  drypoints **9** 307
  engraving **20** 849; **25** 494; **27** 255
  engravings **8** 129; **10** *379*, 379–80
  etchings **9** 697
  gilding **12** *622*
  metalwork **21** *323*, *326*
  printing **17** 274, 275
  prints **25** 612; **28** 290
  relief sculpture **25** 494
  screenprinting **29** 438
  sculpture **27** 16*
  stone-carvings **29** *704*, 704–5
  wood **33** *336*
  wood-carvings **33** *333*
  woodwork **17** 48–50
Toor, Francis **1** 744
Toorenburgh, Gerrit **7** 662; **25** 649
Toorenvliet, Abraham **21** 487; **22** 442
Toorenvliet, Jacob **19** 102; **21** 488; **22** 50
Toorn, Johannes Adrianus van der **22** 891
 works **22** *891*
Toorop, Annie Caroline Pontifex *see* TOOROP, CHARLEY
Toorop, Charley **10** 907; **18** 436; **22** 852; **28** 920; **31** 149*
Toorop, Jan (Theodorus) **22** 850, 854, 908; **31** 147–8*
 collaboration **21** 122
 groups and movements
  Haagsche Kunstkring **14** 43
  Moderne Kunstkring **21** 775
  Neo-Impressionism **19** 792; **21** 851; **22** 746, 747
  Post-Impressionism **25** 358
  Salon de la Rose + Croix **27** 639
  XX, Les **10** 517; **32** 591
 pupils **8** 628; **14** 294
 works **3** 787; **11** 449; **22** 851; **25** 348; **31** *148*
Toot Baldon (Oxon), St Lawrence **27** 131
tooth *see* DOGTOOTH
Tooth, Arthur **2** 234; **6** 519; **10** 362
Tooth, Dudley **29** 384
Tōō Tosa *see* TOSA TŌŌ
Topaia, Villa della *see* VILLA DELLA TOPAIA
topaz **3** *609*; **12** 252, 268, 270, I; **14** 167; **17** 519, 524
Tope Kalan *see* TEPE KALAN
Topelius, Z. **9** 717; **11** 95
Topf, Erhard Christian Johann **23** 312
Topf, Jakob **2** 472
Töpffer, Adam-Wolfgang **1** 449; **12** 276; **21** 135; **31** 149*
 works **30** 133
Töpffer, Rodolphe **31** 149–50*
 works **5** 758; **7** 648; **19** 484; **30** 125, 133
Topham, Richard **3** 380
Top'ian Temple **18** 290
topiary **12** 61, 109, 110, 114, 115; **27** 323; **31** *150*, 150–51*
 see also GARDENS
Topic, John **20** 382
Topic, Theresa **20** 382
Topino, Charles **7** 658; **11** 596; **31** 151*
Topino, Jean-Baptiste **11** 596
Topkapı Palace *see under* ISTANBUL
topknots **22** 652
Toplau, Akimbo Monastery **8** 156
Topler, Mihail **26** 713
toplighting *see under* LIGHTING → types
topographical books **2** 240; **4** 359, 361, 362; **12** 131
topographical illustrations **24** 658
 Britain **2** 240
 China **1** 612
 England **18** 73
 Islamic **16** 347
 Ottoman **16** 347
 South Africa **29** 110, 121
 Turkey **16** 347
topographical maps *see under* MAPS → types
topographical paintings *see under* PAINTING → types
topographical views
 Argentina **2** 399
 Czech Republic **14** *683*; **23** *425*
 England **10** 250–51; **12** 128, 131; **31** 155–6*; **32** 111; **33** *231*
 France **31** 156–7*
 Hong Kong **14** *721*
 Italy **4** *271*, *272*; **24** 841; **31** 155*
 Netherlands, the **31** 154–5*
 Poland **18** *424*
 Scotland **12** 128
 Spain **27** *602*
 see also PAINTING → types → *vedute*
Topographos *see* DEMETRIOS
topography **7** 609; **18** 700, 706, 711; **20** 361–7; **26** 740; **31** 151–7*
 see also ATLASES; CARTOGRAPHY; MAPS
Toporc *see* TOPOREC
Toporec **14** 892; **28** 854
Toppelius, Mikael **11** 95
 works **11** *94*
Toppengiesser, Andreas **28** 696
Töpper, Carl Franz **17** 585
Toprak Kala (Uzbekistan) **6** *182*, 209; **30** 440; **31** *157*, 157–8*, *781*
 architectural decorations **6** 206
 architecture **6** 199; **32** 320
 glass **6** 267
 palace **6** 193; **31** 157–8
  Hall of Kings **6** 218, *218*, 219, *219*
  Hall of Victories **6** 218
  wall paintings **6** *228*
 reliefs **6** 218–19
 sculpture **6** 214
 statuettes **6** 275
 wall paintings **6** 223, *227*, 227–8
Toprakkale (Armenia) **1** *821*; **31** 158–9*, *159*
 architecture **1** 831
 fortress **1** 894; **31** 699
 furniture **31** 700
 ivory-carvings **1** 872
 Mehr Kapısı **31** 699
 metalwork **2** 441
 pottery **1** 838
 sculpture **30** 774; **31** *700*
 temple **1** 830, 890
Toprakkale ware *see under* POTTERY → wares
Topsell, Edward **2** 105; **21** 721
top-side lighting *see* LIGHTING → types → side; top; top-side
Toptani, Murad (Said) **1** 541; **31** 159*
Tor Abbey Jewel **10** 345
Torahs **17** 568*
Toraja **15** 753
 coffins **27** 831
 containers **3** 144
 doors **9** 164
 houses **15** 774, *774*
 jewellery **15** 814
 painting **15** 806, 807
 roofs **3** 144
 textiles **15** 795, 796; **24** 624
Toraja, Sa'dan *see* SA'DAN TORAJA
Toraji Ishikawa *see* ISHIKAWA, TORAJI
Torajirō Kojimo *see* KOJIMO, TORAJIRŌ
Toral, Mario **6** 598; **31** 159–60*
Toral, Octavio *see* TORAL, TABO
Toral, Tabo **23** 905; **31** 160*
Toraldo di Francia, Cristiano **30** 3
T'oramanyan, T. **2** 98, 428, 444
torana **15** 245*
Toranzos, Félix **24** 99
Torao Ōita *see* ŌITA, TORAO
Torarica **30** *12*, 14
Torbay (Devon) **25** 689
Torbido, Francesco (di Marco India) **2** 88; **5** 31; **27** 820; **31** 161*
Torbjörnstorp **26** 639
Torbov, Naum **28** 838
Torcello **16** *618*; **31** 161–3*; **32** 182
 Cathedral of S Maria Assunta **16** 625; **31** 161–3*, *162*
  mosaics **16** 655; **26** 680
  sculpture **26** 622
 glass **9** 645
 S Andrea **32** 215
 S Fosca **4** 774; **16** 625; **31** 163*
Torchiarino, Il *see* ZACCAGNI, BENEDETTO
torchon see under LACE → types
torcs *see* NECK RINGS
Torcy, Jean-Baptiste Colbert de *see* COLBERT DE TORCY, JEAN-BAPTISTE
Torday, Emil **18** 484
Tordesillas, Convento de S Clara **22** 255; **29** 263
 Founder's Chapel **13** 106
 retable **11** 482
 tomb of Elvira de Acebedo **13** 106
 tomb of Elvira de Portocarrero **13** 106
 tomb of Fernán López de Saldaña **13** 106
Tordesillas, Gaspar de **31** 163*
Tōrei *see* MASUDA (YAMAGUCHI) GŪSHO
Tōrei Enji **14** 63; **17** 194
 works **17** *193*
Toreken, Het *see* TANNERS' HOUSE
Torel, William **31** 164*
 patrons and collectors **25** 14
 works **10** 260; **13** 164; **19** 593, 604
Torelli, Antonio **31** 164
Torelli, Felice **31** 164*
 pupils **3** 466; **11** 20; **12** 38, 39
 teachers **29** 33
Torelli, Filippo di Matteo **26** 325, 326; **29** 785; **31** 165*
Torelli, Giacomo **31** 165–6*
 collaboration **30** 660
 reproductive prints by others **2** 853
 works **30** 658, 659, 667, 668, 669
Torelli, Lucia *see* CASALINI, LUCIA
Torelli, Stefano **27** 402; **31** 164*
Toreno, Conde de **25** 225
Toretbat, François **32** 717
toreutic metalwork *see under* METALWORK → types
Torfanini, Giovanni **5** 853
Torgau **12** *360*; **31** 166–7*
 Schloss Hartenfels **12** 366, 368, 402; **29** 522; **31** 166–7*
  Johann-Friedrich-Bau **12** 367
Torgau, Hans von *see* MELTWITZ, HANS
Torgau Altarpiece **8** 114
Torgiano, Bartolomeo Mattioli di *see* BARTOLOMEO MATTIOLI DI TORGIANO
Torhout **3** 588
 chapel **3** 541
 Maere castle **3** 585
tori **23** 478
Tori, Giorgio delle **16** 737
Toribio, Tomas **22** 23; **31** 167*, 753
Toribio de Alcaraz, Hernando **21** 375
Toribio Jerez, Julio y **23** 81
Tori Busshi **17** 418; **31** 167*
 works **14** 773; **17** 97, 108, 320
Toricella, Casa Tonino **30** 129
Torigny, Robert de, Abbot of Mont-Saint-Michel **22** 40
Torihama **17** *11*
Torihama shell-mound **31** 167*
Torii **17** 280–81
Torii, Kotondo **17** 294
Torii, Ryūzō **17** 426
Torii Kiyohide **31** 169
Torii Kiyohiro **31** 170–71*
 teachers **31** 169
 works **17** 282; **31** *170*
Torii Kiyomasu I (*fl* 1697-1722) **31** 168–9*
 works **31** *169*
Torii Kiyomasu II (1706-63) **17** 281, 282; **31** 168, 169–70*
Torii Kiyomine **17** 286
Torii Kiyomitsu I (1735-85) **31** 168, 169–70*
 pupils **31** 170
 teachers **31** 169
 works **17** 282
Torii Kiyomitsu II (1788-1868) **17** 286; **31** 168
Torii Kiyomoto **31** 168
Torii Kiyonaga **17** 281; **31** 168
 teachers **31** 169
 works **17** 276, 283, 285, 286
Torii Kiyonobu I (1664-1729) **31** 168–9*
 pupils **31** 169
 teachers **14** 577
 works **17** 280, *280*, 281
Torii Kiyonobu II (*fl c.* 1725-60) **17** 281, 282; **31** 168, 169, 170
Torii Kiyoshige I **17** 281; **31** 168, 169*
Torii Kiyotada I (*fl c.* 1720-50) **31** 168, 169*
Torii Kiyotada II (*fl* ?1750-1800) **31** 169
Torii Kiyotomo **31** 168
Torii Kiyotsune **17** 282; **31** 169
Torii school **17** 286; **31** 168–70*
Torija, Antonio Torres *see* TORRES TORIJA, ANTONIO
Torija, Juan de **29** 637; **31** 171*
Torim Temple **18** 310
Tōrin Tsutsumi *see* TSUTSUMI TŌRIN
Tori style **31** 167
Torito, Luis Felipe *see* TORO, LUIS FELIPE
Toriyama Sekien **18** 91; **31** 764
Toriyama Sonpo **17** 236
Torksey (Lincs) **10** 301
Torlioni, Bernardo **32** 349
Torlonia (family) **27** 486; **31** 172, 800
Torlonia, Alessandro **4** 42; **7** 528; **17** 444; **25** 62; **31** 171–2*
Torlonia, Carlo **31** 171*
Torlonia, Giovanni **6** 98; **31** 171–2*
Torlonia, Marino **31** 171–2*
Torlopov, Stanislav **27** 434
Torlov **5** 149
Tormo y Monzó, Elías **12** 889; **18** 637; **24** 452; **27** 704; **31** 172–3*
Torna **13** 162
Tornabuoni (family) **12** 551
Tornabuoni, Francesco **31** 173
Tornabuoni, Giovanni **12** 551, 552; **16** 763; **31** 173*
Tornabuoni, Lorenzo **4** 496; **12** 552; **27** 208; **31** 173*
Tornabuoni, Lucrezia **19** 443; **20** 642
Torner, Gustavo **31** 174*
tornesi see under COINS → types

Torness Nuclear Power Station (Highlands) **25** 403
Torni, Jacopo di Lazzaro di Pietro **26** 816; **28** 725
Tornielli, Giovanni Battista **6** 138; **33** 53
Tornini, Jacopo **10** 528; **31** 353
Tornioli, Niccolò **23** 748; **31** 174*
Torn'ov, Anton **28** 838
Tornström, J. **28** 612
Tornyai, János **13** 332, 333; **31** 174*
Tornyai, János, Museum *see under* HÓDMEZŐVÁSÁRHELY
Tornyai Society **31** 174
Toro (Africa) **1** 354
Toro (Japan) **17** 47, 54, 356, 427
  Granary **17** 54
Toro (Spain)
  collegiate church *see* S María la Mayor
  sculpture **26** 642; **29** 291
  S Lorenzo **26** 642
  S María la Mayor **9** 85; **13** 105; **29** 336
Toro, Antonio Herrera *see* Herrera Toro, Antonio
Toro, (Jean-)Bernard (-Honoré) **7** 746; **11** 405; **17** 668; **26** 493; **31** 174–5*
Toro, Francisco de **29** 339
Toro, Luis Felipe **31** 175*
Toro, Osvaldo **25** 701
Toro, Pedro de **21** 375
Torobekov, Suyukbek **18** 569
Toroçko Church **31** 584
torogan *see under* HOUSES → types
Torokin, V. **27** 425
Torollo, Juan **8** 78
Torone **19** 880
Toroni, Niele **5** 193; **11** 552, 553; **21** 892
Toronto **5** *559*, 561; **31** 175–7*, *175*
  architecture **5** 560
  carnivals **5** 788
  City Hall **13** 239; **26** 261; **31** *176*, 243
  CN Tower **5** 648, 649
  Colborne Lodge **5** 560; **14** 810
  collections **5** 589
  Eaton Centre **5** 574
  education (art) **5** 592
  Edward Hanlan memorial **5** 570
  Equity Chambers **5** 562
  interior decoration **5** 576
  Mechanics Institute **5** 590
  Metropolitan Toronto Library **5** 592; **19** 320, *320*; **22** 121
  Metro stations **21** 350
  monument to the Northwest Rebellion **5** 570
  museums and galleries
    Art Gallery of Ontario **5** 591; **8** 528; **31** 176; **32** 794
      archives **2** 370
      collections **5** 589; **20** 109; **31** 177
      Henry Moore Sculpture Centre **22** 57
      library **5** 592
    Art Gallery of Toronto *see* Art Gallery of Ontario
    Art Museum of Toronto *see* Art Gallery of Ontario
    Beth Tzedec Museum **17** 582
    Educational Museum of Upper Canada **5** 570
    Gardner Museum **31** 177
    Grange Mansion *see* Art Gallery of Ontario
    Royal Ontario Museum **8** 528; **31** 176; **32** 794
      Canadiana Gallery **5** 589
      collections **6** 826, 868; **7** 53, 156; **15** 746; **27** 694; **29** 241; **31** 177; **32** 794; **33** 148
      drawings **9** 231
      frames **11** 378
Toronto
  museums and galleries
    Royal Ontario Museum—cont.
      Greek collection **13** 470
      library **5** 592
      reproductions **26** 227
      Samuel, Sigmund Gallery *see* Canadiana Gallery
      sculpture **27** 46
    Sigmund Samuel Canadian Museum **27** 694
    Thomson Gallery **5** 590
  Old City Hall **5** 561
  Ontario College of Art **5** 592; **31** 177
  Ontario Place **5** 563; **30** 468
  Ontario Science Centre **5** 591
  Osgoode Hall **5** 572
  Provincial Legislative Building **5** 570
  Robert Simpson Department Store **5** 562
  Roy Thomson Hall **1** 126
  St Anne's **5** 573
  Scarborough College **5** 562
  South African memorial **5** 570
  Toronto-Dominion Bank **5** 562, 589
  Toronto-Dominion Centre **5** 573
  Toronto Studio Building **14** 194
  Union Station **5** 562
  University of Toronto **2** 370; **5** 590, 592; **19** 321; **29** 435
Toronto Arts and Letters Club **13** 711
Toronto Art Students' League **5** 566, 592
Toros **16** 423
T'oros, King (*reg* 1293-7) **2** 440
T'oros, Prince (1145-68) **2** 440
T'oros Roslin **2** 431; **31** 177*
T'orosyan, D. **2** 428
Torp, Fredrik **23** 602
Torp, Hjalmar **23** 245
Torpa Church **30** 75
Torpo **23** *218*
  church **23** 223
Torquemada, Juan de **2** 39; **31** 505
Torquemada, Tomás de **20** 493
torques *see* NECK RINGS
Torquet, Antoine *see* NAU, JOHN-ANTOINE
Torquim of Ghent **17** 456
Torr, Helen **9** 202
Torralba, Nuraghe Santu Antine **23** 304
Torralva, Diogo de **2** 501; **30** 518; **31** 177–9*
  attributions **25** 291
  patrons and collectors **2** 873
  works **3** 534; **10** 664, *664*; **25** 290, *290*, 291; **27** 823; **31** 102, *178*, *179*
Torralva, Francisco de Arruda *see* ARRUDA TORRALVA, FRANCISCO DE
Torrance Newton, Lilias **5** 567
torre **25** 522
Torre, Anthony **7** 579
Torre, Bartolommeo **14** 886
Torre, Cristoforo della **4** 620
Torre, Francesco della **18** 191
Torre, Giovanni Battista **7** 579
Torre, Giovanni Domenico della **28** 79
Torre, Giulio delle **20** 918
Torre, Giuseppe della **5** 671
Torre, Jerónimo de la **26** 311
Torre, Juan de la **2** 387; **8** 231
Torre, Macedonio de la **24** 510; **31** 179–80*
Torre, Marc'antonio della **12** 719
Torre, Margherita della **16** 723
Torre, Pedro de la **3** 418; **29** 269; **31** 180*
Torre, Pierluigi **15** 826
Torre, Pietro Andrea **20** 371
Torre, Quintín de **29** 295
Torre, Susana **31** 180*
Torrechiara Castle **3** 696
Torrechiara Polyptych **3** *697*
Torre de la Parada **24** 107; **29** 303
  paintings **3** 559; **8** 1; **14** 7; **20** 900; **22** 414; **23** 680; **25** 809; **27** 296; **28** 903; **30** 787; **32** 129
Torre del Greco **16** 750
torre del homenaje *see* SPAIN → donjons
Torre d'en Gaume **3** 105
Torre de Vilela, Parish Church **13** 125
Torre Farfán, Fernando *see* TORRE Y FARFÁN, FERNANDO DE LA
Torreggiani, Alfonso **1** 597; **4** 273; **9** 190; **31** 180–81*
Torreggiani, Antonio **31** 180
Torreggiani, Giuseppe **31** 180
Torrelles, Guillem de *see* GUILLEM DE TORRELLES
Torrelobatón **29** *258*
  Castle **31** *181*, 181–2*
  SS María y Pedro **13** 106
Torremocha del Campo metalwork **29** 337
Torren, A. Van den *see* VAN DEN TORREN, A.
Torrens, José Casademunt *see* CASADEMUNT TORRENS, JOSÉ
Torrentino, Lorenzo **32** 18
Torrentius, Johannes **5** 519; **28** 309; **31** 182*
Torrenuova **27** 62
Torreón, Universidad Iberoamericana **21** 381, 382
Torres, Augusto **30** 275; **31** 184, 755
Torres, Clemente (Fernández) de **31** 182*, 810
Torres, Duilio **23** 753
Torres, Emilio **23** 905
Torres, Francisco Antonio de Guerrero y *see* GUERRERO Y TORRES, FRANCISCO ANTONIO DE
Torres, Gabriel de **31** 183
Torres, Horacio **30** 275; **31** 184, 755
Torres, Joaquín Folch i *see* FOLCH I TORRES, JOAQUÍN
Torres, Juan Bautista Garavelli *see* ANTONELLI, JUAN BAUTISTA (great nephew)
Torres, Julio Romero *see* ROMERO TORRES, JULIO
Torres, Martín de **31** 182*
Torres, Matías de **21** 35; **31** 182–3*
Torres, Pedro de **7** 847
Torres, Ramiro Nuñez de Guzmán, Duque de Medina de las *see* MEDINA DE LAS TORRES, RAMIRO NUÑEZ DE GUZMÁN, Duque de
Torres, Ramón **22** 314; **31** 186*
Torres, Rodolfo Galeotti *see* GALEOTTI TORRES, RODOLFO
Torres, Toribio **14** 714
Torres Agüero, Leopoldo **8** 631
Torresani d'Asola, Andrea dei **12** 734; **17** 481; **20** 350
Torres Balbás, L. **12** 889; **16** 556
Torres Clavé, Josep **3** 217; **12** 177; **29** 273
Torres García, Joaquín **6** 598; **11** 550; **22** 24; **31** 183–4*, 758, 759
  collaboration **18** 397
  groups and movements **2** 400, 525; **6** 342; **21** 854; **30** 275
  patrons and collectors **31** 757, 758
  pupils **11** 249; **31** 755
Torres García, Josep **23** 260
Torres Grau, J. **23** 260
Torres i Clavé, Josep **28** 483; **29** 321; **31** 184*
Torres Martinó, José Antonio **18** 832; **25** 701; **26** 426
Torres Méndez, Ramón **7** 608
Torres Strait Islands **1** *37*; **2** *736*; **31** 184–6*, 891
  canoes **23** 725; **31** 185
  drums (musical instruments) **31** 893
  feathers **31** 186
  headdresses **31** 186
  jewellery **31** 186
  masks **31** *185*, 185–6
  nuts **31** 186
  sculpture **23** 733
  shells **31** 186
  tortoiseshell **31** 185, *185*, 186
  weapons **23** 734
  wood-carvings **31** 186
Torres Torija, Antonio **21** 378
Torres & Velázquez **21** 380; **31** 186*
Torretti, Giuseppe **7** 881; **31** 186–7*
Torretti, il *see* BERNARDI, GIUSEPPE
Torretto, Giuseppe *see* TORRETTI, GIUSEPPE
Torre y Farfán, Fernando de la **31** 811
  works **28** *515*
Torri (family) **19** 816
Torri, Flaminio **5** 635; **31** 187*; **32** 402
Torri, Giorgio delle **9** 57
Torri, Giuseppe Antonio **23** 339; **31** 180
Torricella **31** 756
Torricella, Maria Anna **21** 170
Torricelli (family) **12** 262
Torricelli, Giuseppe Antonio (1659-1719) **11** 234; **12** 260; **26** 148; **31** 187*
Torricelli, Giuseppe Antonio (1710-1808) **19** 781; **30** 132
Torricelli, Bartolomeo **31** 187
Torricelli, Gaetano **31** 187
Torricelli, Giovanni Antonio **19** 781; **30** 132
Torrie, James Erskine **28** 271
Torriente, Fernando de la **31** 187–8*
Torrigiani, Bastiano **9** 340; **25** 257; **31** 188*
Torrigiani, Pietro (di Torrigiano d'Antonio) **13** 905; **29** 289; **31** 188–91*, 205
  assistants **20** 116
  attributions **20** 655, 779
  patrons and collectors **3** 451; **10** 360; **24** 732; **31** 413
  works **4** 870; **10** 260, 270; **16** 695; **19** 605; **20** 116; **27** 447; **30** 498, 502; **31** *190*, *191*; **32** 394
Torrigiani, Pietro, Marchese **8** 597
Torrigiani, Raffaello **29** 728, 729
Torrigiani, Vincenzo **18** 661
Torrigiani collection **4** 209
Torrimpietra Castle **12** 534
Torrini, Girolamo **3** 357
Torrino, Tomás **31** 182
Torriti, Jacopo **13** 135, 144; **16** 655; **31** 192–3*
  collaboration **11** 887; **26** 821
  patrons and collectors **23** 96; **26** 765
  works **2** 482, 624, *624*; **13** 145; **31** 57, *193*
Torroella, Guillem **26** 563
Torroja (Miret), Eduardo **7** 696; **28** 583; **29** 273; **31** 193–4*
Torrone, Angelo **26** 837
Torrs **6** 160
Torrysany, Petir *see* TORRIGIANI, PIETRO (DI TORRIGIANO D'ANTONIO)
Torshalla **30** 103
Tórshavn
  art school **10** 813
  Faröya Sparkassi **10** 813
  SMS shopping centre **10** 813
Torso of Michelangelo *see* BELVEDERE TORSO
Torstensson, Anders **29** 684; **31** 692
Torstensson, Lennart **4** 180; **30** 84
Torsuwan, Rangsan **30** 591
Torte, Hans de La *see* LA TORTE, HANS DE
Tortebat, François **9** 718; **24** 805; **32** 718
Tortelli, Benvenuto **26** 306; **28** 519; **29** 268
Torterel, Jacques **24** 478
tortillons **29** 863
tortoiseshell **25** 23; **31** 194–5*
  historical and regional traditions
    Belgium **3** 583, 585
    China **6** 737, *738*; **31** *194*
    Egypt, ancient **10** 29
    France **11** 590
    Germany **12** 423, 424, *425*
    Indian subcontinent **6** 556
    Islamic **16** 499
    Italy **16** 748*
    Jamaica **16** 888
    Japan **17** 398
    Korea **18** *370*
    Mesoamerica, Pre-Columbian **21** 256
    Ottoman **16** 499
    Papua New Guinea **24** 84
    Peru **33** *332*
    Scotland **28** 246
    Sicily **16** 748
    Spain **29** 314
    Torres Strait Islands **31** 185, *185*, 186
    Vietnam **32** 487
  types
    Greenback **20** 466; **31** 194
    Hawksbill **20** 466; **31** 194
    Loggerhead **31** 194, 195
  uses
    boxes **31** *194*
    cabinets (ii) (furniture) **3** 583; **12** 421, 423
    chess sets **6** 556
    commodes **12** 424, *425*
    desks **29** 314
    furniture **3** 585; **11** 590; **16** 748
    headdresses **31** 186
    inlays **12** 423; **28** 246; **31** 195
    jewellery **10** 29; **32** 487
    lacquer **18** *370*
    marquetry **20** 466; **33** *332*
    masks **31** 185, *185*
    musical instruments **21** 256; **31** 195
    netsuke **17** 398; **31** 195
    scrimshaw **28** 302
    veneers **12** 424, *425*; **16** 499; **31** 195
  watches **7** 447
Tortola **2** 144
Tortolero, Pedro **20** 499; **31** 195*
Tortoletto, Tasto **31** 432
Tortona, Palazzo Vescovile **1** 529
Tortorel, Jacques **33** 357
Tortorino, Francesco **12** 259
Tortosa (Spain) **17** 500
  Castle **21** 564
  Cathedral **11** 480; **13** 67, 123; **17** 505
  College of S Matías and S Luis Gonzaga **29** 267
  glass **29** 330
  University **31** 674
Tortosa (Syria) *see* TARTUS
Tortuna, Master of **20** 774*
Tortuna Church **20** 774
Torulf, Ernst **30** 459
Toruń **25** *92*; **30** 534; **31** 195–6*
  architecture **4** 782
  façade decoration **10** 736
  fortifications **21** 571
  furniture **25** 120
  gold **25** 126, 127
  keep **21** 571
  metalwork **25** 127

Toruń—cont.
museums 25 140
painting 25 101
St James 4 783; 32 93
St John 4 783; 13 189
St Mary 4 783; 13 189
St Nicholas 13 189
Town Hall 4 783; 18 886; 21 820; 25 134; 31 *196*, 237
Torup Castle 30 69
torus mouldings *see under* MOULDINGS → types
Torvalmenningen *see under* BERGEN (NORWAY)
Torvoie, Jean de *see* JEAN DE TORVOIE
Tőry, Emil 25 73–4*
Tory, Geofroy 20 790; 31 196–7*
works 4 358; 31 495
illustrated 24 472
Torzhok, Church of the Resurrection 27 373
Tosa (family) 18 552
groups and movements 31 199
patrons and collectors 17 419
works 1 581; 17 161, 166, 167
Tosa, Lady 17 154; 33 317
Tosa Hiromichi *see* SUMIYOSHI JOKEI
Tosa Mitsumochi 1 581; 17 167; 31 198–200*
Tosa Mitsumoto 31 199
Tosa Mitsunari 31 198, 199, 200
Tosa Mitsunobu 17 163, 780; 31 197–9*
attributions 17 166, *167*
groups and movements 31 199
patrons and collectors 2 598
pupils 23 161
works 17 167, 323, 334; 31 *197*
Tosa Mitsunori 1 581; 16 802; 17 164; 29 924; 31 198, 200
works 31 *200*
Tosa Mitsuoki 31 198–200*
groups and movements 31 199, 200
works 17 792; 29 924
writings 17 416, 439
Tosa Mitsusuke 17 177
Tosa Mitsuyoshi 17 164; 29 924; 31 200
Tosari, René 30 16
Tosa school 7 716; 17 23, 164, 200, 419, 423, 437, 438; 23 594; 31 199–200*
attributions 17 166
members 31 197
treatises 17 416
works 17 163, 167, 168, 419; 28 311; 31 *200*
Tosa Tōō 17 334
Tosca, Juan 8 233
Tosca, Tomás Vicente 31 814
Toscanelli (*fl* 1760) 13 695
Toscanelli, Paolo 11 198; 31 200–201*
Toscani, Cajetan 11 760; 26 258
Toscani, Giovanni (di Francesco) 6 2; 14 517; 24 539; 31 201*
Toscani, Patrick 11 553
Toscano, Bruno 16 775
Toscano, João 4 714
Toschi, Benedetto, Abbot of Pancrazio 22 799
Toschi, Paolo 3 870; 26 232
Tō Seika 17 412
Toshiaki, Leonardo 4 715
Toshiharu Maeda *see* MAEDA TOSHIHARU
Toshihito Hachijō, Prince *see* HACHIJŌ TOSHIHITO, Prince
Toshikata 17 290
Toshiko Furukawa *see* FURUKAWA, TOSHIKO
Toshiko Ichihashi *see* ICHIHASHI, TOSHIKO
Toshimaya Ihei 17 401
Toshimitsu Imai *see* IMAI, TOSHIMITSU
Toshinari *see* FUJIWARA NO SHUNZEI
Toshinobu Okumura *see* OKUMURA TOSHINOBU
Toshio Nagahiro *see* NAGAHIRO, TOSHIO
Toshio Nakanishi *see* NAKANISHI, TOSHIO
Tōshirō Eirakuya *see* EIRAKUYA TŌSHIRŌ
Toshisada Wakao *see* WAKAO, TOSHISADA
Toshitada Hachijō, Prince *see* HACHIJŌ TOSHITADA, Prince
Toshitsuna, Tachibana no *see* TACHIBANA NO TOSHITSUNA
Toshiyama 22 429
Toshi Yoshida *see* YOSHIDA, TOSHI
Toshka *see* TUSHKA
Tōshōdaiji *see under* NARA
Tōshun 31 253
Tō Shunmin 17 412
Tōshūsai Sharaku 31 203–5*
works 17 276, 284; 31 *204*
Tōshū Yamamoto *see* YAMAMOTO, TŌSHŪ
Tosi, Fausta 20 607
Tosi, Paolo, Count 3 904
Tosi, Sergio 20 607
Tosini, Andrea
works 17 *443*
Tosini, Mariotto 25 690
Tosini, Michele 31 205*
pupils 19 672, 871; 25 58
teachers 12 557
works 11 721
Tošković, Jovan Stajić 28 450
Toso (family) 12 795
Toso, Artemio 3 270
Toso, Decio 3 270
Tosŏn 18 268
Toso Sesshū 32 899
Tossa de Montbui, La *see* LA TOSSA DE MONTBUI
Tostes, Celeide 4 722
Tostia 26 206
Tostrup, Jacob 10 195; 23 236
Totagamura, Subhadrarama Vihara 29 461
totai see under BOWLS → types
Tōtarō Miura *see* MIURA TŌTARŌ
Tōtarō Sakuma *see* SAKUMA, TŌTARŌ
Tō Teikan 17 414, 425
totem poles 22 *579*, 668
Toten 23 237
Tóth, Menyhért 13 333
Totila, King of the Ostrogoths (*reg* 541-42) 29 421
Tot'ma 27 *363*, 374
Totnes (Devon) 31 710
Toto del Nunziata, Antonio 20 116; 31 190, 205*
Totoki Baigai 17 190, 237; 23 594
Totoki Hoshō 1 448
Totonac 21 177, 197–8
Totonicapán 13 *758*, 768
S Cristóbal 13 760
theatre 13 762
Totsugen Tanaka *see* TANAKA TOTSUGEN
Tott, Baron de 21 587
Totten, Joseph G. 21 575
Totten, Mary (Betsy)
works 30 VI3
Tottenhill (Norfolk), St Botolph 26 613
Totternhoe stone 29 699
touch *see* HAPTICS
Touche, David Digues de la *see* DIGUES DE LA TOUCHE, DAVID
Touche, Gaston La *see* LA TOUCHE, GASTON
Touche-Ross 31 661
Touchet, Marie 7 *465*
Touggourt 1 304, *376*
Touissant, Bernard 14 59
Toul 19 709
Cathedral *see* St Etienne
St Etienne 13 60; 16 852; 30 778
Toulon
Arsenal 28 612
Hôtel de Ville 25 705
Villa de Mandrot 19 42
Toulon, Cyprian of *see* CYPRIAN OF TOULON
Toulouse 11 *505*, 657; 31 205–12*
Capitole 2 375; 4 536; 10 770; 18 865; 29 522
Collège de Périgord 7 566
colleges 7 566
ecclesiastical buildings
Augustinian priory *see* Musée des Augustins
Cathedral of St Etienne 1 767; 13 43; 20 894; 26 46; 31 211–12*
chapter house 6 467
cloister 7 454
sculpture 26 595, 602; 31 211–12*
Dominican chapel *see* Jacobin church
Franciscan church 13 76
Jacobin church 4 780; 6 464; 9 111; 13 43; 14 82; 31 *206*
La Dalbade 4 780
La Daurade 21 163; 31 210*; 32 618
capitals 31 *211*
cloister 7 454
mosaics 31 210*
sculpture 26 602, 603; 31 210–11*
St Pierre 6 467
St Raymond 4 780
St Romain 9 106
St Sernin 4 780; 11 509, 554; 12 1; 26 585; 31 207–8*, *208*
altar 1 696
cloister 7 454
Porte Miègeville 11 554; 26 607; 31 *209*
restoration 2 320
sculpture 3 820; 26 595, 597, 602; 31 208–10*, *209*
textiles 16 437
wall paintings 11 529
enamel 13 169
faience (ii) (ceramics) 11 605
glass 11 611
Hôtel Assezat 11 514
Hôtel de Beringuier-Maynier 4 780; 11 514
Hôtel du Vieux Raisin *see* Hôtel Béringuier-Maynier
Hôtel de Ville *see* Capitole
metalwork 11 624
Métro stations 21 350
Musée d'Art Moderne 11 665, 666
Musée des Augustins 2 724; 4 780
collections 8 643; 15 843; 19 755; 26 424
Musée Paul Dupuy 27 144
Opéra 2 376
Pont-Neuf 4 801
sarcophagi 9 596
sculpture 13 79
silver 11 620, *621*
tapestries 11 640
Toulouse, Louis-Alexandre de Bourbon (i), Comte de 3 752; 4 536, 537; 11 592; 25 872
Toulouse-Lautrec, Adèle, Comtesse de 20 351
Toulouse-Lautrec, Charles de 31 213
Toulouse-Lautrec (Montfa), Henri (Marie Raymond) de 2 733; 11 667, 672; 31 212–16*, *213*
book jackets 4 369
collaboration 4 325; 15 58; 20 603; 29 612; 31 853
Toulouse-Lautrec (Montfa), Henri (Marie Raymond) de—cont.
dealers 19 10; 26 107
exhibitions 20 351; 31 490
groups and movements 2 562; 15 156; 24 592; 32 591
methods 4 184; 8 128; 17 276, 277
paintings 33 150
patrons and collectors 1 576, 614; 14 569; 22 135, 538; 25 279; 26 488; 30 532; 31 880
Bing, S(iegfried) 4 71
Thiel, Ernest 30 730
periodicals 4 42
prints 25 600, 626
lithographs 4 364; 19 488, 489, 490; 20 *602*; 22 371; 25 601, 607, 615, 620, *620*, 624, 628
monotypes 21 896
posters 25 623
productions 30 685
reproductions in ceramics 22 270
sporting scenes 29 426
stained glass 30 869
teachers 4 329
works 2 107; 10 420, 480; 25 *278*, 346, *347*; 31 *213*, *214*, *215*, *216*, 705
Toulouse-Lautrec, Musée *see under* ALBI
Toulouse-Le-Mirail 5 609, *610*; 30 391
Toumba *see* LEFKANDI
Toungoo 5 *221*
Toungoo, Bayinnaung I *see* BAYINNAUNG I, King
Toupin, Fernand 5 568; 25 28
Tour, André Ivanovich 27 408, 583
Tour, Etienne de La *see* LA TOUR, ETIENNE DE
Tour, Georges de La *see* LA TOUR, GEORGES DE
Tour, Karl Andreievich 27 583
Tour, Louis Ovis de La *see* LA TOUR, LOUIS OVIS DE
Tour, Maurice-Quentin de La *see* LA TOUR, MAURICE-QUENTIN DE
Toura 8 486
Touraine, Jacqueline of Bavaria, Duchesse de 32 823
Touraine, Jean, Duc de 32 823
Tourcoing, Charles VI spinning mills 10 748
Tourhout 3 592
tourism 2 552; 13 809; 24 742
tourist art 2 137; 31 260
Africa 1 239, 251, *252*, 252–3, *253*
Ainu 1 493
Antilles, Lesser 2 153
Asante 1 253
Bali (Indonesia) 15 806, 809; 29 238
Bangwa 3 170
Burma 29 238
Cameroon 3 170
Caribbean Islands 5 754
Côte d'Ivoire 1 252
Easter Island 9 676
Edo (Africa) 1 239
Eskimo 22 575
Gabon 1 252; 11 879, *879*
Ghana 2 588
Haiti 14 59
India, Republic of 15 173, 175
Indian subcontinent 15 732, 750
Kenya 1 252, *252*
Makonde (Mozambique) 1 *253*, 253
Mesoamerica, Pre-Columbian 21 249
Micronesia, Federated States of 21 477
Native North Americans 22 575, 651, 655, 656, 658, 660, 667–70*, *669*; 31 259
tourist art—cont.
Nepal 22 777, *777*, 789
Nupe 23 303
Pacific Islands 23 735–6
Papua New Guinea 24 82
Rwanda 1 252
South-east Asia 29 236, 238–9*
Surinam 30 13
see also COMMERCIAL ART; SOUVENIRS
Tourloti 21 *651*
pottery 21 *669*
tourmaline 12 268, 270, I; 17 514
Tournachon, Adrien 22 424
Tournachon, (Gaspard) Félix *see* Nadar
Tournai 3 *539*; 31 216–23*, *217*
art forms and materials
architecture 3 540, 541
brass 3 603
brasses 4 692
ceramics 3 588; 31 220*
faience (ii) (ceramics) 3 590
fonts (baptismal) 11 253
gold 31 220*
manuscripts 26 563
marble 29 702
marks 3 596, 601; 31 219, 220
metalwork 13 159; 26 683
pewter 3 603
porcelain 3 *590*, 590–91; 22 882; 31 220
sculpture 3 567, 568; 13 99, 110, 111, 112–13; 20 671; 26 630
silver 3 598, 599; 31 220*
stained glass 13 182
stone 10 259
tapestries 3 606; 30 313–14, I2; 31 *218*, 218–19*
textiles 13 195
craftsmen and artists 13 133
ecclesiastical buildings
Abbey of St Martin 3 552
Cathedral of Notre-Dame 3 541; 13 38, 39; 22 819; 26 575; 30 729; 31 220–22*
choir 3 542; 13 42; 31 *221*
epitaph to Canon Jean Lamelin 13 79
ivory-carvings 13 173
mouldings 22 221
nave 31 *221*
Porte Mantile 3 567; 31 *222*
roof 30 907
sculpture 13 99, 100, 110; 26 630; 31 222–3*
shrine of St Eleutherius 28 631
Shrine of the Virgin 3 567; 22 270; 23 98–9
stained glass 13 182
textiles 30 313, 331
wall paintings 3 552; 26 648
Cathedral of St Etienne *see* Cathedral of Notre-Dame
St Jacques 13 99
St Jean 13 113
Ste Marie-Madeleine 3 568; 13 113
St Nicolas 13 110
education (art) 3 618
guilds 3 596
Hôpital de la Planque 13 113
Musée d'Armes 31 217
Musée des Beaux-Arts 6 487; 31 218
tomb of Childeric 21 162; 23 536
town walls 31 216–17
Tournaire, Albert 9 337
tournaments 7 178; 29 488
Tournant, Jacques 19 91
Tournefort, Pitton de
works 31 *303*
Tournehem, Charles-François-Paul Le Normand de *see* LE NORMAND DE TOURNEHEM, CHARLES-FRANÇOIS(-PAUL)
Tournelle, Franciszek 20 397
Tournes, Jean de 1 584; 4 8; 20 793; 23 680; 31 495

Tourneux, Aristide **26** 205
Tourneux, Prosper **18** 816
Tourney **11** 652
Tournier, André **31** 223
Tournier, Nicolas **11** 533, 534; **31** 207, 223*
teachers **20** 267
works **23** 265
Tournières, Robert **6** 549; **31** 223–4*
Tournois, Joseph **28** 349
Tournon, Paul **24** 824; **31** 224*
Tournon, Philippe-Camille-Casimir-Marcellin, Comte de **26** 761
Tournus **10** 776; **11** *505*, 554
St Philibert **11** 509; **12** 5; **23** 491; **26** 582–3, *583*, 601; **31** *224*, 224–5*; **32** 89
ambulatory **1** 767
buttresses **5** 319
crypt **8** 224
roof **27** 131
sculpture **26** 595
vaults **32** 88
westwork **33** 109
Tournus, Abbé **26** *248*
Tourny, Aubert de **4** 389
works **4** *390*
Touront, Hippolyte **21** 363
Tourrisan, Pierre *see* TORRIGIANI, PIETRO (DI TORRIGIANO D'ANTONIO)
Tours **9** *510*; **11** *504*; **19** 709; **26** *908*; **31** *225*, 225–8*
Cathedral of St Gatien **11** 511; **13** 42, 181, 211
ambulatory **1** 767
font **11** 255
stained glass **13** 136, 180; **29** 502
Chapelle des Lazaristes **26** 704
gems **12** 255
glass **11** 611
Hôtel Tristan **4** 780
Hôtel de Ville **3** 464, *465*; **18** 865; **31** 241
manuscripts **9** 603; **20** 334; **21** 637; **22** 520; **28** *303*; **31** *226*, 226–7*
marks **11** 613
Musée des Beaux-Arts **11** 666; **13** 790
museum **11** 665
painting **11** 531
St Julien **26** 655
St Martin **7** 266; **11** 653; **26** 585; **31** 227–8*, *228*
Baptistery **3** 191
coins **7** 535
embroidery **24** 775
manuscript illumination **4** 5; **5** 800, 802–3; **11** 529; **31** *226*, 226–7
manuscripts **20** 330
Tour Charlemagne **26** 599
St Perpétue **11** 653
sculpture **13** 79
silk **11** 644, 645; **28** 716
tapestries **11** 642; **31** 227*
Tours, John of, Bishop of Wells and Abbot of Bath *see* JOHN OF TOURS, Bishop of Wells and Abbot of Bath
tours modèles see under TOWERS → types
Tours-Saint-Laurent, Atelier-Musée Jean Lurçat **19** 808
Tourtellot, Gair **28** 26, 372
Tourtier, Jean **18** 685
Tous, Antonio Juan, Lord of **3** 810
Tous Church **3** 809–10
Tousignant, Claude **22** 39; **31** 228–9*
groups and movements **25** 28
works **5** 568
tous-les-Louis *see* LOUIS REVIVAL
Toussaint, Armand **9** 326
Toussaint Bellanger **21** 823
Toustain de Frontebosc, Guillaume **2** 486
Toutain, Richard **11** 617
Toutenburg, Schenk van **23** 188
Toutin (family) **17** 522
Toutin, Henry **11** 630; **21** 641
works **11** *630*
Toutin, Jean **11** 629; **14** 855; **24** 553; **30** 148
Tou Wan *see* DOU WAN
Tovačov **8** 383
Tovagliari (family) **22** 82
Tovar, Alonso Miguel de **31** 229*
Tovar, Iván **9** 118
Tovars **14** 435
Tovar y Salas **31** 229
Tovar y Tovar, Martín **14** 479; **31** 229*; **32** 173, 178
T'ovmas **23** 355
Tovsta Mogila Pectoral *see* TOLSTAYA MOGILA PECTORAL
Towa **22** 608
Towcester (Northants), Hurlecote Manor **32** 814
towels **19** 416, *416*; **31** 564
tower houses *see under* HOUSES → types
tower keeps *see under* DONJONS → types
Tower of Glass **9** 318, 321; **25** 744; **29** 507; **31** 229*
Tower of the Winds *see under* ATHENS
towers **3** 359; **9** 143; **12** 173–4; **21** 600
historical and regional traditions
Azerbaijan **2** *892*
Belgium **13** 62–3
Cambodia **5** 474
China **3** *519*; **6** *677*
Cuba (Caribbean) **8** 231
Czech Republic **19** *829*; **26** *366*
Denmark **8** 723
Ecuador **9** *711*
England **4** *779*; **10** 227; **21** 560
France **10** *107*; **23** 262
Germany **13** 56; **31** *568*, 569
Gothic
Belgium **13** 62–3
England **4** *779*
Germany **13** 56; **31** *568*
Ireland **5** *915*
Italy **27** *751*
Netherlands, the **13** *62*, 62–3
Spain **13** 68
Greece, ancient **2** *667*
Indian subcontinent **10** *830*; **15** 330
Iran, ancient **33** 707, *707*
Ireland **5** *915*
Islamic **16** 142; **21** 546
Azerbaijan **2** *892*
China **6** *677*
Spain **16** 215, 216
Syria **21** 583
Italy **5** 649; **27** *751*; **31** 442
Netherlands, the **13** *62*, 62–3
Portugal **3** *534*
Prehistoric art **25** 522
Romanesque **10** 227
Rome, ancient **21** 560
Spain **4** *784*; **13** 68; **16** 215, 216
Syria **21** 583
Syria-Palestine **30** 190
Zoroastrianism **33** *707*
materials
brick **4** *779*; **13** 64, 68
masonry **20** 576
mirrors **15** 812
techniques
carving **15** 812
painting **15** 812
types
à bec **6** *54*, 55; **8** 278; **12** 174
Byzantine **9** 555
Czech Republic **24** 462
Early Christian (*c*. AD 250-843) **9** 555
backless **9** 555
towers
types—cont.
bell-towers
Armenia (Europe) **14** *36*; **27** 701
Belgium **4** *924*
Byzantine **9** 549
England **27** 527
Gothic **13** 64; **28** *675*
Italy **4** 855; **8** *134*; **13** 64; **28** *675*
Mudéjar **13** 68
Russia **22** *169*; **27** 374
Spain **13** 68; **16** 143
brochs **21** 546, 552; **22** 241–2; **23** 808; **28** 223
clock **7** 439; **31** 242
cremation **15** 812*
crossing **20** 575–6
face-towers **5** 477
flanking **8** *277*, 278; **12** 173
fortified **9** 553, 554, *555*, 555–6; **30** 695
see also brochs; NURAGHI
great **6** 53–5*; **9** 144; **21** 550
Martello **21** 546, 569, 574
mural **6** 55–6*; **8** 278; **12** 173, 174
nuraghi *see* NURAGHI
pigeon **16** 232
que **6** 648, 697; **23** 773; **25** 800 *800*, 801*
réduits modèles **21** 547, 568
siege **21** 557
signal **21** 559
talayots see TALAYOTS
tomb *see* TOMBS → types → tower
torre see TORRE
tours modèles **21** 547, 568
watch **9** 144
Byzantine **9** 554, 555
Central Asia, Eastern **28** *720*
Early Christian (*c*. AD 250-843) **9** 554, 555
Japan **17** 54, 55, *55*
Rome, ancient **21** 559
Syria-Palestine **21** 553
water **18** 541; **22** *34*
see also PYLONS; ZIGGURATS
tower-sanctuaries
Buddhism **30** 575, 587
Cambodia **5** 465, *466*, *473*, 474
Hinduism **5** *466*
South-east Asia **28** 639
Thailand **4** *795*; **30** 575, 587
Towie Barclay **31** 230
Towler, John **10** 669
Town, Davis & Dakin **8** 574
Town, Harold **5** 568; **23** 791; **31** 177, 231*
Town, Ithiel **2** 734; **8** 573, 575; **31** 231–3*
collaboration **21** 618; **25** 267; **31** 392; **32** 753
personal collection **7** 550
staff **8** 462
works **4** 788; **14** 202, 597; **23** 25; **31** *232*
Town & Davis **8** 573–4; **14** 597; **23** 38
Towne, Francis **1** 24; **13** 304; **28** 614; **31** 233–4*
patrons and collectors **23** 455
works **31** *233*; **32** 900
Towneley (family) **12** 639
Towneley, Charles *see* TOWNLEY, CHARLES
Towneley, Richard **29** 835
Towneley Hall (Lancs) **12** 639; **29** 835
Towneley Lectionary *see under* LECTIONARIES → individual manuscripts
Townend (Cumbria) **8** 107
Townesend, George **31** 235
Townesend, John, I (1648-1728) **31** 234*
Townesend, John, II (1678-1742) **31** 235
Townesend, John, III (1709-46) **31** 235
Townesend, John, IV (*d* 1784) **31** 235
Townesend, William **7** 378; **14** 254; **23** 688; **31** 234–5*
town halls **13** 236; **18** 886; **31** 235–43*
Belgium **31** *238*
Gothic **3** 543, *544*; **4** *925*; **5** *53*; **12** *523*
Renaissance **2** *203*; **12** *523*
Britain **31** 239–41*
Canada **31** *176*
Czech Republic **4** *833*; **25** *444*
Denmark **7** *804*
England **10** 235, 266; **31** 236, 238–9, *240*
Baroque Revival **10** *239*
Gothic Revival **20** *237*
17th cent. **24** *804*
20th cent. **10** *240*
Finland **1** *10*
France **11** *566*; **22** 330; **31** 235, 241–2
Beaux-Arts style **3** *465*
Louis XV style **14** *448*
Germany **19** 746; **31** 237
Baroque **4** *324*; **23** *317*
Mannerism **14** *679*
Renaissance **2** *714*; **19** *110*; **23** 317
20th cent. **12** *380*
Gothic
Belgium **3** *544*; **4** *925*; **5** *53*; **12** *523*
Czech Republic **4** *833*
Italy **13** *773*
Poland **30** *203*; **31** *196*; **33** *417*
Slovakia **3** *224*
Indian subcontinent **31** 241
Italy **13** *773*; **31** 236–7, *237*
Japan **31** 242, *243*
Netherlands, the **31** *239*
Dutch Classicism **22** *825*
Mannerism **8** *666*; **22** *824*
Modern Movement **31** *868*
17th cent. **4** *702*; **13** *893*
Norway **23** *602*
Poland **18** *425*; **25** *409*; **27** *722*; **30** *203*; **31** *196*; **33** *417*
Scotland **28** *229*; **31** 239
Slovakia **3** *224*
Sweden **31** *242*
United States of America **31** 242
Uruguay **31** 753
Wales **5** *731*
see also BOULEUTERIA; CITY HALLS; COUNTY HALLS
town houses *see under* HOUSES → types
Townley, Charles **11** 306; **13** 303; **19** 599; **27** 115; **31** 244–5*; **33** *694*
catalogues **14** 131
collections **10** 79, 365, 487; **17** 475
gems **12** 266
groups and movements **2** 163
house **9** 13
paintings **13** 644; **33** 694
pottery **13** 541
sculpture **4** 886; **6** 97; **9** 24; **10** 368; **27** 46
writings **18** 150
Townley, Fred Laughton **31** 245*
Townley, William **4** 880
Townley and Matheson **31** 245*, 863, 864
Townley Hall (Co. Louth) **16** 9, *9*, 24
Town Palette **14** *407*; **23** 848
town planning *see* URBAN PLANNING
Town Planning Associates **14** 241
Town Planning Institute **12** 229
Town Planning Review **1** 29, 163; **31** 729
Townroe, Reuben **11** 360
towns
historical and regional traditions
Bolivia **29** 893
Britain **31** 722
Crete **21** 664*
England **31** 708, 710
Germany **3** *139*; **12** 471
Greece, ancient **13** 419
Manteño culture **1** 464
Minoan **21** 664*
Mongolia **21** 871*
Native North Americans **5** 386
Prehistoric art **21** 551; **25** 536
Rome, ancient **26** 924
Russia **31** 722
Scotland **31** 710
Swahili **1** 251
United States of America **5** 386; **22** 567; **31** 722
Wales **31** 708, 710
types
fortified **31** 718
Egypt, ancient **21** 554
England **10** 226
France **1** *482*, 482–3
Korea **18** 281–2
Netherlands, the **21** 570, *570*
Rome, ancient **2** 212
garden cities **12** 144–5*; **31** 728
Armenia (Europe) **10** 449
Austria **25** 864
Belgium **4** 577; **8** 681; **9** 759; **11** 724; **25** 190; **31** 875; **32** 380
Britain **12** 144–5, *145*; **31** 728
Czech Republic **18** 405
England **1** 146; **8** 810; **10** 239, 284; **11** 785; **14** 277, 809; **16** 891; **24** 185–6, *186*, 187; **25** 805, *805*; **27** 279
Finland **10** 492
France **2** 391; **3** 226; **11** 526; **12** 145; **24** 128, 129, *129*; **29** 900
Germany **8** 824; **9** 237; **11** 797; **12** 145; **14** 362; **26** 374; **28** 177; **30** 370, 521; **31** 728
Israel **17** 853
Netherlands, the **1** 803; **13** 312, 321, 632; **17** 910
Norway **14** 97; **23** 222; **25** 376
Russia **12** 145; **27** 377, 378; **28** 403; **31** 728
Spain **12** 181
Switzerland **30** 127
United States of America **7** 326, 429; **17** 891; **22** 283; **29** 651; **31** 592
industrial model **31** 713
Britain **31** 725
England **5** 365; **27** 641; **31** *726*
France **11** 724
new **31** 708, 711, 718–21
Algeria **28** 757
Australia **23** 679
Brazil **4** 715; **13** 781–2; **20** 269
Britain **9** 741; **19** 519; **31** 732–3
Canada **20** 890
Denmark **8** 729
England **12** 590, 635; **14** 676; **17** 473; **18** 456; **19** 747
Finland **1** 9
France **2** 11, 700; **4** 227; **5** 609, *610*; **6** 534; **7** 343; **12** 185; **13** 716; **18** 809; **21** 346; **24** 131, *131*; **25** 375; **26** 346–7; **29** 420, 918; **31** 735; **32** 26, 769
Germany **28** 87
Iran **2** 378; **8** 861; **10** 719
Italy **16** 650; **27** *4*; **31** 730
Japan **17** 97
Libya **27** *5*
Netherlands, the **31** 735
Norway **31** 718

towns
 types
  new—cont.
   Poland **25** 100, 135, 136; **31** 718
   Rome, ancient **26** 864, 904, 905; **27** 2–6, *4*, *5*
   Russia **21** 622; **27** 374, 375; **31** 719
   Russia: 18th cent. **5** 520
   Scotland **12** 635
   South Africa **29** 105
   Spain **31** 718
   Sweden **31** 718
   Thailand **17** 686
   Ukraine **31** 552
   United States of America **2** 698; **3** 693; **12** 927; **18** 456; **28** 817; **31** 596, 729
 see also CITIES
townscapes **2** 338; **18** 700; **28** 206; **31** 152, 154–6, 246–9*
 Austria **18** *199*; **32** *433*, *436*
 Barbados **5** *751*
 Belgium **16** *767*; **32** *725*
 Canada **25** *802*; **31** *175*
 England **19** *568*; **31** 155–6
 France **2** *859*; **5** *391*; **31** *156*
  Fauvism **20** *465*
  Impressionism **15** VII; **24** *882*; **28** *796*
  19th cent. **8** *718*
 Germany
  16th cent. **7** *584*; **23** *305*, *307*
  18th cent. **2** *714*; **3** *677*
  19th cent. **3** *793*, *806*; **12** *604*
  20th cent. **11** *735*
 Italy **10** *677*; **20** *414*; **31** 246, 247–9*, *248*; **32** *225*
  20th cent. **26** *777*
 Japan **22** *429*
 Netherlands, the **31** 154–5, 246–7*, *247*
  17th cent. **3** *761*; **8** *667*
 Poland **3** *679*; **12** *223*
 Russia **1** *599*
 Scotland **9** *726*
 Spain **27** *818*
 Turkey **31** *303*
 United States of America **23** *388*; **24** *597*
 see also BIRD'S-EYE VIEWS; CAPRICCIOS; PAINTING → types → *vedute*; TOPOGRAPHY
Townsend (family) **23** 32; **31** 626
Townsend, William (1668-1739) **13** 199
Townsend, William (1909-73) **10** 652
Townsend, Charles Harrison **11** 499; **22** 365; **29** 769; **30** 506; **31** 249–50*
Townsend, Christopher **31** 249
Townsend, Edmund **17** 823; **31** 249
Townsend, Job **12** 834; **31** 249
Townsend, John **29** 120; **31** 249
Townsend, Thomas **29** 120
Townshend, Charlotte, Marchioness of **17** 851
Townshend, George, 4th Viscount and 1st Marquis Townshend **8** 529
town squares *see* SQUARES (TOWN)
town walls *see under* WALLS → types
Towry White Painter **13** 508
Towson (MD), Tilt Showroom **25** 359
Toya, Maxine **22** 608
Toyama, Museum of Modern Art **17** 433
Toyen **25** 433; **30** 22; **31** 250*
 collaboration **29** 884
 groups and movements **8** 393, 829; **30** 23
Toynbee, Arnold **25** 358
Toynton All Saints (Lincs) **10** 302
Toyoaki *see* MATSUMURA GOSHUN
Toyochika Takamura *see* TAKAMURA, TOYOCHIKA
Toyohara Kunichika **17** 290
 works **17** *291*
Toyoharu Utagawa *see* UTAGAWA TOYOHARU
Toyohiko Okamoto *see* OKAMOTO TOYOHIKO
Toyohiro Utagawa *see* UTAGAWA TOYOHIRO
Toyoichi Yamamoto *see* YAMAMOTO, TOYOICHI
Tōyō Iizuka *see* IIZUKA TŌYŌ
Toyō Itō *see* ITŌ, TOYŌ
Toyok **6** *288*, *614*; **31** 250–51*
 manuscripts **6** 306
 reliquaries **6** 319
 sculpture **6** 300
 shrine of the Seven Sleepers **28** 637
 wood-carvings **6** 319
Tōyō Kaneshiga *see* KANESHIGA, TŌYŌ
Tōyō Kaneshige *see* KANESHIGE, TŌYŌ
Toyokazu **17** 401
Toyokumi Utagawa *see* UTAGAWA TOYOKUMI
Toyokuni Utagawa I *see* UTAGAWA TOYOKUNI I
Toyomasa *see* NAITŌ SENSUKE
Toyomasa Ishikawa *see* ISHIKAWA TOYOMASA
Toyonaka
 Nihon Minka Hakubutsukan *see* Open Air Museum of Japanese Farmhouses
 Open Air Museum of Japanese Farmhouses **17** 434; **21** 648
 Ōtsuka Tomb **17** 57, 59
Toyonari Yamamura *see* YAMAMURA, KOKA
Toyonobu Ishikawa *see* ISHIKAWA TOYONOBU
Tōyō Sesshū **17** 29, 409; **18** 552; **31** 251–3*
 patrons and collectors **14** 214; **17** 423, 427
 teachers **30** 466
 works **2** 598; **5** 37, *37*, 120; **17** 24, 173, 323; **31** *252*
Toyoshima, Sōroku **22** 742
Toyosuki irihime no mikoto, Princess **16** 72
Toyota **15** 827
Toyota Hokkei **17** 287, 848; **31** 253*
Toyotarō Tanaka *see* TANAKA, TOYOTARŌ
Toyotomi (family) **23** 554
Toyotomi Hidetsugu **18** 550
Toyotomi Hideyori **16** 812
Toyotomi Hideyoshi, Taikō **23** 592; **31** 253–4*
 architecture **10** 406; **14** 315, 551; **16** 787; **17** 63, 74, 77, 84; **18** 180, 550–51, 557; **21** 827; **23** 596
 castles **14** 551
 coins **17** 370
 collections **17** 428
 dress **17** 315
 food **17** 383
 gardens **12** 98; **18** 557
 metalwork **17** 323
 painting **17** 42
 paintings **14** 215; **17** 423, 728, 784, 785, 786, 796
 prints **17** 271
 saddles **17** 301
 sculpture **17** 127
 seals **17** 409
 standards (vexilloid) **11** 152
 tea ceremonies **17** 336; **28** 411
Toyotomi Kiminobu *see* UKITA IKKEI
Tōyō Unkoku *see* UNKOKU TŌYŌ
Toyozō Arakawa *see* ARAKAWA, TOYOZŌ
toys **6** 276, 277; **7** 143, 147, 835; **15** 724, *726*, 730, 731; **17** 386, 530; **21** 236; **28** 210; **29** 104; **31** 254–9*, *254*, *255*, *256*, *257*, *258*
 see also AUTOMATA; DOLLS; GAMES; KITES; PUPPETS
Toyuq *see* TOYOK
Tōyū Unkoku *see* UNKOKU TŌYŪ
Tōzaian Nanboku **17** 846
Tozeur **32** 312
Tozzi, Mario **16** 680; **31** 268*
Tozzo, Il *see* LARI, ANTONIO MARIA
T-plan mosques *see under* MOSQUES → types
Trabaci, Giovanni Maria **28** 389
Traballesi, Agata **22** 727
Traballesi, Felice **12** 346
Traballesi, Giuliano **2** 232; **21** 527; **24** 758; **31** 268–9*
trabeated construction *see under* ARCHITECTURE → techniques
Trabel, Paul **6** 171
Tra bi Ta **13** 861
Tra bi Tra **13** 861
Trâblous *see* TRIPOLI
Trabzon *see* TREBIZOND
Trac, Frans **18** 171
tracery **31** 270–73*; **32** 88, 92
 historical and regional traditions
  Britain **31** 273
  England **10** 228; **13** 46, 54, 55; **19** 602, 610; **31** 270, 271, 273
  France **11** 153, *154*; **13** 41, 59; **31** 270, 271, 273
  Germany **13** 48, 56, *57*; **31** 270, 271, 273
  Gothic **31** 270
   England **10** 228; **13** 54, 55
   France **11** 153, *154*; **13** 59
   Germany **13** 56, *57*
   Perpendicular **31** 273
   Rayonnant style **31** 273
  Ireland **31** 273
  Islamic **31** 273
  Scandinavia **31** 273
  United States of America **26** 212
 materials
  brick **4** 769
  iron **31** 270
  masonry **31** 270
  mouldings **22** 220
  stone **31** 270
  wood **31** 270
 types
  bar **13** 48; **31** 270, 271*
   curvilinear **31** 271*, *272*
   fan **31** 271*
   Flamboyant **31** 271*
   flowing *see* curvilinear
   Geometric **13** 41; **31** 271*
   Gothic **13** 35, 41, 46, 48, 53, 178; **14** 519
   intersecting **31** 273*
   Kentish **31** 273*
   rectilinear **31** 273*
   reticulated **31** 273*
   Y-tracery **31** 273*
  blind **7** 860; **31** 271, 273*
  curvilinear **31** 270, 273
  fan **31** *272*
  Flamboyant **26** 707; **31** 270, *272*
  Geometric **31** *272*
  intersecting **31** *272*, 273
  Kentish **31** *272*
  mouchettes **22** 210*
  Perpendicular **31** 270
  plate **13** 40; **31** 270–71*, *270*
  rectilinear **31** 271, *272*
  reticulated **31** *272*
 uses
  altarpieces **28** 133
  arcades **31** 271
  screens (i) (architectural) **31** 271
  tombs **31** 271
  vaults (ceiling) **12** 493; **31** 271
  walls **31** 270, 273
tracery
 uses—cont.
  windows **8** 610; **31** 270, *270*, 271, 273
traces **21** 547
Tracey, Ebenezer **31** 625
Tracey, William **4** 289
Trachones Theatre **13** 385
Trachsel, Albert **23** 114
Trachtenbücher *see* COSTUME BOOKS
Trachtová, Eva **28** 856
tracing **7** 109; **24** 659; **25** 281; **31** 273–4*, *274*
tracing floors **28** 497; **31** 270, 274–5*, *275*
tracing houses **31** 274–5*, *275*
tracing-paper *see under* PAPER → types
tracing rooms *see* TRACING FLOORS
Tracy, Arthur **5** 571
Tracy, Everts **30** 62
Tracy, H. de **3** 884
Trad, Farid **19** 7
Tradate, Jacopino da *see* JACOPINO DA TRADATE
trade *see* ART MARKET; COLLECTIONS; CONNOISSEURSHIP; DEALING; INVESTMENT; PATRONAGE
trade cards *see under* CARDS → types
trade fairs **12** 446; **23** 168
trademarks **7** 624
 see also MARKS
Trades, Master of the **19** 421
Tradescant, Hester **31** 276
Tradescant, John, the elder (1590s-1638) **13** 298; **31** 276*; **32** 575
 books **20** 476
 gardens **4** 484; **12** 127
 patrons and collectors **29** 803
 personal collection **10** 364, 368; **19** 582; **22** 675
Tradescant, John, the younger (1608-62) **31** 276*
 collaboration **2** 600
 gardens **4** 484
 horn **7** 125
 patrons and collectors **29** 803
 personal collection **2** 600; **13** 605
 writings **20** 476
trade schools **1** 107; **12** 479
traditions of art *see* ART (TRADITIONS OF)
Traer, Johann Xavier **4** 715
Traetto, Ferrante Gonzaga, Duca di *see* GUASTALLA, FERRANTE GONZAGA, Duca da
Trafalgar chairs *see under* CHAIRS → types
Trafalgar Vases **10** 334
tragacanth **24** 55
tragacanth-sugar **21** 65
Tragana **30** 738
Tragittore, Bastiano **3** 231
Traguiron *see* TROGIR
Tragurio, Ioannes Stephani Duknovich de *see* GIOVANNI DALMATA
Tragurium *see* TROGIR
Traiguera **29** 332
Traikovski, Borislav **19** 884
Trail, Walter, Bishop of St Andrews **27** 530
trailing *see under* GLASS → techniques
Trailokya Mahadevi, Queen (*fl* 1745) (Chalukyas of Badami) **15** 526
Train, Eugène **25** 52; **31** 276*
Trainel, Jean I Jouvenel des Ursins, Baron de **17** 669*
Trainer (family) **14** 513
Traini, Francesco **24** 854; **31** 276–7*
 attributions **5** 124; **20** 776
Traini, Francesco—cont.
 works **9** 107, *107*, 108, 109; **24** 860; **31** *277*
Trajan, Emperor of Rome (*reg* 98-117) **10** *69*; **27** *101*; **31** 277*
 architecture **2** 1; **5** 393; **8** 868; **23** 619; **26** 785, 853, 884, 885, 895, *896*, 896–7*, 906, 910; **31** 349, 350
  military **21** 559
 canals **20** 551
 coins **25** 650; **27** 97
 harbours **23** 619
 reliefs **27** *36*
 sculpture **16** 684, 761; **27** 35, 45
Trajan's Column *see under* ROME → Forum of Trajan
Trakai **19** *494*
 Benedictine Monastery **19** 495
 Castle **3** 527; **19** 495
 church **19** 495
Trakas, George **18** 695
Trakbumde, ruler of Leh (*reg* 15th cent.) **15** 311
Tra Kieu **6** *418*, 429
 citadel **6** 426
 inscriptions **6** 418
 sculpture **6** 428, *429*
Träkumla **26** 647
Tralee Courthouse (Co. Kerry) **16** 9
Tralles **5** 742, 743
 stadium **29** 488
Tralles, Anthemios of *see* ANTHEMIOS OF TRALLES
Trambitsky, A. **12** 856
Tramblin, André **11** 405
Tramello, Alessio **31** 277–8*
 works **24** 695; **31** *278*
Tramezini, Franciscus **4** 443
Tramm, Heinrich **14** 142
Trampota, Jan **8** 393
Tramulles, Francisco **21** 815; **29** 305
Trån **5** 158
Tranakayira **15** 738
Tran dynasty **32** 486
Trang Van Can **32** 482
Trani **16** *621*; **31** 278–9*
 Cathedral of S Nicola Pellegrino **16** 626; **26** 580, 626, 627, 628; **31** 278–9*
  campanile **23** 109
  doors **3** 240; **9** 154
  throne **30** 777
 Ognissanti portals **26** 627
Trani, Anseramo da *see* ANSERAMO DA TRANI
Trani, Pietro, Bishop **31** 162
Tränkner, Erhard **3** 510
Tranquebar **15** *294*, 679, 745; **31** 279*
Transactions of the American Art-Union **24** 431
Transactions of the Apollo Association **24** 431
Transcendental Group of Painters **14** 194
transept basilicas *see under* CHURCHES → types
transepts **9** 530; **31** 279–81*, *280*
transfer (conservation) **24** 7; **29** 892; **31** 281–3*
transfer (printing) **31** 273
 historical and regional traditions
  Belgium **3** 591
  France **11** 606
  Portugal **25** 310
  Scotland **28** 257–8
  Vietnam **32** 482
 materials
  drawings **9** 218
 uses
  ceramics **3** 591; **4** 177; **6** 328; **10** 281, 306; **25** 310; **28** 257–8; **30** 97
  enamel **10** 195, 346, *347*
  fibre art **11** 54
  gilding **12** 621

transfer (printing)
uses—cont.
lacquer **32** 482
papier mâché **24** 61
pottery **11** 606
printing **6** 328
tiles **30** *877*
transfers, oil *see under* DRAWINGS → techniques; PHOTOGRAPHY → processes
Transitional period *see under* NEPAL → periods
Transitional style **20** 859; **22** 269; **31** 283–5*
architecture **31** 283–4
manuscript illumination **26** 677*
painting **13** 139
Transitional ware *see under* PORCELAIN → wares
Transjö **30** 103
translucent enamel *see under* ENAMEL → types
transmission *see* DISSEMINATION
Transoxiana **16** *105*
bronze **16** 370
copper **16** 394
cotton **16** 428
earthenwares **16** 414
jewellery **6** 272
Korans **16** 290
maces **16** *506*
manuscripts **16** 290, 304
silk **16** 428, 435
textiles **16** 435, 443
tiles **6** 207
transparencies **2** 534; **8** 911; **9** 493; **24** 648, 651, 653, 670
see also SLIDES
transparent enamel *see under* ENAMEL → types
transport amphorae *see under* AMPHORAE → types
transporter bridges *see under* BRIDGES → types
transrational language *see* ZAUM
Transvaal Group **1** 319; **20** 484; **29** 106
Transvaal Potteries **29** 116
transverse arches *see under* ARCHES → types
Transylvania, Ferenc II Rákóczy, Prince of *see* FERENC II RÁKÓCZY, Prince of Transylvania
Transylvania, Gabriel Bethlen, Prince of *see* GABRIEL BETHLEN, Prince of Transylvania
Transylvania, George I Rákóczy, Prince of *see* GEORGE I RÁKÓCZY, Prince of Transylvania
Transylvania, Stephen Bathory, Voivode of *see* STEPHEN BATHORY, Voivode of Transylvania
Transylvanian carpets *see under* CARPETS → types
Traoré, Babacar Sadikh **28** 406
Traoré, Ismaila **20** 198
Trapani **16** *103*, *621*; **31** 285*
coral **7** *834*, 835, *835*; **16** 750
Palazzo della Giudecca **28** 657
pottery **16** *416*
Trapani Polyptych, Master of the **28** 656
Trapasso, Cesare **8** 268
Trapezous **4** 112, 113
Traphagen Commercial Textile Studio **7** 873
Trapola, Matteo **18** 693; **19** 751; **33** 259
Trapp (family) **2** 449, 470
Trappeniers, Antoine **7** 480
trappers **14** 182, 404, 425, *426*
trappings **14** 179–87*; **16** 429
materials
bronze **25** 547–8
enamel **25** 547
glass **17** 386
iron **25** 547–8
leather **27** *105*
silver **31** 756
types
buffalo **15** 736
camel **14** 186–7*, *187*
dog **22** *639*
elephant **14** 185–6*
horse **1** 817; **6** 155, 161; **14** 179–81*, 182, *182*, 183–4*, 185*, 233; **17** 386; **23** 803; **25** 547–8*; **27** *105*; **31** 756
Trappists **7** 348
see also CISTERCIAN ORDER
Traprain Law **9** 655
traps **21** 245; **22** 656
Traquair, Phoebe **28** 238
Trarbach, Johann von **14** 627
Trask, Israel **31** 652
Trasmonte, Juan Gómez de *see* GÓMEZ DE TRASMONTE, JUAN
Tratzberg, Schloss *see* SCHLOSS TRATZBERG
Traù *see* TROGIR
Traù, Biagio di Giorgia de *see* BIAGIO DI GIORGIA DE TRAÙ
Trau, Giovanni da *see* GIOVANNI DA TRAU
Traù, Giovanni di *see* GIOVANNI DALMATA
Traun (family) **3** 488
Traungauer (family) **2** 790
Traunstein, St Oswald **32** 822
Trausch, Valentin *see* DRAUSCH, VALENTIN
Traut (von Speyer), Hans I **31** 286
Traut, Wilhelm **18** 43
Traut, Wolf(gang) **23** 310; **31** 286, 287–8*
collaboration **9** 436, 440; **29** 433; **31** 286
patrons and collectors **13** 902; **15** 144
pupils **12** 494
teachers **23** 308
works **12** 386; **28** 57; **31** *287*; **33** 353
Trautschold, (Adolf) Manfred **31** 288
works **25** *805*
Trautschold, (Carl Friedrich) Wilhelm **31** 288*
Traut von Speyer, Hans, II (*d* 1516) **31** 286–7*
works **31** *286*
Traval, Guillaume Thomas **30** 88
Travanca, S Salvador **3** 443; **25** 289; **26** 611
Travancore **15** *294*; **31** 288*
Travani, (Gioacchino) Francesco **20** 921; **31** 289*
Travani, Giovanni Pietro **29** 29
travel books **4** 356, 358; **10** 206; **13** 807; **15** 830; **31** 289–90*
Canada **23** 336
Czech Republic **31** *290*
Egypt, ancient **10** 82
Indian subcontinent **15** 202*
Italy **13** 304
Japan **17** 273
Maya **21** 262
Mesoamerica, Pre-Columbian **21** 262
Spain **4** 443
see also GUIDEBOOKS
Travelling Sketchbook *see under* SKETCHBOOKS → individual manuscripts
travelling watches *see under* WATCHES → types
Traversari, Ambrogio **5** 449; **14** 867, 870; **31** 291*
Traversari, Girolamo **5** 451
Traverse **29** 576
Traverse, Charles de La *see* LA TRAVERSE, CHARLES DE
Traversi, Gaspare **22** 479; **31** 291–2*
works **12** 292; **31** *292*
Traverso, Nicolò Stefano **31** 292*
travertine *see under* LIMESTONE → types
Travessa dos Ladrões **26** 52
Travesseres **26** 642
Travi, Antonio **29** 784; **31** 293*; **32** 826
Traviès, (Charles) Joseph **5** 758; **13** 306; **24** 605; **27** 871; **31** 293*
Trávníček, J. **25** 430
Trawulan **15** *753*, 811
trays
historical and regional traditions
Africa **1** *356*
Buddhism **17** *322*
Central Asia, Western **6** 245, *246*
China **6** 888, 890
Coclé culture **7** *506*
England **24** *62*
Indian subcontinent **15** 727
Iran **16** *372*
Iraq **16** *380*
Islamic **16** 366, 372, *372*, *380*
Japan **17** *322*
Laos **18** 776
Malta (Republic of) **20** 217
Native North Americans **22** 656, 658
Nigeria **1** *356*
Panama **7** *506*
Ryūkyū Islands **27** 471, *471*
South America, Pre-Columbian **7** *506*
Sweden **30** 97
Tajikistan **33** *510*
Yoruba **1** 356, *356*; **33** 558
materials
bark **22** 656
brass **16** *380*
bronze **6** *246*; **17** *322*
faience (ii) (ceramics) **30** 97
grasses **15** 727
inlays **16** *380*
lacquer **27** 471, *471*
metal **6** 245
mother-of-pearl **24** *62*
palm leaves **15** 727
papier mâché **24** 61, 62, *62*
pottery **6** 890; **7** *506*
silver **20** 217
silver-gilt **16** *372*
stone **33** *510*
wood **1** *356*
types
birth trays *see deschi da parto*
deschi da parto **8** 790*; **11** 388; **22** 413
salvers *see* SALVERS
waiters **27** 646
zen **17** 383
Trčka, Anton Josef **28** 90
Trdat (*fl* 989-1001) **2** 97, 426, 444; **14** 36; **16** 592
Trdat, King of Armenia (*reg* AD 54-60; 63-98) **2** 97; **12** 154
Trdat III, King of Armenia (*reg* 287-98) **2** 424; **12** 154
Treacher, William **14** 522
treacle **4** 684
treadle looms *see under* LOOMS → types
Treadwell, E. P. **33** 135
Treadwell, Prentice **26** 474
Treadwell & Martin **25** 688
tread-wheels **7** 764, *765*
Treasure of Attila *see* NAGYSZENTMIKLÓS TREASURE
Treasure of Guarrazar **31** 88
Treasure of the Empress Gisela **17** 519
treasuries **6** 76
Greece, ancient **13** 376, 379, 380, 390; **27** 712; **31** 293*, *294*
6th cent. BC **13** *399*
Rome, ancient **27** 712
Treasury of Atreus *see under* MYCENAE
treasury-temples *see under* TEMPLES → types
Treasuryvala, B. N. **15** 742
treatises **2** 366; **4** 20, 361; **10** 203; **31** 294–303*
historical and regional traditions
Belgium **27** 300
Byzantine **9** 603
China **7** 123; **17** 229
Early Christian (*c.* AD 250-843) **9** 603
England **23** 690
France **19** 9
Germany **30** 709–10
Greece, ancient **13** 394, 554; **24** 414
Indian subcontinent **15** 190, 208–10*; **30** 642
Islamic **16** 136
Italy **8** 609; **27** 894
Byzantine **9** 603
Early Christian (*c.* AD 250-843) **9** 603
Renaissance **29** 738
15th cent. **15** 50
16th cent. **4** 408; **29** 84
Japan **17** 26, 415–17*, 425; **23** 347
Poland **29** 777
Thailand **30** 614
Tibet **30** 813
types
aesthetics **10** 207
China **2** 519
France **2** 15; **9** 372; **31** 197
Greece **5** 215
Indian subcontinent **15** 206
Ireland **15** 37
Islamic **16** 455
Italy **7** 306
Japan **17** 439
Russia **31** 97
Tibet **30** 848
agriculture **26** 884
architecture **10** 204, 205; **31** 294–8*
Austria **15** 166
Belgium **3** 581; **23** 489
Britain **12** 595
China **2** 317; **6** 653, 661
England **6** 411; **9** 367; **10** 231; **13** 298; **18** 742; **21** 620; **25** 713; **28** 645; **31** 297–8*; **33** 387
France **23** 487–8, 489; **28** 371; **31** 296–7*
France: Gothic **31** 835
France: 16th cent. **5** 166; **19** 693–4
France: 17th cent. **2** 168; **6** 417; **10** 489; **12** 310
France: 18th cent. **7** 774, 840; **8** 793; **19** 34
France: 19th cent. **22** 362; **26** 270; **27** 123; **32** 427, 598
Germany **4** 178; **8** 882; **10** 444; **11** 853; **12** 366, 369; **22** 386; **29** 872; **31** 298*
Gothic **12** 619–20; **31** 835
Greece **25** 7
Greece, ancient **13** 408–9; **14** 461; **23** 482
Indian subcontinent **15** 206, 208–10*, 315, 324; **29** 868
Islamic **2** 316; **16** 143, 221
Italy **1** 792; **14** 660; **19** 534; **21** 106; **22** 388; **23** 486, 487, 489, 861; **31** *295*, 295–6*; **32** 550–51, 638
treatises
types
architecture—cont.
Italy: Renaissance **1** 555, 558–60, 568; **3** 850; **7** 863; **11** 71, 72–3, 691; **23** 869; **28** 466, 468–71; **29** 739
Italy: 15th cent. **16** 630; **22** 44; **32** 639
Italy: 16th cent. **2** 167–8; **3** 863; **6** 82; **16** 634; **23** 856; **25** 857; **26** 317; **32** 187
Italy: 17th cent. **13** 753; **23** 870; **28** *31*, 32–3; **32** 594
Italy: 18th cent. **8** 563; **12** 12, 657; **27** 791; **32** 645
Italy: 20th cent. **24** 693
Japan **2** 317; **14** 315; **17** 421
Liechtenstein (i) (country) **19** 336
military **1** 637; **13** 845; **28** 367
Netherlands, the **8** 496; **22** 823
Ottoman **16** 221
Poland **20** 396, 397; **25** 142
Rome, ancient **23** 480, 484; **26** 884, 924; **32** 632
Scotland **28** 252
Spain **23** 487; **31** 297*
Spain: Baroque **29** 269
Spain: Gothic **12** 619–20
Spain: 16th cent. **25** 31; **27** 520
Spain: 17th cent. **5** 411, 700–701, *700*; **24** 350; **27** 763, 765; **31** 171
Turkey **16** 221
see also PATTERN BOOKS → types → architecture
armour **11** 270; **17** 364
art **7** 678; **25** 660
automata **15** 573
bridges **4** 804; **12** 206; **24** 479
calligraphy
China **6** 760
China: Han period (206 BC-AD 220) **6** 769
China: Qing period (1644-1911) **6** 764, 765, 766; **17** 775; **27** 286
China: Tang period (AD 618-907) **30** 2
China: Three Kingdoms (AD 220-80) **6** 769–71
China: 20th cent. **6** 766, 767, 768
Germany **22** 920
Islamic **16** 126, 277*, 284, 286
Japan **17** 224, 226–8, 343; **29** 66, 902
casting **8** 416
Celtic art **16** 830
cemeteries **6** 166
ceramics **6** 17; **16** 394
collections **2** 904
colour **1** 549; **13** 138
design **5** 262; **16** 143
disegno **9** 142; **23** 879
drainage systems **6** 23
drawing **25** 396; **27** 204; **28** 392
engineering **30** 230
engravings
England **10** 393, 757
France **10** 390
Germany **22** 320; **31** 26
Italy **19** 637
epigraphy **12** 656
festivals **23** 769–71
flower arrangements **17** 417
fortifications
Canada **6** 518
France **21** 567; **29** 376
Germany **9** 441; **12** 369; **21** 578
Indian subcontinent **21** 590
Italy **3** 683; **7** 776; **21** 577, 578; **28** 309
Spain **2** 542; **12** 921; **14** 476; **26** 548
fountains **6** 23

treatises
types—cont.
gardens **12** 64, 88, 107, 127
England **6** 411; **12** 61, 64; **30** 123
France **12** 64, 120, 122, 132, 724; **21** 822
Germany **14** 570
Italy **12** 110
Japan **12** 64, 96–7; **17** 417*
Poland **22** 202
gem-engraving **12** 263; **20** 416
gems **15** 701; **16** 412, 527
grottoes **13** 704
hardstones **14** 167
heraldry **7** 780
historiography **3** 98
horse-trappings **19** 337
houses **13** 314
hydraulics **2** 376; **7** 492
iconography **3** 914; **5** 887–8; **10** 209, 211
imitation **5** 526
imprese **9** 142
inks **27** 882
japanning **7** 166; **10** 290; **18** 610, 614; **24** 273; **29** 530
jewellery **17** 524
letters **2** 166
light **19** 354
lithography **19** 479
locks **16** 59
looms **7** 44
maiolica **24** 733
manuscript illumination **2** 430; **13** 136; **20** 324–5
metalwork **6** 139, 147, 148
miniatures (paintings) **14** 547; **21** 639, 640; **23** 208
mosaics **22** 156
mosques **15** 208
optics **7** 627; **33** 721
oratory **25** 824
orders (architecture) **32** 507–8
painting **19** 353, 354; **31** 298–300*
China **6** 754, 784, 785, 804, 824; **7** 148; **14** 820
China: Qing period (1644-1911) **6** 39, 814
China: Song period (AD 960-1279) **6** 804
China: Tang period (AD 618-907) **6** 799
China: Yuan period (1279-1368) **6** 814, 824; **14** 823
encaustic **3** 19; **10** 198, 199
England **5** 271; **26** 278–9; **31** 300
France **31** 300
France: 17th cent. **11** 743; **23** 748; **24** 805
France: 18th cent. **8** 500
France: 19th cent. **10** 199
France: 20th cent **8** 774; **12** 806
fresco **21** 165
Germany **31** 300
Greece, ancient **10** 650; **13** 549; **31** 298
Indian subcontinent **15** 206, 208–10*
Italy **3** 648; **7** 628; **23** 772; **24** 90; **31** 299, 321
Italy: Mannerism **19** 546–7
Italy: Renaissance **1** 555, 557–8; **16** 778
Italy: 14th cent. **30** 425
Italy: 15th cent. **6** 168–9; **7** 627
Italy: 16th cent. **2** 445–6; **12** 571, 629–30; **23** 839–40
Italy: 17th cent. **1** 465; **2** 376; **11** 698; **20** 242; **28** 33–4, 35; **30** 527
Italy: 18th cent. **7** 177; **12** 720
Italy: 20th cent. **25** 568
Japan **17** 416–17, 791; **27** 865
landscape **9** 141; **17** 590; **18** 174; **26** 75; **31** 817
treatises
types
painting—cont.
Mexico **13** 868
Netherlands, the **20** 245–6; **31** 300
Poland **4** 837
Portugal **14** 660
Romanesque **26** 657
Rome, ancient **31** 299
Russia **4** 237; **27** 387
Spain **5** 313; **13** 870
Sweden **28** 68
Tibet **30** 848
palaeography **19** 865
papermaking **24** 40
perspective **19** 354
China **6** 40
England **9** 740; **24** 490
France **8** 786; **24** 335, 490, 494
Greece, ancient **13** 553
Italy **24** 487, 488, 489, 490; **28** 30; **30** 657, 668
Italy: Baroque **25** 416
Italy: Renaissance **1** 557
Italy: 15th cent. **24** 765–6
Italy: 16th cent. **3** 202; **4** 567, 654; **7** 312; **32** 508
Italy: 17th cent. **4** 441; **6** 40; **33** 587
photography **19** 86
pigments **7** 678; **11** 58
portraits **14** 660; **15** 31
pottery **1** 98
prisons **25** 637
proportion
Germany **9** 441
Italy **2** 345; **8** 512; **16** 658; **23** 744; **28** 201
scenography **33** 721
scientific instruments **2** 647
sculpture **31** 301–3*
Greece, ancient **31** 301–2*
Indian subcontinent **15** 206, 208–10*, 541
Italy **31** 302–3*
Italy: Mannerism **6** 147, 148
Italy: Renaissance **1** 555, 558
Italy: 16th cent. **4** 198; **12** 204–5; **28** 509
Tibet **30** 848
seals **7** 130
silk **11** 645
silver **16** 742
stage design **30** 654, 657, 659, 667
stained glass **11** 892; **29** 506
stencilling **29** 628
stereotomy **8** 775; **11** 771; **29** 636–7
stone-cutting **8** 787
stones **19** 178
terracotta **6** 378
theatres **5** 762; **30** 674
topographical drawings **9** 685
urban planning
Austria **28** 800–801
Indian subcontinent **15** 209
Italy **22** 78
Russia **31** 486
Spain **2** 379
varnishing **24** 273; **29** 530
vaults **22** 322; **31** 171
wood **19** 26
wood-engravings **4** 360
see also MANUALS
Trebatti, Paolo Ponzio **25** 208
Il Trebbio **12** 111; **21** 467; **32** 545
Trebeck, George **1** 210
Třebíč **10** 741
St Mary **8** 376; **26** 638
Trebisonda, Andrea da *see* ANDREA DA TREBISONDA
Trebišov Church **28** 853
Trebizond **1** *821*; **6** *623*; **9** *512*, 515; **16** *104*; **31** *303*, 303–4*
carpets **16** 470
coins **9** 638
fortifications **9** 555; **21** 587
Trebizond—cont.
Hagia Sophia **9** 550, 583; **26** 332; **31** 304*
Hagios Eugenios **31** 304*
silk **9** 668
Theotokos Chrysokephalos **31** 304*
Theotokos Theoskepastos **31** 304
urban planning **16** 266
Trebnitz *see* TRZEBNICA
Třeboň
embroidery **8** 420
Monastery **8** 389; **13** 152; **20** 774; **25** *431*
church **8** 376
Třeboň, Master of **20** 774–5*
works **8** 382, 389; **20** *774*; **25** 431, *431*
Treby, George **18** 677
Treccani, Ernesto **13** 872; **21** 528
Treccani, Giovanni **4** 20
Trece, Generación del *see* GENERACIÓN DEL TRECE
Trechsel, Johann **30** 487
Tredgold, Thomas **2** 692; **16** 52
Tree, Herbert Beerbohm **30** 680, 681
Tree, Lambert **6** 575
tree-bark *see* BARK
Tree Carpet **15** 683
tree-carvings **1** 56*; **6** 514
Treeck, Martin van **12** 653
treen **31** 305*
Tree of Jesse in the Buurkerk, Master of the **20** 663
trees **13** *418*, 418–19; **17** 365
tree-shrines *see under* SHRINES (i) (CULT) → types
tree trunks **3** *891*
Trefecca **32** 783
Trefford, Marie Vignon, Marquise de **26** 351
trefid spoons *see under* SPOONS → types
Trefogli, Marc'Antonio **12** 584
trefoil arches *see under* ARCHES → types
trefoil churches *see* CHURCHES → types → triconch
Trefort, Agoston **2** 546
Tregenna Hill Pottery **25** 834
Treglia, Matteo **31** 789
Tréguier, Cathedral of St Tugdual **11** 255
Trehearne and Norman **10** 173
Trehet, Jean **12** 133; **32** 460
Treitzsauerwein, Marx **13** 903; **28** 58; **33** 353
Trélat, Emile **28** 463; **31** 305*
Trelleborg **8** 721; **32** 532–3
trellises **12** 109
Tremadog (Gwynedd) **32** *780*, 782
Peniel **32** 783
Tremanti, Fernando Arbós y *see* ARBÓS Y TREMANTI, FERNANDO
Tremblay, A., Baron du **11** 606
Tremblay, Barthélémy **11** 557; **31** 305*
collaboration **16** 855; **25** 577
works **11** 260, 754; **13** 825
Tremblaye, Guillaume de la **5** 370
Tremecén *see* TLEMCEN
Tremetousia, Hagios Spyridon **8** 357, 358
Tremezzo, Villa Carlotta **12** 118; **16** 677, 719; **30** 764
Tremignon, Alessandro **19** 630; **32** 188, 195
tremisses *see under* COINS → types
Tremithousa **8** 342
Tremlett, David **18** 695; **31** 306*
Tremoille, La (family) *see* LA TREMOILLE (FAMILY)
Trémolières, Pierre-Charles **22** 682; **31** 306*
Trémouille, Marie-Anne de La, Princesse des Ursins *see* URSINS, MARIE-ANNE DE LA TRÉMOUILLE, Princesse des
trempé crayons *see under* CRAYONS
Trencavel, Vicomtes de **5** 727
Trench, Henry **7** 796
Trench, Joseph **28** 900
Trenchard, James **31** 601
Trench & Snook **23** 39; **28** 900
Trenčianské Bohuslavice **28** *848*, 852
wall paintings **28** *852*
Trenčianské Teplice **28** *848*, 850
Trenčín **28** *848*
architecture **28** 849
Castle **28** 849
church **28** 852
Jesuit church **14** 900
Monastery **14** 906
sculpture **28** 855
Trencsén *see* TRENČÍN
Trendall, A. D. **32** 27
Trenka, Stephen **5** 570
Trenkwald, Josef Mathias von **1** 604; **7** 368; **17** 474, 897; **24** 850; **28** 183; **33** 635
Trenque Lauquen Municipal Palace **22** 335
Trenso, Dario da **23** 754
Trent
Buonconsiglio Castle **5** 180–81*; **11** 287; **16** *618*; **26** *727*
frescoes **9** *262*, 262
Magno Palazzo **5** 180, *181*
Museo Provinciale d'Arte **5** 181
Torre Aquila **14** 433; **18** 704
Case Rella **10** 737
Cathedral **30** 331
façade decoration **10** 737
Museo Provinciale d'Arte *see under* Buonconsiglio Castle
S Lorenzo **14** 81
S Pietro **28** *393*
Trenta, Filippo (1731-95) **31** 306–7*
Trenta, Filippo (1892-1976) **31** 307
Trenta, Lorenzo **16** 841; **20** 634
Trentacoste, Domenico **20** 428; **31** 307*
Trentanove, Antonio **12** 584
Trentham Park (Staffs) **3** 689; **12** 139, 177; **20** 868
Trento (family) **22** 388
Trento, Antonio da *see* ANTONIO DA TRENTO
Trento, Giuseppe **22** 388
Trento, Ottavio **22** 388
Trenton (NJ)
ceramics **31** 636, 637, *637*
Jewish Community Center **17** 549
Trenton Pottery **19** 165
Trentowski, K. **32** 879
Trent Tile Co. **4** 863
Trent University *see under* PETERBOROUGH (ONT.; CANADA)
Treo, Wilhelm **19** 516
Trepkowski, Tadeusz **25** 108
Treppenhaus **31** 307*
Trepuco **3** 105
Très Belles Heures *see under* BOOKS OF HOURS → individual manuscripts
Très Belles Heures de Notre-Dame *see under* BOOKS OF HOURS → individual manuscripts
Treschel, Johann(es) **4** 9, 358
Trescore Balneario, Villa Suardi **9** *265*, 266
Tresfjord Church **11** 465
frames **11** *466*
Tresguerras, Francisco Eduardo **21** 378; **25** 815; **31** 95, 307–8*
Tresham, Henry **5** 541; **25** 665; **31** 308*
Tresham, Thomas **32** 551
Tresilian, John **10** 339
Tresini, Domenico *see* TREZZINI, DOMENICO
Treskavac Monastery **19** 882
Church of the Assumption **25** 343; **28** 447, 448
Treskow, Elisabeth **12** 450
works **12** *451*
Trésor du Dauphin **4** 558
Très Petites Heures d'Anne de Bretagne, Master of the **33** 357
Très Riches Heures *see under* BOOKS OF HOURS → individual manuscripts
Tress, Arthur **12** 214; **31** 310*
Tressan, Louis-Elizabeth de la Vergne, Comte de **31** 373
Tressell, Christopher **14** 546
Tressini, Domenico *see* TREZZINI, DOMENICO
trestle tables *see under* TABLES → types
Trestrail, C. Lloyd **31** 335
Treswell, Ralph **19** 568
Treswell, Robert **30** 763
Tres Zapotes **21** *193*, 197, *372*; **23** 416; **31** 310–11*
Burnt Mounds Group **31** 310
colossal heads **21** 219
Mounds 2 Group **31** 310
Mounds 3 Group **31** 310
Mounds I Group **31** 310
New Lands Group **31** 310
Small Farm (Village) Group **31** 310
Stele C **21** 219; **29** 619
Treter, Thomas **18** 177
Tretko, Jan *see* TRICIUS, JAN
Tretower (Brecon) **6** 55; **9** 144
Castle **6** 54
donjon **9** *144*
Tretower Court **32** 781
Tretsch, Aberlin **31** 311*
assistants **3** 870
works **3** 870; **12** 369; **29** 875, *875*
Tretten, De **28** 54
Tret'yakov, Pavel (Mikhaylovich) **4** 489; **24** 247; **31** 311–12*
collections **22** 178; **27** 440
paintings **9** 328; **18** 438; **19** 276; **22** 178; **26** 218; **27** 439; **28** 475
Tret'yakov, Sergey (Mikhaylovich) **27** 439, 440, 441
Tret'yakov State Gallery *see under* MOSCOW → museums
Treumann, Rudolf **24** 592
Trevano, Giovanni **18** 428; **31** 312*
patrons and collectors **32** 5
works **6** 22; **18** 426, 431; **25** 114; **29** 839
Trevejos, Antonio Fernández *see* FERNÁNDEZ TREVEJOS, ANTONIO
Trevelyan, Lady
works **10** *355*
Trevelyan, Julian **5** 531; **20** 590
Trevelyan, Pauline **28** 276
Trevelyan, Walter **28** 276
Treves, Baron **17** 444
Treves, Marco **10** 761; **17** 547
Trèves-Cunault, Notre-Dame **26** 599
Trevethy, Arthur's Quoit **21** *40*
Trevi **16** *620*; **26** *886*
Temple of Clitumnus **13** 300; **26** 625; **31** 312*
Treviglio, S Martino **33** 633
Tréville, Ernest Charton de *see* CHARTON DE TRÉVILLE, ERNEST
Treviño, Fernando Garza *see* GARZA TREVIÑO, FERNANDO
Trevisan, Bernardo **5** 623
Trevisan, Giovanni *see* VOLPATO, GIUSEPPE
Trevisan, Melchior **5** 178
Trevisani, Angelo **7** 779

Trevisani, Francesco 7 682; 13 300, 301; 16 672; 26 774; 31 312–15*, 444
  collaboration 19 816; 20 903
  patrons and collectors
    Carolis, Livio de, Marchese 5 812
    Chigi, Flavio, Cardinal 6 585
    Coke, Thomas, 1st Earl of Leicester of the 1st creation (1697-1759) 7 540
    Elizabeth Farnese, Queen of Spain (1692-1766) 4 560
    Ottoboni, Pietro, Cardinal (1667-1740) 23 637
    Pallavicini, Nicolò, Marchese (1650-1714) 23 874
    Saint-Aignan, Paul-Hippolyte de Beauvillier, Duc de 27 524
    Talbot, Charles, 1st Duke of Shrewsbury (1660-1718) 30 267
    Valenti Gonzaga, Silvio, Cardinal 12 914
    Victor-Amadeus II, 15th Duke of Savoy (*reg* 1675- 1730) and King of Sardinia (*reg* 1720-30) 28 16
  pupils
    Beaumont, Claudio Francesco 3 453
    Carlone (ii), Carlo Innocenzo (1685-1775) 5 774
    Casali, Andrea 5 906, 907
    Costanzi, Placido 8 12
    Duprà, (Giorgio) Domenico 9 402
    Guglielmi, Gregorio 13 802
    Pesci, Girolamo 24 537
    Rotari, Pietro (Antonio) 27 213
    Vieira Lusitano, Francisco 32 424
  reproductive prints by others 6 549; 18 47
  sponsors 26 773
  teachers 14 322; 33 608
  works 3 95; 25 297; 26 810; 31 *313*, *314*
Treviso 16 *618*; 31 315–16*
  Cathedral of S Pietro 4 *738*; 15 137; 26 622
  façade decoration 10 736, 739
  glass 16 740
  Palazzo dei Trecento 31 236
  S Margherita 31 104
  S Nicolò 13 64, 149; 31 103–4, *104*, *316*
  S Vito d'Altivole Cemetery 28 *36*
  Vescovado 5 431
Treviso, Andrea da *see* ANDREA DA TREVISO
Treviso, Dario da *see* DARIO (DI GIOVANNI) DA TREVISO
Treviso, Giovanni Maria da 23 751
Treviso, Girolamo da *see* GIROLAMO DA TREVISO
Treviso, Girolamo Penacchi da *see* PENACCHI DA TREVISO, GIROLAMO
Treviso, Pozzo da *see* TOEPUT, LODEWIJK
Treviso, Vincenzo da *see* DESTRE, VINCENZO DALLE
Trevor, Helen Mabel 16 17
Trew, Christoph Jacob 10 101
Trewhiddle Hoard 31 316–17*
Trewhiddle style *see under* ANGLO-SAXON → styles
Treyman, K. 12 856
Treytz (family) 2 470
Trezini, Domenico *see* TREZZINI, DOMENICO
Trezza, Luigi 32 342
Trezzi, Aurelio 4 426; 26 317
Trezzini, Domenico 27 442; 31 317–18*
  patrons and collectors 26 730
  pupils 33 632
Trezzini, Domenico—cont.
  works 12 134; 25 745; 26 *730*; 27 373, 573, 574, 575, 585, 586; 31 *318*
Trezzini, Pietro Antonio 18 849; 27 586; 33 633
Trezzo, Francesco da 33 274
Trezzo, Jacopo (Nizolla) da, I (1515/9-89) 12 259; 20 919, 920; 31 318–19*
  collaboration 10 502; 20 67
  patrons and collectors 12 260; 14 5
  pupils 17 643; 21 725
  restorations by others 29 343
  works 10 502; 11 486; 20 921; 26 250; 33 274
Trezzo, Jacopo da, II (*d* 1607) 31 319
Trgovište 28 440
TRIAD 7 713
triads *see under* SCULPTURE → types
Trialeti 12 *317*, 318; 25 *471*; 31 319*
  metalwork 12 328
  pottery 12 330
Trianda 26 *289*, 290
  Hagios Nikolaos 26 295
Triande, Toumani 5 217
Triangle: the Art and Psychology Group 18 507
triangular arches *see under* ARCHES → types
Triano, Marqués de 28 884
Trianon Press 7 576; 26 236; 29 628
tribal art 15 731–6*
Tribel, Annie 2 699
Tribel, Jean 2 699
Tribeni, Mosque of Zafar Khan Ghazi 15 351; 16 201
Tribhuvanam 15 333
Tribilia, Antonio *see* TERRIBILIA, ANTONIO
Triblin, Lienhart 13 267
Tribolo, Niccolò 31 320–21*
  assistants 7 331; 22 166
  attributions 24 756
  collaboration 4 280; 7 331; 10 799; 21 16; 22 15; 27 747
    Aimo, Domenico 1 490
    Buglioni, Santi (di Michele Viviano) 5 131; 21 452
    Cosini, Silvio 7 918
    Sangallo, Francesco da 19 688
    Stagi, Stagio 29 496
    Volpaia, Benvenuto di Lorenzo 32 688
  gardens 11 214, 215
  grottoes 13 703
  patrons and collectors 11 893; 12 569; 16 696; 21 20, 21; 23 855; 31 849; 32 22
  pupils 19 672; 24 756
  sculpture 30 495
    allegorical 16 *766*
    fountains 1 791; 8 511; 11 342; 24 756; 31 *321*
    reliefs 19 688, *688*; 26 137; 27 777
    statuettes 29 569
    tombs 3 158
  teachers 27 770
Tribord 18 577
Tribout 31 816
tribunes 12 21; 31 321*
Triburg, Nederlands Textiel Museum 2 371
Tribus 24 430
Trichet de Fresne, Raphaël 4 21; 9 206; 19 197; 31 321–2*
Trichinopoly *see* TIRUCHIRAPALLI
Tricht, Aert van 1 526; 13 160; 28 595; 31 322*
Tricht, Arnt van 17 741; 22 856; 31 322*; 33 458
Tricht, J. van 26 379
Trichur 15 *294*; 31 322–3*
  Vadakkunnatha Temple complex 15 522, 649; 31 322–3
    Vadakkunnatha shrine 15 336; 31 322–3
Tricius, Aleksander (Jan) 17 648; 31 323
Tricius, Jan 17 615; 18 431; 25 104, 105; 31 323*
triclinia 31 323*
triconch churches *see under* CHURCHES → types
Tridacna shells *see under* SHELLS → types
Tridentine style 10 534
Triefenstein, Klosterkirche 33 *672*
Trier 9 *510*; 12 *361*; 23 809; 26 *905*; 31 323–7*
  Altbachtal sanctuary 26 866, 905, *905*
  amphitheatre 26 905
  art forms and materials
    architecture 26 905
    book covers 4 III
    coins 14 419
    gems 12 255
    glass 27 74, 75
    ivory 23 660, *661*
    manuscripts 20 330; 23 653; 26 673; 31 325–6*
    metalwork 23 656; 26 683
    mosaics 9 563, 569; 26 858; 27 62
    painting 12 391; 27 56
    pottery 27 107, 108
    rock crystal 5 811; 26 485
    terracotta 27 110
  Augusta Treverorum 31 323–4*
  Aula Palatina 3 329; 4 776; 26 878, 907, 908; 27 56, 67; 31 *324*
    mosaics 21 III1
  Baptistery 3 192
  Basilica of Constantine *see* Aula Palatina
  baths 26 907; 31 323
  Cathedral of St Peter 2 295; 12 364, 471; 19 709; 26 574; 30 729; 31 *326*, 326–7*
    doors 26 684
    metalwork 6 *174*
    pulpit 12 402; 25 726
    sculpture 14 627
    Treasury 26 646
  Dombezirk 26 908
  double cathedral 9 534; 31 326*
  forum 11 327
  houses 32 281
  Imperial Baths 26 872
  Kornmarkt 27 60
  Liebfrauenkirche 7 257; 12 365; 13 48; 31 326*, 327*, *327*
    tomb of Jakob von Sierck 12 342
    tomb of Karl von Metternich 26 *25*
  Monastery 12 382
  Palais Kesselstatt 30 741
  Palastaula *see* Aula Palatina
  Porta Nigra 7 358, *358*; 21 548; 23 485; 26 573, 907
  roofs 30 909
  St Maximin 7 265; 13 18, 19
    crypt 7 265; 8 223
    Folkardus fountain 26 684
    wall paintings 5 798, *799*; 12 382; 23 651
  westwork 7 265
Trier, Clemens August, Prince-Bishop and Elector of (*fl* 1757) 33 692
Trier, Eduard 31 328
Trier, Gosbertus of *see* GOSBERTUS OF TRIER
Trier, Hann 31 328*
  groups and movements 21 341
  pupils 3 17, 323
  works 3 803, 807
Trier Apocalypse *see under* APOCALYPSES → individual manuscripts
Trier Gospels *see under* GOSPEL BOOKS → individual manuscripts
Trier Mørch, Dea *see* MØRCH, DEA TRIER
Tríes, Antonio Rovira *see* ROVIRA TRÍES, ANTONIO
Triest, Antonine, Bishop of Bruges 9 411; 28 902; 30 461
Trieste (family) 17 444
Trieste 9 *510*; 16 *618*, 776; 26 *886*, *906*; 31 328–9*, 714
  Cathedral of S Giusto 9 529; 31 328–9, *329*
  Museo Civico di Storia ed Arte ed Orto Lapidario 31 329
  Museo Civico Sartorio 31 329
  Palazzo Carciotti 24 496
  S Antonio Nuovo 29 833
  synagogue 17 546
  theatre 26 906
  Villa Sartorio Montebello 4 311
Trifesti, St Nicholas 26 708
Trifolium 14 388; 18 501; 24 674, 738; 32 924
triforia 31 329*
triforium windows *see under* WINDOWS → types
Triga, Giacomo 3 920; 26 827
Trigance (family) 20 218
Trigance, Francesco (*c*. 1660-1737) 31 329
Trigance, Francesco (*fl* 1769) 31 329
Trigance, Gioacchino 31 329
Trigland, Cornelis 20 81
Triglyph Painter 13 536
triglyphs 11 790; 13 377, *378*, 379, 393, 398; 23 478, 481; 31 330*
trigonolites 9 114, *114*; 14 54
Trigt, Hendrik Albert van 22 848
Triik, Nikolai 10 539; 33 566
Trijpweverij 22 899
Triki, Gouider 31 426
Trikkala 16 266
  congregational mosque 16 222
Trikomo, Panagia 8 358, 359; 9 580
trilithons 31 330*
Triller, Erich 30 99
Triller, Ingrid 30 99
Trillo, Lorenzo de 13 731
Trillo, Pero de 25 291
Trim Castle (Co. Meath) 16 22
Trimontium *see* NEWSTEAD
Trinacria *see* SICILY
Trincanato, Egle Renato 27 686
Trincomalee 29 *440*, 448, 452
  fortress 29 452
Tringalvadi, Jaina cave temples 15 315
Trinh Cung 32 483
Trinidad (Bolivia) 4 *255*, 270
Trinidad (Cuba) 8 228, *228*, 236
Trinidad, La *see* LA TRINIDAD
Trinidad and Tobago 2 144; 5 *745*; 31 330–40*, *330*
  architecture 31 333–5*
  bowls 31 *338*
  carnivals 2 146, 147; 5 753, 788, *788*; 31 332, *332*
  ceramics 31 338–9*
  clubs (meeting places) 31 *334*
  collections 31 339–40*
  costumes 31 *332*, 332–3
  dealing 31 339
  education (art) 31 340*
  emblems 8 231
  embroidery 2 146
  exhibitions 5 746
  fringes 31 *332*, 332–3
  furniture 31 *337*, 337–8*
  gongs 31 331
  hats 31 *332*, 332–3
  headdresses 31 *332*
  Hilton Hotel 31 339
Trinidad and Tobago—cont.
  houses 31 334, 335
  interior decoration 31 *337*, 337–8*
  masks 31 332
  metalwork 2 146
  museums 31 339–40*
  musical instruments 31 331
  painting 2 149; 22 *138*; 31 335–6*, *336*
  patronage 31 339*
  postage stamps 25 328
  pottery 31 330–31
  sculpture 31 335–6*
  temples 5 *755*
  trade 31 338
  vases 31 *338*
  wire 31 333
  see also ANTILLES, LESSER
Trinidad Field Naturalists' Club 31 339
Trinidad Pedroza, José 25 321
Trinitarians 31 340–41*
Trinity College Apocalypse *see under* APOCALYPSES → individual manuscripts
Trinity Gospels *see under* GOSPEL BOOKS → individual manuscripts
Trinity of Turin, Master of the 20 775*
Trinquesse, Louis-Rolland 6 563; 31 341*
Trió 30 12, 13
Triolet, Elsa 2 279
Trip, Elias 31 341
Trip, Hendrick 32 586
Trip, Jacob 31 341
Trip, Louys 32 586
tripack processes *see under* PHOTOGRAPHY → processes
Tripartite Machzor *see under* MACHZORS → individual manuscripts
Tripe, Linnaeus 5 261; 31 342*
Tripitaka 18 250
triple arches *see under* ARCHES → types
triple cloth weaving *see under* WEAVING → types
tripods
  Byzantine 9 633
  China 7 86
  Etruscan 10 *626*, *627*
  Greece, ancient 13 *575*, 575–6
  Italy 10 *626*, *627*
  Rome, ancient 27 100
Tripole culture 31 545
tripoli 1 761
Tripoli (County of; Crusader State) 17 500–501
Tripoli (Lebanon) 9 *513*; 16 *104*; 17 501; 30 *180*; 31 342*
  architecture 16 208; 19 7
  St Leontios 9 539
Tripoli (Libya) 1 *376*; 16 *103*
  arch 27 45
  Archaeological Museum 19 324; 27 115
  Arch of Marcus Aurelius 19 323; 26 868, 920, 921; 31 350
  Cathedral of the Sacred Heart of Jesus 7 782; 19 324
  citadel *see* Archaeological Museum; Ethnographical Museum; Natural History Museum
  Ethnographical Museum 19 324
  al-Fatih University 19 324
  Libyan Arab Jamahiriyya Museum 19 324
  medina 19 324
  Natural History Museum 19 324
  paper 24 48
Tripolis (Greece)
  Museum 14 361
Tripolitania *see* LIBYA
Tripol'skaya, Ye. 2 895

Tripol'ye culture **27** 365
copper **25** 516
figurines **25** 512
fortifications **25** 503
houses **25** 501–2*
pottery **25** 514; **27** *366*
Trippel, Alexander **31** 342–3*
pupils **7** 211; **28** 42; **31** 27; **33** 623
works **30** 137
Trippenmeker, Heinrich *see* ALDEGREVER, HEINRICH
Trippet, Henri **11** 166
tripteral temples *see under* TEMPLES → types
Triptolemos Painter **13** 521; **32** 39, 61
Triptych of the Nativity **13** 166
Triptych of the Virgin of Khakhuli *see* KHAKHULI TRIPTYCH
triptychs *see under* ALTARPIECES → types
Tripurantakam **15** 538
Trique **21** 736
Triqueti, Henri-Joseph-François, Baron de **20** 124; **28** 139; **31** 345–6*
patrons and collectors **14** 148
works **23** 522; **31** *345*
Triquetti, Henry **22** 827
works **22** *827*
triradial vaults *see under* VAULTS (CEILING) → types
Triscorni, Agostino **32** 626
Triscorni, Paolo **23** 531
Trisong Detsen, King of Tibet (*reg* 755-94) **19** 293
Trissino, Giangiorgio **23** 862; **31** 346*; **32** 409, 547
Trissino, Pier Francesco **28** 30, 33
Trist, J. H. **14** 849
Tristán de Escamilla, Luis **29** 280; **31** 346–8*
patrons and collectors **5** 871; **27** 724
pupils **5** 553
teachers **13** 344
works **9** 110; **29** 280; **31** 89, *347*
Tristan de Hattonchatel **16** 852
Tristano, Bartolomeo **13** 293
Tristano, Giovanni **17** 510, 511; **26** 822
Tristram, E(rnest) W(illiam) **31** 348*
Triton **7** 576
Triton Painter **13** 513
Triton shells *see under* SHELLS → types
Tritto, Giacomo **23** 87
Tritton, Robert **7** 515
triumphal arches *see under* MONUMENTS → types
triumphal crosses *see* ROODS
Triumph of Death, Master of the **5** 124; **20** 775–6*; **24** 860; **28** 656
works **20** *775*
Triva, Antonio Domenico **22** 302, 308; **33** 276
Trivandrum **15** *294*; **31** 352*
fort **15** 541
Government Museum of Art and Natural History **15** 182
ivory **15** 696
Napier Museum **31** 352
Padmanabhasvami Temple **15** 399, 524
sculpture **15** 541
Sri Chitra Art Gallery **15** 183
trivets **6** 330; **11** 120
Trivikramamangalam Vishnu Temple **15** 523
Trivio, Drudus de *see* DRUDUS DE TRIVIO
Trivulzio, Agostino, Cardinal **8** 503
Trivulzio, Bianca **33** 625
Trivulzio, Gian Giacomo **29** 24; **31** 352*
architecture **21** 517
Trivulzio, Gian Giacomo—cont.
manuscripts **31** 449
paintings **21** 525
sculpture **19** 185
tapestries **4** 653; **16** 757; **21** 525
Trivulzio, Giorgio Pallavicino, Marchese *see* PALLAVICINO TRIVULZIO, GIORGIO, Marchese
Trivulzio knives **16** 742
Trivulzio *Madonna* **20** 312
Trnava **28** *848*; **31** 353–4*
chests **14** 905
Convent of the Poor Clares *see* West Slovak Museum
engravings **14** 899
Municipal Theatre **28** 850
painting **28** 852
prints **28** 852, 853
Town Hall **28** 850
University Church of St John the Baptist **10** 528; **14** 886; **28** 849, 855; **31** 353, *353*
altarpiece **14** 893
sculpture **14** 894
West Slovak Museum **28** 857; **31** 353
Trnava, Michal of *see* MICHAL OF TRNAVA
Trnka, Jiří **8** 393
Trnové Church **28** 852
Troad **13** *363*; **26** *876*; **31** 354–6*
beads **31** 355
bracelets **31** 355
collections **31** 355–6*
cups **31** *355*
earrings **31** 355, *376*
electrum **31** 355, *355*
gold **31** 355*, *376*
granite **26** 877
headdresses **31** *376*
jewellery **31** 354–5*
museums **31** 355–6*
necklaces **31** *376*
pins **31** 355
pottery **31** 354*
silver **31** 355*, *355*
see also ANATOLIA, ANCIENT; TURKEY
Trobriand Islands **23** 713, 735; **24** 64, *64*, 81
Trocchi, Giuseppe **16** 739
Trockel, Rosemarie **31** 356*
Troços **8** 436
Troedel, George, and Co. **29** 767
Trofamonti, Teofilo *see* BIGOT, TROPHIME
Troger, Paul **31** 356–8*; **32** 444
assistants **21** 541
collaboration **33** 629
patrons and collectors **11** 120
pupils **2** 876; **3** 777; **11** 120; **18** 162; **20** 855
works **2** 794, 795; **4** 695; **8** 392; **13** 888; **14** 900; **15** 139; **21** 84; **22** 297; **23** 381; **27** 665; **28** 852, 857; **31** *357*
Troger, Simon **12** 460; **31** 358*
Trogir **8** *174*; **31** 359*; **32** *158*
Cathedral of St Lawrence **8** 178; **26** 594; **31** 359*
Baptistery **1** 604; **8** 175
chapel of Blessed Giovanni Orsini **8** 175, 178
West Portal **8** 177
houses **8** 175
loggia **8** 175
St Barbara **8** 175
St John **23** *93*
sculpture **25** 839–40
Trogiranin, Blaž Jurjev **8** 178
Trogli, Giulio *see* TROILI, GIULIO
Troguéry **32** 280
Tróia
Bishop's Palace **26** 655
Cathedral **16** 626; **26** 580, 627
doors **9** 154; **23** 352
manuscripts **26** 665
pulpit **25** 723; **26** *627*
Troia, Marco di Pietro da *see* MARCO DI PIETRO DA TROIA
Troili, Giulio **30** 668; **31** 359–60*
Troili, Uno **30** 79
trois crayons, aux *see under* DRAWINGS → forms
Trois-Frères **11** *505*; **25** *470*, 475, 478, 480, 481, 484, 487; **31** 360–61*, 410
rock art **31** *360*
Troisi, Aloisio **31** 361
Troisi, Andrea **31** 361
Troisi, Carlo **31** 361
Troisi, Massimiliano **31** 361
Troisi, Pietro Paolo **31** 361
Trois Ilets, Musée de la Pagerie **2** 149
Trois Suisses **11** 584
Troitsko-Lykov, Church of the Trinity **27** 373
Trojan Embellished Jade **16** IV
Trojanowski, Edward **24** 441
Trojer, Ingenuin Albuin *see* EGGER-LIENZ, ALBIN
Trökes, Heinz **3** 803; **31** 361*
Trokhimenko, K. **31** 559
Troll, Johann Heinrich **20** 915
Trolle, Anne-Marie **7** 807
Trolle-Bonde, Gustaf, Count **31** 362*
Trollope, Anthony **4** 363, 885; **14** 680; **21** 602
Trollope, Messrs **7** 406; **8** 831; **32** 865
Trombadori, Francesco **9** 135; **26** 776
Trombarro, Giacomo **2** 417
Trombetta *see* TROMETTA
Trometta **31** 362*
Tromp, Cornelis **21** *510*; **32** 143
trompe l'oeil **15** 135, 140–41*; **17** 303
Belgium **11** 440
England **32** *359*
France **8** 525; **11** *603*; **15** 140; **27** 56; **29** 668
Germany **23** *8*
Greece, ancient **13** 389; **22** 160
Italy **10** 740; **15** IV; **29** 668; **31** *900*
Mexico **10** 737
Netherlands, the **11** 440; **14** *740*; **29** 668
Rome, ancient **22** *159*; **27** 48, *48*, 50, 53, *53*; **29** 665
Spain **29** 668
Sweden **30** 89
United States of America **10** 737; **15** *141*; **24** *555*; **29** 669; **31** 603
see also PAINTING → types → *quadratura*
Trompes, Jan de **8** 552
Tromsø Museum **23** 243
Tronchin, François **8** 210; **12** 277; **19** 436; **31** 362–3*
Tronchón **29** 332
Trøndelag **23** 240
Austerått Palace **23** 220
Trondheim **23** *218*, 219; **31** 363–5*
Archbishop's Palace **23** 219, 224, 231; **31** 363
cathedral school **23** 221
Christ Church Cathedral **13** 50; **22** 217; **23** 217, 219, 229; **26** 593; **31** 363–4*
ballflower **3** 121
sculpture **13** 102; **23** 228, 230; **26** 639; **31** *364*, 365*
crosses **32** 523
Kunstakademi **23** 244
Kunstskole **23** 244
marks **23** 236
metalwork **23** 236
Nordenfjeldske Kunstindustrimuseum **23** 239, 243
Norges Tekniske Høgskole **23** 222, 244
Trondheim—cont.
Norges Tekniske Universitetsbibliotek **23** 244
paintings **23** 223
pottery **23** 234
sculpture **13** 119; **26** 639
Stiftsgård **23** 221, 231
Sverresborg fortress **23** 219
Trondheims Kunstforening **23** 243
wood-carvings **32** 517, 525
tronie see under PORTRAITS → types
tronies **31** 365*
Trono, Niccolò, Doge of Venice (*reg* 1471-3) **7** 537
Troost, Cornelis **22** 846; **25** 49; **31** 365–7*
pupils **5** 322; **30** 297
reproductive prints by others **14** 795
teachers **4** 374
works **1** 807; **7** 787; **11** 448; **21** 416; **31** *366*, *367*
Troost, Elisabeth **31** 365
Troost, Gerdy **22** 710; **31** 368
Troost, Paul Ludwig **31** 367–8*
works **12** 379, 418; **22** 304, 710, *710*, 711
Troost, Sara **31** 365
Troostenberghe, Nicolaas van **3** 609
Troost van Groenendoelen, Jan Hendrik **6** 88
Troostwijk, Wouter Johannes van **20** 400; **22** 847; **31** 368*
teachers **2** 25
works **4** 40; **22** 847, *848*
trophies **31** 368–9*
Greece, ancient **31** 368–9
Italy **31** *369*
Rome, ancient **9** 31; **31** 369, *369*
Trophonios **13** 389
Tropinin, V., and the Moscow Artists of his Time, Museum of *see under* MOSCOW → museums
Tropinin, Vasily (Andreyevich) **22** 178; **27** 442, 579; **31** 369–70*
Tropnina, Nina (Ivanovna) **27** 422
Tropon **25** 347
Troppa, Gerolamo **31** 370*
Troppau, Johann von *see* JAN OF OPAVA
Trosa **30** 111
Troschel, Hans **29** 762; **31** 370–71*
Troschel, Jakob **31** 370
Troschel, Peter Paul **14** 467; **24** 588; **31** 370, 371*
Troso **15** 792
Trost, Henry Charles **7** 619
Trost, Melchior **33** 113
Trost, Ottó *see* KOROKNYAI, OTTÓ
Trotsche, Carl **27** 720
Trotsky, Leon **15** 99; **30** 21; **31** 371*
Trotsky, Noy **27** 378; **31** 371–2*
collaboration **23** 391
pupils **29** 388
works **27** 380, 578
Trotter, William **9** 727; **28** 248, 253–4
Trotti, Giovanni Battista **18** 679; **23** 320; **31** 372*
Trotton, St George **4** 693
brass of Thomas, Lord Camoys **13** 84
Trou, Henri **27** 536
Trou, Henri-Charles **11** 607; **23** 512; **27** 536
Trou, Henri-François **27** 537
Trouard, Louis **31** 372
Trouard, Louis-François **9** 418; **23** 510; **24** 176; **31** 372–3*
Troubadours **11** 665
Troubadour style **2** 848; **26** 334, 738; **31** 373–4*
frames **11** *414*
Troubadour style—cont.
painting **4** *322*; **13** *309*; **26** *265*
Troubetskoy, Gigi **25** *894*
Troubetskoy, Piero **25** *894*
Troubetskoy villa **25** 894
Troubetzkoy, Paolo **5** 127; **16** 706; **20** 849; **25** *894*; **27** 442; **29** 575; **30** 265, 464; **31** 374*
groups and movements **28** 34
pupils **12** 892
works **7** 690
Troubetzkoy, Peter, Prince **28** 705
Troughton & Young **25** 835
trough vaults *see under* VAULTS (CEILING) → types
Trouille, Clovis **7** 842; **30** 21
Troup, F(rancis) W(illiam) **29** 650; **31** 375*
Troup, George **23** 55
works **23** *55*
trousers **9** 290
Africa **1** 348
Byzantine **9** 640
China **7** 74, 144
England **9** 286
Greece **9** 640
Hausa **1** 348
Iran **16** 465, 466
Islamic **16** 460, 461, 462, 465, 466
Ottoman **16** 460, 461, 462
Rome, ancient **9** 251
Turkey **16** 460, 461, 462
Yoruba **1** 348
Troussures **32** 278, 280
Trouvain, Antoine **28** 751
Trouvé, Georges **5** 464
Trouville Pier **24** 747
Trova, Ernest **31** 375*
Trowell, Margaret **1** 432; **31** 528
Troy **1** *821*, 839, *849*, 892; **2** 299, 300; **13** *362*, *363*; **21** 46; **23** 806; **31** 354, 356, 375–7*, 456
architecture **1** 826, 830, 831
cups **31** *355*
excavations **28** 114
figurines **13** 581
gold **1** 874
jewellery **1** 825, 875; **31** 354, 355
looms **1** 880
metalwork **1** 824, 825; **31** 355
pottery **1** 826, 837; **13** 479; **14** 333; **31** 354
sculpture **1** 832
silver **1** 834
statuettes **29** 567
Temple of Athena **13** 405
terracottas **27** 111
trade **14** 335
weapons **1** 834
Troy, Antoine de **31** 377, 378
Troy, François de **9** 8; **31** 378–9*
assistants **9** 301; **26** 385
patrons and collectors **5** 380
pupils **3** 639; **7** 461; **13** 666; **19** 140; **31** 379
reproductions in tapestry **12** 830
reproductive prints by others **9** 296; **19** 144; **28** 756
works **9** 280, *280*; **31** *378*
Troy, Jean-Baptiste (*fl* 1740s) **27** 659
Troy, Jean-Baptiste de (*fl* 1822) **31** 380
Troy, Jean de **31** 377
Troy, Jean-François de **3** 203; **26** 842; **31** 379–80*
collaboration **6** 121; **10** 842
patrons and collectors **2** 154; **4** 513; **14** 395; **24** 256; **27** 524
pupils **1** 105; **8** 499; **9** 370; **10** 843; **17** 684; **19** 543, 796; **24** 772; **31** 852
reproductions in tapestry **22** 726
reproductive prints by others **3** 463; **7** 495; **8** 544; **12** 208
teachers **31** 379
works **11** 407, 459, 538, 577, 594; **23** 381; **24** 135; **30** XIV1; **31** 378, *380*, 684

Troya, Rafael 9 713; 31 380*
Troyan 5 *144*, 158
 Monastery 5 154
  church 5 148, 156
Troye, Edward 2 106; 29 425; 31 380–81*
Troyekurov (family) 22 170
Troyen, Rombout van 31 381*
Troyer, Ferdinand Julio, Count 23 854
Troyes 11 *504*; 31 381–6*
 Cathedral of SS Peter and Paul 6 414; 11 510, 511; 13 42, 59, 61; 22 217; 26 44, 45; 31 383–4*, *383*
  caskets 5 917
  choir 13 40
  collections 7 372
  library 19 313
  silver 11 618
  stained glass 13 141, 180; 26 702; 31 384–5*
  textiles 11 647
  tracing floor 31 275
 Hôtel Dieu *see* museums → Musée de l'Hôtel Dieu
 Hôtel Jean de Mauroy *see* museums → Musée de l'Outil
 Hôtel de Vauluisant *see* museums → Musée Historique de Troyes et de la Champagne
 museums
  Musée d'Art Moderne 19 282; 31 382
  Musée des Beaux-Arts et d'Archéologie 31 382
  Musée de la Bonneterie *see under* Musée Historique de Troyes et de la Champagne
  Musée Historique de Troyes et de la Champagne 31 381, 382
   Musée de la Bonneterie 31 382
  Musée de l'Hôtel Dieu 31 381
  Musée de l'Outil 31 381
 painting 31 382
 Ste Madeleine 11 154; 13 60, 79; 31 *382*
 St Jean-au-Marché 11 154, 155
 St Nicolas 11 154
 St Nizier 11 154
 St Urbain 11 153, 510; 13 42, 43; 22 219, 220; 26 45; 31 *385*, 385–6*
  stained glass 13 136, *136*, 181, 672; 29 502
 sculpture 13 79; 31 382
 silk 11 644, 645
 silver 11 616
 stained glass 31 381–2
Troyes, Chrétien de *see* CHRÉTIEN DE TROYES
Troyo, Ramon Rojas, *see* ROJAS TROYO, RAMON
Troyon, Constant 31 386–7*
 assistants 4 523
 groups and movements 3 212; 26 54
 patrons and collectors 5 57; 6 516; 8 618; 18 869; 21 90; 32 708
 pupils 3 684
 reproductive prints by others 18 658
 works 2 106; 31 *387*
Tršar, Drago 28 862; 31 387*
Trsteno 12 114
Trubert, Georges 2 114, 115; 31 387–8*
 works 2 115; 20 657, 707; 31 *388*
Trubetskoy, Nikita, Prince 31 544
Trubetskoy, Pavel, Prince *see* TROUBETZKOY, PAOLO
Trubillio, Giovanni 28 109
Trübner, (Heinrich) Wilhelm 17 818; 28 170; 31 389*
 dealers 5 924
 groups and movements 3 511; 12 394; 24 591; 26 56; 28 341, 342
Trübner, (Heinrich) Wilhelm—cont.
 pupils 7 855
 works 11 *464*
Trubshaw, Charles 31 389
Trubshaw, Charles Cope 31 389*
Trubshaw, James (1746-1808) 31 389
Trubshaw, James (1777-1853) 31 389*
Trubshaw, James (*b* 1817) 31 389*
Trubshaw, John 31 389*
Trubshaw, Richard 31 389*
Trubshaw, Thomas (*fl* 1632) 31 389*
Trubshaw, Thomas (1802-42) 31 389*
Trubshaw, Wolstan Vyvyan 31 389
Trubshawe, James 4 288, 289
Trubuljak, Goran 8 179
Trubus 15 808
Trucco, Giacomo Matte' *see* MATTE' TRUCCO, GIACOMO
Truchsess, Georg, Abbot of Wetzenhausen 28 60
Truchsess von Waldberg, Otto, Cardinal 4 401; 12 495; 30 800
Truchy, L. 14 520
Trudaine de la Sablière, Charles-Michel 31 390
Trudaine de Montigny, Charles-Louis 31 390
Trudaine de Montigny, Daniel-Charles 24 174; 31 390
 works 26 *347*
Trudaine de Montigny, Jean-Charles-Philibert 31 390
Trudeau, Garry 7 649; 27 872
True, Clarence 31 855
Trueblood, Wilbur T. 9 502
True Pure Land Buddhism *see* BUDDHISM → sects → Jōdo Shin
true script *see* SCRIPTS → types → regular
True View Style 18 314
Truex, Van Day 30 867
Trufemondi *see* BIGOT, TROPHIME
Trugi, Francesco 28 744
Truikys, Liudas 19 499
Trujillo (Honduras) 14 711, *711*, 712, 714
 Cathedral 14 712
 Museo Historico 14 716
Trujillo (Peru) 24 *498*; 31 721
 architecture 24 504
 Cathedral 24 502
 education (art) 24 517
 Universidad Nacional de la Libertad 24 516
Trujillo (Venezuela) 32 177, 178
Trujillo, Alejandro González *see* GONZÁLEZ TRUJILLO, ALEJANDRO
Trujillo, E. 32 568
Trujillo, Guillermo 23 905; 31 390*
Truk *see* CHUUK
Trukhmensky, Afanasy 31 762
Trull, All Saints 25 725
trulli 20 570; 32 *292*, 292
Trumbauer, Horace 19 319; 23 32; 24 598; 31 390*
Trumble & Sons 17 640
Trumbull, Alice (Bradford) *see* MASON, ALICE (BRADFORD) TRUMBULL
Trumbull, John 31 391–2*, 662
 patrons and collectors 12 645; 14 203; 32 753
 personal collection 31 666
 pupils 4 882; 10 145
 reproductive prints by others 7 410; 9 418; 28 558
 teachers 33 92
 works 14 586; 31 *392*, 600, 601
Trumbull Gallery *see under* NEW HAVEN (CT) → Yale University
trumeau (i) (pier) *see under* PIERS (ii) (MASONRY) → types
trumeau (ii) (mirrors) *see under* MIRRORS → types
Trummel, Antoine 11 356
trumpets 22 375
 historical and regional traditions
  Africa 1 292
  Buddhism 28 *582*; 30 *844*
  Cambodia 5 509
  Maya 21 260
  Mesoamerica, Pre-Columbian 21 257*, 260
  Olmec 21 260
  South America, Pre-Columbian 29 217
  Tibet 28 *582*; 30 844, *844*
 materials
  copper 30 *844*
  hardstones 28 *582*
  horn 14 763
  ivory 1 292
  shells 21 257, 260; 28 *582*; 29 217
 techniques
  gilding 30 *844*
Trumpington 14 406
Trümpy, Ivo 12 5
Trunah, Ešetē 10 574
Trunch (Norfolk), St Botolph font 11 254, *254*
Trundholm 25 *470*, 527
 sculpture 25 *527*
Trung Dau 6 426
trunks 6 560
trunnions 21 547
Truphémus, Jean 19 848
Trupin, Johan 7 190
Truppe, Karl 22 711
Truro Methodist Church (Cornwall; UK) 21 347
Truro (MA; USA) 28 536
Truşeşti 30 434
Trushevichi 31 557
Trusler, John 15 57
truss bridges *see under* BRIDGES → types
Trussed Concrete Steel Company 33 204
trussed roofs *see under* ROOFS → types
trusses 32 472
Trusttum, Philip 7 211
Trutat, Félix 8 891; 25 658
Trutnieŭ, Jan 3 529
Trutovsky, Konstantin A. 31 559
Tryavna 5 156, 157, 158
 Church of the Holy Archangels 5 148; 31 393
Tryavna school 31 393*
Tryde Church 26 639, 646
Tryer, Nicholas 19 609
tryfflers 24 579
Tryggvadóttir, Nína 4 807; 15 71; 31 393*
Tryon, Dwight W(illiam) 11 748; 31 141, 393*
Trysa, Heroön 13 458; 20 863
Trzebnica Abbey Church 4 782; 25 *92*, 95, 119; 31 394–5*
 manuscripts 25 101
 St Hedwig's Chapel 25 95, 110; 31 394
 sculpture 25 110; 31 *394*, 395
 tomb of Conrad von Feuchtwangen 31 395
 tomb of Henry I, Prince of Silesia 31 395
Trzemeszno 25 126
 Abbey Church 13 162; 25 95; 26 687
Tsaamba 33 482
Tsageri 12 328
Ts'ai, Chao, Marquis of *see* CAI, ZHAO, Marquis of
Tsai, Wen-Ying 18 63
Ts'ai Ching *see* CAI JING
Tsai-ch'un, Prince *see* TONGZHI, Emperor
Ts'ai Hsiang *see* CAI XIANG
Tsaile (AZ), Navajo Community College 22 568, 670
Ts'ai Lun *see* CAI LUN
Ts'ai Yü *see* CAI YU
Ts'ai Yüan-p'ei *see* CAI YUANPEI
Ts'ai Yung *see* CAI YONG
Tsalenjikha 12 *317*, 330
 Church of the Saviour 9 586; 12 324, *324*
Tsamba (*fl* 1930s) 11 879
Tsangarides, Odysseus 8 364, 894
Ts'ang Chieh *see* CANG JIE
Tsangli 25 500
Tsangli houses *see under* HOUSES → types
Tsan Tai Uk 14 720
Tsantels, Jacob 2 199
Tsanyuv, Zakhari 31 393
Ts'ao Chao *see* CAO ZHAO
Ts'ao Chih-pai *see* CAO ZHIBAI
Ts'ao Pa *see* CAO BA
Ts'ao Pu-hsing *see* CAO BUXING
Ts'ao Tsai-k'uei *see* CAO ZAIKUI
Ts'ao Ts'ao *see* CAO CAO
Ts'ao Yüan-chung *see* CAO YUANZHONG
Tsapakang *see* TSAPARANG
Tsaparang 30 *806*; 31 395*
 castle 21 592
 paintings 15 561
Tsarevo *see* SARAY BERKE
Tsaritsin *see* VOLGOGRAD
Tsaritsin Grad *see* CARIČIN GRAD
Tsaritsyno Palace 3 433; 22 171; 27 377
 bridge 27 *376*
Tsarouhis, Yannis 31 395–6*
 works 13 353, *353*
Tsarparang, Red Chapel 30 833
Tsarskoye Selo *see* PUSHKIN
Tsarsky Kurgan 4 110
Tsas, Hendrik 5 49
Tsa-sah-wee-eh *see* HARDIN, HELEN
Tsatoke, Monroe 22 595
Tsayi 30 418, 419, 420
Tsayutitsa 22 608
Tschachtlan, Bendicht 30 130
Tschaggeny, Charles 32 241
Tschaggeny, Edmond 32 241
Tscharner, Johann (Wilhelm Jan) von 31 396*
Tschering, David 25 106
Tscherny, George 25 353
Tscherte, Hans 2 780
Tschichold, Jan 25 350; 31 396*, 497–8
Tschinkel, Augustin 13 727
Tschirnhaus, Ehrenfried Walther von 4 493; 12 440; 21 63
Tschudi, Hugo von 3 801; 19 112; 22 304; 31 397*
 groups and movements 28 342
Tschumi, Bernard 8 610; 11 528; 24 132; 31 397–8*
Tschumi, Jean 18 874
Tschumi, Otto 30 135
Tschusiya, Tilsa 31 398*
Tselkov, Oleg 8 10; 27 397
Tseng, I, Marquis of *see* ZENG, YI, Marquis of
Tseng Ching *see* ZENG JING
Ts'eng Hsi *see* CENG XI
Tseng Huo-chüeh *see* ZENG HUOJUE
Ts'eng I *see* CENG YI
Tseng Kung-liang *see* ZENG GONGLIANG
Tseng Yuho Ecke 7 157
Tseraerts, Jacob 5 49
Tsereteli, Zurab (Konstantinovich) 12 327; 31 398*
Tsethang 30 846
Tse Tsan *see* VELARDE, PABLITA
T-shaped iwans *see under* IWANS → types
Tshewang Namgyel, Ruler of Basgo (*reg* 16th cent.) 15 311
Tshuma, Zephania 33 679
Tshurphu 5 105
Tsibasov, D. 11 82
Tsichweiler, Robert 12 431
Tsihnahjinnie, Andy 22 595
Tsikalario 13 396
Tsimmerman, A. F. 19 332
Tsimshian 22 547, 564, 580, 620, 632, 640, 645, 657, 668; 28 816
 masks 22 *558*, *664*
Tsingos, Thanos 13 349; 31 398–9*
Tsionglinsky, Yan 2 122; 13 862; 20 850; 32 381
Tsireh, Awa *see* ROYBAL, ALFONSO
Tsitsernavank', basilica 2 425
Tsivoloa 20 36
Tsiv'yan, Alexandr S. 19 13
Tskarostavi Gospels *see under* GOSPEL BOOKS → individual manuscripts
Tskhaltubo 12 320
Ts'o, King of Chung-shan *see* CUO, King of Zhongshan
Tsodilo Hills 4 489
Tsoede 23 302
Tsoghakert, basilica 2 425
Tsogo 1 396; 11 878
Tsokev, Khristo 5 154
Tsolov, Dimiter 8 900; 32 78
Tsonev, Kiril 5 163; 23 16; 31 399*
Tsonga 22 243; 33 723, 724
 dress 29 104
 headrests 1 416–17
 pottery 1 418
 sculpture 1 257, *415*
 staffs 1 417
 wood-carvings 1 414, 416, 417
Tsonga-Shangane 1 415, 416, 419
Tsong Khapa 12 36
Tsonyuv, Simeon 31 393
Tsonyuv, Vitan 31 393
Tsooru 10 *536*
 EKE (Estonian Collective Farm Administrative Building) 10 538
Tso Pai *see* ZUO BAI
Tsotso 1 403
Tsou Che *see* ZOU ZHE
Tsou I-kuei *see* ZOU YIGUI
Tsountas, Christos 1 795; 8 323, 900; 22 698; 28 491; 29 367
T-Square Club 2 572
Tsromi 12 323
 church 12 319
Tsrviz 2 426
Tsubaki Chinzan 17 191
Tsuboi, Shōgorō 17 426
Tsuboi, Yoshikatsu 30 289
Tsuboya *see under* NAHA
tsuchibina *see under* DOLLS → types
Tsuchida, Bakusen 17 201, 202; 31 399*
Tsuchida, Hiromi 31 399*
Tsuchida Sōtaku 14 703, 704
Tsuchiya, Tilsa 24 511; 33 317
Tsuchiya Ichiraku 17 401
Tsuda, Seifū 17 205; 18 96
Tsuda Sōgyū 15 108; 23 347
Tsuda Sōtatsu 4 103
Tsugaru 17 355
tsugarunuri *see* LACQUER → types → marbled *urushi*
Tsuga Teishō 17 410
Tsuguharu Foujita *see* FOUJITA, TSUGOUHARU
Tsuguji Fujita *see* FUJITA, TSUGUJI
Ts'ui Po *see* CUI BO
Ts'ui Yen-shan *see* CUI YANSHAN
Ts'ui Yüan *see* CUI YUAN
Tsuji 17 401
Tsuji, Kakō 17 201
Tsuji, Kyō 17 267
Tsuji, Seimei 17 267
Tsuji, Shindō 31 399–400*

Tsuji Yojirō 17 323; 28 412
Tsukamoto, Kaiji 17 266
Tsukamoto, Seijiro 17 267
Tsukamoto Kaisuke 17 378
Tsukatani Sawaemon 18 537
Tsuki Katsura see under HŌFU
Tsukioka, Kogyo 17 293
Tsukioka Settei 17 177; 23 594
Tsukioka Yoshitoshi 17 177, 200, 290, 293; 31 400–401*
Tsukuba Civic Centre 1 737; 16 564; 17 92
Tsumago 17 83, 97
Tsumaki, Yorinako 3 176; 17 87
Tsunayoshi Tokugawa see TOKUGAWA TSUNAYOSHI, Shogun
Tsuneji Ueda see UEDA, TSUNEJI
Tsunekichi Kaji see KAJI TSUNEKICHI
Tsune Nakamura see NAKAMURA, TSUNE
Tsunenobu see KANŌ TSUNENOBU
Tsunetada see SESONJI TSUNETADA
Tsunetoki Hōjō see HŌJŌ TSUNETOKI, Shogunal Regent
Tsunetomi Kitano see KITANO, TSUNETOMI
Tsuneyuki Kawamata see KAWAMATA TSUNEYUKI
Tsung Ping see ZONG BING
Tsurayuki, Ki no see KI NO TSURAYUKI
Tsurkvishte Church 5 146
Tsurphu 30 818
Tsurugi Shrine 17 320
Tsuru-jo Inagaki see INAGAKI TSURU-JO
Tsuruoka 17 357
Tsuruoka, Masao 17 207; 20 834
Tsuruya, Kokei 17 296
Tsuruzawa Tangei 20 522; 31 764
Tsuruzō Ishii see ISHII, TSURUZŌ
Tsūryū Inaba see INABA TSŪRYŪ
Tsusaka, Jun 11 811
Tsutaya Jūzaburō 17 284; 18 91; 31 203, 204
Tsutsui Sadatsugu 15 108
Tsutsumi 17 373
Tsutsumi kiln 17 258
Tsutsumi pottery see under POTTERY → wares
Tsutsumi Tōrin 17 846
Tsuyazaki-machi 17 59
tsuyazuri 17 276
Tsvetayev, Ivan (Vladimirovich) 18 116; 27 440; 31 401*
Tsvetkov, I. S. 27 439, 441
Tsvetkov, M. Ye. 22 178
Tswana 4 489
  architecture 1 311, 414
  beadwork 1 419
  headrests 1 417
  painting 1 313; 4 489
  sculpture 1 415
  spoons 1 417
  wood-carvings 1 415
Tswett, Mikhail Semenovich 30 401
Tsybikova, Al'bina 27 436
Tsyzkiewicz Painter 13 520
Ttuksom Island 18 283
Tuaillon, Louis 1 763; 12 407; 20 405; 31 401–2*
Tuam 16 5, 19; 31 402–3*
  Cathedral 31 402, 403
  sculpture 26 618
Tuamotu Islands 23 711; 31 403–4*
Tuan-fang see DUANFANG
Tuang 1 313
Tuan Yü-tsai see DUAN YUCAI
Tua Pek Kong Temple 20 166
Tuareg 1 246; 11 829; 23 127; 31 404–7*
  amulets 31 406
  architecture 1 305
  basketwork 31 407*
Tuareg—cont.
  collections 31 404
  craftsmen and artists 1 246
  dress 16 457
  houses 1 306
  jewellery 16 532; 23 127; 31 405–6*
  keys 31 405
  leather 1 299; 23 128; 31 406, 406–7*
  locks 31 405
  mats 31 407
  metalwork 31 405*, 405
  metalworkers 1 286
  palanquins 31 407
  poles 1 306
  saddle-bags 31 406
  saddles 31 407
  stone 1 305
  tents 1 307
  trade 1 251
  veils 1 349
  wood 23 127; 31 407*
Tubatulabal 22 659
Tubbs, H. A. 27 608
Tubbs, Ralph 1 736
tub chairs see under CHAIRS → types
Tubertini, Giuseppe 4 273; 31 180
tubes 29 189
Tubeuf, Jacques 19 145
Tubi, Jean (-Baptiste) see TUBY, JEAN (-BAPTISTE)
Tubières de Grimoard de Pestels de Levis, Anne-Claude-Philippe de see CAYLUS, Comte de
Tübingen 25 545
  Ägyptologisches Institut der Universität 10 93
  Rathaus 33 711
  Schloss Hohentübingen 8 541
  Stiftskirche 12 369
Tübingen, Hans von see HANS VON TÜBINGEN
Tubini, Antonio 1 572
Tübke, Werner 19 112; 31 408*
Tuboeuf, Jacques 6 434
Tubre 26 656
Tubuai Islands see AUSTRAL ISLANDS
tubular steel 10 136
  historical and regional traditions
    Czech Republic 8 402
    Germany 3 402; 12 428
    Spain 29 321
  uses
    chairs 3 402; 6 391; 12 428
    furniture 7 241; 8 402; 29 321; 30 755
    tables 30 218
tubuli 26 871
Tuby, Jean (-Baptiste) (1635-1700) 11 559; 12 832; 31 408–9*
  collaboration 8 93, 94; 11 559; 19 96; 26 91
  patrons and collectors 4 551
  works 7 546; 8 94; 11 344, 344; 12 121; 18 902; 29 571
Tuby, Jean (-Baptiste) (1669-1735) 31 409
Tuca, José 6 595
Tucci, Biagio d'Antonio see BIAGIO D'ANTONIO (TUCCI)
Tucci, Giuseppe 5 308; 30 832, 848, 849; 31 409*
  personal collection 30 849
Tuc d'Audoubert 11 505; 25 470, 477; 26 133; 31 409–10*
  sculpture 25 476
Tu-ch'an see DOKUTAN
Tuch el-Karamus 13 568, 569
Tucher (family) 3 70; 9 432; 16 900; 17 711
Tucher, Anton, II 23 316; 29 729
Tucher, Lorenz 18 511, 511
Tucher Altarpiece, Master of the 20 776*; 23 308
Tu Chin see DU JIN
Tuchkov, A. A. 27 439
Tucholsky, Kurt 27 868
Tuck, Raphael 31 260, 262
Tückelhausen 5 895
Tucker, Albert (Lee) 2 749; 14 493; 31 410*
Tucker, Dudley 28 692
Tucker, Sixtus 14 573
Tucker, Thomas 31 411
Tucker, Tudor St George 11 363
Tucker, William (b 1935) 1 80; 7 697; 10 268; 16 58; 31 411*
Tucker, William Ellis (1800-32) 10 852; 31 411, 637
Tucker China Factory 10 852; 31 411*
Tucker & Hemphill 31 411
Tucker & Hulme 31 411
Tuckerman, Henry T(heodore) 31 411*
Tuckson, Tony 1 67; 20 419; 31 411–12*
Tucson (AZ)
  Arizona State Museum 22 678
  S Xavier del Bac 29 842; 31 589
  University of Arizona
    Center for Creative Photography 2 368; 29 60
    Southwest Indian Art Project 22 596, 677
Tuculescu, Ion 26 716; 31 412*
Tucumán 2 392, 393, 394; 7 606
  Cathedral 2 396
  weaving 2 403
Túcume 29 174
Tuda-i Kalon 6 271
Tudang see CHŎN-KI
Tude see TÚY
Tudela 16 412; 17 561; 26 605
  manuscripts 4 16
Tudela, Martín Gaztelu de see GAZTELU DE TUDELA, MARTÍN
Tudeley (Kent), All Saints 29 508
Tudhaliya IV (reg c. 1260-1230 BC) 2 661; 14 592; 33 513–14
Tudor (House of) 31 412*
Tudor, Catherine Howard, Queen of England see CATHERINE HOWARD, Queen of England
Tudor, Catherine of Aragon, Queen of England see CATHERINE OF ARAGON, Queen of England
Tudor, Catherine Parr, Queen of England see CATHERINE PARR, Queen of England
Tudor, David 5 381; 18 809; 24 407; 29 97, 98
Tudor, Edward VI, King of England see EDWARD VI, King of England
Tudor, Elizabeth I, Queen of England see ELIZABETH I, Queen of England
Tudor, Henry VII see HENRY VII, King of England
Tudor, Henry VIII, King of England see HENRY VIII, King of England
Tudor, Joseph 16 14
Tudor, Mary I, Queen of England see MARY I, Queen of England
Tudoran, Radu 3 88
Tudor arches see under ARCHES → types
Tudor green wares see under POTTERY → wares
Tudor-Hart, (Ernest) Percyval 5 531; 19 878; 27 360; 30 173
Tudosca, Princess 26 721
Tudot, Edmond 25 615
Tudric 10 344; 19 311
Tu Duc 32 476
  tomb 32 475
Tuduk, Teodor 16 546
Tuekta 24 297
Tuer, Andrew White 33 361
Tuerlinckx, Joseph 12 230
tufa
  historical and regional traditions
    Bali (Indonesia) 15 786, 787; 27 831
    Etruscan 10 602
    Greece, ancient 13 387
    Indonesia 15 786, 787
    Islamic 16 269
    Netherlands, the 4 778
    Rome, ancient 26 874; 27 9
    Turkey 16 269
  uses
    architecture 4 778; 16 269; 26 874
    relief sculpture 15 786
    sarcophagi 27 831
    sculpture 15 787; 27 9
Tüfel (family) 30 136
Tufino, Nitza 18 833
Tufiño, Rafael 18 833; 25 702; 26 426; 31 415*
  teachers 18 832
Tufton, Sackville, 8th Earl of Thanet 33 220
Tu Fu see DU FU
Tuganov, Makharbek 27 433
Tugendenkasten see under CHESTS → types
Tugendkhol'd, Yakov (Aleksandrovich) 27 444; 31 416*
Tŭggok see YI IN-NO
Tughluq 8 672; 31 416*
  see also:
    FIRUZ SHAH, Sultan
    GHIYATH AL-DIN TUGHLUQ, Sultan
    MALIK IBRAHIM
    MUHAMMAD IBN TUGHLUQ, Sultan
Tughluqabad see under DELHI
tughras 14 428; 16 135, 514; 31 416–17*
Tugny, Joseph-Antoine Crozat, Marquis de 8 209
Tugwell (family) 3 372
Tuhipua, Teve 23 737
Tui see TÚY
Tuitlán see LA QUEMADA
Tukano 4 707; 7 602, 605
Tuke, Brian 31 417–18*
Tuke, George 31 417
Tuke, Henry Scott 23 26; 31 418*
Tuke, Murray 22 810
Tuke, William 2 658
Tuki (family) 9 676
Tukket 6 379
Tukolor 28 404
Tukulti-Ninurta I (reg 1243-1207 BC) 1 885; 2 637, 639; 17 826; 21 274, 286, 296, 304
Tukulti-Ninurta II 30 492
Tukums 18 847
  Municipal Art Gallery
Tukuna 4 706, 707, 724
Tula (Mexico) 21 186, 193, 200-201, 202–3, 246, 372; 31 97, 418–19*
  architecture 21 211
  ballcourts 3 118
  brick 4 796
  Burnt Palace 23 825
  chacmook 28 640
  coatepantli 7 481, 481
  houses 21 208
  joinery 5 408
  lintels 9 166
  pottery 21 239
  Pyramid B 21 222
  reliefs 21 188
  religion 21 186
  sculpture 21 217, 222–3
  skull racks 31 505
  stucco 29 829
  talud-tablero 30 280
  Temple B 21 211, 211
  Temple of Quetzalcóatl see Temple B
Tula (Mexico)—cont.
  Temple of Tlahuizcalpantecuhtli 5 408, 409; 21 246
  Tula Grande 31 98–9, 418–19*, 419
    Palacio Quemado 31 98–9
    Pyramid B 31 99, 99
Tula (Nigeria) 1 328
  clay 1 381
  pots 1 381
Tula (Russia) 27 387; 31 719
  fireplaces 27 407
  furniture 27 407
  metalwork 27 424, 424
  steel 16 61
Tulasidasa 15 227
Tulbagh 29 105
  law courts 18 887
Tulepbayev, Erbolat 17 867
Tules, Semyon 28 567
tulips 12 76–7, 85
tulip-wood 11 596; 25 307; 26 84
Tulles, Pallister & McDonald 5 578
Tulle theatre 26 480
Tullgarn 30 89
Tulln, Egon Schiele Gesellschaft 2 370
Tullstorp 32 522
Tully, Kivas 29 435
Tullynally Castle (Co. Westmeath) 16 27
Tulmaythah see PTOLEMAIS
Tu Long 7 37
Tulp, Nicolaes 22 902
Tulsa (OK)
  Philbrook Art Center 22 596, 678
  Thomas Gilcrease Institute of American History and Art 12 618
Tulsi 31 420
Tulsi Kalan 31 419–20*
Tulsi Khurd 31 420
Tul'taya 17 866
Tulul al-Shu'aiba 16 149
Tulul al-Ukhaydir 16 149
Tulum 20 882; 21 372; 23 826; 31 420–21*
  architecture 20 884
  fortifications 21 598, 598
  Temple of the Frescoes 31 420
  temples 28 640
  wall paintings 7 636; 21 232; 31 420
T'u Lung see TU LONG
Tulunid 16 113; 31 421*
  see also:
    AHMAD IBN TULUN, Governor
    KHUMARAWAYH, Governor
Tu Luo 2 124
Tum 26 686
  collegiate church 25 95, 101, 109; 26 636, 637
Tumaco see under LA TOLITA
Tumain 15 469
Tuman Bay I, Sultan (reg 1501) (Mamluk) 21 587
Tumarkin, Ygael 16 567; 31 421–2*
tumbaga see under ALLOYS → types
Tumbuka 20 161
Tumbwe 1 403
tumi see under KNIVES → types
Tumm see THUMB
Tumshuk 6 288, 614; 31 422*
  calligraphy 6 307
  moulds 6 298, 298
  sculpture 6 298, 299, 300
  seals 6 315
  Tokkuz-sarai Monastery 6 296, 298, 299, 299, 321
  wall paintings 6 304, 306
  wood-carvings 6 318, 319
tumuli 31 422*
  China 6 696, 698
  Etruscan 10 598
  Greece, ancient 13 383, 384; 31 107

tumuli—cont.
Italy **10** 598
Japan **17** 57
Phrygian **24** 691
Prehistoric art **25** 538; **27** 365
Russia **27** 365–6
see also BARROWS; BURIAL MOUNDS
Tumulus period *see* JAPAN → periods → Kofun
Tuna **16** 432
Tuna el-Gebel **7** 822; **14** 462; **27** 57
funerary temple of Petosiris **9** 892
necropoleis **9** 843
Tunbridge ware *see under* MARQUETRY → types
Tunbridge Wells (Kent) **10** *225*; **20** 469; **31** 422–3*
Calverley Estate **5** 283
Tunbridge Wells Manufacturing Co. **31** 423
Tunca, Muhlis **31** 453
Tuncahuan **29** 151
Tunde Kuye Associates **14** 755
Tune **23** 227; **32** 521, 523
Tunebo **7** 602
Tung An *see* DONG AN
Tungard, Guillem Le *see* LE TUNGARD, GUILLEM
Tung Ch'an *see* DONG CHAN
Tung Ch'i-ch'ang *see* DONG QICHANG
T'ung-chih emperor (Ch'ing; *reg* 1862-74) *see* TONGZHI, Emperor
Tung Chung Fort **14** 719
Tung Lung Island Fort **14** 719
Tung oil *see under* OILS → types
Tung Pai *see* DONG BAI
Tung Pang-ta *see* DONG BANGDA
tungsten **29** 706
tungsten-halogen lamps *see under* LAMPS → types
tungsten lamps *see under* LAMPS → types
Tung Tso-pin *see* DONG ZUOBIN
Tungus **28** 546
dress **28** *546*
Tungutalum, Bede **1** 64
Tung Yu *see* DONG YOU
Tung Yüan *see* DONG YUAN
Tun-huang *see* DUNHUANG
tunicles **32** 389*
tunics **9** 255
Africa **1** *229*
Byzantine **9** *252*, 639, 640, *640*, 641, 643, *644*
Early Christian (*c.* AD 250-843) **9** 639, 640, *640*, 641, 643, *644*
Egypt **9** *640*
Egypt, ancient **30** *563*
Fon **1** 348
Huari culture **29** *181*
Inca **29** 183; **30** IX
Islamic **1** *229*; **16** 454, 458, 461
Malaysia **20** 180
Mexico **21** *394*
Mongolia **21** 876, *876*
Nigeria **1** *229*
Ottoman **16** 461
Peru **29** *181*, *207*; **30** IX
Rome, ancient **9** 246, 251
South America, Pre-Columbian **29** *181*, 188, *207*; **30** IX
Syria **9** *252*
Thailand **30** *626*
Turkey **16** 461
Vietnam **32** 486
Tunis **1** *376*; **5** 891; **16** *103*; **31** 423–7*
Abu Fihr Palace **16** 220
architecture **16** 219; **31** 424
Centre d'Art *see* Ecole des Beaux-Arts
Centre d'Art Vivant **31** 427
congregational mosque *see* Zaytuna Mosque
Tunis—cont.
Dal el Mrabet **32** *312*
Dar al-Hadri **32** 311
Dar el-Mannaii **31** 424
Dar 'Uthman **16** 229; **32** 311
Ecole des Beaux-Arts **31** 425
Great Synagogue **17** 551
Hawa Mosque **16** 219
houses **16** 263; **32** 311–12
jewellery **16** 532; **27** 102
markets **16** 261
mosaics **1** 377
mosque of Sidi Mahrez **16** 229
Mosque of the Qasba **16** 219
Muntasiriyya Madrasa **16** 219
Musée National du Bardo **16** 558; **27** 115; **31** 427
Museum of Popular Arts and Traditions **31** 427
paper **24** 48
pottery **16** 427; **31** 426
printing **16** 361
Qubba Asarak **16** 220
Ras al-Tabiya Palace **16** 220
Shamma'iyya Madrasa **16** 219
Sidi Ben 'Arus *Zāwiya* **16** 220
Sidi Qasim al-Jalizi *Zāwiya* **16** 220, 427
Suq al-'Attarin **16** 220
textiles **16** 447
urban planning **16** 241, 260, 261, 262, 263; **31** 424
Zaytuna Mosque **16** 156, 219; **31** 423
Tunisia **1** *214*, 376; **16** *103*; **31** 424–7*
archaeology **31** 426–7*
architecture **16** 156–7*, 219–20*; **31** 424*
Aghlabid **16** 149, 156–7*
Fatimid **16** 170
Hafsid **16** 219–20
Hammadid **16** 170
Islamic **16** 170–71*
megalithic **21** 43
Ottoman **16** 229
Phoenician **31** 426
vernacular **32** 311–12*
Zirid **16** 170
art schools **31** 425
baths **5** 891
bonnets **16** 459
carpets **16** 486
ceramics **31** 426
circuses **5** 891
coins **16** *512*
coral **7** 834
cotton **18** 48
courtyards **16** *156*
drawings **31** *425*
dress **16** 458
earthenwares **16** 427
engravings **31** *426*
finials (scrolls) **17** 569
fortifications **16** 156
fortresses **16** 156
gardens **12** 70
hair ornaments **27** *102*
headdresses **16** 459
headscarves **16** 459
Institut de Carthage **31** 424
interior decoration **32** *312*
ivory-carvings **16** 525–6*
jewellery **16** 532
khānaqāhs **16** 220
kilims **18** 48
lamps **27** 104, *104*
limestone **27** 14
madrasas **16** 219
maiolica **16** 250
maqṣūras **20** *369*
marble **27** 14
monasteries **16** 156
mosaics **1** *377*; **9** *569*; **16** 256; **32** *543*
mosques **16** *156*, 156–7, *170*, 219
museums **31** 426–7*
painting **31** 424–6*
parchment **31** *425*
Tunisia—cont.
plaster **1** 305
portals **16** *170*, *219*
pottery **31** 426
Islamic **16** 403, 404, 411, 427
Roman **27** 107
ribāṭs **16** 156
sculpture **31** 424–6*
silver **16** *512*
synagogues **17** 543, 551
tattoos **30** 366
textiles **16** 436, 448
tiles **16** 250, 427
tombs **16** 220
trade **16** 400
turbans **16** 459
see also NORTH AFRICA
Tunis School **31** 425–6
Tunja **7** *601*, 603; **31** 427*
Casa de Juan de Castellanos **7** 611
Casa de Juan de Vargas **7** 604, 607, 611
Casa del Fundador **7** 604, 607, 611
Cathedral **7** 604, *604*
Colección de los Padres Dominicanos **31** 427
Convento Concepcionista El Topo **7** 607
Museo Eclesiástico Colonial **31** 427
S Clara la Real **7** 607, 610
S Domingo **7** 604
S Francisco **7** 604
Tunjice Church **28** 859
Tunket **6** 379
Tunma **18** 273
Tunmarch, Erich Gustaf **23** 225
Tunnard, Christopher **19** 891
Tunnard, John (Samuel) **31** 427–8*
tunnel kilns *see under* KILNS → types
tunnels **26** 864; **27** 7*
tunnel tombs *see under* TOMBS → types
tunnel vaults *see* VAULTS (CEILING) → types → barrel
Tunner, Josef (Ernst) **29** 611; **31** 428*
Tunnicliffe, C. F. **32** 791
Tunny, James Good **5** 876
Tuñón, S Adriano **29** 261
Tunstall **29** 495
Tunsukancha **29** 167
Tuohy, Patrick **16** 17; **19** 891
Tuol Dai Buon **5** 484
Tuol Preah Theat **5** 485
Tuoluo *see* BUTKARA
Tuotilo **5** 808, 810
Tupac Inca, Juan Tomás Tuyru *see* TUYRU TUPAC INCA, JUAN TOMÁS
Tupac Inca, Sebastián Acosta *see* ACOSTA TUPAC INCA, SEBASTIÁN
Tupac Inca Yupanqui (*reg* 1471-93) **8** 301; **23** 826
Tupai **28** 921
Tupí **29** 128, 191
Tupič Monastery **3** 528
Tupinamba **29** 194
Tupiza **4** *255*, 270
Tupper, D. **28** 348
Tupperware **25** 26
Tuppo, Francesco del **10** 725
Tuqan, Ja'far **16** 242
Tuquztimur **14** 428
Tur, Etienne le *see* ETIENNE LE TUR
Tura (Egypt) **9** 812; **25** 761, 762, 763
Tura (people)
tools **1** *364*
Tura, Agnolo di *see* AGNOLO DI TURA
Tura, Cosimo **11** 3; **16** 663; **31** 428–33*
attributions **11** 8
Tura, Cosimo—cont.
collaboration **2** 42; **13** 755
patrons and collectors **5** 537; **7** 895; **9** 306; **10** 520; **11** 32; **12** 666; **18** 897
works **11** 4, 5; **13** 195; **30** 314; **31** *429*, *430*, *431*, *432*
Tura, Cosmé *see* TURA, COSIMO
Tura, Pietro del *see* ARETINO, PIETRO
Tur 'Abdin **3** 629; **9** *512*, *513*, 539, 621; **31** 433–6*
architecture **9** 523; **31** *434*, 434–6*, *435*
manuscripts **9** 620; **31** 436*
Turamini (family) **24** 533
Turani, Adnan **31** 454
Turan Malik (Mangujak) **9** 41; **16** 183
Turanshah **16** 377
Turapilli, Ventura di ser Giuliano *see* VENTURA DI SER GIULIANO TURAPILLI
Turaŭ **3** 525, *525*
turbans **16** 429, 452, 454, 455, 456–7, 459, 464, 537, 539; **25** 132; **30** *626*
Turbat-i Shaykh Jam, funerary complex of Shaykh Ahmed **16** 194, 197
Turberville, George **29** 424
Turbessel *see* BASHIR, TELL
Turbino **27** 367; **28** 321
Turcato, Giulio **31** 436*
groups and movements **7** 782; **9** 168; **11** 314, 802; **13** 727; **16** 681
Turchi, Alessandro **31** 436–8*
collaboration **3** 353; **23** 633; **26** 840
patrons and collectors **4** 567; **5** 65; **18** 885; **20** 841; **28** 271
teachers **5** 32
works **31** *437*
Turchi, Giuseppe **31** 679
Turco, Flaminio del **28** 676
tureens **10** 419; **31** 438*
historical and regional traditions
Belgium **3** 589
China **6** *921*
England **15** *820*
France **11** *620*, *622*; **12** *357*; **21** *70*; **32** *583*
Germany **12** *436*
Netherlands, the **22** *882*, *888*
Norway **23** *234*
Portugal **19** *468*
Switzerland **30** *146*
materials
bronze **30** *146*
faience (ii) (ceramics) **23** *234*
porcelain **6** *921*; **12** *436*; **22** *882*; **32** *583*
pottery **15** *820*
quartz **11** *622*
silver **11** *620*, *622*; **12** *357*; **21** *70*; **22** *888*
Tureng Tepe **15** 902, 909
Turenne, Charles-Godefroy de La Tour d'Auvergne, Prince de **7** 640
Turenne, Godefroy-Charles-Henri de La Tour d'Auvergne, Prince de **7** 640
Turenum *see* TRANI
Turfan **6** *288*, *614*; **21** *870*; **28** *719*; **31** 438*
banners **6** 321
calligraphy **6** 307
carpets **5** 833; **7** 68
ceramics **6** 308
dress **6** 310, 311
manuscripts **6** 289, 306
monasteries **5** 102; **6** 296
painting **6** 302, 305
prints **6** 314
roofs **6** 295
sanctuaries **6** 297
sculpture **6** 300–301
Turfan—cont.
silk **28** 721
stupas **6** 297
temples **30** 441
textiles **16** 451
wall paintings **6** 304, 321
turf mazes *see under* MAZES → types
Turgel, Donald **29** 117
Turgenev, Sergey **27** 379
Turgis, Madeleine **12** 832
Turgot, Anne-Robert-Jacques **20** 135
Turgot, Etienne François de **11** 757
Turgunov, B. A. **2** 882
Turhan Sultan **16** 223
Turi, Johan **27** 472
Turin **16** *618*; **31** 438–47*, *441*
Academy (founded 1678) **1** 103
Accademia Albertina di Belle Arti **16** 774
Armeria Reale **2** 462
Biblioteca Reale **31** 446
Casa Fenoglio **16** 721
Casa Miller **16** *721*
Castello degli Acaja *see* palazzi → Palazzo Madama
Castello della Mandria **16** 720
Castello del Valentino **16** 748; **28** 10; **29** 831
churches
Cathedral of S Giovanni Battista **21** 143–4; **31** 439, 447*, *447*
Chapel of the Holy Shroud **7** 258; **12** 790; **13** 749–50, *750*; **16** *642*, 643; **19** 362; **21** 893; **28** 632
Chapel of the Sacra Sindone *see* Chapel of the Holy Shroud
Church of Gran Madre di Dio **7** 258
church of the Carmine **16** 643; **17** 708, *708*
Corpus Domini **32** 631
Madonna del Monte **32** 631
S Cristina **17** 707
S Filippo Neri **17** 707
S Giovanni Battista **31** 447
S Lorenzo **7** 258; **9** 83; **12** 791; **13** 748–9; **16** 643; **19** 362; **30** 649
dome **13** *749*
SS Trinità **32** 631
La Superga **16** 643; **17** 706–7, *707*
portico **25** 266
sculpture **16** 702
Circolo degli Artisti **31** 446
citadel **31** 439–40
Collegio dei Nobili *see* palazzi → Palazzo dell' Accademia delle Scienze
East Gate *see* palazzi → Palazzo Madama
Esposizione Internazionale d'Arte Decorativa, 1902 **29** 843; **31** 446
exhibitions **15** 883; **24** 739
fortifications **31** 439–40
Galleria Civica d'Arte Moderna **2** 10; **31** 445, 446
Galleria Sabauda **8** 584; **31** 446
catalogues **22** 296
collections **5** 405; **11** 393, 396; **16** 774; **28** 3, 15, 18; **31** 444
directors **12** 29
Giardino Reale **12** 118
Gualino office building **16** 649
ketubbot **18** 3
Lingotto Fiat car factory **7** 694; **20** 846
Mole Antonelliana **2** 177*, *177*; **16** 648; **21** 172; **31** 442
monument to Duke Charles-Albert of Savoy **31** 446

Turin—cont.
monument to Duke Emanuel-Philibert of Savoy *see under* Piazza S Carlo
museums **16** 771
Museo Civico **2** 10; **30** 332
Museo Egizio **4** 493; **10** 91; **16** 774; **31** 446
palazzi
Palazzo dell'Accademia delle Scienze **13** 752; **16** 719
see also Galleria Sabauda; museums → Museo Egizio
Palazzo Carignano **13** 750–52, *752*; **16** 643; **23** 836
Palazzo Chiablese **11** 396; **13** 803
Palazzo di Città **18** 729
Palazzo Isnardi di Caraglio **16** 719
Palazzo Madama **12** 791; **16** 643, *644*; **17** 709; **28** 14; **29** 525; **31** 439
paintings **11** 393; **31** 443
Palazzo Reale **8** 12; **15** 148; **18** 618; **26** 500; **28** 12–13; **31** 440, 443
collections **7** 571; **31** 443
frescoes **11** 9; **13** 816; **19** 646; **27** 200
furniture **4** 340; **16** 730; **30** 783
Gabinetto Cinese **3** 453; **28** 18
Gabinetto dei Fiori **28** 18
Galleria delle Armi **3** 453
Galleria delle Battaglie **3** 453; **28** 18
Galleria Beaumont **28** 19
Galleria della Regina *see* Galleria delle Armi
Grande Galleria **28** 6
interior decoration **16** 719, 720; **31** 444
library **28** 19
Medagliere **16** 730
paintings **3** 453, 857; **9** 402; **12** 29; **13** 803; **19** 646; **22** 327; **26** 94; **28** 16; **31** 444
Sala da Ballo **16** 720
Sala del Caffè **4** 46
Sala delle Macchine **22** 326
Sala delle Udienze **16** 720
sculpture **3** 825; **4** 458; **16** 702
Parco del Valentino **16** 647
Piazza d'Armi **17** 710
Piazza Castello **31** *439*, 441
Piazza Reale *see* Piazza S Carlo
Piazza S Carlo **6** 18, *18*; **28** 10; **31** 440
monument to Duke Emanuel-Philibert of Savoy **10** 442; **16** 706; **31** 445
Piazza Vittorio Veneto **31** *442*
Pinacoteca Sabauda *see* Galleria Sabauda
Politecnico
architectural library **16** 776
Porta Aurea **13** 391
Porta Palatina **7** 358; **31** 439
Quartieri Militari **17** 710
Reale Galleria *see* Galleria Sabaudia
Regia Pinacoteca *see* Galleria Sabaudia
sculpture **16** 702*
Stazione Porta Nuova **25** 856; **29** 833
tapestries **16** 758; **30** 324, 328; **31** 446–7*
tapestry factory **3** 454; **16** 758; **30** 326
Teatro Regio **1** 125, 623; **16** 721; **30** 667
urban planning **6** 19; **17** 710; **31** 438–9, 440–41, 714, 731
Valentino Park **7** 696; **22** 805
Venaria Reale *see* VENARIA REALE
Villa della Regina **12** 586
Turin, Holy Shroud of *see* SHROUD OF TURIN
Turin, Pierre **20** 926
Turina, Bartolomeo **3** 687
Turin Crucifixion, Master of the **16** 832; **20** 705
Turin Digest **20** 787
Turin Futurist group **11** 80; **31** 446
Türing, Nikolaus **2** 780; **13** 904; **15** 863, 866
Turinge Church **30** 71
Turini, Baldassare **12** 752; **31** 448*
Turini, Giovanni **16** 842, 843
Turin-Milan Hours *see under* BOOKS OF HOURS → individual manuscripts
Turin Mine Plan **10** 63; **20** 361
Turino, Barna di *see* BARNA DI TURINO
Turino, Giovanni di *see* GIOVANNI DI TURINO
Turino, Lorenzo di *see* LORENZO DI TURINO
Turino di Matteo **28** 677
Turino di Sano **16** 842; **28** 681; **31** 450*
Turino di Vanni **28** 656; **31** 450*
Turjak Castle **28** 859
Turkana **1** 254, 288, 292, 296, 297, 362, 409; **17** 906
beads **1** *297*
headdresses **1** *409*
Turkan-Aga **6** 208
Turkan Khatun **5** 722; **26** 303
Turkeshi, Muharrem **31** 451*
Turkestan (region)
historiography **6** 278–9*
ikat **30** 554
kilims **18** 49
tents **30** 473
textiles **16** 451
Turkestan (town) **6** *182*; **16** *105*; **17** *865*; **31** 451*
architecture **16** 196
shrine of Ahmad Yasavi **6** 190, 203, 285, *286*; **16** 143, 196, 197, *198*, 199, 366; **22** 322; **28** 201, 636; **31** 451
doors **16** 501
metalwork **6** 246; **16** 377
stucco **29** 820
wood-carvings **6** 277
tiles **6** 208
wood-carvings **6** 277
woodwork **16** *501*
Turkestan, Chinese *see* CENTRAL ASIA, EASTERN
Turkey **9** *512*; **13** *362*; **16** *103*, *104*; **21** 266, *267*; **26** *908*; **31** 451–6*
amber **1** 762
aqueducts **16** 224
arches **2** 295
architectural decorations **16** 186, 221, 245
architecture **31** 452–3*
Aqqoyunlu **16** 201, 202
Beylik **16** 202*
brick **16** 186; **26** *912*, *914*
Byzantine **9** 536–7*, 542*, 543–5*, 549–50*
Early Christian (*c.* AD 250-843) **9** 536–7*, 542*
Islamic **16** 183*, 186*, 201–2*, 205–7*, 221*, 227, 265–7*
military **16** 186, 206; **21** 585–6, *586*
Ottoman **16** 205–7*, 221–7*, 265–7*, 604
Qaraqoyunlu **16** 201, 202
Roman **26** *923*
Saljuqs of Anatolia **16** 183
stone **16** 186, 266
vernacular **32** 318–19*
wood **16** 222
architraves **9** *592*
arcosolia **9** *593*
atlantids **10** *426*
barracks **16** 225
Turkey—cont.
basins **6** IV1
bath-gymnasia **26** 912, 914; **27** *837*
baths **3** 376, 377, *377*; **16** 204–5, 224; **26** *912*
bazaars **16** 205, 206
belts **16** 462
belvederes **16** 266
book covers **16** 359
books **16** 360
bowcases **16** 505
brass **16** *388*; **32** *161*
brick **4** *771*, 771; **9** 545; **16** 186, 207; **26** *912*, *914*
bridges **16** 207; **17** *702*
bronze **16** *506*; **31** *700*
calligraphers **16** 285
candlesticks **16** *388*
canteens **16** *542*
capitals **9** *589*
caps **16** 462
caravanserais **5** *723*; **16** 141, 186, 205, 206, 224, 266
carpets **2** 439; **5** 829; **18** 234; **31** 455
animal **16** *470*
Bellini **16** 471
Crivelli **16** 471
Gördes **16** 478
Islamic **16** 430, 466, 469, *470*, 470–72*, *471*, 476–9*
Kirşehir **16** 478
Konya **16** 469
Lâdik **16** *478*, 478
Lotto **16** 471, *471*
Memling **16** 471
Milâs **16** 478
Mucur **16** 478
Ottoman **16** 470–72*, *471*, 476–9*
prayer rugs **16** *478*
Small-pattern Holbein **16** 471
Transylvanian **16** 472
Ushak **5** II; **16** 471–2
cathedrals **16** *592*
cemeteries **14** 515
cenotaphs **6** 172
chapels **9** 544
chargers **16** *418*
chasing **16** *388*
churches
basilicas **9** 536–7, *537*, 542, 544
Byzantine **4** *771*; **8** *777*; **9** 536–7, 543–5*, *545*, 549–50
compact-domed basilicas **9** 542
cross-domed **9** 542
cross-in-square **9** *545*
domed basilicas **9** 537
Early Christian (*c.* AD 250-843) **9** *525*, 536–7; **31** *435*
rock **26** *484*
cisterns **7** *354*
citadels **16** 266
cloisters **16** 184, 204
coats **16** 462
coins **7** 535; **16** *513*, 514
collections **1** 839; **16** 552
colophons **7** *626*
columns **10** *431*; **26** *923*
cotton **16** 462
courtyards **16** 142, 183, 186, 221
craftsmen and artists **16** 346, 387
domes **9** 84; **16** 141, 205, 221, 222–3; **19** *363*
doors **9** 160
doublures **16** 356
dress **16** 453, 458, 460–62*, *462*
dresses **16** 461, 462
dyes **16** 477
earrings **31** *376*
earthenwares **16** 411, 414, 418
education (art) **31** 455–6
emeralds **16** *542*
enamel **2** 575; **9** *633*; **16** 515
engravings
townscapes **31** *303*
façades **16** 221
felt **10** 872, 874; **30** *474*
Turkey—cont.
figurines **1** *729*; **31** *700*
finials (scrolls) **17** 569
forgeries **1** 896
fortifications **16** 155; **21** 585–6, *586*; **31** *700*
fountain courts **16** 202, *203*
fountains **16** 225, *226*, 265
friezes **14** *69*
frit **6** IV1; **16** *418*
gardens **12** 83–5*, *84*
gateways **24** *417*
glass **16** 221, 522
glazes **16** 411
gold **16** *508*, *513*, *542*, *860*; **31** *376*
grilles **16** 257
guidebooks **13** 811
guilds **16** 445
hair **16** 445; **30** 539
hats **16** 462
headdresses **16** 461, 462; **31** *376*
helmets **16** *504*
hospices **16** 202–4
hospitals **16** 184–5, 202–4
houses **16** *266*, 266, 269; **25** 499; **32** 318–19, *319*
ikat **30** 554
imarets **16** 224
incising **16** *388*
inlays **16** 498
inscriptions **16** *137*, 497, 514, 810
iron **16** *504*
ivory **1** *729*
ivory-carvings **27** *101*
iwans **16** 186
jade **16** 860
joinery **16** 497
kaftans **16** *446*, 460, 461
khānaqāhs **16** 265
kilims **5** 830; **16** 477, 478; **18** 48, 49
kiosks **16** *589*
knitting **18** 157
külliye **16** 221
lacquer **16** 535; **18** 609
lamps **13** *603*; **16** 394
leather **16** 544, *544*
Lectionaries **9** *621*
libraries **26** *914*; **31** *453*
limestone **9** 590; **27** 14
linen **16** *137*
lintels **1** *523*
madrasas **10** 493; **16** *184*, 184–5, *185*, 202–4; **20** 56, 57; **27** 632
Beylik **16** 204
Ottoman **16** 222, 223–4, 265, 810
Saljuqs of Anatolia **16** 184
manganese **16** 248
manuscript illumination **9** *621*; **12** *84*; **16** *118*, 304, 307–10*, 329–30*, 346–51*; **23** *642*
manuscripts **16** 304
marble
Byzantine **9** *587*, *592*, *593*
Greece, ancient **8** *870*; **14** *69*, *70*
Islamic **16** 221
Phrygian **27** 13
Prokonnesian **9** *589*, *593*
Roman **2** *220*; **10** *428*; **27** 14
marbling **24** 55
markets **16** 266; **19** 889
masonry **4** 773; **16** 186, 221; **26** *912*
mausolea **14** *71*; **16** 204; **31** *452*
megara (buildings) **13** *7*
metalwork **16** 378, 379, 387–9*
mihrabs **21** 506
minarets **16** 202, 223; **21** 628
minbars **16** *498*; **21** 630
miniatures (manuscript illumination) **16** *446*
Byzantine **7** *228*; **9** *621*
Islamic **16** *329*, *348*, *349*, *454*
Ottoman **16** *348*, *349*, *446*, *454*
mirrors **21** 717
monuments **24** *689*
Turkey—cont.
mortars (building) **22** 159; **26** *912*
mosaics
Byzantine **2** *158*; **7** *220*; **9** *564*, 564–5*, *577*, *583*; **16** *594*, *598*, *601*, *809*; **21** III2; **22** *157*
Early Christian (*c.* AD 250-843) **2** *158*; **9** *564*, 564–5*
Islamic **16** 199
mosques **2** 437; **5** *282*; **16** *179*, 183–4, 202, *203*, *206*, 497
basilica **16** 183, 202
congregational mosques **16** 221
domed **22** *195*, 195–6
hypostyle **16** 183, 202
Islamic **9** *526*
multi-unit **16** 205
Ottoman **9** *730*; **16** 205–6, 221–4, *223*, *224*, 226, 265, 266, 605; **22** *195*
single-domed square **16** 183, 202, 205
single-unit **16** 222
T-plan **16** 205–6, 810
16th cent. **28** *766*, *767*, *768*
moulding **4** 771
mouldings **8** 869
mud-bricks **16** 266
muqarnas (architecture) **22** 323, *323*
museums **1** 839; **16** 557; **31** 456
nakkashane **16** 346
necklaces **31** *376*
nephrite **16** *860*
niches **26** *923*; **31** *434*
opus sectile **16** *596*
orders (architecture) **18** 580; **23** 392
Ottoman Baroque **16** 225–7
painting **16** 535, 536–7*, *537*; **31** 453*
genre **31** *455*
Islamic **16** 221, 497
Ottoman **16** 221
wall
Achaemenid **10** *151*, 151
Anatolia, ancient **2** *504*
Byzantine **9** *581*; **32** II1
Greece, ancient **10** 151
Islamic **16** 254
Ottoman **16** 254
Prehistoric **6** *74*
palaces
block **9** *559*
Byzantine **9** *559*
Islamic **16** 186, 204, 225, 227, 266
Ottoman **16** 225, 227, 266
19th cent. **16** *587*
paper **24** 55, 56
papier mâché **16** 359
parekklesia **9** 544–5
pavilions (buildings) **16** 204, *225*; **23** *638*
pigments **16** 249
porticos **16** 222
portraits **9** *587*; **10** *428*; **14** *70*; **19** *436*
pottery **9** *633*; **16** 406, 411*, 413, 418*, *418*; **31** 455
Abraham of Kütahya ware **16** 418
Baba Nakkaş ware **16** 418
blue-and-white ware **6** IV1; **16** 418, *418*; **30** XIII1
champlevé ware **16** 411
Iznik ware **16** 124
lustreware **16** 411
Miletus ware **16** 414, 418
printing **16** 360
puppets **16** 544, *544*
revetments **16** 599
robes **16** 460, 462
rock crystal **16** *542*
rock reliefs **24** *691*
rubies **16** *542*
rugs **2** 438

Turkey—cont.
salvers **32** *161*
sashes **16** 461, 462; **25** 132
saz **16** 349
scabbards **16** *508*
schools **16** 265
screens (ii) (furniture) **13** *8*
scripts **16** 285
sculpture
architectural **10** *426*
bronze **31** *700*
colossal statues **22** *731*
figure **16** 245
Greece, ancient **14** *70*
marble **8** *870*; **9** *587*; **10** *428*; **14** *69*, *70*
relief
Byzantine **9** *595*
Greece, ancient **10** *431*; **14** *69*
Hittite **4** *231*; **33** *513*
Neo-Hittite **5** *729*
Roman **2** *220*
reserve heads **10** *428*
Roman **10** *428*
Urartian **31** *700*
sgraffito **16** 248, 411
shadow theatre **16** 544–5
shields **31** *159*
shirts **16** *137*, 460
shoes **16** 461
shops **16** 266
silhouettes **24** 56
silk **16** 430, 445, *446*, 446, 462; **23** *639*; **25** 131
silver-gilt **23** *639*
stained glass **16** 257
standards (vexilloid) **11** 151
stands **13** *8*
steel **16** *508*
stelae **29** 618, 619
stone **16** 186, 266
streets **16** 206, *266*
stucco **16** 248, 257
swords **16** *506*, *508*
synagogues **17** 543, 545, *545*, 551
talismans **16** *137*
tankards **16** *860*
tas **17** 569
temples **2** 635; **5** *742*; **8** *869*
tents **30** 473–6*, *474*
textiles **16** 444; **23** *639*
theatres **2** 605, *605*; **21** *543*
tiles **5** *282*; **9** *633*; **16** 206, 221, 248, 418, 604
cuerda seca **16** 199
Islamic **30** XIII1
tin **4** 849
tombs
Islamic **16** 185–6, 206; **31** *114*
iwan **16** 186
Ottoman **16** 206
Qaraqoyunlu **16** 204
tower **16** 185–6, 204; **31** 113
topographical illustrations **16** 347
trade
antiquities **1** 896
carpets **5** 833, 834, 835*, 841; **16** 470, 476, 479
glass **16** 221, 257
porcelain **6** 333; **16** 124
pottery **16** 416, 417, 427
silk **16** 445
treatises **16** 221
trousers **16** 460, 461, 462
tufa **16** 269
tughras **16** 514; **31** 417
tunics **16** 461
underclothes **16** 461
uniforms **16** 461
urban planning **16** 265–7*
vaults (ceiling) **16** 186
velvet **16** 430, 446
waxes **33** 1
weaving **9** 493; **16** 444, 469, 476–7, 478–9
windows **16** 257
women artists **16** 476
wood **9** 160; **13** *8*; **16** 202, 222
wood-carvings **16** 497

Turkey—cont.
woodwork **16** 488, 497–8*, *498*
wool **5** II; **16** *470*, *471*, *478*
workshops **16** 468
writing-tablets **4** 342
see also ANATOLIA, ANCIENT; ANCIENT NEAR EAST; BYZANTINE; CAPPADOCIA; CARIA; LYCIA; OTTOMAN; SYRIA-PALESTINE
Turkey Creek **1** 64
Turkey red *see under* pigments → types
Türkheim **12** 403
Turki, Hedi **31** 457*
groups and movements **31** 426
pupils **31** 426
works **31** 426
Turk'i, Imam (*reg* 1823-34) (Saudi) **26** 433
Turki, Yahia **31** 425
Turki, Zoubeir **31** 426
Turkish Fine Arts Society *see* ASSOCIATION OF OTTOMAN PAINTERS
Turkish knots *see* KNOTS → symmetrical
Turkish script *see under* SCRIPTS → types
Turkish triangles *see* ISLAMIC → consoles
Turkmenistan **6** 181; **16** *105*; **31** 457–60*, *458*
architecture **31** 458–9*
breast-ornaments **31** *459*
carpets **5** III; **6** *253*, 254; **16** 466; **31** 459–60*
ceramics **6** 224
chalk **6** 224
collections **6** 283–4*
cornelian **31** *459*
decorative arts **31** 459–60*
embroidery **31** 460
grounds **6** 224
ivory **6** *271*
ivory-carvings **6** *271*; **23** *160*
jewellery **6** 274
mausolea **21** *169*
museums **6** 283–4*
painting **6** 223–4*; **31** 459*
pottery **6** 255
rhyta **6** *271*; **23** *160*
sand **6** 224
sculpture **31** 459*
silver-gilt **31** *459*
stone **6** 224
tents **30** 473
urban planning **6** 209
wool **5** III; **6** *253*
Turkmenkovyor Company **6** 254
Turkoman **1** 188; **16** 115
carpets **1** 209; **6** 252, 254; **16** 484–5
see also under CARPETS → types
cotton **6** 249
felt **10** 872, 874
jewellery **1** 210
kilims **18** 48
painting **28** 567
pottery **16** 412, 418
tents **16** 485; **30** 474, *474*
textiles **16** 451
Türk ressamlar cemiyeti *see* ASSOCIATION OF OTTOMAN PAINTERS
Turks **16** 108
Türk sanayi i nefise birligi *see* ASSOCIATION OF OTTOMAN PAINTERS
Turku **11** *87*; **31** *460*, 460–62*
Academia Åboensis **11** 90, 91, 94, 113
architecture **11** 89, 90, 91
Art Museum **11** 112; **23** 326; **31** 461; **33** 96
Atrium Apartments **11** 92
Castle **11** 89, 101
paintings **11** 94, 95
pottery **11** 105

Turku—cont.
Cathedral of St Mary and St Henry of Uppsala **4** 781; **11** 87, 98; **31** 461–2*, *462*
altarpieces **11** 714
Ejby chalice **11** 107
monument to Åke Tott **11** 99, *99*
paintings **11** 95
sculpture **11** 98
furniture **11** 104
gold **11** 107, 108
guilds **11** 103
monument to Henrik Gabriel Porthan **11** 99
observatory **23** 340
Old University Building **11** 99
Old University House Square **11** 100
pottery **11** 105
silver **11** *108*
Town Hall **11** 90
Wäinö Aaltonen Museum **1** 12; **31** 461
Turlough O'Connor, King of Ireland (*reg* 1118-56) **7** 459; **31** 402
Turmanin Church **7** 259; **9** 541
Turmel, Charles **11** 659
Turmel, Pierre **31** 462
turmeric **15** 668; **23** 723
Turnbull, Alexander **23** 75
Turnbull, John **13** 712
Turnbull, Stewart & Co **31** 334
Turnbull, Thomas **23** 53, 54; **31** 462–3*; **33** 58
Turnbull, Thomas, & Son **31** 463
Turnbull, William (1868-1941) **31** 463
Turnbull, William (*b* 1922) **25** 628; **31** 463–4*
groups and movements **10** 268; **15** 166; **28** 804
works **10** 268; **16** 58; **28** 240, 300
Turnbull, William (*b* 1935) **22** 52; **27** 730
Turnbull & Stockdale **8** 583
turned chairs *see under* CHAIRS → types
Turner (family) **6** 528
Turner, Benjamin Brecknell **31** 464*
Turner, C(laude) A(llen) P(orter) **2** 740; **7** 694; **31** 464–5*; **32** 861
Turner, Charles **1** 449; **31** 465–7*
collaboration **21** 417
teachers **17** 630
works **31** 467
Turner, Dawson **8** 28, 184; **31** 465*; **32** 379
Turner, Doman **5** 516
Turner, Donald **29** 634
Turner, Elizabeth **31** 465
Turner, H.
works **1** *250*
Turner, Hannah Sarah **31** 465
Turner, Harriet **31** 465
Turner, (Annie) Helen (Nairn) Monro **28** 260; **31** 466*
Turner, Hugh Thackeray **3** 110*
Turner, James (*fl* 1678-1703) **9** 727
Turner, James (*fl* 1770-87) **23** 786; **24** 799
Turner, Jean Edmond **15** 43
Turner, J(oseph) M(allord) W(illiam) **9** 1; **12** 741; **14** 452; **16** 678; **18** 715; **19** 587; **23** 690; **27** 351, 626; **31** 466–75*; **32** 785; **33** 545
attributions **8** 584
book illustrations **26** 541; **28** 286
collaboration **12** 647; **19** 284; **20** 602; **21** 417; **28** 883; **29** 732; **30** 752
collections **9** 19
commentaries **27** 352
dealers **1** 454; **12** 30; **26** 107
drawings **9** 225; **10** 479, 487

Turner, J(oseph) M(allord) W(illiam)—cont.
etchings **25** 619
exhibitions **19** 507
frames **9** 12; **11** *431*, 432, 433
groups and movements **24** 742; **25** 264; **26** 736, 737, 741; **29** 891; **32** 903
methods **4** 184; **5** 658; **7** 629; **13** 708; **19** 355; **23** 379, 788, 789, 792; **24** 495
paintings **10** 251, 252; **20** 424; **22** 730; **23** 690; **26** *741*; **31** *468*, *469*, *472*; **32** 196
landscape **9** 1; **31** *474*
watercolours **9** 24, 217; **10** 251; **31** 155, *470*, *473*; **32** 901, VIII1
patrons and collectors **14** 688
Beckford, William (1760-1844) **3** 476
Bicknell, Elhanan **4** 35
Drummond, George A(lexander) (1827-1910) **9** 305
Egerton, Francis, 3rd Duke of Bridgewater **9** 755
Foster, Myles Birket **11** 331
Frick, Henry Clay **11** 774
George IV, King of Great Britain (*reg* 1820-30) **14** 147
Gillott, Joseph **4** 87; **12** 638
Grosvenor, Hugh Lupus, 1st Duke of Westminster **13** 697
Groult, Camille **13** 705
Hawkins, John Heywood (1803-77) **14** 252
Hoare (i), (Richard) Colt **14** 598
Leicester, John Fleming, Baron de Tabley **10** 365; **19** 98
Loyd-Lindsay, Robert, 1st Baron Wantage **19** 736
McCulloch, Horatio **19** 875
Mellon, Andrew W(illiam) **21** 90
Monro, Thomas **8** 98; **21** 901
Morrison, James **22** 148
Munro (of Novar), H(ugh) A(ndrew) J(ohnstone) **22** 314
Plint, T(homas) E(dward) **25** 41
Prior, Thomas Abiel **25** 635
Ruskin, John **27** 354
Sheepshanks, John **28** 576
Soane, John **28** 908
Tennant, Charles **30** 464
Vaughan, Henry (1809-99) **28** 272
Vernon, Robert **32** 338
William IV, King of Great Britain (*reg* 1830-37) **3** 389; **14** 147
Windus, B(enjamin) G(odfrey) **9** 26; **27** 351; **33** 251
Wyndham, George O'Brien, 3rd Earl of Egremont **9** 24; **10** 361, 365; **33** 453
prints **20** 602; **25** 596; **31** 155
reproductive prints by others **10** 396; **26** 232, 234
Brunet-Debaines, Alfred-Louis **5** 24
Cooke, George **4** 614; **7** 789
Cousen, John **8** 66
Goodall, Edward **12** 925
Hill, John (1770-1850) **14** 536
Landseer, John (George) **18** 721
Lupton, Thomas Goff **19** 806
Prior, Thomas Abiel **25** 635
Pye, John **25** 753
Radclyffe, William **25** 837
Say, William **28** 25
Turner, Charles **31** 465
teachers **20** 220
Turner, John (1739-86) **10** 307, 308
Turner, John (1766-1824) **10** 309; **29** 495
Turner, John B. (*fl* 1974) **24** 534
Turner, Joseph **32** 788
Turner, Llewelyn **5** 373

Turner, Maria (1797-1872) **31** 465
Turner, Mary (*fl* 1960s) **2** 770
Turner, Mary Anne (1803-74) **31** 465
Turner, Nathaniel **1** 772
Turner, Richard **5** 283; **7** 744; **12** 791; **16** 52, 53; **18** 5
works **18** *4*
Turner, Robert **4** 109; **31** 640
Turner, Thomas (1749-1809) **6** 93
Turner, Thomas (1820-91) **9** 297
Turner, W. E. S. **31** 466
Turner, William (*fl* 1600-5) **10** 316
Turner, William (1762-1835; ceramicist) **10** 309; **29** 495
Turner, William (1789-1862; painter) **31** 477*
works **23** 381
Turner, William (*d* 1829) **31** 466
Turnerelli, Peter **31** 477*
Turner of Oxford *see* TURNER, WILLIAM (1789-1862)
Turners Hall **2** 152
Turnhout **3** 610
Turnier, Luce **14** 58
turning *see under* CERAMICS → techniques; POTTERY → techniques; WOODWORK → techniques
Turnock, Enoch H. **17** 476
Turnov **8** 425
Turnovo *see* VELIKO TURNOVO
turnsole **18** 656
Turnstall, W. A. **29** 454
turntables **6** 879; **10** 301; **17** 241
Turnu **26** 707
Turócszentmárton *see* MARTIN (SLOVAKIA)
Turoe **6** *153*, 161
Turone (di Maxio da Camenago) **28** 29; **31** 477*
Turov *see* TURAU
Turow, Nikolaus **20** 852
Turpan *see* TURFAN
turpentine **26** 243; **29** 53; **31** 478*
brushes **5** 34
encaustic paintings **10** 197
etchings **10** 561
inks **25** 598
japanning **18** 610
oil paintings **23** 375, 377
paints **23** 785, 792, 793
paper **24** 55
varnishes **32** 1, 2
waxes **33** 2
turpentine, Chios *see* RESINS → types → terebinth resin
turpentine, larch *see* VENICE TURPENTINE
turpentine, Strasbourg *see* STRASBOURG TURPENTINE
turpentine, Venice *see* VENICE TURPENTINE
Turpilius **27** 52
Turpin, Jean **30** 746
Turpin, John **12** 26
Turpin de Crissé, Lancelot-Théodore, Comte de **31** 478–9*
collaboration **8** 703
patrons and collectors **4** 303, 322; **8** 649
works **31** *479*
turqueries **31** 478–80*
Turquet, Edmond **26** 510
Turquet de Mayerne, Théodore **4** 182; **7** 312; **24** 553; **31** 480*
works **23** 377
writings **4** 101
turquoise
historical and regional traditions
Ancient Near East **1** 873
Aztec **21** 251, 252; **22** 164
Bhutan **3** 914
Buddhism **6** 706
Central Asia, Western **6** 261, 262
China **7** 88, 108
Ming period (1368-1644) **7** 111, *111*

turquoise
historical and regional traditions
China—cont.
Qing period (1644-1911) 6 706; 7 91
Shang period (c. 1600-c. 1050 BC) 6 832, 841; 7 107
Tang period (AD 618-907) 7 109
Yuan period (1279-1368) 7 89
Zhou period (c. 1050-256 BC) 7 107; 21 714
Egypt, ancient 10 28, 38; 12 246
Iran 16 530
Islamic 12 253; 16 507, 530, 531
Kurdistan 16 531
Mesoamerica, Pre-Columbian 1 713; 21 241, 246, 251, 252, 254, 255–6, 737, IV1; 22 158, 164; 33 103
Mexico 21 IV1
Mixtec 21 251, 255–6, 737
Mongolia 3 441; 7 836
Native North Americans 22 615, 668–9
Navajo 22 615
Ottoman 16 507
Peru 28 651
Russia 27 423
Sicán culture 28 651
South America, Pre-Columbian 28 651; 29 155, 217
Thailand 3 441
Tibet 30 839
West Mexico 33 103
uses
amulets 10 38
beads 3 441, 442; 7 88
belthooks 7 88, 107
bracelets 16 530
carvings 7 91
crowns 7 111, 111
daggers 6 261
earrings 7 111
glazes 16 407
hair ornaments 7 108
hairpins 7 109
headdresses 7 836
helmets 16 507
inlays 3 914; 6 832, 841; 7 88
jewellery 7 106, 109, 111; 16 531; 17 525; 22 615; 30 839
knives 28 651
masks 21 251, 737, IV1; 22 158
mirrors 21 714
mosaics 21 254, 255–6, 737, IV1; 22 154, 158, 164; 29 217
pendants (jewellery) 27 423
pins 7 107
sculpture 6 706
shields 21 737
swords 6 261, 262
vessels 7 88
Turreau, (Jean-)Bernard (-Honoré) see TORO, (JEAN-)BERNARD(-HONORÉ)
Turrell, James 10 416; 19 702; 31 480*, 609
patrons and collectors 24 24
works 18 695
turrets 12 175, 176, 222; 15 322, 323; 21 550
Turriano, João 1 591; 7 532; 20 403; 25 291, 292
turris see WESTWORKS
Turris, Nicola De see DE TURRIS, NICOLA
Turrisan, Pedro see TORRIGIANI, PIETRO (DI TORRIGIANO D'ANTONIO)
Turrita, Mino 2 514
Tursi, Carlo Doria (i), Duca di 9 172
Turstan, Abbot of Glastonbury 12 799
Tursun Begi 16 237
Tursunzade 30 252, 252
Turuvekere, Mule-Shankareshvara Temple 15 328
Turvey (Beds), All Saints 9 155
Turzhansky, Leonard 27 392
Tusardi, Bassano 27 483
Tusardi, Paolo 27 483
Tuscaloosa (AL), State Asylum for the Insane 2 658
Tuscan houses see under HOUSES → types
Tuscania 10 613
S Pietro 16 625; 26 624
Tuscan order see under ORDERS (ARCHITECTURAL) → types
Tuscarora 16 61; 22 552
tusche see under CRAYONS → types
Tuscher, (Carl) Marcus 8 733; 31 481*; 32 765
patrons and collectors 29 724
works 7 802; 31 481
Tuscherová, Inez 8 420
Tusculum 9 20; 13 555; 27 58
Tüshaus, Josef 17 2
Tushka 23 279
tusks 25 734
types
boar 16 796; 17 399; 24 79
elephant 1 868; 7 102; 16 796; 17 398; 23 400
mammoth 7 102; 16 796, 799; 25 490
narwhal 16 796; 28 302
China 7 102
Denmark 8 752
Japan 17 398
pig 16 796
walrus 6 557; 16 796; 28 302
China 7 102
France 11 636
Japan 17 398
Norway 6 389
uses
chairs 6 389
chess sets 6 557
horns 16 797
netsuke 17 398, 399
oliphants 16 797; 23 400
scrimshaw 28 302
Tusŏngyŏng see YI AM (ii)
Tusquets Guillem, Oscar 3 217; 29 274, 322, 861
Tussaud, Mme 33 4
works 33 4
Tustar 16 456
Tustin, Charles 5 731
Tustin, Sidney 5 731
Tutankhamun (reg c. 1333-c. 1323 BC) 2 300; 9 777, 782; 10 81, 98; 19 716; 31 107, 482–3*
alabaster (limestone) 1 516
architecture 9 150; 10 803; 17 859; 23 280
beadwork 3 441
canopic chest 10 15
chariot 6 477
chests 6 559
coffin 10 10
collars 17 IV2
daggers 9 817
dress 10 44, 61, 75
Exhibition 10 94, 95
fans 10 775, 775
furniture 9 808, 811, 822, 823; 10 52, 52, 53, 54, 57, 60, 61; 20 466; 23 533; 30 775; 33 III1
glass 10 57, 58
ivory 16 797
jewellery 10 32
metalwork 10 37
models 28 611
mummy 22 284
mummy mask 10 13; 12 865
musical instruments 10 35, 65; 22 372
paintings 14 179
reliefs 9 886
Tutankhamun (reg—cont.
sarcophagus 9 813
sculpture 9 855, 885; 10 20, 91
shabtis 10 18
textiles 10 74, 75, 76
Tutayev, Cathedral of the Resurrection 27 387
Tutbury (Staffs) 1 517
St Mary's 1 517
Tutchone 22 546
tutenag see PAKTONG
Tütenk, Mustafa Akif 2 883
Tuthill, William B. 7 687
works 7 688
Tuthmosis I (reg c. 1493-c. 1482 BC) 9 777
architecture 30 691; 31 483
glass 10 56
jewellery 10 31
mummy 10 80
obelisks 23 329
sculpture 9 880
stelae 29 616
tomb 10 80
Tuthmosis II (reg c. 1482-c. 1479 BC) 9 777, 811; 10 31; 30 691
Tuthmosis III (reg c. 1479-c. 1426 BC) 9 777, 841, 861, 881; 10 5, 31, 80; 25 776; 28 434; 31 483*
architecture 2 690; 3 717; 9 831, 833; 10 803; 18 238; 20 232; 23 279; 30 691, 693, 693
glass 10 56
obelisks 23 330, 331
sarcophagi 27 824
sculpture 1 691; 9 880; 10 54
stelae 29 616
temples 1 506
wall paintings 9 903
Tuthmosis IV (reg c. 1400-c. 1390 BC) 9 777
dress 10 43–4
obelisks 23 330
sculpture 9 860; 10 36
stelae 12 767
textiles 1 880; 10 75, 75
tomb 10 80
Tutin, Mary see GILLICK, MARY
Tutin, Père 19 492
Tutin, Richard 30 741
Tutishcainyo 29 176, 193
Tutrel, François-Alexandre 26 206
Tutsi 1 362; 5 285; 27 458
Tuttin 20 603
Tuttle, Richard 24 213; 31 483–4*
Tuttukkudi 15 294; 31 484*
Tutu (el-Amarna) 9 840
Tutu (Deir Rifa) 9 840
Tutub see KHAFAJEH
Tutuila 27 683
Tutul Xiu 20 888
Tutundjian, Leon 5 776; 7 698, 772; 11 550; 14 329
Tutupec 21 202
Tutxó, Bartomeu 29 332
Tuva 27 436; 28 325
Kokel cemetery 28 325
Tuvalu 10 779; 23 711; 31 484*
Tu Wan see DU WAN
Tuxen, Laurits Regner 18 470; 26 545; 31 485*
Túy 29 258; 31 485–6*
Cathedral 29 262, 334; 31 485–6*
retable 13 69
sculpture 13 103
Tuya 9 822; 10 52, 53, 80; 33 580*, 580
architecture 1 770
furniture 30 775
glass 10 54
Tuylt, Frans van 21 358
Tuyn, J. Van see VAN TUYN, J.
Tuyru Tupac Inca, Juan Tomás 24 502, 507; 31 486*
Tuzhisar 5 722; 16 186
Tuzla 4 459, 462
TVA see TENNESSEE VALLEY AUTHORITY
Tveit, Annanias 23 242
Tveje Merløse Church 8 722
Tver' 27 363, 375, 376; 31 486*
Cathedral of the Transfiguration 27 374, 383
icons 25 338
painting 27 382, 383
Picture Gallery 31 486
pottery 27 411
Regional Local History Museum 31 486
textiles 27 400
urban planning 18 543
Tveraas, Vilhelm 23 227
Tver Factory 27 414
Tverskoy, Lev 27 378
Tvorchestvo 24 451; 27 444
Tvorozhnikov, Ivan 18 482
Tvrdohlaví 25 434
Tvrdošíjní 5 662; 24 440; 25 433; 29 359
Tvrdošíjní skupina see STIFFNECK GROUP
Tvrtković, Paul 8 177
Twa 5 285; 19 72; 27 458
Twachtman, John H(enry) 31 486–8*, 603
groups and movements 15 156; 23 47; 30 452
patrons and collectors 11 141; 24 638; 26 472
pupils 18 895
teachers 9 468
works 9 309; 31 487
Ṭwāfē, Dānē'ēl 10 574
Twain, Mark see CLEMENS, SAMUEL
Twamley, Louisa Ann see MEREDITH, LOUISA ANN
Twana 22 659
Tweed, John 19 600; 28 243; 29 647; 31 488*
works 19 600
Tweed, William Marcy 27 872
Tweeddale-type ware see under POTTERY → wares
Tweedmouth, Lord 28 249
tweeds 16 34; 28 266
Twenké
headdresses 11 758
Twentyman, Lawrence Holme 29 120; 31 488*
Twi 1 235
Twickel Castle 22 813, 872; 31 488*
Twickenham (Middx)
houses 23 857
Marble Hill House 27 131; 32 553, 553
Pope's Villa 12 128, 130; 13 704; 25 233; 32 553
Rugby Football Union 29 426
Strawberry Hill 6 61; 8 48; 10 234, 294, 295, 296; 13 198, 199, 206; 20 277; 23 544; 26 743; 32 554, 824–5, 826
armour 9 31
interior decoration 10 276
library 32 825
miniatures (paintings) 9 27
plaster 29 835
stained glass 29 506, 515
tracery 31 271
twill see under WEAVING → types
twining 3 332; 22 645–6, 655, 659
split-ply 30 550
Twining, Mrs R. H. 23 474
twin lens cameras see under CAMERAS → types
Twin Pillar Tomb 30 913
Twins Seven Seven 1 430; 15 57
works 1 429
Twisden, Thomas 22 387
Twiss (family) 5 578; 31 489*
Twiss, Austin 31 489
Twiss, Benjamin 31 489
Twiss, Greer 23 63
Twiss, Ira 31 489
Twiss, Joseph 31 489
Twiss, Russell 31 489
Twitchell, Ralph 27 313
two-cell tombs see under TOMBS → types
two-centred arches see under ARCHES → types
two-colour glazed ware see under POTTERY → wares
Two Grey Hills (NM) 22 626
Two Grey Hills style 30 368
two-handled cups see under CUPS → types
Twombly, Cy 16 681; 31 489*
dealers 6 23
groups and movements 1 81; 4 110
patrons and collectors 20 524; 21 135
works 9 213; 31 52
Twopenny, William 27 626
two-piece moulding see under MOULDING → types
Tworkov, Jack 4 110; 31 490*
Tworkowski, Władysław 32 879
Twosre, Queen see TAUSERT, Queen
two-stage cabinets see under CABINETS (ii) (FURNITURE) → types
two-tiered arches see under ARCHES → types
two-tiered cupboards see under CUPBOARDS → types
Ty 9 808; 27 812; 31 491*
reliefs 9 819, 820, 820, 822
tomb 27 811
Tybjerg, Peder 29 117
Tybrind Vig 8 720; 25 470; 31 491*
paddles 25 495, 496; 31 491
wood 31 491
Tyche of Antioch 2 156, 157; 13 370, 462; 29 567
Tyddewi see ST DAVID'S
Tye, John de see JOHN DE TYE
Tyers, Jonathan 14 269; 19 619; 27 242
Tyganeshty 21 810
Monastery 21 810
Tyghem, F. Van see VAN TYGHEM, F.
Tygh Valley (OR)
embroidery 22 646
TY Handicrafts Centre 19 241
Tyl, Oldřich 8 380; 25 430; 31 491–2*
Tyldal 6 389; 23 233
Tyler, Doug 14 690
Tyler, James 17 895
Tyler, Kenneth E. 19 492, 493; 20 607, 607–8; 25 626; 28 301; 29 621
works 19 493
Tyler, William 10 264
Tyler Graphics 10 398; 19 493; 20 607, 608–9; 25 626
Tylissos 8 153; 13 362; 21 651; 31 492*
faience (i) (glass) 21 683, 684
figurines 21 691
saws 21 688
villa 21 664
wall paintings 21 674, 675
Tylkowski, Wojciech 31 492*
Tylney, Richard, Viscount Castlemaine 5 907; 8 698
Tylor, Edward Burnett 1 67; 21 264
Tylos see BAHRAIN
Tym, Daniel 32 7, 874
Tyman, Brother 16 832
Tŷ Mawr House 32 782
tympana 31 492–3*
Austria 27 663
Cambodia 5 476
Denmark 26 305
England 10 169; 18 50

tympana—cont.
France **7** *224, 719*; **11** *554*; **26** *600*; **27** *544*; **31** *493*
Gothic **13** *75*; **19** *128*; **27** *543*; **31** *493*
Romanesque **26** *600*
Germany **20** *798*
Gothic **13** *88*
Gothic
France **13** *75*; **19** *128*; **27** *543, 544*; **31** *493*
Germany **13** *88*; **20** *798*
Spain **13** *104*
Italy **11** *6*
Netherlands, the **26** *630*
Poland **25** *109*
Romanesque **7** *224*; **10** *169*; **11** *6, 554*; **18** *50*; **19** *176*; **25** *109*; **26** *305, 600, 630*; **27** *796*
France **7** *719*; **26** *600*
Poland **25** *109*
Serbia **28** *453*
Spain **13** *104*; **19** *176*; **27** *796*
Tympanum, Master of the **32** 396
Ty-Navarro, Virginia **24** 620
Tyndale, William **4** 9
Tyndaris **26** *886*
basilica **28** 655
theatre **26** 873, 888
Týnec nad Sázavou **8** 405
Tynell, Helena **11** 106
Tynemouth Priory (Tyne & Wear) **26** 382
Tyng, Anne Griswold **31** 493–4*
Tyniec Abbey **25** *92*, 95, 109, 126; **26** 636
Tyninghame, Lothian **28** 288
Typaldos, Nikolaos Xydias *see* XYDIAS TYPALDOS, NIKOLAOS
type (movable) **7** 624; **17** 271–2
type-faces **5** 112; **15** 852; **25** 588; **31** 494
forms
Acier **5** 920
American Arabic **16** 361
Auriol Labeur **2** 733
Bembo **31** 494
type-faces
forms—cont.
Bifur **5** 920
Brevier **31** 495
Camelot **13** 223
Centaur **26** 536
Cissarz Latin **7** 346
Decorata **33** 304
Diamond **31** 495
Didot **8** 867
Eckmann **2** 565
Erbar **31** 497
Fontana **20** 404
Forum **13** 224
Française Legère **2** 733
Futura **31** 497
Gill Sans **31** 497
hieroglyphic **8** 570
il Griffo **20** 350
italic **28** 306; **31** 494
Kabel **31** 497
kabinja **28** 382
Kennerley **13** 224
Merrymount **31** 680
Montallegro **31** 680
Nonpareil **31** 495
Pegasus Roman **33** 304
Peignot **5** 921
Pica **31** 495
Riccardi **21** 32
roman **28** 306; **31** 494
Sabon **31** 396, 498
sanserif **31** 497
Tempest **33** 304
Times New Roman **31** 680
Univers **31** 497
universal **3** 402, 422
University of California Old Style **31** *496*
historical and regional traditions
Buddhism **5** 112
China **5** 112; **25** 588
England **31** 494
Italy **4** 217; **31** 494
Japan **17** 270–71
Korea **18** 356; **25** 588
United States of America **31** 680
Typenmöbel **20** 593
typesetting *see under* PRINTING → processes
typewriters **15** *826*; **25** 589
Lettera 22 **15** 826
Lettera De Luxe **15** *826*
Lexicon 80 **15** 826
Valentine typewriter **15** 826
typographical design **31** 496
typography **4** 345, 360; **7** 292; **31** 197, 494–8*, *494, 495, 496, 497*
typological cycles **1** 652; **26** 662; **29** 509–10, *510*; **31** 498–501*, *500*
typology **30** 382*
Typotius, Jacobus **29** 740
TYPSA **27** 523
Tyr, Gabriel **23** 573
Tyranov, Aleksey (Vasil'yevich) **27** 389; **32** 164
Tyras *see* BELGOROD
Tyre **1** *849*, 850; **9** *513*; **16** *104*, 572; **17** 500; **19** 8, 9; **24** 641; **28** *719*, 721; **30** 178, 179, *180*; **31** 501*
Beaufort Castle **19** 9
Cathedral **7** 259, 260, 278; **9** 539, 588; **17** 502
coins **1** 888
dyes **1** 880; **9** 664
figurines **24** 643
fonts (baptismal) **11** 251
fortifications **21** 587
harbour **24** 642
measurements **13** 411
Roman circus **7** 342
screens (i) (architectural) **28** 291
seals **9** 636, *637*
wall paintings **27** 57
Tyrell, Charles **16** 18
Tyrell, James **13** 199
Tyresö **29** 840
Tyrian purple *see under* PIGMENTS → types
Tyringham Hall (Bucks) **13** 608; **20** 868; **28** 906, *907*
Tyritaka **4** 110
Tyrnau *see* TRNAVA
Tyrol **24** 793
furniture **12** *420*
Tyrol, Leopold V, Count of *see* LEOPOLD V, Count of Tyrol
Tyrol, Maximilian, Archduke of Austria and Count of *see* MAXIMILIAN, Count of Tyrol
Tyroll, Hans *see* TIROL, HANS
Tyrone **12** 927
Tyrone Colleries **16** 29
Tyrrell, Lilian **31** 661
Tyrrhenian Group **13** 508
Tyrsa, Nikolay (Andreyevich) **19** 13; **27** 417; **31** 501–2*; **33** 740
Tyrus *see* TYRE
Tyrwhitt, J. **7** 296
Tyrwhitt-Wilson, Gerald Hugh, 14th Baron Berners **11** 242
Tysher, Marcus *see* TUSCHER, (CARL) MARCUS
Tyshler, Aleksandr (Grigor'yevich) **27** 396; **31** 502*
groups and movements **26** 70; **27** 394; **28** 924
Tysoe, Red Horse of *see* RED HORSE OF TYSOE
Tyssen-Amherst, William, 1st Baron Amherst of Hackney **5** 889
Tyszkiewicz (family) **20** 397
Tyszkiewicz, Eustach **10** 90, 94; **19** 498
Tyszkiewicz, Ludwik **17** 756
Tyszkiewicz Painter works **2** *134*
Tytgat, Edgard **2** 516; **4** 619; **5** 44; **31** 502*; **33** 363
Tytgat, Maria **31** 502
Tytler, Mary Fraser **32** 923
Tyttl, Eugen, Abbot of Plasy **8** 398
Tyumen' **27** *362*, 378; **31** 503*
Tyurin, Yevgraf D. **2** 417; **27** 376, 440
Tywcross Church **29** 515
Tyzenhauz, Rajnold **25** 675
Tzanck, Daniel **31** 503*
't Zandt Church **22** 819
Tzaneen **32** 154
Tzanes, Emmanuel **7** 850; **21** 345; **25** 334
Tzanev, Stoyan **31** 503*
Tzanfournaris, Emmanuel **25** 333
Tzankarolas, Stephanos **25** 334
Tzannes, Alexander **2** 743
Tzara, Christian **30** 748
Tzara, Tristan **9** *292*; **11** 549; **24** 405, 427, 428; **31** 503–4*
groups and movements **3** 113, 801; **8** 433, 434, 435, 436, 437, 438, 439; **24** 405; **30** 20, 22
personal collection **1** 438
productions **8** 657; **30** 25
works **8** 437; **19** 653; **20** 287; **21** 176; **24** 405; **30** 20
illustrated **16** 903; **20** 75, 399; **21** 709
Tzaritchingrad *see* CARIČIN GRAD
Tzerstede, Brand von *see* BRAND VON TZERSTEDE
Tzimouris, Athanasios **13** 358
Tzintzuntzan **21** *193, 372*; **31** 504–5*
carvings **30** 341
graves **31** 505
sculpture **21** 225; **31** 505
tombs **31** 118
yácatas **31** 504, *504*
Tzolov, D. **5** 149
tzompantlis see MESOAMERICA, PRE-COLUMBIAN → skull racks
Tzori, N. **3** 883
Tzortzis **22** 228
Tzotzil Maya **21** 249
Tz'u-hsi (empress) *see* CIXI
Tz'u-sheng, Empress *see* CISHENG, Empress
Tzutujil **20** 885
Tzwyfel, Dietrich **26** 407

U

Uahuka *see* MARQUESAS ISLANDS
Uali **17** 866
U.A.M. *see* UNION DES ARTISTES MODERNES
Uapou *see* MARQUESAS ISLANDS
Uata Uata Tjangala No. 2 *see* UTA UTA (JANGALA)
Uaxactún **13** *758*; **20** *882*; **23** 826; **31** 507*
architecture **21** 214
bone-carvings **21** 247
Group E **21** 207
stelae **21** 246
Structure A-V **30** 448
Structure XVIII **21** 214
Temple E-VII sub **21** 213, 215; **25** 764, 765; **30** 448
stucco **29** 828
wall paintings **21** 231
Ubac, Raoul **31** 508*
dealers **20** 75
groups and movements **8** 63; **30** 21
works **3** 462; **19** 491
'Ubad, Tell **9** 543
U-Bahn group **14** 693
Ubaid, Tell al- **21** *267*, 270, 303; **31** 508–9*
copper **4** 849
excavations **33** 373
figurines **21** 293
mosaics **23** 532
pottery **21** 307
stone vessels **2** 272
temple **2** 251; **21** 283; **30** 432
Ubaid culture **21** 270*, 306
Ubaid period *see under* ANCIENT NEAR EAST; MESOPOTAMIA → periods
Ubaldini, Federico **8** 139
Ubaldini, Pietro Paolo *see* BALDINI, PIETRO PAOLO
Ubaldini, Roberto, Cardinal **1** 627
Ubaldini delle Carda, Ottaviano **10** 713
Ubaldino da Campione **5** 549
Ubaldus, G. **30** 657
Ubangi **1** 362
Ubāns, Konrāds **26** 384
U Ba Nyan **5** 246
Ubavkić, Petar **28** 453
'Ubaydallah, Khan (*reg* 1534-9) (Shaybanid) **16** 342, 343
'Ubayd Allah al-Mahdi **20** 105
'Ubayd ibn Ma'ali **6** 171; **16** 490
'Ubaydllah Khan **6** 235
U Ba Zaw **5** 246
al-'Ubbad, Tomb of Abu Madyan **28** 634, 635
Ubbadat-al-Arab **31** 509
Ubbelohde, Otto **33** 174
Ube **17** 138
Ubeda **16** *103*; **29** *258*; **31** 509–10*
Hospital de Santiago **29** 266; **31** *509*
palace of Vázquez de Molina **29** 266
palace of Vela de los Cobos **29** 266
Sacra Capilla del Salvador **29** 266, *266*; **31** *865*
Ubeid, Awad **19** 324
Übelbacher, Hieronymus **31** 510*
Ubeleski, Alexandre **31** 510–11*
Überlingen
Minster **12** 404; **33** 738–9
altar **33** *738*
Rathaus **12** 409; **17** 699
Uberti, Fazio degli **2** 650
Uberti, Lucantonio degli **13** 625; **31** 511*; **33** 356
Uberti, Pietro **24** 894
Ubertini, Francesco *see* BACCHIACCA
Ubertino, Lord of Padua (*reg* 1338-45) **5** 871
Uberto da Piacenza **14** 726
Uberveldt, Jan Braedt von **25** 269
Ubiaja Palace **9** 735
Ubirr **1** *37*, 58; **31** 511*
rock art **31** *511*
Ubisi **12** *317*, 326
church **12** 324, 331
Ubisse, Nurdino **22** 245
Üblher, Johann Georg **31** 511–12*
collaboration **10** 859; **28** 132; **32** 466
Ubong *see* CHO HŬI-RYONG
Ubon Ratchathani **30** 633, 635
Ubriachi, Antonio **10** 180
Ubriachi, Domenico **10** 180
Ubriachi, Geronimo **10** 180
Ubriachi, Giovanni **10** 180
Ubu **24** 626
Ubud **15** 808
Puri Lukisan Museum of Fine Arts **29** 239
Ubud Painters' Club *see* RATNA WARTA
Uçar, Bedri **31** 452
UCC *see* UNIVERSAL COPYRIGHT CONVENTION
Uccello, Antonia **20** 704
Uccello, Paolo **14** 869; **16** 661; **20** 748; **31** 512–17*, 740
assistants **8** 683
attributions **6** 14; **20** 704, 748
collaboration **12** 544; **20** 557
methods **11** 184; **21** 763; **24** 487, 793; **25** 379
paintings
battle **22** 521
frescoes **23** 754; **26** 184
Cathedral of S Maria del Fiore (Florence) **11** 198; **13** 676; **16** 659; **22** 44; **24** 539; **29** 565; **31** *513*
Chiostro Verde (S Maria Novella, Florence) **7** 457; **11** 209; **29** 788; **31** *514*
S Maria degli Angeli (Florence) **5** 450
S Martino (Bologna) **4** 276
panel
battle **11** 149; **16** 660; **31** *515*
hunting scenes **2** 102; **29** 423; **31** *515*
religious **17** 703
patrons and collectors **2** 514; **4** 307; **5** 311, 537; **9** 683; **11** 363; **14** 869; **21** 11; **27** 307
pupils **20** 704
restorations by others **19** 677
stained glass **6** 11; **11** 198; **29** 504
ucchālaka **15** 245*
Uceda Castroverde, Juan de **31** 518*; **32** 99
Uch
tomb of Baba Hatam **15** 338
tomb of Bibi Jiwandi **15** 338
Uchanie Church
tomb of Arnulf and Stanislaus Uchański **25** 113
tomb of Paul and Anna Uchański **25** 113
Uchański, Primate **25** 126
Uchard, François **19** 296, 813
uchen see under SCRIPTS → types
Uchh **15** 686
Uchida **14** 161
Uchida, Iwao **17** 207
Uchida Kūichi **30** 256
Uchidayama Taitani **17** 351
Uchigaiso *see under* NOGATA
Uchii, Shin **31** 518
Uchii, Shōzō **17** 91; **31** 518*
Uchōa, Helio **23** 118
Uch Tepe **14** 128
Uchtomsky, Prince **30** 850
Uci **6** 97
Uç Kilise Church **9** 543
Udabno, Church of the Annunciation and the Ascension **12** 323
Udaipur (Rajasthan) **15** *276*, *597*, 599; **31** 518–19*
Bharatiya Lok Kala Museum **31** 519
City Palace **31** 519
Chitram ki Burj **15** 601
collections **15** 182
Government Museum **31** 519
Museum **31** 519
dyeing **15** 671
fortifications **21** 590
Government Museum *see under* City Palace
houses **32** 323
Jagannatha Temple **15** 385, 491
Jagdish Temple *see* Jagannatha Temple
paintings **15** 597, 598, 599, 600, 643
palace **15** 387, *387*, 390, 693
sculpture **15** 485
Udaipur (Tripura)
temples **15** 396
Udai Singh, Rana of Mewar (*reg* 1536-72) (Rajput) **31** 519
Udalrich, Abbot **1** 4
Udalricus **23** 654
Udal'tsova, Nadezhda (Andreyevna) **9** 296; **31** 519–20*; **32** 661
groups and movements **16** 818; **30** 8
patrons and collectors **8** 10
teachers **21** 364; **33** 577
udambara **15** 245*
Udaya **25** 833
Udayaditya, Ruler (*reg c.* 1080-86) (Paramara) **15** 291
Udayadityavarman II, King of Cambodia (*reg* 1050--66) **2** 55; **5** 472
Udayagiri (i) (Orissa) *see* UDAYGIRI-KHANDAGIRI (ORISSA)
Udayagiri (ii) (Madya Pradesh) **15** 237, *276*, *285*; **31** 520–21*
Cave 1 **15** 254
Cave 4 **15** 467
Cave 5 **15** 468; **31** *520*, 520
Cave 6 **15** 254, 467–8
sculpture **15** *468*
Cave 7 **15** 467
Cave 9 **15** 467
Cave 17 **15** 467
Cave 19 **15** 254, 456, 468; **31** 520–21
reliefs **15** 215
sculpture **15** 218, 231, 416, 455, 467–8, 750
temples **15** 275
Varaha Temple **15** 738
Udayagiri-Khandagiri (Orissa) **3** 908; **5** 96; **15** 505; **18** 18*
apsidal temple **15** 251
Cave 5 **15** *437*
Cave 14 **15** 230
sculpture **15** 437–8*, 503, *505*
Udayamati, Queen (Solanki) **24** 251
Udayapur **15** *285*; **31** 521*
Nilakantheshvara Temple *see* Udayeshvara Temple
temples **15** 738
Udayeshvara Temple **14** 77; **15** *291*, 291–2, 497; **24** 102; **30** 438; **31** 521
sculpture **15** *497*
Udayasena, Ruler (*reg c.* 636) (Maukhari) **15** 261
Udaygiri **15** *279*
Udayi, King (*reg* 5th cent. BC) (Saisunaga) **24** 264
Udaypur, Markuladevi **15** 309
Uddaka **15** 739
Uddandapura **15** 499
Uddiyana **5** 94
Udechukwu, Obiora **23** 136
works **23** *137*
Udegey **27** 436
Udegi **23** 181
terracotta **23** *181*
Udemann, Jakob **20** 692
Uden, Adriaen van **31** 523
Uden, Arnoldus van **31** 523
Uden, Artus van **31** 521
Uden, Jacob van **31** 523
Uden, Lucas van **18** *47*; **25** 808; **31** 521–3*
collaboration **3** 108; **4** 916
works **3** 561; **18** 711; **31** *523*
Uden, Pieter van, (i) (*fl* 1553) **2** 198; **31** 521
Uden, Pieter van, (ii) (*fl* 1673-4) **31** 523
Ūders, Teodors
udgama **15** 245*
Udine, Archbishop's Palace **16** 676; **30** 856
Udine, Giovanni da **13** 658; **26** 769; **31** 523–4*
assistants **24** 419
attributions **10** 349; **26** 61
collaboration **6** 583; **10** 130; **12** 752; **22** 6; **25** 902, 908; **26** 818
paintings
frescoes **25** *907*
patrons and collectors **13** 658; **25** 7
reproductive prints by others **20** 658
works **2** 102; **11** 382; **13** 700; **16** 712, *712*; **21** 17; **26** 817; **27** 649; **29** 829; **31** *523*
Udine, Giovanni Martini da *see* GIOVANNI MARTINI DA UDINE
Udine, Girolamo da *see* GIROLAMO DA UDINE
Udine, Martino da *see* PELLEGRINO DA SAN DANIELE
Udipi **15** 730
Udmurt **27** 435
Udmurtia **27** 434, 435
Udney, John **31** 524–5*
Udney, Robert **9** 740; **10** 366; **31** 524*
Udo, Archbishop of Trier **31** 326
Udoh Umor Aran Ekot
works **15** *64*
Udong (Cambodia) **5** *458*, 507
architecture **5** 481
sculpture **5** 499
stupas **5** 481
Vat Tep Pranam **5** 499
Udong (Korea) **18** 342
Udo-Nwa Matthew Ekpe **15** 64
Udrişte **26** 708
udumbara see UDAMBARA
Uduvil **16** 864
Uebelherr, Johann Georg **13** 853
Ueberfeldt, J. B. van **21** 851
Uecker, Günther **22** 381; **31** 525*
collaboration **20** 11
dealers **26** 193
groups and movements **12** 397; **13** 727; **33** 636
works **10** 178
Ueda, Naokata **17** 267
Ueda, Sōkyū **17** 240
Ueda, Tsuneji **17** 266
Ueda Akinari **17** 197, 414; **23** 594
Ueda Katei **17** 412
Ue Gukei **17** 170, 171
Uele **1** 365
Uelen **27** 436
Uelsmann, Jerry N(orman) **31** 525*
Uelzen, St Viti Leprosenkapelle **13** 187
Uemon *see* NISHIKAWA SUKENOBU
Uemura, Shōen **17** 201, 436; **31** 525*
Uemura Bunrakuken (1737-1810) **17** 350, 407
Uemura Bunrakuken II (1812-87) **17** 407
Ueno (family) **17** 414
Ueno City, Iga-Ueno Castle **15** 108
Ueno Royal Museum *see under* TOKYO → museums
Uenuku **20** 354
Uesugi Kenshin **17** 783; **29** 627
Uesugi Norikata **17** 747
Uesugi Shigekane **17** 747
Uexküll *see* IKŠĶILE
Ufa **27** 434
Bashkirian State Art Museum **4** 313
Regional Museum **27** 440
Uffelen, Lucas van **9** 410; **31** 526*
Uffenbach, Johann Friedrich **11** 734
Uffenbach, Philipp **10** 156; **17** 886; **31** 526*
Uffenbach, Zacharias von **22** 872
Ufficio Fotografico **2** 365
Ufficio per l'Arte Contemporanea **10** 821
Uffington (Oxon)
Castle **31** 527
St Mary **9** 155
Uffington Horse **10** *225*; **14** 544; **25** *470*; **31** 526–7*, *527*
Ufford (Suffolk), St Mary **11** 254
Ufsir **15** 69
Ugalde, Gastón **4** 264
Ugalde, Manuel **4** 262; **31** 527*; **32** 572
Ugāle **18** *847*
church **18** 848
Uganda **1** *214*; **31** 527–9*
architecture **31** 528
bamboo **1** 310
basketwork **1** 295, 296
batik **31** 528
bracelets **1** 362
earplugs **1** 296
education (art) **31** 528
granaries **1** 310
houses **1** 311
musical instruments **31** 528
painting **1** *432*; **31** 528*
palaces **1** 309
papyrus **1** 310
pipes (smoking) **1** 368
rings **1** 362
rock art **1** 374
sculpture **31** 528*

Uganda—cont.
trade **1** 249
Ugarit **1** *821*, 826, *849*, 850; **14** 591; **30** 178, *180*, 185; **31** 529–31*
architecture **4** 772; **5** 557; **30** 191, 192
beads **1** 877
bowls **5** 557
bronze **30** 194; **31** 530
dyes **1** 880
faience (i) (glass) **1** 878, *878*, 879
fortifications **21** 553; **30** 186
glass **1** 865
gold **1** 874; **31** 531
houses **30** 186; **31** 530
ivory-carvings **1** 870*, *870*, 890; **24** 643; **30** 186, 194; **31** 531
jewellery **1** 877
metalwork **30** 195; **31** 530–31
Petit Palais **30** 186
plaster **30** 196
pottery **30** 196, 197
reliefs **30** 193
royal palace **5** 557; **23** 806; **30** 186, 191; **31** 529–30, *530*
scripts **1** 855
sculpture **30** 185; **31** 530
seals **1** 857, 862, 863
stelae **29** 613; **30** 193, *193*, 194; **31** 530
Temple of Baal **31** 530
temples **30** 188; **31** 530
trade **14** 337
writing-tablets **1** 893; **30** 188
Ugarov, Boris (Sergeyevich) **27** 581
Ugarte Eléspuru, Juan Manuel **24** 510; **28** 604; **31** 531*
Ugartemendía, Pedro de **27** 767
Ugelheimer, Peter **4** 397; **17** 481
Ugena, Cristobal de **29** 303
Ugena, Manuel Muñoz de *see* MUÑOZ DE UGENA, MANUEL
Ugento
sculpture **13** 448; **30** 339, *339*
Uggason, Ulfr **32** 523
Uggeri, Angelo **5** 622
Uglich **27** *363*; **31** 531–2*
Castle **4** 783
Historical Museum **31** 532
Ugljen, Zlatko **16** 242
Ugloskaya-Sycheva, Mariya (Alekseyevna) **27** 422
Uglow, Euan **7** 547; **19** 246; **21** 761; **31** 532*
Ugly Realism **31** 532*
Ugo, Margrave of Tuscany (*reg* 961-1001) **11** 175
Ugo da Campione **5** 550
Ugoleto, Taddeo **20** 847
Ugolino da Siena *see* UGOLINO DI NERIO
Ugolino di Nerio **29** 599; **31** 532–4*
collaboration **9** 346, 349
methods **25** 731
patrons and collectors **27** 359
works **11** 184; **13** 146; **25** 463, *730*; **30** *426*; **31** *533*
Ugolino di Prete Ilario **24** 771, 830
Ugolino di Tedice **10** 403; **24** 854
Ugolino di Vieri **28** 676; **31** 534–6*
works **13** 163, 169; **16** 741; **31** *535*
Ugolino-Lorenzetti **5** 164; **14** 570
Ugoni, Mattia **22** 107
Ugonio, Pompeo **31** 536*
Ugryumov, Grigory (Ivanovich) **18** 74; **27** 579; **28** 573; **31** 536–7*; **32** 627
Uguccioni, Benedetto **5** 183
Uğura *see* OLBA
Ugurgieri (family) **28** 681
Uhaimir, Tell *see* KISH
Uhde, (Friedrich Hermann Karl) Fritz von **31** 537–8*
groups and movements **14** 694; **28** 341
Uhde, (Friedrich Hermann Karl) Fritz von—cont.
works **4** 42; **11** 463, *464*; **31** *538*
Uhde, Wilhelm **8** 658; **31** 538–9*
groups and movements **22** 440
paintings **4** 294, 673; **28** 435
patrons and collectors **18** 750
personal collection **24** 720
writings **27** 263
Uhden, Maria **28** 169
Uhemka **9** 872
Uher, Rudolf **28** 855
Uherské Hradiště **8** 378, 388, 425
Uhl, Ottokar **31** 539*
Uhlberger, Hans Thomann **29** 750
Uhle, Max **2** 300; **15** 67; **20** 382; **24** 516; **29** 221; **31** 539*
excavations **21** 750; **23** 702, 703; **29** 218–19, 221
works **29** 157
Uhlhorn, Diedrich **20** 925
Uhlig, Max **31** 539–40*
Uhlmann, Hans **3** 802, 803; **12** 408; **31** 540–41*
Uhrl, Ferenc **14** 895
Uhrovec Glassworks **28** 856
Uhuru **12** 510
Uhyang *see* CHŎNG TAE-YU
UIA *see* UNION INTERNATIONALE DES ARCHITECTES
Uichi Shimizu *see* SHIMIZU, UICHI
Ŭich'ŏn **5** 115
Ŭidoin *see* HŎ PAEK-NYŎN
Ŭijae *see* HŎ PAEK-NYŎN
Ŭijaesanin *see* HŎ PAEK-NYŎN
Ŭijong, King (*reg* 1146-70) **18** 276
Uilenburg, Gerrit *see* UYLENBURGH, GERRIT
Uists, The **28** 229
Uiterwaal, Johan **22** 861
Uiterwijk, John Th., & Co. *see* ARTS AND CRAFTS, JOHN TH. UITERWIJK, & CO.
Uitz, Béla **17** 876; **24** 440; **31** 541–2*
collaborative writings **17** 833
groups and movements **1** 131, 132; **14** 901; **18** 142; **20** 103
works **31** *541*
Ujan **16** 193
Ujantalvölgy Glassworks **29** 249
Ujarma Citadel **12** 319
Ujarrás **8** *15*
church **8** 16
Ujazd **25** *92*
Krzyżtopór Castle **25** 97, 118, 135; **28** 407
Uj föld **24** 441
Uji
Asahiyama *see* Byōdōin
Byōdōin **5** 334–6*; **14** 302; **17** *11*, 52, 68, 598; **30** 446
Amida Hall *see* Phoenix Hall
architecture **5** 118–19
enamel **17** 377
Phoenix Hall **5** 334–6*, *335*; **11** 822; **12** 97; **17** 21, 98, 156, 423
Amida Buddha **17** 21, 100
architecture **5** 335*
sculpture **17** *116*, 117, 119, 397
wall paintings **17** 147; **30** 264
Manpukuji **6** 722; **15** 126; **17** *11*, 75, 231; **20** 285*, 286–7*
Main Buddha Hall **20** *286*
painting **17** 419
Ujichika Imagawa *see* IMAGAWA UJICHIKA
Ujihirō Ōkuma *see* ŌKUMA, UJIHIRŌ
Ujiji **1** *407*, 409; **30** 56
Ujjain **15** *285*, 409; **31** 542–3*
coins **15** 688
ivory **15** 695
Mahakala Temple **15** 498; **31** 542, *542*
sculpture **31** 543
temples **15** 406
Ujong Bukit **5** 11
Ujué, S María **13** 105; **26** 642, 689
Ujung Pandang **15** 775
art schools **15** 819
coins **15** 812
copper **15** 812
figureheads **15** 810
Fort Rotterdam **15** 775; **21** 596
U Khanti **5** 246
Ukhaydir **16** *104*, 152, 549; **23** 815; **31** 543*
brick **4** 791
palace **21** 582; **24** 877
Ukhhotpe **21** 61
reliefs **21** *60*; **24** *88*
Ukhtomsky, Dmitry (Vasil'yevich) **27** 442; **31** 543–4*
assistants **18** 196
collaboration **21** 475; **27** 374
pupils **3** 432; **17** 869; **18** 196
works **22** 171; **27** 374; **28** 465; **31** *544*
Uki **29** 50
UKIC *see* UNITED KINGDOM INSTITUTE FOR CONSERVATION
ukie see under PRINTS → types → *ukiyoe*
Ukil, Sarada **8** 677
Ukita Ikkei **31** 136, 545*
ukiyoe see under JAPAN → painting; prints
Ukon *see* KANŌ TSUNENOBU
Ukraine **27** *363*; **31** 545–65*, *546*
amphorae **28** *324*
architecture **31** 546–50*, 551–3*
armour **31** 563
brass **31** 562
bronze **31** 562
carpets **31** 564
cathedrals **18** *38*; **31** 547
ceramics **31** 563
chapels **19** *836*
churches **7** 274; **18** *36*; **31** *547*, 547, 548, *548*, 550, *552*, 552–4*, *553*
collections **19** 789; **31** 564–5*
copper **31** 562
decorative arts **31** 562*, 563–4*
earthenwares **31** 563
embroidery **31** 564
enamel **31** 562, *562*
exhibitions **2** 634
fortresses **31** *549*
glass **31** 563
gold **31** 562, *562*
hangings **31** 564
houses **25** *501*
icons **25** 341*; **26** *141*; **31** 554–5*, *555*, 557*, 558
jewellery **31** 562*, *562*
manuals **20** 807
manuscript illumination **31** 555–6*, 557–8*
marble **31** 561
marks **31** 547
metalwork **31** 562–3*
miniatures (manuscript illumination) **31** 556, *556*, *558*
monasteries **18** *40*
mosaics **18** *37*, 38–9; **31** 553–4*, *554*
museums **31** 565*
new towns **31** 552
niello **31** 562
painting **31** 553*, 554–6*, 557–60*
wall **18** 39; **25** 344*; **31** 553–4*, 556–7*, 558
20th cent. **4** 605; **31** *559*
patronage **31** 564–5*
sarcophagi **31** 561
sculpture **31** 560–61*
architectural **7** 274
relief **31** *560*
silver **31** 562
silver-gilt **28** *324*
slate **31** *560*
spice-boxes **17** 572
stone **31** 546, 547
synagogues **17** 545, 546; **31** 550
Ukraine—cont.
textiles **31** 563–4
theatres **23** *354*
towels **31** 564
universities **18** *36*
urban planning **31** 547, 549, 551
vernacular art **31** 559, 560, 563
weapons **31** 563
wood **31** 546
wood-carvings **31** 564
see also OLD RUSSIAN; RUS'
U Kya Nyunt **5** 246
Ukyō *see* NISHIKAWA SUKENOBU
Ul, Sebastiano d' *see* VALENTINIS, SEBASTIANO DE
Ulaan Baatar **21** *870*, 871
architecture **21** 874
Central Council of the Trade Unions **21** 875
Central Library **21** 886
Central Museum **21** 875, 886
Drama Theatre **21** 875
Gandantegchinling Monastery *see* Ganden Thekchen Ling Monastery
Ganden Thekchen Ling monastery **21** 872, 883
Megzid Janraiseg temple **21** 875
metalwork **21** *879*
Ih huree **5** 106
monasteries **21** 875
Museum of Fine Arts **21** 877, 879, 886
Museum of Religion **21** 886
Palace Museum **21** 886
State Printing House **21** 875
tents **30** 476
Ulaanbaatar Hotel **21** 875
ULAE (Universal Limited Art Editions) **19** 492, 493; **20** 606, 609; **25** 626
al-'Ula Museum **2** 275
Ulanov, Kirill **22** 177; **27** 387
Ulan-Ude **21** *870*
Ethnographic Museum **21** 886
Museum of Buryat History and Oriental Art **21** 886
museums **27** 436
Ulapmin **24** 73, 74
Ulas, Peeter **10** 540
Ulawa **29** 50
Ulbert, T. **27** 343
Ulceby **6** 161
Ul'chi **27** 436
Ulchu **18** 297
Ulcinj **22** *17*; **28** 452
Ul'delli, S.-I. **12** 633
Ulenborch, Gerrit *see* UYLENBURGH, GERRIT
Ulfstand, Jens **9** 427
Ulf the Painter **11** 94
Uli, Diethelm **20** 803
Ulianskas, Kazimieras **19** 498
Ulich, Anders **11** 94
Ulin, Pierre d' **26** 349
Ulinich, B. Yu. **12** 877
Ulitin, Vasily (Ivanovich) **31** 566*
Ulívarri, Jerónimo **29** 338
Ulivelli, Cosimo **7** 458
Ulivieri della Chiostra **6** 139
Uljayta **24** 48
Uljaytu, Sultan (*reg* 1304-17) (Ilkhanid) **1** 473; **15** 133; **16** 91, 282; **20** 229; **29** 919–20
Ullán, Antonio Ruiz *see* RUIZ ULLÁN, ANTONIO
Ullandhaug **23** 219
Ullas, N. N. **32** 670
Ullastret **10** 190; **21** 551; **25** 536
Ullens de Schooten, Marie-Thérèse **15** 922
Ullevål Garden City **14** 97; **23** 222
Ullman, Micha **31** 566*
Ullman, Vojtěch Ignác **17** 547
Ullmann, Franz **8** 410
Ullmann, Gyula **17** 821*
Ullmann, Ignaz **3** 312; **8** 379; **25** 428, 429
Ulloa, Víctor **9** 118
Ullrich, Dietmar **33** 627
Ullstein **27** 637; **28** 373
Ulm **12** *361*; **31** 566–70*
Dominican monastery church *see* Dreifaltigkeitskirche
Dreifaltigkeitskirche **33** 385
façade decoration **10** 737, 741
gold **12** 443
Hochschule für Gestaltung **4** *61*, 61; **12** 418, 480; **15** 826
Karl Marx School *see* Hochschule für Gestaltung
Minster **4** 189, *189*; **10** 407, 408; **12** 365; **13** 58; **24** 192; **31** 567–9*, *567*, *568*
Besserer Chapel **12** 383; **13** 187; **29** 503
busts **12** 401
choir-stalls **7** 192; **13** 117, *118*; **30** 200
font **11** 254
liturgical furnishings **12** 400
misericords **21** 725
pinnacles **24** 826
sculpture **12** 401; **13** *91*, 91; **31** *569*, 569–70*
spire **20** 581; **29** 414
stained glass **13** 187
vaults **32** 91
painting **12** 384, 387
Podium **30** 684
printing **12** 385
Rathaus **10** 738; **26** 368; **31** 570*
sculpture **13** 91; **19** 831
royal palace **30** 884
St John the Baptist **13** 204
sculpture **13** 85, 117
Spitalkirche *see* Dreifaltigkeitskirche
Ulmer Museum **1** 437; **33** 19
Ulm, Hansen von *see* HANSEN VON ULM
Ulm: Zeitschrift der Hochschule für Gestaltung **24** 429
Ulm Aesop, Master of the **30** 200
Ulmann, Doris **31** 570*
Ulmer, Bastion *see* BASTION ULMER
Ulm Fischkasten **18** 451
Ulner, Peter, Abbot **5** 61
U Lo **30** 626–7
Ulocrino **31** 570*
Ulpiana **28** 439
Ulpius Orestes, M. **27** 27
Ulpius Trajanus **27** 602
Ulrica, Queen of Sweden (1656-93) **10** 773
Ulrica Eleanora, Queen of Sweden (*reg* 1719-20) **30** 114
goblets **30** *101*
Ulricehamn **30** 106
Ulrich, Saint and Bishop of Augsburg **2** 715, 719; **9** 666
Ulrich V, Count of Württemberg (*reg* 1441-80) **4** 187
Ulrich VI, Duke of Württemberg (*reg* 1504 -09; 1534-50) **8** 541; **11** 838; **31** 311; **33** 429
Ulrich, Charles **31** 603
Ulrich, Hans Christian **30** 151
Ulrich, Heinrich **33** 131
Ulrich, Johann Jakob **18** 204; **31** 571*
Ulrich of Braşov **26** 712
Ulrich of Lilienfeld **31** 500
Ulrich of Strasbourg **1** 176
Ulrich von Ensingen *see* ENSINGEN, ULRICH VON
Ulrich von Pottenstein **10** 724
Ulrich von Richental **7** 244; **14** 424; **24** 36
Ulriksdal Castle **30** 90, 96
Ulriksen, Guillermo **18** 810
Ulrych, Josef **8** 423
Ulsan **18** 252
Ulski Aul **28** 323
kurgan 2 **28** 323
Ulster *see* NORTHERN IRELAND
Ulster Fireclay Works **16** 28

Ultimate La Tène *see under* CELTIC → periods
ultramarine *see under* PIGMENTS → types
ultra-violet light *see under* LIGHT
Ultvedt, Per Olof (Jörgensen Hungerholt) **10** 416; **15** 869; **27** 587; **30** 86; **31** 571*
Ulubat, Issız Han **16** 206
Ulu Burun wreck **14** 333; **19** 837; **30** 180
glass **10** 54
seals **17** 836
Ulugh Ajelka Khan **8** 846
Ulughbeg, Sultan (*reg* 1447-9) (Timurid) **16** 197; **23** 338; **30** 917, 920*
architecture **5** 138; **6** 203, 208; **16** 198, 253; **27** 673, 675, 676, 677; **28** 538
jade **6** 272, 285; **15** 699; **16** 527, 552, III1
manuscripts **16** 323
porcelain **16** 413; **27** 674
wood-carvings **6** 277
Ulug Tepe **6** 195
Uluru *see* AYERS ROCK
Ulvik **13** 143
Ul'yanov, Nikolay (Pavlovich) **27** 394; **31** 571–2*; **33** 740
Ul'yanov, V(ladimir) I(l'ich) *see* LENIN, V(LADIMIR) I(L'ICH)
Ul'yanovsk, V. I. Lenin Museum complex **31** 398
Umaid Singh, Maharaja of Marwar (*reg* 1918-47) (Rajput) **17** 600
Umaid Singh, Ruler of Bundi (*reg* 1744-71) (Rajput) **5** 171
Umako, Soga no *see* SOGA NO UMAKO
Umale **15** 109
Uman Deme *see* DEME UMAN
ʻUmar (*fl* 19th cent)
works **16** *508*
ʻUmar, Caliph (*reg* 634-44) (Orthodox Caliphs) **3** 338; **16** 431; **17** 489; **20** 913; **21** 32
ʻUmar, Caliph (*reg* 717-20) (Umayyad) **16** 452
ʻUmar al-Isʻirdi **16** 379
ʻUmar Aqtaʻ **16** 284
Umarbekov, Dzhavlat (Yusupovich) **31** 783
ʻUmar bin Ahmad al-Kazaruni **18** 17
al-ʻUmari **16** 369
ʻUmar ibn al-Khidr **16** 381
Umayyad **16** 112; **31** 572*
banners **11** 146
Umayyad (Spain) **16** 121; **31** 573–4*
architecture **20** 50
palaces **23** 815
silk **28** 716
see also:
AL-HAKAM II, Caliph
ʻABD ALLAH, Amir
ʻABD AL-RAHMAN I, Amir
ʻABD AL-RAHMAN II, Amir
ʻABD AL-RAHMAN III AL-NASIR, Caliph
HISHAM II, Caliph
MUHAMMAD I, Amir
Umayyad (Syria) **16** 121, 122; **31** 572–3*
architecture **4** 464
friezes **31** *573*
palaces **23** 815
stucco **31** *573*
thrones **30** 784
woodwork **17** 496
see also:
AL-WALID I, Caliph
AL-WALID II, Caliph
ʻABD-AL-MALIK, Caliph
HISHAM, Caliph
MARWAN II, Caliph
MUʻAWIYA, Caliph
SULAIMAN, Caliph
Umayyad (Syria)
see also:—cont.
ʻUMAR, Caliph
Umayyad Palace ware *see under* POTTERY → wares
Umbach, Jonas **2** 717, 719; **12** 390; **31** 574*
Um Bau **24** 439
Umbdenstock, Gustave **5** 634; **23** 122; **31** 575*
pupils **8** 131; **10** 689; **24** 824
Umbdenstock, Jean-Pierre **3** 596
umber **11** 763; **15** 855; **24** 792; **28** 339
Umberto I, King of Italy (*reg* 1878-1900) **9** 177; **28** 707
umbrella papers *see under* PAPERS → types
umbrellas **1** 354; **2** 587–8*; **17** 359
Umbrella Trees, Master of the *see* BOQUETEAUX, MASTER OF THE
Umbrian **29** 420
Umbro, Metaurus Suassus **31** 739
Umdurman *see* OMDURMAN
Umeå University **30** 119
Umed Singh, Ruler (*reg* 1748-64) (Pahari) **6** 405
Umehara, Ryūzaburō **17** 207; **30** 241; **31** 575*
exhibitions **17** 436
groups and movements **17** 205; **31** 82
patrons and collectors **23** 179
teachers **2** 579; **17** 205
works **17** *204*
Umehara, Sueji **7** 161
Umělecká Beseda *see* ARTISTIC FORUM
Umělecký měsíčník (Art monthly) **3** 715; **8** 373; **24** 440
Umění **24** 440
Umerkot Museum **23** 804
Umetarō Azechi *see* AZECHI, UMETARŌ
Umm al-Biyarra **9** 737
Umm al-Nar Island **2** *246*
graves **2** 248
jewellery **2** 263
pottery **2** 266
reliefs **2** 253–4
stone vessels **2** 271
Umm al-Nussi **2** 267
Umm al-Qaywayn **2** 275
see also UNITED ARAB EMIRATES
Umm al-Ramadh **2** 267
Umm Dabaghiya **21** *267*, 269; **31** 575–6*
houses **21** 280
pottery **21** 305
wall paintings **21** 308
Umm el-Baragat *see* TEBTUNIS
Umm el-ʻEbeida **28** 810
Temple of Amun **9** 834
Umm el-Halahi **9** 543
Umm el-Kanatir Synagogue **17** 541
Umm er-Rassas **9** 543
St Stephen **9** 568
Umm is-Surab **21** 834
Umm Shegilat **29** 700
Umri, Surya Temple **15** 288
Umriss **24** 439
UMS (Utrechtsche Machinale Stoel- en Meubelfabriek) **22** 876; **31** 576*
works **22** *876*
Umsinn, Anton **31** 510
Un **15** *285*, 292; **24** 102; **31** 576*
Una, Hadrat Shah Pir Dargah **15** 349
Unanimism **1** 21; **26** 558
UNAP *see* UNIÃO NACIONAL DE ARTISTAS PLÁSTICOS
Unas (*reg c.* 2356-*c.* 2325 BC) **9** *776*; **10** 83; **25** 763; **27** 812
Unbertus **26** 595; **27** 534
Uncastillo **29** *259*
S María **26** 607; **31** 577*
S Martín **27** 752
Unchdih **15** 455
Unch'ŏn *see* KIM TU-RYANG
uncial script *see under* SCRIPTS → types
Uncini, Giuseppe **26** 778
Unda, José **9** 713; **16** 806, 834
Undae **18** 342
Undavalli **15** 293, 295, 534
Underadin, Heinrich **12** 223
Underberg, Léon **20** 198
underclothes **16** 458, 461, 464, 466
undercrofts **23** 247
undercutting **21** 878
underdrawings **6** 470; **9** 213, 214; **13** 315; **22** 156; **24** 350; **31** 577–8*
Belgium **31** *577*
England **20** *348*
Gothic **20** *348*
Greece, ancient **13** 543–4
see also DRAWINGS; SINOPIE
underglaze decoration *see under*: CERAMICS; EARTHENWARES; PORCELAIN; POTTERY → techniques;
underground chambers *see* HYPOGEA
Underground Group *see* LONDON PASSENGER TRANSPORT BOARD
underlays **24** 51
underwater archaeology *see* ARCHAEOLOGY → types → marine
underwater foundations *see under* FOUNDATIONS → types
Underwood, Charles **4** 822
Underwood, Leon **1** 448; **5** 531
Underwood, Paul Atkins **9** 527; **16** 597; **31** 578–9*
Underwood, Thomas **25** 264
Underworld Painter **13** 530; **32** 69*
Undi, Carla **12** 839
Undi, Mariska **12** 839
Un'en *see* MASUDA KINSAI
Un enemic del póble **8** 436
UNESCO (United Nations Educational, Scientific and Cultural Organization)
accords **10** 91
archives **2** 365, 369
art policies **2** 556
conservation **7** 743; **10** 81, 83, 95; **24** 602; **31** 424
exhibitions **26** 236
museums **19** 324
restoration **24** 2
sponsorship **2** 323; **27** 601
Únětice **25** 528
Unfertsagt, Georg **20** 146
unfinished works of art *see* ART (UNFINISHED WORKS OF)
Unga, De *see* YOUNG ONES
Ungal **1** 241
Ungarelli, Luigi Maria **13** 629
Ungaro, Michele (*c.* 1400-64) *see* PANNONIO, MICHELE
Ungaro, Michele (*fl* 1680s) **7** 650
Unger, Edmund de **16** 295, 555
Unger, Georg Christian **3** 689, 791; **4** 542; **18** 476; **25** 366
Unger, Gracjan **32** 876
Unger, Johann Friedrich Gottlieb **23** 410; **33** 359
Unger, Johann Georg **33** 359
Unger, Max **28** 52
Unger, Theophile **33** 368
Unger, (Christian) Wilhelm (Jacob) **26** 234; **31** 579*
Unger, William **17** 517, 897
Unger Bros **31** 649
Ungerer, Jacob **3** 511
Ungers, Oswald Mathias **31** 579–80*
assistants **18** 455
collaboration **23** 361
groups and movements **5** 56; **25** 359; **30** 391
pupils **18** 236
Ungers, Oswald Mathias—cont.
works **11** 734, 735; **12** 380, 381, 498, *498*
Ungewitter, Georg Gottlob **31** 580–81*
groups and movements **13** 203, 204, 208
pupils **14** 301; **28** 46; **33** 173
works **8** 400
Unghero, Nanni **3** 683; **31** 320, 581*
Ungjin *see* KONGJU
Ungleich, Philipp **5** 84; **15** 13
unguent vessels **25** 734
U Ngwe Gaing **5** 246
Ŭnhae Temple **18** 311
União Nacional de Artistas Plásticos (UNAP) **2** 87
Uniara
Jagat Shiromani Temple **15** 607
manuscript illumination **15** 607
painting **15** 603
Rangshala **15** 607
UNICO **33** 602
Unicorn (Jednorog) **18** 429
Unicorn, Master of the *see* DUVET, JEAN (*c.* 1485-after 1561)
Unicorn Hunt, Master of the **20** 776–8*; **31** 844, 846
works **20** *777*
UNIDROIT (International Institute for the Unification of Private Law) **2** 556
uniforms **16** 461
Unii, Michele dai *see* PANNONIO, MICHELE
Unik, Pierre **30** 19, 20
Unika-Væv **27** 215
Unimark International **32** 500
Union carpets *see under* CARPETS → types
union carpets *see under* CARPETS → types
union catalogues *see under* CATALOGUES → types
Union Centrale des Beaux-Arts Appliqués à l'Industrie **28** 346
Unión de Arquitectos Socialistas (Mexico) **2** 280; **33** 493
Unión de Orfebres **29** 344
Union des Artistes Modernes **2** 522; **11** 584, 602; **13** 798; **31** 581–2*
members **6** 476; **11** 526; **13** 328; **17** 668; **20** 203; **24** 475; **25** 719; **27** 853
Union des Artistes Russes (France) **12** 894; **18** 793
Union des Arts **10** 517
Union des Femmes Peintres et Sculpteurs **33** 309
unione **6** 570
Unione Cooperativa **29** 486
Union Flint Glass Co. **31** 642
Unionfoto *see* SOYUZFOTO
Union Internationale des Architectes **30** 199
Union Master **20** 674
Union Nationale des Arts Plastiques **1** 635
Union of Active Revolutionary Art **12** 35
Union of Artists (Jednota Umelců Výtvarných) **2** 546
Union of Artists (Soyuz khudozhnikov) **22** 178; **27** 581
Union of Bulgarian Artists *see* NATIONAL ART SOCIETY OF BULGARIA
Union of Czechoslovak Fine Artists (SČVU) **25** 434
Union of Dutch Indies Art Societies **15** 808
Union of Fine Arts (Syria) **30** 177
Union of Friends of the Arts **3** 799
Union of Indonesian Painters *see* PERSAGI
Union of Libyan Artists **19** 324
Union of New Tendencies in Art **30** 363
Union of Plastic Artists, Romania **5** 74; **20** 141
Union of Proletarian Architects *see* VOPRA
Union of Russian Artists **22** 178; **31** 582*
members **27** 392
Arkhipov, Abram (Yefimovich) **2** 417
Bogayevsky, Konstantin (Fyodorovich) **4** 229
Grabar', Igor' (Emmanuilovich) **13** 263
Ivanov, Sergey (Vasil'yevich) **16** 792
Larionov, Mikhail (Fyodorovich) **18** 792
Malyutin, Sergey (Vasil'yevich) **20** 223
Mayakovsky, Vladimir (Vladimirovich) **20** 887
Rylov, Arkady (Aleksandrovich) **27** 463
Serebryakova, Zinaida (Yevgen'yevna) **28** 459
Stepanov, Aleksey (Stepanovich) **29** 631
Ul'yanov, Nikolay (Pavlovich) **31** 571
Yakovlev, Aleksandr (Yevgeniyevich) **33** 486
Yuon, Konstantin (Fyodorovich) **27** 394
Zamyraylo, Viktor (Dmytriyevych) **33** 607
Union of Russian Watercolourists **18** 482
Union of Socialist Architects (Czech Republic) **3** 736; **6** 345; **7** 182; **33** 599
Union of Soviet Architects **9** 73; **21** 622; **32** 383, 695
Union of Soviet Socialist Republics **31** 582*
architecture **29** 529
censorship **6** 176
collections **17** 581
exhibitions **18** 793
government buildings **19** *207*
holograms **14** 690
housing **27** 578
Museums of Painterly Culture **17** 764
paintings **22** 332
periodicals **24** 424, 677
photography **24** 674, 676
photojournalism **11** 775
theories (art) **20** 527
see also ARMENIA; AZERBAIJAN; BELARUS'; ESTONIA; GEORGIA; KYRGYZSTAN; LATVIA; LITHUANIA; MOLDOVA; RUSSIA; TAJIKISTAN; TURKMENISTAN; UKRAINE; UZBEKISTAN
Union of the Art Workers (Soyuz Deyatelei Iskusstv) **18** 536
Union of the Societies of Artists of Bulgaria *see* NATIONAL ART SOCIETY OF BULGARIA
Union of Youth **10** 699; **13** 862; **31** 582–3*
members **5** 220; **18** 141; **20** 440, 851; **25** 374; **27** 283; **30** 361
Union Porcelain Works **31** 583*, 637
Union Steam Saw Moulding, Sash and Door Co. **23** 66
Unión Vidriera de España **29** 330
Unitarianism *see under* CHRISTIANITY → sects
Unitats Fratrum *see under* CHRISTIANITY → sects
United Africa Company **1** 319

United Arab Emirates **2** *246*; **31** 584–5*
architecture **31** 584*
gold **2** *264*
museums **2** 275; **31** 585*
painting **31** 584–5*
sculpture **2** *260*
terracotta **2** *260*
see also ABU DHABI; 'AJMAN; ARABIA; DUBAI; FUJAYRA; RA'S AL-KHAYMA (EMIRATE): SHARJAH; UMM AL-QAYWAYN
United Kingdom (of Great Britain and Northern Ireland) **31** *585*, 585–6*
see also BRITAIN; ENGLAND; NORTHERN IRELAND; SCOTLAND; WALES
United Kingdom Institute for Conservation (UKIC) **7** 744
United Nations **17** 850
United Nations Educational, Scientific and Cultural Organization *see* UNESCO
United Patna and Gaya Society **32** 902
United Shoe Manufacturing Company **25** 893
United Society of Believers in Christ's Second Appearing *see* SHAKERS
United States Glass Co. **14** 603
United States Housing Authority **20** 890
United States Information Agency (USIA) **32** 890
United States Lines Paris Review **20** 815
United States of America **31** 586–673*, *587*
academies **23** 630
acanthus **1** 111
acrylic **22** 336
adobe **4** 786; **22** 567; **31** 588
advertisements **15** 824
aesthetics **8** 839; **27** 787
airports **27** *477*
alabaster (gypsum) **1** 516
alloys **31** 652
alphabets **7** 292
aluminium **31** 654
amber **1** 761, 762
andirons **31** 653
anthropology **22** 673–4
antlers **14** *746*
apartments **7** 436; **22** *53*; **31** *597*
appliqué **1** *425*; **30** VI3; **31** 658
aquatints **31** 599, 602
aqueducts **2** 242
archaeology **2** 299; **22** 671–3*
architects **2** 315–16; **10** 850
architectural decorations **30** *507*
architectural history **22** 283
architecture **4** 786, 788, 789; **12** 221; **30** 505, 507; **31** 588*, 589, 590–98*, 662
cavity-walling **4** 788
Colonial period **31** 588–90*
exhibition **1** *9*; **5** *273*
Franciscan Order **22** 567; **31** 588
Knitlock **13** 648
landscape **9** 205; **24** 742
Mexico **18** 832
military **21** 575–6*
Native North Americans **22** 563–5*, 566–73*, *571*
organic **11** 840; **33** 402
Philippines **24** 614–15
prefabrication **26** 19; **28** 488; **31** 592, *592*, 596
vernacular **32** 300–304*
19th cent. **3** 35; **9** 205; **16** 54; **18** *844*; **27** *642*; **29** 651
archives **2** 365, 366, 367, 368, 369, 371–2*
art (original works of) **20** 605
art criticism **24** 431
United States of America—cont.
art history **2** 532; **4** 477; **22** 359, 674; **31** 669, 671–3*
artists' biographies **9** 396
artists' houses **2** *551*, *552*
art legislation **2** 556
art market **2** 560; **20** 609–10; **22** 660–61; **31** 665
art schools **21** *492*; **26** 466; **27** *314*; **33** 42
assemblages **2** *616*; **7** *874*; **31** 608, 614
assembly rooms **2** 618
asylums **2** 658, *658*
atria (iii) (public buildings) **14** *788*
auction houses **4** 24
banknotes **3** 180, *180*, 181; **5** 916
banks **3** 174–5, *175*, 176, *176*; **17** *621*; **29** *916*
barns **28** *540*; **32** 304
baskets **1** *426*
beadwork **4** I1
beakers **31** *646*
bed hangings **31** 658
beds **31** 623, 624, 627, 629, 631
bird's-eye views **4** 81
bonding **4** 786
bookbindings **4** 347
bookcases **31** 626, *626*, *628*, 629
book illustrations **4** 364–5*, 366, 367, *368*; **24** 672, 673, *673*
19th cent. **4** *365*
bookplates **4** 373
bowls **4** *482*; **22** *601*, *603*; **26** *262*
boxes **31** 624
brass **31** 653*
brick **4** 786, 788, 789
bridges **9** 499; **24** *674*; **27** 565
suspension **23** *42*; **26** *523*, 524; **31** 594
broadsides **27** 872
bronze **7** *875*; **18** *594*; **27** *557*; **31** 611, *612*, *613*, 653*
brooches **31** *655*
building regulations **5** *133*, 136; **7** 429
bureaux **5** 192; **31** 624, 626, *626*, *628*, 629
burial mounds **22** 570, 571–2, *571*
cabinetmaking **31** 623, 625, 628
cabinets (ii) (furniture) **31** 631, *631*
cables **29** *490*
calligraphy **6** 772
canals **2** 242
candlesticks **24** *581*
cane **33** 156
canoes **22** 563
cantilevers **5** *649*
capitols **31** *232*, 236
caricatures **5** 758, 759*, *759*; **25** 651
carpets **5** 830, 832, 839; **16** 466
cars **10** *136*; **15** 822–3, 824–5; **20** 593, *594*
cartoons (comic strips) **25** 653
cartoons (satirical) **27** 872
casinos **18** *821*
cast iron **3** 35; **12** 221; **16** 54; **31** 257, *258*, 592, *592*; **32** *893*
catalogues **4** 22, 23, 24, 27; **24** 820; **31** 671
cathedrals **16** *56*
Federal style **10** *850*
Gothic Revival **17** 877; **26** *214*
19th cent. **4** 215
cemeteries **20** 869
censorship **6** 176
ceramics **10** 852; **31** 634–40*
chairs **4** *761*; **15** *825*; **28** 542, *542*; **31** 623, 625, *625*, 628, 630–31, *632*, 633, *633*; **33** 156
Captain **31** 625
Windsor (Berks; UK) **31** 625
chests **31** 623
United States of America—cont.
chests-of-drawers **31** 623–4, 626, *627*, 629
child art **31** 490
children's books **4** 364
chromium **31** 654
chromium steel **9** 499
chromolithography **25** 449
chronologies **22** 672
churches **31** 588, 589, 592
Colonial period **31** *589*
cruciform **26** 212
Gothic Revival **8** *110*; **12** *927*; **24** *281*; **31** *690*
Greek Revival **21** *617*
Native North Americans **22** 567
Neo-classicism **5** *143*; **24** *209*
Paulist Fathers **24** *281*
Rundbogenstil **31** *691*
19th cent. **18** *845*; **26** *339*
20th cent. **33** *402*, *403*
cinemas **7** 327; **31** 596
city halls **19** *700*; **31** 242
clocks **7** 446*; **20** 593; **31** 624, 629
clubs (meeting places) **7** *470*; **27** *720*; **29** *770*
coins **7** 538
collaboration **20** 604
collages **26** *357*
collections **1** 896; **2** 369, 560; **4** 23, 24; **13** 606; **15** 745–6; **17** 430–31, *431*; **18** 384; **22** 359, 360, 426; **27** 224; **31** 662, 663, 664–6*, 667–9; **32** 889
calligraphy **6** 772
carpets **16** 554–5
casts **22** 359
drawings **9** 231
erotic art **10** 487
Old Masters **22** 359
paintings **7** 563
photography **24** 682–3; **29** 656
reproductions **22** 359
sculpture **9** 298; **13** 469, 470
textiles **22** 400
vernacular art **5** 386
19th cent. **7** 840
collections, public **22** 359
Comic-strip art **7** 648–9, *649*
commercial art **7** 651, 652, 653, 654, 655
competitions (architecture) **7** 666, *669*
conceptual art **31** *609*
concert halls **7** *688*
concrete **7** 326; **22** 336; **25** 892; **27** *128*; **31** 464, 465
connoisseurship **31** 671
conservation **30** 564
conservatories **7** 745
construction machinery **7** *766*, 766
copper **7** 812; **14** *746*; **31** 653*, *653*
corn **31** 260
cotton **1** *425*; **8** 34, 35, 36; **10** 356; **30** VI3; **31** 656, *656*, *657*
couches **31** 623, 628
court-houses **26** *342*; **31** 591
coverlets **31** 656, *656*
craftsmen and artists
Cuba (Caribbean) **18** 834–5*
Latin America **18** 830–31*
Mexico **18** 831–2*
Puerto Rico **18** 832–4*
cranes **7** 766
cupboards **31** 624, *624*
cups **4** *480*
daguerreotypes **22** 150
damask **19** 417
dealers **31** 664–5*
dealing **2** 560
decadence and decline **8** 596
department stores **17** 891; **26** *343*; **28** 900; **29** *915*
United States of America—cont.
derricks **7** *765*, 766
design **8** 802*
designers **15** 824
desks **31** 624, 629, 631; **33** II2
diamonds **31** 654, *655*
display of art **2** 710; **22** 359, 360, 673, 678; **23** *47*, *49*
dolls **31** 260, 261
dolls' furniture **31** *264*
dolls' houses **31** 262, 263
domes **12** *311*; **13** 757; **22** 30; **32** *893*
drawings **28** *541*
architectural **2** 367
Neo-classicism **17** *468*
20th cent. **2** *333*; **13** *326*; **23** 361
presentation **30** *506*
dress **9** 289–90*
drypoints **9** 309, 310
dyeing **30** 558
earthenwares **4** *482*; **31** 634–7, *636*, *638*
earthworks **22** 570–72, *571*
education (art) **3** 271; **18** 831; **22** 678; **31** 638, 669–70*
architecture **31** 669
design **31** 670
industrial drawing **31** 669
embroidery **31** 658
enamel **4** *480*; **31** *636*
engravings **3** *180*; **10** 393, 394, 397; **31** 599, 662; **33** *207*
townscapes **24** *597*
environmental art **7** 237
erotic art **6** 176; **10** 482
etchings **10** 562; **14** 271; **24** *601*; **33** *140*
excavations **2** 299
exhibitions **1** 438; **2** 447, 559; **4** 23, 27; **10** 95, 680, 683–4; **22** 674; **24** 673, 820; **25** 5; **28** 925; **31** 605, 607, 664, 669
architecture **17** 620
ceramics **31** 639
conceptual art **4** 202
international **10** 680
Native North Americans **22** 677
ōtsue **33** 491
20th cent. **23** *47*
façades **23** *39*
factories **10** 749; **17** *722*; **25** 893; **31** *596*
feathers **22** *549*, *653*
feminism **31** 673
fibre art **11** *54*
fibreglass **15** *825*; **18** *831*
figureheads **28** 613, 614, *614*
figurines **22** *669*
films **7** 375; **9** 10; **10** 688; **31** 607
fireproofing **6** 486; **33** 174
flags **7** 408
follies **11** 243
fortifications **21** 575–6
fortresses **27** *532*; **31** 588
forts **21** *575*, 575–6
fountains **11** *345*
frames **11** *496*, 496–9*, *497*, *498*; **31** 627
fur **22** 551
furniture **2** 561; **10** 851–2; **20** 468, 469; **24** 601; **31** 249, 616, 617, 618, 619, 623–34*, *633*; **33** 155, 158
Federal style **31** *628*
Mission furniture **31** 631–2
Neo-classicism **31** *628*
office **31** 633–4
Rococo **31** *627*
vernacular **11** 850
17th cent. **31** *616*
18th cent. **31** *618*
19th cent. **3** 685; **31** *620*
furniture suites **31** 630–31
galleries (iv) (art) **3** 129; **23** 46, *49*; **24** *697*, 820; **31** 665
game-boards **31** 266
United States of America—cont.
gardens **12** 62, 136*, *136*, *142*, 143, *143*
design **9** 204
gay and lesbian art **12** *216*, *217*
glass **10** 852; **12** *794*, *795*, VII2; **20** 593; **28** 488; **31** 641–5*, *641*
glassblowing **19** 501
19th cent. **3** 84; **31** *643*
20th cent. **31** *645*
glazes **31** 636
gnomons **22** 572
goblets **31** *641*
gold **31** 646, *650*, *655*
goldsmiths **31** 646
government buildings **13** *238*
Federal style **31** *591*
Greek Revival **13** *611*
Neo-classicism **26** *352*; **31** *591*
18th cent. **4** *473*
19th cent. **29** *771*
20th cent. **8** *470*; **31** *598*
graffiti **13** *270*; **22** 336; **31** 609
grain elevators **13** 274
grasses **1** *426*; **22** 570
gravestones **31** 610
green belt **7** 326; **22** 283
greenhouses **13** 619
guidebooks **13** 811
guns **15** 822; **20** 593
gypsum **26** *401*
helmets **14** *746*
hemlock **22** 563
heritage **14** 452; **21** 422
historiography **19** 246; **31** 411, 671–3*; **32** 304*
hotels **14** 786, 787–8
Art Deco **21** *421*
Neo-classicism **14** *787*
19th cent. **17** 891
20th cent. **12** *794*; **14** *788*; **25** 270–71
houses **15** 22; **22** 563–5; **31** 589–90, 591–2, 593; **32** 893
bungalows **5** 173; **13** *618*
Chicago school **31** *595*
Colonial period **31** *590*
Colonial Revival **7** *619*
country **9** 204; **15** *22*; **31** 592
hogan **22** 568
model **3** 489
Modernism **10** *120*; **23** *10*; **28** *96*
Modern Movement **2** *551*; **5** *649*; **21** *493*
Native North Americans **22** *567*, 570, 572–3
pithouses **22** 566
prefabricated **26** 19; **31** 596
pueblo **22** 566, *567*
Queen Anne Revival **25** *805*
Romanesque Revival **3** *128*; **23** *40*
Shingle style **20** *17*
terrace **4** 786
town **27** *730*
Usonian House **31** 596; **33** 404, *405*
wikiup **22** 567
18th cent. **6** *486*; **32** *300*, *301*, *302*
19th cent. **15** *22*; **27** *613*; **32** *894*
20th cent. **11** *835*; **12** *632*, *855*; **29** *35*; **30** *870*; **33** *401*, *405*
housing **11** 144
iconography **18** 831–2; **31** 672
illusionism **15** 140
indexes **5** 386
industrial design **15** 822, 824–5*
industrial scenes **15** 829
installations **10** *879*, *881*; **15** *868*
interior decoration **1** *171*; **31** 615–23*, *616*, *618*, *620*, *621*, *622*
iron **4** 228; **29** 651; **31** *264*, 652–3*
jade **16** 861

United States of America—cont.
 jars **22** *601*
 jewellery **31** 654–5*
 joinery **31** 623
 joists **23** 257
 kettles **31** *648*
 kivas **22** 566, 567
 lace **31** 661–2*
 lacquer **18** 614, 615
 lamps **30** *868*, 868–9; **31** 619
 land art **7** *237*; **14** 324; **18** *694*; **28** 890; **31** 615
 law courts **18** 887, 888
 libraries **2** 367; **4** 22, 23, 24; **14** *197*; **31** 666, 670–71*
  Gothic Revival **11** *849*
  public **19** 318, 319; **23** *41*; **25** *666*
  university **19** 319
  19th cent. **20** *18*
  20th cent. **4** *475*; **26** *341*
 lifts **31** 593
 lighting **30** 679
 limestone **19** *437*
 lithography **1** 145; **19** 485, 492–3; **23** 630; **25** *352, 353*
  bird's-eye views **2** *121*; **4** *82*
  Pop art **17** *614*
  19th cent. **8** *276*
  20th cent. **19** *493*; **20** *606, 608*
 locks **15** 822; **20** 593
 lodges **22** 569, 570, 572
 log cabins **31** 589
 machines **15** 822
 mahogany **31** 625, *626*; **33** II2
 mansions **17** 891; **22** 539, *539*
 manuals
  architecture **23** 860; **31** 591
  carpentry **3** 730
  ornament **2** 709
  painting **26** 467
  screenprinting **28** 299
 manufacturing **15** 821–3*, 824–5*; **20** 593
 maple **28** *542*
 maps **11** 331
 marble **1** *441*; **25** *401*
 marks
  furniture **20** 442
  metalwork **20** 443
  pewter **31** 652
 marquetry **20** 468, 469
 masks **22** *558*
 mass production **3** 114; **20** 593, *594*; **31** 619, 656
 master printers **20** 607–10
 mausolea **20** *869*
 medals **7** *875*; **20** 926
 meeting-houses **23** 193; **31** 589
 metal **30** 542
 metalwork **31** 646–7*, 648–9*, 651–4*
 mezzotints **4** 477; **21** 416; **31** 599
 military scenes **24** *666*
 mills (industrial) **10** 748; **21** 601
 mirrors **31** 624, 626–7, 629
 mixed-media **29** *622*
 mobiles **5** 423; **11** *877*; **21** *746*; **31** 613
 models **2** *552*
 Monel metal **31** 654
 monteiths **31** *647*
 monuments **3** *290*; **21** *618*, 619; **31** *611*
 mosaics **19** 878; **22** 336
 mounds **22** 572, 671–2
 museums **2** 368, 369; **4** 23; **6** 772; **15** 745–6; **17** 434; **22** 359*, 360, 365; **26** *480*; **27** 613; **28** *328*; **31** 662, 665–9*, 670–71; **32** 753, 889, *889*
  Jewish art **17** 581–2*
  modern art **12** 15
  natural history **2** 710
  Neo-classicism **7** *429*; **21** *649*
  Romanesque Revival **26** *213*
  20th cent. **2** *694*; **8** *821*; **12** *236*; **17** *724*; **22** *365*; **24** *325*
 narratives **12** *216*
 natural history books **6** 87
 needlework **31** 657–8*
 nude figures **18** *594*; **23** *297*; **26** *430*
  Mexico **18** *831*
  Neo-classicism **25** *401*
  19th cent. **26** 401, *401*; **31** *604*
  20th cent. **19** *844*
 oak **31** *624*
 objets trouvés **31** 608, 614
 observatories **23** 341, *341*
 office buildings **23** *360*
  International Style **15** *887*
  19th cent. **6** *573*; **11** *848*; **27** *138*; **31** *592*
 ottomans (furniture) **31** *632*
 painting **31** 599–610*
  Abstract art **1** *549*; **2** *857*; **8** *635, 871*; **17** *892*; **21** *856*; **26** *126*; **31** *605*
  Abstract Expressionism **1** *86, 87*; **8** *634*; **11** *730*; **13** *215*; **14** *633*; **18** *133*; **22** *206*; **23** *29*; **27** *220, 221*; **29** *663*
  acrylic **1** *129*; **7** *680*; **19** *702*; **32** *862*
  African American art **1** *445*
  allegorical **33** *93*
  cabinet pictures **22** *149*
  collections **7** 840
  colour field **7** III2, VII2(d); **23** 404; **31** *608*
  Cuba (Caribbean) **18** *834*
  fresco **5** 9; **22** 336
  genre **12** 294, 296; **22** *223*; **31** 602
   African American art **1** *443*
   Barbizon school **15** *20*
   18th cent. **25** *453*
   19th cent. **4** *72*; **6** *499*; **17** *617*; **26** *180*; **31** *604*; **32** *327*; **33** *184*
   20th cent. **14** *752*; **25** *553*
  hard-edge **14** *164*; **23** *185*
  history **31** 600
   Romanticism **26** 740
   18th cent. **7** *811*; **31** *392*; **33** *92*
   19th cent. **31** *872*
  hunting scenes **14** *700*
  Japonisme **33** *138*
  Jewish art **17** 578*, *578*
  landscape **18** 715, 718, 719; **31** 601, 602, 603
   Luminism (i) (USA) **14** *276*
   Romanticism **26** 742
   19th cent. **1** *674*; **2** 710; **4** *44*; **7** *285, 550*; **8** *191*; **9** *419*; **12** *606*; **15** *859*; **18** IV1; **22** *75*; **28** 560; **31** *487, 602*
   20th cent. **18** *718*
  literary themes **31** *601*
  marine **20** 425–6*
   19th cent. **18** *726*; **26** *336*; **27** *462*
  murals **15** 830; **22** 335–6*, *336*; **25** 653, 654; **26** *427*; **31** 606
   19th cent. **1** *22*
   20th cent. **3** *748*; **19** 878; **23** *566*
  mythological **14** 492; **32** *109*
  Native North Americans **22** 593–7*
  Op art **7** VIII2(c)
  Photorealism **24** *687*
  Pop art **7** VII2(b), VIII1(b); **12** *217*; **19** *328*
  Post-modernism **25** *360*
  Post-painterly Abstraction **19** *724*
  Precisionism **25** *462*
  Puerto Rico **18** *833*
  Realism (style) **23** *297*
  still-lifes **29** 669, 670, *671*; **31** 603
  Surrealism **20** *838*

United States of America painting—cont.
  townscapes **23** *388*
  urban life **14** *220*
  watercolours **4** *368*; **5** *188*; **14** 698; **31** 603
   19th cent. **2** *710*; **14** *701*; **17** *624*; **18** *627*
  19th cent. **22** *672*
  20th cent. **1** *426, 773*; **2** *596*; **8** *578, 709, 903*; **13** *12, 865*; **17** *615*; **18** *94*; **19** *410*; **21** *795*; **25** *166*; **26** *29*; **30** *173*; **31** *68, 606*
 panelling **31** *616*, 617
 paper **24** 40, 56
 paperweights **24** 57
 papier mâché **24** 62
 parks **23** 256
  public **24** 179, *180*
  19th cent. **23** *420, 422*
 paste **24** 56
 patchwork **24** 253; **31** 658
 patronage **31** 662–3*
 pattern books **20** 878; **24** 275; **31** 592, 593; **32** 555
 pearls **31** *655*
 periodicals **24** 424, 431–4*, 673, 677
  architectural **24** 431–2, 433–4; **28** 844
  photographic **24** 432, 434
 pewter **24** 580, *581*; **31** 651–2*
 photoarchives **2** 365, 371; **24** 682–3; **31** 671
 photograms **24** *654*
 photographic prints **24** *659, 666*
  colour **24** X, XI1, XI2
  platinum prints **24** *739*
 photography **15** 830; **24** 650, 659, 661, 671, 672–3, 674, 676, 679; **25** 653; **31** 602, 605, 606, 662, 663
  cliché-verre **10** 99
  dye transfer **24** XI1
  19th cent. **24** *673*; **29** *655*
  20th cent. **1** *144*; **10** *656*; **11** *728*; **17** *917*; **19** *844*; **21** *794*; **24** *676, 679, 680, 681*; **29** *656, 745*; **33** *105*
 pictographs **13** *332*
 Pictorial photography **24** *739*
 pitchers **22** *602*; **31** 636
 plaster **29** 842*, 845; **31** 611
 plasterboard **24** 51
 platinum **31** *655*
 polychromy **4** 788
 popular culture **9** 10
 porcelain **31** 635, 637–8, 640
  hard-paste **31** 583
  Parian **31** *637*
  soft-paste **31** *635*
  18th cent. **4** 332
  19th cent. **31** *637*
 porches **32** 240
 porringers **31** 648
 porticos **25** 267, *267*; **32** *894*
 portraits
  engravings **10** 393; **30** 853
  group **24** *302, 739*
  painting **23** *45*
   Cubism **14** *204*
   17th cent. **20** *677*
   18th cent. **7** *809*; **11** *496, 497*; **24** *302*; **29** *805*; **31** *600*
   19th cent. **9** *289, 500, 501*; **23** *765*; **24** *301*; **29** *918*
   20th cent. **13** *11*; **25** *167*; **26** *430*
  photography **2** *315*; **24** *659, 671*; **29** *601*
  relief sculpture **27** *557*
  self-portraits **13** *11*; **24** *301*; **25** *167*
  woodcuts **4** *476*
 posters **7** 652; **25** 347, 352, *352, 353, 651*, 652
 posts **22** 572

United States of America—cont.
 pottery **31** 261, 634–7, 638–40
  Native North Americans **22** *603*
  Rockingham ware **31** 636
 pouches **4** I1
 power stations **25** 402
 printing **31** 657, *657*
  colour **14** 616
  offset **20** 609
  photogravure **24** *671, 674*
 print publishers **20** 609–10; **25** 626
 print publishing **8** 276
 prints **20** 604–7; **25** 629*; **31** 599, 601, 602
  monotypes **21** 896, 897
  20th cent. **20** *609*
 prisons **31** 592
 propaganda **25** 651, *651*, 652, 653–4
 property development **25** 655
 quillwork **22** 649–50*
 quilts **1** *425*; **30** VI3; **31** 658
 railways **3** 128; **24** 597
 railway stations **3** 693; **5** *274*; **17** *799*
 ready-mades **13** 891; **26** *51*
 red (*Thuja plicata*) **22** 563
 red-wood **22** 563
 regalia **22** *549*
 religion **22** *557, 558*
 reproductions **26** 227
 rings **31** 654
 rock art **13** 332, *332*; **22** 549
 roofs **27** *128*; **29** *490*
 rose-wood **31** *630, 631*
 rotundas **17** *468*
 rugs **27** 317*, *317*, 318, *318*; **30** VIII2
 samplers **27** 694; **31** 658
 satinet **31** 656
 satires **27** 872*
 schools **26** 19; **28** 157, 159; **32** *827*
 screenprinting **20** 609
 screenprints **1** *444*; **25** *232*
 scrimshaw **28** 302
 scripts **28** 307
 sculpture **3** 114; **31** 610–15*, *612*; **33** 4
  Abstract art **1** *80*; **23** *29*
  African American art **1** *441*
  bronze **18** *594*; **31** 611
  Cubism **19** *437*
  Jewish art **17** 578*
  marble **1** *441*; **25** *401*
  Minimalism **2** *12*; **19** *289*; **21** *646*
  monumental **31** *611*
  Neo-classicism **25** *401*
  relief **31** *612*
  Surrealism **31** *613*
  wood **1** *422*
  19th cent. **15** 23; **26** *401*
  20th cent. **9** *357, 359*; **12** *795*, VII2; **16** *58*; **22** *426*; **23** *12, 397*; **28** *877*; **31** *614, 615*; **33** *97*
 secretaires **31** 631
 service stations **28** 488
 sewing-machines **15** *821*; **20** 593
 shamanism **22** *558*
 ship-decoration **28** 613, 614, *614*
 shopping centres **28** 622–3, *623, 799*; **31** 735
 shops **3** 35; **23** *31*
 shrines (i) (cult) **28** 632
 sideboards **31** 628, 631
 sidewalks **28** 728
 silk **31** 657
 silver **10** 851, *851*; **26** 262, *262*; **28** 737; **31** 646–51*, *646, 647, 648, 651*
 silver-gilt **4** *480*
 silverplate **31** 650
  Sheffield plate **31** 649
 silversmiths **31** 647

United States of America—cont.
 skyscrapers **5** 175; **7** 326; **11** 144; **12** 643; **17** 477; **18** 54; **23** 41; **25** 328; **28** 831–3*; **31** 594, 595, 596, 597, 662
  Art Deco **28** *629, 833*
  International Style **5** *136*
  Post-modernism **25** *359*
  19th cent. **5** 126; **28** *832*; **29** *914*; **30** *506*; **31** *594*
  20th cent. **6** *574*; **11** 25; **12** *614*; **14** 200, *735, 803*; **23** *44*; **26** *488*; **28** *834*; **30** *507*
 sofas **31** 628, 630, *630*, 633
 space-frames **16** *56*
 sponsorship **31** 669
 sporting scenes **3** *680*; **29** 425, 426
 sports centres **23** *272*
 spotlights **3** 537
 spruce **22** 563
 stadia **1** 798; **29** 489, *490*
 stage design **15** 824; **30** 687, 688
 stained glass **18** *101*, 627; **29** 508; **30** 868–9; **31** 689
 statuettes **29** 575–6*
 steel **4** *761*; **16** *56, 58*; **22** 336; **27** 565; **28** 488, *877*; **31** 594, *594, 596, 614*
 stencilling **29** 628, *628*
 stonewares **31** 635–7, *640*
 stoves **31** 652
 stucco **29** 842*, *842*, 845
 studios **15** 21
 surveyors **30** 27
 sweetmeat dishes **31** *635*
 synagogues **14** 198; **17** 545, 547, 548, 549, *549*
 tables **31** 619, 623, 626, 628, 631, *633*
 tapestries **31** 659*, 660–61*
  20th cent. **1** *146*; **31** *660*
 tattoos **30** 366
 tea-urns **10** *851*
 temples **22** *126*, 572; **30** 450
 tension structures **23** *272*, 273
 tepees **22** 568–9, *569*, 570
 terracotta **30** 505*, 507*, *507*
 textiles **10** 852; **21** 601; **31** 616–17, 655–7*, *657*, 659*, 660–62*
  Bangladesh **3** 168
  18th cent. **25** 666
 theatres **1** *158*; **30** 677*
 theories
  architectural **1** 610–11
  art **8** 839; **20** 527, 528; **27** 787; **33** 16
 threads **30** 542
 tiles **30** 887–8*; **31** 637
 timber structures **30** 898; **31** 593; **32** 302
 tin **18** 615; **31** 652–3*
 tombs **22** 571
 town halls **31** 242
 towns **22** 567; **31** 722
  garden cities **7** 326, 429; **17** 891; **22** 283; **29** 651; **31** 592
  new **2** 698; **3** 693; **12** 927; **18** 456; **28** 817; **31** 596, 729
  Pre-Columbian **5** 386
 toys **31** 257, *258*
 tracery **26** 212
 trade **6** 624
  brick **4** 786
  carpets **16** 481, 482
  ceramics **6** 332
  cotton **8** 36; **10** 356
  damask **19** 417
  fur **22** 551
  furniture **2** 150; **16** 36; **19** 592
 treatises
  colour **1** 549
  topographical drawings **9** 685
 trompe l'oeil **10** 737; **15** *141*; **24** *555*; **29** 669; **31** 603
 type-faces **31** 680
 typography **7** 292; **31** *496*

United States of America—cont.
universities 4 474; 20 19; 29 678; 32 235
urban planning 10 684; 23 25; 31 723, 724, 735, 736–7, 738
19th cent. 23 421
20th cent. 13 647; 19 700; 22 283
vases 31 637, 638, 645, 650
veneers 20 468
verandahs 32 240
vernacular art 11 58; 22 426; 32 325, 327, 330
video art 32 420
villages 22 552
villas 8 574, 575; 23 33; 31 620; 32 555
wallpaper 7 168; 24 56; 32 814
walls 4 228
walnut 24 601; 31 625
war artists 24 666
warehouses 32 861, 861
watches 7 448; 15 822; 20 593
waxes 33 4
waxworks 33 4
weathervanes 31 652, 653, 653; 32 325; 33 8
weaving 31 656–7
wicker 31 629; 33 155, 158
window displays 8 809
wire 31 594
women 31 669
women artists 3 489; 10 878; 22 112; 24 305, 671; 25 237; 31 609, 673
wood 1 422; 2 242
wood-carvings 11 321; 31 610
woodcuts 4 476; 11 330; 33 364
woodwork 3 685
wool 30 VIII2; 31 656, 656, 658, 660
wrought iron 32 325
zinc 31 653
see also NATIVE NORTH AMERICANS; NORTH AMERICA
United States Pottery Co. 4 482; 31 636, 637
Unités Pédagogiques 6 see UP6
Unités Pédagogiques 8 see UP8
Unit One 10 258, 267; 19 591; 31 673*
members 5 277; 7 797; 14 401; 22 55, 524; 23 103; 32 754
works 10 257
Univers see under TYPE-FACES → forms
Universal 7 448
universal see under TYPE-FACES → forms
Universal Copyright Convention (UCC) 2 554
Universal Edition 19 69
universal exposition see EXHIBITIONS → types → international
Universal Limited Art Editions see ULAE
Universal Transfer Co. 7 798
Universitas Aurificum, Master of the 31 450
universities 7 565, 566, 567; 31 673–5*
Africa 1 319
Argentina 7 847
Brazil 2 543
Canada 7 858
Chile 27 792
England 24 466; 29 379
Gothic 13 130
Islamic 16 241
Israel 16 566
Italy 13 630; 31 674, 674
Japan 17 420
New Zealand 2 706
Poland 24 699
Portugal 7 531
Russia 22 175
Slovakia 4 694
universities—cont.
Spain 26 520; 27 603
Sweden 30 72
Ukraine 18 36
United States of America 4 474; 20 19; 29 678; 32 235
Venezuela 32 567
Vietnam 32 474
see also COLLEGES; SCHOOLS; PALAZZI DELLA SAPIENZA
University City Pottery 26 287, 471
university libraries see under LIBRARIES → types
University of Alberta see under EDMONTON
University of Arizona see under TUCSON (AZ)
University of Baluchistan see under QUETTA
University of British Columbia see under VANCOUVER
University of California see under BERKELEY (CA); LOS ANGELES (CA); SANTA BARBARA (CA)
University of East Anglia see under NORWICH
University of Fort Hare see under ALICE
University of Garyounis see under BENGHAZI
University of Michigan see ANN ARBOR (MI), UNIVERSITY OF MICHIGAN
University of Nebraska see under LINCOLN (NE)
University of New Brunswick see under FREDERICTON
University of Pennsylvania see under PHILADELPHIA (PA)
University of Texas see under AUSTIN (TX)
University of the Witwatersrand see under JOHANNESBURG
University of Virginia see under CHARLOTTESVILLE (VA)
University of Western Australia see under PERTH-NEDLANDS
University of Zambia see under LUSAKA
Unjitsu 17 126
Unjo 17 124; 31 676
Unka 17 124; 31 676
Unkair, Jörg 33 87, 88
Unkai Yonehara see YONEHARA, UNKAI
Unkei 17 98, 121, 392; 22 492; 31 675–6*
collaboration 17 729; 18 195
groups and movements 17 879
works 17 22, 121, 122, 123, 131, 729; 18 224; 22 497, 499, 502
Unkoku school 17 163; 31 677
Unkoku Tōeki 17 165; 31 677
Unkoku Tōgan 17 164; 31 253, 676–7*
works 17 376; 18 560; 31 676
Unkoku Tōhan 31 677
Unkoku Tōyō 31 677
Unkoku Tōyū 31 677
Unković, Milivoje 4 462
Unmej 31 891
Unmum Temple 18 291
Unna, Meira 16 568
Unno, Kiyoshi 17 324
Unno, Shōmin 17 400
Uno, Sesson 17 240
Unovis 18 181; 29 794; 31 677*; 32 412
members 3 529; 19 475; 20 194; 30 8; 33 522
publications 20 195
Unpō Ōoka see ŌOKA UNPŌ
Unruly Children, Master of the 20 778–9*; 31 189
works 20 778
Unsan 5 114
Unselt, Johann 11 457
Unsere Kunstdenkmäler 24 453
Unshin Ohara see OHARA, UNSHIN
Unsōdō 17 293
Unsong kŏsa see KANG HŬI-MAENG
Untash-Napirisha, King of Anzan and Susa (reg mid-13th cent.) 1 879; 7 187; 10 132; 15 909
stele 10 133
Unterberger, Christoph 31 679*
methods 10 199
patrons and collectors 7 412; 25 8
pupils 12 583; 31 679
works 4 407; 16 644
Unterberger, Franz Sebald 31 678–9*
Unterberger, Giuseppe 31 679
Unterberger, Ignaz 31 679–80*
Unterberger, Michael Angelo 2 794; 26 713; 31 677–9*
assistants 31 679
pupils 18 162; 31 678
works 30 914; 31 678
Unterharz Mining & Foundry Works 18 417
Unterlunkhofen 25 542
Untermeyer Collection see under NEW YORK → museums → Metropolitan Museum of Art
Unteutsch, Friedrich 2 732; 12 422; 31 680*
works 12 422
Unteutsch, Hans 31 680
Untitled 24 434
Unton, Henry 13 298
UNU 4 699; 26 716
Unungе 13 118
Unvaniez ar Seiz Breur (Assembly of the Seven Brothers) 27 888
Unwas, Durga Temple 15 273
Unwin, Raymond 11 785; 12 144; 16 891; 19 576; 20 878; 24 185–7; 31 728
Unwin, Stanley 14 767
Ünye 4 112
Uopie 8 490
works 8 487
Uosikkinen, Raija 11 105
U Otaama Sri 5 250
Uozumi, Iraku 17 324
UP6 14 847
UP8 14 847
Upatissa II, King of Sri Lanka (reg 522) 25 169
Upatnieks, Juris 14 689
Upbargen, Antonis van see OBBERGHEN, ANTONIS VAN
Upcher, Abbot 26 239
Updike, Daniel Berkeley 2 572; 31 680*
up-draught kilns see under KILNS → types
Upendragupta (Vakataka) 15 555; 31 798
Upholsterer 24 431
upholsterers 31 681
upholstery 2 758; 3 585; 6 390; 10 289, 290; 11 587; 18 591; 19 5; 22 866; 24 237; 28 715; 29 314; 30 XIV2, XV, XVI; 31 680–88*, 683, 684, 685, 686, 687
upholstery hide see under LEATHER → types
Uphues, Joseph (Johann Ludwig) 12 407; 31 688*
Upīts, Andrej 4 180
Upjohn, Everard 31 688
Upjohn, Hobart 31 688
Upjohn, Richard 5 124; 23 39; 31 688–91*
assistants 31 691
groups and movements 13 203
pupils 25 371
staff 7 436; 10 103
works 23 32; 31 592, 690, 691
Upjohn, Richard Michell 14 203; 31 690, 691*
Upjohn & Upjohn 3 693
Uplistsikhe 12 320; 31 692*
Upmark, Gustaf 30 120
Ŭpnae 18 273
Upolu 27 683
U Pò Nyun 5 262
Uppark (W. Sussex) 5 899; 9 17; 11 39; 32 540
collections 9 26
dairy 8 461
furniture 7 486; 10 297
paintings 3 382; 8 493; 32 334
restoration 7 729
stucco 29 846
tapestries 9 30; 10 351
Tapestry Bedroom 9 30
Uppenna, Baptistery 9 570
upper case 31 495
upper crypts see under CRYPTS → types
Upper Hardres, SS Peter and Paul 13 183
Upper Rhine, Master of the 18 704
Upper Volta see BURKINA FASO
Uppsala 30 65; 31 692–4*, 718
altarpieces 30 77
architecture 30 70, 71
botanic garden 4 483, 484
Castle 30 68, 72; 32 923
gardens 12 135
stucco 29 840
Cathedral of St Eric 4 781; 10 581; 13 50; 23 462; 30 66, 67; 31 693, 693–4*; 32 923
monument to Gustav Banér 30 84
monument to Gustav I and his Two Wives 30 84, 84
monument to Svante Banér 30 84
sculpture 13 102
silver 30 104
wall paintings 30 79
workshop 13 50
Cathedral School 30 73
Church of the Holy Trinity 30 66
City Library 30 75
Manor 31 692
railway station 30 73
sculpture 30 83
temple 32 524
University 30 73
anatomy theatre 27 308–9; 30 70
Botany Department 30 72, 72
collections 8 649; 14 52, 692
library 20 487; 30 73, 119
Uppukonduru 15 476
Úprka, Joža 8 393
Upsala-Ekeby AB 30 101
Upton, Dell 32 304
Upton, Florence K. 4 368
Upton, Nicholas 14 406
Upton House (Warwicks) 7 194, 579; 8 832, 833; 14 638
Upward, Peter 30 160
ʿUqair, Tell
altar 1 690
architecture 21 270
chapel 21 282
Painted Temple 21 282
wall paintings 21 271, 308
ʿUqaylid, Sharaf al-Dawla Muslim see SHARAF AL-DAWLA MUSLIM, Ruler
Uqba ibn Nafi 17 730
al-Uqsur see THEBES (i) (EGYPT)
Uquía Church 2 398
Ur 1 849, 892, 894; 2 246, 300; 21 267, 273; 31 694–7*
architecture 21 284, 286, 287, 291; 31 694–6
beadwork 3 441
courtyards 8 64
excavations 33 373
faience (i) (glass) 1 878
gilding 12 620
Giparu 21 284
glass 1 868
gold 1 873, 874; 31 696
houses 21 284
Ur—cont.
inlays 31 696, 696
ivory-carvings 24 643
jewellery 1 873, 883; 31 696–7
lamps 19 364
mausolea 31 695–6
metalwork 21 303; 31 696
pottery 21 307
religion 21 277
Royal Cemetery 1 873, 893; 15 902; 21 272, 283, 303, 304, 310; 29 923
metalwork 4 850
musical instruments 1 890–91
seals 1 860, 860
Royal Standard of Ur see ROYAL STANDARD OF UR
sacred enclosure see temenos
sculpture 21 294
seals 1 860
stelae 1 509; 29 614
stone vessels 2 272
temenos 21 273, 552; 30 432; 31 694–5, 695
textiles 1 880, 881
tin 4 849
trade 21 268
veneers 1 869
writing-tablets 1 853, 869
ziggurat of Ur-Nammu 21 283, 283, 284; 29 520, 924; 31 695; 33 675
Ur: Bi-monthly Magazine Devoted to Arab Culture 24 446
Urabe, Shizutarō 18 528–9
Uragami Gyokudō 17 165, 188, 190; 18 60; 31 697–8*
works 31 698
Uragami Shunkin 17 191, 198; 25 867; 33 322
Uraku Oda see ODA URAKU
Ural'skiye samotsvety (Urals gems) works 27 423
Urama 24 76, 78
Urang see KWŎN TON-IN
Uraniborg 4 639–40; 8 725; 23 339
uranium oxides 10 192; 12 782
uranium-series dating see under DATING METHODS → types
Urano Shigekichi 23 367
Urartian 1 822, 827, 851, 852, 854; 15 905; 31 698–701*
animal subjects 1 836
architecture 1 831–2; 21 553; 31 699–700*
bronze 1 836, 836; 31 158, 700, 700–701
canals 31 700
chariots 6 480
figurines 1 729; 31 700
fortifications 21 553; 31 700
fortresses 3 356; 31 699
gold 1 836
harnesses 14 179*
iconography 1 830
inscriptions 1 830
iron 1 836; 31 700
ivory 1 729
ivory-carvings 1 872; 31 701
jewellery 1 836
metalwork 1 835, 836, 836; 2 441; 15 919; 31 700–701
palaces 23 807; 31 699–700
pottery 1 838; 31 701
reliefs 17 878–9
religion 1 830
scripts 1 830
sculpture 31 700, 700
seals 17 879; 31 701
shields 31 159
silver 1 836
temples 1 729, 831; 24 265; 31 700
tombs 31 700
tools 31 700
trappings 14 179*
wall paintings 1 839; 31 700
Urartu
gold 1 875

Urartu—cont.
pottery **1** 838
sculpture **1** 833, 885
seals **1** 863
Urartu, Aytsemnik **2** 436
Ura Tepe *see* URA TYUBE
Ura Tyube **6** *182*; **16** *105*; **30** *252*; **31** 701–2*
architecture **30** 252
Boba-Tago Mosque **6** 278
ceramics **30** 253
jewellery **6** 274
pottery **31** 701
Urawa, Saitama Prefectural Museum of Modern Art **18** 532
Urbain, Claude **27** 593
Urbain, Pierre *see* ARSÈNE, ALEXANDRE
Urban(*fl* 1482-6) **3** 224
Urban, Abbot of Melk (*fl c.*1769-74) **12** 356
Urban, Bishop (*fl* 1120) **26** 617
Urban II, Pope (*reg* 1088-99) **24** 36; **31** 207
Urban IV, Pope (*reg* 1261-65) **23** 460; **31** 381, 385
Urban V, Pope (*reg* 1362-70)
architecture **2** 847; **22** 9, 10, 34; **26** 811
metalwork **8** 412; **24** 36
paintings **2** 863; **11** 891; **12** 697; **20** 774
Urban VIII, Pope (*reg* 1623-44) **3** 205–7*, *207*
architecture **2** 319, 498; **3** 830; **6** 23; **7** 780; **19** 688; **26** 758, 840
coats of arms **14** 416
collections **16** 763
decorative works **7** 620
frescoes **26** 565, 817
ivory-carvings **9** 409
paintings **3** 834; **7** 394, 908; **18** 733; **24** 239
sculpture **3** 829, 830–31; **4** 428; **9** 410; **26** 809; **29** 558
sponsorship **12** 679; **16** 670
Urban, Joseph **31** 632, 702*
collaboration **19** 69; **28** 155
groups and movements **2** 522; **14** 33
staff **17** 838
works **2** 809; **10** 684; **30** 684
Urbanavičius, Vladas **19** 500
Urbaneja, José R. **32** 178
Urbaneta, Abelardo Rodríguez *see* RODRÍGUEZ URBANETA, ABELARDO
Urbania *see* CASTEL DURANTE
Urbanik, Martin **19** 836
Urban Innovations Group **22** 52
urbanisme **1** 447
Urbanistica **24** 448
urban life **31** 703–6*
France **31** *705*
Impressionism **15** VI2; **21** *863*, *864*; **23** III, IV
Neo-Impressionism **28** *501*
Germany **18** *79*
Ireland **16** *16*
Italy **28** *706*; **33** *612*
Netherlands, the **19** *420*; **31** *703*
Russia **18** *791*
Slovakia **28** *853*
United States of America **14** *220*
Vietnam **32** *483*
Urban målare *see* URBAN THE PAINTER
Urbano, Pietro **21** 457
Urbano (di Pietro) da Cortona **9** 130; **12** 705; **28** 681; **31** 707*
urban planning **12** 228; **31** 707–38*
commentaries **1** 29; **28** 800–801
education *see under* EDUCATION (ART) → types
historical and regional traditions
Anglo-Saxon **2** 66
Armenia (Europe) **2** 428
urban planning
historical and regional traditions—cont.
Austria **2** 780; **28** 801; **32** 437, *761*
Aztec **21** 375
Bactria **6** 209
Belgium **30** 47
Bolivia **4** 256*
Brazil **4** 704, 710
Britain **1** 29; **31** 723, 724, 725, 736–7, 738
Indian subcontinent **15** 411
20th cent. **24** 185
Burma **5** 237–8*
Central Asia, Western **6** 208–11*, *210*, *211*; **16** 264
China **6** 662–6*, *663*, *664*
Crete **8** 154
Croatia **8** 175
Cuba (Caribbean) **14** *241*
Cyprus, ancient **8** 336
Denmark **8** 725, 727; **31** 738
Egypt **16** *262*
Egypt, ancient **9** 850–53, *852*, *853*
England **10** 226; **33** 230
Indian subcontinent **20** 52
19th cent. **22** *528*
20th cent. **1** 163; **12** 597
Etruscan **10** 587, 602; **20** *529*
Finland **31** 461
France **8** 217; **31** 724, 737
Modernism **19** *50*
Neo-classicism **22** *34*
16th cent. **29** 376
Germany **12** 471; **31** 724, 737; **33** 51
6th cent. BC **14** 498
17th cent. **12** 368
20th cent. **11** 797; **14** 524
Greece, ancient **13** 382, 401–2, 416, 417, 419–21*, *420*
4th cent. BC **25** 573–5
6th cent. BC **21** 341
Inca **15** 162–3
Indian subcontinent **1** 648; **15** 193, 242, 248, 398, 408–11*
England **20** 52
Gupta **15** 409
Indus civilization **15** 192, 408
Islamic **15** 409–10
Rajput **15** *411*
Indonesia **15** 775–6*
Indus civilization **15** 192, 408
Iran **16** 230, 264*
Iraq **16** 150–51
Ireland **16** 8
Islamic **6** *211*; **16** 260–64*, 268
Central Asia, Western **6** 210–11*; **16** 264
Egypt **16** *262*
Indian subcontinent **15** 409–10
Iran **16** 230, 264–5*
Iraq **16** 150–51
Ottoman **16** 265–7*
Syria **16** *261*
Turkey **16** 265–7*
Israel **17** 854
Italy **11** *271*; **23** *752*; **25** 738; **31** 712
Etruscan **10** 587, 602; **20** *529*
Roman **27** *4*
Somalia **29** 56
15th cent. **16** 629; **27** 182
16th cent. **27** 482
17th cent. **29** *373*
20th cent. **12** 718
Japan **17** 84, 93–7*, *93*, *94*, *95*, *96*
Khmer **30** 592
Korea **18** 281–2*
Libya **27** *5*
Malaysia **20** 169–70*
Mesopotamia **21** 281
Mexico **21** 375
urban planning
historical and regional traditions—cont.
Netherlands, the **9** 746; **14** 39; **31** 737
Brazil **4** 704, 710
13th cent. **3** 504
20th cent. **13** 313
Nigeria **23** 135
North Africa **26** 921
Norway **23** 220
Ottoman **16** 265–7*
Philippines **24** 616–17*
Poland **22** 78; **25** 134; **33** 605, 606
Portugal **19** *465*; **25** 186
Rhodes (city) **26** 291
Rome, ancient **11** 327; **12** 497; **23** 618; **26** 864, 904, 905; **27** 1, 2–6*
Italy **27** *4*
Libya **27** *5*
North Africa **26** 921
Rus' **31** 547
Russia **27** 374, 375, 376, 379; **31** 486
Scotland **28** 227–8, 229
Sicily **28** 654
Singapore **28** 774*
Spain **22** 67; **31** 724, 822
Syria **16** *261*
Syria-Palestine **30** 190, 191
Thailand **30** 592–3*
Turkey **16** 265–7*
Turkmenistan **6** 209
Ukraine **31** 547, 549, 551
United States of America **10** 684; **23** 25; **31** 723, 724, 735, 736–7, 738
19th cent. **23** *421*
20th cent. **13** *647*; **19** 700; **22** 283
Vietnam **32** 477–8*
Urban Planning Workshop **30** 199
Urbański, Jan Jerzy **4** 843; **25** 114; **31** 739*
Urban the Painter **29** 684; **30** 67, 77; **31** 707*
Urbina, Diego de **10** 502; **22** 695; **27** 705; **29** 278
Urbina, José María Fernández *see* FERNÁNDEZ URBINA, JOSÉ MARÍA
Urbina Rivas, Luis **25** 455
Urbini, Francesco **31** 741
Urbino **16** *620*; **31** 739–46*
arks **17** 570
Cathedral **11** 689; **16** 644
Free University **8** 600–601; **16** 650
Galleria Nazionale delle Marche **31** 740, 742
see also Palazzo Ducale
painting **31** *741*
palazzi **16** 629
Palazzo Ducale **4** 643; **11** 688–9; **12** 279; **14** 870; **16** 630, 711; **18** 861–2; **31** 742–6*, *744*
Appartamento dell'Iole **4** 198
carvings **3** 253
cortile **18** *861*
Cortile de Pasquino **31** 745
Cortile d'Onore **31** 744–5
courtyard **8** 65
Facciata ad Ali **31** 746*
Facciata dei Torricini **31** *743*, 745
furniture **16** 722
paintings **14** 517; **17** *704*; **20** 623; **32** 895
Palazzetto della Jole **31** 742*
Porte della Guerra **31** 369
Sala degli Angeli **6** 603
Sala Grande **31** *745*
Scalone d'onore **31** 743*
sculpture **5** 533; **27** 274
stables **29** 485
staircases **29** 521, 522
Urbino
Palazzo Ducale—cont.
Studiolo **3** 844; **15** 136; **16** 659, 711, 723; **20** 467; **22** 13; **29** 665, 859–60, *860*; **31** 740, 744
vaults **32** 94
see also Galleria Nazionale delle Marche
patronage **16** 763
pottery **13** 541
maiolica **6** I1; **16** 734, *734*, 735; **31** 741–2*, *742*
Regional Museum **16** 769
S Bernardino **11** *689*, 690
sculpture **16** 688
tapestries **16** 755
Urbino, Ambrogio da *see* BAROCCI, AMBROGIO (D'ANTONIO)
Urbino, Antonio **21** 459
Urbino, Baldassare da *see* LANCI, BALDASSARE
Urbino (da Crema), Carlo **5** 547; **31** 746*
Urbino, Diego de **26** 249
Urbino, Francesco da **10** 503
Urbino, Gatti da *see* GATTI DA URBINO
Urbino, Nicola da **16** 733; **31** 747*
attributions **6** 18
works **11** 268; **14** 425
Urbino Bible *see under* BIBLES → individual manuscripts
Urbnisi Church **12** 318
Urbot **16** 783
Urcola, Francisco **27** 767
Urcos **24** *498*
church **24** 500
Urdaneta, Alberto **7** 609, 611, 612
Urdaneta, Luciano **32** 169
works **32** *169*
Urdaneta Holgvín, Rafael **21** 4
ūrdhvacchanda **15** 245*
Urdiala **13** 120
Ure, J. F. **4** 799
ureaformaldehydes **6** 336
Urechia, V. A. **26** 723
Uren, Reginald **4** 788; **31** 243
Ureña, Juan Tellez Girón, Count of **23** 625
Ure Smith, Sydney **2** 769; **6** 123; **24** 437
Ureta, Teodoro Núñez *see* NÚÑEZ URETA, TEODORO
ureyite **16** 858
Urfa **9** *512*, *513*; **16** *104*; **17** 499, 502; **31** 747*
architects **16** 173
architecture **9** 542, 548
Baptistery **9** 541
Cathedral (4th cent.) **9** 539
Cathedral of St Sofia (6th cent.) **9** 548
churches **9** 539
congregational mosque **16** 222
manuscripts **9** 619, 620, 621
mosaics **9** 566
St Thomas **9** 539
sculpture **24** 218
silver **9** 654
Urfé, Claude d' **27** 248
Urfé, Honoré d' **18** 812; **25** 833
Urga *see* ULAAN BAATAR
Urga school **21** 880, 881, 883
Urgell, José **2** 397
Urgell, Modesto **2** 62; **21** 705; **32** 97
Urgench **6** *182*, 201; **18** 524; **31** *781*
Urgnano Church **16** 647
Ürgüp **5** 676; **16** 266
Urgut **6** 250
Urhobo **9** 736–7
Uri, Aviva **31** 747*
Uriarte, José Manuel **21** 397
Uriarte, José María **10** 542
Uriatubani Church **12** 318
Uriburu, Nicolás García *see* GARCÍA URIBURU, NICOLÁS
Uric, Gavril **26** 711; **31** 748*
Ur III period *see under* MESOPOTAMIA → periods
Urikki of Cilicia *see* AWARIKUS, King of Adana
Urikki of Que *see* AWARIKUS, King of Adana
urinals **10** 316
urine **9** 492; **16** 330; **24** 799; **29** 813
Urlaub, Georg Anton **31** 748*
Urlaub, Georg Karl **11** 459
Urlaub, Georg Sebastian **31** 748
Urmanche, Baki **27** 434
Ürményi (family) **17** 836
Urmetan **6** 222
mausoleum of Abu'l-Qasim Gurgani **6** 277
Urmia **15** 921
Urmiyya Mosque **16** 162
Ur-Nammu Stele **1** 891; **29** 614
Ur-Nanshe (*reg c.* 2520 BC) **30** 422
Urnes **23** *218*; **31** 748–50*
Stave church **23** 219, 233; **29** 580; **31** 748*, 749–50*; **32** 520
capitals **31** *750*
doors **9** 152, 155
furniture **6** 389
sculpture **23** 228; **26** 647
wood-carvings **31** *749*; **32** 513, 518
Urnes style *see under* VIKING → styles
urns **7** 747
historical and regional traditions
China **6** *877*
England **12** 130; **28** *665*
Etruscan **10** 588, 593, 594
Italy **7** *176*; **10** 588, 593, 594
Native North Americans **22** *611*
Prehistoric art **6** *877*
Russia **14** *172*
Santa María culture **29** 191
Weeden Island culture **22** *611*
materials
alabaster (gypsum) **10** *593*
bronze **8** *796*
malachite **14** *172*
pottery **22** *611*; **29** *191*, *194*
stone **10** 588, 607, 608
terracotta **10** 588, 602–3, *603*; **18** *218*; **27** 9
techniques
gilding **28** *665*
types
biconical **10** *610*
canopic *see* funerary
cinerary *see* funerary
coffee *see* COFFEE-URNS
funerary
Africa **18** *218*
Argentina **29** *191*
Brazil **29** *194*
China **6** *877*
Crete **8** 154
Egypt, ancient **13** 539
Etruscan **7** *176*; **10** 588, 593, *593*, 594, 602–3, *603*, 607, 608, 609; **27** 9
Greece, ancient **13** 539
Indian subcontinent **15** 192
Italy **10** 588, 593, *593*, 594, *603*, 609
Kongo **18** 217, *218*
Korea **18** 273, 335
Mesoamerica, Pre-Columbian **21** 266
Prehistoric art **6** *877*
Rome, ancient **7** 642; **9** 29; **24** *845*; **27** 9, 33, 34
Santa María culture **29** *191*
South America, Pre-Columbian **29** *191*, 193, *194*
Zapotec **21** 266
hut **10** 587, *599*
tea *see* TEA-URNS

urns
  types—cont.
    voting **8** *796*
Urogbo Palace **9** 735
Uromi
  palace **9** 735
  wood-carvings **9** *735*
Uromot **24** 83
Uronarti **9** *774*
  fort **9** 844, 845, *845*, 846, *846*; **10** 81; **21** 554
Urquhart, Thomas **12** 820
Urquijo (family) **21** 81
Urquiza, Domingo **29** 337, 341, 342
Urquiza, Ildefonso **29** 342, 343
Urquiza, Manuel **29** 342, 343
Urrabieta y Ortiz, Vicente **24** 105; **31** 750*
Urrabieta y Vierge, Daniel **4** 364; **14** 853; **31** 750
Urraca, Queen of Castile-León (*reg* 1109-26) **19** 175; **23** 683; **26** 689, 698
Urrea, Francisco Ximénez de *see* XIMÉNEZ DE URREA, FRANCISCO
Urrea, M. de **32** 641
Urrea Abarca de Bolea, Buenaventura de, 9th Conde de Aranda *see* ARANDA, BUENAVENTURA DE URREA ABARCA DE BOLEA, 9th Conde de
Urruchúa, Demetrio **2** 707
Ursel, Duc d' **32** 767
Ursicinus, Bishop of Ravenna **26** 33
Ursins, Jouvenel des *see* JOUVENEL DES URSINS
Ursins, Marie-Anne de La Trémouille, Princesse des **10** 842; **17** 522
Ursinus, Marrius **27** 90
Urso *see* OSUNA
Urso, Archbishop **30** 777
  throne **30** *777*
Urso, Filippo *see* ORSO, FILIPPO
Ursus, Bishop **26** 31
Ursuzio, Antonio **20** 898
Urswick, Christopher **31** 750–51*
Ursy, Giovanni Domenico *see* ORSI, GIOVANNI DOMENICO
Urteaga Alvarado, Mario (Tulio Escipión) **24** 509, 515; **31** 751*
Urtubey, Eduardo **2** 397
Uruguay **29** 128; **31** *751*, 751–9*
  architecture **7** 614–15; **31** 752–4*
  collections **31** 757–8*
  education (art) **31** 758*
    architecture **31** 758
  exhibitions **31** 756
  gold **31** 756*
  government buildings **31** *753*
  libraries **31** 758–9*
  mates **31** 756
  museums **31** 757–8*
  painting **31** 754–6*
    genre **31** *755*
  photoarchives **31** 758–9*
  plastics **31** *757*
  prints **31** 755
  sculpture **31** 754–6*
  silver **31** 756*
  tapestries **31** 755, 757, *757*
  textiles **31** 756–7*
  town halls **31** 753
  trappings **31** 756
  wood-engravings **31** 755
Uruk **1** *849*, 894; **15** 904; **21** *267*; **31** 759–60*
  Anu precinct **31** 759*
    Bit Resh **21** 281; **31** 760
  art forms and materials
    alabaster (gypsum) **21** *293*
    architecture **21** 281–2, 291, 292
    coffins **24** 218
    mosaics **1** 889; **23** 532
    polychromy **25** 171
Uruk
  art forms and materials—cont.
    pottery **21** 271, 306
    sculpture **21** 271–2, 293–4; **31** *760*
    seals **1** 856, *859*, 860
    stelae **22** 510; **29** 613
    stone-carvings **29** 923
    stucco **29** 815
    terracotta **1** 883
    writing-tablets **1** 853; **21** 271, 282
  Cenotaph *see Steingebäude*
  Eanna precinct **21** 270, 271, 281, 282, *282*; **31** 759–60*
    Cone Mosaic Court **21** 282
    gymnasium **21** 282
    Limestone Temple **21** 282; **31** 759
    mosaics **22** 158
    Red Temple **17** 466; **21** 272, 282
    Riemchengebäude **21** 282
    Stone Cone Mosaic Building **21** 282
    Temple D **21** 282
    Temple E **21** 282
  iconography **24** 218
  Kullaba precinct *see* Anu precinct
  Principal Temple *see* Anu precinct → Bit Resh
  religion **21** 277
  Steingebäude **21** 281
  temenos **21** 552
  temples **29** 924; **30** 431–2
    Inanna Temple **17** 836; **21** 281, 286, 287
    Karaindash Temple **21** 296
    Limestone Temple *see under* Eanna Precinct
    Red Temple *see under* Eanna Precinct
    Temple of Anu-Antum **1** 879; **28** 383
    Temple D *see under* Eanna Precinct
    Temple E *see under* Eanna Precinct
    Temple of Gareus **4** *772*
    White Temple **4** 771; **21** 281–2; **30** 431; **31** 759
  terrace **21** 282
  town walls **21** 552
  trade **21** 268
  ziggurat **21** 273; **28** 383; **33** 675
Uruk period *see under* ANCIENT NEAR EAST; MESOPOTAMIA → periods
Urumqi **6** *288*
  ceramics **6** 308
  Museum of the Xinjiang Uygur Autonomous Region **6** 321
Urundi *see* BURUNDI
urushi see under LACQUER → types
urushie see under PRINTS → types → *ukiyoe*
Urville, Dumont d' **23** 57
Urvinum Mataurense *see* URBINO
Uryū **17** 348
Urzecze Glassworks **22** 449; **25** 124; **31** 760*
Urzędowa, Jan Michałowicz z *see* MICHAŁOWICZ Z URZĘDOWA, JAN
Urzúa, Antonio María Bucareli y *see* BUCARELI Y URZÚA, ANTONIO MARÍA
Urzulei **27** 835
USA *see* UNITED STATES OF AMERICA
Usage de la Parole, L' **14** 852
Usa Hachiman Shrine **17** 63
Uşak *see* USHAK
Usan **18** 342
Usaneti **12** 321
Usaquen, S Teresa complex **7** 607
Usa Shrine **17** 127
Usator **6** 380
Usener, Hermann **32** 854
User **10** 75
Userhet **9** 808, 811, 902; **10** 10
Userkaf (*reg c.* 2465–*c.* 2458 BC) **1** 96, 97; **9** *776*, 830, 862, 870; **25** 762; **27** 812
Usermaatre-setepenre *see* RAMESSES II
Useynov, Mikael' **1** 506; **2** 893, 894, 898, 899; **3** 88; **12** 37; **31** 761
Useynova, U. **2** 896
Useynov & Dadashev **2** 894; **31** 761*
Ushak **16** 470, 476, 477, 479
  carpets **5** II
Ushak carpets *see under* CARPETS → types
Ushakov, Pimen *see* USHAKOV, SIMON (FYODOROVICH)
Ushakov, Simon (Fyodorovich) **25** 338; **31** 761–2*
  collaboration **33** 712
  pupils **27** 387
  works **22** 177; **25** 330; **27** 387
Ushimaro *see* HANABUSA ITCHŌ
Ushinoto **17** 353
Ushkur **15** 458
Ushtur-Mullo **6** *182*, 198; **29** 821; **30** *252*; **31** 762*
USIA *see* UNITED STATES INFORMATION AGENCY
Usiai **24** 82
Usimbardi, Lorenzo, Bishop **2** 609; **23** 880; **32** 25
Usina, Sebastián **7** 607; **25** 233
Ušinskas, Stasys **19** 498, 499
'Usiyeh Tomb **14** 21
Usk **18** 615
Uskaf Bani Junayd *see* SUMAKA
Üsküdar *see* ISTANBUL
Üsküdari *see* OKYAY, NECMEDDIN
Uskup *see* SKOPJE
Usmanpur, Sayyid Usman Mosque **1** 473
Usman Zaki **23** 302
US Marine Corps **11** 835; **12** 311
Usol'sk *see* SOL'VYCHEGODSK
Usonian House *see under* HOUSES → types
Usov, A. **21** 812
Uspensky, Aleksei (Aleksandrovich) **27** 417
Uspensky, Pyotr (Dem'yanovich) **30** 7, 711; **31** 763*
Ussher, Beverley **31** 763
Ussher & Kemp **2** 740; **31** 763*
Ussi, Stefano **31** 763–4*
Ussishkin, D. **18** 596
USS Lancaster see under SHIPS → named vessels
USSR *see* UNION OF SOVIET SOCIALIST REPUBLICS
USSR in Construction **7** 653
US Steel **30** 391
Ustad Ahmad Lahauri **2** 317, 729; **3** 238; **15** 365, 366
Ustad 'Ali Akbar **12** 82
Ustad al-Misri **16** 417
Ustad Baba Hajji **16** 326
Ustad Mansur *see* MANSUR
Ustād Muḥammad Siyāh Qalam *see* SIYAH QALAM
Ustad Murad **14** 270
Usta Muhammad **21** 50
Ustehar **15** 632
Usteri, Heinrich **31** 764
Usteri, Jacob Emil **29** 491
Usteri, Johann Martin **29** 73; **30** 133; **31** 764*
Usteri, Martin **33** 737
Ústí nad Labem **8** 426
  Museum of Applied Art **8** 424
Ustí nad Orlicí **8** 380
Ustinov, Plato **4** 63
Ust-Kamenogorsk **17** *865*; **27** 375
Usto Adbulla **18** 195
Ust'-Poluy **25** *471*; **27** 367; **31** 764*
Ust'-Tuba **27** 367
Ustyug(, Veliky) *see* VELIKY USTYUG
Usu **29** 185
Usubaliyev, Altmish **18** 568
Usulután ware *see under* POTTERY → wares
Uta, Abbess of Niedermünster **23** 652, 654
Uta Evangelary **1** 697
Utagawa Hirosada **17** 289
Utagawa Hiroshige *see* ANDŌ HIROSHIGE
Utagawa Kunihiro **17** 288
Utagawa Kunihisa **17** 290
Utagawa Kunimasa **17** 284, 288; **31** 764, 765–6*
Utagawa Kunimasu **17** 289
Utagawa Kuninaga **17** 288
Utagawa Kuninao **17** 288
Utagawa Kunisada I (1786-1864) **17** 287; **31** 766*
  groups and movements **17** 288; **31** 764
  pupils **17** 289, 290
  teachers **31** 765
  works **17** 177, 273, 274, *278*, 279, 288, 290; **31** *766*
Utagawa Kunisada II (1823-80) **31** 766
Utagawa Kunitora **17** 288
Utagawa Kuniyasu **17** 288
Utagawa Kuniyoshi **31** 766–7*
  collaboration **33** 318
  groups and movements **17** 288; **31** 764
  pupils **17** 177, 290, 861; **31** 400
  teachers **31** 765
  works **17** 177, 276, 288, 290, *415*, 415
Utagawa Sadahide **17** 290; **33** 539
Utagawa school **17** 177, 286, 288; **31** 764*
Utagawa Toyoharu **17** 288; **31** 764–6*
Utagawa Toyohiro **17** 287; **31** 766*
  pupils **2** 8; **17** 288
  teachers **31** 764, 765
  works **17** 282
Utagawa Toyokumi
  works **17** *330*
Utagawa Toyokuni I (1769-1825) **31** 765–6*
  attributions **31** 204
  collaboration **31** 765
  pupils **31** 765, 766
  teachers **17** 288; **31** 764, 765
  works **17** 273, 284, 286, 287, 845; **31** *765*
Utagawa Toyokuni II (1777-1835) **17** 288
Utagawa Toyokuni III (1786-1864) *see* UTAGAWA KUNISADA I
Utagawa Yoshiiku **17** 276; **31** 400
Utagawa Yoshikazu **17** 290; **31** 767
Utagawa Yoshitaki **17** 289
Utagawa Yoshitora **17** 290; **31** 767
Utagawa Yoshitoshi **31** 767
Utamaro Kitagawa *see* KITAGAWA UTAMARO
Uta Pericope *see under* PERICOPE BOOKS → individual manuscripts
Utatlán **13** *758*; **20** 886
Uta Uta (Jangala) **31** 767*
Ute **22** 549, 551, 633, 669
Utekač glassworks **28** 856
Utens, Giusto **11** 180, 215; **12** 62, 115, 117; **31** 320
  works **11** *214*; **12** *62*; **32** *546*
Utenwael, Joachim *see* WTEWAEL, JOACHIM
uterine skins *see under* SKINS → types
Utermarke, Dirich **14** 102
Uther, Johan Baptista van **31** 767*
Uther Pendragon **11** 151
Uthina **26** 920
'Uthman, Caliph (*reg* 644-56) (Orthodox Caliphs) **16** 278, 431; **20** 368, 913; **21** 32, 33
'Uthman I, Sultan (*reg* 1281-1324) (Ottoman) **16** 539
'Uthman III, Sultan (*reg* 1754-7) (Ottoman) **16** 226, 610
'Uthman al-Nakhchavani **16** 375
'Uthman ibn Sulayman al-Nakhichivani **2** 899
U Thong **30** *571*, 576, 635
  coins **30** 632
  figurines **30** 510, *511*
  glass **30** 633
  sculpture **30** 595
Utica (Tunisia) **26** 920; **27** 63, 67
Utica Memorial Auditorium (NY; USA) **30** 468
Utili, Andrea **3** 916
Utili, Giovanni Battista *see* BERTUCCI, GIOVANNI BATTISTA
utilitas **2** 362
Utility Scheme **8** 804; **10** 284, 299, 313
Utišenović, D. **9** 331
Utkin, Pyotr **4** 178; **22** 135; **27** 458
Utne, Lars **26** 5
Utne, Sjur **32** 512
Uto kiln **27** 873
Utopia **1** 56, 64; **2** *736*
  textiles **2** 768
  wood-carvings **1** 43
Utpala, Avantivarman *see* AVANTIVARMAN
Utpala, Shankaravarman *see* SHANKARAVARMAN
ut pictura poesis **8** 602; **9** 372; **14** 869; **15** 96; **24** 741; **31** 767–9*
  see also PARAGONI; POETRY
Utrecht **22** *813*, 901; **31** 769–73*
  apartments **22** 831, *831*
  art forms and materials
    architecture **22** 816
    block-books **4** 145
    brass **22** 895
    brick **4** 778
    bronze **22** 894
    ceramics **22** *877*, 878
    earthenwares **22** 877
    glass **22** 884
    gold **22** 889
    guns **2** 464
    manuscript illumination **22** 836
    painting **12** 290; **22** 843–4*, 852
    panel paintings **22** 834
    pewter **22** 893
    sculpture **13** 101, 114; **22** 856; **26** 630–31
    silver **22** 885, 886, 887
    textiles **22** 899
    tiles **22** 881; **30** 878, 879
    tombs **22** 855
  Bioscoop Vreeburg Cinema **19** 367
  Centraal Museum **4** 53; **22** 906; **31** 771
  ecclesiastical buildings
    Benedictine abbey church **22** 817
    Buurkerk **22** 857
    Catharijneconvent *see* Rijksmuseum Het Catharijneconvent
    Cathedral of St Martin and St Saviour **13** 62, *62*; **22** 816, 817, 818, 819, *820*; **31** 770
      sculpture **13** 101; **22** 855, 857
    Mariakerk **22** 817–18
      organ loft **22** 857
      tomb of Jo de Wit **22** 857
    St Gertrudiskerk **4** *444*
    St Jacobikerk **13** 61; **22** 820
    St Janskerk **3** 600; **22** 817; **31** 769
    St Pieterskerk **6** 565; **22** 817; **26** 574, 578; **31** 769
      crypt **8** 223

Utrecht
ecclesiastical buildings
St Pieterskerk—cont.
reliefs **22** *855*
sculpture **22** 855; **26** 631
wall paintings **22** 834
fort **22** 816
Galgenvaard Stadium **29** 490
guilds **13** 823
Het Zandkasteel **4** 790
Huis de Rode Poort **22** 822
Huis Schröder **4** 788; **21** 781, *781*; **22** 830, 868; **32** 555
Instituut **22** 911
Kunstliefde Museum **31** 771
Lofen palace **22** 817
masons' lodges **22** 820
Muziekcentrum Vredenburg **7** 688; **14** 484
Old Canal **31** *770*
Oudaen **6** 57
Oude Gracht *see* Old Canal
Paleis van Justitie **22** 828
Rädemacher-Schorer House **26** 38
Rijksmuseum Het Catharijneconvent **22** 855
Rijksuniversiteit
Bibliotheek **5** 74; **22** 828, 909; **31** 773
collections **8** 150
Stadhuis **22** 828
Vredenburg Castle **17** *884*; **22** 822
Winkel van Sinkel **22** 828
Utrecht, Adriaen van **23** 124; **31** 772*
collaboration **14** 617; **17** 6; **26** 746; **32** 706
patrons and collectors **8** 533; **28** 904
teachers **23** 76
works **3** 561
Utrecht, Casin d' *see* CASIN D'UTRECHT
Utrecht, Cristóvão de **19** 655
Utrecht, Jacob (Claesz.) van *see* JACOB (CLAESZ.) VAN UTRECHT
Utrecht, John van **22** 896
Utrecht Caravaggisti **5** 719; **9** 462; **31** 772*
collections **22** 906
Utrecht Caravaggisti—cont.
members **3** 8; **4** 52, 846; **5** 1; **14** 727; **22** 843
works **4** *52*; **14** *727*, *728*, *729*, *731*
Utrecht Psalter *see under* PSALTERS → individual manuscripts
Utrecht Sacramentary *see under* SACRAMENTARIES → individual manuscripts
Utrechtsche Machinale Stoel- en Meubelfabriek *see* UMS
Utrecht Stone Female Head, Master of the **13** 114
works **13** *115*
Utriainen, Raimo (Arvi Johannes) **31** 774*
Utrillo, Maurice **31** 775–6*, 801
collaboration **20** 603
dealers **13** 826; **33** 627
patrons and collectors **9** 465; **12** 724; **13** 826; **26** 472, 723; **27** 333
works **19** 491; **31** *775*
Utrillo, Miguel **25** 348; **31** 775
Utsond, Gunnar **23** 230
Utsunomiya **17** 433
uttarāṅga **15** 245*
Uttar Madhurā *see* MATHURA
Uttenheim, Master of **20** 779*
Uttenhove, Ermentrude **12** 521
Utter, André **31** 775, 801
Utterslev **17** 485
Utuado, Caguana park **25** 704
Utu Etim Ekpo **15** 61
masks **15** *62*
Utupua **27** 778
Utur *see* ETULO
Utz, Josef (i) (1825-96) **18** 446
Utz, Josef (ii) (1858-1909) **18** 446
Utzon, Jørn (Oberg) **18** 541; **31** 776–7*
collaboration **2** 578; **7** 696; **18** 390; **26** 333
competitions **7** 670
groups and movements **10** 698
house **8** 729
pupils **21** 861
staff **30** 260
works **8** 729, 747; **19** 367; **27** 129; **30** 684; **31** *777*
Utzon-Frank, Einar **8** 741, 760
Uusikaupunki *see* NYSTAD
Uvarov, A. S. **27** 439
Uvarova, P. S., Countess **6** 280
Uvays I, Sultan *see* UWAYS I, Sultan
Uvo **7** 922
Uwanabe **17** 58
Uways I, Sultan (*reg* 1356-74) (Jalayirid) **1** 474; **16** 316, 318; **17** 687; **30** 222
Uwins, Thomas **1** 121; **14** 148; **31** 777–8*
Uxbridge (Middx) **31** 709
Uxmal **20** *882*, 884; **21** *193*, 199, 202, 246, 262, 263, *372*; **23** 826; **31** 778*
architecture **21** 205
Ballcourt **3** 117
causeway **6** 97
lintels **9** 165
mosaics **22** 164
Nunnery Quadrangle **20** 884; **21** 207; **23** 565; **31** 778, *778*
Palace of the Governor **20** 884; **21** 207; **23** 565, *825*; **30** 786; **31** 778
frieze **11** 792
stucco **29** 829
Pyramid of the Magician **21** 214, *214*, 216; **25** 764; **30** 449
skull racks **21** 188; **31** 505
Stele 7 **30** 786
Uxpanapan
sculpture **21** *218*
Uxul **5** 411
Uygarak **2** 101
jewellery **6** 273
Uygur **5** 101; **6** 289, 295, 616, 626, 692; **7** 143, 144
books **6** 314
calligraphy **6** 308
dress **6** 310–11
manuscripts **6** 306
religion **18** 26
scripts **6** 307, 308; **21** 882
scrolls **6** 307
textiles **16** 451
Uygur script *see under* SCRIPTS → types
Uylenborch, Gerrit *see* UYLENBURGH, GERRIT
Uylenbroeck, Gosuin **26** 284
Uylenburch, Saskia van **23** I
Uylenburgh, Abraham **31** 779
Uylenburgh, Gerrit **12** 473, 801; **26** 153, 155, 156, 283; **31** 779*; **32** 155, 262
collaboration **19** 123
paintings **26** 153; **32** 155
printmakers **26** 157
Uylenburgh, Hendrick van **16** 833; **22** 842; **26** 174; **31** 779
Uylenspiegel **24** 439
Uyŏm *see* KWŎN TON-IN
Uytenbogaardt, Roelof (Sarel) **5** 668; **29** 106; **31** 779*
Uytewael, Joachim *see* WTEWAEL, JOACHIM
Uyttenbroeck, Jan (Matheusz.) van **31** 779, 780
Uyttenbroeck, Matheus van **31** 780
Uyttenbroeck, Moses (Matheusz.) van **14** 41; **31** 779–80*
patrons and collectors **23** 465
reproductive prints by others **32** 140
works **22** 844; **31** *780*
Uytterschaut, Victor **8** 63
Uytvanck, Benoît Van *see* VAN UYTVANCK, BENOÎT
Uzairue **9** 735
Uzana Edigi **23** 824
Uzanne, Octave **5** 131
Uzan Shirai *see* SHIRAI, UZAN
Uzbek **6** 252, 253, 254, 274; **7** 144
carpets **1** 209
tents **30** 475
textiles **1** 209; **16** 451
Uzbekistan **6** 181; **16** *105*; **31** 780–84*, *781*
architecture **16** 166; **31** 782*
bowls **6** *188*
carpets **16** 466
clay **6** *187*
collections **6** 283*
cotton **31** *783*
decorative arts **31** 783–4*
dress **31** *783*
manuscript illumination **5** *138*; **6** *234*
minarets **5** *140*
mosques **5** *139*
museums **6** 283*
ossuaries **6** *213*; **31** *76*
painting **6** 302; **31** 782–3*
plaster **31** *76*
portals **6** *203*
Uzbekistan—cont.
pottery **6** *213*
robes **6** *252*
sculpture **31** 782–3*
relief **6** *187*, *276*; **18** *16*
silk **6** *252*; **31** *783*
silver **6** *188*
terracotta **6** *276*
textiles **16** 451
tombs **27** *675*
Uzemchin **21** 870, 876, 878
Uzès, Duc d' **19** 115
Uzès Château **29** 521
Uzgend **6** *182*, 201; **10** 896; **16** *105*; **18** *567*; **31** 781, 784*
architectural decorations **6** 207
mausolea **16** 165, 245; **24** 877
mausoleum of Nasr ibn 'Ali **31** 784
pīshṭāq **16** 164
tiles **6** 208
Uzhhorod **31** *546*, 784*
Museum of Art **31** 784
Transcarpathian Museum of Folk Architecture and Life **31** 784
Transcarpathian Regional Museum **31** 784
Uzielli, G. **28** 707
Uzielli, Matthew **26** 473
Uztáriz, Eduardo Rivero *see* RIVERO UZTÁRIZ, EDUARDO
Üzümlü *see* KADYANDA
Uzun **6** 245
aqueduct **2** 242
Uzuncaburç, Temple of Zeus **13** 405
Uzun Hasan, Sultan (*reg* 1453-78) (Aqqoyunlu) **2** 237; **16** 77, 198, 199, 260, 328, 378; **30** 223, 478
Uzun Köprü **16** 207
Uzunlar *see* ODZUN
Uzunov, Dechko **31** 785*
collaboration **32** 78
patrons and collectors **5** 163
pupils **3** 44
works **5** 154
Uzunov, Sime **19** 885
Uzwil, Waldbühl **3** *75*
Uzzano, Niccolò da *see* NICCOLÒ DA UZZANO

V

Vä **26** 651; **30** 75
St Mary's **26** 593
Va, Barry Le *see* LE VA, BARRY
Vaa, Dyre **23** 230
Vaahsen (, Pastor) **20** 808
Vaardt, Jan van der (*c.* 1653-1727) **21** 416; **31** 786*
collaboration **9** 211, 280; **17** 915; **33** 260
patrons and collectors **23** 468
pupils **28** 881
works **9** *281*
Vaart, Jan van der (1931) **22** 884
Vaasa
Appeal Court **11** 91
furniture **11** 103
Pohjanmaan Museo **11** 111
Vabbe, Ado **10** 539
Vác **14** *881*; **31** 786–7*
Cathedral **14** 885, 887, 888; **31** 786
Dominican church **31** 786
Felsővárosi parish church *see* Dominican church
Piarist school **15** 17
sculpture **26** 638
Triumphal Arch **14** 888
Vaca Duran, Lorgio **4** 263; **22** 335
Văcăresti **26** 708
Vacca, A. **24** 855
Vacca, Flaminio **31** 787*
works **31** *787*
Vacca, Luigi **12** 901, 902; **16** 720
Vaccani, Jacopo de **11** 77
Vaccarini, Giovanni Battista **6** 83; **28** 657; **31** 788*
Vaccaro, Andrea **31** 790–91*
patrons and collectors **1** 690; **4** 619; **10** 115; **17** 893; **22** 486
pupils **10** 803; **32** 593
works **22** 484; **31** *791*
Vaccaro, Domenico Antonio **22** 479; **31** 788, 789–90*
pupils **26** 500
works **16** 640; **22** 473, 485; **26** 500; **31** *790*
Vaccaro, Lorenzo **31** 788–9*
collaboration **31** 789
pupils **31** 789
works **3** 237; **16** 703; **22** 478, 485
Vaccaro, Nicola **22** 479; **31** 791
Vacche, Vincenzo dalle **32** 343
Vače **25** *470*; **28** 806, 807
situlae **28** *806*
Vacek, Ladislav **8** 420
Vach, Hermannus Künig von *see* KÜNIG VON VACH, HERMANNUS
Váchal, Josef **8** 393; **31** 792*; **33** 710
Vaché, Jacques **8** 438
Vache, La *see* LA VACHE
Vacher, Sydney
works **8** *857*
Vachette, Adrien-Jean-Maximilien **11** 630, 633, 636
Vach'e Vach'utian, Prince **27** 701
Vachier, Jaquet le *see* JAQUET LE VACHIER
Vachon, Marius **11** 674
Vachons, Les *see* LES VACHONS
Vachtang I Gorgaslan, King of Iberia (*reg* 447-522) **30** 305
Vacková, J. **8** 426
Václav (14th cent.) **8** 415
Václav (Žlutice) (15th cent.) **26** 131
Václav I, Duke of Bohemia (*reg* 921-9) *see* WENCESLAS, SAINT
Václav I Přemysl, King of Bohemia (*reg* 1230-53) **31** 28
Václav II Přemysl, King of Bohemia (*reg* 1278-1305) **25** 54
Václav IV, King of Bohemia *see* WENCESLAS, Holy Roman Emperor
Václav, František **1** 669
Václav of Budějovice **8** 412
Vacquerie, Auguste **14** 853; **31** 792*
vacuum cleaners **8** *804*; **11** 361
Vad, Poul **8** 762
Vada **10** 586
Vadasz, Christine **31** 792*
Vadaval **15** 487
Vadda **29** 440, 445
Vadder, Hubert de **31** 793
Vadder, Lodewijk de **2** 875; **5** 43; **17** 599; **31** 793*
Vadder, Philippe de **31** 793
Vădeni **26** 708
Vadi, Alberto **25** 702
Vadillo, Francisco Antonio de Salcedo, 1st Marqués de **26** 313
Vadnagar **15** *279*; **31** 793*
torana **31** *160*, 161
Vadodara **15** *276*; **31** 793–4*
Baroda Museum *see* Museum and Picture Gallery
Bhadra **15** 394
Bhaskar Vithalrao's Wada **15** 394
Bhau Shinde's Wada **15** 394
houses **15** 393
Laxmi Vilas Palace **31** 793
Maharaja Fateh Singh Museum **15** 182; **31** 794
Maharaja Sayajirao University **15** 173
collections **15** 182; **31** 794
Faculty of Fine Arts **15** 179
Museum and Picture Gallery **7** 173; **12** 853; **15** 182; **22** 364; **31** 794
Oze Wada **15** 394
Sarkar Wada **15** 394
sculpture **15** 426
Tambekar Wada **15** 394, *394*
Vadstena **30** *65*
Abbey **4** 810; **30** 67; **31** *794*, 794–5*
embroidery **30** 115
manuscripts **30** 77
sculpture **13** 112, 120
tomb of Duke Magnus of Östergötland **30** 84
Castle **27** 279; **30** 68, 87, 92, 109
damask **19** 418; **30** 115
lace **30** 115
Town Hall **30** 67
Vadukkodai **16** 864
Vaduz **20** 788
Liechtenstein Collection **4** 152; **7** 711, *711*; **21** 485; **27** 292, 293, 296; **28** 903
sculpture **32** 731
Vaenius, Otto van *see* VEEN, OTTO VAN
Værnes **3** 775; **23** 224
church **30** *906*, 907
Vaernewijck, Marcus van **12** 519; **31** 795*
Vaerten, Jan **17** 518
Vafflard, Pierre (-Antoine)-Auguste **31** 374, 795–6*
Vågå, St Peter **29** 580
Vaga **24** 419
Vaga, Perino del *see* PERINO DEL VAGA
Vagedes, Adolph von **31** 796*
Vaggelli, Bartolomeo **28** 393
Vaghali, Mudhaidevi Temple **15** 316
Vagharsh, King of Armenia (*reg* AD 117-40) **9** 731
Vagharshapat *see* ĒDJMIADZIN
Vaghela, Visalla *see* VISALLA, Ruler
Vagindra script *see under* SCRIPTS → types
Vagkat *see* URA TYUBE
Vagnet, Leon **27** 322
Vagnetti, Gianni **11** 191
Vágó, József **14** 889; **25** 829; **31** 796–7*
Vágó, Lázló **31** 796–7*
Vago, Pierre **7** 258, 695; **12** 653
Vågø Airport **10** 813
Vago di Lavagno **20** 767
Vahan Mamikonian, Prince of Armenia (*reg c.* 485-505) **2** 425; **9** 731
Vahía, Alejo de **29** 289
Vahland, W(illiam) C(harles) **2** 738; **4** 374; **31** 797*
Vahlen, Johannes **14** 864
Vahram **2** 436
Vahtra, Jaan **10** 542
Vai **1** 256, 387; **19** 309; **21** 115
Vaibhara *see* RAJGIR
Vaikom **15** 336
Vailland, Roger **28** 745
Vaillant, Bernard **19** 381
Vaillant, François Le *see* LE VAILLANT, FRANÇOIS
Vaillant, George C. **21** 739
Vaillant, Wallerant **19** 381; **21** 414; **31** 797*
reproductive prints by others **19** 562
teachers **25** 811
works **4** 96; **15** 140; **21** 350, 415; **22** 916
Vairone, Biagio **24** 286, 287
Vaishali **15** 220, *279*, 409; **31** 798*
pillar **15** 423
ring stones **15** 423
terracotta **15** 453
Vaishampayana **15** 226
Vaishnavism *see under* HINDUISM → sects
Vaison-la-Romaine **11** *505*
Cathedral of Notre-Dame-de-Nazareth **2** 295; **20** 572
altar **1** 693
capitals **26** 603
houses **26** 904
Portico of Pompey **12** 70, *70*
Vasio Vocontiorum **26** *908*; **32** 72*
Vaissel, Guillaume au *see* GUILLAUME AU VAISSEL
Vaitupu **31** 484
Vajai, Imré **10** 472
Vajda, Júlia **14** 902
Vajda, Lajos **3** 111; **31** 798*
groups and movements **10** 650, 651; **14** 901; **30** 207
works **30** 207
Vajdahunyad *see* HUNEDOARA CASTLE
Vajrabodhi **5** 109
Vajragiri **15** 505
Vajrayana Buddhism *see* BUDDHISM → branches → Esoteric
Vajrayogini **27** 755
Vakataka **15** 257; **31** 798*
see also:
HARISHENA, Ruler
PRABHAVATIGUPTA, Queen
UPENDRAGUPTA
Vakhtang VI, King of Georgia (*reg* 1711-14;1719) **12** 331
Vakpent Minaret **16** 248
Vakramyaye, Yuta (Yanovna) **27** 423
Vakurov, Ivan Petrovich **23** 837
Val, François du, Marquis de Fontenay-Mareuil *see* FONTENAY-MAREUIL, FRANÇOIS DU VAL, Marquis de
Valabhi (Indian subcontinent) **5** 95; **15** *276*; **31** 799*
valabhī (roofs) **15** 245*
Valabhi calendar *see* INDIAN SUBCONTINENT → calendars → Gupta
Valabrega, Vittorio **16** 731
Valade, Jean **31** 799*
Valade, Léonard **31** 799
Valadés, Diego de **21** 382
Valadés, Emilio **1** 739
Valadier (family) **11** 394; **16** 729, 743, 776; **26** 148
Valadier, Andrea **31** 799*
Valadier, Filippo **31** 799
Valadier, Giuseppe **31** 800–801*
collaboration **3** 920; **29** 639
groups and movements **22** 741
patrons and collectors **4** 302; **25** 213; **31** 172
pupils **23** 259
restorations **29** 639, 640
works **2** 320; **3** 627; **7** 726; **11** 689; **12** 584; **16** 644, 727; **26** 780, 807; **31** 740, 799, *800*; **32** 554
Valadier, Luigi (1726-85) **16** 727, 743; **25** 8; **26** 389, 780; **31** 799*
Valadier, Luigi, II (*b* 1781) **31** 799
Valadier, Luigi Giovanni **31** 799
Valadier, Tommaso **31** 799
Valadon, Jules-Emmanuel **8** 191
Valadon, René **4** 588; **13** 228
Valadon, Suzanne **31** 775, 801*
Valaitis, Teodoras Kazimieras **19** 499
valances **3** 483, 484; **31** 682
Valashkerteli, Zakaria **12** 325
Valašské Meziříčí Arts and Crafts Centre **8** 420
Valbudea, Ştefan **16** 877; **26** 715; **29** 721; **31** 802*
Valby pottery factory **14** 120
Val Camonica **6** 479; **25** 532, 533
Valcárcel, José Manuel González **18** 810
Valcárcel, Luis (E.) **23** 414; **24** 516; **27** 485, 501
Valcárcel, Roberto **4** 261, 264
Vál Church **14** 888
Valcin, Gérard **14** 58; **31** 802*
Valck **12** 814
Valck, Gerard **12** 812; **21** 415; **31** 802*
collaboration **4** 169
methods **30** 568
printmakers **5** 62
pupils **28** 76
sponsorship **19** 540
works **21** 415
Valck, Leendert Gerritsz. **31** 802
Valck, Leonardus **12** 812; **31** 802
Valck, Peeter *see* VALCKX, PIETER
Valck, Simon de **32** 230
Valckenborch, Frederik van **31** 802, 805–7*
groups and movements **11** 732
patrons and collectors **17** 711
works **31** *805*, *806*
Valckenborch, Geraard van **31** 803
Valckenborch, Gillis van **31** 802, 805
Valckenborch, John Jacob van (1625-75) **31** 803
Valckenborch, Lucas van, I **2** 793; **31** 802, 803–7*
attributions **31** 807
collaboration **11** 165
patrons and collectors **13** 916
works **3** 558; **5** 443; **15** 828; **31** *804*
Valckenborch, Marten van, I (1534-1612) **3** 558; **7** 814; **31** 802, 803*
works **15** 828
Valckenborch, Marten van, II (before 1566-97) **31** 803
Valckenborch, Moritz van **31** 806
Valckenborch, Nicolaus van **31** 806
Valckenburg, Johann van (*d* 1625) **31** 567
Valckenhoven, Cornelis (Harmansz.) **22** 879
Valckenisse, Philip van **22** 201
Valckert, Werner (Jacobsz.) van den **22** 842; **31** 807*
Valcknisse, Filips van **3** 615
Valckx, Abraham **3** 598
Valckx, Pieter **3** 570; **12** 230; **31** 807*; **32** 251
Valdambrino, Francesco di *see* FRANCESCO DI VALDAMBRINO
Valdameri, Rino **30** 513
Val de Aguila, Condesa de **29** 304
Valdeavellano **13** 770
Valdec, Rudolf **8** 178
Valdedíos, S Salvador **2** 653; **29** 261
Valde-Iñigo, Marqués de **31** 808*
Valdelomar, Fernando de Szyszlo *see* SZYSZLO (VALDELOMAR), FERNANDO DE
Valdelvira, Andrés de *see* VANDELVIRA, ANDRÉS DE
Valdemar I, King of Denmark (*reg* 1157-82) **4** 780; **7** 802; **8** 721, 723
Valdemar II, King of Denmark (*reg* 1202-41) **8** 738
Valdemar IV, King of Denmark (*reg* 1340-75) **4** 781; **8** 724
Valdemorillo **29** 329
Valderde **1** 841
Valdés, Cristián **6** 595
Valdés, Fernando **10** 905
Valdés, Lucas de **20** 499; **31** 808, 810, 811*
Valdés, Luisa Raphaela de *see* MORALES, LUISA RAPHAELA
Valdés, Manuel **10** 443; **29** 286
Valdés, María de **31** 808
Valdés, Sebastián de Llanos y *see* LLANOS Y VALDÉS, SEBASTIÁN DE
Valdés Leal, Juan de (1622-90) **20** 234; **28** 515; **31** 808–11*
collaboration **26** 552, 553
groups and movements **30** 456
patrons and collectors **5** 792; **13** 880; **14** 517; **23** 437; **28** 515
pupils **31** 182, 811
works **13** 880; **14** 784; **20** 234; **22** 346; **23** 11; **28** *515*, 520; **29** 281; **31** *809*, *810*, 883
Valdés Leal, Juan de (*b* 1684) **31** 808
Valdés Phillips, Héctor **6** 594
Valdez, Pedro Fernández de *see* FERNÁNDEZ DE VALDEZ, PEDRO

Váldez, Wifredo Díaz see DÍAZ VÁLDEZ, WIFREDO
Valdice Monastery 8 398
Valdina, Laura, Baroness 5 526
Valdivia, Pedro de 6 589, 591; 27 791
Valdivia culture 6 590, 591; 27 609; 29 219; 31 811–12*
figurines 21 241; 31 811–12
iconography 29 134
pottery 29 127, 136, 150; 31 811
sculpture 29 169
shell midden 29 138
stone-carvings 29 155
stools 29 134
textiles 29 152
Universidad Austral 6 602
Valdivieso, Diego de 29 334
Valdivieso, Paulina 6 600
Valdivieso, Raúl 31 812*
Valdor, Jean 19 21
Valdovinos, Mabel 24 99
Valdre, Kalju 30 349
Valdré, Vincenzo 10 199; 13 637
Valdštejn Monstrance 25 443
Vale, Amaro do 25 297; 31 813*; 32 427
Vale, António da Cunha Correia 2 285; 31 813*
Vale, Bruno do 25 814
Vale, H. H. 19 505
Vale, José da Cunha Correia 31 812–13*
Vale, Manuel da Cunha Correia 2 285; 31 813
Valença do Minho 25 304
Valençay Château 11 512
Valence 7 535
Cathedral of St Apollinaire 3 192
Valence, Aymer de, Earl of Pembroke 3 209
Valence Casket 14 419
Valenchine, Jean van see JEAN DE VALENCIENNES
Valencia (Spain) 16 103; 26 904; 29 259; 31 813–16*
Academia de S Bárbara see Real Academia de Bellas Artes de S Carlos
academy 1 105; 29 293
art forms and materials
astrolabes 16 369
brick 4 784
ceramics 30 397, 406
embroidery 29 349, 350
forgeries 16 545
furniture 29 319
leather 19 3
manuscripts 16 291
metalwork 29 332
painting 13 150; 29 276, 280, 282
pottery 6 IV2; 7 XI2; 16 411, 415, 418; 22 256; 29 322, 323, 324, 325, 325
sculpture 13 106
silk 29 348, 348
stage design 30 664
stage machinery 30 664
textiles 16 436
tiles 30 883
Ayuntamiento see museums → Museo Paleontológico Municipal
botanic garden 12 124
Cathedral 13 68; 29 267, 270; 31 814
Capilla de los Covarrubias 23 571
metalwork 29 332
paintings 20 383, 384; 29 277
Puerta de los Apóstoles 13 106
rood screen 13 107
Colegio del Corpus Christi see museums → Museo del Patriarca
Colegio S Pio see museums → Museo de Bellas Artes
Valencia (Spain)—cont.
Corpus Christi College 26 250; 29 268
education (art) 29 357
Instituto Ephialte 29 358
Jardines de la Glorieta, Triton Fountain 29 292
Lonja de la Seda 7 679; 29 263; 31 238, 815
Miguelete 31 814
museums
Casa-Museo Benlliure 31 816
IVAM Centro Julio González 31 816
Museo de Bellas Artes 17 681; 29 357; 31 814, 816
Museo Catedralicio-Diocesano 31 816
Museo Histórico de la Ciudad 31 816
Museo International de Electrografía 10 135
Museo Nacional de Cerámica y de las Artes Suntuarias Gonzáles Marti 29 357, 841, 841; 31 814, 816
Museo Paleontológico Municipal 31 814
Museo del Patriarca 26 300; 31 815, 816
Science Museum 5 414
Olivera Theatre 30 663
painting 29 280
palace of Jerónimo de Vich 29 265
Palacio de la Audiencia see Palacio de la Generalitat
Palacio de la Generalitat 29 326
Palacio del Marqués de Dos Aguas see museums → Museo Nacional de Cerámica y de las Artes
Puente de la Trinidad 29 292
Puente Nuevo see Puente de la Trinidad
Real Academia de Bellas Artes de S Carlos 29 282, 294, 357
S Catalina 29 270
Silk Exchange see Lonja de la Seda
S Martín 29 267
S Miguel de los Reyes 8 79
University 31 674
urban planning 31 815
Valencia (Venezuela) 32 165
academy 32 174*
market 32 169
Valencia, Felipe Gómez de see GÓMEZ DE VALENCIA, FELIPE
Valencia, Jehan de (fl 1332-8) see JEHAN DE VALENCIA
Valencia, Juan de (c. 1530-91) 7 362; 10 535; 29 267
Valencia, Juan de (fl 1714) 3 89
València d'Aneu 26 642
Valencia de Don Juan, Conde de 3 739
Valencia Roman de la Rose, Master of the 7 235
Valenciennes 11 504; 31 816*
art school 11 665
Ecole de Dessin 11 671
Musée des Beaux-Arts 8 123; 11 665
Notre-Dame-la-Grande 13 38
reliquaries 11 616
sculpture 13 113; 26 500
stage design 30 653, 653
tapestries 11 639, 642
textiles 25 315
Valenciennes, Jean de see JEAN DE VALENCIENNES
Valenciennes, Philippe de 18 714
Valenciennes, Pierre-Henri (de) 11 540, 543; 18 713; 31 816–18*
groups and movements 26 741
pupils 3 854; 6 519; 8 771; 21 424
works 11 412; 22 686; 31 817
writings 6 570; 24 495; 31 300
Valenciennes Apocalypse see under APOCALYPSES → individual manuscripts
Valenciennes lace see under LACE → types
Valenge-Chopi 1 415
Valens, Emperor of Rome (East; reg 364-78) 9 560
Valens, E. G. 1 23
Valensi, André 11 552
Valensi, Henri 25 747
Valentano 16 732
Valente, Francesco del see FRANCESCO DEL VALENTE
Valente, Pietro 22 474, 481; 31 818*
Valenti (family) 29 376
Valenti, Carlos 13 765
Valenti, Giuseppe 20 214
Valenti, Italo 7 894
Valentí, Rafael Masó i see MASÓ I VALENTÍ, RAFAEL
Valenti Gonzaga (family) 2 27
Valenti Gonzaga, Arrivabene, Count 12 914
Valenti Gonzaga, Luigi 12 914
Valenti Gonzaga, Silvio, Cardinal 5 354; 12 904, 914*
paintings 26 774, 775; 29 888
Valentijn 30 588
Valentim, Mestre see FONSECA E SILVA, VALENTIM DA
Valentim, Fernando 8 6
Valentim, Rubem 1 425; 4 709, 719
Valentin, Le (1596-1632) see BOULOGNE, VALENTIN DE
Valentin (fl 1677) 28 696
Valentin, Curt 3 481; 31 818–19*
Valentin, Friedrich 26 22
Valentine, DeWain 19 702
Valentine, George D. 23 58
Valentine, James 24 664
valentine cards see under CARDS → types
Valentiner, Wilhelm R(einhold) 14 635; 30 731; 31 819*
Valentine typewriter see under TYPEWRITERS → models
Valentini, Antonio Kuntz y see KUNTZ Y VALENTINI, ANTONIO
Valentini, Francesco 18 900
Valentini, Giuseppe 25 451
Valentini, Pedro Kuntz y see KUNTZ Y VALENTINI, PEDRO
Valentinian I, Emperor of Rome (West; reg 364-75) 21 561
Valentinian II, Emperor of Rome (West; reg 375–92) 9 655; 26 752
Valentinis, Sebastiano de 31 819*
Valentino 5 705
Valentino, Cesare Borgia, Duca di see BORGIA, CESARE, Duca di Valentino
Valentino, Pace di see PACE DI VALENTINO
Valentinois, Charlotte d'Albret, Duchesse de 2 703; 11 639
Valentinois, Diane de Poitiers, Duchesse de see DIANE DE POITIERS, Duchesse de Valentinois
Valentino of Arras 32 205
Valentinus, Basilius 28 714
Valentis, Thoukididis 13 349, 350; 31 819*
Valentius 10 732
Valenza, Francesco Rosso da see ROSSO DA VALENZA, FRANCESCO
Valenzano, Ognissanti 16 626
Valenzuela, Alberto 6 597
works 6 597
Valenzuela, Lautaro 6 600
Vale of Leven 28 266
Vale Press 4 366; 24 885; 26 360
Valera, Lorenzo Coullaut 1 591
Valera, Víctor 32 568
Valeránica 29 275
Valeri, Antonio 5 614; 31 893
Valéri, Salvator 13 856
Valerian, Emperor of Rome (reg 253-60) 15 918; 27 41
Valeriani, Domenico 11 741; 15 139; 22 308
Valeriani, Giuseppe (1708-61) 11 741; 13 626; 15 139; 19 732; 20 147; 22 308
Valeriano, Domenico 24 842
Valeriano, Giuseppe (1542-96) 17 511; 26 770; 31 819–20*
collaboration 25 729
patrons and collectors 17 511
pupils 24 842
works 1 792; 10 800; 26 823
Valeriano, Piero 1 656; 15 83, 87; 26 415; 32 10
Valeriano Dellala di Beinasco, Francesco see DELLALA DI BEINASCO, FRANCESCO VALERIANO
Valerianus Gospels see under GOSPEL BOOKS → individual manuscripts
Valerio, James 19 703
Valério, Théodore 22 17
Valerium, Adrianum 32 232
Valerius Cato, Publius see CATO
Valerius Maximus 7 904; 15 82, 84; 24 788
Valero, Cristóbal 16 49
Valero, István 15 11
Valero, Oscar Bulnes see BULNES VALERO, OSCAR
Valero, Tamás 15 11
Valéry, Paul 18 783; 20 387; 24 801; 29 899; 31 820–21*
Valësh, Good Friday Church 1 540
Valesi, Dionigi 8 267; 31 821*
Valesio, Francesco 29 724
Valesio, Giovanni Luigi 7 857; 25 717
Valeška, Adolfas 19 499
Valetta, Giuseppe 13 541
Valetta collection 14 435
Valette, Adolphe 19 734; 20 240
Valette, Vésian 5 895
Valetz, Jacques 20 138
Valguarnera, Fabrizio 4 538, 540; 5 768; 25 388
Valiani, Bartolomeo 27 204
Valie, Dora 5 164
Valignano, Alessandro 17 182; 18 613
Valī Jān see VELI CAN
Välikangas, Martti 14 371; 31 821*
Valikhanov, Chakan 17 867
Valiūškis, Gediminas 6 134
Valjala 10 536
church 10 536, 538
Valjus, Seppo 26 261
Valk, Gerard see VALCK, GERARD
Valk, Maurits van der 22 850
Valk, Willem 1 647
Valke, Johannes von see JOHANNES VON VALKENBURG
Valkeapää, Guttorm 27 472
Valkeapää, Nils-Aslak 27 472
Valkenauer, Hans 27 664; 31 821*
Valkenburg 27 105
Valkenburg, Dirk 22 383; 30 15; 33 27
Valkenburg, Johannes von see JOHANNES VON VALKENBURG
Valkert, Werner van den 33 358
Valkot, V. F. see WALCOT, WILLIAM
Valla, Lorenzo 13 33; 14 867
Valladares 14 714
Valladares, Clarival do Prado see PRADO VALLADARES, CLARIVAL DO
Valladares, Obed 14 716
Valladolid 16 103; 29 258; 31 822–4*
academy 29 293
Valladolid—cont.
architecture 29 269
Ayuntamiento 29 272
Capitania General see Palacio Real
catafalques 6 71
Colegio Apostólico de Arcas Reales 9 113
Colegio de S Gregorio 9 112; 13 69; 14 420, 578, 579, 579
sculpture 10 743; 13 108
Colegio Mayor de Santa Cruz 14 578; 21 126, 126; 29 264
College of S Gregorio see Museo Nacional de Escultura Religiosa
ecclesiastical buildings
Augustinian convent 29 271
Benedictine Monastery 29 289
Cathedral 10 535; 14 475, 475; 29 268, 270
Church of Las Angustias 29 268
Church of the Passion 29 270
Convent of Las Huelgas Reales 29 268
tomb of María de Molina 13 106
Convent of S Ana 26 642
Convent of S Isabel 17 693
Monastery of S Benito el Real 26 250; 29 268
Monastery of S Francisco choir-stalls 28 689, 689–90; 29 293
S Ana 29 271
S Gregorio 10 476
S Lorenzo 29 336
S María la Antígua 13 68
S María Magdalena 29 265
S Miguel 26 251
S Nicolás de Bari 4 784
S Pablo 10 743, 903; 13 108; 14 578
Vera Cruz church 29 268
education (art) 29 357
gold 31 823–4*
guns 2 458
marks 31 824
metalwork 13 165; 29 333, 335, 335, 336
Museo Nacional de Escultura Religiosa 29 357; 31 823
palace of Fabio Nelli 29 268
Palacio de los Benavente 3 700
Palacio Real 19 3; 32 116
Peñafiel 19 896
Plaza Mayor 31 718
Santiesteban Theatre 30 663
sculpture 13 104; 26 642; 29 291, 295
silver 29 334; 31 823–4
University 29 291; 31 674
urban planning 31 822
Valladolid, Juan de see JUAN DE VALLADOLID
Vallam Cave Temple 15 507
Vallaresso, Zaccaria 33 697
Vallari, Nicholas (de) 30 78, 117; 31 824*
Vallastre, Jean 29 758
Vallaury, Antoine 16 591; 31 452
Vallayer-Coster, Anne 11 228; 29 668; 31 824*; 33 308
Vallbona 29 330
Vallby 30 77
Valle, Amaro do see VALE, AMARO DO
Valle, Andrea da (d ?1577) 31 824–5*
attributions 22 131
teachers 22 131
works 16 770; 22 131
Valle, Andrea della, Cardinal (1463-1534) 19 710; 31 825*; 32 413
Valle, Angel Della see DELLA VALLE, ANGEL
Valle, Aristóbulo del 2 404

Valle, della (family) 23 158; 26 768, 846
  sculpture 26 *768*
Valle, Filippo della 31 826*
  attributions 6 121
  collaboration 3 920
  patrons and collectors 3 707, 708; 4 635; 7 897; 25 301
  pupils 3 899; 6 67; 20 370
  teachers 27 347
  works 16 699; 27 831
Valle, Francisco Perez *see* PEREZ VALLE, FRANCISCO
Valle, Gabriel García del 32 558
Valle, Gino 16 650, 651; 31 826–7*
Valle, Giovanni 17 442
  works 23 *753*
Valle, José de Freitas *see* FREITAS VALLE, JOSÉ DE
Valle, Julio Rosado del *see* ROSADO DEL VALLE, JULIO
Valle, Lázaro Díaz del *see* DÍAZ DEL VALLE, LÁZARO
Valle, Lella *see* VIGNELLI, LELLA
Valle, Louis de (*fl* 16th cent.) 4 161
Valle, Lucio del (1815-74) 4 567
Valle, Marco 7 553
Valle, Matteo da 31 825
Valle, Nani 31 826
Valle, Pedro del (*fl* 1550s) 2 864
Valle, Pietro della (1586-1652) 10 78; 30 479, 480; 31 827*
  inscriptions 1 895
  personal collection 21 310
  works 12 82
Valle, Provino 31 826
Valle, R. 31 823
Vallecas, Primera Escuela de *see* PRIMERA ESCUELA DE VALLECAS
Valle Crucis Abbey 32 781
Valle de los Caídos 10 822
Valle de Oaxaca, Martín Cortés, 2nd Marqués del 10 498
Vallée, Jean De la, *see* DE LA VALLÉE, JEAN
Vallée, Simon De la *see* DE LA VALLÉE, SIMON
Vallejo, Dominguez 29 306
Vallejo, Elias 13 275
Vallejo, Francisco Antonio 21 384; 33 585
Vallejo, Juan de 5 203; 29 265
Vallejo Vivanco, José 26 250
Vallejo ware *see under* POTTERY → wares
Vallejo y Galeazo, José 31 827*
Vallemput, Remigius *see* LEEMPUT, REMI VAN
Vallendar Church 27 335
Vallen de la Motte, Jean-Baptiste-Michel 27 402; 31 827–8*
  collaboration 18 196; 27 402
  patrons and collectors 26 731
  pupils 29 551
  works 18 196; 24 546; 27 575
Vallenilla Echeverría, Pedro 32 178
Valle Romita Altarpiece 12 299, *299*, 302
Vallery Château 12 113
Valle *Satyrs*, della 1 533
Vallet, Edouard 30 134; 31 828*
Vallet, Guillaume 9 362; 14 53
Valletta 18 152; 20 *212*, 218; 21 580; 31 720
  Auberge de Castille 20 *218*
  Auberge de Provence *see* National Museum of Malta
  Auberge d'Italie *see* National Museum of Malta
  churches
    Conventual Church 20 215
    Greek Orthodox Church 20 213
    St John's Co-Cathedral 20 213, 218
      Chapel of the Blessed Sacrament 20 216
Valletta
  churches
    St John's Co-Cathedral—cont.
      gates 20 *217*
      Memorial to Grand Master Perellos 20 214
      Memorial to Louis Charles d'Orléans 20 214
      murals 25 564
      paintings 5 *714*
      reliquary 20 216
      sarcophagus of Grand Master L'Isle Adam 20 214
      sculpture 20 214
    St Paul Shipwrecked 20 216
    St Ursola 20 216
  De Sousa Palace *see* Museum of Fine Arts
  Fort St Elmo 20 214
  foundry 31 329
  Government School of Art 20 213
  Infirmary 20 216
  Jesuit college 20 219
  monument to Queen Victoria 20 214
  Museum of Fine Arts 20 219
  National Museum of Archaeology 20 219
  National Museum of Malta 20 219
  Palace of the Grand Master of the Order of Malta 3 387; 20 213; 22 533; 29 251
  Palazzo Xara *see* National Museum of Malta
  Public Libary, Gabinetto delle Antichità *see* National Museum of Malta
  Royal Mint 31 361
  St John's Museum 20 219
  Upper Barraca Gardens
    Les Gavroches 20 214
    memorial to Admiral Sir Henry Hotham 20 214
Valletta, Francesco 6 109
Vallette, Alfred 24 426
Valley Maidu 22 652
Valley of the Kings *see under* THEBES (i) (EGYPT)
Valley of the Queens *see under* THEBES (i) (EGYPT)
valley temples *see under* TEMPLES → types
Vallgren, Ville 11 100, 106, 108; 31 828–9*
Vallianos brothers 13 359
Vallien, Bertil 30 103
Vallière, J.-O. 25 803
Vallière, Louise de La *see* LA VALLIÈRE, LOUISE DE
Vallin, Auguste 31 829
Vallin, Eugène 2 13, 564; 22 456; 31 829*
Vallin de la Mothe, Jean-Baptiste-Michel *see* VALLEN DE LA MOTTE, JEAN-BAPTISTE-MICHEL
Vallinotto, S Maria della Visitazione 32 644, *644*, *645*
Vallipuram 16 864
Vallmanya, Josep 29 319
Vallmitjana y Barbany, Agapito 3 220; 25 816; 30 3; 31 829
Vallmitjana y Barbany, Venancio 25 816; 29 294; 30 3; 31 829*
Valløby Church 4 781
Vallø Castle 8 740
Vallois, R.
  works 8 *686*
Vallombrosa, Badia 24 523, 525, 527
Vallone, Francesco *see* DIEUSSART, FRANÇOIS
Vallotton, Félix (-Emile-Jean) 3 826; 30 125; 31 830–31*
  groups and movements 17 441; 22 421, 422; 24 592; 25 356; 27 639
Vallotton, Félix (-Emile-Jean)—cont.
  patrons and collectors 4 71; 22 538; 29 604
  pupils 2 122; 6 84; 13 681
  works 4 42; 13 323; 30 134; 31 *830*; 33 361
Vallotton, Paul 31 831
Vallou de Villeneuve, Julien 31 831*
Vallstena Church 5 191; 30 75
Valls Verges, Manuel 13 726
Valltorta, La *see* LA VALLTORTA
vallum 21 547
Vallumbrosan Order 3 709
Valmaggini, Ignazio 28 836
Valmarana (family) 23 868
Valmarana, Benedetto 22 387
Valmarana, Gian Luigi 19 629
Valmarana, Giovann Alvise (Luigi) 31 831
Valmarana, Giovanni Francesco 31 831
Valmarana, Giuseppe di Bernardino 31 831
Valmarana, Leonardo 31 831
Valmaseda, Juan de *see* BALMASEDA, JUAN DE
Valmier, Georges 31 832*
  dealers 27 162
  groups and movements 1 89; 8 240
  works 11 419
Valmiera 18 *847*, 847
  St Simon 18 848
Valmiki 15 226
Valmontone, Palazzo Doria Pamphili 15 138
  frescoes 9 376
  Stanza del Fuoco 8 100
  Stanza dell'Aria 25 563
Valmôr, Viscondessa 30 492
Valnegro, Pietro 2 781; 12 369; 13 329, 918
Valö Church 23 507; 30 77
Valogona, Pedro Juan de *see* PERE JOHAN
Valois (House of) 9 387; 11 655; 31 832–4*, *833*
Valois, Achille 27 548
Valois, Anne de, Duchess of Bourbon *see* ANNE DE VALOIS, Duchess of Bourbon
Valois, Anne de, Queen of France *see* ANNE OF BRITANNY, Queen of France
Valois, Catherine, Queen of France *see* CATHERINE DE' MEDICI, Queen of France
Valois, Charles III, Count of Anjou *see* CHARLES III, Count of Anjou
Valois, Charles V, King of France *see* CHARLES V, King of France
Valois, Charles VI, King of France *see* CHARLES VI, King of France
Valois, Charles VII, King of France *see* CHARLES VII, King of France
Valois, Charles VIII, King of France *see* CHARLES VIII, King of France
Valois, Charles IX, King of France *see* CHARLES IX, King of France
Valois, Charles de, Comte d'Angoulême *see* ANGOULÊME, CHARLES DE VALOIS, Comte d'
Valois, Charles de, Duc de Berry *see* BERRY, CHARLES DE VALOIS, Duc de
Valois, Charles de, Duke of Orléans *see* CHARLES, Duke of Orléans
Valois, Charles the Bold, 4th Duke of Burgundy *see* CHARLES THE BOLD, 4th Duke of Burgundy
Valois, Charlotte of Savoy, Queen of France *see* CHARLOTTE OF SAVOY, Queen of France
Valois, Clementia of Hungary, Queen of France *see* CLEMENTIA OF HUNGARY, Queen of France
Valois, Elizabeth de, Queen of Spain *see* ELIZABETH DE VALOIS, Queen of Spain
Valois, Francis I, King of France *see* FRANCIS I, King of France
Valois, François de, Duc d'Alençon *see* ALENÇON, FRANÇOIS DE VALOIS, Duc d'
Valois, Henry II, King of France *see* HENRY II, King of France
Valois, Henry III, King of France *see* HENRY III, King of France
Valois, Henry of France, Archbishop of Reims *see* HENRY OF FRANCE, Archbishop of Reims
Valois, Isabeau of Bavaria, Queen of France *see* ISABEAU OF BAVARIA, Queen of France
Valois, Isabel de, Queen of England *see* IABEL DE VALOIS, Queen of England
Valois, Jean de, Comte d'Angoulême *see* ANGOULÊME, JEAN DE VALOIS, Comte d'
Valois, Jean de Dunois, Bâtard d'Orléans *see* DUNOIS, JEAN, Comte de, Bâtard d'Orléans
Valois, Jean I de, Duc de Berry *see* BERRY, JEAN I DE VALOIS, Duc de
Valois, Joanna de (*fl c.* 1465) 20 646
Valois, Joanna of Burgundy, Queen of France *see* JOANNA OF BURGUNDY, Queen of France
Valois, Joanna of France, Duchess of Bourbon *see* JOANNA OF FRANCE, Duchess of Bourbon
Valois, John II, King of France *see* JOHN II, King of France
Valois, Louis de, Duc de Guyenne, le Dauphin *see* GUYENNE, LOUIS DE VALOIS, Duc de, le Dauphin
Valois, Louis I de, Duke of Anjou *see* LOUIS I, Duke of Anjou, titular King of Naples, Sicily and Jerusalem
Valois, Louis I de, Duke of Orléans *see* LOUIS I, Duke of Orléans
Valois, Louis XI, King of France *see* LOUIS XI, King of France
Valois, Margaret of Orléans, Comtesse d' Etampes *see* ETAMPES, MARGARET OF ORLÉANS, Comtesse d'
Valois, Marguerite de, Duchesse d'Alençon *see* ALENÇON, MARGUERITE DE VALOIS, Duchesse d'
Valois, Marguerite de, Duchess of Savoy *see* MARGUERITE DE VALOIS, Duchess of Savoy
Valois, Marie de, Princess 27 565
Valois, Marie Marguerite de 20 650
Valois, Nicolas Le *see* LE VALOIS, NICOLAS
Valois, Ninette de 3 119
Valois, Philip the Bold, Duke of Burgundy *see* PHILIP THE BOLD, 1st Duke of Burgundy
Valois, Philip the Good, Duke of Burgundy *see* PHILIP THE GOOD, 3rd Duke of Burgundy
Valois Tapestries 5 814; 14 297; 23 464
Valokuva 24 452
Valori, Baccio 4 408; 21 438; 28 335; 31 851*
Valori, Bartolomeo 6 140
Valori Plastici 8 772; 16 680; 21 87; 24 448; 25 6; 26 776; 31 851–2*
  contributors 5 849; 8 604
  exhibitions 25 6; 29 255
Valori Primordiali group 25 838; 26 289
Valory, Louis-Guy-Henri, Marquis de 31 852*
Valparaíso 6 589, *590*, 591; 31 852–3*
  architecture 6 594
  Exposiciones Municipales 12 917
  Museo Municipal de Bellas Artes 31 853
  Palacio la Rioja 6 601
  trade 6 591
  Universidad Católica 6 601
Valparaiso, Marqués de San Mateo de *see* SAN MATEO DE VALPARAISO, Marqués de
Valperga, Antonio Maurizio 13 748; 20 212; 28 5, 7
Valperga Canavese 27 498
Valpuesta, Pedro de 31 853*
Valpy, Leonard Rowe 23 885
Vals, Hagia Paraskevi 25 336
Valsaín Chapel 13 922
Val-Saint-Lambert company 3 594, 595
Valsamakis, Nikos 13 350; 31 853*
Valsamonero Monastery, Hagios Phanourios 8 156
Valsanzibio, Villa Barbarigo 12 115, 117
Valsequillo Dam 21 192
Valsgärde 14 412
Valştein, Carol 1 750; 26 724, 725
Valtan, Pierre Louis de 25 405
Valtat, Louis 10 839; 11 644; 31 853–4*
Valtellina 16 726
Valters, Jānis Teodors 12 825; 17 743; 18 852; 31 854*
Valtesse de la Bigne, Mme 11 600
Valthjófsstaðir 15 69
Valtice-Lednice 8 379
  Schloss Feldsberg 19 338
Vältin, Gilg 22 918
Valton, Charles 2 642
Valtonen, Osmo 11 101
Valturio, Roberto 21 578; 26 400
Valuraka *see* KARLE
Valvasor, Johann Weikhard 28 860
Valvassori, Gabriele 7 782; 9 175; 23 898; 31 854–5*
Valverde, Bom Jesus 25 291
Valverde, Juan de 3 471; 27 606
Vambéry, A.
  works 10 *545*
vambraces 2 469; 6 262
Vamlingo Church 30 75
Van 2 426; 31 698, 699
  architecture 2 425
  citadel 31 699
  shrine of Sarduri II 31 699, 700
  silver 2 442
  wall paintings 1 839
Van ('t Hoff), Robert *see* HOFF, ROBERT VAN 'T
Vanacken, Joseph *see* AKEN, JOSEPH VAN
Vanadzor 2 428
Vanags, Aleksanders 24 333
Vanaise, Gustave 32 591
Van Alen, William 31 855*
  groups and movements 2 522
  teachers 18 664
  works 16 56; 23 43, 359; 28 833, *833*; 31 596
Van Anderlecht, Englebert 3 565
Van Ao Citadel 6 426
Vanås Castle 30 118
Van Asperen, Jan 31 856
Van Assche, Auguste 3 548, 549, 885; 31 855–6*
Van Averbeke, Emiel 3 550, 551; 31 856*
Van Beerleire, Charles 3 579, 587

Van Bever, Louis 33 598
Vanboucle, Pieter *see* BOUCLE, PIERRE
Van Brée, Andreas 31 856
Van Brée, Mathieu Ignace 31 856–7*
pupils 8 591, 632; 12 12; 19 291; 25 550; 28 77; 32 852; 33 170
teachers 26 83
works 3 562; 14 586
Van Brée, Philippe Jacques 31 856, 857*
Van Breedam, Camiel 3 573
Van Briggle, Artus 31 639
Van Briggle Pottery 2 572; 31 639
Vanbrugh, John 2 314; 4 422; 5 65; 18 *146*; 31 857–62*
architecture
country houses 8 47; 23 857; 33 257
Blenheim Palace (Oxon) 4 *138*; 10 276; 12 128; 25 266; 29 524; 31 234, *859*
Castle Howard (N. Yorks) 6 65, *65*; 8 47; 10 232; 23 812; 31 *858*
Kimbolton Castle (Cambs) 13 200
Kings Weston House 31 235
Seaton Delaval (Northumb.) 31 *861*
Vanbrugh Castle 6 60; 31 *860*
garden buildings 3 689, *689*; 6 66; 7 374; 11 242; 12 128; 14 807; 23 189; 24 290; 25 766; 30 451
mausolea 20 866
military 2 502
orangeries 12 791; 23 *471*
theatres 30 673
assistants 10 278; 14 254
collaboration 4 805; 23 470; 29 835
groups and movements 3 266; 10 96; 23 210
patrons and collectors 4 137, 138; 7 286; 14 127, 485, 807, 808; 21 908; 29 735; 30 451
pupils 23 860
Van Brunt, Henry 31 862–3*; 32 859
assistants 25 152
collaboration 10 683; 15 23; 31 593
Van Brunt & Howe 5 274; 31 863
Van Buren Magonigle, Harold *see* MAGONIGLE, HAROLD VAN BUREN
Van Camp, Camille 4 529; 28 921
Van Cao 32 483
Vancaš, Josip 4 460; 8 176
Vance, Robert 32 909
Vancouver 5 *559*, 561; 31 863–4*
Art Gallery 5 591; 31 863, 864
Dominion Building 5 562
False Creek housing project 5 563
Law Courts 18 890
Marine Building 5 562; 19 869
Public Library 5 592
Sun Tower 5 562
University of British Columbia library 5 592
Museum of Anthropology 5 563; 10 458, *459*; 22 367; 29 241; 31 864
Sedgewick Library 19 321
Vancouver Art, Historical and Scientific Association *see* Vancouver Museums and Planetarium
Vancouver Museums and Planetarium 5 591
Vocational Institute 5 562
Vancouver, George 31 863
Vancouver Island Arts and Crafts Society 32 414
Van Cutsem, Henri 6 487; 23 399
Vandalino, el *see* RUIZ, JUAN
vandalism 13 270
Vandals 21 500, 501
Van Damme, E. 3 619
Van de Cappelle, Jean-Baptiste 31 864*
Van de Casteelen, D. 3 619
Van de Casteyne, O. 3 620
Vandelli, Domenico Agostino 23 454; 25 310, 311; 31 864–5*
Vandelvira, Alonso de 29 268, 637; 31 866
Vandelvira, Andrés de 31 865–6*
attributions 3 45
collaboration 16 898; 29 266
patrons and collectors 7 488
teachers 29 637
works 3 45; 16 863, *863*, 864; 29 266, *266*; 31 *509*, 510, *865*
writings 31 171, 297
Van den Abeele, Albijn 18 626
Van den Berghe, Frits 3 614; 31 866–7*
groups and movements 10 696; 18 626
works 11 450
Vanden Berghe, Louis 19 812
Van den Boogaart, Bram *see* BOGART, BRAM
Vanden Bossche, E. 3 585
Vandenbranden, Guy 5 45
Van den Branden, J. F. 3 619
Vandenbreeden, J. 3 620
Vandenbroeck, P. 3 619
Van den Broek & Bakema 4 814; 28 623; 31 867–8*
works 31 *868*
Van den Driessche, Jan 10 707
Van den Eynde *see* EYNDE, JAN VAN DEN
Vandenhove, Charles 3 551; 18 465; 31 868–9*
Van den Torren, A. 3 602
Vandenyver, J. B. 19 115
Vanderbank, John, the elder (*d* 1717) 10 351; 31 869
Vanderbank, John, the younger (1694-1739) 10 372; 14 637; 19 584; 30 324; 31 869–71*
methods 9 211
patrons and collectors 14 842
pupils 8 501; 14 641; 18 142; 25 210
reproductive prints by others 18 570; 31 871
works 6 65; 10 275; 31 *869*
Vanderbank, Moses 31 870
Vanderbeek, Stanley 4 110; 32 420
Vanderbilt (family) 23 32; 24 183
Vanderbilt, Alva 15 22
Vanderbilt, Cornelius, I (1794-1877) 18 627; 27 137
Vanderbilt, Cornelius, II (1843-99) 4 318; 7 515; 11 143; 15 22; 18 161; 27 557; 31 622
Vanderbilt, George Washington 6 513; 15 22; 23 423
Vanderbilt, Gertrude *see* WHITNEY, GERTRUDE VANDERBILT
Vanderbilt, J. W. 20 60
Vanderbilt, William Henry 18 627; 31 870*
architecture 4 130; 14 482
collections 19 756
groups and movements 1 171
paintings 2 858; 21 69
Vanderbilt, William Kissam 15 22; 21 371; 31 593
Vander Borght *see* BORGHT, VAN DER
Vanderbruggen, Jean 18 626
Vandercam, Serge 5 45
Vandercruse, François 31 870
Vandercruse, Roger 4 524; 11 591, 593; 17 666; 26 375; 31 870*
Van der Donckt (family) 4 530
Van der Grijn, Eric 16 18
Vandergucht, Benjamin 19 587; 31 871*
works 31 *871*
Vandergucht, Gerard 31 870, 871*
collaboration 29 862
groups and movements 14 638
works 1 844; 31 869; 33 409
Vandergucht, John 31 870, 871*
Vandergucht, Michael 25 664; 31 870, 871*
Van der Haegen, V. 3 619
Van der Haert, Hendrik 4 754; 8 841
Vander Hagen, Willem *see* HAGEN, WILLIAM VAN DER
Vanderlyn, John 14 586; 31 872*
patrons and collectors 14 718
reproductive prints by others 9 418
teachers 26 467
works 23 46; 31 600, *872*
Vanderlyn, Pieter *see* GANSEVOORT LIMNER
Van der Mijn *see* MIJN, VAN DER
Van der Nüll, Eduard 31 872*
collaboration 2 786, 808
pupils 3 312; 11 29; 14 216; 21 757; 25 648; 28 175; 29 722; 32 760; 33 687
teachers
works 2 786, 808
Van der Nüll & Siccardsburg 31 872–3*
assistants 33 687
collaboration 32 437
works 2 787; 32 437
Van der Ouderaa, Piet Jan 31 873*
Vanderpoel, John H. 11 322
Vander Roost, Jan *see* ROST, JAN
Van der Stappen, Charles 5 44; 31 874*
groups and movements 14 137
pupils 6 487; 9 326; 27 268; 33 389
teachers 28 756
works 3 572, 573, 602, 604, *604*
Vanderstappen, Harrie 7 161
Van der Straeten, Charles 31 874*
assistants 27 309
works 3 547, 578; 5 41
Van der Swaelmen, Louis 25 190; 31 729, 874–5*
collaboration 9 759; 11 724
groups and movements 3 550
works 3 551
Van der Swaelmen, Louis-Léopold 31 874
Vandervaart, Jan *see* VAARDT, JAN VAN DER
Van Der Zee, James 1 442; 24 671; 31 875*
Vandeuvre, Gabriel de 28 746
Van de Velde, Henry 3 400, 618; 11 526; 12 378; 15 823; 19 137, 260; 20 593; 23 498; 25 190; 28 482; 31 875–7*
architecture 24 473; 33 38
department stores 12 376
garden cities 14 31
house 3 550
houses 14 30
libraries 3 551; 19 320
shops 31 *876*
theatres 7 582; 31 *877*
collaboration 9 759; 14 604; 28 111; 31 888; 32 380
embroidery 3 610
frames 11 449
furniture 3 *586*, 586, 587; 5 193; 12 428; 33 156
groups and movements
Art Nouveau 2 562, 564, 565; 4 48, 74
Arts and Crafts Movement 2 571; 5 44; 12 416
Deutscher Werkbund 8 825
Expressionism 10 697; 21 781
Neo-Impressionism 19 792; 22 746, 747
Van de Velde, Henry
groups and movements—cont.
Rationalism (ii) (style) 26 15
XX, Les 2 563; 3 563; 32 591
interior decoration 3 579
jewellery 3 602, 605
patrons and collectors 4 71; 10 364; 18 466
porcelain 8 802; 12 436; 21 66
posters 25 347
pupils 1 120
sculpture 14 138
silver 12 449
staff 11 805; 29 769
teachers 32 259
Van de Velde, Pieter 24 883
Van de Voorde, A. 31 878
Van de Voorde, Christian 13 182
Van de Voorde, Oscar (-Henri) 3 550; 31 877–8*
Van de Voort, J. 3 620
Van de Walle, A. L. J. 3 620
Van de Woestyne, Gustave 31 878*
groups and movements 2 516; 3 564; 18 626; 21 648
pupils 24 329
Van de Woestyne, Karel 18 626
Vandi, John 28 692
Vandier d'Abbadie, Jean 10 83
Vandières, Abel-François Poisson de, Marquis de Marigny *see* MARIGNY, Marquis de
Van Dissel Co. 19 12
Vandivert, Bill 5 659; 6 603; 20 99
Vandkunsten 8 729
Vandoma, Martin de 11 485
Vandoni, Giuseppe 31 878*
Van-Dúnem, Francisco D. 2 87
Van Dyck, Albert 2 197
Van Dyck, Frans 33 244
Van Dyck, Peter 31 648
Van Dyck brown *see under* PIGMENTS → types
Van Dyke, Ernest 13 877
Van Dyke, J. C. 7 551
works 26 *234*
Van Dyke, Willard 13 710
Vane, Henry, the elder (1589-1655) 10 363
Vane, Henry, 2nd Earl of Darlington (*fl c.* 1785) 10 279
Vaneau, Pierre 31 878–9*
Vanegas, Leonel 25 455
Vanegas Arroyo, Antonio 21 386; 25 321
Vaneijndhoven, Peter 3 647
Vanek 4 460
Vaněk, Jan 8 402
Vaneni, Queen of Armenia (*c.* 1192) 2 436
Van Ertborn, Florent (Joseph) *see* ERTBORN, FLORENT (JOSEPH) VAN
Van Even, E. 3 619
Van Garden 10 782
Vänge Church 26 639, 647; 30 83
Van Geel, Jan Lodewijk 12 230
Vangelder, Peter Mathias 28 242
Vangelisti, Vincenzo 19 636
Van Gierdegom, Jean-Népomucène 31 879
Van Gierdegom, Joseph 31 879
Van Gierdegom, Josephus Franciscus 3 547; 31 879*
Van Ginkel, H. D. P. 27 514
Vang Memorial Stone 26 409; 32 517, *518*, 520
Vang Sang 18 769
Vangsnes
brooches 32 *514*, 515
Vanguard 24 429, 430
Vanguli (family) 30 812
Vanguš, Matthias 16 907
Van Haelen, François 30 727
Van Hecke, Paul-Gustave 3 564; 5 44; 20 100; 31 866
van Heteren (family) 14 42
Van Hoecke, J. 31 855
Van Hoeydonck, Paul 3 565, 573; 31 879*; 33 636
Van Horne, William (Cornelius) 5 588; 22 38; 31 880*
paintings 5 67, 589
photographs 11 743
Van Houten 10 421
Van Hove, Victor 3 572
Van Huffel, Albert 3 550; 7 304; 31 880*
groups and movements 3 587
works 3 579; 5 42
Vani 12 *317*, 328, 330; 21 558
Vanier, Frans 4 153
Vanière, Jacques 12 123
Vani Gospels *see under* GOSPEL BOOKS → individual manuscripts
Vanikoro 27 778, 779
vanishing point 31 880*
see also PERSPECTIVE
vanitas *see under* PAINTING → types
Vanity Fair 5 758
VANK *see* NEDERLANDSCHE VEREENIGING VOOR AMBACHT EN NIJVERHEIDSKUNST
Vankeirsbilck, Jules 11 746
Van Kempen, Begeer & Vos 22 892
Vaňková-Kuchynková, Marie 8 421
Vankovič, Valency *see* WAŃKOWICZ, WALENTY
Van Lau 14 722; 31 883–4*
Van Leemputten, Cornelis 31 884*
Van Leemputten, Frans 31 884*
Van Leemputten, Jan-Frans 31 884
Van Lennep, Henry John 1 520
Van Lerius, Joseph 7 406; 31 873
Vanlimpitt, Remigeus *see* LEEMPUT, REMI VAN
Van Lingen 1 647
Van Lint, Louis 2 545; 3 565; 5 45; 17 518
Vanloo, Carle 11 539, 670; 18 495; 19 645–9*; 22 682; 24 135, 168; 31 444
groups and movements 23 503; 31 373
patrons and collectors 2 724; 4 513, 554, 560; 11 658; 12 312; 14 585; 21 830; 24 256; 25 81, 368; 28 18; 32 898
pupils 8 794; 9 208, 301, 416; 17 681; 18 641; 19 216, 649, 728; 23 416; 26 506; 29 584; 31 26
reproductions in porcelain 6 I3
reproductions in tapestry 12 830; 22 726
reproductive prints by others 3 463; 4 330, 331; 9 407; 11 172; 19 144, 261; 24 480; 27 645
teachers 19 645, 817; 32 670
works 8 893; 9 208; 11 406, 407, 408, 410, 577; 19 644, *647*; 31 445
Van Manen, Hans 10 483
Vanneck, Gerard 4 876; 10 643
Vanni (d'Andrea Salvani), Andrea (di) *see* ANDREA (DI) VANNI (D'ANDREA SALVANI)
Vanni, Francesco 25 867; 28 677; 31 884–5*
collaboration 19 383; 28 529
copies 31 306
patrons and collectors 1 595; 9 173; 27 878
pupils 12 12; 20 264; 31 885
reproductive prints by others 3 199; 17 599
teachers 27 620
works 28 676, 688
Vanni, Giovanni Battista 1 673; 3 631; 7 457

Vanni, Lippo (di) *see* LIPPO (DI) VANNI
Vanni, Mariano *see* TACCOLA, MARIANO (DI JACOPO)
Vanni, Orazio 3 631
Vanni, Raffaele 21 25, 27; 26 810; 31 885*
Vanni, Sam(uel) 11 97; 31 885–6*
 works 11 *97*
Vanni, Stefano d'Antonio 4 30, 31, 32
Vanni, Turino di *see* TURINO DI VANNI
Vannicola, Gaetano 10 641
Vannier, Luigi 28 14
Vannini, Ottavio 31 886*
 collaboration 12 706; 21 26
 patrons and collectors 21 25; 27 205
 works 24 860
 writings 24 25
Vannocci, Oreste 4 83
Vannone, Andrea 3 770
Van Norman, C. B. K., and Associates 31 864
Vannucci, Jacopo, Bishop of Perugia 28 701
Vannucci, Pietro di Cristoforo *see* PERUGINO
Vannuccio, Francesco di *see* FRANCESCO DI VANNUCCIO
Van Osdel, John Mills 6 572; 28 831; 31 887*
Van Overloop, Eugène 3 619
Van Overstraeten, Henri Désiré Louis 3 547, 548; 26 526; 31 887*
Van Phuc
 silk 32 489, *489*
Van Phuc Temple *see under* PHAT TICH
Vanpook, Charles (-François) *see* POUCKE, KAREL VAN
Van Praet, Jules 3 615
Van Rasbourgh, Antoine 26 509
Van Rensselaer, Mariana Griswold 31 887–8*; 33 309
Van Robays, C. 3 578, 585, 884
Van Ryssel, Paul *see* GACHET, PAUL(-FERDINAND)
Van Rysselberghe, Octave 3 550, 579; 23 340; 31 888*
Van Rysselberghe, Théo(phile) 3 614; 31 888–9*
 groups and movements 5 44; 10 517; 19 321; 22 746; 24 592; 25 358; 26 96; 32 591
 pupils 19 792
 studio 31 888
 works 3 563, *614*; 11 449; 14 770; 20 862
Van Sant, Tom 28 829
Vansanzio, Giovanni *see* VASANZIO, GIOVANNI
Van Schoutte, R. 3 619
Van silk *see under* SILK → types
Vansina, Jan 1 232
Vanson, Adrian 7 613; 31 889*
 patrons and collectors 28 234, 268
 works 31 *889*
Van Stapele, François 14 42
Van Stapele, Martinus 14 42
Van Stapele, Reynier 14 42
Van Straten, Henri 2 197; 20 547
Van Strydonck, Guillaume 5 37; 32 591
Vantaa 14 372
 Heureka (Finnish Science Centre) 11 93
Vantini, Rodolfo 4 748
Vantongerloo, Georges 14 437; 31 889–90*
 groups and movements 1 76, 89, 90; 2 525; 6 342; 29 660
 patrons and collectors 2 409
 works 3 573, *574*; 29 *660*
Van Tuyn, J. 3 585
Van Tyghem, F. 3 620
Vanua Lava 31 890
Vanua Levu 11 67
Vanuatu 23 *711*; 25 181; 31 890–93*
 architecture 31 891–2*
 arrows 31 893
 body arts 31 892*
 body ornaments 31 892
 canoes 23 725; 31 893*
 headdresses 31 *891*
 mats 31 892
 musical instruments 31 892–3*
 pottery 23 728; 31 892
 sculpture 23 732
 shells 31 892
 skulls 31 *891*
 slit-drums 31 *892*, 892–3
 weapons 31 893*
 wood-carvings 31 892
 see also POLYNESIAN OUTLIERS
Van Uytvanck, Benoît 3 885
Van Velde, Bram 32 136*
Van Velde, Geer 32 136
Vanvitelli, Carlo 1 574; 11 136; 12 119; 16 646; 24 757; 31 895
Vanvitelli, Gaspare *see* WITTEL, GASPAR VAN
Vanvitelli, Luigi 12 587; 22 479; 31 893–6*; 33 270
 architecture
  bell-towers 19 *685*, 687
  cathedrals 13 199; 21 159, 532
  chapels 12 762
  churches 9 338; 16 644, 645; 21 456; 22 473; 28 676; 29 888
  garden buildings 29 832
  hospitals 31 *894*
  libraries 19 315
  monasteries 24 520; 25 410
  palazzi 5 914, *914*; 19 688; 22 473; 29 525; 31 *895*
  ports 2 1
  restorations 25 144
  squares (town) 22 473
  villas 22 473
 assistants 5 650; 24 757; 27 480
 collaboration 11 136; 12 657; 16 646; 24 885; 25 292; 27 647
 competitions 7 672; 12 657
 gardens 11 345
 interior decoration 22 481
 parks 12 119
 patrons and collectors 3 707; 4 562, 635; 7 897; 11 741; 16 645; 19 777; 22 473
 pupils 8 840; 24 757; 26 403
 reproductions in mosaic 20 70; 26 810
Van Ysendyck 33 567
Van Ysendyck, Antoine 31 896
Van Ysendyck, Jules-Jacques 31 896*
 collaboration 6 482
 teachers 7 480
 works 3 620
 writings 3 549, 579
Van Ysendyck, Maurice 31 896
Van Zeller (family) 23 793
Vapaat 28 105
Vapheio
 cups 21 688
 daggers 14 355
 gold 14 355
 tomb 29 367; 30 738
Vapheio cups *see under* CUPS → types
vāpi see STEPWELLS
Vaprio (family) 28 531
Vaprio, Giovanni Zenone da *see* GIOVANNI ZENONE DA VAPRIO
Vaptsarov, N., Factory 5 158
Vaquelte de Gribeauval, Jean-Baptiste *see* GRIBEAUVAL, JEAN-BAPTISTE VAQUELTE DE
Vaquet, Jean 20 800
Vaquez, Henri 32 740
Varagine, Jacopo da *see* JACOPO DA VORAGINE
Varahadeva 1 500; 15 739; 31 798
Varahamihira 15 209
Varaize Church 26 600
Varakhsha 1 *849*, 882; 6 *182*; 28 *719*; 31 *781*, 896–7*
 helmet 16 505
 palace 6 200; 31 897; 32 321
  friezes 6 *231*
  wall paintings 6 231, 248
 sculpture 6 220
 stucco 29 821
Varalli, Fabrizio Spada, Cardinal *see* SPADA VARALLI, FABRIZIO, Cardinal
Varallo 16 *618*
 Sacro Monte 1 608–9; 15 137; 16 702; 27 497–8, 499, 500; 31 897*, *898*, 898–901*; 33 88
  architecture 31 897–8*
  frescoes 27 *497*
  paintings 30 303, *303*
  Pilate's Palace 31 *900*
Varallo, Niccolò da *see* NICCOLÒ DA VARALLO
Varallo, Tanzio da *see* TANZIO DA VARALLO
Varama 11 878
Varamin 15 *897*; 16 *105*; 31 901–2*
 congregational mosque 16 193; 22 194; 23 562; 24 877
 Friday Mosque 22 *194*
 Imamzada Yahya 1 98, *98*
Varanasi 15 202, *261*, 262, *360*, 409, 414; 16 *105*; 31 902–4*
 American Institute of Indian Studies 15 184
 Bharat Kala Bhavan 15 181, 183; 22 795
 brocades 15 663, *664*
 Durga Kund Temple 31 903
 enamel 15 711
 furniture 15 693
 Great Mosque 31 904
 ikat 15 672
 Karna Meru Temple 15 263
 Laakshmi Narayana Temple 31 *904*
 Manikarnika Ghat 31 *903*
 maps 15 704
 metalwork 15 714
 paintings 15 653–4*
 pillar 15 457
 sculpture 15 454, 455
 stepwells 29 526
 Svami Narayana Mandir 15 406
 textiles 15 664, 665
varaṇḍikā 15 245*
Varano 31 904–5
Varano, Giovanni Maria da 31 905
Varano, Giulio Cesare da 31 904–5
Varas, Alberto 2 397
Văratec Monastery 25 340
Varatojo, Convent of S António 25 304
Varaždin 8 178
Varbanov, Marin 5 161; 31 905*
Varberg 8 725
Varberg Group 3 776; 18 449; 23 206
Vårby 32 517
Varca Church 12 827
Varchi, Benedetto 11 187; 24 91; 25 224; 31 905–6*
 works 11 217, 315; 24 90; 31 302, 768
  on beauty 1 178
Vardanyan, Bart'ugh 2 432
Vardanyan, Varuzhan 2 433
Vardea-Mavromichaeli, Chryssa *see* CHRYSSA
Varde de Bueil, Jacqueline, Comtesse de Moret *see* MORET, JAQUELINE VARDE DE BUEIL, Comtesse de
Vardenega, Gregorio 18 63
Vardi, Aleksander 10 540
Vardier, Jacques 10 84
Vardy, John 31 906*
 collaboration 11 428
 groups and movements 23 858
 works 19 612; 23 859; 33 158
 writings 10 294; 17 902
Vardy, Thomas 11 428; 31 906; 33 98, 99
Vardzia 12 *317*; 31 906–7*
 Ananuri 12 322; 31 906
 Peschernyy Monastery 12 319; 31 906–7
  church 31 *907*
  frescoes 12 323
  icons 12 330
Varea, Miguel 9 714
Varela, Antonio 25 321
Varela, Francisco 31 518, 907*
Varela, Manuel Fernández *see* FERNÁNDEZ VARELA, MANUEL
Varengeville 9 202; 29 508
Varenholz Schloss 33 88
Varennes, Robert de *see* ROBERT DE VARENNES
Varese 27 498, 499, 500
 Hotel Tre Croci 16 648
 Panza di Biumo Collection 16 775
 Sacro Monte 23 320
  Chapel of the Crucifixion 16 701
 Villa Ponti 3 857
Varèse, Edgar 8 435; 11 360
Varga, Imre 14 896
Varga, László 19 31
Vargas 24 518
Vargas, Alberto 1 494
Vargas, Andrés 31 907*
Vargas, Carlos 19 84
Vargas, Cristóbal de 24 502
Vargas, Diego de 12 920
Vargas, Edgar 8 17
Vargas, Enrique Repullés y *see* REPULLÉS Y VARGAS, ENRIQUE
Vargas, Francisco 31 262
Vargas, José María 9 711
Vargas, Juan de (*fl c.* 1505) 31 907
Vargas, Juan de (*fl* mid-16th cent.) 7 607, 611
Vargas, Juan de, Museo Costumbrista *see under* LA PAZ → museums
Vargas, Luis (1887-1976) 6 597
Vargas, Luis de (1505-67) 31 907*; 32 156
 pupils 32 99
 works 29 278
Vargas, Luis Ortiz de (*fl* 1629-47) *see* ORTIZ DE VARGAS, LUIS
Vargas, Max T. 6 413
Vargas, Miguel Díaz *see* DÍAZ VARGAS, MIGUEL
Vargas, Pedro (*fl* 20th cent.) 23 85
Vargas, Pedro de (*b* 1533) 4 102; 24 506
Vargas Carvajal, Gutierre de, Bishop of Plasencia *see* CARVAJAL, GUTIERRE DE VARGAS, Bishop of Plasencia
Vargas Machuca, Manuel de 29 337; 31 90
Vargas Machuca, Manuel Timoteo de 29 337
Vargas Rosas, Luis 22 114
vargueños see DESKS → types → writing-desks
Vari 13 536
Vari, Metello 21 436, 440
variable contrast *see* PHOTOGRAPHY → materials → emulsions; PAPER → uses → photography
Variétés 5 44; 31 866
Varignana, Domenico da *see* AIMO, DOMENICO
Varin, Jean *see* WARIN, JEAN
Varin, Joseph 8 131
 works 30 *670*
Varin, Quentin 24 134; 25 385; 31 908*
Varion, Jean-Pierre 16 738, 739; 23 262
Varisco, Grazia 13 729
Varka 6 206
Varkhuman 6 230
Varlaam, Saint 21 344
Varley, Albert Fleetwood 31 908
Varley, Charles Smith 31 908
Varley, Cornelius 31 908, 909–10*
 groups and movements 32 903
 methods 28 203
 patrons and collectors 21 901
Varley, Cromwell Fleetwood 31 908
Varley, Edgar John 31 908
Varley, Elizabeth 22 276; 31 908
Varley, Fred(erick Horesman) 5 573; 19 878; 31 864, 910*
 groups and movements 5 566, 567; 13 711; 16 818
 patrons and collectors 1 496
 pupils 4 63
Varley, John (1778-1842) 9 766; 31 908–9*
 groups and movements 32 903
 patrons and collectors 18 906; 21 901
 pupils 8 83; 9 55; 11 60; 15 24; 19 426; 22 277; 27 778; 31 477
 works 10 374; 31 *909*
Varley, John, jr (1850-1933) 31 908
Varley, William Fleetwood 31 908
Varlin 31 910–11*; 33 737
Varma, C. Raja Ravi 31 911
Varma, (Raja) Ravi 15 208, 680; 31 911*
 patrons and collectors 15 180, 182
 works 15 657, *657*; 22 404
Varman 15 487
 Surya Temple 15 272–3, 488
Varna 4 110; 5 *144*, 145; 25 *471*; 31 911*
 baths 26 907
 Chayka housing project 5 150
 Cherno More Hotel 5 159
 gold 25 517, *517*; 30 769
 pottery 4 112
Varnanäs 30 89
Varnas, Adomas 19 498
Varnav, Scarlat 26 722
Varnedoe, Kirk 1 234
Varnhagen, Francisco Adolfo de 20 325; 25 319
Varnhem 13 50; 30 66
 Abbey Church 13 102
 sculpture 30 85
Varni, Santo 16 706, 720; 22 22
Varnie (family) 10 621
varnishes 5 33; 8 447; 18 599, 611; 32 1–4*; 33 1
 historical and regional traditions
  Belgium 3 575
  Buddhism 29 462
  Colombia 7 603, *603*
  Egypt, ancient 32 2
  Gothic 13 134
  Greece, ancient 2 217; 13 544
  Islamic 16 356, 533
  Japan 17 297, 384
  Sri Lanka 29 462
 types
  Ropsenfosse 27 140
  spirit 33 335
 uses
  aquatints 2 239, 240
  bookbindings 16 533
  book covers 16 356
  books 8 447
  conservation 32 3–4*
  drawings 32 3
  enamel 32 2
  etchings 10 549, 560, 562; 27 140; 32 3
  fixatives 32 3
  floors 32 2

varnishes
uses—cont.
furniture **7** *603*; **17** 384; **24** 258; **32** 2; **33** 335
leather **3** 575; **8** 447; **19** *1*
mordants (ii) (gilding) **12** 622
painting **2** 217; **27** 321; **32** 2–3, *4*
fresco **11** 764
oil **8** 447; **24** 569
panel **13** 544; **30** 428
secco **28** 339
paints **32** 3
papier mâché **24** 61
pasteprints **24** 245
prints **11** 173
sculpture **24** 258
wallpaper **32** 812, 813
wood **33** 335–6
see also LACQUER
Varnucci, Bartolomeo di Antonio **32** 4*
Varnucci, Chimenti **32** 4
Varnucci, Giovanni **32** 4
Varnum Church **26** 643
Varo, Remedios **21** 388; **30** 22; **32** 5*
Varofari, Alessandro **23** 754
Városlöd **15** 3
Varotari, Alessandro *see* PADOVINO
Varotari, Dario **23** 749; **32** 77
Varotti, Giuseppe **5** 444
Varrese Painter **13** 529
Varro(, Marcus Terrentius)
personal collection **2** 416
works **25** 45
on architecture **2** 344; **32** 633
on gardens **12** 64, 68, 110
on houses **26** 869
on sculpture **8** 262; **13** 467
on weathervanes **33** 8
Varro Atacinus **2** 649
Vartabedjian, Miodrag **28** 452
Vartanesov, I. **2** 894
Vartol **15** 463
Vartsakhan Church **2** 426
Vartu *see* VERTUE
Varvakeion Athena **13** 453; **24** 593; **29** 567
Varzug, Church of the Dormition **27** 373
Vasa (House of) **32** 5*
Vasa, Anne Catherine Constance, Electress Palatine *see* ANNE CATHERINE CONSTANCE, Electress Palatine
Vasa, Charles Philip, Duke of Södermanland *see* SÖDERMANLAND, CHARLES PHILIP, Duke of
Vasa, Erik XIV, King of Sweden *see* ERIK XIV, King of Sweden
Vasa, Gustav I, King of Sweden *see* GUSTAV I, King of Sweden
Vasa, Gustav II Adolf, King of Sweden *see* GUSTAV II ADOLF, King of Sweden
Vasa, Johan Kristiernsson **16** 790
Vasa, John, Duke of Östergötland *see* ÖSTERGÖTLAND, JOHN, Duke of
Vasa, John II (Casimir), King of Poland *see* JOHN II (CASIMIR), King of Poland
Vasa, John III, King of Sweden *see* JOHN III, King of Sweden
Vasa, Juhan, Duke of Finland *see* JOHN III, King of Sweden
Vasa, Karl IX, King of Sweden *see* KARL IX, King of Sweden
Vasa, Maria Eleanora, Queen of Sweden *see* MARIA ELEANORA, Queen of Sweden
Vasa, Sigismund III, King of Poland *see* SIGISMUND III, King of Poland
Vasa, Vladislav IV, King of Poland *see* VLADISLAV IV VASA, King of Poland
Vasak, Prince **2** 444
Vasan, Marquis de **21** 817
Vasantgarh, Jaina Temple **15** 485
Vasanzio, Giovanni **20** 43; **26** 780; **32** 8–9*
collaboration **10** 908; **25** 227
works **4** 405; **11** 741
Vasarely, Jean-Pierre *see* YVARAL
Vasarely, Victor **32** 9–10*
collaboration **17** 833; **20** 607
dealers **26** 193
groups and movements **1** 79; **7** 772; **11** 551; **18** 62; **23** 448
methods **28** 202
patrons and collectors **1** 498; **32** 567
teachers **4** 441
works **3** 462; **12** 437; **13** 888; **29** 787
Vásárhely, István **30** 207
Vasari, Antonio **32** 10
Vasari, Giorgio (1511-74) **4** 276; **6** 90; **8** 612; **9** 21; **11** 179, 185, 187, 674; **16** 778; **19** 666; **21** 452, 759; **24** 91; **26** 769; **32** 10–23*, *19*, 190
academy **11** 215, 216
architecture **5** *183*; **7** 905; **11** *180*, 208, 209; **22** 355; **32** *15*
churches **8** 511; **11** 206
ciboria (ii) (structure) **31** 532
façade decoration **10** 737, 738, 739, *740*, 741
grottoes **13** 703
house **2** 390
loggias **11** 179
museums **2** 365
office buildings **23** 359
palazzi **11** 215; **16** 634, 771; **21** 21
staircases **29** 523
urban planning **24** 852
villas **16** 633
assistants **1** 670; **10** 858; **19** 871
Becerra, Gaspar **3** 471
Carlo di Cesari del Palagio **5** 768
Colle, Raffaello (di Michelangelo di Luca) dal **7** 560
Fontana (i), Prospero **11** 268
Gherardi, Cristofano **12** 527
Naldini, Giovan Battista **22** 447
Poppi **25** 241
Sabatini, Lorenzo **27** 480
Tempesta, Antonio **30** 428
Tito, Santi di **31** 54
Tosini, Michele **31** 205
Zucchi, Jacopo **33** 722
collaboration **4** 408; **5** 605; **11** 720; **16** 724; **27** 275; **29** 741; **32** 504; **33** 717
drawings **9** 220; **21** 763; **32** *13*, *17*
education (art) **24** 91
frames **11** 392
groups and movements **20** 281; **26** 182
houses **1** 662; **2** *548*, 550
interior decoration **11** 179, 212; **21** 21, 22
methods **28** 339
paintings **16** 664; **19** 184
frescoes
Casa Vasari (Florence) **32** *16*
Cathedral of S Maria del Fiore (Florence) **33** 718
Palazzo della Cancelleria (Rome) **12** 719; **20** 279; **25** 71; **26** 836
Palazzo Vecchio **3** 743
Palazzo Vecchio (Florence) **3** 387; **21** *11*
Vatican Palace (Rome) **26** 818
Vasari, Giorgio (1511-74)
paintings—cont.
oil
allegorical **1** 657, 662; **9** 14; **11** 212; **15** 87; **32** *14*
altarpieces **1** 712; **5** 451
ceiling **21** *20*
mythological **32** *17*
portraits **32** *11*
religious **28** 490; **32** *12*
patrons and collectors **16** 763; **32** 386
Altoviti, Bindo **1** 734
Aretino, Pietro **2** 388
Caro, Annibal **5** 789
Cosimo I, Grand Duke of Tuscany (*reg* 1569- 74) **3** 160; **21** 19, 21, 22
Farnese, Alessandro, Cardinal (1520-89) **10** 809
Farnese, Ranuccio, Cardinal **10** 811
Francesco I, Grand Duke of Tuscany (*reg* 1574-87) **15** 828; **21** 22
Gregory XIII, Pope (*reg* 1572-85) **13** 628
Julius III, Pope (*reg* 1550-55) **22** 6
Martelli (family) **20** 482
Medici, Ottaviano de' **21** 18
Pius V, Pope (*reg* 1566-72) **25** 7
Soane, John **28** 908
personal collection **9** 229; **19** 676; **24** 199; **25** 848; **30** 727
drawings **7** 562, 714; **9** 26; **11** 893; **16** 814, 815; **19** 369; **20** 417; **25** 378
Cungi, Leonardo **8** 268
Labacco, Antonio **18** 572
Maiano, Benedetto da **20** 115
mounts **22** 236, *237*; **25** 664
Uccello, Paolo **31** 516
Verrocchio, Andrea del **32** 366
marks **20** 446
mounts **20** 445
paintings **28** 81
sculpture **27** 775
productions **21** 647
pupils **5** 182; **25** 241; **33** 721
sculpture **11** 29
tapestries **11** 193
teachers **2** 390; **13** 827; **27** 846, 851
writings **2** 313, 517, 518, 531; **10** 205; **11** 770; **12** 720; **13** 806; **14** 868; **16** 664, 766, 781; **20** 277, 278; **21** 538; **22** 910; **26** 768; **31** 299
illustrated **4** 408
letters **3** 293
on academies **1** 102
on artists **6** 107; **29** 853
Bottari, Giovanni Gaetano **4** 492
Dürer, Albrecht (1471-1528) **9** 443
Leonardo da Vinci **19** 197
Masaccio **20** 537
Michelangelo (Buonarroti) **2** 558; **21** 459
Michelozzo di Bartolomeo **21** 469
Stefano Fiorentino **29** 599
Veronese, Paolo **32** 351, 355
on artist's models **21** 759
on *camera obscura* **5** 519
on chiaroscuro **6** 569
on death-masks **5** 300; **9** 21
on *disegno e colore* **7** 628; **9** 7
on Dürer Renaissance **9** 445
on Etruscan art **10** 636, 642
on grounds **10** 191; **13** 708
on iconography **15** 89
on Medici Academy **11** 217
on modelli **21** 762
on painting **19** 871
on *paragone* **24** 90, 91
on patronage **16** 763; **28** 916
Vasari, Giorgio (1511-74)
writings—cont.
on *poesie* **25** 71
on pottery **13** 541
on sculpture **31** 302
on sgrafitto **10** 740
on stucco **29** 812
on styluses **29** 884
on tempera **30** 425, 427
translated **8** 525; **24** 300
Vasari, Giorgio, *il giovane* (1562-1625) **32** 10, 22, 25*
Vásári, Miklós, Bishop of Esztergom **14** 898
Vasari Society **25** 238
Vasaro, Giovanni Maria **6** 18; **32** 25*
Vasart Glass Ltd **28** 260
Vasasour-Elder, Irene **24** 457
Vasa style **25** 135
Vasata **15** 284
Vasco, Grão *see* FERNANDES, VASCO
Vasco da Gama **6** 622; **7** 493; **15** 674; **25** 312; **32** 239, 406
Vasco de la Zarza *see* ZARZA, VASCO DE LA
Vasconcellos, Juan de los Santos *see* SANTOS VASCONCELLOS, JUAN DE LOS
Vasconcelos, Constantino de **19** 385; **24** 502; **25** 822; **32** 25–6*
Vasconcelos, Ernani **8** 7; **22** 95; **26** 109
Vasconcelos, Félix Machado da Silva Castro e *see* MACHADO DA SILVA CASTRO E VASCONCELOS, FÉLIX
Vasconcelos, Fernando de Menezes Coutinho e *see* MENEZES COUTINHO E VASCONCELOS, FERNANDO DE
Vasconcelos, Hernani Mendes de *see* MENDES DE VASCONCELOS, HERNANI
Vasconcelos, Joaquim de **25** 320; **32** 26*
Vasconcelos, José **18** 904; **21** 387, 403, 405; **22** 20, 334; **23** 566; **25** 653; **26** 426; **28** 783
Vasconcelos, Maurício de **28** 729
Vasconcelos e Souza, Luiz de **4** 711
Vasconi, Claude **9** 47; **32** 26*
Vasconi, Filippo **13** 626; **19** 732
works **25** *853*
Vascos, Juan **9** 267
Vasco Vescovali **16** 365
Vase carpets *see under* CARPETS → types
Vasegaard, Gertrud **7** 807; **8** 749
Vase Gobelet Monté **9** 399
Vaseline glass *see under* GLASS → types
Vasenzio, Giovanni **26** 807
vase paintings *see under* PAINTING → forms
vases
historical and regional traditions
Ancient Near East **1** *867*
Austria **33** *165*
Byzantine **14** 170
Canada **5** *582*
Celtic **25** *543*
China **6** 890, *890*, *891*, *894*, *898*, 903, *903*, *908*, *909*, *911*; **7** *27*, *79*, *85*, *90*, 103; **16** I; **26** 487
Crete **8** 154; **21** *689*, *690*
Cyprus, ancient **8** 339, 343, 346
Czech Republic **12** VI2
Denmark **8** *750*
Egypt, ancient **10** 28, *28*, 47, *57*
England **10** *311*, *312*
Etruscan **10** 587, 609, 610–16, 631
vases
historical and regional traditions—cont.
France **11** 635, 636; **30** *501*
La Tène culture (*c.* 450-.*c* 50 BC) **25** *543*
19th cent. **11** *610*; **28** *523*
20th cent. **11** *612*; **28** *524*
Germany **21** *66*
Greece, ancient **10** 474; **13** *475*, 477–8, 480, 483, *488*, 489, 590, *590*; **16** 830
Chalcidian **13** 515
Lakonia **13** 512
5th cent. BC **32** *50*
Honduras **29** *153*
Hungary **15** *2*
Islamic **16** 419
Italy **14** 171; **16** *747*
Etruscan **10** 587, 609, 610–16, 631
16th cent. **21** 529
20th cent. **32** *205*
Japan **17** *254*, *263*, *268*, *379*; **18** *554*; **28** *413*
Korea **18** *338*, *339*
La Tène culture (*c.* 450-.*c* 50 BC) **25** *543*
Maya **20** 883; **21** 257, 266
Mesoamerica, Pre-Columbian **21** 266
Mesopotamia **1** *867*; **21** *293*, *303*
Minoan **18** *168*; **21** *689*, *690*
Netherlands, the **8** *668*; **22** *883*
Peru **32** *418*
Poland **25** *123*
Prehistoric art **8** 339; **25** *543*
Russia **27** *418*
Slovenia **28** *863*
South Africa **29** *117*
South America, Pre-Columbian **29** *153*; **32** *418*
Spain **7** XI2; **16** 419; **29** *327*, *330*
Sweden **30** *98*, *100*, *103*
Thailand **30** *610*
Trinidad and Tobago **31** *338*
United States of America **31** *637*, *638*, *645*, *650*
Vicús culture **32** *418*
materials
alabaster (gypsum) **21** *293*
bamboo **28** *413*
brass **33** *165*
earthenwares **16** *419*; **30** *98*; **31** *638*
enamel **7** *27*, *79*; **17** *379*
faience (i) (glass) **10** 48; **13** 590, *590*
faience (ii) (ceramics) **15** *2*
frit **10** 47
glass **1** *867*; **7** *85*; **8** *750*; **10** *57*; **11** *612*; **12** VI2; **27** *418*; **30** *103*; **31** *645*
gold **31** *650*
hardstones **11** 635, 636; **14** 170, 171
ivory **7** 103
jade **16** I
lapis lazuli **16** *747*
marble **29** *153*
obsidian **21** *689*
porcelain
China **6** *898*, *902*, 903, *903*, *908*, *909*, *911*
France **11** *610*; **28** *523*, *524*
Germany **21** *66*
Netherlands, the **22** *883*
Spain **29** *330*
Sweden **30** *100*
United States of America **31** *637*
pottery
China **6** 890, *890*, *891*, III3
Egypt, ancient **10** *28*
Greece, ancient **13** *488*
Netherlands, the **8** *668*
Prehistoric art **25** *543*

vases
  materials
    pottery—cont.
      Spain **7** XI2
      Vicús culture **32** *418*
    quartz **7** *90*
    rock crystal **21** 529; **26** 487
    serpentine **21** *690*
    silver **7** *27*; **21** *303*
    soapstone **18** *168*
    stonewares **10** *312*; **17** *254*, *261*, *268*; **18** *554*; **30** *610*
    terracotta **30** *501*
  techniques
    moulding **13** 480
  types
    Alhambra **16** 419, *419*
    arrow **6** *875*
    baluster **6** *875*, III3
    bilingual **13** 517; **32** 65
    garlic vase *see suantou hu*
    mallet **6** *875*, 893
    meiping **6** 875, *875*, 893, *902*
    Phlyax **26** 873
    plum blossom *see meiping*
    queens' **10** 48
    rouleau **6** *875*
    suantou hu **6** *875*
    yuhuchun **6** *875*, 893
vase stands *see* HOLMOI
Vashishthiputra Camtamula I, King (*reg c.* 350) (Ikshvaku) **15** 233
Vasi, Giuseppe **7** 682; **32** 70*
  illustrated writings **20** *521*
  pupils **20** 513; **24** 842
  works **11** *180*; **19** *685*; **26** *759*, 849; **32** 113
Vasi, Mariano **5** 615; **23** 79; **32** 70
Vasić, Milan **32** 581
Vasil'chikov, A. A. **26** 734
Vasile Lupu, Voivode of Moldavia (*reg* 1634-53) **15** 55; **26** 708, 712, 719, 722; **29** 893
Vasilescu, Paul **23** 757
Vasilev, Asen **5** 158
Vasilev, Slavyan **5** 158
Vasiliki **8** 153; **13** *362*; **21** *651*; **32** 70–71*
  houses **13** 603; **21** 656, 661; **32** 71
Vasiliki ware *see under* POTTERY → wares
Vasiliko *see* SIKYON
Vasiliyev, Danila (Ivanovich) *see* VASSILIEFF, DANILA (IVANOVICH)
Vasil'kovsky, Sergey I.(1884-1917) **28** 838; **31** 559
Vasil'kovsky, S. V. (1892-1960) **12** 234
Vasil'yev, Aleksey **21** 811
Vasil'yev, Alexandr V. **19** 274; **27** 578; **29** 388
Vasil'yev, Fyodor (Aleksandrovich) **27** 391; **28** 41; **32** 71*
Vasil'yev, Gennady **27** 436
Vasil'yev, Grigory (*fl* 1660s) **27** 414
Vasil'yev, Grigory (Vasil'yevich) (1823-64) *see* SROKA, GRIGORY (VASIL'YEVICH)
Vasil'yev, Nikolay (Vasil'yevich) **27** 378, 578; **30** 277; **32** 71–2*
Vasil'yev, Valerian **27** 436
Vasil'yevich, Nikolay
Vasily I, Grand Prince (*reg* 1389-1425) **30** 707
Vasio Vocontiorum *see under* VAISON-LA-ROMAINE
Vasishthipurta (*fl* 1st cent. BC) **1** 500
Vasishthiputra Pulumavi, King (*reg c.* mid-2nd cent. AD) (Satavahana) **27** 866
Vas'ko, Gavrila A. **18** 38; **31** 559
Vaslet, Lewis **3** 373; **9** 199
Vasnetsov, Andrey **27** 397, 405
Vasnetsov, Apollinary (Mikhaylovich) **18** 482; **32** 74*
Vasnetsov, Viktor (Mikhaylovich) **1** 72; **18** 38; **22** 178; **27** 377, 391, 408, 580; **32** 72–4*
  assistants **22** 338
  collaboration **27** 410
  groups and movements **1** 71; **20** 232; **33** 379
  pupils **32** 74
  works **31** 312; **32** *73*; **33** 607
Vasnetsov, Yury (Alekseyevich) **27** 581
Vaspurakan **2** 426
  Museum **2** 444
Vasquez, Bautista **11** 485
Vásquez, Dagoberto **13** 765; **32** 74*
Vásquez, Juan Bautista **32** 247
Vásquez, Julio Antonio **31** 812
Vásquez, Raúl **23** 905
Vásquez Brito, Ramón **32** 74*, 175
Vásquez de Coronado, Juan **8** 15
Vásquez Escobedo, Diego **32** 178
Vass, Elemer **13** 638
Vassal, Bruno **1** 648
Vassal de Saint-Hubert, Jean-Antoine-Hubert **32** 74–5*
Vassall, Elizabeth, Baroness Holland **11** 362
Vassallettus (family) **7** 921, 922; **32** 75*
  collaboration **9** 304
  works **1** 819; **2** 348; **26** 821, 844; **30** 777
Vassallettus, Johannes **32** 75
Vassallettus, Petrus **23** 109; **26** 624; **32** 75
Vassalli, Francesco **7** 409; **10** 278; **12** 595; **28** 878; **29** 835; **31** 862
Vassalli, Luigi **10** 82
Vassallo, Antonio Maria **6** 36; **29** 411; **32** 76*
Vassallo, Gerolamo **20** 924
Vassar, Matthew **26** 213
Vassar College (NY) **9** 231
Vassé, François-Antoine **11** 405, 577, 625; **32** 76
  collaboration **6** 121
  interior decoration **11** 578; **26** 84, 492; **30** 88
  sculpture **11** 405, 626; **32** 76
Vassé, Louis-Claude **11** 561; **32** 76–7*
  patrons and collectors **4** 303
  pupils **8** 650
  works **22** 455
Vasserot, Daniel **30** 148
Vasserot, José **18** 867
Vasseur, Jean Le *see* LE VASSEUR, JEAN
Vasseur, Jehan Le *see* LE VASSEUR, JEHAN
Vasseur, J. S. **11** 410
Vasseur, Paul **3** 366
Vassilacchi, Antonio **5** 533; **31** 15; **32** 77*
  collaboration **9** 74
  patrons and collectors **7** 775; **32** 6
  pupils **26** 363
  works **18** 431; **32** 215
Vassilakis, Panayiotis *see* TAKIS
Vassilieff, Danila (Ivanovich) **2** 753; **32** 77–8*
Vassiliev, Asen **5** 163
Vassiliou, Spyros **13** 353; **32** 78*
Vassilyov, Ivan (Tsokov) **5** 149; **32** 78*
Vassoult, Nicolas **11** 626
Vassouras **4** 712
Vast, Jean **3** 456
Vastagh, György (1868-1946) **14** 896
Västerås **30** *65*, 92
  Castle **30** 92
  Cathedral **4** 781; **30** 67, 76
Vasters, Reinhold **11** 306; **12** 449, 457; **26** 227, 486; **29** 415
  works **11** *307*
Vasto, Marchese del **8** 706
Vastokas, Joan **2** 137
Västra Skrukeby **13** 119
Vastupala **8** 848
Vasulka, Steina **32** 420
Vasulka, Woody **32** 420
Vasvár Benedictine Abbey **14** 883
Vasyurinsky Kurgan **4** 110
Vaszary, János **3** 110; **11** 887; **14** 553, 901; **15** 12; **30** 211
Vatagin, Vasily (Alekseyevich) **27** 411; **32** 78*
Vātāpi *see* BADAMI
Vat Athvea **5** 473, 474
Vat Ban Mang **18** 769
Vat Baset **5** 472
vat dyes *see under* DYES → types
Väte **27** 123, 124
  church **26** 639
  sculpture **26** 647; **30** 83
Väte, Master of **11** 98
Vat Ek **5** 472, 490
Vathi, Hagios Georgios **8** 156
Vathypetro **13** *362*; **21** *651*; **32** 78–9*
  villa **21** 664
Vatican *see* ROME (VATICAN)
Vatican 238, Painter of **10** 615
Vatican 309, Painter of **13** 508; **32** 54
Vatican Astronomical Tables **2** 648
Vatican Biga Painter **10** 615
Vatican Homer, Master of the **12** 171; **18** 872; **27** 807
Vatican Inventory **16** 443
Vatican Mourner, Painter of the **13** 508
Vatican Virgil (Rome, Vatican, Bib. Apostolica, MS. Lat. 3225) **9** 219, 603
Vat Manorom **18** 768
Vat Nahua **18** 769
Vaṭodaka *see* BADOH
Vat Phu **5** 472; **18** 764, 767; **30** 580
Vat Prasat Andet **5** 481
Vat Prasat Phum Prasat **5** 481
Vat Romlok **5** 484, 485
Vats, M. S. **14** 162; **15** 417
Vatsyayana **15** 229, 550
Vattamen, Nicolas **30** 659
Vatuele **11** 69
Vat Xieng Thong **18** 777
Vau, Louis Le *see* LE VAU, LOUIS
Vauban, Sébastien Leprestre de **3** 360; **11** 518, 750; **21** 567–8; **32** 79–80*
  works **2** 242, 337, 495; **3** 873; **7** 362; **19** 380, 827; **20** 472; **21** *567*; **22** 453; **29** 750; **31** 718
  writings **21** 580
Vaucanson, Jacques (de) **2** 837; **16** 850; **22** 726
Vaucelles Abbey **13** 38
Vauchelet, Théophile **1** 28
Vaucher (company) **11** 630
Vaucher, Samuel **30** 127, 154
Vauclair Abbey **30** 907, 908
  roof **30** *906*
Vaucresson, Château Le Butard **6** 509
Vaudechamp, Jean Joseph **23** 32
Vaudémont, François, Comte de **19** 35
Vaudemont, Louise de **31** 478
Vaudemont, Prince de **4** 225
Vaudemont, René II of, Duke of Lorraine *see* RENÉ II OF VAUDEMONT, Duke of Lorraine
Vaudetar, Jean de **4** 525
Vaudey **7** 350, 351
Vaudoyer, Alfred **32** 80, 83
Vaudoyer, Antoine-Laurent-Thomas **32** 80–81*
  assistants **19** 11
Vaudoyer, Antoine-Laurent-Thomas—cont.
  pupils **8** 18; **18** 493, 580, 581; **19** 11; **32** 81
Vaudoyer, Georges **32** 80
Vaudoyer, Jean-Laurent **32** 80
Vaudoyer, Léon **4** 597; **11** 323, 521; **14** 580; **27** 591; **32** 80, 81–3*
  collaboration **6** 511; **9** 312
  groups and movements **28** 345, 346
  pupils **4** 597; **8** 572; **9** 420; **10** 508; **19** 469; **32** 80
  works **5** 905; **8** 565; **10** 508; **11** 324, 521, 522; **18** 688; **20** 473; **25** 173; **32** *82*, *83*
Vaudremer, (Joseph-Auguste-) Emile **32** 84–5*
  collaboration **32** 859
  groups and movements **26** 704
  pupils **3** 6; **14** 458; **29** 913
  teachers **4** 171
  works **11** 521; **32** *84*
Vaudreuil, François, Comte de **8** 561; **11** 663; **19** 25; **32** 85*
Vaudreuil, Joseph-Hyacinthe-François de Paule de Rigaud, Comte de **18** 579
Vaudreuil Château **25** 705
Vaughan, Edward, Bishop of St David's **27** 538
Vaughan, Henry (*fl* 1651) **32** 85
Vaughan, Henry (1845-1917) **4** 475; **32** 887
Vaughan, Herbert, Cardinal **3** 746, 747
Vaughan, (John) Keith **10** 375; **12** 214; **22** 751; **32** 85*
Vaughan, Robert **32** 85–6*
Vaughan, Samuel **29** 805
Vaughan, Thomas (*fl* 1651) **32** 85
Vaughan, Thomas (1839-75) **12** 315
Vaughan, William **32** 790
Vaughan Burns **29** 107
Vaughan-Richards, Alan (Kenneth Hamer) **1** 319; **18** 639; **32** 86*
Vaughn, Henry **29** 516
Vaughn, Lester Howard **4** 481
Vaughton's **4** 87
Vaugondy, Didier de **12** 814
Vaugondy, Gilles Robert de **12** 814
Vau i Dejës Church **1** 542
Vauled, Harry **11** 168
vaults (ceiling) **20** 574; **32** 86–94*, *87*
  historical and regional traditions
    Armenia (Europe) **14** 36
    Assyrian **32** 86
    Britain **4** 778, 779
    Burma **5** 226–7
    Byzantine **9** 524, 526
    Central Asia, Western **6** 202; **16** 199
    Chile **6** 592
    Christianity **32** 86
    Czech Republic **25** 440, *441*; **26** 366
    Early Christian (*c.* AD 250-843) **9** 524
    Egypt, ancient **32** 86
    England **32** 94
      Gothic **10** 228; **13** 54; **19** 402, *402*, 403, *602*
      Gothic: Perpendicular style **19** 602
      Romanesque **9** *449*, *450*; **19** 402; **26** 589
    France **13** 59; **26** 586; **32** *599*
      Gothic **3** 458
    Germany **3** 793; **10** *221*; **12** 366; **26** 575
    Gothic **20** *583*
      Czech Republic **25** *441*
      England **10** 228; **13** 54; **19** 402, *402*, 403, *602*
vaults (ceiling)
  historical and regional traditions
    Gothic—cont.
      England: Perpendicular style **19** 602
      France **3** 458; **13** 59
      Germany **10** *221*; **12** 366
      Poland **13** 57
    Gothic survival **13** 210
    Greece, ancient **13** 391, 403, 404, 407; **29** 488
    Guatemala **13** 760
    Indian subcontinent **15** 343
    Iran **16** 192, 194, 199, *200*
    Iran, ancient **15** 912, 913; **28** 537, *537*
    Iraq **18** 483
    Islamic **16** 140, 142
      Central Asia, Western **6** 202; **16** 199
      Indian subcontinent **15** 343
      Iran **16** 192, 194, 199, *200*
      Spain **16** 217
      Turkey **16** 186
    Italy **26** 796, *878*
    Lithuania **19** *496*
    Macedonia (i) (Greece) **15** 53
    Maya **23** 838
    Mesoamerica, Pre-Columbian **23** 838
    Mesopotamia **21** 275, 284–5; **23** 806
    Netherlands, the **8** 299; **22** *819*
    Peru **24** 501
    Poland **13** 57
    Portugal **9** 104; **22** 14
    Romanesque **26** 569
      England **9** *449*, *450*; **19** 402; **26** 589–90
      France **26** 586
      Germany **26** 575
    Romania **26** 707
    Rome, ancient **26** 864, 873, 874, 878, 880, 911, 923; **27** 47, 51, 55; **32** 86
      Italy **26** 796, *878*
    Sasanian **27** 857
    Spain **16** 217
    Syria-Palestine **30** 190
    Turkey **16** 186
  materials
    amphorae **26** 903
    brick **4** 767, 778, 779; **15** 912; **16** 140, 199, 270; **21** 275; **24** *347*; **26** *878*, 878, 911
    concrete **26** 864
    iron **3** 793; **22** 14
    masonry **20** 576–9*, *577*, *583*
    mud-bricks **23** 806; **28** 537, *537*
    stone **26** 874
    stucco **16** *200*, *233*; **19** *496*
    tas-de-charge **30** 350, *350*
    tiles **26** 878
    wood **13** 54; **32** 94*
  techniques
    centering **6** 178; **28** 498
    mouldings **22** 217, 218, 221
    templates **28** 498
    tracery **12** 493; **31** 271
  types
    annular **32** 86–7*, *87*
    barrel **20** 576–7, *577*, 583, *583*; **32** 86, *87*, 87–8*, 89
      Assyrian **32** 87
      Cistercian Order **32** 88
      Cluniac Order **32** 88
      Croatia **23** 93
      Egypt **16** 270
      Egypt, ancient **32** 87
      England **32** 88
      Germany **22** *307*
      Greece, ancient **8** 694; **32** 87
      Iraq **16** 150, 153
      Islamic **16** 150, 153, 270; **32** 88
      Italy **16** 630
      Romanesque **26** 569, 581; **32** 88
      Rome, ancient **32** 87

vaults (ceiling)
types
barrel—cont.
Spain 26 581
cellular 13 58; 32 87, 88*
cloister 32 87, 88*, 94
corbelled 20 574; 21 205, 207; 32 87, 88*
coved see cloister
cross-vaults see groin
crystal see cellular
curving see rib: curving
domical see cloister; Platzlgewölbe; sail
fan 13 55; 19 602, 602; 20 573, 577, 579, 584; 31 271; 32 87, 88–9*, 93
flat-topped 7 774; 32 89*
groin 20 577, 577–8, 584; 32 87, 89*, 90
Germany 29 392
Romanesque 26 569
Rome, ancient 32 89
Spain 8 79
Guastavino 13 757; 32 89*
jumping see rib: jumping
lierne see rib: lierne
Moldavian 26 707
muqarnas (architecture) 16 142
Algeria 16 190
Iran 16 195, 199
Iraq 16 181
Islamic 22 322–3
Morocco 16 190
Sicily 16 171
Syria 33 614
nave 26 586
net see rib: net
octopartite see rib: octopartite
pendant see rib: pendant
pendentive see sail
pitched-brick 32 87, 87, 89*
Platzlgewölbe 25 34*
ploughshare see rib: ploughshare
pointed 16 153
quadrant 32 87, 89*
quadripartite see rib: quadripartite
reticulated see rib: reticulated
rib 20 573, 577, 578–9, 584; 28 498, 498; 30 350, 350; 32 90*, 91
England 9 449; 26 589
France 13 36; 26 586; 32 90
Germany 14 268
Gothic 6 178; 13 35, 36, 51; 14 268
Iran 16 232, 233
Islamic 16 232, 233
Italy 13 51; 26 578
Romanesque 26 569, 578, 586, 589
Rome, ancient 32 90
rib: curving 32 90*, 91
England 32 90
rib: jumping 13 57; 32 90*, 91
rib: lierne 8 611; 20 579; 32 90–92*, 91, 93
England 13 54; 19 610; 32 90, 91
France 32 90
Gothic 13 54, 69
Spain 13 69
rib: net 20 579; 32 91, 92*
Czech Republic 32 92
England 32 92
France 32 92
Germany 12 366; 32 92
Gothic 12 366
Islamic 16 142
rib: octopartite 5 638; 25 667
rib: pendant 32 92*
England 32 92
rib: ploughshare 32 92*, 93
rib: quadripartite 20 577, 578–9, 583, 583–4; 28 347; 32 91, 92*, 93
rib: reticulated 32 91, 92*
vaults (ceiling)
types—cont.
rib: sexpartite 5 371; 32 91, 92–3*
rib: stalactite 32 93*
rib: star 13 57; 20 579; 24 347, 348; 32 91, 93*; 33 259
rib: stellar see rib: star
rib: tierceron 13 45; 20 579; 32 91, 93*
rib: triradial 12 493; 32 91, 93–4*, 747
Roussillon see flat-topped
sail 9 84*; 32 87, 94*
saucer 22 806
segmental 32 94*
sexpartite see rib: sexpartite
springgewölbe see rib: jumping
stalactite see rib: stalactite
star see rib: star
stellar see rib: star
tierceron see rib: tierceron
triradial see rib: triradial
trough 32 94*
tunnel see barrel
uses
houses 16 270
stadia 29 488
tombs 15 53
vaults (tombs) 6 165; 20 885
Vauquelin, Louis Nicolas 24 149, 794, 799
Vauquer, Jean 11 630; 32 94–5*
Vauquer, Robert 32 95
Vauroze, Jacques Friquet de see FRIQUET DE VAUROZE, JACQUES
Vauthier, Louis 4 711; 26 65
Vauthier, Michel 10 562
Vautier, (Louis) Benjamin (1829–98) 9 461; 17 9; 30 2; 32 95*
Vautier, Benjamin (b 1935) see BEN
vautoir 22 726
Vauvert, Baron de 19 272
Vaux, Calvert 32 95*; 33 263
collaboration 6 573; 9 205; 22 210; 23 39, 40, 419, 420, 422; 24 179; 33 263
works 11 243
writings 32 555
Vaux, Downing 32 95
Vauxcelles, Louis 32 96*
groups and movements 8 239, 246; 10 839
staff 26 44
Vaux Fuller, Meta see FULLER, META VAUX
Vauxhall Glasshouse 10 276, 316; 19 595; 21 720
Vauxhall Pottery 10 306, 308, 309
Vauxhall Walk pottery 9 200
Vaux-le-Vicomte 6 508; 11 356, 504, 516, 657; 19 266, 721; 23 493; 24 290; 32 96–7*, 97
furniture 4 532
gardens 12 120, 121; 19 162, 162–3; 31 480; 32 97*
Allée d'Eau 11 344
Grand Salon 29 833
interior decoration 11 573, 574
sculpture 2 92
stables 29 485
tapestries 11 641
Vaux & Withers 20 13
vav see STEPWELLS
Vavasour (family) 33 547
Vavassore, Giovanni Andrea 2 223
Väversunda 9 156; 26 691
Vavoua Museum 8 23
Vay, Abraham 18 128
Vay, Daniel 18 128
Vay, Miklós, Baron 14 896
Vayer, François de La Mothe le see LA MOTHE LE VAYER, FRANÇOIS DE
Vayreda, Francesc 13 726
Vayreda y Vila, Joaquín 29 284; 32 97–8*
Vaz, Gaspar 10 900; 19 655; 32 98*
Vaz, João 4 386; 32 98*
Vaz, Pero 19 655
Vazcardo, Juan 32 98*
Vaz de Castro, António 25 306
Vaz Dourado, Fernão 32 98–9*
Vázquez, Alonso 23 704; 26 307; 31 518; 32 99*
Vázquez, Bartolomé 32 99*
Vázquez, Diego 29 333
Vázquez, Francisco see COMPOSTELA
Vázquez, Francisco, Museo see under GUATEMALA CITY
Vazquez, Johnny 18 832
Vázquez, José 13 284; 32 99
Vázquez, Juan Bautista 2 865; 14 464; 29 290; 31 89; 32 100*
Vázquez (de Segovia), Lorenzo 32 100–101*
attributions 32 147
groups and movements 25 31
patrons and collectors 21 124, 126; 29 264
works 18 586; 29 264; 31 822
Vázquez, Pedro Ramírez see RAMÍREZ VÁZQUEZ, PEDRO
Vázquez de Arce y Ceballos, Gregorio 4 233; 7 607, 611, 612
Vázquez de Leca, Mateo 22 2
Vázquez Díaz, Daniel 10 822; 20 68; 29 286; 32 101*
pupils 5 341, 613, 622; 14 715; 23 706
Vázquez Molezún, Ramón 29 274
Vázquez y Giralte, Juan 29 338
VBB 18 541
Veale, William 10 757
Veale & Saunders 19 747
Veau, Jean-Jacques (-André) Le see LE VEAU, JEAN-JACQUES(-ANDRÉ)
Veau, Louis Le (d 1661) see LE VEAU, LOUIS
Veau, Victoire-Geneviève Le see LE VEAU, VICTOIRE-GENEVIÈVE
Véber, Jean 19 490
VEB Staatliche Porzellan-Manufaktur Meissen 21 63, 67
Vecchi, Gabriele De see DE VECCHI, GABRIELE
Vecchi, Gaspare de 4 434
Vecchi, Giovanni (Liso) de' 32 101–2*
assistants 26 89
patrons and collectors 10 810
pupils 31 884
works 5 684; 26 809, 823; 32 102
Vecchia, Pietro della 16 675; 32 102–3*
assistants 5 782
collaboration 4 455; 9 489
pupils 18 901; 27 202
reproductive prints by others 25 629
Vecchietta 12 716; 16 662; 28 677; 32 103–5*
assistants 24 781
attributions 4 30; 20 745
collaboration 3 750; 20 557, 558
patrons and collectors 14 764
pupils 2 20; 3 750; 11 687, 692; 18 697
works 9 95; 14 784; 16 662, 691, 692, 843; 20 558; 24 732; 28 682, 683, 687; 29 568; 32 104, 105
Vecchietti, Bernardo 4 408; 32 105–6*
architecture 12 574
collections 11 188
sculpture 12 569, 576, 577
sponsorship 12 568
Vecchio, Boccardino see BOCCARDINO VECCHIO
Vecchio, Floriano 20 607
Vecchio, James Del see DEL VECCHIO, JAMES
Vecchio, Pietro 33 721
Vecchio Bolognese, Il see AIMO, DOMENICO
Vecellio, Cesare 18 590; 24 271; 32 106, 107*
works 11 328; 30 151; 33 356
writings 10 823; 15 84
Vecellio, Fabrizio 32 106
Vecellio, Francesco 31 316; 32 106–7*
Vecellio, Marco 8 766; 13 657; 32 106, 107–8*, 220
Vecellio, Orazio 3 698; 31 41; 32 106, 107*
Vecellio, Tiziano (c. ?1485/90–1576) see TITIAN
Vecellio, Tiziano (1570–1650) 32 106
Vecellio, Tommasso 32 106
Večenaj, Ivan 14 596
Vechkanov, Viktor 27 435
Vechta, Konrad of (patron) see KONRAD OF VECHTA
Vechta, Konrad von (painter) see KONRAD VON VECHTA
Vechte, Antoine 10 335; 11 622
Vechter, Jan 21 789
Vecsei, Andrew 32 108
Vecsei, Eva 32 108*
Vedano, Alessandro da 9 754
Vedara 6 249
Vedat 16 590; 32 108*
works 16 227, 586, 611; 17 893; 23 639; 31 452
Vedavyasa 15 226
vedībandha 15 245*
Vedder, Elihu 23 504; 32 108–9*
works 32 109
Vedernikov, Aleksandr 7 341
vedikā 15 245*
Vedisā see BESNAGAR
Vedova, Emilio 32 109–10*
groups and movements 2 526, 545; 11 802; 13 727; 16 681, 709; 32 197
works 19 491
Vedres, Márk 10 108; 14 896
vedute see under PAINTING → types
vedute ideate see under PAINTING → types
Veen, Otto van 22 902; 26 770; 32 114–16*
assistants 27 288; 33 298
attributions 3 24
collaboration 27 288
patrons and collectors 3 90, 613; 5 427; 13 917; 15 85; 33 252
pupils 3 558; 27 288
reproductive prints by others 15 93; 17 599; 23 908
teachers 30 60
works 1 658; 2 198; 3 558; 10 174, 175; 15 92; 23 381; 28 899; 32 114, 115
illustrated 4 221
Veenwouden 22 822
Veer, Johan de 31 772
Veere
church 22 820
Stadhuis 22 822
Veerendael, Nicolaes van 3 561; 14 290; 32 116*
Vega, Agustín García see GARCÍA VEGA, AGUSTÍN
Vega, Diego González de la see GONZÁLEZ DE LA VEGA, DIEGO
Vega, Eduardo 32 117*
Vega, Félix Lope de see LOPE DE VEGA, FÉLIX
Vega, Francisco Preciado de la see PRECIADO DE LA VEGA, FRANCISCO
Vega, Garcilaso de la 29 179
Vega, Gaspar de 29 267; 32 117*, 559
works 10 498, 501; 24 107
Vega, Jorge de la 2 401; 19 872; 31 758; 32 118*
Vega, José Gutiérrez de la see GUTIÉRREZ DE LA VEGA, JOSÉ
Vega, Juan Talavera y de la see TALAVERA Y DE LA VEGA, JUAN
Vega, La see LA VEGA
Vega, Lorenzo de 26 252
Vega, Luis de 32 116–17*
collaboration 29 266, 267
groups and movements 25 31
patrons and collectors 7 488
pupils 2 375
works 2 284; 8 79; 10 534, 904; 12 920; 20 71; 24 107; 27 481; 31 823; 32 559
Vega, Luís Fernandez de la see FERNANDEZ DE LA VEGA, LUÍS
Vega, Manuel de 18 681
Vega, Marta 18 833
Vega, Pedro Laso de la, 1st Conde de Arcos see ARCOS, PEDRO LASO DE LA VEGA, 1st Conde de
Vega de Alatorre 21 187
Vega de los Rís, Francisco Laso de la see LASO, FRANCISCO
Vega del Pozo, Condesa de la 29 272
Vega el Inca, Garcilaso de la 21 718
Vega Henríquez, Angel 24 517
Vega Marrugal, José de la 30 31
Vega Merlo, Tomás de la 21 159
Vegara, Nicolas de 11 485
Vega y Muñoz (family) 28 516
Vega y Verdugo, José, Conde de Alba Real see ALBA REAL, JOSÉ VEGA Y VERDUGO, Conde de
vegetable fibres see under FIBRES → types
vegetable gardens see under GARDENS → types
vegetable ivory see under IVORY → types
vegetable tannage see under TANNING
Vegetius Renatus, Flavius 21 578
Veghel, St Lambertus 8 299
El Vegón 27 700
Vegter, J. J. M. 3 777; 8 669
Vehap'ar's Gospels see under GOSPEL BOOKS → individual manuscripts
Vehbi
works 16 454
Veheragala 29 478
vehicles see BINDERS
Vehmaa 13 190
Veiga Guignard, Alberto da see GUIGNARD, ALBERTO DA VEIGA
Veii 10 583, 584, 585, 601, 638; 16 620; 26 886; 32 118–19*
Campana Tomb 10 587, 597, 620
houses 10 599
Piazza d'Armi 10 588
Ponto Sodo 10 602
Portonaccio Temple 10 587, 588, 596, 600, 600, 603, 613, 638, 639; 23 480
altar 1 692
sculpture 16 683
terracottas 32 119, 119
Tomb of the Ducks 10 617, 620; 32 118
urban planning 10 602
vase paintings 10 614
vases 10 609, 610, 611, 612, 613
wall paintings 10 617; 16 652
Veii Painter 13 523
Veii School 16 683
Veil, Theodor 11 582
Veil of St Anne 16 432; 31 21, 21
Veil of Veronica 26 141
veils 1 349; 9 644; 16 453; 18 592

Veio *see* VEII
Veit, Johannes **22** 704
Veit, Philipp **32** 119–20*
collaboration **7** 870; **23** 676; **28** 46
groups and movements **12** 393; **22** 703, 704
patrons and collectors **3** 291; **7** 871
pupils **26** 255
works **12** 394; **17** 575; **22** 328; **32** *120*
Veitch, James, & Sons
works **31** *150*
Veith, Antonín, Count **22** 697
Veitshöchheim **12** *133*, 134, *361*; **32** 120–21*
Belvedere grottoes **13** 705
park **26** 497, 498; **32** 758
Vejmluva, Václav, Abbot of Žd'ár **8** 422
Veken, Cornelis van der **32** 121
Veken, Nikolas van der **3** 570; **32** 121*
Vela, Arqeles **10** 543
Vela, Diego Banderas *see* BANDERAS VELA, DIEGO
Vela, Vincenzo **30** 125; **32** 121–2*
works **16** 706; **30** 137; **31** 131; **32** *122*
Velamendi, Juan Miguel de *see* VERAMENDI, JUAN MIGUEL DE
Velarde, Francisco de Herrera *see* HERRERA VELARDE, FRANCISCO DE
Velarde, Pablita **14** 165; **22** 595; **32** 122*
Velasco (family) **5** 201
Velasco, Acisclo Antonio Palomino y *see* PALOMINO Y VELASCO, ACISCLO ANTONIO
Velasco, Antonio Acisclo Palomina y *see* PALOMINA Y VELASCO, ANTONIO ACISCLO
Velasco, Charles Fernandez de **33** 685
Velasco, Cristóbal de **32** 124
Velasco, Diego de **23** 626
Velasco, Fernando Castillo *see* CASTILLO VELASCO, FERNANDO
Velasco, José Manso de *see* MANSO DE VELASCO, JOSÉ
Velasco, José María **21** 385, 405; **32** 122–4*
teachers **18** 696
works **21** 385; **32** *123*
Velasco, Juan Fernández de *see* FERNÁNDEZ DE VELASCO, JUAN
Velasco, Lazaro de **32** 641
Velasco, Luis de **2** 867; **29** 278, 280; **31** 89; **32** 124*
Velasco, Mencia de Mendoza, Condesa de Haro **21** 124
Velasco, Pedro Fernández de, 2nd Conde de Haro *see* HARO, PEDRO FERNÁNDEZ DE VELASCO, 2nd Conde de
Velasquez, Francisco **25** 291
Velásquez, José Antonio **14** 716
works **14** *715*
Velathri *see under* VOLTERRA
Velatice **25** 528
Vela Zanetti, José **9** 117
Velazco, Juan Martínez de *see* MARTÍNEZ DE VELAZCO, JUAN
Velázquez, Alejandro González *see* GONZÁLEZ VELÁZQUEZ, ALEJANDRO
Velázquez, Antonio Gonzalez **23** 381
Velázquez, Castor González *see* GONZÁLEZ VELÁZQUEZ, CASTOR
Velázquez, Cosme **31** 808
Velázquez, Cristóbal **10** 903; **20** 501
Velázquez, Diego (*fl* 1510) **8** 228, 231
Velázquez, Diego (de Silva y) (1599-1660) **1** 629; **5** 738; **13** 869; **20** 66; **22** 478; **26** 772; **28** 515; **29** 279, 281, 302; **32** 125–35*
assistants **24** 109
attributions **20** 899, 900
collaboration **5** 619; **20** 899; **24** 391
dealers **7** 234
dealing **16** 767
frames **11** 486, 488, 489
groups and movements **3** 264; **30** 456
interior decoration **7** 746; **20** 72
methods **13** 708; **23** 377
paintings **11** 491; **24** 107; **29** 345
battle **3** 389
bodegones **4** 209–10, *210*, 211–12; **12** 289; **32** *126*
cabinet pictures **1** 663
cleaned by others **32** 3
frescoes **20** 72
genre **29** 350
history **14** 583
industrial scenes **15** 828
landscape **32** *131*
military scenes **32** *129*
mythological **10** 478; **32** *132*, *133*
portraits **2** 462; **11** *489*; **14** 8, *9*; **17** 516; **20** 71, 109; **32** *128*, *130*, *131*, *134*
religious **5** 778; **32** *127*
still-lifes **29** 340, 667
patrons and collectors **10** 503
Alba, Duques de **1** 528
Alexander I, Emperor of Russia (*reg* 1801-25) **26** 733
Altman, Benjamin **1** 731
Angerstein, John Julius **2** 51
Arce, Pedro de **2** 291; **29** 353
Bankes, William John **3** 179
Bourbon II., Luis Antonio, Infante of Spain **4** 565
Buchanan, William **5** 71
Canino, Lucien Bonaparte, Prince of (1775-1840) **4** 304
Carbonel, Alonso de **5** 725
Carpio, Gaspar de Haro y Guzmán, 7th Marqués del **5** 845
Coats, W. A. **28** 272
Contini Bonacossi, Alessandro, Conte **7** 782
Dennistoun, James **8** 763
Elizabeth Farnese, Queen of Spain (1692-1766) **4** 559
Ensenada, Marqués de **10** 406
Este (i) (family) **21** 771
Farinelli, Carlo Broschi **10** 806
Ferdinand VII, King of Spain (*reg* 1808; 1814-33) **4** 566
Francesco I, 8th Duke of Modena and Reggio (*reg* 1629-58) **10** 526
Frick, Henry Clay **11** 774
Godoy (y Alvárez de Faria), Manuel, Príncipe de la Paz **12** 839
Grosvenor, Robert, 2nd Earl of Grosvenor and 1st Marquess of Westminster **13** 696
Hall, Peter Adolf **14** 80
Hamilton, Alexander, 10th Duke of Hamilton and 7th Duke of Brandon **14** 107
Huntington, Arabella D(uval) **15** 29
Innocent X, Pope (*reg* 1644-55) **23** 899
Iriarte (family) **16** 48
Joseph Bonaparte, King of Naples and Spain (*reg* 1806-8) **4** 304
Jovellanos, Gaspar Melchor de **17** 673
Velázquez, Diego (de Silva y) (1599-1660)
patrons and collectors—cont.
Las Marismas del Guadalquivir, Alejandro María Aguado y Ramírez de Estemoz, Marqués de **18** 811
López Cepero, Manuel **19** 658
Louis-Philippe, King of the French (*reg* 1830-48) **30** 385
Mariette, Pierre-Jean **20** 417
Marquand, Henry G(urdon) **20** 461
Massimo, Camillo (Carlo), Cardinal **20** 588
Medinaceli, Luís de la Cerda Fernández de Córdoba Folch de Cardona y Aragón, 9th Duque de (1660-1711) **21** 35
Medinaceli, Luís de la Soledad Fernández de Córdoba y Figueroa de la Cerda, 13th Duque de **21** 35
National Gallery (London) **5** 283
National Gallery of Scotland, Edinburgh **28** 272
Omazur, Nicolas **23** 437
Oñate y de Villamediana, Conde de **23** 441
Pamphili (family) **23** 898
Pamphili, Benedetto, Cardinal **9** 175
Péreire (family) **24** 396
Philip IV, King of Spain (*reg* 1621-65) **5** 738; **14** 1, 7, 8; **29** 303, 352
Pleydell-Bouverie, Jacob, 2nd Earl of Radnor **25** 39
Rothschild (family) **27** 223
Ruffo, Tommaso, Cardinal, Archbishop of Ferrara **27** 316
Salamanca (y Mayol), José, Marqués de **27** 607
Seymour-Conway, Richard, 4th Marquess of Hertford **20** 875; **28** 527
Standish, Frank Hall **29** 535
Walpole, Robert, 1st Earl of Orford (1676-1745) **32** 824
Weddell, William **33** 20
Wellesley, Arthur, 1st Duke of Wellington **33** 55
Wicar, Jean-Baptiste (-Joseph) **33** 154
Yusupov, Nikolay (Borisovich), Prince (1751- 1831) **33** 579
pupils **1** 621; **20** 899
reproductive prints by others **6** 124; **12** 28; **13** 241, 244; **19** 868; **23** 410; **25** 221; **32** 557
teachers **14** 469; **23** 704
Velázquez, Eugenio Padilla Lucas *see* LUCAS VELÁZQUEZ, EUGENIO PADILLA
Velázquez, González *see* GONZÁLEZ VELÁZQUEZ
Velázquez, Héctor **31** 186*
Velázquez, Juan **10** 903
Velázquez, Miguel **8** 16
Velázquez, Ricardo **28** 513
Velázquez Bosco, Ricardo **16** 550; **20** 71; **29** 272; **32** 125*
Velázquez de Medrano, José **29** 335
Velc *see* VULCI
Velcha (family) **10** 623
Velde (ii), Adriaen van de **32** 141, 144–6*
attributions **14** 15
collaboration **14** 504, 601; **22** 208, 843; **27** 329; **29** 495; **33** 178
copies **21** 170
patrons and collectors **9** 457; **10** 864; **11** 32; **12** 620; **14** 163; **32** 85
pupils **3** 775
Velde (ii), Adriaen van de—cont.
reproductive prints by others **6** 547; **12** 515; **25** *50*
works **14** *601*; **32** *145*
Velde (i), Anthonie van de (1617-72) **32** 137
Velde (i), Anthonie van de (*b c.* 1557) **32** 137
Velde, Bram van **11** 551; **22** 852
dealers **20** 75
groups and movements **24** 144
works **19** 491
Velde (ii), Cornelis van de **32** 141, 144
Velde (i), Esaias van de, the elder (1587-1630) **2** 614; **14** 41; **22** 844; **32** 137–40*
collaboration **3** 352
groups and movements **13** 895
patrons and collectors **5** 679; **23** 465
pupils **13** 255
reproductive prints by others **28** 79; **32** 140, 621
teachers **22** 840
works **10** 553; **11** *460*; **18** 710; **25** 606, *606*; **31** 246; **32** *137*, *138*; **33** 358
Velde (i), Esaias van de, the younger (*b* 1615) **32** 137
Velde, Frans van de **7** 662
Velde, Geer van **22** 852; **32** 136–7*
Velde (i), Hans van de **32** 137
Velde, Henry Van de *see* VAN DE VELDE, HENRY
Velde, Jacob van de **22** 717
Velde (i), Jan van de, I (1568-1623) **32** 137
Velde (i), Jan van de, II (*b c.* 1593-1641) **10** 391; **13** 895; **32** 137, 140*
pupils **13** 222
reproductive prints by others **1** 121; **32** 621
works **5** 324; **10** 553; **13** *893*, 896; **25** 606; **32** *140*, 588
illustrated **11** 794
Velde (i), Jan van de, III (1610-86) **2** 239
Velde (i), Jan van de, IV (1619/20-62) **32** 137
Velde, Joris van de **16** 71
Velde (ii), Willem van de, I (1611-93) **32** 141–4*
assistants **9** 314
collaboration **32** 144
patrons and collectors **5** 679; **32** 143
works **3** 389; **20** 424; **22** 843; **28** 612; **32** *141*
Velde (ii), Willem van de, II (1633-1707) **3** 389; **32** 141, 142–4*
collaboration **9** 719
patrons and collectors **3** 395; **9** 327; **14** 163; **19** 624; **20** 141; **28** 285; **30** 890; **32** 143
personal collection **9** 327
reproductive prints by others **25** 622
teachers **32** 673
works **3** *388*, 389; **20** 424, *425*; **22** 843; **28** 612; **32** *142*, *143*
Velde (ii), Willem van de, III (1667-1708) **32** 141, 144
Veldeke, Heinrich von *see* HEINRICH VON VELDEKE
Velden, Petrus van der **7** 210; **23** 59; **32** 146*
Veldener, Jan **3** 555; **4** 146; **6** 120
Veldhausen, Hans **11** 852
Veldhoen, Aad **22** 854
Veldhuis, Hermanus **20** 275
Veldten, Yuri **27** 402
Vele, Maestro delle *see* ASSISI VAULT, MASTER OF THE
Velehrad Abbey **4** 782; **8** 376
Veleia
basilica **3** 328
Veleia—cont.
baths **3** 375
coins **13** 586, 587
forum **11** 327
urban planning **27** 3
Velen, Ladislav **8** 395
Velenje **28** 860
Veles *see* TITOV VELES
Velesovo Church **28** *858*, 859, 861
Vélez, José Miguel **32** 146*
Vélez, Pedro Fajardo y Chacón, 1st Marqués de los **32** 101, 146
Vélez Blanco Castle **29** *259*, 265; **32** 146–7*
Vélez de Guevara y Tassis, Iñigo *see* OÑATE Y DE VILLAMEDIANA, Conde de
Vel'flin, Genrikh **27** 444
Velgamvehera Image-house **29** 449
Velho, Bartolomeu **32** 147*
Velho, Tomé **32** 147–8*
Velia, Porta Rosa **20** 572
Veli Can **16** 349, 590; **28** 812; **32** 148*
Velicescu, Ana **26** 719
Veličković, Vladimir **28** 451; **32** 148*
Velika Hoca **25** 339
St John **25** 343
St Nicholas **25** 343
Velikanov, Aleksandr (*fl* 1979) **27** 381
Velikanov, A. P. (1900-56) **27** 285
Velike Žablje Mansion **28** 859
Veliki Preslav *see* PRESLAV
Velikiye Sorochintsy *see* VELYKO SOROCHINTSI
Veliko Gradište **28** 439
Veliko Turnovo **5** *144*, 147, 148, 150; **9** *511*; **32** 149*
ecclesiastical buildings **9** 551
Church of the Forty Martyrs **5** 150
Church of the Virgin **5** 154
Forty Martyrs Monastery **5** 147, 150, 162
Great Lavra Monastery **5** 147
St Dimiter **5** 147, 150
SS Peter and Paul **5** 147; **25** 343
St Petka **5** 154, 155
SS Konstantin and Elena **5** 148
Hadji Nikoli Inn **5** 148, *148*
houses **5** 148
icons **25** 339
Library-Museum **5** 150, 162
manuscripts **5** 152, 153, 162
metalwork **5** 160
Museum **5** 163
Sarafkina House **5** 156
sculpture **5** 156
wall paintings **32** 148–9*
Velikovsky, B. M. **3** 685; **22** 174
works **22** *174*
Veliky Ustyug **27** *363*, 389, 426; **32** 149–50*
City Museum of Local Lore **32** 150
Gledensky Monastery of the Trinity **32** *149*
metalwork **27** 420, 422, 423, 424
niello **32** 149–50
silver **27** *420*, 422
Velingrad **5** 158
Velis, Carlos **10** 154
Velislav Bible *see under* BIBLES → individual manuscripts
Veljusa Church **7** 256
Vel'ká Lomnica Church **14** 898; **28** 851
Velké Losiny Castle **8** 395
Velké Meziříčí **8** 382
Velké Uherce
Castle **8** 379
palace **14** 889
Vella Lavella **29** 49
canoes **23** *726*
Vellano, Alberico da **2** 125

Vellay, Lucien *see* PISSARRO, LUCIEN
Vellefaux, Claude 4 548
Velleia *see* VELEIA
Vellert, Dirk (Jacobsz.) 2 195, 206; 3 555, 556; 10 386; 29 504; 32 150–53*; 33 355
groups and movements 19 501
works 5 515; 13 185; 27 256, 257, 258; 29 504; 32 *151*, *152*
Velletri 2 695
Museo Borgia 4 412
Palazzo Ginnetti 19 *634*
Velli, Jean-Louis de 20 147
Vellore 15 *294*; 32 153*
fort 32 153
fortifications 21 590
Jalakanteshvara Temple 15 335, *335*; 32 153
maṇḍapa 32 153
vellum 24 106, 107; 30 6; 32 153*
see also PARCHMENT; SKINS → types → calfskin
vellum paper *see under* PAPER → types
Velmans, Tanya 5 164
Velo, Giacomo 22 387
palazzi 22 *388*
Velonis, Anthony 28 299, 465
velours d'Utrecht see VELVET → types → mock-velvet
Veloz, Mateo, Fray 32 168
Velpen, Roelof van 20 663
Vel Saties 10 623, 636
Velschen, Anna von 30 149
Velserbeek 12 132
Velten, Georg Friderick *see* FEL'TEN, YURY (MATVEYEVICH)
Velthuysen, Diderick van 14 295
Veltoni, Giovanni
works 22 *23*
Veltroni, Stefano 12 527
Veltrusy 8 379
Turkish kiosk 18 73
Velturno Castle 3 56
Veluće Monastery Church 28 442
velvet 28 715; 30 553*
historical and regional traditions
Austria 2 825
Belgium 3 582
Catalonia 29 *313*
Central Asia, Western 6 250
China 7 *50*, *53*, 58
England 10 *290*, 353; 29 *8*
France 7 442
Germany 12 464
Gothic 13 194
Hungary 10 II1; 15 *11*, 12
Indian subcontinent 15 *678*, 716
Iran 16 449
Islamic 16 430, 446, 449; 23 *560*
Italy 16 *753*, 753
Japan 17 315
Ottoman 16 446; 23 *560*
Peru 24 *512*
Spain 29 *349*
Turkey 16 430, 446
types
mock velvet 22 899
uses
armour 7 58
beds 3 483
chairs 3 582
clocks 7 442
desks 29 *313*
dresses 10 II1; 15 *11*
embroidery 6 250; 10 181, 353; 13 194; 15 *11*, 12; 29 *349*
hats 24 *512*
scabbards 15 *678*
settees 29 *8*
stencilling 29 628
tents 15 716; 30 470
upholstery 10 *290*
Velvet Breughel *see* BREUGHEL, JAN, I
velveteen 8 35; 30 553
Velyko Sorochintsi, Church of the Transfiguration 31 559
Velyn, Phillipus 31 856, 857
Velzna *see* ORVIETO → Volsinii Veteres
Venado Beach 29 *136*; 32 153–4*
Vēṇāḍu *see* TRAVANCORE
Venale *see* MONGARDINI, PIETRO
Venant, François 18 227; 25 556, 557
Venantius 25 104
Venantius Fortunatus (530-610) 4 345; 5 779
Venanzio, Giuseppe 28 387
Venaria Reale 17 708; 28 11–12*, *12*
riding house 26 363
stables 29 485
urban planning 6 19
Venasa *see* AVANOS
Venasque
Baptistery 21 163; 26 603
Notre-Dame de Vic
sarcophagus of Bishop Agilbert 21 164
Venatorius, Thomas 9 440
Vence, Chapelle du Rosaire 6 460–61; 11 551, 659; 20 831; 29 508, *509*, 513
stained glass 9 112; 26 140
Vence, Claude-Alexandre de Villeneuve, Comte de 6 527, 547; 7 194; 18 692; 24 772
Venda 1 257; 29 *103*; 32 154–5*
architecture 1 414; 32 154*
beadwork 1 419
bowls 32 *154*, 154–5
doors 32 154
drums (musical instruments) 32 154
mortars (vessels) 1 417
pots 1 418
ritual objects 1 257
sculpture 1 415, 416, 418; 32 155
staffs 1 417
walls 1 414
wood 32 *154*
wood-carvings 1 414, 416; 29 104; 32 154–5
xylophones 32 154
Venda, Osvald Josef 8 385
Vendel 14 412
church 16 790
gate-house 4 781
ship burial 30 83
wall paintings 30 76
Vendelbo Løvenørn, Poul 10 109
Vendelbosch, Carl 23 69
Vendetti, Angelo 29 337
Vendetti, Antonio 29 304, 337, 341, 342
Vendetti, Fabio 29 337
Vendeuvre, Château 11 726
Vendôme, La Trinité 13 179; 26 649
wall paintings 26 *650*
Vendôme, Louis-Joseph, Duc de 8 794, 812
Vendôme, Mathieu de, Abbot of Saint-Denis *see* MATHIEU DE VENDÔME, Abbot of Saint-Denis
Vendôme, Philippe de 8 812; 22 35; 25 895
Vendramin, Andrea 6 76; 22 904; 26 283, 284; 32 155*
Vendramin, Gabriele 32 155–6*
collections 5 535; 16 767; 32 193
drawings 3 651
paintings 12 670, 676; 16 835
prints 25 630
Vendramin, Luca 32 156
Vendramini, Giovanni 32 156*, 198
veneers 32 156*; 33 328
historical and regional traditions
Belgium 3 *583*
Egypt, ancient 9 822; 10 60; 30 775
England 10 281
France 11 588, *588*, 589, 596, *602*; 20 468
Germany 12 421, *421*, 424, *425*, 426; 20 467
Islamic 16 499
Netherlands, the 8 271; 22 *872*, *873*, *874*; 33 IV2
Ottoman 16 499
Rome, ancient 26 875
Scotland 9 727
South Africa 29 115
Switzerland 30 *142*
United States of America 20 468
materials
amber 1 762
birch 12 426
brass 31 195
cherry-wood 11 596; 12 426
ebony 3 *583*; 9 687; 11 596
ivory 10 60; 16 797, 799
king-wood 11 596
mahogany 12 *426*
maple 12 426
marble 26 875
olive-wood 11 596
pear-wood 12 426
rose-wood 11 596
tortoiseshell 12 424, *425*; 16 499; 31 195
tulip-wood 11 596
uses
boullework 20 467
cabinets (ii) (furniture) 11 *588*, 589
cupboards 8 271; 12 *421*; 30 *142*
furniture 11 588, 596, 851; 12 421; 33 332
marquetry 20 465, 466, 467, 468
supports 24 3
tables 11 *602*
thrones 30 775
woodwork 16 499
Venegas, Francisco 19 464; 32 156–7*
collaboration 25 296; 26 253; 30 416
works 32 *157*
Venegas, Miguel 4 701
Venejan 26 603
Veneman, S. L. 28 595
Venenti, Giulio Cesare 5 280
Veneroni, Giannantonio 29 832; 32 157–8*
Venetian carpets *see under* CARPETS → types
Venetian colour *see under* PIGMENTS → types
Venetian Empire 8 155–7; 32 *158*, 158–60*
architecture 8 156; 21 550; 32 159
churches 8 156–7
fortifications 21 550; 32 159, *159*
fortresses 8 156
glass 16 521
icons 8 157, *157*; 32 159
painting 8 156–7; 32 159–60
sculpture 32 160
trade
glass 16 221, 257, 522
lace 11 649
mirrors 21 718
silk 28 716
wood 16 487
Venetian medallist of 1550 13 658
Venetian red *see under* PIGMENTS → types
Venetian Sketchbook *see under* SKETCHBOOKS → individual manuscripts
Venetian stoves *see* STOVES → types → Venetian
Veneto, Bartolomeo *see* BARTOLOMEO VENETO
Veneto, Marco *see* MARCO VENETO
Veneto-Saracenic 32 160–62*
metalwork 32 *161*
Venetsianov, Aleksey (Gavrilovich) 27 389, 442; 32 162–4*
exhibitions 32 724
patrons and collectors 31 312
pupils 27 389; 29 82; 33 621
works 27 579; 32 *163*
Venetus, Sebastianus *see* SEBASTIANO DEL PIOMBO
Veneur, Jacques le, Comte de Carrouges *see* CARROUGES, JACQUES LE VENEUR, Comte de
Venezia *see* VENICE
Venezia, Antonio di Francesco da *see* ANTONIO VENEZIANO
Venezia, Bernardo da *see* BERNARDO DA VENEZIA
Venezia, Francesco 16 651
Venezia, Marco di Martino da *see* MARCO DI MARTINO DA VENEZIA
Venezia, Martino da *see* MARTINO DA VENEZIA
Venezia, Paolino da *see* PAOLINO DA VENEZIA
Venezia, Paolo da *see* PAOLO VENEZIANO
Veneziano, Agostino *see* MUSI, AGOSTINO DEI
Veneziano, Antonio *see* ANTONIO VENEZIANO
Veneziano, Baptista *see* FRANCO, (GIOVANNI) BATTISTA
Veneziano, Bonifazio *see* PITATI, BONIFAZIO DE'
Veneziano, Carlo *see* SARACENI, CARLO
Veneziano, Domenico (*fl* 1438-61) *see* DOMENICO VENEZIANO
Veneziano, Jacometto *see* JACOMETTO VENEZIANO
Veneziano, Lorenzo *see* LORENZO VENEZIANO
Veneziano, Paolo *see* PAOLO VENEZIANO
Veneziano, Sebastiano *see* SEBASTIANO DEL PIOMBO
Veneziano, Stefano *see* STEFANO VENEZIANO
Venezuela 29 125, 128; 32 164–81*, *165*
aluminium 32 171, *171*
apprentices 32 172, 180
arches 32 168
architecture 32 166, 167–72*
auctions 32 179
cathedrals 32 *168*
ceramics 32 166
churches 5 *692*; 32 167–8
collections 32 175, 178–80*
columns 32 168
cotton 32 177, 178
craftsmen and artists 32 172–3, 180
cuatros 32 *166*
dance 32 167
dealing 32 178–9*
drawings 32 172–6*
education (art) 32 172, 180*
festivals 32 167
fortifications 32 168–9
galleries (iv) (art) 32 179
glass 32 171, *171*
gold 32 176–7*
government buildings 32 *169*
hair 32 177
hammocks 32 166
houses 32 166, 169
knitting 18 158
libraries 32 180–81*
linen 32 178
lithography 32 173
markets 32 169
marks 32 177
museums 32 179–80*
Venezuela—cont.
musical instruments 32 *166*, 167
painting 32 172–6*, *175*
battle 32 178
history 32 *174*
landscape 32 175
religious 32 *173*
patios 32 169
patronage 32 165, 178–9*
photoarchives 32 180–81*
plastics 32 171, *171*
portraits 32 178
rugs 32 177, *177*
sculpture 32 172–6*
silver 32 176–7*
textiles 32 166, 177–8*
theatres 32 *171*
trade 32 170, 180
universities 32 *567*
workshops 32 172
Venge Abbey Church 8 721; 26 593
Vengesai, M.C.R 33 678
Venhuizen Church 22 821
Venice 5 765; 9 *510*; 13 298; 16 *616*, *618*; 31 *248*; 32 *158*, 181–229*, *181*
academies 1 105; 21 759
Accademia di Belle Arti
collections 6 151; 16 773; 32 196
directors 11 722; 28 392
drawings 26 323
Galleria dell'Accademia 4 471; 22 357; 32 196, 229
paintings 31 33
see also ecclesiastical buildings → S Maria della Carità
Accademia di Pittura e Scultura 7 881; 10 819; 11 287
archives 32 204
Archivio di Stato 2 371
Archivio Storico dell'Arti Contemporanee della Biennale di Venezia 2 371
library 16 777
Arsenale 2 501; 5 532; 32 183, *183*
Great Gateway 16 631
art forms and materials
altarpieces 9 4
arches 2 298
architecture 16 630
barges 3 231–2
beads 3 441; 32 202
book illustrations 32 198–9
book jackets 24 50
books 4 358; 17 565; 24 707; 32 198–9
brass 16 743, *744*
brick 4 774
candlesticks 16 *541*
cassoni 6 7
centrepieces 32 203–4
ceramics 32 199–200*
chandeliers 32 204
coats of arms 14 410
coins 7 535, 536, 537; 14 419
crowns 26 80
embroidery 10 181; 16 759, 760
enamel 13 170; 32 214
engravings 10 383; 32 199
frames 11 382, *383*, *385*, *386*, 387, 389, *389*, *391*, 395, *395*
furniture 5 *54*, 192; 12 789; 16 *725*, 728, 729
glass 12 782, 786, 787, 788, 790; 16 740; 24 791; 32 200–205*, *201*, *202*, *203*, *205*
see also under MURANO
glazes 12 803
globes 12 *814*
gold 9 657; 16 741, 743
hardstones 16 746
icons 9 622; 19 787; 25 334
incunabula 32 198
ivory-carvings 9 652
jewellery 16 751; 17 519
ketubbot 18 *2*, 3

Venice
art forms and materials—cont.
lace **16** 754; **18** 589, 590, 591, 593; **32** 205–6*
Baroque **16** *754*
needle **32** 205–6
lacquer **18** 614
linen **16** *754*
maiolica **16** 735
manuscripts **7** *188*, 903; **31** 49; **32** 197–8*
maps **20** 363
medals **20** 918, 919
metalwork **13** 163; **16** 741; **32** 160
miniatures (manuscript illumination) **25** *46*
mirror frames **21** 721
mirrors **12** 789; **16** 726; **21** 719, 720; **32** 202, 204
mosaics **22** 157, 158, 163
oliphants **23** 401, *401*; **26** 698
painting **5** 656, 657; **18** 707–8; **22** 413; **32** 110–12, 190–92*, 194–5*
Mannerism **16** 667*
Renaissance **16** 662, 665*
Rococo **16** 675–6
15th cent. **18** 704, 705; **20** 51; **23** 376
16th cent. **9** 7; **16** 661; **18** 705; **24** 3
17th cent. **29** 669
18th cent. **32** *112*
19th cent. **32** *197*
paper **24** 45
pearls **17** 522
pewter **16** 743
pietre dure **16** 747
pilgrim flasks **32** *201*
pitchers **32** *202*
porcelain **6** 924; **32** 200
pottery **6** 333
maiolica **16** 732, 734
printing **16** 360; **22** *370*; **32** 198–9
prints **25** 601, 625
rock crystal **14** 170, 171; **16** 744, 745; **26** 485, 486
sculpture **16** 583, 688, 692–3*, 697*, 702–3*; **30** 497–8*; **32** 192–3*, 195*, 527
silk **13** 197; **16** 714, 752, 753; **28** 716
sprinklers **32** *203*
staircases **29** 523
statuettes **29** 569–70
stucco **4** 776; **29** 831
tapestries **16** 756, *756*, 757, 758; **30** 314; **32** 205*
terracotta **30** 497–8*
textiles **32** 205*
title-pages **10** 389
tombs **5** 302
tortoiseshell **16** 748
vases **32** *205*
woodcuts **32** *181*, 198–9; **33** 347, 350, 355
wrought iron **16** 744
art history **7** 305
art market **2** 558; **32** 190
Ateneo Veneto *see* scuole → Scuola di S Fantin
Biblioteca Nazionale Marciana *see* Libreria Marciana
Biennale **24** 708; **28** 35; **32** 197
archives *see* archives → Archivio Storico dell' Arti Contemporanee della Biennale di Venezia
Biennale, 1986
French Pavilion **10** *416*
bridges **32** *186*
Rialto Bridge **4** 801; **25** 216; **32** *186*
Campiello Argheran **9** 598
carnivals **5** 787
collections **27** 521

Venice—cont.
Collezione Vittorio Cini **5** 594; **7** 782
craftsmen and artists **32** 189–90
Danieli Hotel **14** 786
ecclesiastical buildings
Armenian Monastery
collections **2** 443
Treasury **2** 444
Church of the Angelo Raffaele
paintings **13** *742*
Frari *see* S Maria Gloriosa dei Frari
I Gesuati *see* S Maria del Rosario
Madonna dell'Orto **7** *320*, 320–21; **22** 374; **23** 502; **32** 184
La Pietà **14** 785
Il Redentore **2** 336; **5** 532, 690; **16** 635; **23** 869, *869*; **32** 187
altarpieces **1** 712
S Bartolommeo **9** 434
S Caterina **1** 518
S Chiara
altarpiece **24** 32, *32*
S Clemente al Isola **16** 702
S Francesco della Vigna **16** 635, *636*; **19** 534, *534*; **22** 378; **23** 867
Morsini chapel **10** 771
paintings **11** *721*
sculpture **10** 744
S Giacomo **32** 184
S Giobbe **19** 553
altarpiece **3** 663, *663*; **26** 186
S Giorgio dei Greci **25** 333; **32** 160
S Giorgio Maggiore *see under* ISOLA S GIORGIO
S Giovanni Crisostomo **7** 517; **16** 631
SS Giovanni e Paolo **4** 774; **9** 111; **13** 64; **32** 184, 215–16*
altarpieces **27** 495
Cappella del Rosario **16** 728
frescoes **15** 138
paintings **4** 493; **9** 110; **21** 846
portal **32** *215*
refectory **32** *352*
tomb of Doge Andrea Vendramin **16** 693
tomb of Doge Marco Cornaro **13** 95
tomb of Doge Pietro Mocenigo **16** 693; **19** 553, 555, *555*, 557; **31** *125*, 126
S Giuliano **32** 648–9
altar **32** *649*
Altar of the Deposition **16** 697
S Ilario Abbey **9** 569
S Marco **4** 774; **7** 257, 302; **8** 499; **9** 523, 588; **16** 603, 625; **26** 579; **32** 160, 182, *185*, 189, 206–7*, *206*
altar **16** 693
arches **2** 295; **23** 368
Baptistery **22** 163
campanile **4** 775; **32** *185*
capitals **9** 592
Central Portal **32** *208*
chalices **6** 398
chapel of Cardinal Zen **16** 693; **27** 888
chapel of S Isidore **22** 163
columns **29** 700
dome **9** 84, 85
doors **9** 157, *157*
glass **28** 805
hardstones **14** 170
horses **4** 851; **6** 9; **7** 382; **10** 440, 743; **12** 626; **27** 28; **32** 160
iconostasis **20** *543*, 544, *544*
icons **9** 623, 625
loggetta **10** 744
Mascoli Altar **20** *728*
Mascoli Chapel **12** 580; **22** 163

Venice
ecclesiastical buildings
S Marco—cont.
mosaics **7** 275; **8** 38; **16** 655; **22** 156, 162, 163, 165; **26** 653, 680; **32** 208–12*, *209*, *210*, *211*
organ shutters **23** 502
Pala d'Oro **1** 4, 708; **9** 588, 662; **10** 193; **16** 741, 750; **32** 189, *213*, 213–14*
plaques **9** 590, 593
pulpits **16** 694
reliefs **9** 597
rock crystal **16** 541, 744; **26** 484, 485, 487
sacristy **16** 694
sarcophagus of Doge Marin Morosini **6** 173
sculpture **9** 596, 598; **10** 743; **13** 95; **16** 692, 697; **26** 622; **27** 46; **32** 207–8*, *208*
silver **16** 741
tapestries **16** 757
Tetrarchs **18** 824; **27** 43, *43*
textiles **30** 331
Treasury **9** 657; **16** 553, 765, 770; **19** 886; **32** *212*, 212–13*
Treasury: catalogues **21** 817
Treasury: glass **9** 645, *645*
Treasury: metalwork **9** 657, 660; **13** 163
wall paintings **22** 520; **26** 653
weathervane **33** 8
S Maria Assunta
tomb of Doge Pasquale Cicogna **5** 533
S Maria della Carità **4** 774; **29** 523
campanile **4** 775
see also academies → Accademia di Belle Arti → Galleria dell'Accademia
S Maria del Carmine
reliefs **11** *693*; **26** 137
sculpture **16** 692, 703
S Maria della Fava **23** 472
S Maria Formosa **7** 516–17; **16** 631
S Maria Gloriosa dei Frari **4** 774; **13** 64; **32** 184, 216–17*
altarpiece **1** *710*, 711; **11** 382, *382*; **16** 665
metalwork **8** 412
monument to Paolo Savelli **29** 565
paintings **11** 384; **27** *655*
screen **28** 293
sculpture **16** 691; **32** 647
tie-bars **30** 853
tomb of Doge Francesco Foscari **4** *736*; **13** 95
tomb of Doge Niccolò Tron **16** 693; **26** 439, *439*
S Maria Maddalena **30** 423–4, *424*
S Maria Mater Domini
sculpture **4** *739*
S Maria dei Miracoli **9** 86; **19** 553–4, *554*; **23** 502; **25** 767
S Maria dell'Orto **27** 148–9
S Maria del Rosario **16** 646
frescoes **9** *109*, 110
paintings **24** *705*
S Maria della Salute **7** 258; **16** 641, *641*, 702; **19** 628, *628*; **32** 188, *195*, 217*
altar **7** 900–901
paintings **16** 666
S Maria degli Scalzi **5** 778
S Maria dei Servi **32** 216
S Maria Zobenigo **32** *159*
S Marina **32** 216
S Marziale **26** 320–21
S Michele in Isola **7** 515–16, *516*; **16** 631; **32** 185
screen **28** 293
S Moisè **26** 478

Venice
ecclesiastical buildings—cont.
S Nicolò dei Mendicoli **32** 184
S Nicolò da Tolentino **16** 641, 676; **25** 266; **27** 352
S Pantalon
paintings **24** 30; **32** *353*
S Rocco **32** 227
S Salvador **19** 558; **29** 370
tomb of Caterina Cornaro, Queen of Cyprus **32** 160
S Sebastiano **28** 36; **30** 887; **32** 349
Cappella dell'Annunziata **16** 712
organ shutters **22** 374; **23** *501*, 502
paintings **16** 666
S Simeone Grande **13** 95; **20** 398
SS Simeone e Giuda **16** 641; **25** 266
S Stae
frescoes **30** *855*
paintings **24** *704*
S Stefano **16** 747; **32** 184
tomb of Francesco Morosini **32** 160
S Todaro *see* S Marco
S Trovaso **31** 10, *11*
S Zaccaria **12** 31; **16** 631, *631*
altarpieces **1** 711; **3** 665; **11** 383; **26** 186; **27** 495
chapel of S Tarasio **32** 653
S Zanipolo *see* SS Giovanni e Paolo
exhibitions **16** 766
façade decoration **10** 737
fondachi **32** 184
Fondaco dei Tedeschi **10** 737, 738; **16** 751; **26** 188; **29** 369–70, *370*
frescoes **12** 669
Fondaco dei Turchi **4** 776; **32** 184
foundations
Fondazione Giorgio Cini **7** 331; **32** 214
Fondazione Querini-Stampalia **28** 35
Peggy Guggenheim Foundation **13** 801; **16** 775
Ghetto **32** 186
guidebooks **4** 454; **13** 809; **27** 774
guilds **13** 822, 824; **32** 189–90, 223
Istituto Orientale *see* palazzi → Palazzo Cappella-Layard
Istituto universitario di architettura library **16** 776
Libreria Marciana **5** 532; **16** 635; **19** 313, 315; **27** 771; **32** 222–3*, 349
collections **3** 876; **7** 775, 776, 895; **15** 744
paintings **11** 721; **19** 330; **23** 750; **27** 149; **28** 82; **29** 84
sculpture **16** 770
see also Zecca
Libreria Sansoviniana **10** 744; **32** 94, 647
Molino Stucky **21** 600
monument to Bartolomeo Colleoni **7** 671–2; **10** 440; **16** 690; **26** 186; **29** 565; **32** 160, *363*
museums
Ca' d'Oro **10** 743; **13** 64, *64*; **23** 809; **26** 37; **32** 184
collections **3** 700
furniture **16** 723
Galleria Franchetti **16** 774
paintings **3** 698; **5** 821; **19** 872; **20** 313; **31** 71
sculpture **13** 95; **16** 692
staircase **29** 521
Ca' Rezzonico **8** 193; **32** *187*
chandeliers **6** 443
collections **7** 895

Venice
museums
Ca' Rezzonico—cont.
frescoes **8** *192*
furniture **23** 541
paintings **16** 676
porcelain **16** 738
sculpture **16** 702
Galleria dell'Accademia *see under* academies → Accademia di Belle Arti
Galleria d'Arte Moderna *see* palazzi → Palazzo Pesaro
Museo Archeologico
collections **7** 776; **13** 657; **16** 770; **27** 46
directors **11** 312
Museo d'Arte Orientale **17** 434
see also palazzi → Palazzo Pesaro
Museo Civico di Storia Naturale di Venezia **16** 776
Museo Correr **7** 894; **16** 775; **28** 35
collections **7** 305, 895*; **13** 745; **25** 18; **33** 697
Diziani collection **9** 48
Museo Fortuny **11** 326; **16** 721
Museo Vittorio Fano **17** 582
Statuario Pubblico **2** 162; **16** 770
Ospedale Civile *see* scuole → Scuola Grande di S Marco
Ospedale degli Incurabili **23** 750
Ospedaletto **14** 785
palazzi **16** 631
Ca' Bollani **2** 388
Ca' Cappello *see* Palazzo Cappello-Layard
Ca' da Mosto **32** 184
Ca' d'Oro *see under* museums
Ca' Foscari **13** 64; **16** 650
Ca' Gussoni **31** 7
Ca' Rezzonico *see under* museums
Casa Nuova **21** 747
Doge's Palace **4** 774, 776; **5** 429; **11** 328; **13** 64, 740; **16** 627, 665, 763; **23** 809; **26** 440; **27** 347; **28** 37; **29** 85; **31** 42, 236; **32** 217–22*, *218*
arches **2** 295
Arco Foscari **16** 692, 693; **32** 219, *219*
Cortile dei Senatori **32** 220
ex-votos **8** 836
frescoes **1** 658; **16** 659
interior decoration **16** 712
Magistrato del Proprio **16** 825
paintings **3** 655, 659; **5** 820; **6** 137; **9** 740; **11** 270; **13** 678; **16** 824; **27** 817; **31** 5, 11, 13, 15, 19, 34, 41; **33** 631
Porta della Carta **5** 176, *176*; **13** 95; **16** 692; **29** 712; **32** 218–19
restoration **30** 519
Sala degli Scarlatti **19** 663
Sala dei Tre Capi **25** 209; **32** 349
Sala del Collegio **5** 532; **13** 678; **32** 220, 352
Sala del Consiglio dei Dieci **3** 350; **25** 209; **32** 107, 108, 222, *348*, 348–9
Sala della Bussola **32** 108, 349
Sala dell'Anticollegio **2** 608; **5** 532; **9** 14; **23** 678; **32** 220
Sala dell'Armamento **7** 862
Sala dell'Atrio Quadrato **31** 10
Sala delle Volte **32** 160
Sala delle Quattro Porte **2** 88; **5** 532; **13** 657; **32** 220, 407
Sala dello Scrutinio **2** 88; **3** 349; **26** 321; **32** 108, 407
Sala dello Scudo **3** 660; **20** 365

Venice
palazzi
Doge's Palace—cont.
Sala del Maggior Consiglio 2 88; 3 350, 655, 659; 7 861, 877; 12 299; 13 747; 14 583; 16 666; 19 35; 23 878; 24 523, 861; 31 9, 15; 32 160, *221*, 222, 352–3; 33 719
Sala del Senato 23 879, *879*; 32 108, 220–22
Scala dei Giganti 26 440; 27 *773*; 29 521; 32 *219*, 219–20
Scala d'Oro 13 658; 16 697; 29 831; 32 *193*, 220, 647
sculpture 2 609; 3 162; 5 176, *430*; 6 89; 10 743, *744*; 13 95; 16 692; 27 274, 637; 32 218–20, 648
Palazzo Albrizzi 24 340; 29 831, *832*; 33 608
Palazzo d'Anna 10 736, 739
Palazzo Badoer 8 851
Palazzo Barbarigo 11 287; 13 740
Palazzo Barbaro 3 202
paintings 24 706
Palazzo dei Camerlenghi 13 *649*; 24 888–9; 31 9
Palazzo del Capitano 27 760
Palazzo Cappello-Layard 18 897
Palazzo Cini 13 741
Palazzo Contarini 3 179; 28 *392*; 32 615
Palazzo Corner (campo S Polo) 27 759
Palazzo Corner Ca' Grande 16 635; 23 810; 32 187
Palazzo Corner-Spinelli 7 517
Palazzo Curtis *see* Palazzo Barbaro
Palazzo Ducale *see* Doge's Palace
Palazzo Duodo 11 287
Palazzo Farsetti 23 809
Palazzo Foscarini 26 500
Palazzo Grassi 16 646
Palazzo Grimani 27 649, 759
interior decoration 13 658; 16 712, *712*
sculpture 13 657
Palazzo Gritti 32 184
Palazzo Labia 15 138; 16 676
Palazzo Lando *see* Palazzo Corner-Spinelli
Palazzo Loredan (12th and 13th cent.) 23 809
Palazzo Loredan (16th cent.) *see* Palazzo Vendramin-Calergi
Palazzo Loredan (17th cent.) *see* Palazzo Cini
Palazzo Manfrin 24 390
Palazzo Merati 29 831
Palazzo Orfei *see* museums → Museo Fortuny
Palazzo Pesaro 5 918, 919; 16 679; 20 503; 23 810; 28 395
sculpture 6 89
see also museums → Museo d' Arte Orientale
Palazzo Pisani 10 743; 16 744
Palazzo Sagredo 11 395; 29 831
Palazzo di S Luca 10 818
Palazzo di S Stefano 24 865
Palazzo Vendramin-Calergi 7 517–18, *518*; 16 631; 23 810; 27 654
Palazzo Widmann 20 902
Palazzo Zinelli 33 697
Palazzo Zorzi 7 517
patronage 32 193*, 195–6*, 223, 224
Piazza S Marco 16 635; 27 771; 31 717; 32 *185*
Loggetta 9 158; 16 635, 693; 27 771, *772*

Venice
Piazza S Marco—cont.
sculpture 26 690
Piazzetta 2 *343*; 26 622; 31 717
Procuratie Nuove 28 31
Procuratie Vecchie 13 649
Rialto market 28 36
scuole 32 223–4*
meeting-houses 32 223, 224, 228, 229
Scuola degli Albanesi 5 821
Scuola dell'Angelo Custode 24 703
Scuola dell'Arte dei Pescivendoli 31 7
Scuola dell'Arte dei Sartori 31 7
Scuola Grande di S Giovanni Evangelista 7 517; 32 223, 224–5*, *225*
paintings 16 659; 24 523
Sala dell'Albergo 32 224–5
Scuola Grande di S Marco 7 517; 19 554; 32 223, 225–6*, *226*
gables 11 876
paintings 3 659; 5 820; 31 7, *8*, *9*, 10
Sala dell'Albergo 32 225–6
Sala Grande 25 889; 32 226
sculpture 32 *226*
staircase 32 225
Scuola Grande di S Maria della Carità 32 223, *228*, 229*
Sala dell'Albergo 32 229
see also academies → Accademia di Belle Arti → Galleria dell'Accademia
Scuola Grande di S Maria dei Carmini 5 778; 32 196
Scuola Grande di S Maria della Misericordia 16 692; 32 223, *227*, 227–8*
see also Scuola Vecchia della Misericordia
Scuola Grande di S Rocco 5 177–8; 28 37, *37*; 32 223, 226–7*
coral 16 750
exhibitions 10 676
gates 9 158
interior decoration 16 712
paintings 16 666; 31 7, 8, 11–13, 15
Sala dell'Albergo 31 10; 32 *227*
Sala Superiore 31 11–13
Sala Terrena 31 *12*, 13
staircase 29 522
Scuola Grande di S Teodoro 32 223, 229*
staircase 32 *229*
Scuola dei Mercanti 31 19
Scuola di S Fantin 23 879
Scuola di S Gerolamo 3 659
Scuola di S Giorgio degli Schiavoni 5 821, 822
Scuola di S Nicolò dei Greci 32 160
Scuola di S Orsola 5 819; 16 659
Scuola Spagnola 17 544
Scuola di S Stefano 5 821
Scuola della Trinità 31 8
Scuola Vecchia della Misericordia 32 228
see also Scuola Grande di S Maria della Misericordia
synagogues 17 546
theatres 30 655
La Fenice 16 646; 28 390, *390*; 30 667
Teatro Moisè 30 667
Teatro del Mondo 5 526
Teatro Novissimo 30 667
Teatro S Benedetto 28 390
Teatro di S Cassiano 30 667
Teatro di S Salvador 30 667
Teatro dei SS Giovanni e Paolo 30 667
Torre dell'Orologio 7 439, 518

Venice—cont.
trade
beads 3 441
paintings 16 767
silk 28 716
travel books 7 916
Zecca 16 635; 27 771
see also libraries → Libreria Marciana
Venice Biennale *see* VENICE → Biennale
Venice & Murano Glass & Mosaic Co. 32 204
Venice turpentine 18 610, 611; 26 243; 32 1
japanning 18 611
pigments 24 793
seals 33 5
varnishes 32 1
waxes 33 2, 5
Venier (family) 5 54, 55
furniture 5 *54*
Venier, Francesco 16 835; 19 534
Venier, Leonardo 5 626
Venier, Pietro 16 728
Venieri, Anton Giacomo, Cardinal 20 112
Venini, Paolo 6 443; 8 803; 32 204
works 32 *205*
Venini S.p.A. 8 803; 28 35; 32 500
works 32 *205*
Venius, Otto van *see* VEEN, OTTO VAN
Venkatapa, V. 22 404
Venlo, St Martinus 13 61
Venne, Adriaen (Pietersz.) van de 14 41; 32 230–32*
attributions 32 723
patrons and collectors 23 468; 29 799
reproductive prints by others 1 121; 8 665; 10 *175*; 17 599
works 1 659; 6 88; 22 839, 844; 32 *230*, *231*
Venne, Huybrecht van de 32 232
Venne, Jan van de 32 231
Venne, Pieter van de 32 232
Vennekool, Steven 22 826; 32 232*
Vennes, Jean 12 276; 30 126
Venngarn 30 117, 118; 31 824
Venoaks, Henry A. 30 16
Venosa, SS Trinità Abbey 16 626; 26 580
Venray, St Petruskerk 22 821
Vent, Hans 32 232*; 33 672
Venta, La *see* LA VENTA
Ventana Cave 22 *544*; 32 233*
Ventanas, Las *see* PEÑOL DE JUCHIPILA
Ventayol, Juan 10 509
Ventenat, Etienne-Pierre 4 303; 26 73
Ventia *see* VEII
Venticinque della Campagna Romana 11 12; 27 852
Ventimiglia (family) 23 841
Ventimiglia, Carlo Maria 23 265
Vento, José 13 725
Ventre, André 1 489; 24 129; 31 224
Ventspils 18 *847*
Castle 18 848
church 18 848
Ventura, Agnolo di *see* AGNOLO DI VENTURA
Ventura, Giovanni 11 297
Ventura, Lattanzio 1 637; 19 687
Ventura di Andrea Vitoni *see* VITONI, VENTURA DI ANDREA
Ventura di Moro 11 698; 20 787
Ventura di ser Giuliano Turapilli 28 683
Venturi, Adolfo 4 493; 12 483; 24 423, 448; 30 731; 32 233*
exhibitions 16 774
pupils 12 718; 19 637; 27 635; 31 71
works 16 782

Venturi, Adolfo—cont.
writings 8 146
Venturi, Giovanni Battista 1 17; 19 197
Venturi, Lionello 2 366; 24 449; 26 777; 31 446; 32 234*
groups and movements 11 802; 13 727
pupils 2 391
works 2 517, 518; 16 782; 29 876
Venturi, Rauch & Scott Brown 15 887; 23 490; 31 633; 32 234–6*
staff 11 849
works 3 52; 9 19; 10 242, 371; 14 803; 19 286, 591; 24 598; 28 328, *328*; 32 *235*
Venturi, Robert 16 101; 25 172; 30 391; 32 234
architecture 10 242; 24 598; 25 173; 31 598
competitions 7 670; 16 243
furniture 24 602; 31 633
writings 25 359; 31 598, 735
Venturi, Scott Brown Associates *see* VENTURI, RAUCH & SCOTT BROWN
Venturi, Sergio 3 744
Venturini, Gaspare 28 38
Venturini, Giovanni Francesco 32 236*
Venturino Mercanti da Milano 12 733
Venturi & Scott Brown *see* VENTURI, RAUCH & SCOTT BROWN
Venturoli, Angelo 4 273; 10 446; 17 442
veṇukośa 15 245*
Venur 29 438
Venus and Mercury school *see* VENUSMERC
Venus Colonna *see* APHRODITE EUPLOIA
Venus de' Medici 2 *169*; 23 291; 31 50; 32 236*
acquisition 2 168; 21 23; 23 352
display 13 303; 21 29
Venus de Milo 13 461, 466, *466*, 470, 605; 32 236–7*
acquisition 11 302
discovery 2 171; 21 95
Venus Marine Clock 11 626
Venusmerc 31 74
venus mercenaria shells *see under* SHELLS → types
Venus of Arles 2 418; 4 551
Venus of Cyrene 8 368; 13 470; 31 49
Venus of Knidos 27 46
Venus of the Casa Palmieri-Bolognini 21 27
venustas 2 362; 26 924
Venusti, Marcello 12 558; 26 770; 32 237*
Venuti, Domenico 22 482
Venuti, Ridolfino 3 645; 26 849; 32 237*
Vepsian 27 433
Vera, André 2 520
Vera, Juan de 27 331
Vera, Luis Arías *see* ARÍAS VERA, LUIS
Vera, Ofelia Echagüe *see* ECHAGÜE VERA, OFELIA
Véra, Paul 3 462
Veracini, Agostino 31 268
Veracruz 21 265; 31 721
masks 21 *251*
Museo Regional 21 396
pottery 21 *238*
sculpture 21 185, 219
seals 21 *258*
stele 21 219; 29 620
stone-carvings 5 761
Veragua (family) 21 81
Veraguas culture 7 505; 23 *902*; 32 238–9*
gold 32 238

Veraguas culture—cont.
metalwork 32 238
metates 32 238–9, *239*
pottery 32 238
sculpture 32 238–9
stone 32 238–9, *239*
tombs 31 118
trade
metates 32 239
pottery 32 238
Veralli, Cardinal 26 830
Veramendi, Francisco de 32 239
Veramendi, Juan Miguel de 4 256; 24 501; 29 893; 32 239*
verandahs 1 308; 2 737; 5 173; 13 383; 29 105; 32 239–40*, *240*
Veranneman, E. 3 579, 587
Verano, Francisco 24 620
Verard, Antoine 4 358; 20 699; 23 680
Veraval 15 347
congregational mosque 15 347
Verazzi, Baldassare 19 656
Verband der Museen der Schweiz 30 155
Verband Deutscher Kunsthistoriker 2 533
Verbeeck, Cornelis 32 734
Verbeeck, Pieter Cornelisz. 3 766
Verbeek, Salomon 8 530
Verberchem *see* WITSEN, WILLEM (ARNOLD)
Verberckt, Jacques 3 571; 32 240–41*, 694
patrons and collectors 4 554; 32 370, 374
pupils 19 233; 32 241
works 11 406; 14 791
Verberckt, Jan Baptist, I (1735-1819) 3 600; 32 240, 241*
Verberckt, Jan Baptist, II (1774-1838) 32 240, 241
Verberckt, (Jos) Michiel 32 240, 241*
Verbiest, Ferdinand 7 120
Verbilki, Gardner Porcelain Factory 22 180
Verbitsky, A. M. 18 36
Verboeckhoven, Barthélemy 32 241
Verboeckhoven, Eugène (-Joseph) 32 241*
collaboration 17 642
pupils 32 380
teachers 23 439
works 2 106; 3 562
Verboeckhoven, Louis 32 242
Verboeckhoven, Louis-Charles 32 241–2*
Verboom, Adriaen (Hendricksz.) 3 766; 27 329
Verbruggen (family) 11 227
Verbruggen, Gaspar 29 668
Verbrugghen, Henricus-Franciscus 32 242*
collaboration 17 914; 33 197
works 1 699; 3 570; 7 303; 8 699; 14 24; 25 727, *727*
Verbrugghen, Peeter (i) (1615-86) 3 570; 25 809; 32 242*
assistants 7 500
collaboration 25 727
pupils 3 894; 9 760; 28 63; 32 242
teachers 25 812
works 5 733; 7 703
Verbrugghen, Peeter (ii) (1648-91) 3 570; 7 500; 32 242*
Verburch, Jan 4 846
Verbuys, Arold 4 374
Vercammen, Wout 23 906
Vercelli
Cathedral of S Eusebio 1 624; 26 690
Museo Civico Borgogna 16 774
S Andrea 13 51; 16 625; 26 620
S Cristoforo
frescoes 11 *13*
S Marco 14 81
Vercoutter, Jean 10 81

Vercruysse, Jan 3 574
Verda, Egidio della 32 147
Verda, Pedro 29 341
Verda, Vinzenz de 13 329
verdaccio see under PIGMENTS → types
verde antico see under MARBLE → types
Verdé-Delisle Frères 11 651
Verdelay, Guglielmo di see GUGLIELMO DI VERDELAY
Verdelli (family) 28 677
Verden, St Andrew 4 693
Verden an der Aller Cathedral 13 49; 14 81
Verdenberg, Ferdinand von, Graf 5 771; 25 257
verdetto della Magna see MALACHITE
Verdezotti, Zuan Maria see VERDIZZOTTI, GIOVANNI MARIA
Verdi, Giuseppe 11 283
Verdich & Co. 2 758
Verdier, François 2 708; 18 535; 25 398; 32 242*
Verdier, Louis V. 32 242
verdigris 12 623, 803; 15 852; 24 793
Verdiguier, Jean Michel 1 741
Verdijk, Gerard 14 44
Verdizzotti, Giovanni Maria 32 243*
Verdoel, Adriaen 4 657
Verdugo, José Vega y, Conde de Alba Real see ALBA REAL, JOSÉ VEGA Y VERDUGO, Conde de
Verdun 3 603; 21 577
Verdun, Nicholas of see NICHOLAS OF VERDUN
Verdun, Richard of see RICHARD OF VERDUN
Verdussen, H. 12 885
Verdussen, Jan Peeter 28 18; 29 668; 32 243*
Verdussen, Lenaert Frans 7 832
Verdussen, Peeter 32 243
Vere 6 406
Verecundus 10 875
Vereecken, J.-B. 3 322
Verein Berliner Künstler 3 799, 800; 21 140; 28 342, 343; 32 243–4*
Verein der Berliner Künstlerinnen 33 309
Verein des Vaterländischen Museums für Österreich ob der Enns 2 831
Verein F + F 30 156
Verein für Kunst 32 774
Vereinigte Lausitzer Glaswerke (VLG) 32 757
Vereinigte Werkstätte für Kunst und Handwerk 2 571; 12 416, 427; 22 304
members 23 336; 24 13, 279; 26 374; 31 368
production 24 591; 31 368
Vereinigte Wiener und Gmunder Keramik 2 816, 817; 3 393; 12 821; 19 539; 32 450
Vereinigung Bildender Künstler Österreichs see SECESSION (VIENNA)
Vereinigung der Elf 3 801; 19 112; 28 341; 32 244
Vereinigung Düsseldorfer Künstler 19 94
Vereinigung für Historische Kunst 12 472
Verein Jüngerer Berliner Künstler 3 799; 32 243
Verein zur Förderung des Kunstkandwerks in der Schweiz 14 312
Vereker, John Standish Surtees Prendergast, 6th Viscount Gort 20 217
Vérel 29 628
Verellen, Jan Joseph 14 480
Verelst (family) 10 249
Verelst, Harman 32 244, 245
Verelst, Maria 32 244, 245*
Verelst, Pieter 32 244
Verelst, Simon (Pietersz.) 32 244–5*
patrons and collectors 9 327
pupils 32 245
works 11 228
Verelst, William 32 244, 245*
Verendael, Nicholaes van 11 227
Verenigde Oost-Indische Compagnie (VOC) see DUTCH EAST INDIA COMPANY
Vereniging Rembrandt 1 809; 22 903, 906; 32 708
Vereshchagin, Vasily (Vasil'yevich) 17 776, 867; 27 391; 31 782; 32 245–6*
groups and movements 23 504
works 6 279; 32 *246*
Véret, Jean-Louis 26 192
Veretennikov, Matvei Iakovlevich 27 583
Verevkin, N. N. 24 400
Vereycke, Hans 20 664
Vereysky, Georgy (Semyonovich) 27 396; 32 246–7*
Verfel', Karl F. see WOERFFEL, KARL F.
Verga, Giovanni 32 257
Vergara (family) 29 339
Vergara, Arnao de 32 247
Vergara, Diego de 20 157; 27 330; 29 266
Vergara, Francisco, the elder 31 826; 32 247
Vergara, Ignacio 10 532; 28 389; 31 816; 32 247
Vergara, José 21 815; 29 282, 841; 32 247–8*, *248*
Vergara, Juan de 23 582; 24 107; 32 247
Vergara, Nicolás de (i) (*c.* 1517-74) 32 247*
collaboration 2 23, 868; 29 339
works 13 192; 21 156; 29 339; 31 92
Vergara, Nicolás de (ii) (1540-1606) 32 247*
collaboration 29 339
patrons and collectors 6 44; 14 474
works 10 535; 13 732; 29 267, *268*, 339; 31 92, 180; 32 247
Vergara, Ramón 6 598
Vergara de Flandes, Nicolás de 32 247
Vergé, Jacques see BERGÉ, JACQUES
Verge, John 2 738; 23 53; 30 158; 32 248–9*
Verge, Nicolas 32 248
Vergeaud, Armand 31 425
Vergelli, Tiburzio 9 158; 19 560; 32 249*
Vergennes, Charles Gravier, Marquis de 10 843
Verger de Verville, Jean François Du see DU VERGER DE VERVILLE, JEAN FRANÇOIS
Vergerio, Angelo 10 534
Vergerio, Pietro Paolo 14 866, 867
Vergil, Polydore 15 84
Vergil Augusteus 15 847
Vergina 13 *363*; 19 880; 32 249–50*
couches 13 592
gold 32 250
graves 13 383; 15 53
mosaics 13 560, 564
silver 13 571
summer palace 13 407; 32 249
tombs 13 384; 31 107; 32 249
Prince's Tomb 13 597
Tomb I 13 464
Tomb II see Tomb of Philip II
Vergina
tombs—cont.
Tomb of Persephone 13 544, 548, 551; 31 109
Tomb of Philip II 13 *596*, 597; 15 53; 18 701; 24 604; 31 109
glass 13 594
gold 13 598
metalwork 12 624
wall paintings 13 546, 551
wall paintings 13 375
wall paintings 13 545; 32 250, *250*
Vergne, Louis-Elizabeth de la, Comte de Tressan see TRESSAN, LOUIS-ELIZABETH DE LA VERGNE, Comte de
Vergós, Rafael 14 858
Vergović, Milan 28 453
Vergulde Passer, De 22 272
Verhaecht, Peter 9 489
Verhaecht, Tobias 3 613; 4 915; 7 556; 32 250–51*, 724
collaboration 11 718, 720
patrons and collectors 13 916
pupils 14 23; 27 288
reproductive prints by others 23 908
Verhaegen, Arthur Théodore 3 549; 12 519; 32 251*
collaboration 3 885
teachers 3 548
Verhaegen, L. 3 884
Verhaegen, Pierre-Joseph see VERHAGEN, PIERRE-JOSEPH
Verhaegen, Theodoor 3 571; 31 807; 32 251*
pupils 31 807
teachers 4 220; 17 915
works 7 703, *703*
Verhaeren, Emile (Adolphe Gustave) 3 563; 32 251–2*
groups and movements 1 21
illustrated works 26 97; 31 889
productions 21 410
Verhaert, Piet 32 591
Verhagen, E. Ewout see EWOUT VERHAGEN, E.
Verhagen, Hans (*fl c.* 1554-1600) see VERHAGEN DER STOMME, HANS
Verhagen, Hans (*fl* 1967) 28 103
Verhagen, Pierre-Joseph 3 561, 873; 19 260; 32 252*
Verhagen, Pieter 23 450
Verhagen der Stomme, Hans 32 252*
Verhandlungen des Kunstvereins für die Rheinlände und Westphalen 24 421
Verhanneman, Annekin 21 102
Verhas, Emmanuel 32 253
Verhas, Frans 32 253*
Verhas, Jan Frans 11 448; 32 253*
Verhees, H. 22 821
Verhelst, Egid, I (*c.* 1696-1745) 12 405; 22 302; 32 253–4*
collaboration 31 512
pupils 18 173, 175
works 32 *253*
Verhelst, Egid, II (1733-1818) 32 254
Verhelst, Gillis 32 253
Verhelst, Ignaz Wilhelm 4 375; 32 254
Verhelst, Placidus 2 717; 4 375; 32 254
Verheul, Cornelis 1 803; 32 254
Verheul, Johannes Dirkz. 1 803; 32 254*
Verheyden, Bob 22 877
Verheyden, Isidore 3 562; 5 37; 32 254*, 591
Verheyden, Jean-François 32 254
Verheyden, Pieter see HEYDEN, PIETER VAN DER
Verhoek, Gysbert 25 756
Verhoeven, Artus 17 880
Verhoogen, V. 3 620
Verhulst, Elias 11 226
Verhulst, Martin 3 555
Verhulst, Mayken 4 *895*, 897; 11 226; 32 254*
attributions 20 792
pupils 4 897, 910, 913; 7 518
works 7 519
Verhulst, Pierre-Antoine 14 479
Verhulst, Pieter 33 181
Verhulst, Rombout 3 570; 14 42; 22 858; 32 254–5*
assistants 21 614
attributions 8 834; 22 895, *895*
collaboration 18 11; 22 858; 25 812
pupils 4 158
works 1 813; 8 665; 9 760; 14 44; 19 100; 22 859
Véri, Frédéric 3 460
Véri, Joseph-Alphonse de, Abbé 32 255
Véri (-Raionard), Louis-Gabriel, Marquis de 11 369, 663; 23 778; 32 255*
Veria 29 702
Verino, Benedetto 20 658
Verino, Domenico da 16 725
Verino, Ugolino 14 868; 16 780; 32 255–6*
Veris da Milano, Filippo see FILIPPO VERIS DA MILANO
Veris da Milano, Lanfranco see LANFRANCO VERIS DA MILANO
Verishen Basilica 2 425
Verismo 20 240; 22 98; 32 256–7*
painting 16 *679*; 22 *99*, *100*
sculpture 9 *178*, *403*
Verità, Girolamo 5 533
Verity, Frank (Thomas) 7 327; 26 336; 32 257*
Verity, Robert 16 890
Verity, Thomas 3 367; 32 257
Verity & Beverley 32 257
Verkade, Jan 3 890; 22 421; 25 215; 32 258*
Verkade, Willibrord see VERKADE, JAN
Verkelen, Jan 33 168
Verkhne Pogromnoe 28 325
Verkhny Church 27 432
Verkolje, Jan, I (1650-93) 8 667; 11 445; 22 846; 32 258–9*
frames 11 *443*
pupils 32 259
Verkolje, Nicolaas 21 416; 32 258, 259*
pupils 25 822
reproductive prints by others 14 795; 30 297
works 14 794
Verkruys, Theodor 21 30
Verkuyl, Arie 30 15
Verlach, Johannes 29 5
Verlaine, Paul 2 733; 4 366; 5 69; 18 783, 863; 32 591
illustrated works 19 *513*
Verlat, Charles 32 259*; 33 38
pupils 2 487; 4 657; 12 166; 19 333; 21 167; 23 599
teachers 19 347; 28 68
Verlinde, V. 3 585
Verloop, J. N. 14 625
Verly, Charles 32 259
Verly, François 3 547; 19 381; 32 259*
patrons and collectors 4 302
works 2 193; 3 578; 19 380
Verly, Robert 7 200
Vermandois, Herbert I, Count 25 667
Vermare 5 881
Vermay, Jean-Baptiste 4 303; 8 238; 31 374
Vermay, Jehan see VERMEYEN, JAN CORNELISZ.
Vermeer, Johannes (1632-1675) 11 309; 22 843, 902; 29 375; 32 260–69*
attributions 2 835; 8 427
forgeries by others 3 889; 4 732; 11 306, *306*, 307, 310; 21 39
groups and movements 3 267; 8 669
methods 5 519; 10 191; 24 797; 28 203, 206; 31 578
paintings 8 667; 22 844
allegorical 1 663; 20 109
genre 8 123; 11 444, 446; 12 290, 291; 15 888; 19 354; 20 365; 21 759, *760*; 28 *207*; 30 878; 32 *262*, *264*, *265*
mythological 32 *261*
portraits 32 *263*
religious 14 584, 733
townscapes 2 338; 8 *667*; 22 *844*; 31 246
patrons and collectors
Altman, Benjamin 1 731
Arenberg, Auguste-Marie-Raymond, 6th Duke of 2 382
Bache, Jules Semon 3 18
Caraman, Duc de 5 700
Coats, W. A. 28 272
Frick, Henry Clay 11 774
Gardner, Isabella Stewart 12 147
Gildemeester, Jan (Jansz.) (1744-99) 12 620
Goll van Franckenstein (family) 12 876
Guinness, Edward (Cecil), 1st Earl of Iveagh 13 836
Huntington, Arabella D(uval) 15 29
Kann, Rodolphe 17 777
Lyonet, Pieter 22 905
Marquand, Henry G(urdon) 20 461
Mellon, Andrew W(illiam) 21 90
National Gallery (London) 5 283
National Gallery of Scotland 28 272
Péreire (family) 24 396
Salting, George 27 642
Smith, Joseph, Consul (*c.* 1674-1770) 28 884
Temple, Henry, 2nd Viscount Palmerston 30 451
William I, King of the Netherlands (*reg* 1813-40) 2 229; 23 469
Wrightsman, Charles B(ierer) 33 416
personal collection 10 732
reproductive prints by others 33 677
teachers 4 657
Vermeer, Reynier Jansz. 32 260
Vermeersch, José 3 592; 32 269*
Vermeer van Haarlem, Barent 32 270
Vermeer van Haarlem, Isaak 32 270
Vermeer van Haarlem, Jan, I (*c.* 1600-70) 32 270
Vermeer van Haarlem, Jan, II (1628-91) 17 920; 32 270*
groups and movements 13 895
pupils 32 270
teachers 27 329
Vermeer van Haarlem, Jan, III (1656-1705) 32 270*
Vermeer van Haarlem, Jan, IV (*fl* 1694) 32 270
Vermehren, (Johan) Frederik (Nicolai) 7 805; 32 270*
pupils 1 845; 14 118, 119; 17 646; 18 469; 26 406; 33 594
works 8 735
Vermenton 7 643
Vermeren-Coché (family) 3 591; 5 51
Vermeulen, Cornelis 14 84

Vermeulen, Jan *see* MOLANUS, JOHANNES
Vermexio, Andrea **30** 176; **32** 270–71*
Vermexio, Giovanni **30** 176; **32** 271
Vermey, Jehan *see* VERMEYEN, JAN CORNELISZ.
Vermeyen, Hans **12** 259; **21** 726; **22** 896; **32** 272
works **21** *726*
Vermeyen, Jan **8** 413; **13** 914; **23** 526; **32** 458
works **14** *171*
Vermeyen, Jan Cornelisz. **2** 716; **3** 554, 556; **32** 271–2*
collaboration **16** 831; **24** 15
patrons and collectors **3** 612; **5** 49; **13** 905, 909
tapestries **13** 907, *907*
works **3** 387, 604; **5** *48*; **8** 417; **30** 315, 317; **32** *271*
Vermeylen, François **22** 860
vermiculation *see under* MASONRY → types
vermiculus see under PIGMENTS → types
vermilion *see under* PIGMENTS → types
Vermillion (SD), Shrine to Music Museum **22** 377
Vermont, Hyacinthe Collin de *see* COLLIN DE VERMONT, HYACINTHE
Vermylen, Artus **2** 198
Vernacular Architecture **32** 274
vernacular architecture *see under* ARCHITECTURE → types
Vernacular Architecture Group **32** 273, 274
vernacular art **14** 446; **22** 439–40, 540; **32** 325–30*
collections *see under* COLLECTIONS → types
historical and regional traditions
Burma **5** 262*
Denmark **8** 756–7*
England **32** *324*, *325*, *326*, *327*, *329*
Finland **11** 110–11*
India, Republic of **15** 174–5*, *175*
Indian subcontinent **15** 498, 726–31*
Japan **17** 265–6, *354*, *357*
Malta (Republic of) **32** *328*
Native North Americans **22** 666
Norway **23** 238, 241–2*
Russia **20** 232
Sweden **30** 116–17*
Ukraine **31** 559, 560, 563
United States of America **11** 58; **22** 426; **32** *325*, *327*, *330*
see also VILLAGE ART
vernacular furniture *see under* FURNITURE → types
Vernacular revival *see* OLD ENGLISH STYLE
Vernansal, Guy-Louis **3** 855; **7** 167
Vernay, François **29** 669
Verner, Frederick A(rthur) **5** 566; **32** 331*
vernes **7** 764
Vernet, Antoine **26** 841; **32** 331
Vernet, Antoine-Charles-Joseph *see* VERNET, CARLE
Vernet, Carle **19** 37; **32** 331, 334–5*
collaboration **4** 36, 616; **19** 38, 66
groups and movements **24** 171
pupils **12** 349; **32** 335
reproductive prints by others **8** 595
teachers **19** 217
works **11** 643; **18** 678; **19** 483, 486, *486*; **20** 602; **32** *334*, *335*
Vernet, (Antoine-)François **32** 331
Vernet, (Emile-Jean-) Horace **22** 87; **32** 331, 335–7*
assistants **3** 241
collaboration **19** 38
groups and movements **23** 503; **26** 739
patrons and collectors **4** 106; **11** 542; **23** 521; **28** 527
pupils **1** 449, 774; **3** 528; **7** 408; **8** 883; **16** 573, 904; **18** 678, 744; **26** 455; **30** 384; **32** 852
Bonhommé, (Ignace-) François **4** 319
reproductive prints by others **2** 702; **12** 724; **17** 453
studio **29** 856
teachers **22** 88
works **1** 661; **2** 106; **4** 364; **11** *413*, 543, 544; **18** 678; **19** 483, 486; **20** 602; **28** 170; **30** 385; **32** 333, *336*
Vernet, Jean-Antoine **32** 331
Vernet, (Claude-) Joseph (1714-89) **24** 136; **32** 331–4*
assistants **32** 684; **33** 292
groups and movements **26** 740
patrons and collectors
Azincourt, Barthélémy-Augustin Blondel d' **2** 904
Caraman, Duc de **5** 700
Charles IV, King of Spain (*reg* 1788-1808) **4** 565, 566
Choiseul, Etienne-François, Duc de **7** 194
Creutz, Gustav Filip **8** 161
Fetherstonhaugh, Matthew **11** 39
Harrach, Ernst Guido, Graf von **14** 190
Hoare (i), Henry the younger (1705-85) **14** 598
Howard (ii), Henry, 4th Earl of Carlisle **13** 301
Leeson, Joseph, 1st Earl of Milltown **19** 64
Lowther, William, 3rd Baronet of Marske **19** 735
Marigny, Marquis de **11** 658; **20** 135; **25** 81
Papillon de La Ferté, Denis-Pierre-Jean **24** 63
Paul I, Emperor of Russia (*reg* 1796-1801) **26** 733
Potocki, Wincenty **25** 364
Rushout, John, 2nd Baron Northwick **27** 350
Saint-Aignan, Paul-Hippolyte de Beauvillier, Duc de **27** 524
Terray, Joseph-Marie **30** 514
Véri (-Raionard), Louis-Gabriel, Marquis de **32** 255
Vernet, Joseph (1760-92?) **4** 560
Watelet, Claude-Henri **32** 898
Williams-Wynn, Watkin, 4th Baronet, of Wynnstay (1749-89) **32** 790
Yusupov, Nikolay (Borisovich), Prince (1751- 1831) **33** 579
personal collection **19** 25
pupils **8** 95; **14** 845; **20** 485; **24** 252; **31** 817
reproductions in ceramics **20** 474
reproductive prints by others
Balechou, Jean-Joseph **3** 107
Daudet, Robert (1737-1824) **8** 542
Daullé, Jean **8** 544
Flipart, Jean-Jacques **11** 171
Lebas, Jacques-Philippe **11** 540; **19** 10
Le Mire, Noël **19** 136
Lempereur, Catherine-Elisabeth **19** 144
Longueil, Joseph de **19** 641
teachers **20** 270
Vernet, (Claude-) Joseph (1714-89)—cont.
works **2** 860; **11** *409*, 410, 579, 666; **18** 712; **20** 426; **24** 135; **32** *333*
Vernet, Joseph (1760-92?) **32** 331
Vernet, Louis-François **32** 331
Vernet, Pierre **4** 391
Verneuil, Maurice **23** 693
Verneuil Château **4** 864–5; **6** 506; **11** 514, 515; **12** 120
Verneuil-sur-Avre **6** 54
La Madeleine **13** 79
Vernier, Séraphin **20** 925
Verniquet, Edme **24** 123
vernis Martin see under JAPANNING → types
Vernissage **24** 439
Vernon, Notre-Dame **13** 60
Vernon, (Charles-)Frédéric (-Victor) de **32** 338*
Vernon, Jean de **32** 338*
Vernon, Robert **10** 361; **32** 338*
collections **10** 366, 370
paintings **14** 202, 550; **32** 855
Vernon, Samuel **31** 648
Vernon, Thomas **15** 57
Vernon, W(alter) L(iberty) **23** 36; **32** 339*
works **2** 739, 770; **30** 159
Vernucken, Wilhelm **7** 593; **19** 815; **32** 339*
Verny *see* ALMATY
Veroia **9** 630
Hagios Christos **28** 446
Veroli, Franciscus **28** 92
Veroli, Sulpizio da **2** 346; **19** 256; **32** 639
Veroli Casket **5** 917; **9** 520, 651; **10** 475
Véron, Paul **13** 645
Verona **9** *510*; **16** *618*; **26** *886*, *906*; **27** 820; **32** 340–46*
Amphitheatre *see* Arena
Arena **1** 797; **23** 480; **26** 904, 906; **32** 340
staircases **29** 521
art forms and materials
architecture **16** 635; **28** 28–9
bronze **10** 528
cassoni **6** 5
façade decoration **10** 736, 737, 739
furniture **16** 723
glass **16** 740
painting **16** 661
pigments **24** 793
rock crystal **26** 486
Casa Mazzanti **4** 776
Casa Trevisani-Lonardi **10** 766
Casa Vignola **10** 766
churches **4** 774
Cathedral of S Maria Maggiore **20** 820; **32** 343–4*
altar **1** 695
font **11** 252; **26** 622
sculpture **26** 621, 622
Sacello dei SS Nazaro e Celso **23** 649
S Anastasia **13** 64
Cavalli Chapel **1** *727*
Fregoso altar **6** 89, *90*
Pellegrini Chapel **21** 461; **30** 497
spire **29** 414
S Bernardino
Pellegrini Chapel **27** 236, 760, *761*
S Fermo Maggiore **26** 330
Sarayna Chapel **27** 820
S Maria Antica **14** 421; **20** 865; **32** 345–6*, *346*
tomb of Cangrande I **10** 440; **16** 443
tomb of Cansignorio della Scala **10** 440; **13** 95; **28** *29*
tombs **16** 688
S Maria in Organo **16** 726
Verona churches—cont.
S Nazaro
chapel of S Biagio **10** 765–6
S Teresa degli Scalzi **3** 109
S Zeno Maggiore **4** 141, 774; **10** 742; **16** 625; **20** 767, 820; **26** 579; **32** *342*, 344–5*
altarpiece **11** 382; **20** 308; **26** 185; **27** 495
crypt **8** 224
doors **9** 154; **16** 687
reliefs **26** 622
sculpture **16** 687; **23** 101; **26** 619, 621, 622; **32** *344*
wall paintings **26** 654
Giardino Giusti **12** 115, 116, 117
guidebooks **20** 85
Lazzaretto **27** 760
Loggia del Consiglio **5** 533; **31** 237
Museo Civico di Castelvecchio **16** 775, 776; **28** 35; **32** 341, 342
Museo Lapidario Maffeiano **2** 165; **20** 85; **25** 191; **32** 342, 343
collections **24** 240
palazzi
Bishop's Palace **5** 31
Palace of Theodoric **9** 557
Palazzo Bevilacqua **2** 295; **23** 492; **27** 759; **32** *341*
collections **32** 343
Palazzo Bocca-Trezza **5** 31, 617
Palazzo Canossa **23** 492; **27** *758*, 758–9
Palazzo Fiorio della Seta *see* Palazzo Murari
Palazzo Franchini **10** 766
Palazzo del Governo **1** 725; **16** 710
Palazzo Grimani **27** *760*
Palazzo Lavezola *see* Palazzo Pompei
Palazzo Murari *see* Palazzo Bocca-Trezza
Palazzo Pompei **16** 635; **27** 759
Palazzo Ridolfi **5** 617
Palazzo degli Scaligeri *see* Palazzo del Governo
Palazzo Vescovile **5** 815
Piazza dei Signori **25** 189; **32** 159
Ponte Scaligero **4** 776, 801
Porta de' Gavi **23** 483
Porta dei Borsari **24** 318; **26** 895; **32** *340*
Porta dei Leoni **7** 358
Porta Nuova **7** 359, *360*; **16** 635; **27** 761*
Porta Palio **7** 359; **16** 635; **27** 762*, *762*
Roman theatre **26** 891
S Zeno bastion **3** 359
Teatro Filarmonico **30** 667
Torre del Gardello **4** 776
Verona, Arthur **12** 536
Verona, Giovanni da *see* GIOVANNI DA VERONA
Verona, Guarino da *see* GUARINO DA VERONA
Verona, Jacopo da *see* JACOPO DA VERONA
Verona, Liberale da *see* LIBERALE DA VERONA
Verona, Paolo da *see* PAOLO DA VERONA
Verona, Stefano (di Giovanni) da *see* STEFANO (DI GIOVANNI) DA VERONA
Verone, Pierre de *see* PIERRE DE VERONE
Veronese, Alessandro *see* TURCHI, ALESSANDRO
Veronese, Bonifazio *see* PITATI, BONIFAZIO DE'
Veronese, Guarino *see* GUARINO DA VERONA
Veronese, Paolo **5** 431; **8** 613; **14** 868; **31** 9, 14; **32** 190, 346–56*
assistants **5** 431; **10** 824
attributions **5** 431; **33** 631
collaboration **5** 431, 617; **10** 824; **19** 330; **32** 77; **33** 631
drawings **9** 221; **32** *354*
frames **11** 389, 391, 392, 402, 404, 406, 494
groups and movements **23** 503
interior decoration **16** 666
methods **5** 654, 657; **6** 570; **13** 708; **23** 376; **24** 493, 798; **32** 806
models **21** 766
mosaics **32** 212
musical instruments **22** 374
paintings **16** 666; **32** 191
frescoes
Doge's Palace (Venice) **16** 667; **32** *350*
SS Giovanni e Paolo (Venice) **21** 846
Villa Barbaro (Maser) **5** 887; **9** 265; **11** 387; **13** 676; **15** 137, IV; **18** 708; **20** 279, 546; **23** 678; **32** 191, 550
oil
allegorical **1** 658; **16** 666; **32** 220, 222, *348*
altarpieces **32** 343, *347*
ceiling **9** 14; **32** 220, *221*, 223
history **32** 222
mythological **10** 476; **32** 220
oil sketches **23** 381
organ shutters **23** *501*, 502
portraits **3** *202*; **13** 298; **28** 666; **31** 14
religious **5** 31; **10** 476, 503; **32** 215, 216, *352*, *353*
religious **6** 175
patrons and collectors **25** 137
Augustus III, King of Poland (*reg* 1733-63) **1** 633
Barbaro (family) **3** 203
Benson, R(obert) H(enry) **3** 740
Borghese, Scipione, Cardinal **4** 406
Bourbon I., Louis de, le Grand Dauphin (1661-1711) **4** 553
Bracciano, Livio Odescalchi, Duca di **23** 353
Brienne, Louis-Henri, Comte de **4** 807
Carpio, Gaspar de Haro y Guzmán, 7th Marqués del **5** 844
Carr, Robert **5** 847
Carraquiri, Nazario **5** 871
Cavendish, William, 2nd Duke of Devonshire (1671-1729) **6** 116
Celotti, Luigi, Abbot **6** 151
Charles IV, King of Spain (*reg* 1788-1808) **4** 565
Christina, Queen of Sweden (*reg* 1632-54) **30** 118; **32** 8
Clive, Robert, 1st Baron Clive **7** 437
Contini Bonacossi, Alessandro, Conte **7** 782
Corte, Valerio **5** 456
Créquy, Charles de Blanchefort de **19** 238
Crozat, Pierre **8** 209
Dezallier d'Argenville, Antoine-Joseph **8** 845
Durazzo, Giuseppe M. **4** 811
Eastlake, Charles Lock (1793-1865) **9** 683
Egerton, Francis, 3rd Duke of Bridgewater **9** 755
Este (i) (family) **21** 771
Everdingen, Allart van **10** 660
Ferdinand III, Holy Roman Emperor (*reg* 1637-58) **13** 919
Fitzwilliam, Richard, 7th Viscount Fitzwilliam **11** 141

Veronese, Paolo
patrons and collectors—cont.
Fouquet, Nicolas **11** 356
Francesco I, 8th Duke of Modena and Reggio (*reg* 1629-58) **10** 526
Giustiniani (i), Vincenzo, Marchese **12** 763
Gonzaga, Ercole, Cardinal **10** 805; **12** 910
Habsburg I., Leopold William, Archduke of Austria, Governor of the Netherlands **13** 919
Hesselin, Louis (-Cauchon) **14** 492
Howard (i), Aletheia, Countess of Arundel **14** 807
Howard (i), Thomas, 2nd Earl of Arundel **14** 807
Imperiale, Gian Vincenzo **15** 148
Imstenraedt (brothers) **15** 158
Jabach, Everard **16** 814
Josephine, Empress of the French (1763-1814) **4** 304
Lagoy, Marquis de **18** 641
Lane, Hugh (Percy) **18** 727
Lely, Peter **19** 124
Liechtenstein-Castelkorn, Karel von, Bishop of Olmutz **8** 423
Ludovisi, Ludovico, Cardinal **19** 779
Lumague, Charles **19** 790
Lumague, Marc-Antoine (ii) (1566-1655) **19** 790
Medici, Giovanni Carlo de', Cardinal (1611-63) **21** 27
Medici, Leopoldo de', Cardinal **21** 27
Medinaceli, Luís de la Cerda Fernández de Córdoba Folch de Cardona y Aragón, 9th Duque de (1660-1711) **21** 35
National Gallery (London) **22** 296
Orléans, Philippe II de Bourbon, 2nd Duc d' (1674-1723) **23** 516
Philip II, King of Spain (*reg* 1556-98) **9** 173; **13** 922; **14** 1
Pisani (family) **24** 865
Polignac, Melchior de, Cardinal **25** 150
Poniatowski, Stanisław, Prince **25** 213
Porto, Iseppo da **25** 271
Pourtalès-Gorgier, James-Alexandre, Comte de **25** 383
Reynolds, Joshua **26** 280
Richelieu, Armand-Jean Du Plessis, Cardinal de **26** 348
Rushout, John, 2nd Baron Northwick **27** 350
Sera, Paolo del **28** 433
Seymour-Conway, Francis Charles, 3rd Marquess of Hertford **28** 527
Sheremet'yev, Pyotr (Borisovich), Count **28** 593
Sigismund II Augustus, King of Poland (*reg* 1548-72) **16** 867
Somerset, Henry, 3rd Duke of Beaufort (1707- 49) **13** 301
Strange, John **29** 746
Tallard, Marie-Joseph d'Hostun, Duc de **30** 274
Tessin, Carl Gustav, Count **30** 524
Velázquez, Diego (de Silva y) (1599-1660) **32** 130
Villiers, George, 1st Duke of Buckingham (1592-1628) **32** 575
Winkler, Gottfried **19** 111
pupils **10** 824; **28** 38; **32** 77
reproductive prints by others **3** 308; **5** 857
Baratti, Antonio **3** 199

Veronese, Paolo
reproductive prints by others—cont.
Bertelli, Orazio **3** 851
Carracci, Agostino **5** 856
Dupuis, Nicolas-Gabriel **9** 407
Fontana (ii), Giovanni Battista **11** 270
Jackson, John Baptist **25** 622
Joullain, François **17** 668
Kilian, Lucas **18** 42
Kilian, Philipp **18** 45
Kilian, Wolfgang **18** 44
Lasne, Michel **18** 812; **19** 790
Mellan, Claude **19** 790
Valesi, Dionigi **31** 821
Villamena, Francesco **32** 560
Volpato, Giovanni **32** 689
Zompini, Gaetano Gherardo **33** 697
restorations by others **9** 740; **26** 320
studio **29** 853
teachers **3** 37; **5** 816
workshop **28** 5, 8
Veronese green *see* PIGMENTS → types → green earth
Veronesi, Luigi **22** 242, 381; **32** 358*
Veronica Reliquary **26** 485
Verospi (family) **4** 886; **32** 612
Verotäjs **27** 284
Verovio, Simone **22** 370
Verpoorten, Peter **26** 810
Verrazzano, Admiral da **16** 473
verre églomisé **5** 192; **13** 139; **27** *640*
Verrerie de Munzthal *see* COMPAGNIE DES VERRERIES ET CRISTALLERIES DE SAINT-LOUIS
Verrerie de Nancy **8** 544
Verrerie des Vénitiens **3** 593
Verrerie Impériale et Royale Sainte-Anne **3** 594
Verreries & Cristalleries de Saint-Louis, Co. des *see* COMPAGNIE DES VERRERIES & CRISTALLERIES DE SAINT-LOUIS
Verreries de Sainte-Anne **3** 13
Verreries de Vonêche à Baccarat **3** 595
Verres(, C.) **13** 390; **26** 857; **27** 29
Verreville Crystal-Work **28** 259
Verreville Pottery **28** 257
Verri, Alessandro **21** 527
Verri, Pietro **21** 527
Verrier, Jean **10** 401
Verrier, Johannes **18** 235
verrières see RAFRAÎCHISSOIRS
Verrill, Hyatt **5** 621
Verrio, Antonio **32** 358–9*
assistants **18** 644, 749, 787; **30** 163
collaboration **20** 880
groups and movements **6** 128
patrons and collectors **6** 116, 515; **10** 361; **14** 127; **20** 141
restorations by others **7** 339
works **10** 249, 274; **15** 139; **18** 644; **21** 907; **23** 466; **32** *359*; **33** 249, 250
Verrocchio, Andrea del **16** 689; **19** 188, 555, 676; **32** 359–67*
assistants **3** 298; **24** 521
attributions **6** 14; **8** 798; **11** 694; **19** 188
collaboration **8** 798, 799; **16** 749
competitions **7** 671
drawings **9** 220
frames **11** 382
groups and movements **26** 186
methods **21** 768; **24** 492
paintings **19** 188; **32** *364*, *365*
patrons and collectors **16** 689; **20** 847; **21** 14; **27** 354; **30** 727; **31** 173
pupils **1** 454; **5** 130; **11** 26; **19** 180, 675; **24** 527

Verrocchio, Andrea del—cont.
sculpture **1** 110; **16** 691
busts **16** *691*, 691; **30** 495
equestrian monuments **3** 636; **7** 568; **10** 440; **14** 869; **16** 690, 693; **19** 207; **29** 565; **32** 192, 216, *363*
models **30** 496
reliefs **16** 741, *741*; **25** 159; **30** 497
religious **26** 186; **32** *360*, *362*
statuettes **11** 29; **29** 568
tombs **11** 208; **19** 710; **21** 14; **27** 830; **32** *361*
studio **29** 853
teachers **16** 694
workshop **11** 185; **16** 661
Verrocchio, Francesco di Luca **32** 360
Verrocchio, Giuliano **32** 360
Verroia **9** 555
Verrue, Jeanne-Baptiste d'Albert de Luynes, Comtesse de **3** 760; **4** 166; **11** 338; **17** 684; **18** 692; **23** 513; **30** 274; **32** 368*
Ver sacrum **2** 567; **3** 21; **11** 320; **18** 534; **22** 187; **24** 427, 438; **28** 343, 344
Versailles **11** *504*; **31** 719, *719*
Bibliothèque Municipale **2** 614; **3** 19; **4** 130
Château **3** 264; **6** 60, 508; **7** 545; **11** 508, 517, 659; **12** 898; **19** 23–4, 267, 357, 362, 721; **20** 134, 295–6, 572; **22** 42, 44; **23** 811; **26** 492; **31** 372; **32** 369–71*, *369*, 510
Aile du Gouvernement **11** *883*
Allée Royale **8** 94
Appartement des Bains **4** 535
appartement of Louis-Alexandre **18** 654
appartement of the Duchesse de Chateauroux **11** 407
architecture **4** 785; **19** 233; **24** 177
Ballcourt **3** 118
Bibliothèque du Roi **13** 234
busts **5** 301; **8** 791; **12** 862
Cabinet Intérieur de la Reine **13** 234
Cabinet de la Méridienne **13** 234; **26** 376
furniture **11** 579
Cabinets du Roi **9** 87
carpets **5** 837; **27** 896
catalogues **5** 412
Chambre de la Reine **11** 648; **22** 682; **28** 506
Chambre des Bains du Roi **13** 234
Chambre du Roi **1** 110; **9** 12; **11** 576, *576*, 648
furniture **26** 376
Chapel **7** 422; **11** 657; **20** *297*; **25** 377; **26** 492; **32** 89, 370
frescoes **8** 91
paintings **11** 537; **18** 632; **20** 894; **28** 743
sculpture **16** 702
stained glass **29** 506
chimney-pieces **6** 604
clocks **5** 379, 380
collections **9** 28; **16** 849; **30** 514; **32** 584
copper **29** 572
Cour de Marbre **8** 93; **19** 88
Dauphine's Apartments **32** 338
Dauphin's closet **9** 12
Dauphin's Desk **23** 356
Dauphin's library **11** 596
embroidery **11** 648
Escalier de la Reine **3** 621
Escalier des Ambassadeurs **8** 93; **11** 575; **19** 23; **29** 524
frames **11** 376

Versailles
Château—cont.
furniture **1** 110; **4** 524; **5** 350; **7** 657, 746; **8** 161; **11** 588, 593, 595, 617, 626, 627; **12** 185; **17** 666; **19** 130, 261; **31** 480
Galerie des Antiques **8** 94
Galerie des Batailles **32** 336
Galerie des Glaces **5** 344, 349; **9** 12, 22; **11** 536, 575, 576, 612; **12** 789, 791; **21** 721; **30** 344; **32** 370
furniture **9** 30; **19** 722
interior decoration **19** 721
Galeries Historiques **10** 563; **32** 371
gardens **2** 53; **3** 833; **7** 422; **12** 61, *61*, 105, 120, 121; **14** 174, 804; **19** 163; **20** 897; **26** 449; **28** 314; **31** 408, 480; **32** 369, 371–2*
Allée d'Eau **19** 88, 96
Bain des nymphes **12** 726; **19** 76, 88
Bassin d'Apollon **11** *344*, 344; **12** 121, 725; **20** 480; **31** 408
Bassin de Flore **31** 408
Bassin de Neptune **1** 132, *133*, 133; **4** 509; **11** 560; **19** 141
Bassins des Saisons **32** 373
Demi-lune du Dragon **19** 88
Dragon Fountain **20** 480
Fountain of Enceladus **20** 481
Fountain of Fame **20** 481
Fountain of Latona **20** 480
fountains **9** 22; **11** 344
Grotte de Thétis **11** 344; **12** 725; **13** 703, *704*; **20** 480; **25** 80
Labyrinthe **19** 96
Parterre d'Eau **5** 323; **7** 422; **8** 94; **19** 88, 96, 242; **31** 408
Potager du Roy **12** 121
sculpture **3** 258; **7** 415; **9** 481; **10** 442; **12** 725–6; **18** 902; **19** 76, 96, 242; **20** 481; **25** 706; **26** 91; **28** 845; **29** 564, 711
Siren Fountain **20** 480
Grande Antichambre **11** 576
Grands Appartements **6** 508; **11** 575; **29** 833
interior decoration **19** 721
sculpture **4** 551
Grand Trianon **6** 508; **8** 24; **11** 589; **26** 492; **32** 369, *373*
Chambre de la Duchesse de Bourgogne **26** 492
Chambre du Roi **11** 626
Chapel **18** 643
furniture **4** 532; **7** 657; **19** 115, 130; **20** 467
gardens **7** 422; **12** 121, 123; **14** 174; **20** 480; **32** 373
interior decoration **4** 301; **10** 187; **11** 576
ivory-carvings **11** 637
overdoors **19** 242
paintings **1** 664; **3** 856; **4** 535, 536, 537; **7** 864; **8** 90, 91; **14** 84, 793; **32** 242
Pavillon Français **6** 509; **11** 658, *884*
Salon des Glaces **5** 349
Salon Frais **17** 672
sculpture **11** 754
tapestries **32** 242
theatre **18** 642
Hameau **32** 369, 374
Hamlet *see* Hameau
hardstones **9** 28
hunting-lodge **19** 721; **32** 369
interior decoration **4** 554; **11** 575, *882*; **23** 520–21; **32** 240
japanning **18** 614
Labyrinthe **19** 88; **31** 408
lacquer **18** 614

Versailles
Château—cont.
library of Mme Sophie **6** 509
Ménagerie du Parc **14** 84; **25** 71; **33** 698
Appartement d'Eté **26** 492
paintings **1** 664; **3** 856; **4** 536; **8** 91, 812, 883; **31** 511
metalwork **11** 626, 627
monument to Louis XIV **11** 558
Musée d'Histoire **8** 829; **9** 300; **11** 371, 544, 739; **12** 12, 608; **13** 309; **18** 679; **22** 465; **23** 520; **32** 371
collections **5** 392; **8** 637; **11** 666; **24** 736
paintings **7** 304, 529; **8** 641–2; **19** 37; **26** 264; **27** 143
sculpture **25** 418
Musée National du Château de Versailles et de Trianon **32** 370–71
Opéra **9** 84, 416, *417*; **23** 795; **30** 670
Orangerie **12** 121; **23** 470
sculpture **8** 791; **19** 88
ormolu **29** 572
paintings **4** 744, 808; **24** 168; **30** 343
allegorical **19** 542; **30** 530
architectural **20** 489
battle **20** 489, 873; **21** 367, 368; **32** 243
ceiling **24** 736
Galerie des Batailles **26** 348
genre **8** 883; **18** 693; **19** 115; **31** 379
history **4** 300, 834; **7** 876; **8** 89, 593; **11** 413; **12** 769; **13** 793, 837; **14** 310, 584, 586; **19** 65; **22** 741; **25** 671
hunting scenes **19** 646
mythological **24** 584
portraits **4** 305, 306, 556, 565; **5** 208; **6** 435; **7** 778; **8** 559, 648; **9** 302, 365; **10** 144; **11** 405, 410, 903; **18** 728; **19** 65, 89, 161, 646, 648; **21** 114, 510; **22** 685; **25** 887; **26** 248, 260; **28** 506; **30** 530; **31** 379, 842; **32** 74, 495, 584
religious **11** 406; **28** 743
Pavillon de la Ménagerie **28** 743
Pavillon de Musique **6** 397
Petite Galerie **4** 552; **9** 12
Petit Hameau **8** 461; **11** 658
Petits Appartements **8** 814; **11** 407; **13** 701
paintings **24** 212, 256
Petits Appartements de la Reine **9** 87
Petits Appartements du Roi **4** 513; **9** 87
Petit Trianon **11** 658; **20** 131; **22** 738; **23** 812, 861; **24** 290, 811; **32** 369, 373–4*, *374*, 553
Chambre de Treillage **28** 194
furniture **7** 658; **11** 590
gardens **12** 123, *123*; **22** 210
interior decoration **4** 301
paintings **5** 740; **9** 208; **14** 84; **18** 642; **19** 217
sculpture **23** 795
Temple de l'Amour **21** 893
porcelain **9** 28
portraits **3** 452; **18** 495; **24** 211
reliefs **6** 401
riding house **26** 363
Salle de 1830 **8** 61
Salle de l'hôtel des Menus-Plaisirs **24** *176*
Salle du Grand Couvert **24** 210
Salles des Croisades **8** 641
Salon d'Abondance **11** 404
Salon d'Apollon **4** 552; **23** 542
Salon de Diane **4** 126; **18** 632
Salon de la Guerre **8** 93; **11** 575; **23** 678; **32** *371*

Versailles
Château—cont.
Salon de la Paix **11** 575; **19** 142, *142*
Salon de l'Oeil de Boeuf **26** 492
stucco **11** 156
Vinckenbrinck, Jan (Albertsz.) (*b* 1631) **11** 577
Salon de Mars **11** 404; **32** 718
Salon des Jeux de la Reine **26** 376
Salon des Nobles **7** 864; **11** 305; **13** 234
Salon des Porcelaines **9** 29
Salon d'Hercule **4** 510; **14** 584
paintings **11** 538; **19** 142
Salon Ovale **26** 492
sculpture **7** 876; **11** 156, 559; **13** 790; **15** 34; **19** 225, 242; **29** 571–2
allegorical **4** 458; **20** 481; **31** 56
architectural **2** 375; **5** 379; **11** 156; **20** 480
busts **4** 457; **8** 791; **23** 794; **30** 495
copies **7** 415
portraits **3** 735; **4** 457, 798; **6** 517; **8** 617, 631, 650, 791; **9** 389; **12** 727; **23** 795; **31** 56
stables **29** 485
tapestries **12** 829; **21** 368; **30** 321
Trianon de Marbre *see* Grand Trianon
Trianon de Porcelaine **11** 575; **12** 874; **23** 776; **26** 492; **32** 372–3*
faience (ii) (ceramics) **27** 536
furniture **31** 682, *684*
see also Grand Trianon
Turkish bedroom **26** 182
Château de Groussay **11** 584
Hôtel du Grand Maître **12** 27
Hôtel de la Marine et des Affaires Etrangères *see* Bibliothèque Municipale
Hôtel de Ville **31** 379
mairie **20** 489
Versailles Livy (Paris, Bib. N. Mss. fr. 273-4) **4** 544
Verschaeren, Jan **8** 592; **32** 253
Verschaffelt, Maximilian (Joseph) von **11** 128; **32** 375*; **33** 116
Verschaffelt, Peter Anton von **3** 571; **32** 374–5*; **33** 280
pupils **17** 6; **18** 173; **32** 375
works **12** 405; **13** 832; **20** 282
Verschoten, Floris (Gerritsz.) *see* SCHOOTEN, FLORIS (GERRITSZ.) VAN
Verschuier, Lieve **27** 230
Verschuur, Wim Bos **30** 16
Verschuur, Wouterus **20** 871; **32** 375*
Verschuuring, Willem **32** 258
Verschuyl, P. **2** 318
Vershinin, A. **27** 416
Versigny **13** 211
verso **32** 376*
Verspronck, Cornelis Engelsz. **32** 376
Verspronck, Jan (Cornelisz.) **22** 840; **32** 376*
works **32** *376*
Verspronck, Johannes (Cornelisz.) *see* VERSPRONCK, JAN (CORNELISZ.)
Verstappen, Martin **8** 584; **24** 892
Verstappen, Rombout **32** 254
Versteeg, Gerardus **13** 632; **17** 910
Versteeg, Michiel **30** 412
Versteegh, Dirk **13** 295; **32** 693
Versten Portraits, Master of the **11** 439
Verster, Andrew **9** 427
Verster, Floris (Henric) **19** 102; **22** 850; **32** 376–7*
Verstockt, Marc **3** 574
Verstolk van Soelen, Jan Gijsbert, Baron **32** 377*
paintings **3** 239; **19** 736
prints **26** 453
watercolours **32** 707
Verstraete, Théodore **32** 591
Verstraeten, Willem Jansz. **22** 879
Verstralen, Anthonie **2** 856
versurae **30** 652
Vertangen, Daniel **19** 474; **25** 68
vert de terre *see* PIGMENTS → types → green verditer
Vértebra **5** 356; **13** 765; **25** 826; **26** 549
works **13** *765*
vert émeraude *see under* PIGMENTS → types
Vertès, Marcel **4** 366
Vértesszentkereszr Abbey **26** 638
vertical kilns *see under* KILNS → types
vertical lift bridges *see under* BRIDGES → types
vertical looms *see under* LOOMS → types
vertical scrolls *see* SCROLLS → types → hanging
Vertine Master **9** 349
Vertiz, José Reygadas *see* REYGADAS VERTIZ, JOSÉ
Vertov, Dziga **25** 351
Vertova (family) **6** 343
Vertue, Adam **32** 377
Vertue, George **2** 165; **14** 178; **25** 11; **31** 871; **32** 378–9*
collaboration **14** 795
groups and movements **10** 372; **14** 638
metalwork **17** 768
patrons and collectors **14** 810; **32** 826
teachers **12** 600
writings **9** 26; **10** 377; **14** 178, 538; **19** 585; **23** 690; **30** 772
illustrated **6** 78
Vertue, Robert, I (*d* 1506) **3** 369; **19** 602; **32** 377, 378*
Vertue, Robert, II (*fl* 1506-55) **32** 378
Vertue, William **3** 369; **19** 610; **23** 686; **26** 70; **32** 377, 378*
Verucchio **10** 609
Veruela **29** 263
Verulam, Francis Bacon, 1st Baron *see* BACON, FRANCIS, 1st Baron Verulam & Viscount St Albans
Verulamium *see under* ST ALBANS
Verve **14** 43; **24** 144, 428, 442; **26** 236; **30** 488
Verveer, Salomon Leonardus **32** 379*; **33** 45
Verville, Jean François Du Verger de *see* DU VERGER DE VERVILLE, JEAN FRANÇOIS
Vervloet, Frans **8** 765; **32** 379–80*
Vervloet, J. J. **32** 379
Vervort, Michiel *see* VOORT, MICHIEL VAN DER, I
Vervoz **3** 592
Verwée, Alfred (Jacques) **5** 44; **28** 921; **32** 241, 380*
Verwée, Louis Pierre **32** 241, 380
Verwer, Abraham de **31** 156; **32** 734
Verwey, Margaretha **22** 898
Verwilghen, Raphaël **32** 380*
collaboration **3** 551; **4** 217; **9** 759; **25** 190
staff **9** 759
Ver Wilt, Domenicus **30** 114; **32** 380–81*
Ver y Estimar **2** 405
Verzelini, Giacomo **19** 595
Verzelini, Jacopo **10** 316
works **10** *315*
Verzino *see under* PIGMENTS → types
Vesali (Burma) **2** 280, *281*; **5** *221*, 225
sculpture **5** 239
Vesali (India) *see* VAISHALI
Vesalius, Andreas **32** 381*
methods **28** 206
works **1** 841; **32** 199
illustrated **4** 358, *358*; **5** 415; **21** 6
Vescovado, Master of the **2** 19
Veseer, Johann Joseph **2** 876
Veselovsky, Nikolai I. **6** 278, 279; **20** 892
Veselý, Aleš **8** 388
Veselý, Josef **8** 400
Veshch'/Gegenstand/Objet **19** 476; **24** 450
Veshin, Jaroslav **5** 154
Vésinet, Le *see* LE VÉSINET
Ve Skerries Lighthouse **19** 361
Vesme, Alessandro Baudi di **32** 381*
Vesna **28** 860
Vesnin (family) **3** 88; **15** 886; **22** 174; **23** 529; **32** 685
groups and movements **22** 178
works **3** 88; **31** 459
Vesnin, Aleksandr (Aleksandrovich) **25** 239; **32** 381–3*, 661
collaboration **2** 893; **25** 239; **27** 379
exhibitions **15** 857; **26** 504
groups and movements **7** 769, 770; **23** 590; **27** 379
pupils **5** 276; **19** 206, 732; **28** 747
works **23** 590; **26** 504; **27** 378, 396
writings **27** 405
Vesnin, Leonid (Aleksandrovich) **2** 893; **7** 770; **19** 732; **27** 379; **32** 381–3*, 661
teachers **3** 734
Vesnin, Viktor (Aleksandrovich) **2** 893; **7** 770; **18** 205; **23** 529; **27** 379; **32** 381–3*, 661
Vesontio *see* BESANÇON
Vespa **15** 826
Vespasian, Emperor of Rome (*reg* 69-79) **32** 383–4*
architecture **14** 439, 441; **22** 804; **26** 784, 789, 865, 874, 893, 895
sculpture **25** 43, 45; **27** 34
Vespasiano da Bisticci **16** 658; **20** 333; **22** 13; **31** 740; **32** 384–5*
manuscripts **11** 687
patrons and collectors **13** 328
works **9** 129; **21** 12
Vespasian Psalter *see under* PSALTERS → individual manuscripts
Vespeira, Marcelino **25** 299
Vesperbilder **24** 776
Vespignani, Francesco **32** 385
Vespignani, Renzo **26** 777
Vespignani, Virgilio **32** 385*
collaboration **25** 147
teachers **25** 147
works **3** 644; **26** 761, 833, 834
Vespinis *see* WESPIN(, DE)
Vespremie, A. **26** 719
Vespucci (family) **24** 768
Vespucci, Amerigo **20** 363
Vespucci, Antonia **11** 28
Vespucci, Giorgio Antonio **32** 386*
Vespucci, Giovanni Antonio **28** 928
Vespucci, Guidantonio **32** 386*
Vespucci, Niccolò **32** 386*
Vespucci, Simone **32** 386*
Vessanagara *see* BESNAGAR
vessels
materials
alabaster (gypsum) **2** 272
basalt **10** 72
brass **2** 589, *589*; **23** 303
vessels
materials—cont.
bronze
China **6** 625, 631, 635, 735, 737, 738, *738*, 767, 788, 798, 808, 826, *827*, 827–9*, 830–34, *831*, *833*, 835, *836*, 836–48*, *837*, *838*, *839*, *842*, *843*, *844*, *845*, *846*, *847*, *850*, 850–54*, *851*, *852*, *853*, 857–8, *858*, 859, 861, 864, 865, *865*, *866*, 866, 867, 868; **7** 12, 22, 88; **10** *464*; **21** I4; **23** *155*, 549–50; **24** *14*; **33** *471*
Greece, ancient **13** 574
Rome, ancient **27** 85–7*
copper **7** 88
gold **7** 88; **20** *448*
inlays **6** 853–4, *865*, *866*
inscriptions **6** 826, 836, 840*, 842, 857, 865
jade **7** 3, 9; **16** 527, 528
China **7** 6
Indian subcontinent **16** III2
lacquer **7** 12; **18** *606*
leather **21** 883
limestone **10** 72
malachite **7** 88
metal **10** 37–8*
Azerbaijan **2** 899
Greece, ancient **13** 574–7*
Italy **13** 576
Russia **27** 418, *425*
plaster **30** 196
rock crystal **25** *436*; **26** 485
silver-gilt **30** *146*
stone
Arabia **2** 271–3*
Bahrain **2** 272
Crete **21** 656, 659, 689–90*
Cycladic **8** 308, 317*, *317*
Egypt, ancient **9** *814*, 814–15*, 864; **10** 71–4*, *73*
Minoan **21** 656, 659, 689–90*
turquoise **7** 88
wood **21** 883
types
bian hu **6** *853*
ding **6** *827*, 828, *831*, *833*
dou **6** *827*, 828, *846*
drinking **10** 474; **25** 543
dui **6** *827*
fang ding **6** *827*, 836
fang hu **33** *471*
fang yi **6** *827*, 836, *837*, *844*
fou **6** *827*
fu **6** *827*, 828
gong **6** *827*
gu **6** *827*, 828; **7** *27*
guang see gong
gui **6** *827*, 828, *842*, *843*, 844, *845*, *846*, 851, *851*
he **6** *827*, *836*, *837*
hu **6** *827*, 828, *839*, 845, *846*, *847*, *850*, 853, *853*; **21** I4
jia **6** *827*, *838*
jian **6** *827*, 829, *833*
jiao **6** *827*
jue **6** 827, *827*, *838*, *846*; **10** *464*
lei **6** *827*
li **6** *827*, *846*
pan **6** *827*, *846*
pou **6** *827*
xian see yan
xu **6** *827*
yan **6** *827*
yi **6** *827*, 828
you **6** *827*, 845
yu **6** *827*
zhan **6** *852*
zhi **6** *827*
zun **6** *827*, 828, 845, 851
Vest (family) **8** 160; **12** 430
Vest, Georg **24** 588
Vest, Johann **26** 718
Vestel, Lucian De *see* DE VESTEL, LUCIAN
Vester Vedsted **32** 516
Vestier, Antoine **11** 411; **21** 643; **26** 376; **32** 386–7*
vestments (ecclesiastical) **14** 425; **25** 714; **32** 387–92*
historical and regional traditions
Austria **2** 823; **32** 391
Belgium **3** 609, 610; **32** *389*
Byzantine **9** 641–3*, *643*
Central Asia, Eastern **6** 314
Early Christian (*c*. AD 250-843) **9** 641–3*, *643*
England **32** 392
Germany **32** 391
Gothic **13** 196
Italy **16** *759*
Poland **16** 430
Portugal **25** 316
Russia **16** 430
Serbia **28** 457–8
Spain **32** 391
materials
embroidery **3** 609, 610; **13** 196; **16** *759*
paper **6** 314
silk **32** 391
Vestner, Andreas **32** 392
Vestner, Georg Wilhelm **20** 923; **32** 392*
Vestnik Fotograf **24** 739
Věstonice Venus **8** 381
Vestrcni (family) **10** 623
Vestre Gausdal **13** 119
sculpture **13** *119*
Vestre Slidre **23** 224
Vestri, Michele di Goro **6** 147
vestries *see* SACRISTRIES
Vestris, Eliza **30** 681
Vesy **3** 692; **5** 69
Veszelszky, Béla **14** 902
Veszprém **14** *881*
Cathedral of St Michael
St George's Chapel **14** 891
collections **15** 17
Episcopal Palace **14** 888
Gizella Chapel **14** 898
Petőfi Theatre **14** 890
sculpture **14** 892
Vetera **25** 423
Veth, Jan Pieter **22** 908; **32** 392–3*
groups and movements **19** 654; **33** 266
teachers **1** 650
works **10** 563; **22** 850
writings **8** 778
Vetla Church **8** 376
Vetluna *see* VETULONIA
Vető, János **14** 897
Vetraio, Il *see* BEMBO, GIOVAN FRANCESCO
Vetralla Cathedral **3** *713*
Vetranio, Emperor of Rome (*reg* 350) **9** 635
Vetraro, Gianfrancesco *see* BEMBO, GIOVAN FRANCESCO
Vetri, Domenico (di Polo di Angelo) de' **25** 451; **28** 436; **32** 393*
vetro porcellano *see* GLASS → types → *lattimo*
Vetter, Johann (*fl* 1575) **10** 156
Vetter, Johann (*fl* 1596-1619) **10** 156
Vetter, Konrad **9** 759
Vetterhütte glassworks **19** 522
Vetterswelde **25** 542
Vettewinkel, D. **17** 825
Vettius Cyrus **26** 884
Vetulonia **10** *583*, 585; **16** *620*; **32** 393–4*
bronzes **10** 626, 627
coins **10** 633
gold **10** 631
tombs **32** 393–4
Pietrera **10** 587, 606; **32** 394
Tomba del Duce **10** 626, 631
Tomb of the Cone **10** 626
Tomb of the Lebetes **10** 631
Tomb of the Lictor **10** 631, 639

Vetulonia—cont.
  vases 10 609, 612
Veudre, Le see LE VEUDRE
Veurne 3 539
  St Niklaas 13 99
  St Walburga 13 99
Veuve Perrin factory 20 474
Vever, Henri 13 318; 16 549; 32 394*
  collections 16 557
  prints 20 834
  works 11 637
Vever, Paul 11 637
Vever, Pierre-Paul 32 394
Veveří Castle 8 376, 388
Vewicke, Maynard 31 189; 32 394*
Veyrier, Christophe 25 707; 32 394–5*
Veyrier, François 32 394
Veyrier, Joseph 32 394
Veyrier, Laxare, V 32 394
Veyrier, Louis, I 32 394
Veyrier, Thomas 32 394
Veysberg, Vladimir 27 397
Veysserat 10 781
Vèz 21 549
Vézelay 11 504; 20 562; 26 602
  Ste Madeleine 13 39; 26 584; 32 395–7*, 397
    capitals 26 602
    chapter house 6 467
    nave 32 396
    portal 11 554
    reliefs 26 133, 136
    restorations 2 320; 32 596
    sculpture 7 642; 10 742; 26 602
    tympanum 11 554
Vézelay, Paule 32 395*
Vezo 20 35, 39
Vezzano, Ezechia da 33 587
Vezzi, Francesco 16 737; 32 398
Vezzi, Giovanni 16 737; 32 398
Vezzi Porcelain Factory 8 101; 16 737; 32 200, 398*
Vezzo, Virginia da 32 718
Vezzolano Abbey 26 690
Via 3 772
Via, Agostino dalla 19 732
Via, Arnaud de, Cardinal see ARNAUD DE VIA, Cardinal
Viá, Francesc 29 336
Via, R. de see RAIMON DE BIANYA
Via Aemilia 27 3
Via Amerina 26 887
Via Appia 27 6, 7
Via Aurelia 27 6
Via Cassia 27 6
Viacha 4 255
  church 4 259
viaducts 32 398–9*, 399
Via Flaminia 27 6
Vial, Eugène 19 848
Vialart, Etienne de Bourgevin, Comte de Saint-Morys see SAINT-MORYS, ETIENNE DE BOURGEVIN VIALART, comte de
Vialart, Charles Paul J.-B. Bourgevin de, Comte de Saint-Morys see SAINT-MORYS, CHARLES PAUL JEAN-BAPTISTE DE BOURGEVIN VIALART DE
Viali, Jacques 32 331
Viallat, Claude 11 553; 32 399*
  groups and movements 11 552; 22 35; 30 6
Viana, Eduardo (Afonso) 25 299; 28 781; 32 399–400*
Viana do Alentejo Church 13 192
Viana do Castelo 25 310
  Santa Casa da Misericórdia 26 253
  S Domingos 26 254; 28 911
Viana factory see FÁBRICA DE VIANA
Vianden
  Castle 19 826, 826
  Trinitarian Abbey 19 826
Vianelli, Achille 22 480; 24 893; 28 317; 32 400*
Vianello, Giovanni 5 918
Vianello, Michele 2 181
Vianen, Adam van 22 871; 24 778; 32 401–2*
  groups and movements 2 732
  pupils 5 62; 32 402
  works 13 701; 22 887; 24 271; 25 22; 32 400
Vianen, Christiaen van 19 593; 32 402*
  groups and movements 2 732
  patrons and collectors 29 801
  printmakers 24 271
  pupils 19 583
  works 10 327, 328; 22 887
Vianen, Cornelis van 32 725
Vianen, Ernst Jansz. van 18 8
Vianen, Jan van 14 504; 18 535
Vianen, Paulus van 22 305, 871, 896; 25 432, 731, 867; 32 401–2*
  groups and movements 2 732
  patrons and collectors 8 413; 13 914
  pupils 19 817
  works 8 413; 22 887; 25 22; 32 401
Vianen, van (family) 22 887; 23 540
Vianen Church 22 821
  tomb of Reynout van Brederode and Philippote van der Marck 22 857
Viani, Alberto 11 802; 32 403*
Viani, Antonio Maria 9 15; 32 403–4*
  collaboration 33 274
  patrons and collectors 12 911; 20 318, 320
  works 16 771; 20 320; 32 404
Viani, Domenico Maria 7 898; 10 446; 32 402*
Viani, Giovanni Maria 7 898; 32 402*
Viani, Lorenzo 16 680; 32 405*
Vianini, Antonio Maria see VIANI, ANTONIO MARIA
Vianna, Eduardo see VIANA, EDUARDO
Viano, Giacomo 4 811
Viaplana, Albert 29 274
Viapori see SUOMENLINNA FORTRESS
Viard Glassworks 11 613
Viarecta, Pantaleone see PANTALEONE VIARECTA
Viareggio 5 787
Via Salaria 27 6
Via Tiberina 27 6
Viatiensis see BAEZA
Viatis, Bartholomäus 17 711
Viator see PÉLERIN, JEAN
Viau, Georges 24 883
Viaucourt, Jean de 11 618; 12 832
Viaur Viaduct 30 27
Vibaudan 5 785
Vibert 10 781
Vibert, James A. 3 824; 30 138
Vibert, Théodore 13 228
Vibhutihalli 21 44
Vibius Rufus 27 30
Viborg (Denmark) 8 720
  architecture 32 533
  Cathedral 8 722; 26 593, 640
  sculpture 8 737
Viborg (Russia) see VYBORG
Vic (France), St Martin 26 650
Vic (Catalonia) 16 103
  Cathedral 13 68, 191
    metalwork 29 337
    retable 11 482
    sculpture 26 610
    textiles 16 438
    tomb of St Bernard Calvó 16 436, 437
Vicat, Louis-Joseph 7 693
Vic Cope 23 461
Vicens, Joan 5 909; 29 306
Vicente, Gil 32 406*
  patrons and collectors 2 871; 3 534; 25 312
  works 32 406
Vicente, Manuel 25 294
Vicente, Simón 31 89
Vicentelo de Leca, Miguel Mañara see MAÑARA VICENTELO DE LECA, MIGUEL
Vicente-Maura, Gabriel 25 702
Vicentino, Andrea 31 15; 32 220, 406–7*
Vicentino, (Giuseppe) Niccolò 2 20; 4 195; 32 407*; 33 366, 367
Vicentino, Pasqualino see ROSSI, PASQUALE
Vicentino, Valerio see BELLI, VALERIO
Vicenza 13 298; 16 618; 32 407–11*, 408, 409, 410
  architecture 7 916
  Banca Popolare see palazzi → Palazzo Thiene
  Basilica see palazzi → Palazzo della Ragione
  Centro Internazionale di Studi di Architettura Andrea Palladio 23 862
  glass 16 740
  guidebooks 4 454
  Loggia del Capitaniato 4 776; 23 492, 868–9
  palazzi 5 424
    Palazzo Braghetta sul Corso 3 864
    Palazzo Chiericati 16 635; 23 836, 863–4, 864; 29 523
    Palazzo Folco 3 863
    Palazzo Franceschini see Palazzo Folco
    Palazzo Giustiniani Baggio 12 560
    Palazzo Negri 5 845
    Palazzo da Porto-Festa 23 863
    Palazzo della Ragione 23 865, 865; 27 129; 31 238
    Palazzo Thiene 1 110; 4 776; 23 858, 863
      stucco 32 647
    Palazzo Trissino Baston 12 560
    Palazzo Valmarana 23 492, 868, 868
    Palazzo Velo Vittore 22 388
  Porta Castello 4 776
  S Bartolomeo 21 904
  S Corona 16 747
  S Lorenzo 11 708; 13 64; 24 30
  S Rocco 28 293
  theatres 30 655
    Teatro Berga 30 655
    Teatro Olimpico 1 124; 15 137; 23 869; 30 655, 656, 657
    Teatro Verdi 30 684
  urban planning 32 408
  Villa Almerico-Valmarana see Villa Rotonda
  Villa Caldogne 32 550
  Villa Capra see Villa Rotonda
  Villa Chiericati-Magna 31 71
  Villa Rotonda 14 460; 16 634; 20 280; 23 857, 867, 867–8; 25 265; 27 236; 32 411*, 548
  Villa Valmarana 2 330; 12 292; 32 553
    frescoes 16 719; 30 859–60, 863
Vicenza, Rocco da see ROCCO DA VICENZA
Vicenzo, Alfredo de 18 415
Vich see VIC (CATALONIA)
Vich (family) 26 301
Vich, Jéronimo de 31 815
Vichy 3 226; 11 603
  baths 23 598
Vichy-Chamrond, Marie Anne de, Marquise du Deffand see DEFFAND, MARIE ANNE DE VICHY-CHAMROND, Marquise du
Vich y Mascó, Diego de 31 815
Viciebsk 3 525; 32 411–12*
  art schools 6 384
  Church of the Annunciation 3 526
  Johann Pestalozzi statue 3 531
  Karl Marx statue 3 531
  Museum 3 529; 6 384
  Museum of Antiquity 32 412
  painting 3 529
  Regional Museum of Local History 32 412
  Yury Pen Museum 24 350
Vicino, Giovanni Battista 31 293; 32 754
Vicino da Ferrara 3 93; 11 8
Vicioso, Miki 9 118
Vicitra see BICHITR
Vic-le-Comte, Sainte-Chapelle 27 551
Vico, Enea 10 386, 524; 26 770; 32 412–13*
  groups and movements 10 95
  reproductive prints by others 5 906; 10 487
  works 3 160; 10 477; 13 700; 15 83; 16 778, 779; 24 201; 25 607; 27 275, 606, 650; 32 412
  writings 15 83
Vico, Francesco di see FRANCESCO DI VITO
Vico, Giambattista 10 642; 32 413*
Vico di Val d'Elsa, Palazzo Maioni-Guiccardini 12 706
Vicoforte, Sanctuary of the Madonna 32 631, 631–2
Vicomagistri 27 33, 46
Victoors, Jan see VICTORS, JAN
Victor (fl 1651-97) 25 334, 336
Victor III, Pope (reg 1086-87) see DESIDERIUS, Abbot of Montecassino
Victor, Diane 29 110
Victor, Paul-Emile 2 660
Victor-Amadeus I, 12th Duke of Savoy (reg 1630-37) 4 543; 28 2, 7–8*
  architecture 6 19
  collections 31 443
  paintings 5 405
  sponsorship 5 406
Victor-Amadeus II, 15th Duke of Savoy (reg 1675-1730) and King of Sardinia (reg 1720-30) 11 682; 23 512, 513; 26 322; 28 2, 15–17*
  architecture 6 19; 12 163; 17 706, 708, 709; 26 500; 31 441, 444
  interior decoration 16 716
  metalwork 9 398
  paintings 3 453; 19 524, 645; 20 270; 28 9, 379; 29 41
  sculpture 3 198; 5 525; 18 618
  tapestries 31 446
  urban planning 16 764; 31 441
Victor-Amadeus III, Duke of Savoy and King of Sardinia (reg 1773-96) 4 557; 28 2, 18–19*
  gold 16 742
  sculpture 3 825; 31 445
  wood-carvings 4 340
Victor-Emanuel I, Duke of Savoy and King of Sardinia (reg 1802-21) 28 2
Victor-Emanuel II, Duke of Savoy and King of Sardinia (reg 1849-61), King of Italy (reg 1861-78) 23 829; 28 2, 19–20*
  decorative works 6 20
  paintings 8 716; 12 29, 607; 14 116
  sculpture 3 131; 12 267
Victor-Emanuel III, King of Italy (reg 1900-46) 24 346; 27 303
Victoria (BC; Canada) 5 559; 32 413–14*
  Art Gallery of Greater Victoria 6 826; 7 156
  British Columbia Provincial Museum see Royal British Columbia Museum
  City Hall 5 561
  Emily Carr Art Gallery 32 414
  Government House 5 572
  Maltwood Art Museum and Gallery 32 414
  Royal British Columbia Museum 5 590, 591; 32 414
Victoria (Ecuador) 9 709
Victoria (Gozo)
  Cathedral Museum 20 219
  Museum of Archaeology 20 219
Victoria, Empress of Germany (1840-1901) 14 648, 649, 656*; 15 122
Victoria, Queen of Great Britain (reg 1837-1901) 1 270; 10 362; 14 143, 147–8*; 19 103; 25 193; 33 110
  architecture 8 249
  cameos 27 878
  catalogues 26 69
  ceramics 21 697
  decorative works 30 867
  drawings 9 229
  engravings 9 148
  etchings 25 630
  exhibitions 10 679
  furniture 10 907; 12 172; 13 680; 19 113; 23 65; 24 817; 28 255; 30 783; 31 422
  harnesses 14 186
  interior decoration 28 248; 33 145
  ivory 15 697
  jewellery 6 164; 12 163; 17 516, 527
  lithographs 18 728
  medals 11 812
  paintboxes 23 788
  paintings 5 78; 8 616; 10 367; 14 270, 480; 18 722; 28 509; 33 190
    battle 2 446
    frescoes 10 252
    genre 11 796; 14 680; 23 599; 24 636; 28 77
    hunting scenes 29 425
    marine 4 627; 28 78
    military 5 310
    miniatures 27 173
    portraits 17 673; 32 912
    religious 14 436
    watercolours 4 808; 6 402; 13 891; 14 196; 33 452
  photographs 3 486; 7 403, 435; 20 888; 24 661; 26 131; 33 219
  porcelain 14 449; 15 2
  pottery 26 362
  scissors 8 287
  sculpture 3 509; 4 220; 7 841; 8 472; 10 435; 29 584; 30 703; 31 346; 33 449
  silver 12 612
  teachers 8 652
  tiles 30 504
Victoria, Baltasar de 15 83
Victoria, Francisco Javier de Luna see LUNA VICTORIA, FRANCISCO JAVIER DE
Victoria and Albert Museum see under LONDON → museums
Victoria and Albert Petrarch, Master of the 32 198
Victoria Cabinet Works 28 255
Victoria Eugenia, Queen of Spain (1887-1969) 29 321
Victoria green see under PIGMENTS → types
Victorian Institute of Architects 2 772

Victorian Society **32** 415
Victorian style **32** 414–15*
Victorian Tapestry Workshop **2** 767; **30** 331
Victoria River **1** 43
Victoria Society of Arts **29** 926
Victorica, Miguel Carlos **6** 10; **7** 847; **32** 415*
Victorine Canons **32** 415–16*
Victorinus, Emperor of Rome (*reg* 269-70) **31** 323
Víctor Manuel (García) **8** 233; **32** 416*
Victors, Jacobus **32** 416
Victors, Jan **22** 843; **32** 416–17*
Victors, Victor (*b* 1638) **32** 416
Victors, Victor (*b* 1653) **32** 417
Victory *see under* SHIPS → named vessels
victory gardens *see under* GARDENS → types
Victory of Samothrace *see* NIKE OF SAMOTHRACE
Victricius, Saint **27** 245
Vicuña, Morla **5** *304*
vicuña hair *see under* HAIR → types
Vicuña Mackenna, Benjamín **6** 593; **27** 791
Vicús **29** *156*; **31** 118; **32** 417–18*
Vicús culture **32** 417–18*
gilding **29** 212
metalwork **29** 215
musical instruments **29** 215–16
pottery **32** 417–18
vases **32** *418*
Vic-Wells Ballet *see* ROYAL BALLET (UK)
Vida, Gheza **26** 716; **32** 418–19*
Vidal, Emeric Essex **4** 717; **31** 754; **32** 419*
works **2** 394, 399
Vidal, Francesc **29** 306, 307, 319, 320
Vidal, Gérard **4** 59; **12** 336
Vidal, Joan-Josep Tharrats i *see* THARRATS (I VIDAL), JOAN-JOSEP
Vidal, Miguel Angel **2** 401, 525; **32** 419*
Vidal, Nicolás **29** 341
Vidal, Pedro Antonio **32** 560
Vidal, Teodoro **25** 703
Vidal, Vidal Olivera y *see* OLIVERA Y VIDAL, VIDAL
Vidbergs, Sigismunds **30** 36; **31** 854
Videau, Aymé **10** 332
video art **14** 690; **22** 279, 381; **26** 235; **32** 419–21*
England **10** 258
Germany **23** 777
Netherlands, the **22** 853
United States of America **31** 609; **32** 420
video discs **2** 367; **31** 671
video microscopy *see* TECHNICAL EXAMINATION → types → microscopy (video)
videos **24** 376, 662, 678
Vidigueira Treasure **25** 312
vidimus **29** 498
Vidin **5** *144*, 147, 160
Vidisha *see* BESNAGAR
Vidolenghi, Leonardo **32** 421*
Vidoni, Bartolomeo Soresina *see* SORESINA VIDONI, BARTOLOMEO
Vidor, Emil **32** 421–2*
Vidovszky, László **14** 896
Vidranović, Ilija **28** 450
Vidyadhara, Ruler (*reg c.* 1025-50) (Chandella) **15** 290; **18** 13
Vie des arts **24** 430
Vie et Lumière **2** 197; **7** 405; **14** 507; **19** 791, 792; **22** 136
Viegas Vilhete, Pascoal **27** 809
Viegener, Eberhard **10** 695
Viehweger, Hermann **19** 705*
Vieiera, Custódio **19** 777
Vieil, Guillaume Le *see* LE VIEIL, GUILLAUME
Vieil, Pierre Le *see* LE VIEIL, PIERRE
Vieil-Evreux **27** 2
Vieil-Hesdin **14** 460
Vieira, Affonso Lopes **19** 428
Vieira, Alvaro Siza *see* SIZA VIEIRA, ALVARO
Vieira, Custódio **19** 464; **20** 85; **25** 292; **32** 422*
Vieira, Domingos **4** 633, 634; **25** 297; **32** 422–3*
Vieira, Domingos Francisco **32** 425
Vieira, Jacinto **32** 423*
Vieira, Jorge (Ricardo da Conceição) **25** 302; **32** 423*
Vieira da Cruz, Luís **26** 253
Vieira da Silva(, Marie-Hélène) **4** 719; **19** 468; **25** 310; **30** 882; **32** 423*
collaboration **26** 352
dealers **19** 537
groups and movements **4** 719; **26** 414
teachers **4** 98
works **3** 462; **11** 551; **25** 299; **26** 113
Vieira de Magalhães Porto, Severiano Mário *see* PORTO, SEVERIANO
Vieira Lusitano, Francisco **32** 424–5*
collaboration **8** 858
education (art) **25** 319
patrons and collectors **4** 635; **32** 539
works **25** 297, *297*; **32** *424*
Vieira Matos, Francisco *see* VIEIRA LUSITANO, FRANCISCO
Vieira Portuense, Francisco **3** 816; **32** 425–6*
collaboration **28** 430
patrons and collectors **12** 889; **29** 100
works **11** 395; **25** 298; **32** *425*
Vieira Serrão, Domingos **11** 772; **32** 426–7*
collaboration **25** 297; **26** 253, 516
El Viejón, Monument 1 **29** 619
Viel (de Saint-Meaux), Charles-François **2** 658; **32** 427*
Viel, Victor **10** 682
Vien, Joseph-Marie, Comte (1716-1809) **2** 524; **11** 561; **14** 585; **22** 35; **24** 168; **26** 774; **32** 427–30*
collaboration **6** 121
groups and movements **22** 734; **24** 171
methods **10** 198; **21** 759
patrons and collectors **4** 554; **7** 194; **8** 795; **9** 314; **11** 540, 658; **13** 665; **14** 585; **25** 81, 212
pupils
Aubry, Etienne **2** 702
Cacault, Pierre **5** 356
Cassas, Louis-François **5** 921
Danloux, Henri-Pierre **8** 507
David, Jacques-Louis **8** 555, 560
Debucourt, Philibert-Louis **8** 594
Dunker, Balthazar Anton **9** 395
Floding, Per Gustaf **11** 173
Garnier, Etienne-Barthélemy **12** 158
Hetsch, Philipp Friedrich von **14** 496
Kucharski, Aleksander **18** 495
Losenko, Anton (Pavlovich) **19** 704
Norblin de la Gourdaine, Jan Piotr **23** 202
Roslin, Marie-Suzanne **27** 170
Sablet, François and Jacques **27** 484
Saint-Ours, Jean-Pierre **27** 571
Vien, Joseph-Marie, Comte (1716-1809)
pupils—cont.
Taillasson, Jean-Joseph **30** 238
Vincent, François-André **32** 584
Waldeck, Johann Friedrich (Maximilian), Graf von **32** 774
Wertmüller, Adolf Ulric **33** 86
Wille, Pierre-Alexandre **33** 196
reproductions in tapestry **22** 726
reproductive prints by others **4** 331
sponsors **6** 121
teachers **12** 721
works **1** 898; **11** 368, 540; **21** 825; **24** 135; **25** 192; **32** *428*, *429*
Vien, Joseph-Marie (1762-1848) **32** 427
Vieng Xan-Vieng Kham *see* VIENTIANE
Vienna (Austria) **2** 775, *776*; **26** *906*; **32** 430–61*, *431*, *433*, *435*, *436*, *438*
academies and art schools
Akademie der Bildenden Künste **1** 105; **2** 831; **17** 857; **32** 443, 444, 445
collections **6** 92; **18** 671
Gemäldegalerie **2** 830; **16** 773
Great Hall **2** 797; **11** 47
library **2** 833
paintings **33** 430
see also Graveurakademie; Kupferstichakademie
Akademie der Maler, Bildhauer und Baukünstler **2** 831
Graphische Lehr- und Versuchsanstalt **32** 445
library **2** 833
Graveurakademie **2** 831
see also Akademie der Bildenden Künste
Hochschule für Angewandte Kunst **2** 817, 831, 832; **7** 368; **15** 823, 883; **26** 15
collections **2** 816; **7** 53
library **2** 833
Kaiserliche Akademie **2** 794, 831; **29** 788, 789; **32** 443; **33** 156
Kunstgewerbeschule *see* Hochschule für Angewandte Kunst
Künstlerische Volkshochschule **2** 831
Kupferstichakademie **2** 831
see also Akademie der Bildenden Künste
Manufakturschule **1** 107; **12** 479
Österreichische Akademie der Wissenschaften **2** 784
Wiener Kunstschule **2** 831
Amalienbad **32** 439
apartment blocks **22** 831
Karl-Marx-Hof **10** 98
Kötlergasse/Linke Wienzeile **2** 809
Looshaus **2** 567, 788; **19** 652, *652*; **21** 779
interior decoration **19** 651
Majolika Haus **2** 567; **30** 506, 885, *885*
Arkadenhof **2** 808
art forms and materials
amber **1** 762
architecture **2** 828
armillary spheres **12** *813*
ceramics **2** 816
chasubles **32** *391*
clocks **7** 442
embroidery **2** 824, 825
furniture **2** 812; **32** 448*
glass **2** *818*
gold **2** 819, 820, *820*
jewellery **17** 527
ketubbot **18** 3
Kunstkammern **9** 14
Vienna (Austria)
art forms and materials—cont.
lace **18** 593
majolica **2** 816
manuscript illumination **2** 792; **17** 564
maps **14** 573
medals **20** 925
metalwork **2** 822; **32** 449*
painting **2** 792, 793
ceiling **26** 24
mural **22** 330
panel **2** 792
pigments **24** 794
porcelain **6** 924; **32** 449–50*, *450*
silk **28** 717
silver **2** 821
snuff-boxes **2** 823
textiles **2** 825
Augarten-Portal **2** 785
Bank- und Börsengebäude **2** 786, 808
Belvedere **2** 783, 794, 830; **3** 689; **23** 806, 811; **32** 458–9*
Belvedere Gallery **6** 101; **16** 772; **22** *356*
catalogues **6** 77; **20** 915
collections **22** 356, 357; **32** 446
paintings **9** 18
Bilderzimmer **5** 344
collections **32** 444
frescoes **5** 774
Galerie des Allerhöchsten Kaiserhauses *see under* museums
Galerie des XIX. und XX. Jahrhunderts *see under* museums
gardens **2** 822; **12** 133; **26** 497
gates **2** *822*
Kunsthistorisches Museum *see under* museums
Lower Belvedere **2** 783, 828; **14** 529–30; **32** 458
Marmorsaal **2** 794; **25** 416
Porzellankabinett **5** 348
Sala Terrena **27** 611
sculpture **24** 460
menagerie **33** 698
Moderne Galerie *see under* museums
Museum Mittelalterlicher Kunst *see under* museums
Österreichische Galerie *see under* museums
Österreichisches Barockmuseum *see under* museums
paintings **9** 760; **10** 883
sculpture **13** 922; **21** 313, 314
stucco **29** 839
Upper Belvedere **2** 783; **14** 529–30; **32** 458–9, *459*
Gemahleneskabinett **5** 344
Goldenes Zimmer *see* Spiegelzimmer
interior decoration **2** 806
Marmorierteskabinett **5** 344
paintings **25** 56, *56*
Sala Terrena **2** 695; **27** 610, *611*
Spiegelzimmer **5** 344, 349
stables **29** 485
staircases **29** 525
Börse **10** 669
Britisches Konsulat *see* palaces → Palais Caprara-Geymüller
Bundesdenkmalamt library **2** 832
Bundesmobiliendepot **2** 811
cafés
Café Daum **30** 754
Café Museum **2** 810; **19** 651
Café Nihilismus *see* Café Museum
Kleines Café **2** 789
collections **17** 582
Die Zeit building **2** 814
Dorotheum **2** 829
Vienna (Austria)—cont.
Dürerverein **2** 808
ecclesiastical buildings
Altlerchenfeld parish church **2** 786; **22** 273
Am Steinhof Lunatic Asylum Church **2** 567, 788, 809; **14** 785
Armenian Monastery **2** 443
Augustinerkirche **2** 785, 808; **13** 57
tomb of Maria Christina of Austria **2** 802; **5** 628, *628*; **31** 130; **33** 28
Capuchin church **2** 801
sarcophagus of Charles VI **2** 802
Carmelite church **2** 781; **13** 57
Church of the Comforters of Gethsemane **2** 785
Church of the Holy Ghost **25** 37
Church of the Teutonic Knights **2** 785
Convent of the Order of St Clare **2** 780
Dominican church **2** 780; **26** 24
Franciscan church **2** 780; **23** 501
Gardekirche **2** 784
Greek Orthodox Church **2** 784, 808
Gustav-Adolf-Kirche **2** 786
Jesuit church **2** 780, 794; **15** 139
Jubiläumskirche **2** 787
Karlskirche **2** 782, *782*, 794, 827; **9** 86; **11** 133; **32** 453–4*
frescoes **15** 139
interior decoration **2** 806
portico **25** 266
sculpture **2** 801
Maria am Gestade **32** 454*
Maria Stiegen *see* Maria am Gestade
Maria vom Siege **2** 787; **28** 121
Matzleinsdorf Friedhofskirche **2** 786
Michaelerkirche **2** 784; **32** 433–4, 454*
altarpiece **31** *678*
sculpture **2** 799
Minorite church **2** 785, 808
Peterskirche **2** 782; **25** 728
Piarist church **2** 782, 795
Protestant church **2** 784
Rathauskapelle *see* Salvatorkapelle
Redemptionist Church *see* Church of the Comforters of Gethsemane
St Elisabeth **30** 535
St John Nepomuk **2** 785
St Leopold am Steinhof *see* ecclesiastical buildings → Am Steinhof Lunatic Asylum Church
Salvatorkapelle **2** 779, 800
Schottenkirche **2** 825; **32** *433*
Schwarzspanierkirche **29** 760
pulpit **29** *760*
Servite church **2** 781
Steinhofkirche *see* ecclesiastical buildings → Am Steinhof Lunatic Asylum Church
Stephansdom **2** 777; **13** 58; **14** 81; **32** 450–52*, *451*
bosses **4** 465
choir **13** 49
Giants' Portal **26** 635
marks **20** 441
organ loft **24** 807
pinnacles **24** 826
plans **2** *328*
pulpit **2** 778; **24** 807; **25** 725
roof **30** 909, *910*
sculpture **2** 798, 799, 800; **13** 89; **32** *441*, 453*
spire **29** 414
stained glass **14** 422
Stephansturm **32** 434, 450, 452

Vienna (Austria)
ecclesiastical buildings
Stephansdom—cont.
textiles 2 824
tomb of Frederick III 2 800; 12 344; 13 91
vaults 32 92
Ursulinenkloster 2 824
Votivkirche 2 787, 808; 11 29–30, *30*; 13 202
sculpture 2 802; 13 111, 112
tomb of Count Niclas Salm 2 800
exhibitions
Elektrische Ausstellung, 1883 2 808
Weltausstellung, 1873 2 808; 10 682; 14 908; 15 883; 27 421; 32 438
festivals 23 766
Fledermaus Cabaret 33 166
fortifications 2 780; 21 548; 32 434
galleries 9 19
Galerie Miethke 2 829
Galerie Nächst St Stephan 32 447
Galerie Würthle 2 829; 32 447
Majoratsgalerie *see under* palaces → Stadtpalais Liechtenstein
Gänsehäufel Lido 2 789
gardens 12 133
government buildings
Arsenal 2 786, 808; 21 313
see also museums → Heeresgeschichtliches Museum
Customs Office 2 785
Hauptmünzamt 2 785; 29 431
Landhaus 2 779
Verordnetenstube 13 897
Mint *see* Hauptmünzamt
Parlament 2 787; 3 732; 13 237; 14 *150*, 151
portico 25 268
Revenue Office 2 786
river authority buildings 2 788
Stadthalle 2 810
Grosser Federlhof 2 778
Grosser Musikvereinssaal 7 687
guilds 32 441
Haas-Haus 2 789
Heinrichshof 2 787; 26 190
Hofburg 2 778, 785, *807*; 11 134, *135*; 24 810; 32 454–7*, *455*
Amalienburg 2 778, 782; 13 920; 32 456
Burgtor 2 785, *786*, 787
chapel 27 551
collections 13 921; 32 444
Hofbibliothek *see* Österreichische Nationalbibliothek
Imperial Picture Gallery *see* Stallburg
interior decoration 2 808
Kunstkammer 13 918
Leopoldinischer Trakt 2 782; 32 456
murals 18 419
Neue Burg 2 787; 23 813; 29 843; 32 457
Neue Galerie 2 829
Österreichische Nationalbibliothek 2 370, 782; 13 *278*, 278–9; 19 314, 316; 32 456–7, *457*; 33 116
collections 2 832; 6 78
directors 16 548
frescoes 15 139
interior decoration 2 806
prints 25 631
paintings 13 921; 29 789
Präsidentskanzlei 2 812
Redoutensaal 7 687
Reichskanzleitrakt 32 456

Vienna (Austria)
Hofburg—cont.
Schatzkammer 5 806, 807; 7 179; 13 914
collections 13 921, 922; 26 78, 81; 32 457–8*
Schauräume 14 12
Schweizerhof 2 778; 32 455–6
Schweizertor 2 778, *778*
Schweizertrakt *see* Schweizerhof
Spanish Riding School *see* Winterreitschule
Stallburg 2 778, 782; 9 18; 32 456
collections 13 919
paintings 13 919
sculpture 13 920
Winterreitschule 26 363; 32 456
Zeremoniensaal 2 785
hospitals
Allgemeines Krankenhaus 2 785; 14 783
Narrenturm 2 657, 785
Wilhelminen hospital 30 885
houses
Hasenhaus 2 778; 10 738
Haus L. R. S. 2 *810*
Haus Rufer 2 788
Hüffelbergstrasse 28 30 885
Knips Haus 2 809
Rufer Haus 21 779
Skywa-Primavesi Haus 2 809
Steiner Haus 2 567; 21 779; 26 15; 32 555
Tuchlauben 19 2 792
Zacherl Haus 25 *37*, 37
housing
Pilotengasse Estate 2 789
Schottenhof housing developments 2 785
Veitingergasse Estate 2 789
Josephinum *see under* schools and colleges
Josephsplatz 2 784; 33 624
Justizministerium *see* palaces → Palais Trautson
Karl-Marx-Hof 32 *439*
libraries
Kaiserliche Bibliothek *see* Hofburg → Österreichische Nationalbibliothek
Österreichische Nationalbibliothek *see under* Hofburg
Wiener Stadt und Landesbibliothek
archives 2 370
collections 2 833
Lichtenstein Benefiziatshaus 2 785
masons' lodges 19 532; 32 440
monuments and memorials
memorial to Franz Schubert 2 802
memorial to Ludwig van Beethoven 2 802, *803*
monument to Archduke Charles 2 802; 10 *908*
monument to Emperor Joseph II 2 802
monument to Empress Elizabeth 2 788
monument to Empress Maria-Theresa 33 727
monument to Feldmarschall Carl Schwarzenberg 2 802
monument to Johann Wolfgang von Goethe 2 803
monument to Karl Lueger 2 803
monument to Wolfgang Amadeus Mozart 2 803
Plague Column 2 801; 5 *264*
Trinity Column *see* Plague Column
Mozart fountain 2 803
museums
20iger Haus *see* Museum des 20. Jahrhunderts

Vienna (Austria)
museums—cont.
Albertina 8 502; 22 33; 32 444; 33 110
archives 2 370
catalogues 33 159
collections 2 830; 5 908; 9 426; 13 279; 14 11; 17 434; 24 240; 32 445, 622
directors 3 715
drawings 5 866; 9 230; 14 618
engravings 22 272
furniture 2 813
library 2 832
prints 25 631; 33 116
Ephesos Museum 32 457
Galerie des Allerhöchsten Kaiserhauses
directors 10 703; 18 419
see also Belvedere → Belvedere Gallery; Kunsthistorisches Museum
Galerie des XIX. und XX. Jahrhunderts 2 830; 32 447
Gemäldegalerie der Akademie der Bildenden Künste *see under* academies and art schools → Akademie der Bildenden Künste
Graphische Sammlung Albertina *see* Albertina
Heeresgeschichtliches Museum 2 449, 454, 786; 3 732; 4 106; 14 150; 18 517; 32 437
see also government buildings → Arsenal
Historisches Museum der Stadt Wien 2 808, 831; 14 25; 32 447
archives 2 370
Hofmuseen 3 732; 14 216
Imperial Art Gallery *see* Galerie des Allerhöchsten Kaiserhauses
Imperial Picture Gallery *see* Hofburg → Stallburg
Jüdisches Museum 17 581, 582
Kaiserliche Gemäldegalerie *see* Galerie des Allerhöchsten Kaiserhauses
Kunstgewerbemuseum 11 30; 22 363
Kunsthistorische Sammlungen des Allerhöchsten Kaiserhauses *see* Kunsthistorisches Museum
Kunsthistorisches Museum 2 275, 560, 787; 9 12; 14 12, 216; 20 146; 22 311, 364; 28 400; 29 525, 843; 32 437
Albert Figdor-Stiftung 11 62
archives 2 370
collections 2 830; 3 703; 4 897; 10 85, 91, 93; 14 11, 807; 16 556, 767; 22 357, 696; 25 12; 27 225; 30 331, 519; 32 445, 457
Este Collection 23 333
exhibitions 30 332
Gemäldegalerie 13 919
Greek collection 13 469, 470, 542
interior decoration 2 808; 18 129
library 2 832
Miramare collection 2 830
murals 22 330
musical instruments 22 376
periodicals 24 438
pottery 13 542
Roman collection 27 115
sculpture 27 46
see also Belvedere → Belvedere Gallery
see also Galerie des Allerhöchsten Kaiserhauses
Kupferstichkabinett 19 338
Majoratsgalerie *see under* palaces → Stadtpalais Liechtenstein

Vienna (Austria)
museums—cont.
Moderne Galerie 32 447
Museum des 20. Jahrhunderts 2 810; 22 363; 28 187; 32 447
library 2 832
Museum für Kunst und Industrie *see* Österreichisches Museum für Angewandte Kunst
Museum für Völkerkunde 32 457
collections 2 830; 17 434; 21 250, 264, 265
Museum Mittelalterlicher Kunst 2 830; 32 447
Museum Moderner Kunst 2 830; 12 497; 32 448
collections 14 48
library 2 832
see also palaces → Gartenpalais Liechtenstein in der Rossau
Naturhistorisches Museum 2 *786*, 787; 22 364, 675; 28 400; 30 888; 32 437
collections 2 830
Neue Galerie *see under* Hofburg
Österreichische Galerie 2 830, 832; 32 447, 459
Österreichische Ludwig-Stiftung für Kunst und Wissenschaft 19 779
Österreichisches Barockmuseum 2 830; 32 447
Österreichisches Museum für Angewandte Kunst 2 809, 814, 826, 828, 831; 10 772; 14 12; 32 446, 448
archives 2 370
collections 2 830; 3 703; 8 502; 15 745; 17 441; 30 332
interior decoration 2 808
Kaiser Franz I Zimmer 2 825
Lefler-Zimmer 28 155
library 2 832
Österreichisches Museum für Kunst und Industrie *see* Österreichisches Museum für Angewandte Kunst
Strada's Musaeum 29 737, 739
Waffensammlung *see* Arsenal → Heeresgeschichtliches Museum
Musikvereinsgebäude 1 125
National Bank 2 785, 787; 3 175
Österreichischer Rundfunk 2 789
palaces
Archbishop's Palace
Andreaskapelle 2 800
Gartenpalais Liechtenstein in der Rossau
Belvedere 3 689
furniture 19 113
interior decoration 11 682
paintings 19 338, 339
paintings (ceiling) 3 681
see also museums → Museum Moderner Kunst
see also Stadtpalais Liechtenstein
Gartenpalais Mansfeld-Fondi *see* Palais Schwarzenberg
Geymüller Schlossl 2 808
Lower Belvedere *see under* Belvedere
Majoratspalast *see* Stadtpalais Liechtenstein
Neue Burg *see under* Hofburg
Neugebäude 29 428
Palais Caprara-Geymüller
Pompeii room 2 808
Palais Daun-Kinsky 2 783; 14 529, *529*; 20 842; 23 812
Palais Dietrichstein-Lobkowitz 2 782
Palais Epstein 2 787, 808
Palais Erzherzog Wilhelm 2 787
Palais Fries-Pallavicini 2 785
Palais Hoyos 20 145

Vienna (Austria)
palaces—cont.
Palais Kaunitz-Esterházy 10 530, *530*; 17 857; 18 843
Palais Kinsky *see* Palais Daun-Kinsky
Palais Liechtenstein 9 410
Palais Rasumofsky 2 785, 808
Palais Schönborn 11 131; 23 812
Palais Schwarzenberg 2 782, 801; 12 133; 13 278; 14 528, *528*
Palais Strattmann *see* Palais Windischgrätz
Palais Todesco 2 808
Palais Trautson 11 *132*; 23 812; 29 525
Palais Windischgrätz 11 131; 23 812
Schloss Mirabell 2 783
Schloss Neugebäude 2 778, *779*
Schloss Schönbrunn 2 784, 785, 794, 795, 811; 11 130; 13 852; 14 645; 23 811; 26 496; 32 459*, 460*
belvedere 29 610
Ehrenhof 33 623
frescoes 26 321
gallery 13 802
gardens 2 785, 802; 3 899; 11 123; 18 225; 32 460–61*, *461*
Gloriette 2 785
interior decoration 2 806, 807, 808
Meidlinger Tor 2 822
menagerie 33 698
Millionenzimmer 2 *806*, 807
paintings 15 741, 745; 16 553; 21 512; 26 167; 32 *443*
Rosa rooms 27 136
sculpture 14 32; 25 648
Spiegelkabinett 5 349
Spiegelsaal 5 349
Schönbrunn Palace *see* Schloss Schönbrunn
Stadtpalais Batthyány *see* Palais Schönborn
Stadtpalais Liechtenstein 5 295; 19 337
furniture 2 813
interior decoration 2 808, *809*
Majoratsgalerie 19 337, 338
see also Gartenpalais Liechtenstein in der Rossau
Upper Belvedere *see under* Belvedere
Winter Palace of Eugene of Savoy 2 828; 5 296; 8 141; 11 131; 23 812
Palmenhaus 2 788
Polytechnikum *see* Technische Universität
Postsparkassenamt 2 567, 788, 809, 814; 3 177; 12 792; 21 779; 27 131; 32 *762*, 762–3
Providentia fountain 2 802; 9 146, *146*
Rathaus 2 787; 13 203; 28 121; 31 241
Ringstrasse 14 580
Roman amphitheatre 26 906
Rotunda 32 438
schools and colleges 28 158
Akademisches Gymnasium 2 787; 13 203, *204*
Handelsakademie 2 786
Imperial Gymnasium 28 157
Ingenieurakademie *see* Technische Hochschule
Josephinum 2 *784*, 785
Technische Hochschule 32 436
Veterinary College 2 785
Volksschule Köhlergasse 2 789
sculpture 12 403
Secession building 2 *788*; 22 330; 25 173; 28 343, 344; 30 885
frescoes 18 130

Vienna (Austria)
Secession building—cont.
stucco **29** 843
Shopping-City-Süd **32** 439
shops
Goldmann & Salatsch residential and commercial building *see* apartment blocks → Looshaus
Kerzenladen Retti **2** 789
Modesalon Schwestern Flöge **33** 166
Salon Knize **2** 810
Stadtbahn **2** 567, 788; **32** 761, *761*
see also stations
Stadthalle **2** 789
stations
Karlsplatz Station **1** 111; **2** 567, 809
Metro stations **21** 349
see also Stadtbahn
synagogue **2** 784
Technische Universität **2** 785
see also Universität
theatres **30** 652
Burgtheater **2** 797, 803, 808; **28** *399*
Comödihauss auf der Cortina **5** 264–5; **30** 676
Deutsches Volkstheater **2** 808
Hofoper *see* Staatsoper
Komödienhaus **30** 676
Staatsoper **2** 786, 789, 808; **19** 69; **31** 873
Universität **2** 787; **11** 30
auditorium **13** 802
Aula **18** 129–30
Institut für Kunstgeschichte Library **2** 833
observatory **23** 340
see also Technische Universität
urban planning **31** 715, 723; **32** 437
Villa Hock **2** 788
Villa Vojczik **29** 843
Villa Wassermann **2** 788
Wenzgasse **2** 810
Werkbund-Siedlung **2** 810; **32** 439
Zeiss Factory **23** 358
Zentralfriedhof **17** 555; **31** 131
Vienna (France) *see under* VIENNE
Vienna 1089, Painter of (*fl c.* 400 BC) **32** 65
Vienna Adoration, Master of the **2** 792
Vienna Camera Club **24** 738
Vienna Codex *see under* CODICES → individual manuscripts
Vienna Dioskurides **9** 606, 617–18
Vienna Genesis *see under* BIBLES → individual manuscripts
Vienna green *see* PIGMENTS → types → emerald green
Vienna Hours *see under* BOOKS OF HOURS → individual manuscripts
Vienna Hours of Charles the Bold *see under* BOOKS OF HOURS → individual manuscripts
Vienna Lamentation, Master of the **2** 206
Vienna Painter (*fl c.* 500 BC) **32** 34
Vienna Passion, Master of the **6** 14
Vienna porcelain factory (before 1744) **12** 461; **32** 436
Vienna porcelain factory (after 1744) *see* KAISERLICHE PORZELLANMANUFACTUR (VIENNA; AFTER 1744)
Vienna Regulator *see under* CLOCKS → types
Vienna Rothschild Hours *see under* BOOKS OF HOURS → individual manuscripts
Vienna Schottenstift, Master of the **20** 780*; **32** 441
works **32** *433*
Vienna Secession *see* SECESSION (VIENNA)
Vienna Sketchbook *see under* SKETCHBOOKS → individual manuscripts
Vienne **11** *505*; **26** *904*, *905*; **32** 463–5*
Cathedral
monument to Cardinal de la Tour d'Auvergne and Archbishop Montmorin **28** *846*
gardens **12** 70
mosaics **27** 62
Musée Lapidaire **32** 464
St André-le-Bas **32** 464*
St Maurice **26** 584; **31** 501; **32** 463*
St Pierre **32** *464*, 464–5*
Temple of Livia and Augustus **26** 858; **32** 463
theatre **32** 463
Vienne-en-Bessin **26** 598
Viennelly, Achille *see* VIANELLI, ACHILLE
Viennot, Odette **15** 211
Vienožinskis, Justinas **19** 498, 499
Vientiane **18** *761*; **29** *225*; **32** 465*
dress **18** 772
textiles **18** 771
That Luang **18** 762, 764, 765, 767; **29** 827, 866
Vat Chai Mongkol **18** 767, 769
Vat Chen **18** 777
Vat Ho Phra Kaeo **18** 762, 764, 765
collections **32** 465
sculpture **18** 768
Vat In Peng **18** 765, 766, 769
Vat Sisaket **18** 764, 765, 768, 777
sculpture **18** *768*
Vat Up Mong **18** 770
Vat Xan **18** 765
Vat Yot Kaeo **18** 769
Vieques Island **25** *698*
fort **25** 704
pendants (jewellery) **29** *199*
Viera (family) **2** 133
Viera, Domingos **28** 164
Viereckschanzen **25** 538
Vierendeel, (Jules-)Arthur **3** 550, 618; **32** 465*
Vierge, Daniel Urrabieta y *see* URRABIETA Y VIERGE, DANIEL
Vieri, Ugolino di *see* UGOLINO DI VIERI
Vieria, Custódio **19** 468
Viérin, Jozef **3** 579, 587
Viero, Teodoro **12** 582; **24** 707; **27** 719
Vierpyl, Simon **9** 322; **16** 21; **28** 894
Viertaler, Barthlmä *see* FIRTHALER, BARTHLMÄ
Vierthaler, Ludwig **32** 695
Viervant, Anthony **32** 465
Viervant, Hendrik **32** 465
Viervant, Leendert, II **22** 827; **23** 633; **30** 568; **32** 465–6*
Viervant, Roelofs **23** 633
Vierzehnheiligen **7** 254; **12** *361*, 372; **23** 4–5, 543; **26** 498; **32** 466–7*, *467*
model **2** 336
Viesnik, Peter **23** 70
Viesulas, Romas **10** 178; **19** 499
Viet Bac, Resistance Fine Arts College **32** 482
Viet Khe **29** 230
Vietnam **6** 432–3*; **29** *225*; **32** 467–70*, *468*, *469*, 486*
adhesives **32** 488
altars **1** 706
architecture **6** 420–22*, 423–5*; **32** 471–8*
Buddhism **9** 133
military **6** 425–6*; **21** 595, 596
bamboo-carvings **32** 481
beads **23** 344
Vietnam—cont.
beams **32** 472
bells **32** 489
body ornaments **32** 487*
boots **32** 491
boxes **32** 487, 488
bracelets **32** 487
brick **4** 795; **32** 476
brocades **32** 490
bronze **4** 852; **6** 427, 432; **29** 228, 229; **32** 480, 487–8, *488*
brushes **7** 66
busts **6** *429*
carving **32** 480
casting **32** 480
casuarina **32** 488
ceramics **5** 12; **6** 432*; **29** 232; **32** 481, 484–6*
chinaberry **32** 488
churches **32** 476, *476*
citadels **6** 425–6*
coins **7** 72, 533; **32** 486*
collars **32** 486
colonnettes **6** 421
columns **6** 422, *422*; **32** 472
concrete **32** 477
copper **32** 486
costumes **32** 491
cotton **32** 489, 490
doors **9** 163
dress **32** 486–7*, *487*, 490
drums (musical instruments) **32** 489
dyes **32** 489, 490
earthenwares **32** 484
eaves **32** 472
education (art) **32** 492*
eggshells **32** 482
enamel **32** 485
exhibitions **32** 483
façades **6** *423*
figurines **32** 480
flasks **32** 487
footwear **32** 487, *487*
fortifications **21** 595, 596
furniture **32** 482, 488
gardens **12** 104*
gauze **32** 489
geomancy **32** 471, 477
glazes **32** 484
gold **6** 432; **32** 487
gold leaf **32** 482
hairstyles **32** 486
hats **32** 487, *487*, 491
houses **32** 471, 477*, *477*
iconography **6** 419–20*, 427; **32** 470–71*
incense burners **32** 486, 488
inlays **32** 482, 488*
inscriptions **6** 420
ivory **32** 487
jade **32** 487
jewellery **32** 487*
lacquer **32** 479, *479*, 481, 482*, 489
lamp-holders **32** *488*
limewater **32** 488
lime-wood **32** 488
lithophones **32** 489
looms **32** 489, 490
lost-wax casting **6** 428
lutes **32** 489
marble **32** 477
metalwork **6** 432*; **32** 487–8*
mosaics **32** 481
mother-of-pearl **32** 482, 487, 488*, 489
moulds **32** 486
musical instruments **32** 489*
opera **32** 490, 491
painting **32** 481*, 482–4*, 488
genre **32** *481*
urban life **32** *483*
wall **6** 432*
20th cent. **32** *484*
paper **7** 114; **32** 481
patronage **32** 478
pendants (jewellery) **32** 487
pigments **32** 482
Vietnam—cont.
pilasters **6** 421
pipes (smoking) **32** 481
polishing **32** 482
polychromy **5** *100*
poon **32** 488
porcelain **4** 173
pottery **29** 227; **32** 485–6, *485*
prints **32** 481–2*, *482*
puppets **32** 491, *491*
regalia **6** 432
religion **6** 419–20*; **32** 470–71*
rings **32** 487
robes **32** 486, *487*
roofs **32** 477, 487
sanctuaries **6** 420, *421*
sandalwood **32** 488
sandstone **29** IX2
sculpture **5** 484; **6** 428; **32** 478–81*
architectural **32** 480–81
bronze **32** 480
Buddhism **5** *100*; **6** 427–8*; **9** 133; **32** 478, *478*, *479*, 479–80
Mahayana **6** *428*
Champa **6** 426–7*, 429–30*, 431*
Hinduism **6** 427, 428–9*, 430
Khmer **6** 430
relief **6** 426, *429*; **29** IX2
Socialist Realism **32** *480*
stone **6** *428*; **32** 478
wood **5** *100*; **32** 479, *479*
shrines (i) (cult) **32** 471
silk **32** 489, *489*, 491
silver **32** 487, 488
statuettes **6** 427
stelae **6** 420; **32** 476
funerary **6** 420, 431
stone **6** *428*, *429*; **29** 227–8; **32** 472, 478, 489
stonewares **32** 484
stupas **32** 473, 476
tattoos **32** 487
teak **32** 488
temples **6** 420, 421, *421*, *424*; **32** 471–5*
Buddhism **30** 446; **32** 471–4*, *472*, *473*, *474*
Confucianism **32** *474*, 474–5*
terracotta **6** 426; **32** 472, *472*
textiles **32** 489–90*, *490*
Champa **6** 432–3*
Nhieu **32** 489
The **32** 490
theatre **32** 490–92*, *491*
tiles **6** 432; **32** 485
tombs **31** 115; **32** *475*, 475–6, *476*
tools **29** 227, 228
tortoiseshell **32** 487
trade
bronze **29** 230
ceramics **6** 331; **32** 485–6
dyes **32** 489
fibres **32** 489
furniture **32** 488
lacquer **32** 482
porcelain **4** 175; **6** 622
pottery **6** 331
wool **32** 489
transfer (printing) **32** 482
trusses **32** 472
tunics **32** 486
universities **32** 474
urban planning **32** 477–8*
wood **5** *100*; **32** 479, *479*, 487
zinc **32** 486
zithers **32** 489
see also CHAMPA; SOUTH-EAST ASIA
Vietnamese **5** 459
Vieusseux, Giovan Pietro **11** 189
Vieux, Philippe Des **30** 298
Vieuxpont, Charlotte de **4** 865
View: Through the Eyes of Poets **24** 433
Vieweg, Eduard **28** 400
Vieweg, Friedrich **12** 641
viewers **24** 649, 657
View of St Gudule, Master of the **9** 271; **20** 710, 780–81*
works **20** *780*
Viforiata **25** 340
Vigala **10** *536*
church **10** 539
Vigan, Jean-Pierre **15** 836
Viganò, Bruno **13** 629
Viganó, Vittoriano **5** 57; **16** 650, 651
Vigarani, Carlo **30** 671; **32** 492, 493
Vigarani, Gaspare **32** 492–3*
collaboration **30** 671
patrons and collectors **10** 526, 527
pupils **30** 671
works **30** 669
Vigarani, Lodovico **30** 671; **32** 492
Vigarny, Felipe **13** 108; **23** 487; **29** 289, 290; **32** 493–4*
collaboration **2** 23; **3** 846, 847; **7** 345; **16** 898; **26** 250; **28** 725
groups and movements **25** 30
patrons and collectors **30** 374
pupils **24** 712
retables **29** 289
works **2** 279; **3** 123, 847; **5** 201, 203, 204; **26** *250*; **29** 265; **31** 89, 92; **32** *493*
Vigarny, Gregorio **32** 493
Vigas, Oswaldo **32** 175, 494*
patrons and collectors **32** 568
works **32** *175*
Vigatá, El *see* PLA, FRANCESC
Vigée, Louis **32** 494
Vigée Le Brun, Elisabeth-Louise **19** 25; **22** 86, 480; **26** 841; **32** 85, 494–6*, *496*; **33** 308
groups and movements **24** 136
patrons and collectors **4** 555; **5** 530; **13** 303; **14** 486; **33** 579
pupils **3** 735; **13** 689
reproductive prints by others **1** 645; **4** 807
sponsors **8** 372
works **9** 285; **11** *408*, *409*, 410; **19** 338; **23** 113; **32** *495*
Vigeland, Elisus Thorsen **32** 497
Vigeland, Emanuel **32** 498
Vigeland, Gustav (Adolf) **32** 497–8*
patrons and collectors **30** 730
studio **23** 243
teachers **3** 783
works **23** 230, *230*, 603; **28** 314; **32** *497*
Vigeland, Per **32** 498
Vigeland, Tone **23** 238
Vigenère, Blaise de **5** 814; **13** 878; **14** 546
Vigers, George **25** 688
Vigevano **4** 646; **19** 194
Cathedral of S Vigilo **30** 331
La Sforzesca **32** 545
Viggen Bridge **14** 388
Viggiù, Silla da *see* LONGHI, SILLA
Vígh, Tamás **14** 896; **32** 498–9*
works **14** *897*
Vighen, Claude **32** 716
Vighi, Giacomo *see* ARGENTA
Vigier, Jean **19** 396
Vigil, Evelyn **22** 608
Vigil, Lonnie **22** 606
Vigil, Martina **24** 351
Vigliena, Duke of **23** 841
Vigna, Tommaso della **11** 114
Vignali, Jacopo **5** 179; **9** 76; **32** 499–500*
works **32** *499*
Vignanello **23** 480
Vignas, Antoine de La *see* WYNGAERDE, ANTHONIS VAN DEN
Vignaud, Jean **19** 249
Vignay, Jean (de) **10** 202, 724; **16** 837; **20** 800

Vigne, Charles **12** 468
Vigne, de la (family) **3** 598
Vigne, Edmond De *see* DE VIGNE, EDMOND
Vigne, Edouard De *see* DE VIGNE, EDOUARD
Vigne, Emma De *see* DE VIGNE, EMMA
Vigne, Félix De *see* DE VIGNE, FÉLIX
Vigne, Hugues de la **3** 598
Vigne, Ignace De *see* DE VIGNE, IGNACE
Vigne, Louise De *see* DE VIGNE, LOUISE
Vigne, Malvina De *see* DE VIGNE, MALVINA
Vigne, Paul De *see* DE VIGNE, PAUL
Vigneau, André **9** 71
Vignelli, Lella **32** 500*
Vignelli, Massimo **32** 500–501*
Vignères, Blaise de
illustrated works **10** *130*
Vignerod du Plessis, Louis-François Armand de, Duc de Richelieu *see* RICHELIEU, LOUIS-FRANÇOIS ARMAND DE VIGNEROD DU PLESSIS, Duc de
Vignerot, Marie-Madeleine de, Duchesse d'Aiguillon *see* AIGUILLON, MARIE-MADELEINE DE VIGNEROT, Duchesse d'
vignettes (Egypt) *see* PAPYRI
vignettes (Western decoration) **32** *501*, 501–2*
vignetting *see under* PHOTOGRAPHY → processes
Vignier, Benjamin **26** 347
Vignier, Charles **7** 157; **15** 742, 744; **16** 554
Vignola, Giacinto **32** 505, 506
reproductive prints by others **26** *823*
Vignola, Giovanni Angelo **32** 502
Vignola, Guarnerio **32** 502
Vignola, Jacopo (Barozzi da) **11** 513; **26** 769; **32** 502–8*
architecture
churches **4** 272, 280; **7** 276; **13** 210; **16** 634, 635; **23** 541; **26** 822, *823*; **32** *503*
façades **4** 272; **32** *507*
orders (architecture) **23** 489
palaces **10** 499
palazzi **4** 311; **20** 839; **22** 166; **24** 193, 695; **26** 838
staircases **29** 523
villas **3** 56; **5** 683–4, *683*, 917; **16** 633; **24** 290; **32** *504*, 546, 627
attributions **4** 286; **25** 256; **26** 779; **30** 515
collaboration **11** 318; **18** 573; **26** 806
competitions **7** 665
decorative works **18** 573
drawings **32** 641
gardens **5** 684; **12** *60*, 116; **32** 547
groups and movements **11** 263
interior decoration **5** 684
paintings **16** 673
patrons and collectors **25** 7
Altemps, Marcus Sitticus, Cardinal **11** 740
Farnese, Alessandro, Cardinal (1520-89) **6** 59; **10** 808, 810; **17** 510
Gregory XIII, Pope (*reg* 1572-85) **13** 628
Julius III, Pope (*reg* 1550-55) **22** 6; **32** 546
publications **19** 11
stage design **30** 657
writings
illustrated **32** *502*
on architectural orders **23** 487; **24** 274; **26** 730; **31** 294, 296
on music and art **22** 378
Vignola, Jacopo (Barozzi da)
writings—cont.
on perspective **8** 513; **15** 140; **24** 489
on proportion **2** 356
translated **5** 411; **8** 496; **19** 144
Vignon, Alexandre-Pierre **32** 508–9*
works **7** 254, 774; **8** 75; **10** 745; **11** 519; **25** 268
Vignon, Barthélemy **6** 535; **12** 615
Vignon, Charlotte **32** 510
Vignon, Claude **11** 533, 534; **32** 509–10*
collaboration **33** 669
dealing **11** 662; **18** 745
patrons and collectors **30** 727
pupils **19** 147
reproductive prints by others **8** 77, 525; **20** 415; **27** 269
teachers **5** 172
works **2** 703; **11** 641; **25** 461; **32** *510*
Vignon, Claude-François **32** 510
Vignon, Philippe **32** 510
Vignory, Philibert Orry, Comte de **20** 135; **23** 572*
paintings **22** 682
porcelain **32** 582
sculpture **4** 510
Vignory, Priory Church of St Etienne **13** 79; **26** 586; **30** 907
Vigny, Alfred de **17** 605
Vigny, Pierre de **32** 510–11*
Vigo, Antonio **2** 399
Vigo, Galvano di Rinaldo da *see* GALVANO DI RINALDO DA VIGO
Vigodarzere, Antonio **17** 442
Vigoroso da Siena **1** 709; **2** 623
Viguier, Pierre **13** 79
vihāras **1** 501; **15** 275–7; **22** 792
Viipuri *see* VYBORG
Viiralt, Eduard **10** 539; **32** 511*
Vijaya *see* BINH DINH
Vijayabahu I, King of Sri Lanka (*reg* 1055-1110) **25** 169; **29** 474
Vijayaditya, Ruler (*reg c.* 696-733) (Chalukyas of Badami) **15** 297, 526; **24** 267
Vijayadurga **21** 590
Vijayamandir fort **15** 345
Ba'oli of Khan-i Khanan **15** 346
Dawud Khan Mosque **15** 345
Taleti Mosque **15** 345
Ukha Minar **15** 345
Vijayanagara (Indian city) *see under* HAMPI
Vijayanagara (ii) (Indian dynasty) **14** 124–5; **32** 511–12*
architecture **12** 652
see also:
ACHYUTADEVA, Ruler
DEVA RAYA I, Ruler
KRISHNADEVA RAYA, Ruler
Vijayapura *see* BIJAPUR
Vijayaranga Chokkanatha, Ruler (*reg* 1706-31) (Nayaka) **15** 647
Vijayawada **15** 293, 534, 535
sculpture **15** *534*
Vijayeshvara *see* BEJBEHARA
Vijd, Jodocus **3** 612; **10** 704; **12** 521
Vijf, De **5** 651; **20** 547
Vijinthanasarn, Panya **30** 617
Vijlbrief, Jan **22** 746
Vik, Ingebrigt **23** 230; **32** 512*
Vika **13** 191
Vīka(-Eglīte), Hilda
Viking **8** 527; **32** 512–34*
amber **1** 761
architecture **32** 532–4*
Britain **32** 533
Denmark **8** 721; **32** *533*
England **32** 534
Greenland **32** 533
Iceland **32** 533
Norway **23** 219
Viking—cont.
axes **32** *527*
banners **11** 147
belts **32** 528
benches **32** *519*
bronze **32** *512*, *515*, *516*, *530*
brooches **9** 254; **32** *514*, 515, *516*, 520, 524, 531
camps (military) **8** 721
churches **8** 721; **32** 517, 532
coins **7** 534
craftsmen and artists **32** 529
crosses **2** 71; **32** *529*
cups **32** *516*
decorative arts **32** 514*, 519–24*, 525*, 526–8*, 529, 530*, 531–2*
Borre style **32** 515–16*
Britain **32** 528*
England **32** 528–9*
Ireland **32** 529–30*
Isle of Man **32** 530*
Jelling style **32** 516–17*
Oseberg style **32** 515*
Ringerike style **32** 517*
Scotland **32** 530*
Style III:E **32** 514–15*
Style III:F **32** 515*
Urnes-Romanesque **32** 519*
Urnes style **32** 518–19*
dress **9** 254*, *254*
ex-votos **32** 523
farmhouses **32** 533
figureheads **28** 611, *612*
filigree **32** 524, *530*, 531
gilding **32** *530*
glass **32** *530*
gold **32** *516*, 523, 524, *530*
gold leaf **32** *527*
halls **32** 532
hardstones **32** *530*
harnesses **14** 182
harness-mounts **32** *512*, *513*, *515*
hats **9** 254
historiography **32** 534*
houses **32** 532, 533
human figures **32** 520–21*
iconography **32** 519–24*
iron **32** *527*
jewellery **32** 516, 527, 528
masks **32** 520–21*
mass production **32** 524
memorial stones **32** 517, *517*, 518, *518*, 521–2*, *522*, *523*, *524*, 525
metalwork **32** 513, 515, 516, 524*
monuments **32** 521–2*, 525, 529, 530
narratives **32** 521–4*, *522*, *523*
niello **32** *516*
ornament **23** 537–8; **32** 519–21*
peploi **9** 254
plaques **32** 523
runes **32** 517, 518
rune-stones **31** 748
sculpture **2** 71*; **32** 513, 529
ship-decoration **28** 611, *612*
shrines (i) (cult) **32** *530*
silver **32** *514*, *516*, 524, *527*, *530*, 531
statuettes **32** 524
stone **32** 513, 529
stone-carvings **2** 71*; **17** *474*; **26** *409*; **32** 516, *517*, *518*, *522*, 523, *523*, *524*, 525*, *529*, 530*
styles
Borre style **32** 513, 514, 515–16*, 517, 519, 520, 521, 523, 528, 529, 531
Broa style **32** 515
Jelling style **32** 513, 516–17*, 519, 528, 529, 531
Mammen style **32** 513, 514, 517*, 519, 521, 528, 531, 532
Oseberg style **23** 227; **32** 513, 515*, 519, 520, 521, 531
Ringerike style **1** 110; **26** 409*; **32** 513, 514, 517*, 521, 523, 524, 528, 529, 530, 531, 532
Viking
styles—cont.
Style III:E **32** 513, 514–15*, 520, 521, 531, 534
Style III:F **32** 513, 515*, 531, 534
Urnes-Romanesque **32** 513, 519*, 528
Urnes style **31** 748–9*; **32** 518–19*, 520, 521, 523, 528, 529, 530, 531, 532
Ireland **5** 916
Norway **23** 228; **29** 580
swords **2** 452
textiles **32** 523
trappings **14** 182
weathervanes **33** 8
women **32** 521
wood-carvings **32** 525*
Iceland **32** 524
Norway **23** *228*, *600*; **31** *749*
Sweden **32** *519*
Urnes-Romanesque **32** *519*
workshops **32** 524
Viklau *Virgin* **26** 647; **30** 83
Vik Museum *see under* ØYSTESE
Viková, Jindra **8** 406
Vikrama calendar *see under* INDIAN SUBCONTINENT → calendars
Vikramaditya II, Ruler (*reg c.* 734-47) (Chalukyas of Badami) **15** 297; **24** 267
Vikramaditya Varaguna (*reg c.* 880-920) (Ay) **15** 522
Vikramashila *see* ANTICHAK
Vikrampur **3** *166*; **15** *279*; **32** 534–5*
sculpture **15** *502*
Viksjø, Erling **23** 602
Viksten, Hans **30** 82
Viktring **2** 791
Vila, Doris **14** 690
Vila, Francesc Plá i *see* PLÁ I VILA, FRANCESC
Vila, Joaquín Vayreda y *see* VAYREDA Y VILA, JOAQUÍN
Vila, Victor Masriera y *see* MASRIERA Y VILA, VICTOR
Vila, Waldo **6** 598
Vilabertrán Cross **13** 165
Vila-Bogdanović, Memnuna **4** 462
Vilaça, Francisco **19** 468
Vilaça, José de Santo António Ferreira **26** 254; **30** 799; **32** 535–6*
works **32** *536*
Viladecans, Joan-Pere **3** 220
Vila do Conde, S Clara **13** 192
Viladomat y Manalt, Antonio **29** 282; **32** 536*
Vila Franca de Xira **25** 300
Vila Fresca da Azeitão, Quinta das Torres **30** 880
Vilalobos, Manuel Pinto de **32** 537*
Vilamajo, Julio **22** 24; **24** 297; **31** 753; **32** 537*
Viļāni **18** *847*
St Michael the Archangel **18** 849
Vila Nogueira de Azeitão **30** 880
Vilanova Artigas, João B(atista) *see* ARTIGAS, JOÃO B(ATISTA) VILANOVA
Vila Nova de Gaia **25** 310
Casa-Museu Teixeira Lopes **25** 318; **30** 417
Galerías Diogo de Macedo **25** 318
Vilanova i Geltrú, Ca Pajuol **29** 305
Vilanova y Piera, Juan **25** 474
Vilar, Antonio Ubaldo **2** 396; **21** 783; **32** 538*
Vilar, Carlos **32** 538
Vilar, Jean **24** 800
Vilar, Manuel **7** 408; **21** 385, 397, 404; **32** 538*
pupils **23** 207; **29** 18
Vilar de Frades Abbey Church **26** 253, 611
Vila Real de Santo António **25** 293; **27** 804
Vila Rica *see* OURO PRÊTO
Vilars dehoncort *see* VILLARD DE HONNECOURT
Vilas Boas, Manuel (do) Cenáculo **10** 665; **32** 538–9*
Vilaseca, Josep **29** 272, 308
Vilatobà, Joan **32** 539*
Vila Viçosa **32** 539–40*
Ducal Palace **25** *303*, 308; **30** 880
collections **32** 539
drawings **4** 634
drawings (pastel) **4** 639
Music Room **2** 853
Museu de Arte Sacra **32** 540
S Agostino **25** 292
silk **25** 315
Vilbiss, Alan De *see* DE VILBISS, ALAN
Vilca, Antonio **8** 303; **33** 617
Vilcabamba **15** *161*, 163; **29** 220
Vilcashuamán **29** 166
temple **29** 166
Vilcea **26** *705*
embroidery **26** *721*
Vilches, Amalia de Llano y Dotres, Condesa de **20** *59*
Vilches, Eduardo **6** 598
Vilčinskas, Jonas Kazimieras **7** 244; **19** 498; **27** 348
Vilde, De **8** 759
Vilde, Rudolf **27** 413
Vildrac, Charles **1** 21; **8** 243
Vildžiunas, Vladas **19** 499
works **19** *499*
Vile, William **7** 485; **10** 295; **19** 592; **32** 540*
Vile & Cobb **9** 28; **10** 295; **11** 431; **32** 540
Vilella, Rafael Esteve *see* ESTEVE VILELLA, RAFAEL
Vilém, Jiří **6** 364
Vilém of Avignon **8** 421
Vilém of Pernštejn **24** 108, 462, 463
Vilémovy **8** 407
Vileña, S María la Real **13** 123
tomb of Doña Urraca **13** 123
Vilgertshofen Church **29** 838
Vilhegas, Diogo Ortiz de, Bishop *see* ORTIZ DE VILHEGAS, DIOGO, Bishop
Vilhena, Antonio Manuel de **20** 216; **22** 532
Vilhete, Pascoal Viegas *see* VIEGAS VILHETE, PASCOAL
Vili **1** 274, 402, 405; **2** 85; **11** 878; **18** 217, 219, 221
Viliñjam **15** 522
Vilkumuiža **18** 847
Villa, Claudio de **3** 569; **11** 439; **13** 112; **20** 452
Villa, Edoardo **18** 514; **29** 112; **32** 556–7*
Villa, Emilio **16** 681
Villa, Frederico **33** 183
Villa, Giambattista **31** 131
Villa, José Moreno *see* MORENO VILLA, JOSÉ
Villa, Salvador **4** 258; **25** 365
Villaamil, Arturo **31** 754
Villaamil, Jenaro Pérez *see* PÉREZ VILLAAMIL, JENARO
Villa Barbaro *see* MASER, VILLA BARBARO
Villa Belrespiro *see under* ROME → villas → Villa Doria-Pamphili
Villabrille y Ron, Juan Alonso **32** 557*
pupils **27** 644
works **20** 67; **29** 292, *292*
Villacastín, Antonio de **10** 499; **29** 300; **33** 577
Villacastín, S Sebastián **29** 265

Villacerf, Edouard Colbert, Marquis de 4 550; 7 544; 12 828; 20 134, 139; 23 457
Villacerf, Jean-Baptiste Colbert de, Archbishop of Toulouse 2 375
Villach, Friedrich of *see* FRIEDRICH OF VILLACH
Villach, Thomas Artula von *see* ARTULA VON VILLACH, THOMAS
Villacis, Aníbal 9 713
Villacis, Nicolás de 12 57
Villa Cisneros *see* DAKHLA
Villa de Don Fadrique 29 331
  works 29 *331*
Villa de Guadalupe *see* GUADALUPE
Villa dei Vescovi 32 547
Villa de la Vega *see* SPANISH TOWN
Villa Deliziosa 16 702
Villa dell'Ambrogiana 4 66
Villa della Topaia 4 66
Villa de los Santos 23 *902*
  church 23 904
Villa del Prado 29 333
Villa de Pedrosa de la Vega 9 568
Villafaña, Agustín 8 237
Villafañe, Juan de Arfe y *see* ARFE Y VILLAFAÑE, JUAN DE
Villa Farnese *see under* CAPRAROLA
Villa Farnesina *see under* ROME → villas
Villafeliche 29 327, 328
Villafora, Antonio Maria da *see* ANTONIO MARIA DA VILLAFORA
Villafranca 29 330
Villafranca, Pedro Alvarez de Toledo, Marqués de 2 731; 22 471; 28 308; 31 714
Villafranca (y Malagón), Pedro de 24 475; 32 557*
Villafranca de Duero 26 642
Villagarcía de Campos, S Luis 29 267, 268
village art *see* VERNACULAR ART
Village Letter Foundry 13 224
Village Press 13 223
villages
  Ancient Near East 2 639
  Assyrian 2 639
  Berber 3 754–5*
  Dogon 21 597
  Indonesia 15 772
  Mesopotamia 21 269
  Native North Americans 22 *552*
  Scotland 28 228
  United States of America 22 *552*
  see also COMPOUNDS; SETTLEMENTS
Villa Giovanelli *see under* NOVENTA PADOVANA
Villa Giulia Calyx-krater, Master of the *see* VILLA GIULIA PAINTER
Villa Giulia Painter 13 523; 32 37, 69–70*
Villagómez, Juan Manuel 25 815
Villagra, Agustín
  works 21 *228*
Villagrán (García), José 21 403, 783; 32 557–8*
  collaboration 19 84; 22 69
  groups and movements 33 493
  pupils 19 84; 22 71; 23 369
  works 21 379
Villahermosa (family) 29 342
Villahermosa, Martín Gurrea y Aragón, Duque de 13 862*; 29 352; 33 470
Villahermosa, Serrano Park 21 382
Villahermosa de Arequipa *see* AREQUIPA
Villa Hermosa de la Asunción *see* AREQUIPA
Villahoz, Pedro Perez de *see* PEREZ DE VILLAHOZ, PEDRO
Villain 19 *487*; 20 602
Villa Lante Vase *see* LANTE VASE
Villalaz, Carlos 22 78
Villalba, Darío 32 558*
Villalba del Alcor 22 255
Villalcázar de Sirga, S María la Blanca 13 104; 16 *103*
  tomb of Felipe of Castile 13 104; 16 440
  textiles 16 439, *439*
  tomb of Leonor Ruiz de Castro 16 439
Villalobos (family) 13 104
Villalobos, Lorenzo Nicolás de 24 819
Villalón, Cristóbal de 31 297; 32 558–9*
Villa lo Spedaletto 24 523
Villalpando (family) 29 339
Villalpando, Corral de *see* CORRAL DE VILLALPANDO
Villalpando, Cristobal de 21 383; 32 559*
  patrons and collectors 13 769
  works 13 730, 764
Villalpando, Francisco de 32 559–60*
  collaboration 29 339; 31 87
  patrons and collectors 30 374
  works 10 534; 12 920; 14 474; 29 267, 339, *339*; 31 89
Villalpando, Juan Bautista 23 489; 29 268; 31 297; 32 560*
Villalpando, Juan del Corral de *see* CORRAL DE VILLALPANDO, JUAN DEL
Villalva, Federico 31 187
Villamediana, Conde de Oñate y de *see* OÑATE Y DE VILLAMEDIANA, Conde de
Villamena, Francesco 6 381; 10 390; 32 560*
  assistants 21 85
  reproductive prints by others 30 746
  works 5 867
Villamil, Eugenio Lucas *see* LUCAS VILLAMIL, EUGENIO
Villamil, Jenaro Pérez *see* PÉREZ VILLAMIL, JENARO
Villamil, Julián Lucas *see* LUCAS VILLAMIL, JULIÁN
Villamizar, Eduardo Ramírez *see* RAMÍREZ VILLAMIZAR, EDUARDO
Villamont, Jacques, Seigneur de 10 78
Villa Nazionale Già Pisani *see under* STRA
Villandrando, Rodrigo de 14 7; 32 560–61*
Villandry 11 *504*; 32 561*
Villani, Filippo 32 561*
  works 12 684; 16 780; 29 598
  translated 20 263
Villani, Giovanni 7 243; 12 681, 683
Villani, Konstanty 17 832
Villa Norvada Cerveira, Lima da *see* LIMA DA VILLA NORVADA CERVEIRA
Villanova (Italy) 10 587; 25 *470*; 32 562
Villa Nova (PA; USA), William T. Harris House 7 619
Villanova de São Pedro 21 551; 25 *288*, 503; 32 562*
Villanovan culture 10 584, 625; 25 533; 32 562–3*
  cemeteries 32 562–3
  pottery 32 562, *563*
Villanue, Diego del 7 288
Villanueva, Antonio de 19 659
Villanueva, Carlos Raúl 32 180, 566–8*
  collaboration 22 523
  groups and movements 15 886
  works 5 692; 10 417; 23 629; 32 170, 178, 179, *567*
Villanueva, Diego de 23 746; 31 297; 32 563–4*
Villanueva, Emilio 4 260; 18 778; 32 568*
Villanueva, Jerónimo de 32 568*
Villanueva, Juan de, I (1681-1765) 32 563
Villanueva, Juan de, II (1739-1811) 16 547; 23 413; 29 354; 32 563, 564–6*
  patrons and collectors 4 562, 563, 565
  pupils 24 225
  restorations 20 *62*
  works 2 285; 4 566; 10 501; 14 476; 20 63, 67; 24 108; 29 272, 305, 315; 32 563, *565*, *566*
Villanueva, Leonardo 23 904
Villanueva, Pedro Díaz de *see* DÍAZ DE VILLANUEVA, PEDRO
Villanueva de Alcoran 29 331
Villanueva de los Infantes 26 642
Villa of Helorus 9 568
Villa Pesaro 11 329
Villa Petraia *see under* LA PETRAIA
Villaplana, Albert 32 568
Villaplana & Piñon 32 568–9*
Villar, Francisco P. del 29 344
Villarán Freyre, Manuel 24 506
Villarceau, Yvon 20 573
Villarceaux Château 11 592
Villard, Henry G. 20 16
Villard, Ugo Monneret de *see* MONNERET DE VILLARD, UGO
Villard de Honnecourt 2 313; 14 406; 22 217; 32 569–71*
  drawings 9 219
  methods 28 497
  works 2 325; 3 580; 13 140; 14 *872*, 873; 24 269; 26 114; 30 26; 32 *569*, *570*
  writings 31 295; 32 638
Villard de Honnecourt, Portfolio of 2 325, 348; 7 191; 14 406, *872*; 19 532; 20 565; 22 211, 270; 28 497; 30 430
Villareal, José de 29 269
Villareal, Juan de 31 180
Villareal, Martin de 19 171
Villargut, Giovanni 20 216
Villari, Pasquale 22 97
Villarías, Marques de 23 413
Villar i Lozano, Francesc de Paula del 12 179, 182
Villa Rivero 4 266
Villaro, Carlos Paez *see* PAEZ VILLARO, CARLOS
Villaroel, Francisco de 29 337
Villars, Duchesse de 11 *267*
Villars, Johann Arnold 9 53
Villars, Maréchal de 19 231
villas 21 562; 32 540–56*
  historical and regional traditions
    Australia 32 555
    Britain 26 906, *907*; 32 542, 544, 553, 555
    Bulla Regia 31 426
    Byzantine 8 155; 9 553
    Catalonia 25 II2
    Crete 8 155
    Czech Republic 20 *814*
    Denmark 8 727
    Early Christian (*c.* AD 250-843) 9 553
    England 10 226; 23 781; 32 551, 554
      Orientalism 4 *809*
      Palladianism 23 *858*; 32 *552*, *553*
      19th cent. 32 *555*
    France 32 541, 551, 553–4, 555
      Cubism 11 *525*
      Modernism 19 *42*
      Roman 26 906; 32 543
      20th cent. 32 *556*
    Germany 26 906; 28 *102*; 32 554–5
    Iran 16 230
    Ireland 32 553
    Islamic 16 230, 241
villas
  historical and regional traditions—cont.
    Italy 21 468; 22 413; 32 544–51*
      Mannerism 20 *545*; 23 *863*, *866*, *867*; 32 *547*, *549*
      Neo-classicism 16 *647*, *772*; 20 *393*; 25 *155*
      Renaissance 12 110–12, *278*, *761*; 21 *518*; 24 *530*; 32 *504*, *546*
      Roman 28 496–7; 32 541, *541*
      Veneto 32 547–8
      16th cent. 1 *608*; 2 *357*; 5 *683*; 12 *281*; 31 *64*; 32 *548*
      19th cent. 5 *387*
    Japan 17 *86*
    North Africa 26 870
    Norway 23 602
    Poland 25 *100*
    Rome, ancient 12 110; 26 864, 869–70, 877, 891, 892, 896, 904, 907; 32 540–44*
      Britain 26 906, *907*; 32 542, 544
      France 26 906; 32 543
      Germany 26 906
      Italy 28 496–7; 32 *541*, 541
      Sicily 24 699–701
      Spain 32 543
    Scotland 28 230
    Sicily 24 699–701
    Singapore 28 773
    Spain 32 543
    Sweden 2 *611*
    Switzerland 19 *40*
    United States of America 8 *574*, *575*; 23 *33*; 31 620; 32 555
  types
    double courtyard 32 543
    porticus 26 869
    villa rustica 26 869
    villa suburbana 16 633–4
  see also CHÂTEAUX; HOUSES → types → country
Villasalem, Notre-Dame 26 600, *600*
Villasana, José María 32 571*
Villasandino 13 123
Villa Savoye *see under* POISSY
Villaseca (family) 9 699
Villaseñor, Diego 21 382
Villaseñor, Isabel 29 309; 33 601
Villaseñor, Renaldo 6 598
Villa Serana 31 753
Villasirga 24 808
Villate, François 32 571
Villate, Laurent 32 571
Villate, Pierre 20 632; 25 794, 795, 796; 32 571–2*
Villa Trivulzio, Salone 8 503
Villavechia, Enrique Sagnier i *see* SAGNIER I VILLAVECHIA, ENRIQUE
Villaverde, Marqués de 13 242
Villaverde de Medina Church 4 784
Villavicencio, Antonio 4 262; 32 572*
Villavicencio, Francisca Roldán *see* ROLDÁN VILLAVICENCIO, FRANCISCA
Villavicenco, Pedro Núñez de *see* NÚÑEZ DE VILLAVICENCIO, PEDRO
Villaviciosa 17 515
Villa Volpi *see* MASER, VILLA BARBARO
Villa Widman 16 703
Ville, Antoine de 20 109
Villecocq, de *see* VULCOP, DE
Villedieu-les-Poëles 11 628
Villedo, Michel 18 680
Villedrouin, Pierre-Richard 14 57
Ville e giardini 24 449
Villefosse, Héron de 3 804
Villefranche-de-Conflent, St Jacques 26 610
Villefranche-de-Lauragais Church 4 780
Villefranche-de-Rouergue 5 895; 21 840
Villefranche-sur-Mer, Chapel of St Pierre 6 460
Villegas, Alonso 2 28
Villegas, Armando 7 609; 32 572*
Villegas Marmolejo, Pedro de 32 572*
Villeglé, Jacques Mahé de La *see* LA VILLEGLÉ, JACQUES MAHÉ DE
Ville-Issey (Lorraine), Baron de *see* JADOT DE VILLE-ISSEY, JEAN-NICOLAS
Villejuif, Ecole Karl Marx 11 526
Villelia, Moisés 29 296
Villeminot, Louis 5 825
Villemsens, Jean-Blaise 18 864
Villena, Juan Pacheco, Marqués de (*d* 1474) 13 756
Villena, Marqués de (*fl c.* 1633-6) 29 303
Villeneuve, Comte de 24 352
Villeneuve, Carolus Hubert de 17 187
Villeneuve, Claude-Alexandre de, Comte de Vence *see* VENCE, CLAUDE-ALEXANDRE DE VILLENEUVE, Comte de
Villeneuve, Julien Vallou de *see* VALLOU DE VILLENEUVE, JULIEN
Villeneuve, Victor 6 593
Villeneuve d'Ascq, Musée d'Art Moderne du Nord 28 757
Villeneuve-l'Archevêque, Notre-Dame 13 74
Villeneuve-Lembon Château 11 585
Villeneuve-lès-Avignon 11 *505*; 32 573–4*
  Charterhouse 5 895; 13 150; 32 573–4*
    chapel of Innocent VI 32 *573*
    ivory-carvings 13 174
  Fort St-André 12 173, *174*
  Musée de l'Hospice 32 573
  Musée Municipal 32 573
  Pierre du Luxembourg Museum *see* Musée Municipal
Villeneuve-Saint-Georges 11 612
Villeneuve-sur-Lot
  houses 4 780
  Porte du Pujols 4 780
  Porte Monflanquin 4 780
  Ste Catherine 4 780
Villeneuve-sur-Yonne 11 655; 12 174
Villeneuve-Tolosane 25 502
Villepin 25 492
Villerme, Joseph 11 637
Villeroi, Camille de Neufville de, Archbishop of Lyon *see* NEUFVILLE DE VILLEROI, CAMILLE DE, Archbishop of Lyon
Villeroi, Nicolas de Neufville, 1st Duc de 4 36; 19 263; 32 574*
Villeroy, Duchesses de 13 234
Villeroy, François-Louis de Neufville, Marquis de 11 608
Villeroy, Nicolas 32 574
Villeroy & Boch 3 590, 854; 8 885; 30 885; 32 574–5*
Villers, Claude de 11 618
Villers, François de 4 535
Villers-Cotterêts Château 23 489; 29 833
Villetar, Jean 4 390
Villeval'de, Bogdan (Pavlovich) 4 232; 21 512; 27 685; 28 646
Villiers, Claude de 12 832; 19 543
Villiers, François de 12 832
Villiers, Frederick 3 389
Villiers, Gaston de 3 826

Villiers, George, 1st Duke of Buckingham (1592-1628) 32 575–6*
collections 10 363, 861
decorative works 28 648
etchings 32 377
gardens 31 276
gems 12 266
paintings 2 829; 5 764; 9 477; 10 363; 12 340; 14 729; 18 747; 27 295; 32 379; 33 387
sculpture 9 23; 11 170; 12 577
tapestries 10 349; 22 153
Villiers, George, 2nd Duke of Buckingham (1628-87) 10 316; 21 720
Villiers de La Grolais, Jean, Cardinal 21 434; 24 777
Villiers de l'Isle-Adam, Philippe-Auguste, Comte de 31 889
Villiers-en-Désoeuvre 13 126
Villiers-la-Ville Abbey 3 542
Villoldo, Isidro 32 576*
collaboration 3 847
works 2 865; 29 290; 31 89; 32 100
Villoldo, Juan de 5 902
Villon, François 14 553
Villon, Jacques 5 530; 9 354, 361; 32 576–8*
collaboration 11 525; 12 807
groups and movements 1 90; 8 240; 9 361; 12 806; 19 78; 20 431; 23 569; 25 747; 28 347
methods 8 128
patrons and collectors 2 383
printmakers 8 63
prints 2 241
pupils 11 336
works 9 310; 21 362, 896; 32 *577*
Villot, Frédéric 22 296
Vilmouth, Jean-Luc 11 571
Vilnius 19 *494*; 32 578–9*
Academy 25 140
architecture 25 97, 98
Aušros Gate *see* Dawn Gate
Basil Gate 19 497
bronze 25 129
Dawn Gate 19 495
ecclesiastical buildings 26 498
Calvary church 19 497
Cathedral 4 783; 19 495, 496, 497
St Casimir Chapel 19 496
sculpture 25 115
tomb of Bernardino Zanobi de Gianotsi 3 530
tomb of Bishop Tyszkiewicz 25 114
Cistercian church 19 495, 497
tomb of Stanislaus Radziwiłł 25 113
Dominican church 19 497
Evangelical-Reform Church 19 497
Franciscan Monastery 19 495
St Anne 4 783; 19 495, *495*
St Casimir 19 496
St Catherine 19 497
St Jonas 19 497
St Nicholas 19 495
SS Peter and Paul 3 530; 19 *496*, 497; 25 114
St Teresa 19 496
education (architectural) 25 142
Goštautas monument 19 496
Jašiunai Palace 19 497
Jewish museum 17 581
lithography 25 106
Lower Castle 19 496
Medininkai Gate *see* Dawn Gate
metalwork 25 126
monument to Elizabeth of Hungary 19 496
museums 25 140
Ostra Brama gate 25 128
painting 25 106
Palace of the Grand Dukes 19 496
Vilnius—cont.
Principal School of Lithuania *see* University
Sapieha Palace 19 496
School of Arts 19 499
sculpture 25 116
silver 25 126
synagogue 17 545
Town Hall 19 497
University 19 497; 25 141
Observatory 19 497
University of Stefan Batory
Faculty of Fine Arts 25 141
Upper Castle 19 495
Verkiai Palace 19 497
Wittinghof House 19 497
Vilno *see* VILNIUS
Vilque Church 24 502
Vilsbiburg, Benedikt Eck von 20 730
Vilt, Tibor 14 896; 15 5; 28 39; 32 579*
groups and movements 10 650
Vilutis, Mikas 19 500
Vilvoorde Church 13 110
Vil'yams, Pyotr (Vladimirovich) 27 396; 28 924; 32 579*
Vima Kadphises, Ruler (*reg* 1st cent. AD) (Kushana) 6 197
coins 15 *688*
Vimala 22 224
Vimala Suri 15 226
Vimercate, Martino da 4 654
Vimercate, Tomasino da *see* TOMASINO DA VIMERCATE
Vimercati, Andrea 6 357
Vimercati, Carlo 15 148
Vimercati, Milano 11 280
Vimercati, Ottaviano 5 743
Vimercato, Gasparo, Conte di, Governor of Genoa 19 382
Viminiacum *see* KOSTALAC
Vimperk 17 816
Vinaccia, Antonio 16 748
Vinaccia, Gian Domenico 16 742; 22 477; 32 580*
works 22 *478*
Vinache, Jean-Joseph 4 798; 7 672; 32 580*
Vinache, Joseph 32 580
Viña del Mar 6 *590*
Museo Municipal de Bellas Artes 6 601
Torres de Miramar 6 594
Vinage, Jacques 24 121
works 24 *121*
vinaigrettes 17 526
Viñaque *see* HUARI
Viñaque style pottery *see under* POTTERY → wares
Vinarov, General Ivan, Factory 5 159
Viñas, Antonio de Las *see* WYNGAERDEN, ANTHONIS VAN DEN
Vinatea Reinoso, Jorge 24 509; 29 434; 32 581*
Vinaver, Max 6 384
Vinaya Buddhism *see under* BUDDHISM →sects
Vinča 25 *471*, 499; 28 *437*; 32 581*
figurines 30 434
jewellery 25 517
Vinča culture
clay 25 *464*; 32 *581*
copper 25 516
figurines 25 512; 32 581*, *581*
jewellery 25 517
plaques 25 500
pottery 25 514
sculpture 25 *464*
settlements 25 499–500
shells 25 517
wall paintings 25 500
Vincemala, Giacomino 3 695
Vincenc of Dubrovnik 28 855
Vincennes 32 581–3*
Bois de Vincennes 24 179
Vincennes—cont.
Château 6 54, 504; 7 166; 9 144; 11 512, 655; 24 115; 32 581–2*
Pavillon de la Reine 9 176; 21 891
Sainte-Chapelle 13 76; 24 115; 27 *550*, 550; 32 582
sculpture 8 791
craftsmen and artists 3 590
homes for the aged 11 359
Parc Zoologique de Paris 24 129; 33 699
porcelain 32 582–3*, *583*
Vincennes porcelain factory 3 19; 4 554; 11 608–9; 19 723; 20 388; 23 572; 28 520
designers 4 515, 517; 9 398; 18 804; 30 219
marks 20 441
Vincent 24 473
Vincent, François-André 11 540; 17 627; 18 576; 31 856; 32 584–5*, *585*
competitions 25 638
methods 21 764
patrons and collectors 3 776; 4 554; 33 579
pupils
Bergeret, Pierre-Nolasque 3 775
Guérin, (Jean-Baptiste) Paulin 13 790
Heim, François-Joseph 14 310
Labille-Guiard, Adélaïde 18 575
Landon, Charles Paul 18 699
Mauzaisse, Jean-Baptiste 20 873
Meynier, Charles 21 411
Picot, François-Edouard 24 736
Vanderlyn, John 31 872
Vernet, (Emile-Jean-) Horace 32 335
reproductions in tapestry 12 830
Vincent, François-Elie 18 575; 32 584
Vincent, George 8 185; 23 248; 32 585*
Vincent, James 32 585
Vincent, Johann Nikolaus 29 515
Vincent, Willem, Baron van Wyttenhorst 28 358
Vincent, Zacharie 22 597
Vincent & Co. 22 895
Vincentino, Andrea 32 160
Vincentius Cibiniensis 26 712; 32 586*
Vincent of Beauvais 1 653; 10 202, 724; 15 89
Vincent of Kastav 8 178
Vincenzo I, 4th Duke of Mantua (*reg* 1587-1612) 12 903, *904*, 911–12*
architecture 20 320; 23 746; 32 403
collections 2 558
gold 20 903
paintings 3 179; 9 15; 12 558; 20 322; 21 848; 25 382; 27 288, 289; 31 19
Vincenzo II, 7th Duke of Mantua (*reg* 1626-7) 12 903, *904*, 913*
collections 10 363; 12 913; 19 582
medals 21 805
paintings 23 326; 25 263; 27 723; 29 797, 800
Vincenzo, Antonio di *see* ANTONIO DI VINCENZO
Vincenzo da Treviso *see* DESTRE, VINCENZO DALLE
Vincenzo di Biagio *see* CATENA, VINCENZO
Vinchon, Auguste-Jean-Baptiste 4 106
Vinchy 21 562
Vinci, Castello dei Conti Guidi
Biblioteca Leonardiana 16 776
Vinci, Leo 27 460
Vinci, Leonardo da *see* LEONARDO DA VINCI
Vinci, Pierino da *see* PIERINO DA VINCI
Vincidor, Tommaso (di Andrea) 3 544; 20 658; 32 586*
collaboration 24 230
patrons and collectors 4 732
works 20 658; 22 535, 823
Vincík, M. 25 446
Vinciolo, Federigo de 11 649; 18 590
Vinck, Baron de 11 724
Vinck, Abraham 11 115
Vinck, Antoine De *se* DE VINĆK, ANTOINE
Vinck, Frans 8 62
Vinckboons, David 22 841; 32 586–8*
collaboration 2 875
patrons and collectors 7 584
pupils 32 137, 588
reproductive prints by others 4 282; 5 62; 14 709; 19 564; 32 621
works 11 36; 16 766, *767*; 25 606; 32 *587*
Vinckboons, Philip (*d* 1601) 32 586, 587
Vinckboons, Philips (1607/8-1678) *see* VINGBOONS, PHILIPS
Vinckenbrinck, Abraham 32 590
Vinckenbrinck, Albert Jansz. 32 589–90*
attributions 22 895
works 22 859
Vinckenbrinck, Hendrik 32 590
Vinckenbrinck, Jan (Albertsz.) (*fl c.* 1604) 32 589
Vinckenbrinck, Jan (Albertsz.) (*b* 1631) 32 590
Vinçotte, Thomas 5 44; 32 590*
pupils 17 669
teachers 28 756
works 3 572, 604
Vincque, Carlos 17 649
Vindé, Charles Gilbert Morel de *see* MOREL DE VINDÉ, CHARLES GILBERT
Vindel 29 331
Vindevogel, J. B. 24 885
Vindobona *see* VIENNA (AUSTRIA)
Vindolanda fort 27 112
Vindonissa *see* WINDISCH
vine 17 365
Vine, F. 29 454
Vinea, Ion 8 436
Vinea, Petrus di *see* PETRUS DI VINEA
vine black 6 469; 11 763; 24 789
Vinec Church 8 376
vinegar 7 95; 10 560; 24 56; 28 340, 813
Vineland Flint Glass Works 31 644
works 31 *645*
vine leaves 6 253
Viñes, Hernando 29 286
Viñes, J. Bautista 29 270
vineyards 12 110
Vingboons, Johannes 32 586
Vingboons, Justus 8 660; 9 179; 29 685; 30 70; 31 341; 32 586
works 1 *812*
Vingboons, Philips 1 801; 9 179; 22 825–6; 32 586, 588–9*
patrons and collectors 15 40
works 11 875; 18 11; 32 *589*
writings 12 132
Vingles, Jean de 32 590*
Vingt, Les *see* XX, LES
Vingtrinier, Aimé 19 848
Vinh Yen 32 *468*
Binh Son Temple 32 472–3, 480
Vinitsa 25 501
church 5 146
Viniziano, Sebastiano *see* SEBASTIANO DEL PIOMBO
Vinje 26 646
Vinkeles, Abraham 32 591
Vinkeles, H. 20 400
Vinkeles, Johannes 32 592
Vinkeles, Reinier 1 807, 808; 20 400; 31 856; 32 591–2*
teachers 25 736
works 3 211; 5 322; 10 126; 18 739; 22 846; 25 363
Vinne, Izaak van der 32 592
Vinne, Jacob (Laurensz.) van der 32 592
Vinne, Jan (Vincentsz.) van der (1663-1721) 32 592*
Vinne, Jan (Laurensz.) van der (1699-1753) 32 592
Vinne, Jan (Jansz.) van der (1734-1805) 32 592
Vinne, Laurens (Vincentsz.) van der (1658-1729) 32 592
Vinne, Laurens (Jacobsz.) van der (1712-42) 32 592
Vinne, Vincent (Jansz.) van der 32 592
Vinne, Vincent (Laurensz.) van der (1628-1702) 14 95; 32 592*
pupils 32 592
teachers 22 840
Vinne, Vincent (Laurensz.) van der (1686-1742) 32 592
Vinnen, Carl 33 382
Vinogradov, Dmitri 27 411, 582
Vinogradov, Semyon 27 434
Vinogradova-Benois, Nina A. 12 804
Viñolesco style 10 534
Vinson, Jacob 3 738
Vint 26 718
Vint, Tõnis 10 540; 18 780; 32 593*
Vint, Toomas 10 540
Vintage Painter 32 37
Vinter, Villas 23 235
vinyl 18 612; 28 339; 32 817
vinyl paint *see under* PAINTS → types
Vinzoni, Matteo 18 812
Vioget, Jean 27 729
Viola, Bill 32 421
Viola, Domenico 22 326; 32 593*
Viola, Giovanni Battista 4 340; 9 90, 92; 32 593*
Violani, Andrea 4 562
Violante, Carmelo 32 358
Viola Zanini, Giulio 32 594
Viola Zanini, Giuseppe 32 593–4*
Viole, Pierre 4 126
violet *see under* PIGMENTS → types
violet granite *see* GRANITE → types → *marmor troadense*
violet-wood 11 596
Violi, Bruno 4 233, 234; 7 606
Violier, De 1 809
violins 22 374
Viollet, H. 12 77
Viollet-le-Duc, Eugène-Emmanuel 3 288; 6 605; 11 323; 12 178; 28 345; 32 594–9*, 774
architecture 11 324, 521, 523; 18 873; 20 869; 25 99
assistants 1 13; 8 615; 12 155; 18 688; 21 608; 23 459
book illustrations 11 521
ceramics 22 270
collaboration 3 394, 898; 4 222; 12 313; 18 653, 816
education (art) 11 671, 672, 675
gargoyles 12 150, *150*
groups and movements 13 202, 203, 208; 24 173; 28 345, 346
interior decoration 23 546; 32 *597*
metalwork 11 622
patrons and collectors 28 346
pupils 3 394; 7 170, 896; 9 464; 14 397; 19 469; 31 896
reliquaries 32 *598*
restorations 2 347; 11 659
Autun cathedral 2 841
Carcassonne 5 727; 6 61

Viollet-le-Duc, Eugène-Emmanuel
restorations—cont.
Cathedral of Notre-Dame, Amiens **1** 777
Cathedral of Notre-Dame, Lausanne **18** 874
Notre-Dame, Paris **11** 306, 521; **24** 125, 152, 153; **30** 853
Notre-Dame, Semur-en-Auxois **28** 402
Pierrefonds **6** 510; **19** 896
Sainte-Chapelle, Paris **24** 157
Saint-Denis Abbey **27** 539, 543, 546, 547
Ste Madeleine, Vézelay **32** 396, 397
St Sernin, Toulouse **31** 208
Saint-Thibault-en-Auxois Priory Church **27** 592
St Vincent-de-Paul, Paris **22** 329
Salle Synodale, Sens **32** *595*
sculpture **11** 565
sculpture **3** 290; **21** 608
teachers **19** 35
theories **6** 493
writings
illustrated **30** *350*
on architecture **10** 209–10; **11** 522; **30** 350; **32** *599*
on buttresses **5** 319; **20** *581*
on cathedrals **20** *582*
on Gothic architecture **13** 204; **14** 518; **26** 14
on interior decoration **11** 580
on iron **16** 54
on medieval art **11** 521; **13** 34
on military architecture **21** 565
on pinnacles **24** *825*, 826
on polychromy **4** 788
on proportion **2** 344, 359
on restoration **2** 320
on roofs **30** 899
on thrones **30** 780
on villas **32** 555
on walls **8** *277*
translated **31** 863
viols **22** 374, *374*
Vion, François **11** 627
Vion di Sauroens, Jean **16** 722
Vionnet, Madeleine **9** 292, 391
Vionoja, Veikko **32** 599–600*
Viotti, Giulio **28** 318
Vipiteno, S Maria in Vibitin **2** 799; **13** 117
Vipper, Boris (Robertovich) **27** 444; **32** 600*
Vir **24** 83
Viracochapampa **29** 166
Virágh, Csaba **14** 891
Vira Kerala Varma, Raja of Cochin (*reg* 1537-61) **7** 493
Viramadevi, Crown Princess of Banepa (*c.* 1294) **23** 907
Viram Dev, Ruler of Ghanerao (*reg* 1743-78) (Rajput) **15** 615
Viran Episkopi **8** 155
Vira Nolamba *see* ANNIGA, Ruler
Viranşchir *see* CONSTANTINA
Virasoro, Alejandro **2** 396; **32** 600*
Virbalis Church **19** 497
Vire, Musée Municipal Hôtel Dieu **14** 394
Virey (family) **12** 309
Vîrghis **26** 708
Virgil **20** 321
works **9** 603; **18** 701; **22** 412; **26** 563
on masks **5** 785
on Rome **26** 747
on villas **12** 110; **32** 550
translated **20** 245
Virgil Codex *see under* CODICES → individual manuscripts
Virgil Master *see* APOLLONIO DI GIOVANNI (DI TOMASO)
Virgil of Aghaboe, Bishop of Salzburg **2** 776; **27** 660
Virginia Company **31** 641
Virginia Exhibition Painter **13** 530
Virginia Historical Society **26** 353
Virginia Water (Berks) **27** 715
Virgin Islands **2** 144; **5** 744, *745*
see also ANTILLES, LESSER; LEEWARD ISLANDS
Virgin of Aulne **13** 172
Virgin of Dom Rupert **3** 566
Virgin of Khakhuli triptych *see* KHAKHULI TRIPTYCH
Virgin of Korppoo **11** 98
Virgin of Krużowa **25** 110, *111*
Virgin of Nousiainen **11** 98
Virgin of Noyon **13** 175
Virgin of Ourscamp **13** 172
Virgin of Vladimir **9** 626; **26** 141, *141*; **31** 555
Virgo inter Virgines, Master of the **8** 666; **20** 781–2*; **22** 835
works **20** *782*
viridian **6** 556, *556*; **24** 794
Virilio, Paul **24** 111
Virius, Mirko **14** 595
Virloys, Charles François Roland Le *see* LE VIRLOYS, CHARLES FRANÇOIS ROLAND
Virneburg, Heinrich von, Archbishop of Cologne *see* HEINRICH VON VIRNEBURG, Archbishop of Cologne
Viroconium **19** 889
Virrikh, E. F. **32** 72
Virring Church **26** 593
Virsaladze, Simon (Bagratovich) **12** 327; **32** 601*
Virtaler, Barthlmä *see* FIRTHALER, BARTHLMÄ
Virtue, George **8** 66; **25** 635
Virtuosi al Pantheon **24** 239; **26** 769, 771, 773
Virués, Cristóbal de **30** 664
Viruly, Franciscus *see* VEROLI, FRANCISCUS
Virunum **11** 327
Viry, François **11** 605
Viry, François Gaspard **11** 605
Viry, L. de **25** 777
Vis **8** 174, *174*; **25** 496
Visala *see* UJJAIN
Visalla, Ruler (*reg* 1245-61) (Vaghela) **8** 432
Visavada, Jnan Stepwell **29** 635, *635*, 636
Visayan **24** 625
Visborggård **4** 781
Visby **30** 65, *65*; **32** 601–2*
architecture **30** 66
churches **32** 602
Church of the Holy Spirit **26** 593
metalwork **30** 111
Old Pharmacy **30** 66
St Maria **13** 50, 119, 190
sculpture **30** 83
stained glass **13** 190
town walls **32** *601*
warehouses **32** 861
Viscardi, Bartolomeo **32** 602
Viscardi, Giovanni Antonio **32** 602–3*
collaboration **33** 297
patrons and collectors **22** 308
works **12** 372; **22** 299; **23** 811; **32** 822
Viscardi, Girolamo **32** 603*
collaboration **3** 742; **25** 254; **27** 546
groups and movements **11** 727
patrons and collectors **11** 556
works **3** 742
Visch, Henk **22** 862; **32** 603–4
works **22** *861*
Visch, Mathias de **10** 899; **24** 371; **30** 45
Vische, Francesco Lodovico Birago, Conte di **16** 738
Vischer **31** 262
Vischer (family) **12** 401; **13** 92, 160; **23** 312; **25** 111; **32** 604*
patrons and collectors **8** 384; **25** 137
works **2** 800; **4** 692; **16** 866; **23** 314
workshop **18** 433; **21** 63
Vischer, Georg **9** 446; **32** 604, 608*; **33** 275
Vischer, Georg Matthäus **18** 46
Vischer, Hans **23** 309; **32** 604, 608*
collaboration **11** 223
patrons and collectors **14** 649
works **2** 591; **25** 129; **32** *606*
Vischer, Hermann (i) (*d* 1488) **20** 789; **23** 309, 312; **32** 604*
works **32** *604*
Vischer, Hermann (ii) (1486-1517) **23** 312; **32** 604, 605–8*
works **4** 693; **32** 605, *606*, 608
Vischer, Jacob **32** 604
Vischer, Paulus **32** 604
Vischer, Peter (i) (*c.* 1460-1529) **18** 574, 650; **23** 312; **32** 604, 605–8*
patrons and collectors **13** 904
works **6** 171; **12** 402; **17** 849; **20** 88; **25** 129; **29** 570–71; **32** 604, *605*, 607, *607*, 608
workshop **23** 309
Vischer, Peter (ii) (1487-1528) **23** 312; **32** 604, 606–8*
patrons and collectors **14** 649; **28** 492
works **2** 591; **23** 309; **29** 570–71; **32** 605, *607*
Vischer, Robert **2** 517
Visch van de Capelle, Jan de **10** 703
Visch van de Capelle, Richard de **8** 551
Visconti (i) (family) **28** 531; **32** 609*
architecture **3** 355; **13** 64; **32** 341
manuscripts **4** 395; **20** 634; **21** 464; **26** 564
paintings **18** 704; **20** 95
Visconti, Angelo **22** 384
Visconti, Antonio **6** 357
Visconti (i), Azzo(ne), Lord of Milan *see* AZZO(NE), Lord of Milan
Visconti (i), Bernabò, Lord of Milan *see* BERNABÒ, Lord of Milan
Visconti, Eliseu (d'Angelo) **4** 717; **32** 613–14*
patrons and collectors **4** 726
works **4** 722, 724
Visconti (ii), Ennio Quirino **2** 165; **5** 554; **10** 184; **16** 772; **25** 8; **32** 613*
collaboration **10** 184
reproductive prints by others **11** 319
works **32** 613; **33** 385
illustrated **8** 542
Visconti, Fabio **32** 612
Visconti, Federico, Archbishop of Pisa **24** 867
Visconti (ii), Filippo Aurelio **28** 464; **32** 613
Visconti (i), Galeazzo II, Lord of Milan *see* GALEAZZO II, Lord of Milan
Visconti (i), Gian Galeazzo, 1st Duke of Milan *see* GIAN GALEAZZO, 1st Duke of Milan
Visconti (ii), Giovanni Battista **25** 8; **32** 612–13*
collaboration **6** 98
pupils **32** 613
works **16** 772; **28** 754
Visconti, G. M. **1** 531
Visconti (ii), Louis-Tullius-Joachim **11** 92; **32** 613*
groups and movements **28** 345
patrons and collectors **23** 521
Visconti (ii), Louis-Tullius-Joachim—cont.
pupils **18** 688; **31** 305
teachers **24** 387
works **11** 346, 523; **14** 790; **18** 583; **19** 69; **24** 163, 164; **31** 130, 346
Visconti (i), Lucchino, Lord of Milan *see* LUCCHINO, Lord of Milan
Visconti, Paola **4** 400
Visconti (i), Pirro, Conte **21** 525; **25** 640; **32** 609, 612*
Visconti (i), Prospero **32** 609, 612*
Visconti, Valentina **16** 751
Visconti Hours *see under* BOOKS OF HOURS → individual manuscripts
Visconti Tarocchi, Master of the **3** 695
Visé **3** 601
St Martin
shrine of St Hadelin **26** 146, 682; **28** 630
Visegrád **14** *881*; **26** *906*; **32** 614–15*
bridge **16** 225
Castle **14** 891
fortifications **21** 560
Monastery **26** 638
Royal Palace **12** 114; **14** 883, 884, 885
Visek, Jan **21** 783
Visentin, Giovanni *see* DEMIO, GIOVANNI
Visentini, Antonio **5** 686; **32** 615*
patrons and collectors **4** 611; **28** 884; **32** 195; **33** 714
pupils **12** 914; **33** 444
reproductive prints by others **32** 501
works **5** 597; **24** 705; **32** 111
Vi ser på kunst **24** 452
Viseu **25** *288*; **32** 616–17*
Cathedral **17** 596; **25** 295; **32** *616*
Museu de Grão Vasco **25** 318; **32** 616
Paço dos Tres Escalões *see* Museu de Grão Vasco
painting **25** 295
Viseu, Henry, Duke of **3** 534
Vishakhapatnam **15** *693*, 724
furniture **15** 693
ivory **15** 697
Vishanov, Molera *see* VISHANOV, TOMA
Vishanov, Toma **3** 186; **5** 154; **26** 392
vishap *see under* SCULPTURE → types
Vishniac, Roman **24** 674
Vishnudasa *see* BISHAN DAS
Vishnukumara **2** 57; **5** 470
Vishnusharma **15** 228
Vishnuvardhana *see* BITTIGA, Ruler
Vishnyakov (family) **27** 424
Vishnyakov, Filip Nikitin **27** 427
Vishnyakov, Ivan (Yakolevich) **27** 388, 442, 578; **32** 617*
pupils **2** 188
works **24** 546
Visigothic **8** 527; **32** 617–19*
architectural decorations **32** *619*
carving **32** 618
churches **29** 261
coins **7** 533
crowns **29** 345; **32** *617*, 618*
fibulae **32** 618
gems **32** *617*
gold **32** *617*
marble **32** *618*
metalwork **32** 618*
scripts **28** 305
sculpture **29** 287; **32** *618*
Visigoths **21** 501; **25** 288
Visino **1** 572
Vision **12** 397; **14** 613
Visitación, Pedro de la **31** 823
Visite, Jean le *see* JEAN LE VISITE
visiting cards *see* CARDS → types → *cartes-de-visite*
Vismara, Domenico **32** 619
Vismara, Francesco **32** 619
Vismara, Gaspare **5** 296; **10** 744; **21** 533; **32** 619–20*
Vismara, Giacomo **33** 625
Vismara, Giuseppe **2** 310; **32** 619
Visner, František **8** 411
Visnijica **4** 462
Viṣṇudāsa *see* BISHAN DAS
Viṣṇupura *see* BISHNUPUR
Viso del Marqués Palace **29** *258*, 299; **32** *620*, 620–21*
Visoko, Sherefudin White Mosque **16** 242
Vispré, François-Xavier **2** 240; **13** 676; **32** 621*
Vispré, Saverino *see* VISPRÉ, FRANÇOIS-XAVIER
Vispré, Victor **32** 621
Visscher, Anna Roemer **12** 787; **22** 885, 898
works **22** *885*
Visscher, Arnould de *see* POISSONNIER, ARNOULD
Visscher, Claes Jansz. (1587-1652) **2** 855; **22** 841, 887; **25** 247; **32** 621–2*
printmakers **5** 62; **26** 542
reproductive prints by others **18** 385
works **2** 855; **4** 905; **18** 710; **20** 769; **25** 605, 606; **32** 140, 588, *622*
Visscher, Claes Jansz., II **19** 564
Visscher, Cornelis (de) **8** 665; **32** 377, 622*
works **18** *623*
Visscher, Jan **3** 759; **32** 622
Visscher, Lambert **32** 622
Visscher, Nicolaes **3** 759; **32** 622
Visscher, Pieter **9** 409; **28** 179
Visscher, Roemer **1** 659; **10** 174; **31** 881
Visser, Carel (Nicolaas) **22** 854, 861, 862; **32** 623*
Visser, Martin **22** 876; **32** 623*
Vista, Tomas **2** 87
Vista Alegre, Nossa Senhora da Penha **25** 293
tomb of Manuel de Moura Manuel **18** 782; **25** 301
Vista Alegre factory *see* FÁBRICA DA VISTA ALEGRE
Viste, Jean Le, IV *see* LE VISTE, JEAN, IV
Vistulan Gothic **25** 99
Visual **19** 257
Visum **12** 246
Viswanathan **20** 54
Vita, Fra **8** 599; **28** 441, 453
Vita, Giacomo di *see* GIACOMO DI VITA
Vita, Giovanni di *see* GIOVANNI DI VITA
Vita: Corrente di vita giovanile **24** 448
Vitacura, Comisión Económica para América Latina (CEPAL) **6** 594, *595*
Vita d'arte **24** 448
Vitae Imperatorum, Master of the **12** 718; **20** 783*; **32** 612
Vitagliano, Gioacchino **20** 370
Vital Brazil, Álvaro **4** 713; **32** 624*
Vitale, Alessandro *see* VITALI, ALESSANDRO
Vitale, Filippo **3** 688; **23** 699; **32** 624*
Vitale da Bologna **32** 624–6*
collaboration **28** 753
pupils **31** 103
works **4** 275; **32** *625*
Vitalgiano, Gioacchino **28** 477
Vitali, Alessandro **32** 626*
Vitali, Giovanni Battista **9** 158

Vitali, Ivan (Petrovich) **27** 390; **32** 626–7*
collaboration **4** 599; **12** 633
patrons and collectors **2** 417
Vitalis **27** 887
Vitalis, Bishop of Bologna **5** 797
Vitalis, Ordericus *see* ORDERICUS VITALIS
Vitalis Roll *see under* ROLLS → individual manuscripts
Vita Mathildis (Rome, Vatican, Bib. Apostolica, MS. Lat. 4922) **20** 820
vitāna **15** 245*
Vitanov (family) **5** 158; **31** 393
Vitanov, Koyu **5** 158
Vitanovský, Ignác Jetřich **8** *391*
Vitberg, Aleksandr (Lavrent'yevitch) **32** 627*
Vitebsk *see* VICIEBSK
Viteix (Teixeira, Vitor Manuel) **2** 87
Vítek of Klokota **30** 220
Vítek of Rožmberk **32** 746
Vitelleschi, Ippolito **9** 409
Vitelleschi group **10** 614
Vitelli, Alessandro **7** 542
Vitelli, Camillo Maria **11** 296
Vitelozzi, Annibale **22** 806
works **22** *806*
Viterbese, il *see* ROMANELLI, GIOVANNI FRANCESCO
Viterbo **10** 638; **16** *620*; **32** 627–8*
baths **26** 897
Casa Poscia **13** 98
Museo Civico **10** 640
Palazzo Comunale **8** 182
Palazzo Lunense **27** 182
Palazzo Papale **32** *628*
S Francesco
tomb of Adrian V **31** 124
tomb of Clement IV **7** 303, 919; **13** 97; **24** 783; **31** 121, 124
S Giovanni in Zoccoli **1** 695, *695*
S Maria in Gradi **7** 922; **13** 98
S Maria della Quercia **3** 253
S Maria della Verità **30** 886
Viterbo, Annio of *see* ANNIO OF VITERBO
Viterbo, Antonio da *see* ANTONIO DA VITERBO
Viterbo, Egidio da *see* EGIDIO DA VITERBO
Viterbo, Francesco d'Antonio (Zacchi) da *see* FRANCESCO D'ANTONIO (ZACCHI) DA VITERBO
Viterbo, Francisco Sousa *see* SOUSA VITERBO, FRANCISCO
Viterbo, Lorenzo da *see* LORENZO DA VITERBO
Viterbo, Matteo da *see* GIOVANETTI (DA VITERBO), MATTEO
Viteri, Alicia **23** 905
Viteri, Oswaldo **9** 713; **32** 628–9*
Vitéz, Johannes, Cardinal **32** 629*
architecture **10** 544
manuscripts **4** 76; **20** 413; **26** 326
Vitezović, Pavao Ritter **8** 180
Vithal, B. **4** 291
Viti *see* FIJI
Viti, Timoteo **31** 740; **32** 629*
assistants **10** 653
attributions **6** 583; **31** 744
collaboration **12** 277–8
personal collection **9** 229
Viti Levu **11** 67, 70
Vitko de Welize **25** 434
Vitl, Wolfgang **2** 818
Vito, Francesco di *see* FRANCESCO DI VITO
Vitomir **33** 632
Vitoni, Ventura di Andrea **32** 629–30*
works **32** *630*
Vitória (Brazil) **4** *705*, 722
Vitoria (Spain) **29** *259*; **32** 630*
Cathedral of S María **13** 105; **29** 336
furniture **29** 318
metalwork **29** 333, 341
Museo Provincial de Alava **32** 630
sculpture **13** 105
Vitozzi, Ascanio **32** 630–32*
collaboration **6** 18
patrons and collectors **6** 18; **28** 5, 8; **31** 440
pupils **6** 18
works **13** 748; **31** *439*; **32** *631*
Vitrac, Roger **30** 17
Vitraerius, Laurence *see* LAURENCE VITRAERIUS
Vitra International **12** 472
vitreous tiles *see under* TILES → types
Vitria **29** 118
vitrine cupboards *see under* CUPBOARDS → types
vitriol **15** 851
Vitrolite **12** 854
Vitruvius **2** 312; **32** 632–42*, *639*
architecture **26** 890
reproductive prints by others **20** 457
writings **13** 408; **24** 603; **26** 889; **31** 295
editions
Dutch **4** 868
English **10** 204; **33** 192
Flemish **7** 519
French **7** 195; **13** 225; **20** 488, 489; **24** 468, *468*
German **26** 432
Italian **3** 202; **5** 448; **23** 486, 862; **27** 748; **30** 656; **31** 95; **32** 199
Latin **2** 346; **5** 905; **12** 656; **19** 256; **25** 144
Spanish **27** 331
on acoustics **1** 123
on altars **1** 693
on architects **2** 312; **13** 394; **26** 884–5
on architectural orders **13** 415; **23** 477, 478, 480, 481, 483, 484–5*, 533
on architecture **2** 362; **6** 357–9; **10** 601; **11** 315, 840; **12** 719; **13** 412; **14** 68, 69; **16** 623; **20** 871; **26** 864, 869, 924; **27** 520
on art **2** 518
on astronomy **2** 649
on basilicas **3** 327
on baths **3** 374
on bricks **4** 772; **26** 877
on caryatids **5** 904, 905
on collections **13** 555
on concrete **7** 692; **26** 879
on construction **7** 764; **13** 387
on decorum **8** 613
on display of art **9** 20
on docks **9** 58
on domes **9** 85
on entablatures **13** 414, 415
on entasis **10** 414, 415
on fora **11** 327
on fortifications **21** 577, 578
on geometry **20** 565
on gymnasia **10** 670; **13** 886
on houses **13** 383, 407; **26** 869
on human proportions **14** 870, 871, 874
on hypocausts **15** 51
on hypogea **15** 52
on landscape **18** 700
on landscape painting **18** 701
on libraries **19** 311
on lighting **9** 11
on metalwork **10** 326
on military architecture **21** 547
on painting **10** 197; **13** 699; **15** 135; **27** 50, 51
on palaestrae **23** 828
Vitruvius
writings—cont.
on pediments **24** 318
on perspective **28** 202
on pigments **24** 790, 795; **27** 51
on proportion **2** 344, 350, 353–4*; **13** 412; **20** 565, 567; **25** 575; **26** 924–5; **28** 201; **32** *635*
on stage-painting **30** 651
on stucco **13** 602; **29** 812, 813
on sundials **32** *634*
on surveying **30** 26
on symmetry **30** 171
on temples **2** *355*; **10** 597, 600, 601; **27** 235
on town planning **27** 2
on villas **12** 110
on wall paintings **13** 547
on water systems **11** 339
translated **14** 869
Vitruvius Britannicus **5** 537–8, *538, 539*; **23** 857, 858
Vitry, Bernard **2** 49
Vitry, Jehan de *see* JEHAN DE VITRY
Vitry, Paul **8** 50; **32** 643*
Vitsada **8** 342
Vitsaris, Ioannis **13** 354
Vitskøl Abbey **4** 781; **8** 722
Vitta, Joseph, Baron **3** 875; **4** 626
Vittone, Bernardo Antonio **13** 753; **16** 643; **32** 643–6*
collaboration **25** 886
competitions **25** 886
pupils **4** 422
works **7** 258; **16** 643; **32** *644, 645*
writings **4** 422; **23** *489*; **29** 637; **31** 296
Vittor, Frank **25** 5
Vittore di Matteo *see* BELLINIANO, VITTORE
Vittori (family) **33** 719
Vittoria, Alessandro **23** *878*; **32** 192, 646–50*
architecture **25** 889; **32** 216
attributions **7** 672
collaboration **5** 532; **19** 627; **23** 756; **32** 192
medals **25** 889
patrons and collectors **3** 203; **11** 819; **20** 400; **25** 889; **32** 155, 350
personal collection **22** 696
sculpture **5** 532; **16** 697; **23** 678; **25** 889; **31** 359; **32** 220
altars **32** *649*
architectural **32** 222, 223
busts **5** 302; **30** 495, 498; **32** 215, *648, 649*
façades **27** 772
religious **31** 316
statuettes **29** 569
stucco **11** 721; **29** 831; **32** 193, *193*, 220, 223
teachers **27** 772
workshop **25** 889
Vittoria della Rovere, Grand Duchess of Tuscany (1622-94) **21** *9*, 28*
manuscripts **31** 740
paintings **11** 23, 679, 698
Vittorini, Elio **13** 872
Vittorino da Feltre **14** 866, 869; **20** 319; **28** 156; **32** 650*
pupils **12** 905
Vittoriosa **20** 211, 215
Vittoz, M. **5** 878; **11** 42
Vittskövle Castle **30** 69
Vittskövle group **30** 76
Vitturi **2** 182
Vitullo, Sesostris **2** 400; **32** 651*
Vituya Viejo **6** 380
Viúva Lamego factory **30** 882
Viva, Angelo **32** 651*
Viva, Giacomo **32** 651
Vivaceta Rupio, Fermín **6** 592, 593; **27** 791; **32** 651–2*
works **27** *792*
Viva di Lando **28** 676; **31** 534–6
Vivaldi, Antonio **5** 593
Vivaldis, Dominicus de *see* DOMINICUS DE VIVALDIS
Vivanco, Jorge **4** 315
Vivanco, José Vallejo *see* VALLEJO VIVANCO, JOSÉ
Vivar, Francisco de **29** 333
Vivar, Juan Correa de *see* CORREA DE VIVAR, JUAN
Vivar, Rodrigo de **2** 868
Vivar, Rodrigo Díaz de *see* CID, EL
Vivar del Cid (place) **5** 201
Vivarelli, Carlo **30** 140
Vivares, François **9** 26; **10** 393; **32** 652*
works **5** 295; **14** 856; **28** 755, 879
Vivares, Thomas **32** 652
Vivarini (family) **8** 166; **11** 383; **32** 190, 652–3*
Vivarini, Alvise **32** 652, 657–8*
assistants **3** 316
collaboration **5** 913
pupils **3** 200; **7** 320; **15** 831; **21** 904
works **3** 659, 670; **16** 659; **24** 861; **32** 200, *657, 658*
Vivarini (da Murano), Antonio **16** 662; **32** 652, 653–5*
attributions **11** 684
collaboration **3** 876; **4** 276; **12** 699; **20** 304; **23** 754; **27** 495; **32** 655
restorations by others **24** 343
works **11** 381; **12** 581; **25** 9; **32** 189, *228*, 229, *654*
Vivarini, Armenia **32** 200
Vivarini, Bartolomeo **32** 652, 653, 655–7*
attributions **11** 684; **32** 655
collaboration **4** 276; **32** 653, 654
patrons and collectors **28** 560; **29** 46
pupils **2** 17
restorations by others **4** 493
works **11** 381; **32** 200, 225, *656*
Vivarini, Luigi *see* VIVARINI, ALVISE
Vivarium Monastery **32** 636
Vivar y Mendoza, Rodrigo Díaz de, 1st Marqués del Zenete *see* ZENETE, RODRIGO DÍAZ DE VIVAR Y MENDOZA, 1st Marqués del
Vivas, Fruto **32** 171
Vive-Kapelle, Church of the Nativity of SS Mary and Philip **3** 548; **13** 208, *208*
Vivenel, Antoine **18** 696
Vivenzio, Marchese **2** 40
Vivenzio Hydra **13** 520
Vivero, Gonzalo, Bishop **27** 605
Vivian, Jakob **2** 780
Vivian Bible *see under* BIBLES → individual manuscripts
Viviani, Antonio **19** 383; **26** 837; **32** 658–9*
Viviani, Ludovico **32** 659
Viviani, Michelangelo **22** 15
Vivien, Joseph **22** 302; **32** 659*; **33** 276, 277
methods **24** 242
reproductive prints by others **18** 47
works **10** 884; **11** *457*; **12** 391; **24** 242, *242*
Vivien, P. **29** 752
Vivier, Arnould du *see* ARNOULD DU VIVIER
Vivier, Hennequin du *see* JEAN DU VIVIER
Vivier-en-Brie, Sainte-Chapelle **27** 550
Vivin, Louis **22** 440; **32** 659*
Vivio, Giacomo **4** 654
Vivio dell'Aquila, Giacomo **32** 659–60*
Vivo **14** 779; **17** 860; **22** 503; **31** 106
Vivo, Tommaso De *see* DE VIVO, TOMMASO
Vivonne d'Angennes, Catherine de, Marquise de Rambouillet *see* RAMBOUILLET, Marquise de
Vivulskis, Antanas **19** 498
Vix **11** *504*; **25** *470*; **32** 660*
bronzes **13** 373; **25** 541
brooches **25** 541
gold **25** 542
metalwork **32** *660*
silver **25** 542
Vix Krater **13** 476, 576; **25** 541; **32** 660, *660*
Vixseboxse, J. E. **4** 155
Viyeru, Igor' **21** 811
Vizače *see* NESACTIUM
Vizagapatam *see* VISHAKHAPATNAM
Vizari Basilica **8** 155
Vize
Ayasofya Mosque **7** 252; **9** 542
Hagia Sophia *see* Ayasofya Mosque
Vizgirda, Viktoras **19** 499
Vizille Château **19** 238
Vizzano di Merate, Villa Bagatti Valsecchi **3** 49
Vkhutein **20** 888; **27** 443; **30** 363; **32** 601, 661
Vkhutemas **1** 75; **2** 428; **7** 291, 770; **9** 296; **18** 457, 619; **22** 178; **27** 442–3, 464; **30** 56; **32** 382, 661–2*
directors **10** 843
furniture **27** 405, *409*
pupils **24** 818
teachers **2** 603
Burov, Andrey (Konstantinovich) **5** 276
Dokuchayev, Nikolay (Vasil'yevich) **9** 73
Exter, Alexandra (Alexandrovna) **10** 699
Fal'k, Robert (Rafailovich) **10** 772
Favorsky, Vladimir (Andreyevich) **10** 843
Florensky, Pavel (Aleksandrovich) **11** 218
Golosov, Il'ya (Aleksandrovich) **12** 876
Kardovsky, Dmitry (Nikolayevich) **17** 812
Klucis, Gustav **18** 141
Klyun, Ivan (Vasil'yevich) **18** 141
Konchalovsky, Pyotr (Petrovich) **18** 215
Korolyov, Boris (Danilovich) **18** 388
Korovin, Konstantin (Alekseyevich) **32** 579
Kuprin, Aleksandr (Vasil'yevich) **18** 528
Kushner, Boris (Anisimovich) **18** 536
Leonidov, Ivan (Il'ich) **19** 206
Lissitzky, El **19** 476
Pevsner, Antoine **24** 574
Popova, Lyubov' (Sergeyevna) **25** 239
Rodchenko, Aleksandr (Mikhaylovich) **26** 504
Rylov, Arkady (Aleksandrovich) **27** 464
Shevchenko, Aleksandr (Vasil'yevich) **28** 597
Shterenberg, David (Petrovich) **28** 642
Sokolov-Skalya, Pavel (Petrovich) **29** 19
Stepanova, Varvara (Fyodorovna) **29** 632
Udal'tsova, Nadezhda (Andreyevna) **31** 520
Vlaamsche school, De **24** 439
Vlaams Huis **3** 579, 585
Vlach (family) **12** 429

Vlach, Antonio Ericera 6 363
Vlach, Augustin 25 426
Vlach, Hans 25 426
Vlach, Jan 18 540
Vlach, John Michael
works 1 *421*
Vlach, Mikuláš 18 540
Vlach, Simon 19 500
Vlad, Ion 32 662*
Vladikavkaz 27 433
Vladikavkaz Association of Artists (Vakh) 27 433
Vladimir (Russia) 27 369; 32 662–5*
Cathedral of St Dmitry 26 594, *594*; 27 369, 382; 32 665
Cathedral of the Dormition 27 369, 384; 32 *664*, 664–5
iconostasis 7 279; 28 291
icons 9 626; 31 555
wall paintings 27 305
Church of the Protective Veil of the Virgin 27 369; 32 *663*
Convent of the Princess
Cathedral of the Dormition 25 342; 27 386
enamel 27 426
Golden Gate 27 369; 32 *663*, 663
sculpture 27 382
Silver Gate 27 369
tiles 30 884
Town Hall 31 242
wall paintings 27 382
see also VLADIMIR-SUZDAL
Vladimir (*fl* 1502-08) 8 908; 10 890; 25 342
Vladimir, Prince of Novgorod (*reg* 1036-52) 23 267, 270
Vladimir I Svyatoslavich, Prince of Kiev (*reg* 978-1015) 9 645; 27 368, 437; 31 553, 554; 32 662*
architecture 18 34
Vladimir II Monomach, Prince of Kiev (*reg* 1113-25) 31 548; 32 663, 665
Vladimirescu, Wanda Sachelarie *see* SACHELARIE-VLADIMIRESCU, WANDA
Vladimirov, Iosif 22 177; 27 387
Vladimirov, V. 3 287
Vladimirovka 25 503
Vladimir-Suzdal' 9 *507*; 27 361, *363*, 437; 32 662–7*
churches 7 274
icons 27 382
metalwork 27 418
painting 27 382
sculpture 27 387
see also BOGOLYUBOVO; SUZDAL; VLADIMIR
Vladimir the Saint, Prince of Kiev *see* VLADIMIR I SVYATOSLAVYCH, Prince of Kiev
Vladimir Volynsky *see* VOLODYMYR VOLYNS'KY
Vladislav I, Voivode of Wallachia (*reg* 1364-*c.* 1377) 8 279; 26 719
Vladislav I Herman, Prince of Poland (*reg* 1079-1102) 32 749
Vladislav II Jagiellon, King of Bohemia (*reg* 1471-1516) and King of Hungary (*reg* 1490-1516) 8 383, 390, 422; 16 866*; 18 461; 26 365
architecture 14 885; 25 425, 437, 438
military architecture 1 531
Vladislav II Jagiellon, King of Poland (*reg* 1386-1434) 25 134
architecture 18 424, 430; 19 495
metalwork 25 126
paintings 3 528; 27 722; 33 259
Vladislav II Přemyslid, King of Bohemia (*reg* 1140-73) 8 421; 25 552
architecture 25 444
Vladislav IV Vasa, King of Poland (*reg* 1632-48) 25 134; 32 6–7*
architecture 12 745; 25 135; 30 453; 32 869
collections 25 137
metalwork 20 13; 27 *419*
monuments 30 454
paintings 9 74
prints 25 104
sculpture 32 874
Vlad-Vintilă 26 721
Vlady 21 389
Vladychuk, Alexander (Pavlovich) 31 459
Vlaenderbergh, Barbara van 21 103
Vlahută, Alexandru 26 723
Vlaici 26 723
Vlaminck, Maurice de 32 667–9*
dealers 11 165; 17 725; 32 686
groups and movements 10 839, 840, 842; 16 817; 25 356
methods 7 630
patrons and collectors 7 834
personal collection 1 438; 25 582
reproductive prints by others 32 577
studio 29 858
works 10 *840*; 11 548, 606; 19 491; 28 920; 29 670; 32 *668*; 33 362
Vlasiu, Ion 26 716; 32 669*
Vlasov, Aleksandr (Vasil'yevich) 32 669–70*; 33 518
assistants 3 685
collaboration 9 54; 33 518
groups and movements 32 695
works 22 174
Vlasov, A. S. 27 439
Vleeschouwer, Anthoni de 7 554
Vlerick, Pieter 20 244
Vleughels, Nicolas 4 128; 24 *542*; 32 670*
pupils 17 465; 24 772
works 32 *670*
Vleughels, Philippe 11 587; 32 670
Vlieger, Simon (Jacobsz.) de 27 230; 32 671–3*
assistants 9 314
attributions 13 892
collaboration 5 680
patrons and collectors 5 679; 28 169; 32 377
pupils 32 142
reproductive prints by others 23 191
works 10 553; 20 424; 22 843; 32 *671*, *672*
Vlierbeek Church 3 547
Vlierden, Balten 32 709
Vliet, Elias van 1 810
Vliet, Hendrick (Cornelisz.) van 22 844; 32 673*
groups and movements 8 669
works 2 342; 14 796
Vliet, Jan Jorisz. van 22 843; 26 157, 159; 32 673–4*
Vliet, Willem van 12 532; 32 673
Vliete, Gillis van den 32 674*
Vliete, Jakob van den 26 778
Vlissingen 22 *813*
Beeldenhuis 22 826
monument to Admiral Michiel de Ruyter 22 *860*
Stadhuis 22 826, *826*
van-Dishoeck-huis *see* Stadhuis
Vlissingen, Paul van 17 825
Vlněna 8 420
Vlorë 1 *537*
art schools 1 547
ceramics 1 543
monuments 1 541
Museum of National Independence 1 546
seraglio 1 539
Vlugt, Leendert Cornelis van der
collaboration 4 815*; 30 871
groups and movements 2 318; 15 885; 22 831; 23 450
Vlugt, Leendert Cornelis van der—cont.
staff 29 531
works 4 *815*; 15 886; 22 868; 29 489
Vluten, Guillaume 5 210; 13 79; 32 674*
Vlyndt, Paul, II *see* FLINDT, PAUL, II
VNIIR 7 744
V.N.P. 8 403
Voania Muba 1 329
VOC *see* DUTCH EAST INDIA COMPANY
Vo Canh 6 420
Voce, La 24 427
Vodoca Church 9 579
Vodoun 5 753; 9 115; 14 55
Vodrey, Fredrick 16 29
Voege, Wilhelm *see* VÖGE, WILHELM
Voegeli, Conrad 33 737
Voelcker, John 7 296; 30 391
writings 7 *295*
Voerman, Jan 32 258, 674*
Voerst, Robert van 4 381; 9 482; 14 731
Voet, Alexander 11 358
Voet, Ferdinand 16 82
Voet, Gijsbert 20 81
Voet, Jacob Ferdinand 1 449; 28 13
Vogdt, Arthur 30 370
Vöge, Wilhelm 5 131; 32 675*
Vogel, Andreas (*fl* 1638) 1 6
Vogel (i), Andreas (*fl* 1734) 32 675
Vogel (ii), Carl Christian 32 676
Vogel, Caspar 30 69
Vogel (ii), Christian Leberecht 32 676*
pupils 28 375, 408; 32 675, 676
Vogel, Christoph 32 675
Vogel (i), David 32 676–7*
Vogel (i), Franz Jakob 32 675*
Vogel (i), Heinrich 32 675, 676
Vogel, Hermann Wilhelm 29 654
Vogel, Jean Philippe 19 542; 29 873; 32 677*
Vogel, Johann Caspar 32 675
Vogel (i), Johann Jakob 32 675*
Vogel, J. Ph. 3 825
Vogel, (Georg) Ludwig 32 677*; 33 736
groups and movements 22 703, 704; 23 675; 24 587
works 30 133
Vogel, Peeter (*fl* 1484-6) 4 415
Vogel, Peter (*fl* late 20th cent.) 29 98
Vogel, Sebestyén Antal 14 907; 32 677–8*
Vogel, Sigismund von (*fl* 1636-54) 18 459
Vogel, Susan 1 230
Vogel, Zygmunt (1764-1826) 25 105, 123, 141; 32 678*
Vogelaer, Karel van 23 874; 30 284
Vogeleer, Lieven de *see* VOGHELARIUS, LIVINIUS
Vogeler, (Johann) Heinrich 32 678*; 33 382–3
Vogelgesang, Klaus 3 803; 31 532; 32 678–9*
Vogelherd 12 *361*; 25 *470*; 32 679*
bone-carvings 4 313
figurines 25 488, 489, 490, *490*
ivory-carvings 25 494
Vogelmann, Johann Carl 19 781
Vogels, Guillaume 32 679*
groups and movements 5 44; 7 245; 10 517; 32 591
works 3 563
Vogelsang, W. 1 722; 12 242
Vogel von Vogelstein, Carl Christian 9 236; 32 676*
Vogh, Gergely 29 922
Voghdjaberd Basilica 2 425
Voghel, Willem de 5 210
Voghelarius, Livinius 32 679–80*
Voghele, Herman de *see* HERMAN DE VOGHELE
Voghera, Luigi 8 135
Vogl, Gergely 5 84
Vogl, Konrad 33 746
Vogler, Georg Joseph 25 787
Voglia, Domenico del 11 747
Vogt (family) 24 148
Vogt, Adolphe 22 38
Vogt, Christian (*fl* 1700s) 23 636
Vogt, Christian (*b* 1946) 32 680*
Vogt, Franciszek Antoni 25 115
Vogt, Georges 6 924; 28 524
Vogtherr, Heinrich (i) (1490-1556) 32 680–81*
pupils 32 681
works 32 *680*; 33 354
writings 12 366
Vogtherr, Heinrich (ii) (1513-68) 24 271; 32 680, 681*
Vogt von Wierandt, Caspar 32 681–2*
works 9 235; 18 435
Vogue 10 824
Vogue, La 24 426
Vogüé, (Charles-Jean-) Melchior de 9 464, 527; 10 212; 32 682*
Vohburg, Arnold, Count of 29 501
Vohburg, Counts of 6 525
Vohlin, Ferdinand 26 522
Voigt, A. 8 426
Voigt, Carl Friedrich 32 682*
Voigt, Elisabeth 19 112
Voigt, H. 19 111
Voigt, Otto Eduard Gottfried 21 66
Voigtel, (Karl Eduard) Richard 13 201; 32 682–3*
Voigtländer, Peter Wilhelm Friedrich 24 660
Voigts, Joachim 33 245
Voigt von Wierandt, Caspar *see* VOGT VON WIERANDT, CASPAR
Voijs, Arie de *see* VOIS, ARIE DE
Voinești 26 719
Voinov, Aleksandr 33 585
Voinov, Vsevolod 7 341
Vois, Arie de 19 102; 22 841; 30 425; 32 683*
Voisenon, Abbé de 5 380
Voisinlieu 33 673
Voit, August von 32 683–4*
works 17 547; 22 303, 308, 363; 33 282
Voitländer, František Václav 8 413
works 8 *414*
Vojtěch of Pernštejn 24 462
Vojvodina 28 *437*, 454
Vok, Peter 8 395
Vok of Rožmberk 32 746
Voković, Bozidar 25 339
Volaire, François-Alexis 32 684
Volaire, Jacques 32 684
Volaire, Jean 32 684
Volaire, Marie-Anne 32 684
Volaire, Pierre-Jacques 32 684–5*
patrons and collectors 5 356
teachers 32 333
works 13 304; 18 713; 32 *684*
Volanakis, Konstantinos 13 352, 360
Volant, Au 4 577
Volargne, Villa del Bene 5 816, *816*
Volaterrae *see* VOLTERRA → Velathri
Volaterrano, il *see* MAFFEI, RAFFAELE
Volberg, August 30 349
volcanic andesite *see under* LIMESTONE → types
Volcii *see* VULCI
Volckamer, Paulus 23 314; 29 727
Volckamer, Peter 13 188
Volda Church 11 466
Volders, Karl-Borromäuskirche 2 781
Volders, Lancelot 17 7
Volders, Mattheus, Abbot of Averbode 3 605; 8 204
Voldsted 26 640
Volek, Jan, Bishop of Olomouc 23 424
Volga Bulgar
metalwork 16 *504*
Volga-Don Canal 27 380
Volga Jewellery Factory 27 423
Volgograd 27 *363*, 380; 32 685–6*
Mamayev burial ground 32 737
Monument to the Heroes of the Battle of Stalingrad 32 *685*
urban planning 21 622; 32 383
Volkertsz., Dirck 1 658; 14 293, 869
Volkhov Porcelain Factory 27 413, 414
Volkmann, Artur (Joseph Wilhelm) 20 405; 32 686*
Volkmann, Johann Jakob 13 809
Volkmar, Charles 30 887
Volkonskaya, Zinaida (Aleksandrovna), Princess 27 440
Volkonsky (family) 5 332
Volkonsky, Sergey, Prince 8 849
Volkov, Aleksandr (Nikolayevich) 6 286; 31 783; 32 686*
Volkov, Andrey 27 397
Volkov, Sergey 27 398
Volksbühne 30 686
Volkstedt 30 793
Volkswagen, Stiftung 2 369
Volkswagen Beetle *see under* CARS → models
Vollant, Simon 19 380
Vollard, Ambroise 8 622; 12 193; 15 155; 20 121, 603, 822; 22 422; 24 143; 25 626, 752; 26 209; 27 240, 241, 439; 32 686–7*; 33 362
artists' books 30 488
book illustrations 4 357; 6 384
collections 24 716
dealing 32 669
engravings 28 371
etchings 4 676; 9 373; 24 721
exhibitions 10 680
lithographs 4 326; 19 489, 490; 27 269; 32 739
paintings 6 371, 372, 375; 10 842; 12 194; 22 136
posters 25 623
printmakers 13 829; 24 726; 25 599
writings 4 365; 27 240
illustrated 2 733; 25 752
Vollard Press 20 335
Vollenhoven, Bernart van 18 227
Vollevens, Johannes 3 42; 20 81
Vollgold, Friedrich 32 682
Vollgraff, Wilhelm 2 406
Vollman, Eckhart 22 305
Vollmer, Gottlieb 24 602
Vollmer, Hans 10 212; 15 823; 30 731; 33 156
Vollmer, Johannes 25 856
Vollmer, Philip 8 809
Vollmoeller, Mathilde 25 744
Vollon, Alexis 11 230; 32 687
Vollon, Antoine (1833-1900) 11 230; 29 669; 32 687*
Vollon, Antoine (1865-1945) *see* VOLLON, ALEXIS
Vollschmelz enamel *see under* ENAMEL → techniques
Vollweiler, G. J. 19 483
Volmar, Paul 5 215; 29 578
Volmarijn, Pieter Crijnse 29 79
Volmaryn, Crijn Hendricksz. 29 79; 32 671
Volné směry 20 254; 24 440
Volney, Constantin, Comte de 10 79

Volnukhin, Sergey 2 24; 9 121; 10 493; 12 887; 18 234, 388; 20 849
Volò, Vincenzo 5 378
Volodymyr Volyns'ky 31 545, 550
  Cathedral of the Dormition 27 369; 31 548
  St Basil 31 550
Vologases I (*reg* 51-77) 24 215
Vologasias 24 215
Vologda 27 *363*; 32 687–8*
  Cathedral of St Sophia 27 371, 387; 32 687–8
  lace 32 688
  Local Museum 32 688
  metalwork 27 420
  painting 27 387
  sculpture 27 389
  Vologda Art Gallery 32 688
Volokh, Pyotr 31 563
Volos 23 808
  Athanassakeion Archaeological Museum 14 361
  ceramics 13 358
  Hagios Konstantinos 13 349
  Iolkos 15 891*
  marble 29 702
Voloshin, Maksimilian (Aleksandrovich) 12 875; 18 477; 32 688*
Volotovo 27 383
  Church of the Dormition 27 370, 383
Volotsky, Iosif 15 895
Volpaia, Benvenuto di Lorenzo 32 688
Volpaia, Bernardino della 4 648, 652
Volpaia, Camillo di Lorenzo 32 688
Volpaia, Fruosino di Lorenzo 32 688
Volpaia, Girolamo 32 688
Volpaia, Lorenzo di Benvenuto 32 688–9*
Volpa Synagogue 17 545, *546*
Volpato, Angelo 16 739
Volpato, Giovanni 10 394; 16 739; 32 689*
  assistants 4 84
  collaboration 2 40
  pupils 22 113
  works 23 173
Volpato, Giovanni Battista 6 470; 9 366; 13 701; 32 689–90*
Volpato, Giuseppe 16 739; 32 689
Volpe, Alessandro La *see* LA VOLPE, ALESSANDRO
Volpe, Vincent 20 116; 32 690*
Volpedo, Giuseppe Pellizza da 9 40
Volpi, Alfredo 4 718, 719; 32 690–91*
  works 32 *690*
Volpi, Ambrogio 3 139
Volpi, Elia 11 190
Volpi, Villa *see* MASER, VILLA BARBARO
Volpiano, William of 8 893
Volpicella, Scipione 22 78
Volpini, Giuseppe 22 302
volpinite 29 698
Volpino 29 698
Volpino, Antonio 12 560
Volschenk, J(an) E(rnst) A(braham) 29 108
Volsinii Veteres *see under* ORVIETO
Volstrekt Modernen, De 29 397
Volta, Upper *see* BURKINA FASO
Volta Bridge 4 803
Voltaic 5 216
Voltaire, François-Marie Arouet 10 401; 11 508, *561*; 13 663; 24 787; 27 438; 30 132
  architecture 19 161
  on antiquaries 2 165
  on landscape gardens 12 122
  on Rococo 26 494
Voltaire, François-Marie Arouet—cont.
  works 9 370; 10 118; 13 324; 20 497; 27 868; 30 672
Volten, André 22 861
Volterra 10 *583*, 585, 586, 602, 638; 16 *620*; 32 691–2*
  alabaster (gypsum) 1 517
  Cathedral 26 623, 644
    font 11 254
    Nativity groups 22 680
  coins 10 632, 633
  collections 10 637
  marble 10 602
  Medici fortress 19 896
  metalwork 10 624
  mirrors 10 629
  Museo Diocesano di Arte Sacra 32 692
  Museo Etrusco Guarnacci 10 638, 640, 642; 32 692
  Palazzo Minucci-Solaini 32 692
  Palazzo dei Priori 7 338; 8 503; 14 420; 31 236
  Porta all'Arco 10 602
  sculpture 10 606
  S Francesco
    chapel of the Compagnia della Croce di Giorno 27 *208*
  stele of Avle Tite 10 587
  tombs 31 109
  town walls 10 602
  urns 10 608; 27 9
  vase paintings 10 588, 592, 615, 616
  vases 10 616, 634
  Velathri 32 691*
Volterra, Daniele da *see* DANIELE DA VOLTERRA
Volterra, Francesco da 12 911; 18 689; 25 227; 28 316; 32 692–3*
  patrons and collectors 27 648
  works 20 43
Volterra, Pietro d'Andrea da *see* PIETRO D'ANDREA DA VOLTERRA
Volterrano, il *see* FRANCESCHINI, BALDASSARE
Voltri, Nicolò da *see* NICOLÒ DA VOLTRI
Voltz, Friedrich 2 106; 4 838; 17 885; 28 109
Volubilis 15 103; 22 129; 32 693*
  Arch of Caracalla 26 868, 921; 31 350
  forum 11 328
  houses 26 870, 920, 921
  mosaics 27 63, 67
  textiles 27 113
  tomb of Mulay Idris 28 633
Volumnius, P 10 600
Volusia Cornelia 22 731
volute kraters *see under* KRATERS → types
volutes 8 154; 13 377, 391, 392, 393, 399; 23 478, 480; 32 693*
Volyn' 31 549, 563, 564
Vom Fewerfeld, Küehorn, the elder *see* WALTER, JAKOB
Vomio, Baltasar Maio da *see* MAGGI, BALDASSARE
vomiting sticks 8 229
Vom und Zum Stein, Karl, Reichsfreiherr 15 145–6; 18 813
Vondel, Joost van den 4 250; 10 174; 15 84; 19 *349*; 22 910
Vondráčková, Jaroslava 8 420
Vôneche glassworks 3 13, 595
Von Holst and Fyfe 19 453
Voni 8 342
Vonlynarlyarsky (family) 5 333
Vonwiller, Giovanni 22 98
Voodoo *see* VODOUN
Voogd, Hendrik 2 25; 24 892; 32 693–4*
  works 32 *694*
Voon Fee, Chen 19 384
Voorburg Church 22 821
Voorduin, G. W. M. 30 16
Voorhees, Gmelin & Walker 32 797
Voorhees, Walker, Foley & Smith 32 797
Voorhelm Schneevogt, C(arl) G(ottfried) *see* SCHNEEVOGT, C(ARL) G(OTTFRIED) VOORHELM
Voorst, De *see* DE VOORST
Voorst, John van 22 278
Voorst, Louis van 22 895
Voort, Cornelis van der 3 77; 7 510; 9 470; 18 10; 24 734
Voort, J. Van de *see* VAN DE VOORT, J.
Voort, Michiel van der, I (1667-1737) 3 571; 32 694*
  assistants 10 372; 32 251; 33 460
  attributions 4 220
  collaboration 12 230; 32 251
  pupils 12 637; 14 757; 25 190; 27 466; 32 240
  works 12 230; 25 727
Voort, Michiel van der, II (1704-after 1777) 12 515; 32 694
Voort, Pieter de la Court van der *see* Court van der Voort, Pieter de la
Voortrekker Monument 29 106
VOPRA (All-Union Alliance of Associations of Proletarian Architects) 28 747; 32 669, 695*
Voprosy iskusstvoznaniya 27 444
Vora 15 236
Voragine, Jacobus da *see* JACOPO DA VORAGINE
Vorau Abbey 2 781
  library 19 316
Vorbasse 32 532
Vordemberge-Gildewart, Friedrich 28 197; 32 695*
  groups and movements 7 771; 10 137
  works 32 *695*
Vordingborg Castle 4 781; 8 723
Vore, Richard De *see* DEVORE, RICHARD
Vorhoff, Gerd 1 34
Vorkink, Piet(er) 14 693; 32 696
Vorkink & Wormser 32 696*
Vormal, Timo 13 843
Vornoskov, Vasily 1 71
Vorobevsky, Aleksey 27 414
Vorob'yov, Maksim 2 888; 4 232; 7 244; 19 12
Vorob'yov, Mikhail 14 163
Vorob'yov, Sokrat 9 364; 10 854
Voronca, Ilarie 4 699
Voroneţ 26 *705*, 707, 711; 32 696–7*
  iconostasis 26 718
  Monastery 21 811; 25 344; 26 *711*, 717, 722
Voronikhin, Andrey (Nikoforovich) 27 408, 576, 583; 32 697–8*
  collaboration 27 583
  pupils 21 512; 31 140
  works 12 789; 23 26; 24 291, 292; 27 375, 403, *403*, 404, 416, 428, 575, 582, *583*; 29 778; 32 *698*
Voronin, Nikolay (Nikolayevich) 32 698*
Voronkhin, Andrey 13 611
Voronova, G. 2 901
Vorontsov, Mikhail (Iliaronovich), Count 26 403
Vorontsov-Dashkov (family) 27 439, 441
Vöröskő Castle *see* ČERVENÝ KAMEŇ CASTLE
Vorovsky, Vatslav (Vatslavovich) 27 444
Vorres Museum of Greek Art *see under* PAIANIA
Vorst, St Denis 3 566; 26 645
Vorster, Anna 29 108
Vorster, Margaret 29 110
Vorster, Stauch 9 427
Vorsterman, Jan 19 348; 32 699, 700*
Vorsterman, Lucas, (i) (*c*. 1595-1675) 3 *560*, 561; 10 391; 32 699–700*
  collaboration 9 480; 10 391; 27 299
  pupils 12 851; 25 221; 32 700; 33 262
  works 2 *196*; 4 912; 20 855; 32 *699*
Vorsterman, Lucas, (ii) (1624-66) 32 699, 700*
Vorsterman, Otto 32 699
Vorstermann, Willem 30 61
Vorticism 1 74; 10 255; 11 867; 19 896; 23 23, 437; 26 59; 32 700–702*
  exhibitions 10 547
  members 10 256–7; 13 712
    Dismorr, Jessica 9 9
    Hamilton, Cuthbert 14 107
    Lewis, (Percy) Wyndham 19 287
    Nevinson, Christopher (Richard Wynne) 23 15
    Pound, Ezra (Loomis) 25 380
    Roberts, William (1895-1980) 26 466
    Wadsworth, Edward 32 753
  periodicals 24 427
  production 32 *701*
Vorticists 13 314
Vortography 32 702
Vorträge der Bibliothek Warburg 24 424
Vorwerk 12 469
Vos, Cornelis de 28 901; 32 702–5*
  attributions 10 717
  collaboration 28 904
  patrons and collectors 14 190
  pupils 8 1; 32 712
  reproductive prints by others 23 908; 26 517
  works 3 560; 23 381; 32 *703*, *704*
Vos, Cornelius des 4 847
Vos, Daniel de 32 709
Vos (ii), Jacob de 32 707*
Vos, Jan (1593-1649) 22 910
Vos, Jan (*fl c*. 1655) 15 40; 22 901
Vos, Jan-Baptist de 32 702, 705
Vos, Jan de (*fl* 1489-1521) 10 714; 13 631; 20 676; 32 702
Vos, Jasper de 16 833
Vos, Jodocus de 5 50; 30 324; 31 446
Vos, Johan Hendrik 29 119
Vos, Josse de 3 388
Vos, Maria 22 848
Vos, Marten de, the elder (1532-1603) 25 17; 32 708–12*
  attributions 3 24; 4 897
  collaboration 23 201
  groups and movements 26 728
  patrons and collectors 7 711; 27 501
  pupils 3 107; 7 413, 487; 24 475; 31 70
  reproductive prints by others 3 126; 5 63; 7 556; 12 15, 16; 17 182, 183, 598; 19 564; 24 235; 25 605; 27 502, *502*, 503; 33 169, 170
  works 2 195; 3 558; 4 923; 6 138, 595; 12 881; 17 183, 700; 20 281; 25 604; 32 *710*, *711*
Vos, Marten de, the younger (1576-1613) 32 709
Vos, Paul de 28 901; 32 702, 705–6*
  collaboration 14 616; 32 705
  patrons and collectors 1 690; 4 565; 26 732; 28 903
  teachers 28 904
  works 2 104; 3 561; 32 *706*
Vos, Pieter de (1490-1566) 14 505; 32 708
Vos, Pieter de, the younger (*d* ?1567) 32 709
Vos, Reynier Jansz. *see* VERMEER, REYNIER JANSZ.
Vos, Simon de 32 712–13*
  collaboration 1 161
  pupils 17 919
  reproductive prints by others 7 466
  teachers 32 705
  works 32 *712*
Vos, Willem de 12 243; 30 40
Vose 14 47
Vose, Isaac 4 479; 28 525
Vos (ii) Jbzn, Jacob de (1803-82) 17 841; 32 707–8*
Voskepar 2 425
Voskopojë 1 546
  St Nicholas 1 539, 540
Voskresenk 31 719
Vosmaer, Carel 32 713*
Voss, Hermann 8 513; 13 347; 32 714*
Voss, Knud 8 761
Vossberg, F. A.
  works 14 *410*
Vossius, Gerard 22 415
Vostell, Museo *see* MALPARTIDA DE CÁCERES
Vostell, Wolf 32 714*
  collaboration 1 34; 21 698
  groups and movements 8 609; 11 232
  patrons and collectors 14 48; 29 16
  works 24 407; 32 419
Vosterman, Jan *see* VORSTERMAN, JAN
Vos (ii) Wzn, Jacob de 32 707*
voting urns *see under* URNS → types
votive offerings *see* EX-VOTOS
votive reliefs *see under* RELIEF SCULPTURE → types
votive seals *see under* SEALS → types
votive statues *see under* SCULPTURE → types
votive stelae *see under* STELAE → types
votive stupas *see under* STUPAS → types
Vo Toan 1 527
Votsis, Stelios 8 364
Vottoria, Alessandro 1 110
Vouet, Laurent 32 715
Vouet, Simon 11 533, 534, 558, 587; 24 134; 26 772, 842; 32 715–19*
  assistants 4 521; 19 19; 24 253, 476; 25 70
  attributions 26 94
  collaboration 3 399; 6 434; 9 175; 27 821; 29 623
  groups and movements 30 456
  patrons and collectors
    Archinto (family) 2 310
    Bretonvilliers, Claude le Ragois de 4 756
    Bullion, Claude de 5 168
    Créquy, Charles de Blanchefort de 19 238
    Des Noyers, François Sublet, Baron de Dangu 29 886
    Doria, Gian Carlo, Prince 9 174
    Einden, van den (family) 10 114
    Filomarino, Ascanio, Cardinal 11 81
    Henrietta Maria, Queen of England and Scotland (1609-69) 29 803
    Hesselin, Louis (-Cauchon) 14 492
    La Live de Jully, Ange-Laurent de 18 660
    Louis XIII, King of France (*reg* 1610-43) 4 549

Vouet, Simon
  patrons and collectors—cont.
   Meynier, Charles 21 412
   Orléans, Philippe I de Bourbon, 1st Duc d' (1640-1701) 23 512
   Peiresc, Nicolas-Claude Fabri de 24 330
   Richelieu, Armand-Jean Du Plessis, Cardinal de 11 534; 26 348
   Robien, Christophe-Paul Gautron, Marquis de 26 470
   Roomer, Gaspar 27 133
   Séguier, Pierre 28 370
   Vassal de Saint-Hubert, Jean-Antoine-Hubert 32 74
  pupils 2 724; 9 379; 24 397, 805; 30 530
   Bernard, Jacques-Samuel 3 813
   Blanchet, Thomas 4 128
   Chaperon, Nicolas 6 461
   Corneille, Michel (i) (1601/3-64) 7 863
   Du Fresnoy, Charles-Alphonse 9 371
   François, Claude 11 722
   Le Nôtre, André 19 162
   Lerambert, Louis, II (1620-70) 19 225
   Le Sueur, Eustache 19 246
   Loir, Nicolas-Pierre 19 542
   Mignard, Pierre, I 21 497
   Poërson, Charles 25 70
   Vuibert, Rémy 32 738
   Willaerts, Abraham 33 194
  reproductions in ceramics 20 474
  reproductions in tapestry 1 782
  reproductive prints by others 8 77, 525; 9 175; 17 599; 18 812; 21 85; 32 510
  tapestries 11 *640*, 641
  works 7 569; 11 *534*; 13 701; 22 485; 28 *6*; 30 358; 32 *715*, *716*, *717*, *718*
Vouga, Emil 18 828
Vouga, Paul 18 828
Vougy, Barthélémy Thoynard de *see* THOYNARD DE VOUGY, BARTHÉLÉMY
Vougy, Vicomte de 7 896
Vouillemont, Sébastien 25 833
Vouliagmeni 14 342
Voulkos, Peter 4 110; 19 702; 31 640
  works 31 *640*
Vouni 8 *325*; 13 *362*
  palace 8 332, 335–6, *336*; 32 719*
  sculpture 8 353
  Temple of Athena 8 336
Vounous 8 *325*
  architectural models 8 334
  copper 8 353
  pottery 8 344
  Tomb 19 8 *344*
  Tumulus B 8 *307*, 326, 329
Vounous Bowl 8 *307*, 326, 339
voussoir arch bridges *see under* BRIDGES → types
voussoir arches *see under* ARCHES → types
voussoirs 2 292, *292*; 4 774; 32 719*
Voustre Demeure Hours *see under* BOOKS OF HOURS → individual manuscripts
Voventa Padovano, Villa Giustiniani 16 719
Vovk, F. 31 565
Vox, Marcus de 17 7
Voyer, Marquis de 24 821; 32 719*, 766
  metalwork 9 399
  paintings 7 194; 9 416
  sculpture 24 785
Voyez, François 32 720*
Voyez, Nicolas-Joseph 3 463; 32 719–20*
Vöygh, Jacob *see* FACHT, JACOB
Voys, Arie de *see* VOIS, ARIE DE
Voysey, C(harles) F(rancis) A(nnesley) 20 22; 32 720–22*, 817
  architecture 10 284; 12 177; 25 835; 27 130, 719; 32 834
  collaboration 19 415; 32 835
  furniture 6 391; 10 298; 11 850
  groups and movements 2 562, 569, 575; 9 739; 10 239; 21 779; 23 498; 25 805
  interior decoration 10 283
  patrons and collectors 14 132
  pewter 10 344
  pupils 20 30
  textiles 10 356
  type-faces 2 333
  wallpaper 25 373; 33 372
Voženílek, Jiří 24 226*
Vozmediano, Alonso de *see* ALONSO DE VOZMEDIANO
Vozoulin, Antip 23 168
Vozoulin, Lavrenty 23 168
Vperyod *see* FORWARD GROUP
Vrabiye, Georgy 21 812
vrai drochel see under LACE → types
Vrams Gunnarstorp 30 92
Vrancx (family) 2 199
Vrancx, Sebastiaen 32 722–4*
  collaboration 4 913, 915, 916; 21 830; 22 718; 32 251
  patrons and collectors 23 396
  pupils 28 898
  reproductive prints by others 17 599
  works 5 352; 32 *723*
Vrangel', Nikolay (Nikolayevich), Baron 27 444; 32 724*
Vranje 28 444
Vranov nad Dyjí 27 233
  Castle 8 391; 15 139; 23 812
  pottery 8 405, *405*
Vrantuk 4 460
Vrap 9 654
Vratislav I, Duke of Bohemia (*reg* 895-921) 8 388
Vratislav II, Duke of Bohemia (*reg* 1061-92) 8 421; 25 439, 445
Vratislavice nad Nisou 8 419
Vratislav of Pernštejn 19 500; 24 462, 463
Vratsa 5 160; 25 339; 30 770, 771
Vrbna, Eugen 8 416
Vrbna, Rudolf, Count 8 416
Vredeland, Willem (Backer van) *see* VRELANT, WILLEM (BACKER VAN)
Vredeman de Vries, Hans 3 598; 22 823; 32 724–7*
  architecture 11 875, *875*, 876; 32 860; 33 52
  collaboration 4 147
  paintings 2 340; 5 352; 25 104; 32 *726*
  patrons and collectors 8 395; 12 133; 13 915; 29 429, 799
  prints 13 *701*; 25 606, 607; 29 *748*; 32 *725*
  publications 2 194; 3 484, 569, 576, 581, 582, 609; 6 390; 8 413; 10 745; 12 131; 13 701; 14 709; 22 823, 863, 870, 871; 23 489, 540; 24 271, 274; 29 747; 31 150
  pupils 29 592
  reproductive prints by others 3 558; 7 499; 9 64; 27 504
Vredeman de Vries, Paul 11 444; 22 841; 32 725
  collaboration 11 718; 32 725, 727
  paintings 2 340; 32 725, *726*
  publications 3 582; 22 870; 24 271
Vredeman de Vries, Saloman 32 725
Vreden, St Felicitas 7 265; 13 161
Vredis, Judocus 32 727*
Vreeland, Diana 2 852
Vreeland, Willem (Backer van) *see* VRELANT, WILLEM (BACKER VAN)
Vrees, Jan zonder *see* JAN ZONDER VREES
Vreewijk *see under* ROTTERDAM
Vrefsky, Baroness 14 768
Vrel, Jacobus 22 840; 32 728*
Vrelant, Betkin 32 729
Vrelant, Willem (Backer van) 4 921; 22 836; 32 728–9*
  collaboration 19 252
  paintings 21 102
  patrons and collectors 5 211, 213
  works 3 555; 4 11; 20 724; 26 563; 32 *729*
Vrestena 29 702
Vretblad, Maud 32 730*
Vreyland, Willem (Backer van) *see* VRELANT, WILLEM (BACKER VAN)
Vrhlab 28 440
Vriend, J. J. 8 669
Vriendt, Albert De *see* DE VRIENDT, ALBERT
Vriendt, Cornelius de 3 615
Vriendt, de *see* FLORIS
Vriendt, Jan Florisz. de 11 219
Vriendt, Julian De *see* DE VRIENDT, JULIAN
Vrients, Jan-Baptist 33 169
Vries, Abraham de 8 1; 24 330
Vries, Adriaen de 5 76; 8 390; 14 41, 542; 22 725; 32 730–31*
  collaboration 12 576; 28 60
  patrons and collectors
   Charles I, Prince of Liechtenstein (*reg* 1608-27) 19 336
   Christian IV, King of Denmark and Norway (*reg* 1588-1648) 22 857; 23 396
   Christina, Queen of Sweden (*reg* 1632-54) 32 8
   Colbert, Jean-Baptiste (1619-83) 7 546
   Figdor, Albert 11 62
   Rudolf II, Holy Roman Emperor (*reg* 1576- 1612) 13 914
   Schaumburg, Ernst von, Graf 28 60
   Tessin, Carl Gustav, Count 30 524
   Vilas Boas, Manuel (do) Cenáculo 32 539
  personal collection 27 270
  reproductive prints by others 18 44; 22 272, *272*
  works 2 714; 5 76, 301, *301*; 8 384, 739; 10 436, 502; 12 403; 23 252; 25 432, 438, 445; 26 105; 29 571, 690; 32 *731*
Vries, André R. de 30 16
Vries, Anne Gerard Christiaan de 10 176
Vries, Auke de 14 44
Vries, David Pietersz. de 21 790
Vries, Dirck de 23 112
Vries, Erwin de 30 16
Vries, Hans Vredeman de *see* VREDEMAN DE VRIES, HANS
Vries, Johan de 26 284
Vries, Paul Vredeman de *see* VREDEMAN DE VRIES, PAUL
Vries, Roelof van 27 329
Vries, Saloman Vredeman de *see* VREDEMAN DE VRIES, SALOMAN
Vries, Simon de *see* FRISIUS, SIMON (WYNHOUTSZ.)
Vriesendorp, Jacob 29 773
Vriesendorp, Madelon 18 236; 23 361
Vrij Beelden 22 852
Vrijdag, Daniël 32 592
Vrillière, Marquise de *see* MAZARIN, Duchesse de
Vrindavan 15 *261*, 406; 32 732*
  temple of Govind Dev 15 363
Vrints, Johannes Baptista 32 708
Vrishadeva 5 102
Vrizakis, Theodoros *see* VRYZAKES, THEODOROS
Vṛndāvana *see* VRINDAVAN
Vrokastro 8 154; 21 664
Vroman, Adam Clark 24 666
  works 22 *567*
Vrona, Ivan 2 634
Vrondisi Monastery 8 156
Vronenstein, Mary van 20 663
Vronsky, Makar K. 31 561
Vroom, Cornelis (Hendricksz.), the elder (*fl c.* 1560) 32 732
Vroom, Cornelis (Hendricksz.), the younger (*c.* 1591-1661) 3 766; 20 424; 22 840; 32 732, 734–5*
Vroom, Frederick, I (*d* 1593) 32 732
Vroom, Frederick (Hendricksz.), II (1600-1667) 32 732, 735*
Vroom, Hendrick (Cornelisz.) 13 894; 32 732–5*
  assistants 32 734, 735
  patrons and collectors 20 366; 29 799
  pupils 25 246; 33 167
  works 3 389; 19 613; 22 840; 29 375; 30 318; 32 *733*, *734*
Vroom, Jacob, I (*fl c.* 1620-50) 32 732
Vroom, Jacob, II (*d* 1700) 32 732
Vroutos, Georgios 13 354; 32 735*
Vrouwenpolder Church 4 785
Vrpolje, Ivan Meštrović Memorial Gallery 21 316
Vršac National Museum 28 458
Vrsar 9 565
Vrt'anes K'ert'ogh 2 430, 444
Vrtba, František Josef, Count of 8 405
Vrubel', M. (*fl* 1940-60) 22 178; 27 411
Vrubel', Mikhail (Aleksandrovich) (1856-1910) 1 71; 18 38; 27 391, 392, 408; 30 265; 32 735–6*
  assistants 27 410
  collaboration 12 878; 33 607
  groups and movements 1 71; 4 178; 12 870; 31 582; 33 379
  patrons and collectors 22 135, 331; 27 438, 458, 459; 31 565
  productions 20 232
  sponsors 30 464
  works 28 579; 32 *736*
Vrysi 8 334, 343
Vrysinas 8 153
Vryzakes, Theodoros 13 352; 32 737*
Vsadnik (The Rider) 27 434
Vsekopromsovet (All-Union Council for Craft Cooperatives) 27 422
Vsesoyuznoye Ob'edineniye Assotsiatsii Proletarskikh Arkhitektorov *see* VOPRA
Vsevolod, Prince of Vladimir-Suzdal' (*reg* 1176-1212) 32 665
Vucedol 8 180
Vuchetich, Yevgeny (Viktorovich) 27 396; 32 737*
  collaboration 3 685; 32 685
  works 18 38; 32 *685*
Vuchinich, Vuc 3 64
Vucht, Gerrit van 27 230
Vucht, Jan van der 23 191
Vuechtelin, Johannes *see* WECHTLIN, HANS
Vuez, Arnould de 11 723; 19 381; 32 737–8*
Vufflens Castle 30 126
Vught Church 22 821
Vuibert, Rémy 14 492; 31 382; 32 738*
Vuillamy, Gérard 11 550
Vuillamy, Lewis 17 639
Vuillard, Edouard 11 547, 667; 32 738–43*
  collaboration 4 325; 20 603
  dealers 3 826; 19 10; 26 107; 32 686
  groups and movements 15 156, 888; 22 421, 422; 28 344; 30 169
  lithographs 32 686
  methods 4 184
  patrons and collectors 4 71; 7 832; 22 538; 24 183; 26 472, 534; 33 150
  prints 25 626
  productions 17 449; 30 682, 685
  pupils 3 88, 753, 809; 6 84
  works 9 310; 15 888; 19 489; 25 623; 32 *739*, *740*, *742*
Vuillermet, Charles 18 873
Vuinic, Avessalom 25 340
Vuitton, Louis 2 727
Vujičić, Avesalom 22 17
Vujović, Ksenija 22 18
Vujović, Savo 22 18
Vukan 28 449
Vukanović, Beta 32 743*
Vukotić, Mihailo 22 18
Vukovar 8 *174*
  Bauer Collection and Fine Art Gallery 8 181
  Franciscan Monastery 8 176
  urban planning 8 175
Vuković, Matija 28 454
Vuković-Podgoričanin, Božidar 22 17
Vuković-Podgoričanin, Vićenco 22 17
Vukovo, St Petka 25 343
Vukutu 1 429
Vulas, Šime 8 179
Vulca 8 263; 16 683; 26 860; 32 119
vulcanite 10 346; 17 514; 25 26
Vulchetrun 30 769
Vulci 10 *583*, 585, 601, 637, 638, 640; 16 *620*; 26 *886*; 32 743–4*
  bronze 10 591, 592, 626, *627*, 627
  busts 10 604
  cists 10 630
  coins 10 632
  faience (i) (glass) 13 *590*
  fibulae 12 *868*
  gold 10 631
  group 10 616
  jewellery 10 632
  mirrors 10 629
  monumental 10 591
  Museo Nazionale 10 640
  Ponte dell'Abbadia 7 837
  pottery 10 610, 613; 13 *437*, 542
  sarcophagi 10 588, 607, 608
  sculpture 10 587, 607
  tombs 10 591, 592
   François Tomb 10 586, 595, 596, 636
    wall paintings 10 *622*, 623; 16 653; 32 744
   Isis Tomb 10 606–7
    sculpture 10 *606*
  trade 10 584, 591
  vase paintings 2 *134*; 10 592, 613, 614–15, 616
  vases 10 609, 610, *610*, 611, *611*, 612, 613; 32 33
  wall paintings 10 617
Vulci-Sovana 10 616
Vulcop, Conrad de 31 842; 32 744*
Vulcop, Henri de 7 526; 17 458; 20 652; 32 744*
  collaboration 32 744
Vulgate Bible *see under* BIBLES → types
Vulgrin 2 48; 19 126
Vulliamy, Benjamin 27 197
Vulliamy, Benjamin Lewis 9 31
Vulliamy, Gérard 8 63; 30 135

Vulliamy, Lewis **10** 281; **14** 675
Vung Tao wreck **6** 919
Vungu **11** 878
Vuoksenniska *see* IMATRA
Vuolvinius the Smith **5** 807; **21** 522
Vurnik, Ivan **28** 860; **32** 744*
collaboration **31** 106
groups and movements **28** 860
works **19** 516
Vušković, Dujam **28** 84
Vušković, Miloš **22** 18
Vuvi **11** 878
VVV: Poetry, Plastic Arts, Anthropology, Sociology, Psychology **24** 428, 433; **30** 22
Vyalov, Konstantin **8** 10
Vyatka *see* KIROV
Vyazemsky, Aleksandr **19** 837
Vyborg **11** *87*; **27** *363*; **32** *745*, 745–6*
architecture **11** 90
Castle **11** 101
City Library **1** 125; **11** 92, 104; **19** 320
gold **11** 107
Vyborg—cont.
guilds **11** 103
pottery **11** 105
Vylka, Tyko **27** 434
Vyne, Stephen **23** 460
Vyne, The (Hants) **32** 540
chapel **3** 588; **10** 273; **13** 185
interior decoration **11** 430
portico **25** 265, *266*; **33** 10
tiles **2** 25; **30** 877
Vyner, Mary **5** 195; **13** 645
Vyner, Robert **10** 328
Vyse, Richard **10** 79
Vyšehrad Codex *see under* CODICES → individual manuscripts
Vyšehrad Madonna **25** 432
Vysheslavsky, Gleb **31** 560
Vyshgorod **31** 554
Vyshinsky, F. Ye. **24** 400
Vysoké Mýto **8** 376
Vyšší Brod Abbey **8** *374*, 376; **20** 784; **32** *746*, 746–7*
chapter house **32** 747
collections **8** 423
furniture **8** 398
Vyšší Brod Abbey—cont.
metalwork **8** 412
paintings **8** 389
sculpture **8** 382
Vyšší Brod Altar, Master of the **8** 388; **20** 784*; **25** 431
Vyšší Brod Altarpiece **13** 151
Vytakin, V. L. **6** 279
Vytlačil, Václav **4** 576; **28** 887
Výtvarné snahy **24** 440
Výtvarné umění **24** 440
Výtvarný *see* ARTISTS GROUP
Vyvyan Salt **10** 326; **27** 640, *640*

W

W ♀, Master **20** 803*
W/3 *see* DADA WESTSTUPIDIA 3
Waagen, Carl **10** 720
Waagen, Friedrich Ludwig **32** 748
Waagen, Gustav Friedrich **2** 532; **7** 714; **9** 17; **12** 476; **22** 358; **24** 443; **29** 46; **32** 748*
 exhibitions **10** 679
 works **13** 810, 811; **23** 645
  illustrated **6** 78
  on display of art **9** 19
  translated **9** 683
Waagen's Mostaert *see* ISENBRANDT, ADRIAEN
Waal, Henri van der **4** 27; **15** 91, 97; **22** 911
Waals, Peter van der **12** 650
Waay, Nicolaas van der **1** 808
Wäber, Abraham **33** 13
Wäber, Jakob **29** 644
Wabern, Petermann von **30** 149
Wace, Alan J. B. **4** 137; **18** 668
Wąchock Abbey **25** *92*, 95; **32** 748–50*
 chapter house **32** *749*
Wachs, Sabine **21** 67
Wachsmann, Alois **8** 393
Wachsmann, Konrad (Ludwig) **13** 689; **32** 750*
 assistants **2** 287
 works **26** 19, 20; **29** 250
Wachsmuth, Ernst **4** 740
Wachsmuth, Jeremias **2** 719
Wachtangoff, S. E. **30** 684
Wachtbeke, Provinciaal Molenmuseum **3** 616
Wachtel, Elmer **19** 701
Wachtel, Marian **19** 701
Wächter, (Georg Friedrich) Eberhard **12** 392; **14** 586; **32** 750–51*
Wächter, W. **19** 661
Wachtmeister (family) **29** 366
Wackenfeld, Johann Heinrich **29** 753
Wackenroder, Wilhelm (Heinrich) **9** 443; **26** 738; **32** 751*
Wacker, Otto **11** 308, 309
Wackerbarth, Christoph August von **18** 162; **21** 489; **32** 752*
Wackerle, Joseph **12** 437; **24** 826; **33** 607
Wackernagel, Martin **28** 917; **32** 752–3*
Wacklin, Isak **11** 94
Wacoal Art Centre *see under* TOKYO
Wacquez, Adolphe-André **7** 434
el-Wad **1** 883; **30** *180*, *181*
 antlers **30** 181
 beads **30** 181
wada see under HOUSES → types
Wada, Eisaku **17** 204
 works **17** *203*
Wada, Sanshō **17** 401
Wada, Yoshi **29** 98
Wada Gesshin **22** 119
Wada Yoshimori **31** 675
Wad Ban Naqa **23** *276*
 Isis Temple **23** 282
 palace of Amanishakheto **23** 283
 Temple G **23** 283
Waddell, John **24** 683
Waddesdon Manor (Bucks) **3** 174; **8** 817; **9** 399; **21** 550; **27** 225
 collections **10** 367; **27** 223
 furniture **3** 715; **8** 684; **9** 324; **11** 119, 592, 596; **20** 468; **24** 821, *821*; **26** *84*, 84
 Grey Drawing-room **27** *224*
 interior decoration **19** 231
Waddesdon Manor (Bucks)—cont.
 manuscripts **20** 413, 707
 miniatures (paintings) **21** 643
 overdoors **23** 679
 paintings **2** 722; **3** 785; **4** 882; **9** 193; **11** 410; **18** 692; **28** 50; **32** 494
 panelling **5** 168
 porcelain **20** 388
 sculpture **5** 380; **8** 698
 Sèvres museum **27** 225
 snuff-boxes **22** 205
Waddington, Victor **16** 18
Waddington Graphics **25** 626
Wade, Henry **4** 818
Wade, John **23** 856, 860; **32** 414
Wade, Thomas **6** 612
Wade Cup **16** 365, 368, 374; **23** 559, 563
Wadell, Maj-Brit **30** 120
Wadham **28** 488
Wadham, Dorothy **23** 687
Wadi Atollah **27** 15
Wadi Bahandawaya **21** 301
Wadi Dahr, Dar al-Hajar **33** 519
Wadi Dura **2** *265*
Wadi el-Sebua **23** 280; **25** 776
 churches **23** 287
 cult temples **9** 833; **23** 280; **25** 874; **29** 386
Wadi Fawakhir **29** 700
Wadi Halfa **1** 317
Wadi Hammamat **9** 780, 813; **27** 14; **29** 616
Wadi Hammeh **30** 181
Wadi Kharit **28** 760
Wadi Maghara **9** 868; **28** *760*
 rock reliefs **28** 760
 stelae **29** 615, 616
Wadimu **27** 810, 811
Wadi Natrun
 Deir Abu Maqar *see* Monastery of St Macarius
 Deir al-Anba Bishay *see* Monastery of St Bishai
 Deir al-Baramus *see* Monastery of the Romans
 Deir al-Suryan *see* Monastery of the Syrians
 manuscripts **7** 823; **9** 619
 monasteries **7** 820
 Monastery of St Bishai **7** 820
  church **7** 262
 Monastery of St Macarius **7** 280; **16** 488
 Monastery of the Romans **7** 821
 Monastery of the Syrians **7** *819*, 820
  Church of the Virgin **7** 823, *823*, 824
  screens (i) (architectural) **9** 600
  stucco **29** 817
  wood-carvings **7** 828
Wadi Qututa, Temple of Wadd Dhu Masmaʿ **2** 252, 253
Wadi Sabūʿ *see* WADI EL-SEBUA
Wadi Suq **2** 272
Wadi Wutayya **2** 263
Wadj **9** *776*, 838, 868; **27** 810
Wadsorth, Austin **29** 870
Wadsworth, Daniel **7** 284, 549; **14** 203; **32** 753*
Wadsworth, Edward **5** 531; **10** 374; **20** 425; **24** 427; **32** 753–4*
 groups and movements **8** 265; **10** 256; **13** 712; **19** 622, 623; **23** 23; **25** 380
  Abstraction-Création **1** 90
  Omega Workshops **23** 437
  Rebel Art Centre **26** 59
Wadsworth, Edward
 groups and movements—cont.
  Unit One **31** 673
  Vorticism **32** 700, 701
 works **5** *531*; **10** 256; **30** 426; **32** *701*; **33** 363
Wadsworth, John William **10** 313
Wadsworth Atheneum *see under* HARTFORD (CT)
Wadt, von (family) **30** 312
Wadu, Sane **17** 907, 908
Waechter, John **27** 598
Waehneldt, Carl Friedrich Gustav **26** 414
Wael, Cornelis de **2** 200; **16** 674; **32** 754–5*
 assistants **9** 745
 dealing **31** 526
 paintings **27** 132
 reproductive prints by others **32** 755
 works **2** 200; **13** 896; **32** *755*
Wael, Jan Baptist de, I (1558-1633) **32** 754
Wael, Jan Baptist de, II (1632-? after 1669) **32** 754, 755*
Wael, Lucas de **32** 754*
Waele, Jan van de *see* GOSSART, JAN
Waerniers, Guillaume **11** 642; **19** 382
Waesemann, Herrmann Friedrich **3** 793; **4** 787; **12** 376; **18** 208; **30** 503
Wafa Iyesus Church **10** 569
Wafangzhuang (Nanyang) **7** 98
Wafer, Jeremy **29** 110
Wagemaker, Jaap **20** 846; **22** 852; **32** 755–6*
Wagemans, Henricus **32** 756
Wagemans, Henri-Jean **32** 756
Wagemans, H. J. J. **32** 756
Wagemans, Jules **32** 756
Wagemans Maastricht **32** 756*
Wagenaer, Zacharias **29** 116
Wagenbauer, Max Joseph **19** 482; **22** 303
Wagener, Gottfried **17** 198, 242, 378; **18** 555
Wagener, Zacharias, II **4** 715, 724
Wagenfeld, Wilhelm **11** 852; **15** 826; **32** 756–7*
 groups and movements **3** 402; **7** 772
 works **12** 441; **15** *825*
Wagenfeldt, Otto **32** 757*
Wager, Rhoda **2** 766
Waghemakere, Domien de *see* DOMIEN DE WAGHEMAKERE
Waghemakere, Herman de *see* HERMAN DE WAGHEMAKERE
Waghenaer, Lucas (Jansz.) **9** 64; **20** 364; **31** 153
Wägmann, Hans Heinrich **19** 769; **32** 757
Wägmann, Jakob **32** 757*
Wagmüller, Michael **27** 332; **32** 758*; **33** 283
Wagner **28** 197
Wagner, Abraham **3** 823; **4** 84; **33** 291
Wagner, Alexander (von) **6** 499; **18** 398, 413; **19** 208; **20** 549; **21** 37; **31** 389; **33** 450
Wagner, Anton **16** 737
Wagner, Arthur Douglas **4** 809
Wagner, August **22** 158
Wagner, Christian **12** 452
Wagner, Giuseppe *see* WAGNER, JOSEPH
Wagner, Heinrich **33** 271
Wagner, Henry Mitchell **4** 809
Wagner, Hugo Gari **31** 138
Wagner, Jeremias **22** 918
Wagner, Johann **32** 758
Wagner, Johann Georg **14** 767
Wagner, Johann Peter (Alexander) **32** 758–9*
 collaboration **2** 843
 pupils **32** 759
 teachers **9** 753
 works **12** 405; **32** 120; **33** 434
Wagner, Johann Thomas **32** 758
Wagner, Josef (*fl* 20th cent.) **8** 387
Wagner, Joseph (1706-1780) **1** 784; **3** 199; **5** 55; **10** 394; **11** 172; **12** 582; **24** 842; **32** 759*
 assistants **3** 308
 printmakers **5** 599
 pupils **32** 652
 works **3** 308; **33** 613
Wagner, Konrad **32** 759
Wagner, Leonhard **3** 472; **32** 759*
Wagner, Martin (1885-1956) **13** 688; **14** 632; **26** 405; **31** 728; **32** 759–60*
 collaboration **21** 495; **25** 69
 groups and movements **3** 795; **26** 405
 works **3** 796, *796*; **16** 587
Wagner, (Johann) Martin von (1777-1858) **27** 346; **32** 759*
Wagner, Otto **2** 831; **14** 138; **32** 760–63*
 assistants **14** 749; **23** 393
 collaboration **22** 187; **30** 755
 furniture **6** 391; **18** 192
 groups and movements **2** 566, 567, 787; **21** 779; **26** 14; **28** 344, 670
 house **2** 552
 pupils **2** 568; **13** 330; **18** 467
  Bauer, Leopold **3** 398
  Chochol, Josef **7** 182
  Fabiani, Max **10** 722
  Hoffmann, Josef (Franz Maria) **14** 627
  Janák, Pavel **16** 902
  Kotěra, Jan **18** 404
  Kovačić, Viktor **18** 411
  Medgyaszay, István **21** 4
  Meštrović, Ivan **21** 315
  Plečnik, Jože **25** 37
  Schindler, Rudolph (Michael) **28** 96
  Schönthal, Otto **28** 155
  Vurnik, Ivan **32** 744
 staff **14** 628; **28** 155
 tiles **30** 885, *885*
 works **1** 111; **2** 333, 787, 788, 809, 814; **3** 177; **14** 785; **21** 349; **27** 131, 662; **30** 506; **32** 438, 448, 555, *761*, *762*
Wagner, Péter **14** 890
Wagner, (Wilhelm) Richard **22** 378; **30** 682; **32** 763–4*; **33** 283
 architecture **1** 125; **3** 428; **30** 678
 groups and movements **30** 169
 works **12** 496; **22** 329
Wagner, Sándor **2** 546; **14** 901; **22** 310
Wagner, Siegfried **3** 122
Wagner, Sigmund **24** 453
Wagner, Veit **32** 764*
Wagner, Wieland **30** 687
Wagner Garden Carpet **5** 278, IV; **12** *77*; **16** 475
Wagner-Rieger, Renate **2** 834; **32** 764*
Wagogo **30** 302
wagon roofs *see under* ROOFS → types
wagons **10** 874; **25** 547–8*
 ceremonial **25** 526–7, *527*
 cult **25** *541*
 pageant **30** 653, 662, 665
Wagstaff, Sam **24** 683
Wagstaffe, Thomas R. **25** 688
Wah **10** 29, 46; **22** 284
Wahab, Ahmed Abdel **9** 766
Wahgi **23** 714, 721
 dress **24** *75*
 headdresses **23** *714*
Wahl, Ferdinand von der, Graf **8** 288
Wahl, Johan Soloman **8** 734; **10** 461; **32** 765*
Wahl, Karl **12** 450
Wahl, Theodore **20** 605
Wahlberg, (Herman) Alfred (Leonard) **30** 79; **32** 765*
Wahlis Pottery **8** 406
Wahliss **32** 450
Wahlman, Lars Israel **23** 615; **30** 74; **32** 765–6*
Wähneldt, Gustav **4** 711
Wahorn, András **14** 902
Wah-Pah-Nah-Yah *see* WEST, RICHARD
Wahren, Dorfkirche **9** 156
Waiblingen, Sports Hall **29** 427
Waid, Stefan **4** 186, 188, 190
Waidenlich, Hans **27** 218
Waihi **23** 71
Wailes, William **25** 716
Wailes of Newcastle **29** 766; **30** 533
Wailly, Charles de **22** 93; **32** 766–9*
 collaboration **13** 234; **18** 661; **19** 251; **24** 122, 581–2
 groups and movements **13** 608; **22** 734; **24** 173
 patrons and collectors **29** 411; **32** 719
 pupils **3** 432; **17** 698; **24** 554; **25** 404; **29** 551; **32** 697
 teachers **4** 163; **19** 76
 works **2** 337; **6** 509; **12** 159; **24** 120; **25** 267; **29** *636*; **30** 671; **31** 714; **32** *768*
Waimate North, Mission House **23** 53
Waimea Pottery **23** 69
Wain, Louis **25** 686
Wainewright, Thomas Griffiths **32** 769*
wainscot chairs *see under* CHAIRS → types
wainscoting *see* PANELLING
Wainstein-Krasuk, Olga **2** 397
Wainwright, Ellis **27** 565
Wainwright, John **11** 229; **28** 870
Wainwright, William John **4** 86
Waismith, Master **25** 110
Waismuth **26** 684
waistcoats **8** 35, *35*, 36; **21** 876; **30** X3
Waitangi **23** *52*
 Treaty House **23** 53
Waite, Charles B. **21** 398
Waite, Ezra **6** 485; **32** 303
Waite, Jony **17** 907
Waite, Peter **2** 755
Waite, Richard **31** 176
Waitere, Tene **32** 769–70*
waiters
 England **10** *330*
 materials **10** *330*
Waitt, Richard **9** 724
Waituhi, Meeting House **23** 54

Waitz, Baron 17 835
Waiwai 13 874, 875
Waja
 gourds 1 303
Wajh 16 271; 32 315
Wajid ʿAli Shah, Nawab of Avadh (reg 1847-56) 15 377, 655, 712; 19 775
Wajil ware see under POTTERY → wares
Wajima 17 356
Wakabayashi, Isamu 32 770*
Wakai, Kanezaburō 17 441
wakan 17 781
Wakandar, Vishnu Shridhar 15 551
Wakao, Toshisada 17 267
Wakasugi Isohachi 17 186*
Wakefield (W. Yorks)
 Bretton Hall College
 Yorkshire Sculpture Park 28 315
 Chapel 6 458
 court-house 18 887
 West Riding County Hall 31 242
Wakefield, Cyrus 33 156
Wakefield, Edward Gibbon 2 745; 23 51
Wakefield Rattan Co. 33 156
Wakeley & Wheeler 10 337
Wakelin, Edward 10 332; 14 857; 33 158
Wakelin, John 12 163
Wakelin, Roland (Shakespeare) 2 749, 771; 32 770*
Wakidi 15 807
el-Wakil, Abdel Wahed 27 876; 32 770–71*
 works 9 765; 16 242; 27 876
Wakra 25 776
 museum 25 777
Wakuta 17 262; 27 470
Walafrid Strabo 12 107, 108
Walapai 22 634, 661
Walbaum, Matthias 2 718; 32 771–3*
 collaboration 14 51
 patrons and collectors 4 406
 works 8 739; 12 445; 25 22; 26 148; 32 772
Walbran, John 11 348
Walch, Bernhard 12 366
Walch, Fidelis 23 872
Walch, Niclas 2 817
Walch, Sigmund 12 366
Walchner, Ulrich 12 370
Walcot, William 2 333; 22 173; 32 773*
Walcourt, St Materne 3 566; 26 645
Walcourt, Egidius de see EGIDIUS DE WALCOURT
Walcourt, Gilles de see EGIDIUS DE WALCOURT
Walcourt, Hugo de see HUGO D'OIGNIES
Waldack, Charles 24 669
Waldalgesheim 12 361; 25 470; 32 773–4*
 flagons 6 155
 gold 6 157
Waldauf Altarpiece 26 106
Waldberg, Otto Truchsess von, Cardinal see TRUCHSESS VON WALDBERG, OTTO, Cardinal
Waldberg, Patrick 30 22
Waldburger, Hans 2 801; 27 664
Waldburger, Hans Leonhard 12 404; 14 646; 26 522
Waldburg-Sonnenburg, Endres, Graf von 29 684
Waldeck, Friedrich von, Prince 31 27, 579
Waldeck, Johann Friedrich (Maximilian), Graf von 21 262; 32 774*
Waldegg, Petar 4 462
Waldegrave, William, 1st Baron Radstock 24 571; 32 774*
Waldemar, Otto 16 4
Walden, Herwarth (Georg Lewin) 3 801; 12 472; 17 764; 18 109, 198; 22 304; 24 445; 25 626; 29 871–2; 32 774–5*
 assistants 22 253
 collections 12 474
 groups and movements 3 801; 10 695
 paintings 6 384
 writings 12 395
Walden, Howard de 32 791
Waldenburg 12 428, 430
Waldenstein, Florian Waldauf von 26 105
Wälder, Gyula 14 890; 32 775*
Walderbach Church 14 81; 26 656
Walderdorff, Johann Philipp von, Elector of Trier 26 529; 28 381; 30 866
Waldes, Jindřich 8 423
Waldferdin, Hippolyte 11 369
Waldglas see under GLASS → types
Waldhausen Abbey Church 2 781
Waldherr, František 14 364; 20 875
Waldis, Carlo 18 786
Waldkirch 26 485
Waldmann, Josef 28 163
Waldmann, Kaspar 2 794; 15 865; 32 775*
Waldmann, Michael, I 32 775
Wald Monastery 12 372
Waldmüller, Ferdinand Georg 2 831; 32 775–7*
 exhibitions 2 546
 patrons and collectors 19 339
 pupils 4 438; 18 127; 20 41; 30 205; 33 669
 works 2 796; 11 461; 32 444, 445, 776
Waldner, Hans 2 805; 32 777*
Waldo, Samuel Lovett 32 777–8*
Waldoboro (ME) 27 317
Waldon, Joris 17 648
Waldorp, A. 26 482
Waldpaum, Matthias see WALBAUM, MATTHIAS
Waldport (OR), Alsea Bay Bridge 4 799, 803
Waldré, Vincent 16 14
Waldsassen
 Abbey 19 259; 29 838
 library 19 316
 Pilgrimage Church of the Holy Trinity 8 873
Waldschmidt, E. 18 105
Waldsee, Colleredo, Conte see COLLEREDO WALDSEE, CONTE
Waldseemüller, Martin 12 813
Waldstein, Albrecht von 24 772
Wale, Samuel 10 372; 32 778*
 collaboration 13 884
 reproductive prints by others 19 619, 619
 works 11 907; 19 619
Walenkamp, Herman J(ohannes) M(aria) 18 878; 32 778–9*
Wales 31 585, 585; 32 779–92*, 780
 architecture 26 587–90*; 32 779–84*; 33 208
 capriccios 5 687
 castles 6 56, 61; 21 564
 concentric 21 564
 Gothic 16 896
 Norman Revival 23 210
 13th cent. 5 374
 19th cent. 6 61
 cathedrals 27 537
 ceramics 32 789–90*
 chairs 32 788
 chapels 32 783
 collections 32 790–91*
 crosses 32 786, 787
 dealing 32 790–91*
 dressers 32 788–9
 education (art) 32 792*
 exhibitions 32 791
 fortifications 32 781
Wales—cont.
 furniture 32 788–9*
 gardens 12 131
 glass 32 790
 gold 25 525
 heraldry 14 409
 houses 32 781–2, 782
 interior decoration 32 788*, 788
 law courts 5 731
 manuscript illumination 15 875
 meeting-houses 32 783
 metalwork 32 789*
 mottes 21 562
 museums 32 791*
 painting 32 784–6*
 palaces 27 539
 patronage 32 790–91*
 plates 32 789
 portraits 32 785
 quilts 25 821
 roofs 32 788
 sculpture 26 617–18*; 32 786–8*
 slate 10 236
 stained glass 13 183, 184
 stone 32 787
 textiles 32 790*
 town halls 5 731
 towns 31 708, 710
 see also BRITAIN
Wales, Gerald of see GERALD OF WALES
Wales, Nathaniel Young Armstrong 20 570
Wales-Smith, Anthony 33 678
Walewski, Alexandre 20 498
Waley, Arthur (David) 7 161; 32 792*
Walford, Andrew 29 117; 32 792*
Walgate, C(harles) P(ercival) 29 105; 32 792*
Walhalla see under DONAUSTAUF
Walicki, Michał 25 143
al-Walid I, Caliph (reg 705-15)(Umayyad)
 calligraphy 16 278
 mihrab 18 242
 mihrabs 21 504
 mosques 16 146, 255; 22 193; 27 698
 Damascus 8 479; 16 147
 Jerusalem 17 496
 maqṣūra 20 368
 Masjid al-Haram 20 914
 Medina 21 32, 33, 625
al-Walid II, Caliph (reg 743-4)(Umayyad) 3 376; 16 148, 245; 17 483; 18 21; 22 250; 23 815; 25 830
Walīla see VOLUBILIS
Wali Muhammad 12 204
Wali Muhammad ibn Din Muhammad 16 237
Waliszewski, Zygmunt 17 804; 25 108; 32 793*
Walkelin, Bishop of Winchester 10 166; 26 588
Walkenried Monastery 12 364, 365
Walker (15th cent.) 1 518
Walker (fl 1873) 6 484
Walker, Alan C. 2 766
Walker, Alexander 28 269
Walker, Amy see CARTER, AMY
Walker, Andrew Barclay 19 507
Walker, Anthony 32 793*
Walker, Charles Alvah 21 895, 896
Walker, C(harles) Howard 32 793*
Walker, David 2 766; 19 359
Walker, (Byron) Edmund 5 589; 32 794*
Walker, Emery 7 486, 505; 22 145
Walker, Ethel 32 794*
Walker, Evan 16 819
Walker, Fred(erick) 32 794–5*
 dealers 1 453
 groups and movements 27 564
 reproductive prints by others 19 868
 works 4 868; 10 254; 25 347, 598; 32 795
Walker, George 27 334
Walker, Henry Oliver 7 875
Walker, Horatio 5 566, 593; 32 795–6*
Walker, James (1748-1808) 21 417
Walker, James (1781-1862) 2 690; 5 193
Walker, James (b c. 1950) 23 70
Walker, John (fl c. 1787-1802) 32 793
Walker, John (b 1939) 21 897; 24 213; 32 796*
Walker, John Albert 10 212
Walker, Joseph 9 320
Walker, Kate 10 879
Walker, Nelson 5 586
Walker, Philip 19 734
Walker, Ralph (Thomas) 23 42, 43; 32 797*
Walker, Robert 32 797*
 patrons and collectors 8 186; 10 657, 757
 pupils 3 444
Walker, Robert, Rev. 25 843
Walker, Robin 28 284
Walker, Roger (Nevill) 23 56; 32 797*; 33 58
Walker, Samuel 4 65
Walker, Scott Tallon 11 256
Walker, Thomas 21 832; 32 790
Walker, Thomas Bond 14 397
Walker, Thomas Larkins 11 22; 25 573
Walker, William 32 793
Walker, William Aiken 32 798*
Walker Art Center see under MINNEAPOLIS (MN)
Walker Art Gallery see under LIVERPOOL (MERSEYSIDE)
Walker & Burges 5 193
Walker collection 10 782
Walker & Gillette 3 177
Walker & Hall 21 91; 28 576
Walker & Weeks 7 428, 429
Walkiers, Edouard 23 520
WalkingStick, Kay 22 599
walking-sticks 28 302
Walkley, Albion H. 24 894
Walkolbinger, Manfred 2 804
Walkowitz, Abraham 17 578; 20 605; 21 897; 32 798*
Walks-in-the-Light 22 593
Wall, E. J. 24 648
Wall, John 4 824; 10 309; 14 131; 33 377
Wall, Willem Hendrik van der 22 859; 32 798*
Wall, William Archibald 25 5; 32 799
Wall, William Guy 31 603; 32 799*
 patrons and collectors 14 718
 works 23 46; 31 602
 illustrated 14 536
Wallace, Lady 28 528
Wallace, C. G. 22 608
Wallace, Richard 21 413; 28 527–8*
 architecture 27 768
 armour 7 579; 29 416
 collections 23 126; 28 384, 527
 paintings 21 69
 sculpture 9 451
Wallace, William 5 65; 32 799*
 patrons and collectors 28 268
 works 9 723; 28 225
Wallace Collection see under LONDON → museums
Wallace Monument (Central) 28 288
Wallach Brothers 2 758
Wallaert, Adolphe 3 585
Wallaert, J. B. 3 584
Wallander, Alf 30 98, 100, 102, 884
 works 30 100
Wallbaum, Matthias see WALBAUM, MATTHIAS
Wallberger, Caspar 3 20
Wallberger, Wolfgang 3 20
Wallbrecht, Ferdinand 14 142
wall buttresses see under BUTTRESSES
wall clocks see under CLOCKS → types
wall coverings 3 605; 10 278, 848
wall decorations 22 211, 215
 historical and regional traditions
 Africa 1 312
 Cambodia 5 476
 Greece, ancient 13 383, 392, 393, 393
 Hausa 14 232, 233*
 Malaysia 3 442
 Prehistoric art 25 474
 Rome, ancient 26 863
 Syria-Palestine 30 182
 materials
 beads 3 442
 plaster 29 812
 stucco 29 812
Walle, A. L. J. Van de see VAN DE WALLE, A. L. J.
Walle, Jacobus van der 12 430; 14 131
Walle, Peter van der 19 582
Walleen, C. J. 11 111
Walleghem, Pieter van 24 371
Wallen, John 17 632
Wallenda, Marc 33 597
Wallendorf 25 504; 30 793
Wallenstein (family) 12 473
Wallenstein, Albrecht, Graf von 8 422
 architecture 25 426, 445; 29 371
 paintings 12 473
 sculpture 8 384; 14 306; 32 731
 textiles 8 419
Wallenstein, Johann Friedrich von 20 813
Waller, Edmund 13 299
Waller, Herman 23 589
Waller, John 16 885
Waller, Mervyn Napier 2 763
wallers 20 559
Wallertheim 6 159; 25 547
wall frames see under TIMBER STRUCTURES → types
Wallgrave, Gerhard Cornelius von 30 203
Wallgren, Carl Wilhelm see VALLGREN, VILLE
wall hangings see HANGINGS
Wallinger, Louis 2 116
Wallingford, John of see JOHN OF WALLINGFORD
Wallingford, Richard of, Abbot of St Albans see RICHARD OF WALLINGFORD, Abbot of St Albans
Wallington House (Northumb.) 28 276; 32 415
Wallis, Alfred 32 799–800*
 groups and movements 20 590; 22 441; 27 563
 patrons and collectors 9 716
Wallis, Douglas T. 32 801
Wallis, Frank E. 7 429
Wallis, George Augustus 5 71; 10 366; 11 787
Wallis, Gilbert and Partners 10 749; 32 801
Wallis, Henry 32 800*
 groups and movements 10 253; 25 554
 works 12 295; 14 511
 writings 16 559
Wallis, Thomas 32 801*
Wallis, Whitworth 4 87
Wallman, Johan 8 748
wall maps see under MAPS → types
wall mirrors see under MIRRORS → types
Wall of Media see MEDIAN WALL
Wallop, Isaac Newton, 5th Earl of Portsmouth 2 600
Wallot, Jean 3 544; 4 919
Wallot, Paul 32 801*
 assistants 14 89; 28 119

Wallot, Paul—cont.
competitions **7** 668
pupils **14** 523; **18** 444; **26** 377
staff **11** 129
works **3** 794; **9** 237; **12** 376, *377*, 416; **13** 237, 238, 717; **25** 268; **30** 733
wall paintings **14** 421–2; **30** 5; **32** 802–10*
conservation **10** 618; **32** *807*, 807–10*, *809*, *810*
historical and regional traditions
Achaemenid **10** *151*, 151
Afghanistan **1** 200–203*, *201*, *202*
Africa **1** *246*, 289, *290*, 313, 411
Albania **1** *542*
Anatolia, ancient **1** 838–9*; **2** 504, *504*; **6** *74*
Ancient Near East **2** 504, *504*; **12** *511*; **27** 57; **30** 197
Anglo-Saxon **2** 72–4*, *73*
Angola **1** 313
Arabia **2** 274–5*
Armenia (Europe) **1** 452; **2** *429*, 429–30*
Assyrian **2** 640; **21** 309*, *309*; **31** 700
Austria
Benedictine Order **3** *711*
Gothic **2** 791–2*, *791*; **7** *274*
Renaissance **2** 793, *793*
Romanesque **2** 790*; **3** *711*; **18** 668; **26** 650, *650*, 653
Azerbaijan **2** 896
Bactria **6** 224–6*, *225*, *226*
Belarus' **3** 527–8*
Belgium **3** 551–3*, 577
Romanesque **26** 648
Surrealism **5** *45*
14th cent. **3** *551*
Benedictine Order **3** *711*
Bhutan **3** 914
Bijogo **4** 55*
Britain **27** 56–7
Buddhism
Afghanistan **1** 201–3*, *201*, *202*
Burma **5** 242*, *243*
Central Asia **5** *102*
Central Asia, Eastern **6** *292*, 294, *301*, 301–4*, *303*, *304*, *310*, *312*, 314; **32** 804
Central Asia, Western **6** 225–6*, *226*, 228, 232; **17** *734*
China **6** 776–9, *777*, *822*; **32** 804
Indian subcontinent **1** 500; **15** *562*; **32** 804
Japan **17** 156
Laos **18** 770
Nepal **30** 833
Sri Lanka **5** *97*; **25** 170; **29** 443, 462*
Thailand **30** *615*, 615–16*
Tibet **30** 827, 828, 829–30, 831–2, *832*, 833
Bulgaria **5** 150–51*, *151*, 153–4; **9** *579*, 582; **25** 342–3*
Thracian **30** *768*
Burma **5** 242–4*, *243*; **32** 804
Byzantine **9** 526, 561–2*, 570–81*, 582–6*; **26** 332; **32** 804*
Bulgaria **9** *579*
Cappadocia **5** 675–6*, *676*, *677*, 677–8*
Crete **8** 155; **18** 460–61
Cyprus **7** *229*; **9** 580; **17** 743
Greece **9** 577–9, *578*, *584*, 585; **17** *839*; **22** *406*, *407*, *409*
Italy **9** 581
Macedonia (ii) (former Yugoslavia) **23** 373, *374*
Nubia **10** 803
Serbia **28** *445*, 445–7, *446*
Turkey **9** *581*; **32** III

wall paintings
historical and regional traditions
Byzantine—cont.
Ukraine **18** 39
Cambodia **5** 501, *501*
Cappadocia **5** 675–8*, *676*, *677*
Carolingian **5** 796, 797–8*, *798*, *799*; **22** 385
Catalonia **3** *339*
Central Asia **5** *102*
Central Asia, Eastern **6** 289, 294, *310*
Buddhism **6** *292*, *301*, 301–4*, *303*, *304*, *312*, 314; **32** 804
Central Asia, Western **6** 223*, 224*, 228–33*
Bactria **6** 224–6*, *225*, *226*
Buddhism **6** 225–6*, *226*, 228, 232; **17** *734*
Islamic **6** 202; **16** 200, 252, 253
Khwarazm **6** 223*, *227*, 227–8*, *228*, 233*
Kyrgyzstan **6** 232
Sogdiana **6** 228–32*
Tajikistan **17** *734*
Tokharistan **6** *232*, 232–3*
Turkmenistan **6** 223–4*
Champa **6** 432*
China **6** 698, 700–701, 773, 776, 808
Buddhism **6** 776–9*, *777*, *822*; **32** 804
Daoism **6** *787*
Coptic **3** *420*; **7** 822–3*, *823*
Côte d'Ivoire **1** 313
Crete
Byzantine **8** 155; **18** 460–61
Minoan **8** 153; **21** 657, 659, 660, *660*, 672–7*, *674*, *676*, *677*
Post-Byzantine **25** 334
Venetian Empire **8** 156–7
Cuba (Caribbean) **8** 230
Cycladic **8** 309, 318–21*, *318*, *320*; **30** *713*
Cyprus
Byzantine **7** *229*; **9** 580; **17** 743
Early Christian (*c.* AD 250-843) **8** 358–9*
12th cent. **8** *360*
Cyprus, ancient **8** 356*
Czech Republic **8** *389*; **13** *134*, 151
Daoism **6** *787*
Denmark **8** 729–30, *730*, *731*; **26** 648
Early Christian (*c.* AD 250-843) **1** 707; **9** 561–3*, 570–75*; **26** *799*; **32** 804*
Cappadocia **5** 675–7*, *676*
Cyprus **8** 358–9*
Italy **6** *70*; **9** *563*; **26** *831*
Syria **9** 416
Egypt **1** 313; **3** *420*; **7** 822–3*, *823*; **16** 306
Egypt, ancient **1** 885; **3** 717; **9** 775, *821*, 897–903*; **32** 802*
Amarna style **9** *902*
Early Dynastic (*c.* 2925-*c.* 2575 BC) **9** 899*
First Intermediate Period (*c.* 2130-*c.* 1938 BC) **9** 899–900*; **21** *745*
Middle Kingdom (*c.* 1966-*c.* 1630 BC) **2** *656*; **9** 900*
New Kingdom (*c.* 1539-*c.* 1075 BC) **9** *807*, *809*, *821*, 900–903*, *901*; **14** *179*; **25** 779; **28** *495*; **30** *698*; **32** I1
Old Kingdom (*c.* 2575-*c.* 2130 BC) **9** 899*; **20** *117*
Predynastic (*c.* 6000-*c.* 2925 BC) **14** *514*
Roman **1** *618*; **8** *462*; **27** 57
England **10** 278; **19** 611
Anglo-Saxon **2** 72–4*, *73*

wall paintings
historical and regional traditions
England—cont.
Gothic **13** *128*, 137, 142, 153; **19** *611*, 641
Romanesque **26** 650, 652, *652*
13th cent. **10** 269
Ethiopia **10** 567
Etruscan **10** 587, 616–24*, *618*, *619*, *620*, *621*, *622*, *623*; **32** 118, 744, 803
Finland **11** 94, *94*, *102*
France **27** 56; **32** 806
Gothic **13** 140
Prehistoric **25** 650
Roman **27** *56*
Romanesque **11** *529*; **26** *650*, *651*; **27** 590
Romanticism **15** *88*
17th cent. **11** *755*
19th cent. **11** *158*
Georgia **8** *567*; **12** 322–4*; **30** 305
Post-Byzantine **25** 344*
9th cent. AD **12** *323*
14th cent. **12** *324*
Germany
Carolingian **5** *799*
Gothic **13** 143
Gothic: *Zackenstil* **13** 134, 138, 139; **32** 805
Jewish art **17** *558*
Ottonian **23** 649, *650*, 650–51; **26** 101
Roman **27** 56
Romanesque **26** *649*, 651, 653
16th cent. **33** 278
Ghana **1** 240, *246*, 289, *290*
Gothic **13** 127, 132*, 133–5*, 136, 137, 139, 142; **32** 805*
Austria **2** 791–2*, *791*; **7** *274*
Catalonia **3** *339*
Czech Republic **13** *134*, 151
Denmark **8** *731*
England **13** *128*, 137, 142, 153; **19** *611*, 641
France **13** 140
Germany **13** 143
Germany: *Zackenstil* **13** 134, 138, 139
Italy **13** 144–7*
Spain **13** 144, *150*
Sweden **30** 75–7, *77*
Sweden: *Schöne Stil* **30** *76*
Switzerland **30** 129–30*
Greece
Byzantine **9** 577–9, *578*, *584*, 585; **17** *839*; **22** *406*, *407*, *409*
Post-Byzantine **25** *330*, 334–6*, *335*
Greece, ancient **1** 450; **13** 389, 393, 394, 543–9*, 553–5*; **23** 291; **25** 176–7; **32** 250, 803*
Bronze Age **14** 338
Classical **13** *543*, *546*, 548–9
Hellenistic **13** *547*, 549, *552*
Roman **13** *546*, *547*
Turkey **10** 151
4th cent. BC **32** *250*
Helladic **14** 338, 348–51*, *349*, *350*; **23** 477
Late Helladic (*c.* 1600-*c.* 1050 BC) **14** 338, 340
Hinduism **15** *544*
Hopi **2** 876
Huastec **14** 831; **21** 227
Igbo **1** 289
India, Republic of **15** 174
Indian subcontinent **7** 494; **15** 543–4*, 548*, 551, 553–62*, *559*, 563*, 643–50*, 726; **32** 804
Bengal **15** 563
Bihar **15** 563
Buddhism **1** 500; **15** *562*; **32** 804

wall paintings
historical and regional traditions
Indian subcontinent—cont.
Bundi (Rajasthan) **15** *604*
Bundi school **15** *606*, *608*
Chamba (i) (India) **15** 627
Chola **15** 560
Hinduism **15** *544*
Islamic **15** 354
Karnataka **15** 648
Kerala **15** 649–50
Mysore **15** 649
Orissa **15** 636
Pahari **15** 627
Vijayanagara period **15** *644*, 644–6
5th cent. AD **15** *554*, *556*, *557*, *558*; **32** *322*
6th cent. AD **15** *558*
11th cent. **15** *560*
Iran **16** 200, 233, 253–4, *254*; **32** 804
Safavid **16** 253–4, 331
Iran, ancient **18** *499*
Islamic **12** 625; **16** 250–54*
Central Asia, Western **6** 202; **16** 200, 252, 253
Egypt **16** 306
Indian subcontinent **15** 354
Iran **16** 200, 233, 253–4, *254*, 331
Ottoman **16** 254
Syria **16** 148
Turkey **16** 254
Umayyad (Syria) **16** 252
Italy **7** 275; **12** 621
Byzantine **9** 581
Carolingian **5** *798*
Early Christian (*c.* AD 250-843) **6** *70*; **9** *563*; **26** *831*
Etruscan **10** 587, 616–24*, *618*, *619*, *620*, *621*, *622*, *623*; **32** 118, 744
Gothic **13** 144–7*
Jewish art **17** *534*, 557
Ottonian **23** 649–50
Renaissance **32** *805*, 806
Roman **9** *563*; **12** *69*; **14** *444*; **25** *204*; **26** *788*; **27** *48*, *49*, *51*, *53*, 53–6, *54*; **32** I2
Romanesque **7** *364*; **26** 650–51, *651*, 652–3, *826*
Romanticism **5** *366*
9th cent. AD **27** 806
14th cent. **6** *467*; **16** *656*
17th cent. **20** *841*
Japan **17** 22, 79, 139, 156, 195; **18** 190; **20** *523*; **30** 257; **32** 804
Jewish art **9** *415*; **17** *534*, 556–9*, *557*, *558*
Roman **17** 554
Khwarazm **6** 223*, *227*, 227–8*, *228*, 233*
Kongo **8** 230
Korea **32** 804
Kyrgyzstan **6** 232
Laos **18** 770
Lithuania **19** 495
Macedonia (ii) (former Yugoslavia) **19** 884; **23** 373, *374*
Malaysia **20** *182*
Maya **4** 295–6, *296*; **7** 636, I1; **20** 881, 886; **21** 259; **26** *411*, 411–12; **27** 786; **31** 507
Mesoamerica, Pre-Columbian **21** 226–32*, *229*, *230*, 259, 260; **27** 786; **32** 803*
Huastec **14** 831; **21** 227
Maya **4** 295–6, *296*; **7** I1; **26** *411*, 411–12; **31** 507
Maya region **21** 231–2*
Mexico **4** *296*; **5** *357*; **26** *411*; **30** *484*
Mixtec **21** 231
Olmec **21** 226
Zapotec **21** 230–31*

wall paintings
historical and regional traditions—cont.
Mesopotamia **21** 271, 308*, 309*, *309*; **32** 802–3*
Mexico **4** *296*; **5** *357*; **22** 163; **26** *411*; **30** *484*; **32** 807
Pre-Columbian **7** I1
Minoan **8** 153; **21** 659, 672–7*; **32** 803
Late Minoan (*c.* 1600-*c.* 1050 BC) **21** 659, 660, *660*, *674*, *676*, *677*
Middle Minoan (*c.* 2050-*c.* 1600 BC) **21** 657
Mixtec **21** 231*, 737
Moche (culture) **29** 173, *173*, *174*
Mycenaean **14** 338, 340; **32** 803
Ndebele **1** 289; **22** 712–13
Nepal **22** 785; **30** 833
North Africa **27** 57
Norway **23** *223*
Nubia **10** 803; **23** 284, 288–9, *289*
Olmec **21** 226; **23** 418
Ottoman **16** 254
Ottonian **23** 649–51*, *650*; **26** 101
Parthian **6** 223–4
Peru **19** 385; **24** 506–7; **29** 135
Poland **25** 101, 344*
Post-Byzantine **25** *330*, 334–6*, *335*, 342–4*, *342*
Prehistoric art **1** 838–9*; **6** *74*; **25** 500, 650
Rhodes (island) **26** 293
Rhodes (city) **26** 294–5
Romanesque **6** 564; **26** 648–57*; **32** 805*, 808
Austria **2** 790*; **3** *711*; **18** 668; **26** 650, *650*, 653
Belgium **26** 648
Czech Republic **8** *389*
Denmark **8** *730*; **26** 648
England **26** 650, 652, *652*
France **11** *529*; **26** *650*, *651*; **27** 590
Georgia **8** *567*
Germany **26** 651, 653
Italy **7** *364*; **26** 650–51, *651*, 652–3, *826*
Norway **23** *223*
Serbia **28** 445
Spain **19** *177*; **26** *653*; **28** *695*
Sweden **30** 75
Romania **25** 344*; **26** 707, 710–11, *711*, *712*, 712–13
Rome, ancient **13** 699; **22** 686; **26** 857, 861, *862*; **27** 47–50*, 51–7*; **32** 543, 803–4*
Ancient Near East **27** 57
Britain **27** 56–7
Constantinian **27** 56
Egypt **1** *618*
Egypt, ancient **8** *462*; **27** 57
First Style **15** 135; **27** 53, 69
Fourth Style **14** 444; **26** *788*, 789; **27** *48*, *54*, 54–5; **29** 665
France **27** 56, *56*
Germany **27** 56
Greece, ancient **13** *546*, *547*
Italy **9** *563*; **12** *69*; **14** *444*; **25** *204*; **27** *48*, *49*, *51*, *53*, 53–6, *54*; **32** I2
Jewish art **17** 554, 557
North Africa **27** 57
Ostian **27** 55–6
Pompeian Style **27** *53*, 53–5, *54*
Post-Pompeian **27** 55
Second Style **15** 135; **27** *53*, 53–4; **29** 665
Spain **27** 57
Third Style **27** 54; **29** *664*, 665
3rd cent. AD **26** *799*
Russia **25** 342*, *342*; **27** 381–2, 383, 386, 387; **30** *708*
Sasanian **18** *499*

wall paintings
historical and regional traditions—cont.
Saudi Arabia **2** *274*
Scotland **28** 233
Serbia **22** *79*; **25** 343–4*; **28** *445*, 445–7*, *446*
Sicily **16** 253
Sierra Leone **1** *261*
Slovakia **28** 850–51, *851*, *852*, 852
Sogdiana **6** 228–32*
South America, Pre-Columbian **29** 135, 172–4*, *173*, *174*; **32** 803*
Spain **29** 274–5
Gothic **13** 144, *150*
Roman **27** 56
Romanesque **19** *177*; **26** *653*; **28** *695*
19th cent. **13** *248*
Sri Lanka **5** *97*; **25** 170; **29** 443, 462–5*, *463*, *465*, 466, *466*
Sudan **1** 289
Sweden **30** 75–7, *76*, *77*
Switzerland **30** 129–30*
Syria **9** *415*, 416; **16** 148; **17** 556–7*, *557*
Syria-Palestine **30** 197–8*, *198*
Tajikistan **5** *172*; **17** *734*
Thailand **12** 625; **30** 615–16*, *615*; **32** 804
Thracian **30** *768*
Tibet **30** 827, 828, 829–30, 831–2, *832*, 833–5
Tokharistan **6** *232*, 232–3*
Turkey
Achaemenid **10** *151*, 151
Anatolia, ancient **2** *504*
Byzantine **9** *581*; **32** II1
Greece, ancient **10** 151
Islamic **16** 254
Ottoman **16** 254
Prehistoric **6** *74*
Turkmenistan **6** 223–4*
Ukraine **18** 39; **25** 344*; **31** 553–4*, 556–7*, 558
Urartian **1** 839; **31** 700
Uzbekistan **6** 302
Venetian Empire **8** 156–7
Vietnam **6** 432*
Vinča culture **25** 500
Zapotec **21** 230–31*; **33** 620
materials
arriccio **32** 802
brushes **25** 477
charcoal **6** 302
clay **1** 202; **32** 802
consolidants **7** 747
eggs **6** 227
fixatives **11** 142; **32** 809
gesso **9** 898
glues **1** 202; **32** 808
gold leaf **5** 501; **12** 621; **13** 134; **27** 51
gums **6** 227; **9** 898
gypsum **1** 202
intonaco **27** 51; **32** 802
kaolin **1** 202
pigments **21** 226
plaster **5** 501; **9** 562; **32** 802
pozzolana **27** 51
pumice **27** 51
size **9** 898
stone **13** 543
tempera **1** 200, 202; **21** 226
terracotta **27** 51
waxes **10** 197; **32** 808
restoration **10** 618; **32** 809–10*
technical examination **30** 409
techniques
cartoons (drawings) **32** 805
gilding **12** 625
mass production **6** 314
modelling **10** 617, 623
pouncing **32** 805
sinopie **28** 778; **32** 805
squaring up **11** *762*, 763
stencilling **6** 302; **25** 478
wall paintings—cont.
uses
churches *see under* CHURCHES → decoration
see also FRESCOES; MURALS; PAINTING → forms → tomb; SECCO PAINTINGS
wall panels *see* PANELS (WALL)
wallpaper **10** 275; **32** 810–20*
conservation **32** 819–20*
display **7** 732
historical and regional traditions
Belgium **3** 576, 578
Britain **32** 817
China **10** *278*; **32** 815, 818–19*, *819*, 820, VI
England **10** 272–3, 278, 281; **19** 5; **32** 810, 814, *814*, *816*, V1-3
chinoiserie **7** 168
Gothic Revival **23** *546*
18th cent. **10** *278*
France **9** 370; **24** 63; **32** 810, 814, 815, III, IV1; **33** 711
Germany **19** 429; **32** 810, 817
Sweden **30** 89, 90
United States of America **7** 168; **24** 56; **32** 814
technical examination **30** 395
techniques
embossing **10** 177
flexographic printing **28** 549
gilding **32** 812
painting **32** 810–11*
printing **19** 429; **25** 372, 373; **32** *811*, 811–13*, *813*, *814*, 814–17; **33** 711
screenprinting **19** 415; **32** 813
types
chiaroscuro **16** 820
flock **10** 275; **32** *811*, 812, 813*, 814–15, *815*, IV2, 3
papiers bleus d'Angleterre **32** 814
papiers de tapisserie **24** 63; **32** 814
papiers peints **32** 820
papiers veloutés **32** 815
Perlmuttapeten **32** 816
sanitary **19** 359; **32** 812, 816
stamped **3** 110
stencilled **32** 812*
see also ANAGLYPTA; LINCRUSTA WALTON
uses
appliqué **32** 817
jewellery **17** 530
panoramas **8** 792; **9** 370
Wall Paper Manufacturers Ltd **17** 469; **19** 359; **25** 373; **28** 549; **32** 817
wall passages **5** 371; **26** 569, 574
wall-pillar churches *see under* CHURCHES → types
Wallraf (family) **25** 873
Wallraf, Ferdinand Franz **32** 823*
collections **7** 584; **12** 474; **26** 346
works **15** 145
Wallraff, Heinrich **23** 317
Wallraf-Richartz-Jahrbuch **24** 445
Wallraf-Richartz-Museum *see under* COLOGNE → museums
Wallrave, Gerhard Cornelius von **33** 417
walls
historical and regional traditions
Africa **1** 305, 306, 307
Belgium **3** 575–6, 577–8
Central Asia, Eastern **6** 295
China **7** 98
Colombia **7** 603
Crete **21** 662
England **4** 787
Greece, ancient **13** 388–9, 393, 396; **26** 909
Helladic **14** 340
Inca **15** 162
Japan **17** 47*
Korea **12** 94
Maya **21** 205
walls
historical and regional traditions—cont.
Mesoamerica, Pre-Columbian **21** 205, 255
Minoan **21** 662
Mixtec **21** 255
Mycenaean **14** 340
Rome, ancient **26** *875*, 877–8*, 879–80, 909
Spain **13** 285
Syria-Palestine **30** 182, 190
Venda **1** 414
Zimbabwe **13** 334, 336, *336*
Zirid **13** 285
materials
brick **4** 767
clay **1** 305
iron **7** 98
limestone **26** 879
masonry **20** 574, 576*; **21** 205
mud-bricks **21** 271
palm leaves **1** 306
reeds **7** 603
stone **26** *875*, 879
stucco **13** 389
tiles **4** 787; **26** 877; **30** 874, 876
tracery **31** 270, 273
types
casemates **21** 546
Ancient Near East **21** 552
Mesopotamia **21** 552
Punic **25** 733
Syria-Palestine **30** 190
city *see* town
curtain (i) (castle) **8** 277–8*; **12** 174; **21** 546, 563
Byzantine **9** 553, *554*
Canaanite **5** 557
Early Christian (*c.* AD 250-843) **9** 553, *554*
France **8** *277*
Greece, ancient **21** 557–8
Sweden **32** *601*
curtain (ii) (non-load-bearing) **8** 278–9*; **12** 875
Belgium **8** 681
Denmark **8** 729
England **8** *279*; **10** 240; **19** *576*
Greece **21** 735
New Zealand **23** 56
United States of America **4** 228
defensive **3** 359
Byzantine **9** 557–8
China **13** 333–4
Crete **8** 154
Early Christian (*c.* AD 250-843) **9** 557–8
England **14** 22–3
Greece, ancient **21** 555–6, 557
Ireland **9** 391
Mesopotamia **21** 291
periboli **24** 418*
town **3** 516; **21** 545, 548; **31** 710
Byzantine **9** 553–4
Central Asia, Western **6** 211
China **6** 661, 662; **21** 593, *594*; **22** 458
Early Christian (*c.* AD 250-843) **9** 553–4
Egypt, ancient **9** 844, *850*
England **33** 541
Etruscan **10** 601–2
France **8** *277*
Greece, ancient **13** 389, 403, 404; **21** *312*, 549
Indian subcontinent **15** 409
Islamic **6** 211; **16** 141; **21** 583
Italy **10** 601–2; **26** 887, *902*
Mesopotamia **21** 271; **30** 383
Punic **25** 733
Rome, ancient **21** 549; **26** 874, 887, 901, *902*, 907
Syria **21** 583
Syria-Palestine **30** 190–91
wattle-and-daub *see under* ARCHITECTURE → types
walls, double *see* THICK-WALL STRUCTURES
Walls of the Prince **21** 554
wall tombs *see under* TOMBS → types
wall-walks **8** 277
Walmer **21** 568
Waln, Robert **7** 30
Waln, William **24** 602
Walnaeffer, Jean-Baptiste **13** 805
walnut **33** 324, 334, 335
historical and regional traditions
Austria **7** *447*
Belgium **3** 582, 583
Britain **7** 442
Catalonia **29** *313*
Czech Republic **8** *398*, 399, *402*
England **5** 191; **10** 288, *288*, 290, 292, 293, 297
France **5** *350*; **8** 271; **11** 585, *586*, 587, 589, 595, *600*; **27** *682*; **28** *298*; **33** 326
Germany **5** 191, *191*; **8** 271; **12** 423, 425, 426; **33** 326
Hungary **14** 903, 905, 907
Indian subcontinent **15** 720, 721
Ireland **16** *27*
Islamic **16** *499*
Israel **16** *569*
Italy **2** 459, 465; **3** *483*, 484; **5** 192; **6** 7, *7*; **11** *383*; **16** *722*, *724*, *725*, *730*; **33** 326
Japan **17** 354
Netherlands, the **8** 271
Ottoman **16** *499*
Peru **24** 515
Portugal **25** 306
Scotland **28** 246
Spain **3** *847*; **29** 311, *314*, *317*; **33** 326
United States of America **24** 601; **31** *625*
uses
armoires **8** 271
beds **3** *483*, 484, 582
bookcases **16** *27*
buffets **11** *586*, 587
bureaux **5** 191, *191*, 192; **16** *27*
cabinets (ii) (furniture) **3** 582; **5** *350*
cassoni **6** 7, *7*; **16** *722*, *724*
chairs **8** *402*; **11** 589, *600*; **16** *569*, *725*; **25** 306; **29** *314*; **31** *625*
chests **16** *499*
chests-of-drawers **3** 583
clocks **7** 442, *447*
cupboards **8** 271; **16** *730*; **27** *682*
desks **29** *313*
dolls' furniture **31** 264
doors **9** 157
dyes **17** 354
frames **11** *383*
furniture **8** 399; **10** 288, 290, 292, 293, 297; **11** 585, 595; **12** 425, 426; **14** 903, 905, 907; **24** 601; **28** 246; **29** 311
gun stocks **2** 459, 465
marquetry **20** 467
mirror frames **21** 721
panel paintings **24** 3
relief sculpture **3** *847*
screens (ii) (furniture) **28** *298*
tables **10** *288*; **12** 423; **29** *317*
wardrobes **8** *398*
walnut, Brazilian *see* IMBUIA
walnut oil *see under* OILS → types
walnuts **7** 141
Walois (family) **2** 496
Walois, Huart **32** 823
Walois, Jean **5** 211; **11** 639; **30** 313; **32** 823*
Walpiri **1** 44
Walpole, Edward **28** 284
Walpole, George, 3rd Earl of Orford **32** 824
Walpole, Horace (William), 4th Earl of Orford **8** 481; **19** 165; **32** 824–6*, *825*
architecture **6** 61; **7** 290; **8** 48; **10** 234, 295, 516; **32** 554
collections **2** 559; **20** 911; **32** 379
decorative works **4** 845
drawings **11** 875; **14** 848; **22** 320
furniture **18** 746
glass **13** 302
groups and movements **12** 333; **13** 199, 204; **24** 741; **26** 743; **29** 890
interior decoration **10** 276, 294
methods **5** 519
paintings **13** 301; **15** 45, 47; **24** 213
encaustic paintings **10** 199
miniatures **9** 27; **23** 407
sculpture **20** 277; **31** 826
stained glass **29** 506, 515
weapons **9** 31
writings **6** 77; **8** 471; **9** 740; **10** 377; **12** 65, 128, 130; **13** 301; **32** 824; **33** 387
translated **20** 416
Walpole, Horatio, Baron Walpole of Wolterton **32** 824
Walpole, Robert, 1st Earl of Orford (1676-1745) **18** 677; **32** 824*
architecture **10** 361; **32** 859
collections **2** 559; **10** 368; **27** 438
furniture **17** 902
interior decoration **10** 293
paintings **1** 488; **6** 77; **9** 506; **10** 364, 365, 367; **19** 645; **23** 874; **26** 733
plate **8** 149
sculpture **11** 138
Walpole, Robert, 2nd Earl of Orford (1700-51) **32** 824
Walpole Salver **10** 330; **28** *738*; **32** 824
Walpole Society journal **10** 377
Walrave, Gerhard Cornelius von **21** 571
walrus tusks *see under* TUSKS → types
Wals, Goffredo **7** 389; **32** 826–7*
Walser, Karl **32** 827*
Walser, Robert **32** 827
Walsh, John **22** 370
Walsh, Robert **9** 502
Walsh, Sam **19** 507
Walsh, Timothy **20** 93
Walsh Marais Studio **32** 792
Walsingham, Francis **8** 165
Walsingham, Thomas **4** 177; **27** 528
Walsleben, Emil **18** 116
Walsoken (Cambs), All Saints **11** 253
Walter, Almaric **8** 544
Walter, Bishop of Malonne **33** 416
Walter, Friedrich *see* FRIEDRICH WALTER
Walter, Henry **1** 897; **23** 884
Walter, Hubert, chalice *see* HUBERT WALTER CHALICE
Walter, Jakob **30** 161
Walter, Jean **13** 826; **24** 128
Walter, Johann Heinrich Bartholomäus **10** 537; **30** 349
Walter, John, III **8** 49; **25** 594
Walter, Josef **8** 398
Walter, Joseph **32** 827
Walter, Martin **32** 675
Walter, Master **13** 121; **27** 124
Walter, Paul F. **15** 743, 746
Walter, Plousey and Cassan **14** 783
Walter, Theodora **31** 335
Walter, Thomas U(stick) **21** 619; **32** 827–8*
groups and movements **13** 611
pupils **19** 867
works **7** 666; **9** 86; **13** 237; **16** 54; **17** 626; **24** 597; **32** *827*, 892, *893*

Walter-Guillaume Collection *see under* PARIS → museums → Musée de l'Orangerie
Walter-Kurau, Johann *see* VALTERS, JĀNIS TEODORS
Walter of Colchester 10 141
Walter of Durham 19 607, 611; 30 779
works 30 *780*
Walter of Engelberg 30 150
Walter of Hereford 32 828*
assistants 17 612
works 5 373; 16 894, 895
Walter of Milemete 4 395; 14 423
Walterowna zur Muehlen, Edita 31 852
Walters, Daniel, & Sons 10 357
Walters, Edward 20 237
Walters, Evan 32 786
Walters, Gordon (Frederick) 23 60; 32 829*; 33 58
Walters, Henry (1848-1931) 10 91; 32 829*
collections 15 742; 19 756; 31 667
Walters, Henry (*fl* 1838-57) 13 237
Walters, Henry (1848-1931) 16 554
gems 12 266
stained glass 29 515
Walters, John 32 785
Walters, William T(hompson) 32 828–9*
collections 19 755; 31 664, 667
illustrated writings 25 449
paintings 21 69; 33 371
Walters 219, Master of 20 635
Walters Art Gallery *see under* BALTIMORE (MD) → museums
Walter the Glazier, Master 10 674
Walter von Lomersheim 20 858
Waltham (MA; USA) 31 656
Waltham Abbey (Essex; UK) 6 565; 26 588; 27 125; 30 906
Waltham Cross (Herts) 7 448
Eleanor cross 8 197; 13 82
Walthamstow, Brangwyn Museum *see* LONDON → museums → William Morris Gallery and Brangwyn Gift
Walthard, Beat Ludwig 13 871
Walthausen, Werner von 29 531
Walther (family) 12 402
Walther, Abbot 26 675
Walther, Abbot, Bible *see under* BIBLES → individual manuscripts
Walther, Andreas, I (*d c.* 1560) 32 830
Walther, Andreas, II (*d c.* 1581) 32 830
Walther, Andreas, III (*c.* 1560-96) 32 830, 832*
collaboration 27 168; 32 832
pupils 32 832
works 23 252; 24 208
Walther, Bernhard 23 339
Walther, Christoph, I (*d* 1546) 32 829, 830–31*
works 2 118; 9 238; 32 *830*
Walther, Christoph, II (1534-84) 32 830, 831–2*
works 32 *832*
Walther, Christoph, III (*fl c.* 1550-92) 32 830
Walther, Christoph, IV (*fl c.* 1572-1626) 9 238; 23 252; 32 830, 833
Walther, Christoph Abraham 32 830
Walther, Ernst Hermann 17 441
Walther, Franz Erhard 32 834*
Walther, Hans, I (*fl* 1487-1511) 32 829
Walther, Hans, II (1526-86) 32 829–31*; 33 113
Walther, Henry 4 354
Walther, Johann 4 747
Walther, Michael 23 252; 32 830
Walther, Paul 21 66
Walther, Sebastian 32 830, 832–3*
collaboration 9 238; 14 301
pupils 14 301
works 12 403; 32 *833*
Walther, William 30 506
Walti, Robert 9 759
Waltner, Charles Albert 18 237
Walton, Allan 28 299
Walton, Cecile 28 239
Walton, E(dward) A(rthur) 32 834*
collaboration 8 125
groups and movements 12 779; 19 891; 28 238
Walton, Frederick 32 812
Walton, George 32 834–5*
collaboration 20 23
groups and movements 22 744
works 28 255, 256, 260
Walton, Henry 32 835*
Walton, James 11 59
Walton, John 10 308
Walton, Mary Ann 11 59
Walton, Parry 5 900; 19 124
Walton, William 5 925; 28 808
Walton, W. L. 13 876
Walton-on-the-Hill (Surrey), St Peter 10 338
Walton-Wilson, J. W. 26 476
Waltoś, Jacek 25 116; 29 743
Walz, Liselott 30 145
Wamper, Adolf 22 712
Wamps 30 885
Wamps, Bernard Joseph 19 381
Wamps, Jean-Baptiste 19 382
wampum *see under* BEADWORK → types
Wamser, Christoph 12 369; 32 821
Wan 3 406
Wa Na 23 824
Wana (Sulawesi) 28 545
Wanamaker, John 3 423
Wan'an *see* LIU JUE
Wanbai *see* DENG SHIRU
Wan-chi Hsing-mi *see* WANJI XINGMI
Wancho 15 732, 733
Wanda 12 12
Wandalbert 2 648
Wandelaar, Jan 1 842
works 1 *843*
Wandelaltar see under ALTARPIECES → types
Wander (family) 8 407
Wanderers (Peredvizhniki) 2 633; 17 867; 18 38, 392; 19 276; 22 178; 25 146; 27 364, 390, 579; 29 556; 31 311, 559, 565, 582; 32 835–6*
collections 22 135; 27 439; 28 569
exhibitions 3 529
members
Andreyev, Nikolay (Andreyevich) (i) (1873-1932) 2 24
Arkhipov, Abram (Yefimovich) 2 417
Bialynicki-Birula, Vitaly 3 529
Bogolyubov, Aleksey (Petrovich) 4 232
Dubovskoy, Nikolay (Nikanorovich) 9 328
Ge, Nikolay (Nikolayevich) 12 224
Gintsburg, Il'ya (Yakovlevich) 12 653
Hūns, Kārlis (Teodors) 15 19
Ivanov, Sergey (Vasil'yevich) 16 792
Kasatkin, Nikolay (Alekseyevich) 17 827
Kostandi, Kiriak (Konstyantynovych) 18 399
Kuindzhi, Arkhip (Ivanovich) 18 502
Wanderers (Peredvizhniki) members—cont.
Makovsky, Konstantin (Yegorovich) 20 151
Makovsky, Vladimir (Yegorovich) 20 152
Maksimov, Vasily (Maksimovich) 20 154
Malyutin, Sergey (Vasil'yevich) 20 222
Myasoyedov, Grigory (Grigor'yevich) 22 394
Nevryov, Nikolay (Vasil'yevich) 23 16
Ostroukhov, Il'ya (Semyonovich) 23 624
Perov, Vasily (Grigor'yevich) 24 464
Pimonenko, Mykola (Kornylevych) 24 818
Polenov, Vasily (Dmitriyevich) 25 145
Pozen, Leonid (Volodymyrovych) 25 408
Pryanishnikov, Illarion (Mikhaylovich) 25 674
Repin, Il'ya (Yefimovich) 26 217, 219
Ryabushinsky, Stepan 27 459
Savitsky, Konstantin (Apollonovich) 27 889
Savrasov, Aleksey (Kondrat'yevich) 28 21
Shishkin, Ivan (Ivanovich) 28 617
Stepanov, Aleksey (Stepanovich) 29 631
Vasnetsov, Viktor (Mikhaylovich) 32 72
Vereshchagin, Vasily (Vasil'yevich) 32 245
Yaroshenko, Nikolay (Aleksandrovich) 33 506
works 19 *277*; 22 *177*; 28 919
Wandlebury, Gogmagog 14 544
Wando 18 382
wands 1 493
Wandsbeck 8 824
wanfo bei see under STELAE → types
Wanfried an der Werra 22 878
Wanganui 23 51, *52*
War Memorial Hall 23 56
wood-carvings 23 *731*
Wang Ao 8 458
Wang Baocheng 7 71
Wang C. C. *see* WANG JIQIAN
Wang Chang 6 765
Wang Chao-lung *see* WANG ZHAOLONG
Wang Cheng 7 100
Wang Chen-p'eng *see* WANG ZHENPENG
Wang Chi-ch'ien *see* WANG JIQIAN
Wang Chieh *see* WANG JIE
Wang Chien *see* WANG JIAN
Wang Chih-hsi *see* WANG ZHIXI
Wang Chih-jui *see* WANG ZHIRUI
Wang Ch'i-lei *see* WANG QILEI
Wang Chong 6 759
Wangchuan bieye 12 87
Wang Ch'ung *see* WANG CHONG
Wang Dayuan 7 86
Wangdu
furniture 7 33
paintings 6 808; 7 33
tomb 6 648
wall paintings 6 812
Wang Duo 6 761
Wang E 32 840*; 33 657
wangenbankje see BENCHES → types → wing
Wang Fu (1079-1126) 5 293; 6 867
Wang Fu (1362-1416) 6 817, 820; 32 841–2*; 33 439
works 32 *841*
Wang Gai 7 120; 12 900; 15 854; 17 189, 273; 22 460, 461
Wang Geng 7 119
Wang Geyi 33 421
Wanggŏmsŏng *see* P'YŎNGYANG
Wang Guogi 32 845
Wang Guowei 6 867
Wang Hsiang *see* WANG XIANG
Wang Hsi-chih *see* WANG (i) XIZHI
Wang Hsi-chüeh *see* WANG XIJUE
Wang Hsien-ch'eng *see* WANG XIANCHENG
Wang Hsing-lien *see* WANG XINGLIAN
Wang Hsing-tsu *see* WANG XINGZU
Wang Hsü *see* WANG XU
Wang Hui 6 818, 820; 7 151; 22 460; 25 783; 32 842–3*
collaboration 8 518
groups and movements 23 579, 580; 29 244
patrons and collectors 2 124
teachers 32 838
works 6 541, 791; 32 *843*
Wang I *see* WANG YI
Wang I-jung *see* WANG YIRONG
Wang Ji 12 313
Wang Jian (*d* 918) 6 730; 7 7; 27 832
Wang Jian (1598-1677) 6 818, 820; 25 783; 32 843–4*
collaboration 32 842
groups and movements 23 579, 580; 29 244; 32 842
pupils 23 580; 33 426
teachers 32 842
works 6 541, 791; 32 *844*
Wang Jie 7 117
Wang Jiqian 32 844*
Wang Kai *see* WANG GAI
Wang Keng *see* WANG GENG
Wang Ko-i *see* WANG GEYI
Wang Kŏn 18 250, 391
Wang Kuo-wei *see* WANG GUOWEI
Wang Li (*b c.* 1322) 1 581; 6 798; 33 463
Wang Li (*fl* mid-15th cent.) 6 791
Wang Mang 7 73
Wang Meng 6 773, 790, 819; 23 582; 32 845–7*; 33 646
groups and movements 14 822; 25 73; 29 244
patrons and collectors 30 49; 32 838
works 6 790; 32 *845*, *846*; 33 570
Wang Mian 6 805; 32 847*
works 6 *805*
Wang Mo (*d* 803-4) 30 288
Wangmu gong 29 867
Wang Mu-jih *see* WANG MULI
Wang Muli 14 722
Wang Nie 7 120
Wangnŭngdong, Ch'ŏngnung Temple 18 266, 267
Wang Pao-ch'eng *see* WANG BAOCHENG
Wang Qilei 12 48
Wangshan (Jiangling)
belthooks 3 686
Chu Tomb 1 7 *98*
furniture 7 33
iron 7 97
Tomb 1 7 140
Wang Shen 32 847–8*
Wang Shi 7 120
Wang Shih-chen *see* WANG SHIZHEN
Wang Shih-hsiung *see* WANG SHIXIONG
Wang Shih-min *see* WANG (ii) SHIMIN
Wang Shih-shen *see* WANG SHISHEN
Wang (ii) Shimin 6 818, 820; 25 783; 32 837–8*
collaboration 32 842
groups and movements 23 579, 580; 29 244; 32 842
personal collection 33 427
Wang (ii) Shimin—cont.
pupils 23 580; 32 842, 843; 33 426
works 6 541, 791; 7 148; 32 *838*
Wang Shishen 33 497
works 7 *624*
Wang Shixiong 7 71
Wang Shizhen 6 824; 19 833; 23 580; 32 843, 848*
Wang Tingna 7 119
Wang Tingyun 32 848–9*
works 6 751, *751*, 804, *823*
Wang To *see* WANG DUO
Wang Wei (415-33) 6 796
Wang Wei (701-61) 6 635, 773, 789, 820; 12 87, 88; 23 582; 30 288; 32 849–50*
groups and movements 6 630; 29 244
patrons and collectors 18 752
sponsorship 14 135
works 6 787, 808; 12 87; 25 72; 28 311; 29 68; 32 *849*
Wang Wei-hsien *see* WANG WEIXIAN
Wang Weixian 7 83
Wang Wen 33 439
Wang Wu-hsieh *see* WONG, WUCIUS
Wang Wuxie *see* WONG, WUCIUS
Wang Wuyai 14 722
Wangxian 18 281
Wang Xiancheng 30 49
Wang Xiang 6 767; 12 48
Wang (i) Xianzhi 5 36; 6 743, 747, 770; 32 836, 837*
commentaries 6 770
copies 6 745
patrons and collectors 33 663
works 6 743, *747*
Wang Xijue 7 39; 32 837
Wang Xinglian 7 60
Wang Xingzu 7 10
Wang (i) Xizhi 5 36; 6 743, 745, 764, 770; 7 66, 151; 17 588; 18 329; 23 387; 32 836–7*
attributions 6 744; 30 2
commentaries 6 770
copies 6 745
groups and movements 6 630
patrons and collectors 6 754, 772; 30 251
teachers 33 319
works 6 742, *742*, 770; 11 823; 17 221, 227, 881; 23 581
writings 6 769
Wang Xu 18 366, 373
Wang Yanshou 6 815
Wang Yi 6 812, 814, 824
works 6 *812*
Wang Yirong 6 767
Wang Yuan 6 806; 19 469; 32 850–51*
Wang Yüan-ch'i *see* WANG (ii) YUANQI
Wang (ii) Yuanqi 6 818, 820; 7 151; 25 783; 32 837, 839–42*
collaboration 8 518
groups and movements 23 579, 580–81; 29 244
teachers 32 838
works 7 120, 707; 23 579, *580*; 27 596; 32 *839*
writings 6 824
Wang Yueshang 12 48
Wang Zhaolong 7 130
Wang Zhenpeng 32 851*
Wang Zhirui 2 95
Wang Zhixi 25 800
Wang Ziwei 20 361
Wangzi Wu 33 468
Wani 17 214
Wanitschek, Lajos 14 132
Wanjau, Samwel 17 908
Wanjiabei 8 852
Wanji Xingmi 6 756
Wank, Adams & Slavin 32 851
Wank, Roland (Anthony) 31 596; 32 851*

Wankarani 29 215; 31 45
Wankel, Jindřich 24 332; 25 467
Wańkowicz, Walenty 25 106; 32 579, 851–2*
  teachers 19 497
  works 3 528
Wanla 30 832
Wanley, Humfrey 14 177; 32 852*
Wanli emperor (Ming; reg 1573-1620) 6 703; 7 26, 90, 111, 153; 33 419
  crowns 7 111
  tombs 6 703
Wanly, Adhan 9 768
Wanly, Seif 9 768
Wannebecq Church 13 113
Wannegem-Lede Castle 3 547
Wannenmacher, Joseph 27 554; 33 76
Wanner, Jakob Friedrich 33 735
Wanquelin, Jean 20 333
Wansart, Adolphe 32 852*
Wansart, Eric 32 852
Wanscher, Ole 8 746
Wanscher, Wilhelm 8 760, 761
Wansford (Cambs), St Mary 26 613
Wansleben, Johann Michael 10 78
Wanstead House (Essex) 5 538, 907; 8 47; 10 233; 25 266
Wantage, Harriet Loyd-Lindsay, Baroness see LOYD-LINDSAY, HARRIET, Baroness Wantage
Wantage, Robert Loyd-Lindsay, 1st Baron see LOYD-LINDSAY, ROBERT, 1st Baron Wantage
Wantage Album see under ALBUMS → individual manuscripts
Wanton, Joseph 31 249
Wanyamwezi 30 302
Wapanuckett (MA) 22 570
Wapisiana 13 874, 875
Waplington, Paul 4 790
Wappenstein, Ascher 12 263
Wappers, (Egidius Karel) Gustaf, Baron 14 587; 22 329; 31 857; 32 852–3*
  collaboration 19 291
  groups and movements 26 740
  pupils 1 676; 3 86; 4 754, 877; 6 344; 11 45; 29 848
  teachers 14 480
  works 3 562; 32 853
Wapshott, Thomas 24 86
Waqqas, Tell see HAZOR
War, Jacob Dircksz. 16 831
Warakhshah see VARAKHSHA
Waramin see VARAMIN
Warangal 14 130–31*; 15 294
  carpets 15 684
  citadel 15 541
  figurines 15 731
  metalwork 15 709
  sculpture 15 538, 539
  toraṇas 31 160
Warao 13 874, 875
war artists 3 387; 24 666
Warbourg, Eugene 1 440
Warburg, Aby 2 532, 536; 4 22; 26 63; 28 916; 30 731; 32 854–5*
  assistants 28 23
  personal collection 2 365, 371
  works 12 483; 15 90; 17 583; 27 863
Warburg, Felix M. 7 782; 12 615
Warburg Institute see under LONDON
Warburg school 28 916
Warburton, Joseph 29 495
Warburton, Toni 2 762
war cemeteries 6 166
  see also CEMETERIES
Warchałowski, Jerzy 18 429; 24 441
Warchavchik, Gregori 8 6; 32 855*
  groups and movements 21 783
  pupils 22 95
  works 4 712, 721; 27 808
Ward, Anne, Viscountess Bangor 16 24
Ward, Basil Robert 7 712, 713; 10 241; 23 56
  works 7 712
Ward, Bernard, 1st Viscount Bangor 2 598; 16 24
Ward, Edgar M. 26 477
Ward, Edmund Fisher 12 875
Ward, E(dward) M(atthew) 7 436; 10 351; 19 614; 32 855–6*
Ward, Eva 32 856
Ward, Flora 32 856
Ward, Frank D. 18 890; 28 772
Ward, Frederick 2 756, 759
Ward, George Raphael 32 856
Ward, Henrietta (Mary Ada) 32 856*
Ward, H. H. 33 58
Ward, James 22 122; 32 856–7*
  exhibitions 19 507
  groups and movements 26 740; 29 891
  patrons and collectors 14 146
  pupils 28 25
  works 2 105, 106; 19 487; 23 214; 28 883; 29 425; 32 857
Ward, John 27 613; 28 924
Ward, John Quincy Adams 31 611; 32 857–8*
  collaboration 15 22
  pupils 8 787; 11 755
Ward, John S. M. 29 516
Ward, John William, 1st Earl of Dudley 10 679; 33 448
Ward, Joshua 5 767
Ward, Leslie 19 484; 32 856
Ward, Lindy 3 624
Ward, Marcus 13 615
Ward, Nathaniel Bagshaw 12 137; 13 619
Ward, Robinson 2 148
Ward, Samuel Gray 7 551; 29 870; 31 690, 691
Ward, Seth, Bishop of Salisbury 27 626, 628
Ward, William (1766-1826) 22 122; 29 676; 32 856
Ward, William, 1st Earl of Dudley (1817-1885) 4 209
Wardaman 19 368
Wardell, William Wilkinson 2 738; 32 339, 858–9*
  works 2 738; 7 470; 21 75; 30 158; 32 858
Wardell Johnston, Randolph see JOHNSTON, RANDOLPH WARDELL
Warden Abbey 7 353; 14 419
wardens 20 560, 562
Ward & Grover 24 748
Ward & Hughes 19 406
Wardle, John 23 20
Wardle, Thomas 28 717
Wardour Castle (Wilts) 2 576–7; 10 233
wardrobes 8 271, 398; 18 362
  see also CUPBOARDS
Wardrop, H. M. 19 689
Wardrop and Reid 18 68
Ware (family) 10 356
Ware, George 4 479
Ware, Isaac 32 859–60*
  collaboration 5 520
  groups and movements 14 638; 23 858, 860
  works 4 822; 12 601; 26 474, 499
  writings 2 314; 4 612, 786; 31 298
Ware, Joseph
  works 8 35
Ware, Richard de, Abbot of Westminster 24 783
Ware, William Robert 24 432; 32 859*
  collaboration 31 593, 862
  pupils 12 613; 29 913
Ware, William Rotch 24 432; 32 859*
Wareham (Dorset) 2 66
  Assembly Rooms 2 617
  St Mary 2 65; 10 338
warehouses 21 600; 32 860–61*
  Britain 32 861
  Canada 32 861
  England 14 522
  Islamic 16 141, 262
  Rome, ancient 23 621; 32 860
  United States of America 32 861, 861
Warelwast, William de, Bishop of Exeter see WILLIAM DE WARELWAST, Bishop of Exeter
Warenne (family) 14 425
Warenne, William of, Earl of Surrey see WILLIAM OF WARENNE, Earl of Surrey
Ware Park (Herts) 3 186
Ware & Van Brunt 2 699; 4 474, 788; 7 619; 24 299; 32 859
Wärff, Ann see WOLFF, ANN
Wärff, Göran 30 103
Warham, William, Archbishop of Canterbury 9 28; 10 445; 14 668
war hammers 6 261; 16 504
  see also HAMMERS
Warhol, Andy 25 5; 32 862–3*
  assistants 18 687; 28 624
  collaboration 3 338; 7 413; 20 605, 607
  dealers 6 23
  groups and movements 23 49, 261; 25 232
  methods 10 191
  patrons and collectors 17 620; 18 170; 20 524; 21 135; 27 225, 478; 33 45
  productions 8 270
  studio 29 859
  works 7 649; 10 482, 688; 12 217; 15 869; 25 25, 26, 232, 620, 626; 26 51; 28 52, 300; 29 671; 31 608; 32 862
Wari see HUARI
Warin, Claude 32 864
Warin, François 32 864
Warin, Jean, I (fl 1611-15) 32 863
Warin, Jean, II (c. 1607-72) 3 570; 11 557; 26 95; 32 863–4*
  attributions 4 402
  collaboration 19 250; 24 588
  patrons and collectors 4 551
  works 20 922
Warin, Quentin see VARIN, QUENTIN
Waring, F. 19 483
Waring, John Burley 32 864–5*
Waring & Gillow 6 551; 10 284, 299; 11 242; 16 886
Wark, David 29 835
Warka see URUK
Warka Head 21 294; 31 759, 760
Warka Vase 1 883; 21 272, 277, 293, 293–4; 22 510; 31 759
Warkton (Northants), St Edmund 10 265
Warkworth Castle (Northumb.) 21 549
Warli 15 174, 732
Warlpiri 1 52, 56, 64, 68; 2 137; 19 368
Warmberger, Philipp 12 445
war memorials 6 171; 22 48, 49
  England 22 48
  France 19 823
  see also MONUMENTS → types → public
Warmley (Avon) 4 824; 11 242
Warmond Castle 22 813; 32 865*
Warm Springs Museum (OR) 22 671
Warnars, Jacob 33 391
Warnasuriya, Gamini 29 468
Wärndorfer, Fritz 14 628; 19 876; 22 187; 32 446; 33 165, 166
Warne, Thomas 22 111
Warnecke, John Carl 1 495; 18 193; 32 892
Warner, Albert 17 469
Warner, August 22 163
Warner, Benjamin 10 357; 17 640
Warner, Burns, Toan & Lunde 19 321; 23 427
Warner, Horace 17 469
Warner, Langdon 17 431, 807; 28 663
Warner, Levinus 16 553
Warner, Metford 17 469; 32 816
Warner, Olin Levi 31 611; 32 865*; 33 42
Warner, P.
  works 31 656
Warner, Philip Lee 21 32
Warners, Filip Anne 13 632
Warner & Sons 9 295; 10 357; 30 266
Warnia-Zarzecki, Joseph 13 856
Warnier-David, Jules 26 113
Warnke, M. 28 917
Warnod, André 9 705
Warnsinck, Izaäk 19 116
Warocqué, Raoul 3 616
Waroquier, Henri de 11 550; 13 714
Warou, Daniel 14 894; 32 453
Warpalawas 1 885
Warpechowski, Zbigniew 32 865–6*
warp-faced weaving see under WEAVING → types
warp float see under TEXTILES → types
warp-pile textiles see under TEXTILES → types
warp-printed carpets see under CARPETS → types
warp-weighted looms see under LOOMS → types
Warre, Felix 29 88
Warre, Henry James 5 564
Warren (MI)
  Dodge Half-Ton Truck factory 17 722
  General Motors Technical Center (GMTC) 27 476; 31 597
Warren 28 299
Warren, Charles 17 483
Warren, Edward 13 470
Warren, E. P. 14 743
Warren, Henry 20 421
Warren, H. Langford 13 617
  works 4 480
Warren, John 16 1
Warren, Michael 11 256; 16 22
Warren, (Frederick) Miles 7 210; 23 56; 32 866*
Warren, P. 22 403
Warren, Russell 5 78; 20 438; 25 666; 32 866*
Warren, Samuel 13 470
Warren, S. E. 6 570
Warren, Thomas 10 725
Warren, Whitney 19 260; 32 866, 867
  works 7 470
Warren and Mahoney 1 126; 32 866
Warren & Wetmore 32 866–7*
  collaboration 23 40
  staff 18 779; 32 72
  works 3 464; 7 470; 19 260; 23 40; 31 728
Warrick, Meta Vaux see FULLER, META VAUX
Warring States period see JAPAN → periods → Sengoku
Warrington, George Booth, 2nd Earl of see BOOTH, GEORGE, 2nd Earl of Warrington
Warrington, William 25 712; 29 514
Warrington State Bedstead 6 484
Warrock, George 25 702
Warry, Daniel 3 533
wars 16 438
Warsaw 3 679; 25 92, 93; 32 678, 867–82*, 868
  Academy of Fine Arts 14 499; 25 141
  architecture 25 98, 99, 100, 135
  art forms
    ceramics 25 123; 32 879*
    clocks 32 878
    faience (ii) (ceramics) 32 879
    finials (scrolls) 17 569
    furniture 25 122; 32 878–9*
    lithography 25 106
    metalwork 25 126, 127, 128, 130; 32 878*
    sculpture 25 115; 26 498
  art schools 25 123, 133, 141
  Belvedere Palace 25 99
    faience factory 25 122, 123, 213; 32 879
  central library 12 34
  churches 25 100
    Carmelite church 25 99
    Cathedral
      tomb of Stanisław and Janusz, Dukes of Masovia 32 873
    Church of the Holy Cross 25 130
    Church of the Sister of the Holy Sacrament 25 98
    Franciscan church 25 105
    Lutheran church 25 99
    St Alexander 25 99
    St Anne's 25 105
    Salesian church 25 98
  collections 25 138
  Commercial College 25 100
  education (architectural) 25 142
  Galeria Krzywe Koło 4 234
  Gimnazium Realny 25 141
  Grand Theatre 25 99; 32 871
  Hotel Europejski 25 99
  house of Roesler and Hurtig 33 722
  Jesuit college 25 140
  Krasiński Palace 12 35; 18 440; 25 98; 32 875
    sculpture 28 115
  Kronenberg Palace 26 190
  Łazienki 32 880–81*
    Łazienki Palace 3 15; 23 813; 25 99, 139; 32 881
      chimney-piece 6 605
      stucco 25 99; 29 839
    Myślewicki Palace 25 38
    Old Orangery Theatre 25 38
    White Cottage 25 38
  Marszałkowska Dzielnica Mieszkaniowa (MDM) 29 634
  Ministry Council Building 31 905
  museums
    Asia and Pacific Museum 3 170
    Jewish museum 17 581
    Krasiński Library and Museum 25 139, 142
    Museum of Archaeology 25 140
    Museum of Fine Arts see National Museum
    Museum of Industry and Agriculture 25 140
    Museum of Technology and Industry 25 140
    National Ethnographical Museum 29 241
    National Museum 23 113; 25 139, 140; 31 100
      collections 25 142, 364; 30 332; 33 290
    Polish Army Museum 25 140
    Przezdziecki Library and Museum 25 139, 675
    Silesian Museum 25 140
    State Zoological Museum 25 140
    Zamoyski Museum 25 139
  National Economic Bank 25 100
  Nozyk synagogue 17 548
  Polish Academy of Sciences
    Institute of Art 25 142, 143

Warsaw—cont.
Prymasowski Palace
White Ballroom **29** 839
reconstruction **2** 323
Royal Castle **3** 15; **4** 783; **6** 22; **21** 158; **22** 78; **25** 105, 115, 135, 140; **32** 879–80*; **33** 115–16
academy **25** 140
Great Hall **32** *880*
interior decoration **25** 99, 119, 121
Knights' Hall **25** 118
Marble Room **25** 118; **32** 7, *874*
metalwork **11** 627
museum **25** 140
paintings **32** 6, 7
sculpture **25** 115
Saxon Axis **25** 135
Saxon Garden **25** 98
Sigismund III Column **25** 130; **32** 7
Ujazdow Palace **6** 22; **25** 135
Pillement Room **24** 810
Sale de Canaletto **3** 678
University
Faculty of Education and Fine Art **25** 141
Library **18** 490; **25** 364
urban planning **23** 272
Villa Natolin **32** 554
Wilanów Palace **32** *870*, 881*, *882*
Warsaw School Association of Plastic Artists **10** 872
Warshama **18** 514
Warszawa *see* WARSAW
Warta **25** 102
church **25** 103
Warta, Master from **25** 103
Warta, Vince **33** 710
Wartburg Schloss **12** *361*, 364; **32** 882–3*, *883*
frescoes **28** 195
Palace Hall **26** 575
Warth, Otto **29** 751
Warton, Thomas **31** 283
Wartski Ltd. **19** 596
Waruardus, Johannes **22** 847
Warwick
Castle **3** 209
Caesar's Tower **21** 549
Guy's Tower **21** 549
paintings **14** 268
tapestries **10** 349
wood-carvings **12** 591
furniture **10** 297
law courts **18** 886
Priory **33** 257
St Mary's **10** 341; **32** 90
Beauchamp Chapel **13** 84, 85, 184; **24** 466; **32** 90
sculpture **13** 84
tomb of Richard Beauchamp, Earl of Warwick **2** 449; **10** *260*, 338; **12** 625; **22** 44; **31** 123
Warwick, Charles Greville, 7th Earl Brooke and 7th Earl of *see* GREVILLE, CHARLES, 7th Earl Brooke & 7th Earl of Warwick
Warwick, Francis Greville, 1st Earl Brooke and 1st Earl of *see* GREVILLE, FRANCIS, 1st Earl Brooke and 1st Earl of Warwick
Warwick, Francis Greville, 5th Earl Brooke and 5th Earl of *see* GREVILLE, FRANCIS, 5th Earl Brooke and 5th Earl of Warwick
Warwick, George Greville, 2nd Earl Brooke and 2nd Earl of *see* GREVILLE, GEORGE, 2nd Earl Brooke and 2nd Earl of Warwick
Warwick Candle **10** 195, 346
Warwick Ciborium **10** 322; **26** 694; **31** 499
Warwick Vase **13** 644; **14** 109, 114; **24** 845; **28** 257
Wasa see under SHIPS → named vessels
Wasco **22** 548
Wasen, Hans Am **13** 267
Waser, Anna **32** 883*
Waser, Elizabeth **32** 883
Washburn, Dorothy **2** 137
Washburn, William **30** 741
Washburne, E. G. **31** 653
Washer, F. **3** 610
washers (brush) **5** 34
washes **2** 239; **5** 34; **8** 128; **15** 854; **32** 883*
washing machines **15** 883
Washington (DC; USA) **31** *587*; **32** 883–94*, *885*, *887*
architecture **31** 590–91, 662
Arena Stage Theater **30** 684
Bureau of American Ethnology **22** 677
collections **22** 673, 675
Cabin John Bridge **4** 802
Capitol **5** 143; **7** 666; **10** 850; **13** 237, 610; **18** 844–5; **30** 761; **31** 591, 662; **32** 828, *891*, 891–2*, *893*
capitals **23** 545
columns **11** 231
dome **9** 86; **16** 54
House of Representatives **22** 736
interior decoration **31** 662
orders (architecture) **23** 489
paintings **5** 9
portico **25** 266
Rotunda **13** 621; **22** 47; **31** 392, 872
sculpture **13** 621
Supreme Court Chamber **13** *611*; **18** 887
cemeteries
Arlington National Cemetery **31** 131
Oak Hill Cemetery
Van Ness Mausoleum **20** 869
Rock Creek cemetery
Adams Memorial **33** 28
churches
Basilica of the Immaculate Conception **28** 632
Cathedral of St Peter and St Paul **13** 198; **29** 508
Connecticut Avenue Bridge **4** 803
Dulles International Airport **1** 495; **30** 468; **31** 597
federal buildings
Department of Agriculture **31** 662
Department of the Interior **14** 801
Federal Triangle **31** 662, 663
Old Executive Building **26** 190; **27** 130; **28** 345; **31** 593
Old Patent Office *see* museums → National Portrait Gallery
Old Post Office **13** 611
Pension Building **30** 505
State, War and Navy Building *see* Old Executive Building
Supreme Court **18** 890
Treasury **13** 611; **21** 618; **31** 591, 662
US Naval Observatory **23** 341
Federal Capitol *see* Capitol
Finnish Embassy **11** 93
Georgetown **32** 888
Georgetown College Observatory **23** 340, 341
Institute of Contemporary Arts (ICA) **32** 889
Islamic Center **16** 241
Kennedy Arts Center **29** 716
libraries
Army Medical Library **19** 318
Folger Shakespeare Library **19** 319
Washington (DC; USA)
libraries—cont.
Jimmy Carter Presidential Library **12** 101
Library of Congress **2** 367, 371; **4** 22; **19** 318, 321; **28** 889; **31** 662
collections **1** 442; **2** 382; **3** 170; **17** 625; **24** 364, 682, 683; **27** 166
interior decoration **3** 740
murals **4** 130
Prints and Photographs Division **31** 671
Surgeon-General's Library *see* Army Medical Library
monuments and memorials
Jefferson Memorial **27** 237
Lincoln Memorial **3** 31; **22** 48
Vietnam Veterans Memorial **19** 398; **22** 49
Washington Monument **1** 736; **21** *618*, 618–19; **31** *611*
museums
Archives of American Art **1** 442; **2** 364, 366, 367, 369, 371; **4** 23, 27; **32** 890
Barnett-Aden Gallery **32** 890
B'nai B'rith Klutznick Museum **17** 582
Corcoran Gallery of Art **1** 446; **7** 840; **11** 144; **26** 213; **31** 667; **32** 889, 890
collections **4** 142; **14** 117; **32** 890
exhibitions **24** 683
Dumbarton Oaks **4** 142; **12** 143; **32** 890; **33** 151
gardens **12** *142*
Museum for Pre-Columbian Art **17** 620; **21** 265
Freer Gallery of Art **11** 748; **17** 431, *431*; **25** 33; **31** 668, 670
Chinese collection **6** 735, 826, 868, 925; **7** 156
collections **32** 889
directors **25** 235
etchings **33** 141
exhibitions **18** 384
Indian collection **15** 745
Islamic collection **16** 557
Japanese collection **10** 887; **17** 434
Korean collection **18** 384
laboratory **16** 550
manuscripts **6** 285
paintings **15** 742; **31** 393
Gallery of Modern Art **32** 890
Hirshhorn Museum and Sculpture Garden **5** 176; **28** 314; **31** 668; **32** 888
collections **14** 575; **32** 890
Holocaust Memorial Museum **17** 582
Howard University Gallery of Art **32** 890
Museum of Modern Art Gallery of Washington **32** 890
Museum of Modern Art of Latin America **32** 890
Museum of Temporary Art **32** 890
National Air and Space Museum **22** 366
National Collection of Fine Arts *see* National Museum of American Art
National Gallery of Art **2** 171; **9** 467; **22** 359, 365, *365*, 367; **24** *325*, 326; **27** 166; **31** 668; **32** 886, 888
Architectural Drawings Advisory Group **2** 367
catalogues **6** 78
Centre for Advanced Study in the Visual Arts **2** 371
Washington (DC; USA)
museums
National Gallery of Art—cont.
collections **31** 668; **32** 890
Dale collection **8** 463
drawings **9** 231
exhibitions **15** 748; **23** 741
Garbisch collection **12** 54
Hammer collection **14** 117
Havemeyer collection **14** 244
Kress Collection **7** 336; **9** 298; **18** 448
library **4** 23
Mellon collection **2** 560; **21** 90, 91
photographs **29** 657
plaquettes **25** 19
Rosenwald collection **27** 166
Rothko Foundation collection **27** 222
Schreiber collection **28** 167
Widener collection **33** 159
National Museum (1876) **21** 58
National Museum of African Art **1** 437; **31** 668, 671; **32** *889*
collections **30** 297; **32** 890
exhibitions **1** 438
library **1** 440
National Museum of American Art **31** 662, 668; **32** 890
archives **2** 371
collections **1** 442; **19** 286; **22** 673; **27** 462; **32** 890
National Museum of the American Indian **32** 890
National Museum of Natural History **21** 265; **23** 739; **29** 241
National Museum of Women in the Arts **32** 890; **33** 310
National Portrait Gallery **13** 611; **31** 662, 668; **32** 885, 886, 890
Phillips Collection **24** 638; **32** 889, 890
Project for the Arts **32** 890
Renwick Gallery **26** 213, *213*; **31** 668; **32** 890
Arthur M. Sackler Gallery **27** 493; **32** *889*
collections **6** 868; **7** 156; **15** 745; **16** 557; **32** 394, 889
exhibitions **15** 748
laboratory **16** 550
periodicals **24** 436
Smithsonian Institution **11** 748; **21** 618; **22** 368; **24** 390; **26** 212; **31** 592, 666, 668; **32** 886, 889, *889*
collections **17** 581, 582
conservation **7** 742; **18** 647
exhibitions **5** 746
Freer Collection *see* Freer Gallery of Art
Greek collection **31** 356
Mongolian collection **21** 886
musical instruments **22** 377
Native North American collection **22** 675, 676
Peter A. Juley Collection of Photographic Records **31** 671
see also Archives of American Art; Arthur M. Sackler Gallery; Hirshhorn Museum and Sculpture Garden; National Air and Space Museum; National Gallery of Art; National Museum of American Art; National Museum of Natural History; National Museum of the American Indian; National Portrait Gallery; Renwick Gallery; NEW YORK → museums → Cooper-Hewitt Museum
Washington (DC; USA)
museums—cont.
Textile Museum **32** 890
archives **2** 369
collections **3** 916; **16** 555, 557; **22** 400; **29** 241
National Institute for the Conservation of Cultural Property **7** 744
Octagon House **29** 842; **30** 503
President's House *see* White House
sacromonte **27** 499
Sun Building **26** 704
Union Station **5** *274*; **7** *765*
urban planning **5** 275; **7** 357; **10** 850; **17** 468; **19** 154; **20** 19; **31** 721
US Dept Interior **26** 90
White House **7** 666; **10** 850; **13** 238; **14** 600; **23** 860; **31** 591, 662; **32** 893–4*, *894*
ceramics **19** 165; **33** 22
furniture **18** 749
glass **3** 84; **9** 171; **14** 252; **31** 642
North Portico **25** 267
paintings **19** 538
porcelain **24** 148
silver **13** 9
South Portico **25** 267
Washington (MD; USA), Mormon Temple **22** 126, *126*
Washington, George **25** 655; **31** *611*; **32** 884
architecture **17** 468; **19** 154; **32** 893
gardens **12** 136
glass **1** 769; **31** 642
interior decoration **29** 842
metalwork **31** 652
paintings **11** 59
Washington, Martha **11** 59
Washington Art Club **32** 889
Washington Color Painters **1** 79; **19** 725; **23** 184; **32** 890, 894*
Washington Coronation, Master of the **20** 784–5*; **24** 30
Washington New Town (Tyne & Wear) **19** 519
wash manner **2** 239, 241; **10** 549; **11** 723; **32** 894*
Washoe **22** 549
basketwork **8** 537, *537*; **22** 659, 660, *660*
beadwork **22** 641
dress **22** 633
Wasit **16** 310, 314, 540; **26** 487
coins **16** *512*
congregational mosque **16** 148; **22** 192
al-Wasiti **16** 137
Wasmuth **19** 327
Wasmuth, Ernst **28** 801; **33** 402
Wasmuths Monatshefte für Baukunst **14** 300; **24** 444
Wasow, Eduard **10** 858
Wąsowski, Bartłomiej Nataniel **17** 615; **25** 142, 408; **32** 894–5*
Wąsowski, Erasmus **25** 105
Wasperton Manor (Warwicks) **28** 301
Wassa **1** 503
Wassenaar Obdam, Johan Hendrik van **2** 852; **14** 39; **20** 459
Wassenaer Obdam, Jacob, Baron van **31** 488
Wassenhove, Joos van **3** 553; **12** 519; **17** 702; **32** 895*
Wasserburg, Rathaus **10** 739
Wasserman, Der **10** 756
Wasserschlebe, J. **8** 758
Wasswa, Katongole Kakooza **31** 528
Wastell, John **32** 895*
attributions **24** 546
collaboration **19** 59
works **5** 511, 514, 645; **7** 419; **13** 55; **24** 466

Wastell, Samuel **33** 158
Wasuluka **3** 132
Watam
 drums (musical instruments) **24** *69*
Watanabe (family) **17** 186
Watanabe, Hitoshi **17** 89; **32** 896*
Watanabe, Jin *see* WATANABE, HITOSHI
Watanabe, Setsu **22** 336
Watanabe, Shōzaburō **17** 294
Watanabe, Yoshitomo **17** 135
Watanabe, Yuzuru **17** 87
Watanabe Kazan **17** 191; **30** 295; **32** 896–7*
 works **32** *896*
Watanabe Nangaku **17** 196; **20** 523
Watanabe Ryōkei **17** 785, 788, 797
Watanabe Seiran **23** 390
Watanabe Shikō **17** 179; **23** 365; **32** 897*
 copies **20** 522
 groups and movements **17** 797
 works **17** 195
Watanabe Shūseki **16** 787
Watarai Tomei **17** 792
Wat Ban Khao Ploi Waen **30** 600
Wat Chedi Dok Ngom
 banners **30** 612, *613*
Wat Chedi Si Hong **30** 603
Wat Chedi Sung **30** 583
watches **7** 437–49*; **17** 522, 526
 conservation **7** 729
 historical and regional traditions
  Britain **7** *444*, 447
  England **7** 441; **14** 856
  France **7** 441, *441*, 447; **11** *630*
  Germany **7** 439, *443*
  Switzerland **7** 448; **30** 148
  United States of America **7** 448; **15** 822; **20** 593
 restoration **7** 729
 techniques
  gilding **7** *441*, *443*, 444, *444*
  mass production **7** 447, 448
  repoussé **7** 446
 types
  coach **7** 444
  electric **7** 448
  form **7** 443
  montres de fantaisie **30** 148
  oignon **7** 444
  pair-case **7** 444
  Puritan **7** 443
  quartz crystal **7** 448
  travelling **7** 444
  wrist **7** 448–9, *449*
Wat Chiang Man **30** 586
watch-towers *see under* TOWERS → types
Wat Duang Di **30** 585
Wate, William **23** 884
Watelet, Claude-Henri **32** 897–8*
 collections **23** 778
 gardens **12** 124
 paintings **13** 638
 reproductive prints by others **19** 144
 works **11** 674; **19** 354; **24** 773
 writings **10** 206, 207
Watelet, J.-G. **3** 620
Watelet, Louis-Etienne **1** 641; **8** 653
Watelin, Louis Christian **1** 893; **18** 86
water-buffalo *see under* HIDES → types
Waterbury **7** 448
water-clocks *see under* CLOCKS → types
watercolour paint *see under* PAINTS → types
watercolours **11** 228; **15** 849; **26** 740; **32** 898–902*
 display **9** 26*
 historical and regional traditions
  Algeria **1** *635*
  Argentina **2** 399
  Armenia (Europe) **2** 432
watercolours
 historical and regional traditions—cont.
  Austria **1** *688*; **4** *40*
  Belgium **14** *619*
  Britain **2** 240; **26** 740
  Burma **5** *247*
  Central Asia, Western **16** *132*
  China **7** *122*
  Colombia **7** 609
  Czech Republic **17** *544*
  England **8** 27; **10** 251; **12** 131; **32** 900, 901
   Pre-Raphaelitism **27** *186*
   Romanticism **12** *742*, *743*; **23** *885*
   17th cent. **32** VII1
   18th cent. **26** 76; **27** *278*, *716*; **31** *155*; **32** *825*
   19th cent. **4** *121*, *615*; **8** *27*, *29*, *84*; **10** *280*, *282*; **11** *331*; **31** *470*, *473*, *909*; **32** *901*, VIII1
   20th cent. **10** *285*; **30** *38*
  France
   Art brut **2** *515*
   Orientalism **32** VII2
   Post-Impressionism **6** *373*
   Romanticism **8** *641*
   Symbolism (movement) **22** *91*
   19th cent. **8** *547*; **18** *678*
  Germany **9** 440
   Jewish art **17** *578*
   Renaissance **9** *430*, *433*
   16th cent. **18** *510*; **33** *32*
   20th cent. **12** *215*; **18** *110*
  Guyana **13** 876
  Hinduism **14** *558*
  Hungary **31** *541*
  India, Republic of **15** *175*
  Indian subcontinent
   Bundi school **15** *606*, *607*
   Company painting **15** *652*, *655*
   Hinduism **14** *558*
   Mughal **20** *284*
   17th cent. **1** *583*
  Iran **16** *125*
  Islamic **1** *635*, *636*; **16** *125*, *132*
  Italy **11** *190*
  Jewish art **17** *578*
  Native North Americans **14** *811*; **22** *596*, *599*
  Netherlands, the **22** *866*; **28** *166*; **32** *271*
  New Zealand **23** 57, 58
  Nigeria **23** *137*
  Philippines **24** *621*
  Russia **27** 390
  South Africa **29** 110, 121
  Surinam **30** 15
  Switzerland **12** *500*; **29** *673*; **32** VIII2
  United States of America **4** *368*; **5** *188*; **14** 698; **31** 603
   19th cent. **2** *710*; **14** *701*; **17** *624*; **18** *627*
 materials
  brushes **5** 32, *32*, 34; **32** 898
  glazes **11** 407
  inks **15** 853
  paints *see* PAINTS → types → watercolour
  paper **24** 50, 56; **32** 899
  pigments **18** 656
 techniques
  stopping-out **23** 105
 types
  bistre **4** 101; **15** 852
  sepia **15** 852
 uses
  book illustrations **4** *368*
  conservation **28** 340
  decorative paper **24** I1
  photography **24** 647
  secco paintings **28** 338
  wallpaper **32** 813
watercolour societies **32** 902–3*
Water Colour Society of Ireland **32** 903
water droppers **18** *338*
watered steel *see under* STEEL → types
watered textiles *see under* TEXTILES → techniques
Waterford **16** *5*; **32** 903–4*
 art school **16** 37
 Assembly Rooms **2** 617
 Cathedral **13** 45
 ceramics **16** 28
 court-house **16** 9
 education (art) **16** 37
 furniture **16** 25
 glass **16** 30, *30*
Waterford, Louisa Anne De la Poer, Marchioness of *see* DE LA POER, LOUISA ANNE, Marchioness of Waterford
Waterford Glass House **32** 903–4
Waterford Glass Ltd **16** 30; **32** 904; **33** 23
Waterford Wedgwood **32** 904; **33** 23
water gardens *see under* GARDENS → types
water gilding *see under* GILDING → types
Watergraafsmeer *see under* AMSTERDAM
water-holding mouldings *see under* MOULDINGS → types
Waterhouse, Alfred **7** 668; **11** 785; **14** 420; **32** 904–6*
 architecture
  clubs (meeting places) **7** 470
  colleges **4** 787; **5** 513; **20** 238
  hotels **19** 506
  law courts **18** 888; **33** 375
  museums **10** 371; **11** 360; **22** 363; **30** 504; **32** *905*
  office buildings **19** 506; **23** 258
  town halls **10** 237; **14** 193; **20** *237*, 237; **31** 240, *240*, 241
 collaboration **3** 501; **25** 187; **28** 601
 competitions **7** 667
 groups and movements **13** 204
 patrons and collectors **13** 697
 staff **20** 547; **23** 600
Waterhouse, Ellis (Kirkham) **10** 377; **32** 906*
Waterhouse, G. & S. **6** 164; **16** 32
Waterhouse, John William **9** 54; **25** 556; **32** 906–7*
Waterhouse & Ryland **4** 88
Waterlandt, Claes Simonsz. van **20** 666; **22** 835
Waterlandt, Mouwerijn Simonsz. van **22** 835
Waterlo, Antoni **32** 907–8*
 attributions **13** 892; **27** 330
 catalogues **3** 310; **6** 78
 works **25** 606; **32** *907*
Waterloo Glass House Co. **7** 857
Waterloos, Siegebert **17** 643
Waterlow, Sydney **30** 458
Waterlow's **3** 182
Waterman, Dudley **22** 694
Waterman, L. E. **24** 350
watermarks **7** 116, *117*; **16** 352; **24** 43; **25** 329; **32** 908*, *908*
Water Newton **9** 655
water pipes **13** 419; **27** 7*
waterproof paper *see under* PAPERS → types
water puppets *see under* PUPPETS → types
water puppet theatre *see under* THEATRE → types
Waters, Clara Erskine Clement **10** 211
Waters, Thomas J. **23** 593; **31** 79
Waterschoot, Heinrich von **22** 302
waterspouts **13** 390, 392
Water Stratford (Bucks), St Giles **26** 616
water supply **7** 353–4; **31** 711
 Bosnia **27** 819
 Britain **2** 242
water supply—cont.
 Cambodia **5** 459
 Greece, ancient **2** 241
 Islamic **2** 242
 Mesoamerica, Pre-Columbian **21** 208*
 Rome, ancient **2** 241–2, *242*
 Spain **2** *242*
water towers *see under* TOWERS → types
water-wheels **7** 765
waterworks **12** 61, 62, 115, 116
Watford (Herts), St Mary
 tomb of Charles Morison **1** 520
al-Wathiq, Caliph (*reg* 842-947) (Abbasid) **27** 678
Watjen, Otto van **8** 436
Wat Kamphaeng Laeng **30** 581
Watkeys, William **32** 785
Watkin, David **14** 580; **25** 27
Watkin, Edward **11** 242
Watkin, William Ward **14** 802
Watkins, Carleton E(mmons) **24** 665; **32** 909*
Watkins, David **6** 443
 works **17** *529*
Watkins, Dick **32** 909*
Watkins, Franklin **24** 600
Watkins, J. S. **2** 771
Watkins, Kennett **2** 706; **23** 58
Watkins, Mary Philadelphia *see* MERRIFIELD, MARY PHILADELPHIA
Watkins, Philips, Bynoe and Partners **31** 335
Watkins, W. H. **31** 335
Watkins, William **10** 235
Watkins Grey **15** 56
Watling, Thomas **2** 744; **30** 160; **32** 909*
Watling Street **27** 3
Watlington (Oxon) **14** 544
Wat Phan Tao **30** 585
Wat Phra Boromathat Doi Suthep **30** 585
Wat Phra Phai Luang **30** 581
Wat Phra That **30** 584
Wat Phra That Doi Wao **30** 585
Wat Phra That Lampang Luang **30** 585, 586
Wat Phumin **30** 585
Wat Prang **30** 579
Wat Rampoeng **30** 586
Wat Saen Fang **30** 585
Wat Si Sanphet **29** 867
Wat Si Sawai **30** 581
Watson, Barrington **16** 884; **32** 910*
Watson, Caroline **29** 675; **32** 910*
Watson, Charles (1714-57) **15** 702, 711
Watson, Charles (*c.* 1770-1836) **18** 887
Watson, George **28** 237; **32** 910–12*
Watson, G. W. **18** 888
Watson, Homer (Ransford) **5** 566, 593; **32** 910–11*
Watson, James **21** 416; **26** 278; **32** 909–10*
Watson, James Forbes **10** 580
Watson, Jenny **2** 752
Watson, John *see* WATSON GORDON, JOHN
Watson, John Dawson **4** 868
Watson, John Forbes **4** 82
Watson, J. T. **22** 468
Watson, Musgrave Lewthwaite **6** 457; **29** 926; **32** 911*
Watson, Osmond **16** 889; **32** 911*
Watson, Peter (Victor William) **8** 125; **22** 751; **32** 912*
Watson, Robert **11** 243
Watson, Ruth **23** 62
Watson, Samuel **6** 116, 515; **11** 424
Watson, Thomas **8** 863; **29** 675
Watson, T. L. **28** 231
Watson, William (*b* 1917) **7** 161
Watson, William F. (*fl* mid-19th cent.) **28** 271
Watson, William Smellie **32** 910
Watson Gordon, John **9** 725; **28** 237; **32** 910, 912*
Watson-Wentworth, Charles, 2nd Marquess of Rockingham **32** 912–13*
 coins **5** 337
 paintings **29** 808
 sculpture **4** 886; **23** 189
Watson-Wentworth, Thomas, 1st Earl of Malton and 1st Marquess of Rockingham **11** 138; **31** 826
Watson-Williams, Marjorie *see* VÉZELAY, PAULE
Wat Suphat **30** 579
Watt (company) **6** 484
Watt, Alan **2** 762
Watt, Charles **24** 41
Watt, George **4** 883
Watt, George Frederick **2** 643
Watt, James (1736-1819) **2** 456; **4** 541; **16** 799; **19** 366; **20** 925; **28** 739, 831
Watt, James (1769-1848) **4** 806
Watt, James Henry **10** 396
Watt, John **28** 225
Watt, Richard **5** 169
Watt, William **12** 841; **33** 143
Watteau, (Jean-) Antoine **10** 351; **12** 489; **22** 85; **24** 134, 135, 167; **32** 913–20*
 attributions **14** 846
 collaboration **18** 661
 commentaries **24** 257
 drawings **9** 225, I2; **31** 69
  caricatures **5** 756
  chalk **2** 847; **6** 400, *400*; **32** *918*
 exhibitions **10** 679
 groups and movements **31** 373
 interior decoration **7** 168
 lacquer **18** 614
 methods **9** 216; **31** 578
 musical instruments **22** 373
 paintings **2** 559; **9** 282; **11** 537, 538–9; **12** 638; **13** 701; **26** 493; **28** 776
  cabinet pictures **5** 354; **9** *281*
  conversation pieces **7** 784
  fêtes champêtres **11** 34, 36, *37*
  fêtes galantes **10** 478; **18** 711; **24** 134; **26** 83
  genre **12** 292
  mythological **23** 294, *294*; **32** *914*, *915*, *916*
 patrons and collectors **8** 210
  Arenberg, Auguste-Marie-Raymond, 6th Duke of **2** 382
  Baron, Bernard **3** 259
  Baudot, Claude-Louis-Henri **3** 394
  Beurdeley, (Emmanuel-) Alfred (1847-1919) **3** 889
  Cacault, François **5** 356
  Catherine II, Empress of Russia (*reg* 1762- 96) **26** 732
  Caylus, Comte de **6** 120
  Choiseul, Etienne-François, Duc de **7** 193
  Clark, Robert Sterling **7** 377
  Cognacq, (Théodore-) Ernest **7** 528
  Conti, Louis-François de Bourbon, Prince de (1717-76) **7** 778
  Crozat, Pierre **8** 208, 209; **11** 657
  Denon, (Dominique-) Vivant **8** 764
  Dugléré, Adolphe **9** 378
  Elizabeth Farnese, Queen of Spain (1692-1766) **4** 559
  Fesch, Joseph, Cardinal **11** 32
  Frederick II, King of Prussia (*reg* 1740-86) **3** 798, 806; **12** 473; **14** 652
  Gibbs, James **12** 594

Watteau, (Jean-)Antoine
patrons and collectors—cont.
Groult, Camille 13 705
Hall, Peter Adolf 14 80
Haranger, Pierre-Maurice, Abbé 14 162
Hawkins, John Heywood (1803-77) 14 252
Hohenzollern, Henry, Prince of Prussia 14 653
Jullienne, Jean de 17 684
La Caze, Louis 18 588
Laroon, Marcellus 18 797
La Roque, Antoine de 18 796
Livois, Marquis de 19 510
Mariette, Pierre-Jean 20 417
Marigny, Marquis de 25 82
McLellan, Archibald 28 271
Mead, Richard 10 364; 20 910
Morny, Charles-Auguste, Duc de 22 127
Munro (of Novar), H(ugh) A(ndrew) J(ohnstone) 22 314
Orléans, Philippe II de Bourbon, 2nd Duc d' (1674-1723) 11 631; 23 516
Papillon de La Ferté, Denis-Pierre-Jean 24 63
Périer, Casimir 24 418
Quentin de Lorangère 25 815
Ramsay, John 28 271
Randon de Boisset, (Pierre-Louis-)Paul 25 888
Reynolds, Joshua 26 279
Robien, Christophe-Paul Gautron, Marquis de 26 470
Rothschild (family) 27 223
Rushout, John, 2nd Baron Northwick 27 350
Saint-Morys, Charles Paul Jean-Baptiste de Bourgevin Vialart de 27 568
Schwiter, Louis-Auguste 28 196
Seymour-Conway, Richard, 4th Marquess of Hertford 28 527
Sirois, Pierre 12 489
Soane, John 28 908
Stanislav II Poniatowski, King of Poland (*reg* 1764-95) 25 212
Tessin, Carl Gustav, Count 30 523
Titon du Tillet, Evrard 31 56
Vaudreuil, François, Comte de 32 85
Wernher, Julius 33 84
pattern books 24 271
prints 9 244
pupils 6 120; 24 255; 25 820
reproductions in ceramics 6 462
reproductions in porcelain 14 235; 21 64
reproductions in tapestry 10 *352*
reproductive prints by others 10 391; 11 81; 12 489; 26 230
Audran, Benoît, II (1698-1772) 8 130
Audran, Jean 2 709
Aveline, Pierre (-Alexandre) (1702-60) 2 853
Baron, Bernard 3 259; 20 910
Boucher, François 4 512
Cars, Laurent 5 884
Cochin (ii), Charles-Nicolas, I (1688-1754) 7 495
Huquier, Gabriel 15 31
Joullain, François 17 668
Jullienne, Jean de 17 684
Larmessin, Nicolas de (iii) (1684-1755) 18 795
Lebas, Jacques-Philippe 19 10
Lépicié, (François-) Bernard 18 796
Liotard, Jean-Etienne 7 785; 19 437
Mercier, Philip 21 147
Pond, Arthur 8 130
Watteau, (Jean-)Antoine
reproductive prints by others—cont.
Scotin, Gérard (-Jean-Baptiste), II (1698-after 1755) 28 221
Tardieu, Nicolas-Henry 30 344
Trémolières, Pierre-Charles 31 306
signs (markers) 20 388
sponsors 31 378
teachers 2 708; 12 637
Watteau, François (-Louis-Joseph) 19 381; 32 913, 920–21*
patrons and collectors 19 510
teachers 9 417
works 10 823; 32 *921*
Watteau, Louis (-Joseph) 19 381; 32 913, 920*
assistants 32 920
pupils 14 365; 32 920; 33 153
Watteau de Lille, François *see* WATTEAU, FRANÇOIS(-LOUIS-JOSEPH)
Watteau de Lille, Louis *see* WATTEAU, LOUIS(-JOSEPH)
Wattelé, Henri 9 718
Wat Thong Thua 30 579, 600
wattle-and-daub *see under* ARCHITECTURE → types
Watton Monastery (N. Humberside) 21 840
Watts, David Pike 7 750
Watts, G(eorge) F(rederic) 5 522; 9 290; 32 921–3*
assistants 22 351
frames 11 433, 436
groups and movements 13 297; 19 588
patrons and collectors 3 740; 15 894; 19 875; 24 571; 29 58; 30 359, 464
photographed works 14 688
pupils 17 673; 25 587; 29 537
reproductive prints by others 9 54; 21 418
studio 29 856
teachers 3 509
works 10 254; 11 397, *433*, 434; 19 614; 22 163, 330; 29 426; 31 131; 32 *922*
Watts, John (Cliffe) (i) 2 737; 32 923*
works 2 *737*
Watts, John (1749-92) 17 573
Watts, John William Hurrell 5 572; 23 631
Watts, Reuben 23 71
Watts, Robert 11 232; 29 16
Watts & Co. 4 214
Watts Towers *see under* LOS ANGELES
Watz, Antonius 29 840; 30 87; 31 692; 32 923*
Watzek, Hans (Josef) 14 388; 18 501; 24 738; 32 924*
Watzinger, Carl 17 483
Wauchope, Robert 16 803; 31 507
Wauer, William 29 872
Waulsort 13 182
Waumans, Coenrad 11 699
Wauquelin, Jean 3 555; 5 210; 8 208; 17 454; 20 680; 26 563
Wauquez 3 586
Waurá 4 706
Wauters (family) 30 320
Wauters, Emile (-Charles) 18 134; 32 924*
Wauters, Maria Anna 2 199
Wauters, Michiel 2 200
Wauters, P. (*fl* 1767) 26 285
Wauters, Philip (1617-79) 2 200
Wauwil 30 145
wave mouldings *see under* MOULDINGS → types
Wavere, Jan van 32 924*
Waverley Church (Surrey) 26 590
Waverley, John Anderson, 1st Viscount *see* ANDERSON, JOHN, 1st Viscount Waverley
Waverley, John of *see* JOHN OF WAVERLEY
Wavrin, Jean de, Lord of Forestel *see* FORESTEL, JEAN DE WAVRIN, Lord of
Wavrin, Master of 3 555; 20 785*
Wawra, C. J. 25 729
Waxahachie (TX), Ellis County Court House 18 888
wax crayons *see under* CRAYONS → types
waxed paper *see under* PAPER → types
waxed paper negative process *see under* PHOTOGRAPHY → processes
waxes 33 1–6*
conservation 10 199; 33 6*
historical and regional traditions
Byzantine 33 5
China 7 114, 116
England 19 *580*; 31 *262*; 33 3, *4*, *5*, 6
France 21 *771*; 31 262, 840; 33 3
Germany 10 *702*
Greece, ancient 20 327
Indonesia 15 790
Islamic 33 5
Italy 12 *574*; 16 *706*, 749*; 21 *769*; 27 *207*; 33 2, *3*
Java 15 790
Malaysia 20 176
Rome, ancient 5 298; 20 327; 27 17
United States of America 33 4
technical examination 30 410*
techniques
casting 33 2
moulding 33 2
types
bayberry 5 610
beeswax 1 155, 156; 5 610; 7 747; 8 128; 10 196; 11 764; 14 168; 21 768; 25 23; 26 142; 29 498, 712, 813; 30 558; 33 1, 5
Africa 33 1
Turkey 33 1
candelilla 33 1
carnauba 10 196; 33 1
ceresin 33 1
Chinese insect 33 1
Dorland's Wax Medium 10 197
Japan 8 128; 33 1
microcrystalline 10 196; 26 142; 33 2
mineral 5 610
montan 33 1
ozokerite 33 1
paraffin 7 747; 8 128; 19 364; 23 378; 29 712; 30 558; 33 2
Punic 10 197
sealing 33 1, 5
spermaceti 8 128; 19 364; 23 378; 33 1
stearine 33 2
suint 33 1
uses
batik 3 378
busts 5 298
candles 5 610; 33 1, 2
casts 6 7
consolidants 7 747, 748
crayons 8 127, 128; 33 1
death-masks 31 840
decorative paper 24 112
dolls 31 262*, *262*
dyeing 15 790; 30 558*
ebonite 33 1
écorchés 9 706
enamel 33 1
ex-votos 16 749
fixatives 11 142
frescoes 10 197; 11 764; 33 5
gilding 12 629
waxes
uses—cont.
grounds 10 548; 13 706
lacquer 33 1
leather 33 1
modelli 21 768, *769*, *771*; 33 2
models 16 749
moulds 6 7
painting 33 5*
paintings
encaustic 1 156; 10 196; 33 1, 5
wall 10 197; 32 808
paints 23 378, 784; 33 1, 5
paper 7 114, 116; 24 56; 33 1
pastels 33 1
photographic cylinders 33 1
photography 24 657
see also PHOTOGRAPHY → processes → waxed paper negative process
pietre dure 14 168
plaster 29 813; 33 1
polishes 33 1
polishing 24 258; 29 706
printer's ink 33 1
relief sculpture 12 *574*; 33 2
relining 26 142
restoration 33 1
ropes 33 1
sculpture 10 197, 702; 29 712; 33 1, 2–4*
England 33 *4*
Germany 10 *702*
Italy 16 *706*; 27 *207*; 33 *3*, 725, *726*
relief 16 749
Rome, ancient 27 17
sealants 25 174
seals 19 *580*; 33 *5*, 5–6*
stained glass 29 498
textiles 20 176; 33 1
varnishes 32 3; 33 1
writing-tablets 4 342, *342*; 20 327
wax resist dyeing *see under* DYEING → types
wax resist glazing *see under* GLAZES → techniques
waxworks 33 2, 3–4*, *4*
see also WAXES → uses → sculpture
Way, Thomas, & Son 33 143
Way, T. R. 19 488
Wayampi 11 758
Wayana 11 758, 759; 29 132; 30 12, 13
headdresses 11 *758*
Wayan Tohjiwa 15 808
Wayge, Dietrich zur *see* DIETRICH ZUR WAYGE
Wayname, Church of Kidane Mehret 10 572
Wayne, June (Claire) 1 145; 19 492, 702; 20 606, 608; 31 660; 33 6–7*
Waynesburg (PA), Greene County Court House 18 887
Waynflete, William, Bishop of Winchester 23 474, 686; 30 366; 33 236, 238
Wayō style 17 *73*, 73–4*, 119
wayside monuments *see under* MONUMENTS → types
Wayss, G. A. 7 693
Wayu 7 602
Waywaka 29 212
Waywell, G. B.
works 14 *71*
Waywike, Maynard *see* VEWICKE, MAYNARD
Wayzata (MN), Francis W. Little House 31 *622*
Waza, Jan Albert, Bishop 25 120
Wazaramo 30 302
Wazen Eiraku *see* EIRAKU WAZEN
Wazhaping 6 885
Wazirabad 23 803; 29 824
Wazir Khan 15 366
W‡B, Master 20 804*
WB, Master 20 803*
We 1 313, 339, 391–2; 8 21, 22, 486; 13 860; 19 310
Weale, John 10 208
Weale, W(illiam) H(enry) J(ames) 33 7–8*
weapons 2 447–68*
collections *see under* COLLECTIONS → types
display 9 31*
historical and regional traditions
Aboriginal Australia 1 53–4*, *54*, 55–6*
Africa 1 361–2*
Anatolia, ancient 1 834, 835
Azerbaijan 2 900*
Aztec 21 244, 245, 246, 247
Bamum 3 153
Burma 5 259–60*
Caroline Islands 23 735
Central Asia, Eastern 6 305–6*
Central Asia, Western 6 259–62*
China 6 841, 848–9*; 7 54–8*, 97
Cook Islands 23 734
Crete 8 153, 154; 21 688*
Cyprus, ancient 8 353
Egypt
Mamluk 16 508
Egypt, ancient 10 39*, *40*
Fiji 23 734
Greece, ancient 13 391, 583–5*
Hawaii 23 734
Indian subcontinent 15 676–9*, 696, 712
Mughal 15 678
Rajput 15 678
Indonesia 15 817–18*
Islamic 16 503–10*, *504*, *506*, 528
Japan 2 448, 449; 17 319, 361–4*
Korea 18 345, 353–4*
Maori 23 734
Marquesas Islands 23 734
Maya 21 246, 247
Mesoamerica, Pre-Columbian 21 244–7, *245*
Mesopotamia 21 304
Minoan 8 153; 21 688*
Mongolia 21 875*
Native North Americans 22 573
New Caledonia 23 734
New Guinea 23 734
Olmec 21 246
Ottoman 16 507–9*, 528
Pacific Islands 23 733–5*
Papua New Guinea 23 734; 24 69–70*, *70*
Philippines 24 630–31*, *631*
Rome, ancient 27 94–5*
Santa Cruz Islands 23 734
Scythian 6 261
Sogdiana 16 505
Solomon Islands 23 734
South America, Pre-Columbian 29 204–6*
Sri Lanka 29 468–9*, 471, 474
Syria-Palestine 30 194
Thailand 30 638*
Toltec 21 246
Torres Strait Islands 23 734
Ukraine 31 563
Vanuatu 31 893*
historiography *see under* HISTORIOGRAPHY → types
materials
bone 16 503
bronze
Central Asia, Western 6 260
China 6 841, 848–9*; 7 54, 55, 97
Cyprus, ancient 8 353
Islamic 16 503
Japan 17 319, 361
Korea 18 345, 353
copper 6 260
inlays 15 712

weapons
  materials—cont.
    iron **8** 154, 353; **16** 503; **17** 361; **18** 353; **29** 474
      cast **7** 97
      wrought **7** 97
    ivory **15** 696; **16** 503; **29** 469, 471
    jade **16** 503, 528
    steel **7** 97
    stone **6** 260
    tin **7** 97
    wood **7** 97
Wearnṭ *epitaphios* **26** 720
weasel-hair *see under* HAIR → types
Weatherby, John **4** 600
weathering **24** 258
weathervanes **31** 652, 653, *653*; **32** *325*; **33** 8*
weavers **17** 311–12*
weave stitch *see under* STITCHES
weaving **30** 543–54*, *544, 546, 547*
  guilds *see under* GUILDS → types
  historical and regional traditions
    Africa **1** 246, 250, 293–5*, *294*
    Ancient Near East **1** 879, 880, *882*
    Anglo-Saxon **2** 83
    Angola **2** 87*
    Asante **1** 294
    Australia **2** 767
    Bangladesh **3** 168
    Berber **1** 294; **3** *755*, 756
    Bhutan **3** 915
    Brazil **4** 706, 724
    Brunei **5** 13, *13*
    Burma **5** 247–8*
    Byzantine **9** 665–6
    Cambodia **5** 502
    Canada **5** 586, *587*, 587
    Central Asia, Western **6** 249; **16** 443
    China **7** 43–4, 48
    Czech Republic **8** 418
    Early Christian (*c*. AD 250-843) **9** 665–6
    Egypt **9** 767; **16** 441
    Egypt, ancient **9** 824; **10** 75*
    Etruscan **10** 635
    Fulani **11** 829–30
    Germany **12** 463, 464
    Ghana **1** 293
    Guatemala **13** 766
    Hausa **14** 231
    Hopi **22** 626
    Inca **15** 163
    Indian subcontinent **15** 660*, 727, 732
    Iran **1** *882*; **16** 443
    Iraq **16** 434–5
    Ireland **16** 33
    Iroquois **22** 628
    Islamic **16** 429, 439–40, 441, 443, 444, 447–8, 466, 476–7, 478–9
      Iraq **16** 434–5
      Syria **16** 441
    Italy **10** 635
    Japan **17** 306–8*, 311–12, 317, 354–5*
    Korea **18** 379
    Laos **18** 771
    Madagascar **1** 246, 293, 294; **20** 36
    Malaysia **20** 175–6
    Mali **11** 829–30
    Marshall Islands **20** 479
    Mesoamerica, Pre-Columbian **21** 261
    Micronesia, Federated States of **21** 477
    Morocco **3** *755*; **16** 429
    Native North Americans **22** 620*, 621–2*, 623–4, 627, 665
    Navajo **22** 624–6
    Netherlands, the **22** 899–900*
weaving
  historical and regional traditions—cont.
    New Zealand **23** 74
    Nigeria **1** 246, 293, 294
    North Africa **16** 440, 447–8
    Ottoman **16** 476–7, 478–9
    Paraguay **24** 92
    Philippines **24** 623–4
    Poland **25** 131
    Polynesian outliers **25** 182
    Romanesque **26** 703
    Romania **26** 721–2*
    Rome, ancient **27** 112–13
    South America, Pre-Columbian **29** 159, 194*
    Spain **16** 439–40
    Sri Lanka **29** 476
    Syria **16** 441
    Turkey **9** 493; **16** 444, 476–7, 478–9
    United States of America **31** 656–7
    Zaïre **1** 294, *294*
  materials
    bark **1** 293; **22** 620
    bromelia **24** 92
    cotton **1** 293
    gold **12** 464
    hemp **17** 312
    linen **12** 463, 464
    metal **12** 463
    quills **22** 648
    raffia **1** 293, *294*
    rami (fibre) **17** 312
    silk **1** 293; **9** 665–9; **12** 463; **16** 447–8, 849; **17** 306, 311, 313, 317; **30** 547
    wool **1** 293
  types
    brocading *see* BROCADES
    cannellé **30** 551
    cannetillé see cannellé
    compound tabby **27** 113; **30** 551–2*
    compound twill **30** 552*
    computerized **11** 55
    curved weft **5** 830
    damask *see* DAMASK
    double cloth **5** 830
    eccentric *see* curved weft
    face-to-face **5** 832
    gauze *see* GAUZE
    Gobelins **12** 468
    half-Gobelins **12** 468
    hand **5** 654
    hexamiton **9** 665
      see also tabby
    inweaving **16** 436
    knotted-pile **12** 465; **16** 466–7, *467*, 469
    lampas **30** 552–3*
      Byzantine **9** 666
      China **7** 50
      Early Christian (*c*. AD 250-843) **9** 666
      England **30** 552
      France **30** 552
      Gothic **30** 552
      Iran **16** *444*, 449, *450*
      Islamic **16** *444*, 449, *450*; **30** VII1
      Spain **30** VII1
    machine weaving **5** 654
    pile-weaving **5** 831
    samite *see hexamiton*; tabby
    satin *see* SATIN
    self-patterned tabby **9** 666; **30** 550
    sumak **5** 830, *830*; **18** 49
    tabby **9** 665; **30** 182
    tablet **12** 463; **30** 545*, *545*
    tapestry *see* TAPESTRIES
    tobine **30** 551
    triple cloth **5** 830
    twill **30** 551*
    velvet *see* VELVET
    warp-faced **5** 830
    weft-faced **5** 830
weaving
  types—cont.
    weft-patterned tabby **9** 666
  uses
    baskets **3** 331, 332; **24** 92
    beadwork **3** 440
    carpets **5** *829*, 829–30, *830*, 831–2, *831*, *832*; **16** 466, 476–7, 478–9
    fibre art **11** 54
    mats **15** 727
    rugs **27** 316
    textiles **15** 660*; **16** 429, 434–5
Webb, Aston **32** 773; **33** 9*
  collaboration **4** 85, 835; **10** 267; **18** 890; **23** 34; **26** 316
  groups and movements **3** 269
  pupils **8** 151
  staff **9** 61
  works **4** 170; **5** 513; **9** 317; **10** 371; **16** 11; **22** 527; **23** 814
Webb, Boyd **33** 9*
Webb, Charles (1821-1898; Australia) **33** 9–10*
Webb, Charles (*fl* 1860s; England) **33** 13
Webb, David **31** 655
Webb, Electra Havemeyer **14** 244
Webb, Henry **28** 170
Webb, James **33** 9
Webb, Jane **19** 719
Webb, John (i) (1611-74) **2** 545; **33** 10–11*
  architecture **10** 231
    cathedrals **19** 598
    country houses **8** 45; **14** 435; **25** 265, *266*; **33** *224*, 225
    gates **12** 340
    hospitals **14** 254
    houses **20** 477
    mausolea **20** 866
    palaces **12** 176; **13** 623; **19** 618
    town houses **24** 390
    villas **17** 634; **32** 552, *552*
  interior decoration **10** 292; **23** 678; **33** 225, *225*
  patrons and collectors **7** 378
  productions **24** 752
  stage scenery **30** 662, 674
  teachers **17** 636
  writings **17** 638
Webb, John (1774-1835; industrialist) **33** 13
Webb, John (ii) (1776-1869; antiquarian) **33** 11*
Webb, John (*fl* mid-19th cent.) **13** 207
Webb, Mary **32** 856
Webb, Michael (*fl* 20th cent.) **17** 402
Webb, Mike (*b* 1937) **2** 308, 309
Webb, Peter **10** 482, 486
Webb, Philip (Speakman) **10** 282; **25** 398; **29** 765; **33** 11–13*
  collaboration **22** 142, 143
  groups and movements **10** 239; **13** 204; **21** 779; **23** 498; **25** 804
  patrons and collectors **4** 604; **14** 809; **25** 587; **29** 537
  teachers **29** 765
  works **2** 552; **4** 788, 810; **10** 235, 239, 298, 344; **15** 894, 895; **22** 142, 143, *143*, 146; **27** 131; **33** *12*
Webb, Stephen **26** 190
Webb, Thomas **10** 319, 320, 321; **33** 13*
Webb, Thomas Wilkes **33** 13
Webb, T. T. **1** 66
Webb & Bell **14** 720; **33** 9
Webb Corbett Ltd **10** 321
Webber, Andrew LLoyd **30** 687
Webber, E. Berry **31** 242
Webber, Gordon **21** 816; **25** 635
Webber, Henry **33** 22
Webber, John **33** 13–14*
  works **33** *14*
Webb Head **2** 685
Webb & Knapp, Inc. **24** 325
Webb & Pollock **31** 258
Webb & Richardson **33** 13
Webb's Crystal Glass Co. Ltd **28** 259; **33** 13
Webb Zerafa Menkes **5** 573; **22** 37
Weber, Albert **17** 854
Weber, Antal **3** 412; **14** 889; **33** 15*
Weber, Bruce **33** 15*
Weber, Franz Joseph **11** 731
Weber, Gerhard **30** 684
Weber, Henrik **14** 901; **19** 718
Weber, Josef Leonhard **8** 386
Weber, Karlheinz **3** 510
Weber, Kem **2** 522; **31** 632
Weber, Lorenzo Maria **33** 15*
Weber, Louis **13** 726
Weber, Max (*fl* 1890; zoologist) **14** 817
Weber, Max (1864-1920; sociologist) **28** 917
Weber, Max (1881-1961; artist) **17** 578; **27** 263; **33** 15–16*, 146
  collaboration **20** 605
  exhibitions **31** 490
  patrons and collectors **23** 7; **26** 488; **29** 655; **31** 605, *605*
  pupils **23** 669; **26** 464; **27** 219
  works **17** 578; **31** 612
  writings **29** 655
Weber, Molly **7** *294*
Weber, Paul **14** 215, 396; **26** 335
Weber, Urban, Abbot **1** 160
Weber-Locher, Julius **1** 895
Webley, Henry **30** 384
Webley, Joseph **23** 73
Webster, Burnett **16** 886; **20** 471
Webster, Daniel (*fl* 19th cent; patron) **7** 840
Webster, Daniel T. (*d* 1939; architect) **3** 270
Webster, Godfrey Vassal **4** 806; **5** 169
Webster, Henry **13** 9
Webster, John
  works **2** *758*
Webster, Thomas **33** 16*
  groups and movements **8** 121; **10** 254
  patrons and collectors **12** 638; **32** 338
  reproductive prints by others **29** 691
  works **29** 426
Webster, W. D. **1** 438
Wechelderzande **31** 875
Wechelen, Jan van **8** 464
Wechselburg **12** *360*, *361*
  Schlosskirche **27** 124; **33** 16–17*, *17*
  sculpture **12** 399
Wechsler, Dora **5** 571
Wechsler, Judith **5** 760
Wechter, Georg, I **13** 701; **29** 747; **33** 17–18*
  works **33** *18*
Wechter, Hans **29** 762
Wechtlin, Hans **33** 18–19*, 366
  works **33** *19*
Weckenmann, Johann Georg **10** 859
Wecker, Georg **20** 90
Weckerly, Hans **30** 143
Weckesser, Auguste **7** 896
Weckmann, Claus (*fl* 1504-7) **33** 19
Weckmann, Claus (1450/55-*d* after 1526) *see* WECKMANN, NIKLAUS
Weckmann, Hieronymus **33** 19
Weckmann, Niklaus **30** 201; **31** 569, 570; **33** 19*
Weckström, Björn **11** 109; **17** 530
Weddell, Thomas Philip, 3rd Baron Grantham *see* GREY, THOMAS PHILIP DE, 2nd Earl de Grey
Weddell, William **13** 303; **33** 19–20*
  collections **17** 475
  sculpture **6** 97; **10** 365
Wedderburn, David **3** 908
Wedderburn Castle **24** 845
Wedekind, Carl Wilhelm **4** 204
Wedekind, Frank **8** 596; **28** 54
Wedekind, Franz **8** 709
Wedekind, Johan Heinrich **10** 539
Wedevåg **30** 109
wedge tombs *see under* TOMBS → types
Wedgwood, Aaron (*fl* 1690s) **10** 305
Wedgwood, Aaron (1717-63) **10** 306
Wedgwood, Cecil **33** 22
Wedgwood, Clement Francis **33** 22
Wedgwood, Clement Tom **33** 23
Wedgwood, Francis **33** 22
Wedgwood, Francis Hamilton **33** 22
Wedgwood, Godfrey **33** 22
Wedgwood, Hensleigh Cecil **33** 23
Wedgwood, John **10** 306; **33** 20
Wedgwood, John Hamilton **33** 23
Wedgwood, Josiah (i) (1730-95) **1** 110; **6** 332, 333; **9** 473; **10** 309, 637; **15** 820; **20** 593, 594; **24** 273; **29** 495; **33** 20–22*, 136, 137
  collaboration **4** 541; **7** 814; **10** 306; **29** 809; **33** 99
  groups and movements **2** 163; **10** 96; **22** 739
  methods **10** 199
  personal collection **14** 131; **31** 308
  works **2** 759; **6** 605; **10** 305, 306–7, 345; **11** 162; **15** *820*; **19** 508; **22** 744; **23** 544; **26** 227; **33** *21*
Wedgwood, Josiah (ii) (1769-1843) **33** 22
Wedgwood, Josiah (v) (1899-1968) **33** 23
Wedgwood, Kennard Laurence **33** 22
Wedgwood, Laurence **33** 22
Wedgwood, Mary **33** 20
Wedgwood, Richard **10** 305
Wedgwood, Thomas (1685-1739) **5** 519; **10** 305; **33** 20
Wedgwood, Thomas (1703-76) **10** 306; **33** 20
Wedgwood, Thomas (1717-73) **33** 20
Wedgwood & Bentley **33** 20
Wedgwood ceramics factory **8** 448; **15** 821, 824; **20** 593; **29** 496; **32** 904; **33** 20–23*
  collections **8** 83; **16** 425; **26** 733
  designers **10** 264
    Bacon, John (i) (1740-99) **3** 25
    Burch, Edward (1730-1814) **5** 187
    Carrier-Belleuse, Albert-Ernest **5** 878
    Cheere, John **6** 528
    Crane, Walter **8** 122
    Flaxman, John **11** 162–3
    Follot, Paul **11** 241
    Greatbatch, William **15** 820
    Henning, John (i) (1771-1851) **14** 391
    Howard, Henry **14** 810
    Murray, Keith Day Pearce **10** 313
    Paolozzi, Eduardo **10** 313
    Potter, (Helen) Beatrix **10** 314
    Ravilious, Eric (William) **26** 39
    Tassie, James **30** 356
  marks **20** 442
  production **2** 164; **9** 29; **22** 744; **25** 192
    basaltes **9** 29; **10** 641, 642; **33** *21*
    bone china **10** 310

Wedgwood ceramics factory
production—cont.
creamware **1** 111; **10** 307, *307*; **22** 882
Jasper ware **6** 558; **17** 525; **21** II3
Queen ware **8** 461
Wedgwood Group **7** 798
Wedgwood Museum *see under* BARLASTON
Wedig, Gottfried von **12** 389; **29** 666
Wedll, Don **22** 671
Wednesbury (Staffs) **10** 195, 346
Wednesday Art Group **20** 172
Wedric, Abbot of Liessies **13** 21; **26** 659
Weeber, Carel **22** 832; **31** 867
Weeden Island culture **22** *544*
pottery **22** *611*, 611–12, *612*
Weegee **24** 685; **33** 23*
Weekes, F. **29** 797
Weekes, Henry **3** 509; **6** 456, 457; **29** 926; **33** 24*
Weeks, Edwin Lord **31** 603
Weeks, John **2** 706; **33** 24*
collaboration **14** 784; **19** 519
pupils **28** 888
works **14** *783*; **23** 60; **31** 335
Weeks, Levi **22** 539
Weems, Carrie Mae **10** 882; **33** 314
Weenix, Gillis **33** 24
Weenix, Jan **14** 706; **33** 24, 26–7*
attributions **33** 26
collaboration **32** 908
patrons and collectors **7** 437; **33** 280
teachers **4** 153; **33** 26
works **29** 666; **33** *27*
Weenix, Jan Baptist **14** 706; **26** 772; **33** 24, 25–6*
attributions **33** 26
collaboration **3** 757; **4** 488
groups and movements **9** 462; **28** 92
patrons and collectors **14** 692
pupils **3** 757; **14** 706; **33** 26
teachers **21** 791
works **22** 843; **29** 667; **33** *25*
Weenix, Johannes **33** 24
weepers **33** 28*, *28*
Weerasinghe, Pushpananda **29** 462
Weerden-van Severdonck, van (family) **10** 717
Weerdt, Adriaen de **33** 28–9*
groups and movements **26** 728
reproductive prints by others **7** 799
works **22** 857; **30** 531
Weerdt, Daniel de **11** 731
Weerdt, Hans de **3** 230
Weerelt, Erick van der *see* WILKE, ERICK
Weert, Anna De *see* DE WEERT, ANNA
Weert, Jacob de **33** 169
Weerts, Jean-Joseph **22** 329
Weese, Harry (Mohr) **4** 790; **30** 684, 869; **33** 29*
Weesp
porcelain **22** 882, *882*
weft-faced weaving *see under* WEAVING → types
weft pile *see under* TEXTILES → types
weft-warp openwork *see under* TEXTILES → types
Wegely, Wilhelm Caspar **3** 804; **12** 433
Wegerif, Chris **2** 568
Wegewart, Willem **22** 894
Wegiro **1** *379*
church **1** 315
Wegman, William **32** 420; **33** 29*
Wegmann, Gustav Albert **33** 29–30*, 735
Wegmann, Jacob *see* WÄGMANN, JAKOB
Wegmerange **3** 524
Wegner, Hans J. **8** 747
works **8** *747*
Wegscheider, Joseph Ignaz **29** 399
Wehbé, Rashid **19** 8
Wehrlin, Johann Adam **28** 18
Wehrlin, Pietro Paolo **28** 18
Wei, Xiaowendi, Emperor *see* XIAOWENDI, Emperor
Weiant, C. **31** 310
Weibel, Peter **2** 804
Weibel, Walter **3** 263
Weibermacht, Master of the **20** 620, 785*
Wei Cheng *see* WEI ZHENG
weicher Stil see under GOTHIC → styles
Wei cun (Linfen), Niuwang miao **7** 136
Wei Dan **7** 91
Weidemann, Jakob **23** 227; **33** 30*
Weidemann, Michael **22** 796
Weiden, Cornelis ver **30** 104, 112
Weiden, Petter ver **30** 104
Weidenbach, Ernst **10** 82
Weidenbach, Max **10** 82
Weidenhaupt, Andreas **1** 33
Weidensdorfer, Claus **33** 30–31*
Weiditz, Christof (i) (*b c.* 1500-59) **2** 718; **33** 31, 33*
patrons and collectors **13** 906
works **20** 920; **26** 204; **29** 570
Weiditz, Christof (ii) (*c.* 1517-1572) **12** 402; **33** 31, 33, 34*
Weiditz, Hans (i) (*b c.* ?1475-*d* ?1516) **33** 31–2*
works **1** 658; **29** 570; **33** *31*
Weiditz, Hans (ii) (before 1500-*d c.* 1536) **2** 718; **20** 744; **33** 31, 32–3*
methods **33** 353
works **4** 358; **33** *32*, 353
Weidmann, Karl **12** 441
Weidmann, Leonhard **27** 217; **33** 34*
Wei dynasty *see* CHINA → periods → Wei period
Weie, (Viggo Thorvald) Edvard **8** 736; **33** 35–6*, 595
works **8** *736*
Weifang **7** 113, 147
Wei Fu-jen *see* WEI FUREN
Wei Furen **6** 769; **33** 319
Weiga, M. **22** 245
Weigand, Philip C. **18** 784; **24** 367
Weigandus Glaser **25** 434
Weigel **2** 23
Weigel, Cristoph **18** 47; **19** 832; **21** 415
Weigel, Erhard **12** 812
Weigel, Gotlind **12** 437
Weight, Carel **2** 553; **29** 426; **33** 744
Weightman, John Grey **19** 505; **31** 240
weights
historical and regional traditions
Africa **1** 277–8, *363*, 363–4, 428
Akan **1** 274, 277–8, 363, 392; **2** 590
Asante **1** 240, *363*; **2** 590*
Burma **5** 260*, *260*
Byzantine **9** 645
Côte d'Ivoire **1** 277–8, 363
Cyprus, ancient **8** 353
Early Christian (*c.* AD 250-843) **9** 645
Etruscan **10** 636
Ghana **1** 277–8, 363, 428
Italy **10** 636
Rome, ancient **26** 867
Tarascan **30** 341, 342
materials
brass **1** *363*; **2** 590
bronze **5** 260, *260*
glass **9** 645
gold **1** 392
weights
materials—cont.
pottery **30** 341
uses
clocks **7** 438
looms **10** 636
spinning (textile) **30** 540
Weihe, Ernest **3** 83
Wei Heng **6** 769
Wei ju-fen *see* WEI RUFEN
Weikersheim Schloss **33** 36*
Weil, George **17** 402, 580
Weil, Susan **26** 26
Weil am Rhein, Vitra Design Museum **12** 472
Weiland, Joyce **10** 879
Weilbach, Frederik **8** 761
Weilbach, Philip **8** 761
Weilburg **2** 813
Weiler, Max **2** 797; **15** 866
Weiler-la-Tour **19** 826
Weilhammer glassworks **28** 862
Weilheim **12** 403
Wei Lingchang **19** 469
Weill, Berthe **23** 195; **24** 143, 713; **33** 36*
Weill, Bruno **30** 755
Weill, Kurt **16** 892
Weimar **12** *361*; **33** 36–8*
architecture **12** 376
Atelier für Architektur und Künstgewerbe **29** 600
Donndorf Museum **9** 145
Ducal Museum *see* Landesmuseum
Goethe-Nationalmuseum **33** 37
Hochschule für Angewandte Kunst **12** 416
Landesmuseum **29** 600; **33** 687
Preller-Galerie **25** 550
monument to Goethe and Schiller **26** *377*
painting **12** 394
Rokokomuseum *see* Schloss Belvedere
Schloss **8** 41; **33** *37*
architecture **7** 417
relief sculpture **30** 854
Schloss Belvedere **12** 373; **26** 355
Schlossmuseum **10** 413
Staatliche Kunstsammlungen **33** 37
Stadtmuseum **33** 37
Wittumspalais
Wielandzimmer **25** 550
Weimar school **12** 394
Weimar Secession *see* SECESSION (WEIMAR)
Weinberg, Joseph L. **7** 429
Weinberger, Carmily **6** 176
Weinberger, Paul **4** 832
Weinbrenner, (Johann Jakob) Friedrich **33** 38–40*
collaboration **14** 575
pupils **3** 843; **4** 374; **10** 119, 496; **14** 839; **21** 821; **29** 490; **33** 228
works **11** 346; **12** 374, 375; **14** 305, 786; **17** 547, 816–17; **19** 110; **20** 868; **31** 580; **33** *39*, *40*
Weiner, Lawrence **7** 685
Weiner, Paul Lester **15** 886
Weiner, Richard **8** 250
Weiner, Tibor **14** 890, 891; **33** 41*
Weingart, Wolfgang **25** 354
works **25** *354*
Weingarten Abbey **12** *361*, 369; **33** 41*
collections **21** 250; **27** 617
collegiate church **12** 372, 404; **32** 822
frescoes **2** 580
manuscripts **12** 382; **26** 677; **27** 617
paintings **3** 737
Weinhart, Caspar **9** 750; **22** 302
Weinhausen Abbey **14** 426
Weinher, Peter **33** 271
Weininger, Andor **30** 683
works **30** *683*
Weininger, Andreas **24** 406
Weinles, Franciszka **30** 704
Weinman, Adolph Alexander **30** 62; **33** 41–2*
Weinman, Robert A. **33** 42
Weinmüller, Joseph **19** 781
Weinraub, Munio **16** 565; **20** 299
Weinrib, David **4** 109; **31** 640
Weinsberg, Hermann van **5** 61
Weinstein, Joshua **28** 798
Weintraub, Jakub **25** 127
Weintraub, William H. **25** 887
Weir, John Ferguson **15** 830; **33** 42*
Weir, Julian Alden **31** 603; **33** 43*
groups and movements **2** 633; **15** 156; **23** 47; **30** 452; **31** 487
patrons and collectors **11** 141; **24** 638
pupils **18** 895
works **9** 309
Weir, Lois **23** 670
Weir, Richard **28** 262
Weir, Robert Walter **33** 42–3*, 137
Weir, R. S. *see* SCHULTZ, ROBERT WEIR
Weir, W. **30** 365
Weirotter, Franz Edmund **33** 44*, 196
patrons and collectors **33** 196
reproductive prints by others **20** 914
Wei Rufen **7** 135
Weis, František Ignác **8** 386
Weis, Ignác **16** 817
Weis, Johann Martin (i) (1711-1751) **33** 44*
Weis, Johann Martin (ii) (1738-1807) **33** 44
Weis, Sosthène **19** 827
Weisberg, Gabriel P. **22** 688
Weisberg, Vladimir **8** 10
Weise, Christian Friedrich **10** 176
Weisenborn, Rudolph **6** 575
Weisgerber, Albert **33** 44–5*
Weishui Valley **6** 877
Wei Shuo *see* WEI FUREN
Weiskirchen
metalwork **6** *153*
Weisman, Frederick R. **33** 45*
Weisman, Frederick R., Museum of Art *see under* MINNEAPOLIS (MN) → University of Minnesota
Weisman, Marcia **33** 45*
Weiss, Adolph **5** 381
Weiss, Emil Rudolf **28** 779
Weiss, Jean-Martin **8** 882
Weiss, Johann **28** 854
works **28** *854*
Weiss, María del Rosario **13** 252
Weiss, Marx **11** 838; **29** 787
Weiss, Matthias **11** 766
Weiss, Murry **28** 694
Weiss, Wojciech **18** 428; **25** 108, 141; **33** 45*
pupils **10** 102; **22** 423; **32** 793
Weissbach, Karl Robert **19** 705; **28** 95
Weissenau Codex *see under* CODICES → individual manuscripts
Weissenau Monastery **12** 372
Weissenberger, Lucien **2** 564
Weissen Blätter **5** 924; **24** 427
Weissenbruch, Frederik Adrianus **33** 45
Weissenbruch, Frederik Hendrik **33** 45
Weissenbruch, Isaac **33** 45
Weissenbruch, Jan **22** 848; **33** 45–6*
works **33** *46*
Weissenbruch, Jan Hendrik **14** 42; **33** 45, 46–7*, 677
groups and movements **14** 43, 47
pupils **4** 203
Weissenbruch, Jan Hendrik—cont.
teachers **14** 804
works **11** 448
Weissenbruch, Johan Daniël **33** 45
Weissenbruch, Johannes **33** 45, 46
Weissenbruch, Willem Johannes **33** 45
Weissenburg
jugs **27** *86*
Weissenburger, David **14** 893
Weissenburger, Lucien **22** 456
Weissenfels, Duke of **17** 769
Weissenkircher, Hans Adam **2** 794, 795; **28** 860; **33** 47–8*
Weissenkirchner, Wolf **24** 460
Weisshaupt, Bartolomé **29** 300
Weissman, A(driaan) W(illem) **33** 48*
pupils **29** 483
works **1** 803
illustrated **2** 416
Weissman, Frank **4** 719
Weissmann, Ernst **19** 51
Weisspriach, Burckhard von, Archbishop of Salzburg **18** 650
Weiss-Weingart, Ebbe **12** 451
Weistrach, St Stephen **13** 58
Weisweiler, Adam **7** 658; **11** 595, 597, 627; **24** 150; **33** 48*
patrons and collectors **17** 639
works **9** 29; **11** 593; **12** 831
Wei Tan *see* WEI DAN
Weitersbach Villa **32** 542
Weitling, Otto **8** 729; **16** 828
Weitsch, Anton **33** 49
Weitsch, Friedrich Georg **28** 46; **33** 49
Weitsch, Johann Friedrich **33** 49*
Weitzen *see* VÁC
Weitzmann, Kurt **12** 873; **15** 91; **33** 49*
Weitzmann, Sigfried **18** 386
Weixlbaum, Michael **8** 445
Wei Yan **6** 799
Weiyang *see* YANGZHOU
Wei Yen *see* WEI YAN
Weizenberg, August Ludwig **10** 539; **30** 277
Wei Zheng **33** 477
Wei Zifeng **33** 468
Weizmann, Chaim **21** 120
Wejchart, Alexandra **16** 22
Wejchert, Andrzei **16** 12
Wejchert, Hanna **33** 49*
Wejchert, Kazimierz **33** 49
Welandus M **26** 694
Welbeck Abbey (Notts) **6** 118–19
jewellery **17** 523
miniatures **9** 44; **14** 545, 547; **21** 640; **24** 553
paintings **6** 118; **12** 514; **17** 645; **24** 553; **29** 424
Welby, Selina **25** 712
Welch, Edward **14** 156; **31** 240
Welch, Robert **10** 337; **19** 594; **33** 50*
Welch, Stuart Cary **15** 212, 743, 747, 748
Welcher, Samuel **4** 354
Welches Plantation, Chattel house **2** 147, *147*
Welch & Lander **10** 240
Welcome glasses *see under* GLASSES → types
weld **9** 491; **24** 799
Weld, Charles Goddard **10** 887; **17** 431
Weld-Blundell *see* BLUNDELL (FAMILY)
Welde, W. J. van der **15** 769; **16** 873
Welden, van (family) **2** 199
Weldenck, Melchior **28** 904
Weld-Forester, Cecil George Wilfred, 7th Baron Forester **2** 318
welding **1** 743; **21** 325*; **27** 17
uses **1** 743

Welf (House of) **7** 422; **12** 448, 460; **33** 50–51*
Welf, Anton Ulrich, Duke of Brunswick-Wolfenbüttel *see* ANTON ULRICH, Duke of Brunswick-Wolfenbüttel
Welf, Augustus, Duke of Brunswick-Lüneburg *see* AUGUSTUS, Duke of Brunswick-Lüneburg
Welf, Augustus, Duke of Brunswick-Wolfenbüttel *see* AUGUSTUS, Duke of Brunswick-Wolfenbüttel
Welf, Augustus William, Duke of Brunswick *see* AUGUSTUS WILLIAM, Duke of Brunswick
Welf, Charles I, Duke of Brunswick-Wolfenbüttel *see* CHARLES I, Duke of Brunswick-Wolfenbüttel
Welf, Charles III, Duke of Brunswick-Wolfenbüttel *see* CHARLES III, Duke of Brunswick-Wolfenbüttel
Welf, Christian Ludwig, Duke of Brunswick-Lüneburg *see* CHRISTIAN LUDWIG, Duke of Brunswick-Lüneburg
Welf, Ernest, Duke of Brunswick-Lüneburg *see* ERNEST THE CONFESSOR, Duke of Brunswick-Lüneburg
Welf, Ernest Augustus III, Duke of Brunswick *see* ERNEST AUGUSTUS III, Duke of Brunswick
Welf, Ferdinand Albert, Duke of Brunswick-Bevern *see* FERDINAND ALBERT, Duke of Brunswick-Bevern
Welf, George William, Duke of Calenberg *see* GEORGE WILLIAM, Duke of Calenberg and Celle
Welf, Henry II, Duke of Brunswick-Wolfenbüttel *see* HENRY II, Duke of Brunswick-Wolfenbüttel
Welf, Henry Julius, Duke of Brunswick-Wolfenbüttel *see* HENRY JULIUS, Duke of Brunswick-Wolfenbüttel
Welf, Henry the Lion, Duke of Saxony and Bavaria *see* HENRY THE LION, Duke of Saxony and Bavaria
Welf, Henry XII, Duke of Bavaria *see* HENRY THE LION, Duke of Saxony and Bavaria
Welf, Matilda, Duchess of Saxony and Bavaria *see* MATILDA, Duchess of Saxony and Bavaria
Welf, Otto I, Duke of Brunswick *see* OTTO I, Duke of Brunswick and Lüneberg
Welf, Otto II, Duke of Lüneburg *see* OTTO II, Duke of Lüneburg
Welf, William, Duke of Brunswick-Lüneburg *see* WILLIAM, Duke of Brunswick-Lüneburg
Welf Treasure **5** 29; **14** 570; **26** 146, *146*, 683, 685, 693; **33** 51
Welize, Francz de *see* FRANCZ DE WELIZE
Welize, Laurentius de *see* LAURENTIUS DE WELIZE
Welize, Vitko de *see* VITKO DE WELIZE
Wellcome, Henry S(olomon) **10** 90; **33** 55*
Wellcome *Apocalypse* **21** *6*
Wellcome Collection *see* LOS ANGELES (CA) → University of California → Museum of CulturalHistory
Wellcome Museum of the History of Medicine *see under* LONDON → museums → Science Museum
Welldon, John **11** 119
Welldon, William **11** 119
Weller Pottery **31** 638
Welles, Clara **31** 650
Wellesley, Arthur, 1st Duke of Wellington **5** 631; **10** 334; **33** 55*
architecture **12** 518; **20** 53; **21** 570; **33** 447
ceramics **10** 97
decorative works **29** 723
gold **12** 163
metalwork **4** 638
paintings **4** 304, 330; **9** 17, 19; **21** 35, 723; **24** 811; **28** 370; **33** 189
porcelain **3** 805; **11** 609
silver **16** 32; **25** 314; **28** 431
Wellesley, Arthur Richard, 2nd Duke of Wellington **3** 241; **12** 315
Wellesley, Gerald, 7th Duke of Wellington **33** 55
Wellesley, Henry **9** 231; **33** 56*
Wellesley, Richard **12** 75
Wellesley, Richard Colley, Marquess of Wellesley **5** 418; **15** 741
Wellesley College (MA), Jewett Arts Center **27** 313
Wellge, Henry
works **4** *82*
well-heads **33** 56–7*, *57*
Wellingborough (Northants), All Hallows **13** 109; **29** 508
Wellington **23** 51, *52*; **33** *57*, 57–8*
Alexander Turnbull Library **23** 57, 76
architecture **32** 308
Bank of New Zealand **8** 581
Berhampore Flats **23** 56
Christian Science Church **23** 56
Cox House **23** 56
Dominion Museum *see* Museum of New Zealand Te Papa Tongarewa
furniture **23** 65, 66
Futuna Chapel **23** 56, *56*
General Assembly Library **23** 54
General Post Office **23** 54
Government Buildings **7** 410; **23** 54
Harbour Board Offices **23** 54
Massey House **23** 56
Museum of New Zealand Te Papa Tongarewa **13** 844; **23** 57, 75; **33** 58
collections **2** 94, 371; **5** 282; **22** 439; **23** 76
exhibitions **23** 737
library **23** 76
National Art Gallery *see* Museum of New Zealand Te Papa Tongarewa
National Art Gallery Archives **2** 371
National Museum *see* Museum of New Zealand Te Papa Tongarewa
New Zealand Historic Places Trust **23** 76
Old St Paul's **23** 53
Parliament Buildings **30** 237
Parliament House **5** 541
Public Library **23** 56
Public Trust Office **23** 55
St John **23** 53
School of Design *see* Technical School
State Insurance Building **23** 56
statue of Queen Victoria **23** 62
Sutch House **23** 56
Technical School **23** 75
Victoria University **23** 76
Wellington, Arthur Richard. Wellesley, 2nd Duke of *see* WELLESLEY, ARTHUR RICHARD., 2nd Duke of Wellington
Wellington, Arthur Wellesley, 1st Duke of *see* WELLESLEY, ARTHUR, 1st Duke of Wellington
Wellington, Gerald Wellesley, 7th Duke of *see* WELLESLEY, GERALD, 7th Duke of Wellington
Wellington, Irene **28** 307
Wellington, John B(ooker) B(lakemore) **33** 58*
Wellington and Ward **33** 58
Wellington Art Club **33** 58
Wellington Plate **4** 637; **25** *313*, 314; **28** 429, 431
Wellington Shield **29** 732
wells **12** 109, 126; **13** 381
see also STEPWELLS
Wells (Somerset) **10** *225*; **33** 58–64*
Bishop's Palace **5** 270; **33** 64*, *64*
gate-house **12** 175
Cathedral of St Andrew **9** 669, 670, 671; **10** 227, 228; **13** 44, 46, 54, 55; **17** 673–4; **18** 621; **31** 284; **33** 59–61*
arches **2** 294, 296
capitals **13** 80
chapter house **3** 121; **6** *465*, 466; **33** 60
choir **33** *61*
choir-stalls **7** 190
clock **7** 438
cloister **7** 453
conservation **29** 712
façade **9** 670
Lady Chapel **8** 611, *611*; **18** 622; **32** 93, 94; **33** 59, 60–61, *64*
misericords **21** 724
mouldings **11** 420; **22** 217, 218
nave **33** *59*
piers (ii) (masonry) **24** 751
pulpit **25** 725
retrochoir **33** *60*
roof **30** *906*, 907
sculpture **10** 743; **13** 80, 82, 122; **29** 96, 707; **33** 61*
stained glass **13** 183; **29** 515; **33** 63–4*
stiff-leaf **29** 659
strainer arches **20** 576
throne **30** 779
tomb of Bishop Beckington **10** 339
tracing house **31** 274
vaults **32** 91, 92, 93
west front **33** *62*, 62–3
St Cuthbert **13** 84, 85
Wells, Albert **33** 370
Wells, Henry Tanworth **4** 604; **33** 64
Wells, James **1** 443
Wells, Joanna Mary **4** 604; **33** 64*
Wells, John **22** 36; **27** 563
Wells, Joseph **7** 876
Wells, Randall **25** 634
Wells, William (i) (1768-1847) **14** 550; **33** 65*
Wells, William (ii) **33** 65, 565
Wells Aviation Company **33** 204
Wellz, Josef **26** 708
Wełoński, Pius **18** 430; **25** 115, 130; **32** 877
Wels **2** 815
Welsbach, Alois Auer, Ritter von **32** 449
Welsbach, Carl Auer, Baron von **19** 366
Welsberg, Wilhelm von, Bishop of Brixen **30** 482
Welsch, Maximilian von **29** 630; **33** 65*, 431
collaboration **23** 4
patrons and collectors **28** 146
Welsch, Maximilian von—*cont.*
pupils **18** 495
works **4** 890; **10** 451; **12** 373; **20** 127; **23** 6; **25** 188; **33** 432
welsche Giebel *see under* GABLES → types
Welser, Bartholomäus (*d* 1484) **33** 65
Welser, Bartholomäus, V (1484-1561) **33** 65
Welser, Jacob (1468-1541) **18** 512
Welser, Jakob (*d* 1483) **33** 65
Welser, Lukas **33** 65
Welser, Markus **33** 65–6*
Welser, Matthäus **33** 66
Welser, Ulrich **33** 65
Welser Altar **24** 331
Welsh, Thomas **7** 435
Welshpool (Powys) **32** *780*, 790
Weltausstellung *see* EXHIBITIONS → types → international
Welté, Christian Gottlieb **10** 539
Weltenburg Monastery, SS Georg und Martin **2** 582; **12** 372; **19** 362; **26** 497
altar **19** *364*
frescoes **2** *580*, *583*; **15** 139
sculpture **12** 405
stucco **29** 838
Welter, G. **1** 478
Welti, Albert **3** 824; **30** 133; **33** 66*
Welti-Escher, Lydia **30** 152
Weltring, Heinrich **33** 343
Welwyn (Herts) **6** 162; **27** 81
Welwyn Garden City (Herts) **8** 810; **12** 144, 145; **14** 809; **16** 891; **22** 743; **25** 547; **31** 730
Welz, Jean **29** 109, 110
Welzenbacher, Lois **2** 789; **31** 539; **33** 66*
Wemaëre, Pierre **17** 658
Wembley (Middx)
British Empire Exhibition, 1924 **7** 653; **10** 684; **15** 747; **23** 741; **33** 204
Empire Pool **10** 241
stadium **10** 684; **29** 489
White City **29** 489
Wemyss **28** 241, 259
Wemyss-Charteris-Douglas, Francis, 10th Earl of Wemyss and March **3** 367; **33** 565
Wen Boren **6** 759; **33** 67, 70–71*
works **33** *70*, 437
Wenceslas, Holy Roman Emperor (*reg* 1378-1400) **18** 461; **19** 829, 830*; **25** 431, 437, 441
architecture **8** 376
embroidery **25** 431
manuscripts **8** 422; **33** 71
paintings **8** 390
sculpture **8** 423
(Joseph-)Wenceslas (-Lorenz), Prince of Liechtenstein (*reg* 1748-72) **19** 337–8*; **24** 810
Wenceslas, Saint **8** 421; **25** 439, 552; **26** 80, 82
Wenceslas IV, King of Bohemia *see* WENCESLAS, Holy Roman Emperor
Wenceslas Bible *see under* BIBLES → individual manuscripts
Wenchang *see* XU WEI
Wencheng, Queen (*fl c.* 620) **19** 293
Wenchengdi, Emperor (Wei; *reg* AD 452-65) **6** 709; **33** 574
Wen Cheng-ming *see* WEN ZHENGMING
Wen-ch'eng-ti, Emperor *see* WENCHENGDI, Emperor
Wen Chen-heng *see* WEN ZHENHENG
Wen Chia *see* WEN JIA
Wenck, Ernst (Gustav Alexander) **33** 72*
Wenck, Johannes, Abbot of Heilsbronn **31** 287
Wenckebach, (Ludwig) Willem (Reijmert) **33** 72*
Wenckers, Johann **29** 376
Wenczla, Master **32** 452
Wende, Theodor **12** 450
Wendel, Henri de **8** 30
Wendelin of Speier **11** 722; **28** 306
Wendelinus, Jan *see* WENDELSTAM, JOHAN
Wendell, Jan *see* WENDELSTAM, JOHAN
Wendell Holmes, Oliver **10** 669, 670; **24** 657, 662
Wendelstam, Johan **14** 281; **33** 72–3*
Wendelstein **33** 73*
Wenden *see* CĒSIS
Wendi, Emperor (Han; *reg* 180-157 BC) **14** 133
Wendi, Emperor (Chen; *reg* AD 560-67) **7** 152
Wendi, Emperor (Sui; *reg* 581-604) **7** 152; **29** 905; **33** 645
Wendingen **1** 814; **10** 698; **18** 878; **19** 476; **24** 449; **33** 177, 178
Wendland, Winfried **33** 73*
Wendt, Jochim Matthias **2** 765; **33** 73*
Wendt, Lionel (George Henricus) **2** 21; **29** 455; **33** 73–4*
Wendt, William **19** 701
Wendts **2** 765
Wendu *see* ZHAO ZUO
Wener, F. B.
works **5** *29*
Wen Fong **7** 161
Wenford Bridge pottery **5** 731
Wen Fung *see* WEN FONG
Wenger, Suzanne **1** 331; **15** 57; **23** 136, 138
Weng Tonghe **33** 74*
Weng T'ung-ho *see* WENG TONGHE
Wen-hsüan-ti, Emperor (Northern Qi; *reg* AD 550-60 *see* WENXUANDI, Emperor
Wénilon, Archbishop **28** 413
Wenincx, Jan **33** 26
Wening, Michael **3** 229; **22** 302; **33** 746
works **5** *82*
Wenis **10** 80
Wen Jia **6** 758, 759; **33** 67, 68–70*
sponsors **32** 848
works **33** *69*, 437
Wenlock Priory (Salop) **6** 466
Wen Lou *see* VAN LAU
Wennerberg, Gunnar **30** 98, 100, 102
Wennervirta, Ludwig **11** 113
Wenning, Pieter (Willem Frederick) **17** 603; **29** 108, 110; **33** 74–5*
Wennrich, Wolf **2** 766
Wen Peng **6** 759–60; **7** 130; **33** 67, 69, 70
publications **6** 758
Wen Po-jen *see* WEN BOREN
Wenro **22** 612
Wenselyns, Lambert **7** 708
Wen Shu **33** 320
works **33** *320*
Wenshu Temple *see* MT WENSHU (JIUQUAN)
Wensley (N. Yorks), Holy Trinity Church **24** 576
Went, Louise **24** 332
Wen-ti, Emperor *see* WENDI, Emperor
Wentink, D. E. **4** 155
Wen Tong **6** 804, 818, 823; **33** 75*
works **1** 581; **18** 323
Wen-tsung, Emperor (Yüan; *reg* 1330-32) *see* WENZONG, Emperor
Wen T'ung *see* WEN TONG
Wentworth (Cambs)
Castle **4** 218; **11** 426
St Peter **26** 613

Wentworth (Cambs)—cont.
Stainborough House see Castle
Wentworth, Charles 8 110; 12 926
Wentworth, Richard 30 389; 33 75*
Wentworth, Thomas, 1st Earl of Strafford 9 486; 33 195
Wentworth, William 17 900
Wentworth Woodhouse (S. Yorks) 8 47; 10 294; 32 912
Rockingham Mausoleum 20 868
Wentzel, (Nils) Gustav 33 76*
Wentzel, Hans 29 514
Wentzel, Johann Friedrich 14 651
Wentzinger, Johann Christian 33 76*
house 33 76
works 12 405; 27 554
Wenwu 24 435
Wenxuandi, Emperor (Northern Qi; reg AD 550-60) 6 816
Wenzel, Prince of Liechtenstein see (JOSEPH-)WENCESLAS(-LORENZ), Prince of Liechtenstein
Wenzel, Gusztáv 10 99
Wenzel, Marion 2 137
Wen Zhengming 6 758–9, 774, 820; 7 148; 30 49, 50; 33 67–70*, 320
groups and movements 29 244
patrons and collectors 6 772
pupils 6 547; 33 70, 436
works 1 581; 6 687, 759, 759, 806, 820, 820; 14 825; 33 68, 436
Wen Zhenheng 7 37
Wenzhong see WU BIN
Wenzler, Fedor 28 823
Wenzong, Emperor (Yuan; reg 1330-32) 17 881
Wepener, Franz J. 29 577
Weppa-Wano 9 734, 735
Wepwawetemhet 9 873
Werbauw 10 51
Werbegestälter, Ring Neue see RING NEUE WERBEGESTÄLTER
Werben an der Elbe 13 187
Werchtere, Willem van 3 544
Werden 12 364
St Liudger Abbey Church 7 265; 8 213, 222; 12 399; 23 649; 26 571, 572
crucifixes 12 399
crypt 7 265
tomb of St Liudger 23 646
St Peter 33 108
Werdmüller, Hans Georg 7 396; 33 736
Werdmüller, Hans Rudolf 33 736
Werefkin, Marianne (von) 4 132; 22 921; 33 77*
Werenskiold, Erik (Theodor) 23 225, 602; 33 77–9*
groups and movements 22 540; 23 226; 29 78
pupils 9 750; 29 15
works 33 78
Werfel, K. 25 407
Werfen 2 822
Werff, Adriaen van der 22 846, 846, 910; 33 79–80*
patrons and collectors 4 305; 7 778; 9 460; 11 170; 12 620; 14 652; 22 846; 27 271; 33 280
reproductive prints by others 6 547
teachers 22 720
works 1 664; 11 457; 33 80
Werff, Maria van der 22 846
Werff, Pieter van der 33 80
Wergant, Fortunato see BERGANT, FORTUNAT
Wergeland, Henrik 22 540
Wergman, P. C. 23 231
Werinher, Master 23 659
Werk: Schweizerische Zeitschrift für Baukunst, Gewerbe, Malerei und Plastik, Das 24 453; 27 214
Werkman, Hendrik Nicolaas 22 854; 33 80–81*
Werkring 21 796
Werkstätten für Handwerkskunst 21 780
Werl, Hans 22 302; 30 35; 33 81*, 274
Werl, Heinrich of see HEINRICH OF WERL
Werle, Georg 13 277
Wermuth, Christian 20 923; 33 81*
Werneck, Residenz 23 3, 4
Werner, Alfred 17 583
Werner, Anton (Alexander) von 28 343; 33 82*
assistants 29 578
groups and movements 3 800; 32 244
works 12 394
Werner, August Teodor 20 186
Werner, Caspar 7 441
Werner, Christopher 1 422
Werner, F. B.
works 23 425
Werner, Fritz 21 142
Werner, Hans 3 428
Werner, Heinz 21 67
Werner, Jean-Charles 11 753
Werner, Johan, I (b c. 1600-56) 33 81*
Werner, Johan, II (b c. 1630-91) 33 81–2*
Werner, Joseph, I (fl 1637; d 1675) 33 82
Werner, Joseph, II (1637-1710) 3 823; 12 478; 20 894; 22 308; 33 82, 82–3*
pupils 14 834; 29 644; 32 883
works 3 798; 12 390; 21 641
Werner, Samuel 29 750
Werner, Selmer 32 511
Werner, Sidse 8 750
Werner, Theodor 2 545; 3 803; 12 397; 33 83*
Werner, Woty 12 468
Werner, Zacharias 22 704
Wernher, Bishop of Strasbourg (reg 1002-28) 29 753
Wernher, Provost (fl c. 1181) 31 499
Wernher, Alice Sedgwick 33 84
Wernher, Anastasia (Zia) 33 84
Wernher, Harold Augustus 33 84
Wernher, Julius 33 84*
Wernwag, Lewis 4 802
Wersin, Wolfgang von 12 822; 28 126; 33 84*
Wertheim, Wilhelm 21 311
Wertheimer, Samson 27 224
Wertheimstein (family) 2 829
Wertinger, Hans 22 302; 33 84–6*
works 11 455; 19 107; 33 85
Wertmann, Friedrich 13 727
Wertmüller, Adolf Ulric 4 391; 30 79; 33 86*
patrons and collectors 4 555; 30 524
Werve, Claus de see CLAUS DE WERVE
Wéry, Emile-Auguste 33 86–7*
Weschke, Karl 27 563
Weschler, Adam A., & Son 32 890
Wesdorp, Bob 28 103
Wesel 13 91; 23 354; 24 388, 389
Rathaus 3 40
Wesel, Adriaen van 33 87*
works 13 114, 114; 22 856, 856
Wesel, Andries van see VESALIUS, ANDREAS
Wesel, Herman Wynrich van 33 186
Wesenberg, Jakub 25 121
Weser Renaissance 33 87–8*
Wesley, St Peter 23 53
Wesley, Charles 7 216
Wesley, John (1703-91) 7 216; 23 193
Wesley, John (b 1928) 25 232
Wespelaar Château 12 836
Wespin, Giovanni de see WESPIN, JEAN DE
Wespin, Guillaume de 33 88
Wespin, Jean de 22 81; 27 499; 31 899; 33 88
Wespin, Nicolas de 33 88
Wessel, Henry 23 37
Wessel, Jakub 19 497; 25 841
Wessel, Klaus 10 213
Wesselmann, Tom 33 89*
dealers 16 906
groups and movements 25 232
patrons and collectors 23 7
works 2 617; 10 482; 12 296; 18 719; 23 297
Wessem Church 22 817
Wessén, Natanael 33 89*
Wessex culture 5 292
Wessing, Koen 33 90*
Wessler, Hans 12 439; 23 313
Wessobrun, Diemud of see DIEMUD OF WESSOBRUN
Wessobrunn 12 403
Abbey Church 29 838
Wessobrunn school 28 129
West, Bishop of Ely 10 168
West, Alick 2 553
West, Benjamin 10 361; 14 585; 19 620; 24 599; 26 467; 33 90–94*
assistants 9 395; 24 637; 29 804; 31 139
dealing 7 437
frames 11 429, 429
groups and movements 22 740; 26 737
lithographs 19 483
paintings 31 600
conversation pieces 7 786, 787
history 3 389; 4 601; 7 787; 9 31; 10 250; 11 785; 14 586; 26 53; 33 92
literary themes 4 607
religious 33 93
patrons and collectors
Baring, Francis (1740-1810) 3 239
Boydell, John 10 369
Clive, Robert, 1st Baron Clive 7 437
George III, King of Great Britain (reg 1760-1820) 14 144
Grosvenor, Hugh Richard Arthur, 2nd Duke of Westminster 1 496
Grosvenor, Richard, 1st Earl Grosvenor (1731-1802) 13 696
Hope, Thomas 14 744
Leicester, John Fleming, Baron de Tabley 19 98
Macklin, Thomas 20 26
Neeld, Joseph 22 719
personal collection 9 229; 10 146; 18 895
pupils
Brown, Mather 4 882
Delamotte, William (Alfred) (1775-1863) 8 652
Downman, John 9 205
Earl, Ralph 9 504
Farington, George 10 807
King, Charles Bird 18 64
Morse, Samuel F(inley) B(reese) 22 149
Peale, Charles Willson 24 301
Pratt, Matthew 25 452
Ramberg, Johann Heinrich 25 871
Sargent, Henry 27 839
Trumbull, John 31 391
reproductive prints by others
Anderson, Alexander 2 4
Basire, (John) James, I (1730-1802) 3 329
Cheesman, Thomas 6 528
Clemens, Johan Frederik 7 410
Green, Valentine 13 614; 21 417
West, Benjamin
reproductive prints by others—cont.
Hall, John (1739-97) 14 79
Heath, Charles (i) (1785-1848) 14 280
Heath, James 14 280
Moses, Henry 26 231
Periam, George August 24 418
Sharp, William 28 558
Smith, John Raphael 28 882
Strange, Robert 10 393; 29 747
Woollett, William 4 607; 10 393; 26 230; 33 372
sculpture 7 480
teachers 33 206
West, Francis (?1749-1809) 22 199
West, Francis Robert 28 573
West, Franz (b 1946) 2 804
West, Hans 8 758
West, I. 22 585
West, James (1704-72) 4 845; 14 810; 30 727; 33 94*
West, James, & Son 16 32
West, James G. (fl 1928-33) 16 39
West, John 15 164
West, Margaret 2 766; 33 94*
West, Raphael Lamar 33 90
West, (Walter) Richard 14 538; 22 595; 33 94–5*
West, Robert 16 25, 37; 33 95*
pupils 3 276; 5 216; 14 110; 24 548
works 9 317; 16 24; 29 837
West, William 4 692
West, William Cornwallis 32 791
West Africa Portland Cement 1 319
Westall, Richard 14 147, 280, 744; 18 150; 19 271; 26 541; 33 95*
Westall, William 2 743; 7 789; 25 592; 26 76; 33 95
West bond see under BONDING
Westbroek 22 855
West Bromwich Manor House (Hereford & Worcs) 30 909
Westbury (Wilts)
hill-figure 14 544
Westbury Court 33 199
West Dean Tapestry Studio 10 352; 30 309
Westenak, Adriek 22 884
Westenberg, Pieter George 17 825; 21 58
Westerbaen, Jacob 14 39
Westerbaen, Jan (Jansz.) 14 140
Westerdahl, Eduardo 11 886; 30 22
Westerholm, Victor (Axel) 11 95, 96; 33 95–6*
Westerhout, Arnold van 7 569; 11 770
Westerik, Co 14 43; 22 852, 854; 33 96*
Westerlo Church 13 110
Westermann, H(orace) C(lifford) 6 576; 33 96–7*
works 33 97
Western Central Asia see CENTRAL ASIA, WESTERN
Western Chalukyas see CHALUKYAS OF KALYANA
Westerndorf 27 107
Western Equatoria see under AFRICA → regions
Western Ganga 33 97*
Western Ganga calendar see under INDIAN SUBCONTINENT → calendars
western kufic script see SCRIPTS → types → New Abbasid style
Western New Guinea see IRIAN JAYA
Western Sahara 1 214, 376; 33 97–8*
Western Samoa 27 683
Western Tombs see under YI XIAN
Western Wei period see under CHINA → periods
Westervelt, Abraham van 18 39; 19 496; 25 841
Westervoorde, W. J. van see WITSEN, WILLEM (ARNOLD)
Westfalen, Arnold von see ARNOLD VON WESTFALEN
Westfäling von Meissen see ARNOLD VON WESTFALEN
Westfälische Expressionisten 10 695
West Firle (E. Sussex), St Peter 4 692
Westgate (Kent) 5 173
West Haddon (Northants), All Saints 26 613
West Harling (Norfolk) 4 692
Westhoff, Clara 26 394
Westin, Fredric 33 98*
patrons and collectors 17 814; 30 79
pupils 25 11; 33 697
West Indies 32 240
see also CARIBBEAN ISLANDS; ANTILLES
Westinghouse 15 824; 19 538
West Irian see IRIAN JAYA
West Jersey Society 8 88
West Kennet (Wilts) 25 470, 508
passage tomb 25 508
West Lafayette (IN), Purdue University
Hall of Music 7 687
Westlake, Nathaniel 18 882; 29 514
Westley, John (d c. 1644) 5 511
Westley, John (1702-69) 17 476
West Lothian Glassworks 28 260
Westmacott, Charles Molloy 8 217
Westmacott, F. A. 33 515
Westmacott, George 33 98, 100
Westmacott, Henry 33 98, 100*
Westmacott, James Sherwood 33 98, 100
Westmacott, Richard (i) (1747-1808) 33 98–9*
works 16 24
Westmacott, Richard (ii) (1775-1856) 15 821; 33 98, 99–101*
assistants 5 740; 32 911
collaboration 33 100, 101
patrons and collectors 7 541; 27 357; 28 908
works 5 751; 10 265; 19 599, 600; 29 565; 31 130; 33 100, 448
Westmacott, Richard (iii) (1799-1872) 33 98, 101*
Westmacott Ephebe 25 179
Westman, Carl 13 31; 25 376; 30 74, 96
West Mexico 21 177, 178, 196–7, 200, 203–4; 33 101–4*
architecture 21 216*; 33 101, 102*
Classic (c. AD 250-c. 900) 21 216–17*
Pre-Classic (c. 2000 BC-c. AD 250) 21 216*
ceramics 33 102, 102–3
clay 33 102
figurines 21 196, 236; 33 102, 102
funerary objects 33 103
iconography 33 103
metalwork 33 103
obsidian 21 718
pottery 21 236, 237
rock art 33 103
sculpture 33 103, 103
shaft tombs 21 216*; 33 101, 102
shells 33 103
slate 21 718
stelae 33 101
stone 33 103
turquoise 33 103
Westminster, Hugh Grosvenor, 1st Duke of see GROSVENOR, HUGH LUPUS, 1st Duke of Westminster

Westminster, Hugh Richard Arthur Grosvenor, 2nd Duke of *see* GROSVENOR, HUGH RICHARD ARTHUR, 2nd Duke of Westminster
Westminster, Richard Grosvenor, Earl of Grosvenor and Duke of *see* GROSVENOR, RICHARD, 1st Earl of Grosvenor & Duke of Westminster
Westminster, Robert Grosvenor, 1st Marquess of *see* GROSVENOR, ROBERT, 2nd Earl of Grosvenor and 1st Marquess of Westminster
Westminster, Thomas of *see* THOMAS OF WESTMINSTER
Westminster Abbey *see under* LONDON → ecclesiastical buildings
Westminster Chasuble 13 196
Westminster Psalter *see under* PSALTERS → individual manuscripts
Westminster Retable *see under* LONDON → ecclesiastical buildings → Westminster Abbey
West New Guinea *see* IRIAN JAYA
West of Scotland Cabinet Factory 28 255
Weston, Brett 13 710
Weston, Edward (Henry) 33 104–5*
groups and movements 13 710
patrons and collectors 2 384; 20 142
pupils 21 788
works 24 676, X; 33 *105*
Weston, Richard (*fl c.* 1524-41) 8 44; 10 273
Weston, Richard, 1st Earl of Portland (1557-1635) 12 340; 33 231
Weston, Thomas 4 34
Westover (VA) 31 *590*
West Pakistan University of Engineering and Technology *see under* LAHORE
West Pans Pottery 28 258
Westphalen, Friedrich Wilhelm von, Bishop of Hildesheim 33 49
Westphalia, Guda of *see* GUDA OF WESTPHALIA
Westra, Ans 33 106*
Westreenen van Tiellandt, Willem Hendrik Jacob, Baron van 21 39; 33 106*
West Slope ware *see under* POTTERY → wares
West Stow Hall (Suffolk) 14 73
Westwerk *see* WESTWORKS
Westwood (CA), Armand Hammer Museum of Art and Culture 14 117
Westwood, P. J. 10 173
Westwood, Vivienne 9 294
westworks 33 106–9*
Carolingian 5 795, *795*; 7 264–5; 12 363; 33 *107*
Germany 12 363; 19 697; 26 574; 33 *107*, *108*
Netherlands, the 33 *109*
Ottonian 33 *108*
Romanesque 26 569, 574; 33 *109*
see also CHURCHES
West Wycombe Park (Bucks) 4 413; 8 533; 10 277, 278
paintings 8 533; 20 496
Wet, Gerrit de 33 110
Wet, Jacob (Willemsz.) de, I (1610-71) 33 110*
collaboration 21 827
pupils 3 760; 25 369; 32 270
teachers 26 153
Wet, Jacob (Jacobsz.) de, II (1640-97) 28 234, 246; 33 110
Wet, Jan de 33 110
wet collodion process *see under* PHOTOGRAPHY → processes
Wetherill Mesa 21 174
Wethersfield (CT) 31 623
wet inlay lacquer *see under* LACQUER → types
Wetmore, August 10 669
Wetmore, Charles D. 32 866
Wetmore, James A. 4 475
wet-plate process *see* PHOTOGRAPHY → processes → collodion process
Wetschel, Jan 6 363
Wettenhausen, Mariä Himmelfahrt 23 887
Wettenhausen Altarpiece 28 48
Wetter (family) 13 713
Wetter, Ottmar 2 455
Wetterau ware *see under* POTTERY → wares
Wettergren, Erik 30 98
Wetterhoff, Fredrika 11 110
Wettin (House of) 9 235; 33 *110*, 110*
architecture 12 471; 33 36
collections 12 473
furniture 5 768
ivory-carvings 12 460
metalwork 16 900; 17 888
paintings 12 471
prints 8 114
Wettin, Adelaide, Duchess of Saxe-Meiningen *see* ADELAIDE, Duchess of Saxe-Meiningen
Wettin, Albert, Duke of Saxony *see* ALBERT, Duke of Saxony
Wettin, Albert (Casimir), Herzog von Saxe-Teschen *see* SAXE-TESCHEN, ALBERT (CASIMIR), Herzog von, Governor General of the Netherlands
Wettin, Albert, Prince of Saxe-Coburg and Gotha *see* ALBERT, Prince of Saxe-Coburg-Gotha
Wettin, Anna Amalia, Duchess of Saxe-Weimar *see* ANNA AMALIA, Duchess of Saxe-Weimar
Wettin, Augusta, Queen of Prussia and Empress of Germany *see* AUGUSTA, Empress of Germany
Wettin, Augustus I, Elector of Saxony *see* AUGUSTUS I, Elector of Saxony
Wettin, Augustus II, Elector of Saxony and King of Poland *see* AUGUSTUS II, King of Poland
Wettin, Augustus III, Elector of Saxony and King of Poland *see* AUGUSTUS III, King of Poland
Wettin, Charles Augustus, Grand Duke of Saxe-Weimar *see* CHARLES-AUGUSTUS, Grand Duke of Saxe-Weimar
Wettin, Charles Frederick, Grand Duke of Saxe-Weimar *see* CHARLES FREDERICK, Grand Duke of Saxe-Weimar
Wettin, Christian I, Elector of Saxony *see* CHRISTIAN I, Elector of Saxony
Wettin, Christian II, Elector of Saxony *see* CHRISTIAN II, Elector of Saxony
Wettin, Christina, Queen of Denmark *see* CHRISTINA OF SAXONY, Queen of Denmark
Wettin, Ernest, Duke of Saxe-Gotha-Altenburg *see* ERNEST, Duke of Saxe-Gotha-Altenburg
Wettin, Ernest, Elector of Saxony *see* ERNEST, Elector of Saxony
Wettin, Ernest Augustus, Duke of Saxe-Weimar *see* ERNEST AUGUSTUS, Duke of Saxe-Weimar
Wettin, Ernest I, Duke of Saxe-Coburg and Gotha *see* ERNEST I, Duke of Saxe-Coburg and Gotha
Wettin, Ferdinand II, King of Portugal *see* FERDINAND II, King of Portugal
Wettin, Ferdinand, Prince of Saxe-Coburg-Saalfeld *see* SAXE-COBURG-SAALFELD, FERDINAND, Prince of
Wettin, Francis, Duke of Saxe-Coburg-Saalfeld *see* FRANCIS, Duke of Saxe-Coburg-Saalfeld
Wettin, Francis Xavier, Prince, Regent of Saxony 3 678
Wettin, Frederick-Augustus I, Elector of Saxony *see* AUGUSTUS II, King of Poland
Wettin, Frederick Augustus II, Elector of Saxony *see* AUGUSTUS III, King of Poland
Wettin, Frederick-Augustus III, Elector of Saxony *see* FREDERICK-AUGUSTUS I, King of Saxony
Wettin, Frederick III, Elector of Saxony *see* FREDERICK III, Elector of Saxony
Wettin, George, Duke of Saxony *see* GEORGE, Duke of Saxony
Wettin, George, Margrave of Meissen *see* GEORGE, Duke of Saxony
Wettin, George II, Duke of Saxe-Meiningen *see* GEORGE II, Duke of Saxe-Meiningen
Wettin, Henry, Duke of Saxony *see* HENRY, Duke of Saxony
Wettin, John, Duke of Saxe-Weimar *see* JOHN, Duke of Saxe-Weimar
Wettin, John, Elector of Saxony *see* JOHN, Elector of Saxony
Wettin, John Frederick, Elector of Saxony *see* JOHN-FREDERICK, Elector of Saxony
Wettin, John-George I, Elector of Saxony *see* JOHN-GEORGE I, Elector of Saxony
Wettin, John-George III, Elector of Saxony *see* JOHN-GEORGE III, Elector of Saxony
Wettin, Julius Franz, Herzog von Saxe-Lauenburg *see* SAXE-LAUENBURG, JULIUS FRANZ, Herzog von
Wettin, Leopold I, King of Belgium *see* LEOPOLD I, King of Belgium
Wettin, Leopold II, King of Belgium *see* LEOPOLD II, King of Belgium
Wettin, Maria Amalia, Queen of Spain, *see* MARIA AMALIA, Queen of Naples and Spain
Wettin, Maurice, Elector of Saxony *see* MAURICE, Elector of Saxony
Wettin, Sophie, Electress of Saxony *see* SOPHIE, Electress of Saxony
Wettin, William, Duke of Saxe-Weimar *see* WILLIAM, Duke of Saxe-Weimar
Wettingen
bridge 4 802
Monastery 30 142
Wetwang Slack 6 160
Wetzel, Heinz 4 309; 28 126
Wetzel, Johann Jakob 7 896
Wetzlar, Cathedral of St Maria 14 81
Weusi Nyumba Ya Sanaa 1 445; 23 49
Wewerka, Stefan 14 48; 27 215; 30 391
Wewoke, Maynard *see* VEWICKE, MAYNARD
Wex, Marianne 10 879
Wexford
churches 16 11
memorial to the rebellion of 1798 16 21
pottery 16 28
Weyarn
monastery church 12 370; 32 822
Pfarrkirche St Peter und Paul 26 498
sculpture 13 *851*
Weyde, Henry Van der 19 424
Weyden 27 99
Weyden, Goswijn van der 2 206; 3 554; 33 128–30*
teachers 33 117
works 11 *442*; 33 *129*
Weyden, H. 18 46
Weyden, Pieter van der 20 711; 33 117
Weyden, Rogier van der (*c.* 1399-*d* 1464) 5 548; 8 524; 11 3; 20 711; 26 765; 31 218; 33 117–27*
attributions 4 113, 692; 5 127, 656; 6 565; 17 454; 19 340; 20 747; 29 763
collaboration 8 662; 29 691
copies 2 278
frames 11 439
groups and movements 26 184, 186
methods 12 501, 803; 20 672; 24 492; 25 281
miniatures (manuscript illumination) 5 *211*
paintings 2 339; 3 553, 568; 4 920; 5 884; 20 671; 29 665
altarpieces 1 710; 9 4; 19 530; 31 344, 881; 33 *119*, *122*
grisaille 13 674, 675
justice scenes 17 700
portraits 25 286; 33 *124*, *125*
religious 9 270; 22 862, *863*; 33 *121*, *123*
patrons and collectors 2 178; 3 612
Aders, Carl 1 154
Alfonso I, King of Naples (*reg* 1435-58) 2 276; 7 543; 16 658
Boisserée, Melchior and Sulpiz 4 242
Borbón y Braganza, Sebastián Gabriel 4 379
Chevrot, Jean, Bishop of Tournai 6 565
Ertborn, Florent (Joseph) van 10 491
Este (i) (family) 16 658
Huntington, Arabella D(uval) 15 29
Johnson, John G(raver) (1841-1917) 17 619
Lionello, 13th Marchese of Ferrara (*reg* 1441-50) 10 519
Mary of Hungary, Regent of the Netherlands (1505-58) 13 909
National Gallery (London) 8 571
Nicholas I, Emperor of Russia (*reg* 1825-55) 26 734
Pesaro, Alessandro Sforza, Lord of 28 530
Philip II, King of Spain (*reg* 1556-98) 10 503; 13 922
Philip the Good, 3rd Duke of Burgundy (*reg* 1419- 67) 5 210
Ram, Giovanni 12 676
Rolin, Nicolas 3 612; 14 784; 26 555
Ryerson, Martin A(ntoine) 27 463
Solly, Edward 29 46
William I, King of the Netherlands (*reg* 1813-40) 23 469
Weyden, Rogier van der (*c.* 1399-*d* 1464)
patrons and collectors—cont.
William II, King of the Netherlands (*reg* 1840-49) 23 470
pupils 5 43, 127; 21 101; 28 531
reproductions in tapestry 5 46
reproductive prints by others 7 899; 20 622
restorations by others 27 321
sculpture 12 354
tapestries 7 543
teachers 10 713; 20 671
Weyden, Rogier van der (*fl* 1528-37) 33 127
Weydmann, Hans 10 662
Weyen, Herman 19 154; 24 890
Weyer, Gabriel 12 168; 33 130–31*
works 33 *130*
Weyer, Jacob (Matthias) 12 390; 19 783
Weyerman, Jacob Campo 17 920; 22 910; 30 730; 33 131*
Weyerstall, Albert 31 310
Weygand 4 864
Weyhe, Bernhard Heinrich 12 447
Weyhe, Clemens 19 156
Weymouth Regatta Cup 10 334
Weyr, Rudolf (von) 2 802; 31 401; 32 456; 33 131–2*
Weyrer, Stephan 10 220; 23 204, 205
Weyrother-Mohr-Piepenhagen, Charlotte 24 747
Weyssenburger, Johann 33 85
WG, Master 20 804*
whalebone *see* BALEEN
whale teeth *see under* TEETH → types
Whall, Christopher (Whitworth) 29 497, 507; 33 132*
assistants 31 229
works 12 820
Whall, Veronica 33 132
Whalley, Peter 30 890
Whalley (Lancs), St Mary's 24 577
wharfs *see* DOCKS
Wharncliffe, Edward Montagu Stuart Granville, 3rd Baron and 1st Earl of *see* GRANVILLE, EDWARD MONTAGU STUART
Wharncliffe Hours *see under* BOOKS OF HOURS → individual manuscripts
Wharncliffe viaduct 32 398, *399*
Wharton (i) (family) 32 824
Wharton (ii) (family) 1 184
Wharton, Edith 7 514; 31 680; 33 132*
Whately, Thomas 12 123, 130; 22 202; 33 132–3*
Whatman, James 2 333; 24 50; 30 6
whatnots *see under* TABLES → types
Wheatley (Oxon) 23 684
Wheatley, Francis 10 807; 28 614; 33 133–4*
collaboration 22 153
reproductive prints by others 5 733; 7 579; 14 280; 18 149; 28 86; 29 675, 676; 32 156
teachers 10 372
works 4 601; 7 785; 10 249, 786; 12 293, *293*; 16 15; 33 *133*
wheat starch 16 356; 30 558
Wheatstone, Charles 7 403; 24 651, 657; 33 134*
Wheel carpets *see under* CARPETS → types
wheeled chests *see under* CHESTS → types
wheel engraving *see under* ENGRAVING → types
Wheeler, Candace (Thurber) 15 408; 30 868; 31 657; 33 134*
collaboration 7 577
groups and movements 31 621

Wheeler, Charles 3 82
Wheeler, Douglas 10 416; 19 702
Wheeler, Edward Todd 24 457
Wheeler, Gervase 33 134–5*
Wheeler, John 2 318
Wheeler, (Robert Eric) Mortimer 2 299; 33 135*
excavations 14 162; 20 116
methods 2 300, 301, *303*
pupils 33 465
Wheeler, Orson 5 571
Wheeler, Samuel 31 652
Wheeler, William 28 256
wheel fittings 27 91–2*
wheellocks *see under* GUNS → types
Wheelock, Morton 31 652
wheels 15 193; 25 547
see also BICYCLE WHEELS; POTTERS' WHEELS; PRAYER WHEELS; SPINNING WHEELS
Wheelwright, Edmund M(arch) 20 93; 33 135–6*
Wheelwright, Haven & Hoyt 33 135
Wheelwright & Haven 4 474; 29 382; 33 135
Whelan, Edward 23 600
Whelan, Leo 16 17
Wheler, George 13 608; 33 136*
whelks 9 664
Where We At 26 410
Whessell, John 29 677
Whetenhall, Catherine 18 814
Whethamstede, John, Abbot of St Albans 18 687; 27 528
Whetmore, Charles D.
works 7 *470*
whetstones 30 *45*
Whewell, William 31 284
Whidden, William M(arcy) 33 136*
Whidden & Lewis 33 136*
Whieldon, Thomas 29 495; 33 136–7*
assistants 33 341
collaboration 10 306; 33 20
pupils 29 419
works 10 306, 308
Whin House 2 148
Whipple, John Adams 24 669
Whipsnade Zoo 33 699
Whirlwind 19 589
whisks 17 *341*
Africa 10 779
Asante 1 354
Baule 3 407
Indian subcontinent 10 778
Japan 17 341
Whisler, Francis 8 184
Whistler, Hector 2 154
Whistler, James (Abbott) McNeill 6 499; 10 254; 19 588; 22 51; 24 364; 29 368; 31 603; 32 197; 33 137–44*
collaboration 20 603; 25 628
dealers 4 589; 18 161; 26 107
decorative works 10 283
drawings 9 225
education (art) 22 252
exhibitions 9 19
frames 11 376, 416, 433, *433*, 435
groups and movements 1 181; 26 57
Aesthetic Movement 1 170; 2 530; 10 254; 19 588
Formalism 11 315
Queen Anne Revival 25 805
Société des Trois 19 90
Tonalism 31 141
World of Art (Mir Iskusstva) 33 379
XX, Les 11 83; 32 591
house 10 238; 12 840; 26 360
interior decoration 9 29; 17 467; 22 331
methods 10 556
Whistler, James (Abbott) McNeill—cont.
paintings 10 254; 12 296; 19 588; 22 379; 30 123; 31 141, 156; 33 *138*
portraits 11 774; 33 *139*, *141*, 180
paper 25 597
patrons and collectors 12 779; 20 201, 351; 24 638; 26 107; 28 273, 569; 32 794, 890
Burty, Philippe 5 284
Freer, Charles Lang 11 748
Gallatin, A(lbert) E(ugene) 12 15
Hunterian Museum and Art Gallery, Glasgow 12 777
Ionides, Aleco 15 895
Ionides, Alexander Constantine 15 894
Leyland, F(rederick) R(ichard) 1 171; 9 29; 15 868; 19 290–91
Lucas, George A(loysius) 19 756
Montesquiou (-Fezensac), Robert, Comte de (1855-1921) 22 22
Palmer, Bertha Honoré 23 882
Phillip, John (1817-67) 24 636
Pope, Alfred Atmore 25 234
Whitney, John Hay 33 150, 151
Wilde, Oscar (Fingal O'Flahertie Wills) 33 180
periodicals 4 42
personal collection 10 312; 17 440, 898
prints 9 204; 25 599, 600
drypoints 9 309
etchings 9 468; 10 555; 25 607; 33 *140*
lithographs 19 488; 20 602; 25 624, 628
pupils 2 700
Benois, Alexandre 3 734
Czajkowski, Józef 8 370
Greaves, Walter 13 337
John, Gwen(dolen Mary) 17 607
Menpes, Mortimer 21 138
Ostroumova-Lebedeva, Anna (Petrovna) 23 624
Roussel, Theodore (Casimir) (1847-1926) 27 269
Sickert, Walter Richard 28 659
Somov, Konstantin (Andreyevich) 29 61
Watson, Homer (Ransford) 32 911
studio 29 857
Whistler, Laurence 10 321; 33 145
works 10 *321*
Whistler, Rex (John) 33 145*
patrons and collectors 23 473
productions 30 687
teachers 31 146
works 4 366, 369; 5 *687*, 688; 16 892; 22 332; 28 808; 31 706; 32 502
whistles 17 399; 21 257; 24 359–60
Whitaker, Henry 33 145*
Whitaker, Richard 22 52
Whitaker, Thomas Dunham 18 721; 31 470
Whitbread (family) 21 832
Whitbread, Samuel 12 164, 646; 14 681; 26 85, 282
Whitby (N. Yorks) 10 *225*; 17 516; 33 145*
Abbey 3 708, 709; 10 227; 21 835; 22 217; 26 382; 31 273
piers (ii) (masonry) 24 751
jet 10 346; 17 514, 516
St Mary 25 727
Whitby, John 10 291
Whitchurch (Dyfed), St Marcella tomb of John Salisbury 1 520
Whitcombe & Priestley 12 649
white *see under* PIGMENTS → types
White, Alfred (*fl c.* 1870-1910; cabinet-maker) 23 66
White, Alfred T. (1846-1921; philanthropist) 30 458
White, Canvas 7 693
White, C. & H. 31 260
White, Charles 1 442
White, Clarence H(udson) 33 146*
groups and movements 7 491; 24 688, 739
pupils 4 918; 12 647; 18 738; 31 570
White, D. T. 4 879; 33 251
White, Edward 8 207
White, Elizabeth *see* QOYAWAYMA, POLINGAYSI
White, F. M. 18 185
White, Franklin 29 683
White, Frederick, J. 33 146
White, George (*c.* 1671-1732) 21 416
White, George M. (*fl* 1982) 32 892
White, Gilbert 13 664
White, Henry 25 235
White, Howard Judson 13 271
White, James 33 146
White, John (*fl c.* 1585-93) 19 143; 33 146*
reproductive prints by others 5 62; 6 87; 10 389; 14 855; 22 *637*
works 2 103; 19 143; 22 *552*; 32 899
White, John (*fl* 1790s) 32 909
White, John Forbes 14 47; 28 269, 270, 271
White, Joseph, sr (1799-1870) 33 146*
works 5 581
White, Joseph, jr (1829-1875) 33 146
White, J. P. 3 74
White, Katherine 1 439
White, Katherine, Collection of African Art *see under* SEATTLE (WA) → Art Museum
White, (Anna) Lois 28 888; 33 146*
White, Mark 20 889
White, Minor (Martin) 1 147; 24 434; 33 147*
assistants 5 671
pupils 5 671; 7 917; 20 912; 28 624; 31 525
works 24 678, *679*
White, Robert 33 147*
teachers 19 540
works 18 144; 23 690; 30 892
White, Robin 33 148*
White, Stanford 20 15–20*
collaboration 25 237; 26 339; 27 557
works 8 841; 11 498, *498*; 14 452; 24 281, *281*
White, Stillman 4 481
White, Thomas (*c.* 1674-1748) 31 239
White, Thomas (1736-1811) 33 20
White, William 33 148*
assistants 19 109
groups and movements 10 237, 238
teachers 28 279
works 28 157, 295
White, William Charles, Bishop 7 156; 17 587; 33 148*
White Allom 22 744
White Birch Society 24 436; 33 149*, 491
white bronze *see under* ALLOYS → types
White Brothers and Woods of Perth 7 234
White Canons *see* PREMONSTRATENSIAN CANONS
White Chapel *see under* THEBES (i) (EGYPT) → temples (cult) → Temple of Amun, Karnak
White crosslined ware *see under* POTTERY → wares
Whiteface/Frignano Painter 13 531
Whitefield, Edwin 4 81, 82
Whitefield, George 21 347; 23 193
Whitefriars Glass Ltd 19 595; 25 399
Whitefriars Glass Works 10 320, 321; 24 57; 25 398
white gold *see* ELECTRUM
White-ground pottery *see under* POTTERY → wares
Whitehead, David, & Sons 20 161
Whitehead, John 1 675; 23 453; 25 293; 33 149*
White Heron Group 23 146
Whitehill *see* NEWHAILES
White Hmong 30 624
Whitehorse, Emmi 22 599
white horses *see* HILL-FIGURES
White Horse Society *see* HAKUBAKAI
White House *see under* WASHINGTON (DC)
Whitehouse, David 16 400
Whitehouse, Peter 18 640
White House glassworks 33 13
White Inscriptions, Master of the 20 631
white lead
historical and regional traditions
Greece, ancient 23 141
Italy 7 318
Netherlands, the 24 797
uses
cliché-verre 7 432
etchings 10 560
grounds 13 708; 25 174
lacquer 18 600
paints 31 282
pigments 24 53, 789, 795, 797*; 30 426, 427
secco paintings 28 338
wallpaper 32 811
Whiteleaf Cross 14 544
Whiteley, Brett 2 751, 762; 33 149*
Whiteley, William 26 316
white-line engravings *see under* ENGRAVINGS → types
white-line woodcuts *see under* WOODCUTS → types
White Marmorean Flock 19 286
white metal *see* ALLOYS → types → Britannia metal
White Monastery *see under* SOHAG
white mountain cherry 17 274
White Mountain Redware *see under* POTTERY → wares
White Obelisk 21 298
White-on-dark ware *see under* POTTERY → wares
White Painted ware *see* POTTERY → wares
Whiteread, Rachel 10 882
White Saccos Painter 13 530; 32 33
works 13 *529*
White Scrolls, Master of the 20 413
White Shaved ware *see under* POTTERY → wares
White Slip ware *see under* POTTERY → wares
White Society (Baishe) 24 21
white spirit 5 35; 29 53
White Stag group 16 18
White Sulphur Springs (WV), Greenbrier Hotel 14 787
White Ware 30 182
whiteware porcelain *see under* PORCELAIN → wares
Whiteway, W. T. 5 562
Whiteway and Laidlaw 15 693
whitework *see under* EMBROIDERY → types
Whitfield, Edwin
works 31 *175*
Whitfield, William, & Partners 3 532; 27 527
Whithorn Priory (Dumfries & Galloway) 26 617
Whiting, Cliff 20 359; 33 150*
Whiting, Margaret C. 31 658
Whitland Abbey (Dyfed) 32 781
Whitleigh, Gilbert of *see* GILBERT OF WHITLEIGH
Whitley *Madonna* 7 336
Whitman, Robert 10 416; 24 407
Whitman, Thomas 28 525
Whitman, Walt 11 840
Whitmore, George 7 850
Whitmore, Michael 5 580
Whitney, Anne 6 176; 19 286; 31 611; 33 151*
Whitney, Geoffrey 25 246
Whitney, George (*fl* 1875-84; collector) 26 336
Whitney, George B. (*fl* 1883-5; engineer) 6 573; 17 477
Whitney, Gertrude Vanderbilt 23 48; 31 663; 33 150*
collections 31 665, 668
paintings 27 360
periodicals 24 432
Whitney, James 10 688
Whitney, John 10 688
Whitney, John Hay 29 605; 33 150–51*
Whitney, William 18 627
Whitney Museum of American Art *see under* NEW YORK → museums
Whittemore, Harris 25 234
Whittemore, John Howard 25 234
Whittemore, Thomas 33 151*
Whittingham, Charles, I (1767-1840) 33 152*
Whittingham, Charles, II (1795-1876) 33 152*
Whittle 9 506
Whittle, James 25 626
Whittlesey, Austin 19 700
works 19 *700*
Whittlesey, Julian 20 890
Whittlesford Church (Warwicks) 10 476
Whittock, Nathaniel 4 81
Whitton Place (Middx) 8 587
Whittredge, (Thomas) Worthington 33 152–3*, 185
groups and movements 14 843
sponsors 19 259
works 33 185
Whitty, Samuel Rampson 2 877
Whitty, Thomas (*d* 1792) 2 877; 5 838, 839, 840; 10 358
Whitty, Thomas (1740-99) 2 877
Whitty, Thomas (1775-1810) 2 877
Whitworth, Joseph 20 239
whorls *see* WEIGHTS
Whymper, Josiah Wood 32 794
Whympers 17 877
Whyte, Samuel 22 199
Whythorne, Thomas 25 277, 278
Whytock, Richard 5 840; 28 248
Whytock & Reid 9 727; 28 250, 256
Wiach, Oscar 2 826
Wibald of Stavelot, Abbot 33 153*
enamel 26 692–3
manuscripts 26 660
metalwork 26 683
reliquaries 26 144, 146
Wibaut, F. M. 1 803; 17 910
Wibert, Master 26 685, 686
Wibert, Prior 5 643, 646
Wiblingen Monastery 12 369, 372
Wibyholm Castle 24 21; 30 69
Wicander, August Hjalmar 14 80
Wicar, Jean-Baptiste (-Joseph) 8 772; 19 381; 33 153–4*
collections 8 901
drawings 18 895; 33 345
engravings 6 77

Wicar, Jean-Baptiste (-Joseph)—cont.
patrons and collectors **2** 514; **31** 172
personal collection **9** 229; **23** 634
teachers **8** 556
writings **20** 585
Wich, Carl Heinrich **23** 312
Wich, Johann Christian **23** 312
Wichayen, Chao Phraya *see* PHAULKON, CONSTANTIN
Wicheren, Johan Joeke Gabriel van **16** 573
Wichert, Fritz **12** 476; **21** 407
Wichita **22** 551
Wichman, Erich **22** 852; **33** 154*
Wichmann, Karl **28** 45; **33** 154
Wichmann, Ludwig (Wilhelm) **33** 154–5*
collaboration **26** 22; **28** 98
pupils **3** 497; **28** 91
teachers **28** 45
works **22** 47
Wichterlová, Hana **8** 387
Wiciński, Henryk **18** 433, 434
Wick, Johann Jacob **30** 154
Wicka, P. **25** 100
Wickel, Niclas **23** 314
Wickenberg, Per **30** 79
Wickenburg, Alfred **2** 797
wicker **6** 261, 262, 311; **15** *822*; **16** 507; **22** 663; **30** 775; **31** 629, 684; **33** 155–8*
Wicker, Jacob **9** 505
Wickes, David **10** 398
Wickes, George **10** 329, 332; **12** 163; **19** 593; **33** 158*
patrons and collectors **14** 143
works **10** 332; **29** 432
Wickey, Harry **4** 826
Wickham, John **4** 818; **24** 208
Wickhoff, Franz **2** 532, 833; **12** 483; **33** 158–9*
pupils **2** 834; **18** 187; **26** 531; **28** 114; **30** 867
works **15** 134
Wick-Kmoch, A. **28** 917
Wickramsinghe, Turnour **29** 456
wicks **5** 610
Wicks, Mary **28** 541
Wickstead, Philip **5** 750; **16** 889
Wickström, Hans **30** 116
Wickström, Sigrid **22** 540
Widdicomb **13** 297; **31** 632
Widdowson, J. **4** 541
Widekum **10** 122, 124
Widener (family) **24** 600; **25** 19
Widener, Joseph E. **31** 668; **33** 159*
collections **12** 474; **32** 890
paintings **9** 467
Widener, Peter A. B. **32** 890; **33** 159
Widener Carpet **15** 682
Widerberg, Frans **23** 227
Widerin, Peter **2** 801; **21** 84
Wideville Grotto **13** 703
Widgington, Thomas **14** 522
Widman, Georg **14** 818; **27** 285
Widman, Kristián **8** 385; **33** 159
Widman, Lazar **8** 386; **25** 33; **33** 159*
Widmann, Elias **14** 899
Widmer, Martin **28** 184
Widnmann, Max von **33** 160*
assistants **29** 721
patrons and collectors **12** 406
pupils **14** 207; **18** 527; **32** 758
works **33** 282
Widtsköfle Castle *see* VITTSKÖVLE CASTLE
Wiebenga, Jan Gerko **4** 57, 815; **22** 831
Więcek, Magdalena **33** 160*
Wiedemann, Christian **12** 371, 372
Wiedemann, Guillermo **7** 609; **33** 160–61*
Wiedemann, Josef **12** 477
Wiedenbrück, St Ägidius **11** 253
Wiedewelt, Johannes **8** 760; **31** 342; **33** 161*
patrons and collectors **16** 863
pupils **11** 779; **30** 763
reproductive prints by others **7** 410
works **1** 33; **7** 805; **8** 740; **27** 168
Wiedewelt, Just **33** 161
Wied-Neuwied, Johann Friedrich Alexander, Graf von **26** 529
Wied-Neuwied, Maximilian, Prince of (*reg* 1530-44) **4** 215; **22** 678
Wiegand, Charmion von **21** 855
Wiegand, Theodor **13** 613; **23** 891; **25** 573, 576; **27** 687
Wiegele, Franz **2** 797; **18** 204; **33** 162*
groups and movements **23** 1; **28** 88
Wiegerinck, J. **30** 15
Wiegers, Jan **22** 852, 854; **33** 162*
Wiehl, Antonín **33** 163*
collaboration **25** 151
house **1** 604
works **8** 379, 400
Wieland, Christoph Martin **12** 500; **24** 443; **33** 37, 116
Wieland, Johann Georg **9** 6; **11** 44; **12** 405; **33** 163*
Wieland, Joyce **5** 569; **10** 688; **33** 163*
Wielant, Guillaume *see* VRELANT, WILLEM (BACKER VON)
Wielant, Philip **16** 69
Wielemans, Alexander **13** 330
Wielen, Francis Adolf van der **3** 464
Wieliczka **25** 126
church **25** 126
Wieling, Nicolaas **14** 650; **30** 517
Wielki, Jan **25** 102
Wielopolski, Jan **25** 121
sideboards **25** *121*
Wiemken, Walter Kurt **13** 726
Wienecke, Johann Cornelius **33** 163*
Wiener, Doris **22** 795
Wiener, Léopold **12** 230; **20** 925
Wiener, Oswald **27** 216
Wiener, Paul Lester **4** 713; **7** 606; **23** 117; **28** 483
works **4** *713*
Wiener Altertumsverein zur Erforschung der heimischen Kunstdenkmale **24** 438
Wienerberger **25** 404
Wiener Geschichtesblätter **24** 438
Wiener Gobelin Manufaktur **2** 826
Wiener Jahrbuch für Kunstgeschichte **24** 438
Wiener Keramik **2** 816, 817; **12** 821; **19** 538; **24** 309; **25** 404; **32** 450; **33** 166
see also VEREINIGTE WIENER UND GMUNDENER KERAMIK
Wiener Kunsthefte **24** 439
Wiener Kunst im Hause **20** 152
Wiener Möbelbilder **2** 808
Wiener Möbel Journal **2** 813
Wiener Mosaik Werkstätte **11** 320; **18** 130
Wiener Neustadt **2** *776*; **9** 156; **33** 163–4*
Armoury **2** 778
Burg **2** 778
Georgskapelle **14** 420; **24** 550
Cathedral of Mariae Himmelfahrt **2** 798, 800
Liebfrauenkirche **33** 164
manuscript illumination **2** 792
Neukloster **13** 57
Wiener Neustadt, Michael of *see* MICHAEL OF WIENER NEUSTADT
Wiener Porzellanfabrik Augarten **2** 817; **32** 450
works **32** *450*
Wiener Porzellanmanufaktur *see* KAISERLICHE PORZELLANMANUFACTUR (VIENNA)
Wiener Schmidt *see* SCHMIDT, JOHANN GEORG
Wiener Sezession *see* SECESSION (VIENNA)
Wiener Verlag **19** 539
Wiener Werkbundsiedlung **22** 831
Wiener Werkstätte **2** 520, 567; **8** 825; **33** 165–6*
archives **2** 370
collections **2** 830
designers **14** 628
Baudisch, Gudrun **3** 393
Czeschka, Carl Otto **8** 428
Fellerer, Max **10** 870
Haerdtl, Oswald **14** 25
Hoffmann, Josef (Franz Maria) **14** 630
Jung, Moriz **17** 691
Jungnickel, Ludwig Heinrich **17** 692
Kalvach, Rudolf **17** 744
Klimt, Gustav **18** 130, 132
Löffler, Bertold **19** 539
Makovskaya-Luksh, Yelena (Konstantinovna) **20** 152
Moser, Kolo(man) **2** 826; **22** 187
Peche, Dagobert **24** 309; **32** 817
Powolny, Michael **25** 404
Prutscher, Otto **25** 674
production **2** 571, 803, 814; **8** 802; **32** 446
architecture **2** 567; **29** 693
ceramics **2** 816; **19** 539; **31** 640
furniture **2** 814; **6** 391
interior decoration **2** 809; **14** 628; **17** 692; **24** 309
jewellery **17** 528
lace **18** 593
metalwork **2** 822; **33** *165*
porcelain **2** 817; **32** 450
silver **2** 821
tapestries **30** 327
Wienhausen **13** 186
convent **12** 462
Wienhold, Michał **18** 430
Wierandt, Caspar Vogt von *see* VOGT VON WIERANDT, CASPAR
Wiercińska, Janina **25** 143
Wierda, Sytze Wopkes **25** 565; **29** 105; **33** 166–7*
works **25** *566*
Wieringen, Claes Cornelisz. van **13** 895; **33** 167
Wieringen, Cornelis Claesz. van **32** 734; **33** 167–8*
works **33** *168*
Wierink, Bernard Willem **33** 676
Wierix (family) **2** 195; **11** 717; **20** 455
Wierix, Anton, I (*c.* 1520/25-*c.* 1572) **33** 168*
Wierix, Anton, II (*c.* 1555/9-1604) **6** 596; **10** 389; **33** 168, 169–70*
groups and movements **9** 446
teachers **33** 168
works **3** 558; **12** 848; **29** 431; **32** 711
Wierix, Anton, III (1596-before 1635) **33** 170
Wierix, Hieronymous *see* WIERIX, JEROME
Wierix, Jan **8** 664; **10** 389; **12** 15; **25** 17; **33** 168–70*
groups and movements **9** 446
pupils **14** 709; **33** 168, 169
reproductive prints by others **14** 795
works **2** 411; **3** 558; **4** 911; **6** 596; **11** 222; **27** 502; **32** 711; **33** 168, *169*, *170*
Wierix, Jerome **10** 389; **12** 15; **33** 168, 169–70*
groups and movements **9** 446
pupils **33** 168
Wierix, Jerome—cont.
works **3** 558; **6** 596; **17** 183; **18** 177; **24** 239; **26** 301; **32** 711; **33** 168, 170
Wierts, Johan, II **17** 650
Wiertz, Antoine (Joseph) **3** 613; **31** 857; **33** 170–71*
groups and movements **26** 740
teachers **14** 480
works **3** 562; **33** *171*
Wiertz, Jupp **25** 350
Wiesbaden
Bergkirche **23** 662
Museum Wiesbaden **32** 714
Wies Church **7** 258, 277; **12** *361*, 372; **26** 497, *497*; **29** 838; **33** 172*, 683
frescoes **15** 139
Wièse, Jules **11** 622
Wieselburg, St Ulrichskirche **2** 777, 790; **23** 651
Wieselthier, Vally **12** 821; **31** 640; **32** 450
Wiesentheid Schloss **12** 411
Wieser, Ferenc **33** 172*
Wieser, Wolfgang *see* WISER, WOLFGANG
Wiesiolowski, Krzysztof **25** 131
Wiesner, Arnošt **4** 833; **8** 380, 402; **33** 172–3*
Wiesreither, Hans **22** 302
Wiet, Gaston (Louis Marie Joseph) **16** 549, 557; **33** 173*
Wiethase, Heinrich Johann **33** 173*
Wiethüchter, Gustav **1** 160
Wietrzychowice **25** 507
Wigan **10** 341
Wigand, Albert **33** 174*
Wigand, Ede Thoroczkai **14** 909; **15** 4
Wigand, Georg **26** 359
Wigand, Otto **26** 359
Wigert, Hans **30** 82
Wigge, Gilbert **5** 511
Wiggenhall (Norfolk)
St German **24** 577
St Mary **24** 577, *577*
Wiggin, J. & J. **33** 50
Wigglesworth, H. H. **20** 15
Wiggli, Oskar **30** 140
Wight, Clifford **22** 332
Wight, Peter B(onnett) **27** 137; **28** 830; **30** 505; **33** 174*
staff **5** 273
works **30** 62
Wightwick Manor (W. Midlands) **9** 29
Wight & Wight **17** 799
Wigmore Abbey (Hereford & Worcs) **32** 416
Wignacourt, Alof de, Grand Master **5** 714
wigs **1** 343
Pacific Islands **23** 721
Papua New Guinea **23** 721; **24** 75
18th cent. **9** 282–3
wig stands **7** *166*
Wigstead, Henry **27** 278
Wigström, Henrik **11** 109; **27** 584
Wiig Hansen, Svend **8** 736; **33** 174–5*
Wiik, Maria (Catharina) **33** 175*
Wiinblad, Björn **8** 749
Wiiralt, Eduard *see* VIIRALT, EDUARD
Wiitasalo, Shirley **5** 569
Wijbrandts, Gillis **1** 810
Wijck, Thomas **10** 897; **33** 175–6*
groups and movements **3** 143; **9** 462
patrons and collectors **20** 141
pupils **31** 786
teachers **23** 609
works **33** *176*
Wijdan Ali *see* ALI, WIJDAN
Wijdeveld, Hendrik T(heodorus) **22** 829; **33** 177–8*
groups and movements **1** 815; **10** 698
staff **14** 693
Wijffenbach, Rudolf **11** 224
Wijk, Rikkert **30** 15
Wijk, van **32** *585*
Wijk-bij Duurstede
Castle **22** 822
St Jan Baptistkerk **22** 819
Wijnants, Ernest **3** 573
Wijnants, Jan (*fl* 1626-42) **33** 178
Wijnants, Jan (*c.* 1635-84) **33** 178–9*
collaboration **22** 843; **32** 145
groups and movements **13** 895
patrons and collectors **12** 620; **19** 338; **28** 169
pupils **32** 144
reproductive prints by others **4** 243
works **22** 840; **33** *179*
Wijnblad, Carl **11** 91
Wijnblad, Fridolf **30** 73
Wijnen, Dominicus van **28** 92
Wijnendaele Castle **4** 161
Wijngaard, Hans van den **19** 349
works **28** *595*
Wijngaartrancken, De **13** 895
Wijngaerde, Franz van der **3** 416
Wijntgis, Melchior **24** 261
Wijntrack, Dirck **14** 602; **33** 178
Wijnveld, Barend **2** 487
Wijtman, Mattias **4** 53
Wik Castle **30** 67, *67*
Wikström, Emil **11** 100, 111
works **11** *100*
Wilanów Palace **17** 615; **25** 98, 105, 135, 138
collections **25** 139
gardens **12** 133
interior decoration **25** 118
paintings **25** 364; **28** 743
stucco **29** 839
Wilars dehonecort *see* VILLARD DE HONNECOURT
Wilaya **21** 284
Wilbaut, Jacques
works **11** *409*
Wilber, Donald **16** 548
Wilbernus **26** 684
Wilbour, Charles Edwin **10** 90, 94
Wilcolm, John **2** 578
Wilcop, de *see* VULCOP, DE
Wilcox, Edward **33** 244
Wilcox, Jonathan **33** 244
Wilcox of Birmingham **27** 878
Wilczek, Hans, Count **28** 801
Wild, Charles **7** 548; **29** 632
works **23** *687*; **30** XIV2
Wild, Hans **11** 869
Wild, James William **10** 238; **17** 639; **25** 173; **28** 157
Wild Boar **27** 46
wild cursive script *see under* SCRIPTS → types
Wilde, Bernard de **18** 62; **33** 179*
Wilde, Fred **30** 888
Wilde, Johannes **14** 901; **25** 238, 557; **33** 180*
Wilde, John De *see* DEWILDE, JOHN
Wilde, Oscar (Fingal O'Flahertie Wills) **1** 171; **8** 596; **9** 290; **33** 180–81*
groups and movements **1** 170, 181
productions **19** 428
works **10** 480; **25** 277; **26** 360
illustrated **3** 445; **4** 364; **10** 254–5
Wilde, Samuel De *see* DE WILDE, SAMUEL
Wildenberg, L. van den **28** 751
Wildenborch Castle **22** 822
Wildens, Jan **33** 181–2*
assistants **4** 218

Wildens, Jan—cont.
collaboration **3** 108; **17** 6; **27** 298; **28** 904; **32** 705, 706
reproductive prints by others **14** 709
works **18** 711; **33** *182*
Wildens, Jan Baptist **33** 181
Wildens, Jeremias **33** 181
Wildenstein (family) **2** 559; **33** 182–3*
Wildenstein, Daniel **33** 183*
Wildenstein, Georges **33** 182–3*
Wildenstein, Nathan **11** 664; **31** 664; **33** 182*
Wildenstein, Paul **4** 493
Wildenstein Altar **29** 787
Wildes, Joseph A. **10** 213
Wildey, Samuel Jackman Prescod Polytechnic **2** 154
Wildfire *see* LEWIS, (MARY) EDMONIA
Wild Goat style pottery *see under* POTTERY → wares
Wild Hawthorn Press **7** 699
Wilding, Alison **33** 183*
Wilds, Amon Henry **4** 809; **15** 407
Wildt, Adolfo **33** 183*
groups and movements **16** 708; **21** 528; **23** 264
pupils **11** 281; **21** 95
Wild West and frontier art **33** 183–5*
painting **26** *180*; **33** *184*
Wiley, William T. **19** 492; **22** 690; **27** 731; **31** 609
Wilford, Michael **12** 477; **14** 803; **22** 367; **29** 677–8, 874; **31** 735
works **29** *678*; **31** *736*
Wilfred, Abbot of Marseille **20** 475
Wilfred, Count of Barcelona (*reg* 873-98) **26** 417
Wilfred, Thomas **18** 62; **22** 380
Wilfrid, Saint **2** 65, 69, 83; **14** 501
Wilheim, Jorge **4** 714; **21** 123; **27** 808; **33** 185–6*
Wilhelm, Christian **10** 303
Wilhelm, Gottfried **32** 815
Wilhelm, Heinrich **33** 186*
Wilhelm, J. **31** 298
Wilhelm, Jean-Pierre **13** 727; **14** 620
Wilhelm, Mathias **30** 93
Wilhelm Andstén's Dutch Tile and Faience Factory **11** 105, 106
Wilhelmi & Janssen **22** 275
Wilhelmina, Grand Duchess of Hesse (*fl c.* 1815) **11** 236
Wilhelmina, Margravine of Bayreuth (1709-58) **3** 428; **12** 134, 412; **14** *648*, 649, 651*; **27** 587
Wilhelmina, Queen of the Netherlands (*reg* 1890-1948) **16** 569; **33** 163
Wilhelmina Amalia, Holy Roman Empress (1673-1742) **3** 488
Wilhelmina of Hohenzollern, Queen of the Netherlands (1774-1837) **5** 286; **24** 745; **29** 403
Wilhelmine Baroque *see* NEO-BAROQUE
Wilhelm of Cologne, Master **33** 186*
Wilhelmshaven **31** 724
Wilhelmson, Carl (Wilhelm) **14** 88; **33** 186–7*
Wilhelm von Honstein, Bishop of Strasbourg **8** 541
Wilhering Church **2** 783
Wiligelmo **13** 804; **26** 607, 621; **33** 187–8*
patrons and collectors **20** 820
pupils **25** 109
works **8** 134; **16** 687; **21** 772–3, *772*, *773*; **26** 578, 595, 619
workshop **23** 193
Wilke, Erick **9** 381
Wilke, Hannah **10** 879; **24** 409
Wilkens, M. H., & Söhne **12** 449
Wilkes, John **2** 559; **10** 368
Wilkie, David **14** 587; **19** 587; **33** 188–91*
collaboration **11** 742
dealing **14** 145; **28** 271; **33** 216
groups and movements **23** 503; **26** 740
methods **18** 899
patrons and collectors
Angerstein, John Julius **2** 51
Beaumont, George (Howland) **3** 454
George IV, King of Great Britain (*reg* 1820-30) **14** 146–7
Hawkins, John Heywood (1803-77) **14** 252
Ludwig I, King of Bavaria (*reg* 1825-48) **8** 503
Morrison, James **22** 148
Peel, Robert (1788-1850) **24** 322
Sheepshanks, John **28** 576
Victoria, Queen of Great Britain (*reg* 1837- 1901) **14** 147
Wellesley, Arthur, 1st Duke of Wellington **33** 55
Windus, B(enjamin) G(odfrey) **33** 251
reproductive prints by others **10** 378; **11** 84, 362; **13** 327; **25** 857; **26** 473
teachers **22** 531; **28** 274
works **9** 309, 725; **10** 250, 252; **12** 294; **28** 236, 237, *237*, 238; **33** *189*, *190*
Wilkin, Master **13** 161
Wilkin, Charles **33** 191*
Wilkin, Frank **33** 191
Wilkin, Henry **33** 191
Wilkins, Charles **15** 679
Wilkins, Henry St Clair **4** 288
Wilkins, Ricardo *see* KAYIGA, KOFI
Wilkins, William (i) (1751-1815) **26** 238; **33** 191
Wilkins, William (ii) (1778-1839) **33** 191–2*
competitions **10** 369
groups and movements **13** 607, 609, 610
patrons and collectors **14** 744
staff **11** 22; **12** 26
works **3** 284; **5** 287, 512; **7** 469, 567; **8** 48; **13** *610*; **14** 145; **19** 573, 588, 621; **22** 362; **24** 805; **25** 267, 268; **30** 502; **33** *192*
Wilkinson, A. J., Ltd **7** 434
Wilkinson, Charles (Kyrle) **16** 414; **33** 193*
Wilkinson, Henry **10** 398
Wilkinson, John **29** 88
Wilkinson, John Gardner **10** 78, 82, 83; **13** 810; **22** 352
Wilkinson, J. V. S. **13** 327
Wilkinson, Leslie **2** 772; **7** 619; **9** 62; **33** 193*
Wilkinson, Morris, & Co. **5** 612
Wilkinson, Norman **5** 530; **20** 425
Wilkinson, Rex **13** 225
Wilkinson, Samuel **16** 28
Wilkinson, Thomas **5** 169; **8** 287; **16** 61; **28** 576
Wilkinson, W. B. **7** 693
Wilkinson, William **23** 688
Wilkinson & Co. **28** 577
Wilkowski, Henryk **25** 125
Will, Henry **31** 652
Will, John **31** 651
Will, Philip, jr **24** 457
Will, William **31** 651
Willa, Margravine of Tuscany (*fl* 978) **11** 175
Willading Factory **30** 144
Willaerts, Abraham **4** 53; **24** 236; **33** 193, 194–5*
Willaerts, Adam **22** 843; **33** 193–5*
collaboration **33** 195
pupils **33** 194
works **20** 424; **33** *194*
Willaerts, Cornelis **33** 193
Willaerts, Isaac **33** 193, 195*
Willan, Robert **21** 7
Willard, Aaron **7** 446
Willard, Daniel Wheelock **3** 6*
Willard, Simon **7** 446
Willard, Solomon **4** 472; **33** 195*
assistants **26** 536
attributions **26** 537
groups and movements **3** 730
pupils **4** 312
works **4** 473
Willaume, Adam **33** 195
Willaume, Anne *see* TANQUERAY, ANNE
Willaume, David (1658–*c.* 1740) **10** 328, 329, 330; **19** 593; **33** 195*
patrons and collectors **6** 116
pupils **30** 299
works **14** 856
Willaume, David, II (1692-1761) **25** 4; **30** 299; **33** 195
Willayat Khan **24** 541
Wille, Bruno **8** 824
Wille, Jean-Georges **10** 393; **24** 135, 453; **33** 195–6*
assistants **8** 542; **25** 549
patrons and collectors **8** 481
printmakers **18** 858; **33** 44
pupils **13** 625, 871
Basan, Pierre-François **3** 318
Bervic, Charles-Clément **3** 870
Chevillet, Juste **6** 563
Dorner, Johann Jakob, I (1741-1813) **9** 177
Kobell (i), Ferdinand **18** 173
Longueil, Joseph de **19** 641
Loutherbourg, Philippe Jacques de **19** 728
Massard, Jean **20** 584
Mechel, Christian von **20** 914
Müller, Johann Gotthard von **22** 273
Zick (ii), Januarius **33** 671
works **4** 382; **26** 230; **33** 196
Wille, Pierre-Alexandre **33** 195, 196*
reproductive prints by others **6** 563; **13** 871
Willeboirts, Thomas **14** 617
Willebrand, Hermann **8** 706
Willelmus Martini **32** 464
Willème, François **24** 688*
Willement, Thomas **13** 207; **14** 746; **29** 506
Willement, William **33** 63
Willem of Breda *see* KEY, WILLEM (ADRIAENSZ.)
Willems, Charles-Henri **33** 197
Willems, Florent **29** 645; **33** 196–7*
Willems, Jan **19** 260
Willems, Joseph **6** 533; **10** 308; **29** 432
works **10** *308*
Willemsen, S. **32** 706
Willemsens, Abraham **20** 627
Willemssen, Jan **3** 494
Willemssens, Louis **3** 570; **25** 812; **33** 197*
pupils **25** 52
works **2** 196
Willemstad
Belvédère House **2** 148
Bolo de Bruid **2** 148
Cinelandia **2** 148
Curaçao Museum **2** 145, 149
Fort Amsterdam **2** 148
Fort Church **2** 148
Groot Davelar **2** 148
houses **2** 148
West End cinema **2** 148
Willemsz., Cornelis **14** 291; **22** 835, 837; **28** 215; **32** 271
Willemsz., Jan **22** 835
Willemsz., Willem **21** 485
Willem van Kessel **28** 595
Willem van Montfort, Burggraf **20** 644
Willendorf **2** *776*; **25** *470*; **33** 197–8*
figurines **10** 472; **25** 490
Willendorf *Venus* **33** 197–8, *198*
Willequet, André **3** 574; **5** 45
Willerval, J. **18** 890
Willets Manufacturing Co. **19** 165; **31** 638
Willett, Frank **1** 230; **15** 105; **31** 673
Willette, (Léon) Adolphe **33** 198*
collaboration **20** 602
works **5** 758; **19** 488, 490
Willetts, Duncan
works **19** *859*
Willey, Gordon R. **2** 300; **14** 223; **28** 372
Willey Park (Salop) **33** 448
William (*fl* 1479) **8** 201
William, Abbot of Hirsau (*reg* 1068-91) **7** 231
William, Abbot of Meaux (*reg* 1249-69) **7** 353
William, Abbot of Rievaulx (*fl* 1132) **26** 380
William, Duke of Brunswick-Lüneberg (*fl* 1668-86) **21** 463; **32** 709
William, Duke of Saxe-Weimar (*reg* 1605-62) **33** *110*
William, Holy Roman Emperor (*reg* 1247-56) **14** 37, 44, 45; **22** 822
William , King of Württemberg (*reg* 1816-64) **12** 10; **14** 768; **24** 86; **25** 11; **29** 874; **30** 459; **33** 429, 616
William, Margrave of Baden-Baden (*reg* 1622-77) **21** 640
William I, Elector of Hesse (*reg* 1785-1821) **4** 303; **9** 456; **12** 413; **14** 491; **17** 698, 835; **27** 223
William I, Emperor of Germany (*reg* 1871-88) **14** *648*, 649, 654–5*; **33** *110*
architecture **14** 654; **18** 741; **28** 102; **29** 736
paintings **14** 527
sculpture **14** 207
William I, King of England (*reg* 1066-87), Duke of Normandy (*reg* 1035-87) **17** 684; **26** 586; **33** 198–9*
architecture **3** 709; **5** 369, 370, 510; **9** 203, 451; **13** 850; **14** 75; **19** 608, 615; **21** 562, 563; **23** 258; **26** 615; **29** 532; **33** 230, 235, 247
military **19** 564; **27** 624
oliphants **23** 400
William I, King of Naples and Sicily (*reg* 1154-66) **16** 172; **22** 469; **23** 843
William I, King of Prussia (*reg* 1861-71) *see* WILLIAM I, Emperor of Germany
William I, King of the Netherlands (*reg* 1813-40) **11** 885; **14** 875; **22** 903; **23** 463, *463*, 469*; **31** 856
architecture **5** 41; **22** 828; **24** 885; **30** 47; **31** 874; **32** 259
art policies **3** 617; **10** 93; **22** 907
collections **22** 906
furniture **3** 584
gardens **33** 692
interior decoration **3** 578
paintings **1** 808; **2** 229; **23** 354; **29** 774
porcelain **3** 591
pottery **13** 542
William I, Prince of Orange, Stadholder of the Netherlands *see* WILLIAM THE SILENT, Prince of Orange, Stadholder of the Netherlands
William II, Count of Holland *see* WILLIAM, Holy Roman Emperor
William II, Count of Toulouse (*reg* 1060-88) **31** 207, 208, 209
William II, Duke of Berg (*reg* 1360-1408) **9** 459
William II, Elector of Hesse (*reg* 1821-31) **14** 491; **17** 835; **26** 546
William II, Emperor of Germany (*reg* 1888-1918) **14** *648*, 656*
architecture **6** 51; **14** 649; **15** 122; **22** 250, 319
art policies **10** 413; **28** 343
furniture **3** 152
paintings **4** 639; **10** 760; **12** 394; **28** 40
sculpture **3** 498; **9** 692; **28** 164; **31** 401
silver **5** 57
William II, King of England (*reg* 1087-1100) **13** 850; **14** 75; **19** 615; **26** 81, 616; **33** 550
William II, King of Naples and Sicily (*reg* 1166-89) **14** 240*
architecture **16** 172; **21** 897; **28** 655
mosaics **9** 581
textiles **16** 437
William II, King of the Netherlands (*reg* 1840-49) **15** 40; **23** *463*, 464, 469–70*
architecture **22** 828
collections **22** 903
drawings **33** 154, 345
gardens **29** 8
paintings **18** 481; **22** 905; **24** 745; **26** 734
urban planning **14** 39
William II, Prince of Orange, Stadholder of the Netherlands (*reg* 1647-50) **10** 732; **15** 40; **22** 844; **23** *463*; **30** 463
William II of Albini **6** 54
William II of Villehardouin, Prince of Achaea **22** 405
William III, King of England and Scotland (*reg* 1688-1702) **10** *304*; **14** *289*; **15** 40; **23** 463, *463*, 466–7*; **24** 745; **27** *467*; **28** *50*
architecture **4** 217; **7** 298; **10** 232, 360; **14** 126; **20** 458; **22** 826; **25** 327; **26** 560; **29** 7; **30** 278; **33** 199, 397, 398
clocks **7** 442
decorative works **21** 907
drawings **15** 41
enamel **4** 244
furniture **22** 865; **31** 683
gardens **12** 105, 128, 132; **19** 622
gold **26** 558
guns **2** 466, *466*; **14** 856
interior decoration **10** 274; **14** 855; **20** 458; **22** 864
medals **6** 101; **8** 184
metalwork **30** 871
paintings **3** 570; **9** 14; **12** 801; **18** 144, 652; **19** 859; **22** 846, 904; **23** 447; **26** 394; **27** 263
prints **5** 756
sculpture **7** 298, 500; **22** 859; **23** 253; **33** 197
silver **6** 116; **22** 888
William III, Stadholder of the Netherlands, Prince of Orange *see* WILLIAM III, King of England
William IV, Duke of Bavaria (*reg* 1508-50) **18** 452; **21** 484; **22** 835; **33** *85*, 270–72*, *272*
manuscripts **12** 816
paintings **1** 719; **3** 507; **4** 760; **5** 200; **11** 33; **12** 387; **22** 302; **26** 76; **28** 161
William IV, King of Great Britain (*reg* 1830-37) **9** 148; **10** *319*; **12** 163; **14** 147*; **26** 490
ceramics **33** 378

William IV, King of Great Britain (*reg* 1830-37)—cont.
drawings **7** 431
paintings **3** 389, 490; **6** 402; **14** 849; **29** 632; **33** 190
sculpture **27** 197
William IV, Landgrave of Hesse-Kassel (*reg* 1567-92) **10** 119; **12** 439; **14** 490*; **17** 834; **18** 575; **23** 339; **26** 470; **32** 339
William IV, Stadholder of the Netherlands, Prince of Orange (*reg* 1747-51) **23** 463, *463*, 468*
architecture **14** 39; **20** 459
decorative works **22** 684
paintings **14** 42; **21** 508; **22** 905
sculpture **33** 460
sponsorship **30** 62
William V, Duke of Bavaria (*reg* 1579-98) **22** 302; **33** *272*, 274-5*
architecture **8** 881; **9** 750; **18** 478, 479; **22** 307; **28** 109; **32** 403
collections **30** 35; **32** 612
coral **7** 835
engravings **27** 502
gems **12** 260
gold **22** 305
guns **2** 462
interior decoration **5** 768; **23** 757
ivory-carvings **20** 90
metalwork **12** 446; **32** 771
miniatures (manuscript illumination) **14** 618
paintings **5** 605; **9** 133; **17** 711; **30** 33, 34; **33** 81
sculpture **5** 768; **8** 626; **12** 346-7, 402, 577
silver **19** 152
tombs **26** 103
William V, Duke of Jülich (*reg* 1539-92) **9** 459; **24** 230; **29** 375
William V, Stadholder of the Netherlands, Prince of Orange (*reg* 1751-95) **18** 176; **23** 463, *463*, 468-9*
collections **14** 42
gardens **29** 8
paintings **14** 42; **22** 905; **28** 842
William VI, Margrave of Monferrat (*reg* 1464-83) **22** 104
William VII, Landgrave of Hesse-Kassel (*reg* 1663-70) **15** 47; **17** 834
William VII, Margrave of Baden-Baden (*fl* 1647) **4** 747
William VIII, Landgrave of Hesse-Kassel (*reg* 1751-60) **14** 491-2*
amber **9** 52
architecture **9** 11, 455
collections **8** 887; **12** 473
glass **12** 897
interior decoration **22** 436
paintings **8** 809; **27** 271; **31** 26
William IX, Duke of Aquitaine (*reg* 1086-1127) **31** 207, 209
William IX, Landgrave of Hesse-Kassel *see* WILLIAM I, Elector of Hesse
William, George, 6th Earl of Coventry **18** 746
William and Mary style **10** 360; **14** 855; **22** 872; **23** 463, 466; **33** 199-200*
furniture **31** 623
interior decoration **22** 864-5
William de Brailes **33** 200-201*
works **4** 370, 393; **10** 244; **13** 129, 130, *130*, 141; **23** 689; **24** 478; **33** *200*
William de Luda **14** 416
William de Malton **3** 895
William de Warelwast, Bishop of Exeter **10** 671
William Fehr Collection *see under* CAPE TOWN → Castle of Good Hope
William Joy **33** 236
William Mitchell Design Consultants **4** 789
William of Blois, Bishop of Winchester **23** 461
William of Champeaux **32** 415
William of Conches **10** 202
William of Devon **4** 7, 393; **13** 141
manuscripts **4** *393*
William of Grez, Bishop of Beauvais **3** 458
William of Ireland **13** 81; **27** 629
William of Lyngwode *see* LYNGWODE, WILLIAM
William of Malmesbury **2** 64; **12** 799; **26** 590
William of Marburg **7** 578
William of Montacute **10** 673
William of Prene **33** 201*
William of St Calais, Bishop of Durham **3** 710; **26** 669
William of Sens **2** 313; **33** 201-2*
competitions **7** 664
works **2** 347; **5** 643, 644-5; **9** 70; **13** 45; **22** 211, 218; **33** 209
William of Suffolk **1** 612
William of Towthorpe **10** 340
William of Warenne, Earl of Surrey **7** 473
William of Wykeham **7** 420; **23** 691; **33** 202*, 248
architecture **10** 359; **14** 454; **23** 686; **33** 231, 454, 523
metalwork **10** 322; **13** 164
sculpture **3** 455
stained glass **13** 183; **23** 689, 691; **33** 238
William Rufus, King of England *see* WILLIAM II, King of England
Williams (*fl* 1737) **8** 107
Williams, A. C., Co. **31** 257
Williams, Amancio **2** 397; **29** 641; **33** 202-3*
works **33** *203*
Williams, Arthur **2** 387
Williams, Aubrey **13** 876
Williams, Benjamin Leader *see* LEADER, BENJAMIN WILLIAMS
Williams, Charles **29** 834
Williams, Christopher **32** 786
Williams, Compton **13** 877
Williams, Denis **13** 876
Williams, Dennis **5** 754
Williams, E., Ltd **6** 551
Williams, E. A. **22** 468
Williams, E. F. *see* EDMONDS, FRANCIS W(ILLIAM)
Williams, Emmett **11** 232; **27** 215
Williams, Evan **32** 792
Williams, Fred(erick) **2** 751, 762; **33** 203*
Williams, 'Grecian' *see* WILLIAMS, HUGH WILLIAM
Williams, Harry Hughes **32** 786
Williams, Hugh William **22** 531; **28** 236, 238; **33** 204*
Williams, Iolo **10** 367
Williams, Isaac L. **1** 22
Williams, James **8** 831
Williams, James Watson **3** 395
Williams, Jane **33** 204*
collaboration **30** 516
works **7** 858; **16** 32, *32*
Williams, John (*fl* 1789-1790; writer) **16** 38; **19** 587
Williams, John (1771-1806; silversmith) **33** 204
Williams, Jonathan (*b* 1929) **4** 110
Williams, Julian **10** 512
Williams, Kyffin **32** 786
Williams, Louis R. **20** 437; **23** 212
Williams, Margaret Lindsay **32** 786
Williams, Ora **33** 310
Williams, (Evan) Owen **33** 204-5*
works **10** 240, 241; **13** 615; **23** 258; **33** *205*
Williams, Penry **9** 24; **32** 786
Williams, Pyotr (Vladimirovich) *see* VIL'YAMS, PYOTR (VLADIMIROVICH)
Williams, Sam **23** 67
Williams, Steve **33** 678
Williams, Sue Bennett **3** 62; **10** 882
Williams, Tennessee **30** 687
Williams, T. R. **24** 636
Williams, William (1727-91) **25** 637; **31** 600; **33** 91, 206*
Williams, William Carlos **8** 435
Williams, William Fenwick **21** 587; **30** 27
Williams, William T. (*b* 1942) **1** 444
Williams Bay (WI), Yerkes Observatory **23** 341, *341*
Williamsburg (VA) **2** 322; **30** 502; **31** *587*, 721; **33** 206-7*
Abby Aldrich Rockefeller Folk Art Collection **26** 488
Capitol **18** 887
College of William and Mary **7** 567
Colonial Williamsburg **26** 227
court-house **18** 887
DeWitt Wallace Decorative Arts Gallery **22** 368
furniture **31** 632
Governor's Palace **12** 136, 222; **31** 590; **33** 206-7
Williams-Ellis, (Bertram) Clough **32** 784; **33** 208*, *208*
Williamson, Curtis **5** 593
Williamson, Francis **5** 515
Williamson, Francis John **11** 239; **23** 62
Williamson, John **19** 507
Williamson, Samuel **19** 507
Williamson, Sue **29** 110
Williamson, Thomas **28** 255
Williamson Faulkner Brown & Partners **29** 427
Williamstown (MA)
Hopkins Observatory **23** 341
Sterling and Francine Clark Art Institute **7** 377
Williams College Museum of Art **1** 895; **9** 231; **22** 53
Williams-Wynn, Frances, Lady, of Wynnstay (wife of 3rd Baronet) **27** 468
Williams-Wynn, Henrietta Somerset, Lady, of Wynnstay (wife of 4th Baronet) **14** 382
Williams-Wynn, Watkin, 4th Baronet, of Wynnstay (1749-89) **32** 790; **33** 208-9*
collections **32** 784, 790-91
interior decoration **10** 279
paintings **26** 277, 462; **32** 784; **33** 222
silver **14** 382
Williams-Wynn, Watkin, 5th Baronet, of Wynnstay (*fl* 1789-1830) **12** 598
William the Conqueror *see* WILLIAM I, King of England, Duke of Normandy
William the Englishman **33** 209*
works **5** 643, 644-5; **13** 45; **22** 217
William the Good, King of Naples and Sicily *see* WILLIAM II, King of Naples and Sicily
William the Lion, King of Scotland (*reg* 1165-1214) **28** 260, 267
William the Rich *see* WILLIAM V, Duke of Jülich
William the Silent, Stadholder of the Netherlands, Prince of Orange (*reg* 1572-84) **18** *6*; **23** 462-4*, *463*
architecture **14** 495
engravings **20** 457
stained glass **8** 103
tapestries **14** 297
William the Steadfast, Duke of Bavaria *see* WILLIAM IV, Duke of Bavaria
Willibald **22** 9
Willibald, Maximilian, Herzog von Wolfegg *see* WOLFEGG, MAXIMILIAN WILLIBALD, Herzog von
Willibaldsburg **12** 369
Willibrord, Saint **19** 826; **22** 816; **31** 769
Willigen, Adriaan van der **22** 910
Willigis, Archbishop of Mainz **12** 471; **20** 127; **23** 658
Willing, Victor **26** 96
Willingale Spain (Essex), St Andrew **10** 339
Willinges, Johann **33** 209*
Willink, Albert Carel **22** 852; **33** 210*
Willink, W. E. **19** 506
works **19** *506*
Willink & Thicknesse **21** 371
Willis, Beverly **33** 210*
Willis, Browne **33** 211*
Willis, Fred C. **30** 731
Willis, Nathaniel Parker **8** 66; **25** 837
Willis, Robert **22** 211; **33** 211*
Willis, Thomas **21** 7
Willis, William **19** 424; **24** 655
Willison, George **13** 303; **28** 235
Willits, Ward **33** 401
Williwear **28** 799
Willmann, Michael (Lukas Leopold) **33** 211-12*
patrons and collectors **14** 650
works **8** 391; **12** 390; **19** 748; **24** 108; **25** 445; **33** *212*
Willmann, Peter **33** 211
Willmore, James Tibbetts **4** 87; **10** 396; **25** 836
Willms, Auguste **10** 143
Willoughby **11** 858
Willoughby (NSW) incinerators **2** *741*
Willoughby, Francis **8** 44; **10** 360; **23** 258; **28** 894, 895
Willoughby, Henry, 6th Baron Middleton **33** 447
Willoughby, Percival **28** 894
Willoughby de Eresby, Peter Burrell, 19th Lord *see* BURRELL, PETER, 2nd Lord Gwydyr and 19th Lord Willoughby de Eresby
willow
historical and regional traditions
Austria **33** 156
Belgium **33** 157
Bhutan **3** 913
France **33** 157
Germany **33** 156, 326
India, Republic of **15** 174
Japan **17** 372
Korea **18** 361, 379
Native North Americans **3** 331; **22** 656, *662*, 663
Netherlands, the **33** 157
Switzerland **33** 157
uses
baskets **3** 331, 332; **22** *662*, 663
dolls **17** 372
furniture **18** 361; **33** 156
mats **15** 174
wicker **33** 155
Willow Brook **29** 842
Willow pattern **21** 697
Wills, Frank **4** 823; **5** 561; **22** 36; **33** 212-13*
Wills, G. A. **4** 823
Wills, Royal Barry **29** 807
Wills, W. H. **4** 823
Wills, William John **2** 745
Willson, Edmund R. **25** 666
Willson, Edward James **25** 710; **28** 869
works **25** *711*
Willumsen, Jens Ferdinand **7** 807; **33** 213-14*
groups and movements **7** 805; **11** 790; **28** 814
patrons and collectors **8** 760
Willumsen, Jens Ferdinand—cont.
pupils **11** 798
works **7** *806*; **8** 735, 741, 748; **11** 474, 475, *475*, 790; **33** *214*
Wilm, F. R. **12** 450
Wilmarth, Lemuel **33** 43
Wilmington, Long Man of *see* LONG MAN OF WILMINGTON
Wilmington (DE), Nemours **12** 143
Wilmington, Spencer Compton, Earl of *see* COMPTON, SPENCER, Earl of Wilmington
Wilmore, J.
works **27** *602*
Wilmot, John, 2nd Earl of Rochester **14** 291
Wilmot, Olivia **28** 482
Wilmotte (IL), Bahā'ī temple **30** 450
Wilmotte, Jean-Michel **25** 318
Wilmowsky, Johann Nikolaus von **31** 327
Wilms, Albert **4** 88
Wilms, Fritz **7** 328
Wilmshurst **30** 533, 534
Wilno *see* VILNIUS
Wilpert, Joseph **33** 215*
Wils, Jan **3** 757; **33** 215*
assistants **9** 745
collaboration **3** 757; **9** 62
groups and movements **21** 781; **22** 875; **29** 397, 660
personal collection **29** 57
pupils **3** 757; **4** 216
works **29** 489
Wilshere, Reginald S. **3** 537; **16** 39
Wilsnack **13** 187
Wilson (1692-1723) **14** 110
Wilson, Major **33** 217
Wilson, Alexander **33** 215-16*
collaboration **3** 310; **24** 302
Wilson, Andrew **28** 236, 274; **33** 216*
dealing **28** 271
pupils **14** 208; **18** 855
Wilson, Anthony **33** 678
Wilson, Arnold Manaaki **20** 359; **23** 63; **33** 216-17*
Wilson, Benjamin **33** 217*
assistants **33** 692
patrons and collectors **33** 693
pupils **4** 845; **8** 636; **33** 133
reproductive prints by others **26** 30
works **9** 308
Wilson, Charles **14** 108; **33** 217-18*
works **12** 773, 774; **28** 228, 229; **29** 669
Wilson, Charles Heath **9** 475; **28** 274, 275
Wilson, Colin (Alexander) St John **33** 218-19*
collaboration **19** 321; **20** 491
groups and movements **15** 166
works **4** 789; **5** 513; **10** 242; **19** 321; **23** 689; **33** *218*
Wilson, Daniel **25** 467
Wilson, David **32** 534
Wilson, Edward Arthur **4** 366
Wilson, Erasmus **18** 169
Wilson, Eric **30** 160
Wilson, George **21** 732
Wilson, George Washington **24** 657; **33** 219*
works **1** *30*; **24** *657*
Wilson, Harris, Crain & Associates **17** 620; **33** 604
Wilson, Henry **17** 528; **19** 594; **33** 219*
collaboration **25** 187; **28** 347, 348
groups and movements **2** 570
house **8** 830
methods **12** 869
works **4** 810; **10** 336, 346; **32** 783
Wilson, James **11** 836; **24** 641
Wilson, James Keys **22** 60
Wilson, James Knox **17** 547

Wilson, J. H. 2 739
Wilson, John (*fl* 1790–?1810; dealer) 6 79
Wilson, John (1774–1855; painter) 13 696; 30 680
Wilson, John (*fl* 1838) 24 293
Wilson, Joseph 10 308
Wilson, Judy McIntosh 23 74
works 23 *74*
Wilson, Juliet 14 196
Wilson, Malcolm 29 117
Wilson, Martha Storey 24 409
Wilson, Peter 2 560; 29 88
Wilson, Richard (i) (1713–82) 2 743; 26 774; 32 790; 33 219–23*
exhibitions 10 677; 19 586
groups and movements 22 740; 29 891
paintings 7 572
patrons and collectors
Blundell, Henry 4 181
Butler, Charles (1822–1910) 5 311
Dundas, Lawrence 9 392
Forbes, James Staats 11 301
Ford, Richard 11 304
Foundling Hospital (London) 20 911
Hanover, William Augustus, Duke of Cumberland 14 144
Harvey, Thomas 8 184
Herbert, Henry, 10th Earl of Pembroke 33 226
Hollis, Thomas (1720–74) 14 687
Howard, Ralph, Viscount Wicklow 27 356
Lever, William Hesketh, 1st Viscount Leverhulme 19 270
Locke, William (1732–1810) 19 531
Marsh, Edward (Howard) 20 476
McCulloch, Horatio 19 875
Mellon, Paul 21 91
National Museum of Wales (Cardiff) 5 732
Neeld, Joseph 22 719
Petty, William (Fitzmaurice), 2nd Earl of Shelburne and 1st Marquess of Lansdowne 24 570
Williams-Wynn, Watkin, 4th Baronet, of Wynnstay (1749–89) 32 784; 33 209
Zuccarelli, Francesco 33 714
pupils 10 806; 14 610; 17 640; 22 86; 33 133
reproductive prints by others 4 607; 10 393; 25 618; 26 230; 33 372
sponsors 1 533
works 10 251; 11 *428*, 907; 13 302; 14 785; 18 712, 713; 29 *890*; 32 785; 33 *221*
Wilson, Richard (ii) (*b* 1953) 33 223*
Wilson, Robert 24 409; 33 223*
Wilson, Sam (*fl* 1908–13) 12 612
Wilson, Samuel (*fl* 1920s) 29 843
Wilson, Scottie 30 23
Wilson, Thomas 22 714; 32 377
Wilson, W. D. 2 705
Wilson, W(illiam) Hardy 33 224*
collaboration 9 62
groups and movements 7 619
works 2 741
Wilson, William 28 239, 240, 878
Wilson, W. J. 10 321
Wilson, Woodrow 19 165
Wilson & Aldwinckle 4 171
Wilson Bros & Co. 25 855
Wilstach (family) 24 600
Wilstach, W. P. 4 755
Wilt, Domenicus Ver *see* VER WILT, DOMENICUS
Wilten Monastery 2 781; 6 399
Wilthew, W. 23 70
Wilton (Wilts) 10 *225*; 33 224–6*
carpets 5 831; 10 358; 33 226*
see also under CARPETS → types
Nunnery 2 73
SS Mary and Nicholas 10 238; 29 515
Wilton House 8 45; 10 231; 14 435; 23 859, 860; 33 *224*, 225–6*
collections 10 364; 14 436
Double Cube Room 23 543, 678; 33 *225*
furniture 7 172; 10 290; 17 *902*
garden bridge 4 801
gardens 12 127, 131; 33 225–6
interior decoration 8 45
paintings 3 697; 4 845; 9 375, 377, 481; 14 435; 19 759; 26 344
reliefs 25 665
sculpture 29 714
Triumphal Arch 6 412
wall paintings 24 753
Wilton, Joseph 10 372; 19 157, 585; 33 226–7*
assistants 27 244
patrons and collectors 19 157, 158
personal collection 33 221
sponsors 1 533
works 5 302, 751; 10 264; 28 844; 33 *227*
Wilton, Thomas Egerton, 1st Earl of *see* EGERTON, THOMAS, 1st Earl of Wilton
Wilton, Thomas Grosvenor, 2nd Earl of *see* GROSVENOR, THOMAS, 2nd Earl of Wilton
Wilton, William 33 226
Wilton Cross 10 322
Wilton Diptych 9 4, *4*; 10 245, 359; 11 398; 13 153; 14 423, 436; 18 827; 23 883; 25 17; 26 79; 29 800
Wilton Royal Carpet Co. 5 841
Wilton Royal Carpet Factory 10 279; 14 436; 23 64; 33 225, 226
Wimar, Charles (Ferdinand) 33 227–8*
Wimberger, Johann Cyprian 14 313
Wimbledon (Surrey)
All England Lawn Tennis Association 29 426
Wat Buddhapadipa 30 616, 617
Wimbledon House 6 127; 9 12; 12 127
Wimbledon, Edward Cecil, Viscount *see* CECIL, EDWARD, Viscount Wimbledon
Wimbourne Minster Church (Dorset) 10 286
Wimmel, Carl Ludwig 12 376; 27 335; 33 228*
works 27 *335*
Wimmel, Johann Heinrich 33 228
Wimmer, Dezső *see* CZIGÁNY, DEZSŐ
Wimmer, Hans 33 228–9*
Wimmer-Wisgrill, Eduard Josef 2 826; 33 166
Wimpfeling, Jakob 9 442
Wimpfen im Tal 13 186, *186*
palace 12 364
SS Peter und Paul 13 49; 23 462; 29 510
sculpture 13 86, 87
Wimpole (Cambs)
St Andrew 10 265
Wimpole Hall 13 645
Chapel 10 277
furniture 10 294
gardens 19 622
metalwork 30 872
Yellow Drawing Room 28 905
Winand (family) 3 591
Winans, Ross 20 16
Winans, Thomas 33 137, 138
Wiñay Wayna 29 166
Wincanton (Somerset) 10 305
Winchcombe Abbey (Glos) 2 77; 23 491
Winchcombe Pottery 5 731
Winchcombe Psalter *see under* PSALTERS → individual manuscripts
Winchelsea (E. Sussex) 31 708, 710
Winchendon House (Bucks) 32 824
winches 7 764
Winchester (Hants) 2 66; 10 *225*; 33 229–39*, *231*
art forms
bookbindings 4 351
ivory-carvings 26 698
manuscripts 1 *111*; 9 219; 10 243; 33 232–3*, *233*
painting 26 656
pottery 10 301, *301*
sculpture 26 615
Castle 10 269
Great Hall 14 75, *76*
wall paintings 26 655
Winchester Jubilee Monument 12 610–11
Cathedral of the Holy Trinity, St Peter and St Paul, and St Swithin 2 65, 66, 72; 9 670; 10 227, *228*; 12 5; 13 55; 20 575; 21 839; 26 588; 30 729; 33 108, 233*, 235–7*, *235*, *237*
bosses 4 465
capitals 26 615, 616
Chantry Chapel of Bishop William Wayneflete 13 84
Chantry Chapel of William of Wykeham 6 458
chantry chapels 7 267; 10 260
choir-stalls 7 190, 191
font 11 253; 26 630
furniture 10 288
Great Screen 13 84
Holy Sepulchre Chapel 10 244; 26 653
ivory-carvings 26 697
Lady Chapel 18 621
manuscript illumination 2 75
metalwork 6 76
monument to Joseph Warton 11 *163*
mouldings 22 221
oliphants 23 400
paintings 33 237–8*
presbytery 22 220
Queen Mary's Chair 30 781
retrochoir 22 218; 33 *236*
screen 28 294
sculpture 3 646; 13 80, *81*, 84, 85; 19 405; 33 238*
stained glass 2 83; 29 503; 33 238–9*
tapestries 10 348
transept 31 281
vaults 32 92
vaults (ceiling) 10 228
wall paintings 26 *652*
Hampshire County Records Office 2 323, *324*
Hospital of St Cross 14 781
Hyde Abbey 7 455; 26 673
see also New Minster
maze 18 585
New Minster 2 66, 72, *73*; 10 243
see also Hyde Abbey
Old Minster 26 673; 33 233–4*, *234*
Oram's Arbour 33 229
Palace of William I 14 75
Pilgrim's Hall 30 909
SS Thomas and Swithun *see* Hampshire County Records Office
urban planning 33 229–30
Winchester (Hants)—cont.
Winchester College 7 566; 12 175; 28 156; 29 506; 33 202
Commoners' College 28 156
sculpture 13 82
stained glass 13 182, 183
Winchester Palace 10 232, 360; 33 396
Wolvesey Palace 6 60; 26 616
workshops 29 852
Winchester, Alice 19 439
Winchester Bible *see under* BIBLES → individual manuscripts
Winchester Bible, 'second' *see under* BIBLES → individual manuscripts
Winchester House glasshouse 10 316
Winchester Psalter (London, BL, Cotton MS. Tib. C. VI) *see under* PSALTERS → individual manuscripts → Tiberius Psalter
Winchester Psalter (London, BL, Cotton MS. Nero C. IV) *see under* PSALTERS → individual manuscripts
Winchester School 1 110, 183; 2 74, 75; 10 243; 20 330; 33 232–3
works 33 *233*
Winck, Johann Christian Thomas 12 391; 33 240*
collaboration 10 860
works 12 *391*, 467, 468; 22 303; 28 110
Winck, Joseph Gregor 2 580; 33 240–41*
Winckelmann, Johann Joachim 1 533; 7 384; 10 83, 401, 637; 13 392, 468; 16 772; 22 357; 23 295; 24 443, 453; 26 286, 774, 840, 847; 27 46; 33 241–2*
groups and movements 13 608
personal collection 6 97
pupils 2 94
teachers 5 908
works 2 319, 518, 531; 11 674; 12 391, 406, 413, 482; 13 303, 809
catalogues 12 266; 29 724
illustrated 5 908; 26 230; 31 481
on allegories 1 660; 15 84
on colour 7 629
on gay art 12 214
on Greek art 22 686, 735; 31 300
on Holbein and Dürer 9 443
on iconography 15 89; 22 415
on styles 29 879
on the Antique 2 171
on the Baroque 3 261
translated 10 846; 11 861; 14 835; 25 364; 30 133
Winckh, Joseph Gregor *see* WINCK, JOSEPH GREGOR
Winckler, Bernhard 31 568
Winckler, David 12 444
Winckler, Gottfried 29 376
Winckler, H. 4 229
Wincze, Władysław 25 122
Wind, Edgar 2 536; 26 236; 33 242–3*
Windach, Sebastian Füll von, Pfalzgraf *see* FÜLL VON WINDACH, SEBASTIAN, Pfalzgraf
Windad Ohrmazd 16 371
Windau *see* VENTSPILS
Windberger, Hans 33 278
wind bracing *see* BRACING
wind catchers 16 270; 33 243*
wind chimes 17 386
Winde, William 10 273; 12 341; 23 857; 33 243–4*
Windebank, Francis 33 387
Windemaker, Nikolaus 26 407
Winders, Jean-Jacques 3 549; 33 244*
house 3 579
staff 33 244
Winders, Jean-Jacques—cont.
works 2 194
Winders, Maxime 20 813; 33 244–5*
Windeyer, Richard Cunningham 5 67
Windham, Joseph 8 96
Windham, William 5 295; 32 111
Windhoek 1 *413*; 33 245*
Arts Association Gallery 22 450
Gathemann Building 22 450
National Art Gallery 33 245
Staatsmuseum 22 450
Windige, Bennet 14 624–5
winding drums 7 765
Windisch 3 375; 27 105; 30 144
Windisch, Charles-Christophe 3 591; 5 51
Windisch, Ferenc 24 313
Windisch, Jörg 33 245*
windlasses 7 764
Windmann, Max von 14 66; 28 814
windmill cups *see under* CUPS → types
Windmiller culture 22 553
Windmill Hill (Wilts) 25 504
Windmill Psalter *see under* PSALTERS → individual manuscripts
window displays 6 549; 8 809
window-frames 22 221; 30 846
windows 33 245–6*
historical and regional traditions
Arabia 2 248
Bali (Indonesia) 15 785
Belgium 3 575, 576
Central Asia, Western 6 269
China 6 *689*, 690, *690*; 7 114; 12 92
Egypt 16 257
Egypt, ancient 33 245
England 19 403; 25 *711*
France 9 12
Germany 12 408, 409
Gothic 13 35, 132, 136; 19 403
Indonesia 15 785
Ireland 24 305
Islamic 16 256, 257
Italy 19 *534*; 21 *455*
Japan 17 337
Malta (Republic of) 20 *218*
Nepal 22 792
Netherlands, the 9 12
Norway 23 221
Ottoman 16 257
Rome, ancient 26 871
Somalia 29 *56*
Spain 29 301
Turkey 16 257
materials
alabaster (gypsum) 2 248
glass 6 269; 12 790; 23 221; 26 871
lead 16 257
mouldings 22 216
paper 7 114; 12 408
parchment 12 408; 24 106
textiles 29 301
tracery 8 610; 31 270, *270*, 271, 273
wrought iron 20 *218*
types
band 13 136, *136*, 178, 181, 183; 29 502, VI1, VI1
clerestory 13 179, 181; 19 403
dormer 27 128
French 33 246
lancet 13 181
Málaga (Spain) 20 157
medallion 13 135, *135*, 178, *179*, 181, 183; 29 501
oeil-de-boeuf 23 357*
oriel 25 *711*
rose 13 191; 26 *45*; 31 *270*, 270, 271
sash 10 275
see also MIRADORS
Windrim, James Hamilton 33 246*

Windrim, John T. 33 246
Windrush (Glos), St Peter 6 565
Windsheim, Kilianskirche 26 372
windsocks 6 305
Windsor (Australia)
court-house 18 887
St Matthew's 2 737
Windsor (NS; Canada)
King's College 5 590
Windsor (Berks; UK)
bridge 4 802
Castle 6 53, 55, 57, 407; 10 *225*, 273, 274, 275, 279, 359, 360; 13 202; 14 75, 145; 20 880; 21 563; 23 210; 26 743; 27 *716*; 29 659; 33 247–8*, *247*, 249–50*, *250*
Albert Memorial Chapel 6 171; 31 346
monument to Prince Albert 31 *345*
tomb of Albert Victor, Duke of Clarence 12 611, *611*; 23 34; 25 175, IV; 27 831; 31 132
catalogues 3 81; 23 455; 25 238
ceramics 10 643
Cloister 13 137
decorative works 13 665
etchings 11 329
frames 11 424
furniture 9 28; 10 291, 297; 17 479; 19 261; 20 468, 897; 25 712; 30 779
gardens 8 794; 33 257
gems 12 260, 261
interior decoration 8 106; 33 447
mausoleum of Charles I 20 866
Memorial Chapel tomb model 12 625
paintings 29 799
animal subjects 14 146
cabinet pictures 2 164; 9 14; 13 303; 25 810
genre 12 620; 13 788; 23 107
history 14 147, 586; 26 321
hunting scenes 14 143
landscape 3 758; 27 293
miniatures 9 44; 11 807; 13 309; 14 546; 21 640, 645; 23 407, 408, 409; 29 799
portraits 9 480, 482, 483, 485; 13 314; 14 143, 144, 668, 670; 17 610; 19 384; 26 155, 467; 27 293; 28 313; 29 798, 804; 33 123, 260, 694
religious 9 484; 13 788
vedute 5 595, 597, 598
portraits 14 668, 672
reconstruction 33 447
reliefs 13 29
restoration 7 729
Royal Apartments 6 50; 26 85; 33 248
frescoes 32 358
wood-carvings 12 591
Royal Dairy 14 149
Royal Library
collections 1 31, 532; 3 129; 4 411, 839; 6 87, 115; 8 886; 10 376; 12 214; 20 588; 25 412; 27 264; 33 380
drawings 3 230, 631; 5 598, 854, 866; 7 425, 501; 8 660; 9 220, 230; 11 140; 12 39; 13 786, 788, *788*, 789; 14 144, 683; 15 862; 17 641; 19 546, 707; 20 374; 22 686; 23 349, 745; 24 236, *706*; 25 385, 386, 388, 389, 391, 392, 557, 558; 26 322, 323, 335; 27 491, 521, 693, 715; 28 886; 29 740; 32 588
manuscripts 3 92; 14 761; 20 735; 22 258; 25 873
paintings 26 323
Royal Lodge 8 30
Windsor (Berks; UK)
Castle—cont.
St Edward's Chapel *see* St George's Chapel
St George's Chapel 6 459; 7 179; 10 228, *229*; 13 55; 17 10; 24 466; 33 247–8
altarpieces 1 518
carpets 5 840
choir-stalls 7 192
door fittings 10 339
doors 9 155
misericords 21 725
monument to Edward VII 2 752
monument to Queen Alexandra 2 752
stained glass 13 185
stall plates 14 409
tomb of Edward IV 9 155; 10 339
vaults 32 94
sculpture 4 408; 7 298; 8 481; 14 148, 500; 19 141, 250, 271; 23 874; 30 703; 31 413, 477; 32 730; 33 449
silver 22 728
terracottas 21 489
wall paintings 26 653
Waterloo Chamber 18 893
Frogmore House 20 869
collections 9 26
interior decoration 22 185
paintings 14 145
Royal Mausoleum 31 132
sculpture 10 266
staircase hall 18 644
tomb of Queen Victoria and Prince Albert 31 *131*
Windsor, Anne, Princess Royal 14 511
Windsor, Charles, Prince of Wales 6 483*
interior decoration 14 511
Windsor, Edward VIII, King of England (*reg* 1936) *see* EDWARD VIII, King of England
Windsor, George V, King of England (*reg* 1910-36) *see* GEORGE V, King of England
Windsor, Mary, Queen of Great Britain *see* MARY OF TECK, Queen of Great Britain
Windsor, Philip, Prince, Duke of Edinburgh *see* PHILIP, Prince, Duke of Edinburgh
Windsor, Wallis, Duchess of Windsor
jewellery 17 113
Windsor chairs *see under* CHAIRS → types
Windstosser, Ludwig 29 608
Windus, B(enjamin) G(odfrey) 33 251*
paintings 4 757; 9 27; 21 604; 27 351
Windus, William Lindsay 33 251*
groups and movements 25 554
patrons and collectors 25 41
works 19 507, *507*
Windward Islands 2 144, 146; 5 *745*
see also ANTILLES, LESSER
wine-coolers 3 *590*; 10 *331*; 28 *665*; 33 195
Greece, ancient 13 476
wine-fountains *see under* FOUNTAINS → types
wine-pots 18 *338*
Wines, James 4 790; 25 359; 28 798
wine sets 2 265
Winfield, David 2 602; 18 640
Winfield, R. W., & Co. 26 190; 30 755
Wing (Bucks)
All Saints 2 66
maze 18 585
Wingård, Anders 30 103
wing benches *see under* BENCHES → types
Winge, Eskil 30 110
Winge, Hanna
works 30 *88*
Winge, Sigurd 23 227
Winged Victory of Samothrace *see* NIKE OF SAMOTHRACE
Wingelmüller, Georg 19 55, 339
Wingfield, Mervyn, 7th Viscount Powerscourt (1836-1904) 25 402
Wingfield, Mervyn, 8th Viscount Powerscourt (1880-1947) 25 402
Wingfield, Percy *see* BULLOCK, WYNN
Wingfield, Richard, 1st Viscount Powerscourt (*d* 1751) 25 402
Wingfield, Richard, 3rd Viscount Powerscourt (*fl* 1760s) 26 462
Wingfield, Richard, 6th Viscount Powerscourt (1815-44) 25 402
Wingfield Castle (Suffolk) 12 176
Wingfield Manor House (Derbys) 8 43
Winghe, Jeremias van 29 666; 33 253*
Winghe, Joos van 33 252–3*
pupils 7 413
reproductive prints by others 27 501, 503
works 1 662; 33 *252*
Winghen, Emmanuel van 22 717
Wingles 11 623
wings (theatre) 8 41; 13 385; 25 788; 30 667
see also ALAE
Winiama 5 328; 22 196, 197
masks 5 *329*
Winiarska, Magdalena 25 124
Wink, Johann Christian Thomas *see* WINCK, JOHANN CHRISTIAN THOMAS
Wink, Joseph Gregor *see* WINCK, JOSEPH GREGOR
Winkel & Magnusson 8 759
Winkler, Franz K. *see* SCHUYLER, MONTGOMERY
Winkler, Gottfried 19 111
Winkler, Jerzy 11 739
Winkler, Otto 29 321
Winkler, Ralf *see* PENCK, A. R.
Winkler, Robert 29 602; 33 735
Winkler, Valentin 27 755
Winkles, Henry 11 802
works 33 *445*
Winks & Hall 23 66
Winlock, Herbert 10 80, 81; 30 693
Winn, John 29 515
Winn, Rowland (*fl* 1760s-80s) 7 171, 172; 29 835
Winn, Rowland, 1st Baron St Oswald (*fl* 1867-70) 12 840
Winne, Liévin De *see* DE WINNE, LIÉVIN
Winnebago 22 552
Winner, Gerd 28 300
Winner, William E. 24 600
Winnewisser, Rolf 30 135
Winnicki, A. 18 433
Winnipeg 5 *559*, 561, 562
Art Gallery 5 563, 591
Manitoba Museum of Man and Nature 5 591
warehouses 32 861
Winogrand, Garry 24 678; 33 253*
Winona (MN)
Merchants Bank 3 177
Public Library 8 85
Winqvist, Anja 11 106
Winqvist, Peter 11 106
Winsham (Somerset), St Stephen 27 123
Winslow, Edward 4 479; 31 647, 648
Winslow & Wetherell 13 617; 20 877; 30 507
Winsor, Jacqueline 33 253–4*
Winsor & Newton 23 787; 24 797, 799; 31 300
tubes 23 *787*
Winstanley, Hamlet 9 211; 19 360; 29 32, 807
Winstanley, Henry 1 504
works 10 *230*
Winstanley, Thomas 10 366
Winston, Charles 4 826; 25 398; 29 506, 514
Winston, Harry Lewis 31 654; 33 254
Winston, Lydia 33 254*
Winston-Salem (NC), Museum of Early Southern Decorative Arts 17 626
Wint, Peter De *see* DE WINT, PETER
Winter, Abraham Hendrik de 26 527
Winter, Adrianus de *see* WINTER, JANUS DE
Winter, E. 10 83
Winter, Friedrich 8 409
Winter, Fritz 33 254*
groups and movements 12 397; 14 624; 21 341; 33 635
patrons and collectors 9 121
Winter, G. S. 31 371
Winter, Hendrik de 25 649
Winter, Jacobus de *see* WINTER, JANUS DE
Winter, Janus de 22 852; 33 254–5*
Winter, Joseph 10 703
Winter, Lloyd L.
works 22 *580*
Winter, Martin 4 666; 12 440
Winter, N. S. 32 591
Winter, Parsons & Hall 28 577
Winter Academy *see under* EDINBURGH → academies and art schools
Winterbourne Steepleton (Dorset), St Michael 2 71
winter gardens *see under* GARDENS → types
Wintergerst, Joseph 33 255*
groups and movements 22 703, 704; 23 675; 24 587
Winterhalder, Adam 33 255
Winterhalder, Anton 33 255
Winterhalder, Johann Michael 33 255
Winterhalder, Josef (i) (1702-69) 9 238; 33 255–6*
pupils 33 256
works 8 386, *397*, 398
Winterhalder, Josef (ii) (1743-1807) 20 857; 33 255–6*
Winterhalter, Franz Xaver 4 306; 14 143; 33 256–7*
groups and movements 26 500
patrons and collectors 2 614; 4 306; 10 362; 14 148; 23 126, 521, 523; 28 346
pupils 29 1
reproductive prints by others 2 692; 11 319; 18 728
works 11 432, 463; 14 12; 17 527; 23 *521*; 33 *257*
Winterhalter, Hermann 33 256
Winter King *see* FREDERICK V, Elector Palatine and King of Bohemia
Winternitz, Adolf 24 510, 517; 30 214
Winter Park (FL), Charles Hosmer Morse Museum of American Art 29 516
Winter Queen *see* ELIZABETH, Electress Palatine and Queen of Bohemia
Winterstein, Christian 11 731
Winterthur (Switzerland) 30 *124*, 143, *144*
ceramics 30 143
Winterthur (Switzerland)—cont.
Gottfried Keller-Stiftung 17 886; 30 152
Rikon Institut 30 821
Sammlung Oskar Reinhart 30 152
Stiftung Oskar Reinhart 30 152, 153
Technorama 30 155
Winterthur (DE; USA), H. F. du Pont Winterthur Museum 6 446; 9 401
collections 24 692; 31 616
reproductions 26 227
Winther, Richard 8 736, 742
Winthrop, Grenville 9 231
Winton, Alexander Seton, 3rd Earl of *see* SETON, ALEXANDER, 3rd Earl of Winton
Winton, George Seton, 3rd Earl of *see* SETON, GEORGE, 3rd Earl of Winton
Winton House (Lothian) 28 245
Wipperfurth, St Nicolas 11 614
Wipplinger, Franz 10 865
Wir 29 435
Wiradjuri 1 45, 49
Wirch, Johann Joseph 8 379; 25 428
wire 21 324*, 328
historical and regional traditions
Angola 7 *197*
China 7 *107*, 110, 111, 122
Chokwe 7 *197*
England 10 340; 30 *394*
Japan 17 99; 31 260
Native North Americans 3 331
Trinidad and Tobago 31 333
United States of America 31 594
materials
brass 10 340
gold 7 *107*, 110, 111; 21 324
silver 21 324; 28 738
silver-gilt 7 110
uses
armatures 29 813
baskets 3 331
beadwork 3 440
bridges 31 594
costumes 31 333
crowns 7 110
display of art 9 14
dolls 31 260
fibre art 11 54
furniture 31 629
jewellery 7 111
metalwork 11 76
puppets 7 122
scabbards 30 *394*
sculpture 7 *197*; 17 99
wicker 33 155
wirecutting 4 767
see also under BRICK → techniques
wirelesses *see* RADIOS
wirework *see under* METALWORK → techniques
Wirgin, Jan 33 89
Wirgman, Charles 3 447; 17 198, 420; 18 172; 30 256
Wirgman, Peter 10 348
Wiriot, Pierre *see* WOEIRIOT, PIERRE
Wirkkala, Tapio 8 803; 11 100, 106, 108; 12 437, 796
works 11 *107*
Wirksworth (Derbys), St Mary 2 70
Wirmes, Jean de 31 834
Wirnt von Grafenberg 26 563
Wirsing, Jeremias 32 681
Wirsung, Marx 20 743, 744
Wirth, Karl August 10 176
Wirth, Larry, Collection *see under* KINGSTON (JAMAICA) → National Gallery of Jamaica
Wirth, L. W. K. 4 819
Wiry Geometric style 10 604
Wiryokusumo 15 775

Wirz, Margrit *see* RUPF, MARGRIT
Wisbech Theatre **30** 674
Wisby **2** 449, 469
Wischack, Maximilian **8** 823
Wischnitzer, Rachel **17** 583
Wiscrere, Jacques **14** 780
  works **26** *555*
Wise, George **31** 423
Wise, Henry **33** 257*
  assistants **4** 805; **30** 123
  collaboration **4** 805; **19** 622
  patrons and collectors **4** 137; **6** 116, 515; **7** 286
  works **12** 128
Wise, John R. Capel **8** 121
Wisedell, Thomas **32** 95
Wiser, Wolfgang **18** 478; **33** 258*
Wishxam **22** 548
Wisinger-Florian, Olga **2** 797; **32** 445
Wiskemann **3** 602
Wiskemann, Otto Leonhard **3** 602
Wiślica **25** *92*; **33** 258–9*
  St Mary **13** 57; **25** 95, 110, 134; **31** 557; **33** 258–9*, *259*
Wislicenus, Hermann **13** 19
Wisma Akitek & James Ferrie International **20** 168
Wismar **13** 187; **25** 526
  Fürstenhof **12** 366
  St Marien **4** 777; **13** 56
  Stadtgeschichtliches Museum **4** 667
  tapestries **12** 467
Wiśnicz **25** *92*, 97; **33** 259*
  Carmelite church **25** 97
  Castle **25** 135
  Lubomirski Palace **25** 137
Wiśnicz Nowy *see* NEW WIŚNICZ
Wiśnowiecki, Michael, King of Poland *see* MICHAEL WIŚNOWIECKI, King of Poland
Wisreutter, Hans **33** 271
Wissa Wassef, Ramses **5** 401; **9** 765, 767; **22** 269
Wissa Wassef, Suzanne **9** 767
Wissa Wassef, Yoanna **9** 767
Wissel, Adolf **22** 711
Wisselingh, E. J. van, & Co. **19** 434; **22** 867, 875, 905; **23** 125; **28** 172; **33** 260, 743
Wisselingh, Elbert J. van **3** 397, 398; **4** 588; **13** 228; **14** 47; **20** 434; **23** 1
Wisselingh, van(, & Co.) **1** 811; **33** 260*
Wissembourg Abbey, SS Peter and Paul **26** 700, *700*; **29** 501
Wissing, Willem **33** 260*
  collaboration **9** 211, 280; **31** 786
  patrons and collectors **10** 361
  works **9** *281*; **10** 249; **11** *425*
Wissowa, Georg **10** 211
Wistar, Caspar **29** 654; **31** 641, 653; **33** 260*
Wistar, Richard **33** 260
Wistarburgh factory **31** 641; **33** 260
wisteria **17** 312, 365
Wistow Church (Cambs) **10** 286
Wiszniewski, Adrian **2** 561; **12** 777
Wit, de (family) **2** 696
Wit, Frederick de **5** 62
Wit, Isaac Jansz. de **6** 89
Wit, Jacob de **1** 807; **15** 139; **33** 261–2*
  collaboration **22** 209
  patrons and collectors **4** 618
  pupils **25** 736; **30** 297
  works **1** 802, 813; **13** 676; **22** 846; **25** 736; **33** *262*
Wit, Jacobus de **33** 110
Wit, Jo de **23** 188
Witaskovo **28** 323
Witches' brooches *see under* BROOCHES → types
Witches Pallium **16** 436
Witcombe Villa (Glos) **32** 542
Witdoeck, Hans **28** 180; **32** 700; **33** 262*
Witelo **1** 113, 177; **2** 518; **19** 356; **24** 487; **28** 202
Witéz, Johannes, Cardinal *see* VITÉZ, JOHANNES, Cardinal
Witgarius Cingulum **12** 463
With, Pieter de **33** 262–3*
Witham Friary (Somerset) **26** 660
Witham Pins **26** 303
Withcote Chapel (Leics) **13** 185
Withego I, Bishop **21** 62
Witherington, William Frederick **24** 571; **33** 453
Withers, Frederick Clarke **9** 205; **32** 95; **33** 263*
Withers, George **20** 478
Withers, Robert Jewell **7** 415
Withers, Walter (Herbert) **14** 307; **19** 413; **29** 243; **33** 263–4*
Witholt, Koort **33** 391
Withoos, Alida **33** 264
Withoos, Frans **33** 264
Withoos, Johannes **33** 264
Withoos, Maria **33** 264
Withoos, Matthias **11** 228; **33** 264*, 268
Withoos, Pieter **27** 271; **33** 264
Withypoll, Paul **29** 28, *28*
Witigowo, Abbot of Reichenau **23** 650
Witkamp, Bert **33** 602
Witkiewicz, Stanisław **32** 876; **33** 264, 265
  architecture **25** 100
  groups and movements **25** 107, 119, 122; **28** 838
  works **25** *100*
Witkiewicz, Stanisław Ignacy **11** 317; **25** 108; **33** 264–5*
Witkiewicz-Koszczyc, Jan **17** 874; **25** 100; **28** 839; **33** 265*
Witkin, Isaac **29** 112
Witkin, Joel Peter **33** 265–6*
Witkowski, Romuald Kamil **25** 108, 422; **26** 296
Witney, Thomas of *see* THOMAS OF WITNEY
Wits, Konrad **12** 276
Witsen, Jonas **14** 794; **30** 15
Witsen, Nicolaas **15** 741; **16** 553; **26** 284
Witsen, Willem (Arnold) **1** 808; **19** 654; **22** 854, 908; **33** 266*
  groups and movements **19** 654; **32** 392
  teachers **1** 650
  works **22** 850
Witsenburg, Thierry **3** 589; **5** 50
Witt, Frederick de **25** 10
Witt, George **10** 487
Witt, Giles de **10** 270
Witt, Jacob de **20** 80
Witt, Johannes de **30** 662
  works **30** *662*
Witt, Robert **10** 367, 376
Witte, Adrien De *see* DE WITTE, ADRIEN
Witte, Emanuel de **22** 844; **33** 266–7*
  groups and movements **8** 669
  works **1** 812; **2** 342; **6** 443; **8** 667; **9** 28; **11** *443*, 446; **22** 843; **33** *267*
Witte, Evrard de **22** 717
Witte, Frans de **21** 358
Witte, Gaspard de **15** 43
Witte, Jacob Eduard **33** 268*
Witte, Jan de **19** 836; **20** 788; **25** 98
Witte, J. C. de **32** 706
Witte, Lieven de **33** 268*
Witte, Peter de, I (1586-1651; tapestry designer) **2** 200
Witte, Peter de, II (1617-67; painter) **7** 832
Witte, Pieter de (*fl c.* 1547-62; tapestry weaver) **5** 605
Witte, Pieter de (*c.* 1548-1628; painter, tapestry designer and draughtsman) *see* CANDID, PETER
Wittel, Gaspar (Adriaansz.) van **16** 672, 674; **26** 774, 841; **31** 893; **33** 268–70*
  groups and movements **9** 462
  patrons and collectors **4** 610; **13** 301; **21** 35; **27** 524; **32** 75
  works **2** 342; **31** 247; **32** 111, 112; **33** *269*
Wittelsbach (House of) **33** 270–73*, *272*, *273*, 278*, 281*
  architecture **12** 471; **24** 268
  collections **12** 473
  ivory-carvings **12** 460
  metalwork **16** 900
  objects of vertu **22** 306
  paintings **9** 18; **12** 476
  sculpture **9** 690
  tapestries **19** 705
Wittelsbach, Adelaide Henrietta, Electress of Bavaria *see* ADELAIDE HENRIETTA, Electress of Bavaria
Wittelsbach, Albert I, Duke of Bavaria *see* ALBERT I, Duke of Bavaria-Straubing
Wittelsbach, Albert II, Duke of Bavaria *see* ALBERT II, Duke of Bavaria
Wittelsbach, Albert III, Duke of Bavaria-Munich *see* ALBERT III, Duke of Bavaria
Wittelsbach, Albert IV, Duke of Bavaria *see* ALBERT IV, Duke of Bavaria
Wittelsbach, Albert V, Duke of Bavaria *see* ALBERT V, Duke of Bavaria
Wittelsbach, Albert VI, Duke **1** 36
Wittelsbach, Anna, Duchess of Bavaria *see* ANNA, Duchess of Bavaria
Wittelsbach, Anna Maria Luisa, Electress Palatine *see* ANNA MARIA LUISA DE' MEDICI, Electress Palatine
Wittelsbach, Augustus **33** *272*
Wittelsbach, Charles *see* BIRKENFELD, CHARLES I, Count Palatine of
Wittelsbach, Charles, Elector of Bavaria *see* CHARLES VII, Holy Roman Emperor
Wittelsbach, Charles, Elector Palatine *see* CHARLES, Elector Palatine
Wittelsbach, Charles II Augustus, Duke of Zweibrücken *see* ZWEIBRÜCKEN, CHARLES II AUGUSTUS, Duke of
Wittelsbach, Charles III Philip *see* CHARLES PHILIP, Elector Palatine
Wittelsbach, Charles Ludwig, Elector Palatine *see* CHARLES LUDWIG, Elector Palatine
Wittelsbach, Charles Philip, Elector Palatine *see* CHARLES PHILIP, Elector Palatine
Wittelsbach, Charles Theodore, Elector Palatine *see* CHARLES THEODORE, Elector Palatine and Elector of Bavaria
Wittelsbach, Charles XI, King of Sweden *see* KARL XI, King of Sweden
Wittelsbach, Christian III, Duke of Zweibrücken *see* ZWEIBRÜCKEN, CHRISTIAN III, Duke of
Wittelsbach, Christian IV, Duke of Zweibrücken *see* ZWEIBRÜCKEN, CHRISTIAN IV, Duke of
Wittelsbach, Christopher, Duke of Bavaria *see* CHRISTOPHER, Duke of Bavaria
Wittelsbach, Clemens August, Bishop of Regensburg, Münster and Paderborn, Archbishop of Cologne **7** 584; **8** 288; **33** *273*, 277*
  architecture **5** 7; **8** 289; **11** 124; **19** 268; **23** 5, 458; **24** 740; **28** 105, 106; **33** 277
  coats of arms **14** 420
  collections **12** 473
  drawings (pastel) **32** 659
  frescoes **5** 775
  gardens **12** 723
  paintings **8** 809; **11** 872; **14** 695; **24** 705; **25** 2; **29** 812; **33** 241
  sculpture **13** 680
Wittelsbach, Clemens Franz, Duke of Bavaria *see* CLEMENS FRANZ, Duke of Bavaria
Wittelsbach, Eleanor, Holy Roman Empress *see* ELEANOR OF WITTELSBACH, Holy Roman Empress
Wittelsbach, Elisabeth, Empress of Austria *see* ELISABETH, Empress of Austria-Hungary
Wittelsbach, Elisabeth-Charlotte *see* ORLÉANS, ELISABETH-CHARLOTTE, Duchesse d'
Wittelsbach, Ernest, Bishop of Passau **14** 836
Wittelsbach, Ernest, Duke of Bavaria *see* ERNEST, Duke of Bavaria
Wittelsbach, Ernest, Prince-Bishop of Liège and Archbishop of Cologne **32** 115
Wittelsbach, Ferdinand, Prince-Bishop of Liège and Archbishop of Cologne **9** 198; **12** 238
Wittelsbach, Ferdinand Maria, Elector of Bavaria *see* FERDINAND MARIA, Elector of Bavaria
Wittelsbach, Ferdinand von **12** 348
Wittelsbach, Frederick (1417-80) **33** *272*
Wittelsbach, Frederick, Duke of Bavaria-Landshut *see* FREDERICK, Duke of Bavaria-Landshut
Wittelsbach, Frederick II, Elector Palatine *see* FREDERICK II, Elector Palatine
Wittelsbach, Frederick Michael, Count Palatine of Birkenfeld *see* BIRKENFELD, FREDERICK MICHAEL, Count Palatine of
Wittelsbach, Frederick the Wise, Elector Palatine *see* FREDERICK II, Elector Palatine
Wittelsbach, Frederick V, Elector Palatine *see* FREDERICK V, Elector Palatine and King of Bohemia
Wittelsbach, Isabeau of Bavaria, Queen of France *see* ISABEAU OF BAVARIA, Queen of France
Wittelsbach, John II, Duke of Bavaria *see* JOHN II, Duke of Bavaria-Munich
Wittelsbach, John III, Duke of Bavaria *see* JOHN III, Duke of Bavaria-Straubing
Wittelsbach, John William, Elector Palatine *see* JOHN WILLIAM, Elector Palatine
Wittelsbach, Joseph Clemens, Elector-Archbishop of Cologne **9** 469; **19** 268; **33** *273*, 277*
  architecture **5** 7; **8** 31; **14** 227
Wittelsbach, Ludwig (1429-89) **33** *272*
Wittelsbach, Ludwig I, Duke of Bavaria *see* LUDWIG I, Duke of Bavaria
Wittelsbach, Ludwig I, King of Bavaria *see* LUDWIG I, King of Bavaria
Wittelsbach, Ludwig II, Duke of Bavaria and Count Palatine of the Rhine *see* LUDWIG II, Duke of Upper Bavaria and Count Palatine of the Rhine
Wittelsbach, Ludwig II, King of Bavaria *see* LUDWIG II, King of Bavaria
Wittelsbach, Ludwig IV, Duke of Bavaria *see* LUDWIG IV, Duke of Bavaria and Holy Roman Emperor
Wittelsbach, Ludwig IV, Elector Palatine *see* LUDWIG IV, Elector Palatine
Wittelsbach, Ludwig the Bavarian, Holy Roman Emperor *see* LUDWIG IV, Duke of Bavaria and Holy Roman Emperor
Wittelsbach, Ludwig VI, Elector Palatine *see* LUDWIG VI, Elector Palatine
Wittelsbach, Ludwig VII, Count Palatine of the Rhine *see* LUDWIG VII, Count Palatine of the Rhine
Wittelsbach, Ludwig VII, Duke of Bavaria *see* LUDWIG VII, Duke of Bavaria-Ingolstadt
Wittelsbach, Ludwig X, Duke of Bavaria *see* LUDWIG X, Duke of Bavaria-Landshut
Wittelsbach, Luitpold, Prince Regent of Bavaria **28** 341; **30** 733
Wittelsbach, Margaret of Bavaria *see* MARGARET OF BAVARIA, Duchess of Burgundy
Wittelsbach, Maria Amalia, Electress of Bavaria *see* MARIA AMALIA, Electress of Bavaria
Wittelsbach, Max Friedrich, Elector of Cologne, Prince-Bishop of Paderborn and Münster **28** 106
Wittelsbach, Maximilian-Henry, Prince-Bishop of Liège **11** 166; **14** 392
Wittelsbach, Maximilian I, Duke and Elector of Bavaria *see* MAXIMILIAN I, Duke and Elector ofBavaria
Wittelsbach, Maximilian II, King of Bavaria *see* MAXIMILIAN II, King of Bavaria
Wittelsbach, Maximilian II Emanuel, Elector of Bavaria *see* MAXIMILIAN II EMANUEL, Elector ofBavaria
Wittelsbach, Maximilian III Joseph, Elector of Bavaria *see* MAXIMILIAN III JOSEPH, Elector ofBavaria
Wittelsbach, Maximilian I Joseph, King of Bavaria *see* MAXIMILIAN I JOSEPH, King of Bavaria
Wittelsbach, Maximilian IV Joseph, Elector of Bavaria (*reg* 1799-1806) *see* MAXIMILIAN I JOSEPH, King of Bavaria (*reg* 1806-25)
Wittelsbach, Maximilian Philipp Hieronymus, Prince of Bavaria **10** *702*
Wittelsbach, Otto Henry, Elector Palatine *see* OTTO HENRY, Elector Palatine
Wittelsbach, Otto of, King of Greece *see* OTTO OF WITTELSBACH, King of Greece

Wittelsbach, Philip, Count Palatine of the Rhine *see* PHILIP, Elector Palatine
Wittelsbach, Philipp Ludwig, Count Palatine of Neuburg *see* NEUBURG, PHILIPP LUDWIG, Count Palatine of
Wittelsbach, Philip William of Neuburg, Elector Palatine *see* PHILIP WILLIAM OF NEUBURG, Elector Palatine
Wittelsbach, Renata, Duchess of Bavaria *see* RENATA, Duchess of Bavaria
Wittelsbach, Rudolf, Count Palatine of the Rhine *see* RUDOLF, Count Palatine of the Rhine
Wittelsbach, Rupert, Prince of the Rhine (1619-82) **10** 252, 341, 658; **21** 414, 415; **25** 629; **29** 800; **31** 797; **33** 281
 works **21** *415*
Wittelsbach, Rupert III, Elector Palatine *see* RUPERT, Holy Roman Emperor
Wittelsbach, Sigismund, Duke of Bavaria *see* SIGISMUND, Duke of Bavaria-Munich
Wittelsbach, Stephen **33** *272*
Wittelsbach, Stephen II, Duke of Bavaria *see* STEPHEN II, Duke of Bavaria-Landshut
Wittelsbach, Violante Beatrice *see* MEDICI, VIOLANTE BEATRICE
Wittelsbach, William IV, Duke of Bavaria *see* WILLIAM IV, Duke of Bavaria
Wittelsbach, William the Steadfast, Duke of Bavaria *see* WILLIAM IV, Duke of Bavaria
Wittelsbach, William V, Duke of Bavaria *see* WILLIAM V, Duke of Bavaria
Wittelsbach, Wolfgang (1526-69) **33** *272*
Wittelsbach, Wolfgang William, Count Palatine of Neuburg *see* NEUBURG, WOLFGANG WILLIAM, Count Palatine of
Witten, Hans **12** 401; **20** 683, 711, 797
Wittenberg
 album amicorum **1** 584
 Luther statue **28** 44
 St Marien **32** *604*
Wittenberg, Abraham von **11** 105
Wittenberg Bible *see under* BIBLES → types
Wittenburg **13** 161
Wittenhorst, Willem Vincent, Baron van **25** 65; **33** 26
Wittering (Cambs), All Saints **2** 67; **22** 216
Wittet, George **33** 283*
 works **4** 289, *290*; **7** 361; **22** 364, *364*
Wittewierum, Bloemhof **4** 778
Wittewrongel, Petrus **32** 590
Wittgenstein (family) **33** 166
Wittgenstein, Karl **28** 343; **33** 284*
Wittgenstein, Ludwig (Josef Johann) **8** 428; **28** 343; **33** 284*
Wittgenstein, Oscar **22** 921
Wittig, August **17** 2; **33** 284–5*
Wittig, Edward **25** 130; **33** 285*
 groups and movements **25** 108, 116; **26** 296
Witting, Teodoro **32** 400
Wittingham, William **31** 653
Wittke, Karl Heinz **3** 393
Wittkopf, Rudolf **30** 105
Wittkower, Margot **33** 285
Wittkower, Rudolf **2** 536; **33** 243, 285*
 assistants **12** 485
 works **3** 266; **5** 760; **15** 91; **28** 20
Wittlich, Josef **22** 441
Wittlich, Petr **8** 426
Wittwer, Hans **7** 669; **11** 841; **21** 408; **27** 214; **28** 556
 works **11** *841*
Wittwer, Martin **13** 888; **14** 887; **33** 286*
Witu Islands **24** 84
Witwatersrand **29** 103, 105
 University *see under* JOHANNESBURG
Witz, Konrad **13** 187; **33** 286–8*
 groups and movements **26** 184
 works **3** 335; **10** 713; **12** 384; **18** 704; **20** 614; **29** 665; **30** 129, *130*; **31** 501; **33** *287*
Witzel, Josef **25** 348
Wivenhoe, University of Essex **10** 242
Wiyot **22** 549
W. J. v. W. *see* WITSEN, WILLEM (ARNOLD)
Wlach, Oskar **2** 810, 815; **29** 777
 works **2** *810*
Wladislav II, King of Bohemia and Hungary (*reg* 1061-92) *see* VLADISLAV II, King of Bohemia and Hungary
Władysław of Oporów **8** 429; **25** 126
Wlérick, Robert **7** 839; **11** 569; **12** 148
Wleughels, Nicolas *see* VLEUGHELS, NICOLAS
Włocławek
 Cathedral **13** 189; **25** 102, 126
 faience (ii) (ceramics) **25** 124
 Museum **25** 140
Włodarczyk-Puchała, Regina **25** 125
Włodarski, Marek **2** 528; **33** 288*
Włostowa Church **25** 126
Włostowic, Maria **33** 416
Włostowic, Piotr **24** 698; **25** 134; **33** 416
WMF **32** 757
Wnętrze **24** 441
Wnuk, Marian **14** 219; **25** 116
woad
 historical and regional traditions
  Byzantine **9** 665
  Early Christian (*c.* AD 250-843) **9** 665
  Portugal **25** 315
  Prehistoric art **25** 477
 uses
  dyes **2** 83; **9** 491, 665; **25** 315
  pigments **24** 791*
  rock art **25** 477
Wobe **8** 486
Wobe, M. F. **25** 841
Wobeser, Hilla *see* BECHER, HILLA
Woburn Abbey (Beds) **7** 351; **10** 295; **27** 357; **32** 540
 collections **5** 541; **7** 839; **27** 357
 Conservatory *see* Sculpture Gallery
 dairy **8** 105, 461; **12** 128
 frames **11** 426
 furniture **15** 165
 grotto **11** 242; **13** 704
 interior decoration **26** 85
 paintings **5** 597; **7** 552; **8** 282, 296, 297; **9** 484; **10** 344; **11** 908; **12** 515; **13** 301; **14** 268; **26** 394; **27** 357, 358; **29** 798; **31** 415; **32** 111
 porcelain **30** 219
 sculpture **4** 221; **8** 699; **10** 365; **27** 357; **30** 764
 Sculpture Gallery **7** 744
Wochenblatt für Baukunde **24** 444
Wocher, Marquand **1** 31; **18** 224; **30** 133
Wocke, Richard **4** 155
Wodaabe **11** 827, 828
Wodeyar (dynasty) *see*:
 DODDA DEVARAJA, Raja
 KRISHNARAJA III, Raja
 WODEYAR, Raja
Wodeyar, Raja (*reg* 1578-1617) (Wodeyar) **15** 648
Wodiczko, Krzysztof **33** 288*
Wodlark, Robert **5** 511
Wodon (family) **22** 452
Woeiriot, Pierre **2** 455; **33** 289*
Woelffer, Emerson **19** 492
Woensam, Anton **33** 289–90*
 attributions **20** 790
 works **7** 583, *584*; **33** *290*, 354
Woensam, Jaspar **33** 289
Woerden Castle **22** 822
Woerffel, Karl F. **27** 428
Woestyne, Gustave Van de *see* VAN DE WOESTYNE, GUSTAVE
Woestyne, Karel Van den *see* VAN DEN WOESTYNE, KAREL
Wogensky, André **2** 660; **7** 296; **11** 527; **19** 51; **23** 901; **30** 391, 684
Wogensky, Robert **11** 644
Wohlbrecht, Wawrzyniec **25** 129
Wohlert, Vilhelm **4** 183–4*; **8** 729
Wohlhaupter, Emanuel **30** 536
Wojciechowski, Jarosław **27** 722
Wojciechowski, Tadeusz **2** 528
Wojciechowsky, Konstanty **8** 429
Wojnarowicz, David **12** 218
Wojniakowski, Kazimierz **8** 372; **25** 105; **33** 290*
Wojnowice **4** 783
Wojtkiewicz, Witold **18** 428; **25** 108; **33** 290–91*
Wojtyna-Drouet, Krystyna **25** 134
Woking (Surrey)
 Brookwood Cemetery **6** 166
 Methodist Church **21** 347
Wokingham (Berks)
 Newton's Luckley **9** 739
 school **26** *19*
Wokyndon Cross-orphrey **13** 197
Woland, Franz Pavel Pavlovich de **23** 353
Wolanin, Bronisław **25** 124
Wolbrandt, H. C. **13** 209
Wolcker, Johann Georg **3** 779, 781; **18** 47
Wolcot, John **23** 451
Wold, Roar **13** 726
Wolf, Achille **8** 427; **25** 151
Wolf, Caspar **30** 143; **33** 291–2*
 groups and movements **26** 740
 reproductive prints by others **9** 395
 works **3** 823; **18** 713; **30** 133; **33** *291*
Wolf, Ernesto **4** 725
Wolf, Janez **2** 889; **29** 885
Wolf, Johann Andreas *see* WOLFF, JOHANN ANDREAS
Wolf, LAM de **22** 897
Wolf, Ludwig **18** 484
Wolf, Reinhart **33** 292*
Wolf, Walther **10** 84
Wolfe, Catherine Lorillard **8** 794; **24** 300
Wolfe, Edward **11** 437
 frames **11** *437*
Wolfe, Ernie, III
 works **1** *258*
Wolfe, Ivor de *see* HASTINGS, HUBERT DE CRONIN
Wolfe, John Lewis **3** 281
Wolfe, L. **20** 60
Wolfegg, Maximilian Willibald, Herzog von **8** 126
Wolfegg Codex *see under* CODICES → individual manuscripts
Wolfegg Schloss **2** 607; **12** 369; **14** 665
Wolfenbüttel **12** *360*; **33** 292–3*
 Braunschweigisches Landesmuseum **33** 293
 Bundesakademie für Kulturelle Bildung **33** 293
 churches **14** 82
 Herzog August Bibliothek **19** 314, 315; **33** 51, 293
Wolfenbüttel—cont.
 Lessinghaus **33** 293
 Marienkirche **11** 716
 Niedersächisches Staatsarchiv **33** 293
 pattern books **24** 269
 Schlossplatz **33** *50*
 Schloss Salzdahlum **33** 53, *54*
  Grosse Galerie **33** 53
 tapestries **12** 467
 urban planning **33** 52–3
Wolfenbüttel Model Book (Wolfenbüttel, Herzog August Bib. Cod. Guelf. 61.2. Aug. 8o) **14** 535; **24** 269
Wolfers, Edouard **3** 601
Wolfers, Guillaume **3** 601
Wolfers, Louis **3** 601; **33** 293
Wolfers, Philippe **33** 293–4*
 house **10** 735
 personal collection **3** 586
 works **3** 595, 601–2, *602*, 604, 605; **14** 138
Wolfers Frères **33** 293
Wolff (company) **8** 428
Wolff (ii) (family) *see* WULFF
Wolff, Adolf **8** 435
Wolff, (Carl Konrad) Albert **33** 295–6*
 assistants **28** 51
 pupils **6** 92, 93
  Encke, Erdmann **10** 200
  Herter, Ernst **14** 482
  Klimsch, Fritz **18** 128
  Kruse, (Carl) Max **18** 480
  Küppers, Albert Hermann **18** 527
  Lessing, Otto **19** 244
  Reusch, (Johann) Friedrich **26** 258
  Sinding, Stephan (Abel) **28** 770
  Volkmann, Artur (Joseph Wilhelm) **32** 686
 teachers **12** 406; **26** 23
 works **12** 407
Wolff, Andreas **13** 845
Wolff, Ann **30** 103
Wolff, Christian **5** 381
Wolff, Christian Philipp **33** 295
Wolff, David
 works **12** *786*
Wolff, Eberhard Philipp **4** 374
Wolff, Emil **28** 45, 46; **33** 296*
Wolff, Gustav H(einrich) **33** 296*
Wolff (i), Hans **33** 294, 295*
Wolff, Hans Georg **12** 494
Wolff, Heinrich **3** 796; **24** 591; **29** 638
Wolff, Henning **8** 727
Wolff, Jacob (*fl c.* 1500-1510; print publisher) **20** 793
Wolff (i), Jakob, I (1546-before 1571) **33** 294–5*
 collaboration **5** 763; **33** 295
 pupils **5** 763
 works **12** 368; **23** 307; **33** *294*, 295
Wolff (i), Jakob, II (1571-1620) **12** 370; **33** 294, 295*
 collaboration **5** 763; **33** 294, 295
 works **12** 370; **33** 130
Wolff, Janet **28** 927
Wolff, Jeremias **30** 793
Wolff, J. H. **4** 798
Wolff, Johann **30** 97, 883
Wolff, Johann Andreas **22** 302; **33** 296–7*
 collaboration **32** 603
 pupils **3** 779; **29** 602
 reproductive prints by others **1** 787
Wolff, Johann Caspar **33** 297*
Wolff, Jonas **33** 296
Wolff, Karol **32** 879
Wolff, Kurt **20** 404
Wolff, Martha **6** 78
Wolff, O. **1** 685
Wolff, Thomas **20** 793
Wolff and Bernardi **25** 122
Wolffgang, Johann Georg **10** 857
Wölfflin, Heinrich **2** 532, 535–6; **3** 333; **5** 190; **26** 186, 570; **28** 917; **30** 156, 157; **31** 672; **33** 297–8*
 pupils **4** 143; **11** 737; **12** 47, 601; **14** 99, 383; **21** 478; **26** 405; **28** 23, 165; **29** 613; **30** 120; **32** 752
 works **2** 360, 517; **9** 444; **11** 315; **12** 483; **13** 34; **24** 454; **25** 361; **29** 876, 879
  on the Baroque **3** 262–3, 264
  translated **22** 104
Wolff Metternich, Franz(iskus), Graf von **33** 298*
Wolffort, Artus **19** 430; **33** 298*
Wolffram, Gottfried **8** 752
Wolff Schoemaker, C. P. **15** 770
Wolff von Gudenberg, Wilhelm **22** 883
Wolfganck, Peter **13** 910
Wolfgang (family) **2** 719
Wolfgang, Saint **2** 777
Wolfgang, Georg Andreas (1631-1716) **21** 415; **27** 823; **28** 127
Wolfgang, Georg Anton, I **28** 149
Wolfgang Altarpiece, Master of the **20** 785–6*
Wolfgang von Kaas, Wilhelm Friedrich **7** 584
wolf-hair *see under* HAIR → types
Wolf Heads Painter **10** 614
Wolfhelm, Abbot of Brauweiler **23** 647
Wölfli, Adolf **33** 299*
 groups and movements **2** 516; **30** 23
 patrons and collectors **25** 685
 works **25** *686*
Wolframus (*fl c.* 1160) **26** 685
Wolframus Presbyter (*fl* 1st half of 12th cent.) **26** 684
Wolfram von Eschenbach **26** 563
Wolf Rock Lighthouse **19** 361
Wolfson, Isaac **23** 684
Wolfson, Mitchell, jr **7** 378
Wolfstein Altar **14** 450
wolf teeth *see under* TEETH → types
Wolgemut, Michael **33** 299–302*, 349
 attributions **20** 683
 collaboration **23** 310; **25** 40
 patrons and collectors **14** 485
 pupils **9** 428; **25** 41
 works **12** 385; **23** 308; **27** *660*; **33** *300*, *301*
Wolgemut, Valentin **20** 785; **33** 299
Wolin **25** 124
Woljŏng Temple **18** 293
Wolkenstein, San Micheli **17** 854
Wolkenstein Schloss **33** 113
Wołkowski, Władysław **25** 122
Wollaston, John **3** 700; **23** 46; **31** 600; **33** 302*
Wollaston, William Hyde **5** 518; **28** 203
Wollaston Franks, Augustus **23** 692
Wollaton Hall (Notts) **6** 59; **8** 44; **10** 143, 230, 360; **13** 619; **28** 894–5; **32** 551
 Camellia House **7** 745
 Castle Museum **23** 258
 entrance front **28** *895*
Wolleb, Hans Heinrich **13** 267
Wollek, Carl **2** 803; **28** 155
Wollen, Peter **10** 689
Wollen, William **3** 390
Woller, Jacob **3** 414
Wollfs Erben, Jeremias **18** 120
Wollheim, Richard **1** 174, 183; **7** 715; **10** 692; **14** 459; **29** 876
Wollstonecraft, Mary **4** 117
Wolmar *see* VALMIERA
Wolmark, Alfred **17** 578; **29** 508

Wolmby, Nelson
works **1** *62*
Wolmut, Bonifaz **33** 302–3*
collaboration **10** 889; **25** 426
patrons and collectors **13** 908
works **2** 212, 780; **4** 58; **8** 378; **13** 646; **19** 769; **25** 438, 441; **32** 434; **33** *303*
Wolof **1** 281, 348, 350, 351; **11** 827; **12** 32; **28** 404, 405
Wolpe, Berthold (Ludwig) **22** 117; **33** 303–4*
Wolpert, Ludwig **17** 568
Wolpert, Yehuda **16** 568
Wolrab, Nikolaus **8** 120
Wolryche, John **5** 514; **7** 419
Wols **7** 842; **11** 551; **33** 304–5*
groups and movements **2** 515, 543, 544; **3** 155; **11** 551; **30** 22, 231
patrons and collectors **19** 282; **21** 135; **30** 749
works **9** 310; **32** 902; **33** *305*
Wolsan
jewellery **18** *365*
Wolsey, Thomas, Cardinal **28** 156; **33** 306*
architecture **10** 229, 261; **14** 126; **19** 568, 617; **22** 717; **26** 70
carpets **5** 835; **10** 273
gold **1** 746
manuscripts **14** 760
paintings **10** 362
sculpture **3** 706; **16** 695; **19** 600; **20** 116
tapestries **10** 348
tomb **27** 831
Wolske, Siegfried **4** 324
Wolsong *see* CH'OE PUK
Wolstenholme, Dean **26** 75
Wolters, Matthias-Joseph **3** 548, 578; **33** 306–7*
Wolters, Rudolf **12** 379
Woltmann **24** 423
Woluwe-Saint-Pierre *see under* BRUSSELS
Woluwé-St-Lambert, Université Catholique de Louvain Medical Faculty Building *see under* BRUSSELS
Wolvecamp, Theo **7** 489; **27** 137
Wolvens, Henri-Victor **3** 565; **5** 44
Wolverhampton (W. Midlands)
Art Gallery **10** 370
papier mâché **24** 62
St Peter
Wolverhampton Pillar **2** 70
steel **10** 345
Wolzogen, Ernst von **4** 42; **10** 215
Woman Painter **13** 536
women **10** 682
Africa **1** 246–7*, 256, 340
Assyrian **1** 886
Australia **2** 752
Byzantine **23** 830
Cameroon **1** 259*
Central Asia, Western **30** 917
Early Christian (*c.* AD 250-843) **9** 515
Egypt, ancient **9** 811*, 855, 856, 867, 889-90, 893–4; **22** 722
France **7** 235
Greece, ancient **13** 415, 423; **25** 456
Indian subcontinent **15** 637
Indonesia **15** 771
Islamic **15** 637
Japan **17** 212
Kuba (iii) (Zaïre) **1** 340
Liberia **1** 247, 340
Luba **19** 739*
Mali **1** 247
Mende (Sierra Leone) **1** 236, 247, 340
Netherlands, the **3** 504
Scandinavia **32** 521
Sierra Leone **1** 247, 340
United States of America **31** 669
Viking **32** 521
women—cont.
Yoruba **1** 340
Women and Art **10** 878
Women and Students for Black Liberation **26** 410
women artists **1** 107; **6** 176; **7** 830; **10** 483–4; **24** 662; **33** 307–22*, *311*
Africa **1** *246*, 246–7*
Albania **1** 540
Brazil **33** 316–17
China **33** 317–22*
Denmark **8** 760
England **10** 374, 877–8; **30** 157
17th cent. **5** 766
18th cent. **10** 329
Finland **2** 317
France **4** 318; **10** 197; **11** 672*; **12** 336; **14** 282; **21** 412; **24** 138, 139, 141, 142
Germany **3** 401; **18** 206
Ghana **1** *246*
Gothic **33** *308*
Ijo **1** 247
Islamic **16** 476
Italy **2** 93; **4** 765; **10** 476; **11** 268, 269; **16** 668*, 780
17th cent. **12** 306
Japan **17** 792; **31** 525; **33** 317–22*
Kenya **1** 292
Latin America **33** 316–17*
Mexico **33** 316
Ottoman **16** 476
Peru **24** 509
Portugal **25** 316
Puerto Rico **25** 701
Scotland **28** 235
South Africa **29** 104
Turkey **16** 476
United States of America **3** 489; **10** 878; **22** 112; **24** 305, 671; **25** 237; **31** 609, 673
Yoruba **1** 246
see also FEMINISM
Women's Art Associaton (Montreal) **5** 582
Women's Art Journal **10** 878; **24** 425, 429
Women's Art Magazine **24** 425
Women's Art Registry **9** 385; **10** 878
Womersley, J. **22** 386
Womersley, Peter **28** 232
Wŏnchŏng *see* MIN YŎNG-IK
Wonder, Pieter Christoffel **18** 177; **22** 848; **33** 322–3*
groups and movements **31** 771
works **9** 17, *17*
Wondrous Mountain *see* SAMANDAĞI
Wong, Alfred **28** 772
Wong, Brent **33** 58
Wong, Paul **5** 569
Wong, Wucius **14** 722; **33** 323*
Wongo **18** 484; **24** 357
Wongshing **7** 30
Wong-Upparaj, Damrong **30** 617
Wŏnhyo **5** 115
Woning, De **1** 811; **22** 875; **24** 351; **33** 323*
Wonner, Paul **8** 871
Won-o Temple **18** 266, 267
Wonsam, Anton *see* WOENSAM, ANTON
Wŏnsan **18** *248*, 262
Wŏnsŏng, King (*reg* 785-98) **18** 299
Wŏnwŏn Temple **18** 289
Wŏnyung Buddhism *see* BUDDHISM → sects → Avataṁsaka
wood **33** 323–40*, *323*, *336*
cleaning **33** 339–40
conservation **7** 747, 748; **33** 336–40*
dating methods **11** 309; **30** *403*, 404, *405*
historical and regional traditions
Aboriginal Australia **1** *55*
wood
historical and regional traditions—cont.
Africa **1** 251, 291–2*, 295, 305–7, 321–5*, *322*, *323*, *324*, *325*, *355*, *356*, 365, *398*, *399*, *402*, 402, *403*, *404*, *415*, *427*; **9** 164
Asante **1** *390*
Baga **1** *391*
Baule **1** *233*
Cameroon **1** *277*
Congo, Republic of **1** *399*
Dan (Africa) **1** *368*
Fang **1** *232*
Ibibio **1** *273*
Kenya **1** *411*, *412*
Kissi **1** *359*
Kongo **1** *233*, *275*; **18** *220*
Kuba (iii) (Zaïre) **1** *269*
Lobi **1** *272*
Mossi **1** *384*
Ngumba **1** *397*
Nupe **1** *383*
Senufo **1** *281*
Shona **1** *416*
Surinam **1** *423*
United States of America **1** *422*
Yoruba **1** *270*
Zande **1** *359*
Akan **1** 291; **2** 590
Anglo-Saxon **2** 64, 67
Angola **2** *86*; **7** *197*, *198*
Arabia **2** 248
Asante **2** 588, *588*, 590, *591*
Australia **2** 757
Austral Islands **2** *773*
Austria **9** *152*; **12** *813*; **13** *799*
Aztec **2** 907; **21** 719, *719*
Baga **1** *391*; **3** *46*
Bali (Indonesia) **15** 785–7*, *786*, 806, *812*
Bamana **1** *323*; **3** *132*, 132–3, *133*, *135*; **9** 164
Bamileke **1** *277*; **3** *147*
Bamum **1** 353
Bantu peoples **1** 367, 368
Baule **1** *233*, *324*; **3** *405*, *408*
Belarus' **17** *546*
Belgium **3** 576, 578; **12** *522*; **13** 109–15*, *111*, *112*; **26** 644–5*, *645*
Bembe **3** *694*
Benin Republic **1** *272*
Bhutan **3** 914
Bobo **4** 192
Bolivia **4** 255
Brazil **4** *708*
Buddhism **5** *100*; **6** 298, 300; **17** *116*, 116–26*, *117*, *118*, *120*, *123*, *125*, *126*; **18** *292*, *295*, 295, *296*, 768; **28** *636*; **30** 585–6, *586*, 823; **32** 479, *479*
China **6** 706, 717, 718, 721, 722, *722*
Bulgaria **5** 155–6
Burkina Faso **22** *197*, *198*
Burma **20** 327
Byzantine **1** 694; **9** *521*, 539, 599–602*, *600*
Cambodia **5** 482, 499
Cameroon **1** *277*
Canada **5** 558, 578, 579
Caribbean Islands **5** 748, *748*, 755
Central Asia, Eastern **6** 295, 298, 300, 303, 306, 315, *316*; **28** *636*
Central Asia, Western **6** 220; **16** 199
China **6** 637–43*, 706; **7** 30–31, 94, 109, 122, 126, 128, 138, 143, 145; **20** 326; **28** 310
Han period (206 BC-AD 220) **7** 62–3
Liao period (AD 907-1125) **19** 303
wood
historical and regional traditions
China—cont.
Ming period (1368-1644) **6** 721
Qing period (1644-1911) **6** 722, *722*
Shang period (*c.* 1600-*c.* 1050 BC) **7** 107
Song period (AD 960-1279) **6** 717, 718
Tang period (AD 618-907) **6** 650; **7** 92, 109
Zhou period (*c.* 1050-256 BC) **6** *696*; **7** 62, 97
20th cent. **31** 259
Chokwe **1** 291, *404*; **7** *197*
Congo, Republic of **1** *275*, *399*; **3** *694*
Cook Islands **7** *790*
Côte d'Ivoire **1** *281*; **9** 164; **13** *860*
Czech Republic **8** 376, 379, 383, *383*, *388*
Dan (Africa) **1** *291*, *368*
Denmark **8** 738
Dogon **1** *262*, *322*; **9** *66*, *67*, *68*, *69*, 164
Dominican Order **9** *110*
Early Christian (*c.* AD 250-843) **1** 693; **9** 151–2, 539, 599–602*; **30** 776
Ecuador **9** 710
Egypt **9** 160; **16** 176; **21** 505
Egypt, ancient **9** 775, 819–23*, 824; **10** 70; **29** 614; **30** 775; **31** 259
Early Dynastic (*c.* 2925-*c.* 2575 BC) **14** *494*
Middle Kingdom (*c.* 1966-*c.* 1630 BC) **2** *659*; **10** 10; **20** 327
New Kingdom (*c.* 1539-*c.* 1075 BC) **10** 52, *65*
Old Kingdom (*c.* 2575-*c.* 2130 BC) **10** 8; **14** 494
Predynastic (*c.* 6000-*c.* 2925 BC) **10** 29; **30** 433
Third Intermediate Period (*c.* 1075-*c.* 656 BC) **9** 886; **31** 254
18th Dynasty (*c.* 1539-*c.* 1292 BC) **10** *4*, *5*, 5, *66*
Ejagham **10** *122*, 122–3
England **2** *572*; **10** 288; **13** 121–2*; **14** 198; **23** 809; **26** 643–4*; **30** *778*; **31** 259
Fang **1** *232*; **10** *788*, *789*, *790*, *791*
Fiji **11** 68, *68*
Finland **32** 286–7
Fon **1** *272*
France **4** *661*; **9** 152; **11** 595–6, 598, 601; **13** 125–6*, *126*; **24** *716*, *821*; **26** 641*
Gabon **1** *399*
Gambier Islands **31** *404*
Germany **2** *45*; **3** *672*; **9** *752*; **12** 362; **17** *741*; **22** *303*; **24** *461*; **28** *111*; **31** 255; **32** *253*
Ghana **1** *272*; **12** *509*
Gothic **8** *383*; **13** 109–20*, *111*, *112*, *115*, 115, 121–6*, *122*, *124*, *126*; **14** *892*; **17** *741*
Greece **9** *600*
Greece, ancient **1** 450; **8** 262; **9** 151; **13** 376, 389–90, 433–4*, 442, 543, 592, 604*; **20** 327; **21** 712; **27** 825
Guinea **1** *359*; **3** *46*
Guro **13** *860*
Guyana **13** *877*
Haiti **14** *55*
Hemba **14** *377*, *378*
Hinduism **15** *524*, *783*; **18** *769*
Holy Roman Empire (before 1648) **13** 115–18*; **26** 645–6*; **29** 570
wood
historical and regional traditions—cont.
Hungary **14** *892*
Ibibio **1** *273*
Iceland **15** *72*
Igbo **9** 164; **15** *113*, *115*
Indian subcontinent **15** 412, 414, *524*, 544, 549, 706, 724; **18** 609; **31** 259
Kerala **15** 523–4
Naga (people) **15** *733*
18th cent. **7** *616*
Indonesia **15** 757, *783*, 784, 785–7*, *786*, 789
Iran **6** *172*; **9** 160; **16** 199
Iran, ancient **15** 902
Irian Jaya **16** *43*, *45*, *47*; **23** 715
Islamic **6** 171, 556; **9** 160; **16** 141, 142, 269, 356, *383*, 503; **21** 505, 629–30
Central Asia, Western **16** 199
Egypt **16** 176
Iran **6** *172*; **16** 199
Malaysia **20** 166
Morocco **16** *493*; **21** *630*
North Africa **29** 618
Ottoman **16** 222
Spain **16** 216, *493*, 494–5, *506*
Turkey **16** 202, 222
Yemen **16** *500*, 500–501
Italy **1** 709; **8** *215*; **9** *129*, 151–2; **13** 123–4*, *124*; **26** 644*; **27** *12*; **30** *357*, 667, *776*
18th cent. **5** *54*
Jamaica **5** *748*
Japan **17** 45, 99–100*, 101, 348, 356–7*, 371, 384, 387, 398, 407
Edo period (1600-1868) **17** *126*, *349*, 372, *407*
Heian period (AD 794-1185) **17** *116*, 116–21, *117*, *118*, *120*, *128*
Kamakura period (1185-1333) **17** 121–6*, *123*, *125*, 729
Meiji period (1868-1912) **17** *134*
Nara period (AD 710-94) **17** 116, *391*
Shōwa period (1926-89) **17** *137*
Java **15** 772, *783*
Jewish art **17** *546*
Jukun **17** 680
Kenya **1** *411*, *412*
Khmer **5** 499
Kiribati **23** 717
Kissi **1** *359*
Kongo **1** *233*, *275*; **18** *220*
Korea **18** 264–5, *264*, 266, 271, 277, 281, *292*, 295, *378*, 379; **23** 775
16th cent. **18** *295*
18th cent. **18** *296*
20th cent. **18** 300, 301
Kuba (iii) (Zaïre) **1** *269*; **18** *486*, *488*
Laos **18** 768, *769*, 776–7
Lega **19** *73*
Liberia **1** *291*
Lobi **1** *272*
Luba **1** *325*, *355*; **19** *740*, *742*, *743*, *744*
Lwena **7** *198*
Madagascar **20** *38*, 40
Makonde (Mozambique) **20** *150*
Malaysia **20** 166, 167, 174
Mali **1** *262*, *281*; **9** *68*, 164
Malta (Republic of) **20** *214*
Mangbetu **1** *404*
Maori **23** 717
Mende (Sierra Leone) **1** *282*; **21** *115*, *117*
Mesoamerica, Pre-Columbian **21** *719*
Mesopotamia **9** 539
Mongolia **21** 883–4*
Morocco **16** *493*; **21** *630*

wood
historical and regional traditions—cont.
Mossi **1** *384*; **22** *197*, 198, *198*
Native North Americans **16** *891*; **22** *578*, 582, 586, 662, 663, *664*
Nepal **17** *842*; **22** 774*, *788*
Netherlands, the **13** 109–15*, *115*; **22** *870*, *876*; **26** 644–5*
New Caledonia **23** *18*, *19*
New Zealand **23** *53*, 717
Niger **23** 127
Nigeria **1** *270*, *273*, *356*, *427*; **9** 164, *164*; **15** *113*, *115*
North Africa
Islamic **29** 618
Norway **23** 219, *219*, 220, 221; **31** *750*; **32** 286–7
Nupe **1** *383*; **9** 164
Ottoman **9** 160; **16** 222
Ottonian **23** 647–9
Ovimbundu **7** *199*
Pacific Islands **23** 712, *712*, 715–18*, *717*, *732*
Pakistan **23** 803
Palau **23** 717
Palestine **9** 539
Papua New Guinea **23** 716–17, *717*, *732*; **24** *69*, *71*, *72*, *80*
Paraguay **24** *93*, *97*, *99*
Pende **24** *358*
Peru **24** *498*
Philippines **24** *619*, 626–7*, *630*
Phrygian **13** *8*
Poland **25** *96*
Portugal **13** 124–5*; **25** 303; **26** 648*
Prehistoric art **25** 493, 499, 547
Puerto Rico **5** *750*
Romanesque **9** *152*; **26** 569, 640–41*, 642–7*, *643*, *645*, *647*, 648*
Romania **26** 706, *717*
Rome, ancient **6** 388; **9** 151; **12** 362; **20** 327; **21** 713; **26** 856; **27** 12, *12*
Russia **18** 104; **27** 368; **30** *363*
Samoa **23** 717, 718
Scandinavia **13** 118–20*; **26** 646–7*; **30** 778; **31** 363
Senufo **1** *281*; **9** 164; **28** *419*, *420*, *421*, *422*
Shinto **17** *128*
Shona **1** *416*; **28** *621*
Sierra Leone **1** *282*
Slovenia **28** 862, *862*
Society Islands **23** *712*
Sogdiana **6** 220; **18** *500*
Solomon Islands **29** *49*, *50*
Songo **7** *198*
South America, Pre-Columbian **29** *188*, *189*
South-east Asia **29** 226
Spain **26** 642–3*; **29** 291
Baroque **29** *292*
Gothic **13** *122*, 122–3*
Islamic **16** 216, *493*, 494–5, *506*
Mudéjar **19** 658
Renaissance **3** *846*
Romanesque **26** *643*
15th cent. **2** *529*
17th cent. **9** *110*; **10** *903*; **21** *173*; **22** *2*, *3*, *4*
20th cent. **29** *296*
Sri Lanka **20** *328*; **29** 477–8*
Surinam **1** *423*
Swahili **9** 165; **30** *57*
Sweden **23** *255*; **26** *647*; **32** 286–7
Syria **9** 539
Syria-Palestine **30** 179
Tajikistan **18** *500*
Tanzania **9** 165; **30** *57*
Tarascan **30** 342
Teke **30** *419*, *420*
Thailand **20** 327; **30** 585–6, *586*, *637*, 639

wood
historical and regional traditions—cont.
Tibet **30** 823, 835, 836, *846*, 846–7
Tonga (Pacific Islands) **31** *144*
Tuareg **23** 127; **31** 407*
Turkey **9** 160; **13** *8*; **16** 202, 222
Islamic **16** 222
Ukraine **31** 546
United States of America **1** *422*; **2** 242
Venda **32** *154*
Vietnam **5** *100*; **32** 479, *479*, 487
Yoruba **1** *270*, *283*, 283–4, *356*; **9** 164, *164*
Zaïre **1** *269*, *275*, *359*, *402*; **14** *377*, *378*; **18** *486*, *488*; **19** *73*
Zambia **33** 603
Zande **1** *359*
patinas **11** 307; **24** 258
technical examination **30** 409, 410; **33** 337
techniques
drying **33** 327
painting **33** 335
staining **33** 335, 338
varnishing **33** 335–6
tools **33** *336*
uses
adzes **23** *712*
altarpieces **1** 707, 709; **23** *255*
altars **1** 693, 694, 698; **17** *741*; **18** 777
aqueducts **2** 242
architectural decorations **16** 142; **29** 477–8
architecture **1** 305–7; **20** 167, 560
Anglo-Saxon **2** 64
Belarus' **17** *546*
Cambodia **5** 482
Canada **5** 558
Central Asia, Eastern **6** 295
Central Asia, Western **16** 199
China **6** 637–43*, 650
Czech Republic **8** 376, 379
Egypt **16** 176
Egypt, ancient **9** 775, 824
England **23** 809
Finland **32** 286–7
Indian subcontinent **15** 721
Iran **16** 199
Islamic **16** 141, 176, 199, 269, 491–2, 494–5
Japan **17** 45
Jewish art **17** *546*
Korea **18** 264–5, *264*
Norway **23** 219, 220, 221; **32** 286–7
Pacific Islands **23** 715–18, *717*
Papua New Guinea **23** *717*
Prehistoric art **25** 499
Rome, ancient **26** 856
Russia **18** 104; **27** 368
Scandinavia **31** 363
South-east Asia **29** 226
Spain **16** 494–5
Sweden **32** 286–7
Thailand **30** 585–6, *586*
Ukraine **31** 546
armatures **29** 813
armillary spheres **12** *813*
balconies (houses) **16** 269
barges **30** 639
baskets **1** 295; **22** 662, 663
battens **24** 5, *5*
beads **3** 441
benches **24** *630*
bookbindings **4** 347; **24** 107; **30** 836
bookcases **16** 487
book covers **6** 306; **16** 356; **20** 327; **30** 836, 846, *846*
bowls **1** *356*; **11** 68, *68*; **22** 586; **29** *50*; **31** 305; **32** *154*

wood
uses—cont.
boxes **7** 141; **16** *383*, 487, 497; **30** 847
bridges **4** 802*; **14** 198; **18** 281
brushes **3** 914
brushpots **7** 141, *141*
brush-rests **7** 141
busts **6** *316*; **27** *12*
cabinets (i) (rooms) **5** 346
cabinets (ii) (furniture) **2** *45*
candle holders **18** 777
candlesticks **5** 611
capitals **31** *750*
caskets **9** *521*
catafalques **6** 71
ceilings **2** *529*; **13** 390; **16** 216, 494–5, *495*; **30** *357*
Mudéjar **19** 658
cenotaphs **6** 171, *172*
chairs **1** 291; **2** *572*; **5** *54*; **6** 388, 389; **15** *72*
chalices **31** 305
chariots **30** 639
chess sets **6** 555, 556, 557
churches **2** 67; **12** 362; **23** *53*; **25** *96*; **26** 706; **29** 579
clubs (weapons) **7** *198*; **22** 586
coffins **10** 8, 10; **15** *812*; **30** 639; **33** *580*
columns **16** 502, *502*
combs (hair) **1** *423*; **2** 590; **7** 107, 109
console tables **11** 595
containers **24** 626–7*; **29** *189*
costumes **28** *111*
crosses **8** 203
crucifixes **8** *215*; **13** *122*, 122, 123, *124*; **22** *2*; **23** 647–8; **26** *643*, *647*
cupboards **12** *420*; **18** 777
cups **18** *488*; **31** 305
daggers **16** *506*
diptychs **9** 3
dolls **17** 371, 372; **22** 198, *198*; **31** 259*, 262
dolls' houses **31** 262, 263
domes **16** 496
doors
Africa **9** 164, *164*
Austria **9** *152*
Baule **3** *408*
Byzantine **9** *600*
Early Christian (*c.* AD 250-843) **9** 151–2*, 599–600
France **26** 641
Islamic **9** 160; **16** 492, 495, 501–2
Nigeria **1** *427*
Nupe **1** *383*
Rome, ancient **9** 151
Tanzania **30** *57*
doorways **5** *241*
dressers **22** *870*
drums (musical instruments) **2** *591*; **24** *69*; **30** *637*
écorchés **9** 706
etchings **10** 561
fibre art **11** 54
figureheads **29** *49*
figurines **1** *269*, *270*, *272*, *275*, *277*, *281*; **2** *86*; **3** *694*; **7** 140, 141; **15** *783*; **22** 582
finials (architectural) **23** *18*
floors **3** 578
fonts (baptismal) **11** 252*
fortifications **21** 561–2
frames **11** 373
funerary objects **18** 777
furniture **1** 365; **7** 30–31, 145; **10** 52; **11** 595–6, 598, 601; **13** 592; **14** 494; **16** 498; **17** 384; **18** 776; **20** 40; **22** *876*
game-pieces **31** 266
gates **30** 639
gongs **1** *359*
grilles **16** 487, 496, 502
gun stocks **16** 499
harps **10** *65*

wood
uses—cont.
headdresses **1** *391*; **3** *47*; **15** *124*
headrests **1** *403*, *411*, *416*; **19** *744*; **28** *621*
houses **3** 575; **5** 236; **7** 143; **18** 277; **23** *717*
human figures **16** *43*; **31** *404*
inkstones **7** 94; **17** 387
jewellery **10** 29; **17** 530; **32** 487
keris **20** 174
knife-handles **8** 284, 285
korwar **16** *43*
lacquer **17** 101; **18** 601, 609
ladles **21** *884*
lintels **20** *355*
locks **3** *132*
manuscript covers **15** 544, 549
manuscripts **7** 62–3; **30** 835
maqṣūras **16** 487
marquetry **16** 487, 490; **20** 466, 468
masks
Africa **1** *399*
Asante **1** *390*
Bamana **3** *135*
Bobo **4** 192
Dan (Africa) **8** *487*
Dogon **9** *68*
Ejagham **10** *122*, 122–3
Fang **10** *791*
Gabon **1** *399*
Guro **13** *860*
Ibibio **1** *273*
Indian subcontinent **15** 706
Japan **17** 349, *349*, *391*
Jukun **17** 680
Korea **18** *378*
Kuba (iii) (Zaïre) **18** *488*
Lega **19** *73*
Lwena **7** *198*
Mende (Sierra Leone) **1** *282*; **21** *115*, *117*
Mossi **1** *384*; **22** *197*
Native North Americans **16** *891*; **22** *545*, *573*, *578*, *664*
Nepal **22** *788*
New Caledonia **23** *19*
Papua New Guinea **24** *72*
Pende **24** *358*
Senufo **28** *421*, *422*
meeting halls **17** *842*
mihrabs **16** *492*, 492; **21** 505
minbars **16** 487, *493*, 493–4, 495, 496–7, *498*; **21** 629–30, *630*
mirror frames **21** 719, *719*, 720, 721; **24** *821*
mirror handles **21** 712
mirrors **3** 576; **21** 713
monuments **10** 440
mosques **5** 755; **16** 202, 222; **20** 166
moulds **7** 92
musical instruments **1** *359*; **5** *259*
netsuke **17** 398
pagodas **19** 303; **23** 775
paintings **15** 806
panel **13** 543; **24** *4*, *5*, *6*, *7*, *8*
palettes **10** *4*, 5
paper **24** 40
piers (i) (seaside) **24** 747
pipes (smoking) **1** 368
plaques **7** 140
platters **31** 305
portcullises **12** 174
posts **16** *45*
printing **25** 347; **30** 847
puppets **7** 122; **17** 407, *407*
puzzles **31** 267
queros **24** *499*
relief sculpture **33** *739*
reliquaries **6** *321*
retables **22** *3*
rolls **20** 326
roofs **9** 539; **12** *522*; **15** 772; **16** 141; **26** 569; **30** 894

wood
uses—cont.
sarcophagi **27** 825
sceptres **7** 141
screens (i) (architectural) **16** 496, 500
screens (ii) (furniture) **7** 140; **13** *8*; **15** *125*; **16** 269, 487, 500
scrolls **28** 310, *310*
sculpture **1** *397*; **3** *405*; **9** *67*; **12** *191*; **15** *172*; **17** *693*, 729; **20** *150*; **30** *363*; **33** 325–6*
Africa **1** *232*, *233*, 251, 321–5*, *322*, *323*, *324*, *325*, *359*, *397*, *398*, 402, *404*, *415*, *422*; **18** *220*
Angola **7** *197*, *198*
Asante **2** 588, *588*
Austral Islands **2** *773*
Austria **13** *799*
Aztec **2** 907
Baga **3** *46*
Bali (Indonesia) **15** 784, 785–7*, *786*
Bamana **1** *323*; **3** 132–3, *133*
Baule **1** *233*, *324*
Belgium **13** 109–15*, *111*, *112*; **26** 644–5*, *645*
Bembe **3** *694*
Brazil **4** *708*
Buddhism **18** 295
Buddhism: Central Asia, Eastern **6** 298, 300
Buddhism: China **6** 706, 717, 718, 721, 722, *722*
Buddhism: Japan **17** *116*, 116–26*, *117*, *118*, *120*, *123*, *125*, *126*
Buddhism: Korea **18** *292*, *295*
Buddhism: Laos **18** 768
Buddhism: Tibet **30** 823
Buddhism: Vietnam **5** *100*; **32** 479, *479*
Burkina Faso **22** *197*
Byzantine **9** 599–602*
Cambodia **5** 499
Caribbean Islands **5** *748*
Central Asia, Eastern **6** 298, 300
Central Asia, Western **6** 220
China **6** 706, 717, 718, 721, 722, *722*; **7** 138, 140, 141
Chokwe **1** *404*; **7** *197*
cult statues **8** 261
Czech Republic **8** 383, *388*
Denmark **8** 738
Dogon **1** *262*, *322*; **9** *66*
Dominican Order **9** *110*
Early Christian (*c.* AD 250-843) **9** 599–602*
Egypt, ancient **2** *659*; **9** 886
England **13** 121–2*; **26** 643–4*
Fang **1** *232*; **10** *788*, *789*, *790*
Fiji **11** 68
France **4** *661*; **13** 125–6*, *126*; **24** *716*; **26** 641*
Germany **3** *672*; **9** *752*; **22** *303*; **24** *461*; **32** *253*
Ghana **12** *509*
Gothic **13** 109–20*, *111*, *112*, *115*, 121–6*, *126*; **14** *892*
Greece, ancient **8** 262; **13** 433–4*, 442
Guinea **1** *359*
Guyana **13** *877*
Hemba **14** *377*
Hinduism **15** *524*
Holy Roman Empire (before 1648) **13** 115–18*; **26** 645–6*
Hungary **14** *892*
Igbo **15** *113*, *115*
Indian subcontinent **7** *616*; **15** 412, 414, 523–4, *524*, *733*
Indonesia **15** 784, 785–7*, *786*, 789
Irian Jaya **16** *43*
Italy **9** *129*; **13** 123–4*; **26** 644*
Jamaica **5** *748*

wood
uses
sculpture—cont.
Japan **17** 99–100*, *116*, 116–26*, *117*, *118*, *120*, *123*, *125*, *126*, *128*, *134*, *137*, 348
Khmer **5** 499
Kissi **1** *359*
Kongo **1** *233*; **18** *220*
Korea **18** *292*, 295, *295*, 300, 301
Kuba (iii) (Zaïre) **18** *486*
Laos **18** 768
Luba **1** *325*; **19** *742*, *743*
Madagascar **20** *38*
Mali **1** *262*
Malta (Republic of) **20** *214*
Mangbetu **1** *404*
Mossi **22** *197*
Native North Americans **22** 668
Nepal **22** 774*
Netherlands, the **13** 109–15*, *115*; **26** 644–5*
Nigeria **15** *113*, *115*
Ottonian **23** 647–9*
Ovimbundu **7** *199*
Papua New Guinea **23** *732*; **24** *71*, *80*
Paraguay **24** *93*, *97*, *99*
Philippines **24** *618*, *619*
Portugal **13** 124–5*; **26** 648*
Puerto Rico **5** *750*
relief **8** *383*; **14** *494*; **18** *296*, *769*
Romanesque **26** 640–41*, 642–7*, *643*, *645*, 648*
Rome, ancient **27** 12
Scandinavia **13** 118–20*; **26** 646–7*
Senufo **28** *419*, *420*
Shinto **17** *128*
Slovenia **28** 862, *862*
Sogdiana **6** 220; **18** *500*
Songo **7** *198*
Spain **3** *846*; **9** *110*; **10** *903*; **13** 122–3*; **21** *173*; **22** *4*; **26** 642–3*, *643*; **29** 291, *292*, *296*
Spain: 20th cent. **10** *910*
Tajikistan **18** *500*
Teke **30** *419*, *420*
Tibet **30** 823
United States of America **1** *422*
Vietnam **5** *100*; **32** 479, *479*
Yoruba **1** *283*, 283–4
Zaïre **1** *359*; **14** *377*; **18** *486*
Zambia **33** 603
Zande **1** *359*
seals **6** 315; **7** 128; **10** 70
shields **1** *55*, *412*; **16** *47*, 503
shrines (i) (cult) **18** 776; **28** *636*
shutters (window) **9** *69*
snuff-boxes **1** 367
spoons **1** *291*, *368*; **8** 283, 284, *489*; **10** *66*; **31** 305
staffs **1** *355*, *402*; **7** *790*; **30** 639; **31** *144*
stage design **1** 450
stands **7** 139; **13** *8*; **16** 487, 497, *501*
statuettes **29** 570, 571
stelae **29** 614, 618
stools **1** 365, *366*; **3** *147*; **5** 748; **14** *55*, *378*; **19** *740*
storehouses **23** *219*
supports **6** 303; **13** 543; **24** 3–8, *4*, *5*, *6*, *7*, *8*
tables **2** *572*
tablets **29** *188*
teabowls **30** 847
temples **5** 755; **13** 376; **18** 266; **30** 433; **32** 471
tents **21** 883
theatres **30** 667
thrones **1** 353; **25** *120*; **26** *717*; **30** 775, 776, *776*, 778, *778*

wood
uses—cont.
tombs **6** *696*; **18** 271
tools **25** 493
toys **31** 254, 255, 258
tracery **31** 270
trays **1** *356*
vaults (ceiling) **13** 54; **32** 94*
vessels **21** 883
weapons **7** 97
wheels **25** 547
writing **7** 62; **20** 327
writing boards **10** *5*, 5
writing-tablets **4** 342, *342*; **20** 327
see also WOOD-CARVING; WOODWORK
Wood (ii) (family) **10** 308; **12** 332
Wood (iii), Aaron **33** 137, 341*
Wood, Cecil Walter **6** 527; **33** 342*
staff **24** 224; **32** 866
works **7** 210; **23** 55
Wood, Charles **6** 596
Wood, Charles E. S. **14** 220
Wood, (John) Christopher **10** 257; **27** 563; **28** 506; **32** 328; **33** 342*
Wood, Edgar **20** 238; **23** 194; **33** 342–3*
Wood, Elizabeth Wyn **33** 343*
groups and movements **5** 570
teachers **5** 570
works **5** 570, *571*
Wood (iii), Enoch **33** 341–2*
Wood, Francis Derwent **27** 636; **33** 343*
Wood, Frank P. **5** 589
Wood, Grant **5** 530; **31** 606; **33** 343–4*
collaboration **20** 604
groups and movements **1** 773; **26** 90
patrons and collectors **6** 575
works **12** 296; **18** 718; **19** 492; **27** 872
Wood (iii), John (1746-97) **29** 495
Wood (ii), John, I (1704-54) **2** 316; **33** 340–41*
groups and movements **22** 741
works **2** 324; **3** 370; **4** 821, *822*; **10** 233, 668; **19** 505; **25** 655; **31** 239
writings **31** 298
Wood (ii), John, II (1728-81) **33** 341*
groups and movements **22** 741
works **2** 617; **3** 370; **10** 233; **25** 655; **27** 626; **31** 716
writings **31** 298
Wood, Joseph **17** 450; **32** 889
Wood, J. T. **10** 423, 425, 430
Wood (iii), Ralph, I (1715-72) **29** 495; **33** 341*
Wood (iii), Ralph, II (1748-95) **29** 495; **33** 341*
Wood, Reader **30** 646
Wood, Richard **7** 171
Wood, Robert (*c.* 1717-71) **10** 293; **22** 736; **33** 344–5*
collaboration **8** 581; **23** 891
works **2** 164; **3** 2
Wood, Robert (1839-81) **4** 422; **31** 653
Wood, Thomas **2** 601
Wood, Thomas Waterman **33** 345*
Wood, William **21** 644
Woodall, George **10** 320; **33** 13
Woodall, Thomas **33** 13
woodblock *see under* PRINTING → processes; PRINTS → types
Woodburn, Allen **33** 345
Woodburn, Henry **33** 345
Woodburn, Samuel **9** 230; **18** 895; **33** 345*
drawings **8** 901; **9** 755; **10** 366; **18** 641, 895; **33** 154
paintings **11** 32; **14** 107; **24** 322
prints **23** 777; **25** 631
Woodburn, William **33** 345
Woodbury, Charles **29** 382
Woodbury, Charles Herbert **11** 141
Woodbury, David **4** 627
Woodbury, Walter Bentley **24** 658; **25** 617
Woodburytype *see under* PRINTING → processes
wood-carvers
Africa **1** 246
Asante **1** 435
Ecuador **9** 712
Finland **11** 98
Ghana **1** 435
guilds *see under* GUILDS → types
Ibibio **15** 111, 112
Japan **17** 356
Tibet **30** 847
wood-carvings **28** 302; **31** 305; **33** 333–4*
historical and regional traditions
Aboriginal Australia **1** 42–3*, *43*, *44*, 52, *53*, *55*, 56, *62*
Afghanistan **1** 210
Africa **1** *252*, *253*, 291–2, *366*, 414*; **9** 66; **33** 325
Dan (Africa) **1** *291*
Ainu **1** 493
Akye **1** 515
Alaska **22** *573*
Antilles, Lesser **29** 200
Argentina **2** 398–9
Armenia (Europe) **2** 436
Asante **2** 137, *591*
Austral Islands **2** 774
Azerbaijan **2** 902
Bamana **3** *132*, 132
Bamum **3** 151, *151*, *152*, *153*
Bangwa **3** 170
Baule **3** 406–8, *407*
Belize **3** 624
Bijogo **4** 56*
Buddhism **6** 318–19*, *319*; **17** 100; **18** 295
Bulgaria **5** 155–6
Burma **5** *261*, 261–2*; **12** 626
Cambodia **5** 509*
Cameroon **1** 242; **3** *151*, *152*, *153*
Canada **5** 570; **22** *564*
Celtic **6** 152, 159
Central Asia, Eastern **6** 318–19*, *319*
Central Asia, Western **6** 277–8*; **16** 492
Islamic **6** 277–8
Chican-Taíno culture **29** 200
Chimú **6** 607*
China **7** 138–42*, *139*, *141*, 143; **33** *423*
Chokwe **1** 252, 406; **7** 196
Colombia **7** 602, *608*
Cook Islands **7** 790–91*
Coptic **7** *829*
Côte d'Ivoire **8** 22
Cuba (Caribbean) **8** 229
Dan (Africa) **8** *487*, *488*, *489*, 490
Denmark **25** 495, *496*
Dogon **9** 66, 69, *69*
Dominican Republic **9** 117
Dorset culture **22** 575
Easter Island **9** 675, *676*
Edo (Africa) **9** 734, *734*, *735*, *736*
Egypt **7** *829*; **16** 488
Ejagham **10** 124*
England **19** 510
Eskimo **22** *573*
Fang **10** 792
Finland **11** *98*, 98–9
Fon **11** 247
France **26** 641; **27** *681*
Germany **23** 254
Gothic **13** 143; **30** 136
Guro **13** 861*
Haiti **14** 54
Hausa **14** 233

wood-carvings
historical and regional traditions—cont.
Hawaii **14** 250
Hemba **14** 378–9*
Ibibio **15** 61
Iceland **15** 69; **32** 524
Igalu **15** 109*
Igbo **15** 116
Ijo **15** *124*, 125
Inca **15** 163; **29** 135
Indian subcontinent **15** 309, 336, 491, 541, *722*, 733; **33** 325
Indonesia **15** 757, 776
Iraq **16** 488
Ireland **16** 25
Irian Jaya **16** 43–5, *45*, 46–7, *47*
Islamic **16** 487, 488
Central Asia, Western **6** 277–8; **16** 492
Indonesia **15** 757
Philippines **24** 618
Turkey **16** 497
Yemen **16** 500
Italy **6** 6–7*, *7*; **16** *723*; **30** *357*
Jamaica **16** 882
Japan **17** 99–100*, 104, 215, 350, 356; **33** 325
Jukun **17** 679, *680*
Kenya **1** *252*, 252–3, 292
Kongo **18** 221–2
Korea **18** 295
Laos **18** 769–70
Liberia **8** *487*, *489*
Lobi **19** 522
Luba **14** 378
Lwena **7** 198
Macedonia (i) (Greece) **13** *357*
Madagascar **20** 36–8, *37*
Makonde (Mozambique) **1** 253, *253*; **20** 149
Malaysia **20** 170, 181*, 182–3
Malta (Republic of) **20** 215
Maori **20** *355*, *356*; **23** *731*
Marquesas Islands **20** *463*
Maya **33** 325
Mende (Sierra Leone) **21** 114
Merovingian **21** 164
Mixtec **21** 737
Mongolia **21** 883, *884*
Mossi **1** 291; **22** 197, 198–9*
Native North Americans **11** *321*; **22** *564*, 573, *573*, 575, *577*, *580*; **28** *329*; **33** 325
Nepal **22** 774, 792–4*, *793*; **23** 907
Nigeria **9** *734*, *735*, *736*
Norway **11** *240*; **23** *228*, 229, 241–2
Oseberg style **23** *600*
Urnes style **31** *749*
Nupe **23** 303*
Pacific Islands **23** *731*; **33** 325
Palau **23** *834*
Papua New Guinea **24** 79, *81*, 81–2, *83*, *85*
Paraguay **24** 93, 97
Pende **24** *359*, 360
Philippines **24** 610, 617, 618, 619, *619*, 625, *630*
Portugal **32** 535, *536*
Prehistoric art **13** 5; **25** 495, *496*, 545
Puerto Rico **25** 703
Romanesque **26** 641
Romania **25** *584*; **26** 712
Rome, ancient **27** 29
Russia **13** 5, *14*
Santa Cruz Islands **27** 779
São Tomé and Príncipe **27** 809
Scandinavia **13** 143; **32** *519*, 524, 525*
Scotland **28** 250, *251*, 255
Shona **1** 416, 417
Solomon Islands **29** *49*, 49–51
Somalia **29** 56, *56*
Songye **14** 378

wood-carvings
historical and regional traditions—cont.
South Africa **29** 104
South America, Pre-Columbian **29** 135, 189, 200
Sri Lanka **29** 450, 477–8*, *478*
Surinam **30** 13
Sweden **30** 84; **32** *519*
Switzerland **30** 136
Tabwa **1** *366*; **30** *225*
Thailand **12** 112; **30** 639*
Tibet **30** 836, *846*, 846–7*
Togo **31** 73
Tonga (Pacific Islands) **31** 143–4
Torres Strait Islands **31** 186
Turkey **16** 497
Ukraine **31** 564
United States of America **11** *321*; **31** 610
Vanuatu **31** 892
Venda **1** 414, 416; **29** 104; **32** 154–5
Viking **32** 525*
Iceland **32** 524
Norway **23** *228*
Oseberg style **23** *600*
Sweden **32** *519*
Urnes-Romanesque **32** *519*
Urnes style **31** *749*
Yaka **33** *485*
Yemen **16** 500
Yoruba **1** 291; **33** *554*, *556*
Zaïre **1** *366*; **30** *225*
Zande **33** *610*
Zimbabwe **33** 679
Zulu **1** 414; **33** 724, *724*
technical examination **30** 396
techniques
gilding **5** *261*; **12** 626
tools **33** *333*, 334
see also WOODWORK
Woodchester Villa (Glos) **26** 907; **27** 63
wood-core *see under* LACQUER → techniques
Woodcote Park (Lothian) **28** 231
Wood-Craster, Thomas **9** 55
woodcuts **25** 243, 588, 590, 592, 597, 608, 609–10; **26** 228; **33** 345–67*
historical and regional traditions
Austria **2** 792; **27** *660*
Belarus' **3** 528
Belgium **3** *556*; **17** *471*
Cameroon **5** *524*
China **7** 146
Czech Republic **33** 348
Denmark **8** 731
England **6** 557
15th cent. **33** 350
18th cent. **33** 359*, *359*
19th cent. **7** 413; **25** *244*; **33** 360, 361
France
Post-Impressionism **25** *583*
15th cent. **33** 350*
16th cent. **10** *174*; **33** 357*
18th cent. **25** *243*; **33** 359–60*
19th cent. **6** 491; **17** 441; **19** 214, *215*; **31** 830, *830*; **33** 360, 361, *361*
20th cent. **33** 362
Germany **4** *373*; **10** 695; **12** 383; **14** *182*
Expressionism **10** *695*; **25** *582*
Gothic **12** 385
Lutheranism **19** *814*
Mannerism **4** *864*
Renaissance **1** *721*; **2** *103*, *223*; **5** *199*; **9** *431*; **12** 386; **23** *617*; **26** *79*; **28** *58*; **29** *434*; **33** *19*, *352*
15th cent. **3** *334*; **4** *8*, *357*; **7** 648; **8** *837*; **10** *725*; **25** *589*
16th cent. **2** *719*; **12** *495*; **21** *579*; **28** *144*; **32** *680*

woodcuts
historical and regional traditions
Germany—cont.
17th cent. **33** 358*
19th cent. **26** *256*
20th cent. **4** *893*; **33** 362–3
Gothic **2** 792; **12** 385
Holy Roman Empire (before 1648) **33** *348*, 348–9*, 351–4*, *355*
Italy **28** *214*; **32** *181*
Mannerism **33** *356*
Renaissance **12** *656*
15th cent. **4** *196*; **11** *178*; **33** 350*
16th cent. **31** 43; **33** 355–7*
17th cent. **26** *415*; **33** 358
Japan **11** *146*; **17** 419; **33** 363
Lutheranism **19** *814*
Netherlands, the **2** *136*; **4** *144*, *145*; **33** *168*, 349–50*, 354–5*, 358*
Norway **22** *293*
Poland **25** 106
Romania **26** 716
South Africa **29** 110
Spain **33** 350, 358
Switzerland **4** *358*; **29** *674*
Tahiti **12** *195*
United States of America **4** 476; **11** 330; **33** *364*
Zambia **33** *603*
materials
inks **15** 855
presses **25** 609–10
types
chiaroscuro **6** 569; **22** 723; **25** 610, 619, 622; **26** 229; **32** 199; **33** 365–7*
Germany **5** 199, *294*; **33** 365–6
Italy **5** 843–4; **25** VI; **33** *366*, 366–7
Netherlands, the **12** *883*; **33** 367
images d'Epinal **15** 142*; **25** 244
white-line **25** 610, *610*
uses
Bibles **4** *8*, 9; **25** *589*
block-books **4** 143, *144*, *145*
book illustrations **4** *345*, 356, 357–9, 366; **7** 413; **8** 731; **12** 385; **14** 424; **21** 578; **32** 198–9
bookplates **4** 372, *373*
globes **12** 811
medical books **21** 6
music (printed) **22** 369
wallpaper **32** 815
see also PRINTS → types → flock; tinsel
Woodcut Society **25** 629
wood-drying kilns *see under* KILNS → types
Wooden Framework culture **27** 366
wood-engravings **25** 591, 608, 609, *609*, 610; **26** 231; **33** 367–70*
historical and regional traditions
Brazil **4** 717
Britain **33** 368–9
England **3** *897*; **4** *9*, 366, *367*; **33** *368*
Estonia **10** 539
France **9** *170*; **13** *307*; **29** *857*; **33** 369, *369*
Italy **28** *214*
Japan **10** 485, *485*
Mexico **21** 388
Panama **23** 904
Paraguay **24** 98
Uruguay **31** 755
materials
box-wood **33** 367
uses
Bibles **4** *9*
book illustrations **4** 356, 363, 366, *367*
bookplates **4** 373
Woodford **24** 253
Woodford, James **23** 259
Woodforde, Christopher **29** 514
Woodforde, Samuel **14** 598
Woodgate, Robert **16** 9
Woodhall Park (Herts) **9** 26; **10** 643; **32** 114
Woodhenge (Wilts) **14** 387; **23** 808; **25** 504
Woodhouse, Frederick **2** 772
Woodhouse, G. **31** 241
Woodhouse, John (i) (*d* 1836) **33** 370
Woodhouse, John (ii) (1835-92) **33** 370
Woodhouse, William **33** 370*
Woodlands **22** 669
Woodlark Island **24** *64*, 81
Woodlawn Plantation **29** 842
Woodman, Henry Gillete **28** 879
Woodmason **23** 213
Wood of Pontefract **5** 831
wood-pulp **28** 339
Wood River Post Office (IL) **1** 442
Woodroffe, Edward **14** 743
Woodroffe, Paul **33** 132
Woodrow, Bill **10** 269; **23** 335; **26** 51; **33** 370*
Woodrow, Stephen Tayor **24** 409
Woodruff, Hale (Aspacio) **1** 442, 443, 444; **22** 335; **33** 370–71*
Woods, Corolyn **29** 34
Woods, E. J. **1** 151; **33** 408
Woods, Fanny **11** 75
Woods, George **25** 4
Woods, Henry **11** 75
Woods, Leonora **29** 34
Woods, Peter **23** 72
Woods, Richard **2** 576
Woods, Robert **32** 890
Woods, Shadrach **2** 660; **4** 214; **5** 608–10*; **7** 295; **11** 527; **30** 391
Woods, Thomas H. **7** 233
Wood & Sons **7** 798
Woodstock (South Africa) **29** 118
Woodstock (Oxon; UK) **14** 75
furniture **30** 779
park **24** 178
steel **10** 342, 345; **16** 61
Woodstock (NY; USA) **31** 138
Woodville, R(ichard) Caton (ii) (1856-1927) **3** 389; **9** 461; **33** 371*
Woodville, Richard Caton (i) (1825-1855) **33** 371*
Woodward **24** 791
Woodward, A. M. **18** 668
Woodward, Benjamin **8** 586–7; **16** 11; **23** 600
works **16** *10*
Woodward, Ellsworth **23** 32
woodwork
historical and regional traditions
Afghanistan **1** 210*
Algeria **16** 494
Azerbaijan **2** 902*
Bhutan **3** 913, 916
Buyid **16** 492
Central Asia, Western **16** 491–2*, *492*, *501*, 501–2*
Coptic **7** 828–9*
Egypt **7** 828*; **16** 488–91*, *490*, 496–7*, *496*
England **31** 422–3
Indian subcontinent **15** 720–22*
Iran **16** 491–2*, 501–2*, *502*
Iraq **16** 488–91*, *489*
Islamic **16** 487–95*, *489*, *490*, *492*, *496*, 496–9*, *498*, *499*, *500*, 500–502*, *501*, *502*, 524
Japan **17** 48–50
Kazakhstan **16** *501*
Laos **18** 776–7*
Mongolia **21** 883–4*, *884*
Morocco **16** 494
North Africa **16** 492–5*
Ottoman **16** 498–9*, *499*
woodwork
historical and regional traditions—cont.
Spain **16** 492–5*
Swahili **30** 57
Syria **16** 488–91*, 496–7*
Tajikistan **16** *492*
Turkey **16** 488, 497–8*, *498*
Yemen **16** *500*, 500–501*
materials
inlays **7** 107; **16** 487, 497, 498, 499, 500
inscriptions **16** 492, 497
lacquer **5** 257
mosaics **16** 487
veneers **16** 499
techniques
carving **16** 500
see also WOOD-CARVINGS
gilding **12** 626*
inlays **2** 902
intarsia **16** 524
openwork **3** 585, 685; **7** 140; **11** 764
painting **16** 487, 497
turning **11** 587; **16** 487; **31** 477*
woodworm **24** 7
Woody, Howard **28** 829
Woodyer, Henry **33** 371–2*
wool **7** 735
historical and regional traditions
Africa **1** 293
Ancient Near East **1** 880
Anglo-Saxon **9** 253
Armenia (Europe) **2** 437
Austria **2** 825
Azerbaijan **2** *901*
Belgium **3** *607*; **4** *923*; **30** I2, II1; **31** *218*
Berber **3** *755*
Bhutan **3** 915
Brazil **4** 724
Burma **5** 247, *249*
Byzantine **9** 664
Central Asia, Western **6** 248, 251, 253, *253*; **24** *298*
Chile **6** *599*
China **7** 43, 68
Coptic **30** IV2
Denmark **8** *754*
Early Christian (*c*. AD 250-843) **9** 664
Egypt **9** *767*; **16** 431, *472*; **30** IV2
Egypt, ancient **9** 823
England **8** 36; **10** 275, 278, *350*, *352*, 353; **13** 196; **30** III2, IV1
Etruscan **10** 636
Finland **5** 829; **11** *109*
France **2** *703*; **5** 836, I; **11** *638*, *640*, *648*; **27** *895*; **30** *313*, I1, II2
Fulani **11** *829*, 829–30
Germany **12** 462–3, 464, 465, 467, 469; **18** 158
Gothic **11** *638*; **13** 194
Greece, ancient **9** 246; **13** 604
Guatemala **13** 766
Iceland **15** *74*
Indian subcontinent **15** 665–7*, *666*, *683*
Iran **5** IV; **16** 449, *467*; **18** *48*
Iraq **16** 434, 455
Ireland **16** 33
Islamic **5** II, III, IV; **16** 428, 429, 431, 434, 445, 449, 455, 466, *467*, *470*, *471*, *472*, *478*; **18** *48*
Italy **10** 636; **11** *193*
Japan **17** 356
Korea **18** 303
Madagascar **1** 293
Mali **11** *829*, 829–30
Morocco **3** *755*
Native North Americans **22** *547*, *623*; **30** VIII2
Nepal **22** 791
New Zealand **23** 73–4*, *74*
wool
historical and regional traditions—cont.
Norway **5** 829; **23** *239*
Ottoman **5** II; **16** 445, *471*, *478*
Paraguay **24** 93, 100
Peru **24** *513*; **30** III1
Poland **25** 131, *132*
Portugal **25** 315
Romanesque **26** 703
Rome, ancient **27** 112, *114*
Scotland **28** 265, 266, *267*
Serbia **28** 456
Spain **29** *347*
Tibet **30** 845
Turkey **5** II; **16** *470*, *471*, *478*
Turkmenistan **5** III; **6** *253*
United States of America **30** VIII2; **31** 656, *656*, 658, *660*
techniques
dyeing **9** 490, 491, 492
weaving **1** 293
types
Merino **30** 538
Mouflon **30** 538
pashm **16** 430
Shetland **30** 538
Soay **30** 538
uses
blankets **11** *829*, 829–30; **22** *547*, *623*
brushes **17** 213; **18** 303
carpets **5** 829, 830, 831; **9** 490
Central Asia, Western **6** 248, 253, *253*; **24** *298*
China **7** 68
Finland **11** *109*
France **5** 836, I; **27** *895*
Indian subcontinent **15** *683*
Iran **5** IV
Islamic **16** 466, *467*, *470*, *471*, *472*, *478*
Nepal **22** 791
Poland **25** *132*
Spain **29** *347*
Turkey **5** II; **16** *478*
Turkmenistan **5** III
coverlets **31** *656*
dress **6** 251; **9** 246; **16** 455
embroidery **10** 353; **11** *648*; **12** 462–3; **15** *74*; **28** 265; **31** 658
felt **10** 872
fibre art **11** 54
hangings **5** *249*
kilims **2** *901*; **18** 48, *48*
knitting **18** 158
lace **18** 588
mantles **16** 33; **24** *513*
needlework **17** 356
passementerie **24** 237
patchwork **24** 253
ponchos **2** *403*; **6** *599*
prints **11** 173
rugs **30** VIII2
saddle-bags **3** *755*
sashes **21** *477*
shawls **28** 564
tapestries **9** 490; **30** 308
Belgium **3** *607*; **4** *923*; **5** *47*, *48*, *50*; **30** I2, II1; **31** *218*
Coptic **30** IV2
Denmark **8** *754*
Egypt **9** *767*
England **10** *350*, *352*; **13** 196; **30** III2, IV1
France **2** *703*; **11** *638*, *640*; **30** *313*, I1, II2
Germany **12** 465, 467
Gothic **13** 194
Italy **11** *193*
New Zealand **23** *74*
Norway **23** *239*
Peru **30** III1
Scotland **28** *267*
United States of America **31** *660*
threads **30** 538–9*
wool
uses—cont.
upholstery **31** 682
wallpaper **10** 275; **32** 813
Woolacott, Scott & Hudson **9** 426
Woolavington (Sussex) **10** 273
Woolbury Camp (Hants) **14** 544
Wooldridge, H. E. **25** 398
Woolf, Leonard **4** 168; **19** 591
Woolf, Virginia **3** 631; **4** 168, 169; **10** 547; **19** 591
Woolfe, John **23** 782
Woollams, Henry **33** 372
Woollams, William (1782-1840) **33** 372
Woollams, William (*d* 1859) **33** 372
Woollams & Co. **8** 576; **32** 812, 813, 816; **33** 372*
Woollaston, M(ountford) T(osswill) **11** 59; **23** 60; **33** 372*
Woollen, Evans **17** 605
Woollett, William **4** 607; **10** 393; **33** 372–3*
pupils **4** 886; **14** 279
works **4** 607; **11** 907; **17** 640, 905; **25** 618; **26** 230, 335; **28** 558, 879; **32** 652; **33** 221, 715
Woollett, William W. **19** 700
Woolley, J. W. **2** 758
Woolley, Ken(neth Frank) **33** 373*
collaboration **30** 161
groups and movements **30** 161
works **2** 742
Woolley, (Charles) Leonard **2** 300; **33** 373*
assistants **20** 205
excavations **2** 660
Amarna, (Tell) el- **10** 81
Atchana, Tell **1** 815, 893
Carchemish **1** 893; **5** 728
al-Mina (Syria) **21** 622
Teano **33** 565
Ubaid, Tell al- **31** 508
Ur **1** 509, 880, 881, 893, 894; **21** 284, 310; **29** 923; **31** 694
Woolly Satyrs, Painter of the **13** 522
Woolner, Thomas **2** 752; **33** 373–5*
collaboration **28** 349
groups and movements **25** 554; **32** 415
patrons and collectors **7** 647; **10** 755
pupils **18** 527
teachers **3** 509
works **7** 647; **23** 62; **33** *374*
Woolnough, C. W. **24** 55
Woolsey, D. Kristine **22** 671
Woolston, John **33** 302
Woolworth, Frank W. **12** 615
Woonhuys, 't **22** 875
Wooton, William S. **31** 631
Wootton, John **12** 594; **33** 375–7*
collaboration **8** 455
patrons and collectors **14** 143, 178, 597; **19** 157; **27** 494
teachers **33** 177
works **2** 105, 106; **7** 785; **10** 250, 251; **11** 427; **18** 712; **29** 424; **33** *376*
Wopkeimin **24** 73, 74
Wopkes Wierda, Sytze *see* WIERDA, SYTZE WOPKES
Worcester Law Courts (South Africa) **18** 887
Worcester (UK) **10** *225*; **31** 710; **33** 377–8*
Cathedral of St Mary **4** 63; **10** 266; **13** 44, 45, 55; **18** 621; **21** 839, *840*
alabaster-carvings **1** 519
bosses **29** 659
capitals **26** 611, 616
carpets **5** 839
chapter house **6** 465, 466
cloister **7** 456

Worcester (UK)
Cathedral of St Mary—cont.
crypt **18** 621
misericords **21** 725
mouldings **22** 217
refectory **21** 845
sculpture **13** 80
stained glass **2** 83; **3** 710
stiff-leaf **29** 659
transept **31** 281
Guildhall **31** 239
manuscripts **15** 875
Worcester (MA; USA)
American Antiquarian Society **10** 422
artificial stone **30** 505
Art Museum **13** 470; **15** 745; **27** 47
Worcester Hunt **2** 158; **9** 567
Worcester Panel, Master of the *see* MARTINUS 'OPIFEX'
Worcester Porcelain Company **4** 177, 824; **6** 332; **10** 308, 309; **26** 85; **33** 377–8
collections **28** 168
designers **14** 131
marks **20** 441
painters **6** 408
works **10** *309*; **33** *377*
Worcester Royal Porcelain Co. Ltd **4** 73; **24** 478; **33** 378
Worcester's, Florence of, Chronicle *see* FLORENCE OF WORCESTER'S CHRONICLE
Worcestre, William **22** 211; **33** 378*
Worde, Wynkyn de **6** 120; **20** 142; **31** 494; **33** 94
Word & Image **24** 446
Wordsley Flint glassworks **10** 320; **33** 13
Wordsworth, William **22** 686; **24** 742
Wordwell (Suffolk), All Saints **26** 613
Wores, Theodore **9** 468
work-boxes *see under* BOXES → types
workhouses **3** *536*
Working Architecture Group *see* PAS GROUP
Working Group of Constructivists *see* FIRST WORKING GROUP OF CONSTRUCTIVISTS
works, clerks of *see* CLERKS OF WORKS
Workshop for the Restoration of Unfelt Sensations **33** 378–9*
workshops **1** 102; **21** 600; **25** 627–8*; **29** 850–53*
Anglo-Saxon **29** 851
Belgium **3** 585
Central Asia, Eastern **6** 298
China **6** 787; **7** 147, 150
Egypt, ancient **9** 790, 815, *823*
England **25** *627*
France **29** 852
Germany **3** 399; **28** 492
Gothic **29** *852*
Greece, ancient **13** 371
India, Republic of **15** 179
Indian subcontinent **15** 414–15, 550, 722; **16** 468
Insular art **29** 851
Iran **16** 468
Ireland **29** 851
Islamic **16** 468
Italy **16** 777; **29** 853
Japan **17** 422
Netherlands, the **28** 218
Rome, ancient **26** 861; **27** 55
Scandinavia **32** 524
Spain **29** *852*
Turkey **16** 468
Venezuela **32** 172
Viking **32** 524
see also STUDIOS; BOTTEGE
works of art *see* ART (WORKS OF)
Worksop (Notts)
Priory **3** 878; **9** 155
Worksop Manor **10** 230
Worksop Museum **24** 415
Works Progress Administration (WPA) **23** 12; **24** 182, 674
Farm Security Administration (FSA) **18** 738; **19** 60; **24** 673; **28** 536
photography **24** 685; **25** 653; **28** 919; **31** 606, 663
Federal Arts Project (FAP) **1** 84, 772; **3** 435; **5** 386; **8** 777; **18** 441, 813; **19** 701, 878; **20** 384, 605, 609; **23** 48, 175; **27** 220; **28** 875; **31** 606, 607, 663, 672
architecture **27** 721
ceramics **31** 639
Easel Division **13** 214; **26** 126
lithographs **19** 492
murals **1** 442; **4** 863; **8** 634, 896; **13** 11, 865; **22** 335; **25** 653
paintings **10** 662; **14** 812; **19** 272; **20** 10; **28** 536; **33** 7
photography **33** 147
sculpture **5** 216
Federal Writers' Project **13** 811
Wörl, Hans *see* WERL, HANS
World Bank **18** 647
World Bible *see under* BIBLES → types
World of Art (Mir Iskusstva) **19** 277; **20** 223; **27** 391, 392, 394, 422, 443, 450, 463, 580; **28** 475; **29** 899; **30** 361; **31** 582; **33** 379–80*
members **12** 870
Annenkov, Yury (Pavlovich) **2** 123
Bakst, Léon **3** 86
Benois, Alexandre **3** 734
Bilibin, Ivan (Yakovlevich) **4** 60
Bogayevsky, Konstantin (Fyodorovich) **4** 229
Chekhonin, Sergey (Vasil'yevich) **6** 529
Dobuzhinsky, Mstislav (Valerianovich) **9** 57
Dymshits-Tolstaya, Sof'ya (Isaakovna) **9** 495
Grabar', Igor' (Emmanuilovich) **13** 263
Konashevich, Vladimir (Mikhaylovich) **18** 215
Korovin, Konstantin (Alekseyevich) **18** 389
Lansere, Nikolay (Yevgen'yevich) **18** 749
Lissitzky, El **19** 474
Makovsky, Sergey (Konstantinovich) **20** 152
Mashkov, Il'ya (Ivanovich) **20** 549
Milioti, Nikolay (Dmitriyevich) **21** 544
Ostroumova-Lebedeva, Anna (Petrovna) **23** 624
Petrov-Vodkin, Kuz'ma (Sergeyevich) **24** 566
Roerich, Nicholas **26** 530
Serebryakova, Zinaida (Yevgen'yevna) **28** 459
Ul'yanov, Nikolay (Pavlovich) **31** 571
Vereysky, Georgy (Semyonovich) **32** 247
Yakovlev, Aleksandr (Yevgeniyevich) **33** 486
Yakulov, Georgy (Bogdanovich) **33** 486
Yakunchikova, Mariya (Vasil'yevna) **33** 487
Zamyraylo, Viktor (Dmytriyevych) **33** 607
Žukoŭski, Stanislaŭ **3** 529
works **33** *379*
see also MIR ISKUSSTVA (PERIODICAL)
World of Interiors **10** 284
World Print Council **25** 629
world's fairs *see* EXHIBITIONS → types → international
Worldwide Art Catalogue Bulletin **4** 27
Wörle, Eugen **2** 789, 815; **10** 870
Worlidge, Thomas **4** 601; **9** 308; **33** 380*, 693
Wörlitz **12** *360*; **33** 380–81*
Schloss **12** 374; **33** 380
paintings **4** 154; **10** 825; **19** 525; **20** 456
sculpture **6** 98
Wörlitzer Park **12** 134, 472; **33** 380
cenotaph **6** 171
Gotische Haus **2** 94; **12** 415; **13** 199
Villa Hamilton **32** 554
Worm, Joachim **12** 443
Worm, Olaf **18** 522; **22** 355; **23** 242
works **22** *355*
Wormald, Francis **33** 381*
Wormley, Edward **31** 633
Worms **12** *361*; **33** 381–2*
Baptistery **3** 192
Cathedral of St Peter **9** 86; **12** 364, *364*; **13** 47; **26** 575; **33** 381*
ciborium **7** 303
sculpture **13** 87; **33** 382
façade decoration **10** 736
Jewish cemetery **17** 555
St Pauli **12** 382
synagogues **17** 543, 544, 548
tiles **30** 884
Volkstheater **30** 678
Worms, Anton of *see* WOENSAM, ANTON
Worms, Hans von *see* HANS VON WORMS
Worms, Nikolaus Nievergalt von *see* NIEVERGALT VON WORMS, Nikolaus
Worms, Olaus **2** 104
Wormser, Jacobus **32** 696
Worms Machzor *see under* MACHZORS → individual manuscripts
Worndle, Christoph **33** 587
Wörner, Hans **22** 302; **33** 271
Wornum, (George) Grey **33** 382*
collaboration **8** 810; **11** 808
competitions **7** 670
staff **9** 296
works **10** 240
Wornum, Ralph **10** 679
Wornum, Ralph Nicholson **9** 683
Wornum, Ralph Selden **27** 767; **33** 382
Worpswede **2** 552; **18** 717
Arbeitsgemeinschaft Barkenhoff **32** 678
Brunnenhof **4** 789
Hoetger Hotel **14** 622
Weyerberg *see* Hoetger Hotel
Worpswede colony **21** 494; **33** 382–3*
members **5** 311; **20** 14; **21** 784, 796; **23** 358; **26** 394; **32** 136, 678, 756
works **33** *383*
Worpsweder Werkstätten **33** 383
Worrall, George **29** 835
Worringer, Wilhelm **11** 315; **33** 383–4*
groups and movements **2** 288
writings **13** 33; **26** 49
Worsdale, James **18** 146
Worshipful Company of Founders **19** 594
Worshipful Company of Goldsmiths **19** 593
Worsley, Richard **33** 385*
collections **17** 475
gems **12** 266; **20** 389
writings **10** 365
Worsley, Thomas **23** 858; **29** 485
Worsnop, Thomas **1** 67
wort **8** 127
Wortelmans, Andriaen **23** 11
Wortelmans, Damiaan **4** 812; **14** 467
Worth (company) **18** 659; **25** 78
Worth (Sussex), St Nicholas **2** 66
Worth, Charles Frederick **9** 245, 287–8, 290; **28** 346
Worth, Thomas **8** 276
Worthen, Amy **10** 398
Worthington, (John) Hubert **33** 385
Worthington, Humble & Holland **19** 508
Worthington, J. **25** 264
Worthington, Percy Scott **31** 584; **33** 385
Worthington, Thomas (Locke) **20** 237; **23** 172; **33** 385*
Worthington & Elgood **33** 385
Wortley Hall (W. Yorks) **25** 406
Wortmann, Anton **23** 254
Wörtz, Hans **33** 385*
Woss y Gil, Celeste **9** 117, 119
Wostenholm, George, & Son **28** 576
Wotruba, Fritz **2** 831; **32** 447; **33** 385–6*
pupils **2** 804, 876; **12** 851; **14** 632, 818
teachers **14** 130
works **2** 803, *804*
Wotton, Edward, 1st Baron Wotton **31** 276
Wotton, Henry **9** 12; **10** 363; **13** 298; **29** 800; **33** 386–7*
works **2** 362; **23** 857; **31** 297
Wotton, Thomas **4** 352
Wotton House (Surrey) **4** 249; **12** 128
Wou, Claes (Claesz.) **3** 494; **32** 673
Wouda, Hendrik **22** 868, 875; **23** 908; **33** 387–8*
Wouters, E. **11** 746
Wouters, Frans **33** 388–9*
collaboration **2** 875
pupils **15** 43
teachers **2** 875; **27** 298
works **33** *388*
Wouters, Joseph **3** 590
Wouters, Pieter **2** 199, 875
Wouters, Rik **3** 573, 615; **33** 389*
groups and movements **2** 516; **4** 619; **5** 44
works **3** 564; **11** 450
Woutersz, Jan **3** 193
Woutersz., Reinaut **5** 46; **11** 5; **16** 756; **20** 323; **32** 205
Woutersz., Willem **19** 293
Wouw, Anton van **4** 155; **25** 566; **29** 111
Wouwer, J. R. van de **32** 706
Wouwerman, Johannes **33** 389, 391
Wouwerman, Paulus Joostens **33** 389
Wouwerman, Philips **13** 894, 895; **33** 389–91*
collaboration **27** 329
patrons and collectors **14** 692; **25** 888
Arenberg, Auguste-Marie-Raymond, 6th Duke of **2** 382
Aved, Jacques (-André-Joseph) **2** 852
Boyle, Richard, 3rd Earl of Burlington and 4th Earl of Cork **4** 609
Braamcamp, Gerrit **4** 618
Brukenthal, Samuel, Baron von **5** 9
Catherine II, Empress of Russia (*reg* 1762-96) **26** 732
Choiseul, Etienne-François, Duc de **7** 194
Wouwerman, Philips
patrons and collectors—cont.
Choiseul-(Beaupré-) Gouffier, Marie-Gabriel (-Florent-Auguste), Comte de **7** 193
Conti, Louis-François de Bourbon, Prince de (1717-76) **7** 778
Faesch, Johann Jakob **10** 753
Gildemeester, Jan (Jansz.) (1744-99) **12** 620
Goll van Franckenstein, Pieter Hendrik **12** 876
Josephine, Empress of the French (1763-1814) **4** 304
Jullienne, Jean de **17** 684
La Roque, Antoine de **18** 796
Lowther, William, 1st Earl of Lonsdale **19** 735
Maitland, John, 2nd Earl and 1st Duke of Lauderdale **20** 142
Napoleon III, Emperor of France (*reg* 1852-70) **4** 306
Potocki, Wincenty **25** 364
Seymour-Conway, Francis Charles, 3rd Marquess of Hertford **28** 527
Verrue, Jeanne-Baptiste d'Albert de Luynes, Comtesse de **32** 368
William VIII, Landgrave of Hesse-Kassel (*reg* 1751-60) **12** 473; **14** 492
Yusupov, Nikolay (Borisovich), Prince (1751-1831) **33** 579
pupils **9** 327; **28** 72
reproductions in porcelain **21** 64
reproductive prints by others **18** 866; **19** 10; **21** 800
teachers **14** 95; **22** 840
works **3** 388; **22** 840; **33** *390*
Wouwerman, Pieter **33** 389, 391
Wowake no Omi **15** 160
Woyo **1** 328, 329, 403; **2** 85; **18** 217, 219, 221; **30** 509
Woźniakowic, Grzegorz **25** 121
WPA *see* WORKS PROGRESS ADMINISTRATION
Wprost *see* STRAIGHT AHEAD
Wrangel, Carl Gustaf, Count **2** 95, 463; **10** 458; **12** 421; **14** 52; **21** 152
Wrangell (AK), Chief Shakes's House **22** 581
Wrangelschrank see under MARQUETRY → types
wrapping-paper *see under* PAPER → types
wrappings **20** 327
wraps **1** 348; **15** 792; **16** 459
Wratton Park (Hants) **29** 540
Wrba, Georg **14** 632
wreaths **3** 442; **13** 598, 599; **17** 527; **21** 878
Wrede, Fabian **11** 91; **30** 89
Wredow, August (Julius) **33** 391–2*
Wren, Christopher **2** 314; **14** 420, 742; **23** 362; **24** *753*; **33** 392–9*
architecture
cathedrals **7** 192, 258; **19** 569, 597, 598–9, *599*; **23** 857; **25** 265; **33** *395*
cemeteries **6** 165
chapels **14** 855; **28** 280
churches **1** 123; **4** 786; **7** 254, 270, 277; **8** 224; **10** 360; **19** 566, 576; **24** 752; **29** 414, 835; **33** *394*
colleges **5** 511; **7** 297; **13** 199
domes **9** 86; **15** V; **20** 567, 580, *580*
hospitals **13** 623, *624*; **14** 782; **33** *398*
libraries **19** 314, *315*
mausolea **20** 866; **27** 236
models **2** 336

Wren, Christopher
architecture—cont.
observatories **13** 623; **23** 339
orangeries **23** 470, *471*
palaces **6** 60; **8** 65; **14** 126–7; **19** 617; **23** 466; **33** 231, *397*
parliament buildings **19** 612
restorations **13** 199
theatres **10** 232; **30** 673, *673*
university buildings **23** 687, *688*, 690
urban planning **19** 569; **31** 716, *716*
assistants **10** 263; **20** 477; **30** 872
attributions **23** 212; **28** 295
book illustrations **21** 7
collaboration **4** 79; **5** 336; **10** 657; **12** 591; **23** 470; **24** 753; **29** 843; **31** 239
groups and movements **3** 261, 264, 266, 267; **33** 199
interior decoration **9** 31
metalwork **19** 595
methods **29** 710
patrons and collectors
Bird, Francis **4** 79
Charles II, King of England and Scotland (*reg* 1660-85) **10** 360; **29** 804
Churchill, John, 1st Duke of Marlborough **7** 286
James II, King of Great Britain and Ireland (*reg* 1685-8) **29** 804
Mary II, Queen of England and Scotland (*reg* 1688-94) **10** 360; **23** 467
Soane, John **28** 908
William III, King of England and Scotland (*reg* 1688-1702) **7** 298; **10** 360; **14** 126
prints **25** 629
pulpits **25** 727
pupils **14** 252–4
restorations by others **26** 337
weathervanes **33** 8
writings **13** 34; **27** 628; **31** 298
Wren, Denise **10** 315
Wren, Matthew **33** 393
Wrenk, Franz **6** 92; **21** 417
Wrensted, Benedicte **10** 580
works **10** *578*
Wrenthorpe **33** 399*
Wrestlers **2** 168; **21** 23, 29; **23** 352; **27** 46
Wrest Park (Beds) **1** 784; **5** 827; **9** 327; **10** *282*; **13** 645
Wretman, Fredrik **30** 87
Wrexham (Clwyd) **32** *780*
St Giles **28** 295; **32** 782
memorial to Mary Middleton **32** 787
wrigglework *see under* PEWTER → techniques
Wright, Alf **32** *329*
Wright, Andrew **33** 408*
Wright, Basil **33** 74
Wright, Benjamin **12** 912
Wright, Charles **10** 333; **26** 303
Wright, Christopher **33** 408
Wright, David (*fl* 1920s-50s) **33** 399, 405
Wright, David (*b* 1948) **2** 763; **33** 408*
Wright, Edmund (*fl* 1638) **8** 45
Wright, Edmund (William) (1822-86) **1** 151; **2** 739; **33** 408–9*
Wright, Edward **14** 708; **30** 26; **33** 409*
Wright, Ferdinand von **11** 95; **33** 411–12*
Wright, Frank Lloyd (Lincoln) **2** 315, *315*; **16** 101; **17** 88; **22** 568; **23** 548; **28** 180, 728; **31** 596, 622; **33** 399, 400–408*
architecture **33** 246
banks **3** 176
churches **31** 584; **33** *402*, *403*
hotels **14** 788; **31** 79
Wright, Frank Lloyd (Lincoln)
architecture—cont.
houses **5** 649, *649*; **6** 573; **7** 695; **24** 290; **25** 5; **31** *595*, 596; **33** *401*, *405*
museums **9** 19; **13** 800; **22** 367; **23** 43, 48
office buildings **4** 788, 789; **5** 124; **10** 417; **12** 792; **19** 367, *367*; **23** 360, *360*; **24** 752
roofs **27** 129
service stations **28** 488
skyscrapers **28** 834
synagogues **1** 736; **17** 549
theatres **8** 470; **30** 684
urban planning **19** 700
warehouses **32** 861
collaboration **1** 158; **6** 573; **17** 813; **23** 10; **33** 407
collections **17** 431
furniture **6** 391; **31** 632, 633
groups and movements **2** 572; **6** 578; **11** 840; **21** 780, 781; **23** 498; **25** 446
house **2** *551*, 552; **18** 786; **31** 595
interior decoration **31** *622*
methods **2** 360; **8** 128
personal collection **2** 364, 372
pupils **5** 337; **19** 843; **24** 548; **33** 408
reproductions in textiles **27** 599
staff **9** 305; **13** 647; **22** 187; **26** 42; **28** 96, 887; **29** 34; **33** 408
stained glass **29** 508, 516
typography **2** 333
Wright, G. E. **28** 573
Wright, George **33** 408
Wright, Henry **20** 890; **31** 729
Wright, Horace **3** 62
Wright, James (*fl* 1863-82) **23** 68, 70
Wright, James C. (*fl* 1920s) **23** 904
Wright, John **10** 143; **32** 414
Wright, John Lloyd **33** 399, 408*
Wright, John Michael **9** 724; **28** 234; **33** 409–10*
patrons and collectors **29** 804
pupils **2** 597
teachers **16** 897
Wright, Joseph (1734-97) *see* WRIGHT OF DERBY, JOSEPH
Wright, Joseph (1756-93) **14** 280; **33** 92, 410*
Wright, (Frank) Lloyd **33** 399, 402, 407*
Wright, Magnus von **11** 95; **14** 689; **33** 411*
Wright, Michael **19** 125
Wright, Myles **14** 676
Wright, Olgivanna **33** 404
Wright, Patience Lovell **33** 4, 410
Wright, Philemon **23** 630
Wright, Richard **29** 584; **33** 408
Wright, Russel **1** 738; **31** 653; **33** 410–11*
works **31** 632, 639
Wright, Samuel **30** 877
Wright, Stephen **23** 858, 859
Wright, Thomas (*fl* 1728-37) **11** 243; **25** 635; **33** 220
Wright, Thomas (1711-86) **8** 30; **11** 242
Wright, Thomas (*fl* 1865) **5** 760
Wright, Wilhelm von **33** 411*
Wright, Willard Huntington **30** 173; **33** 412*
Wright, William **10** 263; **33** 412*
Wright & Mansfield **10** 298
Wright of Derby, Joseph **3** 373; **21** 600; **33** 412–15*
exhibitions **19** 507
groups and movements **22** 740; **29** 891
methods **9** 211
patrons and collectors **10** 369; **14** 485; **30** 451
pupils **1** 24
Wright of Derby, Joseph—cont.
reproductive prints by others **9** 506; **21** 417; **24** 551; **26** 231, *231*
teachers **14** 841
works **4** 607; **5** 657; **9** 284; **10** 250, 401, *402*; **11** 141, 428, *430*, 431; **13** 304; **15** 829; **18** 713; **29** 855; **33** *413*, *415*
Wrightsman, Charles B(ierer) **33** 415–16*
Wrightsman, Jayne **33** 415
Wright-Smith, Andrew **2** 754
Wrines, Laurens **31** 843
Wriothesley, Thomas (*d* 1534) **12** 272
Wriothesley, Thomas, 4th Earl of Southampton (*d* 1667) **9** 483; **19** 570
wrist-clasps **9** 253
wristrests **7** 58, 102, *103*
wristwatches *see under* WATCHES → types
writing **25** 467–8; **28** 303
conservation **15** 856
historical and regional traditions
Akkadian (people) **15** 905; **20** 361
Anatolia, ancient **1** 828
Ancient Near East **1** 851, 853–5*, *854*, 893; **10** 1; **20** 326
Arabic **16** 277–8
Assyrian **1** 828; **20** *326*
Buddhism **17** *230*, 231
Burma **20** 327, 329
China **2** 209; **6** 612, *736*, *738*, *739*, *740*, *742*, *743*, *744*, *746*, *747*, *749*, *750*, *751*, *752*, *753*, *754*, *757*, *758*, *759*, *762*, *763*, *765*, *768*; **7** 58, 62, 92, 114, 128; **17** 211, 215, 234–8; **20** 328; **25** 468
Crete **8** 153; **18** 167
Cuba (Caribbean) **8** 231
Cyprus, ancient **8** 331
Easter Island **9** 676
Egypt, ancient **1** 853, 854–5; **10** 1–2*, 3–7*, *3*, *4*, *5*; **20** 329; **24** 88–9
Ejagham **1** 425
Georgia **12** 317
Greece, ancient **13** 369, 490–91; **20** 329
Hittite **4** 230
Indian subcontinent **15** 192, 193, 198–9*; **20** 327, *328*
Indus civilization **25** 468
Iran, ancient **15** 904
Islamic **16** 134–5*, 273–6*, *274*, *275*, 277–8*; **29** 617
Italy **2** 166–7
Japan **17** 210–29*, *212*, *213*, *228*, *230*, 232–40*, *235*, *236*, *237*, *239*, *240*; **28** 625
Kongo **8** 231
Korea **18** *330*
Lydia **19** 840
Maya **20** 883, 885; **27** 607
Mesoamerica, Pre-Columbian **21** 737; **25** 468; **27** 607
Mesopotamia **1** 853–4; **10** 1; **20** *326*, 326; **21** 268, 271; **25** 467; **31** 827
Minoan **18** 167
Mixtec **21** 737
Mongolia **21** 875
Nigeria **8** 231
Philistine **24** 636
Rome, ancient **20** 329
Scandinavia **23** 227
Sri Lanka **20** 329
Sumerian **1** 853; **20** 361; **29** 924*
Tibet **30** 836
materials
bamboo **7** 58, 62
bark **15** 850
writing
materials—cont.
brushes **7** 62; **15** 849, 853; **17** 213
copper **20** *328*
cotton **20** 327
erasers **10** 5
gold *see* CHRYSOGRAPHY
inks **7** 62, 92; **15** 849–52*, 853, 855*; **17** 212–13
lacquer **15** 849; **17** 213; **20** 327
lampblack **17** 213
lead **20** 328
leather **10** 5
metal **20** 328–9
mother-of-pearl **20** 327
ostraca **10** 5
palettes **10** *4*, 5
palm leaves **15** 851
paper **7** 62, 114; **15** 850; **17** 213–14
papyrus **10** 5; **15** 851; **20** 329; **24** 88–9
parchment **15** 851; **24** 106, 107
pens **10** *4*, 5; **15** 850, 853; **24** 348, 349; **28** 303–4
pigments **10** 5
resins **17** 213
sandstone **10** 5
silk **7** 62; **15** 850; **20** 328
silver *see* CHRYSOGRAPHY
size **15** 850
soot **17** 213
styluses **20** 326; **29** 883
wood **7** 62; **20** 327
writing boards **10** 5, *5*; **20** 327
see also BOOKS; CODICES; ROLLS; TABLETS; PSALTERS
writing boards *see under* WRITING → materials
writing-boxes *see under* BOXES → types
Writing-on-Stone, Alta **22** 592
writing sets **1** 762; **18** *522*
writing-tables *see* BUREAUX
writing-tablets **1** 853; **4** 342, *342*; **9** 3; **16** 799; **19** 311; **20** 326, 327
Ancient Near East **1** 851, 865, 868, 895; **19** 311; **20** 326
Assyrian **1** 853; **2** 364; **20** *326*
Babylonian **1** 853; **2** 364
China **6** 740, 767; **20** 327
Greece, ancient **4** 342; **20** 327
Hittite **1** 853, 865
Iran, ancient **1** 854
Mesopotamia **1** 853, 868; **2** 364; **20** 326, *326*, 327; **21** 271, 282; **23** 322; **31** 827
Mitannian **1** 853
Rome, ancient **4** 342; **20** 327, 328
Sumerian **2** 364
Turkey **4** 342
see also BOOKS; MANUSCRIPTS; TABLETS
Writs, Willem **6** 89
Wróblewo **25** 103
Wróblewska, Krystyna **33** 416
Wróblewski, Andrzej **18** 429; **25** 108; **33** 416*
Wrocław **25** *92*; **33** 416–17*
academy **1** 107
Archdiocesan Museum **33** 417
brasses **4** 692
Capitol Cinema **7** 328
churches **4** 782
Augustinian church **4** 782
Cathedral **3** 853; **13** 57; **25** 95, 109, 111
collegiate church **25** 95
Corpus Christi **25** 110
Franciscan church **25** 110
Holy Cross **13** 57; **25** 110
St Barbara **25** 110
St Dorothea **25** 110
St Elizabeth **13** 57, 90; **25** 111
St Martin **25** 110
St Mary Magdalene **4** 782; **13** 57; **25** 110, 111
portal **26** *636*
Wrocław
churches
St Mary Magdalene—cont.
sculpture **26** 636
St Mary-on-the-Sands **13** 57; **26** 637
dioramas **8** 911
fortifications **21** 571
furniture **25** 120
glass **25** 124, 125
guilds **25** 101
Jahrhunderthalle **3** *768*, 769; **7** 694; **9** 86; **10** 697; **19** 365
Jüdisches Museum **17** 581
National Museum **19** 244; **33** 417
archives **2** 371
collections **33** 417
periodicals **24** 441
Neisser house **10** 463
Nowe Miasto **17** 544
observatory **23** 339
Ossolineum **19** 751, 752
Ossoliński Library **33** 417
Ossoliński National Establishment *see* Ossolineum
painting **25** 102
Panorama Building **33** 417
pewter **12** 452, 453
Schlesisches Museum *see* Muzeum Narodowe
State Higher School of Fine Arts **25** 123, 125, 142
Town Hall **4** 782; **10** 738; **25** 111; **31** 238; **33** *417*
Wrocław Group **8** 303
Wrotham (Kent)
pottery **10** 303, *304*, 305
Wrotham Park (Middx) **30** 274
wrought iron **16** 50–54*
historical and regional traditions
Austria **2** 822, *822*
Belgium **3** 580
China **7** 96, 97, 98; **16** 59
England **4** *802*; **10** 236; **16** 53–4, *54*
France **3** 524; **11** 585, 624, 628
Hungary **15** 9, *9*
Igbo **15** 109
Italy **16** 743, 744
Malta (Republic of) **20** *218*
Netherlands, the **22** 895
Rome, ancient **27** 93
Scotland **28** 263; **30** 422
Spain **12** *919*
Syria-Palestine **30** 194
United States of America **32** *325*
uses
arches **16** *54*
architecture **10** 236; **16** 52, 53–4*
bridges **4** 802*, *802*; **30** 422
console tables **7** 747
domes **3** 524
furniture **3** 580; **11** 585
gates **2** *822*; **15** *9*
grilles **22** *455*
knife-handles **8** 284
piers (i) (seaside) **24** 748
roofs **10** 236; **16** *54*
sculpture **12** *919*
tie-bars **30** 853
weapons **7** 97
weathervanes **32** *325*
windows **20** *218*
Wroxham (Norfolk), St Mary **26** 613
Wroxton (Oxon), All Saints **10** 262
Wrschüzky, Jan **8** 399
Wrwd **14** 224
Wrżaskowicz, Łukasz **25** 127
Współczesność **29** 528
W.S. with the Maltese Cross, Master *see* STETTER, WILHELM
Wtenbrouck, Moyses (Matheusz.) van *see* UYTTENBROECK, MOSES (MATHEUSZ.) VAN

Wtewael, Joachim (Anthonisz.) **22** 844; **31** 771; **33** 417–19*
attributions **7** 863
groups and movements **31** 772
patrons and collectors **23** 112
reproductive prints by others **30** 60
works **33** *418*
Wtewael, Peter **33** 419
Wu (family) **14** 823
Wu, Empress (*reg* 684-705) **7** 7, 98, 152; **19** 640, 804; **25** 780; **33** 318
Wu Bin **22** 460; **33** 419–20*
groups and movements **12** 899
works **33** *420*
wucai *see under* PORCELAIN → wares
Wu Changshi **6** 766; **28** 553; **33** 420–21*
groups and movements **28** 553, 555; **33** 497
pupils **17** 413, 861
teachers **26** 216
works **6** 766, 802; **7** 131, *131*
Wu Ch'ang-shih *see* WU CHANGSHI
Wu Changshu *see* WU CHANGSHI
Wu Ch'ang-shuo *see* WU CHANGSHI
Wu Chen *see* WU ZHEN
Wu Chih-fan *see* WU ZHIFAN
Wu-chin *see* WUJIN
Wu Ch'iu-yen *see* WU QIUYAN
Wuchters, Abraham **8** 733; **33** 421–2*
assistants **14** 244
patrons and collectors **23** 396
reproductive prints by others **14** 25
works **8** 733; **33** *421*
Wuchters, Daniel **27** 387
Wu-chun Shih-fan *see* WUZHUN SHIFAN
Wu Dacheng **6** 766, 867; **33** 422*
Wu Dan **22** 460
Wu Daoxuan *see* WU DAOZI
Wu Daozi **6** 635, 785, 808, 816; **30** 288; **33** 422–4*
attributions **33** *423*
methods **6** 821
works **5** 36; **6** 773, 778, 786; **19** 298
Wu Deiyi **12** 49
Wudi, Emperor (Han; *reg* 141-87 BC) **6** 648, 697, 727, 815; **7** 152; **12** 86; **14** 133
Wudi, Emperor (Liang; *reg* AD 502-49) **7** 152; **22** 458
Wudil **23** *129*
Teacher Training Centre **23** 134
Wu Ding **6** 695; **7** 152
Wueluwe, Hendrik van *see* HENDRIK VAN WUELUWE
Wüest, Johann Heinrich **33** 424*
groups and movements **33** 736
pupils **11** 767; **14** 489
works **30** 125, 133, *133*
Wu Fan **6** 817
Wüger, Jacob **3** 890; **22** 329
Wu Guanzhong **7** 158; **33** 424*
Wu Hong **12** 899; **22** 459
Wu Hongyu **14** 823
Wu-hsi *see* WUXI
Wu Hsi-chai *see* WU XIZHAI
Wu Hsiu *see* WU XIU
Wu-hsüeh Tsu-yüan *see* WUXUE ZUYUAN
Wu Hufan **7** 624; **32** 844
Wu Hung *see* WU HONG
Wujae *see* YI (i) I
Wujin **6** *615*; **7** 15; **33** 425*
jade **6** 636
lacquer **7** 15
see also SIDUN; YANGCHENG
Wukari **17** 680; **23** *129*
Wu Lai-hsi *see* WU LAIXI
Wu Laixi **7** 153
Wulcob, de *see* VULCOP, DE
Wulff (family) **12** 405
Wulff, Ebert (i) (*c.* 1535/40-1606/7) **33** 425*
Wulff, Ebert (ii) (*c.* 1560-1609) **5** 76; **8** 629; **12** 410; **28** 60; **33** 425–6*
Wulff, Hans **5** 76; **8** 629; **12** 369; **28** 60; **33** 426*
Wulff, H. E. **16** 550
Wulff, Hermann **33** 87
Wulff, Jonas **5** 76; **8** 629; **12** 410; **28** 60; **33** 425, 426
Wulff, O. **9** 528
Wulfinger, Stephan *see* WULTINGER, STEPHAN
Wulfred, Archbishop of Canterbury **5** 643
Wulfric, Abbot of Canterbury **27** 236
Wulfstan **33** 8
Wu Li **25** 783; **33** 426–7*
groups and movements **23** 579, 580
teachers **32** 838
works **33** *426*
Wulipai **7** 46
Wullekopf, Ernest **21** 600; **32** 188
Wulsinus **27** 527
Wultinger, Stephan **33** 427*
Wülzburg **12** 369
Wulzinger, Stephan *see* WULTINGER, STEPHAN
Wum **3** 148
Wuma **33** 596
Wumbu **11** 878; **18** 401
Wumen Daoren see XIAO YUNCONG
Wunderkammern **5** 345; **6** 76; **9** 14; **18** 520–23*; **22** 355, 376; **29** 861
Austria **2** 812
Germany **12** 475
see also CABINETS (i) (ROOMS); COLLECTIONS → types → curiosities; KUNSTKAMMERN; STUDIOLI
Wunderlich, Hermann **17** 898
Wunderlich, Paul **10** 483; **19** 491; **33** 427*
Wunderlich & Co. **17** 898
Wunderman, Lester **1** 439; **9** 64
Wundji **11** 878
Wünsch, Karel **23** 271
Wunstorp, Johann von *see* JOHANN VON WUNSTORP
Wunuwun, Jack **33** 428*
Wuorio, Salomo **11** 112
Wu Pin *see* WU BIN
Wuppertal **12** 379
Von der Heydt-Museum **14** 506
Wu Qiuyan **7** 130; **17** 413
Wurkun **1** 382; **22** 287
Wurm, Hans **23** 305
works **23** *305*
Wurmser of Strasbourg, Nicholas **17** 820; **25** 431; **33** 428*
Würsch, Johann Melchior *see* WYRSCH, JOHANN MELCHIOR
Wurschbauer, Ignaz **28** 855
Wurstemberger, Simon **12** 468
Wurster, William Wilson **27** 730; **31** 596, 735; **33** 428*
Wurster/Bernardi & Emmons **3** 682
Würtenberger, Ernst **14** 832; **33** 428–9*
Württemberg (House of) **33** 429*
Württemberg, Charles Alexander, Duke of *see* CHARLES ALEXANDER, Duke of Württemberg
Württemberg, Christopher, Duke of *see* CHRISTOPHER, Duke of Württemberg
Württemberg, Dukes of **24** 573; **29** 60
Württemberg, Frederick-Eugene, Duke of *see* FREDERICK-EUGENE, Duke of Württemberg
Württemberg, Frederick I, Duke of *see* FREDERICK I, Duke of Württemberg
Württemberg, Frederick I, King of *see* FREDERICK I, King of Württemberg
Württemberg, Frederick II, Duke of *see* FREDERICK I, King of Württemberg
Württemberg, Georg I, Graf von Mömpelgard *see* MÖMPELGARD, GEORG I, Graf von
Württemberg, Johann Friedrich, Duke of *see* JOHN-FREDERICK, Duke of Württemberg
Württemberg, Ludwig VI, Duke of *see* LUDWIG VI, Duke of Württemberg
Württemberg, Matilda, Countess of *see* MATILDA, Countess of Württemberg
Württemberg, Sophia of *see* MARIA FYODOROVNA, Empress of Russia
Württemberg, Ulrich VI, Duke of *see* ULRICH VI, Duke of Württemberg
Württemberg, William I, King of *see* WILLIAM I, King of Württemberg
Württembergische Metallwaren Fabrik **12** 441, 449, 453
Württembergischer Kunstverein **29** 875
Wurzbach (-Tannenberg), Alfred von **10** 212; **33** 430*
Wurzbach, Wolfgang von **33** 430
Wurzbach Altar **12** 384; **20** 770; **22** 281
Würzburg **12** *361*, 471; **33** 430–34*, *431*
ecclesiastical buildings
Benedictine abbey church **12** 371
Cathedral
Schönborn Chapel **23** 4
textiles **2** 200
Deutschhauskirche **30** 535
Käppele *see* Wallfahrtskirche Mariae Heimsuchung
Marienkapelle **13** 92, *92*
sculpture **26** *370*
Neumünster **10** 745
Stifthaug Church **24** *562*, 562–3
University Church **12** 368; **17** 684
Ursuline Convent **2** 825
Wallfahrtskirche Mariae Heimsuchung **27** 500; **32** 758
glass **23** 6
Jesuit college **32** 758
Julius Hospital **14** 782; **24** 563
Mainfränkisches Museum **32** 758; **33** 430
manuscript illumination **17** 563
painting **12** 391
porcelain **12** 433
Rathaus **26** 372
Residenz **4** 225; **12** 371, 372, 410, 412; **13** 631–2; **14** 530; **15** 139; **23** 811; **26** 495; **33** 431–4*, *432*
Chapel **32** 823
frescoes **30** *858*
Hofkirche **12** 372; **23** 4
Kaisersaal **16** 676; **30** 858
paintings **33** 671
sala terrena **27** 610
sculpture **32** 758
Spiegelkabinett **5** 349
staircase **26** 495
stucco **29** 838
Toskanazimmer **12** 414; **27** 623
Treppenhaus **29** 525; **30** 858–9; **33** *433*, 434
sculpture **13** 117, 118
tapestries **12** 466, 467; **30** 324
University **22** 917; **31** 674; **32** 759
urban planning **23** 5–6
Würzburg—cont.
Women's Prison **12** 375
Würzburg, Konrad von *see* KONRAD VON WÜRZBURG
Wurzel, Ludvík **8** 401
Wurzelbauer, Benedikt **18** 574, 575; **33** 434–5*
works **12** 403; **23** 309; **25** 432; **29** 571; **33** *435*
Wurzelbauer, Johann **18** 574; **23** 309; **33** 435
Wurzinger, Carl **13** 215, 702
Wu Sangui **18** 519
Wusasa **23** 134
Wu school **6** 757–60, 774, 790, 820; **7** 148; **21** 633; **29** 244; **30** 49; **33** 435–9*
collections **19** 833
members **19** 832; **28** 588; **33** 67, 69
works **6** *758*, *759*; **25** 73; **33** *436*
Wu Shifen **6** 867
Wu Shiguang **19** 502
Wu Shih-fen *see* WU SHIFEN
Wu Shunmin **32** 841
Wusi **31** 892
Wüstenfeld, Ferdinand **13** 812
Wustmann, Jakob **8** 529; **19** 815
Wusun **6** 309
Wu Ta-ch'eng *see* WU DACHENG
Wu-t'ai shan *see* MT WUTAI
Wu Taisu **6** 805, 806, 824
Wu Tan *see* WU DAN
Wu Tao-hsüan *see* WU DAOZI
Wu Tao-tzu *see* WU DAOZI
Wuta Wuta Tjangala *see* UTA UTA (JANGALA)
Wüthrich, Friedrich, Studio **27** 215
Wu-ti, Emperor *see* WUDI, Emperor
Wu Ting *see* WU DING
Wu Tingyang **28** 554
Wutki, Michael **14** 17
Wu Tong **14** 820
Wu Tse-t'ien, Empress *see* WU ZETIAN, Empress
Wu Tso-jen *see* WU ZUOREN
Wu-tsung, Emperor (Yüan; *reg* 1307-11) *see* WUZONG, Emperor
Wu Tsung-yüan *see* WU ZONGYUAN
Wu T'ung *see* WU TONG
Wuum **1** 403
Wuvulu **24** 82
Wuwei (China) **6** *615*; **21** *870*; **28** *719*, 720; **33** 438–9*
bronzes **6** 727, *860*, *861*, 862
glass **7** 83
Wenchang temple **33** 439
see also HANTANPO; MOZUIZI
Wu Wei (1459-1508) **6** 817; **22** 460; **33** 437–8*
groups and movements **33** 657
works **6** 810; **33** *438*
Wuxi **6** *615*; **33** 439*
Jichang yuan **12** 89, *89*, 92
Wuxing **7** 119
see also QIANSHANYANG
Wu Xiu **11** 307, 308
Wu Xizhai **12** 48
Wuxue Zuyuan **17** 168, 231, 408, 749
Wu Yaozhong *see* NG YIU-CHUNG
Wuysthoff, Gerrit **18** 764; **32** 465
Wu Yuanyu **14** 859
Wuyue huahui **19** 503
Wu Zetian, Empress (Tang; *reg* 690-705) **6** 698; **30** 288; **33** 477
tomb **6** *698*
Wu Zhen **6** 754, 755, 773, 790, 819; **23** 582; **33** 439–40*
groups and movements **14** 822; **25** 73; **29** 244; **32** 845
patrons and collectors **7** 624; **32** 838
works **1** 581; **6** 790, 805, 819; **25** 72, 73; **33** *440*, 570
Wu Zhifan **7** 60
Wuzhun Shifan **17** 229, 231; **19** 300
Wuzong, Emperor (Yuan; *reg* 1307-11) **7** 151; **33** 318
Wu Zongyuan **6** 809
Wu Zuoren **6** 814; **33** 441*, 467
W with the Key, Master **3** 555; **20** 916
Wyand, S. J. **8** 830
Wyant, Alexander Helwig **31** 141; **33** 441–2*
Wyatt (family) **33** 442–3*, *443*
Wyatt, Benjamin (1709-72) **33** 442, *443*
Wyatt, Benjamin (1744-1818) **33** *443*
Wyatt, Benjamin (1755-1813) **33** *443*
Wyatt, Benjamin Dean **33** *443*, 447*
groups and movements **26** 500
patrons and collectors **33** 55
works **30** 677
Wyatt, Charles **5** 418; **15** 402
Wyatt, Edward **33** *443*, 449
Wyatt, George **33** 448
Wyatt, Henry **33** 448
Wyatt, James (1746-1813) **10** 641; **13** 301; **23** 362, 688; **33** 442, *443*, 444–8*
architecture
assembly rooms **19** 571
clubs (meeting places) **7** 469
concert halls **7** 687
country houses **3** 476; **6** 61; **8** 48; **10** 235; **16** 8; **33** 225, *445*
mausolea **20** 867, 868; **33** *444*
models **2** 337
observatories **23** 340
orangeries **23** 470
palaces **18** 5
parliament buildings **19** 613
restorations **9** 450; **19** 604; **27** 626, 628; **33** 249
theatres **30** 674
town halls **11** 330; **19** 505; **31** 239
assistants **25** 249; **33** 446, 448
collaboration **7** 791; **33** 99, 442
competitions **7** 666
furniture **10** 293; **25** 82
groups and movements **10** 642, 643–4; **13** 200; **26** 743; **29** 890
interior decoration **7** 758; **8** 105; **9** 30; **11** 431; **16** 24, *24*; **25** 192; **33** 225
patrons and collectors **7** 758; **10** 361; **14** 485; **19** 158; **33** 209
plaques **30** 502
pupils **2** 692; **11** 330; **12** 45; **14** 20; **33** 447
silver **4** 540; **10** 333
Wyatt, James (1808-93; sculptor) **33** 448
Wyatt, James (*fl* 19th cent.; painter) **23** 690
Wyatt, Jeffry *see* WYATVILLE, JEFFRY
Wyatt, John **33** *443*
Wyatt, Joseph **33** 442, *443*
Wyatt, Lewis William **33** *443*, 448*
Wyatt, Matthew **33** *443*, 448
Wyatt, Matthew Cotes **33** *443*, 447–8*
collaboration **33** 447
works **10** 266; **22** 47; **29** 565; **33** 99
Wyatt, Matthew Digby **33** *443*, 449–50*
assistants **5** 193; **8** 576
collaboration **5** 13; **12** 791; **19** 575; **25** 857
groups and movements **5** 340
staff **23** 327
works **10** 236; **16** 53; **17** 639; **19** *484*, 485; **24** 293; **25** *856*; **30** 504

Wyatt, Matthew Digby—cont.
writings **24** 273; **32** 864
illustrated **8** 652
Wyatt, Philip William **33** 447
Wyatt, Richard **29** 495
Wyatt, Richard James **3** 79; **30** 703; **33** *443*, 448–9*
Wyatt, Samuel **33** 442–8*, *443*
assistants **33** 446, 448
patrons and collectors **31** 245
works **8** 461; **19** 571; **26** 17; **33** *443*
Wyatt, Thomas **33** *443*
Wyatt, Thomas Henry **26** 541; **33** *443*, 449–50*
pupils **3** 284; **33** 263, 449
works **10** 238; **33** 450
Wyatt, William **33** 442, *443*
Wyatt & Brandon **4** 604
Wyatville, Jeffry **33** *443*, 446–7*
collaboration **8** 106
groups and movements **13** 202; **26** 85
patrons and collectors **6** 117, 515; **14** 145
pupils **11** 330; **14** 260
works **3** 690; **5** 512; **15** 407; **19** 896; **27** 357, 358; **33** 249, *250*, 250, 446, 447
Wyck, Jan **33** 175, 176–7*
collaboration **9** 719; **32** 700
Wyck, Jan—cont.
patrons and collectors **20** 141; **29** 58
pupils **33** 375
works **33** *177*
Wycliffe, John **15** 80
Wyct, Boudewijn van der *see* BOUDEWIJN VAN BATTEL
Wyczółkowski, Leon **18** 428; **25** 107; **32** 876; **33** 450*
pupils **8** 431; **33** 45
Wyditz, Bartholomäus **33** 31
Wydler, Irène **30** 135
Wye (Kent) **14** 545
Wyelant, Guillaume *see* VRELANT, WILLEM (BACKER VON)
Wyeth, Andrew (Newell) **24** 600; **33** 451*
dealers **18** 161
groups and movements **1** 86
methods **12** 501
patrons and collectors **33** 151
works **18** 718, *718*
Wyeth, Newell Convers **33** 451
Wykeham, William of *see* WILLIAM OF WYKEHAM
Wykehampton, Robert de *see* ROBERT DE WYKEHAMPTON
Wyld, William **14** 106; **33** 451–2*
Wyle, Florence **5** 570, 573
Wylie, Robert **25** 214
Wylie, Shanks & Partners **12** 775
Wylie & Lochhead, Ltd **15** 142; **18** 65; **28** 249, 254, 255
Wyllie, Charles **33** 452
Wyllie, Harold **33** 452
Wyllie, William Morrison **33** 452
Wyllie, W(illiam) L(ionel) **4** 81; **20** 424; **33** 452*
Wylsynck, Hynryk **23** 255
Wyman, George Herbert **33** 452–3*
Wyman, William **4** 482
Wymondham Abbey (Norfolk) **1** 723
Wynants, Jan *see* WIJNANTS, JAN (*c.* 1635-84)
Wynantz, Francis **11** 906
Wyndeforth, William *see* WYNFORD, WILLIAM
Wyndham, Charles, 2nd Earl of Egremont **10** 366; **33** 453*
architecture **4** 758
collections **20** 911
sculpture **4** 758, 886; **6** 97
tapestries **33** 715
Wyndham, George O'Brien, 3rd Earl of Egremont **33** 453*
paintings **9** 18; **10** 361, 365; **19** 98, 240; **24** 637; **31** 467
sculpture **3** 79; **5** 740; **27** 197
Wyndham Lewis, Percy *see* LEWIS, (PERCY) WYNDHAM
Wynegaerde, Frans van den **25** 221
Wynfield, David Wilkie **27** 564
Wynford, William **33** 202, 453–4*
collaboration **14** 454
works **13** 55; **23** 691; **33** 60, 231, 236
Wyngaerde, Anthonis van den **31** 154; **32** 899; **33** 454*
Wynn (family) **32** 787
Wynn, David **33** 63
Wynn, John **32** 788
Wynne, Robert **32** 787, 790
Wynnes, James C. **16** 40
works **16** *39*
Wynrich van Wesel, Herman *see* WESEL, HERMAN WYNRICH VAN
Wynstyne, Willem **23** 524
Wynter, Bryan **27** 563
Wyon, Alfred Benjamin **33** 455
Wyon, Allan **33** 455
Wyon, Benjamin **33** 455
Wyon, Edward William **33** 455
Wyon, Joseph Shepard **33** 455
Wyon, Leonard Charles **20** 925; **33** 455
Wyon, Thomas (i) (1767-1830) **33** 455
Wyon, Thomas (ii) (1792-1817) **33** 455
Wyon, William **20** 924, 925; **24** 887; **33** 455
works **20** *924*
Wyrsch, Johann Melchior **4** 755; **33** 455*
pupils **7** 211; **8** 907
works **30** 132
Wysocice Church **26** 637
Wysocki, Mieczysław **2** 528
Wyspiański, Franciszek **33** 455
Wyspiański, Stanisław **18** 428, 429; **24** 441; **25** 141; **33** 455–7*, *456*
collaboration **21** 51
groups and movements **28** 838
productions **27** 451
teachers **20** 810
works **18** 429, 430; **24** 244; **25** 107, 119, 122, 130, *131*
Wyssenbach, Ieremias **4** 179
Wyssenbach, Rudolph **4** 179
Wythenshawe (Lancs) **24** 187
Wytsman, Rodolphe **32** 591
Wywiórski, Michał **18** 398
Wyzewa, Théodore de **32** 591

X

Xabregas see under LISBON
Xala, Conde de San Bartolomé de, see SAN BARTOLOMÉ DE XALA, Conde de
Xanadu see SHANGDU
Xanten 12 360; 26 908; 33 458*
Collegiate Church 7 191; 12 364; 26 908; 33 457, 458*
sculpture 13 87
shrine of St Victor 26 683; 28 630
St Victor (and his Companions) see Collegiate Church
sculpture 13 91
tapestries 30 319
Xanthippos 29 617
stele 29 616
Xanthos 13 362; 19 837; 33 459–60*
Doric arch 19 840
fortifications 19 840
Harpy Tomb 19 838–9; 20 863; 31 109
Inscribed Pillar 19 838
Letoön see Sanctuary of Leto
Lion Tomb 19 838, 839
Nereid Monument 13 384, 458; 19 839–40; 20 863; 31 109; 33 459, 459, 460
acroteria 1 128
frieze 13 426
Sanctuary of Leto 13 405; 33 459–60
sculpture 33 460*
Xanthoudides, Stephanos 14 275
Xaral de Berrio, Marqués de 13 797
Xart, Jaime 8 236
Xauen see CHAOUEN
Xavante 4 706
Xavery, Albertus 33 460
Xavery, Frans 33 460
Xavery, Jacob, IV 4 618; 33 460
Xavery, Jan Baptist 3 570; 14 42; 33 460*
pupils 32 798
works 8 150; 22 859, 895
Xavery, Pieter 19 99; 22 859, 895; 33 460–61*
Xega, Spiro 1 540; 33 461*
Xelhá 6 97
Xell, Georg see GSELL, GEORG
Xenakis, Iannis 2 660; 11 527; 18 809; 19 46, 51
xenia 29 665, 669
Xenokles 13 510
Xenokrates 2 518, 531; 13 467; 25 177; 33 461*
works 13 554; 25 45
Xenophantos 4 112
Xenophon 13 420; 21 552; 33 461–2*
on Achaemenids 1 115
on art 1 175
on Scythians 30 367
xerography see under PRINTING → processes
Xeropolis see LEFKANDI
xeroradiography see under PRINTING → processes; TECHNICAL EXAMINATION → types
Xerox 23 906
Xerxes I (reg 485-465 BC) 2 213; 9 777; 15 906, 914; 24 482; 30 29, 467, 476
X-frame chairs see under CHAIRS → types
Xhosa 1 297, 299, 348, 351, 417, 418, 419; 3 442; 29 104
Xia Gui 3 517; 14 137; 33 462–3*
groups and movements 19 478; 23 215
patrons and collectors 30 465
works 6 773, 789, 817; 33 463
Xiamen 7 104; 28 719, 721
lacquer 18 613
trade 6 624
Xi'an 6 614, 615, 664; 28 718, 719; 33 464, 464–5*
altars 1 702
brick 4 794
caves 6 691
Chang'an 6 662, 663, 664; 29 905
Changle Palace 6 648
College for the Development of Literature 6 745
Daming Palace 6 650, 651, 679
Hanyuan Hall 6 651, 651, 679
Datong dian 33 423
Daxing 6 664
Dayan ta see Great Wild Goose Pagoda
figurines 6 889
Forest of Stelae 29 617; 33 464
gardens 12 86
glass 7 80, 82, 83
Great Mosque 6 677; 33 464
Great Wild Goose Pagoda 6 652, 668; 23 773
hall 6 649, 649
Hong Du Library 6 769
jewellery 7 109
Linde Hall 6 679
manuscripts 6 781
metalwork 7 25
Mingde Gate 7 361
mirrors 6 863
palaces 6 679; 7 152; 23 821
paper 7 114; 24 46
platforms 6 640
pottery 6 882, 888
School of Calligraphy 6 745
sculpture 6 712; 23 216
Shaanxi Provincial Museum 33 464
collections 6 925; 7 154
periodicals 24 435
Small Wild Goose Pagoda 6 652, 668
stelae 6 772
temples 6 626, 667, 671
Anguo Temple 6 715
cosmological temple 7 98
Dongda si see Great Mosque
Kuangzhai Temple, Qibao Terrace 6 714–15
Qinglong Temple 6 652, 667
Qingzhen si see Great Mosque
Temple of Confucius 6 746
Xingjiao Temple 23 773
Xuanzang Pagoda 6 668
tomb of Emperor Jingdi 6 883
tomb of Li Jingxun
glass 7 82
jewellery 6 312; 7 89, 109, 109
tomb of Li Zhongren 7 76
town walls 6 661; 21 594
toys 7 143
wall paintings 6 778
Weiyang Palace 6 648
Xiaoyan ta see Small Wild Goose Pagoda
Xingqing Palace 6 679
see also HANSENZHAI; SHAPO CUN
xian see VESSELS → types → yan
Xia Nai 7 159; 33 465*
Xiangfen 7 38
see also TAOSI
Xiang Jun 17 592
Xiang Kai 6 707
Xiang Shengmo 33 466*
Xiang tu movement see NATIVE SOIL MOVEMENT
Xiang Yu 19 431
Xiang Yuanbian 7 153; 30 49; 33 67, 465–6*
paintings 25 784
writings 5 293
Xiangzhou, Qifa Temple 6 745
Xiantong 33 318
Xianyang 6 615; 33 466–7*
brick 4 794
Palace 1 6 648
palaces 6 679
Qianfo si 7 100
town walls 6 643
see also YANGJIAWAN
Xian Yuanbian 2 124
Xianyu Shu 6 753, 754
works 6 754
Xiao Chen 33 496
Xiao Feng 32 840
Xiaogong 33 466
Xiao Junxian 7 149
Xiao Qin see HSIAO CH'IN
Xiaoshan 6 885
Xiao Shufang 33 467*
Xiaotun (Anyang) 2 209; 7 158
houses 6 647
jade 7 3, 4
palace 6 679
sculpture 7 74
tomb of Fu Hao 6 695, 836; 7 4, 46, 152, 631
bronze 6 828, 836, 840, 841
furniture 7 32
stone-carvings 7 74
Xiaowendi, Emperor (Wei; AD 471-99) 5 108; 6 743; 8 713; 19 803; 33 34
Xiao Xian 13 334
Xiao Yi see YUANDI, Emperor (Liang; reg AD 552-5)
Xiao Yuncong 2 95; 7 119; 33 467–8*
Xiao Zhao 6 817; 19 478; 33 468*
Xiaozong, Emperor (Song; reg 1163-90) 7 8; 29 905; 33 492
Xia period see under CHINA → periods
Xia Shen 33 463
Xiasi (Xichuan) 6 615; 7 247; 33 468–9*
bronze 6 833, 833, 852, 853, 855; 33 468–9*
Tomb M2 7 139
Xia Wenyan 2 519; 6 785, 822; 19 858; 33 649
Xia Yang see HSIA YANG
Xia Zhi 19 514
Xibeigang (Anyang) 2 209; 7 138
tombs 6 646, 694, 694
Xie, Empress (fl mid-13th cent.) 33 462
Xie Bin 18 752
Xie Gongqiao 30 246
Xie He 2 519, 531; 5 35; 6 537, 635, 773, 796, 815, 821; 7 148; 10 693
Xie Huan 6 812; 8 458
Xie Lingyun 6 795
Xieng Dong Xieng Thong see LUANG PRABANG
Xieng Khouang 18 761
Vat Bun Kong 18 764, 765
Xie Son 12 899
Xie Sun 22 460
Xie xian see XIEZHOU
Xie Zhiliu 7 161
Xiezhou, Shrine of Guandi 7 99; 28 638
Xi Gang 7 130
Xigoupan 23 496
XIII, Les 7 405; 21 167
Xi Kang 12 900
Xiling Association of Seal Carvers 7 131
Xilokeratidi 1 795
Ximena y Jurado 2 409
Ximenes, Ettore 5 425; 16 707; 33 469*
Ximénez, Juan 33 469
Ximénez, Miguel 27 818; 33 469*
Ximénez de Urrea, Francisco 33 469–70*
Ximénez Hernández, Domingo 21 377; 33 585
works 21 377
Ximeno, Matías 33 470*
Ximeno y Planes, Rafael 21 384; 33 470*
Xinan see WUXI
Xin'an pai see ANHUI SCHOOL
Xindian culture 6 877
Xindu (Sichuan)
Baoguang Temple 6 782
Guanyin Temple 6 779
tomb of Wang Zhixi 25 800
Xin'gan see DAYANGZHOU (XIN'GAN)
Xinghua Temple 6 779
Xingjing, Yong ling 6 704
Xing kilns 6 885, 886; 7 96
Xinglong 6 830
Xingping 6 709
Mao ling 6 648, 697, 727
tomb of Huo Qubing 6 697, 727, 729
sculpture 6 727
Xingrendong 7 159
Xing Tong 6 761
Xingu 4 94, 706
Xing ware see under PORCELAIN → wares
Xingwu see YANG SHOUJING
Xining 30 847
Xinjian, Prince Deng's Pavilion 24 289
Xinjiang 5 833; 6 248; 7 1; 16 443
Xinjiang Uygur Autonomous region see CENTRAL ASIA, EASTERN
Xinjian wenwu 24 435
Xinle culture 7 159
Xintala 6 308
Xintian see HOUMA
Xinxiang, Tomb of King Lujian 6 732
Xinyang 6 615; 7 247; 33 471*
bronze 6 854
tomb of Changtaiguan 6 648; 7 33, 66
Xin yue see TŌKŌ SHIN'ETSU
Xinzheng 6 615, 851; 33 471–2*
see also LIJIALOU
Xiongnu 10 873; 21 871, 884; 23 495
xipi see LACQUER → types → marbled urushi
Xiu 20 886
Xixia 5 110
pagoda 6 644
Xixian, Xu Guo Fang Gateway 7 361
Xixuan, Marquis 7 111
Xizang Zizhiqu see TIBET
Xizhai Daoren see LI KAN
Xkichmook 21 206
Xochicalco 21 193, 200, 203, 246, 262, 372; 33 472–3*
architecture 21 211
Ballcourt 3 117
fortifications 21 599
Pyramid of the Feathered Serpent 21 211, 221; 23 565; 33 473
talud-tablero 33 473
religion 21 186
sculpture 21 220–21
stelae 29 620
talud-tablero 30 280
tombs 31 117
Xochimilco 10 505; 21 374
Parque Ecológico 21 382
Xochipala 21 260
X(-ray) P(hotoelectron) S(pectroscopy) see under TECHNICAL EXAMINATION → types
Xpuhil 9 165; 21 206; 29 829
X-ray fluorescence spectrometry see under TECHNICAL EXAMINATION → types
X-ray photoelectron spectroscopy see under TECHNICAL EXAMINATION → types
X-ray powder diffraction analysis see under TECHNICAL EXAMINATION → types
X-ray radiography see under TECHNICAL EXAMINATION → types
X-ray style 1 51, 59
Xsell, Georg see GSELL, GEORG
xu see under VESSELS → types
Xuancheng 7 66, 115
Xuande emperor (Ming; reg 1426-35) 4 174; 6 779, 817; 7 90, 153; 8 458
Xuandi, Emperor (reg 74-49 BC) 6 815; 14 133
Xuanhe huapu 18 316
Xuan My 6 430, 431
Xuan paper see under PAPER → types
Xuanping, Yanfu Temple 6 658
Xuantong emperor (Qing; reg 1909-11) see PU YI
Xuanwudi, Emperor (Wei; reg AD 500-515) 19 639
Xuanzang 5 109; 13 812; 33 464
on Ahichchhantra 1 469
on Bamiyan 1 197, 202, 210
on Bodhgaya 15 281
on carpets 15 681
on Central Asia 6 320
on Harshavardhana 15 478
on Kashgar 17 831; 28 720
on Kashmir 30 823
on Kausambi 17 858
on monasteries 21 847
on Nalanda 15 476, 686
on Pataliputra 24 264
on Shotorak 28 625
on shrines 28 637
on Taxila 30 378
on Termez 30 489
on Vadnagar 31 793
on Wuwei 33 438
on Zhambyl 33 640
Xuanzong, Emperor (Tang; reg AD 712-56) 6 786, 816; 7 152; 14 135; 30 288; 33 422, 464
Xu Bangda 7 161
Xu Beihong 6 774; 7 149, 150; 28 553; 33 473–5*
pupils 33 441
works 6 814; 33 474

Xu Bingfang **7** 62
Xu Da **13** 333
Xu Daoning **2** 124; **33** 475–7*
methods **24** 492
works **28** 311; **33** *476*
Xue Ji **33** 477*
Xue Jingshi **7** 44
Xue Shanggong **6** 867
Xue Susu **33** 320
Xuetang *see* LUO ZHENYU
Xue Yao **33** 477
Xu Gu **28** 553
Xu Jianguo
works **6** *775*
Xu Jing **18** 259, 370
Xu Ke **29** 905
Xul Solar **2** 400; **33** 477*
Xultún **30** 786
Xulu, Ruben **29** 112
Xumetra y Ragull, Fernando **25** 786
Xunzi **6** 634
Xuriguera, Josep de **7** 287; **26** 10
Xu Shen **6** 769; **9** 311
Xu Shitai **30** 49
Xu Subai **7** 62
Xu Wei **6** 687; **33** 477–8*
works **6** 760, 785, 807, *807*; **7** 115; **33** *478*
Xu Xi **6** 799, 804; **33** 479*
Xu Yang **3** 517
works **6** *621*
Xuyun **5** 113
Xu Zhenqing **6** 758
Xuzhou **6** 861
Xu Zixiong *see* CHUI TZE-HUNG
XX, Les **2** 197, 562, 571; **3** 563, 564, 572, 586; **9** 40; **11** 83, 746; **14** 43; **19** 321; **22** 747; **32** 590–91*, 679
exhibitions **2** 562; **22** 746; **25** 357
Anquetin, Louis **2** 124
Cézanne, Paul **6** 369
Charpentier, Alexandre (-Louis-Marie) **6** 489
Claus, Emile **7** 405
XX, Les
exhibitions—cont.
Degouve de Nuncques, William **8** 628
Doudelet, Charles **9** 196
Dubois, (Louis-Auguste-) Albert **9** 324
Finch, Alfred William **11** 83
Gauguin, Paul **12** 191
Gausson, Léo **12** 205
Heymans, Adrien Joseph **14** 507
Mellery, Xavier **21** 86
Meunier, Constantin **21** 369
Minne, George **21** 648
Pissarro, (Jacob Abraham) Camille **24** 881
Renan, (Cornelis) Ary **26** 191
Steer, Philip Wilson **29** 595
Stobbaerts, Jan **29** 682
Thorn Prikker, Johan **30** 760
Toulouse-Lautrec (Montfa), Henri (Marie Raymond) de **31** 214
XX, Les
exhibitions—cont.
Van der Swaelmen, Louis **31** 875
Verster, Floris (Henric) **32** 377
members **3** 614; **5** 44; **10** 517; **19** 792; **25** 556; **28** 427
De Groux, Henry (-Jules-Charles) **8** 628
Dubois, Paul (-Maurice) (ii) (1859-1938) **9** 326
Ensor, James (Sidney Edouard), Baron **10** 409
Finch, Alfred William **11** 83
Khnopff, Fernand **18** 23
Lambeaux, Jef (-Marie-Thomas) **18** 670
Lemmen, Georges **19** 137
Maus, Octave **20** 862
Pantazis, Périclès **24** 20
Rops, Félicien (Joseph Victor) **27** 140
XX, Les
members—cont.
Seurat, Georges(-Pierre) **28** 502
Signac, Paul **28** 698
Toorop, Jan (Theodorus) **31** 147
Van Rysselberghe, Théo(phile) **31** 888
Verheyden, Isidore **32** 254
XXe siècle **24** 442
XXX, Les **25** 747
Xydias Typaldos, Nikolaos **33** 479*
xylene **29** 53
xylo **8** 285
xylographs *see* WOODBLOCK
xylography *see* WOODCUTS; WOOD-ENGRAVINGS
Xylonite *see under* IVORY → types
xylophones **5** 508; **15** 817; **30** 636; **32** 154
Xyngopoulos, Andreas **28** 481; **33** 479*

Y

Yaan, Gao Yi que **6** 649, 697; **25** 800
Yabe, Tomoe **17** 206
Yablonevo **31** 557
Church of the Archangel Michael **31** 557
Yablonov Synagogue **17** 559
Yablonskaya, Tat'yana (Nilovna) **31** 559; **33** 480*
Yabu Meizan *see* MEIZAN, YABU
yácatas **31** 504, *504*
Yacimentos Petroliferos Fiscales Bolivanos **4** 260
Yacoubi, Ahmed **22** 129
yad **17** 569, *570*
Yada'il Dharih, King of Saba' (*reg* 8th cent. BC) **2** 252
Yadamsuren **21** 881
Yadanabon Mg Su **5** 246
Yada Shinyōken **18** 87
Yadava **33** 480*
Yadin, Yigael **14** 273; **21** 47
Yadrintsev, Nikolay (Mikhaylovich) **21** 885
Yaemon Nagoshi *see* NAGOSHI YAEMON
Yaeyama islands **27** 469, 471
Yagane **2** 394
Yaghhmurasan **31** 66
Yagi, Issō **33** 480
Yagi, Kazuo **17** 268; **18** 555; **33** 480–81*
Yaguarón **24** *91*
Franciscan mission church **24** 94, *94*, 95, 98
Museo de Yaguarón **24** 102
Yagul **21** *193*, 200, 202, *372*; **33** 481*
fortifications **21** 599
mosaics **21** 255
tombs **31** 118
Yahatabara
sculpture **17** *105*
Yahdun-Lim **30** 197
Yahgan **29** 128
Yahudiya, Tell el- **9** *774*, 830; **10** 80; **33** 481*
pottery **10** 27
Yahya I, Ruler (*reg* 1021-23; 1023-36) (Hammudid) **20** 156
Yahya, Imam (*reg* 1904-48) (Zaydi) **33** 519
Yahya, Tepe **1** 850, 894; **2** *246*; **10** 132; **15** *901*, 902, 903, 904, 907, 909; **33** 482*
bowls **15** 902
figurines **15** *903*, 913
metalwork **15** 919
seals **1** 863
stone vessels **2** 272
Yahya al-Sufi **16** 283; **33** 482*, 503
Yahya ibn Mahmud al-Wasiti **5** 761; **16** 272, 309, 517; **19** 316
works **16** *309*
Yahyalı **9** 555
Yaichi Kusube *see* KUSUBE, YAICHI
Yajnavaraha **2** 57; **5** 470
Yaka **1** 403; **33** 482–5*
divination instruments **1** 356, 357
drums (musical instruments) **1** 357
iconography **1** 262
masks **1** 240, 256, 261, 290, 405; **33** 482, 483–5, *484*
mixed-media **1** 301
patronage **1** 240
sculpture **1** 403; **33** 485, *485*
statuettes **33** 482
wood-carvings **33** *485*
Yakahito, Prince **18** 566
Yakchŏn *see* NAM KU-MAN
yak-hair *see under* HAIR → types
Yakima **22** 671
Yakimine **17** 351
Yakke-Parsan **32** 320
Yakö **1** 310; **10** 122, 124
Yakob, Peter *see* KLODT (VON YURGENSBURG), PYOTR (KARLOVICH)
Yakobson, Adel (Yakovlevna) **27** 417
Yakovlev, Aleksandr (Yevgeniyevich) **27** 392; **33** 486*
collaboration **13** 654; **28** 643
pupils **1** 507
Yakovlev, Postnik **17** 872
Yakovleva, Serafim **27** 414
yakṣa sculpture *see under* SCULPTURE → types
Yaksha Malla **3** 906
yakṣī sculpture *see under* SCULPTURE → types
yak skins *see under* SKINS → types
Yaksu Hermitage **18** 296
sculpture **18** *296*
Yakto
mosaics **2** 156, *158*
Yakuglas *see* JAMES, CHARLIE
Yakulov, Georgy (Bogdanovich) **27** 396; **33** 486–7*
collaboration **26** 504; **31** 519
groups and movements **3** 120; **10** 415; **12** 870; **33** 380
patrons and collectors **8** 10
productions **8** 850; **30** 686
pupils **29** 626
works **2** 432
Yakunchikova, Mariya (Vasil'yevna) **12** 878; **25** 146; **33** 379, 487*
Yakuno-cho, Yakushidō **17** 120
Yakupov, Kharis **27** 434
Yakut **16** 799; **27** 436
Yakutat
beadwork **22** *640*
Yakutsk **27** 436
museum **27** 436
Yalangach **6** 195
Yalangtush Bi Alchin **6** 205; **16** 235, 236; **27** 673, 677
Yalap **6** 380
Yalbay **16** 299, 312
Yale, Elihu **23** 25
Yale Center for British Art *see under* NEW HAVEN (CT)
Yale University *see under* NEW HAVEN (CT)
Yalpanam *see* JAFFNA
Yalyngach **6** 275
Yamaato Kakurei **17** 196
Yamabeta kiln **18** 538
yamachawan see under POTTERY → wares
Yamada (family) **17** 304, 415
Yamada, Kanzan **17** 413
Yamada, Kisai **17** 133
Yamada, Mamoru **14** 761; **15** 885, 886; **17** 88; **33** 488*
Yamada, Matsue **17** 371
Yamada, Shōhei **17** 413
Yamadadera **17** 65, 67; **23** 597
Yamada Dōan **22** 497
Yamada Hikaru *see* HIKARU, YAMADA
Yamada Kyūjō **33** 489
Yamada-Sengoku **30** 258
Yamagata **17** 358
Yamagishi, Kazuo **16** 848
Yamaguchi **17** 138
Prefectural Museum of Art **17** 874
Yamaguchi, Bunzo **17** 88
Yamaguchi, Gen **17** 296
Yamaguchi, Katsuhiro **18** 63; **33** 488*
Yamaguchi, Takeo **17** 860; **27** 594; **33** 488*
Yamaguchi Okatomo **17** 400
Yamaguchi Soken **17** 196, 273
works **17** *271*
yamajiro **21** 547
Yamaki **17** 47
Yamalo-Nenets region **27** 436
Yamamoto, Hōsui **11** 821; **17** 203, 204
Yamamoto, Izuru **17** 267
Yamamoto, Kanae **17** 295, 421; **33** 363
Yamamoto, Riken **17** 91; **33** 488–9*
Yamamoto, Riken, & Field Shop **33** 488
Yamamoto, Shunkyō **17** 201
Yamamoto, Tōshū **17** 267
Yamamoto, Toyoichi **17** 137
Yamamoto, Yohji **9** 294
Yamamoto, Yoshiko **4** 481
Yamamoto Baiitsu **22** 432; **33** 489*
works **17** 191; **33** *489*
Yamamoto Chikuun **17** 413
Yamamoto Fujinobu **17** 283
Yamamoto Joshunsai **22** 118
Yamamoto Ranei **33** 489
Yamamoto Sōken **23** 363
Yamamura, Koka **17** 295
Yamamura, Toyonari *see* YAMAMURA KOKA
Yamanaka, Chiruo **30** 22
Yamanaka, Sadajirō **17** 431; **32** 394
Yamanaka Shinten'ō **17** 238
Yamanobe-no-michi, Tomb of Emperor Sujin **17** 57
Yamanouchi, Sugao **17** 244, 426
Yamanoue Sōji **17** 438
Yamaoka Tesshū **17** 238
Yamasaki, Minoru **33** 489*
collaboration **28** 834
works **8** 821; **17** 549; **19** 701; **27** 216, 876
Yamashita, Kazumasa **17** 91; **33** 490*
Yamashita, Kikuji **33** 490*
Yamashita, Shintarō **17** 205
Yamashita, Shinto **23** 141
Yamato (Japan) **17** 354; **18** 373
Yamato (dynasty) **17** 19, 21, 214
Yamatoe see under JAPAN → painting
Yamato hime no mikoto, Princess **16** 72
Yamato period *see* JAPAN → periods → Kofun
Yamazaki, Chōun **17** 134
Yamazaki, Taihō **17** 240
Yamazaki, Taneji **17** 430
Yambio **1** *379*, *401*; **33** 609
Yambol
market **5** 148
mosque **5** 148; **16** 228
Yambula **14** 376, 377
Yam Fortress **27** 370
Yami **10** 580
Yamoussoukro **1** *386*; **8** 22
Basilica **1** 228; **8** 22
photography **1** *226*
Yamparaes **4** 267
Yampolsky, Mariana **30** 275; **33** 490*
Yamqui, Juan de Santacruz Pachacuti **29** 129, 209
Yamyshevsk **27** 375
yan see under VESSELS → types
Yanagawa (family) **17** 262
Yanagawa Shigenobu **17** 289
Yanagi, Munemichi **21** 635
Yanagi, Muneyoshi **17** 27, 257, 348, 861; **31** 82; **33** 491*
groups and movements **17** 265, 295; **21** 634, 635; **33** 149
personal collection **17** 317
pupils **22** 114
works **17** 344, 429, 440; **23** 554
Yanagi, Sōri *see* YANAGI, MUNEMICHI
Yanagi, Yoshitaka **21** 634
Yanagida, Tairoku **17** 240
Yanagida, Taiun **17** 240
Yanagisawa Kien **17** 411; **33** 491–2*
pupils **15** 126, 127
works **17** 190, 237; **33** *492*
Yanagisawa Yoshiyasu **12** 99
Yanagita, Kunio **17** 345
Yanahuara, S Juan Bautista **24** 503
Yan'an, Lu Xun Academy of Art and Literature **7** 149
Yanase, Masamu **17** 205, 206; **20** 873
Yanbei Jushi *see* DUAN YUCAI
Yanbeta **17** 352
Yan Bi **33** 498
Yanbuʿ **27** 875
fortifications **21** 588
Museum of Yousif Najjar **27** 877
Yancheng (Wujin) **7** 97; **33** 425
Yanchokrak **28** 325
Yan Ciping **33** 492*
Yan Ciyu **33** 492
Yandaishan (Yizheng) **7** 140
Yañez (de la Fuente), Enrique **21** 380, 403; **33** 492–3*
groups and movements **2** 280
works **21** 379, 380
Yañez (de Figueroa), Fernando **14** 516; **19** 516–17*; **29** 277; **31** 815
works **29** *278*
Yáñez, José Anselmo **23** 904
Yañez de la Almedina *see* YAÑEZ (DE FIGUEROA), FERNANDO
Yang, Empress (1162-1232) **1** 581
Yangal-hiti **22** 772
Yang Buzhi **6** 804, 805; **33** 493*
Yang Ch'i-tan *see* YANG QIDAN
Yang-chou *see* YANGZHOU
Yang Chüeh-cheng **1** 126
Yangdi **29** 905; **33** 495
Yang family shrine **28** 638
Yang Guifei **7** 7; **19** 856, 858
Yanghi Urgensh *see* URGENCH
Yang Hsin *see* YANG XIN
Yang Hsüan *see* YANG XUAN
Yang Hŭi-mun **18** 300
Yangi (China) *see* SHORCHUK
Yangi (Kazakhstan) *see* DZHAMBUL
Yangji **33** 493–4*
Yangjiang **7** 113
Yang Jianshan **18** 534
Yangjiawan (Xianyang) **7** 56
Yang Jin **2** 124
Yangji of Silla **18** 257
Yangju, Moknŭng **18** 300
Yang Juezheng *see* YANG CHÜEH-CHENG
Yang Kuei-fei *see* YANG GUIFEI
Yang-le-shod *see* PHARPHING
Yangliuqing **7** 120, 147
Yang Lu **6** 816
Yang Mao **7** 16
Yangmiao (Huaian) **7** 15
Yang Mum **6** 424–5, 430, 431
Yang Ningshi **6** 748
Yangon *see* RANGOON
Yang P'aeng-son **33** 494*
works **33** *494*
Yangping **7** 26
Yang Prung **6** 425
Yang Pu-chih *see* YANG BUZHI
Yangp'yong-gun, Sujong Temple **18** 352
Yangqi Buddhism *see under* BUDDHISM → sects
Yang Qidan **6** 816
Yangsan **18** 341
Yang San-lang **30** 247
Yang Sa-ŏn **18** 329
Yang Shanshen **19** 423
Yangshao **6** 876; **7** 106, 159
Yangshao culture
kilns **6** 870, *870*
pottery **6** 875–7*, *876*, *877*; **7** 159
Yang Shih-ch'i *see* YANG SHIQI
Yang Shiqi **8** 458
Yang shou-ching *see* YANG SHOUJING
Yang Shoujing **17** 414; **18** 534; **33** 494–5*
Yangsondang *see* KIM (i) CHE
Yang Tzu-hua *see* YANG ZIHUA
Yang Wei-chen *see* YANG WEIZHEN
Yang Weizhen **6** 754, 755
Yang Xin **6** 770
Yang Xuan **7** 134
works **7** *134*
Yang Ying-feng **7** 249; **33** 495*
Yang Yinsong **12** 313
Yangyuan, Hutouliang cave **7** 74
Yang Yü-hsüan *see* YANG XUAN
Yang Yuxuan *see* YANG XUAN
Yang Yuyu *see* YANG YING-FENG
Yangzhou **6** *615*, 621; **7** 151; **33** 495–8*
ceramics **6** 915
enamel **7** 71, 79
gardens **12** 89; **33** 495–6*
jade **7** 9
Jixiao shanzhuang **12** 92, *92*
lacquer **7** 18
painting **33** 496–8, *497*
Pao lu **12** 88
Yangzhou Salt Administration **7** 10
Yangzhou school **6** 762–4, 813; **33** 496–8*
members **14** 831; **19** 802; **33** 653
works **19** *802*; **33** *497*
Yang Zihua **6** 816
Yangzishan **1** 702; **6** 482
Yan Hui **6** 783; **33** 498*
Yanhuitlán Monastery **21** 375
Yanik Tepe **15** *901*, 902, 909; **33** 498*
figurines **15** 913
Yaniq, Congregational Mosque **16** 291
Yankilevsky, Vladimir **8** 10; **27** 397
Yankton **22** 551
Yanktonai **22** 551
Yank Wong **14** 722
Yan Liben **6** 730, 816; **7** 108; **33** 498–500*
attributions **6** 808, *809*, *815*, 815, 816; **30** 837
patrons and collectors **30** 251
works **6** 698; **7** 76; **11** 152; **33** *499*
Yan Lide **6** 816
Yanmenguan **13** 334

Yannina see IOANNINA
Yanomani 4 707; 28 547
Yanosuke Iwasaki see IWASAKI, YANOSUKE
Yanovskaya, Yekaterina (Vasil'yevna) 27 417
Yanovsky, Aleksey 31 828
Yano Yoshishige 21 742
Yanshi
 Gong ling 6 699, 730
 tomb of Li Jingyou 7 24
 see also ERLITOU
Yan Shuilong see YEN SHUI-LUNG
Yansi 1 403
Yan Song 7 27; 33 69, 500*
Yantsin 30 476
Yanulis, Petras 17 856
Yan Wengui 6 789; 33 500–502*
 works 33 501
Yanxiadu 6 615, 663; 33 502*
 bronze 6 855
 palace 6 679
 see also YI XIAN
Yan Zhan 6 543
Yan Zhenqing 5 36; 6 746; 33 502–3*
 commentaries 6 770, 771
 copies 6 765
 patrons and collectors 6 772; 33 663
 works 6 746
Yan Zhong 33 492
Yao 1 249; 18 775; 20 161
Yao, Célestin Dogo 8 22, 23
Yaoshan 7 2; 19 302
Yao Song 2 96
Yao Sung see YAO SONG
Yao Tsui see YAO ZUI
Yaoundé 1 394; 5 523
 Bank 5 523
 collections 5 525
 Petit Musée d'Art Camerounais 5 525
 Post Office 5 523
Yao xian 7 25
Yaozhou ware 6 914; 29 67
Yao Zui 6 537, 816, 821
Yap 21 476, 477; 23 711, 717
Yap, Arthur 28 774
Yapahuva 29 440; 33 503*
 architecture 29 450; 33 503
 sculpture 29 460
 town walls 29 450
Yapaí, Joan 2 398
Yapane see JAFFNA
Yapese 23 710
Yaprakhisar, Davullu Kilisesi 5 677
Yāprin see KATHMANDU
Ya'qub 16 253; 23 641
Ya'qub Artin 16 557
Ya'qub Beg, Sultan (reg 1478-90) (Aqqoyunlu) 2 237; 8 533; 16 198, 328, 332; 28 811; 30 223
Ya'qub Beg Albums see under ALBUMS → individual manuscripts
al-Ya'qūbī 13 811; 17 496; 27 678
Ya'qub Shah ibn Sultan Shah 16 222
Yaqut 1 203; 16 485
Yaqut al-Musta'simi 16 284; 33 503–4*
 pupils 1 473; 14 260; 16 283, 284; 33 482
 works 3 53; 16 283; 33 504
Yarborough, Charles Anderson-Pelham, 1st Earl of see ANDERSON-PELHAM, CHARLES, 1st Earl of Yarborough
Yarborough, Charles Pelham, 4th Earl of see PELHAM, CHARLES, 4th Earl of Yarborough
Yarborough, Earls of 33 385
Yardley, Helen 5 842
Yaremich, Stepan (Petrovich) 27 444
Yarets 8 908; 27 400
Yari 16 292
Yarim-Lim 30 185
Yarim Tepe (i) (Iran) 15 901, 902, 904; 33 504*
 houses 21 280
 metalwork 21 269
Yarim Tepe (ii) (Iraq) 33 504–5*
 copper 21 303
 figurines 21 269
 houses 21 280, 281
 kilns 21 269
 pottery 21 270, 305; 33 505*
Yarinovsky, P. 2 894
 works 2 894
Yarkand 7 10; 28 719, 720
Yarkhoto 6 288; 28 720; 33 505*
 architecture 6 296
 fortifications 6 296
 painting 6 304
 prints 6 314
 sculpture 6 298, 300
 stupa 29 867
 Temple 1 30 442
 Temple 1A 30 442
 temples 30 442
Yar Kurgan 6 182, 209, 210; 30 440; 31 781; 33 505–6*
 fortifications 21 591
 minaret 6 201, 206
 sculpture 6 219
 temple 6 200; 30 440
Yarlung dynasty 30 814, 847
Yarlung Valley, Tsechu bumpa 30 815
Yarmamedov, Klychmurad 31 459
Yarm Methodist Church (Cleveland) 21 347
Yar Muhammad Khan 15 372
Yarmuth, Tell Temple 30 188
yarn 15 659, 795; 16 468; 17 316; 22 655
Yarnall, J. 4 27
Yarnold, J. W. 26 125
yarn-sewn rugs see under RUGS → types
Yaroshenko, Nikolay (Aleksandrovich) 27 391; 33 506*
Yaroslav I, Prince of Kiev (reg 1019-54) 18 37, 38; 23 270; 31 555, 561; 33 506
Yaroslavl' 9 507; 27 363, 376; 33 506–7*
 Art Museum 27 440
 Church of the Annunciation 25 342
 Church of the Prophet Elijah 25 342; 27 372
 icon 27 386
 damask 19 418
 icons 15 II2; 27 382, 385
 Lycée 27 376
 Monastery of the Saviour 25 342
 Monastery of the Transfiguration 31 555
 painting 27 382, 386, 387
 St John Chrysostomos 27 372; 33 507
 St John the Baptist 27 372
 St Nicholas the Wet 25 342
 sculpture 27 382
 textiles 27 400
Yaroslav sarcophagus 9 597
Yaroslav the Wise, Prince of Kiev see YAROSLAV I, Prince of Kiev
Yarse 22 199
Yarumela 29 139
Yarwood, Walter 5 571; 23 791
Yarxoto see YARKHOTO
Yas, Juan J. 13 770
Yasa-pabbata see YAPAHUVA
Yaseki see ONO NO MICHIKAZE
Yash see IAŞI
Yasha 17 393
Yashadinna 15 455
Yashar, Yitzhak 10 719; 16 566
Yashbak min Mahdi 5 397; 16 213; 20 230
Yashichirō Zensei Nagoshi see NAGOSHI YASHICHIRŌ ZENSEI
Yashima Gakutei 17 287
Yashirō, Yukio 20 834
Yashodhara 15 550
Yashodharapura see under ANGKOR
Yashodharman, Ruler (reg c. 525-35) (Huna) 15 286, 474; 29 64
Yashovarman, Ruler (reg c. 925-54) (Chandella) 15 290
Yashovarman, Ruler of Kannauj (reg c. 720-50) 15 262
Yashovarman I, King of Cambodia (reg c. 889-900) 2 54, 56, 60; 5 460, 467, 468; 26 558
Yasi see TURKESTAN (TOWN)
Yasiris 5 729
Yasky, Avraham 16 566; 33 507–8*
Yasmah-Adad 30 197
Yass Courthouse 18 887
Yassı Ada 9 632
Yassıhöyük see GORDION
Yasua, Master of the 13 861
 works 13 860
Yasuda, Yukihiko 17 201; 33 508*
Yasuda Fire and Marine Insurance Co. 2 561; 15 888; 17 433
Yasuda Rōzan 17 199
Yasufumi Kijima see KIJIMA, YASUFUMI
Yasuhira, Fujiwara no see FUJIWARA NO YASUHIRA
Yasuhiro Ishimoto see ISHIMOTO, YASUHIRO
Yasui, Sōtarō 17 207; 30 241; 33 508*
 exhibitions 17 436
 groups and movements 17 205; 31 82
 teachers 2 579; 17 205
Yasuji Inoue see INOUE, YASUJI
Yasuji Ogishima see OGISHIMA, YASUJI
Yasukazu Tabuchi see TABUCHI, YASUKAZU
Yasumiya Shrine 17 348
Yasunaga Ishikawa see ISHIKAWA YASUNAGA
Yasunobu Kanō see KANŌ YASUNOBU
Yasuo Kazuki see KAZUKI, YASUO
YAS & Urbanists 18 40
Yasushi Nishikawa see NISHIKAWA, YASUSHI
Yasushi Sugiyama see SUGIYAMA, YASUSHI
Yasutake Funakoshi see FUNAKOSHI, YASUTAKE
Yasutoki Hōjō see HŌJŌ YASUTAKI, Shogunal Regent
Yasuyuki Manno see MANNO, YASUYUKI
Yasuzaemon Matsunaga see MATSUNAGA, YASUZAEMON
Yasuzō Nojima see NOJIMA, YASUZŌ
Yasygin, I. D. 17 744
Yasyin 24 67
Yasyn' Church 31 553
Yatarō Noguchi see NOGUCHI, YATARŌ
Yatayty 24 100
Yatemgētā, Zarihun 10 574
 works 10 575
Yates, Caroline 13 30
Yates, Catherine
 works 29 805
Yates, Frances (Amelia) 33 508–9*
Yates, Joseph Brooks 30 749
Yates, Marie 10 879
Yates, Richard Vaughan 12 598
Yathrib see MEDINA
Yatman Cabinet 5 196
Yatmanov, Grigory 22 508
Yatshing 7 30
Yatsugatake Range 17 245
Yatsuka, Hajime 17 92; 33 509*
Yattendon Guild 32 906
Yaudheya 15 213
Yaunde-Fang 10 787, 791
Yaure 1 357, 392
Yauya Stele 29 620
Yavan 6 182; 30 252; 33 509–10*
 architecture 30 252
 pottery 33 510
 stamps 33 509
Yavapai 22 661
Yavi Church 2 398
Yavi culture 29 191
Yavlensky, Aleksey (Georgevich) see JAWLENSKY, ALEXEI
Yavoh, Malan 1 362
Yavorsky, E. V. 19 13
Yavorsky, Ioan 21 811
Yaxchilán 20 882; 21 193, 199, 246, 264, 372; 23 826; 33 510–11*
 finials (architectural) 21 207
 lintels 9 165; 21 246
 plaques 30 786
 sculpture 21 221
 stele 29 620
 Structure 33 33 510
 Temple 33 21 214
 wall paintings 21 231
Yaxhá 6 97; 21 213
Yaxuná 6 97; 29 829
Yayahuala 21 207
Yayanagi, Go 17 296
Yayoi (people) 17 19
Yayoi culture 17 21
 pottery 17 246, 246*; 33 511
 sculpture 17 97
Yayoi Kusama see KUSAMA, YAYOI
Yayoi period see under JAPAN → periods
Yayvantepe, Mar Gabriel 31 434, 435
Yazd 15 897; 16 105, 366; 33 511–12*
 architecture 16 196
 baths 16 198
 carpets 15 899; 16 482
 Duvazdah Imam 16 159, 160, 161; 22 321; 28 634
 felt 10 874
 Friday Mosque 16 199; 22 194; 33 511–12, 512
 gates 16 160
 houses 16 269, 270
 Khatir Gate 9 160; 21 584
 manuscripts 16 322
 portals 16 194
 stelae 29 618
 textiles 16 449, 450
 tomb of Rukn al-Din 16 195, 250
 Yazdani, Ghulam 16 549
Yazılıkaya (i) (Hittite) 1 821; 14 591; 33 512–14*
 pottery 1 838
 reliefs 1 832, 835, 893; 11 792; 14 592; 15 33; 33 513
 sculpture 1 827
 shrine 1 829
 temple 1 826
 writing-tablets 1 893
Yazılıkaya (ii) (Phrygian)
 altar 24 690
 architecture 1 831; 24 689, 689–90
Yaz Tepe see MERV (UZBEKISTAN)
Yazuri 16 305
Yazz, Beatin 22 595
Yazzie, Sybil 22 595
Ybbs, Nicholas von see NICHOLAS VON YBBS
Ybl, Miklós 14 889, 908; 30 210; 33 514–15*
 assistants 28 87, 118
 collaboration 10 907
 works 5 83, 86; 14 315, 524, 889; 17 858
Yciar, Juan de 28 307
Ycket, Joan see NICQUET, JAN
Ydes 26 602
Ye 23 821
Yeames, William Frederick 14 588; 27 564; 33 515*
yeast black 15 851
Yeates, Alfred Bowman 12 315
Yeats, Elizabeth Corbet 9 318; 16 18; 17 472
Yeats, Jack B(utler) 16 18, 35, 36; 33 515–16*
Yeats, John Butler 16 17; 33 515*
Yeats, Lily 9 318
Yeats, Susan Mary 6 164
Yeats, William Butler 3 446; 19 891; 30 685
Yeavering 2 64; 14 73
Yecheng 12 86
Ye Deyuan 7 36, 37
Yee Bon 14 721
Yefimov, Boris (Yefimovich) 5 759; 33 516*
Yefimov, Il'ya (Konstantinovich) 27 423
Yefimov, Ivan 18 477; 32 661
Yefimov, Lado (Davidovich) 27 422
Yefimov, Nikolay (Yefimovich) 33 516–17*
 works 4 335; 23 168; 27 578, 579
Yefim'yev, Stefan 33 507
Yegerev, Viktor 27 380
Ye'ghishe 2 429
Ye Gongchuo 33 517*
Yegornov, Sergey 9 495
Yegorov, Aleksey 5 25; 16 791; 27 433; 31 537; 32 851
Yegorov, Grigory (Georgiyevich) 27 417
Yegorov, Kristantin 27 434
Yegoshin, German (Pavlovich) 27 581
Yegotov, Ivan (Vasil'yevich) 22 171; 27 375; 33 517*
Yegros, Angel 24 99
Yegüih see LAMBITYECO
Yeha 1 379, 513
 temple 1 378; 10 564
Yehaw-Milk 5 331
Yeh Hsia-an see YE GONGCHUO
Yeh Hsin see YE XIN
Yeh Kung-ch'uo see YE GONGCHUO
Yeh Pulu 15 785
Yeh Te-yüan see YE DEYUAN
Yehudiyah, Tell el- see YAHUDIYA, TELL EL-
Yei 4 489
Yekatarinograd 27 433
Yekaterinburg 27 362, 375, 411, 427; 33 517–18*
 hardstones 27 428
 metalwork 27 422
 Picture Gallery 33 518
Yekaterinhof 27 406, 430; 30 324
Yekaterinoslav see DNIPROPETROVS'K
Yela 1 404; 19 72, 74
Yela Günther, Rafael 13 765; 33 518*
Yela Montanegro, Baldomero 33 518
Yelets 32 527
Yeli 6 406
 masks 6 406
Yeliseyev (family) 17 870
Yeliseyev, G. G. 3 197
Yeliseyev, K. 3 531
Yeliseyevich 27 365
Yelizarov, Viktor (Dimitriyevich) 9 54; 33 518*
Yelizaveta Romanova, Empress of Russia see ELIZABETH, Empress of Russia
Yelles, Bachir 1 635
Yellin, Samuel 16 60; 31 653
yellow see under PIGMENTS → types
Yellow Book 2 562; 3 445
Yellowknife (people) 22 546
Yellowknife (city) 5 559

yellow metal *see* ALLOYS → types → Muntz meta
Yellow Minyan ware *see* POTTERY→ wares → Minyan ware
yellow ochre *see under* OCHRE → types
Yellow Seto ware *see under* POTTERY → wares
yellow-stain *see* SILVER-STAIN
Yemaek **18** 345, 382
Yemaje **3** 728
Yemanu, Barhānu **10** 573
Yemaotai **6** 799
Yemar **30** 829–30
Yemar, Baláččaw **10** 573
Yemen **2** *246*; **16** *104*; **33** 518–20*
  acacia **16** 500
  animal subjects **2** *265*
  architecture **16** 177–8*, 207, 213–15*, 229; **32** 317–18*; **33** 519–20
  book covers **16** 357
  bracelets **16** 532
  bronze **2** *258*, *259*
  cenotaphs **16** *500*, 500–501
  collections **1** 896; **33** 520
  cordia **16** 500
  cotton **16** *438*, 438–9; **31** 21
  domes **16** 214–15
  doors **16** 500
  dyeing **16** 439
  dyes **16** 438
  finials (scrolls) **17** 569
  glass **16** *533*
  grilles **16** 500
  houses **32** *317*; **33** *519*, 519–20
  ikat **16** *438*, 439; **31** 21, 22
  indigo **16** 438
  inlays **16** 500
  inscriptions **16** *438*, 439
  ivory **16** 500
  ivory-carvings **16** 523–4*
  jewellery **16** 532–3*
  *khānaqāh*s **16** 214–15
  lamps **17** 573
  madder **16** 438
  madrasas **16** 214
  metalwork **2** *265*
  mihrabs **16** 178
  minarets **16** 178, 215
  mosques **16** 177, *178*, 213–14, *214*
  mother-of-pearl **16** 500
  mud **33** *519*
  muqarnas (architecture) **16** 215
  nails **16** 500
  necklaces **16** 533, *533*
  portals **16** 178
  screens (i) (architectural) **16** 500
  screens (ii) (furniture) **16** 500
  sculpture **2** *258*, *259*
  shutters (window) **16** 500
  silver **16** 532, *533*
  stucco **16** 214, 215
  synagogues **17** 551
  tamarisk **16** 500
  textiles **16** 438–9*
  tiles **16** 215
  tiraz **16** 438; **31** 21, 22
  tombs **16** 177, 214–15
  trade **16** 417, 438, 527
  wars **16** 438
  wood-carvings **16** 500
  woodwork **16** *500*, 500–501*
  see also ARABIA
Yemeni Artists' Society **33** 520
Yenakiyev, F. Ye. **3** 734; **24** 400
Yencesse, Ovide **20** 925; **25** 214
Yen Chan *see* YAN ZHAN
Yen Chen-ch'ing *see* YAN ZHENQING
Yenen **26** 744
Yener, Ertur **5** 633; **31** 452
  works **31** *453*
Yen-hsia-tu *see* YANXIADU
Yen Hui *see* YAN HUI
Yeni Han **16** 205
Yeni Kaplica *see under* BURSA
Yeniler Grubu *see* NEW GROUP
Yeni Rabat *see* ENI-RABAT
Yeniseysk **27** *362*; **33** 521*
Yen Li-pen *see* YAN LIBEN
Yen Li-te *see* YAN LIDE
Yen Shui-lung **30** 247
Yen Sung *see* YAN SONG
Yen Tz'u-p'ing *see* YAN CIPING
Yen Wen-kuei *see* YAN WENGUI
Yeo, Richard **33** 521*
Yeo, Thomas **28** 774
Yeoh Jin Leng **20** 172
Yeoman Pottery **14** 107; **22** 352
Yeomans, Arthur W.
  works **5** *174*
Yeoryiou, Yeoryios Pol. **8** 364
Yeovil (Somerset) **24** 576
Yepes, Bartolomé de **29** 334
Yepes, Eduardo Díaz *see* DÍAZ YEPES, EDUARDO
Yepes, Tomás *see* HIEPES, TOMÁS
Yerbury, F. R. **10** 240
Yeremin, Yury (Petrovich) *see* YERYOMIN, YURY (PETROVICH)
Yereruyk' **2** *423*, 425; **9** *512*; **33** 521*
  basilica **2** 425
Yerevan *see* EREVAN
Yeriho *see* JERICO
Yer Kurgan *see* YAR KURGAN
Yermenyov, Ivan (Alekseyevich) **27** 389, 579; **33** 522*
Yermolayev, Boris (Nikolayevich) **27** 581
Yermolayeva, Vera (Mikhaylovna) **3** 529; **19** 13; **32** 412; **33** 522*
  groups and movements **30** 8; **31** 677
Yermolin, Rem **27** 434
Yeropkin, Pyotr Mikhailovich **27** 575
Yeroskipos, Hagia Paraskevi **8** 358, 359
Yeroskipou National Museum of Folk Art **8** 366
Yershov, Sofony **27** 433
Yershova, L. **30** 352
Yeryomin, Yury (Petrovich) **33** 522–3*
Yesan, Sudŏk Temple **18** 265, *265*
Yesari *see* ESAD YESARI
Yesemek **1** 827
Yeshe Ö, King of Tibet (*reg* mid-10th cent.) **5** 104; **30** 219, 805, 816
Yeşilova **1** 114
Yestrovich, V. A. **31** 552
Yetik, Sami **2** 634
Yetkin, Suut Kemal **3** 785
Yevangulov, Sergey (Pavlovich) **27** 423
Yevele, Henry **9** 451; **20** 561; **33** 523*
  collaboration **25** 17
  patrons and collectors **25** 16
  works **4** 801; **5** 639, 645; **13** 55; **19** 566, 602, 609, 610; **24** 465
Yevele, Robert **25** 15
Yevlashev, Aleksey Petrovich **27** 373, 374
Yevreinov, Nikolay (Nikolayevich) **1** 453; **2** 123; **18** 507; **26** 530; **28** 570
  productions **24** 405
Yevreinov, Y. N. **9** 54
Yevseyev, S. A. **12** 243; **28** 570
yew **17** 399; **25** *121*
yew, bog *see* BOG YEW
yew oil *see under* OILS → types
Ye Xiaan *see* YE GONGCHUO
Ye Xie **25** 73
Ye Xin **12** 899; **22** 459
Yezd *see* YAZD
Yezhegodnik **27** 580
yi *see under* VESSELS → types
Yialia **8** *325*, 338
  figurines **8** *338*
Yialouusa, Hagia Marina **8** 358
Yi Am (i) (1297-1364) **18** 329; **33** 526*
Yi Am (ii) (*b* 1499) **33** 526–7*
  works **18** *316*, 317; **33** *527*
Yi Bingshou **6** 767; **33** 527*
Yi Chae **18** *322*; **33** 528*
Yi Chae-gwan **26** 482; **33** 528*
Yichang **6** 878
Yi Chang-son **18** 314
Yi Che-hyŏn **33** 528*
Yi (ii) Ching **18** 317, 325; **33** 524, 526*
Yi Chŏng (i) (1541-*d* after 1625) **18** 324; **33** 529*
  works **18** *324*; **33** *529*, 579
Yi Chŏng (ii) (1578-1607) **18** 314; **33** 529–30*
Yi Chong-kŭn (*b* 1531) **33** 577
Yi (ii) Ch'uk **33** 524
Yi Chung-sŏp **18** 326; **33** 530*
Yide, Prince **6** 651, 652; **25** 780
Yi dynasty *see* CHOSŎN DYNASTY
Yi Fujiu **17** 189
Yi Han-ch'ŏl **18** 321
Yi Ha-ŭng **18** 331; **33** 530*
Yi Hou Ze*gui* **6** 845
Yi Hŭi-su **18** 57
Yi Hŭng-hyo **33** 529
Yi Hwang **18** 331
Yi (i) I **18** 331; **33** 523, 524*
Yi In-mun **33** 530–31*
  works **33** *531*
Yi In-no **33** 531*
Yi In-sang **18** 315, 331; **33** 531*
  works **18** 319, 325
Yijae (1330-74) *see* KONGMIN
Yijae (1783-1859) *see* KWŎN TON-IN
Yijing **13** 812; **15** 681, 754; **30** 597
Yi Kang-so *see* KANG SO LEE
Yi Ku *see* MUNJONG
Yi Kuk-chŏn **18** 300
Yi Kwang-p'il **33** 533
Yi Kwang-sa **18** 331; **33** 532*
Yi Kye-ho **33** 532*
Yi Kyŏng **14** 36
Yi (ii) Kyŏng-yun **18** 314, 324; **33** 524–5*
  groups and movements **18** 51
  works **33** *525*
Yi Kyu-bo **18** 324
Yi Kyu-gyŏng **18** 259
Yilan **21** 564
Yıldız *see* ISTANBUL
Yi Man-bong **18** 312
Yi Min-ch'ol **12** 813
Yimsiri, Khien **30** 608
Yi Myŏng-gi **14** 702; **18** 52; **33** 532*
Yi Myŏng-uk **14** 156
Yin *see* ANYANG (CHINA)
Yi'nan **6** *615*, 648, *697*; **33** 532–3*
  reliefs **7** 75; **25** 800
  stone-carvings **7** 33
  tombs **6** 644, *645*, 697
Yinchuan **5** 110; **6** 314
Ying, Prince **6** 707
Ying'a *see* DAI BENXIAO
Yingchuan *see* OKUDA EISEN
Yingqing ware *see under* PORCELAIN → wares
Ying xian **7** 118
  Fogong Temple
    Mu ta *see* Timber Pagoda
    Timber Pagoda **6** 643, 656, 668; **19** 303; **23** 773
      wall paintings **6** 778
  Jingtu Temple **6** 656
Ying Yujian **33** 572
Yintuoluo **2** 599
Yinxu *see* ANYANG (CHINA)
Yi Nyŏng **18** 314; **33** 533*
Yinyuan Longqi *see* INGEN RYŪKI
Yin Yuejiang **23** 365
Yi Pang-un **18** 320
Yipinsoi, Missiem **30** 608
Yi Pul-hae **33** 533*
Yiran *see* ITSUNEN
Yirawala **1** 66, 67; **20** 470; **33** 534*
Yirmisekiz Çelebi, Mehmed **16** 226
Yiroulas
  basilica **22** *698*, 699
  Temple of Demeter and Kore **22** *698*, 699
  kouroi **22** 700
Yirritja **1** 60
Yirrkala **1** 60, 61, 63, 64, 66
  bark painting **1** *51*
Yi Sang-bŏm **18** 326; **25** 760; **33** 534*
Yi Sang-chwa **14** 702; **33** 529, 534*
  attributions **18** 308, *309*
  works **18** 314
Yi Sang-jŏk **18** 331
Yishan *see* LIN LIANG
Yishan Yining **6** 756; **17** 169, 231, 408, 747, 749
Yishu jia **24** 435
Yishu pinglun **24** 435
Yi Sŏng-gye, King *see* T'AEJO, King (*reg* 918-43)
Yi Song-min **33** 534–5*
Yi Su-gwang **18** 259
Yi Su-jang **18** 331
Yi Sukwang **14** 36
Yi Su-mun **18** 314; **29** 13; **33** 535*
Yi Sung-hyo **33** 529
Yi Sŭng-t'aek **18** 301
Yitowo **8** 490
Yi (i) U **18** 331; **33** 523, 524*
Yi (ii) Wi-guk **33** 524
Yi xian
  Fengguo Temple **6** 656
  iron **7** 56
  sculpture **6** 891
  terracotta **30** 509
  tombs **6** 695
  Western Tombs **6** 662, 704, 732
    Mu ling **6** *704*
    pailou **23** 780, *780*
  Xi ling *see* Western Tombs
  see also YANXIADU
Yixing **6** *615*; **33** 535–6*
  pottery **6** 332; **7** 101; **21** 633; **25** 783; **33** *535*
    see also under POTTERY → wares
  stonewares **28** 141
Yi Yŏng **28** 382; **33** 536*
  works **2** 117; **7** 208; **18** 329
Yi Yong-u **25** 760
Yi (ii) Yŏng-yun **18** 314; **33** 524, 525–6*
Yi Youhan **20** 361
Yiyuan chao hua **19** 831
Yiyuan duoying **24** 435
Yi Yu-t'ae **18** 60
Yizheng *see* LI ZAI
Yizhou **6** 717
  ceramics **5** *111*
Ykens, Catharina **33** 537
Ykens, Charles, II **19** 165
Ykens, Frans **3** 494; **11** 227; **28** 904; **33** 536–7*
  works **33** *537*
Ykeus, Simon **7** 708
Ymagier, L' **13** 232; **17** 449; **24** 442; **33** 361
Ymber, Lawrence **31** 413
Ynys Seiriol **32** 780
Yō, Kanji **17** 135
Yoan Iveropulets **3** 21
Yōboku *see* KANŌ TSUNENOBU
Yocavil culture **29** 190
Yōchiku Shinozaki *see* SHINOZAKI YŌCHIKU
Yodaji **18** 309
Yoemon Saitō *see* SAITŌ YOEMON
Yo Ennen **17** 412
yōfūga *see under* JAPAN → painting
Yōga *see under* JAPAN → painting
Yogacara Buddhism *see under* BUDDHISM → sects
Yoganarendra, King (*reg c.* 1684 -*c.* 1705) (Malla) **22** 754
Yogeshvari Cave **15** 708
Yog Man Shakya **22** 776
Yogyakarta **15** *753*, 775; **33** 537–8*
  Akademi Seni Rupa Indonesia *see* Institut Seni Indonesia
  Banguntapan Palace **33** 538
  batik **15** 790
  Candi Ijo **15** 777, *778*
  dance **15** 802
  Fort Vredenburg **15** 775
  Grand Mosque **15** 775
  Hamengkubuwono Palace Museum **29** 239
  Indonesian Academy for the Plastic Arts *see* Institut Seni Indonesia
  Institut Seni Indonesia (ISI) **15** 818
  manuscript illumination **15** 805, 806
  painting **15** 807
  Pakualaman Museum **29** 239
  Pakualam Palace **15** 775
  patronage **29** 238
  puppets **15** 797, *797*, 798, 801
  sculpture **15** *783*
  Sono Budoyo Museum **29** 239; **33** 538
  Sultan's palace **23** 823; **29** 826; **33** 537–8
  Taman Sari **12** 103; **15** 775; **29** 826; **33** 537–8
  textiles **29** 239
  tourist art **29** 239
  Water Castle *see* Taman Sari
Yogyakarta Painters Union **29** 907
Yohachi Nishimurai *see* NISHIMURAI YOHACHI
Yohannes I, Emperor of Ethiopia (*reg* 1667-82) **10** 571
Yohji Yamamoto *see* YAMAMOTO, YOHJI
Yohualtepec **21** 251
Yojirō Tsuji *see* TSUJI YOJIRŌ
yokes (animal) **25** 547
yokes (dress) **7** 77
Yokino **17** 262
Yokogoshi Hoppō Bunka (Northern Culture) Museum **15** 746
Yokohama **17** *11*, 18; **33** 539–40*
  enamel **17** 378
  Gūmyōji **17** 121
  Kanagawa Prefectural Library and Auditorium **17** 89
  Kanagawa Prefectural Museum **33** 539
  Kanazawa Library **17** 430; **19** 317; **33** 539
  Keio University **17** 88
  prints **17** 290; **33** *539*
  Sakuradai Court Village **17** 91
  Sankei'en **14** 161; **17** 433; **33** 539
  Shomyōji **33** 539
  Yokohama Special Bank **17** 87
Yokohamae *see under* PRINTS → types
Yokohama Library (company) **29** 663
Yokoi Kinkoku **17** 190, 830; **33** 540*
Yokoo, Tadanori **25** 354; **33** 540*
Yokotashimo **17** 59
Yokoyama, Misao **17** 202
Yokoyama, Taikan **17** 134, 180; **21** 59; **28** 603, 627; **33** 541*
  collaboration **14** 577
  exhibitions **17** 436
  groups and movements **17** 200, 201
  patrons and collectors **17** 433
  teachers **14** 219
  works **17** 200
Yokoyama Kazan **18** 88
Yokoyama Matsusaburō **17** 198, 420
Yokoyama Seiki **17** 198; **20** 837
Yokut **22** 549, 652, 659
Yōkyŏng *see* KIM HYŎN-SŎNG

Yolanda of France, Duchess of Savoy (*reg* 1212-17) 18 684
Yolande de Soissons 1 782; 8 184
Yolande of Aragon, Duchess of Anjou (1380-1442) 2 49, 51, 111, 113*
  Books of Hours 20 755
Yolande of Flanders, Duchess of Bar (*fl* 1331-62) 3 455; 17 462; 25 694
Yölban Buddhism *see* BUDDHISM → sects → Nirvana
Yolí, Gabriel 22 124
Yolngu 1 44–5, 48, 60–61, 68
  bark painting 1 *51*
  body arts 1 *60*
Yoly, Gerardo *see* JOLY, GABRIEL
Yombe 1 261, 274, 403; 2 85; 18 217, 219, 221
  figurines 1 *275*
  tools 1 *364*
Yombwe, Lawrence 33 602
Yŏm Ch'i-uk 7 203
Yomitan 17 355
Yomiuri Newspaper Company 17 436
Yomudsky, Nazar 31 459
Yomut 6 254; 16 485
Yon, M. 18 98; 27 608
Yŏndam *see* KIM MYŎNG-GUK
Yonehara, Unkai 17 134
Yonekichi Miyake *see* MIYAKE, YONEKICHI
Yŏn'gaek *see* HŎ P'IL
Yŏngch'in 18 57
Yŏngch'ŏn 18 347
Yŏnggok *see* HWANG CHIP-JUNG
Yonghexu 17 594
Yongjia 6 885
Yŏngju, Pusŏk Temple 9 162; 18 265, 268, 279, 321
  calligraphy 18 329
  metalwork 18 349
  sculpture 18 291, *292*
  wall paintings 18 305
Yongkang 18 298
Yongle emperor (Ming; *reg* 1403-24) 6 331, 622, 696, 703, 732; 7 111; 10 776; 22 459; 30 797
  tombs 6 *701*, *702*
Yongming Yanshou 5 110
Yong Mun Sen 20 172
Yongnam, Yongt'ong Temple 18 328
Yongningbao (Hongdong) 7 138
Yŏng'ŏp 18 328
Yongtai, Princess 6 652; 25 780
Yŏngt'ap Temple 18 294
Yongzheng emperor (Qing; *reg* 1723-35) 5 113; 6 39, 40, 704; 7 91
Yŏnong *see* YUN TŎK-HŬI
Yŏnp'o *see* YUN TŎK-HŬI
Yontunç, Kenan 31 454
Yoors, Jan 31 660
Yorakuin *see* KONOE IEHIRO
Yordanov, Kosta, Porcelain Factory 5 159
Yorgan Tepe *see* NUZI
Yorimichi, Fujiwara no *see* FUJIWARA NO YORIMICHI
Yori Saitō *see* SAITŌ, YORI
Yorishige Matsudaira *see* MATSUDAIRA YORISHIGE
Yoritomo *see* MINAMOTO NO YORITOMO, Shogun
York (UK) 2 324; 4 612, *613*; 10 *225*; 26 *905*; 32 528; 33 541–51*, *544*, *546*
  art forms and materials
    alabaster-carvings 1 517
    amber 1 761
    architecture 2 67; 4 770; 26 905; 32 534
    brasses 4 692
    coins 7 534; 14 408
    jet 17 516
    manuscripts 15 875
    metalwork 32 524
York (UK)
  art forms and materials—cont.
    pewter 10 341; 24 579, 580
    roofs 30 907
    sculpture 13 84
    stage design 30 653
    stained glass 29 503, 506
    stone-carvings 32 517
  art schools 10 373
  Assembly Rooms 2 617, 618, *618*; 10 233
  Assize Court 18 887
  Castle 6 52
  Castle Museum 33 544
  City Art Gallery 10 370; 33 545
  Clifford's Tower 6 55; 9 144
  Coppergate 2 67
  craftsmen and artists 10 289
  Eboracum 33 541
  ecclesiastical buildings
    All Saints 29 503
      stained glass 29 II
    Archbishop's Palace Chapel 33 *542*
    Cathedral of St Peter *see* Minster
    Minster 8 610; 9 670; 10 227, 359; 12 5; 13 44, 47, 54, 55; 20 562; 26 382, 570, 588; 33 542–3, 546*, *547*
      architecture 33 546–8*
      capitals 26 614
      Chapter House 13 183
      choir 22 217
      choir-screen 13 84
      choir-stalls 7 192; 29 413
      doors 9 152, 155
      epitaph to Edmund Bunny 10 436
      furniture 10 287, 288; 30 781
      ivory-carvings 16 525
      mouldings 22 221
      nave 33 *548*
      piers (ii) (masonry) 24 751, *751*
      pottery 16 420
      restoration 2 325
      sculpture 13 82; 26 612, 615; 33 548*
      shields 14 420
      stained glass 10 245; 13 127, 142, 149, 152, 183, 184; 26 702; 29 510; 33 *549*, 549–50*
      throne 30 783
      tracery 8 611; 31 271
      tracing floor 2 348; 22 211; 31 270
      tracing house 31 274
      transept 31 281
      vaults 32 94
      wall paintings 7 275
      windows 13 46
      workshops 29 851
    St Margaret 26 614
    St Mary's Abbey 3 709; 10 259; 26 588, 615; 33 550–51*, *551*
      sculpture 13 80; 26 *615*
    St Peter's 2 83
    St Saviourgate Chapel 23 193
  fortifications 21 559, 560
  Guildhall 14 76; 18 886
  guilds 10 287; 24 579
  Jorvik Viking Centre 14 453; 33 544
  Mansion House 33 545
  masons' lodges 13 824
  Merchant Adventurers' Hall 19 508
  Merchant Taylor's Hall 19 508
  National Railway Museum 33 544
  Retreat 2 658
  St Nicholas's Hospital 26 614
  St William's College 33 *545*
  School of Architectural Studies 7 743
  sculptors 10 265
  town walls 31 710; 33 541
  University 10 241
  urban planning 27 3
York (UK)—cont.
  Walmgate Bar 3 209
  workshops 29 852
  Yorkshire Museum 33 544
York (Ont.; Canada) *see* TORONTO
York, Edward P. 20 19
York, Frederica, Duchess of *see* HANOVER, FREDERICA, Duchess of York
York, Frederick Augustus, Duke of *see* HANOVER, FREDERICK AUGUSTUS, Duke of York
York County Court-house (VA) 18 887
Yorke (family) 25 210
Yorke, Francis Reginald Stevens 4 762; 18 386; 24 275; 33 552
Yorke, Francis Walter Bagnell 33 552
Yorke, Joseph 18 628
Yorke, Philip, 1st Baron and 1st Earl of Hardwicke (*d* 1764) 25 882
Yorke, Philip, 2nd Earl of Hardwicke (1720-96) 13 645
Yorke, Philip, 3rd Earl of Hardwicke (1757-1834) 28 905
Yorke, Rosenberg & Mardall 33 552*
  collaboration 2 578
  works 3 537; 16 40; 17 548; 23 258
York Gospels *see under* GOSPEL BOOKS → individual manuscripts
York Helmet 10 338, *338*
York Psalter *see under* PSALTERS → individual manuscripts
York & Sawyer 22 36
Yorkshire school 26 614
Yorkstone *see under* SANDSTONE → types
York Virtuosi 32 902
Yorozu, Tetsugorō 17 205; 30 241; 33 552–3*
Yortan 1 *821*, 824, 837; 33 553*
Yoruba 1 309, 425, 428, 429–30; 3 727; 5 753; 9 115; 14 55; 16 879, 880; 23 128, 132; 31 331; 33 553–9*
  aesthetics 1 235, 239; 33 553–4
  altarpieces 33 557
  altars 33 556
  architecture 23 134; 33 554–5*
  art criticism 2 519
  bags 33 556
  beads 1 298, *298*, 353–4; 33 557–8, *558*, 559
  beadwork 3 442; 4 13
  body arts 1 342; 33 559*
  bowls 1 329, *356*; 33 559
  brass 1 *265*; 15 *106*; 33 558
  caricatures 5 761
  carving 1 239
  cement 1 331, 332
  collections 33 553
  colour 7 635
  copper 15 *104*
  cosmologies 33 554
  costumes 1 270
  crowns 1 *298*, *353*, 353–4; 33 557–8, *558*
  cups 33 558
  dancewands 33 555, *556*
  divination instruments 1 *356*, 356–7
  doors 1 280, 314; 9 164, *164*; 33 554
  dress 1 348, 349
  erotic art 10 473
  fans 10 779
  figurines 1 *270*
  fortifications 21 597
  gesture 1 264, 265, 266
  gourds 1 303
  hairstyles 1 343
  headdresses 1 349; 33 557
  houses 1 311
Yoruba—cont.
  human figures 15 *106*
  iconography 1 261, 276, 280–81, 282–4
  indigo 7 635
  ivory 1 292, 293, 352, *356*; 33 *555*
  masks 1 *239*, 241, *241*, 282, 290, 334, 336, *337*, 340, 341, 423; 5 761; 15 *104*; 33 557*
  painting 33 559*
  palaces 1 242, 309, 314; 23 824; 33 554
  patronage 1 241
  pigments 7 635; 33 556, 559*
  portraits 1 267, 268, 269
  pots 1 328, 329
  regalia 1 352, *353*, 353
  religion 8 230
  robes 1 *353*
  scarification 1 345
  sculpture 1 274, 278, 322, 331, 332, 427; 4 707, 13; 15 *105*, *106*, 106–7*, *107*; 33 555–7*
    equestrian 1 280
    figure 1 231
    Nigeria 15 105*
    wood 1 *283*, 283–4
  shells 1 *283*; 28 581
  shields 33 556
  shrines (i) (cult) 1 289
  staffs 1 *265*; 33 556, 557
  stone-carvings 15 107
  swords 33 *555*
  tattoos 1 346
  temples 1 309
  terracotta 15 *107*; 30 509
  textiles 1 242; 33 559*
  trays 1 356, *356*; 33 558
  trousers 1 348
  women 1 340
  women artists 1 246
  wood 1 *270*, *283*, 283–4, *356*; 9 164, *164*
  wood-carvings 1 291; 33 *554*, *556*
  wraps 1 348
Yoru no Kai (Night Society) 14 129; 23 385
Yosa Buson 17 165, 188, 194; 18 552; 33 560–62*
  collaboration 15 127
  pupils 17 196; 20 836; 23 386
  works 1 582; 17 190, 830; 33 *561*
Yōsai *see* MYŌAN EISAI
Yosemite National Park Service Station (CA) 28 488
Yōsen Kanō *see* KANŌ YŌSEN
Yoshiatsu *see* SATAKE SHOZAN
Yoshida, Hakurei 17 135
Yoshida, Hiroshi 17 204, 294
Yoshida, Hōchiku 17 240
Yoshida, Isoya 17 88; 33 562*
Yoshida, Kenji 17 296
Yoshida, Masaji 17 296
Yoshida, Shōya 21 634
Yoshida, Tetsurō 33 562*
  works 17 88, *88*
Yoshida, Toshio 13 866; 17 294
Yoshida Bungorō III 17 407
Yoshida Bunsaburō 17 406
Yoshida Hanbei 17 280; 23 594
Yoshida Kenkō 17 367
Yoshidaya kiln 18 538
Yoshihara, Jirō 33 562–3*
  groups and movements 13 866; 17 207, 860; 27 594
  works 13 866; 17 207, *207*
Yoshiharu Ashikaga *see* ASHIKAGA YOSHIHARU, Shogun
Yoshihiro Shimazu *see* SHIMAZU YOSHIHIRO
Yoshiiku Utagawa *see* UTAGAWA YOSHIIKU
Yoshikane Ashikaga *see* ASHIKAGA YOSHIKANE
Yoshikawa, Kanpo 17 295
Yoshikazu Utagawa *see* UTAGAWA YOSHIKAZU
Yoshi Kinouchi *see* KINOUCHI, YOSHI
Yoshimasa Ashikaga *see* ASHIKAGA YOSHIMASA, Shogun
Yoshimasa Heinouchi *see* YOSHIMASA HEINOUCHI 17 51
Yoshimatsu Goseda *see* GOSEDA, YOSHIMATSU
Yoshimi-chō 17 58
Yoshimi Hakketsu tombs 17 58
Yoshimitsu Ashikaga *see* ASHIKAGA YOSHIMITSU, Shogun
Yoshimitsu Deme Zekan *see* DEME ZEKAN YOSHIMITSU
Yoshimochi Ashikaga *see* ASHIKAGA YOSHIMOCHI, Shogun
Yoshimori Wada *see* WADA YOSHIMORI
Yoshimoto 17 401
Yoshimune Tokugawa *see* TOKUGAWA YOSHIMUNE, Shogun
Yoshimura (family) 17 82
  houses 17 *82*
Yoshimura, Fumio 24 687
Yoshimura, Junzō 17 88; 33 563*
Yoshimura, Kasen 17 381
Yoshimura, Masunobu 22 742
Yoshimura Kōkei 17 196
Yoshimura Shūzan 17 400
Yoshinaga 17 401
Yoshinao Tokugawa *see* TOKUGAWA YOSHINAO
Yoshinari Shakazuru *see* SHAKUZURU YOSHINARI
Yoshino 17 356
  Mikumari Shrine 17 323
Yoshinobu Ashihara *see* ASHIHARA, YOSHINOBU
Yoshinobu Kanō *see* KANŌ YOSHINOBU
Yoshinogari 17 54–5, *55*, 84
Yoshinori Ashikaga *see* ASHIKAGA YOSHINORI, Shogun
Yoshioka Kinzaburō *see* TSUKIOKA YOSHITOSHI
Yoshiro 18 558
Yoshirō Taniguchi *see* TANIGUCHI, YOSHIRŌ
Yoshisaburō Igusa *see* UTAGAWA KUNIYOSHI
Yoshishige Saitō *see* SAITŌ, YOSHISHIGE
Yoshishige Yano *see* YANO YOSHISHIGE
Yoshitaka Yanagi *see* YANAGI, YOSHITAKA
Yoshitake, Yasumi 23 385
Yoshitaki Utagawa *see* UTAGAWA YOSHITAKI
Yoshitane Ashikaga *see* ASHIKAGA YOSHITANE, Shogun
Yoshitaro Amano *see* AMANO, YOSHITARO
Yoshitoki Hōjō *see* HŌJŌ YOSHITOKI, Shogunal Regent
Yoshitomo Watanabe *see* WATANABE, YOSHITOMO
Yoshitora Utagawa *see* UTAGAWA YOSHITORA
Yoshitoshi Mori *see* MORI, YOSHITOSHI
Yoshitoshi Taiso *see* TSUKIOKA YOSHITOSHI
Yoshitoshi Tsukioka *see* TSUKIOKA YOSHITOSHI
Yoshitoshi Utagawa *see* UTAGAWA YOSHITOSHI
Yoshitsune no Fujiwara *see* GOKYŌGOKU YOSHITSUNE
Yoshiuke Matsui *see* MATSUI, YOSHIUKE
Yoshi Wada *see* WADA, YOSHI
Yoshizaka, Takamasa 33 563*
  collaboration 27 597
  pupils 30 50, 392
  works 17 91

Yoshizumi Ashikaga see ASHIKAGA YOSHIZUMI
Yōshū, Chikanobu 17 290
Yosifova, Mara 5 161
 works 5 162
Yōsō Sōi 17 172
Yotkan 6 288, 614; 33 563–4*
 figurines 6 292, 298
 pottery 6 309
 sculpture 6 298
 seals 6 314
 terracotta 6 315
Yotoco 29 146, 150, 155
 bowls 29 150
Yōtoku see OKUDA EISEN
you see under VESSELS → types
You, Thomas 31 649
Youf, Jean Baptiste 16 729
Youghal (Co. Cork) 18 593
 ceramics 16 28
 pottery 16 28
 Presentation Convent 16 34
 St Mary
  monument to Richard Boyle, 1st Earl of Cork 16 20
Youguo Temple Pagoda 6 645
You Kan 7 126
Youlgreave, All Saints 11 252
Young, The (Fiatalok) 1 131; 13 840, 889; 18 394, 416; 31 541
Young, Alexander 4 589; 14 47
Young, Ammi B(urnham) 4 473; 24 300; 33 564*
Young, Brigham 22 126; 27 642; 30 450
Young, C. D. 26 18
Young, Chic 7 649
Young, Clyde 33 565
Young, Cuyler 33 688
Young, Edward 4 119; 33 152
Young, George (1839-1909) 23 71
 works 23 71
Young, George C. (1898-1981) 27 642
Young, James 10 333
Young, John 10 365; 28 693; 30 160
Young, John B. 30 867
Young, Joseph 27 642
Young, Lamont (1851-1929) 33 564–5*
Young, La Monte (b c. 1930) 11 232; 22 140; 24 407
Young, Mahroni 27 642
Young, M. H. de 27 731
Young, M. H. de, Memorial Museum see under SAN FRANCISCO (CA) → museums
Young, Nelson 3 624
Young, Peter 31 651
Young, Raymond 31 737
Young, Robert (fl 1834; engraver) 4 885
Young, Robert (1822-1917; architect) 33 566*
Young, Robert Magill 33 566
Young, Rodney S. 13 6
Young, T. Cuyler 12 838
Young, Thomas (fl late 17th cent.; carver) 6 515; 11 424
Young, Thomas (fl 1807; writer) 24 376
Young, William (fl 1807-12) 2 153; 4 880; 31 337
Young, William (1801-71) 31 637
Young, William (1843-1900) 3 269; 9 739; 12 774; 33 565*
 works 12 775
Young Artists (Bali) 15 809
Young Artists, The see TINERIMEA ARTISTICĂ
Youngblood, Nathan 22 606
Younge, Gavin 29 112
Younger Balbus 27 46
Youngerman, Jack 24 213; 25 361
Young Estonia (Noor-Eesti) 33 565–6*
Younghusband, Francis 7 159; 30 850
Young & Mackenzie 33 566*
Young Ones 13 719; 27 717; 30 81; 33 566*
Young Painters' Organization 32 483
Young Painting Group 1 636
Young Poland (Młoda Polska) 18 428; 29 791
Youngs, Isaac Newton 28 540
Young & Trotter 9 727; 28 253
Yŏ Un-hyŏng 18 332
Youn Myeung Ro 18 326; 33 566–7*
You Qiu 32 848
Youqua 14 721
Youssoupoff see YUSUPOV
Youssufi, Omar 22 129
Youth see YOUNG, THE (FIATALOK)
Yovnat'anyan see HOVNAT'ANIAN
Yoyokama, Taikan 33 508
Yōyūsai
 works 17 400; 18 I1
Yozgat 16 266
Yozō Hamaguchi see HAMAGUCHI, YOZŌ
Ypre, Nicolas d' see DIPRE, NICOLAS (fl 1492; d 1532)
Ypres 3 539; 33 567–8*
 Cathedral of St Martin 10 710; 16 41; 33 567–8*, 568
 ceramics 3 588
 Cloth Hall see Lakenhalle
 lace 3 610
 Lakenhalle 3 544; 13 110, 824; 20 438; 29 414; 31 238
 marks 3 601
 St Martin 13 41
 silver 3 598
 Stadhuis 31 238
 textiles 25 315
Ypres, André d' see ANDRÉ D'YPRES
Ypres, Jean d' see JEAN D'YPRES
Yrarrázaval, Ricardo 6 598; 33 568–9*
Yriarte, Ignacio de see IRIARTE, IGNACIO DE
YRM see YORKE, ROSENBERG & MARDALL
Yrurtia, Rogelio 2 399; 33 569–70*
 works 33 569
Ysabeau 20 723
Ysambert, Master 28 518
Ysane 30 76
Ysart, Paul 28 260
Ysart, Salvador 28 260
Ysaye, Eugène 19 321
Ysebaert, Adriaen see ISENBRANDT, ADRIAEN
Yselburg, Peter see ISSELBURG, PETER
Yselin, Heinrich see ISELIN, HEINRICH
Ysenbrand, Adriaen see ISENBRANDT, ADRIAEN
Ysendyck, Antoine Van see VAN YSENDYCK, ANTOINE
Ysendyck, Jules-Jacques Van see VAN YSENDYCK, JULES-JACQUES
Ysendyck, Maurice Van see VAN YSENDYCK, MAURICE
Y-shaped cross see under CROSSES → types
Ystad 30 111
 St Peter 8 723; 13 120
Y-tracery see under TRACERY → types → bar
Ytre Moa 32 524
Ytterlännäs 30 76
Yturralde 29 272
Yturralde, José Maria 28 829
yu see under VESSELS → types
Yu, Earl of 7 80
Yu an see MOKUAN REIEN
Yuanbaoshan Tomb 6 701
Yuanchang see CAI JING
Yüan Ch'i see YUAN QI
Yüan Chiang see YUAN JIANG
Yuandi, Emperor (Liang; reg AD 552-5) 6 816; 7 152
Yüan Hsiao-ts'un see YUAN XIAOCUN
Yuan Jiang 12 91; 33 496
 works 12 90
Yuan period see under CHINA → periods
Yuan Qi 10 693
Yuan Shikai 6 908
Yuan the Georgian see YOAN IVEROPULETS
Yüan-ti, Emperor (Liang; reg AD 552-5) see YUANDI, Emperor
Yuanwu Keqin 6 752; 17 342, 343, 344
 works 6 752; 17 343
Yüan-wu K'o-ch'in see YUANWU KEQIN
Yuan Xiaocun 6 733
Yuan Yao 33 496
Yuasa, Megumi 4 722
Yu Ben see YEE BON
Yucatán
 architecture 33 571*
 baths 3 378
 monasteries 33 571*
 sculpture 10 487
 shelters 33 571
 wall paintings 21 226
Yucatán Peninsula 20 882; 21 177, 178, 193
Yucatec 3 621; 21 250
Yucateco 33 571*
Yucay 12 71
yucca 3 331, 332; 22 661, 662
Yuchi 22 552
Yü Chien see YU JIAN
Yü Chien-wu see YU JIANWU
Yü Chih-ting see YU ZHIDING
Yuch'ŏn 18 338, 340
Yuco 7 602
Yūden Taki see TAKI YŪDEN
Yudin, Lev 8 10; 30 8; 31 677
Yudovin, Solomon 3 529; 24 350
Yue 32 468
Yue Fei 6 726; 7 99
Yüeh Fei see YUE FEI
Yuendumu 1 43, 56, 64
Yuen Long 14 720
Yue ware see under POTTERY → wares
Yuezhi see TOKHARIANS
Yufa, Tamara 27 434
Yū Fujiwara see FUJIWARA, YŪ
Yūgai Kō see KŌ YŪGAI
Yu Gongzhu 6 700
Yugoslavia 8 181; 33 571*
 see also BOSNIA; CROATIA; HERZEGOVINA; MACEDONIA (ii); MONTENEGRO; SERBIA; SLOVENIA
Yuhang 6 885
Yu Han-ji 18 331
Yu He 6 754
Yūhi Kumashiro see KUMASHIRO YŪHI
Yūho see MATSUMURA GOSHUN
Yuh of Kom 3 147
Yuhuatai Mountains 6 733
yuhuchun see under VASES → types
Yu Hyŏg-yŏn 33 579
Yūichi Inoue see INOUE, YŪICHI
Yūichi Takahashi see TAKAHASHI YŪICHI
Yuit 22 545, 630, 631
Yujian 6 783, 784; 17 428; 30 465; 33 572*
 works 6 784
Yu Jianwu 6 770
Yūjō 17 195, 417
Yukagir 1 816
Yu K'an see YOU KAN
Yūkei Tejima see TEJIMA, YŪKEI
Yuki 17 408
Yukichi, Fukuzawa 19 319
Yukihiko Soyama see SOYAMA, YUKIHIKO
Yukihiko Yasuda see YASUDA, YUKIHIKO
Yukihiro, Fujiwara no see FUJIWARA NO YUKIHIRO
Yukimoto Ishikawa see ISHIKAWA YUKIMOTO
Yukinari no Fujiwara see FUJIWARA NO KŌZEI
Yukinobu see KANŌ YUKINOBU
Yukinoshita 17 364
Yukitada see KOSE NO YUKITADA
Yukitsune, Fujiwara no see FUJIWARA NO YUKITSUNE
Yūkoku Okamoto see OKAMOTO YŪKOKU
Yü Kung-chu see YU GONGZHU
Yule, Henry 17 798
Yulgok see YI (i) I
Yu Lide 17 235
Yulin Caves 6 719, 778, 779
 Cave 3 6 778
Yulongtai 23 496
Yuma 22 605, 634, 668
Yumachi 17 353
Yumbu Lakhar 21 592
Yume 17 407, 408
Yumeji Takehisa see TAKEHISA, YUMEJI
Yumino 17 351
Yümük Tepe see MERSIN
Yunan, Ramsis 2 511; 5 401; 9 766
Yunapingu, Munggurrawuy 33 573*
Yun Bing 33 321
Yun Che-hong 18 315; 33 574*
Yuncheng 30 443
 temple to Guandi 6 661
Yuncu 16 478
Yungang 5 108; 6 615; 7 151; 23 550; 33 34
 caves 6 650, 709, 717; 29 868; 33 574–5*
  Tanyao Caves 6 709; 30 443; 33 574, 574
 roofs 30 913
 sculpture 6 708, 709; 7 161
Yung-cheng emperor (Ch'ing; reg 1723-35) see YONGZHENG EMPEROR
Yung-le emperor (Ming; reg 1403-24) see YONGLE EMPEROR
Yung-t'ai, Princess see YONGTAI, Princess
Yungur 1 328, 381; 30 509
 gourds 1 302
 terracotta 30 508
Yunhe 6 893
Yün Hsiang see YUN XIANG
Yun Hyo-jung 18 301
Yun Hyong Keun 18 257; 33 575*
Yunjian school 33 652
Yün Jih-ch'u see YUN RICHU
Yün-kang see YUNGANG
Yunkers, Adja 19 492; 20 606; 21 696; 33 575*
Yunkuntjatjara 1 64
Yunmen Buddhism see under BUDDHISM → sects
Yunmeng 6 740; 7 66, 95
Yun Myŏng-no see YOUN MYEUNG RO
Yun Nantian see YUN SHOUPING
Yün Nan-t'ien see YUN SHOUPING
Yün Ping see YUN BING
Yun Richu 33 576
Yun school 33 575
Yun Shouping 6 802, 818; 25 783; 33 321, 575–6*
 collaboration 32 842
 groups and movements 23 579, 580
 pupils 33 321
 works 17 189; 33 576
Yun Sun 18 331; 33 532
Yun Sŭng-uk 18 300
Yun Tŏk-hŭi 18 319; 33 572, 573*
Yun Tu-sŏ 18 331; 33 572–3*
 works 18 319, 322, 322, 325
Yunŭng, Tomb of Emperor Sunjong 18 300
Yun Xiang 23 580
Yun Yong 18 319; 33 572
Yun Yong-gi 18 381
Yun Yong-gu 18 331
Yunyy khudozhnik 27 444
Yuon, Konstantin (Fyodorovich) 27 394; 33 577*
 groups and movements 2 633; 22 178; 27 392
 pupils 32 381
  Bohomazov, Oleksandr (Konstyantynovych) 4 236
  Fal'k, Robert (Rafailovich) 10 771
  Favorsky, Vladimir (Andreyevich) 10 843
  Kuprin, Aleksandr (Vasil'yevich) 18 528
  Popova, Lyubov' (Sergeyevna) 25 238
  Stepanova, Varvara (Fyodorovna) 29 632
  Ternovets, Boris (Nikolayevich) 30 491
  Udal'tsova, Nadezhda (Andreyevna) 31 519
  Vatagin, Vasily (Alekseyevich) 32 78
 teachers 27 889; 28 475
 works 22 178
Yupanqui, Francisco Tito 4 264, 269
Yupe, Lorenzo Muntaner see MUNTANER YUPE, LORENZO
Yupik see YUIT
Yurasov, M. 31 551
Yuri 17 234; 33 577*
Yūrin Maegawa see MAEGAWA YŪRIN
Yurok 22 549, 641, 652, 659, 668, 677
yurts 7 143; 30 474
 see also TENTS
Yury, Prince (d 1434) 33 741
Yūryaku, Emperor (reg 457-90) 16 72
Yur'yev see TARTU
Yur'yev-Pol'sky 27 363
 Cathedral of St George 27 369, 382
Yury I Dolgoruky, Prince of Vladimir-Suzdal (reg 1125-57) 9 51; 13 14; 33 741
Yury II, Prince of Vladimir-Suzdal' (reg 1212-38) 32 665
Yury Vsevolodovich, Prince of Vladimir 23 168
Yūsai Hosokawa see HOSOKAWA YŪSAI
Yusaku Kamekura see KAMEKURA, YUSAKU
Yüsekli Church 5 678
Yūsetsu Kaihō see KAIHŌ YŪSETSU
Yūsetsu Munenobu see KANŌ YŪSETSU MUNENOBU
Yü Shih-nan see YU SHINAN
Yūshi Ishizaki see ISHIZAKI YŪSHI
Yu Shinan 6 745–6, 770; 30 251
Yūshō see KAIHŌ YŪSHŌ
Yūshō Ojio see OJIO YŪSHŌ
Yusi 17 732
Yu Sŏng-ŭp 33 577*
Yussef Ahmad 25 777
Yuste Monastery 14 516; 29 258; 33 577–8*
Yustman, Ricardo 24 99
Yusuf (Iran) 1 97, 98*; 16 412
Yusuf (Syria) 16 415
Yusuf I, Sultan (reg 1333-54) (Nasrid)
 architecture 4 784; 13 282, 287; 20 156–7; 22 535
 inscriptions 13 287

Yusuf III, Sultan (*reg* 1407-17) (Nasrid) **13** 288; **16** 419; **20** 158; **22** 535
Yusuf al-Bahili **15** 696; **16** 523
Yusuf ʻAli **15** 594
Yusuf Efendi **21** 50
Yūsuf ibn ʻAli ibn Muḥammad ibn Abī Ṭāhir *see* YUSUF
Yusuf ibn Naghrallah **33** 686
Yusuf ibn Taj al-Din **16** 232
Yusuf ibn Tashufin, Ruler (*reg* 1061-1106) (Almoravid) **1** 683; **11** 49; **20** 470; **31** 66
Yusuf Koç Kilisesi **5** 678
Yusuf Mashhadi **16** 283
Yu Suk **7** 203; **18** 321; **33** 578*
Yusupov (family) **26** 449; **27** 404, 441
Yusupov, Boris (Nikolayevich), Prince **33** 578
Yusupov, Nikolay (Borisovich), Prince (1751-1831) **27** 438; **33** 578, 579*
ceramics **22** 180
collections **2** 417; **27** 439
paintings **7** 916
Yusupov, Nikolay, Prince (1794-1849) **13** 793; **27** 213
Yusupov, Nikolay (Borisovich), Prince (*d* 1891) **33** 578
Yusupova, Zinaida (Nikoylayevna) **33** 579
Yutaishan (Jiangling)
cemetery **6** 696
furniture **7** 33
Tomb 471 **7** 140
weapons **7** 97
Yutaka Izue *see* IZUE, YUTAKA
Yūtei Ishida *see* ISHIDA YŪTEI
Yu Ťok-chang **33** 579–80*
Yu Un-hong **18** 320
Yu xian **6** 895
Yu xin **25** 72
Yuya **9** 822; **10** 52, 53, 80; **33** 580*
architecture **1** 770
coffin **10** 11
furniture **30** 775
glass **10** 54
Yuyang dongtian **12** 88
Yuyao **6** 885
Yuyao wreck **6** 914
Yu Yong-guk **18** 326
Yu Youren *see* YÜ YU-JEN
Yü Yu-jen **6** 767; **33** 581*
yuzen *see under* TEXTILES → types
Yu Zhiding **6** 813
Yuz Oba **4** 110
Yūzō Kondō *see* KONDŌ, YŪZŌ
Yūzō Saeki *see* SAEKI, YŪZŌ
Yuzō Seiki *see* SEIKI, YUZŌ
Yuzuru Tominaga *see* TOMINAGA, YUZURU
Yva **23** 37
Yvaral **13** 709; **21** 746; **26** 193
Yvart, Bandrin **12** 828, 832
Yvart, Joseph **12** 828, 832; **26** 260
Yver, Jaime **6** 600
Yverni, Jacques *see* IVERNI, JACQUES
Yves de Vergy, Abbot of Cluny **7** 476
Yvon, Adolphe **4** 306; **11** 48; **14** 717; **33** 581–2*
Yvonnet de la Motte **31** 842
Ywyns, Michiel **33** 582*
Yxwerth, William **10** 259; **13** 81; **19** 604
works **10** *259*

Z

Zaachila 21 202
bowls 21 *240*
funerary objects 21 254
pottery 21 188
sculpture 21 221
Tomb 1 21 737; 29 829
Tomb 2 21 737
Zaagmolen, Martinus 19 832; 22 383
Zaalberg, Maarten 29 117
Zaalberg Potterij 29 117
Zaandam 7 442
Zabad 16 278
Zabala, Bruno Mauricio de 31 752
Zabala, Eduardo Zamacois y *see* ZAMACOIS Y ZABALA, EDUARDO
Zabala, Romulo 2 405
Zabaleta, Ignacio Zuloaga y *see* ZULOAGA (Y ZABALETA), IGNACIO
Zabaleta, Juan de 29 302
Zabaleta, Rafael 33 583*
Zabalza, Diego de 29 335
Zabalza, Luis de 29 336
Zabani, Moshe 17 567
Zabarella, Francesco 23 92
Záběhlice 18 405
Zabelin, Ivan (Yegorovich) 27 443; 33 583*
Zabern *see* SAVERNE
Zabid 16 *104*; 33 583–4*
architecture 16 213
Great Mosque 16 178, 215
houses 33 520
madrasas 16 214
towers 16 178
Zabłocki, Wojciech 33 584*
Zabludovsky, Abraham 33 584*
collaboration 12 921; 21 381, 397, 404
works 21 381, *381*
Zabłudow Synagogue 17 544
Zabolotsky, Nikolay 33 522
Záboří, St Procopius 8 381; 26 637
Zaborsky, Georgy (Vladimirovich) 33 585*
Zabrat 2 893
Zacatecas 21 *372*, 393; 33 585*
Cathedral 21 377, *377*
Monastery of S Luis Gonzaga 7 877
Museo Francisco Goitia 33 585
Museo Pedro Coronel 21 395; 33 585
Museo Rafael Coronel 21 395
museums 21 396
Zaccagni, Benedetto 33 585, 586
Zaccagni, Bernardino 24 196; 33 585–6*
Zaccagni, Gian Francesco 24 196; 33 585, 586
Zaccaria, Antonio 3 249
Zaccaria, Benedetto 12 281
Zacchi, Francesco d'Antonio *see* FRANCESCO D' ANTONIO (ZACCHI) DA VITERBO
Zacchi, Giovanni 33 586–7*
Zacchi (da Volterra), Zaccaria 4 280; 5 180; 33 586
Zacchia, Lorenzo 19 190; 33 587*
Zacchia *il vecchio* *see* VEZZANO, EZECHIA DA
Zaccolini, Matteo 6 570; 24 493; 33 587*
Zach, Andreas 14 191
Zach, Bruno 29 576
Zach, František de Paula 8 410
Zách, Joseph 9 754; 18 417
Zacharias, Archbishop of Iberia 9 657
Zacharias, Pope (*reg* 741-52) 9 111; 20 365
Zachariáš of Hradec 8 395; 14 818*
Zacharjewicz, Julian 30 279
Zächerle, Franz 33 587–8*
Zachrisson, Julio (Augusto) 23 905; 33 588*
Zachtleven *see* SAFTLEVEN
Zack 5 589
Zack, Léon 33 588*
Zackenstil (13th cent.) *see under* GOTHIC → styles
Zackenstil (20th cent.) 12 450
Žačko, Askold 28 856
Zacks, Sam 16 570
Zacks Abramov, Ayala 16 570
Zacolini, Matteo *see* ZACCOLINI, MATTEO
Zacuala 21 207
Zacualpa 4 796
Zaculeu 13 *758*; 20 *882*; 33 588–9*
Museo Arqueológico 13 769
Temple I 21 213
temples 28 640
Zadar 8 174
Archaeological Museum 8 180
Cathedral of St Anastasia 26 594
clock-tower 8 175
convent of St Mary 8 180
fortifications 32 159, *159*
forum 26 906
guilds 8 180
loggia 8 175
monastery of St Francis 8 180
mosaics 9 566
St Donat 7 256; 8 175; 26 594
St Krševan 8 175
St Mary 8 175
St Nediljica 8 177
St Simeon 13 161
St Stošija 8 175
Zara 8 *174*; 32 *158*
Zmajević Palace 8 176
Zadar, Nicolò of *see* NICOLÒ OF ZADAR
Zadek, Peter 29 420
Zadikow-Lohsing, Hilde 17 816
Zadkine, Ossip 11 568, 569; 17 577; 33 589–91*
assistants 8 515; 23 403
collaboration 30 33
groups and movements 4 109; 8 240; 10 696; 11 568; 27 307
pupils
Cimiotti, Emil 7 325
Colvin, Marta 7 645
Gerstein, Noemí 12 490
Hasior, Władysław 14 219
Helgadóttir, Gerður 14 328
Kemble, Kenneth 17 894
Kohn, Gabriel 18 192
Noland, Kenneth 23 183
Parsons, Betty (Bierne) 24 213
Penalba, Alicia 24 352
Reddy, Krishna 26 67
Sklavos, Yerasimos 28 820
Stankiewicz, Richard 29 539
Sugarman, George 29 900
Tajiri, Shinkichi 30 255
studio 29 858
works 11 568; 13 328; 19 491; 22 49; 29 576; 33 *590*
Zadorin, Aleksandr (Yevgen'yevich) 27 411
Zaenredam *see* SAENREDAM
Zaer, Kaetzaert van *see* KAETZAERT VAN ZAER
Zaeslin, Karl 2 512
Zafar 2 *246*, 257, 263
Zafar, Aftab 23 803
Zafar Dhibin
mosque 16 177, 178
tombs 16 177, 215
Zaffaronio, Ambrogio 23 368
Zafferblau see under PIGMENTS → types
Zaffran, Lodovico 5 180
Zafimaniry 20 35, 36, 38, 39, 40
Zafouk, Dominik 8 416
Zafuris, Nikolaos 20 52; 25 332
Zagala, Juan 29 340
Zaganelli, Bernardo 33 591
Zaganelli, Francesco (di Bosio) 3 868; 33 591*
Zağanos Pasha 16 498
Zagar, Jacob 3 700
Zagarolo, Camillo Rospiglioso, Duca di 27 172
Zagarolo, Giovanni Battista Rospigliosi, Duca di 27 171, 172
Zagayski, Michael 17 582
Zaghawa 1 285
Zagheh, Tepe 15 903, 918
Zaghouan 26 920
Zagłębie Staropolskie 25 130
Zagora 1 *376*; 13 *363*; 33 591–2*
fortifications 13 396
houses 13 382, 396
town walls 21 555
Zagorsk *see* SERGIYEV POSAD
Zagreb 8 *174*, 178; 33 592–3*
Academy of Art 8 180, 181
architecture 19 749
Art Pavilion 8 178
Crafts School *see* museums → Museum of Arts and Crafts
crematorium 8 177
Croatian Academy of Arts and Sciences 8 176
Domotörffy Palace 8 176
Drašković-Jelačić Palace 8 176
ecclesiastical buildings
Archbishop's Palace 8 176
Cathedral 8 175, 176; 33 592
choir-stalls 14 904
collections 8 180
paintings 8 178
St Stephen's Chapel 14 898
Convent of the Poor Clares *see* museums → Museum of the City of Zagreb
St Blaise 8 *176*, 176
St Catherine 8 176, 178; 33 *592*
St Mark's 8 175
embroidery 8 180
French Pavilion 30 468
Grič-Zagreb 8 175
House of Fine Arts *see under* museums → Museum of the Revolution of Croatian Peoples
Ivan Meštrović Studio 8 181; 21 316
Kaptol-Zagreb 8 175
Kulmer Palace 8 176
museums
Archaeological Museum 8 180; 33 593
Benko Horvat Gallery of Renaissance Drawings 33 593
Cathedral Museum 33 593
Ethnographic Museum 14 724; 33 593
Gallery of Modern Art 8 176, 180; 18 473; 33 593
Gallery of Primitive Art 8 179, 180; 14 596
Historical Museum of Croatia 33 592
Mimara Museum 8 180
Zagreb
museums—cont.
Municipal Art Gallery 8 181
Museum of Arts and Crafts 4 270; 8 180; 18 473; 33 593
Museum of the City of Zagreb 33 592
Museum of the Revolution of Croatian Peoples 21 315
Strossmayer Gallery of Old Masters 8 178, 180; 33 593
Theatre Museum 8 180
National University Library Graphic Arts Collection 8 180
new city hall 8 175
Old Theatre 8 176
Opera House 8 176
Oršić-Rauch Palace 8 176
School of Arts and Crafts 8 180
University 8 177
urban planning 8 175, 176
Vraniczany Mansion *see* museums → Gallery of Modern Art
Zagreb School 15 66
Zagros 15 903, 919
Zagros culture 21 269*
Zagwe 1 314
Zaharovič, Vladimir 10 667
al-Zahir, Caliph (*reg* 1021-36) (Fatimid) 16 256; 31 22
al-Zahir, Caliph (*reg* 1225-26) (Abbasid) 17 496, 497
al-Zahir Ghazi, Sultan (*reg* Aleppo 1186-1216) (Ayyubid) 1 602; 2 888
al-Ẓāhir Rukn al-Dīn Baybars al-Bunduqdārī *see* BAYBARS I
al-Ẓāhir Sayf al-Dīn Barqūq ibn Anas *see* BARQUQ
Zahn, Anton 7 210
Zahn, J. György 15 4
Zahn, Wilhelm 25 623
Zahner, Andreas 17 585; 23 425
Zahner, Joseph 13 850
Zahos, Aristotelis 13 349, 358
Zahra, (Vincenzo) Francesco 5 131; 20 213; 31 361; 33 593*
Zahra, Pietro Paolo 33 593
Zahrani Church 9 567
Zähringen (family) 17 817
Zähringen, Carolina Luise, Margravine of Baden-Durlach *see* CAROLINE LOUISE, Margravine of Baden-Durlach
Zähringen, Charles-Frederick, Grand Duke of Baden *see* CHARLES-FREDERICK, Grand Duke of Baden
Zähringen, Charles William, Margrave of Baden-Durlach *see* CHARLES III, Margrave of Baden-Durlach
Zähringen, Christoph I, Margrave of Baden *see* CHRISTOPHER I, Margrave of Baden
Zähringen, Filibert, Margrave of Baden-Baden *see* PHILIBERT, Margrave of Baden-Baden
Zähringen, Frances Sibyl Augusta, Margravine of Baden-Baden *see* FRANCES SIBYL AUGUSTA, Margravine of Baden-Baden
Zähringen, Frederick I, Grand Duke of Baden *see* FREDERICK I, Grand Duke of Baden
Zähringen, Frederick V, Margrave of Baden-Durlach *see* FREDERICK V, Margrave of Baden-Durlach
Zähringen, Leopold, Grand Duke of Baden *see* LEOPOLD, Grand Duke of Baden
Zahringer, Berchtold V 3 822
Zahrtmann, (Peder Henrik) Kristian 14 595; 33 594–5*
groups and movements 11 790; 18 470
patrons and collectors 14 572
pupils 8 735
Adrian-Nilsson, Gösta 1 161
Christiansen, Poul S(imon) 7 233
Egedius, Halfdan 9 751
Eiebakke, August 10 105
Erichsen, Thorvald 10 457
Find, Ludvig (Frederik) 11 84
Giersing, Harald 12 602
Isakson, Karl (Oskar) 16 67
Larsen Stevns, Niels 18 799
Nielsen, Ejnar (August) 23 116
Scharff, (Niels) William 28 54
Sohlberg, Harald Oskar 29 15
Sørensen, Henrik (Ingvar) 29 78
Stefánsson, Jón 29 599
Swane, Sigurd 30 59
Syberg, Fritz (Christian Friedrich Wilhelm Heinrich), Baron von 30 157
Weie, (Viggo Thorvald) Edvard 33 35
Zahrtmanns Skole 8 760
Zaïane 16 486
Zaichun, Prince *see* TONGZHI EMPEROR (Qing; *reg* 1862-74)
Zaim, Turgut 31 454; 33 595*
Zaimov, Dimo 5 161
Zaimović, Mehmed 4 461
Zain al-Abidin, Sultan of Kashmir (*reg* 1420-70) (Shah Miri) 15 650
Zainer, Günther 2 718; 3 150; 4 9
Zainer, Hieronymus 12 444
Zainer, Johann 10 725
Zaini 15 808
Zaïre 1 *214*; 11 880; 33 595–8
basketwork 1 295, 296, *296*
beads 18 *488*
beadwork 3 440
beds 1 296
bells 1 360
body arts 1 285, 288, *343*
burial practices 1 259*
cement 1 331
ceramics 1 328, *329*
chairs 1 366
cicatrices 1 *346*
craftsmen and artists 1 *338*
crucifixes 1 *228*
cups 18 *488*
currency 1 363
divination instruments 1 357
drums (musical instruments) 1 360; 22 *375*
education (art) 33 597–8*
feathers 1 *405*
fibres 1 *405*
figurines 1 *269*, 273, *275*; 19 *72*
gesture 1 265, 266
hairstyles 1 *343*
harps 1 359
hats 1 296
houses 1 295
huts 1 311
iconography 1 261, 262, 263, 282
ivory 1 293; 19 *72*; 29 575
looms 1 294, *294*
masks 1 261, *301*, *336*, *338*, *405*; 18 *488*; 19 *73*; 29 *70*; 33 *484*
meeting-houses 1 310
megaphones 1 360
mixed-media 1 301, *301*

Zaïre—cont.
monuments 1 331
mud 1 285
museums 33 598*
musical instruments 1 *359*
mythology 1 282
niombos 1 259
nude figures 18 *486*
painting 1 430, *430, 432*; 33 595*, *596, 597*
palm leaves 1 *296*
portraits 1 268, 269
pots 1 *329*
raffia 1 *294*; 3 440
religion 1 230
sculpture 1 *359*; 14 *377*; 18 *486*; 29 *69*; 30 *225*
shells 18 *488*
shelters 1 306
shields 1 296
staffs 1 *402*
stools 1 *366*; 14 *378*
textiles 1 349
tools 1 *364*
trade 1 249
ivory 3 604
weaving 1 294, *294*
wood 1 *269, 275, 359, 402*; 14 *377, 378*; 18 *486, 488*; 19 *73*
wood-carvings 1 *366*; 30 *225*
Zais, Giuseppe 32 194; 33 598–9*
works 11 37; 24 865; 29 736
Zaječar National Museum 28 459
Żak, Eugeniusz 25 108; 26 296
Žák, Ladislav 8 402; 33 599*
Zakanitch, Robert 1 81
Zak'arian, Ivanē, Prince 12 235
Zak'arian, Zak'arē, Prince 12 235
Zakari Awang 20 171
Zak'arids 2 435
Zakariya Khan 15 375
Zakariyya' ibn Muhammad al-Qazwini 2 650
Zakhariev (family) 31 393
Zakhariev, Krustyo 31 393
Zakhariev, Tsanyu 31 393
Zakhariev, Vassil 5 155; 33 599*
Zakharina, Natal'ya 27 381
Zakharov, Andreyan (Dmitriyevich) 27 579; 33 599–600*
groups and movements 13 611; 22 741
pupils 21 91
works 6 552; 12 173; 13 238; 27 375, 576; 28 568; 31 553; 33 *600*
Zakharov, Gury 27 397
Zakharov, Pyotr 27 433
Zakharov, U. D. 31 551
Zakharov, Vadim 27 398
Zaki, Muhammad Salih 16 2
Zakim 17 879
Zakkichō 20 834
zakomary see under ARCHES → types
Zakopane 25 *92*
art schools 25 133
Tatra Museum 25 140
villa Pod Jedlami 25 100, *100*
Zakopane style 25 122, 123
villas 25 *100*
Zakro *see* KATO ZAKRO
Zakro Master 21 686
Zakros Palace 8 153
Zakrzewski, Włodzimierz 25 108
Zákupy 8 400
Zakynthos
Ayios Dionysios 13 358; 26 149
icons 25 334
Zala, György 5 83, 85; 14 896; 15 14; 28 87
Zalaczyński & Herodek 32 879
Zalaegerszeg, Göcsej Museum 18 86
Zalameda, Oscar 24 623
Zalavár Church 21 501
Zaļā Vārna
Zalaváry, Lajos 14 891
Zalavruga 25 *471*; 27 *363*; 33 600*
rock art 27 365
Zalavár Abbey 26 638
Zalce, Alfredo 30 275; 33 600–601*
Zaldestani Associates 27 613
Zāle, Kārlis 26 383; 33 601*
Zaleman, Gugo 33 601
Zaleśsie, Ahinski Palace 3 527
Zales'ye *see* ZALEŚSIE
Zālīte, Kārlis *see* ZĀLE, KĀRLIS
Zaļkalns, Teodors 12 825; 28 534; 33 601*
Zalktis 27 284
Zallinger, A. 31 353
Zaloumis, George
works 1 *350*
Zaltbommel 22 *813*
Huis van Marten van Rossum 22 822
St Maartenskerk 22 820, 821, 856
Zaltieri, Bolognino 5 888
Zaltsman, Peter 12 265
Žaludak 3 527
Załuski (family) 25 142
Załuski, Andrzej Chrzyzostom 25 135
Załuski, Andrzej Stanisław 18 524
Zama *see* TULUM
Zamacois y Zabala, Eduardo 6 66
Zamahe *see* RIMAH, TELL EL-
Zamalek
Akhnaten Halls and Art Complex *see* Centre of Arts
Centre of Arts 9 768
Egyptian Centre of International Cultural Cooperation 9 768
Zaman, Muhammad *see* MUHAMMAD ZAMAN
Zamarev, G. T. 12 633
Zambaccian, K. H. 26 723, 724
Zambaldini, Pietro di Francesco 21 413
Zambeccari, Marchese 24 227
Zambeccari, Emilio 5 852
Zambeccari, Paolo 11 700
Zambelli, Alfonso 1 554
Zambelli da Bergamo, Damiano 16 725; 32 502
Zamberlan, Francesco 25 216
Zambia 1 *214*; 11 880; 33 601–3*
architecture 33 602*
basketwork 1 296, 310
caves 1 304
collections 33 603
education (art) 33 603*
houses 4 *792*
iconography 1 282
limestone 33 603
masks 1 296
metal 1 287
mud-bricks 4 792, *792*
museums 33 603*
musical instruments 1 358
painting 33 602–3*
patronage 33 603*
prints 33 602
religion 1 230
rock art 1 375
sculpture 1 261; 33 603*
shrines (i) (cult) 1 289, 310
stools 1 365
trade 1 249
wood 33 603
woodcuts 33 *603*
Zámbó, István ef 14 902
Zamboanga 24 617
Nuestra Señora del Pilar de Zaragoza 21 596
Zamboni, Baldassare Camillo 3 385
Zambrano, L. 21 396
Zambrano, S. 21 396
Zambrów Church 25 126
Zambujal 21 551; 25 522
Zamecznik, S. 10 793
Zamet, Sébastien, Bishop of Langres 25 790
Žametas-Žemaitis, Albertas 19 498
Zamil, Irshad 23 802
Zam'jan 21 880
Zammit, Giuseppe 20 219
Zammit, Themistocles 20 210, 219
Zamojski, Jan 10 871
Zamoner Neto, Guilhermo 4 715
Zamora 29 *258*; 33 604–5*
Cathedral of S Salvador 9 85; 29 263; 33 *604*, 604–5*
choir-stalls 7 192, *192*; 13 123
dome 9 84
furniture 29 317, *317*
retable 13 69
tapestries 31 219
textiles 13 195; 30 314, 331
embroidery 29 350
S Pedro de la Nave 29 261; 32 619
Zamora, Carlos Fonseca *see* FONSECA ZAMORA, CARLOS
Zamora, María de la Salud Madrid Alcalá *see* SALUD MADRID ALCALÁ-ZAMORA, MARÍA DE LA
Zamora, Mario 14 716
Zamora, Sancho de *see* SANCHO DE ZAMORA
Zamość 22 78; 25 *92*, 97, 135; 31 718; 33 605–6*
urban planning 33 605, 606
Zamoyski's Academy 25 142
Zamoyska, Gryzelda Celestyna *see* DZIAŁYŃSKI, GRYZELDA CELESTYNA, Countess
Zamoyski (family) 25 135
Zamoyski, Count (*fl* early 20th cent.) 14 498
Zamoyski, Andrzej 20 397
Zamoyski, August 11 317; 25 116; 26 266; 33 607*
Zamoyski, Jan 33 606*
architecture 22 78; 25 97; 31 718; 33 605
works 25 135
Zamoyski, Stanisław 20 397; 25 136; 33 607*
Zamoyski's Academy *see under* ZAMOŚĆ
Zamuco 24 93, 100
Zamudio, Enrique 6 600
Zamurro *see* AZEMMOUR
Zamyraylo, Viktor (Dmytriyevych) 12 875; 33 607–8*
Zan (Andrade, José zan) 2 86
Zan, Bernhard 23 310; 25 731; 29 747; 33 608*
Zanabazar, Ondor Gegen 5 106; 21 873, 880, 883; 30 812
Zanaga
sculpture 18 *402*
Zañartu, Enrique 6 598
Zañartu, Juan José de Goicoles y *see* GOICOLES ZAÑARTU, JUAN JOSÉ DE
Zañartu, Luis Manuel de 6 592
Zanazabar 21 878
works 21 *879*
Zanchi, Antonio 32 194, 196; 33 608*
collaboration 6 29; 22 308; 28 340
pupils 21 816; 31 313
teachers 25 227
works 3 229; 5 450; 33 276
Zanchi, Giovanni Battista 21 579, 580
Zancon 5 617
Zancon, Gaetano 32 350
Zand 33 609*
Zand, Muhammad Karim Khan *see* MUHAMMAD KARIM KHAN, Ruler
Zanda *see* THOLING
Zandana 6 248, 249; 16 435; 28 721
zandanījī see under TEXTILES → types
Zande 33 609–10*
bells 1 360
gongs 33 610
harps 33 610
houses 1 308
knives 33 610
musical instruments 1 *359*; 33 610
paddles 1 365
pots 1 328
pottery 33 610
sculpture 1 *359*, 404; 29 895; 33 609–10*
shields 33 610
terracotta 30 509
tools 1 *364*
wood 1 *359*
wood-carvings 33 *610*
Zandomeneghi, Federico 16 678; 20 482; 33 611–12*
works 33 *612*
Zandomeneghi, Luigi 16 705; 32 196, 217
Zandomeneghi, Pietro 32 196, 217
Zane, Carlo 32 205
Zaneletti, Pietro 16 731
Zanelli, Siro 10 763; 16 701
Zanetti (family) 8 764; 10 770; 24 706
Zanetti, Alesandro *see* ZANETTI, ANTON MARIA (ii)
Zanetti, Anton Maria (Girolamo) (i), Conte (1680-1767) 6 91; 10 394; 33 612–13*
dealing 8 209; 13 746; 30 523
paintings
personal collection 12 355
personal collection 6 36; 22 236; 26 323; 33 697, 700
drawings 3 308; 9 230; 10 769; 16 815
etchings 5 598; 30 857
gems 13 10
reproductive prints by others 32 759
writings 5 756; 12 669; 25 664; 26 323; 33 367
Zanetti, Anton Maria (Alesandro) (ii) (1706-78) 6 91; 33 612, 613*
reproductive prints by others 32 759
works 31 7; 32 196; 33 613
writings 16 768
Zanetti, Domenico 22 919; 33 280
Zanetti, Girolamo (i) (1680-1767) *see* ZANETTI, ANTON MARIA (i)
Zanetti, Girolamo (ii) (*fl* 1750s) 33 612, 613
Zanetti, Vincenzo 32 204
Zanetti, Vittore 1 453
Zanettini, Siegbert 33 613*
Zangaroli *see* AYIA TRIADA
Zangid 22 202; 33 614*
see also:
'IMAD AL-DIN, Ruler
NUR AL-DIN, Ruler
Zanguidi, Jacopo *see* BERTOIA, JACOPO
Zang Yingxuan 17 589
Zanhuang, Tomb of Li Xizong 7 23
Zani, Pietro 16 782; 23 115; 33 614*
Zanine Caldas, José 4 714, 722
Zanini *see* VIOLA ZANINI, GIUSEPPE
Zanini, Bernardo 14 646
Zanini, Gigiotto 23 263
Zanini, Marco 29 90
Zanino di Francia (*fl* 1422-42) 20 323
Zanino di Francia (*fl c.* 1491-1507) *see* ZOHANNE DE FRANZA
Zanino di Pietro 7 903; 12 302; 32 205; 33 614*
Zanjan 15 *897*
congregational mosque 16 234
Zankle 13 586
Zannacchini, Giovanni 28 319
Zanobi (de Gianotis), Bernardino 25 96, 113; 32 578; 33 614–15*
works 19 496; 32 *873*, 874
Zanobi, Jacopo di 12 575
Zanobi da Firenze 20 637
Zanobi degli Strozzi *see* STROZZI, ZANOBI (DI BENEDETTO DI CAROCCIO DEGLI)
Zanobi di Bartolo 13 94
Zanobi di Comenico 22 801
Zanobi di Migliore 19 894; 24 537
Zanobi Picardi, Andrea di 12 575
Zanoia, Giuseppe 1 758; 2 176; 16 562, 647; 21 532; 25 155
Zanotta 2 727
Zanotti, Giovan Pietro (Cavazzoni) 5 444; 12 559; 24 227; 33 615*
Zanskar 15 311
Zanstra, Giesen, Sijmons 33 616
Zanstra, Piet 1 804; 29 484; 33 616*
Zanten, Giovanni Van *see* VASANZIO, GIOVANNI
Zanth, Ludwig von 22 59; 29 874; 33 616*
Zanthier 17 834
Zantvoort, Dirck (Dircksz.) *see* SANTVOORT, DIRCK (DIRCKSZ.)
Zantzinger, C. Clark 31 390
Zanuoli, Ottaviano 2 793
Zanusi, Jacob 11 120
Zanuso, Marco 16 651; 33 616*
Zanzibar (island) *see* TANZANIA
Zanzibar (town) 1 315, *407*
architecture 1 410; 30 300
doors 30 300
museum 30 56
Old Fort Museum 30 302
Zaor, Jan 19 497
Zaortiga, Bonanat 27 818
Zao Wou-Ki 12 830; 19 491, 537; 33 616–17*
Zapaca Inga, Juan 6 596
Zapata, Cardinal 24 394; 26 375
Zapata, José Antonio 10 509
Zapata, Marcos 8 303; 24 507; 33 617*
Zapata Gollán, Agustín 2 399
Zapher Papoura 21 681, 682
Zapiain, Luis Antonio 12 921; 33 584
Zapkus, Keytutis 19 499
Zaporizhzhya 31 552, 564
Zaporozh'ye *see* ZAPORIZHZHYA
Zapotal 21 *193, 372*; 33 617–18*
pottery 21 238
religion 21 188
sculpture 33 *618*
temple 33 617
sculpture 33 617
Zapotec 8 460; 21 177, 192, 195, 198, 736, 738; 33 618–20*
bone-carvings 21 248
clay 33 *619*
figurines 33 *619*
forgeries 21 266
headdresses 21 249
jade 21 251
masks 21 251
observatories 23 338
painting 21 *230*, 230–31*; 33 620
portraits 18 *675*
pottery 21 238, 249
sculpture 21 217; 33 619
Classic (*c.* AD 250-*c.* 900) 21 221*
Pre-Classic (*c.* 2000 BC-*c.* AD 250) 21 218, 219*
relief 8 *460*; 21 219*
stone 8 *460*
stone-carvings 22 *8*
stucco 18 *675*
tombs 18 675–6; 31 118
urns 21 266
Zappas, Evangelos 13 359
Zappi, Gian Paolo 11 269

zappler clocks see under CLOCKS → types
Zapyškis 19 494
St Jonas 19 495
Zar, Johann Gregor del see SCHARDT, JOHANN GREGOR VAN DER
Zara see under ZADAR
Zaragoza see SARAGOSSA
Zaragoza, Lorenzo 11 481
Zaragoza, Miguel 24 622
Zaragoza y Ebri, Agustín Bruno see BRIZGUZ BRU, ATHANASIO GENARO
Zaramo 1 410; 17 907
Zarang 16 401
Zaranj see NAD 'ALI
Zaranou Museum 8 23
Zárate, Manuel Ortiz de see ORTIZ DE ZÁRATE, MANUEL
Zaraut-Kamar 6 222–3
Zara Yakob, Emperor of Ethiopia (reg 1434–68) 10 570
Zardaryan, Horhannes 2 432
Zarhy, Moshe 26 64, 65
Zaria 1 381; 14 231; 23 129
Emir's Palace 1 315; 23 133
fortifications 21 597
Friday Mosque 1 316, 383; 23 133
houses 1 318
painting 23 137
University 1 432; 23 135
wall decorations 14 233
Zaria Art Society 23 136, 137
Zarić, Sretan 3 621
Zarin, Aleksandar 28 453
Zariñena, Juan see SARIÑENA, JUAN
Zaripov, Il'dar 27 435
Zaritsky, Yossef 17 577; 33 620*
groups and movements 16 567; 17 579; 23 25
pupils 18 525
works 16 567, 567
Žarković, Milenko 22 18
Zarlino, Gioseffo 22 378
Żarnów Church 25 129
Żarnower, Teresa 4 148; 7 772; 25 422; 30 199, 204
Zarotto see LUZZO, LORENZO
Zarov, Kliment 19 883
al-Zarqali 2 647
Zárraga, Angel 21 386, 387, 397
Zárraga, Guillermo 23 369
Zarriņš, Rihards 12 825; 18 852
Zar Tepe 6 182, 209; 31 781; 33 620–21*
medallion 6 244
wall paintings 6 232
Zarudny, Ivan (Petrovich) 33 621*
attributions 27 373
works 22 171; 27 374; 30 277; 31 317
Zaryanko, Sergey (Konstantinovich) 20 151, 152; 24 464; 33 621–2*
Zarza, Diogo de see SARÇA, DIOGO DE
Zarza, Vasco de la 27 823; 33 622*
collaboration 3 846
works 2 864, 865; 29 290; 31 89
Zarzian period see under IRAN, ANCIENT → periods
Zarzma 12 317, 328
church 12 320, 324
Zasaragi 17 19
Zasche, Ivan 33 622*
Zasche, Josef 8 379
Zasinger, Matthäus 20 801
Zaslaŭe Palace 3 530
Zaslava Palace see ZASLAŬE PALACE
Zaslavsky, Abram 32 695
Žatec 8 376
bridge 8 379
Zator Church 25 129
Zatta, Antonio 32 501; 33 697
Zattara, Cesare 10 803
Zau see SAIS
Zauch, Hans 2 95; 33 622*
Zaudy 26 379
Zauerveid, Aleksander 10 855
Zauffaly, Anton Franz 33 692
Zauffaly, Johannes Josephus see ZOFFANY, JOHAN (JOSEPH)
Zauli, Giuseppe 4 291; 21 623
zaum 18 22, 474; 30 7; 31 763
Zauner, Franz Anton 32 444; 33 623–4*
pupils 8 502; 16 61
works 2 802; 14 645; 32 457
Zauphaly, John see ZOFFANY, JOHAN (JOSEPH)
Zaurbekova, Batima 17 868
Zaushkevich, I. 7 174; 21 810
Zavadovsky (family) 31 564
Zavadovsky, P. V. 25 791
Zavadsky, Lidia 16 568
Zavala (Bosnia & Herzegovina) 4 459, 459
Zavala (fl 1928) 7 294
Zavara 16 105; 33 624*
congregational mosque 16 162, 165; 22 194; 33 624
mihrab 16 165
Pa Minar Mosque 33 624
Zavargna see LOMAZZO, GIOVANNI PAOLO
Zavarov, A. I. 9 54; 33 518
Zavattari (family) 9 262; 33 624–6*
frescoes 33 625
Zavattari, Ambrogio (di Franceschino) 33 625
Zavattari, Cristoforo (di Francesco) 33 624
Zavattari, Franceschino (di Cristoforo) 33 624, 625, 626
Zavattari, Francesco (di Giovanni) 33 625
Zavattari, Gerolamo (di Giovanni) 33 625
Zavattari, Giovanni (di Franceschino) 33 624, 625
Zavattari, Giovanni Angelo (di Ambrogio) 33 625
Zavattari, Gregorio (di Franceschino) 33 624, 625
Zavattari, Guido (di Giovanni) 33 625
Zaventem 8 681
Závist 21 551; 25 536, 538
hill-fort 25 535
Zavordas Monastery 25 335
Zawadzki, Stanisław 25 99, 212, 213, 364
Zawar
brass 4 682, 684
Zawareh see ZAVARA
Zawi Chemi Shanidar 21 280
Zawichost, Franciscan Church 4 782
al-Zawiya (The Religious Fraternity) 10 833; 14 221; 16 2
zāwiyas see KHĀNAQĀHS
zawiya-type mosques see MOSQUES → types → T-plan
Zawyat el-Mayitin 9 779
Zawyet el-Aryan, Layer Pyramid 25 761
Zawyet Umm el-Rakham 9 848
Zayadine, F. 27 669
Zayan
saddle-bags 3 755
Zayas, Gabriel de 14 661; 22 71
Zayas, Marius de 2 383; 8 433, 435; 29 655, 656
Zayas, Miguel de 21 110
Zaydi 33 626*
see also:
AL-MANSUR AL-HUSAYN, Imam
AL-MUTAWAKKIL, Imam
YAHYA, Imam
Zayd ibn Thabit 18 239
Zaymov, Dimo 5 159
Zayn al-'Abidin 16 337, 338, 339; 27 514; 33 626*
Zayn al-'Abidin ibn Muhammad al-Katib al-Shirazi
works 16 284
Zaynal Beg (Aqqoyunlu) 2 237
Zayn al-Din (fl 15th/16th cent.) 32 160, 161
Zayn al-Din (fl 1777–82) 15 653
works 15 654
Zayn al-Din ibn Abi Rashid 2 892; 3 87
Zaytsev, Yury 27 434
Zay-Ugrócz Glassworks 15 4; 29 249
Zbarazh 25 115
Zbigniew of Oleśnica see OLEŚNICKI, ZBIGNIEW
Zborowski, Léopold 10 680; 17 577; 18 445; 21 787; 29 246; 33 626–7*
paintings 10 838
Zbraslav
Cathedral 8 376
Monastery 8 384
Zbrożyna, Barbara 9 394
Zdanevich, Il'ya 8 437, 438, 439
Zdanevich, Kirill 9 144
Zdeněk Lev of Rožmitál 26 367
Zdeslav 6 364
Zdík, Jindřich, Bishop of Olomouc 8 421; 23 424; 25 444
Zdrój 25 141; 26 266
Zea 24 327–8
Zea, Francisco Antonio, Museo de Antioquia see under MEDELLÍN
Zeami, Motokiyo see MOTOKIYO ZEAMI
Zeban Ona Libanos 1 373, 376
Zebed see ZABAD
Zebegény Church 14 890; 18 394
Žebera, Karel 25 467
Zeberiņš, Indriķis
Žebnice 13 187
Zebo da Firenze 20 637
Zebra 12 397; 33 627*
Žebrák Lamentation, Master of the 8 383
Zebra's Voice 24 430
zebra-wood 10 297; 33 325
Żebrowski, Walenty 25 105
Zec, Safet 4 461
Zecca, Giuseppe 20 352
Zecchin, Vittorio 32 204
Zech 3 585
Zech, Jacob 7 439
Zech, Paul 24 427
Zechlin glass factory 4 666; 12 440, 441
Zeckel, Johann 12 447
Zeckendorf, William 24 325
Zeckhorn, Heinrich 28 144
Zedelgem 26 630
zedi see BURMA → stupas
Zee, Harry van der 4 507
Zeegen, Christina van 22 899
Zeeman, Reinier see NOOMS, REINIER
Zeerijp 22 813
church 22 819
Zeeu, Cornelis de
works 9 275
Zeeus, Jacob 14 794
Zeevaert, Adolfo 15 887
Zefarović, Hristofor 28 450
Zefat see SAFED
Zeffirelli, Franco 31 396
Zeffis, Giovanni 3 108
Zefirov, Konstantin K. 20 151
Zege, Sigismund 18 851
Zegers, Gerard see SEGHERS, GERARD
Zeggin, Georg 33 271
Zeggin, Paul 1 36
Zeherin, Karl see CARLO DI CESARI DEL PALAGIO
Zehlendorf Planungsamt 3 797
Zehnerring see RING, DER
Żehra Church 28 851
Zehrfuss, Bernard (Louis) 19 848; 24 130; 33 627–8*
assistants 20 450
collaboration 11 527; 22 806
works 7 696; 28 583, 583
Zeicher, Felix 29 75
Zeid, Fahrelnissa 17 655; 31 454; 33 628*
Zeidenberg, Savely 2 122
Zeidler, Eberhard (Heinrich) 31 864; 33 628*
Zeidler Partnership 31 176
Zeidler Roberts Partnership 33 628
Zeijlemaker, Jack 15 818
Zeilenbau 20 879
Zeiller, Franz Anton 13 258; 23 636; 25 560; 33 629
Zeiller, Johann Jakob 33 629*
collaboration 23 636
pupils 25 560; 33 744
teachers 31 358
works 11 125, 127; 15 139; 33 270
Zeiller, Martin 13 809; 21 152
Zeiller, Paul 33 629
Zeil Schloss 12 369; 30 34
Zeiner, Peter 14 160
Zeisenis, Bartholomeus 22 828
Zeising, Adolf 14 874
Zeisler, Claire 11 54
Zeiss 23 358; 24 669
Zeissig, Johann Elias 9 407; 21 65; 26 98; 32 676
Zeiss-Ikon 29 52
Zeist 12 132
Castle 22 826
Rijksdienst voor Monumentenzorg 22 909
Zeitblom, Bartholomäus 20 693; 31 566; 33 629–30*
assistants 20 745
attributions 21 157
collaboration 10 455; 29 773
pupils 20 191
works 12 384; 33 630
Zeit-Echo 24 427
Zeitgeist 33 630*
Zeitler, Rudolf 30 120
Zeitner, Herbert 12 451
Zeitschrift des Architekten- und Ingenieur-Vereins für das Königreich Hannover 24 444
Zeitschrift des Vereins zur Ausbildung der Gewerbe in München 24 444
Zeitschrift für Baukunde see WOCHENBLATT FÜR BAUKUNDE
Zeitschrift für Bauwesen 14 594; 24 444
Zeitschrift für bildende Kunst 24 423, 444, 445
Zeitschrift für christliche Kunst 24 444
Zeitschrift für Ethnologie 24 429
Zeitschrift für Geschichte der Architektur 24 444
Zeitschrift für Innendekoration
Haus eines Kunstfreundes (Art Lover's House) 3 398; 20 24
Zeitschrift für Kunstgeschichte 24 424, 445
Zeitschrift für Kunstwissenschaft 24 424
Zeitschrift für praktische Baukunst 18 161; 24 444
Zeitschrift für schweizerische Archäologie und Kunstgeschichte/Revue suisse d'art et d'archéologie 24 453
Zekkai Chūshin 17 169, 663
Zela 1 403
Zelada, Francesco Saverio, Cardinal 6 111
Zelata, Cardinal 8 172
Zelaya Sierra, Pablo 14 715
Żelazowa Wola, Fryderyk Chopin Museum 25 140
Zel'dich, Asya (Davydovna) 27 418
Zelená Hora, St John Nepomuk 27 798, 798
Zelenak, Ed 5 571
Zelenitziotos, David 25 336
Zelentsov, Kapiton 27 389
Zelezny, Franz 2 803
Železný Brod 8 374, 411, 425; 33 630–31*
Železný Brod Glass 33 630
Zelger, Joseph 33 727
Želibský, Ján 28 853
Zelinger, Anton 8 399
Želiv Monastery 8 379; 27 797
Zelking, Christoph von 18 451; 20 705
Zelking, Wilhelm von 18 452
zelkova 7 31; 17 399; 18 361, 363; 33 IV1
Zell, Christoph 28 144
Zell, Wilhelm von 4 372
Zell am See, Haus Gadenstätter 2 789
Zellenmosaik see under HARDSTONES → techniques
Zeller, Jakob 33 631*, 670
Zeller, Jiří 8 413
Zeller, Pankraz 33 631
Zel'ma, Georgy (Anatol'yevich) 33 631*
Zelotti, Battista 16 667; 33 631–2*
collaboration 5 617; 10 824; 32 348
patrons and collectors 32 348
works 23 332, 867; 32 191, 349
Zeltiņš, Voldemārs
Zeltschach-Gurk, Hemma von 13 857
Zeltweg, Der 8 436
Zemarkhos 33 640
Zemborain, Eduardo 2 397
Zemdega, Kārlis
Zemen 5 144, 146; 9 511; 33 632*
monastery of St John the Evangelist 33 632*
St John the Theologian 5 146–7, 151
Zemenkov, Boris 8 437
Zement 21 67
Zemła, Gustav 25 116; 33 632*
Zemlja see EARTH GROUP
Zemlyanitsyn, Boris 27 409; 32 661
works 27 409
Zemmour 16 486
Zemono Mansion 28 859
Zempoala see CEMPOALA
Zemtsov, Mikhail (Grigor'yevich) 20 839; 33 632–3*
collaboration 18 543
pupils 23 76
teachers 31 318
works 6 562; 25 745; 27 401, 574, 575; 29 778
Zemun 3 620
zen see under TRAYS → types
Zen, Carlo 16 731
Zen, Francesco 28 467
Zen, Giovanni Battista, Cardinal 33 633*
Zen 49 1 77; 2 545; 22 305; 33 635*
members 10 825; 12 237; 13 217; 20 833; 29 65; 31 328; 33 83, 254
Zenale, Bernardo 33 633–4*
collaboration 5 307; 21 525
patrons and collectors 3 49
pupils 3 137
restorations by others 21 825
works 6 357; 11 294; 22 107; 33 634
writings 24 493
Zen Buddhism see under BUDDHISM → sects
Zendan-i Sulayman 30 262

Zenderoudi, Hussein **15** 898; **27** 810; **33** 634*
works **15** *899*
Zendrini, Bernardino **25** 144
Zen'emon Kinkōzan *see* KINKŌZAN ZEN'EMON
Zenen **17** 125
Zenete, Rodrigo Díaz de Vivar y Mendoza, 1st Marqués del (1464-1523) **18** 586; **21** 124; **29** 299; **32** 100
Zenetos, Takis Ch. **33** 634–5*
works **13** 350, *350*
Zeng, Yi, Marquis of
bells **3** 626; **6** 829
bowls **7** 139
bronzes **6** 828, 830, 834, 852; **7** 247; **23** 550
eyebeads **7** 80
gold **7** 21
jade **7** 5
lacquer **7** 13
stands **7** 139
tomb **6** 648, 695
Zenga see under JAPAN → painting
Zengerler *see* LIMYRA
Zeng Gongliang **21** 594
Zenghelis, Elia **18** 235, 236; **23** 361
Zenghelis, Zoe **18** 236; **23** 361
Zeng Huojue **7** 71
Zeng Jing **6** 813
Zengo, Androniqi **1** 540
Zengo, Sofia **1** 540
Zengövárkönye **25** 516
Zen group *see* ZEN 49
Zenica **4** *459*
basilica **4** 459
Zenil, Alfonso Medellín *see* MEDELLÍN ZENIL, ALFONSO
Zenil, Nahum B. **21** 390
Ženíšek, František **1** 604; **25** 433; **29** 885; **33** 635–6*
Zenit **8** 178
Zenjan *see* ZANJAN
Zenji Miyashita *see* MIYASHITA, ZENJI
Zenkei **17** 125
Zenkevičius, Jonas **19** 498
Zen'kov, A. P. **1** 678; **18** 568
Zennaro, Mario **16** 755
Zennstrom, Petter **30** 82
Zeno, Bishop of Kourion **18** 408
Zeno, Emperor of Byzantium (*reg* 474-91) **9** 540; **25** 771
Zeno, Apostolo **15** 50
Zeno, Simon **23** 325
Zenobia *see under* HALABIYEH
Zeno da Campione **5** 551
Zenodoros **26** 764; **27** 28, 32; **33** 636*
Zenon **27** 28
Zenone da Vaprio, Giovanni *see* GIOVANNI ZENONE DA VAPRIO
Zenon Papyrus **1** 616; **13** 556, 557, 558
zenpōkōen see TOMBS → types → keyhole
Zensaburō Kojima *see* KOJIMA, ZENSABURŌ
Zenshun **17** 125
Zen style **17** 72*
Zentarō Kojima *see* KOJIMA, ZENTARŌ
Zentner, Anton **11** 852
Zentralblatt **24** 444
Zepeda **14** 714
Zepita **24** *498*
S Pedro **24** 504
Zepner, Ludwig **21** 67
Zerafa, Menkes, Housden **22** 36
Zerarti, Arezki **1** 635
Zerbe, Karl **10** 199
Zerbo, Pietro **29** 831
Zerelia **14** 351
Zeri **15** 862; **23** 323
Zeri, Federico **7** 715; **16** 782
Zerletti **6** 91
Zerletti, Guglielmo **21** 831
Zermani, Paolo **16** 651
Zermatt **30** 142
Zero **1** 79; **13** 727; **23** 298; **33** 636–7*
members **12** 397
Castellani, Enrico **6** 21
Dorazio, Piero **9** 168
Graubner, Gotthard **13** 322
Klein, Yves **18** 118
Mack, Heinz **20** 11
Piene, Otto **24** 744
Schmela, Alfred **28** 120
Uecker, Günther **31** 525
Zero **24** 428
Zerohour **20** 8
Żeroński, Piotr **32** 6
Zeror, Tell **24** 634
Žerotín (family) **8** 422
Žerotín, Jan **33** 637*
Žerotín, Karel **8** 422; **33** 637*
Žerotín, Ladislav Velen **33** 637–8*
Zerpa, Pedro **19** 659
Zerubbabel **17** 487
Zerun, Antonius von **33** 113
Zervos, Christian **11** 550; **30** 488
Zeshin Shibata *see* SHIBATA ZESHIN
Zethelius, Adolf **30** 107
Zethelius, Frederik **30** 108, 113
works **30** *108*
Zethelius, Pehr **30** 107
works **30** *106*
Zethelius, Wilhelm **30** 108, 113
works **30** *108*
Zettervall, Helgo **19** 795; **30** 73; **33** 638–9*
Zeugheer, Leonhard **33** 30, 639*
Zeus statue *see under* OLYMPIA
Zeuxias **24** 337
Zeuxippus ware *see under* POTTERY → wares
Zeuxis **2** 523; **7** 673; **10** 675; **13** 548; **16** 658; **18** 587; **25** 44; **26** 223; **33** 639–40*
competitions **29** 665
forgeries by others **11** 307
methods **21** 757
works **13** 545, 550, 553, 561; **15** 135; **19** 771; **23** 291; **25** 44
writings **13** 554
Zevaco, Jean-François **1** 319
Zevallos, Andrés **24** 511
Zevi, Bruno **16** 650; **23** 498; **25** 792
Zeylmans van Emmichhoven, F. W. **14** 295
Zeytinbagi, Fatih Cami **9** *526*, 526
Žeželj, Branko **28** 445
Zezuru **28** 620
Zhabka **21** *810*
Monastery **21** 810
Zhaksylykov, M. **17** 867
Zhakypov, Zh. **18** 568
Zhalu *see* SHALU
zhamatun see HALLS → types → *gavit'*
Zhambyl **6** *182*; **16** *105*; **17** *865*; **33** 640*
architecture **17** 866
Historical and Regional Museum **6** 284
mausoleum of 'Aysha Bibi **6** 207
ossuaries **23** 607
Zhamhayr **27** 701
Zhang (family) **6** 922
Zhang Cheng **7** 16
Zhang Daojun **6** 542
Zhang Daoling **6** 626
Zhang Daqian **7** 158; **14** 825; **30** 249; **33** 640–41*
works **6** 781; **30** 249; **33** *641*
Zhang Dunli **19** 504
Zhang Feng **22** 460; **33** 642*
Zhang Fu **32** 848
Zhang Geng **22** 459
Zhang Heng **12** 812
Zhang Hong **33** 642–3*
works **33** *643*
Zhanghua *see* CHANG-HUA
Zhanghuai, Prince **6** 652; **25** 780
Zhang Huaiguan **32** 836
Zhangjiapo **6** *615*; **33** 643–4*
Zhang Jizhi **6** 752; **14** 703; **17** 231; **25** 892
Zhang Kun **17** 189
Zhang Lian **12** 88
Zhanglingshan **19** 302
Zhang Lu **33** 644*, 657
Zhang Meixi **14** 826
Zhang Mingqi **6** 866
Zhang Qian **6** 320; **28** 718
Zhang Ran **12** 88
Zhang Ruitu **6** 761; **33** 644–5*
zhang sceptres *see under* SCEPTRES → types
Zhang Sengyou **6** 635, 803, 808; **30** 49
Zhang Shanzi **33** 640
Zhang Sheng **7** 35
Zhang Shengwen **6** 780
Zhang Shicheng **7** 50, 77
Zhang Tongzhi **7** 26
Zhang Wanfu **6** 786
Zhang Wu **6** 810
Zhang Xie (calligrapher) **6** 765
Zhang Xie (*fl c.* 1618) **7** 87
Zhang Xihuang **7** 59, 60
Zhang Xu **5** 36; **6** 747
Zhang Xuan **6** 808, 816; **33** 645*
Zhang Yanyuan **6** 630
works **2** 519; **6** 631, 816; **7** 148; **30** 288
on art **6** 821
on collectors **7** 152
on hanging scrolls **28** 311
on landscape painting **6** 796
on painters **6** 635
on painting **2** 519, 539; **6** 815
Zhang Yi *see* CHEUNG YEE
Zhang Yinwen **7** 152, 153
Zhang Yousheng **31** 251
Zhang Yu **6** 754
Zhang Yuguang **19** 502
Zhang Zeduan **6** 687, 789; **7** 36; **29** 67; **31** 704
Zhang Zhi **6** 770
Zhangzhou **7** 104
Zhangzi, Chongqing Temple **6** 717, 718
Zhang Zi **19** 856
Zhang Ziwan **6** 792
Zhangzong, Emperor (Jin; *reg* 1190-1234) **6** 817
Zhan Jingfeng **2** 95; **6** 824
Zhan Ziqian **33** 645–6*
Zhao Bingwen **6** 804
Zhao Boju **14** 137; **23** 215; **33** 648–9*
Zhao Bosu **33** 648
Zhao Buzhi **25** 72
Zhao Chang **33** 649*
Zhaocheng
Guangsheng Temples **6** 657; **30** 443
Lower Temple
Buddha Hall **14** 78
Feihong ta (Flying rainbow Pagoda) **6** 660
Upper Temple
Buddha Hall **6** 658
Feihong ta (Flying rainbow Pagoda) **23** 773
Zhao Danian *see* ZHAO LINGRANG
Zhao Feng **33** 646
Zhao Gan **33** 649–50*
works **33** *650*
Zhao Hong **21** 885
Zhao Lanbo **7** 152
Zhao Lin **33** 646
Zhao Lingrang **14** 859; **18** 752; **33** 650–51*
works **33** *651*
Zhao Mengfu **3** 516; **6** 752, 753–4, 773, 790, 800, 801, 809, 819, 824; **7** 66, 148, 151; **18** 327; **32** 845; **33** 319, 646–8*
groups and movements **23** 215
Zhao Mengfu—cont.
patrons and collectors **33** 319, 663
pupils **14** 822; **28** 586; **30** 287; **32** 850
works **6** *753*, 754, 755, 790, *790*, 800, 805; **7** 129, 632, IV1; **12** 50; **17** 231, 881; **33** 465, 570, *647*
Zhao Mengjian **6** 751, 803, 804, 805, 806; **33** 663
Zhao Qianli *see* ZHAO BOJU
Zhao Shaoang **7** 208; **14** 722; **19** 423
Zhaosu *see* MONGOLKURE
Zhao Wuji *see* ZAO WOU-KI
Zhao Xigu **19** 299
Zhao Yan **12** 88
works **12** *87*
Zhaoyang **7** 37
Zhao Yi **6** 769; **33** 646
Zhao Yong **32** 845; **33** 319, 646, 648*
Zhao Yuan **6** 817
Zhao Zhao **33** 320
Zhao Zhichen **7** 130
Zhao Zhifeng **6** 718
Zhao Zhiqian **6** 766, 802; **7** 131; **33** 651–2*
groups and movements **28** 554
patrons and collectors **17** 861
Zhao Zhong **6** 806
Zhao Zong **33** 661
Zhao Zuo **28** 588; **33** 652–3*
Zharkov, Pyotr (Gerasimovich) **27** 426
Zhar-tsvet *see* HEAT-COLOUR
Zha Shibiao **2** 95; **25** 73; **33** 496, 653*
works **25** *73*
Zhaxilhünbo *see* TASHILHUNPO
Zhdan-Nikolay **18** 35; **31** 546
Zhdanov *see* MARIUPOL'
Zhdanov, A. A., State University *see under* ST PETERSBURG
Zhdanov, Andrey **28** 917
Zhe *fang yi* **6** 844
Zhegin, Lev F. **6** 530; **20** 151; **27** 394
Zhejiang school **7** 130
Zhemchuzhnikov, Lev M. **31** 559
Zhendov, Alexandar **23** 16
Zheng, King (Qin) *see* QIN SHI HUANGDI
Zheng, Madam **33** 318
Zheng Banqiao *see* ZHENG XIE
Zheng Chenggong **30** 243
Zheng Daozhao **6** 744
Zhengding
Dacheng dian **6** 674
Longxing Temple **6** 654, *654*, 667, 669; **24** 289
Dabei Pavilion **6** 669
Maitreya Pavilion **27** 129
stele **6** 745
Yanghe Tower **6** 657
Zheng Fu **6** 763
Zheng He **6** 622
Zheng Min **2** 96
Zheng pai see ORTHODOX SCHOOL
Zheng Pei **17** 184
Zheng Shanxi *see* CHENG SHAN-HSI
Zheng Sixiao **6** 631, 806; **30** 49
works **6** *806*
Zheng Weiguo *see* CHENG WEI KWOK
Zheng Wenlin **33** 657
Zheng Xie **6** 801; **33** 653–4*
groups and movements **33** 497
works **6** 763; **25** 73; **33** *654*
Zheng Zhenduo **7** 121
Zheng Zhong **2** 95
Zhengzhou **6** *615*; **13** 333; **28** 603; **33** 654–6*
altars **1** 701
architecture **6** 646
bone **4** 314
Zhengzhou—cont.
bronze **4** 852; **6** 636, 835; **33** 655
graves **6** 694
Henan Provincial Museum **6** 734; **33** 656
jade **7** 3
oracle bones **33** 655–6
palace **6** 679
pottery **6** 869, 880, *880*; **33** 655
town walls **6** 663; **21** 593
see also DAHE CUN; GUXING ZHEN
Zhenjiang, Ganlu Temple **7** 24, 99
Zhenke **5** 112
Zhenla **18** 762
zhenyao kilns *see under* KILNS → types
Zhen Yuanyun **17** 189; **28** 495
Zherebtsov, Ivan **27** 374
Zhe school **6** 774; **19** 857; **21** 633; **23** 215, 582; **33** 435, 656–7*
members **6** 817; **18** 51, 751; **19** 426; **32** 840; **33** 437, 644, 667
works **6** 790; **33** *656*
Zhestovo Troitsky **27** 427
Zheverzheyev, Lerky **31** 583
Zheyi **5** 108
Zhezong, Emperor (Song; *reg* 1086-1101) **6** 699
tomb **6** *699*
zhi see under VESSELS → types
Zhi Cian **7** 62
Zhifangtou (Baoji) **3** 187
Zhilinsky, Dmitry (Dmitrevich) **27** 397; **33** 658*
zhilkombinat **12** 877
Zhi Loujiachan **5** 107
Zhilyardi, Dementy Ivanovich *see* GILLARDI, DOMENICO
Zhirovichi *see* ŻYRAVICY
Zhisheng *see* YOU KAN
Zhitkova, Marta (Dmitriyevna) **27** 411
Zhitomir **31** 545
Zhivotkov, Aleksandr **31** 560
Zhivskul'ptarkh **2** 603; **18** 388, 457, 619; **26** 504
Zhixian *see* WU BIN
Zhiyong **6** 745, 746, 770
Zhmuydzinavichyus, Antanas (Ionasovich) *see* ŽMUIDZINAVIČIUS, ANTANAS
Zhokhov, Vladimir **27** 418
Zholkva *see* NESTEROV
Zholtovsky, Ivan (Vladislavovich) **27** 378; **32** 661; **33** 658–9*
assistants **12** 876
collaboration **11** 358; **12** 878; **22** 173
competitions **7** 670
groups and movements **11** 358; **29** 529
pupils **18** 205; **21** 92
staff **3** 287
works **27** 379, 380, *380*
Zholudok *see* ŽALUDAK
Zhongbin *see* LI KAN
Zhongding **33** 655
Zhongdu *see* FENGYANG
Zhongfeng Mingben **5** 112; **6** 756; **17** 804
Zhong Li **33** 657
Zhongren **6** 783, 804
Zhongyan **7** 114
Zhong You **5** 36; **6** 755, 770
Zhongyuan wenwu **24** 435
Zhostovo **27** 424
Zhou Bin **7** 133, 134
works **7** *134*
Zhou Chen **33** 659–60*
pupils **25** 784; **30** 293
works **6** 810; **33** *659*
Zhou Daguan **2** 60, 61; **5** 459, 460, 472, 508; **6** 432
Zhou Enlai **19** 376
Zhou Fang **6** 808, 816; **33** 661–2*
attributions **33** *662*
Zhou Fenglai **25** 784

Zhou Hao **7** 61
Zhou Hu **33** 320
Zhou Jichang **6** 783
Zhoukoudian **7** 106, 159
  bone **4** 313
  houses **6** *689*
  windows **6** *690*
Zhou Kouren **7** 49
  works **7** *48*
Zhou Li **6** 817
Zhou Lianggong **1** 581; **2** 95; **22** 460; **33** 662–3*
Zhou Lijing **6** 820
Zhou Luyun *see* CHOU, IRENE
Zhou Mi **7** 153; **33** 663*
Zhou period *see under* CHINA → periods
Zhou Shangjun *see* ZHOU BIN
Zhou Shuren *see* LU XUN
Zhou Wenjing **33** 657
Zhou Wenju **6** 809; **33** 663–4*
Zhou Wenshu **7** 126
  works **7** *126*
Zhou Xi **33** 320
Zhou xian, Tomb of Zhu Tan **7** 38
Zhou Yu **7** 76
  dress **7** *76*
Zhou Yue **5** 407
Zhuangbai **6** *615*; **33** 664–5*
  bells **3** 626, *626*; **6** 849
  bronzes **6** 842, 844, *846*, 847, 848; **33** 664–5*
  ladles **6** *849*
Zhuang Su **19** 857; **33** 468
Zhuang Zhe *see* CHUANG CHE
Zhuangzi **6** 625, 634
Zhu Bang **33** 657
Zhu Bishan **7** 124; **33** 570
Zhu Ciqi **17** 775
Zhu Da **6** 687, 762, 791, 818; **25** 783; **33** 665–6*
  works **6** 762, 785, 801, *802*, 807; **33** *666*
Zhu Derun **18** 714; **33** 666–7*
Zhu Duan **33** 657, 667*
Zhudzden' Mausoleum **17** 866
Zhu Gui **7** 120
Zhu Haogu **6** 779
Zhu He **7** 59, 60
Zhuhong **5** 112
Zhujiaji *see under* SHOU XIAN
Zhu Jian **7** 101
Zhu Jingxuan **6** 822
Zhukov, A. F. **6** 526
Zhukov, Konstantin N. **28** 838
Zhukov, Pavel (Semyonovich) **33** 667*
Zhukov, V. G. **30** 467
Zhukovsky, Stanislav **25** 238
Zhukovsky, S. Yu **27** 392
Zhukovsky, Vasily (Andreyevich) **6** 279; **33** 667–8*
Zhumaty, Ivan **21** 811
Zhu Ming *see* CHU MING
Zhuping **33** 535
Zhu Qizhan **28** 553; **33** 668*
Zhuravlyov, B. N. **11** 245
Zhurnal izyashchnykh iskusstv **27** 443
Zhu Rui **6** 817
Zhu Sansong *see* ZHU ZHIZHENG
Zhu Shoucheng **7** 60
  works **7** *60*
Zhu Shunshui **31** 84
Zhu Tan **7** 38
Zhu Weibi **6** 867
Zhu Xi **5** 111; **6** 626, 800
Zhuxian **6** 621
Zhu Xiaosong *see* ZHU YING
Zhu Yan **5** 293
Zhu Ying **7** 59, 60
Zhuyuangou (Baoji) **3** 187; **6** 848, 849
Zhu Yuanzhang *see* HONGWU emperor
Zhu Yunming **6** 758; **33** 668*
  patrons and collectors **6** 772
  works **6** *758*; **14** 825; **17** 236
Zhu Zhizheng **7** 59, 60
  works **7** *59*
Zhwa lu *see* SHALU
Zia (NM) **22** 607
Ziani, Sebastiano, Doge of Venice (*reg* 1172-78) **5** 429; **32** 182
Zianzhen *see* GANJIN
Ziapur, Jalil **15** 898
Ziar nad Hronom
  Benedictine abbey church **14** 884
  Szentbenedek Castle **14** 904
Ziarnki, Jana **25** 675; **33** 668–9*
Zibliyat Ziggurat **33** 675
Zibo
  ceramic factory **6** 913
  glassworks **7** 82, 83
  porcelain **6** 907
Ziborghi, Giovanni **32** 549
Žiča **28** *437*
  Church of the Ascension **28** 446
  Church of the Saviour **9** 585; **28** 441
Žiče Monastery **5** 894; **28** 857, *858*, 861
Zichem, Viglius de **17** 643
Zichem Church **13** 182
Zichy (family) **14** 899; **15** 13
Zichy, Charlotte, Comtesse **28** 527
Zichy, Ferenc **13** 888; **20** 856
Zichy, István **12** 839
Zichy, Mihály **5** 876; **12** 326; **30** 915; **33** 669*
Zick (ii), Alexander **33** 671
Zick (i), Caspar, I (1623-82) **33** 670
Zick (i), Caspar, II (1650-1731) **33** 670
Zick (i), Christoph **33** 670
Zick (i), David, I **33** 670
Zick (ii), Gustav **33** 671
Zick (ii), Januarius **33** 671–2*
  collaboration **26** 529; **33** 671
  pupils **18** 498
  works **4** 891; **12** 391, 424; **33** *672*
Zick (ii), Johann (1702-62) **33** 671*
  patrons and collectors **13** 631
  pupils **33** 671
  works **4** 891; **15** 139; **27** 610; **33** 434
Zick (i), Johannes (*b* 1627) **33** 670
Zick (ii), Konrad **33** 671
Zick (i), Lorenz **33** 669–70*
  workshop **33** *670*
Zick (i), Peter, I (1571-1629) **12** 460; **33** 669
Zick (ii), Peter, II (1596-after 1652) **33** 670
Zick (i), Stephan **33** 670
Zickelbein, Horst **33** 672*
Zidanku, Tomb 1 **28** 310
Ziebland, Georg Friedrich **33** 673*
  collaboration **25** 789
  pupils **14** 227; **22** 273
  works **18** 123; **33** 282
Ziegelman, Robert **13** 763
Ziegler, Adolf **10** 413; **12** 396; **22** 710, 711
Ziegler, Gerhard **18** 186
Ziegler, Jakob **33** 673*
Ziegler, Johann **2** 512
Ziegler, Jörg **33** 674
Ziegler, Jules-Claude **3** 422; **8** 40, 654; **33** 673*
Ziegler, Karlheinz **13** 729
Ziegler, M. **32** 597
Ziegler, Nikolaus **28** 59
Ziegler, Walter **10** 563
Ziegler, Wilhelm **33** 673–4*
Ziegler carpets *see under* CARPETS → types
Ziegler & Co. **15** 899; **16** 482
Ziegler-Pellis Factory **30** 144
Zieliński, Tadeusz **17** 825
Zieliński, Tomasz **25** 138
Zielke, Willy **5** 535
Ziem, Félix (-François-Georges-Philibert) **33** 674*
Ziemski, Rajmund **32** 878
Zierglas see under GLASS → types
Ziericsen, Claes **26** 269
Zierikzee, St Lieven **13** 63; **22** 820
Ziesel, Eva **31** 639
Ziesenis, Anthonie **1** 808; **22** 859; **26** 30; **33** 268, 674
Ziesenis, Barthold W(ilhelm) H(endrik) **1** 813; **13** 607; **33** 674–5*
Ziesenis, (Johann) Friedrich Blasius **9** 753; **12** 405
Ziesenis, Johann Georg **11** 459; **12** 391; **23** 469; **33** 675*
Ziffer, Sándor **22** 434; **32** 419
Zifroni, Israel ben Daniel **14** 35; **17** 565
ziggurats **2** *236*; **15** *910*; **21** *283*, 283–4, 286; **23** 338; **33** 675–6*
Zigrosser, Carl **2** 366; **28** 465
Zigui **6** 878
Zijdebalen **8** 149; **12** 132; **33** 676*
Zijl, Gerrit Pietersz. van **32** 258
Zijl, Lambertus **22** 860; **33** 676*
  collaboration **18** 469; **21** 122
  groups and movements **4** 891; **21** 122
  works **22** 860, 861, 883
Zikaras, Juozas **19** 498
Zikaras, Teisutis **2** 754; **18** 64
Zikhron Ya'aqov, Mivtachim Resort Hotel **16** 566
Zil al-Sultan **12** 82
Zil'bershteyn, Il'ya **27** 440, 441
Zil'bershteyn, I. S. **27** 439
Zilcken, (Charles Louis) Philip **10** 563; **33** 677*
Zilcken, R. H. L. **33** 677
Zileti, Innocente **10** 868
Žilina **28** *848*, 849
  Franciscan church **28** 849
  synagogue **17** 548
Žilinčanová, Viera **28** 853
Zilio, Carlos **4** 720
Žilius, Vlacas **19** 500
Zille, (Rudolf) Heinrich **22** 430; **24** 671; **27** 871; **33** 677*
Ziller, Ernst (Moritz Theodor) **13** 358; **33** 677*
  villa **29** 885
  works **13** 349, 360
Zillmann, Adolf **33** 636
Zilveti, Luis Calderón *see* CALDERÓN ZILVETI, LUIS
Zilzer, Hajnalka **5** 86
Zimba **1** 404; **14** 378; **19** 72, 74
Zimbabwe **1** *214*; **33** 678–80*
  architecture **13** *336*; **33** 678
  education (art) **33** 680
  exhibitions **33** 680
  houses **1** 320
  masonry **1** 305; **13** 334, 336
  metal **1** 287
  museums **1** 440
  nephrite **16** 861
  painting **33** 678–9
  palaces **1** 308
  patronage **33** 679–80
  poles **1** 307
  rock art **1** 375; **27** 695–6
  sculpture **33** 679, *679*
  serpentine **33** 679, *679*
  stone **1** 292, 305; **33** 679
  walls **13** 334, 336, *336*
  wood-carvings **33** 679
Zimbabwe Insight **24** 430
Zimbalo, Giuseppe **16** 640; **19** 28
Zimblytė, Kazimiera **19** 500
Zimdal, Helge **1** 475
Zimenko, Vladislav **25** 653
Zimitrov, Zakhary (Khristovich) *see* ZOGRAPH, ZAKHARY (KHRISTOVICH)
Zimmer, Bernd **12** 397
Zimmer, Hans-Peter **29** 435
Zimmer, Heinrich R(obert) **15** 211; **32** 120; **33** 680*
Zimmer, Klaus **2** 763; **33** 680–81*
Zimmer, Salomé **12** 397
Zimmerman, Friedrich **10** 396
Zimmerman, Jack **22** 795
Zimmerman, Johann Georg von **23** 423
Zimmerman, Josef, & Co. **9** 703
Zimmerman, Marie **31** 651
Zimmermann, Albert **4** 838; **21** 317; **23** 697
Zimmermann, Clemens **8** 790
Zimmermann, Dominikus **33** 681, 683–4*
  collaboration **33** 172, 681, 682
  groups and movements **26** 497
  pupils **9** 183
  works **7** 258; **10** 215; **12** 372; **23** 636; **29** 838; **32** 823; **33** *683*
Zimmermann, Elias **33** 681*
Zimmermann, Franz Dominikus **33** 681*
Zimmermann, Franz Michael **33** 681*
Zimmermann, Johann Baptist **22** 302; **33** 681–3*
  assistants **10** 860
  collaboration **8** 288, 290; **9** 746; **29** 761; **31** 511; **33** 172, 683
  groups and movements **26** 497, 498
  patrons and collectors **22** 309; **33** 278
  pupils **31** 26
  works **11** 125; **12** 405, 411; **15** 139; **22** 309; **28** 110; **29** 838, *838*; **33** 172, *682*
Zimmermann, Johann Joseph **33** 681*
Zimmermann, Jorg F. **12** 441
Zimmermann, Joseph Anton **12** 170
Zimmermann, Juliette **9** 332
Zimmermann, Robert **26** 369
Zimmermann & Co. **12** 452
Zimmern, von (family) **29** 787
Zimmerreimer, Paul **27** 657
Zimnicea **30** 772
Zimno, Church of the Dormition **31** 550
Zinacantan **21** 249
Zinat al-Nisa Begum **8** 675
zinc **4** 688; **21** 320; **33** 684*
  alloys
    copper **4** 680–81, 848; **12** 621; **21** 319; **24** 61
    gold **12** 865
  historical and regional traditions
    Bantu peoples **1** 368
    Indian subcontinent **15** 713
    Islamic **16** 363
    United States of America **31** 653
    Vietnam **32** 486
  patinas **21** 330*
  uses
    coins **32** 486
    dolls' furniture **31** 265
    dyeing **30** 558
    gilding **24** 55
    glazes **6** 329
    lithography *see* ZINCOGRAPHS
    mouldings **22** 211
    papier mâché **24** 61
    pigments **24** 797–8*
    pipes (smoking) **1** 368
    printing plates **10** 379, 548, 562; **25** 612
zinc green *see under* PIGMENTS → types
Zincgref, Julius Wilhelm **21** 152
Zincirli **1** *821*, 893; **2** 283; **30** *180*, 194; **31** 456; **33** 684–5*, *685*
  architecture **1** 831
  ivory-carvings **1** 870
  reliefs **13** 487; **30** 187, 190
  sculpture **1** 833; **21** 301; **29** 395; **30** 187, 189
  seals **1** 858
Zincke, Christian Friedrich **21** 641; **33** 685*
  pupils **21** 409
  teachers **4** 245; **10** 857
Zincke, Christian Friedrich—cont.
  works **7** 814
Zincke, Otmar **8** 422
Zincke, Paul Christian **10** 857
zincographs **19** 488; **33** 685
zinc oxide **10** 559; **23** 786; **24** 797; **30** 558
zinc yellow *see under* PIGMENTS → types
Zinder **1** *381*
  museum **23** 128
Zingaro, Lo *see* SOLARIO, ANTONIO
Zingg, Adrian **12** 392, 500; **20** 914
Zini, Filippo **6** 361
Ziniare **22** 198
  dolls **22** *198*
Žinkovy **8** 400
Zinner, Bartholomäus **5** 40; **13** 832
Zinner, Jan Anton **6** 363
Zinnick, Gilbert van **3** 546; **33** 685–6*
Zinnow, Gustav **14** 87
Zinov'yev, Nikolay Mikhaylovich **23** 837
Zinov'yev, Stepan **27** 387
Zinquevie **32** 205
Zinther **32** 775
Zintner, Bartoloměj **13** 661, 662
Zintu Museum *see under* LUSAKA
Zinzendorf (family) **4** 507
Zinzendorf, Erdmuth Dorothea, Gräfin von **22** 80
Zinzendorf, Nikolaus Ludwig, Graf von **22** 80
Zio, Francesco **16** 835; **23** 355, 876; **28** 216
Zipaquirá Cathedral **7** 605
Zipelius, Georges **33** 711
Ziranek, Silvia **33** 686*
Zirc Cistercian Abbey **14** 887
zirconium **12** 270, I; **17** 530
ziricote **3** *624*
Zirid **13** 281, 285; **33** 686*
  see also:
    AL-MU'IZZ IBN BADIS, Ruler
    BADIS, Ruler
    BULUGGIN, Ruler
Zirnack, Arthur **30** 103
Ziros, Hagia Paraskevi **8** 157
Zisenis, Johann Georg *see* ZIESENIS, JOHANN GEORG
zitan **7** 30, *41*, 141
Zítek, Josef **33** 687*
  assistants **10** 795; **28** 175
  collaboration **25** 429; **28** 133, 176
  pupils **16** 902; **29** 652; **33** 162
  staff **25** 151
  works **8** 379, 400; **25** 429, *429*; **29** 600; **33** 37
Žitence **26** 638
zithers **5** 509; **15** 817; **17** 396, 397, *397*; **22** 376; **32** 489
Žitňanský, M. **28** 850
Zittau, Weberei Neumann **25** 402
Zitterbarth (family) **14** 889
Zitterbarth, Henrik **33** 687
Zitterbarth, János, I (1776-1824) **33** 687
Zitterbarth, János, II (1826-82) **33** 687
Zitterbarth, Mátyás, I (*fl* 1789-1803) **33** 687
Zitterbarth, Mátyás, II (*fl* 1804-18) **33** 687
Zitterbarth, Mátyás, III (1803-67) **5** 82; **33** 687*
Zitzmann, Julius **18** 237
Ziveri, Alberto **16** 680; **21** 87; **28** 319
Zīverts, Ernest **12** 825
Zıviyya *see* ZIWIYEH
Živković, Bogosav **22** 441
Život **2** 546; **7** 772
Život a mythus **2** 546
Zívr, Ladislav **8** 387

Ziwiyeh 2 102; 15 *901*, 905, 922; 33 688*
  bowls 33 *688*
  forgeries 1 896
  ivory-carvings 1 870
  metalwork 15 919; 17 879; 28 322
Ziwiyeh Treasure 1 875, 894
Zix, Benjamin 9 13, 18
Ziya *see* GÜRAN, NAZMI ZIYA
Ziyadat Allah, Governor (*reg* 817-38) (Aghlabid) 16 156; 17 730
Ziyad ibn Abihi 16 145
Ziyad ibn Abi Sufyan 3 338
Ziyadid 33 583
  see also:
  HUSAYN IBN SALAMA, Ruler
  MUHAMMAD IBN ZIYAD, Ruler
Ziyar, Khusrawgird minaret 21 *627*, 627
Zizhao *see* SHENG MAO
Zlatá Koruna Monastery 8 376; 13 57
Zlatar, Matey 5 160
  works 5 *160*
Zlati, Zafir 5 160
Zlatnó glassworks 15 4; 28 856
  works 15 *4*
Zlatny Pyasutsy 5 150
Žleby Castle 8 379
Zlēkas Church 18 848
Zlín 8 380, 423, 425
Zliten 27 57, 63
Zlobina-Stroganova, Anna 29 54
Zloković, Milan 19 883; 28 444
Zmajević, Andrija, Archbishop of Bar 18 196
Zmeiny Kurgan 4 111
Zmeivki 31 556
Zmeták, Ernest 28 853, 854
Zmeyskaja Dolmen 27 432
Zmierhrodski, K. 3 530
Žmuidzinavičius, Antanas 26 403
Żmurko, Franciszek 25 107
Znaim Altar, Master of the 2 799
Znamensk'y Monastery
  Church of the Trinity 31 550
Znojmo 8 376, 377
  chapel of St Catherine 8 388, *389*
Zoagli 12 285
Zōami Hisatsugu 17 393
Zoan Andrea 10 384; 20 322; 24 248; 33 689*
Zobel, Eberhard, Abbot of Fiecht 14 834
Zóbel, Fernando 29 354; 31 174; 33 689–90*
Zobel, George 24 637
Zobernig, Heimo 2 804
Zobole, Ernest 32 786
Zoboli, Giacomo 33 690*
Zocchi, Giuseppe 16 674; 33 690–91*
  patrons and collectors 11 192; 12 355
  reproductive prints by others 11 *180*; 12 582; 21 831
Zocha, Friedrich Wilhelm von 12 372, 373
Zocha, Johann Wilhelm von 11 886; 12 372; 33 691
Zocha, Karl Friedrich von 11 886; 26 257; 33 691*
Zocher, Jan David, the elder (1763-1817) 12 132; 22 828; 29 8; 33 691
Zocher, Jan David, the younger (1791-1870) 22 828; 28 132; 33 691–2*
  works 1 803; 22 828; 29 8, 433; 31 488, 770
Zocher, Karel George 33 691
Zocher, Louis Paul 1 803; 11 885; 31 488; 33 691, 692
Zocolino, Matteo *see* ZACCOLINI, MATTEO
Zodchiy 27 580; 28 628; 30 202
Zodiac 24 449
zodiacs 2 648; 5 427; 9 603
Žodžiks, Imants 33 378
Zoe, Empress of Byzantium (*reg* 1028-50) 9 *577*, 638
Zōen 17 417
Zoffany, Johan (Joseph) 5 419; 8 83; 15 654; 17 575; 33 692–5*
  collaboration 33 217
  exhibitions 19 586
  methods 9 212
  paintings 9 *15*
  patrons and collectors 3 179; 7 786; 8 83; 12 164; 14 144; 26 335; 31 245
  pupils 3 489; 8 20; 32 835
  reproductive prints by others 9 506; 21 417
  works 2 164; 7 785, 786, 787; 9 14, 17; 10 249, 365; 11 *429*; 13 302, 303, 541; 19 *620*, 621; 30 783; 33 *693*, *694*
Zoffoli, Giacomo 13 303; 29 572
Zogolovitch, Roger 13 225
Zograf, Pimen 25 343
Zograf, Radul 25 340
Zografi, Athanas 1 540
Zografi, Kostandin 1 540
Zografski, Ǵorǵi 19 884
Zograph 26 719
Zograph, Zakhary (Khristovich) 26 392; 27 686; 33 695*
Zographos, Panagiotis 13 359
Zographski, Khristo 5 163
Zohanne de Franza 20 323
Zohar, Israel 33 695–6*
Zohn, Alejandro 13 731; 21 381; 33 696*
Zoilos, Gaius Julius 2 220
Zoïs, A. 32 71
Zois, Žiga 28 862
Zōkei bijutsuka kyōkai (Plastic Artists' Association) 17 759
Zōkin 17 125
Zōkyū Gakuō *see* GAKUŌ ZŌKYŪ
Zola, Emile 15 153, 157; 24 671; 33 696*
  collaboration 29 612
  collections 17 440
  groups and movements 26 55
  personal collection 6 366; 27 206
  works 2 530; 11 545; 22 685, 686, 687
  illustrated 7 690; 14 457; 15 58
Zola Predosa, Villa Albergati 5 281
  frescoes 5 *280*
Zoldhalompuszta 28 323
Żołkwia 25 122
Zoll, Kilian (Christoffer) 18 800; 30 79; 33 697*
Zoller, Franz Anton 31 358
Zollern, Joseph Niclas II, Graf von 33 674
Zollikofen Mormon Temple 30 450
Zollikon 30 143
Zöllner, Louis 12 634
Zolotova, Ekaterina 5 159
Zolotoye Runo *see* GOLDEN FLEECE
Zolotoy vek 27 444
Zoltán Veress Factory 15 5
Zólyom *see* ZVOLEN
Zombo 33 485
Zombory, Lajos 30 211
Zomer, Jan Pietersz. *see* ZOOMER, JAN PIETERSZ.
Zompini, Gaetano Gherardo 6 36; 33 613, 697–8*
Zona, Antonio 8 135
zonaria 9 643, *644*
  see also CINGULA
Zondadari, Chigi, Cardinal *see* CHIGI ZONDADARI, Cardinal
Zong Bing 6 787, 796
Zongolopoulos, George 13 355; 33 698*
Zonjić, Jovan 22 18
zonseinuri *see* LACQUER → types → filled-in *urushi*
Zontal, Jorge 12 275
Zoo, Team *see* TEAM ZOO
zoological books 28 206
Zoom 24 449
Zoomer, Jan Pietersz. 22 904; 25 631; 33 345, 700*
zoomorphic calligraphy *see under* CALLIGRAPHY → types
zoophori 33 700*
zoopraxiscope *see* PHOTOGRAPHY → instruments
zoos 12 61; 33 698–700*, *699*
  see also MENAGERIES
Zopfstil 12 425; 28 859
Zoppelli, Giovanni Maria 26 818
Zoppo *see* BENEDETTO DI BINDO
Zoppo, Marco 4 276; 33 700–703*
  patrons and collectors 5 792
  teachers 23 754; 29 436
  works 33 *701*, *702*
Zoppo, Rocco 20 684; 24 525
Zora, Giovanni Gregori de *see* SCHARDT, JOHANN GREGOR VAN DER
Zorach, Marguerite 7 875; 26 488; 33 703*
Zorach, William 7 875; 33 703*
Zorava Church 9 539
Zoravar 2 426
Zorawar Singh, Maharaja of Bikaner (*reg* 1736-45) (Rajput) 15 609
Żórawski, Juliusz 32 872; 33 703–4*
Zorés, Ferdinand 16 53
Zorio, Gilberto 2 526; 33 704*
Zoritchak, Jan 3 595
Zorn (family) 30 311
Zorn, Anders (Leonard) 30 79, 80, 81, 91, 114, 120; 33 704–5*, *705*
  groups and movements 3 628
  patrons and collectors 30 730
  teachers 30 275
  works 11 475, *475*; 30 113
Zoroastrianism 15 908; 33 705–8*
  art forms
    dress 16 453
    fire-holders 33 *708*
    iconography 6 192–3*, *193*; 33 706–8*
    ossuaries 6 193; 23 606–9*, *608*
    relief sculpture 23 *608*; 33 *707*
    sanctuaries 15 913
    towers 33 *707*
  regional traditions
    Afghanistan 1 188
    Central Asia, Western 6 186, 192–3*
    Indian subcontinent 15 202, 204
Zoroku Hata *see* HATA ZOROKU
Zōroku I (1735-94) 17 412; 33 709*
  works 33 *709*
Zōroku II (1772-1819) 17 412; 33 709*
Zōroku III (1791-1843) 17 413; 18 191; 33 709*
Zōroku IV (1826-75) 33 709*
Zōroku V (1866-1909) 33 709*
Zorrilla de San Martin, José Luis 31 755, 758
Zorrilla de San Martin, Juan, Museo *see under* MONTEVIDEO → museums
Zorzi, Marco 3 660; 7 517
Zorzi da Castelfranco *see* GIORGIONE
Zorzis 25 335
Zorzon *see* GIORGIONE
Zoser *see* DJOSER
Zosima 29 51
Zosimos 21 330
Zötl, Aloys 30 23
Zotov, Vladimir (Alekseyevich) 27 423
Zotto, Antonio da 29 885
Zoubaloff Sketchbook *see under* SKETCHBOOKS → individual manuscripts
Zoubek, Olbram 8 388
Zouch, Edward 10 316
Zou Che 12 899
Zoude, Louis 3 595; 24 57
Zoude, Louis & Cie 3 595
Zoude, Sébastien 3 594
Zoukes, Demetrios 21 345
Zoumbaria 2 160
Zoutleeuw, St Leonardus 3 569; 13 160; 26 645; 30 732
  sculpture 13 110
  tabernacle 3 *568*
Zoutsloot 22 881
Zou xian 6 877
Zou Yigui 6 39; 13 839
Zou Zhe 22 459
Zovodovsky, Ivan 31 563
Zovuni, SS Paul and Peter 2 425, 426
Zozaya, J. 28 511
Zozlov, Sergey 27 427
Zrenjanin 28 456
  National Museum 28 459
Zríny, Miklós 14 886
Zrinyi (family) 15 15
Zrinyi, Miklós 14 899; 15 15
Zrumeczky, Dezső 18 394; 33 699
Zrzavý, Jan 25 433; 33 710*
  groups and movements 2 546; 8 250, 393; 31 792
  works 8 249, 393, 394
Zrze
  Monastery 9 630; 19 882; 28 448
  St Nicholas 28 449
Zschokke, Alexander 22 921
Zsennye 3 111
Zsolnay 22 59
Zsolnay, Ignác 15 2; 33 710
Zsolnay, Miklós (*fl* 1851) 15 2; 33 710
Zsolnay, Miklós (*d* 1922) 33 710
Zsolnay, Vilmos 15 2; 19 30; 33 710
Zsolnay Ceramics Factory 5 85; 15 2, 3; 20 447; 33 710*
  designers 20 518; 26 419
  works 15 *2*
Zuan da Milano *see* RUBINO, GIOVANNI
Zuan de Cologna 17 481
Zuane Giacomo 10 765
Zuanne, Jacopo di *see* JACOPO DI ZUANNE
Zuazo (Ugalde), Secundino 12 58; 29 273; 33 711*
Zubara Museum 25 777
Zubaru (family) 21 81
Zubayda (Arabia) 2 268
Zubayda (Abbasid) 17 830
Zuber, Czesław 25 125
Zuber, Jean 33 711
Zuberbühler, Carlos 2 404
Zuber & Cie 10 187; 27 319; 32 812, 816; 33 711*
  works 32 IV3
Zuberi, Rabia 23 802
Züberlin, Jakob 33 711–12*
  works 33 *712*
al-Zu'bi, Hazim 17 655
Zubi, Ozzir 23 800, 802, 803
Zubieta, Pedro de 29 334
Zubkov, N. 21 811
Zubov, Aleksey (Fyodorovich) 27 389, 442; 33 713*
  works 27 *574*
Zubov, Fyodor 27 387; 33 712–13*
  pupils 33 712
  works 22 177
Zubov, Ivan 33 712–13*
Zubov, Osip 33 712
Zubov, Platon, Prince 14 222
Zucca, Edward 31 634
Zuccalli (family) 12 370; 32 435
Zuccalli, Domenico Christoferus 33 713
Zuccalli, Enrico 2 782; 33 276, 713–14*
  architecture 3 229; 4 324; 8 32; 12 371, 372; 22 299; 28 836; 33 276
    palaces 8 290; 22 308; 23 811; 33 277
  assistants 32 602
  patrons and collectors 22 308; 28 109, 110
Zuccalli, Gaspare 33 713
Zuccalli, Giovanni Battista 33 713
Zuccalli, Johann Kaspar 2 781; 27 661; 28 199; 32 822; 33 276, 713
Zuccarelli, Francesco 32 194; 33 714–15*
  patrons and collectors 12 355
    Augustus III, King of Poland (*reg* 1733-63) 1 633
    Borromeo, Vitaliano VI, Conte (1620-90) 4 427; 16 562
    Cowper, George Nassau Clavering, 3rd Earl 8 83
    Curzon, Nathaniel, 1st Baron Scarsdale 8 281
    Fetherstonhaugh, Matthew 11 39
    George III, King of Great Britain (*reg* 1760-1820) 14 144
    List, Herbert 19 478
    Smith, Joseph, Consul (*c.* 1674-1770) 28 884
    Tessin, Carl Gustav, Count 30 523
  reproductive prints by others 3 308; 6 91; 12 582; 32 652, 689
  teachers 2 26
  works 10 351; 18 711; 24 865; 28 755; 32 615, 900; 33 *715*
Zuccaro, Federico 1 102; 2 523; 16 665; 21 759; 24 489; 26 770, 841, 842; 29 280; 31 740; 33 716, 718–20*
  architecture 16 771
  assistants 5 735; 26 89
  collaboration 1 551; 3 101, 858; 5 172; 8 4, 268; 19 371; 20 840; 21 849; 22 6, 716; 29 428; 33 718
  drawings 1 *663*; 9 221; 26 *770*; 33 *720*
  frames 11 391
  house 1 662; 2 547, *547*
  interior decoration 5 684; 19 687; 33 718
  methods 21 766
  paintings
    frescoes
      Cappella Pucci (Santa Trinità dei Monti, Rome) 24 419
      Cathedral of S Maria del Fiore (Florence) 11 198
      Frangipani Chapel (S Marcello al Corso, Rome) 33 717
      Grimani Chapel (S Francesco della Vigna, Venice) 11 722
      Oratory of S Luca del Gonfalone (Rome) 33 *719*
      Palazzo Farnese (Rome) 26 838
      Palazzo Mattei di Paganica (Rome) 20 839
      Palazzo Sodalizio Piceni (Rome) 2 493
      Vatican Palace (Rome) 26 818; 27 480
      Villa Aldobrandini (Frascati) 1 596
      Villa Farnese (Caprarola) 3 858; 5 684; 15 84; 32 506
    oil
      allegorical 1 664
      altarpieces 10 503
      ceiling 26 770
      portraits 30 358
      religious 10 502; 26 823
    religious 14 517

Zuccaro, Federico—cont.
patrons and collectors
Charles-Emanuel I, 11th Duke of Savoy (reg 1580-1630) 28 6; 31 443
Dudley, Robert, 1st Earl of Leicester (c. 1532-88) 9 367
Farnese, Alessandro, Cardinal (1520-89) 10 810
Francesco-Maria II, Duke of Urbino 27 274
Gregory XIII, Pope (reg 1572-85) 13 628
Grimani, Giovanni, Patriarch of Aquileia 13 659
Grimani, Marino, Cardinal, Patriarch of Aquileia 13 658
Guidobaldo II, 4th Duke of Urbino (reg 1538-74) 27 274
Lely, Peter 19 124
Mattei, Alessandro 20 840
Philip II, King of Spain (reg 1556-98) 13 922; 28 709
Pius IV, Pope (reg 1559-66) 25 7
Ribera (i), Juan de, Archbishop of Valencia 26 306
Vecchietti, Bernardo 32 106
pupils 6 364; 12 532; 22 715; 24 239; 28 61; 32 114
reproductive prints by others 1 551, 662; 7 899; 19 257; 27 212
restorations 26 818
writings 9 7; 13 808; 31 16, 299
Zuccaro, Francesco 31 362
Zuccaro, Ottaviano 33 716
Zuccaro, Taddeo 26 770; 33 716–20*
assistants 33 718
collaboration 3 858; 8 268; 11 268; 22 6; 28 658; 33 718, 720
drawings 9 221
patrons and collectors 10 753, 810, 811; 19 124; 20 839; 25 7; 27 274
pupils 31 362
reproductive prints by others 1 551; 7 899; 20 812
works 5 684, 789, 887; 10 130; 15 84; 20 839; 24 419; 26 818, 838; 27 653; 32 506; 33 716, 717, 719
Zuccati, Sebastiano 31 32
Zucchi, Andrea 10 394; 19 732; 30 676; 32 356, 689; 33 721
Zucchi, Antonio 17 851; 33 721*
collaboration 1 140; 5 687; 33 721
groups and movements 10 643
patrons and collectors 8 281; 11 430
pupils 14 115
teachers 1 784
works 10 643
Zucchi, Carlo (1682-1767) 18 849; 19 732; 24 842; 33 721
Zucchi, Carlos (d 1856) 2 395; 31 753
works 31 753
Zucchi, Francesco 3 385; 6 343; 22 388; 32 501; 33 721
Zucchi, Giuseppe Carlo 33 721
Zucchi, Jacopo 3 231; 33 721–2*
attributions 26 827
collaboration 32 14, 17
works 26 818
Zucchi, Lorenzo 11 241; 33 721
Zucchi, Marco Antonio 33 586
Zucco, Accio 10 725
Zuccoli, Luigi 30 512, 513
Zucconi, Giovanni Battista 22 481
Zudrazil, Adolf 17 897
Zuetina 30 181
Zug 30 124
fountains 30 136
St Oswald 30 126
Zug, Szymon Bogumił 12 134; 32 871; 33 722*
assistants 18 490
patrons and collectors 2 414–15; 25 121, 211, 212
pupils 32 678
works 1 482; 18 693; 23 113; 25 99
Zügel, Heinrich von 19 283
Zugno, Francesco 33 721
Zugravul, Radu 26 713
al-Zuhra 33 520
Zuhrs, Hugo 30 81
Zuichō Tachibana see TACHIBANA, ZUICHŌ
Zuid-Holland factory 7 552; 22 884
Zuivere Beelding 5 44
Zukas, Cynthia 33 602
Žukas, Vaidas 19 500
Zukau Church 1 519
Žukoŭski, Stanislaŭ 3 529
Zukowo Kartuzy 25 111
Zula 14 376, 378
Żuławska, Hanna 25 123
Zuleta, Guillermo González see GONZÁLEZ ZULETA, GUILLERMO
Zulian, Girolamo 5 626
Zulkifli Dahlan 20 172
zulla 16 144
Zulliani, Candido 28 859
Züllich, Rudolf Czélkúti 14 895, 896
Zuloaga, Blas 29 343
Zuloaga, Daniel 30 506; 32 125
Zuloaga, Eusebio 2 456, 468; 29 343
Zuloaga (y Zabaleta), Ignacio 20 68; 21 387; 29 285; 33 722–3*
groups and movements 10 822
patrons and collectors 1 529; 28 569; 31 757
pupils 8 132
Zuloaga, Plácido 2 457, 468; 29 343
Zuloaga, Ramón 29 343
Zülow, Franz von 33 723*
Zulu 33 723–5*, 724, 725
aprons 1 348; 3 442; 33 724
architecture 1 414
armlets 1 351
beads 1 297; 29 104; 33 723, 724–5
beadwork 1 418, 419; 3 442
brass 33 723
buckets 33 724
clubs (weapons) 1 362
colour 7 635
dolls 1 419
dress 33 724–5, 725
figurines 1 273
headdresses 1 351; 33 724
headrests 1 366, 416, 417; 33 724, 724
huts 1 308, 311
leather 33 724
plates 1 417; 33 724
pots 1 369, 418
sculpture 1 323; 29 104
shields 1 362
skirts 33 724
spoons 1 369
staffs 1 417, 417; 33 724
wood-carvings 1 414; 33 724, 724
Zulu, Vuminkosi 29 112
Zumárraga, Juan 21 395
Zumárraga, Miguel de 29 268
Zumaya, Francisco de 9 695
Zumaya, Villa Zuloaga 33 723
Zumbigo y Salcedo, Bartolomé 10 498
Zumbo, Gaetano (Giulio) 33 725–6*
patrons and collectors 16 749; 21 29
pupils 31 187
Zumbo, Gaetano (Giulio)—cont.
works 33 3, 726
Zumbusch, Kasper Clemens 2 803; 32 445; 33 726–7*
pupils 14 525
works 2 802, 803
Zumbusch, Ludwig von 33 727
Zummo, Gaetano (Giulio) see ZUMBO, GAETANO (GIULIO)
Zum schwarzen Ferkel 22 291
zun see under VESSELS → types
Zünd, Amman 16 901
Zünd, Matthias 16 901
Zünd, Robert 30 125, 134; 33 727*
Zündt, Matthias 12 455; 23 310, 312; 33 727*
Zünfte see GUILDS
Zungu, Tito 1 430; 29 110
works 1 431
Zunhua
Dong ling see Eastern Tombs
Eastern Tombs 6 662, 704, 732
Dong ding ling 6 705
pailou 23 780
Tai ling 6 704
Yu ling 6 705
Zuni (NM; USA) 22 544, 567, 568
metalwork 22 614
pottery 22 607
water pots 22 608
Zuni (people) 22 360, 676
craftsmen and artists 22 676
historiography 22 673
jewellery 22 615, 629, 669
metalwork 22 614
pottery 22 608, 608–9, 668, 676
Zunie, Catalina 22 608
Zúñiga, Diego Ortiz de see ORTIZ DE ZÚÑIGA, DIEGO
Zúñiga, Francisco 1 783; 8 17; 33 493, 728*
Zúñiga, Inés-Francisca de 22 21
Zuñiga, Juan de, Viceroy of Naples 6 98
Zúñiga, Lorenzo Bautista de 31 195
Zúñiga, Manuel de Acevedo y, 6th Conde de Monterrey see MONTERREY, MANUEL, 6th Conde de
Zúñiga, Manuel María 33 728
Zúñiga, Mateo de 13 764; 33 728*
Zúñiga Figueroa, Carlos 14 715
Zuno, José Guadalupe see GUADALUPE ZUNO, JOSÉ
Zuntz-Harag, Hanna 16 568
Zuo Bai 7 114
Zuojiakongshan 7 46
Župansky, Vladimir 28 836
Zurbarán, Francisco de 11 710; 28 515; 29 281; 33 728–33*
attributions 18 840
collaboration 2 291; 25 91
frames 11 488, 488, 490–91
groups and movements 30 456
paintings 20 71; 24 391
battle 32 129
bodegones 29 667
history 14 516
mythological 29 303
portraits 2 411
religious 9 110; 13 732; 14 469; 24 506; 33 729, 731
still-lifes 29 340, 667; 33 730
patrons and collectors 28 515; 32 129
Alexander I, Emperor of Russia (reg 1801-25) 26 733
Bankes, William John 3 179
Butler, Charles (1822-1910) 5 311
Cambó y Batlle, Francisco de Asís 5 509
Carol I, King of Romania (reg 1866-1914) 5 792
Carraquiri, Nazario 5 871
Zurbarán, Francisco de
patrons and collectors—cont.
Esterházy, Pál, Prince (1786-1866) 10 530
Ferdinand VII, King of Spain (reg 1808; 1814-33) 4 566
Ford, Richard 11 304
Galliera, Maria de Ferrari, Duchessa di 4 811
Gardner, Isabella Stewart 12 147
Godoy (y Alvárez de Faria), Manuel, Príncipe de la Paz 12 839
Gomes Figueira, Baltazar 2 878
Hieronymites 14 517
Jovellanos, Gaspar Melchor de 17 673
Las Marismas del Guadalquivir, Alejandro María Aguado y Ramírez de Estemoz, Marqués de 18 811
Lázaro Galdiano, José 18 899
López Cepero, Manuel 19 658
Louis-Philippe, King of the French (reg 1830-48) 23 521; 30 385
Marquand, Henry G(urdon) 20 461
Montpensier, Antoine-Marie-Philippe-Louis de Bourbon, Duc de 23 523
Museo Provincial (Cádiz) 5 368
Pourtalès-Gorgier, James-Alexandre, Comte de 25 383
Salamanca (y Mayol), José, Marqués de 27 607
Soult (Jean de Dieu), Maréchal 29 96
Standish, Frank Hall 29 535
pupils 19 658; 33 733
reproductive prints by others 12 28
Zurbarán, Juan de 33 733*
Zürcher Arbeitsgruppe für Städtebau 28 190
Zürcher Konkreten 30 135; 33 737
Zürcher Kunstgesellschaft 33 736
Zürcher Werkbund 14 24
Zurich 26 908; 30 124; 33 733–7*, 735
Alberto Giacometti Collection 33 737
Anker Bank 30 153
art forms and materials
architecture 4 789; 30 140
Bibles 4 9
ceramics 30 143; 33 737*
fountains 30 136
furniture 30 142
gold 30 145
heraldry 14 416
interior decoration 30 141
manuscript illumination 12 382
metalwork 30 146, 147
painting 30 131, 135
stucco 30 136
wall paintings 30 129
Bank Julius Bär 30 153
Bibliothek des Instituts für Schweizerische Kunstgeschichte 30 156
Bleicherhof 27 658
Cabaret Pantagruel 8 433
clergy house 4 790
collections 17 582
education (art) 30 155
Eidgenössische Technische Hochschule (ETH) 21 406; 30 127
Galerie Koller 30 153
Grosser Tonhallesaal 7 687
Grossmünster 7 269; 26 635; 30 134
Haus zum Loch 14 420
houses 30 128
Kunstgewerbeschule 30 155–6*
Muraltengut 30 127
Zurich—cont.
museums
Kunstgewerbemuseum 15 745; 30 155
Kunsthaus 30 127, 155
archives 2 371
collections 5 132; 21 406, 710; 30 153
exhibitions 15 747
Museum für Gestaltung 30 156
Museum Rietberg 15 748; 16 789
collections 1 437; 6 735, 826; 7 155; 15 742, 745; 29 240
Schweizerisches Landesmuseum 13 842; 30 127, 154, 155; 33 736
collections 29 516; 30 332
library 30 156
Weapons Room 14 614
Völkerkundemuseum der Universität see under ZURICH → Universität Zurich
Polytechnikum 23 340
Rathaus 9 754
Schweizerisches Institut für Kunstwissenschaft 30 152, 153
Siedlung Neubühl 30 128, 128
Stiftung Sammlung E. G. Bührle 30 153
Swiss Provinces Exhibitions, 1939
Zementhalle 7 696
Union Bank of Switzerland 30 152, 153
Universität Zürich 30 127
Völkerkundemuseum der Universität 29 240
Zoologisches Museum 30 155
Weber, Heidi, Haus see Zentrum Le Corbusier-Heidi Weber
Zentralbibliothek 2 371; 30 154
Zentrum Le Corbusier-Heidi Weber 30 128
Zunfthaus zur Meisen 30 127
Zürich, Hans von 2 606
Zurich Faience and Porcelain Factory 29 73; 30 144; 33 737
Zurita, José Lorenzo 32 172
Zurlauben, Beát 13 871; 19 9
Zurletta, Giovanni Antonio 13 293
Zurlinger, Wolfgang 2 819
works 2 820
Zur Mühlen, Rudolf Julius von 10 539
Zürn (family) 2 801; 12 402, 403; 23 425
Zürn, David 12 404; 33 738, 739
Zürn, Hans, the elder (1555/60-1631) 33 738, 739
Zürn, Hans, the younger (1585/90-1624) 33 738
Zürn, Hans Jakob 8 626; 33 738, 739, 740
Zürn, Jörg 28 75; 33 738–9*
works 12 404; 33 738, 739
Zürn, Martin 33 738, 739–40*
Zürn, Michael 8 386; 12 404; 33 738, 740*
collaboration 33 739
works 18 447; 33 739, 740
Zurn, Unica 3 673
Zurreño, Antonio 29 341
Zurreño, Damián 29 336
Zutman, Henri 29 885
Zutman, Lambert see SUAVIUS, LAMBERT
Zutphen 22 813
glass 22 884
pewter 24 578
St Walburgiskerk 13 160; 19 313; 22 818, 820
town walls 22 822
Zuun-kherem 21 885
Zuyev, Grigory (Grigor'yevich) 27 425
Zuyev, V. F. 27 439
Zuzan 16 161
madrasa 16 163, 248

Zuzan—cont.
squinches **16** 169
Zvantseva, Yelizaveta (Nikolayevna) **3** 86; **24** 566; **31** 571; **33** 740*
Zvart'nots **2** *423*; **9** *512*; **33** 740–41*
Cathedral **2** 426, 434, 444; **7** 256; **33** 740–41
mosaics **2** 429
sculpture **2** 434
Zvečan **28** 440
Zvenigorod **27** *363*; **33** 741*
Cathedral of the Dormition **27** 370; **33** 741, *741*
Museum of History and Ethnography **33** 741
Savvino-Storozhevsky Monastery Cathedral **27** 370
Storozhevsky Monastery of St Savva *see* Museum of History and Ethnography
Zvenigorodskoi, A. **12** 331
Zverev, Anatoly (Timofeyevich) **8** 10; **27** 397; **33** 741–2*
Zverin Monastery, St Simeon Bogopriimets **25** 342
Zvezdochetov, Konstantin **27** 398
Zvíkov Castle **8** *374*, 376; **24** 462; **33** 742–3*
chapel of St Wenceslas **33** *742*, 742–3*
tiles **8** 404
Zvíkov Lamentation, Master of the **8** 383
Zvolen **14** 884; **28** *848*
Castle **28** 849
collections **28** 857
Zvono **4** 462
Zwaan, Willem de **25** 566
Zwaansvliet **10** 734
Zwart, Piet **33** 743*
groups and movements **23** 450
works **7** 655; **24** 686; **25** 351
Zwart, Willem de **14** 43; **33** 743*
groups and movements **14** 47
pupils **3** 490
teachers **20** 434
Zwartjes, Niek **22** 877
Zwätzen **26** 686
Zweck, C. W. **19** 111
Zweder van Culemborg, Bishop of Utrecht **20** 786
Zweder van Culemborg, Master of **10** 713; **20** 786*; **22** 835
pupils **20** 644
workshop **31** 771
Zweibrücken **33** 281
Zweibrücken, Charles II Augustus, Duke of **30** 783; **33** *273*, 281*
Zweibrücken, Christian III, Duke of **33** *272*
Zweibrücken, Christian IV, Duke of **33** *272*, *273*, 281*
paintings **20** 282; **22** 271
Zweibrücken, Dukes of **20** 283
Zwelidumile Geelboi Mgxaji Mslaba Feni *see* DUMILE (FENI)
Zwemmer, Anton **33** 744*
Zwengs, Bartholomeus (Jakob) **18** 505; **29** 422
Zwenkau-Harth **14** 73
Zwerger, Georg, II **32** 822
Zwerger, Philipp Jakob **28** 110
Zwettl **2** *776*
Klosterkirche Mariae Himmelfahrt **2** 777, *777*
Monastery **2** 781, 800
church **2** 783
cloister **7** 453
ivory-carvings **13** 173
Zwiefalten Monastery **11** 125; **12** 371
Abteikirche **7** 211–12; **10** 859; **12** 372, 497; **29** 838
pulpit **25** 728
frescoes **15** 139
Zwiefalten Monastery—cont.
manuscripts **10** 201; **26** 661, 674
sculpture **12** 405
Zwiener, Joseph **11** 600
Zwiener, Julius **3** 485
Zwijndrecht **22** 831
Zwimpfer, Hans **11** 304
Zwinck, Franz Seraph **33** 270, 744*
Zwinck, Johann Joseph **33** 744
Zwine, Jacques **4** 925
Zwinger, Christoph **1** 141
Zwinger, Gustav Philipp **18** 115
Zwingli, Huldrych **7** 269, 277; **14** 868; **15** 80; **33** 745
Zwinglianism **33** 745*
Zwirner, Ernst Friedrich **33** 745*
assistants **32** 682
groups and movements **13** 201
works **2** 321; **7** 589; **17** 547; **26** 102; **32** 683
Zwitzel, Bernhard **29** 738; **33** 745, 746*
collaboration **22** 307
Zwitzel, Jakob **29** 738; **33** 745–6*
Zwitzel, Simon **9** 750; **33** 745, 746*
collaboration **22** 307
Zwolle **22** *813*
brass **22** 895
Zwolle—cont.
glass **22** 884
Grote Kerk *see* St Michaelkerk
patronage **22** 886
pewter **22** 893
St Michaelkerk **13** 61; **22** 820
sculpture **22** 855
silver **22** 886, 890
Stadhuis **22** 870
Zwolle, Arnt van *see* ARNT VAN KALKAR
Zwolle, Master IAM of *see* IAM OF ZWOLLE, MASTER
Zwollo, Frans (1872-1945) **18** 878; **22** 892, 895; **23** 120
Zwollo, Frans (1896-1989) **22** 892
Zyablin, L. **1** 504
Zych, Władysław **25** 125
Życie **24** 441; **33** 457
Zyfflich, St Martin **23** 647
Zygouries **13** *363*; **14** *332*; **33** 746*
pottery **14** 342
sculpture **14** 351
Zypen, Julius van der **29** 221
Żyravicy
St George **3** 526
Uniate Monastery **3** 528
Żywi **18** 433

Appendix

NON-WESTERN DYNASTIES AND PEOPLES

For further information on the following non-Western dynasties and peoples, the reader should consult the main index for the dynastic or tribal name or the relevant culture, country or civilization entry.

I. Dynasties

Indian Subcontinent
- ʻAdil Shahi
- Bahmani
- Barid Shahi
- Chahamana
- Chalukyas of Badami
- Chalukyas of Kalyana
- Chalukyas of Vengi
- Chandella
- Chola
- Dandan
- Durrani
- Eastern Ganga
- Gauda
- Ghaznavid
- Ghurid
- Gupta
- Gurjara-Pratahira
- Haihaya
- Hoysala
- Huna
- Ikshvaku
- Kachchhapaghata
- Kakaitya
- Karkota
- Khalji
  - Delhi
  - Malwa
- Kulashekhara
- Kushana
- Lichchhavi
- Line of Habashi
- Line of Ilyas Shah
- Line of Sayyid Husayn Shah
- Lodi
- Mamluk
- Maurya
- Mughal
- Nawabs of Avadh
- Nawabs of Bengal
- Nayaka
- Nizam Shahi
- Nolamba
- Pahari
  - Basohli
  - Bilaspur
  - Chamba
  - Guler
  - Jasrota
  - Kangra
  - Kulu
  - Mandi
  - Nurpur
- Pala
- Pahlava
- Pallava
- Pandya
- Qutb Shahi
- Rajput
  - Amer
  - Bikaner
  - Bundi

Indian Subcontinent—cont.
- Rajput—cont.
  - Dig
  - Ghanerao
  - Indargarh
  - Kishangarh
  - Kota
  - Kachchh
  - Marwar
  - Mewar
  - Orchha
  - Rawats of Deogarh
  - Tomara
- Rashtrakuta
- Saisunaga
- Satavahana
- Sayyid
- Sena
- Shah Miri
- Shaka
- Sharqi
- Shunga
- Sikh
- Sultans of Gujarat
- Sur
- Vaghela
- Vakataka
- Vijayanagara
- Western Ganga
- Wodeyar
- Yadava

Islamic
- Abbasid
- ʻAdil Shahi
- Afsharid
- Aghlabid
- ʻAlawi
- Almohad
- Almoravid
- Aqqoyunlu
- Artuqid
- Ayyubid
- Bahmani
- Barid Shahi
- Bawandid
- Barakzay
- Beylik
- Buyid
- Danishmendid
- Durrani
- Fatimid
- Ghaznavid
- Ghurid
- Giray Khans
- Great Khans
- Hafsid
- Hamdanid
- Hammadid
- Hammudid
- Hashimid
- Kart
- Khalji
  - Delhi
  - Malwa

Islamic—cont.
- Idrisid
- Ilkhanid
- Jalayrid
- Khwarazmshahs
- Kakuyid
- Line of Habashi
- Line of Ilyas Shah
- Line of Sayyid Husayn Shah
- Lodi
- Mamluk
  - Egypt and Syria
  - Indian Subcontinent
- Muhammad Ali's Line
- Marinid
- Mughal
- Muzaffarid
- Nasrid
- Nizam Shahi
- Ottoman
- Orthodox Caliphs
- Palhavi
- Qajar
- Qarakhanid
- Qaraqoyunlu
- Qutb Shahi
- Rasulid
- (al-) Sabah
- Saffarid
- Saljuqs (Great)
- Saljuqs of Anatolia
- Samanid
- Saudi
- Sayyid
- Shah Miri
- Sharqi
- Shaybanid
- Shaddadid
- Sulayhid
- Sultans of Gujarat
- Sur
- Tahirid
- Timurid
- Tulunid
- Umayyad
  - Spain
  - Syria
- ʻUqaylid
- Zand
- Zangid
- Zaydi
- Zirid

South-east Asia
- Chakri
- Malla
- Myohaung

II. Peoples

AFRICA

Algeria
- Harakta

Algeria—cont.
- Kabyles
- Nemencha
- Tuareg

Angola
- Bantu
- Boma
- Chokwe
- Holo
- Kakongo
- Kongo
- Kwanyama
- Luwa
- Lwena
- Nkanu
- Ovimbundu
- Pelende
- Shinji
- Songo
- Suku
- Tsaamba
- Vili
- Woyo
- Yaka
- Yombe
- Zombe

Benin
- Bariba
- Batammaliba
- Edo
- Fon
- Gelede
- Gun
- Yemaje
- Yoruba

Botswana
- Kalanga
- Kgatla
- Mbukushu
- Ndebele
- San
- Tswana
- Yei

Burkina Faso
- Bobo
- Bwa
- Dodo
- Fulani
- Gurunsi
- Jula
- Kassena
- Lobi
- Mande
- Marka
- Mossi
- Senufo
  - Nafara
- Somolo
- Yoruba

Burundi
- Hutu
- Tutsi
- Twa

Cameroon
- Bafut
- Bamileke
- Bamum
- Bangwa
- Bantu
- Beti
- Bulu
- Chamba
- Douala
- Efik
- Efut
- Ejagham
- Eton
- Ewondo
- Fali
- Fulani
- Hausa
- Mofou
- Tsogho
- Yaunde-Fang

Central African Republic
- Gbaya
- Zande

Chad
- Sara

Congo
- Bantu
- Bembe
- Boma
- Bwende
- Fumu
- Kakongo
- Kongo
- Kukuya
- Ladi
- Mbembe
- Ngungulu
- Nkanu
- Nzabi
- Nziku
- Sese
- Teke
- Vili
- Woyo
- Yombe

Côte d'Ivoire
- Abe
- Akan
- Akye
- Anyi
- Attie
- Baule
- Bedu
- Bete

Côte d'Ivoire—cont.
- Dan
- Dida
- Dyula
- Ebrie
- Gur
- Guro
- Kru
- Kulango
- Kyaman
- Lagoon
- Lobi
- Malinke
- Mande
- Nzima
- Senufo
- Toura
- Wan
- We
- Yaure

Egypt
- Berber

Djibuti
- Afar
- Issa

Equatorial Guinea
- Bubi
- Fang
- Kissi

Ethiopia
- Amhara
- Chencha
- Dorze
- Oromo
- Sidama
- Somali
- Tigre

Gabon
- Adjuma
- Aduma
- Apindji
- Bantu
- Enenga
- Eshira
- Fang
- Galwa
- Kota
- Kwele
- Lali
- Lumbo
- Mahongwe
- Myene
- Ndambomo
- Ndassa
- Ngove
- Njabi
- Obamba
- Ondumbo

Gabon—cont.
Punu
Sango
Sangui
Shake
Shamay
Shira-Punu
Tégé
Teke
Tsayi
Tsogo
Varama
Vili
Vungu
Vuvi
Wumbu
Wundji

Gambia
Fulani
Jola
Mandingo
Serahuli
Wolof

Ghana
Akan
Akuapem
Aowin
Asante
Brong
Dagomba
Ewe
Fante
Frafra
Gurensi
Hausa
Koma
Krobo
Tallensi
Twi
Wassa
Yoruba

Guinea
Baga
Bassari
Buluñits
Coniagui
Dan
Fulani
Kakissa
Kalum
Kissi
Koba
Landuma
Malinke
Mandori
Mmami
Nalu
Pukur
Sitemu
Susu
Temne

Guinea-Bissau
Balanta
Beafada-Nalu
Bijogo
Diola
Fulani
Mande
Manjaco

Kenya
Baluyia
Borana
Gabra
Kamba
Kikuyu
Luo
Mijikenda
Maasai
Okiek
Samburu
Somali
Swahili
Turkana

Lesotho
Basotho
Rolong
San
Sotho
Taung

Liberia
Dan
De
Gbande
Gola
Grebo
Kissi
Kpalla
Loma
Mande
Mano
Mende
Vai
We

Libya
Berber
Tuareg

Madagascar
Antaimoro
Antandroy
Antanosy
Arab-Swahili
Bara
Betsileo
Betsimisaraka
Mahafaly
Masikoro
Merina
Sakalava
Sihanaka
Vezo
Zafimaniry

Malawi
Chewa
Maravi
Ngoni
Tonga
Tumbuka
Yao

Mali
Bamana
Bobo
Bwa
Dan
Dogon
Dyula
Fulani
Gurunsi
Mande
Senufo
Nafara
Songhai
Sorko
Tellem
Tuareg

Mauritania
Berber
Fulani
Soninke

Morocco
Glaoua
Kal'a
Udaya
Zaiane

Mozambique
Makonde
Makua-Lomwe
Shona
Tsonga

Namibia
San

Niger
Bororo

Niger—cont.
Djerma
Fulani
Hausa
Kanuri
Songhai
Tuareg
Wodaabe

Nigeria
Adamawa
Ahoada
Akweya
Alago
Avianwu
Awka
Bata
Bena
Bini
Borgu
Bororo
Bussa
Cham
Chamba
Dakakari
Doma
Edo
Efik
Ejagham
Ekiti
Ekperi
Etulo
Etung
Fulani
Ga'anda
Gwari
Hausa
Higis
Ibibio
Idoma
Ife
Igala
Igbo
Igbomina
Igede
Ijo
Kalabari
Isoko
Jen
Jukun
Keana
Kyaman
Kwa
Longuda
Mambila
Mumuye
Ndoki
Nok
Nupe
Ohafia
Okpella
Olodiama
Tiv
Tula
Ungal
Urhobo
Uzairue
Vere
Waja
Weppa-Wano
Wodaabe
Wurkun
Yakö
Yoruba
Ijebu
Yungur

Rwanda
Hutu
Tutsi
Twa

Senegal
Bassari
Fouta Djallon
Fulani
Serer
Tukolor
Wolof

Sierra Leone
Bullom
Gola
Fulah
Fulani
Kissi
Krio
Madingo
Mende
Temne
Yoruba

Somalia
Swahili
Issa
Afar
Somali

South Africa
Bantu
Boers
Cele
Cunu
Manala
Malay
Ndebele
Ndzundza
Nguni
Rozwi
Shona
Sotho
Tembu
Tsonga
Venda
Xhosa
Zulu

Sudan
Baggara
Belanda
Dinka
Hausa
Kababish
Lango
Makaraka
Moro
Nuba
Mesakin
Nuer
Shilluk
Zaghawa
Zande
Adio

Tanzania
Barungi
Chagga
Hadza
Iraqw
Maasai
Makonde
Nguu
Nyasa
Swahili
Wagogo
Wanyamwezi
Wazaramo

Togo
Bassari
Batammaliba
Chamba
Ewe
Gourma
Kaybe
Kotokoli
Lamba
Mina
Moba
Sanga
Tchokossi
Tofinou
Yoruba

Tunisia
Beni Mguild
Beni M'tir
Hamama
Mahadba
Marmoucha

Uganda
Baganda
Bahima
Kiga
Toro

Western Sahara
Bedouin
Berber

Zaïre
Babemo
Baka Kinga
Bala
Bangubangu
Bantu
Batali
Bembe
Bieng
Binja
Binji
Biombo
Bole
Boma
Boyo
Bulang
Buli
Bushong
Bwaka
Chofwe
Chokwe
Coofa
Cwa
Dondo
Ebombo
Eki
Ekolombi
Hemba
Holo
Hombo
Honga
Hunde
Hungana
Iding
Ilande
Kaam
Kagulu
Kagulu Kamalungu
Kahela
Kakongo
Kalebwe
Kanu
Katego
Kayungu
Kayuweng
Kel
Kete
Kongo
Konjo
Kuba
Kusu
Kwame
Lega
Leka
Lele
Lengola
Lobo
Lub
Luika Niembo
Lulua
Lunda
Luwa
Lwena
Maluk
Mambwe
Mangbetu
Mbala
Mbengi
Mbole
Mbuti
Milembwe
Mitoko
Mogasa
Mongo
Muhona
Nbaka
Ndengese
Ngbaka
Ngbandi

Zaïre—cont.
Ngelima
Ngende
Ngenga
Ngengele
Ngombe
Ngongo
Niembo
Nkanu
Nkuvu
Nonda
Nyanga
Ooli
Ovimbundu
Pelende
Pende
Pere
Pyang
Pyang Ibaam
Sayi
Sengele
Shoowa
Songo
Songola
Songye
Suku
Tabwa
Teke
Tembo
Tsaamba
Twa
Vili
Wongo
Woyo
Yaka
Yambula
Yela
Yombe
Zande
Zimba
Zombo
Zula

Zambia
Bemba
Chewa
Chokwe
Ila
Lala
Lozi
Lwena
Ovimbundu
Songo
Tabwa
Tonga

Zimbabwe
Bantu
Mambo Mutota
Ndebele
Nguni
San
Shona
Sotho

AMERICAS

Argentina
Araucano
Atacameño
Diaguita
Guaraní
Ona
Querandíe
Selk'nam
Tehuelche
Yagane

Aruba
Caquetios
Ciboney

Bahamas
Lucayo

Bay Islands
Garifuna

Belize
- Carib
- Creole
- Garífuna
- Kekchi
- Maya
- Mopan
- Yucatec

Bolivia
- Atacameño
- Aymara
- Callahuaya
- Yamparaes

Bonaire
- Caquetios
- Ciboney

Brazil
- Ananatuba
- Anago
- Aruã
- Bororo
- Desana
- Kaapor
- Kadiwéu
- Karajá
- Kayabi
- Mangueiras
- Marajoara
- Mundurucú
- Paresi
- Tabajares
- Tapajó
- Timbira
- Tiriyo
- Tukano
- Tukuna
- Tupinamba
- Waurá
- Xavante
- Yanomani
- Yoruba

Canada
- Ahtna
- Aleut
- Beaver
- Bella Bella
- Carrier
- Chilcotin
- Chinooka
- Chipewyan
- Clallam
- Cree
- Cree-Metis
- Dogrib
- Eskimo
- Eyak
- Gitskan
- Haida
- Haihai
- Haisla
- Han
- Hare
- Heiltsuk
- Huron
- Ingalik
- Inuit
- Kaska
- Kwakwaka'wakw
- Kwakiutl
- Kolchan
- Koyukon
- Kutchin
- Makah
- Metis
- Montagnais
- Mountain People
- Naskapi
- Nishga
- Nitinaht
- Nuu-chah-nuulth
  - Northern
- Nuxalk
- Ojibwa
  - Eastern
  - Northern

Canada—cont.
- Petun
- Quileute
- Quinault
- Sahaptian
- Salish
- Saulteaux
- Sekani
- Slavey
- Tagish
- Tahltan
- Tanaina
- Tanana
- Thule
- Tlingit
- Tsimshian
- Tutchone
- Wasco
- Wishxam
- Yellowknife

Chile
- Atacameño
- Mapuche
- Selk'nam

Columbia
- Ambalo
- Arawak
- Arhuaco
- Capulí
- Carare
- Carib
- Catio
- Chami
- Chibcha
- Coconuco
- Creole
- Cubeo
- Cuiba
- Desana
- Embera
- Guajibo
- Guajiro
- Guambiano
- Huitoto
- Ica
- Kogi
- Kogui
- Kuna
- Motilone
- Musica
- Noanama
- Paez
- Paniquita
- Putumayo
- Quillacinga
- Qimbaya
- Sanka
- Sibundoy
- Tairona
- Tolima
- Tukano
- Tunebo
- Wayu
- Yuco

Cuba
- Arawak
- Ciboney
- Creole
- Taíno

Curaçao
- Caquetios
- Ciboney

Dominican Republic
- Arawak
- Bantu
- Carib
- Ciboney
- Taíno
- Yoruba

Ecuador
- Guangala
- Jama-Coaque

Ecuador—cont.
- Manteño
- Otovala
- Quechua
- Valdivia

French Guiana
- Aluku
- Arawak
- Galibi
- Emerillon
- Hmong
- Ndjuka
- Palikur
- Samaraka
- Wayampi
- Wayana

Guatemala
- Garífuna
- Maya

Guyana
- Akawaio
- Arawak
- Arecuna
- Carib
- Creole
- Kapon
- Karinyas
- Lokono
- Makusi
- Patamona
- Pemon
- Waiwai
- Wapisiana
- Warao

Haiti
- Akan
- Arawak
- Bamana
- Ciboney
- Ewe
- Igbo
- Mande
- Taíno
- Yoruba

Honduras
- Garífuna

Jamaica
- Asante
- Anago
- Ibo
- Kikongo
- Kongo
- Kumina
- Mandingo
- Maroon
- Taíno
- Yoruba

Mesoamerica, Pre-Columbian
- Amuzgo
- Aztec
- Chichimec
- Chinantec
- Chocho-Popoloca
- Cuicatec
- Huastec
- Ichcatec
- Izapan
- Matlazinca
- Maya
  - Ajaw
  - Cakchiquel
  - Cawek
  - Chiapanec
  - Chontal (Putún)
  - Cocom
  - Itzá
  - Puuc
  - Quiché
  - Tamub
  - Toltecat
  - Tutul Xiu

Mesoamerica, Pre-Columbian—cont.
- Maya—cont.
  - Tzotzil
  - Tzutujil
  - Xiu
  - Yucatec
- Mazatec
- Mixtec
- Náhuatl
- Nonoalca
- Olmec
- Otami
- Tarascan
- Tlaxcaltec
- Toltec
- Totonac
- Trigue
- Zapotec

Panama
- Kuna

Paraguay
- Aché
- Ayoresi
- Cario

Paraguay—cont.
- Chamacoco
- Chirigano
- Chiripá
- Guaraní
- Lengua
- Manjui
- Mashco
- Mataco
- Mbyá
- Tomáharo
- Zamuco

Peru
- Chimú
- Huarpa
- Inca
- Shipibo
- Usu

Puerto Rico
- Carib
- Taíno

St Vincent
- Carib
- Maroon

São Tomé Príncipe
- Creole

South America, Pre-Columbian
- Alacaluf
- Araucano
- Aruã
- Atacameño
- Bedulu
- Bribri
- Caduveo
- Cañari
- Capulí
- Chanka
- Chibcha
- Chimú
- Chincha
- Chono
- Cocama
- Cuismancu
- Diaguita
- Guana
- Guaraní
- Huari
- Huarpa
- Huitoto
- Hupa-iya
- Inca
- Jama-Coaque
- Jívaro
- Kogi
- Konduri
- Manteño
- Mapuche

South America, Pre-Columbian—cont.
- Marajoara
- Moche
- Mundurucú
- Musica
- Omagua
- Ona
- Punáes
- Quechua
- Querandíe
- Selk'nam
- Sicán
- Sinu Carib
- Suazey
- Tabajares
- Tairona
- Tapajó
- Tehuelche
- Tolima
- Tupí
- Tupinamba
- Usu
- Wayana
- Yagane
- Yahgan
- Yotoco

Surinam
- Akuriyo
- Aluku
- Arawak
- Aucaner
- Bush Creoles (Bush Negroes)
- Carib
- Djuka
- Kwinti
- Matuariér
- Paramaccaner
- Saramaccaner
- Saramaka
- Trió
- Wayana

Trinidad and Tobago
- Arawak
- Carib
- Creole
- Dahomian Rada
- Igbo
- Kumar
- Nepuyos
- Yoruba

United States of America
- Abnaki
- Achomawi
- Ahtna
- Aleut
- Algon
  - Delaware
  - North Carolina
  - Virginia
- Anasazi
- Apache
  - Cibecue
  - Chiricahua
  - Jicarilla
  - Kiowa
  - Lipan
  - Mescalero
- Arapaho
- Arikara
- Assiniboin
- Athapaskan
- Atsugewi
- Attu
- Bacavi
- Beaver
- Bella Bella
- Biloxi
- Birnirk
- Blackfoot
- Caddo
- Cahuilla
- Calusa
- Carrier
- Catawba

United States of America—cont.
- Cayuga
- Chemehuevi
- Cherokee
- Cheyenne
- Chicano
- Chickasaw
- Chilcotin
- Chinooka
- Chipewyan
- Chippewa
- Chitimacha
- Choctaw
- Chumash
- Comanche
- Costanoan
- Cree
  - Plains
- Creek
- Crow
- Dakota
- Delaware
- Dogrib
- Erie
- Eskimo
- Flathead
- Fox
- Gabrielino
- Gitskan
- Gros Ventre
- Haida
- Haihai
- Haisla
- Halkomelem
- Han
- Hare
- Havasupai
- Heiltsuk
- Hidatsa
- Hohokam
- Hopi
- Hoteville
- Hupa
- Huron
- Ipai
- Illinois
- Ingalik
- Inuit
- Inupiaq
- Inuvialuit
- Ipiutak
- Iroquois
- Iowa
- Kansa
- Kansas
- Karoc
- Kaska
- Kawaiisu
- Keres
- Klamath
- Klickitat
- Kolchan
- Koso
- Koyukon
- Kutchin
- Kwakwaka'wakw
- Lumbee
- Maidu
- Makah
- Mandan
- Menominee
- Metlakatla
- Miami
- Mimbres
- Mission
- Missouri
- Miwok
- Modoc
- Moenkopi
- Mogollon
- Mohave
- Mohawk
- Monache
- Montagnais
- Mountain People
- Muskogean
- Naskapi

United States of America—cont.
- Natchez
- Navajo
- Nez Percé
- Nisenan
- Nishga
- Nitinaht
- Neutral
- Nuu-chah-nuulth
- Nuxalk
- Ocotillo
- Ojibwa
- Okvik
- Omaha
- Oneida
- Onondaga
- Ootam
- Osage
- Oto
- Ottawa
- Paiute
  - Northern
  - Owen's Valley
  - Southern
- Papago
- Pastolik
- Patayan
- Patwin
- Pawnee
- Penobscot
- Pima
- Pomo
- Ponca
- Potawatomi
- Powhatan
- Pueblo
- Punuk
- Quapaw
- Quechan
- Quileute
- Quinault
- Sahaptian
- Salish
  - Coast
- Sarsi
- Sauk
- Saulteaux
- Sekani
- Seminole
- Seneca
- Shawnee
- Shoshone
  - Panamint
  - Northern
  - Western
- Slavey
- Sioux
  - Santee
  - Yankton
  - Yanktonai
- Taensa
- Tagish
- Talhtan
- Tanaina
- Tanana
- Teton
- Tewa
- Thule
- Timuca
- Tipai
- Tiwa
- Tlingit
- Tohono O'Odham
- Tolowa
- Tonkawa
- Towa
- Tubatulabal
- Tuscarora
- Tutchone
- Ute
- Valley Maidu
- Walapai
- Wasco
- Washoe
- Wichita
- Winnebago
- Wishxam
- Wiyot

United States of America—cont.
- Yakima
- Yakutat
- Yavapai
- Yellowknife
- Yokut
- Yuchi
- Yuit
- Yuma
- Yurok
- Zuni

Uruguay
- Chanáe
- Charrúa
- Guaraní

Venezuela
- Arawak
- Cubagua
- Margarita
- Timoto-Cuicas
- Yanomani

Asia

Afghanistan
- Aimaq
- Baluch
- Hazara
- Kirghiz
- Nuristani
- Pathan
- Pushtun
- Tajik
- Turkoman

Bangladesh
- Bengali
- Chakma
- Garo
- Hajong
- Khasi
- Mogh
- Santal
- Tipra

Bhutan
- Drukpa

Brunei
- Iban
- Malay
- Penan

Burma
- Akha
- Haka Chin
- Karen
- Lahu
- Lisu
- Mon
- Padaung
- Pyu

Cambodia
- Cham
- Khmer Tam
- Jarai Khmer
- Rhadé

China
- Hakka
- Han
- Hui
- Lolo
- Miao
- Mongol
- Qiang
- Qidan
- Ruzhen
- Shu
- Tangut
- Uygur
- Xiongnu
- Yami

India
- Ahir
- Baiga
- Bhil
- Bhuiya
- Bhutia
- Birhor
- Dokra
- Dorla
- Gond
- Jat
- Juang
- Kathi
- Khampti
- Kondh
- Konyak
  - Thendu
  - Thenkoh
- Kuttia Kondh
- Lakher
- Lhota
- Lushai
- Mahajan
- Maria
- Mina
- Mongpa
- Muduva
- Muria
  - Bastar
- Naga
  - Adi
  - Angami
  - Ao
  - Apa Tani
  - Ara Juang
  - Manipur
  - Mishmi
  - Nocte
  - Sema
  - Wancho
- Oraon
- Pradhan Gond
- Purum
- Rabari
- Saora
- Santal
- Thadou Kuki
- Toda
- Warli

Indonesia
- Alor
- Angkola
- Asmat
- Atoni
- Badui
- Batak
  - Karo
  - Pakpak
  - Simalungun
  - Toba
- Bidayuh
- Buginese
- Dayak
- Duri
- Ema
- Gayo
- Iban
- Kayan
- Kenyah
- Kroes
- Lamahalot
- Ma'anyan
- Marind-Anim
- Minangkabau
- Ngada
- Ngaju
- Ot Danum
- Pantar
- Sa'dan Toraja
- Sumba
- Sundanese
- Tetum
- Wana

Iran
- Afshar
- Baluch
- Bakhtiari

Iran—cont.
- Qashqa'i

Japan
- Ainu
- Burakumin
- Okinawan
- Ryūkyū

Korea
- Koguryŏ
- Okcho
- Samhan
- Yemaek

Laos
- Akha
- Hmong
- Khmer
- Ko
- Nu Kuay
- Tai
  - Dam
  - Daeng
  - Khao
  - Lue
  - Muai
  - Neua
  - Phuan
  - Phu Tai
- Yao

Malaysia
- Baba Nyonya
- Bajau
- Bidayuh
- Bugis
- Dayak
- Dusun
- Iban
- Jah Heut
- Jakun
- Kadazan
- Kayan
- Kelabit
- Kenyah
- Mah Meri
- Malay
- Maloh
- Melanau
- Minangkabau
- Murut
- Negrito
- Orang Asli
- Orang Ulu
- Penan
- Rungu
- Sakai
- Semang
- Senoi
- Straits Chinese

Mongolia
- Altai Uriankhai
- Barga
- Buryat
- Chahar
- Dalai Choinkor
- Dariganga
- Derbet
- Hun
- Kalmak
- Khalka
- Mongol
- Oirat
- Ordos
- Uygur
- Uzemchin
- Xiongnu

Nepal
- Gopala
- Gurung
- Kirata
- Magar
- Newar
- Nipa
- Rai
- Sherpa
- Tamang

Pakistan
- Kafir
- Kalash
- Pathan

Philippines
- Badjau
- Bagobo
- Batak
- Bontoc
- Bukidnon
- Gaddang
- Ifugao
- Igorot
- Ilongot
- Isinai
- Isneg
- Kalinga
- Kankanay
- Mandaya
- Maguindanao
- Mangyan
- Maranao
- Negrito
- Pala'wan
- Samal
- Tausug
- T'boli
- Tinguian
- Toraja
- Ubu
- Visayan

Russian Federation
- Adygeya
- Agul
- Aleut
- Altay
- Arabatchi
- Avar
- Balkar
- Bashkir
- Buryat
- Chechen
- Chodor
- Chukchi
- Chuvash
- Circassian
- Dargin
- Eskimo
- Evenky
- Ingush
- Inuit
- Izhorian
- Kabardin
- Kalmyk
- Karachay-Circassian
- Karachayev
- Khanty
- Komi-Zyryan
- Koryak
- Kyrgyz
- Lak
- Lezgin
- Mansi
- Nanay
- Nenets
- Orkhon Turk
- Salor
- Samoyed
- Saryk
- Tatar
- Tekke
- Tungus
- Udegey
- Udmurt
- Ul'chi
- Vespian
- Yakut
- Yomut
- Yuit
- Yukagir

Sri Lanka
- Dravidian
- Indo-Aryan
- Sinhalese
- Tamil
- Vadda

Thailand
- Akha
- Hmong
  - Blue
  - White
- Karen
- Khmer
- Lahu
  - Na
  - Nyi
  - Sheh Leh
  - Shi
- Lao
  - Khang
- Loimi
- Lua
- Miao
- Mien
- Phami
- Pwo
- Sgaw
- Tai
  - Dam
  - Lao
  - Lue
  - Phuan
  - Phu Tai
  - Yai
  - Yuan
- U Lo

Tibet
- Mi-nyag

Turkey
- Turkoman
- Yuncu

Turkmenistan
- Baluch

Vietnam
- Bahnar
- Cham
- Jarai Arap
- Katu
- Khmou
- Lat
- Lolo
- Maa
- Monom
- Muong
- Rhadé
- Sedang
- Stieng
- Thai

Australia and Pacific Islands

Australia
- Warlpiri

Chatham Islands
- Moriori

Fiji
- Jiajau
- Lenaki

Mariana Islands
- Chamarro

New Caledonia
- Kanak

New Zealand
- Maori

Papua New Guinea
- Abelam
- Agarabi
- Angkeiakmin
- Arapesh
- Baining
- Barli
- Berepa
- Boiken

Papua New Guinea—cont.
- Breri
- Buang
- Bundi
- Chachet
- Elema
- Falamin
- Fregolmin
- Gahuku
- Hagener

Papua New Guinea—cont.
- Iatmul
- Kara
- Karawari
- Kairak
- Kerewa
- Keruru
- Kilenge
- Kiwai
- Kominimung

Papua New Guinea—cont.
- Kwanga
- Kwoma
- Lakalai
- Lavongai
- Madak
- Manus
- Matankor
- Maring
- Mengen

Papua New Guinea—cont.
- Murik
- Nagatman
- Nalik
- Namau
- Nggala
- Notsi
- Nukuma
- Oksapmin
- Patpator-Tolai

Papua New Guinea—cont.
- Rao
- Sawos
- Sulka
- Tabar
- Telefolmin
- Tifalmin
- Tigak
- Tolai
- Ulapmin

Papua New Guinea—cont.
- Urama
- Uromot
- Usiai
- Vir
- Watam
- Wopkeimin
- Yasyin

Solomon Islands
- Lapita